ASLIB

DIRECTORY OF INFORMATION SOURCES IN THE UNITED KINGDOM

ASLIB

DIRECTORY OF INFORMATION SOURCES IN THE UNITED KINGDOM

15th EDITION

Routledge
Taylor & Francis Group

LONDON AND NEW YORK

First published 1928
Fifteenth edition 2008

©Routledge 2008
Albert House, 1–4 Singer Street, London, EC2A 4BQ
(Routledge is an imprint of the Taylor & Francis Group, an **informa** business)

ISBN 978-1-85743-488-0
ISSN 1743–8616

Editors: Sheila Garrard, Alison Neale

Proofreaders: Christopher Bell, Jonathan Derrick, Sheila Garrard, Justin Lewis

Research: James Middleton

Senior Editor, European Directories: Michael Salzman

Editorial Director: Paul Kelly

Typeset in 7pt Palatino

FSC
Mixed Sources
Product group from well-managed
forests and other controlled sources
Cert no. SGS-COC-003788
www.fsc.org
© 1996 Forest Stewardship Council

Typeset by AMA DataSet Limited, Preston
Printed and bound in Great Britain by Polestar Wheatons, Exeter

FOREWORD

The 15th edition of the ASLIB DIRECTORY OF INFORMATION SOURCES IN THE UNITED KINGDOM offers the reader a wealth of information sources on a potentially limitless range of topics. The pursuers of great learning and of minority hobbies, the great collections, the charitable organisations, the statutory bodies and the defenders of individual rights are there, ready and willing to pass on help, advice, erudition and entertainment.

The information in the directory can be used in a variety of ways. Browsing can, of course, be fun, and an hour might well go by unnoticed as the reader discovers organisations where answers can be obtained to longstanding questions.

Where a named institution is sought, the Main Directory offers entries listed alphabetically, by the name of the organisation, while the Index of Abbreviations and Acronyms, which follows the Main Directory, can provide a full name for a puzzling acronym.

However, the reader who is seeking a source of information on a specific topic may prefer to turn first to the extensive Subject Index which forms the final section of the book. Organisations are grouped there by subject and, in the case of broad topics, under sub-headings.

Most of the information that appears in this directory has been provided by the organisations concerned and we are very grateful to those individuals who have given their time to check and update their entry for the new edition.

November 2008

CONTENTS

Main Directory

1 STOP DATA LIMITED

1 Stop Data House, 46 High Street, Ewell, Surrey, KT17 1RW

Tel: 020 8786 9111
Fax: 020 8786 9115
E-mail: info@1stopdata.com

Enquiries:
Enquiries to: Managing Director

Founded:
2001

Formerly called:
Graham and Trotman; Gale Direct (part of the Gale Group) (year of change 2001)

Incorporates the former:
Graham & Whiteside Limited (year of change 2001)

Organisation type and purpose:
Service industry, publishing house.
Business and professional information supplier.

Subject coverage:
Business, professional, academic.

Printed publications:
Trade Associations and Professional Bodies of the UK (15th ed)

Electronic and video publications:
International Associations Database
International Libraries Database
International Major Marketer's Datafile
International Research Centre's Database
Major Companies Database
UK Medical File
UK Companies Database
Ward's Database of US Companies

Publications list:
Available in print

Access to staff:
Contact by letter, by telephone, by fax, by e-mail and via website
Hours: Mon to Fri, 0900 to 1700

100 BLACK MEN OF LONDON

The Bridge, 12–16 Clerkenwell Road, London, EC1M 5PQ

Tel: 0870 121 4100
E-mail: info@100bmol.org.uk

Website:
http://www.100bmol.org.uk

Founded:
2001

Organisation type and purpose:
A non-profit organisation formed by a group of African–Caribbean men who aim to help the youth of their community to achieve their full potential, supported by programmes with an emphasis on mentoring, education, economic development and health and wellbeing.

Links with:
100 Black Men of America Inc.
  website: http://www.100blackmen.org

1745 ASSOCIATION

Ferry Cottage, Corran, Ardgour, Fort William, Inverness-shire, PH33 7AA

Tel: 01855 841306
E-mail: c.aikman@btinternet.com

Website:
http://www.1745association.org.uk

Enquiries:
Enquiries to: Honorary Secretary

Founded:
1946

Organisation type and purpose:
Membership association (membership is by subscription), present number of members: 300, voluntary organisation.

Subject coverage:
History of the whole Jacobite Movement from 1688 to 1788, particularly with reference to Scotland; the Risings of 1715 and 1745 and their aftermath.

Printed publications:
Brochure (on the Association)
Muster Roll of Prince Charles Edward Stuart's Army 1745–46 (1984, Aberdeen University Press, enlarged edition 2001)
Reports of Association's Meetings, etc
The Jacobite (3 times a year)

Access to staff:
Contact by letter and by telephone
Hours: Mon to Fri, 0900 to 1700

2ND AIR DIVISION MEMORIAL LIBRARY

The Forum, Millennium Plain, Norwich, Norfolk, NR2 1AW

Tel: 01603 774747
E-mail: 2admemorial.lib@norfolk.gov.uk

Website:
http://www.2ndair.org.uk

Organisation type and purpose:
Library administered by the Board of Governors of the Memorial Trust, a UK registered charity, working in consultation with Norfolk County Council Library Authority and the Executive Committee of the 2nd Air Division Association.

Subject coverage:
Books, periodicals and videos on all aspects of American history, culture and life, and specialised material about the Second World War in the air and about the special relationship between the peoples of the UK (particularly East Anglia) and the USA. The Library does not hold any official military personnel records.

Access to building, collection or gallery:
Mon to Sat, 0900 to 1700. Closed on bank holidays.

3M UNITED KINGDOM PLC

3M House, PO Box 1, Bracknell, Berkshire, RG12 1JU

Tel: 01344 858000
Fax: 01344 858278

Website:
http://www.3M.com
Profiles on subsidiaries, global company and product information, innovations and new products, press releases.

Enquiries:
Enquiries to: Business Intelligence Manager

Founded:
1902

Organisation type and purpose:
Manufacturing industry.

Subject coverage:
Manufacture and marketing of adhesives, adhesive tape, medical products, coated abrasives, reflective products, electrical products, fluorochemicals, reinforced plastics, static eliminators, film cleaners, traffic control, and decorative and recreational products.

Part of:
Minnesota Mining and Manufacturing Company
  USA

ABBEYFIELD SOCIETY

53 Victoria Street, St Albans, Hertfordshire, AL1 3UW

Tel: 01727 857536

Fax: 01727 846168
E-mail: post@abbeyfield.com

Website:
http://www.abbeyfield.com
Details of services and current information on topics relating to older people.

Enquiries:
Enquiries to: Public Relations
Direct tel: 01727 734091
Direct e-mail: j.burder@abbeyfield.com

Founded:
1956

Organisation type and purpose:
To provide housing and innovative services for older people across the UK in 750 sheltered houses and 80 care homes.

Subject coverage:
Legal and financial information for starting and running Abbeyfield societies and houses, including housing for older and frail older people.

Museum or gallery collection, archive, or library special collection:
Books, journal articles, photographs

Trade and statistical information:
The Abbeyfield Profile (latest statistics).

Library catalogue:
All or part available in-house

Printed publications:
What is Abbeyfield? (leaflet)
Any Questions? (leaflet)
Focus (6 times a year)
Manual of Information (free to each Society)
The Abbeyfielder (2 times a year)

Publications list:
Available in print

Access to staff:
Contact by letter, by telephone, by fax, by e-mail and via website. Appointment necessary. All charged.
Hours: Mon to Fri, 0900 to 1700

Access to building, collection or gallery:
No prior appointment required

ABC-CLIO EUROPE

PO Box 1437, Oxford, X4 9AZ

Tel: 01844 238448
E-mail: salesinternational@abc-clio.com

Website:
http://www.abc-clio.com/international

Enquiries:
Enquiries to: Marketing Manager
Other contacts: International Sales Director for sales.

Founded:
1971

Formerly called:
Clio Press Limited

Organisation type and purpose:
Publishing house.

Subject coverage:
Own publications of abstracts and bibliographies in history, politics, American studies, international organisations, general reference.

Printed publications:
America: History and Life
Clio Montessori Series
Historical Abstracts
Reference books
World Bibliographical Series

Electronic and video publications:
America: History and Life (CD-ROM and web)
Historical Abstracts (CD-ROM and web)
World Geography (web)
World History FullText (web)

Publications list:
Available in print

continued overleaf

Access to staff:
Contact by letter, by telephone, by fax, by e-mail and via website
Hours: Mon to Fri, 0900 to 1700

Parent body:
ABC-CLIO Inc
   USA

ABERDEEN AND GRAMPIAN CHAMBER OF COMMERCE

Greenhole Place, Bridge of Don, Aberdeen, AB23 8EU

Tel: 01224 343900
Fax: 01224 343943
E-mail: info@agcc.co.uk

Website:
http://www.agcc.co.uk

Enquiries:
Enquiries to: Policy and Communications Manager
Direct tel: 01224 343913
Direct fax: 01224 343943
Direct e-mail: kate.yuill@agcc.co.uk

Founded:
1877

Formerly called:
Aberdeen Chamber of Commerce (year of change 2001)

Organisation type and purpose:
Membership association (membership is by subscription), present number of members: 1300.

Printed publications:
Business Alert (free to members)
Business Bulletin (free to members)
Scottish Chambers of Commerce Directory (free to members, £50 non members)

Access to staff:
Contact by letter, by telephone, by fax, by e-mail, in person and via website
Hours: Mon to Fri, 0900 to 1700

Other address:
Information Centre
   27 Albyn Place, Aberdeen, AB10 1DB; tel: 01224 252727; fax: 01224 580055; e-mail: sbg -grampian@scotent.co.uk

ABERDEEN AND NORTH EAST SCOTLAND FAMILY HISTORY SOCIETY

Acronym or abbreviation: ANESFHS

The Family History Research Centre, 158–164 King Street, Aberdeen, AB24 5BD

Tel: 01224 646323
Fax: 01224 639096
E-mail: enquiries@anesfhs.org.uk

Website:
http://www.anesfhs.org.uk
Publications list, society details, membership application form, ancestor chart index, monumental inscriptions index, meetings syllabus, projects.

Enquiries:
Enquiries to: Secretary
Other contacts: Press Officer (press.office@anesfhs.org.uk)

Founded:
1978

Organisation type and purpose:
Membership association (membership is by subscription), present number of members: 5,000, voluntary organisation, registered charity (charity number SCO 12478).

Subject coverage:
Genealogy relating to the North East of Scotland, census, parish register information for North East parishes, family history.

Museum or gallery collection, archive, or library special collection:
Reference library of books on local and family history
Collection of ancestor charts submitted by members
Historical maps of the area
Parish information
Microfiche of major indexes e.g. IGI, General Register House, Scottish Record Office, BMD for England from 1837
1881 Census (CD-ROM)
Members' research interests
Deryk Cameron Memorial Collection: OPRs and Census (microfilm) for Shetland

Library catalogue:
All or part available online and in-house

Printed publications:
Journal (quarterly, members)
Membership List
Monumental inscriptions
Census 1851
Aberdeenshire Poll Book 1696
Books on church history and other local subjects

Electronic and video publications:
Master index to surnames relating to graveyard inscriptions gathered from publications (actual and draft form, £5 disc supplied by Society)

Publications list:
Available online and in print

Access to staff:
Contact by letter, by telephone, by fax, by e-mail, in person and via website. Non-members charged.
Hours: Mon to Fri, 1000 to 1600; Sat, 1000 to 1300
Members only Tue to Fri, 1900 to 2200
Special comments: Reference library for members only.

Access for disabled people:
At no. 160 entrance

Member organisation of:
Aberdeen and Grampian Tourist Board
   Exchange House, 26–28 Exchange Street, Aberdeen, AB11 6PH; tel: 01224 288828; fax: 01224 288838; e-mail: aberdeen.information@ visitscotland.com; website: http://www .visitscotland.com
Scottish Association of Family History Societies
   website: http://www.safhs.org.uk

ABERDEEN ANGUS CATTLE SOCIETY

Pedigree House, 6 King's Place, Perth, Tayside, PH2 8AD

Tel: 01738 622477
Fax: 01738 636436
E-mail: info@aberdeen-angus.co.uk

Website:
http://www.aberdeen-angus.com

Enquiries:
Enquiries to: Chief Executive

Founded:
1879

Organisation type and purpose:
Breed Society.

Subject coverage:
Pedigree Aberdeen Angus cattle.

Printed publications:
Aberdeen Angus Herdbook (annually)
Aberdeen Angus Review (annually)

Access to staff:
Contact by telephone, by e-mail and via website
Hours: Mon to Fri, 0900 to 1700

ABERDEEN CITY ARCHIVES

The Town House, Broad Street, Aberdeen, AB10 1AQ

Tel: 01224 522513; 01224 522381 (minicom)

Fax: 01224 638556
E-mail: archives@aberdeencity.gov.uk

Website:
http://www.aberdeencity.gov.uk/archives

Enquiries:
Enquiries to: City Archivist
Other contacts: Duty Archivist for general enquiries.

Founded:
1980

Organisation type and purpose:
Local government body.

Subject coverage:
History of Aberdeen and its local government institutions, including schools.
History of North East Scotland, local government institutions (Old Aberdeen Branch).

Information services:
Library available for reference; Aberdeen City Councils Neighbourhood Services (Central Learning); Culture and Library Information Services

Museum or gallery collection, archive, or library special collection:
Local authority archives within Aberdeen City and former Grampian region
Some deposited business, church and private collections
Town House Library – 19th-century collection of local history, books and pamphlets selectively updated

Non-library collection catalogue:
All or part available in-house

Library catalogue:
All or part available in-house

Printed publications:
Information Leaflets (free)

Microform publications:
Council Registers 1600 to 1883 (microfilm)
Burgh Sasine Registers (microfilm)
Microfilm of other council records

Access to staff:
Contact by letter, by telephone, by fax, by e-mail and in person. Appointment necessary.
Hours: Town House: Wed to Fri, 0930 to 1630
Old Aberdeen House: Mon to Wed, 0900 to 1300, 1400 to 1630
Special comments: Researchers by prior appointment.

Also at:
Aberdeen City Archives – Old Aberdeen House Branch
   Old Aberdeen House, Dunbar Street, Aberdeen, AB24 1UE; tel: 01224 481775; fax: 01224 495830; e-mail: archives@aberdeencity.gov.uk

ABERDEEN CITY LIBRARY AND INFORMATION SERVICES

Acronym or abbreviation: ACL

Central Library, Rosemount Viaduct, Aberdeen, AB25 1GW

Tel: 01224 641985
Fax: 01224 636811

Website:
http://www.aberdeencity.gov.uk

Enquiries:
Enquiries to: Business & Technical Librarian
Direct tel: 01224 652502
Direct fax: 01224 641985
Direct e-mail: businesstechnicallibrary@ aberdeencity.gov.uk

Founded:
1887

Formerly called:
Aberdeen Arts & Recreation Division – Library Services

Organisation type and purpose:
Public library.

Business and Technical Dept.

Subject coverage:
Public library service covering all subjects including audio-visual lending service. Scottish history, genealogy and tartans.
Specialist business and technical department provides company product information, technical standards, patents and trademarks and reference and lending services covering all aspects of business management, science and technology.

Museum or gallery collection, archive, or library special collection:
British and other technical standards
British, European and USA Patents
Cosmo Mitchell Collection on dancing
Collection of company and product directories
George Washington Wilson Collection of photographs
Health and safety data on CD-ROM
Oil and gas collection
Statistics and market research
Walker Collection of music
Patents and Trade Marks

Trade and statistical information:
Data on oil and gas explorations including technical standards.
Patent information centre for north of Scotland.
Company and product information relating to UK, Europe, and USA.

Electronic and video publications:
Community Contacts (CD-ROM)

Access to staff:
Contact by letter, by telephone, by fax, by e-mail and in person. Appointment necessary.
Hours: Mon to Thu, 0900 to 2000; Fri, Sat, 0900 to 1700
Lending Dept: Mon to Thu, 0900 to 1900; Fri, Sat, 0900 to 1700

Access for disabled people:
Yes

ABERDEEN COLLEGE

Gallowgate, Aberdeen, AB25 1BN

Tel: 01224 612000 ext 2138
Fax: 01224 612001
E-mail: gallowlib@abcol.ac.uk
Website:
http://www.abcol.ac.uk/library

Enquiries:
Enquiries to: Librarian
Direct tel: 01224 612138
Direct e-mail: kapp@abcol.ac.uk

Founded:
1992

Formerly called:
Aberdeen College of Commerce, Aberdeen College of Further Education, Aberdeen Technical College (year of change 1992)

Organisation type and purpose:
College of further education.

Subject coverage:
Business and commercial, technical, at further education level.
Art, social sciences, catering.

Library catalogue:
All or part available in-house

Access to staff:
Contact by telephone and by e-mail
Hours: Mon to Thu, 0830 to 2130; Fri, 0830 to 1700; Sat, Sun, 0900 to 1700

Access for disabled people:
Parking provided, ramped entry, toilet facilities

ABERDEEN INTERNATIONAL YOUTH FESTIVAL

Acronym or abbreviation: AIYF

Custom House, 35 Regent Quay, Aberdeen, AB11 5BE

Tel: 01224 213800
Fax: 01224 213833
E-mail: info@aiyf.org
Website:
http://www.aiyf.org
Full information about the Aberdeen International Youth Festival, its associated summer schools, programme of events, how to buy tickets, etc.

Enquiries:
Enquiries to: Director
Other contacts: General Manager

Founded:
1982

Organisation type and purpose:
Registered charity (charity number SCO 14935), suitable for ages: 12 to 25.
Annual international youth arts festival welcoming youth orchestras, choirs, jazz, dance and theatre groups from around the world to take part in a non-competitive festival. Up to 1000 young participants up to the age of 25 reside at the University, give public performances and experience different cultures and art forms.

Subject coverage:
Youth orchestras, choirs, jazz and wind bands, all forms of youth dance groups and theatre companies worldwide. Education: ballet summer school plus Scottish traditional music summer school and opera project.

Publications list:
Available online and in print

Access to staff:
Contact by letter, by telephone, by fax, by e-mail and via website
Hours: Mon to Fri, 0900 to 1700

Access to building, collection or gallery:
Hours: Mon to Fri, 0900 to 1700

ABERDEENSHIRE COUNCIL

Woodhill House, Westburn Road, Aberdeen, AB16 5GB

Tel: 01467 620981
Fax: 01224 665444
E-mail: agcampbell@aberdeenshire.gov.uk
Website:
http://www.aberdeenshire.gov.uk

Enquiries:
Enquiries to: Public Relations Manager
Direct tel: 01224 664405
Direct fax: 01224 665204
Direct e-mail: bill.neish@aberdeenshire.gov.uk

Founded:
1996

Formed from:
Banff and Buchan District Council, Gordon District Council, Grampian Regional Council, Kincardineshire and Deeside District Council

Organisation type and purpose:
Local government body.

Subject coverage:
The Grampian region: social, economic, educational, business and commercial information, Aberdeenshire council, services and amenities.

Printed publications:
Grampian Regional Official Guide

Access to staff:
Contact by letter, by telephone and by fax
Hours: Mon to Fri, 0900 to 1700

Other addresses:
Aberdeenshire Council
Gordon House, Inverurie, AB51 3WE; tel: 01467 620981
Aberdeenshire Council
View Mount, Stonehaven, AB39 2DQ; tel: 01567 762001

Aberdeenshire Council
St Leonards, Sandyhill Road, Banff, AB45 1BH; tel: 01261 813200

ABERDEENSHIRE HERITAGE

Station Road, Mintlaw, Peterhead, Aberdeenshire, AB42 5EE

Tel: 01771 622807
Fax: 01771 623558
E-mail: heritage@aberdeenshire.gov.uk
Website:
http://www.aberdeenshire.gov.uk/ahc.htm
Details of the museums.

Enquiries:
Enquiries to: Curatorial Officer, Documentation and Conservation
Direct tel: 01771 622807
Direct fax: 01771 623558
Direct e-mail: david.bertie@aberdeenshire.gov.uk
Other contacts: Senior Museums & Heritage Officer

Founded:
1996

Formed by the amalgamation of:
North East of Scotland Agricultural Heritage Centre, North East of Scotland Museums Service (NESMS) (year of change 1996)

Organisation type and purpose:
Local government body, museum.

Subject coverage:
Northeast Scotland local history, geology, archaeology, natural history, fishing, shipping and whaling of northeast Scotland, Banff silver, numismatics, details of museums in the north east of Scotland.

Museum or gallery collection, archive, or library special collection:
Large photograph collection relating to the north east of Scotland
Peterhead Port Books
Some fishing boat records on microfilm

Printed publications:
Literary Families (Bertie D M, 50p)
Master and Pupil (Bertie D M, 50p)

Access to staff:
Contact by letter, by telephone, by fax and by e-mail. Appointment necessary.
Hours: Mon to Fri, 0900 to 1630

Branch museums:
Aberdeenshire Farming Museum
Aden Country Park, Mintlaw, Peterhead, AB42 5FQ
Arbuthnot Museum
St Peter Street, Peterhead, AB42 1LA; tel: 01771 622807
Banchory Museum
Bridge Street, Banchory, Kincardineshire, AB31 5SX; tel: 01771 622807
Banff Museum
High Street, Banff, Banffshire, AB45 1AE; tel: 01771 622807
Brander Museum
The Square, Huntly, Aberdeenshire, AB54 8AE; tel: 01771 622807
Carnegie Museum
The Square, Inverurie, Aberdeenshire, AB51 3SN; tel: 01771 622807
Fordyce Joiner's Workshop Visitor Centre
Church Street, Fordyce, Banffshire, AB45 2SL; tel: 01771 622807
Garlogie Mill Power House Museum
Garlogie, Skene, Aberdeenshire, AB32 6RX; tel: 01771 622807
Maud Railway Museum
Maud Railway Station, Maud, Aberdeenshire, AB42 5LY; tel: 01771 622807
Sandhaven Meal Mill
Sandhaven, Fraserburgh, Aberdeenshire, AB43 4EP; tel: 01771 622807
Tolbooth Museum
The Harbour, Stonehaven, Kincardineshire, AB39 2JU; tel: 01771 622807

continued overleaf

Parent body:
Aberdeenshire Council

ABERDEENSHIRE LIBRARY AND INFORMATION SERVICE

Acronym or abbreviation: ALIS

Meldrum Meg Way, Oldmeldrum, Inverurie, Aberdeenshire, AB51 0GN

Tel: 01651 872707
Fax: 01651 872142
E-mail: alis@aberdeenshire.gov.uk

Website:
http://www.aberdeenshire.gov.uk/libraries

Enquiries:
Enquiries to: Principal Librarian

Founded:
1996

Organisation type and purpose:
Public library.
Covers the District of Aberdeenshire.

Subject coverage:
Local history, community information, leisure, educational and cultural, open learning through links with colleges.

Museum or gallery collection, archive, or library special collection:
George MacDonald Collection (manuscripts and books)
Strichen Local History Collection (estate papers)

Library catalogue:
All or part available online

Printed publications:
What's at your library (information leaflet)
Welcome to your library (guide to services)
Family History Research Guide

Electronic and video publications:
Clubs Directory (online)

Access to staff:
Contact by letter, by telephone, by fax, by e-mail, in person and via website
Hours: Headquarters: Mon to Fri, 0900 to 1700; Sat, 0900 to 1630
Special comments: Opening hours in branches vary.

Constituent part of:
Education, Learning and Leisure Service of Aberdeenshire Council

ABERTAY HISTORICAL SOCIETY

c/o SUAT Ltd (Archaeological Contractors), 55 South Methven Street, Perth, PH1 5NX

Tel: 01738 622393
Fax: 01738 631626
E-mail: csmith@suat.co.uk

Website:
http://www.scan.org.uk/bookshop/abertay.htm
Bookshop.

Enquiries:
Enquiries to: Honorary Sales Secretary

Founded:
1947

Organisation type and purpose:
Membership association (membership is by subscription, present number of members: 150, voluntary organisation.

Subject coverage:
History of Dundee, Tayside and Fife.

Library catalogue:
All or part available online and in print

Printed publications:
Dundee's Literary Lives, vols 1 and 2, (Andrew Murray Scott, 2003, £7 each plus p&p)
Victorian Dundee at Worship (Ian McCraw, 2002, £7 plus p&p)

Patrons, Poverty & Profit – Organised Charity in Nineteenth-Century Dundee (Lorraine Walsh, 2000, £3 plus p&p)
The Demands of the People – Dundee Radicalism 1850–1870 (Michael St John, 1997, £2.50 plus p&p)
The Nine Trades of Dundee (Annette M. Smith, 1995, £6 plus p&p)
Making the Vote Count: The Arbroath Women Citizens' Association, 1931–1945 (Sarah F. Browne, 2007, £6.00 plus p&p)
A Noble and Potent Lady: Katherine Campbell, Countess of Crawford (Mary Verschuur, 2006, £7.50 plus p&p)
The Guildry of Dundee (Annette M. Smith, 2005, £7.50 plus p&p)
The Schoolmaster Engineer: Adam Anderson of Perth and St Andrews (Kenneth Cameron, 2006, £7.50 plus p&p)
One Artful and Ambitious Individual: Alexander Riddoch (1745–1822) (Enid Gauldie, 1989, £3.00 plus p&p)
Order printed publications from: The Sales Secretary e-mail: csmith@suat.co.uk

Publications list:
Available online and in print

Access to staff:
Contact by letter, by telephone, by fax and by e-mail
Hours: Mon to Fri, 0900 to 1700

ABERYSTWYTH LIBRARY

Corporation Street, Aberystwyth, Ceredigion, SY23 2BU

Tel: 01970 633703
Fax: 01970 625059
E-mail: llyfrgell.library@ceredigion.gov.uk

Website:
http://www.ceredigion.gov.uk/libraries

Enquiries:
Enquiries to: Librarian
Direct tel: 01970 633713
Direct e-mail: williamh@ceredigion.gov.uk

Organisation type and purpose:
Public library.

Subject coverage:
Welsh local history (Ceredigion); Welsh language publications; Welsh literature.

Museum or gallery collection, archive, or library special collection:
Local history

Library catalogue:
All or part available online and in-house

Access to staff:
Contact by letter, by telephone, by fax, by e-mail and in person
Hours: Mon to Fri, 0900 to 1700

Access to building, collection or gallery:
No access other than to staff

Also at:
Ceredigion County Council
Bibliographical Department

Branch libraries:
Aberaeron Library
County Hall, Aberaeron, Ceredigion, SA46 0AT; tel: 01545 570382; e-mail: aeronllb@ceredigion.gov.uk
Cardigan Library
Cardigan, Ceredigion, SA43 1JL; tel: 01239 612578; fax: 01239 612285; e-mail: teifillb@ceredigion.gov.uk
Lampeter Library
Market Street, Lampeter, Ceredigion, SA48 7DR; tel: 01570 423606; e-mail: pedrllb@ceredigion.gov.uk
Llandysul Library
Llandysul, Ceredigion, SA44 4QS; tel: 01559 362899; e-mail: tysulllb@ceredigion.gov.uk
New Quay Library
Church Street, New Quay, Ceredigion

Tregaron Library
Secondary School, Tregaron, Ceredigion, SY25 6HG; tel: 01974 298009; e-mail: caronllb@ceredigion.gov.uk

ABERYSTWYTH UNIVERSITY – HUGH OWEN LIBRARY

Penglais, Aberystwyth, Ceredigion, SY23 3DZ

Tel: 01970 622391
Fax: 01970 622404
E-mail: library@aber.ac.uk

Website:
http://www.voyager.aber.ac.uk
Library OPAC.
http://www.aber.ac.uk
Information about the University and library. Links to useful information services.

Enquiries:
Enquiries to: Director of Information Services

Founded:
1872

Formerly called:
University College of Wales, Aberystwyth (year of change 1994)

Organisation type and purpose:
University library.

Subject coverage:
Accounting and business studies, economics, applied plant biology; genetics and plant breeding; botany; zoology; physical geography including meteorology; biochemistry, biometry, biology, microbiology, cell and immune biology, physics, mathematics, computer science, business studies, theatre, film and television studies, sports science. English and American literature, European literature/languages (French, Spanish, Italian, German), classical studies, history, visual art, social sciences, education. Agriculture and agricultural botany and biochemistry, agricultural economics, law, Celtic studies; Welsh, Irish, Breton, Gaelic, Cornish and Manx; politics, international politics, library and information studies.

Museum or gallery collection, archive, or library special collection:
18th and 19th century Legal Texts (microfiche Inter Documentation Zug)
Archive of British Master Potters
British Official Publications and Statistical Collection
British Sessional Papers 1801–1930 (Readex microprint)
British Society of Rheology Collection
Canadian Official Publications. Selective Depository 1979-.
Celtic Collection
David De Lloyd papers (original compositions and material on Welsh folksongs)
Diplomatic documents
Duff Collection of pamphlets on classical studies
Early American Imprints from 1639 to 1800 (Readex Microprint)
English Legal Sources (microfiche Inter Documentation Zug)
Gregynog Press Collection
George Powell Collection
J C Hotten publications. (Victorian publisher 1856–1873)
J O Francis archive (prompt copies etc of his plays)
Learning materials for Welsh Language schools
Lily Newton papers on water pollution
Richard Ellis papers (relating to Edward Lhuyd)
Rudler Collection of 19th century geological pamphlets
T F Roberts MSS (UCW during his Principalship, 1891–1919)
Thomas Webster Letters (19th century British geologists)
Three Centuries of Drama: English section 1500–1800 (Readex Microprint) UN and League of Nations publications
David Davies Memorial Library (international politics)

Trade and statistical information:
Statistics Collection, official publications, European documentation, Celtic collection.

Non-library collection catalogue:
All or part available online and in-house

Library catalogue:
All or part available online

Printed publications:
Aberystwyth and District: a bibliography of the earth and environmental sciences, 1991
Bible in Welsh and the vernacular, 1988
Bibliographical Handlists
Books printed before 1701 in the Hugh Owen Library (1972, out of print)
Catalog Adnoddau Addysg (Catalogue of Educational Resources in Welsh) 1987
Catalogue of the Scott Blair Collection (British Society of Rheology), 1991
Electronic Information Resources, 1999
Exhibition Catalogues
Glossary of library terms, 1991
Print Collection of the University College of Wales/ Casgliad Printiau Coleg Prifysgol Cymru, 1984
Richard Ellis Papers: handbook and schedule (compiled by Brynley F Roberts, 1983)
The College Library 1872–1976 (T G Lloyd, 1977)
Information Services Guide 2006/2007

Access to staff:
Contact by letter and by telephone. Appointment necessary. Access for members only. Letter of introduction required.
Hours: Term time: Mon to Fri, 0900 to 2200; Sat, 1200 to 1800; Sun, 1200 to 1800
Vacations: Mon to Fri, 0900 to 1730
Special comments: No reference service on weekends.

Access for disabled people:
Hours: Term time: Mon to Fri, 0900 to 2200; Sat, 1200 to 1800; Sun, 1200 to 1800
Vacations: Mon to Fri, 0900 to 1730

Constituent institution of the:
University of Wales

ABERYSTWYTH UNIVERSITY – THOMAS PARRY LIBRARY

Llanbadarn Fawr, Aberystwyth, Ceredigion, SY23 3AS

Tel: 01970 622417
Fax: 01970 621868
E-mail: parrylib@aber.ac.uk

Website:
http://edina.ac.uk/landlifeleisure
Land, Life and Leisure – rural information database
http://www.irs.aber.ac.uk
Institute of Rural Sciences.

Enquiries:
Enquiries to: Site Librarian
Direct e-mail: eet@aber.ac.uk
Other contacts: Rural Studies Librarian for agricultural and rural studies enquiries.

Founded:
1996

Formerly called:
Welsh Institute of Rural Studies Library Aberystwyth; Information and Library Studies Library, University of Wales Aberystwyth (year of change 1991)

Subject coverage:
Librarianship; information science; Welsh librarianship; African librarianship; archives and records management; library buildings, planning; children's literature; physical and historical bibliography; publishing, printing and book trade. Agriculture as practised in the UK (animal production; crop production; farm management; farm mechanisation); forestry; organic husbandry; rural planning; countryside management and conservation; tourism; equine studies.

Museum or gallery collection, archive, or library special collection:
Appleton Collection (Victorian colour printing and publishers binding)
Bibliographical collection (private presses and fine printing)
Children's Collection including Horton Collection of early children's books and ephemera
Library literature (library annual reports and guides)
Press cuttings (librarianship and related subjects)
Simon Collection (Curwen Press and related material)
Welsh Studies Collection
Whittinghams Collection (Chiswick Press)
Agricultural and countryside grant information
Agricultural press notices
Countryside management press notices

Non-library collection catalogue:
All or part available in-house

Library catalogue:
All or part available online

Electronic and video publications:
Land Life and Leisure: farming and countryside index

Access to staff:
Contact by letter, by telephone, by fax and by e-mail. Appointment necessary.
Hours: Term time: Mon to Thu, 0900 to 2100; Fri, 0900 to 1930; Sat, 1200 to 1800
Vacations: Mon to Fri, 0900 to 1730

Access for disabled people:
Ramped entry

Parent body:
University of Wales Aberystwyth
Directorate of Information Services

ABILITYNET

PO Box 94, Warwick, CV34 5WS

Tel: 01926 312847/0800 269545
Fax: 01926 407425
E-mail: enquiries@abilitynet.org.uk

Website:
http://www.abilitynet.org.uk

Enquiries:
Enquiries to: Information Officer

Formerly called:
Foundation for Communication for the Disabled, The Computability Centre

Organisation type and purpose:
Registered charity (charity number 1067673), consultancy.
Providing information on making computers accessible for people with disabilities.

Subject coverage:
Computer access for people with disabilities

Printed publications:
Factsheets

Access to staff:
Contact by letter, by telephone, by fax, by e-mail, in person and via website
Hours: Mon to Fri, 0900 to 1700

ABINGDON AND WITNEY COLLEGE

Witney Campus, Library and Resource Centre, Holloway Road, Witney, Oxfordshire, OX28 6NE

Tel: 01993 208010
Fax: 01993 703006

Website:
http://www.oxfe.ac.uk/witney/home.htm
College prospectus, etc.

Enquiries:
Enquiries to: Librarian

Formerly called:
West Oxfordshire College Learning Resources Centre

Organisation type and purpose:
Suitable for ages: 16+.
College of further education.

Subject coverage:
General further education; stud and stable husbandry; racing industry.

Museum or gallery collection, archive, or library special collection:
Thoroughbred horse management

Non-library collection catalogue:
All or part available in-house

Library catalogue:
All or part available in-house

Access to staff:
Contact by letter, by telephone, by fax and in person
Hours: Mon to Thu, 0830 to 1900; Fri, 0830 to 1630
Special comments: Non-students reference only.

Access for disabled people:
Parking provided, ramped entry, toilet facilities

Member organisation of:
COLRIC
Open University Study Centre

ABORTION RIGHTS

The Print House, 18 Ashwin Street, London, E8 3DL

Tel: 020 7923 9792
Fax: 020 7923 4979
E-mail: choice@abortionrights.org.uk

Website:
http://www.gn.apc.org/nac/
http://www.abortionrights.org.uk/

Enquiries:
Enquiries to: Administrator

Founded:
2003

Created by the merger of:
the National Abortion Campaign (NAC) and the Abortion Law Reform Association (ALRA)

Organisation type and purpose:
National organisation, membership association (membership is by subscription), voluntary organisation.
Campaigning for equal access to safe, free abortion on request.

Subject coverage:
Abortion in the UK and worldwide; contraception; new reproductive technology; not counselling.

Printed publications:
Books, pamphlets (prices vary)
Abortion: Facts & Figures (Lloyd L, £2.50 plus p&p)
NAC Comic – It's My Choice – Jill, 16, gets pregnant – her story (50p plus p&p)
Voices for Choice: women recollect their experiences of abortion in Britain 1936–97 (£2.50 plus p&p)

Publications list:
Available in print

Access to staff:
Contact by letter, by telephone, by fax, by e-mail and via website. Appointment necessary.
Hours: Varies each week

Links with:
Co-ordinating Committee to Defend the 1967 Abortion Act (Co-ord)
Education for Choice
European Network for a Woman's Right to Abortion and Contraception (ENWRAC)
Pro-Choice Alliance (PCA)
Voice For Choice (VFC)
  tel: 020 7636 4619; fax: 020 7436 9011; e-mail: vfc@mailbox.co.uk

ABP – PORT OF IPSWICH

Old Custom House, Key Street, Ipswich, Suffolk, IP4 1BY

Tel: 01473 231010
Fax: 01473 230914
E-mail: Ipswich@ABPorts.co.uk

Website:
http://www.ABPorts.co.uk
Port facilities, etc.

Enquiries:
Enquiries to: Sales Manager
Direct fax: 01473 225364

Founded:
1997

Formerly called:
Port of Ipswich; Ipswich Port Authority (year of change 1997)

Organisation type and purpose:
Service industry.

Subject coverage:
Port facilities and operation; discharge and loading of containers, roll-on/roll-off, general cargo, bulk solid and bulk liquid vessels.

Printed publications:
Development Notes (History of the Port)
Port of Ipswich Handbook (annually)

Parent body:
Associated British Ports (ABP)

ABP MARINE ENVIRONMENTAL RESEARCH

Acronym or abbreviation: ABP Research

Suite B, Waterside House, Town Quay, Southampton, S014 2AQ

Tel: 023 80711 840
Fax: 023 80711 841
E-mail: enquiries@abpmer.co.uk

Website:
http://www.abpmer.co.uk
ABP Research – capability profile, current news items, project experience, case studies, recent reports and publications.

Enquiries:
Enquiries to: Technical Marketing Manager
Other contacts: Library and Information Services

Founded:
1950

Formerly called:
British Transport Docks Board (year of change 1983); ABP Research and Consultancy Limited (year of change 2002)

Organisation type and purpose:
Consultancy, research organisation.
Specialists in water environment consultancy.

Subject coverage:
Dock and harbour engineering; rivers, estuaries and coastal research; maritime hydraulics and structures; hydrographic surveying and dredging research; port operations and management.

Museum or gallery collection, archive, or library special collection:
Comprehensive library covering all aspects of water environment science and hydraulics research inclusive of over 400 reports and technical guidance notes

Printed publications:
Annual Report, brochures (free)
Technical Reports (for purchase subject to client permission)

Electronic and video publications:
Environmental Risk Assessment Package
Estuary Database – UK wide Directory/Information system describing a wide range of estuary features, resources etc

Access to staff:
Contact by telephone, by fax, by e-mail and via website
Hours: Mon to Fri, 0900 to 1700
Special comments: Library searches will be charged at commercial rates, available on application.

Parent body:
Associated British Ports Holdings plc
150 Holborn, London, EC1N 2LR; tel: 020 7430 1177; fax: 020 7430 1384

AC OWNERS' CLUB LIMITED

Acronym or abbreviation: ACOC

Thatch End, Godmanstone, Dorset, DT2 7AQ

Tel: 01300 342058
Fax: 01799 522513
E-mail: rish.morpeth@virgin.net

Website:
http://www.racecar.co.uk/acoc

Enquiries:
Enquiries to: Membership Secretary

Founded:
1949

Organisation type and purpose:
Membership association (membership is by subscription), present number of members: 700.

Subject coverage:
The AC motor car.

Museum or gallery collection, archive, or library special collection:
The Club Library contains: documents, publications, etc, concerning AC cars from the early years of the 20th century to date

Library catalogue:
All or part available in-house

Printed publications:
Magazine (monthly, by subscription only)
Registers 1910–2001 (£50)

Access to staff:
Contact by letter, by telephone and by e-mail
Hours: Mon to Sat, 0900 to 2000

ACADEMY OF ANCIENT MUSIC

Acronym or abbreviation: AAM

10 Brookside, Cambridge, CB2 1JE

Tel: 01223 301509
Fax: 01223 327377
E-mail: info@aam.co.uk

Website:
http://www.aam.co.uk
History, news, feature articles, concert listings and a complete discography of the orchestra's recordings.

Enquiries:
Enquiries to: Administrator

Organisation type and purpose:
Registered charity (charity number 1085485).
Period instrument orchestra.

Subject coverage:
Performance of classical and baroque music.

Electronic and video publications:
Extensive CD discography
Order electronic and video publications from: record shops

Access to staff:
Contact by e-mail
Hours: Mon to Fri, 0900 to 1800

ACADEMY OF EXECUTIVES AND ADMINISTRATORS

Acronym or abbreviation: AEA

Warwick Corner, 42 Warwick Road, Kenilworth, Warwickshire, CV8 1HE

Tel: 01926 855498
Fax: 01926 513100
E-mail: info@group-ims.com

Website:
http://www.group-ims.com

Founded:
2002

Organisation type and purpose:
Professional body (membership is by subscription, qualification), range of professional diploma courses available.

Printed publications:
The Academy of Executives and Administrators Journal

Access to staff:
Contact by letter, by telephone, by fax and by e-mail
Hours: Mon to Fri, 0900 to 1700

Links with:
Institute of Management Specialists
  at the same address
Institute of Manufacturing and Professional
Business and Technical Management
  at the same address
The Academy of Multi-Skills
  at the same address

ACADEMY OF EXPERTS

Acronym or abbreviation: TAE

3 Gray's Inn Square, Gray's Inn, London, WC1R 5AH

Tel: 020 7430 0333
Fax: 020 7430 0666
E-mail: admin@academy-experts.org

Website:
http://www.academy-experts.org

Enquiries:
Enquiries to: Secretary General

Founded:
1987

Organisation type and purpose:
Professional body (membership is by qualification), consultancy.

Subject coverage:
All matters pertaining to experts, especially in contentious matters. Accreditation of practising experts and qualified dispute resolvers. Matters involving alternative dispute resolution (ADR) including training, accreditation and appointments. Cost-efficient dispute resolution, provision of standards for experts, mediators and others.

Museum or gallery collection, archive, or library special collection:
Directory of Experts
Register of Qualified Dispute Resolvers

Printed publications:
The Model Form of Experts Report (£10)
Resolving Your Disputes by Mediation (£7)
The Expert (£60)
Order printed publications from: Website

Access to staff:
Contact by letter and by e-mail
Hours: Mon to Fri, 0900 to 1700

Access to building, collection or gallery:
Prior appointment required

ACADEMY OF MULTI-SKILLS

Acronym or abbreviation: AMS

Warwick Corner, 42 Warwick Road, Kenilworth, Warwickshire, CV8 1HE

Tel: 01926 855498
Fax: 01926 513100
E-mail: info@group-ims.com

Website:
http://www.group-ims.com

Enquiries:
Enquiries to: Administrator

Founded:
1995

Organisation type and purpose:
International organisation, professional body (membership is by qualification), training organisation, range of professional diploma courses available.
All groups and types of people who are multi-skilled. The multi-skilled should register with the academy.

Subject coverage:
The principal aim of the Academy is to bring together and help the people who have multi-skilled potential, those who wish to lift themselves to higher positions in life by perfecting and securing recognition for their skills. Most people possess more potential than they realise, are already multi-skilled, or have never had their hidden multi-skills recognised. The Academy can help to support and expand their careers.

Printed publications:
Journals from any of the international, professional bodies (£7 per copy to non members)
Journals issued to members

Access to staff:
Contact by letter, by telephone, by fax, by e-mail and via website
Hours: 24 hours by fax

Links with:
Professional Business and Technical Management (founded 1983) (PBTM)
    at the same address
The Academy of Executives & Administrators (founded 2002) (AEA)
    at the same address
The Institute of Management Specialists, The International Group (founded 1971) (IMS)
    at the same address
The Institute of Manufacturing (founded 1978) (Imanf)
    at the same address

ACAS

Formal name: Advisory, Conciliation and Arbitration Service

Brandon House, 180 Borough High Street, London, SE1 1LW

Tel: 020 7210 3613
Fax: 020 7210 3615
E-mail: library@acas.org.uk

Website:
http://www.acas.org.uk
Press releases, details of ACAS publications including full text of some publications. Local public enquiry telephone numbers.

Enquiries:
Enquiries to: Librarian
Direct tel: 020 7210 3917

Founded:
1974

Organisation type and purpose:
Statutory body.

Subject coverage:
Industrial relations, industrial arbitration and conciliation, trade unions, employee involvement, organisational behaviour, employment law, quality of working life, total quality management, stress, personnel management, management of change.

Printed publications:
Advisory booklets
Advisory Handbooks
Annual Reports
Ask ACAS leaflets
Codes of Practice
Advice Leaflets

Getting It Right – Guides for small firms
Self Help Guides
Research Papers
Order printed publications from: ACAS Publications PO Box 235, Hayes, Middlesex, UB3 1HF, tel: 0870 242 9090, fax: 020 8867 3225, e-mail: acas@eclogistics.co.uk

Publications list:
Available online and in print

Access to staff:
Contact via website. Appointment necessary.
Hours: Mon to Fri, 1000 to 1600

Has::
11 regional centres.

ACCOUNTS COMMISSION FOR SCOTLAND

110 George Street, Edinburgh, EH2 4LH

Tel: 0131 477 1234
Fax: 0131 477 4567

Website:
http://www.audit-scotland.gov.uk
Audit Scotland publications published on behalf of Accounts Commission and Auditor General.
http://www.accounts-commission.gov.uk
Commission's publications.

Enquiries:
Enquiries to: Corporate Service Department
Other contacts: Secretary; Audit Scotland Reception

Founded:
1975

Organisation type and purpose:
Statutory body.

Subject coverage:
The performance of Scottish Councils, and police and fire boards. Audit and value for money review in local government in Scotland.

Library catalogue:
All or part available online

Printed publications:
Annual Report and Accounts
A selection of publications relating to local government, most of which are available free of charge from the Accounts Commission (see website)
Order printed publications from: www.audit-scotland.gov.uk

Publications list:
Available online and in print

Access to staff:
Contact by letter, by telephone, by fax and by e-mail
Hours: Mon to Fri, 0900 to 1700

ACCRINGTON CENTRAL LIBRARY

St James' Street, Accrington, Lancashire, BB5 1NQ

Tel: 01254 872385
Fax: 01254 301066
E-mail: library@lcl.lancscc.gov.uk

Website:
http://www.lancashire.gov.uk/libraries
Includes library catalogue.

Enquiries:
Enquiries to: Reference Librarian
Direct tel: 01254 306905
Direct e-mail: accrington.reference@lcl.lancscc.gov.uk

Founded:
1908

Formerly called:
Hyndburn Central Library (year of change 1994)

Organisation type and purpose:
Public library.

Subject coverage:
Local history of the Hyndburn District of Lancashire, and the county of Lancashire; history of the Accrington Pals (11th Service Battalion, East Lancashire Regiment) in World War I and generally; World War I collection (includes war graves, memorial registers and official histories).

Museum or gallery collection, archive, or library special collection:
Commonwealth War Graves Commission Registers for World War I
Funder Finder computerised database, for groups in need, provides an index to trusts who can supply funding to voluntary organisations

Trade and statistical information:
Small area statistics for Hyndburn district of Lancashire. Census figures for Lancashire. General statistics, eg: Annual Abstract of statistics.

Non-library collection catalogue:
All or part available online

Library catalogue:
All or part available online

Printed publications:
Leaflets (irregular)

Access to staff:
Contact by letter, by telephone, by fax, by e-mail and in person
Hours: Mon and Tue, 0930 to 1930; Wed, 0930 to 1230; Thu and Fri, 0930 to 1700; Sat, 0930 to 1600

Part of:
Lancashire County Library & Information Service

ACE CREDIT UNION SERVICES

Acronym or abbreviation: NFCU

3rd Floor, 20 Great North Road, Newcastle upon Tyne, NE2 4PS

Tel: 0191 257 2219
Fax: 0191 259 1884

Enquiries:
Enquiries to: Chairman
Other contacts: National Co-ordinator

Founded:
1964

Formerly called:
National Federation of Credit Unions

Organisation type and purpose:
Advisory body.

Subject coverage:
Information, technical advice and training in the registering and operating of credit unions for communities, organisations and employees.

Printed publications:
Newsletter (4 times a year)
Leaflets available on request

Electronic and video publications:
Available on request

Publications list:
Available in print

Access to staff:
Contact by letter, by telephone and by fax.
Appointment necessary.
Hours: Mon to Fri, 0900 to 1700

ACE STUDY TOURS

Babraham, Cambridge, CB2 4AP

Tel: 01223 835055
Fax: 01223 837394
E-mail: ace@study-tours.org

Website:
http://www.study-tours.org

Enquiries:
Enquiries to: Secretary

continued overleaf

Founded:
1958

Formerly called:
Association for Cultural Exchange

Organisation type and purpose:
Service industry.
Tour operator for educational study tours and courses in England, Europe and worldwide.

Subject coverage:
International adult education.

Printed publications:
Annual brochure
Summer Newsletter
Winter/Spring brochure
Bulletins
Newsletter

Access to staff:
Contact by letter, by telephone, by fax and by e-mail
Hours: Mon to Fri, 0900 to 1700

ACEVO

Formal name: Association of Chief Executives of Voluntary Organisations

83 Victoria Street, London, SW1H 0HW

Tel: 0845 345 8481
Fax: 0845 345 8482
E-mail: info@acevo.org.uk

Website:
http://www.acevo.org.uk

Enquiries:
Enquiries to: Receptionist/Publications Officer
Other contacts: Head of Policy & Communications for press and policy.

Founded:
1987

Formerly called:
Association of Chief Executives of National Voluntary Organisations (ACENVO)

Organisation type and purpose:
Professional body, present number of members: c. 1,800, voluntary organisation, training organisation.
Networking organisation.

Subject coverage:
All matters relating to chief executives of voluntary organisations, training, education, legal advice, support, mentoring, twinning, fundraising, helpline.

Library catalogue:
All or part available online

Printed publications:
Basic Guides to Good Practice
Appraising the Chief Executive: A Guide
Chief Executive Remuneration Survey
Codes of Conduct for Chief Executives and Trustees
Model Contract for Chief Executives
Model Job Descriptions
Partners in Leadership: a New Style of Governance and Management for Professionally Managed Charities
Planning for Partnership: the Relationship between Chairs and Trustees

Publications list:
Available online and in print

Access to staff:
Contact by letter, by telephone, by fax, by e-mail and via website
Hours: Mon to Fri, 0900 to 1700

ACNE SUPPORT GROUP

Acronym or abbreviation: ASG

PO Box 9, Newquay, Cornwall, TR9 6WG

Tel: 0870 870 2263

Website:
http://www.stopspots.org
Loads of factual information on acne, Agony Aunt and Doctor contribute.

Enquiries:
Enquiries to: Chief Executive
Direct tel: 020 8841 8400

Founded:
1992

Organisation type and purpose:
Membership association (membership is by subscription), present number of members: 7000 (charity number 1026654).

Subject coverage:
Acne and Rosacea.

Printed publications:
Acne – The Facts
Face Forward (magazine, 3 times a year, membership fees apply)
Membership pack contains a selection of specially written information
Rosacea – The Facts

Publications list:
Available in print

Access to staff:
Contact by letter and by telephone
Hours: Mon to Fri, 0900 to 1630

ACPPLD

Formal name: Association of Chartered Physiotherapists for People with Learning Disabilities

Physiotherapy Department, SEHST, Lightwood House, Lightwood Lane, Sheffield, South Yorkshire, S8 8BG

Tel: 0114 271 6551
Fax: 01709 545570

Website:
http://www.acppld.org.uk
All about the association, membership, overview of service provision.

Enquiries:
Enquiries to: Honorary Chairperson
Direct e-mail: joan.green@tiscali.co.uk
Other contacts: Secretary

Founded:
Mid 1980s

Formerly called:
Association of Chartered Physiotherapists to Mental Handicap

Organisation type and purpose:
Professional body (membership is by subscription), present number of members: 250.

Subject coverage:
Physiotherapy for people with learning disabilities.

Museum or gallery collection, archive, or library special collection:
Rebound Standards
Standards and Audit of Standards Documents

Printed publications:
Reference List available
Newsletter (3 times a year)
Order printed publications from: Honorary Research Officer, ACPPLD
Physiotherapy Department, Royal Hants County Hospital, Romsey Road, Winchester, Hampshire, tel: 01962 824917

Access to staff:
Contact by letter, by telephone, by fax, by e-mail and via website. Appointment necessary.
Hours: Mon to Fri, 0900 to 1700

Clinical interest group within the:
Chartered Society of Physiotherapy

Other addresses:
ACPPLD
CIG Liaison Officer, Chartered Society of Physiotherapy, 14 Bedford Row, London; tel: 020 7306 6611

ACT

Formal name: Association for Children's Palliative Care

Orchard House, Orchard Lane, Bristol, BS1 5DT

Tel: 0845 108 2201 (helpline)
Fax: 0117 930 4707
E-mail: info@act.org.uk

Website:
http://www.act.org.uk

Enquiries:
Enquiries to: Information and Administration Officer

Founded:
1993

Subject coverage:
ACT (Association for Children's Palliative Care) aims to provide information on support services available for families whose children have life-threatening or terminal conditions, regardless of the particular disease involved. It is involved in consultation and contact between service providers and campaigns to encourage the development of children's palliative care services.

Trade and statistical information:
National information service on support services available for families with a child/children with life-limiting or life-threatening conditions.

Library catalogue:
All or part available online and in-house

Printed publications:
See website

Publications list:
Available online and in print

Access to staff:
Contact by letter, by telephone, by fax, by e-mail and via website. Appointment necessary.
Hours: Access to Families/Health Professionals: Mon to Fri, 0900 to 1700

Access to building, collection or gallery:
Prior appointment required

Access for disabled people:
Special comments: Situated on first floor, access by stairs

ACTION AGAINST ALLERGY

Acronym or abbreviation: AAA

PO Box 278, Twickenham, Middlesex, TW1 4QQ

Tel: 020 8892 2711/4949
Fax: 020 8892 4950
E-mail: aaa@actionagainstallergy.freeserve.co.uk

Website:
http://www.actionagainstallergy.co.uk

Enquiries:
Enquiries to: Executive Director
Direct e-mail: actionagainstallergy@btinternet.com

Founded:
1978

Organisation type and purpose:
Registered charity (charity number 276637), patient support organisation.
Provides information about allergic illness and related conditions to patients and professionals in the health care field.

Subject coverage:
Allergies, allergy-related illness.

Museum or gallery collection, archive, or library special collection:
Information leaflets list available on request with sae
Various papers on different aspects of allergic illness

Printed publications:
AAA Directory of Suppliers (£2.95, including postage within the UK)
Allergy Newsletter (3 times a year, £15 per annum UK, US$30, or Sterling equivalent, Overseas, free to members)
Information packs (£3 each)
Names and addresses of specialists (search fee of £5)
Various leaflets

Publications list:
Available online and in print

Access to staff:
Contact by letter, by telephone, by fax, by e-mail and via website
Hours: Mon to Fri, 0930 to 1700

ACTION ASTHMA

Allen & Hamburys Limited, Department G, Freepost DR83, Ashford, Kent, TN24 0YX

Tel: 020 8990 3011/2430

Subject coverage:
Asthma.

Access to staff:
Contact by letter
Hours: Mon to Fri, 0900 to 1700

Access to building, collection or gallery:
No access other than to staff

Access for disabled people:
Access to all public areas

Other address:
GlaxoSmithKline
Building 10, Stockley Park West, Uxbridge, UB11 1BT

ACTION CENTRE FOR EUROPE LIMITED

Acronym or abbreviation: ACE

29 Tufton Street, London, SW1P 3QL

Tel: 020 7976 7706
Fax: 020 7976 8331
E-mail: info@actioncentreeurope.org.uk

Website:
http://www.actioncentreeurope.org.uk

Enquiries:
Enquiries to: Chief Executive
Direct tel: 01257 276992
Direct fax: 01257 231254
Direct e-mail: mwelsh@UKIP.com.uk

Founded:
1995

Organisation type and purpose:
Membership association (membership is by subscription), present number of members: 225, research organisation, publishing house.
Policy studies network.

Subject coverage:
European policy studies.

Printed publications:
Printed material available free or for purchase directly
Order printed publications from: ACE
29 Tufton Street, London, SW1P 3QL, tel: 020 7976 7706, fax: 020 7976 8331

Publications list:
Available online and in print

Access to staff:
Contact by letter, by telephone, by fax and by e-mail

Hours: Mon to Fri, 0930 to 1500
Special comments: Part-time office opening.

Access to building, collection or gallery:
Prior appointment required

Other addresses:
Action Centre for Europe Limited
181 Town Lane, Whittle-le-Woods, Chorley, Lancashire, PR6 8HG; tel: 01257 276992; fax: 01257 231254

ACTION FOR BLIND PEOPLE

Information & Advice Centre, 14–16 Verney Road, London, SE16 3DZ

Tel: 020 7635 4800; National Freephone Helpline 0800 915 4666
Fax: 020 7635 4900
E-mail: info@actionforblindpeople.org.uk

Website:
http://www.actionforblindpeople.org.uk

Enquiries:
Enquiries to: Information Officer

Founded:
1857

Organisation type and purpose:
Voluntary organisation, registered charity (charity number 205913).
To provide services for visually impaired people.

Subject coverage:
Visual impairment: service provision, general awareness, aids and equipment, accommodation and residential care, leisure and holidays, education, employment and training, welfare rights and grants.

Library catalogue:
All or part available in-house

Printed publications:
Brochures or leaflets on most of the following subject headings: Information and Advice, Accommodation, Holidays, Employment, Leisure, Welfare Rights, Benefit Briefings

Electronic and video publications:
Most publications available on audio tape, or via email

Publications list:
Available online and in print

Access to staff:
Contact by letter, by telephone, by fax, by e-mail and via website. Appointment necessary.
Hours: Mon to Fri, 0900 to 1700

Access for disabled people:
Ramped entry, toilet facilities

ACTION FOR KIDS, CHARITABLE TRUST

Acronym or abbreviation: AFK

Ability House, 15A Tottenham Lane, Hornsey, London, N8 9DJ

Tel: 020 8347 8111\ Minicom no. 020 8347 3486
Fax: 020 8347 3482
E-mail: info@actionforkids.org

Website:
http://www.actionforkids.org
Remit and service provision of the charity, and news updates.

Enquiries:
Enquiries to: Information Officer

Founded:
1992

Organisation type and purpose:
Registered charity (charity number 1068841).
Provides grants for the provision of mobility aid, provider of work experience programmes for disabled young people, assists children and young people suffering physical and mental disability to lead full and independent lives.

Subject coverage:
The relief of physical and mental disability – through independence, created by provision of mobility aids supplied which are not available on the NHS and supported into work learning programmes, both in-house and outreach, for disabled young people. Equipment provided for those up to age 21. Work-related training for those up to age 26.

Printed publications:
Annual Review
Booklets (free)
Newsletter (3 times a year)

Electronic and video publications:
Videos

Access to staff:
Contact by letter, by telephone, by fax, by e-mail and via website. Appointment necessary.
Hours: Mon to Fri, 0900 to 1730

Access for disabled people:
Parking provided, access to all public areas
Special comments: Full disabled access and facilities.

ACTION FOR ME

Formal name: Action for Myalgic Encephalomyelitis
Acronym or abbreviation: AfME

Third Floor, Canningford House, 38 Victoria Street, Bristol, BS1 6BY

Tel: 0845 123 2314
Fax: 0117 9279552
E-mail: admin@afme.org.uk

Website:
http://www.afme.org.uk
Information on ME and the services provided by Action for ME.

Enquiries:
Enquiries to: Administrator
Direct e-mail: media@afme.org.uk

Founded:
1987

Formerly called:
ME Action

Organisation type and purpose:
National organisation, membership association (membership is by subscription), present number of members: 8000+, voluntary organisation, registered charity (charity number 1036419).
Over 150 local support groups.
Provides information and support to people with ME and campaigns to government and the medical profession for better understanding and treatment.

Subject coverage:
Information on myalgic encephalomyelitis (ME), chronic fatigue syndrome, and post-viral fatigue syndrome.

Library catalogue:
All or part available in-house and in print

Printed publications:
Please contact us for details.
Order printed publications from: AfME Information Service
PO Box 1302, Wells, Somerset, BA5 1YE

Publications list:
Available in print

Access to staff:
Contact by letter, by telephone, by fax and by e-mail
Hours: Mon to Fri, 9.30am – 5pm
Special comments: Please telephone initially

Access to building, collection or gallery:
No access other than to staff

Access for disabled people:
Special comments: Please telephone initially

continued overleaf

Also at:
Action for ME
73 Watling Street, London, EC4M 9BL; tel: 020 7329 2299; fax: 020 7329 3600; e-mail: london@afme.org.uk

ACTION FOR SOUTHERN AFRICA

Acronym or abbreviation: ACTSA

28 Penton Street, London, N1 9SA

Tel: 020 7833 3133
Fax: 020 7837 3001
E-mail: actsa@actsa.org

Website:
http://www.actsa.org

Enquiries:
Enquiries to: Office Manager

Founded:
1994

Formerly called:
Anti-Apartheid Movement

Organisation type and purpose:
Membership association (membership is by subscription), voluntary organisation. Lobbying support of Southern Africa, campaigning for peace, democracy and development in Southern Africa.

Subject coverage:
Peace, democracy and development in Southern Africa, South Africa, Lesotho, Swaziland, Botswana, Namibia, Angola, Zambia, Zimbabwe, Mozambique, Malawi, Tanzania, Mauritius, Democratic Republic of Congo, Seychelles.

Printed publications:
ACTSA News (quarterly)

Publications list:
Available online

Access to staff:
Contact by letter, by telephone, by fax, by e-mail and via website
Hours: Mon to Fri, 0930 to 1730

Access to building, collection or gallery:
Prior appointment required

ACTION ON ELDER ABUSE

Acronym or abbreviation: AEA

Astral House, 1268 London Road, London, SW16 4ER

Tel: 020 8765 7000
Fax: 020 8679 4074
E-mail: enquiries@elderabuse.org.uk

Website:
http://www.elderabuse.org.uk

Founded:
1993

Organisation type and purpose:
International organisation, membership association (membership is by subscription), present number of members: 550, voluntary organisation, registered charity (charity number 1048397).
To prevent the abuse of older people by raising awareness, encouraging education and research, and collecting and disseminating information.

Subject coverage:
The abuse of older people by someone in any relationship of trust at home or in care settings.

Non-library collection catalogue:
All or part available in-house

Library catalogue:
All or part available in-house

Printed publications:
Action on Elder Abuse
Briefing Pack
Elder abuse – what is it?

Publications list:
Available online and in print

Access to staff:
Contact by letter, by telephone, by fax, by e-mail and via website
Hours: Mon to Fri, 0900 to 1700

ACTION ON PRE-ECLAMPSIA

Formal name: Action on Pre-eclampsia
Acronym or abbreviation: APEC

84–88 Pinner Road, Harrow, Middlesex, HA1 4HZ

Tel: 020 8863 3271 (Administration)\ 020 8427 4217 (Helpline) Mon to Fri, 1000 to 1300
Fax: 020 8424 0653
E-mail: info@apec.org.uk

Website:
http://www.apec.org.uk

Enquiries:
Enquiries to: Chief Executive

Founded:
1991

Organisation type and purpose:
Membership association (membership is by subscription), present number of members: 1000, voluntary organisation, registered charity (charity number 1013557).
To prevent or ease suffering from pre-eclampsia by means of enhanced public awareness, increased professional knowledge and skill, and the provision of immediate and continuing support for affected families.

Subject coverage:
Pre-eclampsia.

Printed publications:
Information pack, available to order
Leaflet, send an sae

Publications list:
Available online

Access to staff:
Contact by letter, by telephone, by fax, by e-mail and via website. Non-members charged.
Hours: Mon to Fri, 0900 to 1700

ACTION ON SMOKING AND HEALTH

Acronym or abbreviation: ASH

First Floor, 144–145 Shoreditch High Street, London, E1 6JE

Tel: 020 7739 5902
Fax: 020 7613 0531
E-mail: enquiries@ash.org.uk

Website:
http://www.ash.org.uk

Enquiries:
Enquiries to: Research Manager

Founded:
1971

Organisation type and purpose:
National organisation, voluntary organisation, registered charity (charity number 262067).

Subject coverage:
Smoking and its effect on health, tobacco industry, tobacco control activities, statistics on tobacco and smoking, covering the UK and other countries.

Printed publications:
Publications include reports on Smoking & Health, Tobacco Industry, Tobacco Advertising, Tobacco Policy, Tobacco & Economics and Resource Guides
28 Factsheets
Regular Reports

Electronic and video publications:
All published items are on the website

Publications list:
Available online and in print

Access to staff:
Contact by letter, by telephone and via website
Hours: Mon to Fri, 0900 to 1700
Special comments: No public access to office.

Access to building, collection or gallery:
No access other than to staff

ACTION WITH COMMUNITIES IN RURAL KENT

15 Manor Road, Folkestone, Kent, CT20 2AH

Tel: 01303 850816
Fax: 01303 850244
E-mail: info@ruralkent.org.uk

Website:
http://www.ruralkent.org.uk

Enquiries:
Enquiries to: Director

Founded:
1923

Organisation type and purpose:
Membership association (membership is by subscription), present number of members: 400, registered charity (charity number 212796).

Subject coverage:
All rural issues.

Printed publications:
Oast to Coast (magazine)
Rural News (newsletter)

Publications list:
Available in print

Access to staff:
Contact by letter, by telephone, by fax and by e-mail
Hours: Mon to Fri, 0900 to 1700

Access to building, collection or gallery:
Prior appointment required

ACTIONAID SCHOOLS AND YOUTH

Acronym or abbreviation: AA

Chataway House, Leach Road, Chard, Somerset, TA20 1FR

Tel: 01460 238000
Fax: 01460 67191
E-mail: deved@actionaid.org.uk

Website:
http://www.actionaid.org
Education resource catalogue.

Enquiries:
Enquiries to: Schools Co-ordinator
Other contacts: Press Officer

Founded:
1972

Formerly called:
ActionAid Education

Organisation type and purpose:
International organisation, registered charity. Non-governmental organisation. Development education unit for the charity.

Subject coverage:
Development, geographical and environmental information for Key Stages 1 to 4 of the National Curriculum.

Non-library collection catalogue:
All or part available online, in-house and in print

Printed publications:
Education Catalogue

Electronic and video publications:
CD-ROMs of educational resources for Key Stages 1–4

Publications list:
Available online

Access to staff:
Contact by letter, by telephone, by fax, by e-mail, in person and via website. Appointment necessary.
Hours: Mon to Fri, 0900 to 1700

Access for disabled people:
Parking provided, toilet facilities

Parent body:
ActionAid UK
Hamlyn House, MacDonald Road, Archway, London, N19 5PG

Subsidiary body:
Azione Aiuto
Via Trincea delle Frasche 2, Milano, I-20136, Italy

ACUMEDIC CENTRE FOR CHINESE MEDICINE

1 Wyle Cop, Shrewsbury, Shropshire, SY1 1UT

Tel: 01743 236100
Fax: 01743 236100

Enquiries:
Enquiries to: Manager

Founded:
1989

Formerly called:
Acumedic Ltd

Organisation type and purpose:
Service industry.

Subject coverage:
Acupuncture and traditional Chinese herbal medicine.

Access to staff:
Contact by telephone
Hours: Mon to Fri, 0900 to 1700

Affiliated to:
Acumedic
17 Carlisle Road, Colindale, London, NW9 0HD

Parent body:
Acumedic Centre
101 Camden High Street, London, NW1 7JN; tel: 020 7388 6704; fax: 020 7387 5766; e-mail: infon@acumedic.com

ADAM SMITH COLLEGE

Library, St Brycedale Avenue, Kirkcaldy, Fife, KY1 1EX

Tel: 01592 223411
Fax: 01592 640225
E-mail: library@adamsmith.ac.uk

Website:
http://www.adamsmithcollege.ac.uk

Enquiries:
Enquiries to: Learner Resources Manager

Created by the merger of:
Fife College of Further and Higher Education, and Glenrothes College (year of change 2005)

Organisation type and purpose:
College of further and higher education

Subject coverage:
General

Non-library collection catalogue:
All or part available in-house

Library catalogue:
All or part available online

Access to staff:
Contact by telephone, by e-mail and in person
Hours: Mon to Thu, 0850 to 2100; Fri, 0850 to 1620; Sat, 0900 to 1200

ADAM SMITH LIBRARY

University of Glasgow, 40 Bute Gardens, Glasgow, G12 8RT

Tel: 0141 330 5648
E-mail: adamsmith@lib.gla.ac.uk

Enquiries:
Enquiries to: Adam Smith Librarian
Direct e-mail: k.ross@lib.gla.ac.uk

Founded:
1968

Organisation type and purpose:
University library.
Library of the Faculty of Law, Business & Social Sciences.

Subject coverage:
Anthropology, economics, politics, psychology, sociology, town and regional planning.

Non-library collection catalogue:
All or part available online and in-house

Library catalogue:
All or part available online and in-house

Access to staff:
Contact by letter, by telephone and by e-mail. Appointment necessary.
Hours: Term time: Mon to Thu, 0900 to 2100; Fri, 0900 to 1700
Vacations: Mon to Fri, 0900 to 1700

Access for disabled people:
Parking provided, ramped entry

ADAMSON PUBLISHING

8 The Moorings, Norwich, NR3 3AX

Tel: 01603 623336
Fax: 01603 624767
E-mail: sales@adamsonbooks.com

Website:
http://www.adamsonbooks.com

Enquiries:
Enquiries to: Managing Director

Founded:
1984

Organisation type and purpose:
Publishing house.

Subject coverage:
Information for school governors and teaching assistants.

Non-library collection catalogue:
All or part available online and in print

Printed publications:
TheToolkit for Effective Governance (3rd edn, 2004)
The School Governors' Yearbook (annually)
Parent Governors (2006)
Staff Governors (2006)
Community Governors (2006)
Foundation Governors (2006)
Local Authority Governors (2006)
Inspection and School Self-Evaluation (2005)
Being Strategic (2005)
Monitoring and Evaluation (2004)
Exclusions (2005)
Recruitment and Selection (2005)
Policies (3rd edn, 2008)
Teaching Assistants: The Complete Handbook (2004)
Joined-up Governance (2002)
Start Here (rev. edn 2006)
Accountability (2007)
Performance Management Revisited (2007)
The Green School (2008)
Headteachers and Governing Bodies (2007)
Order printed publications from: Marston Book Services

Publications list:
Available online

ADAS UK LIMITED

Acronym or abbreviation: ADAS

Woodthorne Wergs Road, Wolverhampton, West Midlands, WV6 8TQ

Tel: 01902 754190
Fax: 01902 743602
E-mail: mark.talbot@adas.co.uk

Website:
http://www.globalfarmers.com
E-commerce agricultural trading exchange.
http://www.adas.co.uk
Information about ADAS.
http://www.rbnet.co.uk
RBN (Rural Business network) joint venture between ADAS, CLA and the NFU.

Enquiries:
Enquiries to: Facilities
Direct tel: 01902 693483
Direct fax: 01902 693438
Direct e-mail: Mark.Talbot@adas.co.uk

Founded:
1997

Formerly called:
ADAS Executive Agency from 1992 to 1997; MAFF (year of change 1992)

Organisation type and purpose:
Architectural and environmental consultancy.

Subject coverage:
Land-based industries, agricultural and environment-related subjects, food.

Printed publications:
ADAS Research (annually, free)
Insight (4 times a year, free)

Access to staff:
Contact by letter, by telephone, by fax and by e-mail. Appointment necessary. All charged.
Hours: Mon to Fri, 0830 to 1700

Access to building, collection or gallery:
Hours: Mon to Fri, 0830 to 1700 (by invitation only)

Access for disabled people:
Mon to Fri, 0830 to 1700
Hours: Phone before visit

ADDACTION

67–69 Cowcross Street, London, EC1M 6PU

Tel: 020 7251 5860
Fax: 020 7251 5890
E-mail: info@addaction.org.uk

Website:
http://www.addaction.org.uk
Information including: press releases, news clippings, fundraising news and donor forms, information about Addaction, research reports.

Enquiries:
Enquiries to: Administrator
Other contacts: Press Office for media enquiries.

Founded:
1967

Formerly called:
Association for Prevention of Addiction (APA) (year of change 1997)

Organisation type and purpose:
Registered charity (charity number 1001957). Addaction provides drug and alcohol treatment services at over 70 projects throughout the country. To solve drug and alcohol problems and to campaign for innovative approaches to solving drug and alcohol problems.

Subject coverage:
Drug and alcohol addiction and misuse.

continued overleaf

Non-library collection catalogue:
All or part available online

Printed publications:
Annual Report (£2)
Information booklets: including, Parents' Guide to
Drugs

Publications list:
Available online

Access to staff:
Contact by letter, by telephone, by fax and by e-mail
Hours: Mon to Fri, 0900 to 1700

Founder member of:
Alcohol Concern
SCODA

ADFAM

Formal name: National Charity for Families and
Friends of Drug Users

25 Corsham Street, London, N1 6DR

Tel: 020 7553 7640
Fax: 020 7253 7991
E-mail: admin@adfam.org.uk

Website:
http://www.adfam.org.uk
Information and list of resources for families and
drug users, database and services for families.

Enquiries:
Enquiries to: Chief Executive

Founded:
1984

Organisation type and purpose:
Voluntary organisation, registered charity (charity
number 1067428), training organisation.
A national organisation working with families
affected by drugs and alcohol and a leading
agency in substance-related family work; provides
a range of publications and resources for families
about substances and criminal justice and operates
an online message board and searchable database
of local support groups that helps families hear
about and talk to people who understand their
situation; runs a range of training programmes on
substances and family support; also operates direct
support services at London prisons for families of
prisoners with drug problems.

Subject coverage:
Families and drug use, family dynamics, effects of
drug use on the family, training in family support
skills, setting up family support groups, drug
education for parents, help for families of drug-using prisoners.

Printed publications:
Prison Drugs and You – For the families and
friends of prisoners using drugs
Are you worried about your Mum, Dad or Carer
using Drugs or Alcohol (for children)
Living with a Drug User – A booklet for parents of
drug users
Living with a Drug User – A booklet for partners
of drug users
A Guide to Setting Up a Family / Friend Support
Group
Families in Focus – England
Journeys (leaflets)
Selection of Criminal Justice Posters

Electronic and video publications:
Reality Bites (Video, DVD, £5 plus p&p)
Putting It into Words – Family Support (Video, £5
plus p&p)

Publications list:
Available online and in print

Access to staff:
Contact by letter, by telephone, by fax and by e-mail
Hours: Mon to Fri, 0900 to 1700
Special comments: Donations welcomed for
provision of information.

Board member of:
Drugscope
National Council for Voluntary Organizations

ADHESIVE TAPE MANUFACTURERS ASSOCIATION

Acronym or abbreviation: ATMA

Sussex House, 8–10 Homesdale Road, Bromley,
Kent, BR2 9LZ

Tel: 020 8464 0131
Fax: 020 8464 6018
E-mail: tradeassn@craneandpartners.com

Enquiries:
Enquiries to: Secretary

Organisation type and purpose:
Trade association.

Subject coverage:
Pressure-sensitive tapes, technical aspects and
applications of adhesive tapes.

Publications list:
Available in print

Affiliated to:
European association (AFERA)

ADOPTION UK

46 The Green, South Bar Street, Banbury,
Oxfordshire, OX16 9AB

Tel: 01295 752240
Fax: 01295 752241
E-mail: admin@adoptionuk.org.uk

Website:
http://www.adoptionuk.org
Information about Adoption UK and includes
printable membership form.

Enquiries:
Enquiries to: Helpline Adviser

Founded:
1970–71

Formerly called:
Parent to Parent Information on Adoption Services
(PPIAS) (year of change 1999)

Organisation type and purpose:
Membership organisation for prospective adopters
and adoptive parents, present number of members:
over 4500, registered charity (charity number
326654).
Membership subscription £20-£40 per annum.To
provide information, advice, support, and training.

Subject coverage:
Adoption for children (permanent family
placement), especially for those who are racially
mixed, who have a physical or mental disability or
who are older than the usual age for adoption;
support and information service for prospective
and existing adoptive families.

**Museum or gallery collection, archive, or library
special collection:**
Adoptive families willing to speak to members
about any given experience (adoption)

Non-library collection catalogue:
All or part available in-house

Library catalogue:
All or part available in print

Printed publications:
Adoption Today (6 times a year)
Children Who Wait (monthly)
Oh, Brother (£5)
Adoption Law for Adopters (£10)

Electronic and video publications:
Attachment in Adopted and Foster Children
(Hughes D, tape)
Annual General Meeting 2001 (Hughes D, tape)

Publications list:
Available online and in print

Access to staff:
Contact by letter, by telephone, by fax, by e-mail,
in person and via website. Appointment necessary.
Access for members only.
Hours: Mon to Fri, 0900 to 1700 office; Mon to Fri,
1000 to 1600 helpline
Special comments: Helpline Telephone is answered
in person during office hours and by answerphone
at all other times.

Access for disabled people:
Access to all public areas, toilet facilities

Links with:
all adoption agencies and local authorities in the
UK

ADULT RESIDENTIAL COLLEGES ASSOCIATION

Acronym or abbreviation: ARCA

6 Bath Road, Felixstowe, Suffolk, IP11 7JW

Tel: 01394 278161
Fax: 01394 271083
E-mail: arcasec@aol.com

Website:
http://www.arca.uk.net
Information on ARCA colleges and courses

Enquiries:
Enquiries to: Honorary Secretary

Founded:
1983

Organisation type and purpose:
Membership association (membership is by
subscription, qualification), present number of
members: 30 institutions, voluntary organisation,
suitable for ages: adults.
To promote residential short-term liberal adult
education for the benefit of the general public.

Subject coverage:
First stop call to member colleges for public
enquiries.

Access to staff:
Contact by letter, by telephone, by fax and by e-mail
Hours: Mon to Fri, 0900 to 1700

ADVERTISING ASSOCIATION

Acronym or abbreviation: AA

7th Floor North, Artillery House, 11–19 Artillery
Row, London, SW1P 1RT

Tel: 020 7340 1100
Fax: 020 7222 1504
E-mail: aa@adassoc.org.uk

Website:
http://www.adassoc.org.uk/inform/content.html
Student briefings, links to list, position papers,
publications list, press releases, information sheets,
reading lists, 'Getting into advertising: a careers
guide'.

Founded:
1926

Organisation type and purpose:
The Advertising Association is a federation of
trade bodies and organisations representing the
advertising and promotional marketing industries,
including advertisers, agencies, the media and
support services in the UK.

Subject coverage:
Advertising, marketing, public relations,
communications, sales promotion, the media.

Library catalogue:
All or part available in-house

Printed publications:
Books
Research monographs and statistical publications
See website for full list

Electronic and video publications:
Getting Into Advertising: Careers Booklet (website)
Student Briefings on advertising (website)

Publications list:
Available online and in print

Access to staff:
Contact by letter, by telephone, by e-mail and via website. Appointment necessary.
Special comments: See AA website for details.

Members:
Cinema Advertising Association (CAA)
Communication Advertising and Marketing Education Foundation (CAM)
Data Publishers Association (DPA)
Direct Marketing Association (UK) Limited (DMA)
Direct Selling Association (DSA)
Incorporated Society of British Advertisers (ISBA)
Institute of Practitioners in Advertising (IPA)
Institute of Sales Promotion (ISP)
Interactive Advertising Bureau (UK) (IAB)
Internet Advertising Association – UK Chapter (IAA UK Chapter)
ITV plc (ITV)
Mail Order Traders' Association (MOTA)
Market Research Society (MRS)
Marketing Communication Consultants Association
Newspaper Publishers Association Limited (NPA)
Newspaper Society (NS)
Outdoor Advertising Association of Great Britain Limited (OAA)
Periodical Publishers Association (PPA)
Point of Purchase Advertising International (POPAI)
Radio Centre
Royal Mail (RM)
Satellite and Cable Broadcasters' Group (SCBG)
Scottish Newspaper Publishers Association (SNPA)

ADVERTISING STANDARDS AUTHORITY

Acronym or abbreviation: ASA

Mid City Place, 71 High Holborn, London, WC1V 6QT

Tel: 020 7492 2222
Fax: 020 7242 3696
E-mail: enquiries@asa.org.uk

Website:
http://www.asa.org.uk
Advertising standards codes plus information about the role and remit of the Authority.

Enquiries:
Enquiries to: Enquiries Team

Founded:
1962

Organisation type and purpose:
Advisory body, professional body, trade association.
Regulates UK advertising.

Subject coverage:
Pre-publication advice on interpretation of the advertising codes available for advertisers, agencies and the media.

Museum or gallery collection, archive, or library special collection:
Various research and briefing notes

Trade and statistical information:
Data on the number and nature of complaints about advertising.

Printed publications:
Guide to the Advertising Standards Authority
Annual Report
Background Briefings
Advertising Codes
Complaints Procedure

Access to staff:
Contact by letter, by telephone, by fax, by e-mail and via website

Hours: Mon to Fri, 0900 to 1730

Access to building, collection or gallery:
No access other than to staff

Access for disabled people:
Ramped entry

Links with:
Committee of Advertising Practice
Mid City Place, 71 High Holborn, London, WC1V 6QT; tel: 020 7492 2222; fax: 020 7242 3696; e-mail: enquiries@cap.org.uk; website: www.cap.org.uk
European Advertising Standards Alliance
website: www.easa-alliance.org

ADVICE SERVICE CAPABILITY SCOTLAND

11 Ellersly Road, Edinburgh, EH12 6HY

Tel: 0131 313 5510
Fax: 0131 346 1681
E-mail: ascs@capability-scotland.org.uk

Website:
http://www.capability-scotland.org.uk

Enquiries:
Enquiries to: Advice Worker

Founded:
1946

Organisation type and purpose:
A national disability information and advice service, specialising in information on cerebral palsy.

Subject coverage:
Information on a range of disability issues including cerebral palsy.

Museum or gallery collection, archive, or library special collection:
A wide range of books, videos, audio-cassettes and journals about cerebral palsy and other disabilities, which can be borrowed.

Library catalogue:
All or part available online

Publications list:
Available online and in print

Access to staff:
Contact by letter, by telephone, by fax, by e-mail and in person
Hours: Mon to Fri, 0900 to 1700

Access for disabled people:
Parking provided, ramped entry, toilet facilities

ADVISORY CENTRE FOR EDUCATION

Acronym or abbreviation: ACE

1c Aberdeen Studios, 22 Highbury Grove, London, N5 2DQ

Tel: 020 7354 8318 (Business line only)
Fax: 020 7354 9069
E-mail: enquiries@ace.dialnet.com

Website:
http://www.ace-ed.org.uk/pdf/publications.pdf
Publications list.
http://www.ace-ed.org.uk/advice.html
Advice pages including downloadable booklets on bullying, SEN, exclusion, school admissions, choosing a school and taking matters further.
http://www.ace-ed.org.uk
Home page.

Enquiries:
Enquiries to: Information Officer
Direct tel: 020 7354 8318

Founded:
1960

Organisation type and purpose:
National organisation (membership is by subscription), voluntary organisation, registered charity (charity number 313142), publishing house. Advises on parents' rights in education. Independent national education advice service for parents.

Subject coverage:
Education in the statutory school years 5 to 16, guidance for parents, special education, exclusion from school, education law, governors' duties, choosing a school. Advice available for England and Wales only.

Museum or gallery collection, archive, or library special collection:
Education 5–16 books, pamphlets, cuttings

Non-library collection catalogue:
All or part available in-house

Printed publications:
ACE Bulletin (6 times a year, free to members)
Stop Press (monthly)
A range of books and information leaflets for parents, teachers and governors including:
Governors' briefings (6 titles)
Governors' Handbook (5th ed., 2001)
Home Education Pack
Index to the School Standards and Framework Act (1999)
Outside, Looking In: children's and families' experiences of exclusion (The Children's Society, 2001)
School Governors: a plain guide for people like you (Sallis J, 1999)
Special Educational Handbook – The law on children with special needs (Updated 2002)
The Special Educational Needs and Disability Discrimination Act 2001
Order printed publications from: e-mail: enquiries@ace.dialnet.com

Publications list:
Available online and in print

Access to staff:
Contact by telephone. Appointment necessary.
Hours: Free telephone advice line, Mon to Fri, 1400–1700: tel 0808 800 5793
Special comments: Advice is given by telephone only. Internet Web pages also provide downloadable information.

Access to building, collection or gallery:
No access other than to staff

ADVISORY COMMITTEE ON PROTECTION OF THE SEA

Acronym or abbreviation: ACOPS

11 Dartmouth Street, London, SW1H 9BN

Tel: 020 7799 3033
Fax: 020 7799 2933
E-mail: acopsorg@netcomuk.co.uk

Website:
http://www.acops.org

Enquiries:
Enquiries to: Programme Officer

Founded:
1952

Organisation type and purpose:
Advisory body, registered charity.
Non-Governmental Organisation.

Subject coverage:
Protection of the marine environment.

Printed publications:
ACOPS Brochure
Annual Oil Pollution Survey around the coasts of the UK
Newsletters
Reports of Conferences
Yearbook (every 2 years)

continued overleaf

Access to staff:
Contact by letter, by telephone, by fax and by e-mail
Hours: Mon to Fri, 0900 to 1700

ADVISORY SERVICE FOR SQUATTERS

Acronym or abbreviation: ASS

Angel Alley, 84b Whitechapel High St, London, E1 7QX

Tel: 020 3216 0099
Fax: 020 3216 0098
E-mail: advice@squat.freeserve.co.uk

Website:
http://www.squatter.org.uk

Enquiries:
Enquiries to: Information Officer

Founded:
1975

Organisation type and purpose:
Advisory body, voluntary organisation.

Subject coverage:
Squatting history, housing struggles, surveys of squatters and their lifestyles (1970), law relating to squatting, practical and legal advice to squatters and homeless persons.

Museum or gallery collection, archive, or library special collection:
Books, photographs, some files on family squatting associations
Documents, relating to squatting in Europe, mainly Holland, France and Germany
Late 1970s bibliography of articles on squatting

Trade and statistical information:
Files on squatting in Europe and the world.

Printed publications:
Squatters Handbook (12th ed., £1.50 plus 50p postage)

Access to staff:
Contact by letter, by telephone, by fax, by e-mail, in person and via website
Hours: Mon to Fri, 1400 to 1800

Connections with:
COHRE
Hauikstraat 38 bis, Utrecht, 3514 TR, The Netherlands
Droit au Logement
3 bis rue de Vaucouleurs, Paris, F-75011, France

ADVOCACY RESOURCE EXCHANGE

Acronym or abbreviation: ARX

Unit 3, 60 Duke Street, Liverpool, L1 5AA

Tel: 0151 734 3047
E-mail: chris@advocacyresource.net

Website:
http://www.leevalley.co.uk/cait
Information on CAIT and citizen advocacy.
http://www.citizenadvocacy.org.uk

Enquiries:
Enquiries to: Information Officer

Founded:
1988

Formerly called:
Citizen Advocacy Information & Training (CAIT); Advocacy Alliance; National Citizen Advocacy (year of change 1994)

Organisation type and purpose:
Voluntary organisation, registered charity (charity number 1035082), training organisation.
CAIT supports the development of local citizen advocacy schemes, through the provision of information, training and networking.
The support of people disadvantaged through age, mental or physical health, or learning difficulties.

Subject coverage:
Citizen advocacy.

Museum or gallery collection, archive, or library special collection:
Collection of policies, publicity material and training programmes used by local citizen advocacy schemes
Small library of books and articles on citizen advocacy

Printed publications:
CAIT Newsletter (quarterly)
CAPE: Standards for Citizen Advocacy Program Evaluation (1979, £11.50)
Citizen Advocacy – A Powerful Partnership (1998, £15.40)
List of Citizen Advocacy and Related Advocacy Groups (£3)
Standing By Me – a collection of stories of citizen advocacy partnerships (1998, £8)

Publications list:
Available online and in print

Access to staff:
Contact by letter, by telephone, by fax and via website. Appointment necessary.
Hours: Mon to Fri, 0900 to 1700

Access to building, collection or gallery:
No prior appointment required

Access for disabled people:
Parking provided, access to all public areas, toilet facilities

Funded by:
London Boroughs Grants Committee

Has:
some 200 schemes in the UK

ADVOCATES FOR ANIMALS

10 Queensferry Street, Edinburgh, EH2 4PG

Tel: 0131 225 6039
Fax: 0131 220 6377
E-mail: info@advocatesforanimals.org

Website:
http://www.advocatesforanimals.com

Enquiries:
Enquiries to: Campaign Officer

Founded:
1912

Formerly called:
Scottish Society for the Prevention of Vivisection (year of change 1990)

Organisation type and purpose:
International organisation, voluntary organisation.
Campaigning pressure group.
The protection of animals from cruelty, the prevention of the infliction of suffering and the abolition of vivisection.

Subject coverage:
Use of living animals for research, development of alternatives, humane methods of research, other fields of animal exploitation and cruelty, and protection/welfare of animals so exploited.

Information services:
Office Assistant

Museum or gallery collection, archive, or library special collection:
Photographic archive
Video loan library

Trade and statistical information:
Data on the use and abuse of animals in the United Kingdom and abroad.

Printed publications:
Campaign Update (three times a year)

Access to staff:
Contact by letter, by telephone, by fax, by e-mail and via website. Appointment necessary.
Hours: Mon to Fri, 0900 to 1700

Links with:
Animal Aid (AAG)
The Old Chapel, Bradford Street, Tonbridge, Kent, TN9 1AW; tel: 01732 364546; fax: 01732 366533

Sister organisation:
St Andrew Animal Fund
10 Queensferry Street, Edinburgh, EH2 4PG; tel: 0131 225 2116; fax: 0131 220 6377

ADVOCATES LIBRARY

Faculty of Advocates, Parliament House, Edinburgh, EH1 1RF

Tel: 0131 260 5683
Fax: 0131 260 5663
E-mail: inqdesk@advocates.org.uk

Website:
http://www.advocates.org.uk/library/index.html

Enquiries:
Enquiries to: Reader Services Librarian

Founded:
1689

Organisation type and purpose:
Professional body (membership is by qualification), present number of members: 460.
The Advocates Library is a private library servicing members of the Scottish bar.
Legal deposit law materials for Scotland.

Subject coverage:
Law, jurisprudence, Roman law and civil law.

Museum or gallery collection, archive, or library special collection:
Materials from other common law and Commonwealth jurisdictions, Roman, Canon and Civil Law
Roman-Dutch collection
Session Papers (printed pleadings)

Non-library collection catalogue:
All or part available online

Library catalogue:
All or part available online

Access to staff:
Contact by letter, by telephone, by fax, by e-mail and via website. Access for members only.
Hours: Mon to Fri, 0900 to 1700
Special comments: Private library, stock made available to public via NLS

Access to building, collection or gallery:
Prior appointment required

AEA TECHNOLOGY ENVIRONMENT

Culham, Abingdon, Oxfordshire, OX14 3ED

Tel: 0870 190 1900
Fax: 0870 190 6318
E-mail: environment.help1@aeat.co.uk

Website:
http://www.aeat-env.com

Enquiries:
Enquiries to: Information Officer

Founded:
April 1994

Formerly called:
National Environmental Technology Centre; Environmental Safety Centre, Warren Spring Laboratory (year of change 1994)

Organisation type and purpose:
Environmental consultancy.

Subject coverage:
Air pollution, marine pollution, industrial effluent, waste management, recycling, cleaner technology, contaminated land, biotechnology, project hubs, future energy solutions, environmental and risk consultancy, chemical emergency response, environmental policy and climate change.

Publications list:
Available online and in print

Access to staff:
Contact by letter, by telephone, by fax, by e-mail and via website
Hours: Mon to Fri, 0900 to 1700

Registered office:
AEA Technology plc
329 Harwell, Didcot, Oxfordshire, OX11 0QJ

AERO INDEX LIMITED

39 Waylands Mead, The Knoll, Beckenham, Kent, BR3 5XT

Tel: 020 8650 3973

Website:
http://www.aeroindex.com

Enquiries:
Enquiries to: Managing Director
Direct e-mail: jr@aeroindex.freeserve.co.uk

Founded:
1993

Organisation type and purpose:
Publishing house.

Subject coverage:
World aerospace industry.

Printed publications:
Aero Index (3 vols, 2002)

Access to staff:
Contact by fax
Hours: Mon to Fri, 0900 to 1700

AEROPLANE COLLECTION LIMITED

Acronym or abbreviation: TAC

7 Mayfield Avenue, Stretford, Manchester, M32 9HL

Tel: 0161 866 8255

Enquiries:
Enquiries to: Chairman
Direct e-mail: mayfieldsparkes@aol.com

Founded:
1962

Formerly called:
Northern Aircraft Preservation Society

Organisation type and purpose:
Registered charity.
Preservation of aviation related artefacts.

Subject coverage:
Aircraft and aero engine preservation, historical aviation research.

Museum or gallery collection, archive, or library special collection:
Very detailed collections of books, pictures, photographs and some drawings, all relating to aviation

Access to staff:
Contact by letter, by e-mail and in person
Hours: Mon to Fri, 1730 to 2200

AETHELFLAED

1 Auckland Road, London, SW11 1EW

Tel: 020 7924 5868

Enquiries:
Enquiries to: Honorary Treasurer

Founded:
1999

Organisation type and purpose:
Learned society (membership is by subscription), present number of members: 23, voluntary organisation, research organisation.

To encourage research and awareness concerning Aethelflaed, Lady of the Mercians, daughter of Alfred The Great.

Subject coverage:
Anglo-Saxon England, Aethelflaed, Lady of the Mercians, Old English, Alfred The Great.

Printed publications:
Newsletter (members only)
Bibliography (members only)

Access to staff:
Contact by letter
Hours: Mon to Fri, 0900 to 1700

AETHERIUS SOCIETY

Formal name: The Aetherius Society

757 Fulham Road, London, SW6 5UU

Tel: 020 7736 4187 or 7731 1094
Fax: 020 7731 1067
E-mail: info@aetherius.co.uk

Website:
http://www.aetherius.org

Enquiries:
Enquiries to: Executive Secretary
Other contacts: Media Relations Officer

Founded:
1955

Organisation type and purpose:
International organisation, membership association, voluntary organisation, training organisation, publishing house.
Religious and educational organisation.
Service to humanity.

Subject coverage:
UFOs, cosmic contacts and life on other planets, aspects of metaphysics, new age thought, use of prayer, spiritual healing, self-development, psychic development and yoga.

Education services:
Workshops and lectures.

Printed publications:
Wide range of literature including:
Contact With a Lord of Karma (£9.99)
Operation Space Power (£9.99)
The Nine Freedoms (£14.99)
Visit to the Logos of Earth (£9.99)
The Twelve Blessings (£12.99)
Contacts with the Gods from Space (£9.99)
Realise Your Inner Potential (£9.99)
Order printed publications from: Postal address

Electronic and video publications:
Unique CD library of lectures by George King, DSc, PhD (individual CDs for sale)
DVDs
Order electronic and video publications from: Postal address

Publications list:
Available online and in print

Access to staff:
Contact by letter, by telephone, by fax, by e-mail, in person and via website. Appointment necessary.
Hours: Mon to Fri, 0900 to 2100; weekends, variable hours

Also at:
The Inner Potential Centre
36 Kelvedon Road, London, SW6 5BW; tel: 020 7736 4187; e-mail: info@innerpotential.org

Has:
13 other member groups in England

Northern Centre is:
The Aetherius Society
Northern UK Branch, 350 Sheffield Road, Birdwell, Barnsley, South Yorkshire, S70 5TU; tel: 01226 744659

AFASIC

1st Floor, 20 Bowling Green Lane, London, EC1R 0BD

Tel: 020 7490 9410
Fax: 020 7251 2834
E-mail: info@afasic.org.uk

Website:
http://www.afasic.org.uk

Enquiries:
Enquiries to: Information Officer
Other contacts: Helpline Manager for individual support for parents seeking help.

Founded:
1968

Formerly called:
Association for All Speech Impaired Children

Organisation type and purpose:
Membership association (membership is by subscription), voluntary organisation, registered charity (charity number 1045617).
Afasic is the UK charity representing children and young adults with speech, language and communication impairments, working for their inclusion in society and supporting their parents and carers.

Subject coverage:
Speech and language difficulties. Speech and language impairments in children and young people; special educational facilities; speech and language therapy provision; advice to parents.

Printed publications:
Newsletter (3 times a year)
Publications include:
Choosing a School (£3)
Glossary Sheets: individual sheets explaining terms (50p each)
Principles for Education Provision (£1.50)
The Proposed Statement (£1)
Leaflets on a variety of subjects (free)

Publications list:
Available online and in print

Access to staff:
Contact by letter, by telephone, by fax and by e-mail
Hours: Office: Mon to Thu, 0900 to 1700; Fri, 0900 to 1600
Helpline: Mon to Fri, 1030 to 1430

Access to building, collection or gallery:
Prior appointment required

Also at:
Afasic Cymru
1st Floor, The Exchange Building, Mount Stuart Square, Cardiff Bay, Cardiff, CF10 5EB; tel: 029 2046 5854; fax: 029 2046 5861
Afasic Scotland
1, Prospect 3, Gemini Crescent, Dundee Technology Park, Dundee DD2 1TY; tel: 01382 561891; fax: 01382 568391; e-mail: afasicscotland@btopenworld.com

AFFINITY

PO Box 246, Bridgend, CF31 9FD

Tel: 01656 646152
E-mail: admin@affinity.org.uk

Website:
http://affinity.org.uk/

Enquiries:
Enquiries to: Director

Founded:
1952

Organisation type and purpose:
Membership association, registered charity (charity number 258924).
Council of Churches; consultancy service.

continued overleaf

Subject coverage:
Evangelical Christianity, especially the co-ordination of churches outside the Ecumenical Movement.

Printed publications:
Table Talk (3 times a year, £3)
Foundations (theological journal, 2 times a year, £4 per issue)
Affinity (magazine, 3 times a year, free)
Bulletin (3 times a year, online)

Access to staff:
Contact by letter, by telephone and by e-mail. Appointment necessary.

AFGHAN ACADEMY IN UK

PO Box 1570, London, W7 3ZJ

Tel: 020 8579 8436\ 07952 578473
Fax: 020 8579 8436

Enquiries:
Enquiries to: Director
Other contacts: Co-ordinator for reports and works of the other committees within Afghan Academy.

Founded:
1991

Formerly called:
Afghan Link Association (year of change 1991); Afghanistan, Centre for Research and Development of Thoughts (year of change 1995); Afghan Academy (year of change 1997)

Organisation type and purpose:
Membership association (membership is by subscription), voluntary organisation.
Cultural and welfare.
Afghan Academy provides educational, cultural and welfare services to the Afghan Community. It promotes art and artistic activities among Afghans and works to present Afghan art and culture.

Subject coverage:
Afghanistan; Afghan refugees in UK; Afghanistan's cultural heritage; Afghan societies in and outside Afghanistan.

Museum or gallery collection, archive, or library special collection:
Publications in Persian/Pushto languages

Printed publications:
Almost all publications are in Persian/Pushto languages

Electronic and video publications:
The selection of videos covers the monthly seminars which have been held since 1995

Publications list:
Available online and in print

Access to staff:
Contact by letter, by telephone and by fax. Appointment necessary.
Hours: 24-hour emergency telephone and fax

Access to building, collection or gallery:
Prior appointment required

AFRICA CENTRE

38 King Street, Covent Garden, London, WC2E 8IT

Tel: 020 7836 1973
Fax: 020 7836 1975

Website:
http://www.africacentre.org.uk

Organisation type and purpose:
The Centre seeks to project a positive face of Africa in London, providing a focal point for all forms of cultural and social activities related to Africa through meetings, talks, visual arts exhibitions, cinema, literature and the performing arts.

Subject coverage:
Contemporary African culture and creativity.

Access to building, collection or gallery:
The Centre's premises were undergoing redevelopment in 2008, with core offices concentrated on one floor.

AFRICAN BIRD CLUB

Acronym or abbreviation: ABC

c/o Birdlife International, Wellbrook Court, Girton Road, Cambridge, CB3 0NA

E-mail: secretary@africanbirdclub.org

Website:
http://www.africanbirdclub.org
Aims of the club, membership details and club news, selected articles from previously published bulletins.

Enquiries:
Enquiries to: Secretary
Other contacts: Chairman, email chairman@ africanbirdclub.org

Founded:
1994

Organisation type and purpose:
Membership association (membership is by subscription), present number of members: 1200, registered charity (charity number 1053920).
To promote African ornithology.

Subject coverage:
African ornithology and all activities related to the study and conservation of African birds.

Printed publications:
Bulletin of the African Bird Club (journal, 2 times a year, £9 per issue)

Access to staff:
Contact by letter, by e-mail and via website
Hours: Mon to Fri, 0900 to 1700

AFRICAN STUDIES ASSOCIATION OF THE UNITED KINGDOM

Acronym or abbreviation: ASAUK

SOAS, University of London, Thornhaugh Street, Russell Square, London, WC1H 0XG

Tel: 020 7898 4390
Fax: 020 7898 4389
E-mail: asa@soas.ac.uk

Enquiries:
Enquiries to: Honorary Secretary

Founded:
1963

Organisation type and purpose:
Learned society.

Subject coverage:
Symposia and conferences on topics of current importance in Africa.

Printed publications:
African Affairs (quarterly, membership includes subscription)
African Studies Association Newsletter (quarterly with African Affairs)

Access to staff:
Contact by letter, by telephone and by e-mail
Hours: Mon to Fri, 0900 to 1700

Affiliated to:
Royal African Society
at the same address

AGE CONCERN ENGLAND

Acronym or abbreviation: ACE

Astral House, 1268 London Road, London, SW16 4ER

Tel: 020 8765 7200\ Minicom no. 020 8679 2832 (text phone)
Fax: 020 8765 7211
E-mail: ace@ace.org.uk

Website:
http://www.ageconcern.org.uk
Large website giving information about the organisation, news, fact sheets, reading lists, etc.

Enquiries:
Enquiries to: Library Resources Manager

Formerly called:
National Council on Ageing

Organisation type and purpose:
Registered charity (charity number 261794).
Hub of a network of about 1400 Age Concern organisations which provide services on a local basis.
National charity which aims to promote the well-being of all older people, and involve them in all aspects of society.

Subject coverage:
All aspects of the welfare of older people including: housing, health and social services, income maintenance, welfare rights, heating, transport and consumer affairs.

Museum or gallery collection, archive, or library special collection:
Library of books, journals and a large amount of grey material

Library catalogue:
All or part available in-house

Printed publications:
Book List
Books and videos on a wide range of subjects
Briefings
Factsheets
Monthly Information Bulletin

Publications list:
Available in print

Access to staff:
Contact by letter, by telephone, by fax, by e-mail and via website. Appointment necessary.
Hours: Mon to Fri, 0930 to 1700
Special comments: Reference only.

Access to building, collection or gallery:
Prior appointment required

Access for disabled people:
Ramped entry, toilet facilities

AGE CONCERN LONDON

Acronym or abbreviation: ACL

21 St. George's Road, London, SE1 6ES

Tel: 020 7820 6770
Fax: 020 7820 1063
E-mail: general@aclondon.org.uk

Website:
http://www.ageconcern.org.uk

Enquiries:
Enquiries to: Communication Officer
Direct e-mail: pwoodward@aclondon.org.uk

Founded:
1966

Formerly called:
Greater London Conference on Old People's Welfare

Organisation type and purpose:
Voluntary organisation, registered charity (charity number 249335), research organisation.
Working across the capital to improve the quality of life for older people and to enhance their status and influence.

Subject coverage:
Referral to local Age Concern organisations in the London boroughs. Details available via website or by calling National Age Concern Information Line 0800 009966. Also available in phone book.

Printed publications:
Directories including:
Age Concern in London Directory
Elders' Health: The Voice of Experience (2000, £4)

Hospital Aftercare Schemes in London (£3)
AGE Factsheets (free, also see
    www.ageconcern.org.uk)
Primary Care Briefings (free – SAE)
Poverty and Ethnic Minority Elders (1996, £4)
Reports (various titles, £5 each)
Getting Transport to Health Services in London
    (leaflet)
Older People and Housing Benefit Administration
    in London
A helicopter would be nice – transport to health
    services for older Londoners (£10)
Order printed publications from: Publications
Administrator, Age Concern London
e-mail: vduncan@aclondon.org.uk

Publications list:
Available online and in print

Access to staff:
Contact by letter, by telephone, by fax, by e-mail
and via website
Hours: Mon to Fri, 0930 to 1700
Telephone answered: Mon to Fri, 1100 to 1200 and
1500 to 1600
Answerphone at all other times
Special comments: Building not accessible.

Links with:
Age Concern organisations in London

AGE CONCERN NORTHERN IRELAND

Acronym or abbreviation: ACNI

3 Lower Crescent, Belfast, BT7 1NR

Tel: 028 9024 5729
Fax: 028 9023 5497
E-mail: info@ageconcernni.org

Website:
http://www.ageconcernni.org

Enquiries:
Enquiries to: Director

Formerly called:
Northern Ireland Old People's Welfare Council

Organisation type and purpose:
Voluntary organisation.
For the welfare of older people.

Subject coverage:
Welfare rights and services available for older
people and carers throughout Northern Ireland.
Policy analysis and research on all aspects of
ageing and older people.

Printed publications:
Annual Report (free)
Agenda for the Age (free)
Work of Age Concern (free)
Your Rights (annually)
Ageing Well (leaflets)

Access to staff:
Contact by letter, by telephone, by fax and by e-
mail
Hours: Mon to Fri, 0900 to 1700

AGE CONCERN SCOTLAND

113 Rose Street, Edinburgh, EH2 3DT

Tel: 0131 220 3345
Fax: 0131 220 2779
E-mail: enquiries@acscot.org.uk

Enquiries:
Enquiries to: Information Officer
Direct tel: 0131 625 9331
Direct e-mail: pamela.stewart@acscot.org.uk

Founded:
1943

Formerly called:
Scottish Old People's Welfare Council (year of
change 1974)

Organisation type and purpose:
Membership association (membership is by
subscription), present number of members: 512,
voluntary organisation, training organisation,
consultancy, research organisation.
To promote the interests of older people in
Scotland.

Subject coverage:
Housing; residential accommodation; welfare
rights; health; income maintenance; day services;
needs of older people and those who work with
them or care for them; voluntary services; ageing;
statutory services; community care; insurance
services.

Library catalogue:
All or part available in-house

Printed publications:
Adage (newsletter, 6 times a year)
Leaflets on money, health, housing, care training
    and community care
Books for personal use, including:
Better Health in Retirement (Roberts Dr A, 2001)
The Retirement Handbook (New Edition)
Using Your Home as Capital 2000–2001
Your Rights 2000–2001, a guide to money benefits
    for older people
Carers Handbook Series (12 titles)
Books and training packs for professional use
Policy Books

Electronic and video publications:
Home Maintenance Video for Older Householders
    (Free, 2000)

Publications list:
Available in print

Access to staff:
Contact by letter, by telephone, by fax and by e-
mail. Appointment necessary.
Hours: Mon to Fri, 0900 to 1700

Access to building, collection or gallery:
Prior appointment required
Hours: Mon to Fri, 0900 to 1700

Access for disabled people:
Toilet facilities
Special comments: Chairlift entry

AGE ENDEAVOUR FELLOWSHIP

Registered Office, The Old Well House, 130
Holland Park Avenue, London W11 4VE

Enquiries:
Enquiries to: Chairman

Formerly called:
Employment Fellowship

Organisation type and purpose:
Registered charity.

Subject coverage:
Funding of elderly and respite care.

AGECARE – THE ROYAL SURGICAL AID SOCIETY

Formal name: Royal Surgical Aid Society

47 Great Russell Street, London, WC1B 3PB

Tel: 020 7637 4577
Fax: 020 7323 6878
E-mail: enquiries@agecare.org.uk

Website:
http://www.agecare.org.uk
General information about the Society and its two
homes.

Enquiries:
Enquiries to: Chief Executive

Founded:
1862

Formerly called:
RSAS AgeCare

Organisation type and purpose:
Registered charity (charity number 216613).
Service provider and facilitator.

Subject coverage:
Improvement of the care and well-being of older
people, who are physically frail or suffering from
dementias, through continuous development of
good practice in our own homes, seeking pre-
eminence in training, supporting research,
promoting awards for excellence and contributing
to the exchange of knowledge.

Printed publications:
Annual Report
Information on Homes
Newsletter

Access to staff:
Contact by letter, by fax and by e-mail
Hours: Mon to Fri, 0900 to 1700

Homes for the elderly in:
Crowborough, Droitwich, Sevenoaks and
Shepperton

AGRICULTURAL ECONOMICS SOCIETY

Acronym or abbreviation: AES

The Mount Lodge, Church Street, Whitchurch,
Hampshire, RG28 7AR

Tel: 01256 892705
Fax: 01256 893090
E-mail: aes@cingnet.org.uk

Website:
http://www.aes.ac.uk
Information about the Society, its journal, etc.
Membership application information.

Enquiries:
Enquiries to: Administrator

Founded:
1926

Organisation type and purpose:
Learned society (membership is by subscription),
present number of members: c. 900.

Subject coverage:
Agricultural economics.

Printed publications:
EuroChoices (3 times a year)
Journal of Agricultural Economics (3 times a year)

Access to staff:
Contact by letter, by telephone, by fax and by e-
mail
Hours: Mon to Fri, 0900 to 1700

AGRICULTURAL ENGINEERS ASSOCIATION

Acronym or abbreviation: AEA

Samuelson House, Paxton Road, Orton Centre,
Peterborough, Cambridgeshire, PE2 5LT

Tel: 01733 362925
Fax: 01733 370664
E-mail: dg@aea.uk.com

Website:
http://www.aea.uk.com
Membership details, statistics of industry; industry
news; directory of members' products for export.
http://www.ope-groundscare.co.uk
Details of Association, news and statistics.
http://www.aea-farm-machinery.co.uk
Details of Association, news and statistics.

Enquiries:
Enquiries to: Director General

Founded:
1875

continued overleaf

Organisation type and purpose:
Trade association. To provide a service to
agricultural machinery manufacturers and outdoor
power turfcare, landscape, forestry and leisure
industries.

Subject coverage:
European and national technical legislation and
regulations relating to agriculture and outdoor
power vehicles, agricultural tractors, machinery
and equipment, including construction and use,
health and safety, standards, type approval, vehicle
licensing and environmental issues, economics,
statistics, technical and legal aspects.

Trade and statistical information:
Data on UK and European markets for agricultural
machinery and tractors, economics, statistics,
overseas export technical; legal; standards;
related to industries (agricultural machinery
manufacturers and outdoor power turfcare),
landscape, forestry and leisure industries and
sole importers.

Printed publications:
OPE Directory and Price Guide (twice a year, £45
hard copy, £30 (CD) annual UK subscription, £35
annual EU and £65 annual rest of world)

Access to staff:
Contact by letter, by telephone, by fax, by e-mail
and via website. Non-members charged.
Hours: Mon to Fri, 0900 to 1700
Special comments: Directory of members on web
page.

Access for disabled people:
Parking provided, toilet facilities

AGRICULTURAL INDUSTRIES CONFEDERATION

Acronym or abbreviation: AIC

Confederation House, East of England
Showground, Peterborough, PE2 6XE

Tel: 01733 385230
Fax: 01733 385270
E-mail: enquiries@agindustries.org.uk

Website:
http://www.agindustries.org.uk/
Fertiliser statistics, publications available, press
releases, background briefing to fertilisers.

Founded:
2003

Created by the merger of:
the Fertiliser Manufacturers Association (1875) and
the UK Agricultural Supply Trade Association
(1917)

Organisation type and purpose:
Trade association (membership is by election or
invitation), present number of members: 34.
To represent its membership to government and to
co-operate with other organisations with shared
interests. To promote an understanding of the
issues relating to plant nutrients.

Subject coverage:
Fertilisers: production, storage, transport, safety,
statistics, use and environmental effects.

Trade and statistical information:
Summary of fertiliser use in the UK, including
historical data.

Printed publications:
Nutrients for Plants (free)
Understanding Garden Fertilisers (free)
Mineral Fertiliser Manufacture (free)
Crop Production
Good Earth – The Science of Arable Farming (£5)
Fertiliser Review (annual, free)
Guidance leaflets on best fertiliser practice, quality
and advice
Health & Safety Handbook

Publications list:
Available in print

Access to staff:
Contact by letter
Hours: Fri, 0900 to 1600

Access to building, collection or gallery:
No prior appointment required

Links with:
European Fertilizer Manufacturers Association
tel: + 322 675 3550; fax: + 322 675 3961; e-mail:
main@efma.be
International Fertilizer Industry Association
tel: 00 33 1 539 30500; fax: 00 33 1 539 30547; e-
mail: ifa@fertilizer.org

AGRICULTURAL MANPOWER SOCIETY

Department of Agriculture, University of Reading,
Earley Gate, Reading, Berkshire, RG6 6AT

Tel: 0118 931 8492
Fax: 0118 935 2421

Enquiries:
Enquiries to: Honorary Secretary

Formerly called:
British Society for Agricultural Labour Science

Organisation type and purpose:
Learned society.

Subject coverage:
Efficiency, safety, health and job satisfaction in
agriculture, horticulture and forestry.

Printed publications:
Journal of Rural Enterprise and Management

Access to staff:
Contact by letter
Hours: Mon to Fri, 0900 to 1700

AHMADIYYA MUSLIM ASSOCIATION (UK)

Acronym or abbreviation: AMA(UK)

The London Mosque, 16 Gressenhall Road,
London, SW18 5QL

Tel: 0202 8875 4321
Fax: 020 8874 4779

Website:
http://www.al-islam.org

Enquiries:
Enquiries to: National Secretary, Publications
Direct tel: 01438 231311/0797 420 2225
Direct fax: 01438 231311
Direct e-mail: arshadahmedi@hotmail.com

Founded:
1889

Formerly called:
Jamaat Ahmadiyya, London Mosque

Organisation type and purpose:
International organisation, present number of
members: over 200 million worldwide, registered
charity (charity number 299081).
Religious Community.

Subject coverage:
Philosophy and teachings of Islam, correct
interpretation of the Holy Qur'an and sayings of
the Holy Prophet of Islam, facility in many western
and eastern European languages.

**Museum or gallery collection, archive, or library
special collection:**
Approximately 1000 books on Islam and related
subjects in English, Arabic and Urdu
Past editions of the Muslim Herald
Translation and Exegesis of the Qur'an in various
European and Eastern languages

Printed publications:
Selected sayings of the Holy Prophet – in 90
different languages (50p each)
Translations of the Holy Qur'an – in 50 different
languages (between £5 and £10 depending on
language)

Review of Religions (monthly, in English)
Many other books on Islam available at cost
Order printed publications from: Secretary,
Publications
at the same address, e-mail: ishaatuk@aol.com

Publications list:
Available in print

Access to staff:
Contact by letter, by telephone and by fax.
Appointment necessary.
Hours: Mon to Fri, 1030 to 1930; calls may remain
unattended during prayers
Special comments: Library and consulting facility
available by prior arrangement.

Access to building, collection or gallery:
No prior appointment required

Subsidiary body:
Lajna Imaullah (UK)
at the same address
Majlis Ansarullah (UK)
at the same address; tel: 020 8687 7845
Majlis Khuddamul Ahmadiyya (UK)
at the same address; tel: 020 8687 7904

AHMED IQBAL ULLAH RACE RELATIONS RESOURCE CENTRE

Ground Floor, Devonshire House, Precinct Centre,
Oxford Road, Manchester, M13 9PL

Tel: 0161 275 2920
E-mail: rrarchive@manchester.ac.uk

Website:
http://www.racearchive.org.uk

Founded:
1999

Organisation type and purpose:
Resource centre founded to combat racist ideas
about black people.

Subject coverage:
Books, periodical articles, cuttings, video and
audio tapes and ephemeral material on key themes
of history, politics, culture and identity, women,
education and employment, housing, immigration,
social services, and criminal justice; also an
expanding local history section focused on the
history of Manchester's African, Asian and
Caribbean communities.

Access to building, collection or gallery:
Hours: Mon to Fri, 0930 to 1630
Special comments: Appointment requested for
group visits.

AIIC (UNITED KINGDOM AND IRELAND REGION)

Formal name: International Association of
Conference Interpreters (Association Internationale
des Interprètes de Conférence)
Acronym or abbreviation: AIIC

12 Vicars Road, London, NW5 4NL

Tel: 020 7284 3112
Fax: 020 7284 0240
E-mail: info@aiic-uk-ireland.com

Website:
http://www.aiic.net
Advice for users of interpretation, for would-be
interpreters, for interpreters, for venues, etc.

Enquiries:
Enquiries to: Administrator

Formerly called:
AIIC (British Isles Region) (year of change 1999)

Organisation type and purpose:
International organisation, professional body,
service industry, consultancy.
Promotes high standards for conference
interpreters.

Subject coverage:
Interpreting, especially conference interpreting, including: training, research, qualifications, requirements, practice.

Museum or gallery collection, archive, or library special collection:
Bibliography of publications
Research in the field of interpreting

Access to staff:
Contact by letter, by telephone, by fax, by e-mail and via website. Appointment necessary.
Hours: Mon to Fri, 0900 to 1700

Parent body:
AIIC
10 Avenue de Sécheron, Geneva, CH-1202, Switzerland; tel: +41 22 908 1540; fax: +41 22 732 4151; e-mail: info@aiic.net

AIM25: ARCHIVES IN LONDON AND THE M25 AREA

C/o Director of Archive Services, King's College London, Strand, London, WC2R 2LS

E-mail: aim25@ulcc.ac.uk

Website:
http://www.aim25.ac.uk

Enquiries:
Enquiries to: Project Dir
Direct tel: 020 7848 2187
Direct e-mail: aim25@ulcc.ac.uk

Organisation type and purpose:
To provide electronic access to collection level descriptions of the archives of over ninety higher education institutions and learned societies within the greater London area.

Subject coverage:
Social sciences, military history, teaching, medicine, overseas development, vocational history, history of higher education, biography, literary history.

Non-library collection catalogue:
All or part available online

Access to staff:
Contact by letter, by telephone, by e-mail and via website

AIR TRANSPORT USERS COUNCIL

Acronym or abbreviation: AUC

CAA House, 45–59 Kingsway, London, WC2B 6TE

Tel: 020 7240 6061
Fax: 020 7240 7071

Website:
http://www.auc.org.uk

Enquiries:
Enquiries to: Chief Executive

Founded:
1973

Formerly called:
Air Transport Users Committee

Organisation type and purpose:
Independent consumer group, supported by an annual grant from the Civil Aviation Authority.
To represent effectively the requirements of all transport users by means of consultation, advocacy or campaigning, as appropriate.

Subject coverage:
All matters concerning and affecting air transport users.

Printed publications:
Annual Report
Flight Plan (booklet, passenger guide to the planning and use of air travel)

Access to staff:
Contact by letter and by telephone
Hours: Mon to Fri, 0900 to 1700

Access to building, collection or gallery:
No access other than to staff

Member of:
Federation of Air Transport User Representatives in Europe (FATURE)

AIRCRAFT RESEARCH ASSOCIATION LIMITED

Acronym or abbreviation: ARA

Manton Lane, Bedford, MK41 7PF

Tel: 01234 350681
Fax: 01234 328584
E-mail: ara@ara.co.uk

Website:
http://www.ara.co.uk
Publicity material.

Enquiries:
Enquiries to: Librarian
Direct e-mail: library@ara.co.uk

Founded:
1954

Organisation type and purpose:
Research organisation.
Association of major companies.

Subject coverage:
Aerodynamics, wind tunnel testing, mathematical modelling, analysis and computing code generation, model design and manufacture.

Library catalogue:
All or part available in-house

Access to staff:
Contact by letter, by telephone, by fax and by e-mail
Hours: Mon to Fri, 0800 to 1600

AIRSHIP ASSOCIATION LIMITED

The Light House, Barton Road, Keinton Mandeville, Somerset, TA11 6EA

Tel: 01458 223332
E-mail: secretary@airship-association.org

Website:
http://www.airship-association.org
Information about the Airship Association and forthcoming events, e.g., conferences, symposia.

Enquiries:
Enquiries to: Secretary

Founded:
1972

Organisation type and purpose:
Professional body.
To promote the use of airships for surveillance, load-carrying, advertising and scientific purposes.

Subject coverage:
Design, construction and operation of all types of modern airships; provision of information about airship designers and manufacturers, aeronautical engineers.

Printed publications:
Airship Journal (quarterly)
Various airship-related information sheets

Access to staff:
Contact by letter, by telephone, by e-mail and via website. Non-members charged.
Hours: Mon to Fri, 0900 to 1700

AL-ANON FAMILY GROUPS UK AND EIRE AND ALATEEN

61 Great Dover Street, London, SE1 4YF

Tel: 020 7403 0888
Fax: 020 7378 9910
E-mail: enquiries@al-anonuk.org.uk

Website:
http://www.al-anonuk.org.uk

Publication list, general information about the organisation, some extracts from the literature.

Enquiries:
Enquiries to: Public Information Secretary
Other contacts: General Secretary

Founded:
1951

Organisation type and purpose:
International organisation, membership association (membership is by qualification), voluntary organisation, registered charity.
Al-Anon is active worldwide and offers understanding and support for families and friends of problem drinkers, whether the alcoholic is still drinking or not. Alateen, a part of Al-Anon, is for young people aged 12 to 20 who have been affected by someone else's drinking, usually that of a parent.

Subject coverage:
Alcoholics, alcoholism, and its effects on family and friends.

Information services:
Confidential helpline, tel: 020 7403 0888 daily, 1000 to 2200

Printed publications:
Prices do change and literature is subject to availability:
Al-Anon Community Resource Book
Al-Anon's Twelve Steps & Twelve Traditions (£7.60)
Alateen – Hope for Children of Alcoholics
Al-Anon Family Groups – Classic Edition (£10.70)
ALATEEN: A Day at a Time (£6.85)
Courage to Change (£12)
From Survival to Recovery: Growing Up in an Alcoholic Home (£12.70)
One Day at a Time in Al-Anon (£6.60, or in large print £10.65)
A wide range of Al-Anon leaflets, pamphlets and posters, including some in Asian languages
A wide range of leaflets and pamphlets from Alateen

Publications list:
Available online and in print

Access to staff:
Contact by letter, by telephone, by fax, by e-mail and via website
Hours: Mon to Fri, 1000 to 1600
Confidential Helpline 020 7403 0888: daily, 1000 to 2200

Has:
almost 1000 self-help groups meet in UK and Eire, and 30,000 worldwide

Parent body:
Al-Anon Family Groups UK and Eire

ALBANY TRUST

239a Balham High Road, London, SW17 7BE

Tel: 020 8767 1827
E-mail: info@albanytrust.org

Website:
http://www.albanytrust.org.uk/

Enquiries:
Enquiries to: Administrator

Founded:
1958

Organisation type and purpose:
Learned society, registered charity (charity number 233564).
Counselling and psychotherapy service.

Subject coverage:
Relationships, personal and sexual counselling.

Access to staff:
Contact by telephone
Hours: Mon to Fri, 0900 to 1700

Incorporates the:
Sexual Law Reform Society

ALBINISM FELLOWSHIP

PO Box 77, Burnley, Lancashire, BB11 5GN

Tel: 01282 771900
E-mail: info@albinism.org.uk

Website:
http://www.albinism.org.uk

Founded:
1979

Organisation type and purpose:
National organisation, membership association
(membership is by subscription), present number
of members: 450, voluntary organisation,
registered charity (charity number SCO 09443).
Aims to provide information, advice and support
to people with albinism, their families and the
professionals working with them.

Subject coverage:
Albinism.

Printed publications:
Introductory leaflet (free)
Six-monthly newsletters (members only)
Albinism Lives: Personal and Photographic
   Perspectives on Albinism
Order printed publications from: Via website or
fellowship address

Publications list:
Available online

Access to staff:
Contact by letter, by telephone, by e-mail and via
website
Hours: answerphone

ALBION VEHICLE PRESERVATION TRUST

Acronym or abbreviation: AVPT

18 Netherdale Drive, Paisley, Renfrewshire, PA1
3DA

E-mail: albionregister@yahoo.co.uk

Website:
http://www.albion-trust.org.uk

Organisation type and purpose:
Preservation trust (Scottish charity no. SC028791)
maintaining a 1950 Albion Valiant heavy coach
and a 1967 Viking coach. Keeps a register of more
than 1,000 surviving Albion vehicles worldwide.

Subject coverage:
Albion vehicles.

Links with:
Biggar Albion Foundation
   The Albion Club, 9 Edinburgh Road, Biggar,
   Lanarkshire, ML12 6AX

ALCOHOL CONCERN

64 Leman Street, London, E1 8EU

Tel: 020 7264 0510
Fax: 020 7488 9213
E-mail: contact@alcoholconcern.org.uk

Website:
http://www.alcoholconcern.org.uk/
Work of organisation, press releases, factsheets.
http://ourworld.compuserve.com/homepages/
dolomite_publishing
Directory of Alcohol Services.

Enquiries:
Enquiries to: Information Team
Direct e-mail: info@alcoholconcern.org.uk

Founded:
1984

Organisation type and purpose:
Membership association (membership is by
subscription), present number of members: 1,000,
voluntary organisation, registered charity (charity
number 291705).

To raise public awareness of the problems of
alcohol abuse; to improve services for problem
drinkers and to promote preventive action.
National agency on alcohol misuse. Works to
reduce the incidence and costs of alcohol-related
harm and to increase the range and quality of
services available to people with alcohol-related
problems. Provides information and encourages
debate on the wide range of public policy issues
affected by alcohol, including public health,
housing, children and families, crime and
licensing. Supports specialist and non-specialist
service providers helping to tackle alcohol
problems at a local level, whilst also working to
influence national alcohol policy.

Subject coverage:
Alcohol use and misuse, treatment, health and
social effects, policies.

Information services:
Factsheets, directory of alcohol services, leaflets
and extensive library database of journal articles,
books, research papers, booklets and leaflets.

Special visitor services:
Office not open to the public.

Printed publications:
Alcohol Concern Straight Talk Magazine
   (quarterly)
Alcohol Education Booklets
Alcohol Services Directory 2007 (price £25 incl.
   p&p, from http://www.ris.org.uk)
A number of book titles on alcohol-related topics
Leaflets
Order printed publications from: The online
bookshop

Publications list:
Available online and in print

Access to staff:
Contact by letter, by telephone, by fax, by e-mail
and via website. Appointment necessary.

Access to building, collection or gallery:
Office is not open to the public
Hours: Mon to Fri, 0930 to 1630

ALCOHOL FOCUS SCOTLAND

Acronym or abbreviation: AFS

2nd Floor, 166 Buchanan Street, Glasgow, G1 2LW

Tel: 0141 572 6700
Fax: 0141 333 1606
E-mail: enquiries@alcohol-focus-scotland.org.uk

Website:
http://www.alcohol-focus-scotland.org.uk

Enquiries:
Enquiries to: Chief Executive

Founded:
1973

Formerly called:
Scottish Council on Alcohol (SCA); Scottish
Council on Alcoholism (year of change 1985)

Organisation type and purpose:
Voluntary organisation, registered charity (charity
number SCO 09538), training organisation.

Subject coverage:
All issues relating to alcohol misuse and abuse,
counselling and training.

**Museum or gallery collection, archive, or library
special collection:**
Information service
Collection includes: journals, conference reports
   and proceedings, educational materials and
   videos

Printed publications:
Annual Report
UK Alcohol Statistics Book (every two years)
Young People and Alcohol in Scotland (report)
Many publications on alcohol and alcohol related
   problems.

Publications list:
Available online and in print

Access to staff:
Contact by letter, by telephone, by fax, by e-mail
and via website. Appointment necessary.
Hours: Mon to Fri, 0900 to 1700

Local councils:
Alcohol & Drugs Support – South West
   The Sun Project, Unit 4, Kelloholm Business
   Estate, Greystone Avenue, Sanquhar, DG4 6RB;
   tel: 01659 67137; fax: 01659 67484; e-mail: mail@
   sunproject.ssbusiness.co.uk
Alcohol & Drugs Support – South West Scotland
   82 King Street, Castle Douglas, DG7 1AT; tel:
   01556 503550; fax: 01556 503550; e-mail: alcohol
   .info@virgin.net
Alcohol Advisory and Counselling Service
   62 Dee Street, Aberdeen, AB11 6DS; tel: 01224
   573887; fax: 01224 213479; e-mail: info@aacs.co
   .uk
Alcohol Counselling – Inverness
   34A Tomnahurich Street, Inverness, IV3 5DS; tel:
   01463 220995; fax: 01463 729292
Alcohol Counselling Service – Ross/Sutherland
   4 Ardross Road, Alness, Ross-Shire, IV17 0PU;
   tel: 01349 880771; fax: 01349 880771; e-mail:
   alness@acsras.org
Alcohol Counselling Service Ross/Sutherland
   Estate Office, 1 Duke Street, Golspie, Sutherland,
   KW10 6RF; tel: 01408 634200; fax: 01408 634200;
   e-mail: golspie@acsras.org
Ayrshire Council on Alcohol
   3rd Floor, 64 Fort Street, Ayr, KA7 3EH; tel:
   01292 281238; fax: 01292 290355
Ayrshire Council on Alcohol
   2 Bridge Lane, Kilmarnock, KA1 1QH; tel: 01563
   541155; fax: 01563 573232
Borders Council on Alcohol
   42 High Street, Galashiels, TD1 1RZ; tel: 01896
   757657; fax: 01896 757657
Bute Council on Alcohol & Drugs
   26 Bishop Street, Rothesay, PA20 9DG; tel: 01700
   505855
Caithness Council on Alcohol
   Rhind House Annexe, West Banks Avenue, Wick,
   KW1 5LU; tel: 01955 603462; fax: 01955 603462
Counselling & Support Service for Alcohol &
Drugs
   13 Pitt Terrace, Stirling, FK8 2EZ; tel: 01786
   450721; fax: 01786 449671; e-mail: info@
   counsellingservices.ssnet.co.uk
Cowal Council on Alcohol
   Ballochyle House, Kirk Street, Dunoon, PA23
   7DP; tel: 01369 704406
Cumbernauld & Lancashire Counselling Services
   2nd Floor, Carron House, Town Centre,
   Cumbernauld, G67 1ER; tel: 01236 738689; fax:
   01236 780538; e-mail: info@ckas.fsnet.co.uk
Dumbarton Area Council on Alcohol
   West Bridgend Lodge, West Bridgend,
   Dumbarton, G82 4AD; tel: 01389 731456; fax:
   01389 734690; e-mail: email@daca0.fsnet.co.uk
Dumbarton Area Council on Alcohol
   82 Dumbarton Road, Clydebank, G81 1UG; tel:
   0141 952 0881; fax: 0141 952 0124; e-mail: email@
   daca0fsnet.co.uk
Edinburgh & Lothian Council on Alcohol
   40 Shandwick Place, Edinburgh, EH2 4RT; tel:
   0131 225 8888; fax: 0131 220 4090; e-mail:
   alcoholcounselling@elca.fsbusiness.co.uk
Fife Alcohol Advisory Service
   17 Tolbooth Street, Kirkcaldy, KY1 1RW; tel:
   01592 206200; fax: 01592 206201; e-mail: faas@
   fass.org.uk
Glasgow Council on Alcohol
   1st Floor, Bristol & West House, 82 Union Street,
   Glasgow, G1 3QS; tel: 0141 226 3883; helpline
   4774; fax: 0141 226 3014; e-mail: info.gca@virgin
   .net
Inverclyde Counselling Service
   2A Newton Street, Greenock, PA16 8UJ; tel:
   01475 786695
Islay Council on Alcohol
   The Claddich Centre, Shore Street, Bowmore, Isle
   of Islay, PA43 7JB; tel: 01496 810226
Kintyre Alcohol & Drugs Advisory Service
   Castlehill, Campbeltown, PA28 2AN; tel: 01586
   553555; fax: 01586 553555

Lochaber Council on Alcohol
Caol Shopping Centre, Caol, Fort William, Inverness-shire, PH33 7DR; tel: 01397 702340; fax: 01397 702304; e-mail: lca@lochaber84 .freeserve.co.uk
Mid Argyll Council on Alcohol
PO Box 9559, Lochgilphead, Argyll, PA30 8YE; tel: 01546 602880; fax: 01546 602880
Monklands Council on Addictions
81C Hallcraig Street, Airdrie, ML6 6AN; tel: 01236 753263; fax: 01236 767937
Moray Council on Addictions
252 High Street, Elgin, IV30 1BE; tel: 01343 552211; fax: 01343 547000; e-mail: mca@moray .gov.uk
Oban Council on Alcohol
Market Street Centre, Market Street, Oban, PA34 4HR; tel: 01631 566090
Orkney Council on Alcohol
43 Junction Road, Kirkwall, Orkney, KW15 1AF; tel: 01856 874738; fax: 01856 873937; e-mail: oacas@btclick.com
Renfrew Council on Alcohol
Mirren House, Back Sneddon Street, Paisley, PA3 2AF; tel: 0141 887 0880; fax: 0141 887 8063; e-mail: rcapaisley@compuserve.com
Ross-shire Council on Alcohol
66 High Street, Invergordon, IV18 0DH; tel: 01349 852438
Shetland Alcohol Trust, Alcohol Advice Centre
44 Commercial Street, Lerwick, Shetland, ZE1 0AB; tel: 01595 695363; fax: 01595 692801; e-mail: aac@care4free.net
Skye & Lochalsh Council on Alcohol
Highland Council Offices, Dunvegan Road, Portree, Isle of Skye, IV51 9HD; tel: 01478 612633
Tayside Council on Alcohol
13 King Street, Dundee, DD1 2JD; tel: 01382 223965; fax: 01382 227142; e-mail: enquiries@tca .sol.co.uk

ALCOHOLICS ANONYMOUS

Acronym or abbreviation: AA

PO Box 1, Stonebow House, Stonebow, York, YO1 7NJ

Tel: 01904 644026
Fax: 01904 629091

Website:
http://www.alcoholics-anonymous.org.uk
General information.

Enquiries:
Enquiries to: General Secretary

Founded:
1935

Organisation type and purpose:
International organisation, voluntary organisation, registered charity (charity number 226745).

Subject coverage:
Alcoholism, recovery from alcoholism.

Printed publications:
40 plus leaflets on all aspects of AA's work and organisation including:
A Newcomer Asks (50p)
Is there an Alcoholic in your life? (50p)
This is AA (80p)
Books include:
Alcoholics Anonymous (£8)
Twelve Steps and Twelve Traditions (£6)

Electronic and video publications:
Message to Young People (video, £10)
One Day at a Time (video, £10)

Publications list:
Available in print

Access to staff:
Contact by letter, by telephone and by fax
Hours: Mon to Thu, 0900 to 1700; Fri, 0900 to 1630

Also at:
Northern Service Office (Scotland)
tel: 0141 226 2214
Southern Service Office (London)
tel: 020 7833 0022

ALEXANDER STUDIO

Danceworks, 16 Balderton Street, London, W1K 6TN

Tel: 020 7629 1808

Enquiries:
Enquiries to: Managers

Organisation type and purpose:
Professional body.

Subject coverage:
Stress management, psychophysical health, poise and grace for performing artists, relief from muscular aches and pains.

Electronic and video publications:
From Stress to Freedom (1990, video, from STAT Books)

All teachers are members of the:
Society of Teachers of the Alexander Technique (STAT)

ALFA LAVAL LIMITED

Acronym or abbreviation: A-L; Alfa

7 Doman Road, Camberley, Surrey, GU15 3DN

Tel: 01276 63383
Fax: 01276 685035

Website:
http://www.alfalaval.com

Enquiries:
Enquiries to: Public Relations Manager
Direct tel: 01276 413632
Direct fax: 01276 413524
Direct e-mail: peter.rose@alfalaval.com

Founded:
1923

Formerly called:
Alfa-Laval Flow Ltd, Alfa-Laval Separation Ltd, Alfa-Laval Sharples Ltd, Alfa-Laval Thermal Ltd

Organisation type and purpose:
Manufacturing industry.

Subject coverage:
Heat transfer technology, sanitary pumps, valves and fittings.

Access to staff:
Contact by letter, by telephone, by fax, by e-mail and via website
Hours: Mon to Fri, 0900 to 1700

Access for disabled people:
Level entry, toilet facilities

Other addresses:
Alfa Laval Limited
8H May Brook Road, Sutton Coldfield, West Midlands, B76 1AL; tel: 0121 351 3131; fax: 0121 351 7888
Alfa Laval Limited
Office 5 – 9th Floor, Salveson Tower, Blaikies Quay, Aberdeen, AB11 5PW; tel: 01224 424300; fax: 01224 424315

ALFA ROMEO 1900 REGISTER

Mariners, 14 Lower Station Road, Billingshurst, West Sussex, RH14 9SX

E-mail: ar.01177@yahoo.co.uk

Website:
http://www.ar1900reg.org

Enquiries:
Enquiries to: Factotum

Founded:
1977

Organisation type and purpose:
International organisation, membership association (membership is by qualification), present number of members: 500.

Register – The register lists cars rather than owners, i.e. cars with owners, not owners with cars.
Record all Alfa Romeo 6C2300, 6C2500 and 1900 still extant and to provide information on these models.

Subject coverage:
The Register of Alfa Romeo 6C2300, 6C2500 and 1900 also tries to assist on other uncommon post-war Alfa Romeos, including brochure information.

Printed publications:
Photocopies of handbooks, manuals, parts books and brochures

Access to staff:
Contact by letter and by telephone

Also at:
North American Register
302 Brown Thrush Road, Savannah, Georgia, 31419, USA

ALFA ROMEO GIULIA 105 REGISTER

144 Sussex Way, Enfield, Cockfosters, Barnet, Hertfordshire, EN4 0BG

Tel: 020 8351 8565

Enquiries:
Enquiries to: Secretary

Organisation type and purpose:
Membership association.

Subject coverage:
Alfa Romeo Giulia 105 cars.

Access to staff:
Contact by letter, by telephone and by fax. Appointment necessary.
Hours: Mon to Fri, 0900 to 1700

Parent body:
Alfa Romeo Owners Club

ALL ENGLAND LAWN TENNIS & CROQUET CLUB

Church Road, Wimbledon, London, SW19 5AE

Tel: 020 8944 1066
Fax: 020 8947 3354

Website:
http://www.wimbledon.org

Enquiries:
Enquiries to: Club Secretary
Direct tel: 020 8971 2252
Other contacts: Curator for Wimbledon Lawn Tennis Museum.

Founded:
1868

Organisation type and purpose:
Membership association (membership is by election or invitation), present number of members: 375 plus honorary members. Private tennis club.

Subject coverage:
Lawn tennis and croquet.

Access to staff:
Contact by letter, by telephone and by fax. Appointment necessary.
Hours: Mon to Fri, 0900 to 1700

ALL ENGLAND NETBALL ASSOCIATION LIMITED

Acronym or abbreviation: AENA Ltd

Netball House, 9 Paynes Park, Hitchin, Hertfordshire, SG5 1EH

Tel: 01462 442344
Fax: 01462 442343
E-mail: info@aena.co.uk

continued overleaf

Website:
http://www.england-netball.co.uk
Chat pages, structure of AENA, where to play,
calendar of events.
Departmental sections: development, umpiring,
coaching, England squads.

Enquiries:
Enquiries to: Communications Officer
Direct e-mail: siobhana@aena.co.uk

Founded:
1926

Merged with:
English Schools Netball Association (year of
change 1994)

Organisation type and purpose:
National organisation, membership association
(membership is by subscription, election or
invitation), present number of members: 55,000
individual members.
Governing body of netball in England.

Subject coverage:
International, national, regional, county and club
netball; development, performance, disability,
coaching, umpiring, awards.

**Museum or gallery collection, archive, or library
special collection:**
Archives and photographs

Printed publications:
Coaching Manual
First Step Netball
High Five
Know the Game
Netball Magazine (quarterly)
Official Netball Rules
Planning a Tournament
Netball Skills
With Netball in Mind
Order printed publications from: The Sports Motive
fax: 01926 888832

Electronic and video publications:
Umpiring and coaching videos (see merchandise
catalogue)

Publications list:
Available in print

Access to staff:
Contact by letter, by e-mail and via website
Hours: Mon to Fri, 0900 to 1700

Member of:
International Federation of Netball Associations
tel: 0121 446 4451; fax: 0121 446 5857; e-mail:
ifna@btinternet.com

ALL NATIONS CHRISTIAN COLLEGE

Acronym or abbreviation: ANCC

Easneye, Ware, Hertfordshire, SG12 8LX

Tel: 01920 461243
Fax: 01920 462997
E-mail: library@allnations.ac.uk

Website:
http://www.allnations.ac.uk
Information about college facilities, courses and
faculty members.

Enquiries:
Enquiries to: Librarian
Direct tel: 01920 443503
Direct e-mail: s.bruce@allnations.ac.uk

Founded:
1971

Formed from:
All Nations Bible College (year of change 1962);
All Nations Missionary College, Mount Hermon
Missionary Training College, Ridgelands Bible
College (year of change 1971)

Organisation type and purpose:
Suitable for ages: 18+.
International Christian college.

Subject coverage:
Christianity, Islam, Judaism and other religions,
missiology, anthropology, cross-culture studies.

**Museum or gallery collection, archive, or library
special collection:**
Archives of constituent colleges

Library catalogue:
All or part available in-house

Electronic and video publications:
Pocket catalogue on disk; renewable every 6
months

Access to staff:
Contact by letter, by telephone and by e-mail.
Appointment necessary. Letter of introduction
required. Non-members charged.
Hours: Mon to Fri, 0915 to 1715
Special comments: External readership restricted to
ministers, church leaders, mission leaders,
theological students.

Access for disabled people:
Ramped entry, access to all public areas, toilet
facilities

ALL WHEEL DRIVE CLUB

Acronym or abbreviation: AWDC

Registered Office: c/o Vallance Lodge & Co, Units
082–086, 555 White Hart Lane, London, N17 7RN

E-mail: secretary@awdc.co.uk

Website:
http://www.awdc.co.uk
General club information. Club magazine
information. Rights of Way information.

Enquiries:
Enquiries to: Membership Administrator
Direct tel: 01825 731875

Founded:
1968

Organisation type and purpose:
National organisation, membership association
(membership is by subscription), present number
of members: 2600, voluntary organisation.
Organisation of off-road motorsport events and
other activities for 4x4 vehicles.

Subject coverage:
Off-road motor sport, its environmental impact,
guidance for landowners, unsurfaced vehicular
rights of way, their existence and usage.
Recreational use of cross-country motorised
vehicles.

Access to staff:
Contact by letter and by e-mail
Hours: Mon to Fri, 0900 to 1700

Affiliated to:
Motor Sports Association

Has:
branches throughout the country

ALLARD OWNERS CLUB

1 Brooklyn Court, Woking, Surrey, GU22 7TQ

Tel: 01483 773428
Fax: 01483 773428

Enquiries:
Enquiries to: Secretary

Founded:
1951

Organisation type and purpose:
Membership association.

Subject coverage:
Allard cars.

Printed publications:
Newsletter (monthly, members only)

Access to staff:
Contact by letter

Hours: Mon to Fri, 0900 to 1700

Access to building, collection or gallery:
No access other than to staff

ALLEGRO CLUB INTERNATIONAL

23 Birchview Close, Yateley, Hampshire, GU46
6DL

Website:
http://www.allegroclubint.org.uk
Membership application and club news.

Enquiries:
Enquiries to: Membership Secretary
Direct e-mail: ian.sc@dial.pipex.com

Founded:
1990

Organisation type and purpose:
Membership association.
Car owners club.

Subject coverage:
Providing parts for Allegro cars, helping those
who wish to buy or sell such cars, organising
gatherings, pooling information for owners,
gathering history of Allegro cars. The club has an
archive of Allegro-related material.

Printed publications:
Quartic (magazine, several times a year, members)
List of Allegro parts for sale (members)
Used Allegro listings for sale (members)

Access to staff:
Contact by letter. Access for members only.
Hours: Mon to Fri, 0900 to 1700

Access to building, collection or gallery:
No access other than to staff

ALLERGY UK

3 White Oak Square, London Road, Swanley, Kent,
BR8 7AG

Tel: 01322 619898
Fax: 01322 663480
E-mail: info@allergyuk.org

Website:
http://www.allergyuk.org/
http://www.allergyfoundation.com

Enquiries:
Enquiries to: Membership Enquiries
Direct e-mail: raegan@allergyuk.org
Other contacts: Chairman

Founded:
1991

Formerly called:
British Allergy Foundation (BAF), date of change,
May 2001

Organisation type and purpose:
Membership association, present number of
members: 5600, registered charity (charity number
1003726).
To raise awareness of allergy, provide information
for sufferers and raise funds for research.

Subject coverage:
All allergy-related disorders including: respiratory
(nose and lungs), dermatological, eye disorders,
food-related problems, venom allergy, drug
allergy, occupational allergic diseases.

**Museum or gallery collection, archive, or library
special collection:**
Data on prevalence of allergic disorders

Printed publications:
What is Allergy? – Allergy Testing (free)
10 leaflets and 20 factsheets (A supply of 30 copies
of 5 assorted leaflets available £15)
Freedom for your Senses
Hayfever Advice for Sufferers
Hayfever (Read C)
House Dust Mite Avoidance Measures for Allergy
Sufferers
What is The British Allergy Foundation (free)

Publications list:
Available in print

Access to staff:
Contact by letter, by telephone, by fax, by e-mail
and in person. Appointment necessary.
Hours: Mon to Fri, 0900 to 1700
Special comments: Helpline: Mon to Fri, 0900 to
2100; Sat, Sun, 1000 to 1300.

Affiliated to:
British Society for Allergy and Clinical
Immunology
tel: 020 8398 9240; fax: 020 8398 2766; e-mail: s
.duff@co.puserve.com

Has:
Local support groups at various UK locations
(contact via main office)

Member of:
European Federation of Asthma & Allergy
Associations (EFA)

ALLIANCE OF INDEPENDENT RETAILERS

Acronym or abbreviation: AIR

Bank Chambers, 5–9 St Nicholas Street, Worcester,
WR1 1UW

Tel: 01905 612733 or 613106
Fax: 01905 21501
E-mail: alliance@indretailer.co.uk

Website:
http://www.indretailer.co.uk

Enquiries:
Enquiries to: General Secretary

Founded:
1983

Organisation type and purpose:
Trade association (membership is by election or
invitation), present number of members: 24,750,
publishing house.

Subject coverage:
Retailing: small to medium enterprises; publishing:
magazines, brochures, newsletters, etc; mailing:
complete mailing and distribution services;
political: approaches to government.

Trade and statistical information:
Information Technology Roadshows.

Printed publications:
Hotelier (magazine, free to members)
Independent Retailer (magazine, free to members)

Access to staff:
Contact by letter, by telephone, by fax, by e-mail
and via website. Appointment necessary.
Hours: Mon to Fri, 0900 to 1700

Subsidiary body:
Alliance Mailing Services
Alliance Publishing Ltd
Design Connection

ALLIANCE OF LITERARY SOCIETIES

Acronym or abbreviation: ALS

59 Bryony Road, Selly Oak, Birmingham, B29 4BY

Tel: 0121 475 1805
E-mail: l.j.curry@bham.ac.uk

Website:
http://www.allianceofliterarysocieties.org.uk/
Information about member societies with details of
contacts and future events, also leads to other sites
for each society, e-texts and general literary items
of interest. A gazetteer for the member ALS
Societies.

Enquiries:
Enquiries to: Membership Secretary
Direct e-mail: johnshorland@aol.com

Founded:
1973

Organisation type and purpose:
Membership association (membership is by
subscription), present number of members: 108,
suitable for ages: 10+.
Uniting literary societies.
Provides mutual help and advice on the running of
societies, funding, etc., and encourages working
together to save threatened places of literary
significance.

Subject coverage:
Addresses of member societies; literary enquiries;
literary society etc.

Printed publications:
The Open Book (£2 for non-members, £1.50 for
members, both inc. p&p)
Newsletter (2 times a year, 4 x 2nd class stamps,
free to member societies)

Access to staff:
Contact by letter, by telephone, by fax, by e-mail
and via website
Hours: Mon to Fri, 0700 to 1500

ALPINE CLUB LIBRARY

55 Charlotte Road, London, EC2A 3QF

Tel: 020 7613 0745
Fax: 020 7613 0755
E-mail: library@alpine-club.org.uk

Website:
http://www.alpine-club.org.uk
Description of Alpine Club, calendar of events and
expedition reports, Himalayan Index, a database of
references to the literature of attempts and ascents
of peaks over 6000m in the Himalayas and
adjacent areas.

Enquiries:
Enquiries to: Librarian
Other contacts: Archivist; Photo Librarian

Founded:
1857

Organisation type and purpose:
Membership association (membership is by
subscription), registered charity (charity number
313051).
Mountaineering club.
Caters specifically for those who climb in the Alps
and the Greater Ranges of the world.

Subject coverage:
Historical and current information on
mountaineering and mountain ranges worldwide
including Himalayan database, ski
mountaineering, walking, high altitude medicine
and climbing equipment.

**Museum or gallery collection, archive, or library
special collection:**
Alpine Club Records
The library has one of the most comprehensive
collections of mountaineering literature in the
world including journals, early books,
photographs, manuscripts, newspaper cuttings
from 1891, diaries and correspondence, guide
books and reports
Expedition Reports
Records of the former Ladies' Alpine Club

Non-library collection catalogue:
All or part available in print

Library catalogue:
All or part available in-house

Printed publications:
The Alpine Club (corporate author) Alpine Club
Library Catalogue: Books and Periodicals
(Volume one, London, Heinemann, 1982)
Alpine Journal: annual record of mountain
exploration and achievement (free to members)
Guide Books: cover most popular regions of the
Alps (detailed English language guide books of
the region)
Newsletter
Year Books of the Ladies' Alpine Club 1910–1975
(Merz J, index Alpine Club Library, 2000)

Access to staff:
Contact by letter, by telephone, by fax and by e-
mail. Appointment necessary. Non-members
charged.
Hours: Tue, Wed, 1000 to 1700

Access for disabled people:
Special comments: Library on first floor, no lift.

Affiliated to:
British Mountaineering Council
177–179 Burton Road, Manchester, M20 2BB; tel:
0870 010 4878; fax: 0161 445 4500; e-mail: info@
thebmc.co.uk

Parent body:
Alpine Club
at the same address

ALPINE GARDEN SOCIETY

Acronym or abbreviation: AGS

AGS Centre, Avon Bank, Pershore, Worcestershire,
WR10 3JP

Tel: 01386 554790
Fax: 01386 554801
E-mail: ags@alpinegardensociety.org

Website:
http://www.alpinegardensociety.org
Information on the Society, news, updated
information, show reports, extracts from
publications. Forthcoming events, expeditions, etc.
Members' seed exchange.

Enquiries:
Enquiries to: Director and Secretary to the Society

Founded:
1929

Organisation type and purpose:
International organisation, membership
association (membership is by subscription),
present number of members: 13,850, voluntary
organisation, registered charity (charity number
207478), suitable for ages: all.
Specialist horticultural plant society.
To disseminate knowledge of alpine and rock
garden plants – alpines is a generic term to
encompass small hardy plants, including
perennials, bulbs, ferns, dwarf conifers, etc.

Subject coverage:
Horticultural, with specialist knowledge of the
cultivation of alpines and rock plants, small hardy
plants, including perennials, bulbs, ferns, dwarf
conifers etc. Locations: where to travel in the world
to find alpine specimens. Conservation: the Society
encourages conservation and discourages
indiscriminate collecting.

**Museum or gallery collection, archive, or library
special collection:**
Specialist Library – reference books
Slide Library – hire/loan service

Non-library collection catalogue:
All or part available in-house

Library catalogue:
All or part available in-house

Printed publications:
Bulletin (quarterly)
Encyclopaedia of Alpines
Leaflets
Newsletter (quarterly)
Seed list
Booklist contains over 100 titles covering:
Bulbous plants
Specific Genera
Floras and Guides to Continents and Countries

Electronic and video publications:
The Plant Finder Reference Library 1999/2000 (CD-
ROM)

Publications list:
Available online and in print

Access to staff:
Contact by letter, by telephone, by fax, by e-mail,
in person and via website. Appointment necessary.

continued overleaf

Hours: Mon to Thu, 0900 to 1730; Fri, 0900 to 1700

Access for disabled people:
Parking provided, ramped entry, toilet facilities

Has:
60 local groups

Seed Distribution Limited:
Alpine Garden Society
11 Boston Close, Culcheth, Warrington, WA3
4LW

ALUMINIUM FEDERATION

Formal name: Aluminium Federation Limited
Acronym or abbreviation: ALFED

National Metalforming Centre, 47 Birmingham
Road, West Bromwich, West Midlands, B70 6PY

Tel: 0121 601 6363
Fax: 0870 183 9714
E-mail: alfed@alfed.org.uk

Website:
http://www.alfed.org.uk

Enquiries:
Enquiries to: Librarian
Direct tel: 0121 601 6746
Other contacts: Technical Executive

Founded:
1963

Formerly called:
Aluminium Development Association

Organisation type and purpose:
Trade association (membership is by subscription),
present number of members: 200.
Information centre.

Subject coverage:
Technical and commercial information on
aluminium and its alloys, extrusion, coating,
anodizing, rolling.

Museum or gallery collection, archive, or library special collection:
Library with largest collection in the world on
aluminium; full range of traditional library
services

Non-library collection catalogue:
All or part available online

Library catalogue:
All or part available in-house

Printed publications:
Handbooks and videos
The Properties of Aluminium and its Alloys (9–2
edn, £30 (UK) incl. p&p)
UK Aluminium Industry Fact Sheets
Technical and promotional brochures on rolled
products, extrusions, anodising and finishing
and safety

Publications list:
Available online and in print

Access to staff:
Contact by letter, by telephone, by fax, by e-mail
and via website
Hours: Mon to Fri, 0900 to 1700
Special comments: Members and bona fide students
only.

Member organisations:
Aluminium Alloys Recycling and Melting
Association (AARMA)
    at the same address
Aluminium Extruders Association (AEA)
    at the same address
Aluminium Finishing Association (AFA)
    at the same address
Aluminium Primary Producers Association
(APPA)
    at the same address
Aluminium Rolled Products Manufacturers
Association (ARPMA)
    at the same address
Aluminium Stockholders Association (ASA)
    at the same address; tel: 0121 601 6716; fax: 0121
    601 6375

Diecasting Society (DCS)
    at the same address
European Aluminium Particulate Association
    at the same address

ALUMINIUM PACKAGING RECYCLING ORGANISATION

Acronym or abbreviation: ALUPRO

1 Brockhill Court, Brockhill Lane, Redditch,
Worcestershire, B97 6RB

Tel: 01527 597757
Fax: 01527 594140
E-mail: info@alupro.org.uk

Website:
http://www.alupro.org.uk
All information on aluminium can and aluminium
foil recycling in the United Kingdom.

Enquiries:
Enquiries to: Communications Director

Founded:
1994

Formerly called:
Aluminium Can Recycling Association (ACRA),
Aluminium Foil Recycling Campaign (AFRC)
(year of change 1999)

Organisation type and purpose:
Membership association.
Promotes collection of aluminium packaging
through all routes: local authority collection and
kerbside systems, 'cash for cans' recycling centres.

Subject coverage:
Viable collection opportunities for aluminium,
recycling technology, foil in energy from waste
plants. Packaging waste legislation.

Printed publications:
Information pack (free)
Education pack (free)

Access to staff:
Contact by letter, by telephone, by fax, by e-mail
and via website
Hours: Mon to Fri, 0900 to 1700

ALVIS OWNER CLUB

4 Field Lane, Normanby-By-Spital, Market Rasen,
Lincolnshire, LN8 2HB

Tel: 01673 878148
E-mail: gensec@alvisoc.org

Website:
http://www.alvisoc.org

Enquiries:
Enquiries to: General Secretary

Founded:
1951

Organisation type and purpose:
Membership association (membership is by
subscription).

Subject coverage:
Technical information, historic information, help
and advice on matters concerning the use and
restoration of Alvis vehicles.

Printed publications:
Bulletin (monthly)

Access to staff:
Contact by e-mail and via website. Appointment
necessary.
Hours: Mon to Fri, 0900 to 1700

ALVIS REGISTER

The Vinery, Wanborough Hill, Wanborough,
Guildford, Surrey, GU3 2JR

Tel: 01483 810308
Fax: 01483 810308

Enquiries:
Enquiries to: Registrar

Founded:
1948

Organisation type and purpose:
Membership association (membership is by
subscription), present number of members: 520.

Subject coverage:
Alvis cars.

Access to staff:
Contact by letter and by telephone
Hours: Mon to Fri, 0900 to 1700

ALZHEIMER SCOTLAND

22 Drumsheugh Gardens, Edinburgh, EH3 7RN

Tel: 0131 243 1453
Fax: 0131 243 1450
E-mail: alzheimer@alzscot.org

Website:
http://www.alzscot.org/local/index.html
Information about the organisation, about
dementia itself and caring for people who have
dementia.
http://www.alzscot.org/pages/regions/index.htm
Database of services
http://www.alzscot.org/pages/publications.htm
Publications list

Enquiries:
Enquiries to: Information Manager
Direct e-mail: mthom@alzscot.org

Founded:
1994

Organisation type and purpose:
Membership association, voluntary organisation,
registered charity (charity number SC022315).
Has a network of branches and services across
Scotland, for information contact the Regional
Office.
Provision and promotion of services for people
with dementia and their carers.

Subject coverage:
Information relating to statistics on numbers of
people in Scotland with dementia. Range of
services offered in Scotland. Information on
medical and caring aspects of dementia and on
government policy.

Printed publications:
Annual Report
A variety of reports, including:
Creating dementia-friendly communities: a guide
(2001)
You're not alone: dementia awareness in Scotland
(2002)
Making the journey brighter: early diagnosis and
support services for people with dementia and
their carers (2003)
Signposts to support: Understanding the special
needs of carers of people with dementia (2003)
Short break services for people with dementia and
their carers in Scotland (2004)
This is my home: quality of care for people with
dementia living in care homes (2005)
Various booklets and leaflets about coping with
dementia, including:
Branches and Services of Alzheimer
Scotland(information sheet, 25p standard print,
40p large print)
Dementia: Money and Legal Matters – a guide for
carers (booklet)
We Care About Dementia: about the work of
Alzheimer Scotland(leaflet, free)
What is Dementia? (leaflet, 10p)
Newsletter: Dementia in Scotland (4 times a year,
£1.50, free to members)

Electronic and video publications:
Audio and video tapes

Publications list:
Available online and in print

Access to staff:
Contact by letter, by telephone, by fax, by e-mail and via website. Appointment necessary.
Hours: 24-hour helpline

Regional office:
Alzheimer Scotland, Argyll & Clyde Regional Headquarters
32 Riccartsbar Avenue, Paisley, PA2 6BG; tel: 0141 887 4902; fax: 0141 840 1815; website: http://www.alzscot.org/pages/regions/argyll.htm
Alzheimer Scotland, Ayrshire and Dumfries & Galloway
1 Gordon Street, Dumfries, DG1 1EG; tel: 01387 261303; fax: 01387 251899; website: http://www.alzscot.org/pages/regions/ayrshiredumf.htm
Alzheimer Scotland, Forth Valley & Lanarkshire
Lanarkshire Information and Advice Centre, Old Town Hall, High Road, Motherwell, ML1 3HU; tel: 01698 275300; fax: 01698 251867; website: http://www.alzscot.org/pages/regions/forth.htm
Alzheimer Scotland, Glasgow and East Dunbartonshire
81 Oxford Street, Glasgow, G5 9EP; tel: 0141 418 3930; fax: 0141 418 3945; website: http://www.alzscot.org/pages/regions/glasgow.htm
Alzheimer Scotland, Grampian, Tayside and Shetland
27 Huntly Street, Aberdeen, AB10 1TJ; tel: 01224 644077; fax: 01224 644088; website: http://www.alzscot.org/pages/regions/grampian.htm
Alzheimer Scotland, Highland, Western Isles and Orkney
3 Gordon Terrace, Inverness, IV2 3HD; tel: 01463 711707; fax: 01463 711715; website: http://www.alzscot.org/pages/regions/highland.htm

ALZHEIMER'S SOCIETY

Acronym or abbreviation: AS

Gordon House, 10 Greencoat Place, London, SW1P 1PH

Tel: 020 7306 0606
Fax: 020 7306 0808
E-mail: info@alzheimers.org.uk

Website:
http://www.alzheimers.org.uk
Description of services.

Enquiries:
Enquiries to: Director of Information and Education
Other contacts: 1. Press Officer, 2. Librarian for (1) comments on news and articles (2) library enquiries only.

Founded:
1979

Formerly called:
Alzheimer's Disease Society (ADS) (year of change 1999)

Organisation type and purpose:
National organisation, membership association (membership is by subscription), present number of members: 22,000, voluntary organisation, registered charity (charity number 296645), research organisation.
Serves England, Wales and Northern Ireland.
To provide care for people with Alzheimer's disease and other forms of dementia and research into the condition.
To provide support for their carers and families.

Subject coverage:
Dementia and dementia care.

Museum or gallery collection, archive, or library special collection:
Ann Brown Memorial Library with over 6000 items including pictures, slides and videos

Library catalogue:
All or part available in-house

Printed publications:
Annual Report
Fact sheets, booklets
General leaflets (available in 16 languages)
Carers resource pack
Current Awareness Bulletin: Alzheimer's Update

If you are looking after a confused relative (practical tips on caring)
I'm told I have dementia: what you can do ... who you can turn to
Information pack for GPs
Newsletter (monthly)
Young People with Dementia: care resource book 1996

Electronic and video publications:
Caring for the Person with Dementia (audiotape, £3.50, free to the visually impaired)
Freephone Information on Dementia (audiotape, £3.50, free to the visually impaired)
Looking at Alzheimer's Disease (video, £10)

Publications list:
Available online and in print

Access to staff:
Contact by letter, by telephone, by fax, by e-mail, in person and via website. Appointment necessary. Non-members charged.
Hours: Mon to Fri, 0900 to 1700

Access to building, collection or gallery:
No access other than to staff
Hours: Mon to Fri, 0900 to 1700

Access for disabled people:
Toilet facilities

Regional Offices:
Alzheimer's Society, Central (Bedfordshire, Berkshire, Buckinghamshire, Hertfordshire, Northamptonshire and Oxfordshire)
16 North Bar Street, Banbury, Oxfordshire, OX16 0TF; tel: 01295 273401; fax: 01295 275724; e-mail: roc@alzheimers.org.uk
Alzheimer's Society, Eastern (Cambridgeshire, Essex, Norfolk and Suffolk)
Abbey House, 30 Angel Hill, Bury St Edmunds, Suffolk, IP33 1LS; tel: 01284 725045; fax: 01284 725052; e-mail: roe@alzheimers.org.uk
Alzheimer's Society, London (London and Middlesex)
45–46 Lower Marsh, London, SE1 7RG; tel: 020 7620 3020; fax: 020 7401 7352; e-mail: rol@alzheimers.org.uk
Alzheimer's Society, Midlands (Hereford & Worcester, West Midlands, Shropshire, Staffordshire and Warwickshire)
Drawbridge House, 44a Worcester Road, Bromsgrove, Worcestershire, B61 7AE; tel: 01527 871711; fax: 01527 870771; e-mail: rom@alzheimers.org.uk
Alzheimer's Society, North Wales Office
2 Glanrafon, Bangor, Gwynedd, LL57 1LH; tel: 01248 353 608; fax: 01248 353 605; e-mail: rown@alzheimers.org.uk
Alzheimer's Society, North West (Cheshire, Isle of Man, Lancashire, Greater Manchester and Merseyside)
Healey House, Withington Hospital, West Didsbury, Manchester, M20 2LR; tel: 0161 448 2039; fax: 0161 448 7457; e-mail: ronw@alzheimers.org.uk
Alzheimer's Society, Northern (Cleveland, Cumbria, Co Durham, Northumberland and Tyne & Wear)
The Bungalow, Sheriff Leas, Springfield Road, Newcastle upon Tyne, NE5 3DS; tel: 0191 271 4040; fax: 0191 271 2233; e-mail: ron@alzheimers.org.uk
Alzheimer's Society, Northern Ireland
403 Lisburn Road, Belfast, BT9 7EW; tel: 028 9066 4100; fax: 028 9066 4440; e-mail: roni@alzheimers.org.uk
Alzheimer's Society, South West (Bristol, Cornwall, Devon, Gloucestershire and Somerset)
11–15 Dix's Field, Exeter, EX1 1QA; tel: 01392 274327; fax: 01392 274235; e-mail: rosw@alzheimers.org.uk
Alzheimer's Society, Southern (Dorset, Hampshire, Isle of Wight, Kent, Surrey, East Sussex, West Sussex, Wiltshire and Channel Islands)
90b The Street, Ashtead, Surrey, KT21 1AW; tel: 01372 276989; fax: 01327 274857; e-mail: ros@alzheimers.org.uk

Alzheimer's Society, Trent (Derbyshire. Leicestershire, Lincolnshire, Nottinghamshire and South Yorkshire)
Penmore House Precinct, Hasland Road, Chesterfield, Derbyshire, S41 0SJ; tel: 01246 557370; fax: 01246 556421; e-mail: rot@alzheimers.org.uk
Alzheimer's Society, Wales
Tonna Hospital, Neath, West Glamorgan, SA11 3LX; tel: 01639 641938; fax: 01639 639608; e-mail: row@alzheimers.org.uk
Alzheimer's Society, Yorkshire (Humberside, North Yorkshire and West Yorkshire)
The Retreat, Heslington Road, York, YO1 5BN; tel: 01904 431265; fax: 01904 431257; e-mail: roy@alzheimers.org.uk

AMATEUR BOXING ASSOCIATION OF ENGLAND LIMITED

Acronym or abbreviation: ABA

Crystal Palace, National Sports Centre, London, SE19 2BB

Tel: 020 8778 0251
Fax: 020 8778 9324

Website:
http://www.amateurboxingassociation.co.uk

Enquiries:
Enquiries to: Secretary

Founded:
1993

Formerly called:
Amateur Boxing Association

Organisation type and purpose:
Membership association (membership is by election or invitation), voluntary organisation, training organisation.
Governing body of amateur boxing in England.

Subject coverage:
History of boxing, coaching, officials, membership.

Museum or gallery collection, archive, or library special collection:
Literature on the Association

Printed publications:
Boxing News

Access to staff:
Contact by letter. Appointment necessary.
Hours: Mon to Fri, 0900 to 1600

Affiliated to:
European Boxing Association (EABA)
International Amateur Boxing Association (AIBA)

AMATEUR FOOTBALL ALLIANCE

Acronym or abbreviation: AFA

55 Islington Park Street, London, N1 1QB

Tel: 020 7359 3493
Fax: 020 7359 5027
E-mail: a.f.a@dial.pipex.com

Website:
http://www.amateur-fa.org

Enquiries:
Enquiries to: General Secretary

Founded:
1907

Organisation type and purpose:
Membership association (membership is by election or invitation, subscription, qualification), present number of members: 320 affiliated clubs, 340 affiliated referees.
Regional governing body for association football.

Subject coverage:
Recreational amateur football.

Printed publications:
Handbook (annually)
AFA Record (magazine, 3 times a year, £4)

continued overleaf

Access to staff:
Contact by letter, by telephone, by fax, by e-mail and via website
Hours: Mon to Fri, 0915 to 1645

Parent body:
The Football Association

AMATEUR ROWING ASSOCIATION

Acronym or abbreviation: ARA

The Priory, 6 Lower Mall, Hammersmith, London, W6 9DJ

Tel: 020 8237 6700
Fax: 020 8237 6749

Website:
http://www.ara-rowing.org

Enquiries:
Enquiries to: Information Officer

Founded:
1882

Organisation type and purpose:
Membership association, voluntary organisation, publishing house, training organisation.
Governing body of the sport in England.

Subject coverage:
All aspects of rowing: learning, training, coaching, rules, organisation, clubs, international and Olympic representation.

Museum or gallery collection, archive, or library special collection:
British Rowing Almanack & Year Book (from 1869)
Reference library of historic and contemporary books associated with rowing

Library catalogue:
All or part available in-house

Printed publications:
British Rowing Almanack (annually in March) TBC
Regatta (monthly, subscription £25 for UK and £35 for rest of Europe, £40 for rest of the world or through membership)

Access to staff:
Contact by letter, by telephone, by fax and in person
Hours: Mon to Fri, 0900 to 1700
Special comments: Library by prior appointment.

Members:
British Olympic Association
  tel: 020 8871 2677; fax: 020 8871 9104
Central Council of Physical Recreation
  tel: 020 7854 8500; fax: 020 7854 8501
Commonwealth Games Federation
  tel: 020 7388 6643
Fédération Internationale des Sociétés d'Aviron
  tel: +41 21 617 8373; fax: +41 21 617 8375; e-mail: info@fisa.org

AMATEUR SWIMMING ASSOCIATION

Acronym or abbreviation: ASA

Harold Fern House, Derby Square, Loughborough, Leicestershire, LE11 5AL

Tel: 01509 618700
Fax: 01509 618701
E-mail: customerservices@swimming.org

Enquiries:
Enquiries to: Customer Services Manager

Founded:
1869

Organisation type and purpose:
Governing body of swimming.

Subject coverage:
Swimming; diving; water polo; synchronised swimming; competitive swimming; examinations and awards; education and teaching; student research; swimming for people with a disability; aquatic exercise.

Printed publications:
ASA Handbook
Books and handbooks on swimming and coaching, babies and children, synchronised swimming, diving, special needs, masters, survival, aquafit, water polo, nutrition
Information brochures
Swimming (monthly)
Order printed publications from: ASA Merchandising Ltd
Unit 1, Kingfisher Enterprise Park, 50 Arthur Street, Redditch, Worcestershire, B98 8LG, tel: 0800 220292, fax: 01527 514277, e-mail: sales@asa-awards.co.uk

Electronic and video publications:
Videos

Publications list:
Available in print

Access to staff:
Contact by letter, by telephone, by fax and by e-mail
Hours: Mon to Fri, 0900 to 1700

Houses the:
Institute of Swimming Teachers and Coaches

Member of:
Central Council of Physical Recreation
Sports Council

AMATEUR SWIMMING ASSOCIATION, WATER POLO COMMITTEE

Acronym or abbreviation: ASA

177 Urmston Lane, Stretford, Manchester, M32 9EH

Tel: 0161 866 8588
Fax: 0161 865 6041
E-mail: juliemikepolo@supanet.com

Enquiries:
Enquiries to: Committee Administrator

Organisation type and purpose:
Membership association.

Subject coverage:
Water polo.

Access to staff:
Contact by letter, by telephone, by fax and by e-mail
Hours: Sun to Sat, 0900 to 2000

Access to building, collection or gallery:
No access other than to staff

Connections with:
Amateur Swimming Association
  Harold Fern House, Derby Square, Loughborough, LE11 5AL; tel: 01509 618700; fax: 01509 618701

AMBER VALLEY BOROUGH COUNCIL

Acronym or abbreviation: AVBC

PO Box 15, Town Hall, Market Place, Ripley, Derbyshire, DE5 3XE

Tel: 01773 570222\ Minicom no. 01773 841490
E-mail: enquiry@ambervalley.gov.uk

Website:
http://www.ambervalley.gov.uk
Information about Amber Valley and the services which the council provides.

Enquiries:
Enquiries to: Chief Executive

Organisation type and purpose:
Local government body (membership is by election or invitation), present number of members: 45.

Subject coverage:
Local government issues.

Printed publications:
Amber Valley News (free, early March)

Access to staff:
Contact by letter, by telephone, by fax, by e-mail and in person. Appointment necessary.
Hours: Mon to Fri, 0900 to 1700

Access for disabled people:
Parking provided, toilet facilities

AMBLESS

Shalom House, Lower Celtic Park, Enniskillen, Co Fermanagh, BT74 6HP

Tel: 028 6632 0320
Fax: 028 6632 0320

Enquiries:
Enquiries to: Secretary
Other contacts: Chief Executive

Founded:
1984

Formerly called:
I Am Blessed Ministries (year of change 1990)

Incorporates the former:
DAP, Disasters, Accidents Involving People (year of change 1996)

Organisation type and purpose:
Non-profit-making organisation. Ambless is a national charity with a Christian ethos, which works to alleviate distress, suffering, heartache, grief, loneliness and trauma that accidents can cause. The services provided are confidential and discreet and are available to patients, their families and carers. Ambless relies entirely on the free-will support of the general public. Operates the 24-hour Ambless Accident Supportline (028 66320321 – tel, fax, SMS text and voicemail) and Ambless Care Car (tel 0792 0793456).

Subject coverage:
Professional counselling, befriending, information and advice and practical support for people who have suffered an accident, and for their families and carers.

Museum or gallery collection, archive, or library special collection:
I am Blessed (newsletter)
Our Companion (newsletter)

Printed publications:
Fundraising Ideas (annually)
Ambless Inspirational Catalogue (quarterly)
Healthy Living Factsheet (annually)
Our Companion (newsletter, 8 times a year)
Info Pack (free)
SOS Helpcards, leaflets etc.

Access to staff:
Contact by letter, by telephone, by fax and in person. Appointment necessary.
Hours: Mon to Sat, 1000 to 2200

Access for disabled people:
Parking provided

AMBULANCE SERVICE INSTITUTE

Acronym or abbreviation: ASI

2 Appletree Close, Oakley, Basingstoke, Hampshire, RG23 7HL

Fax: 01256 782650
E-mail: ambservinst.uk@virgin.net

Website:
http://www.asi-international.com

Enquiries:
Enquiries to: Honorary Secretary

Founded:
1976

Formerly called:
Institute of Ambulance Officers, Institute of Certified Ambulance Personnel, National Institute of Ambulance Instructors

Organisation type and purpose:
International organisation, professional body, registered charity, training organisation.

Subject coverage:
Ambulance Service organisation, administration and operation; training and qualifying examinations.

Printed publications:
asi International (official publication)

Publications list:
Available online

Access to staff:
Contact by letter, by fax, by e-mail and via website
Hours: Mon to Fri, 0900 to 1700

AMBULANCE SERVICE NETWORK

The NHS Confederation, 3rd Floor, 29 Bressenden Place, London, SW1E 5DD

Tel: 020 7074 3200
E-mail: liz.kendall@nhsconfed.org

Website:
http://www.nhsconfed.org/ambulance-trusts/index.cfm

Enquiries:
Enquiries to: Information Officer

Founded:
1994

Created by the merger of:
the Ambulance Service Association (ASA) and the NHS Confederation (NHSC)

Formerly called:
Association of Chief Ambulance Officers (ACAO) (year of change 1994)

Organisation type and purpose:
National organisation, trade association (membership is by qualification), present number of members: 39 Corporate members.
Corporate membership for NHS Ambulance Services.

Subject coverage:
NHS Ambulance Services.

Trade and statistical information:
Data on Ambulance personnel, finance and operations.

Printed publications:
The Future of the Ambulance Services in the UK to 2010 (£5)
Operational Arrangements for Civil Emergencies (£25)
Guidance on Chemical Incidents (£25)
Mailing list of UK Ambulance Services (£25)
Order printed publications from: Administrative Assistant, Ambulance Service Association
As main address

Access to staff:
Contact by letter
Hours: Mon to Fri, 0900 to 1730

Access to building, collection or gallery:
Prior appointment required

Access for disabled people:
Parking provided, ramped entry, access to all public areas, toilet facilities

AMERICAN AUTO CLUB UK

Acronym or abbreviation: AAC UK

2 Cumbers Cottage, Sandy Lane, Hanmer, Whitchurch, Shropshire, SY13 3DL

Tel: 01948 830754
Fax: 01948 830754
E-mail: secaacuk@aol.com

Website:
http://www.american-auto-club.co.uk
Membership and events details.

Enquiries:
Enquiries to: Chief Executive Officer
Other contacts: Membership Secretary, President

Founded:
1981

Organisation type and purpose:
International organisation, membership association (membership is by subscription), present number of members: 2600.
To expand interest and ownership of American automobiles in the UK.

Subject coverage:
Technical information on American automobiles, registrations, valuations for insurance purposes, location of parts. Recognised by DVLA for providing vehicle data to obtain year-related registrations. There are 47 area representatives covering the United Kingdom and the United States to locate spares etc.

Museum or gallery collection, archive, or library special collection:
Collection of books relating to production and data of American cars, trucks and motor cycles

Printed publications:
Magazine (monthly, free to members)

Access to staff:
Contact by letter, by telephone, by fax and by e-mail
Hours: Mon to Fri, 0900 to 1700

Access to building, collection or gallery:
No access other than to staff

AMERICAN CHURCH IN LONDON

Acronym or abbreviation: ACL

Whitefield Memorial Church, Tottenham Court Road, London, W1T 4TD

Tel: 020 7580 2791
Fax: 020 7580 5013

Enquiries:
Enquiries to: Secretary
Direct e-mail: churchsecretary@amchurch.fsnet.co.uk
Other contacts: (1) Senior Pastor; (2) Associate Pastor; (3) Church Secretary

Organisation type and purpose:
Church.

Access to staff:
Contact by telephone, by fax and by e-mail
Hours: Mon to Fri, 0900 to 1700

Member of:
The United Reform Church (URC)

AMERICAN EMBASSY

Formal name: Embassy of The United States of America

Information Resource Centre, American Embassy, 24 Grosvenor Square, London, W1A 1AE

Tel: 020 7894 0925 (1000 to 1200); 020 7894 0643
Fax: 020 7629 8288
E-mail: reflond@state.gov

Website:
http://london.usembassy.gov

Enquiries:
Enquiries to: Resource Centre Director
Direct tel: 020 7499 5684

Organisation type and purpose:
National government body.
Embassy unit.

Respond to enquiries about the US from journalists, media researchers, academics, libraries, members of parliament, government departments.

Subject coverage:
United States government, politics, legislation, society, current affairs.

Museum or gallery collection, archive, or library special collection:
Approximately 30 US journal subscriptions in appropriate subject areas (news, current affairs, politics etc)
Approximately 2000 books
CIS (Congressional Information Service) microfiche collection
Selected US Government reports and documents

Trade and statistical information:
Only basic economic and trade-related statistical data on the US.
Market survey-type information is not held.

Library catalogue:
All or part available in print

Access to staff:
Contact by letter, by telephone, by fax and by e-mail. Appointment necessary.
Hours: Mon to Fri, 0900 to 1700

Access to building, collection or gallery:
Prior appointment essential

Parent body:
Department of State
Washington DC, 20520, United States of America; website: http://www.america.gov; http://www.state.gov

AMERICAN TECHNICAL PUBLISHERS LIMITED

Acronym or abbreviation: ATP

IHS, Willoughby Road, Bracknell, Berkshire, RG12 8FB

Tel: 01344 328039
Fax: 01344 328005 emeastore@ihs.com
E-mail: emeastore@ihs.com

Website:
http://www.ameritech.co.uk/
Search facility for technical book and standards.
http://www.ihsatp.com/

Enquiries:
Enquiries to: Managing Director

Founded:
1980

Organisation type and purpose:
Distributor of standards and technical information.

Subject coverage:
Providers of technical standards and books of USA engineering societies and publishers.

Printed publications:
Engineering Publications Catalogues

Electronic and video publications:
ASTM Standards on CD-ROM

Access to staff:
Contact by letter, by telephone, by fax, by e-mail and via website
Hours: Mon to Fri, 0800 to 1730

AMERICAN UNIVERSITY IN LONDON

97–101 Seven Sisters Road, London, N7 7QP

Tel: 020 7263 2986
Fax: 020 7281 2815
E-mail: aul@ukbusiness.com or info@aul.edu

Website:
http://www.aul.edu

Enquiries:
Enquiries to: Registrar
Direct e-mail: aul@ukbusiness.com or inf@aul.edu

continued overleaf

Founded:
1986

Organisation type and purpose:
University department or institute.

Non-library collection catalogue:
All or part available online

Library catalogue:
All or part available in-house

Access to staff:
Contact by letter, by telephone, by fax, by e-mail and in person. Appointment necessary.
Hours: Mon to Fri, 0900 to 1700

Access to building, collection or gallery:
No prior appointment required

AMICUS – MSF SECTION

MSF Centre, 33–37 Moreland Street, London, EC1V 8HA

Tel: 020 7505 3271
Fax: 020 7505 3282
E-mail: info@msf.org.uk

Website:
http://www.msf.org.uk

Enquiries:
Enquiries to: Head of Research

Founded:
1988

Formerly called:
Association of Scientific, Technical and Managerial Staffs (ASTMS), Manufacturing Science Finance (MSF), Technical and Supervisory Staffs Union (TSSU)

Organisation type and purpose:
Trade union, present number of members: 416,000.

Subject coverage:
Trade Union representing professional, managerial and technical staff in a wide range of industries including engineering, aerospace, oil and chemicals, electronics and computing, vehicle manufacture, food, drink and tobacco, universities, the health service, insurance and banking and the voluntary sector.

Printed publications:
AMICUS-MSF Works
AMICUS-MSF Report
NHS News
Common Ground
Community Practitioner (CPHVA)
Finance Sector Update
Selling Today

Access to staff:
Contact by e-mail
Hours: Mon to Fri, 0900 to 1700

Access for disabled people:
Access to all public areas, toilet facilities

Affiliated to:
Trades Union Congress and the Labour Party

AMIIS

Formal name: Advocacy, Mediation and Independent Investigation Service
Acronym or abbreviation: AMIIS

Astolat, Coniers Way, Guildford, Surrey, GU4 7HL

Tel: 01483 531308
Fax: 01483 301072
E-mail: mediation@amiis.com

Website:
http://www.amiis.com
Description of services.

Enquiries:
Enquiries to: Head of Service
Direct e-mail: david@amiis.com

Organisation type and purpose:
Membership association (membership is by election or invitation), voluntary organisation.
Resolving problems/complaints for social service users and carers in Surrey.

Subject coverage:
Social service users and carers.

Access to staff:
Contact by letter, by telephone, by fax, by e-mail and in person
Hours: Mon to Fri, 0900 to 1700

Access for disabled people:
Parking provided
Special comments: Access via separate door and lift.
Please telephone to make arrangements.

AMNESTY INTERNATIONAL (UNITED KINGDOM)

Acronym or abbreviation: AI

1 Easton Street, London, WC1X 0DW

Tel: 020 7413 5500
Fax: 020 7956 1157
E-mail: sct@amnesty.org.uk

Website:
http://www.amnesty.org/en/library
Library
http://www.amnesty.org.uk/news/index.html
Press releases, Amnesty magazine, letter writing activities.
http://www.amnesty.org.uk/amnesty/index.html
Introduction to AIUK.
http://www.amnesty.org.uk/support/index.html
Events and fundraising.
http://www.amnesty.org.uk/action/index.html
Campaigning news.

Enquiries:
Enquiries to: Information Officer
Direct e-mail: press@amnesty.org.uk

Founded:
1961

Organisation type and purpose:
International organisation, membership association (membership is by subscription), voluntary organisation.
Human rights campaigning.
Seeks release of prisoners of conscience; against death penalty, torture, political killings and disappearances; for fair trials for political prisoners.

Subject coverage:
Human rights violations worldwide.

Museum or gallery collection, archive, or library special collection:
Collection of recent AI reports on human rights issues

Library catalogue:
All or part available online

Printed publications:
Amnesty (magazine)
Books and video catalogue

Microform publications:
AI reports available on microfiche

Electronic and video publications:
Videos available for purchase

Publications list:
Available online and in print

Access to staff:
Contact by letter, by telephone, by fax, by e-mail and via website
Hours: Mon to Fri, 0900 to 1700

Access to building, collection or gallery:
No prior appointment required

AMSPAR LIMITED

Formal name: Association of Medical Secretaries, Practice Managers, Administrators and Receptionists Limited
Acronym or abbreviation: AMSPAR

Tavistock House North, Tavistock Square, London, WC1H 9LN

Tel: 020 7387 6005
Fax: 020 7388 2648
E-mail: info@amspar.co.uk

Website:
http://www.amspar.com

Enquiries:
Enquiries to: Membership Secretary

Founded:
1964

Organisation type and purpose:
Professional body (membership is by subscription, qualification, election or invitation), present number of members: 4,000, registered charity (charity number 313310), suitable for ages: 16+.
National registered awarding body for professional qualifications.

Subject coverage:
Professional qualifications for General Practice Managers, medical secretaries, medical receptionists, delivered via a network of approved centres and colleges throughout the United Kingdom.

Printed publications:
Quarterly Magazine
Careers leaflets
College lists

Access to staff:
Contact by letter, by telephone, by fax and by e-mail. Appointment necessary.
Hours: Mon to Fri, 0900 to 1700

ANAESTHETIC RESEARCH SOCIETY

Acronym or abbreviation: ARS

University Department of Anaesthesia and Intensive Care, Queen's Medical Centre, Nottingham, NG7 2UH

Tel: 0115 823 1002
Fax: 0115 970 0739

Website:
http://www.ars.ac.uk

Enquiries:
Enquiries to: Honorary Secretary
Direct e-mail: jonathan.hardman@nottingham.ac.uk

Founded:
1958

Organisation type and purpose:
Learned society.
Presentation and publication of ongoing research in anaesthesia and related subjects.

Subject coverage:
Anaesthesia; intensive care; acute and chronic pain relief.

Museum or gallery collection, archive, or library special collection:
Abstracts published twice a year in the British Journal of Anaesthesia

Printed publications:
British Journal of Anaesthesia (abstracts only)

Access to staff:
Contact by letter, by fax, by e-mail and via website
Hours: Mon to Fri, 0900 to 1700

ANAPHYLAXIS CAMPAIGN

PO Box 275, Farnborough, Hampshire, GU14 6SX

Tel: 01252 542029 (Helpline)\ 01252 546100
(Administration)
Fax: 01252 377140
E-mail: info@anaphylaxis.org.uk

Website:
http://www.anaphylaxis.org.uk
http://www.allergyinschools.org.uk

Founded:
1994

Organisation type and purpose:
Membership association (membership is by
subscription), present number of members: 7800,
registered charity (charity number 1085527).
Offer support and guidance to those with life
threatening allergies, raise awareness in food
industry, medical profession etc, promote research.

Subject coverage:
Anaphylaxis, allergic reactions.

Printed publications:
Cyril the Squirrel (children's book, £5.25)

Electronic and video publications:
Action for Anaphylaxis (information video, £16.50,
DVD, £18 both incl p&p)
The New Kid (children's information video, £2 incl
p&p)

Access to staff:
Contact by letter, by telephone, by fax, by e-mail
and via website
Hours: Mon to Fri, 0900 to 1700
Special comments: Answerphone outside office
hours; membership queries to PO Box address.

Office at:
Anaphylaxis Campaign
1 Alexandra Road, Farnborough, Hampshire,
GU14 6BU; tel: 01252 542029; fax: 01252 377140;
e-mail: info@anaphylaxis.org.uk

ANATOMICAL SOCIETY OF GREAT BRITAIN AND IRELAND

Acronym or abbreviation: ASGBI

Department of Anatomy, University College, Cork,
Republic of Ireland

Tel: 00 35321 4902115
Fax: 00 35321 4273518
E-mail: anatomy@ucc.ie

Website:
http://www.blackwell-science.com
Information on the society.
http://www.journals.cup.org
Information on the Journal of Anatomy.

Enquiries:
Enquiries to: Honorary Secretary
Other contacts: (1) Membership Secretary (2)
Treasurer for (1) membership queries (2) financial
queries.

Founded:
1887

Organisation type and purpose:
Learned society.

Subject coverage:
Gross anatomy, anthropology, histology, cell
biology, developmental biology, pathological
anatomy, biomechanics and related topics.

**Museum or gallery collection, archive, or library
special collection:**
Human embryology database

Printed publications:
Journal of Anatomy (8 times a year, pub.
Blackwells)
Order printed publications from: Blackwell Science
Limited
Osney Mead, Oxford, OX2 0EL, tel: 01865 206206,
fax: 01865 721205

Access to staff:
Contact by letter, by e-mail and via website
Hours: Mon to Fri, 0900 to 1700

ANCIENT AND HONOURABLE GUILD OF TOWN CRIERS

Formal name: The Ancient and Honourable Guild of
Town Criers
Acronym or abbreviation: AHGTC

10 Weston Road, Guildford, Surrey, GU2 8AS

Tel: 01483 833489
Fax: 01483 833489
E-mail: secretary@ahgtc.org.uk

Website:
http://www.ahgtc.org.uk
History, How to Join, Events.

Enquiries:
Enquiries to: Honorary Secretary
Other contacts: Membership Secretary (for
appointment of new Town Criers, new members)

Founded:
1978

Organisation type and purpose:
International organisation, membership
association.

Subject coverage:
Town crying for local authorities and commercial
interests, non-political. Town Crying competitions,
information, history and organisation; charters the
World Town Criers Championship, the European
Towncriers Championship.

Printed publications:
Newsletter (quarterly, members only)

Access to staff:
Contact by letter, by telephone, by fax, by e-mail
and via website
Hours: Mon to Fri, 0900 to 2200

Access to building, collection or gallery:
No access other than to staff

Subsidiary body:
World Town Criers Championships Limited
at the same address

ANCIENT MONUMENTS SOCIETY

Acronym or abbreviation: AMS

St Ann's Vestry Hall, 2 Church Entry, London,
EC4V 5HB

Tel: 020 7236 3934
E-mail: office@ancientmonumentssociety.org.uk

Website:
http://www.ancientmonumentssociety.org.uk

Enquiries:
Enquiries to: Secretary

Founded:
1924

Organisation type and purpose:
National organisation, learned society
(membership is by subscription), present number
of members: 2,000, voluntary organisation,
registered charity (charity number 209605).
Study and conservation of ancient monuments,
historic buildings of all ages and fine old
craftsmanship.

Subject coverage:
Historic buildings of all ages and types, their
dating, conservation and care, new uses, planning;
law as it relates to them; sources of money for their
restoration.

Library catalogue:
All or part available in-house

Printed publications:
Newsletters (three times a year)
Transactions (annually)

Publications list:
Available in print

Access to staff:
Contact by letter, by telephone and by e-mail
Hours: Mon to Fri, 0900 to 1700

Access to building, collection or gallery:
No access other than to staff

Links with:
Friends of Friendless Churches

ANDREA ADAMS TRUST

Acronym or abbreviation: AAT

Hova House, 1 Hova Villas, Hove, East Sussex,
BN3 3DH

Tel: 01273 704900
Fax: 01273 704900
E-mail: elaine@andreaadamstrust.org

Website:
http://www.andreaadamstrust.org

Enquiries:
Enquiries to: Office Manager

Founded:
1997

Organisation type and purpose:
Registered charity (charity number 1064539),
training organisation, consultancy.
National Workplace Bullying Advice Line, training
and mediation for business and industry.

Subject coverage:
Workplace bullying.

Trade and statistical information:
Statistical information on workplace bullying and
rates of occurrence.

Printed publications:
Bullying at Work (Adams A and Crawford N,
1992, pub Virago)
Factsheet on workplace bullying (£3 with A4 sae)
Guide to Workplace Bullying: The Legal Position
Guide to Workplace Bullying: Summary of latest
research

Publications list:
Available in print

Access to staff:
Contact by letter, by telephone, by fax, by e-mail
and via website
Hours: Mon to Fri, 0900 to 1700
Special comments: No visitors.

Access to building, collection or gallery:
No access other than to staff

ANGELA THIRKELL SOCIETY

54 Belmont Park, London, SE13 5BN

Tel: 020 8244 9339
E-mail: penny.aldred@ntlworld.com

Website:
http://www.angelathirkellsociety.com

Enquiries:
Enquiries to: Secretary

Founded:
1980

Organisation type and purpose:
Membership association.
Literary society.

Subject coverage:
Life and works of Angela Thirkell and her family.

Printed publications:
Publications for members only

Publications list:
Available in print

Access to staff:
Contact by letter, by telephone and by e-mail
Hours: Mon to Fri, 0900 to 1700

Links with:
Alliance of Literary Societies (ALS)
22 Belmont Grove, Bedhampton, Havant,
Hampshire, PO9 3PU; tel: 02392 475855; fax:
02392 788842; e-mail: rosemary@sndc.demon.co
.uk

ANGLESEY ANTIQUARIAN SOCIETY AND FIELD CLUB

Acronym or abbreviation: AAS

Llangefni Library, Education and Leisure Department, Isle of Anglesey County Council, Lôn y Felin, Llangefni, Anglesey, LL77 7RT

Tel: 01248 752092
Fax: 01248 750197
E-mail: hanesmon@btinternet.com

Website:
http://www.hanesmon.btinternet.co.uk
Who we are, membership, publications, meetings, excursions, transactions, constitution, committees.

Enquiries:
Enquiries to: Honorary Librarian and Curator
Other contacts: Honorary General Secretary for general information regarding the Society.

Founded:
1911

Organisation type and purpose:
Learned society, registered charity (charity number 507837).

Subject coverage:
Anglesey; its history, antiquities, archaeology, natural science, geology and literature.

Museum or gallery collection, archive, or library special collection:
Collection of printed materials, manuscripts and artefacts pertaining to Anglesey
Lucy Williams, Holyhead Collection
Transactions and Proceedings of various historical and antiquarian societies
William Williams, Pentraeth (1839–1915) Collection

Non-library collection catalogue:
All or part available in-house

Printed publications:
A New Natural History of Anglesey (Jones W E ed, 1990, £7.50 plus p&p)
Index to Transactions 1913–1985 (Jones D comp, 1987, £3 plus p&p)
Newsletter (2 times a year, free to members)
Prehistoric Anglesey (Lynch F, 2nd ed., 1991, £17 plus p&p)
Portraits of an Island (Ramage H, 2nd ed., 2001, £12.95 plus p&p)
Transactions (annually, free to members, some back issues available £6 per volume)
Order printed publications from: Publications Officer, Anglesey Antiquarian Society and Field Club Bryn Eglwys, Llanddyfnan, Llangefni, Anglesey, LL75 8UL, tel: 01248 450310

Publications list:
Available online

Access to staff:
Contact by letter, by telephone and by fax.
Appointment necessary.
Hours: Mon to Fri, 0900 to 1700

Access for disabled people:
Parking provided, level entry, toilet facilities
Special comments: Lift available.

ANGLESEY COUNTY ARCHIVE SERVICE

Formal name: Gwasanath Archifau Ynys Mon/ Anglesey County Archive Service

Shire Hall, Glanhwfa Road, Llangefni, Anglesey, LL77 7TW

Tel: 01248 752080
Fax: 01248 751289
E-mail: archifau@anglesey.gov.uk

Website:
http://www.ynysmon.gov.uk
Summary of holdings and purpose of Record Office.

Enquiries:
Enquiries to: Archivist

Founded:
1974

Formerly called:
Llangefni Area Record Office of Gwynedd Archives and Museums Service (year of change 1996)

Organisation type and purpose:
Local government body.
Record Office.

Subject coverage:
Usual holdings of a county record office including parish records, quarter sessions records, poor law unions, local authorities, family and business collections.

Non-library collection catalogue:
All or part available in-house

Access to staff:
Contact by letter, by telephone, by fax, by e-mail and in person
Hours: Mon, Wed, Thur, Fri, 0900 to 1700; Tue, 1400 to 1700 (1400 to 1900 every 2nd and 4th Tue)
Special comments: Member of the County Archives Research Network, tickets issued on day of visit with suitable identification.

Access to building, collection or gallery:
No prior appointment required
Hours: Mon, Wed, Thur, Fri, 0900 to 1700; Tue, 1400 to 1700 (1400 to 1900 every 2nd and 4th Tue)
Special comments: Closed: first full week in November; St David's day. No prior appointment required except for microform.

Access for disabled people:
Toilet facilities
Hours: Mon, Wed, Thur, Fri, 0900 to 1700; Tue, 1400 to 1700 (1400 to 1900 every 2nd and 4th Tue)
Special comments: Stairlift, with prior arrangement access to a ground floor room can be arranged.

ANGLIA RUSKIN UNIVERSITY

Acronym or abbreviation: ARU

University Library, Queen's Building, Rivermead Campus, Bishop Hall Lane, Chelmsford, Essex, CM1 1SQ

Tel: 01245 493131
Fax: 01245 490835
E-mail: username@nglia.ac.uk

Website:
http://www.libweb.anglia.ac.uk
Information page and prospectus of university (projected). Library catalogue and links to other sources.

Enquiries:
Enquiries to: University Librarian

Formerly called:
Cambridge College of Arts & Technology, Essex Institute

Organisation type and purpose:
University library.

Subject coverage:
Law, business, management, telecommunications, languages, built environment, computing, education, nurse education, social welfare, humanities, technology, science, art, design, music, social science, English, women's studies, forensic science, chemistry, communications and media, history, optometry, psychology, politics

Museum or gallery collection, archive, or library special collection:
French Resistance Archive (Cambridge)

Library catalogue:
All or part available online

Access to staff:
Contact by letter, by fax, by e-mail, in person and via website
Hours: Varies between sites, telephone for details or see web pages
Special comments: Appropriate identification should be carried.

Access for disabled people:
Parking provided, level entry, toilet facilities

Other address:
Anglia Ruskin University
University Library, Cambridge Road Campus, East Road, Cambridge, CB1 1PT; tel: 01223 363271; fax: 01223 352973

ANGLIA SUPPORT PARTNERSHIP

Acronym or abbreviation: ASP

Kingfisher House, Hinchingbrooke Business Park, Huntingdon, Cambridgeshire, PE29 6FH

Tel: 01480 398708
Fax: 01480 398501
E-mail: asplibrary@asp.nhs.uk

Website:
http://www.nowledge.asp.nhs.uk
Information about the health authority, its partners, local information, demographics, full text Public Health Report and HIMP

Enquiries:
Enquiries to: Head of Knowledge Services
Direct tel: 01480 398622
Direct e-mail: hilary.jackson@cambs-ha.nhs.uk

Founded:
1999

Formerly called:
Cambridge and Huntingdon Health Authority, Cambridge Health Authority, Cambridgeshire Family Health Services Authority, Huntingdon Health Authority, North West Anglia Health Authority, Cambridgeshire Health Authority

Organisation type and purpose:
Shared Services Organisation

Subject coverage:
Health management, evidence-based health care, public health, social care.

Library catalogue:
All or part available online

Access to staff:
Appointment necessary.
Hours: Mon to Fri, 0900 to 1700

Access to building, collection or gallery:
No prior appointment required

Access for disabled people:
Access to all public areas

ANGLICAN SOCIETY FOR THE WELFARE OF ANIMALS

Acronym or abbreviation: ASWA

PO Box 7193, Hound Green, Hook, Hampshire, RG27 8GT

Tel: 01252 843093
Fax: 01252 843093
E-mail: angsocwelanimals@aol.com

Website:
http://www.aswa.org.uk

Enquiries:
Enquiries to: Honorary Secretary

Founded:
1970

Organisation type and purpose:
Membership association, registered charity (charity number 1087270).
An Anglican, Christian animal welfare organisation.

Subject coverage:
Animal welfare, religious, educational, aiming to raise awareness of animal welfare issues amongst clergy and Christians.

Printed publications:
Pamphlets on a variety of animal issues written from a Christian perspective, eg use of animals for experimentation, hunting etc

Publications list:
Available in print

Access to staff:
Contact by letter, by telephone, by fax, by e-mail and via website. Appointment necessary.
Hours: Mon to Fri, 0900 to 1700

Access to building, collection or gallery:
Prior appointment required

ANGLO ARGENTINE SOCIETY

Acronym or abbreviation: AAS

2 Belgrave Square, London, SW1X 8PJ

Tel: 020 7235 9505
Fax: 020 7235 9505
E-mail: angloargentinesociety@hotmail.co.uk

Enquiries:
Enquiries to: Secretary

Founded:
1948

Organisation type and purpose:
International organisation, membership association (membership is by subscription), present number of members: 1,100, registered charity (charity number 208002).
To develop relationships between Argentina and the United Kingdom.

Subject coverage:
Anglo-Argentine relations.

Access to staff:
Contact by letter, by telephone, by fax, by e-mail and in person
Hours: Mon, Wed and Thu, 1330 to 1730

ANGLO BRAZILIAN SOCIETY

32 Green Street, London, W1K 7AU

Tel: 020 7493 8493
Fax: 020 7493 8493
E-mail: anglo@braziliansociety.freeserve.co.uk

Enquiries:
Enquiries to: General Secretary

Founded:
1943

Organisation type and purpose:
Membership association (membership is by subscription), registered charity.
To promote close and friendly relations between Brazil and the UK.

Subject coverage:
Brazil: its people, intellectual, artistic and cultural life.

Museum or gallery collection, archive, or library special collection:
Library of Brazilian books

Access to staff:
Contact by letter, by telephone and by e-mail
Hours: Tue, Wed, Thu, 1000 to 1600

Member of:
Hispanic and Luso-Brazilian Council
2 Belgrave Square, London, SW1X 8PJ

ANGLO EUROPEAN COLLEGE OF CHIROPRACTIC

Acronym or abbreviation: AECC

13–15 Parkwood Road, Bournemouth, BH5 2DF

Tel: 01202 436200
E-mail: library@aecc.ac.uk

Website:
http://www.aecc.ac.uk
Course information; college prospectus; clinic and research information.

Enquiries:
Enquiries to: Librarian
Direct tel: 01202 436307

Direct fax: 01202 436308
Direct e-mail: doneill@aecc.ac.uk

Founded:
1965

Organisation type and purpose:
University department or institute.

Subject coverage:
Chiropractic.

Library catalogue:
All or part available in-house

Access to staff:
Contact by letter, by telephone, by fax, by e-mail and via website. Appointment necessary. Non-members charged.
Hours: Mon to Fri, 0900 to 1700

Access to building, collection or gallery:
Prior appointment required

Access for disabled people:
Parking provided, ramped entry, level entry

ANGLO GERMAN FOUNDATION FOR THE STUDY OF INDUSTRIAL SOCIETY

Acronym or abbreviation: AGF

34 Belgrave Square, London, SW1X 8DZ

Tel: 020 7823 1123
Fax: 020 7823 2324
E-mail: info@agf.org.uk

Website:
http://www.agf.org.uk

Enquiries:
Enquiries to: Press and Publications Officer
Direct tel: +49 30 20634985
Direct fax: +49 30 20648466

Founded:
1973

Organisation type and purpose:
Registered charity.
Grant awarding body.
Funding British-German comparative research, conferences and seminars in in the fields of Innovation, Productivity and Growth; Environment and Resources; Welfare, Employment and Social Justice.

Subject coverage:
British-German comparative research in the fields of innovation, productivity and growth; environment and resources; welfare, employment and social justice.

Printed publications:
Various publications (books and reports) on industry, economics and social consequences; all reports are listed and can be downloaded from the Foundation's website at http://www.agf.org.uk.
Order printed publications from: Anglo-German Foundation, London

Publications list:
Available in print

Access to staff:
Contact by letter, by telephone, by fax and by e-mail. Appointment necessary.
Hours: Mon to Thu, 0900 to 1700; Fri, 0900 to 1600

Branches:
AGF
Anna-Louisa-Karsch-Straße 2, 10178 Berlin, Germany; tel: +49 30 20634985; fax: +49 30 20648466

ANGLO JEWISH ASSOCIATION

Acronym or abbreviation: AJA

Suite 5, 107 Gloucester Place, London, W1U 6BY

Tel: 020 7486 5055
Fax: 020 7486 5155
E-mail: info@anglojewish.co.uk

Website:
http://www.anglojewish.co.uk

Founded:
1871

Organisation type and purpose:
Voluntary organisation, registered charity (charity number 256946), suitable for ages: undergraduates and postgraduate students at university.

Subject coverage:
Jewish affairs, grants and loans for higher education.

Museum or gallery collection, archive, or library special collection:
Archives since 1871 (held at Southampton University)

Access to staff:
Contact by letter, by telephone and by fax
Hours: Mon to Thu, 0900 to 1500

Affiliated to:
Consultative Council of Jewish Organisations (UN)

ANGLO NORSE SOCIETY

25 Belgrave Square, London, SW1X 8QD

Tel: 020 7235 9529

Enquiries:
Enquiries to: Honorary Secretary

Organisation type and purpose:
Membership association (membership is by subscription), present number of members: 500, registered charity (charity number 263933).
A society promoting understanding between Britain and Norway.

Subject coverage:
Encouraging exchanges of an artistic, social, literary and scientific nature. Teaching of Norwegian in UK.

Printed publications:
Textbooks for the teaching of Norwegian
Anglo-Norse Review (2 times a year)
Newsletter (quarterly)

Access to staff:
Contact by letter and by telephone
Hours: Tue and Thu only, 1100 to 1600

ANGLO SCOTTISH FAMILY HISTORY SOCIETY

c/o Manchester & Lancashire FHS, Clayton House, 59 Piccadilly, Manchester, M21 2AQ

Tel: 0161 236 9750
Fax: 0161 237 3812
E-mail: office@mlfhs.org.uk

Website:
http://www.mlfhs.org.uk
Full catalogue and price list – subject index.

Enquiries:
Enquiries to: General Secretary

Founded:
1964

Organisation type and purpose:
Membership association (membership is by subscription), present number of members: c. 4500, registered charity (charity number 515599 (M&LFHS)).
Promotion of family history research.

Subject coverage:
Genealogy.

Museum or gallery collection, archive, or library special collection:
Extensive collection of genealogical material

Non-library collection catalogue:
All or part available in-house

Library catalogue:
All or part available in-house

continued overleaf

Printed publications:
Extensive list of indexes and transcripts

Microform publications:
Extensive list of indexes and transcripts

Electronic and video publications:
Specialist indexes and transcripts (CD-ROM)

Publications list:
Available online and in print

Access to staff:
Contact by letter, by telephone, by fax, by e-mail, in person and via website
Hours: Mon, Fri, 1015 to 1300; Tue, Thu, 1015 to 1600

Parent body:
Manchester & Lancashire FHS (M&LFHS)
   At the same address

ANGLO THAI SOCIETY

9 Old Hay Close, Dore, Sheffield, South Yorkshire, S17 3GP

Enquiries:
Enquiries to: Secretary

Organisation type and purpose:
Voluntary organisation.

Subject coverage:
Relations between Thailand and Great Britain; history, culture, economy, national institutions and external relations of Thailand.

Access to staff:
Contact by letter
Hours: Mon to Fri, 0900 to 1700

ANGLO TURKISH SOCIETY

43 Montrose Place, London, SW1X 7DU

Tel: 020 7235 8148 or 01420 562506
Fax: 01420 562506

Enquiries:
Enquiries to: General Secretary
Direct tel: 01420 562506

Founded:
1953

Organisation type and purpose:
Membership association (membership is by subscription), voluntary organisation, registered charity (charity number 278727).

Subject coverage:
Cultural and social Anglo-Turkish links.

Access to staff:
Contact by letter
Hours: Mon to Fri, 0900 to 1700

ANGLO-AUSTRIAN MUSIC SOCIETY

Acronym or abbreviation: AAMS

158 Rosendale Road, London, SE21 8LG

Tel: 020 8761 0444
Fax: 020 8766 6151
E-mail: info@aams.org.uk

Website:
http://www.aams.org.uk

Enquiries:
Enquiries to: General Secretary

Founded:
1942

Organisation type and purpose:
Membership association, registered charity (charity number 219021).
Concerts by Austrian artists. The Richard Tauber Prize for singers.

Access to staff:
Contact by letter, by fax and by e-mail
Hours: Mon to Fri, 0900 to 1700

ANGLO-HELLENIC LEAGUE

Acronym or abbreviation: AHL

1618 Paddington Street, London, W1U 5AS

Tel: 020 7486 9410
Fax: 020 7486 4254
E-mail: anglohellenic.league@virgin.net

Enquiries:
Enquiries to: Administrator

Founded:
1913

Organisation type and purpose:
Membership association (membership is by subscription), present number of members: 710, registered charity (charity number 278892).
To strengthen the ties between Great Britain and Greece, and promote social and cultural relations between the peoples of the two countries.

Subject coverage:
Great Britain and Greece relationships.

Printed publications:
The Anglo-Hellenic Review (ISSN 1351–9107, 2 times a year, £2 each issue, free to members)

Access to staff:
Contact by letter and by telephone
Special comments: Closed during August.

ANGLO-ISRAEL ASSOCIATION

Acronym or abbreviation: AIA

PO Box 47819, London, NW11 7WD

Tel: 020 8458 1284
Fax: 020 8458 3484
E-mail: info@angloisraelassociation.com

Website:
http://www.angloisraelassociation.com

Enquiries:
Enquiries to: Executive Director

Founded:
1949

Organisation type and purpose:
Membership association (membership is by subscription), present number of members: 250, voluntary organisation, registered charity (charity number 313523).
Friendship organisation promoting Anglo-Israel relations in the UK.

Subject coverage:
Israel and its place in the Middle East, Israeli life, scholarships.

Printed publications:
Annual newsletter
Pamphlets
Publicity material

Publications list:
Available in print

Access to staff:
Contact by letter, by telephone, by fax, by e-mail and via website. Appointment necessary.
Hours: Mon to Thu, 1000 to 1630

Access to building, collection or gallery:
No access other than to staff

Links with:
Israel, Britain and the Commonwealth Association Tel-Aviv, Israel

ANGLO-NORMAN TEXT SOCIETY

Acronym or abbreviation: ANTS

School of Languages, Birkbeck College, Malet Street, London, WC1E 7HX

E-mail: i.short@bbk.ac.uk

Website:
http://www.bbk.ac.uk/ants

Enquiries:
Enquiries to: Honorary Secretary

Founded:
1938

Organisation type and purpose:
Learned society, research organisation, publishing house.

Subject coverage:
Anglo-Norman language and literature; mediaeval French language and literature; publication of texts of historical, legal, linguistic and literary value.

Printed publications:
Annual Texts Series
Occasional Publications Series
Plain Texts Series
Medieval French Textual Studies (Vols 1–4, occasional)

Publications list:
Available online and in print

Access to staff:
Contact by letter, by e-mail and via website

ANGUS ARCHIVES

Hunter Library, Restenneth Priory, Forfar, DD8 2SZ

Tel: 01307 468644
E-mail: angus.archive@angus.gov.uk

Website:
http://www.angus.gov.uk/history/archives
Features on Angus people, places and documents. Resources listed for archives, photographs and books.
Contacts for Angus libraries and museums.

Enquiries:
Enquiries to: Archivist

Founded:
1989

Formerly called:
Angus Local Studies Centre

Organisation type and purpose:
Local government body.

Subject coverage:
Burgh and county history, village history, family history, Angus people, archives of Angus.

Museum or gallery collection, archive, or library special collection:
Over 800 sets of manuscript collections comprising papers belonging to individuals, businesses and societies in Angus, Arbroath, Brechin, Carnoustie, Edzell, Ferryden, Forfar, Kirriemuir, Montrose and Newtyle. These include:
Antiquities of Forfarshire, 19th century
Poems of Betty Stuart, Kinnaird Castle, 1911
Arbroath Ladies Clothing Society, 1840–1927
Papers of William Dorward, mariner in Arbroath, 1803–1871
Royal Naval Lifeboat Institute, Arbroath Branch, 1854–1983
Brechin Dispensary 1823–1870
Papers of Frederick A Ferguson, Town Clerk of Brechin, 1925–1959
Brechin Guildry papers, 1628-c.1900
Caledonian Railway – Carnoustie Station Lavatory charges, 1920–1974
Carnoustie Townswomen's Guild, 1964–1984
Papers concerning Rev Robert Inglis and Inglis Memorial Hall, 1837–1903
Forfar Baptist Church, 1872–1926
Forfar Tract Society, 1858–1940
Correspondence of J M Barrie, Kirriemuir, 1844–1892
Monifieth Scouts minute book, 1950–1969
Montrose Trades Library, 1855–1904
George Fairweather, Funeral Director, Baltic Street, Montrose, 1911–1971
Correspondence of George Paton, merchant in Montrose, 1762–1766
Newtyle Collection of William Murdoch Duncan, 1970s

Non-library collection catalogue:
All or part available online, in-house and in print

Library catalogue:
All or part available online and in-house

Printed publications:
Indexes to a large number of records, collections, and photographs

Electronic and video publications:
6,000 photographs

Access to staff:
Contact by letter, by telephone, by e-mail, in person and via website. Appointment necessary.
Hours: Mon to Fri, 1000 to 1600

Access to building, collection or gallery:
Hours: Mon to Fri, 1000 to 1600

ANGUS COUNCIL

Cultural Services, Administration Unit, County Buildings, Market Street, Forfar, Tayside, DD8 3WF

Tel: 01307 461460
Fax: 01307 462590
E-mail: cultural@angus.gov.uk

Website:
http://www.angus.gov.uk
Information on council services, events, departments, etc.

Enquiries:
Enquiries to: Senior Cultural Services Manager
Other contacts: Libraries Manager

Founded:
1996

Formerly a part of:
Angus District Council; Tayside Regional Council; Dundee City Council (year of change 1996)

Organisation type and purpose:
Local government body.
Public library, archives, art galleries and exhibition, museum, education resources service, halls and theatre.
The Libraries and Museums Service is a major community facility within Angus whose purpose is to give unbiased access to information.

Subject coverage:
General, Scottish and local history.

Museum or gallery collection, archive, or library special collection:
John C. Ewing, Forfar Library (Scottish Material)
Montrose Library (original Montrose Subscription Library)
R. W. Inglis Free Library, Edzell
On microfiche and available for consultation are the following:
British Standards
Census and Parish Records
Evaluation Volumes
International Genealogical Index
Local Newspapers

Library catalogue:
All or part available online and in-house

Publications list:
Available in print

Access to staff:
Contact by letter, by telephone, by fax, by e-mail and in person
Hours: Mon to Fri, 0900 to 1700

Links with:
Chartered Institute of Library and Information Professionals (CILIP)
Chartered Institute of Library and Information Professionals, Scotland (CILIPS)
Scottish Museums Council
SLIC

ANIMAL CONCERN

PO Box 5178, Dumbarton, Strathclyde, G82 5YJ

Tel: 01389 841639
Fax: 01389 841639

E-mail: animals@jfrobins.force9.co.uk

Website:
http://www.animalconcern.com

Enquiries:
Enquiries to: Campaigns Consultant
Direct tel: 07721 605521
Direct e-mail: animals@jfrobins.force9.co.uk

Founded:
1988

Formerly called:
Scottish Anti-Vivisection Society (SAVS) (year of change 1988)

Organisation type and purpose:
Membership association (membership is by subscription), present number of members: 302, voluntary organisation, suitable for ages: students. Pressure group.
The elimination of animal exploitation.

Subject coverage:
All animal rights and welfare issues.

Printed publications:
Animal Concern News (2 or 3 times a year, free)
Annual Report (free)
Range of fact sheets
Range of leaflets

Access to staff:
Contact by letter, by telephone, by fax, by e-mail and via website. Appointment necessary.
Hours: 24-hour access

Access to building, collection or gallery:
No access other than to staff

ANIMAL HEALTH TRUST

Acronym or abbreviation: AHT

Lanwades Park, Kentford, Newmarket, Suffolk, CB8 7UU

Tel: 08700 502424
Fax: 08700 502425
E-mail: library@aht.org.uk

Enquiries:
Enquiries to: Librarian

Founded:
1947

Organisation type and purpose:
Registered charity (charity number 209642), research organisation.
The advancement of veterinary science.

Subject coverage:
Veterinary science includes cancer, skin diseases, eye problems, genetics, haematology, immunology, clinical chemistry, microbiology, mycology, pathology, radiography, surgery and epidemiology.

Non-library collection catalogue:
All or part available in-house

Library catalogue:
All or part available in-house

Printed publications:
Animal Health Trust News (Quarterly)
Annual Report

Publications list:
Available online

Access to staff:
Contact by letter, by telephone, by fax and by e-mail. Appointment necessary.
Hours: Tues to Thurs, 0900 to 1700

Access to building, collection or gallery:
Prior appointment required

ANNE FRANK TRUST UK

Acronym or abbreviation: AFTUK

Star House, 104–108 Grafton Road, London NW5 4BA

Tel: 020 7284 5858

E-mail: info@annefrank.org.uk

Website:
http://www.annefrank.org.uk

Enquiries:
Enquiries to: Executive Director
Other contacts: Administrator

Founded:
1990

Formerly called:
Anne Frank Educational Trust (AFETUK)

Organisation type and purpose:
Membership association (membership is by subscription), registered charity (charity number 1003279), suitable for ages: all.

Subject coverage:
Holocaust education, anti-racism education, citizenship education.

Printed publications:
Dear Anne (magazine for Young Friends of the Anne Frank Educational Trust)
Diary (journal)
Anne Frank: A History for Today
Anne Frank Journal
Beyond the Diary

Electronic and video publications:
Dear Kitty (video)
A Book of Dreams (video)
Eyewitnesses (video)
Anne Frank Remembered (video)

Publications list:
Available online and in print

Access to staff:
Contact by letter, by telephone, by fax and by e-mail
Hours: Mon to Fri, 0900 to 1700

Access to building, collection or gallery:
No access other than to staff
Hours: Mon to Fri, 0930 to 1630

ANNUITY BUREAU, THE

The Tower, 11 York Road, London, SE1 7NX

Tel: 020 7902 2300
Fax: 020 7621 1888
E-mail: web-enquiry@annuity-bureau.co.uk

Website:
http://www.annuity-bureau.co.uk

Enquiries:
Enquiries to: Head of Marketing
Direct tel: 020 7902 2328
Direct fax: 020 7902 0388
Direct e-mail: david@bureauxltd.co.uk

Founded:
1991

Organisation type and purpose:
Service industry.

Subject coverage:
Financial service and advice at retirement.

Printed publications:
Income Drawdown (free)
You and Your Annuity (free)

Publications list:
Available online and in print

Access to staff:
Contact by letter, by telephone, by fax, by e-mail and via website
Hours: Mon to Fri, 0900 to 1700

Access for disabled people:
Parking provided, ramped entry

Northern Region Branch:
Annuity Bureau
Sunhill Laithe, Sunhill, Fleets Lane, Rystone, Skipton, BD23 6NA; tel: 01756 731 900; fax: 01756 730 443

ANTARCTIC ENVIRONMENTAL DATA CENTRE

Acronym or abbreviation: AEDC BAS

British Antarctic Survey, High Cross, Madingley Road, Cambridge, CB3 0ET

Tel: 01223 221400
Fax: 01223 362616
E-mail: aedc@bas.ac.uk

Website:
http://www.antarctica.ac.uk/aedc
Information on facilities and projects/support provided by the AEDC. Access to the AEDC's Metadata System for information on NERC's Antarctic data sets.

Organisation type and purpose:
Research organisation.
A virtual data centre proving a gateway to the distributed data holdings of the British Antarctic Survey. One of the Designated Centres of the UK Natural Environment Research Council (NERC).
The UK National Data Centre within the International Antarctic Data Directory Systems (ADDS).
Responsible for ensuring the secure, long-term management of BAS data holdings, individually managed by Principal Investigators and Programme Data Managers.

Subject coverage:
Information on data sets collected by BAS and other NERC sponsored organisations in the Antarctic covering: the physical, biological and geological sciences.

Trade and statistical information:
Under Article III(1)(c) of the Antarctic Treaty, data are to be freely exchanged between Treaty parties. Therefore, within the Antarctic scientific community data are made freely available.

Non-library collection catalogue:
All or part available online

Electronic and video publications:
Information on access to data sets from AEDC web pages, via BAS Metadata Management Systems (MDMS)

Access to staff:
Contact by e-mail and via website
Hours: Mon to Fri, 0900 to 1700
Special comments: Email is primary preferred form of contact.

Memberships:
One of the Designated Data Centres of the UK Natural Environment Research Council (NERC)
The UK National Antarctic Data Centre within the International Antarctic Data Directory Systems (NADC ADDS)

Parent body:
British Antarctic Survey
at the same address

ANTHROPOLOGY LIBRARY

British Museum Department of Ethnography, 6 Burlington Gardens, London, W1S 3EX

Tel: 020 7323 8031
Fax: 020 7323 8013

Website:
http://www.thebritishmuseum.ac.uk
http://lucy.ukc.ac.uk/AIO.html
The Index to the Anthropology Library's journal collection is available through Anthropological Index online, a free internet service.

Enquiries:
Enquiries to: Senior Librarian
Other contacts: Reading Room Supervisor for Reading Room enquiries, appointments, bibliographical information etc.

Formerly called:
British Museum Ethnography Library, Museum of Mankind Library (year of change 2001)

Organisation type and purpose:
National government body, museum.
The Anthropology Library is a major anthropological collection with its origins in the nineteenth century. It incorporates the former library of the Royal Anthropological Institute (RAI).

Subject coverage:
Its scope is worldwide and covers every aspect of anthropology: cultural anthropology, archaeology, some biological anthropology, linguistics, and related fields such as history, sociology and description and travel.
Material culture, ethnography, tribal art and anthropology of indigenous African, American, Asian, Oceanic and some European societies.
Archaeology of the New World.

Museum or gallery collection, archive, or library special collection:
Incorporates former library of the Royal Anthropological Institute
The library includes the Henry Christy and the Sir Eric Thompson collections and a significant Pictorial Collection
The collection contains around 120,000 books and pamphlets and 4000 journal titles (of which 1450 are current)

Library catalogue:
All or part available online

Access to staff:
Contact by letter, by telephone and by fax.
Appointment necessary.
Hours: Mon to Fri, 0900 to 1700
Special comments: Visitors by prior appointment except Fellows and Junior Fellows of the RAI.
Fellows and Junior Fellows of the RAI can borrow items donated by the RAI.
Other visitors and researchers may have access, by appointment, for reference purposes only.

Departmental library of the:
British Museum
currently housed in the former Museum of Mankind; tel: 020 7323 8031; fax: 020 7323 8013; e-mail: ethnography@thebritishmuseum.ac.uk

ANTHROPOSOPHICAL SOCIETY IN GREAT BRITAIN

Acronym or abbreviation: AS IN GB

Rudolf Steiner House, 35 Park Road, London, NW1 6XT

Tel: 020 7723 4400
Fax: 020 7724 4364

Website:
http://www.anth.org.uk
Anthroposophical Society; Rudolf Steiner Press Catalogue; Steiner Waldorf Education.

Enquiries:
Enquiries to: Librarian
Direct tel: 020 7224 8398
Direct fax: 020 7224 8398
Direct e-mail: rsh-library@anth.org.uk
Other contacts: Executive Secretary

Founded:
1923

Organisation type and purpose:
International organisation, learned society, registered charity (charity number 220480).

Subject coverage:
Anthroposophy (science of the spirit and the spiritual world); every field of art, science, religion, philosophy and social life from that aspect, including education, special needs education, medicine, agriculture and social sciences.

Museum or gallery collection, archive, or library special collection:
Art prints, photographs, archive material, eg: letters, journals
Books and MSS relating to Rudolf Steiner (1861–1925) and his work

Library catalogue:
All or part available in-house

Printed publications:
Catalogues of related publishers
Catalogue of Rudolf Steiner Press Publications
Information leaflets based on aspects of Steiner-based work
New View (magazine)
Rudolf Steiner House Programme (termly)

Electronic and video publications:
Small selection of videos

Access to staff:
Contact by letter, by telephone, by fax, by e-mail and in person
Hours: Office: 1030 to 1800
Bookshop: Mon to Fri, 1030 to 1400 and 1500 to 1800; Sat, 1030 to 1400 and 1500 to 1700
Library: Tue to Thu, 1100 to 1300 and 1400 to 1700 (Tue, 1930 term time); Fri, 1300 to 1800; Sat, 1200 to 1700

Associated with:
Anthroposophical Medical Association
tel: 01299 861561; fax: 01299 861375
Association of Camphill Communities
tel: 01653 694197; fax: 01653 600001; e-mail: info@camphill.org.uk
Bio-Dynamic Agricultural Association
tel: 01453 759501
Committee for Steiner Special Education
Emerson College (Forest Row)
tel: 01342 822238; fax: 01342 826055; e-mail: mail@emerson.org.uk
Peredur Centre for the Arts (Schools) of Eurhythmy and Speech Formation (East Grinstead)
Rudolf Steiner Press
Steiner Waldorf Schools Fellowship
tel: 01342 822115; fax: 01342 826004; e-mail: mail@waldorf.compulink.co.uk
Tobias School of Art (East Grinstead)
tel: 01342 313655; fax: 01342 313655
Triodos Bank (Bristol), and others
tel: 0117 973 9339; fax: 0117 973 9303

ANTI-SLAVERY INTERNATIONAL

Thomas Clarkson House, The Stableyard, Broomgrove Road, London, SW9 9TL

Tel: 020 7501 8920
Fax: 020 7738 4110
E-mail: antislavery@antislavery.org

Website:
http://www.antislavery.org
ASI website, with details of campaigns, news, resources (including the library, publications etc).
http://www.antislavery.org/breakingthesilence
UNESCO's Breaking the Silence free educational portal on the Transatlantic Slave Trade

Enquiries:
Enquiries to: Librarian
Direct tel: 020 7501 8939
Direct e-mail: j.howarth@antislavery.org

Founded:
1839

Organisation type and purpose:
Registered charity (charity number 1049160), research organisation.

Subject coverage:
Modern forms of slavery, child labour, child prostitution, indigenous peoples, domestic workers, child domestic workers, history of slavery, female genital mutilation, servile marriage, bonded labour, descent-based slavery, migrant labour, forced prostitution, child prostitution, codes of conduct, trafficking of people, Transatlantic Slave Trade, abolition.

Museum or gallery collection, archive, or library special collection:
A collection of eighteenth and nineteenth century tracts on slavery including Transatlantic Slavery Binns Collection and supplementary historical and slavery collection (also in microfilm)

Books, documents and research papers on modern forms of slavery
Collection of ILO publications on slavery
Collection of United Nations publications on slavery
Large collection of literature on child labour, bonded labour and trafficking.
Slides and photography relevant to exploited labour including Congo atrocities c. 1900

Non-library collection catalogue:
All or part available in-house

Library catalogue:
All or part available in-house

Printed publications:
Anti-Slavery Reporter (4 times a year, free to members, subscription £25, annually)
Redefining Prostitution as Sex Work on the International Agenda
Slavery in Sudan
The Cocoa Industry in West Africa: A history of exploitation
The Migration-Trafficking Nexus: Combating trafficking through the protection of migrants' human rights
Order printed publications from: Publications Officer tel: 020 7501 8922, fax: 020 7738 4110, e-mail: b .shand@antislavery.org

Microform publications:
Aborigines Protection Society
Anti-Slavery Reporter 1825 to date
Binns Collection and supplementary historical and slavery collection (microfilm from Academic Microforms)
Annual Reports 1880–2000 and Publications and Reports of Anti-Slavery International and predecessors, 1880–1979 by Adam Matthews

Electronic and video publications:
The Changing Face of Slavery (video and teacher's pack, £15)
Our News Our Views (video and teacher's pack, £14)

Publications list:
Available online and in print

Access to staff:
Contact by letter, by telephone, by e-mail and via website. Appointment necessary.
Hours: Mon to Fri, 1000 to 1700

Member of:
End Child Prostitution, Pornography and Trafficking (ECPAT, Ethical Trading Initiative (ETI) at the same address; tel: 020 7501 8927; e-mail: ecpatuk@antislavery.org

ANTIGUA AND BARBUDA TOURIST OFFICE

2nd floor, 45 Crawford Place, London, W1H 4LP

Tel: 020 7258 0070
Fax: 020 7258 3826
E-mail: tourisminfo@antigua-barbuda.com

Website:
http://www.antigua-barbuda.com

Enquiries:
Enquiries to: Director of Tourism

Organisation type and purpose:
To promote Antigua and Barbuda's tourist industry.

Subject coverage:
History of the islands, tourism including: weddings and honeymoons, water sports, sightseeing, golf, tennis, maps, sailing, special events, meetings and incentives, family holidays.

Trade and statistical information:
Tourism statistics.

Printed publications:
General information leaflets

Electronic and video publications:
CD-ROM, videos, available on loan
Slides available on Leonardo databank

Access to staff:
Contact by letter, by telephone, by fax, by e-mail, in person and via website
Hours: Mon to Fri, 0930 to 1500
Special comments: Contact by telephone is from 0900 to 1700.

Links with:
Ministry of Tourism, Culture and Environment

ANTIQUARIAN BOOKSELLERS ASSOCIATION

Acronym or abbreviation: ABA

Sackville House, 40 Piccadilly, London, W1J 0DR

Tel: 020 7439 3118
Fax: 020 7439 3119
E-mail: admin@aba.org.uk

Website:
http://www.aba.org.uk

Enquiries:
Enquiries to: Administrator

Founded:
1906

Organisation type and purpose:
Trade association.

Printed publications:
List of members, with fields of specialisation

Access to staff:
Contact by letter, by telephone, by fax and by e-mail
Hours: Mon to Fri, 0930 to 1730

Access to building, collection or gallery:
No access other than to staff

Affiliated to:
International League of Antiquarian Booksellers website: http://www.ilab.org

ANTIQUARIAN HOROLOGICAL SOCIETY

Acronym or abbreviation: AHS

New House, High Street, Ticehurst, Wadhurst, East Sussex, TN5 7AL

Tel: 01580 200155
Fax: 01580 201323
E-mail: secretary@ahsoc.demon.co.uk

Website:
http://www.ahsoc.demon.co.uk

Enquiries:
Enquiries to: Administrator

Founded:
1953

Organisation type and purpose:
Learned society, registered charity (charity number 260925).
Practises and promotes the study of antiquarian horology and allied disciplines in 13 countries.

Subject coverage:
Promotes the study of clocks and watches, and the history of time measurement in all its forms. The society has grown to be the premier Society in the English-speaking world devoted to antiquarian horology.

Museum or gallery collection, archive, or library special collection:
Library is housed at the Guildhall Library, London

Printed publications:
Antiquarian Horology (quarterly)
Books on horology including:
Norfolk & Norwich Clocks & Clockmakers (Bird C and Y, eds)
Suffolk Clocks & Clockmakers (Haggar and Miller)
The Clockmakers of Hertfordshire (Tyler E J)

Publications list:
Available online and in print

Access to staff:
Contact by letter, by telephone, by fax and by e-mail
Hours: Mon to Fri, 0900 to 1700

ANTIQUE COLLECTORS' CLUB

Acronym or abbreviation: ACC

Sandy Lane, Old Martlesham, Woodbridge, Suffolk, IP12 4SD

Tel: 01394 389950
Fax: 01394 389999
E-mail: sales@antique-acc.com

Website:
http://www.antique-acc.com

Enquiries:
Enquiries to: Marketing Director
Direct tel: 01394 389966
Direct e-mail: sarah.smye@antique-acc.com

Founded:
1966

Organisation type and purpose:
Publishing house.

Subject coverage:
Art, antiques, architecture, design, fashion, gardens and gardening.

Printed publications:
Antique Collecting (10 times a year)
Guide to the Antique Shops of Britain (annually)
An extensive range of titles covering:
Jewellery
Textiles
Horology
Glass
Art Reference, etc.

Publications list:
Available online and in print

Access to staff:
Contact by letter, by telephone, by fax, by e-mail and in person
Hours: Mon to Fri, 0900 to 1730

Also at:
Antique Collectors' Club
5 Church Street, Woodbridge, Suffolk, IP12 1DS; tel: 01394 385501; fax: 01394 384434

ANTRIM COURT SERVICE

30 Castle Way, Antrim, BT41 4AQ

Tel: 028 94 462661
Fax: 028 94 463301
E-mail: antrimcourthouse@courtsni.gov.uk

Enquiries:
Enquiries to: The Clerk of Petty Sessions

Formerly called:
Northern Ireland Court Service

Organisation type and purpose:
National government body.

Access for disabled people:
Parking provided, access to all public areas, toilet facilities

ANXIETY UK

Zion CRC, 339 Stretford Road, Hulme, Manchester, M15 4ZY

Tel: 0844 477 5774
Fax: 0161 226 7727
E-mail: info@anxietyuk.org.uk

Website:
http://www.anxietyuk.org.uk
National anxiety disorders charity.

Enquiries:
Enquiries to: Chief Executive

Founded:
1970

continued overleaf

Formerly called:
National Phobics Society

Organisation type and purpose:
Registered charity, voluntary organisation (charity number 1113403).

Subject coverage:
Anxiety disorders, of which there are over 400 classifications, specific help for those suffering from anxiety disorders ie phobias, agoraphobia, obsessional and compulsive disorders; depression. Help for people with tranquillisers – withdrawal and/or addiction. Panic attacks. Body Dysmorphic Disorder, social phobia, Generalised Anxiety Disorder (GAD).

Printed publications:
Bibliographies and self-help papers
Clinical Hypnotherapy
Contacts lists
Fact sheets
Network of Self-help Groups
Person-Centred Counselling
Quarterly magazine: Anxious Times
Cognitive Behavioural Therapy
Complementary Therapies

Publications list:
Available online and in print

Access to staff:
Contact by letter, by telephone, by fax, by e-mail, in person and via website. Appointment necessary. Access for members only. Non-members charged.
Hours: Mon to Fri, 0930 to 2100; message service outside office hours
Special comments: When corresponding by letter please enclose an sae.

Access for disabled people:
Access to all public areas

APACS

Formal name: APACS Administration Ltd

Mercury House, Triton Court, 14 Finsbury Square, London, EC2A 1LQ

Tel: 020 7711 6200
Fax: 020 7256 5527
E-mail: press@apacs.org.uk

Website:
http://www.apacs.org.uk

Enquiries:
Enquiries to: Director of Corporate Communications
Direct tel: 020 7711 6234
Direct e-mail: corpcomms@apacs.org.uk

Founded:
1985

Formerly called:
Association for Payment Clearing Services (year of change 2001)

Organisation type and purpose:
UK payments association. Provides the forum for the UK's financial institutions to come together on non-competitive issues, to develop banking systems for the future and to provide innovation and developments in payments.

Subject coverage:
UK payments issues including plastic cards, card fraud, cheques, electronic payments and cash.

Printed publications:
See online

Publications list:
Available online

Access to staff:
Contact by letter and by e-mail
Hours: Mon to Fri, 0900 to 1700

APEX TRUST

Formal name: Apex Charitable Trust Limited

7th Floor, 3 London Wall Buildings, London Wall, London EC2M 5PD

Tel: 020 7638 5931
Fax: 020 7638 5977
E-mail: jobcheck@apextrust.com

Website:
http://www.apextrust.com
Full description of the work of the Apex Trust – mission, services, operation, staff profiles, publications, how to make donations.

Enquiries:
Enquiries to: Chief Executive

Founded:
1965

Organisation type and purpose:
National organisation, registered charity (charity number 284736).
The Trust aims to reduce overall crime in society by the appropriate employment of people with a criminal record by operating 28 projects in prisons and the community giving direct advice to ex-offenders; by raising this issue with employers; and by working with other statutory and voluntary organisations in raising this issue.

Subject coverage:
Employment of ex-offenders; placing techniques; social skills training; careers advice; training in probation and after-care service, social services and prison service; attitudes and policies of professional bodies; unemployment and crime.

Museum or gallery collection, archive, or library special collection:
No library or collections

Printed publications:
Apex Fidelity Bond (free)
People Management (£1 plus 70p per copy p&p)
Releasing the Potential (£2.50 plus 70p per copy p&p)
Straight for Work (£3.50 plus 70p per copy p&p)
Work Matters (£3.50 plus 70p per copy p&p)

Publications list:
Available online and in print

Access to staff:
Contact by letter, by telephone, by fax, by e-mail and via website. Appointment necessary.
Hours: Mon to Fri, 1000 to 1800

Access to building, collection or gallery:
Prior appointment required
Hours: Mon to Fri, 1000 to 1800

APOSTROPHE PROTECTION SOCIETY

Acronym or abbreviation: APS

23 Vauxhall Road, Boston, Lincolnshire, PE21 0JB

Tel: 01205 350056
E-mail: john.richards2@virgin.net

Enquiries:
Enquiries to: Chairman

Founded:
2001

Organisation type and purpose:
Voluntary organisation.
To urge the correct use of the apostrophe and to give advice.

Subject coverage:
Correct use of the apostrophe.

Access to staff:
Contact by letter and by e-mail
Hours: Mon to Fri, 0900 to 1700

APPLIED ARTS SCOTLAND

ECA, School of Design and Applied Arts, Hunter Building, Lauriston Place, Edinburgh, EH3 9DF

Tel: 0131 221 6143
E-mail: office@appliedartsscotland.org.uk

Enquiries:
Enquiries to: Administrator
Other contacts: Convenor for policy matters.

Founded:
1992

Formerly called:
Association for Applied Arts (AAS) (year of change 2000)

Organisation type and purpose:
Membership association (membership is by subscription), present number of members: 300, voluntary organisation, registered charity (charity number SCO 22604).
To promote contemporary applied arts produced in Scotland.

Subject coverage:
Applied Arts Scotland holds a commissioning register of slides and information from around 300 makers in Scotland. They offer a commissioning service to public and private companies, galleries, retail outlets etc.

Printed publications:
The Bulletin (monthly)

Publications list:
Available in print

Access to staff:
Contact by letter, by telephone and by e-mail.
Access for members only. Non-members charged.
Hours: Mon, 0930 to 1730

Access to building, collection or gallery:
No prior appointment required
Special comments: Commissioning register.

ARAB HORSE SOCIETY

Acronym or abbreviation: AHS

Windsor House, The Square, Ramsbury, Marlborough, Wiltshire, SN8 2PE

Tel: 01672 520782
Fax: 01672 520880

Enquiries:
Enquiries to: Honorary Secretary
Direct tel: 01323 811385
Direct fax: 01323 811533
Direct e-mail: jean-mary.crozier@virgin.net

Founded:
1918

Organisation type and purpose:
Membership association (membership is by subscription), present number of members: 3950, registered charity (charity number 213366).
Breeding of Arabian horse and its derivatives, horse shows, amateur flat racing.

Subject coverage:
Stud book and race records for Arab, Anglo-Arab and part bred Arab horses.

Museum or gallery collection, archive, or library special collection:
Library mainly on breed stud books from 1918 when the Society was founded

Trade and statistical information:
World data on Arab horse registration.

Printed publications:
Journal (2 times a year, free to members)
Newsletter (3 times a year, free to members)

Access to staff:
Contact by letter, by telephone, by fax, by e-mail and in person
Hours: Mon to Fri, 0900 to 1700

Access to building, collection or gallery:
No prior appointment required

Affiliated to:
British Horse Society
ECAHO
WAHO

ARAB WORLD DOCUMENTATION UNIT

IAIS Building, Exeter University, Stocker Road, Exeter, Devon, EX4 4ND

Tel: 01392 264041
Fax: 01392 264035
E-mail: awdu@exeter.ac.uk

Website:
http://www.library.ex.ac.uk/awdu/bombaydiaries.htm
Descriptive listing of the extracts from the Bombay Diaries held at the centre.
http://www.library.ex.ac.uk/awdu
Introduction to the the Arab World Documentation Unit and summary of holdings.
http://www.library.ex.ac.uk/awdu/KeyTitlesList.html
Key Titles List: A detailed catalogue of major holdings.
http://lib.exeter.ac.uk/
University of Exeter Library online catalogue.

Enquiries:
Enquiries to: AWDU Librarian
Direct tel: 01392 264016
Direct e-mail: ahmed.zayed@exeter.ac.uk
Other contacts: Library Assistant (AWDU)

Founded:
1979

Formerly called:
Centre for Arab Gulf Studies Documentation Unit (CAGS); Arab World Documentation Unit (AWDU) (year of change 2001)

Organisation type and purpose:
University library, research organisation.
Reference and research library; Documentation Unit.
To further the study of the Gulf and Arabian Peninsula region, Arab countries and other Middle East topics.

Subject coverage:
Arab Countries, especially Arabian Peninsula and Gulf region: current documentation (often including back-runs to the mid-20th century) with emphasis on statistical material, economic reports, development plans, etc from governments and official sources including international organisations, commercial sources: banks, monetary agencies, commerce and industry, and also from academic and political sources and news media. History of the region, 16th to 20th century, including published, microform and photocopied archives.
Middle East studies: especially economic, political and sociological. Palestine and the Arab-Israeli Conflict.
International petroleum studies.

Museum or gallery collection, archive, or library special collection:
Archives held as photocopies or films:
Bombay Archives 1780–1830 (15,000 pages selected for relevance to the Gulf, Red Sea and Arabian Peninsula region, with typed transcripts and detailed index (this collection is unique, being the only copy in Europe)
Some Portuguese archives of the region 1560–1752
French consular correspondence on Muscat 1783–1810
Relevant selections from the National Archives of US, National Archives of India, UK Foreign Office and India Office records 1800–1959
Microfiche edition Palestine: the British Mandate. Also published books from Archive Editions of the region
A substantial library on Palestine, Israel and the Arab-Israeli conflict including governmental, international, commercial, academic and political publications, plus unpublished and archival materials and research documentation eg papers on Arrabeh 1850–1950
Press cuttings: classified microfiche collection on the Middle East 1957–82

Trade and statistical information:
Trade information for countries of the region and regional trade (Middle East)
Statistical information, on every aspect of the countries and the Middle East region. Primary countries covered: Bahrain, Iraq, Kuwait, Oman, Saudi Arabia, UAE, Yemen, Iran, Palestine, Israel, (also Lebanon, Jordan, Syria and Egypt).

Non-library collection catalogue:
All or part available online

Library catalogue:
All or part available online

Printed publications:
Catalogues of the Unit including Key Titles List (detailed list of major holdings)
Descriptive listings of extracts from the Bombay Diaries (available on request or from website)
New Arabian Studies (journal, available for sale from Exeter UP)

Access to staff:
Contact by letter, by telephone, by fax, by e-mail, in person and via website
Hours: Mon to Fri, 0900 to 1700
Special comments: A prior appointment for visitors is useful but not essential.

Access for disabled people:
Parking provided, level entry, toilet facilities

Parent body:
Exeter University Library
    Stocker Road, Exeter, EX4 4PT; tel: 01392 264051; fax: 01392 263871; e-mail: j.p.c.auchterlonie@ex.ac.uk

ARBORICULTURAL ASSOCIATION

Acronym or abbreviation: AA

Ampfield House, Winchester Road, Ampfield, Romsey, Hampshire, SO51 9PA

Tel: 01794 368717
Fax: 01794 368978
E-mail: admin@trees.org.uk

Website:
http://www.trees.org.uk

Enquiries:
Enquiries to: Chief Executive

Founded:
1964

Incorporates the former:
Association of British Tree Surgeons and Arborists

Organisation type and purpose:
National organisation, professional body, membership association (membership is by subscription), present number of members: 2000, registered charity.
To advance the science of arboriculture for the public benefit.

Subject coverage:
Production, selection, planning and maintenance of ornamental trees, shrubs and amenity woodlands; tree surveys, inspection, pathology; legal matters.

Non-library collection catalogue:
All or part available online

Printed publications:
Arboricultural Journal (quarterly)
Directories of Registered Consultants and Approved Contractors
Newsletter (4 times a year)
A Guide to Tree Pruning
Tree Survey and Inspection
A Guide to Good Climbing Practice
Twelve Leaflets to be purchased as a set, including:
Trees Suitable for Small Gardens
A Guide to Tree Planting
Trees, Subsidence, and other Structural Damage (A Householder's Guide)
Guide to the Use of MEWPs in Arboriculture
Order printed publications from: Postal address

Publications list:
Available online and in print

Access to staff:
Contact by letter, by telephone, by fax, by e-mail and via website
Hours: Mon to Fri, 0900 to 1700

Access to building, collection or gallery:
No prior appointment required

Access for disabled people:
Parking provided

Has:
8 regional branches

ARC

Formal name: Association for Real Change

ARC House, Marsden Street, Chesterfield, Derbyshire, S40 1JY

Tel: 01246 555043
Fax: 01246 555045
E-mail: contact.us@arcuk.org.uk

Website:
http://www.arcuk.org.uk

Enquiries:
Enquiries to: Chief Executive

Founded:
1976

Formerly called:
Association of Residential Communities

Organisation type and purpose:
Professional body (membership is by subscription), present number of members: 300 organisations, voluntary organisation, registered charity (charity number 285575), training organisation, publishing house.

Subject coverage:
Learning disability (mental handicap), social care, vocational training in health and social care, management, sexual abuse.

Non-library collection catalogue:
All or part available in-house and in print

Publications list:
Available online

Access to staff:
Contact by letter, by telephone, by fax, by e-mail and via website. Appointment necessary.
Hours: Mon to Fri, 0900 to 1700

Access to building, collection or gallery:
No prior appointment required
Hours: Mon to Fri, 0900 to 1700
Special comments: Library, members only.

Also at:
ARC Cymru
    Unit 3A, MENTEC, Deiniol Road, Bangor, LL57 2UP; tel: 01248 361990
ARC Northern Ireland
    43 Marsden Gardens, Cave Hill, Belfast, BT15 5AL; tel: 028 9022 9020; fax: 028 9020 9300; e-mail: arc.ni@arcuk.org.uk
ARC Scotland
    Unit 13, Hardengreen Business Centre, Eskbank, Dalkeith, Midlothian, EH22 3NX; tel: 0131 663 4444; fax: 0131 663 5522; e-mail: arc.scotland@arcuk.org.uk
ARC Training Consortium
    ARC House, Marsden Street, Chesterfield, Derbyshire, S40 1JY; tel: 01246 564970; fax: 01246 55504; e-mail: consortium@arcuk.org.uk

ARC ANTENATAL RESULTS & CHOICES

Acronym or abbreviation: ARC

73 Charlotte Street, London, W1P 1LB

Tel: 020 7631 0280
Fax: 020 7631 0280
E-mail: info@arc-uk.org

continued overleaf

Website:
http://www.arc.uk.org

Enquiries:
Enquiries to: Director

Founded:
1988

Formerly called:
Support Around Termination for Abnormality
(SATFA) (year of change 1998)

Organisation type and purpose:
Membership association, present number of
members: 1400, voluntary organisation, registered
charity (charity number 299770).

Subject coverage:
Helping parents through antenatal testing,
decision-making, offering continued support to
parents whatever decision they make about the
future of the pregnancy, training of health care
professionals to provide appropriate services.

Printed publications:
Another Pregnancy
Help for Fathers
Help for Grandparents
Talking to Children
Parents' Handbook – Support Around Termination
   For Abnormality
Parents handbook – Continuing a pregnancy after
   the diagnosis of an abnormality
ARC Information leaflet
ARC News
Supporting Parents' Decisions

Publications list:
Available online and in print

Access to staff:
Contact by letter, by telephone, by fax, by e-mail
and in person. Appointment necessary.
Hours: Mon to Fri, 1000 to 1700

ARCHAEOLOGY SCOTLAND

Formal name: Council for Scottish Archaeology
Acronym or abbreviation: CSA

Causewayside House, 160 Causewayside,
Edinburgh, EH9 1PR

Tel: 0131 668 4189
Fax: 0131 668 4275
E-mail: info@scottisharchaeology.org.uk

Website:
http://www.scottisharchaeology.org.uk

Enquiries:
Enquiries to: Director
Other contacts: Assistant Director for co-ordinator
of Young Archaeologists' Club Scottish network

Founded:
1944

Formerly called:
The Council for British Archaeology Scotland
(CBA Scotland)

Organisation type and purpose:
National organisation, membership association
(membership is by subscription), present number
of members: c. 900, voluntary organisation,
registered charity (charity no. SCO 001723),
suitable for ages: 8 to 16.
To promote informed opinion concerning the
conservation of Scotland's archaeological heritage.

Subject coverage:
Archaeology, including education, careers,
excavations, sources of information on sites,
cultural resource management and integrated
environmental approaches, who to contact in other
bodies etc.

**Museum or gallery collection, archive, or library
special collection:**
Inventory of the Scottish Church Heritage – A
   database of all sites in Scotland and how to
   access further details

Printed publications:
Discovery & Excavation in Scotland (annually,
   some out of print)
Scottish Archaeological News (3 times a year)

Publications list:
Available in print

Access to staff:
Contact by letter, by telephone and by fax.
Appointment necessary.
Hours: Mon to Fri, 0900 to 1700

Sister body of the:
Council for British Archaeology

ARCHDEACON SHARP LIBRARY

The College, Durham, DH1 3EH

Tel: 0191 386 2489
Fax: 0191 386 4267 (Durham Chapter Office)
E-mail: library@durhamcathedral.co.uk

Enquiries:
Enquiries to: Assistant Librarian

Organisation type and purpose:
Theological library.
A library of modern theology in English.

Subject coverage:
Theology : 20th century printed theology in
English.

Non-library collection catalogue:
All or part available online

Library catalogue:
All or part available online

Access to staff:
Contact by letter, by telephone, by e-mail and in
person
Hours: Mon to Fri, 0900 to 1300 and 1400 to 1700
Special comments: Closed for first two weeks of July.

Parent body:
Trustees of Lord Crewe's Charities
   c/o Chapter Clerk, Durham Cathedral, The
   College, Durham, DH1 3EH; tel: 0191 386 4266;
   fax: 0191 386 4267

ARCHERY GB

Lilleshall National Sports Centre, Near Newport,
Shropshire, TF10 9AT

Tel: 01952 677888
Fax: 01952 606019
E-mail: enquiries@archerygb.org

Website:
http://www.archerygb.org

Enquiries:
Enquiries to: Enquiries Officer

Founded:
1861

Formerly called:
Grand National Archery Society (year of change
2008)

Organisation type and purpose:
Membership association (membership is by
subscription), present number of members: 30,000.
Governing body for the sport of archery in the
United Kingdom.

Subject coverage:
Target archery; field archery; clout and flight
shooting; coaching; addresses of UK Clubs and of
overseas associations.

**Museum or gallery collection, archive, or library
special collection:**
Archers Register 1864–1915
Colonel Walrond Photographs Collection

Printed publications:
Archery UK (quarterly, free to members)
Does Fitness Count
Principles of Practice and Preparation for
   Tournaments

Electronic and video publications:
Coaching DVD

Access to staff:
Contact by letter, by telephone, by fax and by e-
mail
Hours: Mon to Fri, 0900 to 1700

Member organisation of:
AAS
   tel: 01295 721463
British Olympic Association
   tel: 020 8871 2677; fax: 020 8871 9104
Central Council of Physical Recreation
   tel: 020 7828 3163; fax: 020 7630 8820
English Federation of Disability Sport
   tel: 0161 247 5294; fax: 0161 247 6895
Fédération Internationale de Tir à l'Arc (FITA)
   tel: + 4121 614 3050; fax: + 4121 614 3055

ARCHIFDY CEREDIGION ARCHIVES

County Offices, Marine Terrace, Aberystwyth,
Ceredigion, SY23 2DE

Tel: 01970 633697/8
Fax: 01970 633663 (Attention: Archives)
E-mail: archives@ceredigion.gov.uk

Enquiries:
Enquiries to: Archivist

Founded:
1974

Formerly called:
Dyfed Archives; Cardiganshire Record Office
(year of change 1996)

Organisation type and purpose:
Local government body.

Subject coverage:
Historical information, often in manuscript form,
concerning the County of Ceredigion, formerly
Cardiganshire.

Access to staff:
Contact by letter, by telephone, by fax, by e-mail
and in person
Hours: Mon to Fri, 1000 to 1300 and 1400 to 1600

Access for disabled people:
Toilet facilities
Special comments: Disability lift and separate
entrance.

ARCHIFDY MEIRIONNYDD ARCHIVES

Ffordd y Bala, Dolgellau, Gwynedd, LL40 2YF

Tel: 01341 424681/424682
Fax: 01341 424683
E-mail: archives.dolgellau@gwynedd.gov.uk

Website:
http://www.gwynedd.gov.uk/Archives

Enquiries:
Enquiries to: Area Archivist

Organisation type and purpose:
Local government body.

Subject coverage:
Local history.

Non-library collection catalogue:
All or part available online and in-house

Library catalogue:
All or part available in-house

Access to staff:
Contact by letter, by telephone, by fax, by e-mail
and in person
Hours: Wed closed
Special comments: Closed first full week in
November.

ARCHITECTS REGISTRATION BOARD

Acronym or abbreviation: ARB

8 Weymouth Street, London, W1W 5BU

Tel: 020 7580 5861
Fax: 020 7436 5269
E-mail: info@arb.org.uk

Website:
http://www.arb.org.uk

Enquiries:
Enquiries to: Policy Adviser
Direct e-mail: suey@arb.org.uk

Founded:
1997

Formerly called:
Architects Registration Council of the United Kingdom (ARCUK) (year of change 1997)

Organisation type and purpose:
Statutory body.
UK statutory regulator of the architects' profession.

Printed publications:
Register of Architects (for purchase)

Publications list:
Available in print

Access to staff:
Contact by letter, by telephone, by fax and by e-mail
Hours: Mon to Fri, 0900 to 1700

Access for disabled people:
Ramped entry, toilet facilities

ARCHITECTURAL AND SPECIALIST DOOR MANUFACTURERS ASSOCIATION

Acronym or abbreviation: ASDMA

3 Coates Lane, High Wycombe, Buckinghamshire, HP13 5EY

Tel: 01494 447370
Fax: 01494 462094
E-mail: info@asdma.com

Enquiries:
Enquiries to: General Secretary

Founded:
1989

Organisation type and purpose:
Trade association (membership is by qualification, election or invitation), present number of members: 14 full, 7 associate, 2 associate installer, 1 sponsoring.
To promote the use of and correct fitting of specialist timber doorsets, through the adoption of quality and BS Standards, and fair conditions of contract.

Subject coverage:
Specialist timber doors, particularly fire, smoke, security and sound attenuating.

Printed publications:
Members' list – free

Access to staff:
Contact by letter, by telephone, by fax and by e-mail
Hours: Mon to Fri, 0900 to 1700

ARCHITECTURAL ASSOCIATION

Acronym or abbreviation: AA

34–36 Bedford Square, London, WC1B 3ES

Tel: 020 7887 4032
Fax: 020 7414 0782

Website:
http://www.aaschool.ac.uk/library/
Address for the library.
http://www.aaschool.ac.uk/photolib/
Photo Library.

http://www.aaschool.ac.uk/publications/
Publications.
http://www.aaschool.ac.uk
Main address for the AA.

Enquiries:
Enquiries to: Librarian
Direct tel: 020 7887 4035
Direct e-mail: hsklar@aaschool.ac.uk

Founded:
1847

Organisation type and purpose:
Professional body, membership association (membership is by subscription).
School of architecture.

Subject coverage:
Architecture, building, planning, landscape design.

Museum or gallery collection, archive, or library special collection:
AA Slide Collection
Early works on architecture
History of the Association
Material on the Architectural Association from 1847 onwards
Material on the Modern Movement
Rare and early works on architecture

Library catalogue:
All or part available online

Printed publications:
AA Association/School of Architecture:
AA Quarterly
AA School of Architecture Prospectus (annually)
Annual Review
Architectural Association Annual Review
Architectural Association Library Annual Report
Architectural Association Library Bibliographies (irregular)
Architectural Association Papers (irregular)
Architectural Association Quarterly
Exhibition Catalogues
Files: Annals of the AA School of Architecture
Guide to the Architectural Association Library (annually)
Projects Review (annually)
School of Architecture AA Cahiers
School of Architecture Projects Review (annually)
School of Architecture Prospectus (annually)
AA Library:
Annual Report
Online bibliographies
Guide to the Library
History of the AA Library from 1862
Periodicals and Serials in the AA Library
Theses and Essays in the AA Library
AA Slide Library:
History of the Slide Library
Introduction to the Slide Library

Publications list:
Available online and in print

Access to staff:
Access for members only. Non-members charged.
Hours: Term time: Mon to Fri, 1000 to 2100; Sat, 1100 to 1600
Vacations: 1000 to 1700; closed August to mid-September.

Includes the:
AA Photo Library

ARCHITECTURAL CLADDING ASSOCIATION

Acronym or abbreviation: ACA

60 Charles Street, Leicester, LE1 1FB

Tel: 0116 253 6161
Fax: 0116 251 4568
E-mail: aca@britishprecast.org

Website:
http://www.britishprecast.org/aca

Enquiries:
Enquiries to: Secretary

Organisation type and purpose:
Trade association.

Subject coverage:
Precast concrete architectural cladding.

Printed publications:
Cast in Concrete: reconstructed stone and precast concrete – a guide for architects (£25)
Code of Practice for the Safe Erection of Precast Concrete Cladding (£25)
Façade (newsletter)

Access to staff:
Contact by letter, by telephone, by fax and by e-mail
Hours: Mon to Fri, 0900 to 1700

Product association of the:
British Precast Concrete Federation

ARCHITECTURAL GLAZING SERVICES

Acronym or abbreviation: AGS

PO Box 2210, London, W1A 1WF

Tel: 0800 028 3708
Fax: 020 7535 5676
E-mail: info@cobaltco.co.uk

Website:
http://www.vanceva.com

Enquiries:
Enquiries to: Information Officer
Direct tel: 020 7535 5678
Direct e-mail: wendy@cobaltco.co.uk

Founded:
October 2001

Incorporated:
Laminated Glass Information Centre (formed in 1990) (LGIC), date of change, October 2001

Organisation type and purpose:
Private venture information centre, sponsored by Solutia SA/NV.
To offer advice to architects, specifiers, trade and industry, media and general public.

Subject coverage:
Safety, security, acoustic, solar-resistant laminated glass, also coloured and patterned laminated glass, laminated glass. Available in automotive and architectural sectors.

Printed publications:
Bulletin
Factsheets on regulations, safety, security etc
Questions and Answers on Laminated Glass

Electronic and video publications:
Variety of information (CD-ROM)

Publications list:
Available in print

Access to staff:
Contact by letter, by telephone, by fax and by e-mail
Hours: Mon to Fri, 0900 to 1700

Access to building, collection or gallery:
No access other than to staff

ARCHITECTURAL HERITAGE FUND

Acronym or abbreviation: AHF

Alhambra House, 27–31 Charing Cross Road, London, WC2H 0AU

Tel: 020 7925 0199
Fax: 020 7930 0295
E-mail: ahf@ahfund.org.uk

Website:
http://www.ahfund.org.uk
Details of services and publications available along with history objects and activities.

Enquiries:
Direct e-mail: ahf@ahfund.org.uk

continued overleaf

Founded:
1976

Organisation type and purpose:
Registered charity (charity number 266780).
To promote the preservation of historic buildings
for beneficial new uses by assisting the
establishment of suitable charitable trusts, and by
offering grants and working capital loans to such
charities.

Subject coverage:
The permanent preservation of buildings,
monuments or other edifices or structures, of
particular beauty or historical or constructional
interest in all parts of the United Kingdom.

**Museum or gallery collection, archive, or library
special collection:**
Back issues of own publications

Printed publications:
Annual Review (for sale)
How to Rescue a Ruin – by setting up a Buildings
Preservation Trust (1997, for sale)

Electronic and video publications:
Standard Governing documents for a Buildings
Preservation Trust (on disc) (£5)

Publications list:
Available in print

Access to staff:
Contact by letter, by telephone, by fax, by e-mail
and via website. Appointment necessary.
Hours: Mon to Fri, 0900 to 1700

Access to building, collection or gallery:
Mon to Fri, 0900 to 1700

Member of:
UK Association of Preservation Trusts (APT)
tel: 020 7930 1629; fax: 020 7930 0295; e-mail:
apt@ahfund.org.uk; website: http://www.ukapt
.org.uk

ARCHITECTURAL HERITAGE SOCIETY OF SCOTLAND

Acronym or abbreviation: AHSS

The Glasite Meeting House, 33 Barony Street,
Edinburgh, EH3 6NX

Tel: 0131 557 0019
Fax: 0131 557 0049
E-mail: nationaloffice@ahss.org.uk

Website:
http://www.ahss.org.uk

Enquiries:
Enquiries to: Director

Formerly called:
Scottish Georgian Society

Organisation type and purpose:
Learned society (membership is by subscription),
present number of members: 1440, voluntary
organisation, registered charity (charity number
SCO 07554).
The Society exists to promote the study and
protection of Scottish architecture.

Subject coverage:
Architectural conservation and history, planning
for listed buildings, protection of the built
environment, heritage.

Printed publications:
Architectural Heritage (journal, annually, free to
members, price varies, about £20)
Magazine (2 times a year, free to members, £5 each
plus p&p to non-members)

Access to staff:
Contact by letter, by telephone, by fax, by e-mail
and via website. Appointment necessary.
Hours: Mon to Fri, 0900 to 1700

ARCHITECTURE AND SURVEYING INSTITUTE

Acronym or abbreviation: ASI

St Mary House, 15 St Mary Street, Chippenham,
Wiltshire, SN15 3WD

Tel: 01249 444505
Fax: 01249 443602
E-mail: mail@asi.org.uk

Website:
http://www.asi.org.uk

Enquiries:
Enquiries to: Chief Executive

Founded:
1926

Amalgated with the:
Guild of Incorporated Surveyors (GIS), date of
change, October 1999

Formerly called:
Architects and Surveyors Institute (ASI),
Construction Surveyors Institute (CSI), Faculty of
Architects and Surveyors (FAS)

Organisation type and purpose:
International organisation, professional body
(membership is by subscription, qualification),
present number of members: 5500, service
industry, suitable for ages: all.
To promote and extend the practice, knowledge
and study of architecture and surveying.

Subject coverage:
Architecture, surveying, building contracts and
associated documentation, careers, examinations.

Printed publications:
ASI Journal (6 times a year, free to members, others
on subscription)
Build Safe (An Aid to C.D.M.)
Contract Administration Forms
Contract Documents
European Single Market: Matters Affecting the
Construction Industry
Newsletters (ad hoc)
Private Practice Register
Order printed publications from: ASI Services
Limited, St Mary House, 15 St Mary Street,
Chippenham, Wiltshire, SN15 3JN, tel: 01249
658262, fax: 01249 443602, e-mail: asinst@aol.com

Publications list:
Available in print

Access to staff:
Contact by letter, by telephone, by fax and by e-
mail. Appointment necessary.
Hours: Mon to Fri, 0930 to 1600

Member of:
Construction Industry Council
Construction Industry Standing Conference
European Group of Surveyors

Subsidiary body:
ASI Services Limited

ARCHITECTURE FOUNDATION

60 Bastwick Street, London, EC1V 3TN

Tel: 020 7253 3334
Fax: 020 7253 3335
E-mail: mail@architecturefoundation.org.uk

Website:
http://www.architecturefoundation.org.uk

Enquiries:
Enquiries to: Press and PR Co-ordinator
Direct e-mail: claire@architecturefoundation.org.uk

Founded:
1991

Organisation type and purpose:
Membership association (membership is by
subscription), present number of members: 150,
voluntary organisation, registered charity (charity
number 1006361), suitable for ages: all, research
organisation.

Access to staff:
Contact by letter, by telephone, by e-mail and via
website. Appointment necessary.
Hours: Tue to Sun, 1200 to 1800

Access for disabled people:
Ramped entry, toilet facilities

ARCHITECTURE+DESIGN SCOTLAND

Acronym or abbreviation: A+DS

Bakehouse Close, 146 Canongate, Edinburgh, EH8
8DD

Tel: 0131 556 6699
Fax: 0131 556 6633
E-mail: info@ads.org.uk

Website:
http://www.ads.org.uk/

Founded:
1927

Organisation type and purpose:
To promote good architecture, design and
planning in Scotland's built environment.

Subject coverage:
Planning, design of building, urban environment,
architecture, all aspects of planning and design of
our environment.

Non-library collection catalogue:
All or part available online

Library catalogue:
All or part available online

Access to staff:
Contact by letter, by fax and by e-mail
Hours: Mon to Fri, 0900 to 1700

Access for disabled people:
Level entry, toilet facilities
Special comments: Ground floor only.

Sponsor department:
Scottish Executive Education Department (SEED)

ARCHIVE OF ART AND DESIGN

Acronym or abbreviation: AAD

Word and Image Department, Victoria and Albert
Museum, 23 Blythe Road, London, W14 0QX

Tel: 020 7602 0281 ext 209
Fax: 020 7602 0980
E-mail: archive@vam.ac.uk

Website:
http://www.vam.ac.uk/resources/archives

Enquiries:
Enquiries to: Archivist

Founded:
1978

Organisation type and purpose:
Museum.
Archive collection of principally 20th-century
archives of designers, design associations and
companies involved in the design process.

Subject coverage:
British design, design, graphic design, product
design, illustration, textiles, fashion, ephemera.

**Museum or gallery collection, archive, or library
special collection:**
Over 250 archives, including:
Krazy Kat Arkive of 20th-century popular culture
Papers of individual designers, crafts people and
artists
Heal & Son Ltd, bedding and furniture
manufacturers and retailers
Edward Barnard & Sons Ltd, silversmiths
Art and Crafts Exhibition Society
John French, fashion photographer
Eileen Gray, interior and furniture designer and
architect
Ambassador, the British export magazine for
textiles and fashion

Non-library collection catalogue:
All or part available online and in-house

Library catalogue:
All or part available online

Printed publications:
Cumulative list of titles of the archive groups
collected by the Archive from 1978–August 1991
(published in Journal of Design History vol. 4,
no. 4, 1991 pp. 255–8)
Annual returns and updates
Guide to the Archive of Art and Design, Victoria &
Albert Museum (2001, £45)
Order printed publications from: Fitzroy Dearborn
Publishers, 310 Regent Street, London, W1B 3AX
Publications Department, V & A Museum, South
Kensington, SW7 2RL; tel. 020 7942 2000

Publications list:
Available in print

Access to staff:
Contact by letter, by telephone, by fax and by e-
mail. Appointment necessary.
Hours: Tue to Fri, 1000 to 1630

Access to building, collection or gallery:
Prior appointment required
Hours: Tue to Fri, 1000 to 1630
Special comments: Reference only.

Constituent part of:
Victoria and Albert Museum's Word and Image
Department

Links with:
Artists' Papers Register
    website: http://www.apr.ac.uk
National Register of Archives

ARG EUROPE LIMITED

Formal name: Asbestos Removal (Groves) Limited

Unit 2, 58a Alexandra Road, Ponders End, Enfield,
Middlesex, EN3 7EH

Tel: 020 8804 8008
Fax: 020 8805 7600
E-mail: enquiries@arggroup.org

Website:
http://www.asbestos-removal.co.uk
All aspects of work carried out by the company.

Enquiries:
Enquiries to: Managing Director

Founded:
1984

Formerly called:
Asbestos Removal (Groves) Limited (year of
change 1997)

Organisation type and purpose:
Service industry.
Asbestos removal, asbestos surveys.

Subject coverage:
Asbestos in buildings, advice on treatment,
removal and identification. Asbestos surveys.

Non-library collection catalogue:
All or part available in-house

Library catalogue:
All or part available in-house

Access to staff:
Contact by letter, by e-mail and via website
Hours: Mon to Fri, 0900 to 1700

Access to building, collection or gallery:
No access other than to staff

ARGYLL & BUTE COUNCIL

Kilmory, Lochgilphead, Argyll, PA31 8RT

Tel: 01546 602127
Fax: 01546 604138

Website:
http://www.argyll-bute.gov.uk

Founded:
1996

Organisation type and purpose:
Local government body.

Subject coverage:
Argyll and Bute Council, services and amenities,
corporate services, education, environmental
services, finance, housing, legal services, personnel
services, planning development and tourism,
property and technical services, roads and
transportation, social services, council tax and
other payments, registration of births, deaths and
marriages.

Printed publications:
ABC News: The Newspaper of Argyll and Bute
Council

Access to staff:
Contact by letter, by telephone and by fax.
Appointment necessary.
Hours: Mon to Fri, 0900 to 1700

ARGYLL & BUTE COUNCIL LIBRARY AND INFORMATION SERVICE

Highland Avenue, Sandbank, Dunoon, Argyll,
PA23 8PB

Tel: 01369 703214 or 703735
Fax: 01369 705797

Website:
http://www.argyll-bute.gov.uk
Includes list of own publications

Enquiries:
Enquiries to: Culture and Libraries Manager
Other contacts: Head of Community Regeneration
for overall responsibility for libraries, museums
and arts.

Founded:
1996

Formed from:
Argyll and Bute District Library, Helensburgh and
Lomond Area of Dumbarton District Library (year
of change 1996)

Organisation type and purpose:
Public library.

Subject coverage:
Argyll and Bute local studies.

**Museum or gallery collection, archive, or library
special collection:**
MacGrory Collection (photographs of
    Campbeltown and Kintyre, 1890 to 1910)
Robertson Collection (local history)

Non-library collection catalogue:
All or part available in-house

Printed publications:
Local history publications (various titles, listed
online)

Access to staff:
Contact by letter, by telephone, by fax, by e-mail
and in person. Appointment necessary.
Hours: Mon to Fri, 0900 to 1700

Access for disabled people:
Hours: Mon to Fri, 0900 to 1700

Parent body:
Argyll and Bute Council
    Kilmory, Lochgilphead, Argyll, PA31 8RT; tel:
    01546 602127; fax: 01546 604138

ARGYLL, THE ISLES, LOCH LOMOND, STIRLING & TROSSACHS TOURIST BOARD

Acronym or abbreviation: AILLSTTB

Old Town Jail, St John Street, Stirling, FK8 1EA

Tel: 01786 445222
Fax: 01786 471301

Website:
http://www.scottish-heartlands.org
Information on general area and accommodation
providers.

Enquiries:
Enquiries to: Chief Executive

Founded:
1996

Formerly called:
Bute & Cowal Tourist Board, Forth Valley Tourist
Board, Loch Lomond, Stirling & Trossachs Tourist
Board, West Highlands & Islands of Argyll Tourist
Board (year of change 1996)

Organisation type and purpose:
Statutory body, membership association
(membership is by subscription).
To promote the area through marketing and visitor
services activities at home and abroad.

Subject coverage:
Advice to members on marketing, business
planning and development.
Accommodation bookings through local and
national schemes, promotion through the Board's
publications e.g. accommodation guide.

**Museum or gallery collection, archive, or library
special collection:**
Slide library available for hire

Printed publications:
Accommodation Guide
Holiday and short breaks guide
Visitor guides
What's On Guides

Publications list:
Available in print

Access to staff:
Contact by letter, by telephone, by fax and by e-
mail
Hours: Mon to Fri, 0900 to 1700

Access to building, collection or gallery:
No prior appointment required

Tourist Information Centres:
Aberfoyle (April to October)
    Main Street, Aberfoyle; tel: 01877 382352
Alva (all year)
    Mill Trail Visitor Centre, West Stirling Street,
    Alva; tel: 01259 769696
Ardgartan (April to October)
    Glen Croe, Ardgartan; tel: 01301 702432
Balloch (April to October)
    Balloch Road, Balloch; tel: 01389 753533
Bo'ness (April to September)
    Car Park, Seaview Place, Bo'ness; tel: 01506
    826626
Bowmore (all year)
    The Square, Isle of Islay, Bowmore; tel: 01496
    810254
Callander (March to December and weekends only
during January and February)
    Rob Roy & Trossachs Visitor Centre, Ancaster
    Square, Callander; tel: 01877 330342
Campbeltown (all year)
    MacKinnon House, The Pier, Campbeltown; tel:
    01586 552056
Craignure (all year)
    The Pier, Isle of Mull; tel: 01680 812377
Drymen (May to September)
    Drymen Library, The Square, Drymen; tel: 01306
    660068
Dumbarton (all year)
    Milton, A82 Northbound; tel: 01389 742306
Dunblane (May to September)
    Stirling Road, Dunblane; tel: 01786 824428
Dunoon (all year)
    7 Alexandra Parade, Dunoon; tel: 01369 703785
Falkirk (all year)
    2–4 Glebe Street, Falkirk; tel: 01324 620244
Helensburgh (April to October)
    Clock Tower, The Pier, Helensburgh; tel: 01436
    672642
Inveraray (all year)
    Front Street, Inveraray; tel: 01499 302063

continued overleaf

Killin (March to November)
Breadalbane Folklore Centre, Falls of Dochart,
Killin; tel: 01567 820254
Lochgilphead (April to October)
Lochnell Street, Lochgilphead; tel: 01546 602344
Oban (all year)
Argyll Square; tel: 01631 563122
Rothesay (all year)
Isle of Bute, Rothesay; tel: 01700 502151
Stirling (all year)
Royal Burgh of Stirling, Visitor Centre, Castle
Esplanade; tel: 01786 479901
Stirling (all year)
41 Dumbarton Road, Stirling; tel: 01786 475019
Stirling (April to October)
M9/M80 Junction 9, Motorway Service Area,
Stirling; tel: 01786 814111
Tarbet (Loch Fyne) (April to October)
Harbour Street, Tarbet (Loch Fyne); tel: 01880
820429
Tarbet (Loch Lomond) (April to October)
Main Street, Tarbet (Loch Lomond); tel: 01301
702260
Tobermory (April to October)
The Pier, Isle of Mull, Tobermory; tel: 01688
302182
Tyndrum (April to October)
Main Street, Tyndrum; tel: 01838 400246

ARIC

Formal name: aric

Department of Environmental and Geographical
Sciences, Manchester Metropolitan University,
Chester Street, Manchester, M1 5GD

Tel: 0161 247 1593
Fax: 0161 247 6332
E-mail: aric@mmu.ac.uk

Website:
http://www.doc.mmu.ac.uk/aric/
Factsheets, newsletters on air quality issues.

Enquiries:
Enquiries to: Information Officer
Other contacts: All enquiries to the Information
Officer

Founded:
1984

Formerly called:
Acid Rain Information Centre (ARIC) (year of
change 1991); Atmospheric Research and
Information Centre (ARIC) (year of change 1999)

Organisation type and purpose:
Consultancy, research organisation.
Information centre.
To provide world class research and education in
atmospheric and sustainability issues to encourage
responsible development.

Subject coverage:
Air quality issues, acid rain, greenhouse effect,
ozone depletion, transport, waste, sustainability,
energy efficiency.

**Museum or gallery collection, archive, or library
special collection:**
Many reference books on acidification, global
climate change and urban air quality

Library catalogue:
All or part available in-house

Printed publications:
A wide range of publications on acid rain, air
pollution, global change and ozone depletion

Electronic and video publications:
Educational material: Atmosphere, Climate &
Environment (by aric for teachers and librarians,
CD-ROM, £20 plus VAT)

Publications list:
Available in print

Access to staff:
Contact by letter, by telephone, by fax, by e-mail
and via website. Appointment necessary.
Hours: Mon to Fri, 0900 to 1700

Supported by:
Department for Environment, Food and Rural
Affairs (DEFRA)

ARMAGH PUBLIC LIBRARY

Abbey Street, Armagh, BT61 7DY

Tel: 028 3752 3142
Fax: 028 3752 4177
E-mail: armroblib@aol.com

Enquiries:
Enquiries to: Assistant Keeper
Other contacts: Administration Officer for access to
cataloguing of collection.

Founded:
1771

Organisation type and purpose:
Registered charity, museum, public library, historic
building, house or site, research organisation.

**Museum or gallery collection, archive, or library
special collection:**
17th and 18th century books on theology,
philosophy, classic and modern literature,
voyages and travels, history, medicine, law
Medieval and 17th and 18th century manuscripts
Engravings by Piranesi, Hogarth and Bartolozzi

Library catalogue:
All or part available online

Access to staff:
Contact by letter, by telephone and by e-mail.
Appointment necessary.
Hours: Mon to Fri, 1000 to 1300 and 1400 to 1600
Special comments: Other times by prior
arrangement.

Access to building, collection or gallery:
No prior appointment required

Access for disabled people:
Ramped entry
Special comments: Chairlift to library.

ARMENIAN GENERAL BENEVOLENT UNION (LONDON)

Formal name: Armenian General Benevolent Union
(London)
Acronym or abbreviation: AGBU

25 Cheniston Gardens, London, W8 6TG

E-mail: arline.medazoumian@agbu.org.uk

Website:
http://www.agbu.org.uk

Enquiries:
Enquiries to: Hon. Sec.
Direct e-mail: arline.medazoumian@agbu.org.uk

Founded:
1910

Organisation type and purpose:
To support the educational, cultural and social life
of the UK Armenian community and promote
Armenian culture and heritage within the UK.

Printed publications:
Hoosharar (4 a year, in English and Armenian)

Access to staff:
Contact by letter and by e-mail

Branch of:
Armenian General Benevolent Union (AGBU)
55 East 59th Street, New York, NY 10022–1112,
USA; tel: (212) 319–6383; fax: (212) 319–6507; e-
mail: agbuwb@agbu.org; website: http://www
.agbu.org

ARMITT GALLERY, LIBRARY AND MUSEUM

Formal name: Armitt Gallery, Library and Museum

Rydal Road, Ambleside, Cumbria, LA22 9BL

Tel: 01539 431212

Fax: 01539 431313
E-mail: info@armitt.com

Website:
http://www.armitt.com

Enquiries:
Direct e-mail: info@armitt.com

Founded:
1909

Organisation type and purpose:
Art, literature and artefacts relating to Lake District
and famous inhabitants

Subject coverage:
Art, archaeology, archives, books, geology,
photography and local history of the Lake District

**Museum or gallery collection, archive, or library
special collection:**
Library of 10,000 items relating to the Lake District
Archives (manuscripts, letters, folk songs, local
account books, poor-law records and deeds)
Newspapers and parish magazines
Beatrix Potter illustrations

Access to staff:
Contact by letter, by telephone, by fax, by e-mail
and via website

Access to building, collection or gallery:
Hours: Museum: Mon to Sun, 1000 to 1700; library:
Mon to Fri, 1000 to 1630

ARMY RECORDS SOCIETY

Acronym or abbreviation: ARS

Heritage House, PO Box 21, Baldock,
Hertfordshire, SG7 5SH

Tel: 01462 896688
Fax: 01462 896677
E-mail: ars@hall-mccartney.co.uk

Website:
http://www.armyrecordssociety.org.uk
Membership information, publication information,
society news.

Enquiries:
Enquiries to: Honorary Secretary
Direct tel: 020 7848 2112
Direct fax: 020 7848 2026
Direct e-mail: william.philpott@kcl.ac.uk

Founded:
1985

Organisation type and purpose:
Learned society (membership is by subscription), .
National organisation for publishing volumes of
historical documents relating to history of the
British Army.

Subject coverage:
British army history (by publications).

Printed publications:
Annual volumes:
At Wellington's Right Hand. The letters of Lt. Col.
Sir Alexander Gordon, 1808–15 (2004)
Rawlinson in India (2003)
The Journal of Corporal Todd (2002)
Sir Hugh Rose and the Central India Campaign
1858 (1999)
Lord Roberts and the War in South Africa 1899–
1902 (2000)
The Journal of Corporal William Todd, 1745–1762
(2001)
An Eighteenth Century Secretary at War (1988)
Colonel Samuel Bagshawe and the Army of
George II (1990)
John Peebles' American War, 1776–82 (1997)
Letters of a Victorian Army Officer: Edward
Wellesley, 1840–1854 (1995)
Lord Chelmsford's Zululand Campaign, 1878–1879
(1994)
Military Miscellany 1 (1996)
Montgomery and the English Army (1991)
Roberts in India, 1876–1893 (1993)
The Army and the Curragh Incident, 1914 (1986)
The British Army and Signals Intelligence in the
First World War (1992)

The Napoleonic War Journal of Captain Thomas Brown (1987)

The Maratha War Papers of Arthur Wellesley, 1803 (1998)

The Military Correspondence of Field Marshal Sir William Robertson, Chief of the Imperial General Staff, 1915–1918 (1989)

The Military Correspondence of FM Sir Henry Wilson (1985)

Order printed publications from: Publications Department, Army Records Society, Heritage House, PO Box 21, Baldock, Hertfordshire, SG7 5SH, tel: 01462 896688, fax: 01462 896677, e-mail: ars@hallmccartney.co.uk

Publications list:
Available online and in print

Access to staff:
Contact by letter and via website
Hours: Mon to Fri, 0900 to 1700

Membership Administrators:
Hall McCartney Limited
Heritage House, PO Box 21, Baldock, Hertfordshire, SG7 5SH; tel: 01462 896688; fax: 01462 896677; e-mail: ars@hall-mccartney.co.uk

AROMATHERAPY COUNCIL

Acronym or abbreviation: AOC

PO Box 6522, Desborough, Kettering, Northamptonshire, NN14 2YX

Tel: 0870 7743477
E-mail: info@aromatherapy-regulation.org.uk

Website:
http://www.aromatherapycouncil.co.uk

Enquiries:
Enquiries to: Secretary

Founded:
1991

Formerly called:
Aromatherapy Organisations Council (AOC); Aromatherapy Consortium (year of change 2006)

Organisation type and purpose:
Regulatory authority.

Subject coverage:
Aromatherapy.

Publications list:
Available online

Access to staff:
Contact by letter, by telephone and by e-mail

Access to building, collection or gallery:
No access other than to staff

AROMATHERAPY TRADE COUNCIL

Acronym or abbreviation: ATC

PO Box 387, Ipswich, Suffolk, IP2 9AN

Tel: 01473 603630
Fax: 01473 603630
E-mail: info@a-t-c.org.uk

Website:
http://www.a-t-c.org.uk
Background information to the ATC, list of members, the regulation and responsible marketing of essential oils and aromatherapy products.

Enquiries:
Enquiries to: Administrator

Founded:
1992

Organisation type and purpose:
Trade association for the specialist aromatherapy essential oil trade.

Subject coverage:
The regulation and responsible marketing of essential oils and aromatherapy products.

Trade and statistical information:
Data on responsible marketing of essential oils. Guidelines on the regulation of essential oils and aromatherapy products.

Printed publications:
General information booklet (free on receipt of A5 sae)
Membership list (free as above)
ATC Guidelines on the Regulation, Labelling, Advertising & Promotion of Aromatherapy Products (Cost £100 incl p&p)

Access to staff:
Contact by letter, by telephone, by fax, by e-mail and via website
Hours: Mon to Fri, 0900 to 1700

ARON VECHT AND ASSOCIATES

95 Corringham Road, London, NW11 7DL

Tel: 020 8316 8429
Fax: 020 8316 8405
E-mail: phosphors@vecht.com

Website:
http://www.aronvechtandassociates.com
http://www.vecht.com

Enquiries:
Enquiries to: Principal
Direct tel: 020 8455 4361
Direct fax: 020 8201 9555
Direct e-mail: phosphor@vecht.com

Founded:
1987

Formerly called:
Phosphor Consultants (year of change 1987)

Organisation type and purpose:
International organisation, consultancy, research organisation.

Subject coverage:
Materials science, semiconductors, phosphors, displays and thin films, as well as ultra-pure chemicals used in the electronics industry, assessment of new technologies in these areas for investment and marketing. Specific areas of expertise include: chemical vapour deposition of thin films, electro-luminescence, liquid crystals and cathode ray phosphors.

Printed publications:
See website

Electronic and video publications:
Specialist phosphors prepared on request (purchase order)

Publications list:
Available in print

Access to staff:
Contact by letter, by telephone, by fax, by e-mail and via website
Hours: Mon to Fri, 0900 to 2400

ART AND ARCHITECTURE SOCIETY

Acronym or abbreviation: A&A

70 Cowcross Street, London, EC1M 6EJ

Tel: 020 7733 2436
Fax: 020 7733 2436
E-mail: A&A@tsib.demon.co.uk

Website:
http://www.artandarchitecture.co.uk
Full information on events, current activities, artists' network, and links for the A & A Society.

Enquiries:
Enquiries to: Honorary Secretary

Founded:
1982

Organisation type and purpose:
Learned society (membership is by subscription), present number of members: c 400, voluntary organisation.
Furthering artistic collaboration between those creating the built environment.

Subject coverage:
Public art, art works, commissions, policy, environmental art, urban design, artists and craftsmen working on architectural commissions, sculpture parks.

Printed publications:
Brochure (free)
Journal of Art and Architecture (4 times a year, free to members)
Manifesto (£3)
Register of Artists and Craftsmen in Architecture (£10 plus p&p)

Access to staff:
Contact by letter, by telephone, by fax, by e-mail and via website
Hours: Mon to Fri, 0900 to 1700

ART DIRECTORS & TRIP PHOTO LIBRARY

57 Burdon Lane, Cheam, Surrey, SM2 7BY

Tel: 020 8642 3593
Fax: 020 8395 7230
E-mail: images@artdirectors.co.uk

Website:
http://www.artdirectors.co.uk

Enquiries:
Enquiries to: Manager

Organisation type and purpose:
Commercial slide library.

Subject coverage:
Photography, usage of colour pictures for printing, brochures, advertising, audiovisuals etc. Areas covered: worldwide geographical, lifestyle, business and economic, nature and ecology, landscapes, holiday travel, religion and backgrounds.

Non-library collection catalogue:
All or part available online

Library catalogue:
All or part available online

Access to staff:
Contact by letter, by telephone, by fax and by e-mail. Appointment necessary.
Hours: Mon to Fri, 0900 to 1800

Member organisation of:
British Association of Picture Libraries and Agencies (BAPLA)

ART FUND

Formal name: National Art Collections Fund
Acronym or abbreviation: NACF

Millais House, 7 Cromwell Place, London, SW7 2JN

Tel: 020 7225 4800
Fax: 020 7225 4848
E-mail: info@artfund.org

Website:
http://www.artfund.org

Enquiries:
Enquiries to: Communications Department
Direct fax: 020 7225 4808/4848

Founded:
1903

Organisation type and purpose:
National organisation, membership association (membership is by subscription), present number of members: 80,000, registered charity (charity number 209174). Art charity giving to museums and galleries across the country for the purchase of works of art. The Art Fund is entirely self funded,

continued overleaf

raising the money from membership subscriptions, donations and legacies. It also campaigns on behalf of museums and galleries, particularly on issues such as free admission to national collections and funding for acquisitions.

Subject coverage:
Art current affairs, art history, bequests, grants.

Non-library collection catalogue:
All or part available online

Printed publications:
Art Quarterly (quarterly, members only)
Members' Guide (list of over 500 museums, galleries and historic houses with free entry to the permanent collections for members)
Review (annual, members only)

Access to staff:
Contact by letter, by telephone, by fax, by e-mail and via website
Hours: Mon to Fri, 0930 to 1730

ART LIBRARIES SOCIETY OF THE UK AND IRELAND

Acronym or abbreviation: ARLIS/UK & Ireland

Word and Image Department, Victoria and Albert Museum, South Kensington, London, SW7 2RL

Tel: 020 7942 2317
Fax: 020 7942 2394
E-mail: arlis@vam.ac.uk

Website:
http://www.arlis.org.uk

Enquiries:
Enquiries to: Business Manager

Founded:
1969

Organisation type and purpose:
International organisation, professional body, registered charity (charity number 1048642). Corporate voice of art and design libraries in the UK and Ireland, making their views known to the appropriate professional and educational bodies.

Subject coverage:
Art, architecture and design librarianship.

Printed publications:
Artists' books: A cataloguers' manual (2006)
First Steps in Archives: A Practical Guide (2004)
Trade Literature: Cataloguing and Classification Guidelines (2004)
A Library and Information Plan for the Visual Arts (1993)
Art Libraries Journal vols 1–29, 1976–2004 (prices on application)
Art Libraries Journal and ARLIS News-sheet: Ten Year Indexes, 1976–85 and 1986–95
Art Libraries Journal (quarterly)
Directory of members (annually)
Art Exhibition Documentation in Libraries: cataloguing guidelines (2000)
Guidelines on stock disposal (2000)
News-sheet (6 times a year)

Publications list:
Available online and in print

Access to staff:
Contact by letter, by telephone, by fax, by e-mail, in person and via website. Appointment necessary.
Hours: Mon to Fri, 1000 to 1700

ARTHRITIC ASSOCIATION

One Upperton Gardens, Eastbourne, East Sussex, BN21 2AA

Tel: 01323 416550
Fax: 01323 639793
E-mail: info@arthriticassociation.org.uk

Website:
http://www.arthriticassociation.org.uk
General.

Enquiries:
Direct e-mail: info@arthriticassociation.org.uk

Founded:
1942

Organisation type and purpose:
Membership association (membership is by subscription), present number of members: 4000, registered charity (charity number 292569).
To relieve the suffering from arthritis and allied illnesses using complementary techniques.

Subject coverage:
Arthritis and allied illnesses.

Non-library collection catalogue:
All or part available in-house

Printed publications:
Home Treatment Book and Dietary Guidance Chart
The Arthritic Association News (magazine, spring and autumn)
Books by the late Charles de Coti-Marsh
Arthritis – The Conquest
Diet for Arthritis
Prescription for Energy

Electronic and video publications:
Tapes of the Home Treatment for Blind and Partially Sighted

Access to staff:
Contact by letter, by telephone, by fax, by e-mail and via website. Appointment necessary.
Hours: Mon to Fri, 1000 to 1300 and 1400 to 1600

ARTHRITIS CARE

18 Stephenson Way, London, NW1 2HD

Tel: 0808 800 4050 (answerphone helpline)
Fax: 020 7380 6505
E-mail: helpline@arthritiscare.org.uk

Website:
http://www.arthritiscare.org.uk

Enquiries:
Enquiries to: Information Manager
Direct tel: 020 7380 6577
Direct e-mail: info@arthritiscare.org.uk

Founded:
1947

Formerly called:
British Rheumatism Association (year of change 1980)

Organisation type and purpose:
Membership association (membership is by subscription), present number of members: 44,000, voluntary organisation, registered charity (charity number 206563).
National voluntary organisation with over 580 branches.

Subject coverage:
Health and well-being of people with arthritis, exercise, self-management, aids and equipment, and holidays.

Trade and statistical information:
Statistics on impact of arthritis

Library catalogue:
All or part available in-house

Printed publications:
Arthritis News (6 times a year for members)
Booklets and factsheets

Electronic and video publications:
Arthritis News Magazine on tape for people with sight impairments
All booklets are available on audio CD

Publications list:
Available in print

Access to staff:
Contact by letter, by telephone, by fax, by e-mail and via website. Appointment necessary.
Hours: Mon to Fri, 0900 to 1700
Special comments: Helpline hours are 1000 to 1600

Access to building, collection or gallery:
Prior appointment required

Access for disabled people:
Toilet facilities

ARTHRITIS RESEARCH CAMPAIGN EPIDEMIOLOGY UNIT

Acronym or abbreviation: ARC Unit

School of Epidemiology and Health Sciences, Stopford Building, University of Manchester, Oxford Road, Manchester, M13 9PT

Tel: 0161 275 3235
Fax: 0161 275 5043
E-mail: arcstaff@fs1.ser.man.ac.uk

Website:
http://www.arc.org.uk
Official website of the Arthritis Research Campaign, background to the ARC, information about arthritis, publications.
http://www.arc.man.ac.uk
Background to work of unit, staff and publications, courses and job vacancies.

Enquiries:
Enquiries to: Information Officer

Founded:
1954

Formerly called:
Arthritis and Rheumatism Council

Organisation type and purpose:
Registered charity (charity number 207711), university department or institute, research organisation.
Research into the epidemiology of the rheumatic diseases.

Subject coverage:
Epidemiology of rheumatic diseases i.e. incidence and prevalence data on rheumatic diseases.

Museum or gallery collection, archive, or library special collection:
Rheumatic disease journals

Printed publications:
Leaflets, booklets and information sheets for patients
Health Care Needs Assessment
Medical Student handbook
Reports on Rheumatic Diseases: Series 3 (for medical professionals)
Order printed publications from: ARC Trading Ltd Brunel Drive, Northern Road Industrial Estate, Newark, Nottinghamshire, NG24 2DE

Electronic and video publications:
Teaching Slides (4 sets)
Video : Help is at Hand (£4.95)
Video: Reaching a Balance – Arthritis and the Family (£4.95)

Publications list:
Available in print

Access to staff:
Contact by letter, by telephone, by fax, by e-mail and via website. Appointment necessary. Non-members charged.
Hours: Mon to Fri, 0800 to 1600

Parent body:
Arthritis Research Campaign
Copeman House, St Mary's Court, Chesterfield, Derbyshire, S41 7TD; tel: 01246 558033; fax: 01246 558007

ARTIFICIAL INTELLIGENCE APPLICATIONS INSTITUTE

Acronym or abbreviation: AIAI

University of Edinburgh, 80 South Bridge, Edinburgh, EH1 1HN

Tel: 0131 650 2732
Fax: 0131 650 6513
E-mail: aiai@ed.ac.uk

Website:
http://www.aiai.ed.ac.uk/
Complete description of AIAI and its work.

Enquiries:
Enquiries to: Commercial Director
Other contacts: Training Secretary; Publications
Secretary

Founded:
1984

Organisation type and purpose:
University department or institute, consultancy,
research organisation.
Technology transfer.

Subject coverage:
Artificial intelligence, knowledge-based systems,
modelling, methods, planning, scheduling,
information management, process management,
intelligent workflow.

**Museum or gallery collection, archive, or library
special collection:**
Edinburgh AI Library
Exchange arrangements with international AI
Research centres has led to a collection of over
15,000 AI research papers

Printed publications:
Institute Reports
Newsletter
Project Reports
Technical Reports

Electronic and video publications:
Many technical reports available via ftp

Publications list:
Available online

Access to staff:
Contact by letter, by telephone, by fax, by e-mail
and via website. Appointment necessary.
Hours: Mon to Fri, 0900 to 1700

Parent body:
University of Edinburgh
tel: 0131 650 1000; fax: 0131 650 2147; e-mail:
communications.office@ed.ac.uk

ARTS AND BUSINESS

Acronym or abbreviation: A&B

Nutmeg House, 60 Gainsford Street, Butlers
Wharf, London, SE1 2NY

Tel: 020 7378 8143
Fax: 020 7407 7527
E-mail: head.office@AandB.org.uk

Website:
http://www.aandb.org.uk

Enquiries:
Enquiries to: Information Officer

Founded:
1975

Formed from:
Association for Business Sponsorship of the Arts
(ABSA) (year of change 2000)

Organisation type and purpose:
National organisation, membership association,
service industry, registered charity (charity number
274040), consultancy.
To help business people support the arts and the
arts to inspire business people, because good
business and great art enrich society.

Subject coverage:
Arts sponsorship advice to businesses and arts
organisations, tax advice, evaluation, research,
consultancy, arts funding, the Board Bank, Skills
Bank and mentoring placements. Corporate art
collections and creative and development training.

Trade and statistical information:
Business Investment (of the arts) figures since 1990
Archive surveys.

Library catalogue:
All or part available in-house

Printed publications:
A Creative Education
A&B Literature & Statistics
Art Collecting
Business Investment in the Arts 2002/2003
Creative Connections
Cultural Sponsorship in Europe
Did it Deliver?
Did it Make A Difference?
Did it Work for You?
Funding and Friendship
It Worked for Them
Recreating Communities: Business, the Arts and
Regeneration
The Sponsorship Manual

Publications list:
Available online and in print

Access to staff:
Contact by letter, by telephone, by fax, by e-mail
and via website. Appointment necessary.
Hours: Mon to Fri, 0930 to 1730

Access to building, collection or gallery:
Prior appointment required
Hours: Thu, Fri, 0930 to 1730

Arts & Business Offices and Staff:
Arts & Business Cymru/Wales
16 Museum Place, Cardiff, CF10 3BH; tel: 029
2030 3023; fax: 029 2030 3024; e-mail: cymru@
AandB.org.uk
Arts & Business East
67 Regent Street, Cambridge, CB2 1AB; tel: 01223
321421; fax: 01223 365536; e-mail: east@AandB
.org.uk
Arts & Business East Midlands
Carlton Studios, Lenton Lane, Nottingham, NG7
2NA; tel: 0115 964 5648; fax: 0115 964 5488; e-
mail: nottingham@AandB.org.uk
Arts & Business North West
127–129 Portland Buildings, Portland Street,
Manchester, M1 4PZ; tel: 0161 236 2058; fax:
0161 236 2068; e-mail: north.west@AandB.org.uk
Arts & Business Northern Ireland
53 Malone Road, Belfast, BT9 6RY; tel: 028 9066
4736; fax: 028 9066 4500; e-mail: northern
.ireland@AandB.org.uk
Arts & Business Scotland
6 Randolph Crescent, Edinburgh, EH3 7TH; tel:
0131 220 2499; fax: 0131 220 2296; e-mail:
scotland@AandB.org.uk
Arts & Business South East, Brighton Office
4 Frederick Terrace, Frederick Place, Brighton,
East Sussex, BN1 1AX; tel: 01273 738333; fax:
01273 738666; e-mail: south.east@AandB.org.uk
Arts & Business South East, Eastleigh Office
The Point Dance and Arts Centre, Leigh Road,
Eastleigh, Hampshire, SO50 9DE; tel: 023 8061
9172; fax: 023 8061 9173; e-mail: south.east@
AandB.org.uk
Arts & Business South West
61 Park Street, Bristol, BS1 5NU; tel: 0117 929
0522; fax: 0117 929 1756; e-mail: south.west@
AandB.org.uk
Arts & Business South West, Exeter Office
Civic Centre, Paris Street, Exeter, Devon, EX1 1JJ;
tel: 01392 434272
Arts & Business West Midlands
Suite 16–18, 21 Bennetts Hill, Birmingham, B2
5QP; tel: 0121 248 1200; fax: 0121 248 1202; e-
mail: midlands@AandB.org.uk
Arts & Business Yorkshire
Dean Clough, Halifax, West Yorkshire, HX3 5AX;
tel: 01422 367860; fax: 01422 363254; e-mail:
yorkshire@AandB.org.uk
Cumbria
Arts & Business North West, Community
Foundation, Unit 6B, Lakeland Business Park,
Cockermouth, Cumbria, CA13 0QT; tel: 01900
829376; e-mail: elaine/wise@AandB.org.uk
Highlands and Islands Office
Suites 4/5 – 4th Floor, Ballantyne House, 84
Academy Street, Inverness, IV1 1LU; tel: 01463
720886; fax: 01463 720895; e-mail: inverness@
AandB.org.uk

North Wales Office
1–2 Chapel Street, Llandudno, LL30 2SY; tel:
01492 574003; e-mail: lorraine.hopkins@AandB
.org.uk
North Wales Office
Room 40, The Town Hall, Lloyd Street,
Llandudno, LL30 2UP; tel: 01492 574003; e-mail:
lorraine.hopkins@AandB.org.uk
The Sponsors Club for Arts & Business
Cale Cross House, 156 Pilgrim Street, Newcastle
upon Tyne, NE1 6SU; tel: 0191 222 0945; fax:
0191 230 0689; e-mail: northern@AandB.org.uk

Member of:
Comité Européen pour le Rapprochement de la
Culture (CEREC)
c/Tuset, 8, 1°, 2°, Barcelona, 08006, Spain; tel: 00
34 93 237 2682; fax: 00 34 93 237 22 84; e-mail:
contact@cerec.org

ARTS AND HUMANITIES
RESEARCH COUNCIL

Formal name: Arts and Humanities Research
Council

Whitefriars, Lewins Mead, Bristol, BS1 2AE

Tel: 0117 987 6500
Fax: 0117 987 6544

Website:
http://www.ahrb.ac.uk

Founded:
1998
Arts and Humanities Research Board (date of
change, 1st April 2005)

Organisation type and purpose:
To fund research and postgraduate study within
the UK's higher education institutions and
museums, galleries and collections that are based
in, or attached to, higher education institutions in
England.

Access to staff:
Contact by letter, by telephone, by fax, by e-mail
and via website

ARTS COUNCIL ENGLAND,
LONDON

2 Pear Tree Court, London, EC1R 0DS

Tel: 020 7608 6100\ Minicom no. 020 7608 4101\
0845 300 6200
Fax: 020 7608 4100
E-mail: firstname.surname@artscouncil.org.uk

Website:
http://www.artscouncil.org.uk/regions

Enquiries:
Enquiries to: Administrator
Other contacts: Publishing Administrator

Organisation type and purpose:
Registered charity (charity number 1036733).
London Arts Board is the arts funding and
development agency for the capital.

Printed publications:
Annual Reports: 1998/99; 1999/00; 2000/01 London:
The Creative City
Artists in Residence – A Teachers' Handbook
(1997, £5 plus £1.50 p&p)
Creative Partnerships
Dance Rehearsal Space Use in London (1996)
Getting On-Line (1997)
A Guide to the London Arts Board
Funding Programmes 1999/00; 2000/01; 2001/02;
2002/03
Musicians Go to School (1998, £10)
Large number of reports and guides including:
Local Authority Arts & Education Directory (1997/
98)
Refugee Directory

Publications list:
Available online and in print

continued overleaf

Access to staff:
Contact by letter, by telephone, by fax and by e-mail
Hours: Mon to Fri, 0900 to 1700
Special comments: Access to staff also by textphone.

ARTS COUNCIL ENGLAND, SOUTH EAST

Sovereign House, Church Street, Brighton, BN1 1RA

Tel: 0845 300 6200
Fax: 0870 242 1257 0845 300 6200
E-mail: enquiries@artscouncil.org.uk

Website:
http://www.artscouncil.org.uk/regions/
The official website of the English Regional Arts Boards. Grants information, information menu, staff list, snapshot of region covered, background to South East Arts.

Enquiries:
Enquiries to: Press Officer
Direct tel: 01273 763053
Direct e-mail: chloe.barker@artscouncil.org.uk

Founded:
1992

Formerly called:
Southern & South East Arts

Organisation type and purpose:
Advisory body, registered charity.
Arts funding body, range of information sheets, website, annual review, bi-monthly newsletter. Regional Arts Development.

Subject coverage:
All areas of arts funding for professional artists and art organisations, arts grants, local authority contacts, venues and promoters and National Lottery applications.

Museum or gallery collection, archive, or library special collection:
South East Arts Visual Art and Craft Collection (catalogue available)

Trade and statistical information:
Arts research data (available to clients only). Local authority contacts, press contacts.

Printed publications:
Annual Report
Arts Resources leaflet
Festivals! Festivals!: The South East Arts Guide to Arts Festivals
General Information leaflet
Getting On-line, guide to the Internet
Information Services Menu
Literature supplement
Marketing Guides
Newsletter (once every two months, free) with the following 2 supplements:
Visual Arts and Crafts supplement
South East Arts Gallery Guide
Various arts strategies

Publications list:
Available in print

Access to staff:
Contact by letter, by telephone, by fax, by e-mail and via website
Hours: Mon to Thu, 0900 to 1730; Fri, 0900 to 1700

Access to building, collection or gallery:
Prior appointment required
Hours: As above

Access for disabled people:
Ramped entry
Special comments: Third floor, lifts available.

Also at:
Southern & South East Arts
Union House, Eridge Road, Tunbridge Wells, Kent, TN4 8HF; tel: 01892 507200; fax: 0870 2421259; e-mail: infotw@ssea.co.uk

Parent body:
Arts Council of England
14 Great Peter Street, London, SW1P 3NQ; tel: 020 7333 0100; text phone: 020 7973 6564; fax: 020 7973 6590; e-mail: enquiries@artscouncil.org.uk; website: http//www.artscouncil.org.uk

ARTS COUNCIL OF ENGLAND

Acronym or abbreviation: ACE

Library, 14 Great Peter Street, London, SW1P 3NQ

Tel: 020 7333 0100\ Minicom no. 020 7973 6564
Fax: 020 7973 6590
E-mail: enquiries@artscouncil.org.uk

Website:
http://www.artscouncil.org.uk
Aims and objectives, information regarding funding programmes, new initiatives, gateway to key arts support organisations.

Enquiries:
Enquiries to: Information Officer
Direct tel: 020 7973 6517

Founded:
1945

Formerly called:
Arts Council of Great Britain (year of change 1994)

Organisation type and purpose:
National government body.
Non-Departmental Public Body (NDPB)
Government grant aided institution, incorporated under Royal Charter, national body for funding and development of the arts.
Develop and improve knowledge, understanding and practice of the arts; increase the accessibility of the arts; advise and co-operate with government, local authorities and other bodies.

Subject coverage:
Cultural policy, marketing, management, economy and financing of the arts, fundraising and sponsorship.

Museum or gallery collection, archive, or library special collection:
Market research reports on the arts

Trade and statistical information:
Data on the level of central government funding of the arts.

Printed publications:
Information leaflets available in large print, audio tape or Braille
Range of bibliographies and fact sheets on cultural policy
Order printed publications from: Marston Book Services
PO Box 269, Abingdon, Oxfordshire, OX14 4YN, tel: 01235 465500, fax: 01235 465555

Publications list:
Available online

Access to staff:
Contact by letter, by telephone, by fax and via website
Hours: Mon to Fri, 1000 to 1300 and 1400 to 1700
Special comments: Due to limited space, priority is given to artist and art administrator groups, for other categories it is a library of last resort.

Access to building, collection or gallery:
Prior appointment required

Regional Arts Boards:
East England Arts Area covered: Bedfordshire, Cambridgeshire, Essex, Hertfordshire, Norfolk, Suffolk, Lincolnshire; unitary authority of Luton
Eden House, 48–49 Bateman Street, Cambridge, CB2 1LR; tel: 01223 454400; fax: 01223 248075
East Midlands Arts Board Area covered: Derbyshire (excluding High Peak District), Leicestershire, Northamptonshire, Nottinghamshire; unitary authorities of Derby, Leicester, Rutland
Mountfields House, Epinal Way, Loughborough, Leicestershire, LE11 0QE; tel: 01509 218292; fax: 01509 262214

London Arts Board Area covered: The area of the 32 London Boroughs and the City of London
Elme House, 133 Long Acre, Covent Garden, London, WC2E 9AF; tel: 020 7240 1313; fax: 020 7240 4580
North West Arts Area covered: Lancashire, Cheshire, Merseyside, Greater Manchester and High Peak Districts of Derbyshire
Manchester House, 22 Bridge Street, Manchester, M3 3AB; tel: 0161 834 6644; fax: 0161 834 6969
Northern Arts Area covered: Cumbria, Durham, Northumberland; unitary authorities of Darlington, Hartlepool, Middlesbrough, Redcar & Cleveland, Stockton; metropolitan districts of Newcastle, Gateshead, North Tyneside, Sunderland & South Tyneside
9–10 Osborne Terrace, Jesmond, Newcastle upon Tyne, NE2 1NZ; tel: 0191 281 6334; fax: 0191 281 3276
South East Arts Board Area covered: Kent, Surrey, East and West Sussex, unitary authority of Brighton and Hove
10 Mount Ephraim, Tunbridge Wells, Kent, TN4 8AS; tel: 01892 515210; fax: 01892 549383
South West Arts Area covered: Cornwall, Devon, Dorset (except districts of Bournemouth, Christchurch & Poole), Gloucestershire and Somerset; unitary authorities of Bristol, Bath and North East Somerset, South Gloucestershire, North Somerset
Bradninch Place, Gandy Street, Exeter, EX4 3LS; tel: 01392 218188; fax: 01392 413554
Southern Arts Board Area covered: Berkshire, Buckinghamshire. Hampshire, Isle of Wight. Oxfordshire, Wiltshire; unitary authorities of Bournemouth, Milton Keynes, Poole, Southampton, Swindon
13 St Clement Street, Winchester, Hampshire, SO23 9DQ; tel: 01962 855099; fax: 01962 861186
West Midlands Arts Board Area covered: Hereford & Worcester, Shropshire, Staffordshire, Warwickshire; metropolitan districts of Birmingham, Coventry, Dudley, Sandwell, Solihull, Walsall, Wolverhampton; unitary authority of Stoke-on-Trent
82 Granville Street, Birmingham, B1 2LH; tel: 0121 631 3121; fax: 0121 643 7239
Yorkshire & Humberside Arts Board Area covered: North Yorks; unitary authorities of York, Hull, East Riding, North Lincs; metropolitan districts of Barnsley, Bradford, Calderdale, Doncaster, Kirklees, Leeds, Rotherham, Sheffield, Wakefield
21 Bond Street, Dewsbury, West Yorkshire, WF13 1AX; tel: 01924 455555; fax: 01924 466 522

ARTS COUNCIL OF ENGLAND (NORTHERN ARTS)

Central Square, Forth Street, Newcastle upon Tyne, NE1 3PJ

Tel: 0845 300 6200
Fax: 0191 230 1020

Website:
http://www.arts.org.uk/directory/regions/northern

Enquiries:
Enquiries to: Communications Officer
Direct e-mail: kathryn.goodfellow@artscouncil.org.uk

Formerly called:
Northern Arts

Organisation type and purpose:
Local government body, advisory body, professional body (membership is by subscription), registered charity (charity number 517711), training organisation, consultancy, research organisation.
Art funding body.
Regional arts board responsible for almost all national and regional arts funding in the North.

Subject coverage:
Music, drama, performing arts, visual arts, crafts, literature, film, photography, video, community arts, arts funding and organisation, Millennium Fund and lottery.

Museum or gallery collection, archive, or library special collection:
Fundraising library
Slide library (artists index)

Library catalogue:
All or part available in-house and in print

Printed publications:
Annual Report
Northern Review (monthly)

Access to staff:
Contact by letter, by telephone, by fax, by e-mail and via website. Appointment necessary.
Hours: Mon to Fri, 0900 to 1700
Special comments: First floor access only, stairs above not accessible by lift.

Access to building, collection or gallery:
No prior appointment required

ARTS COUNCIL OF WALES

Acronym or abbreviation: ACW

9 Museum Place, Cardiff, CF10 3NX

Tel: 029 2037 6500\ Minicom no. 029 2039 0027
Fax: 029 2022 1447
E-mail: information@artswales.org.uk

Website:
http://www.artswales.org.uk

Enquiries:
Enquiries to: Information Officer

Founded:
1994

Formerly called:
Welsh Arts Council (year of change 1994)

Organisation type and purpose:
National government body, advisory body, statutory body (membership is by election or invitation), present number of members: 18 members on ACW's Council, 150+ on panels and committees, registered charity (charity number 1034245).
Distributes National Assembly for Wales and National Lottery funds for the arts in Wales.

Subject coverage:
Development of all art forms in Wales, funding for arts activities from National Assembly for Wales and National Lottery sources.

Library catalogue:
All or part available online and in print

Printed publications:
Annual Report and Corporate Plan summary 1999–2002
Artists Notes (newsletter, quarterly, for visual artists)
ArtsFile (bi-monthly newsletter for the arts in Wales)
Crefft (quarterly newsletter for craftspeople)
Building a Creative Society – consultation paper and responses to strategic proposals to develop a practical way forward for the arts in Wales from 1999–2004
Directory of Publishers in Wales
The Arts and Young People in Wales
The Economic Impact of the Arts and Cultural Industries in Wales

Publications list:
Available online and in print

Access to staff:
Contact by letter, by telephone, by fax, by e-mail and via website
Hours: Carmarthen and Colwyn Bay Offices: Mon to Fri, 0900 to 1700
Cardiff Office: Mon to Fri, 0900 to 1730

Other addresses:
Arts Council of Wales
   Cardiff; tel: 029 2037 6500; fax: 029 2022 1447; e-mail: information@ccc-acw.org.uk
Arts Council of Wales
   36 Prince's Drive, Colwyn Bay, LL29 8LA; tel: 01492 533440 Minicom 01492 532288; fax: 01492 533677; e-mail: information@ccc-acw.org.uk
Arts Council of Wales
   6 Gardd Llydaw, Jackson's Lane, Carmarthen, SA31 1QD; tel: 01267 234248; fax: 01267 233084; e-mail: information@ccc-acw.org.uk

ARUN DISTRICT COUNCIL

Arun Civic Centre, Maltravers Road, Littlehampton, West Sussex, BN17 5LF

Tel: 01903 737500\ Minicom no. 01903 732765
Fax: 01903 730442

Website:
http://www.arun.gov.uk
General information about Arun District, including tourism and visitor information, What's New, council information.

Enquiries:
Enquiries to: Public Relations Manager

Founded:
1974

Organisation type and purpose:
Local government body.

Subject coverage:
Tourism, strategy co-ordination, consultation processes, customer care.

Printed publications:
Annual report (free)
Arun's Customer Panel (free)
Civic Guide (free)
Customer Care handbooks for staff (price on application)
Tourism Brochure (free)
Order printed publications from: Head, Strategy Unit at the same address, e-mail: strategy.unit@arun.gov.uk

Access to staff:
Contact by letter, by telephone, by fax and by e-mail. Appointment necessary.
Hours: Mon to Thu, 0845 to 1715; Fri, 0845 to 1645

ASBESTOS CONTROL AND ABATEMENT DIVISION

Acronym or abbreviation: ACAD

Tica House, Allington Way, Yarm Road Business Park, Darlington, Co Durham, D21 4QB

Tel: 01325 466704
Fax: 01325 487691
E-mail: enquiries@tica-acad.co.uk

Website:
http://www.tica-acad.co.uk
Membership information, current news and developments, etc.

Enquiries:
Enquiries to: Operations Manager
Other contacts: ACAD Training Co-ordinator for training enquiries.

Founded:
1994

Formed from:
Insulation and Environmental Training Association (IETA), Insulation and Environmental Training Trust Limited (IETTL)

Organisation type and purpose:
Advisory body, trade association (membership is by subscription), present number of members: 117 members, 39 associate members, service industry, training organisation, consultancy, research organisation.

Subject coverage:
Safe removal of asbestos using latest technology, technical, health and safety advice, training courses. National Vocational Qualifications (NVQs).

Trade and statistical information:
Data on health and safety matters relating to asbestos products, removal and waste handling, for the United Kingdom, Europe and some international information.

Printed publications:
Best Practical Means (series of advice documents)
Practical Information Sheets
Quarterly magazine
Technical publications
Monthly newsletter

Publications list:
Available in print

Access to staff:
Contact by letter, by telephone, by fax, by e-mail, in person and via website. Appointment necessary. Non-members charged.
Hours: Mon to Fri, 0900 to 1700

Access to building, collection or gallery:
Prior appointment required

Access for disabled people:
Parking provided

Parent body:
Thermal Insulation Contractors Association (TICA)

ASCEND

Formal name: Ascend Worldwide

Cardinal Point, Newall Road, Heathrow Airport, Hounslow, Middlesex, TW6 2AS

Tel: 020 8564 6700
Fax: 020 8897 0300
E-mail: info@ascendworldwide.com

Website:
http://www.ascendworldwide.com
Lists of all services available; loss adjusting; consultancy; database; publications, valuations etc.
https://online.ascendworldwide.com//Login/PortalLogin.aspx
Aviation information on fleets, aircraft, prices, news and publications
http://www.ascendv1.com
Aircraft valuations
http://www.ascendspacetrak.com/Home/Login.aspx
Detailed information on insurance losses, launches and satellites

Enquiries:
Direct e-mail: uk@ascendworldwide.com

Founded:
1964

Formerly a part of:
Airclaims Limited (year of change 2006)

Organisation type and purpose:
International organisation, service industry, consultancy, publishing house.
Aviation Loss Adjuster and Information Provider.

Subject coverage:
Commercial aviation, including airline fleets, aircraft, current and future values, accidents, information on communications satellites and launchers (ie commercial astronautics).

Non-library collection catalogue:
All or part available in-house

Library catalogue:
All or part available in-house

Printed publications:
Ascend fast track ™ (bi-monthly)
V1EWPoint (quarterly)
Aviation Pocket Book
Space Intelligence News (monthly)
Space Review (monthly)

continued overleaf

Electronic and video publications:
Airline Finance & Traffic (2 times a year, CD-ROM and disc)
Airline Order Backlog (4 times a year, disc)
Fleet Developments (2 times a year, CD-ROM and disc)
Jet Scoresheet (2 times a year, CD-ROM)
Aircraft Programmes (annually, CD-ROM and disc)
Jet Storage Update (monthly)
Major Loss Record (updated every other month, CD-ROM)
Market Intelligence, MI (monthly)
SpaceTrak (database, monthly)
Turbine Airliner Fleet Survey (2 times a year)

Publications list:
Available online and in print

Access to staff:
Contact by letter, by telephone, by fax, by e-mail, in person and via website
Hours: Mon to Fri, 0900 to 1700

Headquarters address:
Ascend Asia
35/F Central Plaza, 18 Harbour Road, Wanchai, Hong Kong; tel: +852 2813 6366; fax: +652 2813 6357; e-mail: asia@ascendworldwide.com; website: http://www.ascendworldwide.com
Ascend USA
380 Lexington Avenue, 17th Floor, New York, NY 10168, USA; tel: +1 212 551 1118; fax: +1 212 551 1001; e-mail: usa@ascendworldwide.com; website: http://www.ascendworldwide.com

ASHFIELD DISTRICT COUNCIL

Council Offices, Urban Road, Kirkby-in-Ashfield, Nottinghamshire, NG17 8DA

Tel: 01623 450000
Fax: 01623 457590
E-mail: info@ashfield-dc.gov.uk

Website:
http://www.ashfield-dc.gov.uk

Enquiries:
Enquiries to: Chief Executive

Founded:
1974

Organisation type and purpose:
Local government body.

Subject coverage:
Local government services.

Access for disabled people:
Parking provided, toilet facilities
Special comments: Audio Loop System.

ASHFORD BOROUGH COUNCIL

Acronym or abbreviation: ABC

Civic Centre, Tannery Lane, Ashford, Kent, TN23 1PL

Tel: 01233 637311\ Minicom no. 01233 637311
Fax: 01233 645654
E-mail: media@ashford.gov.uk

Website:
http://www.ashford.gov.uk

Enquiries:
Enquiries to: Chief Executive
Direct e-mail: david.hill@ashford.gov.uk
Other contacts: Marketing and Communications Manager for press issues and general publicity.

Organisation type and purpose:
Local government body.

Subject coverage:
Local government services.

Printed publications:
Ashford Borough Guide
Ashford Borough Review
Holiday Guide 2000
Millennium Guide 2000

Electronic and video publications:
Tourism (CD-ROM)

Access to staff:
Contact by letter and by e-mail. Appointment necessary.
Hours: Mon to Fri, 0900 to 1700

ASHFORD LIBRARY

Church Road, Ashford, Kent, TN23 1QX

Tel: 01233 620649
Fax: 01233 646580
E-mail: ashfordlibrary@kent.gov.uk

Website:
http://www.kent.gov.uk/libs
Kent Libraries website with access to online catalogue

Enquiries:
Enquiries to: Librarian

Organisation type and purpose:
Public library.

Subject coverage:
General, railways, local studies.

Museum or gallery collection, archive, or library special collection:
Railway Collection. A dedicated room of books, maps, videos, cassettes, plans, original documents that relate to railway matters in general, but specifically concentrating on railways in the South-East; the area covered by the Southern Railway, its predecessors and successors.
Local studies

Library catalogue:
All or part available online

Access to staff:
Contact by letter, by telephone, by fax, by e-mail, in person and via website
Hours: Mon to Wed and Fri, 0900 to 1800; Thu, 0900 to 1700; Sat, 0900 to 1700

ASIA HOUSE

63 New Cavendish Street, London, W1G 7LP

Tel: 020 7307 5454
Fax: 020 7307 5459
E-mail: enquiries@asiahouse.co.uk

Website:
http://www.asiahouse.org

Founded:
1996

Organisation type and purpose:
A non-profit, non-political organisation serving as a focal point for the development of understanding of business, and of diplomatic and cultural interaction, between Asia and Britain. Runs a programme of events for the public.

Subject coverage:
The organisation's geographical scope extends west–east from Iran to Japan and north–south from the central Asian republics to Indonesia

Access to building, collection or gallery:
Hours: Mon to Fri, 0900 to 1900; Sat (only when there is an exhibition in the gallery), 1000 to 1800

ASIAN ART IN LONDON

Acronym or abbreviation: AAL

32 Dover Street, London, W1S 4NE

Tel: 020 7499 2215
Fax: 020 7499 2216
E-mail: info@asianartinlondon.com

Website:
http://www.asianartinlondon.com
Full list of participating galleries and auction houses, calendar of events.

Enquiries:
Enquiries to: Project Manager

Founded:
1998

Organisation type and purpose:
Membership association (membership is by subscription), present number of members: 40–50. Annual event.
AAL is an annual event which promotes private dealers, auction houses, societies, academic institutions and museums, which deal in and provide Asian Art.

Subject coverage:
Chinese, Japanese, Islamic and Middle Eastern, Indian, South East Asian, Himalayan and Tibetan, Korean Art, antique and contemporary art.

Non-library collection catalogue:
All or part available in-house

Printed publications:
AAL Journal 2000
AAL Journal 2001
AAL Guidebook (annually)
AAL Leaflet (annually)

Access to staff:
Contact by letter, by telephone, by fax, by e-mail, in person and via website. Appointment necessary.
Hours: Mon to Fri, 0900 to 1800

Access to building, collection or gallery:
Prior appointment required
Hours: Mon to Fri, 0900 to 1800

ASIAN FAMILY COUNSELLING SERVICE

Acronym or abbreviation: AFCS

Suite 51, The Lodge, Windmill Place, 2–4 Windmill Lane, Southall, Middlesex, UB2 4NJ

Tel: 020 8571 3933
Fax: 020 8571 3933
E-mail: afcs@btconnect.com

Website:
http://www.asianfamilycounselling.org.uk

Enquiries:
Enquiries to: Administrator

Founded:
1985

Organisation type and purpose:
Voluntary organisation, registered charity (charity number 517595), training organisation, consultancy.

Subject coverage:
Marital and family counselling service.

Access to staff:
Contact by letter, by telephone, by fax and by e-mail. Appointment necessary.
Hours: Mon to Fri, 1000 to 1600

Access for disabled people:
Wheelchair access not available.

ASIAN STUDIES CENTRE

Acronym or abbreviation: ASC

St Antony's College, Oxford, OX2 6JF

Tel: 01865 274559
Fax: 01865 274559
E-mail: asian@sant.oc.ac.uk

Website:
http://www.sant.ox.ac.uk/areastudies/asian/shtml

Enquiries:
Enquiries to: Secretary

Founded:
1982

Formerly called:
Far East Centre (year of change 1982)

Organisation type and purpose:
Research organisation.
A scholarly Centre for Asian Studies within St Antony's College conducting seminars and special talks on Asia; funded by endowment at St Antony's College.

Subject coverage:
History; anthropology; international relations; politics; economics; Asia, with special reference to Japan, Korea, China (including Hong Kong, Taiwan and Tibet), India and Southeast Asia.

Museum or gallery collection, archive, or library special collection:
A collection of c. 4000 books and periodicals; access restricted to members of St Antony's College
The Asian Studies Collection is held in the St Antony's College Library (books primarily related to international relations in Asia)

Access to staff:
Contact by letter, by telephone, by fax, by e-mail, in person and via website. Appointment necessary.
Hours: Mon, Tue, Thu, Fri, 0815 to 1430

ASIAN WOMEN'S RESOURCE CENTRE

Acronym or abbreviation: AWRC

108 Craven Park, London, NW10 8QE

Tel: 020 8961 6549
Fax: 020 8838 1823
E-mail: asianwomencentre@aol.com

Website:
http://www.asianwomencentre.org.uk

Enquiries:
Enquiries to: Director
Direct tel: 020 8961 5701

Founded:
1980

Organisation type and purpose:
Voluntary organisation, registered charity (charity number 1049058).
Advice centre.

Subject coverage:
Educational and social resources for Asian women living in England.

Printed publications:
Asian Women at Risk of Self-Harm and Suicide
Gender Equality Duty
HIV/Sexual Health Posters (available, free)
Posters about domestic violence

Access to staff:
Contact by letter, by telephone, by fax, by e-mail, in person and via website. Appointment necessary.
Hours: Mon to Fri, 1000 to 1700

Access for disabled people:
Ramped entry

ASKHAM BRYAN COLLEGE

Askham Bryan, York, YO23 3FR

Tel: 01904 772277
Fax: 01904 772288

Website:
http://www.askham-bryan.ac.uk
General college website.

Enquiries:
Enquiries to: Learning Resources Manager
Direct tel: 01904 772234
Direct fax: 01904 772287
Direct e-mail: JA@askham-bryan.ac.uk
Other contacts: Librarian for general library enquiries.

Founded:
1948

Organisation type and purpose:
College of further and higher education – landbased.

Subject coverage:
Agriculture, agricultural engineering, horticulture, landscape design, arboriculture, greenkeeping, agribusiness, business, management, forestry, equine management, animal care/management, environmental management and conservation, food technology, community education, design, biosciences, IT, food production, botany, veterinary sciences, nursing; careers information.

Library catalogue:
All or part available in-house

Printed publications:
Farming in Yorkshire (annually)
Order printed publications from: Rural Business Research Unit, Askham Bryan College
tel: 01904 772218, fax: 01904 700129, e-mail: ml@askham-bryan.ac.uk

Electronic and video publications:
Videotapes, photoslides, CD-ROM, DVDs

Access to staff:
Contact by letter, by telephone, by fax, by e-mail, in person and via website. Appointment necessary.
Hours: Term Time: Mon to Thu, 0845 to 2100; Fri, 0845 to 1900; Sat, Sun, 1245 to 1630
Vacations: Mon to Fri, 0900 to 1700
Special comments: Non-members of the college may use the library for reference only.

Access for disabled people:
Parking provided, ramped entry, power-assisted front door

Affiliated to:
University of Leeds, Harper Adams University College, University College York St John

Campus also at:
Askham Bryan College
Bedale Centre, Benkhill Drive, Bedale, Yorkshire, DL8 2EA; tel: 01677 422344

In collaboration with:
Middlesborough College (NECAM), Wakefield College, Yorkshire Coast College, Norton College

Other addresses:
Askham Bryan College
Guisborough Centre, Avenue Place, Redcar Road, Guisborough, Cleveland, TS14 6AX; tel: 01287 633870
Askham Bryan College
Harrogate Centre, Great Yorkshire Showground, Harrogate, North Yorkshire, HG2 8BW; tel: 01423 870600
Askham Bryan College
Pickering Centre, Swainsea Lane, Pickering, Yorkshire, YO18 8NE; tel: 01751 473431

Part of:
DEFRA Farm Management Survey Organisation

ASLIB PROFESSIONAL RECRUITMENT LIMITED

Acronym or abbreviation: APR

Holywell Centre, 1 Phipp Street, London, EC2A 4PS

Tel: 020 7613 3031
Fax: 020 7613 5080
E-mail: recruit@aslib.com

Website:
http://www.aslib.com
Recruitment application form, APR literature and job advertisements.

Enquiries:
Enquiries to: Manager
Other contacts: Recruitment Consultant

Organisation type and purpose:
Library and Information Recruitment Specialists.

Subject coverage:
Recruitment of both temporary and permanent library and information staff for placement in all sectors.

Printed publications:
Brochures
CVs and Interview guidelines

Access to staff:
Contact by letter, by telephone, by fax, by e-mail and via website. Appointment necessary.
Hours: Mon to Fri, 0915 to 1715

Wholly owned subsidiary of:
Aslib

ASLIB, THE ASSOCIATION FOR INFORMATION MANAGEMENT

Holywell Centre, 1 Phipp Street, London, EC2A 4PS

Tel: 020 7613 3031
Fax: 020 7613 5080
E-mail: aslib@aslib.com

Website:
http://www.aslib.com
Home page. Open Learning programme – constructing a thesaurus
http://www.managinginformation.com
Information update and Copyright Courier

Founded:
1924

Organisation type and purpose:
International organisation, membership association (membership is by subscription), members in some 70 countries, registered charity (charity number 290809).
Aslib actively promotes best practice in the management of information resources. It lobbies on all aspects of the management of, and legislation concerning, information at local, national and international levels.

Subject coverage:
Information management, information science, librarianship, applications of information technology, automation of information and library services, online information retrieval, information sources, records management, CD-ROM, thesaurus and database construction.

Printed publications:
Aslib corporate members receive discounts on titles published under the Aslib imprint by Emerald and Taylor & Francis
Managing Information (10 times a year)

Publications list:
Available online and in print

Access to staff:
Contact by letter, by telephone, by fax, by e-mail and via website. Appointment necessary. Non-members charged.
Hours: Mon to Fri, 0915 to 1715

Links with:
CEC DG XIIIE

Member of:
European Council of Information Associations (ECIA)

ASPARAGUS GROWERS' ASSOCIATION

133 Eastgate, Louth, Lincolnshire, LN11 9QG

Tel: 01507 602 427
Fax: 01507 607165
E-mail: crop.association@pvga.co.uk

Website:
http://www.british-asparagus.co.uk

Enquiries:
Enquiries to: Membership Secretary

Founded:
1984

Organisation type and purpose:
National organisation, trade association.

Access to staff:
Contact by letter, by telephone, by fax and by e-mail
Hours: Mon to Fri, 0900 to 1700

ASSIST UK

Redbank House, 4 St Chad's Street, Manchester,
M8 8QA

Tel: 0870 770 2866
Fax: 0870 770 2867
E-mail: info@assist-uk.org

Website:
http://www.assist-uk.org

Enquiries:
Enquiries to: Chief Executive
Other contacts: Communications Officer for
communications enquiries.

Founded:
1985
Disabled Living Centres Council (DLCC)

Organisation type and purpose:
Membership association (membership is by
qualification), present number of members: 40,
voluntary organisation, registered charity (charity
number 1039444), suitable for ages: all.
National voice for disabled living centres.

Subject coverage:
Creating a Disabled Living Centre, providing
contact with Disabled Living Centres, working
with other organisations to provide access to their
services for disabled living.

Printed publications:
Briefing (monthly, free to members)
Newsletter (quarterly, free to members)
Community equipment services why we should
care? (£35 plus £1.35 p&p)
Disability Equipment Services: What's the
Problem? (Winchcombe M, 1997, £5 plus £1 p&p)
Equipped for Change (£5 plus £1 p&p)
Equipped for Life (£5 plus £2.50 p&p)
Who's for an Easier Life? (Winchcombe M, 1996, £5
plus £1 p&p)

Electronic and video publications:
Copy of summary of Community equipment
services why we should care? (tape)
Your Disabled Living Centre (video, £10 to buy, £5
to rent for two weeks, both plus £1 p&p)

Publications list:
Available online and in print

Access to staff:
Contact by letter, by telephone, by fax, by e-mail
and via website. Appointment necessary.
Hours: Mon to Fri, 0900 to 1700

Access to building, collection or gallery:
Prior appointment required

Access for disabled people:
Parking provided, level entry, access to all public
areas, toilet facilities

Members:
43 disabled living centres

ASSOCIATED BRITISH PORTS HOLDINGS PLC

Acronym or abbreviation: ABPH

150 Holborn, London, EC1N 2LR

Tel: 020 7430 1177
Fax: 020 7430 1384
E-mail: pr@abports.co.uk

Website:
http://www.abports.co.uk

Enquiries:
Enquiries to: Corporate Communications Manager
Direct e-mail: mcollins@abports.co.uk

Founded:
1983

Formerly called:
British Transport Docks Board (year of change
1983)

Organisation type and purpose:
Service industry.
Ports, transport and property company.

Ports owner and operator; subsidiaries include
property, ferry, transport services, auto-processing
terminals, computer and research companies, and
dredging division.

Subject coverage:
Transport, the port industry, property
development and investment, shipping, auto-
processing, research, computing, dredging.

Trade and statistical information:
In 1998, 121 million tonnes of cargo was handled at
23 United Kingdom ports owned by Associated
British Ports Holding's major subsidiary,
Associated British Ports.

Printed publications:
Annual Report
Fact Book
Ports '99 and 2000 – A Guide to ABP's 23 Ports
(fact book, free of charge)
Interim Report
Port Brochures
Ports Magazine

Access to staff:
Contact by letter, by telephone and by fax
Hours: Mon to Fri, 0830 to 1800

ASSOCIATION FOR ARCHERY IN SCHOOLS

Acronym or abbreviation: AAS

Bloxham School, Banbury, Oxfordshire, OX15 4PE

Tel: 01295 721463
Fax: 01295 721463

Website:
http://www.aasinfo.demon.co.uk

Enquiries:
Enquiries to: Secretary
Direct tel: 01295 724338
Direct e-mail: cfe@blockhamschool.com

Founded:
1963

Organisation type and purpose:
Membership association (membership is by
subscription), voluntary organisation, suitable for
ages: Under 18.
Promotion of Archery in schools and colleges.

Subject coverage:
Archery achievement (a Badge Scheme); formation
of archery clubs; equipment; coaching;
tournaments.

Printed publications:
Directory (annually, free)
Junior Archery World – JAW
Newsletter (3 times a year, free)

Access to staff:
Contact by letter, by telephone, by fax, by e-mail
and via website
Hours: Answerphone/Fax during working day;
personal contact late night, 2300 to 0200

Affiliated to:
Fédération Internationale de Tir à l'Arc (FITA)
Grand National Archery Society (GNAS)
National Council for School Sports (NCSS)

ASSOCIATION FOR ASTRONOMY EDUCATION

Formal name: Association for Astronomy Education
Acronym or abbreviation: AAE

Royal Astronomical Society, Burlington House,
Piccadilly, London, W1J 0BQ

Website:
http://www.aae.org.uk
General introduction to Association for Astronomy
Education.

Enquiries:
Enquiries to: Secretary
Direct e-mail: secretary@aae.org.uk

Founded:
1981

Organisation type and purpose:
Membership association (membership is by
subscription), present number of members: 120,
registered charity (charity number 1046041).
To promote astronomy education at all levels and
to support teachers through training, information
and resources.

Subject coverage:
Astronomy education.

Printed publications:
Earth and Beyond – Resources for primary
teachers
Earth and Space – Resources for secondary
teachers
Order printed publications from: ASE Publications
College Lane, Hatfield, Hertfordshire, AL10 9AA,
tel: 01707 283000

Access to staff:
Contact by letter, by e-mail and via website
Hours: Mon to Fri, 0900 to 1700

ASSOCIATION FOR BETTER LIVING AND EDUCATION

Acronym or abbreviation: ABLE

Saint Hill Manor, East Grinstead, West Sussex,
RH19 4JY

Tel: 01342 301902
Fax: 01342 327539

Website:
http://www.able.org

Enquiries:
Enquiries to: Executive Director

Founded:
1985

Organisation type and purpose:
Membership association, voluntary organisation, .
To work in the field of eradicating drug abuse,
crime, illiteracy and forwarding a non-religious
moral code.

Printed publications:
10 Things your friends may not know about
DRUGS
Solutions Magazine
The Way to Happiness (booklet)

Access to staff:
Contact by letter, by telephone and by fax
Hours: Mon to Sat, 1000 to 2200

ASSOCIATION FOR CERAMIC TRAINING & DEVELOPMENT

Acronym or abbreviation: ACTD

St James House, Webberley Lane, Stoke-on-Trent,
Staffordshire, ST3 1RJ

Tel: 01782 597016
Fax: 01782 597015
E-mail: actd@actd.co.uk

Enquiries:
Enquiries to: Director

Founded:
1993

Organisation type and purpose:
National training organisation.

Non-library collection catalogue:
All or part available in-house

Library catalogue:
All or part available in-house

Access to staff:
Contact by letter
Hours: Mon to Fri, 0900 to 1700

ASSOCIATION FOR CLINICAL BIOCHEMISTRY

Acronym or abbreviation: ACB

130–132 Tooley Street, London, SE1 2TU

Tel: 020 7403 8001
Fax: 020 7403 8006
E-mail: enquiries@acb.org.uk

Website:
http://www.acb.org.uk
General information about the Association.
General information for careers in clinical biochemistry.

Enquiries:
Enquiries to: Administrator

Founded:
1953

Organisation type and purpose:
Professional body, trade union, present number of members: 2200.

Subject coverage:
Clinical biochemistry, chemical pathology, biochemical medicine, clinical chemistry, clinical sciences.

Museum or gallery collection, archive, or library special collection:
Archives of the Association

Non-library collection catalogue:
All or part available in-house

Library catalogue:
All or part available online

Printed publications:
Annals of Clinical Biochemistry (6 times a year, for sale)
News Sheet (monthly, free to members and for sale)
Diabetes & Laboratory Medicine
Neonatology & Laboratory Medicine
A Practical Guide to Accreditation in Laboratory Medicine
Poisoning & Laboratory Medicine
Biochemical Investigations in Laboratory Medicine
Liver Disease and Laboratory Medicine
Cancer and Clinical Biochemistry
Clinical Investigations and Statistics in Laboratory Medicine
Primary Care and Laboratory Medicine
Intensive Care & Clinical Biochemistry
Therapeutic Drug Monitoring & Clinical Biochemistry

Electronic and video publications:
Clinical Cases (CD-ROM, for purchase):
Calcium Cases
Diabetes Cases
Proteins Cases

Publications list:
Available online and in print

Access to staff:
Contact by letter, by fax and by e-mail
Hours: Mon to Fri, 0900 to 1700

Access for disabled people:
Ramped entry, access to all public areas, toilet facilities

Associated, for professional matters, with the:
Association of Clinical Cytogeneticists (ACC)
Association of Clinical Microbiologists (ACM)

Linked, for scientific and educational matters, with the:
International Federation of Clinical Chemistry and Laboratory Medicine (IFCC)

ASSOCIATION FOR COACHING

Acronym or abbreviation: AC

66 Church Road, London, W7 1LB

Tel: 0845 225 5048 or 020 8566 2400
Fax: 0845 225 5049
E-mail: enquiries@associationforcoaching.com

Website:
http://www.associationforcoaching.com
Information on the organisation and its members

Enquiries:
Enquiries to: Chairman
Direct tel: 07884 434547
Direct e-mail: ktulpa@associationforcoaching.com

Founded:
2002

Organisation type and purpose:
National organisation, advisory body, professional body (membership is by qualification, election or invitation).

Subject coverage:
Advancing education and best practice in coaching; executive, business, performance, private.

Access to staff:
Contact by telephone, by fax, by e-mail, in person and via website
Hours: Mon to Fri, 0900 to 1700

ASSOCIATION FOR CONTINENCE ADVICE

Acronym or abbreviation: ACA

c/o Fitwise Management Ltd, Drumcross Hall, Bathgate, EH48 4JJ

Tel: 020 8692 4680
Fax: 020 8692 6217
E-mail: info@aca.uk.com

Enquiries:
Enquiries to: Membership Secretary
Other contacts: Development Manager for professionals only.

Founded:
1981

Organisation type and purpose:
International organisation, advisory body, membership association (membership is by subscription), present number of members: 817, voluntary organisation, registered charity, training organisation, consultancy.
Membership organisation for healthcare professionals working with people with bladder and bowel dysfunction.

Printed publications:
Journal (quarterly, £6, £22 annual subscription inc. p&p, available direct)

Access to staff:
Contact by letter, by telephone, by fax, by e-mail and via website
Hours: Mon to Fri, 0900 to 1700

ASSOCIATION FOR EDUCATION WELFARE MANAGEMENT

Acronym or abbreviation: AEWM

1 The Boundary, Bradford, West Yorkshire, BD8 0BQ

Tel: 01924 305519 (daytime), 01274 542295 (evening)
Fax: 01924 305646
E-mail: jprice@wakefield.gov.uk

Enquiries:
Enquiries to: General Secretary
Other contacts: Assistant Secretary (Publicity)

Founded:
1917

Organisation type and purpose:
National organisation, professional body (membership is by subscription), present number of members: 150.
Promotes good practice and provides professional support, responds to government initiatives.

Subject coverage:
Education welfare management.

Access to staff:
Contact by letter and by e-mail
Hours: Mon to Fri, 0900 to 1700

ASSOCIATION FOR GROUP AND INDIVIDUAL PSYCHOTHERAPY

Acronym or abbreviation: AGIP

1 Fairbridge Road, London, N19 3EW

Tel: 020 7272 7013
Fax: 020 7272 6945
E-mail: office@agip.org.uk

Website:
http://www.ag.p.org.uk

Enquiries:
Enquiries to: Administrator

Founded:
1974

Organisation type and purpose:
Registered charity (charity number 1083030), training organisation.
Provision of services in psychotherapy.

Subject coverage:
Psychoanalytic psychotherapy, training, clinical and supervision services.

Special visitor services:
Low fee psychotherapy clinic.

Education services:
Education and training in psychotherapy.

Services for disabled people:
By arrangement.

Access to staff:
Contact by letter, by telephone, by fax, by e-mail and via website
Hours: Mon to Fri, 0900 to 1500

Member of:
United Kingdom Council for Psychotherapy

ASSOCIATION FOR HUMANISTIC PSYCHOLOGY IN BRITAIN

Acronym or abbreviation: AHPB

BM Box 3582, London, WC1N 3XX

Tel: 08457 078506
E-mail: admin@ahpb.org.uk

Website:
http://www.ahpb.org.uk
Outline of organisation, index pages of journal, links to American Association.

Enquiries:
Enquiries to: Administrator

Founded:
1969

Organisation type and purpose:
Professional body, voluntary organisation, registered charity (charity number 290548).

Subject coverage:
Humanistic psychology; counselling and psychotherapy; training.

Printed publications:
Newsletter
Self and Society (journal)
Order printed publications from: admin@ahpb.org.uk

Electronic and video publications:
Guide to Humanistic Psychology (online)

Access to staff:
Contact by letter, by telephone, by e-mail and via website
Hours: 24-hour answering machine.

ASSOCIATION FOR INDUSTRIAL ARCHAEOLOGY

Acronym or abbreviation: AIA

continued overleaf

The Wharfage, Coach Road, Coalbrookdale,
Telford, Shropshire, TF8 7DQ

Tel: 01952 432141
Fax: 01952 432237

Enquiries:
Enquiries to: Secretary
Other contacts: Correspondence Secretary

Founded:
1973

Organisation type and purpose:
Advisory body, learned society (membership is by
subscription), voluntary organisation, research
organisation, publishing house.

Subject coverage:
Industrial archaeology; conservation; preservation.

Education services:
Group education facilities, resources for Further or
Higher Education.

Printed publications:
IA News (4 times a year)
Industrial Archaeology Review (2 times a year)
Order printed publications from: Sales Officer
Barn Cottage, Bridge Street, Bridgnorth,
Shropshire, WV15 6AF, tel: 01746 765159

Publications list:
Available in print

Access to staff:
Contact by letter, by telephone and by fax
Hours: Mon to Fri, 0900 to 1700

Access to building, collection or gallery:
No prior appointment required

Also at:
AIA Liaison Officer
School of Archaeological Studies, University of
Leicester, University Road, Leicester, LE1 7RH;
tel: 0116 252 5337; fax: 0116 252 5005; e-mail:
aia@le.ac.uk

Links with:
Ironbridge Gorge Museum Trust
tel: 01952 433522

ASSOCIATION FOR LANGUAGE LEARNING

Acronym or abbreviation: ALL

150 Railway Terrace, Rugby, Warwickshire, CV21
3HN

Tel: 01788 546443
Fax: 01788 544149
E-mail: info@all-languages.org.uk

Website:
http://www.all-languages.org.uk

Enquiries:
Enquiries to: Manager
Other contacts: Advertising, Courses and
Conference Assistant for advertising enquiries.

Founded:
1990

Organisation type and purpose:
Professional body, membership association
(membership is by subscription), present number
of members: 4800, registered charity (charity
number 1001826).
Support for teachers of all modern foreign
languages in all sectors of education.

Subject coverage:
Modern foreign language teaching and learning at
all levels of education from primary to university,
adult education and training, Asian languages,
Dutch, French, German, Italian, Portuguese,
Russian, Spanish teaching in schools and
universities, teaching materials and sources of
auxiliary teaching materials.

Printed publications:
Language Learning Journal (twice a year)
Francophonie (journal, twice a year)
German Teaching (journal, twice a year)
Rusistika (journal, twice a year)

Tuttitalia (journal, twice a year)
Vida Hispánica (journal, twice a year)
Language World (newsletter, quarterly)

Publications list:
Available in print

Access to staff:
Contact by letter, by telephone, by fax, by e-mail
and in person
Hours: Mon to Fri, 0900 to 1700

Affiliated to:
Fédération Internationale de Professeurs de
Français (FIPF)
Fédération Internationale de Professeurs de
Langues Vivantes (FIPLV)
IDV
MAPRYAL

ASSOCIATION FOR LATIN LITURGY

Acronym or abbreviation: ALL

47 Western Park Road, Leicester, LE3 6HQ

Tel: 0116 285 6158
E-mail: enquiries@latin-liturgy.org

Website:
http://www.latin-liturgy.org
Full information on the association and its
publications.

Enquiries:
Enquiries to: Chairman
Direct e-mail: enquiries@latin-liturgy.org

Founded:
1969

Organisation type and purpose:
Learned society, membership association
(membership is by subscription), present number
of members: 300.
Religious (Roman Catholic). Shares aims with the
Latin Liturgy Assoc. (USA), the Vereniging voor
Latijnse Liturgie (Netherlands) and Pro Liturgia
(France). There is a formal Federation of the three
European associations.
To promote understanding of the value of the
Catholic liturgy and its music in Latin, and in a
practical way to encourage its use.

Subject coverage:
The Latin liturgy of the Roman Catholic Church
and its associated music in the past and at the
present day. The teaching of ecclesiastical Latin.
Advice on printed texts connected with the above.

Printed publications:
Adoremus (£1.50)
A New Approach to Latin for the Mass (£12) (CD
[Orate Fratres] is available for use with this book
or separately £12)
A Voice for all Time (£6)
Latin Gregorian Chant Sung Mass Booklets:
Lux et Origo (Mass I, 75p)
Cunctipotens genitor Deus (Mass IV, 75p)
Kyrie magnae (Mass V, 75p)
Cum Jubilo (Mass IX, 75p)
De Angelis (Mass VIII, 75p)
Orbis Factor (Mass XI, 75p)
Advent and Lent (Mass XVII, 75p)
Requiem (75p)
Organ Accompaniment (Mass VIII, £5)
Latin in the Liturgy (1988, available free on
request)
Newsletter (3 times a year, members)
Orders from outside UK: Please add 25%
Order printed publications from: Publications
Manager
31 Netherfield Road, Sheffield, S10 1RA; e-mail:
sales@latin-liturgy.org.uk

Electronic and video publications:
CD: Orate Fratres (Pronunciation and singing of
Latin at Mass) (£12)
Orders from outside UK: Please add 25%
Order electronic and video publications from:
Publications Manager

31 Netherfield Road, Sheffield, S10 1RA; e-mail:
sales@latin-liturgy.org.uk

Publications list:
Available online and in print

Access to staff:
Contact by letter, by e-mail and via website
Hours: Mon to Fri, 0900 to 1700

ASSOCIATION FOR LEARNING TECHNOLOGY

Acronym or abbreviation: ALT

Gipsy Lane, Headington, Oxford, OX3 0BP

Tel: 01865 484125
Fax: 01865 484165
E-mail: admin@alt.ac.uk

Website:
http://www.alt.ac.uk

Enquiries:
Enquiries to: Director of Development
Other contacts: Administrator for membership
enquiries or conference booking information.

Founded:
1993

Organisation type and purpose:
Learned society (membership is by subscription),
present number of members: 700, registered
charity (charity number 1063519).

Subject coverage:
Innovative teaching and learning in further and
higher education, application of learning
technology, interchange and representation of the
membership.

Printed publications:
ALT-J (journal, 3 times a year)
ALT-N (newsletter, quarterly, subscription
included in membership fee)
An Introduction to Learning Technology Within
Tertiary Education in the UK (Handbook)
Enabling Active Learning (Conference abstracts)
Changing Education, Changing Technology
(Conference abstracts)
Changing Face of Learning Technology (book)
Integrating Technology into the Curriculum
(Conference abstracts)
Virtual Campus, Real Learning (Conference
abstracts)

Electronic and video publications:
Media Active 94: Conference Proceedings (CD-
ROM)
Harnessing Multimedia for Higher Education (CD-
ROM, £20)

Publications list:
Available in print

Access to staff:
Contact by letter, by telephone, by fax, by e-mail
and via website
Hours: Mon to Fri, 0900 to 1700

Access to building, collection or gallery:
No access other than to staff

ASSOCIATION FOR LOW COUNTRIES STUDIES IN GREAT BRITAIN AND IRELAND

Acronym or abbreviation: ALCS

Department of Germanic Studies, University of
Sheffield, Sheffield, S10 2TN

Tel: 0114 222 4396
E-mail: alcs@sheffield.ac.uk

Website:
http://alcs.group.shef.ac.uk

Enquiries:
Enquiries to: Administrator

Founded:
1995

Organisation type and purpose:
Learned society (membership is by subscription). To promote the scholarly study of the language, culture, history and society of the Low Countries; to encourage research in Low Countries Studies; to increase the public awareness of the Low Countries, and especially the Dutch Language, and Dutch and Flemish culture, history and society; to represent the interests of Low Countries Studies in higher education at national and international level.

Subject coverage:
Study of language, literature, history, art, politics, geography and culture of the Low Countries, i.e. the Netherlands and Belgium (particularly Flanders).

Printed publications:
ALCS Newsletter (2 times a year to members only)
Dutch Crossing: A Journal for Low Countries Studies (2 times a year; individuals £25 per year, institutions £45 per year, ALCS members £15 per year)

Publications list:
Available online

Access to staff:
Contact by letter, by telephone, by e-mail and via website. Appointment necessary.
Hours: Mon to Fri, 0900 to 1700

Links with:
University Council for Modern Languages in Higher Education (UCML)

ASSOCIATION FOR MANAGEMENT EDUCATION AND DEVELOPMENT

Acronym or abbreviation: AMED

1st Floor, 62 Paul Street, London, EC2A 4NA

Tel: 020 7613 4121
Fax: 01923 859999
E-mail: ahatherill@aol.com

Website:
http://www.amed.org.uk
Articles from journal.
http://www.amed.co.uk
Current events, news, chat rooms, e-newsletters.

Enquiries:
Enquiries to: Membership Secretary
Direct tel: 01923 859999
Direct e-mail: allyson@management.org.uk
Other contacts: Office Manager

Founded:
1978

Organisation type and purpose:
Membership association (membership is by subscription), present number of members: 1200. For the development and propagation of management, organisational learning and education.

Subject coverage:
Learning, knowledge management, change management, board and director development, organisation developments, management development, management consultancy.

Library catalogue:
All or part available online

Printed publications:
AMED News (newsletter, monthly)
Conference Proceedings
Organisations and People (journal, quarterly)
Order printed publications from: AMED
The Gardeners Cottage, Shenley Park, Radlett Lane, Shenley, WD7 9DW

Electronic and video publications:
Conference Proceedings (CD-ROM)

Publications list:
Available in print

Access to staff:
Contact by letter, by telephone, by fax, by e-mail and via website
Hours: Mon to Fri, 0900 to 1700

ASSOCIATION FOR MEDICAL OSTEOPATHY

8–10 Boston Place, London, NW1 6QH

Tel: 020 7262 5250
Fax: 020 7723 7492

Enquiries:
Enquiries to: Honorary Secretary
Other contacts: Membership Secretary

Founded:
1911

Formerly called:
Association of Medical Osteopaths, British Osteopathic Association (BOA), London College of Osteopathic Medicine

Organisation type and purpose:
Professional body (membership is by qualification), present number of members: 120. Medically qualified osteopaths trained at the London College of Osteopathic Medicine.

Subject coverage:
Osteopathic medicine; UK sources of treatment.

Library catalogue:
All or part available in-house

Printed publications:
Directory of Osteopathic Physicians (biennial)
Newsletter (quarterly)

Access to staff:
Contact by letter, by telephone and by fax. Access for members only.
Hours: Mon to Fri, 0930 to 1700

Access to building, collection or gallery:
No access other than to staff

Access for disabled people:
Level entry, toilet facilities

At the same address is the:
Osteopathic Association Clinic
tel: 020 7262 1128; fax: 020 7723 7492

Close links with:
Osteopathic Trusts Limited
tel: 020 7262 5250; fax: 020 7723 7492

ASSOCIATION FOR PALLIATIVE MEDICINE OF GREAT BRITAIN AND IRELAND

Acronym or abbreviation: APM

76 Botley Road, Park Gate, Southampton, SO31 1BA

Tel: 01489 565665
E-mail: sabine.tuck@palliative-medicine.org

Website:
www.palliative-medicine.org

Enquiries:
Enquiries to: Administrator

Founded:
1985

Organisation type and purpose:
Professional body, membership association (membership is by subscription, qualification), present number of members: 700, registered charity (charity number 1053572).

Subject coverage:
Palliative Medicine.

Printed publications:
Clinical governance documents
APM newsletter (for members)
SpR research documents
Manual for trainers in palliative medicine
Palliative medicine curriculum

Access to staff:
Contact by letter, by telephone and by e-mail
Hours: Mon to Fri

ASSOCIATION FOR PASTORAL CARE OF THE MENTALLY ILL

Acronym or abbreviation: APCMH

Cornerstone House, 14 Willis Road, Croydon, Surrey, CR0 2XX

Tel: 020 8665 6718
Fax: 020 8665 1972
E-mail: apcmh@croydononline.org

Enquiries:
Enquiries to: Development Officer

Founded:
1984

Organisation type and purpose:
Voluntary organisation.

Subject coverage:
Mental health especially spirituality and mental health promotion.

Printed publications:
General information leaflet and information on mental health including in minority languages

Access to staff:
Contact by letter, by telephone, by fax and by e-mail
Hours: Mon, Wed, Fri, 0830 to 1530

Access to building, collection or gallery:
No access other than to staff

National Office:
APCMH
c/o Marylebone Park Church, Marylebone Road, London, NW1 5LT; tel: 01483 538936

ASSOCIATION FOR PERIOPERATIVE PRACTICE

Acronym or abbreviation: AFPP

Daisy Ayris House, 6 Grove Park Court, Harrogate, North Yorkshire, HG1 4DP

Tel: 01423 508079
Fax: 01423 531613
E-mail: hq@afpp.org.uk

Website:
http://www.afpp.org.uk
Information about the association, job forum, updated daily, main articles from journal each month, journal index, join membership online and application form, discussion forum, list of national events.

Enquiries:
Enquiries to: Chairman

Founded:
1964

Formerly called:
National Association of Theatre Nurses (year of change 2005)

Organisation type and purpose:
Advisory body, membership association (membership is by subscription), training organisation.

Subject coverage:
Operating theatre nursing (all surgical specialisations); theatre technique; staffing of operating theatres; non-nursing staff in theatres; planning; patient care; anaesthetic room nursing; recovery room nursing; legal implications of patients' safety and accidents; sterilisation.

Museum or gallery collection, archive, or library special collection:
Journals on nursing (national)
Journals on perioperative nursing (national and international)
Books on theatre nursing and related topics

continued overleaf

Printed publications:
British Journal of Theatre Nursing (monthly)
Journal of Perioperative Practice (monthly)
Journal of Advanced Perioperative Care (twice a
 year)
Order printed publications from: AFPP directly or
website

Publications list:
Available online and in print

Access to staff:
Contact by letter, by telephone, by fax, by e-mail
and via website
Hours: Mon to Fri, 0830 to 1630

ASSOCIATION FOR PHYSICAL EDUCATION

Acronym or abbreviation: AFPE

Building 25, London Road, Reading, Berkshire,
RG1 5AQ

Tel: 0118 378 6240
Fax: 0118 378 6242
E-mail: enquiries@afpe.org.uk

Website:
http://www.afpe.org.uk

Enquiries:
Enquiries to: Chief Executive

Founded:
2006

Organisation type and purpose:
Professional body (membership is by subscription),
registered charity (charity number 1114673),
research organisation.

Subject coverage:
Physical education, continuing professional
development, health and fitness education.

**Museum or gallery collection, archive, or library
special collection:**
PEA Archives in the Library, Sheffield University

Printed publications:
PE Matters
Assessment for Learning in Physical Education
Case Law in Physical Education and School Sport
Achieving Excellence
Self-evaluation in Physical Education
Developing the Process
A guide to Self-review in Physical Education

Publications list:
Available in print

Access to staff:
Contact by letter, by telephone, by fax, by e-mail
and via website. Appointment necessary.
Hours: Mon to Fri, 0900 to 1700

Access to building, collection or gallery:
Prior appointment required

Access for disabled people:
Parking provided

ASSOCIATION FOR POST NATAL ILLNESS

Acronym or abbreviation: APNI

145 Dawes Road, London, SW6 7EB

Tel: 020 7386 0868
Fax: 020 7386 8885
E-mail: info@apni.org

Website:
http://www.apni.org
Details of Association and leaflets.

Enquiries:
Enquiries to: Information Officer

Founded:
1979

Organisation type and purpose:
Membership association, present number of
members: 1800, voluntary organisation, registered
charity (charity number 280510).
Provides information and support to mothers
suffering from postnatal depression, information
for health professionals, supports research into
postnatal illness.

Subject coverage:
The management and treatment of postnatal
illness.

Printed publications:
Coping with Postnatal Depression (Marshall F,
 Shelden Press 1993, £5.99)
Depression after Childbirth (Dalton K, OUP)
Leaflets including:
Puerperal Psychosis (10p per copy, not suitable for
 general display)
Postnatal Depression (75p each, over 200, 60p each)
The Baby Blues and Postnatal Depression (100
 copies £10)
Health Visitors Notes for Guidance (75p per copy,
 only available to Health Visitors, Midwives and
 Community Psychiatric Nurses)

Publications list:
Available in print

Access to staff:
Contact by letter, by telephone, by fax, by e-mail
and via website
Hours: Mon to Fri, 1000 to 1400

ASSOCIATION FOR PROFESSIONALS IN SERVICES FOR ADOLESCENTS

Acronym or abbreviation: APSA

1 Arun House, River Way, Uckfield, East Sussex,
TT22 1SL

Tel: 01825 760 886
Fax: 01825 768 864
E-mail: apsa@bhm.co.uk

Website:
http://www.apsa-web.uk
Information about the Association and its
publications.

Enquiries:
Enquiries to: Administrator
Other contacts: Membership Secretary for
subscription enquiries.

Founded:
1970

Organisation type and purpose:
Professional body (membership is by subscription),
present number of members: 605, registered
charity.
Promote the study, understanding, and care of
adolescents.

Subject coverage:
Subjects related to disturbed adolescents.

Printed publications:
Journal of Adolescence (6 times a year)
Newsletters (3 times a year, members)
Rapport Journal (4 times a year)

Access to staff:
Contact by letter, by telephone, by fax, by e-mail
and via website
Hours: Mon to Fri, 0900 to 1700

ASSOCIATION FOR PROJECT MANAGEMENT

Acronym or abbreviation: APM

150 West Wycombe Road, High Wycombe,
Buckinghamshire, HP12 3AE

Tel: 0845 458 1944
Fax: 01494 528937
E-mail: info@apm.org.uk

Website:
http://www.apm.org.uk

Details of the Association.

Enquiries:
Enquiries to: Chief Executive
Direct e-mail: cro@apm.org.uk
Other contacts: Head of Professional Development;
Head of Membership; Head of Marketing

Founded:
1972

Formerly called:
Association of Project Managers (year of change
1997)

Organisation type and purpose:
National organisation, professional body
(membership is by subscription), present number
of members: 17,000, registered charity (charity
number 290927).
Promotion of the professions of Project
Management both in the UK and internationally
and the development of the art and science of
project management.

Subject coverage:
Project management across all sectors of business
and industry.

Printed publications:
International Journal of Project Management (8
 times a year by subscription)
Project Magazine (10 times a year, members: free)
Project Risk Analysis and Management Guide 2nd
 edition
APM Body of Knowledge 5th Edition
Standard Terms for the Appointment of a Project
 Manager
Starting out in Project Management – A Study
 Guide for the APM Introductory Certificate in
 Project Management 2nd edition
Project Management Pathways
APM Competence Framework
APM Yearbook 2006–7 The Business of Projects
APM Yearbook 2005–6 Insights in Project and
 Programme Management
Earned Value Management – Guideline for the
 United Kingdom
Contract Strategy for Successful Project
 Management
Directing Change: A Guide to the Governance of
 Project Management
Co-Directing Change: Guide to the Governance of
 Multi-Owned Projects
Models to Improve the Management of Projects
APM Introduction to Programme Management
Order printed publications from: Turpin Distribution:
01767 604951

Electronic and video publications:
APM/BSi product containing BS6079, the APM
 Body of Knowledge and the APMP Examination
 Syllabus
APM Project Management Standards
A Guide to Knowledge Management
Order electronic and video publications from: Turpin
Distribution: 01767 604951

Access to staff:
Contact by letter, by telephone, by fax and by e-
mail
Hours: Mon to Fri, 0900 to 1700

Access to building, collection or gallery:
Mon to Fri, 0900 to 1700
Hours: Mon to Fri, 0900 to 1700

Access for disabled people:
Parking provided, level entry
Hours: Mon to Fri, 0900 to 1700

Affiliated to:
International Project Management Association
(IPMA)
 Service Secretariat, PO Box 30, Monmouth, NP5
 4YZ; tel: 01594 531007; fax: 01594 531008; e-mail:
 ipma@btinternet.com; website: http://www.ipma
 .co.uk

ASSOCIATION FOR PUBLIC SERVICE EXCELLENCE

Acronym or abbreviation: APSE

2nd floor Washbrook House, Lancastrian Office Centre, Talbot Road, Old Trafford, Manchester, M32 0FP

Tel: 0161 772 1810
Fax: 0161 772 1811
E-mail: enquiries@apse.org.uk

Website:
http://www.apse.org.uk
APSE's services.

Enquiries:
Enquiries to: Chief Executive
Direct e-mail: po'brien@apse.org.uk
Other contacts: Research and Advisory Officer for publications, press releases, briefing notes

Founded:
1981

Formerly called:
Association of Direct Labour Organisations (ADLO) (year of change 2000)

Organisation type and purpose:
Local government body, advisory body, professional body (membership is by subscription), present number of members: 270, training organisation, consultancy, research organisation. To consult, develop, promote and advise on best practice in the delivery of public services.

Subject coverage:
Public sector contracting, service delivery issues such as quality, structures etc, best value, PFI, TUPE, housing stock transfers, best value consultancy, local government benchmarking.

Museum or gallery collection, archive, or library special collection:
Small library and resource unit

Trade and statistical information:
Data on local government direct service provision.

Non-library collection catalogue:
All or part available online

Library catalogue:
All or part available online

Printed publications:
Housing Stock Transfer: The Only Answer?
Internal Service Provision: The Best Value Option?
Report on Hand-Arm Vibration
Structuring towards Best Value
Inspecting Best Value
New Millennium Service Provider
The Involvement of DLOs and DSOs in Local Authority PFI Scheme
Pursuing Excellence in Local Government (Volumes 1 to 3)
Housing Options
The Ingredients for Success
The Future Role of Elected Members
The Composting and Disposal of Green Waste
A Guide to Local Authority Charging and Trading
Construction Skill Shortages in the Public Sector
Environmental Services: At the Heart of Every Community
Delivering the Liveability Agenda
Soft FM
Maximising Local Potential
Towards a Future for Public Employment
The Future of Local Government in Wales
Governance, Neighbourhoods & Service Delivery
Order printed publications from: e-mail: enquiries@apse.org.uk

Publications list:
Available online and in print

Access to staff:
Contact by letter, by telephone, by fax, by e-mail and via website. Appointment necessary. Access for members only. Non-members charged.
Hours: Mon to Fri, 0900 to 1700

Access to building, collection or gallery:
No access other than to staff

Access for disabled people:
Access to all public areas

Also at:
Association for Public Service Excellence (Scottish APSE)
11th Floor, Council Offices, Almada Street, Hamilton, ML3 0AL; tel: 01698 454015; fax: 01698 454183; e-mail: enquiries@apse.org.uk

ASSOCIATION FOR RATIONAL EMOTIVE BEHAVIOUR THERAPY

PO Box 39207, London, SE3 7XH

Tel: 020 8293 4334
Fax: 020 8293 4114
E-mail: rebtadmin@managingstress.com

Website:
http://rebt.bizland.com
Information about the Association, membership details, recognised courses, publications

Enquiries:
Enquiries to: Honorary Secretary
Other contacts: Membership Secretary

Founded:
1993

Formerly called:
Association for Rational Emotive Behaviour Therapists (year of change 2002)

Organisation type and purpose:
Professional body (membership is by subscription, qualification), present number of members: 85.
To promote the art and science of rational emotive behaviour therapy.

Non-library collection catalogue:
All or part available online

Printed publications:
The Rational Emotive Behaviour Therapist Journal

Electronic and video publications:
Online journal

Access to staff:
Contact by letter, by telephone, by e-mail and via website
Hours: Mon to Fri, 1000 to 1700

ASSOCIATION FOR ROAD TRAFFIC SAFETY AND MANAGEMENT

Acronym or abbreviation: ARTSM

Office 8, Epic House, 128 Fulwell Road, Teddington, TW11 0RQ

Tel: 020 8977 6952
Fax: 020 8977 8339

Website:
http://www.artsm.org.uk

Enquiries:
Enquiries to: General Secretary
Direct e-mail: philip.crickmay@artsm.org.uk

Founded:
1933

Formerly called:
Association of Road Traffic Sign Makers (ARTSM) (year of change 1995)

Organisation type and purpose:
Trade association (membership is by subscription, qualification), present number of members: 41.

Subject coverage:
Transport, road safety, pedestrian safety, road traffic signs, permanent and portable variable message signs, portable traffic signals, sign luminaires, street lighting, street name plates, traffic cones and lamps, sign erection, sign design-computer systems, vehicle detection and control.

Printed publications:
Brochure of members and products (free)

Access to staff:
Contact by letter, by telephone, by fax, by e-mail and via website. Appointment necessary.
Hours: Mon, Tue, Thu, 0900 to 1700

ASSOCIATION FOR SCIENCE EDUCATION

Acronym or abbreviation: ASE

College Lane, Hatfield, Hertfordshire, AL10 9AA

Tel: 01707 283000
Fax: 01707 266532
E-mail: info@ase.org.uk

Website:
http://www.ase.org.uk
Membership information, safety, publications, Association policies.

Enquiries:
Enquiries to: Chief Executive
Other contacts: Executive Director (Professional and Curriculum Innovation) – bookselling operations; Co-ordinator Journals – magazines

Founded:
1901

Organisation type and purpose:
Professional body (membership is by subscription), present number of members: 15,000, registered charity (charity number 313123), suitable for ages: 3 to 19, publishing house.
Educational organisation.

Subject coverage:
Primary, secondary and further education science education, study for its improvement, school safety issues.

Printed publications:
Education in Science (5 times a year)
Many publications for teachers of science
Primary Science (5 times a year)
Science Teacher Education (3 times a year)
School Science Review (4 times a year)

Electronic and video publications:
Videos

Publications list:
Available online and in print

Access to staff:
Contact by letter, by telephone, by fax, by e-mail and via website. Appointment necessary.
Hours: Mon to Fri, 0900 to 1700

Links with:
40 International Science Teacher Education Associations

ASSOCIATION FOR SCOTTISH LITERARY STUDIES

Acronym or abbreviation: ASLS

Department of Scottish Literature, 7 University Gardens, University of Glasgow, Glasgow, G12 8QH

Tel: 0141 330 5309
Fax: 0141 330 5309
E-mail: office@asls.org.uk

Website:
http://www.asls.org.uk
The ASLS website contains on-line articles, teaching materials, information on our publications and conferences, and links to other sites of interest.

Enquiries:
Enquiries to: Manager

Founded:
1970

Organisation type and purpose:
International organisation, membership association (membership is by subscription), present number of members: 600, registered charity (charity number SC006535), publishing house.
ASLS is an educational charity promoting the languages and literature of Scotland, from the study of classic texts to encouraging contemporary talent.

continued overleaf

Subject coverage:
Languages and literature of Scotland.

Printed publications:
Books and edited editions
ASLS Annual Volumes Series
New Writing Scotland Series
ASLS Occasional Papers Series
Scotnotes (24 titles relating to specific authors or books)
ScotLit (2 times a year)
Scottish Language (annually)
Scottish Literary Review (2 times a year)

Electronic and video publications:
The International Journal of Scottish Literature at http://www.ijsl.stir.ac.uk
The Bottle Imp at http://www.thebottleimp.org.uk

Publications list:
Available online and in print

Access to staff:
Contact by letter, by telephone, by fax, by e-mail and via website
Hours: Mon to Fri, 0900 to 1700

ASSOCIATION FOR SHARED PARENTING

Acronym or abbreviation: A.S.P.

PO Box 2000, Dudley, West Midlands, DY1 1YZ

Tel: 01789 751157
Fax: 01789 751081
E-mail: spring.cott@btopenworld.com

Website:
http://www.sharedparenting.org.uk
http://www.sharedparenting.f9.co.uk/

Enquiries:
Enquiries to: Honorary Secretary
Direct e-mail: owner@sharedparenting.org.uk

Founded:
1993

Formerly called:
Families Need Fathers (West Midlands Branch) (FNF) (year of change 1993)

Organisation type and purpose:
Membership association (membership is by subscription), present number of members: 80, voluntary organisation, registered charity (charity number 1042874).
To promote the right of children to have sufficient contact with both parents after separation or divorce.

Subject coverage:
The Children Act 1989, parental responsibility, family court procedures, divorce and children, maintaining contact with children after separation or divorce, how to manage your solicitor, use of child contact centre.

Printed publications:
Leaflets and occasional magazine

Access to staff:
Contact by letter and by telephone
Hours: Daily, 0800 to 2200

Other branches in:
Leicestershire
    tel: 0116 254 8453

ASSOCIATION FOR SPECIALIST FIRE PROTECTION

Acronym or abbreviation: ASFP

Tournai Hall, Evelyn Woods Road, Aldershot, Hampshire, GU11 2LL

Tel: 01252 357832
Fax: 01252 357831
E-mail: info@asfp.org.uk

Website:
http://www.asfp.org.uk

Enquiries:
Enquiries to: Secretary
Direct e-mail: john.fairley@asfp.org.uk

Founded:
1975

Organisation type and purpose:
Trade association, present number of members: 64.
Represents UK manufacturers, distributors, contractors, consultants, testing houses and others involved in passive fire protection products and services. Produces a wide range of relevant publications.

Subject coverage:
Represents UK manufacturers, distributors, contractors, consultants, testing houses and others involved in passive fire protection products and services.

Printed publications:
On-site Measurement of Intumescent Coatings
Spray Coatings for Fire Protection of Concrete Floors
Spray Coatings for Fire Protection of Structural Steel
List of members and services (free)
Fire Stopping & Penetration Seals for the Construction Industry (Red Book)
Fire Protection for Structural Steel in Buildings (Yellow Book with supplement)
Fire Protection for Timber Floors (Green Book)
Fire Protection of Roof Components & Secondary Structural Steelworks of Portal Frame Buildings

Publications list:
Available in print

Access to staff:
Contact by letter, by telephone, by fax, by e-mail and via website
Hours: Mon to Fri, 0900 to 1700

ASSOCIATION FOR SPINA BIFIDA AND HYDROCEPHALUS

Acronym or abbreviation: ASBAH

ASBAH House, 42 Park Road, Peterborough, Cambridgeshire, PE1 2UQ

Tel: 01733 555988
Fax: 01733 555985
E-mail: helpline@asbah.org

Website:
http://www.asbah.org
Information on the disabilities (spina bifida/hydrocephalus), topic sheets.

Enquiries:
Enquiries to: Helpline and Information Service
Direct tel: 0845 450 7755

Founded:
1966

Organisation type and purpose:
Voluntary organisation, registered charity (charity number 249338).
40 affiliated local associations in UK.
Provides information, advice and support to families/individuals with spina bifida and/or hydrocephalus.

Subject coverage:
Spina bifida, hydrocephalus, (antenatal testing, welfare and help as to benefit entitlement, education, mobility, continence, training and employment, aids and appliances in relation to spina bifida or hydrocephalus only).

Printed publications:
Link (journal, bi-monthly, £6.80 annual subscription)
Annual Report
Below the Belt (ASBAH, £7)
Benny Bear Books (£2 each)
Hydrocephalus and its implications for teaching and learning (£9)
Hydrocephalus and YOU (Holgate, L and Batchelor, R, £7.50)

The Statementing Process for Children with Special Needs (ASBAH)
Information sheets
Your Child and Hydrocephalus (£9.99)

Publications list:
Available online and in print

Access to staff:
Contact by letter, by telephone, by fax, by e-mail and via website
Hours: Mon to Fri, 0900 to 1700. Helpline: Mon to Fri, 1000 to 1600

ASSOCIATION FOR THE CONSERVATION OF ENERGY

Acronym or abbreviation: ACE

Westgate House, Prebend Street, London, N1 8PT

Tel: 020 7359 8000
Fax: 020 7359 0863
E-mail: info@ukace.org

Website:
http://members.aol.com/aceuk/home.htm
Access to briefing notes, general information.

Enquiries:
Enquiries to: Office Manager
Other contacts: Research Director for research function.

Founded:
1981

Organisation type and purpose:
Membership association (membership is by subscription, election or invitation), present number of members: 18, research organisation.
Campaigning organisation.
To increase investment in energy conservation.

Subject coverage:
Energy conservation (policy rather than product related), greenhouse effect, CO_2 emissions, fuel poverty.

Museum or gallery collection, archive, or library special collection:
Material on energy conservation policy

Publications list:
Available in print

Access to staff:
Contact by letter, by telephone, by fax, by e-mail and via website
Hours: Mon to Fri, 0930 to 1730
Special comments: Strictly no personal callers.

Links with:
British Energy Efficiency Federation

ASSOCIATION FOR UNIVERSITY AND COLLEGE COUNSELLING

Acronym or abbreviation: AUCC

British Association for Counselling and Psychotherapy, 15 St John's Business Park, Lutterworth, Leicestershire, LE17 4HB

Tel: 01455 883300 Minicom no. 01455 0307
Fax: 01455 550243
E-mail: bacp@bacp.co.uk

Website:
http://www.bacp.co.uk
http://www.counselling.co.uk

Enquiries:
Enquiries to: Administrator

Founded:
1971

Formerly called:
Association for Student Counselling (ASC) (year of change 1997)

Organisation type and purpose:
Voluntary organisation.
To promote counselling in institutions of post-compulsory education.

Subject coverage:
Provision of counselling services in post-compulsory education, practice of student counselling, careers counselling, training and professional development of members, advisory service to members for their institutional provision, appropriate conditions of service for counsellors in institutions.

Trade and statistical information:
Statistical survey of institutions (available to contributing members only).

Printed publications:
Advisory Service for Institutions (free)
Association for Student Counselling (free)
Directory of Training Courses (via BACP)
Executive Council (free)
Guidelines for the ASC Recognition of Training Courses (free)

Access to staff:
Contact by letter, by telephone, by fax, by e-mail and via website. Appointment necessary.
Hours: Mon to Fri, 0900 to 1700

Access to building, collection or gallery:
Prior appointment required
Hours: Mon to Fri, 0900 to 1700

Access for disabled people:
Parking provided, ramped entry, toilet facilities

Constituent part of:
British Association for Counselling and Psychotherapy

ASSOCIATION OF ACCOUNTING TECHNICIANS

Acronym or abbreviation: AAT

154 Clerkenwell Road, London, EC1R 5AD

Tel: 020 7837 8600
Fax: 020 7837 6970
E-mail: info@aat.org.uk

Website:
http://www.aat.org.uk

Enquiries:
Enquiries to: Communications Manager
Direct tel: 020 7415 7670
Direct fax: 020 7415 7699
Direct e-mail: kate.martin@aat.org.uk

Founded:
1980

Organisation type and purpose:
International organisation, professional body (membership is by subscription, qualification), present number of members: 105,000, registered charity (charity number 1050724), suitable for ages: 16+.
The Association of Accounting Technicians is the only dedicated professional body approved to award National Vocational Qualifications (NVQs) and Scottish Vocational Qualifications (SVQs) in Accounting.
The Association was established in 1980 to provide a recognised qualification body for Accounting Technicians.

Subject coverage:
Training as an Accounting Technician – NVQs/SVQs in Accounting AAT Qualifications.
Membership of the AAT and Continuing Professional Development.

Printed publications:
The Guide (free)
Approved Assessment Centres (free)
Accounting for Success (free)
Skillcheck leaflet (free)
Student Records (free)
Accounting Portfolio Leaflet (free)

Publications list:
Available online and in print

Access to staff:
Contact by letter, by telephone, by fax, by e-mail, in person and via website. Appointment necessary.
Hours: Mon to Fri, 0900 to 1700

ASSOCIATION OF AMERICAN DANCING

Acronym or abbreviation: AAD

Aspenshaw Hall, Thornsett, High Peak, Derbyshire, SK22 1AU

Tel: 01663 744986
E-mail: email@a-a-d.wanadoo.co.uk

Website:
http://www.the-aad.org.uk

Enquiries:
Enquiries to: Assistant Director

Founded:
1934

Organisation type and purpose:
Professional body, membership association (membership is by qualification), training organisation.
Examination and teaching body in dance disciplines.

Subject coverage:
Most dance forms, particularly ballet, mime, tap, acrobatic and modern stage dancing.

Library catalogue:
All or part available in-house

Printed publications:
Many publications on theory, enchainements, ballet, including:
Tap, Acrobatic, Modern, Ballet, Mime Syllabus
Mime Vocabulary Grades 1, 2 and preliminary
Mime Vocabulary Elementary, Intermediate, Advanced
Authentic Time Steps and Breaks Theory and Dance
The Theory of Tap Dancing for the Graduate
The Theory of Ballet, Each Grade
Order printed publications from: General Secretary, Association of American Dancing

Electronic and video publications:
Audio tapes, CD-ROMs available for purchase, members only

Publications list:
Available in print

Access to staff:
Contact by letter and by telephone. Appointment necessary.
Hours: Mon to Fri, 1000 to 1700

Access to building, collection or gallery:
Mon to Fri, 1000 to 1700

Access for disabled people:
Hours: Mon to Fri, 1000 to 1700

Affiliated to:
Council for Dance Education and Training (UK) London

Member of:
Modern Art Group

ASSOCIATION OF APPLIED BIOLOGISTS

Acronym or abbreviation: AAB

C/o Warwick HRI, Wellesbourne, Warwickshire, CV35 9EF

Tel: 01789 470382
Fax: 01789 470234
E-mail: carol.aab@warwick.ac.uk

Website:
http://www.aab.org.uk/
Home page: Details about Association, contents list for Annals of Applied Biology, programmes and booking forms for Association's meetings. Instructions to authors for Annals, publications list.

Enquiries:
Enquiries to: Executive Officer

Founded:
1904

Organisation type and purpose:
International organisation, learned society (membership is by election or invitation), present number of members: 800, registered charity (charity number 275655), training organisation, publishing house.

Subject coverage:
Plant breeding, pathology, physiology, virology, entomology, nematology, host plant resistance to diseases and pests, plant microbial interactions, bio-control, crop physiology, weeds and crop agronomy, post-harvest biology, pesticide application.

Printed publications:
AAB News (newsletter, members, 2 times a year)
Annals of Applied Biology (6 times a year)
Aspects of Applied Biology (papers and contributions from meetings)

Electronic and video publications:
Description of Plant Viruses (CD-ROM)
Molecular Biology Notebook (CD-ROM)

Publications list:
Available online and in print

Access to staff:
Contact by letter, by telephone, by fax and via website. Appointment necessary.
Hours: Mon to Fri, 0900 to 1700

Access to building, collection or gallery:
Prior appointment required

Access for disabled people:
Parking provided, toilet facilities

Affiliated to:
Institute of Biology

ASSOCIATION OF ART & ANTIQUES DEALERS

Formal name: The Association of Art & Antiques Dealers
Acronym or abbreviation: LAPADA

535 Kings Road, London, SW10 0SZ

Tel: 020 7823 3511
Fax: 020 7823 3522
E-mail: lapada@lapada.org

Website:
http://www.lapada.org

Enquiries:
Enquiries to: Chief Executive

Founded:
1974

Formerly called:
London and Provincial Antique Dealers Association (LAPADA)

Organisation type and purpose:
Trade association (membership is by qualification), present number of members: 600.

Subject coverage:
Trade in art and antiques.

Publications list:
Available online and in print

Access to staff:
Contact by letter, by telephone, by fax, by e-mail and via website
Hours: Mon to Fri, 0900 to 1700

Member organisation of:
Confédération Internationale des Négociants en Oeuvres d'Art (CINOA)

ASSOCIATION OF ART HISTORIANS

Acronym or abbreviation: AAH

Cowcross Court, 70 Cowcross Street, London, EC1M 6EJ

Tel: 020 7490 3211
E-mail: admin@aah.org.uk

continued overleaf

Website:
http://www.aah.org.uk
Association information and publications.

Enquiries:
Enquiries to: Administrator

Founded:
1974

Organisation type and purpose:
Membership association.

Subject coverage:
Art history, art, design, architecture, photography, film and media, museum studies, conservation, cultural studies.

Printed publications:
Art History (5 times a year)
The Art Book (4 times a year)
Bulletin (3 times a year, free to members)
Order printed publications from: Wiley-Blackwell Publishing

Electronic and video publications:
Available via the publishers' website to members

Publications list:
Available online

Access to staff:
Contact by letter, by telephone, by fax and by e-mail
Hours: Mon to Fri, 0930 to 1730

Links with:
College Art Association (CAA)
USA
Scottish Society of Art Historians (SSAH)

ASSOCIATION OF BAKERY INGREDIENT MANUFACTURERS

Acronym or abbreviation: abim

4a Torphichen Street, Edinburgh, EH3 8JQ

Tel: 0131 229 9415
Fax: 0131 229 9407
E-mail: abim@abim.org.uk

Website:
http://www.abim.org.uk

Enquiries:
Enquiries to: Executive Secretary

Founded:
1917

Formerly called:
Bakery Allied Traders' Association (BATA) (year of change 1999)

Organisation type and purpose:
Trade association (membership is by subscription). Acts as lobbying organisation for trade sector.

Subject coverage:
Bakery ingredients.

Printed publications:
Code of Good Hygiene Practice (£2.50 plus 75p p&p)
Occupational Allergy Guidelines and Material Safety Data Sheets (£5 plus £1 p&p)

Publications list:
Available online

Access to staff:
Contact by letter, by telephone, by fax, by e-mail and via website. Appointment necessary. Access for members only.
Hours: Mon to Fri, 0900 to 1700

Access to building, collection or gallery:
Prior appointment required

Member of:
FEDIMA
FMBRA
Food and Drink Federation
UKBICC

ASSOCIATION OF BLIND PIANO TUNERS

Acronym or abbreviation: ABPT

31 Wyne Crescent, Darwen, Lancashire, BB0 J9

Tel: 01254 776148
Fax: 01254 773158
E-mail. abpt@uk-piano.org

Website:
http://www.uk-piano.org

Enquiries:
Enquiries to: General Secretary

Founded:
1954

Organisation type and purpose:
Trade association, service industry.

Subject coverage:
Piano tuning and repairs.

Access to staff:
Contact by letter, by telephone, by e-mail and via website
Hours: Mon to Fri, 0900 to 1700

ASSOCIATION OF BREASTFEEDING MOTHERS

Acronym or abbreviation: ABM

PO Box 207, Bridgwater, Somerset, TA6 7YT

Tel: 08444 122948 (admin); 08444 122949 (helpline)
E-mail: info@abm.me.uk

Website:
http://www.abm.me.uk

Enquiries:
Enquiries to: Administrator

Founded:
1979

Organisation type and purpose:
Membership association (membership is by subscription), registered charity (charity number 280537). Promotion of breastfeeding and provision of counselling for mothers with breastfeeding problems, training breastfeeding counsellors.

Subject coverage:
Support and information on breastfeeding for mothers and health professionals, counsellor training available.

Printed publications:
A series of leaflets on breastfeeding
Magazine (to members, 3 times a year)

Publications list:
Available online and in print

Access to staff:
Contact by letter, by telephone, by e-mail and via website
Hours: Daily: 0930 to 2230

ASSOCIATION OF BRITISH & IRISH WILD ANIMAL KEEPERS

Acronym or abbreviation: ABWAK

Twycross Zoo, Burton Road, Atherstone, Warwickshire, CV9 3PX

Tel: 01827 880250
Fax: 01827 880700
E-mail: amy.hulse@twycrosszoo.org

Website:
http://www.abwak.co.uk

Enquiries:
Enquiries to: Honorary Secretary
Direct fax: 01827 881049

Founded:
1974

Organisation type and purpose:
Professional body.

Subject coverage:
Animal husbandry and zoos.

Printed publications:
Careers leaflet
Management Guidelines
Proceedings of Symposia (annually)
RATEL members' journal (quarterly)
Order printed publications from: Publications Officer, Leeds Castle, Maidstone, Kent, ME17 1PL

Publications list:
Available in print

Access to staff:
Contact by letter, by e-mail and via website
Hours: Mon to Fri, 0900 to 1700

ASSOCIATION OF BRITISH CERTIFICATION BODIES LIMITED

Acronym or abbreviation: ABCB

Sandover Centre, 129A Whitehorse Hill, Chislehurst, Kent, BR7 6DQ

Tel: 020 8295 1128
Fax: 020 8467 8095
E-mail: tinman@abcb.org.uk

Website:
http://www.abcb.org.uk/
Members list, SME Workbook for 1S0 9000:2000.

Enquiries:
Enquiries to: Chief Executive

Founded:
1984

Organisation type and purpose:
National organisation, trade association (membership is by subscription, qualification), present number of members: 25.
To promote ABCB as the UK's centre of excellence for product, quality management and environmental certification for the benefit of its members.

Trade and statistical information:
List of members.

Printed publications:
Newsletter (periodic, free)

Access to staff:
Contact by letter, by telephone, by fax and by e-mail
Hours: Mon to Fri, 0900 to 1700

ASSOCIATION OF BRITISH CLIMATOLOGISTS

Acronym or abbreviation: ABC

School of Environmental Science, University College Northampton, Park Campus, Boughton Green Road, Northampton, NN2 7AL

Tel: 01604 735500
Fax: 01604 720636
E-mail: chris.holt@northampton.ac.uk

Website:
http://itu.reading.ac.uk/rms/abcgroup.html

Enquiries:
Enquiries to: Honorary Secretary

Founded:
1970

Organisation type and purpose:
Learned society (membership is by subscription).

Subject coverage:
All aspects of climatology, e.g. building climatology, agricultural climatology; climatic change.

Printed publications:
Directory of British Climatologists
Mailings (3 times a year, to members)

Access to staff:
Contact by letter, by fax and by e-mail
Hours: Mon to Fri, 0900 to 1700

Specialist group of the:
Royal Meteorological Society
104 Oxford Road, Reading, Berkshire

ASSOCIATION OF BRITISH CORRESPONDENCE COLLEGES

Acronym or abbreviation: ABCC

PO Box 17926, London, SW19 3WB

Tel: 020 8544 9559
Fax: 020 8540 7657
E-mail: info@homestudy.org.uk

Website:
http://www.homestudy.org.uk

Enquiries:
Enquiries to: Secretary

Founded:
1955

Organisation type and purpose:
Trade association (membership is by qualification),
present number of members: 22.

Subject coverage:
Distance education; academic, professional,
commercial and technical courses.

Access to staff:
Contact by letter, by telephone, by fax, by e-mail
and via website
Hours: Mon to Fri, 1430 to 1800 (variable)

ASSOCIATION OF BRITISH CYCLING COACHES, THE

Acronym or abbreviation: ABCC

19 Forbes Avenue, Beverley High Road, Hull, East
Yorkshire, HU6 7AJ

Tel: 01482 857774
E-mail: jim@jsampson.karoo.co.uk

Website:
http://www.abcc.freeserve.co.uk

Enquiries:
Enquiries to: Administrator

Founded:
before 1970

Formerly called:
British Cycling Coaches Association (BCCA), date
of change, c. 1990

Organisation type and purpose:
Membership association (membership is by
qualification), present number of members: 702,
voluntary organisation, training organisation.
Educate, qualify, and maintain a register of cycling
coaches.

Subject coverage:
Cycling coaching.

Printed publications:
Cycle Coaching (4 times a year, non-ABCC coaches
£20)

Access to staff:
Contact by letter, by telephone and by e-mail
Hours: Mon to Fri, 0900 to 1700

ASSOCIATION OF BRITISH DISPENSING OPTICIANS

Acronym or abbreviation: ABDO

Godmersham Park, Godmersham, Canterbury,
Kent, CT4 7DT

Tel: 01227 738829
Fax: 01227 733900
E-mail: general@abdo.org.uk

Website:
http://www.abdo.org.uk

Enquiries:
Enquiries to: Reception
Direct tel: 01227 733901

Direct fax: 01227 733900
Other contacts: Head of distance learning
department for education matters.

Founded:
1989

Formerly called:
Association of Dispensing Opticians

Organisation type and purpose:
Professional body (membership is by subscription,
qualification), present number of members: 6,400,
training organisation.

Subject coverage:
Optics and opticians.

Printed publications:
Books (available for purchase)
Dispensing Optics (journal)
Order printed publications from: ABDO College
Bookshop

Publications list:
Available online and in print

Access to staff:
Contact by letter, by telephone, by fax and via
website. Appointment necessary. Access for
members only.
Hours: Mon to Fri, 0900 to 1700

Access for disabled people:
Parking provided, ramped entry, toilet facilities

ASSOCIATION OF BRITISH FIRE TRADES LIMITED

Acronym or abbreviation: ABFT

Neville House, 55 Eden Street, Kingston Upon
Thames, Surrey, KT1 1BW

Tel: 020 8549 5855
Fax: 020 8547 1564

Enquiries:
Enquiries to: Secretary

Founded:
1979

Organisation type and purpose:
Service organisation for the fire trade, in particular
for the Fire Industry Council, Fire Extinguishing
Trades Association, British Fire Protection Systems
Association, British Approvals for Fire Equipment.
Provides administrative and secretarial services to
the fire protection industry's own trade
associations.

Subject coverage:
Organisation and interests of fire trade
associations.

Access to staff:
Contact by letter, by telephone and by fax
Hours: Mon to Fri, 0900 to 1700

ASSOCIATION OF BRITISH HEALTHCARE INDUSTRIES

Acronym or abbreviation: ABHI

111 Westminster Bridge Road, London, SE1 7HR

Tel: 020 7960 4360
Fax: 020 7960 4361
E-mail: enquiries@abhi.org.uk

Website:
http://www.abhi.org.uk

Founded:
1988

Created by the merger of:
British Health Care Export Council (BHEC) and
British Health Care Trade and Industry
Confederation (BHTIC) (year of change 1988)

Organisation type and purpose:
Trade association (membership is by subscription,
qualification), present number of members: 200.

To promote medical technology and systems for
better health care and to be a facilitator of industry
growth and health-care development by
supporting the industry.

Subject coverage:
The medical devices industry, technical and
regulatory affairs, NHS, overseas trade.

Printed publications:
Annual Report
Focus (journal, quarterly)

Publications list:
Available online

Access to staff:
Contact by letter, by telephone, by fax, by e-mail
and via website. Appointment necessary.
Hours: Mon to Fri, 0900 to 1700

Access to building, collection or gallery:
No prior appointment required
Hours: Mon to Fri, 0900 to 1700
Special comments: Members can use the library.

Access for disabled people:
Access to all public areas

ASSOCIATION OF BRITISH INSURERS

Acronym or abbreviation: ABI

51 Gresham Street, London, EC2V 7HQ

Tel: 020 7600 3333
Fax: 020 7696 8999
E-mail: info@abi.org.uk

Website:
http://www.abi.org.uk
Site has three main sections providing information
to different audiences:
(a) All site visitors – explanation of ABI's role,
ability to view and print a range of consumer
information sheets, press releases, details of ABI
members, hot links to insurance company sites
(b) Insurance information service (by subscription)
– most newsletters, circulars, daily press summary,
ability to view and download ABI's statistical
publications
(c) members – all the above plus information
confidential to the membership, all newsletters,
copies of ABI briefings, representations and
submissions.

Enquiries:
Enquiries to: Consumer Support Adviser
Direct tel: 020 7216 7416

Founded:
1985

Formerly called:
British Insurance Association, Fire Offices
Committee, Life Offices Association

Organisation type and purpose:
Trade association (membership is by subscription,
qualification).

Subject coverage:
UK insurance industry, EC insurance sector,
statistics.

Printed publications:
Annual Report (free)
Consumer advice leaflets, information sheets,
reports (prices vary)
Order printed publications from: Download from
website or ring 020 7216 7617 after consulting
website publications list

Publications list:
Available online

Access to staff:
Contact by letter, by telephone, by fax, by e-mail
and via website. Access for members only.
Hours: Mon to Fri, 0900 to 1700 (Closed 1 to 2pm)

ASSOCIATION OF BRITISH INTRODUCTION AGENCIES

Acronym or abbreviation: ABIA

Suite 109, 315 Chiswick High Rd, Chiswick, London, W4 4HH 020 8742 0386

Tel: 020 8742 0386

Website:
http://www.abia.org.uk
List of member agencies, code of practice, general information for members of the public.

Enquiries:
Enquiries to: Press Officer
Direct tel: 07530 415 388
Direct e-mail: press@abia.org.uk

Founded:
1981

Organisation type and purpose:
Trade association, membership association (membership is by qualification), present number of members: 30, research organisation.
To monitor, regulate and disseminate information regarding the industry, enforcing the code of conduct supported by the Office of Fair Trading.

Subject coverage:
Introduction agencies, including marriage bureaux and introduction and dating agencies.

Trade and statistical information:
Available upon request.

Printed publications:
Code of Practice (free)
List of current members (free)

Access to staff:
Contact by letter, by fax, by e-mail and via website
Hours: Telephone between 0930 to 1700
Special comments: No visitors.

ASSOCIATION OF BRITISH INVESTIGATORS

Acronym or abbreviation: ABI

48 Queens Road, Basingstoke, Hampshire, RG21 7RE

Tel: 01256 816390
Fax: 01256 479547
E-mail: abi@globalnet.co.uk

Website:
http://www.theabi.org.uk
Membership listing, history, information regarding publications.

Enquiries:
Enquiries to: Company Secretary
Other contacts: President for Administrative Head of organisation.

Founded:
1913

Organisation type and purpose:
International organisation, trade association (membership is by qualification), present number of members: 400.
Association for private investigators.
Representation and training.

Subject coverage:
Any legally obtainable information about individuals, corporations, associations, trusts etc worldwide.

Printed publications:
Investigate (4 times a year, members or by subscription)
Directory of Members (annually, £25)
Process Servers Guide (£30)
Best Practice Guide for Professional Investigators

Access to staff:
Contact by letter, by telephone, by fax and by e-mail
Hours: Mon to Fri, 0900 to 1700

ASSOCIATION OF BRITISH ORCHESTRAS

Acronym or abbreviation: ABO

20 Rupert Street, London, W1D 6DF

Tel: 020 7287 0333
Fax: 020 7287 0444
E-mail: info@abo.org.uk

Website:
http://www.abo.org.uk
General information about the ABO, its membership, events and activities.

Enquiries:
Enquiries to: Director
Direct e-mail: mark@abo.org.uk

Founded:
1947

Organisation type and purpose:
The ABO exists to support, develop and advance the interests and activities of the orchestral profession in the UK.
The ABO's key activities centre around Advocacy, Services, Information and Learning and are delivered through conferences, seminars, negotiations, training opportunities, education initiatives and representation.
Full membership is open to professional orchestras that have been in existence for more than two years and have given at least 24 performances. Associate, Corporate and Individual membership is also available.

Subject coverage:
Professional orchestras in the UK.

Library catalogue:
All or part available online

Printed publications:
ABO Update (monthly newsletter for members only)
Factsheets
Annual Report
Other reports on specialist subjects

Publications list:
Available online and in print

Access to staff:
Contact by letter, by telephone, by fax, by e-mail and via website. Appointment necessary.
Hours: Mon to Fri, 0930 to 1730

Access to building, collection or gallery:
Prior appointment required

ASSOCIATION OF BRITISH PEWTER CRAFTSMEN

Acronym or abbreviation: ABPC

Unit 10, Edmund Road Business Centre
135 Edmund Road, Sheffield, S2 4ED

Tel: 0114 252 7550
Fax: 0114 252 7555
E-mail: enquiries@abpcltd.co.uk

Website:
http://www.abpcltd.co.uk

Enquiries:
Enquiries to: Secretary

Organisation type and purpose:
Trade association.

Subject coverage:
Manufacture of articles of pewter.

Museum or gallery collection, archive, or library special collection:
Collections at Pewter Hall, Oat Lane, London

Printed publications:
Pewter Review (3 times a year)

Access to staff:
Contact by letter, by telephone and by fax
Hours: Mon to Fri, 0900 to 1700

ASSOCIATION OF BRITISH PHILATELIC SOCIETIES LIMITED, THE

Formal name: Association of British Philatelic Societies
Acronym or abbreviation: ABPS

66 Crafts End, Chiltern, OX11 0SB

E-mail: abpssec@ukphilately.org.uk

Website:
http://www.ukphilately.org.uk/abps

Enquiries:
Enquiries to: Publicity and Publications Officer
Direct tel: 01692 598844
Direct e-mail: abps.phil@elics.co.uk

Founded:
1994

Formerly called:
British Philatelic Federation (BPF) (year of change 1994)

Organisation type and purpose:
National organisation, advisory body, membership association (membership is by subscription), present number of members: 372 federations and societies.
Federation of collectors, societies, etc.

Subject coverage:
Philately generally, stamp collecting, postal history.

Printed publications:
ABPS News (quarterly)
Congress Handbook (annually)
ABPS Directory (alternate years)
Speakers' List (alternate years)

Publications list:
Available in print

Access to staff:
Contact by letter, by telephone and via website
Hours: Mon to Fri, 0900 to 1700

Affiliated to:
Fédération Internationale de Philatélie (FIP)
Federation of European Philatelic Federations (FEPA)

ASSOCIATION OF BRITISH PICTURE RESTORERS

Formal name: The Association of British Picture Restorers
Acronym or abbreviation: ABPR

PO BOX 258 , Norwich, NR13 4WY

Tel: 01603 516237
Fax: 0160 351 0985
E-mail: office@bapcr.org.uk

Website:
http://www.bapcr.org.uk/
Future meetings, journals, training, information about ABPR and conservation enquiries.

Enquiries:
Enquiries to: Secretary

Founded:
1943

Organisation type and purpose:
Professional body.

Subject coverage:
Restoration and conservation of oil paintings; professional training.

Printed publications:
Conference Preprints
Journal (2 times a year)
Newsletter
Training leaflet

Access to staff:
Contact by letter, by telephone, by fax and by e-mail
Hours: Mon to Fri, 0930 to 1730

Affiliated to:
IIC

IPC
SSCR

ASSOCIATION OF BRITISH RIDING SCHOOLS

Acronym or abbreviation: ABRS

Queen's Chambers, 38–40 Queen Street, Penzance, Cornwall, TR18 4BH

Tel: 01736 369440
Fax: 01736 351390
E-mail: office@abrs-info.org

Website:
http://www.abrs-info.org
All exam syllabi, information from ABRS handbook, membership information.

Enquiries:
Enquiries to: General Secretary

Founded:
1954

Organisation type and purpose:
National organisation, advisory body, professional body (membership is by subscription), present number of members: 550, voluntary organisation, training organisation.
Professional association for proprietors, managers and staff of riding establishments.

Subject coverage:
Standards of instruction; horsemastership, welfare of horses and ponies in riding establishments, problems of riding establishments.

Printed publications:
ABRS Tests Guidelines Book (£7.00 inc. p&p)
ABRS Tests Summary syllabi (£1 inc. p&p)
An Instructor's Pocket Guide to Safe and Interesting Hacking (£3 inc. p&p)
Cereals (£2.50 inc. p&p)
Drills and Formation Riding (£7.50 inc. p&p)
Fundamentals of Riding (£5.50 inc. p&p)
Grooms Certificate Training Logbook (£6.00 inc. p&p)
Official Handbook (£5 inc. p&p)
Wintering Out (£2.50 inc. p&p)
Order printed publications from: ABRS

Publications list:
Available online and in print

Access to staff:
Contact by letter, by telephone, by fax and by e-mail
Hours: Mon to Fri, 0930 to 1730

Member organisation of:
British Equestrian Federation (BEF)
British Equestrian Trade Association (BETA)
Central Council of Physical Recreation (CCPR)
SEA
SSA

ASSOCIATION OF BRITISH THEATRE TECHNICIANS

Acronym or abbreviation: ABTT

55 Farringdon Road, London, EC1M 3JB

Tel: 020 7242 9200
Fax: 020 7242 9303
E-mail: office@abtt.org.uk

Website:
http://www.abtt.org.uk
Theatre – technical, careers and training.

Enquiries:
Enquiries to: Administrator

Founded:
1961

Organisation type and purpose:
Membership association (membership is by subscription), voluntary organisation, registered charity, training organisation.

Subject coverage:
Technical aspects of theatre; design and planning of theatre buildings; training and careers in the technical theatre.

Library catalogue:
All or part available in-house

Printed publications:
ABTT Codes of Practice (for sale to members and non-members):
Technical Standards for Places of Entertainment (pub Jun 2008, £45 members, £50 non-members)
Modern Rules of Management for Places of Public Entertainment (£20 members, £25 non-members)
Flying (£15 members, £20 non-members)
Fibre Ropes (£10 members, £15 non-members)
Wire Ropes (£10 members, £15 non-members)
A Modern Approach to Emergency Lighting in Theatre (£6 members, £10 non-members)
Firearms and Ammunition: Acquisition, Possession and Use (£6 members, £10 non-members)
Pyrotechnics & Smoke Effects (£6 members, £10 non-members)
Design Guide – Guard Rails (£5 members, £10 non-members)
Guidance Note on Exit Signs (free)
Guidance Note on Water and check list (free)
Plus other publications
Time & Space (Exhibition Catalogue 1999 SBTD, £17.95 members, £18.95 non-members)

Publications list:
Available online and in print

Access to staff:
Contact by letter, by telephone, by fax and by e-mail
Hours: Mon to Fri, 1000 to 1700

Affiliated to and at the same address as:
Society of British Theatre Designers

ASSOCIATION OF BRITISH THEOLOGICAL AND PHILOSOPHICAL LIBRARIES

Acronym or abbreviation: ABTAPL

Website:
http://www.newman.ac.uk/abtapl/index.html
http://www.le.ac.uk/abtapl/
Union list of Periodicals.

Enquiries:
Enquiries to: Honorary Secretary
Other contacts: Chairman

Founded:
1954

Organisation type and purpose:
National organisation, professional body (membership is by subscription), present number of members: 200.

Subject coverage:
Theology, religious studies, philosophy, librarianship.

Printed publications:
Bulletin (3 times a year)
Guide to the Theological Libraries of Great Britain and Ireland
Union List of Theological Periodicals

Access to staff:
Contact by letter, by fax and by e-mail
Hours: Mon to Fri, 0900 to 1700
Special comments: Voluntary organisation, no paid staff.

Links with:
American Theological Libraries Association
Conseil International des Associations des Bibliothèques de Théologie
Library Association

ASSOCIATION OF BRITISH TRAVEL AGENTS

Acronym or abbreviation: ABTA

67–71 Newman Street, London, W1T 3AH

Tel: 020 7637 2444
Fax: 020 7637 0713
E-mail: abta@abta.co.uk

Website:
http://www.abta.com

Enquiries:
Enquiries to: Information Officer
Direct tel: 0901 201 5050 (charged at 50p per min)
Direct fax: 020 7307 1992
Other contacts: Policy and Research Executive for research.

Founded:
1950

Organisation type and purpose:
Trade association.

Subject coverage:
Travel destinations, travel advice, details of ABTA members.

Printed publications:
Annual Report
ABTA Codes of Conduct (£25)
ABTA Magazine (monthly £24)
ABTA Members Handbook (£40)
ABTA Members List (£30)
Order printed publications from: ABTA Magazine, Absolute Publishing
197–199 City Road, London, EC1V 1JN

Electronic and video publications:
ABTA Members Database

Access to staff:
Contact by telephone. All charged.
Hours: Mon to Fri, 0830 to 1800

Access for disabled people:
Ramped entry, toilet facilities

Subsidiary body:
ABTA National Training Board
Waterloo House, 11–17 Chertsey Road, Woking, Surrey; tel: 01483 727321; fax: 01483 756698

ASSOCIATION OF BROADCASTING DOCTORS

Acronym or abbreviation: ABD

PO Box 15, Sindalthorpe House, Ely, Cambridgeshire, CB7 4SG

Tel: 01353 688456 or 688588
Fax: 01353 688451
E-mail: soundplanltd@netscapeonline.co.uk

Website:
http://www.broadcasting-doctor.org
Medical news, members' specialities, aims, medical links.

Enquiries:
Enquiries to: Director
Other contacts: Administrator

Founded:
1988

Organisation type and purpose:
Professional body (membership is by election or invitation), present number of members: 755, voluntary organisation, training organisation, consultancy.
Support for clinicians who also broadcast.

Subject coverage:
Medical broadcasting, all medical specialities. The provision of medical practitioners and specialists as contributors to radio and television, and of producers and journal editors.

Museum or gallery collection, archive, or library special collection:
Library of written and recorded material

Printed publications:
Newsletter (monthly)

Electronic and video publications:
Various audio tapes on medical topics

continued overleaf

Access to staff:
Contact by letter, by telephone, by fax, by e-mail and via website
Hours: 0600 to 1900, seven days a week

Administered by:
Soundplan Broadcasting Services Limited
at the same address

ASSOCIATION OF BUILDING COMPONENT MANUFACTURERS LIMITED

Acronym or abbreviation: ABCM

Clark House, 3 Brassey Drive, Aylesford, Kent, ME20 7QL

Tel: 01622 715577
Fax: 08700 54 39 15
E-mail: abcm@building-components.org

Website:
http://www.building-components.org

Enquiries:
Enquiries to: Director

Founded:
1965

Organisation type and purpose:
Trade association (membership is by subscription).

Access to staff:
Contact by letter, by telephone, by fax, by e-mail and via website
Hours: Mon to Fri, 0900 to 1700

ASSOCIATION OF BUILDING ENGINEERS

Acronym or abbreviation: ABE

Lutyens House, Billing Brook Road, Weston Favell, Northampton, NN3 8NW

Tel: 01604 404121
Fax: 01604 784220
E-mail: building.engineers@abe.org.uk

Website:
http://www.abe.org.uk

Enquiries:
Enquiries to: Chief Executive
Other contacts: Editor ABE Journal

Founded:
1925

Formerly called:
Incorporated Association of Architects and Surveyors (IAAS) (year of change 1993)

Organisation type and purpose:
Professional body.
To specialise in the technology of building.

Subject coverage:
Building surveying and construction in general, architecture, technology of building, town planning, valuation, estate management.

Printed publications:
Building Engineer (journal, monthly, £40 a year incl. p&p)

Access to staff:
Contact by letter, by telephone, by fax, by e-mail and via website. Appointment necessary. Non-members charged.
Hours: Mon to Fri, 0900 to 1700

Member organisation of:
Construction Industry Council
Construction Industry Standing Conference
L'Association d'experts européens du bâtiment et de la construction

ASSOCIATION OF BUSINESS RECOVERY PROFESSIONALS

Acronym or abbreviation: R3

120 Aldersgate Street, London, EC1A 4JQ

Tel: 020 7566 4200
Fax: 020 7566 4224
E-mail: association@r3.org.uk

Website:
http://www.r3.org.uk

Enquiries:
Enquiries to: Chief Operating Officer
Direct tel: 020 7566 4219

Founded:
1990

Organisation type and purpose:
National organisation, professional body, trade association, membership association (membership is by subscription), present number of members: 4000.
A strong voice for all those who work with underperforming businesses and people in financial difficulty.

Subject coverage:
Business recovery, rescue and renewal, including insolvency.

Printed publications:
The Ostrich's Guide to Business Survival
Understanding Insolvency
Making a Career as an Insolvency Practitioner
Creditors' Guides
Is a Voluntary Arrangement Right For Me?
Order printed publications from: www.r3.org.uk

Electronic and video publications:
Business Recovery Training Package

Publications list:
Available online and in print

Access to staff:
Contact by letter, by telephone, by fax and by e-mail
Hours: Mon to Fri, 0900 to 1700

Access to building, collection or gallery:
Prior appointment required

Access for disabled people:
Access to all public areas, toilet facilities

ASSOCIATION OF CATERING EXCELLENCE

Acronym or abbreviation: ACE

Bourne House, Horsell Park, Woking, Surrey, GU21 4LY

Tel: 01483 765111
Fax: 01483 751991
E-mail: admin@acegb.org

Enquiries:
Enquiries to: Administrator

Founded:
1948

Organisation type and purpose:
Professional body (membership is by subscription, qualification), service industry.

Subject coverage:
Contract catering and all subjects allied to staff catering.

Access to staff:
Contact by letter, by telephone, by fax and by e-mail. Non-members charged.
Hours: Mon to Fri, 0900 to 1700

ASSOCIATION OF CEREAL FOOD MANUFACTURERS

Acronym or abbreviation: ACFM

6 Catherine Street, London, WC2B 5JJ

Tel: 020 7836 2460
Fax: 020 7836 0580

Enquiries:
Enquiries to: Executive Secretary

Organisation type and purpose:
Trade association.
Lobbying organisation.

Subject coverage:
Breakfast cereal products and related legislation.

Access to staff:
Appointment necessary. Access for members only.
Hours: Mon to Fri, 0900 to 1700

Affiliated to:
CEEREAL
Rond Point, Schuman 9 bte 11, Brussels, B-1040, Belgium

Umbrella organisation:
Food and Drink Federation
6 Catherine Street, London, WC2B 5JJ

ASSOCIATION OF CERTIFIED FRAUD EXAMINERS (UK)

Acronym or abbreviation: ACFE(UK)

840 Melton Road, Thurmaston, Leicester, LE4 8BN

Tel: 0116 260 6961
Fax: 0116 2604 0141
E-mail: acfe@associationhq.org.uk

Website:
http://www.acfe.org.uk

Enquiries:
Enquiries to: Executive Secretary

Founded:
January 1997

Organisation type and purpose:
Membership association (membership is by subscription, qualification), present number of members: 500.
UK Chapter.

Printed publications:
The Beacon
The White Paper (journal, 6 times a year)
Fraud Examiners Manual

Electronic and video publications:
Self-study video/workbook courses
Fraud Examiners Manual
Occupational Fraud and Abuse

Publications list:
Available online and in print

Access to staff:
Contact by letter, by telephone, by fax and by e-mail. Appointment necessary.
Hours: Mon to Fri, 0900 to 1700

Headquarters:
ACFE
The Gregor Building, 716 West Avenue, Austin, Texas, 78701, USA

ASSOCIATION OF CHARITABLE FOUNDATIONS

Acronym or abbreviation: ACF

Central House, 14 Upper Woburn Place, London, WC1H 0AE

Tel: 020 7255 4499
Fax: 020 7255 4496
E-mail: acf@acf.org.uk

Website:
http://www.acf.org.uk
General information about ACF and about UK trusts and foundations, including guidance on applying for funding, publications.

Enquiries:
Enquiries to: Chief Executive

Founded:
1989

Organisation type and purpose:
Membership association (membership is by subscription), voluntary organisation, registered charity (charity number 1105412).

Membership body for more than 300 charitable grant-making trusts and foundations.

Subject coverage:
Philanthropy, charitable grant-making, relevant aspects of charity and investment law.

Printed publications:
Annual Report
Trust and Foundation News (magazine, 4 times a year, free to members)
Funders' News (monthly bulletin only for members)
Variety of texts on charitable and grant-making issues (see website for details)

Publications list:
Available online

Access to staff:
Contact by letter, by e-mail and via website. Appointment necessary.
Hours: Mon to Fri, 0930 to 1730

ASSOCIATION OF CHARITY OFFICERS

Acronym or abbreviation: ACO

Five Ways, 57–59 Hatfield Road, Potters Bar, Hertfordshire, EN6 1HS

Tel: 01707 651777
Fax: 01707 660477
E-mail: info@aco.uk.net

Enquiries:
Enquiries to: Chief Executive
Other contacts: Administrative Officer; Helpline Co-ordinator (for queries relating to grants and from a member charity).

Founded:
1946

Incorporates the former:
Occupational Benevolent Funds Alliance (OBFA)

Organisation type and purpose:
Professional body, membership association (membership is by subscription), present number of members: over 200 charities, registered charity (charity number 1118605).
Association of over 200 charities who give non-contributory relief by means of financial grants and in other ways. ACO itself has no funds for grant aid.
The professional association for benevolent funds and charities helping people in need.

Subject coverage:
Charities; benevolent funds, residential and nursing home care of older people in the voluntary sector; effects of legislation, interest of members. ACO offers training on Access to Benevolence to all those charities and benevolent funds helping people in need. Also gives guidelines and information on best practice.

Museum or gallery collection, archive, or library special collection:
ACO holds details of a large number of grant-making charities which might help individuals in need (not projects)

Trade and statistical information:
Database of member funds.

Printed publications:
Annual Review
Benchmarks – How much do charities pay in grants?
Helping Charities Helping People
Directory of members (for members only)
GP Healthcare for older people in care and sheltered accommodation managed by charities
Individuals in Need – Guidelines for Grantmakers
News-sheet (for members only)
Sheltered Housing for Older People – The Occupational Benevolent Funds Alliance (OBFA) – GP charges
Benevolence in the 21st century (survey)

Access to staff:
Contact by letter, by telephone, by fax and by e-mail. Appointment necessary.
Hours: Mon to Fri, 1000 to 1600

ASSOCIATION OF CHARTERED PHYSIOTHERAPISTS IN INDEPENDENT HOSPITALS & CHARITIES

14 Bedford Row, London, WC1R 4ED

Tel: 020 7306 6666
E-mail: acpihc@acpihc.net

Enquiries:
Enquiries to: Honorary Secretary
Other contacts: Chairman

Formerly called:
Association of Chartered Physiotherapists in Independent Hospitals (ACPIH)

Organisation type and purpose:
National organisation, advisory body, professional body.
To assist Chartered Physiotherapists working in independent hospitals and give information about physiotherapy within independent hospitals.

Subject coverage:
Physiotherapy in independent hospitals or charities.

Printed publications:
Regular newsletter for members
Standards & Guidelines Document

Access to staff:
Contact by letter, by telephone and by e-mail
Hours: Mon to Fri, 0900 to 1700

Group within the:
Chartered Society of Physiotherapy

ASSOCIATION OF CHARTERED PHYSIOTHERAPISTS IN MANAGEMENT

Acronym or abbreviation: ACPM

14 Bedford Row, London, WC1R 4ED

Tel: 020 7306 6666
Fax: 020 7306 6611

Enquiries:
Enquiries to: Honorary Secretary
Other contacts: Chairman

Founded:
1944

Formerly called:
Association of District and Superintendent Chartered Physiotherapists (ADSCP)

Organisation type and purpose:
Professional body.

Subject coverage:
Physiotherapy.

Printed publications:
Guidelines for External Assessors (£5)

Access to staff:
Contact by letter, by telephone and by fax
Hours: Mon to Fri, 0900 to 1700

Group within the:
Chartered Society of Physiotherapy

ASSOCIATION OF CHARTERED PHYSIOTHERAPISTS IN OCCUPATIONAL HEALTH AND ERGONOMICS

Acronym or abbreviation: ACPOHE

c/o Chartered Society of Physiotherapy, 14 Bedford Row, London, WC1R 4ED

Tel: 020 7242 1941

Website:
http://www.acpohe.org.uk

Enquiries:
Enquiries to: Chairman
Direct tel: 01332 785915
Direct e-mail: fran.polak@derbyhospitals.nhs.uk

Founded:
1948

Formerly called:
Association of Chartered Physiotherapists in Occupational Health (ACPOH)

Organisation type and purpose:
National organisation, professional body (membership is by subscription, qualification), present number of members: 450.
Specific interest group of the Chartered Society of Physiotherapy.

Subject coverage:
Occupational health physiotherapy, ergonomics, education and training, health promotion and fitness in the workplace, work hardening and conditioning, functional capacity evaluation, pre-employment screening, health and safety (risk assessment and risk management), moving and handling, workplace design, rehabilitation.

Printed publications:
Guidelines for Practice
Information leaflets (on request)
Newsletter (3 times a year, for members)

Access to staff:
Contact by letter, by telephone and by e-mail
Hours: Mon to Fri, 0900 to 1700

Constituent part of:
Chartered Society of Physiotherapy

ASSOCIATION OF CHARTERED PHYSIOTHERAPISTS IN RESPIRATORY CARE

Acronym or abbreviation: ACPRC

School of Health Science – Physiotherapy, University of Birmingham, Morris House, Edgbaston, Birmingham, B15 2TT

Tel: 0121 605 2020
Fax: 0121 605 2021
E-mail: c.r.liles@bham.ac.uk

Enquiries:
Enquiries to: Journal Editor

Organisation type and purpose:
Membership association (membership is by subscription), present number of members: over 500.

Subject coverage:
Respiratory diseases, cardiorespiratory physiotherapy, education, research, audit, management, physiotherapy techniques.

Printed publications:
ACPRC Journal (annually)
Newsletter (4 times a year)
Respiratory Review (annually)

Access to staff:
Contact by letter, by telephone and by fax
Hours: Mon to Fri, 0900 to 1700

Special Interest Group within the:
Chartered Society of Physiotherapy
tel: 020 7306 6666; fax: 020 7306 6611

ASSOCIATION OF CHARTERED PHYSIOTHERAPISTS IN WOMEN'S HEALTH

Acronym or abbreviation: ACPWH

14 Bedford Row, London, WC1R 4ED

Tel: 020 7306 6666

Website:
http://www.acpwh.org.uk

continued overleaf

Enquiries:
Enquiries to: Secretary
Direct e-mail: juliabraytq@hotmail.com
Other contacts: Chairman for when Secretary is unavailable.

Founded:
1948

Formerly called:
Association of Chartered Physiotherapists in Obstetrics and Gynaecology (year of change 1993)

Organisation type and purpose:
National organisation, professional body (membership is by subscription), present number of members: 700.

Subject coverage:
Physiotherapy in obstetrics and gynaecology; antenatal education and advice; postnatal education advice and exercise, female and male bladder and bowel dysfunction; musculoskeletal problems relating to pregnancy or gynaecological in nature, particularly pelvic floor weakness.

Printed publications:
Information leaflets (lists available through the Secretary)
Journal (2 times a year)

Publications list:
Available in print

Access to staff:
Contact by letter and by e-mail

Group within the:
Chartered Society of Physiotherapy at the same address; tel: 020 7306 6666

ASSOCIATION OF CHARTERED PHYSIOTHERAPISTS INTERESTED IN NEUROLOGY

Acronym or abbreviation: ACPIN

14 Bedford Row, London, WC1R 4ED

Tel: 020 7306 6666
Fax: 020 7306 6611
E-mail: enquiries@csp.org.uk

Website:
http://www.acpin.net

Enquiries:
Enquiries to: Professional Adviser

Organisation type and purpose:
Professional body.

Subject coverage:
Physiotherapy; neurology.

Printed publications:
Synapse (Apr and Nov)
Guidance on manual handling for treatment
Recommendations of Physiotherapy Practice in Neurology
Standards of Physiotherapy Practice in Neurology

Access to staff:
Contact by telephone and via website
Hours: Mon to Fri, 0900 to 1700

Group within the:
Chartered Society of Physiotherapy

ASSOCIATION OF CHRISTIAN COMMUNITIES AND NETWORKS

Acronym or abbreviation: NACCAN

Community House, Eton Road, Newport, Gwent, NP19 0BL

Tel: 01633 265486
E-mail: moderator@naccan.freeserve.com.uk

Enquiries:
Enquiries to: Moderator

Founded:
1971

Formerly called:
National Association of Christian Communities and Networks (year of change 1999)

Organisation type and purpose:
International organisation, membership association (membership is by subscription), present number of members: 286, voluntary organisation, registered charity (charity number 283972), training organisation.
Links together Networks, Groups, Communities and individuals from a wide variety of Christian traditions committed to living out the implications of what Christian Community means.

Subject coverage:
Linking, informing, affirming Christian communities and networks in Britain, particularly those taking new initiatives in the local scene, with some contacts overseas also.

Trade and statistical information:
Information provided on communities and networks in membership.

Printed publications:
Christian Community (newsletter, 4 times a year, free to members, otherwise donation for p&p)
Directory of Christian Communities and Groups (£5 including p&p, on request)
Results of research projects

Access to staff:
Contact by letter, by telephone and by e-mail.
Appointment necessary.
Hours: Mon, Thu, 1000 to 1600; Tue, Wed, and Fri, 0900 to 1700. Ansaphone 24 hours

Affiliated to:
CCBI
CYTUN

ASSOCIATION OF CHRISTIAN COUNSELLORS

Acronym or abbreviation: ACC

29 Momus Boulevard, Coventry, Warwickshire, CV2 5NA

Tel: 0845 124 9569
Fax: 0845 124 9571
E-mail: office@acc-uk.org

Website:
http://www.acc-uk.org
General and specific information, joining, accreditation, links with ACC Europe, training organisations.

Enquiries:
Enquiries to: Chief Executive
Direct e-mail: ceo@acc-uk.org

Founded:
1992

Organisation type and purpose:
Professional body, registered charity (charity number 1018559).

Subject coverage:
Christian counselling, training in Christian counselling, accreditation for Christian counsellors, affiliation for Christian Counselling agencies, referrals for those requiring Christian counselling.

Printed publications:
Information Pack
Personal Counselling Porfolio
Code of Ethics
Training Criteria (for courses)
Accreditation Applications
Accord (magazine, quarterly)

Electronic and video publications:
Accreditation forms

Access to staff:
Contact by letter, by telephone, by fax, by e-mail, in person and via website
Hours: Mon to Fri, 0900 to 1700

Access to building, collection or gallery:
No prior appointment required

ASSOCIATION OF CIRCUS PROPRIETORS OF GREAT BRITAIN

Acronym or abbreviation: ACP

PO Box 131, Blackburn, Lancashire, BB1 9GJ

Tel: 01254 814789
Fax: 01254 814789
E-mail: malcolmclay@talk21.com

Enquiries:
Enquiries to: Secretary

Founded:
1932

Organisation type and purpose:
Advisory body, trade association (membership is by election or invitation), present number of members: 14.
To monitor the circus industry in the UK. To advise on standards of animal welfare, and the training and keeping of performing animals.

Subject coverage:
Circus training and career opportunities in the circus. The welfare of performing animals and the ethics of animal training.

Printed publications:
Say Yes to the Highest Standards of Animal Welfare 1990

Access to staff:
Contact by letter, by telephone and by fax.
Appointment necessary.
Hours: Mon to Fri, 0900 to 1700

Member of:
Variety and Entertainments Council (VAEC)

ASSOCIATION OF CLINICAL PATHOLOGISTS

Acronym or abbreviation: ACP

189 Dyke Road, Hove, East Sussex, BN3 1TL

Tel: 01273 775700
Fax: 01273 773303
E-mail: info@pathologists.org.uk

Website:
http://www.pathologists.org.uk
Membership information, meetings, etc.

Enquiries:
Enquiries to: General Administrator

Founded:
1927

Organisation type and purpose:
International organisation, learned society, professional body (membership is by election or invitation), registered charity (charity number 209555).

Subject coverage:
Clinical pathology.

Printed publications:
ACP News (quarterly)
Journal of Clinical Pathology (monthly)
Programme of Postgraduate Education (annually)
Year Book

Access to staff:
Contact by letter, by telephone, by fax, by e-mail and via website. Appointment necessary. Access for members only.
Hours: Mon to Fri, 0900 to 1700

ASSOCIATION OF COLLEGES

Acronym or abbreviation: AoC

5th Floor, Centre Point, 103 New Oxford Street, London, WC1A 1RG

Tel: 020 7827 4600
Fax: 020 7827 4650
E-mail: communications@aoc.co.uk

Website:
http://www.aoc.co.uk

Enquiries:
Enquiries to: Director of Communications

Founded:
1997

Formerly called:
Association for Colleges (AfC), Colleges'
Employers Forum (CEF) (year of change 1996)

Organisation type and purpose:
Membership association (membership is by
subscription), present number of members: 450,
service industry, suitable for ages: 16+.
Colleges of Further Education.
Representation of the interests of further education
colleges, sixth form colleges, tertiary and specialist
colleges throughout the UK by lobbying, member
consultations, conferences and seminars and
research.

Subject coverage:
Further education, 16 to 19 years education, sixth
form colleges, general further education and
specialist colleges, adult education, lifelong
learning, training.

**Museum or gallery collection, archive, or library
special collection:**
The Association does not hold a historical library
of information

Printed publications:
Regular bulletins are issued to the sector on
matters related to current Further Education
delivery
Weekly bulletins on all aspects of colleges' activity
are published free
FE Now (magazine, 4 times a year, £25
subscriptions to non-members)

Publications list:
Available online and in print

Access to staff:
Contact by letter, by telephone, by fax, by e-mail
and via website. Appointment necessary.
Hours: Mon to Fri, 0900 to 1700

ASSOCIATION OF COMMONWEALTH ARCHIVISTS AND RECORD MANAGERS

Acronym or abbreviation: ACARM

c/o IRMT, 4th Floor, 7 Hatton Garden, London,
EC1N 8AD

Tel: 020 7831 4101
E-mail: newsletter@acarm.org

Website:
http://www.acarm.org

Enquiries:
Enquiries to: Membership Secretary
Direct fax: 020 7831 6303

Founded:
1984

Organisation type and purpose:
Individual and institutional membership
organisation (membership by subscription).
ACARM seeks to promote professional
development and the sharing of solutions to the
problems of managing records and archives (in
paper and electronic formats) throughout the
Commonwealth.

Printed publications:
Newsletter (3 times a year)

Access to staff:
Contact by letter, by telephone, by e-mail and via
website

ASSOCIATION OF COMMONWEALTH UNIVERSITIES

Acronym or abbreviation: ACU

John Foster House, 36 Gordon Square, London,
WC1H 0PF

Tel: 020 7380 6700
Fax: 020 7387 2655
E-mail: info@acu.ac.uk

Website:
http://www.acu.ac.uk
Full range of information about the ACU and its
services.
http://www.csfp-online.org
http://www.obhe.ac.uk

Enquiries:
Enquiries to: Secretary General

Founded:
1913

Organisation type and purpose:
International organisation, membership
association (membership is by subscription),
present number of members: 487 universities,
registered charity (charity number 314137), age
range: Higher.
Voluntary association of universities which aims to
strengthen through international co-operation and
understanding its 487 members in 35
Commonwealth countries or regions including the
UK.

Subject coverage:
Commonwealth-wide university / higher
education information; administers several
scholarship and fellowship schemes; advertises
academic, administrative and technical job
vacancies at HE institutions in the Commonwealth.
Hosts Policy and Research Unit. Hosts the
Observatory on Borderless Higher Education
(OBHE).

**Museum or gallery collection, archive, or library
special collection:**
18,500 volume reference library

Printed publications:
ACU Bulletin; controlled circulation (ACU
member universities only) (5 times a year)
International Awards
Commonwealth Universities Yearbook
Community of Universities: An Informal Portrait
of the Association of Universities of the British
Commonwealth 1913–1963
Mapping borderless higher education: policy,
markets and competition: selected reports from
the Observatory on Borderless Higher Education
(OBHE)
The Commonwealth of Universities: the Story of
the ACU 1963–1988
Universities and development: a report on the
socioeconomic role of universities in the
developing countries of the Commonwealth
Who's Who of Executive Heads: Vice-Chancellors,
Presidents, Principals, Rectors

Publications list:
Available online and in print

Access to staff:
Contact by letter, by telephone, by e-mail and via
website. Appointment necessary.
Hours: Mon to Fri, 0930 to 1730

Access to building, collection or gallery:
No prior appointment required
Hours: Library: Mon to Fri, 1000 to 1300 and 1400
to 1700

Formal consultative relations with:
UNESCO

Works closely with:
Commonwealth Secretariat

ASSOCIATION OF COMMUNITY HEALTH COUNCILS FOR ENGLAND AND WALES

Acronym or abbreviation: ACHCEW

Tel: 020 7609 8405
Fax: 020 7700 1152
E-mail: mailbox@achcew.org.uk

Website:
http://www.achcew.org.uk

Enquiries:
Enquiries to: Director

Founded:
1977

Organisation type and purpose:
Membership association.
Providing forum, support and research facilities.

Subject coverage:
Community Health Councils: constitution,
research and activities, representation of the
patient/consumer in primary and institutional
health care services, NHS complaints procedures.

**Museum or gallery collection, archive, or library
special collection:**
Library of Reports published by individual
Community Health Councils

Printed publications:
Health News Briefings (over 40)
Health Perspectives – topic papers
Patients' Rights Factsheets
Distance Learning Pack – Skills for CHC Chairs
Nationwide Casualty Watch 2001
Why are we waiting? Snapshot surveys of the
impact of emergency pressures on patient care
(2000)
Directory of Community Health Councils (2000)

Publications list:
Available in print

Access to staff:
Appointment necessary.
Hours: Mon to Fri, 0900 to 1700
Special comments: No disabled access.

ASSOCIATION OF COMMUNITY WORKERS

Acronym or abbreviation: ACW

Stephenson Buildings, Elswick Road, Newcastle
upon Tyne, NE4 6SQ

Tel: 0191 272 4341
E-mail: lesleyleach@acw1.fsbusiness.co.uk

Enquiries:
Enquiries to: Information Officer

Founded:
1969

Organisation type and purpose:
Membership association (membership is by
subscription), voluntary organisation.

Subject coverage:
Community work, organisation and practice,
collective action, policies and activities.

Printed publications:
Community Work Skills Manual
Community Work (monthly newsletter)
Talking Point (monthly discussion paper)

Publications list:
Available in print

ASSOCIATION OF CONSULTANT ARCHITECTS LTD

Acronym or abbreviation: ACA

98 Hayes Road, Bromley, Kent, BR2 9AB

Tel: 020 8325 1402
Fax: 020 8466 9079
E-mail: office@acarchitects.co.uk

Website:
http://www.acarchitects.co.uk

Enquiries:
Enquiries to: Secretary-General

Founded:
1975

Organisation type and purpose:
Membership association (membership is by
qualification, subscription), present number of
members: 200.

continued overleaf

Represents the interests of architects in private practice.

Subject coverage:
Architectural practices and practice.

Trade and statistical information:
Data on specialist services provided by member architectural practices.

Library catalogue:
All or part available online

Printed publications:
ACA Form of Building Agreement (3rd edn 1998, 2003 revision, £14.00)
ACA Form of Subcontract (3rd edn 1998, 2003 revision, £10.00)
GUIDE to ACA Form of Building Agreement (3rd edn 1998, 2003 revision, £12.00)
ACA98 – The Appointment of a Consultant Architect for Small Works (£5.00)
PPC 2000 – ACA Standard Form of Contract for Project Partnering (amended 2008, £20.00)
SPC2000 – ACA Standard Form of Specialist Contract for Project Partnering (amended 2008, £20.00)
TPC2005 – ACA Standard Form of Contract for Term Partnering (amended 2008, £20.00)
GUIDE to ACA Project Partnering Contracts PPC2000 and SPC2000 (£20.00)
Introduction to Pricing under PPC2000 (£5.00)
SPC International – ACA Standard Form of Specialised Contract for Project Partnering (£20.00)
PPC International – ACA Standard Form of Contract for Project Partnering (£20.00)
ACA Conciliation Agreement 1998 (£4.00)
ACA Certificate – Agreeing Extended Period for the Consideration of a Planning Application (£12.00)
ACA Architect's Instruction (pad of 100, £14.00)
ACA Interim Certificate (for 2003 revision, pad of 100, £14.00)
ACA Taking-Over Certificate (pad of 50, £10.00)
ACA Final Certificate (pad of 50, £10.00)
ACA SFA/08 – ACA Standard Form of Agreement for the Appointment of an Architect (£20.00)

Publications list:
Available online and in print

Access to staff:
Contact by letter, by telephone, by fax, by e-mail and via website
Hours: Mon to Fri, 0900 to 1730

ASSOCIATION OF CONSULTING ACTUARIES

Acronym or abbreviation: ACA

1 Wardrobe Place, London, EC4V 5AG

Tel: 020 7248 3163
Fax: 020 7236 1889
E-mail: acahelp@aca.org.uk

Enquiries:
Enquiries to: Honorary Secretary

Founded:
1952

Organisation type and purpose:
Trade association (membership is by subscription, qualification), present number of members: 1000. Association of Fellows of the Institute or Faculty of Actuaries engaged in consulting work.

Subject coverage:
Consultancy in retirement benefits and pension arrangements, sickness and hospital benefit schemes, investment policy, financial planning of funds, operational research and other statistical applications, mergers, life and general insurance, damages and divorce settlements.

Printed publications:
Annual Review
List of Members
Newsletters

Publications list:
Available online and in print

Access to staff:
Contact by letter, by telephone, by fax, by e-mail and via website
Hours: Mon to Fri, 0900 to 1700

Access to building, collection or gallery:
Prior appointment required

ASSOCIATION OF CONSULTING SCIENTISTS LIMITED

Acronym or abbreviation: ACS

PO Box 4040, Thorpe-le-Soken, Clacton-on-Sea, Essex, CO16 0EL

Tel: 01255 862526
Fax: 01255 862526
E-mail: secretary@consultingscientists.co.uk

Website:
http://www.consultingscientists.com
Directory of members and services

Enquiries:
Enquiries to: Secretary

Founded:
1958

Organisation type and purpose:
Advisory body, professional body (membership is by election or invitation), present number of members: 21, consultancy, research organisation. The Association provides a forum for all member scientists practising as consultants.

Subject coverage:
Consulting activities – expert witnesses, health and safety, microbiological testing, laboratory testing.

Printed publications:
Newsletter (online)

Access to staff:
Contact by letter, by telephone and by fax
Hours: Mon to Fri, 0900 to 1700
Special comments: Part time.

Subsidiary body:
Forensic and Expert Witness Group
Testing Laboratories Group

ASSOCIATION OF CONTACT LENS MANUFACTURERS

Acronym or abbreviation: ACLM

PO Box 735, Devizes, Wiltshire, SN10 3TQ

Tel: 01380 860418
Fax: 01380 860863
E-mail: secgen@aclm.org.uk

Website:
http://www.aclm.org.uk
Contact lens information for consumers and practitioners

Enquiries:
Enquiries to: Secretary General

Founded:
1962

Organisation type and purpose:
National organisation, trade association (membership is by subscription, election or invitation), present number of members: 25, manufacturing industry.
Members represent over 95% of the UK market. To promote and increase the wearing of contact lenses.

Subject coverage:
Contact lenses, contact lens care products, contact lens materials.

Non-library collection catalogue:
All or part available online and in print

Printed publications:
ACLM Year Book

Publications list:
Available online

Access to staff:
Contact by letter, by telephone, by fax, by e-mail and via website
Hours: Mon to Fri, 0900 to 1700

ASSOCIATION OF CORPORATE TREASURERS

Acronym or abbreviation: ACT

51 Moorgate, London, EC2R 6BH

Tel: 020 7847 2540
Fax: 020 7374 8744
E-mail: enquiries@treasurers.org

Website:
http://www.treasurers.org

Enquiries:
Enquiries to: Director of Communications
Direct tel: 020 7847 2545
Direct e-mail: khoyle@treasurers.org
Other contacts: Chief Executive for enquiries relating to the ACT or treasury profession.

Founded:
1979

Organisation type and purpose:
Professional body (membership is by qualification).

Subject coverage:
Treasury, risk management, corporate finance

Education services:
Provider of treasury qualifications

Library catalogue:
All or part available in-house

Printed publications:
Order printed publications from: http://www.global-investor.com

Electronic and video publications:
The International Treasurer's Handbook (online)

Publications list:
Available online

Access to staff:
Contact by letter, by telephone, by fax and by e-mail
Hours: Mon to Fri, 0900 to 1700

Access to building, collection or gallery:
No prior appointment required

Access for disabled people:
Level entry, access to all public areas, toilet facilities

ASSOCIATION OF CRICKET STATISTICIANS AND HISTORIANS

Acronym or abbreviation: ACS

Archives Department, Glamorgan Cricket, Sophia Gardens, Cardiff, CF11 9XR

Tel: 0115 945 5407
E-mail: office@acscricket.com

Website:
http://acscricket.com

Enquiries:
Enquiries to: Secretary

Founded:
1973

Formerly called:
Association of Cricket Statisticians (year of change 1994)

Organisation type and purpose:
International organisation, learned society (membership is by subscription), present number of members: 1300, voluntary organisation, suitable for ages: all, research organisation, publishing house.

To research and publish all aspects of cricket history and statistical record.

Subject coverage:
Cricket and cricketers at all levels throughout the world, both historical and contemporary.

Printed publications:
Journal (quarterly free to members)
ACS International Cricket Year Book
Second Eleven Annual
Books (two or three per annum, free to members) total over 200 including:
County and State Booklets
Famous Cricketers series of 100
First Class Match Scores (16 books by groups of years or single years 1801 to 1910)
Statistical Surveys by year 1862 to 1880

Access to staff:
Contact by letter, by telephone, by fax and in person

Access for disabled people:
Level access, ground floor, direct access to street, wide door

ASSOCIATION OF DIRECTORS OF SOCIAL SERVICES

Acronym or abbreviation: ADSS

ADSS Office, London Borough of Hammersmith and Fulham, 145 King Street, Hammersmith, London, W6 9XY

Tel: 020 8741 8147
Fax: 020 8753 5739
E-mail: anne.martin@lbhf.gov.uk

Website:
http://www.adss.org.uk
ADSS branches, policy statements. ADSS offices, forthcoming events and values statements.

Enquiries:
Enquiries to: Honorary Secretary
Other contacts: Administrator

Organisation type and purpose:
Local government body, professional body.

Subject coverage:
Social services.

Printed publications:
Publications include:
ADSS Handbook (£25)
ADSS Inform (approx quarterly, £20 a year)
Selection of ADSS Guidelines, Policy Statements and Reports (no charge)

Publications list:
Available in print

Access to staff:
Contact by letter, by telephone, by fax and by e-mail
Hours: Mon to Fri, 0900 to 1700

ASSOCIATION OF DISABLED PROFESSIONALS

Acronym or abbreviation: ADP

BCM ADP, London, WC1N 3XX

Tel: 01204 431638
Fax: 01204 431638
E-mail: adp.admin@ntlworld.com

Website:
http://www.adp.org.uk
http://www.disabled-entrepreneurs.net

Enquiries:
Enquiries to: Development Officer

Founded:
1971

Organisation type and purpose:
Voluntary organisation, registered as a charitable company limited by guarantee (company number 6390586; charity number 1121706).

Subject coverage:
Education, training and employment opportunities for disabled people, career prospects. Also provides support to disabled people in self-employment.

Printed publications:
Quarterly (house bulletin, free to members)
Occasional surveys
The Employment of Disabled Teachers (£4.05 including p&p)
Setting up in business? A Resource Guide for disabled people and their advisors (£2.00 including p&p to disabled people/£10.00 to organisations)
What Happens When Nurses Become Disabled? (£5 including p&p)

Access to staff:
Contact by letter, by telephone, by fax and by e-mail
Hours: 24-hour answerphone

Also at:
Association of Disabled Professionals
Beechers Brook, 16 Aintree Drive, Waterlooville, Hampshire, PO7 8NG

ASSOCIATION OF DOMESTIC MANAGEMENT

Acronym or abbreviation: ADM

3 Hagg Bank Cottages, Wylam, Northumberland, NE41 8JT

Tel: 01661 853097
Fax: 01661 853097
E-mail: adm@adom.demon.co.uk

Website:
http://www.adom.demon.co.uk
Summary of publications, magazine, information on conferences. exhibitions and membership.

Enquiries:
Enquiries to: Business Manager

Founded:
1974

Organisation type and purpose:
Professional body.

Subject coverage:
Facilities management.

Printed publications:
Excel (quarterly, magazine)
Standards for Environmental Cleanliness in Hospitals (£25, joint publication with Infection Control Nurses Association)
Minimum Frequencies (publ. Dec 2001, £5)

Publications list:
Available in print

Access to staff:
Contact by letter, by telephone, by fax, by e-mail and via website. Appointment necessary.
Hours: Tue, Thu and Fri, 0830 to 1515

Access to building, collection or gallery:
No access other than to staff

Founder member of:
ADM Conference & Exhibition Ltd
British Cleaning Council

Has links with:
CAMRASO
Hefma
NHS Estates
The Knowledge Centre

ASSOCIATION OF DRAINAGE AUTHORITIES

Acronym or abbreviation: ADA

12 Cranes Drive, Surbiton, Surrey, KT5 8AL

Tel: 0844 209 0089
Fax: 020 8399 9368
E-mail: admin@ada.org.uk

Enquiries:
Enquiries to: Chief Executive

Founded:
1937

Organisation type and purpose:
Advisory body, membership association.

Subject coverage:
Flood risk-management, lowland drainage, water level management.

Printed publications:
ADA Gazette (official journal of the Association, 4 times a year)

Access to staff:
Contact by letter
Hours: Mon to Fri, 0900 to 1700

ASSOCIATION OF DRUM MANUFACTURERS

Acronym or abbreviation: ADM

St John's House, 4 London Road, Crowborough, East Sussex, TN6 2TT

Tel: 01892 654414
Fax: 01892 654981
E-mail: enquiries@the-adm.co.uk

Website:
http://www.the-adm.co.uk

Enquiries:
Enquiries to: Secretary

Founded:
1896

Organisation type and purpose:
Trade association, present number of members: 15.

Subject coverage:
Drum manufacturing.

Access to staff:
Contact by letter
Hours: Mon to Fri, 0900 to 1700

ASSOCIATION OF EASTERN MOTOR CLUBS

Acronym or abbreviation: AEMC

9 Dales Court, Dales Road, Ipswich, IP1 4JR

Tel: 01473 463444
Fax: 01473 463444

Website:
http://www.aemc.co.uk
Clubs in association, events and championships, marshals information.

Enquiries:
Enquiries to: Honorary Secretary

Founded:
1950

Organisation type and purpose:
Membership association (membership is by qualification), voluntary organisation.

Subject coverage:
Motor car sports in East Anglia for amateur enthusiasts.

Access to staff:
Contact by letter, by telephone and by fax
Hours: Mon to Fri, 0900 to 1700

Recognised by the:
Motor Sports Association (MSA)
Riverside Park, Colnbrook, Slough, SL3 0HG; tel: 01753 765000; fax: 01753 682938; website: www .msauk.org

ASSOCIATION OF ELECTORAL ADMINISTRATORS

Acronym or abbreviation: AEA

PO Box 201, South Eastern, Liverpool, L16 5HH

continued overleaf

Tel: 0151 281 8246
Fax: 0151 281 8246
E-mail: gina.armstrong@aea-elections.co.uk

Website:
http://www.aea-elections.co.uk
General information about the Association, members' area with frequently asked questions, diary, etc.

Enquiries:
Enquiries to: National Executive Officer

Founded:
1987

Organisation type and purpose:
Advisory body, professional body (membership is by subscription), present number of members: 1000, training organisation, consultancy.
To offer impartial and professional advice on electoral arrangements and the democratic process at Central and Local Government.

Subject coverage:
Elections, electoral processes, electoral registration, training.

Museum or gallery collection, archive, or library special collection:
Basic practice publications
Archival records of Association business

Printed publications:
Quarterly bulletin (free)

Access to staff:
Contact by letter, by telephone, by fax, by e-mail and via website
Hours: Mon to Fri, 0900 to 1700

Other address:
Association of Electoral Administrators
    PO Box 184, Leicester, LE4 4EL; tel: 0116 267 2015; fax: 0116 267 2015

ASSOCIATION OF ELECTRICITY PRODUCERS

Acronym or abbreviation: AEP

1st Floor, 17 Waterloo Place, London, SW1Y 4AR

Tel: 020 7930 9390
Fax: 020 7930 9391
E-mail: enquiries@aepuk.com

Enquiries:
Enquiries to: Chief Executive
Direct tel: 020 7747 2931
Direct e-mail: sam@aepuk.com (personal assistant)

Founded:
1987

Organisation type and purpose:
Trade association (membership is by subscription), present number of members: 100, service industry.

Subject coverage:
Electricity generation, competition in electricity production, liberalised electricity markets, renewable energy.

Publications list:
Available in print

Access to staff:
Contact by letter, by telephone, by fax and by e-mail. Appointment necessary.
Hours: Mon to Fri, 0900 to 1700

ASSOCIATION OF EUROPEAN BRAND OWNERS

Acronym or abbreviation: MARQUES

840 Melton Road, Thurmaston, Leicester, LE4 8BN

Tel: 0116 264 0080
Fax: 0116 264 0141
E-mail: info@marques.org

Website:
http://www.marques.org

Enquiries:
Enquiries to: Secretary General

Founded:
1987

Formerly called:
Association of European Trade Mark Proprietors (year of change 1997)

Organisation type and purpose:
International organisation, trade association (membership is by subscription).

Subject coverage:
Brand names, trade mark protection.

Access to staff:
Contact by letter, by telephone, by fax, by e-mail and via website
Hours: Mon to Fri, 0900 to 1700

ASSOCIATION OF EVENT ORGANISERS LIMITED

Acronym or abbreviation: AEO

119 High Street, Berkhamsted, Hertfordshire, HP4 2DJ

Tel: 01442 285810
Fax: 01442 875551
E-mail: info@aeo.org.uk

Website:
http://www.aeo.org.uk

Enquiries:
Enquiries to: Director General
Other contacts: Commercial Manager for administration, membership, exhibition enquiries.

Founded:
1930

Formerly called:
Association of Exhibition Organisers Ltd (year of change 2006)

Organisation type and purpose:
Trade association.

Subject coverage:
Exhibitions and events world-wide, when, where and who; career information for exhibition organisers.

Printed publications:
AEO brochure
Careers Information (free)
Code of Practice (free)
Exhibition Issues
How to Exhibit

Electronic and video publications:
Make a Stand (DVD)
How to Exhibit (e-learning)

Access to staff:
Contact by letter, by telephone, by fax, by e-mail and via website. Appointment necessary.
Hours: Mon to Fri, 0900 to 1700

Member organisation of:
Union des Foires Internationales (UFI)
    35 bis rue Jouffroy d'Abbans 5F, Paris 75017, France

ASSOCIATION OF FLIGHT ATTENDANTS

Acronym or abbreviation: AFA

AFA Council 07, United Airlines Cargo Centre, Shoreham Road East, Heathrow Airport, Hounslow, Middlesex, TW6 3UA

Tel: 020 8276 6723
Fax: 020 8276 6706
E-mail: afalhr@unitedafa.org

Website:
http://www.afalhr.org.uk

Enquiries:
Enquiries to: General Secretary

Organisation type and purpose:
International organisation, trade union (membership is by qualification), present number of members: 800.

Subject coverage:
Airline safety and security, cabin crew issues.

Access to staff:
Contact by letter, by telephone, by fax, by e-mail, in person and via website
Hours: Mon to Fri, 0900 to 1700

Access to building, collection or gallery:
Prior appointment required

Access for disabled people:
Parking provided, access to all public areas, toilet facilities

ASSOCIATION OF FRIENDLY SOCIETIES

Acronym or abbreviation: AFS

Denzell House, Denzell Gardens, Dunham Road, Bowden, Cheshire, WA14 4QE

Tel: 0161 952 5051
Fax: 0161 929 5163
E-mail: info@afs.org.uk

Website:
http://www.afs.org.uk
About the movement, its members, what they do, what the AFS is doing, private site for member societies.

Enquiries:
Enquiries to: Administrator

Founded:
1995

Formed by the merger of:
Association of Collecting Friendly Societies and other existing organisations of Friendly Societies, National Conference of Friendly Societies

Organisation type and purpose:
Trade association.

Subject coverage:
Matters relating to member societies and the Friendly Society Movement, particularly information on legislation and regulation applying to them, financial services and welfare state reform.

Printed publications:
Newsletter (6 times a year, annual subscription)
Yearbook (for sale)

Access to staff:
Contact by letter, by telephone, by fax and by e-mail. Appointment necessary.
Hours: Mon to Fri, 0900 to 1700

Access to building, collection or gallery:
Prior appointment required

ASSOCIATION OF GENEALOGISTS AND RESEARCHERS IN ARCHIVES

Acronym or abbreviation: AGRA

29 Badgers Close, Horsham, West Sussex, RH12 5RU

E-mail: agra@agra.org.uk

Website:
http://www.agra.org.uk
Details of members, advice on using a professional researcher, events organised by AGRA

Enquiries:
Enquiries to: Secretary

Founded:
1968

Organisation type and purpose:
National organisation, professional body
(membership is by subscription, qualification),
present number of members: 100, consultancy,
research organisation.

Subject coverage:
Family history, family trees, locating missing
relatives, translations, surname studies, manorial
records, histories of properties, palaeography,
census and probate research, baptism and
marriage indexes, army and navy records.

Printed publications:
List of Members (annually £2.50 inc. p&p, or 6
International Reply Coupons, available from
Post Offices worldwide, to overseas enquirers)
Newsletter (members only)

Access to staff:
Contact by letter, by e-mail and via website
Hours: Mon to Fri, 0900 to 1700

ASSOCIATION OF GEOTECHNICAL AND GEOENVIRONMENTAL SPECIALISTS

Acronym or abbreviation: AGS

Forum Court, 83 Copers Cope Road, Beckenham,
Kent, BR3 1NR

Tel: 020 8658 8212
Fax: 020 8663 0949
E-mail: ags@ags.org.uk

Website:
http://www.ags.org.uk
Full information about the AGS, newsletters,
members, etc. Also edition III of the AGS
Electronic Format for SI data – download
(Acrobat) plus discussion forum.

Enquiries:
Enquiries to: Administrator

Founded:
1990

Organisation type and purpose:
Trade association.

Subject coverage:
Geotechnics e.g. foundations (design and
construction), site investigation, laboratory testing,
geoenvironment testing, remediation, monitoring,
geotechnical design, geoenvironmentalism.

Printed publications:
Collateral Warranties (members £15, non-members
£20)
Electronic Transfer of Geotechnical Data from
Ground Investigation (3rd ed., members £20,
non-members £40)
Guide to the Selection of Geotechnical Soil
Laboratory Testing (£40 members, £55 non-
members)
Guidelines for Combined Geoenvironmental and
Geotechnical Investigation (members £28, non-
members £45)

Access to staff:
Contact by letter, by telephone, by fax and by e-
mail
Hours: Mon to Fri, 0900 to 1700

Members of:
Ground Forum

ASSOCIATION OF GOLF WRITERS

Acronym or abbreviation: AGW

1 Pilgrims Bungalow, Mulberry Hill, Chilham,
Kent, CT4 8AH

Tel: 01227 732496
Fax: 01227 732496
E-mail: andyfarrell292@btinternet.com

Enquiries:
Enquiries to: Honorary Secretary

Founded:
1938

Organisation type and purpose:
Membership association.

Subject coverage:
Golf; sports writing.

Access to staff:
Contact by letter, by telephone, by fax and by e-
mail
Hours: Mon to Fri, 0900 to 1700

ASSOCIATION OF GRACE BAPTIST CHURCHES (SE)

Acronym or abbreviation: AGBC(SE)

7 Arlington Way, London, EC1R 1XA

Tel: 020 7278 1200
Fax: 020 7278 3598
E-mail: assoc@agbcse.org.uk

Website:
http://www.agbcse.org.uk

Enquiries:
Enquiries to: Association Secretary
Other contacts: Company Secretary for finance and
legal.

Founded:
1871

Organisation type and purpose:
Registered charity (charity number 276352).
To promote the unity and prosperity of associated
churches and devise and employ means for the
furtherance of the Gospel in London, Berkshire,
Buckinghamshire, Essex, Hampshire,
Hertfordshire, Kent, Oxfordshire, Surrey and
Sussex.

Access to staff:
Contact by letter, by telephone, by fax and by e-
mail
Hours: Mon to Fri, 0900 to 1700

Access to building, collection or gallery:
Prior appointment required

Access for disabled people:
Ramped entry

ASSOCIATION OF GRADUATE RECRUITERS

Acronym or abbreviation: AGR

The Innovation Centre, Warwick Technology Park,
Gallows Hill, Warwick, CV34 6UW

Tel: 01926 623236
Fax: 01926 623237
E-mail: info@agr.org.uk

Website:
http://www.agr.org.uk

Enquiries:
Enquiries to: Chief Executive

Founded:
1968

Organisation type and purpose:
Professional body.

Subject coverage:
Graduate recruitment from the employer's
viewpoint.

Trade and statistical information:
Graduate vacancies and salaries information.

Printed publications:
Graduate Recruiter (magazine, six times a year, for
the graduate recruitment market)

Publications list:
Available online and in print

Access to staff:
Contact by letter, by telephone, by fax, by e-mail
and via website

Hours: Mon to Fri, 0900 to 1700

Access for disabled people:
Parking provided, access to all public areas, toilet
facilities

ASSOCIATION OF HEAD TEACHERS AND DEPUTES IN SCOTLAND

Acronym or abbreviation: AHDS

PO Box 18532, Inverurie, AB51 0WS

Tel: 0845 260 7560
E-mail: info@ahds.org.uk

Website:
http://www.ahds.org.uk

Enquiries:
Enquiries to: General Secretary

Founded:
1975

Organisation type and purpose:
Trade union

Subject coverage:
Trade Union support for headteachers and deputes
from Scotland's nursery, primary and special
schools

Access to staff:
Contact by letter, by telephone, by e-mail, in
person and via website. Appointment necessary.
Hours: Mon to Fri, 0900 to 1700

ASSOCIATION OF ILLUSTRATORS

Acronym or abbreviation: AOI

81 Leonard Street, London, EC2A 4QS

Tel: 020 7613 4328
Fax: 020 7613 4417
E-mail: info@a-o-illustrators.demon.co.uk

Website:
http://www.aoisupplement.co.uk
Images Annual online.

Enquiries:
Enquiries to: Membership Secretary

Founded:
1974

Organisation type and purpose:
Trade association (membership is by subscription).

Subject coverage:
Illustration and illustrators; ethics, copyright law,
fees and standard practice.

Printed publications:
AOI Booklet: Listing Services (free)
Despatch: (journal, monthly, free, members only)
Images: Yearbook of the Best of British Illustration
Rights: The Illustrator's Guide to a Professional
Practice (for sale to non-members)
Survive: A Guide to Starting in Illustration

Access to staff:
Contact by telephone, by fax and by e-mail.
Appointment necessary.
Hours: Mon to Fri, 0900 to 1700

Within the:
Joint Ethics Committee for the Visual Arts

ASSOCIATION OF INDEPENDENT COMPUTER SPECIALISTS

Acronym or abbreviation: AICS

Honeyhill, Bismore, Eastcombe, Stroud,
Gloucestershire, GL6 7DG

Tel: 0701 0701 118
E-mail: honsec@aics.org.uk

Website:
http://www.aics.org.uk

continued overleaf

Full information about the Association and business profiles of a subset of members who may be contacted by email.

Enquiries:
Enquiries to: Honorary Secretary
Direct tel: 0845 123 5399

Founded:
1972

Organisation type and purpose:
Trade association.
A trade association for individuals and independent firms whose main business is the supply of computer-related services, including consultancy.

Subject coverage:
Introduction to members offering specific specialist computer-related services.

Printed publications:
Newsletter (quarterly)

Electronic and video publications:
Electronic newsletter to members

Access to staff:
Contact by telephone, by e-mail and via website
Hours: Mon to Fri, 0900 to 1700

Access to building, collection or gallery:
No access other than to staff

ASSOCIATION OF INDEPENDENT LIBRARIES

Acronym or abbreviation: AIL

The Leeds Library, 18 Commercial Street, Leeds, West Yorkshire, LS1 6AL

Tel: 0113 245 3071

Enquiries:
Enquiries to: Honorary Secretary
Direct tel: 01473 253992

Founded:
1989

Organisation type and purpose:
National organisation.
To promote an interest in libraries, reading, literature generally and in the many and varied special collections.

Access to staff:
Contact by letter and by telephone. Appointment necessary.
Hours: Mon to Fri, 0900 to 1700

ASSOCIATION OF INDEPENDENT MUSEUMS

Acronym or abbreviation: AIM

4 Clayhall Road, Gosport, PO12 2BY

Tel: 023 9258 7751
E-mail: aimadmin@aim-museums.co.uk

Website:
http://www.aim-museums.co.uk

Founded:
1977

Organisation type and purpose:
Professional body, trade association (membership is by subscription), present number of members: 800, voluntary organisation.
National museum association for those institutions not directly administered by central or local government.

Subject coverage:
Museum development; management; administration; fundraising; marketing; display; publications, particularly for the independent sector.

Printed publications:
AIM Bulletin (6 times a year for members)

AIM Guidelines on specific topics, generally relating to establishment of specific roles within museums

Access to staff:
Contact by letter, by telephone and by e-mail
Hours: Mon to Fri, 0900 to 1700

ASSOCIATION OF INDEPENDENT PSYCHOTHERAPISTS

PO Box 1194, London, N6 5PW

Tel: 020 7700 1911
E-mail: referrals@aip.org.uk

Website:
http://www.aip.org.uk

Founded:
1988

Organisation type and purpose:
Professional body (membership is by election or invitation), voluntary organisation, suitable for ages: 30 to 60, training organisation, consultancy.

Subject coverage:
Psychotherapy.

Access to staff:
Contact by letter, by telephone and by e-mail
Hours: Mon to Fri, 0900 to 1700

Other address:
Association of Independent Psychotherapists
8 Victoria Mansions, 135 Holloway Road, London, N7 8LZ

ASSOCIATION OF INDEPENDENT TOUR OPERATORS LIMITED

Acronym or abbreviation: AITO

133a St Margaret's Road, Twickenham, Middlesex, TW1 1RG

Tel: 020 8744 9280
Fax: 020 8744 3187
E-mail: info@aito.co.uk

Website:
http://www.aito.co.uk
AITO members.

Enquiries:
Enquiries to: Chairman

Founded:
1976

Organisation type and purpose:
Trade association (membership is by subscription), present number of members: 157.

Subject coverage:
Overseas tour operations.

Printed publications:
Consumer Handbook 2007

Publications list:
Available online and in print

Access to staff:
Contact by letter, by telephone, by fax and by e-mail
Hours: Mon to Thu, 0900 to 1730; Fri, 0900 to 1700

ASSOCIATION OF INTERIOR SPECIALISTS LIMITED

Acronym or abbreviation: AIS

Olton Bridge, 245 Warwick Road, Solihull, West Midlands, B92 7AH

Tel: 0121 707 0077
Fax: 0121 706 1949
E-mail: info@ais-interiors.org.uk

Website:
http://www.ais-interiors.org.uk
General information.

Enquiries:
Enquiries to: Chief Executive

Founded:
1998

Formed by the merger of:
Partitioning & Interiors Association Limited (PIA), Suspended Ceilings and Interiors Association Limited (SCIA) (year of change 1998)

Organisation type and purpose:
A single source serving the interiors fit-out industry, the AIS is a trade association that represents some 466 companies involved in the manufacture, supply and installation of all aspects of interior fit-outs and refurbishments, with particular emphasis on ceilings and partitions. Its members operate in retail and commercial offices, the public sector, banks and building societies, hotels and leisure, airports and hospitals.

Subject coverage:
All aspects of interior fit-out, including industrial and commercial partitioning, operable walls, suspended ceilings, drylining, access flooring. Manufacture, supply and installation.

Printed publications:
AIS – Serving the Interiors Sector (promotional leaflet)
Ceilings Site Guide
Directory of products and services
Fact File Information Sheets on various topics
Health and Safety Handbook
Interiors Focus (journal, 2 times a year, aimed at specifiers of commercial/interior design)
Interiors Insight (4 times a year)
Occasional market research on system partitioning
Partitioning Site Guide
Register of members
Raised Access Flooring Guide
Wallcoverings Guide
Drylining Guide

Access to staff:
Contact by letter, by telephone, by fax, by e-mail and via website
Hours: Mon to Fri, 0900 to 1700

Access to building, collection or gallery:
No prior appointment required

Members of:
National Specialist Contractors Council (NSCC) Construction House, 54–56 Leonard Street, London, EC2A 4JX; tel: 020 7608 5090; fax: 020 7608 5081

ASSOCIATION OF INTERNATIONAL ACCOUNTANTS

Acronym or abbreviation: AIA

AIA Head Office, Staithes 3, The Watermark, Metro Riverside, Newcastle upon Tyne, NE11 9SN

Tel: 0191 493 0277
E-mail: aia@aiaworldwide.com

Website:
http://www.aiaworldwide.com/
AIA prospectus, press releases, syllabus, reading lists, structure, membership information, examinations, events, recruitment.

Enquiries:
Enquiries to: Membership Services
Direct e-mail: membership.services@aiaworldwide.com

Founded:
1928

Organisation type and purpose:
International organisation, professional body (membership is by qualification).
Accounting body.
Under the Companies Act 1989 the AIA Accountancy qualification is a recognised professional qualification for company auditors in the United Kingdom.

Subject coverage:
Financial and management accountancy, investigations, auditing, management consultancy, taxation.

Printed publications:
International Accountant (available to all
members) and those wishing to subscribe

Publications list:
Available online

Access to staff:
Contact by letter, by telephone, by fax, by e-mail
and via website
Hours: Mon to Fri, 0900 to 1700

Access to building, collection or gallery:
No access other than to staff

Access for disabled people:
Parking provided

Affiliated to:
Asociación Española de Expertos Contables y
Fiscales
European Accounting Association (EAA)
International Association for Accounting and
Research (IAAER)
International Institute of Accountants (New
Zealand)

Other addresses:
AIA Hong Kong Branch
Room 1003, 10F Emperor Group Centre, 288
Hennessy Road, Wanchai, Hong Kong; tel: 00
852 2845 4982; fax: 00 852 2845 7495; e-mail:
aiahkbr@netvigator.com
Persatuan Alumni Akauntan – Cawangan
Malaysia
Suite 20–10, Level 20, Wisma Uoa II, 21 Jalan,
Pinang, 50450 Kuala Lumpur, Malaysia; tel: 00
60 3 2166 3020; fax: 00 60 3 2166 4020; e-mail:
paaicm@tm.net.my

ASSOCIATION OF JEWISH REFUGEES IN GREAT BRITAIN

Acronym or abbreviation: AJR

1 Hampstead Gate, 1A Frognal, London, NW3
6AL

Tel: 020 7431 6161
Fax: 020 7431 8454
E-mail: carol@ajr.org.uk

Website:
http://www.ajr.org.uk

Enquiries:
Enquiries to: Administrator

Founded:
1941

Organisation type and purpose:
Membership association, present number of
members: 3500, voluntary organisation, registered
charity (charity number 211239).
Representation and welfare for Jewish refugees
from Nazi persecution, and their families.

Subject coverage:
Matters pertaining to former Jewish refugees from
Nazi persecution in fields of restitution,
compensation, social welfare, old age homes,
accommodation, historical and political matters.

Printed publications:
AJR Journal (monthly, £3 to non-members, free to
members)

Access to staff:
Contact by letter, by telephone, by fax, by e-mail
and via website
Hours: Mon to Thu, 0930 to 1700; Fri, 0930 to 1330

Access to building, collection or gallery:
No prior appointment required

Access for disabled people:
Toilet facilities

Affiliated to:
AJR Charitable Trust
at the same address

Also:
Association of Jewish Refugees Day Centre
15 Cleve Road, London, NW6 3RL; tel: 020 7328
0208

ASSOCIATION OF KI AIKIDO

Acronym or abbreviation: AKA

17 Langland Gardens, London, NW3 6QE

Tel: 020 7435 1330
E-mail: charlie@harris.u-net.com

Website:
http://www.happyaikido.com
Information about Aikido.

Enquiries:
Direct tel: 020 7435 1330
Direct e-mail: ki@footloosefilms.com

Founded:
1987

Organisation type and purpose:
Training organisation.
Training in martial art of Aikido, self-defence and
calmness under pressure in daily life.

Subject coverage:
Martial art of Ki Aikido.

Access to staff:
Contact by telephone and by e-mail. Appointment
necessary.
Hours: Wed, 2000 to 2140; Sun, 1700 to 1900

Access to building, collection or gallery:
Prior appointment required

Access for disabled people:
Yes
Hours: Wed, 2000 to 2140; Sun, 1700 to 1900

ASSOCIATION OF LANDSCAPE CONTRACTORS OF IRELAND (NORTHERN REGION)

Acronym or abbreviation: ALCI

22 Summerhill Park, Bangor, BT20 5QQ

Tel: 028 9127 2823
Fax: 028 9127 2823
E-mail: secretary@alci.org.uk

Enquiries:
Enquiries to: Secretary

Founded:
1971

Organisation type and purpose:
Trade association.
Representation of the landscape contracting
industry in Ireland.

Subject coverage:
Training needs and educational matter relating to
the landscaping industry, including contract
procedures, standards of quality and
workmanship, and management.

Printed publications:
Who's Who 2001/2002 (brochure with the aims,
objectives, conditions of membership and list of
members, available free, direct)

Access to staff:
Contact by letter, by telephone, by fax and by e-
mail. Appointment necessary.
Hours: Mon to Fri, 0900 to 1700

Access to building, collection or gallery:
Prior appointment required

Works closely with:
British Association of Landscape Industries
Institute of Groundsmen

ASSOCIATION OF LASER USERS

Acronym or abbreviation: AILU

100 Ock Street, Abingdon, Oxfordshire, OX14 5DH

Tel: 01235 539595
Fax: 01235 550499
E-mail: admin@ailu.org.uk

Website:
http://www.ailu.org.uk

Directory, technical information on laser
processing, product guide, United Kingdom
statistics.

Enquiries:
Enquiries to: Executive Secretary

Founded:
1995

Organisation type and purpose:
Professional body, membership association
(membership is by subscription), present number
of members: 350, manufacturing industry.
To disseminate information and aid networking.

Subject coverage:
Laser use in industry. Manufacturers and supplies
of laser and laser-related equipment and services.
Laser applications topics, including materials
processing and measurement.

Trade and statistical information:
Centres for UK laser activity.

Printed publications:
Introduction to Laser Materials Processing (£18)
Laser Materials Processing: Challenge and
Opportunities in Europe (proceedings, 1997, £45)
The Industrial Laser User (magazine, 4 times a
year, members only)

Access to staff:
Contact by letter, by telephone, by fax, by e-mail
and via website
Hours: Mon to Fri, 0900 to 1700

ASSOCIATION OF LAW COSTS DRAFTSMEN

Acronym or abbreviation: ALCD

Church Cottage, Church Lane, Stuston, Diss,
Norfolk, IP21 4AG

Tel: 01379 741404
Fax: 01379 742702
E-mail: enquiries@alcd.org.uk

Website:
http://www.alcd.org.uk
Details of the Association and information on
joining.

Enquiries:
Enquiries to: Administrator

Founded:
1977

Organisation type and purpose:
Professional body (membership is by
qualification), present number of members: 850.
Membership subscription is required.
Law Costs Draftsmen are specialists in the law
who operate by advising upon and applying laws
and directions which relate to the evaluation and
recovery of solicitors' fees.

Printed publications:
ALCD (monthly)

Publications list:
Available in print

Access to staff:
Contact by letter, by telephone, by fax, by e-mail
and via website
Hours: Mon to Fri, 0900 to 1700

ASSOCIATION OF LAW TEACHERS

Acronym or abbreviation: ALT

City Law School, 4 Gray's Inn Place, London,
WC1R 5DX

Tel: 020 7404 5787, ext 368
E-mail: amanda.fancourt.1@city.ac.uk

Enquiries:
Enquiries to: Honorary Secretary

Founded:
1965

continued overleaf

Organisation type and purpose:
Professional body (membership is by subscription), present number of members: 500, research organisation.

Subject coverage:
Legal education, academic law.

Printed publications:
ALT Bulletin and e-newsletter
The Law Teacher (3 times a year)
Order printed publications from: Nigel Duncan (Editor The Law Teacher), City Law School, 4 Gray's Inn Place, London, WC1R 5DX

Access to staff:
Contact by letter, by telephone, by fax and by e-mail
Hours: Mon to Fri, 0900 to 1700

ASSOCIATION OF LEADING VISITOR ATTRACTIONS

Acronym or abbreviation: ALVA

4 Westminster Palace Gardens, Artillery Row, London, SW1P 1RL

Tel: 020 7222 1728
E-mail: info@alva.org.uk

Website:
http://www.alva.org.uk

Enquiries:
Enquiries to: Information Officer

Founded:
1989

Organisation type and purpose:
Trade association.

Access to staff:
Contact by letter, by telephone, by fax, by e-mail, in person and via website. Appointment necessary.
Hours: Mon to Fri, 0900 to 1700

Access to building, collection or gallery:
Prior appointment required

ASSOCIATION OF LEARNED AND PROFESSIONAL SOCIETY PUBLISHERS

Acronym or abbreviation: ALPSP

1 Abbey Cottages, The Green, Sutton Courtenay, Oxfordshire, OX14 4AF

Tel: 01235 847776
Fax: 0870 706 0332
E-mail: ian.russell@alpsp.org

Website:
http://www.alpsp.org

Enquiries:
Enquiries to: Chief Executive

Founded:
1972

Organisation type and purpose:
Trade association, suitable for ages: 18+, training organisation.
Offers an extensive programme of education, training and development.
ALPSP is the international association for the community of not-for-profit scholarly and professional publishers and those who work with them. ALPSP advocates best practice, carries out research and other projects, monitors national and international issues and represents members' interests to the wider world. The Association provides co-operative services such as the ALPSP Learned Journals Collection and the ALPSP e-books Collection.

Subject coverage:
Learned and professional publishing; not-for-profit publishing (e.g. learned societies, university presses, non-governmental organisations etc.).

Printed publications:
Learned Publishing (quarterly, non-members institutional rate: £180 per year (2009 price), print plus electronic. Full prices on website)
Various research reports, white papers etc.
Order printed publications from: Nick Evans (Chief Operating Officer), 9 Stanbridge Road, Putney, London, SW15 1DX; 020 8789 2394; nick.evans@alpsp.org

Electronic and video publications:
Learned Publishing (quarterly)
ALPSP Alert (electronic newsletter)

Publications list:
Available online

Access to staff:
Contact by letter, by telephone, by fax, by e-mail, in person and via website. Appointment necessary.
Hours: Mon to Fri, 0900 to 1700

Links with:
Publishing Skills Group

ASSOCIATION OF LIBERAL DEMOCRAT COUNCILLORS

Acronym or abbreviation: ALDC

Birchcliffe Centre, Birchcliffe, Hebden Bridge, West Yorkshire, HX7 8DG

Tel: 01422 843785
Fax: 01422 843036
E-mail: aldc@cix.co.uk

Website:
http://www.aldc.org

Enquiries:
Enquiries to: Information Officer

Organisation type and purpose:
Membership association (membership is by subscription).

Access to staff:
Contact by letter, by telephone, by fax, by e-mail and via website. Access for members only.
Hours: Mon to Fri, 0900 to 1700

ASSOCIATION OF LONDON CHIEF LIBRARIANS

Acronym or abbreviation: ALCL

c/o London Libraries Development Agency, 6 Charing Cross Road, London. WC2H 0HF

Tel: 020 7641 5266
Fax: 020 7641 5266
E-mail: andy.ryan@llda.org.uk

Website:
http://www.llda.org.uk

Enquiries:
Enquiries to: Honorary Secretary
Other contacts: President

Founded:
1965

Organisation type and purpose:
Local government body, professional body, public library.

Subject coverage:
London public libraries.

Access to staff:
Contact by letter, by telephone, by fax and by e-mail
Hours: Mon to Fri, 0900 to 1700

ASSOCIATION OF LONDON GOVERNMENT

Acronym or abbreviation: ALG

59½ Southwark Street, London, NW6 7NE

Tel: 020 7934 9999
Fax: 020 7934 9991
E-mail: info@alg.gov.uk

Website:
http://www.alg.gov.uk

Enquiries:
Enquiries to: Press and Publications Manager

Founded:
2000

Formerly called:
London Borough Grants Committee (LBGC) (year of change 1997); London Boroughs Grants Unit (LBGU) (year of change 2000)

Organisation type and purpose:
Local government body.
Grant-making body, as defined by Section 48 of the Local Government Act 1985.
To distribute grants to voluntary organisations on a London-wide basis.

Subject coverage:
Strategic funding of the voluntary sector in London, grant applications and monitoring processes; funding initiatives; the LBG and London Boroughs Grant Committee; advice and guidance for voluntary organisations; funding sources and other information.

Printed publications:
Information Pack
London Grants News (quarterly)
A variety of other publications

Publications list:
Available in print

Access to staff:
Contact by letter, by telephone, by fax, by e-mail, in person and via website
Hours: Mon to Fri, 0915 to 1715

Access for disabled people:
Parking provided, ramped entry, access to all public areas, toilet facilities

ASSOCIATION OF MANUFACTURERS OF POWER GENERATING SYSTEMS

Acronym or abbreviation: AMPS

Samuelson House, 62 Forder Way, Hampton, Peterborough, PE7 8JB

Tel: 0845 644 8748
Fax: 01733 314767
E-mail: ab@amps.org.uk

Website:
http://www.amps.org.uk

Enquiries:
Enquiries to: Director General

Founded:
1977

Organisation type and purpose:
Trade association (membership is by subscription).
The international promotion of the UK power generation systems industry.

Subject coverage:
Promotion of the interests and sales of the United Kingdom's manufacturers of diesel and gas driven electrical generating systems worldwide. By representation on British, European and International Standards Committees, EUROPGEN and other bodies, to speak with one voice on all issues of technical standards, legislation and commercial policy which affect members' interests. To help members maintain the highest technical standards, quality and customer support.

Trade and statistical information:
Data on worldwide market for diesel and gas turbine electrical power generating systems – volume and value.

Printed publications:
Directory of Members
A Guide to Earthing of Private Generating Sets up to 5MW – single and parallel operation
Technical guidelines to the first 6 parts of the Generating Set Standard ISO 8528

Electronic and video publications:
Directory of AMPS members, activities and
products (CD-ROM, free of charge)

Publications list:
Available in print

Access to staff:
Contact by letter, by telephone, by fax and by e-
mail
Hours: Mon to Fri, 0830 to 1700

Member of:
British Electrotechnical and Allied Manufacturers'
Association (BEAMA)
Electrical Generating System Association, USA
(EGSA)
Electricity Supply Association of Australia Limited
(ESSA)
European Generating Set Association
(EUROPGEN)
Institution of Diesel and Gas Turbine Engineers
(IDGTE)

ASSOCIATION OF MBAS

Formal name: Association of Masters in Business
Administration

25 Hosier Lane, London, EC1A 9LQ

Tel: 020 7246 2686
Fax: 020 7246 2687
E-mail: info@mbaworld.com

Website:
http://www.mbaworld.com

Enquiries:
Enquiries to: Company Secretary
Direct e-mail: p.north@mbaworld.com
Other contacts: Membership Secretary

Founded:
1967

Formerly called:
Business Graduates Association (BGA) (year of
change 1987)

Organisation type and purpose:
Professional body, membership association
(membership is by subscription, qualification),
present number of members: 9,000, registered
charity (charity number 313412), suitable for ages:
24+.
To promote and improve management standards.

Subject coverage:
MBA courses worldwide, accreditation of MBA
courses, funding for MBA courses.

Trade and statistical information:
Data on the number of MBA courses available and
the numbers of students graduating each year.
Salary and careers data of MBAs.

Printed publications:
Annual address book of members (free to members
only)
Annual Report (free)
Official MBA Handbook (2003 edition, annually,
£35)
MBAs: Salaries and Careers 2001 (biennially, £75)

Access to staff:
Contact by letter, by telephone, by fax, by e-mail,
in person and via website. Appointment necessary.
Hours: Mon to Fri, 0900 to 1700

ASSOCIATION OF MEDICAL RESEARCH CHARITIES

Acronym or abbreviation: AMRC

61 Gray's Inn Road, London, WC1X 8TL

Tel: 020 7269 8820
Fax: 020 7269 8821
E-mail: info@amrc.org.uk

Website:
http://www.amrc.org.uk

Enquiries:
Enquiries to: Chief Executive

Founded:
1987

Organisation type and purpose:
Membership association of charities that fund
medical research in the UK.
Membership is by application.
Members must use peer review, have a research
strategy in place, and sign up to AMRC position
statements in order to qualify for membership.
Present number of members: 114.
Registered charity (charity no. 296772), company
limited by guarantee (company no. 2107400).
Aims to further medical research in the UK
generally; in particular to further effectiveness of
those charities in which a principal activity is
medical research.

Subject coverage:
Advice and guidance on best practice in medical
research. Information on the contribution of
charities to UK medical research.

Trade and statistical information:
Data on the funding of medical research charities,
including distribution and types of funds.

Electronic and video publications:
Online guide to member charities
Guidance documents on best practice in medical
research funding available to download from
website

Access to staff:
Contact by letter, by telephone, by fax, by e-mail
and via website. Appointment necessary.
Hours: Mon to Fri, 0930 to 1730

Access to building, collection or gallery:
Prior appointment required

Access for disabled people:
Toilet facilities

ASSOCIATION OF MOTOR RACING CIRCUIT OWNERS LTD

Acronym or abbreviation: AMRCO Ltd

BARC, Thruxton Circuit, Andover, Hampshire,
SP11 8PN

Tel: 01264 882200
Fax: 01264 882233
E-mail: amrco@barc.net

Website:
http://www.motorsportsuk.co.uk

Enquiries:
Enquiries to: Honorary Secretary

Founded:
1962

Organisation type and purpose:
Trade association, membership association
(membership is by subscription, qualification),
present number of members: 18.
To represent the interests of UK motor sport circuit
owners.

Subject coverage:
Motor sport organisation and race circuit
management. Circuits include: Anglesey, Brands
Hatch, Cadwell Park, Castle Combe, Croft,
Donington Park, Goodwood, Kirkistown,
Knockhill, Lydden Hill, Mallory Park, Mondello
Park, Oulton Park, Pembrey, Rockingham,
Silverstone, Snetterton and Thruxton.

Access to staff:
Contact by letter
Hours: Mon to Fri, 0900 to 1700

ASSOCIATION OF MUSLIM RESEARCHERS

Acronym or abbreviation: AMR

PO Box 8715, London, SE23 3ZB

Tel: 020 8699 1887
E-mail: amr.org@btinternet.com

Website:
http://www.amr.org
Introduction to the organisation, aims and
objectives, forthcoming events, publications,
membership information, etc.

Enquiries:
Enquiries to: Executive Officer

Founded:
1989

Organisation type and purpose:
Membership association (membership is by
subscription), present number of members: 75,
voluntary organisation, registered charity (charity
number 1069744).
Generation, application and dissemination of
knowledge. Learned societies in the fields of
education, humanities and science and technology.

Subject coverage:
Islam. Islam and education/science and
technology/humanities. Specific information in the
fields of art and Islam, music and Islam. GCSE/AS/
A level Islamic Studies. Science courses.
Networking services. Providing referrals,
knowledge of British Muslim community.

Printed publications:
AMR News (quarterly)
Annual reports, proceedings
Publications/recordings (available direct and book
order agencies)
Non-registered publications/recordings (only
available direct)

Electronic and video publications:
Tapes of selected talks

Publications list:
Available online and in print

Access to staff:
Contact by telephone and by e-mail
Hours: Thu, 1200 to 1400; Fri, 0900 to 1200
Answer machine at other times, response usually
within 3 hours

Access to building, collection or gallery:
No access other than to staff

Affiliated to:
Muslim Council of Britain (MCB)
PO Box 52, Wembley, HA9 0XW; tel: 020 8903
9024

ASSOCIATION OF MUSLIM SCHOOLS

Acronym or abbreviation: AMS

512 Berridge Road West, Nottingham, NG7 5JU

Tel: 0115 841 1919
Fax: 0115 841 5806
E-mail: ams@webstar.co.uk

Enquiries:
Enquiries to: Director

Founded:
1992

Organisation type and purpose:
Membership association (membership is by
subscription), present number of members: 52
schools, training organisation, consultancy.
Members are full-time Muslim schools.
To enhance the development of Muslim schools.

Subject coverage:
Muslim schools, Islamic education, general
education, Islam.

Printed publications:
Al Madaris (termly, free)

Access to staff:
Contact by letter, by telephone and by fax
Hours: Mon to Fri, 0900 to 1700

Connections with:
Association of Muslim Schools
PO Box 537, Lenasia, 1820, South Africa

ASSOCIATION OF NATIONAL TOURIST OFFICE REPRESENTATIVES

Acronym or abbreviation: ANTOR

ANTOR Executive Secretary, 39 Pennington Close, Colden Common, Winchester, Hampshire, SO21 1UR

Tel: 0870 241 9084
Fax: 01962 711239
E-mail: esther@antor.com

Website:
http://www.antor.com

Enquiries:
Enquiries to: Executive Secretary

Founded:
1952

Organisation type and purpose:
International organisation, professional body (membership is by subscription, election or invitation), present number of members: over 90 National Tourist Office members, voluntary organisation.

Subject coverage:
Tourism in each member country, tourist planning facilities.

Access to staff:
Contact by letter, by telephone, by e-mail and via website. Appointment necessary.
Hours: Telephone has an answering machine

ASSOCIATION OF NATURAL BURIAL GROUNDS

12A Blackstock Mews, London, N4 2BT

Tel: 0871 288 2098
E-mail: contact@naturaldeath.org.uk

Website:
http://www.naturaldeath.org.uk
Addresses and descriptions of all woodland burial sites; criteria for association members.

Enquiries:
Enquiries to: General Secretary

Founded:
1994

Organisation type and purpose:
Registered charity.

Subject coverage:
Association for the 240+ green burial grounds (and 50 more at planning stage) where body is buried with a tree planted instead of a headstone; legal, ecological, and other issues pertaining to such a burial method.

Trade and statistical information:
Details of sites run by councils, farmers and wildlife trusts.

Printed publications:
The Natural Death Handbook (4th ed, £15.50 inc. p&p), lists all the woodland burial grounds in the UK, recommended funeral directors, suppliers of cardboard coffins, how to arrange a funeral without a funeral director, green, DIY funerals etc, plus information on how to set up a woodland burial ground.

Access to staff:
Contact by letter, by telephone, by e-mail and via website
Hours: Mon to Fri, 1100 to 1400

Connections with:
Natural Death Centre
at the same address

ASSOCIATION OF NEWSPAPER AND MAGAZINE WHOLESALERS

Acronym or abbreviation: ANMW

PO Box 40, 4 Acre Road, Reading, Berkshire RG2 0XZ

Tel: 0845 1213210
E-mail: enquiries@anmw.co.uk

Website:
http://www.anmw.co.uk/

Enquiries:
Enquiries to: Chairman
Direct e-mail: adrian.smith@anmw.co.uk

Founded:
1904

Organisation type and purpose:
Trade association.

Subject coverage:
Wholesaling of newspapers and magazines within the United Kingdom.

Access to staff:
Contact by letter, by telephone, by fax and by e-mail
Hours: Mon to Fri, 0900 to 1700

ASSOCIATION OF NOISE CONSULTANTS

Acronym or abbreviation: ANC

105 St Peter's Street, St Albans, Hertfordshire, AL1 3EJ

Tel: 01727 896092
Fax: 01727 896026
E-mail: anc@kingstonsmith.co.uk

Website:
http://www.association-of-noise-consultants.co.uk

Enquiries:
Enquiries to: Honorary Secretary

Founded:
1973

Organisation type and purpose:
Professional body, present number of members: 88 corporate members.

Subject coverage:
To help potential clients identify the services of consultancy advice in the fields of noise and vibration.

Non-library collection catalogue:
All or part available online

Printed publications:
Aims and Objectives
Membership Directory
Information sheet on the Noise at Work Regulations 1989
ANC Guidelines – Noise Measurement in Buildings
ANC Guidelines – Measurement and Assessment of Groundborne Noise and Vibration

Publications list:
Available online

Access to staff:
Contact by telephone
Hours: Mon to Fri, 0900 to 1700

Access to building, collection or gallery:
No access other than to staff

ASSOCIATION OF NORTHUMBERLAND LOCAL HISTORY SOCIETIES

Acronym or abbreviation: ANLHS

c/o The Black Gate, Castle Garth, Newcastle upon Tyne, NE1 1RQ

E-mail: mail@anlhs.org.uk

Website:
http://www.anlhs.org.uk

Enquiries:
Enquiries to: Secretary
Direct tel: 0191 284 0555

Founded:
1966

Formerly called:
Northumberland Local History Society (year of change 1979)

Organisation type and purpose:
Membership association (membership is by subscription), present number of members: 130 individual, 53 societies, voluntary organisation, registered charity (charity number 251179). Umbrella organisation supporting affiliated local history societies in Northumberland and Newcastle. Annual research project, lectures and meetings.

Subject coverage:
History of the geographic county of Northumberland (including Tyne and Wear and North Tyneside), excluding family history.

Museum or gallery collection, archive, or library special collection:
At Northumberland Collection Service:
War Memorials Index of Northumberland
Shops and Businesses of Northumberland

Printed publications:
Tyne and Tweed (annually autumn, £4.50 plus p&p)
Order printed publications from: The Secretary

Access to staff:
Contact by letter, by telephone, by e-mail and via website

Affiliated to:
British Association for Local History

ASSOCIATION OF NURSES IN SUBSTANCE ABUSE

Acronym or abbreviation: ANSA

37 Star Street, Ware, Hertfordshire, SG12 7AA

Tel: 0870 241 3503
Fax: 0192 0462 730
E-mail: info@ansauk.org

Website:
http://www.ansa.uk.net

Enquiries:
Enquiries to: Chairman

Founded:
1983

Organisation type and purpose:
Membership association (membership is by subscription).
Membership organisation for nurses and other allied professions working in the field of substance misuse or with an interest in this area of work.

Subject coverage:
All aspects of substance misuse, its effects and treatment.

Printed publications:
List on the website

Publications list:
Available in print

Access to staff:
Contact by letter, by telephone, by e-mail and via website

ASSOCIATION OF OPTOMETRISTS

Acronym or abbreviation: AOP

61 Southwark Street, London, SE1 0HL

Tel: 020 7261 9661
Fax: 020 7261 0228
E-mail: postbox@aop.org.uk

Website:
http://www.aop.org.uk
About the Association, our activities and services.

Enquiries:
Enquiries to: Chief Executive

Founded:
1946

Formerly called:
Association of Optical Practitioners (AOP) (year of change 1987)

Organisation type and purpose:
Professional body (membership is by subscription), present number of members: 9000.

Subject coverage:
Optometry, including eye care and protection in industry, DIY, drivers' vision, sports vision, eye care for the elderly, children, road safety.

Printed publications:
Annual Report
General selection of leaflets on aspects of eye care
Insider (members newsletter, quarterly)
Optometry Today (fortnightly)
Order printed publications from: Editor, Optometry Today
Victoria House, 178–180 Fleet Road, Fleet, Hampshire, GU13 8DA, tel: 01252 816266, fax: 01252 816176, e-mail: info@optometry.co.uk

Access to staff:
Contact by letter, by telephone, by fax, by e-mail and via website. Appointment necessary.
Hours: Mon to Fri, 0830 to 1730

Access to building, collection or gallery:
Prior appointment required

Houses the:
Optical Functional Whitley Council
Optometric Fees Review Committee

ASSOCIATION OF PAEDIATRIC CHARTERED PHYSIOTHERAPISTS

Acronym or abbreviation: APCP

42 Cammo Grove, Edinburgh, EH4 8EX

Tel: 0131 339 7555
Fax: 0131 476 3388
E-mail: c.h.shaw@cableinet.co.uk

Enquiries:
Enquiries to: Secretary
Other contacts: Chairman

Founded:
1973

Organisation type and purpose:
Advisory body, professional body.

Subject coverage:
Physiotherapy treatment for children in areas of speciality i.e. respiratory care, neuro-developmental, cerebral palsy, learning disability, dyspraxia, orthopaedic, neonatal care.

Publications list:
Available in print

Access to staff:
Contact by letter, by telephone, by fax and by e-mail
Hours: Mon to Fri, 0900 to 1700

Parent body:
Chartered Society of Physiotherapy
tel: 020 7306 6666

ASSOCIATION OF PHOTOGRAPHERS LIMITED

Acronym or abbreviation: AOP

81 Leonard Street, London, EC2A 4QS

Tel: 020 7739 6669
Fax: 020 7739 8707
E-mail: general@aophoto.co.uk

Website:
http://www.aophoto.co.uk

Enquiries:
Enquiries to: Membership Secretary
Other contacts: Chief Executive

Founded:
1968

Formerly called:
Association of Fashion, Advertising and Editorial Photographers (AFAEP)

Organisation type and purpose:
Trade association (membership is by subscription, election or invitation), present number of members: 1900.
To support and promote the interests of photographers in the areas of fashion, editorial and advertising photography.

Subject coverage:
Copyright, standards and ethics, education.

Museum or gallery collection, archive, or library special collection:
Careers Information
Photographic Reference Books

Printed publications:
Beyond The Lens
Image Magazine (monthly)
The Awards Book (annually)
Order printed publications from: Ventura BHP
The Plant Shop, Lenham Road, Kingswood, Maidstone, Kent, ME17 1LZ, tel: 01622 844417, fax: 01622 844418

Electronic and video publications:
Careers Information for Libraries

Access to staff:
Access for members only.
Hours: Mon to Fri, 0930 to 1800

Access for disabled people:
Level entry

ASSOCIATION OF PHYSICAL & NATURAL THERAPISTS

Acronym or abbreviation: APNT

27 Old Gloucester Street, London, WC1N 3XX

Tel: 07966 181 588
E-mail: apntsource@lineone.net

Website:
http://www.apnt.org.uk
Therapy schools links, news, membership information.

Enquiries:
Enquiries to: General Secretary

Founded:
1986

Organisation type and purpose:
National organisation, membership association (membership is by subscription), training organisation.

Access to staff:
Contact by telephone and by e-mail
Hours: Mon to Fri, 0900 to 1700

Member of:
Aromatherapy Organisations Council
British Complementary Medicine Association

ASSOCIATION OF PIONEER MOTOR CYCLISTS

Acronym or abbreviation: APMC

Heather Bank, May Close, Liphook Road, Headley, Bordon, Hampshire, GU35 8LR

Tel: 01428 712666

Enquiries:
Enquiries to: Honorary Secretary
Direct e-mail: john@barraclough40.freeserve.co.uk
Other contacts: News Editor

Organisation type and purpose:
International organisation, membership association.

All members have held motorcycle driving licences for 50 years for Pioneer Status and 40 years for Companion Member.
For motorcyclists to combine knowledge and meet socially during the year.

Subject coverage:
History of motor cycles and motorcycling.

Museum or gallery collection, archive, or library special collection:
Available only to members on application
Large collection of books, bound volumes of periodicals and other ephemera relating to the history of motor cycles and motorcycling (personal property of the present secretary)

Printed publications:
Newsletter (quarterly)
Rules and Register of Members (revised and updated in alternate years)

Access to staff:
Contact by letter and by telephone. Letter of introduction required.
Hours: Mon to Fri, 0900 to 1700

ASSOCIATION OF PLAY INDUSTRIES

Acronym or abbreviation: API

Federation House, National Agricultural Centre, Stoneleigh Park, Warwickshire, CV8 2RF

Tel: 024 7641 4999
Fax: 024 7641 4990
E-mail: api@api-play.org

Enquiries:
Enquiries to: Association Manager
Direct tel: 024 7641 4999 ext 208

Founded:
1984

Organisation type and purpose:
Trade association (membership is by subscription), present number of members: 60.

Subject coverage:
Manufacturers and suppliers of play equipment and impact-absorbing surfaces.

Printed publications:
Directory of Members
Guide to the Provision of Rubber Impact Absorbing Surfaces
Guide to Installation
Standard Form of Contract

Access to staff:
Contact by letter, by telephone, by fax and by e-mail
Hours: Mon to Fri, 0900 to 1700

Member of:
Federation of European Play Industries (FEPI)

Part of:
The Federation of Sports and Play Associations

Subsidiary body:
Constructors Section
Indoor Play Section
Outdoor Play Section
Surfacing Section

ASSOCIATION OF PLEASURE CRAFT OPERATORS / CANAL BOATBUILDERS ASSOCIATION

Acronym or abbreviation: APCO/CBA

Parkland House, Audley Avenue, Newport, Shropshire, TF10 7BX

Tel: 01952 813572
Fax: 01952 820363

Website:
http://www.britishmarine.co.uk
Lists activities and Group Associations of British Marine Federation.

continued overleaf

Enquiries:
Enquiries to: Administrator

Founded:
1954

Organisation type and purpose:
Trade association.
Operation of hireboats, passenger, hotel boats and all business involved in the inland waterways of England & Wales, including boat building and maintenance.

Subject coverage:
Information about boating holidays on the inland waterways of England and Wales and other businesses on the inland waterways. General information about the Association's aims.

Printed publications:
Membership List (annually, free)

Access to staff:
Contact by letter, by telephone and by fax
Hours: Mon to Fri, 0900 to 1600

Group Associations of the:
British Marine Federation (BMF)
tel: 01784 473377; fax: 01784 439678; e-mail: info@britishmarine.co.uk

ASSOCIATION OF PLUMBING AND HEATING CONTRACTORS

Acronym or abbreviation: APHC

Ensign House, Ensign Business Centre, Westwood Way, Coventry, Warwickshire, CV4 8JA

Tel: 024 7647 0626
Fax: 024 7647 0942
E-mail: enquiry@aphc.co.uk

Website:
http://www.licensedplumber.co.uk
Member company details. Association details.

Enquiries:
Enquiries to: National Director
Other contacts: Commercial Director for membership, PR, publications, database information, business development and marketing.

Founded:
1925

Formerly called:
National Association of Plumbing and Domestic Engineers; National Association of Plumbing Heating and Mechanical Services Contractors (year of change 1997)

Organisation type and purpose:
Trade association, consultancy.

Subject coverage:
Plumbing, heating, air conditioning, sprinkler systems, building dynamics and building maintenance services.
Training (BPEC certification), modern apprenticeships, training grants to employers, trainee placement (BSI Training Limited).

Museum or gallery collection, archive, or library special collection:
Archive of trade association journals relating to plumbing

Trade and statistical information:
List of member firms including sole traders.

Printed publications:
Bulletin (monthly, for members)
Members' Reference Book

Electronic and video publications:
Members list (disc format, for purchase)

Access to staff:
Contact by letter, by telephone, by fax, by e-mail and via website. Appointment necessary. Non-members charged.
Hours: Mon to Fri, 0900 to 1700

Affiliated to:
British Plumbing Employers Council (BPEC)

British Plumbing Employers Council Certification Limited (BPEC)
Joint Industry Board (JIB)
Union Internationale de la Couverte et Plomberie (UICP)
9 Rue la Pérouse, Paris Cedex 16, F-75784, France

ASSOCIATION OF POLICY MARKET MAKERS

Acronym or abbreviation: APMM

Holywell Centre, 1 Phipp Street, London, EC2A 4PS

Tel: 020 7739 3949
Fax: 020 7613 2990
E-mail: enquiries@apmm.org

Website:
http://www.apmm.org
Full description of market. Ability to access the market. Links to members' sites.

Enquiries:
Enquiries to: Executive Director

Founded:
1992

Organisation type and purpose:
Trade association (membership is by subscription), present number of members: 8 companies.
To establish and maintain an orderly market in Traded Endowment Policies (TEPs). To provide objective information. To act as a focus and a voice for the market.

Trade and statistical information:
Market turnover £500 million in 2000 and rising.

Printed publications:
A Fair Deal for All
The Association of Policy Market Makers

Access to staff:
Contact by letter, by telephone, by fax, by e-mail and via website
Hours: Mon to Fri, 0830 to 1745

ASSOCIATION OF PORT HEALTH AUTHORITIES

Acronym or abbreviation: APHA

Dutton House, 46 Church Street, Runcorn, Cheshire, WA7 1LL

Tel: 08707 444505
Fax: 01928 581596
E-mail: apha@cieh.org.uk

Enquiries:
Enquiries to: Executive Secretary

Founded:
1898

Organisation type and purpose:
Local government body, membership association (membership is by subscription).
Health control of ships, aircraft and imported food control.

Subject coverage:
EU and UK law relating to public health, food control and pollution. Environmental health relating to ships, and aircraft, fish and shellfish production.

Museum or gallery collection, archive, or library special collection:
Minutes and Papers from 1898 to date

Printed publications:
Codes of Practice
Control of Infectious Disease on Aircraft
Imports of Fishery from Third World Countries
Newsletter (monthly)
Port Health Handbook
Quarterly bound edition of minutes

Access to staff:
Contact by letter, by telephone, by fax and by e-mail. Appointment necessary. Access for members only.

Hours: Mon to Fri, 0830 to 1630

Access for disabled people:
Ramped entry, toilet facilities

ASSOCIATION OF PRACTISING ACCOUNTANTS

Acronym or abbreviation: APA

Devonshire House, 60 Goswell Road, London, EC1M 7AD

Tel: 020 7566 4000
Fax: 020 7566 4010

Website:
http://www.apa-uk.co.uk

Enquiries:
Enquiries to: Secretary
Direct tel: 01727 896030
Direct fax: 020 7689 6329
Direct e-mail: pneale@kingstonsmith.co.uk

Founded:
1988

Organisation type and purpose:
Membership association (membership is by election or invitation).

Subject coverage:
Accountancy.

Access to staff:
Contact by letter and by e-mail
Hours: Mon to Fri, 0900 to 1700

ASSOCIATION OF PRESERVATION TRUSTS

Acronym or abbreviation: APT

9th Floor, Alhambra House, 27–31 Charing Cross Road, London, WC2H 0AU

Tel: 0207 930 1629
Fax: 0207 930 0295
E-mail: apt@ahfund.org.uk

Website:
http://www.ukapt.org.uk/
Information on APT, information about building preservation trusts and completed projects.

Enquiries:
Enquiries to: Administrator
Other contacts: Chairman

Founded:
1989

Formerly called:
United Kingdom Association of Preservation Trusts

Organisation type and purpose:
Advisory body, membership association (membership is by subscription), present number of members: 235, registered charity (charity number 1027919).
Membership open to building preservation trusts.
To improve effectiveness of building preservation trusts through advice and information. To represent their views and to provide the public with information about them.

Subject coverage:
Guidance on setting up a preservation trust, information about building preservation trusts and their projects. Advice on rescuing buildings at risk through partnering building preservation trusts.

Trade and statistical information:
Various research data compiled ad hoc. Please ask for further information.

Printed publications:
APT Newsletter
Guidance Notes for Building Preservation Trusts

Publications list:
Available in print

Access to staff:
Contact by letter, by telephone, by fax, by e-mail and via website
Hours: Mon to Fri, 0900 to 1700

Has:
9 Area Committees contactable through the London office

ASSOCIATION OF PRINTING MACHINERY IMPORTERS

Acronym or abbreviation: APMI

65 Hazlewell Road, London, SW15 6UT

Tel: 020 8780 2966
Fax: 020 8780 2864

Enquiries:
Enquiries to: Secretary

Founded:
1959

Organisation type and purpose:
Trade association (membership is by election or invitation), present number of members: 39.

Subject coverage:
Printing machinery and equipment imported into the United Kingdom.

Printed publications:
For members only

Access to staff:
Contact by letter, by telephone and by fax
Hours: Mon to Fri, 0900 to 1700

ASSOCIATION OF PRIVATE CLIENT INVESTMENT MANAGERS AND STOCKBROKERS

Acronym or abbreviation: APCIMS

1st Floor, 114 Middlesex Street, London, E1 7JH

Tel: 020 7247 7080
Fax: 020 7377 0939
E-mail: info@apcims.co.uk

Website:
http://www.apcims.co.uk
Information about APCIMS members, services they offer and directory of firms across UK and Ireland.

Enquiries:
Enquiries to: Head of Information

Founded:
1990

Organisation type and purpose:
Trade association.

Subject coverage:
Investment and stockbroking for private individuals.

Printed publications:
Annual Report (information on APCIMS' activities throughout the year, free)
Directory (of over 200 members with an outline of services, annually, free)

Access to staff:
Contact by letter, by telephone, by fax, by e-mail and via website
Hours: Mon to Fri, 0900 to 1730

Access to building, collection or gallery:
No access other than to staff

ASSOCIATION OF PROFESSIONAL LANDSCAPERS

Acronym or abbreviation: APL

19 High Street, Theale, Reading, Berkshire, RG7 5AH

Tel: 0118 9303132
Fax: 0118 9303453

E-mail: apl@the-hta.org.uk

Enquiries:
Enquiries to: Administrator
Other contacts: Publicity Officer for PR & Publicity.

Founded:
1994

Organisation type and purpose:
Trade association (membership is by subscription), present number of members: 114.

Subject coverage:
Landscape gardening.

Access to staff:
Contact by letter, by telephone, by fax, by e-mail and via website

Specialist group within:
Horticultural Trades Association (HTA)
19 High Street, Theale, Reading, Berkshire, RG7 5AH; tel: 01189 303132; fax: 01189 323453; e-mail: info@the-hta.org.uk

ASSOCIATION OF PROFESSIONAL MUSIC THERAPISTS

Acronym or abbreviation: APMT

24–27 White Lion Street, London, N1 9PD

Tel: 020 8440 4153
E-mail: apmtoffice@aol.com

Website:
http://www.apmt.org

Enquiries:
Enquiries to: Administrator

Founded:
1976

Organisation type and purpose:
Professional body (membership is by qualification), present number of members: 600.
To maintain high standards of practice and training. To assist music therapists in development and all matters pertaining to their profession.

Subject coverage:
Music therapy; learning difficulties; mental health disabilities; autism; special needs; career literature.

Printed publications:
Journal (2 times a year)
Music Therapy and Mental Health
Music Therapy for People with Learning Disabilities
Music Therapy Research Register (1993)
Careers and information leaflets
Documents on music therapy in mental health, education and mental handicap

Publications list:
Available online and in print

Access to staff:
Contact by letter, by telephone, by fax and by e-mail
Hours: Mon to Fri, 0930 to 1530

Links with:
British Society for Music Therapy
tel: 020 8441 6226; fax: 020 8441 6226; e-mail: info@bsmt.org

ASSOCIATION OF PROFESSIONAL RECORDING SERVICES LIMITED

Acronym or abbreviation: APRS

PO Box 22, Totnes, Devon, TQ9 7YZ

Tel: 01803 868600
Fax: 01803 868444
E-mail: info@aprs.co.uk

Website:
http://www.aprs.co.uk
Details about Association, members services and exhibition.

Enquiries:
Enquiries to: Executive Director

Other contacts: Administration for Head Office.

Founded:
1947

Formerly called:
Association of Professional Recording Studios

Organisation type and purpose:
International organisation, trade association (membership is by subscription, qualification), present number of members: 350.
Membership is by subscription for individuals and by qualification for companies.
Furthering standards and needs of companies and individuals in audio-related industries.

Subject coverage:
Professional sound recording and related technology.

Printed publications:
APRS
Handbook (members)
Sound Recording Practice (5th edn, 2007)
The Master Tape Book (currently out of print, but being updated)
APRS Quarterly Bulletin

Access to staff:
Contact by letter, by telephone, by fax, by e-mail and via website. Appointment necessary.
Hours: Mon to Fri, 0900 to 1700

Access to building, collection or gallery:
No access other than to staff

Links with:
Music Producers Guild (MPG)

ASSOCIATION OF PROFESSIONAL TOURIST GUIDES

Acronym or abbreviation: APTG

33–37 Moreland Street, London, EC1V 8HA

Tel: 020 7780 4060
Fax: 020 7780 4142
E-mail: aptg@aptg.org.uk

Website:
http://www.aptg.org.uk
Details of the association, information about Blue Badge tourist guides and some tourism events.

Enquiries:
Enquiries to: Administrator

Founded:
1989

Organisation type and purpose:
Professional body (membership is by qualification), present number of members: 470.
Membership association for Blue Badge Tourist Guides.

Subject coverage:
Tourism issues.

Printed publications:
Register of Members – A listing of London-based Blue Badge tourist guides
Tourist Guide's Directory – Opening times and admission prices of historic sites, stately homes, cathedrals etc across the UK

Publications list:
Available in print

Access to staff:
Contact by letter, by telephone and by e-mail
Hours: Mon to Fri, 1000 to 1530

Access to building, collection or gallery:
No access other than to staff

ASSOCIATION OF PROFESSIONAL VIDEOMAKERS

Acronym or abbreviation: APV

Ambler House, Helpringham, Lincolnshire, NG34 0RB

Tel: 01529 421717

continued overleaf

Fax: 01529 421742
E-mail: jan@videomakers.com

Website:
http://www.apv.org.uk

Enquiries:
Enquiries to: Information Officer

Founded:
1995

Organisation type and purpose:
Membership association (membership is by subscription), present number of members: 500.

Subject coverage:
Video production and associated trades, skills.

Access to staff:
Contact by letter, by telephone, by fax and by e-mail
Hours: Mon to Fri, 0900 to 1700

ASSOCIATION OF PUBLISHING AGENCIES

Acronym or abbreviation: APA

Queens House, 55–56 Lincoln's Inn Fields, London, WC2A 3LJ

Tel: 020 7404 4166
Fax: 020 7404 4167
E-mail: info@apa.co.uk

Website:
http://apa.co.uk

Enquiries:
Enquiries to: Director
Direct tel: 020 7400 7516
Other contacts: Marketing Executive for other principal contact.

Founded:
1993

Organisation type and purpose:
Trade association (membership is by subscription, qualification), present number of members: 32.

Subject coverage:
Customer magazine publishing. Publishing agencies.

Trade and statistical information:
Statistics on the size of the UK contract publishing market. Data on customer magazines published by UK agencies.

Printed publications:
Annual Directory of Publishing Agencies (free)
APA Information Pack (free)
APA Membership Pack (free)

Access to staff:
Contact by letter, by telephone, by fax, by e-mail and via website
Hours: Mon to Fri, 0900 to 1730

Parent body:
Periodical Publishers Association (PPA) at the same address

ASSOCIATION OF RADICAL MIDWIVES

Acronym or abbreviation: ARM

16 Wytham Street, Oxford, OX1 4SU

Tel: 01865 248159
E-mail: sarahmontagu@gmail.com

Website:
http://www.midwifery.org.uk
General information, reprints from journals, links to useful organisations.

Enquiries:
Enquiries to: Secretary

Founded:
1976

Subject coverage:
Midwifery, maternity care, childbirth, breast feeding, postnatal care.

Printed publications:
Midwifery Matters (journal, quarterly, £30 a year subscription)
What is a Midwife? (leaflet, free for single copies, p&p for bulk supplies)
Choices in Childbirth (leaflet, free for single copies, p&p for bulk supplies)

Publications list:
Available online

Access to staff:
Contact by letter, by telephone and by e-mail
Hours: Mon to Fri, 0900 to 1700

ASSOCIATION OF REFLEXOLOGISTS (UK)

Acronym or abbreviation: AoR

5 Fore Street, Taunton, TA1 1HX

Tel: 0870 5673320
E-mail: info@aor.org.uk

Website:
http://www.aor.org.uk
Reflexology organisations worldwide, information on courses, training standards, career opportunities.

Enquiries:
Enquiries to: Executive Director
Direct tel: 01278 733393
Direct fax: 01278 733665
Direct e-mail: aoreo@reflexology.org
Other contacts: Chairman for policy.

Founded:
1984

Organisation type and purpose:
Professional body, membership association (membership is by qualification).
Awarding Body for Practitioner Qualification in Reflexology.
Accrediting Body for Practitioner Courses in Reflexology.

Subject coverage:
Reflexology, complementary therapies, integrated health.

Trade and statistical information:
Information on courses, reflexology organisations worldwide, training standards, career opportunities.

Printed publications:
Journal (quarterly)
Leaflets on Reflexology
List of Accredited Practitioners Courses in Reflexology (free)
Register of Practitioners (free)
Sales Catalogue

Publications list:
Available in print

Access to staff:
Contact by letter, by telephone, by fax and by e-mail
Hours: Mon to Fri, 0900 to 1700

Member of:
International Council of Reflexologists
Reflexology in Europe Network

Other departments at:
AoR Administration
    Katepwa House, Ashfield Park Avenue, Ross-on-Wye, Herefordshire, HR9 5AX; tel: 01989 567667; fax: 01989 567676; e-mail: aor@assocmanagement.co.uk
AoR Training and Education
    19 Benson Road, Henfield, West Sussex, BN5 9HY; tel: 01273 492385; fax: 01273 495920; e-mail: aor@reflexology.org

ASSOCIATION OF RELOCATION AGENTS

Acronym or abbreviation: ARA

PO Box 189, Diss, Norfolk, IP22 1PE

Tel: 08700 737475
Fax: 08700 718719
E-mail: info@relocationagents.com

Website:
http://www.relocationagents.com
Details of different services available from relocation companies and a geographic database of member and other relocation companies worldwide.

Enquiries:
Enquiries to: Chief Executive

Founded:
1986

Organisation type and purpose:
Trade association.

Subject coverage:
Relocation services, setting up relocation agencies, relocation industry.

Printed publications:
Directory of Members (annually, free)
Guide to Homesearch: information pack for those considering setting up a relocation agency (annually, £75)
The ARA Guide to the UK (once every two years, £12)

Access to staff:
Contact by letter, by telephone, by fax, by e-mail and via website
Hours: Mon to Fri, 0900 to 1700

ASSOCIATION OF RESEARCHERS IN MEDICINE & SCIENCE

Acronym or abbreviation: ARMS

c/o Henry Wellcome, LINE, Dorothy Hodgkin Building, Whitson Street, University of Bristol, Bristol, BS1 3NY.

Tel: 0117 331 3050
Fax: 0117 331 3049
E-mail: david.jessop@bris.ac.uk

Website:
http://www.hop.man.ac.uk/arms/arms.html
Membership, committee, interests and newsletters, aims, links.

Enquiries:
Enquiries to: Chairman
Direct tel: 07973 675422

Founded:
1978

Organisation type and purpose:
Voluntary organisation, research organisation.

Subject coverage:
Medical and scientific research, contract research, science policy, conditions of employment etc.

Printed publications:
Newsletter (4 times a year)
Surveys of contract research

Access to staff:
Contact by letter, by fax, by e-mail and via website
Hours: Mon to Fri, 0900 to 1700

ASSOCIATION OF RESIDENTIAL LETTING AGENTS

Acronym or abbreviation: ARLA

Arbon House, 6 Tournament Court, Edgehill Drive, Warwick, CV34 6LG

Tel: 01926 496800
Fax: 01926 417788
E-mail: info@arla.co.uk

Website:
http://www.arla.co.uk

Enquiries:
Enquiries to: Administrator

Founded:
1981

Organisation type and purpose:
Trade association (membership is by subscription). National professional and regulatory body for agents specialising in residential letting and management.

Subject coverage:
Private sector residential rental property; law and property; management and administration.

Printed publications:
Members Magazine (every other month)

Access to staff:
Contact by letter, by telephone, by fax and by e-mail
Hours: Mon to Fri, 0900 to 1730

Access to building, collection or gallery:
No access other than to staff

ASSOCIATION OF RESIDENTIAL MANAGING AGENTS LTD

Acronym or abbreviation: ARMA

178 Battersea Park Road, London, SW11 4ND

Tel: 020 7978 2607
Fax: 020 7498 6153
E-mail: info@arma.org.uk

Website:
http://www.arma.org.uk

Enquiries:
Enquiries to: Secretary

Founded:
1991

Organisation type and purpose:
Trade association (membership is by subscription), present number of members: 200+, service industry.
Trade association representing managers of residential leasehold blocks of flats in England and Wales.

Subject coverage:
Matters relating to block management of residential property.

Printed publications:
See publications online

Publications list:
Available online

Access to staff:
Contact by letter, by fax, by e-mail and via website
Hours: Mon to Fri, 0900 to 1700

Access to building, collection or gallery:
No access other than to staff

ASSOCIATION OF SCHOOL AND COLLEGE LEADERS

Acronym or abbreviation: ASCL

130 Regent Road, Leicester, LE1 7PG

Tel: 0116 299 1122
Fax: 0116 299 1123

Website:
http://www.ascl.org.uk

Founded:
1977

Organisation type and purpose:
Professional body, trade union. Represents more than 14,000 senior leaders in secondary schools and colleges.

Subject coverage:
Secondary and further education.

Printed publications:
Magazine, poilcy and guidance papers, books.

Publications list:
Available in print

Access to staff:
Contact by letter, by telephone and by fax
Hours: Mon to Fri, 0900 to 1700

ASSOCIATION OF SCOTTISH COMMUNITY COUNCILS

Acronym or abbreviation: ASCC

28 Bank Street, Brechin, DD9 6AX

Tel: 01356 623330
E-mail: secretary@ascc.org.uk

Website:
http://www.ascc.org.uk
General information

Enquiries:
Enquiries to: Secretary

Founded:
1993

Organisation type and purpose:
Membership association (membership is by subscription), present number of members: 600, voluntary organisation.

Subject coverage:
Scottish Community Councils.

Museum or gallery collection, archive, or library special collection:
Complete database for all Scottish community councils

Printed publications:
Newsletter (quarterly, free, direct)
1999 Survey (£5, direct)

Access to staff:
Contact by letter, by telephone, by fax and by e-mail. Appointment necessary.
Hours: Mon to Fri, 0900 to 1700

ASSOCIATION OF SCOTTISH VISITOR ATTRACTIONS

Acronym or abbreviation: ASVA

Argyll's Lodging, Castle Wynd, Stirling, FK8 1EG

Tel: 01786 475152
Fax: 01786 474288
E-mail: info@asva.co.uk

Website:
http://www.asva.co.uk

Enquiries:
Enquiries to: Administrator
Other contacts: Development Manager

Founded:
1989

Organisation type and purpose:
Trade association (membership is by subscription), present number of members: 400.

Subject coverage:
All aspects of visitor attraction in Scotland, development, operations and marketing.

Publications list:
Available in print

Access to staff:
Contact by letter, by telephone, by fax, by e-mail and via website
Hours: Mon to Fri, 0900 to 1700

ASSOCIATION OF SEA TRAINING ORGANISATIONS

Acronym or abbreviation: ASTO

Unit 10, North Meadow, Royal Clarence Yard, Gosport, Hampshire, PO12 1BP

Tel: 023 9250 3222
Fax: 023 9250 3222
E-mail: office@asto.org.uk

Website:
http://www.asto.org.uk
Exact copy of brochure including links to ASTO members website.

Enquiries:
Enquiries to: Business Manager

Founded:
1971

Organisation type and purpose:
Membership association (membership is by election or invitation), registered charity, training organisation.

Subject coverage:
Sail training for young people and adults, able-bodied or disabled, personal development for young people.

Printed publications:
Publicity material
Sail to Adventure, directory of sail training opportunities (updated every 2 years)

Access to staff:
Contact by letter, by telephone and by fax
Hours: Mon to Fri, 0900 to 1700

Supported by:
Royal Yachting Association

ASSOCIATION OF SHOW AND AGRICULTURAL ORGANISATIONS

Acronym or abbreviation: ASAO

PO Box 4575, Sherborne, Dorset, DT9 4XA

Tel: 07711 205833
Fax: 01749 823169
E-mail: asaosecretary@asao.co.uk

Website:
http://www.asao.co.uk
List of members events.

Enquiries:
Enquiries to: Secretary

Founded:
1923

Organisation type and purpose:
National organisation, trade association (membership is by subscription), present number of members: 187, voluntary organisation, registered charity (charity number 1023932).

Subject coverage:
Organisation of agricultural and similar shows.

Publications list:
Available in print

Access to staff:
Appointment necessary.
Hours: Mon to Fri, 0900 to 1700

ASSOCIATION OF SINGER CAR OWNERS

Acronym or abbreviation: ASCO

39 Oakfield, Rickmansworth, Hertfordshire, WD3 8LR

Tel: 01923 778575

Website:
http://www.asco.org.uk
General information about the club, photographs of Singer cars, membership form.

Enquiries:
Enquiries to: General Secretary

Founded:
1976

continued overleaf

Organisation type and purpose:
Membership association (membership is by subscription), present number of members: 200.

Subject coverage:
Restoration, technical advice, source materials on all aspects of Singer cars.

Printed publications:
Magazine (once every two months, free to members)

Access to staff:
Contact by letter and by telephone
Hours: Mon to Sun, 1000 to 1900

ASSOCIATION OF SOCIAL ANTHROPOLOGISTS OF THE COMMONWEALTH

Acronym or abbreviation: ASA

50 Fitzroy Street, London, W1T 5BT

E-mail: admin@theasa.org

Website:
http://www.theasa.org

Enquiries:
Enquiries to: Administrator

Organisation type and purpose:
Professional body (membership is referenced).

Subject coverage:
Social anthropology and its various sub-fields.

Printed publications:
ASA Monographs (annually, pub. Berg)
ASA Research Methods (published periodically by Academic Press and Berg)

Electronic and video publications:
Annals (online)
ASAonline
ASAfilm (online)

Publications list:
Available online

Access to staff:
Contact by letter and by e-mail
Hours: Mon to Fri, 0900 to 1700
Special comments: Office is remote so best access is via e-mail

Links with:
Association of Learned Societies in the Social Sciences

ASSOCIATION OF STAINLESS FASTENER DISTRIBUTORS

Acronym or abbreviation: ASFAD

Ikon Trading Estate, Droitwich Road, Hartlebury, DY10 4EU

E-mail: info@bafd.org

Website:
http://www.bafd.org

Enquiries:
Enquiries to: General Secretary

Founded:
1984

Organisation type and purpose:
Trade association (membership is by qualification, election or invitation).

Subject coverage:
Sources of supply of stainless fasteners and distribution.

Access to staff:
Contact by letter, by telephone, by fax and by e-mail. Access for members only.
Hours: Mon to Fri, 0900 to 1700

Members of:
European Fastener Distributors Association (EFDA)
Germany

Parent body:
British Association of Fastener Distributors (BAFD) at the same address

ASSOCIATION OF SUPERVISORS OF MIDWIVES

Acronym or abbreviation: ASM

West Yorkshire Health Authority, Bleneim House West One, Duncombe Street, Leeds, West Yorkshire, LS14PL

Tel: 0113 295 2094
Fax: 0113 295 2222
E-mail: jean.duerden@westyorks.nhs.uk

Enquiries:
Enquiries to: Honorary Secretary

Founded:
1910

Subject coverage:
Supervision of midwives.

Printed publications:
Journal (annually, members only)

Access to staff:
Contact by letter, by telephone, by fax and by e-mail
Hours: Mon to Fri, 0900 to 1700

ASSOCIATION OF SURGEONS OF GREAT BRITAIN AND IRELAND

Acronym or abbreviation: ASGBI

The Royal College of Surgeons, 35–43 Lincoln's Inn Fields, London, WC2A 3PN

Tel: 020 7973 0300
Fax: 020 7430 9235

Website:
http://www.asgbi.org.uk

Enquiries:
Enquiries to: Chief Executive
Direct e-mail: admin@asgbi.org.uk

Founded:
1920

Organisation type and purpose:
Professional body, membership association (membership is by subscription, election or invitation), present number of members: 1100, registered charity (charity number 1068016). The advancement of the science and art of surgery.

Subject coverage:
General surgery and the specialities thereof: upper and lower GI, vascular, endocrine, transplant, breast, laparascopic surgery.

Access to staff:
Contact by letter, by telephone and by fax
Hours: Mon to Fri, 0900 to 1700

ASSOCIATION OF TANK AND CISTERN MANUFACTURERS

Acronym or abbreviation: ATCM

22 Grange Park, St Arvans, Chepstow, Monmouthshire, NP16 6EA

Tel: 01291 623634
E-mail: imcc@atcmtanks.org.uk

Website:
http://www.atcmtanks.org.uk
Purpose, objectives, information, members, links for ATCM.

Enquiries:
Enquiries to: Chairman
Other contacts: Secretary

Founded:
1969

Formerly called:
Plastic Tanks and Cisterns Manufacturers Association (year of change 1992)

Organisation type and purpose:
Trade association (membership is by subscription), present number of members: 12, manufacturing industry.
The ATCM is a group of like-minded manufacturers who co-operate and promote with common interest the manufacture of tanks and cistern products conforming to highest-possible standards of quality.
Co-operation between members in technical matters, standard production in UK and Europe, and action on behalf of members when making representations to government and regulatory authorities.

Subject coverage:
Manufacture and installation of tanks and cisterns for the storage of water, oil or chemical products.

Access to staff:
Contact by letter, by telephone, by e-mail and via website
Hours: Mon to Fri, 0900 to 1700

Links with:
Institute of Plumbing

ASSOCIATION OF TAXATION TECHNICIANS

Acronym or abbreviation: ATT

12 Upper Belgrave Street, London, SW1X 8BB

Tel: 020 7235 2544
Fax: 020 7235 2562
E-mail: info@att.org.uk

Website:
http://www.att.org.uk
Website of the ATT.

Enquiries:
Enquiries to: Head of Education Department

Founded:
1989

Organisation type and purpose:
Professional body, registered charity (charity number 803480), training organisation.

Subject coverage:
Taxation.

Museum or gallery collection, archive, or library special collection:
Tax Library located at King's College, London (members only)

Printed publications:
Annual Report (free on written request)
Essential Accounting for the Tax Technician (£25)
Essential Law for the Tax Adviser (£35 to non-members, £30 to members or students)
List of members (apply for cost)
Tax Adviser (journal, monthly, £64 subscription to non-members)

Access to staff:
Contact by letter, by telephone, by fax, by e-mail and via website
Hours: Mon to Fri, 0900 to 1700

Access to building, collection or gallery:
No access other than to staff

Associated with:
Chartered Institute of Taxation
12 Upper Belgrave Street, London, SW1X 8BB; tel: 020 7235 9381; fax: 020 7235 2562; e-mail: post@ciot.org.uk

ASSOCIATION OF TEACHERS OF MATHEMATICS

Acronym or abbreviation: ATM

Unit 7, Prime Industrial Park, Shaftesbury Street, Derby, DE23 8YB

Tel: 01332 346599
Fax: 01332 204357
E-mail: admin@atm.org.uk

Website:
http://www.atm.org.uk

Enquiries:
Enquiries to: Administrative Officer

Founded:
1952

Organisation type and purpose:
International organisation, membership association (membership is by subscription), present number of members: 3500, registered charity (charity number 293125). Mathematics Association.

Subject coverage:
Mathematics education at primary, secondary and tertiary levels.

Printed publications:
Software products
Mathematics Teaching incorp Micromath (6 times a year)
E-Newsletter and many other publications

Publications list:
Available online and in print

Access to staff:
Contact by letter, by telephone, by fax and by e-mail
Hours: Mon to Fri, 0900 to 1630

ASSOCIATION OF TECHNICAL LIGHTING AND ACCESS SPECIALISTS

Acronym or abbreviation: ATLAS

4c St Mary's Place, The Lace Market, Nottingham, NG1 1PH

Tel: 0115 955 8818
Fax: 0115 941 2238
E-mail: info@atlas-1.org.uk

Website:
http://www.atlas-1.org.uk

Enquiries:
Enquiries to: Secretary

Founded:
1946

Formerly called:
National Federation of Master Steeplejacks and Lightning Conductor Engineers (NFMS&LCE)

Organisation type and purpose:
Trade association.

Subject coverage:
Steeplejacking and lightning conductor engineering.

Member organisation of:
National Specialist Contractors Council

ASSOCIATION OF THE BRITISH PHARMACEUTICAL INDUSTRY

Acronym or abbreviation: ABPI

12 Whitehall, London, SW1A 2DY

Tel: 0870 890 4333
Fax: 020 7747 1400
E-mail: abpi@abpi.org.uk

Website:
http://www.abpi.org.uk
Information about ABPI, press area, publications, education and training, associated links, member services.

Enquiries:
Enquiries to: Information Officer
Direct e-mail: ccoomber@abpi.org.uk
Other contacts: Information Services Executive

Founded:
1929

Organisation type and purpose:
Trade association.

Represents the pharmaceutical industry operating in the UK in a way that assures patients access to the best available medicines, creates a favourable political, economic and regulatory environment, encourages innovative research and development, and affords fair commercial returns.

Subject coverage:
General information on the UK pharmaceutical industry, careers, education and training.

Library catalogue:
All or part available in-house

Printed publications:
Annual Review (free)
Books, briefings and leaflets
Resources for Schools (Key Stage 3 and 4), list of schools and careers materials
Order printed publications from: abpi@edist.co.uk

Publications list:
Available online

Access to staff:
Contact by letter, by telephone, by fax, by e-mail and via website. Access for members only.
Hours: Mon to Fri, 0830 to 1630
Special comments: Priority given to members.

Access to building, collection or gallery:
No access other than to staff
Special comments: Members only.

Also at:
ABPI Cymru Wales
   2 Caspian Point, Pierhead Street, Cardiff Bay, CF10 4DQ; tel: 0870 890 4333; fax: 029 2045 4298; e-mail: wales@abpi.org.uk
ABPI Northern Ireland
   224 Lisburn Road, Belfast, BT9 6GE; tel: 029 2045 4297
ABPI Scotland
   Third Floor East, Crichton House, 4 Crichton's Close, Canongate, Edinburgh, EH8 8DT; tel: 0870 890 4333; fax: 0131 523 0491

Associated with:
Office of Health Economics
   tel: 020 7747 8850; fax: 020 7747 8851; e-mail: ohegeneral@ohe.org; website: www.ohe.org

Member organisation of:
European Federation of Pharmaceutical Industry's Associations (EFPIA)
   Brussels; tel: +32 2 6262555; fax: +32 2 6262566
International Federation of Pharmaceutical Manufacturers' Associations (IFPMA)
   Geneva; tel: +41 22 338 32 00; fax: +41 22 338 32 99

ASSOCIATION OF TRANSLATION COMPANIES LIMITED

Acronym or abbreviation: ATC

5th Floor Greener House, 66 – 68 Haymarket, London, SW1Y 4RF

Tel: 020 7930 2200
Fax: 020 7451 7051
E-mail: info@atc.org.uk

Website:
http://www.atc.org.uk

Enquiries:
Enquiries to: General Secretary

Founded:
1976

Organisation type and purpose:
Professional body, trade association (membership is by subscription, qualification), present number of members: 85.
To provide the use of professionally produced translations by commerce and industry and to regulate translation companies who are members.

Subject coverage:
Information on the sourcing of translation, matching language and specialist subject matter.

Museum or gallery collection, archive, or library special collection:
Libraries, of some members, on unusual subjects, of specialist technical and other glossaries, of translations of foreign technical standards

Trade and statistical information:
The ATC conducts regular surveys of the translation profession, some of the results may be purchased by interested parties.

Printed publications:
ATC Members' Directory (free to those purchasing translations, £25 plus VAT to those selling their services to others).

Access to staff:
Contact by letter, by telephone, by fax, by e-mail and via website. Appointment necessary.
Hours: Mon to Fri, 0900 to 1700

ASSOCIATION OF TUTORS, THE

Acronym or abbreviation: AOT

Sunnycroft, 63 King Edward Road, Northampton, NN1 5LY

Tel: 07000 268835
Fax: 07000 268329

Website:
http://www.tutor.co.uk

Enquiries:
Enquiries to: Secretary

Founded:
1958

Organisation type and purpose:
Professional body (membership is by election or invitation).

Subject coverage:
All aspects of tutoring.

Access to staff:
Contact by letter
Hours: Mon to Fri, 0900 to 1700

ASSOCIATION OF UK MEDIA LIBRARIANS

Acronym or abbreviation: AUKML

PO Box 14254, London, SE1 9WL

E-mail: aukml@brighton.ac.uk

Website:
http://www.AUKML.org.uk
Membership info, quarterly newsletters excerpts, mailing list, conference details.

Enquiries:
Enquiries to: Chairman

Founded:
1986

Organisation type and purpose:
Membership association (membership is by subscription, qualification).
To create links between librarians and information workers in all areas of the media industry. Members come from newspaper and magazine publishing, broadcasting organisations and academic institutions. Overseas members welcome.

Subject coverage:
Information provision in the media industry.

Printed publications:
Deadline (4 times a year for members)

Access to staff:
Contact by letter and by e-mail
Hours: Mon to Fri, 0900 to 1700

ASSOCIATION OF VETERINARY TEACHERS AND RESEARCH WORKERS

Acronym or abbreviation: AVTRW

continued overleaf

Department of Agriculture for Northern Ireland, Veterinary Sciences Division, Stoney Road, Stormont, Belfast, BT4 3SD

Tel: 02890 525606
Fax: 02890 525754
E-mail: john.mcevoy@dardni.gov.uk

Website:
http://www.avtrw.org.uk
Information on the Association and the annual conferences.

Enquiries:
Enquiries to: Honorary Secretary
Other contacts: Affiliated to British Veterinary Association

Founded:
1946

Organisation type and purpose:
International organisation, professional body (membership is by subscription), present number of members: 850.

Subject coverage:
Veterinary teaching and research.

Printed publications:
Proceedings for the 2000 Annual Conference: Research in Veterinary Science, Vol 68, Supp; A, June 2000.
Proceedings for the 2001 Annual Conference: Research in Veterinary Science, Vol 70, Supp; A, April 2001.
Guidelines for the recognition and assessment of pain in animals (1989, ISBN 0 900767 56 1)
Order printed publications from: UFAW
8 Hamilton Close, Potters Bar, Hertfordshire, EN6 3QD

Access to staff:
Contact by letter, by telephone, by fax and by e-mail
Hours: Mon to Fri, 0900 to 1700

Affiliated to:
British Veterinary Association
tel: 020 7636 6541; fax: 020 7436 2970; e-mail: bvahq@bva.co.uk

ASSOCIATION OF WHEELCHAIR CHILDREN

Acronym or abbreviation: AWC

6 Woodman Parade, North Woolwich, London E16 2LL

Tel: 0844 544 1050
Fax: 0844 544 1055
E-mail: headoffice@wheelchairchildren.org.uk

Website:
http://www.wheelchairchildren.org.uk
Comprehensive, up to date list of all training course locations and how to attend courses. How to help the charity.

Enquiries:
Enquiries to: Fundraising Co-ordinator
Direct tel: 0870 121 0053
Direct fax: 0870 121 0051

Founded:
1990

Organisation type and purpose:
Registered charity (charity number 1057894).
To provide expert training and advice for wheelchair-using children throughout the UK, to help them become more independently mobile, both in the home and out of doors.

Subject coverage:
Information, support and training for children in wheelchairs throughout the UK.

Printed publications:
Annual Report
Get Mobile (leaflet)

Access to staff:
Contact by letter, by telephone, by fax, by e-mail, in person and via website
Hours: Mon to Fri, 0900 to 1700

Special comments: First floor office.

National Headquarters at:
Association of Wheelchair Children
6 Woodman Parade, North Woolwich, London, E16 2LL; tel: 0870 121 0050; fax: 0870 121 0051; e-mail: hq@awc.btinternet.com

ASSOCIATION OF WOMEN BARRISTERS

Acronym or abbreviation: AWB

Administrator, General Council of The Bar, 2–3 Cursitor Street, London, EC4A 1NE

Tel: 020 7242 1289
Fax: 020 7242 1107
E-mail: jbradley@barcouncil.org.uk

Website:
http://www.womenbarristers.co.uk

Enquiries:
Enquiries to: Chairwoman
Other contacts: Administrator for contact details.

Founded:
1991

Organisation type and purpose:
National organisation, membership association (membership is by subscription), present number of members: c. 500.

Subject coverage:
Women barristers.

Printed publications:
Order printed publications from: Administrator

Electronic and video publications:
Newsletters online

Publications list:
Available online

Access to staff:
Contact by letter, by telephone, by e-mail and via website
Hours: Mon to Fri, 0900 to 1700
Special comments: Personal visits not recommended to Administrator's office.

ASSOCIATION OF YOUNG PEOPLE WITH ME

Acronym or abbreviation: AYME

9a Vermont Place, Tongwell, Milton Keynes, MK15 8JA

Tel: 08451 232389
E-mail: info@ayme.org.uk

Website:
http://www.ayme.org.uk

Enquiries:
Enquiries to: Manager

Founded:
1995

Organisation type and purpose:
National organisation, membership association (membership is by qualification), present number of members: 2000, registered charity (charity number 1082059).

Subject coverage:
Advice and information for young people with ME / CFS aged 0 to 25 years and their families.

Printed publications:
Information Resource Pack
Somebody Help M.E. (Moss J)
My Daughter and M.E. (Davies S)

Electronic and video publications:
What do you know about ME? (video)

Publications list:
Available online and in print

Access to staff:
Contact by letter, by telephone, by fax, by e-mail, in person and via website

Hours: Mon to Fri, 1000 to 1400

Access to building, collection or gallery:
No prior appointment required

Access for disabled people:
Parking provided, ramped entry, toilet facilities

ASTA BEAB CERTIFICATION SERVICES

Intertek House, Cleeve Road, Leatherhead, Surrey, KT22 7SB

Tel: 01372 370900
Fax: 01372 370999
E-mail: info@beab.co.uk

Website:
http://www.uk.intertek-etlsemko.com/
Currently offers contacts information, services and buyers guide. Future intention is to offer a more comprehensive service for customers, business partners and the general public.

Enquiries:
Enquiries to: Administrative Officer

Founded:
2004

Created by the merger of:
the Association of Short-circuit Testing Authorities (ASTA) and the British Electrotechnical Approvals Board (BEAB)

Organisation type and purpose:
Trade association.

Subject coverage:
Safeguarding and protection of the public by testing and approving electrical appliances and electrotechnical equipment to British Standards.

Printed publications:
Mark of Safety (leaflet)
Update (magazine, quarterly)
BEAB Product and Services Guide
BEAB Brochure Pack

Publications list:
Available online and in print

Access to staff:
Contact by letter, by telephone, by fax, by e-mail and via website. Appointment necessary.
Hours: Mon to Thu, 0900 to 1700; Fri, 0900 to 1630

Constituent part of:
Intertek Testing Services (ITS)

ASTHMA UK

Summit House, 70 Wilson Street, London, EC2A 2DB

Tel: 020 7786 4900
Fax: 020 7256 6075
E-mail: info@asthma.org.uk

Website:
http://www.asthma.org.uk

Enquiries:
Enquiries to: Administrator

Founded:
1990

Organisation type and purpose:
Membership association (membership is by subscription), voluntary organisation, registered charity (charity number 802364).
Provides information, advice and support to people with asthma and their carers; provides funding for research into asthma and related allergies.

Subject coverage:
Asthma, medication, anyone involved, e.g. people with asthma, family, health professionals.

Printed publications:
Annual Report
Asthma News (4 times a year)

General Information on Asthma in adults, babies and children for health professionals and for primary and secondary schools

Electronic and video publications:
Managing Your Asthma (video only in Bengali, Gujerati, Hindi, Punjabi, Urdu)

Publications list:
Available online and in print

Access to staff:
Contact by letter
Hours: Helpline only: 0900 to 1900

Access to building, collection or gallery:
No access other than to staff

Other address:
Asthma UK Scotland
2A North Charlotte Street, Edinburgh, EH2 4HR; tel: 0131 226 2544; fax: 0131 226 2401

ASTM

Formal name: American Society for Testing and Materials
Acronym or abbreviation: ASTM

European Office, 27–29 Knowl Piece, Wilbury Way, Hitchin, Hertfordshire, SG4 0SX

Tel: 01462 437933
Fax: 01462 433678
E-mail: atp@ameritech.co.uk

Website:
http://www.ameritech.co.uk
Technical books and standards.

Enquiries:
Enquiries to: Managing Director

Founded:
1980

Organisation type and purpose:
International organisation, learned society, professional body (membership is by subscription), publishing house.
Development of standards for testing and materials.

Subject coverage:
Standards on testing of materials and general technical information related to materials.

Electronic and video publications:
ASTM Standards on costing of materials (CD-ROM)

Publications list:
Available in print

Access to staff:
Contact by letter, by telephone, by fax and by e-mail
Hours: Mon to Fri, 0900 to 1700

Head office:
ASTM
100 Barr Harbor Drive, West Conshohoeken, PA 19428–2959, USA; tel: 00 1 610 832 9500; fax: 00 1 610 832 9555

ASTON MARTIN OWNERS CLUB LIMITED

Acronym or abbreviation: AMOC

Drayton St Leonard, Wallingford, Oxfordshire, OX10 7BG

Tel: 01865 400400
Fax: 01865 400200
E-mail: hqstaff@amoc.org

Website:
http://www.amoc.org
Details of Club. News of activities. Contacts.

Enquiries:
Enquiries to: Secretary

Founded:
1935

Organisation type and purpose:
International organisation, membership association (membership is by subscription), present number of members: 5000.
To provide for the needs and interests of owners of Aston Martin cars.

Subject coverage:
Aston Martin history, technical information.

Museum or gallery collection, archive, or library special collection:
Large archive of material relating to Aston Martins including: drawings for pre-war cars; racing history; brochures; etc

Printed publications:
AM Magazine (4 times a year)
AM Register (every 4 years)
News sheet (11 times a year)

Access to staff:
Contact by letter, by telephone, by fax, by e-mail and via website. Appointment necessary. Non-members charged.
Hours: Mon to Fri, 0900 to 1700

Access to building, collection or gallery:
Special comments: Wed PM, open to public

ASTON UNIVERSITY, LIBRARY & INFORMATION SERVICES

Library & Information Services, Aston Triangle, Birmingham, B4 7ET

Tel: 0121 204 3000
Fax: 0121 204 4530
E-mail: library@aston.ac.uk

Website:
http://library.aston.ac.uk
Web catalogue
http://www.aston.ac.uk/lis/general.htm
Times of opening
http://www.aston.ac.uk/lis/
Home page containing Annual Report, link to Library catalogue, general information

Enquiries:
Enquiries to: Enquiries
Direct tel: 0121 204 4525

Founded:
1895

Organisation type and purpose:
University Library.

Subject coverage:
Applied psychology, environmental health, ophthalmic optics, sociology and social history, political and economics studies, environmental planning and design, biological sciences, chemistry and chemical engineering, computer studies, electrical and electronic engineering, languages and linguistics, management, mathematics, mechanical engineering, pharmacy and pharmacology, production technology, international business and company information.

Library catalogue:
All or part available online

Printed publications:
Library information leaflets

Access to staff:
Contact by e-mail and via website. Access for members only.
Hours: Term time: Service hours; Mon, Tue, Thu, 0900 to 1800; Wed, 1000 to 1800; Fri, 0900 to 1700; Sat, 1000 to 1300; reference hours are longer
Vacations: Mon to Fri; 0900 to 1700
For full details – see website at http://www.aston.ac.uk/lis/
Special comments: An access control system is in use, for details see website at http://www.aston.ac.uk/lis/
Non-members of the university can use printed resources only.

ASTRA ZENECA UK LIMITED

Brixham Environmental Laboratory, Freshwater Quarry, Brixham, Devon, TQ5 8BA

Tel: 01803 882882
Fax: 01803 882974
E-mail: claire.coleman@brixham.astrazeneca.com

Website:
http://www.brixham.astrazeneca.com
Available services and points of contact.

Enquiries:
Enquiries to: Marketing Officer
Direct e-mail: keith.moore@brixham.astrazeneca .com

Formerly called:
ICI Brixham Laboratory; ICI Group Environmental Laboratory (year of change 1993); Brixham Environmental Laboratory, Zeneca (year of change 2000)

Organisation type and purpose:
Research organisation.
Company Laboratory of Zeneca Limited providing a service to Zeneca business and external clients.

Subject coverage:
Ecology, effluents, environment and environmental sciences, estuaries, marine sciences, mathematics, oceanography, hydrology, waste treatment, toxicology, environmental assessment, groundwater monitoring.

Museum or gallery collection, archive, or library special collection:
Ray Society publications

Non-library collection catalogue:
All or part available online

Library catalogue:
All or part available in-house

Printed publications:
Cadmium as an environmental pollutant (1980) – Bibliography
Mercury Bibliography (over 1,000 references on mercury as an environmental pollutant, 1975)
Reports on the flora and fauna of estuaries
Summary of the Data on the Toxicity of Various Materials to Aquatic Life (16 titles)

Publications list:
Available online

Access to staff:
Contact by letter, by telephone, by fax, by e-mail and via website. All charged.
Hours: Mon to Fri, 0900 to 1700

ASTROLOGICAL ASSOCIATION, THE

Acronym or abbreviation: AA

BCM 450, London, WC1N 3XX

Tel: 0208 625 0098
E-mail: office@astrologicalassociation.com

Website:
http://www.astrologicalassociation.com
Information about the AA and general astrological information.

Enquiries:
Enquiries to: Media Enquiries
Direct e-mail: media@astrologicalassociation.com

Founded:
1958

Organisation type and purpose:
International organisation, membership association (membership is by subscription), present number of members: 1600, voluntary organisation, suitable for ages: all.
To give out information on astrology. To inform members of current trends and developments. A forum for the exchange of astrological research.

continued overleaf

Subject coverage:
Astrology, history of astrology, historical studies, research practice, data collection of natal data on famous and infamous.

Printed publications:
Astrology & Medicine Newsletter (for astrologers who are interested in healing, 3 times a year)
Astrological Journal (6 times a year)
Correlation: journal of research into astrology (biennial)
Culture & Cosmos (looks at the social & historical setting of astrology, 2 times a year)

Electronic and video publications:
Collection of cassette tapes of conference seminars list available direct from the AA office (£7 each, £18 for 3)

Access to staff:
Contact by letter, by telephone, by fax, by e-mail and via website. Non-members charged.
Hours: Mon, Tue, Wed, Fri, 1100 to 1700; closed Thu

ASTRONOMICAL SOCIETY OF EDINBURGH

Acronym or abbreviation: ASE

105–19 Causewayside, Edinburgh, EH9 1QG

Tel: 0131 556 4365
E-mail: secretary@astronomyedinburgh.org

Website:
http://www.astronomyedinburgh.org
Membership information, dates and times of meetings, open days, observing nights, etc.

Enquiries:
Enquiries to: Secretary
Direct tel: 0131 667 0647
Direct e-mail: graham.rule@ed.ac.uk

Founded:
1924

Organisation type and purpose:
Membership association (membership is by subscription).
Amateur Scientific Society.

Subject coverage:
Teaching of astronomy; most fields of astronomy at a fairly elementary level, specialist information on aurorae, meteors, noctilucent clouds, via members specialising in these fields.

Museum or gallery collection, archive, or library special collection:
Antiquarian astronomical telescopes and clocks
Library of astronomical books

Printed publications:
Annual Report
Journal (2 times a year, free to members)

Access to staff:
Contact by letter, by telephone and by e-mail.
Appointment necessary.
Hours: Mon to Fri, 0900 to 1700
Special comments: Please telephone before midnight.

Address for meetings:
Astronomical Society of Edinburgh
City Observatory, Calton Hill, Edinburgh, EH7 5AA

Affiliated to:
British Astronomical Association
Federation of Astronomical Societies

ASUCPLUS

Acronym or abbreviation: ASUC

Tournai Hall, Evelyn Woods Road, Aldershot
Hampshire GU11 2LL

Tel: 01252 357833
Fax: 01252 357831
E-mail: admin@asuc.org.uk

Website:
http://www.asuc.org.uk

Enquiries:
Enquiries to: Secretary

Founded:
March 1992

Organisation type and purpose:
Trade association, present number of members: 21.
Members of ASUCplus are specialists in Subsidence Repair Techniques and Engineered Foundation Solutions, including new build foundations and basement development.

Subject coverage:
Subsidence Repair. Foundations.

Access to staff:
Contact by letter, by telephone, by fax, by e-mail and via website
Hours: Mon to Fri, 0900 to 1700

ATAXIA GROUP OF GREAT BRITAIN AND NORTHERN IRELAND, THE

Acronym or abbreviation: ATAXIA UK

Room 9 Winchester House, Kennington Park,
Cranmer Road, London, SW9 6EJ

Tel: 020 7582 1444
Fax: 020 7582 9444
E-mail: office@ataxia.org.uk

Website:
http://www.ataxia.org.uk

Enquiries:
Enquiries to: Administrator

Founded:
1964

Formerly called:
Friedreich's Ataxia Group (FAG) (year of change 2001)

Organisation type and purpose:
Membership association (membership is by subscription), registered charity (charity number 102391).
Helpline, limited welfare grants for those who have ataxia, local branches, contacts and meetings.
To raise money for research into ataxias and to provide information, advice and support to sufferers and their families, carers, professionals, and the general public.

Subject coverage:
Ataxias, Friedreich's, Cerebellar and other diseases of the nervous system, beginning in childhood or early adulthood, research projects funded by the Group, management and care of sufferers.

Printed publications:
Leaflets for information purposes
The Ataxian (magazine, quarterly)

Publications list:
Available in print

Access to staff:
Contact by letter, by telephone, by fax, by e-mail and via website
Hours: Mon to Fri, 0900 to 1700
Special comments: Answerphone available out of office hours.

Has:
11 local branches throughout the UK

ATHENAEUM LIVERPOOL

Church Alley, Liverpool, L1 3DD

Tel: 0151 709 7770
Fax: 0151 709 0418
E-mail: library@athena.force9.net

Website:
http://www.athena.force9.co.uk
Description and brief history of the club and library with three illustrations.

Enquiries:
Enquiries to: Librarian

Founded:
1797

Organisation type and purpose:
Membership association (membership is by subscription, election or invitation), present number of members: 543.

Subject coverage:
General collection; Merseyside, Lancashire and Cheshire, including maps, views, playbills.
Genealogy, 19th century economic pamphlets, 18th century individual plays, natural history.

Museum or gallery collection, archive, or library special collection:
18th century plays
Blanco White and South American Collection
Eshelby Collection
Genealogy
Jackson pamphlets
Liverpool playbills
Robert Gladstone pamphlets and 17th century law
Roscoe Collection
Teignmouth Bibles
Topography
Yorkshire history

Non-library collection catalogue:
All or part available in-house and in print

Library catalogue:
All or part available in-house

Printed publications:
Catalogue of the Library 1864 (£35 post free)
The Athenaeum Liverpool 1797 to 1997 (Carrick N and Ashton E L, 1997, £13.75 post free)
The Athenaeum Liverpool 1928 (McKenna, £2 post free)

Microform publications:
Diary ... of the Brig Henricus 1807–20 (Piper R, 1994, 7 microfiche, £14)

Access to staff:
Contact by letter, by telephone, by fax, by e-mail, in person and via website. Appointment necessary.
Letter of introduction required.
Hours: Members: 0900 to 1600; others: Tue to Thu, 1300 to 1600

ATLANTIC SALMON TRUST LIMITED

Acronym or abbreviation: AST

Suite 3/11, King James VI Business Centre, Friarton Road, Perth, PH2 8DG

Tel: 01738 472032
E-mail: director@atlanticsalmontrust.org

Website:
http://www.atlanticsalmontrust.org

Enquiries:
Enquiries to: Deputy Director (England & Wales)
Direct e-mail: ivorllewelyn@atlanticsalmontrust.org

Founded:
1967

Formed from:
Atlantic Salmon Research Trust (ASRT) (year of change 1980)

Organisation type and purpose:
Voluntary organisation.
Conservation and enhancement of stocks of wild Atlantic salmon and sea trout.

Subject coverage:
Wild Atlantic salmon and sea trout management and conservation.

Printed publications:
Atlantic Salmon Facts
Blue Books on salmon and sea trout matters
Posters
Journal (2 times a year)

Publications list:
Available in print

Access to staff:
Contact by letter, by telephone and by fax.
Appointment necessary.
Hours: Mon to Fri, 0930 to 1630

Associated with:
Association Internationale de Défense du Saumon Atlantique (France)
International Atlantic Salmon Foundation (Canada)
tel: 00 1 506 529 4581; fax: 00 1 506 529 4438

ATOMIC WEAPONS ESTABLISHMENT

Acronym or abbreviation: AWE

Aldermaston, Reading, Berkshire, RG7 4PR

Tel: 0118 981 4111
Fax: 0118 981 5320

Website:
http://www.awe.co.uk
Background information on Company, services, contacts.

Enquiries:
Enquiries to: Librarian
Direct tel: 0118 982 5722
Direct e-mail: library@awe.co.uk

Formerly called:
Atomic Weapons Research Establishment (AWRE)

Organisation type and purpose:
Research organisation.

Subject coverage:
Science, technology and engineering supporting the Company's programme.

Library catalogue:
All or part available in-house

Access to staff:
Contact by telephone and by e-mail. Appointment necessary.
Hours: Mon to Fri, 0830 to 1600

Access to building, collection or gallery:
Prior appointment required

Access for disabled people:
Parking provided, ramped entry

AUDAX UNITED KINGDOM

Acronym or abbreviation: AUK

8 Nap View, Awliscombe, Honiton, Devon, EX14 3PL

Tel: 01404 46588 (day)
Fax: 01404 46501
E-mail: ian@audax.uk.net

Website:
http://www.audax.uk.net/cal/
Calendar of Events.
http://www.audax.uk.net/faq.htm
FAQ.
http://www.audax.uk.net
Homepage.

Enquiries:
Enquiries to: Honorary Secretary

Founded:
1976

Organisation type and purpose:
National organisation, membership association (membership is by subscription), present number of members: 3800.
Produces calendars of, validates and keeps records of long-distance cycle rides registered as Brevets de Randonneurs.

Subject coverage:
Calendar of Brevets de Randonneurs cycling events in the UK; links to international events and cycling related information.

Museum or gallery collection, archive, or library special collection:
Results of successful Brevets de Randonneurs cycle rides in the UK from 1987

Trade and statistical information:
365 events of between 50 and 1,400 km calendared in 2001, in the UK, with 14,000 successful riders.

Non-library collection catalogue:
All or part available in-house

Printed publications:
Arrivée (magazine, quarterly, available to members only)
Calendar/Handbook (annually, £4)
Order printed publications from: Audax United Kingdom
10 Huntingdon Drive, The Park, Nottingham, NG7 1BW, e-mail: young@lineone.net

Access to staff:
Contact by letter, by telephone, by fax, by e-mail and via website
Hours: Mon to Fri, 0900 to 1700

Affiliated with:
The Cyclist Touring Club

Associated with:
Audax Club Parisien

Member of:
Les Randonneurs Mondiaux

AUDIO ENGINEERING SOCIETY LTD

Acronym or abbreviation: AES

PO Box 645, Slough, Berkshire, SL1 8BJ

Tel: 01628 663725
Fax: 01628 667002
E-mail: uk@aes.org

Website:
http://www.aes.org

Enquiries:
Enquiries to: Administrator

Founded:
1970

Organisation type and purpose:
International organisation, professional body.

Subject coverage:
Audio engineering.

Museum or gallery collection, archive, or library special collection:
Society's Publications

Printed publications:
AES Standards, Drafts and Information Documents
Anthology Series: collected papers of archival quality reproduced exactly as they appeared in the Journal and other authoritative sources
Conference Proceedings and Collected Papers
Cumulative Indices
Directory of Educational Programs, 1998
Journal Issues
CD-ROM Preprints

Electronic and video publications:
An Afternoon with Jack Mullin (video)

Publications list:
Available online and in print

Access to staff:
Contact by telephone
Hours: Mon to Fri, 0900 to 1700

Access to building, collection or gallery:
No access other than to staff

Affiliated to:
Audio Engineering Society Inc
60 East 42nd Street, New York, NY, 10165, USA; tel: 00 1 212 661 8528; fax: 00 1 212 682 0477; e-mail: hq@aes.org

AUDIO VISUAL ASSOCIATION

Acronym or abbreviation: AVA

156 High Street, Bushey, Watford, Hertfordshire, WD23 3HF

Tel: 020 8950 5959
Fax: 020 8950 7560

Enquiries:
Enquiries to: Chairman

Founded:
1977

Organisation type and purpose:
Membership association.
To represent professionals involved in audiovisual, video and multimedia.

Subject coverage:
Professional audiovisual up to broadcast standard including multimedia.

Access to staff:
Contact by letter and by telephone
Hours: Mon to Fri, 0900 to 1700

Specialist interest group of the:
British Institute of Professional Photography

AUDIT COMMISSION

1st Floor, Millbank Tower, Millbank, London, SW1P 4HQ

Tel: 0844 798 1212
Fax: 0844 798 2945
E-mail: communications@audit-commission.gov.uk

Website:
http://www.audit-commission.gov.uk

Enquiries:
Enquiries to: Information Officer

Founded:
1982

Organisation type and purpose:
Statutory body.

Subject coverage:
Local government and health service.

Printed publications:
Order printed publications from: Audit Commission Publications, PO Box 99, Wetherby, LS23 7JA, tel: 0800 502030, fax: 0870 121 4217, e-mail: audit-com-publications@capita.co.uk

Publications list:
Available online and in print

Access to staff:
Contact by letter, by telephone, by fax, by e-mail and via website. Appointment necessary.
Hours: Mon to Fri, 0900 to 1700

AUSTIN 3 LITRE OWNERS' CLUB

78 Croft Street, Ipswich, Suffolk, IP2 8EF

Tel: 01473 684867
E-mail: n.kidby@virgin.net

Enquiries:
Enquiries to: Secretary

Organisation type and purpose:
International organisation, membership association (membership is by subscription), present number of members: 45.
To provide a service to owners of 1967–1971 Austin 3 litre cars, provide bimonthly newsletter and a spares service.

Subject coverage:
All mechanical information on Austin 3 litres, details of part numbers for spares, history of Austin 3 litres.

Museum or gallery collection, archive, or library special collection:
Selected archive material i.e. road tests, period advertisements, magazine articles

continued overleaf

Printed publications:
Newsletter (issued to members)
Austin 3 Litre Owners Club Newsletter (6 times a
  year)

Access to staff:
Contact by letter, by telephone and by fax.
Appointment necessary.
Hours: Mon to Fri, 0900 to 2100

AUSTIN A40 FARINA CLUB

2 Ivy Cottages, Fullers Vale, Headley Down,
Bordon, Hampshire, GU35 8NR

E-mail: thinton@surrart.ac.uk

Website:
http://www.a40farinaclub.org

Enquiries:
Enquiries to: Events and Publicity Officer
Direct tel: 01628 673472
Direct e-mail: the.minters@btopenworld.com

Founded:
1979

Organisation type and purpose:
Membership association.
Actively pursuing the recognition of the A40 in its
true light and seeking to ensure its continuing
place in the history of British motor cars.

Subject coverage:
All aspects of the Austin A40 Farina MkI and MkII
(1958–1967), including history, information,
owners' register, technical advice.

**Museum or gallery collection, archive, or library
special collection:**
Archives, books and magazines on the A40

Printed publications:
Farina News (magazine, quarterly)

Access to staff:
Contact by letter, by e-mail and via website
Hours: Mon to Fri, 1800 to 2200; Sat, Sun, any
reasonable time

Other addresses:
Austin A40 Farina Club
  26 Wootton Way, Maidenhead, Berkshire, SL6
  4QU; tel: 01628 673472; e-mail: the.minters@
  btopenworld.com
Austin A40 Farina Club
  75 Tennal Road, Harbourne, Birmingham, B32
  2JB
Events & Publicity Officer
Membership Secretary

AUSTIN BIG SEVEN REGISTER

101 Derby Road, Chellaston, Derby, DE73 5SB

Enquiries:
Enquiries to: Registrar

Founded:
1969

Organisation type and purpose:
Membership association.
Car club for 1937/39 Austin Big Seven.
To register all cars of this marque which have
survived and are being restored or used.

Subject coverage:
Technical information, advice and information,
spares advice.

**Museum or gallery collection, archive, or library
special collection:**
Books, documents, technical information, relating
  to 1937–1939 Austin Big Sevens

Printed publications:
Hand Books & Technical Journal sheets
Newsletter (2 or 3 times a year)

Access to staff:
Contact by letter and by telephone
Hours: Mon to Sat, 1800 to 2000

Member organisation of:
Austin Seven Clubs Association
Federation of Austin Clubs, Registers and
Associations
  e-mail: austinfederation@aol.com
Federation of British Historic Motor Vehicle Clubs

AUSTIN CAMBRIDGE/ WESTMINSTER CAR CLUB

Acronym or abbreviation: CROWW

4 Russell Close, East Budleigh, Budleigh Salterton,
Devon, EX9 7EH

Tel: 01395 446210
E-mail: acwcc@blueyonder.co.uk

Website:
http://www.acwcc.org

Enquiries:
Enquiries to: Information Officer

Founded:
1981

Organisation type and purpose:
International organisation, membership
association (membership is by subscription),
present number of members: 177.

Subject coverage:
Austin Cambridge 1954–71, Morris Oxford 1959–
71, MG Magnette 1958–68, Riley 1959–68, Wolseley
1959–69, Austin Westminster 1954–68, 3L Austin
1968–70; spares, stockists, advice.

Printed publications:
Newsletter

Access to staff:
Contact by letter, by telephone and by e-mail
Hours: Mon to Fri, 0900 to 2100

AUSTIN MAXI CLUB

Formal name: Austin Maxi Owners Club

27 Queen Street, Bardney, Lincolnshire, LN3 5XF

Tel: 01526 398377
Fax: 01526 398377

Website:
http://www.austinmaxiclub.org

Enquiries:
Enquiries to: Membership Secretary

Founded:
1989

Organisation type and purpose:
Membership association.

Subject coverage:
Austin Maxi, its continuation of use, availability of
spares.

Access to staff:
Contact by letter
Hours: Mon to Fri, 0900 to 1700

AUSTRALASIAN PLANT SOCIETY

Acronym or abbreviation: APS

1 Iffin Cottages, Iffin Lane, Canterbury, Kent, CT4
7BE

Tel: 01227 780038
E-mail: secretary@anzplantsoc.org.uk

Website:
http://www.anzplantsoc.org.uk

Enquiries:
Enquiries to: Honorary Secretary

Founded:
1988

Formerly called:
Australian Plant Society (year of change 1992)

Organisation type and purpose:
National organisation (membership is by
subscription), present number of members: 200.

Subject coverage:
Details about wild plants of Australia and New
Zealand.

**Museum or gallery collection, archive, or library
special collection:**
Colour slides
Books about Antipodean plants

Non-library collection catalogue:
All or part available in-house

Printed publications:
Newsletter (two times a year, to members only)
Seed Germination information (to members only)
Information pack (members only)

Access to staff:
Contact by letter, by telephone and by e-mail
Hours: Daily, 0900 to 1700

AUSTRALIA'S NORTHERN TERRITORY TOURIST COMMISSION

Acronym or abbreviation: NTTC

1st Floor, Beaumont House, Lambton Road,
London, SW20 0LW

Tel: 020 8944 2992
Fax: 020 8944 2993
E-mail: info@nttc.co.uk

Website:
http://www.ntholidays.com
Holiday and touring information for Australia's
Northern Territory.

Enquiries:
Enquiries to: Manager

Organisation type and purpose:
Marketing office for Australia's Northern Territory.

Subject coverage:
Holiday information for Australia's Northern
Territory.

Printed publications:
Tour Guides (free)

Electronic and video publications:
Some videos (available on loan for travel agent
  training)

Access to staff:
Contact by letter, by telephone, by fax and by e-
mail
Hours: Mon to Fri, 0900 to 1700
Special comments: Office not open to the general
public.

Parent body:
Northern Territory Tourist Commission
  PO Box 1155, Darwin, NT 0801, Australia

AUSTRALIAN BUSINESS

Swire House, 59 Buckingham Gate, London, SW1E
6AJ

Tel: 0870 8900720
Fax: 020 7379 0721
E-mail: enquiries@australianbusiness.co.uk

Website:
http://www.australianbusiness.co.uk

Enquiries:
Enquiries to: Director

Organisation type and purpose:
Membership association.

Subject coverage:
Trade between Australia and New Zealand, and
the UK.

Access to staff:
Contact by fax and by e-mail. Non-members
charged.
Hours: Mon to Fri, 0900 to 1700

AUSTRALIAN WINE BUREAU

Acronym or abbreviation: AWB

Australia Centre, Strand, London, WC2B 4LG

Tel: 020 7887 5259
Fax: 020 7240 9429
E-mail: awb@australianwinebureau.com

Website:
http://www.australianwinebureau.com

Enquiries:
Enquiries to: Chief Executive

Founded:
1987

Organisation type and purpose:
Generic marketing organisation.

Subject coverage:
Australian wine.

Trade and statistical information:
World data on export/import of Australian wines –
value and volume.

Printed publications:
Promotional leaflets, posters

Electronic and video publications:
6 minute promotional video (to rent or buy)
20 minute promotional video (to rent or buy)

Access to staff:
Contact by letter, by telephone, by fax, by e-mail
and via website
Hours: Mon to Fri, 0900 to 1700

Access to building, collection or gallery:
Prior appointment required

Parent company:
Australian Wine & Brandy Corporation
tel: 00 61 8 8228 2000; fax: 00 61 8 8228 2022; e-
mail: awbc@awbc.com.au

AUSTRIAN CULTURAL FORUM

Acronym or abbreviation: ACF

28 Rutland Gate, London, SW7 1PQ

Tel: 020 7225 7300
Fax: 020 7225 0470
E-mail: culture@austria.org.uk

Enquiries:
Enquiries to: Librarian

Founded:
1956

Formerly called:
Austrian Cultural Institute (ACI) (year of change
2001)

Organisation type and purpose:
National government body.
Cultural affairs body.

Subject coverage:
Cultural aspects of Austrian life, studying in
Austria.

Printed publications:
Leaflets from Foreign Ministry on various subjects
Own small series on Austrian themes, issues

Access to staff:
Contact by letter, by telephone and by e-mail.
Appointment necessary.
Hours: Mon to Fri, 0900 to 1700

Access to building, collection or gallery:
via Rutland Gate
Hours: Mon to Fri, 0900 to 1700

Constituent part of:
Austrian Embassy

AUSTRIAN EMBASSY

18 Belgrave Mews West, London, SW1X 8HU

Tel: 020 7235 3731/2/3 and 7344 0290
Fax: 020 7344 0292
E-mail: embassy@austria.org.uk

Website:
http://www.austria.org.uk
General information on Austria, information on
consular matters, information for Austrians living
in the UK, information on culture, trade and
tourism.

Enquiries:
Enquiries to: Information Officer
Other contacts: Consul General for consular
matters.

Organisation type and purpose:
Embassy and Consulate.

Subject coverage:
General information on Austria, consular service,
assistance to Austrian citizens living in the UK.

**Museum or gallery collection, archive, or library
special collection:**
Information material (booklets, pamphlets etc.)
available by letter or fax to the Information
Officer

Library catalogue:
All or part available in-house

Electronic and video publications:
Video on Austria (for short term loan, contact the
Austrian Cultural Forum)

Access to staff:
Contact by letter, by telephone, by fax, by e-mail,
in person and via website. Appointment necessary.
Hours: Consulate: Mon to Fri, 0900 to 1200

Connections with:
Austrian Cultural Forum
28 Rutland Gate, London, SW7 1PQ; tel: 020 7584
8653; fax: 020 7225 0470; e-mail: culture@austria
.org.uk
Austrian Trade Commission
45 Princes Gate, Exhibition Road, London, SW7
2QA; tel: 020 7584 4411; fax: 020 7584 2565; e-
mail: london@wko.at

Parent body:
Austrian Federal Ministry of Foreign Affairs
Ballhausplatz 2, Wien, A-1014, Austria; tel: + 43 1
53115; website: http://www.bmaa.gv.at

AUSTRIAN TRADE COMMISSION

45 Princes Gate, Exhibition Road, London, SW7
2QA

Tel: 020 7584 4411
Fax: 020 7584 7946
E-mail: london@austriantrade.org

Website:
http://www.advantageaustria.org/gb

Enquiries:
Enquiries to: Information Officer

Subject coverage:
Trade-related information.

AUTHORS' LICENSING &
COLLECTING SOCIETY LIMITED

Acronym or abbreviation: ALCS

Marlborough Court, 14–18 Holborn, London,
EC1N 2LE

Tel: 020 7395 0600
Fax: 020 7395 0660
E-mail: alcs@alcs.co.uk

Website:
http://www.alcs.co.uk
Information on ALCS.

Enquiries:
Enquiries to: Communications Manager

Founded:
1977

Organisation type and purpose:
International organisation, membership
association, present number of members: 18,000
full members, 35,000 associate members.

British collecting society for all writers. Ensures
hard-to-collect revenues due to authors are
efficiently collected and speedily distributed.
Campaigns to raise awareness of copyright issues
and authors' rights among writers.

Subject coverage:
Database of film, broadcasting and literary
information containing information on British
writers and film and television works including
foreign episode titles, details of daily programming
in the United Kingdom and several other European
Countries which relate to writers' works. Also a
database of books holding details of works
photocopied since licensing introduced in 1984.
Information on literary estates and literary agents.

Printed publications:
Information leaflets
Newsletter (members and interested parties only)

Access to staff:
Contact by letter, by telephone, by fax, by e-mail
and via website. Appointment necessary.
Hours: Mon to Fri, 0930 to 1750

Affiliations with:
NUJ and other writers' organisations
Society of Authors
Writers Guild of Great Britain

Constituent member of:
Copyright Licensing Agency (CLA)
Educational Recording Agency (ERA)

Lead partner in:
BCC
CISAC
EU Imprimatur Project
European Writers' Congress
IFRRO

AUTISM INDEPENDENT UK

Acronym or abbreviation: SFTAH

199–203 Blandford Avenue, Kettering,
Northamptonshire, NN16 9AT

Tel: 01536 523274
Fax: 01536 523274
E-mail: autism@autismuk.com

Website:
http://www.autismuk.com

Enquiries:
Enquiries to: Chief Executive
Direct e-mail: keithlovett@ntlworld.com

Founded:
1987

Formerly called:
Society for the Autistically Handicapped

Organisation type and purpose:
National organisation, voluntary organisation,
registered charity (charity number 803003),
training organisation.

Subject coverage:
Specialised information: autism, Asperger's
Syndrome, education, care and treatment, training,
statementing.

Library catalogue:
All or part available online and in print

Printed publications:
Society leaflets, fact file (Autism) and Holiday
Home brochure (free – send SAE)
In-depth Autism, specialised areas and general
information

Publications list:
Available online

Access to staff:
Contact by letter, by telephone, by fax, by e-mail,
in person and via website. Appointment necessary.
Hours: Every day, 0900 to 1700, answerphone at
other times
Special comments: Appointments necessary for
reference library.

continued overleaf

Access to building, collection or gallery:
Prior appointment required

Access for disabled people:
Special comments: One step

AUTO-CYCLE UNION

Acronym or abbreviation: ACU

ACU House, Wood Street, Rugby, Warwickshire,
CV21 2YX

Tel: 01788 566400
Fax: 01788 573585
E-mail: admin@acu.org.uk

Website:
http://www.acu.org.uk

Enquiries:
Enquiries to: Communications Officer

Founded:
1903

Organisation type and purpose:
Governing body of British motorcycle sport.

Subject coverage:
Motorcycle events from youth to world
professional status, the Isle of Man TT races and all
home grand prix for road racing, moto cross, hill
climbing and off-road racing; proposed road, path,
right-of-way or land alterations; access rights for
sport purposes; insurance risks; off-road training.

Printed publications:
Sportmoto (magazine)
Annual Handbook
Rules on safety, noise, machinery, etc.
Standing Orders
Starting motorcycle sport

Publications list:
Available online

Access to staff:
Contact by letter, by telephone, by fax, by e-mail
and via website
Hours: Mon to Fri, 0900 to 1700

Access for disabled people:
Ramped entry, access to all public areas, toilet
facilities

AUTOMATIC DOOR SUPPLIERS ASSOCIATION LIMITED

Acronym or abbreviation: ADSA

411 Limpsfield Road, Warlingham, Surrey, CR6
9HA

Tel: 01883 624961
Fax: 01883 626841
E-mail: nas@clara.net

Enquiries:
Enquiries to: Director

Founded:
1985

Organisation type and purpose:
Trade association, consultancy.

Subject coverage:
Supply/installation of automatic doors and the
safety aspects of these.

Printed publications:
British Standard – BS 7036 1996: Code of Practice
for Provision and Installation of Safety Devices
for Automatic Power Operated Pedestrian Door
Systems (copies from BSI, Chiswick)

Access to staff:
Contact by letter, by telephone and by fax
Hours: Mon to Fri, 0900 to 1700

AUTOMATIC VENDING ASSOCIATION

Acronym or abbreviation: AVA

1 Villiers Court, 40 Upper Mulgrave Road, Cheam,
Surrey, SM2 7AJ

Tel: 020 8661 1112
Fax: 020 8661 2224

Website:
http://www.ava-vending.co.uk
AVA services and members. AVEX 2009 –
International Vending and Water Exhibition
www.avex2009.co.uk. Refreshment vending.
General information. Links to members, technical
information.

Enquiries:
Enquiries to: Director
Direct e-mail: janette@ava-vending.co.uk

Founded:
1929

Formerly called:
Automatic Vending Association of Britain (AVAB)
(year of change 2000)

Organisation type and purpose:
Trade association.

Subject coverage:
Availability and suitability of automatic vending
machines systems for catering or retailing services,
UK vending market, explaining refreshment
vending.

Trade and statistical information:
Size of the installed vending machine base and the
products being sold through it, available as the
AVA Census.

Electronic and video publications:
AVA Census (CD-ROM)
Water – Don't let the bugs get you down (DVD)

Publications list:
Available online

Access to staff:
Contact by letter, by telephone, by fax, by e-mail
and via website
Hours: Mon to Fri, 0900 to 1700

Access for disabled people:
Parking provided, level entry, toilet facilities

AUTOMOBILE ASSOCIATION, THE

Acronym or abbreviation: AA

Norfolk House, Priestley Road, Basingstoke,
Hampshire, RG24 9NY

Tel: 0990 448866
Fax: 01256 493389
E-mail: customer.services@theAA.com

Website:
http://www.theaa.com

Enquiries:
Enquiries to: Public Relations Manager

Founded:
1905

Organisation type and purpose:
Service industry.

Subject coverage:
Motoring developments (non-commercial):
technical, statistical, legislative, environmental and
related transport and travel.

**Museum or gallery collection, archive, or library
special collection:**
Archives of the Association from 1905

Publications list:
Available in print

Access to staff:
Contact by letter, by telephone, by fax, by e-mail
and via website
Hours: Mon to Fri, 0900 to 1700

AUTOMOTIVE DISTRIBUTION FEDERATION

Acronym or abbreviation: ADF

68 Coleshill Road, Hodge Hill, Birmingham, B36
8AB

Tel: 0121 784 3535
Fax: 0121 784 4411
E-mail: admin@adf.org.uk

Enquiries:
Enquiries to: Secretary

Founded:
1930

Formerly called:
Motor Factors Association (MFA) (year of change
1990)

Organisation type and purpose:
Trade association (membership is by subscription),
present number of members: 340 companies.
The Automotive Distribution Federation
represents the opinions of manufacturers,
importers and wholesale distributors (motor
factors) of vehicle parts and accessories.

Subject coverage:
Manufacturers, importers and wholesale
distributors (motor factors) of vehicle parts and
accessories.

Printed publications:
Eyes and Ears (newsletter, 6 times a year, free to
members, £15 annual subscription)

Access to staff:
Contact by letter, by telephone, by fax, by e-mail
and via website. Appointment necessary.
Hours: Fri, 0900 to 1630

AUTOVIA CAR CLUB

Pond Cottage, 67 Bentfield Green, Stansted, Essex,
CM24 8HY

Tel: 01279 813124
E-mail: marionalan@aol.com

Enquiries:
Enquiries to: Secretary

Founded:
1990

Organisation type and purpose:
National organisation.

Subject coverage:
Riley Autovia cars.

Access to staff:
Contact by letter and by telephone
Hours: Mon to Fri, 0900 to 1700

AVECIA BIOTECHNOLOGY

PO Box 2, Billingham, Cleveland, TS23 1YN

Tel: 01642 363511
Fax: 01642 364463

Enquiries:
Enquiries to: Librarian
Direct tel: 01642 364432
Direct fax: 01642 364454

Founded:
1993

Formerly called:
Avecia Lifescience Molecules, ICI Bio Products,
Zeneca Lifescience Molecules

Organisation type and purpose:
Research organisation.

Subject coverage:
Healthcare, bioscience.

Access to staff:
Contact by letter, by telephone and by fax
Hours: Mon to Fri, 0900 to 1700

Parent body:
Avecia Limited

AVERT

4 Brighton Road, Horsham, West Sussex, RH13
5BA

Tel: 01403 210202
Fax: 01403 211001
E-mail: info@avert.org

Website:
http://www.avert.org
Wide range of material on HIV/AIDS including
United Kingdom and US AIDS statistics,
educational material, medical and self-help
information. Links to other HIV/AIDS related sites.

Enquiries:
Enquiries to: Information Officer

Founded:
1986

Formerly called:
Aids Education and Research Trust

Organisation type and purpose:
Registered charity (charity number 1074849).
To combat HIV and AIDS world-wide.

Subject coverage:
HIV and AIDS information.

**Museum or gallery collection, archive, or library
special collection:**
Reference library

Trade and statistical information:
Statistics on epidemiology of HIV and AIDS in
United Kingdom especially.

Printed publications:
All publications are now available for free online,
including:
HIV and AIDS: Information for Young People
Sex and Sexual Relationships
Teens, STDs and HIV/AIDS
Changing Times: Information about Puberty
STD Booklet
Information about contraception

Publications list:
Available online and in print

Access to staff:
Contact by letter, by telephone, by fax, by e-mail
and via website
Hours: Mon to Fri, 0900 to 1700

Access to building, collection or gallery:
Prior appointment required
Hours: Mon to Fri, 0900 to 1700

Access for disabled people:
Parking provided, ramped entry, level entry, access
to all public areas, toilet facilities

AVIATION ENVIRONMENT FEDERATION

Acronym or abbreviation: AEF

Broken Wharf House, 2 Broken Wharf, London,
EC4V 3DT

Tel: 020 7248 2223
Fax: 020 7329 8160
E-mail: info@aef.org.uk

Website:
http://www.aef.org.uk
Summary of objectives, membership information,
summary of newsletters/members briefing notes.
http://www.aef.org.uk/publications.htm

Enquiries:
Enquiries to: Information Officer

Founded:
1975

Formerly called:
Airfields Environment Federation (year of change
1993)

Organisation type and purpose:
National organisation, membership association
(membership is by subscription), present number
of members: 110, voluntary organisation,
consultancy, research organisation.
Addresses all the environmental impacts of aircraft
and aerodrome operations.

Subject coverage:
Environmental and amenity effects and impacts of
aviation.

**Museum or gallery collection, archive, or library
special collection:**
Environmental statements
Industry and government reports
Papers, journals
Planning inquiry documents

Trade and statistical information:
World data on the environmental performance of
the aviation industry.

Printed publications:
Annual Report
Newsletter (6 times a year)
Aviation and its Environmental Effects (Logan M,
1995, £5 plus 50p p&p)
Aviation, the Environment & Planning Law: An
AEF Handbook (Bingham A, Johnson T ed., 1995,
£20 plus £1 p&p)
The Development of Surface Access Links to
Airports: The Environmental Issues (Johnson T,
1997, £5 plus 50p p&p)
The Environmentalist Viewpoint (Logan M, 1997,
£5 plus 50p p&p)
Papers, briefings and reports

Publications list:
Available online and in print

Access to staff:
Contact by letter, by telephone, by fax, by e-mail
and via website. Appointment necessary. Non-
members charged.
Hours: Mon to Fri, 0930 to 1630

Access to building, collection or gallery:
Prior appointment required

Co-ordinator of:
Green Skies
tel: 020 7248 2223; e-mail: info@greenskies.org

Member of:
European Environment Bureau
Brussels, Belgium

AVON LOCAL HISTORY AND ARCHAEOLOGY

Acronym or abbreviation: ALHA

5 Parrys Grove, Bristol, BS9 1TT

Tel: 0117 968 4979
Fax: 0117 968 4979
E-mail: william.evans@uwe.ac.uk

Website:
http://www.jonathanalha.pwp.blueyonder.co.uk
Activities, and contacts of member groups and
societies

Enquiries:
Enquiries to: Honorary Secretary
Other contacts: Treasurer

Founded:
1976

Organisation type and purpose:
Membership association.
County local history liaison.
Promotion of local history in the region and a co-
ordinating forum.

Subject coverage:
Local history in Avon (Bristol and Bath) area;
especially contacts and club collections.

Printed publications:
Newsletter (quarterly, annual subscription £5)

Publications list:
Available in print

Access to staff:
Contact by letter, by telephone, by fax and by e-
mail

Links with:
some 80 affiliated groups and societies

AVON PARK INTERNATIONAL RACING ASSOCIATION

Acronym or abbreviation: APIRA

The Annex, Half Moon Farm, Rushall, Diss,
Norfolk, IP21 4QD

Tel: 01379 740100
Fax: 01379 740100
E-mail: wendy@apira.org.uk

Website:
http://www.shakespearecountyraceway.com
Race dates, contacts, information on the area, news
updates.

Enquiries:
Enquiries to: General Secretary
Direct fax: 01789 252030
Direct e-mail: wendy@shakespearecountyraceway
.org.uk
Other contacts: Events Information and Race-
Meetings Secretary; Membership Secretary

Founded:
1990

Formerly called:
NDRC-NDRA

Organisation type and purpose:
International organisation, membership
association (membership is by subscription),
present number of members: 350
Motor sports racing organisation for drag racing.

Subject coverage:
Drag car racing covered by the Motorsport
Association and the Auto Cycle Union.

Printed publications:
Newsletters (website)
Order printed publications from: LA Performance
Services
60 Berry Road, Paignton, Devon, TQ3 3QJ, tel:
01803 554308, e-mail: la.racing@virgin.net

Publications list:
Available online

Access to staff:
Contact by letter, by telephone, by fax, by e-mail,
in person and via website. Letter of introduction
required.
Hours: Mon to Fri, 0900 to 1700

Access to building, collection or gallery:
No prior appointment required
Hours: Racing commences 1000 to 1800

Access for disabled people:
Parking provided, level entry, access to all public
areas, toilet facilities
Special comments: Viewing ramp for disabled
wheelchair persons and their carers.

Affiliated to:
Auto Cycle Union
ACU House, Wood Street, Rugby, Warwickshire,
CV21 2YX; tel: 01788 566400; fax: 01788 573585;
website: http://www.acu.org.uk
The Motor Sports Association (MSA)
Motor Sports House, Riverside Park, Colnbrook,
Slough, Berkshire, SL3 0HG; tel: 01753 681736;
fax: 01753 682936; website: http://www.msauk
.org

Track Owner:
Avon Park International Racing Association
Airfield House, Long Marston, Stratford Upon
Avon, Warwickshire, CV37 8LL; tel: 01789
414119; fax: 01789 262030; website: http://www
.shakespearecountyraceway.org.uk

AWDURDOD PARC CENEDLAETHOL ERYRI / SNOWDONIA NATIONAL PARK AUTHORITY

Acronym or abbreviation: APCE / SNPA

Swyddfa'r Parc Cenedlaethol, Penrhyndeudraeth, Gwynedd, LL48 6LF

Tel: 01766 770274
Fax: 01766 771211
E-mail: parc@eryri-npa.gov.uk

Website:
http://www.eryri-npa.gov.uk

Founded:
1951

Organisation type and purpose:
Local government body.

Subject coverage:
Farming; woodland management; ecology; planning; visitor services; conservation; demography; education; agriculture.

Printed publications:
Maps, guides, walking routes

Microform publications:
Photographs

Access to staff:
Contact by letter, by telephone, by fax, by e-mail and via website
Hours: Mon to Fri, 0900 to 1700

Access for disabled people:
Parking provided, level entry, toilet facilities

AXIS

Formal name: Axis – for information on Visual Artists

Round Foundry Media Centre, Foundry Street, Leeds, LS11 5QP

Tel: 0845 362 8230
Fax: 0845 362 8231
E-mail: info@axisweb.org

Website:
http://www.axisartists.org.uk
Includes a description of Axis, the Axis Database, how to join, how to use Axis, exhibitions of artists, list of all artists on the database, Axis CD-ROMS, Axis points around the UK and Axis future plans.

Enquiries:
Enquiries to: Communications Manager
Direct e-mail: kara@axisweb.org

Founded:
1991

Formerly called:
Axis – visual arts information service

Organisation type and purpose:
International organisation, registered charity (charity number 10022841).
Arts Information Service. Visual information service, on-line gallery.
Axis is a contemporary visual arts service that provides information about artists and crafts people living/working in Britain to a national and international audience.

Subject coverage:
National Artists' Register, visual arts information service. On-line gallery.

Trade and statistical information:
National database of contemporary visual artists and makers.

Non-library collection catalogue:
All or part available online

Printed publications:
Axis leaflets, free
Axisnotes (newsletter, free to artists)

Electronic and video publications:
ACE Arts Council Collection Acquisitions 1989 – 1995 (CD-ROM)

Axis database on CD-ROM 1999
Range of CD-ROMS of artists on Axis Database 1998

Access to staff:
Contact by letter, by telephone, by fax, by e-mail, in person and via website. Appointment necessary.
Hours: Mon to Fri, 0900 to 1700

Access to building, collection or gallery:
No prior appointment required
Hours: Mon to Thu, 0900 to 1600

AXREM

Formal name: Association of Healthcare Technology Providers for Imaging, Radiotherapy and Care
Acronym or abbreviation: AXrEM

Broadwall House, 21 Broadwall, London, SE1 9PL

Tel: 020 7207 9660
Fax: 020 7642 8096
E-mail: peter.lawson@axrem.org.uk

Website:
http://www.axrem.org.uk/

Enquiries:
Enquiries to: Director

Organisation type and purpose:
Trade association.

Subject coverage:
Commerce and technology of the medical diagnostic imaging and radio-therapy equipment.

AYRSHIRE CATTLE SOCIETY OF GREAT BRITAIN AND IRELAND

17 Barns Street, Ayr, Scotland, KA7 1XB

Tel: 01292 267123
Fax: 01292 611973
E-mail: society@ayrshirescs.org

Website:
http://www.ayrshirescs.org/
Details of services and breed.

Enquiries:
Enquiries to: General Manager

Founded:
1877

Organisation type and purpose:
International organisation, advisory body, membership association (membership is by subscription), present number of members: 1000, registered charity (charity number SC007015). Breed Society.

Subject coverage:
Ayrshire cattle breeding and pedigrees; production records; linear type evaluations; AI use with Ayrshire cattle; livestock pedigree record systems.

Museum or gallery collection, archive, or library special collection:
books, microfilm and tape journals since 1923
Herd books since 1877

Printed publications:
Herd Directory (2 yearly)
Ayrshire Journal (April and September)

Access to staff:
Contact by letter, by telephone, by fax, by e-mail and via website. Appointment necessary.
Hours: Mon to Fri, 0900 to 1700

Affiliated to:
World Federation of Ayrshire Breed Societies

BA, THE

Formal name: British Association for the Advancement of Science

Wellcome Wolfson Building, 165 Queen's Gate, London, SW7 5HE

Tel: 0870 770 7101
Fax: 0870 770 7102

E-mail: info@the-ba.net

Website:
http://www.the-ba.net
Description of the British Association and its key projects, including young people's activities, extensive information about all activities, searchable database.

Enquiries:
Enquiries to: Chief Executive
Other contacts: (1) Membership Department (2) Young Peoples Programme Officer for (1) Membership enquiries (2) Schools enquiries.

Founded:
1831

Organisation type and purpose:
National organisation, membership association, present number of members: 3500, voluntary organisation, registered charity (charity number 212479), suitable for ages: 8+ 12+ 16+. The UK's nationwide, open membership organisation dedicated to connecting science with people, so that science and its applications become accessible to all. The BA aims to promote openness about science in society and to engage and inspire people directly with science and technology and their implications. Established in 1831, the BA organises major initiatives across the UK, including the annual BA Festival of Science, National Science Week, programmes of regional and local events, and an extensive programme for young people in schools and colleges.

Subject coverage:
Public understanding awareness and appreciation of science and technology, science education and promotion, sections cover agriculture and forestry, anthropology and archaeology, biological sciences, chemistry; economics, engineering, education, geography, geology, history of science, mathematics, medical sciences, physics, psychology and sociology.

Printed publications:
Annual Report
Information packs for school science clubs
BAnter (member's newsletter, monthly for members)
Science and Public Affairs (4 times a year, for members and subscribers)

Publications list:
Available in print

Access to staff:
Contact by letter, by telephone, by fax and by e-mail. Appointment necessary.
Hours: Mon to Fri, 0930 to 1700

Access to building, collection or gallery:
No access other than to staff

Has:
33 branches throughout the UK

Parent body:
The British Association
at the same address

BACH CHOIR, THE

33 Upham Park Road, London, W4 1PQ

Tel: 020 8742 3661
Fax: 020 8742 3661
E-mail: genman@thebachchoir.org.uk

Website:
http://www.thebachchoir.org.uk
Information about the choir, concerts, booking information, how to join, etc.

Enquiries:
Enquiries to: General Manager

Founded:
1876

Organisation type and purpose:
Membership association (membership is by subscription, qualification), present number of members: 250, registered charity (charity number 238287).

Choral Society.

Subject coverage:
The performance of choral music.

Access to staff:
Contact by letter, by telephone, by fax and by e-mail. Appointment necessary. Letter of introduction required.
Hours: Mon to Fri, 0900 to 1700

BACKCARE

16 Elmtree Road, Teddington, Middlesex, TW11 8ST

Tel: 020 8977 5474\Helpline: 0845 130 2704
Fax: 020 8943 5318
E-mail: info@backcare.org.uk

Website:
http://www.backcare.org.uk

Enquiries:
Enquiries to: Communications Manager

Founded:
1968

Formerly called:
Back Pain Association (BPA); National Back Pain Association (NBPA) (year of change 1999)

Organisation type and purpose:
Advisory body, membership association, voluntary organisation, registered charity (charity number 256751).
Charity dedicated to educating people on how to avoid preventable back pain, and supporting those living with back pain.
Research.

Subject coverage:
Back pain, encouragement of research into causes and treatment, prevention of damage by proper use of the body, formation of branches to inform and aid people with back pain.

Printed publications:
Annual Report
Training, advisory and educational publications including:
Advisory posters
Better Backs for Children
Information Packs
Manual Handling: an ergonomic approach
Talkback (magazine, quarterly, free to supporters)
The Handling of Patients (guide for health professionals, 4th ed.)

Electronic and video publications:
Fighting Back (video, £15.99)
Catering for Lifters (training video, £24.95)

Publications list:
Available online and in print

Access to staff:
Contact by letter, by telephone, by fax, by e-mail and via website
Hours: Mon to Fri, 0900 to 1700

BACKPACKERS CLUB

49 Lyndhurst Road, Exmouth, Devon, EX8 3DS

Tel: 01395 265159
E-mail: wjbeed@genie.co.uk

Website:
http://www.catan.demon.co.uk/backpack/
Club information.

Enquiries:
Enquiries to: General Secretary

Founded:
1972

Organisation type and purpose:
National organisation, membership association (membership is by subscription).
Leisure, camping club.

Subject coverage:
Specialist organisation for lightweight camping, catering for walkers, cyclists and canoeists (national/international).

Museum or gallery collection, archive, or library special collection:
Extensive Club Library of camping books and walking guides

Library catalogue:
All or part available in-house

Printed publications:
Backpack (magazine, quarterly, members)
Camp Site Directories, Farm and Long Distance Paths (members only)

Electronic and video publications:
Camp Site Directories, Farm and Long Distance Paths (members only)

Access to staff:
Contact by letter and by telephone
Hours: Mon to Fri, 0900 to 1700 and answerphone

BACTA

Formal name: British Amusement Catering Trades Association

Bacta House, Regent's Wharf, 6 All Saints Street, London, N1 9RQ

Tel: 020 7713 7144
Fax: 020 7713 0446
E-mail: sgreenman@bacta.org.uk

Enquiries:
Enquiries to: Public Relations Manager
Direct tel: 020 7841 3234

Founded:
1974

Organisation type and purpose:
Trade association.
Represents Britain's pay-to-play leisure machines industry.

Subject coverage:
Manufacture and operation of coin-operated leisure machines.

Trade and statistical information:
Data on pay-to-play leisure machines.

Printed publications:
Amusing Britain
Booklet on the industry
Guide to the Gaming Act 1968 (updated periodically)
History of BACTA

Access to staff:
Contact by letter, by telephone, by fax and by e-mail
Hours: Mon to Fri, 0900 to 1700

Access to building, collection or gallery:
No prior appointment required

Links with:
Euromat
National Amusements Council

BACUP NATURAL HISTORY SOCIETY

Acronym or abbreviation: BACUP 'NAT'

24 Yorkshire Street, Bacup, Lancashire, OL13 9AE

Enquiries:
Enquiries to: General Secretary
Direct tel: 01706 873042
Other contacts: Museum Curator, Tel: 01706 873961

Founded:
1878

Organisation type and purpose:
Learned society (membership is by subscription), present number of members: 70, voluntary organisation, registered charity, museum.

Subject coverage:
Natural history – flora, fauna, fossils, local history and domestic bygones.

Museum or gallery collection, archive, or library special collection:
Library of over 2000 books
Copies of Bacup newspapers from 1863
Some 4000 photographs of old Bacup and its mills, houses, farms, churches, public houses etc

Non-library collection catalogue:
All or part available in-house

Library catalogue:
All or part available in-house

Printed publications:
Nat, snap and whit – 125 years of the Nat (£1.95)

Access to staff:
Contact by letter and in person
Hours: Mon to Fri, 0900 to 1700

Has a section:
Bacup Camera Club
at the same address

BADMINTON ENGLAND

Formal name: Badminton Association of England Ltd

National Badminton Centre, Bradwell Road, Loughton Lodge, Milton Keynes, Buckinghamshire, MK8 9LA

Tel: 01908 268400
Fax: 01908 268412
E-mail: enquiries@badmintonengland.co.uk

Website:
http://www.badmintonengland.co.uk
General information and contacts.

Enquiries:
Other contacts: Press Officer

Founded:
1893

Organisation type and purpose:
Professional body.
Governing body of the sport of badminton in England.

Subject coverage:
Badminton: rules-regulations, courts, lighting, playing facilities, shuttles, coaching, events, championships, players, general information.

Museum or gallery collection, archive, or library special collection:
A number of historic books on badminton

Printed publications:
Badminton (magazine 4 times a year)
BADMINTON England Handbook (annually)
Power & Precision (coaching magazine)
The Diary (annually)
The Laws (annually)

Electronic and video publications:
Videos, DVDs

Publications list:
Available online and in print

Access to staff:
Contact by letter, by telephone, by fax, by e-mail and in person. Appointment necessary.
Hours: Mon to Thu, 0900 to 1700; Fri, 0900 to 1530

Affiliated to:
British Olympic Association
Central Council of Physical Recreation
Commonwealth Games Council
European Badminton Union
    tel: + 49 2151 503020; fax: + 49 2151 503111; e-mail: ebu.gen.sec@t-online.de
International Badminton Federation
    tel: 00603 92837 155; e-mail: info@intbadfed.org
Sport England

BADMINTONSCOTLAND

Formal name: Scottish Badminton Union Ltd

The Cockburn Centre, 40 Bogmoor Place, Glasgow, G51 4TQ

Tel: 0141 445 1218
Fax: 0141 425 1218
E-mail: enquiries@badmintonscotland.org.uk

Website:
http://www.badmintonscotland.org.uk
All about badminton in Scotland.

Founded:
1911

Organisation type and purpose:
Governing body of the sport of badminton in Scotland.

Printed publications:
Scottish Badminton (4 times a year, £6 a year)

Access to staff:
Contact by letter, by telephone, by e-mail and via website
Hours: Mon to Fri, 0900 to 1700

Access to building, collection or gallery:
Prior appointment required

BAE SYSTEMS

Advanced Technology Centre, West Hanningfield Road, Great Baddow, Chelmsford, Essex, CM2 8HN

Tel: 01245 473331
Fax: 01245 242388
E-mail: arthur.jones@baesystems.com

Enquiries:
Enquiries to: Senior Information Officer
Direct tel: 01245 242394
Direct e-mail: baddow.library@baesystems.com

Formerly called:
GEC Marconi Research Centre, Marconi Research Centre

Organisation type and purpose:
Manufacturing industry, research organisation.

Subject coverage:
Electronics, communications, radar, avionics, antennas, microwave research, remote sensing, radio propagation.

Library catalogue:
All or part available in-house

Access to staff:
Contact by letter, by telephone, by fax and by e-mail
Hours: Mon to Fri, 0900 to 1600

Access to building, collection or gallery:
Prior appointment required

BAHA'I COMMUNITY OF THE UK

27 Rutland Gate, London, SW7 1PD

Tel: 020 7584 2566
Fax: 020 7584 9402
E-mail: opi@bahai.org.uk

Website:
http://www.bahai.org.uk/
Information about the Baha'i faith and links to local communities.
http://www.bahai-publishing-trust.co.uk
Information about Baha'i publications.

Enquiries:
Enquiries to: National Public Information Officer
Direct tel: 020 7590 8785
Direct e-mail: carmel.momen@bahai.org.uk

Organisation type and purpose:
Registered charity (charity number 250851). Faith community.

Subject coverage:
Babi and Baha'i religions.

Printed publications:
UK Baha'i Review (3 times a year, £2 per issue, available direct)
Order printed publications from: The Manager, Baha'i Books UK
4 Station Approach, Oakham, Rutland, LE15 6QW, tel: 01572 722780 / 0800 092 4149, fax: 01572 724280, e-mail: reception@bahai-publishing-trust.co.uk

Electronic and video publications:
Audio-visual material

Publications list:
Available online and in print

Access to staff:
Contact by letter, by telephone, by fax, by e-mail, in person and via website. Appointment necessary.
Hours: Mon to Fri, 1000 to 1600

Access for disabled people:
Toilet facilities

National governing council and registered charity:
National Spiritual Assembly of the Baha'is of the UK
At the same address

BALINT SOCIETY

Tollgate Health Centre, 220 Tollgate Road, London, E6 5JS

Tel: 020 7439 9399
Fax: 020 7473 9388
E-mail: david.watt@gp-f84093.nhs.uk

Website:
http://www.balint.co.uk
Membership, FAQ, programme.

Enquiries:
Enquiries to: Honorary Secretary

Founded:
1969

Organisation type and purpose:
Learned society, professional body, registered charity, training organisation, research organisation.

Subject coverage:
Research and education on the doctor-patient relationship.

Museum or gallery collection, archive, or library special collection:
Balint Archives

Printed publications:
Journal of the Balint Society

Access to staff:
Contact by letter, by telephone, by fax and by e-mail
Hours: Mon to Fri, 0900 to 1700

Associated with:
International Balint Federation

BALLIOL COLLEGE LIBRARY

Balliol College, Oxford, OX1 3BJ

Tel: 01865 277709
Fax: 01865 277803
E-mail: library@balliol.ox.ac.uk

Website:
http://www.balliol.ox.ac.uk/library

Enquiries:
Enquiries to: Librarian
Direct tel: 01865 277770

Founded:
1263

Organisation type and purpose:
College of University of Oxford

Subject coverage:
Information relating to collections.

Museum or gallery collection, archive, or library special collection:
Archives
Early printed books
Mediaeval manuscripts
Modern manuscripts
Special collections relating to history of Balliol and to former members

Non-library collection catalogue:
All or part available online, in-house and in print

Library catalogue:
All or part available online and in-house

Printed publications:
Catalogue of Jowett Papers

Microform publications:
Mediaeval manuscripts available from World Microfilms

Access to staff:
Contact by letter, by e-mail and via website. Appointment necessary.
Hours: Mon to Fri, 0900 to 1700

BALTIC EXCHANGE

38 St Mary Axe, London, EC3A 8BH

Tel: 020 7623 5501
Fax: 020 7369 1622
E-mail: enquiries@baltic exchange.co.uk

Website:
http://www.balticexchange.com
General information on the Baltic Exchange; specific market information for members only.

Enquiries:
Enquiries to: Chief Executive
Other contacts: Development Manager for membership, marketing, press and PR.

Founded:
1900

Organisation type and purpose:
International organisation, professional body, trade association, membership association (membership is by subscription), present number of members: 700 corporate.
Shipping Exchange.
To match bulk ships and bulk cargoes, and to buy and sell bulk vessels.

Subject coverage:
Shipping, including chartering, freight rates, sale and purchase of ships.

Trade and statistical information:
Four daily bulk shipping indices and daily market reports.

Printed publications:
Shipping (magazine, 6 times a year)

Access to staff:
Contact by letter, by telephone, by fax, by e-mail and via website. Appointment necessary.
Hours: Mon to Fri, 0900 to 1700

BANGOR UNIVERSITY – ARCHIVES DEPARTMENT

Bangor, Gwynedd, LL57 2DG, Cymru

Tel: 01248 382966
Fax: 01248 382979
E-mail: e.w.thomas@bangor.ac.uk

Website:
http://www.archiveshub.ac.uk
http://www.bangor.ac.uk/is/library/archives.html

Enquiries:
Enquiries to: Archivist

Founded:
1884

Organisation type and purpose:
University library.
Archives Department within University Library.

Subject coverage:
University of Wales, Bangor; North Wales –
history, people, topography; estate and family
papers from counties of Anglesey, Caernarfon,
Flint, Denbigh and Merioneth. Subject areas
include: literary, historical and antiquarian
manuscripts; industrial and business enterprises
records e.g. mines and quarries; records of
religious and educational bodies; records of
ownership of land and property; personal and
family archives; farming and agricultural records;
records of a political nature; genealogical records;
records of plantations in Jamaica and the West
Indies; hunting records.

Non-library collection catalogue:
All or part available in-house

Library catalogue:
All or part available online

Access to staff:
Contact by letter, by telephone, by fax, by e-mail
and in person
Hours: Mon to Fri, 0900 to 1300, 1400 to 1700

BANGOR UNIVERSITY – LIBRARY AND ARCHIVE SERVICE

Acronym or abbreviation: UWB

College Road, Bangor, Gwynedd, LL57 2DG

Tel: 01248 382981
Fax: 01248 382979
E-mail: library@bangor.ac.uk

Website:
http://www.bangor.ac.uk/library

Enquiries:
Enquiries to: Librarian
Direct tel: 01248 383772
Direct e-mail: g.griffiths@bangor.ac.uk
Other contacts: Library Secretary for departmental
secretary.

Formerly called:
Bangor University College of North Wales Library
(year of change 1997)

Organisation type and purpose:
University library.

Subject coverage:
Accountancy, banking, finance, administration and
social policy, environmental planning, leisure and
tourism, communication and media studies;
agriculture and forest studies, biological sciences,
chemistry; education, ITT – primary and
secondary; electronic engineering and computing
systems;
English and linguistics; health and physical
education; health and midwifery, radiography;
history, Welsh history, archaeology; mathematics;
modern languages (French, German, Spanish,
Russian, Italian); music; ocean studies; psychology;
sociology, social policy, criminology; theology and
religious studies; Welsh and Celtic language,
literature and traditions.

**Museum or gallery collection, archive, or library
special collection:**
Archive of Welsh Music
Bangor Cathedral Library (on deposit)
Frank Brangwyn Collection
G S Evans Collection of botanical materials
Local (North Wales) estate records
Welsh material (particularly historical, religious,
literary; printed and manuscript)

Non-library collection catalogue:
All or part available in-house

Access to staff:
Contact by letter, by fax, by e-mail and via
website. Appointment necessary.
Hours: Hours vary from library to library, please
phone or see web pages

Access to building, collection or gallery:
No prior appointment required

Other addresses:
Adeilad Deiniol Library
University of Wales, Bangor, Adeilad Deiniol,
Deiniol Road, Bangor, Gwynedd, LL57 2UX; tel:
01248 382963; fax: 01248 383826; e-mail: library@
bangor.ac.uk
Dean Street Library (School of Electronics)
University of Wales, Bangor, Dean Street,
Bangor, Gwynedd, LL57 1UT; tel: 01248 382986;
e-mail: library@bangor.ac.uk
Fron Heulog Library (School of Healthcare
Sciences)
University of Wales, Bangor, Ffriddoedd Road,
Bangor, Gwynedd, LL57 2EF; tel: 01248 383131;
e-mail: library@bangor.ac.uk
Normal Site Library
University of Wales, Bangor, Ffordd Caergybi,
Bangor, Gwynedd, LL57 2PX; tel: 01248 383048;
fax: 01248 383976; e-mail: library@bangor.ac.uk
Wolfson Library (School of Ocean Sciences)
School of Ocean Sciences, University of Wales,
Bangor, Askew Street, Menai Bridge, Anglesey,
LL59 5EY; tel: 01248 382985; e-mail: library@
bangor.ac.uk
Wrexham Maelor Library (School of Healthcare
Sciences)
School of Nursing and Midwifery Studies,
Archimedes Centre, Technology Park, Wrexham,
Clwyd, LL13 7YP; tel: 01978 316370; fax: 01978
311154; e-mail: library@bangor.ac.uk

BANK OF ENGLAND

Information Centre, Threadneedle Street, London,
EC2R 8AH

Tel: 020 7601 4846 or 4715
Fax: 020 7601 4356
E-mail: library@bankofengland.co.uk

Website:
http://www.bankofengland.co.uk/
General information about the Bank, press
releases, publications.

Enquiries:
Enquiries to: Information Centre Manager

Founded:
1694

Organisation type and purpose:
National government body.
Central bank.

Subject coverage:
UK and overseas banking and financial economics,
history of British banking, banking and monetary
statistical data, central banking.

**Museum or gallery collection, archive, or library
special collection:**
19th century government reports on banking and
finance
Acts of Parliament from 1693
Collections include United Kingdom 17th to 19th
century economic tracts
Sets include:
The Course of the Exchange (Castaing, Shergold,
Lutyens and Wetenhall) from 1698 to 1898

Printed publications:
Bank of England Discussion Papers
Bank of England Inflation Report
Bank of England Panel of Academic Consultants.
Papers (occasional)
Bank of England Quarterly Bulletin
Bank of England Report (annually)
Financial Stability Review
Practical Issues Arising from the Euro
Order printed publications from: Publications Group,
Bank of England
Threadneedle Street, London, EC2R 8AH, tel: 020
7601 4886

Electronic and video publications:
Magnetic tape service providing banking and
monetary statistical data, containing machine
readable data of longer runs and, in some cases,
more frequent observations and additional
details than published in the BoE Quarterly
Bulletin

Data available on website

Access to staff:
Appointment necessary.
Hours: Mon to Fri, 0930 to 1700
Special comments: Disabled access very restricted.

BANKRUPTCY ASSOCIATION

4 Johnson Close, Abraham Heights, Lancaster, LA1
5EU

Tel: 01539 469474
E-mail: mcqueen314@btinternet.com

Website:
http://www.theba.org.uk

Enquiries:
Enquiries to: Founder

Founded:
1983

Formerly called:
Association of Bankrupts (year of change 1991);
Bankruptcy Association of Great Britain and
Ireland (year of change 2000)

Organisation type and purpose:
Membership association (membership is by
subscription).
To provide advice and support to those who
experience bankruptcy and its long-term effects.

Subject coverage:
Insolvency in general, but particularly personal
bankruptcy, debt, liquidation and reform of
insolvency law.

Printed publications:
Newsletter (quarterly)
Bankruptcy Explained (£14.95)
Boom to Bust: The Great 1990s Slump (£12.95)
How to Settle Debts with Creditors (£9.95)
Saving the Family Home in Bankruptcy (£14.95)
Choosing the Correct Legal Format for Running a
Business (£14.95)

Publications list:
Available online and in print

Access to staff:
Contact by letter, by telephone, by e-mail and via
website. Appointment necessary. Access for
members only.
Special comments: Helpline for general enquiries:
Mon to Fri, 1230 to 1700

BAPTIST HISTORICAL SOCIETY

Acronym or abbreviation: BHS

Baptist House, PO Box 44, 129 Broadway, Didcot,
Oxfordshire, OX11 8RT

Tel: 01235 517700
Fax: 01235 517715
E-mail: stephen.bhs@dsl.pipex.com

Website:
http://www.baptisthistory.org.uk

Enquiries:
Enquiries to: Honorary Secretary

Founded:
1908

Organisation type and purpose:
Learned society (membership is by subscription),
present number of members: 550, registered
charity (charity number 271367).
Study and recording of Baptist Church history and
theology.

Subject coverage:
Baptist Church history and theology, including
original church records and published
bibliographies.

Printed publications:
Baptist Quarterly (journal, quarterly)

Publications list:
Available online and in print

continued overleaf

Access to staff:
Contact by letter, by telephone, by e-mail and via website
Hours: Mon to Fri, 0900 to 1700

Also at:
Angus Library
Regents Park College, Oxford, OX1 2LB; tel: 01865 288120; e-mail: angus.library@regents.ox .ac.uk
Honorary Secretary
Baptist Historical Society, 60 Strathmore Avenue, Hitchin, Hertfordshire, SG5 1ST; tel: 01462 431816; e-mail: stephen.bhs@dsl.pipex.com

BAPTIST UNION OF SCOTLAND

14 Aytoun Road, Glasgow, G41 5RT

Tel: 0141 423 6169
Fax: 0141 424 1422
E-mail: admin@scottishbaptist.org.uk

Website:
http://www.scottishbaptist.org.uk

Enquiries:
Enquiries to: General Secretary
Other contacts: Publications Secretary

Founded:
1869

Organisation type and purpose:
Voluntary organisation, registered charity (charity number SC 004960).
Church organisation.

Subject coverage:
Baptist Church life and organisation; current ministerial conditions and persons; denominational budget, policies, programmes and development.

Trade and statistical information:
Statistics of Baptist Churches in Scotland.

Printed publications:
Scottish Baptist Yearbook (directory of members' churches and reports of committees)

Publications list:
Available in print

Affiliated to:
Baptist World Alliance
European Baptist Federation
Evangelical Alliance
Fellowship of British Baptists

BAR ASSOCIATION FOR COMMERCE, FINANCE AND INDUSTRY, THE

Acronym or abbreviation: BACFI

PO Box 4352, Edlesborough, Dunstable, Bedfordshire, LU6 9EF

Tel: 01525 222244
E-mail: secretary@bacfi.org

Website:
http://www.bacfi.org/

Enquiries:
Enquiries to: Secretary

Organisation type and purpose:
Membership association (membership is by subscription).

BARBICAN LIBRARY

Barbican Centre, Silk Street, London, EC2Y 8DS

Tel: 020 7638 0569
Fax: 020 7638 2249
E-mail: barbicanlib@cityoflondon.gov.uk

Website:
http://www.cityoflondon.gov.uk/barbicanlibrary
Description of services, events and activities.
http://www.musicpreserved.org
Music Preserved.

Enquiries:
Enquiries to: Librarian

Founded:
1982

Organisation type and purpose:
Local government body, public library.

Subject coverage:
Marxism, London history, fine and performing arts, including art history, painting, sculpture, ceramics, photography, cinema, film and theatre, music, conservation and finance.

Museum or gallery collection, archive, or library special collection:
Crime fiction collection
Libraries of the Gilbert and Sullivan Society
Music Performance Research Centre (MPRC) studio of live performance recordings (audio and video) not available commercially, includes interviews with artists
The Society of Technical Analysts

Non-library collection catalogue:
All or part available online and in-house

Library catalogue:
All or part available online and in-house

Access to staff:
Contact by letter, by telephone, by fax, by e-mail and in person. Appointment necessary.
Hours: Mon, Wed, 0930 to 1730; Tue, Thu, 0930 to 1930; Fri, 0930 to 1400; Sat, 0930 to 1600

Access to building, collection or gallery:
No prior appointment required

Access for disabled people:
Parking provided, level entry, access to all public areas, CCTV Magnifier, Large and trackerball keyboards
Special comments: Stairlift to Music Library; Jaws and Zoom text available on some PCs.

Branch libraries:
City of London Libraries, Archives and Guildhall Art Gallery Dept
Guildhall Library, Aldermanbury, London; tel: 020 7332 1852

Parent body:
City of London
tel: 020 7332 1852

BARBOUR

Building B, Kingswood, Kings Ride, Ascot, Berkshire, SL5 8AS

Tel: 01344 884121
Fax: 01344 884845
E-mail: barbour-marketing@cmpi.biz

Website:
http://www.barbour.info

Enquiries:
Enquiries to: Marketing Executive
Direct tel: 01344 899385

Founded:
1947

Organisation type and purpose:
Publishing house.
Information providers.

Subject coverage:
Design, editorial and production of formulated technical product data, building and construction materials product information; electronic libraries on building design and health and safety.
Food safety, health and safety, environmental management, environmental health, trading standards.

Museum or gallery collection, archive, or library special collection:
Trade literature collection on building products and materials

Non-library collection catalogue:
All or part available online and in print

Library catalogue:
All or part available online and in print

Printed publications:
Barbour Compendium
Opus Building Services

Access to staff:
Contact by letter, by telephone, by fax, by e-mail and via website
Hours: Mon to Fri, 0900 to 1700

Access to building, collection or gallery:
Hours: Mon to Fri, 0900 to 1700

Access for disabled people:
Accessible
Hours: Mon to Fri, 0900 to 1700

Links with:
Barbour ABI
The Chapter House, Hinderton Hall Estate, Neston, Cheshire, CH64 7UX; tel: 0151 353 3500; fax: 0151 353 3501; e-mail: info@barbour-abi .com; website: http://www.barbour-abi.com

BARING FOUNDATION

60 London Wall, London, EC2M 5TQ

Tel: 020 7767 1348
Fax: 020 7767 7121
E-mail: baring.foundation@uk.ing.com

Website:
http://www.baringfoundation.org.uk

Enquiries:
Enquiries to: Administration Officer

Founded:
1969

Organisation type and purpose:
Registered charity (charity number 258583).
Grant-making charity.

Subject coverage:
Three grant programmes: Strengthening the Voluntary Sector Independence programme; Arts programme; International Development programme

Printed publications:
A full list of publications can be found on the website, or requested by e-mail

http://www.baringfoundation.org.uk/ publications.htm

Publications list:
Available online and in print

Access to staff:
Contact by letter, by telephone, by fax, by e-mail and via website
Hours: Mon to Fri, 0900 to 1700

Access for disabled people:
Access to all public areas, toilet facilities

BARKING AND DAGENHAM ADULT & COMMUNITY SERVICES DEPARTMENT

Central Library, Barking, Essex, IG11 8DQ

Tel: 020 8724 8723
Fax: 020 8724 8733
E-mail: reference@lbbd.gov.uk

Website:
http://www.lbbd.gov.uk/4-libraries/lib-menu.html

Enquiries:
Enquiries to: Librarian

Founded:
1888

Organisation type and purpose:
Local government body, public library.

Subject coverage:
Printing, journalism, publishing and newspapers, local history.
Fiction (Joint Fiction Reserve) B-BAI.

Museum or gallery collection, archive, or library special collection:
Fanshawe manuscripts and portraits

Non-library collection catalogue:
All or part available online and in-house

Library catalogue:
All or part available online and in-house

Publications list:
Available online and in print

Access to staff:
Contact by letter, by telephone, by fax, by e-mail, in person and via website. Appointment necessary.
Hours: Barking Library: Mon to Thu, 0900 to 2130; Fri, 0900 to 1900; Sat, 0900 to 1700; Sun, 1000 to 1600

Access to building, collection or gallery:
No prior appointment required

Access for disabled people:
Access to all public areas

Also at:
Local History Collection housed at Local Studies Centre, Valence House Museum
    Becontree Avenue, Dagenham, Essex, RM8 3HT; tel: 020 8270 6896
Valence Library
    Becontree Avenue, Dagenham, Essex, RM8 3HT; tel: 020 8270 6896

Parent body:
London Borough of Barking and Dagenham

BARNABAS TRUST

Freepost TN2186, Tonbridge, Kent, TN11 9BR

Tel: 01732 366766
Fax: 01732 366767
E-mail: headoffice@barnabas.org.uk

Website:
http://www.barnabas.org.uk

Enquiries:
Enquiries to: Chief Executive

Founded:
1978

Formerly called:
Belgrave Trust (year of change 1978)

Organisation type and purpose:
Registered charity (charity number 276346).

Subject coverage:
Holiday centres for groups of young people including church, secular and school.

Access to staff:
Contact by letter, by telephone, by fax, by e-mail and via website. Appointment necessary.
Hours: Mon to Fri, 0900 to 1700

BARNARDO'S

Tanners Lane, Barkingside, Ilford, Essex, IG6 1QG

Tel: 020 8550 8822
Fax: 020 8551 6870

Website:
http://www.barnardos.co.uk

Enquiries:
Enquiries to: Information Officer
Direct tel: 020 8498 7556
Direct e-mail: barninfo@compuserve.com
Other contacts: Librarian

Founded:
1867

Formerly called:
Dr Barnardo's (year of change 1988)

Organisation type and purpose:
Voluntary organisation, registered charity (charity number 216250).
Child care organisation.

To help the most vulnerable children and young people transform their lives and fulfil their potential.

Subject coverage:
Social welfare policy and practice. Child care, social services with families, neighbourhoods and communities.

Museum or gallery collection, archive, or library special collection:
Archives, dating from 1860s (held by Liverpool University, restricted access)
Films, dating from 1920s
History of Barnardo's
Photographs, dating from 1874 (estimated 500,000)

Printed publications:
Annual Review
Barnardo's Today (twice a year)
Library Bulletin (monthly)
Order printed publications from: Child Care Publications
Barnardo's Trading Estate, Paycocke Road, Basildon, Essex, SS14 3DR, tel: 01268 520224, fax: 01268 284804

Electronic and video publications:
Videos (large number)

Publications list:
Available in print

Access to staff:
Appointment necessary.
Hours: Mon to Fri, 0930 to 1630

Access for disabled people:
Parking provided, level entry, toilet facilities

BARNET AND DISTRICT LOCAL HISTORY SOCIETY

Barnet Museum, 31 Wood Street, Barnet, Hertfordshire, EN5 4BE

Tel: 020 8440 8066
E-mail: secretary@barnetmuseum.co.uk

Website:
http://www.barnetmuseum.co.uk

Enquiries:
Enquiries to: Honorary Secretary

Founded:
1927

Organisation type and purpose:
Learned society, voluntary organisation, museum.

Subject coverage:
Local history of Barnet and District, historical and archaeological records.

Museum or gallery collection, archive, or library special collection:
Books, documents, maps, costumes, exhibitions and artefacts relating to history of Barnet

Library catalogue:
All or part available in-house

Printed publications:
Bulletins (list available)
Educational materials
Newsletter (occasional)
A range of titles on local history including:
800 years of Barnet Market (Cobben J L and Willcocks D, 1999, £5)
Barnet and District Local History
Barnet at War (Reboul P and Heathfield J, £7.99 plus £1 p&p)
Historic Barnet, Gelder W
Monumental Inscriptions in Chipping Barnet Church (50p)
Monumental Inscriptions in East Barnet Church (50p)
The Book of Totteridge (Griffiths D, £10 plus 80p p&p)

Publications list:
Available in print

Access to staff:
Contact by letter and in person

Hours: Tue, Wed, Thu, 1430 to 1630; Sat, 1030 to 1230 and 1400 to 1600
Special comments: Donations appreciated

Affiliated to:
Hertfordshire Association for Local History
London and Middlesex Archaeological Society

BARNET LIBRARIES, MUSEUMS AND LOCAL STUDIES

Building 4, North London Business Park, Oakleigh Road South, London, N11 1NP

Tel: 020 8359 7774
E-mail: hendon.library@barnet.gov.uk

Website:
http://www.barnet.gov.uk/libraries
General description of services.
http://www.libraries.barnet.gov.uk
Library catalogue.

Enquiries:
Enquiries to: Reference Librarian, Hendon Library
Direct tel: 020 8359 2628
Direct fax: 020 8359 2885
Direct e-mail: hendon.library@barnet.gov.uk
Other contacts: Information and Heritage Manager for borough-wide reference and information services.

Founded:
1965

Organisation type and purpose:
Local government body, public library.

Subject coverage:
General, local studies.

Museum or gallery collection, archive, or library special collection:
Local history including the
C O Banks Collection on Finchley

Non-library collection catalogue:
All or part available online

Library catalogue:
All or part available in-house

Printed publications:
Various local history and local information publications

Publications list:
Available in print

Access to staff:
Contact by letter, by telephone, by fax, by e-mail and via website. Appointment necessary.
Hours: Mon to Fri, 0900 to 1700

BARNET LOCAL STUDIES & ARCHIVES CENTRE

Formal name: London Borough of Barnet Local Studies and Archives Centre

80 Daws Lane, London, NW7 4SL

Tel: 020 8359 3960
E-mail: library.archives@barnet.gov.uk

Website:
www.barnet.gov.uk/archives
Contact details and location, brief list of holdings, link to useful resources, entry to Barnet Image database.

Enquiries:
Enquiries to: Local Studies Manager
Other contacts: Heritage Officer; Local Studies Assistant

Founded:
1974

Organisation type and purpose:
Local government body.

Subject coverage:
Local history.

Information services:
Public computers with internet access.

continued overleaf

Special visitor services:
Arranged individually.

Education services:
Relevant work undertaken with local primary, secondary and further education establishments.

Services for disabled people:
Disabled access to all public facilities.

Museum or gallery collection, archive, or library special collection:
Local reference collections
Local archive/MSS collections
Photographic and maps collections

Non-library collection catalogue:
All or part available online and in-house

Library catalogue:
All or part available online and in-house

Access to staff:
Contact by letter, by telephone, by e-mail and in person. Appointment necessary.
Hours: Tue, Wed, Fri, 0930 to 1630; Thu, 1300 to 1900; first and third Sat of each month, 0930 to 1630

Access to building, collection or gallery:
Prior appointment required
Special comments: Fully accessible, sited on ground floor.

Access for disabled people:
Low level ramp to entry; all public areas on ground floor and accessible

BARNETT RESEARCH CENTRE AT TOYNBEE HALL

Formal name: Toynbee Hall

28 Commercial Street, London, E1 6LS

Tel: 020 7392 2939
Fax: 020 7377 5964
E-mail: info@toynbeehall.org.uk

Website:
http://www.toynbeehall.org.uk
History of organisation; description of services; details of events; news page; message board.

Enquiries:
Enquiries to: Librarian/Archivist
Direct tel: 020 7392 2939
Direct e-mail: barnettresearchcentre@toynbeehall.org.uk

Founded:
1884

Organisation type and purpose:
Voluntary organisation.

Museum or gallery collection, archive, or library special collection:
Specialist library on the history of social policy and welfare, archives of Toynbee Hall

Non-library collection catalogue:
All or part available online and in-house

Library catalogue:
All or part available in-house

Printed publications:
Annual Report
Magazine (2 times a year)
The Toynbee Journal (onnline)

Electronic and video publications:
Photographs, oral history collection

Access to staff:
Contact by letter, by telephone, by e-mail, in person and via website. Appointment necessary.
Hours: Tues to Thurs, 0930 to 1630

Access to building, collection or gallery:
No appointment required, but we welcome enquiries in advance of visits

BARNSLEY ARCHIVE AND LOCAL STUDIES DEPARTMENT

Central Library, Shambles Street, Barnsley, South Yorkshire, S70 2JF

Tel: 01226 773950
Fax: 01226 773955
E-mail: archives@barnsley.gov.uk

Website:
http://www.barnsley.gov.uk/educat/libraries/index.html

Enquiries:
Enquiries to: Archives and Local Studies Officer
Other contacts: Local Studies Librarian (for local studies enquiries)

Organisation type and purpose:
Local government body.

Subject coverage:
Relating to Barnsley Metropolitan Borough Council.

Museum or gallery collection, archive, or library special collection:
Census enumeration returns (microfilm or microfiche)
IGI for northern counties of England and Ireland
GRO Index for births, marriages and deaths
Local newspapers (mainly on microfilm)
Local publications such as annual reports and newsletters of organisations, church magazines, council minutes
Parish register copies (printed or microfilm)
Deeds, wills, estate papers
Local photographs and maps

Non-library collection catalogue:
All or part available online, in-house and in print

Library catalogue:
All or part available in-house

Printed publications:
The Family History Handbook (new publication this year)
Family History Starter Pack (£5.00)

Publications list:
Available online and in print

Access to staff:
Contact by letter, by telephone, by fax, by e-mail, in person and via website

Access to building, collection or gallery:
Hours: Mon, 0930 to 1300 and 1400 to 1700; Tue, Thu and Fri, 0930 to 1300 and 1400 to 1730; Wed, 0930 to 1300 and 1400 to 1800; Sat, 0930 to 1300

BARNSLEY CHAMBER OF COMMERCE AND INDUSTRY

Acronym or abbreviation: BCCI

Business Innovation Centre, Innovation Way, Wilthorpe, Barnsley, South Yorkshire, S75 1JL

Tel: 01226 217770
Fax: 01226 215729
E-mail: info@barnsleychamber.co.uk

Enquiries:
Enquiries to: Chief Executive

Founded:
1882

Organisation type and purpose:
Membership association (membership is by subscription), present number of members: 800, service industry.
Chamber of Commerce.

Subject coverage:
Policy, representation, export service, debt recovery, general business advice.

Trade and statistical information:
Trade surveys.

Publications list:
Available in print

Access to staff:
Contact by letter, by telephone, by fax, by e-mail and in person
Hours: Mon to Fri, 0900 to 1700

Access for disabled people:
Parking provided, ramped entry, level entry, toilet facilities

BARNSLEY METROPOLITAN BOROUGH COUNCIL

Town Hall, Barnsley, South Yorkshire, S70 2TA

Tel: 01226 770770
Fax: 01226 773099
E-mail: townhall@barnsley.gov.uk

Website:
http://www.barnsley.gov.uk
Pages on economic development, tourism, newsline, events, best value.

Enquiries:
Enquiries to: Chief Executive

Founded:
1974

Organisation type and purpose:
Local government body.

Subject coverage:
Local government services provided to 227,000 citizens covering education, housing, social services, planning, highways, economic development and training.

Printed publications:
Order printed publications from: Public Relations officer
at the same address, tel: 01226 773400, fax: 01226 773399

Access to staff:
Contact by letter, by telephone, by fax, by e-mail, in person and via website
Hours: Mon to Fri, 0900 to 1700

Access for disabled people:
Ramped entry

BARNSLEY METROPOLITAN BOROUGH LIBRARY SERVICES

Central Library, Shambles Street, Barnsley, South Yorkshire, S70 2JF

Tel: 01226 773930
Fax: 01226 773955
E-mail: librarian@barnsley.gov.uk

Website:
http://www.barnsley.gov.uk/service/libraries/index.asp

Enquiries:
Enquiries to: Librarian
Direct tel: 01226 773926

Organisation type and purpose:
Public library.

Subject coverage:
General; local studies and archives (historical and other information on the Barnsley Metropolitan District).

Museum or gallery collection, archive, or library special collection:
Barnsley Archive Collection
Barnsley Local History Collection
Dransfield Collection (local history of Penistone)

Printed publications:
Local Societies' List
Speakers' List
Translators' List
Variety of reading lists

Access to staff:
Contact by letter, by telephone, by fax, by e-mail and in person
Hours: Mon, Wed, 0930 to 1900; Tues, Fri, 0930 to 1730; Sat, 0930 to 1600 for Central Library

Special comments: Hours for specific departments vary.

Access for disabled people:
Level entry, access to all public areas, toilet facilities

Parent body:
Barnsley Metropolitan Borough Council

BARWICK-IN-ELMET HISTORICAL SOCIETY

G. Thornton (Chairman), 8 Richmondfield Lane, Barwick-in-Elmet, Leeds, LS15 4EZ

Tel: 01132 812407
E-mail: hjsmith@claranet.co.uk

Website:
http://www.barwickinelmethistoricalsociety.com
The society's site is devoted to the publication of the history of the Yorkshire parish of Barwick-in-Elmet.

Enquiries:
Enquiries to: Secretary
Direct tel: 01132 867341
Direct e-mail: gday63@googlemail.com

Founded:
1984

Organisation type and purpose:
Membership assocation, current mems: over 60. To record, research and publish on the history of this Yorkshire parish

Museum or gallery collection, archive, or library special collection:
The society has a resource centre in Barwick-in-Elmet of a wide range of documents and photographs, mostly secondary copies.

Non-library collection catalogue:
All or part available in-house

Printed publications:
The Barwicker (quarterly journal)
Books:
Bygone Barwick
Pen Sketches of Barwick-in-Elmet
The Maypole Stayed Up
A Greater Wonder: A History of Methodism in the village
Barwick School: Education in a Yorkshire Village
Map of Barwick-in-Elmet (2000)
Brief History (2000)

Publications list:
Available online

Access to staff:
Contact by letter, by telephone, by e-mail and via website

BASEC

Formal name: British Approvals Service for Cables
Acronym or abbreviation: BASEC

23 Presley Way, Crownhill, Milton Keynes, Buckinghamshire, MK8 0ES

Tel: 01908 267300
Fax: 01908 267255
E-mail: mail@basec.org.uk

Website:
http://www.basec.org.uk
Cable certification.
http://www.env-basec.org.uk
Environmental certification.

Enquiries:
Enquiries to: Chief Executive

Founded:
1971

Formerly called:
British Approvals Service for Electric Cables (BASEC)

Organisation type and purpose:
Service industry.

Certification Body.

Subject coverage:
ISO 9000 certification, cable, ancillary product, instruments, installation, rod rolling, stockists; quality certification; product certification for cables; UK cable market certificate holders; new product assessment (cables). Environmental certification to ISO 14001 and/or EMAS. Certification of Health and Safety management systems to OHSAS 18001.

Museum or gallery collection, archive, or library special collection:
Worldwide ISO 9000 cable manufacturers listings

Printed publications:
List of Certificate Holders for Cables (certified product plus ISO 9000)

Access to staff:
Contact by letter, by telephone, by fax, by e-mail and via website
Hours: Mon to Thu, 0900 to 1700; Fri, 0900 to 1300

BASIC SKILLS AGENCY AT NIACE

Acronym or abbreviation: BSA at NIACE

21 DeMontfort Street, Leicester, LE1 7GE

Tel: 0116 204 4200
Fax: 0116 285 4515
E-mail: enquiries@niace.org.uk

Website:
http://archive.basic-skills.co.uk/aboutus

Enquiries:
Enquiries to: Information Officer
Other contacts: Director (Literacy, Language and Numeracy & Workplace)

Founded:
1975

Formerly called:
ALBSU; Basic Skills Agency (year of change 2008)

Organisation type and purpose:
The BSA became an independent charity with government support in 1990. The Agency's work was critical for developing a strategy for literacy, language and numeracy and a range of work in the schools sector. In the light of changing circumstances the BSA's board sought an effective partner to take forward its work with adults and young people. Following competition, NIACE, working with Tribal, was successful in offering a way forward. The BSA's work in Wales will be assimilated into the Welsh Assembly Government in line with Welsh Assembly policy.

Subject coverage:
Basic literacy (including English for speakers of other languages, ESOL), numeracy and related basic skills.

Trade and statistical information:
Data on the scale of need in England and Wales.

Printed publications:
Approximately 250 titles including:
Basic Skills Research
Basic Skills Resources, posters, books, teaching-packs
Magazine (quarterly, free)
Order printed publications from: Basic Skills Agency Prolog-UK, PO Box 5050, Sherwood Park, Annesly, Nottingham, NG15 0DL

Electronic and video publications:
Video and audio cassettes, computer software

Publications list:
Available online and in print

Access to staff:
Contact by letter, by telephone, by fax, by e-mail and via website
Hours: Mon to Fri, 0900 to 1730

Constituent part of:
NIACE
website: www.niace.org.uk

Links with:
Basic Skills Cymru
website: http://www.basic-skills-wales.org/bsastrategy/en/home/index.cfm
Tribal
website: http://www.tribalgroup.co.uk

BASILDON DISTRICT COUNCIL

The Basildon Centre, St Martin's Square, Basildon, Essex, SS14 1DL

Tel: 01268 533333
Fax: 01268 294350

Website:
http://www.basildondistrict.com

Enquiries:
Enquiries to: Public Relations Manager
Direct tel: 01268 294157
Direct fax: 01268 294148
Direct e-mail: marketingcommunications@basildon.gov.uk

Organisation type and purpose:
Local government body.

Subject coverage:
Detailed information about Basildon Council services and policies. General information about Basildon. The District Council is responsible for providing a wide range of services in a thriving district of 165,000 people. It is helping lead a significant set of partnerships to regenerate the area, the most important examples being: Community Safety, Thames Gateway, South Essex, and Gardener's Lane South.

Printed publications:
District Diary (council newspaper)
Miscellaneous information leaflets and lists
Press Releases

Access to staff:
Contact by letter, by telephone, by fax and by e-mail
Hours: Mon to Fri, 0900 to 1715

BASINGSTOKE AND DEANE BOROUGH COUNCIL

Civic Offices, London Road, Basingstoke, Hampshire, RG21 4AJ

Tel: 01256 844844
Fax: 01256 844707
E-mail: information@basingstoke.gov.uk

Website:
http://www.basingstoke.gov.uk
General information about the council, tourism and leisure, business information, local services, what's going on?

Enquiries:
Enquiries to: Head of Corporate Communications
Direct tel: 01256 845485
Direct e-mail: m.reid@basingstoke.gov.uk

Founded:
1974

Organisation type and purpose:
Local government body.

Subject coverage:
Local government including: environmental health, leisure, events, housing needs, planning, development, local plans, policy and committees, business development.

Printed publications:
General information leaflets on many subjects

Access to staff:
Contact by letter, by telephone, by fax, by e-mail, in person and via website
Hours: Mon to Thu, 0830 to 1700; Fri, 0830 to 1630

Access for disabled people:
Parking provided, ramped entry, level entry, toilet facilities

BASINGSTOKE COLLEGE OF TECHNOLOGY

Acronym or abbreviation: BCOT

Worting Road, Basingstoke, Hampshire, RG21 8TN

Tel: 01256 354141
Fax: 01256 306444
E-mail: information@bcot.ac.uk

Website:
http://www.bcot.ac.uk

Enquiries:
Enquiries to: Learning Resources Manager
Direct tel: 01256 306383
Direct e-mail: learning.resources@bcot.ac.uk

Organisation type and purpose:
College of further education.

Subject coverage:
General library to support GCSE A levels NVQs, BTEC, some HND and HNC. Engineering; building; business studies.

Access to staff:
Contact by letter, by telephone, by fax, by e-mail and in person
Hours: Term time: Mon to Thu, 0845 to 2100; Fri, 0845 to 1700; Sat closed
Vacations: Mon to Fri, 0845 to 1700; Sat closed

Associate college:
University of Portsmouth
Winston Churchill Avenue, Portsmouth, Hampshire, PO1 2UP

BASKETMAKERS' ASSOCIATION

Highlanes Farm, Brockton, Eccleshall, Staffordshire, ST21 6LY

Tel: 01630 620363
Fax: 01630 620363
E-mail: isobeledge@hotmail.com

Website:
http://www.basketassoc.org
General information, membership details, sales and course details.

Founded:
1975

Organisation type and purpose:
Membership association (membership is by subscription), present number of members: 1000–1200.
To promote the craft of basketmaking and chair seating.

Subject coverage:
All forms of basketry; willow work, cane work, rush work, coil work; hedgerow basketry; chair seating; straw work; growth and preparation of materials; history, tools, books and equipment, courses list nationwide (send large sae to publications sales).

Printed publications:
Newsletter (quarterly, members only)
Basketwork Through the Ages (Bobart H H, reprinted by the Basketmakers Association)
An Introduction to the Art of Basketmaking (Okey T, 1911, classic reprinted by the BA)
The Basketmakers List, Wage Rates and Specifications at 1956 (reprinted by the BA)
Order printed publications from: Sales, Basketmakers Association
216 Walton Road, East Molesey, Surrey, KT8 0HR

Electronic and video publications:
How To Make Round Baskets (video)
How to Make Oval Willow Baskets with Cross Handles (video)
Lowestoft Trawl (documentary video)
Devon Maund (documentary video)
Willow Class (documentary video)
George Chambers making a Porthleven Lobster Pot (video)
Colin Manthorpe making a Quarter Aran Herring Basket (video)

Access to staff:
Contact by letter, by telephone, by fax and by e-mail
Hours: Mon to Fri, 0900 to 1700

BAT CONSERVATION TRUST

Acronym or abbreviation: BCT

15 Cloisters House, 8 Battersea Park Road, London, SW8 4BG

Tel: 020 7627 2629
Fax: 020 7627 2628
E-mail: enquiries@bats.org.uk

Website:
http://www.bats.org.uk
Information about bats and the Bat Conservation Trust.

Enquiries:
Enquiries to: Chief Executive

Founded:
1991

Organisation type and purpose:
National organisation, membership association (membership is by subscription), present number of members: 4000, voluntary organisation, registered charity (charity number 1012361), training organisation, consultancy, research organisation.
BCT is the UK organisation solely devoted to the conservation of bats and their habitats through: conservation projects, research, supporting and educating people who find bats in their property, and encouraging appreciation of these animals.

Subject coverage:
Biology and conservation of bats.

Library catalogue:
All or part available in-house

Printed publications:
Bat News (newsletter, quarterly, free to BCT members)
Bats (leaflet, free with sae)

Publications list:
Available in print

Access to staff:
Contact by letter, by telephone, by fax, by e-mail and via website
Hours: Mon to Fri, 0900 to 1700

Umbrella group for:
over 90 voluntary bat groups in the UK

BATH AND NORTH EAST SOMERSET COUNCIL

Formal name: Bath and North East Somerset
Acronym or abbreviation: B&NES

Riverside, Temple Street, Keynsham, Somerset, BS31 1CA

Tel: 01225 477000
E-mail: communications_marketing@bathnes.gov.uk

Website:
http://www.bathnes.gov.uk
General Council information on Bath and North East Somerset Council and surrounding areas.

Enquiries:
Enquiries to: Information and Publications Officer
Direct tel: 01225 477413
Direct fax: 01225 477499
Other contacts: Communications & Marketing Manager

Founded:
April 1996

Formed from:
Avon County Council, Bath City Council, Wansdyke District Council (year of change 1996)

Organisation type and purpose:
Local government body.

Local authority.
To provide local services.

Subject coverage:
Education, environmental health, economic development, housing, libraries, planning, roads, social services and many others.

Printed publications:
Annual Reports (free)
Bath and Beyond (free)
Council News (free)
Your Guide to Council Services (free)
Performance Plan
Order printed publications from: Information and Publicity Officer, Bath and North East Somerset Council
Guildhall, High Street, Bath, Somerset, BA1 5AW, e-mail: juliet_williams@bathnes.gov.uk

Access to staff:
Contact by letter, by telephone, by fax, by e-mail and in person. Appointment necessary.
Hours: Mon to Thu, 0830 to 1700; Fri, 0830 to 1630

Access for disabled people:
Parking provided

Other addresses:
Guildhall
High Street, Bath, BA1 5AW; tel: 01225 477000
The Hollies
Midsomer, Wotton, BA3 2OP

BATH AND NORTH EAST SOMERSET RECORD OFFICE

Guildhall, High Street, Bath, BA1 5AW

Tel: 01225 477421
Fax: 01225 477439
E-mail: archives@bathnes.gov.uk

Website:
http://www.batharchives.co.uk
Introductory information, family history, house history and principal collections, leaflets and link to on-line catalogue.

Enquiries:
Enquiries to: Archivist

Formerly called:
Bath City Record Office (year of change 1996)

Organisation type and purpose:
Local government body.
Record office.

Subject coverage:
History of Bath and district.

Museum or gallery collection, archive, or library special collection:
Official records of the City of Bath from the 12th century
Records of local businesses, families and organisations
Collections of photographs, maps and plans

Non-library collection catalogue:
All or part available online and in-house

Access to staff:
Contact by letter, by telephone, by fax, by e-mail and in person
Hours: Tue to Thu, 0900 to 1300 and 1400 to 1700; Fri, 0900 to 1300 and 1400 to 1630

Access for disabled people:
By prior arrangement

BATH PRESERVATION TRUST

Acronym or abbreviation: BPT

No 1 Royal Crescent, Bath, BA1 2LR

Tel: 01225 338727
Fax: 01225 481850
E-mail: admin@bptrust.demon.co.uk

Website:
http://www.bath-preservation-trust.org.uk

Enquiries:
Enquiries to: Administrator
Other contacts: Director

Founded:
1934

Organisation type and purpose:
Membership association (membership is by
subscription), present number of members: 1070,
registered charity (charity number 203048).
Buildings preservation trust.

Subject coverage:
The trust exists to preserve the historic character
and amenities of Bath.

Printed publications:
Annual Report
Newsletter (annual)

Access to staff:
Contact by letter
Hours: Mon to Fri, 0900 to 1700

Access to building, collection or gallery:
Prior appointment required

BATH ROYAL LITERARY AND SCIENTIFIC INSTITUTION

16–18 Queen Square, Bath, Somerset, BA1 2HN

Tel: 01225 312084
Fax: 01225 442460
E-mail: admin@brlsi.org

Website:
http://www.brlsi.org

Enquiries:
Enquiries to: Administrator

Founded:
1824

Organisation type and purpose:
Membership organisation (membership by
donation/subscription).
Research institution, museum and library.

Subject coverage:
Literature, geology, natural history, archaeology,
fine art, photography, social history and local
history of Bath.

Museum or gallery collection, archive, or library special collection:
Library:
Rev. Leonard Jenyns Collection (science and
natural history)
Christopher Edmund Broome Collection (botany,
especially the lower plants, fungi and algae)
Parliamentary Collection
Libraries of the Bath Natural History and
Antiquarian Field Club and the Bath District of
the Somerset Archaeological and Natural
History Society
Geology:
Moore Collection (32 Plesiosaurs and
Ichthyosaurs)
William Lonsdale Collection (rocks and fossils)
Natural history:
Jenyns Herbarium of British Plants (3,000
specimens)
Broome Herbarium (6,600 British and European
specimens)
Shell Collection (17,000 specimens)
Other collections for archaeology, social history,
fine art, photography and archives

Non-library collection catalogue:
All or part available online and in-house

Access to staff:
Contact by letter, by telephone, by fax, by e-mail
and via website

BATH SPA UNIVERSITY

Library, Newton Park, Bath, BA2 9BN

Tel: 01225 875490
Fax: 01225 875493

Website:
http://www.bathspa.ac.uk/srvices/library/

Enquiries:
Enquiries to: Head of Library and Information
Services

Created by the merger of:
Bath College of Education (Home Economics),
Newton Park College and Bath Academy of Art

Organisation type and purpose:
The university is an accredited institution for the
award of its own degrees up to taught Masters
level.

Subject coverage:
Education (primary and secondary), English,
history, study of religions, environmental biology,
geography, creative arts, fine art, ceramics, graphic
design, social sciences, psychology, food
management, music, visual culture, health studies,
business studies, dance.

Library catalogue:
All or part available online

Access to staff:
Contact by letter and by telephone. Appointment
necessary. Non-members charged.
Hours: Mon to Fri, 0900 to 1700

Access for disabled people:
Level entry via ramp, lifts

Library is part of the:
UK Libraries Plus

BATHROOM MANUFACTURERS ASSOCIATION

Acronym or abbreviation: BMA

Federation House, Station Road, Stoke-on-Trent,
Staffordshire, ST4 2RT

Tel: 01782 747123
Fax: 01782 747161
E-mail: info@bathroom-association.org.uk

Website:
http://www.bathroom-association.org.uk

Enquiries:
Enquiries to: Commercial Director

Formerly called:
Council of British Ceramic Sanitaryware
Manufacturers (CBCSM) (year of change 1987);
British Bathroom Council (BBC) (year of change
1999); Bathroom Association (BA) (year of change
2001)

Organisation type and purpose:
Trade association.

Subject coverage:
Information on bathroom products sold in the UK,
including sanitaryware, baths, taps and showers,
and bathroom refurbishment.

Museum or gallery collection, archive, or library special collection:
Factsheets on bathroom refurbishment

Printed publications:
Factsheets (notes on bathroom design and
suppliers of equipment, sae 43p)

Access to staff:
Contact by letter, by fax, by e-mail and via
website
Hours: Mon to Fri, 0900 to 1700

BATTERSEA DOGS & CATS HOME

4 Battersea Park Road, London, SW8 4AA

Tel: 020 7622 3626
Fax: 020 7622 6451
E-mail: info@battersea.org.uk

Website:
http://www.battersea.org.uk

Features include online rehoming application
form, reporting of a lost dog or cat to our Lost
Dogs & Cats Line. Downloadable Battersea leaflets
and a selection of current canine and feline
residents.

Founded:
1860

Formerly called:
The Temporary Home for Lost & Starving Dogs;
The Dogs Home Battersea; Battersea Dogs Home
(year of change 2005)

Organisation type and purpose:
Registered charity (charity number 206394).
Animal rescue and rehoming.

Subject coverage:
Practical problems, help to owners of lost dogs and
cats, and subsequent rehoming of animals, advice
on pet ownership and behavioural problems.

Printed publications:
Annual Report
Lots of leaflets for new dog and cat owners and
advice for people thinking about taking on a dog
or cat (also downloadable from the website)
Paws Magazine (in-house supporter publication)
and Fantail (for supporters under the age of 16
years)

Publications list:
Available in print

Access to staff:
Contact by letter, by telephone, by fax, by e-mail,
in person and via website. Appointment necessary.
All charged.
Hours: Office hours

Access to building, collection or gallery:
at postal address
Hours: 24 hours, for stray dogs and cats only

Access for disabled people:
Hours: Opening hours

Also at:
Battersea Dogs & Cats Home
Crowhurst Lane, Ash, Kent; tel: 01474 874994
Battersea Dogs & Cats Home
Priest Hill, Old Windsor, Berkshire, SL4 2JN; tel:
01784 432989

Member organisation of:
Association of Dogs and Cats Homes

BATTERY VEHICLE SOCIETY

Acronym or abbreviation: BVS

Sorgwm, Cwmdu, Powys, NP8 1RT

Tel: 01874 730320
E-mail: battery@zetnet.co.uk

Website:
http://www.bvs.org.uk
Current Society activities and other relevant
activities.

Enquiries:
Enquiries to: Enquiries Officer
Other contacts: Secretary

Founded:
1973

Organisation type and purpose:
Learned society (membership is by subscription),
present number of members: 350, voluntary
organisation, research organisation.

Subject coverage:
Battery, hybrid and solar electric traction: technical,
commercial, recreational and historic aspects.

Museum or gallery collection, archive, or library special collection:
Books, periodicals, brochures, drawings, diagrams,
photographs

Trade and statistical information:
Data on the availability of battery-electric cars
and light commercials, and parts thereof.

continued overleaf

Printed publications:
Battery Car Conversions & Supplement
Battery Road Vehicles: Brief History
Battery Vehicle Review (6 times a year)
Serendipity (Competition Car)

Access to staff:
Contact by letter, by telephone and by e-mail
Hours: Mon to Fri, 0800 to 2200

Affiliated to:
Royal Automobile Club
Transport Trust

BBC HAYMARKET EXHIBITIONS LIMITED

2–14 Shortlands, London, W6 8DJ

Tel: 020 8267 8300
Fax: 020 8267 8350

Website:
http://www.haymarketgroup.com

Enquiries:
Enquiries to: Operations Director

Organisation type and purpose:
Exhibition organisers.

Subject coverage:
Organisation of consumer exhibitions.

Access to staff:
Contact by letter
Hours: Mon to Fri, 0930 to 1730

Connections with:
Haymarket Exhibitions Limited
 At the same address

BBC INFORMATION AND ARCHIVES

Acronym or abbreviation: BBC (I&A)

Unit 7, Ariel Way, London, W12 7SL

Website:
http://www.bbc.co.uk

Enquiries:
Enquiries to: Marketing Manager

Formerly called:
BBC Libraries and Archives

Organisation type and purpose:
National government body.
Broadcasting archive and information service.
Maintenance of the BBC's archives and provision
of a research service to support broadcasters and
programme-makers.

Subject coverage:
The subjects are covered by the extent of the
archive collections based on particular specialist
subject areas as well as unique information
research services and tools tailored to programme-
makers and researchers, such as negative name
checks, events and anniversaries lists, topical
pronunciation guides and quiz question checking.

**Museum or gallery collection, archive, or library
special collection:**
Document Archive: 570,000 files and rolls of
 microfilm
Music Archive: 1.2M commercial music recordings
 from the earliest sound recordings on wax
 cylinders up to the present, 4.5M items of sheet
 music ranging from mss arrangements to song
 copies, and from orchestral scores to vocal scores
 with an archive of compositions and
 arrangements, specially commissioned for the
 BBC since 1936
Picture Archive: 3M photo stills
Radio Sound Archive: 750,000 audio recordings
 going back to the 1880s, 25,000 individual sound
 effect recordings
Research Materials: 22.5M newspaper cuttings
 from the 1930s onwards; 500,000 phonetic
 pronunciations in any language of words and
 names of places, politicians, musicians, sports
 personalities etc; 160,000 books and periodicals

Television Archive: 1.5M items of film and
 videotape mainly from the 1930s onwards

Trade and statistical information:
The service deals with over 600,000 enquiries a
year and issues more than 900,000 items from the
archives a year.

Printed publications:
More information on BBC Information and
Archives can be found in the Handbook
available free of charge from the Commercial
Unit, Bush House

Publications list:
Available in print

Access to staff:
Contact by letter, by telephone, by fax and by e-
mail. Appointment necessary. All charged.
Hours: Mon to Fri, 0900 to 1700
Special comments: Access to some collections is
limited due to copyright, transmission, legal or
other restrictions.
All commercial licensing of audiovisual material
for re-use by non-BBC and overseas customers
must be arranged through BBC Worldwide Library
Sales on tel: 020 8576 8612, fax: 0020 8576 2939.
Any other copyright and contractual clearance of
materials issued by Information and Archives is
the responsibility of the customer. Please refer
specific queries to the research staff dealing with
the enquiry.

All non-BBC commercial research enquiries:
BBC Information and Archives
 Commercial Unit, Room LG29, Centre Block,
 Bush House, The Strand, London, WC2B 4PH;
 tel: 020 7557 2452; fax: 020 7557 2728

Main television and radio archive:
BBC Information and Archives
 Brentford

Other addresses:
BBC Information and Archives
 Television Centre, Wood Lane, London, W12 7RJ;
 tel: 020 8576 1540

Research Centre at:
BBC Information and Archives
 Room LG26, Centre Block, Bush House, The
 Strand, London, WC2B 4PH; tel: 020 7557 2154;
 fax: 020 7379 6588
BBC Information and Archives
 Room G067, Broadcasting House, Portland Place,
 London, W1A 1AA; tel: 020 7765 4850; fax: 020
 7765 2599
BBC Information and Archives
 Records and Programme Information Centre
 (Rapic), Unit 5, London, W12 7SL; tel: 020 8576
 8877; fax: 020 8746 2424

BBC MONITORING

Acronym or abbreviation: BBC

Caversham Park, Reading, Berkshire, RG4 8TZ

Tel: 0118 948 6289
Fax: 0118 946 3823
E-mail: marketing@mon.bbc.co.uk

Website:
http://www.monitor.bbc.co.uk

Enquiries:
Enquiries to: Marketing Department

Founded:
1939

Organisation type and purpose:
International organisation, publishing house.
Foreign Affairs news service compiled from
international news media monitoring.

Subject coverage:
Continually updated political and economic news
from more than 140 countries. Coverage includes
government policy, international relations, security
issues, globalisation, energy, trade, investment and
human rights.

Printed publications:
All former printed publications are now only
 available on electronic formats

Microform publications:
Microfiche and microfilm of the SWB publications
 can be purchased from UMI (USA) and
 Information Publications International Limited
 (UK)

Electronic and video publications:
Subscribers can choose from a variety of 'push' and
 'pull' formats
Global Newsline – daily news, available on
 different regions of the world, sent by email
International Reports – news service tailored to
 individual needs, sent by email
BBC Monitoring Online – searchable internet news
 database with email alerts, archive and reference
 materials
Additional specialist reports are available for
 Central Asia and the international broadcast
 industry

Publications list:
Available online

Access to staff:
Contact by letter, by telephone, by fax, by e-mail
and via website. All charged.
Hours: Open 24 hours; main office 0900 to 1730

Access to building, collection or gallery:
No access other than to staff

Connections with:
BBC World Service, BBC

BBC RESEARCH CENTRAL

Formal name: British Broadcasting Corporation

B116 Television Centre, Wood Lane, London, W12
7RJ

Tel: 020 7557 2452
Fax: 020 8576 7020
E-mail: research-central@bbc.co.uk

Website:
http://www.bbcresearchcentral.com

Founded:
1932

Organisation type and purpose:
Media.
International broadcaster.

Printed publications:
Anniversaries Lists (p.o.a.)
Future Events Lists (p.o.a.)
Chronology of the Gulf Crisis (pub. Longmans)

Access to staff:
Contact by telephone, by fax and by e-mail.
Appointment necessary. All charged.
Hours: Mon to Fri, 0930 to 1800

BBC SCOTLAND

40 Pacific Quay, Glasgow, G51 1DA

Tel: 0141 422 6000
E-mail: enquiries.scot@bbc.co.uk

Website:
http://www.bbc.co.uk/scotland/

Enquiries:
Enquiries to: Organiser, Library Services

Organisation type and purpose:
National government body.
Broadcasting organisation.

Subject coverage:
Information relevant to BBC Scotland broadcast
output, Scotland and related topics form the basis
of all collections.

**Museum or gallery collection, archive, or library
special collection:**
BBC Scotland radio broadcasts from 1949 onwards
 (tape and disc)

BBC Scotland TV broadcasts from 1952 onwards
(film and tape)
Scottish press cuttings from 1968 onwards
(microform)

Access to staff:
Contact by letter and by fax. All charged.
Hours: Mon to Fri, 0900 to 1700

Access to building, collection or gallery:
No access other than to staff

Access for disabled people:
Parking provided, level entry, toilet facilities
Special comments: Access to most areas

Also at the same address::
BBC Radio Scotland, BBC Alba, Radio nan
Gaidheal

BBC WALES

Acronym or abbreviation: BBC

Research & Archives, Ty Oldfield – MO28,
Llandaff, Cardiff, CF5 2YQ

Tel: 029 2032 3309
Fax: 029 2032 2798
E-mail: edith.hughes@bbc.co.uk

Website:
http://www.bbc.wales.com
General information on all departments.

Enquiries:
Enquiries to: Resource & Archive Manager

Founded:
1928

Organisation type and purpose:
National broadcaster.

Subject coverage:
TV film and videotape, radio productions, film
transfer servcice (fee payable).

**Museum or gallery collection, archive, or library
special collection:**
Film and TV archive
News cuttings
Radio Times – 1928 to the present
Sound archive
Stills collection

Electronic and video publications:
Hanes BBC Wales / BBC Wales: A History
(bilingual, CD-ROM)

Access to staff:
Contact by letter, by telephone, by fax and by e-
mail. Appointment necessary.
Hours: Mon to Fri, 0930 to 1730

BBC WRITTEN ARCHIVES CENTRE

Formal name: British Broadcasting Corporation
Acronym or abbreviation: BBC

Caversham Park, Reading, Berkshire, RG4 8TZ

Tel: 0118 948 6281
Fax: 0118 946 1145
E-mail: heritage@bbc.co.uk

Website:
http://www.bbc.co.uk/heritage
History of the BBC and information about the
archives.
http://www.bbc.co.uk/info/
General information and contacts for all aspects of
the BBC's work and programmes.

Founded:
1922

Organisation type and purpose:
International organisation.
Broadcasting organisation.

Subject coverage:
Correspondence, minutes of meetings, news
bulletins, scripts, press cuttings and other detailed
information relating to the whole of the BBC's
output, regional and national, at home and

overseas; papers relating to the history and
development of the BBC, including technical
development, from 1922, constitute a major source
for 20th-century social and political history,
biography, music, drama and the arts in the 20th
century, as well as broadcasting itself.

**Museum or gallery collection, archive, or library
special collection:**
Collection of press cuttings on all aspects of
broadcasting (1922–mid 1960s)
Complete sets of Radio Times from 1923
The Listener and all BBC Schools publications

Non-library collection catalogue:
All or part available in-house

Library catalogue:
All or part available in-house

Printed publications:
Order printed publications from: BBC Worldwide, 80
Wood Lane, London, W12 0TT; tel: 0870 600 7080

Access to staff:
Contact by letter, by telephone, by fax, by e-mail
and via website. Appointment necessary.
Hours: Mon to Fri, 0930 to 1730
Special comments: No loans.

Access to building, collection or gallery:
Prior appointment required
Hours: Wed to Fri, 0945 to 1700

Access for disabled people:
Parking provided, access to all public areas, toilet
facilities

BBC YOUNG MUSICIAN OF THE YEAR

Room 3223, White City, 201 Wood Lane, London,
W12 7TS

Tel: 020 8752 4212
Fax: 020 8752 4050
E-mail: young.musician@bbc.co.uk

Website:
http://www.bbc.co.uk/youngmusician

Enquiries:
Enquiries to: Artistic Administrator

Founded:
1978

Organisation type and purpose:
National organisation.
Music competition.

Subject coverage:
Competition for young classical musicians.

Access to staff:
Contact by letter, by telephone, by fax, by e-mail
and via website
Hours: Mon to Fri, 0900 to 1700

BEAFORD ARTS

Greenwarren House, Beaford, Winkleigh, Devon,
EX19 8DU

Tel: 01805 603201
Fax: 01805 603202
E-mail: lyn@beaford-arts.co.uk

Website:
http://www.beaford-arts.co.uk

Enquiries:
Enquiries to: Director
Direct tel: 01805 603734

Founded:
1972

Formerly called:
Beaford Archive, Beaford Photographic Archive

Organisation type and purpose:
Registered charity (charity number 279784).
Photographic Archive.

Subject coverage:
Old North Devon from 1850 to present day,
including all aspects of life from domestic to
industrial and from childhood to old age; images
of farming, transport, leisure, costume, trades and
crafts, landscapes and streetscapes.

**Museum or gallery collection, archive, or library
special collection:**
The Old Archive of 9000 negatives and prints of
images taken from the 1850s until World War II
and after
The New Archive, the lifetime's study of North
Devon by James Ravilious, 8300 negatives and
prints
Contemporary collection currently 4000 negatives
and prints

Printed publications:
Publicity Leaflet (free, 3 time year)

Access to staff:
Contact by letter, by telephone, by fax and by e-
mail. Appointment necessary.
Hours: Mon to Fri, 0900 to 1800

Access to building, collection or gallery:
Prior appointment required
Hours: Telephone for information on access to
library and archive.

Access for disabled people:
Toilet facilities
Special comments: Wheelchair access to archive

BEAT

Formal name: Eating Disorders Association
Acronym or abbreviation: BEAT

1st Floor, Wensum House, 103 Prince of Wales
Road, Norwich, Norfolk, NR1 1DW

Tel: 0870 770 3256
Fax: 01603 664915
E-mail: info@edauk.com

Website:
http://www.b-eat.co.uk

Enquiries:
Enquiries to: Information Officer
Direct tel: 0870 770 3221
Direct e-mail: media@edauk.com

Founded:
1989

Incorporates the former:
Anorexic Aid, Anorexic Family Aid

Organisation type and purpose:
Membership association (membership is by
subscription), present number of members: 3,200,
registered charity (charity number 801343).
Help and understanding for anorexia and bulimia.

Subject coverage:
Anorexia nervosa and bulimia nervosa; offers help,
understanding and support to people with an
eating disorder and their family and friends, and
provides education, training and research.

Printed publications:
European Eating Disorders Review (members £25,
non-members £45 every 3 months)
Signpost (free to members, non-members £1.50,
every 3 months)
Understand Anorexia & Bulimia Nervosa/Join Us
(pair of leaflets, also available in Welsh)

Publications list:
Available in print

Access to staff:
Contact by telephone, by e-mail and via website
Hours: Administration only: 0900 to 1700
Special comments: Youth Helpline: Mon to Fri, 1600
to 1800, 01603 765050
Adult Helpline: Mon to Fri, 0900 to 1830, 01603
621414.

BEAULIEU ARCHIVES

John Montagu Building, Beaulieu, Brockenhurst, Hampshire, SO42 7ZN

Tel: 01590 612345
Fax: 01590 612624
E-mail: info@beaulieu.co.uk

Website:
http://www.beaulieu.co.uk

Enquiries:
Enquiries to: Archivist

Founded:
1952

Organisation type and purpose:
Museum.
Montagu family & Beaulieu estate private archives.
Private estate and leisure destination.

Subject coverage:
Family of Lords Montagu of Beaulieu, Beaulieu Estate and Parish Buckler's Hard 18th century shipbuilding village, Beaulieu Abbey. Ditton Park Estate, Slough, Buckinghamshire.

Museum or gallery collection, archive, or library special collection:
Beaulieu History
Archive of the Montagu family

Non-library collection catalogue:
All or part available in-house

Printed publications:
Wheels Within Wheels: An Unconventional Life (Lord Montagu of Beaulieu)
An Album of Old Beaulieu & Buckler's Hard (Susan Tomkins)
Beaulieu: The Finishing School for Secret Agents (Cyril Cunningham)
Buckler's Hard guidebook
Buckler's Hard: a rural shipbuilding centre (A J Holland)
John Montagu of Beaulieu (Paul Tritton)
Palace House & Beaulieu Abbey (guidebook)
The Beaulieu Record (H E R Widnell)
all prices from Shop Manager
Order printed publications from: Shops Manager, Beaulieu Enterprises Limited
John Montagu Building, Beaulieu, Brockenhurst, Hampshire, SO42 7ZN, tel: 01590 614639, fax: 01590 612624, e-mail: info@beaulieu.co.uk

Access to staff:
Contact by letter, by telephone, by fax, by e-mail and via website. Appointment necessary.
Hours: Mon to Fri, 1000 to 1500

Access for disabled people:
Parking provided, ramped entry, toilet facilities
Special comments: Access to Archives by ramped entry and lift.

BEAUMONT SPECIALIST FABRICATIONS LIMITED

Woodlands Road, Mere, Wiltshire, BA12 6BT

Tel: 01747 860481
Fax: 01747 861076
E-mail: sales@beaumont-chimneys.co.uk

Website:
http://www.beaumont-chimneys.co.uk

Enquiries:
Enquiries to: Director

Founded:
2001

Formerly called:
Beaumont Chimneys (year of change 1949); F E Beaumont Limited (year of change 2001)

Organisation type and purpose:
Manufacturing industry.
Design, manufacturing, installation, inspection and maintenance of steel chimneys and associated items.

Subject coverage:
Steel chimneys, flue liners, flue ducting, aerodynamic stabiliser vanes, counterbalance dampers.

Printed publications:
General sales literature

Access to staff:
Contact by letter, by telephone and by fax
Hours: Mon to Thu, 0845 to 1700; Fri, 0845 to 1600

BEAVERBROOK FOUNDATION

11 Old Queen Street, London, SW1H 9JA

Tel: 020 7222 7474
Fax: 020 7222 2198

Website:
http://www.beaverbrookfoundation.org

Enquiries:
Enquiries to: Secretary

Organisation type and purpose:
Registered charity.

Access to staff:
Contact by letter
Hours: Mon to Fri, 0900 to 1700

BEDFORD CENTRAL LIBRARY

Harpur Street, Bedford, MK40 1PG

Tel: 01234 350931\ 01234 270102, Reference Library
Fax: 01234 342163
E-mail: via website

Website:
http://www.bedfordshire.gov.uk
Click on Libraries for Bedfordshire Libraries Virtual Library.

Enquiries:
Enquiries to: The Library Manager

Organisation type and purpose:
Local government body, public library.

Subject coverage:
Local community information, business information, local studies, family history, John Bunyan.

Museum or gallery collection, archive, or library special collection:
Bedford Old Library
Bedfordshire Local Studies Library
Fowler Collection
Frank Mott Harrison Collection (John Bunyan)
George Offor Collection
General Registrar's Index to Births, Marriages and Deaths, including the overseas index (microfiche)
Mark Rutherford Collection 1837–2002

Non-library collection catalogue:
All or part available online

Library catalogue:
All or part available online

Printed publications:
Local studies bulletin (3 times a year)

Access to staff:
Contact by letter, by telephone, by fax, by e-mail, in person and via website
Hours: Mon, Tue, Wed, Fri, 0900 to 1800; Thu, 0900 to 1300; Sat, 0900 to 1700

Access for disabled people:
Lift, wide doors, toilet facilities

Parent body:
Bedfordshire County Council

BEDFORD COLLEGE

Library and Resource Centre, Cauldwell Street, Bedford, MK42 9AH

Tel: 01234 291321
Fax: 01234 342674

Website:
http://www.bedford.ac.uk
College website.

Enquiries:
Enquiries to: Library and Resource Centre Manager
Direct e-mail: hcjones@bedford.ac.uk

Founded:
1993

Organisation type and purpose:
Suitable for ages: 14+.

Subject coverage:
Engineering (mechanical, electrical, electronic, motor vehicle, aeronautical engineering), construction, business studies, art and design, English as a foreign language, leisure, sport, tourism, catering, computing, performing arts, health, social and child care, hair, beauty and holistic therapies.

Museum or gallery collection, archive, or library special collection:
Learning and Skills Council information and reports

Non-library collection catalogue:
All or part available in-house

Library catalogue:
All or part available online and in-house

Access to staff:
Contact by letter, by telephone, by e-mail and via website. Appointment necessary.
Hours: Term time: Mon to Thu, 0830 to 1915; Fri, 0830 to 1630
Vacations: 1000 to 1600

Access for disabled people:
Access to all public areas, toilet facilities, parking provided, ramped entry

BEDFORDSHIRE AND LUTON ARCHIVES AND RECORDS SERVICE

Acronym or abbreviation: BLARS

Riverside Building, County Hall, Cauldwell Street, Bedford, MK42 9AP

Tel: 01234 228833; 01234 228777
Fax: 01234 228854
E-mail: archive@bedscc.gov.uk

Website:
http://www.bedfordshire.gov.uk/archive

Enquiries:
Enquiries to: County Archivist

Founded:
1913

Organisation type and purpose:
Local government body.
Archive repository.
The Service collects and preserves a comprehensive and evolving archive illustrating all aspects of Bedfordshire life and history, including contemporary records of archival value; facilitates public and community access to the records; and promotes their use for business, education, cultural and recreational purposes.

Subject coverage:
Bedfordshire history – all aspects.
Documents recording or illustrating: the topography, ownership, occupations and use of land in Bedfordshire; human activity in Bedfordshire e.g. the social, economic, religious, cultural, political, administrative life and history of the County's inhabitants, communities, organisations and government at all levels.

Museum or gallery collection, archive, or library special collection:
Unique archive material from a variety of sources.
Major holdings include Quarter Sessions Archives, County Council, District and Parish Council Archives, Bedford Estate Papers, Lucas (Wrest Park) Collection, Whitbread Family Papers, Bedford Archdeaconry Records,

Ecclesiastical Parish Records, Pym Family Papers and Estate Archives, Orlebar Estate, Methodist Church, Beds and Herts Regiment, Poor Law Unions, London Brick Company

Non-library collection catalogue:
All or part available online

Printed publications:
Many titles, including:
Guides to Holdings – specific subject areas (e.g. family history, property history, educational sources, women's and ethnic minority sources), as produced
Newsletter (quarterly)
Bedfordshire 1851 Census Index (several vols, those out of print available on microfiche)
Series of free service leaflets, including: Summary List of Archive Holdings, Guide for Visitors, Service Charter, Enquiries and Research Services
Bedfordshire Parish Register series (all places up to 1812)

Microform publications:
Bedfordshire Parish Register Series (vols 1–44)

Publications list:
Available online

Access to staff:
Contact by letter, by telephone, by fax, by e-mail, in person and via website
Hours: Mon 0900 to 1900, Tue, Wed and Fri, 0900 to 1700
Closed Thu and weekend

Access for disabled people:
Access to all public areas
Special comments: Access possible, please contact the service in advance.

Parent body:
Bedfordshire County Council

BEDFORDSHIRE FAMILY HISTORY SOCIETY

PO Box 214, Bedford, MK42 9RX

E-mail: bfhs@bfhs.org.uk

Website:
http://www.bfhs.org.uk

Enquiries:
Enquiries to: Honorary Secretary

Founded:
1977

Organisation type and purpose:
Membership association (membership is by subscription), present number of members: 1,000, registered charity (charity number 281677).
To bring together those interested in family history, genealogy and heraldry, primarily in Bedfordshire.

Printed publications:
Bedfordshire Parish Registers Series (as the microfiche, in hard copy from Bedfordshire and Luton Archives and Records Service)
Bedfordshire Parish Registers Series
Bedfordshire Strays Index Vols 1 and 2
Poor Law Papers 1622–1834
Index to 1851 Census of Bedfordshire
Bedfordshire Churches in the Nineteenth Century (4 vols)
Bedfordshire Wills 1531–1539

Microform publications:
Bedfordshire Parish Registers Series (microfiche, over 120 parishes, i.e. all the pre-1812 parish registers)
Bedfordshire Parish Registers Series (microfiche)
Monumental Inscriptions for 86 parishes

Electronic and video publications:
Luton General Cemetery (Rothesay Road) Registers 1854–2003
Bedfordshire Parish Registers Index (PRIME, CD)

Publications list:
Available in print

Access to staff:
Contact by letter, by e-mail and via website
Hours: Mon to Fri, 0900 to 1700

BEDFORDSHIRE HISTORICAL RECORD SOCIETY

Acronym or abbreviation: BHRS

48 St Augustine's Road, Bedford, MK40 2ND

Tel: 01234 309548
E-mail: rsmart@ntlworld.com

Website:
http://www.bedfordshirehrs.org.uk
Publications list

Enquiries:
Enquiries to: Honorary Secretary

Founded:
1913

Organisation type and purpose:
Learned society (membership is by subscription), present number of members: 300, registered charity (charity number 1098629).
Record publishing society (historical source materials for Bedfordshire).
Publication of materials for the history of Bedfordshire.

Subject coverage:
Bedfordshire local history, archival sources.

Museum or gallery collection, archive, or library special collection:
The Fowler Library (owned by BHRS but housed by the University of Northampton)

Non-library collection catalogue:
All or part available online and in print

Printed publications:
Historical source materials, edited records, monographs, diaries and documents.

Microform publications:
Some titles available on microfiche (Chadwyck-Healey)

Publications list:
Available online and in print

Access to staff:
Contact by letter, by telephone, by e-mail and via website
Hours: Mon to Fri, 0900 to 1700

BEDFORDSHIRE LIBRARIES

Bedfordshire County Council, County Hall, Cauldwell Street, Bedford, MK42 9AP

Tel: 01234 228752
Fax: 01234 213006
E-mail: bedfordshire.libraries@bedscc.gov.uk

Website:
http://www.galaxy.bedfordshire.gov.uk/cgi-bin/vlib.sh
Bedfordshire's Virtual Library

Enquiries:
Enquiries to: Head of Libraries
Direct e-mail: barry.george@bedscc.gov.uk

Organisation type and purpose:
Local government body.
Public library service.

Subject coverage:
Public library service offering access to information, books, spoken word, DVDs and CDs for all ages and interests. Plus local information on Bedfordshire and its history, agriculture, local government information, life and works of John Bunyan, medieval English history; aeronautics; automobile engineering.

Education services:
Homework centres and a virtual homework centre

Museum or gallery collection, archive, or library special collection:
Fowler Collection of Printed Sources in Medieval English History (Bedford Central Library)
Frank Mott-Harrison Collection of John Bunyan (Bedford Central Library)
George Offer Collection of John Bunyan Books and Ephemera (Bedford Central Library)
Old Bedford Library (Bedford Central Library)
Yieldon Parish Library (County Hall)

Non-library collection catalogue:
All or part available online and in-house

Library catalogue:
All or part available online

Printed publications:
Asian Bedford and European Bedfordshire
Order printed publications from: Download for free from the Virtual Library

Microform publications:
Catalogue of holdings

Access to staff:
Contact by letter, by telephone, by fax, by e-mail, in person and via website
Hours: Mon to Sat

BEES FOR DEVELOPMENT

Acronym or abbreviation: BfD

Troy, Monmouth, NP25 4AB

Tel: 01600 713648
Fax: 01600 716167
E-mail: info@beesfordevelopment.org

Website:
http://www.beesfordevelopment.org

Enquiries:
Enquiries to: Director

Founded:
1993

Organisation type and purpose:
International organisation, training organisation, consultancy.

Subject coverage:
Beekeeping in developing countries.

Library catalogue:
All or part available in-house

Access to staff:
Contact by letter, by telephone, by fax, by e-mail and via website. Appointment necessary.
Hours: Mon to Fri, 0900 to 1700
Special comments: Strictly by prior appointment.

Access to building, collection or gallery:
Prior appointment required

BEIT MEMORIAL FELLOWSHIPS FOR MEDICAL RESEARCH

The Beit Trust, Grove Road, Woking, Surrey GU21 5JB

Tel: 01483 725833
E-mail: beit.fellowships@hammer.imm.ox.ac.uk

Website:
http://www.beittrust.org.uk/

Enquiries:
Enquiries to: Honorary Secretary
Direct e-mail: sec@beittrust.org.uk

Founded:
1909

Organisation type and purpose:
Registered charity, research organisation.

Subject coverage:
Advancement by research of medicine and of the allied sciences in their relation to medicine.

BELARUS EMBASSY

Formal name: The Embassy of the Republic of Belarus

6 Kensington Court, London, W8 5DL

Tel: 020 7937 3288
Fax: 020 7361 0005
E-mail: uk@belembassy.org

Enquiries:
Enquiries to: Ambassador

Organisation type and purpose:
National government body.
Embassy.

Subject coverage:
Belarus and Belarusian governmental matters, economy and trade.

Trade and statistical information:
Belarusian market.

Access to staff:
Contact by letter, by telephone, by fax and by e-mail
Hours: Mon to Fri, 0900 to 1800

Access to building, collection or gallery:
No access other than to staff

BELFAST CARERS' CENTRE

Unit 1, The Spires, Fisherwich Place, Belfast, BT1 6DU

Tel: 028 9043 4700
Fax: 028 9024 9999
E-mail: info@carerscentre.org

Website:
http://www.carerscentre.org

Enquiries:
Enquiries to: Manager
Direct e-mail: r.devlin@carerscentre.org

Founded:
2002

Formerly called:
Princess Royal Trust Limited

Organisation type and purpose:
Registered charity.

Subject coverage:
Information and support for carers.

Museum or gallery collection, archive, or library special collection:
Range of information material pertinent to carers.

Publications list:
Available online and in print

Access to staff:
Contact by letter, by telephone, by fax, by e-mail and via website. Appointment necessary.
Hours: Mon to Fri, 0900 to 1700

Access to building, collection or gallery:
No prior appointment required
Hours: Mon to Fri, 0900 to 1700

BELFAST CITY COUNCIL

Development Department, The Cecil Ward Building, 8–10 Linenhall Street, Belfast, BT2 8BP

Tel: 028 9032 0202\ Minicom no. 028 9027 0405
Fax: 028 9027 0325

Website:
http://www.development.belfastcity.gov.uk
Arts, projects, markets, planning and development, tourism, events, industrial, economic development, estates, gasworks site, procurement.

Enquiries:
Enquiries to: Director
Direct e-mail: shawa@belfastcity.co.uk
Other contacts: Head of Capital Works, Tourism Manager, Events Manager, Culture and Arts Manager,

Organisation type and purpose:
Local government body.

Subject coverage:
Economic development, arts, tourism development and events in Belfast.

Printed publications:
Arts Strategy and Arts Directory
Relocation Brochure
Strategy for economic development
Tourism guides for Belfast

Access to staff:
Contact by letter, by telephone, by fax and by e-mail. Appointment necessary.
Hours: Mon to Fri, 0900 to 1700

Access to building, collection or gallery:
Prior appointment required

Connections with:
Belfast First Stop Business Shop (First Stop Shop)
    tel: 028 9027 8399
Belfast Visitor & Convention Bureau (BVCB)
    tel: 028 9023 9026
Investment Belfast Limited (IBL)
    tel: 028 9031 136

BELFAST INSTITUTE OF FURTHER AND HIGHER EDUCATION

Acronym or abbreviation: BIFHE

Gerald Moag Campus, Millfield, Belfast, BT1 1HS

E-mail: information-servicesbelfastinstitute.ac.uk

Website:
http://www.belfastinstitute.ac.uk
All relevant information about courses and services is either available now or will be shortly.

Enquiries:
Enquiries to: Information Officer
Direct e-mail: information_services@belfastinstitute.ac.uk
Other contacts: Director

Founded:
1991

Formerly called:
College of Business Studies, College of Technology, Rupert Stanley College

Subject coverage:
Education and training at all levels in all subjects except mining, agriculture and marine technology.

Printed publications:
Adult Education News (twice a year, free)
Annual Report (free)
General Prospectus (annually, free)
Higher Education Prospectus (annually, free)

Access to staff:
Contact by letter, by telephone, by fax, by e-mail and in person
Hours: Mon to Thu, 0900 to 1700; Fri, 0900 to 1600

BELFAST PUBLIC LIBRARIES

Royal Avenue, Belfast, BT1 1EA

Tel: 028 9050 9150
Fax: 028 9033 2819
E-mail: info@libraries.belfast-elb.gov.uk

Enquiries:
Enquiries to: Chief Librarian

Founded:
1888

Formerly called:
Belfast City Libraries

Organisation type and purpose:
Local government body, public library.

Subject coverage:
Departmentalised as follows:
General Reference Library; social sciences, philosophy, religion, history, arts, literature, science, medicine, law
Local History Library; local studies and Irish material
Music Library; music, records, cassettes, CDs, scores
Business Library; business information
Electronic Information Services; internet access, CD-ROM, on-line searching, software application, email.

Museum or gallery collection, archive, or library special collection:
Belfast Theatre Posters
Early Belfast printed books
F J Bigger Collection
Grainger, Moore, Riddell and Horner Collections
Irish and Belfast Newspapers from 1761
Irish folksong and music records
Irish history, archaeology and antiquarian material
J S Crone Collection
UN Depository Library

Printed publications:
Reading lists on specific topics

Access to staff:
Contact by letter, by telephone, by fax, by e-mail and in person
Hours: Mon, Thu, 0900 to 2000; Tue, Wed, Fri, 0900 to 1730; Sat, 0900 to 1300

Access for disabled people:
Level entry, access to all public areas, toilet facilities

BELGIAN EMBASSY

103 Eaton Square, London, SW1W 9AB

Tel: 020 7470 3700
Fax: 020 7259 6213
E-mail: info@belgium-embassy.co.uk

Website:
http://belgium.fgov.be
Guide to the Federal Administration, decisions of the Federal Council of Ministers, information from the Federal Information Service, all about Belgium, hyperlinks to other sites, an address for all questions.
http://www.belgium.fgov.be
Belgium on the Internet (Federal information service).
http://www.belgium-embassy.co.uk
Belgian Events (in-house publication), general information.

Enquiries:
Enquiries to: Information Officer

Organisation type and purpose:
Diplomatic mission.

Subject coverage:
General (politics, media, monarchy, etc), culture, economics, working and living in Belgium, visas and passports.

Printed publications:
Bulletin of Belgian Events in Great Britain (6 times a year)

Heads or is associated with the:
Anglo-Belgian Club
    60 Knightsbridge, London, SW1X 7LF; tel: 020 7235 2121; fax: 020 7243 9470
Belgian Consulates
Belgian Tourist Office Brussels-Ardennes
    217 Marsh Wall, London, E14 9FJ; tel: 020 7531 0390; fax: 020 7531 0393; e-mail: info@belgium-tourism.net
Belgo-Luxembourg Chamber of Commerce
    Riverside House, 27–29 Vauxhall Grove, London, SW8 1SY; tel: 020 7820 7839; fax: 020 7793 1628
Tourism Flanders-Brussels
    31 Pepper Street, London, E14 9RW; tel: 020 7867 0311; fax: 020 7458 0045; e-mail: info@flanders-tourism.org

BELIZE HIGH COMMISSION

Third Floor, 45 Crawford Place, London, W1H 4LP

Tel: 020 7723 3603
Fax: 020 7723 9637
E-mail: bzhc-lon@btconnect.com

Website:
http://www.belizehighcommission.com/

Enquiries:
Enquiries to: High Commissioner
Other contacts: The First Secretary for Consular and Administrative Affairs.

Organisation type and purpose:
National government body.
Diplomatic mission of the government of Belize.

Subject coverage:
Belize: economics, tourism, politics, investment, trade, social structure, citizenship and visas.

Printed publications:
Free information packs on Belize (on request)
Application forms (visa, passports)

Access to staff:
Contact by letter, by telephone, by fax and by e-mail. Appointment necessary.
Hours: Mon to Fri, 1000 to 1800

Access to building, collection or gallery:
Prior appointment required
Hours: Consular Hours: Mon to Fri, 1000 to 1300

BELL COLLEGE TECHNICAL INFORMATION SERVICE

Acronym or abbreviation: BECTIS

Bell College of Technology, Almada Street, Hamilton, South Lanarkshire, ML3 0JB

Tel: 01698 285658
Fax: 01698 286856
E-mail: bectis@bell.ac.uk

Website:
http://www.bell.ac.uk

Enquiries:
Enquiries to: Information Officer

Organisation type and purpose:
Commercial information service.
To make the resources of Bell College Library available to the industrial community.

Subject coverage:
Industrial, commercial and public authorities information, technical and managerial subjects, British Standards.

Printed publications:
BECTIS Bulletin (10 times a year)

Access to staff:
Contact by letter, by telephone, by fax, by e-mail and in person
Hours: Mon to Fri, 0830 to 1630

Access to building, collection or gallery:
No access other than to staff
Hours: Term time: Mon to Thu, 0830 to 2100; Fri, 0830 to 1630; Sat 0900 to 1300

BENESH INSTITUTE

36 Battersea Square, London, SW11 3RA

Tel: 020 7326 8031
Fax: 020 7924 3129
E-mail: beneshinstitute@rad.org.uk

Website:
http://www.benesh.org

Enquiries:
Enquiries to: Director

Founded:
1962

Formerly called:
Institute of Choreology

Organisation type and purpose:
Professional body (membership is by subscription), registered charity (charity number 312826), suitable for ages: 16+.

Education and research institute in movement notation.

Subject coverage:
Benesh Movement Notation, anthropology, choreography, computer research, dance techniques, dance repertoire, ethnic dance, physiotherapy.

Museum or gallery collection, archive, or library special collection:
Choreographic scores in Benesh Movement Notation

Library catalogue:
All or part available online

Printed publications:
A range of publications relating to Benesh Movement Notation, including the following:
Movement Study and Benesh Movement Notation
Benesh Movement Notation Elementary Solo Syllabus
Order printed publications from: http://www.radenterprises.co.uk

Electronic and video publications:
Benesh Notation Editor computer software
Order electronic and video publications from: http://www.radenterprises.co.uk

Publications list:
Available online

Access to staff:
Contact by letter, by telephone, by fax and by e-mail. Appointment necessary. Non-members charged.
Hours: Mon to Thu, 1000 to 1800; Fri, 1000 to 1730

Access to building, collection or gallery:
Prior appointment required
Hours: Mon to Thu, 1000 to 1800; Fri, 1000 to 1730

Access for disabled people:
Ramped entry, toilet facilities
Special comments: Wheelchair access to first two floors.

Links with:
The Royal Academy of Dance
at the same address; tel: 020 7326 8000; fax: 020 7924 3129; e-mail: info@rad.org.uk; website: http://www.rad.org.uk

BERKELEY ENTHUSIASTS CLUB

41 Gorsewood Road, St Johns, Woking, Surrey, GU21 1UZ

Tel: 01483 475330

Enquiries:
Enquiries to: Secretary

Founded:
1963

Organisation type and purpose:
Membership association (membership is by subscription), present number of members: 300, voluntary organisation.

Subject coverage:
Preservation of all types of 3 and 4 wheeled Berkeley sports cars, sources of cars, parts, technical advice.

Printed publications:
Newsletter (monthly, members)

Access to staff:
Contact by letter
Hours: Mon to Fri, 0900 to 1700

BERKSHIRE ARCHAEOLOGICAL SOCIETY

Acronym or abbreviation: BAS

43 Laburnham Road, Maidenhead, Berkshire, SL6 4DE

Tel: 01628 631225

Enquiries:
Enquiries to: Honorary Secretary

Founded:
1871

Organisation type and purpose:
Learned society.

Subject coverage:
Berkshire archaeology and history.

Museum or gallery collection, archive, or library special collection:
Library of rare books on Berkshire
Pre-1998 archaeological periodicals from UK mostly, some from elsewhere, for sale from October 1998, please apply for catalogue

Printed publications:
Berkshire Archaeological Journal

Access to staff:
Contact by letter
Hours: Mon to Fri, 0900 to 1700
Special comments: International reply coupon requested if outside UK.

Member of:
Council for British Archaeology

Practical Arm:
Berkshire Field Research Group

BERKSHIRE LOCAL HISTORY ASSOCIATION

Acronym or abbreviation: BLHA

The Bailiwick, Tag Lane, Hare Hatch, Twyford, Reading, Berkshire, RG10 9ST

Tel: 0118 940 2376
E-mail: peter@bailiwick1.co.uk

Enquiries:
Enquiries to: Chairman
Other contacts: Newsletter Editor

Founded:
1976

Organisation type and purpose:
Membership association (membership is by subscription), present number of members: 40 corporate bodies, 80 individuals, voluntary organisation.
Acts to liaise and disseminate information about the activities of its members interested in local and family history, and archaeology.

Subject coverage:
Various aspects of the history of Berkshire, its towns, parishes, people, landscape, etc depending on research and interests of members.

Printed publications:
Berkshire Old and New (annually for sale to non-members, free to members)
Newsletter (3 times a year, free to members)

Access to staff:
Contact by letter, by telephone and by e-mail
Hours: Mon to Fri, 0900 to 1700

Affiliated to:
British Association of Local History

Members include:
Berkshire Archaeological Society
tel: 01628 631225
Berkshire Family History Society
tel: 0118 984 3995
Berkshire Industrial Archaeology Group
tel: 0118 978 5234
Berkshire Library Service
Berkshire Record Office
tel: 0118 901 5132; fax: 0118 901 5131; e-mail: arch@reading.gov.uk
many local history and historical societies in the county

Other addresses:
Berkshire Local History Association
18 Foster Road, Abingdon, Oxfordshire, OX14 1YN

BERKSHIRE RECORD OFFICE

9 Coley Avenue, Reading, Berkshire, RG1 6AF

Tel: 0118 901 5132
Fax: 0118 901 5131
E-mail: arch@reading.gov.uk

Website:
http://www.berkshirerecordoffice.org.uk

Enquiries:
Enquiries to: County Archivist

Founded:
1948

Organisation type and purpose:
Local government body.

Subject coverage:
Family and local history relating to Berkshire
(including area now in Oxfordshire).

**Museum or gallery collection, archive, or library
special collection:**
Business Archives
Charity Archives
Church Archives
Estate and Family Archives
Local Government Archives
Public Records

Non-library collection catalogue:
All or part available in-house

Access to staff:
Contact by letter, by telephone, by fax, by e-mail
and in person. Appointment necessary.
Hours: Mon, closed; Tue, Wed, 0900 to 1700; Thu,
0900 to 2100; Fri, 0900 to 1630
Special comments: Two weeks stocktaking, usually
first two weeks in Nov. Reader's ticket required.

Access for disabled people:
Parking provided, level entry, access to all public
areas, toilet facilities

Parent body:
Bracknell Forest Borough Council
Reading Borough Council
Royal Borough of Windsor and Maidenhead
Slough Borough Council
West Berkshire Council
Wokingham District Council

BERKSHIRE, BUCKINGHAMSHIRE AND OXFORDSHIRE WILDLIFE TRUST

Acronym or abbreviation: BBOWT

The Lodge, 1 Armstrong Road, Littlemore, Oxford,
OX4 4XT

Tel: 01865 775476
Fax: 01865 711301
E-mail: info@bbowt.org.uk

Website:
http://www.bbowt.org.uk

Enquiries:
Enquiries to: Information Officer
Direct e-mail: wildinfo@bbowt.org.uk

Founded:
1961

Formerly called:
Berkshire, Buckinghamshire and Oxfordshire
Naturalists' Trust (BBONT) (year of change 1999)

Organisation type and purpose:
Voluntary organisation, registered charity (charity
number 204330).
Environmental, conservation, wildlife
organisation.

Subject coverage:
All aspects of wildlife in Berkshire,
Buckinghamshire and Oxfordshire.

**Museum or gallery collection, archive, or library
special collection:**
Guides to nature reserves in these three counties

Printed publications:
Where to go for wildlife in Berkshire,
Buckinghamshire and Oxfordshire (available free
on joining)

Access to staff:
Contact by letter, by telephone, by fax, by e-mail
and via website. Appointment necessary.
Hours: Mon to Fri, 0900 to 1700

Parent body:
Wildlife Trusts
UK Office, The Kiln, Waterside, Mather Road,
Newark, Notts, NG24 1NT; tel: 0870 036 7711;
fax: 0870 036 0101; e-mail: enquiry@
wildlifetrusts.org

BERLIOZ SOCIETY

c/o 49 Amerland Road, London, SW18 1QA

Tel: 020 8870 4931
Fax: 020 8877 3841

Website:
http://www.hberlioz.com/berliozsociety.html
http://www.hberlioz.com
Host homepage.

Enquiries:
Enquiries to: Honorary Secretary
Direct e-mail: sqing@btinternet.com

Founded:
1952

Organisation type and purpose:
Membership association (membership is by
subscription), present number of members: 240.

Subject coverage:
Music of Berlioz, life of Berlioz, performances of
Berlioz' work, Berlioz' writing.

Non-library collection catalogue:
All or part available in-house

Library catalogue:
All or part available in-house

Printed publications:
Bibliography (by Michael Wright)
The Society Bulletin (approximately 3 times a year,
£10 a year, free to members)
Order printed publications from: Bulletin, Berlioz
Society
9 Bridgemar Avenue, Wood Green, London, N22
7BY

Access to staff:
Contact by letter, by telephone, by fax, by e-mail
and via website

Access to building, collection or gallery:
No access other than to staff

Also at:
Hon. Secretary, Berlioz Society
450B Lea Bridge Road, Leyton, E10 7DY

BERMUDA TOURISM

26 York Street, London, W1U 6PZ

Tel: 0207 096 4246
Fax: 0207 096 0509
E-mail: bermudatourism@cibgroup.co.uk

Enquiries:
Enquiries to: Manager
Other contacts: Sales Administration Co-ordinator

Founded:
1985

Formerly called:
Bermuda Tourism BCB Limited

Organisation type and purpose:
National Tourist Office.

Subject coverage:
Bermuda, tourism and travel.

Printed publications:
Tourist literature and brochures on Bermuda
updated annually

Access to staff:
Contact by e-mail
Hours: Mon to Fri, 0900 to 1700

Access to building, collection or gallery:
No access other than to staff

BERTRAND RUSSELL PEACE FOUNDATION LIMITED

Acronym or abbreviation: BRPF

Russell House, Bulwell Lane, Nottingham, NG6
0BT

Tel: 0115 978 4504
Fax: 0115 942 0433
E-mail: elfeuro@compuserve.com

Website:
http://www.russfound.org
http://www.spokesmanbooks.com

Enquiries:
Enquiries to: Secretary
Direct tel: 0115 970 8318
Direct e-mail: julia@brpf.demon.co.uk

Founded:
1963

Organisation type and purpose:
International organisation (membership is by
election or invitation), research organisation,
publishing house.
To investigate the causes of international and social
conflict and to work for peace and disarmament.

Subject coverage:
International relations, politics, economics, civil
liberties.

Printed publications:
Journal
Spokesman Books
Order printed publications from:
www.spokesmanbooks.com

Publications list:
Available online and in print

Access to staff:
Contact by letter, by telephone, by fax, by e-mail
and via website
Hours: Mon to Fri, 0900 to 1700

Access to building, collection or gallery:
Prior appointment required

BERWICK-UPON-TWEED RECORD OFFICE

Council Offices, Wallace Green, Berwick-upon-
Tweed, Northumberland, TD15 1ED

Tel: 01289 301865 or 330044 ext 265
Fax: 01289 330540
E-mail: lb@berwick-upon-tweed.gov.uk

Website:
http://www.northumberland.gov.uk/collections
Contains information about the office and sources
kept.

Enquiries:
Enquiries to: Archivist

Founded:
1980

Organisation type and purpose:
Local government body
Record office.

Subject coverage:
Local and family history of North Northumberland
including Berwick-upon-Tweed.

**Museum or gallery collection, archive, or library
special collection:**
Berwick Borough Archives, 16th to 20th centuries
Berwick Salmon Fisheries Company records
Ford and Etal Estate records
IGI (England, Scotland and Ireland, microfiche)
North Northumberland census returns, 1841 to
1901 (microfilm)

North Northumberland parish registers
(microfilm)
GRO Birth, Marriage and Death Indexes, 1837 to
1955 (microfiche)

Non-library collection catalogue:
All or part available in-house

Printed publications:
Berwick-on-Tweed Illustrated, 1894–1994 (£5, inc.
p&p)

Microform publications:
Printed list of microfiche publications (transcripts
of parish registers and census) available on
receipt of sae

Publications list:
Available online and in print

Access to staff:
Contact by letter, by telephone, by fax, by e-mail
and in person
Hours: Only Wed, Thu, 0930 to 1300 and 1400 to
1700

Access for disabled people:
Level entry, toilet facilities

Parent body:
Berwick-upon-Tweed Borough Council
Council Offices, Wallace Green, Berwick-upon-
Tweed; tel: 01289 330044; fax: 01289 330540;
website: www.berwick-upon-tweed.gov.uk
Northumberland County Council
County Hall, Morpeth, NE61 2EF; website: www
.northumberland.gov.uk

BEVIN BOYS ASSOCIATION

Acronym or abbreviation: BBA

c/o Warwick Taylor MBE, 1 Rundlestone Court,
Poundbury, Dorchester, Dorset, DT1 3TN

Tel: 01305 261269

Enquiries:
Enquiries to: Archivist
Other contacts: Vice President

Founded:
1989

Organisation type and purpose:
Voluntary organisation.
To encourage comradeship, and organise reunions
and events throughout the UK for all ex Bevin
Boys who worked in the coal mines to serve their
National Service in lieu of service in the Forces
during WWII. Bevin Boys were so named after
Ernest Bevin the wartime Minister of Labour and
National Service.

Printed publications:
Newsletter (members only)

Access to staff:
Contact by letter, by telephone and by fax
Hours: Mon to Fri, 0900 to 1700

BEXLEY LIBRARY SERVICE

Central Library, Townley Road, Bexleyheath, Kent,
DA6 7HJ

Tel: 020 8303 7777 ext. 3450
Fax: 020 8304 7058
E-mail: centrallibrary@bexley.gov.uk

Website:
http://www.bexley.gov.uk

Enquiries:
Enquiries to: Library Manager

Organisation type and purpose:
Local government body, public library.

Subject coverage:
General.

**Museum or gallery collection, archive, or library
special collection:**
Government publications

Non-library collection catalogue:
All or part available online

Library catalogue:
All or part available online

Access to staff:
Contact by letter, by telephone, by fax, by e-mail
and in person
Hours: Mon, Tue, Wed, Fri, 0930 to 1730; Thu 0930
to 2000; Sat, 0930 to 1700; Sun 1000 to 1400

Branch of:
South East Area Libraries Information Co-
operative (SEAL)

BEXLEY LOCAL STUDIES AND ARCHIVE CENTRE

Central Library, Townley Road, Bexleyheath, Kent,
DA6 7HJ

Tel: 020 8303 7777 ext. 7470
Fax: 020 8304 7058
E-mail: archives@bexley.gov.uk

Website:
http://www.bexley.gov.uk/localstudies/index.html

Enquiries:
Enquiries to: Local Studies Manager
Other contacts: Archivist (for archive collection
enquiries)

Founded:
1972

Formerly called:
Bexley Local Studies Society

Organisation type and purpose:
Public library.
Diocesan Record Office for Rochester and
Southwark.
Local Authority Record Office for Bexley

Subject coverage:
Historical information for area now covered by
London Borough of Bexley.

Non-library collection catalogue:
All or part available online and in-house

Library catalogue:
All or part available online and in-house

Printed publications:
Publications on the history of Bexley, Sidcup,
Crayford, Erith

Microform publications:
Local Parish registers, census, GRO indexes and
newspapers (for reference only)

Electronic and video publications:
Image Database for the local area (online)

Publications list:
Available online

Access to staff:
Contact by letter, by telephone, by fax, by e-mail,
in person and via website
Hours: Mon to Fri, 0930 to 1730; Thu, 0930 to 2000;
Sat, 0930 to 1700

Access for disabled people:
Access to all public areas, toilet facilities

Branch libraries:
Bexley Council
Environment and Regeneration, Civic Offices,
Bexleyheath, Kent; tel: 020 8303 7777; website:
http://www.bexley.gov.uk

BFMS

Formal name: British False Memory Society

Bradford on Avon, Wiltshire, BA15 1NF

Tel: 01225 868682
Fax: 01225 862251
E-mail: bfms@bfms.org.uk

Website:
http://www.bfms.org.uk

Enquiries:
Enquiries to: Administrator

Founded:
1993

Formerly called:
ACAP, British False Memory Society

Organisation type and purpose:
Registered charity (charity number 1040683).
Formed in 1993 to raise awareness of dangers of
'recovered memory therapy' which has given rise
to an epidemic of decades-delayed,
uncorroborated allegations, against parents, of
childhood sexual abuse. Comprehensive archive
on damage to patients and families as a result of
false allegations influenced by therapy and
associated beliefs; legal implications of 'recovered
memory' and unreliable allegations in the criminal
and civil courts, with case histories and contacts.

Subject coverage:
False memory/recovered memory including legal
implications.

**Museum or gallery collection, archive, or library
special collection:**
Books, videos, audio cassettes, academic papers
and newspaper, journal and magazine cuttings

Non-library collection catalogue:
All or part available in-house

Library catalogue:
All or part available in-house

Printed publications:
Fractured Families (book)
List of academic articles (by request)
Brochure
Newsletters
Booklet

Electronic and video publications:
Various videos related to false memories

Access to staff:
Contact by letter, by telephone, by fax, by e-mail
and via website. Appointment necessary. Access
for members only.
Hours: Mon to Fri, 0900 to 1700
Special comments: Lift serves the first two flights of
stairs, not the third flight of stairs.

Access for disabled people:
Ramped entry
Special comments: Lift to 1st floor only.

BFWG CHARITABLE FOUNDATION

Formal name: FfWG

20 Fern Road, Storrington, Pulborough, West
Sussex, RH20 4LW

Tel: 01903 746723
Fax: 01903 746723
E-mail: valconsidine@toucansurf.com

Website:
http://www.ffwg.org.uk

Enquiries:
Enquiries to: Company Secretary
Direct e-mail: jean.c@blueyonder.co.uk (re grants)
Other contacts: Grants Administrator for details
relating to grant applications.

Founded:
1925

Formerly called:
Crosby Hall (year of change 1993)

Organisation type and purpose:
Registered charity (charity number 312903).
Grant awarding charity.
Grants to help women graduates with their living
expenses while registered for study or research at
an approved institution of higher education in
Great Britain.

Access to staff:
Contact by letter, by telephone, by fax, by e-mail,
in person and via website. Appointment necessary.

continued overleaf

Hours: Mon to Fri, 0900 to 1645

Member of:
International Federation of University Women
(IFUW)
    8 rue de l'ancien port, 1201, Geneva, Switzerland;
    tel: +4122 731 1280; fax: +4122 738 0440; e-mail:
    ifuw@ifuw.org
University Women of Europe (UWE)

Parent body:
British Federation of Women Graduates (BFWG)
    4 Mandeville Courtyard, 142 Battersea Park
    Road, London, SW11 4NB; tel: 020 7498 8037;
    fax: 020 7498 8037; e-mail: bfwg@bfwg.demon.co
    .uk

BG GROUP PLC

Information Centre, 100 Thames Valley Park Drive,
Reading, Berkshire, RG6 1PT

Tel: 0118 929 2496
Fax: 0118 929 2482
E-mail: padraig.cronin@bg-group.com

Enquiries:
Enquiries to: Commercial Intelligence Manager
Other contacts: Information Analyst

Formerly called:
BG plc, date of change, December 1999; British Gas
(year of change 1997)

Organisation type and purpose:
International organisation.
Industrial commercial company.
Gas exploration and production, overseas gas-
related ventures.

Subject coverage:
Oil/gas exploration and production, LNG, power
generation, gas transmission and distribution.

Library catalogue:
All or part available in-house

Access to staff:
Contact by letter, by telephone and by fax
Hours: Mon to Fri, 0900 to 1700

Access to building, collection or gallery:
Prior appointment required

Access for disabled people:
Parking provided, access to all public areas

BHF GROUP

225 Bristol Road, Edgbaston, Birmingham, B5 7UB

Tel: 0121 446 6688
Fax: 0121 446 5215
E-mail: info@bhfgroup.co.uk

Website:
http://www.bhfgroup.co.uk

Enquiries:
Enquiries to: Information Officer

Founded:
1899

Organisation type and purpose:
Trade association.
Trade Federation.
Represents more than 4,000 primary retail outlets
in hardware, ironmongery, DIY, building supplies
and agricultural machinery.

Subject coverage:
Finance clearing house, merchandising company,
insurance, inter-firm comparison, computer
systems, information service, training, shop
design, direct mail.

Printed publications:
Grey List (monthly)
Hardware Today (monthly)
Home Décor & Furnishings (bi-monthly)
CHA Times (bi-monthly)
BAGMA Bulletin (bi-monthly)
Garden Machinery Price Guide (monthly)
Members Handbook (Annual)

Access to staff:
Contact by letter and by e-mail. Access for
members only.
Hours: Mon to Fri, 0900 to 1700

Links with:
British Retail Consortium
DTI De-Regulation Task Force
Eurocommerce Limited
International Hardware Association
Rainy Day Trust

BHR GROUP LIMITED

The Fluid Engineering Centre, Cranfield,
Bedfordshire, MK43 0AJ

Tel: 01234 750422
Fax: 01234 750074
E-mail: contactus@bhrgroup.com

Website:
http://www.bhrgroup.com

Enquiries:
Enquiries to: Manager – Information Service

Founded:
1947

Organisation type and purpose:
Consultancy, research organisation.
Independent technology organisation.

Subject coverage:
Fluid dynamics and process engineering, more
specifically: pumps and other fluid machines, fluid
power, tribology, abrasive waterjet and plain water
jet cutting and cleaning technology, fluid sealing
and containment integrity, multiphase flow,
pipeline technology; flow in pipes, cavitation, flow
measurement and control, hydraulic transport of
solid materials in pipelines, open channel flow,
civil engineering, hydraulic structures (dams,
spillways, flood defences, cooling systems, etc.)
fluid effects on structures, industrial
aerodynamics, biotechnology; process technology,
process intensification, fluid control, valves, oil and
gas production improvement, oil and gas
transport, water and waste water treatment, water
supply modelling software systems, knowledge-
based software tools for water resource allocation
planning, biodiesel production. Knowhow for
reduction of emissions, computational fluid
dynamics (CFD), pipeline pigging and pipe
protection, mixing – batch and inline, filtration and
separation.

Non-library collection catalogue:
All or part available online and in-house

Library catalogue:
All or part available in-house

Publications list:
Available online

Access to staff:
Contact by letter, by telephone, by fax, by e-mail,
in person and via website
Hours: Mon to Fri, 0900 to 1700
Special comments: Charges, either by subscription or
one-off, for certain services; details on request.

BIAB ONLINE – THE BRITISH AND IRISH ARCHAEOLOGICAL BIBLIOGRAPHY

Acronym or abbreviation: biab online

c/o The British Academy, 10 Carlton Terrace,
London, SW1Y 5AH

Tel: 020 7969 5223 or 5444
Fax: 020 7969 5300 (shared)
E-mail: info@biab.ac.uk

Website:
http://www.biab.ac.uk
Site includes searchable database of c. 200,000
bibliographic references from 1695 to the present
day, organisational information for biab online,
also information on archaeological publishers and

journals and other helps and standards. biabonline
is a free service. A full system and service upgrade
will be launched at end-2008.

Enquiries:
Enquiries to: Chief Bibliographer & Editor
Direct e-mail: office@biab.ac.uk

Founded:
1997

Formerly called:
British Archaeological Abstracts (year of change
1991); British Archaeological Bibliography (year of
change 1996)

Organisation type and purpose:
Research organisation.
biab online is a service provided by the Council for
British Archaeology (CBA) with the support of
funding from English Heritage, Society of
Antiquaries of London, Cadw, the Heritage
Council of the Republic of Ireland and others. It
provides the abstracts and indexing service for
British and Irish Archaeology and is now available
online at http://www.biab.ac.uk.
To compile and publish a comprehensive
bibliography for the archaeology of Great Britain
and Ireland.

Subject coverage:
Archaeology of Great Britain and Republic of
Ireland; publications relating to the archaeology of
Great Britain and Ireland.

**Museum or gallery collection, archive, or library
special collection:**
Electronic data on archaeology bibliography from
    1695 to 1980, citations only; 1967 to present,
    citations and abstracts

Printed publications:
Standard update .pdf available as print-on-
demand
Order printed publications from: http://
www.biab.ac.uk

Electronic and video publications:
Online database & web pages

Access to staff:
Contact by letter, by telephone, by fax and by e-
mail. Appointment necessary.
Hours: Mon to Fri, 0900 to 1700

Connections with:
Council for British Archaeology (CBA)
    St Mary's House, 66 Bootham, York, YO30 7BZ;
    tel: 01904 671 417; fax: 01904 671 384; website:
    http://www.britarch.ac.uk

BIBIC

Formal name: British Institute for Brain Injured
Children

Knowle Hall, Bridgwater, Somerset, TA7 8PJ

Tel: 01278 684060
Fax: 01278 685573
E-mail: info@bibic.org.uk

Website:
http://www.bibic.org.uk

Enquiries:
Enquiries to: Marketing Co-ordinator
Other contacts: Family Services Director

Founded:
1972

Organisation type and purpose:
National organisation, voluntary organisation,
registered charity (charity number 1057635). Caters
for children from the age of 6 months to 18 years.
BIBIC exists to maximise the potential of children
with conditions affecting their social, sensory
communication, motor and learning abilities.

Subject coverage:
BIBIC's home-based therapy helps rehabilitate
children variously diagnosed as having autism,
autistic tendencies, brain damage, brain injury,
cerebral palsy, developmental delay, Downs
syndrome, dyslexia, epilepsy, hydrocephalus,

learning difficulties, learning disability, microcephalus, dyspraxia, attention deficit hyperactivity disorders (ADHD). It draws not only on sensory-motor techniques but also incorporates aspects derived from speech therapy, physiotherapy and occupational therapy in a medically overseen environment. Bursary funding for children from disadvantaged backgrounds is available.

Printed publications:
Milestones (newsletter, 2 times a year, free)

Electronic and video publications:
CD and DVD

Access to staff:
Contact by letter, by telephone, by fax, by e-mail and via website. Appointment necessary.
Hours: Mon to Fri, 0900 to 1700

Access for disabled people:
Parking provided, ramped entry, toilet facilities, lift, stair lift.
Special comments: Access to most public areas

BIBLE SOCIETY

Formal name: British & Foreign Bible Society
Acronym or abbreviation: BFBS

Contact Centre, Stonehill Green, Westlea, Swindon, Wiltshire, SN5 7DG

Tel: 01793 418100
Fax: 01793 418118
E-mail: contactus@biblesociety.org.uk

Website:
http://www.biblesociety.org.uk

Founded:
1804

Organisation type and purpose:
Registered charity (charity number 232759).
Helping church people to own, use, value and share the Bible.

Subject coverage:
Bible translation and distribution of the scriptures throughout the world, printing history, linguistics, church growth, mission, bible commentaries, social and religious trends, research reports relating to these.

Museum or gallery collection, archive, or library special collection:
Catalogue of manuscripts
Historical catalogue of printed Bibles with sectional revisions for African, English, Indian and Chinese scriptures
Scriptures Library and Archive (28,000 volumes in more than 2000 languages) now housed in Cambridge University Library, access via Contact Centre, Swindon

Printed publications:
Bibles
Bible Translations – update and background
Word in Action (3 times a year, free)
Bible in TransMission (3 times a year, free to clergy)
Resources relating to projects
Order printed publications from: Visit website bibleresources.org.uk

Electronic and video publications:
Complete Bible on microchip in pocket computer
New Testament on diskette
Cassettes
Videos

Access to staff:
Contact by letter, by fax and by e-mail.
Appointment necessary.
Hours: Mon to Fri, 0900 to 1700

Access for disabled people:
Parking provided, ramped entry, access to all public areas, toilet facilities

Founder member of:
United Bible Society – a fellowship of national bible societies around the world (UBS)

BIBLIOGRAPHICAL SOCIETY

Formal name: The Bibliographical Society

C/o Institute of English Studies, Room 306, Senate House, Malet Street, London, WC1E 7HU

E-mail: secretary@bibsoc.org.uk

Website:
http://www.bibsoc.org.uk

Enquiries:
Enquiries to: Hon. Sec.

Founded:
1892

Organisation type and purpose:
Learned society.
Membership organisation (membership by subscription)
To promote and encourage study and research in the fields of: historical, analytical, descriptive and textual bibliography, and the history of printing, publishing, bookselling, bookbinding and collecting.
To hold meetings at which papers are read and discussed. To print and publish a journal and books concerned with bibliography.
To maintain a bibliographical library.
To support bibliographical research by awarding grants and bursaries.

Museum or gallery collection, archive, or library special collection:
Society's library is housed at Stationers' Hall.
Members wishing to borrow books should apply to the Hon. Librarian: Robin Myers, Stationers' Company, Stationers' Hall, London EC4M 7DD.
The catalogue for the library is now available electronically, via the catalogue of the School of Advanced Study at the University of London (go to http://catalogue.ulrls.lon.ac.uk/ and select Bibliographical Society from the options).

Library catalogue:
All or part available online

Publications list:
Available online

Access to staff:
Contact by letter and by e-mail

BIBRA TOXICOLOGY ADVICE & CONSULTING LTD

Westmead House, 123 Westmead Road, Sutton, Surrey, SM1 4JH

Tel: 020 8722 4701
Fax: 020 8722 4706
E-mail: info@bibratoxadvice.co.uk

Website:
http://www.bibra-information.co.uk/
General information on services.

Enquiries:
Enquiries to: Information Officer
Other contacts: Sales Manager

Founded:
1960

Created by the merger of:
BIBRA Information Services Ltd and Toxicology Advice & Consulting Ltd (year of change 2007)

Formerly called:
TNO BIBRA International Limited

Organisation type and purpose:
Consultancy, research organisation.
Independent research and advice on the health effects of chemicals.

Subject coverage:
Chemical toxicology and ecotoxicology and safety in use, including industrial chemicals, food additives, food contaminants such as packaging migrants, pesticides, feed additives and other agricultural chemicals, cosmetics and toiletry components, dry excipients, surgical products, tobacco additives and air and water pollutants,

international legislation on the foregoing subjects, need for and design of toxicological tests on specific materials.

Museum or gallery collection, archive, or library special collection:
Unique collection of over 400,000 specially selected up-to-date research papers, reports, expert comment, and legislative material relating to the health effects of chemicals

Printed publications:
Toxicology and Regulatory News (monthly; formerly TNO BIBRA Bulletin)
Food and Chemical Toxicology
Toxicity Profiles
Toxicology In Vitro

Access to staff:
Contact by letter, by telephone, by fax and by e-mail
Hours: Mon to Fri, 0900 to 1715

Parent body:
TNO Nutrition and Food Research Institute
Utrechtseweg 48, PO Box 360, Zeist, Netherlands; tel: +31 3 694 4754; fax: +31 3 695 7928; e-mail: infodesk@tno.nl

BICYCLE ASSOCIATION OF GREAT BRITAIN LIMITED

Acronym or abbreviation: BA

Starley House, Eaton Road, Coventry, Warwickshire, CV1 2FH

Tel: 024 7655 3838
Fax: 024 7622 8366
E-mail: office@ba-gb.com

Enquiries:
Enquiries to: Secretary

Organisation type and purpose:
Trade association.

Subject coverage:
British bicycle industry, manufacture, statistics, imports, accessories.

Trade and statistical information:
UK market for bicycles.

Printed publications:
Order printed publications from: Secretary

Publications list:
Available in print

Access to staff:
Contact by letter and by telephone
Hours: Mon to Fri, 0900 to 1700

Access to building, collection or gallery:
No access other than to staff

BIGGAR ALBION FOUNDATION

The Albion Club, 9 Edinburgh Road, Biggar, Lanarkshire, ML12 6AX

E-mail: albionregister@yahoo.co.uk

Website:
http://www.albion-trust.org.uk

Organisation type and purpose:
Foundation responsible for the Albion Club (membership is open to all those interested in Albion vehicles), the Albion Archive, the Biggar Rally and the Albion museum.

Subject coverage:
Albion vehicles.

Museum or gallery collection, archive, or library special collection:
Albion archive of material relating to Albion commercial vehicles

Printed publications:
Albion Magazine (quarterly)

continued overleaf

Links with:
Albion Vehicle Preservation Trust
 18 Netherdale Drive, Paisley, Renfrewshire, PA1
 3DA

BILLINGS NATURAL FAMILY PLANNING CENTRE

Acronym or abbreviation: The BOM Trust

The Basement, 58b Vauxhall Grove, London, SW8
1TB

Tel: 020 7793 0026
Fax: 020 7793 0026

Enquiries:
Enquiries to: Director General
Other contacts: Secretary for book and literature
orders.

Founded:
1987

Formerly called:
Billings Family Life Centre, Billings Natural Family
Planning Centre

Organisation type and purpose:
International organisation, national organisation,
professional body (membership is by qualification,
election or invitation), voluntary organisation,
registered charity (charity number 10077245),
suitable for ages: 12 to 22, training organisation,
consultancy.

Subject coverage:
Literature, teaching and teacher training in the
Billings Ovulation Method providing a means of
natural family planning for the achievement or
avoidance of pregnancy. Teacher training and
education courses in human sexuality which, while
addressing all aspects of the human person
including fertility, teach chastity.

Access to staff:
Contact by letter, by telephone and by fax.
Appointment necessary.
Hours: Mon, Tue, Wed, Fri, 1000 to 1800
Special comments: Evening and weekend
appointments.
Charges made to all users (with exceptions).
May close during state school holidays.

Access to building, collection or gallery:
Prior appointment required
Hours: Mon to Fri, 1000 to 1700; plus some
evenings and Sats
Special comments: Closed on some evenings, some
weekends and some school holidays.

Affiliated with the:
World Organisation of Ovulation Method Billings
(WOOMB)

Other addresses:
Billings NFP Centre (Hours: Tue and Thu, 0930 to
1230)
 Margaret House, 132 Huntley Street, Aberdeen,
 AB10 1SU; tel: 01224 643300; e-mail:
 mariesandison@hotmail.com

Parent body:
Billings Family Life Centre (WOOMB)
 27 Alexandra Parade, North Fitzroy, 3068,
 Australia; tel: (00 61 3) 948 1722 / 1 800 336 860;
 fax: (00 61 3) 9482 4208; e-mail: billings@ozemail
 .com.au; website: http://www.woomb.org

BINGO ASSOCIATION, THE

Lexham House, 75 High Street North, Dunstable,
Bedfordshire, LU6 1JF

Tel: 01582 860921
Fax: 01582 860925
E-mail: info@bingo-association.co.uk

Website:
http://www.bingo-association.co.uk
Industry news; press releases.

Enquiries:
Enquiries to: Chief Executive

Other contacts: Administration Manager for centre
of activity.

Founded:
1985

Formerly called:
Bingo Association of Great Britain (year of change
1998)

Organisation type and purpose:
Trade association (membership is by qualification,
election or invitation), present number of
members: 125.

Subject coverage:
Licensed bingo in Great Britain; Gaming Act 1968
and the law appertaining to licensed bingo, where,
how and when you can play; history of bingo.

Printed publications:
Industry Factsheet
Code of Practice
Management Guide (£10 per copy plus postage)

Access to staff:
Contact by letter, by telephone, by fax, by e-mail,
in person and via website. Appointment necessary.
Hours: Mon to Fri, 0900 to 1700

BIO INDUSTRY ASSOCIATION SCOTLAND

Acronym or abbreviation: BIA Scotland

Centre House, Midlothian Innovation Centre,
Pentlandfield, Roslin, Midlothian, EH25 9RE

Tel: 0131 440 6161
Fax: 0131 440 2871
E-mail: scotland@bioindustry.org

Website:
http://www.bioindustry.org

Enquiries:
Enquiries to: Director

Founded:
2001

Formerly called:
Scottish Biomedical Association (SbA) (year of
change 2001)

Organisation type and purpose:
Trade association.

Subject coverage:
All aspects associated with the promotion of the
healthcare industry, biomedical and biotechnology
sectors in Scotland.

Printed publications:
Annual Review
Membership directory (members only)
Membership Information
Order printed publications from: Bio Industry
Association
14/15 Belgrave Square, London, SW1X 8PS, tel: 020
7565 7192, fax: 020 7565 7191, e-mail: rgrant@
bioindustry.org

Electronic and video publications:
BIS-Database of biotech industry in the UK –
 contains details of companies, products (CD-
 ROM)

Publications list:
Available in print

Access to staff:
Contact by letter, by telephone, by fax and by e-
mail. Appointment necessary.
Hours: Mon to Fri, 0900 to 1700

Parent body:
BIA
 14–15 Belgrave Square, London, SW1X 8PS; tel:
 020 7565 7190; fax: 020 7565 7191

BIO-WISE

Formal name: BIO-WISE – Biotechnology at Work

PO Box 83, Didcot, Oxfordshire, OX11 0BR

Tel: 0800 432100 Freephone helpline
Fax: 01235 432997
E-mail: biowise.help@aeat.co.uk

Website:
http://www.dti.gov.uk/biowise
The BIO-WISE website carries regularly updated
information on the Programme and its activities. It
also signposts to other websites and information
sources which may be useful.

Enquiries:
Enquiries to: BIO-WISE Helpline
Direct tel: 0800 4732100

Founded:
1999

Formerly called:
Biotechnology Means Business (BMB) (year of
change 1999)

Organisation type and purpose:
National government body, advisory body.
BIO-WISE is a major UK Government Programme,
funded by the Department of Trade and Industry.
BIO-WISE aims to improve the competitiveness of
UK industry and to support the development of
the UK biotechnology supply industry.

Subject coverage:
BIO-WISE offers free independent and practical
advice on how biotechnology can be used to
potentially reduce business costs, improve product
quality and/or reduce environmental impact.
Sources of information include a Helpline, website,
publications and events.

**Museum or gallery collection, archive, or library
special collection:**
The BIO-WISE Helpline has access to a wealth of
 information relating to the use of biotechnology

Printed publications:
For details of BIO-WISE publications call the
 freephone Helpline or visit the website. All
 publications are free of charge

Access to staff:
Contact by letter, by telephone, by fax, by e-mail
and via website
Hours: Mon to Fri, 0900 to 1700

BIOCHEMICAL SOCIETY

Third Floor, Eagle House, 16 Procter Street,
London, WC1V 6NX

Tel: 020 7280 4100
Fax: 020 7280 4170
E-mail: genadmin@biochemistry.org

Website:
http://www.biochemistry.org
http://www.portlandpress.com

Enquiries:
Enquiries to: Membership Secretary
Direct e-mail: membership@biochemistry.org

Founded:
1911

Organisation type and purpose:
National organisation, learned society
(membership is by election or invitation), present
number of members: 7200, registered charity
(charity number 253894), publishing house.

Subject coverage:
Biochemistry, biotechnology, biomolecular
sciences, molecular biology, genetics, cell biology.

**Museum or gallery collection, archive, or library
special collection:**
Contact Archivist at: genadmin@biochemistry.org

Printed publications:
Biotechnology and Applied Biochemistry (6 times
 a year)
Biochemical Journal (fortnightly)
Biochemical Society Transactions (quarterly)
Essays in Biochemistry (2 times a year)
Graduate Employment Survey (annually)
Symposia (annually)
The Biochemist (6 times a year)

Biology of the Cell (12 times a year)
Order printed publications from: Portland Press
Commerce Way, Colchester, CO2 8HP, tel: 01206
796351, fax: 01206 799331, e-mail: sales@portland
-services.com

Publications list:
Available online and in print

Access to staff:
Contact by letter, by telephone, by fax, by e-mail
and via website
Hours: Mon to Fri, 0900 to 1700

Links with:
Portland Press
   tel: 020 7580 5530; fax: 020 7323 1136; e-mail:
   editorial@portlandpress.com

Members of:
Association of Learned and Professional Society
Publishers
Federation of European Biochemical Societies
International Union of Biochemistry and Molecular
Biology

Other address:
Biochemical Society
   Commerce Way, Colchester, CO2 8HP; tel: 01206
   796351; fax: 01206 799331; e-mail: membership@
   biochemistry.org

BIOLOGICAL RECORDS CENTRE & LUDLOW MUSEUM

Acronym or abbreviation: SBRC

Ludlow Museum Resource Centre, Parkway,
Ludlow, Shropshire, SY8 2PG

Tel: 01584 813666
Fax: 01584 813601
E-mail: ludlow.museum@shropshire-cc.gov.uk

Website:
http://www.shropshire.gov.uk/museums.nsf

Enquiries:
Enquiries to: Curator

Founded:
1833

Organisation type and purpose:
Museum.
Formed in 1833 as a museum.

Museum or gallery collection, archive, or library special collection:
Biological and geological records
Geological, biological, social history collections

Non-library collection catalogue:
All or part available in-house

Library catalogue:
All or part available in-house

Access to staff:
Contact by letter, by telephone, by fax, by e-mail
and in person. Appointment necessary.
Hours: Mon to Fri, 0900 to 1700

Access to building, collection or gallery:
Prior appointment required

Access for disabled people:
Parking nearby

Other addresses:
Ludlow Museum Display
   Castle Street, Ludlow; e-mail: ludlow.museum@
   shropshire-cc.gov.uk

BIOMEDICAL RESEARCH EDUCATION TRUST

Acronym or abbreviation: BRET

25 Shaftesbury Avenue, London, W1D 7EG

Tel: 020 7287 2595
Fax: 020 7287 2595
E-mail: t.g@bret.org.uk

Website:
http://www.bret.org.uk

Information otherwise found in leaflets,
information about obtaining speakers.

Enquiries:
Enquiries to: Director
Direct e-mail: ted@tgriffiths.net

Founded:
1988

Organisation type and purpose:
Service industry, registered charity (charity
number 292366), training organisation.
Information for schools and other interested
groups about why animals are used for medical
research.

Subject coverage:
Animal welfare, information for schools,
biomedical research.

Printed publications:
Information About Animal Research (leaflet, free)
Schools Resources Guide (leaflet, free)
Why Is Animal Research Necessary? (leaflet, free)

Electronic and video publications:
Animals and Human Kidney (video, free to schools
   on request)
Choices (video, free to schools on request)
Inside the Animal House (video available for
   viewing only with a speaker)
The Use of Animals in Medical Research (video,
   free to schools on request)
What About People? (video, free to schools on
   request)

Access to staff:
Contact by letter, by telephone, by fax, by e-mail
and via website
Hours: Mon to Fri, 0900 to 1700

Parent body:
Research Defence Society

BIOSS INTERNATIONAL

Acronym or abbreviation: BIOSS

Box 3, Brunel Science Park, Kingston Lane,
Uxbridge, Middlesex, UB8 3PQ

Tel: 01895 270072
Fax: 01895 254760
E-mail: post@bioss-international.com

Website:
http://www.bioss.com
EDAC, a website which provides organisation and
individual development procedures on-line, based
on the analysis by trained practitioners from three
instruments known as MCPA, an executive
development instrument, Launchpad, a
psychometric instrument, a modified version of
CPA (Career Path Appreciation).

Enquiries:
Enquiries to: Secretary General
Other contacts: Secretary & Registrar (Finance and
Legal)

Founded:
1968

Formerly called:
Bioss International Ltd; Brunel Institute of
Organisation and Social Studies (year of change
2001)

Organisation type and purpose:
International organisation, advisory body,
membership association (membership is by
qualification, election or invitation), present
number of members: over 200, registered charity
(charity number 1016381).

Subject coverage:
Social policy, social organisation, social
relationships, social institutions, social
stratification and mobility, individual behaviour
and capacity, education, church and the
community, youth in society.
Career path appreciation, mapping and appraisal.
The use and management of strategic information
and the management of change and Organisation
Mapping.

Printed publications:
Conference papers, books, working papers
A list of locally produced papers is held at the
   address

Access to staff:
Contact by letter, by telephone, by fax, by e-mail
and via website. Appointment necessary.
Hours: Mon to Fri, 0900 to 1700

Other officers worldwide:
BIOSS International
   Information at same address

BIOTECHNOLOGY AND BIOLOGICAL SCIENCES RESEARCH COUNCIL

Acronym or abbreviation: BBSRC

Polaris House, North Star Avenue, Swindon,
Wiltshire, SN2 1UH

Tel: 01793 413200
Fax: 01793 413201
E-mail: external.relations@bbsrc.ac.uk

Website:
http://www.bbsrc.ac.uk
Information on the organisation, funding, research
committees, studentships, fellowships and special
initiatives. Oasis database of recent BBSRC-funded
research.

Formerly called:
AFRC, Science and Engineering Research Council
(year of change 1994)

Organisation type and purpose:
Research organisation.

Subject coverage:
Agriculture, food, biotechnology, pharmaceutical,
chemical and healthcare industries.

Printed publications:
Annual Report
BBSRC Business Strategic Plan

Electronic and video publications:
Oasis database of recent BBSRC-funded research

Access to staff:
Contact by e-mail. Appointment necessary.
Hours: Mon to Fri, 0900 to 1700

BIRDLIFE INTERNATIONAL

Wellbrook Court, Girton Road, Cambridge, CB3
0NA

Tel: 01223 277318
Fax: 01223 277200
E-mail: birdlife@birdlife.org

Website:
http://www.birdlife.org
Information about the organisation. How to
contact Partners. Publications. Information on
important bird areas and globally threatened bird
species.

Enquiries:
Enquiries to: Communications Manager
Direct tel: 01223 279813
Direct e-mail: martin.fowlie@birdlife.org.uk
Other contacts: Information Scientist & Librarian

Founded:
1922

Formerly called:
International Council for Bird Preservation (year of
change 1993)

Organisation type and purpose:
International organisation (membership is by
subscription), registered charity (charity number
1042125), research organisation.
Carries out field projects, research and advocacy
relating to threatened bird species and their
habitats.

continued overleaf

Subject coverage:
Status of bird species throughout the world especially all endangered species; conservation problems and priorities concerning threatened bird species and their habitats.

Museum or gallery collection, archive, or library special collection:
Library and reprint collection relating to threatened birds

Trade and statistical information:
World data on threatened bird species.

Library catalogue:
All or part available in-house

Printed publications:
Books:
Bird Conservation series (12 titles)
Birds in Europe
Important Bird Areas
Red Data Books (3 titles)
Threatened Birds of the World
Periodical publications:
Annual Report
BirdLife International Africa (newsletter, 2 times a year)
BirdLife International Asia (newsletter, quarterly)
World Birdwatch (magazine, quarterly, annual subscription £25)
Order printed publications from: For books only: NHBS Limited, 2–3 Wills Road, Totnes, Devon, tel: 01803 865913, fax: 01803 865280, e-mail: sales@nhbs.co.uk
For Threatened Birds of the Worl: Lynx Edicions, Passeig de Gràcia, Barcelona, 12 E-08007, Spain, tel: +34 93 301 07 77, fax: +34 93 302 1475, e-mail: lynx@hbw.com

Access to staff:
Contact by letter, by telephone, by fax, by e-mail and via website
Hours: Mon to Fri, 0900 to 1700

Access to building, collection or gallery:
By prior appointment only
Hours: Mon to Fri, 0900 to 1700

Access for disabled people:
Toilet facilities

Partnership of:
National conservation organisations worldwide, present in more than 100 countries or territories

BIRKBECK COLLEGE LIBRARY

Library, Malet Street, London, WC1E 7HX

Tel: 020 7631 6064
Fax: 020 7631 6066
E-mail: library-help@bbk.ac.uk

Website:
http://www.bbk.ac.uk/lib/
Library services.

Enquiries:
Enquiries to: Librarian
Direct tel: 020 7631 6250
Direct e-mail: p.dolphin@bbk.ac.uk

Founded:
1823

Organisation type and purpose:
University library.

Subject coverage:
Applied linguistics, economics, English, film studies, French, geography, German, history, history of art, philosophy, politics, psychology, occupational psychology, sociology, Spanish, chemistry, botany, zoology, statistics, computer science, crystallography, geology, law, management and business studies.

Library catalogue:
All or part available online

Printed publications:
Leaflets on Library services – all on Web

Access to staff:
Contact by letter, by telephone, by fax, by e-mail and via website. Non-members charged.
Hours: Malet Street: Term time; Mon to Thu, 1000 to 2230; Fri, 1100 to 2230; Sat, 1000 to 2000; Sun, 1200 to 2000
Gresse Street: Term time: Mon to Thu, 1000 to 2130, Fri, 1100 to 2130; Sat, 1000 to 1700
Vacations: times vary, check website

Other addresses:
Birbeck College Library
    Gresse Street, London, W1P 2LL; tel: 020 7631 6492; fax: 020 7631 6435
Continuing Education Library
    39 Gordon Square, London, WC1H 0PD; tel: 020 7631 6167; fax: 020 7631 6163

Parent body:
University of London

BIRMINGHAM AND DISTRICT BUTCHERS ASSOCIATION

Acronym or abbreviation: BBA

30 Manor House, Moat Lane, Birmingham, B5 5BD

Tel: 0121 622 4900

Enquiries:
Enquiries to: Secretary

Founded:
1878

Organisation type and purpose:
Trade association.

Subject coverage:
All aspects relating to the running of a retail butcher's shop, including current legislation and consumer opinion on a daily basis.

Access to staff:
Contact by letter and by telephone
Hours: Mon to Fri, 0900 to 1300, with 24-hour answering service

BIRMINGHAM AND MIDLAND INSTITUTE

Acronym or abbreviation: BMI

9 Margaret Street, Birmingham, B3 3BS

Tel: 0121 236 3591
Fax: 0121 212 4577
E-mail: admin@bmi.org.uk

Enquiries:
Enquiries to: Administrator

Founded:
1854

Incorporated:
The Birmingham Library (year of change 1955)

Organisation type and purpose:
Learned society (membership is by subscription), present number of members: 500, registered charity (charity number 522852).
Founded by Act of Parliament in 1854 for the Diffusion and Advancement of Science, Literature and Art amongst all Classes of Persons resident in Birmingham and the Midland Counties.

Subject coverage:
Science, literature and art.

Museum or gallery collection, archive, or library special collection:
18th century volumes
19th and 20th century volumes on history, literature, natural history, science, travel, biography, autobiography, poetry
Late 19th and early 20th century fiction
Classical music books, records, CDs

Non-library collection catalogue:
All or part available in-house

Library catalogue:
All or part available in-house

Printed publications:
BMI Insight (annual magazine, free to members)

Access to staff:
Contact by letter, by telephone, by fax and in person. Appointment necessary. Non-members charged.
Hours: Mon to Fri, 0900 to 1800

Access to building, collection or gallery:
Prior appointment required
Hours: Library: Mon to Fri, 1000 to 1800
Special comments: Members only. Charge for non-members research. Reference only for non-members.

Access for disabled people:
Ramped entry

Includes:
The Birmingham Library, founded in 1779

BIRMINGHAM ASSOCIATION OF YOUTH CLUBS

Acronym or abbreviation: BAYC

Hilda Simister House, 581 Pershore Road, Selly Park, Birmingham, B29 7EL

Tel: 0845 241 0923
Fax: 0845 241 0924
E-mail: info@bayc.org

Enquiries:
Enquiries to: Chief Executive
Other contacts: Principal Development Officer for affiliations and support services.

Founded:
1898

Organisation type and purpose:
Membership association, voluntary organisation, registered charity (charity number 1090789).
Youth Club Association.
Servicing agency for mixed youth groups in Birmingham and the Black Country.

Subject coverage:
Good practice in youth work; networks and contacts; volunteering opportunities for young people; project design and development; curriculum development; specialist work with young women and young men; accreditator of young people's voluntary activity, capacity building for youth groups.

Museum or gallery collection, archive, or library special collection:
Resources on work with girls and young women, boys and young men, youth work policy and practice, residential centres and projects, action research with young people, involving disabled young people as volunteers

Trade and statistical information:
Profile of youth groups in Birmingham and surrounding areas.

Printed publications:
Annual Report
Newsletter (monthly)
Promotional material for specific projects
Publications available through national body, UK Youth

Access to staff:
Contact by letter, by telephone, by fax and by e-mail. Appointment necessary.
Hours: Mon to Fri, 0915 to 1800

Access for disabled people:
Parking provided, ramped entry

Affiliated to:
UK Youth
    2nd Floor, Kirby House, 20–24 Kirby Street, London, EC1N 8TS; tel: 020 7242 4045; fax: 020 7242 4125; e-mail: info@ukyouth.org

BIRMINGHAM AUTOMOTIVE SAFETY CENTRE

Acronym or abbreviation: BASC

School of Engineering (Mechanical and Manufacturing Engineering), University of Birmingham, Edgbaston, Birmingham, B15 2TT

Tel: 0121 414 5156
Fax: 0121 414 4180

Website:
http://barc.bham.ac.uk

Enquiries:
Enquiries to: Manager
Direct tel: 0121 414 7384
Direct e-mail: a.m.hassan@bham.ac.uk

Founded:
1970

Formerly called:
Accident Research Centre; Accident Research Unit (year of change 1999)

Organisation type and purpose:
University department or institute, training organisation, consultancy, research organisation.

Subject coverage:
Injuries and vehicle design, accident causation, transport, safety, product liability.

Access to staff:
Contact by letter, by telephone, by fax, by e-mail and via website. Appointment necessary.
Hours: Mon to Fri, 0900 to 1700

BIRMINGHAM BIBLIOGRAPHICAL SOCIETY

c/o Information Services, The University of Birmingham, Edgbaston, Birmingham, B15 2TT

Tel: 0121 414 3132
E-mail: a.l.dover@bham.ac.uk

Enquiries:
Enquiries to: Honorary Secretary

Organisation type and purpose:
Learned society.

Subject coverage:
Bibliographical and allied subjects, printing, booktrade etc; West Midlands Bibliography; local history of the book trade. On-going research project on the West Midlands book trade.

Printed publications:
West Midlands Book Trade Project; Working papers 1–7 covering the period to 1839, published 1975–1987

Access to staff:
Contact by e-mail
Hours: Mon to Fri, 0900 to 1700

BIRMINGHAM BOTANICAL GARDENS AND GLASSHOUSES

Acronym or abbreviation: BBHS

Westbourne Road, Edgbaston, Birmingham, B15 3TR

Tel: 0121 454 1860
E-mail: admin@birminghambotanicalgardens.org.uk

Website:
http://www.birminghambotanicalgardens.org.uk

Enquiries:
Enquiries to: Director
Other contacts: Curator for scientific and educational.

Founded:
1832

Formerly called:
Birmingham Botanical and Horticultural Society Limited

Organisation type and purpose:
Membership association (membership is by subscription), present number of members: 5,000, registered charity (charity number 528981), suitable for all ages.

The Company, which is limited by guarantee, is an educational charity whose aims are: to further public education in botany, horticulture and zoology, and provide facilities for research; to maintain and operate the Birmingham Botanical Gardens and Glasshouses for the above purpose, and for the recreation of the public.

Subject coverage:
Horticulture, history of Birmingham Botanical Gardens.

Non-library collection catalogue:
All or part available in-house

Library catalogue:
All or part available in-house

Printed publications:
Annual report and accounts (online)
Information sheets (10p to £1.50)
Newsletters (quarterly, £1)
Souvenir Guide (£3)

Electronic and video publications:
Guides (audio, braille and large print, free of charge)

Publications list:
Available online

Access to staff:
Contact by letter, by telephone, by fax, by e-mail and via website. Appointment necessary.
Hours: Mon to Fri, 0900 to 1700 (variable according to season)

Access for disabled people:
Parking provided, ramped entry, access to all public areas, toilet facilities

BIRMINGHAM BOYS AND GIRLS UNION

Acronym or abbreviation: BBGU

Woodlands Camp, Bournevale, Walsall, West Midlands, WS9 0SH

Tel: 0121 353 7329
Fax: 0121 353 7329

Enquiries:
Enquiries to: Warden

Founded:
1906

Organisation type and purpose:
Registered charity (charity number 522487), suitable for ages: 7+.
Residential outdoor activity centre giving priority to disadvantaged and handicapped groups.

Subject coverage:
Outdoor education; animal sanctuary; environmental.

Printed publications:
Brochures
Newsletter

Access to staff:
Contact by letter, by telephone and in person. Appointment necessary.
Hours: Mon to Fri, 0900 to 1700

Access for disabled people:
Parking provided, ramped entry, toilet facilities

BIRMINGHAM BURNS CENTRE

Selly Oak Hospital, Raddlebarn Road, Birmingham, B29 6JD

Tel: 0121 627 1627
Fax: 0121 627 8782

Enquiries:
Enquiries to: Clinical Lead in Burns
Direct tel: 0121 627 8784
Direct e-mail: remopapini@doctors.org.uk
Other contacts: Burns & Plastic Surgery Co-ordinator for clinical service lead in burns.

Founded:
1944

Formed from:
Birmingham Accident Hospital, date of change, October 1995

Formerly called:
West Midlands Regional Burns Unit (year of change 1993)

Organisation type and purpose:
Hospital.
Hospital department specialising in care of burn victims.

Subject coverage:
Care of burns, epidemiology, pathology, acute care, aftercare and rehabilitation, aspects of clinical use of cultured skin and skin substitutes.

Access to staff:
Contact by letter, by telephone, by fax and by e-mail. Appointment necessary.
Hours: 24 hours

Access for disabled people:
Toilet facilities

Part of:
National Health Service

BIRMINGHAM CHAMBER OF COMMERCE AND INDUSTRY

Acronym or abbreviation: BCI

75 Harborne Road, Edgbaston, Birmingham, B15 3DH

Tel: 0121 454 6171\ Minicom no. 0845 606 2666
Fax: 0121 455 8670
E-mail: info@birminghamchamber.org.uk

Website:
http://www.bci.org.uk

Enquiries:
Enquiries to: Information Officer

Founded:
1813

Organisation type and purpose:
Trade association, membership association (membership is by subscription).

Subject coverage:
Business information, export documentation, export advice and trade missions, business management and policy.

Museum or gallery collection, archive, or library special collection:
Business directories and databases
British Standards

Printed publications:
Newspaper/Bulletin (monthly)
Surveys, reports and handbooks
Members Directory (annually)

Access to staff:
Contact by letter, by telephone, by fax, by e-mail, in person and via website. Non-members charged.
Hours: Mon to Fri, 0900 to 1700

Access for disabled people:
Parking provided, ramped entry, access to all public areas, toilet facilities

Member of:
Association of British Chambers of Commerce

Partner in:
Birmingham Economic Development Partnership
Business Link Birmingham

BIRMINGHAM CHINESE SOCIETY

11 Allcock Street, Birmingham, B9 4DY

Tel: 0121 773 0099 / 0870 2030100
Fax: 0121 733 3636
E-mail: ichu@jobs4brum.org.uk

Website:
http://website.lineone.net/~b.chinese.s

Enquiries:
Enquiries to: Manager

continued overleaf

Founded:
1988

Organisation type and purpose:
Voluntary organisation, registered charity (charity number 1049035), training organisation.
Umbrella organisation.

Subject coverage:
Information and advice centre, employment, business; training, ESOL, IT, Chinese input, basic food hygiene course, intermediate food hygiene course, first aid, home maintenance course; health, mental health, men and women; business offering advice to local Chinese businesses; translation and interpreting service, Cantonese, Mandarin, Haka, Vietnamese to English.

Access to staff:
Contact by letter, by telephone, by fax, by e-mail, in person and via website. Appointment necessary.
Hours: Mon to Fri, 1000 to 1700

BIRMINGHAM CITY ARCHIVES

Birmingham Central Library, Chamberlain Square, Birmingham, B3 3HQ

Tel: 0121 303 4217
E-mail: archives@birmingham.gov.uk

Website:
http://www.birmingham.gov.uk
Part guide to records held.

Enquiries:
Enquiries to: Senior Archivist
Other contacts: Archivist

Organisation type and purpose:
Local government body, public library.
Archives, record office.
To collect, preserve and make available for research archival collections relating to the City of Birmingham, 12th to 20th centuries.

Subject coverage:
Sources for local and family history in the Birmingham area including local authority records, church records, business records, estate and family records and public records (eg courts, coroners, hospitals etc); some records relating to wider West Midlands area.

Museum or gallery collection, archive, or library special collection:
Original archival materials including documents, photographs etc, too many and varied to list

Non-library collection catalogue:
All or part available online and in-house

Access to staff:
Contact by letter, by telephone, by fax, by e-mail, in person and via website
Hours: Tue,Wed, 1000 to 1700; Thu, 1000 to 2000; Fri, Sat, 1000 to 1700; Closed Mon
Special comments: Official proof of ID required.

BIRMINGHAM CITY UNIVERSITY

Acronym or abbreviation: BCU

Kenrick Library, Perry Barr, Birmingham, B42 2SU

Tel: 0121 331 5000
Fax: 0121 356 2875

Website:
http://library.bcu.ac.uk

Enquiries:
Enquiries to: Director of Library and Learning Resources
Direct tel: 0121 331 5300
Direct e-mail: judith.andrews@bcu.ac.uk

Organisation type and purpose:
University library.

Subject coverage:
Construction technology, quantity surveying, computer studies, architecture, economics, management, communications studies, english, nursing, midwifery and community health, law,

sociology, social work, accounting, finance, speech therapy, town planning, landscape architecture, housing, government, banking, fine art, art education, fashion and textiles, foundation and community studies, jewellery, silversmithing and horology, three-dimensional design, visual communication, education, music, psychology, media, electrical engineering, mechanical engineering, acting, drama

Museum or gallery collection, archive, or library special collection:
Birmingham Flute Society Library
Royal College of Organists Library
Early Printed Music Collection (pre c.1850)
Material samples from late 19th century to mid-20th century
Piranesi engravings (15 vols)

Library catalogue:
All or part available online

Publications list:
Available online and in print

Access to staff:
Contact by letter, by telephone, by fax, by e-mail, in person and via website. Appointment necessary.
Hours: Mon to Fri, 0900 to 1700

Access to building, collection or gallery:
No prior appointment required. Kenrick Library has controlled access and identification is required.

BIRMINGHAM CIVIL JUSTICE CENTRE

Formal name: Ministry of Justice, Midlands Region Library and Information Service

The Library, The Priory Courts, 33 Bull Street, Birmingham, B4 6DW

Tel: 0121 681 3446
Fax: 0121 681 3444
E-mail: mike.troon@dca.gsi.gov.uk

Organisation type and purpose:
National government body.
Ministry of Justice (MoJ) Regional Library Service.
To provide a legal information service for judiciary and MoJ staff throughout the Midlands Region (including all court libraries).

Subject coverage:
Law reports, public general acts and measures, statutory instruments, legal books and periodicals.

Information services:
Library Information Service provided by Ministry of Justice Library and Information Services, Judicial and Court Libraries

Library catalogue:
All or part available in-house

Access to staff:
Appointment necessary.
Hours: Mon to Fri, 0830 to 1530
Special comments: The Priory Courts Library is primarily for the use of the judiciary and staff of the Ministry of Justice in the Midlands Region.

Access to building, collection or gallery:
Prior appointment required

BIRMINGHAM EARLY MUSIC FESTIVAL LTD

PO Box 9442, Birmingham, B15 3QA

Tel: 0870 241 6441
Fax: 0870 241 6441

Website:
http://www.bemf.net

Enquiries:
Enquiries to: Administrator

Founded:
1992

Organisation type and purpose:
Registered charity (charity number 1039399).

Runs annual festival of early music.

Subject coverage:
Early music.

Access to staff:
Contact by letter
Hours: Mon to Fri, 0900 to 1700

Access to building, collection or gallery:
No access other than to staff

BIRMINGHAM ECONOMIC STRATEGY

Development Strategy, 18th Floor Alpha Tower, Suffolk Street, Queensway, Birmingham, B1 1TR

Tel: 0121 303 3719
Fax: 0121 303 3076
E-mail: BEIC.Enquiry.Line@birmingham.gov.uk

Website:
http://www.birminghameconomy.org.uk

Enquiries:
Enquiries to: Information Service
Other contacts: Business Centre Manager for major projects, strategies, analysis.

Founded:
1994

Organisation type and purpose:
Local government body, research organisation.
Source of information and analysis on the operation of the Birmingham economy and labour market.

Subject coverage:
The Birmingham economy and labour market.

Museum or gallery collection, archive, or library special collection:
Wide variety of reports and information on the Birmingham economy

Trade and statistical information:
Data on the Birmingham economy, economic forecasts, volume of investment, employment (occupation, sector), unemployment, impact & evaluation studies.

Access to staff:
Contact by letter, by telephone, by fax, by e-mail and via website. Appointment necessary.
Hours: Mon to Fri, 0900 to 1700
Special comments: Charges made for some services.

Access for disabled people:
Level entry, access to all public areas

Affiliated to:
Birmingham Economic Development Partnership Limited

Parent body:
Birmingham City Council

BIRMINGHAM FOCUS ON BLINDNESS

Acronym or abbreviation: Birmingham Focus

48–62 Woodville Road, Harborne, Birmingham, B17 9AT

Tel: 0121 478 5200; 0121 478 5222 (helpline)
Fax: 0121 478 5280
E-mail: info@birminghamfocus.org.uk

Website:
http://www.birminghamfocus.org.uk

Enquiries:
Enquiries to: Chief Executive
Direct tel: 0121 478 5201
Direct e-mail: rob@birminghamfocus.org.uk
Other contacts: Marketing Manager

Founded:
1846

Formerly a part of:
Birmingham Royal Institution for the Blind (BRIB) (year of change 1997)

Formerly called:
BRIB – Working with Blind People (year of change 1998)

Organisation type and purpose:
Registered charity (charity number 1065745). Welfare organisation.

Subject coverage:
Welfare of blind and partially sighted people in Birmingham, training and development, low vision assessment, rehabilitation and aids, blindness with multiple disabilities.

Printed publications:
In Focus News (quarterly; large print, audio, Braille)
Focal Bulletin
Leaflets on Services and Volunteers, Legacies, etc.

Electronic and video publications:
All publications available in large print, audio, Braille or e-mail

Access to staff:
Contact by letter, by telephone, by fax, by e-mail, in person and via website. Appointment necessary.
Hours: Mon to Fri, 0900 to 1700

Member organisation of:
National Association of Local Societies for Visually Impaired (NALSVI)
Queen Alexandra College

BIRMINGHAM LAW SOCIETY

8 Temple Street, Birmingham, B2 5BT

Tel: 0121 633 6901
Fax: 0121 633 3507
E-mail: info@birminghamlawsociety.co.uk

Website:
http://www.birminghamlawsociety.co.uk

Founded:
1818

Organisation type and purpose:
Professional body (membership is by subscription).

Subject coverage:
Law.

Library catalogue:
All or part available in-house

Access to staff:
Contact by letter, by telephone, by fax and by e-mail. Appointment necessary. Access for members only.
Hours: Mon to Fri, 0900 to 1700

Access to building, collection or gallery:
Prior appointment required

BIRMINGHAM LIBRARIES

Acronym or abbreviation: BLS

Central Library, Chamberlain Square, Birmingham, B3 3HQ

Tel: 0121 303 4511\ Minicom no. 0121 235 4511
Fax: 0121 233 4458
E-mail: centrallibrary@birmingham.gov.uk

Website:
http://www.birmingham.gov.uk/libraries

Enquiries:
Enquiries to: Librarian
Direct tel: 0121 303 4220
Direct e-mail: centrallibrary@birmingham.gov.uk
Other contacts: Information Officer for fee based business information service.

Founded:
1866

Formerly called:
Birmingham Public Libraries (BPL); Birmingham Library Services (BLS) (year of change 2001)

Organisation type and purpose:
Public library.

Subject coverage:
Local studies and history; Birmingham information, history, geography, maps, genealogy, photographs; science, technology management, environment, engineering, motor manuals, information technology, building, manufacturing, general and production management; social sciences, politics, economics, law, education (including open learning, school governor information), community information, health information, philosophy, religion, transport; arts, languages and literature; fine and performing arts, music, scores, sets of vocal scores, sound recordings; business information, telephone and trade directories, company information, annual reports, statistics, market research reports, marketing, company histories; archives.

Museum or gallery collection, archive, or library special collection:
Archives (of Birmingham)
Baskerville Collection
Boulton and Watt and Priestley collections
British Standards
Early and fine printing
Francis Bedford Collection of photographs
Francis Frith Collection of photographs
Kings Norton and Sheldon Parochial libraries
Local history of Birmingham and surrounding counties
Marston Rudland Collection of engraved portraits
Milton, Johnson, Cervantes, War poetry collections
National organ archive
Official publications
Parker Collection of early children's books and games
Patents (British, European, US and PCT)
Railway collection
Shakespeare
Stone Collection of Victorian and Edwardian photographs
Trade union collection
UN depository library

Non-library collection catalogue:
All or part available in-house

Library catalogue:
All or part available online

Printed publications:
Literature and art bibliographies
Local history publications
Statistics and market research
Building the City – a series of fourteen books to date, tracing the history of different areas of the city, each title is illustrated with over 200 photographs mainly drawn from the Birmingham Central Library Archives, £9.99 each volume:
Acocks Green
Northfield
Moseley, Balsall Heath and Highgate
Yardley
Old Harbourne
Kings Heath
Kings Norton
Edgbaston
Erdington
Handsworth, Hockley and Handsworth Wood
Sutton Coldfield
Sutton Coldfield the Second Selection
Hall Green
Aston and Perry Barr
The Heart of the City – a series of books
Birmingham Transport
Birmingham Pubs
Contrasts in a Victorian City
Birmingham Between The Wars
Central Birmingham 1870–1920
Central Birmingham 1920–1970
Other series include Sounds of the City, Shaping the City, Capturing the City, The Man from the City, Life and Death in the City, news from the City
Order printed publications from: Room Bookings and Sales, Birmingham Library Services
tel: 0121 303 2868

Electronic and video publications:
Birmingham – A Journey Through Time (1932–1945, £12.99, video)
Birmingham – A Journey Through Time Part 2 (1946–1969, £12.99, video)
Sutton Coldfield – A Journey Through Time (£12.99, video)

Publications list:
Available in print

Access to staff:
Contact by letter, by telephone, by fax, by e-mail, in person and via website
Hours: Mon, Tue, Thu, Fri, 0900 to 2000; Sat, 0900 to 1700
Special comments: Archives section has restricted opening hours, closing at 1700 each day and all day Wednesday.

Houses the:
Diocesan Record Office
Information Direct

Member of:
UK Patents Information Network

Parent body:
Birmingham City Council

BIRMINGHAM LOCAL MEDICAL COMMITTEE

36 Harborne Road, Edgbaston, Birmingham, B15 3AF

Tel: 0121 454 5008
Fax: 0121 455 0758

Enquiries:
Enquiries to: Executive Secretary / Business manager
Other contacts: Doctors

Founded:
1911

Organisation type and purpose:
Professional body.

Subject coverage:
Advice on range of medical and medico/legal matters to GPs.

Access to staff:
Contact by letter and by fax
Hours: Mon to Fri, 1030 to 1530

Access to building, collection or gallery:
Appointment required

Access for disabled people:
Parking provided, ramped entry

BIRMINGHAM LOCAL STUDIES AND HISTORY SERVICE

Birmingham Central Library, Chamberlain Square, Birmingham, B3 3HQ

Tel: 0121 303 4220 or 4549
Fax: 0121 464 0993
E-mail: local.studies.library@birmingham.gov.uk

Website:
http://www.birmingham.gov.uk
Information on central library as a whole but including local studies and genealogy.

Enquiries:
Enquiries to: Librarian

Organisation type and purpose:
Public library.

Subject coverage:
History and development of Birmingham, general world history/geography, military history, world tourist guides, archaeology, ancient history and genealogy.

Museum or gallery collection, archive, or library special collection:
Benjamin Stone Photographic Collection (microform and original)
Dyche

continued overleaf

Francis Bedford (microform)
Francis Frith Collection (microform)
Photographic Collections
Priestley Collection (books written by and about
  Joseph Priestley)
Warwickshire Photographic Society

Non-library collection catalogue:
All or part available online

Library catalogue:
All or part available online

Printed publications:
Bella Brum – A History of Birmingham's Italian
  Community
Brum Undaunted – Birmingham during the Blitz
Contrasts in a Victorian City – Sources and Notes
  for a study of Victorian Birmingham
Sources for the Study of the History of Black
  People in Birmingham
Range of leaflets on family history (free)

Publications list:
Available in print

Access to staff:
Contact by letter, by telephone, by fax, by e-mail,
in person and via website
Hours: Mon to Fri, 0900 to 2000; Sat, 0900 to 1700

BIRMINGHAM ROYAL BALLET

Acronym or abbreviation: BRB

Thorp Street, Birmingham, B5 4AU

Tel: 0121 245 3500
Fax: 0121 245 3571
E-mail: info@brb.org.uk

Website:
http://www.brb.org.uk
General information on the company, its dancers
and productions.

Enquiries:
Enquiries to: Communications Director
Direct e-mail: keithlongmore@brb.org.uk

Founded:
1990

Formed from:
Sadler's Wells Royal Ballet (SWRB) (year of change
1989)

Organisation type and purpose:
Ballet company.

Subject coverage:
Information concerning Birmingham Royal Ballet
and its history.

**Museum or gallery collection, archive, or library
special collection:**
Cast lists, photographs, programmes

Trade and statistical information:
Casting, performance dates.

Non-library collection catalogue:
All or part available in-house

Library catalogue:
All or part available in-house

Electronic and video publications:
Some videos of performances available

Access to staff:
Contact by letter and by e-mail
Hours: Mon to Fri, 0900 to 1700

Access to building, collection or gallery:
Prior appointment required
Hours: Mon to Fri, 0930 to 1730

Access for disabled people:
Level entry

BIRMINGHAM SCHOOL OF ACTING

Acronym or abbreviation: BSA

Level 0 – Millennium Point, Curzon Street,
Birmingham, B4 7XG

Tel: 0121 331 7220
Fax: 0121 331 7221

Website:
http://www.bsa.bcu.ac.uk

Enquiries:
Enquiries to: Director
Direct tel: 0121 331 7224
Direct e-mail: stephen.simms@bcu.ac.uk
Other contacts: Registrar, Admissions Manager,
Marketing Manager

Founded:
1936

Formerly called:
Birmingham School of Speech and Drama;
Birmingham School of Speech Training & Dramatic
Art Ltd

Organisation type and purpose:
Birmingham School of Acting is a small specialist
institution offering full-time higher education
courses at undergraduate and postgraduate level
and part-time and summer school courses for
adults, young people and children. Birmingham
School of Acting is a faculty of Birmingham City
University and its acting courses are accredited by
the National Council for Drama Training (NCDT).

Subject coverage:
Acting technique, extending natural talent for the
professional theatre, dance, fencing and stage
fighting, stage management, radio technique, voice
production and speech training, relaxation and
stress management.

**Museum or gallery collection, archive, or library
special collection:**
Drama and play collection

Library catalogue:
All or part available in-house

Printed publications:
Prospectus (also at http://www.bsa.bcu.ac.uk/
  Contact/BSA%20Prospectus%202008%20-
  %2009.pdf)

Electronic and video publications:
CD-ROM

Publications list:
Available in print

Access to staff:
Contact by letter, by telephone, by fax, by e-mail
and via website. Appointment necessary.
Hours: Mon to Fri, 0900 to 1700

Access for disabled people:
All levels entry, toilet facilities

BIRTH DEFECTS FOUNDATION

Acronym or abbreviation: BDF

BDF Centre, Hemlock Way, Cannock,
Staffordshire, WS11 2GF

Tel: 01543 462777
Fax: 01543 468999
E-mail: enquiries@birthdefects.co.uk

Website:
http://www.birthdefects.co.uk

Enquiries:
Enquiries to: Chief Executive

Founded:
1991

Also known as:
BDF Newlife

Formerly called:
Happy Birthday Appeal

Organisation type and purpose:
Registered charity (charity number 1001817).

Subject coverage:
Birth defects.

Printed publications:
Publications available free of charge

Publications list:
Available online and in print

Access to staff:
Contact by letter, by telephone, by fax, by e-mail,
in person and via website. Appointment necessary.
Hours: Helpline: Mon to Fri, 0930 to 1900; Sat, 0930
to 1700
Office: Mon to Fri, 0900 to 1700

Access for disabled people:
Parking provided, level entry, access to all public
areas, toilet facilities

BISCUIT, CAKE, CHOCOLATE & CONFECTIONERY ASSOCIATION

Acronym or abbreviation: BCCCA

6 Catherine Street, London, WC2B 5JJ

Tel: 020 7420 7200
Fax: 020 7420 7201
E-mail: office@bccca.org.uk

Website:
http://www.bccca.org.uk

Enquiries:
Enquiries to: Director

Founded:
1901

Organisation type and purpose:
Trade association.

Subject coverage:
Cocoa, chocolate, confectionery products, cakes
and biscuits.

Trade and statistical information:
Data on the sales of biscuits, cakes, chocolate and
confectionery for the home market and for
export.

Printed publications:
Annual Review

Electronic and video publications:
Microbiology & Hygiene Factsheets (CD-ROM,
£10)

Member of:
CAOBISCO, the corresponding EC professional
organisation
Food and Drink Federation

BISHOP AUCKLAND COLLEGE LIBRARY

Woodhouse Lane, Bishop Auckland, Co Durham,
DL14 6JZ

Tel: 01388 443000
Fax: 01388 609294
E-mail: enquiries@bacoll.ac.uk

Website:
http://www.bishopaucklandcollege.ac.uk
Courses available.

Enquiries:
Enquiries to: Learning Resources Manager
Direct tel: 01388 443000 ext 2264

Formerly called:
Bishop Auckland College Student Resource Centre
(year of change 1998)

Organisation type and purpose:
Suitable for ages: 16+.
College library.

Subject coverage:
Engineering, construction, business studies,
creative and community subjects, hairdressing,
crafts, caring, art and design, information
technology, leisure and tourism.

Non-library collection catalogue:
All or part available in-house

Library catalogue:
All or part available in-house

Access to staff:
Contact by letter, by telephone, by fax and by e-mail
Hours: Term time: Mon to Thu, 0900 to 1930; Fri, 0900 to 1600
Vacations: Mon to Thu, 0900 to 1630; Fri, 0900 to 1600

Access for disabled people:
Parking provided, ramped entry, level entry, access to all public areas, toilet facilities
Special comments: Library is on first floor.

BISHOPSGATE INSTITUTE

230 Bishopsgate, London, EC2M 4QH

Tel: 020 7392 9270
Fax: 020 7392 9275
E-mail: library@bishopsgate.org.uk

Website:
http://www.bishopsgate.org.uk/library

Enquiries:
Enquiries to: Library Special Collections Manager
Other contacts: Library Learning and Public Services Manager

Founded:
1894

Organisation type and purpose:
Independent free public library.

Subject coverage:
London history and topography, labour and trade union history, economic and political history, co-operation and the co-operative movement in London and the South East, secularism, humanism, republicanism, pacifism, anarchism.

Museum or gallery collection, archive, or library special collection:
London Collection (50,000 volumes); Howell Collection (5000 volumes); Holyoake Collection (1000 items); Bradlaugh Papers (3000 items); London Cooperative Society Collection (20,000 items); archives of: Raphael Samuel; Republic; British Humanist Association; Rationalist Association; Stop the War Coalition.

Non-library collection catalogue:
All or part available online and in-house

Library catalogue:
All or part available online and in-house

Printed publications:
James Ince (Umbrellas): two centuries of an East London family business

Access to staff:
Contact by letter, by telephone, by e-mail and in person
Hours: Mon, Tue, Thu and Fri, 1000 to 1730; Wed, 1000 to 2000

Access to building, collection or gallery:
No prior appointment required

Access for disabled people:
Yes

BISHOPTHORPE LOCAL HISTORY GROUP

39 Acaster Lane, Bishopthorpe, York, YO23 2SA

Tel: 01904 704584
E-mail: historygroup@bishopthorpe.net

Website:
http://www.bishopthorpe.net/mt/history

Enquiries:
Enquiries to: Chairman

Founded:
1998

Organisation type and purpose:
Membership association (membership is by subscription), present number of members: 11, voluntary organisation.

Subject coverage:
Local and family history relating to the parish of Bishopthorpe.

Museum or gallery collection, archive, or library special collection:
Bishopthorpe photographs, ephemera and administration records of local groups.

Non-library collection catalogue:
All or part available in-house

Printed publications:
Bishopthorpe: Reaping the Past, 1800–1900 (£4.95 plus p&p, out of print)
Bishopthorpe Remembered (£2.95 plus 75p p&p)
Bishopthorpe History Trail (Free)

Access to staff:
Contact by letter, by telephone and by e-mail
Hours: Mon to Fri, 0900 to 1700

BITTER OWNERS CLUB

Treasurer and Membership Secretary, 6 Swanston Field, Whitchurch on Thames, RG8 7HP UK

Tel: 01189 845214
E-mail: info@bitter-owners-club.com

Website:
http://www.bitter-owners-club.com/

Enquiries:
Enquiries to: Secretary

Founded:
1988

Organisation type and purpose:
Membership association (membership is by subscription), present number of members: 55, service industry.
Classic car club.
To promote and encourage Bitter owners and prospective buyers of the cars.

Subject coverage:
Bitter cars.

Museum or gallery collection, archive, or library special collection:
Collection of over 5000 pictures of Bitter cars
Collection of archive press articles and road tests

Trade and statistical information:
Values and numbers of Bitter cars.

Non-library collection catalogue:
All or part available in-house

Printed publications:
Club magazine (6 times a year, included in £34 membership fee)
Bitter the Cars (Griffith P B, A4 100pp, £12.95 plus £2 p&p)

Access to staff:
Contact by letter, by telephone, by fax and by e-mail. Appointment necessary.
Hours: Mon to Sun, 0900 to 2100

Member of:
Classic Car Association

BITUMEN WATERPROOFING ASSOCIATION (UK) LTD

Acronym or abbreviation: BWA

19 Regina Crescent, Ravenshead, Nottingham, NG15 9AE

Tel: 01623 430574
Fax: 01623 798098
E-mail: info@bwa-europe.com

Website:
http://www.bwa-europe.com
Membership, meetings, general activities, congress.

Enquiries:
Enquiries to: Chief Executive

Founded:
1968

Organisation type and purpose:
International organisation, trade association (membership is by subscription, qualification, election or invitation), manufacturing industry, service industry.

Subject coverage:
Technical investigations, market survey projects, PR role.

Printed publications:
Newsline (newsletter, quarterly)
Past Congress Book of Proceedings (£39)

Access to staff:
Contact by letter, by telephone, by fax, by e-mail, in person and via website
Hours: Mon to Fri, 0900 to 1700

UK registered office:
Bitumen Waterproofing Association (UK) Ltd
Newstead House, Pelham Road, Nottingham, NG5 1AP; tel: 0115 960 8412; fax: 0115 969 1878

BLABY DISTRICT COUNCIL

Council Offices, Desford Road, Narborough, Leicestershire, LE9 5EP

Tel: 0116 275 0555\ Minicom no. 0116 284 9786
Fax: 0116 275 0368

Website:
http://www.blaby.gov.uk
Publications and leaflets, and ordering.

Enquiries:
Enquiries to: Public Relations Manager
Direct tel: 0116 272 7556
Direct e-mail: djm@blaby.gov.uk

Organisation type and purpose:
Local government body.

Subject coverage:
Local government services.

Printed publications:
A range of publications and leaflets available from the Council Offices covering services and leisure activities

Publications list:
Available online

Access to staff:
Contact by letter, by telephone, by fax, by e-mail, in person and via website
Hours: Mon to Thu, 0845 to 1715; Fri, 0845 to 1645

Access for disabled people:
Parking provided, level entry, access to all public areas, toilet facilities
Special comments: Access to all public areas.

BLACK COUNTRY CHAMBER OF COMMERCE

Formal name: Black Country Chamber & Business Link
Acronym or abbreviation: BCCBL

Dudley Court South, Waterfront East, Level Street, Brierley Hill, West Midlands, DY5 1XW

Tel: 0845 113 1234
Fax: 01384 360560
E-mail: info@bccbl.com

Website:
http://www.bccbl.com

Enquiries:
Enquiries to: Information Officer

Founded:
2001

Organisation type and purpose:
Membership association (membership is by subscription), present number of members: 2500, service industry.

Subject coverage:
Business information and services for business.

continued overleaf

Non-library collection catalogue:
All or part available online

Library catalogue:
All or part available online and in-house

Access to staff:
Contact by letter, by telephone, by fax, by e-mail, in person and via website. Non-members charged.
Hours: Mon to Thu, 0830 to 1730; Fri, 0830 to 1700
Special comments: SME business within the Black Country and members of the Black Country Chamber of Commerce.

Access for disabled people:
Access to all public areas, toilet facilities

BLACK COUNTRY INVESTMENT

The Deckhouse, Waterfront West, Dudley Road, Brierley Hill, DY5 1LW

Tel: 0845 815 1515
E-mail: enquiries@bci-uk.com

Website:
http://www.bci-uk.com
Black Country property location facility, general information concerning the Black Country.

Enquiries:
Enquiries to: Enquiry Officer
Direct e-mail: jane_mcgreen@
blackcountryconsortium.co.uk

Founded:
2001

Formerly called:
Business Link Sandwell (year of change 2001)

Organisation type and purpose:
Local government body.

Subject coverage:
Property location information within the Black Country, general information concerning the Black Country.

Printed publications:
Black Country Investment Property Finder
Black Country Investment Services Brochure
Newsletter (quarterly)

Access to staff:
Contact by letter, by telephone, by fax, by e-mail and via website
Hours: Mon to Fri, 0900 to 1700

BLACK COUNTRY SOCIETY

Acronym or abbreviation: BCS

PO Box 71, Kingswinford, West Midlands, DY6 9YN

Tel: 01384 295606

Website:
http://www.blackcountrysociety.co.uk

Enquiries:
Direct e-mail: editor@blackcountrysociety.co.uk
Other contacts: Membership Secretary for subscriptions

Founded:
1967

Organisation type and purpose:
Learned society (membership is by subscription), present number of members: 2000, voluntary organisation.
To foster interest in the Black Country past, present and future.

Subject coverage:
Local history, industrial archaeology, geography and culture; the past, present and future of the Black Country region.

Museum or gallery collection, archive, or library special collection:
Photographic collection (now deposited in the Black Country Living Museum)

Printed publications:
Black Countryman (quarterly, £2.75)
Booklets on local topics including:
Black Country Humour
Black Country Stories
William Fowler's Kingswinford
The Gospels in Black Country Dialect
The Black Country as seen through Antique Maps
– a survey from 1579 (Richardson E, £5.95)
Bostin' Fittle
Order printed publications from: Publications, BCS PO Box 71, Kingswinford, West Midlands, DY6 9YN, tel: 01384 295606

Publications list:
Available online and in print

Access to staff:
Contact by letter, by telephone, by e-mail and via website
Hours: Mon to Fri, 0900 to 1700

Access to building, collection or gallery:
No access other than to staff

Also at:
Advertising/Distribution/Publications
32 Lawnswood Avenue, Wordsley, Stourbridge, West Midlands, DY8 5LP; tel: 01384 295606

Has:
four subsidiary groups, all with same contact details as BCS

BLACK WELSH MOUNTAIN SHEEP BREEDERS ASSOCIATION

Touch Stone, 3 Quarry Cottages, Bourton on the Hill, Moreton-in-Marsh, Gloucestershire, GL56 9AJ

Tel: 01386 701538
Fax: 01386 701383

Enquiries:
Enquiries to: Secretary

Founded:
1920

Organisation type and purpose:
Membership association (membership is by subscription), present number of members: 250, registered charity.
Sheep breeders association.

Access to staff:
Contact by letter, by telephone and by fax
Hours: Mon to Fri, 0900 to 1700

BLACKBURN COLLEGE LIBRARY

Feilden Street, Blackburn, Lancashire, BB2 1LH

Tel: 01254 292120
Fax: 01254 682700

Website:
http://catalogue.blackburn.ac.uk

Enquiries:
Enquiries to: Learning Resources Manager

Organisation type and purpose:
College of Further Education.

Subject coverage:
Wide subject coverage for FE and HE in FE curriculum.

Library catalogue:
All or part available online

Printed publications:
Library guide
Study skills and projects and assignments guides
Available for library users only

Access to staff:
Contact by letter, by telephone and in person.
Appointment necessary. Non-members charged.
Hours: Term time: Mon to Thu, 0845 to 2000; Fri, 0845 to 1500; Sat, 0900 to 1230
Vacations: Mon to Fri, 0900 to 1630

Special comments: Associate membership is available (annual subscription) to members of the public; occasional users may prefer single admission fee for each visit.

Access for disabled people:
Access to all public areas

Associate college of:
Lancaster University

BLACKBURN WITH DARWEN BOROUGH COUNCIL

Town Hall, Blackburn, Lancashire, BB1 7DY

Tel: 01254 585585
Fax: 01254 680870

Website:
http://www.council.blackburnworld.com

Enquiries:
Enquiries to: Public Relations Manager

Organisation type and purpose:
Local government body.

BLACKFRIARS LIBRARY

64 St Giles, Oxford, OX1 3LY

Tel: 01865 278400
Fax: 01865 278403

Website:
http://www.bfriars.ox.ac.uk

Enquiries:
Enquiries to: Librarian
Direct e-mail: librarian@blackfriars.ox.ac.uk

Organisation type and purpose:
Library.

Subject coverage:
Philosophy, theology and scripture (particularly in relation to the Roman Catholic tradition and the medieval contribution of Dominican authors such as St Thomas Aquinas); life, work and history of the Dominican Order.

Museum or gallery collection, archive, or library special collection:
1 papyrus, 5 MSS, some cuneiform tablets, 26 incunabula and some 350 books printed before 1700, including many Dominican authors
Autograph letters of George Tyrrell SJ
Private press items, including many from St Dominic's Press
Works from the Library of André Raffalovich

Access to staff:
Contact by letter
Hours: Mon to Fri, 0900 to 1700

Access to building, collection or gallery:
Prior appointment required

A permanent private hall of:
Oxford University

In collaboration with other libraries of the:
English Dominicans

Serves a priory and *studium generale* of the:
English Province of the Friars of the Order of Preachers (Dominicans)

BLACKHEATH SCIENTIFIC SOCIETY

Mycenae House Community Centre, Mycenae Road, London, SE3

Enquiries:
Other contacts: Honorary Secretary, 1 The Orchard, London, SE3 0QU, tel: 020 8852 6117, email: bruceandjune@btopenworld.com

Founded:
1857

Organisation type and purpose:
Learned society (membership is by subscription, election or invitation), voluntary organisation.

Airing of information on developments in science and technology to qualified and non-qualified public; members.

Subject coverage:
Current scientific and technological developments. Coverage is wide and does include occasionally an historical lecture.

Printed publications:
Minutes of meetings and agendas

Access to staff:
Contact by letter, by telephone and by e-mail. Appointment necessary.
Hours: Mon to Fri, 0900 to 2200

BLACKPOOL AND THE FYLDE COLLEGE

Ashfield Road, Bispham, Blackpool, Lancashire, FY2 0HB

Tel: 01253 352352
Fax: 01253 356127
E-mail: lrc@blackpool.ac.uk

Website:
http://www.blackpool.ac.uk

Enquiries:
Enquiries to: Learning Resources
Direct tel: 01253 352352
Direct e-mail: lrc@blackpool.ac.uk

Founded:
1934

Organisation type and purpose:
Education for ages 16+.

Library catalogue:
All or part available online

Access to staff:
Contact by letter, by telephone, by fax and by e-mail. Appointment necessary.
Hours: Mon to Fri, 0900 to 1700

BLACKPOOL CENTRAL LIBRARY

Queen Street, Blackpool, Lancashire, FY1 1PX

Tel: 01253 478080
Fax: 01253 478082
E-mail: central.library@blackpool.gov.uk

Website:
http://www.blackpool.gov.uk
General council services and information.

Enquiries:
Enquiries to: Assistant Director (Cultural Services)

Organisation type and purpose:
Local government body, public library.

Subject coverage:
General, local history of Blackpool and Fylde area.

Library catalogue:
All or part available online

Access to staff:
Contact by letter, by telephone, by fax, by e-mail and in person
Hours: Mon, Fri, 0900 to 1700; Tue, Thu, 0900 to 1900; Wed, Sat, 1000 to 1700
Special comments: Local history items are for use in the library only.

Access for disabled people:
Access to all public areas

BLACKWELL PUBLISHING LIMITED

9600 Garsington Road, Oxford, OX4 2DQ

Tel: 01865 776868
Fax: 01865 714591

Website:
http://www.blackwell-science.com
Catalogue of books and journals.
http://www.blackwellpublishers.co.uk

Catalogue of books and journals.
http://www.blackwellpublishing.com
Merger site
http://www.blackwell-synergy.com
Journals online.

Enquiries:
Enquiries to: Marketing Co-ordinator
Direct e-mail: laura.dolphin@oxon.blackwellpublishing.com

Founded:
1939

Formerly called:
Blackwell Scientific Publications Limited (BSPL) (year of change 1995); Blackwell Publishers Limited (BPL), Blackwell Science Limited (BSL) (year of change 2001)

Organisation type and purpose:
Publishing house.

Subject coverage:
Books and journals in medicine, humanities, life and social sciences, as listed in catalogues.

Printed publications:
Catalogues and journal lists

Electronic and video publications:
Roists Essential Immunology (CD-ROM)
Rook's Textbook of Dermatology (CD-ROM)
Synergy (journals online)

Publications list:
Available online and in print

Access to staff:
Contact by letter and by telephone
Hours: Mon to Fri, 0900 to 1700

Other addresses:
Blackwell Publishing Asia
    54 University Street, Carlton South 3053, Victoria, Australia; tel: 00 61 3 9374 0300; fax: 00 61 3 9347 5001
Blackwell Publishing Limited
    108 Cowley Road, Oxford, OX4 1JF
Blackwell Publishing Limited
    10 rue Casimir Delavigne, 75006 Paris, France; tel: +33 1 53 10 33 10; fax: +33 1 53 10 33 15; e-mail: AboydSquires@compuserve.com
Blackwell Publishing, Inc
    Commerce Place, 350 Main Street, Malden, MA 02148–5018, USA; tel: 00 1 781 388 8250; fax: 00 1 781 388 8255
Blackwell Wissenschaft-Verlag
    Kurfürstendamm 57, Charlottenburg, Berlin, D-10707, Germany; tel: +49 30/32 79 06 -0; fax: +49 30/32 79 06 -10; e-mail: verlag@blackwis.de

Sister company:
B H Blackwell Limited

BLACKWELL UK LIMITED

Acronym or abbreviation: Blackwell's

Beaver House, Hythe Bridge Street, Oxford, OX1 2ET

Tel: 01865 792792
Fax: 01865 200285
E-mail: sales@blackwell.co.uk

Website:
http://www.blackwell.com
Databases of books, series and CD-ROMs.

Enquiries:
Enquiries to: International Sales Manager
Direct fax: 01865 200285

Founded:
1879

Also known as:
Blackwell's, Blackwell's Book Services

Organisation type and purpose:
International organisation, service industry.
Booksellers.
Academic Library Suppliers

Subject coverage:
Academic books, CD-ROM, music, microform, cataloguing and bibliographic services, eBook services.

Non-library collection catalogue:
All or part available online

Printed publications:
Advance information on books not yet published
Subject bibliographies
Trade catalogues

Electronic and video publications:
EBooks
Collection Manager (Web-based library Collection Development/Acquisitions service)

Publications list:
Available online

Access to staff:
Contact by letter, by telephone, by fax, by e-mail and via website. Appointment necessary.
Hours: Mon to Fri, 0900 to 1700

BLAENAU GWENT COUNTY BOROUGH COUNCIL

Municipal Offices, Civic Centre, Ebbw Vale, Gwent, NP23 6XB

Tel: 01495 350555
Fax: 01495 301255

Website:
http://www.blaenau-gwent.gov.uk

Enquiries:
Enquiries to: Public Relations Officer
Direct tel: 01495 355112
Direct fax: 01495 355093

Organisation type and purpose:
Local government body.
Unitary authority.

Subject coverage:
Local government services.

Printed publications:
Valley's Voice (magazine)
Official guide and street atlas
A-Z guide to services

Access to staff:
Contact by letter, by telephone and by fax
Hours: Mon to Fri, 0900 to 1700

BLAENAU GWENT COUNTY BOROUGH LIBRARIES

c/o Ebbw Vale Library, 21 Bethcar Street, Ebbw Vale, Gwent, NP23 6HH

Tel: 01495 303069
Fax: 01495 350547

Enquiries:
Enquiries to: Principal Librarian
Direct tel: 01495 355950
Direct fax: 01495 355900
Direct e-mail: sue.white@blaenau-gwent.gov.uk

Organisation type and purpose:
Local government body, public library.

Subject coverage:
General subjects, local studies and self-help, European information, adult basic information.

Museum or gallery collection, archive, or library special collection:
Main information collections housed at Ebbw Vale Library
European information housed at Ebbw Vale Library
Main local history collections housed at Tredegar Library
National Assembly Information housed at Ebbw Vale Library

Non-library collection catalogue:
All or part available online and in-house

continued overleaf

Library catalogue:
All or part available online and in-house

Printed publications:
History of Ebbw Vale

Publications list:
Available in print

Access to staff:
Contact by letter, by telephone, by fax, by e-mail
and in person. Appointment necessary.
Hours: Mon to Fri, 0900 to 1700; Sat 0900 to 1600

Library HQ:
Blaenau Gwent County Borough Council
Leisure Services, Anvil Court, Church Street,
Abertillery, NP13 1DB; tel: 01495 355950; fax:
01495 355900; e-mail: sue.white@blaenau-gwent
.gov.uk

BLATCHINGTON COURT TRUST

Acronym or abbreviation: BCT

Ridgeland House, 165 Dyke Road, Hove, East
Sussex, BN3 1TL

Tel: 01273 727222
Fax: 01273 722244
E-mail: blatchington.court@virgin.net

Website:
http://www.blatchington-court.co.uk

Enquiries:
Enquiries to: Client Services Manager

Founded:
1993

Organisation type and purpose:
Voluntary organisation, registered charity (charity
number 306350), suitable for ages: 0 to 30.
Primarily grant giving charity to promote
education and employment and provide grants for
young visually impaired people for computers and
sensory equipment. Also help with Family Support
and Advocacy.

Subject coverage:
Services and facilities for visually impaired young
people, mainly in Sussex; help includes: family
support service, advocacy service, IT training,
education and employment.

Printed publications:
Information Packs about the specific work of BCT
(free of charge)

Access to staff:
Contact by letter, by telephone, by fax, by e-mail,
in person and via website
Hours: Mon to Fri, 0900 to 1700

Access to building, collection or gallery:
No prior appointment required

Access for disabled people:
Parking provided, ramped entry

BLC LEATHER TECHNOLOGY CENTRE

Acronym or abbreviation: BLC

Leather Trade House, Kings Park Road, Moulton
Park, Northampton, NN3 6JD

Tel: 01604 679999
Fax: 01604 679998
E-mail: info@blcleathertech.com

Website:
http://www.blcleathertech.com
Services, training, member directory, consultancy.

Enquiries:
Enquiries to: Information Officer

Founded:
1920

Formerly called:
British Leather Confederation

Organisation type and purpose:
International organisation, trade association,
training organisation, consultancy, research
organisation.

Subject coverage:
Manufacture and use of leather; raw hides and
skins; fellmongering; treatment and disposal of
industrial wastes; chemistry and testing of leather;
tanning; physical and mechanical testing of leather;
leather dyes and surface coatings: safety in the
leather industry; cleaner processing in the leather
industry.

Printed publications:
BLC Journal (monthly, confidential to members)
Farming and Abattoir Practices Leading to
Impaired Leather Quality
Guide to Fellmongering
Leather Clothing; its manufacture and
maintenance
Leather Descriptions and Definitions
Leather under the Microscope
Member/Product Directory

Electronic and video publications:
Leather Online CD-ROM (available to members
only)

Access to staff:
Contact by letter, by telephone, by fax, by e-mail
and via website
Hours: Mon to Fri, 0900 to 1700

Incorporates the:
British Leather Confederation

BLENHEIM PROJECT

321 Portobello Road, London, W10 5SY

Tel: 020 8960 5599
Fax: 020 8960 0508
E-mail: blenpro@dircon.co.uk

Website:
http://www.theblenheimproject.org

Enquiries:
Enquiries to: Administrator

Founded:
1966

Organisation type and purpose:
Voluntary organisation, registered charity (charity
number 1015237).
Drugs counselling.

Subject coverage:
Counselling for drug users, their friends and
family, use and effects, alternative therapies, detox
teas.

Printed publications:
Changing Gear (£1.20 plus p&p)
Drugs – Check This Out (£1.20 plus p&p)
How to Help (£1.20 plus p&p)
How to Stop (£1.20 plus p&p)
What's the Crack – Professional – Information on
how to help crack and cocaine users (£5)
What's the Crack – User's Guide – Information for
crack and cocaine users (£1.50)

Publications list:
Available in print

Access to staff:
Contact by letter, by telephone, by fax, by e-mail,
in person and via website
Hours: Mon to Fri, 1000 to 1700; Drop in: Mon to
Fri, 1300 to 1600; Tue, 1800 to 2100

BLOOMSBURY HEALTHCARE LIBRARY

Ground Floor, Bonham Carter House, 52 Gower
Street, London, WC1E 6EB

Tel: 020 7436 1414
Fax: 020 7436 5111

Website:
http://www.chllib.demon.co.uk

Library services, NVQ's, external sources, services
to region.

Enquiries:
Enquiries to: Librarian

Founded:
1997

Organisation type and purpose:
NHS Library.
Library services for all healthcare staff in
associated organisations.

Subject coverage:
Nursing, midwifery, health visiting, sociology,
psychology, education, management,
physiotherapy, occupational therapy, dietetics,
clinical governance, NHS policy, radiography,
librarianship.

Non-library collection catalogue:
All or part available online

Library catalogue:
All or part available online

Printed publications:
Current Awareness Bulletin (monthly)

Access to staff:
Contact by letter, by telephone and by fax.
Appointment necessary. Non-members charged.
Hours: Mon to Fri, 0900 to 1700

Access to building, collection or gallery:
No prior appointment required

BLUEFACED LEICESTER SHEEP BREEDERS ASSOCIATION

Acronym or abbreviation: BFLSBA

Furmiston, Carsphairn, Castle Douglas DG7 3TE

Tel: 01644 460647
Fax: 01644 460647
E-mail: info@blueleicester.co.uk

Website:
http://www.blueleicester.co.uk

Enquiries:
Enquiries to: President
Direct e-mail: janecruik21@hotmail.co.uk

Founded:
1962

Organisation type and purpose:
National government body, membership
association (membership is by subscription).
Sheep Breeders Association.
Sheep registration.

Subject coverage:
Leicester sheep.

Access to staff:
Contact by letter, by telephone, by fax, by e-mail
and via website
Hours: Mon to Fri, 0900 to 1500

Access to building, collection or gallery:
Prior appointment required

BMS WORLD MISSION

PO Box 49, Baptist House, 129 Broadway, Didcot,
Oxfordshire, OX11 8XA

Tel: 01235 517700
Fax: 01235 517601
E-mail: mail@bmsworldmission.org

Website:
http://www.bmsworldmission.org
Information about mission personnel, prayer
requests, ways to support BMS, resources and five
channels for user groups: ministers, BMS reps in
churches, those seeking mission opportunities, 24:7
Partners and campaigners.

Enquiries:
Enquiries to: General Director

Founded:
1792

Formerly called:
Baptist Missionary Society (BMS)

Organisation type and purpose:
Voluntary organisation, registered as a charity in England and Wales (number 233782) and in Scotland (number SC037767).
BMS World Mission is a Christian mission organisation aiming to share life in all its fullness with the world's peoples by: enabling them to know Christ, alleviating suffering and injustice, improving the quality of life with people as the primary agent of change – motivating, training, sending and resourcing them. Has missions in 4 continents.

Subject coverage:
Christian missions worldwide involving church planting and evangelism; development initiatives; disaster relief; educational programmes; health programmes; and other specialised activities.

Museum or gallery collection, archive, or library special collection:
Archives of the 19th century relating to the establishment of missions and some rare books at Regents Park College, Oxford

Printed publications:
engage magazine
Mission Catalyst (for ministers)
The Equipment (for BMS Reps)
FACE (resource for all-age church events)
Prayer Guide
Order printed publications from: Resources 01235 517617 or e-mail resources@bmsworldmission.org

Publications list:
Available online

Access to staff:
Contact by letter, by telephone, by fax, by e-mail and via website. Appointment necessary.
Hours: Mon to Fri, 0900 to 1700

BMT GROUP LTD

Goodrich House, 1 Waldegrave Road, Teddington, Middlesex, TW11 8LZ

Tel: 020 8943 5544
Fax: 020 8943 5347
E-mail: dgriffiths@bmtmail.com

Website:
http://www.bmt.org
http://www.marinescienceandtechnology.com
http://www.marinetechnologyabstracts.com/
The Marine Technology Abstracts database contains bibliographic information providing a reference and description for over 90,000 technical articles, reports, books, conference and transaction papers and other material on all aspects of maritime technology

Enquiries:
Enquiries to: Librarian
Direct tel: 020 8614 4277

Founded:
1985

Organisation type and purpose:
Consultancy, research organisation.

Subject coverage:
Fluid mechanics, naval architecture, ocean engineering, industrial aerodynamics as related to the commercial shipping, maritime defence, ports and harbours, and offshore oil and gas industries.

Museum or gallery collection, archive, or library special collection:
Report material of former National Maritime Institute
Report material of former ship, aero and maritime science divisions of the National Physical Laboratory
Transactions of Royal Institution of Naval Architects, Society of Naval Architects and Marine Engineers, North-east Coast Institution of Engineers and Shipbuilders, Institution of Engineers and Shipbuilders in Scotland

Library catalogue:
All or part available in-house

Printed publications:
40 Years of Progress: A History of the Wallsend Research Station 1945–1985 (£25)
BMT Abstracts: 1946 to date (monthly, £220 per year)
BMT Focus (3–4 times a year, free)
Codes of Practice (£50)
Engineering Economics and Ship Design (£30, students £15)
NMI Technical Reports (from £40 each)
Research reports and technical memoranda (from £40)
Shipbuilding Industry and Steelwork Manufacturing Standards
Ship Design Manuals (£1,000 each)
Ships in the Making: a history of ship model testing at Teddington and Feltham 1910–1994 (D. Bailey, Lloyd's of London Press, 1995, £45)

Electronic and video publications:
Marine Technology Abstracts (online)

Publications list:
Available in print

Access to staff:
Contact by letter, by telephone, by fax, by e-mail and via website. All charged.
Hours: Mon to Thu, 0830 to 1700; Fri, 0830 to 1630

Access to building, collection or gallery:
No prior appointment required

Also at:
BMT Group Ltd
Northumbria House, Davy Bank, Wallsend, Tyne and Wear, NE28 6UY; tel: 0191 263 6899; fax: 0191 263 8754; e-mail: gsmith@bmtmail.com

BOARD OF DEPUTIES OF BRITISH JEWS

Community Issues Division, 6 Bloomsbury Square, London, WC1A 2LP

Tel: 020 7543 5400
Fax: 020 7543 0010
E-mail: info@bod.org.uk

Website:
http://www.kosher.org.uk
Information on Kosher restaurants, food products and ingredients.

Enquiries:
Enquiries to: Director of Community Issues
Direct e-mail: es.rosen@bod.org.uk
Other contacts: (1) Education Officer (2) Research Officer for (1) specific education enquiries (2) statistical information.

Organisation type and purpose:
Membership association (membership is by election or invitation), voluntary organisation, registered charity.
Lay representative body for Jewish community in the UK.

Subject coverage:
Judaism in RE, Jewish issues in education, inspecting Jewish schools, information on Holocaust, demographic and general social information on British Jewry.

Museum or gallery collection, archive, or library special collection:
Jewish Way of Life Exhibition

Printed publications:
Publications and off-prints under the following headings:
Overviews
Demography
Synagogue
Women
Area Studies
Identity
Research and Methodology

Publications list:
Available online and in print

Access to staff:
Contact by letter, by telephone, by fax and by e-mail. Appointment necessary.
Hours: Mon to Fri, 0930 to 1730 (early closing on Friday in winter months)

Access to building, collection or gallery:
Prior appointment required

BOARD OF GRADUATE STUDIES

Formal name: University of Cambridge Board of Graduate Studies
Acronym or abbreviation: BGS

University of Cambridge, 4 Mill Lane, Cambridge, CB2 1RZ

Tel: 01223 760606
Fax: 01223 338723
E-mail: admissions@gradstudies.cam.ac.uk

Website:
http://www.admin.cam.ac.uk/univ/gsprospectus
Prospectus and orders
http://www.admin.cam.ac.uk/offices/gradstud

Enquiries:
Enquiries to: Admissions Office

Founded:
1284

Organisation type and purpose:
University department or institute.
University graduate admissions.

Subject coverage:
All academic subjects studied at the university: arts, humanities, social sciences, physical sciences, biological sciences, engineering, management, technology.

Printed publications:
Prospectus (online)

Access to staff:
Contact by letter, by telephone, by fax and by e-mail
Hours: Mon to Fri, 1000 to 1600

Access to building, collection or gallery:
Mon to Fri, 1000 to 1600

Access for disabled people:
Mon to Fri, 1000 to 1600

Parent body:
University of Cambridge
Cambridge; website: www.cam.ac.uk

BOARDING SCHOOLS' ASSOCIATION

Acronym or abbreviation: BSA

Grosvenor Gardens House, 35–37 Grosvenor Gardens, London, SW1W 0BS

Tel: 020 7798 1580
Fax: 020 7798 1581
E-mail: bsa@boarding.org.uk

Website:
http://www.boarding.org.uk

Enquiries:
Enquiries to: National Director

Founded:
1965

Organisation type and purpose:
National professional society of schools with boarding facilities.

Subject coverage:
Boarding school education in both independent and maintained sectors, with specialist areas in: training, publication, information, National Boarding Standards.

Printed publications:
Magazine (2 times a year)
For full list of publications see website

Publications list:
Available online and in print

continued overleaf

Access to staff:
Contact by letter, by telephone, by fax, by e-mail, in person and via website. Appointment necessary. Access for members only. Non-members charged.
Hours: Mon to Fri, 0900 to 1700

Links with:
GSA
HMC
IAPS
ISA
ISC
SHMIS
State Boarding Schools' Association (SBSA)

BOBATH CENTRE FOR CHILDREN WITH CEREBRAL PALSY

Bradbury House, 250 East End Road, London, N2 8AU

Tel: 020 8444 3355
Fax: 020 8444 3399
E-mail: info@bobathlondon.co.uk

Website:
http://www.bobathlondon.co.uk

Enquiries:
Enquiries to: Director for Referrals
Other contacts: (1) Course Organiser (2) Appointments Organiser for (1) training (2) treatment information.

Founded:
1957

Formerly called:
Western Cerebral Palsy Centre

Organisation type and purpose:
Registered charity (charity number 229663), treatment organisation, training organisation, research organisation.
Treatment of children with cerebral palsy and related conditions; training of therapists; research. Treatment of adults with neurological disability.

Subject coverage:
Cerebral palsy, brain damage, treatment of these conditions.

Printed publications:
A Neurodevelopmental Treatment of Cerebral Palsy
The Bobath Concept Evolution and Application
The Motor Disorders of Infantile Hemiplegia and their Treatment
The Neuro-Developmental Treatment (Bobath K & B)
The Prevention of Mental Retardation in Patients with Cerebral Palsy
Treatment Principals and Planning in Cerebral Palsy

Electronic and video publications:
Teaming with Success (video, £49.95, £20 a month to hire)
The Bobath Approach to the Treatment of Children with Cerebral Palsy (video, £50 to buy, £20 a month to hire)

Publications list:
Available online and in print

Access to staff:
Contact by letter, by telephone, by fax, by e-mail and via website. Appointment necessary.
Hours: Mon to Fri, 0900 to 1700

Access for disabled people:
Parking provided, level entry, access to all public areas, toilet facilities

Connections with:
Bobath Children's Therapy Centre Wales
19 Park Road, Whitchurch, Cardiff, CF4 7BP; tel: 029 2052 2600; fax: 029 2052 1477
Bobath Scotland
Golden Jubilee National Hospital, Beardmore Street, Clydebank, G81 4HX; tel: 0141 435 3270; fax: 0141 435 3279
British Association of Bobath Trained Therapists

BODLEIAN JAPANESE LIBRARY

Acronym or abbreviation: BJL

27 Winchester Road, Oxford, OX2 6NA

Tel: 01865 284506
Fax: 01865 284500
E-mail: japanese@bodley.ox ac.uk

Website:
http://www.bodley.ox.ac.uk/dept/oriental/
http://library.ox.ac.uk
Oxford Library Information System (OLIS)

Enquiries:
Enquiries to: Librarian

Founded:
1993

Created by the merger of:
The Japanese collections of the Bodleian Library and the former Nissan Institute Library (year of change 1993)

Organisation type and purpose:
University library.

Subject coverage:
Japanese studies.

Non-library collection catalogue:
All or part available online

Library catalogue:
All or part available online

Access to staff:
Contact by letter, by telephone, by fax, by e-mail, in person and via website. Non-members charged.

Access to building, collection or gallery:
Hours: Term time: Mon to Fri, 0915 to 1900; Sat, 1000 to 1300
Vacations: Mon to Fri, 0915 to 1700
Special comments: Must be accredited readers of the Bodleian Library

Access for disabled people:
Ramped entry, toilet facilities

Parent body:
Bodleian Library
Broad Street, Oxford, OX1 3BG; tel: 01865 277000; fax: 01865 277182; website: http://www .ouls.ox.ac.uk/bodley/home

BODLEIAN LAW LIBRARY

St Cross Building, Manor Road, Oxford, OX1 3UR

Tel: 01865 271462
Fax: 01865 271475
E-mail: law.library@bodley.ox.ac.uk

Website:
http://www.ouls.ox.ac.uk/law

Enquiries:
Enquiries to: Law Librarian
Other contacts: Academic Services Librarian for services offered by the library, ILL, copies of materials.

Founded:
c.1602

Organisation type and purpose:
University library.

Subject coverage:
Law; criminology; legal bibliography.

Museum or gallery collection, archive, or library special collection:
Law from the jurisdiction of the British Isles, most Commonwealth countries, USA, most European countries
Public international law
European Documentation Centre

Non-library collection catalogue:
All or part available online

Library catalogue:
All or part available online

Access to staff:
Contact by letter, by telephone, by fax, by e-mail and via website. Appointment necessary.
Hours: Mon to Fri, 0900 to 1700

Access for disabled people:
Ramped entry, toilet facilities
Special comments: Lift

Constituent part of:
Oxford University Library Service
Broad Street, Oxford, OX1 3BG; website: http:// www.ouls.ox.ac.uk

BODLEIAN LIBRARY

Broad Street, Oxford, OX1 3BG

Tel: 01865 277000
Fax: 01865 277182
E-mail: enquiries@bodley.ox.ac.uk

Website:
http://www.lib.ox.ac.uk/olis/
OLIS Oxford University Library Information Service.
http://www.ouls.ox.ac.uk/bodley
Bodleian library information.

Enquiries:
Enquiries to: Librarian
Other contacts: Director of University Library Services and Bodley's Librarian

Founded:
1598

Organisation type and purpose:
University library.
University and Copyright library, of the University of Oxford.

Subject coverage:
Comprehensive range of a university and copyright library dating from 1602; strong coverage in Orientalia, Hebraica, medieval mss, incunabula, English 16th and 17th century literature and history, modern political papers, music (manuscripts and printed); maps.

Museum or gallery collection, archive, or library special collection:
Clarendon State Papers
Douce, Francis (1757–1834) Collection (MSS and early printed works)
Gough, Richard (1735–1809) Collection (British topography)
Harding Collection (music, scores and libretti)
John Johnson Collection of Printed Ephemera
Locke, John (1632–1704) Papers and library
Malone Collection of Shakespearean and British drama
Opie, Peter Mason (1918–1982) Collection (children's literature)
Rawlinson, Richard (1690–1755) Collection
Rawlinson, Thomas (1681–1725) Collection
Selden, John (1584–1654) Collection
UN and EC documents

Non-library collection catalogue:
All or part available online and in print

Library catalogue:
All or part available online and in print

Printed publications:
Catalogues, Union Lists, Histories, Picture books
Order printed publications from: Marketing and Publishing Division, Bodleian Library
Broad Street, Oxford, OX1 3BG, tel: 01865 277091, fax: 01865 277218, e-mail: sales@bodley.ox.ac.uk

Microform publications:
Colour transparencies and film strips

Electronic and video publications:
Pre-1920 catalogue on CD-ROM (OUP)
A tour of the Bodleian Library (The Library, 1998, 25 minute video, PAL/NTEC)

Publications list:
Available online and in print

Access to staff:
Contact by letter, by telephone, by fax and by e-mail. Non-members charged.
Hours: Mon to Fri, 0900 to 1900 or 2200
Special comments: Admission Form (available on web) required. No access below undergraduate level; access to undergraduates of other universities only during vacations.

Central Bodleian site:
Admissions Office (for enquiries about becoming a reader at the library)
tel: 01865 277180; fax: 01865 277105; e-mail: admissions@bodley.ox.ac.uk
Bodleian Japanese Library at the Nissan Institute (for Japanese collections)
27 Winchester Road, Oxford, OX2 6NA; tel: 01865 284506; fax: 01865 284500; e-mail: japanese@bodley.ox.ac.uk
Bodleian Law Library (for law, excluding ecclesiastical law)
Manor Road, Oxford, OX1 3UR; tel: 01865 271463; fax: 01865 271475; e-mail: law.library@bodley.ox.ac.uk
Department of Oriental Books and Manuscripts (books and manuscripts in Oriental languages, except Japanese and the languages of the Indian subcontinent)
tel: 01865 277034; fax: 01865 277029; e-mail: oriental@bodley.ox.ac.uk
Department of Special Collections & Western Manuscripts (manuscripts, rare and early printed books, modern political papers in Western languages)
tel: 01865 277158; fax: 01865 277182; e-mail: western.manuscrpts@bodley.ox.ac.uk
Eastern Art Library
Pusey Lane, Oxford, OX1 2LE; tel: 01865 278202; fax: 01865 278190; e-mail: eastern.art.library@bodley.ox.ac.uk
European Documentation Centre (receives all European Union publications)
Bodleian Law Library, Manor Road, Oxford, OX1 3UR; tel: 01865 271463; fax: 01865 271475; e-mail: edc@bodley.ox.ac.uk
Hooke Library (for science)
South Parks Road, Oxford, OX1 3UB; tel: 01865 272812; fax: 01865 272821; e-mail: hooke@bodley.ox.ac.uk
Imaging Services (all photocopy and photographic enquiries)
tel: 01865 277061; fax: 01865 287127; e-mail: repro@bodley.ox.ac.uk
Indian Institute Library (for books and manuscripts from the Indian subcontinent)
Bodleian Library, Broad Street, Oxford, OX1 3BG; tel: 01865 277081; fax: 01865 277182; e-mail: indian.institute@bodley.ox.ac.uk
Institute for Chinese Studies Library
Walton Street, Oxford, OX1 2HG; tel: 01865 280430; fax: 01865 280431; e-mail: chinese.studies.library@bodley.ox.ac.uk
John Johnson Collection (printed ephemera)
tel: 01865 277047; fax: 01865 277182; e-mail: jjcoll@bodley.ox.ac.uk
Map Room (for maps and geography-related resources)
tel: 01865 277013; fax: 01865 277139; e-mail: maps@bodley.ox.ac.uk
Marketing & Publishing Division (library publications and merchandise, publication of material from the library)
tel: 01865 277091; fax: 01865 277218; e-mail: sales@bodley.ox.ac.uk
Modern Papers (modern political papers)
tel: 01865 277046; fax: 01865 277182; e-mail: modern.papers@bodley.ox.ac.uk
Music Room (for music resources)
tel: 01865 277063; fax: 01865 277182; e-mail: music@bodley.ox.ac.uk
Oriental Institute Library
Pusey Lane, Oxford, OX1 2LE; tel: 01865 278202; fax: 01865 278190; e-mail: library@orinst.ox.ac.uk
Philosophy Library (admission restricted to University members)
10 Merton Street, Oxford, OX1 4JJ; tel: 01865 276927; fax: 01865 276932; e-mail: philosophy.library@bodley.ox.ac.uk

Preservation & Conservation Department (preservation and conservation of the collections)
tel: 01865 277086; fax: 01865 277182; e-mail: prescons@bodley.ox.ac.uk
Radcliffe Science Library (for science, covering the physical and life sciences)
Parks Road, Oxford, OX1 3QP; tel: 01865 272800; fax: 01865 272821; e-mail: rsl.enquiries@bodley.ox.ac.uk
Reader Services Department (reader services relating to printed books and journals in Western languages)
tel: 01865 277162; fax: 01865 287112; e-mail: reader.services@bodley.ox.ac.uk
Rhodes House Library (for African and Commonwealth history and politics)
South Parks Road, Oxford, OX1 3RG; tel: 01865 270908; fax: 01865 270912; e-mail: rhodes.house.library@bodley.ox.ac.uk
Systems Section (Bodleian's database network and www pages)
tel: 01865 277074; fax: 01865 277182; e-mail: systems@bodley.ox.ac.uk
Technical Services Department (status of items on order, receipt of legal deposit material, reporting errors in the Oxford union catalogue, OLIS)
tel: 01865 277017; fax: 01865 277036; e-mail: technical.services@bodley.ox.ac.uk
Vere Harmsworth Library (for American history and politics)
South Parks Road, Oxford, OX1 3TG; tel: 01865 282700; fax: 01865 282709; e-mail: vhl@bodley.ox.ac.uk

Parent body:
University of Oxford
tel: 01865 270000; fax: 01865 270708

BODLEIAN LIBRARY OF COMMONWEALTH AND AFRICAN STUDIES AT RHODES HOUSE

South Parks Road, Oxford, OX1 3RG

Tel: 01865 270908
Fax: 01865 270912
E-mail: rhodes.house.library@bodley.ox.ac.uk

Website:
http://www.bodley.ox.ac.uk/dept/rhodes Library website.

Enquiries:
Enquiries to: Subject Consultant or Archivist

Founded:
1929

Organisation type and purpose:
University library.

Subject coverage:
History of the Commonwealth (excluding the Indian sub-continent) and Africa south of the Sahara.

Museum or gallery collection, archive, or library special collection:
C J Rhodes Papers
Colonial Records (collection of papers of colonial servants)
Papers of the Anti-Apartheid Movement
Papers of the Anti-Slavery Society
Papers of the United Society for the Propagation of the Gospel
Scicluna Collection (Malta)
Sir Roy Welensky Papers

Library catalogue:
All or part available online

Printed publications:
African medical history: a guide to personal papers on Rhodes House Library, Oxford
Manuscript collections in Rhodes House Library: accessions 1978 to 1994
Papers of Sir Roy Welensky, 1907–1991 in Rhodes House Library: a catalogue

Microform publications:
Manuscript catalogues available from the Bodleian Library

Publications list:
Available in print

Access to staff:
Contact by letter, by telephone, by fax, by e-mail and in person. Letter of introduction required. Non-members charged.
Hours: Term time: Mon to Fri, 0900 to 1900; Sat, 0900 to 1300
Vacations: Mon to Thu, 0900 to 1900; Fri, 0900 to 1700; Sat, 0900 to 1300

Access for disabled people:
Access difficult due to steps at building entrance and within building. Please contact staff in advance for material to be moved to an accessible reading room.

Constituent part of:
Bodleian Library
Oxford University

BOLSOVER DISTRICT COUNCIL

Acronym or abbreviation: BDC

Sherwood Lodge, Bolsover, Derbyshire, S44 6NF

Tel: 01246 242424\ Minicom no. 01246 242450
Fax: 01246 24242
E-mail: enquiries@bolsover.gov.uk

Website:
http://www.bolsover.gov.uk

Enquiries:
Enquiries to: Chief Executive
Direct tel: 01246 242400
Direct e-mail: wes.lumley@bolsover.gov.uk

Founded:
1974

Organisation type and purpose:
Local government body.

Printed publications:
Intouch Newspaper (free, direct)
Street Map Guide (free, direct)
Days Out (pocket guide, free, direct)
Various tourism publications (free, direct)
Business and Industry Directory (free, direct)

Electronic and video publications:
Intouch Newspaper (online)

Publications list:
Available online and in print

Access to staff:
Contact by letter, by telephone, by fax, by e-mail, in person and via website
Hours: Mon to Fri, 0900 to 1700

Access for disabled people:
Parking provided, ramped entry, toilet facilities

BOLTON COMMUNITY COLLEGE

Library and Learning Resource Centre, Manchester Road, Bolton, Lancashire, BL2 1ER

Tel: 01204 907325
Fax: 01204 907321
E-mail: info@bolton.community.college.ac.uk

Website:
http://www.boltoncommunitycollege.ac.uk

Enquiries:
Enquiries to: Learning Centre Manager

Founded:
1937

Formerly called:
Bolton Metropolitan College; Bolton Technical College; Bolton College

Organisation type and purpose:
Suitable for ages: 14 to 19 + Adult, training organisation.
College of further education, Access, Vocational. Also has school links with 14 to 16 year olds and part-time mature students. Community College including Adult Education.

continued overleaf

Subject coverage:
Building; construction; electrical engineering; food preparation and service; food technology; industrial safety; business studies, hairdressing and beauty therapy, science, maths, computing. All subjects at further education technical level only, not research level. Some HNC, HND, craft subjects, basic skills, ESOL, adult education. Developmental education, community care, humanities/communication, motor vehicle – at Horwich Centre.

Museum or gallery collection, archive, or library special collection:
Bolton College archives

Non-library collection catalogue:
All or part available online and in-house

Library catalogue:
All or part available online and in-house

Access to staff:
Contact by letter, by telephone, by fax, by e-mail and via website. Appointment necessary. Access for members only.
Hours: Members (Registered Students), term time: Mon to Thu, 0900 to 2000; Fri, 1000 to 1600; vacations: Mon to Fri, 0900 to 1600; Sat, 0900 to 1300

Other addresses:
Horwich Library and LRC Centre
 Bolton Community College, Victoria Road, Horwich, Lancashire; tel: 01204 907520; e-mail: @ bolton.community.college.ac.uk
Study Library
 Bolton Community College, Clarence Street Centre, Clarence Street, Bolton

BOLTON LIBRARIES

Central Library, Civic Centre, Le Mans Crescent, Bolton, Lancashire, BL1 1SE

Tel: 01204 333173
Fax: 01204 332225
E-mail: josie.butterworth@bolton.gov.uk

Website:
www.bolton.gov.uk/libraries
Includes access for library members to online information resources

Enquiries:
Enquiries to: Team Librarian
Direct tel: 01204 332853
Direct e-mail: central.library@bolton.gov.uk

Founded:
1853

Organisation type and purpose:
Local government body, public library.

Subject coverage:
General, science and technology, textiles, local studies, business information, childcare information, career information.

Information services:
In-depth Information Service, Tourist Information Service, Primary Care Trust Library

Museum or gallery collection, archive, or library special collection:
Textiles Collection, Special Periodicals Collection, Rare Books Collection, Lancashire Collection, British Standards, Childcare Information, Careers

Trade and statistical information:
Mainly official British statistics, EU statistics, UN statistics.

Library catalogue:
All or part available online

Access to staff:
Contact by letter, by telephone, by fax, by e-mail and in person
Hours: Mon, Tue and Thu, 0900 to 1930; Wed and Fri, 0900 to 1730; Sat, 0900 to 1700

Access to building, collection or gallery:
Hours: Mon, Tue and Thu, 0815 to 1930; Wed and Fri, 0815 to 1730; Sat, 0815 to 1700

Access for disabled people:
Ramped entry, toilet facilities
Hours: Mon, Tue and Thu, 0815 to 1930; Wed and Fri, 0815 to 1730; Sat, 0815 to 1700

BOLTON METROPOLITAN BOROUGH COUNCIL

Town Hall, Bolton, Lancashire, BL1 1RU

Tel: 01204 333333
Fax: 01204 392808
E-mail: bolton@bolton.gov.uk

Website:
http://www.bolton.gov.uk

Organisation type and purpose:
Local government body.

Subject coverage:
Local government services.

BOND OWNERS' CLUB

Acronym or abbreviation: BOC

42 Beaufort Avenue, Hodge Hill, Birmingham, B34 6AE

Tel: 0121 784 4626
Fax: 0121 784 4626

Website:
http://www.bondownersclub.co.uk
Details of the club, Bond cars and includes membership form.

Enquiries:
Enquiries to: General Secretary

Founded:
1951

Organisation type and purpose:
International organisation, membership association.

Subject coverage:
Information on Bond cars and the Bond Owners' Club, spares availability and technical advice.

Museum or gallery collection, archive, or library special collection:
Production records and original archive material

Printed publications:
Bond Related Information, Handbooks and Parts Lists

Access to staff:
Contact by letter, by telephone and by fax. Appointment necessary.
Hours: Evenings and weekends

BOOK AID INTERNATIONAL

39–41 Coldharbour Lane, London, SE5 9NR

Tel: 020 7733 3577
Fax: 020 7978 8006
E-mail: info@bookaid.org

Website:
http://www.bookaid.org
Information about the organisation and its work, copies of our newsletter, interchange and details of how people can support our work.

Enquiries:
Enquiries to: Administrator

Founded:
1954

Organisation type and purpose:
Registered charity (charity number 313869). Working in partnership with organisations in developing countries to support their work in literacy, education, training and publishing.

Subject coverage:
Education, book provision and publishing in developing countries, especially Africa.

Printed publications:
Annual Review and Three Year Plan
Newsletter (irregular)
Posters and pamphlets

Access to staff:
Contact by letter, by telephone, by fax, by e-mail and via website. Appointment necessary.
Hours: Mon to Fri, 0900 to 1700

BOOK PRODUCTION CONSULTANTS LTD

Acronym or abbreviation: BPC

25–27 High Street, Chesterton, Cambridge, CB4 1ND

Tel: 01223 352790
Fax: 01223 460718
E-mail: enquiries@bpccam.co.uk

Website:
http://www.bpccam.co.uk

Enquiries:
Enquiries to: Marketing Manager
Direct e-mail: jl@bpccam.co.uk

Founded:
1973

Organisation type and purpose:
Service industry, publishing house.
Complete one-stop publishing service, from conception to distribution, for books, magazines, institutional journals, guides, catalogues, brochures, newsletters, catalogues and company histories.

Subject coverage:
Service publishing including: guides and magazines, corporate manuals and brochures, books and journals, all subjects covered.

Publications list:
Available in print

Access to staff:
Contact by letter, by telephone, by fax and by e-mail
Hours: Mon to Fri, 0900 to 1730

Constituent bodies:
Granta Editions

BOOK TRUST

Formal name: Book Trust

Book House, 45 East Hill, London, SW18 2QZ

Tel: 020 8516 2977
Fax: 020 8516 2978
E-mail: query@booktrust.org.uk

Website:
http://www.booktrust.org.uk

Organisation type and purpose:
To provide reviews, information and advice giving readers the widest possible access to books.

Subject coverage:
Books, publishing, reading, literary prizes

Access to staff:
Contact by letter, by telephone, by fax, by e-mail and via website

BOOKPLATE SOCIETY

Yarkhill, Upper Bucklebury, Reading, Berkshire, RG7 6QH

E-mail: publications@bookplatesociety.org

Website:
http://www.bookplategb.org
Membership details, list of publications.

Enquiries:
Enquiries to: Honorary Secretary

Founded:
1972

Organisation type and purpose:
International organisation, membership association (membership is by subscription), present number of members: 250, registered charity (charity number 295678), publishing house. Voluntary association of bookplate collectors, artists and bibliophiles.
To promote the collection and study of bookplates.

Subject coverage:
History of bookplates, bookplate artists, bookplate literature.

Museum or gallery collection, archive, or library special collection:
Society Archive

Printed publications:
Newsletter (twice a year)
The Bookplate Journal
Books about bookplates (usually biennually) including:
The Bookplates of Edward Gordon Craig (Blatchley, J, 1997)
Bookplates by Robert Osmond (Lee, B N, 1998)
The Bookplates of Edmund Hort New (Lee, B N, 1999/2000)
Scottish Bookplates (Lee, B N and Campbell, I, 2006)
Bookplates in the Trophy Style (Latcham, P, 2006)
Some Bookplates of Heralds (Lee, B N, 2003)
Order printed publications from: The Bookplate Society
Address as above

Publications list:
Available online

Access to staff:
Contact by letter and by e-mail
Hours: Weekends and evenings

Affiliated to:
Fédération Internationale des Sociétés d'Amateurs d'Ex-Libris (FISAE)

BOOKS EXPRESS

PO Box 10, Saffron Walden, Essex, CB11 4EW

Tel: 01799 513726
Fax: 01799 513248
E-mail: info@books-express.co.uk

Website:
http://www.books-express.co.uk
Ordering information, lists of specialist publications.

Enquiries:
Enquiries to: Managing Director
Direct e-mail: john@books-ex.demon.co.uk
Other contacts: Bibliographic Services Manager for website enquiries, bibliographic enquiries.

Founded:
1983

Organisation type and purpose:
Service industry.
Specialist bookseller and information service.

Subject coverage:
Official publications, government documents and electronic information from Commonwealth of Australia (AGPS), Federal Government of Canada (CCG-P), Federal Government of USA (USGPO), Queensland Department of Primary Industry and Library Cataloguing Materials from United States Library of Congress. North American and European academic publishers.

Museum or gallery collection, archive, or library special collection:
Comprehensive database of official publications for sale from Australia, Canada, USA and Queensland
US and European academic publications

Printed publications:
Over 60,000 titles and journals including:

USA government books, documents and grey literature
Canadian government books, documents and grey literature
Australian government books, documents and grey literature
Queensland Department of Primary Industries
US Code of Federal Regulations
English-French French-English bilingual glossaries and vocabularies in over 60 subjects

Access to staff:
Contact by letter, by telephone, by fax, by e-mail and via website. Appointment necessary.
Hours: Mon to Fri, 1000 to 1800

Other addresses:
Books Express Technical
Newell House, Church Road, Ryton on Dunsmore, Coventry, CV8 3ET; tel: 01203 307627; fax: 01203 307627

BOOKSELLERS ASSOCIATION OF THE UK & IRELAND LIMITED

Acronym or abbreviation: BA

272 Vauxhall Bridge Road, London, SW1V 1BA

Tel: 020 7802 0802
Fax: 020 7802 0803
E-mail: mail@booksellers.org.uk

Website:
http://www.booksellers.org.uk

Enquiries:
Enquiries to: Chief Executive

Founded:
1895

Organisation type and purpose:
Trade association, present number of members: 4400 mostly retail outlets.
Representing and promoting retail booksellers nationwide.

Subject coverage:
Book trade regulations, market conditions, legislation, shopfitting, distribution, national book tokens, careers etc.

Printed publications:
The Complete Guide to Starting and Running a Bookshop (£28.00)
Bookselling Essentials (magazine)
Directory of BA Members (annually, £34)
Directory of UK amd Irish Book Publishers
Labels of special interest booksellers and publishers

Publications list:
Available in print

Wholly owned companies:
batch.co.uk
    e-mail: mail@batch.co.uk
Book Tokens Limited
    e-mail: mail@booksellers.co.uk

BORD BIA (IRISH FOOD BOARD)

Clanwilliam Court, Lower Mount Street, Dublin 2, Ireland

Tel: 00 353 1 668–5155
Fax: 00 353 1 668–7521
E-mail: info@bordbia.ie

Website:
http://www.bordbia.ie
http://www.foodisland.com

Enquiries:
Enquiries to: UK Manager

Founded:
1994

Organisation type and purpose:
Bord Bia is the market development and promotions body for the Irish food and drink industry set up in 1994 by the Government of Ireland. Its role is to work in partnership with Irish

companies, bringing them and prospective buyers together to build sales of Irish food and drink in export markets.

Subject coverage:
Can provide comprehensive presentations on the Irish food and drink industry. Extensive database of Irish companies, strategic market information.

Non-library collection catalogue:
All or part available in-house

Library catalogue:
All or part available online and in-house

Electronic and video publications:
Videos

Access to staff:
Contact by letter, by telephone, by fax, by e-mail and via website
Hours: Mon to Fri, 0900 to 1700

Access to building, collection or gallery:
No access other than to staff

BORDER HERITAGE

Loophill, Canonbie, Dumfries & Galloway, DG14 0XF

Tel: 01387 371780
Fax: 01387 381243
E-mail: info@borderheritage.co.uk

Website:
http://www.borderheritage.com
Family history on video.

Enquiries:
Enquiries to: Managing Director

Founded:
1997

Subject coverage:
Scottish/English Border history, films, books.

Museum or gallery collection, archive, or library special collection:
Extensive video tape collection on Border family history
Books

Non-library collection catalogue:
All or part available online

Printed publications:
Various publications (available direct or via website)
Various products (available direct or via website)

Publications list:
Available online

Access to staff:
Contact by letter, by telephone, by fax and by e-mail
Hours: Mon to Fri, 0900 to 1700

Access to building, collection or gallery:
Prior appointment required

BORDER UNION AGRICULTURAL SOCIETY

Showground Office, Springwood Park, Kelso, Borders, TD5 8LS

Tel: 01573 224188
Fax: 01573 226778
E-mail: bordunion@aol.com

Enquiries:
Enquiries to: Secretary

Founded:
1813

Organisation type and purpose:
Voluntary organisation, publishing house.
Agricultural Society.
Organisation and promotion of agricultural, rural and canine activities.

continued overleaf

Subject coverage:
Shows and exhibitions, agricultural, canine and general, rural life. Access to rural historical records for the locality. Information on present day rural activities.

Museum or gallery collection, archive, or library special collection:
Society records dating from 1813

Printed publications:
Border Union Show: Catalogue (annually in July, charge)
Border Union Show: Prize Schedule (annually in April, free)
Championship Dog Show: Schedule and Catalogue (annually, Schedule February, free, Catalogue June, charge)
Kelso Ram Sales: Catalogue (annually in September, charge)

Access to staff:
Contact by letter, by telephone and by fax
Hours: Mon to Fri, 0900 to 1700

Member of:
Association of Show and Agricultural Organisations

BORGWARD DRIVERS' CLUB

158 Willow Avenue, Edgbaston, Birmingham, B17 8HG

Tel: 0121 429 7169
E-mail: borgwardclub@btinternet.com

Website:
http://www.borgward.org.uk
History of company and description of cars plus pictures.

Enquiries:
Enquiries to: Secretary

Founded:
1980

Organisation type and purpose:
Membership association (membership is by subscription), present number of members: 70, voluntary organisation.
To further the promotion of Borgward, Lloyd, Goliath, and Hansa cars in the United Kingdom.

Subject coverage:
Borgward cars, Lloyd cars, Goliath cars, Hansa cars and spares for same.

Printed publications:
Newsletters (6 times a year)

Access to staff:
Contact by letter, by telephone, by e-mail and via website
Hours: Sun to Sat, 0900 to 2000

BORTHWICK INSTITUTE FOR ARCHIVES

University of York, Heslington, York, YO1 5DD

Tel: 01904 642315

Website:
http://www.york.ac.uk/inst/bihr
Summary details of holdings, publications and access, list of publications.

Enquiries:
Enquiries to: Keeper of Archives

Founded:
1953

Organisation type and purpose:
University department or institute.
Historical research institute and archives.

Subject coverage:
Ecclesiastical, social, economic, local and political history, medical history, architectural history and the history of Southern Africa.

Museum or gallery collection, archive, or library special collection:
Archives of the Archbishopric of York c. 1200 to present day
Archives of the Centre for Southern African Studies
Archives of the Earls of Halifax
Atkinson-Brierley architectural archive
Geoffrey Elton Reference Library (moved to Raymond Burton Library, University of York)
York Health Trust Archives
The Institute houses c. 500,000 wills and inventories 1320–1858, for Yorkshire

Non-library collection catalogue:
All or part available online, in-house and in print

Printed publications:
Borthwick Papers (many relate to the history of York, 2 times a year, annual subscription £5, or individually at £4 plus 50p p&p)
Borthwick Texts and Calendars (annually) including:
Archbishop Drummond's Visitation Returns 1764: I Yorkshire Parishes A-G (ed Annesley C and Hoskin P, 1997 £11.50 plus £1.15 p&p)
Archbishop Drummond's Visitation Returns 1764: II Yorkshire Parishes H-R (ed Annesley C and Hoskin P, 1998 £14.50 plus £1.50 p&p)
Archbishop Drummond's Visitation Returns 1764: III Yorkshire Parishes S-Y (ed Annesley C and Hoskin P, 2001 £15 plus £1.20 p&p)
Borthwick Studies in History
Borthwick Wallets includes eg:- English Medieval Handwriting and The Reformation in the North (8 Titles £4 plus 65p p&p)
Occasional Papers
A Guide to Genealogical Sources in the Borthwick Institute of Historical Research (Webb C C, 3rd ed., 1996)
Writers in Yorkshire (Webb C C 1984, 50p plus 35p p&p)

Publications list:
Available online and in print

Access to staff:
Contact by letter. Appointment necessary.
Hours: Mon to Fri, 0930 to 1650

Affiliated to:
University of York

BOTANICAL SOCIETY OF SCOTLAND

Acronym or abbreviation: BSS

c/o Royal Botanic Garden Edinburgh, 20a Inverleith Row, Edinburgh, EH3 5LR

Tel: 0131 552 7171
Fax: 0131 248 2901

Website:
http://www.botsocscot.org.uk

Enquiries:
Enquiries to: General Secretary

Founded:
1836

Organisation type and purpose:
Learned society (membership is by subscription, election or invitation), voluntary organisation, recognised Scottish charity, no. 016283).
Incorporates the Cryptogamic Society of Scotland.

Subject coverage:
Plant science; Scottish flora: plant identification, ecological studies and botanical conservation.

Museum or gallery collection, archive, or library special collection:
Library is incorporated within that of the Royal Botanic Garden Edinburgh

Printed publications:
Plant Ecology and Diversity: previously Botanical Journal of Scotland (twice a year)
BSS News (twice a year)
Checklists of the Flowering Plants and Ferns of East Lothian, West Lothian and Midlothian
Flora of Sutherland (J. Anthony)

A Map of the Flora of Mainland Inverness-shire (in collaboration with the Botanical Society of the British Isles)
Plant Life of South West Asia
Plant Life of Edinburgh and the Lothians (2002)

Access to staff:
Contact by letter

BOTANICAL SOCIETY OF THE BRITISH ISLES

Acronym or abbreviation: BSBI

Department of Botany, Natural History Museum, Cromwell Road, London, SW7 5BD

Tel: 020 7492 5002 (answerphone only)
E-mail: dpearman4@aol.com

Website:
http://www.bsbi.org.uk
General information about the Society.

Enquiries:
Enquiries to: Honorary General Secretary for specific plant enquiries
Other contacts: Honorary Assistant Secretary for all general enquiries

Founded:
1836

Organisation type and purpose:
Learned society (membership is by subscription), present number of members: 2800 approx, voluntary organisation, research organisation, publishing house.
The study and conservation of the British and Irish vascular plant and charophyte flora, its form and distribution. Research into the taxonomy, ecology, biogeography of the flora, maintenance of a botanical recording network and collaboration with other statutory and voluntary bodies.

Subject coverage:
British flowering plants and ferns, identification of wild plants, local floras.

Museum or gallery collection, archive, or library special collection:
Database at University of Leicester c/o Dr R J Gornall, University Road, Leicester LE1 7RH

Printed publications:
Large number of publications including:
BSBI News (3 times per annum, to members only)
Conference Reports
Handbooks on Identification, etc including:
Dandelions of Great Britain and Ireland (235 species, £17.50)
Plant Crib 1998 (£18.50)
Roses of Great Britain and Ireland (£12.50)
Willows and Poplars of Great Britain and Ireland (£12.50)
Watsonia: Journal and Proceedings of the Botanical Society of the British Isles (2 parts annually)
Order printed publications from: Botanical Society of the British Isles Publications
c/o Summerfield Books, 3 Phoenix Park, Skelton, Penrith, Cumbria, CA11 95DE, tel: 01768 484909, fax: 01768 484910, e-mail: info@summerfieldbooks.com

Publications list:
Available in print

Access to staff:
Contact by letter, by telephone and by e-mail
Hours: Mon to Fri, 0900 to 1700
Special comments: Answerphone provides a letter reply only.

BOTANIX LIMITED

Hop Pocket Lane, Paddock Wood, Tonbridge, Kent, TN12 6DQ

Tel: 01892 833415
Fax: 01892 836905
E-mail: intray@botanix.co.uk

Website:
http://www.botanix.co.uk

Enquiries:
Enquiries to: Managing Director

Founded:
1987

Organisation type and purpose:
International organisation, manufacturing industry.

Subject coverage:
Marketing of English hops and hop products; processors and suppliers of English essential oils.

Access to staff:
Contact by letter, by telephone, by fax, by e-mail and via website
Hours: Mon to Fri, 0900 to 1700

Subsidiary body:
Elizarome Limited
at the same address; tel: 01892 833334; fax: 01892 833335; e-mail: arthur@aroma-oils.co.uk
H G Hesselberger and Co Ltd
at the same address

BOUNDARY COMMISSION FOR SCOTLAND

3 Drumsheugh Gardens, Edinburgh, EH3 7QJ

Tel: 0131 538 7510
Fax: 0131 538 7511
E-mail: secretariat@scottishboundaries.gov.uk

Website:
http://www.bcomm-scotland.gov.uk
Information on boundaries of constituencies in Scotland for Scottish and Westminster parliaments, and on the periodic reviews of those boundaries.

Enquiries:
Enquiries to: Secretary

Founded:
1945

Organisation type and purpose:
Statutory body.
Advisory non-departmental public body, constituted under the Parliamentary Constituencies Act 1986, reporting to the Scotland Office.

Subject coverage:
Parliamentary boundaries.

Printed publications:
Periodical and Interim Reports
Order printed publications from: The Stationery Office

Electronic and video publications:
Reports available from website as PDF files

Publications list:
Available online

Access to staff:
Contact by letter, by telephone, by fax, by e-mail and via website
Hours: Mon to Fri, 0900 to 1700

BOURNEMOUTH AND POOLE COLLEGE

North Road, Parkstone, Poole, Dorset, BH14 0LS

Tel: 01202 747600
Fax: 01202 205477
E-mail: gokane@bpc.ac.uk

Website:
http://www.thecollege.co.uk

Enquiries:
Enquiries to: Librarian
Direct tel: 01202 205631

Subject coverage:
FE courses (GCSE, A-level, AS-level, AVCE, GMVQ, NVQ) in the following subjects: construction, engineering, social care, child care, theatre and performing arts, hairdressing, floristry, beauty therapy, catering, tourism, hotel operations,

business studies, computing, media studies, management, teacher training, art and design, science, languages, social sciences, law.
HE courses (BSC and BEng Foundation, HND, HNC) in the following subjects: conservation sciences, computing, electronics, design engineering, business, business information technology, computer-aided design, geography and coastal conservation, popular music, tourism and leisure management, mechanical and production engineering, building studies.

Museum or gallery collection, archive, or library special collection:
249 journals
6000 audio visual items (videos, tapes)
70,776 books to support courses listed

Library catalogue:
All or part available in-house

Access to staff:
Contact by letter and by e-mail
Hours: Mon to Thu, 0900 to 1900; Fri, 0900 to 1700

Access for disabled people:
Parking provided, ramped entry, access to all public areas, toilet facilities

BOURNEMOUTH UNIVERSITY

Library and Learning Centre, Talbot Campus, Fern Barrow, Poole, Dorset, BH12 5BB

Tel: 01202 524111
Fax: 01202 513293

Website:
http://www.bournemouth.ac.uk/library
Information about all library services

Enquiries:
Enquiries to: University Librarian
Direct tel: 01202 965044
Direct fax: 01202 965475
Direct e-mail: jascott@bmth.ac.uk
Other contacts: Deputy University Librarian

Founded:
1979

Organisation type and purpose:
University library.

Subject coverage:
Computing, IT, electronics and information systems, psychology, communications and sociology, economics and industry, finance, taxation and accountancy, law, management, marketing, retailing, advertising and public relations, health and community studies, social policy, nursing and midwifery, biological and environmental sciences, design, production and manufacture, food hospitality, tourism, recreation and leisure, media studies, archaeology and heritage conservation.

Museum or gallery collection, archive, or library special collection:
Wedlake and Greening: Archaeology
Ernst and Young: Taxation and Revenue Law
BBC Radio 4 Analysis Programme
Broadcasting Audience Research
Independent Local Radio Programme Sharing Digitization Project Archive
Segrue Journalism Collection
TV Times Project
Printed and electronic sources covering history of broadcasting, public relations and advertising; product design, interior design and engineering

Trade and statistical information:
Collection of government and EC official statistics. A range of unofficial statistics.
Business information.
Company data.
Market Research.

Printed publications:
Bournemouth University Occasional Papers on Library and Information Services (BUOPOLIS)
British Nursing Index
Conference Proceedings

Order printed publications from: Academic Services, Bournemouth University
tel: 01202 965725, fax: 01202 965475, e-mail: gfowler@bournemouth.ac.uk

Electronic and video publications:
British Nursing Index online and on CD-ROM

Access to staff:
Contact by letter, by e-mail and via website.
Appointment necessary.
Hours: Term time: Mon to Thu, 0900 to 2100; Fri, 0915 to 1715; Sat, 1200 to 1800; Sun 1200 to 1700

Members:
Southern Universities Purchasing Consortium (SUPC)

BOVIS LEND LEASE LIMITED (EUROPE)

Acronym or abbreviation: BLLE

142 Northolt Road, Harrow, Middlesex, HA2 0EE

Tel: 020 8271 8000
Fax: 020 8271 8188
E-mail: liz.barnes-downing@eu.bovislendlease.com

Website:
http://www.bovislendlease.com
Information on Bovis Lend Lease worldwide.

Enquiries:
Enquiries to: Librarian
Direct tel: 020 8271 8124 (Information Centre)

Founded:
1885

Organisation type and purpose:
Service industry.
Construction company.
Project and construction management, consultancy, creative solutions.

Subject coverage:
Building construction.

Library catalogue:
All or part available in-house

Access to staff:
Contact by letter, by e-mail and via website.
Appointment necessary.
Hours: Mon to Fri, 0900 to 1700

Access to building, collection or gallery:
No access other than to staff

Parent body:
Lend Lease Limited

Regional offices in:
Birmingham, Bristol, Edinburgh, Glasgow, Manchester, Dublin, Belfast

BOWLS ENGLAND

Acronym or abbreviation: BE

Lyndhurst Road, Worthing, West Sussex, BN11 2AZ

Tel: 01903 820222
Fax: 01903 820444
E-mail: enquiries@bowlsengland.com

Website:
http://www.bowlsengland.com

Enquiries:
Enquiries to: Chief Executive

Founded:
1903

Organisation type and purpose:
National organisation, professional body, present number of members: 132,000.
National governing body of the game.

Subject coverage:
The game of bowls.

Access to staff:
Contact by letter, by telephone and by fax.
Appointment necessary.
Hours: Mon to Fri, 0900 to 1700

continued overleaf

Access for disabled people:
Parking provided, level entry

Also at:
Bowls England
Victoria Park, Archery Road, Royal Leamington Spa, Warwickshire, CV31 3PT; tel: 01926 430686; fax: 01926 332024

BOX CULVERT ASSOCIATION

Acronym or abbreviation: BoxCA

60 Charles Street, Leicester, LE1 1FB

Tel: 0116 253 6161
Fax: 0116 251 4568
E-mail: boxca@britishprecast.org
Website:
http://www.boxculverts.org.uk

Enquiries:
Enquiries to: Secretary

Organisation type and purpose:
Trade association.

Subject coverage:
Precast concrete box culverts.

Printed publications:
Brochure (free)
Site Use Guide (free)
Specification (1991, £3)

Access to staff:
Contact by letter, by telephone, by fax and by e-mail
Hours: Mon to Fri, 0900 to 1700

Product association of the:
British Precast Concrete Federation

BOYS BRIGADE

Acronym or abbreviation: BB

Felden Lodge, Felden Lane, Hemel Hempstead, Hertfordshire, HP3 0BL

Tel: 01442 231681
Fax: 01442 235391
E-mail: felden@boys-brigade.org.uk
Website:
http://www.boys-brigade.org.uk
History, events, guestbook.

Enquiries:
Enquiries to: Chief Executive

Founded:
1883

Organisation type and purpose:
Voluntary organisation.
Youth organisation.

Subject coverage:
Church-based youth work with boys and young men in nearly 3000 churches of most denominations.

Museum or gallery collection, archive, or library special collection:
Archives relating to the founding (in 1883) and subsequent history of the Brigade

Printed publications:
Annual Report
BB Gazette (6 times a year)
Order printed publications from: The Supplies Manager, The Boys' Brigade Alington Road, Eynesbury, St Neots, Cambridgeshire, PE19 2RD, tel: 01480 470515, fax: 01480 470516, e-mail: bus-cent@boys-brigade.org.uk

Access to staff:
Contact by letter, by fax and by e-mail
Hours: Mon to Fri, 0900 to 1700

BP VIDEO LIBRARY

52–54 Southwark Street, London, SE1 1UN

Tel: 020 7357 7521
Fax: 020 7357 9953
E-mail: bpvl@bp.com
Website:
http://www.bpvideolibrary.com

Enquiries:
Enquiries to: Librarian

Organisation type and purpose:
Suitable for ages: all.
Distribution library.

Subject coverage:
Oil industry, refining, exploration, energy, environment, motoring, power and engineering.

Museum or gallery collection, archive, or library special collection:
Video programmes covering wide area of the oil industry

Library catalogue:
All or part available in print

Electronic and video publications:
Videos

Publications list:
Available in print

Access to staff:
Contact by letter, by telephone, by fax and by e-mail
Hours: Mon to Fri, 0900 to 1700

BPA CONSULTING LIMITED

Atlas House, Spring Court, Station Road, Dorking, Surrey, RH4 1EB

Tel: 01306 875500
Fax: 01306 888179
E-mail: bpa@bpaconsulting.com

Enquiries:
Enquiries to: Director

Founded:
1971

Organisation type and purpose:
Consultancy.

Subject coverage:
Strategic consultants to the electronics industry, specialising in inter-connection and packaging.

Publications list:
Available online and in print

Access to staff:
Contact by letter, by telephone, by fax and by e-mail
Hours: Mon to Fri, 0900 to 1730

BRACKENHURST LIBRARY

The Nottingham Trent University, Brackenhurst, Nottingham Road, Southwell, Nottinghamshire, NG25 0QF

Tel: 01636 817000 Switchboard; 817049 Library
Fax: 01636 815404

Enquiries:
Enquiries to: Information Specialist
Direct tel: 01636 817049
Direct e-mail: beth.gibbs@ntu.ac.uk

Organisation type and purpose:
University library, suitable for ages: 16+.

Subject coverage:
Agriculture, food science, horticulture and floristry, equine studies and horse management, land management, small animal care.

Access to staff:
Contact by telephone
Hours: Term time: Mon to Thu, 0830 to 1900; Fri, 0830 to 1730

Department of:
Nottingham Trent University

Links with:
Nottinghamshire County Library
Other colleges of further education

BRACKNELL AND WOKINGHAM COLLEGE

Church Road, Bracknell, Berkshire, RG12 1DJ

Tel: 01344 460200
Fax: 01344 420360
E-mail: study@bracknell.ac.uk
Website:
http://www.bracknell.ac.uk
General and course information.

Enquiries:
Enquiries to: Learning Resources Centre Manager
Direct tel: ext 239/240
Direct e-mail: lrc@bracknell.ac.uk

Founded:
1962

Organisation type and purpose:
Suitable for ages: 16+.

Subject coverage:
General education up to and including A Level; AVCE and BTEC National Diploma; art, design and media studies, business and leisure; marketing, personnel and accountancy; computing and IT; engineering; health and social care; EFL; modern languages; access; teacher training, including PGCE.

Library catalogue:
All or part available in-house

Access to staff:
Contact by letter, by telephone, by e-mail, in person and via website
Hours: Mon to Thu, 0900 to 1930; Fri, 0900 to 1500
Special comments: Limited opening in College vacation.

Access for disabled people:
Parking provided, ramped entry, access to all public areas, toilet facilities

Other addresses:
Bracknell & Wokingham College
Montague House, Broad Street, Wokingham, Berkshire, RG11 1AU; tel: 0118 902 9150; fax: 0118 902 9160
Bracknell & Wokingham College
Wick Hill Centre, Wick Hill, Sandy Lane, Bracknell, RG12 2JG; tel: 01344 390400 ext 421 or 422; fax: 01344 390490
Bracknell & Wokingham College
Woodley Hill House, Eastcourt Avenue, Earley, Reading, RG6 1HH; tel: 0118 926 1621; fax: 0118 966 0321

BRACKNELL FOREST BOROUGH COUNCIL

Easthamstead House, Town Square, Bracknell, Berkshire, RG12 1AQ

Tel: 01344 424642\ Minicom no. 01344 352045
Fax: 01344 352810
E-mail: 106005.521@compuserve.com
Website:
http://www.bracknell-forest.gov.uk

Enquiries:
Enquiries to: Public Relations Manager
Other contacts: Borough Administrator

Organisation type and purpose:
Local government body.

Subject coverage:
Leisure, environmental health, housing services, planning, development and control, council tax, refuse collection, street lighting, landscape maintenance, drains, sewer clearance and cesspools, services for residents of the borough of Bracknell Forest.

Trade and statistical information:
Data on the local population of Bracknell, amenities, services and employment.

Printed publications:
Annual Report
Bracknell 'The Making of Our New Town' (book)
Community plan
Guide to the Borough of Bracknell Forest

Electronic and video publications:
Live, work and play, the Bracknell Forest way (video)
What's Important to You? (video)

Access to staff:
Contact by letter, by telephone and by fax
Hours: Mon to Fri, 0900 to 1700

BRACKNELL FOREST BOROUGH COUNCIL LIBRARY AND INFORMATION SERVICE

Bracknell Central Library, Town Square, Bracknell, Berkshire, RG12 1BH

Tel: 01344 423149
Fax: 01344 411392
E-mail: bracknell.library@bracknell-forest.gov.uk

Website:
http://www.bracknell-forest.gov.uk/libraries

Organisation type and purpose:
Local government body, public library.

Museum or gallery collection, archive, or library special collection:
Photographic collection of the development of Bracknell town, and local studies collection.

Library catalogue:
All or part available online

Access to staff:
Contact by letter, by telephone, by fax, by e-mail and in person
Hours: Mon, Wed, 0930 to 1700; Tue, Thu, Fri, 0930 to 1900; Sat, 0930 to 1600

Access to building, collection or gallery:
Special comments: No lift access at Bracknell Library

Access for disabled people:
Ramp and automatic doors

BRACKNELL FOREST HERITAGE

Formal name: Bracknell Forest Heritage

Environment & Leisure, Time Square, Market Street, Bracknell, RG12 1JD

Tel: 01344 351754
E-mail: heritage@bracknell-forest.gov.uk

Website:
http://www.bfheritage.org.uk

Enquiries:
Enquiries to: Heritage Officer
Direct tel: 01344 351754
Direct e-mail: heritage@bracknell-forest.gov.uk

Access to staff:
Contact by letter, by telephone and by e-mail

BRADFORD CATHEDRAL

Formal name: Cathedral Church of St Peter, Bradford

Cathedral Office, Stott Hill, Bradford, West Yorkshire, BD1 4EH

Tel: 01274 777720
Fax: 01274 777730
E-mail: dean@bradford.anglican.org

Enquiries:
Enquiries to: Education Officer or Cathedral Secretary
Direct e-mail: secretary@cathedral.bradford.anglican.org

Other contacts: Dean of Bradford for special permissions; major events.

Founded:
7th Century

Organisation type and purpose:
Cathedral: place of worship, historic listed building, concert and exhibition venue, education resource – visits programme, Bradford heritage.

Subject coverage:
Christian worship and faith; local history; William Morris Glass.

Access to staff:
Contact by letter, by telephone, by fax, by e-mail and in person
Hours: Mon to Fri, 0900 to 1700; Sun, services only
Special comments: Groups by prior appointment.

Access to building, collection or gallery:
Hours: Mon to Fri, 0900 to 1630; Sat, 0900 to 1600 (phone ahead for confirmation)

Access for disabled people:
Parking provided, level entry, toilet facilities
Special comments: Access for most areas.

BRADFORD CHAMBER OF COMMERCE & INDUSTRY

Acronym or abbreviation: CMS

Devere House, Vicar Lane, Little Germany, Bradford, West Yorkshire, BD1 5AH

Tel: 01274 772777
Fax: 01274 771081
E-mail: information@bradfordchamber.co.uk

Website:
http://www.bradfordchamber.co.uk

Enquiries:
Enquiries to: Chief Executive
Other contacts: Enterprise and Marketing Manager

Organisation type and purpose:
Trade association (membership is by subscription), present number of members: 1100.
Chamber of Commerce.
Provision of business services to members.

Subject coverage:
All business information, international trade documentation, business representation, training services.

Printed publications:
Contact (annually)
Construction Review (annually)
Directory of members (annually)
Export/Import Guide (annually)

Access to staff:
Access for members only. Non-members charged.
Hours: Mon to Fri, 0900 to 1700

BRADFORD LIBRARIES, ARCHIVES AND INFORMATION

Central Library, Princes Way, Bradford, West Yorkshire, BD1 1NN

Tel: 01274 433600
Fax: 01274 395108
E-mail: public.libraries@bradford.gov.uk

Website:
http://www.bradford.gov.uk

Enquiries:
Enquiries to: Head of Service: Libraries Archives & Information

Founded:
1872

Organisation type and purpose:
Local government body, public library.

Subject coverage:
Business information; local studies including oral history; photography; Indic languages especially Urdu; multicultural material, particularly children's material.

Museum or gallery collection, archive, or library special collection:
Arthur Blackburn Monumental Inscriptions Collection
Bradford Heritage Recording Unit (local oral history)
Dickons Collection (mainly Bradford history)
Federer Collection (Yorkshire books and pamphlets)
Lees Botanical Collection (19th century flora)
Snowdon Collection (political and social history of the late 19th and early 20th centuries)

Library catalogue:
All or part available online

Printed publications:
Key Companies in Bradford (directory of 1300 companies in Bradford, for purchase)
DIVA database of community and voluntary organisations in the Bradford district

Electronic and video publications:
Key Companies in Bradford (directory of 1300 companies in Bradford, CD-ROM, for purchase)

Publications list:
Available in print

Access to staff:
Contact by letter, by telephone, by fax, by e-mail and in person

Access for disabled people:
Access to all public areas, toilet facilities

Houses the library of:
Bradford Antiquarian Society

BRADFORD MECHANICS' INSTITUTE LIBRARY

76 Kirkgate, Bradford, West Yorkshire, BD1 1SZ

Tel: 01274 722857
E-mail: bmi-library@tiscali.co.uk

Enquiries:
Enquiries to: Administrator

Founded:
1832

Organisation type and purpose:
Registered charity (charity number 509231).
Independent subscription library.

Subject coverage:
Lending library; local history collection, history of Bradford and environs, history of the Institute.

Printed publications:
Newsletter (quarterly, members only)

Access to staff:
Contact by letter and by telephone. Access for members only.

Access to building, collection or gallery:
Hours: Mon to Fri, 0900 to 1630; Sat, 0900 to 1200
Special comments: Library open to members only by subscription.

Member organisation of:
Association of Independent Libraries

BRADFORD SCHOOL OF MANAGEMENT

Heaton Mount, Keighley Road, Bradford, West Yorkshire, BD9 4JU

Tel: 01274 234485
Fax: 01274 234444
E-mail: edp.ubmc@bradford.ac.uk

Website:
http://www.brad.ac.uk
All brochures, full course details.
http://www.brad.ac.uk/acad/management

Enquiries:
Enquiries to: Director
Direct tel: 01274 234466
Other contacts: Programme Administrators

continued overleaf

Founded:
1962

Organisation type and purpose:
University department or institute.
Creation and delivery of executive education and development programmes.

Subject coverage:
Management development; marketing; finance and accounting; human resource management; strategic management; negotiation skills; effective manager programmes; company programmes.

Museum or gallery collection, archive, or library special collection:
Business Library

Printed publications:
Open courses brochure (annually, free)

Publications list:
Available online and in print

Access to staff:
Contact by letter, by telephone, by fax, by e-mail and in person
Hours: Mon to Fri, 0900 to 1700

Access to building, collection or gallery:
No prior appointment required
Hours: Mon, Tue, Thu, Fri, 0900 to 1700; Wed, 0900 to 2100; Sat, 0900 to 1200

Access for disabled people:
Parking provided, level entry, toilet facilities

Parent body:
University of Bradford
 tel: 01274 232323

BRADFORD UNIVERSITY SCHOOL OF MANAGEMENT LIBRARY

Emm Lane, Bradford, West Yorkshire, BD9 4JL

Tel: 01274 234402
Fax: 01274 234398
E-mail: j.finder@bradford.ac.uk

Website:
http://www.brad.ac.uk/lss/library
Library services, catalogue, subject guides.

Enquiries:
Enquiries to: Librarian

Founded:
1962

Organisation type and purpose:
University library, consultancy.

Subject coverage:
All aspects of management.

Museum or gallery collection, archive, or library special collection:
Research publications, projects and theses on a wide variety of management topics
Library with business information services

Library catalogue:
All or part available online

Access to staff:
Contact by letter, by telephone, by fax, by e-mail and in person. Non-members charged.
Hours: Mon to Fri, 0900 to 1700

Access to building, collection or gallery:
No prior appointment required
Hours: Term Time: Mon, Tue, Thu, Fri, 0845 to 1730; Wed, 0845 to 2000; Sat, 1000 to 1400
Vacation: Mon to Fri, 0845 to 1730

Parent body:
University of Bradford Library
 Richmond Road, Bradford, West Yorkshire, BD7 1DP; tel: 01274 233400; fax: 01274 233398; e-mail: j.j.horton@bradford.ac.uk (university librarian)

BRAIN AND SPINE FOUNDATION

7 Winchester House, Kennington Park, Cranmer Road, London, SW9 6EJ

Tel: 020 7793 5900
Fax: 020 7793 5939
E-mail: info@brainandspine.org.uk

Website:
http://www.brainandspine.org.uk
General information about the services provided.

Enquiries:
Enquiries to: Administrator

Founded:
1992

Organisation type and purpose:
Registered charity (charity number 1098528).
To improve the prevention, treatment and care of disorders of the brain and spine, funds medical research and develops an education programme to increase the knowledge and understanding of neurological disorders for the profession and general public.

Subject coverage:
Disorders of the brain and spine.

Printed publications:
Leaflets and information booklets for patients and carers covering a wide range of neurological disorders (free to patients and carers, for purchase by all others, various prices)

Electronic and video publications:
Disability and Rehabilitation (training video for medical students, free to medical students, available for purchase to all others)

Publications list:
Available online and in print

Access to staff:
Contact by letter, by telephone, by fax, by e-mail and via website. Appointment necessary.
Hours: Mon to Fri, 0900 to 1700

Member organisation of:
Association of Medical Research Charities (AMRC)
National Council for Voluntary Organisations (NCVO)
Neurological Alliance
Spinal Injuries Forum

BRAIN RESEARCH TRUST

Acronym or abbreviation: BRT

15 Southampton Place, London, WC1A 2AJ

Tel: 020 7404 9982
Fax: 020 7404 9983
E-mail: thebrt@aol.com

Website:
http://www.brt.org.uk

Enquiries:
Enquiries to: Director

Founded:
1971

Organisation type and purpose:
Registered charity (charity number 263064).
Promotes and supports neurological research at the Institute of Neurology, Queen Square, London.

Subject coverage:
Neurological research.

Printed publications:
Annual Report
Newsletter

Access to staff:
Contact by letter, by telephone, by fax and by e-mail. Appointment necessary.
Hours: Mon to Fri, 0900 to 1700

BRAINTREE DISTRICT COUNCIL

Causeway House, Braintree, Essex, CM7 9HB

Tel: 01376 552525\ Minicom no. 01376 557766
Fax: 01376 552626

Website:
http://www.braintree.gov.uk

Elections, local services, local information.

Enquiries:
Enquiries to: Public Relations Manager
Direct tel: 01376 557752

Founded:
1974

Organisation type and purpose:
Local government body.

Publications list:
Available online

Access to staff:
Contact by letter and by telephone. Appointment necessary.
Hours: Mon to Fri, 0900 to 1700

Access for disabled people:
Parking provided, ramped entry, access to all public areas, toilet facilities

BRAM STOKER SOCIETY, THE

Acronym or abbreviation: B S Society

c/o 43 Castle Court, Killiney Hill Road, Killiney, Co. Dublin, Ireland

E-mail: gothicalbert@eircom.net

Website:
http://www.bibliomania.com
http://www.vampyreempire.com
Summary of our activites and contact address

Enquiries:
Enquiries to: Registrar & Journal Editor

Founded:
1980

Organisation type and purpose:
Learned society (membership is by subscription), present number of members: 120.
The promotion of the serious study and appreciation of Bram Stoker, his works, and influence in the areas of fiction, cinema, theatre and music, as well as his importance in the Gothic Horror literary genre.

Subject coverage:
The Vampire in fiction, Count Dracula, Bram Stoker, the Gothic Horror genre in film and literature and the Irish Supernatural tradition in folklore and literature.

Museum or gallery collection, archive, or library special collection:
An archive of 5000 books, mss and documents relating to Bram Stoker held at The Chairperson's address

Printed publications:
Newsletter (quarterly, to members by subscription)
Journal of scholarly articles (annually, to members by subsription)
Order printed publications from: Editor (Dr Albert Power), The B S Society Journal
43 Castle Court, Killiney Hill Road, Killiney, County Dublin, Ireland

Publications list:
Available in print

Access to staff:
Contact by letter, by e-mail and in person. Appointment necessary. Access for members only. Non-members charged.
Hours: Mon to Fri, 0900 to 1700

Access to building, collection or gallery:
Prior appointment required
Special comments: Prior appointment by application to Chairperson in advance, to consult archives held at his private house.
The Annual Summer School held in Dublin, 1st weekend of July.

Affiliated to:
The Bram Stoker Club
 Trinity College, Dublin
The Bram Stoker Memorial Association of New York

Chairperson's address:
The B S Society
1 Lakelands Close, Stillergan, County Dublin, Ireland; tel: 00 35 31 288 1970; fax: 00 35 31 288 1970

Close links with:
Dracula Society of London

BRANCH LINE SOCIETY

Acronym or abbreviation: BLS

73 Norfolk Park Avenue, Sheffield, South Yorkshire, S2 2RB

Tel: 0114 275 2303
Fax: 0114 275 2303

Website:
http://www.branchline.org.uk
Details of society activities plus news archive.

Enquiries:
Enquiries to: General Secretary
Other contacts: Sales Officer (for sales and membership recruitment enquiries only)

Founded:
1955

Organisation type and purpose:
Membership association (membership is by subscription), present number of members: 900, voluntary organisation.

Subject coverage:
Minor and branch railway lines, primarily in the British Isles but also in the rest of Europe and other parts of the world.

Printed publications:
Branch Line News (twice monthly, Members only)
List of occasional publications available from the Society
Order printed publications from: Sales Officer, Branch Line Society
37 Osberton Place, Sheffield, S11 8XL, tel: 0114 268 0429, fax: 0114 263 1094, e-mail: bls.sales@tesco.net

Access to staff:
Contact by letter, by telephone and by fax. Appointment necessary.
Hours: Mon to Sun, 0900 to 2200

BRASS BAND HERITAGE TRUST

Acronym or abbreviation: BBHT

1 Clumber Close, Poynton, Cheshire, SK12 1PG

E-mail: peh@paulhindmarsh.com

Enquiries:
Enquiries to: Director

Founded:
1996

Organisation type and purpose:
Registered charity (charity number 1037552).
To promote, present activities and foster the future of the Brass Band movement in the UK. The Trust is an active commissioner of new repertoire for brass bands.

Subject coverage:
Commissioning new works for brass band for national and regional events. A partner with the British Federation of Brass Bands in supporting the activities of youth brass bands, nationwide.

Access to staff:
Contact by letter, by telephone and by e-mail
Hours: Mon to Fri, 0900 to 1700

BREAKTHROUGH DEAF/HEARING INTEGRATION

Acronym or abbreviation: Breakthrough

Alan Geale House, The Close, Westhill Campus, Bristol Road, Birmingham, B29 6LN

Tel: 0121 415 2289 (voice and text)
Fax: 0121 415 2323

E-mail: info@breakthrough-dhi.org.uk

Website:
http://www.breakthrough-dhi.org.uk

Enquiries:
Enquiries to: Information Officer

Founded:
1971

Organisation type and purpose:
National organisation, voluntary organisation, registered charity (charity number 261951), training organisation.
Self help group.
Development of innovative work with deaf and hearing people through contact, information and training.

Subject coverage:
Integration between deaf and hearing adults through contact, information and training.

Museum or gallery collection, archive, or library special collection:
Information service on all aspects of deafness

Printed publications:
An OBE Investiture at Buckingham Palace (Michael Jackson, booklet, £2.50)
Have You Heard? (information booklet, £4)
Hear my Silence (Jacqui Parkes, selected poems, £4)
Laminated Fingerspelling Mats (A3 £3, A4 £2.50)
Summary of Services, Information and Publications on Deafness in the United Kingdom (booklet, £4)

Access to staff:
Contact by letter and via website
Hours: Mon to Fri, 0900 to 1700

Access for disabled people:
Parking provided, toilet facilities

Regional centres at:
Breakthrough (London) Ealing & Hammersmith & Fulham
2 Erconwald Street, East Acton, London, W12 0BS; tel: 020 8749 4111 (voice/fax); 020 8749 8186 (text); 020 8749 7854 (video); e-mail: london .ealing@breakthrough-dhi.org.uk and london .hammersmith
Breakthrough (London) Ealing & Hammersmith & Fulham
The Hall, Peyton Place, Greenwich, London, SE10 8RS; tel: 020 8853 5661; 020 8858 7689 (text); 020 8858 2954 (video); fax: 020 8853 5661; e-mail: london.greenwich@breakthrough-dhi.org.uk
Breakthrough (London) Harrow
2nd Floor, Premier House, 1 Canning Road, Wealdstone, HA7 7TS; tel: 020 8424 0983 (voice/ fax); 020 8424 4626 (text); 020 8861 4625 (video); e-mail: london.harrow@breakthrough-dhi.org.uk
Breakthrough (London) Tower Hamlets
Trinity Centre, Key Close, London, E1 4HG; tel: 010 7790 8478 (voice/fax); 020 7791 0105 (text); 020 7790 7453 (video); e-mail: london.tower .hamlets@breakthrough-dhi.org.uk
Breakthrough (North)
John Haswell House, 8/9 Gladstone Terrace, Gateshead, Tyne and Wear, NE8 4DY; tel: 0191 478 7920 (voice/fax) 0191 478 6363 (text) 0191 478 4369 (video phone); e-mail: north@breakthrough -dhi.org.uk
Breakthrough (Southern Counties)
Farnborough Centre, 67 Albert Road, Farnborough, Hampshire, GU14 6SL, Text 01252 372978 (video); tel: 01252 510051; 522765; fax: 01252 524642; e-mail: southern.counties@ breakthrough-dhi.org.uk
Breakthrough (Southern Counties)
Aldershot Centre, Princess Gardens, 2A High Street, Aldershot, Hants, GU11 1BJ; tel: 01252 313882 (voice/text) 01242 310041 (video); fax: 01252 337546; e-mail: southern.counties@ breakthrough-dhi.org.uk
Breakthrough (West Midlands)
1 College Walk, Bristol Road, Selly Oak, Birmingham, B29 6LE; tel: voice/fax 415 5900, Minicom 0121 472 5488

Breakthrough London Services Team
The Hall, Peyton Place, London, SE10 8RS; tel: 020 8269 0307 (voice/fax); 020 8269 0287 (text); 020 8269 0242 (video); e-mail: london.services@ breakthrough-dhi.org.uk

BREAST CANCER CARE – GLASGOW

Acronym or abbreviation: BCC

2nd Floor, 40 St Enoch Square, Glasgow, G1 4DH

Tel: 0141 221 2244
Fax: 0141 221 9499
E-mail: sco@breastcancercare.org.uk

Website:
http://www.breastcancercare.org.uk

Enquiries:
Enquiries to: Head of National Development
Other contacts: National Manager responsible for all services provided in Scotland.

Founded:
1973

Organisation type and purpose:
National organisation, voluntary organisation, registered charity (charity number 1017658).

Subject coverage:
Breast cancer in women and men, information, help and support.

Library catalogue:
All or part available online and in print

Printed publications:
Breast Cancer and Breast Care (£6)
A range of leaflets and booklets on subjects related to breast cancer (free)
Order printed publications from: Publications Department, Breast Cancer Care
Kiln House, 210 New Kings Road, London, SW6 4NZ, tel: 0808 800 6000 or 0141 221 2244, fax: 020 7384 3387, e-mail: bcc@breastcancercare.org.uk

Electronic and video publications:
Treating Breast Cancer (audio tape)

Publications list:
Available online and in print

Access to staff:
Contact by letter, by telephone, by fax, by e-mail and via website. Appointment necessary.
Hours: Mon to Fri, 0900 to 1700

Access for disabled people:
Level entry, toilet facilities

BREAST CANCER CARE – LONDON

Acronym or abbreviation: BCC

Kiln House, 210 New Kings Road, London, SW6 4NZ

Tel: 020 7384 2984\ Minicom no. 020 7731 6395
Fax: 020 7384 3387
E-mail: info@breastcancercare.org.uk

Website:
http://www.breastcancercare.org.uk
Full range of patient information, ordering publications, making donations, discussion forums, ask the nurse email service, news, fundraising, press, recruitment.

Enquiries:
Enquiries to: Administrator

Founded:
1973

Organisation type and purpose:
National organisation, membership association, present number of members: 400, voluntary organisation, registered charity (charity number 1017658).
To provide information and support to those affected by breast cancer.

continued overleaf

Subject coverage:
Breast cancer; treatments, general information, prostheses, after-care, support groups.

Printed publications:
Newsletter (quarterly)
Several booklets and 30 factsheets dealing with breast cancer, its treatment and support for sufferers (free but charge for bulk order postage), all publications are available in large print on request

Electronic and video publications:
Treating Breast Cancer (tape)
Diagnosing and Treating Breast Cancer (URDU) (tape)

Publications list:
Available online and in print

Access to staff:
Contact by letter, by telephone, by fax, by e-mail and via website
Hours: Helpline: Mon to Fri, 1000 to 1700; Sat, 1000 to 1400

Access to building, collection or gallery:
Prior appointment required

Access for disabled people:
Parking provided, ramped entry, toilet facilities
Special comments: Parking must be requested prior to visit.

Also at Northern Office:
Breast Cancer Care
   Volsenc House, 14–18 West Bar Green, Sheffield, S1 2DA; tel: 0114 276 0296; fax: 0114 276 0293

Also at Scotland Office:
Breast Cancer Care
   46 Gordon Street, Glasgow, G1 3PU; tel: 0141 221 2244; fax: 0141 221 9499

Subsidiary body:
Lavender Trust Charity

BRECON BEACONS NATIONAL PARK AUTHORITY

Acronym or abbreviation: BBNPA

Plas y Ffynnon, Cambrian Way, Brecon, Powys, LD3 7HP

Tel: 01874 624437
Fax: 01874 622574
E-mail: enquiries@breconbeacons.org

Enquiries:
Enquiries to: Public Relations Officer
Other contacts: Chief Executive for statutory and legal matters.

Founded:
1957

Organisation type and purpose:
Local government body, advisory body, statutory body, present number of members: 24, public library, research organisation, publishing house.
National park authority, two thirds of the authority members are appointed by the constituent unitary authorities; one third are appointed by the Welsh Assembly.
To protect and conserve wildlife, landscape and cultural heritage; to promote opportunities for quiet enjoyment of the countryside; a local planning authority.

Subject coverage:
Landscape conservation and countryside recreation within the Brecon Beacons National Park. Ecology/archaeology/planning, local area knowledge.

Printed publications:
Guided Walks Programme
Park Update Newsletter
Welcome Guide
Tourism Newsletter
Unitary Development Plan
State of the Park report
Leaflets, books and maps for walkers, cavers, cyclists, horseriders, and tourism employees.

Publications list:
Available in print

Access to staff:
Contact by letter, by telephone, by fax, by e-mail and in person. Appointment necessary.
Hours: Mon to Fri, 0900 to 1700

BRECON BEACONS NATIONAL PARK VISITOR CENTRE

Libanus, Brecon, Powys, LD3 8ER

Tel: 01874 623366
Fax: 01874 624515
E-mail: visitor.centre@breconbeacons.org

Website:
http://www.breconbeacons.org
Events, education, location map.

Enquiries:
Enquiries to: Information Officer

Founded:
1957

Organisation type and purpose:
Local government body, service industry, suitable for ages: all.
To provide an information and education service relating to the Brecon Beacons National Park.

Subject coverage:
Activities within the Brecon Beacons National Park, specialised publications on offer, education resources.

Library catalogue:
All or part available in-house

Printed publications:
Various leaflets and small books on walks and sites of interest within the Brecon Beacons National Park under the headings: Maps, Recreational, Cultural, Historical, Nature Guides.

Publications list:
Available in print

Access to staff:
Contact by letter, by telephone, by fax, by e-mail, in person and via website
Hours: Sun to Sat, 0930 to 1700

Access to building, collection or gallery:
No prior appointment required
Hours: Sun to Sat, 0930 to 1700

Access for disabled people:
Parking provided, ramped entry, access to all public areas, toilet facilities
Special comments: Hearing loop/induction installed.

Other addresses:
Brecon Beacons National Park Authority
   Plas y Ffynnon, Cambrian Way, Brecon, Powys, LD3 7HP; tel: 01874 624437

BRENT ARCHIVE

152 Olive Road, Cricklewood, London, NW2 6UY

Tel: 020 8937 3541
Fax: 020 8450 5211
E-mail: archive@brent.gov.uk

Website:
http://www.brent.gov.uk/archive

Enquiries:
Enquiries to: Museum and Archive Manager

Founded:
1976/7

Organisation type and purpose:
Local government body.
Archive.

Subject coverage:
Local history of London Borough of Brent and predecessors (Willesden, Wembley, etc).

Non-library collection catalogue:
All or part available online and in-house

Library catalogue:
All or part available online

Publications list:
Available online and in print

Access to staff:
Contact by letter, by telephone, by fax, by e-mail, in person and via website. Appointment necessary.
Hours: Mon, 1300 to 1800; Tue, 0900 to 1800; Thu, 1300 to 2000; Sat, 0900 to 1700

Access for disabled people:
Public area on ground floor

Links with:
Brent Museum
   Willesden Green Library Centre, 95 High Street, Willesden, NW10 2SF; tel: 020 937 3600

BREWERS' COMPANY

Formal name: Brewers' Company

Brewers' Hall, Aldermanbury Square, London, EC2V 7HR

Tel: 020 7606 1301
Fax: 020 7796 3557
E-mail: clerk@brewershall.co.uk

Website:
http://www.brewershall.co.uk

Enquiries:
Enquiries to: The Clerk
Direct e-mail: clerk@brewershall.co.uk

Founded:
1515

Organisation type and purpose:
Membership association (membership is by election or invitation).
City of London Livery Company.

Access to staff:
Contact by letter, by telephone, by fax, by e-mail and via website

BREWERY HISTORY SOCIETY

10 Ringstead Court, Ringstead Road, Sutton, Surrey, SM1 4SH

Tel: 020 8642 7189

Enquiries:
Enquiries to: Archivist

Founded:
1971

Organisation type and purpose:
Membership association (membership is by subscription), present number of members: 700, voluntary organisation, research organisation, publishing house.

Subject coverage:
History of the British brewery industry.

Museum or gallery collection, archive, or library special collection:
Histories of brewing industry, yearbooks, directories, periodicals

Non-library collection catalogue:
All or part available in-house

Library catalogue:
All or part available in-house

Printed publications:
Brewery History Journal (quarterly)
Wide variety of books including:
Beers and Brewing
Brewery Histories, by region
Brewery Transport
Bottles
Historical Research
Hops and Maltings
Inns and Pubs
Inn Signs
Order printed publications from: Paul Travis
Long High Top, Heptonstall, Hebden Bridge, West Yorkshire, HX7 7PF

Publications list:
Available in print

Access to staff:
Contact by letter, by telephone and in person.
Appointment necessary.
Hours: Mon to Fri, 0900 to 1700

BREWING, FOOD & BEVERAGE INDUSTRY SUPPLIERS ASSOCIATION

Acronym or abbreviation: BfBi

3 Brewery Road, Wolverhampton, West Midlands, WV1 4JT

Tel: 01902 422303
Fax: 01902 795744
E-mail: info@bfbi.org.uk

Website:
http://www.bfbi.org.uk

Enquiries:
Enquiries to: Chief Executive

Founded:
1907

Organisation type and purpose:
Trade association (membership is by subscription), present number of members: 430.

Printed publications:
Annual Directory of Members and classified listings (pub June, £95, direct)

Publications list:
Available in print

Access to staff:
Contact by letter, by telephone, by fax and by e-mail
Hours: Mon to Fri, 0900 to 1700

BRIDGEMAN ART LIBRARY LIMITED

17–19 Garway Road, London, W2 4PH

Tel: 020 7727 4065
Fax: 020 7792 8509
E-mail: info@bridgeman.co.uk

Website:
http://www.bridgeman.co.uk
A searchable archive of thousands of images from the collection.

Enquiries:
Enquiries to: Marketing Manager

Founded:
1972

Organisation type and purpose:
Service industry.
Commercial company; formerly Cooper-Bridgeman Library; fine art photographic library/agency; agency agreements with photographic libraries outside the UK.
Fine art photo archive (commercial).

Subject coverage:
Large format colour transparencies of paintings, sculpture, prints, manuscripts, the decorative arts, antiques and antiquities.

Museum or gallery collection, archive, or library special collection:
Over 150,000 large format colour transparencies growing by more than 500 new pictures each week, of the works from more than 1000 museums, galleries and private collections, including contemporary artists

Library catalogue:
All or part available online and in print

Printed publications:
Catalogues of complete collections

Electronic and video publications:
Catalogue (online, free registration)

Publications list:
Available online and in print

Access to staff:
Contact by telephone, by fax, by e-mail and via website. Appointment necessary.
Hours: Mon to Fri, 0930 to 1730

Access to building, collection or gallery:
Prior appointment required

Members of:
British Association of Picture Libraries & Agencies (BAPLA)
    Vine Hill, London, EC1

Other address:
Bridgeman Art Library International
    65 East 93rd Street, New York, NY 10128, USA; tel: 00 1 212 828 1238; fax: 00 1 212 828 1255; e-mail: info@bridgemanart.com
Bridgeman Giraudon
    36 rue des Bourdonnais, 75001 Paris, France; tel: + 33 1 55 80 79 10; fax: + 33 1 55 80 79 11; e-mail: paris@bridgeman.fr

BRIDGEND COUNTY BOROUGH COUNCIL

Civic Offices, Angel Street, Bridgend, Mid Glamorgan, CF31 1LX

Tel: 01656 643643
Fax: 01656 646966

Website:
http://www.bridgend.gov.uk
Tourism and general information.

Enquiries:
Enquiries to: Public Relations Manager
Direct tel: 01656 643210/17
Direct fax: 01656 643215

Founded:
April 1996

Organisation type and purpose:
Local government body.

Subject coverage:
Economic and business database, traffic surveys, transport infrastructure, trading standards, public protection, planning, local plan, mineral extraction, design and print, information technology, demographic information.

Access to staff:
Contact by letter, by telephone, by fax and by e-mail
Hours: Mon to Thu, 0830 to 1700; Fri, 0830 to 1630

Access for disabled people:
Ramped entry, toilet facilities

BRIDGEND LIBRARY AND INFORMATION SERVICE

Coed Parc, Park Street, Bridgend, Mid Glamorgan, CF31 4BA

Tel: 01656 754800
Fax: 01656 645719
E-mail: blis@bridgend.gov.uk

Website:
http://www.bridgend.gov.uk/libraries

Enquiries:
Enquiries to: Librarian

Founded:
1996

Organisation type and purpose:
Public library.

Subject coverage:
Local history (Mid Glamorgan), family history (Glamorgan area).

Museum or gallery collection, archive, or library special collection:
Local studies (Mid Glamorgan and areas surrounding Bridgend County Borough)

Non-library collection catalogue:
All or part available online

Library catalogue:
All or part available online

Access to staff:
Contact by letter, by telephone, by fax, by e-mail and in person
Hours: Mon to Fri, 0830 to 1900; Sat, 0830 to 1700

Access for disabled people:
Parking provided, ramped entry

BRIDGNORTH & DISTRICT HISTORICAL SOCIETY

Barn Cottage, Bridge Street, Bridgnorth, Shropshire, WV15 6AF

Tel: 01746 765159

Enquiries:
Enquiries to: Treasurer and Publicity

Organisation type and purpose:
Membership association (membership is by subscription), present number of members: 120, voluntary organisation, registered charity.

Subject coverage:
History of Bridgnorth and district.

BRIDGNORTH DISTRICT COUNCIL

Westgate, Bridgnorth, Shropshire, WV16 5AA

Tel: 01746 765131
Fax: 01746 764414

Website:
http://www.bridgnorth.gov.uk

Enquiries:
Enquiries to: Public Relations Manager
Direct tel: 01746 713111
Direct e-mail: lscreen@bridgnorth-dc.gov.uk

Founded:
1974

Organisation type and purpose:
Local government body.

Access to staff:
Contact by letter, by telephone, by fax, by e-mail and in person
Hours: Mon to Fri, 0900 to 1700

Access for disabled people:
Ramped entry

BRIDLEDOWN CHILDREN'S FARM AND WILDLIFE CENTRE

Bridledown, West Hougham, Dover, Kent, CT13 7AG

Tel: 01304 201382
Fax: 01304 204757
E-mail: bridledown.dover@virgin.net

Enquiries:
Enquiries to: Information Officer

Founded:
1968

Organisation type and purpose:
Suitable for ages: Key Stages 1 and 2.
Stray dogs' kennels and children's activity farm.
Finding homes for stray dogs.

Subject coverage:
Teaching the importance of wildlife, farming in the community and hands-on fun for the family.

Access to staff:
Contact by letter, by telephone, by fax, by e-mail, in person and via website
Hours: Daily, 1000 to 1700

Access for disabled people:
Access to all public areas

BRIGHTON AND HOVE CITY LIBRARIES

Jubilee Library, Jubilee Street, Brighton, BN1 1GE

Tel: 01273 296969; 01273 290800
Fax: 01273 296976
E-mail: libraries@brighton-hove.gov.uk

Website:
http://www.citylibraries.info

Enquiries:
Enquiries to: Librarian

Founded:
1869

Organisation type and purpose:
Local government body, public library.

Subject coverage:
Local studies, fine arts, early printed books, business and European studies.

Museum or gallery collection, archive, or library special collection:
Bloomfield Collection (rare books)
Cobden Collection (2,500 items from Richard Cobden's library)
Elliot Collection (3,000 Greek and Hebrew texts)
Lewes Collection (3,000 European language books in fine arts)
Long Collection (3,000 classical texts)
Matthews Collection (3,500 oriental (Middle East) books)
Wolseley Collection (late 19th-century British military history and horticulture and topography of Sussex, including Field Marshal Wolseley's letters)

Library catalogue:
All or part available online

Access to staff:
Contact by letter, by telephone, by fax, by e-mail and in person

Access to building, collection or gallery:
Hours: Mon and Tue, 1000 to 1900; Wed, Fri and Sat, 1000 to 1700; Thu, 1000 to 2000; Sun, 1100 to 1600
Special comments: Some special collections materials and rare books require membership of rare books scheme. Baby changing area available.

Access for disabled people:
Jubilee Library is fully accessible and has adult change facilities. Guide dogs are welcome.

BRINSBURY COLLEGE

Pulborough, West Sussex, RH20 1DL

Tel: 01798 877400
Fax: 01798 875222
E-mail: student-services@brinsbury.ac.uk

Website:
http://www.brinsbury.ac.uk
General.

Enquiries:
Enquiries to: Information Officer

Organisation type and purpose:
Suitable for ages: 16+, training organisation.

Subject coverage:
Land-based training.

Printed publications:
Course Directory
Section Leaflets

Access to staff:
Contact by letter, by telephone, by fax, by e-mail and in person
Hours: Mon to Fri, 0900 to 1700

Access for disabled people:
Parking provided, ramped entry, toilet facilities

BRISTOL AND GLOUCESTERSHIRE ARCHAEOLOGICAL SOCIETY

Acronym or abbreviation: BGAS

Stonehatch, Oakridge Lynch, Stroud, Gloucestershire, GL6 7NR

Tel: 01285 760460
E-mail: john@loosleyj.freeserve.co.uk

Website:
http://www.bgas.org.uk

Enquiries:
Enquiries to: General Secretary
Other contacts: Chairman (for special correspondence); Editor

Founded:
1876

Organisation type and purpose:
Learned society (membership is by subscription), present number of members: 900, voluntary organisation, registered charity (charity number 202014), suitable for ages: 18+, publishing house. Promotes the study of the history and antiquities of Bristol and Gloucestershire, including South Gloucestershire; encourages their conservation and publishes records, reports and papers.

Subject coverage:
History, archaeology and antiquities of Gloucestershire including South Gloucestershire and Bristol.

Museum or gallery collection, archive, or library special collection:
Archaeological Library: Bristol, Gloucestershire and neighbouring counties

Non-library collection catalogue:
All or part available online

Library catalogue:
All or part available online

Printed publications:
Newsletter (twice a year)
Monographs (occasional)
Transactions (annually)
Record Series (vols of edited texts) including:
Historic Churches and Church Life in Bristol (ed. J. Bettey)
Archives and Local History in Bristol and Gloucestershire (ed. J. Bettey)
Bigland's Historical Monumental and Genealogical Collections Relative to the County of Gloucester (four parts, ed. B. Firth, each part £30)
Cheltenham Probate Records 1660–1740 (ed. A. J. H. Sale, £30)
Original Acta of St Peter's Abbey, Gloucester, c.1122–1263 (ed. R. B. Patterson, £30)
The Cartulary of St Augustine's Abbey, Bristol (ed. D. Walker, £30)
Register of Llanthony Priory, 1457–65, 1501–25 (ed. J. Rhodes, £30)
Transportees from Gloucestershire to Australia 1783–1842 (ed. I. Wyatt, £20)
A Calendar of the Registers of Apprentices of the City of Gloucester 1595–1700 (ed. J. Barlow, £30)
Abstracts of Feet of Fines for Gloucestershire, 1199–1299 (ed. C. R. Elrington, £30)
Catalogue of Medieval Muniments at Berkeley Castle (ed. B. Wells-Furby, two vols, £30 each)
Notes on the Diocese of Gloucester by Chancellor Richard Parsons c.1700 (ed. J. Fendley, £30)
Abstracts of Feet of Fines for Gloucestershire, 1200–1359 (ed. C. R. Elrington, £30)
Gloucester Cathedral Chapter Act Book 1616–1687 (ed. S. Eward, £30)
Order printed publications from: Stockholder, Bristol and Gloucestershire Archaeological Society, 17 Estcourt Road, Gloucester, GL1 3LU; tel. 01452 528930

Publications list:
Available online and in print

Access to staff:
Contact by letter, by telephone, by e-mail and via website

Links with:
Committee for Archaeology in Gloucestershire (CAG)
Same address

BRISTOL AND WESTERN ENGINEERING MANUFACTURERS ASSOCIATION LIMITED

Acronym or abbreviation: BEMA

Engineers House, The Promenade, Clifton Down, Bristol, BS8 3NB

Tel: 0117 906 4830
Fax: 0117 906 4827
E-mail: enquiries@bema.co.uk

Enquiries:
Enquiries to: Director

Founded:
1936

Organisation type and purpose:
Trade association.
Engineering Companies in South West and South Wales.

Subject coverage:
Personnel matters including employment law, wage rates, technical and business matters affecting small engineering companies, health and safety legislation and training courses.

Trade and statistical information:
Sources of engineering products and services in the South West and South Wales.

Printed publications:
Engineering Handbook (quarterly)
Bulletin (quarterly)

Access to staff:
Contact by letter and by fax
Hours: Mon to Fri, 0900 to 1700

Affiliated to:
Engineering Industries Association

Member of:
CBI

BRISTOL CENTRAL LIBRARY

Central Library, College Green, Bristol, BS1 5TL

Tel: 0117 903 7200
Fax: 0117 922 1081
E-mail: bristol_library_service@bristol-city.gov.uk

Website:
http://www.bristol-city.gov.uk/librarycatalogue

Enquiries:
Enquiries to: Reference enquiries
Direct tel: 0117 903 7202
Direct e-mail: refandinfo@bristol-city.gov.uk

Founded:
1613

Organisation type and purpose:
Local government body, public library.
Central lending, music, reference and business libraries.

Subject coverage:
Bristol local history; slave trade; modern literature; caving and potholing; doctrinal theology; genealogy; British Standards and British Patents; non-performing arts, both fine and applied.

Museum or gallery collection, archive, or library special collection:
Private Press books; Early Printed books (Bristol)
Stuckey Lean Collection (folklore and proverbs) (Bristol)
Thomas Chatterton Collection (Bristol)

Non-library collection catalogue:
All or part available online

Library catalogue:
All or part available online

Access to staff:
Contact by letter, by telephone, by fax, by e-mail and in person. Appointment necessary.
Hours: Mon, Tue and Thu, 0930 to 1930; Wed 1000 to 1700, Fri and Sat, 0930 to 1700; Sun, 1300 to 1700

Access for disabled people:
Ramped entry, toilet facilities

Parent body:
Bristol City Council
Culture and Leisure Services

BRISTOL CITY COUNCIL

The Council House, College Green, Bristol, BS1 5TR

Tel: 0117 922 2000
Fax: 0117 922 2024
E-mail: simon_caplan@bristol-city.gov.uk

Website:
http://www.bristol-city.gov.uk

Enquiries:
Enquiries to: Head of Corporate Communications
Direct tel: 0117 922 2650
Direct fax: 0117 922 4330

Organisation type and purpose:
Local government body.

Subject coverage:
Full range of local authority information.

Access to staff:
Contact by letter, by telephone, by fax, by e-mail, in person and via website. Appointment necessary.
Hours: Mon to Fri, 0900 to 1700

BRISTOL RECORD OFFICE

B Bond Warehouse, Smeaton Road, Bristol, BS1 6XN

Tel: 0117 922 4224
Fax: 0117 922 4236
E-mail: bro@bristol.gov.uk

Website:
http://www.bristol.gov.uk/recordoffice

Enquiries:
Enquiries to: Archivist

Organisation type and purpose:
Local government body.

Subject coverage:
Historical archives relating to the city of Bristol from the 12th century to the present day.

Non-library collection catalogue:
All or part available online and in-house

Library catalogue:
All or part available online and in-house

Printed publications:
Handlists and Aids to Research
Introductory leaflet
Registers and Bishop's Transcripts of births, baptisms, marriages and burials in Bristol Record Office, includes Anglican and Nonconformist registers
Index to Bristol's wills 1793–1858
Bristol: The Home Front, records in Bristol Record Office relating to World War II
The Poor Law in Bristol: a handlist of records
Information leaflets, books and pamphlets including:
Bristol Record Office: what we do and how to use us
Family History at Bristol Record Office
Sources for Ships, Seaman and Emigrants
Sources for the History of Buildings
Records relating to Slavery
Maps: Bristol Parish Boundaries c.1900; Ancient parishes of Bristol; South Gloucestershire and North Somerset Parishes, 1830; Mathews' New and Correct plan of the City and suburbs of Bristol, 1794
Antiquaries of Gloucestershire and Bristol (Gray I, 1981)

Bristol Apprentice Books 1566–1593
Bristol Cathedral: history and architecture (ed. J. Rogan, 2000)
Historic Churches and Church Life in Bristol
Views of Bristol Churches (43 city churches, 6 country churches and 10 nonconformist churches)
Bristol Record Society Publications
Historical Association (Bristol Branch) Publications

Electronic and video publications:
Bristol: Bristol's VE Day: a City celebrates (DVD)
Bristol Historical Sources (CD)
Wills index 1791–1858 (online)
List of parish register holdings (online)

Publications list:
Available in print

Access to staff:
Contact by letter, by telephone, by fax, by e-mail and in person
Hours: Tue to Fri, 0930 to 1630; first two Thu of month, 0930 to 1900; first two Sat of month, 1000 to 1600

Access for disabled people:
Parking provided, ramped entry, access to all public areas, toilet facilities

BRISTOL SOCIETY, THE

Leigh Court, Abbots Leigh, Bristol, BS8 3RA

Tel: 0117 915 2335
Fax: 01275 374423

Enquiries:
Enquiries to: Membership Secretary
Direct e-mail: sally.allen@bcci.westec.co.uk
Other contacts: Chairman

Founded:
1992

Organisation type and purpose:
Learned society (membership is by subscription), present number of members: 300.
Lecture society.

Access to staff:
Contact by letter and by telephone
Hours: Mon to Fri, 0900 to 1700

Other addresses:
The Bristol Society
Somerset House, 18 Canynge Road, Clifton, Bristol, BS8 3JX; tel: 0117 923 9234; fax: 0117 923 9237

BRISTOL-MYERS SQUIBB PHARMACEUTICALS LIMITED

141–149 Staines Road, Hounslow, Middlesex, TW3 3JA

Tel: 020 8572 7422
Fax: 020 8754 3789

Website:
http://www.b-ms.co.uk/

Enquiries:
Enquiries to: Librarian
Direct tel: 020 8754 3610
Direct fax: 020 8572 7370

Organisation type and purpose:
Manufacturing industry.

Subject coverage:
Pharmaceutical industry, cardiovascular disease, oncology.

Library catalogue:
All or part available in-house

Access to staff:
Contact by letter
Hours: Mon to Fri, 0900 to 1700

Access to building, collection or gallery:
No access other than to staff

BRITAIN-AUSTRALIA SOCIETY

c/o Swire House, 59 Buckingham Gate, London, SW1E 6AJ

Tel: 020 7630 1075
Fax: 020 7828 2260
E-mail: britaus@britain-australia.org.uk

Website:
http://www.britain-australia.org.uk

Enquiries:
Enquiries to: National Director
Direct e-mail: natdir@britain-australia.org.uk

Founded:
1971

Organisation type and purpose:
Membership association (membership is by subscription).
Society for development of strong Anglo-Australian relations.

Subject coverage:
All aspects of life in Australia.

Printed publications:
BritOz Magazine (3 times a year, members only)

Access to staff:
Contact by letter, by telephone, by fax, by e-mail and via website. Appointment necessary.
Hours: Mon to Fri, 1000 to 1630

BRITAIN-RUSSIA CENTRE

Acronym or abbreviation: BRC

Willcox House, 42 Southwark Street, London, SE1 1UN

Tel: 020 7378 8222
Fax: 020 7378 8333
E-mail: mail@bewc.org

Website:
http://www.bewc.org/

Enquiries:
Enquiries to: Information Officer

Founded:
1959

Organisation type and purpose:
Membership association (membership is by subscription), present number of members: 1400.
To promote understanding and contacts between UK and countries of former USSR, excluding Baltic States.

Subject coverage:
General Information on Russia and other republics of former USSR; arts and humanities, literature, history, geography and travel, politics and society.

Museum or gallery collection, archive, or library special collection:
Reference library

Library catalogue:
All or part available in-house

Printed publications:
The British East – West Journal (3 times a year)

Access to staff:
Contact by letter, by telephone, by fax, by e-mail and via website. Appointment necessary. Access for members only. Non-members charged.
Hours: Tue, 1300 to 1900, other times by appointment only
Special comments: All non-members by appointment only.

Also known as:
British East-West Centre (BEWC)
at the same address; tel: 020 7823 1990

Other addresses:
Britain-Russia Centre (Scotland)
3 Bruntsfield Crescent, Edinburgh, EH10 4HD; tel: 0131 452 8132; e-mail: jas@briteastwest.easynet.co.uk

BRITISH & EUROPEAN GERANIUM SOCIETY

Acronym or abbreviation: BEGS

1 Bishopsteignton, Shoeburyness, Southend-on-Sea, Essex, SS3 8AD

Tel: 01702 584329
E-mail: pelargoniums.begs@care4free.net

Website:
http://www.fitzjohn.linkuk.co.uk

Enquiries:
Enquiries to: Honorary Secretary

Founded:
1970

Organisation type and purpose:
National government body, membership association (membership is by subscription), present number of members: 800, registered charity (charity number 1055072).

Subject coverage:
Geraniums and pelargoniums: culture, propagation, hybridisation and grafting techniques; judging standards; classification, nomenclature and sources of named varieties.

Printed publications:
The Geranium Gazette (quarterly)
Year Book

Publications list:
Available in print

Access to staff:
Contact by letter, by telephone and by e-mail
Hours: Mon to Fri, 0900 to 1700

Affiliated to:
Royal Horticultural Society

BRITISH & INTERNATIONAL FEDERATION OF FESTIVALS FOR MUSIC, DANCE AND SPEECH

Festivals House, 198 Park Lane, Macclesfield, Cheshire, SK11 6UD

Tel: 0870 774 4290
Fax: 0870 774 4292
E-mail: liz@federationoffestivals.org.uk

Website:
http://www.festivals.demon.co.uk

Enquiries:
Enquiries to: Chief Executive
Direct tel: 01625 611578

Founded:
1921

Organisation type and purpose:
Membership association (membership is by qualification), voluntary organisation, registered charity (charity number 213125), training organisation.
Consists of festival organisers, adjudicators, accompanists and private members.

Subject coverage:
Amateur festivals, all aspects of the performing arts, particularly music, speech, drama and dance, adjudication in all these disciplines.

Printed publications:
Newsletter (3/4 per annum, free, for members only)
Year Book (annually, for sale)

Access to staff:
Contact by letter, by telephone, by fax and by e-mail
Hours: Mon to Fri, 0930 to 1730

Headquarters of the:
Amateur Competitive Festival Movement

BRITISH ABRASIVES FEDERATION

Acronym or abbreviation: BAF

Toad Hall, Hinton Road, Horst, Berkshire, RG10 0BS

Tel: 08456 121380
Fax: 08456 121380
E-mail: info@thebaf.org.uk

Website:
http://www.the-british-abrasives-federation.org.uk
The BAF, its organisation, objectives, membership, technical pages and access to the FEPA site.

Enquiries:
Enquiries to: Secretary General

Organisation type and purpose:
Trade association.

Subject coverage:
Use, care and protection of grinding wheels and other abrasive products; British and European safety standards.

Printed publications:
Abrasive Grain Booklets
Diamond and Superabrasive Wheel and Grain Booklets
FEPA Safety Code for the use, care and protection of Abrasive Wheels (£9.50)

Access to staff:
Contact by letter, by telephone, by fax, by e-mail and via website
Hours: Mon to Fri, 0900 to 1700

Affiliated to:
Fédération Européenne des Fabricants de Produits Abrasifs (FEPA)
  Secretariat, 20 Avenue Reille, Paris, F-75014; tel: 00 331 4581 2590; fax: 00 331 4581 6294; e-mail: fepa@compuserve.com

Product groups:
Abrasive Grain
Bonded Abrasives
Coated Abrasives
Superabrasives

BRITISH ACADEMIC CONFERENCE IN OTOLARYNGOLOGY

Acronym or abbreviation: BACO

c/o BAO – HNS, The Royal College of Surgeons, 35–43 Lincoln's Inn Fields, London, WC2A 3PE

Tel: 020 7404 8373
Fax: 020 7404 4200
E-mail: admin@entuk.org

Website:
http://www.baco2003.co.uk

Enquiries:
Enquiries to: Secretary

Founded:
1975

Organisation type and purpose:
Professional body, registered charity (charity number 270672), training organisation, research organisation.

Subject coverage:
Ear, nose and throat surgery.

Access to staff:
Contact by letter, by telephone, by fax and by e-mail
Hours: Mon to Fri, 0930 to 1730

BRITISH ACADEMY

Formal name: British Academy: The National Academy for the Humanities and Social Sciences

10 Carlton House Terrace, London, SW1Y 5AH

Tel: 020 7969 5200
Fax: 020 7969 5300
E-mail: secretary@britac.ac.uk

Website:
http://www.britac.ac.uk

Information about the British Academy as a learned society; its funding programmes for humanities and social sciences.

Enquiries:
Enquiries to: Secretary
Direct fax: 020 7969 5414

Founded:
1902

Organisation type and purpose:
National organisation, learned society (membership is by election or invitation), present number of members: 851 ordinary, 307 corresponding, 18 hon fellows, registered charity (charity number 233176).
Directory of all UK Learned Bodies in the social sciences and humanities.
Promotes advanced research in humanities and social sciences.

Subject coverage:
Humanities and social sciences.

Printed publications:
Lectures and Symposia
Research Series
Policy Documents

Publications list:
Available online and in print

Access to staff:
Contact by letter, by fax and by e-mail
Hours: Mon to Fri, 0930 to 1730

Access to building, collection or gallery:
No access other than to staff

Access for disabled people:
Access to all public areas

BRITISH ACADEMY OF COMPOSERS AND SONGWRITERS

British Music House, 26 Berners Street, London, W1T 3LR

Tel: 020 7636 2929
Fax: 020 7636 2212
E-mail: info@britishacademy.com

Website:
http://www.britishacademy.com
News, events, links page, register of members

Enquiries:
Enquiries to: Information Officer
Direct e-mail: julian@britishacademy.com

Founded:
1999

Organisation type and purpose:
Professional body, trade association.

Subject coverage:
Advice on publishing contracts in classical music, recommended commissioning fees, copyright advice, music hire fees, competitions.
Music, songwriting; music industry; copyright; authors' royalties from broadcast and public performances; music publishing; creative workshops.

Printed publications:
The Works (quarterly, members on subscription)

Access to staff:
Contact by letter, by telephone, by fax and by e-mail. Appointment necessary.
Hours: Mon to Fri, 1000 to 1700

BRITISH ACADEMY OF DRAMATIC COMBAT

Acronym or abbreviation: BADC

3 Castle View, Helmsley, North Yorkshire, YO62 5AU

Tel: 01439 770546
E-mail: info@badc.co.uk

Website:
http://www.badc.co.uk

Enquiries:
Enquiries to: Secretary

Organisation type and purpose:
Professional body.

Subject coverage:
Stage and screen combats of all kinds; weapons for use in the theatre; safety in stage fighting; history of armed combat, training in stage and screen combat.

Library catalogue:
All or part available in-house

Access to staff:
Contact by letter, by telephone, by e-mail and via website
Hours: Any reasonable time

BRITISH ACADEMY OF FILM AND TELEVISION ARTS

Acronym or abbreviation: BAFTA

195 Piccadilly, London, W1J 9LN

Tel: 020 7734 0022
Fax: 020 7734 1792

Website:
http://www.bafta.org

Enquiries:
Enquiries to: Public Relations Manager
Direct fax: 020 7734 1009
Other contacts: Membership Officer

Founded:
1947

Organisation type and purpose:
Professional body (membership is by subscription, qualification, election or invitation), registered charity (charity number 216726).

Access to staff:
Contact by letter and by fax. Appointment necessary.
Hours: Mon to Fri, 0900 to 1700

Access to building, collection or gallery:
Prior appointment required

Access for disabled people:
Level entry

Also at:
BAFTA Cymru
Chapter Arts Centre, Market Road, Canton, Cardiff, CF5 1QE; tel: 029 2022 3898; fax: 029 2066 4189
BAFTA East Coast
31 West 56th Street, New York, NY 10019, USA; tel: 00 1 212 254 2681; fax: 00 1 212 258 2653
BAFTA LA
930 South Robertson Boulevard, Los Angeles, California, CA 90035–1626, USA; tel: 00 1 310 652 4121; fax: 00 1 310 854 6002
BAFTA North
International Media Centre, Adelphi House, The Crescent, Salford, Manchester, M3 3EN; tel: 0161 831 9733; fax: 0161 831 9733
BAFTA Scotland
74 Victoria Crescent Road, Glasgow, G12 9JN; tel: 0141 357 4317; fax: 0141 337 1432

BRITISH ACCREDITATION COUNCIL

Formal name: British Accreditation Council for Independent Further and Higher Education
Acronym or abbreviation: BAC

44 Bedford Row, London, WC1R 4LL

Tel: 020 7447 2584
Fax: 020 7447 2585
E-mail: info@the-bac.org

Website:
http://www.the-bac.org

Enquiries:
Enquiries to: Chief Executive
Other contacts: Head of Administration

Founded:
1984

Organisation type and purpose:
Registered charity (charity number 326652). Inspection and accreditation of privately funded institutions of further and higher education.

Printed publications:
Leaflet about BAC (free)
Accreditation Handbooks (free)
Review (free)

Publications list:
Available online

Access to staff:
Contact by letter, by telephone, by fax, by e-mail and via website
Hours: Mon to Fri, 0830 to 1630

Access for disabled people:
Lift
Hours: Mon to Fri, 0830 to 1630

BRITISH ACTIVITY HOLIDAY ASSOCIATION

Acronym or abbreviation: BAHA

The Hollies, Oak Bank Lane, Hoole Village, Chester, CH2 4ER

Tel: 01244 301342
E-mail: info@baha.org.uk

Website:
http://www.baha.org.uk
Information about members and required standards.

Enquiries:
Enquiries to: Secretary

Founded:
1986

Organisation type and purpose:
Trade association (membership is by qualification), present number of members: 31, service industry, suitable for ages: all.

Subject coverage:
Activities offered by members; recommended standards of safety in activity holidays; legislation covering activity holidays.

Printed publications:
Guide to members (free)
Members' manual (for members only)

Access to staff:
Contact by letter, by telephone, by fax and by e-mail
Hours: Mon to Thu, 0930 to 1230

Access to building, collection or gallery:
No access other than to staff

BRITISH ACUPUNCTURE COUNCIL

Acronym or abbreviation: BAcC

63 Jeddo Road, London, W12 9HQ

Tel: 020 8735 0400
Fax: 020 8735 0404
E-mail: info@acupuncture.org.uk

Website:
http://www.acupuncture.org.uk
Training, research, membership, how to find a practitioner, health and safety; general acupuncture information.

Enquiries:
Enquiries to: Administrator

Founded:
1995

Organisation type and purpose:
Advisory body, professional body, membership association (membership is by subscription, qualification), present number of members: 2035, research organisation.

Governing body of the acupuncture profession working to maintain common standards of education, ethics, discipline and codes of practice to ensure the health and safety of the public at all times. It is committed to promoting research and enhancing the role that traditional acupuncture can play in the health of the nation.

Subject coverage:
Acupuncture, ethics, practice, research, training and educational developments.

Museum or gallery collection, archive, or library special collection:
Code of Ethics
Code of Practice
Guidelines for Acupuncture Education

Trade and statistical information:
Data on the number of acupuncture practitioners, registered with BACC.

Printed publications:
Code of Ethics
Code of Practice
Code of Professional Conduct
European Journal of Oriental Medicine (EJOM)
Information leaflet
Reading List
Register of Practitioner Members (annually, £5)
Training List
Disciplinary Procedures

Access to staff:
Contact by letter, by telephone, by fax, by e-mail and via website. Appointment necessary.
Hours: Mon to Fri, 0930 to 1730
Special comments: Office not open to the public.

Links with:
Acupuncture Research Resource Centre (ARRC) Thames Valley University; tel: 020 8280 5277; e-mail: arrc@tvu.ac.uk
British Acupuncture Accreditation Board (BAAB) at the same address; tel: 020 8735 0466; fax: 020 8735 0477; e-mail: baab@acupuncture.org.uk; website: www.acupuncture.org.uk

BRITISH ADHESIVE AND SEALANTS ASSOCIATION

Acronym or abbreviation: BASA

5 Alderson Road, Worksop, Nottinghamshire, S80 1UZ

Tel: 01909 480888
Fax: 01909 473834
E-mail: secretary@basaonline.org

Website:
http://www.basaonline.org

Enquiries:
Enquiries to: Secretary

Organisation type and purpose:
Trade association.

Subject coverage:
Information on the manufacturers and suppliers of adhesives and sealants.

Printed publications:
Members Handbook (annually)
Adhesives and Sealants, A Resource Pack for Schools (free)
Information on other publications available at website www.basaonline.org

Access to staff:
Contact by letter
Hours: Mon to Fri, 0900 to 1700

BRITISH AEROSOL MANUFACTURERS' ASSOCIATION

Acronym or abbreviation: BAMA

Kings Buildings, Smith Square, London, SW1P 3JJ

Tel: 020 7828 5111
Fax: 020 7834 8436
E-mail: enquiries@bama.co.uk

continued overleaf

Website:
http://www.bama.co.uk

Enquiries:
Enquiries to: Director
Other contacts: PR Manager for press, statistics.

Founded:
1961

Organisation type and purpose:
Trade association.

Subject coverage:
Aerosols.

Trade and statistical information:
Data on UK production of aerosols.

Printed publications:
The BAMA Standard for Consumer Safety and
    Good Manufacturing Practice
BAMA Annual Report
BAMA Test Methods
Guides to Safety

Access to staff:
Contact by letter, by telephone, by fax and by e-
mail
Hours: Mon to Fri, 0900 to 1700

Access to building, collection or gallery:
Prior appointment required

Affiliated to:
European Aerosol Federation
    Brussels

BRITISH AGENTS REGISTER

Acronym or abbreviation: BAR

24 Mount Parade, Harrogate, North Yorkshire,
HG1 1BP

Tel: 01423 560608
Fax: 01423 561204
E-mail: info@agentsregister.com

Website:
http://www.agentsregister.com

Enquiries:
Enquiries to: Director
Other contacts: Membership Secretary

Founded:
1963

Organisation type and purpose:
Membership association (membership is by
subscription), service industry.

Subject coverage:
Commercial sales agents and their advantages in
developing sales plus payable services to assist
manufacturers in finding sales agents and a
monthly publication detailing agencies, available
by annual subscription.

Printed publications:
Handbook for the Manufacturers Agents (£10)
Operating an Agency Sales Force (£45)
The EC Guide to Agency Agreements and
    Contracts (£25)

Access to staff:
Contact by letter, by telephone, by fax, by e-mail
and via website
Hours: Mon to Fri, 0900 to 1700

Access to building, collection or gallery:
Prior appointment required

BRITISH AGRICULTURAL &
GARDEN MACHINERY
ASSOCIATION

Acronym or abbreviation: BAGMA

Entrance B, Level 1, Salamander Quay West, Park
Lane, Harefield, Middlesex, UB9 6NZ

Tel: 0870 205 2834
Fax: 0870 205 2835
E-mail: info@bagma.com

Website:
http://www.bagma.com

Enquiries:
Enquiries to: Information Officer
Direct e-mail: information@bhfgroup.co.uk
Other contacts: Director General

Founded:
1917

Organisation type and purpose:
Trade association (membership is by subscription,
qualification), service industry, training
organisation.

Subject coverage:
Agricultural and garden machinery dealer
industry.

Printed publications:
Garden Machinery Price Guide
Market Guide to Used Farm Tractors and
    Machinery
Technical Specification
Order printed publications from: Indices Publications
Ltd
14–16 Church Street, Rickmansworth,
Hertfordshire, WD31 1RQ, tel: 01923 711434, fax:
01923 896063

Access to staff:
Contact by letter, by telephone, by fax and by e-
mail. Appointment necessary.
Hours: Mon to Fri, 0900 to 1700

BRITISH AGRICULTURAL
HISTORY SOCIETY

Acronym or abbreviation: BAHS

University of Exeter, Department of History,
Amory Building, Rennes Drive, Exeter, Devon,
EX4 4RJ

Tel: 01392 263284
Fax: 01392 263305
E-mail: bahs@exeter.ac.uk

Website:
http://www.bahs.org.uk

Enquiries:
Enquiries to: Membership Secretary
Other contacts: Editorial, tel no: 0118 931 8662

Founded:
1952

Organisation type and purpose:
Learned society (membership is by subscription),
present number of members: 970.
To further the study of rural and agricultural
history.

Subject coverage:
British agricultural history and rural economics.

Printed publications:
Agricultural History Review (1 volume per
    annum, in two parts)

Access to staff:
Contact by letter, by e-mail and via website
Hours: Mon to Fri, 0900 to 1700

BRITISH AIKIDO BOARD

6 Halkingcroft, Langley, Slough, Berkshire, SL3
7AT

Tel: 01753 577878
Fax: 01753 577331

Enquiries:
Enquiries to: General Secretary

Founded:
1975

Organisation type and purpose:
National government body, membership
association (membership is by subscription),
voluntary organisation, training organisation.
Governing body for Aikido in UK.

Subject coverage:
Aikido.

Access to staff:
Contact by letter and by telephone
Hours: Mon to Fri, 0900 to 1700
Special comments: Enclose an sae for reply to letter.

BRITISH AMATEUR RUGBY
LEAGUE ASSOCIATION

Acronym or abbreviation: BARLA

West Yorkshire House, 4 New North Parade,
Huddersfield, West Yorkshire, HD1 5JP

Tel: 01484 544131
Fax: 01484 519985
E-mail: info@barla.org.uk

Website:
http://www.barla.org.uk
Everything related to Rugby League

Enquiries:
Enquiries to: Membership Secretary
Direct e-mail: msd@barla.org.uk

Founded:
1973

Organisation type and purpose:
Membership association (membership is by
subscription), present number of members: 42
leagues.
Controlling body of the sport.

Subject coverage:
Rugby League.

Printed publications:
The Bulletin (journal, bi-monthly, free to clubs,
    £1.50 per issue to others, £6 a year)

Publications list:
Available online and in print

Access to staff:
Contact by letter, by telephone, by fax, by e-mail
and in person
Hours: Mon to Fri, 0900 to 1700

Access to building, collection or gallery:
No prior appointment required

Access for disabled people:
Parking provided

Links with:
Rugby League Coach Education Programme
(RLCEP)

BRITISH AMBULANCE SOCIETY

21 Victoria Road, Horley, Surrey, RH6 9BN

Tel: 01293 776636 (answerphone)
Fax: 01293 776636
E-mail: basochq@aol.com

Website:
http://www.britambsoc.org.uk

Enquiries:
Enquiries to: General Secretary

Founded:
1974

Organisation type and purpose:
International organisation, advisory body,
membership association (membership is by
subscription), present number of members: 300,
voluntary organisation, museum, research
organisation.
To encourage the research of the British
Ambulance Service and its vehicles. To provide an
educational medium for all ambulance-related
subjects. To create a museum appertaining to the
history of the British ambulance service.

Subject coverage:
Ambulances, the ambulance service, history and
operation, (past, present and future).

Museum or gallery collection, archive, or library special collection:
Vehicles and uniforms
Reference library of model and badge collection
Journals, documents, pictures, photographs, publications, statistical information, videos

Printed publications:
Ambulance Scene (newsletter, 5 times a year)
Ambulance World (journal, formerly Bells & Beacons International, quarterly)

Access to staff:
Contact by letter, by telephone, by fax and by e-mail. Appointment necessary. Non-members charged.
Hours: After 2000 for phone contact or 24-hour answerphone
Special comments: Access by prior appointment.

Access to building, collection or gallery:
No prior appointment required

Links with:
Council Vehicle Society / Fleet Data Register
Fire Service Preservation Group
Professional Car Society (USA)
St John Ambulance Brigade

Membership Secretary:
British Ambulance Society
Falklands, 251 Kings Drive, Eastbourne, East Sussex, BN21 2UR; tel: 01323 508233

Public Relations Officer:
British Ambulance Society
25 West Rise, Tonbridge, Kent, TN9 2PG; tel: 01732 508525; e-mail: chrisbatten@virgin.net

BRITISH AMERICAN BUSINESS INC

Acronym or abbreviation: BABi

75 Brook Street, London, W1K 4AD

Tel: 020 7467 7400
Fax: 020 7493 2394
E-mail: ukinfo@babinc.org

Website:
http://www.babinc.org

Enquiries:
Enquiries to: Director – Commercial
Direct e-mail: cwells@babinc.org
Other contacts: Director – Membership

Founded:
2000

Organisation type and purpose:
International organisation, membership association (membership is by subscription), present number of members: 630 corporate, 2400 individuals, service industry, suitable for ages: 20 to 60.
Leading transatlantic business organisation dedicated to helping its member companies build and expand their international business.
As a not-for-profit organisation, BABi's mission is to provide practical business benefits for its member companies.

Subject coverage:
Focuses closely on US and UK company information and trading relationships. Through BABi's collection of databases, it is possible to trace and highlight the ownership of company affiliates and subsidiaries worldwide, including information on US subsidiaries in the UK and UK subsidiaries in the US.

Trade and statistical information:
US company data.

Printed publications:
Network New York London (quarterly, available to members and selected journalists, organisations etc)
British American Business – publication giving information and advice to companies looking to expand into or open offices in the UK (handbook, annually)

Membership Directory – lists all member companies (annually, members only)
UK and USA (magazine)
Order printed publications from: Publications Manager, BABi

Publications list:
Available online and in print

Access to staff:
Contact by letter, by telephone, by fax, by e-mail and via website. Appointment necessary. Non-members charged.
Hours: Mon to Fri, 0900 to 1700

Affiliated to:
British-American Business Inc
20th Floor, 52 Vanderbilt Avenue, New York, NY, 1022, USA; tel: + 1 212 661 4060; fax: + 1 212 661 4074; e-mail: info@babinc.org

BRITISH AMERICAN TOBACCO

Acronym or abbreviation: BAT

Regent's Park Road, Southampton, SO15 8TL

Tel: 023 8079 3603
Fax: 023 8079 3800
E-mail: val_rice@britamtob.com

Website:
http://www.bat.com
Company information, tobacco history.

Enquiries:
Enquiries to: Information Manager

Founded:
1956

Organisation type and purpose:
Manufacturing industry.

Subject coverage:
Tobacco growing, cigarette manufacture, tobacco history.

Library catalogue:
All or part available in-house

Access to staff:
Contact by letter, by fax and by e-mail
Hours: Mon to Fri, 0900 to 1700

Parent body:
British American Tobacco (Investments) Limited
tel: 020 7845 1000; fax: 020 7845 0555

BRITISH AND FOREIGN SCHOOL SOCIETY

Acronym or abbreviation: BFSS

Maybrook House, Godstone Road, Caterham, Surrey, CR3 6RE

Tel: 01883 331177

Website:
http://www.bfss.org.uk
On the Society and its Archive catalogue.

Enquiries:
Enquiries to: Director
Direct e-mail: bfss.archive@brunel.ac.uk
Other contacts: Archivist for archive, holdings, research.

Founded:
1808

Organisation type and purpose:
Membership association (membership is by subscription), present number of members: 154, registered charity (charity number 314286).

Subject coverage:
Archive Centre: History of education as contained in records of the Society from 1800 to the present day.

Museum or gallery collection, archive, or library special collection:
Records of the Society's Schools and Colleges, mainly 1830–1976, including Borough Road College, Saffron Walden College, Stockwell College and Darlington College
Surviving records of the Society from the beginning of the nineteenth century including minute books 1808–1834, correspondence of the Secretaries of the Society 1814–1897, overseas correspondence
Letters of Joseph Lancaster 1810–1812
Nineteenth and twentieth century records of the Society
Student registers and other official records of student progress including Teaching Practice
Prints and photographs, paintings and engravings, architects' plans

Non-library collection catalogue:
All or part available online

Access to staff:
Contact by letter, by telephone, by fax, by e-mail and in person. Appointment necessary.
Hours: Wed, Fri, 1000 to 1600

Access for disabled people:
Hours: Wed, Fri, 1000 to 1600
Special comments: None

Archives:
BFSS Archive Centre
Haywood Building, Runnymede Campus, Brunel University, Egham, Surrey, TW20 0JZ; tel: 020 8891 0121 ext 2615; fax: 020 8891 8211; e-mail: bfss.archive@brunel.ac.uk

BRITISH AND IRISH ASSOCIATION OF LAW LIBRARIANS

Acronym or abbreviation: BIALL

Lincoln's Inn Library, London, WC2A 3TN

Tel: 020 7242 4371
Fax: 020 7404 1864
E-mail: susanfrost@compuserve.com

Website:
http://www.biall.org.uk

Enquiries:
Enquiries to: Administrator

Founded:
1969

Organisation type and purpose:
Professional body.
To provide better administration and exploitation of law libraries and legal information units; unite and co-ordinate the interests, opinions and activities of legal information professionals into a single influential voice.

Subject coverage:
Law librarianship, exchange of information and improvement of service, history of law and the courts, legal bibliography. Salary information in legal information sector.

Trade and statistical information:
Salary survey.

Printed publications:
Bibliography of Commonwealth Law Reports
Directory of Law Libraries (5th ed.)
History of the British and Irish Association of Law Librarians 1969–1999 (Blake, M)
Manual of Law Librarianship (Moys E ed., 2nd ed.)
Newsletter (4 times a year)
Legal Information Management (4 times a year)
Sources of Biographical Information on Past Lawyers (Holborn, G)
Order printed publications from: BIALL Administrator, BIALL
26 Myton Crescent, Warwick, CV34 6QA, tel: 01926 491717, fax: 01926 491717, e-mail: susanfrost@compuserve.com

Access to staff:
Contact by letter, by telephone, by fax, by e-mail and via website

continued overleaf

Hours: Administrator available Mon to Fri, 0900 to 1200, or answerphone available

Administrator's Office:
British and Irish Association of Law Librarians (BIALL)
26 Myton Crescent, Warwick, CV34 6QA; tel: 01926 491717; fax: 01926 491717; e-mail: susanfrost@compuserve.com

Cooperation with:
other national law librarianship associations such as CALL and AALL

BRITISH AND IRISH BASKETBALL FEDERATION

Acronym or abbreviation: BIBF

Carnegie National Sports Development Centre, Beckett Park, Leeds, West Yorkshire, LS6 3QS

Tel: 0113 283 7418
Fax: 0113 283 3170
E-mail: m.welch@lmu.ac.uk

Enquiries:
Enquiries to: Secretary

Founded:
1970

Organisation type and purpose:
Membership association.

Subject coverage:
Basketball.

Access to staff:
Contact by letter, by fax and by e-mail. Appointment necessary.
Hours: Mon to Fri, 0900 to 1700

Affiliated to:
British Olympic Association and the Central Council of Physical Recreation

BRITISH AND IRISH ORTHOPTIC SOCIETY

Acronym or abbreviation: BIOS

Tavistock House North, Tavistock Square, London, WC1H 9HX

Tel: 020 7387 7992
Fax: 020 7383 2584
E-mail: bios@orthoptics.org.uk

Website:
http://www.orthoptics.org.uk

Enquiries:
Enquiries to: Executive Officer

Founded:
1937

Organisation type and purpose:
Professional body, trade union, present number of members: 1400.

Subject coverage:
Orthoptics, binocular vision, amblyopia.

Museum or gallery collection, archive, or library special collection:
National archive of orthoptics

Printed publications:
British and Irish Orthoptic Journal (annually)
Newsletter (monthly, for members)

Access to staff:
Contact by e-mail
Hours: Mon to Fri, 0900 to 1700

Access to building, collection or gallery:
Prior appointment required

Access for disabled people:
Ramped entry

BRITISH ANTARCTIC SURVEY

Acronym or abbreviation: BAS

High Cross, Madingley Road, Cambridge, CB3 0ET

Tel: 01223 221400
Fax: 01223 362616
E-mail: information@bas.ac.uk

Website:
http://www.antarctica.ac.uk

Enquiries:
Enquiries to: Information Officer

Organisation type and purpose:
International organisation, national government body, research organisation.

Subject coverage:
Antarctic research as follows:- atmospheric sciences: upper air and surface meteorology (including ozone observations), geomagnetism, aurora and airglow, ionosphere and whistlers; earth sciences: glaciology and physical oceanography, marine and land geophysics (including seismology), geology (including economic geology), topographical survey, hydrography and hydrographic surveys, quaternary studies; life sciences: taxonomy, biogeography, bioclimatology, marine biology, freshwater biology, pedology, terrestrial ecology, physiology (including human physiology); also: polar equipment and travel techniques, including the operation of ships, aircraft and vehicles.

Museum or gallery collection, archive, or library special collection:
BAS Archive Collection – Expeditions from 1943
BAS Herbaria – Code: AAS (Antarctic and Sub-Antarctic plants)
Geology Rock Collection
Sea ice records, and field data and maps for all scientific work carried out

Library catalogue:
All or part available in-house

Printed publications:
Antarctic Science (journal from 1989, quarterly, pub CUP)
BAS Annual Report
British Antarctic Survey Bulletin (collections of shorter papers, ceased publication 1988)
British Antarctic Survey Scientific Reports (monographs, ceased publication 1991)
Leaflets, booklets, posters and postcards

Electronic and video publications:
CD-ROM for polar bibliographies

Access to staff:
Contact by letter, by fax, by e-mail and via website
Hours: Mon to Fri, 0900 to 1700

Access to building, collection or gallery:
Prior appointment required
Special comments: Access to library by prior appointment only.

Access for disabled people:
Parking provided, level entry, toilet facilities

Funded institute of the:
Natural Environment Research Council (NERC)
Polaris House, North Star Avenue, Swindon, SN2 1EU; tel: 01793 411500; fax: 01793 411501

BRITISH ANTIQUE DEALERS' ASSOCIATION

Acronym or abbreviation: BADA

20 Rutland Gate, London, SW7 1BD

Tel: 020 7589 4128
Fax: 020 7581 9083
E-mail: info@bada.org

Website:
http://www.bada.org

Enquiries:
Enquiries to: Secretary-General

Founded:
1918

Organisation type and purpose:
Trade association (membership is by election or invitation), present number of members: 400.

Subject coverage:
Buying, selling, valuation and care of antiques.

Printed publications:
Handbook (annual)
Consumer information sheets, including:
Buying Antiques with Confidence
Care of Antiques
Careers in Antiques
Information on Shippers
List of members
Newsletter (for members)

Publications list:
Available in print

Access to staff:
Contact by letter, by telephone, by fax, in person and via website
Hours: Mon to Fri, 0930 to 1700

Links with:
Confédération des Négociants en Oeuvres d'Art

BRITISH ANTIQUE FURNITURE RESTORERS ASSOCIATION

Acronym or abbreviation: BAFRA

Head Office, The Old Rectory, Warmwell, Dorchester, Dorset, DT2 8HQ

Tel: 01305 854822
Fax: 01305 854822
E-mail: headoffice@bafra.org.uk

Website:
http://www.bafra.org.uk

Enquiries:
Enquiries to: Executive Secretary
Other contacts: Chief Executive Officer

Founded:
1979

Organisation type and purpose:
International organisation, national organisation, advisory body, professional body, trade association (membership is by subscription, qualification), present number of members: 102 in all categories, suitable for ages: 18 to 60, publishing house. Although a trade association, BAFRA is also a professional body in the conservation and restoration field.
To provide the public and private heritage sector and antique trade with a network of highly skilled and accredited conservators/restorers across Britain.

Subject coverage:
Furniture conservation and restoration, furniture history, training in furniture conservation and restoration.

Printed publications:
BAFRA Directory of Members
BAFRA (Journal, 2 times a year)
Order printed publications from: BAFRA Head Office

Publications list:
Available in print

Access to staff:
Contact by letter, by telephone, by fax, by e-mail and via website. Appointment necessary.
Hours: Mon to Fri, 0900 to 1700

BRITISH APPAREL & TEXTILE CONFEDERATION

Acronym or abbreviation: BATC

5 Portland Place, London, W1B 1PW

Tel: 020 7636 7788
Fax: 020 7636 7515
E-mail: batc@dial.pipex.com

Website:
http://www.batc.co.uk

Enquiries:
Enquiries to: Director General

Organisation type and purpose:
Trade association.

Subject coverage:
Apparel and textile industry.

Access to staff:
Contact by letter, by fax and by e-mail
Hours: Mon to Fri, 0900 to 1700

Access to building, collection or gallery:
Prior appointment required

Member of:
European Clothing and Textile Association
(EURATEX)

BRITISH APPROVALS FOR FIRE EQUIPMENT

Acronym or abbreviation: BAFE

Neville House, 55 Eden Street, Kingston Upon
Thames, Surrey, KT1 1BW

Tel: 020 8541 1950
Fax: 020 8547 1564

Enquiries:
Enquiries to: General Secretary
Other contacts: BAFE Scheme Administrator

Founded:
1984

Organisation type and purpose:
The organisation writes and adopts schemes of
third party accreditation for the fire protection
industry.

Subject coverage:
Active fire protection equipment, services.

Printed publications:
BAFE brochure/supplement (free)
List of approved manufacturers/suppliers (free)

Access to staff:
Contact by letter, by telephone and by fax
Hours: Mon to Fri, 0900 to 1700

BRITISH ARACHNOLOGICAL SOCIETY

Acronym or abbreviation: BAS

31 Duxford Close, Redditch, Worcestershire, B97
5BY

E-mail: secretary@britishspiders.org.uk

Website:
http://www.britishspiders.org.uk
Information about the Society and its publications.

Enquiries:
Enquiries to: Honorary Secretary

Organisation type and purpose:
Learned society (membership is by subscription),
present number of members: 700, registered
charity (charity number 260346).

Subject coverage:
Arachnida (spiders, harvestmen,
pseudoscorpions).

**Museum or gallery collection, archive, or library
special collection:**
Library of books, papers and microfiche available
to members

Printed publications:
Bulletin of the British Arachnological Society (3
times a year)
How to Begin the Study of Spiders (booklet)
Newsletter (3 times a year)
Society Handbook
Specialist Books
Order printed publications from: Francis Farr-Cox
1 Winchester Road, Burnham on Sea, Somerset,
TA8 1HY; e-mail: sales@britishspiders.org.uk

Access to staff:
Contact by letter, by e-mail and via website

Hours: Mon to Fri, 0900 to 1700

Links with:
American Arachnological Society
Centre de Documentation Arachnologique

BRITISH ARCHITECTURAL LIBRARY

Acronym or abbreviation: BAL

Royal Institute of British Architects, 66 Portland
Place, London, W1B 1AD

Tel: 020 7580 5533
Fax: 020 7631 1802
E-mail: info@inst.riba.org

Website:
http://www.architecture.com
Information regarding library holdings, on-line
catalogue.

Enquiries:
Enquiries to: Director
Other contacts: Archivist, Curator of Drawings

Founded:
1834

Organisation type and purpose:
Professional body.
Library of a professional organisation; the title
given above was designated in 1975; includes the
Sir Banister Fletcher Library.

Subject coverage:
Architecture; architectural history; building;
construction; planning; landscape architecture;
conservation; design; applied and decorative arts;
interior design; topography.

**Museum or gallery collection, archive, or library
special collection:**
Biography Files (over 15,000 vertical files on
architects and others)
Books Collection (some 135,000 volumes)
Collection on the Modern Movement
Drawings and Archives Collection (some 500,000
drawings, predominantly British from the 15th
century onwards, at the RIBA Study Rooms in
the Victoria and Albert Museum)
Early Imprints Collection (some 4000 books on
architecture, printed before 1841)
Handley-Read Collection on Victorian decorative
arts
Manuscripts Collection (important papers of
architects, architectural historians, practices,
firms and societies, 17th century to present, at
the RIBA Study Rooms in the Victoria and Albert
Museum)
Periodicals Collection (700 current titles and 1400
which have ceased publication)
Photographs Collection (some 1.5 million images
including postcards and slides)

Non-library collection catalogue:
All or part available online and in print

Library catalogue:
All or part available online and in-house

Printed publications:
Architectural Keywords
Architectural Publications Index (quarterly)
Architecture Database
British Architectural Library Guides
RIBA Drawings Collection Catalogue (20 volumes)
RIBA List of Recommended Books (annually)
Order printed publications from: Directory of British
Architects 18341914 (2001)

Microform publications:
Microfiche and microfilm of catalogues, drawings,
manuscripts, rare books and early journals

Electronic and video publications:
Architecture database on Dialog (file 179)
Architectural publications index, on disc (APId)
available on CD-ROM

Publications list:
Available online

Access to staff:
Contact by letter, by telephone, by fax, by e-mail,
in person and via website. Non-members charged.
Hours: Mon, closed; Tue, 1000 to 2000; Wed, Thu,
Fri, 1000 to 1700; Sat, 1000 to 1330

Access for disabled people:
Ramped entry, level entry

BRITISH ART MEDAL SOCIETY

Acronym or abbreviation: BAMS

c/o Department of Coins and Medals, British
Museum, London, WC1B 3DG

Tel: 020 7323 8568
Fax: 020 7323 8171
E-mail: jlarkin@thebritishmuseum.ac.uk

Website:
http://www.bams.org.uk
Activities of the Society and medals issued by it.

Enquiries:
Enquiries to: Secretary

Founded:
1982

Organisation type and purpose:
Learned society, voluntary organisation, registered
charity (charity number 288869).
To encourage, develop and support the practice
and study of medallic art.

Subject coverage:
Medals and coins; commissioning of medals;
sculpture; history of art; contemporary art.

Printed publications:
The Medal (twice a year)
Contemporary art medals: the BAMS student
medal project (annual, £2)
The Pingo family and medal making in 18th-
century Britain (Eimer, C. £19.95)
Designs on Posterity: drawings for medals (Jones,
M. £35)
Christian Wermuth: a German medallist of the
Baroque age (Wohlfahrt, C. £95)
Modern Hungarian medals (£3)
British art medals 1982–2002 (Attwood, P. £10)
The British Columbia medals of John Lobban
(£8.50)
Order printed publications from: Galata Print Ltd,
The Old White Lion, Market Street, Llanfyllin,
Powys, SY22 5BX; fax: 01691 648765

Publications list:
Available in print

Access to staff:
Contact by letter, by telephone, by fax and by e-
mail. Appointment necessary.
Hours: Mon to Fri, 1000 to 1700

BRITISH ARTS FESTIVALS ASSOCIATION

Acronym or abbreviation: BAFA

2nd Floor, 28 Charing Cross Road, London, WC2H
0DB

Tel: 020 7240 4532
Fax: 020 7247 5010
E-mail: info@artsfestivals.co.uk

Website:
http://www.artsfestivals.co.uk
Map, calendar and A-Z directory for over 100 arts
festivals in the UK with direct links to their
websites and links to European festival networks.

Enquiries:
Enquiries to: Co-ordinator

Founded:
1970

Organisation type and purpose:
Membership association (membership is by
subscription), present number of members: 110,
voluntary organisation, registered charity (charity
number 1010867).

continued overleaf

BAFA is the meeting point of arts festivals in the UK, and is a point of information for member festivals.
Promotes and co-ordinates information in more than 100 arts festivals.

Subject coverage:
Arts festivals, dates, and programmes etc.

Printed publications:
Free annual arts festivals calendar published each winter for succeeding year
Festivals Mean Business (research report, 2001, £30 inc. p&p)

Publications list:
Available in print

Access to staff:
Contact by letter, by telephone, by fax, by e-mail and via website
Hours: Mon to Fri, 0900 to 1700

Access to building, collection or gallery:
No access other than to staff

Affiliated to:
European Festivals Association (EFA)
Chateau di Coppet, Case Postale 26, Coppet, CH 1296, Switzerland; tel: 00 41 22 776 8673; fax: 00 41 22 776 4275; e-mail: geneva@euro-festival.net; website: www.euro-festival.net

BRITISH ASSOCIATION FOR AMERICAN STUDIES

Acronym or abbreviation: BAAS

Department of English and American Studies, University of Leicester, University Road, Leicester, LE2 7RH

Tel: 0116 223 1068
E-mail: catherine.morley@baas.ac.uk

Website:
http://www.baas.ac.uk

Enquiries:
Enquiries to: Secretary
Other contacts: Chair

Founded:
1955

Organisation type and purpose:
Learned society, professional body.
To promote, support and encourage the study of the USA in the United Kingdom.

Subject coverage:
History, literature, politics, sociology, geography, film, culture of the USA.

Printed publications:
Journal of American Studies (3 times a year)
BAAS American Studies paperbacks series
Newsletter (twice a year)
Pamphlets in American Studies (no longer published, backlist in print)
Ryburn/BAAS Reprint Library
US Studies Online (BAAS Postgraduate Journal)

Microform publications:
BRRAM series (British Records Relating to America)

Publications list:
Available in print

Access to staff:
Contact by letter, by telephone, by fax and by e-mail
Hours: Variable hours

Links with:
American Studies Association (US)
Canadian Association for American Studies
European Association for American Studies
International American Studies Association
Irish Association for American Studies

BRITISH ASSOCIATION FOR APPLIED LINGUISTICS

Acronym or abbreviation: BAAL

c/o Dovetail Management Consultancy, London, SE15 3WB

Tel: 020 7639 0090
Fax: 020 7635 6014
E-mail: admin@baal.org.uk

Website:
http://www.baal.org.uk

Enquiries:
Enquiries to: Administrator

Founded:
1967

Organisation type and purpose:
Learned society, membership association (membership is by subscription), present number of members: 750 individual, 13 associate (publishers), 16 university departments and libraries.
To promote the study of language in use, to foster interdisciplinary collaboration and to provide a common forum for those engaged in the theoretical study of language and those interested in its practical use.

Subject coverage:
Applied linguistics.

Printed publications:
The following publications are available to members only:
Membership list
Newsletter (3 times a year)
Proceedings of Annual Meeting (pub. John Benjamin Publishing Company)

Access to staff:
Contact by letter, by fax and by e-mail
Hours: Thu, 0900 to 1700 (call to confirm)

Links with:
Association Internationale de Linguistique Appliquée (AILA)

BRITISH ASSOCIATION FOR CANADIAN STUDIES

Acronym or abbreviation: BACS

31 Tavistock Square, London, WC1H 9HA

Tel: 020 7862 8687
Fax: 020 7117 1875
E-mail: jodie.robson@canadian-studies.net

Website:
http://www.canadian-studies.net
About BACS: conferences and other events; British Journal of Canadian Studies and BACS Newsletter; Access Canada.

Enquiries:
Enquiries to: Administrator

Founded:
1975

Organisation type and purpose:
Learned society.

Subject coverage:
General information on Canadian studies in Britain, on Canadian academics visiting the UK, travel grants to scholars, specialist groups on Canada/UK architecture, business and economic studies, Canada in schools, history, social policy, library and resources, Aboriginal studies.

Printed publications:
BACS Newsletter (two issues per annum, winter and summer)
British Journal for Canadian Studies (two issues per annum)
Occasional workshop and bibliographical publications
Order printed publications from: BACS

Access to staff:
Contact by letter, by telephone, by e-mail and via website. Appointment necessary.
Hours: Mon to Fri, 0900 to 1700

Member organisation of:
International Council for Canadian Studies
250 City Centre Avenue, Suite 303, Ottawa, Ontario, K1R 6K7, Canada; website: http://www .iccs-ciec.ca

BRITISH ASSOCIATION FOR CANCER RESEARCH

Acronym or abbreviation: BACR

c/o Institute of Cancer Research, 15 Cotswold Road, Sutton, Surrey, SM2 5NG

Tel: 020 8722 4208
Fax: 020 8770 1395
E-mail: bacr@icr.ac.uk

Website:
http://www.bacr.org.uk

Enquiries:
Enquiries to: Administrator

Founded:
1960

Organisation type and purpose:
National organisation, learned society (membership is by election or invitation), present number of members: 1,100, representing all aspects of clinical and experimental research.
Registered charity (charity number 289297).
Organises scientific meetings/workshops on cancer research within the United Kingdom, and provides a platform for presentation of original clinical and experimental research. Funds exchanges between laboratories to encourage knowledge transfer and engender collaborations both nationally and internationally; provides opportunities for senior investigators to undergo further training to enable them to keep abreast of new investigative/research methods, and opportunities for junior investigators and research students to present their work at other meetings/conferences.

Subject coverage:
Cancer research.

Printed publications:
Newsletter (annual)

Access to staff:
Contact by letter, by telephone, by fax, by e-mail and via website
Hours: Mon to Fri, 0900 to 1700

Links with:
European Association for Cancer Research
Institute of Biology

BRITISH ASSOCIATION FOR CEMETERIES IN SOUTH ASIA

Acronym or abbreviation: BACSA

135 Burntwood Lane, London, SW17 0AJ

E-mail: rosieljai@clara.co.uk

Website:
http://members.ozemail.com.au/~clday/bacsa.htm
http://www.bacsa.org.uk

Enquiries:
Enquiries to: Honorary Secretary

Founded:
1976

Organisation type and purpose:
Membership association (membership is by subscription), present number of members: over 1800, registered charity (charity number 273422), research organisation, publishing house.

Subject coverage:
Information on cemeteries in South Asia (excluding war graves).

Museum or gallery collection, archive, or library special collection:
An archive maintained in the British Library – Oriental and India Office Collections

Printed publications:
Chowdikar (journal, twice a year, members)
Over 30 books and booklets on Records,
  Monumental Inscriptions and Biographical
  Details published by BACSA (prices vary, 50p
  p&p per item)
Series of paperback books about the lives of
  Europeans in South Asia: written by BACSA
  members (prices vary, £1 p&p per item)
  including:
Canals and Campaigns: An Engineer Officer on
  India, 1877 (Moncrieff, Maj-Gen Sir George,
  1987)
India Served and Observed (Archer W and M,
  1994)
Memoirs of an Adventurous Dane in India: 1904–
  1947 (Hansen A P, 1999)
The Calcutta of Begum Johnson (Edwards-Stuart I,
  1990)
Statues of the Raj (Steggles M, 2000)
A Railway Family in India (Stevenage P, 2001)
Who Was Dr Jackson: Two Calcutta Families
  (Benett, 2002)
Willingly to War (Norris, 2004)

Publications list:
Available in print

Access to staff:
Contact by letter, by e-mail and via website
Hours: Mon to Fri, 0900 to 2000

BRITISH ASSOCIATION FOR CENTRAL AND EASTERN EUROPE

Formal name: British Association for Central and
Eastern Europe
Acronym or abbreviation: BACEE

10 Westminster Palace Gardens, Artillery Row,
London, SW1P 1RL

Tel: 020 7976 0766
Fax: 020 7976 8831
E-mail: bacee@bacee.org.uk

Website:
http://www.bacee.org.uk

Enquiries:
Enquiries to: Deputy Director
Direct e-mail: bacee@bacee.org.uk

Organisation type and purpose:
Corporate and individual membership
organisation (membership by subscription).
To promote a closer understanding between the
British people and the countries of Central and
Eastern Europe and beyond and to support them
in developing democratic systems and civil society.

Printed publications:
Newsletter (2 times a year)

Access to staff:
Contact by letter, by telephone, by fax and by e-
mail

Affiliated to:
Foreign and Commonwealth Office (FCO)

BRITISH ASSOCIATION FOR CHEMICAL SPECIALITIES

Acronym or abbreviation: BACS

Simpson House, Windsor Court, Clarence Drive,
Harrogate, HG1 2PE

Tel: 01423 700249
Fax: 01423 520297
E-mail: enquiries@bacsnet.org

Website:
http://www.bacsnet.org
General data about the Associates and programme
of events.

Enquiries:
Enquiries to: Secretariat

Founded:
1977

Organisation type and purpose:
Trade association (membership is by subscription),
present number of members: 155.

Subject coverage:
The British Association for Chemical Specialities
(BACS) is the trade association representing
manufacturers and formulators of speciality
chemicals and intermediates. Major classes of
performance and effect chemicals covered by
BACS include maintenance products for consumer
and industrial use, disinfectants and industrial
biocides, including water treatment chemicals and
services, speciality surfactants and personal care
and cosmetic ingredients.

Printed publications:
Proceedings of Chemical Symposia for current and
  previous years
BACS Code of Practice on the Control of
  Legionellae
BACS Guide to the Choice of Disinfectants
BACS Review of Worldwide Disinfectant Test
  Methods
BACS Annual Review
Understanding Germs, Hygiene and Health

Publications list:
Available online

Access to staff:
Contact by letter, by telephone, by fax and by e-
mail. Appointment necessary.
Hours: Mon to Fri, 0900 to 1700

BRITISH ASSOCIATION FOR COMMUNITY CHILD HEALTH

Acronym or abbreviation: BACCH

5–11 Theobalds Road, London, WC1X 8SH

Tel: 020 7092 6084
Fax: 020 7092 6194
E-mail: bacch@rcpch.ac.uk

Website:
http://www.bacch.org.uk

Enquiries:
Enquiries to: Administrator

Subject coverage:
Community paediatrics, child development.

Printed publications:
Standards for Child Development Services (free)
Directory of Child Development Centres (£6)
Child Health Rights: a Practitioners Guide (£5)

Publications list:
Available online

Access to staff:
Contact by letter, by telephone, by fax, by e-mail,
in person and via website
Hours: Mon to Fri, 0900 to 1700

Groups in the organisation:
British Academy for Childhood Disability (BACD)
  at the same address
Child – Public Health Interest Group (C-PHIG)
  at the same address
Child Protection Interest Group (CPIG)
  at the same address

BRITISH ASSOCIATION FOR COUNSELLING & PSYCHOTHERAPY

Acronym or abbreviation: BACP

15 St John's Business Park, Lutterworth LE17 4HB

Tel: 01455 883300 01455 550243 \ Minicom 01455
550307
E-mail: enquiries@bacp.co.uk

Website:
http://www.counselling.co.uk
Membership details, accreditation criteria, Code of
Ethics, publications, services available.
http://www.bacp.co.uk/

Enquiries:
Enquiries to: Information Officer
Other contacts: (1) Membership Services Manager
(2) Accreditation Manager for (1) membership (2)
accreditation.

Founded:
1977

Organisation type and purpose:
National organisation, learned society, professional
body (membership is by subscription), present
number of members: 15,000 individuals, 800+
organisations, registered charity (charity number
298361).
Counselling help in local areas of England, Wales,
Scotland and Northern Ireland; agencies and
individuals, available on the website or on receipt
of an SAE.

Subject coverage:
Counselling, psychotherapy, training, personal
development, stress management, employee
assistance programmes, post-trauma.

Printed publications:
Variety of books and pamphlets on counselling
  and psychotherapy, research, special interests
  and careers and training, including:
Counselling & Psychotherapy Directory 2006
Good Practice Guidance for Counsellors in Schools
  (£9 members, £11 non-members)
Counselling Journal (monthly)
Divisional journals or newsletters (7)
Handbook of Counselling (2nd ed., 1997, £17.99
  members, £18.99 non-members)
List of counsellors and counselling organisations in
  your area (on receipt of an A5 sae or on website)
Research Study I False Memory Syndrome (£3
  members, £3.50 non-members)
Research Study II Child Sexual Abuse (£3
  members, £3.50 non-members)
Training and Careers in Counselling (pamphlet, on
  receipt of an A5 sae)
United Kingdom Counselling & Psychotherapy
  Directory
List of publications and audio-visual aids, on
  request

Electronic and video publications:
Videos available through the Concord Video and
  Films Council
Order electronic and video publications from: Concord
Films
201 Felixstowe Road, Ipswich, Suffolk, IP3 9BJ

Publications list:
Available online and in print

Access to staff:
Contact by letter, by fax and by e-mail
Hours: Mon to Fri, 0845 to 1700

Divisions of BAC:
Association for Counselling at Work (ACW)
Association for Pastoral Care and Counselling
  (APCC)
Association for Student Counselling (ASC)
Counselling in Education (CIE)
Counselling in Medical Settings (CMS)
Personal/Sexual/Relationship/Family Counselling
  (PSRF)
Race and Cultural Education in Counselling
  (RACE)

Member of:
Standing Conference for the Advancement of
Counselling

BRITISH ASSOCIATION FOR CRYSTAL GROWTH

Acronym or abbreviation: BACG

BAE Systems Infra-red Limited, PO Box 217,
Millbrook Industrial Estate, Southampton, SO15
0EG

Tel: 023 8070 2300
Fax: 023 8031 6777
E-mail: pete.capper@baesystems.com

continued overleaf

Website:
http://bacg.newi.ac.uk

Enquiries:
Enquiries to: Honorary Secretary

Founded:
1969

Organisation type and purpose:
International organisation, national organisation, membership association (membership is by qualification), present number of members: 400, registered charity (charity number 261780), suitable for ages: 21+.
Interdisciplinary in nature and representing crystal growth in industry, research laboratories and higher education in the UK.
To encourage scientific and technological communication on crystal growth including all types of inorganic and organic crystals.

Subject coverage:
Crystal growth of inorganic and organic crystalline materials including metals, ceramics, polymers and electronic-device materials.

Printed publications:
Newsletter (2 times a year, free to members)

Access to staff:
Contact by letter, by telephone, by fax and by e-mail
Hours: Mon to Fri, 0900 to 1700

Affiliated to:
International Organisation for Crystal Growth (IOCG)

BRITISH ASSOCIATION FOR EMERGENCY MEDICINE

Acronym or abbreviation: BAEM

Royal College of Surgeons of England, 35–43 Lincoln's Inn Fields, London, WC2A 3PE

Tel: 020 7831 9405
Fax: 020 7405 0318
E-mail: baem@emergencymedicine.uk.net

Website:
http://www.baem.org.uk

Enquiries:
Enquiries to: Administrator

Founded:
1967

Organisation type and purpose:
Advisory body, learned society (membership is by subscription, qualification), present number of members: 1600, registered charity (charity number 273876).

Subject coverage:
Emergency medicine.

Printed publications:
Guidelines produced by the:
Clinical Effectiveness Committee
Central Consultants and Specialists Committee (CCSC)

Publications list:
Available in print

Access to staff:
Contact by letter, by telephone, by fax and by e-mail
Hours: Mon to Fri, 0900 to 1730

BRITISH ASSOCIATION FOR IMMEDIATE CARE

Acronym or abbreviation: BASICS

Turret House, Turret Lane, Ipswich, Suffolk, IP4 1DL

Tel: 0870 1654999
Fax: 0870 1654949
E-mail: admin@basics.org.uk

Website:
http://www.basics.org.uk

Enquiries:
Enquiries to: Chief Executive

Founded:
1977

Organisation type and purpose:
Membership association (membership is by subscription), present number of members: 1400, registered charity (charity number 276054), training organisation.

Subject coverage:
Emergency medical care.

Printed publications:
Newsletter (3 times a year)
Other publications on immediate medical care

Access to staff:
Contact by letter, by telephone, by fax, by e-mail and via website
Hours: Mon to Thu, 0900 to 1700; Fri, 0900 to 1630

BRITISH ASSOCIATION FOR INFORMATION AND LIBRARY EDUCATION AND RESEARCH

Acronym or abbreviation: BAILER

Department of Information Management, Liverpool Business School, Liverpool John Moores University, 98 Mount Pleasant, Liverpool, L3 5UZ

Tel: 0151 231 3425
Fax: 0151 707 0423
E-mail: l.s.ashcroft@livjm.ac.uk

Website:
http://www.bailer.ac.uk
The official pages of the Association, contains details of all Bailer members as well as links to departmental websites and documents of relevance to Bailer members.

Enquiries:
Enquiries to: Chairman

Founded:
1992

Organisation type and purpose:
Professional body, university department or institute.
Comprising teaching and research staff of information and library schools and departments in the UK.

Subject coverage:
Education and research in library and information studies.

Printed publications:
Directory of Courses in Information and Library Studies in the UK

Access to staff:
Contact by e-mail
Hours: Mon to Fri, 0900 to 1700

BRITISH ASSOCIATION FOR LOCAL HISTORY

Acronym or abbreviation: BALH

PO Box 6549, Somersal Herbert, Ashbourne, DE6 5WH

Tel: 01283 585947
E-mail: info@balh.co.uk

Website:
http://www.balh.co.uk
Details of BALH and abstracts of recent articles in The Local Historian available.

Enquiries:
Enquiries to: Secretary General
Direct e-mail: mail@balh.co.uk

Founded:
1982

Organisation type and purpose:
Membership association (membership is by subscription), present number of members: 2500, voluntary organisation, registered charity (charity number 285467), publishing house.

Subject coverage:
Local history, family history, genealogy, industrial archaeology, vernacular architecture, archive services, library services, museum services.

Printed publications:
Annual Report
Publications include:
The Local Historian (journal, quarterly)
Concise Index to the Local Historian Volumes 1–27
From Chantry to OXFAM – A short history of charities and charity legislation (Alvey N, 1996)
Local History News (magazine, quarterly)
How Much is that Worth? (Munby L, 1996)
Local History Catalogue
Newspapers and Local History (Murphy M, 1991)
Reading Tudor and Stuart Handwriting (Munby L, 1988)
The Late Victorian Town (Grace F, 1991)
Writing Local History: A Practical Guide (Dymond D, 2000)

Publications list:
Available online and in print

Access to staff:
Contact by letter and by fax
Hours: Mon to Fri, 0900 to 1700

BRITISH ASSOCIATION FOR PAEDIATRIC NEPHROLOGY

Acronym or abbreviation: BAPN

Renal Unit, Royal Hospital for Sick Children, Yorkhill, Glasgow, G3 8SJ

Tel: 0141 201 0122
Fax: 0141 201 0859

Website:
http://bapn.uwcm.ac.uk

Enquiries:
Enquiries to: Speciality Coordinator

Organisation type and purpose:
Professional body.

Subject coverage:
All aspects of kidney disease in children, including the treatment of renal failure; research.

Printed publications:
Paediatric Nephrology in the nineties (1995)
Reports, 1974 and 1979, on the siting of units for the care of children with chronic renal failure in the United Kingdom
The Provision of Services in the UK for Children and Adolescents with Renal Disease (1995)

Access to staff:
Contact by letter
Hours: Mon to Fri, 0900 to 1700

Close links with:
Renal Association
Royal College of Paediatrics and Child Health

BRITISH ASSOCIATION FOR PERFORMING ARTS MEDICINE

Acronym or abbreviation: BAPAM

4th Floor, Totara Park House, 34–36 Gray's Inn Road, London, WC1X 8HR

Tel: 020 7404 5888
Fax: 020 7404 3222
E-mail: admin@bapam.org.uk

Website:
http://www.bapam.org.uk
Basic information about BAPAM.

Enquiries:
Enquiries to: Chief Executive

Other contacts: (1) Administrator; (2) Clinic Manager; for (1) Membership; (2) Volunteering, helpline, clinic.

Founded:
1984

Organisation type and purpose:
National organisation, membership association, registered charity (charity number 10823295), training organisation, research organisation.
To provide medical assessment and diagnosis for performers with performance-related injury and/or illness.

Subject coverage:
Medical and psychological problems of performing artists.

Museum or gallery collection, archive, or library special collection:
Small specialist library

Trade and statistical information:
Data on specific medical problems of performers.

Printed publications:
Journal (2 times a year)
Newsletter (quarterly)
Journal, Newsletter and Membership (£35 a year)

Access to staff:
Contact by letter, by telephone and by e-mail.
Appointment necessary.
Hours: Tues to Fri, 0900 to 1830; Mon, 0900 to 1500

Access to building, collection or gallery:
Prior appointment required

Access for disabled people:
Lift and level floors

Subsidiary body:
Association of Medical Advisors to British Orchestras

BRITISH ASSOCIATION FOR PERINATAL MEDICINE

Acronym or abbreviation: BAPM

50 Hallam Street, London, W1W 6DE

Tel: 020 7307 5627
Fax: 020 7307 5601
E-mail: bapm@rcpch.ac.uk

Website:
http://www.bapm-london.org
All information on the Association including publications

Enquiries:
Enquiries to: Administrator

Founded:
1976

Organisation type and purpose:
Professional body.

Subject coverage:
All aspects of perinatal medicine.

Printed publications:
Various documents available for purchase and for free download from the website including:
Guidelines Relating to the Birth of Extremely Immature Babies (March 2000)
National Census of Availability of Neonatal Intensive Care (September 2000)
Standards for Hospitals Providing Neonatal Intensive and High Dependency Care (2nd ed December 2001)
Training Needs of Professionals Responsible for Resuscitation of Babies at Birth (October 1998)

Publications list:
Available online

Access to staff:
Contact by letter, by telephone, by fax and by e-mail
Hours: Mon to Fri, 0900 to 1700

BRITISH ASSOCIATION FOR PRINT AND COMMUNICATION

Acronym or abbreviation: BAPC

Catalyst House, 720 Centennial Road, Centennial Park, Elstree, Herts, WD6 3SY

Tel: 020 8736 5862
Fax: 020 8224 9090
E-mail: info@bapc.co.uk

Website:
http://www.bapc.co.uk

Enquiries:
Enquiries to: Executive Director
Other contacts: Chairman for public relations.

Founded:
1978

Organisation type and purpose:
National organisation, trade association (membership is by subscription, qualification).

Subject coverage:
Trade association within the print sector, providing its members with a wide range of facilities and benefits to help printers survive and succeed, including free legal advice, marketing support, technical assistance, product assessment, seminars, conferences, magazines and newsletters, tailored insurance and credit-check scheme, health, safety and employment hotline, arbitration, mentoring and distance-learning schemes.

Access to staff:
Contact by letter, by telephone, by e-mail and via website
Hours: Mon to Fri, 0900 to 1700

Access to building, collection or gallery:
Prior appointment required

BRITISH ASSOCIATION FOR PSYCHOLOGICAL TYPE

Acronym or abbreviation: BAPT

17 Royal Crescent, Cheltenham, Gloucestershire, GL50 3DA

Tel: 01242 282990
Fax: 01242 282990
E-mail: office@bapt.org.uk

Website:
http://www.bapt.org.uk

Enquiries:
Enquiries to: General Secretary

Founded:
1989

Organisation type and purpose:
Professional body (membership is by subscription), present number of members: 200, voluntary organisation, registered charity (charity number 1045772), consultancy.

Subject coverage:
Advice on Psychological Type including workshops and register of practitioners.

Information services:
Library of Psychological Type

Library catalogue:
All or part available in-house and in print

Publications list:
Available online

Access to staff:
Contact by letter, by telephone and by e-mail
Hours: Mon to Fri, 0900 to 1700

Access to building, collection or gallery:
No access other than to staff

BRITISH ASSOCIATION FOR PSYCHOPHARMACOLOGY

Acronym or abbreviation: BAP

36 Cambridge Place, Hills Road, Cambridge, CB2 1NS

Tel: 01223 358395
Fax: 01223 321268
E-mail: susan@bap.org.uk

Website:
http://www.bap.org.uk

Enquiries:
Enquiries to: Administrator
Direct tel: 01223 358428

Founded:
1974

Organisation type and purpose:
International organisation, learned society (membership is by subscription), present number of members: 1050, registered charity (charity number 277825).

Subject coverage:
Psychopharmacology: behavioural pharmacology, neurochemical pharmacology, psychopharmacological treatment in psychiatry.

Printed publications:
Journal of Psychopharmacology (8 times a year, free to members, on subscription to others)
Newsletters (for members)

Access to staff:
Contact by letter, by fax, by e-mail and via website
Hours: Mon to Fri, 0900 to 1700

BRITISH ASSOCIATION FOR SEXUAL AND RELATIONSHIP THERAPY

Acronym or abbreviation: BASRT

PO Box 13686, London, SW20 9ZH

Tel: 020 8543 2707
Fax: 020 8543 2707
E-mail: info@basrt.org.uk

Website:
http://www.basrt.org.uk

Enquiries:
Enquiries to: Administrator

Founded:
1976

Organisation type and purpose:
National organisation, membership association (membership is by subscription, qualification), present number of members: 730, voluntary organisation, registered charity (charity number 1101961).
Professional body for clinicians and therapists who treat sexual and relationship problems.
To further education of professionals working in field of sexual and relationship therapy, to set and maintain ethical standards, to promote research and raise public awareness of sexual and relationship therapy.

Subject coverage:
A professional body for clinicians and therapists who treat sexual and relationship problems.

Printed publications:
Sexual and Relationship Therapy (journal, quarterly)
List of qualified practitioners
Order printed publications from: Taylor & Francis plc Rankine Road, Basingstoke, RG24 8PR, tel: 020 7017 6318, e-mail: info@tandf.co.uk

Publications list:
Available in print

Access to staff:
Contact by letter, by telephone, by fax, by e-mail and via website
Hours: Mon to Fri, 0900 to 1430

BRITISH ASSOCIATION FOR SHOOTING AND CONSERVATION

Marford Mill, Chester Road, Rossett, Wrexham, Clwyd, LL12 0HL

Tel: 01244 573000
Fax: 01244 573001
E-mail: enq@basc.org.uk

Website:
http://www.basc.org.uk
About shooting and British Association for Shooting and Conservation.

Enquiries:
Enquiries to: Head of Media and Communications
Direct tel: 01244 573032
Direct fax: 01244 573040
Other contacts: Press Officer

Founded:
1908

Organisation type and purpose:
Membership association (membership is by subscription), present number of members: 120,000.
Cross-party lobbying organisation, representing United Kingdom shooting sports.

Subject coverage:
Firearms, political lobbying, public relations, land management, education and training, ecology, quarry species management, research.

Trade and statistical information:
Data on shooting sports, quarry species, firearms ownership, access issues, and shooting and conservation.

Printed publications:
Codes of Practice
Factsheets
Guides
Handbook of Shooting
Magazine (quarterly)
Specialist newsletters

Publications list:
Available in print

Access to staff:
Contact by letter, by telephone, by fax, by e-mail and via website
Hours: Mon to Fri, 0900 to 1700

Other addresses:
BASC Northern Ireland
   Courtyard Cottage, Galgorm Castle, Ballymena, Co Antrim, BT42 1HL
BASC Scotland
   Trochry, Dunkeld, Tayside, PH8 0DY; tel: 01350 723226; fax: 01350 723227; e-mail: scotland@basc.org.uk

BRITISH ASSOCIATION FOR THE STUDY AND PREVENTION OF CHILD ABUSE AND NEGLECT

Acronym or abbreviation: BASPCAN

17 Priory Street, York, YO1 6ET

Tel: 01904 613605
Fax: 01904 642239
E-mail: baspcan@baspcan.org.uk

Website:
http://www.baspcan.org.uk

Founded:
1979

Organisation type and purpose:
Professional body (membership is by subscription), present number of members: 1,800, registered charity (charity number 279119).
Networking.
Multi-disciplinary networking association for professionals working in the field of child protection. Membership applications invited.

Subject coverage:
Child abuse.

Printed publications:
Child Abuse Review (newsletter, quarterly, free to members)
Journal (6 times a year, free to members)

Access to staff:
Contact by letter, by telephone, by e-mail and via website
Hours: Mon to Fri, 0900 to 1700

BRITISH ASSOCIATION OF ADVISERS AND LECTURERS IN PHYSICAL EDUCATION

Acronym or abbreviation: BAALPE

Sports Development Centre, Loughborough University, Loughborough, Leicestershire, LE11 3TU

Tel: 01509 228378
Fax: 01509 228378
E-mail: baalpe@lboro.ac.uk

Website:
http://www.baalpe.org

Enquiries:
Enquiries to: General Secretary
Direct tel: 01746 769487
Direct fax: 01746 769487
Other contacts: 1) Finance and Membership Officer; 2) Continuing Professional Development (CPD) Manager for (1) Finance and membership issues (2) CPD/training.

Founded:
1921

Organisation type and purpose:
National organisation, professional body, trade union (membership is by qualification, election or invitation), present number of members: 450.
The development and maintenance of high standards in all areas and all phases of physical education in schools.

Subject coverage:
Teaching and coaching of physical activities; equipment and apparatus; training of teachers in primary and secondary schools; health of young people; safety in physical activities; consultancy on safe practice providing expert witnesses for court cases related to physical education/leisure; recreation, leisure, health, safety related to physical education and recreation; curriculum and management issues in physical education; initial teacher's training and CPD for PE.

Museum or gallery collection, archive, or library special collection:
Bulletin copies since 1920s (foundation time)

Non-library collection catalogue:
All or part available online

Printed publications:
Bulletin of physical education (quarterly)
Order printed publications from: Dudley LEA (BAALPE Publications)
Saltwells EDC, Bowling Green Road, Dudley, West Midlands, tel: 01384 813706/7, fax: 01384 813801

Electronic and video publications:
Videos

Publications list:
Available online and in print

Access to staff:
Contact by letter, by telephone, by fax, by e-mail and via website
Hours: Permanent 24-hour answerphone on 01509 228378.

Affiliated to:
Central Council of Physical Recreation
Fédération Internationale Éducation Physique

BRITISH ASSOCIATION OF ART THERAPISTS

Acronym or abbreviation: BAAT

5 Tavistock Place, London, WC1H 9SN

Tel: 020 7383 3774
Fax: 020 7431 2450
E-mail: baat@ukgateway.net

Website:
http://www.baat.co.uk

Enquiries:
Enquiries to: Honorary Secretary

Founded:
1964

Organisation type and purpose:
Professional body, voluntary organisation.

Subject coverage:
Art therapy and art education in special schools; training in art therapy; research in art therapy; professional standards; conditions of work; art therapy in all areas of child, adult and elderly care; mental health; learning disabilities; physical and neurological problems; dementia; autism etc.

Printed publications:
BAAT Register of Art Therapists (price £5)
Code of Ethics and Principles of Professional Practice (price £2.50)
Inscape (journal of BAAT twice a year, Individual subscription £11; Institutional subscription £21)

Access to staff:
Contact by letter, by telephone, by fax, by e-mail and via website
Hours: Mon to Fri, 0900 to 1700

Access to building, collection or gallery:
No access other than to staff

BRITISH ASSOCIATION OF AUDIOLOGICAL PHYSICIANS

Acronym or abbreviation: BAAP

c/o Department of Neuro-otology, The National Hospital for Neurology and Neurosurgery, Queen Square, London, WC1N 3BG

Tel: 020 7837 3611 ext 3386
Fax: 029 7829 8775
E-mail: honsec.baap@virgin.net

Website:
http://www.baap.org.uk
Information regarding the hospital speciality of audiological medicine. Names of contacts and some physicians. Curriculum for trainees; constitution, policy document.

Enquiries:
Enquiries to: Honorary Secretary

Founded:
1976

Organisation type and purpose:
National organisation, professional body (membership is by subscription, qualification, election or invitation), present number of members: 90.

Subject coverage:
Audiological medicine; audiology; hearing aids; auditory rehabilitation; hearing loss; balance disorders; neuro-otology; auditory electrophysiology. Vestibular medicine; vestibular rehabilitation; noise-induced hearing loss; cochlear implants; universal newborn screening for hearing loss; auto-immune inner ear disease.

Printed publications:
Career's Focus Article: BMJ
Careers leaflet
Policy document
Guidelines for referral
Promotional poster

Publications list:
Available online

Access to staff:
Contact by letter, by telephone, by fax, by e-mail and via website
Hours: Mon to Fri, 0900 to 1700

Connections with:
National Council for Professionals in Audiology (NCPA)
c/o Ellen Godden BSA, Brighton Road, Reading

BRITISH ASSOCIATION OF AVIATION CONSULTANTS

Acronym or abbreviation: BAAC

Queen Anne's Gate Buildings, London, SW1H 9HP

Tel: 0207 630 5358
Fax: 0207 828 0667
E-mail: committee@baac.org.uk

Website:
http://www.baac.org.uk

Enquiries:
Enquiries to: Chairman
Other contacts: Honorary Secretary for administration.

Founded:
1972

Organisation type and purpose:
Professional body (membership is by qualification), present number of members: 80.
Aviation consultancy.

Subject coverage:
Aviation worldwide.

Printed publications:
Register of Members (annual)

Publications list:
Available online and in print

Access to staff:
Contact by e-mail
Hours: Mon to Fri, 0900 to 1700

BRITISH ASSOCIATION OF COLLIERY MANAGEMENT, TECHNICAL, ENERGY AND ADMINISTRATIVE MANAGEMENT

Acronym or abbreviation: BACM-TEAM

17 South Parade, Doncaster, South Yorkshire, DN1 2DR

Tel: 01302 815551
Fax: 01302 815552
E-mail: enquiries@bacmteam.org.uk

Website:
http://www.bacmteam.org.uk

Enquiries:
Enquiries to: General Secretary
Other contacts: Office Manager

Founded:
1947

Organisation type and purpose:
Trade union (membership is by subscription), present number of members: 4300.

Subject coverage:
Mining, European energy, employment law.

Printed publications:
BACMTEAM Focus (quarterly newsletter to members)

Access to staff:
Contact by letter, by telephone and by e-mail
Hours: Mon to Fri, 0830 to 1700

Access to building, collection or gallery:
No prior appointment required

Affiliated to:
TUC

Member of:
ECSC
FICME
MIF

BRITISH ASSOCIATION OF COMMUNICATORS IN BUSINESS LTD

Acronym or abbreviation: CiB

42 Borough High Street, London, SE1 1XW

Tel: 020 7378 7139
Fax: 020 7378 7140
E-mail: enquiries@bacb.org

Website:
http://www.bacb.org

Enquiries:
Enquiries to: Secretary General

Founded:
1949

Organisation type and purpose:
Professional body (membership is by subscription), present number of members: 1000.

Subject coverage:
Corporate media management and practice.

Museum or gallery collection, archive, or library special collection:
Library of current house journals

Printed publications:
CIB News (monthly, for members)
Communicators in Business Magazine (4 times a year)
Membership directory and occasional surveys

Access to staff:
Contact by letter, by telephone, by fax and by e-mail. Appointment necessary.
Hours: Mon to Fri, 0900 to 1700

Access to building, collection or gallery:
No prior appointment required

Access for disabled people:
Level entry

Liaison with:
International Association of Business Communicators
USA

Member of:
Federation of European Industrial Editors Associations

BRITISH ASSOCIATION OF CONFERENCE DESTINATIONS

Acronym or abbreviation: BACD

6th Floor, Charles House, 148–149 Great Charles Street, Birmingham, B3 3HT

Tel: 0121 212 1400
Fax: 0121 212 3131
E-mail: info@bacd.org.uk

Website:
http://www.bacd.org.uk

Enquiries:
Enquiries to: Executive Director
Other contacts: Marketing Executive for library and information services.

Founded:
1969

Organisation type and purpose:
Trade association.
Association of local authorities, convention bureaux and tourist boards.
To promote the British Isles as a conference destination.

Subject coverage:
Conference and exhibition facilities in British Isles, information/research on the conference industry, consultancy advice on conference infrastructure developments.

Museum or gallery collection, archive, or library special collection:
Library of reports and publications

Trade and statistical information:
Data on the value, size, and trends etc, in the conference and business tourism sectors.

Printed publications:
Surveys and papers including:
BACD Library Index
British Conference Destinations Directory (2002 ed., £15 plus £1.50 p&p)
Conferences: A 21st Century Industry (1998, Longmans)

Electronic and video publications:
Conference organiser database information available for purchase on disk

Access to staff:
Contact by letter, by telephone, by fax and by e-mail. Appointment necessary.
Hours: Mon to Fri, 0900 to 1700

Member of:
The Council for Travel and Tourism
LGM House, Mill Green Road, Haywards Heath, West Sussex, RH16 1XQ; tel: 01444 452277; fax: 01444 452244

BRITISH ASSOCIATION OF DENTAL NURSES

Acronym or abbreviation: BADN

11 Pharos Street, Fleetwood, Lancashire, FY7 6BG

Tel: 01253 778631
Fax: 01253 773266
E-mail: admin@badn.org.uk

Website:
http://www.badn.org.uk

Enquiries:
Enquiries to: Executive Secretary
Direct tel: 01253 778800
Direct e-mail: xs@badn.org.uk

Founded:
1940

Organisation type and purpose:
Professional body, trade union (membership is by subscription).

Subject coverage:
Education, training, employment, salaries and conditions of employment, advice seminars, annual conference, local group network, national groups for DNs in specific areas of dentistry.

Museum or gallery collection, archive, or library special collection:
Library available to members

Printed publications:
British Dental Nurses Journal (quarterly, UK £35, overseas £40)

Publications list:
Available in print

Access to staff:
Contact by letter, by telephone, by fax, by e-mail and via website
Hours: Mon to Fri, 0900 to 1700

BRITISH ASSOCIATION OF DERMATOLOGISTS

Acronym or abbreviation: BAD

4 Fitzroy Square, London, W1T 5HQ

Tel: 020 7383 0266
Fax: 020 7388 5263
E-mail: admin@bad.org.uk

Website:
http://www.skinhealth.co.uk
Information on skin disease and dermatology in the UK.

Enquiries:
Enquiries to: Executive Officer

Founded:
1920

continued overleaf

Organisation type and purpose:
Learned society, professional body (membership is by qualification, election or invitation), present number of members: 800.
A body of international specialists of dermatology formed to promote and represent the best interests of dermatologists and patients affected by diseases of the skin. Its objects are: to promote for public benefit greater knowledge and understanding of diseases of the skin, and improve the teaching of dermatology at all levels by organising and sponsoring scientific meetings, conferences and seminars; to stimulate and promote appropriate medical and scientific research; to collect, evaluate and disseminate data and information on all matters relating to the well-being of patients.

Subject coverage:
Dermatology.

Museum or gallery collection, archive, or library special collection:
A small specialised library of historically significant books in relation to dermatology, which can only be viewed privately since it is a private collection controlled from the Association's offices
Willan Library

Printed publications:
British Journal of Dermatology

Access to staff:
Contact by letter
Hours: Mon to Fri, 0900 to 1700

BRITISH ASSOCIATION OF DOMICILIARY CARE

Acronym or abbreviation: BADCO

6 Meadow View, Winnersh, Berkshire, RG41 5PD

Tel: 0118 977 2878
Fax: 0118 977 2878
E-mail: ruth.foster@virgin.net

Website:
http://www.badco.org

Enquiries:
Enquiries to: Director
Other contacts: Secretariat

Founded:
1988

Organisation type and purpose:
Professional body (membership is by subscription), consultancy.
To promote professional practice; to raise the status of Domiciliary Care.

Subject coverage:
Domiciliary care, community care, house care, care at home in the public, private and voluntary sectors.

Printed publications:
Good Practice Guidelines series to assist Managers in the provision of good quality home care services (£3 each inc. p&p):
Caring for Staff
Charter of Rights for Home Care Service Users
Code of Practice for the Management of
    Domiciliary Care Services
A guide for commissioners
Handling Service Users Money and Valuables
Managing Absence
Medication
Professional/Personal Boundaries
Safe Hygiene Practice
Staff Support, Supervision and Appraisal

Publications list:
Available in print

Access to staff:
Contact by letter, by telephone, by fax, by e-mail and via website. Appointment necessary.
Hours: Mon to Fri, 0900 to 1700

BRITISH ASSOCIATION OF DRAMATHERAPISTS

Acronym or abbreviation: BADth

Waverley, Battledown Approach, Cheltenham, Gloucestershire, GL52 6RE

Tel: 01242 235515
E-mail: enquiries@badth.org.uk

Website:
http://www.badth.org.uk

Enquiries:
Enquiries to: Administrator

Founded:
1977

Organisation type and purpose:
Professional body (membership is by qualification, election or invitation), present number of members: 650, voluntary organisation, training organisation, research organisation, publishing house.

Information services:
Information about dramatherapy and dramatherapy training

Printed publications:
The Dramatherapy Journal (3 times per year)
The Prompt Newsletter (quarterly)
Order printed publications from:
enquiries@badth.org.uk

Publications list:
Available in print

Access to staff:
Contact by letter, by telephone, by e-mail and via website
Hours: Mon to Fri, variable hours

BRITISH ASSOCIATION OF FASTENER DISTRIBUTORS

Acronym or abbreviation: BAFD

Ikon Trading Estate, Droitwich Road, Hartlebury, DY10 4EU

Tel: 07801 030543
Fax: 07092 310932
E-mail: info@bafd.org

Website:
http://www.bafd.org

Enquiries:
Enquiries to: General Secretary

Founded:
1945

Organisation type and purpose:
National organisation, trade association (membership is by subscription), present number of members: 80.

Subject coverage:
Sources of supply of fasteners and distribution.

Printed publications:
Training Manuals (available for purchase)

Access to staff:
Contact by letter, by telephone, by fax, by e-mail and via website
Hours: Mon to Fri, 0900 to 1700

Affiliated to:
European Fastener Distributors Association (EFDA)
    Germany

BRITISH ASSOCIATION OF FRIENDS OF MUSEUMS

Acronym or abbreviation: BAFM

c/o Deborah Woodland MSc, BAfM Hon. Secretary, The Shrubbery, 14 Church Street, Whitchurch, Hampshire, RG28 7AB

Tel: 0870 224 8904
E-mail: secretary@bafm.org.uk

Website:
http://www.bafm.org.uk

Enquiries:
Enquiries to: Honorary Secretary
Other contacts: Administrator

Organisation type and purpose:
National organisation, membership association, voluntary organisation, registered charity (charity number 270253), museum, art gallery, historic building, house or site, consultancy.
To inform, encourage and support all those, whether in groups or as individuals, who wish to work in and for museums in a voluntary capacity.

Subject coverage:
Museums, the organisation and management of friends, groups, supporters and volunteers in museums of all kinds. Setting up a group, good practice, model constitution, contacts worldwide.

Printed publications:
The Handbook for Heritage Volunteer Managers
    and Administrators (£5)
Handbook for Friends – How to set up and Run a
    Group of Friends for your Local Museum, Art
    Gallery, Theatre, Historic House, Garden or
    Archaeological Site (£6.80)
Insurance for Friends of Museums (£2)
Newsletter (3 times a year, free to members)
Information Sheets (14, free to members)

Publications list:
Available online and in print

Access to staff:
Contact by letter, by telephone, by fax, by e-mail and via website. Appointment necessary.
Hours: Mon to Fri, 0900 to 1700

Links with:
Association of Independent Museums
Museum Association
World Federation of Friends of Museums
    Paris, France

BRITISH ASSOCIATION OF GREEN CROP DRIERS LIMITED

Acronym or abbreviation: BAGCD

March Hares, Montagu Road, Canwick, Lincoln, LN4 2RW

Tel: 01522 523322
Fax: 01522 568539
E-mail: info@bagcd.org

Website:
http://www.bagcd.org

Enquiries:
Enquiries to: Secretary

Founded:
1963

Organisation type and purpose:
National organisation, trade association (membership is by election or invitation), present number of members: 30, manufacturing industry.

Subject coverage:
All production, political and nutritional aspects of drying grass and lucerne for animal feed.

Access to staff:
Contact by letter, by telephone, by fax and by e-mail
Hours: Mon to Fri, 0900 to 1700

Access to building, collection or gallery:
No access other than to staff

Links with:
European Dehydrators Association – Commission Intersyndicale des Deshydrateurs Européens (CIDE)
    tel: +33 2 33 85 12 38; fax: +33 2 33 85 12 38; e-mail: ericguillemot@aol.com

BRITISH ASSOCIATION OF LANDSCAPE INDUSTRIES

Acronym or abbreviation: BALI

Landscape House, NAC, Stoneleigh Park, Warwickshire, CV8 2LG

Tel: 024 7669 0333
Fax: 024 7669 0077
E-mail: membership@bali.co.uk

Website:
http://www.bali.co.uk

Enquiries:
Enquiries to: Chief Executive

Founded:
1972

Organisation type and purpose:
Trade association (membership is by subscription, qualification), present number of members: 645, training organisation.
Industry training organisation for landscaping.
BALI is the national body representing Landscape Contractors in the UK.

Subject coverage:
Environmental landscaping, all landscape work and supplies, all facets of landscaping.

Printed publications:
BALI Who's Who Membership Directory is available to potential clients, architects and designers on request
Model tender documents

Access to staff:
Contact by letter and by telephone
Hours: Mon to Fri, 0900 to 1700

Founder member of:
Confederation of British Industry (CBI)
Industry Lead Body for Amenity Horticulture (ILBAH)
Joint Council for Landscape Industries (JCLI)
National Specialist Contractors Council (NSCC)

BRITISH ASSOCIATION OF LIBERTARIAN FEMINISTS

25 Chapter Chambers, Esterbrook Street, London, SW1P 4NN

Tel: 020 7821 5502
Fax: 020 7834 2031
E-mail: admin@libertarian.co.uk

Website:
http://www.libertarian.co.uk

Enquiries:
Enquiries to: Director
Direct e-mail: chris@rand.demon.co.uk

Publications list:
Available online

BRITISH ASSOCIATION OF MOUNTAIN GUIDES

Acronym or abbreviation: BMG

Siabod Cottage, Capel Curig, Conwy, LL24 0ES

Tel: 01690 720386
Fax: 01690 720248
E-mail: guiding@bmg.org.uk

Website:
http://www.bmg.org.uk

Enquiries:
Enquiries to: Honorary Secretary
Direct tel: 07878 303229
Other contacts: President (for discipline, conduct.)

Founded:
1975

Organisation type and purpose:
Professional body (membership is by qualification), present number of members: 170, service industry.

Subject coverage:
Guides for climbing and mountaineering, climbing instruction, advice and consultancy on mountaineering affairs.

Printed publications:
News from the Mountains (broadsheet, 3 times a year, in-house, members only)

Access to staff:
Contact by letter, by telephone, by fax and by e-mail
Hours: Mon to Fri, 0900 to 1700

Links with:
Union Internationale des Associations de Guides de Montagne (The International Federation of Mountain Guide Associations)
Armin Oehrli, Sekretar IVBV/UIAGM, Badweidli, 3780 Gstaad, Switzerland; tel: +41 (0)33 744 54 77; fax: +41 (0)33 744 54 77; website: htp://www.ivbv.info

BRITISH ASSOCIATION OF NUMISMATIC SOCIETIES

Acronym or abbreviation: BANS

General Services, 42 Campbell Road, Bow, London, E3 4DT

Tel: 020 8980 5672
E-mail: bans@mernicks.com

Website:
http://www.coinclubs.freeserve.co.uk
Lists member societies, publications and conferences.

Enquiries:
Enquiries to: Honorary Secretary

Founded:
1953

Organisation type and purpose:
National organisation, membership association (membership is by subscription), present number of members: 60.
A coordinating body for liaison and research among local numismatics societies.

Subject coverage:
Numismatics.

Museum or gallery collection, archive, or library special collection:
Collections of slides of coins for lecturing purposes (for loan to affiliated societies)

Printed publications:
Doris Stockwell Memorial Papers

Electronic and video publications:
Videotaped Lectures

Publications list:
Available in print

Access to staff:
Contact by letter, by telephone and by e-mail
Hours: Mon to Fri, 0900 to 1700

BRITISH ASSOCIATION OF PAPER HISTORIANS

Acronym or abbreviation: BAPH

c/o Ian Hendry, 27 North End, Longhoughton, Alnwick, NE66 3JG

Tel: 01665 577988
E-mail: ifhendry@btinternet.com

Website:
http://www.baph.org.uk

Enquiries:
Enquiries to: Membership Secretary

Founded:
1989

Organisation type and purpose:
Membership association (membership is by subscription).

Subject coverage:
Paper making history, paper mill sites, raw materials, communities; paper watermarks, users and conservation.

Printed publications:
BAPH (quarterly)
BAPH News
Conference Papers

Publications list:
Available online

Access to staff:
Contact by letter, by e-mail and via website
Hours: Mon to Fri, 0900 to 1700

BRITISH ASSOCIATION OF PHARMACEUTICAL WHOLESALERS

Acronym or abbreviation: BAPW

90 Long Acre, London, WC2E 9RA

Tel: 020 7031 0590
Fax: 020 7031 0591
E-mail: mail@bapw.net

Website:
http://www.bapw.net/

Enquiries:
Enquiries to: Executive Director

Founded:
1967

Organisation type and purpose:
Trade association (membership is by subscription).

Subject coverage:
Pharmaceuticals.

Printed publications:
Members Directory

Access to staff:
Contact by letter, by telephone, by fax and by e-mail. Appointment necessary.
Hours: Mon to Thu, 0900 to 1700; Fri, 0900 to 1600

Affiliated to:
Groupement International de la Répartition Pharmaceutique Européenne (GIRP)
International Federation of Pharmaceutical Wholesalers (IFPW)

BRITISH ASSOCIATION OF PICTURE LIBRARIES AND AGENCIES

Acronym or abbreviation: BAPLA

18 Vine Hill, London, EC1R 5DZ

Tel: 020 7713 1780
Fax: 020 7713 1211
E-mail: enquiries@bapla.org.uk

Website:
http://www.bapla.org
Search accredited libraries and agencies by name or subject. Details of vacancies in the industry, the work of BAPLA and our publications.

Enquiries:
Enquiries to: Administrator

Founded:
1975

Organisation type and purpose:
National organisation, advisory body, trade association (membership is by subscription), present number of members: 400.
Free referral service to picture researchers to assist them locate best source of photographic imagery.
To develop and maintain a professional framework for the industry.

Subject coverage:
Picture libraries.

Museum or gallery collection, archive, or library special collection:
Members' specialist collections

continued overleaf

Trade and statistical information:
1999 UK Picture Library Industry Survey. Data on UK Picture Industry.
2000 European Picture Library Industry Survey. Pricing Trends Survey 2001

Non-library collection catalogue:
All or part available online

Printed publications:
BAPLA Directory of Members (annually, £25)

Access to staff:
Contact by letter, by telephone, by fax, by e-mail and via website. Appointment necessary.
Hours: Mon to Fri, 0930 to 1800

Access to building, collection or gallery:
By appointment only

Member of:
British Copyright Council
British Photographers Liaison Committee (BPLC)
9–10 Domingo Street, London, EC1Y 0TA
CEPIC
Picture Agency Council of America
Picture Industry Council

BRITISH ASSOCIATION OF PSYCHOTHERAPISTS

Acronym or abbreviation: BAP

37 Mapesbury Road, London, NW2 4HJ

Tel: 020 8452 9823
Fax: 020 8452 5182
E-mail: library@bap-psychotherapy.org

Website:
http://www.bap-psychotherapy.org

Enquiries:
Enquiries to: Librarian

Founded:
1951

Organisation type and purpose:
National organisation, professional body, membership association (membership is by qualification, election or invitation), present number of members: 500, registered charity (charity number 281720), training organisation.

Subject coverage:
Analytic psychotherapy (child, adolescent and adult), registration of psychotherapists, training in adult and child psychotherapy (Jungian and Freudian), clinical assessment and referral service.

Museum or gallery collection, archive, or library special collection:
Books and journals on psychotherapy

Library catalogue:
All or part available in-house

Printed publications:
Journal
Details of short courses
General information booklet
List of qualified practitioners
Monographs of papers from public conferences
Pamphlets on the Clinical Service and Reduced Fee Scheme
Training Prospectus – Child and Adult
What is Psychotherapy?
Order printed publications from: Administrator

Publications list:
Available in print

Access to staff:
Contact by letter, by telephone, by fax, by e-mail and via website. Appointment necessary.
Hours: Mon to Fri, 0930 to 1700

Access for disabled people:
Parking provided, toilet facilities
Special comments: No lift to the 1st floor.

Includes the:
British Confederation of Psychotherapists
tel: 020 8830 5173; fax: 020 8452 3684; e-mail: mail@bcp.org.uk

Clinical Assessment and Referral Service
tel: 020 8452 9183; fax: 020 8452 5282; e-mail: mail@gap.org

BRITISH ASSOCIATION OF REMOVERS

Acronym or abbreviation: BAR

Tangent House, 62 Exchange Road, Watford, Herts, WD18 0TG

Tel: 01923 699480
Fax: 01923 699481
E-mail: info@bar.co.uk

Website:
http://www.bar.co.uk
The British Association of Removers is the largest and most established trade association for the professional removals and storage industry in the UK.

Enquiries:
Enquiries to: General Secretary
Direct e-mail: robert.syers@bar.co.uk
Other contacts: Executive Assistant

Founded:
1900

Organisation type and purpose:
Trade association.

Subject coverage:
Removal, storage, shipping etc, of household goods and effects and commercial, office furniture and effects.

Printed publications:
Removals and Storage (monthly)

Access to staff:
Contact by letter, by telephone, by fax, by e-mail and via website
Hours: Mon to Fri, 0900 to 1700

Affiliated to:
Fédération des Entreprises de Déménagement du Marché Commun (FEDEMAC)
Fédération Internationale des Déménageurs Internationaux (FIDI)

Associated with:
Freight Transport Association
Road Haulage Association

BRITISH ASSOCIATION OF SETTLEMENTS AND SOCIAL ACTION CENTRES

Acronym or abbreviation: bassac

33 Corsham Street, London, N1 6DR

Tel: 0845 241 0375
Fax: 0845 241 0376
E-mail: info@bassac.org.uk

Website:
http://www.bassac.org.uk

Enquiries:
Enquiries to: Administrator

Founded:
c. 1919–20

Organisation type and purpose:
National organisation, membership association (membership is by subscription), present number of members: 100, voluntary organisation, registered charity (charity number 1028784). Network of 70 independent organisations.

Subject coverage:
Social welfare, community development, member settlements and social action centres, inner-city projects, urban regeneration, community work, funding (members only).

Library catalogue:
All or part available in-house

Printed publications:
see website

Publications list:
Available online

Access to staff:
Contact by letter, by telephone, by fax, by e-mail and via website. Appointment necessary.
Hours: Mon to Fri, 0930 to 1730
Special comments: Primarily, information provided to members.

Access for disabled people:
Level entry, access to all public areas, toilet facilities; lift

Member organisation of:
International Federation of Settlements (IFS)
Canada; tel: +1 416 469 5711; e-mail: ifs.agnes@woodgreen.org

BRITISH ASSOCIATION OF SKI PATROLLERS (BASP UK LTD)

Acronym or abbreviation: BASP

20 Lorn Drive, Glencoe, Ballachulish, Argyll, PH49 4HR

Tel: 01855 811443
E-mail: firstaid@basp.org.uk

Website:
http://www.basp.org.uk
Ski patrol. First aid training, membership, international ski patrol, newsletters.

Enquiries:
Enquiries to: Administrator

Founded:
1987

Organisation type and purpose:
Professional body (membership is by subscription), present number of members: 120, education, suitable for ages: 18+, training organisation. Training and grading of ski patrollers. First Aid training.

Subject coverage:
Ski patrolling, first aid training, specialist advanced mountain medicine.

Printed publications:
BASP Outdoor First Aid and Safety Manual (ISBN 09528435 52)

Publications list:
Available in print

Access to staff:
Contact by letter, by telephone, by e-mail and via website
Hours: Mon to Fri, 0900 to 1700

BRITISH ASSOCIATION OF SNOWSPORTS INSTRUCTORS

Acronym or abbreviation: BASI

Morlich House, 17 The Square, Grantown-on-Spey, Morayshire, PH26 3HG

Tel: 01479 861717
Fax: 01479 861718
E-mail: basi@basi.org.uk

Website:
http://www.basi.org.uk

Enquiries:
Enquiries to: Chief Executive

Founded:
1963

Organisation type and purpose:
Membership association (membership is by subscription, qualification), present number of members: 4500, training organisation.

Subject coverage:
Training and grading of snowsport instructors; skiing and ski teaching; snowboard teaching.

Printed publications:
Alpine Manual: features more than 200
    photographs and diagrams and reference
    material for professionals (£25 plus £5 p&p)
BASI News (quarterly, members)
Information Pack
Snowboard Handbook (£10)
Telemark handbook (£10)

Electronic and video publications:
Various technical skiing videos
Boarding Skool 1 – beginners s/b (video, £19.95
    plus p&p)
Central Theme Video: designed to complement
    manual (£10 plus £2 p&p)
Boarding Skool 2 – advanced s/b (video, £19.95
    plus p&p)
CD-ROM Manual (£30 plus £1 p&p)
Ski Skool – beginners ski video (£14.95)
Ski Skool again – advanced ski video (£19.95)

Publications list:
Available in print

Access to staff:
Contact by letter, by telephone, by fax, by e-mail,
in person and via website
Hours: Mon to Fri, 0900 to 1700

Access for disabled people:
Parking provided, ramped entry

Affiliated to:
Snowsports GB

BRITISH ASSOCIATION OF SOCIAL WORKERS

Acronym or abbreviation: BASW

16 Kent Street, Birmingham, B5 6RD

Tel: 0121 622 3911
Fax: 0121 622 4860

Website:
http://www.basw.co.uk

Enquiries:
Enquiries to: Chief Executive
Direct e-mail: i.johnston@basw.co.uk

Founded:
1970

Organisation type and purpose:
Professional body.

Subject coverage:
Social work and social welfare in all field and
residential settings (public, charitable and private
agencies and independent practice), including
child care, child abuse, mental health, learning
disabilities, old age, physical handicap, personal
and family problems, adult and juvenile offenders,
community work, poverty, social services
management, education and training in social
services, social services employment.

**Museum or gallery collection, archive, or library
special collection:**
Archives of the founding associations

Printed publications:
BASW Publications (books and pamphlets)
British Journal of Social Work (8 times a year)
Practice (4 times a year)
Professional Social Work (monthly)
Venture Press Books
Practitioner Guides Series (Expanding Horizons
    Series)

Publications list:
Available in print

Access to staff:
Contact by letter, by telephone, by fax and by e-
mail

Affiliated to:
International Federation of Social Workers

BRITISH ASSOCIATION OF SPORTS AND EXERCISE SCIENCES

Acronym or abbreviation: BASES

Chelsea close, off Amberley road, Armley, Leeds,
LS12 4HP

Tel: 0113 289 1020
Fax: 0113 231 9606 and 0113 289 1020
E-mail: jbairstow@bases.org.uk

Website:
http://www.bases.org.uk

Enquiries:
Enquiries to: Executive Officer
Direct e-mail: cpalmer@bases.org.uk
Other contacts: Office Manager for general
information and membership.

Founded:
1983

Organisation type and purpose:
Learned society, professional body, membership
association (membership is by subscription,
qualification), present number of members: 2855.

Subject coverage:
Sport and exercise sciences; psychology,
physiology, biomechanics, nutrition, elite sport,
health promotion, exercise and associated careers.

Printed publications:
Annual Report (free)
BASES Newsletter (4 times a year)
Accreditation Sheets
Advice List/Career Information
Biomechanical Analysis of Movement in Sport and
    Exercises (£20)
Members Handbook
Physiological Testing Guidelines (£30)

Access to staff:
Contact by letter, by telephone, by fax, by e-mail
and via website
Hours: Mon to Fri, 0830 to 1645

Access to building, collection or gallery:
No prior appointment required
Hours: Mon to Fri, 0900 to 1700

Access for disabled people:
Parking provided, ramped entry, toilet facilities

Affiliated to:
European Federation of Sports Psychology
International Society of Biomechanics

BRITISH ASSOCIATION OF SURGICAL ONCOLOGY

Acronym or abbreviation: BASO~ACS

at the Royal College of Surgeons, 35–43 Lincoln's
Inn Fields, London, WC2A 3PE

Tel: 020 7405 5612
Fax: 020 7404 6574

Website:
http://www.baso.org.uk

Enquiries:
Enquiries to: Honorary Secretary

Founded:
1972

Organisation type and purpose:
Learned society (membership is by subscription),
present number of members: 650, registered
charity (charity number 269736).

Subject coverage:
Cancer surgery; oncology.

Library catalogue:
All or part available online

Printed publications:
European Journal of Surgical Oncology

Access to staff:
Contact by letter
Hours: Mon to Fri, 0900 to 1700

BRITISH ASSOCIATION OF TEACHERS OF DANCING

Acronym or abbreviation: BATD

23 Marywood Square, Glasgow, G41 2BP

Tel: 0141 423 4029
Fax: 0141 423 0677
E-mail: enquiries@batd.co.uk

Website:
http://www.batd.co.uk

Enquiries:
Enquiries to: General Secretary

Founded:
1892

Organisation type and purpose:
International organisation, professional body
(membership is by qualification, election or
invitation), present number of members: 3000,
suitable for ages: 16+.
Registered Friendly Society, no. 11SA(S).
To promote the art of dancing and aid members in
times of distress.

Subject coverage:
All dancing activities.

Printed publications:
Printed syllabus and books available for sale to
    qualified dance teachers

Access to staff:
Contact by letter, by telephone, by fax, by e-mail,
in person and via website
Hours: Mon to Fri, 0900 to 1700

Affiliated to:
Central Council of Physical Recreation

Representation on:
British Council of Ballroom Dancing
Scottish Official Board of Highland Dancing
Stage Dance Council International

BRITISH ASSOCIATION OF TEACHERS OF THE DEAF

Acronym or abbreviation: BATOD

175 Dashwood Avenue, High Wycombe,
Buckinghamshire, HP12 3DB

Tel: 01494 464190
Fax: 01494 464190
E-mail: secretary@batod.org.uk

Website:
http://www.batod.org.uk
Whole range of our interests plus formal
submissions to government bodies.

Enquiries:
Enquiries to: Secretary
Other contacts: Magazine Editor and Publications
Editor for matters related to magazine and
publications.

Founded:
1977

Organisation type and purpose:
National organisation, professional body
(membership is by subscription), present number
of members: 1650, voluntary organisation, suitable
for ages: all, training organisation, consultancy,
research organisation, publishing house.

Subject coverage:
National curriculum (hearing impaired),
communication, teacher of deaf training,
examination special arrangements, special
education (hearing impaired), educational
audiology, educational legislation.

**Museum or gallery collection, archive, or library
special collection:**
Archived history Birmingham University

Printed publications:
BATOD journal (4 times a year, free to members)
BATOD magazine (5 times a year, free to members)
Information leaflets and guidelines

continued overleaf

Publications list:
Available online and in print

Access to staff:
Contact by letter, by telephone, by fax, by e-mail and via website. Appointment necessary.
Hours: Answerphone 24-hours

Affiliated to:
European Federation of Associations of Teachers of the Deaf (FEAPDA)
C/o 175 Dashwood Avenue, High Wycombe, Buckinghamshire, HP12 3DB; tel: 01494 464190; fax: 01494 464190; e-mail: president@feapda.org; website: www.feapda.org

BRITISH ASSOCIATION OF UROLOGICAL SURGEONS

Acronym or abbreviation: BAUS

Royal College of Surgeons of England, 35–43 Lincoln's Inn Fields, London, WC2A 3PE

Tel: 020 7869 6950
Fax: 020 7404 5048
E-mail: admin@baus.org.uk

Enquiries:
Enquiries to: Chief Executive

Founded:
1945

Organisation type and purpose:
Professional body.

Subject coverage:
Urology; urological surgery.

Access to staff:
Contact by letter, by fax and by e-mail
Hours: Mon to Fri, 0900 to 1700

BRITISH AUTOMOBILE RACING CLUB LIMITED

Acronym or abbreviation: BARC

Thruxton Circuit, Andover, Hampshire, SP11 8PN

Tel: 01264 882200
Fax: 01264 882233
E-mail: info@barc.net

Website:
http://www.barc.net

Enquiries:
Enquiries to: Chief Executive

Founded:
1912

Organisation type and purpose:
Membership association.
Motor Sport Organisation.

Subject coverage:
Motor racing, motor sport organisation and motor racing safety.

Museum or gallery collection, archive, or library special collection:
Early photographs, motoring books, minutes, Brooklands programmes, etc

Printed publications:
Race Meeting Programmes
Startline magazine (6 times a year, for members)
Programme of Events booklet (yearly)

Access to staff:
Contact by letter, by telephone, by fax, by e-mail, in person and via website
Hours: Mon to Fri, 0900 to 1700
Special comments: By appointment for research.

Access for disabled people:
Parking provided, toilet facilities

Affiliated to:
Royal Automobile Club Motor Sports Association
tel: 01753 681736; fax: 01753 682938

BRITISH AVIATION PRESERVATION COUNCIL

Acronym or abbreviation: BAPC

c/o Museum of Science and Industry, Liverpool Road, Castlefield, Manchester, M3 4JP

Tel: 0161 832 2244
Fax: 0161 834 5135
E-mail: n.forder@msim.org.uk

Enquiries:
Enquiries to: Chairman

Founded:
1967

Organisation type and purpose:
International organisation, advisory body, membership association (membership is by subscription), present number of members: 162. Co-ordinating body.
To link national, local authority, independent and service museums with private collections, voluntary groups and other organisations in the advancement of the preservation of Britain's aviation heritage.

Subject coverage:
Preservation, restoration and exhibition of historic aviation, archives and associated records.

Printed publications:
All publications are free to members, non-members will be charged postage and packing at cost
Logbook: BAPC Members' Manual
National Aviation Heritage Register
Register of Historic Aero Engines (internal draft document)
Stopping the Rot (seminar papers)
Wants, Disposals and Sales listings: distributed quarterly
Order printed publications from: British Aviation Preservation Council
1 Calfe Fen Close, Soham, Ely, CB7 5GD

Access to staff:
Contact by letter, by telephone, by fax and by e-mail
Hours: Mon to Fri, 0900 to 1700

Affiliated to:
Association of British Transport Museums
European Aviation Representation Council
Transport Trust

There are some:
6 observers, 3 honorary members, 139 member organisations and 12 affiliated member organisations

BRITISH BALLET ORGANIZATION

Acronym or abbreviation: BBO

39 Lonsdale Road, Barnes, London, SW13 9JP

Tel: 020 8748 1241
Fax: 020 8748 1301
E-mail: info@bbo.org.uk

Website:
http://www.bbo.org.uk

Enquiries:
Enquiries to: Director

Founded:
1930

Organisation type and purpose:
Membership association, registered charity (charity number 277177), suitable for ages: all. Examining body for ballet, tap, jazz and modern dancing at all ages. Teaching qualifications in ballet and tap dancing. Teacher training programme.

Subject coverage:
Examinations in ballet, tap, jazz and modern dancing, in the UK, Australia, New Zealand, Spain, Cyprus, Jordan and Kuwait. Dance and teacher training and examinations.

Museum or gallery collection, archive, or library special collection:
Archives of the British Ballet Organization

Archives of the Espinosa Family (founders)

Printed publications:
Bulletin (2 times a year)
Magazine (once a year)
Syllabus: Ballet and tap dancing (primary to advanced)
Syllabus: Modern (primary to intermediate)
Syllabus: Jazz (primary to elementary)
Order printed publications from: BBO Dance Supplies Limited
39 Lonsdale Road, Barnes, London, SW13 9JP, tel: 020 8748 1241, fax: 020 8748 1301, e-mail: info@bbo .org.uk

Electronic and video publications:
Ballet: Primary to advanced (tape)
Grade 1 to 5 (CD)
Jazz: Primary to Grade 7 (tape)

Access to staff:
Contact by letter, by fax and by e-mail
Hours: Mon to Fri, 0900 to 1700
Special comments: Open to anyone wishing to join and study the British Ballet Organisation method.

Access for disabled people:
Parking provided

Registered with:
The Council for Dance Education and Training (CDET(UK))

BRITISH BANDSMAN

SP&S Building, Campfield Road, St Albans, AL1 5HY

Tel: 01727 894783
Fax: 01727 894956
E-mail: info@britishbandsman.com

Website:
http://www.britishbandsman.com

Enquiries:
Enquiries to: Information Officer
Other contacts: Managing Editor

Founded:
1887

Organisation type and purpose:
Publishing house.

Subject coverage:
Brass bands.

Printed publications:
By subscription and newsagent

Access to staff:
Contact by letter
Hours: Mon to Fri, 0900 to 1630

Parent body:
Kapitol Media and Events Limited
64 London End, Beaconsfield, Buckinghamshire, HP18 9QH; tel: 01494 674411; fax: 01494 670932; e-mail: info@britishbandsman.com

BRITISH BANKERS' ASSOCIATION

Acronym or abbreviation: BBA

Pinners Hall, 105–108 Old Broad Street, London, EC2N 1EX

Tel: 020 7216 8800
Fax: 020 7216 8905
E-mail: info@bba.org.uk

Website:
http://www.bba.org.uk
General banking information sheets, British Bankers' Association information, publications list.

Founded:
1919

Organisation type and purpose:
Trade association.

Subject coverage:
Banks and banking; specific information for member banks; some limited information for general public.

Trade and statistical information:
Monthly statistical information of bank lending (available on website).

Printed publications:
Abstract of Banking Statistics (annually, May)

Publications list:
Available online and in print

Access to staff:
Contact by letter
Hours: Mon to Fri, 0900 to 1700

Access to building, collection or gallery:
By appointment only

Member of:
European Banking Federation

BRITISH BANKING HISTORY SOCIETY

Acronym or abbreviation: BBHS

71 Mile Lane, Cheylesmore, Coventry, Warwickshire, CV3 5GB

Tel: 024 7650 3245
Fax: 01484 425658
E-mail: info@cheque-collectors.co.uk

Website:
http://www.banking-history.co.uk
General information.

Enquiries:
Enquiries to: Honorary Secretary

Founded:
1980

Organisation type and purpose:
Membership association (membership is by subscription).

Subject coverage:
The collection of cheques and research into banking history.

Printed publications:
Counterfoil (journal, quarterly, available by subscription only to members of the society)

Access to staff:
Contact by letter, by telephone, by fax and by e-mail
Hours: Mon to Fri, 0900 to 1700

BRITISH BATTERY MANUFACTURERS ASSOCIATION

Acronym or abbreviation: BBMA

3 London Wall Buildings, London Wall, London, EC2M 5SY

Tel: 020 7826 2690
Fax: 020 7826 2601
E-mail: info@bbma.co.uk

Website:
http://www.bbma.co.uk

Enquiries:
Enquiries to: Secretary
Other contacts: Executive

Founded:
1986

Organisation type and purpose:
Trade association.

Subject coverage:
Standards, safety, statistics, UK and European legislation, environmental interest, disposal and recycling of portable batteries, both primary (non-rechargeable) and secondary (rechargeable).

Printed publications:
Battery Compartment Guidelines
Battery Ingestion Guidelines
Battery Safety Guidelines
Powering Everyday Life: An introduction to the BBMA
Environmental Initiatives by the Battery Industry

Publications list:
Available online and in print

Access to staff:
Contact by letter, by telephone, by fax and by e-mail
Hours: Mon to Fri, 0900 to 1700

Member of:
European Portable Battery Association

BRITISH BAVARIAN WARMBLOOD ASSOCIATION

Acronym or abbreviation: BBWA

Sittyton, Straloch, Newmachar, Aberdeen, AB21 0RP

Tel: 01651 882226
Fax: 01651 882313
E-mail: bbwa@bbwa.co.uk

Website:
http://www.bbwa.co.uk
Information on the various aspects of the Association.

Enquiries:
Enquiries to: Secretary

Founded:
1987

Organisation type and purpose:
Membership association (membership is by subscription), present number of members: 80.

Subject coverage:
Bavarian Warmblood horses, breeding, registration, grading and performance testing.

Access to staff:
Contact by telephone
Hours: Mon to Fri, 0900 to 1700

Parent body:
Landesverband Bayerischer Pferdezuechter eV Landshamer Str.11, Munich, D-81929, Germany; tel: 00 49 89 926967; fax: 00 49 89 907405

BRITISH BEEKEEPERS ASSOCIATION

Acronym or abbreviation: BBKA

National Agricultural Centre, Stoneleigh Park, Warwickshire, CV8 2LG

Tel: 024 7669 6679
Fax: 024 7669 0682
E-mail: bbka@britishbeekeepers.com

Website:
http://www.britishbeekeepers.com

Enquiries:
Enquiries to: General Secretary

Founded:
1874

Organisation type and purpose:
Membership association (membership is by subscription), present number of members: 12,521, registered charity (charity number 212025).
To further the craft of beekeeping.

Subject coverage:
Bees and beekeeping; examinations in beekeeping.

Museum or gallery collection, archive, or library special collection:
AVA library of slides, tapes etc
Library of numerous collections

Printed publications:
Honey Recipe leaflets (50p)
Advisory leaflets on many aspects of beekeeping (50p)
Leaflets of bee management (50p)
BBKA News (for members)
Bee Craft (monthly by subscription)
First Steps in Beekeeping
Honeybee Swarms – What to Do?
Bees in the Curriculum – Schools pack (£15 inc. p&p in United kingdom; £30 inc. p&p overseas)

Microform publications:
Honeybee Anatomy, 8 coloured transparency plates in folder complete with index (£4)

Publications list:
Available in print

Access to staff:
Contact by letter, by telephone, by fax and by e-mail. Appointment necessary.
Hours: Mon to Fri, 0930 to 1230 and 1300 to 1430

BRITISH BEER & PUB ASSOCIATION

Market Towers, 1 Nine Elms Lane, London, SW8 9NQ

Tel: 020 7627 9191
Fax: 020 7627 9123
E-mail: enquiries@beerandpub.com

Website:
http://www.beerandpub.com
Career information.

Enquiries:
Enquiries to: Secretary

Founded:
1904

Organisation type and purpose:
Trade association.

Subject coverage:
Beer, brewing, the brewing industry, public houses, licensing system.

Museum or gallery collection, archive, or library special collection:
Trade periodicals and annuals back to 1880

Printed publications:
Statistical Handbook (annually)

Publications list:
Available in print

Access to staff:
Contact by letter
Hours: Mon to Fri, 0900 to 1700

Access for disabled people:
Level entry

Member of:
Confederation of British Industry

BRITISH BELGIAN BLUE CATTLE SOCIETY

Fell View, Blencarn, Penrith, Cumbria, CA10 1TX

Tel: 01768 88775
E-mail: info@belgianblue.co.uk

Website:
http://www.belgianblue.co.uk

Enquiries:
Enquiries to: Secretary

Founded:
1983

Organisation type and purpose:
Membership association (membership is by subscription), present number of members: 430.

Publications list:
Available online and in print

Access to staff:
Contact by letter, by telephone, by fax, by e-mail and via website
Hours: Mon to Fri, 0900 to 1700

BRITISH BERRICHON DU CHER SHEEP SOCIETY LIMITED

Acronym or abbreviation: BdC

The Lodge, Sutton Bassett, Market Harborough, Leicestershire, LE16 8HL

Tel: 01858 462427
Fax: 01858 462427

Enquiries:
Enquiries to: Secretary

Founded:
1986

Organisation type and purpose:
Membership association (membership is by subscription).
Breed Society.

Subject coverage:
British Berrichon Du Cher sheep breed.

Printed publications:
Promotional leaflets available free

Access to staff:
Contact by letter, by telephone and by fax
Hours: Mon to Fri, 0900 to 1700

BRITISH BIOMAGNETIC ASSOCIATION

Acronym or abbreviation: BBA

31 St Marychurch Road, Torquay, Devon, TQ1 3JF

Tel: 01803 293346
Fax: 01803 293346
E-mail: secretary@britishbiomagneticassoc.fsnet.co.uk

Enquiries:
Enquiries to: Secretary
Other contacts: Course Administrator

Founded:
1976

Organisation type and purpose:
Professional body (membership is by qualification), present number of members: 250, training organisation, research organisation.
Postgraduate Training.

Subject coverage:
Magnetic effects on acupuncture points, acupuncture at postgraduate level, radionic practice.

Access to staff:
Contact by letter, by telephone, by fax and by e-mail
Hours: Not Wed or Fri afternoon

BRITISH BIRD COUNCIL

Acronym or abbreviation: BBC

1st Floor Offices, 1159 Bristol Road South, Northfield, Birmingham, B31 2SL

Tel: 0121 476 5999

Website:
http://www.britishbirdcouncil.com

Enquiries:
Enquiries to: Administrator
Direct tel: 01902 700319
Direct fax: 01902 701140
Direct e-mail: rogercaton@birdexpert.fsnet.co.uk

Founded:
1970

Organisation type and purpose:
Non-governmental organisation.
Department for the Environment, Food & Rural Affairs approved supplier of rings for birds.

Subject coverage:
Rings to identify British birds.

Access to staff:
Contact by letter
Hours: Mon to Fri, 0900 to 1700

Access to building, collection or gallery:
No access other than to staff

Affiliated society:
Cleveland British Bird Club
Eastern Federation of British Bird Fanciers
Lancashire British Bird & Hybrid Club
London & Home Counties British Bird & Mule Club
National British Bird & Mule Club
North Derbyshire British Bird & Mule Club
Sandwell British Bird & Hybrid Club
Scottish British Bird & Mule Club
Severn Counties Foreign & British Bird Society
South Coast British Bird & Hybrid Club
Staffordshire British Bird & Mule Club
Welsh British Bird & Mule Club
Yorkshire British Bird & Hybrid Club

Affiliated to:
National Council for Aviculture

BRITISH BIRDWATCHING FAIR

Acronym or abbreviation: BBWF

Fishponds Cottage, Stamford Road, Oakham, Rutland, LE15 8AB

Tel: 01572 771079
Fax: 01572 756611
E-mail: bbwf@rutlandwater.clara.net

Website:
http://www.birdfair.org.uk

Enquiries:
Enquiries to: Administrator

Founded:
1989

Organisation type and purpose:
Voluntary organisation.
Conservancy organisation.
Three day event at Egleton Nature Reserve, Rutland Water, the purpose of which is a celebration of birdwatching and a way of raising funds for international bird conservation.

Subject coverage:
Birdwatching and conservation.

Trade and statistical information:
Approximately 250 exhibitions and 15,000 visitors.

Access to staff:
Contact by letter, by telephone, by fax and by e-mail
Hours: Mon to Fri, 0900 to 1700
Special comments: Preferred access order: email, letter, fax, telephone.

Access for disabled people:
Parking provided, toilet facilities

Connections with:
Leicestershire and Rutland Trust for Nature Conservation
  tel: 0116 270 2999; fax: 0116 270 9555; e-mail: leicswt@cix.compulink.co.uk
Royal Society for the Protection of Birds
  tel: 01767 680551

BRITISH BLIND AND SHUTTER ASSOCIATION

Acronym or abbreviation: BBSA

42 Heath Street, Tamworth, Staffordshire, B79 7JH

Tel: 01827 52337
Fax: 01827 310827
E-mail: info@bbsa.org.uk

Website:
http://www.bbsa.org.uk
Members' details, technical product information.

Enquiries:
Enquiries to: Secretary

Founded:
1919

Organisation type and purpose:
National organisation, advisory body, trade association (membership is by subscription), present number of members: 390.
Represents manufacturers and suppliers.

Subject coverage:
Internal and external blinds, awnings and security grilles and shutters.

Printed publications:
Blinds and Shutters Buyers Guide 2006/7
Blinds and Shutters (quarterly)
Openings (trade journal)

Access to staff:
Contact by letter, by telephone, by fax and by e-mail
Hours: Mon to Thu, 0900 to 1700; Fri, 0900 to 1630

BRITISH BLIND SPORT

Acronym or abbreviation: BBS

4–6 Victoria Terrace, Leamington Spa, Warwickshire, CV31 3AB

Tel: 01926 424247
Fax: 01926 427775
E-mail: info@britishblindsport.org.uk

Website:
http://www.britishblindsport.org.uk

Enquiries:
Enquiries to: Admin. Manager

Founded:
1975

Organisation type and purpose:
Membership association, voluntary organisation, registered charity (charity number 271500).
Providing sport and recreation for blind and partially sighted people.

Subject coverage:
General information about sports for the blind and partially sighted, specialist sports, classification of sight categories.

Printed publications:
Newsletter (4 times a year)

Electronic and video publications:
Tape copy of newsletter

Access to staff:
Contact by letter and by e-mail
Hours: Mon to Thu, 0900 to 1700; Fri, 0900 to 1630

Affiliated to:
International Blind Sport Association

BRITISH BOARD OF AGRÉMENT

Acronym or abbreviation: BBA

Bucknalls Lane, Garston, Watford, Hertfordshire, WD25 9BA

Tel: 01923 665300
Fax: 01923 665301
E-mail: mail@bba.star.co.uk

Website:
http://www.bbacerts.co.uk
Information on the BBA. Listings of approved products and installers. Test services information.

Enquiries:
Enquiries to: Information Officer
Direct e-mail: athomas@bba.star.co.uk
Other contacts: Sales and Marketing Director

Founded:
1966

Organisation type and purpose:
Approvals body for the construction industry.

Subject coverage:
Testing and approval of building and civil engineering products (successful assessments are published as Agrément Certificates, which contain essential technical data for designers and users).

Museum or gallery collection, archive, or library special collection:
3500 agrément certificates dating from 1966

Non-library collection catalogue:
All or part available online

Library catalogue:
All or part available online

Printed publications:
Directory of Approved Installers
Index of Certificates (quarterly with monthly
 updates)
Methods of Assessment and Testing
Supplement to the Approved Documents
 supporting the Building Regulations

Microform publications:
All publications available on microfiche

Electronic and video publications:
Agrément Certificates

Publications list:
Available in print

Access to staff:
Contact by letter, by fax, by e-mail and via
website
Hours: Mon to Fri, 0900 to 1730

Access to building, collection or gallery:
Hours: Mon to Fri, 0900

UK member of:
European Organisation for Technical Approvals
(EOTA)
 tel: +32 2 502 6900; fax: +32 2 502 3814; e-mail:
 info@eota.be
European Union of Agrément (UEATC)
 tel: 01923 665412; fax: 01923 665301; e-mail:
 jblaisdale@bba.star.co.uk

BRITISH BOTTLERS' INSTITUTE

Acronym or abbreviation: BBI

c/o Binsted Group, Attwood House, Mansfield
Park, Four Marks, Hampshire, GU34 5PZ

Tel: 01420 568901
Fax: 01420 565994
E-mail: bbi@binstedgroup.com

Website:
http://www.bbi.org.uk

Enquiries:
Enquiries to: President

Founded:
1953

Organisation type and purpose:
Trade association (membership is by election or
invitation), present number of members: 135.

Subject coverage:
Bottling, canning and packaging of beverages,
including beers, mineral waters, soft drinks, fruit
juices, ciders, wines, spirits.

Access to staff:
Contact by letter, by telephone, by fax and by e-
mail
Hours: Mon to Fri, 0900 to 1700

BRITISH BRICK SOCIETY

Acronym or abbreviation: BBS

Brick Development Association, 26 Store Street,
London, WC1E 7BT

Tel: 020 7323 7030
Fax: 020 7580 3795
E-mail: michael@mhammett.freeserve.co.uk

Website:
http://www.britishbricksoc.free-online.co.uk

Enquiries:
Enquiries to: Honorary Secretary
Direct tel: 01494 520599

Founded:
1972

Organisation type and purpose:
Learned society (membership is by subscription),
present number of members: c.300.
To promote the study and recording of all aspects
of the archaeology and history of bricks,
brickmaking and brickwork.

Subject coverage:
Historical aspects of brickmaking in the United
Kingdom and of brickwork structures.

Printed publications:
INFORMATION (newsletter, c.20pp, members, 3
 times a year)
All book issues kept in print and Index available

Access to staff:
Contact by letter, by telephone, by fax and by e-
mail
Hours: Mon to Fri, 0900 to 1700

Also at:
Honorary Secretary
 9 Bailey Close, High Wycombe,
 Buckinghamshire, HP13 6QA; tel: 01494 520299;
 e-mail: michael@mhammett.freeserve.co.uk

Links with:
British Archaeological Association, Brick Section

BRITISH BRYOLOGICAL SOCIETY

Acronym or abbreviation: BBS

Ivy House, Wheelock Street, Middlewich,
Cheshire, CW10 9AB

Website:
http://www.britishbryologicalsociety.org.uk
Meetings, referees and recording, Tropical
Bryology Group, membership enquiries.

Enquiries:
Enquiries to: General Secretary

Founded:
1896

Organisation type and purpose:
Learned society (membership is by subscription),
present number of members: 604, registered
charity (charity number 228851).
To promote a wide interest in bryology.

Subject coverage:
Study and conservation of mosses and liverworts
(bryophytes) worldwide.

**Museum or gallery collection, archive, or library
special collection:**
Bryological library
Herbarium of approximately 30,000 dried
 specimens of bryophytes

Printed publications:
Census Catalogue of British Bryophytes
Bulletin of the British Bryological Society (2 times a
 year)
Journal of Bryology (4 times a year)
Occasional publications: BBS Special Volumes

Access to staff:
Contact by letter
Hours: Mon to Fri, 0900 to 1700

BRITISH BUDDHIST ASSOCIATION

Acronym or abbreviation: BBA

11 Biddulph Road, London, W9 1JA

Tel: 020 7286 5575
Fax: 020 7289 5545

Enquiries:
Enquiries to: Director

Founded:
1974

Organisation type and purpose:
Voluntary organisation.
Specialists in teaching and practice of early
Buddhism. The BBA is non-sectarian and seeks to
express devotion in ways suitable to Western
practitioners.

Subject coverage:
Educational, religious and meditation aspects of
the Buddha's teaching. The Association promotes
educational, religious and meditation aspects of
the Buddha's teaching at evening and weekend
sessions both in London and at country retreats, to
augment private study and practice. The BBA is
non-sectarian and seeks to express devotion in
ways suitable to Western practitioners.

Access to staff:
Contact by letter and by fax
Hours: Mon to Fri, 0900 to 1700

Access to building, collection or gallery:
Prior appointment required

BRITISH BULGARIAN CHAMBER OF COMMERCE

Acronym or abbreviation: BBCC

PO Box 123, Bromley, Kent, BR1 4ZX

Tel: 020 8464 5007
E-mail: info@bbcc.bg

Website:
http://www.bbcc.bg

Enquiries:
Enquiries to: Executive Director

Founded:
1993

Organisation type and purpose:
International organisation, membership
association (membership is by subscription).

Subject coverage:
Promotion of business between the United
Kingdom and Bulgaria.

Electronic and video publications:
BBCC Weekly Newsletter (E-mail)

Access to staff:
Contact by e-mail
Hours: Mon to Fri, 0900 to 1700

Access to building, collection or gallery:
No access other than to staff

BRITISH BURN ASSOCIATION

Acronym or abbreviation: BBA

Research and Education Office, Burn Centre,
Wythenshawe Hospital, Southmoor Road,
Wythenshawe, Greater Manchester, M23 9LT

Tel: 0161 291 6323
Fax: 0161 291 6323
E-mail: bba@uhsm.nhs.uk

Website:
http://www.britishburnassociation.co.uk

Enquiries:
Enquiries to: Honorary Secretary

Founded:
1967

Organisation type and purpose:
Professional body (membership is by subscription,
qualification), registered charity (charity number
260167).
Disseminate knowledge and research into the care
of, recovery from and prevention of burns.

Subject coverage:
Burn prevention; burn treatment, care and
rehabilitation.

Printed publications:
Burncare (newsletter)

Access to staff:
Contact by letter, by telephone, by fax and by e-
mail
Hours: Mon to Fri, 0900 to 1700

Affiliated to:
International Society for Burn Injuries

BRITISH BUSINESS AWARDS ASSOCIATION

The Stables, Highfield Park, Creaton, Northampton, NN6 8NT

Tel: 01604 505480

Enquiries:
Enquiries to: Information Officer

BRITISH BUTTON SOCIETY

Acronym or abbreviation: BBS

E-mail: british.button.society@care4free.net

Website:
http://www.britishbuttonsociety.org

Enquiries:
Enquiries to: Secretary
Other contacts: Membership Secretary for information regarding membership.

Founded:
1976

Organisation type and purpose:
Membership association (membership is by subscription), present number of members: 350 (approx).
Members, collect and research the background to old, interesting buttons; uniform and dress.

Subject coverage:
History of button manufacturers, collection and research into all types of buttons i.e. modern/antique dress, military/service uniform, all types of civilian uniform, livery. Not present day manufacturers or sources of supply.

Printed publications:
Button Lines (quarterly, to paid-up members only)

Access to staff:
Contact by letter
Hours: Mon to Fri, 0900 to 1700

Membership Secretary:
British Button Society
  Jersey Cottage, Parklands Road, Patchway, Bower Ashton, Bristol, BS3 2JR

BRITISH CABLES ASSOCIATION

Acronym or abbreviation: BCA

37a Walton Road, East Molesey, Surrey, KT8 0DH

Tel: 020 8941 4079
Fax: 020 8783 0104
E-mail: admin@bcauk.org

Enquiries:
Enquiries to: Secretary General

Organisation type and purpose:
Trade association.

Subject coverage:
Insulated cables.

Access to staff:
Contact by e-mail
Hours: Mon to Fri, 0900 to 1700

Access to building, collection or gallery:
No access other than to staff

BRITISH CACTUS AND SUCCULENT SOCIETY

Acronym or abbreviation: BCSS

49 Chestnut Glen, Hornchurch, Essex, RM12 4HL

Tel: 01708 447778
Fax: 01444 454061
E-mail: bcss@cactus-mall.com

Website:
http://www.bcss.org.uk
World-wide information on events related to cactus and succulents. Branch programmes and events. Nurseries.

Enquiries:
Enquiries to: Membership Secretary
Direct tel: 01904 410512
Direct e-mail: membership@bcss.org.uk
Other contacts: Secretary (for general enquiries); Publicity Officer

Founded:
1983

Organisation type and purpose:
Learned society (membership is by subscription), present number of members: 3,700, registered charity (charity number 290786).
To educate the general public on all aspects of the subject.

Subject coverage:
All aspects concerned with the growing, propagation and conservation of succulent plants.

Printed publications:
Journal (quarterly, members only)
Publications available for purchase
Order printed publications from: Publications Manager, BCSS, Brenfield, Bolney Road, Ansty, West Sussex, RH17 5AW, tel: 01444 441193, fax: 01444 454061, e-mail: bcss@cactus.mall.com

Publications list:
Available online

Access to staff:
Contact by letter, by telephone, by fax, by e-mail and via website
Hours: Mon to Fri, 0900 to 1700

Access to building, collection or gallery:
No prior appointment required
Special comments: Members only for reference library, no borrowing.

Also at:
Membership Secretary, British Cactus and Succulent Society
  15 Brentwood Crescent, Hull Road, York, YO10 5HU; tel: 01904 410512

BRITISH CALCIUM CARBONATES FEDERATION

Acronym or abbreviation: BCCF

c/o Omya UK Ltd, Omya House, Stephensons Way, Wyvern Business Park, Chaddesden, Derby, DE21 6LY

Tel: 01332 887435
Fax: 01332 887043
E-mail: mike.nocivelli@omya.com

Website:
http://www.calcium-carbonate.org.uk

Enquiries:
Enquiries to: Secretary

Founded:
1943

Organisation type and purpose:
Trade association.

Subject coverage:
Calcium carbonates (chalk whiting), production and uses.

Printed publications:
List of members

Access to staff:
Contact by letter, by telephone, by fax and by e-mail
Hours: Mon to Fri, 0900 to 1700

BRITISH CANOE UNION

Acronym or abbreviation: BCU

John Dudderidge House, Adbolton Lane, West Bridgford, Nottingham, NG2 5AS

Tel: 0115 982 1100
Fax: 0115 982 1797

Website:
http://www.bcu.org.uk

General information on the sport and recreation of canoeing and kayaking.

Enquiries:
Enquiries to: Chief Executive
Other contacts: PA to Chief Executive

Organisation type and purpose:
Membership association (membership is by subscription), present number of members: 23,000.
Governing body for the sport and recreation of canoeing and kayaking.

Subject coverage:
All aspects of canoeing.

Museum or gallery collection, archive, or library special collection:
Archival films

Printed publications:
Booklets on canoeing
Canoe Focus
Coaching Handbook

Access to staff:
Contact by letter and by e-mail
Hours: Mon to Fri, 0900 to 1700

Access to building, collection or gallery:
No prior appointment required

Affiliated to:
British Olympic Association
  tel: 020 8871 2677; fax: 020 8871 9104
Central Council of Physical Recreation
  tel: 020 7828 3163; fax: 020 7630 8820
Commonwealth Games Federation for England
  tel: 020 7388 6643; fax: 020 7388 6744
European Canoe Association
International Canoe Federation

BRITISH CARTOGRAPHIC SOCIETY

Acronym or abbreviation: BCS

c/o Royal Geographical Society, 1 Kensington Gore, London, SW7 2AR

Tel: 01823 665775
Fax: 01823 665775
E-mail: admin@cartography.org.uk

Website:
http://www.cartography.org.uk
News, membership, job vacancies, directories (corporate members, freelance cartographers, students), publications.

Enquiries:
Enquiries to: Administrator

Founded:
1963

Organisation type and purpose:
Learned society (membership is by subscription), present number of members: 700, registered charity (charity number 240034).
To promote the art and science of map-making.

Subject coverage:
Cartography, history of cartography, map libraries curatorship, GIS, technical developments and automation in cartography, design, technology, education and careers in cartography.

Museum or gallery collection, archive, or library special collection:
Library housed at the National Library of Scotland
Exchange and subscription journals
Map design awards entries
Reference works

Printed publications:
Working in The Map industry (2007) brief guide for young people seeking a career in the map world. The full version (Careers in Cartography) may be viewed on the Society's website.
The Cartographic Journal (4 times a year, free to members and on subscription to non-members)
Maplines (Society newsletter for members, 3 times a year)

Cartographiti (Map Curators' Group newsletter, up to 3 times a year, free to members and on subscription to non-members)

Directory of UK Map Collections (1995, £10 members, £15 non-members). An updated version may be viewed on the Society's website

Index to the Cartographic Journal 1964–1996 (£10 members, £15 non-members)

Military Publisher's Designations: a list of publishers' designations appearing on military maps past and present (£1.20)

Qualifications: a collection of papers, discussions and proposals from the 1991 meeting of RICS on qualifications in Mapping and Surveying (Lawrence, P., ed., £5.50)

Recording our Changing Landscape (1994, £9)

Order printed publications from: The Cartographic Journal, Maney Publishing, 0113 243 2800, www.maney.co.uk

All other publications from the Administration address.

Publications list:
Available in print

Access to staff:
Contact by letter, by telephone, by fax, by e-mail and via website
Hours: Mon to Fri, 0900 to 1700; answerphone when absent

Also at:
British Cartographic Society (Administration)
12 Elworthy Drive, Wellington, Somerset, TA21 9AT; tel: 01823 665775; fax: 01823 665775

BRITISH CARTON ASSOCIATION

Farringdon Point, 29–35 Farringdon Road, London, EC1M 3JF

Tel: 020 7915 8300
Fax: 020 7405 7785
E-mail: sigs@bpif.org.uk

Website:
http://bpif.org.uk
General information about BPIF, current press releases.

Enquiries:
Enquiries to: Manager

Founded:
1933

Organisation type and purpose:
Trade association.
To represent manufacturers of printed folding cartons.

Subject coverage:
Cartons, folding cartons, carton board, employment affairs, technical, legal, training advice, statistics, health and safety, environment.

Trade and statistical information:
Printing industry statistics, consumption and production of cartons.

Printed publications:
ECMA Folding Carton Dictionary (five languages)
European Carton Manufacturers Association Code
Glossary of folding carton terms
Handbook of Carton Board and Carton Test Procedures

Publications list:
Available in print

Access to staff:
Contact by letter and by e-mail
Hours: Mon to Fri, 0900 to 1700

Affiliated to:
British Printing Industries Federation
tel: 020 7915 8300; fax: 020 7405 7784

BRITISH CARTOON ARCHIVE

Templeman Library, University of Kent, Canterbury, Kent, CT2 7NU

Tel: 01227 823127

Fax: 01227 823127
E-mail: j.m.newton@kent.ac.uk

Website:
http://library.kent.ac.uk/cartoons

Founded:
1973

Formerly called:
Centre for the Study of Cartoons and Caricature

Organisation type and purpose:
Created as a research centre and picture library with the objectives of conserving and cataloguing cartoons; encouraging research into all aspects and periods of cartooning; planning and promoting exhibitions of cartoon originals; and servicing teaching in a variety of disciplines.

Subject coverage:
Cartoons.

Museum or gallery collection, archive, or library special collection:
Archive of 100,000 cartoons, of which more than 80,000 are available for viewing online on the Archive's database.
Library of more than 5,000 books, periodicals, cuttings, slides, videos and cassettes about cartoons, caricature and humour.

BRITISH CATTLE VETERINARY ASSOCIATION

Acronym or abbreviation: BCVA

The Green, Frampton on Severn, Gloucester, GL2 7EP

Tel: 01452 740816
Fax: 01452 741117
E-mail: office@cattlevet.co.uk

Website:
http://www.bcva.org.uk

Enquiries:
Enquiries to: Secretariat

Organisation type and purpose:
Learned society.

Subject coverage:
Veterinary science related to cattle and cattle production.

Printed publications:
Abstracts
Meetings Papers

Access to staff:
Contact by letter, by telephone, by fax, by e-mail and via website
Hours: Mon to Fri, 0900 to 1700

Affiliated to:
British Veterinary Association

BRITISH CAVE RESEARCH ASSOCIATION

Acronym or abbreviation: BCRA

The Old Methodist Chapel, Great Hucklow, Buxton, Derbyshire, SK17 8RG

Tel: 01298 873800
E-mail: enquiries@bcra.org.uk

Website:
http://www.bcra.org.uk
Full description of BCRA services, meetings, publications. Contents list of Caves and Caving, Cave and Karst Science.

Enquiries:
Enquiries to: Secretary

Founded:
1973

Organisation type and purpose:
National organisation, membership association (membership is by subscription), present number of members: 1000, registered charity (charity number 267828), research organisation, publishing house.
The national organisation for the study of sciences associated with caving, caves and karst.

Subject coverage:
Speleology (British and foreign), biospeleology, hydrology, cave chemistry, physics and geophysics, cave archaeology and palaeontology, cave survey and photography, regional studies (NW Yorkshire, Derbyshire, Mendip, South Wales and Devon limestone regions); geology, geomorphology, erosion of limestones, cave rescue and medicine, ropes, ladders, lights.

Museum or gallery collection, archive, or library special collection:
National Caving Library, including old and rare works, British and foreign publications virtually a complete collection of published material on speleology

Non-library collection catalogue:
All or part available in-house

Printed publications:
Caves and Caving (quarterly, formerly BCRA Bulletin up to 1978)
Cave and Karst Science (quarterly to vol.12, 1986 then 3 times a year)
Cave Studies, series of occasional booklets
Current Titles in Speleology CTS/BBS/SA (annually up to 1993, now incorporated within the Bulletin Bibliographique Spéléologique/Speleological Abstracts)
Several books, full list on request
Order printed publications from: Publications Sales Officer, BCRA
Village Farm, Great Thirkleby, Thirsk, YO7 2AT, tel: 01845 501424

Electronic and video publications:
CTS/BBS/SA (CD-ROMS)

Access to staff:
Contact by letter, by telephone and by e-mail
Hours: Usually 0900 to 2100 but not guaranteed

Access to building, collection or gallery:
Prior appointment required for access to library
Hours: Mon to Fri, 0900 to 1700
Special comments: Contact: BCRA, Holt House, Holt Lane, Lea, Matlock, Derbyshire, DE4 5GQ, tel: 01629 534775, email: librarian@bcra.org.uk

Associated with the:
British Caving Association

BRITISH CAVING ASSOCIATION

Acronym or abbreviation: BCA

The Old Methodist Chapel, Great Hucklow, Buxton, Derbyshire, SK17 8RG

E-mail: secretary@british-caving.org.uk

Website:
http://www.british-caving.org.uk
Information on organisation, members training, conservation, access.

Enquiries:
Enquiries to: Publications and Information Officer
Direct e-mail: publications@british-caving.org.uk
Other contacts: Training coordinator for leadership qualification queries.

Founded:
1969

Organisation type and purpose:
Advisory body, statutory body, membership association (membership is by subscription), present number of members: 5000, voluntary organisation, training organisation.
Governing body of the sport of caving in the UK.

continued overleaf

Subject coverage:
Caving training and equipment, cave conservation and access, research and science, rescue, registry data, diving; mine history, overseas caving expeditions, caving in general, caving clubs.

Trade and statistical information:
Statistics on caving accidents.

Printed publications:
Cave Conservation Handbook
Cave Conservation Policy
Equipment, library and film lists
Instructor and Leadership Qualifications in caving
Legal Aspects of Access Underground (£1)
National Caving Code
Protect our Caves
Radon Underground
So You Want to Go Caving
Speleoscene (newsletter, 6 times a year)
Weil's Disease Leaflet

Electronic and video publications:
Lost Caves of Britain (video, £10)

Publications list:
Available online and in print

Access to staff:
Contact by letter, by telephone, by e-mail, in person and via website
Hours: 24 hours every day
Special comments: Voluntary organisation, officers have other occupations.

Affiliated to:
European Speleological Federation
International Speleological Union

Umbrella organisation of the:
5 Regional Caving Councils
British Cave Rescue Organisation
British Cave Research Association
National Association on Mining History Organisations
William Pengyelly Cave Studies Trust

BRITISH CERAMIC CONFEDERATION

Acronym or abbreviation: BCC

Federation House, Station Road, Stoke-on-Trent, Staffordshire, ST4 2SA

Tel: 01782 744631
Fax: 01782 744102
E-mail: bcc@ceramfed.co.uk

Website:
http://www.ceramfed.co.uk

Enquiries:
Enquiries to: Chief Executive

Organisation type and purpose:
Trade association.
Representative body for UK ceramics manufacturing industry.

Subject coverage:
Ceramics manufacturing industry.

Printed publications:
Careers Brochure
List of Member Companies

Access to staff:
Contact by letter, by fax and by e-mail
Hours: Mon to Fri, 0900 to 1700
Special comments: No personal callers. Information available to members only.

Links with:
Cerame Unie

BRITISH CERAMIC PLANT AND MACHINERY MANUFACTURERS ASSOCIATION

Acronym or abbreviation: BCPMMA

Founded:
1962

Organisation type and purpose:
Trade association (membership is by subscription), present number of members: 75, manufacturing industry, publishing house.
Exhibition Organisers.

Subject coverage:
Plant, machinery and raw materials and/or turn-key projects for the manufacture of the complete range of ceramic products, including building bricks, sewer pipes, roofing/wall/floor tiles, tableware, sanitary ware, art pottery, porcelain insulators, refractories etc.

Printed publications:
Global Ceramic Review (quarterly)

Access to staff:
Contact by letter, by telephone, by fax, by e-mail, in person and via website. Appointment necessary.
Access for members only. Non-members charged.
Hours: Mon to Fri, 0900 to 1700

Affiliated to:
British Ceramic Confederation

BRITISH CHAMBERS OF COMMERCE

Acronym or abbreviation: BCC

4 Westwood House, Westwood Business Park, Coventry, Warwickshire, CV4 8HS

Tel: 024 7669 4484
Fax: 024 7669 5844
E-mail: enquiry@britishchambers.org.uk

Website:
http://www.britishchambers.org.uk

Enquiries:
Enquiries to: Managing Director

Organisation type and purpose:
Membership association.
Chamber of commerce.

Subject coverage:
Export advice and guidance, international trade advice, links to local and overseas chambers of commerce.

Trade and statistical information:
European economics.
UK economics and business statistics.

Printed publications:
British Chambers of Commerce Quarterly Economic Survey
European Economic Survey
Other specific policy reports
Small Firms Survey
Order printed publications from: 65 Petty France, St James's Park, London, SW1H 9EU

Publications list:
Available online and in print

Access to staff:
Contact by letter, by telephone, by fax, by e-mail and via website. Appointment necessary.
Hours: Mon to Fri, 0845 to 1645 (Coventry Office), 0900 to 1700 (London Office)

Parent body:
The British Chambers of Commerce
65 Petty France, St James Park, London, SW1H 9EU; tel: 020 7654 5800; fax: 020 7654 5819; e-mail: info@britishchambers.org.uk

BRITISH CHEMICAL ENGINEERING CONTRACTORS ASSOCIATION

Acronym or abbreviation: BCECA

1–4 Regent Street, London, SW1Y 4NR

Tel: 020 7839 6514
Fax: 020 7930 3466
E-mail: ian.corbidge@bceca.org.uk

Website:
http://www.bceca.org.uk

Enquiries:
Enquiries to: Director

Founded:
1966

Organisation type and purpose:
Trade association (membership is by subscription, qualification, election or invitation), present number of members: 20.

Subject coverage:
Process plant contracting and the activities of member companies, their qualifications and experience.

Trade and statistical information:
Industry statistics, member companies order, intake and exports.

Printed publications:
Target – Careers Information and Graduate Employers

Access to staff:
Contact by letter, by telephone and by e-mail
Hours: Mon to Thu, 1000 to 1600

BRITISH CHINESE ARTISTS' ASSOCIATION

Acronym or abbreviation: BCAA

Tel: 020 7813 0086
Fax: 020 7482 5292

Enquiries:
Enquiries to: Information Officer
Other contacts: Arts & Education for education work.

Founded:
1991

Organisation type and purpose:
Voluntary organisation, registered charity (charity number 1059823), suitable for ages: 5+, training organisation, consultancy, research organisation. To raise the profile of Chinese arts and artists through education for the public benefit through the promotion of the full spectrum of arts practised by artists of Chinese origins in Britain.

Subject coverage:
Database of Chinese artists in London and UK, in performing arts, visual arts, design, music and film. Education projects, research, general advice to public, media sector.

Access to staff:
Contact by letter, by telephone, by fax and by e-mail. Appointment necessary.
Hours: Mon to Fri, 0900 to 1700

BRITISH CHIROPODY AND PODIATRY ASSOCIATION

Acronym or abbreviation: BChA

The New Hall, Bath Road, Maidenhead, Berkshire, SL6 4LA

Tel: 01628 632449
Fax: 01628 674483
E-mail: smae_institute@compuserve.com

Enquiries:
Enquiries to: Membership Secretary

Founded:
1959

Organisation type and purpose:
Professional body (membership is by qualification, election or invitation), present number of members: over 10,000, service industry, training organisation, consultancy, research organisation, publishing house.

Subject coverage:
Chiropody, chiropodists, podiatry, all matters pertaining to feet and footware care.

Printed publications:
Fact sheets on: verruca and calluses, diabetes and footsore, flat foot, bunions, general advice on footcare
Magazine (on subscription)

Publications list:
Available in print

Access to staff:
Contact by letter, by telephone, by fax, by e-mail and via website
Hours: Mon to Fri, 0900 to 1700

Access to building, collection or gallery:
No prior appointment required

Affiliated to:
School of Surgical Chiropody

BRITISH CHIROPRACTIC ASSOCIATION

Acronym or abbreviation: BCA

59 Castle Street, Reading, Berkshire, RG1 7SN

Tel: 0118 950 5950
Fax: 0118 958 8946
E-mail: enquiries@chiropractic-uk.co.uk

Website:
http://www.chiropractic-uk.co.uk
Information on chiropractic research data; membership of BCA.

Enquiries:
Enquiries to: Press Officer
Direct e-mail: jdoyle@publicasity.co.uk

Founded:
1925

Organisation type and purpose:
Advisory body, statutory body, professional body (membership is by subscription), present number of members: 816, voluntary organisation.

Subject coverage:
Chiropractic within the UK.

Museum or gallery collection, archive, or library special collection:
Library of resource material
Photographs and slides of chiropractors, their work and related topics

Printed publications:
Annual Report
Register of all BCA members
Variety of leaflets (available on request)

Access to staff:
Contact by letter, by telephone, by fax, by e-mail and via website. Appointment necessary. Access for members only.
Hours: Mon to Fri, 0900 to 1700

Access to building, collection or gallery:
No access other than to staff

BRITISH CHRISTMAS TREE GROWERS ASSOCIATION

Acronym or abbreviation: BCTGA

13 Wolrige Road, Edinburgh, EH16 6HX

Tel: 0131 664 1100
Fax: 0131 664 2669
E-mail: rogermhay@btinternet.com

Website:
http://www.bctga.co.uk/

Enquiries:
Enquiries to: General Secretary

Founded:
1979

Organisation type and purpose:
National organisation, trade association (membership is by subscription), present number of members: 380.
Promotion of Real Christmas Trees.

Subject coverage:
Growing, cultivations and marketing real Christmas trees.

Printed publications:
Newsletter
Care of Tree Leaflets
History of Christmas Trees

Access to staff:
Contact by letter, by telephone, by fax and by e-mail
Hours: Mon to Fri, 0900 to 1700

BRITISH CLEANING COUNCIL LIMITED

Acronym or abbreviation: BCC Ltd

PO Box 1328, Kidderminster, Worcestershire, DY11 5ZJ

Tel: 01562 851129
Fax: 01562 851129

Enquiries:
Enquiries to: General Secretary/Treasurer
Direct e-mail: info@britishcleaningcouncil.org
Other contacts: Press Office, tel no: 01942 612616 for public relations

Founded:
1982

Organisation type and purpose:
Trade association (membership is by election or invitation), research organisation.
Co-ordinating body for UK cleaning industry.

Subject coverage:
All matters relating to cleaning and hygiene, including cleaning of buildings, internally and externally, and cleaning of outside areas.

Publications list:
Available in print

Access to staff:
Contact by letter, by telephone, by fax and by e-mail. Appointment necessary. Non-members charged.
Hours: Mon to Fri, 0900 to 1700

Member organisations:
18 member organisations

BRITISH CLOTHING INDUSTRY ASSOCIATION LIMITED

Acronym or abbreviation: BCIA

5 Portland Place, London, W1B 1PW

Tel: 020 7636 7788
Fax: 020 7636 7515
E-mail: bcia@dial.pipex.com

Enquiries:
Enquiries to: Director

Organisation type and purpose:
Trade association.

Subject coverage:
Clothing industry.

Printed publications:
News sheets (for members)
UK Fashion Exhibition Calendar

BRITISH COFFEE ASSOCIATION

Acronym or abbreviation: BCA

Federation House, 6 Catherine Street, London, WC2B 5JJ

Tel: 020 7836 2460
Fax: 020 7836 0580

Enquiries:
Enquiries to: Executive Secretary

Organisation type and purpose:
Trade association.

Subject coverage:
Coffee.

Access to staff:
Access for members only.
Hours: Mon to Fri, 0900 to 1700

Member of:
Food and Drink Federation

BRITISH COLOSTOMY ASSOCIATION

Acronym or abbreviation: BCA

15 Station Road, Reading, Berkshire, RG1 1LG

Tel: 0118 939 1537
Fax: 0118 956 9095
E-mail: sue@bcass.org.uk

Website:
http://www.bcass.org.uk

Enquiries:
Enquiries to: Secretary

Founded:
1967

Organisation type and purpose:
Membership association, voluntary organisation, registered charity (charity number 298299).
25 area organisers, to help people who have, or are about to have, a colostomy.

Subject coverage:
Help and advice to anyone who has, or is about to have, a colostomy.

Printed publications:
Literature available from Head Office or from 25 area organisers (free of charge)

Publications list:
Available in print

Access to staff:
Contact by letter, by telephone, by fax, by e-mail and via website. Appointment necessary.
Hours: Mon to Thu, 0900 to 1700; Fri, 0900 to 1500

Access to building, collection or gallery:
Prior appointment required

Connections with:
Macmillan Cancer Relief (MCR)
tel: 020 7840 7840; fax: 020 7840 7841; website: www.macmillan.org.uk

BRITISH COMPLEMENTARY MEDICINE ASSOCIATION

Acronym or abbreviation: BCMA

PO Box 5122, Bournemouth, BH8 0WG

Tel: 0845 345 5977
Fax: 0845 345 5978
E-mail: office@bcma.co.uk

Website:
http://www.bcma.co.uk
General.

Enquiries:
Enquiries to: General Secretary

Founded:
1992

Organisation type and purpose:
National organisation, professional body, membership association (membership is by subscription, qualification), present number of members: 86 organisations, voluntary organisation.

Subject coverage:
Complementary therapies and medicines generally.

Trade and statistical information:
No commercial trading.

Printed publications:
Code of Conduct

continued overleaf

Complaint Investigation and Disciplinary
Procedure
Membership list
Helping you to be Better Informed about Comp.
Therapies (leaflet, free)
Protecting Patients, Promoting Professionalism
(leaflet, free)

Access to staff:
Contact by letter, by telephone, by fax, by e-mail
and via website
Hours: Mon to Fri, 0900 to 1700

Access to building, collection or gallery:
No access other than to staff

BRITISH COMPRESSED AIR SOCIETY

Acronym or abbreviation: BCAS

33–34 Devonshire Street, London, W1G 6PY

Tel: 020 7935 2464
Fax: 020 7935 3077
E-mail: society@britishcompressedair.co.uk

Website:
http://www.britishcompressedair.co.uk

Enquiries:
Enquiries to: Executive Director

Organisation type and purpose:
Trade association.
Technical body for the compressed air industry.

Subject coverage:
Compressed air, gas and vacuum equipment and
use; European and British legislation affecting the
industry.

Printed publications:
Installation guide
Tools guide -pneumatic
Condensate publication booklet
Pipe joined guide
Publications on services, legislation, regulations,
tools, terminology, symbols, product liability

Publications list:
Available in print

Access to staff:
Contact by letter, by telephone, by fax and by e-
mail. Appointment necessary.
Hours: Mon to Fri, 0900 to 1700

BRITISH COMPRESSED GASES ASSOCIATION

Acronym or abbreviation: BCGA

1 Gleneagles House, Vernongate, Derby, DE1 1UP

Tel: 01332 225120
Fax: 01332 225101
E-mail: enquiries@bcga.co.uk

Website:
http://www.bcga.co.uk

Enquiries:
Enquiries to: Secretary

Founded:
1971

Organisation type and purpose:
National organisation, trade association.
Representation of about 35 companies who
manufacture or distribute gases, or manufacture
cylinders to contain them or equipment to use
them. It does not represent the interests of the
compressed air or natural gas industries.

Subject coverage:
Compressed and liquefied industrial, medical and
food gases e.g. oxygen, nitrogen, carbon dioxide,
acetylene, chlorine etc; cylinders, regulators, valves
etc; safety in handling, transport and use.

Printed publications:
Codes of Practice
Guidance notes
Technical Reports

A Method for Estimating the Offsite Risks from
Bulk Storage of Liquefied Oxygen
Avoidance and Detection of Internal Corrosion of
Gas Cylinders
Carriage of Gas Cylinders by Road in Cars and
Vans – Guidance for Drivers at Work: 1996
(leaflet)
The Safe Handling of Gas Cylinders at Waste
Facilities (leaflet
The Safe Use of CO2 and CO2/N2 Cylinders in the
Beverage Dispense Industry
The Safe Use of Non-Refillable Gas Containers
(Cylinders)

Publications list:
Available online

Access to staff:
Contact by e-mail
Hours: Mon to Fri, 0900 to 1700

Affiliated to:
European Industrial Gases Association (EIGA)

BRITISH COMPUTER ASSOCIATION OF THE BLIND

Acronym or abbreviation: BCAB

c/o RNIB, 58–72 John Bright Street, Birmingham,
B1 1BN

Tel: 0845 430 8627
E-mail: secretary@bcab.org.uk

Website:
http://www.bcab.org.uk
General information; membership and contact
details.

Enquiries:
Enquiries to: Administrator

Founded:
1969

Organisation type and purpose:
National government body, professional body,
membership association (membership is by
subscription, qualification), present number of
members: 250, voluntary organisation, registered
charity (charity number SCO232324), suitable for
ages: all, training organisation.
A society pursuing all matters of interest to blind
people in the computer field.

Subject coverage:
Training, advice on computer access devices for the
visually impaired, support groups.

Printed publications:
Newsletter (quarterly)

Electronic and video publications:
Membership CD (3 times a year)

Access to staff:
Contact by letter, by telephone, by fax and by e-
mail
Hours: Mon to Fri, 0900 to 1700

Access to building, collection or gallery:
No access other than to staff

BRITISH COMPUTER SOCIETY

Acronym or abbreviation: BCS

1st Floor, block D, North Star House, North Star
Avenue, Swindon, SN2 1FA

Tel: 01793 417417
Fax: 01793 417444
E-mail: bcshq@bcs.org.uk

Website:
http://www.bcs.org.uk

Enquiries:
Enquiries to: Public Relations Manager
Direct tel: 01793 417433
Direct e-mail: aduckworth@hq-bcs.org.uk

Founded:
1957

Organisation type and purpose:
Professional body.

Subject coverage:
Computers and their applications, commercial
data processing, programming and programming
languages, information technology, safety-critical
and business-critical systems, computers for the
disabled and computer misuse (including hacking
and viruses).

**Museum or gallery collection, archive, or library
special collection:**
The Society's Library is online

Library catalogue:
All or part available online

Printed publications:
Computer Bulletin (6 times a year)
Distributed Systems Engineering Journal
(quarterly, jointly with the IEE and the IoP)
Formal Methods in Computing (quarterly, pub.
jointly with Springer-Verlag)
HCI Journal (4 times a year, pub. jointly with
Butterworth)
High Integrity Systems (4 times a year, pub. jointly
with Oxford University Press)
Information Technology and Nursing (pub. BCS
Nursing Specialist Group)
Software Engineering Journal (10 times a year, pub.
jointly with OUP)
The Computer Journal (6 times a year)

Publications list:
Available in print

Access to staff:
Contact by letter, by telephone, by fax and by e-
mail
Hours: Mon to Fri, 0915 to 1715

Associated with:
numerous similar Information Technology
Societies

Member of:
Council of European Professional Information
Societies

UK member of:
IFIP

BRITISH CONSTRUCTIONAL STEELWORK ASSOCIATION LIMITED

Acronym or abbreviation: BCSA

Head Office, 4 Whitehall Court, Westminster,
London, SW1A 2ES

Tel: 020 7839 8566
Fax: 020 7976 1634
E-mail: postroom@steelconstruction.org

Website:
http://www.steelconstruction.org

Enquiries:
Enquiries to: Director General
Direct fax: 020 7839 4729
Direct e-mail: derek.tordoff@steelconstruction.org

Founded:
1906

Organisation type and purpose:
Trade association.

Subject coverage:
Constructional steelwork.

Publications list:
Available online and in print

Access to staff:
Contact by letter, by telephone, by fax and by e-
mail
Hours: Mon to Fri, 0900 to 1700

BRITISH CONTRACT FURNISHING ASSOCIATION

Acronym or abbreviation: BCFA

Project House, 25 West Wycombe Road, High Wycombe, Buckinghamshire, HP11 2LQ

Tel: 01494 896790
Fax: 01494 896779
E-mail: enquiries@bcfa.org.uk

Website:
http://www.bcfa.org.uk
Members benefits, list of members.

Enquiries:
Enquiries to: Chief Executive

Founded:
1970

Organisation type and purpose:
Trade association.

Subject coverage:
British manufactured goods and services for the contract furnishing sector.

Printed publications:
Contract Furnishing Magazine
Contract Furnishing Export Directory
Contract Furnishing Directory

Access to staff:
Contact by telephone, by fax, by e-mail and via website
Hours: Mon to Fri, 0900 to 1700

Access for disabled people:
Ramped entry

BRITISH COPYRIGHT COUNCIL

Acronym or abbreviation: BCC

29–33 Berners Street, London, W1T 3AB

Tel: 01986 788122
E-mail: secretary@britishcopyright.org

Website:
http://www.britishcopyright.org

Enquiries:
Enquiries to: Secretary

Organisation type and purpose:
Membership association (membership is by subscription), present number of members: 31.
Liaison committee.
Discussion forum for the Council's member associations on matters of common concern relating to copyright in literary, musical, dramatic and artistic works.

Subject coverage:
Copyright and rights in performances in the UK.

Access to staff:
Contact by letter and by e-mail

BRITISH CORRESPONDENCE CHESS ASSOCIATION

Acronym or abbreviation: BCCA

61 Swanswell Road, Solihull, West Midlands, B92 7ET

Tel: 0121 707 3850
E-mail: s.grayland@sky.com

Website:
http://www.bcca.info
Current activities and tournaments taking place within the association

Enquiries:
Enquiries to: General Secretary

Founded:
1906

Organisation type and purpose:
Membership association (membership is by subscription), present number of members: 250, voluntary organisation.

Subject coverage:
Postal chess, e-mail chess and chess in general.

Printed publications:
Correspondence Chess (quarterly)

Access to staff:
Contact by letter, by telephone, by e-mail and via website
Hours: Mon to Fri, 0900 to 1700

Links with:
British Federation for Correspondence Chess
tel: 01206 542753

BRITISH COUNCIL – INFORMATION CENTRE

Acronym or abbreviation: BC

Bridgewater House, 58 Whitworth Street, Manchester, M1 6BB

Tel: 0161 957 7755\ Minicom no. 0161 957 7188
Fax: 0161 957 7762
E-mail: general.enquiries@britishcouncil.org

Website:
http://www.britishcouncil.org
The work of the British Council in general.

Founded:
1934

Organisation type and purpose:
International organisation, service industry, registered charity (charity number 209131).
Non-government organisation.
Promoting art, cultural, and educational co-operation between Britain and other countries.

Subject coverage:
British education system, English language teaching and learning, higher education courses, English literature, visual arts, science and technology education, overseas development, work of the British Council overseas, environment, government, law and social development.

Museum or gallery collection, archive, or library special collection:
The unit holds small collections of leaflets, prospectuses, reports, etc. in its fields of interest, but it has no major holdings of books or runs of periodicals

Printed publications:
Address book of British Council offices overseas
Information sheets on studying and living in Britain
British Council Annual Report
English language courses and schools in UK (brochure)

Access to staff:
Contact by letter, by telephone, by fax, by e-mail and via website
Hours: Mon to Fri, 1000 to 1645

Access to building, collection or gallery:
No access other than to staff
Hours: Mon to Fri, 1000 to 1700

Funded by:
Foreign and Commonwealth Office

BRITISH COUNCIL – VISUAL ARTS DEPARTMENT

10 Spring Gardens, London, SW1A 2BN

Tel: 020 7389 3050
Fax: 020 7389 3101
E-mail: visual.arts@britishcouncil.org

Website:
http://www.britishcouncil.org/arts

Enquiries:
Enquiries to: Resources Officer
Other contacts: Research Officer for bibliographic enquiries.

Founded:
1934

Organisation type and purpose:
International organisation, national organisation, registered charity (charity number 209131).

To develop and enlarge overseas knowledge and appreciation of British achievements in the fields of contemporary visual art.

Subject coverage:
Painting, sculpture, printmaking, design, photography, crafts, architecture, video, installation, performance.

Museum or gallery collection, archive, or library special collection:
Art collection specialising in British Art, especially post-1945

Non-library collection catalogue:
All or part available online, in-house and in print

Library catalogue:
All or part available online and in-house

Printed publications:
Distributed by Cornerhouse, Manchester
Order printed publications from: Cornerhouse Publications
70 Oxford Street, Manchester, M1 5NH, tel: 0161 200 1503, fax: 0161 200 1504, e-mail: publications@ cornerhouse.org

Publications list:
Available online

Access to staff:
Appointment necessary.
Hours: Mon to Fri, 1000 to 1700
Special comments: Library: by appointment only.
Art Collection: online only.

Access to building, collection or gallery:
By appointment only
Hours: Mon to Fri, 1000 to 1700

BRITISH COUNCIL EDUCATION AND TRAINING GROUP

10 Spring Gardens, London, SW1A 2BN

Tel: 0161 957 7755
Fax: 0161 957 7762
E-mail: education.enquiries@britishcouncil.org

Website:
http://www.educationuk.org
Advice and information on studying in the UK.
http://www.globalgateway.org
Advice and information on international school linking, including an interactive database where schools can register and look for partners.
http://www.britishcouncil.org/montageworld
Global internet projects for education.
http://www.britishcouncil.org/learning
Information on the British Council's range of services in the area of education and training.

Enquiries:
Enquiries to: Information Officer
Other contacts: Director

Organisation type and purpose:
International organisation, registered charity (charity number 209131).
The British Council Education and Training Group promotes and enhances quality education and training in the UK and worldwide by strengthening education, training and youth co-operation between the UK and other countries; increasing international recognition of the range and quality of learning opportunities, including English language teaching, provided by the UK; supporting education and training reform; sharing creativity, innovation and best practice between the UK and other countries; delivering a range of quality programmes in international education, training, youth and sport.

Subject coverage:
For international students: information and advice on studying in the UK and on British courses, qualifications and examinations.
For the UK education and training field: information and advice on working internationally, setting up educational partnerships, international professional development and exchange opportunities, the promotion of UK education and training overseas.

continued overleaf

Access to staff:
Contact by letter, by telephone, by fax, by e-mail and via website
Hours: Mon to Fri, 1000 to 1645

Other addresses:
Belfast Office
  Norwich Union Building, 7 Fountain Street, Belfast, BT1 5EG; tel: 028 9024 8220; fax: 028 9023 7592
Cardiff Office
  28 Park Place, Cardiff, CF10 3QE; tel: 029 2039 7346; fax: 029 2023 7494
Edinburgh Office
  3rd Floor, The Tun, 4 Jackson's Entry, Holyrood Road, Edinburgh, EH8 8PJ; tel: 0131 524 5700; fax: 0131 524 5701
Manchester Office
  Bridgewater House, 58 Whitworth Street, Manchester, M1 6BB; tel: 0161 957 7755; fax: 0161 957 7762

Parent body:
British Council
  10 Spring Gardens, London, SW1A 2BN

BRITISH COUNCIL FOR OFFICES

Acronym or abbreviation: BCO

78–79 Leadenhall Street, London, EC3A 3DH

Tel: 020 7283 0125
Fax: 020 7626 1553
E-mail: mail@bco.org.uk

Website:
http://www.bco.org.uk

Enquiries:
Enquiries to: Chief Executive
Other contacts: Assistant Secretary

Founded:
1990

Organisation type and purpose:
Membership association (membership is by subscription), present number of members: 1,553. The British Council for Offices' mission is to research, develop and communicate best practice in all aspects of the office sector. It delivers this by providing a forum for the discussion and debate of relevant issues.

Printed publications:
Best Practice in the Specification for Offices
Good Practice in the Selection of Construction Materials
Management Guidance – Security
International Benchmarking
Annual Review
Members' Handbook (available to members only)
Order printed publications from: http://www.bco.org.uk/research

Publications list:
Available online

Access to staff:
Contact by letter, by telephone, by fax, by e-mail and via website. Appointment necessary.
Hours: Mon to Fri, 0930 to 1730

BRITISH COUNCIL OF CHINESE MARTIAL ARTS

c/o 110 Frensham Drive, Nuneaton, Warwickshire, CV10 9QL

Tel: 0906 302 1036
Fax: 024 7639 4642
E-mail: info@bccma.com

Website:
http://www.bccma.com

Enquiries:
Enquiries to: Secretary General

Organisation type and purpose:
Membership association (membership is by subscription, qualification).
Governing body of the sport.

Subject coverage:
Traditional Chinese martial arts, freestyle martial arts, Tai Chi and Chi Gung and Chinese boxing (Sanshou).

Access to staff:
Contact by letter, by telephone, by e-mail and via website
Hours: Mon to Fri, 1000 to 1600

Affiliated to:
European Wu Shu Federation
International Wu Shu Federation

Member of:
Sports Council

BRITISH COUNCIL OF DISABLED PEOPLE

Acronym or abbreviation: BCODP

Suites 1–2, Litchurch Plaza, Litchurch Lane, Derby, DE24 8AA

Tel: 01332 295551\ Minicom no. 01332 295581
Fax: 01332 295580
E-mail: bcodp@bcodp.org.uk

Website:
http://www.bcodp.org.uk

Enquiries:
Enquiries to: Chief Executive

Founded:
1981

Organisation type and purpose:
Registered charity.

Subject coverage:
Campaigning and lobbying, representing the interests of disabled people at national level and above; supporting new and existing organisations run by and for disabled people to represent their interests.

Printed publications:
Making Your Own Choices
Cashing in on Independence
From Local to National
Demolishing Special Needs
Everything You Need to Know About Getting & Using Direct Payments
The Way Forward – a BCODP Resource Pack
Users' Ability to Manage Direct Payments
Notes on the Disability Discrimination Act as at April 2000

Publications list:
Available in print

Access to staff:
Contact by letter, by telephone, by fax and by e-mail
Hours: Mon to Fri, 0900 to 1700

Access for disabled people:
Parking provided, ramped entry, access to all public areas, toilet facilities

BRITISH COUNCIL OF SHOPPING CENTRES

Acronym or abbreviation: BCSC

1 Queen Anne's Gate, Westminster, London, SW1H 9BT

Tel: 020 7222 1122
Fax: 020 7222 4440
E-mail: info@bcsc.org.uk

Website:
http://www.bcsc.org.uk

Enquiries:
Enquiries to: Head of Secretariat
Other contacts: Events Manager for BCSC Events.

Founded:
1984

Organisation type and purpose:
Membership association.

To provide a forum for all those involved in the development and management of shopping centres.

Subject coverage:
Matters relating to shopping centres.

Publications list:
Available in print

Access to staff:
Contact by letter, by telephone and by e-mail
Hours: Mon to Fri, 0900 to 1730

Access to building, collection or gallery:
No access other than to staff

BRITISH COUNTRY MUSIC ASSOCIATION

Acronym or abbreviation: BCMA

PO Box 240, Harrow, Middlesex, HA3 7PH

Tel: 01273 559750
Fax: 01273 559750
E-mail: jimars@globalnet.co.uk

Enquiries:
Enquiries to: Secretary

Founded:
1969

Organisation type and purpose:
Membership association.

Subject coverage:
Country music.

Printed publications:
BCMA Yearbook
Bulletin (6 times a year, members)

Access to staff:
Contact by letter, by telephone, by fax and by e-mail
Hours: Mon to Fri, 0900 to 1700

Access to building, collection or gallery:
No access other than to staff

BRITISH CROWN GREEN BOWLING ASSOCIATION

Acronym or abbreviation: BCGBA

94 Fishers Lane, Pensby, Wirral, Merseyside, CH61 8SB

Tel: 0151 648 5740
Fax: 0151 648 0733
E-mail: jac21up@aol.com

Website:
http://www.bowls.org

Enquiries:
Enquiries to: Chief Executive
Other contacts: Financial Officer

Founded:
1907

Organisation type and purpose:
Membership association.
Governing body of crown green bowls.

Subject coverage:
Crown green bowls; coaching; manufacture and maintenance of crown greens.

Printed publications:
Handbook (annually, £1.75)

Access to staff:
Contact by letter, by telephone and by fax
Hours: Mon to Fri, 0900 to 1700

BRITISH CUTLERY AND SILVERWARE ASSOCIATION

Acronym or abbreviation: BCSA

Unit 10 Edmund Road Business Centre, Sheffield, S2 4ED

Tel: 0114 252 7850

Fax: 0114 252 7855
E-mail: enquiries@secas.co.uk

Website:
http://www.secas.co.uk
Under construction.

Enquiries:
Enquiries to: Chief Executive

Organisation type and purpose:
Trade association.

Subject coverage:
Trade marks, patterns, care of cutlery and silverware, sources of supply.

Printed publications:
Buyers Guide
History of the Industry

BRITISH CYCLING FEDERATION

Acronym or abbreviation: BCF

National Cycling Centre, Stuart Street, Manchester, M11 4DQ

Tel: 0870 871 2000
Fax: 0870 871 2001
E-mail: info@britishcycling.org.uk

Website:
http://www.britishcycling.org.uk

Enquiries:
Enquiries to: Company Secretary
Direct tel: 0161 274 2038

Founded:
1959

Organisation type and purpose:
Membership association (membership is by subscription), present number of members: 20,000.
Promotional and governing body for the sport and pastime of cycling.

Subject coverage:
All forms of cycling, including cycle racing, coaching, touring, leisure cycling.

Printed publications:
BCF Quarterly Handbook 2002 (£10 annually)

Access to staff:
Contact by letter, by telephone, by fax, by e-mail, in person and via website. Non-members charged.
Hours: Mon to Thu, 0845 to 1700; Fri, 0845 to 1545

Access for disabled people:
Access to all public areas

BRITISH DANCE COUNCIL

Acronym or abbreviation: BDC

Terpsichore House, 240 Merton Road, South Wimbledon, London, SW19 1EQ

Tel: 020 8545 0085
Fax: 020 8545 0225
E-mail: secretary@british-dance-council.org

Website:
http://www.british-dance-council.org
Information about the BDC

Enquiries:
Enquiries to: Manager

Founded:
1929

Organisation type and purpose:
Membership association.
Official Board of Ballroom Dancing.
Promotion and regulation of ballroom dancing, dance sport and social dancing in Great Britain.

Subject coverage:
Ballroom dancing.

Printed publications:
Ballroom Dancing as a Career
Ballroom Dancing in Great Britain
Researching into Dance
Leaflets, include:

Charts, scripts and books
Let's Dance – fun, health, sports, making friends

Publications list:
Available in print

Access to staff:
Contact by letter, by telephone, by fax, by e-mail and via website. Appointment necessary.
Hours: Mon to Fri, 1000 to 1600

Corporate member:
Allied Dancing Association
71 Haileybury Road, Woolton, Liverpool, L25 8SN; tel: 0151 428 1312
British Association of Teachers of Dancing
23 Marywood Square, Glasgow, G41 2BP; tel: 0141 423 4029
Imperial Society of Teachers of Dancing
Imperial House, 22/26 Paul Street, London, EC2A 4QE; tel: 020 7377 1577; fax: 020 7247 8979
International Dance Teachers Association
International House, 76 Bennett Road, Brighton, BN2 5JL; tel: 01273 685652/3; fax: 01273 674388; e-mail: idta@fastnet.co.uk
National Association of Teachers of Dancing
44–47 The Broadway, Thatcham, Berkshire, RG19 3HP; tel: 01635 868888; fax: 01635 872301
National Resource Centre of Dance
University of Surrey, Guildford, Surrey, GU2 5HX; tel: 01483 259316
Northern Counties Dance Teachers' Association
67 Elizabeth Drive, Palmersville, Newcastle upon Tyne, NE12 9QP; tel: 0191 268 1830
Scottish Dance Teachers' Alliance
339 North Woodside Road, Glasgow, G20 6ND; tel: 0141 339 8944
United Kingdom Alliance
Centenary House, 30/40 Station Road, Blackpool, FY4 1EU; tel: 01253 408828; fax: 01253 408066

Member of:
World Dance and Dance Sport Council
at the same address; tel: 020 8545 0223; fax: 020 8544 9825

BRITISH DARTS ORGANISATION

Acronym or abbreviation: BDO

2 Pages Lane, Muswell Hill, London, N10 1PS

Tel: 020 8883 5544
Fax: 020 8883 0109
E-mail: britishdarts.org@btconnect.com

Website:
http://www.bdodarts.com

Enquiries:
Enquiries to: Director

Founded:
1973

Organisation type and purpose:
Membership association (membership is by subscription), voluntary organisation.
Incorporates 66 member county darts organisations in England, Scotland and Wales; plus associations with over 60 countries worldwide.
Promoters of darts.

Subject coverage:
Promotion and organisation of the sport of darts at all levels, i.e. local darts league, Inter County Championships and International and World Championships; rules and regulations governing the sport of darts (updated annually). Promoters of the BBC televised Lakeside World Professional Darts Championships and Winmau World Masters annually.

Printed publications:
Annual Yearbook and Darts Diary (published 1 September)
Current Playing Rules for the Sport of Darts

Access to staff:
Contact by letter
Hours: Mon to Fri, 0900 to 1700

Member of:
Central Council of Physical Recreation
World Darts Federation (WDF)

BRITISH DEAF ASSOCIATION

Acronym or abbreviation: BDA

1–3 Worship Street, London, EC2A 2AB

Tel: 0870 770 3300 (voice, national rate)\ 0800 6522965 (text, free)\ 020 7496 9539 (videophone)
Fax: 020 7588 3527
E-mail: helpline@bda.org.uk

Website:
http://www.bda.org.uk

Enquiries:
Enquiries to: Helpline Office

Founded:
1890

Organisation type and purpose:
Membership association, voluntary organisation, registered charity.
Membership-led charity campaigning on behalf of nearly 70,000 deaf people in Britain.
To advance and protect the interests of the Deaf Community, to increase deaf people's access to the facilities and lifestyles of hearing people, and to ensure a greater awareness of their rights and responsibilities as members of society.

Subject coverage:
Profound deafness; British sign language; deaf community, culture and heritage.

Printed publications:
Publication list available on website
British Deaf News (monthly)
Information Directory
Information pack

Publications list:
Available online

Access to staff:
Contact by letter, by telephone, by fax, by e-mail, in person and via website
Hours: Mon to Fri, 0900 to 1700
Textphone also available during evening hours.
Special comments: Voice and textphone also available for access.

Access for disabled people:
Level entry, toilet facilities

Has regional offices in:
Belfast, Cardiff, Edinburgh and Warrington

Representative organisation of UK on the:
European Union of the Deaf
World Federation of the Deaf (affiliated to the United Nations)

BRITISH DEAF HISTORY SOCIETY

Acronym or abbreviation: BDHS

11–13 Wilson Patten Road, Warrington, Cheshire, WA1 1PG

Tel: 01925 632463
Fax: 01606 593142
E-mail: info.bdhs@btconnect.com

Website:
http://www.bdhs.org.uk

Organisation type and purpose:
Membership organisation focusing on history related to deafness.

Subject coverage:
History related to deafness.

BRITISH DEAF SPORTS COUNCIL

Acronym or abbreviation: BDSC

Bridge Street, Otley, West Yorkshire, LS21 1B

Tel: 01943 850214 / Minicom: 01943 850081
Fax: 01943 850828
E-mail: enquiries@britishdeafsportscouncil.org.uk

Website:
http://www.britishdeafsportscouncil.org.uk/

continued overleaf

Enquiries:
Enquiries to: Administrator

Founded:
1930

Organisation type and purpose:
Membership association (membership is by subscription), registered charity (charity number 1014541).

Subject coverage:
Sports for hearing impaired people.

Access to staff:
Contact by letter, by telephone and by fax
Hours: Mon to Thu, 0930 to 1330 and 1430 to 1730; Fri, 0930 to 1330 and 1430 to 1700
Special comments: Stamped addressed envelope preferred.

BRITISH DEER FARMERS ASSOCIATION

Acronym or abbreviation: BDFA

Old Stoddah, Penruddock, Penrith, Cumbria, CA11 0RY

Tel: 01768 483810
Fax: 01768 483809
E-mail: bdfa@old-stoddah.demon.co.uk

Website:
http://www.deer.org.uk

Enquiries:
Enquiries to: Secretary

Organisation type and purpose:
National organisation, trade association (membership is by subscription).
National association representing deer farmers and venison processors.

Subject coverage:
Deer farming; farmed venison.

Printed publications:
Deer Farming (journal, quarterly by subscription direct from BDFA)

Access to staff:
Contact by e-mail and via website
Hours: Mon to Fri, 0900 to 1700

BRITISH DENTAL ASSOCIATION

Acronym or abbreviation: BDA

64 Wimpole Street, London, W1G 8YS

Tel: 020 7563 4545
Fax: 020 7935 6492
E-mail: r.farbey@bda.org

Website:
http://www.bda.org

Enquiries:
Enquiries to: Librarian
Other contacts: Head of Library Services

Founded:
1880

Organisation type and purpose:
National organisation, professional body (membership is by subscription).

Subject coverage:
Dentistry and the dental profession.

Museum or gallery collection, archive, or library special collection:
Rare historical dental texts
DVD and video collection

Printed publications:
British Dental Journal (2 times a month)
Occasional publications
BDA News

Access to staff:
Contact by letter. Appointment necessary. Letter of introduction required.
Hours: Mon to Fri, 0900 to 1800

Access to building, collection or gallery:
Prior appointment required for non-members, except to museum
Hours: Mon to Fri, 0900 to 1800

BRITISH DENTAL HEALTH FOUNDATION

Acronym or abbreviation: BDHF

Smile House, 2 East Union Street, Rugby, Warwickshire, CV22 6AJ

Tel: 0870 770 4000
Fax: 0870 770 4010
E-mail: feedback@dentalhealth.org.uk

Website:
http://www.dentalhealth.org.uk
Dental health advice, press releases, on-line shopping.
http://www.dentalhelpline.org
Public enquiry service, individual response to personal enquiries on dental issues.

Enquiries:
Enquiries to: Public Relations Department
Direct tel: 0870 770 4014
Direct e-mail: pr@dentalhealth.org.uk

Founded:
1971

Organisation type and purpose:
International organisation (membership is by subscription, election or invitation), present number of members: 1400, voluntary organisation, registered charity (charity number 263198).
To promote dental health to the public.

Subject coverage:
Free, impartial and independent advice on dental health for the public and the media.

Library catalogue:
All or part available online and in print

Printed publications:
Annual Report
Foundation Focus (members newsletter)
Word of Mouth Yearbook (for health professionals)
Patient information leaflets (for the general public)

Electronic and video publications:
Do I Have to Go to the Dentist? (audio book)
Happy & Gappy (audio tape)
Just Five Minutes a Day (video)
Everything you always wanted to know about mouth cancer, but were afraid to ask (CD-ROM)
Other titles cover tooth whitening, implants and bad breath (CD-ROM)

Publications list:
Available online and in print

Access to staff:
Contact by letter, by telephone, by fax and by e-mail
Hours: Mon to Fri, 0900 to 1700

BRITISH DISABLED WATER SKI ASSOCIATION

Acronym or abbreviation: BDWSA

The Tony Edge National Centre, Heron Lake, Hythe End, Wraysbury, Middlesex, TW19 6HW

Tel: 01784 483664
Fax: 01784 482747
E-mail: southern@bdwsa.org

Website:
http://www.bdwsa.org

Enquiries:
Enquiries to: Honorary Secretary
Other contacts: Chairman

Founded:
1979

Organisation type and purpose:
Membership association (membership is by subscription), present number of members: 200, registered charity (charity number 1063678).

Teaching disabled people to water ski.

Subject coverage:
Tuition and equipment for disabled water skiers.

Printed publications:
Brochures

Publications list:
Available in print

Access to staff:
Contact by letter, by telephone, by fax, by e-mail, in person and via website
Hours: Mon to Fri, 0900 to 1700

Access for disabled people:
Parking provided, level entry, access to all public areas, toilet facilities

Parent body:
British Water Ski Federation
390 City Road, London, EC1V 2QA; tel: 020 7833 2856

BRITISH DRAGON BOAT RACING ASSOCIATION

Acronym or abbreviation: BDA

13 The Prebend, Northend, Southam, Warwickshire, CV47 2TR

Tel: 01295 770734
Fax: 01295 770734
E-mail: dacogswell@aol.com

Website:
http://www.dragonboat.com

Enquiries:
Enquiries to: Company Secretary and Treasurer

Founded:
1987

Organisation type and purpose:
National government body, membership association (membership is by subscription), present number of members: 867, voluntary organisation.
Governing body of the sport.

Subject coverage:
The BDA in general, dragon boat racing, boats, sponsoring of dragon boat racing, dragon boat purchase and specification, dragon boat events.

Printed publications:
BDA Handbook
BDA Magazine
Calendar of events
Various leaflets on specific subjects

Access to staff:
Contact by letter, by telephone, by fax, by e-mail and via website
Hours: Mon to Fri, 0900 to 2100

Access to building, collection or gallery:
Prior appointment required

Parent body:
International Dragon Boat Federation
HKTA , 35th Floor, Jardine House, Central, Hong Kong

Subsidiary body:
Dragon Boats UK

BRITISH DRILLING ASSOCIATION LIMITED

Acronym or abbreviation: BDA

Wayside, 55 London End, Upper Boddington, Daventry, Northamptonshire, NN11 6DP

Tel: 01327 264622
Fax: 01327 264623
E-mail: info@britishdrillingassociation.co.uk

Website:
http://www.britishdrillingassociation.co.uk

Enquiries:
Enquiries to: Executive Secretary

Founded:
1975

Organisation type and purpose:
Professional body, trade association.

Subject coverage:
Ground drilling, including ground investigation, ground improvement, water well drilling, mining and quarrying, mineral exploration and some aspects of tunnelling.

Printed publications:
Newsletter (6 times a year)

Access to staff:
Contact by letter, by telephone, by fax, by e-mail and via website
Hours: Mon to Fri, 0900 to 1700

BRITISH DRIVING SOCIETY

Acronym or abbreviation: BDS

83 New Road, Helmingham, Stowmarket, Suffolk, IP14 6EA

Tel: 01473 892001
Fax: 01473 892005
E-mail: email@britishdrivingsociety.co.uk

Website:
http://www.britishdrivingsociety.co.uk
Various

Enquiries:
Enquiries to: Executive Secretary

Founded:
1957

Organisation type and purpose:
Membership association (membership is by subscription), present number of members: 6000, voluntary organisation.
To encourage and assist those interested in the driving of horses and ponies.

Subject coverage:
Driving of horses and ponies.

Printed publications:
Annual book of driving shows/trials/competitions (for members)
Annual journal (for members)
Book List
Newsletter (quarterly, for members)

Publications list:
Available online and in print

Access to staff:
Contact by letter, by telephone, by fax, by e-mail and via website
Hours: Mon to Fri, 0900 to 1700

Affiliated to:
Joint National Horse Education and Training Council

BRITISH DYSLEXIA ASSOCIATION

Acronym or abbreviation: BDA

Unit 8, Bracknell Beeches, Old Bracknell Lane, Bracknell, RG12 7BW

Tel: 0845 251 9002 (helpline); 0845 251 9003 (office)
Fax: 0845 215 9005
E-mail: helpline@bdadyslexia.org.uk

Website:
http://www.bdadyslexia.org.uk

Founded:
1960

Organisation type and purpose:
Membership association, voluntary organisation, registered charity (charity number 289243), training organisation.
Co-ordinates 120 independent local associations.

Subject coverage:
Dyslexia; education and training for the young, adults and professionals in education, health and employment, medical and psychological

information. The charity offers advice, information and help to dyslexic people, their families and the professionals who support them, and works to raise awareness and understanding and to effect change.

Printed publications:
Achieving Dyslexia-Friendly Schools (available as a download)
Code of Practice for Employers
Conference proceedings (every 2 or 3 years)
Dyslexia – An International Journal of Research and Practice
Dyslexia Contact (magazine, 3 times a year)
Dyslexia Handbook

Publications list:
Available online and in print

Access to staff:
Contact by letter, by telephone, by fax, by e-mail and via website
Hours: Mon to Fri, 1000 to 1600; Wed, 1700 to 1900

Member organisations:
local dyslexia associations and corporate members

BRITISH EARTH SHELTERING ASSOCIATION

Acronym or abbreviation: BESA

15 Maes-y-Fron Terrace, Abercrave, Swansea Valley, SA9 1XE

Tel: 01639 730006
E-mail: caerllan@compuserve.com, undergroundwoods@hotmail.co.uk

Enquiries:
Enquiries to: Honorary Secretary

Founded:
1981

Organisation type and purpose:
Membership association.

Subject coverage:
Design and construction of earth sheltering structures, energy efficiency and architecture.

Printed publications:
Newsletter (3–4 times a year, £2 non-members, free to members)

Access to staff:
Contact by letter, by telephone, by fax, by e-mail and via website. Appointment necessary.
Hours: Mon to Fri, 0900 to 1700

BRITISH ECOLOGICAL SOCIETY

Acronym or abbreviation: BES

26 Blades Court, Putney, London, SW15 2NU

Tel: 020 8871 9797
Fax: 020 8871 9779
E-mail: info@BritishEcologicalSociety.org

Website:
http://www.BritishEcologicalSociety.org
Details of the society's activities.

Enquiries:
Enquiries to: Executive Secretary

Founded:
1913

Organisation type and purpose:
Learned society.
To promote the science of ecology through research, and to use the findings of such research to educate the public and influence policy decisions which involve ecological matters.

Subject coverage:
Ecology, as a branch of natural science.

Printed publications:
Ecological Issues Booklets (1 or 2 each year)
Journal of Animal Ecology (6 times a year)
Journal of Applied Ecology (6 times a year)
Journal of Ecology (6 times a year)
Journal of Functional Ecology (6 times a year)

Symposium volumes

Publications list:
Available in print

BRITISH EDITORIAL SOCIETY OF BONE AND JOINT SURGERY

Acronym or abbreviation: BESBJS

22 Buckingham Street, London, WC2N 6ET

Tel: 020 7782 0010
Fax: 020 7782 0995
E-mail: info@jbjs.org.uk

Website:
http://www.jbjs.org.uk
Information about all publications and content hosted online.

Enquiries:
Enquiries to: The General Manager
Other contacts: Circulation Manager for ordering subscriptions.

Founded:
1948

Organisation type and purpose:
Registered charity (charity number 209299), publishing house.
The advancement and improvement of education in orthopaedic surgery and allied branches of surgery.

Subject coverage:
Bone and joint surgery.

Museum or gallery collection, archive, or library special collection:
Watson-Jones Library Bequest

Non-library collection catalogue:
All or part available online

Library catalogue:
All or part available in-house

Printed publications:
Journal of Bone and Joint Surgery
The History of the ABC Club of Travelling Fellows

Microform publications:
Journal of Bone and Joint Surgery

Electronic and video publications:
Journal of Bone and Joint Surgery

Publications list:
Available online and in print

Access to staff:
Contact by letter, by telephone, by fax, by e-mail and via website. Appointment necessary.
Hours: Mon to Fri, 0900 to 1700

Access to building, collection or gallery:
Prior appointment required

BRITISH EDUCATIONAL SUPPLIERS ASSOCIATION LIMITED

Acronym or abbreviation: BESA

20 Beaufort Court, Admirals Way, London, E14 9XL

Tel: 020 7537 4997
Fax: 020 7537 4846
E-mail: besa@besa.org.uk

Website:
http://www.besa.org.uk

Enquiries:
Enquiries to: Information Manager / Research Assistant

Founded:
1933

Organisation type and purpose:
Trade association.

continued overleaf

Subject coverage:
Educational equipment and materials, home and export.

Printed publications:
Annual Report
BESA Book – UK Education and Training: The directory of products and Suppliers (annual, free on request)
Memorandum and Articles of Association
Promotional literature (all free on request):
ETEMA Brochure
ESPA Brochure
eIC Factfile
UK Show Brochures
BETT
The Education Show
Education Show London
Special Needs London
Specialist Schools Trust National Conference Exhibition
BESA International Conference
ICT in UK State Schools 2003 (full report, members free, non-members £250)
ICT in UK State Schools 2003 (summary report, free)
ICT in UK Schools 2002 Full report (Jan 2003, members free, non-members £250)
English Schools Budgets 2003–04 (released May 2003, members free, non-members £250)
Early Years Resourcing report (released April 2003, members free, non-members £250)
Resources in English Schools – Full Report 2004 (released April 2004, members free, non-members £250)
Resources in English Schools – Summary Report 2004 (released February 2004, free)
Resources in English Schools – Full Report (April 2003, members free, non-members £250)
Resources in English Schools – Summary report (first published February 2003, free)
BESA CD Rom – available to overseas enquirers
Single-issue reports on a variety of subjects, such as the Licensing Survey Report commissioned by ESPA
BESA Licensing Survey Report 2000
A variety of BESA commissioned foreign market reports

Electronic and video publications:
BESA CD Rom (available to overeseas enquirers / potential trade partners) BESA Members directory (online) UK Education and Training: The directory of products and Suppliers
UK Show Brochures – BETT
The Education Show

Access to staff:
Contact by letter, by telephone, by fax, by e-mail and via website
Hours: Mon to Fri, 0900 to 1700

Special interest group the:
British Educational Distributors and Contractors Group
British Educational Furniture Manufacturers Group
Educational Software Publishers Association

BRITISH ELASTIC ROPE SPORTS ASSOCIATION

Acronym or abbreviation: BERSA

33a Canal Street, Oxford, OX2 6BQ

Tel: 01865 311179
Fax: 01865 426007
E-mail: info@bersa.org

Website:
http://www.bersa.org

Enquiries:
Enquiries to: Chairman

Founded:
1989

Organisation type and purpose:
Professional body.

National governing body for the safety and regulation of bungee jumping and other sports involving elastic ropes.

Subject coverage:
General and specialist information on current clubs and their locations, history of the sport and of the Association, recognised equipment and its safe use. Training of operatives within clubs, insurance and accident investigation, inspection of sites, risk assessment and product development to BERSA Certification Mark standard.

Printed publications:
The BERSA Code of Safe Practice (£42)

Access to staff:
Contact by letter, by telephone, by fax and by e-mail. Appointment necessary.
Hours: Mon to Fri, 0900 to 1700
Special comments: Charges made for some services.

BRITISH ELECTROTECHNICAL COMMITTEE

Acronym or abbreviation: BEC

389 Chiswick High Road, London, W4 4AJ

Tel: 020 8996 7458
Fax: 020 8996 7460
E-mail: mike.graham@bsi-global.com

Website:
http://www.bsi-global.com

Enquiries:
Enquiries to: Secretary

Founded:
1908

Organisation type and purpose:
Advisory body.
Represents the UK in European and International Electrotechnical bodies.

Subject coverage:
International and European Electrotechnical Standardization and its relationship with British Standards.

Museum or gallery collection, archive, or library special collection:
Full Collection of British, European and International Standards

Library catalogue:
All or part available in-house

Printed publications:
Order printed publications from: Customer Services, BSI
at the same address

Microform publications:
Order microform publications from: Technical Indexes Ltd
Willoughby Road, Bracknell, Berkshire, RG12 4DW

Publications list:
Available online and in print

Access to staff:
Contact by letter, by telephone, by fax and by e-mail
Hours: Mon to Fri, 0900 to 1700

Access to building, collection or gallery:
Prior appointment required

Access for disabled people:
Parking provided, ramped entry, level entry, access to all public areas, toilet facilities

Links with:
BSI
at the same address

BRITISH ENERGY

Barnett Way, Barnwood, Gloucester, GL4 3RS

Tel: 01452 652769
Fax: 01452 654163

Website:
http://www.british-energy.co.uk
General information about the company including details of power stations. Graduate positions also noted.

Enquiries:
Enquiries to: Corporate Librarian

Organisation type and purpose:
Electricity generator.

Subject coverage:
Nuclear engineering, electrical engineering, heat transfer, physics and mechanical engineering, health and safety, management.

Access to staff:
Appointment necessary.
Hours: Mon to Thu, 0900 to 1700; Fri, 0900 to 1600

BRITISH ENERGY PLC

Acronym or abbreviation: BE

Corporate Library, British Energy, Barnett Way, Barnwood, Gloucester, GL4 3RS

Tel: 01452 652222
Fax: 01452 654163

Website:
http://www.british-energy.com

Enquiries:
Enquiries to: Library and Information Officer
Direct tel: 01452 652769; 01452 653660
Direct e-mail: bwd.library@british-energy.com

Founded:
1996

Organisation type and purpose:
Service industry.
Electricity generator.

Subject coverage:
Power generation; nuclear technology; electricity supply industry.

Library catalogue:
All or part available in-house

Access to staff:
Contact by telephone and by e-mail. Appointment necessary.
Hours: Mon to Fri, 0900 to 1600

Access to building, collection or gallery:
Prior appointment required

BRITISH ENGINEERS' CUTTING TOOLS ASSOCIATION

Acronym or abbreviation: BECTA

c/o Institute of Spring Technology, Henry Street, Sheffield, S3 7EQ

Tel: 0114 278 9143

Enquiries:
Enquiries to: Secretary

Organisation type and purpose:
Trade association.

Subject coverage:
Cutting tools manufactured from high-speed steel.

Access to staff:
Contact by letter, by telephone, by fax and by e-mail
Hours: Mon to Fri, 0900 to 1700

Affiliated to:
Federation of British Engineers' Tool Manufacturers

BRITISH EQUESTRIAN FEDERATION

Acronym or abbreviation: BEF

National Agricultural Centre, Stoneleigh, Kenilworth, Warwickshire, CV8 2RH

Tel: 024 7669 8871
Fax: 024 7669 6484
E-mail: info@bef.co.uk

Website:
http://www.bef.co.uk
General information on the work of the BEF, international competitions in the UK and articles of equestrian interest.

Enquiries:
Enquiries to: Chief Executive

Organisation type and purpose:
International organisation, national government body, advisory body, membership association (membership is by election or invitation). Represents the sport on the National Olympic Committee of the British Olympic Association.

Subject coverage:
BEF provides knowledge regarding international equestrian matters concerning competition, rules and regulations. Member disciplines provide specialist discipline knowledge.

Access to staff:
Contact by letter, by telephone, by fax, by e-mail and via website. Appointment necessary.
Hours: Mon to Fri, 0900 to 1700

Access to building, collection or gallery:
Prior appointment required

Access for disabled people:
Level entry

Member disciplines:
Association of British Riding Schools (ABRS)
    tel: 01736 369440; fax: 01736 351390; e-mail: office@abrs.org
British Dressage Limited
    tel: 024 7669 8843; e-mail: name.surname@ britishdressage.co.uk
British Equestrian Trade Association (BETA)
    tel: 01937 587062; fax: 01937 582728; e-mail: clairewilliams@beta-uk.org
British Equestrian Vaulting Limited
    tel: 0976 421789; fax: 01203 463027; e-mail: julievaulting@hotmail.com
British Eventing
    tel: 024 7669 8856; e-mail: name.surname@ britisheventing.com
British Horse Driving Trials Association
    tel: 01347 878789; e-mail: BHDTA@dial.pipex .com
British Horse Society
    tel: 01926 707700; fax: 01926 707800
British Reining Horse Association (BRHA)
    tel: 01342 892203; fax: 01342 893441
British Show Jumping Association
    tel: 024 7669 8800; e-mail: nameinitial@bsja.co.uk
Endurance GB
    tel: 024 7669 8863
Pony Club
    tel: 024 7669 8300; fax: 024 7669 6386; e-mail: name@pcuk.org
Scottish Equestrian Association (SEA)
    tel: 01475 540687; fax: 01475 540348; e-mail: patsypup@aol.com

BRITISH EQUESTRIAN TRADE ASSOCIATION

Acronym or abbreviation: BETA

East Wing, Stockeld Park, Wetherby, West Yorkshire, LS22 4AW

Tel: 01937 587062
Fax: 01937 582728
E-mail: info@beta-uk.org

Enquiries:
Enquiries to: Secretary
Direct e-mail: tinar@beta-int.com

Founded:
1977

Organisation type and purpose:
Trade association.

Subject coverage:
Equestrian business and trade, including saddlery, pharmaceutical products, breeding, feedstuffs, transport, stalling, exporting, importing and other related matters.

Information services:
BETA International Trade Fair

Printed publications:
British Equestrian Directory and Trade Supplement
Equestrian Trade News (monthly)
Newsletter

Access to staff:
Contact by letter, by telephone, by fax and by e-mail
Hours: Mon to Fri, 0900 to 1700

Links with:
EMC Limited, publishers

Subsidiary body:
BETA Trade Fairs

BRITISH ESSENCE MANUFACTURERS ASSOCIATION

Acronym or abbreviation: BEMA

PO Box 172, Cranleigh, GU6 8WU, England

Tel: 01483 275411
E-mail: secretariat@bemaorg.org

Website:
http://www.bemaorg.org

Enquiries:
Enquiries to: Secretary

Founded:
1917

Organisation type and purpose:
Trade association.

Subject coverage:
Food and drink flavourings, UK, EEC and global legislation.

Access to staff:
Contact by letter and by e-mail
Hours: Mon to Fri, 0900 to 1700

Links with:
British Fragrance Association
Food and Drink Federation

BRITISH EXPERTISE

1 Westminster Palace Gardens, 1–7 Artillery Row, London, SW1P 1RJ

Tel: 020 7222 3651
Fax: 020 7222 3664
E-mail: mail@britishexpertise.org

Website:
http://www.britishexpertise.org/

Enquiries:
Enquiries to: Executive Director

Founded:
1965

Formerly called:
BCCB (British Consultants & Construction Bureau)

Organisation type and purpose:
Trade association.
Bureau of multi-disciplined consultants. Primary information source on business prospects worldwide.
Promotion of British Consultancy of all disciplines worldwide.

Subject coverage:
Overseas projects and British Consultancy expertise in all disciplines and specialisations; engineers, architects, planners, management and economics, surveyors, agriculture, mining, healthcare, education and training, environment, tourism, security, legal, banking, catering, energy, transportation, leisure, IT, maritime, water engineering, fire, telecommunications, corrosion, acoustics, chemical, contractors and construction.

Trade and statistical information:
Knowledge of all countries and multi lateral funding agencies.

Printed publications:
BCCB Directory (every two years)
Mission reports

Electronic and video publications:
BCCB Directory 2005–2006 (CD-ROM)

Access to staff:
Contact by letter, by telephone, by fax, by e-mail and via website. Appointment necessary. Access for members only.
Hours: Mon to Fri, 0915 to 1715

BRITISH EXPORTERS ASSOCIATION

Acronym or abbreviation: BExA

Broadway House, Tothill Street, Westminster, London, SW1H 9NQ

Tel: 020 7222 5419
Fax: 020 7799 2468
E-mail: hughbailey@bexa.co.uk

Website:
http://www.bexa.co.uk

Enquiries:
Enquiries to: Director

Founded:
1940

Organisation type and purpose:
Trade association.
Lobby organisation.

Subject coverage:
Exporting.

BRITISH FALCONERS' CLUB

Acronym or abbreviation: BFC

Westfield, Meeting Hill, Worstead, North Walsham, Norfolk, NR28 9LS

Tel: 01692 404057
Fax: 01692 404057
E-mail: admin@britishfalconersclub.co.uk

Website:
http://www.britishfalconersclub.co.uk

Enquiries:
Enquiries to: Director
Other contacts: Public Relations Officer for publicity and press releases.

Founded:
1927

Organisation type and purpose:
Membership association (membership is by subscription), present number of members: 1,266.

Subject coverage:
Promotion of falconry in the British Isles and promotion of captive breeding for birds of prey.

Museum or gallery collection, archive, or library special collection:
The Alexander Library, Oxford University Zoological Department Library
The A. K. Bell Library, Perth

Printed publications:
Journal (annually, free to members)
Newsletter (2 times a year, free to members)

Access to staff:
Contact by letter, by telephone, by fax, by e-mail and via website
Hours: Mon to Fri, 0900 to 1300

Access to building, collection or gallery:
No access other than to staff

Branches:
11 regional clubs in the United Kingdom, and overseas members

continued overleaf

Member organisation of:
Countryside Alliance
Federation of Field Sports Associations of the EEC
(FACE)
International Association of Falconry and
Conservation of Birds of Prey (IAF)
Standing Conference on Countryside Sports
(SCCS)

BRITISH FASHION COUNCIL

Acronym or abbreviation: BFC

5 Portland Place, London, W1B 1PW

Tel: 020 7636 7788
Fax: 020 7636 7515

Website:
http://www.britishfashioncouncil.com
http://www.londonfashionweek.co.uk

Enquiries:
Enquiries to: Administrator

Organisation type and purpose:
Trade association.

Subject coverage:
Fashion; fashion exhibitions and London Fashion
Week.

Printed publications:
UK Fashion Exhibition Calendar

BRITISH FEDERATION OF BRASS BANDS

Acronym or abbreviation: BFBB

Unit 12, Maple Estate, Stocks Lane, Barnsley, South
Yorkshire, S75 2BL

Tel: 01226 771015
Fax: 01226 732630
E-mail: natoffice@bfbb.co.uk

Website:
http://www.bfbb.co.uk/
General information and contact points of the
Federation.

Enquiries:
Enquiries to: Membership Secretary
Direct tel: 01226 711316

Founded:
1968

Organisation type and purpose:
Membership association (membership is by
subscription), present number of members: 310,
registered charity (charity number BFBB 1065181;
BBHT 1037552).
National umbrella body.
Working for all brass bands in the UK.

Subject coverage:
Amateur brass band movement in the UK.

**Museum or gallery collection, archive, or library
special collection:**
Brass Band Music Library

Non-library collection catalogue:
All or part available in-house

Library catalogue:
All or part available in-house

Printed publications:
Directory of British Brass Bands (annually, for
purchase by non-members)

Publications list:
Available online and in print

Access to staff:
Contact by letter, by telephone, by fax, by e-mail,
in person and via website
Hours: Mon to Fri, 0900 to 1700

Other address:
British Federation of Brass Bands (BFBB)
122 Main Street, Bingley, BD16 2HL; tel: 01274
511280; fax: 01274 511281

BRITISH FEDERATION OF WOMEN GRADUATES

Acronym or abbreviation: BFWG

4 Mandeville Courtyard, 142 Battersea Park Road,
London, SW11 4NB

Tel: 020 7498 8037
Fax: 020 7498 5213
E-mail: hq@bfwg.demon.co.uk

Website:
http://www.bfwg.org.uk
Scholarships and social events.

Enquiries:
Enquiries to: Executive Secretary
Other contacts: President

Founded:
1907

Organisation type and purpose:
International organisation, membership
association (membership is by subscription),
present number of members: 1500 in UK (excl.
Northern Ireland); 180,000 Worldwide, voluntary
organisation, registered charity (charity number
273043).
BFWG is a non-profit, international non-
governmental organisation working locally,
nationally and globally to improve the status of
women and girls, to promote lifelong education,
and to enable graduate women to use their
expertise to effect change.

Subject coverage:
National pre-doctoral research scholarships for
women entering their final year towards a PhD
degree, lobbying of government, EU, UN;
educational exchange plus international
fellowships for members of IFUW.

**Museum or gallery collection, archive, or library
special collection:**
Archives held in The Women's Library, Old Castle
Street, London E1 7NT

Printed publications:
BFWG News (5 times a year, free to members)

Access to staff:
Contact by letter, by telephone, by fax, by e-mail
and via website. Appointment necessary.
Hours: Mon to Fri, 0945 to 1545
Special comments: Reference library at BFWG
Charitable Foundation.

Access to building, collection or gallery:
Prior appointment required

Other branches:
Approximately 40 Associations in Great Britain in
different locations

Other offices in:
70 Countries

Parent body:
International Federation of University Women
10 Rue de Lac, Geneva, CH-1207; tel: 00 41 22
731 2380; fax: 00 41 22 738 0440; e-mail: ifuw@
ifuw.org; website: http://www.ifuw.org

Subsidiary:
British Federation of Women Graduates Charitable
Foundation (BFWG (CF))
28 Great James Street, London, WC1N 3ES; tel:
020 7404 6447; fax: 020 7404 6505; e-mail: bfwg
.charity@btinternet.com

BRITISH FILM INSTITUTE – NATIONAL FILM ARCHIVE

Formal name: British Film Institute
Acronym or abbreviation: NFTVA

Curatorial Unit, 21 Stephen Street, London, W1P
1LN

Tel: 020 7255 1444
Fax: 020 7580 7503
E-mail: information.unit@bfi.org.uk

Website:
http://www.bfi.org.uk/collections/catalogues

http://www.bfi.org.uk
General information on the bfi Collections.

Founded:
1935

Organisation type and purpose:
National government body.
Cultural Organisation.

Subject coverage:
Art and history of the cinema and of television, the
documentary record of the 20th century. Films,
video and TV programmes produced, shown,
distributed or transmitted in the UK; preservation
and restoration; cataloguing of film and TV
material.

**Museum or gallery collection, archive, or library
special collection:**
The Archive holds approximately 450,000 titles
dating from 1895 to the present day
The Collection comprises features and short films,
animation, documentaries, newsreels, television
programmes, amateur films and videos

Non-library collection catalogue:
All or part available online and in-house

Printed publications:
See bfi website

Access to staff:
Contact by letter, by telephone, by fax, by e-mail
and in person
Hours: Mon to Fri, 1000 to 1730

Access to building, collection or gallery:
Appointment required

BFI – Imax Cinema:
1 Charlie Chaplin Walk, South Bank, Waterloo,
London, SE1 8XR; tel: 020 7902 1234

Founder member of:
International Federation of Film Archives

BRITISH FILM INSTITUTE – NATIONAL LIBRARY

Acronym or abbreviation: BFI

21 Stephen Street, London, W1T 1LN

Tel: 020 7255 1444
Fax: 020 7436 2338
E-mail: library@bfi.org.uk

Website:
http://www.bfi.org.uk/library

Enquiries:
Enquiries to: Information Officer
Direct fax: 020 7436 0165
Other contacts: Curator of Special Collections for
access to special collections

Founded:
1933

Organisation type and purpose:
National organisation, registered charity.
Grant-aided education/cultural body.
To enable everyone to experience, enjoy and
discover more about the world of film and
television.

Subject coverage:
All aspects of world cinema; UK broadcast
television, with some restrictions.

**Museum or gallery collection, archive, or library
special collection:**
Rare and old books on cinema and pre-cinema
The following are accessed via the library:
Collections, over 200, donated by organisations
associated with film and TV
Newspaper cuttings (over 1.5m. dating back to
1930s)
Includes the former ITC (Independent Television
Commission) Library collection
Periodicals collection (believed to be largest of its
kind in the world)
Published and unpublished scripts (over 20,000)

Trade and statistical information:
Film production statistics, television viewing figures.

Non-library collection catalogue:
All or part available online and in-house

Library catalogue:
All or part available online and in-house

Printed publications:
see website for details
Order printed publications from: Some items from BFI only

Microform publications:
Order microform publications from: Cinema Pressbooks 1920–40 (via Proquest Chadwyck-Healey)
Film Weekly
Picturegoer (via Proquest Chadwyck-Healey)

Electronic and video publications:
Order electronic and video publications from: Film Index International (via Proquest Chadwyck-Healey)

Publications list:
Available online and in print

Access to staff:
Contact by letter, by telephone, by fax, by e-mail, in person and via website. Non-members charged.

Access to building, collection or gallery:
No prior appointment required
Hours: Reading room: Mon and Fri, 1030 to 1730; Tue and Thu, 1030 to 2000; Wed, 1300 to 2000; closed Sat and Sun; information line: Mon to Fri, 1000 to 1200 and 1500 to 1700; special collections by appointment.
Special comments: Special collections; users required to be annual-pass holders. Charges made to some users.
Visitors travelling from a great distance recommended to reserve place.

Access for disabled people:
Level entry, toilet facilities

Constituent bodies:
Collections and Information: National Film and Television Archive

BRITISH FIRE ADVISORY SERVICES LIMITED

3 Otterbourne Place, Willington, Maidstone, Kent, ME15 8JL

Tel: 01622 755365
Fax: 01622 755365
E-mail: bfas@zoom.co.uk

Enquiries:
Enquiries to: Director
Other contacts: Senior Consultant

Founded:
2000

Organisation type and purpose:
Consultancy.
A non-political organisation not funded by public money.

Subject coverage:
Fire risk assessment; advice on all fire safety-related legislation; fire fighting procedures; means of escape from fire for disabled persons.

Access to staff:
Contact by letter, by telephone, by fax and by e-mail. Appointment necessary. All charged.
Hours: Mon to Fri, 0900 to 1700

BRITISH FIRE PROTECTION SYSTEMS ASSOCIATION LIMITED

Acronym or abbreviation: BFPSA

Neville House, 55 Eden Street, Kingston Upon Thames, Surrey, KT1 1BW

Tel: 020 8549 5855

Fax: 020 8547 1564

Website:
http://www.bfpsa.org.uk
Members products and services, Association information.

Enquiries:
Enquiries to: General Manager
Other contacts: Technical Manager, Marketing Manager

Founded:
1966

Organisation type and purpose:
Trade association.

Subject coverage:
Automatic fire detection; manual alarm systems; fire warning; fixed fire extinguishing systems; chemical extinguishing systems; fire fighting equipment.

Printed publications:
Annual Review
BFPSA Manual (for sale)
List of Members
Code of Practice for Category 1 Aspirating Detection Systems (£45)
Code of Practice for Gaseous Fire Fighting Systems (£45)
Code of Practice for the Design, Installation and Servicing of Voice Alarm Systems Associated with Fire Detection Systems (£35)
Guidance for Power Supplies for Use in Fire Detection Systems (£30)

Electronic and video publications:
Fighting Fires with Foam (CD-ROM, £55)

Access to staff:
Contact by letter, by telephone and by fax
Hours: Mon to Fri, 0900 to 1700

Member of:
European Association of Fire Alarm Manufacturers
Fire Industry Confederation

Premises and secretarial services are shared with the:
Association of British Fire Trades Limited
British Approvals for Fire Equipment
Fire Extinguishing Trades Association

BRITISH FLUE AND CHIMNEY MANUFACTURERS' ASSOCIATION

Acronym or abbreviation: BFCMA

2 Waltham Court, Milley Lane, Hare Hatch, Reading, Berkshire, RG10 9TH

Tel: 0118 940 3416
Fax: 0118 940 6258
E-mail: info@feta.co.uk

Website:
http://www.feta.co.uk

Enquiries:
Enquiries to: Commercial Manager

Founded:
1977

Organisation type and purpose:
Trade association.

Subject coverage:
Natural draught flues and chimneys for all fuels.

Printed publications:
Guide to Choosing and Using Flues and Chimneys for Domestic Solid Fuel and Woodburning Appliances (2007)
Guide to Flues and Chimneys for Gas Appliances (2007)

Publications list:
Available online

Access to staff:
Contact by letter, by telephone, by fax and by e-mail
Hours: Mon to Thu, 0830 to 1630; Fri, 0830 to 1600

Links with:
Federation of Environmental Trade Associations at the same address

BRITISH FLUID POWER ASSOCIATION

Acronym or abbreviation: BFPA

Cheriton House, Cromwell Park, Chipping Norton, Oxfordshire, OX7 5SR

Tel: 01608 647900
Fax: 01608 647919
E-mail: enquiries@bfpa.co.uk

Website:
http://www.bfpa.co.uk
Trade association profile, members' products guide, publications, news, training information.

Enquiries:
Enquiries to: Director

Founded:
1959

Organisation type and purpose:
Trade association.
Trade association for manufacturers and distributors of hydraulic and pneumatic equipment.

Subject coverage:
Hydraulic and pneumatic equipment.

Trade and statistical information:
General production and trade statistics UK and Europe (specific data available to members only), technical information, product sourcing, exhibitions.

Printed publications:
Annual Membership Directory & Year Book
Guides, guidelines, data sheets, codes of practice, etc. (over 40 titles)

Publications list:
Available online and in print

Access to staff:
Contact by letter, by telephone, by fax, by e-mail and via website
Hours: Mon to Thu, 0900 to 1700; Fri, 0900 to 15.20

Access for disabled people:
Parking provided

Sister association:
British Fluid Power Distributors Association at the same address

BRITISH FLUORIDATION SOCIETY

Acronym or abbreviation: BFS

Ward 4, Booth Hall Children's Hospital, Charlestown Road, Manchester, M9 7AA

Tel: 0161 918 5223
E-mail: bfs@bfsweb.org

Website:
http://www.bfsweb.org/
History of fluoridation, BFS publications.

Enquiries:
Enquiries to: Information Officer
Direct e-mail: w.ross.thomson@ntlworld.com
Other contacts: Administrator, tel no: 01565 872445, fax: 01565 873936

Founded:
1969

Organisation type and purpose:
Learned society (membership is by subscription), research organisation.

Subject coverage:
Fluoridation of public water supplies; safety, benefits, effectiveness; fluoride supplements.

Printed publications:
Booklets on legal cases and scientific cases
Fluoridation – Safety First

continued overleaf

Fluoride – The Dental Benefits
How Fluoridation Works
News and Information Bulletin
Society Briefings
Reading List

Electronic and video publications:
Five, six minute videos on fluoridation and dental
decay

Publications list:
Available in print

Access to staff:
Contact by letter, by telephone, by fax, by e-mail
and via website
Hours: Mon to Fri, 0900 to 1700

BRITISH FLUTE SOCIETY

Acronym or abbreviation: BFS

The Nook, How Mill, Brampton, Cumbria, CA8
9JY

Tel: 01228 670306
E-mail: membership@bfs.org.uk

Enquiries:
Enquiries to: Membership Secretary

Organisation type and purpose:
Membership association.
To promote the flute and flute playing, provide an
opportunity for enthusiasts to contact each other.

Subject coverage:
Flutes and flute making, music, instruments,
history, players, events worldwide.

Printed publications:
Pan (journal, quarterly)

Access to staff:
Contact by letter, by telephone and by e-mail
Hours: Mon to Fri, 0900 to 1700

BRITISH FOOTWEAR ASSOCIATION

Acronym or abbreviation: BFA

3 Burystead Place, Wellingborough,
Northamptonshire, NN8 1AH

Tel: 01933 229005
Fax: 01933 225009
E-mail: infor@britfoot.com

Website:
http://www.britfoot.com
Industry summary, consumer information, details
of member firms.

Founded:
1890

Organisation type and purpose:
National organisation, trade association
(membership is by subscription), present number
of members: 80, manufacturing industry, service
industry.

Subject coverage:
Footwear manufacture: labour relations, working
conditions, environmental and safety legislation,
export information and labelling.

Access to staff:
Contact by letter, by telephone, by fax, by e-mail
and via website. Non-members charged.
Hours: Mon to Fri, 0900 to 1700

Access to building, collection or gallery:
Prior appointment required

BRITISH FRANCHISE ASSOCIATION

Acronym or abbreviation: BFA

Thames View, Newtown Road, Henley-on-
Thames, Oxfordshire, RG9 1HG

Tel: 01491 578050
Fax: 01491 573517

E-mail: mailroom@british-franchise.org.uk

Website:
http://www.british-franchise.org.uk
Comprehensive information on franchising and
publication ordering service.

Enquiries:
Enquiries to: Director General

Founded:
1977

Organisation type and purpose:
Advisory body, trade association (membership is
by subscription), present number of members: 280,
training organisation, research organisation,
publishing house.
To develop and continuously improve the
standards of good practice in franchising.

Subject coverage:
Franchising: an introduction to franchising to
individuals looking to invest in a franchise
opportunity.
Guidance to businesses on how to franchise their
business.

Trade and statistical information:
Annual survey and statistics on the extent and
performance of franchising in the UK.

Printed publications:
The Franchisee Guide (to purchase, direct from the
BFA)
The Franchisor Guide (to purchase, direct from the
BFA)

Electronic and video publications:
Your Introduction to Franchising (video, £9.95 or
free with Franchisee or Franchisor Guide, direct)

Publications list:
Available online

Access to staff:
Contact by letter, by telephone, by fax, by e-mail
and via website
Hours: Mon to Fri, 0900 to 1700

BRITISH FRIENDS OF RAMBAM MEDICAL CENTRE

Formal name: The British Friends of Rambam
Medical Center
Acronym or abbreviation: BFRMC

The Director, 10 North Crescent, London, N3 3LL

Tel: 020 8371 1500
Fax: 020 8271 1501
E-mail: alexanderpasse@dsl.pipex.com

Enquiries:
Enquiries to: Director

Founded:
1993

Organisation type and purpose:
Registered charity (charity number 1028061).
The purchase of medical equipment for all
departments of the Rambam Medical Centre.

Access to staff:
Contact by letter
Hours: Mon to Fri, 0900 to 1700

BRITISH FRIESLAND SHEEP SOCIETY

Weir Park Farm, Christow, Exeter, Devon, EX6 7PB

Tel: 01647 252549
E-mail: 1nf0@baber.co.uk

Founded:
1980

Subject coverage:
British Friesland sheep.

BRITISH FUCHSIA SOCIETY, THE

Acronym or abbreviation: BFS

PO Box 178, Evesham, Worcestershire, WR11 3WY

Tel: 01386 45158
E-mail: editor@thebfs.org.uk

Website:
http://www.thebfs.org.uk
Society details and news, pictures of fuchsias,
cultural information.

Enquiries:
Enquiries to: Honorary Secretary

Founded:
1938

Organisation type and purpose:
Membership association (membership is by
subscription), present number of members: 5300,
registered charity (charity number 1038334).
To encourage, improve and research the cultivation
of fuchsias and their various cultivars.

Subject coverage:
All matters related to the culture of Fuchsias,
availability of specific cultivars (limited to those
grown in the UK).

Printed publications:
Fuchsia Annual (free to members, limited quantity
may be available to non-members)
Bulletins (2 times a year, free to members, limited
quantity may be available to non-members)

Access to staff:
Contact by letter and by telephone
Hours: Mon to Fri, 0900 to 1700

Affiliated to the:
Royal Horticultural Society

Has:
300 affiliated local societies

BRITISH FURNITURE MANUFACTURERS FEDERATION

Members:
High Wycombe Furniture Manufacturers Society
London and South Eastern Furniture
Manufacturers Association
Midlands and North West Furniture
Manufacturers Association
Northern Furniture Manufacturers Association
Scottish Furniture Manufacturers Association
West of England & South Wales Furniture
Manufacturers Association

BRITISH GEAR ASSOCIATION

Acronym or abbreviation: BGA

Suite 43, Imex Business Park, Shobnall Road,
Burton-on-Trent, Staffordshire, DE14 2AU

Tel: 01283 515521
Fax: 01283 515841
E-mail: admin@bga.org.uk

Website:
http://www.bga.org.uk

Enquiries:
Enquiries to: Office Manager
Other contacts: Technical Executive for technical
enquiries.

Organisation type and purpose:
Trade association, membership association
(membership is by subscription).
Association for the Mechanical Power
Transmission Industry.

Subject coverage:
Technical, research, education, training and
economic aspects related to the mechanical power
transmissions industry.

**Museum or gallery collection, archive, or library
special collection:**
Congress papers on mechanical power
transmission subjects

Trade and statistical information:
Statistical Profile of the Power Transmission
Industry, members: 1 CD copy free of charge, UK
non-members: £250 for hard copy, £120 + VAT for
CD, outside UK: please ask for quote.

Printed publications:
Buyers Guide & Members Handbook
Gear Technology Manual
Gear Technology Teaching Pack
Technical Publications

Publications list:
Available online and in print

Access to staff:
Contact by letter, by telephone, by fax, by e-mail
and via website
Hours: Mon to Fri, 0900 to 1700

Member of:
European Committee of Associations of
Manufacturers of Gears and Transmission Parts
tel: + 49 69 66 03 1526; fax: + 49 69 66 03 1459

BRITISH GEOLOGICAL SURVEY

Acronym or abbreviation: BGS

Natural History Museum, Cromwell Road,
London, SW7 5BD

Tel: 020 7589 4090
Fax: 020 7584 8270
E-mail: bgslondon@bgs.ac.uk

Website:
http://www.bgs.ac.uk
BGS publications.
http://www.geologyshop.com

Enquiries:
Enquiries to: Manager

Founded:
1845

Organisation type and purpose:
Research organisation.
Scientific research (earth sciences).

Subject coverage:
Geological sciences, earth sciences, geology and
associated subjects, economic resources,
environmental geology, hydrogeology,
geochemistry, regional geology (UK and overseas),
geophysics, palaeontology, engineering geology,
minerals, remote sensing, seismology, volcanology,
petrology, biostratigraphy, petroleum geology,
fluid processes, marine geology, coastal geology,
geological maps, natural hazards.

**Museum or gallery collection, archive, or library
special collection:**
1:10,000 / 1:10,560 National Grid and County Series
Geological maps of the British Isles and other
scale geological maps
Indexes to field notebooks and BGS archives
Manuscript graphic indexes to BGS maps
All BGS publications including:
BGS Memoirs, open file, technical and research
reports

Trade and statistical information:
World mineral statistics.
UK Minerals Year-book.

Library catalogue:
All or part available online

Printed publications:
Catalogue of Geological Maps and Books
Sale collection of BGS and some non-BGS
publications, including maps
Guide to the London BGS Information Office
New Releases list
Various leaflets on the Services of the Survey
Printed publications list of the most popular items

Publications list:
Available online and in print

Access to staff:
Contact by letter, by telephone, by fax, by e-mail,
in person and via website

Hours: Mon to Fri; tel., 0900 to 1700; visitors, 1000
to 1700

Access for disabled people:
Toilet facilities
Special comments: Lift available to office level.

BRITISH GEOLOGICAL SURVEY –
MARINE OPERATIONS AND
ENGINEERING

Formal name: British Geological Survey
Acronym or abbreviation: BGS

2A Nivensknowe Road, Loanhead, Midlothian,
EH20 9AU

Tel: 0131 448 2700
Fax: 0131 448 2545
E-mail: A.Skinner@bgs.ac.uk

Website:
http://www.bgs.ac.uk
Description of all facilities available from BGS with
further specific information on help index.

Enquiries:
Enquiries to: Information Officer
Direct tel: 0131 667 1000 Murchison House; 01159
363 100 Keyworth
Direct fax: 0131 668 4140 Murchison House; 01159
363 200 Keyworth
Other contacts: Head of Marine Operations for
offshore surveys/coring equipment.

Founded:
1835

Organisation type and purpose:
National government body, professional body,
research organisation.
National onshore and offshore data archive for
geology and geoscience.
Geological survey, geophysical survey and
monitoring (geomagnetism and earthquakes).

Subject coverage:
Geological, geophysical, geotechnical field data
maps, reports, computer databased archive files
and maps, seismic hazards. Geomagnetic
observations and predictions. Offshore geophysical
and geological surveys. Specialised offshore
sampling and coring equipment. Coastal and
environmental monitoring and data collection.

Trade and statistical information:
Documentation relating to mineral statistics,
earthquake statistics and similar data.

Non-library collection catalogue:
All or part available in-house

Library catalogue:
All or part available in-house

Printed publications:
Publications available from bookshops at the
offices in London, Keyworth and Edinburgh,
HMSO and some outdoor sports/hillwalking/
climbing shops
Annual Reports
Geological and geophysical reports
Maps and surveying documents
Order printed publications from: Information Officer,
British Geological Survey, Murchison House, West
Main Road, Edinburgh, EH9 3LA, tel: 0131 667
1000, fax: 0131 668 2683
Information Officer, British Geological Survey,
Keyworth, Nottingham, NG12 5GG, tel: 0115 936
3100, fax: 0115 936 3200

Microform publications:
Contact BGS Keyworth and Murchison House

Electronic and video publications:
Contact BGS or website

Publications list:
Available online and in print

Access to staff:
Contact by letter, by fax and by e-mail.
Appointment necessary. All charged.
Hours: Mon to Thu, 0900 to 1700; Fri, 0900 to 1630

Special comments: There may be data exchange
arrangements.
Access times may vary. Please check with staff
concerned.

Access for disabled people:
Parking provided
Special comments: Access varies dependent on
building.

Main Office:
British Geological Survey
Platt Lane, Nicker Hill, Keyworth, Nottingham,
NG12 5GG; tel: 01159 363 100; fax: 01159 363
200; e-mail: @bgs.ac.uk

North UK Office:
British Geological Survey
Murchison House, West Main Road, Edinburgh,
EH19 3LA; tel: 0131 667 1000; fax: 0131 668 4140;
e-mail: pmgg@bgs.ac.uk

Part of:
The Natural Environment Research Council
(NERC)
Polaris House, North Star Avenue, Swindon,
Wiltshire, SN2 1EU; tel: 01793 411500; fax: 01793
411501

BRITISH GEOLOGICAL SURVEY –
RESEARCH KNOWLEDGE
SERVICES

Acronym or abbreviation: BGS

Kingsley Dunham Centre, Keyworth,
Nottinghamshire, NG12 5GG

Tel: 0115 936 3205
Fax: 0115 936 3015
E-mail: libuser@bgs.ac.uk

Website:
http://www.bgs.ac.uk
Access to the high-level data index and to OPAC.
http://nora.nerc.ac.uk
NERC Open Research Archive

Enquiries:
Enquiries to: Head of Research Knowledge Services

Founded:
1835

Organisation type and purpose:
National government body, consultancy, research
organisation, publishing house.
The mission of the BGS is to: advance geoscientific
knowledge of the United Kingdom landmass and
its adjacent continental shelf; provide
comprehensive, objective and up-to-date
geoscientific information, advice and services;
enhance the United Kingdom science base.

Subject coverage:
Earth sciences and related subjects.

**Museum or gallery collection, archive, or library
special collection:**
500,000 volumes
14,000 serials also world-wide
BGS archives
National collection of field survey records (NGRC)
Survey and British Association Geological
photographs (80,000)
World-wide collections of geological maps and
related texts (200,000)

Trade and statistical information:
Minerals statistics.

Non-library collection catalogue:
All or part available online and in-house

Library catalogue:
All or part available online

Printed publications:
BGS Catalogue of geological maps, books, and
data
Earthwise (House magazine)
Earthworks (House magazine)
Order printed publications from: Sales Desk, British
Geological Survey

continued overleaf

Electronic and video publications:
BGS Publications on OPAC geolib.bgs.ac.uk
  (GEOLIB)
Order electronic and video publications from: Sales at
http://www.bgs.ac.uk/contacts/sales.html

Publications list:
Available online and in print

Access to staff:
Contact by letter, by telephone, by fax, by e-mail,
in person and via website
Hours: Mon to Thu, 0900 to 1700; Fri, 0900 to 1630

Access to building, collection or gallery:
Prior appointment required
Hours: Mon to Thu, 0900 to 1700; Fri, 0900 to 1630
Special comments: Library available for reference
only.

Access for disabled people:
Parking provided, ramped entry, level entry, toilet
facilities

Also at:
British Geological Survey
  Maclean Building, Crowmarsh Gifford,
  Wallingford, Oxfordshire, OX10 8BB; tel: 01491
  838800; fax: 01491 692345; website: http://www
  .bgs.ac.uk/contacts/sites/wallingford/wahome
  .html
British Geological Survey
  Columbus House, Greenmeadow Springs,
  Tongwynlais, Cardiff, CF15 7NE; tel: 029 2052
  1962; fax: 029 2052 1963; website: http://www
  .bgs.ac.uk/contacts/sites/cardiff/home.html
British Geological Survey
  Hydrogeological Enquiries and National Wells
  Records Archive; tel: 01491 692299; fax: 01491
  692345; e-mail: hydro@bgs.ac.uk
British Geological Survey
  Murchison House, West Mains Road, Edinburgh,
  EH9 3LA; tel: 0131 667 1000; fax: 0131 668 2683;
  e-mail: enquiry@bgs.ac.uk; website: http://www
  .bgs.ac.uk/contacts/sites/edinburgh/mhhome
  .html
British Geological Survey
  London Information Office, Natural History
  Museum Earth Galleries, Exhibition Road, South
  Kensington, London, SW7 2DE; tel: 020 7589
  4090; fax: 020 7584 8270; e-mail: bgslondon@bgs
  .ac.uk; website: http://www.bgs.ac.uk/contacts/
  sites/london/liohome.html
Geological Survey of Northern Ireland
  Colby House, Stranmills Court, Belfast, BT9 5BF;
  tel: 028 9038 8462; fax: 028 9038 8461
National Geological Records Centre (North)
  tel: 0131 650 0307; fax: 0131 667 2785; e-mail:
  ngrcn@bgs.ac.uk
National Geological Records Centre (South)
  tel: 0115 936 3109; fax: 0115 936 3276; e-mail:
  ngis@bgs.ac.uk

Parent body:
Natural Environment Research Council
  Polaris House, North Star Avenue, Swindon,
  SN2 1EU; tel: 01793 411500; fax: 01793 411501;
  website: http://www.nerc.ac.uk

BRITISH GEOTECHNICAL ASSOCIATION

Acronym or abbreviation: BGA

Institution of Civil Engineers, 1 Great George
Street, London, SW1P 3AA

Tel: 020 7665 2233
Fax: 020 7799 1325
E-mail: bga@icc.org.uk

Website:
http://www.ice.org.uk
Meetings of the British Geotechnical Society.

Enquiries:
Enquiries to: Administrator

Organisation type and purpose:
Learned society.

Subject coverage:
Soil mechanics; foundation engineering; rock and
ice mechanics; geotechnical engineering; details of
conferences and proceedings in the field.

Printed publications:
Geotechnique (quarterly)

Access to staff:
Contact by letter
Hours: Mon to Fri, 0900 to 1700

Affiliated to:
Institution of Civil Engineers

Member of:
International Society for Rock Mechanics
International Society for Soil Mechanics and
Ground Engineering

BRITISH GERIATRICS SOCIETY

Acronym or abbreviation: BGS

Marjory Warren House, 31 St John's Square,
London, EC1M 4DN

Tel: 020 7608 1369
Fax: 020 7608 1041
E-mail: general.information@bgs.org.uk

Website:
http://www.bgs.org.uk

Enquiries:
Enquiries to: Administrator

Founded:
1947

Organisation type and purpose:
Advisory body, professional body (membership is
by qualification), voluntary organisation,
registered charity (charity number 268762).
Voluntary association of physicians and scientists
concerned with improving standards of treatment,
and encouraging research in the illnesses of elderly
people.

Subject coverage:
Promotion of high standards of health and
treatment for the elderly, the teaching of geriatric
medicine, the training of medical and paramedical
staff, and research into age-related disease.

Printed publications:
Compendium of Guidelines, Policy Statements and
  Statements of Good Practice
Fact sheets on a range of practical issues (keeping
  warm, eating well, etc)
Publications for Carers, NHS Decision Makers and
  Researchers

Publications list:
Available online and in print

Access to staff:
Contact by letter, by telephone, by fax, by e-mail
and via website
Hours: Mon to Fri, 0900 to 1700
Special comments: The society does not deal
specifically with the public, but aims its activities
at doctors with an interest in elderly care.

BRITISH GLASS MANUFACTURERS CONFEDERATION

Acronym or abbreviation: BGMC

Northumberland Road, Sheffield, South Yorkshire,
S10 2UA

Tel: 0114 268 6201
Fax: 0114 268 1073
E-mail: info@britglass.co.uk

Website:
http://www.britglass.co.uk

Enquiries:
Enquiries to: Librarian
Other contacts: Recycling Officer

Founded:
1959

Organisation type and purpose:
Advisory body, trade association (membership is
by subscription, qualification), present number of
members: 144, training organisation, consultancy,
research organisation.

Subject coverage:
Glass, recycling, statistics, education, economics,
legislation, safety, specifications, HSE, training and
consultancy, environmental services.

Trade and statistical information:
Production and recycling statistics.

Library catalogue:
All or part available in-house

Printed publications:
Digest of Information and Patent Review
  (quarterly, on subscription)
Making Glass
Teachers' Notes on Recycling
Technical Manuals
TEC Publications
Wall Charts

Electronic and video publications:
Video on bottle banks
First Glass Packaging
Ollie Recycles (CD-ROM)

Publications list:
Available in print

Access to staff:
Contact by letter, by telephone and by e-mail.
Appointment necessary. Non-members charged.
Hours: Mon to Fri, 0900 to 1700

Access to building, collection or gallery:
Prior appointment required
Hours: Mon to Fri, 0900 to 1700

Access for disabled people:
Parking provided, toilet facilities

Member of:
(ETSU)
British Standards Institution
European Domestic Glassware Organisation
European Glass Manufacturers
Scientific Glassware Association

BRITISH GLIDING ASSOCIATION

Acronym or abbreviation: BGA

Kimberley House, 47 Vaughan Way, Leicester, LE1
4SE

Tel: 0116 253 1051
Fax: 0116 251 5939
E-mail: bga@gliding.co.uk

Website:
http://www.gliding.co.uk

Enquiries:
Enquiries to: Secretary

Founded:
1929

Organisation type and purpose:
Membership association (membership is by
election or invitation), present number of
members: 9500, voluntary organisation.
Governing body for the sport.

Subject coverage:
Gliding.

Printed publications:
Sailplane and Gliding (6 times a year)

Access to staff:
Contact by letter, by telephone, by fax, by e-mail
and in person
Hours: Mon to Fri, 0900 to 1700

Affiliated to:
Fédération Aéronautique Internationale
Royal Aero Club of the United Kingdom

BRITISH GLOVE ASSOCIATION

Acronym or abbreviation: BGA

Sussex House, 8–10 Homesdale Road, Bromley, Kent, BR2 9LZ

Tel: 020 8464 0131
Fax: 020 8464 6018
E-mail: tradeassn@craneandpartners.com

Website:
http://www.gloveassociation.org

Enquiries:
Enquiries to: Secretary

Organisation type and purpose:
Trade association.

Subject coverage:
Glove production, glove types (dress, sports, industrial and protective).

Museum or gallery collection, archive, or library special collection:
The Worshipful Company of Glovers is responsible for two glove collections, both at the Museum of Costume, Bath
The Duplicate Royal Coronation Gloves Collection
The Spence Collection

Sponsors the:
Worshipful Company of Glovers

BRITISH GOAT SOCIETY

Acronym or abbreviation: BGS

34–36 Fore Street, Bovey Tracey, Newton Abbot, Devon, TQ13 9AD

Tel: 01626 833168
Fax: 01626 834536
E-mail: secretary@allgoats.com

Website:
http://www.allgoats.com

Enquiries:
Enquiries to: Secretary

Founded:
1879

Organisation type and purpose:
Voluntary organisation.
Registration body, over 90 local and regional societies are affiliated.

Subject coverage:
Goat husbandry and management; registration of stock.

Printed publications:
Books on husbandry, etc
Leaflets or pamphlets on goatkeeping, feeding, goats' milk, etc
Monthly Journal
Year Book and Herd Book

Publications list:
Available in print

Access to staff:
Contact by letter, by telephone and by e-mail
Hours: Mon to Fri, 0900 to 1700

BRITISH GRASSLAND SOCIETY

Acronym or abbreviation: BGS

PO Box 237, The Department of Agriculture, The University of Reading, Reading, Berkshire, RG6 6AR

Tel: 0118 931 8189
Fax: 0118 966 6941
E-mail: office@britishgrassland.com

Website:
http://www.i-way.co.uk/~bgs

Enquiries:
Enquiries to: Administrator

Founded:
1945

Organisation type and purpose:
Learned society, present number of members: 800, registered charity (charity number 261800).

BGS is a forum for those with an active interest in the science and practice of temperate grassland production and utilisation.

Subject coverage:
The advancement of methods of production and utilisation of grass and forage crops for the promotion of agriculture and the public benefit; the advancement of education and research in grass and forage crop production, and utilisation and the publication of the results of such research.

Publications list:
Available in print

Access to staff:
Contact by letter, by fax and via website
Hours: Mon to Fri, 0900 to 1700

BRITISH GREYHOUND RACING BOARD LIMITED

Acronym or abbreviation: BGRB

32 Old Burlington Street, London, W1S 3AT

Tel: 020 7292 9900
Fax: 020 7292 9909

Enquiries:
Enquiries to: Chief Executive

Founded:
1976

Organisation type and purpose:
Advisory body, statutory body, trade association.

Subject coverage:
Greyhound racing.

Trade and statistical information:
Information and statistics on greyhound racing.

Access to staff:
Contact by letter and by telephone
Hours: Mon to Fri, 0930 to 1700

BRITISH GUILD OF TRAVEL WRITERS

Acronym or abbreviation: BGTW

51B Askew Crescent, London, W12 9DN

Tel: 020 8749 1128
Fax: 020 8181 6663
E-mail: secretariat@bgtw.org

Website:
http://www.bgtw.org
About the Guild, current committee, membership criteria, code of conduct, Guild awards, purchase the yearbook.

Enquiries:
Enquiries to: Administrator

Founded:
1960

Organisation type and purpose:
Membership association (membership is by election or invitation), present number of members: 250.
Professional travel writers, authors broadcasters and photographers.

Subject coverage:
Travel, tourism, journalism, photography, radio, television, video.

Printed publications:
Yearbook (£108 to purchase via website)

Publications list:
Available in print

Access to staff:
Contact by letter, by telephone, by fax and by e-mail
Hours: Mon to Fri, 0900 to 1700

BRITISH GYMNASTICS

Acronym or abbreviation: BG

Ford Hall, Lilleshall National Sports Centre, Newport, Shropshire, TF10 9NB

Tel: 01952 822300
Fax: 01952 820326
E-mail: information@british-gymnastics.org

Website:
http://www.baga.co.uk

Enquiries:
Enquiries to: Public Relations Manager
Direct fax: 01952 822338
Direct e-mail: vera.a@british-gymnastics.org
Other contacts: Chief Executive for policy of the association.

Founded:
1888

Organisation type and purpose:
Membership association (membership is by subscription), present number of members: 100,000, training organisation.
National governing body of the sport.

Subject coverage:
Gymnastics, women's and men's; rhythmic gymnastics, trampolining, sports acrobatics, general gymnastics, gymnastics for people with disabilities, sports aerobics, competitions, courses, membership, technical information, awards and publications, events, promotion and publicity, judging.

Museum or gallery collection, archive, or library special collection:
Large library

Non-library collection catalogue:
All or part available in-house

Printed publications:
Books, guides, training and teaching materials
Calendar of Events
Gymnast (magazine, 6 times a year, subscription agents, telephone: 01580 200657)
Gym News (6 times a year)
Wall charts
Order printed publications from: World Wide Subscription Ltd, Unit 4, Gibbs Reed Farm, Pashley Road, Ticehurst, Wadhurst, East Sussex, TN5 7HE, tel: 01580 200657

Electronic and video publications:
Videos

Publications list:
Available in print

Access to staff:
Contact by letter, by telephone, by fax, by e-mail, in person and via website. Appointment necessary.
Hours: Mon to Thu, 0900 to 1700; Fri, 0900 to 1630

Access to building, collection or gallery:
Prior appointment required
Hours: Mon to Thu, 0900 to 1700; Fri, 0900 to 1630
Special comments: Library at Lilleshall HQ may be visited on request, for information and research.

Access for disabled people:
Parking provided

Constituent part:
British Trampoline Federation (BTF)

European governing body is:
UEG
Switzerland; tel: +41 21 613 7332; fax: +41 21 613 7331; e-mail: info@ueg.org

World governing body is:
FIG
Switzerland; tel: +41 32 494 6410; fax: +41 32 494 6419; e-mail: fig.gymnastics@worldsport.org

BRITISH HALLMARKING COUNCIL

No 1 Colmore Square, Birmingham, B4 6AA

Tel: 0870 763 2000
Fax: 0870 763 1814
E-mail: david.gwyther@martineau-uk.com

continued overleaf

Website:
http://www.britishhallmarkingcouncil.gov.uk/

Enquiries:
Enquiries to: Secretary

Founded:
1973

Organisation type and purpose:
Statutory body.
Created by the Hallmarking Act of 1973;
supervisory body for the activities of the
Independent Assay Offices.

Subject coverage:
Hallmarking in the United Kingdom.

Printed publications:
Annual Report

Access to staff:
Contact by letter
Hours: Mon to Fri, 0900 to 1700

BRITISH HANG GLIDING AND PARAGLIDING ASSOCIATION

Acronym or abbreviation: BHPA

Old Schoolroom, Loughborough Road, Leicester,
LE4 5PJ

Tel: 0116 261 1322
Fax: 0116 261 1323
E-mail: office@bhpa.co.uk

Website:
http://www.bhpa.co.uk
Skywings magazine.

Enquiries:
Enquiries to: Public Relations Manager
Direct tel: 01366 324346
Direct fax: 01366 324346
Direct e-mail: dw@dw-photography.co.uk

Founded:
1992

Organisation type and purpose:
Membership association.
Governing body of the sport.

Subject coverage:
Hang gliding and paragliding; availability,
training, licensing of instructors, safety regulations,
national competitions, development of new
techniques and equipment, courses, conventions.

Printed publications:
Directory of Clubs
Leaflets, posters, handbooks and textbooks
Safety Standards Manuals and Codes of Practice
Skywings Magazine (monthly)

Access to staff:
Contact by letter, by telephone, by fax and by e-mail
Hours: Mon to Fri, 0900 to 1700

Affiliated to:
Fédération Aéronautique Internationale

Includes the:
British Association of Parascending Clubs
British Hang Gliding Association

Representation on:
Royal Aero Club of the United Kingdom

BRITISH HARDMETAL ASSOCIATION

Acronym or abbreviation: BHA

c/o Institute of Spring Technology, Henry Street,
Sheffield, S3 7EQ

Tel: 0114 278 9143

Enquiries:
Enquiries to: Secretary

Organisation type and purpose:
Trade association.

Subject coverage:
Hardmetal and associated products.

Access to staff:
Contact by letter, by telephone, by fax and by e-mail
Hours: Mon to Fri, 0900 to 1700

Affiliated to:
Federation of British Engineers' Tool
Manufacturers

BRITISH HEALTH CARE ASSOCIATION

Acronym or abbreviation: BHCA

Unit 8, Cherry Hall Rd, Kettering, Northampshire,
NN14 1UE

Tel: 01536 519960
Fax: 01536 519379
E-mail: steve.fritz@bhcaservices.co.uk

Website:
http://www.bhca.org.uk
Full details of the BHCA, together with a list of
Member Organisations. Access to members
benefits etc is also available.

Enquiries:
Enquiries to: Chief Executive
Other contacts: President

Founded:
1947

Organisation type and purpose:
Trade association (membership is by subscription).
To promote and advance the interest of Member
Organisations; lobby, consult and negotiate on
their behalf and undertake and arrange for the
arbitration of disputes. To determine and
administer an ethical Code of Conduct for the
resolution of disputes.

Subject coverage:
Health care insurance.

Museum or gallery collection, archive, or library special collection:
History of the Association

Library catalogue:
All or part available online and in print

Printed publications:
Information brochure (free)
Annual Report (free)

Publications list:
Available in print

Access to staff:
Contact by letter, by telephone and by fax
Hours: Mon to Fri, 0900 to 1700

Member Organisation:
BHSF Limited (BHSF Ltd)
Gamgee House, 2 Darnley Road, Birmingham,
B16 8TE; tel: 0121 454 3601; fax: 0121 454 7725; e-mail: sales@bhsf.co.uk; website: http://www.bhsf
.co.uk
Bolton and District Hospital Saturday Council
Coronation House, 16 Silverwell Street, Bolton,
Lancashire, BL1 1PP; tel: 01204 22775; fax: 01204
522452; e-mail: sales@hospital-saturday.org.uk;
website: http://www.hospital-saturday.org.uk
Forester Health
Forester House, Cromwell Avenue, Bromley,
Kent, BR2 9BF; tel: 020 8628 3434; fax: 020 8628
3535; e-mail: Foresterhealth@Forester.co.uk;
website: http://www.Foresterhealth.co.uk
Gwent Hospitals Contributory Fund
13 Cardiff Road, Newport, Gwent, NP20 2EH;
tel: 01633 266152; fax: 01633 262456
Healthsure Group
43–45 Lever Street, Manchester, M60 7HP; tel:
0161 236 1901; fax: 0161 237 5578; e-mail:
marketing@healthsure.org.uk; website: http://
www.healthsure.org.uk
Hospital Contributory Scheme
140 Eddleston Road, Crewe, Cheshire, CW1 7EZ;
tel: 01270 212940

Hospital Saving Association Limited
Hambledon House, Waterloo Court, Andover,
Hampshire, SP10 1LQ; tel: 01264 353211; fax:
01264 333650; e-mail: communications@has.co
.uk; website: http://www.has.co.uk
Leeds Hospital Fund Limited
Riverside House, 7 Canal Wharf, Leeds, LS11
5WA; tel: 0113 245 0813; fax: 0113 234 0815; e-mail: customer.services@lhfhealthplan.org.uk;
website: http://www.lhfhealthplan.org.uk
Medicash Health Benefits
Merchants Court, 2–12 Lord Street, Liverpool, L2
1TS; tel: 0151 702 0202; fax: 0151 702 0250; e-mail: info@medcash.org; website: http://www
.medicash.org
Patient's Aid Association
Paycare House, George Street, Wolverhampton,
WV2 4DX; tel: 01902 371000; fax: 01902 371030;
e-mail: enquiries@paycare.org; website: http://
www.paycare.org
Premier Health Benefits
35 Peterson Road, Wakefield, West Yorkshire,
WF1 4DU; tel: 01924 373552; fax: 01924 200377;
e-mail: phb@wdhcs.com; website: http://www
.wdhcs.com
Simplyhealth
Stag House, Old London Road, Hertford, SG13
7LA; tel: 01992 515515; fax: 01992 515516; e-mail:
enquiries@simplyhealth.uk.com; website: http://
www.simplyhealth.uk.com
Sovereign Health Care
Royal Standard House, 26 Manningham Lane,
Bradford, West Yorkshire, BD1 3DN; tel: 01274
729472; fax: 01274 722252; e-mail: mail@
sovereignhealth.co.uk; website: http://www
.sovereignhealth.co.uk
The Health Scheme
15 Freetown Way, Kingston upon Hull, HU2 8JP;
tel: 01482 327376; fax: 01482 327379; e-mail:
info@the-health-scheme.co.uk; website: http://
www.the-health-scheme.co.uk
The Hospital Saturday Fund
24 Upper Ground, London, SE1 0PQ; tel: 020
7928 6662; fax: 020 7928 0446; e-mail: sales@hsf
.co.uk; website: http://www.hsf.co.uk
The Western Provident Association Limited
Rivergate House, Blackbrook Park, Taunton,
Somerset, TA1 2PE; tel: 01823 623000; fax: 01823
623050; e-mail: ppd@wpa.org.uk; website: http://
www.wpa.org.uk
WHA Healthcare
60 Newport Road, Cardiff, CF2 1YG; tel: 029
2048 5461; fax: 029 2048 8859; e-mail: mail@
whalhealthcare.co.uk; website: http://www
.whalhealthcare.co.uk

BRITISH HEALTHCARE TRADES ASSOCIATION

Acronym or abbreviation: BHTA

1 Webbs Court, Buckhurst Avenue, Sevenoaks,
Kent, TN13 1LZ

Tel: 01732 458868
Fax: 01732 459225
E-mail: bhta@bhta.com

Website:
http://www.bhta.com
List of members.

Enquiries:
Enquiries to: Director

Founded:
1917

Organisation type and purpose:
Trade association (membership is by subscription),
present number of members: 320.

Subject coverage:
BHTA's aim is to be seen as the body that
effectively represents the sector of the British
health care industry that serves those with special
physical needs.

Trade and statistical information:
Membership lists available for general circulation.
All other information available to members only.

Printed publications:
Exporters List (free)
General membership list (free)
Surgical Instrument Directory (free)
Wheelchair Distributors Membership List (free)

Publications list:
Available in print

Access to staff:
Contact by letter, by telephone, by fax, by e-mail and via website
Hours: Mon to Fri, 0900 to 1700

Access to building, collection or gallery:
No access other than to staff

BRITISH HEART FOUNDATION

Acronym or abbreviation: BHF

14 Fitzhardinge Street, London, W1H 6DH

Tel: 020 7935 0185
Fax: 020 7486 5820

Website:
http://www.bhf.org.uk

Enquiries:
Enquiries to: Director of Communications
Direct tel: 020 7487 7183
Direct fax: 020 7224 5082
Other contacts: Editor

Founded:
1961

Organisation type and purpose:
Registered charity (charity number 225971), research organisation.
Medical research charity working in the field of cardiovascular disease. Producers of a statistical database.
Funds vital research, rehabilitation programmes, life-saving cardiac equipment and educational initiatives, BHF nurses and co-ordinates heart support groups. Encourages people to learn emergency life support skills.

Subject coverage:
Research into the causes, diagnosis, treatment and prevention of heart disease, public education and information, information to the medical profession, rehabilitation, heart support groups, emergency life support skills training.

Trade and statistical information:
Coronary heart disease statistics.

Printed publications:
Annual Medical and Research Reports (free to members of the medical profession)
Annual Review, Report and Accounts
Heart Information Series (constantly updated and available)
Leaflets, newsletters and booklets for children and adults (some available in Welsh and Asian versions, free)
Cardiopulmonary resuscitation (CPR)
Diet information
Exercise information
Heart information series

Electronic and video publications:
Educational videos, including those for patients, available for a donation of approximately £5

Publications list:
Available online and in print

Access to staff:
Contact by letter and by telephone. Appointment necessary.
Hours: Mon to Fri, 0900 to 1700

Has:
9 regional offices

Member of:
International Society and Federation of Cardiologists

Regional Offices:
Region 1
4–6 Bridge Street, Tadcaster, North Yorkshire, LS24 9AL; tel: 01937 835421
Region 10
6 Terrace Walk, Bath, BA1 1LN; tel: 01225 463616
Region 2
2 Kiln House Yard, Baldock Street, Royston, Hertfordshire, SG8 5AY; tel: 01763 242414
Region 3
4 Shore Place, Edinburgh, EH6 6UU; tel: 0131 555 5891
Region 5
Oak House B, Ransom Wood Business Park, Southwell Road West, Mansfield, Nottinghamshire, NG21 0HJ; tel: 01623 624558
Region 6
21 Cathedral Road, Cardiff, CF11 9HA; tel: 029 2038 2368
Region 7
7 Queen Avenue, Dale Street, Liverpool, L2 4TZ; tel: 0151 236 6988
Region 8
239A High Street, Erdington, Birmingham, B23 6SS; tel: 0121 382 3168
Region 9
33 High Street, Ticehurst, Wadhurst, East Sussex, TN5 7AS; tel: 01580 200443

BRITISH HEDGEHOG PRESERVATION SOCIETY

Acronym or abbreviation: BHPS

Hedgehog House, Dhustone, Ludlow, Shropshire, SY8 3PL

Tel: 01584 890801
Fax: 01584 891313
E-mail: info@britishhedgehogs.org.uk

Enquiries:
Enquiries to: Chief Executive

Founded:
1982

Organisation type and purpose:
National organisation, membership association (membership is by subscription), present number of members: 11,000, registered charity (charity number 326885).
National organisation with some foreign members. To heighten awareness of needs of hedgehogs.

Subject coverage:
Hedgehog care.

Printed publications:
Background to the BHPS
Education packs
Leaflets (12 titles)
Newsletter (2 times a year, for members)
Project packs
Treating Sick Hedgehogs (intended for Veterinary Surgeons)

Access to staff:
Contact by letter, by telephone, by e-mail and via website
Hours: Mon to Fri, 0900 to 1700

BRITISH HELICOPTER ADVISORY BOARD LIMITED

Acronym or abbreviation: BHAB

Graham Suite, West Entrance, Fairoaks Airport, Chobham, Woking, Surrey, GU24 8HX

Tel: 01276 856100
Fax: 01276 856126

Website:
http://www.bhab.demon.co.uk

Enquiries:
Enquiries to: Chief Executive
Other contacts: Executive Assistant for information regarding membership or helicopter charter, services.

Founded:
1969

Organisation type and purpose:
Trade association (membership is by subscription).
To promote and advise on civil helicopter operations.

Subject coverage:
All aspects of helicopter operations.

Printed publications:
Code of Flight Conduct for Helicopter Pilots
Information Handbook (annually)
Pilot Training Leaflet
The Civil Helicopter in the Community

BRITISH HERBAL MEDICINE ASSOCIATION

Acronym or abbreviation: BHMA

PO Box 583, Exeter, EX1 9GX

Tel: 0845 680 1134
Fax: 0845 680 1136
E-mail: secretary@bhma.info

Website:
http://www.bhma.info

Enquiries:
Enquiries to: Secretary

Founded:
1964

Organisation type and purpose:
Trade association.
BHMA provides an advisory service to government and is involved in scientific research and legislation.

Subject coverage:
Herbs and herbal medicine; herbal products; Medicines Act (1968); advertising regulations on herbs, suppliers etc.; training facilities for herbal practitioners; research.

Printed publications:
British Herbal Compendium (1992 and 2005)
British Herbal Pharmacopoeia (1983, 1990, 1996)
A Guide to Traditional Herbal Medicines
Code of Advertising
Occasional Papers

Access to staff:
Contact by letter, by telephone, by fax and by e-mail
Hours: Mon to Fri, 1000 to 1600

BRITISH HERNIA CENTRE

87 Watford Way, Hendon Central, London, NW4 4RS

Tel: 020 8201 7000
E-mail: experts@hernia.org

Website:
http://www.hernia.org
Comprehensive information, including explanations on hernia in plain English.
Award winning website.

Enquiries:
Enquiries to: Chief Executive

Founded:
1990

Organisation type and purpose:
Specialist hospital.
The largest tension-free specialist hernia centre in the world.

Subject coverage:
All aspects of hernias, treatment and cure.

Library catalogue:
All or part available online

Printed publications:
Explanatory booklets on all types of Hernia
Various academic publications

Publications list:
Available online

Access to staff:
Contact by letter, by telephone, by fax, by e-mail and via website. Appointment necessary.

continued overleaf

Hours: Mon to Fri, 0900 to 1700
Special comments: Telephone lines open 24 hours.

Links with:
BHC – Grosvenor Hospitals Group Limited

BRITISH HERPETOLOGICAL SOCIETY

Acronym or abbreviation: BHS

Zoological Society of London, Regent's Park, London, NW1 4RY

Tel: 01674 671676
E-mail: secretary@thebhs.org

Website:
http://www.thebhs.org

Enquiries:
Enquiries to: Secretary

Founded:
1947

Organisation type and purpose:
Learned society (membership is by subscription), present number of members: 600, voluntary organisation, registered charity.
Study of herpetology.

Subject coverage:
Herpetology, study and protection of amphibians and reptiles, particularly British and European; captive breeding of species in vivaria as a conservation tool.

Museum or gallery collection, archive, or library special collection:
Scientific journal from various countries
Corkhill Collection of books and bound papers

Printed publications:
Bulletin (4 times a year)
Herpetological Journal (4 times a year)
NatterJack newsletter (12 times a year)
The Care and Breeding of Captive Reptiles
The Reptiles and Amphibians of Dorset

Access to staff:
Contact by letter, by telephone and by e-mail
Hours: Mon to Fri, 1730 to 1930

Constituent bodies:
conservation committee, research committee, captive breeding committee, education committee including a young members group (Young Herpetologists Club)

BRITISH HOLIDAY AND HOME PARKS ASSOCIATION

Acronym or abbreviation: BH & HPA Ltd

6 Pullman Court, Great Western Road, Gloucester, GL1 3ND

Tel: 01452 526911
Fax: 01452 508508

Enquiries:
Enquiries to: Director General

Founded:
1950

Organisation type and purpose:
Trade association.

Subject coverage:
The interests of owners and managers of holiday and residential parks nationwide.

Printed publications:
BH & HPA Journal
BH & HPA Members' Handbook (free for qualifying individuals)

Access to staff:
Contact by letter
Hours: Mon to Fri, 0900 to 1700

BRITISH HOLISTIC MEDICAL ASSOCIATION

Acronym or abbreviation: BHMA

PO Box 371 Bridgwater Somerset, TA6 9BG

Tel: 01278 722000
E-mail: admin@bhma.org

Website:
http://www.bhma.org

Enquiries:
Enquiries to: Chairman

Founded:
1983

Organisation type and purpose:
Membership association (membership is by subscription), present number of members: 650, voluntary organisation, registered charity (charity number 289459), training organisation, research organisation, publishing house.
BHMA is an organisation of professionals and members of the public who care about the future of healthcare and want to adopt a more holistic approach in their own life and work.
The BHMA is furthering the development of holistic healthcare through bringing together the many people who can contribute to a system for the 21st century by holding conferences, workshops, seminars and by facilitating a network of regional groups.

Subject coverage:
Holistic medical practice; complementary therapies, their application in and outside orthodox medical practice; training.

Printed publications:
Journal of Holistic Healthcare (quarterly)

Electronic and video publications:
Self help CDs: Coping with Stress, The Breath of Life, Getting to Sleep, Introducing Meditation, Imagery for Relaxation, Coping with Persistent Pain

Access to staff:
Contact by letter, by telephone, by e-mail and via website
Hours: Mon to Fri, 1000 to 1600
Answerphone checked regularly
Special comments: If contacting by letter please enclose an sae.

Access to building, collection or gallery:
Prior Appointment Required

BRITISH HOMEOPATHIC ASSOCIATION

Acronym or abbreviation: BHA

Hahnemann House, 29 Park Street West, Luton, LU1 3BE

Tel: 0870 444 3950
Fax: 0870 444 3960
E-mail: info@trusthomeopathy.org

Website:
http://www.trusthomeopathy.org

Enquiries:
Enquiries to: Chief Executive

Founded:
1902

Organisation type and purpose:
Membership association, registered charity (charity number 235900).
To promote homeopathy and raise funds for research and education.

Subject coverage:
Homeopathy practised by statutorily registered healthcare professionals – doctors, dentists, nurses, vets, pharmacists, podiatrists, midwives, osteopaths

Information services:
Information on medical homeopathy.

Printed publications:
Health & Homeopathy (4 times a year, free to members, subscription £25)
Order printed publications from: British Homeopathic Association

Access to staff:
Contact by letter, by telephone, by e-mail and via website. Appointment necessary.
Hours: Mon to Fri, 0900 to 1700

Access to building, collection or gallery:
Prior appointment required

Access for disabled people:
Hours: Mon to Fri, 0900 to 1700

BRITISH HOROLOGICAL FEDERATION

Acronym or abbreviation: BHF

Upton Hall, Upton, Newark, Nottinghamshire, NG23 5TE

Tel: 01636 813795
Fax: 01636 812258
E-mail: clocks@bhi.co.uk

Website:
http://www.bhi.co.uk/bhfhome.htm

Enquiries:
Enquiries to: Secretary General

Founded:
1932

Organisation type and purpose:
Trade association.

Subject coverage:
Clocks and watches, manufacturers and suppliers, horological technology (including standards), horological trade fairs, European directives for the horological industry.

Printed publications:
Horological Journal (monthly, members only)

Access to staff:
Contact by fax
Hours: Mon to Fri, 0900 to 1700

Member of:
European Committee for the Industry

Other address:
British Horological Federation
tel: 01636 706965; fax: 01636 706965; e-mail: gevansbhf@aol.com

Sister organisation at the same address the:
British Horological Institute

BRITISH HOROLOGICAL INSTITUTE

Acronym or abbreviation: BHI

Upton Hall, Upton, Newark, Nottinghamshire, NG23 5TE

Tel: 01636 813795
Fax: 01636 812258
E-mail: clocks@bhi.co.uk

Website:
http://www.bhi.co.uk

Enquiries:
Enquiries to: General Manager
Other contacts: Education Team for education related services and facilities.

Founded:
1858

Organisation type and purpose:
Professional body, membership association (membership is by subscription), present number of members: 3500, museum, historic building, house or site, training organisation.
To protect and further the science and art of horology.

Subject coverage:
Horology.

Museum or gallery collection, archive, or library special collection:
Library and museum

Printed publications:
Horological Journal

Access to staff:
Contact by letter, by telephone, by fax, by e-mail and via website. Appointment necessary. Letter of introduction required. Non-members charged.
Hours: Mon to Fri, 0900 to 1700

Access to building, collection or gallery:
Prior arrangement necessary
Hours: By appointment for members only. Group visits for non-mems by prior arrangement

Access for disabled people:
Parking provided, level entry, toilet facilities
Special comments: Access to ground floor only.

Houses the:
British Horological Federation

BRITISH HOROLOGICAL INSTITUTE LTD

Acronym or abbreviation: BHI

Upton Hall, Upton, Newark, Nottinghamshire, NG23 5TE

Tel: 01636 813795
Fax: 01636 812258

Website:
http://www.bhi.co.uk

Founded:
1858

Organisation type and purpose:
A company limited by guarantee (no. 130649). Membership by subscription is open to anyone with an interest in horology, whether professional, academic or recreational; also corporate membership. The Institute organises examinations accredited by the Qualifications and Curriculum Authority, leading to certificates in Clock and Watch Servicing and in the Repair, Restoration and Conservation of Clocks / Watches.

Subject coverage:
Clocks and watches.

BRITISH HORSE SOCIETY

Acronym or abbreviation: BHS

Stoneleigh Deer Park, Kenilworth, Warwickshire, CV8 2XZ

Tel: 01926 707700 / 0844 848 1666
Fax: 01926 707800
E-mail: enquiry@bhs.org.uk

Website:
http://www.bhs.org.uk
Information on the BHS and its work for every horse and rider
http://www.britishhorse.com
The BHS bookshop online.

Enquiries:
Enquiries to: Communications Director
Direct tel: 01926 707738
Direct fax: 01926 707746
Other contacts: Chief Executive

Founded:
1947

Created by the merger of:
Institute of the Horse and Pony Club and the National Horse Association of Great Britain

Organisation type and purpose:
Membership association (membership is by subscription), registered charity (charity number 210504 and SC038516). Represents all equine interests and has the following objectives: to promote and advance the education, training and safety of the public in all matters relating to the horse; to promote the use, breeding, well-being, safety, environment, health and management of

the horse for the public benefit; to promote community participation in healthy recreation involving the horse; to promote and facilitate the prevention of cruelty, neglect or harm to horses and to promote the relief, safety, sanctuary, rescue and welfare of horses in need of care, attention and assistance; to promote and secure the provision, protection and preservation of rights of way and of access for ridden and driven horses over public roads, highways, footpaths, bridleways, carriageways, public paths and other land.

Subject coverage:
Equine welfare, equestrian safety, access and riding rights of way, qualifications, training and careers, riding schools, horse and pony breeds, riding clubs, competitions.

Museum or gallery collection, archive, or library special collection:
Library deposited with Warwickshire College, Moreton Morrell

Trade and statistical information:
Data on statistics relating to equestrian activities.

Printed publications:
A large range of books on all the subjects above including:
British Horse (magazine, 6 times a year)
Riding and Road Safety Manual
Where to Ride, Train & Stable your Horse (inc. register of Instructors)
Year Book
Order printed publications from: http://www.britishhorse.com

Electronic and video publications:
Tapes for teaching
Videos of events, training and entertainment

Access to staff:
Contact by letter, by telephone, by fax, by e-mail and in person
Hours: Mon to Thu, 0835 to 1700; Fri, 0835 to 1500

Access for disabled people:
Ramped entry, level entry, toilet facilities

Affiliated to the BHS:
British Riding Clubs
The British Horse Society, Stoneleigh Deer Park, Kenilworth, Warwickshire, CV8 2XS; tel: 01926 707700; fax: 01926 707764

BHS is affiliated to:
British Equestrian Federation (BEF)
National Agriculture Centre, Stoneleigh Park, Kenilworth, Warwickshire, CV8 2RH; tel: 01203 698871; fax: 01203 696484

Represented by the BEF in matters concerned with the:
Fédération Equestre Internationale (FEI)

BRITISH HORSEBALL ASSOCIATION

Acronym or abbreviation: BHA

67 Clifford Road, New Barnet, Barnet, Hertfordshire, EN5 5NZ

Tel: 020 8441 1799
Fax: 020 8441 1060
E-mail: horseball@showmobiles.demon.co.uk

Website:
http://www.horseball.org.uk

Enquiries:
Enquiries to: Chairman
Direct e-mail: jim@horseball.org.uk

Founded:
1991

Organisation type and purpose:
Membership association.
National governing body.
To control and develop the game of horseball.

Subject coverage:
The game of horseball.

Printed publications:
Newsletter (free to members)
Rule Book for Horseball

Publications list:
Available online and in print

Access to staff:
Contact by letter, by telephone, by fax, by e-mail and via website. Appointment necessary.
Hours: Mon to Fri, 0900 to 1700

BRITISH HOSPITALITY ASSOCIATION

Acronym or abbreviation: BHA

Queen's House, 55–56 Lincoln's Inn Fields, London, WC2A 3BH

Tel: 020 7404 7744
Fax: 020 7404 7799
E-mail: bha@bha.org.uk

Website:
http://www.bha-online.org.uk
FAQs, information research bank, key personnel, mission statement.

Enquiries:
Enquiries to: Information Officer
Direct e-mail: bill@bha.org.uk

Founded:
1910

Organisation type and purpose:
Trade association (membership is by subscription).

Subject coverage:
Hotels, restaurants, industrial catering, motorway catering, employment in the hotel and catering industry (legislation and conditions), computer software for hotels etc, licensing law, food hygiene.

Trade and statistical information:
Contract catering survey.
Starting a small hotel or restaurant business.

Printed publications:
British Hospitality Trends and Statistics
Contract Catering Survey
Hospitality Matters (magazine, 6 times a year)
Starting a Small Hotel or Restaurant Business
Statutory Notices and Stationery
Systematic Assessment of the Food Environment (SAFE)
Order printed publications from: Office Manager

Publications list:
Available in print

Access to staff:
Contact by letter, by telephone, by fax, by e-mail and via website. Access for members only.
Hours: Mon to Fri, 0900 to 1700

Access to building, collection or gallery:
No prior appointment required

Member of:
European Federation of Contract Catering Organisations (FERCO)
Brussels
European Hotel, Restaurant and Catering Association (HOTREL)
Brussels
International Hotel and Restaurants Association (IHRA)
Paris

Other addresses:
British Hospitality Association
c/o Dundas & Wilson, Saltire Court, Edinburgh, EH1 2EN; tel: 0131 200 7484; fax: 0131 228 8888; e-mail: john.a.loudon@dundas.wilson.com

BRITISH HUMANIST ASSOCIATION

Acronym or abbreviation: BHA

1 Gower Street, London, WC1E 6HD

Tel: 020 7079 3580
Fax: 020 7079 3588

continued overleaf

E-mail: info@humanism.org.uk

Website:
http://www.humanism.org.uk
Introductory information to main beliefs and areas of work.

Enquiries:
Enquiries to: Reception
Other contacts: Membership Officer for general information.

Founded:
1896

Organisation type and purpose:
Learned society, membership association (membership is by subscription), present number of members: 4000, service industry, registered charity (charity number 285987), suitable for ages: all.

Subject coverage:
Humanism, moral education, ethics, law as it relates to religious privilege, reform of religious education and collective worship, non-religious funerals, weddings and baby namings.

Museum or gallery collection, archive, or library special collection:
Archive, books, international journals

Printed publications:
BHA News (six times a year)
Books on naming ceremonies, weddings and funerals and other topics, including:
Humanism
Humanist Anthology
Problems with Arguments for the Existence of God

Electronic and video publications:
The Great Detective Story (video)

Publications list:
Available online and in print

Access to staff:
Contact by letter, by telephone, by fax, by e-mail and via website. Appointment necessary.
Hours: Mon to Fri, 0900 to 1700

Affiliated to:
Religious Education Council

Has:
50 regional and local groups, parliamentary group; branch details are available from Head Office

Member organisation of:
European Humanist Federation
International Humanist and Ethical Union

BRITISH HUMANITARIAN AID

11 Devon Road, Canterbury, Kent, CT1 1RP

Tel: 01227 453434
Fax: 01227 787728
E-mail: office@britishhumanitarianaid.co.uk

Enquiries:
Enquiries to: Director
Direct tel: 07774 100 273 (mobile)

Founded:
1992

Organisation type and purpose:
Voluntary organisation, registered charity (charity number 1031547).
Aid to the needy abroad, mainly children, presently Ukraine.

Subject coverage:
Convoying of humanitarian aid to those in need, Ukraine, supplying aid. Ukraine – centre for adults and children in need, helping 4 orphanages in Ukraine for physically and mentally handicapped children.

Printed publications:
Newsletter (3 times a year)

Access to staff:
Contact by letter, by telephone, by fax, by e-mail and via website
Hours: Mon to Fri, 0900 to 1700

BRITISH HYPNOTHERAPY ASSOCIATION

Acronym or abbreviation: BHA

67 Upper Berkeley Street, London, W1H 7QX

Tel: 020 7723 4443
E-mail: therapy@the-wordsmith.co.uk

Website:
http://www.british-hypnotherapy-association.org

Enquiries:
Enquiries to: Secretary

Founded:
1958

Organisation type and purpose:
International organisation, national organisation, advisory body, learned society, professional body (membership is by qualification), present number of members: 348, training organisation, consultancy, research organisation.
The organisation of practitioners who have had at least four years of relevant training and who comply with professional standards of competence and ethics in psychotherapy involving hypnotherapy.
To maintain a register of competent qualified practitioners and raise standards in the treatment of nervous problems.

Subject coverage:
Hypnotherapy; hypno-analysis; psychotherapy; psychodynamics; nervous problems; emotional problems; birth; parenthood; human relationships; phobias; compulsions, lack of confidence; fears; learning difficulties; parent problems; migraine; psoriasis; psychosexual problems; anxiety etc.

Printed publications:
Amongst many are:
British Medical Hypnotists and the General Medical Council
Choosing a Hypnotherapist
How to Assess Therapy Organisations
Hypnosis in Psychotherapy
The Hypnotherapy Handbook

Publications list:
Available in print

Access to staff:
Contact by letter and by telephone. Appointment necessary.
Hours: Mon to Fri, 0900 to 1700

BRITISH IMAGING AND PHOTOGRAPHIC ASSOCIATION

Acronym or abbreviation: BIPA

Ambassador House, Brigstock Road, Thornton Heath, Surrey, CR7 7JG

Tel: 020 8665 5395
Fax: 020 8665 6447
E-mail: bipa@admin.co.uk

Website:
http://www.bipa.org

Enquiries:
Enquiries to: Chief Executive

Founded:
1918

Organisation type and purpose:
Trade association.

Subject coverage:
Photographic and imaging products.

Access to staff:
Contact by letter, by fax and by e-mail
Hours: Mon to Fri, 0900 to 1700

BRITISH IN VITRO DIAGNOSTIC ASSOCIATION

Acronym or abbreviation: BIVDA

1 Queen Anne's Gate, London, SW1H 9BT

Tel: 020 7957 4633
Fax: 020 7957 4644
E-mail: enquiries@bivda.co.uk

Website:
http://www.bivda.co.uk

Enquiries:
Enquiries to: Director-General

Founded:
1992

Organisation type and purpose:
Trade association (membership is by subscription), present number of members: 113 companies.

Subject coverage:
In vitro diagnostics; laboratory medicine.

Access to staff:
Contact by letter, by telephone, by fax and by e-mail
Hours: Mon to Fri, 0900 to 1700

BRITISH INDEPENDENT PLASTIC EXTRUDERS' ASSOCIATION

Acronym or abbreviation: BIPEA

89 Cornwall Street, Birmingham, B3 3BY

Tel: 0121 236 1866
Fax: 0121 200 1389

Enquiries:
Enquiries to: Secretary

Founded:
1981

Organisation type and purpose:
Trade association (membership is by election or invitation), present number of members: 26.

Subject coverage:
Details of main areas of manufacture of members and materials extruded.

Printed publications:
Members Brochure

Access to staff:
Contact by letter, by telephone and by fax
Hours: Mon to Fri, 0900 to 1700

BRITISH INDUSTRIAL FURNACE CONSTRUCTORS ASSOCIATION

Acronym or abbreviation: BIFCA

National Metalforming Centre, 47 Birmingham Road West Bromwich B70 6PY

Tel: 0121 601 6350
Fax: 0121 601 6387
E-mail: enquiry@bifca.org.uk

Website:
http://www.bifca.org.uk
List of members, products and services, exhibitions and conferences, members area, recruitment area, useful links.

Enquiries:
Enquiries to: Secretary

Organisation type and purpose:
Trade association.

Subject coverage:
Design and manufacture of furnaces, refurbishment, ancillary equipment and control systems.

Access to staff:
Contact by letter, by telephone, by fax, by e-mail and via website. Appointment necessary.
Hours: Mon to Fri, 0900 to 1700

Access to building, collection or gallery:
Prior appointment required

Federated member of the:
Metcom Organisation (Mechanical and Metal Trades Confederation) (METCOM)
tel: 0141 332 0826; fax: 0141 332 5788; website: www.metcon.org.uk

Founder member of:
European Committee of Furnace and Heating Equipment Associations (CECOF)
Frankfurt, Germany; tel: 0 69 66 03 14 13; fax: 0 69 66 03 16 92; e-mail: cecof@vdma.org

BRITISH INDUSTRIAL TRUCK ASSOCIATION

Acronym or abbreviation: BITA

5–7 High Street, Sunninghill, Berkshire, SL5 9NQ

Tel: 01344 623800
Fax: 01344 291197
E-mail: info@bita.org.uk

Enquiries:
Enquiries to: Secretary General
Other contacts: Technical Officer for technical matters.

Founded:
1942

Organisation type and purpose:
Trade association, present number of members: 130.
Represents UK manufacturers of industrial trucks, UK suppliers to the industry and importers of trucks, components and accessories.

Subject coverage:
Industrial trucks (lift trucks), operator safety, code books and guidance notes for the industry.

Printed publications:
Publications on operational safety and training

Publications list:
Available online and in print

Access to staff:
Contact by letter, by telephone, by fax and by e-mail
Hours: Mon to Thur, 0900 to 1700; Fri, 0900 to 1630

Member of:
British Materials Handling Federation
tel: 0121 200 2100; fax: 0121 200 1306

BRITISH INFECTION SOCIETY

Acronym or abbreviation: BIS

Department of Infection and Tropical Medicine, Leicester Royal Infirmary, Infirmary Square, Leicester, LE1 5WW

Tel: 0116 258 6952
Fax: 0116 258 5067
E-mail: martin.wiselka@uhl-tr.nhs.uk

Website:
http://www.britishinfectionsociety.org

Enquiries:
Enquiries to: Honorary Secretary

Founded:
1997

Organisation type and purpose:
Learned society.

Subject coverage:
Infection and communicable diseases and within that general context, public health, microbiology, zoonoses.

Printed publications:
Journal of Infection (12 times a year, free to society members, otherwise on subscription, pub. W B Saunders Company)

Access to staff:
Contact by letter, by fax and by e-mail
Hours: Mon to Fri, 0900 to 1700

BRITISH INSTITUTE AT ANKARA

Acronym or abbreviation: BIAA

10 Carlton House Terrace, London, SW1Y 5AH

Tel: 020 7969 5204
Fax: 020 7969 5401

E-mail: biaa@britac.ac.uk

Website:
http://www.biaa.ac.uk

Enquiries:
Enquiries to: Administrator

Founded:
1948

Organisation type and purpose:
Learned society, registered charity (charity number 313940), research organisation, publishing house. The British Institute at Ankara (BIAA) supports, promotes and publishes British research focused on Turkey and the Black Sea littoral in all academic disciplines within the arts, humanities and social sciences, whilst maintaining a centre of excellence in Ankara focused on the archaeology and related subjects of Turkey.

Subject coverage:
British research focused on Turkey and the Black Sea littoral in all academic disciplines within the arts, humanities and social sciences.

Museum or gallery collection, archive, or library special collection:
Library (40,000 vols), maps, inscription squeezes, pottery, botanical and bone collections, field work archives, photographs and slides

Non-library collection catalogue:
All or part available online and in-house

Library catalogue:
All or part available online and in-house

Printed publications:
BIAA Monographs :
A Catalogue of Glass Vessels in Afyon Museum (C. S. Lightfoot, 1989)
Anatolian Iron Ages 2 (ed. A. Çilingiroglu and D. French, 1991)
Anatolian Iron Ages 3 (ed. A. Çilingiroglu and D. French, 1994)
Anatolian Iron Ages 5 (ed. A. Çilingiroglu and G. Darbyshire, 2005)
An Epigraphical Survey in the Kibyra-Olbasa Region Conducted by A. S. Hall: Regional Epigraphic Catalogues of Asia Minor III (N. P. Milner, 1998)
Canhasan Sites 1, Canhasan I: Stratigraphy and Structures (D. French, 1998)
Canhasan Sites 2, Canhasan I: The Pottery (D. French, 2005)
Greek and Latin Inscriptions in the Konya Archaeological Museum (B. H. McLean, 2002)
Greek, Roman and Byzantine Coins in the Museum at Amasya (Ancient Amaseia), Turkey (S. Ireland, 2000)
Inhabiting Çatalhöyük: Reports from the 1995–99 Seasons (ed. I. Hodder, 2005)
On the Surface: Çatalhöyük 1993–1995 (ed. I. Hodder, 1997)
Recent Turkish Coin Hoards and Numismatic Studies (ed. C. S. Lightfoot, 1991)
Roman Bath Buildings in Lycia (A. Farrington, 1995)
Roman Roads and Milestones of Asia Minor 2: An Interim Catalogue of Milestones (D. French, 1988)
Studies in the Ancient Coinage of Turkey (ed. R. Ashton, 1996)
Studies in the History and Topography of Lycia and Pisidia. In Memoriam A. S. Hall (ed. D. French, 1994)
Survey of Medieval Castles of Anatolia I: Kutahya (C. Foss, 1985)
Survey of Medieval Castles of Anatolia II: Nicodma (C. Foss, 1996)
The Asvan Sites 3 (A. G. Sagona, 1994)
The Black Sea: Past, Present and Future (Erkut and Mitchell, 2007)
The Eastern Frontier of the Roman Empire (ed. D. French and C. S. Lightfoot, 1989)
The Greek and Latin Inscriptions in the Burdur Archaeological Museum (Horsley, 2007)
The Madra River Delta: Regional Studies on the Aegean Coast of Turkey (Lambrianides and Spencer, 2007)

The Ottoman House; Papers of the Amasya Symposium 24–27 September 1996 (ed. S. Ireland and W. Bechhoefer, 1998)
Tille Hôyük I, The Medieval Period (J. Moore, 1993)
Tille Hôyük IV, The Late Bronze Age and the Iron Age Transition (G. D. Summers, 1993)
Towards Reflexive Method in Archaeology: The Example at Çatalhöyük (ed. I. Hodder, 2000)
BIAA Occasional Publications:
A Classical Map of Asia Minor (W. M. Calder and G. E. Bean, 1958)
Beycesultan Vol. I, Vol. II, Vol. III.1, Vol. III.2
The Sultantepe Tablets Vol. I (O. R. Gurney and J. J. Finkelstein, 1957)
The Sultantepe Tablets Vol. II (O. R. Gurney and P. Hullin, 1964)
BIAA Annual Publications:
Anatolian Studies, Vols 1 (1951) to 57 (2007), prices vary
The Indexes to Anatolian Studies Vols 1–10, 11–20, 21–30, 31–40
Anatolian Archaeology, Vols 1 (1995) to 13 (2007)
Special Anniversary Volume: Fifty Years' Work by the British Institute of Archaeology at Ankara (ed. R. Matthews, 1997)
Order printed publications from: Oxbow Books, Park End Place, Oxford, OX1 1HN; tel. 01865 241249; website http://www.oxbowbooks.com

Publications list:
Available online and in print

Access to staff:
Contact by letter, by telephone, by fax, by e-mail, in person and via website. Appointment necessary.
Hours: Mon, Tue and Thu, 0900 to 1300

Also at:
British Institute at Ankara
Tahran Caddesi 24, Kavaklidere, Ankara, TR-06700, Turkey; tel: +90 312 427 5487; fax: +90 312 428 0159

Parent body:
British Academy
10 Carlton House Terrace, London, SW1Y 5AH

BRITISH INSTITUTE FOR ALLERGY AND ENVIRONMENTAL THERAPY

Ffynnonwen, Llangwyryfon, Aberystwyth, Ceredigion, SY23 4EY

Tel: 01974 241376
Fax: 01974 241795
E-mail: allergy@onetel.com

Enquiries:
Enquiries to: Principal

Founded:
1987

Organisation type and purpose:
Professional body.

Subject coverage:
Allergies; clinical ecology.

Access to staff:
Contact by letter, by telephone and by fax
Hours: Mon to Fri, 0900 to 1600

BRITISH INSTITUTE FOR LEARNING & DEVELOPMENT

Acronym or abbreviation: BILD

Trym Lodge, 1 Henbury Road, Westbury on Trym, Bristol, BS9 3HQ

Tel: 0117 959 6517
Fax: 0117 959 6518
E-mail: info@thebild.org

Website:
http://www.thebild.org/
On-line database of members' products, services and courses.

Enquiries:
Enquiries to: Marketing and Development Manager

continued overleaf

Other contacts: General Manager

Founded:
1990

Formerly called:
the British Learning Association (formed by merger in 2003 of the British Association for Open Learning and The Forum for Technology in Training) (year of change 2007)

Organisation type and purpose:
International organisation, national organisation, trade association, membership association (membership is by subscription), present number of members: 300, registered charity (charity number 328229).
To build a dynamic community, with global reach, committed to inculcating excellence and best practice in learning.

Subject coverage:
Open, flexible and distance learning and e-learning. All aspects associated with this area.

Printed publications:
Guide to the BAOL Quality Mark-UK (£26.25, UK inc. p £28.83, Europe inc. p&p)
Ensuring Quality in open learning (£41.45, UK inc. p £42.25, Europe inc. p&p)
Open Learning Today (journal, 4 times a year, £55 per annum, £65 per annum overseas)

Access to staff:
Contact by letter, by telephone, by fax, by e-mail and via website. Appointment necessary.
Hours: Mon to Fri, 0900 to 1700

BRITISH INSTITUTE IN EASTERN AFRICA

Acronym or abbreviation: BIEA

10 Carlton House Terrace, London, SW1Y 5AH

Tel: 020 7969 5201
Fax: 020 7969 5401
E-mail: biea@britac.ac.uk

Enquiries:
Enquiries to: Secretary

Founded:
1960

Organisation type and purpose:
Learned society (membership is by subscription), registered charity (charity number 1061622).

Subject coverage:
Research into the history, archaeology and related subjects of eastern Africa.

Printed publications:
Azania (journal, free to members)
Archaeology at Aksum, Ethiopia 1993–7 (Phillipson DW, 2000, 2 vols)
Early Pastoralists of South-western Kenya (Robertshaw P, 1990)
Excavations at Aksum: Research at the Ancient Ethiopian Capital by the Late Dr Neville Chittick (Munro-Hay S, 1989)
Kibiro: The Salt of Bunyoro, past and present (Connah G, 1996)
Kilwa: an Islamic Trading City on the East African Coast (Chittick N, 1974)
Manda: Excavations at an Island Port on the Kenya Coast (Chittick N, 1984)
Shanga: The archaeology of a Muslim trading community on the coast of East Africa (Horton M, 1996)
Soba: Archaeological Research at a Medieval Capital on the Blue Nile (Welsby D A and Daniels C M, 1991)
Soba II: Renewed Excavations within the metropolis of the Kingdom of Alwa in Central Sudan (Welsby D A, 1998, £70)
The Growth of Farming Communities in Africa from the Equator Southwards (ed. Sutton J E G, 1996)
The Monuments of Aksum (ed. Phillipson D W)
The Prehistory of Eastern Zambia (Phillipson D W, 1976)

Order printed publications from: Members order through the Institute to obtain their discount
Oxbow Books
Park End Place, Oxford, OX1 1HN, tel: 01865 241249, fax: 01865 794449

Publications list:
Available in print

Access to staff:
Contact by letter, by telephone, by fax and by e-mail
Hours: Mon to Fri, 1400 to 1800

Other addresses:
British Institute in Eastern Africa
PO Box 30710, Nairobi, Kenya; tel: 00 254 2 43721; fax: 00 254 2 43365; e-mail: britinst@insightkenya.com

BRITISH INSTITUTE OF AGRICULTURAL CONSULTANTS

Acronym or abbreviation: BIAC

The Estate Office, Torry Hill, Milstead, Sittingbourne, Kent, ME9 0SP

Tel: 01795 830100
Fax: 01795 830243
E-mail: info@biac.co.uk

Website:
http://www.biac.co.uk

Enquiries:
Enquiries to: Chief Executive
Direct e-mail: anthony.hyde@farmline.com

Founded:
1957

Organisation type and purpose:
Professional body.

Subject coverage:
Agriculture, horticulture, forestry, silviculture, arboriculture, crop production, livestock production, mechanisation, land drainage and reclamation, landscape planning, chemicals and fertilisers, plant pathology, farm and estate management, farm buildings, pollution, soils, management, finance, planning appeals, agricultural education and law, fish farming, photography, snail farming, deer farming, historic houses and gardens, leisure and amenity, environment and conservation, arbitration.

Printed publications:
Curricula Vitae of Overseas Consultants
Curricula Vitae of Business Management Consultants
List of members and their specialist services

Electronic and video publications:
Membership List
Overseas Consultants List

Access to staff:
Contact by letter, by telephone, by fax, by e-mail and via website
Hours: Mon to Fri, 0900 to 1700

BRITISH INSTITUTE OF CLEANING SCIENCE

Acronym or abbreviation: BICSc

9 Premier Court, Boarden Close, Moulton Park, Northampton, NN3 6LF

Tel: 01604 678710
Fax: 01604 645988
E-mail: info@bics.org.uk

Website:
http://www.bics.org.uk

Enquiries:
Enquiries to: Executive Director
Direct tel: 01604 678715
Direct e-mail: stan@bics.org.uk
Other contacts: Business Development Manager

Founded:
1961

Organisation type and purpose:
Membership association (membership is by qualification), present number of members: 5,000, service industry, suitable for ages: 18+.
Education and training body for the cleaning industry.

Subject coverage:
Education, training and general information regarding the cleaning industry, cleaning of buildings, internally and externally; cleaning of outside areas; education and training.

Printed publications:
Cleaning Industry Handbook (pub. Market Place Publishing for the Institute, annually, free to members)
Newsletter (quarterly, members only)
BICSc supply a number of educational products connected with the Cleaning Operator Proficiency Certificate (COPC), Food Premises Cleaning Certificate (FPCC), Healthcare Professional Cleaning Certificate (HPCC), Cleaning Supervisors Skills Certficate (CSSC) and the Car Valeting Certificate (CVC). Also specialist manuals. Some items are restricted to members.

Electronic and video publications:
2 training DVDs

Publications list:
Available online and in print

Access to staff:
Contact by letter, by telephone, by fax, by e-mail and via website. Appointment necessary.
Hours: Mon to Fri, 0830 to 1700

Links with:
British Cleaning Council

BRITISH INSTITUTE OF FACILITIES MANAGEMENT

Acronym or abbreviation: BIFM

67 High Street, Saffron Walden, Essex, CB10 1AA

Tel: 01799 508606
Fax: 01799 513237
E-mail: admin@bifm.org.uk

Website:
http://www.bifm.org.uk
General information, publications for members only.

Enquiries:
Enquiries to: Membership Secretary
Direct tel: 01799 508610
Direct e-mail: membership@bifm.org.uk

Founded:
1993

Organisation type and purpose:
Professional body (membership is by subscription, election or invitation), present number of members: 6000.
To promote awareness of facilities management and provide support, education, training and information to members.

Subject coverage:
All aspects of facilities management including space planning, lighting, business continuity planning, measurement protocol.

Trade and statistical information:
Survey of members' responsibilities.
Research Directory.

Printed publications:
The Bulletin (fortnightly)
Best practice guides on: Space Planning, Lighting, Business Continuity Planning, Measurement Protocol
Conference Proceedings
Measurement Protocol (£15)

Publications list:
Available online and in print

Access to staff:
Contact by letter, by telephone, by fax, by e-mail and via website. Appointment necessary.
Hours: Mon to Fri, 0900 to 1700

BRITISH INSTITUTE OF GRAPHOLOGISTS

Acronym or abbreviation: BIG

PO Box 3060, Gerrards Cross, Buckinghamshire, SL9 9XP

Tel: 01753 891 241

Website:
http://www.britishgraphology.org
Example analysis on monthly basis, history, background, free lesson on monthly basis, mailing list, information pack available, services offered, details of library, lectures and membership.

Enquiries:
Enquiries to: General Secretary

Founded:
1983

Organisation type and purpose:
Learned society.
To promote understanding and recognition of graphology.

Subject coverage:
Graphology consultancy in: vocational guidance; information and professional training; personnel selection etc.

Printed publications:
Books and monographs
The Graphologist (quarterly)

Access to staff:
Contact by letter, by telephone and by e-mail
Hours: Mon to Fri, 0900 to 1700

Also at:
Association of Disabled Professionals
Netley Lodge, 134 Old Woking Road, Woking, Surrey, GU22 8NY

Subsidiary body:
Graphology Research & Education Trust (GRET)
55 Whitton Avenue East, Greenford, Middlesex, UB6 0BQ; tel: 020 8902 4183

BRITISH INSTITUTE OF HOMEOPATHY

Acronym or abbreviation: BIH

Endeavour House, 80 High Street, Egham, Surrey, TW20 9HE

Tel: 01784 473800
Fax: 01784 473801
E-mail: britinsthom@compuserve.com

Website:
http://www.britinsthom.com
All course information.

Enquiries:
Enquiries to: Managing Director

Founded:
1986

Organisation type and purpose:
International organisation, training organisation.

Subject coverage:
Homoeopathic medicine, homoeopathic pharmacy, herbal medicine, anatomy, physiology, pathology, nature of disease. Bach flower therapy, nutrition, differential diagnosis, aromatherapy.

Printed publications:
International Newsletter (3 times a year)

Electronic and video publications:
Audio and videotapes and CD-ROM which form an integral part of the courses

Access to staff:
Contact by letter, by telephone, by fax, by e-mail and in person. Appointment necessary.

Hours: Mon to Fri, 0900 to 1700

Access to building, collection or gallery:
No prior appointment required

Parent body:
The British Institute of Homeopathy Limited
tel: 01784 440467; fax: 01784 449887; e-mail: britinsthom@compuserve.com

BRITISH INSTITUTE OF HUMAN RIGHTS

Acronym or abbreviation: BIHR

School of Law, King's College London, 3rd Floor, 26–29 Drury Lane, London, WC2B 5RL

Tel: 020 7848 1818
Fax: 020 7848 1814
E-mail: admin@bihr.org

Website:
http://www.bihr.org

Enquiries:
Enquiries to: Administrator

Founded:
1970

Organisation type and purpose:
Registered charity (charity number 1101575).
Conducting research, organising lectures, conferences, etc. in the human rights field.

Subject coverage:
Human rights with particular application to education; European Convention on Human Rights.

Printed publications:
Aspects of incorporation of the European Convention on Human Rights into Domestic Law
The Best Interests of the Child: International Co-operation on Child Abduction
Human Rights for the New Millennium
Human Rights Protection

Access to staff:
Contact by letter and by e-mail
Hours: Mon to Fri, 0930 to 1730

Close links with:
King's College, London

Connections with:
Council of Europe
Other human rights organisations through the Human Rights Network

BRITISH INSTITUTE OF INDUSTRIAL THERAPY

Acronym or abbreviation: BIIT

243 Shelley Road, Wellingborough, Northamptonshire, NN8 3EN

Tel: 01933 675327
Fax: 01933 675327

Enquiries:
Enquiries to: Administrator

Founded:
1981

Organisation type and purpose:
Professional body (membership is by subscription), present number of members: 110, voluntary organisation, registered charity (charity number 283951), consultancy.
National charitable organisation with members from both statutory and voluntary sector units.

Subject coverage:
Rehabilitation through work therapy and associated social education and training for the relief and rehabilitation of the mentally disabled. Advancement of science and practice of industrial therapy. Educational courses for those working in the field of industrial therapy. Consultancy service on work rehabilitation for members.

Printed publications:
Specialised information leaflets (members only)

Access to staff:
Appointment necessary.
Hours: Mon to Fri, 0900 to 1700
Special comments: Answerphone if not available.

Chairman:
British Institute of Industrial Therapy
Lewin Cottage, Jeremy's Lane, Bolney, Haywards Heath, West Sussex, RH17 5QE; tel: 01444 881054

BRITISH INSTITUTE OF INNKEEPING

Acronym or abbreviation: BII

Wessex House, 80 Park Street, Camberley, Surrey, GU15 3PT

Tel: 01276 684449
Fax: 01276 23045
E-mail: info@bii.org

Website:
http://www.bii.org
Information on all BII products and services.
http://www.barzone.co.uk
Careers information for the sector.

Enquiries:
Enquiries to: Reception
Direct fax: 01276 682214
Direct e-mail: reception@bii.org

Founded:
1981

Organisation type and purpose:
Professional body (membership is by qualification, election or invitation), present number of members: 16,000, registered charity (charity number 283945), training organisation.
BII is the professional body for the licensed retail sector. BII's aim is to provide skills, information and qualifications to help members run more successful businesses. BIIAB is a wholly-owned subsidiary awarding qualifications for licensed hospitality.

Subject coverage:
Qualifications for those entering or already in the licensed retail sector (pubs) and off licences.
Information on careers in licensed retailing.

Trade and statistical information:
Data relating to careers in the licensed retail sector (pubs).

Printed publications:
biiBusiness (business magazine, 10 times a year, members and on subscription)
Handbooks for specific qualifications

Publications list:
Available online

Access to staff:
Contact by letter, by telephone, by fax, by e-mail, in person and via website
Hours: Mon to Fri, 0900 to 1700

Links with:
BIIAB – qualifications for licensed hospitality
tel: 01276 684449; fax: 01276 23045; e-mail: info@bii.org

BRITISH INSTITUTE OF INTERNATIONAL AND COMPARATIVE LAW

Acronym or abbreviation: BIICL

Charles Clore House, 17 Russell Square, London, WC1B 5JP

Tel: 020 7862 5151
Fax: 020 7862 5152
E-mail: info@biicl.org

Website:
http://www.biicl.org
Details of services offered by the Institute.

continued overleaf

Enquiries:
Enquiries to: Director

Founded:
1952

Organisation type and purpose:
International organisation, consultancy, research organisation.
Commonwealth Legal Advisory Service.

Subject coverage:
Public international law; EC law; human rights law; private international law; comparative law; Commonwealth law.

Printed publications:
Bulletin of Legal Developments (fortnightly)
International and Comparative Law Quarterly (ICLQ)
Newsletter (quarterly)
Various monographs, please contact to order catalogue

Publications list:
Available online and in print

Access to staff:
Contact by letter, by telephone, by fax and by e-mail
Hours: Mon to Fri, 0930 to 1730

BRITISH INSTITUTE OF LEARNING DISABILITIES

Acronym or abbreviation: BILD

Campion House, Green Street, Kidderminster, Worcestershire, DY10 1JL

Tel: 01562 723010
Fax: 01562 723029
E-mail: enquiries@bild.org.uk

Website:
http://www.bild.org.uk

Enquiries:
Enquiries to: Information Administrator
Direct tel: 01562 723014
Direct e-mail: k.brackley@bild.org.uk

Founded:
1972

Organisation type and purpose:
Professional body (membership is by subscription), registered charity (charity number 1019663), training organisation, consultancy, research organisation, publishing house.
Receives financial support from the Department of Health.
Aims to improve the quality of life of people with learning disabilities, through advancing education, research and practice and by promoting better ways of working with and for children and adults with learning difficulties.

Subject coverage:
Learning disability and multi-handicap, medical, nursing, social, educational and environmental needs.

Library catalogue:
All or part available in-house

Printed publications:
A selection of books and journals relating to all aspects of disability; research, good practice, everyday living and study materials, including:
British Journal of Learning Disabilities (quarterly)
Current Awareness Service (monthly)
Good Autism Practice (2 times a year)
Journal of Applied Research in Intellectual Disabilities (quarterly)
Learning Disability Bulletin (quarterly)
The SLD Experience (3 times a year)
A Place at the Table? (Simons K)
Crossing Boundaries (Edited by Brighman L, Atkinson D, et al, 2000)
Forgotten Lives: Exploring the History of Learning Disability (Edited by Atkinson D, Jackson M, Walmsley J)
Pathways to Citizen Advocacy (Brooke J, 16 training units)

Shared Ownership for People with Learning Difficulties (Dixon T, 2001)
Order printed publications from: BookSource 32 Finlas Street, Cowlair's Estate, Glasgow, G22 5DU, tel: 08702 402182, fax: 0141 557 0189

Publications list:
Available online and in print

Access to staff:
Contact by letter, by telephone, by fax, by e-mail and via website. Appointment necessary.
Hours: Mon to Thu, 0900 to 1300 and 1400 to 1700; Fri, 0900 to 1300 and 1400 to 1630

Access to building, collection or gallery:
Prior appointment required

Access for disabled people:
Parking provided, level entry, access to all public areas, toilet facilities

BRITISH INSTITUTE OF MUSCULOSKELETAL MEDICINE

Acronym or abbreviation: BIMM

34 The Avenue, Watford, Hertfordshire, WD17 4AH

Tel: 01923 220999
Fax: 01923 249037
E-mail: bimm@compuserve.com

Website:
http://www.bimm.org.uk

Enquiries:
Enquiries to: Honorary Secretary
Other contacts: Secretary for non-medical enquiries.

Founded:
1992

Organisation type and purpose:
Professional body (membership is by subscription), present number of members: 340, registered charity, training organisation, research organisation.
Dissemination of knowledge to medical profession of musculoskeletal medicine.

Subject coverage:
Musculoskeletal medicine, including manual/manipulative medicine, all aspects of mechanical disorders of the spine and peripheral joints, and sports injuries. This specifically includes soft tissue disorders/injuries of muscles, ligaments, tendons and fascia.

Printed publications:
Patient Information Leaflets
Journal of Orthopaedic Medicine (4 times a year)
Membership list of Practitioners
Newsletter (4 times a year)

Access to staff:
Contact by letter, by telephone, by fax and by e-mail
Hours: Mon to Fri, 0900 to 1700

Access to building, collection or gallery:
No access other than to staff

Affiliated to:
British League Against Rheumatism (BLAR)
Fédération Internationale de Médecine Manuel/Musculoskeletal (FIMM)

BRITISH INSTITUTE OF NON-DESTRUCTIVE TESTING

Acronym or abbreviation: BINDT

1 Spencer Parade, Northampton, NN1 5AA

Tel: 01604 630124
Fax: 01604 231489
E-mail: info@bindt.org

Website:
http://www.bindt.org
Membership data, details of publications, events, certification.

Enquiries:
Enquiries to: Secretary

Founded:
1954

Organisation type and purpose:
Learned society.
Includes a Condition Monitoring Research and Development Group and a Research Group.
To promote the science and practice of non-destructive testing and all other associated materials testing disciplines.

Subject coverage:
Non-destructive testing, condition and health monitoring and all other materials and quality testing disciplines. Various specialist groups for NDT application e.g. aerospace, service inspection, research. Condition monitoring and diagnostic technology group.

Printed publications:
Insight (journal, monthly with quarterly European issues)
NDT News (monthly)
NDT Yearbook (annually)
A wide range of technical titles on related subjects including:
Basic Metallurgy for Non-Destructive Testing (ed Taylor J L)
Mathematics and formulae in NDT (Halmshaw R)
Series: The Capabilities and Limitations of NDT (8 parts, ed Hanstead P D)
Non-Destructive Testing for Engineering Design (Birchon D, rev ed Halmshaw R)

Publications list:
Available in print

A nominated body of the:
Engineering Council

Member of:
British National Committee for Non-Destructive Testing
European Council of Non-Destructive Testing

Wholly owned subsidiary:
Personnel Certification in Non-Destructive Testing

BRITISH INSTITUTE OF OCCUPATIONAL HYGIENISTS

Acronym or abbreviation: BIOH

5–6 Melbourne Business Court, Millennium Way, Pride Park, Derby, DE24 8LZ

Tel: 01332 298101
Fax: 01332 298099
E-mail: admin@bohs.org

Website:
http://www.bioh.org

Enquiries:
Enquiries to: Media Enquiries
Direct tel: 01332 250701
Direct e-mail: anthea@bohs.org

Founded:
1997

Organisation type and purpose:
Professional body (membership is by subscription, qualification), registered charity (charity number 1066537).

Subject coverage:
Occupational hygiene.

Access to staff:
Contact by letter, by telephone, by fax and by e-mail
Hours: Mon to Fri, 0830 to 1630

Access to building, collection or gallery:
No access other than to staff

BRITISH INSTITUTE OF ORGAN STUDIES

Acronym or abbreviation: BIOS

39 Church Street, Haslingfield, Cambridge, CB23
1JE

Tel: 01223 872190
Fax: 01223 872190
E-mail: bios@drawstop.plus.com

Website:
http://www.bios.org.uk
Current officers, National Pipe Organ Register
with search facilities, British Organ Archive
Handlist.
Directory of British Organ-builders.

Enquiries:
Enquiries to: Secretary
Direct e-mail: c.kearl@blueyonder.co.uk
Other contacts: Hon. Archivist; Membership
Secretary

Founded:
1976

Organisation type and purpose:
Learned society (membership is by subscription),
present number of members: c. 650, voluntary
organisation, registered charity (charity number
283936), suitable for ages: 11–80.

Subject coverage:
Conservation, history and restoration of historic
British pipe organs; information on its repertoire
and performance practice.

**Museum or gallery collection, archive, or library
special collection:**
British Organ Archive (largest single collection of
original records, order books, designs, working
drawings, etc. of organ builders from 1820;
housed in Birmingham Central Library)

Non-library collection catalogue:
All or part available online

Printed publications:
BIOS Journal (annually)
BIOS Reporter (quarterly)
Directory of British Organ-builders
Guidance Leaflets:
Sound Advice – The Care of your Pipe Organ
Grants – Funding for work on historic instruments
Order printed publications from: Positif Press, British
Institute of Organ Studies
130 Southfield Road, Oxford, OX4 1PA, tel: 01865
243 220, fax: 01865 243 272, e-mail: john.f.brennan@
btinternet.com

Publications list:
Available online

Access to staff:
Contact by letter, by fax, by e-mail and via
website. Appointment necessary. Letter of
introduction required.
Hours: Mon to Fri, 0900 to 1700
Special comments: Visitors to British Organ Archive
require a letter of introduction and should arrange
a prior appointment with Birmingham Central
Library (City Archives) where the Archive is held.

Access to building, collection or gallery:
Prior appointment required
Hours: Mon, Tue, Fri, Sat, 0900 to 1700; Thu, 0900
to 2000

Parent body of:
British Organ Archive (BOA)
National Pipe Organ Register (NPOR)

BRITISH INSTITUTE OF
PROFESSIONAL PHOTOGRAPHY

Acronym or abbreviation: BIPP

Fox Talbot House, Amwell End, Ware,
Hertfordshire, SG12 9HN

Tel: 01920 464011
Fax: 01920 487056
E-mail: info@bipp.com

Website:
http://www.bipp.com

Enquiries:
Enquiries to: Executive Secretary

Founded:
1901

Organisation type and purpose:
Professional body.

Subject coverage:
Imaging.

Printed publications:
The Photographer (monthly, £39.95)
Directory of Professional Photography (annually,
£20)

Access to staff:
Contact by letter, by telephone, by fax and by e-
mail
Hours: Mon to Fri, 0900 to 1700

BRITISH INSTITUTE OF
RADIOLOGY

Acronym or abbreviation: BIR

36 Portland Place, London, W1B 1AT

Tel: 020 7307 1405
Fax: 020 7307 1414
E-mail: infocentre@bir.org.uk

Website:
http://www.bir.org.uk
British Institute of Radiology home page and
sample journal pages, library and archives pages.

Enquiries:
Enquiries to: General Secretary
Direct tel: 020 7307 1406
Other contacts: Information Centre Manager

Founded:
1897

Organisation type and purpose:
Professional body, registered charity (charity
number GB 233 7553 63).

Subject coverage:
Radiology, radiography, diagnostic imaging,
ultrasound, radiation protection, radiation physics,
radiotherapy and oncology, computed
tomography, radiobiology, nuclear medicine,
NMR, MRI (magnetic resonance imaging), history
of radiology.

**Museum or gallery collection, archive, or library
special collection:**
Hugh Davies Bequest
KC Clark Slide Collection of 3,500 glass slides

Library catalogue:
All or part available online

Printed publications:
Annual Report
British Journal of Radiology (monthly with a
Congress supplement)
Imaging
Dentomaxillofacial Radiology
Special Reports

Publications list:
Available online and in print

Access to staff:
Contact by letter, by telephone, by fax and by e-
mail. Appointment necessary. All charged.
Hours: Mon, Wed and Fri, 0900 to 1700; Tue and
Thu, 1000 to 1800

BRITISH INSURANCE BROKERS'
ASSOCIATION

Acronym or abbreviation: BIBA

BIBA House, 14 Bevis Marks, London, EC3A 7NT

Tel: 020 7623 9043
Fax: 020 7626 9676
E-mail: enquiries@biba.org.uk

Website:
http://www.biba.org.uk
Consumers can get details of local insurance
brokers.

Enquiries:
Enquiries to: Chief Executive

Founded:
1978

Organisation type and purpose:
Trade association.
Representing insurance brokers and independent
intermediaries for the sale of general insurance.

Subject coverage:
The sale of general insurance products through an
insurance broker or independent intermediary.

Printed publications:
The Broker (Quarterly)

Access to staff:
Contact by letter, by telephone, by fax, by e-mail
and via website
Hours: Mon to Fri, 0830 to 1730

BRITISH INSURANCE LAW
ASSOCIATION

Acronym or abbreviation: BILA

London Metropolitan University, 84 Moorgate,
London, EC2M 6SQ

Tel: 020 7320 1490
Fax: 020 7320 1497
E-mail: bila@lgu.ac.uk

Website:
http://www.bila.org.uk

Enquiries:
Enquiries to: Administrator

Founded:
1964

Organisation type and purpose:
Learned society.
Education and exchange of ideas.

Subject coverage:
Law affecting any branch of insurance.

Printed publications:
Bulletin (3 times per annum)
Technical papers, including government and law
reforms

Access to staff:
Contact by letter, by fax, by e-mail and via
website
Hours: Mon to Fri, 0900 to 1700

Affiliated to:
International Insurance Law Association (AIDA)

BRITISH INTERIOR TEXTILES
ASSOCIATION

Acronym or abbreviation: BITA

5 Portland Place, London, W1B 1PW

Tel: 020 7636 7788
Fax: 020 7636 7515
E-mail: bita@dial.pipex.com

Website:
http://www.interiortextiles.co.uk

Enquiries:
Enquiries to: Secretary

Founded:
1917

Organisation type and purpose:
Trade association.

Subject coverage:
Furnishing textiles industry, manufacture and
distribution. UK and EC legislation affecting the
industry.

Printed publications:
Directory of Products and Services
Newsletter

Electronic and video publications:
CD-ROM of members and services

continued overleaf

Publications list:
Available in print

Access to staff:
Contact by letter, by fax, by e-mail and via website. Appointment necessary.
Hours: Mon to Fri, 0900 to 1730

Access to building, collection or gallery:
Prior appointment required

BRITISH INTERNATIONAL FREIGHT ASSOCIATION

Acronym or abbreviation: BIFA

Redfern House, Browells Lane, Feltham, Middlesex, TW13 7EP

Tel: 020 8844 2266
Fax: 020 8890 5546
E-mail: bifa@bifa.org

Website:
http://www.bifa.org
Background information to BIFA, its organisation, aims, structure, news, members, associate organisations, trading conditions, etc, as well as detailed information on the range of training services available.

Enquiries:
Enquiries to: Information Officer
Direct tel: 020 8844 3639
Direct e-mail: information@bifa.org

Founded:
1944

Organisation type and purpose:
Trade association.
To represent the international freight services industry.

Subject coverage:
Practical help and advice on any aspect of running a freight forwarding business or any industry related issues which may affect member companies.

Publications list:
Available online and in print

Access to staff:
Contact by letter, by telephone, by fax and by e-mail. Access for members only. Non-members charged.
Hours: Mon to Fri, 0900 to 1700

Incorporates:
Institute of Freight Professionals

BRITISH INTERNATIONAL STUDIES ASSOCIATION

Acronym or abbreviation: BISA

16 Ridge Croft, Stone, Staffordshire, ST15 8PN

Tel: 01785 818788
Fax: 01785 818788
E-mail: pkellybisa@compuserve.com

Website:
http://www.bisa.ac.uk

Enquiries:
Enquiries to: Administrator

Founded:
1975

Organisation type and purpose:
Membership association (membership is by subscription), present number of members: c. 1000, registered charity.
To promote the study of International Relations and related subjects through teaching, research and the facilitation of contact between scholars.

Subject coverage:
International studies, IR theory, strategy, IPE, environment, UN and International organisations.

Printed publications:
Review of International Studies (Academic Journal and BISA Newsletter available free to members, review available for purchase)

Publications list:
Available in print

Access to staff:
Contact by letter, by e-mail and via website
Hours: Mon to Fri, 0900 to 1700

BRITISH INTERPLANETARY SOCIETY

Acronym or abbreviation: BIS

27–29 South Lambeth Road, London, SW8 1SZ

Tel: 020 7735 3160
Fax: 020 7820 1504
E-mail: mail@bis-spaceflight.com

Website:
http://www.bis-spaceflight.com

Enquiries:
Enquiries to: Executive Secretary

Founded:
1933

Organisation type and purpose:
Learned society, registered charity (charity number 250556).
Promotion of studies in space research, technology and applications.

Subject coverage:
Space research and technology, space applications and astronomy.

Museum or gallery collection, archive, or library special collection:
Specialised library contains about 8000 books and reports (members only)

Printed publications:
Journal of the British Interplanetary Society (6 times a year)
Spaceflight (monthly)
Space Chronicle (2 times a year)

Electronic and video publications:
Space videos

Access to staff:
Contact by letter, by telephone, by fax, by e-mail and via website
Hours: Mon to Fri, 0930 to 1700

Founder member of:
International Astronautical Federation

BRITISH INVESTMENT CASTING TRADE ASSOCIATION

Acronym or abbreviation: BICTA

National Metalforming Centre, 47 Birmingham Road, West Bromwich, West Midlands, B70 6PX

Tel: 0121 601 6390
Fax: 0121 601 6391
E-mail: admin@cmfed.co.uk

Enquiries:
Enquiries to: Manager

Founded:
1958

Organisation type and purpose:
Trade association.

Subject coverage:
All aspects of the foundry process known as investment (or lost wax) casting – technology of process, markets for investment castings, equipment and consumables used in process, related (foundry) subjects.

Museum or gallery collection, archive, or library special collection:
Books on investment casting

Copies of proceedings of: BICTA Conferences, EICF (European Investment Casters' Federation) Conferences, World Investment Casting Conference, US Investment Casting Institute Conferences
Miscellaneous technical papers

Trade and statistical information:
Data on output of investment castings.

Printed publications:
Abstracts (members only)
Bicta Bulletin (3 times a year, magazine issued to members and others interested in investment casting)

Publications list:
Available online and in print

Access to staff:
Contact by letter, by telephone, by fax and by e-mail. Appointment necessary. Non-members charged.
Hours: Mon to Thu, 0900 to 1700; Fri, 0900 to 1530

BRITISH IRIS SOCIETY

Acronym or abbreviation: BIS

1 Sole Farm Close, Great Bookham, Leatherhead, Surrey, KT23 3ED

Tel: 01372 454581
E-mail: sheila@ecklin.fsnet.co.uk

Enquiries:
Enquiries to: Honorary Secretary

Founded:
1922

Organisation type and purpose:
Voluntary organisation, registered charity (charity number 261896), research organisation.

Subject coverage:
Irises and iridaceae: origins, breeding, cultivation, taxonomy, history.

Museum or gallery collection, archive, or library special collection:
The Genus Iris: original paintings by W R Dykes
Miscellaneous printed material not available in public libraries
Slide library
Paintings by Paul Furse
Paintings by Caparne

Printed publications:
Alphabetical Table and Cultivation Guide to the Species of the Genus Iris and other titles
Cultivation of Irises (2 parts)
First Steps in Iris Growing
Irises for the Water Garden
Year Books (1929 to date)
Introducing Iris
List of Iris Suppliers
Order printed publications from: Publications Officer, British Iris Society
8 Wicket Road, Kinson, Bournemouth, Dorset, BH10 5LT

Access to staff:
Contact by letter and by telephone
Hours: Mon to Fri, 0900 to 1700

Affiliated to:
iris societies around the world
Royal Horticultural Society

Enrolment Secretary:
British Iris Society
47 Station Road, New Barnet, Hertfordshire, EN5 1PR; tel: 020 8441 1300; fax: 020 8441 1300; e-mail: britirissoc@aol.com

Member of the:
National Plant Societies Federation

Membership Secretary:
British Iris Society
15 Parkwood Drive, Rawtenstall, Lancashire, BB4 6RP; tel: 01706 212840; e-mail: joymet@dircon.co.uk

BRITISH JEWELLERS' ASSOCIATION

Acronym or abbreviation: BJA

10 Vyse Street, Birmingham, B18 6LT

Tel: 0121 237 1110
Fax: 0121 237 1113
E-mail: info@bja.org.uk

Website:
http://www.bja.org.uk

Enquiries:
Enquiries to: Senior Co-ordinator

Organisation type and purpose:
Membership association (membership is by subscription).

Subject coverage:
Jewellery manufacturing and silversmithing, designers, jewellery tools, members who supply these services.

Printed publications:
Retail Jeweller & British Jeweller (magazine)
The British Jeweller Yearbook
Jewellery in Britain
Order printed publications from: British Jewellers' Association
338 Goswell Road, London, EC1V 7QP

Access to staff:
Contact by letter, by telephone, by fax, by e-mail and via website
Hours: Mon to Fri, 0900 to 1700

BRITISH JIGSAW PUZZLE LIBRARY

Acronym or abbreviation: BJPL

Clarendon, Parsonage Road, Herne Bay, Kent, CT6 5TA

Tel: 01227 742222
E-mail: jigsawman@britishjigsawpuzzlelibrary.co.uk

Website:
http://www.britishjigsawpuzzlelibrary.co.uk
Subscription information, brief history, types of jigsaw puzzles, contact information.

Enquiries:
Enquiries to: Secretary

Founded:
1933

Organisation type and purpose:
Membership association (membership is by subscription), present number of members: 350.
Library of wooden jigsaw puzzles.
Leisure and therapy.

Subject coverage:
Jigsaw puzzles (subscription loan service).
Lending library of wooden jigsaw puzzles.
Puzzles exchanged by post.
Stock contains jigsaws with large pieces suitable for stroke victims and people with disabilities.

Trade and statistical information:
Collection of over 3500 high quality craftsman cut wooden puzzles.

Printed publications:
History of The Jigsaw Puzzle Library (£4)

Access to staff:
Contact by letter, by telephone, by e-mail and via website. Appointment necessary.
Hours: Mon to Fri, 0900 to 1700

Access to building, collection or gallery:
No access other than to staff

BRITISH JUDO COUNCIL

Acronym or abbreviation: BJC

1A Horn Lane, Acton, London, W3 9NJ

Tel: 020 8992 9454
Fax: 020 8993 3526

Enquiries:
Enquiries to: General Secretary

Organisation type and purpose:
Voluntary organisation.

Subject coverage:
Judo.

Access to staff:
Contact by letter and by telephone. Appointment necessary.
Hours: Mon to Fri, 0900 to 1500

BRITISH KENPO KARATE UNION

Acronym or abbreviation: BKKU

16 York Road, Exeter, Devon, EX4 6BA

Tel: 07778 921623
E-mail: info@bkku.com

Website:
http://www.bkku.com

Enquiries:
Enquiries to: Secretary

Founded:
1981

Organisation type and purpose:
Membership association (membership is by subscription), present number of members: 100, service industry, training organisation.

Subject coverage:
Kenpo karate.

Access to staff:
Contact by e-mail
Hours: Mon to Fri, 0900 to 1700

BRITISH KIDNEY PATIENT ASSOCIATION

Acronym or abbreviation: BKPA

Bordon, Hampshire, GU35 9JZ

Tel: 01420 472021/2
Fax: 01420 475831

Enquiries:
Enquiries to: Chief Executive

Organisation type and purpose:
National Charity.
To help kidney patients and their families.

Subject coverage:
Renal dialysis and transplantation, material and physical needs of patients and their relatives, lobbying for more facilities.

Printed publications:
Questions & Answers on Series: Kidney Transplantation, Donation, Failure, CAPD, Nephrotic Syndrome in Children, Polycystic Disease, Alport's Syndrome, Renal Diabetes, Haemolytic Uraemic Syndrome
Silver Lining Appeal (annually)
The Home Dialysis Patient
Timbo: A Struggle for Survival by Mrs E D Ward
The Kidney Question – education pack (free of charge, £5.30 p&p)
Work of the BKPA

Electronic and video publications:
Videos

Publications list:
Available in print

Access to staff:
Contact by letter, by telephone and by fax.
Appointment necessary.
Hours: Mon to Fri, 0900 to 1700

BRITISH KORFBALL ASSOCIATION

Acronym or abbreviation: BKA

Registrations Officer, 50 Mayfair Avenue, Worcester Park, Surrey, KT4 7SL

Tel: 020 8337 6729
E-mail: registrations@korfball.co.uk

Website:
http://www.korfball.co.uk
Links to IKF and other national body sites including UK.
Rules of the sport, contact person for clubs and areas, noticeboard, national league fixtures and results.

Enquiries:
Enquiries to: General Secretary
Direct e-mail: secretary@korfball.co.uk
Other contacts: Development Officer

Founded:
1946

Organisation type and purpose:
Voluntary organisation.
Governing body for the sport.

Subject coverage:
Rules of Korfball, lists of clubs, coaches and referees, coaching and refereeing courses.

Printed publications:
Handbook of Clubs
Korfball Magazine

Access to staff:
Contact by letter and by e-mail
Hours: Answerphone, if unavailable during office hours; personal contact by phone, normally in the evenings

Affiliated to:
International Korfball Federation
PO Box 85394, 3508 AJ Utrecht, The Netherlands; tel: 00 31 30 656 6354; fax: 00 31 30 657 0468; e-mail: office@ihf.org; website: www.ihf.org

General Secretary:
British Korfball Association
PO Box 179, Maidstone, Kent, ME14 1LU; e-mail: secretary@korfball.co.uk

BRITISH LEPROSY RELIEF ASSOCIATION

Acronym or abbreviation: LEPRA

Leprosy Charity, Fairfax House, Causton Road, Colchester, Essex, CO1 1PU

Tel: 01206 562286
Fax: 01206 762151
E-mail: lepra@lepra.org.uk

Website:
http://www.lepra.org.uk
Information about the Charity and its work.

Enquiries:
Enquiries to: Information Officer
Direct e-mail: irene_allen@lepra.org.uk

Founded:
1924

Organisation type and purpose:
Registered charity (charity number 213251).
Eradication of leprosy.

Subject coverage:
Research into treatment of the disease of leprosy.

Printed publications:
Leprosy Review (quarterly: Mar, Jun, Sep, Dec £34)

Access to staff:
Contact by letter, by telephone, by fax and in person
Hours: Mon to Fri, 0900 to 1700

Subsidiary body:
Lepra India
Post Box 1518, Krishnapuri Colony, West Marredpally, Secunderabad, 500 026, India

BRITISH LIBRARY – ASIA, PACIFIC AND AFRICA COLLECTIONS

Acronym or abbreviation: APAC

96 Euston Road, London, NW1 2DB

Tel: 020 7412 7873
Fax: 020 7412 7641
E-mail: apac-enquiries@bl.uk

Website:
http://www.bl.uk/collections/asiapacificafrica.html

Enquiries:
Enquiries to: Reference Services

Founded:
1753

Organisation type and purpose:
Non-departmental public body.

Subject coverage:
Languages, literature, religion, art, social and political life of the various regions of Asia and North Africa, both historical and contemporary; principal linguistic and geographical sections are: Hebrew (with Coptic, Syriac, Ethiopian, etc), Islamic (Arabic, Turkish, Iranian, etc.), South Asian, South-East Asian, Far Eastern.
Official British records relating to the Indian sub-continent from 1600 to 1947, humanities and social sciences relating to the sub-continent, activities of the British in the sub-continent and in other areas of Asia where the East India Company was active, material in Indian vernacular languages, Indian studies in the broadest sense.

Education services:
Free monthly training sessions for first-time users of the family history sources

Museum or gallery collection, archive, or library special collection:
Drawings and prints, including miniatures (over 29,000 items)
Each language section contains rare and specialised collections of manuscripts and printed books
East India Company material, including collections on factories or early trading stations, and the Company's maritime activities
Government of India Publications (70,200 vols)
Manuscripts in European languages (over 100 major collections)
Manuscripts in Oriental languages (over 27,000 items)
Maps: topographical, subject (railways, canals, irrigation, etc.)
Oriental language newspapers and official publications
Photographs, including some 187,000 photographs of scenes in India, pre-1947 and 2,300 negative plates of Indian inscriptions and antiquities
Records of the Crown Representative and of the Residents in the Indian Princely States

Non-library collection catalogue:
All or part available online, in-house and in print

Library catalogue:
All or part available online, in-house and in print

Printed publications:
Annual Report
Detailed catalogues of the collections
Guide to the Department of Oriental Manuscripts and Printed Books (1977)
Guide to the India Office Library
Guide to the India Office Records (1982)
List of catalogues is available from the Department Newsletter

Publications list:
Available in print

Access to staff:
Contact by letter, by telephone, by fax, by e-mail and in person
Hours: Mon, 1000 to 1700; Tue to Sat, 0930 to 1700

Access for disabled people:
Ramped entry, access to all public areas, toilet facilities

Special comments: Parking spaces for disabled people are in Midland Road.

Constituent part of:
British Library

BRITISH LIBRARY – BIBLIOGRAPHIC DEVELOPMENT

Acronym or abbreviation: Bib Dev

Boston Spa, Wetherby, West Yorkshire, LS23 7BQ

Tel: 01937 546548
Fax: 01937 546586
E-mail: bd-info@bl.uk

Website:
http://www.bl.uk
British Library website (collections, catalogues and services), including the British Library Integrated Catalogue (online).

Founded:
2002

Formerly called:
National Bibliographic Service

Organisation type and purpose:
National government body, public library.
To develop bibliographic standards with reference to their application in British Library bibliographic products and services, and in a variety of EC and other projects.

Subject coverage:
The development of bibliographic standards at national and international levels; the British National Bibliography; support for bibliographic products and services; projects in support of the UK library and information community.

Museum or gallery collection, archive, or library special collection:
Bibliographic Development does not hold collections but provides information relating to the national imprint (British National Bibliography) and the British Library collections

Printed publications:
British National Bibliography (BNB): lists by subject all forthcoming and new books and serials published in the UK and Ireland with full author and title indexes (options include weekly list, cumulations, annual vol.)
Serials in the British Library (SBL): lists all serials acquired through legal deposit together with titles purchased by the London Reading Rooms (three printed issues and an annual cumulative vol.)
Current Serials Received (CSR): over 60,000 current serial titles received by the British Library and available for document supply (annual vol.)
Index of Conference Proceedings (ICP): newly acquired by the British Library and available for document supply (annual vol.)
The UKMARC Exchange Record Format (1997) (also available online)
The UKMARC Manual: a cataloguer's guide to the bibliographic format (4th ed., 1996, with updates 1997–2002) (also available online)
Order printed publications from: Available from: Extenza-Turpin, Stratton Business Park, Pegasus Drive, Biggleswade, Bedfordshire, SG18 8QB; tel: 01767 604955; fax: 01767 601640; e-mail: turpin@extenza-turpin.com

Electronic and video publications:
Exchange data services:
BNB MARC Weekly File
British Library holdings (Humanities & Social Sciences, Science Technology and Business)
British Library Document Supply Centre Monographs / Conferences / Serials files
Library of Congress weekly 'Books All' file (distribution in the UK and Europe)
Order electronic and video publications from: The British Library, Bibliographic Data Licensing, Boston Spa, Wetherby, West Yorkshire, LS23 7BQ; tel: 01937 546797; fax: 01937 546586; email: data-licensing@bl.uk

Publications list:
Available in print

Access to staff:
Contact by letter, by telephone, by fax and by e-mail. Appointment necessary.
Hours: Mon to Fri, 0900 to 1700

BRITISH LIBRARY – BUSINESS AND INTELLECTUAL PROPERTY CENTRE

Acronym or abbreviation: BL

96 Euston Road, London, NW1 2DB

Tel: 020 7412 7454 (enquiries and holdings information)
Fax: 020 7412 7453
E-mail: bipc@bl.uk

Website:
http://www.bl.uk/bipc

Organisation type and purpose:
Information service.

Subject coverage:
Business and intellectual property information on patents, designs, trademarks, copyright, markets, companies, and products covering all sectors in the United Kingdom and overseas.

Museum or gallery collection, archive, or library special collection:
Various electronic databases, patent specifications, market research reports, trade directories, trade journals and trade literature collection

Trade and statistical information:
Range of national and international trade statistics.

Non-library collection catalogue:
All or part available online and in-house

Library catalogue:
All or part available online

Access to staff:
Contact by letter, by telephone, by fax, by e-mail, in person and via website

Access to building, collection or gallery:
Hours: Mon, 1000 to 2000; Tue to Thu, 0930 to 2000; Fri to Sat, 0930 to 1700
Special comments: No access to first-time users after 1700

Access for disabled people:
Ramped entry, toilet facilities
Special comments: Parking spaces for disabled people are in Midland Road.

BRITISH LIBRARY – DEPARTMENT OF MANUSCRIPTS

Formal name: British Library Department of Western Manuscripts
Acronym or abbreviation: BL MSS

96 Euston Road, London, NW1 2DB

Tel: 020 7412 7513
Fax: 020 7412 7745
E-mail: mss@bl.uk

Website:
http://www.bl.uk/collections/manuscripts.html
Information on the manuscripts reading room and collections.

Enquiries:
Enquiries to: Reading Room Manager
Other contacts: Manuscripts Librarian for subject enquiries.

Founded:
1753

Organisation type and purpose:
Non-departmental public body.

Subject coverage:
Primarily material written by hand in Western languages, covering virtually all aspects of history, literature and culture, including maps dating from the classical period to the present day and early (pre-1500) music.

Museum or gallery collection, archive, or library special collection:
Additional MSS
Arundel MSS
Ashley MSS
Burney MSS
Collections of Charters, Rolls, Seals, Papyri and Ostraca
Cotton MSS
Egerton MSS
Hargrave MSS
Harley MSS
King's MSS
Lansdowne MSS
Lord Chamberlain's Plays
Modern Playscripts
Photocopies of exported manuscripts
Royal MSS
Sloane MSS
Stowe MSS
Yates Thompson MSS
Zweig MSS
Facsimile collection

Non-library collection catalogue:
All or part available online and in print

Printed publications:
Guide to the Catalogues and Indexes of the Department of Manuscripts (M. A. E. Nickson, 3rd edn, London 1998)
Index of Manuscripts in the British Library (10 vols, Chadwyck-Healey, 1984–86 and supplements)
Manuscripts Collections
Using the Manuscripts Reading Room
Other collection guides

Access to staff:
Contact by letter, by telephone, by fax, by e-mail and via website
Hours: Mon, 1000 to 1700; Tue to Sat, 0930 to 1700

Access for disabled people:
Ramped entry, access to all public areas, toilet facilities
Special comments: Parking spaces for disabled people are in Midland Road.

BRITISH LIBRARY – DIALTECH

96 Euston Road, London, NW1 2DB

Tel: 020 7412 7951 or 7946
Fax: 020 7412 7947
E-mail: dialtech@bl.uk

Website:
http://www.gemcatcher.com
Gives a description of the GEM service provided by EINS, details of costs, training courses available etc. Also gives access to the GEM databases if the GEM customer has a password.
http://www.bl.uk/
Services provided by Dialtech.

Enquiries:
Enquiries to: Manager
Direct e-mail: roy.kitley@bl.uk

Organisation type and purpose:
To provide the UK national centre for EINS (European Information Network Services) which gives access to the GEM online information service in science, technology and business information. Support is also given to customers in Australia, New Zealand, Ireland, Canada and the USA.

Subject coverage:
Bibliographic and factual databases in science, technology and business information.

Printed publications:
Newsletter (irregular, free)

Access to staff:
Contact by letter, by telephone, by fax, by e-mail and via website. Appointment necessary. All charged.
Hours: Mon to Fri, 0930 to 1700

Access for disabled people:
Ramped entry, toilet facilities
Special comments: Parking spaces for disabled people are in Midland Road.

Represents the:
European Information Network Services (EINS)

BRITISH LIBRARY – DOCUMENT SUPPLY

Acronym or abbreviation: BLDS

Boston Spa, Wetherby, West Yorkshire, LS23 7BQ

Tel: 01937 546060
Fax: 01937 546333
E-mail: dsc-customer-services@bl.uk

Website:
http://www.bl.uk/catalogue
Free access to Integrated Catalogue. Includes online document ordering link for both registered and non-registered customers.
http://www.bl.uk/docsupply
Web pages dedicated to British Library Document Supply service.
http://www.bl.uk/inside
A fully integrated searching and ordering service based on the British Library's Document Supply collection.
http://www.bl.uk
General British Library site.

Enquiries:
Enquiries to: Customer Services
Direct tel: 01937 546060
Direct fax: 01937 546333
Direct e-mail: dsc-customer-services@bl.uk

Founded:
1962

Organisation type and purpose:
National Library Service.
To provide a document supply and loan service to researchers in every field of enquiry anywhere in the world. A small Reading Room also operates on-site (open Mon to Fri, 0930 to 1600: tel: 01937 546070).

Subject coverage:
Science, technology, law, finance, industry, medicine, humanities, social sciences and all allied subjects.

Museum or gallery collection, archive, or library special collection:
Over 250,000 journal series in total (50,000 current subscriptions)
Over 3 million books
All British official publications since 1962
All EC official publications since 1973
Conference Proceedings (over 370,000)
Local authority material (28,000)
Music (over 129,000 scores)
Reports (over 4,300,000, mainly US and in microform)
Russian science and technology monographs (over 220,000)
Theses and Dissertations (over 580,000 UK, US, and some European)
Translations (over 570,000)
Microform research collections – includes one of the largest medieval manuscript collections in Europe
Access to all United Kingdom and international patents

Non-library collection catalogue:
All or part available online and in print

Printed publications:
British Library publications can be purchased online from www.bl.uk/bookshop
Order printed publications from: Turpin Distribution Services Ltd

Blackhorse Road, Letchworth, Hertfordshire, SG6 1HN, tel: 01462 488900, fax: 01462 480947, e-mail: turpin@rsc.org
Or www.bl.uk/bookshop

Electronic and video publications:
British National Bibliography

Publications list:
Available in print

Access to staff:
Contact by letter, by telephone, by fax, by e-mail, in person and via website
Hours: Document supply staff are working around the clock: 0800, Mon to 0200, Sat (except for English public holidays)
Customer Services open: Mon to Fri, 0830 to 1700 (except for English public holidays)
Special comments: Charges made for document supply and interlibrary loan. Orders must be sent online or by email.

Access for disabled people:
For visitors to the Boston Spa site, parking provided, ramped entry, toilet facilities

Affiliated to:
National Bibliographic Service
Boston Spa; tel: 01937 546585; fax: 01937 546586; e-mail: nbs-info@bl.uk

Parent body:
British Library
tel: 020 7412 7111; fax: 020 7412 7168; e-mail: press-and-pr@bl.uk

BRITISH LIBRARY – ECCLES CENTRE FOR AMERICAN STUDIES

Acronym or abbreviation: BL

96 Euston Road, London, NW1 2DB

Tel: 020 7412 7551
Fax: 020 7412 7792
E-mail: eccles-centre@bl.uk

Website:
http://www.bl.uk/ecclescentre

Enquiries:
Enquiries to: Director

Founded:
1991

Organisation type and purpose:
Information agency.
To support the study and understanding of North America in the United Kingdom through the resources of the British Library.

Subject coverage:
North American collections in the British Library, North American educational activities in the United Kingdom, general information on the USA and Canada.

Museum or gallery collection, archive, or library special collection:
Many and varied collections

Non-library collection catalogue:
All or part available online

Library catalogue:
All or part available online

Publications list:
Available online

Access to staff:
Contact by letter, by telephone, by fax, by e-mail, in person and via website. Appointment necessary.
Hours: Mon to Fri, 0900 to 1700
Special comments: Please telephone for opening times.

Access to building, collection or gallery:
No prior appointment required

Parent body:
The British Library
96 Euston Road, London, NW1 2DB; tel: 020 7412 7000

BRITISH LIBRARY – ENVIRONMENTAL INFORMATION SERVICE

Acronym or abbreviation: EIS

96 Euston Road, London, NW1 2DB

Tel: 020 7412 7477
Fax: 020 7412 7954
E-mail: eis@bl.uk

Website:
http://www.bl.uk/environment
Environmental Information Service at the British
Library: lists of environmental organisations by
topic and A-Z, all hypertext linked, and resources
on the Internet.

Enquiries:
Enquiries to: Information Officer
Other contacts: Head of Science and Technology
Information Services

Founded:
1989

Organisation type and purpose:
Consultancy, research organisation.
Information service.

Subject coverage:
Scientific and technological aspects of
environmental information.

**Museum or gallery collection, archive, or library
special collection:**
Access to all British Library collections including
environmental newsletters and corporate
environmental reports

Printed publications:
Amongst many are:
How to Find Information – Environment (1998)

Publications list:
Available in print

Access to staff:
Contact by letter, by telephone, by fax and by e-
mail
Hours: Mon to Fri, 0930 to 1700
Special comments: Reader Pass needed.
Charges made for on-line searches and detailed
enquiries.

Access for disabled people:
Ramped entry, toilet facilities
Special comments: Parking spaces for disabled
people are in Midland Road.

Part of:
British Library (same address)

BRITISH LIBRARY – HEALTH CARE INFORMATION SERVICE

Acronym or abbreviation: HCIS

96 Euston Road, London, NW1 2DB

Tel: 020 7412 7489
Fax: 020 7412 7954
E-mail: hcis@bl.uk

Website:
http://www.bl.uk/health
British Library website, Healthcare information
page.
http://www.bl.uk/services/publications/onlineshop
.html
Publications list.

Enquiries:
Enquiries to: Information Officer
Direct fax: 020 7412 7947
Direct e-mail: fiona.mclean@bl.uk
Other contacts: Head of HCIS

Founded:
1995

Organisation type and purpose:
Non-departmental public body.

Subject coverage:
Biomedicine and healthcare, medical information,
consumer health information, complementary
medicine, allied healthcare, occupational therapy,
physiotherapy, palliative care, rehabilitation,
nursing, health informatics.

**Museum or gallery collection, archive, or library
special collection:**
UK Publications (and selected overseas) including
patents and historical material, as well as a wide
range of relevant books, journals, grey literature
and databases

Trade and statistical information:
Health Care Statistics for the United Kingdom.

Non-library collection catalogue:
All or part available in-house

Library catalogue:
All or part available online

Printed publications:
AMED Thesaurus
Complementary Medicine Index (monthly, also in
electronic format)
Employment Health: Psychosocial Stress in the
Workplace (Grimshaw J, 1999)
Directory of Organisations in Allied and
Complementary Health Care (Madge D, 2000)
Guide to Libraries and Information Sources in
Medicine and Health Care (Dale P, 3rd ed., 2001)
List of Journals Indexed for AMED
Health Care Updates – 29 titles including
Alcoholism, Asthma, Depression, Drug
Dependence, Eating Disorders, Obesity,
Parkinson's Disease, Epilepsy, Health Care in
Britain, Dementia, Schizophrenia, Smoking and
Women's Health (monthly, also in electronic
format)
Occupational Therapy Index (monthly, also in
electronic format)
Palliative Care Index (monthly, also in electronic
format)
Physiotherapy Index (monthly, also in electronic
format)
Podiatry Index (quarterly, also in electronic format)
Rehabilitation Index (monthly, also in electronic
format)
How to Find Information series (brief guides):
Social Sciences (Grimshaw J, 2000)
Health Care (Madge D, 2001)
Complementary and Alternative Health Care
(Madge D, 2001)
Genetically Modified Foods (Lee, 2000)
Order printed publications from: Health Care
Information Service (North)
Boston Spa, Wetherby, West Yorkshire, LS23 7BQ,
tel: 01937 546361, fax: 01937 546458, e-mail: anita
.jackson@bl.uk

Electronic and video publications:
Allied and Alternative Medicine Database (AMED)
(CD-ROM)

Publications list:
Available online and in print

Access to staff:
Contact by letter, by telephone, by fax, by e-mail
and via website. Appointment necessary.
Hours: Mon to Fri, 1000 to 1700
Special comments: Voicemail out of hours.

Access for disabled people:
Ramped entry, toilet facilities
Special comments: Parking spaces for disabled
people are in Midland Road.

Other address:
Health Care Information Service (North) and
Reading Room (North)
The British Library
Boston Spa, Wetherby, West Yorkshire, LS23
7BQ; tel: 01937 546364; fax: 01937 546458

Parent body:
British Library

BRITISH LIBRARY – IFLA INTERNATIONAL PROGRAMME FOR UAP

Formal name: Universal Availability of Publications
Acronym or abbreviation: IFLA

c/o British Library, Boston Spa, Wetherby, West
Yorkshire, LS23 7BQ

Tel: 01937 546123
Fax: 01937 546478
E-mail: ifla@bl.uk

Website:
http://www.ifla.org/V1/Z/uap.htm
Overview of programme.

Enquiries:
Enquiries to: Programme Officer

Organisation type and purpose:
Research organisation.
Professional unit of the International Federation of
Library Associations and Institutions.

Subject coverage:
Improvement of the availability of publications,
from their initial supply from producers,
acquisition policies and systems, national and
international interlending systems, to repository
policies and systems.

Printed publications:
Newsletter (irregular)
Charging for Document Delivery and Interlending
(workshop 1996, Gould S ed., £5)
Copyright in Libraries: Global Concerns, Local
Solutions (seminar 1996, Watkins J ed., £5)
Guide to Centres of International Document
Delivery (5th ed., Barwick M and Connolly P
eds, 1996, £20)
Guide to Centres of International Lending (5th ed.,
Barwick M and Connolly P eds, 1995, £15)
Various publications related to copyright,
document supply, lending, copying

Publications list:
Available in print

Access to staff:
Contact by letter, by telephone, by fax, by e-mail
and via website
Hours: Mon to Fri, 0900 to 1700

BRITISH LIBRARY – IFLA OFFICE FOR INTERNATIONAL LENDING

Formal name: International Federation of Library
Associations and Institutions
Acronym or abbreviation: IFLA

Boston Spa, Wetherby, West Yorkshire, LS23 7BQ

Tel: 01937 546123
Fax: 01937 546478
E-mail: ifla@bl.uk

Website:
http://www.ifla.org/v1/2/uap.htm
Overview of work of the office and information
about the IFLA Voucher Scheme.

Enquiries:
Enquiries to: Research Officer

Organisation type and purpose:
Research organisation.
Professional unit of the International Federation of
Library Associations and Institutions, supported
by the British Library, for the furtherance and
development of international lending and
document supply.

Subject coverage:
Present nature and potential improvement in
national and international lending and document
supply systems and procedures.

Printed publications:
Charging for Document Delivery and Interlending
(Gould S, ed, 1997, £5)
Copyright in Libraries: Global Concerns, Local
Solutions (Watkins J ed., 1997, £5)
Guide to Centres of International Document
Delivery (5th ed, 1996, £20)

Guide to Centres of International Lending (5th ed, 1995, £15)

Model Handbook for Interlending and Copying (Cornish G P, 1991, £5)

National Libraries of the World: an Address List (updated regularly)

The Role of Libraries in Economic Development (Watkins J and Connolly P, 1997, £10)

The Digital Library. Challenges and Solutions for the New Millennium (Connolly P and Reidy D, 2000, £20)

Solving Collection Problems through Repository Strategies (Connolly P, ed, 1999, £20)

Interlending and Document Supply: Proceedings of the 3rd, 4th, 5th, 6th and 7th Conferences, 1994 to 2002

Publications list:
Available in print

Access to staff:
Contact by letter, by telephone, by fax, by e-mail and via website
Hours: Mon to Fri, 0900 to 1700

BRITISH LIBRARY – LIBRARIANSHIP AND INFORMATION SCIENCES SERVICE

Acronym or abbreviation: LIS

96 Euston Road, London, NW1 2DB

Tel: 020 7412 7676
Fax: 020 7412 7691
E-mail: lis@bl.uk

Website:
http://www.bl.uk
Description of services and collections; recent accessions lists including journal holdings; links to useful sites and services.
http://catalogue.bl.uk
British Library Integrated Catalogue

Enquiries:
Enquiries to: Reference Specialist

Organisation type and purpose:
National library

Subject coverage:
All aspects of librarianship and information science.

Museum or gallery collection, archive, or library special collection:
Collections include British material acquired by legal deposit and selected non-British material on librarianship, information science and related subjects

Non-library collection catalogue:
All or part available online

Library catalogue:
All or part available online

Printed publications:
Leaflet and reader guide

Access to staff:
Contact by letter, by telephone, by fax, by e-mail and in person
Hours: Mon, 1000 to 2000; Tue, Wed, Thu, 0930 to 2000; Fri, Sat, 0930 to 1700
Special comments: A Reader Pass is required for entry to the Reading Rooms, see details on website.

Access for disabled people:
disabled access

BRITISH LIBRARY – MAP COLLECTIONS

Acronym or abbreviation: BL

96 Euston Road, London, NW1 2DB

Tel: 020 7412 7702
Fax: 020 7412 7780
E-mail: maps@bl.uk

Website:
http://www.bl.uk

Enquiries:
Enquiries to: Head of Map Collections
Direct tel: 020 7412 7701
Direct e-mail: peter.barber@bl.uk

Organisation type and purpose:
Non-departmental public body.

Subject coverage:
Cartographic materials (atlases, maps, globes), cartobibliography, celestial atlases and maps, history of cartography, remotely sensed imagery, topographical views and panoramas, gazeteers.

Museum or gallery collection, archive, or library special collection:
Crace Collection (maps of London)
King George III Topographical and Maritime Collections
Ministry of Defence mapping archive
Ordnance Survey manuscript drawings
Ordnance Survey publications, including large-scale plans (the United Kingdom's definitive collection)
Royal United Services Institution map collection

Non-library collection catalogue:
All or part available online, in-house and in print

Library catalogue:
All or part available online, in-house and in print

Printed publications:
County Atlases of the British Isles Vol III – the period 1764–1789 (D. Hodson, 1997, £35)
Images and Icons of the New World – Essays on American Cartography (K. S. Cook, 1996, £17.50)
Lie of the Land: The Secret Life of Maps (A. Carlucci and P. Barber, 2001, £9.95)
Mappa Mundi: The Hereford World Map (P. D. A. Harvey, 1996, £17.95 or £10.95 paper)
Mapping Time and Space: How Medieval Mapmakers Viewed Their World (E. Edson, 1997, £19.95 paper)
Maps as Prints in the Italian Renaissance (D. Woodward, 1996, £16)
The Charting of the Oceans – Ten Centuries of Maritime Maps (P. Whitfield, 1996, £20)
The Dictionary of Land Surveyors and Local Mapmakers of Great Britain and Ireland 1530–1850 (S. Bendall, 1997, £75)
The Image of the World – 20 Centuries of World Maps (P. Whitfield, 1997, £12.95)
The Mapping of the Heavens (P. Whitfield, 1997, £12.95)
Order printed publications from: Turpin Distribution Ltd, Blackhorse Road, Letchworth, Hertfordshire, SG6 1HN; tel. 01462 672555; fax 01462 480497; e-mail turpin@turpinltd.com

Access to staff:
Contact by letter, by telephone, by fax, by e-mail, in person and via website. Appointment necessary.
Hours: Mon, 1000 to 1700; Tue to Sat, 0930 to 1700

Access for disabled people:
Ramped entry, toilet facilities
Special comments: Parking spaces for disabled people are in Midland Road.

BRITISH LIBRARY – MUSIC COLLECTIONS

Acronym or abbreviation: BL

96 Euston Road, London, NW1 2DB

Tel: 020 7412 7772
Fax: 020 7412 7751
E-mail: music-collections@bl.uk

Website:
http://www.bl.uk/collections/music/music.html

Enquiries:
Enquiries to: Head of Music Collections
Direct tel: 020 7412 7529

Founded:
1973

Organisation type and purpose:
Non-departmental public body.

Subject coverage:
All aspects of printed and manuscript music, including music history, music printing, bibliography of music, availability of music, music copyright, popular music, etc. NB for recorded music see British Library Sound Archive.

Museum or gallery collection, archive, or library special collection:
Hirsch Collection
Royal Music Library
Royal Philharmonic Society Archive

Non-library collection catalogue:
All or part available in-house

Library catalogue:
All or part available online and in print

Printed publications:
Catalogue of Printed Music in the British Library to 1980 (62 vols, 1980–87)
Stefan Zweig Collection: catalogue of the music manuscripts (1999)

Electronic and video publications:
CPM PLUS (2nd ed., CD-ROM catalogue of printed music in the British Library to 1996)

Publications list:
Available in print

Access to staff:
Contact by letter, by telephone, by fax, by e-mail and via website. Appointment necessary.
Hours: Mon, 1000 to 2000; Tue, Wed, Thu, 0930 to 2000; Fri, Sat, 0930 to 1700
Special comments: Reader's Pass required to use reading rooms.

Access for disabled people:
Ramped entry, access to all public areas, toilet facilities.
Special comments: 3 parking bays in Ossulton Street.

BRITISH LIBRARY – NATIONAL PRESERVATION OFFICE

Acronym or abbreviation: NPO

96 Euston Road, London, NW1 2DB

Tel: 020 7412 7612
Fax: 020 7412 7796
E-mail: npo@bl.uk

Website:
http://www.bl.uk/npo/
Basic information via the British Library's home pages; lists of publications, etc.
http://www.bl.uk/services/npo/npo.html

Enquiries:
Enquiries to: Information Officer
Other contacts: Director

Founded:
1984

Organisation type and purpose:
Research organisation.
Independent national advisory body.
Independent national focus for debate and information on preservation, conservation and security in libraries and archives.

Subject coverage:
Preservation, conservation, disaster control, security, surrogacy.

Printed publications:
see website for details, http://www.bl.uk/services/npo/publications.html

Access to staff:
Contact by letter, by telephone, by fax, by e-mail and via website
Hours: Mon to Fri, 0900 to 1700
Special comments: Visitors by prior appointment only (no casual callers).

Funded by:
British Library
Cambridge University Library

continued overleaf

The Bodleian Library, Oxford University
The National Archives
The National Library of Scotland
The National Library of Wales
Trinity College Library, Dublin

Policies guided by the:
National Preservation Office Board

BRITISH LIBRARY – NEWSPAPERS

Colindale Avenue, London, NW9 5HE

Tel: 020 7412 7353
Fax: 020 7412 7379
E-mail: newspaper@bl.uk

Website:
http://www.bl.uk/collections/newspapers.html

Organisation type and purpose:
The national archive collections in the United
Kingdom of British and overseas newspapers; the
only large, integrated national newspaper service
in the world, combining facilities for the collection,
preservation, and use of newspapers all on one
site.
Our collections, which also include popular
magazines and periodicals, are made available in
hard copy, in microform, and on CD-ROM in the
Newspaper Reading Rooms in Colindale, north
west London. Subject to restrictions, facilities are
available for the photocopying, microfilming, and
photographic and film reproduction of items from
the collections in our care.

**Museum or gallery collection, archive, or library
special collection:**
British Library Newspapers Web Catalogue
The British Library Online Newspaper Archive
  (Pilot version only)
British and Irish Newspapers
Overseas Newspapers
Periodicals and Comics
Visual Arts collections
Microform Series
Chatham House Press Cuttings
Special collections:
British and Irish Cinema and Film Periodicals
British Comics Collection
British Football Programmes
British Military History Collections 1801–1945
The Burney Collection of Newspapers
Current Foreign (Non-British Isles) Newspapers
The Dutch Underground Press 1940–1945
Early American Newpapers
Early English Newspapers
Early Indian Newspapers
The Francis Place Collection (British Politics and
  Economics)
General Strike Newspapers 1926
German-language Newspapers and Journals
  Published in London since 1810
Modern Music Periodicals: Pop and Jazz
Northern Ireland Politicial Literature: Periodicals
  1966–1989
The Thomason Tracts (English Newsbooks, 1640–
  61)
Tuskegee Institute News Clippings File (African-
  Americans 1899–1966)
Victorian Illustrated Newspapers and Journals

Printed publications:
Newsletter

Electronic and video publications:
Abstracts and Indexes to Newspapers and Journals
Full-Text, Word-Searchable Newspapers and
  Journals
Chronological and Subject Guides based on News
  and Newspapers
Other databases

Access to staff:
Hours: Mon to Fri, 0900 to 1700

BRITISH LIBRARY – PATENTS INFORMATION/PATENTS ONLINE

Acronym or abbreviation: BL

96 Euston Road, London, NW1 2DB

Tel: 020 7412 7903
Fax: 020 7412 7930
E-mail: patents-information@bl.uk

Website:
http://www.bl.uk/patents

Enquiries:
Enquiries to: Information Officer

Organisation type and purpose:
Information service.

Subject coverage:
Patents information – national and international.
Patents documentation – national and
international.
Trademark and designs information.

**Museum or gallery collection, archive, or library
special collection:**
Extensive collection of patent documentation, both
  national and international
Other intellectual property literature also collected
  widely

Printed publications:
History of Science and Technology:
British Patents of Invention, 1617–1977: A Guide
  for Researchers
The Indefatigable Mr Woodcroft: The Legacy of
  Invention
Inventing the 19th Century: The Great Age of
  Victorian Inventions
Inventing the 20th Century: 100 Inventions that
  Shaped the World
James Watt and the Patent System
Michael Hill on Science, Invention and Information
New and Improved: Inventors and Inventions that
  Have Changed the Modern World
Rooms near Chancery Lane: The Patent Office
  under the Commissioners, 1852–1883
Patents:
How to Find Information: Patents on the Internet
International Guide to Official Industrial Property
  Publications (3rd edn)
Introduction to Patents Information (4th edn, 2002)
Trade Marks: An Introductory Guide and
  Bibliography (2nd edn)
Order printed publications from: Turpin Distribution
Services, Blackhorse Road, Letchworth,
Hertfordshire, SG6 1HN; tel. 01462 672555; fax
01462 480947; e-mail turpin@turpinltd.com

Publications list:
Available online and in print

Access to staff:
Contact by letter, by telephone, by fax, by e-mail,
in person and via website

Access to building, collection or gallery:
Hours: Mon to Fri, 1000 to 1300 and 1400 to 1700
Special comments: Reader Pass required by visitors.
Ring for details of admission procedure.

Access for disabled people:
Ramped entry, toilet facilities

BRITISH LIBRARY – PHILATELIC COLLECTIONS

96 Euston Road, London, NW1 2DB

Tel: 020 7412 7635
Fax: 020 7412 7780
E-mail: philatelic@bl.uk

Website:
http://www.bl.uk/collections/philatelic
http://www.collectbritain.co.uk/collections/
philatelic

Founded:
1973

Organisation type and purpose:
Non-departmental public body.

Subject coverage:
Philately, postal history, philatelic literature,
history of philately.

**Museum or gallery collection, archive, or library
special collection:**
Over 50 main collections, including:
Board of Inland Revenue Stamping Department
  Archive
Crown Agents Philatelic and Security Printing
  Archive
Fletcher Collection
Foreign and Commonwealth Office Collection
Harrison Collection
Tapling Collection (perhaps the most important
  and unique)

Non-library collection catalogue:
All or part available in-house

Printed publications:
Newsletter
Catalogue of the Crawford Library of Philatelic
  Literature at the British Library (Sir E. Bacon,
  £90)
Stamps (R. F. Schoolley-West, 1987, £6.95)
The Care and Preservation of Philatelic Materials
  (T. J. Collings and R. F. Schoolley-West, £12.95)

Access to staff:
Contact by letter, by telephone, by fax and by e-
mail. Appointment necessary.
Hours: Mon to Fri, 0900 to 1700

Access to building, collection or gallery:
Prior appointment required
Hours: Mon to Fri, 1000 to 1600
Special comments: Reader's Pass required

Access for disabled people:
Ramped entry, toilet facilities

BRITISH LIBRARY – READER REGISTRATION OFFICE

Acronym or abbreviation: BL

96 Euston Road, London, NW1 2DB

Tel: 020 7412 7677
Fax: 020 7412 7794
E-mail: reader-registration@bl.uk

Website:
http://www.bl.uk
Admissions information.

Enquiries:
Enquiries to: Curator

Founded:
1973

Organisation type and purpose:
Non-departmental public body.

Subject coverage:
Applications for a Reader's Pass and information
about access to the Library.

Printed publications:
Application for a Reader's Pass

Access to staff:
Contact by letter, by telephone, by fax, by e-mail
and in person
Hours: Mon, 1000 to 1800; Tue, Wed, Thu, 0930 to
1800; Fri, Sat, 0930 to 1630

Access for disabled people:
Ramped entry, toilet facilities
Special comments: Parking spaces for disabled
people are in Midland Road and Ossulton Street

BRITISH LIBRARY – READING ROOMS AT ST PANCRAS

96 Euston Road, London, NW1 2DB

Tel: 020 7412 7676
Fax: 020 7412 7609
E-mail: reader-services-enquiries@bl.uk

Website:
http://www.bl.uk

Organisation type and purpose:
Non-departmental public body.

Access to staff:
Contact by letter, by telephone, by fax, by e-mail, in person and via website
Hours: Mon to Fri, 0900 to 1700
Special comments: Reader's Pass required, apply to the Reader Admissions Office.

Direct lines:
General enquiries; reader services and advance reservations
   tel: 020 7412 7676; fax: 020 7412 7789; e-mail: reader-services-enquiries@bl.uk
Humanities 1 and 2; includes the Library and Information Sciences Service and the Recorded Sound Information Service
   Humanities and LISS; 0171 412 7440, RSIS; tel: 020 7412 7676
Manuscripts
   tel: 020 7412 7513
Maps
   tel: 020 7412 7702
Oriental and India Office
   tel: 020 7412 7873
Rare Books and Music; includes the Music Service and the Listening and Viewing Service
   Early Printed Collections; 0171 412 7772, Music Service; tel: 020 7412 7673
Reader Admissions Office; information about access to the Library
   tel: 020 7412 7677; fax: 020 7412 7794
Readers' Advisor; information about assistance for users with disabilities
   tel: 020 7412 7666; fax: 020 7412 7557; e-mail: lydia.butler@bl.uk
Science, Technology & Innovation Information Services; British and EPO patents
   tel: 020 7412 7919
Science, Technology & Innovation Information Services; Business
   tel: 020 7412 7454/7977
Science, Technology & Innovation Information Services; Foreign patents
   tel: 020 7412 7902
Science, Technology & Innovation Information Services; Science and Technology
   tel: 020 7412 7288/7494/7496
Science, Technology & Innovation Information Services; Social Sciences
   tel: 020 7412 7536

BRITISH LIBRARY – RESEARCH SERVICE

Acronym or abbreviation: BL

96 Euston Road, London, NW1 2DB

Tel: 020 7412 7903
Fax: 020 7412 7480
E-mail: research@bl.uk

Website:
http://www.bl.uk
Describes the service; provides search request form.

Enquiries:
Enquiries to: Information Expert

Organisation type and purpose:
Information service.

Subject coverage:
All aspects of science, technology and medicine, including science policy; physical property data; intellectual property information; business information; humanities; social sciences; government materials

Non-library collection catalogue:
All or part available online

Printed publications:
How to Find Information: Genetically Modified Foods
Order printed publications from: Turpin Distribution Services Limited, Blackhorse Road, Letchworth, Hertfordshire, SG6 1HN, tel: 01462 672555, fax: 01462 480947, e-mail: turpin@turpinltd.com

Publications list:
Available in print

Access to staff:
Contact by letter, by telephone, by fax and by e-mail. Appointment necessary. All charged.
Hours: Mon to Fri, 0930 to 1700

Constituent part of:
Operations and Services

BRITISH LIBRARY – SOCIAL SCIENCES AND OFFICIAL PUBLICATIONS REFERENCE SERVICE

96 Euston Road, London, NW1 2DB

Tel: 020 7412 7676 (general enquiry line)
Fax: 020 7412 7761
E-mail: social-sciences@bl.uk

Website:
http://catalogue.bl.uk
The British Library integrated catalogue.
http://www.bl.uk/socialsciences
Description of collections and services, including collection guides and finding aids

Enquiries:
Enquiries to: Social Sciences Reference Service

Founded:
1753

Organisation type and purpose:
Non-departmental public body.

Subject coverage:
Government, national and local; politics and administration; sociology; economics; education and training policy and administration; transport and the environment; social care, health and welfare services; social security; theory of management; housing and homelessness; law

Museum or gallery collection, archive, or library special collection:
Legal deposit collection of British official publications
Electoral registers for whole of United Kingdom from 1947 and extensive earlier collection
Depository for United Nations publications, some UN agencies, World Bank, International Labour Organization, European Union, OECD and World Health Organization
World-wide collections of publications of governments and inter-governmental organisations, including microfiche of US Federal GPO publications (both depository and non-depository) from 1982 (extensive earlier collection in hard copy) and full text electronic resources including Congressional Serial Set Online, Congressional Hearings Digital Collection 1823–1979, Congressional Record, Declassified Documents Reference System and Digital National Security Archive.
Reading room open access collections include:
National Statistics Collection
Social Sciences collection of recent English-language books and serials
UK Parliamentary materials and legislation
NOTE: The British Library has one of the largest collections of social science publications world-wide, accessible through the Social Sciences Reading Room, but this is not organised as a discrete collection

Trade and statistical information:
The National Statistics Collection based in SS&OP (focus on social and demographic statistics for the UK).

Library catalogue:
All or part available online

Electronic and video publications:
Welfare Reform on the Web: free current awareness service, available at the website, http://www.bl.uk/welfarereform/index.html

Access to staff:
Contact by letter, by telephone, by fax, by e-mail and in person
Hours: Telephone enquiries: Mon to Fri, 0930 to 1700

Access to building, collection or gallery:
No access other than to reading rooms
Hours: Reading Room: Mon, 1000 to 2000; Tue, Wed, Thu, 0930 to 2000; Fri, Sat, 0930 to 1700
Special comments: Reader's Pass required.

Access for disabled people:
Ramped entry, access to all public areas, toilet facilities

Constituent part of:
British Library, Operations and Services

BRITISH LIBRARY FOR DEVELOPMENT STUDIES

Acronym or abbreviation: BLDS

Institute of Development Studies, University of Sussex, Falmer, Brighton, East Sussex, BN1 9RE

Tel: 01273 678263
Fax: 01273 621202 or 691647
E-mail: blds@ids.ac.uk

Website:
http://www.ids.ac.uk
Devline: IDS research, teaching, publishing and operational programmes.
http://www.eldis.org
ELDIS is the electronic gateway to information on the environment or development plus host for other databases and library catalogues.
http://blds.ids.ac.uk
BLDS services, BLDS catalogue and journal articles database.

Enquiries:
Enquiries to: Enquiries Librarian
Direct tel: 01273 873067

Founded:
1966

Organisation type and purpose:
University department or institute.
Research organisation library.
Services to researchers, postgraduate students, and developing country users.

Subject coverage:
Socio-economic aspects of developing countries and third world relations with world economy; subjects include: health, education, communication, industrial development, rural development, debt and adjustment, population studies, development theory, lender issues, political development, environment.

Museum or gallery collection, archive, or library special collection:
Collection of contemporary (1966 to date) government publications of most African, Asian, and Latin American countries including statistical information
Third World publications including grey literature
Third World serials

Non-library collection catalogue:
All or part available online

Library catalogue:
All or part available online

Printed publications:
Books on agriculture and rural problems, environment, political and economic development, gender, health and education, employment and technology, and international issues
IDS Bulletin (quarterly)
IDS Discussion Papers
IDS Research Reports
IDS Working Papers
Order printed publications from: via http://www.ids.ac.uk/ids/bookshop
Mail order: Intermediate Technology Publications, 103/105 Southampton Row, London, WC1B 4HH, tel: 020 7436 9761, fax: 020 7436 2013, e-mail: orders@itpubs.org.uk

Publications list:
Available online and in print

continued overleaf

Access to staff:
Contact by letter, by telephone, by fax, by e-mail, in person and via website
Hours: Mon to Fri, 0930 to 1700

Funded by:
Department for International Development
Institute of Development Studies

Parent body:
Institute of Development Studies (IDS)

BRITISH LIBRARY OF POLITICAL AND ECONOMIC SCIENCE

Acronym or abbreviation: BLPES

London School of Economics and Political Science (LSE), 10 Portugal Street, London, WC2A 2HD

Tel: 020 7955 7229
Fax: 020 7955 7454
E-mail: library@lse.ac.uk

Website:
http://www.library.lse.ac.uk
Library home page and link to on-line catalogue.

Enquiries:
Enquiries to: Librarian and Director of Information Services
Other contacts: Archivist

Founded:
1896

Organisation type and purpose:
University library.

Subject coverage:
Accounting; anthropology; economics; geography; government; history; industrial relations; law; philosophy; politics; population studies; psychology; social administration; sociology; statistics.

Museum or gallery collection, archive, or library special collection:
Archives and private papers on recent political, social and economic history, social anthropology and the history of the London School of Economics; including papers of the Liberal Party, the Independent Labour Party, John Stuart Mill, Beatrice and Sidney Webb, Fabian Society, William Beveridge, George Lansbury, Hugh Dalton, Walter Citrine, Bronislaw Malinowski, C A R Crosland and the Hall-Carpenter Archives of lesbian and gay activism
Collections of rare books on political, economic and social subjects from the 16th century to the present day
The Library is a depository for the United Nations, the United States Government and is a European Documentation Centre
A large collection of publications from intergovernmental organisations and national governments worldwide, with particular emphasis on statistics

Non-library collection catalogue:
All or part available online

Library catalogue:
All or part available online

Printed publications:
Annual Report
Various free guides to the Library
International Bibliography of the Social Sciences

Electronic and video publications:
International Bibliography of the Social Sciences (CD-ROM, Silverplatter)
International Bibliography of the Social Sciences (online, available via BIDS)

Access to staff:
Contact by letter, by telephone, by fax, by e-mail, in person and via website. Non-members charged.
Hours: Core Hours: Mon to Fri, 0900 to 2000
Hours vary throughout year, full details on website
Special comments: Charges to commercial/business users.
Letter of introduction required in certain circumstances.

Access for disabled people:
Level entry, access to all public areas, toilet facilities

Administers the:
Edward Fry Library of International Law

Parent body:
London School of Economics and Political Science

BRITISH LIBRARY SOUND ARCHIVE

Acronym or abbreviation: BLSA

96 Euston Road, London, NW1 2DB

Tel: 020 7412 7676
Fax: 020 7412 7441
E-mail: sound-archive@bl.uk

Website:
http://www.bl.uk/soundarchive
Information on collections and services; online sounds; the current issue of Playback.
http://cadensa.bl.uk
Catalogue of the British Library Sound Archive.

Enquiries:
Enquiries to: Head of the Sound Archive
Direct tel: 020 7412 7424
Direct fax: 020 7412 7422
Direct e-mail: richard.ranft@bl.uk

Founded:
1955

Organisation type and purpose:
Registered charity (charity number 292096).
Non-departmental public body.

Subject coverage:
All aspects of recorded sound, in particular music, including classical music, world and traditional music, popular music and jazz; spoken word, including poetry and drama, oral history, language and dialect; wildlife sounds including birds, mammals, insects, reptiles, amphibians and fish; sound effects; also the United Kingdom music business, broadcasting and the technology of recording.

Museum or gallery collection, archive, or library special collection:
Classical Music Collection
Drama and Literature Collection
Library of printed reference sources
Music video
National Deposit Collection of published phonograms
Oral History Collection
Popular Music Collection
Radio recordings
Record catalogues, national and international
Wildlife Sounds
World and Traditional Music Collection

Trade and statistical information:
Data on the United Kingdom record industry.

Non-library collection catalogue:
All or part available online

Library catalogue:
All or part available online

Printed publications:
Numerous publications, see website

Publications list:
Available online

Access to staff:
Contact by letter, by telephone, by fax, by e-mail and in person
Hours: Mon, 1000 to 2000; Tue, Wed and Thu, 0930 to 2000; Fri and Sat, 0930 to 1700
Special comments: Listening and viewing service by appointment.

Access to building, collection or gallery:
Special comments: Reader's Pass required.

Access for disabled people:
Ramped entry, access to all public areas, toilet facilities

Special comments: Parking spaces for disabled people are in Midland Road.

Parent body:
British Library

BRITISH LIMBLESS EX-SERVICEMEN'S ASSOCIATION

Acronym or abbreviation: BLESMA

Frankland Moore House, 185–187 High Road, Chadwell Heath, Romford, Essex, RM6 6NA

Tel: 020 8590 1124
Fax: 020 8599 2932
E-mail: headquarters@blesma.org

Website:
http://www.blesma.org
Comprehensive details of the charity, including Members' activities and reports, fundraising events, reports, and pensions advice.

Enquiries:
Enquiries to: General Secretary
Other contacts: National Welfare Officer for all welfare matters.

Founded:
1932

Organisation type and purpose:
National organisation, membership association (membership is by subscription), present number of members: 5000 including widows, voluntary organisation, registered charity (charity number: England – 1084189; Scotland – SCO10315). National charity dealing specifically with amputation and rehabilitation. Operates residential and nursing homes. Grant-making organisation providing advice on pensions and allowances.

Subject coverage:
Amputation and rehabilitation, general welfare, prosthetics and orthotics, pension advice and casework, financial grants, research and development, residential homes, counselling.

Printed publications:
Better Health for the Amputee, 1987
BLESMAG – House Journal (3 times a year)
Driving After Amputation (2001)
Newsletter (2 times a year, members)
Out on a Limb, 1982
The Amputee Guide 1997

Electronic and video publications:
Welfare video

Publications list:
Available in print

Access to staff:
Contact by letter, by telephone, by fax, by e-mail and via website
Hours: Mon to Fri, 0900 to 1700

Access for disabled people:
Parking provided, ramped entry, toilet facilities

Associated with:
International Society of Prosthetics and Orthotics (ISPO)
Royal Association for Disability and Rehabilitation (RADAR)
World Veterans Federation (WVF)

Has:
44 branches

Other addresses:
The Ancaster BLESMA Home, Crieff
  Alligan Road, Crieff, Perthshire, PH7 3JU; tel: 01764 652480; fax: 01764 652550; e-mail: crieff@blesma.org
The Elizabeth Frankland Moore Home
  539 Lytham Road, Blackpool, Lancashire, FY4 1RA; tel: 01253 343313; fax: 01253 408994; e-mail: blackpool@blesma.org

BRITISH LIME ASSOCIATION

Acronym or abbreviation: BLA

156 Buckingham Palace Road, London, SW1W 9TR

Tel: 020 7730 8194
Fax: 020 7730 4355

Website:
http://www.bla.org
http://www.britishlime.org
http://www.qpa.org

Enquiries:
Enquiries to: Public Relations Manager
Direct e-mail: clements@qpa.org
Other contacts: Lime Product Officer

Organisation type and purpose:
Trade association.

Subject coverage:
Lime, limestone, chalk dolomite, health and safety, environmental matters.

Trade and statistical information:
Data on industry statistics.

Printed publications:
Lime Posters for schools
Lime Stabilisation Manual

Publications list:
Available in print

Access to staff:
Contact by letter, by telephone, by fax, by e-mail and via website
Hours: Mon to Fri, 0900 to 1700

Parent body:
Quarry Products Association (QPA)
tel: 020 7730 8194; fax: 020 7730 4355; e-mail: info@qpa.org

BRITISH LIVER TRUST

2 Southampton Road, Ringwood, Hampshire, BH24 1HY

Tel: 01425 481320
Fax: 01425 481335
E-mail: info@britishlivertrust.org.uk

Website:
http://www.britishlivertrust.org.uk

Founded:
1988

Organisation type and purpose:
National organisation. Registered charity (charity number 298858). Suitable for adults. Research organisation. Education on liver disease. The charity produces information on all aspects of liver disease and funds research.

Subject coverage:
Information on liver disease.

Information services:
Liver disease information helpline 0800 652 7330

Printed publications:
Bulletin (newsletter, twice a year)
Publications on liver disease (order form and price list available from the British Liver Trust)
Order printed publications from:
publications@britishlivertrust.org.uk

Publications list:
Available online and in print

Access to staff:
Contact by letter, by telephone, by fax, by e-mail and via website
Hours: Mon to Fri, 0900 to 1700

Access to building, collection or gallery:
No access other than to staff

BRITISH LLAMA AND ALPACA ASSOCIATION

Acronym or abbreviation: BLAA

Banks Way House, Effingham Common, Leatherhead, Surrey, KT24 5JB

Tel: 01372 458350
Fax: 01372 451131

Website:
http://www.llama.co.uk
Information on all four species of camelid and camels, breeding, breeders list, events, conference, links, etc.
http://www.alpaca.co.uk
Information on all four species of camelid and camels, breeders list, events, conference, links, etc.

Enquiries:
Enquiries to: Honorary Secretary

Founded:
1987

Organisation type and purpose:
Membership association (membership is by subscription), present number of members: 432, registered charity (charity number 802688). Owners and breeders association.
To promote good husbandry and the establishment of sound breeding programmes to improve and increase British stock; to guide and foster the growing interest in camelids.

Subject coverage:
Welfare guidelines, trekking, sheep guarding, pets, information from conference proceedings, social days, showing and judging camelids, contacts to visit, camelid fibre.

Printed publications:
Books available mainly imports from USA, but stocks usually held:
Along Came A Llama (Ruck R J, £7.95)
Caring for Llamas (Hoffman C, £17)
GALA: The Guanaco, Alpaca and Llama Advertiser (constantly updated, free initially then £1 per update)
Llama and Alpaca Neonatal Care (Smith B and Timms R, £20.95)
Medicine and Surgery of South American Camelids, Llama, Alpaca, Vicuna, Guanacos (Fowler M E, £75)
The Veterinary Clinics of North America: Llama Medicine (ed La Rue Johnson, £35)

Publications list:
Available in print

Access to staff:
Contact by letter, by telephone and by fax
Hours: Mon to Fri, 0900 to 1700

Access to building, collection or gallery:
No access other than to staff

BRITISH LUGGAGE AND LEATHERGOODS ASSOCIATION

Acronym or abbreviation: BLLA

Federation House, 10 Vyse Street, Birmingham, B18 6LT

Tel: 0121 237 1107
Fax: 0121 236 3921
E-mail: enquries@blla.org.uk

Website:
http://www.blla.org.uk
Product search available, members area, consumers area, retailer and product/brand search.

Enquiries:
Enquiries to: Chief Executive
Direct e-mail: diana.fiveash@blla.org.uk

Founded:
1918

Organisation type and purpose:
Trade association (membership is by subscription, election or invitation), present number of members: 102.
National trade body for those manufacturing and supplying luggage, travel goods, briefcases, handbags, small leathergoods and accessories.

Subject coverage:
Luggage, travel goods, briefcases, handbags, small leathergoods and accessories.

Printed publications:
Buyer's Guide (£20)
BLLANews (newsletter, free)

Fashion Extras

Publications list:
Available online

Access to staff:
Contact by letter, by telephone, by fax, by e-mail and via website. Appointment necessary.
Hours: Mon to Thu, 0930 to 1630; Fri, 0900 to 1600

Access to building, collection or gallery:
Prior appointment required

Access for disabled people:
Parking provided, access to all public areas, toilet facilities

Parent body:
British Jewellery and Giftware Federation Limited
Federation House, 10 Vyse Street, Birmingham, B18 6LT; tel: 0121 236 2657; fax: 0121 236 3921

BRITISH LUNG FOUNDATION

73–75 Goswell Road, London EC1V 7ER

Tel: 020 7831 5831
Fax: 020 7831 5832

Website:
http://www.lunguk.org/

Enquiries:
Enquiries to: Press Officer
Direct tel: 020 7688 5564
Direct e-mail: casey.purkiss@blf-uk.org

Founded:
1984

Organisation type and purpose:
Registered charity (charity number 326730). Raising funds for, and promoting research into, diseases of the lung.

Subject coverage:
Diseases of the chest and lungs, their prevalence, treatment, social and economic effects and research into these diseases; maintaining healthy lungs; effects of atmospheric pollution and occupational respiratory disease.

Printed publications:
Annual Report with research reports (free)
Breathe Easy Club (free)
Leaflets on specific lung disorders (free)
Press releases on research work in lung disease

Publications list:
Available online and in print

Access to staff:
Contact by letter, by telephone, by fax and by e-mail
Hours: Mon to Fri, 0900 to 1700

Member of:
Association of Medical Research Charities
Long-Term Medical Conditions Alliance

Regional Offices:
British Lung Foundation
The Nuffield House, Queen Elizabeth Hospital, Birmingham, B15 2TH; tel: 0121 627 2260; fax: 0121 697 8323
British Lung Foundation
Orchard Street Business Centre, 3 Charles Place, Bristol, BS8 4QW; tel: 0117 925 5810; fax: 0117 925 5809; e-mail: susan@blfsw.fsnet.co.uk
British Lung Foundation
Sir G B Hunter Memorial Hospital, The Green, Wallsend, Tyne & Wear, NE28 7PB; tel: 0191 263 0276; fax: 0191 262 2660
British Lung Foundation (North West)
Moroney House, Cardiothoracic Centre, Thomas Drive, Liverpool, L14 3LB; tel: 0151 228 4723; fax: 0151 228 4723
British Lung Foundation Scotland
The Beacon, 176 St Vincent Street, Glasgow, G2 5SG; tel: 0141 249 6810; e-mail: redballoon@blfscotland.org.uk

BRITISH LYMPHOLOGY SOCIETY

Acronym or abbreviation: BLS

continued overleaf

PO Box 196, Shoreham, Sevenoaks, TN13 9BF

Tel: 01959 525524
Fax: 01959 525524
E-mail: admin@blsac.demon.co.uk

Website:
http://www.lymphoedema.org/bls

Enquiries:
Enquiries to: Administrator

Founded:
1985

Organisation type and purpose:
Professional body (membership is by subscription), present number of members: 600, registered charity (charity number 1042561).

Subject coverage:
Lymphoedema.

Printed publications:
Introduction Leaflet (p&p only)
Screening Tools
Equipment Catalogue
Directory of Lymphoedema Treatment Centres (2000–2001)
Guidelines for the use of Manual Lymphatic Drainage and Self-Administered Massage in Lymphoedema

Publications list:
Available online and in print

Access to staff:
Contact by letter, by telephone, by fax, by e-mail and via website
Hours: Tue to Thu, 0900 to 1700

Access to building, collection or gallery:
Prior appointment required

BRITISH MARINE INDUSTRIES FEDERATION SCOTLAND

Acronym or abbreviation: BMIF Scotland

Westgate, Toward, Dunoon, Argyll, PA23 7UA

Tel: 01369 870251
Fax: 01369 870251
E-mail: bmif-s@clydemarinepress.co.uk

Website:
http://www.bmif.co.uk

Enquiries:
Enquiries to: Administrator

Founded:
1921

Organisation type and purpose:
Trade association (membership is by election or invitation), present number of members: 55, training organisation.
Representing members of the Scottish Marine industry.

Subject coverage:
Yacht and boat building in Scotland, chandlery manufacture, wholesale and retail, marina operations, marine electronics, yacht chartering and other related marine operations in Scotland.

Access to staff:
Contact by letter, by telephone, by fax and by e-mail
Hours: Mon to Fri, 0900 to 1700

Member of:
British Marine Industries Federation
Meadlake Place, Thorpe Lea Road, Egham, Surrey, TW20 8HE

BRITISH MARITIME TECHNOLOGY

Acronym or abbreviation: BMT

Northumbria House, Davy Bank, Wallsend, Tyne and Wear, NE28 6UY

Tel: 0191 262 5242
Fax: 0191 263 8754

E-mail: gsmith@bmtshipdes.demon.co.uk

Website:
http://www.bmt.org
http://www.marinescienceandtechnology.com

Enquiries:
Enquiries to: Librarian

Founded:
1985

Organisation type and purpose:
Consultancy, research organisation.

Subject coverage:
Maritime and civil engineering research, naval architecture, fluid mechanics, ocean engineering, marine engineering, wind engineering, offshore technology, industrial aerodynamics, marine traffic operations, port and harbour design operations and related subjects.

Museum or gallery collection, archive, or library special collection:
Stock/Holdings: 1000 books and 10,000 reports on related subjects
Reports and Technical Memoranda of British Ship Research Association (BSRA)
Special Collections:
Transactions of Royal Institution of Naval Architects
Transactions of Society of Naval Architects & Marine Engineers
Transactions of North East Coast Institution of Engineers and Shipbuilders
Transactions of Engineers and Shipbuilders in Scotland
Reports and Technical Memoranda of British Ship Research Association (BSRA)
Transactions of Engineers and Shipbuilders in Scotland
Transactions of North East Coast Institution of Engineers and Shipbuilders
Transactions of Royal Institution of Naval Architects
Transactions of Society of Naval Architects & Marine Engineers

Library catalogue:
All or part available in-house

Printed publications:
BMT Abstracts (monthly, £220 p.a.)
BMT News (quarterly)
BMT Focus (quarterly)
Code of Procedure for Marine Instrumentation and Control Equipment
Engineering Economics and Ship Design
Recommended Practice for the Protection and Painting of Ships
Ship Design Manual: Hydrodynamics (5 volumes, £1000)
Ship Design Manual: Marine Structures (7 volumes, £1000)
Ship Design Manual: Noise (£1000)
Technical Reports (list available)

Electronic and video publications:
Marine Technology Abstracts (CD-ROM, jointly with Institute of Marine Engineers)

Publications list:
Available in print

Access to staff:
Contact by letter, by telephone, by fax and by e-mail. All charged.
Hours: Mon to Thu, 0830 to 1700; Fri, 0830 to 1630

Access to building, collection or gallery:
Prior appointment required

Other addresses:
British Maritime Technology Limited
Orlando House, 1 Waldegrave Road, Teddington, Middlesex, TW11 8LZ; tel: 020 8943 5544; fax: 020 8943 5347; e-mail: davidg@bmtlib.demon.co.uk; website: http://www.bmt.org
British Maritime Technology Limited
Ceres House, Davy Bank, Wallsend, Tyne & Wear, NE28 6UY; tel: 0191 262 5242; fax: 0191 263 8754; e-mail: g.sbmtlib@britishlibrary.net; website: http://www.bmt.org

Part of:
British Maritime Technology (BMT)
Orlando House, 1 Waldegrave Road, Teddington, Middlesex, TW11 8LZ; tel: 020 8943 5544; fax: 020 8943 5347; e-mail: davidg@bmtlib.demon.co.uk

BRITISH MATCHBOX LABEL AND BOOKLET SOCIETY

Acronym or abbreviation: BML&BS

122 High Street, Melbourn, Cambridgeshire, SG8 6AL

Tel: 01763 260399
E-mail: secretary@phillumeny.com

Website:
http://www.phillumeny.com

Enquiries:
Enquiries to: Secretary

Founded:
1945

Organisation type and purpose:
Membership association (membership is by subscription), present number of members: 500.

Subject coverage:
Matchbox labels and bookmatch collecting, hardware, advertising and other material pertaining to the hobby of collecting these items.

Printed publications:
Books and catalogues by collectors
Magazine (6 times a year)
Membership list (to members only)
Order printed publications from: Bookshop Manager, BML&BS, 53 Trafford Road, Norwich, Norfolk, NR1 2QR

Access to staff:
Contact by letter, by telephone, by e-mail and via website
Hours: Mon to Fri, 0900 to 1700

BRITISH MATERIALS HANDLING FEDERATION

Acronym or abbreviation: BMHF

National Metalforming Centre, 47 Birmingham Road West Bromwich B70 6PY

Tel: 0121 601 6350
Fax: 0121 601 6387
E-mail: enquiry@bmhf.org.uk

Website:
http://www.bmhf.org.uk
Overview of BMHF, details of member associations, products/services, useful links, recruitment facility.

Enquiries:
Enquiries to: General Secretary

Organisation type and purpose:
Trade association.
The UK's voice in Europe on materials handling matters.

Subject coverage:
Heavy lifting and handling equipment, continuous handling equipment, industrial trucks, mobile cranes, lifts, escalators, passenger conveyors, series lifting equipment, storage equipment and methods, powered access vehicles.

Printed publications:
English language versions of FEM's technical publications

Access to staff:
Contact by letter, by telephone, by fax and by e-mail
Hours: Mon to Fri, 0900 to 1700

BRITISH MEASUREMENT AND TESTING ASSOCIATION

Acronym or abbreviation: BMTA

East Malling Enterprise Centre, New Road, East Malling, Kent, ME19 6BJ

Tel: 01732 897452
Fax: 01732 897453
E-mail: kgb@bmta.co.uk

Website:
http://www.bmta.co.uk
Membership list, member company information, meeting notices and reports, etc.

Enquiries:
Enquiries to: Executive Secretary
Other contacts: Assistant Secretary

Founded:
1990

Organisation type and purpose:
Membership association (membership is by subscription), present number of members: 90.
An Association for organisations concerned with measurement or testing.

Subject coverage:
Testing and calibration; European issues relating to testing and product conformity.

Printed publications:
Newsletter
Directory of European Testing and Analytical
    Laboratories
Measurement Good Practice Guide No 36,
    Estimating Uncertainties in Testing

Access to staff:
Contact by telephone, by fax, by e-mail and via website
Hours: Mon to Fri, 0900 to 1700

UK member of:
EUROLAB

BRITISH MEDICAL ACUPUNCTURE SOCIETY

Acronym or abbreviation: BMAS

BMAS House, 3 Winnington Court, Northwich, Cheshire, CW8 1AQ

Tel: 01606 786782
Fax: 01606 786783
E-mail: admin@medical-acupuncture.org.uk

Website:
http://www.medical-acupuncture.co.uk

Enquiries:
Enquiries to: Support Manager to Medical Director
Direct e-mail: bmaslondon@aol.com

Founded:
1980

Organisation type and purpose:
National organisation, professional body (membership is by subscription, election or invitation), registered charity (charity number 1057942).

Subject coverage:
Medical acupuncture; medically qualified practitioners who practise acupuncture.

Printed publications:
Acupuncture in Medicine (quarterly)
Newsletter (2 times a year)
Patient information leaflet

Electronic and video publications:
Electronic Journal available

Publications list:
Available online

Access to staff:
Contact by letter, by telephone, by fax, by e-mail and via website
Hours: Mon to Fri, 0900 to 1700 (Head Office); Mon to Fri, 1000 to 1800 (London office)

Access to building, collection or gallery:
No access other than to staff

Also at:
Medical Director
BMAS, The Royal London Homoeopathic Hospital, 60 Great Ormond Street, London, WC1N 3HR; tel: 020 7713 9437; fax: 020 7713 6286; e-mail: bmaslondon@aol.com; website: http://www.medical-acupuncture.co.uk

Links with:
International Council for Medical Acupuncture and Related Techniques (ICMART)
    62 rue de l'Amazone, Bruxelles, 1050, Belgium

BRITISH MEDICAL ASSOCIATION

Acronym or abbreviation: BMA

BMA House, Tavistock Square, London, WC1H 9JP

Tel: 020 7383 6625
Fax: 020 7388 2544
E-mail: bma.library@bma.org.uk

Website:
http://www.bma.org

Enquiries:
Enquiries to: Librarian

Organisation type and purpose:
Professional body, trade union.

Subject coverage:
Current clinical information, medical ethics, computers and medicine.

Museum or gallery collection, archive, or library special collection:
Hastings, Sir Charles (1794–1866) Collection (c. 400 volumes pre-1866 which belonged to the founder of the Association)

Access to staff:
Contact by letter. Appointment necessary. Access for members only. Letter of introduction required. Non-members charged.
Hours: Mon to Fri, 0900 to 1700

BRITISH MEDICAL ASSOCIATION IN SCOTLAND

Acronym or abbreviation: BMA

14 Queen Street, Edinburgh, EH2 1LL

Tel: 0131 247 3000
Fax: 0131 247 3001
E-mail: bmascotland@bma.org.uk

Website:
http://www.bma.org.uk
http://www.bma.org.uk/scotland

Enquiries:
Enquiries to: Scottish Secretary

Founded:
1832

Organisation type and purpose:
National organisation, professional body, trade union (membership is by subscription).
Represents the interests of and provides services for 140,044 members in UK, including 19,000 medical students and 3,000 overseas members.

Access to staff:
Contact by letter, by telephone, by fax and by e-mail. Access for members only.
Hours: Mon to Fri, 0900 to 1700

Access to building, collection or gallery:
Prior appointment required

Access for disabled people:
Parking provided, disabled lift, toilet facilities

Headquarters address:
BMA
    BMA House, Tavistock Square, London, WC1H 9JP; tel: 020 7387 4499

BRITISH MEDICAL ULTRASOUND SOCIETY

Acronym or abbreviation: BMUS

36 Portland Place, London, W1B 1LS

Tel: 020 7636 3714
Fax: 020 7323 2175
E-mail: secretariat@bmus.org

Website:
http://www.bmus.org

Enquiries:
Enquiries to: General Secretary

Founded:
1984

Organisation type and purpose:
Learned society, present number of members: 2,400.
The advancement of science and technology in medical ultrasound; maintenance of the highest standards in these fields; to advance and encourage education and research in these areas.

Subject coverage:
Diagnostic medical ultrasound.

Printed publications:
BMUS Journal (quarterly)

Access to staff:
Contact by letter, by telephone, by fax, by e-mail and via website
Hours: Mon to Fri, 0900 to 1700

Links with:
European Federation of Ultrasound in Medicine & Biology (EFSUMB)
    36 Portland Place, London, W1B 1LS; fax: 020 7099 7140; e-mail: 020 7436 7934; website: www .efsumb.org

BRITISH MENSA LIMITED

Acronym or abbreviation: MENSA

St John's House, St John's Square, Wolverhampton, West Midlands, WV2 4AH

Tel: 01902 772771
Fax: 01902 392500
E-mail: enquiries@mensa.org.uk

Website:
http://www.mensa.org.uk
How to join, puzzles, general information.

Enquiries:
Enquiries to: Financial Controller
Direct e-mail: info@mensa.org.uk
Other contacts: PA to GM

Founded:
1946

Organisation type and purpose:
Learned society, membership association (membership is by qualification), present number of members: 27,000.
Society for people with high IQ.
Association for people of high intelligence (IQ scope above 98th percentile).

Subject coverage:
Measurement of intelligence, gifted children, puzzles.

Printed publications:
Home Test
Invigilated Test
Books via bookshops

Access to staff:
Contact by letter, by telephone, by fax and by e-mail
Hours: Mon to Fri, 0830 to 1630

BRITISH MENSWEAR GUILD

Acronym or abbreviation: BMG

5 Portland Place, London, W1B 1PW

Tel: 020 7580 8783

continued overleaf

Fax: 020 7436 8833
E-mail: director@british-menswear-guild.co.uk

Website:
http://www.british-menswear-guild.co.uk
Information about members, listing of relevant
trade shows and special events, information on
joining the BMG.

Enquiries:
Enquiries to: Director

Founded:
1959

Organisation type and purpose:
Trade association.

Subject coverage:
Manufacturing of top quality men's clothing and
accessories, clothing trade exhibitions in the United
Kingdom and Europe.

Trade and statistical information:
Available from the Department of Trade and
    Industry.

Printed publications:
List of member companies (free)
Press releases with information about the Guild
    and its member companies (free)
Year book (annually, free)

Access to staff:
Contact by letter, by telephone, by fax and by e-
mail
Hours: Mon to Fri, 0900 to 1700

BRITISH METALS RECYCLING ASSOCIATION

Acronym or abbreviation: BMRA

16 High Street, Brampton, Huntingdon,
Cambridgeshire, PE28 4TU

Tel: 01480 455249
Fax: 01480 453680
E-mail: admin@recyclemetals.org

Website:
http://www.britmetrec.org.uk
Educational literature, membership list, annual
report, benefits, code of practice, history.

Enquiries:
Enquiries to: Director General

Founded:
1919

Organisation type and purpose:
Trade association.

Subject coverage:
Ferrous and non-ferrous scrap metal recycling.

Access to staff:
Contact by letter, by telephone, by fax, by e-mail
and via website
Hours: Mon to Fri, 0900 to 1700

Access to building, collection or gallery:
No access other than to staff

BRITISH MICROCIRCULATION SOCIETY

Acronym or abbreviation: BMS

c/o Department of Bioengineering, Imperial
College of Science, Technology and Medicine,
London, SW7 2BY

Tel: 020 7594 5172
Fax: 020 7594 5177
E-mail: m.j.lever@ic.ac.uk

Website:
http://www.microcirculation.org.uk
Full information about the Society and full
updates.

Enquiries:
Enquiries to: Honorary Secretary

Founded:
1963

Organisation type and purpose:
Learned society, present number of members: 225.
Promotion of all aspects of research into
microvascular function.

Subject coverage:
Microcirculation, blood flow in small vessels,
capillary function, endothelial function, tissue fluid
balance, vessel growth, vasculature in disease,
nitric oxide, inflammation, oedema.

**Museum or gallery collection, archive, or library
special collection:**
Annual proceedings

Printed publications:
Constitution, Rules and List of Members
    (containing a summary of members' research
    interests, every 2 years)
Scientific abstracts (annually)
Journal of Vascular Research

Access to staff:
Contact by fax and by e-mail
Hours: Mon to Fri, 0900 to 1700

Affiliated to:
European Society for Microcirculation

BRITISH MICROLIGHT AIRCRAFT ASSOCIATION

Acronym or abbreviation: BMAA

Bullring, Deddington, Banbury, Oxfordshire, OX15
0TT

Tel: 01869 338888
Fax: 01869 337116
E-mail: general@bmaa.org

Website:
http://www.bmaa.org

Enquiries:
Enquiries to: Chief Executive

Founded:
1978

Organisation type and purpose:
National organisation, membership association
(membership is by subscription), present number
of members: 4,000, service industry.
Promotion of affordable aviation in microlight
aircraft.

Subject coverage:
Information on every aspect of microlight flying.

Access to staff:
Contact by letter, by telephone, by fax, by e-mail
and via website
Hours: Mon to Fri, 0900 to 1700

Authorised company of:
Civil Aviation Authority (CAA)

Links with:
Fédération Aéronautique Internationale (FAI)
Royal Aero Club of Great Britain

BRITISH MILKSHEEP SOCIETY

Acronym or abbreviation: BMS

The Row, Roweltown, Carlisle, Cumbria, CA6 6LX

Tel: 01697 748217
E-mail: parsonstherow@freenetname.co.uk

Enquiries:
Enquiries to: Secretary

Founded:
1982

Organisation type and purpose:
Membership association (membership is by
subscription, qualification, present number of
members: 131, voluntary organisation.
To promote the British Milksheep, advertise the
breed, assist members with exports, collate
pedigree breeding data, organise meetings for
members.

Subject coverage:
Information on the British Milksheep, on milking
sheep and pedigree data of British Milksheep.

Affiliation to:
National Sheep Association (NSA)
    Sheep Centre, Malvern, Worcestershire

BRITISH MODEL FLYING ASSOCIATION

Acronym or abbreviation: BMFA

Chacksfield House, 31 St Andrews Road, Leicester,
LE2 8RE

Tel: 0116 244 0028
Fax: 0116 244 0645
E-mail: admin@bmfa.org

Website:
http://www.bmfa.org
News, clubs, calendar of events, resources, what's
new?

Enquiries:
Enquiries to: Chief Executive

Founded:
1922

Organisation type and purpose:
Membership association (membership is by
subscription, election or invitation), present
number of members: 28,000, voluntary
organisation.
National governing body for model flying.

Subject coverage:
Model flying legislation, model aircraft building
and flying, flying site retention, national and
international model flying competitions.

Printed publications:
Acquisition and Retention of Flying Sites – Book
BMFA/BHPA Code for Shared Use of Sites
BMFA: Why Join (annually)
BMFA: Members Handbook (annually)
BMFA News (6 times a year)
BMFA: Your voice
Leaflets on wide range of model flying topics

Access to staff:
Contact by letter, by telephone, by fax, by e-mail,
in person and via website
Hours: Mon to Fri, 0900 to 1700

Links with:
Fédération Aéronautique Internationale (FAI)
General Aviation Awareness Council (GAAC)
Royal Aero Club of the United Kingdom (RAeC)

BRITISH MODEL SOLDIER SOCIETY

Acronym or abbreviation: BMSS

12 Savay Lane, Denham, Buckinghamshire, UB9
5NH

Tel: 01895 832757
E-mail: model.soldiers@btinternet.com

Website:
http://www.model.soldiers.btinternet.co.uk
Description of the society; details of branches,
meetings and shows; advice on modelling and
painting; photos of model soldiers; how to join the
society.

Enquiries:
Enquiries to: Honorary Secretary

Founded:
1935

Organisation type and purpose:
International organisation, voluntary organisation.
Promote research and scholarship of military
history, weaponry, uniforms, etc. through the
media of military models.

Subject coverage:
Collecting, making and painting model soldiers, military vehicles and weapons, military uniforms and operations of all periods, campaigns of all military bodies of all nationalities and periods.

Museum or gallery collection, archive, or library special collection:
The Society's National Collection of all types of figures of a military nature

Printed publications:
Bulletin (quarterly, free to members)
Bulletin Extra (quarterly, free to members)
Handbook sheets (when published, free to members)

Access to staff:
Contact by letter, by telephone and by e-mail. Access for members only.
Hours: Mon to Fri, 0900 to 1700

BRITISH MOTORSPORT MARSHALS CLUB

Acronym or abbreviation: BMMC

22 Adlington Drive, Sandbach, Cheshire, CW11 1DX

Tel: 07715 377 887
Fax: 0161 455 9001

Website:
http://www.marshals.co.uk

Enquiries:
Enquiries to: Chairman

Founded:
1957

Organisation type and purpose:
International organisation, membership association (membership is by subscription), present number of members: 2200, voluntary organisation, training organisation, consultancy. To provide training and improve safety at all categories of motor sport. The members of the club marshall at most of the motorsport events in the UK.

Subject coverage:
The provision of training in all aspects of motorsport from event organisation, fire training, flag signalling etc.

Printed publications:
Club information leaflet (free to all)
Safety precautions (free, members)

Access to staff:
Contact by letter, by telephone and by fax
Hours: Mon to Fri, 0900 to 1900

Member of:
Royal Automobile Club Motor Sports Association

BRITISH MUSEUM

Acronym or abbreviation: BM

Great Russell Street, London, WC1B 3DG

Tel: 020 7323 8000\ Minicom no. 020 7323 8920
Fax: 020 7323 8616
E-mail: information@thebritishmuseum.ac.uk

Website:
http://www.thebritishmuseum.ac.uk
General information about galleries, opening times, access for disabled visitors.
http://www.britishmuseum.co.uk
British Museum Company (retail and mail order).

Enquiries:
Enquiries to: Information Officer
Direct tel: 020 7323 8299
Other contacts: Visitor Information Manager

Founded:
1753

Organisation type and purpose:
Museum.
National museum.

Subject coverage:
The history, culture and ethnography of much of the world from prehistoric times to the present day. The collections are displayed in the following departments:
Greek and Roman Department
Ancient Near East Department
Oriental Department
Japanese Department
Prehistory and Early Europe Department
Medieval and Modern Europe Department
Coins and Medals Department
Egyptian Department
Ethnography Department
Prints and Drawings Department.

Information services:
Helpline available, tel no: 020 7323 8299.

Special visitor services:
Guided tours, tape recorded guides, materials and/ or activities for children.

Education services:
Group education facilities, resources for Key Stages 1 and 2, 3 and 4.

Services for disabled people:
For the visually impaired; for the hearing impaired.

Museum or gallery collection, archive, or library special collection:
Records of the buildings, staff and administration, 1753 to the present day, are in the Central Archives
The departments hold manuscript records relating to the history of the collections
These include the papers of Charles Townley relating to his collection of classical antiquities, 1760–1805

Non-library collection catalogue:
All or part available online and in-house

Printed publications:
Books, children's books, scholarly titles
Full list of publications is available from the British Museum Company Limited, The British Museum Press
Order printed publications from: British Museum Company Ltd
46 Bloomsbury Street, London, WC1B 3QQ, tel: 020 7323 1234, fax: 020 7436 7315, e-mail: sales.products@bmcompany.co.uk

Publications list:
Available in print

Access to staff:
Contact by letter, by telephone, by fax, by e-mail, in person and via website
Hours: Mon to Sun, 0900 to 1730

Access for disabled people:
Parking provided, ramped entry, level entry, access to all public areas, toilet facilities
Special comments: Pre-booking required for parking.

BRITISH MUSIC HALL SOCIETY

Acronym or abbreviation: BMHS

82 Fernlea Road, London, SW12 9RW

Tel: 020 8673 2175

Enquiries:
Enquiries to: Honorary Secretary

Founded:
1963

Organisation type and purpose:
Learned society (membership is by subscription), present number of members: 950, consultancy, research organisation.
Study group.
To preserve the history of British Music Hall and Variety, and recall the artists who created it.

Subject coverage:
The British music halls and variety theatre from 1800 to present day.

Museum or gallery collection, archive, or library special collection:
Removed from Passmore Edwards Museum, now in storage awaiting a new venue, information from the Historian/Archivist

Printed publications:
The Call Boy (quarterly, for members only)

Access to staff:
Contact by letter and by telephone. Non-members charged.
Hours: Mon to Fri, 1830 to 2230

Access to building, collection or gallery:
No prior appointment required
Special comments: Contact Historian/Archivist, 76 Royal Close, Chichester, West Sussex, PO19 2FL, enclose sae, tel 01243 783322.

BRITISH MUSIC INFORMATION CENTRE

Acronym or abbreviation: BMIC

Lincoln House, 75 Westminster Bridge Road, London SE1 7HS

Tel: 020 7928 1902
Fax: 020 7928 2957
E-mail: info@bmic.co.uk

Website:
http://www.bmic.co.uk
About BMIC, counterpoints, information pages on publishers, composers, ensembles (contemporary music), funding bodies.

Enquiries:
Enquiries to: Director
Other contacts: Production and Services Manager

Founded:
1967

Organisation type and purpose:
International organisation, national organisation, registered charity (charity number 326829), public library.
Resource centre for British contemporary classical music.

Subject coverage:
British classical music written from 1900 to present day, including background information about composers and repertoire suggestions.

Museum or gallery collection, archive, or library special collection:
Archives of press cuttings, reviews, articles covering individual composers
Scores and recordings covering more than 45,000 works

Non-library collection catalogue:
All or part available online and in-house

Library catalogue:
All or part available online

Printed publications:
Counterpoints (newsletter of the 'Friends' organisation, 4 times a year, free)

Publications list:
Available online

Access to staff:
Contact by letter, by telephone, by fax, by e-mail, in person and via website. Appointment necessary.
Hours: Mon to Fri, 1200 to 1700

Access for disabled people:
Lift to first floor

Member of:
International Association of Music Information Centres (IAMIC)
e-mail: gratzl@iamic.net

BRITISH MUSIC SOCIETY

Acronym or abbreviation: BMS

7 Tudor Gardens, Upminster, Essex, RM14 3DE

Tel: 01708 224795

continued overleaf

E-mail: sct.bms1943@amserve.com

Website:
http://www.britishmusicsociety.co.uk
Membership and catalogue.

Enquiries:
Enquiries to: Honorary Treasurer

Founded:
1978

Organisation type and purpose:
Membership association (membership is by subscription), present number of members: 600, voluntary organisation, registered charity (charity number 1043838).
To promote an interest in the music of lesser-known British composers of serious music, especially between 1850 and 1975 and where they do not have their own society or trust.

Subject coverage:
Promotion of British composers from about 1800 to the present day, especially between 1850 and 1975.

Printed publications:
Publications include:
Aspects of British Song (£6)
British Composer Profiles (£6.25)
British Music (journal, annual, 29 volumes, £5 per volume)
British Opera in Retrospect (£6)
Monographs (occasional series, £5)
Newsletter (quarterly, free to members)
British Choral Music (£8.95)
Goodnight to Flamboro (Baines W, £10.99)
Parrotcisms: the autobiography of Professor Ian Parrott (£8.99)

Electronic and video publications:
British choral and instrumental music (cassette tapes and CDs)

Publications list:
Available online and in print

Access to staff:
Contact by letter, by telephone and by e-mail.
Appointment necessary.
Hours: Mon to Fri, 0900 to 1700

BRITISH MYCOLOGICAL SOCIETY

Acronym or abbreviation: BMS

Joseph Banks Building, Royal Botanic Gardens, Kew, Richmond-upon-Thames, Surrey, TW9 3AB

Tel: 020 8332 5720
Fax: 020 8332 5720
E-mail: info@britymycolsoc.org.uk

Website:
http://www.britmycolsoc.org.uk
Information about society and its activities, links to other scientific sites.

Enquiries:
Enquiries to: General Secretary
Direct tel: 0151 231 2203
Direct fax: 0151 207 4726
Direct e-mail: g.p.sharples@livjm.ac.uk
Other contacts: Membership Secretary for membership application.

Founded:
1896

Organisation type and purpose:
Learned society, registered charity (charity number 276503).
To promote mycology in all its aspects by publications, meetings and such other means as the society deems appropriate.

Subject coverage:
Mycology, biodiversity, biotechnology, conservation, ecology, genetics, fungal pathogens of plants and animals, systematics.

Museum or gallery collection, archive, or library special collection:
Books

Printed publications:
Field Mycology (quarterly)
Guides and Keys (variable)
Mycologist (quarterly)
Mycological Research (monthly)
Symposium Volumes (annually)
Order printed publications from: Books, The Librarian and Archivist
British Mycological Society, c/o Herbarium, Royal Botanic Gardens, Kew, Richmond, Surrey, TA9 3AE, tel: 020 8332 5720, e-mail: v.barkham@rbgkew.org.uk

Publications list:
Available in print

Access to staff:
Contact by letter, by fax and by e-mail
Hours: Mon to Fri, 0900 to 1700

Book collection housed with:
Librarian and Archivist
British Mycological Society, c/o Herbarium, Royal Botanic Gardens, Kew, Richmond-upon-Thames, Surrey, TW9 3AE; tel: 020 8332 5720; e-mail: v.barkham@rbgkew.org.uk

BRITISH NATIONAL CARNATION SOCIETY

Acronym or abbreviation: BNCS

Linfield, Duncote, Towcester, Northamptonshire, NN12 8AH

Tel: 01327 351594
E-mail: betty@induncote.freeserve.co.uk

Enquiries:
Enquiries to: Membership Secretary

Founded:
1948

Organisation type and purpose:
National organisation, membership association (membership is by subscription), present number of members: c 400, voluntary organisation.

Subject coverage:
Carnations and pinks (Dianthus family); culture and hybridisation; exhibitions and competitions.

Printed publications:
The following publications are available for purchase:
How to Grow Border Carnations
How to Grow Perpetual Flowering Carnations
How to Grow Pinks
Newsletter (two times a year)
Rules for judging, standards and classifications
The Carnation Yearbook

Access to staff:
Contact by e-mail
Hours: Evenings

Affiliated to:
Royal Horticultural Society

BRITISH NATIONAL LYMPHOMA INVESTIGATION

Acronym or abbreviation: BNLI

UCL & CRC Cancer Trials Centre, 222 Euston Road, London, NW1 2DA

Tel: 020 7679 8060
Fax: 020 7679 6061
E-mail: bnli@ctc.ucl.ac.uk

Website:
http://www.bnli.ucl.ac.uk/
Trial information, staff information, links to other sites.

Enquiries:
Enquiries to: Senior Data Manager

Founded:
1970

Organisation type and purpose:
Professional body, registered charity (charity number 263424).

Subject coverage:
Lymphoma investigation.

Publications list:
Available in print

Access to staff:
Contact by letter and by e-mail
Hours: Mon to Fri, 0900 to 1700

BRITISH NATIONAL TEMPERANCE LEAGUE

Acronym or abbreviation: BNTL

30 Keswick Road, Worksop, Nottinghamshire, S81 7PT

Tel: 01909 477882
E-mail: bntl@btconnect.com

Website:
http://www.bntl.org

Enquiries:
Enquiries to: Chief Executive Officer

Founded:
1834

Organisation type and purpose:
Voluntary organisation, registered charity (charity number 224555), suitable for ages: 5–18.
Promoting drug-free lifestyles; providing education and resources on the subject.

Subject coverage:
Alcohol and drug education, history of temperance organisations (general), training.

Museum or gallery collection, archive, or library special collection:
Livesey Library held at the University of Central Lancashire in Preston: temperance history and 19th-century social reform, includes items bequeathed by William E. Moss

Printed publications:
Annual Report
Drugs and their Dangers (Key Stage 1)
Alcohol and Your Body (Key Stage 2)
Basic Drug Awareness (Key Stage 2)

Electronic and video publications:
Basic Drug Awareness Resource Box (suitable for ages: 14+)
Basic Alcohol Awareness Resource Box (suitable for ages: 14+)

Access to staff:
Contact by letter, by telephone, by e-mail and in person
Hours: Mon to Thu, 0900 to 1700

BRITISH NATURALISTS' ASSOCIATION

Acronym or abbreviation: BNA

PO Box 5682, Corby, Northamptonshire, NN17 2ZW

Tel: 01536 262977
Fax: 01536 262977
E-mail: secretary@bna-naturalists.org

Website:
http://www.bna-naturalists.org
General natural history; branch details.

Enquiries:
Enquiries to: General Secretary

Founded:
1905

Organisation type and purpose:
Membership association (membership is by subscription), registered charity (charity number 296551).
One of the oldest natural history societies in the UK.
Educational charity.

Subject coverage:
Natural history in general.

Museum or gallery collection, archive, or library special collection:
Books, records and documents

Printed publications:
British Naturalist (2 times a year)
Country-Side magazine (2 times a year)
How to Begin the Study series (3 titles)
Spiders, Amphibians, Slugs and Snails

Access to staff:
Contact by letter, by telephone, by fax and by e-mail
Hours: Mon to Fri, 1830 to 2200

Has:
12 branches
24 affiliated societies

BRITISH NON-FERROUS METALS FEDERATION

Acronym or abbreviation: BNFMF

5 Grovelands Business Centre, Boundary Way, Hemel Hempstead, HP2 7TE

Tel: 01442 275705
Fax: 01442 275716
E-mail: bnfmf@copperuk.org.uk

Enquiries:
Enquiries to: Technical Secretary

Founded:
1945

Organisation type and purpose:
Trade association.

Subject coverage:
Production and supply of semi-manufactures in copper and copper alloys.

Access to staff:
Contact by letter, by fax and by e-mail
Hours: Mon to Fri, 0900 to 1700

Administered by:
Copper Development Association
5 Grovelands Business Centre, Boundary Way, Hemel Hempstead, HP2 7TE; tel: 01442 275705; fax: 01442 275716; website: http://www.cda.org.uk

BRITISH NUCLEAR ENERGY SOCIETY

Acronym or abbreviation: BNES

Institution of Civil Engineers, 1–7 Great George Street, London, SW1P 3AA

Tel: 020 7665 2241
Fax: 020 7799 1325
E-mail: ianandrews@ice.org.uk

Website:
http://www.bnes.org.uk
Details of BNES, Nuclear Energy journal, events.

Enquiries:
Enquiries to: Secretary

Founded:
1962

Organisation type and purpose:
Learned society, professional body (membership is by subscription), present number of members: 1100, registered charity (charity number 261687).

Subject coverage:
Nuclear energy for power generation; fuel; safety.

Printed publications:
Conference Proceedings
Nuclear Energy (6 times a year)
Order printed publications from: Stk Publishing Ltd
6 Yarde Hill Orchard, Sidmouth, Devon, EX10 9J2

Access to staff:
Contact by letter, by telephone, by fax and by e-mail
Hours: Mon to Fri, 0900 to 1700

Affiliated to:
European Nuclear Society
tel: + 41 31 382 6111; fax: + 41 31 382 6845
Institution of Civil Engineers
tel: 020 7222 7722; fax: 020 7222 7500

Constituent bodies:
Institute of Energy
tel: 020 7580 7124; fax: 020 7580 4420
Institute of Marine Engineers
tel: 020 7382 2600; fax: 020 7382 2670; e-mail: imare@imare.org.uk
Institute of Materials
tel: 020 7839 4071; fax: 020 7839 1702
Institute of Measurement and Control
tel: 020 7387 4989; fax: 020 7388 8431
Institute of Physics
tel: 020 7470 4800; fax: 020 7470 4848
Institution of Chemical Engineers
tel: 01788 578214; fax: 01788 560833
Institution of Civil Engineers
tel: 020 7222 7722; fax: 020 7222 7500
Institution of Electrical Engineers
tel: 020 7240 1871
Institution of Incorporated Engineers
Institution of Mechanical Engineers
tel: 020 7222 7899; fax: 020 7222 4557
Institution of Nuclear Engineers
tel: 020 8698 1500; fax: 020 8695 6409
Royal Society of Chemistry
tel: 020 7437 8658; fax: 020 7437 8883

BRITISH NUCLEAR FUELS PLC

Magnox Generation, Berkeley Centre, Berkeley, Gloucestershire, GL13 9PB

Tel: 01453 810451
Fax: 01453 812529

Enquiries:
Enquiries to: Information Officer
Direct tel: 01453 812562
Direct fax: 01453 813914

Founded:
1996

Organisation type and purpose:
Electricity generator.

Subject coverage:
Nuclear engineering, electrical engineering, physics, mechanical engineering, health and safety, robotics.

Access to staff:
Contact by telephone and by fax
Hours: Mon to Fri, 0900 to 1700

BRITISH NUCLEAR MEDICINE SOCIETY

Acronym or abbreviation: BNMS

Regent House, 291 Kirkdale, London, SE26 4QD

Tel: 020 8676 7864
Fax: 020 8676 8417
E-mail: office@bnms.org.uk

Website:
http://www.bnms.org.uk

Enquiries:
Enquiries to: Administrator

Founded:
1969

Organisation type and purpose:
Learned society.
Affiliated to the European Nuclear Medicine Society and to the World Federation of Nuclear Medicine; the British Association for Radiopharmacy is an affiliate society.

Subject coverage:
Nuclear medicine; clinical uses of unsealed radioactive isotopes and radiopharmaceuticals.

Printed publications:
Nuclear Medicine Communications

Electronic and video publications:
Myocardial Perfusion (CD-ROM)

BRITISH NUMBER PLATE MANUFACTURERS ASSOCIATION

Acronym or abbreviation: BNMA

PO Box 23, South Shore, Blackpool, Lancs FY4 3DA

Tel: 01253 345287
Fax: 01253 344595
E-mail: jhartley@bnma.org

Website:
http://www.bnma.org/

Enquiries:
Enquiries to: Press Officer
Direct e-mail: tsanders@bnma.org

Organisation type and purpose:
Trade association.

Subject coverage:
Road vehicle number plates.

Access to staff:
Contact by letter, by fax and by e-mail
Hours: Mon to Fri, 0900 to 1700

BRITISH NUMISMATIC SOCIETY

Acronym or abbreviation: BNS

c/o Warburg Institute, Woburn Square, London, WC1H 0AB

Tel: 01223 332915
E-mail: secretary@britnumsoc.org

Website:
http://www.britnumsoc.org

Enquiries:
Enquiries to: Honorary Secretary

Founded:
1903

Organisation type and purpose:
Learned society.

Subject coverage:
British numismatics: coins, currency, medals and tokens of Great Britain and Ireland, Empire and Commonwealth; numismatics more generally, especially the literature; history of minting techniques.

Museum or gallery collection, archive, or library special collection:
Library

Printed publications:
British Numismatic Journal (annually, free to members)
British Numismatic Society Special Publications (occasional)

Affiliated to:
British Association of Numismatic Societies

BRITISH NUMISMATIC TRADE ASSOCIATION

Acronym or abbreviation: BNTA

PO Box 2, Rye, East Sussex, TN31 7WE

Tel: 01797 229988
Fax: 01797 229988
E-mail: bnta@lineone.net

Website:
http://www.numis.co.uk

Enquiries:
Enquiries to: General Secretary

Founded:
1973

Organisation type and purpose:
Trade association.

continued overleaf

Subject coverage:
The purchase and sale of numismatic items including coins, medals and decorations.

Printed publications:
Membership Directory (dealers who specialise in purchase and sale of numismatic items, annually, free)

Publications list:
Available in print

Access to staff:
Contact by letter, by telephone, by fax and by e-mail
Hours: Mon to Fri, 0900 to 1700

BRITISH NURSING ASSOCIATION

Acronym or abbreviation: BNA

The Colonnades, Beaconsfield Close, Hatfield, Hertfordshire, AL10 8YD

Tel: 01707 263544 or 0800 657575
Fax: 01707 272250
E-mail: info@bna.co.uk

Website:
http://www.bna.co.uk

Enquiries:
Enquiries to: Marketing Director
Direct fax: 01707 255659

Founded:
1949

Organisation type and purpose:
Professional body, service industry.
Provision of nurses and carers to support people in their own homes, hospitals, NHS Trusts, social services departments, prisons and industry.

Subject coverage:
Nursing, staffing, occupational health, first aid courses, social services, nursing homes, family health services authorities, insurance companies, GP practices, prisons, individual clients in their own homes.

Printed publications:
BNA branch address list
Brochures about services available

Access to staff:
Contact by letter, by telephone, by e-mail, in person and via website
Hours: Mon to Fri, 0900 to 1700
Special comments: 24 hour emergency on-call at local BNA branches.

Has:
over 160 Branches Nationwide

Holding Group:
Nestor Healthcare Group
The Colonnades, Beaconsfield Close, Hatfield, Hertfordshire; tel: 01707 255635; fax: 01707 255633

Member of:
REC
UKHCA

Other companies in the group include:
Abigail Care
At Home Care
Forensic Medical Services
Grosvenor Nursing Agency
Home Nursing Agency
Kensington and Knightsbridge Nurses Bureau
Mayfair Specialist Nurses
Medic International
Medico Nursing
Nestor Medical Duty Services
Nestor Primecare
Nightingales
United Kingdom Underwriting Services
Worldwide Healthcare Exchange

BRITISH NUTRITION FOUNDATION

Acronym or abbreviation: BNF

High Holborn House, 52–54 High Holborn, London, WC1V 6RQ

Tel: 020 7404 6504
Fax: 020 7404 6747
E-mail: postbox@nutrition.org.uk

Website:
http://www.nutrition.org.uk
Nutrition information. Information on resources, press contacts and events.
http://www.teachingfoodsafety.org.uk
Primary school food safety issues.

Enquiries:
Enquiries to: Education Secretary

Founded:
1967

Organisation type and purpose:
National organisation, registered charity (charity number 251681), suitable for ages: 5 to 18, consultancy, publishing house.
Independent scientific charity.
Provides scientifically based information on nutrition and related health matters, also provides health education resources for Primary and Secondary schools.

Subject coverage:
Nutrition and related health matters, science of nutrition and its application, food and diet, diet-related health problems, nutrition education, food labelling, food safety.

Printed publications:
BNF Briefing Papers (19 titles)
BNF Nutrition Bulletin and Conference Proceedings
BNF Nutrition Facts
Diet and Heart Disease: A round table of factors (2nd ed., 1996, £29.99)
Food – A Fact of Life (educational materials for 11 to 16 year olds, prices vary)
McCance and Widdowson – A Scientific Partnership of 60 years (book, 1993, £10)
Task Force Reports – comprehensive and authoritative reviews of a particular area of nutrition science (7 titles)

Electronic and video publications:
Teaching Food Safety (primary)
Interactive Food Facts (secondary)

Publications list:
Available online and in print

Access to staff:
Contact by letter, by fax, by e-mail and via website
Hours: Mon to Fri, 0900 to 1700
Special comments: Stamped addressed envelope is useful for information.

BRITISH OAT AND BARLEY MILLERS ASSOCIATION

Acronym or abbreviation: BOBMA

4A Torphichen Street, Edinburgh, EH3 8JQ

Tel: 0131 229 9415
Fax: 0131 229 9407
E-mail: andrew.jack@sfdf.org.uk

Enquiries:
Enquiries to: Executive Secretary

Organisation type and purpose:
Trade association.
Acts as a lobbying organisation for trade sector.

Subject coverage:
Supply of oats and barley.

Access to staff:
Contact by telephone and by e-mail. Appointment necessary. Access for members only.
Hours: Mon to Fri, 0900 to 1700

Affiliated to the European organisation:
CEEREAL
Rond-Point Schuman 9, bte 11, Brussels, B-1040, Belgium; tel: 00 3 22 230 4354; fax: 00 3 22 230 9493

Umbrella organisation:
Food and Drink Federation (FDF)
6 Catherine Street, London, WC2B 5JJ; tel: 020 7836 2460; fax: 020 7836 0580; e-mail: fdf@fdf.org.uk

BRITISH OCCUPATIONAL HYGIENE SOCIETY

Acronym or abbreviation: BOHS

5–6 Melbourne Business Court, Millennium Way, Pride Park, Derby, DE24 8LZ

Tel: 01332 298101
Fax: 01332 298099
E-mail: admin@bohs.org

Website:
http://www.bohs.org

Enquiries:
Enquiries to: Press Officer
Direct e-mail: anthea@bohs.org

Founded:
1953

Organisation type and purpose:
Learned society, registered charity (charity number 801417).

Subject coverage:
Occupational hygiene; recognition, evaluation and control of the workplace; physical and chemical factors affecting the health or well-being of workers or the community, emphasis on health hazards at work and indoor air quality.

Printed publications:
Annals of Occupational Hygiene (pub. OUP)
Newsletter (Joint publication with the British Institute of Occupational Hygienists)

Access to staff:
Access for members only.
Hours: Mon to Thu, 0830 to 1630; Fri, 0830 to 1600

Access to building, collection or gallery:
No access other than to staff

BRITISH ORCHID COUNCIL

Acronym or abbreviation: BOC

Hall Farm House, Shelton, Newark on Trent, NG23 5JG

Tel: 01949 850713
E-mail: bocsecretary@tiscali.co.uk

Website:
http://www.british-orchid-council.info
Details of the organisation.

Enquiries:
Enquiries to: Secretary

Founded:
1971

Organisation type and purpose:
Membership association (membership is by subscription), registered charity (charity number 1002945).

Subject coverage:
Orchids: their study, cultivation, breeding and conservation.

Museum or gallery collection, archive, or library special collection:
Slide (35mm) Library

Library catalogue:
All or part available in-house

Printed publications:
Grower's and Buyer's Guide (annually)

Access to staff:
Contact by letter, by telephone and by e-mail
Hours: Sun to Sat, 0800 to 2100

BRITISH ORGAN DONOR SOCIETY

Acronym or abbreviation: BODY

Balsham, Cambridge, CB1 6DL

Tel: 01223 893636
Fax: 01223 893636 (telephone first)
E-mail: body@argonet.co.uk

Website:
http://www.argonet.co.uk/body

Enquiries:
Enquiries to: Administrator

Founded:
1984

Organisation type and purpose:
Voluntary organisation, registered charity (charity number 294925).

Subject coverage:
Aspects of transplantation and organ donation other than specific medical details; help available to donor recipient and waiting recipient families, especially where there are emotional problems; information to nurses and researchers about the emotional side of organ donation.

Printed publications:
Information Pack (free upon request)
Newsletter (2 times a year)
The Gift of Life (3 vols, £4.95 each)
Whole Body Donation and Society

Electronic and video publications:
The Race for Life (video, £17.50 incl. p&p)

Access to staff:
Contact by letter, by telephone, by fax, by e-mail and via website
Hours: Mon to Fri, 0900 to 1700
Special comments: 24 hour answerphone, no office access or personal answers.

Member organisation of:
Council of TIME (transplants in mind)

BRITISH ORIENTEERING FEDERATION

Acronym or abbreviation: BOF

Riversdale, Dale Road North, Darley Dale, Matlock, Derbyshire, DE4 2HX

Tel: 01629 734042
Fax: 01629 733769
E-mail: mail@bof.cix.co.uk

Website:
http://www.britishorienteering.org.uk/index.html

Enquiries:
Enquiries to: Secretary General
Other contacts: (1) Director of Coaching (2) Marketing and Membership Manager

Founded:
1967

Organisation type and purpose:
Governing body of the sport.

Subject coverage:
Orienteering, maps, forests and adventure; competitive events, specialised coaching awards, teachers' and leaders' certificates, NVQ qualifications.

Publications list:
Available in print

Access to staff:
Contact by letter, by telephone, by fax and in person
Hours: Mon to Fri, 0900 to 1700

Affiliated to:
International Orienteering Federation (IOF)
Radio Katu 20, FI-00093 SLU, Finland

BRITISH ORNITHOLOGISTS' UNION

Acronym or abbreviation: BOU

The Natural History Museum, Akeman Street, Tring, Hertfordshire, HP23 6AP

Tel: 01442 890080
Fax: 020 7942 6150
E-mail: bou@bou.org.uk

Website:
http://www.bou.org.uk
Information on the organisation, publications, conferences and meetings, etc.

Enquiries:
Enquiries to: Administrator
Direct tel: 01733 390392
Direct fax: 01733 390408
Direct e-mail: stevedudley@bou.org.uk

Founded:
1858

Organisation type and purpose:
International organisation, learned society, registered charity (charity number 249877).

Subject coverage:
Ornithology.

Printed publications:
A Dictionary of Birds
Checklist Series (19 in series)
Status of Birds in Britain and Ireland 1971
The Ibis (quarterly)

Electronic and video publications:
Ibis (online)

Publications list:
Available online and in print

Access to staff:
Contact by letter, by telephone, by fax and by e-mail
Hours: Mon to Fri, 0900 to 1700

Member of:
Biological Council

BRITISH OVERSEAS TRADE BOARD

Acronym or abbreviation: BOTB

China and Hong Kong Branch:
China
tel: 020 7215 5252 or 4827
Hong Kong
tel: 020 7215 4829

Exports to North America Branch:
consumer goods
tel: 020 7215 4595 or 4593
industrial goods
tel: 020 7215 4608 or 4606

Latin America, Caribbean and Australasia Branch:
Australia, Papua New Guinea
tel: 020 7215 5319/21
Caribbean
tel: 020 7215 5297
Latin America
tel: 020 7215 5059
New Zealand, the Pacific Islands
tel: 020 7215 4760

Market branches:
East Europe Branch
tel: 020 7215 5258
Exports to Europe Branch
tel: 020 7215 5336

Middle East Branch:
Arabian Gulf
tel: 020 7215 5096
Egypt
tel: 020 7215 4947
North Africa
tel: 020 7215 5358
other Middle East countries
tel: 020 7215 5501

South Asia and Far East Branch:
Burma, Indonesia
tel: 020 7215 4738
India, Sri Lanka
tel: 020 7215 4825
Indo-China, North Korea
tel: 020 7215 4736
Japan
tel: 020 7215 4804
Pakistan, Bangladesh, Nepal
tel: 020 7215 4821/4
Singapore, Malaysia, Brunei
tel: 020 7215 5143
South Korea
tel: 020 7215 4808
Thailand, the Philippines
tel: 020 7215 5253

Sub-Saharan Africa Branch:
tel: 020 7215 4969/70

BRITISH PARACHUTE ASSOCIATION

Acronym or abbreviation: BPA

5 Wharf Way, Glen Parva, Leicester, LE2 9TF

Tel: 0116 278 5271
Fax: 0116 247 7662
E-mail: skydive@bpa.org.uk

Website:
http://www.bpa.org.uk
Operations manual governing the sport
http://www.skydivemag.com
Subscription and advertising information

Enquiries:
Enquiries to: Membership Services

Founded:
1962

Organisation type and purpose:
Membership association.
Governing body for Sport Parachuting in the United Kingdom.
Parachuting in the UK.

Subject coverage:
Sport parachuting, technical information, safety information, diary of events, skydiving and people in the sport.

Printed publications:
Skydive – magazine (6 times a year, members and by subscription)

Electronic and video publications:
UK Sport Parachuting (Skydiving) Operations Manual, governing the conduct of the sport in the United Kingdom (available online).

Publications list:
Available online

Access to staff:
Contact by letter, by telephone, by fax, by e-mail, in person and via website
Hours: Mon to Fri, 0900 to 1700

Links with:
Fédération Aéronautique Internationale, through the Royal Aero Club of the United Kingdom

BRITISH PEST CONTROL ASSOCIATION

Acronym or abbreviation: BPCA

1 Gleneagles House, Vernon Gate, Derby, DE1 1UP

Tel: 0870 609 2687
Fax: 01332 295904
E-mail: enquiry@BPCA.org.uk

Website:
http://www.BPCA.org.uk
Post code searchable database to find members, training course and exams, open discussion forum, members-only section.

Enquiries:
Enquiries to: Public Relations Manager

continued overleaf

Direct tel: 01332 225114
Direct e-mail: christine@bpca.org.uk

Founded:
1942

Organisation type and purpose:
National organisation, trade association
(membership is by qualification), present number
of members: 420, training organisation.

Subject coverage:
Public hygiene, pest control.

Printed publications:
Newsletter
Professional Pest Controller (magazine)

Publications list:
Available online

Access to staff:
Contact by letter, by telephone, by fax, by e-mail
and via website
Hours: Mon to Thu, 0830 to 1700; Fri, 0830 to 1600

Access to building, collection or gallery:
No access other than to staff

Access for disabled people:
Parking provided, ramped entry, level entry, access
to all public areas, toilet facilities

BRITISH PÉTANQUE ASSOCIATION

Acronym or abbreviation: BPA

Coventry Enterprise Centre, Bilton Industrial
Estate, Humber Avenue, Coventry, Warwickshire,
CV3 1JL

Tel: 024 7645 7815
Fax: 024 7645 7815
E-mail: bpa@britishpetanque.co.uk

Enquiries:
Enquiries to: National Secretary

Founded:
1974

Organisation type and purpose:
Membership association.
Governing body of the sport.

Subject coverage:
Pétanque: starting a club, facilities, equipment,
coaching, umpiring, competition organisation,
leagues.

Printed publications:
BPA Competition Organisers Manual (£15 inc.
  p&p)
Pétanque/Boules Explained (£2)
Directory of Officers and Clubs (£1 inc. p&p)
Pétanque: A Comprehensive and Structured
  Coaching Course (£8 inc. p&p)
The Official Rules of the Game of Pétanque (£2 inc.
  p&p)
Pétanque – The Game of Boules (£6.50)

Publications list:
Available in print

Access to staff:
Appointment necessary.
Hours: Mon to Fri, 0900 to 1700

Member of:
CCPR
Fédération Internationale de Pétanque et Jeu
Provençal
Sports Council

BRITISH PHARMACOLOGICAL SOCIETY

Acronym or abbreviation: BPS

16 Angel Gate, City Road, London, EC1V 2PT

Tel: 020 7417 0110
Fax: 020 7417 0114
E-mail: ks@bps.ac.uk

Website:
http://www.bps.ac.uk
Information about BPS and about pharmacology.

Enquiries:
Enquiries to: Executive Assistant

Founded:
1931

Organisation type and purpose:
Learned society (membership is by qualification,
election or invitation), present number of
members: 2700, registered charity (charity number
1030623).
To promote and advance pharmacology, (including
without limitation clinical pharmacology).

Subject coverage:
Pharmacology, drug use.

Printed publications:
British Journal of Clinical Pharmacology (monthly)
British Journal of Pharmacology (twice a month)
Careers in Pharmacology

Access to staff:
Contact by letter, by telephone, by fax and by e-
mail
Hours: Mon to Fri, 0900 to 1700
Special comments: Press enquiries only – no general
information service.

Access to building, collection or gallery:
No access other than to staff

BRITISH PHOTOGRAPHIC & IMAGING ASSOCIATION

Acronym or abbreviation: BPIA

Ambassador House, Brigstock Road, Thornton
Heath, Surrey, CR7 7JG

Tel: 020 8665 6181
Fax: 020 8665 6447
E-mail: bpia@admin.co.uk

Website:
http://www.bpia.co.uk
List of members and products with hot links to
their sites and description of Association activities.

Enquiries:
Enquiries to: Secretary General

Founded:
1952

Organisation type and purpose:
Trade association.

Subject coverage:
Imported photographic and imaging products and
accessories.

Access to staff:
Contact by e-mail
Hours: Mon to Fri, 0900 to 1700

BRITISH PIG ASSOCIATION

Acronym or abbreviation: BPA

Trumpington Mews, 40B High Street,
Trumpington, Cambridge, CB2 2LS

Tel: 01223 845100
Fax: 01223 846235
E-mail: bpa@britishpigs.org

Website:
http://www.britishpigs.org.uk

Enquiries:
Enquiries to: Chief Executive

Founded:
1884

Organisation type and purpose:
Trade association.
Representative body for the UK pig industry and
pedigree recording society.

Subject coverage:
Pig industry matters; non-technical aspects of pig
breeding and production in the UK; UK pedigree
pig breeds.

**Museum or gallery collection, archive, or library
special collection:**
Herd Books for Pedigree Pig Breeds from 1884

Printed publications:
Pig Industry (magazine, monthly)
Publicity and membership leaflets

Access to staff:
Appointment necessary.
Hours: Mon to Fri, 0900 to 1700

BRITISH PLASTICS FEDERATION

Acronym or abbreviation: BPF

6 Bath Place, Rivington Street, London, EC2A 3JE

Tel: 020 7457 5000
Fax: 020 7457 5045
E-mail: bpf@bpf.co.uk

Website:
http://www.bpf.co.uk/bpf/books_online/
bpf_publications/

Enquiries:
Direct e-mail: mcairns@bpf.co.uk

Founded:
1933

Organisation type and purpose:
National organisation, trade association
(membership is by subscription), present number
of members: 400 companies.
To promote and safeguard the UK plastics
industry.

Subject coverage:
Plastics industry, commercial and technical;
economic trends and statistics, biological safety,
environmental information, fire hazards and
prevention, industrial health and safety, plastics in
building, processing and moulding, reinforced
plastics, thermoplastics, thermosets.

**Museum or gallery collection, archive, or library
special collection:**
Many and varied publications, photographs,
  illustrations related to the plastics industry

Non-library collection catalogue:
All or part available online

Library catalogue:
All or part available online

Printed publications:
Factsheets
Many publications on market information,
  material and processing, health and safety,
  windows, doors and conservatories
Product Information for the Plastics Industry

Publications list:
Available online and in print

Access to staff:
Contact by letter, by telephone, by fax, by e-mail
and via website
Hours: Mon to Fri, 0900 to 1700

Access for disabled people:
Parking provided, ramped entry, access to all
public areas, toilet facilities

Affiliated associations:
Association of Flexible Calendared uPVC Sheet
Manufacturers
British Laminated Fabricators Association Limited
British Rigid Urethane Foam Manufacturers
Association
Flexible Packaging Association
Gauge and Toolmakers Association
Northern Ireland Polymers Association
Packaging and Industrial Films Association
Plastics Consultancy Network
Polymer Machinery Manufacturers and
Distributors Association
Scottish Plastics and Rubber Association

Member of:
European Plastics Converters Association

BRITISH POLAROGRAPHIC RESEARCH INSTITUTE

Acronym or abbreviation: BPRI

6 Beechvale, Hillview Road, Woking, Surrey, GU22 7NS

Enquiries:
Enquiries to: Director of Research

Founded:
1955

Organisation type and purpose:
Advisory body, research organisation.

Subject coverage:
Polarographic operational-research (theory and methodology); polarographic mathematical, physical and chemophysical, depolarisational processes and phenomena; polarophilosophy, polarology, polaronomy, polarometry, polaroscopy, polarography, polarological sciences; polaroengineering sciences, radiopolarography, communication-radiopolarography, medical communication-radiopolarography, deaf-mute communication radiopolarography, stroke-communication radiopolarography. Cardiopolarographic therapy, cardiac-immobility polarography, cancer diagnostic polarography, psychoanalytical polarography, psychomotivation polarography. Space-communication radiopolarography, fog-prevention gas-phase polarography, fog and (CO) jet-stream-dispersal polarography, cot death (CO) poisoning (prevention) polarography, learning disabilities, (communication), photon-polarography, and very many other applications and uses of polarography.

Printed publications:
Reprints of Research Papers, following Journal publication

Access to staff:
Contact by letter
Hours: Mon to Fri, 0900 to 1700

Links with:
Institute of Pure Polarology Research
National Institute of Applied Polarology Research
Polarographic Society
UK Polaromatics R E:- National Centre for Polarological and Polarographic Operational Research

Parent body:
British Polarological Research Society (BPRS)
6 Beechvale, Hillview Road, Woking, Surrey, GU22 7NS

BRITISH POLIO FELLOWSHIP

Acronym or abbreviation: BPF

Ground Floor Unit A, Eagle Office Centre, The Runway, South Ruislip, Middlesex, HA4 6SE

Tel: 0800 0180586
Fax: 020 8842 0555
E-mail: info@britishpolio.org.uk

Website:
http://www.britishpolio.org.uk

Enquiries:
Enquiries to: Chief Executive
Other contacts: Information and Benefits Manager for support and information

Founded:
1939

Organisation type and purpose:
Registered charity (charity number 1108335, England, Scotland, SC038863).

Subject coverage:
Support for people who have had polio and their carers, information available on the late effects of polio, often referred to as post-polio syndrome.

Information services:
Information in relation to post-polio syndrome, benefits.

Printed publications:
The Bulletin (6 times a year, free to members)
Information on the late effects of polio

Electronic and video publications:
Living with the Late Effects of Polio (video, £8 inc p&p)

Publications list:
Available online and in print

Access to staff:
Contact by letter, by telephone, by fax, by e-mail and in person. Appointment necessary.
Hours: Mon to Thu, 0900 to 1700; Fri, 0900 to 1600

Access for disabled people:
Parking provided, level entry, access to all public areas, toilet facilities

BRITISH PORTS ASSOCIATION

Acronym or abbreviation: BPA

Africa House, 64–78 Kingsway, London, WC2B 6AH

Tel: 020 7242 1200
Fax: 020 7430 7474
E-mail: info@britishports.org.uk

Website:
http://www.britishports.org.uk

Enquiries:
Enquiries to: Director
Other contacts: Association Secretary

Founded:
1993

Organisation type and purpose:
Trade association.

Subject coverage:
Port industry and policy.

Access to staff:
Contact by letter, by telephone, by fax, by e-mail and via website. Appointment necessary.
Hours: Mon to Fri, 0900 to 1700

Affiliated to:
European Seaports Organisation (ESPO)
International Association of Ports and Harbours (IAPH)

BRITISH POSTAL MUSEUM AND ARCHIVE

Acronym or abbreviation: BPMA

Freeling House, Phoenix Place, London, WC1X 0DL

Tel: 020 7239 2570
Fax: 020 7239 2576
E-mail: info@postalheritage.org.uk

Website:
http://www.postalheritage.org.uk

Enquiries:
Enquiries to: Archive Assistant
Other contacts: Head of Archive/Collections Manager (for offers of donation of records/objects); Philatelic Curator (for appointments for access to philatelic collections)

Founded:
1896

Formerly called:
Post Office Heritage (year of change 2001)

Incorporates the former:
National Postal Museum; Post Office Archives (year of change 1998); Consignia Heritage Services (year of change 2004)

Organisation type and purpose:
Archive and museum service.

Subject coverage:
All aspects of British postal history.

Museum or gallery collection, archive, or library special collection:
An archive of historical records of Royal Mail Group plc, from 1636 to the present day, including working files, staff records, reports and visual records such as maps, posters, artwork and photographs.
Stamps of Great Britain from the Penny Black onwards, and their artwork, and British postal markings from 1661.
Museum collection: letter boxes, vehicles, uniforms, postal equipment, paintings, signs, etc.

Non-library collection catalogue:
All or part available online and in-house

Printed publications:
Postal Reform and the Penny Black: A New Appreciation (D. Muir, 1990)
Moving the Mail: By Road (J. Stray, 2006)
Range of information sheets and leaflets on various aspects of postal history (available free of charge)

Publications list:
Available online

Access to staff:
Contact by letter, by telephone, by fax, by e-mail and in person
Hours: Mon, Tue, Wed, Fri, 1000 to 1700; Thu, 1000 to 1900; Sat, see website
Special comments: Philatelic collections available by appointment only. Cannot undertake research on behalf of members of the public, although will provide access to the records.

Access for disabled people:
Level entry, access to all public areas, toilet facilities

BRITISH POSTMARK SOCIETY

Acronym or abbreviation: BPS

12 Dunavon Park, Strathaven, Lanarkshire, ML10 6LP

Tel: 01357 522430
E-mail: johlen@stracml10.freeserve.co.uk

Enquiries:
Enquiries to: General Secretary

Founded:
1958

Organisation type and purpose:
Membership association (membership is by subscription), present number of members: 243, voluntary organisation; registered charity (charity number 1102748).

Subject coverage:
British postmarks, postal history, postal mechanisation markings.

Museum or gallery collection, archive, or library special collection:
Cuttings and reprints (10 titles by W G Stitt-Dibden and 29 titles by J A Mackay)
Cuttings collected under subject headings, available for loan to members; information provided to non-members by the Librarian
Postmark Library

Library catalogue:
All or part available in-house

Printed publications:
Bulletin (4 times a year, £13 UK, £18 overseas)
Special Event Postmarks of the United Kingdom (3 volumes, price for 3 volumes £21.50 plus £3 p&p)
Special Event Postmarks of the United Kingdom, volume 4 1994–2003, Finch A and Peachey Cm 2004, (£9.50 plus £2 p&p)
Twenty Years of First Day Postmarks (£3.50 plus 75p p&p)
Skeleton Postmarks of England and Wales, 3rd edn, Awcock P and Frost L (£18.50 plus £2.50 p&p)
Order printed publications from: Publications, British Postmark Society

continued overleaf

19 Moorland Road, Hemel Hempstead,
Hertfordshire, HP1 1NH

Publications list:
Available in print

Access to staff:
Contact by letter, by telephone and by e-mail
Hours: Mon to Fri, 0900 to 1700

BRITISH POTATO TRADE ASSOCIATION

Acronym or abbreviation: BPTA

14 Britannia House, Bentwaters Park, Rendlesham,
Suffolk, IP12 2TW

Tel: 01394 460075
Fax: 01394 461117
E-mail: dfradd@bpta.org.uk

Website:
http://www.bpta.org.uk

Enquiries:
Enquiries to: Secretary

Founded:
1940

Created by the merger of:
the National Association of Seed Potato Merchants
(NASPM) and the Scottish Potato Trade
Association (SPTA) (year of change 2006)

Organisation type and purpose:
Trade association (membership is by subscription,
election or invitation), present number of
members: 148.

Subject coverage:
All matters pertaining to seed potato merchanting.

Access to staff:
Contact by letter, by telephone, by fax, by e-mail
and in person
Hours: Mon to Fri, 0900 to 1400

BRITISH POULTRY COUNCIL

Acronym or abbreviation: BPC

Europoint House, 5 Lavington Street, London, SE1
0NZ

Tel: 020 7202 4760
Fax: 020 7928 6366
E-mail: bpc@poultry.uk.com

Website:
http://www.poultry.uk.com

Enquiries:
Enquiries to: Chief Executive

Founded:
2001

Organisation type and purpose:
Trade association (membership is by election or
invitation).

Subject coverage:
Poultry meat industry.

Access to staff:
Contact by letter, by telephone and by e-mail.
Appointment necessary.
Hours: Mon to Fri, 0900 to 1700

Subsumed into British Poultry Council:
BCA (Co-operative & Export) Limited
British Chicken Association
British Goose Producers Association
British Poultry Breeders and Hatcheries
Association
British Turkey Federation
Duck Producers Association
Hen Packers Association
Poultry Industry Conference

BRITISH PRECAST CONCRETE FEDERATION

Acronym or abbreviation: BPCF

60 Charles Street, Leicester, LE1 1FB

Tel: 0116 253 6161
Fax: 0116 251 4568
E-mail: info@britishprecast.org

Website:
http://www.britishprecast.org.uk

Enquiries:
Enquiries to: Secretary

Organisation type and purpose:
Trade association.

Subject coverage:
Precast concrete.

Publications list:
Available online

Access to staff:
Contact by letter, by telephone, by fax, by e-mail
and via website
Hours: Mon to Fri, 0900 to 1700

Access to building, collection or gallery:
No access other than to staff

Members:
Concrete Lighting Column Association
Concrete Lintel Association

BRITISH PREGNANCY ADVISORY SERVICE

Acronym or abbreviation: bpas

20 Timothy's Bridge Road, Stratford Enterprise
Park, Stratford upon Avon, CV37 9BF

Tel: 0845 730 4030
Fax: 0845 365 5051
E-mail: info@bpas.org

Website:
http://www.bpas.org
Full details of bpas services.

Founded:
1968

Organisation type and purpose:
National organisation, advisory body and
registered charity (charity number 289145). bpas is
the UK's leading provider of abortion care.

Subject coverage:
Pregnancy testing; pre- and post-abortion
counselling; abortion assessment, treatment and
aftercare; vasectomy; female sterilisation;
vasectomy reversal; contraception; unplanned
pregnancy and online STI testing and treatment.

Printed publications:
Information leaflets: general; abortion; other
services and other resources
Order printed publications from: marketing@bpas.org

Publications list:
Available online and in print

Access to staff:
Contact by letter, by telephone, by fax, by e-mail
and via website
Hours: Mon to Fri, 0800 to 2100; Sat, 0830 to 1800;
Sun, 0930 to 1430

Branches:
For branches nationwide
tel: 0845 730 4030

BRITISH PRINTING INDUSTRIES FEDERATION

Acronym or abbreviation: BPIF

Farringdon Point, 29–35 Farringdon Road,
London, EC1M 3JF

Tel: 0870 240 4085
Fax: 020 7405 7784
E-mail: info@bpif.org.uk

Website:
http://www.britishprint.com

Careers, information about the industry, members
services, training and news.

Enquiries:
Enquiries to: Director of Corporate Affairs
Direct tel: 020 7915 8378
Direct fax: 020 7915 8395
Direct e mail: andrew.brown@bpif.org.uk

Founded:
1901

Organisation type and purpose:
National organisation, advisory body, trade
association, present number of members: 2500,
training organisation, consultancy.
The British Printing Industries Federation is the
leading trade association and business support
organisation for the UK printing industry. The
BPIF runs a strong regional network of advisors
and business centres to support printing
companies in the UK, offering a 'one-stop shop' for
skills solutions, and delivering expert assistance
across the full range of business activities from
sales and marketing to environmental and risk
management, from training to insurance and
pensions.
As a leading trade association the BPIF also works
closely with government and international
institutions. Regularly consulted by government
and other national and international trade
associations, the BPIF is in a strong position to
lobby and influence public policy on behalf of the
industry both in the UK, in Europe and other parts
of the globe.

Subject coverage:
British printing industry and paper; employment
affairs, education and training, industrial relations,
technical, consultancy, environment, health and
safety, waste management.

Trade and statistical information:
Surveys for the UK printing industry.

Printed publications:
Action (newsletter, fortnightly)
Company staff salaries (Salary Survey), UK
Directions – Survey of Trends in the Printing
Industry (quarterly)
Manpower Survey Report (annually)
Print & Profitability Survey
Printing for Profit Report (annually)
Salary Survey Report (annually)
Wages Survey (Manpower Survey)
Order printed publications from: Information Officer

Publications list:
Available in print

Access to staff:
Contact by letter, by telephone, by fax, by e-mail
and via website. Appointment necessary. Non-
members charged.
Hours: Mon to Fri, 0900 to 1700

Access to building, collection or gallery:
No access other than to staff
Hours: Mon to Fri, 0930 to 1630

Access for disabled people:
Parking provided, ramped entry, access to all
public areas, toilet facilities

Affiliated to:
Intergraf

Regional business centres:
BPIF Eastern (Bedfordshire, Buckinghamshire,
Cambridgeshire, Essex (East and North),
Hertfordshire, Norfolk and Suffolk)
7 Kings Court, Willie Snaith Road, Newmarket,
Suffolk, CB8 7SG; tel: 01638 565180; fax: 01638
665235; e-mail: east@bpif.org.uk
BPIF Midland (Derbyshire (except High Peak and
Chesterfield areas), Leicestershire, Lincolnshire,
Northamptonshire, Nottinghamshire, Shropshire,
Staffordshire, Warwickshire, West Midlands and
Worcestershire)
Unit 2 Villiers Court, Meridien Business Park,
Birmingham Road, Coventry, West Mids, CV5
9RN; tel: 01676 526030; fax: 01676 526033; e-
mail: mid@bpif.org.uk

BPIF North Eastern (Cleveland, Derbyshire (Chesterfield area), Durham, Humberside, Northumberland, Tyne and Wear, North Yorkshire, South Yorkshire and West Yorkshire)
142 Thornes Lane, Wakefield, West Yorkshire, WF2 7XG; tel: 01924 203330; fax: 01924 290092; e-mail: ne@bpif.org.uk
BPIF North Western (Cheshire, Cumbria, Derbyshire (High Peak district), Lancashire, Greater Manchester, Merseyside, Isle of Man, Clwyd, Gwynedd and Northern Ireland)
8th Floor, Trafford House, Chester Road, Stretford, Manchester, M32 0RS; tel: 0161 886 8400; fax: 0161 877 4455; e-mail: nw@bpif.org.uk
BPIF South Eastern (Berkshire, Hampshire, Kent, Greater London, Surrey, Sussex and the Isle of Wight)
Farringdon Point, 29–35 Farringdon Road, London, EC1M 3JF; tel: 020 7915 8400; fax: 020 7404 7304; e-mail: se@bpif.org.uk
BPIF South Western (Avon, Cornwall, Devon, Dorset, Gloucestershire, Herefordshire, Oxfordshire, Somerset, Wiltshire, Dyfed, Mid Glamorgan, South Glamorgan, West Glamorgan, Gwent and Powys)
Lindsey House, Oaklands Business Park, Bristol, BS37 5NA; tel: 01454 333 331; fax: 01454 333 331; e-mail: sw@bpif.org.uk

Subsidiary of BPIF, access through BPIF Head Office:
Book Production Section
British Binders and Finishers Association (BBFA)
British Carton Association (BCA)
British Engraved Stationery Association (BESA)
British Roll Label Association (BRLA)
Business Documents Section
Digital Interest Group
Direct Marketing Special Products Section
Heidelberg Users Group
Inplant Printers
Magazine & Media Section
Promotional Finishers Association (PFA)
Young Managing Printers (YMP)

BRITISH PROMOTIONAL MERCHANDISE ASSOCIATION

Formal name: British Promotional Merchandise Association Limited
Acronym or abbreviation: BPMA

Arena House, 66–68 Pentonville Road, London, N1 9HS

Tel: 020 7689 5555
Fax: 020 7837 5326
E-mail: enquiries@bpma.co.uk

Website:
http://www.bpma.co.uk

Enquiries:
Enquiries to: Secretary

Founded:
1965

Organisation type and purpose:
Trade association, present number of members: 800. Members are manufacturers and suppliers of products and services to the sales promotion industry.

Printed publications:
BPMA Yearbook (trade journal for the sales promotion industry)
Promotion News (trade journal, 12 times a year)

Access to staff:
Contact by letter, by telephone, by fax, by e-mail and via website
Hours: Mon to Fri, 0900 to 1700

BRITISH PROPERTY FEDERATION

Acronym or abbreviation: BPF

7th Floor, 1 Warwick Row, London, SW1E 5ER

Tel: 020 7828 0111
Fax: 020 7834 3442

E-mail: info@bpf.org.uk

Enquiries:
Enquiries to: Operations Manager
Direct tel: 020 7802 0105
Direct e-mail: asinclair@bpf.org.uk

Founded:
1974

Organisation type and purpose:
Trade association, present number of members: 450.

Subject coverage:
Property taxation (direct and indirect) accounting standards, private rented sector, planning and environment, property legislation, landlord/tenant relationship, impact of development on archaeology.

Printed publications:
BPF Short-Term Commercial Lease
TBPF Research Report Conversion of Redundant Commercial Space to Residential Use
BPF Research Report: Business Parking Standards: The effects of PPG13 (2001, free to members, £15 non-members)
BPF/IPD Annual Lease Review 2001
Form of Agreement for Collateral Warranty Co Wa/F (3rd ed)
Form of Agreement for Collateral Warranty Co Wa/P&T (2nd ed)
Good Practice in the Selection of Construction Materials
An Independent report on the nature of the commercial property industry in the UK – prepared for the BPF by London Economics
Manual of the British Property Federation System for Building Design and Construction
Changes in Institutional Leases; A response to market circumstances (research report)
Survey of Member Attitudes to PFI
The British Archaeologists & Developers Liaison Group Codes of Practice

Electronic and video publications:
BPF Short-Term Commercial Lease

Publications list:
Available in print

Access to staff:
Contact by letter, by telephone, by fax and by e-mail
Hours: Mon to Fri, 0930 to 1700

Access for disabled people:
Access to all public areas

Subsidiary company:
BPF Commercial Ltd
at the same address
British Property Federation (Europe) Ltd
at the same address; tel: 020 7828 0111; fax: 020 7828 0111; e-mail: info@bpf.org.uk

BRITISH PSYCHIC AND OCCULT SOCIETY

Acronym or abbreviation: BPOS

PO Box 1112, London, N10 3XE

Tel: 020 8442 1233
Fax: 020 8442 1233

Website:
http://www.dfarrant.co.uk
Brief description of BPOS.

Enquiries:
Enquiries to: General Secretary

Founded:
1967

Organisation type and purpose:
Learned society, present number of members: 374, research organisation.
Psychic research and investigation, including ghosts, poltergeists, unexplained apparitions and other phenomena, unsolved mysteries etc.

Subject coverage:
Psychic research in general, i.e. unexplained phenomena, psychic disturbances, mysterious or unexplained events relating to 'ghosts', 'vampires' etc.

Printed publications:
Dark Journey: True Cases of Ghostly Phenomena from the Files of the BPOS
Vampyre Syndrome: The Truth Behind the Highgate Vampire Legend (publ BPOS)
Shadows in the Night: Distant Dreams and Lost Reality (publ BPOS)
Beyond the Highgate Vampire (1997, publ BPOS)
Dark Secrets (2001, publ BPOS)
Man, myth and Manchester, Ser. 1–8 (2001–2004, publ BPOS)
Order printed publications from: BPOS Publications

Electronic and video publications:
In Search of the Highgate Vampire (video 45 mins, £9.99 plus £1.50 p&p)
The British Psychic and Occult Society (Electronic Press Kit, CD-ROM, £4.99 plus 50p p&p)

Access to staff:
Contact by letter and by fax
Hours: Mon to Fri, 0900 to 1700

Access to building, collection or gallery:
No access other than to staff

BRITISH PSYCHOANALYTIC COUNCIL

Formal name: The British Psychoanalytic Council
Acronym or abbreviation: BPC

West Hill House, 6 Swains Lane, London, N6 6QS

Tel: 020 7267 3626
Fax: 020 7267 4772
E-mail: mail@psychoanalytic-council.org

Website:
http://www.psychoanalytic-council.org
Information on training, finding a therapist, registration of psychotherapists, member institutions, issues relating to psychoanalysis and psychodynamic psychotherapy.

Enquiries:
Enquiries to: Honorary Secretary
Other contacts: Chief Executive Officer; Head of Services

Founded:
1993

Formerly called:
British Confederation of Psychotherapists (year of change 2005)

Organisation type and purpose:
Professional body, voluntary organisation.
To publish a register of appropriately qualified psychotherapists.

Subject coverage:
Register lists psychoanalysts, Jungian analysts, psychoanalytic psychotherapists and child psychotherapists.

Printed publications:
Register, includes brief description of psychotherapy and how to find a therapist; lists referral services and reduced-fee schemes offered by member societies

Access to staff:
Contact by letter, by telephone, by fax, by e-mail and via website
Hours: Mon to Fri, 0930 to 1730

Members:
British Association of Psychotherapists
37 Mapesbury Road, London, NW2 4HJ; tel: 020 8452 9823; fax: 020 8452 5182; e-mail: admin@ bap-psychotherapy.org; website: http://www .bap-psychotherapy.org
British Psychoanalytical Society and the Institute of Psychoanalysis
112A Shirland Road, London, W9; tel: 020 7563 5000; fax: 020 7563 5001; website: http://www .psychoanalysis.org.uk

continued overleaf

Lincoln Clinic and Centre for Psychotherapy
23 Abbeville Mews, 88 Clapham Park Road, London, SW4 7BX; tel: 020 7978 1545; fax: 020 7720 4721; e-mail: info@lincoln-psychotherapy .org.uk

London Centre of Psychotherapy
32 Leighton Road, London, NW5 2QE; tel: 020 7482 2002; fax: 020 7482 4222; e-mail: info@lcp -psychotherapy.org.uk; website: http://www.lcp -psychotherapy.org.uk

North of England Association of Psychoanalytic Psychotherapists
Claremont House, off Framlington Place, Newcastle upon Tyne, NE2 4AA; tel: 0191 282 4547; fax: 0191 282 4542

Northern Ireland Association for the Study of Psycho-Analysis
32 Upper Malone Park, Upper Malone Road, Belfast, BT9 6PP; tel: 028 9047 3254

Scottish Association of Psychoanalytical Psychotherapists
172 Leith Walk, Edinburgh, EH6 5EA; tel: 0131 454 3240; fax: 0131 454 3241

Scottish Institute of Human Relations
172 Leith Walk, Edinburgh, EH6 5EA; tel: 0131 226 9610; fax: 0131 454 3241; e-mail: info@sihr .org.uk; website: http://www.sihr.org.uk

Severnside Institute for Psychotherapy
11 Orchard Street, Bristol, BS1 5EH; tel: 0117 923 2354; fax: 0117 923 2354; e-mail: sipsychotherapy@blueyonder.co.uk

Society of Analytical Psychology
1 Daleham Gardens, London, NW3 5BY; tel: 020 7435 7696; fax: 020 7731 1495; e-mail: office.sap@ btconnect.com; website: http://www.jungian -analysis.org

Tavistock Clinic and Tavistock Society of Psychotherapists
120 Belsize Lane, London, NW3 5BA; tel: 020 7435 7111; fax: 020 7447 3709; e-mail: info@tavi -port.org; website: http://www.tavi-port.org

Partner organisation:
Association of Psychoanalytic Psychotherapists in the National Health Service
5 Windsor Road, London, N3 3SN; tel: 020 8349 9873; fax: 020 8343 3197; e-mail: joycepiper@ compuserve.com

BRITISH PSYCHOLOGICAL SOCIETY

Acronym or abbreviation: BPS

St Andrews House, 48 Princess Road East, Leicester, LE1 7DR

Tel: 0116 254 9568
Fax: 0116 247 0787
E-mail: mail@bps.org.uk

Website:
http://www.bps.org.uk
Information pages being developed.

Enquiries:
Enquiries to: Help Desk

Founded:
1901

Organisation type and purpose:
Learned society, professional body.
Empowered to maintain Register of Chartered Psychologists; 20 specialist divisions or sections.

Subject coverage:
Psychology, specialist groups in educational, medical, clinical, criminological and legal, mathematical, statistical and computing, social, developmental, cognitive, consciousness and experimental psychology, counselling psychology, occupational psychotherapy, history and philosophy of psychology, neuropsychology, teaching of psychology, psychology of women, transpersonal psychology.

Museum or gallery collection, archive, or library special collection:
Archives

Printed publications:
British Journal of Clinical Psychology (quarterly)
British Journal of Developmental Psychology (quarterly)
British Journal of Educational Psychology (3 times a year)
British Journal of Mathematical and Statistical Psychology (2 times a year)
British Journal of Medical Psychology (quarterly)
British Journal of Psychology (quarterly)
British Journal of Social Psychology (quarterly)
Directory of Chartered Psychologists (annually)
Information sheets (list available from the Society)
Journal of Occupational and Organisational Psychology (quarterly)
Register of Chartered Psychologists (annually)
Selection and Development Review (6 times a year)
The Psychologist: incorporating the Bulletin of the British Psychological Society (monthly)

Access to staff:
Contact by telephone, by e-mail and via website
Hours: Mon to Fri, 0900 to 1700

Affiliated to:
European Federation of Professional Psychological Associations
International Union of Psychological Science

BRITISH PTERIDOLOGICAL SOCIETY

Acronym or abbreviation: BPS

Department of Botany, Natural History Museum, Cromwell Road, South Kensington, London, SW7 5BD

Tel: 020 8850 3218
Fax: 020 8850 3218
E-mail: secretary@eBPS.org.uk

Website:
http://www.eBPS.org.uk
Information about the Society and about ferns generally.

Enquiries:
Enquiries to: Honorary Secretary
Direct e-mail: horticulturalinformation@eBPS.org .uk
Other contacts: Horticultural Information Officer for horticultural information.

Founded:
1891

Organisation type and purpose:
International organisation, learned society (membership is by subscription), present number of members: 760, voluntary organisation.
Membership comprises amateur and professional pteridologists.
To promote the growing, study and conservation of ferns and fern allies, both of wild species and cultivated varieties and to encourage interest in their taxonomy, distribution and ecology.

Subject coverage:
Ferns and fern allies: their morphology, ecology, distribution, taxonomy, conservation. All aspects of fern growing.

Printed publications:
BPS Bulletin (annually, free to members)
Fern Gazette (twice a year, free to members)
Occasional Pamphlets, for sale
Pteridologist (annually, free to members)
Special Publication Series produced at irregular intervals, for sale

Access to staff:
Contact by letter, by telephone, by fax and by e-mail
Hours: Mon to Fri, 0900 to 1700

Affiliated to:
National Council for the Conservation of Plants and Gardens
National Plant Societies Federation
Plantlife
Royal Horticultural Society

BRITISH PUMP MANUFACTURERS ASSOCIATION

Acronym or abbreviation: BPMA

National Metalforming Centre, 47 Birmingham Road, West Bromwich, B70 6PY

Tel: 0121 601 6350
Fax: 0121 601 6387
E-mail: enquiry@bpma.org.uk

Website:
http://www.bpma.org.uk
LIst of Members. Pump Search facility. Events.

Enquiries:
Enquiries to: Administration
Direct e-mail: admin@bpma.org.uk
Other contacts: Technical Director

Founded:
1941

Organisation type and purpose:
Trade association, present number of members: 80.

Subject coverage:
Manufacture and marketing of pumps.

Education services:
Training in pump technology.

Printed publications:
Buyers Guide
Order printed publications from: http:// www.bpma.org.uk or admin@bpma.org.uk

Publications list:
Available online and in print

Access to staff:
Contact by telephone, by fax, by e-mail and via website
Hours: Mon to Fri, 0900 to 1700

Affiliated to:
European Committee of Pump Manufacturers (EUROPUMP)

Parent body:
Mechanical and Metal Trades Confederation (METCOM)

BRITISH PUPPET AND MODEL THEATRE GUILD

Acronym or abbreviation: BPMTG

65 Kingsley Avenue, West Ealing, London, W13 0EH

Tel: 020 8997 8236
Fax: 020 8997 8236
E-mail: peter@peterpuppet.co.uk

Website:
http://www.puppetguild.org.uk

Enquiries:
Enquiries to: Honorary Chairman
Direct tel: 07931 550365

Founded:
1924

Organisation type and purpose:
Membership association (membership is by subscription), voluntary organisation.
To promote and encourage the art of puppetry in all its forms.

Subject coverage:
Puppetry, model theatre, workshops, technical assistance, festivals, exhibitions.

Museum or gallery collection, archive, or library special collection:
Books on puppetry
Puppet archives

Non-library collection catalogue:
All or part available online

Printed publications:
Newsletter (monthly)
Puppet Master (magazine, annual)

Access to staff:
Contact by letter, by telephone and by fax. Non-members charged.
Hours: Any reasonable time.

Access to building, collection or gallery:
Prior appointment required

BRITISH RACING SPORTS CAR CLUB

Acronym or abbreviation: BRSCC

Westway House, Castle Combe, Chippenham, Wiltshire, SN14 7EY

Tel: 01249 782417
Fax: 01249 782392
E-mail: southwest@brscc.co.uk

Website:
http://www.castlecombecircuit.co.uk

Enquiries:
Enquiries to: Vice President

Founded:
1946

Organisation type and purpose:
Membership association (membership is by subscription), present number of members: 4500.

Access to staff:
Contact by letter, by telephone, by fax, by e-mail and via website
Hours: Mon to Fri, 0900 to 1700

BRITISH RECORDS ASSOCIATION

Acronym or abbreviation: BRA

c/o Finsbury Library, 245 St John Street, London, EC1V 4NB

Tel: 020 7833 0428
Fax: 020 7833 0416
E-mail: britrecassoc@hotmail.com

Website:
http://www.britishrecordsassociation.org.uk

Enquiries:
Enquiries to: Honorary Secretary
Direct tel: 01924 305980
Direct fax: 01924 305983
Direct e-mail: cathtaylor@waitrose.com
Other contacts: Chairman, Vice-Chair, Chair – Records Preservation Section; Administrative Officer

Founded:
1932

Organisation type and purpose:
National organisation, membership association (membership is by subscription), present number of members: 800, registered charity (charity number 227464). Council includes representatives of the British Academy, the Library Association, the National Archives, the Society of Archivists, etc.
Preservation and promotion of archival material as an historical source.

Subject coverage:
Archive management, archive services, use of documentary sources
(in general), information management, preservation, conservation, care;
deposit and use of historical records, manuscripts and archives, advice to
record owners and keepers, friends of record offices, publication of records
and archive user guides.

Printed publications:
Archives (journal, 2 times a year)
Sources for the History of London 1939–45: a Guide and Bibliography (Creaton H)
Guidelines series on records preservation
Irish History from 1700. A Guide to the Sources in the Public Record Office (Prochaska A)

Materials for the Local and Regional Study of Schooling, 1700–1900 (Stephens WB and Unwin RW)
Newsletter (2 times a year)
Sources for the History of English Nonconformity 1660–1830 (Mullet M)
Indexing for Editors (Hunnisett RF, out of print)
Records of the Established Church in England, excluding Parochial Records (Owen DM)
Manorial Records (Harvey PDA)
Documenting the History of Houses (Alcock NW)
Sources for the History of Policing (Bridgeman I, in preparation)
Order printed publications from: BRA

Publications list:
Available online and in print

Access to staff:
Contact by letter, by telephone, by fax and by e-mail. Appointment necessary.
Hours: Mon, 0930 to 1930; Tue, 0930 to 1630; Thu, 0930 to 1930
Special comments: Please telephone for an appointment.

Constituent bodies:
Records Preservation Section

Links with:
Scottish Records Association

BRITISH RED CROSS SOCIETY

Acronym or abbreviation: British Red Cross

UK Office, 44 Moorfields, London, EC2Y 9AL

Tel: 0844 871 1111
Fax: 020 7562 2000
E-mail: information@redcross.org.uk

Website:
http://www.redcross.org.uk

Enquiries:
Enquiries to: Information Officer
Direct tel: 0844 412 2804

Founded:
1870

Organisation type and purpose:
Voluntary organisation, registered charity (England and Wales charity number 220949; Scotland charity number SC037738).

Subject coverage:
Improvement of health, prevention of disease, first aid, nursing, welfare, training, community services, family reunions, transport, medical equipment loans, fundraising, voluntary work.

Museum or gallery collection, archive, or library special collection:
Collection of international humanitarian law documents and Red Cross policies, practices and procedures

Printed publications:
Lifeline: update of work (quarterly)

Publications list:
Available online and in print

Access to staff:
Contact by letter, by telephone, by fax, by e-mail and via website. Appointment necessary.
Hours: Mon to Fri, 0930 to 1730

Access to building, collection or gallery:
Prior appointment required
Hours: Mon to Fri, 0900 to 1700

Access for disabled people:
Ramped entry, access to all public areas, toilet facilities

Also at:
British Red Cross Museum and Archives
same address; tel: 020 7201 5153; e-mail: enquiry@redcross.org.uk; website: http://www.redcross.org.uk/museumandarchives

Links with:
International Committee of the Red Cross
International Federation of Red Cross and Red Crescent Societies

BRITISH REED GROWER'S ASSOCIATION

Acronym or abbreviation: BRGA

c/o Brown & Co, Old Bank of England Court, Queen Street, Norwich, Norfolk, NR2 4TA

Tel: 01603 629871
Fax: 01603 760756
E-mail: i.lonsdale@brown-co.com

Website:
http://www.mhp-ltd.co.uk
On line general information on the BREA, copies of Buying and Selling Reed and Norfolk Reed Roofing Today as well as general updates on reed.

Enquiries:
Enquiries to: Secretary

Founded:
1965

Organisation type and purpose:
Trade association (membership is by subscription), present number of members: 50, suitable for ages: all.
Promotion of reed and sedge growing; co-ordination of supply to thatchers, monitoring supply and demand; promotion of research into improved production, maintaining close links with the thatching trade, environmental groups, government agencies and local authorities; lobbying over important relevant issues.

Subject coverage:
Reed bed management and creation, marketing reed and sedge.

Trade and statistical information:
Guideline information on cost of reed and sedge.

Printed publications:
Buying and Selling Reed (free)
New Wetland Harvests – New Life for the Broads Fens (free)
Norfolk Reed, Roofing Today (free)
Reedbed Management for Bitterns
Reedbed Management for Commercial and Wildlife Interests (Hawke C J and José P V, published in conjunction with RSPB £14.95)

Publications list:
Available in print

Access to staff:
Contact by letter, by telephone, by fax, by e-mail and via website. Non-members charged.
Hours: Mon to Fri, 0900 to 1700

BRITISH REFLEXOLOGY ASSOCIATION

Acronym or abbreviation: BRA

Monks Orchard, Whitbourne, Worcester, WR6 5RB

Tel: 01886 821207
Fax: 01886 822017
E-mail: bra@britreflex.co.uk

Website:
http://www.britreflex.co.uk

Enquiries:
Enquiries to: Chairman

Founded:
1985

Organisation type and purpose:
Membership association, training organisation.

Subject coverage:
Reflexology and reflexology training.

Printed publications:
Footprints (magazine, quarterly, £10 per year)
Reflexology: A Way to Better Health (Nicola Hall, £9.99 plus p&p)

continued overleaf

Reflexology for Women (Nicola Hall, £9.99 plus p&p)
Register of Reflexologists (£3 plus 50p p&p)

Electronic and video publications:
Reflexology: A Way to Better Health – The
  Practical Technique (DVD, £15.99 plus p&p)
Reflexology: A Way to Better Health – The
  Practical Technique (video, £14.99 plus p&p)

Publications list:
Available online and in print

Access to staff:
Contact by letter, by telephone, by fax, by e-mail
and via website
Hours: Mon to Thu, 0900 to 1600

Official teaching body:
The Bayly School of Reflexology
  Monks Orchard, Whitbourne, Worcestershire,
  WR6 5RB; tel: 01886 821207; fax: 01886 822017;
  e-mail: bayly@britreflex.co.uk

BRITISH REFRACTORIES & INDUSTRIAL CERAMICS ASSOCIATION

Acronym or abbreviation: BRICA

Federation House, Station Road, Stoke-on-Trent,
Staffordshire, ST4 2SA

Tel: 01782 744631
Fax: 01782 744102
E-mail: ragb@ceramfed.co.uk

Website:
http://www.ceramfed.co.uk

Enquiries:
Enquiries to: Secretary
Direct e-mail: andrewm@ceramfed.co.uk

Organisation type and purpose:
Trade association.

Subject coverage:
Refractory and ceramics materials industry,
commercial and industrial relations within it.

Printed publications:
Refractories Industry of Great Britain (1991)

Access to staff:
Contact by letter, by telephone, by fax and by e-mail
Hours: Mon to Fri, 0900 to 1700

Member of:
British Ceramic Confederation
  at the same address

BRITISH REGISTER OF COMPLEMENTARY PRACTITIONERS

PO Box 194, London, SE16 7QZ

Tel: 020 7237 5165
Fax: 020 7237 5157
E-mail: infor@i-c-m.org.uk

Website:
http://www.i-c-m.org.uk

Enquiries:
Enquiries to: General Secretary
Direct e-mail: clive.teal@i-c-m.org.uk

Founded:
1982

Organisation type and purpose:
Professional body (membership is by
qualification), registered charity (charity number
326258).

Subject coverage:
Complementary medicine.

Printed publications:
Journal

Access to staff:
Contact by letter, by telephone and by e-mail

Hours: Mon to Fri, 1000 to 1500

Access to building, collection or gallery:
No access other than to staff

BRITISH RETAIL CONSORTIUM

Acronym or abbreviation: BRC

Second Floor, 21 Dartmouth Street, London, SW1H
9BP

Tel: 020 7854 8900
Fax: 020 7854 8901
E-mail: info@brc.org.uk

Website:
http://www.brc.org.uk

Enquiries:
Enquiries to: Marketing and Business Information
Director
Direct e-mail: gill.cronin@brc.org.uk

Founded:
1992

Organisation type and purpose:
Trade association.

Subject coverage:
Retailing, consumer affairs.

Trade and statistical information:
Retailing.

Publications list:
Available online

Access to staff:
Contact by letter, by fax, by e-mail and via
website
Hours: Mon to Fri, 0900 to 1700

Branch office:
Scottish Retail Consortium
  PO Box 13737, Gullane, EH31 2WX; tel: 07830
  152423; e-mail: src@brc.org.uk

BRITISH RETINITIS PIGMENTOSA SOCIETY

Acronym or abbreviation: BRPS

PO Box 350, Buckingham, MK18 1GZ

Tel: 01280 821334
Fax: 01280 815900
E-mail: info@brps.org.uk

Website:
http://www.brps.org.uk
http://www.fightingblindness.org.uk

Enquiries:
Enquiries to: Chief Executive Officer

Founded:
1975

Organisation type and purpose:
Membership association (membership is by
subscription), present number of members: 3000,
charity, research organisation.
Run by volunteers, it aims to raise funds for
scientific research to provide treatments leading to
a cure for RP.
Provides welfare support and guidance service to
members and their families.

Subject coverage:
Retinitis pigmentosa (RP), medical advice,
progress of research, aids to sufferers.

Printed publications:
Quarterly Newsletter (available in large print and
Braille)

Electronic and video publications:
Monthly e-bulletin
Quarterly Newsletter (available on tape, by e-mail
  or computer diskette)

Publications list:
Available in print

Access to staff:
Contact by letter, by telephone, by fax and by e-mail

BRITISH RIGID URETHANE FOAM MANUFACTURERS' ASSOCIATION LIMITED

Acronym or abbreviation: BRUFMA

12a High Street East, Glossop, Derbyshire, SK13
8DA

Tel: 01457 855884
Fax: 01457 855884
E-mail: brufma@brufma.co.uk

Website:
www.brufma.co.uk

Enquiries:
Enquiries to: Chief Executive
Direct e-mail: mel.price@brufma.co.uk

Founded:
1967

Organisation type and purpose:
Trade association.

Subject coverage:
BRUFMA is the trade association that was
established in 1978 to represent the manufacturers
of the wide range of PIR/PUR insulation products
produced in the UK. Its membership comprises the
major companies in the industry, both
manufacturers of finished insulation products and
suppliers of the various raw materials.

Publications list:
Available online

Access to staff:
Contact by e-mail and via website. Appointment
necessary.
Hours: Mon to Fri, 0915 to 1700

Affiliated to:
Construction Products Association

BRITISH ROSE GROWERS ASSOCIATION

Acronym or abbreviation: BRGA

c/o Horticultural Trades Association, 19 High
Street, Theale, Reading, Berkshire, RG7 5AH

Tel: 0118 930 3132
Fax: 0118 930 4989
E-mail: info@the-hta.org.uk

Enquiries:
Enquiries to: Administrator
Direct e-mail: info@the-hta.org.uk

Founded:
1976

Organisation type and purpose:
Trade association (membership is by election or
invitation), present number of members: 70.

Printed publications:
Find That Rose (2006/07, £3.00, inc. p&p, available
  from Editor)
Order printed publications from: The Editor, British
Rose Growers Association
303 Mile End Road, Colchester, CO4 5EA

Access to staff:
Contact by letter, by telephone and by fax
Hours: Mon to Fri, 0900 to 1700

BRITISH ROSE TRADE ASSOCIATION

Acronym or abbreviation: RTA

The Royal National Rose Society, Chiswell Green,
St Albans, Hertfordshire, AL2 3NR

Tel: 01727 850461
Fax: 01727 850360
E-mail: mail@rnrs.org.uk

Enquiries:
Enquiries to: Director General

Organisation type and purpose:
Trade association.
To encourage and extend the growing of
ornamental plant varieties under licence in the UK.
(i.e. under Plant Breeders' Rights).

Subject coverage:
All aspects of roses and the rose industry. Breeding
roses; details of new roses; distribution of varieties;
ornamental plant varieties.

Trade and statistical information:
Production figures for roses and hardy ornamental
nursery stock under PBRs in UK. Members' data
is confidential and not available outside the
association.

Printed publications:
Find That Rose (annually)

Access to staff:
Contact by letter and by e-mail
Hours: Mon to Fri, 0900 to 1700

Subordinate organisations are the:
British Association Representing Breeders (BARB)
    tel: 01553 773094
British Rose Growers Association (BRGA)
    tel: 01328 851950; fax: 01328 851960

BRITISH SAFETY COUNCIL

Acronym or abbreviation: BSC

70 Chancellors Road, London, W6 9RS

Tel: 020 8741 1231
Fax: 020 8741 4555
E-mail: mail@britsafe.org

Website:
http://www.britsafe.org
Information on the Council, its services and
products.

Founded:
1957

Organisation type and purpose:
Advisory body, professional body (membership is
by subscription), present number of members:
10,000, registered charity, training organisation.
To promote health, safety and environmental best
practice for the increase of productivity and the
benefit of society.

Subject coverage:
Occupational health, safety and environmental
issues, training, risk management, audits, award
schemes, advisory and assessment schemes, and
related publications.

Printed publications:
Health and Safety at Work Act Newsletter
Safety Management (magazine, 11 times a year,
    free to members or £60 annual UK Subscription)
British Safety Council Guides and posters
    (monthly, free to members)

Access to staff:
Contact by letter, by telephone, by fax, by e-mail
and via website. Appointment necessary.
Hours: Mon to Fri, 0900 to 1700

Access for disabled people:
Level entry, access to all public areas, toilet
facilities

BRITISH SAFETY INDUSTRY FEDERATION

Acronym or abbreviation: BSIF

93 Bowen Court, St Asaph Business Park, Glascoed
Road, St Asaph, Denbighshire, LL17 0JE

Tel: 01745 585600
Fax: 01745 585800
E-mail: b.s.i.f@virgin.net

Enquiries:
Enquiries to: Secretary General

Founded:
1994

Organisation type and purpose:
Trade association (membership is by qualification),
present number of members: 180, service industry.
Single voice for UK safety industry.

Subject coverage:
Lead association for the PPE directive, access to
supply chain for safety products, access to
information on safety industry.

Access to staff:
Contact by letter, by telephone and by fax. Non-
members charged.
Hours: Mon to Fri, 0900 to 1600

Access to building, collection or gallery:
No access other than to staff

Access for disabled people:
Parking provided, ramped entry, toilet facilities

BRITISH SCHOOL OF OSTEOPATHY

Acronym or abbreviation: BSO

275 Borough High Street, London, SE1 1JE

Tel: 020 7407 0222
Fax: 020 7089 5300
E-mail: admin@bso.ac.uk

Website:
http://www.bso.ac.uk
Information on the BSc Hons course in osteopathy
and about the clinic.

Enquiries:
Enquiries to: Librarian
Direct tel: 020 7089 5324
Direct e-mail: willp@bso.ac.uk

Founded:
1917

Organisation type and purpose:
Registered charity (charity number 312873).
Private institution of higher education.

Subject coverage:
Medicine, complementary medicine, osteopathy.

**Museum or gallery collection, archive, or library
special collection:**
J. M. Littlejohn collection of osteopathic books
Special collection of osteopathic books and
    periodicals

Library catalogue:
All or part available online

Printed publications:
Bibliography on palpation
How to do research
Spinal Outcomes
Study methods

Access to staff:
Contact by letter, by telephone, by fax, by e-mail
and in person. Non-members charged.
Hours: Mon to Fri, 0900 to 1700

Access for disabled people:
Parking provided, ramped entry, access to all
public areas, toilet facilities

Links with:
University of Bedfordshire
    Park Square, Luton, Bedfordshire, LU1 3JU; tel:
    01234 793006; website: http://www.beds.ac.uk

BRITISH SCHOOL OF SHIATSU-DO

Acronym or abbreviation: BSS-Do

Unit 3, Thane Works, Thane Villas, London, N7
7NU

Tel: 020 7700 3355
Fax: 020 7700 3355
E-mail: london@shiatsu-do.co.uk

Website:
http://www.shiatsu-do.co.uk

Enquiries:
Enquiries to: Registrar
Direct tel: 020 7700 3355

Founded:
1983

Organisation type and purpose:
Training organisation.

Subject coverage:
Shiatsu-Do, Shiatsu.

Printed publications:
British School of Shiatsu-Do handbook (£6.99)

Electronic and video publications:
BSS-Do video (£14.99)

Access to staff:
Contact by letter, by telephone, by fax, by e-mail
and in person
Hours: Mon to Fri, 1100 to 1300 and 1400 to 1800

Access to building, collection or gallery:
No prior appointment required
Hours: Mon to Fri, 0900 to 1900

Access for disabled people:
Parking provided
Special comments: No wheelchair access

BRITISH SCHOOL OF YOGA

Acronym or abbreviation: BSY GROUP

Stanhope Square, Holsworthy, Devon, EX22 6DF

Tel: 0800 731 9271
E-mail: info@bsygroup.co.uk

Website:
http://www.bsygroup.co.uk

Enquiries:
Enquiries to: Information Officer

Founded:
1946

Organisation type and purpose:
Learned society (membership is by qualification),
training organisation.

Subject coverage:
Complementary therapies, stress management,
counselling, alternative therapies, self
improvement, beauty therapies, yoga, new age,
fitness training.

Publications list:
Available online and in print

Access to staff:
Contact by letter, by telephone, by fax, by e-mail
and via website. Appointment necessary.
Hours: Mon to Fri, 0900 to 1800

BRITISH SCHOOLBOY MOTORCYCLE ASSOCIATION

20 Glenpark Crescent, Kingscourt, Stroud,
Gloucestershire, GL5 5DT

Tel: 01453 766516
Fax: 01453 764877

Enquiries:
Enquiries to: Information Officer

Founded:
1969

Organisation type and purpose:
Membership association.

Subject coverage:
Motorcycling for those of school age.

Access to staff:
Contact by letter
Hours: Mon to Fri, 0900 to 1700

BRITISH SCHOOLS CYCLING ASSOCIATION

Acronym or abbreviation: BSCA

21 Bedhampton Road, North End, Portsmouth, Hampshire, PO2 7JX

Tel: 023 9264 2226
Fax: 023 9266 0187
E-mail: susanknight@bsca.fsnet.co.uk

Website:
http://www.bsca.org.uk

Enquiries:
Enquiries to: General Secretary

Founded:
1967

Organisation type and purpose:
Membership association (membership is by subscription).
School sports governing body.

Access to staff:
Contact by letter, by telephone and by fax
Hours: Answerphone in operation

Connections with:
National Council for Schools' Sport

BRITISH SCHOOLS EXPLORING SOCIETY

Acronym or abbreviation: BSES Expeditions

Royal Geographical Society, 1 Kensington Gore, London, SW7 2AR

Tel: 020 7591 3141
Fax: 020 7591 3140
E-mail: info@bses.org.uk

Website:
http://www.bses.org.uk

Enquiries:
Enquiries to: Executive Director

Founded:
1932

Organisation type and purpose:
Learned society (membership is by qualification), registered charity (charity number 802196), suitable for ages: 16 to 24, training organisation. The British Schools Exploring Society is a pioneering youth development charity undertaking scientific research expeditions. For over 75 years its aim has been to recruit, train and develop the leaders and scientists of the future who are able to inspire others.

Subject coverage:
Expeditions to areas such as Svalbard, Greenland, northern Norway, Peruvian Amazon, Ladakh and South Georgia. Other destinations include Canada, Kenya, Botswana, Zimbabwe, Australia, Papua New Guinea, Iceland and Namibia. Field work in associated sciences eg glaciology, geology, botany, survey, art and photography. All associated expedition planning and logistics, including budgets.

Museum or gallery collection, archive, or library special collection:
Library (private) of exploration books
Slides of past expeditions
Video collection made from 8mm/16mm film etc, of BSES expeditions, mainly Arctic areas, since 1932

Printed publications:
Annual Report (details of expeditions run by Society since 1932)
Expedition Reports (annually)
The Explorer Newsletter (2 times a year)
Scientific Reports from expeditions

Electronic and video publications:
Videos of expeditions since 1932 to present day

Access to staff:
Contact by letter, by telephone, by fax, by e-mail and in person. Appointment necessary.

Hours: Mon to Fri, 0930 to 1730

Links with:
Royal Geographical Society
at the same address

BRITISH SCHOOLS GYMNASTIC ASSOCIATION

Acronym or abbreviation: BSGA

Orchard House, 15 North Common Road, Uxbridge, Middlesex, UB8 1PD

Tel: 01895 233377
Fax: 01895 814031
E-mail: crhamilton@lineone.net

Enquiries:
Enquiries to: General Secretary

Organisation type and purpose:
National organisation, voluntary organisation.
National schools sports organisation – voluntarily staffed.

Subject coverage:
Coaching of gymnastics for boys and girls; organisation of national gymnastic competitions.

Printed publications:
Annual Handbook

Affiliated to:
British Amateur Gymnastics Association

BRITISH SCIENCE FICTION ASSOCIATION LIMITED

Acronym or abbreviation: BSFA

8 West Avenue Road, London, E17 9SE

E-mail: bsfachair@gmail.com

Website:
http://www.bsfa.co.uk
BSFA website.
http://www.mjckeh.demon.co.uk/
BSFA magazine index.

Enquiries:
Enquiries to: Administrator

Founded:
1958

Organisation type and purpose:
Voluntary organisation.
Amateur association and company limited by guarantee dedicated to the enjoyment and promotion of science fiction.

Subject coverage:
Science fiction in general; publication sources; writers' forum; book reviews.

Museum or gallery collection, archive, or library special collection:
BSFA Library (based at Science Fiction Foundation, Liverpool University)

Printed publications:
Focus (2 times a year, for writers)
Matrix (news magazine, 6 times a year)
Vector (critical journal, 6 times a year)
A Very British Genre (a critical history of UK Science Fiction, Chapbook, free to members, non-members £5)
Omegatropic – Collection of fiction and non-fiction (Baxter S, £8 paperback, £20 hardback)

Publications list:
Available online

Access to staff:
Contact by letter, by e-mail and via website
Hours: Mon to Fri, 0900 to 1700

BRITISH SECURITY INDUSTRY ASSOCIATION LIMITED

Acronym or abbreviation: BSIA

Kirkham House, John Comyn Drive, Worcester, WR3 7NS

Tel: 0845 389 3889
Fax: 0845 389 0761
E-mail: info@bsia.co.uk

Website:
http://www.bsia.co.uk
Members' list, news, articles, events, information.

Enquiries:
Enquiries to: Press contacts
Direct e-mail: k.gray@bsia.co.uk

Founded:
1967

Organisation type and purpose:
Trade association (membership is by subscription).
To promote and encourage high standards of ethics, equipment and service throughout the industry.

Subject coverage:
All aspects of security, including, guard and patrol services, security equipment manufacture and installation, physical and electronic, access control, closed circuit television, locks and safes.

Trade and statistical information:
UK security industry market size by sector.

Printed publications:
Codes of practice
Information Pack (free)
Guidelines on legislation etc
Security Direct
Spectrum (newsletter, 2 times a year, free)

Publications list:
Available online and in print

Access to staff:
Contact by letter, by telephone, by e-mail and via website
Hours: Mon to Fri, 0900 to 1715

Connections with:
Security Industry Training Organisation (SITO)
tel: 01905 20004

BRITISH SHOOTING SPORTS COUNCIL

Acronym or abbreviation: BSSC

PO Box 53608, London, SE24 9YN

Tel: 020 7095 8181
Fax: 020 7095 8181
E-mail: djpbssc@btconnect.com

Website:
http://www.bssc.org.uk

Enquiries:
Enquiries to: Secretary

Founded:
1956

Organisation type and purpose:
Advisory body.
To promote and safeguard the lawful use of firearms and air weapons for sporting and recreational purposes in the United Kingdom amongst all sections of the community, to co-ordinate and present the views of member associations and other bodies.

Subject coverage:
The lawful manufacture and use of firearms, air weapons and ammunition in the United Kingdom, for sporting and recreational purposes. National policy for the use of firearms and air weapons.

Museum or gallery collection, archive, or library special collection:
Archive of Council

Printed publications:
Annual Report
Order printed publications from: BSSC, PO Box 53608, London, SE24 9YN

Electronic and video publications:
Annual Report and miscellaneous publications on website.

Access to staff:
Contact by letter, by telephone and by e-mail
Hours: Mon to Fri, 0900 to 1700

Access to building, collection or gallery:
No access other than to staff

Links with:
Home Office Consultee on Shooting Issues
tel: 020 7273 2623; fax: 020 7273 4284
World Forum of Shooting Sports Associations
(WFSA)
tel: +39 06 592 5971; fax: +39 06 322 0016

Member organisations:
Association of Professional Clay Target Shooting
Grounds
tel: 01295 678141; fax: 01295 670100
British Association for Shooting and Conservation
tel: 024 4457 3000; fax: 024 4457 3001
Clay Pigeon Shooting Association
tel: 01483 485400; fax: 01483 485410
Countryside Alliance
tel: 020 7582 5432; fax: 020 7793 8484
Gun Trade Association
tel: 01684 291865; fax: 01684 291864
Muzzle Loaders Association
tel: 01734 590080; fax: 01734 590080
National Rifle Association
tel: 01483 797777; fax: 01483 797285
National Small Bore Rifle Association
tel: 01483 485500; fax: 01483 476392
Sportsman Association
tel: 01772 863900; fax: 01772 866373
United Kingdom Practical Shooting Association
tel: 01702 342501; fax: 01702 431775

BRITISH SHOW JUMPING ASSOCIATION

Acronym or abbreviation: BSJA

British Equestrian Centre, National Agricultural
Centre, Stoneleigh Park, Kenilworth,
Warwickshire, CV8 2LR

Tel: 024 7669 8800
Fax: 024 7669 6685
E-mail: bsja@bsja.co.uk

Website:
http://www.bsja.co.uk

Enquiries:
Enquiries to: Chief Executive

Founded:
1925

Organisation type and purpose:
Membership association.
National governing body.

Subject coverage:
National and international show jumping.

Printed publications:
Directory (monthly)
Rules Year Book (annually)
Show Jumper (magazine, quarterly)

Access to staff:
Contact by letter, by telephone, by fax and by e-mail
Hours: Mon to Fri, 0900 to 1700

BRITISH SIGN & GRAPHICS ASSOCIATION

Acronym or abbreviation: BSGA

5 Orton Enterprise Centre, Bakewell Road, Orton
Southgate, Peterborough, Cambridgeshire, PE2
6XU

Tel: 01733 230033
Fax: 01733 230993
E-mail: bsa@sign.u-net.com

Website:
http://www.bsga.co.uk

Enquiries:
Enquiries to: Director

Founded:
1978

Organisation type and purpose:
Trade association.

Subject coverage:
Illuminated and non-illuminated signs.

Trade and statistical information:
Data on UK and European sign manufacturing
markets.

Printed publications:
BSA News (bi-monthly)
Sign Directions Magazine (bi-monthly)

Publications list:
Available in print

Access to staff:
Contact by letter, by telephone, by fax, by e-mail
and via website. Appointment necessary.
Hours: Mon to Fri, 0900 to 1700

Affiliated to:
European Federation of Illuminated Signs and the
Outdoor Advertising Council

BRITISH SIKH FEDERATION

Acronym or abbreviation: BSF

PO Box 242, Wolverhampton, West Midlands,
WV4 5DH

Tel: 01242 226517
Fax: 01242 226517
E-mail: british_sikh_fed@btopenworld.com

Website:
http://www.british-sikh-federation.org

Enquiries:
Enquiries to: General Secretary
Direct tel: 07221 507055 (mobile)

Founded:
1984

Organisation type and purpose:
Voluntary organisation.
Tackle major UK political and religious issues of a
serious nature for the British Sikh community.

Subject coverage:
Politics, religion, legal and business issues as they
relate to the Sikh community, contacts for other
Sikh organisations, interests of 600,000 British
Sikhs.

Access to staff:
Contact by letter and by e-mail. Access for
members only.
Hours: Mon to Fri, 0900 to 1700

BRITISH SIMMENTAL CATTLE SOCIETY

National Agricultural Centre, Stoneleigh Park,
Kenilworth, Warwickshire, CV8 2LG

Tel: 024 7669 6513
Fax: 024 7669 6724
E-mail: information@britishsimmental.co.uk

Website:
http://www.britishsimmental.co.uk

Enquiries:
Enquiries to: General Secretary

Founded:
1970

Organisation type and purpose:
Membership association (membership is by
subscription), registered charity (charity number
985570).
Registration and promotion of Simmentals.

Subject coverage:
Breeds of beef cattle.

Printed publications:
Annual Review (free to members)

Access to staff:
Contact by letter, by telephone and by fax.
Appointment necessary.
Hours: Mon to Fri, 0900 to 1700

BRITISH SMALL ANIMAL VETERINARY ASSOCIATION

Acronym or abbreviation: BSAVA

Woodrow House, 1 Telford Way, Waterwells
Business Park, Quedgeley, Gloucestershire, GL2
4AB

Tel: 01452 726700
Fax: 01452 726701
E-mail: adminoff@bsava.com

Website:
http://www.bsava.com

Enquiries:
Enquiries to: Administration Officer

Founded:
1957

Organisation type and purpose:
Membership association (membership is by
subscription, qualification), present number of
members: 5700, registered charity (charity number
1024811).
To foster and promote high scientific and
educational standards of small animal medicine
and surgery in practice, teaching and research.

Subject coverage:
Health, welfare and diseases of small animals,
birds and fish; veterinary science and medicine.

Printed publications:
An Introduction to Veterinary Anatomy and
Physiology
Flea Allergic Skin Disease in Cats (£1 plus p&p)
Journal of Small Animal Practice (monthly)
Manual of Anaesthesia in Small Animal Practice
Manual of Canine Behaviour (£30.50 plus p&p)
Manual of Companion Animal Nutrition and
Feeding (£60 plus p&p)
Manual of Exotic Pets
Manual of Feline Behaviour (£17 plus p&p)
Manual of Ornamental Fish
Manual of Psittacine Birds
Manual of Reptiles
Manual of Small Animal Neurology (2nd ed., 1995)
Practical Veterinary Nursing (3rd ed.)

Electronic and video publications:
BSAVA Congress Lectures 1995–2001 are available
on CD-ROM

Parent body:
British Veterinary Association

BRITISH SNORING AND SLEEP APNOEA ASSOCIATION LIMITED

Acronym or abbreviation: BSSAA

1 Duncroft Close, Reigate, Surrey, RH2 9DE

Tel: 01737 245638
Fax: 01737 248744
E-mail: helpline@britishsnoring.co.uk

Website:
http://www.britishsnoring.co.uk

Enquiries:
Enquiries to: Helpline staff
Other contacts: Information Officer, Help Line
Manager

Founded:
1991

Organisation type and purpose:
International organisation, national organisation,
membership association, voluntary organisation.

Subject coverage:
Snoring and sleep apnoea and related topics,
including surgery, treatment and prevention.

continued overleaf

Printed publications:
Information leaflets available (A4 sae plus £2.50
donation cheque)
Sound Asleep (quarterly, £10 a year)
Library articles (£1.50 each)
Back issues of Sound Asleep (£5 each)

Access to staff:
Contact by letter, by telephone, by fax, by e-mail
and via website
Hours: Mon to Fri, 0900 to 1700

BRITISH SOCIETY FOR ALLERGY AND CLINICAL IMMUNOLOGY

Acronym or abbreviation: BSACI

BSACI Secretariat, 66 Weston Park, Thames Ditton,
Surrey, KT7 0HL

Tel: 020 8398 9240
Fax: 020 8398 2766
E-mail: SusanMDuff@cs.com

Website:
http://www.bsaci.soton.ac.uk/bsaci/
Membership information.

Enquiries:
Enquiries to: Administrator
Other contacts: President, Secretary, Newsletter
Editor

Founded:
1948

Organisation type and purpose:
Learned society (membership is by qualification),
present number of members: 580, registered
charity.
The recognition of allergy and clinical immunology
as a specialised branch of medicine; to advance
and encourage study of the subject.

Subject coverage:
Allergy, clinical immunology.

Printed publications:
Clinical and Experimental Allergy (journal,
monthly)

Access to staff:
Contact by letter, by telephone, by fax and by e-
mail
Hours: Mon to Fri, 0900 to 1700

Affiliated to:
EAACI
IAACI

BRITISH SOCIETY FOR CELL BIOLOGY

Acronym or abbreviation: BSCB

School of Biosciences, Faculty of Medical Sciences,
University of Newcastle, Newcastle upon Tyne,
NE2 4HH

Tel: 0191 222 5264
Fax: 0191 222 6706
E-mail: michael.whitaker@ncl.ac.uk

Website:
http://www.bscb.org
News, information about scientific meetings,
contact details, educational content.

Enquiries:
Enquiries to: Secretary

Founded:
1965

Organisation type and purpose:
Learned society.

Subject coverage:
Research in the general field of cell and molecular
biology and cytology, applications of cell biology
in the commercial and biomedical fields.

Printed publications:
BSCB Handbook of Members

Access to staff:
Contact by letter, by telephone, by fax and by e-
mail. Appointment necessary.
Hours: Mon to Fri, 0900 to 1700

Constituent society of the:
European Cell Biology Organization

BRITISH SOCIETY FOR CLINICAL CYTOLOGY

Acronym or abbreviation: BSCC

PO Box 352, Uxbridge, Middlesex, UB10 9AU

Tel: 01895 274020
Fax: 01895 274080
E-mail: lesley.couch@btopenworld.com

Website:
http://www.clinicalcytology.co.uk

Enquiries:
Enquiries to: Secretariat

Organisation type and purpose:
Learned society.

Subject coverage:
Clinical cytology; diagnostic cytopathology;
education and training for medical and non-
medical personnel.

Printed publications:
Newsletter (3 times a year)

Access to staff:
Contact by letter, by telephone, by fax and by e-
mail
Hours: Mon, Wed, Thu, 0900 to 1700

Access to building, collection or gallery:
No access other than to staff

Affiliated to:
International Academy of Cytology

Has:
9 affiliated regional cytology societies

Member of:
European Federation of Cytology Societies

BRITISH SOCIETY FOR DENTAL RESEARCH

Acronym or abbreviation: BSDR

Restorative Dentistry, The Dental School,
Framlington Place, Newcastle upon Tyne, NE2
4BW

Tel: 0191 222 7823
Fax: 0191 222 8191
E-mail: a.w.g.walls@ncl.ac.uk

Website:
http://www.bsdr.org.uk
Details of meetings, registration, constitutions,
management committee members, BSDR Research
Groups – Contacts, newsletter, BSDR competitions.

Enquiries:
Enquiries to: Honorary Secretary

Founded:
1952

Organisation type and purpose:
International organisation, learned society,
registered charity, research organisation.

Subject coverage:
Dental public health, forensic dentistry, oral and
dental sciences, dental materials, implant research,
restorative dentistry, oral medicine, oral
microbiology and immunology, oral pathology,
oral surgery, mineralised tissues, oral anatomy and
histology, oral biochemistry and physiology.

Printed publications:
Journal of Dental Research (monthly, from IADR
Headquarters 1619 Duke Street, Alexandria, VA,
USA)
Newsletter (annually)

Access to staff:
Contact by letter, by telephone, by fax, by e-mail
and via website
Hours: Mon to Fri, 0900 to 1700

Affiliated to:
International Association for Dental Research
1619 Duke Street, Alexandria, VA, USA

BRITISH SOCIETY FOR DEVELOPMENTAL BIOLOGY

Acronym or abbreviation: BSDB

Department of Developmental Neurobiology,
UMDS, Guy's Hospital, London, SE1 9RT

Tel: 020 7955 4798
Fax: 020 7955 4886
E-mail: bsdb@kcl.ac.uk

Website:
http://www.ana.ed.ac.uk/BSDB

Enquiries:
Enquiries to: Secretary
Direct tel: 020 7848 6547
Direct fax: 020 7848 6550
Direct e-mail: ivor.mason@kcl.ac.uk

Founded:
1964

Organisation type and purpose:
Learned society.

Subject coverage:
Developmental biology.

Printed publications:
Newsletter

Access to staff:
Contact by letter
Hours: Mon to Fri, 0900 to 1700

Affiliated to:
United Kingdom Life Sciences Council

BRITISH SOCIETY FOR GEOMORPHOLOGY

Acronym or abbreviation: BSG

Royal Geographical Society (with IBG), 1
Kensington Gore, London, SW7 2AR

E-mail: bsg@rgs.org

Website:
http://www.geomorphology.org.uk

Enquiries:
Enquiries to: Honorary Secretary
Other contacts: Administrator

Founded:
1960

Organisation type and purpose:
Learned society.

Subject coverage:
Geomorphology: landforms, earth surface
processes, sedimentology, earth materials,
hydrology, Quaternary stratigraphy, Quaternary
studies; fluvial, coastal, glacial, periglacial, tropical
and arid environment processes and landforms;
land deposits.

Printed publications:
BGRG Technical Bulletins (30 titles, Hardisty,
University of Hull)
Earth Surface Processes and Landforms (journal,
13 times a year, John Wiley)
Symposium Series (John Wiley)
Order printed publications from: John Wiley & Sons,
43 Leinster Gardens, London, W2 3AN

Access to staff:
Contact by letter and by e-mail
Hours: Mon to Fri, 0900 to 1700

Links with:
Royal Geographical Society (with IBG)

BRITISH SOCIETY FOR HAEMATOLOGY

Acronym or abbreviation: BSH

2 Carlton House Terrace, London, SW1Y 5AF

Tel: 020 8643 7305
Fax: 020 8770 0933
E-mail: janice@bshhya.demon.co.uk

Website:
http://www.blackwell.science.com/uk/society/bsh/default.htm

Enquiries:
Enquiries to: Administrator

Founded:
1962

Organisation type and purpose:
Learned society, registered charity (charity number 1005735).

Subject coverage:
General haematology, including diagnosis and treatment of blood diseases, leukaemia, haemophilia and other bleeding diseases, lymphomas. Equipment used in haematological laboratories, quality control and standards in haematological laboratories, blood transfusion and blood products (preparation and clinical use).

Printed publications:
Newsletters
Publicity material

Access to staff:
Contact by letter, by fax and by e-mail
Hours: Flexible

BRITISH SOCIETY FOR IMMUNOLOGY

Acronym or abbreviation: BSI

Vintage House, 37 Albert Embankment, London, SE1 7TL

Tel: 020 3031 9800
Fax: 020 7582 2882
E-mail: bsi@immunology.org

Website:
http://www.immunology.org
Society activities, publications, meetings, conferences and events, immunology-related jobs.

Founded:
1956

Organisation type and purpose:
Learned society (membership is by subscription, qualification, election or invitation), present number of members: 4,000, registered charity (charity number 1043255).

Subject coverage:
Immunology; biochemical immunology, materno-foetal immunology, comparative and veterinary immunology, mucosal immunology, neuroimmunology, histocompatibility and immunogenetics, clinical immunology.

Printed publications:
Clinical & Experimental Immunology (monthly)
Immunology (monthly)
Immunology News (6 times a year)

Electronic and video publications:
Immunology online
Clinical & Experimental Immunology online

Publications list:
Available in print

Access to staff:
Contact by letter, by e-mail and via website.
Appointment necessary.
Hours: Mon to Fri, 0900 to 1700

Affiliated to:
European Federation of Immunological Societies
International Union of Immunological Societies

BRITISH SOCIETY FOR MEDICAL AND DENTAL HYPNOSIS

Acronym or abbreviation: BSMDH (MET&S)

(Metropolitan and South), Flat 23, Broadfield Heights, Broadfield Avenue, Edgware, Middlesex, HA8 8PF

Tel: 020 8905 4342
Fax: 020 8958 8069

Enquiries:
Enquiries to: Referral Secretary

Founded:
1960

Organisation type and purpose:
Learned society.

Subject coverage:
Use of hypnosis in dentistry and medicine. Training of doctors, dentists and clinical psychologists. Referral service for members of public, medical and dental practitioners.

Access to staff:
Contact by letter and by telephone
Hours: Mon to Fri, 0900 to 1700
Special comments: Telephone for referral requests.

Links with:
European Society for Hypnosis
International Society of Hypnosis

BRITISH SOCIETY FOR MERCURY FREE DENTISTRY

Acronym or abbreviation: BSMFD

225 Old Brompton Road, London, SW5 0EA

Tel: 020 7373 3655
Fax: 020 7736 2480

Enquiries:
Enquiries to: President

Organisation type and purpose:
Advisory body, professional body, registered charity.

Subject coverage:
Mercury poisoning from dental amalgam filling.

Access to staff:
Contact by letter and by telephone. All charged.
Hours: Mon to Fri, 0900 to 1700

BRITISH SOCIETY FOR MUSIC THERAPY

Acronym or abbreviation: BSMT

61 Church Hill Road, East Barnet, Herts, EN4 8SY

Tel: 020 8441 6226
Fax: 020 8441 4118
E-mail: info@bsmt.org

Website:
http://www.bsmt.org
Information on music therapy, training and publications.

Enquiries:
Enquiries to: Administrator
Other contacts: Chairperson

Founded:
1958

Organisation type and purpose:
International organisation, learned society (membership is by subscription), present number of members: 850, registered charity (charity number 260837).
To promote the use and development of music therapy.

Subject coverage:
Use and development of music therapy.

Non-library collection catalogue:
All or part available online, in-house and in print

Library catalogue:
All or part available online, in-house and in print

Printed publications:
BSMT Bulletin (3 times a year, members)
BSMT Information Booklet
BSMT Booklist
Index of Articles in the British Journal of Music Therapy
British Journal of Music Therapy (2 times a year, members)
Conference Paper – 'Changes' Exploring clinical, professional and global perspectives BSMT/APMT Conference – February 2004 (conference paper £12 plus £2 p&p)
Conference Paper – Community, Relationship and Spirit: Continuing the dialogue and debate BSMT/APMT Conference February 2004 (conference paper £12 plus £2 p&p)
BSMT also sells large number of books on music therapy

Electronic and video publications:
Music for Life (CD. £11.70)
Music Therapy at the Child Development Centre, Cambridge (video £16 plus £2 p&p)
Timothy – Music therapy with a little boy who has Asperger Syndrome (video £16 plus £2 p&p)
Training as a Music Therapist, the MA in Music Therapy at APU (video £16 Plus £2 p&p)
Music Therapy for Children on the Autistic Spectrum (video £16 plus £2 p&p)
Joshua and Barry – Music Therapy with a Partially sighted little boy with cerebral Palsy (video £16 plus £2 p&p)
Sounds and Meaning – Group Music Therapy with People with Profound Learning Difficulties and their Carers (video £19 plus £2 p&p)
CD – Ice Calm – Background Patterns for Improvisation (CD £9 plus £2 p&p)
Music Therapy with Children (CD Rom £15.95 plus £2 p&p)

Publications list:
Available online and in print

Access to staff:
Contact by letter, by telephone, by fax and by e-mail. Appointment necessary.
Hours: Mon to Thurs, 0930 to 1530

Access to building, collection or gallery:
No access other than to staff

Connections with:
Association of Professional Music Therapists
tel: 020 8440 4153; fax: 020 8440 4153

BRITISH SOCIETY FOR PARASITOLOGY

Acronym or abbreviation: BSP

24 The Paddock, Hitchin, SG4 9EF

Tel: 01462 624081; 01462 451618
Fax: 01462 648693
E-mail: hedgepigs@aol.com

Website:
http://www.bsp.uk.net

Enquiries:
Enquiries to: Honorary Secretary
Direct e-mail: john@troproject.com

Founded:
1962

Organisation type and purpose:
International organisation, national organisation, learned society (membership is by subscription), present number of members: 800, registered charity (charity number 206847), suitable for ages: 18 to 26.

Subject coverage:
All aspects of parasitology including human, animal, fish and plant diseases caused by parasites; study of parasites including physiology, biochemistry, immunology, ecology, pathology.

Printed publications:
Autumn Symposium Proceedings (annually, Cambridge University Press)
Newsletter (for members, quarterly)

continued overleaf

Access to staff:
Contact by letter, by telephone, by fax, by e-mail
and via website
Hours: Mon to Fri, 0900 to 1700

BRITISH SOCIETY FOR RESTORATIVE DENTISTRY

Acronym or abbreviation: BSRD

Department of Restorative Dentistry, The Royal
London Hospital, Whitechapel, London, E1 1BB

Enquiries:
Enquiries to: Honorary Secretary

Organisation type and purpose:
Learned society.

Subject coverage:
General or specialised information on restorative
dentistry, the conservation of teeth and the
improvement of their appearance (the Society does
not recommend by name individual dentists able
to carry out this work).

Printed publications:
European Journal of Prosthodontics and
   Restorative Dentistry (quarterly)
Members Newsletter

Access to staff:
Contact by letter
Hours: Mon to Fri, 0900 to 1700

BRITISH SOCIETY FOR RHEUMATOLOGY

Acronym or abbreviation: BSR

Bride House, 18–20 Bride Lane, London, EC4Y 8EE

Tel: 020 7842 0900
Fax: 020 7842 0901
E-mail: bsr@rheumatology.org.uk

Website:
http://www.rheumatology.org.uk

Enquiries:
Enquiries to: Chief Executive

Founded:
1984

Organisation type and purpose:
Learned society, registered charity.

Subject coverage:
Rheumatology, education for medical staff,
research conferences, information for providers/
purchasers of rheumatology services, also runs
British Health Professionals in Rheumatology
(BHPR) and Arthritis and Musculoskeletal Alliance
(ARMA).

**Museum or gallery collection, archive, or library
special collection:**
The Heberden Library – based at the Royal College
   of Physicians

Trade and statistical information:
Can provide access to epidemiological information
eg number of people with osteoarthritis in UK.

Printed publications:
Annual Report
Rheumatology (journal, monthly, free to members,
   on subscription to others)
BSR Newsletter (3 times a year)
Handbook (annually, members only)
Information for Purchasers of Rheumatology
   Services

Access to staff:
Contact by letter
Hours: Mon to Fri, 0830 to 1730

Access to building, collection or gallery:
Prior appointment required

Access for disabled people:
Parking provided

Member of:
Arthritis & Musculoskeletal Alliance (ARMA)
   at the same address
European League Against Rheumatism (EULAR)

BRITISH SOCIETY FOR STRAIN MEASUREMENT

Acronym or abbreviation: BSSM

71 Hillview Drive, Clarkston, Glasgow, G76 7JJ

Tel: 0141 577 6297
Fax: 0141 577 6281
E-mail: bssmsec@moragmac.clara.net

Enquiries:
Enquiries to: Honorary Secretary

Founded:
1964

Organisation type and purpose:
Learned society.

Subject coverage:
Strain measurement by strain gauges, brittle
lacquers, photoelasticity extensometers, strain
transducers and other optical methods;
experimental stress analysis and other
experimental engineering evaluation, theoretical
analysis, engineering measurements by
transducers; data logging and data handling.

Printed publications:
Strain (quarterly)

Access to staff:
Contact by letter, by telephone, by fax and by e-
mail
Hours: Mon to Fri, 0900 to 1700

BRITISH SOCIETY FOR THE HISTORY OF PHARMACY

Acronym or abbreviation: BSHP

840 Melton Road, Thurmaston, Leicester, LE4 8BN

Tel: 0116 264 0083
Fax: 0116 264 0141
E-mail: bshp@associationhq.org.uk

Website:
http://www.bshp.org

Enquiries:
Enquiries to: Secretary

Founded:
1967

Organisation type and purpose:
Learned society.

Subject coverage:
History of pharmacy in Britain, pharmaceutical
antiques.

Printed publications:
Pharmaceutical Historian (4 times a year)
Transactions (occasional)

Access to staff:
Contact by letter and by e-mail
Hours: Mon to Fri, 0900 to 1700

Affiliated to:
Royal Pharmaceutical Society of Great Britain

BRITISH SOCIETY FOR THE HISTORY OF SCIENCE

Acronym or abbreviation: BSHS

PO Box 3401, Norwich, Norfolk, NR7 7JF

Tel: 01603 516236
E-mail: office@bshs.org.uk

Website:
http://www.bshs.org.uk
History of science information and activities.

Enquiries:
Enquiries to: Executive Secretary

Founded:
1947

Organisation type and purpose:
International organisation, learned society
(membership is by subscription), present number
of members: 700, registered charity (charity
number 258854).
To promote and further the study of the history
and philosophy of science.

Subject coverage:
History and philosophy of science.

Non-library collection catalogue:
All or part available online

Printed publications:
British Journal for the History of Science (4 times a
   year, free to members, £134 a year to non-
   members)
List of Theses in History of Science in British
   Universities and Polytechnics online)
Monograph Series (12 current titles)
Newsletter (3 times a year, free to members, £10 a
   year to non-members)
Viewpoint
Order printed publications from: British Journal for
the History of Science, Cambridge University
Press, FREEPOST, The Edinburgh Building,
Shaftesbury Road, Cambridge, CB2 1BR

Electronic and video publications:
British Journal for the History of Science (Online by
   arrangement with Cambridge University Press)
Wheeler Library online project (in preparation)

Publications list:
Available online and in print

Access to staff:
Contact by letter, by telephone, by fax, by e-mail
and via website. Appointment necessary.
Hours: Mon to Fri, 0900 to 1700

Links with:
Association for Science Education
History of Science Society (USA)
   e-mail: info@hssonline.org; website: http://www
   .hssonline.org

BRITISH SOCIETY FOR THE STUDY OF PROSTHETIC DENTISTRY

Acronym or abbreviation: BSSPD

Division of Restorative Dentistry, University
Dental School and Hospital, Wilton, Cork,
Republic of Ireland

Tel: 00 353 21 490 1186
Fax: 00353 21 434 5737
E-mail: finbarralen@hotmail.com

Website:
http://www.derweb.ac.uk/bsspd/

Enquiries:
Enquiries to: Honorary Secretary

Organisation type and purpose:
Learned society.

Subject coverage:
Prosthetic dentistry.

Access to staff:
Contact by letter, by fax and by e-mail
Hours: Mon to Fri, 0900 to 1700

Affiliated to:
European Prosthodontic Association

Conference organiser:
British Society for the Study of Prosthetic Dentistry
   Birmingham Dental School, St Chad's
   Queensway, Birmingham; e-mail: c.w.barclay@
   bham.ac.uk

BRITISH SOCIETY OF AESTHETICS

Acronym or abbreviation: BSA

c/o Kathleen Stock, Dept. of Philosophy, University of Sussex, Falmer, Brighton, BN1 9QN

E-mail: kathleen@british-aesthetics.org

Website:
http://www.british-aesthetics.org

Enquiries:
Enquiries to: Honorary Secretary

Founded:
1965

Organisation type and purpose:
International organisation, learned society (membership is by subscription).

Subject coverage:
Aesthetics, philosophy of the arts and criticism, theory of beauty.

Printed publications:
British Journal of Aesthetics
BSA Newsletter

Access to staff:
Contact by letter, by e-mail and via website
Hours: Mon to Fri, 0900 to 1700

Member of:
British Philosophical Association
International Association of Aesthetics

Organisers of the:
Collaborative European Conferences

BRITISH SOCIETY OF ANIMAL SCIENCE

Acronym or abbreviation: BSAS

PO Box 3, Penicuik, Midlothian, EH26 0RZ

Tel: 0131 445 4508
Fax: 0131 535 3120
E-mail: bsas@ed.sac.ac.uk

Website:
http://www.bsas.org.uk

Enquiries:
Enquiries to: Secretary
Direct tel: 01848 331437
Direct fax: 01848 331437
Other contacts: Finance Officer for membership and financial matters.

Founded:
1943

Organisation type and purpose:
National organisation, learned society (membership is by subscription), present number of members: 1100, service industry, registered charity, suitable for ages: 18+.
Educational society.

Subject coverage:
Animal science in most areas and species, research, welfare, nutrition, breeding/genetics.

Trade and statistical information:
Our journal 'Animal Science' is sent to libraries and institutes all over the world.

Printed publications:
Animal Science (6 times a year)
Occasional Publications (proceedings of conferences or meetings, 1 or 2 times a year) including:
Animal Choices
Animal Production in Developing Countries
Hill and Upland Livestock Production
Safety & Quality of Food from Animals
Metabolic Stress in Dairy Cows
Milk Composition
Fertility in the High Producing Dairy Cow
Animal Welfare – Who Writes The Rules
Challenge of Genetic Change in Animal Production

Electronic and video publications:
Various CD-ROMs to purchase, direct
Annual Meeting Proceedings (CD-ROM)
Animal Science – BSAS Journal (CD-ROM)

Publications list:
Available in print

Access to staff:
Contact by letter, by telephone, by fax and by e-mail
Hours: Mon to Fri, 0900 to 1700

Member of:
Biological Society
European Association for Animal Production (EAAP)
Via A Torlonia 15/A, Rome, I-00161, Italy

BRITISH SOCIETY OF AUDIOLOGY

Acronym or abbreviation: BSA

80 Brighton Road, Reading, Berkshire, RG6 1PS

Tel: 0118 966 0622
Fax: 0118 935 1915
E-mail: bsa@thebsa.org.uk

Website:
http://www.thebsa.org.uk
Information about the society.

Enquiries:
Enquiries to: Administrator

Founded:
1966

Organisation type and purpose:
National organisation, professional body (membership is by subscription), present number of members: 1400, registered charity (charity number 261060).
Umbrella organisation in audiology services.

Subject coverage:
Audiology; otology; hearing; hearing loss; clinical audiological practice.

Museum or gallery collection, archive, or library special collection:
Hearing aid museum (now at Thackray Museum, Leeds)

Library catalogue:
All or part available in-house

Printed publications:
International Journal of Audiology (12 times a year, pub. Informa)
BSA News (3 times a year)
Careers in Audiology
Educational pamphlets and booklets
Procedures in Audiology

Access to staff:
Contact by letter, by telephone, by fax and by e-mail
Hours: Mon to Fri, 0900 to 1400

Access to building, collection or gallery:
No access other than to staff

BRITISH SOCIETY OF DOWSERS

Acronym or abbreviation: BSD

2 St. Ann's Road, Malvern, Worcestershire, WR14 4RG

Tel: 01684 576969
Fax: 01684 576969
E-mail: info@britishdowsers.org

Website:
http://www.britishdowsers.org
Full details of the society and its activities.

Enquiries:
Enquiries to: Director

Founded:
1933

Organisation type and purpose:
International organisation, learned society (membership is by subscription), present number of members: 1420, registered charity (charity number 295911), training organisation.

Subject coverage:
Dowsing (water divining) for geophysical, medical, agricultural and other purposes; radiesthesia; professional operators.

Museum or gallery collection, archive, or library special collection:
Library of books on dowsing, radiesthesia and allied subjects

Non-library collection catalogue:
All or part available online

Printed publications:
Dowsing Today (quarterly, to members only)

Access to staff:
Contact by letter, by telephone, by fax, by e-mail, in person and via website. Appointment necessary.
Hours: Mon to Fri, 0900 to 1300, 1400 to 1700

Access to building, collection or gallery:
Mon to Fri, 1030 to 1500

BRITISH SOCIETY OF GASTROENTEROLOGY

Acronym or abbreviation: BSG

3 St Andrews Place, Regent's Park, London, NW1 4LB

Tel: 020 7935 3150
Fax: 020 7487 3734
E-mail: enquiries@bsg.org.uk

Website:
http://www.bsg.org.uk
Information on membership. Working Party Reports and Guidelines all produced in-house.

Enquiries:
Enquiries to: Chief Executive

Founded:
1937

Organisation type and purpose:
Learned society, professional body (membership is by qualification), registered charity (charity number 258713), research organisation.

Subject coverage:
Clinical and scientific aspects of the structure and function of the gastrointestinal system and its appendages; liver disease; gastrointestinal endoscopy.

Printed publications:
GUT (monthly, free to members)

Electronic and video publications:
Various clinical guidelines available (website)

Access to staff:
Contact by letter, by telephone, by fax, by e-mail and via website
Hours: Mon to Fri, 0900 to 1700

BRITISH SOCIETY OF GERONTOLOGY

Acronym or abbreviation: BSG

Department of Applied Social Science, University of Stirling, Stirling, FK9 4LA

Tel: 01786 467701
E-mail: susan.tester@stir.ac.uk

Website:
http://www.soc.surrey.ac.uk/bsg

Enquiries:
Enquiries to: Honorary Secretary

Founded:
1971

Organisation type and purpose:
Learned society (membership is by subscription), present number of members: 650, registered charity (charity number 264385).

Subject coverage:
Quality of life in old age. Implications of ageing societies and populations. Social care of older people.

continued overleaf

Printed publications:
Ageing and Society (6 times a year, Cambridge University Press)
Ageing in Society: An introduction to social gerontology (1993, Sage Publications)
Directory of Members' Research (2002, BSG)
Generations Review (quarterly, free to members, BSG)

Publications list:
Available in print

Access to staff:
Contact by letter, by telephone and by e-mail
Hours: Mon to Fri, 0900 to 1700

Member organisation of:
Academy of Learned Societies for the Social Sciences (ALSISS)
   tel: 020 7468 2296; fax: 020 7468 2296; e-mail: andy.cawdell@the-academy.org.uk
International Association of Gerontology – European Region
   tel: + 34 91 807 0874; fax: + 34 91 807 5637
International Association of Gerontology (IAG)
   tel: + 61 8 8201 7552; fax: + 61 8 8201 7551; e-mail: cas@flinders.edu.au

BRITISH SOCIETY OF HEARING AID AUDIOLOGISTS

Formal name: British Society of Hearing Aid Audiologists Limited
Acronym or abbreviation: BSHAA

9 Lukins Drive, Great Dunmow, Essex, CM6 1XQ

Tel: 01371 876623
Fax: 01371 876623
E-mail: secretary@bshaa.com

Website:
http://www.bshaa.com
General information on hearing difficulty, directory of Hearing Aid Dispensers.

Enquiries:
Enquiries to: Executive Secretary

Founded:
1954

Organisation type and purpose:
Professional body, trade association, membership association (membership is by subscription), present number of members: 650.

Subject coverage:
Hearing aid audiology; education and research in acoustics relating to hearing aids.

Printed publications:
Newsletter (quarterly)

Access to staff:
Contact by letter and by telephone
Hours: Mon to Sun, 0900 to 1700

Approved education body for the examinations of the:
Hearing Aid Council

BRITISH SOCIETY OF HYPNOTHERAPISTS

Acronym or abbreviation: BSH

37 Orbain Road, Fulham, London, SW6 7JZ

Tel: 020 7385 1166
Fax: 020 7385 1166
E-mail: syhyp@onetel.net

Website:
http://www.bsh1950.fsnet.co.uk

Enquiries:
Enquiries to: Secretary

Founded:
1950

Organisation type and purpose:
Professional body.

Subject coverage:
Clinical and educational applications of hypnotherapy; information on training courses, training standards and qualifications; hypnotherapy for patients suffering from functional nervous problems and unwanted habits such as smoking; phobias, depression and insomnia; stammering, asthma etc (psychosomatic conditions); hypnotherapy as complementary to orthodox medicine.

Access to staff:
Contact by letter, by telephone, by fax and by e-mail
Hours: Mon to Fri, 0900 to 1700

Access to building, collection or gallery:
No access other than to staff

BRITISH SOCIETY OF MASTER GLASS PAINTERS

Acronym or abbreviation: BSMGP

5 Tivoli Place, Ilkley, West Yorkshire, LS29 8SU

E-mail: bsmgp@cix.co.uk

Website:
http://www.bsmgp.org.uk
Events, courses, portfolios of work.

Enquiries:
Enquiries to: Honorary Secretary

Founded:
1921

Organisation type and purpose:
Learned society, voluntary organisation.
To promote and elevate the art and craft of glass painting and staining and the conservation and appreciation of historic stained glass.

Subject coverage:
Glass painting, use of decorative glass in churches and secular buildings, conservation and restoration services by accredited craftsmen.

Printed publications:
Directory of members' work
Newsletter (quarterly)
The Journal of Stained Glass

Access to staff:
Contact by letter, by e-mail and via website
Hours: Mon to Fri, 0900 to 1700
Special comments: Please enclose sae for reply.

BRITISH SOCIETY OF NEURORADIOLOGISTS

Acronym or abbreviation: BSNR

Department of Radiology, Hull Royal Infirmary, Anlaby Road, Hull, East Yorkshire

Tel: 01482 674083
Fax: 01482 320137
E-mail: rjvbartlett50@hotmail.com

Enquiries:
Enquiries to: Honorary Secretary

Founded:
1970

Organisation type and purpose:
Learned society.

Subject coverage:
Neuroradiology: training, post availability and career prospects.

Printed publications:
Effective Neuroradiology

Access to staff:
Contact by letter, by telephone, by fax and by e-mail
Hours: Mon to Fri, 0900 to 1700

Recognised by the:
Royal College of Radiologists

BRITISH SOCIETY OF PERIODONTOLOGY

Acronym or abbreviation: BSP

BSP Administrative Manager, 44 Pool Road, Hartley Wintney, Hook, Hampshire, RG27 8RD

Tel: 01252 843598
Fax: 01252 607800
E-mail: bspadmin@btinternet.com

Website:
http://www.bsperio.org.uk

Enquiries:
Enquiries to: Administrator

Founded:
1949

Organisation type and purpose:
Learned society, registered charity (charity number 265815).

Subject coverage:
Dentistry, periodontology, periodontics, periodontal diseases, dental hygiene.

Printed publications:
Newsletter
Policy document on periodontology in general dental practice (revised Mar 2001)

Access to staff:
Contact by letter, by telephone, by fax, by e-mail and via website
Hours: Mon to Fri, 0900 to 1700

BRITISH SOCIETY OF PLANT BREEDERS LIMITED

Acronym or abbreviation: BSPB

Woolpack Chambers, Market Street, Ely, Cambridgeshire, CB7 4ND

Tel: 01353 653200
Fax: 01353 661156
E-mail: enquiries@bspb.co.uk

Website:
http://www.bspb.co.uk
Introduction to plant breeding and the work and role of the BSPB.

Enquiries:
Enquiries to: Chief Executive
Other contacts: Technical Liaison Manager

Organisation type and purpose:
Membership association (membership is by subscription, qualification).
To liaise with official bodies and other organisations on technical and legislative matters concerning plant breeding, issue licences and to collect and redistribute royalties.

Subject coverage:
Plant breeding, technical and legislative matters.

Printed publications:
Leaflets (free)

Access to staff:
Contact by letter, by telephone, by fax and by e-mail
Hours: Mon to Fri, 0900 to 1700

Access to building, collection or gallery:
Prior appointment required

BRITISH SOCIETY OF SOIL SCIENCE

Acronym or abbreviation: BSSS

c/o Macaulay Land Use Research Institute, Craigiebuckler, Aberdeen, AB9 2QJ

Tel: 01224 318611
Fax: 01224 208065
E-mail: j.gauld@mluri.sari.ac.uk

Enquiries:
Enquiries to: Administrator

Organisation type and purpose:
Learned society (membership is by subscription), voluntary organisation.

Subject coverage:
Soil science, soil management, environmental management, education, agriculture, agricultural management.

Printed publications:
European Journal of Soil Science (quarterly)
Intermittent publications in relation to soil science in school curriculum and careers
Soil Use and Management (quarterly)

Access to staff:
Contact by telephone, by fax and by e-mail
Hours: Mon to Fri, 0900 to 1700

BRITISH SOCIOLOGICAL ASSOCIATION

Acronym or abbreviation: BSA

Bailey Suite, Palatine House, Belmont Business Park, Belmont, Durham, DH1 1TW

Tel: 0191 383 0839
Fax: 0191 383 0782
E-mail: enquiries@britsoc.org.uk

Website:
http://www.britsoc.org.uk

Enquiries:
Enquiries to: Enquiries
Other contacts: Membership Development Administrator for member enquiries; Events Organiser for events; Publications Assistant for publications.

Founded:
1951

Organisation type and purpose:
National organisation, learned society (membership is by subscription), present number of members: 2,500, registered charity (charity number 1080235), age range: higher.
To represent the intellectual and sociological interests of its members.

Subject coverage:
Sociology.

Information services:
Website/IT Officer

Printed publications:
Newsletter (members only)
Sociology (journal, for purchase through SAGE Publications or free with membership)
Work, Employment and Society (journal, subscriptions through SAGE Publications or free with membership)
Cultural Sociology (journal, subscriptions through SAGE Publications)
Order printed publications from: via http://www.britsoc.co.uk/publications/pubsjournals.htm

Electronic and video publications:
The World of Sociology (DVD)

Access to staff:
Contact by letter, by telephone, by e-mail and via website
Hours: Mon to Fri, 0900 to 1700

Access to building, collection or gallery:
Prior appointment required

Access for disabled people:
Parking provided

BRITISH SOFT DRINKS ASSOCIATION LIMITED

Acronym or abbreviation: BSDA

20–22 Stukeley Street, London, WC2B 5LR

Tel: 020 7430 0356
Fax: 020 7831 6014
E-mail: bsda@britishsoftdrinks.com

Website:
http://www.britishsoftdrinks.com

Enquiries:
Enquiries to: Public Relations Manager
Other contacts: Administration for publications.

Founded:
1987

Organisation type and purpose:
Trade association.

Subject coverage:
UK soft drinks, fruit juices, bottled water industries.

Publications list:
Available online and in print

Access to staff:
Contact by letter, by telephone, by fax, by e-mail and via website. Appointment necessary. Non-members charged.
Hours: Mon to Fri, 0900 to 1700

Member of:
AIJN
EFBW
UNESDA

Subsections are:
Bottled Waters Group
Fruit Juice Committee

BRITISH SOFTBALL FEDERATION

Acronym or abbreviation: BSF

Birchwood Hall, Storridge, Malvern, Worcestershire, WR13 5EZ

Tel: 01886 884204
Fax: 01886 884204
E-mail: bfromer@netcomuk.co.uk

Website:
http://www.baseballsoftballuk.com
Comprehensive information on softball in the UK.

Enquiries:
Enquiries to: Chief Executive

Founded:
1984

Organisation type and purpose:
Membership association.
Governing body of the sport.

Subject coverage:
Playing and coaching of softball, umpiring, team locations, award schemes for schools, national teams.

Printed publications:
Softball Starter Pack
Schools/Youth Starter Pack
Idiot's Guide to Softball
Softball Scoring Guide
How to Run a Tournament
Basic Skills Coaching Manual

Electronic and video publications:
Slowpitch Coaching Video
Softball Strategy and Tactics Video

Publications list:
Available online and in print

Access to staff:
Contact by letter, by e-mail and via website
Hours: Mon to Fri, 0900 to 1700

Affiliated to:
European Softball Federation
International Softball Federation

Other address:
c/o Baseball Softball UK
  Ariel House, 74a Charlotte Street, London, W1T 4QJ; tel: 020 7453 7055; fax: 020 7453 7007; e-mail: info@baseballsoftballuk.com

BRITISH SPORTING ART TRUST

Acronym or abbreviation: BSAT

99 High Street, Newmarket, Suffolk, CB8 8JL

Tel: 01638 664429
E-mail: bsatrust@btconnect.com

Website:
http://www.bsat.co.uk

Founded:
1977

Organisation type and purpose:
An independent registered charity (no. 274156) with membership by subscription.

Subject coverage:
Sporting art.

Museum or gallery collection, archive, or library special collection:
Representative collection of British sporting paintings
Library of books, transparencies, catalogues, magazines and archive material

Printed publications:
A Bibliography of British Sporting Artists

BRITISH STAMMERING ASSOCIATION

Acronym or abbreviation: BSA

15 Old Ford Road, London, E2 9PJ

Tel: 020 8983 1003
Fax: 020 8983 3591
E-mail: mail@stammering.org

Website:
http://www.stammering.org
Information about BSA and about stammering.

Enquiries:
Enquiries to: Director

Organisation type and purpose:
National organisation, membership association (membership is by subscription), present number of members: 1600, voluntary organisation, registered charity (charity number 278170), suitable for ages: School Age.
To help stammerers help themselves and promote wider understanding of stammering.

Subject coverage:
Stammering, speech therapy, disability, special needs, medical/health, self-help.

Museum or gallery collection, archive, or library special collection:
Postal library
Regional directories of speech therapy provision
Research information database

Library catalogue:
All or part available online

Printed publications:
Books for professionals, teachers, parents and pupils
Newsletter (quarterly)
Selection of leaflets providing information about stammering for all age ranges
The Adult Who Stammers (leaflet)
The Child Who Stammers

Electronic and video publications:
Audio tape Slow Prolonged Speech tape (£4.95)

Publications list:
Available online and in print

Access to staff:
Contact by letter, by telephone, by fax, by e-mail and via website. Appointment necessary.
Hours: Mon to Fri, 0900 to 1700

Member of:
European League of Stuttering Associations (ELSA)
VOCAL

BRITISH STANDARDS SOCIETY

Acronym or abbreviation: BSS

continued overleaf

389 Chiswick High Road, London, W4 4AL

Tel: 020 8996 7081
Fax: 020 8996 7091
E-mail: bss@bsi-global.com

Website:
http://www.bsi.global.com/

Enquiries:
Enquiries to: Secretary
Direct tel: 01923 252361
Direct fax: 01923 252361
Direct e-mail: pam.hall@bsi-global.com

Founded:
1960

Organisation type and purpose:
Professional body (membership is by subscription), present number of members: 500.
Voluntary association of individuals concerned with the application of standards; established and administered by BSI.

Subject coverage:
Application of standards in design, manufacturing, services, quality assurance, information technology and in-service support; special interest groups on building, electronics and management systems, health and environment, consumer products and services, information technology.

Museum or gallery collection, archive, or library special collection:
Library of papers on various aspects of standardisation available to members only

Printed publications:
Members' Handbook (annually)
Newsletter (quarterly)
PD 3542: 1998 Standards and Quality Management: an integrated approach (BSI, £50, members of BSI and BSS £25)
PD 6614: 1999 Obsolescence Management: guide to the subscription of components in electronic equipment (BSI, £50, members of BSI and BSS £25)
PD 6615: 1998 Guide to setting up a parts database (BSI, £36, members of BSI & BSS £15)
PD 6667: 2000 Obsolescence Management: suppliers guide to the substitution of components in electronic equipment (BSI, £36, members of BSS & BSI £18)
Programme of meetings (annually)
Order printed publications from: Customer Services, BSI
389 Chiswick High Road, London, W4 4AL, tel: 020 8996 9001, fax: 020 8996 7001, e-mail: www.bsi-global.com

Access to staff:
Contact by letter, by telephone, by fax and by e-mail
Hours: Mon to Fri, 0900 to 1700

Parent body:
British Standards Institution
tel: 020 8996 9000; fax: 020 8996 7001; website: http://www.bsi-global.com

UK member of:
International Federation of Standards Users (IFAN)
tel: +41 22 749 0331; fax: +41 22 749 0155; e-mail: ifan@iso.ch

BRITISH STARCH INDUSTRY ASSOCIATION

Acronym or abbreviation: BSIA

Federation House, 6 Catherine Street, London, WC2B 5JJ

Tel: 020 7836 2460
Fax: 020 7836 0580

Enquiries:
Enquiries to: Executive Secretary
Direct e-mail: bob.price@fdf.org.uk

Organisation type and purpose:
Trade association.

Subject coverage:
Maize refining and wheat refining, production of starch, glucose and other derived products.

Access to staff:
Contact by letter, by fax and by e-mail
Hours: Mon to Fri, 0930 to 1730

BRITISH SUNDIAL SOCIETY

4 New Wokingham Road, Crowthorne, Berkshire, RG45 7NR

Tel: 01344 772303
E-mail: douglas.bateman@btinternet.com

Website:
http://www.sundials.co.uk/bsshome.htm
Types of dials, books in print, equation of time, national sundial societies, information about the British Sundial Society.

Enquiries:
Enquiries to: Secretary

Founded:
1989

Organisation type and purpose:
Learned society (membership is by subscription), present number of members: 500, voluntary organisation, registered charity (charity no. 1032530).
A society for those interested in gnomonics and sundials generally.

Subject coverage:
Constructing sundials, makers of sundials, sundial bibliography, history of sundials, location of sundials (British), restoration of sundials, gnomonics, speakers' panel.

Museum or gallery collection, archive, or library special collection:
Photographs of existing sundials
Records of existing sundials
Books on sundials

Trade and statistical information:
List of dial makers in the UK who are members of the society.

Non-library collection catalogue:
All or part available in print

Printed publications:
Make a Sundial (Book for Schools, 70pp)
Sundial Books in English from 1900 (A4 sheet)
Sundial Makers (D/S A4 sheet)
Sundial Register (Locations, Details, 210pp)
Sundial Glossary (terminology, equations, 84pp)
Biographical Index of British Sundial Makers from the Seventh Century to 1920 (117pp)
Order printed publications from: British Sundial Society

Microform publications:
Sets of Slides for lectures:
Basic Theory
Early History
Early British Dials

Electronic and video publications:
Looking at Sundials (education video available for purchase direct)
Sundial Calculations

Publications list:
Available online

Access to staff:
Contact by letter, by telephone, by e-mail and via website. Appointment necessary.
Hours: Mon to Sat, 0900 to 1900

Connections with:
European sundial societies
North American Sundial Society
Public Monuments and Sculpture Association

BRITISH SURFING ASSOCIATION

Acronym or abbreviation: BSA

c/o The International Surfing Centre, Fistral Beach, Newquay, Cornwall, TR7 1HY

Tel: 01637 876474
Fax: 01637 878608
E-mail: info@britsurf.co.uk

Website:
http://www.nationalsurfingcentre.com
http://www.gbsurf.org
http://www.britsurf.co.uk

Enquiries:
Enquiries to: National Director
Other contacts: Assistant to National Director

Founded:
1966

Organisation type and purpose:
Membership association.
Governing body of the sport.

Subject coverage:
Surfing; courses for beginners, teachers and coaches.

Trade and statistical information:
Information on surfing related business available.

Printed publications:
BSA Guide to Surfing in Britain (£3.95)
General fact sheets on surfing
Newsletters

Access to staff:
Contact by letter, by telephone, by fax and by e-mail
Hours: Mon to Fri, 0900 to 1700

Access to building, collection or gallery:
No prior appointment required

Affiliated to:
Central Council of Physical Recreation
International Surfing Association

BRITISH SUZUKI INSTITUTE

Acronym or abbreviation: BSI

Kensington Charity Centre, 4th Floor, Charles House, 375 Kensington High Street, London W14 8QH

Tel: 020 7471 6780
Fax: 020 7471 6778
E-mail: info@britishsuzuki.com

Website:
http://www.britishsuzuki.org.uk/

Enquiries:
Enquiries to: General Secretary

Founded:
1978

Organisation type and purpose:
Membership association (membership is by subscription), present number of members: c. 1600, registered charity (charity number 278005), training organisation.
To further education by Suzuki method.

Subject coverage:
Information about the Suzuki approach to instrumental teaching, provision of training courses in music and general education. The emphasis is on teaching very young children with parental involvement.

Museum or gallery collection, archive, or library special collection:
A small library on Suzuki method includes musical tapes and CDs

Printed publications:
Ability Development (journal, 3 times a year)
Annual Report
Music, books
Suzuki method pamphlets and information

Electronic and video publications:
Tapes and CDs relating to Suzuki method

Publications list:
Available in print

Access to staff:
Contact by letter, by telephone, by fax and by e-mail. Appointment necessary.
Hours: Mon to Fri, 0930 to 1630
Special comments: 24 hour answerphone.

Affiliated to:
European Suzuki Association
at the same address
International Suzuki Association
3–10–3 Fukhshi, Matsumoto, Nagawo, 390, Japan

BRITISH TARANTULA SOCIETY

Acronym or abbreviation: BTS

81 Phillimore Place, Radlett, Hertfordshire, WD7 8NJ

Tel: 01923 856071

Website:
http://www.bts.ndirect.co.uk
Details of Society and its services, articles and photographs.

Enquiries:
Enquiries to: Honorary Secretary

Founded:
1984

Organisation type and purpose:
Membership association (membership is by subscription), present number of members: over 700, voluntary organisation, suitable for ages: all, research organisation.
Membership is predominantly UK but is also worldwide.

Subject coverage:
Keeping, conservation, captive breeding and management of tropical arachnids (tarantulas and scorpions).

Museum or gallery collection, archive, or library special collection:
Reference library

Library catalogue:
All or part available online

Printed publications:
Journal (quarterly, members only)
Publicity material

Access to staff:
Contact by letter and by telephone. Non-members charged.
Hours: 24-hour answerphone

BRITISH TAXPAYERS ASSOCIATION LIMITED

Acronym or abbreviation: British Taxpayers

Barclays House, 51 Bishopric, Horsham, West Sussex, RH12 1BS

Tel: 01403 271919
Fax: 01403 271912
E-mail: enquiries@britishtaxpayers.com

Website:
http://www.britishtaxpayers.com

Enquiries:
Enquiries to: Managing Director
Direct fax: 01403 271912

Founded:
1919

Organisation type and purpose:
Consultancy.

Subject coverage:
Income, capital gains and inheritance tax, overseas income and trusts, expatriate taxation, national insurance contributions, tax return preparation, personal financial planning, remuneration planning, employee benefits, revenue investigations, incentive schemes.

Museum or gallery collection, archive, or library special collection:
Research library on all UK taxation matters

Trade and statistical information:
Full data on UK personal taxation.

Printed publications:
Publications available online via
www.britishtaxpayers.com

Publications list:
Available online

Access to staff:
Contact by letter, by telephone, by fax, by e-mail and in person
Hours: Mon to Fri, 0900 to 1700

Affiliated to:
British Taxpayers Financial Planning
tel: 020 7456 0450; fax: 020 7247 0411; e-mail: mail@british-taxpayers.com
The Taxpayers' Society
tel: 01403 271919; fax: 01403 271912; e-mail: tps@british-taxpayers.com

Also at:
British Taxpayers
78 Park Street, Horsham, West Sussex, RH12 1BS; tel: 01403 271919; fax: 01403 271912; e-mail: mail@british-taxpayers.co.uk

BRITISH TECHNION SOCIETY

62 Grosvenor Street, London, W1K 3JF

Tel: 020 7495 6824
Fax: 020 7355 1525
E-mail: bts62@apl.com

Website:
http://www.britishtechnionsociety.org
Full history of BTS.

Enquiries:
Enquiries to: Executive Director

Founded:
1951

Organisation type and purpose:
Registered charity (charity number 206922).
To raise funds for Technion, Haifa, Israel.

Subject coverage:
Promotion of Technion, fund-raising for Technion.

Printed publications:
Newsletter and other printed material (no charge)

Access to staff:
Contact by letter, by telephone, by fax and in person
Hours: Mon to Fri, 0900 to 1700

Parent body:
Technion
Israel Institute of Technology, Haifa, 32000, Israel

BRITISH TEXTILE MACHINERY ASSOCIATION

Acronym or abbreviation: BTMA

Mount Pleasant, Glazebrook Lane, Glazebrook, Warrington, WA3 5BN

Tel: 0161 775 5740
Fax: 0161 775 5485
E-mail: btma@btma.org.uk

Website:
http://www.btma.org.uk

Enquiries:
Enquiries to: Director
Direct e-mail: eric.france@btma.org.uk

Founded:
1940

Organisation type and purpose:
Trade association (membership is by subscription), present number of members: 100, manufacturing industry.

To promote the British textile machinery industry worldwide.

Subject coverage:
Textile machinery for natural and synthetic products.

Printed publications:
Directory of Members and Products (annually, free)

Access to staff:
Contact by letter, by telephone, by fax, by e-mail and via website. Appointment necessary.
Hours: Mon to Fri, 0900 to 1700

BRITISH THYROID FOUNDATION

Acronym or abbreviation: BTF

2nd Floor, 3 Devonshire Place, Harrogate, HG1 4AA

Tel: 01423 709707

Website:
http://www.btf-thyroid.org

Enquiries:
Enquiries to: Membership Secretary

Founded:
1991

Organisation type and purpose:
Voluntary organisation, registered charity.
To support sufferers of thyroid disorders.

Subject coverage:
Thyroid disorders.

Printed publications:
General introductory leaflet: contains membership information (free)
Newsletter: includes telephone numbers of local support groups (quarterly, members)
Pamphlets on thyroid disorders (members)

Access to staff:
Contact by letter and by telephone
Hours: Mon to Fri, 1000 to 1400

BRITISH TINNITUS ASSOCIATION

Acronym or abbreviation: BTA

Acorn Business Park, Woodseats Close, Sheffield S8 0TB

Tel: 0114 250 9933 \ Minicom 0114 258 5694
Fax: 0114 258 2279
E-mail: info@tinnitus.org.uk

Website:
http://www.tinnitus.org.uk/

Enquiries:
Enquiries to: Operations Manager
Direct tel: 0114 273 0122
Other contacts: Membership Secretary

Founded:
1992

Organisation type and purpose:
Membership association (membership is by subscription), present number of members: 10,000, voluntary organisation, registered charity (charity number 1011145).
The sole national voluntary organisation for people with tinnitus, close links with tinnitus associations in other countries, self-help groups.
To raise an increasing awareness to the condition, support new research, promote better medical services and provide support for sufferers.

Subject coverage:
Tinnitus; help or treatments available; information on research in progress.

Printed publications:
Information leaflets
Medical Leaflets (6, free for sae)
Quiet (journal, quarterly; £10 a year)

Electronic and video publications:
New World relaxation tapes
Video cassette for hire

continued overleaf

Publications list:
Available in print

Access to staff:
Contact by letter, by telephone, by fax and by e-mail
Hours: Mon to Fri, 0930 to 1630 (plus 24hr answerphone)

BRITISH TOY & HOBBY ASSOCIATION LIMITED

Acronym or abbreviation: BTHA

80 Camberwell Road, London, SE5 0EG

Tel: 020 7701 7271
Fax: 020 7708 2437
E-mail: admin@btha.co.uk

Website:
http://www.btha.co.uk

Enquiries:
Enquiries to: Director General

Founded:
1944

Organisation type and purpose:
Trade association.

Subject coverage:
Toys and hobbies, toy industry, UK toy exports and imports, toy safety, advertising of toys and responsible manufacturing.

Printed publications:
Advertising Toys to Children in the UK and
    Europe (£4.50)
BTHA Sourcebook
British Toys and Hobbies Briefing
Directory of Members (annually)
Games (£4.50)
Hundred popular toys and games for blind and
    partially sighted children (1996, free)
Intergenerational Play (£4.50)
Play Value (£4.50)
Television Advertising and Children (£25)
Toys and Play in Child Development (£4.50)
War Toys (£4.50)

Access to staff:
Contact by letter, by telephone, by fax and by e-mail
Hours: Jun to Sep, Mon to Thu, 0830 to 1700; Fri, 0830 to 1630

Houses the:
British Toy Council
British Toy Fairs (International) Limited
    website: http://www.toyfair.co.uk

Member of:
International Council of Toy Industries
    website: http://www.toy-icti.org
Toy Industries of Europe
    website: http://www.tietoy.org

BRITISH TOY COUNCIL LIMITED

80 Camberwell Road, London, SE5 0EG

Tel: 020 7701 7271
Fax: 020 7708 2437
E-mail: admin@btha.co.uk

Enquiries:
Enquiries to: Secretary

Founded:
1967

Organisation type and purpose:
Trade association.

Subject coverage:
Standards of design, development, quality and safety of toys; preparation and implementation of these standards UK and international.

Museum or gallery collection, archive, or library special collection:
Some international toy safety standards

Access to staff:
Contact by letter
Hours: Mon to Fri, 0900 to 1700

Subsidiary of:
British Toy and Hobby Association
    website: http://www.btha.co.uk

BRITISH TOYMAKERS GUILD

Acronym or abbreviation: BTG

PO Box 240, Uckfield, TN22 9AS

Tel: 01225 442440
E-mail: info@toymakersguild.co.uk

Website:
http://www.toymakersguild.co.uk
News on traditional toys, toymakers and forthcoming events.

Enquiries:
Enquiries to: Manager

Founded:
1955

Organisation type and purpose:
International organisation, trade association (membership is by subscription, qualification), present number of members: 200.

Subject coverage:
Toys.

Trade and statistical information:
Data on the traditional toy sector.

Printed publications:
A Closer Look at the Traditional Toy Sector
A Guide to Self Certification
Marketing Traditional Toys
Yearly Catalogue

Access to staff:
Contact by letter, by telephone, by e-mail and via website. Appointment necessary.
Hours: Mon to Fri, 0900 to 1700

BRITISH TROLLEYBUS SOCIETY

Acronym or abbreviation: BTS

2 Josephine Court, Southcote Road, Reading, Berkshire, RG30 2DG

Tel: 0118 958 3974

Enquiries:
Enquiries to: Honorary Secretary

Founded:
1961

Organisation type and purpose:
Membership association (membership is by subscription), present number of members: 320, voluntary organisation, registered charity (charity number 1033666).

Subject coverage:
History and development of British trolleybus systems in particular, and foreign systems in general; history and development of bus operation in the Thames Valley area, development of public transport in West Yorkshire area.

Printed publications:
Bus Fare (monthly)
Trolleybus (monthly)
Wheels (monthly)

Access to staff:
Contact by letter and by telephone
Hours: Mon to Fri, 0900 to 1700

Associated with:
Sandtoft Transport Centre

There are groups in:
Bradford and Reading

BRITISH TROUT ASSOCIATION

Acronym or abbreviation: BTA

British Trout Association, The Rural Centre, West Mains, Ingliston, EH28 8NZ

Tel: 0131 472 4080
Fax: 0131 472 4083
E-mail: mail@britishtrout.co.uk

Website:
http://www.britishtrout.co.uk
Information on organisation, list of members and their addresses.

Enquiries:
Enquiries to: Honorary Secretary

Organisation type and purpose:
National organisation, trade association (membership is by subscription).
Information for members only.

Access to staff:
Contact by e-mail
Hours: Mon to Fri, 0900 to 1700

BRITISH TRUST FOR CONSERVATION VOLUNTEERS SCOTLAND

Acronym or abbreviation: BTCV Scotland

Balallan House, 24 Allan Park, Stirling, FK8 2QG

Tel: 01786 479697
Fax: 01786 465359
E-mail: scotland@btcv.org.uk

Website:
http://www.btcv.org.uk/scotland

Enquiries:
Enquiries to: Administrator

Founded:
1984

Organisation type and purpose:
National organisation, membership association (membership is by subscription), present number of members: 5,000, voluntary organisation, registered charity (charity number 261009), training organisation.
Environmental organisation.
To involve people in improving the quality of Scotland's environment through practical conservation.

Subject coverage:
Information provided on all aspects of practical conservation and community regeneration work.

Printed publications:
Annual Review
Environmental Skills books
Conserver Magazine
CLAN Bulletin Magazine

Electronic and video publications:
Green Gym (video)

Access to staff:
Contact by letter, by telephone, by fax, by e-mail, in person and via website
Hours: Mon to Fri, 0900 to 1700

Access to building, collection or gallery:
No prior appointment required

Access for disabled people:
Parking provided, toilet facilities

Also at:
Edinburgh, Glasgow, Falkirk, Aberdeen, Inverness, Fife

Constituent bodies:
285 affiliated local conservation groups, collectively known as Community Local Action Network (CLAN)

Constituent part of:
British Trust for Conservation Volunteers (BTCV)

Links with:
Action Recycle
    27 Winchester Avenue, Denny, FK6 6QE; tel: 01324 826826; fax: 01324 882533; e-mail: action-recycle@btcv.org.uk

BRITISH TRUST FOR ORNITHOLOGY

Acronym or abbreviation: BTO

The Nunnery, Thetford, Norfolk, IP24 2PU

Tel: 01842 750050
Fax: 01842 750030
E-mail: btostaff@bto.org

Website:
http://www.bto.org

Enquiries:
Enquiries to: Director of Development
Direct e-mail: nick.carter@bto.org

Founded:
1933

Organisation type and purpose:
Membership association (membership is by subscription), present number of members: 12,500, registered charity (charity number 216652), research organisation.

Subject coverage:
British and migratory birds, their habitats and population levels, breeding season, mortality, migration, using information gathered by members. Understanding, appreciation and conservation of birds.

Museum or gallery collection, archive, or library special collection:
Largest data collection on British birds in the UK
Second largest ornithological library of books and journals in the UK
Breeding Bird Survey (data from 1994 onwards)
Common Birds Census (data from 1962 to 2000)
Ornithological Sites Register (data from 1960s onwards)
Waterway Bird Survey (data 1974 onwards)
Wetland Bird Survey (data from 1993 onwards)
Nest Record Scheme (data from 1930s onwards)
National Ringing Scheme (data from 1909 onwards)

Non-library collection catalogue:
All or part available online, in-house and in print

Library catalogue:
All or part available in-house

Printed publications:
Contact BTO for price details
Bird Study (3 times a year)
BTO News (6 times a year)
Bird table (4 times a year)
Occasional technical guides, books
Research reports
Ringing and Migration (2 times a year)
The New Atlas of Breeding Birds in Britain and Ireland: 1988–1991

Publications list:
Available online and in print

Access to staff:
Contact by letter, by telephone, by fax and by e-mail
Hours: Mon to Fri, 0900 to 1700

Access to building, collection or gallery:
Prior appointment required
Special comments: Members only, preferably by prior appointment.

Access for disabled people:
Parking provided, level entry, toilet facilities

Other office:
British Trust for Ornithology (Scottish Office) (BTO Scotland)
School of Biological & Environmental Sciences, Cottrell Building, University of Stirling, Stirling, FK9 4LA.; tel: 01786 466560; fax: 01786 466561

BRITISH TUNNELLING SOCIETY

Acronym or abbreviation: BTS

Institution of Civil Engineers, 1–7 Great George Street, London, SW1P 3AA

Tel: 020 7665 2233

Fax: 020 7799 1325
E-mail: bts@ice.org.uk

Website:
http://www.ice.org.uk
http://www.britishtunnelling.org
Meetings of the British Tunnelling Society listed.

Enquiries:
Enquiries to: Co-ordinator

Founded:
1971

Organisation type and purpose:
Learned society.

Subject coverage:
All aspects of tunnel design, construction and maintenance.

Museum or gallery collection, archive, or library special collection:
Library tunnelling section of the ICE library

Printed publications:
Tunnels and Tunnelling (10 times a year, free to members)

Access to staff:
Contact by letter, by telephone and via website
Hours: Mon to Fri, 0900 to 1700
Special comments: Access to library/archives of Institution of Civil Engineers on payment of a fee.

Affiliated to:
Institution of Civil Engineers

National section of the:
International Tunnelling Association

BRITISH TURNED PARTS MANUFACTURERS ASSOCIATION

Acronym or abbreviation: BTMA

PTC, Snitterfield Lane, Norton Lindsey, Warwick, CV35 8JQ

Tel: 01789 730877
Fax: 01789 730899
E-mail: iangold@btma.org

Website:
http://www.btma.org

Enquiries:
Enquiries to: Director

Organisation type and purpose:
Trade association.

Subject coverage:
Precison-turned parts and machined components.

Education services:
CNC setter training courses for members

Non-library collection catalogue:
All or part available online and in print

Printed publications:
Buyer's Guide
Order printed publications from: Postal address

Access to staff:
Contact by letter, by telephone, by fax, by e-mail and via website

Access to building, collection or gallery:
Special comments: No access

BRITISH UNIDENTIFIED FLYING OBJECT RESEARCH ASSOCIATION

Acronym or abbreviation: BUFORA

41 Castlebar Road, Ealing, London, W5 2DJ

Tel: 020 8997 3496
E-mail: enquiries@bufora.org.uk

Website:
http://www.bufora.org.uk

Founded:
1962

Organisation type and purpose:
Non-membership Association conducting objective/scientific based investigative research into the UFO phenomenon.

Subject coverage:
Field investigations, research, investigator training, support in all areas pertaining to UFOs and related paranormal phenomena

Printed publications:
Website with free access to all material therein, unless otherwise stated.

Access to staff:
Contact by letter, by telephone, by e-mail and via website
Hours: Access via e-mail 24 hours
Special comments: Telephone evenings after 1830 and weekends

BRITISH UNION CONFERENCE OF SEVENTH-DAY ADVENTISTS

Acronym or abbreviation: BUC

Stanborough Park, Garston, Watford, Hertfordshire, WD25 9JZ

Tel: 01923 672251
Fax: 01923 893212
E-mail: info@adventist.org.uk

Website:
http://www.adventist.org.uk
General information about the Seventh-day Adventist Church, links to other sites and to other Christian sites.

Enquiries:
Enquiries to: Communications Director
Direct e-mail: vhulbert@adventist.org.uk

Organisation type and purpose:
Registered charity (charity number 209780). British Isles Headquarters of the Seventh-day Adventist Church.

Subject coverage:
Seventh-day Adventist beliefs and history, health and temperance.

Museum or gallery collection, archive, or library special collection:
Rare collections relating to Church history are housed at the denominational college, Newbold College, Binfield, nr Bracknell, Berkshire, RG42 4AN

Printed publications:
Encounter Youth Magazine, Messenger, Life.info Focus Magazine

Electronic and video publications:
Satellite Television Channel – The Hope Channel – on Hotbird, www.hopetv.org.uk

Access to staff:
Contact by letter, by telephone, by fax, by e-mail and via website
Hours: Mon to Thu, 0900 to 1700; Fri, 0900 to 1200

Access to building, collection or gallery:
Hours: Mon to Thu, 0900 to 1700; Fri, 0900 to 1200

Access for disabled people:
Disabled access available

Also at the same address:
Seventh-day Adventist Association Limited website: http://www.adventist.org.uk

Parent body:
General Conference of Seventh-day Adventists 12501 Old Columbia Pike, Silver Spring, MD 20904–6600, USA

Subsidary body:
Adventist Development and Relief Agency (ADRA-uk)
at the same address; tel: 01923 681723; website: http://adra.org.uk

BRITISH UNION FOR THE ABOLITION OF VIVISECTION

Acronym or abbreviation: BUAV

16a Crane Grove, Islington, London, N7 8NN

Tel: 020 7700 4888
Fax: 020 7700 0252
E-mail: info@buav.org

Website:
http://www.buav.org

Enquiries:
Other contacts: Media Manager for media enquiries

Founded:
1898

Organisation type and purpose:
The BUAV works to create a world where nobody wants to or believes in the need to experiment on animals. It campaigns peacefully to end animal testing. Through undercover investigations, political lobbying, the promotion of cruelty-free products, legal and scientific expertise and media activities, it works to make the world a better place for animals.

Subject coverage:
Animal protection, campaigning, Cruelty Free, laboratory animals and the campaign against vivisection.

Museum or gallery collection, archive, or library special collection:
BUAV archive material (1898 to present day) held at Brynmor Jones Library, University of Hull, available to bona fide researchers by appointment

Library catalogue:
All or part available in-house

Printed publications:
Annual Report
BUAV Update, supporter newsletter
Fact sheets on campaign issues

Access to staff:
Contact by letter, by telephone, by fax, by e-mail and via website. Appointment necessary. Letter of introduction required.
Hours: Mon to Fri, 0900 to 1700

Access to building, collection or gallery:
Hours: Mon to Fri, 0900 to 1700

Affiliated to:
European Coalition to End Animal Experiments at the same address

BRITISH UNION OF SOCIAL WORK EMPLOYEES

Acronym or abbreviation: BUSWE

BUSWE House, 208 Middleton Road, Manchester, M8 4NA

Tel: 0161 720 7727
Fax: 0161 795 4524
E-mail: buswe@buswe.fsnet.co.uk

Enquiries:
Enquiries to: General Secretary

Founded:
1976

Organisation type and purpose:
Trade union, present number of members: 3500+.

Subject coverage:
UK social work structure and services, industrial relations.
Development of a broad knowledge base; education of the public and others as to the purpose and impact of social care practices and procedures; creation of the optimal circumstances for the employment of social care practitioners; participation in the setting and evolution of professional standards of social care; support of initiatives which promote the expansion of opportunities within which individuals can expand their development potential; re-

establishment of education and training of social care employees in order that the demands of evolving standards and practices can be met.

Access to staff:
Contact by letter, by telephone and by e-mail.
Appointment necessary.
Hours: Mon to Fri, 0900 to 1700

Access to building, collection or gallery:
Prior appointment required
Hours: Mon to Fri, 0900 to 1700

Access for disabled people:
Parking provided

BRITISH UNIVERSITIES FILM & VIDEO COUNCIL

Acronym or abbreviation: BUFVC

77 Wells Street, London, W1T 3QJ

Tel: 020 7393 1500
Fax: 020 7393 1555
E-mail: ask@bufvc.ac.uk

Website:
http://www.bufvc.ac.uk
Annual information on BUFVC membership, services and publications. HERMES, RGO, BUND, MIGr and TRILT databases.

Enquiries:
Enquiries to: Head of Information
Direct tel: 020 7393 1508
Direct e-mail: luke@bufvc.ac.uk
Other contacts: Library and Database Manager for general Information. Also newsreels@bufvc.ac.uk and rgo@bufvc.ac.uk

Founded:
1948

Merged with:
Learning on Screen (year of change 2004)

Organisation type and purpose:
Registered charity (no. 313582), research organisation, publishing house.
Reference Library founded 1972; instrumental in founding the Consortium for Drama and Media in Higher Education, providing the secretariat since 1974; assumed responsibility for administration of Slade Film History Register, 1975; took over production of HELPIS catalogue from Council for Educational Technology, 1976; Audio-Visual Reference Centre opened, 1978; took over distribution of the films of the Interuniversity History Film Consortium, 1981, launched British Universities Newsreel Project 1995; launched British Universities Newsreel (Scripts) Project 1999; launched Researcher's Guide Online and Moving Image Gateway (2001); launched Television & Radio Index for Learning and Teaching (2002).

Subject coverage:
Audio-visual media, including computer-based multi-media, materials and techniques for degree-level teaching and research, resource lists on the history of science and invention, Shakespeare, post-war British history, physics and astronomy, teaching, guides to film, and newsreel collections.

Museum or gallery collection, archive, or library special collection:
BKSTS book library
Issue sheets for all British newsreels and cinemagazines, as well as details of unissued material, held in the Slade Film History Register
Newsreel commentary scripts, dope sheets and other original documents from Reuters Television
Records of the Scientific Film Association
Subject index to television documentary programmes broadcast by BBC and ITV from 1987 to 2001

Printed publications:
Annual Report
As You Like It: Audio Visual Shakespeare (3rd ed.)
Buying and Clearing Rights: Print, Broadcast and Multimedia

Film and Television Collections in Europe: The MAP-TV Guide
Filming History: BUFVC Handbook (3rd ed.)
Researchers' Guide to British Film and Television Collections (6th ed. 2001)
Researchers' Guide to British Newsreels vol. I, (1983); vol. II, (1988); vol. III, (1993)
Viewfinder (4 times per annum)

Microform publications:
British Newsreels Issue Sheets 1913–1970 on Microfiche

Electronic and video publications:
The BUFVC Newsreel Project (CD-ROM)
Origins of the Cold War (CD-ROM)

Publications list:
Available in print

Access to staff:
Contact by letter, by telephone, by fax and by e-mail. Appointment necessary. Non-members charged.
Hours: Mon to Fri, 0930 to 1730
Special comments: Information service open for enquiries 1200 to 1730.

Supported by:
the Joint Information Systems Committee (JISC)

BRITISH UNIVERSITIES SPORTS ASSOCIATION

Acronym or abbreviation: BUSA

8 Union Street, London, SE1 1SZ

Tel: 020 7357 8555
Fax: 020 7403 1218
E-mail: office@busa.org.uk

Website:
http://www.busaresults.org.uk
Results of sports matches and league information. Contact information and sponsor information.

Enquiries:
Enquiries to: Public Relations Manager

Organisation type and purpose:
National government body, membership association (membership is by qualification), present number of members: 147, registered charity (charity number 223324).

Subject coverage:
Governing body for University Sport in the UK. Organise tournaments in 42 sports for 147 member institutions.

BRITISH URBAN REGENERATION ASSOCIATION

Acronym or abbreviation: BURA

63–66 Hatton Garden, London, EC1N 8LE

Tel: 020 7539 4030
Fax: 020 7404 9614
E-mail: info@bura.org.uk

Website:
http://www.bura.org.uk

Enquiries:
Enquiries to: Business Development Director

Founded:
1990

Organisation type and purpose:
Trade association (membership is by subscription, election or invitation), present number of members: 550, voluntary organisation.
Promoting an integrated approach to improving the quality of life in urban areas, taking fully into account the interdependence of the social, economic and environmental issues involved.

Subject coverage:
Urban regeneration; contaminated land; sustainable development; annual awards: BURA Award for Best Practice in Urban Regeneration; The Secretary of State for the Environment,

Transport and the Regions' Award for Partnership in Regeneration; Best Practice in Community Regeneration Awards; Best Practice in Promoting Sport in the Community Awards.

Printed publications:
Urban Regeneration Handbook
Research Papers
Newsletter (quarterly)
Conference Reports

Access to staff:
Contact by letter, by telephone, by fax and by e-mail. Appointment necessary.
Hours: Mon to Fri, 0930 to 1730

Standing committees and working groups include:
Contaminated Land Working Group
Urban Policy Group

Works in partnership with:
Association of Town Centre Management
Civic Trust
Local Government Association
Royal Town Planning Institute
Town and Country Planning Association
Urban Villages Forum

BRITISH URUGUAYAN SOCIETY

Shreelane, 222 Brooklands Road, Weybridge, Surrey, KT13 0RJ

Tel: 01932 847455
Fax: 01932 847455

Enquiries:
Enquiries to: Secretary

Founded:
1945

Organisation type and purpose:
Membership association (membership is by subscription), present number of members: 270, registered charity (charity number 275362). Educational charity promoting knowledge of Uruguay in Britain and of Britain in Uruguay.

Subject coverage:
History, geography and culture of Uruguay; educational contacts for students; some limited information on business, trade and travel, not specialists but have contacts and are willing to help wherever possible.

Museum or gallery collection, archive, or library special collection:
The Society's library is on permanent loan to the Library of the Hispanic and Luso-Brazilian Council at 2 Belgrave Square, London, SW1, where it is open to the public weekdays 0930 to 1730

Printed publications:
El Hornero (journal, 2 times a year, in English with some Spanish articles, free to members, otherwise £2 per copy)
History of the British Uruguayan Society 1945–1995 (1997) (£5 inc. p&p)
Tales of Uruguay (anthology of members' reminiscences, 1988, £5 inc. p&p)
History of the Uruguayan Short Story (Adams J, in preparation)

Access to staff:
Contact by letter and by telephone
Hours: Mon to Fri, 0900 to 1700

Affiliated to:
Hispanic and Luso-Brazilian Council
 tel: 020 7235 2303; fax: 020 7235 3587

BRITISH VALVE & ACTUATOR ASSOCIATION

Acronym or abbreviation: BVAMA

9 Manor Park, Banbury, OX16 3TB

Tel: 01295 221270
Fax: 01295 268965
E-mail: enquiry@bvaa.org.uk

Website:
http://www.bvaa.org.uk
Members information, product locator, members only information.

Enquiries:
Enquiries to: Director

Founded:
1939

Organisation type and purpose:
Trade association.

Subject coverage:
Industrial valves for the control of fluids.

Printed publications:
Valve Users Manual
Valves and Actuators from Britain (sale item only, 7th ed.)

Publications list:
Available online and in print

Access to staff:
Contact by letter, by telephone, by fax and by e-mail
Hours: Mon to Fri, 0900 to 1700

Access to building, collection or gallery:
Prior appointment required

BRITISH VENDEEN SHEEP SOCIETY

Formal name: British Vendeen Sheep Society Ltd
Acronym or abbreviation: BVSS

Darkes House, Conderton, Tewkesbury, Gloucestershire, GL20 7PP

Tel: 01386 725229
E-mail: info@vendeen.co.uk

Website:
http://www.vendeen.co.uk
Subscribing, flocks, sheep for sale.

Enquiries:
Enquiries to: Secretary

Founded:
1985

Organisation type and purpose:
National organisation, membership association (membership is by subscription), present number of members: 40, registered charity.
To promote and improve the breed of British Vendeen sheep.

Subject coverage:
Breeding and breeding from British Vendeen sheep.

Printed publications:
Flock Book

Access to staff:
Contact by letter, by telephone, by fax, by e-mail and in person
Hours: Any reasonable time

BRITISH VETERINARY ASSOCIATION

Acronym or abbreviation: BVA

7 Mansfield Street, London, W1G 9NQ

Tel: 020 7636 6541
E-mail: bvahq@bva.co.uk

Website:
http://www.bva.co.uk
General information on BVA services including annual congress.

Enquiries:
Enquiries to: Head of Media
Direct e-mail: press@bva.co.uk

Founded:
1882

Organisation type and purpose:
Professional body (membership is by subscription, election or invitation), present number of members: 10,000.
Houses the BVA Animal Welfare Foundation.
There are 2 branches (Scottish and Welsh), 30 territorial divisions and 20 specialist divisions within the Association.
The national representative body for the British veterinary profession.

Subject coverage:
Veterinary science, including animal health and welfare and public health.

Printed publications:
Handbooks, guidelines, etc
In Practice (monthly)
Journal of the Association of Veterinary Students (quarterly)
Veterinary Record (weekly)
Off The Record (monthly)
Publication list available for purchase
Order printed publications from: Ten Alps Subscriber Services, Coach House, Turners Drive, Thatcham, Berkshire RG19 4QB
6 Bourne Enterprise Centre, Wrotham Road, Borough Green, Wrotham, Kent, TN15 8DG, tel: 01732 884023, fax: 01732 884034

Publications list:
Available online and in print

Access to staff:
Contact by letter, by telephone, by e-mail and via website. Access for members only.
Hours: Mon to Fri, 0930 to 1700

Member organisation of:
Commonwealth Veterinary Association
Federation of Veterinarians in Europe
Inter-Professional Group
Parliamentary and Scientific Committee
Pet Advisory Committee
Pet Health Council
World Veterinary Association

Specialist divisions at the same address:
Association for Veterinary Teaching and Research Work
Association of Government Vets
Association of Veterinarians in Industry
Association of Veterinary Students
British Cattle Veterinary Association
British Equine Veterinary Association
British Laboratory Animals Veterinary Association
British Small Animal Veterinary Association
British Veterinary Hospitals Association
British Veterinary Poultry Association
British Veterinary Zoological Society
Fish Veterinary Society
Goat Veterinary Society
Pig Veterinary Society
Royal Army Veterinary Corps Division
Sheep Veterinary Society
Society for the Study of Animal Breeding
Society of Greyhound Veterinarians
Society of Practising Veterinary Surgeons
Veterinary Deer Society
Veterinary Public Health Association

BRITISH VIDEO ASSOCIATION

Acronym or abbreviation: BVA

167 Great Portland Street, London, W1W 5PE

Tel: 020 7436 0041
Fax: 020 7436 0043
E-mail: general@bva.org.uk

Website:
http://www.bva.org.uk

Enquiries:
Enquiries to: Director General

Founded:
1980

Organisation type and purpose:
Trade association.
Represent the interests of UK video rights owners.

continued overleaf

Subject coverage:
Trends in market of video rental and retail sales.

Trade and statistical information:
Quarterly statistical press release.

Printed publications:
British Video Association Yearbook

Access to staff:
Contact by letter, by telephone, by fax, by e-mail and via website. Appointment necessary.
Hours: Mon to Fri, 0930 to 1730

Affiliated to:
British Screen Advisory Council
  tel: 020 7287 1111
International Video Federation
  tel: 00 322 503 4063

BRITISH VOICE ASSOCIATION

Acronym or abbreviation: BVA

330 Grays Inn Road, London, WC1X 8EE

Tel: 020 7713 0064
Fax: 020 7915 1388
E-mail: bva@dircon.co.uk

Website:
http://www.british-voice-association.com

Enquiries:
Enquiries to: Administrator

Founded:
1991

Organisation type and purpose:
Professional body, registered charity.
An umbrella group for all professionals involved with the care of the human voice – from laryngologists and speech and language therapists to voice and singing teachers.

Subject coverage:
Multidisciplinary voice; otolaryngology; speech and language therapy; teachers of singing; singers; voice trainers, students of all of the above.

Printed publications:
List of voice clinics in the UK
Newsletter (3 times a year and published in print and web form)
Logopedics Phoniatrics Vocology (journal, 4 times a year)
List of members (members only)

Electronic and video publications:
Newsletter (online, 3 times a year)

Publications list:
Available online and in print

Access to staff:
Contact by letter, by telephone, by fax, by e-mail and via website
Hours: Mon to Fri, 0900 to 1700

Access for disabled people:
Parking provided, ramped entry, toilet facilities
Special comments: Please check for parking availability.

BRITISH WATCH AND CLOCKMAKERS GUILD

Acronym or abbreviation: BWCMG

PO Box 2368, Romford, Essex, RM1 2YZ

Tel: 01708 750616
Fax: 01708 750616

Enquiries:
Enquiries to: Honorary Secretary

Founded:
1907

Organisation type and purpose:
Trade association (membership is by election or invitation).
Trade organisation to protect the interests of those engaged in the watch, clock and general horological industry.

Subject coverage:
Horological and allied crafts.

Printed publications:
Newsletter (2 times a year)

Access to staff:
Contact by letter, by telephone and by fax
Hours: Mon to Fri, 1300 to 1800

BRITISH WATER

1 Queen Anne's Gate, London, SW1H 9BT

Tel: 020 7957 4554
Fax: 020 7957 4565
E-mail: info@britishwater.co.uk

Website:
http://www.britishwater.co.uk

Enquiries:
Enquiries to: Chief Executive
Other contacts: (1) International Director (2) Technical Director (3) UK Director for (1) inward/ outward trade missions (2) standards/regulations/ technology (3) industrial/municipal/domestic (POU) equipment.

Founded:
1993

Organisation type and purpose:
Trade association (membership is by subscription).
The British water and waste water industry worldwide.

Subject coverage:
Plant for the treatment of water for potable or industrial use; disinfection of swimming pools; plant for the treatment of domestic and municipal sewage and liquid industrial waste, and for industrial and waterworks sludges; domestic water softeners etc; statistics. With some 200 members, it promotes the involvement of all sectors in water-related projects, working closely with government and government departments at home and overseas; it organises outward and inward missions, seminars, exhibitions and other platforms to promote the technical, financial and administrative expertise of the British water sector. The organisation operates technical committees concerned with all aspects of the industry's activities and collaborates with British and European agencies in the development of standards.

Non-library collection catalogue:
All or part available online and in-house

Library catalogue:
All or part available online

Printed publications:
Annual Report
Codes of Practice for Swimming Pool Ozone Plant and Water Softeners
Guidance documents
Membership list including products, services and buyers' guide
Standards

Publications list:
Available online

Access to staff:
Contact by letter, by telephone, by fax, by e-mail and via website. Appointment necessary.
Hours: Mon to Fri, 0900 to 1700

Access to building, collection or gallery:
Prior appointment required

Links with:
Aqua Europa
  Geelseweg 56, B-2250, Olen, Belgium
METCOM
  Savoy Tower, Glasgow, G2 3BZ; tel: 0141 332 5788; fax: 0141 332 0826

BRITISH WEIGHT LIFTERS ASSOCIATION LIMITED

Acronym or abbreviation: BWLA

Lilleshall National Sports Centre, near Newport, Shropshire, TF10 9AT

Tel: 01952 604201
Fax: 01952 604265
E-mail: steve.cannon@uklifting.demon.co.uk

Website:
http://www.bwla.netcalm.co.uk
General information.

Enquiries:
Enquiries to: Chief Executive Officer

Organisation type and purpose:
Membership association (membership is by subscription), present number of members: 4,000, voluntary organisation.
Sports governing body.

Subject coverage:
Weightlifting, powerlifting, weight training and fitness training with weights.

Printed publications:
The BWLA Safe Weight Training Manual
The BWLA Handbook
The British Weight Lifter (magazine)
Training books

Publications list:
Available in print

Access to staff:
Contact by letter, by telephone and by fax
Hours: Mon to Fri, 0900 to 1700

Affiliated to:
European Powerlifting Federation
European Weightlifting Federation
International Powerlifting Federation
International Weightlifting Federation

Links with:
British Olympic Committee
Central Council of Physical Recreation
Commonwealth Games Council

Welsh Divisional Association:
British Amateur Weight Lifters Association
  Pennant Blaenau, Ammanford, Dyfed, SA18 3BZ

BRITISH WEIGHTS AND MEASURES ASSOCIATION

Acronym or abbreviation: BWMA

PO Box 590, London, WC1 X0U

Tel: 020 8922 0089 (24-hour answer machine)

Website:
http://www.bwmaonline.com
http://www.footrule.org

Enquiries:
Enquiries to: Director
Other contacts: Press Officer, tel no: 01568 708820, fax 01568 708765

Founded:
c1868

Organisation type and purpose:
Membership association.
To oppose compulsory metrication and to explain the good reasons for using traditional weights and measures.

Subject coverage:
The advantages of British weights and measures and the disadvantages of metrication.

Printed publications:
The Yardstick (quarterly, £10 a year)
The Footrule (newsletter, free to members)

Access to staff:
Contact by letter, by telephone and by fax
Hours: Mon to Fri, 0900 to 1700

Access to building, collection or gallery:
Prior appointment required

Access for disabled people:
Level entry, toilet facilities

BRITISH WHEEL OF YOGA, THE

25 Jermyn Street, Sleaford, Lincolnshire, NG34
7RU

Tel: 01529 306851
Fax: 01529 303233
E-mail: office@bwt.org.uk

Website:
http://www.bwy.org.uk

Enquiries:
Enquiries to: Central Office Manager
Direct tel: 01529 303881
Direct e-mail: office@bwy.org.uk

Founded:
1965

Organisation type and purpose:
National organisation, membership association
(membership is by subscription), present number
of members: 8400, registered charity (charity
number 264993), training organisation.
The governing body for yoga in Great Britain, non-
political, non-sectarian.
To encourage and help all persons to a greater
knowledge and understanding of all aspects of
Yoga and its practice by the provision of study,
education and training, to maintain and improve
the standard of teaching.

Subject coverage:
Yoga: philosophy involving meditation and
physical discipline; training of yoga teachers; yoga
for therapy and for the elderly and less able.

Printed publications:
Quarterly Regional Newsletter
Spectrum: quarterly magazine (for members)
Order printed publications from: BWY Services
e-mail: office@bwy.org.uk

Electronic and video publications:
British Wheel of Yoga (video/DVD)

Access to staff:
Contact by letter, by telephone, by fax, by e-mail
and via website
Hours: Mon to Fri, 0900 to 1700

Affiliated to:
European Union of National Federations of Yoga

Member of:
Central Council of Physical Recreation

BRITISH WHEELCHAIR SPORTS FOUNDATION

Acronym or abbreviation: BWSF

Guttmann Road, Stoke Mandeville, Aylesbury,
Buckinghamshire, HP21 9PP

Tel: 01296 395995
Fax: 01296 424171
E-mail: infos@bwsf.org.uk

Website:
http://www.bwsf.org.uk

Enquiries:
Enquiries to: Chief Executive
Other contacts: Head of Public Relations

Founded:
1952

Organisation type and purpose:
National organisation, membership association
(membership is by subscription, election or
invitation), present number of members: 1500,
voluntary organisation, registered charity (charity
number 265498).
National body for wheelchair sport – sport for
disabled people.

Subject coverage:
Wheelchair sports; archery, athletics, basketball,
bowls, fencing, rugby, shooting, snooker,
swimming, table tennis, tennis, weightlifting,
wintersports – sledge hockey and handcycling.

Printed publications:
Handbook (annually, free)
Newsletter (quarterly, free to members)

Access to staff:
Contact by letter, by telephone, by e-mail and via
website. Appointment necessary.
Hours: Mon to Fri, 0900 to 1700

Access to building, collection or gallery:
Prior appointment required

Access for disabled people:
Access to all public areas

Affiliated to:
British Paralympic Association
tel: 020 8681 9655

Member of:
International Paralympic Committee
International Stoke Mandeville Wheelchair Sports
Federation
tel: 01296 436179
Royal Association for Disability and Rehabilitation
tel: 020 7250 3222

BRITISH WILDLIFE PUBLISHING

The Old Dairy, Milton on Stour, Gillingham,
Dorset, SP8 5PX

Tel: 01747 835511
Fax: 01747 835522
E-mail: enquiries@britishwildlife.com

Website:
http://www.britishwildlife.com
Details of BW magazine.

Enquiries:
Enquiries to: Information Officer

Founded:
1989

Organisation type and purpose:
Publishing house.

Subject coverage:
Natural history, environment, conservation.

Printed publications:
British Wildlife (magazine, 6 times a year, for
  purchase)
Enact (magazine, 4 times a year, for purchase)

Access to staff:
Contact by letter
Hours: Mon to Fri, 0900 to 1700

BRITISH WILDLIFE RESCUE CENTRE

Acronym or abbreviation: BWRC

Amerton Working Farm, Amerton, Stafford, ST18
0LA

Tel: 01889 271308
E-mail: ahardy@thebwrc.co.uk

Website:
http://www.britishwildliferescue.co.uk

Enquiries:
Enquiries to: Owner

Founded:
1991

Organisation type and purpose:
Voluntary organisation, suitable for ages: all.

Subject coverage:
Rescue and rehabilitation of British wildlife,
animal hospital, centre open to the public, school
parties welcome, visits to schools, national
curriculum subjects covered.

Printed publications:
Newsletter (quarterly, free on receipt of sae)

Access to staff:
Contact by letter, by telephone and in person
Hours: Summer: Sun to Sat, 1000 to 1800
Winter: Sun to Sat, 1000 to 1700
Special comments: Closed Christmas Day, New
Year's Day

Access for disabled people:
Hours: Summer: Sun to Sat, 1000 to 1800
Winter: Sun to Sat, 1000 to 1700

Member and working links with:
Royal Society for the Prevention of Cruelty to
Animals (RSPCA)

Member of:
British Wildlife Rehabilitation Council
  website: www.bwrc.co.uk

Postal address only:
British Wildlife Rescue Centre
  35 Marston Road, Stafford, ST16 3BT; tel: 01785
  247486; e-mail: ahardy@thebwrc.org.uk; website:
  http://www.thebwrc.co.uk

BRITISH WIRELESS FOR THE BLIND FUND

Acronym or abbreviation: BWBF

10 Albion Place, Maidstone, Kent, ME14 5DZ

Tel: 01622 754757
Fax: 01622 751727
E-mail: info@blind.org.uk

Website:
http://www.blind.org.uk
Information and details of products and services
provided by the charity.

Enquiries:
Enquiries to: Chief Executive
Other contacts: Fundraiser

Founded:
1929

Organisation type and purpose:
Registered charity (charity number 211849).
To provide the comfort of radio listening to the
registered blind in need.

Subject coverage:
Free permanent loan of radio, radio/cassette
players and CD/radio/cassette players for
registered blind people.

Services for disabled people:
Provision of radios and associated equipment to
registered blind and registered partially sighted
people resident in the United Kingdom, over the
age of 8 and in need. Sets can be sold to those who
do not qualify through the trading arm of the
charity.

Printed publications:
Annual Report and Accounts
Deed of Covenant (brochures)
Make a Will (brochures)
Talkabout (newsletter)
Who We Are, What We Do and How You Can
  Help (brochures)

Access to staff:
Contact by letter, by telephone, by fax, by e-mail
and via website. Appointment necessary.
Hours: Mon to Fri, 0900 to 1700

Access for disabled people:
full disabled access

BRITISH WOMEN PILOTS' ASSOCIATION

Acronym or abbreviation: BWPA

Brooklands Museum, Brooklands Road,
Weybridge, Surrey, KT13 0QN

E-mail: info@bwpa.co.uk

Website:
http://www.bwpa.co.uk

Enquiries:
Enquiries to: Chairman
Direct fax: 020 8763 2922

Founded:
1955

Organisation type and purpose:
Membership association (membership is by
subscription).

continued overleaf

Subject coverage:
Women in aviation. Careers in Aviation.

Printed publications:
Annual Gazette
Newsletter (members only)

Access to staff:
Contact by letter and via website
Hours: Mon to Fri, 0900 to 1700

BRITISH YOUTH COUNCIL

Acronym or abbreviation: BYC

Downstream Building, The Mezzanine 2, 1 London Bridge, SE1 9BG

Tel: 0845 458 1489
Fax: 0845 458 1847
E-mail: mail@byc.org.uk

Website:
http://www.byc.org.uk
What BYC does; outline of activities; list of publications.

Enquiries:
Enquiries to: Policy and Press Officer
Direct tel: 0845 458 1489
Direct e-mail: helen.deakin@byc.org.uk

Founded:
1948

Organisation type and purpose:
Membership association (membership is by subscription), present number of members: 130 member organisations, voluntary organisation, registered charity (charity number 305973).
The British Youth Council is the independent voice of young people in the UK.
Representing the views of young people in government and decision-makers at national and international levels.

Subject coverage:
Interests and views of young people, advocacy for the increased participation of young people in society.

Printed publications:
Publications include:
BYC News – Quarterly Newsletter
A Young Person's Guide to Lobbying
Listening to the Unheard: The National Youth
 Consultation for the European Youth Policy
 (2000)
Peer Education – The British Youth Council's
 Manual
State of the Young Nation – A Report by the British
 Youth Council (1998)
Youth Index – an information and analysis service
 with 2 publications:
Youth Agenda (monthly)
Youth Update (monthly)
Order printed publications from: Policy and Research Officer, British Youth Council
at the same address, tel: 020 7422 8644, e-mail: louise.king@byc.org.uk

Publications list:
Available in print

Access to staff:
Contact by letter, by telephone, by e-mail and via website. Appointment necessary.
Hours: Mon to Fri, 0930 to 1800

Access to building, collection or gallery:
Prior appointment required

Access for disabled people:
Ramped entry

BRITISH-GERMAN ASSOCIATION

Acronym or abbreviation: BGA

34 Belgrave Square, London, SW1X 8QB

Tel: 020 7235 1922
Fax: 020 7235 1902
E-mail: BGALondon@compuserve.com

Enquiries:
Enquiries to: Honorary Treasurer
Direct tel: 020 7244 7663
Direct fax: 020 7373 3415

Founded:
1951

Organisation type and purpose:
Membership association (membership is by subscription), present number of members: 1000, registered charity (charity number 206062).
Promotion of Anglo-German relations on an educational and cultural basis.

Subject coverage:
All aspects of German affairs and British-German cultural and educational relations.

Printed publications:
British-German Review (quarterly, for members)
Diary of Activities (for members)
Order printed publications from: Editor-in-Chief, British-German Review
April House, Balcombe, Sussex, RH17 6LF, tel: 01444 811237, fax: 01444 811237

Access to staff:
Contact by letter, by telephone and by fax
Hours: Mon to Fri, 1100 to 1600

Connected with:
Deutsch Englische Gesellschaft (DEG)
Jaegerstrasse 54/5, Berlin, D10112, Germany; tel: 030 203 983

BRITISH-ISRAEL-WORLD FEDERATION

Acronym or abbreviation: BIWF

121 Low Etherley, Bishop Auckland, DL14 0HA

Tel: 01388 834395
Fax: 01388 835957
E-mail: admin@britishisrael.co.uk

Website:
http://www.britishisrael.co.uk
Publications catalogue, basis outline of belief/research, membership details.

Enquiries:
Enquiries to: Administrator

Founded:
1919

Organisation type and purpose:
International organisation, national organisation (membership is by subscription), present number of members: 300, registered charity (charity number 208079), research organisation, publishing house.
Christian heritage research into Anglo-Saxon-Celtic peoples as the modern-day descendants of the ancient Hebrew race and nation of Israel which spread to the west from the Assyrian and Babylonian Captivities.

Subject coverage:
Migrations of Israel in Europe; scriptural evidence, bible prophecy, early Christian Church, 1st century in Britain, charts of royal descent, heraldry showing British links with Israel, current events.

Museum or gallery collection, archive, or library special collection:
Books in library, not open to public

Printed publications:
The following are published by The Covenant
 Publishing Company Limited
The Origin and Early History of Christianity in
 Britain
Eating for Life
Celt, Druid and Culdee
The Hidden Treasure of the Parables
Royal House of Britain an Enduring Dynasty
Order printed publications from: The Covenant Publishing Company Limited
at the same address

Publications list:
Available online and in print

Access to staff:
Contact by letter, by telephone, by fax, by e-mail and via website. Appointment necessary.
Hours: Mon to Fri, 0900 to 1700

Access to building, collection or gallery:
Prior appointment required
Hours: Access for publications by prior appointment

Access for disabled people:
Parking provided, toilet facilities
Special comments: Level entry at rear from parking area.

Associated with similar:
Christian Israel Organisations in: Australia, Canada, Holland, New Zealand, South Africa and USA

BRITISH-ITALIAN SOCIETY

The Offices of Venice in Peril Fund, Hurlingham Studios (Unit 4), Ranelagh Gardens, London, SW6 3PA

Tel: 020 8150 9167
E-mail: jj@british-italian.org

Website:
http://www.british-italian.org

Enquiries:
Enquiries to: General Secretary

Founded:
1941

Organisation type and purpose:
Learned society, membership association (membership is by subscription), present number of members: 500, registered charity (charity number 253386).
To increase understanding of Italy in this country and to promote friendship between Great Britain and Italy.

Subject coverage:
General information on Italy.
No employment contacts.

Printed publications:
Rivista (quarterly, for members or by subscription)

Access to staff:
Contact by letter, by telephone, by fax and by e-mail
Hours: 3 days per week variable

Access to building, collection or gallery:
Prior appointment required

BRITISH-KAZAKH SOCIETY

Formal name: British-Kazakh Society

105 Salisbury Road, London, NW6 6RG

Tel: 020 7596 5176
Fax: 020 7596 5115
E-mail: info@bksoc.org.uk

Website:
http://www.bksoc.org.uk

Founded:
2002

Organisation type and purpose:
Individual and corporate membership organisation (membership by subscription)
To promote relations between the UK and Kazakhstan.

Access to staff:
Contact by letter, by telephone, by fax, by e-mail and via website

BRITISHSERBIAN BENEVOLENT TRUST

Acronym or abbreviation: B-SBT

Glebelands, Star Lane, Rockland St Mary, Norwich, NR14 7BX

Tel: 01508 480262
Fax: 01508 480262
E-mail: orns@lineone.net

Enquiries:
Enquiries to: Chairman

Founded:
1917

Organisation type and purpose:
National organisation, registered charity (charity number 254179).
Charitable trust.

Subject coverage:
The relief of children resident in Serbia who are in conditions of need, hardship or distress.

Access to staff:
Contact by letter, by telephone, by fax and by e-mail. Appointment necessary.
Hours: Mon to Fri, 0900 to 1700

BRITTEN-PEARS LIBRARY

The Red House, Golf Lane, Aldeburgh, Suffolk, IP15 5PZ

Tel: 01728 451700
Fax: 01728 453076
E-mail: bpl@britten-pears.co.uk

Website:
http://www.britten-pears.co.uk
General information; access; collections; catalogue; exhibitions; publications; bibliography.

Enquiries:
Enquiries to: Director
Other contacts: Curator for Reader Services for reader admissions.

Founded:
1980

Organisation type and purpose:
Registered charity (charity number 295595), research organisation, publishing house.
Private research library.

Subject coverage:
Benjamin Britten's life, career and music, Peter Pears's life and career, English song (books and music), Gustav Holst's music, English Opera Group/English Music Theatre, Aldeburgh Festival, music in general.

Museum or gallery collection, archive, or library special collection:
Benjamin Britten's manuscripts (some on permanent loan from the British Library)
Britten's collection of printed music
Britten's personal papers (including correspondence and diaries)
Printers' copies, proofs and early editions of Britten's works
Peter Pears's collection of printed music
Pears's personal papers (including correspondence)
Extensive collection of sound recordings and video cassettes (chiefly relating to Britten and Pears)
English Opera Group/English Music Theatre Archive
Aldeburgh Festival Archive
Archive of press cuttings and programmes (chiefly relating to Britten and Pears)
Photographic archives (chiefly relating to Britten and Pears)
Manuscripts of works by other composers, including Bax, Bedford, L Berkeley, M Berkeley, Bridge, Crosse, Maxwell Davies, C A Gibbs, Greene, Harvey, Henze, G Holst, I Holst, Knussen, Lehmann, Lutoslawski, Maconchy, C Matthews, D Matthews, Maw, Moeran, Nash, Oldham, Quilter, Rainier, Saxton, Seiber, Shostakovich, Stanford, Tippett, Turnage, Weir, Wellesz, Williamson
Literary manuscripts, including those of W H Auden, Ronald Duncan, E M Forster, Thomas Hardy, Wilfred Owen, Myfanwy Piper, William Plomer, Edith Sitwell
English Song (from 16th century to present day)
Julian Herbage material relating to Thomas Arne

Holst Library, a lending library for use of students attending the Britten-Pears School for Advanced Musical Studies

Non-library collection catalogue:
All or part available online

Printed publications:
Benjamin Britten: A Catalogue of the Published Works
Britten and the Far East: Asian Influences in the Music of Benjamin Britten
The Making of Peter Grimes: A Facsimile of Benjamin Britten's Composition Draft
On Mahler and Britten: Essays in Honour of Donald Mitchell on His Seventieth Birthday
The Travel Diaries of Peter Pears
Britten's Gloriana: Essays and Sources
A Britten Source Book
Music of Forty Festivals: A list of works performed at the Aldeburgh Festivals from 1948 to 1987
Transcripts of the Prince of Hesse Memorial Lectures 1990 to 2000

Publications list:
Available online and in print

Access to staff:
Contact by letter, by telephone, by fax, by e-mail and via website. Appointment necessary.
Hours: Mon to Fri, 1000 to 1300 and 1415 to 1715, closed on bank holidays

Access to building, collection or gallery:
Prior appointment required

Access for disabled people:
Level entry, toilet facilities

Administers the:
Holst Library

BRITTEN-PEARS YOUNG ARTIST PROGRAMME

Acronym or abbreviation: BPP

Snape Maltings Concert Hall, Snape, Saxmundham, Suffolk, IP17 1SP

Tel: 01728 688671
Fax: 01728 688171
E-mail: britten-pears@aldeburgh.co.uk

Website:
http://www.aldeburgh.co.uk
Information about the Britten-Pears Young Artist Programme, including courses for 2005 and an on-line application form.

Enquiries:
Enquiries to: Assistant
Other contacts: Administrator for orchestral enquiries.

Founded:
1972

Organisation type and purpose:
Music school.
The Britten-Pears Programme offers a unique opportunity for young professionals and advanced students to study intensively with some of the world's most respected musicians.

Access to staff:
Contact by letter, by telephone, by fax, by e-mail and via website
Hours: Mon to Fri, 0930 to 1730

Parent body:
Aldeburgh Productions
Snape Maltings Concert Hall, Snape, Saxmundham, Suffolk, IP17 1SP; tel: 01708 687100; fax: 01728 687120; e-mail: info@aldeburgh.co.uk

BRITTLE BONE SOCIETY

Acronym or abbreviation: BBS

Grant-Paterson House, 30 Guthrie Street, Dundee, DD1 5BS

Tel: 01382 204446 Freephone 08000 282459

Fax: 01382 206771
E-mail: bbs@brittlebone.org

Enquiries:
Enquiries to: Chief Executive

Founded:
1968

Organisation type and purpose:
Registered charity (Scottish registered charity SCO10951).
Promoting research and providing information and support for people and their relatives.

Subject coverage:
The society seeks to promote research into the causes, inheritance and treatment of osteogenesis imperfecta, characterised by excessive fragility of the bones. It also provides advice, encouragement and practical help for patients and their relatives facing the difficulties of living with brittle bones, practical aspects of living with brittle bones, education, wheelchairs and other equipment.

Publications list:
Available in print

Access to staff:
Contact by letter, by telephone and by e-mail. Appointment necessary.
Hours: Mon to Fri, 0900 to 1630

Access to building, collection or gallery:
Hours: Mon to Fri, 0900 to 1630

Charity Shop:
BBS Shop
112 City Road, Dundee; tel: 01382 667603

BROADCASTING GROUP OF THE SOCIETY OF AUTHORS

Acronym or abbreviation: SoA

84 Drayton Gardens, London, SW10 9SB

Tel: 020 7373 6642
Fax: 020 7373 5768
E-mail: info@societyofauthors.org

Enquiries:
Enquiries to: Assistant General Secretary

Organisation type and purpose:
Trade union.

Subject coverage:
Writing for radio and television.

Access to staff:
Contact by letter and by e-mail
Hours: 0930 to 1730

BROADCASTING, ENTERTAINMENT, CINEMATOGRAPH AND THEATRE UNION

Acronym or abbreviation: BECTU

373–377 Clapham Road, London, SW9 9BT

Tel: 020 7346 0900
Fax: 020 7346 0901
E-mail: info@bectu.org.uk

Website:
http://www.bectu.org.uk

Enquiries:
Enquiries to: Administrator

Founded:
1991

Incorporates the former:
ABS, ACTT, FAA, NATTKE (year of change 1991)

Organisation type and purpose:
Trade union, present number of members: 26,000.

Subject coverage:
The interests of workers in broadcasting, film, theatre and related areas of the arts and media.

continued overleaf

Museum or gallery collection, archive, or library special collection:
Documents of the Unions dating back to 1890 (uncatalogued)

Printed publications:
Stage, Screen and Radio (journal, 10 times a year)

Access to staff:
Contact by letter, by telephone, by e-mail and via website. Access for members only.
Hours: Mon to Fri, 0900 to 1700

Access for disabled people:
Wheelchair lift, toilet facilities, induction loop

Affiliated via Federation of Entertainment Unions to:
Irish Congress of Trade Unions

Affiliated to:
Trades Union Congress

Affiliated via Federation of Entertainment Unions to:
Labour Party
Uni-Media Entertainment International
Wales Trades Union Congress

Member organisations:
Scottish Trades Union Congress

BROADLAND DISTRICT COUNCIL

Thorpe Lodge, 1 Yarmouth Road, Thorpe St Andrew, Norwich, Norfolk, NR7 0DU

Tel: 01603 431133\ Minicom no. 01603 703399
Fax: 01603 300087
E-mail: business@broadland.gov.uk

Website:
http://www.broadland.gov.uk
Services for local people, tourism and business development information.

Enquiries:
Enquiries to: Communications Manager
Direct tel: 01603 430523
Direct fax: 01603 430614
Direct e-mail: angi.day@broadland.gov.uk

Founded:
1974

Organisation type and purpose:
Local government body.

Subject coverage:
Broadland District Council area, services and amenities.

Printed publications:
Training Prospectus & Business Directory
Broadland News (3 times a year)
Property Register

Access to staff:
Contact by letter, by telephone, by fax, by e-mail and via website. Appointment necessary.
Hours: Mon to Fri, 0900 to 1700

Access for disabled people:
Parking provided, ramped entry

BROADS AUTHORITY, THE

18 Colegate, Norwich, Norfolk, NR3 1BQ

Tel: 01603 610734
Fax: 01603 765710
E-mail: broads@broads-authority.gov.uk

Website:
http://www.broads-authority.gov.uk
General and Press.

Enquiries:
Enquiries to: Information Officer

Founded:
1989

Organisation type and purpose:
Local government body.
Equivalent to national park.

Subject coverage:
The Broads: conservation (including planning), recreation, navigation.

Printed publications:
Broads Authority Research Series
Broads Design and Management Information
Project Design Series (prices vary)
Research Series (prices vary)
The Broads Plan 2004 (£5, inc. p&p)
Various general titles including:
Broads Fact pack: two books covering all aspects of the Broads life and landscape (£2.99)
Broad Walks: maps and guides to eight walks in the Bure Valley (£2.50)
Hathor, goddess of love and joy: the story of a Norfolk pleasure wherry (£2)

Publications list:
Available online and in print

Access to staff:
Contact by letter, by telephone, by fax and by e-mail. Appointment necessary.
Hours: Mon to Fri, 0900 to 1700

BROADS SOCIETY

Solar Via, Happisburgh, Norwich, Norfolk, NR12 0QU

Tel: 01692 651321
E-mail: broads_society.admin@bigfoot.com

Website:
http://www.broads-society.org.uk
Description of Broads environment, ecology, recreation, navigation and role of Society in preservation and enhancement.

Enquiries:
Enquiries to: Administrator

Founded:
1956

Organisation type and purpose:
Membership association (membership is by subscription), present number of members: 1700, voluntary organisation, registered charity (charity number 1078434).
Voluntary body dedicated to securing a sustainable future for The Broads as a unique and protected landscape in which leisure, tourism and the local economy can thrive in harmony with the natural environment.

Subject coverage:
Wetland conservation, navigation on inland waters.

Museum or gallery collection, archive, or library special collection:
Collection of all back issues of quarterly magazine

Printed publications:
The Harnser (magazine, quarterly, ISSN 1368–5554, free to members, back issues available free from administrator)

Access to staff:
Contact by letter, by telephone, by e-mail and via website
Hours: Any reasonable time; 24-hour answering service

Chairman at:
Broads Society
at the main address

Editor at:
Broads Society Editor
Grebe Cottage, New Road, Catfield, Great Yarmouth, NR29 5BQ; tel: 01692 584179; e-mail: harnser2006@yahoo.co.uk

BROMLEY COLLEGE OF FURTHER AND HIGHER EDUCATION

Acronym or abbreviation: BCFHE

Rookery Lane, Bromley, Kent, BR2 8HE

Tel: 020 8295 7000
Fax: 020 8295 7099

E-mail: library@bromley.ac.uk

Website:
http://www.bromley.ac.uk
Qualifications offered; international information; information request form; College news; course list and course details.

Enquiries:
Enquiries to: Librarian
Direct tel: 020 8295 7024
Direct e-mail: judym@bromley.ac.uk

Founded:
1959

Organisation type and purpose:
Suitable for ages: all.
Library of a college of further and higher education.

Subject coverage:
Life science, engineering (electrical, mechanical and motor vehicle), social work, business, finance, law, IT, software engineering, hairdressing and beauty therapy, leisure, travel and tourism, counselling, teaching and training, media, built environment, sport.

Library catalogue:
All or part available online and in-house

Access to staff:
Contact by telephone, by e-mail and via website. Appointment necessary.
Hours: Mon to Fri, 0900 to 1700

Access for disabled people:
Parking provided, ramped entry, toilet facilities

Other addresses:
Old Town Hall Site
Tweedy Road, Bromley, BR2 8HE; tel: 020 8295 7091

BROMLEY HOUSE LIBRARY

Acronym or abbreviation: BHL

Bromley House, Angel Row, Nottingham, NG1 6HL

Tel: 0115 947 3134
E-mail: enquiries@bromleyhouse.org

Website:
http://www.bromleyhouse.org

Enquiries:
Enquiries to: Librarian

Founded:
1816

Organisation type and purpose:
Membership association (membership is by subscription), present number of members: 1000, registered charity (charity number 1074752).
Private library for research purposes.

Subject coverage:
Victorian fiction, history, local history, biography, travel, theology.

Printed publications:
Bromley House 1752–1991 (ed Coope R and Corbett J, £6, pbk)

Access to staff:
Contact by letter, by telephone and by e-mail. Appointment necessary. Access for members only. Letter of introduction required.
Hours: Mon to Fri, 0930 to 1700

Access for disabled people:
No disabled access
Special comments: Situated on first floor and above.

BROMLEY PUBLIC LIBRARIES

Central Library, High Street, Bromley, Kent, BR1 1EX

Tel: 020 8460 9955
Fax: 020 8466 7860
E-mail: reference.library@bromley.gov.uk

Website:
http://www.bromley.gov.uk/libraries

Enquiries:
Enquiries to: Principal Library Service Manager

Organisation type and purpose:
Local government body, public library.

Subject coverage:
General; geography, travel and history of all countries, excluding Europe, history and studies of the London Borough of Bromley, business information.

Museum or gallery collection, archive, or library special collection:
Crystal Palace Collection
H. G. Wells Collection
Harlow Bequest (Orpington and Kent)
Walter de la Mare Collection

Library catalogue:
All or part available online

Printed publications:
Bibliographies
Catalogue of the H. G. Wells Collection
Various local history publications
Order printed publications from: Local Studies Librarian, Central Library, High Street, Bromley, BR1 1EX; tel. 020 8461 7170; fax 020 8466 7860; e-mail localstudies.library@bromley.gov.uk

Access to staff:
Contact by letter, by telephone, by e-mail and in person
Hours: Central Library: Mon, Wed, Fri, 0930 to 1800; Tue, Thu, 0930 to 2000; Sat, 0930 to 1700
Branch Libraries: open at 0930 but are all closed one day a week (Burnt Ash three days, Hayes three days), so telephone first

Branch libraries:
Anerley Library
  Anerley Town Hall, Anerley Road, Anerley, SE20 8BD; tel: 020 8778 7457
Beckenham Library
  Beckenham Road, Beckenham, BR3 4PE; tel: 020 8650 7292
Biggin Hill Library
  Church Road, Biggin Hill, TN16 3LB; tel: 01959 574468
Burnt Ash Library
  Burnt Ash Lane, Bromley, BR1 5AF; tel: 020 8460 3405
Chislehurst Library
  Red Hill, Chislehurst, BR7 6DA; tel: 020 8467 1318
Hayes Library
  Hayes Street, Hayes, BR2 7LH; tel: 020 8462 2445
Mottingham Library
  31 Mottingham Road, Mottingham, SE9 4QZ; tel: 020 8857 5406
Orpington Library
  The Priory, Church Hill, Orpington, BR6 0HH; tel: 01689 831551
Penge Library
  186 Maple Road, Penge, SE20 8HT; tel: 020 8778 8772
Petts Wood Library
  Frankswood Road, Petts Wood, BR5 1BP; tel: 01689 821607
Shortlands Library
  110 Shortlands Road, Bromley, BR2 0JP; tel: 020 8460 9692
Southborough Library
  Southborough Lane, Bromley, BR2 8HP; tel: 020 8467 0355
St Paul's Cray Library
  Mickleham Road, St Paul's Cray, Kent, BR5 2RW; tel: 020 8300 5454
West Wickham Library
  Glebe Way, West Wickham, BR4 0SH; tel: 020 8777 4139

Parent body:
The London Borough of Bromley

BROMYARD AND DISTRICT LOCAL HISTORY SOCIETY

5 Sherford Street, Bromyard, Herefordshire, HR7 4DL

Tel: 01885 488755
E-mail: bromyard.history@virgin.net

Website:
http://www.bromyardhistorysociety.org.uk

Founded:
1966

Organisation type and purpose:
A registered charity (no. 1051572), with a Local History Centre at 5 Sherford Street run by volunteers.

Subject coverage:
History of Bromyard and the surrounding area.

Museum or gallery collection, archive, or library special collection:
Archive of documents, books, maps, newspapers and photographs

Printed publications:
Newsletter

Access to building, collection or gallery:
Hours: Thu and Fri, 1000 to 1300 and 1400 to 1630; Sat, 1000 to 1230

BRONTË SOCIETY

The Brontë Parsonage Museum, Church Street, Haworth, Keighley, West Yorkshire, BD22 8DR

Tel: 01535 642323
Fax: 01535 647131
E-mail: bronte@bronte.org.uk

Website:
http://www.bronte.info
Information about the Brontë Parsonage Museum and the Brontë Society.

Enquiries:
Enquiries to: Library and Information Officer
Direct tel: 01535 640199
Direct fax: 01535 647131
Direct e-mail: sarah.laycock@bronte.org.uk
Other contacts: Director, Brontë Parsonage Museum for all matters concerning the museum.

Founded:
1893

Organisation type and purpose:
Learned society (membership is by subscription), present number of members: 1750, voluntary organisation, registered charity (charity number 529952), suitable for ages: all.
Entrusted with the ownership and care of the Brontë Parsonage Museum.
To stimulate interest in the writing and the history of the Brontë Family and to promote understanding of their contemporary significance as an integral part of the intellectual, cultural and historical heritage of world literature.

Subject coverage:
The writings of the Brontës and those associated with them; interpretations of their lives and works, subsequent biographies, monographs and scholarly criticism.

Museum or gallery collection, archive, or library special collection:
Books, manuscripts, drawings, furnishings and artefacts owned by the Brontës
Bonnell Collection: archive of manuscripts, drawings, first editions, Brontës' own books
Brontë Society General Collection: archive of manuscripts, letters, drawings, first editions, Brontës' own books, furniture, personal memorabilia
Grolier Collection of manuscripts
Seton Gordon Collection of manuscripts

Non-library collection catalogue:
All or part available in-house

Printed publications:
The Art of The Brontës (catalogue)
Journal of the Brontë Studies (journal, 3 times a year, by subscription, reduced rate for members)
The Brontë Parsonage Museum (Guide to the house, with Brontë chronology)
The Brontë Society Gazette (newsletter, free to members)

Access to staff:
Contact by letter, by telephone, by fax, by e-mail and via website. Appointment necessary.
Hours: Mon to Fri, 1000 to 1630
Special comments: Visitors to the research library by prior appointment. Academic reference required in advance for access to primary sources.

Affiliated to:
Irish Brontë Society

Member of:
Alliance of Literary Societies (ALS)
Association of Independent Museums (AIM)
Yorkshire and Humberside Museums Council (YMHC)

BROOKLANDS SOCIETY LIMITED

Rudgelands, 4 Blackstone Hill, Redhill, Surrey, RH1 6BE

Tel: 01737 217221
Fax: 01737 764401
E-mail: reynolds@rudgelands.prestel.co.uk

Website:
http://www.brooklands.org.uk

Enquiries:
Enquiries to: Assistant Secretary

Founded:
1967

Organisation type and purpose:
International organisation, learned society, membership association (membership is by subscription), present number of members: 1350, voluntary organisation.

Subject coverage:
Brookland motor course and airfield, history and preservation of relics.

Museum or gallery collection, archive, or library special collection:
Large archive of films, photographs and artefacts related to the Brooklands motor course and the personalities involved for the period 1907–1987

Printed publications:
The following are available free or for purchase direct:
Occasional Historic Publications
Quarterly Gazette
Quarterly Newsletter

Publications list:
Available online and in print

Access to staff:
Contact by letter, by telephone, by fax, by e-mail and via website. Appointment necessary.
Hours: Mon to Fri, 0900 to 1700

Access to building, collection or gallery:
Prior appointment required

Affiliated to:
Brooklands Museum Trust
  Brooklands Museum, Brooklands Road, Weybridge, Surrey, KT13 0QN

Website management:
Brooklands Society Limited
  Hartland, Copse Corner, 38 Coxheath Road, Church Crookham, Hampshire, GU13 0QC; tel: 01252 408877; fax: 01252 408878; e-mail: brooklands@hartland.co.uk

BROOM'S BARN RESEARCH STATION

Higham, Bury St Edmunds, Suffolk, IP28 6NP

continued overleaf

Tel: 01284 812200
Fax: 01284 811191

Website:
http://www.broomsbarn.ac.uk
Advisory information for UK sugar beet growers
and advisers, areas of research, job vacancies.

Enquiries:
Enquiries to: Information Officer
Direct tel: 01284 812230
Direct e-mail: mike.may@bbsrc.ac.uk

Organisation type and purpose:
Research organisation.
Agricultural research station for English sugar beet
crop.

Subject coverage:
Sugar beet crop rotation: seed quality, fertiliser
practice, irrigation, crop agronomy; sugar beet
crop protection: seedling pests and diseases, beet
cyst nematode, virus yellows and vector aphids,
leaf diseases, rhizomania, weed control.

Library catalogue:
All or part available in-house

Printed publications:
Growers Guide (every 4 to 5 years)
Reprints of Scientific Papers (free)
Station Guide (free)

Access to staff:
Contact by letter, by telephone, by fax and by e-
mail
Hours: Mon to Thu, 0830 to 1700; Fri, 0830 to 1630

Funded by:
Biotechnology and Biological Sciences Research
Council

BROUGH SUPERIOR CLUB

Flint Cottage, St Pauls Walden, Hitchin,
Hertfordshire, SG4 8DN

Tel: 01438 871714

Enquiries:
Enquiries to: Secretary

Organisation type and purpose:
Voluntary organisation.

Subject coverage:
Preservation and use of W.E. Brough and Brough
Superior Motorcycles, and any knowledge relating
to these.

BROUGHAM HALL CHARITABLE TRUST

Acronym or abbreviation: BHCT

Brougham Hall, Brougham, Penrith, Cumbria,
CA10 2DE

Tel: 01768 868184
Fax: 01768 862306
E-mail: juliachurchill@btinternet.com

Website:
http://www.broughamhall.co.uk

Enquiries:
Enquiries to: Administrator

Founded:
1986

Organisation type and purpose:
Registered charity (charity number 517943),
museum, historic building, house or site, suitable
for ages: school leavers and undergraduates;
training organisation, consultancy, research
organisation, publishing house.

Subject coverage:
Vernacular crafts, architecture, stone masonry,
political history.

**Museum or gallery collection, archive, or library
special collection:**
A collection of books, documents, manuscripts,
pictures, photographs and other materials

Library catalogue:
All or part available in-house

Printed publications:
A History of Brougham Hall and Highhead Castle
(Philimore, 1992, £30, direct)
Windsor of the North (Ross, 1999, £9, direct)
Order printed publications from: Brougham Hall,
Brougham, Penrith, Cumbria, CA10 2DE

Publications list:
Available in print

Access to staff:
Contact by letter
Hours: Mon to Fri, 0900 to 1700
Special comments: Prior appointment preferred.

Access to building, collection or gallery:
No prior appointment required
Hours: Mon to Fri, 0900 to 1700

Access for disabled people:
Parking provided, ramped entry, level entry, toilet
facilities
Special comments: Access to most areas, including
cafe

BROXBOURNE BOROUGH COUNCIL

Borough Offices, Bishops' College, Churchgate,
Cheshunt, Hertfordshire, EN8 9XQ

Tel: 01992 785555\ Minicom no. 01992 785581
Fax: 01992 785578
E-mail: enquiry@broxbourne.gov.uk

Website:
http://www.broxbourne.gov.uk

Enquiries:
Enquiries to: Senior Communications Officer

Founded:
1974

Organisation type and purpose:
Local government body.

Subject coverage:
Local information, tourism, recycling, refuse,
environment, leisure facilities, social housing,
building control, planning and development,
council tax.

Access to staff:
Contact by letter, by telephone, by fax, by e-mail
and via website
Hours: Mon, Wed, Thu, 0800 to 1800; Tue, 0800 to
1930; Fri, 0800 to 1730; Sat, 0900 to 1300

Access for disabled people:
Parking provided, level entry, access to all public
areas, toilet facilities

Also at:
Broxbourne Borough Council
Unit 5, Broxbourne Business Centre, New River
Estate, Cheshunt, Waltham Cross, Hertfordshire,
EN8 0NP; tel: 01992 642240; fax: 01992 642216; e-
mail: broxserv@broxbourne.gov.uk

BRUNEL INSTITUTE FOR BIOENGINEERING

Acronym or abbreviation: BIB

Information Unit, Brunel University, Uxbridge,
Middlesex, UB8 3PH

Tel: 01895 266926
Fax: 01895 274608
E-mail: dawn.brandl@brunel.ac.uk

Website:
http://www.brunel.ac.uk

Enquiries:
Enquiries to: Information Officer

Founded:
1983

Organisation type and purpose:
University department or institute.

Commercial institute attached to Brunel
University.

Subject coverage:
mainly countercurrent chromatography and
centrifugal partition chromatography, but will
compile bibliographies on any relevant subject

Printed publications:
Bibliography of counter-current chromatography
1964–2004 (£50)

Access to staff:
Contact by letter, by telephone, by fax, by e-mail
and in person. Appointment necessary. Non-
members charged.
Hours: Fri, 0730 to 1500

Access for disabled people:
Toilet facilities

BRUNEL UNIVERSITY

Library, Uxbridge, Middlesex, UB8 3PH

Tel: 01895 266154
Fax: 01895 203263
E-mail: library@brunel.ac.uk

Website:
http://www.brunel.ac.uk/lite/study/library

Enquiries:
Direct tel: 01896 266154

Founded:
1965

Organisation type and purpose:
University library.

Subject coverage:
Biology, computer science, economics, electrical
engineering, government, human sciences, law,
mathematics, health sciences, arts and media,
education, design, management, government,
social work, sports science, occupational therapy,
physiotherapy, sports medicine, sports science,
education, social work, arts and humanities.

**Museum or gallery collection, archive, or library
special collection:**
Collection of Working Class autobiographies
Channel Tunnel Library and Archive (Runnymede
Campus)
Clinker and Garnett Railway Collection
(Runnymede Campus)
I K Brunel photographs (please direct enquiries to
Library Office)
Maria Grey Archives (Runnymede Campus)
Murray Collection (Victorian children's books)
(Runnymede Campus)
Salmon Collection (books and pamphlets on
Joseph Lancaster in the British and Foreign
School Society Archives) (Runnymede Campus)

Library catalogue:
All or part available online

Access to staff:
Contact by letter, by telephone and by e-mail.
Appointment necessary.
Hours: Hours may vary during weekends,
vacations and semesters

Access for disabled people:
Access to all public areas, toilet facilities

BSA FRONT-WHEEL DRIVE CLUB

Acronym or abbreviation: BSAFWDC

93 Barkby Road, Syston, Leicestershire, LE7 2AH

Tel: 0116 260 9663

Website:
http://www.bsafwdc.co.uk

Enquiries:
Enquiries to: Information Officer

Founded:
1959

Organisation type and purpose:
To preserve the BSA front-wheel drive car and to maintain its position in the history of motor-engineering.

Subject coverage:
BSA front-wheel drive 3- and 4-wheel cars produced from 1929 to 1939. Also caters for RWD cars.

Printed publications:
Front Wheels (bulletin, monthly, members)

BSA OWNERS' CLUB

Formal name: Birmingham Small Arms Owners' Club

PO Box 27, Crewe, Cheshire, CW1 6GE

E-mail: bsaoc@bsaoc.demon.co.uk

Website:
http://www.bsaoc.demon.co.uk
General information on club and news of forthcoming events. Links to like-minded URLs.

Enquiries:
Enquiries to: National Secretary

Founded:
1958

Organisation type and purpose:
Membership association (membership is by subscription), present number of members: 4000. Support for owners of BSA Motorcycles worldwide in terms of technical help and opportunity to get together with other motorcyclists.

Subject coverage:
Information and technical advice on motorcycles produced by the Birmingham Small Arms Co. This includes original factory machine dispatch books, an archive of technical and publicity material. The club also offers social events for BSA owners through regional branch meetings and national and international rallies. International branches also exist.

Library catalogue:
All or part available in-house

Printed publications:
The Star (magazine, monthly, members)
Occasional handbook for members

Access to staff:
Contact by letter, by e-mail and via website. Non-members charged.
Hours: Mon to Fri, 0900 to 1700

BSEM

Formal name: British Society for Ecological Medicine

c/o New Medicine Group, PO Box 3AP, London, W1A 3AP

Tel: 020 7100 7090
E-mail: info@ecomed.org.uk

Website:
http://www.ecomed.org.uk

Enquiries:
Enquiries to: Administrator

Founded:
1993

Organisation type and purpose:
Membership association (membership is by subscription), present number of members: 160, registered charity (charity number 326372).

Subject coverage:
Nutritional and environmental medicine.

Publications list:
Available in print

Access to staff:
Contact by letter, by telephone and by e-mail
Hours: Mon, Tue and Thu, 0900 to 1700

BSI

Formal name: British Standards Institution
Acronym or abbreviation: BSI

389 Chiswick High Road, London, W4 4AL

Tel: 020 8996 7004, Library
Fax: 020 8996 7005
E-mail: library@bsi-global.com

Website:
http://www.bsi-global.com
Information on BSI's products and services. On-line catalogue of BSI publications. British Standards on-line (subscription service).

Enquiries:
Enquiries to: Librarian
Direct tel: 020 8996 7041
Direct e-mail: mary.yates@bsi-global.com

Founded:
1901

Organisation type and purpose:
Professional body (membership is by subscription), present number of members: 20,000. National Standards body.

Subject coverage:
British, international and overseas standards and technical requirements covering most subject areas, certification schemes, European Community legislation, environmental issues.

Museum or gallery collection, archive, or library special collection:
BSI current and obsolete standards
Books on quality and environmental management
International and overseas national standards and related specifications (Library)

Printed publications:
British Standards
Business Standards (monthly)
BSI Root Thesaurus
BSI Standards Catalogue (annually, with supplement monthly, cumulative)
BSI Update (monthly)

Microform publications:
British Standards on microform, available from Technical Indexes

Electronic and video publications:
Electronic catalogue (monthly)
British Standards are available online via web site on a subscription basis
PERINORM, CD-ROM (updated monthly)
Various electronic books of standards

Publications list:
Available online and in print

Access to staff:
Contact by letter, by telephone, by fax, by e-mail, in person and via website. Non-members charged.
Hours: Mon to Fri, 0900 to 1700
Special comments: Free to members and students.

Access for disabled people:
Parking provided, access to all public areas, toilet facilities

Controls:
BSI Product Services, Hemel Hempstead

Member of:
European Committee for Electrotechnical Standardization (CENELEC)
European Committee for Standardization (CEN)
International Electrotechnical Commission (IEC)
International Organization for Standardization (ISO)

BSI PRODUCT SERVICES

Formal name: British Standards Institution Product Services
Acronym or abbreviation: BSI

Kitemark House, Maylands Avenue, Hemel Hempstead Industrial Estate, Hemel Hempstead, Hertfordshire, HP2 4SQ

Tel: 08450 765600

Fax: 01442 278630
E-mail: product.services@bsigroup.com

Website:
http://www.bsigroup.com
Corporate website of BSI
http://www.kitemark.com
Dedicated web portal for Kitemark (UK symbol of quality and trust)

Enquiries:
Enquiries to: Customer Service

Founded:
1901

Organisation type and purpose:
Service industry.
Product testing and certification services.

Subject coverage:
Product testing information in the following areas: construction, engineering, fire, personal protective equipment, electrical and electronic, lighting, environmental, healthcare, services, automotive services, combustion equipment, building and construction products, engineering and scientific products, transport and recreation, electronics, communications systems, electrical machines, lighting, cables, Canadian Standards Association, electromagnetic compatibility, electrical and mechanical calibration. Support for product development, product certification, voluntary (Kitemark schemes) and mandatory (CE marking).

Museum or gallery collection, archive, or library special collection:
National and International Standards
National Standards Body Library based at HQ Chiswick

Library catalogue:
All or part available online and in print

Printed publications:
Annual BSI Buyers Guide (listing all certified and registered products and licensees; free)
Catalogue of THE documents (2 a year, free)
Order printed publications from: BSI Customer Services
389 Chiswick High Road, London, W4 4AL, tel: 020 8996 9001

Access to staff:
Contact by letter, by telephone, by fax, by e-mail and via website. Appointment necessary.
Hours: Mon to Fri, 0900 to 1700

Access for disabled people:
Parking provided, ramped entry

Parent body:
British Standards Institution
389 Chiswick High Road, London, W4 4AL; tel: 020 8996 9000; website: http://www.bsigroup.com

BSI-DISC

389 Chiswick High Road, London, W4 4AL

Tel: 020 8996 9000
Fax: 020 8996 7448
E-mail: disc.enquiries@bsi-global.com

Website:
http://www.brainstorm.co.uk/reg/DISC
Basic information on a variety of activities, products and services.

Enquiries:
Enquiries to: Membership Secretary
Direct tel: 020 8996 7180

Founded:
1990

Organisation type and purpose:
International organisation, membership association (membership is by subscription), present number of members: 5000, training organisation, publishing house.
The standards development and publishing service for the information and communications technology sector.

continued overleaf

Subject coverage:
Information management systems, data protection, document scanning and storage, IT service management, risk assessment, disaster recovery, training and workshops, records management, telecommunications.

Printed publications:
Publications and standards (for purchase, price on application)

Electronic and video publications:
Data Protection (interactive CD-ROM)
TickIT Guide v5.0 (interactive CD-ROM)

Publications list:
Available online and in print

Access to staff:
Contact by letter, by telephone, by fax, by e-mail and via website
Hours: Mon to Fri, 0900 to 1700

Access to building, collection or gallery:
Prior appointment required

Access for disabled people:
Parking provided, level entry, access to all public areas, toilet facilities

Parent body:
British Standards Institution

BSS

Formal name: Broadcasting Support Services
Acronym or abbreviation: bss

Head Office, Suite C International House, 7 High Street, Ealing, London, W5 5DB

Tel: 020 8799 9000
Fax: 020 8799 9099
E-mail: marketing@bss.org

Website:
http://www.bss.org
Information about bss.

Enquiries:
Enquiries to: Business Development Executive
Direct tel: 0845 600 1317
Direct fax: 020 8799 9099
Direct e-mail: marketing@bss.org

Founded:
1975

Organisation type and purpose:
National organisation, registered charity (charity number 282264), consultancy.
BSS provides tailored communications solutions to broadcasters, charities and organisations, through the provision of helplines, and distribution services. BSS also processes credit card and online donations.

Subject coverage:
Charity providing communications solutions through: helplines provision, donation processing for appeals, design, print and distribution services.

Printed publications:
BSS leaflet (available on request)

Electronic and video publications:
Presentation of BSS services

Access to staff:
Contact by telephone, by fax, by e-mail and via website
Hours: Mon to Fri, 0930 to 1730

Access to building, collection or gallery:
Prior appointment required

Access for disabled people:
Parking provided

Offices in:
Leicester, Manchester and London

BT ARCHIVES

Formal name: British Telecommunications Archives

Third Floor, Holborn Telephone Exchange, 268–270 High Holborn, London, WC1V 7EE

Tel: 020 7440 4220
Fax: 020 7242 1967
E-mail: archives@bt.com

Website:
http://www.btplc.com/archives/
Information on BT Archives, facilities, and the history of the BT Group.
http://www.connected-earth.com

Enquiries:
Enquiries to: Customer Services Adviser

Founded:
1984

Organisation type and purpose:
Service industry.
Telecommunications provider, BT Archives is the company archive and historical information resource.

Subject coverage:
History of telecommunications, particularly on development of products and services of BT, Post Office Telecommunications and their predecessors dating back to the 1840s.

Museum or gallery collection, archive, or library special collection:
Archives of British Telecommunication plc and its predecessors, including private telegraph and telephone companies, Post Office Telecommunications and BT (public corporation)
Major collections include:
Phone book collection, 1880 to date
Photographic, film and video library, 19th century to date
Historical telecommunications library of printed sources, including several hundred publications, 1769 to date
Numerous in-house and external periodicals
Some Oftel reports

Non-library collection catalogue:
All or part available online and in-house

Library catalogue:
All or part available in-house

Printed publications:
Guide to Events in Telecommunications History (free)

Microform publications:
Copies of telephone directories and phone books, 1880–1982 (for purchase)
Microfilm copies of documents as requested (for purchase)

Access to staff:
Contact by letter, by telephone, by fax, by e-mail and via website. Appointment necessary.
Hours: Mon to Fri, 0900 to 1700

Access to building, collection or gallery:
Special comments: Research visits by appointment: Tue, Thu, 1000 to 1600

BT GROUP

Antares Building, Room 1/3, Martlesham Heath, Ipswich, Suffolk, IP5 3RE

E-mail: library@bt.com

Website:
http://www.bt.com

Enquiries:
Enquiries to: Information Officer

Organisation type and purpose:
Research organisation.

Subject coverage:
Telecommunications, electronics, computing, Internet, information technology, business, management, learning and development.

Library catalogue:
All or part available in-house

Access to staff:
Contact by e-mail

Hours: Mon to Fri, 0900 to 1700

Access to building, collection or gallery:
No access other than to staff

BTCV – BARN COUNTRYSIDE CENTRE

Formal name: British Trust for Conservation Volunteers

Philips Park, Whitefield, Manchester, M45 7QJ

Tel: 0161 796 6404
Fax: 0161 796 8846

Website:
http://www.btcv.org
All aspects of the charity locally and nationally.

Enquiries:
Enquiries to: Manager

Founded:
1959

Organisation type and purpose:
Membership association (membership is by subscription), voluntary organisation, registered charity.

Access to staff:
Contact by letter, by telephone and by fax
Hours: Mon to Fri, 0900 to 1700

Access for disabled people:
Parking provided, ramped entry, access to all public areas, toilet facilities

BTCV – WALLINGFORD

Formal name: British Trust for Conservation Volunteers
Acronym or abbreviation: BTCV

36 St Mary's Street, Wallingford, Oxfordshire, OX10 0EU

Tel: 01491 821600
Fax: 01491 839646
E-mail: information@btcv.org.uk

Website:
http://www.btcv.org

Enquiries:
Enquiries to: Information Officer
Other contacts: PR Manager for media contacts.

Founded:
1959

Organisation type and purpose:
Membership association (membership is by subscription), present number of members: 5000, voluntary organisation, registered charity (charity number 261009), training organisation.
BTCV is the UK's leading practical conservation charity supporting people from all sectors of the community in positive action to improve our environment.
BTCV's purpose is to ensure that the potential of voluntary action for the environment is fully realised.

Subject coverage:
Volunteering, particularly in relation to conservation and the environment. Practical conservation operations in woodlands, waterways, wetlands, footpaths and sand dunes, hedging, dry stone walling and fencing. Environmental skills training, e.g. hedge-laying, dry stone walling. Community groups – support network for groups involved in conservation. BTCV is the UK's leading conservation charity supporting over 84,000 volunteers each year in action to improve their local environment. Information on conservation working holidays both in Britain and abroad.

Museum or gallery collection, archive, or library special collection:
Slide-photo library

Printed publications:
BTCV Conservation Holidays
Practical handbooks and educational material

The Conserver (quarterly, free to members)
A range of titles on conservation and related
  subjects including:
Drystone Walling (Brooks A, 1999)
Fencing (Agate E)
Footpaths (Agate E)
Trees and Aftercare (ed Kiser B)
Waterways and Wetlands (Agate E)
Woodlands (Brooks A)
Order printed publications from: BTCV Enterprises,
The Conservation Centre, Balby Road, Doncaster,
South Yorkshire, DN4 0RH, tel: 01302 572200, fax:
01308 310167

Publications list:
Available in print

Access to staff:
Contact by letter, by telephone, by fax, by e-mail
and via website
Hours: Mon to Fri, 0900 to 1700

Has:
130 offices throughout the UK

BTTG

Formal name: British Textile Technology Group
Acronym or abbreviation: BTTG

Wira House, West Park Ring Road, Leeds, West
Yorkshire, LS16 6QL

Tel: 0113 259 1999
Fax: 0113 278 0306
E-mail: info@bttg.co.uk

Website:
http://www.bttg.co.uk
Services available from BTTG.

Enquiries:
Enquiries to: Customer Services
Direct tel: 0161 445 8141
Direct fax: 0161 434 9957
Other contacts: Pat Widdowson

Founded:
1988

Organisation type and purpose:
International organisation, membership
association (membership is by subscription),
present number of members: 120, training
organisation, consultancy, research organisation.
Specialised centre of excellence in textile-related
testing, investigation and evaluation.
UKAS accredited textile testing laboratory.
Research and technical services for the textile and
related industries.

Subject coverage:
Textiles of all types (sourcing, processing, use,
performance), carpets, cleaning science,
biotechnology, polymers, testing of textiles and
many other products including toys, flammability
research, forensic science, water, effluent, energy,
noise, safety etc.
Technical textiles, personal protective equipment,
fire testers, chemical and biochemical sciences,
laundry products, textile ecology (Oeko-Tex),
microscopy, toys, spinning and non-wovens,
certification, training etc.

**Museum or gallery collection, archive, or library
special collection:**
Research results

Printed publications:
Books on textile topics (15 titles for purchase)
BTTG Independent (news magazine, 4 times a
  year, free subscription)
Services promotional literature (free)

Access to staff:
Contact by letter, by telephone, by fax, by e-mail
and via website
Hours: Mon to Fri, 0900 to 1700

Other addresses:
BTTG (British Textile Technology Group) (BTTG)
  Shirley House, Wilmslow Road, Didsbury,
  Manchester, M20 2RB; tel: 0161 445 8141; fax:
  0161 434 4957; e-mail: info@bttg.co.uk

BTTG Fire Technology Services
  Unit 4B, Stag Industrial Estate, Atlantic Street,
  Broadheath, Altrincham, Cheshire, WA14 5DW;
  tel: 0161 929 8056; fax: 0161 929 8070; e-mail:
  pmeaton@bttg.co.uk
BTTG Spinning and Non-Wovens
  Unit B6, Newton Business Park, Talbot Road,
  Hyde, SK14 4UQ; tel: 0161 368 2630; fax: 0161
  368 1305; e-mail: info@bttg.co.uk

BUCKINGHAMSHIRE
ARCHAEOLOGICAL SOCIETY

Formal name: Buckinghamshire Archaeological and
Architectural Society
Acronym or abbreviation: BAS

County Museum, Church Street, Aylesbury,
Buckinghamshire, HP20 2QP

Tel: 01296 671184
E-mail: bucksas@buckscc.gov.uk

Enquiries:
Enquiries to: Honorary Librarian/Archivist
Direct tel: 01296 678114 (Wed only)

Founded:
1847

Organisation type and purpose:
Learned society (membership is by subscription),
present number of members: 569 plus 16 affiliated
societies.

Subject coverage:
History of Buckinghamshire in all aspects.

Non-library collection catalogue:
All or part available in-house and in print

Printed publications:
Newsletter (2 times a year)
Records of Buckinghamshire (annually, since 1857)
Addington Church, Critchley D (2004)
Buckinghamshire in the 1760s and 1820s: The
  County Maps of Jefferys & Bryant (2001, £15 plus
  £3 p&p)
Bucks in 1851: evidence of the Census, Thorpe D
  (2002)
Catalogue of the BAS Archives, Head L (2002)
Historic Views of Buckinghamshire (2004)
A History of Upton Park and Herschel Park,
  Hunter J (2002)
An Atlas of Gerrards Cross 1840–1940, Thorpe D
  (2006)
Making the Road from Princes Risborough to
  Thame, Gulland P (2006)
Milton Keynes Monograph Series: (all plus £3 p&p)
3. Excavations at Great Linford
4. Pennylands and Hartigans
6. Excavations on Medieval and Later Sites in
  Milton Keynes
7. Bancroft (2 vols)
8. Tattenhoe and Westbury
9. Caldecotte
10. Wavendon Gate

Access to staff:
Contact by letter, by telephone, by e-mail and in
person. Appointment necessary. Non-members
charged.
Hours: Members only: Mon to Sat, 1000 to 1700;
Sun, 1400 to 1700
Non-members: Wed, 1000 to 1600

Access for disabled people:
Parking provided
Special comments: Ramped entry to building; level
entry to library.

BUCKINGHAMSHIRE CHILTERNS
UNIVERSITY COLLEGE

Queen Alexandra Road, High Wycombe,
Buckinghamshire, HP11 2JZ

Tel: 01494 522141
Fax: 01494 524392
E-mail: advice@bcuc.ac.uk

Website:
http://www.bcuc.ac.uk

Enquiries:
Enquiries to: Marketing Officer
Direct fax: 01494 471585

Organisation type and purpose:
College of higher education; formerly High
Wycombe College of Technology and Art and
Newland Park College of Education; connection
with Missenden Abbey Management Centre.

Subject coverage:
Art and design, arts and social sciences, built
environment, business and management,
computing, engineering and technology, furniture,
health studies, leisure and tourism.

Printed publications:
College Prospectus, updated annually, distributed
  freely

Publications list:
Available in print

Access to staff:
Contact by letter
Hours: Mon to Fri, 0900 to 1700

Access to building, collection or gallery:
Prior appointment required

Access for disabled people:
Parking provided, ramped entry

BUCKINGHAMSHIRE FAMILY
HISTORY SOCIETY

PO Box 403, Aylesbury, Buckinghamshire, HP21
7GU

Subject coverage:
Buckinghamshire family history.

Access to staff:
Contact by letter
Hours: Mon to Fri, 0900 to 1700

BUCKINGHAMSHIRE LIBRARY
SERVICE

The Gallery Suite, County Hall, Walton Street,
Aylesbury, Buckinghamshire, HP20 1UU

Tel: 0845 2303232
E-mail: library@buckscc.gov.uk

Website:
http://www.buckscc.gov.uk/bcc/content/index
  .jsp?contentid=-342380260

Enquiries:
Enquiries to: Head of Culture and Learning

Organisation type and purpose:
Local government body, public library.

Subject coverage:
General, Buckinghamshire, business information,
careers and courses information.

Information services:
Libraries Information Service (see below)

**Museum or gallery collection, archive, or library
special collection:**
Buckinghamshire Collection (at the Centre for
  Buckinghamshire Studies, Aylesbury)
Early Children's Book Collection (at Chesham),
  County Museum (Aylesbury)

Library catalogue:
All or part available online

Access to staff:
Contact by letter, by telephone, by fax, by e-mail,
in person and via website
Hours: Mon to Fri, 0900 to 1700
Special comments: Access hours to libraries vary.

Branch libraries:
Aylesbury Study Centre
  County Hall, Walton Street, Aylesbury,
  Buckinghamshire, HP20 1UU; tel: 0845 2303132
Centre for Buckinghamshire Studies
  County Hall, Walton Street, Aylesbury,
  Buckinghamshire, HP20 1UU; tel: 01296 382250;
  fax: 01296 382771

continued overleaf

Chesham Study Centre
  Chesham Library, Elgiva Lane, Chesham,
  Buckinghamshire, HP5 2JD; tel: 0845 2303132
High Wycombe Study Centre
  High Wycombe Library, 5 Eden Place, High
  Wycombe, Buckinghamshire, HP11 2DH; tel:
  0845 2303132

Member organisation of:
Buckinghamshire Culture and Learning
Department
European Public Information Centre Network
(EPIC)
  County Hall, Walton Street, Aylesbury,
  Buckinghamshire, HP20 1UU; tel: 01296 383252;
  fax: 01296 382405; e-mail: lib-info@buckscc.gov
  .uk
Libraries Information Service
  County Hall, Walton Street, Aylesbury,
  Buckinghamshire, HP20 1UU; tel: 0845 2303132;
  fax: 01296 382405; e-mail: lib-info@buckscc.gov
  .uk; website: http://www.bucks.gov.uk

BUCKINGHAMSHIRE RECORD SOCIETY

Centre for Buckinghamshire Studies, County Hall,
Aylesbury, Buckinghamshire, HP20 1UU

Tel: 01296 383013
Fax: 01296 382771
E-mail: archives@buckscc.gov.uk

Website:
http://www.bucksinfo.net/brs

Enquiries:
Enquiries to: Honorary Secretary

Founded:
1947

Organisation type and purpose:
Learned society (membership is by subscription),
voluntary organisation, registered charity (charity
number 262004).
To publish volumes based on original records
illustrative of the history of Buckinghamshire; to
concern itself with the collection, preservation and
listing of public and private records relating to the
county, including, if necessary, the raising of
separate funds for this purpose.

Subject coverage:
Local history of Buckinghamshire.

Printed publications:
Vols include:
Vol. 19 The Courts of the Archdeaconry of
  Buckingham 1483–1525 (edited with an
  introduction, E. M. Elvey, 1975)
Vol. 23 The Autobiography of Joseph Mayett of
  Quainton 1783–1839 (edited with an
  introduction, A. Kussmaul, 1986)
Vol. 26 Descriptions of Lord Cobham's Gardens at
  Stowe 1700–1750 (edited by G. B. Clarke)
Vol. 28 Buckinghamshire Dissent and Parish Life
  1669–1712 (edited by J. Broad, 1993)
Vol. 31 Recollections of Nineteenth Century
  Buckinghamshire (edited by I. Toplis, G. Clarke,
  I. Beckett and H. Hanley, 1998)
Vol. 32 An Index to Buckinghamshire Probate
  Records, 1420–1660 (edited by J. Hunt, R.
  Bettridge and A. Toplis, with introduction by H.
  Hanley, 2001)
Vol. 33 The Household Book (1510–51) of Sir
  Edward Don (edited by R. A. Griffiths, 2004)
Vol. 34 The Buckinghamshire Eyre of 1286 (edited
  by L. Boatwright, 2006)
Order printed publications from: From the Society

Electronic and video publications:
Vols 1–22 in digital format.
Vol. 8 The Subsidy Roll for Buckinghamshire 1524
  (edited by A. B. Chibnall and A. V. Woodman,
  1950, with index by G. M. de Fraine)
Vol. 17 The Certificate of Musters for
  Buckinghamshire 1522 (edited by A. B. Chibnall,
  1973)
Vol. 22 The Buckinghamshire Posse Comitatus
  1798 (edited by I. F. W. Beckett, 1985)

Order electronic and video publications from: From the
Society

Publications list:
Available in print

Access to staff:
Contact by letter, by telephone, by fax and by e-
mail. Appointment necessary.
Hours: Tue to Fri, 0900 to 1715

Access for disabled people:
Ramped entry, access to all public areas, toilet
facilities

BUDDHIST SOCIETY

58 Ecclestone Square, London, SW1V 1PH

Tel: 020 7834 5858
Fax: 020 7976 5238
E-mail: info@thebuddhistsociety.org

Website:
http://www.the buddhistsociety.org.uk
Online library catalogue.

Enquiries:
Enquiries to: Librarian (for enquiries related to the
literature of Buddhism)
Direct e-mail: library@thebuddhistsociety.org

Founded:
1924

Organisation type and purpose:
Membership association (membership is by
subscription), present number of members: 2,000.
Religious society.

Subject coverage:
All aspects of Buddhism.

Library catalogue:
All or part available online and in-house

Printed publications:
Leaflets on Buddhism and the Society's activities
Middle Way (quarterly, free to members)

Electronic and video publications:
CD and cassette recordings, mostly of lectures
  given at the Society

Publications list:
Available online and in print

Access to staff:
Contact by letter, by telephone, by fax, by e-mail
and in person
Hours: Mon to Fri, 1400 to 1800; Sat, 1400 to 1700

Links with:
European Buddhist Union
World Federation of Buddhists

BUGATTI OWNERS' CLUB LIMITED

Prescott Hill, Gotherington, Cheltenham,
Gloucestershire, GL52 9RD

Tel: 01242 673136
Fax: 01242 677001
E-mail: club@bugatti.co.uk

Website:
http://www.prescott-hillclimb.com
http://www.prescott-hillclimb-school.uk

Enquiries:
Enquiries to: Secretary

Founded:
1929

Organisation type and purpose:
Membership association (membership is by
subscription).

Subject coverage:
Speed Hill Climb meetings, Speed Hill Climb
driver school, Bugatti information.

Access to staff:
Contact by letter, by telephone, by fax and by e-
mail

Hours: Mon to Fri, 0900 to 1700

Access for disabled people:
Parking provided, toilet facilities

BUILDERS CONFERENCE

Unilink House, 21 Lewis Road, Sutton, Surrey,
SM1 4BR

Tel: 020 8770 0111
Fax: 020 8770 7736
E-mail: info@buildersconf.co.uk

Enquiries:
Enquiries to: Chief Executive
Direct tel: 020 8643 4452

Founded:
1935

Organisation type and purpose:
Trade association, registered charity (charity
number 281742), research organisation.

Subject coverage:
Building.

Trade and statistical information:
A comprehensive tender reporting and market
  information service in the UK market.

Access to staff:
Contact by letter, by telephone, by fax and by e-
mail. Appointment necessary.
Hours: Mon to Fri, 0900 to 1700

BUILDING COST INFORMATION SERVICE

Acronym or abbreviation: BCIS

Royal Institution of Chartered Surveyors, 12 Great
George Street, Parliament Square, London, SW1P
3AD

Tel: 020 7695 1500
Fax: 020 7695 1501
E-mail: bcis@bcis.co.uk; bmi@bcis.co.uk

Website:
http://www.bcis.co.uk
Information about BCIS and BMI publications and
services.

Enquiries:
Enquiries to: Executive Director
Direct tel: 020 7695 1502

Founded:
1961

Organisation type and purpose:
Membership association, consultancy, research
organisation.
Voluntary association for the exchange of
information; open to all those willing to exchange
information.
To provide information on the construction and
property markets.

Subject coverage:
Construction industry information; statistical and
econometric studies, facilities management
information, building cost information, building
economic forecasting, analysis of prices; property
occupancy and costs; building maintenance
management and costs; facilities management; life
cycle costs.

Trade and statistical information:
Statistics on price and cost trends in UK
  construction.
Statistics on the level of prices for UK building
  construction.
Data on occupancy costs.
Data on expenditure on maintenance of buildings
  in the UK.

Printed publications:
BCIS Bulletin Service
BMI Building Maintenance Price Book (annually,
£110)
Guide to Dayworks

Guide to House Rebuilding Costs for Insurance
Valuation (annually, £99)
Quarterly Review of Building Prices (quarterly,
£450)
Standard Form of Cost Analysis
BMI Quarterly Cost Briefing (£175)
Studies on building maintenance (c. 100 titles)

Electronic and video publications:
BCIS Online data service

Access to staff:
Contact by letter, by telephone, by fax, by e-mail
and via website. Access for members only. All
charged.
Hours: Mon to Fri, 0900 to 1700

Division of:
Royal Institution of Chartered Surveyors

BUILDING RESEARCH ESTABLISHMENT LIMITED

Acronym or abbreviation: BRE

Bucknalls Lane, Garston, Watford, Hertfordshire,
WD25 9XX

Tel: 01923 664000
Fax: 01923 664010
E-mail: enquiries@bre.co.uk

Website:
http://www.bre.co.uk
Home page.
http://www.brebookshop.com
On-line book shop.
http://www.bre.co.uk/askbre
On-line advice service.

Enquiries:
Enquiries to: Administrator

Founded:
1921

Organisation type and purpose:
Consultancy, research organisation.

Subject coverage:
Building materials, building services, construction
industry, structural design, fire science, timber
construction, radioactive waste disposal, indoor
environment (sick building syndrome), energy
conservation, contaminated land.
Fire statistics; self-heating, ignition and growth of
fire; structural aspects of fire in buildings;
detection, extinction and suppression of fire; heat
and smoke detectors; explosion hazards;
combustion products, smoke, toxicity; smoke
control and ventilation; human behaviour, escape
and risk; combustion theory and modelling;
sprinklers and extinguishing agents; special fire
hazards in industries and materials.

Library catalogue:
All or part available in-house

Printed publications:
Publications list available on-line
Order printed publications from: BRE Press,
distributed by IHS, Willoughby Road, Bracknell,
Berkshire, RG12 8FB, tel: 01344 328038, fax: , e-
mail: brepress@ihsatp.com
url: www.BREbookshop.com

Publications list:
Available online and in print

Access to staff:
Contact by letter, by telephone, by fax, by e-mail
and via website. All charged.
Hours: Mon to Fri, 0900 to 1700
Special comments: Not normally open to visitors.

Access to building, collection or gallery:
No access other than to staff
Special comments: Collections not open to the public

Access for disabled people:
Access to all public areas, toilet facilities

Member of:
Construction Industry Information Group (CIIG)
26 Store Street, London, WC1E 7BT

European Network of Building Research
Institutions (ENBRI)
International Council for Research and Innovation
in Building and Construction (CIB)
International Network for Fire Information and
Reference Exchange (INFIRE)

Other addresses:
Scottish Laboratory
Kelvin Road, East Kilbride, Glasgow, G75 0RZ;
tel: 01355 233001

BUILDING SERVICES RESEARCH AND INFORMATION ASSOCIATION

Acronym or abbreviation: BSRIA

Old Bracknell Lane West, Bracknell, Berkshire,
RG12 7AH

Tel: 01344 465600
Fax: 01344 465626
E-mail: bsria@bsria.co.uk

Website:
http://www.bsria.co.uk/bookshop
Publications, searching and ordering.
http://www.bsria.co.uk
Full information covering all BSRIA activities.

Enquiries:
Enquiries to: Marketing Manager
Direct tel: 01344 465521
Direct e-mail: information@bsria.co.uk

Founded:
1955

Organisation type and purpose:
Membership association (membership is by
subscription), present number of members: 720,
consultancy, research organisation.
An independent research testing and information
organisation offering laboratory facilities, site
investigations and consultancy for building
services.

Subject coverage:
Heating; ventilation and air conditioning; building
and energy management; technical information;
equipment consultancy and testing; water quality
and legionella; research; marketing research;
management consultancy.

Trade and statistical information:
Market research facilities for building service
industry.

Library catalogue:
All or part available online

Printed publications:
Publications Index (complete list of titles)
Guides
Building Services Legislation, 2003
Illustrated guide to building services, 2002
International Building Services Abstracts (6 times a
year)
Order printed publications from: BSRIA Bookshop
Address as before

Publications list:
Available online and in print

Access to staff:
Contact by letter, by telephone, by fax, by e-mail
and via website. Appointment necessary. Non-
members charged.
Hours: Mon to Fri, 0830 to 1700

Access to building, collection or gallery:
Prior appointment required
Hours: Mon to Fri, 0830 to 1700
Special comments: Members only.

Access for disabled people:
Parking provided, level entry, access to all public
areas

BUILDING SOCIETIES ASSOCIATION

Acronym or abbreviation: BSA

6th Floor, York House, 23 Kingsway, London,
WC2B 6UJ

Tel: 020 7520 5900
Fax: 020 7240 5290
E-mail: simon.rex@bsa.org.uk

Website:
http://www.bsa.org.uk

Enquiries:
Enquiries to: Information Services Manager

Organisation type and purpose:
Trade association.

Subject coverage:
Building society industry, housing finance, the
mortgage market, savings markets, related
financial services.

Library catalogue:
All or part available in-house

Publications list:
Available online

Access to staff:
Contact by letter, by telephone, by fax, by e-mail
and via website. Appointment necessary.
Hours: Mon to Fri, 0900 to 1700

Access to building, collection or gallery:
Appointment required
Hours: Mon to Fri, 0900 to 1700

BURDEN NEUROLOGICAL INSTITUTE

Acronym or abbreviation: BNI

Frenchay Park Road, Bristol, BS16 1JB

Tel: 0117 918 6720
E-mail: burdeninstitute@hotmail.com

Enquiries:
Enquiries to: Director
Direct e-mail: n.j.scolding@bris.ac.uk

Founded:
1939

Organisation type and purpose:
University department or institute, research
organisation.

Subject coverage:
Research in neurological diseases and stem-cell
therapies.

**Museum or gallery collection, archive, or library
special collection:**
Research journals in the fields of neurology,
neurophysiology, neuropsychology, psychiatry,
psychophysiology

Access to staff:
Contact by letter, by telephone and by e-mail
Hours: Mon to Fri, 0900 to 1700

Access to building, collection or gallery:
Prior appointment required

Access for disabled people:
Level entry, access to all public areas, toilet
facilities

Associated institute of the:
University of Bristol

BUREAU OF ANALYSED SAMPLES LIMITED

Acronym or abbreviation: BAS

Newham Hall, Newby, Middlesbrough, Cleveland,
TS8 9EA

Tel: 01642 300500
Fax: 01642 315209
E-mail: enquiries@basrid.co.uk

Website:
http://www.basrid.co.uk

Enquiries:
Enquiries to: Managing Director

continued overleaf

Founded:
1935

Organisation type and purpose:
Manufacturing industry.

Subject coverage:
Certified reference materials (CRM), sources of supply.

Non-library collection catalogue:
All or part available online, in-house and in print

Library catalogue:
All or part available online, in-house and in print

Printed publications:
Catalogue of Certified Reference Materials produced by BAS and other leading CRM producers

Publications list:
Available online and in print

Access to staff:
Contact by letter, by telephone, by fax, by e-mail and via website
Hours: Mon to Thu, 0900 to 1700; Fri, 0900 to 1630

BUREAU VAN DIJK ELECTRONIC PUBLISHING LIMITED

Northburgh House, 10 Northburgh Street, London, EC1V 0PP

Tel: 020 7549 5000
Fax: 020 7549 5010
E-mail: uk@bvdep.com

Website:
http://www.bankscope.bvdep.com
Detailed information for over 23,000 banks worldwide.
http://www.cameo.bvdep.com
UK Electoral Roll on the internet.
http://www.mintforbusiness.com
Companies, news, industry research and directors in a single easy to use business information database
http://www.fame.bvdep.com
Detailed information for 3m UK and Irish companies.
http://www.bvdep.com
Information on our products and services.
http://www.amadeus.bvdep.com
Detailed information for over 8m European companies.

Enquiries:
Enquiries to: Marketing Manager

Founded:
1970

Organisation type and purpose:
Publishing house.
Provider of business information solutions on disk and via the Internet.

Subject coverage:
Company information for the UK, Europe and Worldwide.
Detailed information on Banks Worldwide.
Detailed information on Insurance Companies Worldwide.
UK Electoral Roll on the internet.

Access to staff:
Contact by letter, by telephone, by fax, by e-mail and via website
Hours: Mon to Fri, 0830 to 1830

BURNLEY BOROUGH COUNCIL

Town Hall, Manchester Road, Burnley, Lancashire, BB11 1JA

Tel: 01282 425011
Fax: 01282 438772

Enquiries:
Enquiries to: Public Relations Manager
Direct tel: 01282 477180
Direct fax: 01282 424764
Direct e-mail: srichardson@burnley.gov.uk

Organisation type and purpose:
Local government body.

Subject coverage:
Local government services.

BURTON COLLEGE LIBRARY

Lichfield Street, Burton-on-Trent, Staffordshire, DE14 3RL

Tel: 01283 494431
Fax: 01283 494800
E-mail: library@burton-college.ac.uk

Enquiries:
Enquiries to: Librarian

Subject coverage:
Electrical, electronic, mechanical and automobile engineering, plastics and rubber technology, mathematics and pure sciences, construction, business and management studies, computer science, nursery nursing, catering, art, drama and design.

Library catalogue:
All or part available online

Affiliated to:
College Librarians in Staffordshire (COLLIS)
Forum for Information Resources in Staffordshire (FIRST)
LA/CoFHE (West Midlands Circle)

BURTON UPON TRENT FAMILY AND LOCAL HISTORY CENTRE

Burton upon Trent Public Library, Riverside, High Street, Burton upon Trent, Staffordshire, DE14 1AH

Tel: 01283 239556
Fax: 01283 239571
E-mail: burton.library@staffordshire.gov.uk

Website:
http://www.staffordshire.gov.uk/libraries

Enquiries:
Enquiries to: Librarian

Organisation type and purpose:
Public library.

Subject coverage:
Civic, educational, Burton Workhouse, and church (including some nonconformist) records, etc. Also copies of census from 1841–1901 inclusive, pre- and post-WWII local newspapers, and a range of material relating to Burton and the surrounding areas in East Staffordshire and South Derbyshire.

Non-library collection catalogue:
All or part available online and in-house

Library catalogue:
All or part available online

Access to staff:
Contact by letter, by telephone, by fax, by e-mail and in person
Hours: Mon, Wed and Fri, 0830 to 1800; Tue, 1000 to 1800; Thu, 0830 to 2000; Sat, 0830 to 1630

Access to building, collection or gallery:
Hours: Mon, Wed and Fri, 0830 to 1800; Tue, 1000 to 1800; Thu, 0830 to 2000; Sat, 0830 to 1630

Access for disabled people:
Parking provided, ramped entry, access to all public areas, toilet facilities

BURY ARCHIVE SERVICE

Moss Street, Bury, BL9 0DR

Tel: 0161 253 6782
Fax: 0161 253 5878
E-mail: archives@bury.gov.uk

Website:
http://www.bury.gov.uk
Interim guide to holdings.

Enquiries:
Enquiries to: Archivist

Founded:
1986

Organisation type and purpose:
Public Archive Service.

Subject coverage:
Local history, geography, government of Bury and district, other local information.

Museum or gallery collection, archive, or library special collection:
The archives of local authorities in the Bury area, 1675 to present
Deposited archives of various local organisations (business, trade union, church, voluntary, sports etc) and individuals, mostly c.1780 to present

Non-library collection catalogue:
All or part available online, in-house and in print

Printed publications:
Interim Guide to Holdings (£2.50)
Newsletter (quarterly, free)

Access to staff:
Contact by letter, by telephone, by fax, by e-mail and in person. Appointment necessary.
Hours: Tue, Wed, 1300 to 1600; Thu, Fri, 1000 to 1600; Sat, 2nd of the month, 1000 to 1600
Special comments: Appointment strongly recommended, except on Tuesdays.

Access to building, collection or gallery:
Prior appointment required
Hours: Mon to Fri, 1000 to 1300 and 1400 to 1700

Access for disabled people:
Ramp and lift access, bathrooms.

Location:
Bury Metro Borough Council (Personal and Community Services Dept)
Athenaeum House, Market Street, Bury; tel: 0161 253 5863; fax: 0161 253 5915

BURY COLLEGE

Learning Resources Centre, Bury Centre, Market Street, Bury, Lancashire, BL9 0TE

Tel: 0161 280 8280

Website:
http://www.burycollege.ac.uk

Enquiries:
Enquiries to: Resource Librarian
Direct tel: 0161 280 8446/447
Direct fax: 0161 280 8403
Direct e-mail: angela.walker@burycollege.ac.uk
Other contacts: Learning Resources Manager

Organisation type and purpose:
Suitable for ages: 16+.
Further Education College.

Subject coverage:
Paper-making, health studies, catering, computing, business studies, hairdressing.

Library catalogue:
All or part available in-house

Access to staff:
Contact by letter, by telephone, by fax and by e-mail. Appointment necessary.
Hours: Mon to Fri, 0900 to 1700

Access to building, collection or gallery:
No prior appointment required

Access for disabled people:
Access to all public areas

BURY METROPOLITAN BOROUGH LIBRARIES

Reference and Information Services, Bury Library, Manchester Road, Bury, BL9 0DG

Tel: 0161 253 5871
Fax: 0161 253 5857
E-mail: information@bury.gov.uk

Website:
http://www.bury.gov.uk/libraries
Libraries pages include community contacts
database, guide to web, branch libraries, archives,
library catalogue, magazines, online library
services.

Enquiries:
Enquiries to: Reference and Information Services
Librarian

Founded:
1901

Organisation type and purpose:
Local government body, public library.

Subject coverage:
General, business, local history and genealogical
information, careers, social science.

Information services:
Online library services.

Services for disabled people:
Visual impairment unit, hearing impairment unit,
housebound library service.

Non-library collection catalogue:
All or part available online

Library catalogue:
All or part available online

Printed publications:
Local Contacts Lists (20p each)
Routes: Guide to sources for family historians (£5)
Order printed publications from: Reference
Information Services, Bury Library

Electronic and video publications:
Bury Community Contacts
Order electronic and video publications from: Website

Publications list:
Available online and in print

Access to staff:
Contact by letter, by telephone, by fax, by e-mail,
in person and via website

Access to building, collection or gallery:
Hours: Mon, Tue, Thu, Fri, 0930 to 1730; Wed, 0930
to 1930; Sat, 0930 to 1630

Access for disabled people:
Disabled access available
Hours: As above

Branch libraries:
14 branch libraries throughout
Bury MBC, incl Radcliffe, Prestwich,
Ramsbottom

BUS USERS UK

PO Box 2950, Stoke on Trent, ST4 9EW

Tel: 01782 442855
Fax: 01782 442856
E-mail: enquiries@bususer.org

Website:
http://www.bususers.org
Details of work of Bus Users UK and membership
application, good practice guide, guide to making
a complaint about bus services.

Enquiries:
Enquiries to: Chairman

Founded:
1985

Formerly called:
National Federation of Bus Users (year of change c.
2004)

Organisation type and purpose:
National organisation, membership association,
voluntary organisation.

Printed publications:
BUS USER (newsletter, 4 times a year, for
members)
Good Practice Guide (free)

Access to staff:
Contact by letter

Hours: Mon to Fri, 0900 to 1300

Access to building, collection or gallery:
No access other than to staff

BUSINESS AND PROFESSIONAL WOMEN UK LIMITED

Acronym or abbreviation: BPW UK Ltd

74 Fairfield Rise, Billericay, Essex, CM12 9NU

Tel: 01225 837251
E-mail: hq@bpwuk.co.uk

Website:
http://www.bpwuk.co.uk

Founded:
1938

Organisation type and purpose:
Membership association (membership is by
subscription), present number of members: 500,
voluntary organisation.
Lobbying and networking organisation.

Subject coverage:
The interests of all working women, equality,
women in the workplace and public life, support
for them personally or in their work, assisted by a
networking system.

Printed publications:
Annual Review
BPW News (quarterly, free to members,
subscription)
Monthly Bulletin

Access to staff:
Contact by letter, by telephone, by e-mail and via
website

Links with:
International Federation of Business and
Professional Women
tel: +41 1 252 1742; fax: +41 1 252 6562; e-mail:
president@bpw-international.org

Member organisations:
There are 30 clubs in the United Kingdom

BUSINESS AND TRADE STATISTICS LIMITED

Acronym or abbreviation: BTS

Lancaster House, More Lane, Esher, Surrey, KT10
8AP

Tel: 01372 463121
Fax: 01372 469847
E-mail: info@worldtradestats.com

Website:
http://www.worldtradestats.com

Enquiries:
Enquiries to: Managing Director

Founded:
1986

Organisation type and purpose:
Service industry.

Subject coverage:
External trade statistics for the UK, all the
European Community countries and Switzerland,
Norway, USA, Canada, Mexico, Japan, Hong
Kong, South Korea, Taiwan, Singapore, Australia,
New Zealand.

**Museum or gallery collection, archive, or library
special collection:**
Historical data back to 1979

Trade and statistical information:
Statistical databases.
Production Statistics (PRODCOM) for UK.
UK consumption statistics for beer, wine, spirits,
tobacco, hydrocarbons and expenditure in
betting and gambling.

Printed publications:
Printed reports

Electronic and video publications:
Online, CD-ROM and floppy disks provision

Publications list:
Available in print

Access to staff:
Contact by letter, by telephone, by fax and by e-
mail. Appointment necessary.
Hours: Mon to Fri, 0900 to 1700

BUSINESS ARCHIVES COUNCIL OF SCOTLAND

Acronym or abbreviation: BACS

c/o Glasgow University Archive Services, 77
Dumbarton Road, Glasgow, G11 6PW

Tel: 0141 330 4159
Fax: 0141 330 4158
E-mail: bacs@archives.gla.ac.uk

Website:
http://www.gla.ac.uk/archives/bacs

Enquiries:
Enquiries to: Surveying Officer

Founded:
1960

Organisation type and purpose:
National organisation, membership association
(membership is by subscription), registered charity
(charity number SCO 02565).

Subject coverage:
Scottish business history, locating records of
Scottish business history, preserving, appraising
and listing.

Printed publications:
Scottish Business and Industrial History
Order printed publications from: Editor, Scottish
Business and Industrial History, c/o Business
Archives Council of Scotland; e-mail: bacs@
archives.gla.ac.uk

Electronic and video publications:
Publications online, including detailed index to the
journal Scottish Business and Industrial History

Publications list:
Available online

Access to staff:
Contact by letter, by telephone, by fax, by e-mail,
in person and via website. Appointment necessary.
Hours: Mon to Fri, 0900 to 1700

Access to building, collection or gallery:
No access other than to staff

BUSINESS IN THE COMMUNITY

Acronym or abbreviation: BITC

137 Shepherdess Walk, London, N1 7RQ

Tel: 0870 600 2482
Fax: 020 7253 1877

Website:
http://www.bitc.org.uk

Enquiries:
Enquiries to: Executive Secretary
Other contacts: Information Officer for publications

Founded:
1982

Organisation type and purpose:
Membership association (membership is by
subscription, election or invitation), present
number of members: 650 companies, voluntary
organisation, registered charity (charity number
297716).
BITC's mission is to inspire businesses to increase
the quality and extent of their contribution to social
and economic regeneration by making corporate
social responsibility an essential part of business
excellence.

continued overleaf

Subject coverage:
Development of companies' positive impact on society through specialised campaigns.

Printed publications:
Information pack (free)
Specialist publications available upon request

Publications list:
Available in print

Access to staff:
Contact by telephone
Hours: Mon to Fri, 0900 to 1700

Offices at:
Business in the Community, East Midlands
  3rd Floor, 30–34 Hounds Gate, Nottingham, NG1 7AB; tel: 0115 911 6666; fax: 0115 911 6667
Business in the Community, East of England
  PO Box 93, 58 High Street, Newmarket, CB8 8ZN; tel: 01638 663272; fax: 01638 666841
Business in the Community, North East
  Design Works, William Street, Felling, Tyne & Wear, NE10 0JP; tel: 0191 469 5333; fax: 0191 469 5353
Business in the Community, North West
  Suite 17, St James Court, Wilderspool Causeway, Warrington, WA4 6RS; tel: 01925 230317; fax: 01925 652644
Business in the Community, Northern Ireland
  c/o TK-ECC Limited, 770 Upper Newtownards Road, Dundonald, Belfast, BT16 1UL; tel: 028 9041 0410; fax: 028 9041 9030
Business in the Community, South East
  137 Shepherdess Walk, London, N1 7RQ; tel: 0870 600 2482; fax: 020 7253 1877
Business in the Community, South West
  165 Whiteladies Road, Bristol, BS8 2RN; tel: 0117 923 8750; fax: 0117 923 8270
Business in the Community, Wales
  Fourth Floor, Empire House, Mount Stuart Square, Cardiff, CF10 5FN; tel: 029 2048 3348; fax: 029 2046 1513
Business in the Community, West Midlands
  c/o Cadbury Limited, 83 Bournville Lane, Birmingham, B30 2HP; tel: 0121 451 2227; fax: 0121 451 2782
Business in the Community, Yorkshire & Humberside
  Progress House, 99 Bradford Road, Pudsey, Leeds, LS28 6AT; tel: 0113 236 1888; fax: 0113 236 0555

Sister organisation:
Scottish Business in the Community
  PO Box 408, Bankhead Avenue, Edinburgh, E11 4EX; tel: 0131 442 2020; fax: 0131 442 3555

BUSINESS INFORMATION SERVICES & EURO INFO CENTRE

Acronym or abbreviation: EIC

Invest Northern Ireland, LEDU House, Upper Galwally, Belfast, BT6 8TB

Tel: 028 9049 0486
Fax: 028 9049 0490
E-mail: eic@investni.com

Website:
http://www.investni.com
Guide to InvestNI services and products, free company database for NI sector information.

Enquiries:
Enquiries to: Manager
Direct e-mail: mandy.mills@investni.com
Other contacts: (1) Business Information Executive (2) European Information Executive

Founded:
1989

Organisation type and purpose:
National government body.
Advisory and financial support organisation for businesses in Northern Ireland.

Subject coverage:
Export promotion; market information, local, national and international; European market information; European legislation; Small Business

Advisory Information; company information, local, national and international; regional development and inward investment; research and technology.

Museum or gallery collection, archive, or library special collection:
EU Legislation databases
Grants Information on CD-ROM
An extensive collection of European Business Information databases
A wide range of information, factsheets, databases and directories are available as CD-ROMs on such subjects as market research, company information, funding, legislation, tenders and government bodies, phone directories

Trade and statistical information:
Marketing data for a wide range of industries and countries.

Non-library collection catalogue:
All or part available online and in-house

Library catalogue:
All or part available in-house

Publications list:
Available in print

Access to staff:
Contact by letter, by telephone, by fax, by e-mail and via website. Appointment necessary.
Hours: Mon to Thu, 0900 to 1700; Fri, 0900 to 1630

Access to building, collection or gallery:
No prior appointment required

Access for disabled people:
Parking provided, level entry, access to all public areas, toilet facilities

Has:
3 sites in Belfast and one each in Lisburn, Newry, Ballymena, Omagh and Derry

Parent body:
Invest Northern Ireland (INI)
  at the same address

BUSINESS INSTITUTE

University of Ulster at Jordanstown, Shore Road, Newtownabbey, Co Antrim, BT37 0QB

Tel: 028 9036 6417
Fax: 028 9036 6831
E-mail: e.oneilln@ulster.ac.uk

Website:
http://www.tmi.ulst.ac.uk
Description and breakdown of all activities.

Enquiries:
Enquiries to: Director
Direct tel: 028 9036 8091

Founded:
1984

Organisation type and purpose:
University department or institute, training organisation, consultancy, research organisation.
Provider of management development, management education and research.

Subject coverage:
Training and education in all areas of business, small business research, personal and organisational development.

Printed publications:
Course brochures available on request

Access to staff:
Contact by letter, by telephone, by fax, by e-mail and via website
Hours: Mon to Fri, 0900 to 1700

Access to building, collection or gallery:
No prior appointment required

BUSINESS LINK

Acronym or abbreviation: CBE

Churchgate House, 56 Oxford Street, Manchester, M60 7HJ

Tel: 0161 237 4018
Fax: 0161 236 9945
E-mail: businfo@blgm.co.uk

Website:
http://www.blgm.co.uk/

Enquiries:
Enquiries to: Information Manager

Organisation type and purpose:
Business support organisation.

Printed publications:
Foreign Owned Companies in the North West (various, charged)
North West Top 100 Companies (annual, charged)

Electronic and video publications:
Mailing lists, credit reports, market research and publications available at a cost and usually delivered by email
British Standards Institution publications and overseas standards available at a cost and delivered by post

Access to staff:
Contact by letter, by telephone, by fax, by e-mail and via website
Hours: Mon to Thurs, 0900 to 1700, Fri 0900 to 1630
Special comments: Charges on some services.

BUSINESS LINK BIRMINGHAM

Acronym or abbreviation: BLB

75 Harborne Road, Edgbaston, Birmingham, B15 3DH

Tel: 0121 607 0809\ Minicom no. 0845 606 2666
Fax: 0121 607 9899
E-mail: info@birmingham.businesslink.co.uk

Enquiries:
Enquiries to: Customer Services Adviser

Founded:
1993

Organisation type and purpose:
Advisory body.
Business support organisation.

Subject coverage:
Business advice, business information, on-line services, international marketing advice, training, legal and employment advice, European information centre.

Museum or gallery collection, archive, or library special collection:
British Standards
Business directories
Business databases

Electronic and video publications:
Mailing list information (available for purchase)

Access to staff:
Contact by letter, by telephone, by fax, by e-mail, in person and via website. Non-members charged.
Hours: Mon to Fri, 0830 to 1730
Special comments: Charges to non-chamber members.

Access for disabled people:
Parking provided, ramped entry, access to all public areas, toilet facilities

Parent body:
Birmingham Chamber of Commerce

BUSINESS LINK COUNTY DURHAM

1st Floor, IMEX Business Centre, Abbey Road, Pity Me, Durham, DH1 5JZ

Tel: 0191 374 4000
Fax: 0191 374 4010

Website:
Information service of Business Link County Durham.

Enquiries:
Enquiries to: Information Services Manager
Other contacts: General Manager

Founded:
1995

Organisation type and purpose:
Service industry, consultancy.
To provide advice and information to local business.

Subject coverage:
Product and company sourcing, market research, worldwide company information, Europe, financial assistance, regulations, codes of practice, credit checking, legislation, directives and general business information.

Museum or gallery collection, archive, or library special collection:
Business CD-ROMs
Directories
Health and Safety Manuals
IDS Pay Reviews

Trade and statistical information:
International trade services provided by Trade Partners UK.

Non-library collection catalogue:
All or part available in-house

Library catalogue:
All or part available in-house

Access to staff:
Contact by letter, by telephone, by fax, by e-mail, in person and via website
Hours: Mon to Thu, 0830 to 1700; Fri, 0830 to 1630

Access for disabled people:
Parking provided, ramped entry, access to all public areas, toilet facilities

BUSINESS LINK DERBYSHIRE

Commerce Centre, Canal Wharf, Chesterfield, Derbyshire, S41 7NA

Tel: 0845 601 1038
E-mail: info@derbyshirebusinesslink.co.uk

Website:
http://www.businesslinkderbyshire.co.uk

Enquiries:
Enquiries to: Information Officer

Founded:
1995

Organisation type and purpose:
Advisory body.
Business advice and support.

Subject coverage:
Business information and support.

Trade and statistical information:
Local economic information, company information worldwide.

Access to staff:
Contact by letter, by telephone, by fax, by e-mail and via website. Appointment necessary.
Hours: Mon to Fri, 0900 to 1700
Special comments: Some charges made, mainly for incurred costs and research time.

Access to building, collection or gallery:
No prior appointment required
Hours: Mon to Fri, 0700 to 1700

Services are delivered jointly by:
North Derbyshire Chamber of Commerce and Industry
Canal Wharf, Chesterfield, Derbyshire, S41 7NA
Southern Derbyshire Chamber of Commerce
Innovation House, Riverside Park, Raynesway, Derby, DE21 7BF

BUSINESS LINK FOR LONDON – NEW BRIDGE STREET

6 New Bridge Street, London, EC4V 6AB

Tel: 020 7010 1000
Fax: 020 7010 0000
E-mail: info@bl4london.com

Website:
http://www.bl4london.com
Summary of all Business Link services and those of the partner organisations.

Enquiries:
Enquiries to: Information Manager

Founded:
2001

Organisation type and purpose:
Service industry.
Business information and advice service.
To provide information and advice to small and medium sized businesses.

Subject coverage:
General business advice, advice on sources of finance, health and safety, export, law, premises, solicitors, accountants, ISO 9000, environment, copyright, patents, regional supply network, markets, company information, marketing, innovation, design, technology, investors in people, quality consultancy, market sector analysis, export advice, individually tailored research service.

Printed publications:
Business Factsheets
Market Sector Reports
Company Reports

Access to staff:
Contact by letter, by telephone, by fax, by e-mail, in person and via website
Hours: Mon to Fri, 0900 to 1730
Special comments: Charges for most services, business counselling and business advice services by appointment.

Head Office:
Business Link for London
Centre Point, 103 New Oxford Street, London, WC1A 1DP

BUSINESS LINK FOR NORTH MANCHESTER

Acronym or abbreviation: BLNM

Wigan Investment Centre, Waterside Drive, Wigan, Lancashire, WN3 5BA

Tel: 01942 705750
Fax: 01942 705296
E-mail: info@businesslinknw.co.uk

Website:
http://www.businesslinknorthmanchester.org.uk

Enquiries:
Enquiries to: Information Officer
Direct tel: 01942 705259
Direct e-mail: mgore@blnm.co.uk

Founded:
1886

Organisation type and purpose:
Local government body, advisory body, manufacturing industry, service industry, suitable for ages: all, training organisation, consultancy.
Business support, business advice.

Subject coverage:
Business information, support services, funding for businesses, export, training, technology and innovation, doing business in Europe.

Museum or gallery collection, archive, or library special collection:
Resource library, containing a wide range of publications, periodicals, marketing publications, reference books and directories (available to the public)

Printed publications:
North West Chambers of Commerce Members Directory
Wigan Business Directory
Wigan Chamber of Commerce Training and Enterprise Ltd Members' Directory

Access to staff:
Contact by letter, by telephone, by fax, by e-mail, in person and via website
Hours: Mon to Thu, 0830 to 1700; Fri, 0830 to 1600

Access to building, collection or gallery:
Prior appointment required

Access for disabled people:
Parking provided, access to all public areas, toilet facilities

Parent body:
North Manchester Chambers Business Services Limited

Partners are:
Bolton & Bury Chamber
Oldham Chamber
Rochdale Borough Chamber
Wigan Borough Partnership (WBP)

Registered office:
Bury Office
Link House, 35 Walmersley Road, Bury, BL9 5AE; tel: 0845 608 3388; fax: 0845 600 9989; e-mail: info@blnm.co.uk
Business Link for North Manchester

Satellite offices:
Bolton Enterprise Services
Washington Street, Bolton, BL3 5EY; tel: 01204 336173
Bolton Office
Oldham Business Centre
Cromwell Street, Oldham, OL1 1BB; tel: 0161 615 5012; fax: 0161 633 6333
Oldham Office
Rochdale Office
The Post Office, The Esplanade, Rochdale, OL16 1AE; tel: 01706 868586; fax: 01706 649979

BUSINESS LINK FOR SUFFOLK LIMITED

Acronym or abbreviation: BLS

Felaw Maltings, 42 Felaw Street, Ipswich, Suffolk, IP2 8PN

Tel: 01473 417000\ Minicom no. 01473 417009
Fax: 01473 417070
E-mail: info@bls.org.uk

Website:
http://www.bls.org.uk
Home pages and current awareness bulletins.

Enquiries:
Enquiries to: Information Manager
Direct tel: 01473 417005
Other contacts: Senior Information Officer

Founded:
1995

Organisation type and purpose:
Advisory body, service industry, consultancy.
Business support aimed at small to medium sized businesses.

Subject coverage:
Information, support and advice to businesses, especially SMEs, financial assistance, starting a business, premises, training, markets, marketing, exporting, staff development, supplier information, company information, general business information.

Museum or gallery collection, archive, or library special collection:
Reference library

Trade and statistical information:
Computer database of Suffolk businesses for mailing lists.
IT training, market research reports, company reports.

continued overleaf

Library catalogue:
All or part available in-house

Printed publications:
British Standards (for purchase)
Leaflets covering all aspects of Business Link
Suffolk's services

Electronic and video publications:
Business Information and News (newsletter, email,
monthly, free to Suffolk businesses)
UK Mailing List Data (for purchase)

Access to staff:
Contact by letter, by telephone, by fax, by e-mail,
in person and via website
Hours: Mon to Fri, 0830 to 1700
Special comments: Some services are chargeable,
others are free.

Access to building, collection or gallery:
Prior appointment required

Access for disabled people:
Ramped entry, access to all public areas, toilet
facilities

Other addresses:
Business Link for Suffolk
The Vision Centre, 5 Eastern Way, Bury St
Edmunds, IP32 7AB

BUSINESS LINK FOR WEST YORKSHIRE

Acronym or abbreviation: BLfWY

Unit 4 Meadow Court, Millshaw Business Park,
Millshaw, Leeds, West Yorkshire, LS11 8LZ

Tel: 0113 383 7744
Fax: 0113 383 7700
E-mail: info@blwy.co.uk

Website:
http://www.blwy.co.uk
Information about services, events, case studies,
etc.

Enquiries:
Enquiries to: Information Officer

Founded:
March 2001

Organisation type and purpose:
Service industry.
Business support to start-ups and small and
medium size enterprises.

Subject coverage:
Business support. Business information.

Printed publications:
Sources of Finance – information on grants and
loans in each local authority area of West
Yorkshire

Access to staff:
Contact by letter, by telephone, by e-mail and via
website
Hours: Mon to Fri, 0800 to 1730

Access for disabled people:
Level entry, toilet facilities

BUSINESS LINK IN LONDON

Link House, 1st and 2nd Floor, 292–308 Southbury
Road, Enfield, EN1 1TS

Tel: 0845 6000 787
E-mail: info@bllondon.co.uk

Website:
www.businesslink.gov.uk/london

Enquiries:
Enquiries to: Information Officer

Organisation type and purpose:
National government body, local government
body, consultancy.
Training business support services for SMEs in
South London (boroughs of Bexley, Greenwich,
Lewisham, Sutton, Bromley and Croydon).

Subject coverage:
Business advisory service for SMEs in London.

Trade and statistical information:
Access to a wide range of trade and statistical
information pertinent to London SMEs.

Printed publications:
A range of booklets, pamphlets, fact sheets etc,
pertinent to London SMEs

Electronic and video publications:
A range of CD-ROM and Online services available
directly and via partner organisations

Access to staff:
Contact by letter, by telephone, by fax and by e-
mail
Hours: Mon to Fri, 0900 to 1730

Access to building, collection or gallery:
Prior appointment required

BUSINESS LINK IN THE NORTH EAST

Acronym or abbreviation: BLTV

Spectrum 6, Spectrum Business Park, Seaham,
Durham, SR7 7TT

Tel: 0845 600 9006
E-mail: enquiries@businesslinknortheast.co.uk

Website:
http://www.teesbusinesslink.co.uk/

Enquiries:
Enquiries to: Customer Liaison Officer
Other contacts: Information Researcher for
Information Research Service.

Founded:
1995

Formerly called:
Business Link Teesside (year of change 1998);
Business Link Tees Valley (year of change 2007)

Organisation type and purpose:
Service industry.
Business support organisation, a partnership of
local public and private business support
organisations throughout Tees Valley.
To provide a single point of access to the business
support network for all Tees Valley businesses.

Subject coverage:
All business-related topics including business
information on companies, markets, products,
finance, legislation. Business Information Research
Service offered on chargeable basis, plus mailing
lists, company financial reports, financial
assistance searches.

**Museum or gallery collection, archive, or library
special collection:**
Local business information including literature on
business support services
Business information directories, CD-ROM and
online services, including Kompass, Corporate
Profound, Equifax, Experian, Grantfinder

Trade and statistical information:
Access to online services, including Corporate
Profound for market research. International
Trade team access DTI services.

Library catalogue:
All or part available in-house

Printed publications:
Promotional literature only

Access to staff:
Contact by letter, by telephone, by fax, by e-mail,
in person and via website
Hours: Mon to Thu, 0830 to 1700; Fri, 0830 to 1630
Special comments: Charges made for some services.

Access to building, collection or gallery:
No prior appointment required
Special comments: Access restricted, by appointment
only.

Branch Office:
Business Link Tees Valley Limited
Training & Enterprise House, 2 Queens Square,
Middlesbrough, TS2 1AA

BUSINESS LINK IN THE SOUTH WEST

Great Western Business Centre, Emlyn Square,
Swindon, Wiltshire SN1 5BP

Tel: 0845 600 9966
E-mail: enquiry@businesslinksw.co.uk

Website:
http://www.businesslink.gov.uk/southwest/

Enquiries:
Enquiries to: Information Manager
Other contacts: Information Officer

Founded:
2007

Created by the merger of:
Business Link Devon and Cornwall and Business
Link Somerset (1997)

Organisation type and purpose:
Service industry.
Access point for those in Somerset wishing to start,
run or develop a business.

Subject coverage:
Company information, market information, legal
and technical information, financial information,
business information.

Access to staff:
Contact by letter, by telephone, by fax and by e-
mail
Hours: Mon to Fri, 0830 to 1700

Access to building, collection or gallery:
Prior appointment required
Hours: Mon to Fri, 0900 to 1700

Access for disabled people:
Yes
Hours: Mon to Fri, 0900 to 1700

BUSINESS LINK LINCOLNSHIRE & RUTLAND

Welton House, Lime Kiln Way, Lincoln, LN2 4WH

Tel: 0845 7574000\ Minicom no. 01522 574111
Fax: 01522 574005
E-mail: enquiries@matrixbusinesslink.co.uk

Website:
http://www.matrixbusinesslink.co.uk
Information of services available from Business
Link Lincolnshire and Rutland.

Enquiries:
Enquiries to: Information Manager
Other contacts: Information Officers

Founded:
1994

Formerly called:
Business Link Lincolnshire (year of change 2001)

Organisation type and purpose:
Service industry.
Business support organisation.
To help small and medium size firms in
Lincolnshire to compete effectively through the
provision of a comprehensive range of business
support services.

Subject coverage:
General business information, business advice
services.

Trade and statistical information:
General statistical information. General market
data.

Access to staff:
Contact by letter, by telephone, by fax, by e-mail,
in person and via website
Hours: Mon to Fri, 0830 to 1700
Special comments: Charges made for some services.

Parent body:
Mercian Matrix Limited

BUSINESS LINK NORTH & WESTERN LANCASHIRE

Leyland House, Lancashire Enterprise Business Park, Centurion Way, Preston, Lancashire, PR26 4TY

Tel: 01772 790200
Fax: 01772 450501

Website:
http://www.nwlbusinesslink.co.uk
About the organisation, advice, support, sign posting.

Enquiries:
Enquiries to: Information Manager
Direct e-mail: info@nwl.businesslink.co.uk

Founded:
1999

Formerly called:
Business Link Central Lancashire (year of change 1999)

Organisation type and purpose:
Advisory body, consultancy.

Subject coverage:
Business information.

Non-library collection catalogue:
All or part available online and in print

Library catalogue:
All or part available online and in print

Publications list:
Available in print

Access to staff:
Contact by letter and by e-mail
Hours: Mon to Fri, 0830 to 1730

Access to building, collection or gallery:
No prior appointment required

Access for disabled people:
Parking provided, ramped entry, access to all public areas, toilet facilities

BUSINESS LINK NORTHWEST

City Office Park, Bluebell Way, Preston, Lancashire, PR2 5PZ

Tel: 0845 0066 888
E-mail: info@businesslinknw.co.uk

Website:
www.businesslink.gov.uk/northwest/
About us, what's new, services, press releases, events diary, case studies, contacts and how to find us.

Enquiries:
Enquiries to: Information Officer
Direct tel: 01228 613271
Direct fax: 01229 877413
Direct e-mail: jhughes@businesslinkcumbria.co.uk
Other contacts: Export Manager for International Trade.

Founded:
1991

Formerly called:
Business Link for Cumbria (year of change 2007)

Organisation type and purpose:
Advisory body, service industry.

Subject coverage:
Business information, export and trade, Cumbrian companies and area.

Printed publications:
e-zine – www.get-theedge.com
Cumbria At Work (business directory, charge)

Access to staff:
Contact by letter, by telephone, by fax, by e-mail and in person
Hours: Mon to Thu, 0830 to 1700; Fri, 0830 to 1630

Access for disabled people:
Parking provided, ramped entry, access to all public areas

Connections with:
Quality Guild
tel: 0870 757 1188

Parent body:
Activ8 Business Solutions Limited
As main address

BUSINESS LINK SOUTH EAST ESSEX

Acronym or abbreviation: BLSEE Ltd

Ground Floor, Chamber House, 845 London Road, Westcliff on Sea, Essex, SS0 9SZ

Tel: 01702 477080
Fax: 01702 477985
E-mail: info@businesslinksee.co.uk

Enquiries:
Enquiries to: Manager

Formerly called:
Business Link (Essex) (BLE), UK Online for Business (UKOB) (year of change 2001)

Organisation type and purpose:
National organisation, training organisation.

Subject coverage:
UK Online for Business authorised learning studio. Part of the government initiative to get businesses online by 2005. All types of computing, internet and business practice courses subsidised to be affordable.

Printed publications:
BLSEE (newsletter, quarterly)
Booklets including:
E-Commerce – Trading Online
Tax Information
Course details

Publications list:
Available in print

Access to staff:
Contact by telephone, by fax, by e-mail and in person
Hours: Mon to Fri, 0900 to 1700

Access to building, collection or gallery:
No access other than to staff

BUSINESS LINK SOUTH YORKSHIRE

Acronym or abbreviation: BLSY

Reresby House, Bow Bridge Close, Templeborough, Rotherham, South Yorkshire, S60 1BY

Tel: 0800 073 7474
Fax: 01709 386330
E-mail: info@blsy.com

Website:
http://www.blsy.com

Enquiries:
Enquiries to: Business Information Adviser

Founded:
2001

Formed from:
Business Link Barnsley, Business Link Doncaster, Business Link Rotherham, Business Link Sheffield (year of change 2001)

Organisation type and purpose:
Business support, advice and information.

Subject coverage:
Business-related topics.

Access to staff:
Contact by letter, by telephone, by fax, by e-mail, in person and via website
Hours: Mon to Thu, 0830 to 1730; Fri, 0830 to 1700

Other offices:
Business Link South Yorkshire
  Enterprise House, White Rose Way, Hyde Park, Doncaster, South Yorkshire, DN4 5ND
Business Link South Yorkshire
  Beevor Court, Pontefract Road, Barnsley, South Yorkshire, S71 1HG
Business Link South Yorkshire
  Albion House, Savile Street, Sheffield, South Yorkshire, S4 7UD

BUSINESS LINK TYNE & WEAR

Business and Innovation Centre, Wearfield, Sunderland Enterprise Park, Sunderland, Tyne and Wear, SR5 2TA

Tel: 0191 516 6700\ Minicom no. 0191 516 6704
Fax: 0191 516 6777

Website:
http://www.businesslinktw.co.uk

Enquiries:
Enquiries to: Information Officer

Founded:
2001

Formerly called:
Business Link Sunderland (year of change 2001)

Organisation type and purpose:
Local government body, service industry.
To assist local businesses with advice and information.

Subject coverage:
Business, companies, credit, health and safety, grants, funding and employment.

Non-library collection catalogue:
All or part available in-house

Access to staff:
Contact by letter, by telephone, by fax, by e-mail and in person
Hours: Mon to Thu, 0900 to 1700; Fri, 0900 to 1630

BUSINESS LINK WESSEX – GILLINGHAM

The Town Hall, School Road, Gillingham, Dorset, SP8 4QR

Tel: 01747 821761
Fax: 01747 821613
E-mail: enquiries@businesslinkwessex.co.uk

Website:
http://www.businesslink.org
http://www.businesslinkwessex.co.uk

Founded:
2001

Formerly called:
Business Link Dorset (year of change 2001)

Organisation type and purpose:
National government body, advisory body.
Business development and support.

Subject coverage:
Business advice and information.

Access to staff:
Appointment necessary.

Satellite of the main office:
Business Link Wessex
  Wates House, Wallington Hill, Fareham, Hampshire, PO16 7BJ; tel: 08454 588558

BUSINESS LINK WESSEX – NEWPORT IOW

Mill Court, Furlong, Newport, Isle of Wight, PO30 2AA

Tel: 01983 534501

Founded:
1994

continued overleaf

Formerly called:
Business Link Isle of Wight

Organisation type and purpose:
Advisory body, service industry.
A one-stop shop for business advice and information.

Subject coverage:
Every aspect of information, advice and support for start-up and existing businesses on the Isle of Wight.

Access to staff:
Contact by letter, by telephone and in person
Hours: Mon to Fri, 0830 to 1715

Head Office:
Business Link Wessex
Fareham, Hampshire

BUSINESS LINK WEST

Leigh Court Business Centre, Abbots Leigh, Bristol, BS8 3RA

Tel: 01275 373373
Fax: 01275 370706
E-mail: info@businesswest.co.uk

Website:
http://www.businesswest.co.uk

Enquiries:
Enquiries to: Information Manager

Founded:
1995

Organisation type and purpose:
National government body.
Headquarters office of Business Link West.

Subject coverage:
Business information and support services.

Printed publications:
Link magazine

Access to staff:
Contact by letter, by telephone, by fax, by e-mail, in person and via website. Appointment necessary. Non-members charged.
Hours: Mon to Fri, 0900 to 1700

Access to building, collection or gallery:
No prior appointment required

Outlets at:
Bath, South Gloucestershire, North Somerset

Partners are:
Bath & North East Somerset, South Gloucestershire & North Somerset Councils

BUSINESS LINK WEST (NORTH SOMERSET)

Formal name: Business Link West (North Somerset) is the trading name of the North Somerset Enterprise Agency
Acronym or abbreviation: BLW or NSEA

The Link Centre, Oldmixon Crescent, Weston-Super-Mare, Somerset, BS24 9AY

Tel: 01934 418118
Fax: 01934 629541
E-mail: enquiries@businesswest.co.uk

Website:
http://www.northsomersetenterpriseagency.co.uk

Enquiries:
Enquiries to: Chief Executive

Founded:
1987

Formerly called:
Weston and Woodspring Enterprise Agency (year of change 1996)

Organisation type and purpose:
Service industry.
Non-profit making organisation set up to give business advice and training in the community.

Subject coverage:
Export, finance, grants, inward investment, starting a business, legal, networking, marketing, health and safety, sourcing, planning, premises, legislation, BS EN ISO 9000.

Museum or gallery collection, archive, or library special collection:
Business directories
DTI literature, export and business
Inland Revenue, Employment Service and Customs and Excise literature

Printed publications:
Various leaflets
Business Matters Newsletter (free)
Business Link Magazine (free)

Access to staff:
Contact by letter, by telephone, by fax, by e-mail and via website. Appointment necessary.
Hours: Mon to Fri, 0900 to 1700

Access to building, collection or gallery:
Mon to Fri, 0900 to 1700

Access for disabled people:
Ramped entry

Also houses the:
North Somerset Enterprise Agency

BUSINESS LINK WEST MIDLANDS

Advantage House, 19 Ridgeway, Quinton Business Park, Quinton, Birmingham, West Midlands, B32 1AL

Tel: 0845 113 1234
E-mail: info@businesslinkwm.co.uk

Website:
http://www.businesslinkwm.co.uk/
Guide to services

Enquiries:
Enquiries to: Business Support Team
Other contacts: Marketing Manager

Founded:
1995

Formerly called:
Business Link Staffordshire (year of change 2007)

Organisation type and purpose:
Service industry.

Subject coverage:
General business advice, grants, legislation, mailing lists, published market research.

Access to staff:
Contact by letter, by telephone, by fax, by e-mail, in person and via website
Hours: Mon to Fri, 0830 to 1730

Access to building, collection or gallery:
Prior appointment required

Access for disabled people:
Parking provided, level entry, toilet facilities

Other office:
Business Link Staffordshire
Cannock

BUSINESS LINK YORKSHIRE

1 Capitol Court, Capitol Business Park, Dodworth, Barnsley, S75 3TZ

Tel: 0845 6 048 048
E-mail: info@businesslinkyorkshire.co.uk

Website:
http://www.businesslink.gov.uk/yorkshire/

Enquiries:
Enquiries to: Managing Director
Other contacts: Information Adviser for all enquiries.

Founded:
1998

Formerly called:
Business Link (Boothferry) Limited, Business Link (Grimsby and Cleethorpe) Limited, Business Link (Hull and East Riding) Limited, Business Link (North Lincolnshire) Limited (year of change 1998); Business Link (Humberside) Limited (year of change 2001); Business Link Humber (year of change 2008)

Organisation type and purpose:
Local government body, research organisation.
Business information service, market intelligence and research.
To help SMEs increase their competitiveness by access to market information and business advisory services.

Subject coverage:
Business information, credit ratings, mailing lists, market research UK and international.

Access to staff:
Contact by letter, by telephone, by fax, by e-mail, in person and via website
Hours: Mon to Fri, 0800 to 1700
Special comments: Businesses in the Humberside area (North Lincolnshire, North East Lincolnshire, Hull, East Riding of Yorkshire).

Other offices:
Business Link Humber
10–14 Hainton Square, Grimsby, DN32 9BB; tel: 01472 312121; fax: 01472 312131
Business Link Humber
Kingsway Centre, Kingsway, Scunthorpe, DN17 1AL; tel: 01724 867190
Business Link Humber
Bridlington Business Centre, Bessingby Industrial Estate, Bridlington, YO16 4SF; tel: 01262 401399; fax: 01262 401633; e-mail: info@blhumber.co.uk
Business Link Humber
East Riding Small Business Centre, Annie Reed Road, Beverley, HU17 0LF; tel: 01482 880460; fax: 01482 880442
Business Link Humber
Berkeley House, Doncaster Road, Scunthorpe, DN15 7DQ; tel: 01724 270444; fax: 01724 276773
Business Link Humber
The Old Goole Shipyard, Swinefleet Road, Goole; tel: 01405 722630
Business Link Humber (HABAC)
Samman House, Bowlalley Lane, Hull, HU3 1XR; tel: 01482 607100; fax: 01482 607102

Parent body:
A4E Consult

Part of:
Business Link Network

BUSINESS SERVICES ASSOCIATION

Acronym or abbreviation: BSA

Warnford Court, 29 Throgmorton Street, London, EC2N 2AT

Tel: 020 7786 6300
Fax: 020 7786 6309
E-mail: holly.edwards@bsa-org.com

Website:
http://www.bsa-org.com

Enquiries:
Enquiries to: Director General
Direct tel: 020 7786 6301
Direct e-mail: norman.rose@bsa-org.com

Founded:
1993

Organisation type and purpose:
Trade association (membership is by subscription), present number of members: 19, service industry.
Leading representative of major companies in the business services industry. BSA is secretary of the Parliamentary All Party Group for Business Services and represents the views of the industry to government.

Has close links with UK and EU government monitoring policies and legislation. It develops policy papers on issues of employment and social policy including Best Value in local government contracting, public sector pensions and National Minimum Wage.

Subject coverage:
Support services, public sector market testing, employment legislation, government tendering, EU markets, PFI, local government contracting, pensions, training.

Trade and statistical information:
Data on private companies competing for public sector markets.

Printed publications:
Briefing brochure on the BSA
Newsletter (quarterly)

Access to staff:
Contact by letter, by telephone, by fax and by e-mail
Hours: Mon to Fri, 0900 to 1700

Access to building, collection or gallery:
No access other than to staff

BUSINESS SOFTWARE ALLIANCE

Acronym or abbreviation: BSA

79 Knightsbridge, London, SW1X 7RB

Tel: 020 7245 0304
Fax: 020 7245 0310

Website:
http://www.bsa.org

Enquiries:
Enquiries to: Communications Manager

Founded:
1988

Organisation type and purpose:
International organisation, trade association. Alliance of Microsoft, Novell/WordPerfect, Adobe, Autodesk, Bentley Systems, Apple, Borland, CNC/ Mastercam, Macromedia, Symantec and Unigraphics Solutions.

Subject coverage:
Software piracy, its occurrence and prevention, software management.

Trade and statistical information:
Statistics on software piracy and what this has cost in jobs and taxes in Europe.

Electronic and video publications:
Audit Disk (for purchase)

Access to staff:
Contact by letter, by telephone and by fax
Hours: Mon to Fri, 0900 to 1700

Access to building, collection or gallery:
No access other than to staff

Headquarters of the:
BSA
1180 18th Street NW, Suite 700, Washington, DC, 20036, USA; tel: + 1 202 872 5500; fax: + 1 202 872 5501

BUSINESS WEST

Formal name: Bristol Chamber of Commerce and Initiative (trading as Business West)

Leigh Court Business Centre, Abbots Leigh, Bristol, BS8 3RA

Tel: 01275 373373
Fax: 01275 370706
E-mail: info@businesswest.co.uk

Website:
http://www.businesswest.co.uk

Enquiries:
Enquiries to: Information Services Manager

Founded:
1826

Organisation type and purpose:
Membership association (membership is by subscription), present number of members: 2400, service industry.
Business Link.

Subject coverage:
Industrial, commercial and financial affairs in Bristol and region: overseas trade, travel and marketing; overseas trade documentation; transport and shipping procedures; general business information; export credit insurance; EU legislation and public sector tenders information; credit referencing.

Museum or gallery collection, archive, or library special collection:
Company Information and Market Information, UK and worldwide
EC legislation: Official journal (LC and S series)
Electronic Database Information
Standard reference material for business information

Trade and statistical information:
UK and European statistics.
CSO data.
Tradstats.

Printed publications:
Directory of Members

Access to staff:
Contact by telephone, by fax and by e-mail. Non-members charged.
Hours: Mon to Fri, 0900 to 1700

Affiliated to:
Bristol Euro Info Centre (EIC)
at the same address

BUSINESS-COMMUNITY CONNECTIONS, CRAIGMILLAR AND SOUTH EDINBURGH

Castlebrae Community High School, 2a Greendykes Road, Edinburgh, EH16 4DP

Tel: 0131 652 0367
Fax: 0131 661 9811
E-mail: janet@ednet.co.uk

Website:
http://www.craigmillarinfo.co.uk

Enquiries:
Enquiries to: Manager

Founded:
1991

Formerly called:
Friends of Craigmillar (year of change 2000)

Organisation type and purpose:
Registered charity.
To act as a link between the business and community sector to generate jobs for local people and to create innovative working links.

Subject coverage:
Links between community groups and the private sector.

Printed publications:
Newsletter (quarterly, free)

Microform publications:
Slides

Access to staff:
Contact by letter, by telephone and by fax
Hours: Mon to Fri, 0900 to 1700

Access to building, collection or gallery:
Prior appointment required

Access for disabled people:
Parking provided, level entry

BUTTERFLY CONSERVATION

Acronym or abbreviation: BC

Manor Yard, East Lulworth, Wareham, Dorset, BH20 5QP

Tel: 0870 7744 309
Fax: 0870 7706 150
E-mail: info@butterfly-conservation.org

Website:
http://www.butterfly-conservation.org

Enquiries:
Enquiries to: Publicity Officer
Direct e-mail: cmallinson@butterfly-conservation .org

Founded:
1968

Formerly called:
British Butterfly Conservation Society Limited (BBCS)

Organisation type and purpose:
Membership association (membership is by subscription), present number of members: 11,500, registered charity (charity number 254937), the UK charity taking action to save butterflies, moths and their habitats.
Conservation society.

Subject coverage:
Butterfly and moth conservation, species information, habitat information, research, monitoring, nature reserves.

Printed publications:
Butterfly Magazine (3 times a year, free to members)
Species Action Plans for each of 22 threatened species (£5 each inc. p&p)
Booklets, occasional papers
Saving Butterflies – a practical guide to the conservation of butterflies (ed Dunbar D, £5 soft, £7 hard inc. p&p)

Publications list:
Available in print

Access to staff:
Contact by letter, by telephone, by fax and by e-mail
Hours: Mon to Fri, 0900 to 1700

Associated with:
Butterfly Recording Scheme
English Nature
JCCBI
Wildlife Link

Has:
32 branches

BUTTERFLY HOUSE

Formal name: Seaforde Gardens and Tropical Butterfly House

Seaforde Demense, Seaforde, Downpatrick, Co Down, BT30 8PG

Tel: 028 4481 1225
Fax: 028 4481 1370
E-mail: plants@seafordegardens.com

Enquiries:
Enquiries to: Owner

Founded:
1988

Subject coverage:
Gardens, maze and tropical butterfly house

Access to staff:
Contact by letter, by fax and by e-mail

Access to building, collection or gallery:
Hours: Easter to end September: Mon to Sat, 1000 to 1700; Sun, 1300 to 1800

Access for disabled people:
Parking provided, access to all public areas, toilet facilities

BUTTERWORTH-HEINEMANN

Linacre House, Jordan Hill, Oxford, OX2 8DP

Tel: 01865 310366
Fax: 01865 314519

continued overleaf

E-mail: bhmarketing@repp.co.uk

Website:
http://www.bh.com
Comprehensive details of all available and
forthcoming titles.

Enquiries:
Enquiries to: Administrator
Direct tel: 01865 314492
Direct e-mail: maggie.harte@repp.co.uk

Founded:
1990

Formerly called:
Butterworth Scientific Limited, Heinemann
Professional Publishing

Organisation type and purpose:
Publishing house.
Books and electronic products. An Imprint of
Elsevier Science.

Subject coverage:
Software development; information systems;
strategy formulation and implementation,
architecture, networking, data communications,
programming, IS/IT management, personal
computing, internet, business, open learning fields
for tertiary and professional qualification.

Printed publications:
Numerous titles under the following headings:
IS/IT Management
Networking and Data Communications
Personal Computing
Software Development/Programming
Systems/Intervals/Architecture
Order printed publications from: Customer Services
Department, Reed Publishers, Oxford
PO Box 382, Halley Court, Jordan Hill, Oxford,
OX2 8RU, tel: 01865 888110, fax: 01865 314029, e-
mail: bhuk.orders@repp.co.uk

Publications list:
Available online and in print

Access to staff:
Contact by letter, by fax, by e-mail and via
website
Hours: Mon to Fri, 0900 to 1700

Parent body:
Elsevier Science

BUTTONHOOK SOCIETY

2 Romney Place, Maidstone, Kent, ME15 6LE

Tel: 01622 752949
Fax: 01622 752949
E-mail: buttonhooksociety@tiscali.co.uk

Website:
http://www.thebuttonhooksociety.com

Enquiries:
Enquiries to: Chairman

Founded:
1979

Organisation type and purpose:
International organisation, learned society
(membership is by subscription), research
organisation.
Archives of over 70,000 buttonhooks.
Research into origins and social history associated
with buttonhooks.

Subject coverage:
Buttonhooks, their origins, history, social context,
materials and construction, costume, sources of
information and areas of further research.

Information services:
Speakers list available

**Museum or gallery collection, archive, or library
special collection:**
Computerised archival material on known
buttonhooks in collections, sorted by type and
material

Non-library collection catalogue:
All or part available in-house

Printed publications:
Antique buttonhooks (Bettersley B)
Buttonhooks and Shoehorns (Sue Brandon, pub.
 Shire Books)
Buttonhooks (Booker J)
Collecting Buttonhooks (Compton C)
Compendium of Buttonhooks
Glovehook in Colour (Moorehead P G)
Newsletter (6 times a year, for members)
The Boutonneur
Buttonhooks to Trade, to Treasure (Bettersley B)
Specialities & Novelties in Shoe Store Supplies
 (1920 US Catalogue reprint)

Publications list:
Available in print

Access to staff:
Contact by letter, by telephone, by e-mail and via
website
Hours: Mon to Fri, 0900 to 1700

Associated with:
Button Society
Costume Society

Other addresses:
Overseas coordinator for American members
 Box 287, White Marsh, Maryland, 21162–0287,
 USA

BYRON SOCIETY

Byron House, 6 Gertrude Street, London, SW10
0JN

Tel: 020 7352 5112

Enquiries:
Enquiries to: Honorary Director

Founded:
1972

Organisation type and purpose:
Learned society.

Subject coverage:
Lord Byron's life and works, and those of his
contemporaries (1788–1824).

Printed publications:
The Byron Journal (annually, £5 per copy)

Access to staff:
Contact by letter
Hours: Mon to Fri, 0900 to 1700

Includes the:
International Byron Society; maintains contact with
many literary societies

CAB INTERNATIONAL

Formal name: Centre for Agriculture and
Biosciences International
Acronym or abbreviation: CABI

Wallingford, Oxfordshire, OX10 8DE

Tel: 01491 832111
Fax: 01491 833508
E-mail: cabi@cabi.org

Website:
http://www.cabi.org/
Full range of products and services, together with
information on our scientific institutes, developing
country initiatives and training programmes.

Enquiries:
Enquiries to: Director General

Founded:
1929

Formerly called:
Imperial Agricultural Bureaux (year of change
1948); Commonwealth Agricultural Bureaux (year
of change 1985)

Incorporates:
Bureau of Hygiene and Tropical Diseases (year of
change 1993)

Organisation type and purpose:
International organisation, membership
association (membership is by election or
invitation), present number of members: 41
countries, training organisation, consultancy,
research organisation.
Intergovernmental organisation, granted
international status under the International
Organisations Act of 1985.
Provides information, scientific and development
services in the applied life sciences.

Subject coverage:
Agriculture, forestry and forest products, field
crops, grasslands, horticulture, crop protection,
plant and animal breeding, veterinary science,
water pollution and quality, leisure, recreation and
tourism. Rural sociology and development. Public
health, communicable diseases, tropical diseases,
community health and medicine, environmental
science, soils, land and water management,
biotechnology, biodiversity, biosystematics,
integrated pest management, biological control,
human and animal nutrition, human and animal
parasitology, AIDS.

Printed publications:
Abstract Journals (over 50 current titles)
Primary Journals
Review Journals
Annotated Bibliographies (over 3,000 titles)
Annual Report
Directories
Distribution maps of pests
Identification keys
Newsletters
Review articles
Reference Textbooks
Training manuals etc
Order printed publications from: Publishing Division,
CAB INTERNATIONAL
Wallingford, Oxfordshire, OX10 8DE

Microform publications:
Contact marketing department

Electronic and video publications:
CABCD (CAB ABSTRACTS database) series in CD
 format
Electronic multimedia compendium on CD-ROM
 eg Crop Protection Compendium
Many abstract products on CD-ROM and diskette
CD-ROM Topics in International Health (resource
 collection for researchers, professionals and
 students, more titles available in 1999)

Publications list:
Available in print

Access to staff:
Contact by letter, by fax, by e-mail and via
website
Hours: Mon to Fri, 0900 to 1700

Access for disabled people:
Parking provided, level entry

Member countries:
Australia, Bahamas, Bangladesh, Belize, Botswana,
Brunei Darussalam, Canada, People's Republic of
China, Chile, Colombia, Cyprus, Fiji, Gambia,
Ghana, Guyana, Hungary, India, Indonesia,
Jamaica, Kenya, Malawi, Malaysia, Mauritius,
Myanmar, New Zealand, Nigeria, Pakistan, Papua
New Guinea, Philippines, Sierra Leone, Solomon
Islands, South Africa, Sri Lanka, Tanzania,
Trinidad & Tobago, Uganda, United Kingdom, UK
Dependent Territories, Vietnam, Zambia,
Zimbabwe

Other addresses:
CAB INTERNATIONAL
 Headquarters, CABI Publishing, Wallingford,
 Oxfordshire, OX10 8DE; tel: 01491 832111; fax:
 01491 829292; e-mail: publishing@cabi.org
CAB International Africa Regional Centre
 ICRAF Complex, PO Box 633, Village Market,
 Nairobi, Kenya; tel: + 254 2 524462; fax: + 254 2
 522150; e-mail: arc@cabi.org
CAB International Caribbean Regional Centre
 Gordon Street, Curepe, Trinidad & Tobago, West
 Indies; tel: + 1 868 645 7628; fax: + 1 868 663 2859;
 e-mail: crc@cabi.org

CAB International North America
CABI Publishing, 10 East 40th Street, Suite 3203, New York, NY 10016, USA; tel: +1 212 481 7018 and +1 800 528 4841; fax: +1 212 686 7993; e-mail: cabi-nao@cabi.org

CAB International South-East Asia Regional Centre
MARDI, PO Box 210, 43409 UPM Serdang, Malaysia; tel: +60 3 894 32921; fax: +60 3 894 36400; e-mail: searc@cabi.org

CABI Bioscience Switzerland Centre
1 Rue des Grillons, CH-2800 Delémont, Switzerland; tel: + 41 32 421 4870; fax: + 41 32 421 4871; e-mail: swiss.centre@cabi-bioscience.ch

CABI Bioscience UK Centre
Bakeham Lane, Egham, Surrey, TW20 9TY; tel: 0178 470111; fax: 01491 829100; e-mail: bioscience.egham@cabi.org

CABI Bioscience UK Centre
Silwood Park, Buckhurst Road, Ascot, Berkshire, SL5 7TA; tel: 01491 829129; fax: 01212 686 7993

Registered with the:
United Nations

CACDP

Mersey House, Mandale Business Park, Belmont, Durham, DH1 1TH

Tel: 0191 383 1155\ Minicom no. 0191 383 7915
Fax: 0191 383 7914
E-mail: durham@cacdp.org.uk

Website:
http://www.cacdp.org.uk
Publications, factsheets, NVQ information, subscribing to CACDP, examinations, diary dates, links.

Enquiries:
Enquiries to: Communications Team Support
Direct tel: 0191 383 7922
Direct e-mail: claret@cacdp.org.uk

Founded:
1982

Organisation type and purpose:
Registered charity. A UK awarding body accredited by the Qualifications and Curriculum Authority offering a wide range of high quality qualifications in British Sign language and other forms of communication used by deaf and deafblind people. Also conducts the selection, training and monitoring of assessors. Promotes the importance of professional standards and working practices amongst those offering linguistic access services. Maintains a register of qualified and trainee interpreters and publishes a national directory of Sign Language Interpreters, Lipspeakers and Interpreters for deafblind people. To provide knowledge and recognise skills in the languages and communication methods used by deaf people.

Subject coverage:
Communicating with deaf or deafblind people, British sign language, lipspeaking, communicating and guiding skills with deafblind people, sign language interpreting, deaf awareness, deafblind awareness.

Printed publications:
Annual Report (free)
Deaf Awareness Curriculum (£5)
Directory 2001/02 (£17)
Fact sheets – communicating with deafblind people, communicating with social workers, lipspeaking, NVQs, sign language interpreting
General Information Leaflet
Interpreting (Manual Alphabet) Pack (£150)
Newsletter (quarterly)
Note-taking teaching Pack (£50)
Review (annually)

Electronic and video publications:
Sign language videos – which give practice in signing for students
Lipspeaking (video £25)

Publications list:
Available online and in print

Access to staff:
Contact by letter, by telephone, by fax, by e-mail and via website
Hours: Mon to Thu, 0900 to 1700; Fri, 0900 to 1630
Special comments: All enquiries to Durham office.

Northern Ireland Office:
CACDP
Wilton House, 5 College Square North, Belfast, BT1 6AR; tel: 028 9043 8161 (voice and text); fax: 028 9043 8161

CADOGAN TIETZ LIMITED

14 Clerkenwell Close, London, EC1R 0PQ

Tel: 020 7490 5050
Fax: 020 7490 2160
E-mail: info@tietz.co.uk

Website:
http://www.tietz.co.uk

Enquiries:
Enquiries to: Managing Director

Founded:
1959

Formerly called:
S B Tietz & Partners (year of change 1999)

Organisation type and purpose:
Consultancy.
Consulting civil, structural, process, energy, mechanical and electrical engineers. Forensic engineers and project managers.

Subject coverage:
Civil, structural and traffic engineering, mechanical and electrical engineering, energy efficiency, industrial process design and waste disposal.

Access to staff:
Contact by letter, by telephone, by fax, by e-mail and via website
Hours: Mon to Fri, 0900 to 1700

CAERNARFON AREA RECORD OFFICE

County Offices, Shirehall Street, Caernarfon, Gwynedd, LL55 1SH

Tel: 01286 679088
Fax: 01286 679637
E-mail: AnnRhydderch@gwynedd.gov.uk

Website:
http://www.llgc.org.uk/cac/cac0053.htm
Basic information, telephone numbers, classes of records, services to public.
http://www.gwynedd.gov.uk/archives

Enquiries:
Enquiries to: Archivist

Founded:
1947

Organisation type and purpose:
Local government body.

Subject coverage:
Local government archives, parish material, estates, industrial (predominantly slate), maritime records.

Non-library collection catalogue:
All or part available online

Printed publications:
Several publications of Gwynedd historical interest
Maritime Wales (journal, annually)

Publications list:
Available online

Access to staff:
Contact by letter, by telephone, by fax, by e-mail and in person
Hours: Mon, closed; Tue, Thu, Fri, 0930 to 1230, 1330 to 1700; Wed, 0930 to 1230, 1330 to 1900

Special comments: CARN Reader's ticket required.

Access for disabled people:
Level entry, access to all public areas, toilet facilities

CAERNARVONSHIRE HISTORICAL SOCIETY

County Offices, Caernarfon, Gwynedd, LL55 1SH

Tel: 01286 679088
Fax: 01286 679637

Enquiries:
Enquiries to: Honorary Secretary

Founded:
1939

Organisation type and purpose:
Learned society, voluntary organisation, registered charity.
Historical Society.

Subject coverage:
Local history in the former county of Caernarvon (now Gwynedd).

Printed publications:
Transactions (annually)

Access to staff:
Contact by letter, by telephone and by fax
Hours: Mon to Fri, 0900 to 1700

Member of:
Federation of Local History Societies in Caernarvonshire

CAERPHILLY COUNTY BOROUGH COUNCIL

Nelson Road, Tredomen, Ystrad Mynach, Mid Glamorgan, CF82 7WF

Tel: 01443 815588 or 01495 226622
Fax: 01443 863029

Website:
http://www.caerphilly.gov.uk
Information on the area: tourism, business opportunities, training. Information on the Council; news and views.

Enquiries:
Enquiries to: Communications Manager
Direct tel: 01443 864262
Direct fax: 01443 864246
Direct e-mail: rosemarymathews@caerphilly.gov.uk

Founded:
1996

Formerly called:
Gwent County Council, Islwyn Borough Council, Mid Glamorgan County Council, Rhymney Valley District Council

Organisation type and purpose:
Local government body.

Subject coverage:
Socio-economic data about the county borough.

Printed publications:
Caerphilly County Borough Ward Profiles based on census of population conducted every 10 years
Caerphilly Street Atlas
Caerphilly Insight: A Profile of Caerphilly County Borough

Access to staff:
Contact by letter
Hours: Mon to Thu, 0830 to 1700; Fri, 0830 to 1630

CAIRNGORM REINDEER CENTRE, THE

Glenmore Forest Park, Visitors Centre, Aviemore, Inverness-shire, PH22 1QU

Tel: 01479 861228
Fax: 01479 861228

continued overleaf

E-mail: reindeerinfo@btinternet.com

Enquiries:
Enquiries to: Director

Founded:
1952

Organisation type and purpose:
Promotion and research of reindeer.

Subject coverage:
Reindeer breeding and general husbandry, training to harness, import/export of reindeer to and from the UK.

Printed publications:
Rangifer Tarandus, Reindeer (small booklet)
Velvet Antlers, Velvet Noses (Smith T, pub. Hodder and Stoughton)

Publications list:
Available in print

Access to staff:
Contact by letter, by fax and by e-mail
Hours: Mon to Fri, 0900 to 1700

CALDERDALE COLLEGE

Learning Resources Centre, Francis Street, Halifax, West Yorkshire, HX1 3UZ

Tel: 01422 399312
Fax: 01422 399320
E-mail: kenp@calderdale.ac.uk

Website:
http://www.calderdale.ac.uk
Details of college departments, courses and facilities.

Enquiries:
Enquiries to: Head of Learning Resources

Formerly called:
Percival Whitley College of Further Education Library and Resources

Organisation type and purpose:
Further educational college

Subject coverage:
All subjects covered by the further education curriculum; building construction; information technology; health and safety; further and adult education; chemistry; physics; biology; mathematics; computing; commercial art; business; strongest subjects are business and social care, graphic and fine arts, photography, service industries, health and caring.

Library catalogue:
All or part available online

Access to staff:
Contact by letter, by telephone, by fax and by e-mail. Appointment necessary. Letter of introduction required.
Hours: Mon to Thu, 0845 to 2000; Fri, 0915 to 1600; Sat, 1000 to 1300 (term only).
Special comments: Restricted hours during college vacations.

Access for disabled people:
Level entry, access to all public areas, toilet facilities

Member organisation of:
Leeds Metropolitan University Regional University Network
website: http://www.leedsmet.ac.uk/regional/new
Welcome!
website: http://welcome.hud.ac.uk

CALDERDALE FAMILY HISTORY SOCIETY

Acronym or abbreviation: CFHS

288 Halifax Road, Hove Edge, Brighouse, West Yorkshire, HD6 2PB

Tel: 01484 718576
E-mail: mail@cfhsweb.co.uk

Website:
http://www.cfhsweb.co.uk
Full information concerning the Society, our publications and ability to become a member.

Enquiries:
Enquiries to: Chairman

Founded:
1985

Organisation type and purpose:
Membership association (membership is by subscription).
The Society exists to encourage interest in, and assist in, matters relating to genealogy and family history, and to record and preserve genealogical material for future generations.

Subject coverage:
Genealogy, family history, particularly with relation to Halifax (West Yorkshire) and surrounding areas.

Museum or gallery collection, archive, or library special collection:
Calderdale War Dead
Other local summary information

Non-library collection catalogue:
All or part available in print

Library catalogue:
All or part available in-house

Printed publications:
Halifax St. John's Parish Church Baptisms 1813–1838, Marriages 1754–1837 and Burials 1813–1937
Elland St. Mary's Parish Church Baptisms 1559–1850, Marriages 1559–1837 and Burials 1559–1843
1851 Census – All areas within the Halifax Registration District
Monumental Inscriptions
Order printed publications from: Publications Officer, Calderdale Family History Society
22 Well Grove, Hove Edge, Brighouse, HD6 2LT
tel: 01484 714311, e-mail: publications@cfhsweb.co.uk

Microform publications:
Halifax Parish Church Baptisms 1813–1838, Marriages 1754–1837 and Burials 1813–1937
Elland St. Mary's Parish Church Baptisms 1559–1850, Marriages 1559–1837 and Burials 1559–1843
1851 Census Hebden Bridge
1841 and 1851 Census Todmorden

Electronic and video publications:
CDs:
Halifax Census (1881)
St Mary Elland Births, Deaths and Marriages (1558–1837)
St John Halifax Births, Deaths and Marriages (1812–1837)
Censuses (1801–1831)

Publications list:
Available in print

Access to staff:
Contact by letter, by telephone and by e-mail
Hours: Sun to Sat, 1000 to 2100; Research Room, Brighouse Library Tues 13:30 to 16:30 & Thurs 10:00 to 13:00

CALDERDALE LIBRARIES

Central Library, Northgate, Halifax, West Yorkshire, HX1 1UN

Tel: 01422 392630
Fax: 01422 392615
E-mail: libraries@calderdale.gov.uk

Website:
http://www.calderdale.gov.uk

Enquiries:
Enquiries to: Information Services Team Leader
Direct tel: 01422 392631
Direct fax: 01422 349458
Direct e-mail: reference.library@calderdale.gov.uk

Founded:
1882

Formerly called:
Halifax Central Library, Halifax Public Libraries

Organisation type and purpose:
Local government body, public library, suitable for all ages.

Subject coverage:
General; Calderdale local history.

Services for disabled people:
Access to all unit, including assistive technology for full access to IT services

Museum or gallery collection, archive, or library special collection:
Edwards Bindings (Halifax late 18th and early 19th centuries)
Horsfall Turner Local History Collection (Calderdale)
Milner Collection (publications of William Milner dating 1834–1913)
Phyllis Bentley Collection (MS books and work books)
Some incunabula

Library catalogue:
All or part available online and in-house

Access to staff:
Contact by letter, by telephone, by fax, by e-mail and in person
Hours: Mon, Tue, Thu and Fri, 0930 to 1900; Sat, 0930 to 1700

Access for disabled people:
Access to all public areas

Branch libraries:
21 local branches, 2 mobile libraries

Parent body:
Calderdale Metropolitan Borough Council
Town Hall, Crossley Street, Halifax, HX1 1UJ; tel: 01422 357257; fax: 01422 393102

CALEDONIAN RAILWAY ASSOCIATION

Acronym or abbreviation: CRA

63 Andrew Drive, Clydebank, Dunbartonshire, G81 1BU

E-mail: dwhind@ukonline.co.uk

Website:
http://www.crassoc.org.uk

Enquiries:
Enquiries to: Secretary

Founded:
1983

Organisation type and purpose:
Voluntary organisation, research organisation.

Subject coverage:
Research and study of former Caledonian Railway Company, including locomotive drawings, coach and wagon drawing, signal box track diagrams, industrial relations, architecture, publicity material, shipping services, tickets and history.

Printed publications:
Locomotive Drawings (quarterly)
Signal Box Track Diagrams (quarterly)
The True Line (journal, quarterly)
Timetable reprints (periodically)
Wagon Drawings (quarterly)
Order printed publications from: Sales Officer, Caledonian Railway Association, 73 Victoria Park Drive North, Glasgow, G14 9PS

Access to staff:
Contact by letter, by telephone and by e-mail.
Non-members charged.
Hours: Mon to Fri, 0900 to 1700
Special comments: Sample publications sent in return for two 2nd class stamps.

CALOUSTE GULBENKIAN FOUNDATION

98 Portland Place, London, W1B 1ET

Tel: 020 7636 5313
Fax: 020 7908 7580
E-mail: info@gulbenkian.org.uk

Website:
http://www.gulbenkian.org.uk
Information on how to apply for grants,
Foundation priorities for grants and recent
publications

Enquiries:
Enquiries to: Information Officer

Founded:
1956

Organisation type and purpose:
Charitable foundation.

Subject coverage:
Arts, education, social welfare, Anglo-Portuguese
cultural relations.

Printed publications:
Advice to applicants (free)
Annual report (free)
Reports include:
Art not Chance: Nine artists' diaries
Centres for Curiosity and Imagination
Children and Violence
Creating Chances: Arts interventions in Pupil
  Referral Units and Learning Support Units
Experience and Experiment: The UK Branch of the
  Calouste Gulbenkian Foundation 1956–2006
Fit to Dance? The Report of the National Inquiry
  into Dancers' Health and Injury
Hospice Without Walls
Joining In: An Investigation into Participatory
  Music
Let's Act Locally – The Growth of Local Exchange
  Trading Systems
Mediation in Action
Passport: A framework for personal and social
  development
Public Interest: New models for delivering public
  services?
Rethinking Families
Science, not Art: Ten scientists' diaries
Serious Play: An evaluation of arts activities in
  Pupil Referral Units and Learning Support Units
Social Enterprise in Anytown
Strange and Charmed: Science and the
  contemporary visual arts
Taking Children Seriously: A Proposal for a
  Children's Rights Commissioner (New edition)
The Arts in Schools: – principles, practice and
  provision
The Turning World: Stories from the London
  International Festival of Theatre
Tomorrow's Parents: Developing Parenthood
  Education in Schools
UK Review of Effective Government Structures for
  Children 2001
Understanding the Stranger: Building Bridges
  Commmunity Handbook
Why Restorative Justice? Repairing the harm
  caused by crime
Wild Reckoning: An anthology provoked by
  Rachel Carson's 'Silent Spring'
Wise Before the Event – coping with crises in
  school
Plus others – see Publications List (free)
Order printed publications from: Central Books Ltd,
99 Wallis Road, London E9 5LN, tel: 0845 458 9911,
fax: 0845 458 9912; e-mail:
orders@centralbooks.com website:
www.centralbooks.co.uk

Publications list:
Available online and in print

Access to staff:
Contact by letter, by telephone, by fax and by e-
mail
Hours: Mon to Fri, 0930 to 1730
Special comments: Telephone messages taken all
day.

Parent body:
Calouste Culbenkian Foundation
  Avenida de Berna 45A, Lisbon, 1067–001,
  Portugal; tel: 00 35121 782 3000; fax: 00 35121 782
  3021; e-mail: info@gulbenkian.pt; website: www
  .gulbenkian.pt

CAMANACHD ASSOCIATION

Alton House, 4 Ballifeary Road, Inverness, IV3 5PJ

Tel: 01463 715931
E-mail: admin@shinty.com

Website:
http://www.shinty.com
Fixtures, leagues, contacts, news, etc.

Enquiries:
Enquiries to: Executive Officer
Direct e-mail: executive@camanachd.co.uk

Founded:
1893

Organisation type and purpose:
Membership association (membership is by
subscription).
National governing body of the game.
To foster and develop the game of Shinty.

Subject coverage:
The game of Shinty.

Access to staff:
Contact by fax
Hours: Mon to Fri, 0900 to 1700

CAMBERWELL COLLEGE OF ARTS

Peckham Road, London, SE5 8UF

Tel: 020 7514 6302
Fax: 020 7514 6310
E-mail: enquiries@camberwell.arts.ac.uk

Website:
http://www.camberwell.arts.ac.uk/

Enquiries:
Enquiries to: Head of Learning Resources
Direct tel: 020 7514 6350

Founded:
1898

Formerly called:
Camberwell College of Arts and Crafts

Organisation type and purpose:
College of higher and further education.

Subject coverage:
Fine art (painting and sculpture); ceramics; textiles;
graphic design; printing; print making;
typographic design; bookbinding; silversmithing
and metalwork; conservation of prints, drawings,
textiles and artefacts; book illustration;
photography and film.

**Museum or gallery collection, archive, or library
special collection:**
Books and ephemera by and about Walter Crane
Books on poster art
Thorold Dickinson Cinema Collection

Non-library collection catalogue:
All or part available online

Library catalogue:
All or part available online

Access to staff:
Contact by letter. Appointment necessary. Access
for members only.
Hours: Mon, Fri, 1000 to 1700; Tue, Thu, 1000 to
2000; Wed, 1000 to 1930

Parent body:
University of the Arts London

CAMBRIDGE ASSESSMENT

Syndicate Buildings, 1 Hills Road, Cambridge, CB1
2EU

Tel: 01223 553311
Fax: 01223 460278

Enquiries:
Enquiries to: Chief Executive

Founded:
1857

Formerly called:
University of Cambridge Local Examinations
Syndicate

Organisation type and purpose:
Examining body established 1858.
UK Examinations offered through OCR (which is
part of Cambridge Assessment) include GCSE,
GCE at A/AS, and vocational qualifications

Subject coverage:
Specifications and question papers in all subjects
for which papers are set, numerous examinations
and assessment services.

Printed publications:
Occasional Publications on specification or
  research matters
Past Papers – generally previous 3 years available
Regulations and specifications (annually)

Subsidiary body:
Oxford Cambridge and RSA Examinations (OCR)
  1 Hills Road, Cambridge; tel: 01223 552552; fax:
  01223 552553

CAMBRIDGE BIBLIOGRAPHICAL SOCIETY

University Library, West Road, Cambridge, CB3
9DR

Tel: 01223 333123
Fax: 01223 333160
E-mail: nas1000@cam.ac.uk

Website:
http://www.lib.cam.ac.uk/cambibsoc

Enquiries:
Enquiries to: Secretary
Other contacts: Treasurer (for subscription
enquiries)

Founded:
1949

Organisation type and purpose:
Learned society.

Subject coverage:
Bibliography (historical), rare books, manuscripts,
book collecting.

Printed publications:
Transactions Vol II Part 1 (1954) to Vol XII, pt 1
  (2000) 1954–99 (£8 each part), 2000– (£12 each
  part)
Monographs (occasional) including:
A Hand-List of English Provincial Newspapers,
  1700–1760 (G. A. Cranfield, reprint with two
  supplements, £4.50)
A Hand-List of Irish Newspapers, 1685–1750 (R. L.
  Munter, £4.50)
English Embossed Bindings 1825–1850 (£8.50)
The Caxton Master and his Patrons (£8.50)
Sir Frederick Madden at Cambridge (£7)
A catalogue of books belonging to Dr Jonathan
  Swift (£9)
Andrew Perne Quatercentenary studies (£7)
Garrett Godfrey's accounts (£8)
The Recovery of the Past in Elizabethan England
  (£8)
Order printed publications from: The Secretary
(address as above)

Publications list:
Available in print

Access to staff:
Contact by letter, by telephone and by e-mail
Hours: Mon to Fri, 0930 to 1245 and 1400 to 1730

CAMBRIDGE CRYSTALLOGRAPHIC DATA CENTRE

Acronym or abbreviation: CCDC

12 Union Road, Cambridge, CB2 1EZ

Tel: 01223 336408
Fax: 01223 336033
E-mail: admin@ccdc.cam.ac.uk

Website:
http://www.ccdc.cam.ac.uk
Overview of the Cambridge Structural Database System, organisation of CCDC, contact information.

Enquiries:
Enquiries to: Executive Director

Founded:
1987

Organisation type and purpose:
Registered charity (charity number 800579).
Research organisation.
Independent non-profit institution.

Subject coverage:
Chemical structure and substructure searching, crystal structures of organic, organometallic compounds.

Museum or gallery collection, archive, or library special collection:
Reprint collection
Structural data on CD-ROM

Access to staff:
Contact by e-mail and via website
Hours: Mon to Fri, 0900 to 1700
Special comments: Academic and industrial scientists.

Access to building, collection or gallery:
No access other than to staff

Access for disabled people:
Level entry

Links with:
International Union of Crystallography
University of Cambridge

CAMBRIDGE PHILOSOPHICAL SOCIETY

Bene't Street, Cambridge, CB2 3PY

Tel: 01223 334743
E-mail: philosoc@hermes.cam.ac.uk

Website:
http://www.cambridgephilosophicalsociety.org
Enquiries:
Enquiries to: Executive Secretary

Founded:
1819

Organisation type and purpose:
Learned society.
To promote scientific enquiry.

Subject coverage:
Science, biology and mathematics.

Printed publications:
Biological Reviews (1 volume, 4 issues a year, £118 per volume, 2002)
Mathematical Proceedings (2 volumes, 3 issues each a year, £326 per volume, 2002)

Microform publications:
Transactions (available on microfilm, £77)

Access to staff:
Contact by letter and by e-mail. Appointment necessary.
Hours: Mon to Fri, 0900 to 1630

CAMBRIDGE REFRIGERATION TECHNOLOGY

Acronym or abbreviation: CRT

140 Newmarket Road, Cambridge, CB5 8HE

Tel: 01223 365101
Fax: 01223 461522
E-mail: dgoddard@crtech.demon.co.uk

Website:
http://www.crtech.co.uk
Newsletters, refrigerant information, commodity information, CRT services.

Enquiries:
Enquiries to: Information Officer
Direct tel: 01223 461352

Founded:
1965

Organisation type and purpose:
Research organisation.
Research association; connection with IIR (Paris), RIB, Institute of Refrigeration.

Subject coverage:
Transportation of perishable cargoes; specialist knowledge on all storage and stowage techniques of fruits and vegetables; transport, both road vehicles and sea freight – reefers and containers; refrigeration equipment; refrigerants; CFCs; food legislation.

Museum or gallery collection, archive, or library special collection:
Early books and ship drawings from 1850s of refrigeration equipment and refrigerated ships

Trade and statistical information:
Data on UNEP and all environmental organisations, especially connected with use of solvents, refrigerants, and foams.

Non-library collection catalogue:
All or part available online

Printed publications:
Evaluation of Refrigerant R502 Alternative for use in Air Cooled Refrigeration Equipment
Instrumentation for Transport Equipment
Pressure Drops through Loaded Containers
Refrigerated Transport for the Grocery Industry
Transport of Perishable Foodstuffs 3 vols.

Publications list:
Available in print

Access to staff:
Contact by letter, by telephone, by fax, by e-mail and via website. Appointment necessary. Non-members charged.
Hours: Mon to Fri, 0900 to 1700

Access to building, collection or gallery:
Prior appointment required

Access for disabled people:
Parking provided

CAMBRIDGE UNION SOCIETY

Acronym or abbreviation: CUS

Keynes Library, Bridge Street, Cambridge, CB2 1UB

Tel: 01223 568439
Fax: 01223 566444
E-mail: eak12@cus.cam.ac.uk

Enquiries:
Enquiries to: Assistant Librarian

Founded:
1815

Organisation type and purpose:
Membership association (membership is by subscription), registered charity, historic building, house or site.
To provide services for members, including debates, bar, meeting rooms and library.

Subject coverage:
Strong subjects: music, biography, fiction, travel, leisure interests.

General subjects: history, geography; English, French, German and Italian literature; art, architecture, politics, sociology, anthropology, theology, philosophy.

Museum or gallery collection, archive, or library special collection:
Erskine Allon Music Library
Fairfax Rhodes Collection (mainly art and literature)
Extensive collection of biographies and memoirs

Non-library collection catalogue:
All or part available online

Library catalogue:
All or part available in-house

Access to staff:
Contact by letter, by telephone, by e-mail and in person. Appointment necessary. Access for members only. Letter of introduction required.
Hours: Term time: Mon to Fri, 1300 to 1800
Special comments: Open to non-members by prior appointment only.

Access to building, collection or gallery:
Prior appointment required

CAMBRIDGE UNIVERSITY LIBRARY

West Road, Cambridge, CB3 9DR

Tel: 01223 333000
Fax: 01223 333160
E-mail: library@lib.cam.ac.uk

Website:
http://www.lib.cam.ac.uk

Founded:
1400

Organisation type and purpose:
University library.
Legal Deposit Library.

Subject coverage:
Extensive and general.

Museum or gallery collection, archive, or library special collection:
Acton Library
Adversaria
Almanacks
Armorial bindings
Bible Society Library and Archives
Book sales (English Sales catalogues)
Bookplates and book stamps
Bradshaw Collection (Irish books)
Cambridge Collection
Chapbooks
Darwin Library and papers
Early English printed books
Ely Diocesan and Chapter Records
Gerhardie Collection
Hunter-McAlpine Collection (history of psychiatry)
Incunabula
Jardine-Matheson Archives
Keynes Collection (Sir Geoffrey Keynes' personal library)
Madden Collection of Ballads
Madden Collection of Maps
Music
Norton Collection (early European printing 1501–1520)
Official Publications
Peterborough Cathedral Library
Portraits
Royal Commonwealth Society's Library
Royal Greenwich Observatory Archives
Taylor-Schechter Genizah Collection
University Archives
Vickers Archives
Wade Collection (Chinese books)
War Collection 1914–1919

Non-library collection catalogue:
All or part available online, in-house and in print

Printed publications:
Cambridge University Libraries Directory

Exhibition catalogues
General books
Genizah series
Specialised catalogues
Order printed publications from: Library Offices,
Cambridge University Library
tel: 01223 333048, e-mail: admin@lib.cam.ac.uk

Publications list:
Available online and in print

Access to building, collection or gallery:
Prior appointment required
Hours: Mon to Fri, 0900 to 1915; Sat, 0900 to 1700;
Easter Full Term: Mon to Fri, 0900 to 2200
Special comments: Closed between Christmas and
New Year, Bank Holidays, Sept. 16 to 23. A prior
appointment is advised to obtain reader's ticket.

Access for disabled people:
Parking provided, ramped entry, toilet facilities
Special comments: Recommended to contact Library
before first visit.

Also at the same address:
Cambridge Bibliographical Society
University Archives
tel: 01223 333147/8

Organisationally, it includes the:
Betty & Gordon Moore Library
  Centre for Mathematical Sciences, Wilberforce
  Road, Cambridge, CB3 0WD; tel: 01223 765670;
  fax: 01223 765678; e-mail: moore-library@lib.cam
  .ac.uk
Cambridge University Medical Library
  Clinical School Building, Box 111,
  Addenbrooke's Hospital, Hills Road, Cambridge,
  CB2 2SP; tel: 01223 336750; fax: 01223 331918; e-
  mail: library@medschl.cam.ac.uk
Central Science Library
  Bene't Street, Cambridge, CB2 3PY; tel: 01223
  334742; fax: 01223 334748; e-mail: lib-spl
  -inquiries@lists.cam.ac.uk
Squire Law Library
  10 West Road, Cambridge, CB3 9DZ; tel: 01223
  330077; fax: 01223 330048; e-mail: dfur1003@cus
  .cam.ac.uk

CAMBRIDGE UNIVERSITY PRESS

Acronym or abbreviation: CUP

The Edinburgh Building, Shaftesbury Road,
Cambridge, CB2 8RU

Tel: 01223 312393
Fax: 01223 325959
E-mail: information@cambridge.org

Website:
http://www.cambridge.org

Enquiries:
Enquiries to: Sales Manager

Founded:
1534

Organisation type and purpose:
University department or institute, publishing
house.

Subject coverage:
The Press publishes in all main academic and
educational subject areas, including English
Language Teaching, Schoolbooks, Humanities,
Social Sciences, STM and Reference books, Bibles
and prayer books, educational software and CD-
ROMs.

Printed publications:
About 1500 titles a year
230 learned journals
Online catalogue; also subject lists and lists of
  journals

Publications list:
Available online and in print

Access to staff:
Contact by letter, by telephone, by fax, by e-mail
and via website
Hours: Mon to Fri, 0900 to 1700

CAMBRIDGESHIRE ARCHIVES SERVICE

County Record Office, Castle Hill, Cambridge, CB3
0AP

Tel: 01223 717281
Fax: 01223 718823
E-mail: county.records.cambridge@cambridgeshire
.gov.uk

Website:
http://www.cambridgeshire.gov.uk/leisure/
archives

Enquiries:
Enquiries to: Senior Archivist Public Services
Other contacts: Archives and Local Studies
Manager for matters of general policy, broad
issues.

Founded:
1930

Organisation type and purpose:
Local government body.
Record office.

Subject coverage:
Historical matters of all kinds relating to the area
of the former county of Cambridgeshire and the
Isle of Ely; matters relating to the County Council
of Cambridgeshire since 1974.

**Museum or gallery collection, archive, or library
special collection:**
Cambridge Borough, 13th to 20th century
Land drainage authorities including the former
  Bedford Level Corporation 1663–1920

Non-library collection catalogue:
All or part available online and in-house

Library catalogue:
All or part available in-house

Printed publications:
A Century of Cambridgeshire Parish Councils
  (Batcheler K C, 1994, £4.95)
Archaeology of Cambridgeshire 1. South-West
  Cambridgeshire (Taylor A, 1997, £9.95)
Archaeology of Cambridgeshire 2. South-East
  Cambridgeshire and the Fen Edge (Taylor A,
  1998, £11.95)
Changing Landscapes: The Ancient Fenland (Coles
  J and Hall D, 1998, £4.95)
Guide to Education Records in the County Record
  Office Cambridge (Black A, 1972, £1)
Reproduction posters, prints and maps

Microform publications:
Microform of parish register transcripts (about 80
  sets) in office available from Cambridge Family
  History Society

Publications list:
Available in print

Access to staff:
Contact by letter, by telephone, by e-mail and in
person
Hours: Tue, Wed and Thu, 0900 to 1245, 1345 to
1715; Fri 0900 to 1245, 1345 to 1615; Tue, 1715 to
2100 by appointment only

Branch office:
County Record Office Huntingdon
  tel: 01480 375842

Parent body:
Cambridgeshire County Council
  tel: 01223 717111

CAMBRIDGESHIRE CHAMBERS OF COMMERCE

Vision Park, Histon, Cambridge, CB24 9ZR

Tel: 01223 237414
Fax: 01223 237405
E-mail: enquiries@cambscci.co.uk

Enquiries:
Enquiries to: Chief Executive

Founded:
1917

Please select:
Cambridge and District Chamber of Commerce
and Industry

Organisation type and purpose:
Membership association (membership is by
subscription), present number of members: 1100.
Chamber of Commerce.

Subject coverage:
International trade services, relevant information
and back-up services.

**Museum or gallery collection, archive, or library
special collection:**
UK, Local and International Trade Library

Trade and statistical information:
On-line access to trade statistics.

Printed publications:
Cambridge Directory of Industry and Commerce
  (annually)
Cambridge Chamber Newsletter (12 times a year)
Export Newsletter (monthly)

Access to staff:
Contact by letter, by telephone, by fax, by e-mail
and in person
Hours: Mon to Fri, 0900 to 1700

Access to building, collection or gallery:
No access other than to staff
Hours: Mon to Fri, 0900 to 1700

Member of:
Association of British Chambers of Commerce

CAMBRIDGESHIRE RECORDS SOCIETY

Cambridgeshire Archives, Box RES1009, Shire
Hall, Castle Hill, Cambridge, CB3 0AP

Tel: 01223 716858/699399
Fax: 01223 718823
E-mail: cambs.archives@cambridgeshire.gov.uk

Website:
http://www.cambsrecordsociety.co.uk/index.php

Enquiries:
Enquiries to: Secretary

Founded:
1972

Formerly called:
Cambridge Antiquarian Records Society (year of
change 1987)

Organisation type and purpose:
A not-for-profit record publishing society of
around 120 individual and institutional members
publishing texts of documentary sources and
reproductions of maps, etc., relating to
Cambridgeshire and adjoining areas.

Subject coverage:
History of Cambridgeshire, documentary sources.

Printed publications:
Edited texts and documents including:
A Cambridgeshire Lieutenancy Letter Book 1595–
  1605 (ed. E. J. Bourgeois)
Romilly's Cambridge Diary 1842–47 and 1848–64
  (ed. M. E. Bury and J. D. Pickles)
Edmund Pettis's Survey of St Ives 1728 (ed. M.
  Carter)
Churchwardens' Book of Bassingbourn 1496–
  c.1540 (ed. D. Dymond)
Cartulary of the Hospital of St John Cambridge
  (ed. M. G. Underwood)
Order printed publications from: from the Society

Publications list:
Available online and in print

Access to staff:
Contact by letter, by telephone, by fax and by e-
mail

Links with:
Cambridge Antiquarian Society (CAS)
  Haddon Library, Faculty of Archaeology and
  Anthropology, Pembroke Street, Cambridge, CB2
  3RA

CAMDEN LOCAL STUDIES AND ARCHIVES CENTRE

Holborn Library, 32–38 Theobalds Road, London, WC1X 8PA

Tel: 020 7974 6342
Fax: 020 7974 6284
E-mail: localstudies@camden.gov.uk

Website:
http://www.camden.gov.uk/localstudies

Enquiries:
Enquiries to: Principal Officer: Local Studies and Archives

Organisation type and purpose:
Local government body, public library.
Archives service.

Subject coverage:
Local studies, local history of Camden including Hampstead, Holborn and St Pancras, archives, conservation.

Museum or gallery collection, archive, or library special collection:
Local books and printed materials
Local newspapers
Ephemera
Local directories
Electoral registers
Illustrations
Maps
Census returns for Camden Area 1841–1901 (microfilm)
Archives of the London Borough of Camden and its predecessor bodies
Deposited archives including Highgate Cemetery registers (microfilm)
Special collections including:
Bellmoor Collection (compiled by Hampstead historian Thomas J. Barratt)
Eleanor Farjeon Collection
Heal Collection (compiled by local historian Sir Ambrose Heal on St Pancras to 1913)
Kate Greenaway Collection (available by special application only)

Non-library collection catalogue:
All or part available in-house

Printed publications:
A large number of books about the history of the area and particular places, including:
Beating the Bounds of Camden: A long distance walk (M. J. Holmes, ISBN 0 901389 79 X)
Camden Celebrates Cinema 100 – A guide to film locations in Camden (ISBN 0 901 389 86 2)
Camden Town 1791–1991: a pictorial record (V. Hart, R. Knight, L. Marshall, ISBN 0 901389 70 6)
The Cinemas of Camden (M. Aston, ISBN 0 901389 88 9)
Hampstead and Highgate Directory 1885/1886 (ISBN 0901389 48X)
A History of Camden: Hampstead, Holborn and St Pancras (J. Richardson, ISBN 0 948667 58 3)
Memories of Holborn (ed. M. Waugh, ISBN 0 901389 53 6)
Somers Town: A record of change (M. J. Holmes, ISBN 0 901389 50 1)
Twelve Views of Camden: A portfolio of prints (ISBN 0 901389 09 9)
Wartime Camden (ed. V. Hart and L. Marshall, ISBN 0 901389 40 4)
Camden Past and Present: A guide to the Camden Local Studies and Archives Centre (M. Aston, M. J. Holmes, R. G. Knight, ISBN 0 901389 99 4)
Studying Camden: A students' guide to Camden Local Studies and Archives Centre (M. Aston, ISBN 1 900846128)
King's Cross: A tour in time (M. Aston and L. Marshall, ISBN 1900846187)
Little Italy: The story of London's Italian quarter (T. Allen, ISBN 9781900846219)

Publications list:
Available online and in print

Access to staff:
Contact by letter, by telephone, by fax, by e-mail, in person and via website

Hours: Mon, Thu, 1000 to 1900; Tue, Fri, 1000 to 1800; Sat, 1000 to 1300 and 1400 to 1700; Wed closed. (Hours to be revised Autumn 2008)
Special comments: Appointments needed for some archives held in outstore.

Parent body:
London Borough of Camden
    Culture and Environment Directorate

CAMPAIGN AGAINST ARMS TRADE

Acronym or abbreviation: CAAT

11 Goodwin Street, London, N4 3HQ

Tel: 020 7281 0297
Fax: 020 7281 4369
E-mail: enquiries@caat.org.uk

Website:
http://www.caat.org.uk

Enquiries:
Enquiries to: Research Co-ordinator

Founded:
1974

Organisation type and purpose:
Voluntary organisation.

Subject coverage:
UK arms exports.

Publications list:
Available in print

Access to staff:
Appointment necessary.
Hours: Mon to Fri, 1030 to 1730

CAMPAIGN FOR AN INDEPENDENT BRITAIN

Acronym or abbreviation: CIB

81 Ashmole Street, London, SW8 1NF

Tel: 020 8340 0314
Fax: 020 7582 7021
E-mail: info@cibhq.co.uk

Website:
http://www.cibhq.co.uk

Enquiries:
Enquiries to: Honorary Secretary
Direct tel: 020 8348 3784
Direct fax: 020 8347 8246
Other contacts: Chairman

Founded:
1976

Formerly called:
Safeguard Britain Campaign (year of change 1983); British Anti-Common Market Campaign (year of change 1989)

Organisation type and purpose:
Membership association (membership is by subscription), present number of members: 3000.
To recoup self-government from the European Union.

Subject coverage:
European Community and its impact on the United Kingdom.

Printed publications:
A price not worth paying: the economic cost of EMU (Burkitt B et al, £4.50)
The Common Fisheries Policy – End or Mend? (Mitchell A, £2.50)
There IS an Alternative: Britain and its relationship with the EU (Burkitt B, et al, £4.50 inc. p&p)

Publications list:
Available in print

Access to staff:
Contact by letter, by telephone and by fax
Hours: Mon to Fri, 0900 to 1700

CAMPAIGN FOR FREEDOM OF INFORMATION

Acronym or abbreviation: CFoI

Suite 102, 16 Baldwins Gardens, London, EC1N 7RJ

Tel: 020 7831 7477
Fax: 020 7831 7461
E-mail: admin@cfoi.demon.co.uk

Website:
http://www.cfoi.org.uk

Founded:
1984

Organisation type and purpose:
Not-for-profit organisation working to improve public access to official information and ensure that the Freedom of Information Act is implemented effectively.

Subject coverage:
Freedom of information. Data protection/access to personal files.

Printed publications:
Various publications available free via website or to purchase in paper form

Publications list:
Available online and in print

Access to staff:
Contact by letter, by telephone, by fax and by e-mail
Hours: Mon to Fri, 1000 to 1600

Access to building, collection or gallery:
Prior appointment required

CAMPAIGN FOR HOMOSEXUAL EQUALITY

Acronym or abbreviation: CHE

PO Box 342, London, WC1X 0DU

Tel: 07702 326151
Fax: 020 8743 6252
E-mail: secretary@c-h-e.fsnet.co.uk

Enquiries:
Enquiries to: Secretary

Founded:
1969

Organisation type and purpose:
Membership association (membership is by subscription), present number of members: 200, voluntary organisation.
Pressure group.
To promote acceptance of homosexuality.

Subject coverage:
Discrimination against homosexuals and bisexuals.

Printed publications:
Annual Report
Newsletter
Variety of leaflets on the subject (free)

Electronic and video publications:
Audio Cassette: Coming Out (£6)

Publications list:
Available in print

Access to staff:
Contact by letter and by telephone
Hours: Mon to Fri, 0900 to 1700

CAMPAIGN FOR NATIONAL PARKS

Acronym or abbreviation: CNP

6–7 Barnard Mews, London, SW11 1QU

Tel: 020 7924 4077
Fax: 020 7924 5761
E-mail: info@cnp.org.uk

Website:
http://www.cnp.org.uk

General information.

Enquiries:
Enquiries to: Chief Executive

Founded:
1936

Organisation type and purpose:
Voluntary organisation, registered charity (charity number 295336).

Subject coverage:
National Parks of England and Wales; conservation and protection.

Printed publications:
Various – list on receipt of sae

Publications list:
Available in print

Access to staff:
Contact by letter, by telephone, by e-mail and via website. Appointment necessary. Non-members charged.
Hours: Mon to Fri, 0900 to 1700

Access to building, collection or gallery:
Prior appointment required

Links with:
over 40 organisations

CAMPAIGN FOR PRESS AND BROADCASTING FREEDOM

Acronym or abbreviation: CPBF

2nd Floor, Vi & Garner Smith House, 23, Orford Road, Walthamstow, London, E17 9NL

Tel: 020 8521 5932
Fax: 020 8521 5932
E-mail: freepress@cpbf.org.uk

Website:
http://www.cpbf.org.uk
All you want to know about the Campaign for Press and Broadcasting Freedom.

Enquiries:
Enquiries to: National Organiser

Founded:
1979

Organisation type and purpose:
Membership association, voluntary organisation, research organisation.
Campaign for diversity and democracy in the media.

Subject coverage:
Media ownership, right of reply, new media technologies, democracy and diversity in the media.

Museum or gallery collection, archive, or library special collection:
Books and videos on the issues

Printed publications:
Free Press (6 times a year, £1)
Media Catalogue – Into The Millennium (publications from many publishers in paper and video)

Publications list:
Available in print

Access to staff:
Contact by letter, by telephone, by fax and by e-mail. Appointment necessary.
Hours: Mon to Fri, 1000 to 1800

Access to building, collection or gallery:
Prior appointment required

Access for disabled people:
Level entry

CAMPAIGN FOR REAL ALE LIMITED

Acronym or abbreviation: CAMRA

230 Hatfield Road, St Albans, Hertfordshire, AL1 4LW

Tel: 01727 867201
Fax: 01727 867670
E-mail: camra@camra.org.uk

Website:
http://www.camra.org.uk

Enquiries:
Enquiries to: Research and Information Manager
Other contacts: iain.loe@camra.org.uk

Founded:
1971

Organisation type and purpose:
National organisation, membership association (membership is by subscription), present number of members: 82,000, voluntary organisation, publishing house.
Consumer organisation.
To act as the champion of the consumer in relation to the UK drinks industry.

Subject coverage:
Brewing industry, traditional beer and public houses, consumer protection, foreign breweries and beer.

Museum or gallery collection, archive, or library special collection:
Issues of What's Brewing – the newspaper of the campaign – back to the early 70s
Good Beer Guides back to 1st edition 1974

Trade and statistical information:
Some statistics on the UK Brewing Industry.

Printed publications:
Beer, Bed & Breakfast
Brew Your own Real Ale at Home
Good Beer Guides (annually, 1974–2002)
Good Beer Guide to Belgium & Holland
Good Beer Guide to Prague & the Czech Republic
Good Beer Guide to Munich & Bavaria
The Best Pubs (series of local guides)
What's Brewing (monthly, available to members)
Good Bottled Beer Guide
Dictionary of Beer
London Pub Guide
CAMRA's Good Cider Guide
Good Beer Guide to Germany

Access to staff:
Contact by letter, by fax and by e-mail.
Appointment necessary.
Hours: Mon to Fri, 0900 to 1700

Access to building, collection or gallery:
Prior appointment required

Access for disabled people:
Parking provided

Links with:
European Beer Consumer Union (EBCU)
230 Hatfield Road, St Albans, Hertfordshire, AL1 4LW; tel: 01727 867201; fax: 01727 867670; e-mail: ebcu@camra.org.uk

CAMPAIGN FOR STATE EDUCATION

Acronym or abbreviation: CASE

98 Erlanger Road, London, SE14 5TH

Tel: 07932 149942
E-mail: case@casenet.org.uk

Website:
http://www.casenet.org.uk

Enquiries:
Enquiries to: Contact

Founded:
1963

Formerly called:
Campaign for the Advancement of State Education

Organisation type and purpose:
Membership association (membership is by subscription), voluntary organisation.

Education campaign group.

Subject coverage:
State education, funding, class size, contacts, government policy, comprehensive education.

Printed publications:
Parents and Schools (5 times a year, £20 year's subscription, £15 members)

Publications list:
Available online and in print

Access to staff:
Contact by letter, by telephone, by fax and by e-mail

Access to building, collection or gallery:
No access other than to staff

CAMPAIGN FOR THE PROTECTION OF RURAL WALES

Acronym or abbreviation: CPRW

Ty Gwyn, 31 High Street, Welshpool, Powys, SY21 7YD

Tel: 01938 552525 or 556212
Fax: 01938 552741
E-mail: deb@cprwmail.org.uk

Website:
http://www.cprw.org.uk
General information.

Enquiries:
Enquiries to: Liaison Officer

Founded:
1928

Formerly called:
Council for the Protection of Rural Wales

Organisation type and purpose:
Voluntary organisation, registered charity (charity number 239899).
Protection of Wales countryside and coasts from inappropriate development.

Subject coverage:
Active protection of the Welsh countryside and its villages; planning; amenities; legislation.

Museum or gallery collection, archive, or library special collection:
Library of environmental publications

Printed publications:
Rural Wales (magazine, 3 times a year, free to members, others on request)

Access to staff:
Contact by e-mail and via website. Appointment necessary.
Hours: Mon to Fri, 0900 to 1700

CAMPAIGN TO PROTECT RURAL ENGLAND – DORSET BRANCH

Acronym or abbreviation: CPRE Dorset

The Little Keep, Bridport Road, Dorchester, Dorset, DT1 1SQ

Tel: 01305 265808
Fax: 01305 265808
E-mail: info@dorset-cpre-office.org.uk

Website:
http://www.dorset-cpre-office.org.uk

Enquiries:
Enquiries to: Executive Director

Founded:
1937

Organisation type and purpose:
Membership association (membership is by subscription), voluntary organisation, registered charity (charity number 211974). To improve, protect and preserve for the benefit of the public, the countryside, and the country towns and villages of the county of Dorset.

continued overleaf

Subject coverage:
Planning procedures appropriate to county structure plan, minerals and waste local plans, district and borough local plans and planning applications within the county. Issues relevant to the protection of the countryside, transport issues.

Museum or gallery collection, archive, or library special collection:
Government (DoE) Planning Policy Guidance

Printed publications:
Dorset Review (2 times a year, free)

Access to staff:
Contact by letter, by telephone, by fax, by e-mail and via website. Appointment necessary.
Hours: Tue, 0900 to 1600; and most Thu, 0900 to 1200
Special comments: 24 hour answerphone and fax.

National office:
Campaign to Protect Rural England (CPRE)
    128 Southwark Street, London, SE1 0SW; tel: 020 7981 2800; fax: 020 7981 2899; e-mail: info@cpre.org.uk

CAMPAIGN TO PROTECT RURAL ENGLAND – OXFORDSHIRE BRANCH

Acronym or abbreviation: CPRE Oxfordshire

Punches Barn, Waterperry Road, Holton, Oxfordshire, OX33 1PP

Tel: 01865 874780
E-mail: campaign@cpreoxon.org.uk

Website:
http://www.cpreoxon.org.uk
Campaign news and advice on protecting the countryside.

Enquiries:
Enquiries to: Campaign Manager
Direct e-mail: campaign@cpreoxon.org.uk

Founded:
1931

Organisation type and purpose:
Membership association (membership is by subscription).
A company limited by guarantee, registered in England, no. 04443278.
Registered charity (charity no. 1093081).
Branch of the national charity.

Subject coverage:
Protection of the local countryside, planning applications, transport, development, conservation issues relating to rural environment, hedgerows, dry stone walls.

Printed publications:
The Oxford Green Belt Way (£5 plus £1 p&p)
Order printed publications from: Order directly from the office. Please send cheques payable to CPRE Oxfordshire.

Access to staff:
Contact by letter, by telephone, by e-mail and via website. Appointment necessary.
Hours: Mon, Tue, Thu and Fri, 1000 to 1300
Special comments: Officer is only part-time.

CAMPAIGN TO PROTECT RURAL ENGLAND – SHROPSHIRE BRANCH

Acronym or abbreviation: CPRE

Bear Steps Office, St Alkmond's Square, Shrewsbury, Shropshire, SY1 1UH

Tel: 01743 356511
Fax: 01743 344994
E-mail: cpre@civic.plus.net

Enquiries:
Enquiries to: Secretary

Founded:
1926

Organisation type and purpose:
Membership association (membership is by subscription), present number of members: 550, voluntary organisation, registered charity (charity number 218782), suitable for ages: all.
The care and improvement of the whole of the countryside.

Subject coverage:
Environmental conservation.

Access to staff:
Contact by letter, by telephone, by fax and by e-mail
Hours: Mon to Fri, 1000 to 1600
Special comments: Shrewsbury office open on Monday and Thursday only. National office is open Monday to Friday inclusive.

National Office at:
Campaign to Protect Rural England
    128 Southwark Street, London, SE1 0SW; tel: 020 7981 2800; fax: 020 7981 2899

CAMPBELL HOOPER

35 Old Queen Street, London, SW1H 9JD

Tel: 020 7222 9070
Fax: 020 7222 5591
E-mail: danieleilon@campbellhooper.com

Website:
http://www.campbellhooper.com
Information relating to the firm.

Enquiries:
Enquiries to: Partner
Direct tel: 020 7654 5115
Direct fax: 020 7654 5226

Founded:
1760

Organisation type and purpose:
Solicitors.
Legal advice, transactional work and litigation.

Subject coverage:
Computer software copyright issues, intellectual property advice and litigation, employment, commercial property, company law and commercial law, private client and trust issues.

Printed publications:
Order printed publications from: Marketing Administrator, Campbell Hooper
35 Old Queen Street, London, SW1H 9JD; tel: 020 7222 9070, fax: 020 7222 5591, e-mail: marketing@campbellhooper.com

Publications list:
Available online

Access to staff:
Contact by letter, by telephone, by fax, by e-mail and via website. Appointment necessary.
Hours: Mon to Fri, 0900 to 1800

CAMPDEN AND CHORLEYWOOD FOOD RESEARCH ASSOCIATION

Acronym or abbreviation: CCFRA

Chipping Campden, Gloucestershire, GL55 6LD

Tel: 01386 842000
Fax: 01386 842100
E-mail: information@campden.co.uk

Website:
http://www.campden.co.uk

Enquiries:
Enquiries to: Information Officer

Founded:
1919

Created by the merger of:
Campden Food and Drink Research Association, Flour Milling and Baking Research Association (year of change 1995)

Formerly called:
Campden Food and Drink Research Association

Organisation type and purpose:
Consultancy, research organisation.

Subject coverage:
Food science and technology associated with the preservation (canning, aseptic, chill, modified atmosphere packaging, freezing, dehydration) of foods, microbiology, chemistry, biochemistry and sensory quality evaluation of processed foods, suitability of raw materials for processing.

Museum or gallery collection, archive, or library special collection:
Old books on milling and baking equipment and products

Publications list:
Available online

Access to staff:
Contact by letter, by telephone, by fax, by e-mail and via website. Non-members charged.
Hours: Mon to Fri, 0900 to 1700

CAMPING AND CARAVANNING CLUB, THE

Greenfield House, Westwood Way, Coventry, Warwickshire, CV4 8JH

Tel: 024 7647 5448
Fax: 024 7669 4886

Website:
http://www.campingandcaravanningclub.co.uk
Information about the Club's services and sites.

Enquiries:
Enquiries to: Public Relations Officer
Direct tel: 024 7647 5204

Founded:
1901

Formerly called:
Camping Club of Great Britain and Ireland

Organisation type and purpose:
Membership association.
Owning and running around 100 campsites on behalf of members, although most sites are also open to non-members.

Subject coverage:
Technical assistance to members with tents, caravans, trailer tents, motor caravans. General assistance on camping law and information to official bodies, media, trade etc.

Museum or gallery collection, archive, or library special collection:
Historical archives relative to the club and camping in general

Printed publications:
Camping and Caravanning (magazine, monthly)
Carefree International Travel Service Brochure (annually)
Club Handbook (free to all members)
Member Services Directory (annually)
Your Big Sites Book (every 2 years)
Your Place in the Country (annually)

Access to staff:
Contact by letter
Hours: Mon to Fri, 0845 to 1645

Access for disabled people:
Parking provided, lift
Special comments: Access to all floors

CAMPING FOR THE DISABLED

Mobility Information Service, 20 Burton Close, Dawley, Telford, TF4 2BX

Tel: 01743 340269
E-mail: mis@nmcuk.freeserve.co.uk

Enquiries:
Enquiries to: Administrator

Founded:
1981

Organisation type and purpose:
International organisation, advisory body, membership association (membership is by subscription), voluntary organisation, suitable for ages: all.

Subject coverage:
Data on adapted campsites for disabled people, advice on modifications to camping equipment, adapting or building a motor home or caravan, route planning in Europe.

Printed publications:
Guides to Adapted Sites in Austria, France, Germany, Holland (50p each)
UK Guide to Adapted Sites (£1.50)

Publications list:
Available in print

Access to staff:
Contact by letter, by telephone and by fax. Appointment necessary. Non-members charged.
Hours: Mon to Fri, 0900 to 1700

Access to building, collection or gallery:
Prior appointment required

Access for disabled people:
Parking provided, ramped entry, access to all public areas, toilet facilities

Administration shared with the:
Mobility Information Service

CANADA WOOD UK

PO Box 1, Farnborough, Hampshire, GU14 6WE

Tel: 01252 522545
Fax: 01252 522546
E-mail: office@canadawooduk.org

Website:
http://www.canadawood.info

Enquiries:
Enquiries to: UK Consultant

Formed from:
Canadian Lumbermans' Association (CLA), Canadian Plywood Association (Canply), Council of Forest Industries (COFI), Forest Products Association of Canada (FPAC), Maritime Lumber Bureau (MLB), Quebec Wood Export Bureau (QWEB), Western Red Cedar Export Association (WRCEA).

Organisation type and purpose:
Advisory body (membership is by subscription, qualification), manufacturing industry.
Industry association representing in the United Kingdom, Canadian timber and plywood manufacturers through various agencies and associations.
Providing technical information and advice on member company products to architects, engineers, specifiers and the construction and wood utilising industries generally.

Subject coverage:
Technical advisory service for application and use of wood and plywood in construction.

Trade and statistical information:
Worldwide exports of Canadian timber and plywood.

Printed publications:
Technical literature on Canadian timber species, plywood, structural grading (free of charge)

Access to staff:
Contact by letter, by telephone, by fax and by e-mail. Appointment necessary.
Hours: Mon to Fri, 0900 to 1700

Other address:
Maritime Lumber Bureau
PO Box 459, Amherst, Nova Scotia, B4H 4A1, Canada; tel: 00 1 902 667 3889; fax: 00 1 902 667 0401

CANADA-UNITED KINGDOM CHAMBER OF COMMERCE

38 Grosvenor Street, London, W1K 4DP

Tel: 020 7258 6576 or 020 7258 6578
Fax: 020 7258 6594
E-mail: info@canada-uk.org

Website:
http://www.canada-uk.org
About the Chamber, its services and resource links.

Enquiries:
Enquiries to: Manager
Direct tel: 020 7258 6576

Founded:
1921

Organisation type and purpose:
Membership association (membership is by subscription), present number of members: 330.

Subject coverage:
Enquiries about trade and investment between Canada and the United Kingdom in both directions.

Printed publications:
Link Newsletter (faxed/e-mailed monthly)

Access to staff:
Contact by letter, by telephone, by fax, by e-mail and via website. Appointment necessary. Non-members charged.
Hours: Mon to Fri, 0900 to 1700

CANCER PREVENTION RESEARCH TRUST

Cobden House, 231 Roehampton Lane, London, SW15 4LB

Tel: 020 8785 7786
Fax: 020 8785 6466
E-mail: cprt@talk21.com

Website:
http://www.cancerpreventionresearch.org.uk

Enquiries:
Enquiries to: Director

Founded:
1973

Organisation type and purpose:
International organisation, national organisation, voluntary organisation, registered charity (charity number 265985), research organisation.

Subject coverage:
Cancer prevention, cancer research.

Printed publications:
Cancer Prevention and Health News (newsletter, monthly, free with sae)

Access to staff:
Contact by letter, by telephone, by fax, by e-mail, in person and via website
Hours: Mon to Fri, 0900 to 1700

Access to building, collection or gallery:
No prior appointment required

Access for disabled people:
Toilet facilities

CANCER RESEARCH UK

Beatson Laboratories, Garscube Estate, Switchback Road, Bearsden, Glasgow, G61 1BD

Tel: 0141 330 3953
Fax: 0141 942 6521
E-mail: library@beatson.gla.ac.uk

Website:
http://www.beatson.gla.ac.uk/index.html

Enquiries:
Enquiries to: Librarian
Direct tel: 0141 330 4801

Founded:
1912

Formerly called:
CRC Beatson Laboratories; Beatson Institute for Cancer Research (year of change 1967)

Organisation type and purpose:
Research organisation.

Subject coverage:
Molecular biology, cell biology, molecular pathology, cancer research, proteomics, pharmacology, medical oncology, radiation oncology.

Museum or gallery collection, archive, or library special collection:
Historical collection relating to Sir George Beatson and the founding of the Royal Glasgow Cancer Hospital

Non-library collection catalogue:
All or part available in-house

Library catalogue:
All or part available in-house

Printed publications:
Cancer Research UK Beatson Laboratories Scientific Report (annual, contains a list of papers by staff)

Publications list:
Available in print

Access to staff:
Contact by letter, by telephone, by fax and by e-mail. Appointment necessary.
Hours: Mon to Wed, 0930 to 1500; Thu 1215 to 1730

Access to building, collection or gallery:
Prior appointment required

Access for disabled people:
Parking provided, level entry, toilet facilities

Links with:
University of Glasgow

CANCERBACUP

Formal name: British Association of Cancer United Patients
Acronym or abbreviation: CancerBACUP

3 Bath Place, Rivington Street, London, EC2A 3JR

Tel: 020 7696 9003
Fax: 020 7696 9002
E-mail: info@cancerbacup.org

Website:
http://cancerbacup.org.uk
Details of CancerBACUP's services on cancerhelp UK.

Enquiries:
Enquiries to: Public Relations Officer
Direct tel: 020 7920 7219
Direct e-mail: cmoore@cancerbacup.org

Founded:
1985

Formerly called:
British Association of Cancer United Patients (BACUP), date of change, 5 January 1998

Organisation type and purpose:
Voluntary organisation, registered charity (charity number 1019719).
Supporting cancer patients, their families and friends by providing information and support.

Subject coverage:
Cancer and related medical conditions, treatment of cancer, support for carers, services available for people with cancer, their families and friends, information on any aspect of cancer for anyone affected by cancer, counselling, education and training for health professionals.

Printed publications:
CancerBACUP News (3 times a year)
Over 56 publications on specific cancers, site-specific cancers, how to live with cancer and treatments available (free to individuals, health professionals charged £2.50 with discounts for bulk orders); these include:
Diet and the Cancer Patient

continued overleaf

Facing the Challenge of Advanced Cancer
Lost for Words – how to talk to someone with
  cancer
What do I Tell the Children?
Who Can Ever Understand?
Making a Will

Electronic and video publications:
Video about the services
CD-ROM available containing all booklets
Talking About Cancer (audio tape)

Publications list:
Available online and in print

Access to staff:
Contact by letter, by telephone, by fax, by e-mail
and via website
Hours: Mon to Fri, 0900 to 1730

Access for disabled people:
Access to all public areas

Links with:
Cancer Education Coordinating Group
major cancer charities

Other addresses:
CancerBACUP Scotland (Cancer Counselling
Service)
  30 Bell Street, Glasgow, G1 1LG; tel: 0141 553
  1553

CANNING HOUSE LIBRARY

Formal name: Hispanic and Luso-Brazilian Council
Acronym or abbreviation: HLBC

Hispanic & Luso-Brazilian Council, Canning
House, 2 Belgrave Square, London, SW1X 8PJ

Tel: 020 7235 2303
Fax: 020 7838 9258
E-mail: library@canninghouse.com

Website:
http://www.canninghouse.com

Enquiries:
Enquiries to: Library and Information Services
Manager
Direct tel: ext 208
Direct e-mail: abiggins@canninghouse.com

Founded:
1943

Organisation type and purpose:
Registered charity.
Cultural lending and reference library.
Promotes relations between the UK and Latin
America, Spain and Portugal.

Subject coverage:
Most subjects relating to Latin America, the
Caribbean, Portugal and its former colonies, and
Spain, including history, archaeology, politics,
economics, sociology, anthropology, religion,
geography, natural history, travel, literature,
language, art, music, cinema, food and drink.

**Museum or gallery collection, archive, or library
special collection:**
R. B. Cunninghame Graham Collection
W. H. Hudson Collection
George Canning Collection
Rare books (travel accounts, history, literature and
  language, religion, anthropology, natural history,
  etc.)
Feature films from Latin America, Spain and
  Portugal, on DVD and video

Non-library collection catalogue:
All or part available online and in-house

Library catalogue:
All or part available online

Printed publications:
British Bulletin of Publications on Latin America,
  the Caribbean, Portugal and Spain (twice a year)
Cultural Centre Newsletter (electronic, bi-monthly)
Information leaflets
Printed catalogue (to 1973, subject and author)

Order printed publications from: Worldwide
Subscription Services; admin@
worldwidesubscriptions.com

Publications list:
Available online

Access to staff:
Contact by letter, by telephone, by fax, by e-mail,
in person and via website
Hours: Mon to Fri, 1400 to 1800

Links with:
ACLAIIR, REDIAL, SALALM

CANTERBURY CATHEDRAL ARCHIVES

Acronym or abbreviation: CCA

The Precincts, Canterbury, Kent, CT1 2EH

Tel: 01227 865330\ Minicom no. 01622 605249
Fax: 01227 865222
E-mail: archives@canterbury-cathedral.org

Website:
http://www.canterbury-cathedral.org/archives
.html
Main archives site.

Enquiries:
Enquiries to: Archivist
Other contacts: Canon Librarian

Founded:
597

Organisation type and purpose:
Local government body.
Cathedral archives.

Subject coverage:
Archives relating to Canterbury, especially the
Cathedral, City, Diocese and Archdeaconry
parishes.

**Museum or gallery collection, archive, or library
special collection:**
Archives of Christ Church, dating from the 8th
  century, including charters, financial records and
  manorial records
Archives of the post-Reformation Dean and
  Chapter, to the present day, including
  photographs and architectural drawings
Records of the City of Canterbury, dating from the
  12th century
Records of the Diocese of Canterbury
Parish records for Church of England parishes in
  the Archdeaconry of Canterbury
Records of individuals, families, businesses and
  organisations in the district of Canterbury
Collections of artefacts

Non-library collection catalogue:
All or part available online and in-house

Printed publications:
Canterbury Sources Series (Shaw, Dr D J, Editor):
The Oxford Movement (Canterbury Sources 1)
  (1999, £10 plus £1.75 p&p)
In Foreign Parts (Canterbury Sources 2) (2000, £12
  plus £1.75 p&p)
The Slave Trade (Canterbury Sources 3) (2001, £12
  plus £1.75 p&p)
Handlist of parish records

Microform publications:
Stock of microfilm of deposits, especially
  genealogical sources (available for purchase)

Publications list:
Available online and in print

Access to staff:
Contact by letter, by telephone, by fax, by e-mail,
in person and via website. Appointment necessary.
Hours: Mon to Thu, 0900 to 1700; 1st and 3rd Sat,
0900 to 1300

Access for disabled people:
Parking provided, subject to availability
Special comments: Lift to search room; hearing loop.

Parent body:
Dean and Chapter of Canterbury
  Cathedral House, The Precincts, Canterbury, CT1
  2EH; tel: 01227 762862; fax: 01227 865222
Kent County Council
  Sessions House, County Hall, Maidstone, Kent,
  ME14 1XQ; tel: 01622 671411; fax: 01622 697186

CANTERBURY CATHEDRAL LIBRARY

Acronym or abbreviation: CCL

The Precincts, Canterbury, Kent, CT1 2EH

Tel: 01227 865287
Fax: 01227 865222
E-mail: library@canterbury-cathedral.org

Website:
http://www.canterbury-cathedral.org
Summary of collections, opening hours, history of
the library.
http://opac.ukc.ac.uk
Catalogue.

Enquiries:
Enquiries to: Librarian
Direct tel: 01227 865288
Direct e-mail: librarian@canterbury-cathedral.org
Other contacts: Canon Librarian

Founded:
597

Organisation type and purpose:
Registered charity.
Cathedral library.

Subject coverage:
Church history, Kentish history, bibliography, anti-
slavery literature, early natural science books,
printed historical sources, Oxford Movement,
Roman Catholic controversy.

**Museum or gallery collection, archive, or library
special collection:**
50,000 books in total: 30,000 pre-19th century
  books and pamphlets held on computer database
Anti-slave trade tracts (19th century)
Herbals and other natural history books
Howley-Harrison Library (12,800 books
  bequeathed by Benjamin Harrison, Archdeacon
  of Maidstone, 1887)
Local history and cathedral history collection
Mendham Collection on Roman Catholic
  Controversy
Parish collections for Elham and Preston-next-
  Wingham

Library catalogue:
All or part available online and in print

Printed publications:
The Slave Trade: bibliography of the collection
  (revised ed. 2001, £12)
In Foreign Parts: books and pamphlets on the
  World Beyond Western Europe printed before
  1900 (2000, £12)
The Oxford Movement: 19th century books and
  pamphlets in the Cathedral Library (1999, £10)
Catalogue of Canterbury Cathedral Library's pre-
  1801 books (1998)
Catalogue of the Mendham Collection (1994)
Order printed publications from:
CanterburySources@canterbury-cathedral.org
Adam Matthews Publications, Marlborough,
Wiltshire (for the Cathedral pre-1801 catalogue)

Access to staff:
Contact by letter, by telephone, by e-mail and via
website. Appointment necessary.
Hours: Mon to Thu, 0900 to 1700; 1st and 3rd Sat,
0900 to 1300

Access for disabled people:
Parking provided
Special comments: Lift to first floor where library is
situated.

Affiliated to the:
University of Kent at Canterbury
  tel: 01227 764000

Parent body:
Dean and Chapter of Canterbury Cathedral
tel: 01227 762862

CANTERBURY CHRIST CHURCH UNIVERSITY

North Holmes Road, Canterbury, Kent, CT1 1QU

Tel: 01227 767700
Fax: 01227 470442

Website:
http://www.cant.ac.uk

Enquiries:
Enquiries to: Director of Library Services
Direct tel: 01227 782232
Direct fax: 01227 767530
Direct e-mail: a.d.conyers@canterbury.ac.uk

Founded:
1962

Organisation type and purpose:
University library.
University sector College of Higher Education.

Subject coverage:
American studies, applied social sciences, art and design, business and management studies, education, English, geography, history, language studies, mathematics, IT, nursing and midwifery studies, occupational therapy, radio, film and TV studies, radiography, religious studies, social work, and sports science.

Museum or gallery collection, archive, or library special collection:
Elizabeth Gaskell Collection

Access to staff:
Contact by letter, by telephone and by e-mail.
Non-members charged.
Hours: Mon to Fri, 0900 to 1700

CANTERBURY CITY COUNCIL

Military Road, Canterbury, Kent, CT1 1YW

Tel: 01227 862000
Fax: 01227 862020
E-mail: firstname.familyname@canterbury.gov.uk

Website:
http://www.canterbury.co.uk

Enquiries:
Enquiries to: Chief Executive

Founded:
1974

Organisation type and purpose:
Local government body.

Subject coverage:
Local government.

Access to staff:
Contact by letter, by telephone, by fax, by e-mail, in person and via website. Appointment necessary.
Hours: Mon to Fri, 0900 to 1700

CAPEL

Formal name: Capel: The Chapels Heritage Society

5 Cuffnell Close, Liddell Park, Llandudno, Conwy, LL30 1UX

Tel: 01492 860449
E-mail: obadiah1@btinternet.com

Website:
http://www.capeli.org.uk
General information about the society and list of forthcoming events in English and Welsh.

Enquiries:
Enquiries to: Honorary Secretary
Other contacts: Treasurer for subscription/ membership

Organisation type and purpose:
Membership association (membership is by subscription), present number of members: 300, voluntary organisation, registered charity (charity number 518411).
Presentation of the nonconformist heritage of Wales.

Subject coverage:
Nonconformist history, chapels in Wales.

Printed publications:
Newsletter (twice a year)

Publications list:
Available online and in print

Access to staff:
Contact by letter and by e-mail
Hours: Mon to Fri, 0900 to 1700

CAPEL MANOR COLLEGE

Bullsmore Lane, Enfield, Middlesex, EN1 4RQ

Tel: 08456 122122
Fax: 01992 717544
E-mail: enquiries@capel.ac.uk

Website:
http://www.capel.ac.uk/

Enquiries:
Enquiries to: Student Registrar

Formerly called:
Capel Manor Horticultural and Environmental Centre

Organisation type and purpose:
Further education college.
Specialist horticultural college and gardens open to the public.

Subject coverage:
Horticulture, garden design, arboriculture, countryside management, floristry, balloon artistry.

Library catalogue:
All or part available in-house

Access to staff:
Contact by letter, by telephone and by e-mail.
Appointment necessary.
Hours: Mon to Fri, 0900 to 1700

Access for disabled people:
Parking provided, level entry, access to all public areas, toilet facilities

Also at:
Capel Manor College at Castle Green
  Gale Street, Dagenham, RM9 4UN; tel: 020 8724 1528
Capel Manor College at Crystal Palace
  Crystal Palace Park, Ledrington Road, SE19 2BS; tel: 020 8778 5572
Capel Manor College at Gunnersbury Park
  Popes Lane, Gunnersbury Park, Acton, W3 8LQ; tel: 020 8993 6266; fax: 020 8993 6266
Capel Manor College at Regent's Park
  The Store Yard, Inner Circle, Regent's Park, NW1 4NR; tel: 020 7486 7930

CAPRI CLUB (INTERNATIONAL)

Acronym or abbreviation: CCI

Capri Club HQ, Badgers Hill, Sheriffs Lench, Evesham, Worcestershire, WR11 4SN

Tel: 01386 860860
Fax: 01386 861455
E-mail: capriclub@btclick.com

Website:
http://www.capriclub.co.uk/

Enquiries:
Enquiries to: Membership Secretary

Founded:
1983

Formerly called:
Capri 70 Owners Club, Capri Owners Club

Organisation type and purpose:
Membership association (membership is by subscription), present number of members: 8000.

Subject coverage:
Ford Capris 1969 to 1987.

Printed publications:
Catalogue (annually to members)
Club Magazine (monthly to members)
Mk3 Biography Book (£12.95 plus postage)

Electronic and video publications:
Capri – Documentary (video, £14.95 plus postage)
Convention '97 (video, £14.95, plus postage)
Summer Camp '97 (video, £14.95, plus postage)
Summer Camp '98 (video, £14.95 plus postage)
Summer Camp '99 (video, £14.95 plus postage)
Summer Camp '00 (video, £14.95 plus postage)
Summer Camp '01 (video, £14.95 plus postage)

Access to staff:
Contact by letter, by telephone, by fax, by e-mail and in person
Hours: Mon to Fri, 0900 to 1700

CARADON DISTRICT COUNCIL

Luxstowe House, Liskeard, Cornwall, PL14 3DZ

Tel: 01579 341000\ Minicom no. 01579 341010
Fax: 01579 341001
E-mail: postroom@caradon.gov.uk

Website:
http://www.caradon.gov.uk
Gives information about Caradon District Council and about the area.

Enquiries:
Enquiries to: Chief Executive
Direct tel: 01579 341022
Direct fax: 01579 341002
Other contacts: Corporate Communications Officer for public relations and media enquiries.

Founded:
1974

Organisation type and purpose:
Local government body.

Access to staff:
Contact by letter, by telephone, by fax, by e-mail and in person. Appointment necessary.
Hours: Mon to Fri, 0830 to 1700

Access for disabled people:
Parking provided, ramped entry, toilet facilities

CARDIFF COUNTY LIBRARIES

Cardiff Central Library, John Street, Cardiff, CF10 5BA

Tel: 029 2038 2116
Fax: 029 2087 1599
E-mail: centrallibrary@cardiff.gov.uk

Website:
http://www.cardiff.gov.uk/libraries
Service point profiles, opening hours, catalogue, fines and charges.

Enquiries:
Enquiries to: Central Library Manager
Direct e-mail: rboddy@cardiff.gov.uk
Other contacts: Bibliographic Services Officer

Founded:
1882

Formerly called:
South Glamorgan County Libraries (year of change 1996)

Organisation type and purpose:
Local government body, public library.

Subject coverage:
Humanities department:
business, law, education, history, art, language and literature, military studies, social sciences, religion and philosophy.
Sciences department:

continued overleaf

transport, life sciences, geography, environmental studies, science and technology.
Music department.
Information department:
business and commercial directories: UK and worldwide; telephone directories: UK, Eire, Jersey and Guernsey; British Standards; statistical information, European Union information, census statistics, maps and atlases, community information, local studies and genealogy, census returns, bibliographical information, National Assembly for Wales; trade journals; market research.
Leisure Library including: fiction, talking books, DVDs, CD-ROMs, popular non-fiction, newsroom.
Children's and Schools Library Service.
Community Languages Department

Museum or gallery collection, archive, or library special collection:
Mackworth Collection (early music)
Manuscripts, fine bindings, private press books, early printed books, limited editions
Cardiff Local Collection including photographs, maps and newspapers

Non-library collection catalogue:
All or part available in-house

Library catalogue:
All or part available online

Access to staff:
Contact by letter, by telephone, by fax, by e-mail, in person and via website
Hours: Mon, Tue, Wed, Fri, 0900 to 1800; Thu, 0900 to 1900; Sat, 0900 to 1730

Access for disabled people:
Level entry, access to all public areas, toilet facilities
Special comments: Lifts to all floors.

Parent body:
Cardiff County Council
  Culture, Leisure and Parks

CARDIFF NATURALISTS SOCIETY

The Library, National Museum Wales, Cathays Park, Cardiff, CF10 3NP

Tel: 029 2057 3202
Fax: 029 2057 3216
E-mail: library@museumwales.ac.uk

Enquiries:
Enquiries to: Librarian

Founded:
1867

Organisation type and purpose:
Learned society.

Subject coverage:
Natural history of the Glamorgan area; zoology; ornithology; botany; entomology.

Museum or gallery collection, archive, or library special collection:
Library, mainly periodicals via exchange agreements
Morrey Salmon Ornithology Archive

Library catalogue:
All or part available in-house

Printed publications:
Newsletter (quarterly)

Access to staff:
Contact by letter, by telephone and by fax.
Appointment necessary.
Hours: Tue to Fri, 1000 to 1700

Access for disabled people:
Parking provided, ramped entry, toilet facilities
Special comments: Lift.

CARDIFF UNIVERSITY – INFORMATION SERVICES

PO Box 430, Cardiff, CF24 0DE

Tel: 029 2087 9362
Fax: 029 2037 1921
E-mail: library@cardiff.ac.uk

Website:
http://www.cardiff.ac.uk/insrv

Enquiries:
Enquiries to: University Librarian and Senior Assistant Director, Information Services
Direct e-mail: petersjm@cardiff.ac.uk

Founded:
1883

Formerly called:
University of Wales, Cardiff, Library

Organisation type and purpose:
University library.
Information service.

Subject coverage:
Humanities, religious studies, education, music, social sciences, law, Welsh language, literature, history and culture, archaeology, language, literature and history of other Celtic countries, engineering, biosciences, optometry, pharmacy, physics, chemistry, earth sciences, architecture, business studies, town planning, computer studies, journalism, mathematics, medicine, nursing and health care.

Museum or gallery collection, archive, or library special collection:
British Government, EC and UN publications
Carmarthen Presbyterian College Library
Architecture rare books collection
Companies information (business studies)
Pre-1800 and fine or rare post-1800 books, including some manuscripts (those of the poets Edward Thomas and Anne Griffiths in particular)
Salisbury Library (Welsh and Celtic material)
Tennyson Collection
Welsh Hymnology collection
Welsh Ballads collection
History of Medicine
China Studies
Cochrane Archive
Centre for the History of Evaluation in Healthcare (CHEHC)
Osman Collection (photojournalism)
Cudlipp Collection (journalism)
Richard Stott Daily Mirror papers (journalism)
Tom Harrison Mass Observation Collection
Mackworth Collection (Music)
Aylward Collection (Music)
UN Deposit Collection

Non-library collection catalogue:
All or part available online

Library catalogue:
All or part available online

Publications list:
Available online

Access to staff:
Contact by letter, by telephone, by e-mail and in person
Hours: 0900 to 1700

Access to building, collection or gallery:
No prior appointment required

Access for disabled people:
Parking provided, ramped entry, level entry, toilet facilities
Special comments: Cardiff University Information Services are distributed across the campus. All areas are accessible but by different means – some areas ramped or level entry.

CARDIFF UNIVERSITY – RESEARCH AND COMMERCIAL DIVISION

Acronym or abbreviation: CU

7th Floor, 30–36 Newport Road, Cardiff, CF24 0DE

Tel: 029 2087 5834
Fax: 029 2087 4189

E-mail: whittinghamj@cf.ac.uk

Website:
http://www.cardiff.ac.uk/racdv

Enquiries:
Enquiries to: Research Information Officer

Formerly called:
Cardiff University, Research and Consultancy Division, Cardiff University

Organisation type and purpose:
University Division, consultancy, research policy, research support, research funding, University expertise, technology transfer, IP, business development, commercial support.

Subject coverage:
Architecture, semiconductors, engineering, pharmacy, computing, geology, marine research, magnetics technology, aerospace, chemistry, motors, astronomy, insect biology, systems dynamics, EDI, Cardiff University Innovation Network, planning, optometry, medicine, dentistry, nursing, health care, social sciences, history, archaeology, religion, politics, music, Welsh, journalism, English, philosophy, business, physics, biosciences, languages, psychology, law.

Library catalogue:
All or part available online

Printed publications:
Annual Reports
University Prospectuses

Access to staff:
Contact by e-mail and via website
Hours: Mon to Fri, 0800 to 1600

CARE FOR THE WILD INTERNATIONAL

Acronym or abbreviation: CFTWI

1 Ashfolds, Horsham Road, Rusper, West Sussex, RH12 4QX

Tel: 01293 871596
Fax: 01293 871022
E-mail: info@careforthewild.org.uk

Website:
http://www.careforthewild.org.uk
Details of our latest appeals and information on our animal fostering programmes. Our gift catalogue.

Enquiries:
Enquiries to: Public Relations Manager

Founded:
1984

Organisation type and purpose:
Registered charity (charity number 288802).
To alleviate suffering and the exploitation of wildlife around the world.

Subject coverage:
Care for the Wild International works with local people and government bodies in an attempt to alleviate suffering of wild animals around the world. In Britain it funds rescue centres and animal protection groups throughout the county helping a wide range of wildlife such as badgers, otters, foxes, sea-birds and birds of prey, seals and dolphins. Overseas it helps projects in Africa and Asia, supporting their initial work to protect tigers, elephants, rhinos, gorillas, turtles, gibbons, chimpanzees and hippos.

Printed publications:
Care for the Wild News (annually)
Care for the Badger (£3.50)
Care for the Wild (£4.95)
Life with Bluebell and Other Tales from an Animal Orphanage (£14.99)
My Secret World (£14.99)
Tigers (£4.99)
Trapping Animals for Fur (£1.50)
With My Soul Amongst Lions (£15.99)

Electronic and video publications:
Lifeline ...The Last Hope for the African Elephant
(video, £24.95)
The Elephant Harvest (video, £9.99)

Publications list:
Available in print

Access to staff:
Contact by letter, by telephone, by fax and by e-mail
Hours: Mon to Fri, 0800 to 1700

Also at:
Care for the Wild Denmark
    Ordrupvej 101, 2920 Charlottenlund, Denmark;
    tel: 00 45 3963 2360; fax: 00 45 3963 2360
Care for the Wild Germany
    Landauer Str 57/A, 70499 Stuttgart, Germany;
    tel: 00 49 711 838 6715; fax: 00 49 711 838 6719
Care for the Wild Kenya
    PO Box 34334, Nairobi, Kenya; tel: 00 254 2
    21977/8; fax: 00 254 2 219717
Care for the Wild Thailand
    PO Box 228, Klong Chan Post Office, Bangkapi,
    Bangkok, 10240, Thailand; tel: 00 2 662 732 7617;
    fax: 00 2 662 732 7618
Care for the Wild USA
    3705 Sequoia Trail, Verona, Wisconsin, 53593,
    USA; tel: 00 1 608 798 2801; fax: 00 1 608 798 2513

CARE PROGRAMME APPROACH ASSOCIATION

Walton Hospital, Whitecoats Lane, Chesterfield,
Derbyshire, S40 3HW

Tel: 01246 515975
Fax: 01246 515976
E-mail: cpa.association@derbysmhservices.nhs.uk

Enquiries:
Enquiries to: Administrator
Direct fax: 01246 515974
Other contacts: Secretary

Founded:
April 1996

Subject coverage:
Application of CPA in mental health, CPAA
standards and criteria.

Printed publications:
The Approach (quarterly)
CPA Handbook (2004)

Access to staff:
Contact by letter, by telephone, by fax and by e-mail
Hours: Mon to Fri, 0900 to 1700

Access to building, collection or gallery:
No access other than to staff, prior appointment
required

Access for disabled people:
Parking provided, toilet facilities

Regional Representatives addresses:
obtainable from CPAA

CAREERS GROUP, UNIVERSITY OF LONDON

Stewart House, 32 Russell Square, London, WC1B
5DN

Tel: 020 7863 6014
Fax: 020 7863 6003
E-mail: careers@careers.lon.ac.uk

Website:
http://www.careers.lon.ac.uk

Enquiries:
Enquiries to: Information & Research Specialist

Organisation type and purpose:
University department or institute.
Careers service.

Subject coverage:
Careers advice, recruitment information,
occupational information.

Printed publications:
How to write a CV
How to complete an application form
How to change your career
How to analyse and promote your skills for work
How to succeed at interviews
Graduate entry into medicine
Getting into international development
Recruitment agencies

Access to staff:
Contact by letter, by telephone, by fax, by e-mail
and via website. Non-members charged.
Hours: Mon to Thu, 0930 to 1700; Fri, 1100 to 1700

CARERS UK

20 Great Dover Street, London, SE1 4LX

Tel: 020 7490 8818; 0808 808 7777 (carers' line)
Fax: 020 7490 8824
E-mail: info@carersuk.org

Website:
http://www.carersuk.org

Enquiries:
Enquiries to: Chief Executive
Other contacts: Information Officer for professional
enquiries; Advice Officer/Carers' line (for carers)

Founded:
1988

Formerly called:
Carers National Association (year of change 2001)

Organisation type and purpose:
National organisation, voluntary organisation,
registered charity (charity number 246329).
Campaigning organisation.
To give information and advice to carers and
professionals, develop support groups, campaign
at all levels of national and local government, and
with service providers on behalf of carers.

Subject coverage:
Information on any subject of concern or interest to
carers, e.g. benefits, community care, residential
care, practical caring, money worries, emotional
support, housing, holdings, council tax, etc.

Trade and statistical information:
Data on the numbers of carers in the United
Kingdom.

Printed publications:
Leaflets
Information booklets
Caring (magazine)

Publications list:
Available online and in print

Access to staff:
Contact by letter, by telephone, by fax and by e-mail
Hours: Mon to Fri, 0900 to 1700
Carers' line: Wed, Thu, 1000 to 1200 and 1400 to
1600

Branches:
Carers Northern Ireland
    58 Howard Street, Belfast, BT1 6PJ; tel: 028 9043
    9843; fax: 028 9032 9299; e-mail: info@carersni.co
    .uk; website: http://www.carersni.org
Carers Scotland
    91 Mitchell Street, Glasgow, G1 3LN; tel: 0141
    221 9141; fax: 0141 221 9140; e-mail: info@
    carerscotland.org; website: http://www
    .carerscotland.org
Carers UK North of England
    23 New Mount Street, Manchester, M4 4DE; tel:
    0161 953 4233; fax: 0161 953 4092; e-mail: info@
    carersuk.org
Carers Wales
    River House, Ynys Bridge Court, Gwaelod-y-
    Garth, Cardiff, CF15 9SS; tel: 029 2081 1370; fax:
    029 2081 1575; e-mail: info@carerswales.org;
    website: http://www.carerswales.org

CARITAS – SOCIAL ACTION

Acronym or abbreviation: CCWC

39 Eccleston Square, London, SW1V 1BX

Tel: 020 7901 4875
E-mail: caritas@cbcew.org.uk

Website:
http://www.caritas-socialaction.org.uk

Enquiries:
Enquiries to: Director

Founded:
2002
Catholic Child Welfare Council

Organisation type and purpose:
Membership association, present number of
members: 22 corporate members, voluntary
organisation, registered charity.
Umbrella organisation for Roman Catholic
agencies concerned with the care and welfare of
children and families.

Subject coverage:
Services to children and families provided by
Catholic Children's Societies and other Catholic
social care agencies. Adoption and fostering of
children, post-adoption support work, birth
records counselling, family support projects,
support of children through Catholic schools and
parishes, child migration.

Printed publications:
Directory of Catholic Diocesan Children's Societies
    and other Caring Services (every 2–3 years,
    current ed. 2000, £1.50)
Other occasional publications

Access to staff:
Contact by letter, by telephone and by e-mail.
Appointment necessary.
Hours: Mon to Fri, 1000 to 1700
Special comments: Office is not always staffed.

Member organisations are:
Catholic Childrens Societies
diocesan care agencies
some religious congregations

CARLISLE CITY COUNCIL

Civic Centre, Carlisle, Cumbria, CA3 8QG

Tel: 01228 817000
Fax: 01228 817013
E-mail: customerservices@carlisle.gov.uk

Website:
http://www.carlisle.gov.uk

Organisation type and purpose:
Local government body.

Subject coverage:
Policy and performance, property, community
services, building and mechanised services, leisure
and amenity services and housing, environmental
services.

Access to staff:
Contact by letter, by telephone, by fax and by e-mail
Hours: Mon to Thu, 0900 to 1700; Fri, 0900 to 1600

CARLISLE COLLEGE LEARNING RESOURCE CENTRE

Acronym or abbreviation: Carlisle College LRC

Victoria Place, Carlisle, Cumbria, CA1 1HS

Tel: 01228 822760
Fax: 01228 822710
E-mail: lrc@carlisle.ac.uk

Website:
http://www.carlisle.ac.uk

Enquiries:
Enquiries to: Library Manager
Direct tel: 01228 822763

continued overleaf

Formerly called:
Carlisle College Learning Resource Centre; Carlisle Technical College

Organisation type and purpose:
College of further and higher education.

Library catalogue:
All or part available online

Access to staff:
Contact by letter, by telephone and by e-mail. Appointment necessary.
Hours: Term time: Mon, Tue, Thu, 0830 to 1900; Wed, 0830 to 1700; Fri, 0830 to 1600
Special comments: For reference only.

CARLISLE PUBLIC LIBRARY

11 Globe Lane, Carlisle, Cumbria, CA3 8NX

Tel: 01228 227310
Fax: 01228 607333
E-mail: carlisle.library@cumbriacc.gov.uk

Website:
www.cumbria.gov.uk/libraries

Enquiries:
Enquiries to: Area Library Manager

Organisation type and purpose:
Local government body, public library.

Subject coverage:
General.

Library catalogue:
All or part available online

Access to staff:
Contact by letter, by telephone, by fax, by e-mail and in person
Hours: Mon, Wed and Fri, 0930 to 1730, Tue and Thu, 0930 to 1900, Sat 0930 to 1600, Sun 1200 to 1600

Parent body:
Cumbria Library Services

CARMARTHENSHIRE ARCHIVE SERVICE

Parc Myrddin, Richmond Terrace, Carmarthen, SA31 1DS

Tel: 01267 228232
Fax: 01267 228237
E-mail: archives@carmarthenshire.gov.uk

Enquiries:
Enquiries to: Archivist

Founded:
1959

Formerly called:
Dyfed Archives Services (year of change 1996)

Organisation type and purpose:
Local government body.

Subject coverage:
Aspects of the history of Carmarthenshire, church and chapel records 16th-20th century, estate records 13th-20th century, business records 18th-20th century, local government records 16th-20th century, maps of the county 18th-20th century.

Museum or gallery collection, archive, or library special collection:
Cawdor Collection containing the Golden Grove Book, an 18th century collection of pedigrees relating to the whole of Wales
Records of local historical interest, including parish registers

Printed publications:
Carmarthen Book of Ordinances 1569–1606 (£3.95 with p&p £5)
Leaflets and booklets
Summaries of the holdings of the Offices
Topic lists

Publications list:
Available in print

Access to staff:
Contact by letter, by telephone, by fax, by e-mail and in person. Appointment necessary.
Hours: Mon, closed; Tue, 0930 to 1930 (1700 to 1930 by appointment only); Wed to Fri, 0930 to 1700
Special comments: For reservations at other times phone for appointment

Links to:
Carmarthen Reference Library
  St Peter's Street, Carmarthen; tel: 01267 224822
Carmarthenshire Museums Service
  Abergwili, Carmarthen; tel: 01267 231691

CARMARTHENSHIRE COLLEGE (COLEG SIR GAR)

Graig Campus, Sandy Road, Llanelli, Carmarthenshire, SA15 4DN

Tel: 01554 748000
Fax: 01554 756088
E-mail: admissions@colegsirgar.ac.uk

Website:
http://www.colsirgar.ac.uk
Course details and college information.

Enquiries:
Enquiries to: Marketing Officer
Direct tel: 01554 748112
Direct e-mail: debbie.williams@colegsirgar.ac.uk

Founded:
1984

Formerly called:
Llanelli Technical College

Organisation type and purpose:
Suitable for ages: 16+.
Higher and further education establishment.

Subject coverage:
Access and general education; business, management, and office technology, catering, hairdressing and beauty therapy, computing and applied science, creative and performing arts, engineering and construction, foundation and community education, health, social and child care, sport, leisure, tourism and land-based studies.

Printed publications:
Prospectus (free)
Faculty leaflets (free)
Course leaflets (free)

Access to staff:
Contact by letter, by telephone, by fax, by e-mail, in person and via website. All charged.
Hours: Mon to Thu, 0845 to 2100; Fri, 0845 to 1630

Access for disabled people:
Parking provided, toilet facilities

Has:
5 sites (11,000 students, 500 staff)

Parent body:
Funding Council for Wales
  Lambourne House, Cardiff Business Park, Llanishen, Cardiff, CF4 5GL

Subsidiary body:
CCTA Enterprises Ltd

CARMARTHENSHIRE COUNTY LIBRARIES

Block 1, Parc Myrddin, Richmond Terrace, Carmarthen, SA31 1DS

Tel: 01267 228337
Fax: 01267 238584
E-mail: dpthomas@carmarthenshire.gov.uk

Enquiries:
Enquiries to: Libraries and Heritage Manager

Founded:
1996

Formerly called:
Dyfed County Library, Llanelli Borough Library (year of change 1996)

Organisation type and purpose:
Local government body, public library.

Subject coverage:
General, local history and other matters relating to the county of Carmarthenshire, history of Wales, Welsh languages and literature.

Museum or gallery collection, archive, or library special collection:
Carmarthenshire Antiquarian Society Collection
Video collection on physical and mental disabilities

Library catalogue:
All or part available online and in-house

Printed publications:
Coal Mining in the Llanelli Area vol 1 16th Century (Simons M V, £5)
Booklets and Exhibition Catalogues and other publications including:
Facsimile copies of classic local history studies previously out of print
Dyfed in old photographs (10 volumes, £7.95 each)
Historic Carmarthenshire Homes and their Families (Major F Jones, 1986, £15)
A History of Gorslas 1804–2007(£12)
Llanarthney Past and Present (Jones T & D £12)

Publications list:
Available online and in print

Access to staff:
Contact by letter, by telephone, by fax, by e-mail and in person
Hours: Mon to Wed, Fri, 0900 to 1900; Thu and Sat, 0900 to 1700

Access to building, collection or gallery:
No prior appointment required

Access for disabled people:
Ramped entry

CARNEGIE DUNFERMLINE TRUST

Abbey Park House, Abbey Park Place, Dunfermline, Fife, KY12 7PB

Tel: 01383 723638
Fax: 01383 721862
E-mail: admin@carnegietrust.com

Enquiries:
Enquiries to: Secretary

Founded:
1903

Organisation type and purpose:
Registered charity (charity number SCO 15710). Recreational and cultural purposes within Dunfermline.

Subject coverage:
The Trust's own activities and policies; life and career of Andrew Carnegie.

Printed publications:
Annual Report
Occasional other publications
My Own Story (hardback, £4.95, paperback, £1.95)
Auld Grey Toun (£8.95)
Elgin or Charlestown Railway (£4)
Townhill (£2)
50 Years of Carnegie Hall (£3)
Story of Erskine Beveridge (£4.95)
and others

Access to staff:
Contact by letter, by telephone, by fax and by e-mail
Hours: Mon to Fri, 0900 to 1700

Links with:
Andrew Carnegie Birthplace Memorial
  tel: 01383 723302; fax: 01383 721862
Carnegie Hero Fund Trust
  tel: 01383 724638; fax: 01383 721862

CARNEGIE HERO FUND TRUST

Abbey Park House, Dunfermline, Fife, KY12 7PB

Tel: 01383 723638

Fax: 01383 721862
E-mail: herofund@carnegietrust.com

Enquiries:
Enquiries to: Secretary

Founded:
1908

Organisation type and purpose:
Registered charity (charity number SCO 00729).

Subject coverage:
The Trust's own activities and policies in providing, if needed, monetary and other help to people who have been injured or sustained financial loss, or to the families of people who have lost their lives, in heroic endeavour to save human life in peaceful pursuits in the British Isles.

Museum or gallery collection, archive, or library special collection:
Roll of Heroes and Heroines, 1908 to date

Printed publications:
Annual Report

Access to staff:
Contact by letter, by telephone and by fax
Hours: Mon to Fri, 0900 to 1700

Parent body:
Carnegie Dunfermline Trust
tel: 01383 723638; fax: 01383 723638; e-mail: admin@carnegietrust.com

CARNEGIE UNITED KINGDOM TRUST

Comely Park House, New Row, Dunfermline, Fife, KY12 7EJ

Tel: 01383 721445
Fax: 01383 620682
E-mail: raji@carnegieuk.org

Website:
http://www.carnegieuktrust.org.uk
Publications and general information.

Enquiries:
Enquiries to: Chief Executive
Other contacts: Communications Director

Founded:
1913

Organisation type and purpose:
Registered charity (charity number SCO 12799).

Museum or gallery collection, archive, or library special collection:
Archives (held in National Archives of Scotland)

Printed publications:
Annual Report, obtainable in all main public and reference libraries, ISBN prefix 0900259
Policy Guidelines, available free from Trust office on receipt of an sae

Electronic and video publications:
The following are also available on our website:

Publications list:
Available online and in print

Access to staff:
Contact by letter, by telephone and by e-mail
Hours: Mon to Fri, 0900 to 1700

CARNIVOROUS PLANT SOCIETY

Acronym or abbreviation: CPS

1 Orchard Close, Ringwood, Hampshire, BH24 1LP

Enquiries:
Enquiries to: Chairman
Other contacts: Membership Secretary for membership enquiries.

Founded:
1978

Organisation type and purpose:
Membership association (membership is by subscription), present number of members: 600, voluntary organisation, registered charity (charity number 281423).
To bring together all those interested in carnivorous plants whether beginners or experts. To increase people's knowledge both in horticulture and in the wild, including conservation.

Subject coverage:
Botany and horticulture of carnivorous plants; seed bank; conservation of carnivorous plants in their habitats.

Printed publications:
Guide to Carnivorous Plants
Journal (annual)
Newsletters (4 times a year)

Access to staff:
Contact by letter
Hours: Mon to Fri, 0900 to 1700

Affiliated to:
Royal Horticultural Society

Membership Secretary:
Carnivorous Plant Society
100 Lambley Lane, Burton Joyce, Nottingham, NG14 5BL

CARPENTERS' COMPANY

Carpenters' Hall, Throgmorton Avenue, London, EC2N 2JJ

Tel: 020 7588 7001
Fax: 020 7638 6286
E-mail: theclerk@carpentersco.com

Website:
http://www.thecarpenterscompany.co.uk
Building Crafts College, Rustington Convalescent Home, Wyatts Almshouses, Timber Industry Awards, Carpenters Craft Competititon.

Enquiries:
Enquiries to: The Clerk

Founded:
1271

Organisation type and purpose:
Professional body (membership is by election or invitation), present number of members: 150.
City of London Livery Company which supports the construction industry, craft of carpentry and charitable giving.

Access to staff:
Contact by letter
Hours: Mon to Fri, 0900 to 1700

CARPET FOUNDATION, THE

MCF Complex, 60 New Road, Kidderminster, Worcestershire, DY10 1AQ

Tel: 01562 755568
Fax: 01562 565405
E-mail: info@carpetfoundation.com

Website:
http://www.carpetfoundation.com

Enquiries:
Enquiries to: Commercial Director

Founded:
1999

Organisation type and purpose:
Membership association (membership is by subscription), present number of members: 12.
To promote the image of carpets and to improve knowledge about them to this end.

Subject coverage:
Pile carpets (especially wool carpets), carpet tiles and most other wall-to-wall textile floor coverings – but NOT oriental or machine washable rugs.

Printed publications:
CarpetCare

Carpet Foundation Brochure

Access to staff:
Contact by letter, by telephone, by fax, by e-mail and via website
Hours: Mon to Fri, 0900 to 1700

CARSHALTON COLLEGE

Nightingale Road, Carshalton, Surrey, SM5 2EJ

Tel: 020 8770 6800
Fax: 020 8770 6898

Website:
http://www.carshalton.ac.uk
General introduction to the college; information on courses.

Enquiries:
Enquiries to: Learning Centres Manager
Direct tel: 020 8770 6895
Other contacts: Systems Librarian, RBL Librarian

Subject coverage:
Leisure and tourism, business studies, media, catering, motor vehicle engineering, electrical installation, health and social care, history, art, literature, Spanish, early years, art and design, information technology and entry level vocational studies.
Level 4 courses in management, computing, teacher training, multimedia and performing arts.

Library catalogue:
All or part available in-house

Printed publications:
Course leaflets
Prospectus

Access to staff:
Contact by telephone
Hours: Mon to Fri, 0900 to 1700

Access to building, collection or gallery:
Prior appointment required

Access for disabled people:
Parking provided, level entry, toilet facilities

CAST METALS FEDERATION

Acronym or abbreviation: CMF

National Metalforming Centre, 47 Birmingham Road, West Bromwich, West Midlands, B70 6PY

Tel: 0121 601 6390
Fax: 0121 601 6391

Website:
http://www.castmetalsfederation.com
Casting enquiries, supplier enquiries, technical enquiries, casting processes, members section.

Enquiries:
Enquiries to: Chief Executive

Founded:
2001

Formed from:
British Foundry Association (BFA), British Investment Casting Trade Association (BICTA), British Metal Castings Association (BMCA) (year of change 2001)

Organisation type and purpose:
National organisation, trade association (membership is by subscription).
The single trade body for the UK cast metals sector.

Subject coverage:
Promotion of Best Of British castings, influencing and forming legislation, guidance and information on environmental, health, safety, statistics, markets, costs, prices, contracts, best practice, benchmarking.

Printed publications:
CMF Newsletter

Access to staff:
Appointment necessary.
Hours: Mon to Fri, 0900 to 1700

CASTINGS TECHNOLOGY INTERNATIONAL

Advanced Manufacturing Park, Brunel Way, Rotherham, S60 5WG

Tel: 0114 254 1144
Fax: 0114 254 1155
E-mail: info@castingstechnology.com

Website:
http://www.castingstechnology.com
Services provided by the organisation, Cti.

Enquiries:
Enquiries to: Information Officer

Founded:
1996

Formerly called:
British Cast Iron Research Association and the Castings Development Centre (year of change 2001)

Organisation type and purpose:
International organisation, membership association (membership is by subscription), present number of members: 300, research organisation.

Subject coverage:
Cast metals technology includes environmental and working conditions, melting and molten metal treatment, moulding and coremaking, process and quality control, NDE guaranteed quality, automation and advanced manufacturing technology (AMT), new cast materials, new applications for castings, casting design and choice of materials ferrous and non-ferrous, operating economics, design and production control, and costing.

Museum or gallery collection, archive, or library special collection:
National and International Standards
The Cti Library is devoted solely to the technology of metal castings production

Non-library collection catalogue:
All or part available in-house

Library catalogue:
All or part available in-house

Publications list:
Available online and in print

Access to staff:
Contact by letter, by telephone, by fax and by e-mail. Access for members only.
Hours: Mon to Fri, 0800 to 1600

CASTLE BROMWICH HALL GARDENS TRUST

Acronym or abbreviation: CBHGT

Chester Road, Castle Bromwich, Birmingham, B36 9BT

Tel: 0121 749 4100
Fax: 0121 749 4100
E-mail: enq@cbhgt.swinternet.co.uk

Website:
http://www.cbhgt.swinternet.co.uk
Admission/opening hours, special events, friends' organisation, photographs and history.

Enquiries:
Enquiries to: Secretary

Founded:
1985

Organisation type and purpose:
Registered charity (charity number 516855), historic building, house or site.
Historic gardens and maze.
Restoration of walled gardens to their 18th century glory.

Subject coverage:
Historical and horticultural. The Hall and Gardens were built in 1599 by Sir Edward Devereux who was MP for Tamworth. In 1657 the estate was purchased by Sir John Bridgeman I and later extended by his son Sir John Bridgeman II to its present boundaries. The gardens are of some 10 acres and include a 19th century holly maze.

Information services:
Lectures by special arrangement.

Special visitor services:
Guided tours.

Library catalogue:
All or part available in-house

Printed publications:
Brochure

Access to staff:
Contact by letter and by telephone
Hours: Mon to Fri, 0900 to 1700

Access for disabled people:
Level entry, access to all public areas, toilet facilities

CASTLE COMBE CIRCUIT LIMITED

Castle Combe, Chippenham, Wiltshire, SN14 7EY

Tel: 01249 782417
Fax: 01249 782392
E-mail: sales@castlecombecircuit.co.uk

Website:
http://www.castlecombecircuit.co.uk
Full programme of events, availability of courses/content/etc, services provided

Enquiries:
Enquiries to: Managing Director

Founded:
1950

Organisation type and purpose:
Service industry.
Racing circuit.

Subject coverage:
All usages of the circuit, racing and other, motorsports, learning to race.

Printed publications:
Annual fixtures and courses (free)
Race school brochures (free)

Access to staff:
Contact by letter, by telephone, by fax, by e-mail, in person and via website
Hours: Mon to Fri, 0900 to 1700; Sat, 0900 to 1600

Subsidiary body:
Castle Combe Exhibitions Limited
  tel: 01249 782417; fax: 01249 782392; e-mail: sales@castlecombecircuit.co.uk
Castle Combe Racing School
  tel: 01249 782929; fax: 01249 782392; e-mail: sales@castlecombecircuit.co.uk

CASTOR MANUFACTURERS ASSOCIATION

Acronym or abbreviation: CMA

1 Perch Close, Marlow, Buckinghamshire, SL7 2BQ

Tel: 01628 475648
Fax: 01628 475648

Enquiries:
Enquiries to: General Secretary

Founded:
1963

Organisation type and purpose:
Trade association.

Subject coverage:
Furniture, hospital and industrial castors.

Printed publications:
CMA Brochure detailing aims and objectives of the association and a list of members with products classified into industry types

Access to staff:
Contact by letter, by telephone and by fax
Hours: Mon to Fri, 0900 to 1700

Member of:
British Materials Handling Federation
BSI
FIRA

CASUALTIES UNION

Acronym or abbreviation: CU

PO Box 1942, London, E17 6YU

Tel: 08700 780590
Fax: 08700 780590
E-mail: hq@casualtiesunion.org.uk

Website:
http://www.casualtiesunion.org.uk

Enquiries:
Enquiries to: Honorary General Secretary
Other contacts: Honorary Treasurer (for financial matters)

Founded:
1942

Organisation type and purpose:
Membership association (membership is by subscription or invitation), present number of members: 450, voluntary organisation, registered charity (charity number 234672), suitable for ages: 8+.
To advance for the public benefit education and training in first aid, the treatment of illness, nursing, rescue, accident prevention, care in the community and similar activities, particularly through casualty simulation.

Subject coverage:
Casualty simulation, training and provision of skilled acting casualties, demonstrations and emergency exercises for training first aid, rescue, ambulance and hospital personnel.

Printed publications:
Casualty Simulation (quarterly, free to members including associates)
More Ways Than One of Fighting a War (E. Claxton, £3)
The Struggle for Peace – the history of CU's founding and early development (E. Claxton, £3 each or the pair for £5)

Access to staff:
Contact by letter, by telephone, by fax and by e-mail
Hours: Mon to Fri, 1100 to 2100

CATERING EQUIPMENT DISTRIBUTORS ASSOCIATION OF GREAT BRITAIN

Acronym or abbreviation: CEDA

PO Box 683, Inkberrow, Worcestershire, WR7 4WQ

Tel: 05602 618485
E-mail: peterkay@ceda.co.uk

Website:
http://www.ceda.co.uk

Enquiries:
Enquiries to: Director

Founded:
1972

Organisation type and purpose:
Trade association, membership association (membership is by subscription).
The official organisation of the catering equipment dealer and supply industry.

Subject coverage:
Provision, installation, service and design of commercial kitchens, catering equipment and kitchen utensils.

Printed publications:
Membership List (free of charge)
Newsletter (free of charge)

Association Information (free of charge)

Publications list:
Available online

Access to staff:
Contact by letter, by telephone, by e-mail and via website. Appointment necessary.
Hours: Mon to Fri, 0900 to 1700

CATES

Formal name: Campaign Against the Trade of Endangered Species
Acronym or abbreviation: CATES

23 Clifton Road, Henlow, Bedfordshire, SG16 6BL

Enquiries:
Enquiries to: Secretary
Other contacts: Director

Founded:
1985

Formerly called:
North Herts FOE Endangered Species Campaign (year of change 1985)

Organisation type and purpose:
Advisory body (membership is by subscription), present number of members: 200, voluntary organisation, research organisation.

Subject coverage:
Environmental subjects including: tropical rainforests, endangered species campaign, tree planting/woodland management, introduction/reintroduction (ie plant or animal species), behavioural and genetic extinction, pesticides and architecture.

Museum or gallery collection, archive, or library special collection:
Earth Matters Magazines (Friends of the Earth)
TRAFFIC Bulletins

Non-library collection catalogue:
All or part available in-house

Printed publications:
CATES membership and all publications £7, or:
Behavioural and Genetic Extinction (free, sae)
Campaign sheets
Housing Policy/Development (£1.50)
Information material
Pesticide Infractions/HSE's Response portfolio (£1.50)
Reintroduction/Introduction (free, sae)
Tree Planting/Woodland Management (£3)

Publications list:
Available in print

Access to staff:
Contact by letter
Hours: Mon to Fri, 0900 to 1700

CATHEDRAL ORGANISTS' ASSOCIATION

Acronym or abbreviation: COA

Royal School of Church Music, Cleveland Lodge, Westhumble Street, Dorking, Surrey, RH5 6BW

Tel: 01722 424848
Fax: 01722 424849
E-mail: coa@rscm.com

Enquiries:
Enquiries to: Secretary

Founded:
1946

Organisation type and purpose:
Professional body.
To provide opportunities for all cathedral organists to meet at 2 conferences per year and for the exchange of useful information.

Subject coverage:
Cathedral music today, education of choristers and the choir school situation today.

Access to staff:
Contact by letter, by telephone and by fax. Access for members only.
Hours: Mon to Fri, 0900 to 1700

CATHEDRALS AND CHURCH BUILDINGS LIBRARY

Formal name: Cathedrals and Church Buildings Division of the Archbishops' Council of the Church of England

Church House, Great Smith Street, London, SW1P 3AZ

Tel: 020 7898 1866
Fax: 020 7898 1881
E-mail: enquiries.ccb@c-of-e.org.uk

Website:
http://www.churchcare.co.uk
Advice on care of church buildings
http://www.cofe.anglican.org/about/librariesandarchives
Libraries and Archives of the Church of England

Enquiries:
Enquiries to: Honorary Librarian

Founded:
1921

Organisation type and purpose:
The Library supports the work of the Church Buildings Council (CBC) and the Cathedrals Fabric Commission for England (CFCE). The CBC advises churches and dioceses on matters relating to architecture and ecclesiastical planning regulations; also dispenses grants, for conservation of furnishings of historical or artistic significance in Church of England churches, on behalf of charitable organisations. The CFCE oversees the Church's own system of planning controls for cathedrals and provides guidance and advice on such issues.

Subject coverage:
Ecclesiastical art and architecture, with special reference to the cathedral and church buildings and furnishings of the Church of England; conservation of works of art in Church of England churches, general and specific information on a wide range of topics relating to churches and their contents including ecclesiology; liturgy; heraldry; ecclesiastical history; symbolism; hagiography.

Museum or gallery collection, archive, or library special collection:
Library of c.13,000 books and over 100 periodical titles on ecclesiastical art and architecture; liturgy; ecclesiology; National Association of Decorative and Fine Arts Society (NADFAS) church recorders reports; National Survey of English Churches, with documentary and photographic material, postcards and guide books relating to about 18,000 churches

Library catalogue:
All or part available in print

Access to staff:
Contact by letter, by telephone, by fax and by e-mail. Appointment necessary.
Hours: Tue, Wed, 1000 to 1600

Constituent part of:
Cathedrals Fabric Commission for England
Church Buildings Council

Parent body:
Archbishops' Council of the Church of England

CATHEDRALS FABRIC COMMISSION FOR ENGLAND

Acronym or abbreviation: CFCE

Church House, Great Smith Street, London, SW1P 3NZ

Tel: 020 7898 1866
Fax: 020 7898 1881
E-mail: enquiries@cfce.c-of-e.org.uk

Enquiries:
Enquiries to: Secretary

Founded:
1991

Formerly called:
Cathedrals Advisory Committee (CAC) (year of change 1991)

Organisation type and purpose:
Advisory and research body.
Statutory church body.

Subject coverage:
Care of cathedrals in England.

Library catalogue:
All or part available in-house

Access to staff:
Contact by letter
Hours: Mon to Fri, 0930 to 1630
Special comments: By appointment only.

Access to building, collection or gallery:
Prior appointment required

Access for disabled people:
Ramped entry, access to all public areas

Parent body:
Archbishops' Council of the Church of England

CATHOLIC AGENCY FOR OVERSEAS DEVELOPMENT

Acronym or abbreviation: CAFOD

Romero Close, Stockwell Road, London, SW9 9TY

Tel: 020 7733 7900
Fax: 020 7274 9630
E-mail: hqcafod@cafod.org.uk

Website:
http://www.cafod.org.uk
Information about CAFOD, its publications, campaigns, contact, library and information centre.

Enquiries:
Enquiries to: Information Services Manager
Direct tel: 020 7326 5600

Founded:
1962

Organisation type and purpose:
Voluntary organisation, registered charity (charity number 285776).
Specialised library.
Development and relief NGO working in the third world.

Subject coverage:
Computing, development economics, debt, trade, environment, land, information technology, theology, women, children in Africa, Asia, the Pacific, Latin America, the Caribbean and Eastern Europe.

Trade and statistical information:
A number of UN and World Bank statistical reports.

Library catalogue:
All or part available in-house

Printed publications:
An extensive selection of educational material relevant to Third World environmental, economic, justice and religious issues
CAFOD Bulletin
CAFOD Reports
Fruits of the Earth
Food and Land
Order printed publications from: e-mail: afarragh@cafod.org.uk

Electronic and video publications:
Videos on all aspects of the work

Publications list:
Available in print

Access to staff:
Contact by letter, by telephone, by fax, by e-mail and via website. Appointment necessary.

continued overleaf

Hours: Mon to Fri, 1030 to 1630

Access to building, collection or gallery:
No access other than to staff

Regional Offices:
CAFOD East
  Chigwell Convent, 803 Chigwell Road,
  Woodford Green, Essex, IG8 8AX; tel: 020 8502
  9722
CAFOD East Midlands
  61 Staton Road, Rearsby, Leicestershire, LE7 4YY;
  tel: 01664 424346
CAFOD Leeds and Hallam
  St William of York, Eccleshall Road, Sheffield,
  S11 8TL; tel: 0114 268 7817
CAFOD Liverpool
  St Joseph's, Upholland, Lancashire, WN8 0PZ;
  tel: 01695 633284
CAFOD North East
  Ushaw College, Durham, DH7 9BJ; tel: 0191 373
  5001
CAFOD North West
  St Walburge, Weston Street, Preston, Lancashire,
  PR2 2QE; tel: 01772 733310
CAFOD South
  St John's Seminary, Wonersh, Surrey, GU5 0QX;
  tel: 01483 898866
CAFOD South West
  The Mount, Taunton, Somerset, TA1 3NR; tel:
  01823 338903
CAFOD Southwark
  Hubert House, Mallard Close, Temple Hill,
  Dartford, Kent, DA1 5HU; tel: 01322 294924; fax:
  01322 279223; e-mail: southwark@cafod.org.uk
CAFOD Wales
  St Mary's Parish Centre, Union Street,
  Carmarthen, Dyfed, SA31 3DE; tel: 01267 221549
CAFOD West Midlands
  23 Glebe Street, Walsall, West Midlands, WS1
  3NX; tel: 01922 722944
CAFOD Westminster
  The Benedictine Centre for Spirituality, 29
  Bramley Road, Cockfosters, London, N14 4HE;
  tel: 020 8449 6970

CATHOLIC AGENCY TO SUPPORT EVANGELISATION AND THE CATHOLIC ENQUIRY OFFICE

Acronym or abbreviation: CASE-CEO

114 West Heath Road, London, NW3 7TX

Tel: 020 8458 3316
Fax: 020 8905 5780
E-mail: info@caseresources.org.uk

Website:
http://www.caseresources.org.uk
http://www.life4seekers.co.uk

Enquiries:
Enquiries to: Administrator
Direct tel: 020 8458 3316
Direct e-mail: jc@cms.org.uk

Founded:
2003

Formerly called:
Catholic Enquiry Office; Catholic Missionary
Society

Organisation type and purpose:
To support Catholic communities and individuals
in England and Wales.

Printed publications:
Evangelisation Directory

Publications list:
Available online

Access to staff:
Contact by letter, by telephone, by fax and by e-
mail. Appointment necessary.
Hours: Mon to Fri, 0900 to 1700

Access to building, collection or gallery:
Prior appointment required

CATHOLIC BISHOPS' CONFERENCE OF ENGLAND AND WALES

Department for International Affairs, 39 Eccleston
Square, London, SW1V 1BX

Tel: 020 7901 4861
Fax: 020 7901 4821

Enquiries:
Enquiries to: Secretary

Founded:
1968

Formerly called:
Commission for International Justice and Peace

Organisation type and purpose:
Advisory body, professional body, registered
charity.
Promotion of international justice and peace
including development. The Department is an
advisory body for the Catholic Bishops of England
and Wales, and has four analytical groups dealing
with: international justice and peace, European
affairs, refugees and migrants, environmental
issues.

Subject coverage:
Catholic teaching on international affairs,
development, and justice and peace issues.

Access to staff:
Contact by letter
Hours: Mon to Fri, 0900 to 1700

Subsidiary body:
National Liaison Committee of Diocesan Justice
and Peace Groups

CATHOLIC CENTRAL LIBRARY

Lancing Street, London, NW1 1ND

Tel: 020 7383 4333
Fax: 020 7388 6675
E-mail: librarian@catholic-library.org.uk

Website:
http://www.catholic-library.org.uk
Membership details, periodical holdings, latest
new book list, mission register holdings (baptism,
marriage etc).

Enquiries:
Enquiries to: Librarian
Other contacts: Director

Organisation type and purpose:
Registered charity (charity number 1064460/0).
A theological library.

Subject coverage:
Catholic Church in England and in countries of the
world, Roman Catholic current affairs, theology,
ecumenism, scripture, ecclesiastical history,
comparative religion and Christian sociology.

**Museum or gallery collection, archive, or library
special collection:**
19th century Roman Catholic pamphlets, tracts
  and directories
Ecumenism
Papal documents and magisterial statements
Post-Reformation English Catholic history
Vatican Council II

Printed publications:
List of additions to the library (3 times a year)

Access to staff:
Contact by letter, by telephone, by fax, by e-mail,
in person and via website
Hours: Mon, Tue, Thu, Fri, 1030 to 1700; Wed, 1030
to 1900

Access for disabled people:
Level entry, access to all public areas, toilet
facilities

CATHOLIC CHILDREN'S SOCIETY

Formal name: Catholic Children's Society (Arundel
& Brighton, Portsmouth and Southwark)

49 Russell Hill Road, Purley, Surrey, CR8 2XB

Tel: 020 8668 2181
Fax: 020 8763 2274
E-mail: info@cathchild.org

Website:
http://www.cathchild.org
Information on the work of the society and how
people can support the organisation.

Enquiries:
Enquiries to: Executive Director

Founded:
1887

Organisation type and purpose:
The Catholic Children's Society is a regional social
care agency. It works primarily in disadvantaged
communities helping to improve the emotional
wellbeing and outcomes for children, young
people and families. It supports people from a
diverse range of backgrounds, cultures and faiths.
It places children's needs at the centre of
everything it does.

Subject coverage:
Adoption, fostering, schools counselling,
community projects and catechetical programmes
and residential care for people with learning
difficulties.

Access to staff:
Contact by letter, by telephone, by fax and by e-
mail
Hours: Mon to Fri, 0900 to 1700

Access to building, collection or gallery:
Hours: Mon to Fri, 0900 to 1700

Also at:
Hove Adoption, Catholic Children's Society
Adoption
  Linkline House, 65 Church Road, Hove, BN3
  2BD; tel: 01273 821234; e-mail: hoveadoption@
  cathchild.org
Purley Adoption, Catholic Children's Society
Adoption
  49 Russell Hill Road, Purley, CR8 2XB; tel: 020
  8668 2181; e-mail: info@cathchild.org
Reading Adoption, Catholic Children's Society
Adoption
  50 Mount Pleasant, Reading, RG1 2TD; tel: 0118
  987 5121; e-mail: reading@cathchild.org
Winchester Adoption, Catholic Children's Society
Adoption
  7 Bridge Street, Winchester, SO23 0HN; tel:
  01962 842024; e-mail: adoption,winchester@
  cathchild.org
Winchester Fostering, Catholic Children's Society
Fostering
  7a Bridge Street, Winchester, SO23 0HN; tel:
  01962 842024; e-mail: fostering.winchester@
  cathchild.org

Cabrini Residential Care:
Cabrini
  3a Healy Drive, Orpington, Kent, BR6 9LB; tel:
  01689 891401; e-mail: cabrini@cathchild.org

Catechetical Programmes:
Fountains Centre
  24 Knebworth Road, Bexhill on Sea, TN39 4JJ;
  tel: 01424 730536; e-mail: fountainscentre@
  cathchild.org

Dartford Community Project:
Hubert House, Dartford
  Mallard Close, Knights Manor Estate, Dartford,
  DA1 5HU; tel: 01322 224500; e-mail:
  huberthouse@cathchild.org

Peckham Community Project:
Bird in Bush, Peckham
  616 Old Kent Road, Peckham, London, SE15 1JB;
  tel: 020 7639 3030; e-mail: birdinbush@cathchild
  .org

Schools Counselling:
Schools Counselling
   49 Russell Hill Road, Purley, CR8 2XB; tel: 020
   8668 2181; e-mail: info@cathchild.org

Vauxhall Community Project:
St Anne's, Vauxhall
   42–46 Harleyford Road, Vauxhall, London, SE11
   5AY; tel: 020 7735 7049; e-mail: vauxhall@
   cathchild.org

CATHOLIC EDUCATION SERVICE

Formal name: Catholic Education Service for
England and Wales
Acronym or abbreviation: CES

39 Eccleston Square, London, SW1V 1BX

Tel: 020 7901 4880
Fax: 020 7901 4893
E-mail: general@cesew.org.uk

Website:
http://www.cesew.org.uk

Enquiries:
Enquiries to: Office Manager
Direct fax: 0807 901 4893

Founded:
1847

Formerly called:
Catholic Poor Schools Committee

Organisation type and purpose:
Promoting and supporting Catholic education in
England and Wales.

Subject coverage:
Catholic education.

Printed publications:
http://www.cesew.org.uk
Order printed publications from:
general@cesew.orguk

Publications list:
Available online and in print

Access to staff:
Contact by letter, by telephone, by fax, by e-mail
and via website. Appointment necessary.
Hours: Mon to Fri, 0900 to 1700

The education agency of the:
Bishops' Conference of England and Wales

CATHOLIC INSTITUTE FOR INTERNATIONAL RELATIONS

Acronym or abbreviation: CIIR

Unit 3 Canonbury Yard, 190a New North Road,
London, N1 7BJ

Tel: 020 7288 8600
Fax: 020 7359 0017
E-mail: info@ciir.org

Website:
http://www.ciir.org
Information on all aspects of CIIR's work.

Enquiries:
Enquiries to: Information Officer
Other contacts: Advocacy Officer for issue/region
based information request.

Organisation type and purpose:
Membership association (membership is by
subscription), registered charity (charity number
294329).
CIIR works for justice, development and the
eradication of poverty through a combination of
technical assistance and advocacy for political
change.

Subject coverage:
Social, economic, cultural and political analysis
and expertise in geographic regions: Dominican
Republic, El Salvador, Nicaragua, Honduras,
Ecuador, Peru, Namibia, Zimbabwe, Somalia,
Yemen, East Timor.

Printed publications:
Burma's Excluded Majority: Women, dictatorship
   and the democracy movement (briefing,
   O'Shannassy T)
Contagion and Cure: Tackling the crisis in global
   finance (comment series, Woodward D)
Education for the Future: Environment and
   sustainable development in Peru (ed Chauvin L
   O)
Families in the War on Drugs: Peasant families,
   alternative development and the war on drugs in
   Bolivia (Blickman T)
Reaping the Whirlwind: Economic reform and
   food security in Zimbabwe (Chisvo M, Jimat
   Consultants)
Storm Warnings: Hurricanes Georges and Mitch
   and the lessons for development (Mowforth M)
Thinking Strategically about Politics and Poverty
   (Moore M and Putzel J)
Trade and Food Security: An assessment of the
   Uruguay Round Agreement on Agriculture
   (discussion paper, Murphy S)

Publications list:
Available in print

Access to staff:
Contact by e-mail and via website. Appointment
necessary.
Hours: Mon to Fri, 0930 to 1730

Access to building, collection or gallery:
Prior appointment required

Other addresses:
International Cooperation for Development (ICD)
   At the same address

CATHOLIC RECORD SOCIETY

Acronym or abbreviation: CRS

12 Melbourne Place, Wolsingham, Co Durham,
DL13 3EH

Tel: 01388 527747

Website:
http://www.catholic-history.org.uk/crs

Enquiries:
Enquiries to: Honorary Secretary
Direct e-mail: leogooch@wolsingham.DL133EH
.freeserve.co.uk

Founded:
1905

Organisation type and purpose:
Learned society, present number of members: 700.

Subject coverage:
Catholic history of England and Wales from the
Reformation (not genealogical).

Non-library collection catalogue:
All or part available online

Printed publications:
Annual Report
Newsletter (annually)
Recusant History (2 times a year)
Volume of Records or a Monograph (approx. every
   two years)

Access to staff:
Contact by letter, by telephone and by e-mail
Hours: Mon to Fri, 0900 to 1700

CATHOLIC YOUTH SERVICES

Acronym or abbreviation: CYS

39 Eccleston Square, London, SW1V 1BX

Tel: 020 7901 4870
Fax: 020 7901 4873
E-mail: cys@btinternet.com

Enquiries:
Enquiries to: Director

Organisation type and purpose:
Statutory body, voluntary organisation, registered
charity.
Training agency.

Subject coverage:
Youth, youth service, youth work.

Printed publications:
CYS News (quarterly)
Catholic Curriculum Youth Work Document (£3)
Ecumenical Pack (£2)
Guidelines to Good Practice (£3.95)
Induction Pack for Youth Workers (£3.95)
National Youth Sunday Pack (£2)

Access to staff:
Contact by letter, by telephone and by fax.
Appointment necessary.
Hours: Mon to Fri, 0900 to 1700

Also at:
Assistant Director
   Newman College, Genners Lane, Bartley Green,
   Birmingham, B32 3NT; tel: 0121 411 1033; fax:
   0121 475 0012

Member of:
British Youth Council
Council of Churches for Britain and Ireland (Youth
Unit)
National Council for Voluntary Youth Services

Sponsored by:
Roman Catholic Bishops' Conference

CBD RESEARCH LIMITED

Chancery House, 15 Wickham Road, Beckenham,
Kent, BR3 5JS

Tel: 020 8650 7745
Fax: 020 8650 0768
E-mail: cbd@cbdresearch.com

Website:
http://www.cbdresearch.com

Enquiries:
Enquiries to: Company Secretary

Founded:
1961

Organisation type and purpose:
Publishing house.

Subject coverage:
Sources of business information; directories and
guides to associations, societies and institutions of
all kinds in Great Britain and Europe.

Library catalogue:
All or part available online

Printed publications:
Amongst many are:
American Companies: A Guide to Sources of
   Information
Asian and Australian Companies: a Guide to
   Sources of Information
Centres, Bureaux and Research Institutes
Councils, Committees and Boards including
   Government Agencies and Authorities
Current British Directories
Current European Directories
Directory of British Associations and Associations
   in Ireland
Directory of European Industrial and Trade
   Associations
Directory of European Professional and Learned
   Societies
European Companies: A Guide to Sources of
   Information
Pan-European Associations
Statistics-Europe: Sources for social, economic and
   market research

Electronic and video publications:
Directory of British Associations and Associations
   in Ireland (18th edn, 2008, CD-ROM)
Mailing lists of associations to the client's
   specifications, in print or mailing label format.

Publications list:
Available online and in print

Access to staff:
Contact by letter, by telephone, by fax, by e-mail
and via website. Appointment necessary.
Hours: Mon to Fri, 0800 to 1700

continued overleaf

Member organisation of:
Data Publishers Association (DPA)
Independent Publishers Guild (IPG)

CCDU LIMITED

Churchwood House, Headingley Campus, Leeds
Metropolitan University, Leeds, LS6 3QS

Tel: 0113 283 6117
Fax: 0113 275 5927
E-mail: info@ccdu.co.uk

Enquiries:
Enquiries to: Business Manager
Direct tel: 0113 283 8611
Other contacts: Managing Director for shares
responsibility with the Business Manager.

Founded:
1976

Organisation type and purpose:
Training organisation, consultancy.
Personal and Professional Leadership and
Management Development for individuals and
organisations in education, and children's services

Subject coverage:
Training and consultancy provision for: managing
diversity, people management, personal
management and organisational management and
development. Recruitment assessment and testing.

Printed publications:
Getting it Right Series of practical guides:
Succesful Presentations
Facilitation: getting the most out of working with
groups
Mentoring in Organisations
Mentoring in Medicine

Publications list:
Available online and in print

Access to staff:
Contact by letter, by telephone, by fax and by e-mail
Hours: Mon to Fri, 0900 to 1700

CCLRC DARESBURY LABORATORY

Formal name: Council for the Central Laboratory of
the Research Councils

Daresbury, Warrington, Cheshire, WA4 4AD

Tel: 01925 603189
Fax: 01925 603779
E-mail: library@dl.ac.uk

Website:
http://www.clrc.ac.uk/Activity/LIS
Description of library services available including
access to library catalogue.

Enquiries:
Enquiries to: Library Services Development
Manager

Organisation type and purpose:
Research organisation.

Subject coverage:
Atomic, molecular and condensed matter physics,
synchrotron radiation, nuclear structure,
accelerator physics, computing and computational
science, biological sciences, materials science.

Library catalogue:
All or part available online

Printed publications:
Annual Report

Access to staff:
Appointment necessary.
Hours: Mon to Fri, 1000 to 1600

Laboratory of the:
Council for the Central Laboratory of the Research
Councils

CCUSA

Formal name: Camp Counsellors USA
Acronym or abbreviation: CCUSA

1st Floor North, Devon House, 171–177 Great
Portland Street, London, W1W5PQ

Tel: 020 7637 0779
Fax: 0207 580 6209
E-mail: info@ccusa.co.uk

Website:
http://www.ccusa.com
Information and application forms

Enquiries:
Enquiries to: Marketing Manager
Direct e-mail: jamiem@ccusa.co.uk

Founded:
1986

Formerly called:
Camp Counsellors USA (CCUSA) (year of change
2001)

Organisation type and purpose:
International organisation.
Student work & travel specialists.
Recruitment for summer work placements in the
USA and gap years to Australia or New Zealand,
work experience in Brazil or Russian summer
camps.

Subject coverage:
Work experience placements and travel.

Printed publications:
Brochure (free, on request)

Access to staff:
Contact by letter, by telephone, by fax, by e-mail,
in person and via website
Hours: Mon to Fri, 0900 to 1700

Also at the same address:
Work Experience USA (WEUSA)

CDC ENTERPRISE AGENCY AND BUSINESS LINK COUNTY DURHAM

Formal name: Chester-le-Street and Durham City
Enterprise Agency, and Business Link County
Durham

Newcastle Road, Chester-le-Street, Co Durham,
DH3 3TS

Tel: 0191 389 2648
Fax: 0191 387 1684

Enquiries:
Enquiries to: Chief Executive

Formerly called:
Business Link County Durham

Branch office of:
Business Link County Durham
First Floor, Imex Business Centre, Abbey Road,
Pity Me, Durham, DH1 5JZ

CEEBIS

Formal name: Central and East European Business
Information Service

Glasgow University Library, Hillhead Street,
Glasgow, G12 8QE

Tel: 0141 330 6735
Fax: 0141 330 4952
E-mail: T.Konn@lib.gla.ac.uk

Enquiries:
Enquiries to: Information Officer

Founded:
1990

Formerly called:
Soviet and East European Business Information
Service

Organisation type and purpose:
University library, consultancy.

Subject coverage:
Economic, social and political background for all
countries of Eastern Europe and the former Soviet
Union, general and specialised business
information services.

**Museum or gallery collection, archive, or library
special collection:**
50 current newspaper titles
75,000 monographs
600 journals
Back runs of newspapers held on microfilm

Trade and statistical information:
Statistics, company data, legislation.

Access to staff:
Appointment necessary. All charged.
Hours: Mon to Fri, 0900 to 1700

CELTIC FILM AND TELEVISION FESTIVAL

249 West George Street, Glasgow, G2 4QE

Tel: 0141 302 1737
Fax: 0141 302 1738
E-mail: mail@celticfilm.co.uk

Website:
http://www.celticfilm.co.uk

Enquiries:
Enquiries to: Chief Executive

Founded:
1980

Formed from:
Celtic Film and Television Association

Organisation type and purpose:
International organisation, trade association
(membership is by subscription, election or
invitation), registered charity (charity number SC
028708).
Celebrates and showcases the best of film and
broadcasting from the Celtic countries and regions
of Scotland, Ireland, Wales, Cornwall and Brittany.
The festival is a unique platform for debate and
international co-production development.

Access to staff:
Contact by letter, by telephone, by fax and by e-mail
Hours: Mon to Fri, 0930 to 1730

CEMENT ADMIXTURES ASSOCIATION

Acronym or abbreviation: CAA

38a Tilehouse Green Lane, Knowle, West
Midlands, B93 9EY

Tel: 01564 776362
Fax: 01564 776362
E-mail: info@admixtures.org.uk

Website:
http://www.admixtures.org.uk
Comprehensive range of information, technical
and environmental sheets for free download.

Enquiries:
Enquiries to: Secretary

Organisation type and purpose:
Trade Association.

Subject coverage:
Admixtures for concrete, mortar, grout and
sprayed concrete; curing compounds for concrete.

Printed publications:
Admixture Information Sheets
Admixture Technical Sheets
Admixture Environmental Sheets

Member organisation of:
European Federation of Concrete Admixtures
Associations (EFCA)
Cobblers Cottage, Chester Road, Daresbury,
Warrington, Cheshire, WA4 4AJ; tel: 01925
740581; fax: 01925 740581; e-mail: roland
.harbron@talktalk.net; website: www.efca.info

CENTER FOR AUTISM & RELATED DISORDERS

Acronym or abbreviation: CARD

Acorn House, 13 Moorfield Road, Orpington, Kent, BR6 0HG

Tel: 01689 837373
Fax: 01689 896656
E-mail: carduk@kentseuk.freeserve.co.uk

Website:
http://www.cardhq.com

Enquiries:
Enquiries to: Clinic Supervisor

Founded:
1998

Organisation type and purpose:
National organisation, suitable for ages: 2–8.
Special Needs Education.

Subject coverage:
Design and implementation of home-based teaching programmes for children with autism and related disorders based on the Lovaas technique.

Printed publications:
Brochures (on application)

Access to staff:
Contact by letter, by telephone and by e-mail
Hours: Mon to Fri, 0900 to 1700

Access to building, collection or gallery:
Prior appointment required

Headquarters:
Center for Autism & Related Disorders
2330 Ventura Boulevard, Woodland Hills, California, CA 91364, USA; tel: +1 818 223 0123

CENTRAL & WEST LANCASHIRE CHAMBER OF COMMERCE AND INDUSTRY

Acronym or abbreviation: CWLCCI

9–10 Eastway Business Village, Oliver's Place, Fulwood, Preston, Lancashire, PR2 9WT

Tel: 01772 653000
Fax: 01772 655544
E-mail: info@lancschamber.co.uk

Website:
http://www.lancschamber.co.uk

Enquiries:
Enquiries to: Chief Executive
Direct e-mail: mwhittle@nwi.businessint.co.uk

Founded:
1916

Organisation type and purpose:
Membership association, present number of members: 1400.
To promote, protect and develop the local business community at local national and international level.

Subject coverage:
Export, training, market research, business information, library, databases.

Printed publications:
Chamber Directory/Desk Diary
NetWork Magazine

Electronic and video publications:
NetWork Magazine (CD-ROM)

Publications list:
Available in print

Access to staff:
Contact by letter, by telephone, by fax, by e-mail and via website. Non-members charged.
Hours: Mon to Fri, 0800 to 1800

Access to building, collection or gallery:
Prior appointment required

Access for disabled people:
Parking provided, ramped entry, toilet facilities

CENTRAL ARBITRATION COMMITTEE

Acronym or abbreviation: CAC

PO Box 51547, London, SE1 1ZG

Tel: 020 7904 2300
Fax: 020 7904 2301
E-mail: enquiries@cac.gov.uk

Website:
http://www.cac.gov.uk
Press releases, information about organisation, latest applications, decisions and hearings, annual report, guidelines.

Founded:
1976

Organisation type and purpose:
National government body.
Permanent independent arbitration body.
To promote fair and efficient arrangements in the work place, by resolving collective disputes (in England, Scotland and Wales), either by voluntary agreement or, if necessary, through adjudication.

Subject coverage:
Disclosure of information (Trade Union and Labour Relations (Consolidation) Act 1992: Section 183); voluntary arbitration (1992 Act: Section 212); industrial relations. Statutory recognition (Employment Relations Act 1999). Considers applications and complaints under the Information and Consultation of Employees Regulations 2004 and a similar role in relation to European Works Councils, European Companies, European Co-operative Societies and Cross-Border Mergers.

Museum or gallery collection, archive, or library special collection:
Copies of past awards as issued by the Industrial Court, Industrial Arbitration Board and Central Arbitration Committee, from 1919
Applications and decisions on all case load
Guidelines to Statutory Recognition Procedures

Printed publications:
CAC Annual Report (free)
CAC information leaflet (free)
Statutory Guidelines to Recognition (free)
Information and Consultation Guidance (free)

Publications list:
Available online

Access to staff:
Contact by letter, by telephone, by fax, by e-mail and via website. Appointment necessary.
Hours: Mon to Fri

Access to building, collection or gallery:
Prior appointment required

Access for disabled people:
Parking provided, ramped entry, access to all public areas, toilet facilities

CENTRAL COUNCIL FOR BRITISH NATURISM

Acronym or abbreviation: CCBN or British Naturism

30–32 Wycliffe Road, Northampton, NN1 5JF

Tel: 01604 620361
Fax: 01604 230176
E-mail: headoffice@british-naturism.org.uk

Website:
http://www.british-naturism.org.uk

Enquiries:
Enquiries to: Secretary General
Other contacts: Public Relations Office, 07799 677732, Archivist 01223 840907

Founded:
1964

Organisation type and purpose:
National organisation, membership association (membership is by subscription), present number of members: 20,000, voluntary organisation.
National organisation of clubs and individuals.

Subject coverage:
History of, and present facilities for, naturism and naturist sunbathing throughout the world.

Museum or gallery collection, archive, or library special collection:
Archives of CCBN and its predecessors
Magazines and books concerning naturism throughout the world

Printed publications:
British Naturism (quarterly)
Members Handbook (approximately every other year)

Publications list:
Available online and in print

Access to staff:
Contact by letter, by telephone, by fax, by e-mail and via website
Hours: Mon to Fri, 0900 to 1630

Affiliated to:
International Naturist Federation

CENTRAL COUNCIL OF CHURCH BELL RINGERS

Acronym or abbreviation: CCCBR

E-mail: honsec@cccbr.org.uk

Website:
http://www.cccbr.org.uk
Information about the Council, its committees, publications and affiliated societies, and Doves' Guide to the Church Bells of Britain and Ringing Peals of the World.

Enquiries:
Enquiries to: Honorary Secretary
Other contacts: Honorary Librarian email: honlib@cccbr.org.uk URL: www.cccbr.org.uk/lib/lib.php

Founded:
1891

Organisation type and purpose:
Advisory body, membership association (membership is by election or invitation), present number of members: 230, voluntary organisation, registered charity (charity number 270036).
To promote and foster the ringing of church bells for Christian worship and on other occasions, to represent ringers to national bodies etc, to advise on all matters concerned with bells and bellringing.

Subject coverage:
Bells and their fittings (both historical and engineering aspects); technical aspects of change ringing; history of change ringing; assistance with disposal of bells from redundant churches; advice on fund-raising for bells and their maintenance.

Museum or gallery collection, archive, or library special collection:
Unique collection of books and manuscripts on bells,
bellfounders, bell-ringers and bell-ringing in the English tradition, covering the British Isles and overseas

Non-library collection catalogue:
All or part available online, in-house and in print

Printed publications:
Available from The Editor, The Ringing World, Eagleside House, 7–8 Chantry Street, Andover, Hampshire, SP10 1DE tel: 01264 366620, email: editor@ringingworld.co.uk URL: www.ringingworld.co.uk:
The Ringing World (weekly journal)
Available from Central Council Publications: email: pubs@cccbr.org.uk URL: www.cccbr.org.uk/pubs/ccpb.php :
Towers and Bells Handbook
Change Ringing History (3 volumes)
Publications on various aspects of bell ringing under the following general headings:
Technical – learning
Technical – teaching

continued overleaf

Recruiting
Maintenance, restoration, etc
History
Method collections etc

Electronic and video publications:
Also available from Central Council Publications:
Bell Handling – A Tutor's Companion (video)
Listening to Ringing (two cassettes or CDs)

Publications list:
Available online

CENTRAL GURDWARA LONDON

Formal name: The Central Gurdwara (Khalsa Jatha) London

62 Queensdale Road, London, W11 4SQ

Tel: 020 7603 2789
Fax: 0207 480 7636
E-mail: ksg@khalsa.com

Website:
http://www.centralgurdwara.org.uk

Enquiries:
Enquiries to: General Secretary
Direct tel: 020 7481 8176

Founded:
1908

Formerly called:
Central Gurdwara (British Isles Khalsa Jatha) London

Organisation type and purpose:
Membership association (membership is by subscription), present number of members: 1,000, registered charity (charity number 258324), public library, suitable for all ages.
Sunday school.
Religious congregations; education; births, marriages, death rites; library; music.

Subject coverage:
Sikhism

Non-library collection catalogue:
All or part available in-house

Library catalogue:
All or part available in-house

Printed publications:
Newsletter (monthly)

Access to staff:
Contact by letter, by telephone, by fax, by e-mail and in person
Hours: Access to the Executive Committee by phone, or Sunday evening on the premises. Wed and Fri, 1900 to 2030

Access to building, collection or gallery:
No access other than to staff
Hours: Daily, 0500 to 2030

CENTRAL LIBRARY, DERBY

The Wardwick, Derby, DE1 1HS

Tel: 01332 641702
Fax: 01332 369570
E-mail: central.library@derby.gov.uk

Enquiries:
Direct e-mail: askusaquestion@derby.gov.uk

Founded:
1879

Organisation type and purpose:
Local government body, public library.

Museum or gallery collection, archive, or library special collection:
An extensive manuscript collection, files of newspapers, Derbyshire census (both on microfilm), photographs, engravings, maps and family records
Local studies collection incorporates the Devonshire and Bemrose family libraries

The collection of printed books and pamphlets includes works published in 17th, 18th, 19th and 20th centuries. This is housed at the Local Studies Library, 25B Irongate, Derby, DE1 3GL

Library catalogue:
All or part available online and in-house

Access to staff:
Contact by letter, by telephone, by fax, by e-mail, in person and via website

Access for disabled people:
Ramped entry, access to all public areas, toilet facilities

Part of:
Derby City Libraries
   website: http://www.derby.gov.uk/libraries

CENTRAL SCHOOL OF BALLET

Acronym or abbreviation: CSB

10 Herbal Hill, Clerkenwell Road, London, EC1R 5EG

Tel: 020 7837 6332
Fax: 020 7833 5571
E-mail: info@csbschool.co.uk

Website:
http://www.centralschoolofballet.co.uk

Enquiries:
Enquiries to: Assistant Administrator
Other contacts: Senior School Administrator for admission process

Founded:
1982

Organisation type and purpose:
Registered charity (charity number 285398), dance training organisation.
Affiliate Member of the Conservatoire for Dance & Drama.

Access to staff:
Contact by letter, by telephone, by fax, by e-mail, in person and via website
Hours: Mon, Wed, Fri, Sat, 0900 to 1830; Tue, Thu, 0900 to 2100

Access to building, collection or gallery:
Prior appointment required

Graduate touring company:
Ballet Central
   at the same address; e-mail: info@csbschool.co .uk; website: http://www.balletcentral.co.uk

CENTRAL SCHOOL OF SPEECH AND DRAMA

Acronym or abbreviation: CSSD, Central

Embassy Theatre, 64 Eton Avenue, London, NW3 3HY

Tel: 020 7559 3942
Fax: 020 7722 4132
E-mail: library@cssd.ac.uk

Website:
http://www.cssd.ac.uk/pages/library.htmll
Library pages.

Enquiries:
Enquiries to: Head of Library Services
Direct tel: 020 7559 3942
Other contacts: Library, Media, Computer Services Managers for library, media, computer enquiries.

Founded:
1906

Organisation type and purpose:
University library.
H E College library.
Higher education.

Subject coverage:
Theatre, drama, art and design, drama education.

Museum or gallery collection, archive, or library special collection:
Library of c. 32,000 vols

Library catalogue:
All or part available online

Electronic and video publications:
DVD and video collections

Access to staff:
Contact by telephone. Appointment necessary. Non-members charged.
Hours: Telephone for hours as times vary for term time and holidays

Access to building, collection or gallery:
Prior appointment required
Hours: Hours vary, see website for details
Special comments: Charges for borrowing and copying

Access for disabled people:
Toilet facilities
Special comments: Access via side-entrance, phone beforehand.

CENTRAL SCIENCE LABORATORY

Acronym or abbreviation: CSL

Sand Hutton, York, North Yorkshire, YO41 1LZ

Tel: 01904 462000
Fax: 01904 462111
E-mail: science@csl.gov.uk

Website:
http://www.csl.gov.uk

Enquiries:
Enquiries to: Information Centre Manager
Direct tel: 01904 462272

Founded:
1992

Organisation type and purpose:
National government body, research organisation.

Subject coverage:
Plant pathology (bacteriology, plant health and disease assessment, disease control, mycology, virology), agricultural entomology (general entomology, vertebrate pest assessment, biology and control, fumigation, insect systematics), crop protection, biochemistry, chemistry (biological efficiency, analytical methods for pest formulations and residues in crops, safety to users), toxicology and industrial hygiene related to pesticides. Biology and control of invertebrate pests of stored products, moulds on stored products, mycotoxins. Food safety, food quality, food authenticity, pesticide residues in food and water. Microbiology. Alternative crops, GMOs. Conservation, environmental protection and environmental effects of pesticides, ecotoxicology. Mammal and bird ecology, invasive species, avian risks to aviation ('birdstrike'), animal health and welfare, zoonoses. Risk assessment, epidemiology, modelling and bioinformatics relevant to the above areas.

Museum or gallery collection, archive, or library special collection:
Cowan collection on Bees and Beekeeping – a collection containing works from the 17th century to date. Original drawings of invertebrate pest species. Photographic images of pest species and plant diseases.

Trade and statistical information:
Annual Pesticide Usage Survey Reports.

Printed publications:
Annual Pesticide Usage Survey Reports
Annual Report and Accounts (priced, TSO)
Insect Identification Cards (priced, available directly)
Photographs (priced, available directly)
Research papers
Science Review (priced, TSO)

Publications list:
Available online

Access to staff:
Contact by letter, by telephone and by e-mail.
Appointment necessary.
Hours: Mon to Thu, 0900 to 1700, Fri 0900 to 1630
Special comments: Some charges may be made.

Access to building, collection or gallery:
Appointment necessary.

Constituent part of:
Department for Environment, Food and Rural
Affairs (DEFRA)

CENTRAL SCOTLAND FAMILY HISTORY SOCIETY

Acronym or abbreviation: CSFHS

11 Springbank Gardens, Dunblane, Perthshire,
FK15 9JX

Website:
http://www.csfhs.org.uk

Enquiries:
Enquiries to: Honorary Secretary

Founded:
1990

Organisation type and purpose:
Membership association (membership is by
subscription).

Subject coverage:
Family history of the area.

Printed publications:
Stirling Burgess Lists
Various 1851 Census Indexes

Publications list:
Available online

CENTRAL ST MARTINS COLLEGE OF ART AND DESIGN

Acronym or abbreviation: CSM

Southampton Row, London, WC1B 4AP

Tel: 020 7514 7000
Fax: 020 7514 7033

Website:
http://www.csm.arts.ac.uk
College website including pages on the Museum
and Study Collection (this collection holds the
college archives and other special collections).
http://www.arts.ac.uk/library
Library website including catalogue.

Enquiries:
Enquiries to: Head of Learning Resources
Direct tel: 020 7514 7029
Direct e-mail: j.conway@csm.arts.ac.uk
Other contacts: Library Manager for requests for
access by potential external users.

Founded:
1896
ILEA Art Schools; Central School of Art and
Design, St Martins School of Art (year of change
1989); Drama Centre London (year of change
2000); Byam Shaw School of Art (year of change
2003)

Organisation type and purpose:
University department or institute, suitable for
ages: 18+.
College of Higher Education.

Subject coverage:
fine arts, graphic design, product and industrial
design, fashion design, textile design, jewellery
design, ceramic design, photography, animation,
film and video, theatre design and scenography,
performing arts

**Museum or gallery collection, archive, or library
special collection:**
Materials and Products Collection.
Artists books
Fashion files

Non-library collection catalogue:
All or part available online

Library catalogue:
All or part available online

Printed publications:
Guide to the Special Collections and Archives
within the Libraries of the London Institute

Publications list:
Available online

Access to staff:
Contact by letter, by telephone, by fax, by e-mail
and via website. Appointment necessary.
Hours: Mon to Fri, 0900 to 1700

Other addresses:
Central St Martins College of Art and Design
109 Charing Cross Road, London, WC2H 0DU;
tel: 020 7514 7190; fax: 020 7514 7189

Parent body:
University of the Arts London
65 Davies Street, London, W1; tel: 020 7514 6000;
fax: 020 7514 8073; e-mail: p.christie@arts.ac.uk

CENTRAL SUSSEX COLLEGE

Learning Resource Centre (LRC), Crawley
Campus, College Road, Crawley, West Sussex,
RH10 1NR

Tel: 01293 442281
Fax: 01293 442399
E-mail: lrc@centralsussex.ac.uk

Enquiries:
Enquiries to: Manager of Learning Resource Centres
Other contacts: Deputy Manager of Learning
Resource Centres

Organisation type and purpose:
Further education, Higher education

Subject coverage:
Business and finance, beauty therapy, catering,
computing and IT, engineering, construction,
hairdressing, health and social care, languages,
management, education, the arts, social sciences,
travel and tourism.

Library catalogue:
All or part available in-house

Access to staff:
Contact by letter, by telephone and by e-mail.
Appointment necessary.
Hours: Mon to Fri, 1000 to 1600

Access for disabled people:
Access to most areas

CENTRE FOR ACCESSIBLE ENVIRONMENTS

Acronym or abbreviation: CAE

Nutmeg House, 60 Gainsford Street, London, SE1
2NY

Tel: 020 7357 8182\ Minicom no. 020 7357 8182
Fax: 020 7357 8183
E-mail: info@cae.org.uk

Website:
http://www.cae.org.uk

Enquiries:
Enquiries to: Information Officer
Other contacts: Technical Officer for help on design
or access audit requests.

Founded:
1970

Formerly called:
Centre on Environment for the Handicapped

Organisation type and purpose:
Registered charity (charity number 1050820).

Subject coverage:
Information and advice on the design of the built
environment for disabled and older people.

**Museum or gallery collection, archive, or library
special collection:**
Specialist library on the environment and disability

Library catalogue:
All or part available in-house

Printed publications:
Access by Design (journal, 4 times a year)

Electronic and video publications:
Designing for Accessibility (available via our
website and access audits and in alternative
formats)
Keeping up with the Past (38 minute video on
making access improvements to historic
buildings)

Publications list:
Available in print

Access to staff:
Contact by letter, by telephone, by fax, by e-mail
and via website. Appointment necessary.
Hours: Mon to Fri, 0900 to 1700

CENTRE FOR AGRICULTURAL STRATEGY

Acronym or abbreviation: CAS

The University of Reading, PO Box 237, Earley
Gate, Reading, Berkshire, RG6 6AR

Tel: 0118 931 8150
Fax: 0118 935 3423
E-mail: casagri@reading.ac.uk

Website:
http://www.rdg.ac.uk/AgriStrat
Staff, aims of the centre, publications, forthcoming
conferences.

Enquiries:
Enquiries to: Director

Founded:
1980

Organisation type and purpose:
University department or institute, research
organisation.

Subject coverage:
Agriculture, including food, horticulture, forestry,
agroforestry, fish production; environment; long-
term planning and forecasting for the agricultural
industries, worldwide.

Printed publications:
Papers, contributed by outside authors
Reports, prepared by the Centre staff
Order printed publications from: Publications
Department, Centre for Agricultural Strategy
at the same address, tel: 0118 931 8152, fax: 0118
935 3423, e-mail: t.m.hicks@rdg.ac.uk

Publications list:
Available in print

Access to staff:
Contact by letter, by telephone, by fax, by e-mail,
in person and via website
Hours: Mon to Fri, 0900 to 1700

Established by the:
Nuffield Foundation as an independent, non-profit
distributory organisation

Part of:
University of Reading within the Faculty of
Agriculture and Food

CENTRE FOR ALTERNATIVE TECHNOLOGY

Acronym or abbreviation: CAT

Machynlleth, Powys, SY20 9AZ

Tel: 01654 705989 or 0845 330 8355
Fax: 01654 702782
E-mail: info@cat.org.uk

Website:
http://www.cat.org.uk

continued overleaf

Information about services provided by CAT, description of visitors centre, on-line mail order catalogue, details of courses, education, training, consultancy and publications.

Enquiries:
Enquiries to: Free Information Service

Founded:
1975

Organisation type and purpose:
International organisation, national organisation, membership association (membership is by subscription), registered charity (charity number 265239), suitable for ages: all, training organisation, consultancy, research organisation, publishing house.
Visitor Centre.
Display and research in sustainable, environmental, alternative technology and energy conservation issues.

Subject coverage:
Small scale renewable energy, wind, water and solar energy, energy efficiency, environmentally sound buildings, organic gardening, alternative sewage systems, reed beds, compost toilets, green tourism, environmental visitor centres, green building technology.

Printed publications:
Clean Slate (journal, quarterly)
Do-It-Yourself Plans
Educational material (10 titles)
Periodic publication of information sheets on all aspects of alternative technology
Resource Lists
Books
Order printed publications from: C.A.T. Mail Order at the same address, tel: 01654 705959 or 0845 330 4592, fax: 01654 705999, e-mail: mail.order@cat.org.uk

Publications list:
Available online and in print

Access to staff:
Contact by letter, by telephone, by fax, by e-mail, in person and via website
Hours: Mon to Fri, 0930 to 1730
Also Sat, Sun for visitors to the centre)
Special comments: In person access may be restricted – please phone for details.

Access to building, collection or gallery:
No prior appointment required
Hours: Mon to Sun, 1000 to 1730
Special comments: Entrance fee.

Access for disabled people:
Parking provided, level entry, access to most public areas, toilet facilities

CENTRE FOR APPLIED RESEARCH IN EDUCATION

Acronym or abbreviation: CARE

School of Education and Professional Development, University of East Anglia, Norwich, Norfolk, NR4 7TJ

Tel: 01603 456161
Fax: 01603 451412
E-mail: c.stephens@uea.ac.uk

Website:
http://www.uea.ac.uk/care/
CARE Web has information on research projects/initiatives, personnel and publications. Details of research degree programmes.

Enquiries:
Enquiries to: Director's Secretary
Direct tel: 01603 592638

Founded:
1970

Organisation type and purpose:
University department or institute, consultancy, research organisation.

University policy and curriculum research centre with degree teaching function; a constituent of the School of Education while maintaining its own identity.

Subject coverage:
Curriculum research, evaluation, development, dissemination, particularly in relation to centralised innovation projects; policy research and evaluation; information technology in education; computer-based education; bilingual education; in-service teacher education, particularly school-focused with an action research element; naturalistic methods of inquiry; problems and effects of teaching about race relations; library access and independent study for sixth-form students; performing arts evaluation; police training; AIDS/HIV education; research on youth; funding and contracting of social research, higher education research, disaffected pupils and curriculums; research/evaluation of nurse, midwife and GP education.

Museum or gallery collection, archive, or library special collection:
Archive of major research and curriculum development projects

Printed publications:
CARE publications on methodology
Monographs (24 titles published commercially)
Prospectus
Research and Evaluation Reports (40 titles)

Publications list:
Available in print

Access to staff:
Contact by e-mail
Hours: Mon to Fri, 0900 to 1700

CENTRE FOR ARMENIAN INFORMATION AND ADVICE

Formal name: Centre for Armenian Information and Advice

Hayashen, 105a Mill Hill Road, London, W3 8J

Tel: 020 8992 4621
Fax: 020 8993 8953
E-mail: info@caia.org.uk

Website:
http://www.caia.org.uk

Founded:
1986

Organisation type and purpose:
To enhance the quality of life for disadvantaged members of the Armenian community in London, specifically those in poverty and isolation, through the provision of welfare, educational and cultural services.
To promote understanding of the Armenian heritage, history and culture among the Armenian community and the wider public.
Registered charity (charity number 1088534)

Printed publications:
Armenian Voice (4 times a year, in English and Armenian)

Access to staff:
Contact by letter, by telephone, by fax, by e-mail and via website. Appointment necessary.
Hours: Mon to Fri, 0900 to 1600 (phone for appointment)

CENTRE FOR BUCKINGHAMSHIRE STUDIES

County Hall, Aylesbury, Buckinghamshire, HP20 1UU

Tel: 01296 382587 (Archives); 01296 382250 (Local Studies)
Fax: 01296 382771
E-mail: archives@buckscc.gov.uk and localstudies@buckscc.gov.uk

Website:
http://www.buckscc.gov.uk/archives
Introductory information, family history information, conservation leaflet, Internet links, list of newspapers, house history information
http://www.buckscc.gov.uk (click on P in A-Z index, then Photographs of Buckinghamshire)
Database for images of over 20,000 photographs.
http://www.nationalarchives.gov.uk/a2a
Many of the Centre's archive catalogues are available online on the Access to Archives website.
http://www.buckscc.gov.uk/libraries
Local Studies Library stock is on the main Library catalogue

Enquiries:
Enquiries to: Archivist

Founded:
1938

Formed from:
Buckinghamshire Records and Local Studies Service (year of change 2002)

Formerly called:
Buckinghamshire Record Office (year of change 1997)

Organisation type and purpose:
Local government body.

Subject coverage:
Local authority records, including Buckinghamshire Quarter Sessions (from1678) and County Council (from 1889), Church of England parish records, also records of non-Conformist churches, records of Archdeaconry of Buckinghamshire (including wills 1483–1858) etc, family and estate records.

Museum or gallery collection, archive, or library special collection:
Microfiche copies of National Probate Index, 1858–1943
Microfiche copies General Register Office index to births, deaths and marriages, 1837–2004
Microfilm copies of most of the Buckinghamshire Parish Registers held in the archives are available in the Local Studies Library

Non-library collection catalogue:
All or part available online and in-house

Library catalogue:
All or part available online and in-house

Printed publications:
Newsletter (4 times a year)
The Buckinghamshire Sheriffs (992–1992) (Hanley H. A., 1992)
Leaflets:
Your County Archives
Genealogical Sources
Local History Sources
Public House History Sources
How to Care for Your Family Archives

Publications list:
Available online and in print

Access to staff:
Contact by letter, by telephone, by fax, by e-mail, in person and via website. Appointment necessary.
Hours: Tue, Wed and Fri, 0900–1730; Thu 0900–2000; Sat, 0900–1600.
(Archive Searchroom closes 1715 Tue-Fri, 1545 Sat)
Special comments: CARN Readers Ticket required for archive searchroom, can be issued on presentation of proof of identity, name, address, signature.
A reservation is strongly advised for a microfilm/microfiche reader in the Local Studies Library and for a seat in the archive searchroom.

Access for disabled people:
Ramped entry, toilet facilities
Special comments: Access to all public areas.

Part of the:
Culture and Learning Service of Buckinghamshire County Council

CENTRE FOR BUSINESS AND PUBLIC SECTOR ETHICS

Acronym or abbreviation: CBPSE

Suite 131, 23 King Street, Cambridge, CB1 1AH

Tel: 01954 710086
Fax: 01954 710103
E-mail: info@ethicscentre.org

Website:
http://www.ethicscentre.org
http://www.ethicspress.com

Enquiries:
Enquiries to: Director

Founded:
1988

Organisation type and purpose:
International organisation, registered charity (charity number 1045986), training organisation, consultancy, research institute, publishing house.

Subject coverage:
Business ethics, corporate governance, government and political ethics, corporate and social responsibility, ethical systems, ethical audit, public administration and policy, environmental ethics, sustainable development, anti-corruption.

Non-library collection catalogue:
All or part available online and in print

Library catalogue:
All or part available online and in print

Printed publications:
See www.ethicspress.com
Business Ethics
Environmental Ethics
Espionage and Secrecy
Government Ethics
The British Philosophy of Administration
Ethics and Anti-corruption

Publications list:
Available online and in print

Access to staff:
Contact by letter, by telephone, by fax, by e-mail and via website. Appointment necessary.
Hours: Mon to Fri, 0900 to 1700

Access to building, collection or gallery:
No access other than to staff

Also at:
Centre for Business and Public Sector Ethics
St Andrew's Castle, St Andrew's Street South, Bury St Edmunds, IP33 3PH; tel: 01954 710086; fax: 01954 710103; e-mail: info@ethicscentre.org

CENTRE FOR CELL & TISSUE RESEARCH

Acronym or abbreviation: CCTR

Department of Biology, University of York, PO Box 373, York, YO10 5YW

Tel: 01904 432936
Fax: 01904 432936
E-mail: cmj4@york.ac.uk

Enquiries:
Enquiries to: Marketing Coordinator
Other contacts: Director

Founded:
1981

Organisation type and purpose:
University department or institute.
Commercial Unit.
The development and use of equipment.

Subject coverage:
Low temperature preparation techniques for electron microscopy, rapid freezing, cryo-sem, cryo ultra-microtomy freeze fracture for transmission electron microscopy, freeze-etching, low temperature embedding.

Access to staff:
Contact by letter, by telephone, by fax and by e-mail
Hours: Mon to Fri, 0900 to 1700

CENTRE FOR CLASSICAL HOMOEOPATHY

Homoeopathy Clinic, 2a Meal Market, Hexham, Northumberland, NE46

Tel: 01434 322084
E-mail: francishannon@hotmail.com

Website:
http://www.hompath.club24.co.uk
Introduction to Principal and information about service and email address.
http://www.yell.co.uk/sites/homeopathy
Addresses and telephone numbers of clinics.

Enquiries:
Enquiries to: Director

Founded:
1979

Formerly called:
Hannon Clinic of Natural Medicine

Organisation type and purpose:
Service industry, consultancy. To treat sick people by means of homoeopathic medicine. Specialising in chronic diseases such as arthritis, asthma, eczema and psoriasis.

Subject coverage:
Treatment of chronic diseases by means of homoeopathic medicine.

Printed publications:
Brief Introduction to Homeopathy (leaflet)
Guide to Self-help with Homeopathy (leaflet)

Access to staff:
Contact by letter, by telephone, by e-mail and via website. Appointment necessary.
Hours: Mon to Fri, 0900 to 1700

Also at:
Homoeopathy Clinic
Lindisfarne, 71 Westgate Road, Newcastle Upon Tyne
Homoeopathy Clinic
1 Red Gables, Chatsworth Road, Carlisle, CA1

CENTRE FOR COACHING

156 Westcombe Hill, London, SE3 7DH

Tel: 020 8293 4334
Fax: 020 8293 4114
E-mail: admin@centreforcoaching.com

Website:
http://www.centreforcoaching.com
Details of training courses, services, consultancy and products

Enquiries:
Enquiries to: Director

Founded:
2001

Organisation type and purpose:
Training organisation, consultancy, research organisation.

Subject coverage:
Coaching, life coaching, performance coaching, business coaching, executive coaching, stress management coaching, psychological coaching, cognitive coaching, training.

Non-library collection catalogue:
All or part available online

Printed publications:
Life Coaching: A Cognitive Behavioural Approach
Dealing with People Problems at Work
Conquer Your Stress
Creating a Balance: Managing Stress

Electronic and video publications:
Articles available online

Publications list:
Available online

Access to staff:
Contact by letter, by telephone, by fax and by e-mail. Appointment necessary.
Hours: Mon to Fri, 0900 to 1700

Links with:
Centre for Stress Management
156 Westcombe Hill, London, SE3 7DH

Member organisation of:
Association for Coaching

CENTRE FOR COMBUSTION AND ENERGY STUDIES

University of Leeds, Leeds, West Yorkshire, LS2 9JT

Tel: 0113 343 2498
Fax: 0113 244 0572

Website:
http://www.mech-eng.leeds.ac.uk/cces/ce.html

Enquiries:
Enquiries to: Deputy Director
Direct tel: 0113 343 2108
Direct fax: 0113 242 4611
Direct e-mail: comb-energy@mech-eng.leeds.ac.uk

Organisation type and purpose:
University department or institute, consultancy, research organisation.
Consortium of University Departments of Chemistry, Fuel and Energy Engineering and Mechanical Engineering.

Subject coverage:
Combustion; fundamentals and applications in engines, furnaces, power generation; flames; control and diagnostics. Heat transfer; pollution emission control; energy; analysis, conservation, cogeneration; alternative sources; fuels; analysis, reserves, conversion technologies; fire and explosion hazards.

Printed publications:
Research Project Summaries
Short Course Information (2 times a year)
Specialist MSC Course brochures

Access to staff:
Contact by letter, by telephone and by e-mail
Hours: Mon to Fri, 0900 to 1700

Access for disabled people:
Access to all public areas

CENTRE FOR COMPLEMENTARY AND INTEGRATED MEDICINE

56 Bedford Place, Southampton, SO15 2DT

Tel: 023 8033 4752
Fax: 023 8023 1835
E-mail: info@complemed.co.uk

Website:
http://www.complemed.co.uk
Services the centre provides.

Enquiries:
Enquiries to: Manager

Founded:
1982

Organisation type and purpose:
Service industry, training organisation, research organisation.
Medical Practice.
To provide services, planning and research within complementary medicine.

Subject coverage:
A multi-disciplinary, medically based clinical practice within the field of complementary medicine encompassing training and research in homoeopathy, osteopathy, acupuncture, environmental medicine, clinical ecology (food and chemical sensitivity).

continued overleaf

Printed publications:
Books of interest to doctors and therapists
including:
Modern Chinese Acupuncture (a review, Lewith G
and N, £12.99)
Books of interest to the lay public including:
Allergy and intolerance (Lewith G et al, £8.99)

Publications list:
Available in print

Access to staff:
Contact by letter, by telephone, by fax and via
website
Hours: Mon to Thu, 0900 to 1300

Also at:

21 Harcourt House, 19 Cavendish Square,
London W1G 0PL; tel: 020 7935 7848

CENTRE FOR COMPOSITE MATERIALS

Imperial College of Science, Technology and
Medicine, Prince Consort Road, London, SW7 2BY

Tel: 020 7594 5084
Fax: 020 7594 5083
E-mail: composites@ic.ac.uk

Website:
http://www.cm.ic.ac.uk
General.

Enquiries:
Enquiries to: Director

Founded:
1983

Organisation type and purpose:
University department or institute.
MSc in composite materials, research degrees,
contract research and testing for industry.

Subject coverage:
Testing, characterisation, design, mathematical
modelling of fibre-reinforced plastics, metals and
ceramics.

Printed publications:
Annual Report
Newsletter (2 times a year)
Post-experience courses (annually)
Postgraduate research brochure (annually)

Access to staff:
Contact by letter, by telephone, by fax and by e-
mail. Appointment necessary.
Hours: Mon to Fri, 0900 to 1700

CENTRE FOR CONSERVATION STUDIES

Department of Archaeology, University of York,
The Kings Manor, York, YO1 7EP

Tel: 01904 433963
Fax: 01904 433902
E-mail: pab11@york.ac.uk

Website:
http://www.york.ac.uk/depts/arch
Information on the department, research, staff,
courses.

Enquiries:
Enquiries to: Postgraduate Administrator

Formed from:
Institute of Advanced Architectural Studies
(IAAS), Institute of Advanced Architectural
Studies Centre for the Conservation of Parks and
Gardens

Organisation type and purpose:
University department or institute, suitable for
ages: 18+.
Award of MA and DPhil degrees. Short courses
open to the public.

Subject coverage:
Architectural conservation, archaeological heritage
management, landscape studies.

**Museum or gallery collection, archive, or library
special collection:**
Library housed at the Kings Manor Library,
University of York

Library catalogue:
All or part available online

Publications list:
Available in print

Access to staff:
Contact by letter, by telephone, by fax, by e-mail,
in person and via website. Appointment necessary.
Hours: Mon to Fri, 0900 to 1700

Access to building, collection or gallery:
No access other than to staff
Hours: Mon to Fri, 0900 to 1700
Special comments: Borrowing restricted to
university members and subscribers, but access is
free.

CENTRE FOR CONTEMPORARY ART AND THE NATURAL WORLD

Acronym or abbreviation: CCANW

Haldon Forest Park, Exeter, Devon, EX6 7XR

Tel: 01392 832277
E-mail: info@ccanw.co.uk

Website:
http://www.ccanw.co.uk

Founded:
2001

Organisation type and purpose:
A registered limited company (no. 4141506) and
registered charity (no. 1092019), seeking to increase
access to the arts by breaking down physical,
psychological and intellectual barriers, while
working with different communities, embracing
cultural diversity and social inclusion.

Subject coverage:
Man's artistic relationship with the natural world.

CENTRE FOR CONTEMPORARY ARTS

Acronym or abbreviation: CCA

350 Sauchiehall Street, Glasgow, G2 3JD

Tel: 0141 332 7521
Fax: 0141 332 3226
E-mail: gen@cca-glasgow.com

Website:
http://www.cca-glasgow.com

Enquiries:
Enquiries to: Head of Administration & Resources

Founded:
1993

Organisation type and purpose:
Voluntary organisation, registered charity, art
gallery.
Arts centre.
To support artists in making possible the creation
of original works, increasing the accessibility and
strengthening the understanding of contemporary
arts through a range of activities including talks,
tours, writers' events, classes and workshops.

Subject coverage:
Contemporary visual and performing arts
especially in Scotland.

Printed publications:
Catalogues for CCA commissioned or joint
commissioned exhibitions 1993–1998

Publications list:
Available in print

Access to staff:
Contact by telephone and by e-mail
Hours: Mon to Fri, 0900 to 1700

Access for disabled people:
Access to all public areas

CENTRE FOR COUPLE RELATIONSHIPS

Acronym or abbreviation: TCCR

Tavistock Centre, 120 Belsize Lane, London, NW3
5BA

Tel: 020 8938 2353
Fax: 020 7435 1080
E-mail: tccr@tccr.org.uk

Website:
http://www.tccr.org.uk

Enquiries:
Enquiries to: Information Officer
Other contacts: Director

Founded:
1948

Organisation type and purpose:
Voluntary organisation, registered charity (charity
number 211058), training organisation,
consultancy, research organisation.
Psychotherapy Organisation working nationally
and internationally; learned institute concerned
with the couple relationship.

Subject coverage:
Training, consultancy and research organisation
offering psychotherapy to couples, teaching,
training and consultancy to other practitioners
working with couples, research. Areas of particular
interest: couple psychotherapy, divorce, infertility,
unemployment, family transitions, divorce court
welfare, mediation, inter-agency collaboration.

Printed publications:
Annual Report
In Brief (newsletter, annually)
Training Prospectus (annually)
In House publications include:
Brief Casework with a Marital Problem (Guthrie L
and Mattinson J, 1975, £4.50, ISBN: 901882–03–8)
Marital Interaction and Some Illnesses in Children
(Mainprice J, 1977, £4.50, ISBN: 901882–09–7)
The Reflection Process in Casework Supervision
(Mattison J, 2nd ed 1991)
Marriage and Mental Handicap (Mattison J, 1975,
£9.50, ISBN: 90188212–7)
Mate and Stalemate: Working with Marital
Problems in a Social Services Department
(Mattinson J and Sinclair I, 1981, £9.50 ISBN 0–
901882–16-X)
Shared Fantasy in Marital Problems (Bannister K
and Pincus L, 1975, £4.50)
Staff Supervision in a Turbulent Environment
(Hughes L and Pengelly P, 2nd ed. 1991 £14.95)
Order printed publications from: Karnac (Books) Ltd
58 Gloucester Road, London, SW7 4DQ, tel: 020
7584 3303, fax: 020 7823 7743

Electronic and video publications:
Teaching videos

Publications list:
Available online and in print

Access to staff:
Contact by letter, by telephone, by fax, by e-mail
and via website. Appointment necessary.
Hours: Mon to Fri, 0900 to 1700

Member of:
International Union of Family Organisations
United Kingdom Council for Psychotherapy

Parent body:
Tavistock Institute of Medical Psychology

CENTRE FOR CRIME AND JUSTICE STUDIES, THE

Acronym or abbreviation: CCJS

King's College London, Strand, WC2R 2LS

Tel: 020 7848 1688
Fax: 020 7848 1689
E-mail: info@crimeandjustice.org.uk

Website:
http://www.kcl.ac.uk/ccjs
http://www.crimeinfo.org

http://www.kcl.ac.uk/istd

Enquiries:
Enquiries to: Director
Other contacts: Research and Development Officer

Founded:
1931

Formerly called:
Institute for the Study and Treatment o'
Delinquency (ISTD)

Organisation type and purpose:
Membership association (membership is by
subscription), present number of members: 926,
voluntary organisation, registered charity (charity
number 251588), research organisation.
To promote the exchange of knowledge, experience
and understanding of criminal justice matters
among interested individuals and to provide an
independent, objective and non-campaigning
forum for debate.

Subject coverage:
Criminology, criminal justice, delinquency.

**Museum or gallery collection, archive, or library
special collection:**
The E T Jensen Library (over 2000 volumes on
Criminology) now in the King's College Library

Printed publications:
Annual Report
British Journal of Criminology (quarterly, pub.
OUP)
Conference Reports (for sale)
Criminal Justice Matters (newsletter, quarterly)
Occasional papers (for sale)

Publications list:
Available online and in print

Access to staff:
Contact by letter, by telephone, by fax, by e-mail
and via website
Hours: Mon to Fri, 0900 to 1700

CENTRE FOR CRIMINOLOGY

Formal name: The Centre for Criminology
Acronym or abbreviation: CCR

Manor Road Building, Manor Road, Oxford, OX1
3UQ

Tel: 01865 274444/8
Fax: 01865 281924
E-mail: ccr@crim.ox.ac.uk

Website:
http://www.crim.ox.ac.uk
Information about CCR, its research activities,
staff, visiting academics and graduate
programmes.
http://www.lib.ox.ac.uk/olis
Oxford University's online union library catalogue.

Enquiries:
Enquiries to: Administrator

Founded:
1996

Formerly called:
Penal Research Unit (year of change 1973); The
Centre for Criminological Research and Probation
Studies Unit (year of change 2004)

Organisation type and purpose:
University department or institute, research
organisation.
Research centre. Provider of graduate programmes
at Master's and DPhil level

Subject coverage:
Policing and security; sentencing and punishment;
public opinion, politics and crime control; victims;
extra-legal governance and organized crime, and
crime, rehabilitation and desistance.

Printed publications:
Bullying in Prisons (O'Donnell I and Edgar K,
1998, Occasional Paper No.18, £15.50)
The Changing Face of Crime and Criminal Policy
in Europe (Hood R and Courakis N E eds, 1999,
£10)

Victims with Learning Disabilities: Negotiating the
Criminal Justice System (Sanders A et al, 1997,
Occasional Paper No.17, £14.50)
Paroling with New Criteria: Evaluating the Impact
and Effects of Changes in the Parole System:
Phase Two (Hood R and Shute S, 1995,
Occasional Paper No.16, £10.50)
Armed Robbery: A Study in London (Morrison S
and Ian O'Donnell, 1994, Occasional Paper
No.15, £5)
Parole in Transition: Evaluating the Impact and
Effects of Changes in the Parole System: Phase
One, Establishing the Base-Line (Hood R and
Shute S, 1994, Occasional Paper No.13, £10)
Reported and Unreported Racial Incidents in
Prisons (Burnett R and Farrell G, 1994,
Occasional Paper No.14, £12.50)

Access to staff:
Contact by letter, by telephone, by fax, by e-mail
and via website. Appointment necessary.
Hours: Mon to Fri, 0915 to 1700

Access to building, collection or gallery:
Please arrange appointment in advance
Hours: Mon to Fri, 0900 to 1700
Special comments: University card required.

Access for disabled people:
Please arrange appointment in advance
Hours: Mon to Fri, 0900 to 1700
Special comments: University card required.

CENTRE FOR DEFENCE AND INTERNATIONAL SECURITY STUDIES

Acronym or abbreviation: CDISS

Cartmel College, University of Lancaster, Bailrigg,
Lancaster, LA1 4YL

Tel: 01524 594254
Fax: 01524 594258
E-mail: cdiss@lancaster.ac.uk

Website:
http://www.cdiss.org
CDISS Research Programme, 450 pages on Ballistic
Missile Defence, details of all CDISS publications.

Enquiries:
Enquiries to: Executive Secretary
Direct e-mail: p.elliott@lancaster.ac.uk
Other contacts: Director

Founded:
1990

Formed by the merger of:
Centre for Defence and Security Analysis (CDSA),
Centre for the Study of Arms Control and
International Security (CSACIS) (year of change
1990)

Organisation type and purpose:
Membership association (membership is by
election or invitation), present number of
members: 54, university department or institute,
research organisation.

Subject coverage:
Ballistic missile defence; defence management;
civil-military relations; military technology;
maritime and naval policy.

**Museum or gallery collection, archive, or library
special collection:**
150+ Defence Journal Titles 1983–1999 as Abstracts
and indexed in The Lancaster Index

Non-library collection catalogue:
All or part available online and in print

Library catalogue:
All or part available in-house

Printed publications:
Bailrigg Debating Points
Bailrigg Memoranda
Bailrigg Papers including:
Future Conditional: War & Conflict after Next (ed
Edmonds M, 2002, £15)
Bailrigg Studies including:

Landmarks in Defense Literature (Edmunds M and
Gray B, 2001 £9.95)
100 Years of the Trade. RN Submarines: Past,
Present & Future (ed Edmonds M, 2001, £25)
Defense & Security Analysis

Electronic and video publications:
Lancaster Index (CD-ROM for purchase with the
search programme (Windows format))

Publications list:
Available in print

Access to staff:
Contact by letter, by telephone, by fax, by e-mail
and via website
Hours: Mon to Fri, 0900 to 1700

Access to building, collection or gallery:
No access other than to staff
Hours: University Library: 0900 to 2100 term time
Special comments: Permission required.

Connections with:
ANEPE
Santiago, Chile
CERSA Toulouse University
CISSM Maryland University
Defence Research Centre
Tokyo, Japan
SIIA
Johannesburg, South Africa

CENTRE FOR DEVELOPMENT STUDIES

Acronym or abbreviation: CDS

University of Wales, Swansea, Singleton Park,
Swansea, West Glamorgan, SA2 8PP

Tel: 01792 295332
Fax: 01792 295682
E-mail: h.lewis@swansea.ac.uk

Website:
http://www.swan.ac.uk/cds/index.htm
http://www.swan.ac.uk/cds/devres/index.htm
For publications.

Enquiries:
Enquiries to: Admissions Secretary

Founded:
1976

Organisation type and purpose:
International organisation, university department
or institute, training organisation, consultancy,
research organisation, publishing house.

Subject coverage:
Development planning, in particular social
development; monitoring, evaluation and impact
assessment; development policy; regional
development; rights-based approaches;
development management; environmental
planning; population and development;
participatory development; health planning; sexual
and reproductive health; crime and justice systems;
children's rights; governance; poverty reduction;
sustainable livelihoods; corporate social
responsibility.

Printed publications:
CDS Prospectus
Papers in International Development
Resources in Social Development Practice
Research Issues in Natural Resource Management

Publications list:
Available online and in print

Access to staff:
Contact by letter, by telephone, by fax, by e-mail,
in person and via website. Appointment necessary.
Hours: Mon to Fri, 0900 to 1700

Links with:
Resource Centre for Department for International
Development, in the fields of social development,
health and population

CENTRE FOR ECOLOGY AND HYDROLOGY – EDINBURGH RESEARCH STATION

Acronym or abbreviation: CEH

Bush Estate, Penicuik, Midlothian, EH26 0QB

Tel: 0131 445 4343
Fax: 0131 445 3943
E-mail: bulib@ceh.ac.uk

Website:
http://www.ceh.ac.uk
Comprehensive information on the work of the Institute and its research stations, publications lists.

Enquiries:
Enquiries to: Librarian
Direct tel: 0131 445 8509

Founded:
2000

Created by the merger of:
Institute of Freshwater Ecology (IFE), Institute of Hydrology (IH), Institute of Terrestrial Ecology (ITE), Institute of Virology and Environmental Microbiology (IVEM) (year of change 2000)

Formerly a part of:
Nature Conservancy Council

Organisation type and purpose:
Research organisation.

Subject coverage:
Factors determining the structure, composition and processes of terrestrial ecological systems and the abundance and performance of individual species and organisms, scientific bases for predicting and modelling future environmental trends, human impact, land use, conservation and the protection and management of the environment.

Library catalogue:
All or part available online

Printed publications:
Annual Report
Provisional atlases of the flora and fauna of Britain and Ireland
Research publications series (pub HMSO)
Symposium series (pub HMSO)
Order printed publications from: Publications Section, ITE Monks Wood, Abbots Ripton, Huntingdon, PE17 2LS

Access to staff:
Contact by letter, by telephone, by fax, by e-mail and via website. Appointment necessary.
Hours: Mon to Fri, 0900 to 1700
Special comments: Researchers only

Also at:
Banchory Research Station
    Hill of Brathens, Banchory, Kincardineshire, AB31 4BY; tel: 01330 823434
Bangor Research Unit
    University College of North Wales, Deiniol Road, Bangor, Gwynedd, LL57 2UW; tel: 01248 370045
CEH Lancaster
    Lancaster Envionment Centre, Library Avenue, Bailrigg, LA1 4AP; tel: 01524 595906; fax: 01539 534705
Centre for Ecology and Hydrology
    Mansfield Road, Oxford, OX1 3SR; tel: 01865 281630
Centre for Ecology and Hydrology
    Maclean Building, Crowmarsh Gifford, Wallingford, Oxfordshire, OX10 8BB; tel: 01491 838800
Centre for Ecology and Hydrology
    Ferry House, Far Sawrey, Ambleside, Cumbria, LA22 0LP; tel: 015394 42468
Dorset Technology Station
    Winfrith Research Centre, Dorchester. DT2 8ZD; tel: 01305 213500
Monks Wood Research Station
    Abbots Ripton, Huntingdon, Cambridgeshire, PE17 2LS; tel: 01487 773381

Parent body:
Natural Environment Research Council

CENTRE FOR ECOLOGY AND HYDROLOGY – MONKS WOOD

Acronym or abbreviation: CEH

Abbots Ripton, Huntingdon, Cambridgeshire, PE28 2LS

Tel: 01487 772400
Fax: 01487 773467

Website:
http://www.ceh.ac.uk/html/unicorn.htm
Library catalogue

Enquiries:
Enquiries to: Librarian
Direct tel: 0131 445 8512
Direct fax: 0131 445 4343
Direct e-mail: sjpr@ceh.ac.uk

Founded:
2000

Formed from:
Institute of Freshwater Ecology (IFE), Institute of Hydrology (IH), Institute of Terrestrial Ecology (ITE), Institute of Virology and Environmental Microbiology (IVEM) (year of change 2000)

Organisation type and purpose:
Research organisation.
One of the Centres and Surveys of the Natural Environment Research Council, and is the leading UK body for research, survey and monitoring in terrestrial and freshwater environments.

Subject coverage:
Environmental science, aquatic ecology, terrestrial ecology, hydrology, microbiology, environmental chemistry, hydrobiology.

Museum or gallery collection, archive, or library special collection:
Various collections of original (unpublished) data

Library catalogue:
All or part available online

Publications list:
Available online

Access to staff:
Contact by letter, by telephone, by fax and by e-mail. Appointment necessary.
Hours: Mon to Fri, 0900 to 1700

Access to building, collection or gallery:
Prior appointment required
Special comments: Any bona fide researcher with a scientific not-for-profit research need which cannot easily be met through their own organisation's resources may use the libraries at the discretion of the Site Director

Access for disabled people:
Parking provided

Other addresses:
CEH Bangor
    Orton Building, Bangor, Deiniol Road, Bangor, Gwynedd, LL57 2UP; tel: 01248 370045; fax: 01248 3553656; e-mail: bae@ceh.ac.uk
CEH Dorset
    Winfrith Technology Centre, Dorchester, Dorset, DT2 8ZD; tel: 01305 213500; fax: 01305 213600
CEH Edinburgh
    Bush Estate, Penicuik, Midlothian, EH26 0QB; tel: 0131 445 4343; fax: 0131 445 3943
CEH Lancaster
    Lancaster Environment Centre, Library Avenue, Bailrigg, Lancaster, LA1 4AP; tel: 01524 595 800; fax: 01524 61536; e-mail: lanacaster@ceh.ac.uk
CEH Oxford
    Mansfield Road, Oxford, OX1 3SR; tel: 01865 281630; fax: 01865 281696; e-mail: oxford-enquiries@ceh.ac.uk
CEH Wallingford
    Maclean Building, Crowmarsh Gifford, Wallingford, Oxfordshire, OX10 8BB; tel: 01491 838800; fax: 01491 692424
CEU Banchory
    Hill of Brathens, Banchory, Aberdeenshire, AB31 4BW; tel: 01330 826303; fax: 01330 823303

Parent body:
Natural Environment Research Council (NERC)
    Polaris House, North Star Avenue, Swindon, SN2 1EY; tel: 01793 411500; fax: 01793 411501

CENTRE FOR ECOLOGY AND HYDROLOGY – NATIONAL HYDROSCIENCES LIBRARY

Acronym or abbreviation: CEH

Maclean Building, Crowmarsh Gifford, Wallingford, Oxfordshire, OX10 8BB

Tel: 01491 838800
Fax: 01491 692424
E-mail: wllibrary@wpo.nerc.ac.uk

Website:
http://www.ceh.ac.uk
CEH homepage.
http://library.ceh.ac.uk/html/unicorn.htm
On-line library catalogue.
http://www.ceh.ac.uk/library/index.html
CEH Library Service homepage.

Enquiries:
Enquiries to: Librarian

Founded:
1962

Formerly called:
Institute of Hydrology (IH) (year of change 2000)

Organisation type and purpose:
Research organisation.

Subject coverage:
Hydrology, including groundwater, soil science, meteorology, climatology, climate change, mathematical modelling, regional water resources, flow prediction, agricultural hydrology, remote sensing, conservation, environmental sciences.

Museum or gallery collection, archive, or library special collection:
Hurst Collection (Nile hydrology)
Rofe Collection (water legislation)

Library catalogue:
All or part available online

Printed publications:
Report Series (irregular, free, these are not library publications, though despatched by us, also online)
One-off special publications eg Flood Estimation Handbook 2000
Further information available at the CEH website

Publications list:
Available online and in print

Access to staff:
Appointment necessary.
Hours: Mon to Fri, 0900 to 1700

Houses the editorial office of the:
International Association of Hydrological Sciences

Parent body:
Centre for Ecology and Hydrology (CEH)
Natural Environment Research Council (NERC)

CENTRE FOR ECONOMIC PERFORMANCE

Acronym or abbreviation: CEP

London School of Economics, Houghton Street, London, WC2A 2AE

Tel: 020 7955 7048
Fax: 020 7955 7595
E-mail: cep_info@lse.ac.uk

Website:
http://cep.lse.ac.uk
http://cep.lse.ac.uk/papers/
Publications list.

Enquiries:
Enquiries to: Administrator

Founded:
1990

Organisation type and purpose:
University department or institute, research organisation.
Researching the factors affecting the economic performance of nations and firms.

Subject coverage:
Economic aspects of the labour market, including employment, unemployment, inflation and income distribution; economics of education and human capital, economic growth, corporate performance, industrial relations, skills and job satisfaction, globalisation, internet economy, productivity and innovation, and wellbeing.

Library catalogue:
All or part available online

Publications list:
Available online and in print

Access to staff:
Contact by e-mail and via website
Hours: Mon to Fri, 0900 to 1700

Access to building, collection or gallery:
No access other than to staff

Access for disabled people:
Access to all public areas

Parent body:
London School of Economics (LSE)
  Houghton Street, London, WC2A 2AE

CENTRE FOR ECONOMIC POLICY RESEARCH

Acronym or abbreviation: CEPR

90–98 Goswell Road, London, EC1V 7RR

Tel: 020 7878 2900
Fax: 020 7878 2999
E-mail: cepr@cepr.org

Website:
http://www.cepr.org

Enquiries:
Enquiries to: External Relations Manager

Founded:
1983

Organisation type and purpose:
Registered charity, research organisation.

Subject coverage:
Economic policy.

Printed publications:
Books
CEPR Bulletin (4 times a year)
CEPR Discussion Papers
Economic Policy (journal, 2 times a year)
European Economic Perspectives (newsletter, 6 times a year)
Order printed publications from: tel: 020 7878 2903, e-mail: orders@cepr.org

Publications list:
Available online and in print

Access to staff:
Contact by e-mail
Hours: Mon to Fri, 0900 to 1700

Links with:
Centre for Economic Policy Research International Foundation (US)

CENTRE FOR EFFECTIVE DISPUTE RESOLUTION

Acronym or abbreviation: CEDR

70 Fleet Street, London, EC4Y 1EU

Tel: 020 7536 6000
Fax: 020 7536 6001
E-mail: info@cedr.co.uk

Website:
http://www.cedr.co.uk

Enquiries:
Enquiries to: Administration Manager, Corporate Resources

Founded:
1990

Organisation type and purpose:
International organisation, advisory body, membership association (membership is by subscription), present number of members: 450, registered charity (charity number 106369), training organisation, consultancy, research organisation.
Experts in mediation and other forms of effective dispute resolution for commercial disputes.
CEDR is an independent organisation supported by industry and professional advisers and founded to promote and encourage more effective commercial resolution of disputes.

Subject coverage:
Alternative dispute resolution (ADR) information services and training, negotiating training, mediation and alternative dispute resolution techniques, mediation training for lawyers, UK and worldwide, commercial alternative dispute resolution services, extensive mediation and conflict resolution training.

Printed publications:
Booklets and research reports (annually)
Newsletter (quarterly)
International Mediation: the art of business diplomacy
Commercial Dispute Resolution – An ADR Practice Guide
Court Referred ADR – a guide for the judiciary
ADR for Corporate Counsel and Executives

Electronic and video publications:
CEDR ADR video

Publications list:
Available online and in print

Access to staff:
Contact by letter, by telephone, by fax, by e-mail, in person and via website. Appointment necessary.
Hours: Mon to Fri, 0900 to 1800

CENTRE FOR ENERGY PETROLEUM AND MINERAL LAW AND POLICY

Acronym or abbreviation: CEPMLP

University of Dundee, Carnegie Building, Geddes Quadrangle, Dundee, DD1 4HN

Tel: 01382 348302
Fax: 01382 385854
E-mail: r.m.carstairs@dundee.ac.uk

Website:
http://www.cepmlp.org

Enquiries:
Enquiries to: Information Services Manager

Formerly called:
Centre for Petroleum and Mineral Law and Policy (CPMLP) (year of change 1997)

Organisation type and purpose:
University library, training organisation, consultancy, research organisation, publishing house.

Subject coverage:
Oil and gas law, policy and economics; mineral law, policy and economics; natural resources law, policy and economics; environmental law and policy.

Education services:
Access given to external research scholars, but by prior arrangement only

Museum or gallery collection, archive, or library special collection:
Petroleum, mining and environmental laws, world-wide. Contracts and agreements collection.

Library catalogue:
All or part available online and in-house

Printed publications:
Books
Conference Proceedings
Professional Papers Series
Seminar Papers Series

Electronic and video publications:
DVD available
Order electronic and video publications from: Order our publications from online store

Publications list:
Available online and in print

Access to staff:
Contact by letter, by telephone, by fax, by e-mail, in person and via website. Appointment necessary.
All charged.
Hours: Mon to Fri, 0930 to 1230 and 1400 to 1700

CENTRE FOR ENGLISH LANGUAGE TEACHING

Acronym or abbreviation: CELT

Airthrey Castle, University of Stirling, Stirling, FK9 4LA

Tel: 01786 467934
Fax: 01786 466131
E-mail: celt@stir.ac.uk

Website:
http://www.celt.stir.ac.uk/
CELT course information.

Enquiries:
Enquiries to: Associate Director
Other contacts: Director

Founded:
1981

Organisation type and purpose:
University department or institute.
Provides English language courses for non-native speakers of English.

Subject coverage:
Courses in English as a foreign language lasting from 4 weeks to 3 years for anyone over the age of 17; courses in the teaching of English as a foreign language.

Printed publications:
Full publicity material on all courses prepared each November and available throughout the year to enquirers

Access to staff:
Contact by letter, by telephone, by fax, by e-mail and via website
Hours: Mon to Fri, 0900 to 1700

CENTRE FOR ENVIRONMENT, FISHERIES AND AQUACULTURE SCIENCE, THE

Acronym or abbreviation: Cefas

Lowestoft Laboratory, Lowestoft, Suffolk, NR33 0HT

Tel: 01502 562244
Fax: 01502 524525
E-mail: lowlibrary@cefas.co.uk

Website:
http://www.cefas.co.uk

Enquiries:
Enquiries to: Librarian

Organisation type and purpose:
National government body.
Main Cefas laboratory.

Subject coverage:
Fisheries, fishing and aquatic environmental research; marine biology; oceanography; aquaculture; marine pollution; fish diseases; marine radiobiology.

continued overleaf

Printed publications:
Annual Report
Shellfish News
Trout News
Order printed publications from: tel: 01502 524380, fax: 01502 542525, e-mail: lowlibrary@cefas.co.uk

Publications list:
Available online and in print

Access to staff:
Contact by letter, by telephone, by fax and by e-mail. Appointment necessary.
Hours: Mon to Thu, 0900 to 1700; Fri, 0900 to 1600

Access to building, collection or gallery:
No access other than to staff

Access for disabled people:
Parking provided, ramped entry, toilet facilities

Also at:
Cefas Weymouth Laboratory
  Barrack Road, The Nothe, Weymouth, Dorset, DT4 8UB; tel: 01305 206600; e-mail: weylibrary@cefas.co.uk

Constituent part of:
Department for Environment, Food and Rural Affairs (DEFRA)

CENTRE FOR ENVIRONMENTAL DATA AND RECORDING

Acronym or abbreviation: CEDaR

Ulster Museum, 12 Malone Road, Belfast, BT9 5BN

Tel: 028 9038 3154/3153
Fax: 028 9038 3103
E-mail: damien.mcferran.um@nics.gov.uk

Website:
http://www.ulstermuseum.org.uk/cadar

Enquiries:
Enquiries to: Records Centre Manager

Organisation type and purpose:
National government body, museum, university department or institute, research organisation. Grant aided by the Environment Service: Countryside and Wildlife (Environment and Heritage Service (DoE)(NI)).

Subject coverage:
Natural history, flora and fauna, and geology of Northern Ireland and its coastal waters.

Museum or gallery collection, archive, or library special collection:
Databases of the location, date, vice-county, recorder, species and grid reference
Over 200,000 local natural history records
Over 1 million species and site records

Access to staff:
Contact by letter, by telephone, by fax and by e-mail. Appointment necessary.
Hours: Mon to Fri, 0900 to 1700

Access to building, collection or gallery:
No prior appointment required

CENTRE FOR ENVIRONMENTAL INITIATIVES

Acronym or abbreviation: The CEI

Old School House, Mill Lane, Carshalton, Surrey, SM5 2JY

Tel: 020 8770 6611
Fax: 020 8647 0719
E-mail: info@thecei.org.uk

Website:
http://www.thecei.org.uk
Newsletters, reports and community projects.

Enquiries:
Enquiries to: Director

Founded:
1987

Formerly called:
Centre for Environmental Information (year of change 1993)

Organisation type and purpose:
Voluntary organisation, registered charity (charity number 800377), suitable for ages: all, training organisation, consultancy, research organisation. Local agenda 21, sustainable development, community involvement in sustainability. The CEI's aim's to achieve and sustain strong, vibrant communities within a healthy environment.

Subject coverage:
Local agenda 21, sustainable development, community involvement and participation in sustainable development, community consultation techniques.

Printed publications:
Available for purchase directly

Publications list:
Available in print

Access to staff:
Contact by letter. Appointment necessary.
Hours: Mon to Fri, 1000 to 1630
Special comments: Building accessible to the disabled, but there are no disabled toilets.

Access to building, collection or gallery:
Prior appointment required
Hours: Mon to Fri, 1000 to 1630

CENTRE FOR ENVIRONMENTALLY RESPONSIBLE TOURISM

PO Box 14, Benfleet, Essex, SS7 3LW

Tel: 01268 752827
Fax: 0870 139 2802
E-mail: cert.desk@virgin.net

Enquiries:
Enquiries to: Chief Executive

Founded:
1994

Organisation type and purpose:
International organisation (membership is by subscription), voluntary organisation.

Access to staff:
Contact by e-mail
Hours: Mon to Fri, 0900 to 1700

Access to building, collection or gallery:
No access other than to staff

CENTRE FOR EPIDEMIOLOGY AND HEALTH SERVICES RESEARCH

Formal name: Centre for Epidemiological Research CER
Acronym or abbreviation: CEHSR

Brunel University, School of Health Sciences and Social Care, Mary Seacole Building (Room 301B), Uxbridge, Middlesex, UB8 3PH

Tel: 01895 268818
Fax: 01895 269853

Website:
http://www.brunel.ac.uk/research/centres/cehsr

Enquiries:
Enquiries to: Centre Director
Direct e-mail: janet.peacock@brunel.ac.uk
Other contacts: Senior Investigator

Founded:
1992

Formerly called:
Centre for Evaluation Research (CER) (year of change 1992)

Organisation type and purpose:
Professional body (membership is by subscription), university department or institute, consultancy, research organisation.
To undertake evaluative research in the field of healthcare and welfare.

Subject coverage:
Evaluation research investigating the quality and effectiveness of health and welfare (including education and training) services. Also methods and techniques of evaluation and quality assurance.

Printed publications:
Welfare or Welfare State (Marsland D, hardback, £45; paperback, £14.99)
Regular publications on research methods, social policy and evaluation studies

Publications list:
Available in print

Access to staff:
Contact by letter and by telephone. Appointment necessary.
Hours: Mon to Fri, 0900 to 1700

Parent body:
Brunel University

CENTRE FOR FACILITIES CONSULTANCY LIMITED

PO Box 7490, Chelmsford, CM2 8YW

Tel: 0870 607 0201
Fax: 01245 403 262
E-mail: centre@globalnet.co.uk

Website:
http://www.facilities-centre.com

Enquiries:
Enquiries to: Chairman
Other contacts: Office Manager for absence of the Chairman.

Founded:
1992

Organisation type and purpose:
Service industry, training organisation, consultancy.
Facilities management consulting and training.

Subject coverage:
All aspects of facilities management consultancy including strategic reviews, accommodation strategy, outsourcing, cost savings, business continuity, performance measurement, health and safety, skills training, specifications, impartial advice and information on facilities management in UK and overseas. Training in non-clinical aspects of NHS Trusts, eg: violence, aggression, quality aspects.

Printed publications:
UK FM Overview (newsletter)

Access to staff:
Contact by letter, by telephone, by fax, by e-mail and via website. Appointment necessary.
Hours: Mon to Fri, 0900 to 1700

Access for disabled people:
Access to all public areas

CENTRE FOR GLOBAL ENERGY STUDIES

Acronym or abbreviation: CGES

17 Knightsbridge, London, SW1X 7LY

Tel: 020 7235 4334
Fax: 020 7235 4338
E-mail: marketing@cges.co.uk

Website:
http://www.cges.co.uk

Enquiries:
Enquiries to: Marketing Manager
Direct tel: 020 7309 3610
Direct e-mail: jenni.wilson@cges.co.uk

Founded:
1990

Organisation type and purpose:
International organisation, research institute (oil and gas).

Subject coverage:
Oil market subscription reports, studies, special reports, events and oil market consulting.

Trade and statistical information:
Oil and gas/energy.

Printed publications:
Global Oil Report (6 times a year, annual subscription £1500)
Monthly Oil Report (market analysis and comment, monthly, annual subscription £500)
Special Reports on specific areas of oil and gas
Order printed publications from: website: http://www.cges.co.uk, e-mail: marketing @cges.co.uk

Publications list:
Available online and in print

Access to staff:
Contact by letter, by telephone, by fax, by e-mail and via website
Hours: Mon to Fri, 0930 to 1730

CENTRE FOR HEALTH ECONOMICS

Acronym or abbreviation: CHE

University of York, Heslington, York, YO10 5DD

Tel: 01904 433707
Fax: 01904 433644
E-mail: jmg1@york.ac.uk

Website:
http://www.york.ac.uk/inst/che/welcome.html
Descriptions of organisations and staff, projects, publications.

Enquiries:
Enquiries to: Information Service Manager
Direct e-mail: cheweb@york.ac.uk
Other contacts: Director for research opportunities.

Founded:
1983

Organisation type and purpose:
University department or institute, training organisation, research organisation.
Centre for research and training in the factors affecting the demand for and supply of health, and the consequences for the provision of care.

Subject coverage:
Health economics, health technology assessment, community care, economics of addiction, health services manpower, quality of life.

Museum or gallery collection, archive, or library special collection:
Health economics working papers

Library catalogue:
All or part available in-house

Printed publications:
Discussion Papers (over 100)
Occasional Papers
Technical Papers
Order printed publications from: Publications Office, Centre for Health Economics
at same address, tel: 01904 433648, fax: 01904 433644, e-mail: chepub@york.ac.uk

Publications list:
Available online and in print

Access to staff:
Contact by letter, by telephone, by fax, by e-mail and via website. Appointment necessary.
Hours: Mon to Fri, 0900 to 1700
Special comments: Closed 23 Dec to 2 Jan.

Connections with:
NHS Centre for Reviews and Dissemination (CRD)
tel: 01904 433707; fax: 01904 433661; e-mail: revdis@york.ac.uk

Parent body:
University of York
tel: 01904 430000; fax: 01904 433433

Part of:
Institute for Research into the Social Sciences (IRISS)
tel: 01904 433523; fax: 01904 433524

CENTRE FOR HEALTH INFORMATICS

Acronym or abbreviation: CHI

City University, Northampton Square, London, EC1V 0HB

Tel: 020 7040 8367
Fax: 020 7040 8364
E-mail: a.v.roudsari@city.ac.uk

Website:
http://www.city.ac.uk/chi

Enquiries:
Enquiries to: Director

Founded:
1983

Formerly called:
Centre for Measurement and Information in Medicine (year of change 2005)

Organisation type and purpose:
University department or institute, research organisation.

Subject coverage:
e-Health and telecare, high-dependency medicine and public health; decision support systems (including computer-aided learning); integrated policy modelling for ICT-enhanced public health care; health care technologies, with emphasis upon methodologies for assessment and evaluation.

Museum or gallery collection, archive, or library special collection:
Annual Reports

Printed publications:
Annual Report
Occasional Technical Reports

Access to staff:
Contact by letter, by telephone, by fax, by e-mail and via website. Appointment necessary.
Hours: Mon to Fri, 0900 to 1700; other times by arrangement

Constituent part of:
Cass Business School of the City University

Links with:
School of Engineering and Mathematical Sciences of City University
School of Informatics of City University

CENTRE FOR HUMAN GENETICS

Children's Hospital, Western Bank, Sheffield, South Yorkshire, S10 2TH

Tel: 0114 271 7000
Fax: 0114 273 7467
E-mail: o.quarrell@sheffield.ac.uk

Enquiries:
Enquiries to: Director
Other contacts: Head of Department

Organisation type and purpose:
Professional body.

Subject coverage:
Genetics, medical genetics, cytogenetics.

Access to staff:
Contact by letter
Hours: Mon to Fri, 0900 to 1700

Links with:
Sheffield Children's Hospital

CENTRE FOR INDEPENDENT TRANSPORT RESEARCH IN LONDON

Acronym or abbreviation: CILT

Room 208, The Colourworks, 2 Abbot Street, London, E8 3DP

Tel: 020 7275 9900\ Minicom no. 020 7275 9123
Fax: 020 7254 6777
E-mail: cilt@dial.pipex.com

Website:
http://www.cilt.dial.pipex.com/
Descriptions of work; archive of papers and articles generated by that work; selected articles from the magazine; links to other useful web sites.

Enquiries:
Enquiries to: Researchers

Founded:
1983

Formerly called:
The Campaign to Improve London's Transport (CILT) (year of change 1988)

Organisation type and purpose:
Membership association (membership is by subscription), present number of members: 30, voluntary organisation, registered charity (charity number 1001580), consultancy, research organisation, publishing house.
Research and resource unit.
To explore ways of making public transport more accessible, efficient and safe for all those who want to use it.

Subject coverage:
Transport, environment, transport planning, operational issues, women's transport needs, disability access, related issues.

Museum or gallery collection, archive, or library special collection:
Books, documents, reports, own publications, transport journals

Printed publications:
Variety of publications including:
Accessible Transport in East London (S Bell & D Hardle, 1998, £30, £10 for community groups)
Can the Boroughs Keep London Moving? (1992, £3)
The Complete 'Green Transport Plan' for Local Authorities (D Hurdle, 1998, £15)
Green Commuter Plans – London Boroughs' Progress (£10)
Lewisham Community Transport Study (A Peck et al, 1993, £13)
Motorcycling – Time to Apply the Brakes (£10)
Red Routes into Green Routes (G Smith, 1993)
Traffic and Transport: a guide to understanding and influencing the transport system (UK £10.50 inc. p&p, overseas £34 inc. p&p)
Stage or Terminus: a review of 50 years of London's public transport (K Fuller, 1985, £1)
Street Trams for London (C Wood, 1994, £12.50)
Transition (journal, replaces CILT Journal, quarterly, UK £18 a year, overseas £23, free to affiliates)

Electronic and video publications:
Transition (available on tape, on request)

Publications list:
Available online and in print

Access to staff:
Contact by letter, by telephone, by fax, by e-mail and via website. Appointment necessary.
Hours: Mon to Fri, by arrangement

Access to building, collection or gallery:
Prior appointment required

Access for disabled people:
Ramped entry, access to all public areas, toilet facilities
Special comments: Lift to second floor. Heavy gates and doors, but staff will come down to assist if requested. Very poor pavements in the surroundings.

CENTRE FOR INFORMATION QUALITY MANAGEMENT

Acronym or abbreviation: CIQM

Penbryn, Bronant, Aberystwyth, Ceredigion, SY23 4TJ

Tel: 01974 251441
Fax: 01974 251441
E-mail: lisqual@cix.co.uk

Website:
http://www.i-a-l.co.uk/index.htm

Enquiries:
Enquiries to: Managing Director

Founded:
1993

Organisation type and purpose:
Professional body, training organisation, consultancy, research organisation.
CIQM represents the professional interests of the information community with respect to the quality, evaluation and selection of informational resources and databases.

Subject coverage:
CIQM acts as a clearing house for database and internet resource quality issues, and as a research and consulting organisation for all matters concerning the provision of good quality electronic information. Has worked to establish a methodology for database resource and internet resource quality assurance: database labelling.

Publications list:
Available online and in print

Access to staff:
Contact by letter, by telephone, by fax, by e-mail and via website. Appointment necessary.
Hours: Mon to Fri, 0900 to 1700

Access to building, collection or gallery:
Prior appointment required

Access for disabled people:
Parking provided

Affiliated to:
CILIP
 7 Ridgmount Street, London
UKeIG: UK electronic Information Group
 7 Ridgmount Street, London

Parent body:
Information Automation Limited (IAL)
 at the same address; tel: 01974 251302

CENTRE FOR INSTITUTIONAL STUDIES

Acronym or abbreviation: CIS

Duncan House, Stratford High Street, London, E15 2JB

Tel: 020 8223 3333 \ Minicom 020 8223 2853

Website:
http://www.uel.ac.uk

Enquiries:
Enquiries to: Press Officer
Direct tel: 020 8223 8194
Direct e-mail: h.esselink@uel.ac.uk

Founded:
1970

Organisation type and purpose:
University department or institute, research organisation.

Subject coverage:
Public policy and institutions, education policy, administration, local government, the voluntary sector, volunteering, urban regeneration, management of voluntary organisations, youth justice, community safety, social enterprise, community action, philosophy of Karl Popper.

Museum or gallery collection, archive, or library special collection:
Reference library

Printed publications:
CIS Commentaries on public policy issues
 (occasional)
Working papers (occasional)

Publications list:
Available in print

Access to staff:
Contact by letter, by telephone, by fax and by e-mail
Hours: Mon to Fri, 0900 to 1700

Access for disabled people:
Ramped entry, toilet facilities

CENTRE FOR INTER-CULTURAL DEVELOPMENT

Acronym or abbreviation: CI-CD

Diversity Works Ltd, 27 Langland Gardens, London, NW3 6QE

Tel: 020 7431 1712
E-mail: johntwitchin@diversityworks.co.uk

Website:
http://www.diversityworks.co.uk
(see CI-CD pages).

Enquiries:
Enquiries to: Director
Other contacts: Co-Director

Founded:
1993

Organisation type and purpose:
Consultancy, research, training provision.

Subject coverage:
Managing diversity, awareness and skills of Cross Cultural Communication, training video production, equal opportunities policy implementation, anti-discrimination law, performance measuring and appraisal, customer care across cultures, recruitment across cultures, institutional racism and/or sexism.

Museum or gallery collection, archive, or library special collection:
Library of Training Resources: Research papers, books and video packages

Non-library collection catalogue:
All or part available online

Printed publications:
Appraisal Interviewing across Cultures (training manual)
Attitudes to Islam (training manual)
Counselling and Advice across Cultures (training manual)
Crosstalk (training manual)
Equal Opps at Work – Race (training manual)
Evidence Unseen (training manual)
Information sheets (free)
Recruitment Interviewing Across Cultures (training manual)
Multicultural Education, Staff Development in Multicultural Practice (book)
The Black and White Media Book (£10.95)
What Makes You Say That? – Cultural Diversity at Work (training manual)

Publications list:
Available online

Access to staff:
Contact by letter, by telephone, by e-mail, in person and via website. Appointment necessary.
Hours: Mon to Fri, 0900 to 1700

Associates in:
Australia, Malaysia, Hong Kong, USA, Finland, South Africa

CENTRE FOR INTERFIRM COMPARISON

Acronym or abbreviation: CIFC

32 St Thomas Street, Winchester, Hampshire, SO23 9HJ

Tel: 01962 844144
Fax: 01962 843180
E-mail: enquiries@cifc.co.uk

Website:
http://www.cifc.co.uk

Enquiries:
Enquiries to: Managing Director

Founded:
1959

Organisation type and purpose:
Consultancy, research organisation.
To organise benchmarking projects and properly conducted interfirm comparisons between firms or organisations in the same industry or trade as each other, as a service to them.

Subject coverage:
Benchmarking studies, interfirm comparison, management ratios, financial information systems, industry surveys, industry statistics.

Access to staff:
Contact by letter, by telephone, by fax, by e-mail and via website. Appointment necessary.
Hours: Mon to Fri, 0900 to 1700

CENTRE FOR JAPANESE AND EAST ASIAN STUDIES

Acronym or abbreviation: CJEAS

PO Box 427, Pinner, Middlesex, HA5 3FX

Tel: 020 8429 2839
E-mail: ruth.taplin@btinternet.com

Website:
www.jie.org.uk
Access to the Journal of Interdisciplinary Economics

Enquiries:
Enquiries to: Director

Founded:
1989

Organisation type and purpose:
Consultancy, research organisation, translation (Japanese, Chinese, Korean interpreters)

Subject coverage:
East and South-East Asia. Specialised translations and interpretations of the languages of the region, bespoke marketing strategies, research, cultural training such as company briefings. Content analysis of medical and pharmaceutical clinical trials, and legal reports. Japanese, Chinese and Korean Intellectual Property Law consultancy.

Printed publications:
The Journal of Interdisciplinary Economics (editor, Dr Ruth Taplin)
Order printed publications from: Other publications by Dr Taplin from Routledge, 2 Park Square, Milton Park, Abingdon, Oxford, OX14 4RN

Access to staff:
Contact by letter, by telephone and by fax. Appointment necessary.
Hours: Mon to Fri, 0900 to 1700

CENTRE FOR LAW AND SOCIETY

Formal name: Criminology & Law
Acronym or abbreviation: CLS

Faculty of Law, University of Edinburgh, Old College, South Bridge, Edinburgh, EH8 9YL

Tel: 0131 650 2025
Fax: 0131 650 2005
E-mail: elizabeth.goodwin-andersson@ed.ac.uk

Enquiries:
Enquiries to: Director

Formerly called:
Centre for Criminology and the Social and Philosophical Study of Law

Organisation type and purpose:
University department or institute.

Subject coverage:
Official data on crime, crime surveys, policy analysis on crime and punishment, policy advice on crime and punishment, comparative knowledge on criminal justice policy, legal theory.

Access to staff:
Contact by letter, by telephone, by fax and by e-mail
Hours: Mon to Fri, 0900 to 1700

Access for disabled people:
Ramped entry, toilet facilities
Special comments: Lifts.

CENTRE FOR LEBANESE STUDIES

Acronym or abbreviation: CLS

c/o 14a Airlie Gardens, London, W8 7AL

Tel: 020 7221 3809
E-mail: info@lebanesestudies.com

Website:
http://lebanesestudies.com

Enquiries:
Enquiries to: Director
Direct e-mail: shehadi@herald.ox.ac.uk

Founded:
1984

Organisation type and purpose:
Learned society (membership is by subscription), registered charity (charity number 298375), research organisation, publishing house.

Subject coverage:
The Centre initiates and publishes research papers and books on relevant historical, economic, political, sociological and cultural issues affecting Lebanon.

Printed publications:
A Vision of the Middle East: An Intellectual Biography of Albert Hourani (Al-Sudairi A)
CLS Bulletins report on various conferences and seminars (3 vols)
Index to the Archives of the Centre for Lebanese Studies (Shultz K)
Papers on Lebanon – 17 analytical essays dealing with historical, political and economic issues
Prospects for Lebanon – 9 analytical essays dealing with policy aspects of relevant and current issues
The Breakdown of the State in Lebanon 1967 to 1976 (El Khazen F)
The Politics of Interventionism in Ottoman Lebanon, 1830 to 1861 (Farah C)
Titles of more recent publications available on request

Publications list:
Available in print

Access to staff:
Contact by letter, by telephone, by fax, by e-mail and via website. Appointment necessary.
Hours: Mon to Fri, 1030 to 1730

Access to building, collection or gallery:
Prior appointment required

Access for disabled people:
Ramped entry, access to all public areas, toilet facilities

CENTRE FOR LOCAL ECONOMIC STRATEGIES

Acronym or abbreviation: CLES

Express Networks, 1 George Leigh Street, Manchester, M4 5DL

Tel: 0161 236 7036
Fax: 0161 236 1891
E-mail: info@cles.org.uk

Website:
http://www.cles.org.uk

Enquiries:
Enquiries to: Information Officer

Founded:
1986

Organisation type and purpose:
Membership association, registered charity (charity number 1089503).

Subject coverage:
Regeneration, economic development, local government, employment and labour markets, sector studies, urban and regional economics, community initiatives, European issues, European legislation and links.

Museum or gallery collection, archive, or library special collection:
Large collection of local government publications, published, semi-published, grey literature, committee reports etc

Library catalogue:
All or part available in-house

Publications list:
Available online

Access to staff:
Contact by letter, by telephone, by fax and by e-mail. Appointment necessary. Non-members charged.
Hours: Mon to Fri, 0900 to 1700

Subsidiary body:
CLES European Research Network (CERN)

CENTRE FOR MANAGEMENT CREATIVITY

Acronym or abbreviation: CMC

High Trenhouse, Malham Moor, Settle, North Yorkshire, BD24 9PR

Tel: 01729 830322
Fax: 01729 830519
E-mail: helen@centreformanagementcreativity.com

Website:
http://www.centreformanagementcreativity.com

Enquiries:
Enquiries to: Business Development Manager

Founded:
1985

Organisation type and purpose:
Service industry, training organisation, consultancy. Managing change.

Subject coverage:
Strategic thinking, team development, culture change, management techniques, personal development.

Printed publications:
Newsletters (members only)
MagNotes for structuring thoughts

Electronic and video publications:
Visual Concept software

Access to staff:
Contact by letter, by telephone, by fax, by e-mail and via website. Appointment necessary.
Hours: Mon to Fri, 0900 to 1700

Access for disabled people:
Parking provided, ramped entry, toilet facilities

CENTRE FOR MANX STUDIES

Formal name: School of Archaeology, Classics and Egyptology, University of Liverpool
Acronym or abbreviation: CMS

6 Kingswood Grove, Douglas, Isle of Man, IM1 3LX

Tel: 01624 695150
Fax: 01624 678752
E-mail: cms@liv.ac.uk

Website:
http://www.liv.ac.uk/manxstudies

Enquiries:
Enquiries to: Director
Other contacts: Lecturer in Manx Studies; Secretary (mornings only)

Founded:
1992

Organisation type and purpose:
Centre for the academic sudy of anything Manx; undergraduate and postgraduate research organisation.

Subject coverage:
Research related to the Isle of Man, particularly earth sciences, archaeology, architecture, history, music, language and social studies.

Education services:
BA in History and Heritage Management (with IOM Dept Education); MA in Manx Studies; MPhil; PhD

Museum or gallery collection, archive, or library special collection:
Collection of reference-only books on Manx topics.

Non-library collection catalogue:
All or part available online

Library catalogue:
All or part available online

Printed publications:
for list of publications see http://www.liv.ac.uk/manxstudies
Order printed publications from: Secretary

Publications list:
Available online and in print

Access to staff:
Contact by letter, by telephone, by fax, by e-mail, in person and via website
Hours: Mon to Fri, 0900 to 1700
Special comments: Secretary: Mon to Fri, 0930 to 1300

Access to building, collection or gallery:
No prior appointment required

Access for disabled people:
Level entry at back door (please phone if you need to enter this way)

Links with:
Isle of Man Department of Education
St George's Court, Upper Church Street, Douglas, Isle of Man, IM1 2SG
Manx National Heritage
Kingswood Grove, Douglas, Isle of Man, IM1 3LY

Parent body:
School of Archaeology, Classics and Egyptology, University of Liverpool
PO Box 147, Liverpool, L69 3BX; tel: 0151 794 2000; fax: 0151 708 6502; website: http://www.liv.ac.uk

CENTRE FOR MARINE TECHNOLOGY

University of Salford, 43 The Crescent, Salford, Manchester, M5 4WT

Tel: 0161 295 5081
Fax: 0161 295 5380
E-mail: r.hughes@salford.ac.uk

Enquiries:
Enquiries to: Director

Organisation type and purpose:
University department or institute.

Subject coverage:
Offshore processing of oil and gas; enhanced oil recovery; simulation of oil and gas production; underwater life support systems.

Access to staff:
Contact by letter, by telephone, by fax and by e-mail
Hours: Mon to Fri, 0900 to 1700

continued overleaf

Associated with:
Marinetech North West

CENTRE FOR MASS COMMUNICATION RESEARCH

Acronym or abbreviation: CMCR

University of Leicester, 104 Regent Road, Leicester, LE1 7LT

Tel: 0116 252 5293
Fax: 0116 252 5276
E-mail: cmcr@le.ac.uk

Website:
http://www.le.ac.uk/cmcr/
General departmental website and useful links.
http://www.le.ac.uk/cmcr/dl
Information on the MA in Mass Communications (by Distance Learning).

Enquiries:
Enquiries to: General Office Manager/PA to Head of Department
Direct e-mail: hlh7@leicester.ac.uk

Founded:
1966

Organisation type and purpose:
University department or institute, suitable for ages: 18+, research organisation.

Subject coverage:
Mass media, sociological research on mass media and communications, media and health, science communications, media and environment, media and politics, popular music industry, film, globalisation, culture, national identity, television and food.

Museum or gallery collection, archive, or library special collection:
Current and pre-current year British national newspapers, limited access available

Trade and statistical information:
Data on use of media in health education, structure of the media industries, viewing, listening, reading behaviour.

Access to staff:
Contact by telephone and by e-mail. Appointment necessary.
Hours: Mon to Fri, 0900 to 1700

Access to building, collection or gallery:
Prior appointment required

CENTRE FOR MEDICAL EDUCATION

Acronym or abbreviation: CME

Tay Park House, 484 Perth Road, Dundee, DD2 1LR

Tel: 01382 631968
Fax: 01382 645748
E-mail: p.a.wilkie@dundee.ac.uk

Website:
http://www.dundee.ac.uk/meded/

Enquiries:
Enquiries to: Director
Direct tel: 01382 631973
Direct e-mail: r.m.harden@dundee.ac.uk
Other contacts: AMEE Administrator for membership of Association for Medical Education in Europe.

Organisation type and purpose:
University department or institute.

Subject coverage:
Medical education: curriculum design, development and assessment; teaching and learning methods, evaluation management and administration, technology-based learning in medicine and health sciences, distance learning, vocational training and continuing medical and nursing education; diploma and masters of

medical education; diploma in advanced nursing studies, degree in nursing studies, masters in palliative care.

Museum or gallery collection, archive, or library special collection:
Extensive collection of books and journals on medical and general education

Library catalogue:
All or part available in-house

Printed publications:
Distance learning programmes on a variety of topics in medicine and health care
Newsletter (free)

Publications list:
Available in print

Access to staff:
Contact by letter, by telephone, by fax, by e-mail and via website. Appointment necessary.
Hours: Mon to Fri, 0900 to 1700

Access for disabled people:
Parking provided, ramped entry

CENTRE FOR MEDIEVAL STUDIES

Acronym or abbreviation: CMS

King's Manor, York, YO1 7EP

Tel: 01904 433910
Fax: 01904 433918
E-mail: gmg501@york.ac.uk

Website:
http://www.york.ac.uk/inst/cms
Information on centre and courses offered.

Enquiries:
Enquiries to: Administrator

Founded:
1968

Organisation type and purpose:
University department or institute.

Subject coverage:
Medieval studies.

Library catalogue:
All or part available in print

Access to staff:
Contact via website

CENTRE FOR MULTIMODAL THERAPY

156 Westcombe Hill, Blackheath, London, SE3 7DH

Tel: 020 8228 1185
E-mail: admin@managingstress.com

Website:
http://www.centreforcoaching.com
http://www.managingstress.com
Books, articles, course details. Details about staff.

Enquiries:
Enquiries to: Director
Other contacts: Co-ordinator

Founded:
1990

Organisation type and purpose:
Training organisation, consultancy, research organisation, publishing house.

Subject coverage:
Multimodal therapy, stress management, stress counselling, training for counsellors, psychologists and therapists.

Electronic and video publications:
Audio tapes for relaxation and hypnosis
Some articles are freely available to download from the website

Publications list:
Available online

Access to staff:
Contact by letter, by telephone, by fax, by e-mail and via website. Appointment necessary.
Hours: Mon to Fri, 1000 to 1700

Parent body:
Centre for Stress Management

CENTRE FOR ORGANISATIONAL MANAGEMENT

Acronym or abbreviation: COM

Zenith House, Craigholm, Shooters Hill, London, SE18 3RR

Tel: 020 8319 1449
Fax: 020 8319 1449
E-mail: almeric@dircon.co.uk

Website:
http://www.organisational-leadership.co.uk

Enquiries:
Enquiries to: Director

Founded:
1985

Formerly called:
Centre for Performance Improvement (year of change 1990)

Organisation type and purpose:
International organisation, training organisation, consultancy, research organisation.
Using an organisational design and development approach to improve organisational leadership skills, team and systems performance. These techniques are all focused on significantly improving an organisation's business performance.

Subject coverage:
Organisational leadership skills, motivational decision making, organisational design and development, team development, reduction of organisational stress, consequences and impact of introducing information technology on the culture and performance of business organisations.

Access to staff:
Contact by letter, by telephone, by fax, by e-mail, in person and via website. Appointment necessary.
Hours: Sun to Sat, 0900 to 1700

Access for disabled people:
Parking provided, ramped entry

CENTRE FOR PERSONAL AND PROFESSIONAL DEVELOPMENT

The Brewery, High Street, Twyford, Winchester, Hampshire, SO21 2RG

Tel: 01962 715838
Fax: 01962 711419
E-mail: ann@cppd.co.uk

Enquiries:
Enquiries to: Managing Director
Other contacts: Administrator

Founded:
1994

Organisation type and purpose:
Training organisation, consultancy.
Counselling services.
To provide counselling, training and consultancy services to both individuals and organisations, personal and professional development.

Subject coverage:
Counselling, psychotherapy, family and marital therapy, hypnotherapy, personal and professional development, training.

Access to staff:
Contact by letter, by telephone and by e-mail. Appointment necessary.
Hours: Mon to Fri, 0900 to 1700

Access to building, collection or gallery:
Prior appointment required

Access for disabled people:
Parking provided

CENTRE FOR POLICY ON AGEING

Acronym or abbreviation: CPA

25–31 Ironmonger Row, London, EC1V 3QP

Tel: 020 7553 6500
Fax: 020 7553 6501
E-mail: ageinfo@cpa.org.uk

Website:
http://www.cpa.org.uk
AGEINFO – bibliographic database updated monthly, NDAR – National database of ageing research, SAP – Single Assessment Process national resource.

Enquiries:
Enquiries to: Director
Other contacts: Librarian

Founded:
1947

Organisation type and purpose:
Registered charity (charity number 207163). Independent policy and information unit promoting and formulating effective policies to improve services etc for older people.

Subject coverage:
Social aspects of gerontology in Britain and, to a lesser extent, Europe, USA, etc; includes health care, housing, adult education/leisure, employment, retirement, social policy etc for older people.

Museum or gallery collection, archive, or library special collection:
Reference library (by appointment only)
International collection on gerontology, over 500 core journals and 49,000 monographs, reports, statistical sources, legislation, etc

Library catalogue:
All or part available online and in-house

Printed publications:
Many books and reports including:
Ageing and Society (5 times a year)
Directory of Services for Elderly People
European Directory of Old Age
New Literature on Old Age (6 times a year)
Old Age: a register of social research 1985–1990 (biennial)
Order printed publications from: Central Books, 99 Wallis Road, London, E9 5LN, tel: 020 8986 5488, fax: 020 8533 5821, e-mail: peter@centralbooks.com

Electronic and video publications:
AGEINFO (CD-ROM with quarterly updates, Internet with monthly updates, comprises three databases: 50,000 plus bibliographic items; 4,500 national and international organisations; calendar of events)

Publications list:
Available online and in print

Access to staff:
Contact by letter, by telephone, by fax and by e-mail. Appointment necessary.
Hours: Mon, 1400 to 1700; Tue to Fri, 1000 to 1700

Access to building, collection or gallery:
Prior appointment required

Established by:
Nuffield Foundation

CENTRE FOR PUBLISHING STUDIES

University of Stirling, Stirling, FK9 4LA

Tel: 01786 467510
Fax: 01786 466210
E-mail: engl1@stir.ac.uk

Website:
http://www.stir.ac.uk/publishing/
Centre information, staff, course content.
http://www.stir.ac.uk
University home page and links.

Enquiries:
Enquiries to: Director
Direct tel: 01786 467511
Other contacts: Secretary for general course enquiries.

Founded:
1982

Organisation type and purpose:
University department or institute, training organisation, consultancy, research organisation, publishing house.
Research and teaching in publishing studies (mainly contemporary) on an international basis.

Subject coverage:
Publishing industry, book trade, Scottish publishing industry, textual and scholarly editing, Sir Walter Scott, James Hogg, public support for literature, authorship and the book trade, publishing in Africa, China, Malaysia, developmental issues.

Library catalogue:
All or part available online

Printed publications:
Publishing Studies course leaflet (free)
University Postgraduate Prospectus (annually, free)

Access to staff:
Contact by letter, by telephone, by fax, by e-mail and via website
Hours: Mon to Fri, 0900 to 1700

Cooperative links with similar bodies in:
North America, Far East, Australia, Europe

Member of:
International Association for Publishing Education
UK Association of Publishing Educators

CENTRE FOR RADIOGRAPHIC AND MEDICAL STUDIES

Cranfield University, Shrivenham, Swindon, Wiltshire, SN6 8LA

Tel: 01793 785756
Fax: 01793 785744
E-mail: j.laxon@rmcs.cranfield.ac.uk

Enquiries:
Enquiries to: Director
Direct tel: 01793 785227
Direct e-mail: berridge@rcms.cranfield.ac.uk
Other contacts: Undergraduate Admissions Officer for undergraduate admissions through UCAS.

Founded:
1992

Formed from:
Joint Services School of Radiography, Northampton School of Radiography, Oxford Regional School of Radiography

Formerly called:
Oxford Centre for Radiographic Studies (year of change 1997)

Organisation type and purpose:
University department or institute.

Subject coverage:
Radiography, radiobiology, radiation physics, radiation dosimetry, medical ultrasound, veterinary radiography and ultrasound, dental radiography, radiation protection, imaging, oncology, forensic radiography, radiation effects on materials.

Printed publications:
Course literature and undergraduate and post-graduate prospectus (free on request)

Publications list:
Available in print

Access to staff:
Contact by letter, by telephone, by fax and by e-mail
Hours: Mon to Fri, 0900 to 1700

Access for disabled people:
Parking provided, ramped entry, access to all public areas, toilet facilities

CENTRE FOR RATIONAL EMOTIVE BEHAVIOUR THERAPY

Broadway House, 3 High Street, Bromley, Kent, BR1 1LF

Tel: 020 8228 1185
E-mail: admin@managingstress.com

Website:
http://www.managingstress.com
Course details, books, articles.

Enquiries:
Enquiries to: Director
Other contacts: Co-ordinator

Founded:
1990

Formerly called:
Centre for Rational Emotive Therapy

Organisation type and purpose:
Training organisation, consultancy, research organisation, publishing house. Counselling and training centre.

Subject coverage:
Rational emotive behaviour therapy, counselling, coaching and training.

Printed publications:
Rational Interviews (£6.95 plus 75p p&p)
Think Rationally (£1.95 inc. p&p)

Electronic and video publications:
Audio tapes for relaxation and self hypnosis

Publications list:
Available online

Access to staff:
Contact by letter, by telephone, by e-mail and via website. Appointment necessary.
Hours: Mon to Fri, 1000 to 1700

Affiliated to:
Centre for Coaching
Centre for Multimodel Therapy
Centre for Problem Focused Training and Therapy
Centre for Stress Management

CENTRE FOR RESEARCH IN ETHNIC RELATIONS

Acronym or abbreviation: CRER

University of Warwick, Coventry, Warwickshire, CV4 7AL

Tel: 024 7652 3605
Fax: 024 7652 4324
E-mail: CRER@warwick.ac.uk

Website:
http://www.warwick.ac.uk/CRER
Searchable citations of reports and pamphlets including ethnic minority health from medical literature. Information about CRER research and postgraduate teaching. Publications ordering information.

Enquiries:
Enquiries to: Librarian
Direct tel: 024 7652 2972
Other contacts: Publications Manager for publications.

Organisation type and purpose:
University department or institute, research organisation.

continued overleaf

Subject coverage:
All aspects of British, and increasingly of European, race and ethnic relations: employment, health, housing, education, politics, social services, etc; migrant workers in Europe; refugees; community studies.

Museum or gallery collection, archive, or library special collection:
Large indexed press clippings collection; videos and ephemera collection
Over 200 periodicals and newspapers
Over 8000 pamphlets and reports
Resources Centre maintained and staffed part-time, reinforcing the university library's collection of material on race and ethnic relations

Trade and statistical information:
National Ethnic Minority Data Archive (statistical, survey and census data, primarily for Britain).

Library catalogue:
All or part available online

Printed publications:
British Pakistanis – Demographic, Social and Economic Position (Muhammad Anwar, £10)
National Ethnic Minority Archive: 1991 Census Statistical Papers
Making Monitoring Work (Jones A, £20)
Research Papers, Bibliographies and Monographs in Ethnic Relations
Order printed publications from: Publications Manager, Centre for Research in Ethnic Relations
tel: 024 7652 3607, fax: 024 7652 4324, e-mail: Bains@warwick.ac.uk

Publications list:
Available online and in print

Access to staff:
Contact by letter, by telephone, by fax and by e-mail
Hours: Mon to Fri, 0900 to 1600

Access for disabled people:
Ramped entry, toilet facilities

Parent body:
University of Warwick
tel: 024 7652 3523

CENTRE FOR REVIEWS AND DISSEMINATION

Acronym or abbreviation: CRD

University of York, Heslington, York, YO10 5DD

Tel: 01904 321846
Fax: 01904 321041
E-mail: crd-info@york.ac.uk

Website:
http://www.york.ac.uk/inst/crd/
Descriptions of organisation and staff, projects, publications.
Full text of selected publications.
Searchable databases: NHS Economic Evaluation Database, Database of Abstracts of Reviews of Effects.
Health Technology Assessment database.

Enquiries:
Enquiries to: Information Service Manager

Founded:
1994

Organisation type and purpose:
University department or institute, training organisation, consultancy, research organisation.
To provide information to the NHS on the effects of treatments and the delivery and organisation of care.

Subject coverage:
Systematic reviews of the effects of health care interventions. Cost-effectiveness information.

Museum or gallery collection, archive, or library special collection:
Clinical effectiveness materials, including systematic reviews
Technology assessment (health) reports

Library catalogue:
All or part available online and in-house

Printed publications:
CRD Reports
Also available full text on website
Order printed publications from: Publications Officer, Centre for Reviews and Dissemination at same address, tel: 01904 321441, fax: 01904 321035

Electronic and video publications:
Database of Abstracts of Reviews of Effects (Cochrane Library CD-ROM, and free at website)
NHS Economic Evaluation Database (Cochrane Library CD-ROM, and available free at website)
Health Technology Assessment database (Cochrane Library CD-ROM, and free at website)

Publications list:
Available online and in print

Access to staff:
Contact by letter, by telephone, by fax, by e-mail and via website
Hours: Mon to Fri, 0900 to 1700, closed 23 Dec to 2 Jan

Parent body:
University of York
York, YO10 5DD; tel: 01904 430000; fax: 01904 433433

CENTRE FOR SOCIAL ANTHROPOLOGY AND COMPUTING

Acronym or abbreviation: CSAC

University of Kent, Canterbury, Kent, CT2 7NS

Tel: 01227 764000
Fax: 01227 827289
E-mail: csa-c@lucy.ukc.ac.uk

Website:
http://www.lucy.ukc.ac.uk/
http://www.csac.anthropology.ac.uk/
http://www.era.anthropology.ac.uk/
http://www.lucy.ukc.ac.uk/online_pubs.html
Summary of online publications.
http://www.lucy.ukc.ac.uk/AIO.html
Anthropological Index Online – online bibliography.
http://www.aio.anthropology.org.uk/
Registration for updates to AIO.

Enquiries:
Enquiries to: Director
Direct e-mail: m.d.fischer@ukc.ac.uk
Other contacts: Deputy Director

Organisation type and purpose:
University department or institute.

Subject coverage:
Anthropology, anthropological computing, teaching and learning materials.

Printed publications:
CSAC Monographs (prices on request from CSAC Office)
South-East Asian Studies Occasional Paper Series
Order printed publications from: CSAC Office
Eliot College, University of Kent, Canterbury, CT2 7NS

Electronic and video publications:
Experience Rich Anthropology (CD-ROM and via www)
Era Sampler (CD-ROM)

Publications list:
Available online and in print

Access to staff:
Contact by letter, by e-mail and via website
Hours: Mon to Fri, 0900 to 1700

Affiliated to:
Department of Anthropology
University of Kent, Canterbury, CT2 7NS; tel: 01227 764000

CENTRE FOR SOCIO-LEGAL STUDIES

Acronym or abbreviation: CSLS

Oxford University, Wolfson College, Linton Road, Oxford, OX2 6UD

Tel: 01865 284220
Fax: 01865 284221
E-mail: admin@csls.ox.ac.uk

Website:
http://www.cslc.ox.ac.uk
History of centre; events; research staff and profiles; areas of research; student programme; visitors programme; directions; library information.

Enquiries:
Enquiries to: Administrator

Founded:
1972

Organisation type and purpose:
University department or institute, research organisation.

Subject coverage:
Role and function of law in societies, law and the media, human rights, social history, procedures for adjudication and dispute settlement, law and psychology, law and economics, families and the law especially divorce, compensation for illness and injury, medicine and law, regulation of health and safety at work, regulation of public and private sector, regulation of business practice.

Museum or gallery collection, archive, or library special collection:
Small specialised socio-legal library, open for outside use by appointment

Printed publications:
Annual Reports (including details of current research projects)
Bibliographies in socio-legal studies
Oxford Socio-Legal Studies series (pub. OUP)
Research Reviews of subject areas (eg law and economics)
Working papers and conference papers

Publications list:
Available in print

Access to staff:
Contact by letter, by fax, by e-mail and via website. Appointment necessary.
Hours: Mon to Fri, 0900 to 1700

CENTRE FOR SPEECH TECHNOLOGY RESEARCH

Acronym or abbreviation: CSTR

University of Edinburgh, 2 Buccleuch Place, Edinburgh, EH8 9LW

Tel: 0131 650 2804
Fax: 0131 650 4587
E-mail: evelcen@cogsci.ed.ac.uk

Website:
http://www.cstr.ed.ac.uk/
Home page.

Enquiries:
Enquiries to: Secretary

Founded:
1984

Organisation type and purpose:
University department or institute, research organisation.

Subject coverage:
Phonetics, dialogue engineering, speech synthesis, speech signal processing and coding, hidden markov modelling, neural networks, transputer DSP and PC prototyping, speaker verification, expert software.

Printed publications:
Annual published papers volume
Annual Report

Access to staff:
Contact by letter, by telephone, by fax and by e-mail
Hours: Mon to Fri, 0900 to 1700

Links with:
research organisations throughout Europe

Member of:
European Network in Language and Speech (ELSNET)

CENTRE FOR STRESS MANAGEMENT

Acronym or abbreviation: CFSM

Broadway House, 3 High Street, Bromley, BR1 1LF

Tel: 020 8228 1185 or 020 8318 4448
E-mail: admin@managingstress.com

Website:
http://www.managingstress.com
Information about the centre including courses and staff. Also articles about stress, stress management and relaxation methods.

Enquiries:
Enquiries to: Director
Other contacts: Co-ordinator

Founded:
1987

Organisation type and purpose:
Training organisation, consultancy, research organisation, publishing house.

Subject coverage:
Stress management, stress counselling, stress audits, positive approaches to managing pressure and stress, assertion and communication skills, self-esteem and self-acceptance, challenging irrational beliefs and public beliefs.

Printed publications:
General Information and Training Programme
Conquer your Stress (£8.99)
How to Deal with Stress ISBN 10: 0–7494–4866–0

Electronic and video publications:
Audio tapes – relaxation, hypnosis

Publications list:
Available in print

Access to staff:
Contact by letter, by telephone, by fax, by e-mail and via website. Appointment necessary.
Hours: Mon to Fri, 1000 to 1700

Affiliated to:
Centre for Cognitive Behaviour Therapy
Centre for Multimodal Therapy
   tel: 020 8318 4448
Centre for Problem Focused Training and Therapy
Centre for Rational Emotive Behaviour Therapy
Institute for Complementary Medicine

Also at:
Centre for Stress Management
   Porthleven, Cornwall

CENTRE FOR STUDIES ON INCLUSIVE EDUCATION LIMITED

Acronym or abbreviation: CSIE

New Redland, Frenchay Campus, Coldharbour Lane, Bristol, BS16 1QU

Tel: 0117 328 4007
Fax: 0117 328 4005

Enquiries:
Enquiries to: Director

Founded:
1982

Formerly called:
Centre for Studies on Integration in Education (CSIE) (year of change 1994)

Organisation type and purpose:
Voluntary organisation, registered charity (charity number 327805), suitable for ages: 0 to 19.
The Centre is committed to working towards an end to segregated education and developing inclusive education, with support, for all in the mainstream.
The Centre publishes the Index for Inclusion, which helps break down barriers to learning and participation. The Index facilitates inclusive school development by investigating the culture, policy and practice of a school.

Subject coverage:
Inclusion of all children with disabilities or difficulties in learning into society during school years from nurseries to colleges; parental involvement in assessment and placement; the 1996 and 2001 Education Acts; LEA policy and practice on inclusion.

Printed publications:
A wide range of leaflets, publications and free material on Inclusive Education is available
Booklets, survey reports, factsheets including:
Human Rights and School Change – The Newham Story
Inclusive Education – The Right to Belong to the Mainstream
Index for Inclusion: developing learning and participation in schools
Index for Inclusion – developing learning participation and play in early years and childcare
Learning supporters and inclusion

Microform publications:
ERIC, Virginia, USA

Electronic and video publications:
Inclusion in Action (Audio tape. £12)
Talking Inclusion (Audio tape, £5)

Publications list:
Available online and in print

Access to staff:
Contact by letter, by telephone and by fax.
Appointment necessary.
Hours: Mon to Fri, 0900 to 1700
Special comments: Redland Close (house) is on a hill.

Access to building, collection or gallery:
Prior appointment required

Access for disabled people:
Parking provided, ramped entry, access to all public areas, toilet facilities

Has links with:
Council for Exceptional Children (ERIC)
   1920 Association Drive, Reston, Virginia, 20191–1589, USA

CENTRE FOR SUSTAINABLE ENERGY

Acronym or abbreviation: CSE

3 St Peter's Court, Bedminster Parade, Bristol, BS3 4AQ

Tel: 0117 929 9950
E-mail: info@cse.org.uk

Website:
http://www.planningrenewables.org.uk/
http://www.cse.org.uk/

Enquiries:
Enquiries to: Information Officer
Direct e-mail: info@planningrenewables.org.uk
Other contacts: Renewable Energy Enquiries Bureau

Founded:
1979

Organisation type and purpose:
National government body.
Established to stimulate the development of new and renewable energy sources wherever they have the prospect of being economically attractive and environmentally acceptable, in order to contribute to diverse, secure and sustainable energy supplies,

reduction in the emission of pollutants, and encouragement of internationally competitive industries.

Subject coverage:
Biosciences, commercialisation, energy from waste, solar energy, wave and tidal energy, wind energy.

Printed publications:
The programme has produced over 1700 publications in the last ten years including brochures, technology status reports, case studies, factsheets, newsletters, project summaries and contractor reports. With the exception of contractor reports these are sent to enquirers free of charge and do not need to be returned. A loan service operates for contractor reports

Publications list:
Available online and in print

Access to staff:
Contact by letter, by telephone, by fax and by e-mail. Appointment necessary.
Hours: Mon to Fri, 0815 to 1700

Parent body:
Department of Trade and Industry

CENTRE FOR THE ECONOMICS AND MANAGEMENT OF AQUATIC RESOURCES

Acronym or abbreviation: CEMARE

University of Portsmouth, Boathouse No. 6, College Road, HM Naval Base, Portsmouth, PO1 3LJ

Tel: 023 9284 4082
Fax: 023 9284 4614
E-mail: christopher.martin@port.ac.uk

Website:
http://www.port.ac.uk/cemare
Home page; reading room; research; consultancy; training; publications.

Enquiries:
Enquiries to: Librarian

Founded:
1970

Formerly called:
Centre for Marine Resource Economics, Marine Resources Research Unit

Organisation type and purpose:
University department or institute, consultancy, research organisation.

Subject coverage:
Fisheries economics, agricultural economics, environmental economics, coastal zone management, aquaculture, recreational fisheries.

Museum or gallery collection, archive, or library special collection:
2000 books, 10,000 reports, 5000 reprints, 165 serial titles (60 current)
Large collection of FAO Fisheries publications on hard copy and microfiche

Non-library collection catalogue:
All or part available online and in-house

Printed publications:
CEMARE Miscellaneous Papers (irregular)
CatchUp Alumni Newsletter (irregular)
CEMARE Reports (irregular)
CEMARE Research Papers (irregular)

Publications list:
Available online and in print

Access to staff:
Contact by e-mail and via website. Appointment necessary.
Hours: Mon to Fri, 1000 to 1700

Member of:
BIASLIC
EURASLIC
IAALD
IAMSLIC

CENTRE FOR THE HISTORY OF TECHNOLOGY, SCIENCE AND SOCIETY

University of Bath, Claverton Down, Bath, BA2 7AY

Tel: 01225 311508
E-mail: hssraab@bath.ac.uk

Enquiries:
Enquiries to: Honorary Director

Founded:
1964

Organisation type and purpose:
University department or institute, research organisation.
The National Cataloguing Unit for the Archives of Contemporary Scientists is now in the University Library.

Subject coverage:
History of technology in all periods and all forms, technology and society, history of engineering, especially in Britain, engineering biography, Victorian engineering, history of stationary steam power, industrial archaeology, national heritage and conservation.

Museum or gallery collection, archive, or library special collection:
Watkins collection (photographs and documentation of stationary steam engines), now with the National Buildings Record, English Heritage, Swindon

Printed publications:
Papers in scientific journals
Research reports
Works on industrial archaeology, the steam engine, engineering biographies, especially I K Brunel, gunpowder history etc. (12 titles, independently published)

Access to staff:
Contact by letter and by e-mail
Hours: Mon to Fri, 0900 to 1700

CENTRE FOR THE STUDY OF FINANCIAL INNOVATION

Acronym or abbreviation: CSFI

5 Derby Street, London, W1J 7AB

Tel: 020 7493 0173
Fax: 020 7493 0190
E-mail: info@csfi.org.uk

Website:
http://www.csfi.org.uk
Information about the centre, future events and past events. Minutes of past meetings, publications and how to purchase. Information about our sponsors.

Enquiries:
Enquiries to: Director
Direct e-mail: andrew@csfi.org.uk
Other contacts: (1) Director of Studies; (2) Sponsorship Manager for (1) research, themes; (2) membership.

Founded:
1993

Organisation type and purpose:
Membership association (membership is by subscription), present number of members: c. 70, registered charity (charity number 1017352), research organisation.

Subject coverage:
Banking, regulation, risk, e-finance, SMEs, development finance, Europe, insurance, technology.

Printed publications:
Reports (10 to 12 per annum, for purchase)

Electronic and video publications:
Pdfs available for purchase

Publications list:
Available online and in print

Access to staff:
Contact by letter, by fax and by e-mail
Hours: Mon to Fri, 0900 to 1700

Access to building, collection or gallery:
Prior appointment required

CENTRE FOR THE STUDY OF GLOBALISATION AND REGIONALISATION

Acronym or abbreviation: CSGR

Department of Economics, University of Warwick, Coventry, Warwickshire, CV4 7AL

Tel: 024 7657 2533
Fax: 024 7657 2548
E-mail: csgr@warwick.ac.uk

Website:
http://www.warwick.ac.uk/fac/soc/CSGR
http://www.csgr.org

Enquiries:
Enquiries to: Research Fellow

Organisation type and purpose:
University department or institute, research organisation.

Subject coverage:
Globalisation, regionalisation, trade, finance

CENTRE FOR THE STUDY OF INTERRELIGIOUS RELATIONS

Acronym or abbreviation: CSIR

University of Birmingham, Elmfield House, Bristol Road, Birmingham, B29 6LQ

Tel: 0121 415 8373
Fax: 0121 415 8376
E-mail: d.r.thomas.1@bham.ac.uk

Website:
http://www.bham.ac.uk/theology

Enquiries:
Enquiries to: Administrative Secretary
Direct e-mail: h.ingram@bham.ac.uk

Founded:
2007

Formerly called:
Centre for the Study of Islam and Christian-Muslim Relations (year of change 2007)

Organisation type and purpose:
University department, research organisation

Subject coverage:
Interreligiuos relations; Christian-Muslim relations; philosophy of religion; religion in South Asia.

Museum or gallery collection, archive, or library special collection:
Mingana Collection of Islamic Arabic, Christian Arabic and Syriac Manuscripts

Library catalogue:
All or part available online

Printed publications:
Islam and Christian-Muslim Relations (journal)
Newsletter
Order printed publications from:
h.ingram@bham.ac.uk

Electronic and video publications:
Islam and Christian-Muslim Relations (journal)
Order electronic and video publications from: Taylor & Francis

Publications list:
Available online and in print

Access to staff:
Contact by letter, by telephone, by fax, by e-mail, in person and via website. Appointment necessary.
Hours: Mon to Fri, 0900 to 1700

Access to building, collection or gallery:
Doors security locked; wall phone to secretaries available
Hours: 0900 to 1700

Access for disabled people:
Parking provided, toilet facilities

CENTRE FOR THE STUDY OF PUBLIC POLICY

Acronym or abbreviation: CSPP

Edward Wright Building, University of Aberdeen, Aberdeen, AB24 3QY

Website:
http://www.cspp.strath.ac.uk
http://www.russiavotes.org
http://www.socialcapital.strath.ac.uk

Enquiries:
Enquiries to: Director
Direct e-mail: cspp@abdn.ac.uk

Founded:
1976

Organisation type and purpose:
University department or institute, research organisation.
Concerned with the problems of public policy, especially post-Communist societies and new democracies. Specialised databases of public opinion, surveys of 20 countries.

Subject coverage:
Public policy generally; the growth of government; public finance and political economy; elections, transformation of post-Communist societies. Social capital.

Museum or gallery collection, archive, or library special collection:
A variety of machine-readable data sets

Non-library collection catalogue:
All or part available online and in print

Printed publications:
CSPP Monograph series: Studies in Public Policy (about 16 times a year)
Journal of Public Policy (pub. CUP)

Electronic and video publications:
Massive survey database on 20 countries

Publications list:
Available online and in print

Access to staff:
Contact by letter and via website
Hours: Mon to Fri, 0900 to 1700

Collaborates with:
research institutes in Eastern and Western Europe and the United States

CENTRE FOR THE STUDY OF REGULATED INDUSTRIES (CRI)

Acronym or abbreviation: CRI

School of Management, University of Bath, Bath, BA2 7AY

Tel: 01225 386271 Director; 01225 383197 Office
Fax: 01225 383221
E-mail: p.vass@bath.ac.uk

Website:
http://www.bath.ac.uk/cri
Publications list, recently published. Staff, other links, reference library, conferences, contact details, information.

Enquiries:
Enquiries to: Administrator
Direct e-mail: mnsjsm@management.bath.ac.uk

Founded:
1991

Organisation type and purpose:
International organisation, research organisation.

Independent research centre of the University of Bath.

The CRI is an interdisciplinary research centre investigating how regulation and competition are working in practice, both in the UK and abroad. It is independent and politically neutral. It aims to produce authoritative, practical contributions to regulatory policy and debate, which are put into the public domain. The CRI focuses on comparative analyses across the regulated industries.

Subject coverage:
Accounting and information, competition and performance, regulation and management incentives, accountability, quality and the environment – issues connected with regulation and regulated (ie network) industries. Such industries include: electricity, water, telecoms, airports, rail, gas and postal services. Some focus has also been given to European liberalisation and regulation.

Printed publications:
Include regulatory briefs, industry briefs, regulatory reviews, statistics series, international series, research reports, discussion papers, and seminar and conference papers

Publications list:
Available online and in print

Access to staff:
Contact by letter, by telephone, by fax, by e-mail and via website. Appointment necessary.
Hours: Mon to Fri, 0900 to 1700

CENTRE FOR TRADITIONAL CHINESE MEDICINE

78 Haverstock Hill, London, NW3 2BE

Tel: 020 7284 2898
Fax: 020 7485 8875
E-mail: centcm@netcomuk.co.uk

Enquiries:
Enquiries to: Director

Founded:
1992

Organisation type and purpose:
Professional body, consultancy.

Subject coverage:
Chinese herbal medicine, acupuncture and Chinese massage.

Museum or gallery collection, archive, or library special collection:
Chinese herbal samples
Chinese medical books

Access to staff:
Contact by letter, by telephone, by fax and by e-mail
Hours: Mon to Fri, 0930 to 1730

CENTRE OF AFRICAN STUDIES, LIBRARY

University of Cambridge, Mond Building Free School Lane, Cambridge, CB2 3RF

Tel: 01223 334398
Fax: 01223 769325
E-mail: afrlib@hermes.cam.ac.uk

Website:
http://www.african.cam.ac.uk/library.htm
library guide and information, library news, links to electronic sources

Enquiries:
Enquiries to: Librarian
Direct tel: 01223 334398
Direct fax: 01223 769325
Direct e-mail: meg23@cam.ac.uk
Other contacts: assistant librarian

Organisation type and purpose:
University department or institute.

Subject coverage:
Africa: its history, geography, literature, economics and politics and its social, developmental, cultural and artistic affairs.

Library catalogue:
All or part available online

Publications list:
Available in print

Access to staff:
Contact by letter, by telephone, by fax, by e-mail, in person and via website. Appointment necessary.
Hours: Mon to Fri, 0900 to 1730
Special comments: The library hours may be shortened during the summer vacation so please check before visiting.

Access to building, collection or gallery:
Hours: 9 – 5.30 open access
Special comments: after hours and at weekend authorised card entry only (no access to library)

Access for disabled people:
by side door – intercom to request door opening
Hours: 9–5.30
Standing Conference on Library Materials on Africa (SCOLMA)

CENTRE OF CANADIAN STUDIES

University of Edinburgh, 21 George Square, Edinburgh, EH8 9LD

Tel: 0131 650 4129
Fax: 0131 650 4130
E-mail: centreofcanadianstudies@ed.ac.uk

Website:
http://www.cst.ed.ac.uk

Enquiries:
Enquiries to: Administrator
Other contacts: Director

Organisation type and purpose:
University department or institute.

Subject coverage:
Canada.

Publications list:
Available online

Access to staff:
Contact by letter, by telephone, by fax, by e-mail, in person and via website. Appointment necessary.
Hours: Mon to Thu, 0900 to 1700; Fri, 0900 to 1230

Access to building, collection or gallery:
No access other than to staff

CENTRE OF MEDICAL LAW AND ETHICS

Formal name: Centre of Medical Law and Ethics
Acronym or abbreviation: CMLE

King's College London, Strand, London, WC2R 2LS

Tel: 020 7848 2382
Fax: 020 7848 2575
E-mail: cmle.enq@kcl.ac.uk

Website:
http://www.kcl.ac.uk/cmle

Enquiries:
Enquiries to: Administrator
Other contacts: Director

Founded:
1978

Organisation type and purpose:
University department or institute.

Subject coverage:
Medical ethics, medical and healthcare law.

Museum or gallery collection, archive, or library special collection:
Specialist collection of medical, law and ethics books and periodicals held by King's College Library, Chancery Lane, London WC2

Printed publications:
Advance Directives and AIDS (£5)
Dispatches (newsletter, 3 issues per academic year, £12.50)
Manual for Research Ethics Committees (updated annually)
Occasional Papers Series (frequency and price varies; OPS1 £12, OPS2 £8, OPS3 £13)

Publications list:
Available in print

Access to staff:
Contact by letter, by telephone, by fax and by e-mail. Appointment necessary.
Hours: Mon to Fri, 0930 to 1300, 1400 to 1730

Part of:
School of Law
    King's College London, London

CENTRE OF SOUTH ASIAN STUDIES

Laundress Lane, Cambridge, CB2 1SD

Tel: 01223 338094
Fax: 01223 767094
E-mail: webmaster@s-asian.cam.ac.uk

Website:
http://www.s-asian.cam.ac.uk
Library Guide.
List of microfilms held of South Asian newspapers.
List of collections in Archive.
List of memoirs in Archive.
List of microforms held of government archives.
Handlist of Archive
Databases of film and photographic collections.

Enquiries:
Enquiries to: Librarian

Founded:
1964

Organisation type and purpose:
University library, university department or institute, research organisation.

Subject coverage:
South Asia (India, Sri Lanka, Pakistan, Bangladesh, Nepal) and Southeast Asia (Burma, Thailand, Laos, Cambodia, Vietnam, Malaysia, Singapore, Indonesia, Philippines); social sciences, history (17th century onwards), geography, agriculture, economics, development etc.

Museum or gallery collection, archive, or library special collection:
7500 microforms on South and South East Asia
30,000 monographs on South and South East Asia
Cambridge South Asian Archive of the personal papers relating to the British period in India
Indian Newspapers on microfilm from the 19th century onwards
50 Hours of Cinefilm now on DVD

Non-library collection catalogue:
All or part available online and in print

Library catalogue:
All or part available online

Printed publications:
Archive Guides and Handlists
Cambridge South Asian Archive (pub. Chadwyck-Healey; 5 volumes, continuing)
Cambridge South Asian Studies (pub. Cambridge University Press; some 60 titles)
Central Government of India publications held by libraries in London, Oxford and Cambridge
Centre's Annual Reports
Government of Ceylon publications held by libraries in London, Oxford and Cambridge
Government of Pakistan publications held by libraries in London, Oxford and Cambridge
Library Quarterly Accessions Lists
Serial publications of the Indian Government held by libraries in London, Oxford and Cambridge
Union Catalogues

Access to staff:
Contact by letter and via website. Appointment necessary. Letter of introduction required.

continued overleaf

Hours: Mon to Fri, 0930 to 1730
Special comments: Closed Christmas and Easter.

Part of:
University of Cambridge

CENTRE OF WEST AFRICAN STUDIES

Acronym or abbreviation: CWAS

University of Birmingham, Edgbaston, Birmingham, B15 2TT

Tel: 0121 414 5128
Fax: 0121 414 3228
E-mail: cwas@bham.ac.uk

Website:
http://www.bham.ac.uk/WestAfricanStudies

Enquiries:
Enquiries to: Director
Direct tel: 0121 414 5125
Direct e-mail: tmccaskie@aol.com
Other contacts: Secretary, CWAS for routine requests for information, publications.

Founded:
1963

Organisation type and purpose:
Museum, university department or institute, suitable for ages: 18+, research organisation.

Subject coverage:
History (social, Islamic, South African), geography, political science, Yoruba language, literature (African and Caribbean), popular culture, sociology – all related to West Africa and, in some cases, Eastern or Southern Africa. Specialisms in Benin, Ghana, Mali, Nigeria, Senegambia and Sierra Leone, African development studies, African cultural anthropology.

Museum or gallery collection, archive, or library special collection:
Cadbury Papers
CMS archives
Danford Collection of African Art and Artefacts
Early West African newspapers
Extensive holdings of books on Africa
John Figueroa Papers
Joseph Chamberlain Papers
R E Bradbury Papers (Benin)
William Bascom Collection (Yoruba)

Printed publications:
Birmingham University African Studies series nos 1–5 (for purchase, direct)
Sierra Leone Studies (volume produced 1987 and 1990, for purchase, direct)

Publications list:
Available online

Access to staff:
Contact by letter, by e-mail and via website. Appointment necessary.
Hours: Mon to Fri, 0930 to 1700

Access to building, collection or gallery:
Prior appointment required

CENTREPOINT

Neil House, 7 Whitechapel Road, London, E1 1DU

Tel: 020 7426 5300

Website:
http://www.centrepoint.org.uk

Enquiries:
Enquiries to: Information Officer

Organisation type and purpose:
Voluntary organisation, registered charity.

Subject coverage:
Housing and support to homeless 16–25 year olds, research with young people at risk.

Publications list:
Available online and in print

Access to staff:
Contact by letter and by telephone
Hours: Mon to Fri, 0900 to 1700

Access to building, collection or gallery:
No prior appointment required

CEP ASSOCIATES

1st Floor NYMCA, North View, Ashington, Northumberland, NE63 9XQ

Tel: 01670 521805
Fax: 01670 521805
E-mail: patdreyer@cepassociates.fsnet.co.uk

Website:
http://www.cepassociates@fsnet.co.uk
Course information; company information; application forms.

Enquiries:
Enquiries to: Information Officer

Founded:
1991

Formerly called:
Community Education Project

Organisation type and purpose:
Suitable for ages: 18+, training organisation, consultancy.

Subject coverage:
Community education.

Access to staff:
Contact by letter, by telephone, by fax, by e-mail, in person and via website. Appointment necessary.
Hours: Mon to Fri, 0900 to 1700

Access for disabled people:
Ramped entry

CERAM RESEARCH LTD

Queens Road, Penkhull, Stoke-on-Trent, Staffordshire, ST4 7LQ

Tel: 01782 764444
Fax: 01782 412331
E-mail: enquiries@ceram.com

Website:
http://www.ceram.com
Services available.

Enquiries:
Enquiries to: Information Manager
Direct tel: 01782 764241
Direct e-mail: ann.pace@ceram.com

Founded:
1948

Organisation type and purpose:
Membership association (membership is by subscription), present number of members: 300, research organisation.
Research and technology organisation for ceramics and materials industries.

Subject coverage:
Production and service behaviour of ceramic materials and pottery (tableware, tiles, sanitary ware, electrical porcelain); refractories; technical ceramics for engineering and electrical applications; clay and calcium silicate-based building products (bricks, sewer pipes) and their behaviour in structures; evaluation of properties, and physical and chemical testing methods.

Museum or gallery collection, archive, or library special collection:
Graves Library (on bricks and building)
Mellor Memorial Library

Trade and statistical information:
Statistical information on ceramics industry (worldwide).
Material information on ceramics industry (worldwide).

Non-library collection catalogue:
All or part available in-house

Library catalogue:
All or part available in-house

Printed publications:
Progress (two a year, members only)

Electronic and video publications:
World Ceramics (database internet subscription – Cambridge Scientific Abstracts)

Publications list:
Available online and in print

Access to staff:
Contact by letter, by telephone, by fax, by e-mail, in person and via website. Appointment necessary. Access for members only. Letter of introduction required. Non-members charged.
Hours: Mon to Thu, 0845 to 1715; Fri, 0845 to 1645

CEREDIGION ARCHIVES

County Office, Marine Terrace, Aberystwyth, Ceredigion, SY23 2DE

Tel: 01970 633697
Fax: 01970 633663
E-mail: archives@ceredigion.gov.uk

Website:
http://www.archifdy-ceredigion.org.uk

Enquiries:
Enquiries to: Archivist

Founded:
1974

Formerly called:
Dyfed Archives, Cardiganshire Area Office (year of change 1996)

Organisation type and purpose:
Local government body.
Local government county record office.

Non-library collection catalogue:
All or part available online and in-house

Access to staff:
Contact by letter, by telephone, by fax, by e-mail, in person and via website
Hours: Mon, 1400 to 1900; Tue, Wed, 1400 to 1630; Thu, Fri, 1400 to 1630

Access to building, collection or gallery:
No prior appointment required

Access for disabled people:
Toilet facilities
Special comments: Disability lift

Parnet body:
Ceredigion County Council

CEREDIGION COUNTY COUNCIL

Neuadd Cyngor Ceredigion, Penmorfa, Aberaeron, Ceredigion, SA46 0PA

Tel: 01545 570881
Fax: 01545 572009
E-mail: info@ceredigion.gov.uk

Website:
http://www.ceredigion.cix.co.uk/cyngor/
General, tourism, economic development.

Enquiries:
Enquiries to: Public Relations Manager
Direct tel: 01545 572002
Direct e-mail: marke@ceredigion.gov.uk

Founded:
1996

Formerly called:
Cardiganshire County Council, Dyfed County Council; Cyngor Dosbarth Ceredigion (year of change 1996)

Organisation type and purpose:
Local government body.

Access to staff:
Contact by letter, by telephone, by fax, by e-mail, in person and via website
Hours: Mon to Fri, 0900 to 1700

CERTIFICATION OFFICE FOR TRADE UNIONS AND EMPLOYERS' ASSOCIATIONS, THE

Brandon House, 180 Borough High Street, London, SE1 1LW

Tel: 020 7210 3734
Fax: 020 7210 3612
E-mail: enquiries@certoffice.org

Website:
http://www.certoffice.org

Enquiries:
Enquiries to: Manager
Direct tel: 020 7210 3735

Founded:
1976

Organisation type and purpose:
National government body.
Independent statutory body.
To ensure trade unions and employers' associations comply with the relevant legislation.

Subject coverage:
Information on financial returns of trade unions and employers' associations, mergers between trade unions and employers' associations, trade union independence, elections for trade unions officers and members of executive, trade union political fund rules.

Museum or gallery collection, archive, or library special collection:
Certification Officers annual reports from 1976
Trade union and employers' associations annual returns, rules and constitutions from 1976
Trade union and employers' associations merger documents from 1976

Printed publications:
Annual Report
A guide to political fund review ballots (2000 free)
Financial irregularities in trade unions and employers associations. The approach of the Certification Officer in exercising his powers of investigation (2000)
Guidance for trade unions and employers' associations wishing to establish a political fund (1994 free)
Guidance for trade unions wishing to apply for a certificate of independence (2000 free)
Making a complaint to the Certification Officer against a trade union (1999 free)
Mergers: a guide to the statutory requirements for transfers of engagements and amalgamation of employers' associations (2000 free)
Mergers: a guide to the statutory requirements for transfers of engagements and amalgamations of trade unions (2000 free)

Publications list:
Available in print

Access to staff:
Contact by letter and by telephone
Hours: Mon to Fri, 0900 to 1700

Access to building, collection or gallery:
No prior appointment required
Hours: Mon to Fri 0930 to 1630

Access for disabled people:
Ramped entry, toilet facilities

CHAMBER BUSINESS

The Business Competitiveness Centre, Kimpton Road, Luton, Bedfordshire, LU2 0LB

Tel: 01582 522448
Fax: 01582 522450

Enquiries:
Enquiries to: Information Officer
Direct e-mail: infow@chamber-business.com

Founded:
2001

Formerly called:
Bedfordshire & Luton Chamber of Commerce,
Business Link Bedfordshire (year of change 2001)

Organisation type and purpose:
Membership association (membership is by subscription), present number of members: 1400, service industry, training organisation, consultancy, research organisation.

Subject coverage:
Business, companies, grants, funding, employment, exporting, HR, credit.

Access to staff:
Contact by e-mail
Hours: Mon to Fri, 0900 to 1700

Access for disabled people:
Parking provided, ramped entry, access to all public areas, toilet facilities

CHAMBER OF COMMERCE HEREFORDSHIRE & WORCESTERSHIRE

Head Office, Severn House, Prescott Drive, Warndon Business Park, Worcester, WR4 9NE

Tel: 0845 641 1641
Fax: 0845 641 4641
E-mail: enquiries@hwchamber.co.uk

Website:
http://www.hwchamber.co.uk

Enquiries:
Enquiries to: Manager

Founded:
1985

Formerly called:
Redditch, Bromsgrove and District Chamber of Commerce and Industry

Organisation type and purpose:
Membership association, service industry.
Chamber of Commerce.

Subject coverage:
Business information, export documentation.

Printed publications:
Directory of Local Companies (yearly)

Access to staff:
Contact by letter, by telephone and by fax. Non-members charged.
Hours: Mon to Fri, 0900 to 1700

Also at:
Hereford Office
Crossway House, Holmer Road, Hereford, HR4 9SS

CHAMBER OF COMMERCE HEREFORDSHIRE AND WORCESTERSHIRE

Head Office, Severn House, Prescott Drive, Warndon Business Park, Worcester, WR4 9NE

Tel: 0845 641 1641
Fax: 0845 641 4641
E-mail: enquiries@hwchamber.co.uk

Website:
http://www.hwchamber.co.uk

Enquiries:
Enquiries to: Information & On-line Services Executive

Founded:
1993

Formerly called:
HAWTEC Hereford & Worcester (year of change 1996/97); Business Link Herefordshire and Worcestershire (year of change 1998/99)

Organisation type and purpose:
National organisation, advisory body, professional body, membership association (membership is by subscription), present number of members: 2700.

Business support services, business advice and information, membership services.

Subject coverage:
Information on Herefordshire and Worcestershire.

Information services:
Business Reference Library for Chamber Members.
On-line Resource Centre.

Museum or gallery collection, archive, or library special collection:
Business Reference library

Library catalogue:
All or part available online

Printed publications:
New Direction (6 times a year)
Chamber Quarterly Economic Survey (quarterly survey of members' views on the economy, etc.)
Economic Assessment (annual report in conjunction with Worcestershire County Council)

Access to staff:
Contact by letter, by telephone, by fax, by e-mail, in person and via website. Appointment necessary. Access for members only. Non-members charged.
Hours: Mon to Fri, 0830 to 1730

Access for disabled people:
Parking provided, ramped entry, level entry, access to all public areas, toilet facilities

Affiliated to:
British Chamber of Commerce Accredited Chamber (BCC)

Also at:
Chamber of Commerce Herefordshire and Worcestershire
Crossway House, Holmer Road, Hereford, HR4 9SS; tel: 0845 641 1641; e-mail: enquiries@ hwchamber.co.uk

CHAMBER OF COMMERCE TRAINING COMPANY LIMITED

Enterprise House, Castle Street, Worcester, WR1 3EN

Tel: 01905 744450
Fax: 01905 744451

Enquiries:
Enquiries to: Chief Executive
Direct e-mail: jennyj@hwchamber.co.uk
Other contacts: Administrator

Founded:
1982

Organisation type and purpose:
Training organisation.

Subject coverage:
Offers broad range of training services from IT internet training through to MIG and TIG welding training.

Printed publications:
Products, services brochures, on request

Access to staff:
Contact by letter, by telephone, by fax and by e-mail
Hours: Mon to Fri, 0830 to 1730

Access for disabled people:
Parking provided, ramped entry, level entry, access to all public areas, toilet facilities

CHANGING FACES

The Squire Centre, 33/37 University Street, London, WC1E 6JN

Tel: 0845 4500 275
Fax: 0845 4500 276
E-mail: info@changingfaces.org.uk

Website:
http://changingfaces.org.uk

continued overleaf

Enquiries:
Enquiries to: National Infomation and Advice Worker

Founded:
1992

Organisation type and purpose:
Registered charity (charity number 1011222). To provide information, advice and counselling to children, adults (and families) affected by disfigurement. Also provides training and resources to health and social care professionals, schools and employers.

Subject coverage:
Facial disfigurement.

Library catalogue:
All or part available in-house

Printed publications:
Reading list available to purchase
Up to three books available free to clients, at a charge to all others
Handling other people's reactions
Managing the effects of burns
When a medical skin condition affects the way you look
When facial paralysis affects the way you look
Talking to health professionals about disfigurement
Also a selection of other guides and booklets for adults, children and professionals
Order printed publications from: Full details on website; available from same address

Electronic and video publications:
Video on managing day-to-day challenges of living with disfigurement (available at cost)

Publications list:
Available online and in print

Access to staff:
Contact by letter, by telephone, by fax, by e-mail, in person and via website. Appointment necessary.
Hours: Mon to Fri, 0900 to 1700
Special comments: online counselling via young people website www.iface.org.uk

Access for disabled people:
full access

CHANNEL CROSSING ASSOCIATION, THE

Acronym or abbreviation: CCA

Bolden's Wood, Fiddling Lane, Stowting, Ashford, Kent, TN25 6AP

Tel: 01303 812011
Fax: 01303 812011
E-mail: channelcrossings@aol.com

Website:
http://www.channelcrossingassociation.com

Enquiries:
Enquiries to: Information Officer

Founded:
2001

Organisation type and purpose:
International organisation, membership association (membership is by subscription). To act as a body competent to organise and/or control selected sporting activities which take place in the Channel (eg Channel swims and crossings undertaken by unorthodox craft) and to liaise with the British and French Coastguards and Maritime Authorities, to maintain a register of professional pilots with experience of providing escort and pilotage for these activities.

Subject coverage:
Professional escort and pilotage across Strait of Dover and effective liaison with coastguard agencies of UK and France.

Printed publications:
Information/Registration Pack (available for purchase, direct)

Access to staff:
Contact by telephone, by e-mail and via website
Hours: Mon to Fri, 0900 to 1700

Access to building, collection or gallery:
No access other than to staff

Wholly-owned subsidiary of:
Channel Crossings Association Limited at the same address

CHANNEL SWIMMING ASSOCIATION LIMITED

Acronym or abbreviation: CSA

Bolden's Wood, Fiddling Lane, Stowting, Ashford, Kent, TN25 6AP

Tel: 01303 814788
Fax: 01303 813835
E-mail: swimsecretary@aol.com

Website:
http://www.channelswimmingassociation.com

Enquiries:
Enquiries to: General Secretary

Founded:
1927

Organisation type and purpose:
Voluntary organisation.

Subject coverage:
All information on Channel swimming since 1875, assistance for channel swimmers, observation and ratification of swims.

Museum or gallery collection, archive, or library special collection:
Photographs and press cuttings from 1875

Printed publications:
Handbook
Information Pack
Captain Webb and 100 Years of Channel Swimming

Access to staff:
Contact by telephone and by e-mail
Hours: Mon to Fri, 0900 to 1700

CHANNEL VIEW PUBLICATIONS LTD

Acronym or abbreviation: CVP

St Nicholas House, 31–34 High Street, Bristol, BS21 2AW

Tel: 0117 315 8562
Fax: 0117 315 8563
E-mail: info@multilingual-matters.com

Website:
http://www.multilingual-matters.com

Enquiries:
Enquiries to: Managing Director

Founded:
1980

Formerly called:
Multilingual Matters Limited (year of change 2008)

Organisation type and purpose:
Publishing house.

Subject coverage:
Languages, linguistics, translations, education, bilingualism, travel and tourism.

Printed publications:
A large selection of publications covering each of the above topics including:
A Parents and Teachers' Guide to Bilingualism
Culture-specific Language Styles (Minami M)
Current Issues in Language Planning (journal)
Dyslexia (Payne T, Turner E)
Encyclopedia of Bilingualism & Bilingual Education (Baker C and Jones S P)
Foundations of Bilingual Education and Bilingualism (Barker C)
Journal of Multilingual and Multicultural Development (journal)
Language, Culture and Curriculum (journal)
Power, Prestige and Bilingualism (de Mejia A M)
Translation-mediation Communication in a Digital World (O'Hargan M, Ashworth D)
Tourism and Development (Sharpley R)

Publications list:
Available online and in print

Access to staff:
Contact by letter, by telephone, by fax, by e-mail and via website
Hours: Mon to Fri, 0900 to 1700

Subsidiary body:
Multilingual Matters Limited
tel: as above; fax: as above

CHANTRAINE SCHOOL OF DANCE

25a Menelik Road, London, NW2 3RJ

Tel: 020 7435 4247
Fax: 020 7435 4247

Enquiries:
Enquiries to: Director

Founded:
1978

Organisation type and purpose:
International organisation.
Dance school.
Teaches the Chantraine Dance of Expression, created in France by Alain and Françoise Chantraine, for the harmony and development of the person through rhythm, interiority, technique, creativity and choreography.

Subject coverage:
Chantraine Dance of Expression: movement and dance as aids to the development of the person. An approach to dance created in France by Alain and Françoise Chantraine since 1958.

Printed publications:
La Danse de la Vie (F Chantraine, 1998, Cerf, £5.75)
Leaflets describing the Chantraine approach to dance and listing the classes available (revised annually, free)
Poems/Poèmes by Alain Chantraine, translated (Woodall P, £3 from Chantraine School)

Access to staff:
Contact by letter, by telephone and by fax
Hours: Daily, 0830 to 2130

Other branches at:
High Wycombe Centre
13 Queens Road, High Wycombe, Buckinghamshire, HP13 6AQ; tel: 01494 447741
Wanstead Centre
27 Blake Hall Crescent, London, E11 3RH; tel: 020 8989 8604

Parent body:
Ecole de Danse Chantraine
12 Avenue Ste-Foy, Neuilly sur Seine, 92200, France; tel: + 33 1 46 24 01 89; fax: + 33 1 46 24 64 11

CHAPELS SOCIETY

c/o 47 Salisbury Drive, Midway, Swadlincote, DE11 7LD

Tel: 01283 558169
E-mail: chapelssociety@googlemail.com

Website:
http://www.britarch.ac.uk/chapelsoc/index.html

Enquiries:
Enquiries to: Honorary Secretary

Founded:
1988

Organisation type and purpose:
Learned society (membership is by subscription),
voluntary organisation, registered charity (charity
number 1014207).
The Chapels Society seeks to promote knowledge
of the architectural and historical importance of
places of worship outside the established Church,
primarily the buildings of Christian bodies
(Protestant, Roman Catholic, and Orthodox) but
also those of other faiths.

Subject coverage:
Nonconformist (ie non-Anglican) places of
worship in England and comparable buildings
throughout UK.

Printed publications:
Occasional Publications (series)
Newsletter (3 times a year, members)
Order printed publications from: Honorary Editor,
Chapels Society
c/o 31 Melrose Avenue, Reading, RG6 7BN

Publications list:
Available online

Access to staff:
Contact by letter, by e-mail and via website
Special comments: Please make contact by e-mail.

Links with:
Capel (Welsh Chapels Heritage Society)
Historic Chapels Trust

CHARITIES AID FOUNDATION

Acronym or abbreviation: CAF

Kings Hill, West Malling, Kent, ME19 4TA

Tel: 01732 520000
Fax: 01732 520001
E-mail: enquiries@cafonline.org

Website:
http://www.cafonline.org/research
Latest research on the Voluntary Sector.
http://www.cafonline.org/info
Practical informtion on CAF and the Sector.
http://www.cafonline.org
Dynamic interactive guide to the services and
activities of CAF worldwide. Other sites include
information resources for the non-profit sector and
facilities for online giving to charity.

Enquiries:
Enquiries to: Information Officer
Direct tel: 01732 520081/2/3
Other contacts: Press Officer for PR enquiries.

Founded:
1924

Organisation type and purpose:
International organisation, registered charity
(charity number 268369), consultancy, research
organisation.
CAF provides a range of services to charities and
their supporters worldwide.
Exists to increase the flow of funds to the voluntary
sector. We advise on how to give tax-effectively
and provide charities with banking, investment
and administration services.

Subject coverage:
Tax-effective giving, resources in the voluntary
sector, loans for charities, international giving,
administration and investment services for
charities. Information on the charitable sector, lists
of specific areas of charities, advice and support for
charities seeking to use the Internet.

Trade and statistical information:
Income and expenditure of top 500 charities.
Size and scope of UK voluntary sector.
Levels of individual giving.
Corporate giving in the UK.
Local Authority and central government support
for the voluntary sector.
Grant-making Trusts in the UK.

Printed publications:
A Lot of Give – trends in charitable giving for the
21st century (£14.99 plus p&p)

Coming Full Circle – the role of charitable funds in
London's health (Pharaoh C and Mocroft I, £10
plus p&p)
Dimensions 2000 Series:
Income From Government Sources (£10 plus p&p)
An Update on CAF's Top 500 Fundraising
Charities (£6 inc. p&p)
Patterns of Independent Grant-Making in the UK
(£25 plus p&p)
Healthy Relationships (1998, £12 plus p&p)
Benchmarking Charity Costs (1998, £10 plus p&p)

Publications list:
Available in print

Access to staff:
Contact by letter, by telephone, by fax, by e-mail
and via website. Appointment necessary.
Hours: Mon to Fri, 0900 to 1700

Access for disabled people:
Parking provided, level entry, access to all public
areas, toilet facilities

Offices also at:
Charities Aid Foundation
114–118 Southampton Row, London, WC1B
5AA; tel: 020 7400 2300; fax: 020 7831 0134; e-
mail: enquiries@cafonline.org

Overseas offices:
CAF America
King Street Station, 1800 Diagonal Road, Suite
150, Alexandria, Virginia 22314–2840, USA; tel:
00 1 703 549 8931; fax: 00 1 703 549 8934; e-mail:
info@cafamerica.org
CAF Brussels
Rue Dejonckerstraat 46, Brussels, B-1060,
Belgium; tel: 00 32 2 544 0050; fax: 00 32 2 544
0880; e-mail: cafbrussels@cafonline.org
CAF Bulgaria
65 Vitosha Blvd, 2nd Floor, Sofia, 100, Bulgaria;
tel: 00 359 2 981 1901; fax: 00 359 2 981 1901; e-
mail: bcaf@cafonline.org
CAF India
25 Navjeevan Vihar, Ground Floor, New Delhi,
110017, India; tel: 00 91 11 652 2206; fax: 00 91 11
618 6646; e-mail: cafindia@cafonline.org
CAF Russia (based in Moscow)
14/6 Ulitsa Sadovnicheskaya 57, Moscow,
113035, Russia; tel: 00 7 095 792 5929; fax: 00 7
095 792 5929; e-mail: cafrussia@cafonline.org
CAF Southern Africa
41 de Korte Street, Braamfontein 2017, Gauteng,
South Africa; tel: 00 27 11 339 1136; fax: 00 27 11
339 1152; e-mail: cafsouthafrica@cafonline.org
CAF West Africa
F-146/5 Second Soula Street, North Labone
Estates, PO Box 05–2956, OSU, Accra, Ghana; tel:
00 233 21 771 953; fax: 00 233 21 7011 260; e-mail:
cafwestafrica@cafonline.org

CHARITIES EVALUATION SERVICES

Acronym or abbreviation: CES

4 Coldbath Square, London, EC1R 5HL

Tel: 020 7713 5722
Fax: 020 7713 5692
E-mail: enquiries@ces-vol.org.uk

Website:
http://www.ces-vol.org.uk

Enquiries:
Enquiries to: Information Officer

Organisation type and purpose:
Registered charity (charity number 803602),
training organisation.

Access to staff:
Contact by letter, by telephone, by fax, by e-mail
and via website. Appointment necessary.
Hours: Mon to Fri, 0900 to 1730

Access for disabled people:
Parking provided, level entry, toilet facilities

CHARITY COMMISSION FOR ENGLAND AND WALES

Charity Commission Direct, PO Box 1227,
Liverpool, L69 3UG

Tel: 0845 300 0218
Fax: 0151 703 1555
E-mail: enquiries@charitycommission.gsi.gov.uk

Website:
http://www.charitycommission.gov.uk

Organisation type and purpose:
Central government body; includes the Central
Register of Charities.

Subject coverage:
General advice to charity trustees, information on
the Commission to members of the public, effective
use of charitable monies, charity law, history,
administration and management.

**Museum or gallery collection, archive, or library
special collection:**
19th-century reports of the former Commissioners
for Inquiring concerning Charities
Unreported vols concerning charities (mid-19th
century to 1947)

Library catalogue:
All or part available in-house

Printed publications:
Annual Report
Guidance leaflets on charity administration
Order printed publications from: The Stationery
Office

Publications list:
Available online

Access to staff:
Contact by letter, by telephone, by fax, by e-mail,
in person and via website. Appointment necessary.
Hours: Mon to Fri, 0900 to 1700
Special comments: Central Register of Charities open
1000 to 1600 by appointment only.

Access to building, collection or gallery:
Prior appointment required
Hours: 1000 to 1600

Access for disabled people:
Level entry, access to all public areas, toilet
facilities

CHARLES WILLIAMS SOCIETY

Flat 8, 65 Cadogan Gardens, London, SW3 2RA

Tel: 020 7581 9917
E-mail: brian.horne2@btinternet.com

Website:
http://www.charleswilliamssociety.org.uk

Enquiries:
Enquiries to: Librarian

Founded:
1976
Dormant

Organisation type and purpose:
Learned society.
To promote interest in, and provide opportunities
for, study of Charles Williams' writings.

Subject coverage:
Life and works of Charles Walter Stansby
Williams, author, theologian and poet, 1886–1945.

**Museum or gallery collection, archive, or library
special collection:**
Members' lending and reference libraries are
located at CMRS, St Michael's Hall, Shoe Lane,
Oxford, OX1 2DP

Printed publications:
Quarterly (newsletter for members, 4 a year)
Occasional publications

Access to staff:
Contact by letter, by telephone, by e-mail and via
website
Hours: Mon to Fri, 0900 to 1700

CHARLOTTE M. YONGE FELLOWSHIP

Acronym or abbreviation: CMYF

8 Anchorage Terrace, Durham, DH1 3DL

Tel: 0191 384 7857
E-mail: c.e.schultze@durham.ac.uk

Website:
http://www.cmyf.org.uk

Enquiries:
Enquiries to: Membership Secretary

Founded:
1995

Organisation type and purpose:
Membership association (membership is by subscription), present number of members: 160. Literary society for all those interested in the work of Victorian novelist, Charlotte M. Yonge.

Subject coverage:
The works, life and milieu of Victorian novelist, Charlotte M. Yonge (1823–1901).

Museum or gallery collection, archive, or library special collection:
Collection of books by and relating to Charlotte M. Yonge, accessible to members, located in Oxford, United Kingdom

Printed publications:
Review (twice a year, to members; individual issues available for purchase by non-members)
Journal (approx. biennial, to members; also available for purchase by non-members)
Books (essay vol. on Yonge, 2007)
Reprinted works by Yonge (forthcoming)
Order printed publications from: Details on website

Publications list:
Available online

Access to staff:
Contact by letter, by e-mail and via website
Hours: Mon to Fri, 0900 to 1700

Access to building, collection or gallery:
No access other than to staff

CHARTERED INSTITUTE OF ARBITRATORS

Acronym or abbreviation: CIArb

International Centre for Arbitration and Mediation, 12 Bloomsbury Square, London, WC1A 2LP

Tel: 020 7421 7444
Fax: 020 7404 4023
E-mail: info@ciarb.org

Website:
http://www.ciarb.org
Information about the Institute, dispute resolution and details about education and training, membership and resources for practitioners.

Enquiries:
Enquiries to: Member Services Assistant
Direct tel: 020 7421 7439
Direct e-mail: kmurray@ciarb.org
Other contacts: The Legal Counsel (for legal enquiries)

Founded:
1915

Organisation type and purpose:
The Institute is globally recognised as the professional home for all dispute resolvers and is a resource centre for those who benefit from cost effective, private dispute resolution; present number of members: 11,000 world-wide; the CIArb is one of the leading global authorities on dispute resolution. CIArb membership offers individuals from a variety of sectors internationally recognised standards of excellence. The Institute also provides dispute resolution services for public sector, consumer and commercial markets, providing bespoke solutions for the efficient settlement of disputes.

Subject coverage:
Commercial arbitration, mediation, adjudication, dispute resolution, aspects of law, arbitration clauses, appointment of arbitrators, arbitration acts, international arbitration, international conventions on arbitration, enforcement of arbitration awards, training of arbitrators, duties of expert witnesses and advocacy, alternative dispute resolution procedures.

Museum or gallery collection, archive, or library special collection:
Volumes on arbitration procedure and practice throughout the world
Legal texts covering dispute resolution

Library catalogue:
All or part available online and in-house

Printed publications:
Arbitration Journal, Institute Newsletter (quarterly, arbitration rules)

Access to staff:
Contact by letter, by telephone, by fax, by e-mail and via website. Appointment necessary.
Hours: Mon to Fri, 0830 to 1730

Access to building, collection or gallery:
Library available to members
Hours: Mon to Fri, 0830 to 1730

Access for disabled people:
Toilet facilities
Special comments: Lifts

Branches:
30 branches world-wide

CHARTERED INSTITUTE OF ARCHITECTURAL TECHNOLOGISTS

Acronym or abbreviation: CIAT

397 City Road, Islington, London, EC1V 1NH

Tel: 020 7278 2206
Fax: 020 7837 3194
E-mail: info@ciat.org.uk

Website:
http://www.ciat.org.uk

Enquiries:
Enquiries to: Communications Director
Other contacts: Assistant Communications Director

Founded:
1965

Formerly called:
British Institute of Architectural Technologists; Society of Architectural & Associated Technicians (year of change 1986); British Institute of Architectural Technicians (year of change 1994)

Organisation type and purpose:
Professional body (membership is by subscription), present number of members: 8500.
International qualifying body for Chartered Architectural Technologists and Professional Architectural Technicians.

Subject coverage:
Careers advice, practice and technical advice, education guidance, recognition of the CIAT qualifications, continuing professional development, consultative panel for construction documents, architecture and construction awards.

Printed publications:
Architectural Technology (journal, 6 times a year)
Becoming a Member (free)
Careers Handbook (free)
Code of Conduct (free)

Publications list:
Available in print

Access to staff:
Contact by letter, by telephone, by fax, by e-mail and via website
Hours: Mon to Fri, 0900 to 1700

Access to building, collection or gallery:
Prior appointment required

Member of:
Construction Industry Council

CHARTERED INSTITUTE OF BANKERS IN SCOTLAND, THE

Acronym or abbreviation: CIOBS

38b Drumsheugh Gardens, Edinburgh, EH3 7SW

Tel: 0131 473 7777
Fax: 0131 473 7788
E-mail: info@ciobs.org.uk

Website:
http://www.ciobs.org.uk
General information on who we are and what we do, full details of the educational programmes.

Enquiries:
Enquiries to: Chief Executive
Other contacts: (1) Director of Education (2) Business Development Manager for (1) information on qualifications and courses (2) marketing and development issues.

Founded:
1875

Formerly called:
Institute of Bankers in Scotland (year of change 1991)

Organisation type and purpose:
Professional body (membership is by subscription, qualification, election or invitation), present number of members: 11,500, registered charity (charity number SCO 13927).

Subject coverage:
Banking and finance, administration and management.

Museum or gallery collection, archive, or library special collection:
Scottish Bank Notes from 1727 to the present

Printed publications:
Handbooks on Scottish banking practice
Workbooks relating to the financial services sector
Scottish Banker (6 times a year)

Publications list:
Available in print

Access to staff:
Contact by letter, by telephone, by fax, by e-mail and via website. Appointment necessary.
Hours: Mon to Fri, 0900 to 1700

CHARTERED INSTITUTE OF BUILDING

Acronym or abbreviation: CIOB

Englemere, Kings Ride, Ascot, Berkshire, SL5 7TB

Tel: 01344 630700
Fax: 01344 630777
E-mail: reception@ciob.org.uk

Website:
http://www.constructors.org
Membership access for library database, membership database.
http://www.ciob.org.uk
Public access for the CIOB and its services plus members-only area.

Enquiries:
Enquiries to: LIS Manager
Direct fax: 01344 630764
Direct e-mail: lis@ciob.org.uk

Founded:
1834

Organisation type and purpose:
International organisation, professional body (membership is by qualification), present number of members: 38,000 individuals, 320 firms, registered charity (charity number 280795), suitable for ages: 18+, research organisation, publishing house.

Subject coverage:
Processes of management in construction: eg, law; contracts; human resources; costs; planning and programming; education and training.

Museum or gallery collection, archive, or library special collection:
Photographic collection on Construction Management Processes (small)
Building Law Reports
Conference Proceedings, 1970 to date
Construction Law Reports

Library catalogue:
All or part available online

Printed publications:
Construction History (annually)
Construction Information Quarterly (4 times a year)
Construction Manager (formerly Chartered Builder, 10 times a year)
Order printed publications from: Construction Books Direct, Englemere Limited
The White House, Englemere, Kings Ride, Ascot, SC5 7JR, tel: 01344 630810

Publications list:
Available online

Access to staff:
Contact by letter, by telephone, by fax, by e-mail and via website. Appointment necessary. Access for members only. Non-members charged.
Hours: Mon to Fri, 0830 to 1700 (phone)

Access to building, collection or gallery:
Appointment required
Hours: Mon to Fri, 0930 to 1630
Special comments: Members only.

Access for disabled people:
Parking provided, ramped entry, access to all public areas, toilet facilities

Affiliated to:
CIRIA
    tel: 020 7222 8891
Conseil International du Bâtiment (CIB)
Construction Industry Computing Association
    tel: 01223 236336; e-mail: postmaster@cica.org.uk

CHARTERED INSTITUTE OF ENVIRONMENTAL HEALTH

Acronym or abbreviation: CIEH

Chadwick Court, 15 Hatfields, London, SE1 8DJ

Tel: 020 7928 6006
Fax: 020 7827 5866
E-mail: info@cieh.org

Website:
http://www.cieh.org
Information about the Chartered Institute, including press releases and policy statements.

Enquiries:
Enquiries to: Information Officer
Direct tel: 020 7827 5821
Direct fax: 020 7827 6322

Founded:
1883

Organisation type and purpose:
Professional body (membership is by qualification), registered charity (charity number 290350).
Registration board and examining body for Environmental Health Officers.

Subject coverage:
Environmental health, housing, pollution control, food safety, health and safety at work, and noise.

Museum or gallery collection, archive, or library special collection:
Complete set of the CIEH journal: Environmental Health Practitioner 1895 to date

Library catalogue:
All or part available in-house

Printed publications:
Environmental Health Practitioner (monthly)
Environmental Health News (weekly)
Food Forum (quarterly)
Journal of Environmental Health Research (twice a year)
Books and reports on environmental protection, food hygiene, general environmental health, health and safety, housing, and pest control

Publications list:
Available online

Access to staff:
Contact by letter, by telephone, by fax, by e-mail and via website. Appointment necessary.
Hours: Mon to Fri, 0900 to 1700

Access to building, collection or gallery:
Library access for CIEH members and researchers, by appointment
Hours: Library: Mon to Fri, 0900 to 1700

CHARTERED INSTITUTE OF HOUSING

Acronym or abbreviation: CIH

Octavia House, Westwood Way, Coventry, Warwickshire, CV4 8JP

Tel: 024 7685 1700
Fax: 024 7669 5110

Website:
http://www.cih.org
Some information on policy, training and publications.

Enquiries:
Enquiries to: Information Officer
Other contacts: Good Practice Manager

Formerly called:
Institute of Housing

Merged with:
Institute of Rent Officers and Rental Valuers, date of change, February 1999

Organisation type and purpose:
Professional body (membership is by subscription), present number of members: over 17,000, registered charity (charity number 244067/R), training organisation, research organisation.

Subject coverage:
Housing (social and private rented sector), housing finance, CCT, homelessness, housing management and good practice.

Museum or gallery collection, archive, or library special collection:
15,000 books and reports and about 35 journal titles held in library

Trade and statistical information:
Housing statistics, stock sizes, tenure type.

Printed publications:
Briefing papers on current topics of housing interest
Housing (magazine, monthly)
Inside Housing (magazine, weekly)
Yearbook
Many good practice books, guides and manuals including:
Manual on Housing Benefit and Valuation
Order printed publications from: Publications Officer
tel: 02476 851700

Electronic and video publications:
Housing Management Standards Manual: Hypertext edition

Publications list:
Available online and in print

Access to staff:
Contact by letter, by telephone and by e-mail.
Access for members only.
Hours: Mon to Fri, 0900 to 1700
Special comments: Members only.

Access to building, collection or gallery:
No prior appointment required

Other addresses:
CIH London
    9 White Lion Street, Islington, London, N1 9XJ; tel: 020 7837 4280; fax: 020 7278 2705
CIH Scotland
    6 Palmerston Place, Edinburgh, EH12 5AA; tel: 0131 225 4544; fax: 0131 225 4566
CIH Wales
    4 Purbeck House, Lambourne Crescent, Cardiff Business Park, Llanishen, Cardiff, CF4 5GJ; tel: 029 2076 5760; fax: 029 2076 5761

CHARTERED INSTITUTE OF JOURNALISTS, THE

Acronym or abbreviation: CIOJ

2 Dock Offices, Surrey Quays Road, London, SE16 2XU

Tel: 020 7252 1187
Fax: 020 7232 2302
E-mail: memberservices@cioj.co.uk

Website:
http://www.ioj.co.uk

Enquiries:
Enquiries to: General Secretary
Other contacts: Treasurer for all financial matters.

Founded:
1884

Formerly called:
Institute of Journalists (IOJ) (year of change 1978)

Organisation type and purpose:
International organisation, professional body, trade union (membership is by subscription, election or invitation), present number of members: 1150.

Subject coverage:
Journalism, broadcasting.

Museum or gallery collection, archive, or library special collection:
Newspaper and journalistic library

Printed publications:
CIOJ Journal (quarterly, free to members)
Directory of Chartered Institute of Freelance Journalists
CIOJ Update (newsletter)

Access to staff:
Contact by letter, by telephone, by fax, by e-mail and via website. Appointment necessary.
Hours: Mon to Fri, 0900 to 1700

Access to building, collection or gallery:
No prior appointment required

Links with:
British Copyright Council
Campaign for Freedom of Information
Independent Unions Training Council
Journalists' Copyright Fund
Media Society
National Council for the Training of Journalists

CHARTERED INSTITUTE OF LIBRARY AND INFORMATION PROFESSIONALS

Acronym or abbreviation: CILIP

7 Ridgmount Street, London, WC1E 7AE

Tel: 020 7255 0500; 020 7255 0505 (minicom, textphone)
Fax: 020 7255 0501
E-mail: info@cilip.org.uk

Website:
http://www.cilip.org.uk

Enquiries:
Enquiries to: Information Services
Direct tel: 020 7255 0620
Other contacts: Chief Executive

Founded:
1877

continued overleaf

Formerly called:
The Institute of Information Scientists (IIS), The Library Association (LA) (year of change 2002)

Organisation type and purpose:
CILIP is the leading professional body for librarians, information specialists and knowledge managers. CILIP forms a community of around 36,000 people engaged in library and information work, of whom approximately 21,000 are CILIP members and about 15,000 are regular customers of CILIP Enterprises.

Subject coverage:
Librarianship, libraries, information science and services, education for the profession, salaries and conditions, qualifications and professional development, service provision guidelines and standards, databases, copyright, legislation, local authorities, recruitment agency.

Library catalogue:
All or part available in-house

Printed publications:
Library and Information Gazette
Directories and published works from Facet Publishing
Library and Information Update
Chartered Institute of Library and Information Professionals' Yearbook

Publications list:
Available in print

Access to staff:
Contact by letter, by telephone, by fax and by e-mail. Appointment necessary.
Hours: Mon to Fri, 0900 to 1700

CHARTERED INSTITUTE OF LIBRARY AND INFORMATION PROFESSIONALS IN SCOTLAND

Acronym or abbreviation: CILIP

1st Floor Building C, Brandon Gate, Leechlee Road, Hamilton, ML3 6AU

Tel: 01698 458888
Fax: 01698 283170
E-mail: sla@slainte.org.uk

Website:
http://www.slainte.org.uk
Gateway to Scottish authors, gateway to community information, Scottish Earl News, SLIC/SLA News.

Enquiries:
Enquiries to: Director
Direct tel: 01698 458888
Direct e-mail: e.fulton@slainte.org.uk

Founded:
1908

Formed by the unification of:
The Scottish Library Association and the Institute of Information Scientists (IIS) (year of change 2002)

Organisation type and purpose:
Professional body, registered charity (charity number 313014).

Subject coverage:
Librarianship and library resources in Scotland.

Printed publications:
Bonnie Fechters (women in Scotland 1900–1950)
Discovering Scottish Writers
Exploring Scottish History (2nd edition)
Scotland 1939
Scotland 1945
The Scot and his Maps
Voyage of the Pharos
Working Lives (photographs of workers and their work in Scotland 1897–1997)

Publications list:
Available in print

Affiliated to:
Library Association

CHARTERED INSTITUTE OF LINGUISTS

Acronym or abbreviation: IoL

Saxon House, 48 Southwark Street, London, SE1 1UN

Tel: 020 7940 3100
Fax: 020 7940 3101
E-mail: info@iol.org.uk

Website:
http://www.iol.org.uk
Membership, examinations, assessments, employment possibilities, the Linguist, Members' Discussion Forum, Find-a-Linguist service, Chartered Linguist site.

Enquiries:
Enquiries to: Director of Communications
Direct tel: 020 7940 3135
Direct fax: 020 7940 3121
Direct e-mail: cetty.zambrano@iol.org.uk
Other contacts: (1) Central Registration Department (2) Registrar for (1) examination queries (2) membership eligibility.

Founded:
1910

Organisation type and purpose:
International organisation, professional body (membership is by qualification), present number of members: 6500.
To promote the interests of professional linguists and maintain standards within the language world.

Subject coverage:
Language learning; courses; methods; availability and training of translators and interpreters; qualifications; language grammar books and dictionaries; employment of translators; examinations in languages; careers with languages; language in general; public service interpreters; language assessments.

Museum or gallery collection, archive, or library special collection:
Journals and magazines relating to languages or linguistics received from appropriate organisations overseas
Monolingual minor language works
Technical and/or specialised multilingual dictionaries

Trade and statistical information:
Survey of freelance notes for translators and interpreters.

Library catalogue:
All or part available in-house

Printed publications:
Publications for language and translator's qualifications available
1998 Freelance Rates Survey (full report, £15 plus p&p)
Informations sheets for translators
The Linguist (6 times a year)
Translator's Information Pack (members free, non-members £5 plus p&p)
Order printed publications from: Membership Department

Publications list:
Available online and in print

Access to staff:
Contact by letter, by telephone, by fax, by e-mail and via website
Hours: Mon to Fri, 0900 to 1700

Access to building, collection or gallery:
By appointment with a contact
Hours: Mon to Fri, 0900 to 1700

Access for disabled people:
Wheelchair access not available due to the heritage condition and age of the building, disabled persons can be assisted by staff at the main entrance

CHARTERED INSTITUTE OF LOGISTICS AND TRANSPORT (UK)

Acronym or abbreviation: CILT (UK)

Logistics and Transport Centre, Earlstrees Court, Earlstrees Road, Corby, Northamptonshire, NN17 4AX

Tel: 01536 740100
Fax: 01536 740101
E-mail: enquiry@ciltuk.org.uk

Website:
http://www.ciltuk.org.uk
Services, products and activities.

Enquiries:
Enquiries to: Chief Executive
Other contacts: Director Corporate Communications

Founded:
1999

Organisation type and purpose:
Professional body (membership is by qualification), present number of members: 23,000, registered charity (charity number 1004963).

Subject coverage:
Information technology, logistics, warehousing, transport, materials management, materials handling, inventory systems, stock control, storage, distribution, road, rail, air and sea transport, transport planning, transport operations, transport infrastructure provision.

Library catalogue:
All or part available online and in-house

Printed publications:
Logistics and Transport Focus (10 times a year, free to members)

Publications list:
Available in print

Access to staff:
Contact by letter, by telephone, by fax, by e-mail and via website. Appointment necessary.
Hours: Mon to Fri, 0900 to 1700

Access to building, collection or gallery:
No access other than to staff and members
Hours: Mon to Fri, 0900 to 1700
Special comments: Charge to non-members.

Other address:
The Chartered Institute of Logistics and Transport (CILT)
Earlstrees Industrial Estate, Corby, NN17 4AX; tel: 01536 740100; fax: 01536 740101; e-mail: enquiry@ciltuk.org.uk

CHARTERED INSTITUTE OF LOSS ADJUSTERS

Acronym or abbreviation: CILA

Warwick House, 65/66 Queen Street, London EC4R 1EB

Tel: 020 7337 9960
Fax: 020 7929 3082
E-mail: info@cila.co.uk

Website:
http://www.cila.co.uk

Enquiries:
Enquiries to: Executive Director

Founded:
1941

Organisation type and purpose:
Professional body (membership is by qualification), present number of members: Approx 2600.

Subject coverage:
Insurance, loss adjusting, property, liability.

Printed publications:
Publication list available direct

Publications list:
Available in print

Access to staff:
Contact by letter
Hours: Mon to Fri, 0900 to 1700

CHARTERED INSTITUTE OF MARKETING

Acronym or abbreviation: CIM

Moor Hall, Cookham, Maidenhead, Berkshire, SL6 9QH

Tel: 01628 427500
Fax: 01628 427499
E-mail: marketing@cim.co.uk

Website:
http://www.cim.co.uk
Outline of CIM services and events.

Enquiries:
Enquiries to: Information Services Manager
Direct tel: 01628 427333
Direct fax: 01628 427349
Direct e-mail: library@cim.co.uk
Other contacts: Head of Communications

Founded:
1911

Organisation type and purpose:
Professional body.

Subject coverage:
Consumer and industrial products and services, retail, wholesale and distribution sectors, marketing planning, implementation and control techniques, marketing communications, marketing support services, human resources.

Museum or gallery collection, archive, or library special collection:
6000 books held on marketing and management specifically, relevant marketing journals, market research reports, miscellaneous other reports. Members also have access to online journals from their desktops.

Trade and statistical information:
Market research reports and government statistics.

Non-library collection catalogue:
All or part available in-house

Library catalogue:
All or part available online and in-house

Printed publications:
Books, marketing and sales texts (joint ventures and own publications)
The marketer (magazine, 11 times a year). Twice yearly papers published on topics such as segmentation, marketing law, communications, sponsorship and technology.
Order printed publications from: CIM Direct at the same address, tel: 01628 427427, fax: 01628 427439, e-mail: cimdirect@cim.co.uk

Publications list:
Available online and in print

Access to staff:
Contact by letter, by telephone, by fax, by e-mail, in person and via website. Appointment necessary. Non-members charged.
Hours: Mon to Fri, 0900 to 1700 for telephone and email enquiries and Wed to Fri, 0900 to 1700 for personal visits
Special comments: Charges may be made to non-members for usage, prior appointment required. Some services free to members.

Member of:
European Marketing Council (EMC)
  tel: + 32 2 7421780; fax: + 32 2 7421785; e-mail: infodesk@emc.be

Other addresses:
Chartered Institute of Marketing (Scotland)
  3rd Floor, 100 Wellington Street, Glasgow, G2 6DH; tel: 0141 221 7700; fax: 0141 221 7766

Chartered Institute of Marketing Ireland
  13 Harbour Court, Heron Road, Belfast, BT3 9HB; tel: 028 9045 1005; fax: 028 9046 9004

CHARTERED INSTITUTE OF PATENT ATTORNEYS

Acronym or abbreviation: CIPA

95 Chancery Lane, London, WC2A 1DT

Tel: 020 7405 9450
Fax: 020 7430 0471
E-mail: mail@cipa.org.uk

Website:
http://www.cipa.org.uk
General basic information on patents, trademarks, designs and copyright, careers information, lists of firms of patent attorneys (also known as patent agents), general news, links to other relevant sites.

Enquiries:
Enquiries to: Institute Manager

Founded:
1882

Formerly called:
The Chartered Institute of Patent Agents (year of change 2006)

Organisation type and purpose:
Professional body.

Subject coverage:
Patents, designs, trademarks, copyright.

Printed publications:
CIPA – Journal of the CIPA (£100 a year)
Directory of Firms of Patent Agents (free, and on the internet)
Information Pack for Inventors (free, and on the internet)
Membership list (£25)
Register of Patent Agents (annually, £25, free on the internet)

Electronic and video publications:
What is a Patent Agent? (video, £20 plus VAT)

Access to staff:
Contact by letter, by telephone, by fax, by e-mail and via website
Hours: Mon to Fri, 0900 to 1730

CHARTERED INSTITUTE OF PERSONNEL AND DEVELOPMENT

Acronym or abbreviation: CIPD

151 The Broadway, London, SW19 1JQ

Tel: 020 8612 6200
Fax: 020 8612 6232
E-mail: cipd@cipd.co.uk

Website:
http://www.cipd.co.uk/
2000 pages on CIPD services and access for members to the LIS webcat.

Enquiries:
Enquiries to: Head of Library and Information Services
Direct tel: 020 8612 6210
Direct fax: 020 8612 6232
Direct e-mail: lis@cipd.co.uk

Founded:
2000

Organisation type and purpose:
Professional body, registered charity (charity number 1079797), training organisation, research organisation.

Subject coverage:
Personnel management, industrial relations, employment law, training.

Museum or gallery collection, archive, or library special collection:
Comprehensive collection of publications for the European Centre for the Development of Vocational Training (CEDEFOP)

Printed publications:
People Management (journal, fortnightly)
Wide range of publications on personnel development and general management for managers and students

Electronic and video publications:
Careers information (cipd.co.uk)
Case Studies (cipd.co.uk)
Quick Facts (cipd.co.uk)
Reports (cipd.co.uk)
Surveys (cipd.co.uk)

Publications list:
Available in print

Access to staff:
Contact by letter, by telephone, by fax, by e-mail, in person and via website. Non-members charged.
Hours: Mon to Fri, 0900 to 1730
Special comments: Primarily for members only.

UK contact for:
European Centre for the Development of Vocational Training (CEDEFOP)
International Federation of Training and Development Organisations (IFTDO)

CHARTERED INSTITUTE OF PUBLIC FINANCE AND ACCOUNTANCY

Formal name: The Chartered Institute of Public Finance and Accountancy
Acronym or abbreviation: CIPFA in Scotland

Fettes Park, Second Floor, West Wing, 496 Ferry Road, Edinburgh, EH5 2DL

Tel: 0131 551 2100
Fax: 0131 551 2223
E-mail: scotland@cipfa.org

Website:
http://www.cipfascotland.org.uk

Enquiries:
Enquiries to: Director

Founded:
1885

Organisation type and purpose:
Professional body (membership is by qualification), present number of members: 13,000, registered charity (charity number 231060).

Subject coverage:
Financial management in the public services, especially as regards Scotland.
Accountancy training and qualifications.

Trade and statistical information:
Information published on the expenditure and income of all Scottish local authorities; two annual publications of statistics (Rating Review).

Printed publications:
Publications and newsletters regarding financial management in the public services in Scotland.
Scottish News (quarterly)

Publications list:
Available in print

Access to staff:
Contact by letter, by telephone, by fax, by e-mail and via website
Hours: Mon to Fri, 0900 to 1700
Special comments: Not a public office.

Other address:
CIPFA (CIPFA)
  3 Robert Street, London, WC2N 6BH; tel: 020 7543 5600; fax: 020 7543 5700; e-mail: info@cipfa.org.uk

CHARTERED INSTITUTE OF PUBLIC RELATIONS

Acronym or abbreviation: CIPR

32 St James's Square, London, SW1Y 4JR

Tel: 020 7766 3333

continued overleaf

Fax: 020 7766 3344
E-mail: info@cipr.co.uk

Website:
http://www.cipr.co.uk

Founded:
1948

Organisation type and purpose:
Professional body, present number of members:
9000.

Subject coverage:
Public relations practice in central and local
government, industry and commerce,
consultancies and voluntary organisations.

Printed publications:
Annual Report (free)
Profile (magazine, members)
The CIPR Planning, Research and Evaluation
Toolkit (£35 members, £85 non-members, plus £1
p&p)
Other publications include:
The PR in Practice series
Order printed publications from: www.cipr.co.uk/
publications

Publications list:
Available in print

Access to staff:
Contact by letter, by telephone, by fax, by e-mail
and via website. Appointment necessary.
Hours: Mon to Fri, 0900 to 1800

Member organisation of:
European Confederation of Public Relations
(CERP)
Global Alliance

CHARTERED INSTITUTE OF TAXATION

Acronym or abbreviation: CIOT

12 Upper Belgrave Street, London, SW1X 8BB

Tel: 020 7235 9381
Fax: 020 7235 2562
E-mail: post@ciot.org.uk

Website:
http://www.tax.org.uk
Information on taxation and the Institute.

Enquiries:
Enquiries to: Head of Education Department

Founded:
1930

Formerly called:
Institute of Taxation (year of change 1994)

Organisation type and purpose:
Professional body, registered charity (charity
number 1037771), training organisation.

Subject coverage:
UK taxation, information on examinations in
taxation and careers in the profession.

**Museum or gallery collection, archive, or library
special collection:**
Tax Library at King's College London (members
only)

Printed publications:
Annual Report (free)
Essential Law for the Tax Adviser
Essential Accounting for the Tax Technician
Directory of Chartered Tax Advisers
Tax Adviser (journal, monthly, free to members,
subscription for non-members)

Access to staff:
Contact by letter, by telephone, by fax, by e-mail
and via website
Hours: Mon to Fri, 0900 to 1700

Access to building, collection or gallery:
No access other than to staff

Sister body to:
Association of Taxation Technicians
at the same address; tel: 020 7235 2544; fax: 020
7235 4571; e-mail: info@att.org.uk

UK Representative Body on the:
Confédération de Fiscale Européenne

CHARTERED INSTITUTION OF BUILDING SERVICES ENGINEERS

Acronym or abbreviation: CIBSE

222 Balham High Road, London, SW12 9BS

Tel: 020 8675 5211
Fax: 020 8675 5449

Website:
http://www.cibse.org

Enquiries:
Enquiries to: Information Officer

Founded:
1977

Formerly called:
Illuminating Engineering Society (IES), Institution
of Heating and Ventilating Engineers (IHVE) (year
of change 1977); Chartered Institution of Building
Services (CIBS) (year of change 1982)

Organisation type and purpose:
Professional body, registered charity (charity
number 278104).
Provides the Secretariat of the National
Illumination Committee of Great Britain.

Subject coverage:
All engineering services within buildings: design,
installation, commissioning, maintenance,
acoustics, air conditioning, communications,
controls, electrical services, energy management,
fire protection, heating, internal transportation,
lighting, maintenance, public health, refrigeration,
safety, security, ventilating, facilities management.

Printed publications:
Building Services (technical journal, monthly)
Building Services Engineering Research and
Technology (technical journal, quarterly)
Lighting Research and Technology (technical
journal, quarterly)
Lighting Register (annual)
Minimising the risk of Legionnaires' disease (2000)
Register of Building Services Consultants
(annually and online)
A comprehensive range of information on building
services including: guides, reference books,
technical memoranda, commissioning and
building energy codes, application manuals and
research publications

Electronic and video publications:
Register of Building Services Consultants (online,
annually)
CIBSE Guide C: Reference data (2001) (CD-ROM)
CIBSE Guide J: Weather, solar and illuminance
data (CD-ROM)

Publications list:
Available online and in print

Access to staff:
Contact by letter, by telephone, by fax and by e-
mail
Hours: Mon to Fri, 0900 to 1700

CHARTERED INSTITUTION OF WASTES MANAGEMENT

Acronym or abbreviation: CIWM

9 Saxon Court, St Peter's Gardens, Northampton,
NN1 1SX

Tel: 01604 620426
Fax: 01604 621339
E-mail: technical@ciwm.co.uk

Website:
http://www.ciwm.co.uk

Enquiries:
Enquiries to: Technical Officer

Founded:
1898

Formerly called:
Institute of Public Cleansing (IPC), Institute of
Solid Wastes Management (ISWM), Institute of
Wastes Management (IWM)

Organisation type and purpose:
National organisation, professional body,
registered charity, training organisation, research
organisation.

Subject coverage:
Refuse collection; refuse disposal; street cleaning;
litter abatement and control; resource recovery;
incineration of waste and heat utilisation; analysis
of wastes, best practice and technical articles and
publications on waste and resource management,
biological treatment, strategy, healthcare waste.

**Museum or gallery collection, archive, or library
special collection:**
Comprehensive technical library on all aspects of
wastes management

Library catalogue:
All or part available online

Printed publications:
Briefing Notes and Technical Publications
(irregular)
Scientific & Technical Review (quarterly)
CIWM (monthly)

Electronic and video publications:
CD-ROM access in library
Videos on environmental and waste management
issues (for hire)

Publications list:
Available online and in print

Access to staff:
Contact by letter, by telephone, by fax, by e-mail
and via website. Appointment necessary.
Hours: Mon to Fri, 0900 to 1630

Access to building, collection or gallery:
Prior appointment required
Hours: Mon to Fri, 0900 to 1700

Access for disabled people:
Toilet facilities

UK national member of:
International Solid Waste Association (ISWA)
Overgarden Oven Vandet 48E, Copenhagen, DK-
1415; tel: + 0045 3296 1588; fax: + 0045 3296 1584;
e-mail: iswa@inet.vni2.dk

CHARTERED INSTITUTION OF WATER AND ENVIRONMENTAL MANAGEMENT

Acronym or abbreviation: CIWEM

15 John Street, London, WC1N 2EB

Tel: 020 7831 3110
Fax: 020 7405 4967
E-mail: admin@ciwem.org.uk

Website:
http://www.ciwem.org.uk

Enquiries:
Enquiries to: Executive Director

Founded:
1895

Formed by the merger of:
Institute of Water Pollution Control, Institution of
Public Health Engineers, Institution of Water
Engineers and Scientists (year of change 1987)

Formerly called:
Institution of Water and Environmental
Management (year of change 1995)

Organisation type and purpose:
Professional body (membership is by
qualification), present number of members: 11,500,
registered charity (charity number 1043409).

Subject coverage:
Water treatment, water pollution control, treatment and disposal of sewage and trade waste, sewers and sewerage waste disposal, environmental issues.

Library catalogue:
All or part available in-house

Printed publications:
International Directory of Members (annually)
Journal of the Chartered Institution of Water and Environmental Management (4 times a year)
Water and Environment Manager (magazine, 10 times a year)
Proceedings of Conferences and Symposia
Information Booklet on CIWEM
Manuals (on waste water treatment, river engineering, etc)
A large selection of publications on environmental issues

Publications list:
Available in print

Access to staff:
Contact by letter, by telephone, by fax, by e-mail and via website. Appointment necessary.
Hours: Wed, 1000 to 1600

Access to building, collection or gallery:
Prior appointment required

Access for disabled people:
Hours: Mon to Fri, 0900 to 1700

Founder member of:
Society of Environment

Nominated body of:
Engineering Council
Science Council

CHARTERED INSURANCE INSTITUTE

Acronym or abbreviation: CII

20 Aldermanbury, London, EC2V 7HY

Tel: 020 7417 4416/5
Fax: 020 7417 0110
E-mail: knowledge@cii.co.uk

Website:
http://www.cii.co.uk
http://www.cii.co.uk/knowledge
CII Knowledge Services

Founded:
1934

Organisation type and purpose:
Professional body for those working in the insurance and financial services industry, with 92,000 members.

Subject coverage:
Insurance, United Kingdom and overseas, risk, financial services and related subjects.

Trade and statistical information:
Overseas insurance markets, UK insurance market.

Non-library collection catalogue:
All or part available online

Library catalogue:
All or part available online

Printed publications:
Research reports
Textbooks
The Journal (6 times a year)
Financial Solutions (6 times a year)
Order printed publications from: 31 Hillcrest Road, London, E18 2JB, tel: 020 8989 8464, fax: 020 8530 3052, e-mail: customer.serv@cii.co.uk

Electronic and video publications:
Online market and technical information on the CII Knowledge Services website (mostly members only)

Access to staff:
Contact by letter, by telephone, by fax, by e-mail, in person and via website. Non-members charged.
Hours: Mon to Fri, 0900 to 1700

Access for disabled people:
Ramped entry, access to all public areas, toilet facilities

Branches:
Insurance Institute of London and 60 others

Constituent bodies:
Personal Finance Society
    same address; tel: 020 8989 8464
Society of Mortgage Professionals
    same address; tel: 020 8989 8464

CHARTERED MANAGEMENT INSTITUTE

Acronym or abbreviation: CMI

Management House, Cottingham Road, Corby, Northamptonshire, NN17 1TT

Tel: 01536 204222
Fax: 01536 201651
E-mail: mic.enquiries@managers.org.uk

Website:
http://www.managers.org.uk
Information on the Institute, its services and membership; links to other useful sites.
http://www.managers.org.uk/bookshop
Publications catalogue.

Enquiries:
Enquiries to: Head of Information Services
Direct tel: 01536 207423
Direct fax: 01536 401013
Direct e-mail: bob.norton@managers.org.uk

Founded:
1992

Organisation type and purpose:
Professional body, membership association (membership is by subscription, qualification, election or invitation), present number of members: 74,000, registered charity (charity number 1091035), research organisation.

Subject coverage:
Techniques, skills, theories and practices of management.

Non-library collection catalogue:
All or part available online

Printed publications:
Annual Report
Business in a Week (series)
Checklists
Professional Manager (6 times a year)
Reading lists, fact sheets
The Management Thinkers

Electronic and video publications:
Checkpoint (checklists and thinkers, CD-ROM)

Publications list:
Available online

Access to staff:
Contact by letter, by telephone, by fax, by e-mail, in person and via website
Hours: Mon to Fri, 0900 to 1700
Special comments: Non-members may use the library for reference free of charge. Use of other services will incur a charge.

Access for disabled people:
Parking, level entry, access to all areas, toilet facilities
Special comments: Ramped fire exits

Administrative Office:
Chartered Management Institute
    3rd Floor, 2 Savoy Court, London, WC2R 0EZ; tel: 020 7497 0580; fax: 020 7497 0463; e-mail: secretariat@managers.org.uk

CHARTERED PHYSIOTHERAPISTS IN MENTAL HEALTHCARE

Acronym or abbreviation: CPMH

14 Bedford Row, London, WC1R 4ED

Tel: 020 7306 6666

E-mail: enquiries@csp.org.uk

Website:
http://www.csp.org.uk

Enquiries:
Enquiries to: General Secretary

Formerly called:
Association of Chartered Physiotherapists in Psychiatry (ACPP) (year of change 1994)

Organisation type and purpose:
International organisation, advisory body, professional body (membership is by subscription, qualification, election or invitation), present number of members: 150, training organisation.

Subject coverage:
Physiotherapy, psychiatry, mental healthcare.

Access to staff:
Contact by letter, by telephone and by fax
Hours: Mon to Fri, 0900 to 1700

Group within the:
Chartered Society of Physiotherapy

CHARTERED QUALITY INSTITUTE

Acronym or abbreviation: CQI

12 Grosvenor Crescent, London, SW1X 7EE

Tel: 020 7245 6722
Fax: 020 7245 6788
E-mail: info@thecqi.org

Website:
http://www.thecqi.org

Formerly called:
Institute of Quality Assurance (year of change 2007)

Organisation type and purpose:
Professional body.

Subject coverage:
All aspects of quality assurance and quality management.

Printed publications:
Quality World Monthly Magazine
Order printed publications from: via website

Publications list:
Available in print

Access to staff:
Contact by letter, by telephone, by fax, by e-mail and via website. Appointment necessary.
Hours: Mon to Thu, 0900 to 1700; Fri, 0900 to 1600

Access to building, collection or gallery:
Prior appointment required

Constituent part of:
International Register of Certificated Auditors
    tel: 020 7245 6722; fax: 020 7245 6788; e-mail: iqa@iqa.org

CHARTERED SOCIETY OF DESIGNERS

Acronym or abbreviation: CSD

1 Cedar Court, Royal Oak Yard, Bermondsey Street, London, SE1 3GA

Tel: 020 7357 8088
Fax: 020 7407 9878
E-mail: info@csd.org.uk

Website:
http://www.csd.org.uk

Enquiries:
Enquiries to: Director

Founded:
1930

Formerly called:
Society of Industrial Artists & Designers (year of change 1977)

continued overleaf

Organisation type and purpose:
Professional body (membership is by subscription, qualification, election or invitation). Registered charity (no. 279393).

Subject coverage:
Industrial, product and engineering design, fashion and textile design, interior and exhibition design, graphic design and illustration, professional practice in all the foregoing, design copyright and registration, intellectual property law.

Printed publications:
A Guide to Business Practice: Graphic, Textile, Product and Interior
Chartered Designers Newsletter (6 times a year, free to members)
Introductory Pack
Protecting Your Designs
The Professional Practice of Design

Electronic and video publications:
Electronic forms

Access to staff:
Contact by letter, by fax and by e-mail
Hours: Mon to Fri, 0930 to 1730

Member of:
Bureau of European Designers Association (BEDA)

CHARTERED SOCIETY OF PHYSIOTHERAPY

Acronym or abbreviation: CSP

14 Bedford Row, London, WC1R 4ED

Tel: 020 7306 6666
Fax: 020 7306 6611
E-mail: enquiries@csp.org.uk

Website:
http://www.csp.org.uk
Information on the society and its role. Resources include information papers, online library catalogue, careers information and Physiotherapy Frontline magazine. CSP Members can access the full text of the Physiotherapy Journal.

Enquiries:
Enquiries to: Chief Executive

Founded:
1894

Organisation type and purpose:
Professional body, educational body, trade union (membership is by subscription, qualification), present number of members: 47,000 with 50 groups, research organisation.

Subject coverage:
Physical rehabilitation and therapy, treatment techniques, conditions such as back pain, physiotherapy.

Services for disabled people:
Facilities in the Learning Resource Centre for literature searching, reading documents and accessing the Internet are available for blind, visually impaired, dyslexic and disabled members. These include a scanner and speech synthesis system (Cicero), a magnifier/screen reader (Zoomtext 8.0) and a screen reader (JAWS for windows 8.0). A CCTV is also available.

Museum or gallery collection, archive, or library special collection:
CSP Learning Resource Centre holding 180 English language journals; Society's Journals from 1916; foreign language journals; CSP specific interest group literature; books; documents; theses and dissertations

Non-library collection catalogue:
All or part available in-house

Library catalogue:
All or part available in-house

Printed publications:
Annual Report
Factsheets and Guidelines, mainly for members
Frontline (magazine, 2 a month)

Information papers
Physiotherapy (journal, quarterly)
Standards of Physiotherapy Practice

Electronic and video publications:
Electronic Library on website

Publications list:
Available online and in print

Access to staff:
Contact by letter, by telephone, by fax, by e-mail and via website. Appointment necessary.
Hours: Mon to Fri, 0900 to 1700

Connections with:
Universities for validation of courses

Groups at the same address:
Acupuncture Association of Chartered Physiotherapists
 website: http://www.aacp.uk.com
Aquatic Therapy Association of Chartered Physiotherapists
Association of Chartered Physiotherapists for People with Learning Disabilities
 website: http://www.acppld.org.uk
Association of Chartered Physiotherapists in Animal Therapy
 website: http://www.acpat.org.uk
Association of Chartered Physiotherapists in Cystic Fibrosis
Association of Chartered Physiotherapists in Electrotherapy
Association of Chartered Physiotherapists in Energy Medicine
 website: http://www.energymedphysio.org.uk
Association of Chartered Physiotherapists in Independent Hospitals and Charities
Association of Chartered Physiotherapists in Management
 website: http://www.physiomanagers.org.uk
Association of Chartered Physiotherapists in Occupational Health and Ergonomics
 website: http://www.acpohe.org.uk
Association of Chartered Physiotherapists in Oncology and Palliative Care
 website: http://www.acpopc.org.uk
Association of Chartered Physiotherapists in Orthopaedic Medicine and Injection Therapy
 website: http://www.acpom.org.uk
Association of Chartered Physiotherapists in Reflex Therapy
Association of Chartered Physiotherapists in Respiratory Care
 website: http://www.acprc.org
Association of Chartered Physiotherapists in Sports Medicine
 website: http://www.acpsm.org
Association of Chartered Physiotherapists in the Community
Association of Chartered Physiotherapists in Therapeutic Riding
Association of Chartered Physiotherapists in Vestibular Rehabilitation
Association of Chartered Physiotherapists in Women's Health
 website: http://www.acpwh.org.uk
Association of Chartered Physiotherapists interested in Cardiac Rehabilitation
Association of Chartered Physiotherapists interested in Massage
Association of Chartered Physiotherapists interested in Neurology
 website: http://www.acpin.net
Association of Chartered Physiotherapists working with Older People
 website: http://www.agile-uk.org
Association of Orthopaedic Chartered Physiotherapists
 website: http:// www.aocp.co.uk
Association of Paediatric Chartered Physiotherapists
British Association of Bobath Trained Therapists
 website: http://www.bobath.org.uk/babtt/index.html
British Association of Chartered Physiotherapists in Amputee Rehabilitation
 website: http://www.bacpar.org.uk
British Association of Hand Therapists Ltd
 website: http://www.hand-therapy.co.uk

Chartered Physiotherapists in International Health and Development
Chartered Physiotherapists in Mental Healthcare (CPMH)
 website: http://www.cpmh.org.uk
Chartered Physiotherapists Promoting Continence
 website: http://www.cppc.org.uk
Chartered Physiotherapists working as Extended Scope Practitioners
Craniosacral Therapy Association of Chartered Physiotherapists
 website: http://www.craniosacral.co.uk
Manipulation Association of Chartered Physiotherapists
 website: http://www.macp-online.co.uk
McKenzie Institute Mechanical Diagnosis and Therapy Practitioners
 website: http://www.mckenzieinstitute.co.uk
Medico Legal Association of Chartered Physiotherapists
 website: http://www.mlacp.org.uk
Physio First
 website: http://www.physiofirst.org.uk
Physiotherapy Pain Association for Chartered Physiotherapists
 website: http://www.ppaonline.co.uk
Physiotherapy Research Society
 website: http://www.prs-uk.org/
Rheumatic Care Association of Chartered Physiotherapists
 website: http://www.rheumatology.org.uk

Umbrella group:
Manipulation Association of Chartered Physiotherapists
 website: http://www.macpweb.org

CHARTERED SURVEYORS TRAINING TRUST

Acronym or abbreviation: CSTT

Downstream Building, 1 London Bridge, London SE1 9BG

Tel: 020 7785 3850
Fax: 020 7785 3856
E-mail: cstt@cstt.org.uk

Website:
http://www.cstt.org.uk/

Enquiries:
Enquiries to: Chief Executive

Organisation type and purpose:
Registered charity (charity no. 327456), training organisation.
Training for the professions of the built environment.

Access to staff:
Contact by letter, by telephone, by fax and by e-mail
Hours: Mon to Fri, 0900 to 1700

CHARTERED SURVEYORS' COMPANY

Formal name: Chartered Surveyors' Company

75 Meadway Drive, Horsell, Woking, Surrey, GU21 4TF

Tel: 01483 727113
E-mail: wccsurveyors@btinternet.com

Website:
http://www.surveyorslivery.org.uk

Enquiries:
Enquiries to: The Clerk
Direct tel: 01483 727113
Direct e-mail: wccsurveyors@btinternet.com

Founded:
1977

Organisation type and purpose:
Membership association (membership is by election or invitation).
City of London Livery Company.

Access to staff:
Contact by letter, by telephone, by e-mail and via website

CHATHAM DOCKYARD HISTORICAL SOCIETY

Acronym or abbreviation: CDHS

The Museum of The Royal Dockyard, The Historic Dockyard, Chatham, Kent, ME4 4TZ

Tel: 01634 832028

Enquiries:
Enquiries to: Honorary Secretary
Direct tel: 01634 250647

Founded:
1980

Organisation type and purpose:
Learned society, registered charity (charity number 287263), museum, historic building, house or site, suitable for ages: 8+, research organisation.
To spread the knowledge of the dockyard and promote the museum.

Subject coverage:
To do with history of the Navy and its men, ships etc. Workers and trades in the dockyard.

Information services:
Catalogue in preparation.

Special visitor services:
Guided tours, materials and/or activities for children.

Services for disabled people:
Displays and/or information at wheelchair height.

Museum or gallery collection, archive, or library special collection:
Extensive reference library
Reserve Collection of artefacts in addition to those on show

Printed publications:
Research papers Nos 1 to 26 (available direct):
No. 1 The Royal Marines in Chatham (40p)
No. 2 Convicts in the Dockyard (40p)
No. 3 Chatham Built Submarines (40p)
No. 4 Naval Cannon (40p)
No. 5 Bugler Timmins (15p)
No. 6 HMS Chatham (40p)

Access to staff:
Contact by letter, by telephone and in person
Hours: Mon to Fri, 1030 to 1700

Access to building, collection or gallery:
No prior appointment required
Hours: Apr to end Oct: Daily, 1030 to 1800
Nov, Feb, Mar: Wed, Sat, Sun, 1030 to 1800
Special comments: Closed to the public Dec and Jan.

Access for disabled people:
Parking provided, level entry, toilet facilities

CHELMSFORD BOROUGH COUNCIL

Civic Centre, Duke Street, Chelmsford, Essex, CM1 1JE

Tel: 01245 606606
Fax: 01245 606747
E-mail: mailbox@chelmsfordbc.gov.uk

Website:
http://www.chelmsford bc.gov.uk
General information.

Enquiries:
Enquiries to: Chief Executive
Other contacts: Head of Publicity and Marketing

Organisation type and purpose:
Local government body.

Subject coverage:
All local authority services.

Museum or gallery collection, archive, or library special collection:
Chelmsford Museum
Essex Regiment Museum

Printed publications:
Economic development information
Tourism and Information leaflets (free)

Access to staff:
Contact by letter and by telephone. Appointment necessary.
Hours: Mon to Thu, 0845 to 1645; Fri, 0845 to 1615
Special comments: Closed until 1000 last Wed of month for staff training.

CHELMSFORD CATHEDRAL LIBRARY

The Cathedral Centre, New Street, Chelmsford, Essex, CM1 1TY

Tel: 01245 294489
Fax: 01245 294499
E-mail: office@chelmsfordcathedral.org.uk

Website:
http://www.chelmsfordcathedral.org.uk

Enquiries:
Enquiries to: Librarian
Other contacts: Canon Theologian

Organisation type and purpose:
Voluntary organisation, suitable for ages: adults.
Theological library.
Mainly reference only, together with those Cathedral Archives that are not in the County Record Office.

Subject coverage:
19th- and early 20th-century theology; contemporary works in biblical, liturgical, missionary, ecumenical and behavioural, inter-faith studies; Essex church history.

Museum or gallery collection, archive, or library special collection:
Appointment required to view the collections marked *:
Ante-Nicene Fathers, 10 vols
*Historic Collection
*Essex Church History
*Knightbridge Library (mainly Puritan theology and patristics: 571 vols of 16th and 17th centuries)
Nicene; Past Nicene Fathers, 2 series, 28 vols

Non-library collection catalogue:
All or part available in-house

Library catalogue:
All or part available in-house

Access to staff:
Contact by letter, by telephone, by fax, by e-mail, in person and via website
Hours: Mon to Fri, 0900 to 1600
Special comments: Appointment required for certain collections.

Access to building, collection or gallery:
No prior appointment required
Hours: Mon to Fri, 0900 to 1600
Special comments: Prior appointment is required for Historic and Essex Collections.

Access for disabled people:
Level entry, toilet facilities

Constituent part of:
Chelmsford Cathedral
Cathedral Centre, New Street, Chelmsford, CM1 1TY; tel: 01245 294489; fax: 01245 294499; e-mail: office@chelmsfordcathedral.org.uk; website: http://www.chelmsfordcathedral.org.uk

Member organisation of:
Cathedral Libraries and Archives Associations

CHELSEA PHYSIC GARDEN

66 Royal Hospital Road, London, SW3 4HS

Tel: 020 7352 5646

Fax: 020 7376 3910
E-mail: enquiries@chelseaphysicgarden.co.uk

Website:
http://www.cpgarden.demon.co.uk
Visual promotion of work and activities of the Garden.

Enquiries:
Enquiries to: Curator
Direct tel: 020 7352 5646 ext .3

Founded:
1673

Organisation type and purpose:
Registered charity (charity number 286513), research organisation.
Botanic garden.
Research and education in botany, horticulture especially medicinal plants.

Subject coverage:
Medicinal plants and herbalism, history of plant introductions, history of the Chelsea Physic Garden and its curators.

Services for disabled people:
One wheelchair available to reserve.

Museum or gallery collection, archive, or library special collection:
Library ex Society of Apothecaries
Thomas Moore Clematis Herbarium
Photographic archive of the Chelsea Physic Garden

Non-library collection catalogue:
All or part available in-house

Library catalogue:
All or part available in-house

Printed publications:
Guide Books
Research Publications relating to previous Curators
Seed List (annually)
Work of Garden

Publications list:
Available in print

Access to staff:
Appointment necessary.
Hours: Mon to Fri, 0900 to 1700

Access to building, collection or gallery:
Hours: Public openings: April to October, Wed, Thurs, Fri. 1200 to 1700, Sun and Bank Holidays 1200 to 1800. Members: all year Mon to Fri 0930 to 1700 (or dusk if earlier), Sun 1200 to 1800 April to October.

Access for disabled people:
Through 66 Royal Hospital Road

CHELTENHAM LIBRARY

Clarence Street, Cheltenham, Gloucestershire, GL50 3JT

Tel: 01242 532686/7
Fax: 01242 532684
E-mail: cheltenham.library@gloucestershire.gov.uk

Website:
http://www.gloucestershire.gov.uk
All Gloucestershire libraries, details of Cheltenham special collections.

Enquiries:
Enquiries to: Librarian
Direct tel: 0845 230 5421
Direct e-mail: ask@gloucestershire.gov.uk

Founded:
1897

Organisation type and purpose:
Local government body, public library.

Subject coverage:
General reference, local studies – Cheltenham and environs, art.

continued overleaf

Museum or gallery collection, archive, or library special collection:
Art collection – 6000 items covering fine and applied arts

Library catalogue:
All or part available online

Access to staff:
Contact by letter, by telephone, by fax, by e-mail and in person
Hours: Mon, Wed, Fri, 0900 to 1900; Tue, Thu, 0900 to 1730; Sat, 0900 to 1600

Access for disabled people:
Ramped entry

Member of:
ARLIS

Parent body:
Gloucestershire County Council, Libraries & Information

CHEMICAL INDUSTRIES ASSOCIATION

Acronym or abbreviation: CIA

Kings Buildings, Smith Square, London, SW1P 3JJ

Tel: 020 7834 3399
Fax: 020 7834 4469
E-mail: enquiries@cia.org.uk

Website:
http://www.chemistry-industry.org.uk
Overview of the chemical industry and its products.
http://www.sourcerer.co.uk
Sourcerer, a directory of products and services. News about chemicals.
http://www.cia.org.uk
Overview of the association, its activities and the industry it serves.

Enquiries:
Enquiries to: General Secretary
Other contacts: Head of Media Relations for press enquiries.

Founded:
1965

Organisation type and purpose:
National organisation, advisory body, trade association, membership association (membership is by subscription), present number of members: 200, manufacturing industry, training organisation, publishing house.
Employers' Federation.

Subject coverage:
Chemical and allied industries economic aspects, e.g. production, investment, employees and employment, safety, law, trade, tariffs, statistics; not information on individual companies, technical information limited to the extent of staff expertise. Comprehensive product information on Sourcerer (See Internet home pages), health, safety, and environment.

Printed publications:
Publications dealing with: safety, health and environment, public affairs, community relations, business development, science and technology, employment, schools liaison etc
Directory of Chemical Products and Buyers Guide (annually)
Directory of Chemical Services (annually)
Responsible Care
Guidance manuals, codes of practice, statistics, etc
Order printed publications from: Publications Orders at the same address, fax: 020 7834 4469, e-mail: publications@cia.org.uk

Electronic and video publications:
Audio and video programmes:
Chemicals with Care
Policy Against Pollution
PSGO – Product Stewardship reference and guide (CD-ROM)

Publications list:
Available in print

Access to staff:
Contact by letter, by telephone, by fax, by e-mail and via website. Appointment necessary. Access for members only.
Hours: Mon to Fri, 0900 to 1700
Special comments: No library facilities available. CIA and Sourcerer on www 24 hours a day.

Access to building, collection or gallery:
Prior appointment required

Affiliated associations:
Association of the British Pharmaceutical Industry (ABPI)
  tel: 020 7930 3477; fax: 020 7747 1411
British Aerosol Manufacturers Association (BAMA)
  tel: 020 7828 5111; fax: 020 7834 8436; e-mail: bama@compuserve.com
British Agrochemicals Association (BAA)
  tel: 01733 349225; fax: 01733 562523; e-mail: reception@brit-agro.prestel.co.uk
British Association for Chemical Specialities (BACS)
  tel: 01524 849606; fax: 01524 849194
British Chemical Distributors & Traders Association (BCDTA)
  tel: 020 8686 4545; fax: 020 8686 7768
Fertiliser Manufacturers Association (FMA)
  tel: 01733 331303; fax: 01733 332909
National Sulphuric Acid Association (NSAA)
  tel: 01244 322200; fax: 01224 345155
Picon Ltd
  tel: 01372 824513; fax: 01372 824628
Soap and Detergent Industry Association (SDIA)
  tel: 01444 450884; fax: 01444 450951
Solvents Industry Association (SIA)
  tel: 01206 252268; fax: 01206 252268

Member of:
Confederation of British Industry (CBI)
  tel: 020 7395 8247; fax: 020 7240 1578
European Chemical Industry Council (CEFIC)
  Brussels, Belgium; tel: 00 32 2 676 7211; fax: 00 32 2 676 7300; e-mail: mde@cefic.be

CHERWELL DISTRICT COUNCIL

Bodicote House, Bodicote, Banbury, Oxfordshire, OX15 4AA

Tel: 01295 252535\ Minicom no. 01295 221572
Fax: 01295 270028
E-mail: pat.simpson@cherwell.dc.gov.uk

Website:
http://www.cherwell-dc.gov.uk

Enquiries:
Enquiries to: Communications Manager
Direct tel: 01295 221577
Direct e-mail: pat.simpson@cherwell.dc.gov.uk

Organisation type and purpose:
Local government body.

Subject coverage:
Local government services.

Access to staff:
Contact by letter, by telephone, by fax, by e-mail and via website. Appointment necessary.
Hours: Mon to Thu, 0840 to 1715; Fri, 0840 to 1620

CHESHIRE AND CHESTER ARCHIVES AND LOCAL STUDIES SERVICE

Cheshire Record Office, Duke Street, Chester, Cheshire, CH1 1RL

Tel: 01244 972574
Fax: 01244 973812
E-mail: recordoffice@cheshire.gov.uk

Website:
http://www.cheshire.gov.uk/recordoffice
General information and index of Cheshire wills 1492–1940; publications; online catalogue; tithe maps online; family history pages

Enquiries:
Enquiries to: County Archivist

Founded:
1949

Organisation type and purpose:
Local government body.

Subject coverage:
History of ancient county of Cheshire, development of Cheshire and its communities.

Museum or gallery collection, archive, or library special collection:
Antiquarian Collections
Archives of local authorities, courts, the diocese, parishes, nonconformist churches, private estates and businesses
Central Local Studies Collection includes books, journals, maps, pamphlets, etc.

Non-library collection catalogue:
All or part available online, in-house and in print

Library catalogue:
All or part available online

Printed publications:
Census Indexes of Cheshire 1851, 1881, 1891
Township Packs, selected material from the standard printed sources
Cheshire in the Civil War – A learning resource pack with contemporary documents intended for school use (£7.50 plus 93p p&p)
Cheshire Parish Registers – A summary guide (B. Langston, 2002)
The Ancient Parishes, Townships and Chapelries of Cheshire (booklet and map, F. I. Dunn, £4.50 plus 45p p&p)
Various local history publications

Microform publications:
Directories for Cheshire and Lancashire (some 15, 1789–1924)

Publications list:
Available online and in print

Access to staff:
Contact by letter, by telephone, by fax, by e-mail, in person and via website
Hours: Mon, 1300 to 1700; Tue to Fri, 0900 to 1700; 3rd Sat in month, 0900 to 1600

Access to building, collection or gallery:
Special comments: CARN Readers' Ticket required, booking recommended.

Access for disabled people:
Ramped entry, level entry, access to all public areas, toilet facilities
Special comments: Parking available

Parent body:
Cheshire County Council

CHESHIRE COMMUNITY ACTION

Acronym or abbreviation: CCA

96 Lower Bridge Street, Chester, Cheshire, CH1 1RU

Tel: 01244 323602
Fax: 01244 401036
E-mail: enquiries@cheshireaction.org.uk

Website:
http://www.cheshireaction.org.uk

Enquiries:
Enquiries to: Chief Executive
Direct e-mail: alison.roylance@cheshireaction.org.uk
Other contacts: Assistant Chief Executive

Founded:
1930

Formerly called:
Cheshire Community Council (year of change 2008)

Organisation type and purpose:
Advisory body, membership association (membership is by subscription), voluntary organisation, registered charity (charity number 1074676).

To promote the quality of life in Cheshire communities, especially rural communities.

Subject coverage:
Management and funding of charities and voluntary bodies, community development and voluntary action, rural community services.

Information services:
Community development, grants, funding.

Museum or gallery collection, archive, or library special collection:
Data on rural communities and services in Cheshire
Directories of funding sources
Grantfinder national computer database on funding sources

Printed publications:
Village Halls Newsletter (sample free)
Cheshire Community Action Newsletter (quarterly, by subscription)
Rural Briefings (send an sae)
Annual Report
Order printed publications from: Website, or see contact details

Electronic and video publications:
Order electronic and video publications from: Website

Publications list:
Available online

Access to staff:
Contact by letter, by telephone, by fax, by e-mail, in person and via website. Appointment necessary.
Hours: Mon to Thu, 0900 to 1630; Fri, 0900 to 1600

Access to building, collection or gallery:
Hours: Mon to Fri, 0900 to 1700
Special comments: Parking can be a problem.

Access for disabled people:
No disabled access
Special comments: Stairs; no lifts or ramps.

Also at:
Satellite office
Unit 20, Blakemere Craft Centre, Chester Road, Sandiway, Cheshire, CW8 2EB

Parent body:
ACRE (Action with Communities in Rural England)
Somerford Court, Somerford Road, Cirencester, Gloucestershire, GL7 1TW

CHESHIRE COUNTY COUNCIL

Acronym or abbreviation: EDS

Economic Development & Environment Policy Service, County Hall, Chester, Cheshire, CH1 1SF

Tel: 01244 602624
Fax: 01244 603003
E-mail: econdev@cheshire.gov.uk

Website:
http://www.cheshire.gov.uk/edubus

Enquiries:
Enquiries to: Economic Information Officer

Founded:
1989

Organisation type and purpose:
Local government body, research organisation.

Subject coverage:
Economic development; small business; statistics; training; Europe; company information sectors, tourism.

Printed publications:
Cheshire Property Market Assessment
Directory of Information Sources
Business Parks

Electronic and video publications:
Online Business Directory

Publications list:
Available online and in print

Access to staff:
Contact by letter, by telephone, by fax, by e-mail, in person and via website. Appointment necessary.
Hours: Mon to Thu, 0900 to 1700; Fri, 0900 to 1630

CHESHIRE COUNTY COUNCIL RESEARCH LIBRARY

Room 243, County Hall, Chester, Cheshire, CH1 1SF

Tel: 01244 602246
Fax: 01244 602754
E-mail: researchlib@cheshire.gov.uk

Website:
http://www.cheshire.gov.uk
Basic information about Cheshire.

Enquiries:
Enquiries to: Senior Librarian
Direct tel: 01244 602247
Direct e-mail: shannonm@cheshire.gov.uk
Other contacts: Librarian for legal, education.

Founded:
1972

Formerly called:
Cheshire County Information and Records Service (CCIRS) (year of change 1998)

Organisation type and purpose:
Local government body, public library.
Local information service of Cheshire County Council.

Subject coverage:
Local government, education, law, finance, social services, environmental planning.

Printed publications:
Review Series: Current awareness bulletins (monthly)
Todays Press: Newspaper cutting service (daily)

Access to staff:
Contact by letter, by telephone, by fax, by e-mail and via website
Hours: Mon to Fri, 0900 to 1700

Access to building, collection or gallery:
Prior appointment required

Information service of the:
Cheshire Libraries and Archives Department

CHESHIRE LIBRARIES

Macclesfield Library, Jordangate, Macclesfield, Cheshire, SK10 1EE

Tel: 01625 374000
Fax: 01625 612818
E-mail: macclesfield.infopoint@cheshire.gov.uk

Formerly called:
Cheshire Libraries and Archives

Organisation type and purpose:
Local government body, public library.

Subject coverage:
Full range of general reference and information from local to international, e.g. community, business, travel, law, leisure.

Museum or gallery collection, archive, or library special collection:
Collection of books written by, and with paintings or drawings by, Charles F. Tunnicliffe, bird artist
Extensive local history collection including works on the Silk Industry of Macclesfield

Library catalogue:
All or part available online

Access to staff:
Contact by letter, by telephone, by fax, by e-mail, in person and via website
Hours: Mon, Tue, Thu, 0930 to 1900; Wed, Fri, 0930 to 1700; Sat, 0900 to 1300

Access to building, collection or gallery:
No access other than to staff

Access for disabled people:
Level entry, access to all public areas, toilet facilities

Headquarters address:
Cheshire County Council
Libraries and Culture, Room 286, County Hall, Chester, CH1 1SF

CHESHIRE MUSEUMS SERVICE

162 London Road, Northwich, Cheshire, CW9 8AB

Tel: 01606 271640
Fax: 01606 350420
E-mail: cheshiremuseums@cheshire.gov.uk

Website:
http://www.saltmuseum.org.uk

Enquiries:
Enquiries to: Heritage and Museums Officer

Founded:
1974

Organisation type and purpose:
Local government body, museum.

Subject coverage:
Archaeology and field monuments, excavations at Northwich and Middlewich, museology, curatorship, history of the salt industry.

Museum or gallery collection, archive, or library special collection:
Main collections relate to the industrial and social history of Mid-Cheshire with particular emphasis on salt. Material held ranges from industrial equipment, packaging, domestic items and art, to photographs, also archaeological excavation archives for Cheshire, excluding Chester district

Non-library collection catalogue:
All or part available in-house

Publications list:
Available online and in print

Access to staff:
Contact by letter, by telephone and by e-mail
Hours: Mon to Fri, 0900 to 1700

Access for disabled people:
Parking provided, ramped entry, toilet facilities lift access to first floor

Administers:
Salt Museum
Stretton Watermill

CHEST, HEART & STROKE SCOTLAND

Acronym or abbreviation: CHSS

65 North Castle Street, Edinburgh, EH2 3LT

Tel: 0131 225 6963
Fax: 0131 220 6313
E-mail: admin@chss.org.uk

Website:
http://www.chss.org.uk

Enquiries:
Enquiries to: Finance Director

Founded:
1959

Formerly called:
Chest Heart and Stroke Association (year of change 1991)

Organisation type and purpose:
Registered charity (charity number SC 018761).

Information services:
Advice Line, tel: 0845 077 6000

Printed publications:
Order printed publications from: Website, e-mail or telephone

Publications list:
Available online and in print

continued overleaf

Access to building, collection or gallery:
No access other than to staff

Regional Offices:
Glasgow
  tel: 0141 633 1666
Inverness
  tel: 01463 713433

CHESTER COMMUNITY HISTORY & HERITAGE

Formal name: Chester Community History & Heritage
Acronym or abbreviation: CHH

St Michael's Church, Bridge Street Row East, Chester, Cheshire, CH1 1NW

Tel: 01244 402110
Fax: 01244 312243
E-mail: e.stewart@chester.gov.uk

Website:
http://www.chester.gov.uk/heritage/history/home
.html
Chester history and heritage
http://www.chester.gov.uk/heritage/history/family
-history.html
Internet tutorials for family history enthusiasts.
1901 Census vouchers for sale
http://www.chesterimagebank.com
Image Bank online

Enquiries:
Enquiries to: Community Heritage Officer

Founded:
2000

Formerly called:
Chester Archives, Chester City Record Office (year of change 2000)

Organisation type and purpose:
Local government body, suitable for ages: all.

Subject coverage:
Family history, local history, community history, conservation archaeology.

Information services:
Library available for reference (for conditions see Access above); Guided tours for parties – walks and talks.

Special visitor services:
Materials and/or activities for children.

Education services:
Group education facilities, resources for Key Stages 1 and 2.

Museum or gallery collection, archive, or library special collection:
General Register Office Index 1837–1969
Census for Chester District 1841–1901
1881 census for UK
Electoral registers for Chester, IGI for Cheshire, Lancashire, Shropshire, Staffordshire, Derbyshire and Wales.
Parish registers for Chester
Local newspapers, maps
Chester photographic survey team, street by street ongoing record since 1950s with some early photographs
Local history library
Archaeological library

Printed publications:
Books, pamphlets and leaflets on Chester and surrounding district including:
Our House
History of the ROWS
Tudor Chester
Millennium Trail of Chester
History of Chester (Ormerod G)

Electronic and video publications:
Chester Revealed (CD-ROM)

Access to staff:
Contact by letter, by telephone, by fax, by e-mail and in person

Hours: Mon to Thu, 1000 to 1600

Access to building, collection or gallery:
Hours: Mon to Thu, 1000 to 1600

CHESTER-LE-STREET AND CITY OF DURHAM ENTERPRISE AGENCY

Acronym or abbreviation: CDC Enterprise Agency

7 Millennium Place, Durham City, DH1 1WA

Tel: 0191 384 5407
Fax: 0191 386 3934
E-mail: enquiries@cdcbp.org.uk

Website:
http://www.cdcbp.org.uk

Enquiries:
Enquiries to: Chief Executive

Founded:
1986

Organisation type and purpose:
Voluntary organisation, consultancy, training organisation.
Business advice, information and training.

Subject coverage:
Business information.

Printed publications:
Available free

Access to staff:
Contact by letter, by telephone, by fax, by e-mail, in person and via website. Appointment necessary.
Hours: Mon to Fri, 0900 to 1700

Access for disabled people:
Ramped entry, full disabled access

Also at:
Chester-le-Street and City of Durham Enterprise Agency
  Mile House, Newcastle Road, Chester-le-Street, Co Durham, DH3 3RA; tel: 0191 389 2648; fax: 0191 387 1684; e-mail: enquiries@cdcbp.org.uk

Links with:
Chester-le-Street District Council
  tel: 0191 387 1919
Durham City Council
  tel: 0191 386 6111

CHESTERFIELD BOROUGH COUNCIL

Acronym or abbreviation: CBC

Town Hall, Chesterfield, Derbyshire, S40 1LP

Tel: 01246 345345
Fax: 01246 345252
E-mail: info@chesterfieldbc.gov.uk

Website:
http://www.chesterfieldbc.gov.uk
Details of Chesterfield Council services, economic development, tourism.

Enquiries:
Enquiries to: Public Relations Manager

Organisation type and purpose:
Local government body.

Subject coverage:
Local government services and amenities.

Printed publications:
A-Z of Council Services
Chesterfield Tourist Guide
Community Housing News (twice a year)
Our Town (newspaper, 4 times a year, free)

Access to staff:
Contact by letter, by e-mail and via website
Hours: Mon to Fri, 0900 to 1700

CHESTERFIELD LIBRARY

New Beetwell Street, Chesterfield, Derbyshire, S40 1QN

Tel: 01246 209292\ Minicom no. 01246 229538
Fax: 01246 209304
E-mail: chesterfield.library@derbyshire.gov.uk

Website:
http://www.derbyshire.gov.uk/librar/
librarysystem.htm
Not all local studies materials included otherwise comprehensive.

Enquiries:
Enquiries to: District Librarian

Organisation type and purpose:
Local government body, public library.

Subject coverage:
Marketing information, disabled services, music and drama.

Museum or gallery collection, archive, or library special collection:
Asa Lees collection (dogs, especially s.c. fox terriers): a collection of printed items (including Kennel Gazette 1880–1973 and Stud Book 1859–1973) and manuscript correspondence, pedigrees and show reports
Stephenson Collection (railway history)

Non-library collection catalogue:
All or part available online

Library catalogue:
All or part available online

Access for disabled people:
Level entry, access to all public areas, toilet facilities

CHESTERTON LTD

10 Gillingham Street, London, SW1V 1HJ

Tel: 020 3040 8240

Website:
http://www.chesterton.co.uk
Details of range of services offered by Chesterton, commercial properties in United Kingdom, job vacancies.

Enquiries:
Enquiries to: Senior Information Officer

Organisation type and purpose:
Service industry, consultancy.
Commercial Company.
Property agents and consultants.

Subject coverage:
Property, including offices, retail, industrial, residential, leisure, investment, UK, Europe, USA, Japan, South East Asia, companies.

Library catalogue:
All or part available in-house

Printed publications:
Commercial Property Bulletin (available on a monthly basis by email)
Licensed Leisure Bulletin (available on a quarterly basis by email)
Retailer News Property Bulletin (available on a quarterly basis by email)
Banking & Finance Property Bulletin (available on a quarterly basis by email)
Various Property related research reports – details on application

Publications list:
Available online

Access to staff:
Contact by letter, by telephone, by fax and by e-mail
Hours: Mon to Fri, 0900 to 1730

Access to building, collection or gallery:
No prior appointment required

Other addresses:
Chesterton Ltd
    Head Office, 54 Brook Street, London, W1A 2BU;
    tel: 020 7499 0404; fax: 020 7629 7804

CHESTERTON SOCIETY, THE

11 Lawrence Leys, Bloxham, Near Banbury,
Oxfordshire, OX15 4NU

Tel: 01295 720869\ 07766 711984 (Mobile)
Fax: 01295 720869
E-mail: roberthughes11@talktalk.net@onetel.com

Enquiries:
Enquiries to: Honorary Secretary

Founded:
1964

Organisation type and purpose:
International organisation, national organisation,
learned society (membership is by subscription),
present number of members: 1500, voluntary
organisation.
To inform and educate members on the writing of
G K Chesterton.

Subject coverage:
Words and writings of G K Chesterton.

Non-library collection catalogue:
All or part available in-house and in print

Library catalogue:
All or part available in-house and in print

Printed publications:
The G K Chesterton Quarterly (for purchase)
Order printed publications from: Secretary,
Chesterton Society
As main address

Publications list:
Available in print

Access to staff:
Contact by letter, by telephone, by fax, by e-mail
and in person
Hours: Any reasonable time

CHETHAM'S LIBRARY

Long Millgate, Manchester, M3 1SB

Tel: 0161 834 7961
Fax: 0161 839 5797
E-mail: librarian@chethams.org.uk

Website:
http://www.chethams.org.uk
Archival finding aids.

Enquiries:
Enquiries to: Librarian
Other contacts: Archivist (for archival enquiries);
Senior Librarian (for systems)

Founded:
1653

Organisation type and purpose:
Registered charity (charity number DG/526702C-1/
E), museum, historic building, house or site.
Free public library, founded in 1653, for research
and consultation.

Subject coverage:
History and topography of the North-West of
England, rare books.

**Museum or gallery collection, archive, or library
special collection:**
Archival Collections re Manchester
Halliwell-Phillipps Collection of broadsides
History of Lancashire and Cheshire
Incunabula
John Byrom's Collection

Non-library collection catalogue:
All or part available online

Library catalogue:
All or part available online

Printed publications:
A Catalogue of Proclamations, Broadsides, Ballads,
    and Poems, presented to the Chetham Library by
    James O. Halliwell (Phillipps) (London, privately
    printed, 1851)
A Catalogue of the Collection of Tracts for and
    against Popery (published in or about the reign
    of James II) in the Manchester Library founded
    by Humphrey Chetham (Thomas Jones ed.,
    Manchester, 1859–65, 2 vols, Chetham Society,
    Original Series, 48 and 64)
A Catalogue of the Library of John Byrom
    (Compiled by B. B. B. R. Wheatley, privately
    printed, 1848)
A selection from the list of historical manuscripts
    in the Chetham Library (compiled in 1930 by G.
    H. Tupling, in Bulletin of the Institute of
    Historical Research, vol. X (1932–33), pp. 69–72)
Bibliothecae Chethamensis Catalogus (Manchester,
    1701–1883, 6 vols)
Catalogue of the John Radcliffe Collection
    (compiled by C. T. E. Phillips, Manchester, 1937)

Access to staff:
Contact by letter, by telephone, by fax and by e-
mail. Appointment necessary.
Hours: Mon to Fri, 0930 to 1630

Access for disabled people:
Parking provided, ramped entry

CHEVIOT SHEEP SOCIETY

Holm Cottage, Langholm, Dumfries & Galloway,
DG13 0JP

Tel: 013873 80222

Website:
http://www.cheviotsheep.org

Enquiries:
Enquiries to: General Secretary

Organisation type and purpose:
Membership association (membership is by
subscription), present number of members: 114,
registered charity.
To promote and encourage the breeding of Cheviot
sheep.

Subject coverage:
South country Cheviot sheep; record of ram
pedigrees.

Printed publications:
British Sheep Book (8th ed., pub. National Sheep
    Association)
Flock Book (annually, includes list of members, for
    members only)
Information booklets and pamphlets

Member of:
National Sheep Association
    The Sheep Centre, Malvern, Worcestershire

CHICHESTER CHAMBER OF COMMERCE & INDUSTRY

Acronym or abbreviation: CCCI

3 Chapel Street, Chichester, West Sussex, PO19
1BU

Tel: 01243 531765
Fax: 01243 531765
E-mail: office@chichestercci.org.uk

Enquiries:
Enquiries to: Membership Secretary

Founded:
1970

Organisation type and purpose:
Advisory body, membership association
(membership is by subscription), voluntary
organisation.

Subject coverage:
Local business information.

Printed publications:
Chichester Business News
Chichester Chamber Business Directory

Access to staff:
Contact by letter, by telephone, by fax and by e-
mail. Appointment necessary.
Hours: Mon to Fri, 0900 to 1700

CHICHESTER DISTRICT COUNCIL

East Pallant House, 1 East Pallant, Chichester, West
Sussex, PO19 1TY

Tel: 01243 785166
Fax: 01243 776766
E-mail: helpline@chichester.gov.uk

Website:
http://www.chichester.gov.uk

Enquiries:
Enquiries to: Information Services Officer
Direct tel: 01243 534679

Founded:
1974

Organisation type and purpose:
Local government body.

Subject coverage:
Archaeology in Chichester district, tourist
information, local government information,
business information, housing needs,
environmental health, waste management,
recycling, development control and building
control, council tax, business and economic
development.

Trade and statistical information:
Local business information (including statistics),
local tourism information (including statistics),
crime audit information (including statistics).

Printed publications:
Initiatives – the magazine of Chichester District
    Council
Archaeological Report
Community Safety Strategy
Chichester District Community Plan
Business Directory
Tourism Leaflet/Guide
Order printed publications from: Information Services
Officer, Chichester District Council
tel: 01234 534679

Electronic and video publications:
Initiatives (tape, free, for the partially sighted)

Access to staff:
Contact by letter, by telephone, by fax and by e-
mail
Hours: Mon to Thu, 0845 to 1710; Fri, 0845 to 1700

Access for disabled people:
Parking provided, ramped entry, level entry, toilet
facilities

Other area offices:
Midhurst Area Office
    North Street, Midhurst, West Sussex, GU29
    9DW; tel: 01730 812251
Petworth Area Office
    The Old Bakery, Golden Square, Petworth, West
    Sussex, GU28 0AP; tel: 01798 342241

CHILD ACCIDENT PREVENTION TRUST

Acronym or abbreviation: CAPT

22–26 Farringdon Lane, London, EC1R 3AJ

Tel: 020 7608 3828
Fax: 020 7608 3674
E-mail: safe@capt.org.uk

Website:
http://www.capt.org.uk

Founded:
1981

Organisation type and purpose:
Advisory body, voluntary organisation, registered
charity (charity number 1053549), consultancy,
research organisation.

continued overleaf

Researches childhood accidents, examines modes of prevention, promotes the importance of a child's safe environment, spreads information about nature and prevention of accidents to children and young people.

Subject coverage:
Prevention of children's accidents, child development, child's environment, road accidents, home accidents, leisure accidents, injury types (burns, scalds, poisonings, falls, suffocations, etc.), accident prevention (United Kingdom, international), product safety, accident prevention and health services, safety education, accident compensation and post-accident disability.

Publications list:
Available in print

Access to staff:
Contact by letter, by telephone, by fax and via website. Appointment necessary.
Hours: Mon to Fri, 0930 to 1700

CHILD BEREAVEMENT CHARITY

Acronym or abbreviation: CBC

Aston House, High Street, West Wycombe, Buckinghamshire, HP14 3AG

Tel: 01494 446648 (information and support)
Fax: 01494 440057
E-mail: enquiries@childbereavement.org.uk

Website:
http://www.childbereavement.org.uk

Enquiries:
Enquiries to: Chief Executive

Founded:
1994

Formerly called:
Child Bereavement Trust (year of change 2007)

Organisation type and purpose:
Supporting families, educating professionals

Subject coverage:
The Child Bereavement Charity provides support to families and professionals when a child dies or when a child is bereaved of someone important in their lives. Services offered include a support and information line, interactive website with a Families and Professionals Forum, resources and Professionals Training Programme.

Information services:
Support and information for bereaved families and the professionals who care for them.

Education services:
Educating professionals and offering bereavement training in schools

Museum or gallery collection, archive, or library special collection:
Resources include DVDs, CD-ROMs, books, leaflets, research

Printed publications:
Resources available from www.childbereavement.org.uk

Publications list:
Available online and in print

Access to staff:
Contact by letter, by telephone, by fax, by e-mail and via website. Appointment necessary.
Hours: Mon to Fri, 0900 to 1700

Access to building, collection or gallery:
No access other than to staff

Access for disabled people:
Parking provided

CHILD DEATH HELPLINE

York House, 37 Queen Square, London, WC1N 3BH

Tel: 0800 282986 (helpline)
Fax: 020 7813 8516

E-mail: contact@childdeathhelpline.org

Website:
http://www.childdeathhelpline.org.uk

Enquiries:
Enquiries to: Head of Department
Direct tel: 020 7813 8551
Other contacts: Administrator

Founded:
1995

Organisation type and purpose:
Voluntary organisation.
A national freephone service for all those affected by the death of a child of any age, from pre-birth to adult, under any circumstances, however recently or long ago.

Subject coverage:
Support for those bereaved by the death of a child whether recent or many years ago.

Printed publications:
Information Pack

Publications list:
Available online and in print

Access to staff:
Contact by letter, by telephone, by fax and by e-mail
Hours: Mon to Fri, 0900 to 1700
Special comments: Helpline open: Mon, Thu and Fri, 1000 to 1300 and 1900 to 2200; Tue and Wed, 1000 to 1600 and 1900 to 2200

Also at:
Child Death Helpline Department
Great Ormond Street Hospital NHS Trust, London, WC1N 3JH; tel: 020 7813 8551; fax: 020 7813 8516
The Alder Centre
Alder Hey Children's Hospital, Eaton Road, Liverpool, L12 2AP; tel: 0151 252 5391; fax: 0151 252 5513

CHILD GROWTH FOUNDATION

Acronym or abbreviation: CGF

2 Mayfield Avenue, Chiswick, London, W4 1PW

Tel: 020 8994 7625 or 8995 0257
Fax: 020 8995 9075
E-mail: cgflondon@aol.com

Website:
http://www.heightmatters.org.uk
General information on growth, assessing appropriateness.
http://www.tss.org.uk
Turner Syndrome, assessing appropriateness.

Enquiries:
Enquiries to: Administrator

Founded:
1977

Organisation type and purpose:
Membership association (membership is by subscription), present number of members: 1100, registered charity (charity number 274325).
Parent support and to promote public and professional awareness of growth and growth related problems.

Subject coverage:
All aspects of growth disorders and related problems, including Silver Russell Syndrome; Soto's Syndrome; Turner's Syndrome; growth hormone deficiency and insufficiency, multiple pituitary hormone deficiency, achondroplasia and bone dysplasias, premature sexual maturation, intrauterine growth retardation.

Printed publications:
Baby Check (a checklist to determine whether babies up to six months old need medical attention)
Leaflets for all growth disorders
Newsletter (2 times a year, members, annual membership UK £15, overseas £22.50)

Publications list:
Available in print

Access to staff:
Contact by letter, by telephone and by fax
Hours: Mon to Fri, 0900 to 1600

CHILD POVERTY ACTION GROUP

Acronym or abbreviation: CPAG

94 White Lion Street, London, N1 9PF

Tel: 020 7837 7979
Fax: 020 7837 6414
E-mail: staff@cpag.co.uk

Website:
http://www.cpag.org.uk

Enquiries:
Enquiries to: Information Officer

Founded:
1965

Organisation type and purpose:
Membership association (membership is by subscription), voluntary organisation, registered charity (charity number 294841), training organisation, research organisation, publishing house.
Promotes action for relief of poverty among families with children.

Subject coverage:
Poverty in the United Kingdom; social policy and administration; welfare rights and benefits; social security; children; social security law, appeals and reviews.

Museum or gallery collection, archive, or library special collection:
CPAG Library

Library catalogue:
All or part available in-house

Printed publications:
Child Support Handbook (annual)
Benefits for Students Handbook
Poverty Journal
Housing Benefit and Council Tax Legislation
Welfare Rights Bulletin (6 times a year)
Paying for Care Handbook
Welfare Benefits and Tax Credits Handbook (annual)
Order printed publications from: CPAG

Electronic and video publications:
Welfare Benefits and Tax Credits Handbook (CD-ROM, online)

Publications list:
Available online and in print

Access to staff:
Contact by letter, by telephone, by fax and by e-mail. Appointment necessary.
Hours: Mon to Fri, 0900 to 1700

Access to building, collection or gallery:
Prior appointment required
Hours: Mon to Fri, 0900 to 1700

Access for disabled people:
Parking provided, ramped entry, access to all public areas, toilet facilities
Hours: Mon to Fri, 0900 to 1700

Also at:
Child Poverty Action Group in Scotland
Unit 9, Ladywell, 94 Duke St, Glasgow, G4 0UW; tel: 0141 552 3303; fax: 0141 552 4404; e-mail: staff@cpagscotland.org.uk

Links with:
Citizens' Rights Office
Department for Welfare Benefits and Tax Credits, at the same address

CHILD PSYCHOTHERAPY TRUST

Acronym or abbreviation: CPT

Star House, 104–108 Grafton Road, Kentish Town, London, NW5 4BD

Tel: 020 7284 1355
Fax: 020 7284 2755
E-mail: cpt@globalnet.co.uk

Website:
http://www.childpsychotherapytrust.org.uk

Enquiries:
Enquiries to: Administrator

Founded:
1987

Organisation type and purpose:
Voluntary organisation, registered charity (charity number 327361).
Provide information on children's behaviour and emotional development, promote understanding of psychoanalytic work, promote the training of child psychotherapists, and increase the access of children in need of help to child psychotherapy provision.

Subject coverage:
Concerned with providing information about child psychotherapy within the National Health Service. Child and adolescent mental health, emotional and behavioural problems, and supporting psychotherapists through providing training awards.

Library catalogue:
All or part available in-house

Printed publications:
The Child Psychotherapy Review (newsletter, subscription)
Putting child psychotherapy on the map (booklet)
Won't they just grow out of it? (factsheet)
Attending to difficult behaviour (leaflet)
Crying and sleeping (leaflet)
Divorce and separation (leaflet)
Separations in early years (leaflet)
Sibling rivalry (leaflet)
Tempers and tears (leaflet)
Your new baby, your family and you (leaflet)
Key Stages in Your Child's Emotional Development (booklet)

Electronic and video publications:
Won't they just grow out of it? (video)

Publications list:
Available in print

Access to staff:
Contact by letter, by telephone, by fax and by e-mail
Hours: Mon to Fri, 0900 to 1700

CHILDLINE

2nd Floor, Royal Mail Building, Studd Street, London, N1 0QW

Tel: 020 7239 1000 (Admin only)
Fax: 020 7239 1001 (Admin only)
E-mail: info@childline.org.uk (Admin only)

Website:
http://www.childline.org.uk

Enquiries:
Enquiries to: Executive Director
Other contacts: Information Officer

Founded:
1986

Organisation type and purpose:
Voluntary organisation, registered charity (charity number 1003758).
To provide help and support to children and young people in trouble or danger. It also brings to public attention issues affecting children's welfare and rights.

Subject coverage:
ChildLine is the free, national helpline for children and young people in danger and distress. It provides a confidential phone counselling service for any child with any problem 24 hours a day, every day. It listens, comforts and protects. Trained counsellors provide support and advice, and refer children in danger to appropriate helping agencies. ChildLine also raises public awareness of issues affecting children's welfare and rights.

Printed publications:
A selection of literature related to trauma in youg people, including:
Beyond the Limit – Children who live with parental alcohol misuse (Houston A, Kork S, Macleod M)
No Home and Alone – Runaway and homeless young people calling ChildLine (Keep G)
Saving Young Lives – Calls to ChildLine about Suicide (McConville B)

Publications list:
Available online and in print

CHILDLINK ADOPTION SOCIETY

10 Lion Yard, Tremadoc Road, Clapham, London, SW4 7NQ

Tel: 020 7501 1700
Fax: 020 7498 1791
E-mail: enquires@adoptchildlink.org.uk

Website:
http://www.adoptchildlink.org.uk

Enquiries:
Enquiries to: Administrator

Founded:
1913

Formerly called:
Church Adoption Society (year of change 1990)

Organisation type and purpose:
Voluntary organisation, registered charity (charity number 211419).
Adoption.

Subject coverage:
Adoption; counselling for children, parents and adopters; relevant childcare.

Printed publications:
Brochure
Newsletter

Access to staff:
Contact by letter, by telephone, by fax, by e-mail and via website
Hours: Mon to Fri, 0930 to 1700

Access to building, collection or gallery:
No access other than to staff

CHILDREN 1ST

83 Whitehouse Loan, Edinburgh, EH9 1AT

Tel: 0131 446 2300
Fax: 0131 446 2339
E-mail: info@children1st.org.uk

Website:
http://www.children1st.org.uk

Enquiries:
Enquiries to: Chief Executive

Founded:
1884

Organisation type and purpose:
Voluntary organisation (charity number SCO 16092).

Subject coverage:
Child protection, child abuse and neglect, parent support.

Printed publications:
Factsheets (also available online)

Access to staff:
Contact by letter, by telephone, by e-mail and via website. Appointment necessary.
Hours: Mon to Fri, 0900 to 1700

Links with:
NSPCC
tel: 020 7825 2500

CHILDREN IN SCOTLAND

Princes House, 5 Shandwick Place, Edinburgh, EH2 4RG

Tel: 0131 228 8484
Fax: 0131 228 8585
E-mail: info@childreninscotland.org.uk

Website:
http://www.childreninscotland.org.uk/children

Enquiries:
Enquiries to: Information & Publications Manager

Formerly called:
Scottish Child and Family Alliance

Organisation type and purpose:
Membership association (membership is by subscription), present number of members: 320, voluntary organisation, registered charity (charity number SCO 03527).
National coordinating agency of over 300 members who work with children and families throughout Scotland.

Subject coverage:
Information relevant to children and families in Scotland, e.g. education, welfare, health, services, special needs, early years and rural development.

Printed publications:
Publications catalogue available on application

Publications list:
Available online and in print

Access to staff:
Contact by letter, by telephone, by fax, by e-mail and via website. Appointment necessary.
Hours: Mon to Fri, 0900 to 1700

Affiliated to:
Children in Wales
National Children's Bureau

CHILDREN LAW UK

44 Queen Anne Street, London, W1G 8HG

Tel: 020 7224 3566
Fax: 020 7224 3577
E-mail: info@childrenlawuk.org.uk

Enquiries:
Enquiries to: Secretary

Founded:
1974

Formerly called:
British Juvenile and Family Courts Society (BJFCS) (year of change 2001)

Organisation type and purpose:
Registered charity (charity number 265966).
Working for children and families in legal proceedings throughout the UK.
We aim to inform and educate professionals, to commission research and disseminate findings and to enrich national policy development in order to foster a judicial process that works in the interests of children, young people, families and the wider community.

Subject coverage:
Forum for information and debate on national and international policy and practice; best European practice and research; authoritative and independent contribution to youth and family court policy across the UK.

Access to staff:
Contact by letter, by telephone, by fax and by e-mail
Hours: Mon to Fri, 0900 to 1700

Affiliated to:
The International Association of Juvenile and Family Court Magistrates

CHILDREN WITH AIDS CHARITY

Acronym or abbreviation: CWAC

continued overleaf

Calvert House, 5 Calvert Avenue, London
E2 7JP

Tel: 020 7033 8620
Fax: 020 7739 3902
E-mail: info@cwac.org

Website:
http://www.cwac.org
News and events website.

Enquiries:
Enquiries to: Administrator
Other contacts: (1) Transport Co-ordinator (2)
Grants Administrator for (1) transport information
(2) Hardship Fund enquiries.

Founded:
1992

Organisation type and purpose:
Membership association (membership is by
subscription), present number of members: 100,
voluntary organisation, registered charity (charity
number 1027816), suitable for ages: under 18.
Leaflets, videos and resources available re
paediatric HIV in the UK.

Subject coverage:
Medicine, HIV/Aids.

Non-library collection catalogue:
All or part available in-house

Library catalogue:
All or part available in-house

Printed publications:
Booklet on Disclosure
Talking with Children about Illness and HIV
(£2.50)
Voices of Young People (£3.50)

Electronic and video publications:
Problem video (for 7 to 10 year olds, HIV
transmission and hygiene)
The Cloakroom video (for all teenagers on keeping
secrets)
HIV: Risky Business (for 12–15 year olds, on HIV
transmission)

Access to staff:
Contact by letter, by telephone, by fax and by e-
mail. Appointment necessary.
Hours: Mon to Fri, 1000 to 1700

Access to building, collection or gallery:
No access other than to staff
Special comments: HIV Resources Library.

CHILDREN WITH LEUKAEMIA TRUST

51 Great Ormond Street, London, WC1N 3JQ

Tel: 020 7404 0808
Fax: 020 7404 3666
E-mail: info@leukaemia.org

Website:
http://www.leukaemia.org.uk/

Enquiries:
Enquiries to: Media Enquiries
Direct e-mail: tina@tinapriceconsultants.com

Founded:
1991

Part of:
Cancer and Leukaemia in Childhood (CLIC), date
of change, October 1998

Organisation type and purpose:
Voluntary organisation, registered charity (charity
number 1035538).

Subject coverage:
Leukaemia in children.

Access to staff:
Contact by letter, by telephone and by fax
Hours: Mon to Fri, 0900 to 1700

CHILDREN'S AID DIRECT

c/o Ray McElroy, Concern, Camden Street, Dublin
2, Ireland

Tel: 353 1 417 7700

Website:
http://www.cad.org.uk
Overseas programmes, appeals, mountain
challenge events.

Enquiries:
Enquiries to: Communications Manager
Direct e-mail: enquiries@cad.tele2.co.uk

Founded:
1990

Formerly called:
Feed the Children (year of change 1996)

Organisation type and purpose:
Registered charity (charity number 803236).
International aid agency.

Subject coverage:
Children in North Korea, Burundi, Kosovo,
Liberia, Azerbaijan, Albania, Sierra Leone,
Tajikistan, Macedonia, Afghanistan.

Access to staff:
Contact by letter, by telephone, by fax, by e-mail
and via website. Appointment necessary.
Hours: Mon to Fri, 0900 to 1700

CHILDREN'S CLINIC AT DOLPHIN HOUSE

Formal name: Dolphin House Children's Clinic

14 New Road, Brighton, East Sussex, BN1 1UF

Tel: 01273 324790
Fax: 01273 729491
E-mail: info@thechildrensclinic.org.uk

Enquiries:
Enquiries to: Practice Manager

Founded:
1983

Formerly called:
Foundation for Traditional Medicine

Organisation type and purpose:
Registered charity (charity number 288174),
suitable for ages: 0 to 18.
Only registered charity in the UK which focuses on
providing a comprehensive range of
complementary therapies to babies, children and
young people, regardless of family means, mainly
focusing on familes and children who are socially
and economically excluded.

Subject coverage:
Complementary therapies for children: treating
children with acupuncture, homoeopathy,
paediatric/cranial osteopathy, creative art therapy,
nutritional advice, herbal medicine, reflexology,
healing.

Access to staff:
Contact by letter, by telephone, by fax and in
person
Hours: Mon to Sat, 0900 to 1730

CHILDREN'S LEGAL CENTRE

Acronym or abbreviation: CLC

The University of Essex, Wivenhoe Park,
Colchester, Essex, CO4 3SQ

Tel: 01206 872466 (administration)
Fax: 01206 874026
E-mail: clc@essex.ac.uk

Website:
http://www.childrenslegalcentre.com

Enquiries:
Enquiries to: Director
Direct tel: 01206 872561

Founded:
1981

Organisation type and purpose:
Advisory body, registered charity (charity number
281222).
Independent national charity concerned with law
and policy affecting children and young people.
To give free and confidential advice for children,
young people and their advisers, on any aspect of
children's legal rights; to lobby for changes in the
law.

Subject coverage:
Law and policy affecting children and young
people in England and Wales, welfare and rights of
children and young people.

Printed publications:
Childright (a bulletin of law and policy affecting
children and young people, 10 times a year, £60
to institutions, £50 to individuals)
Legal guides and information sheets (21 titles)
Reports and handbooks (12 titles)
Working with Young People (£14.95)
You and the Police: fact cards for young people

Access to staff:
Contact by letter, by telephone, by fax, by e-mail
and via website
Hours: Mon to Fri, 0900 to 1700

CHILDREN'S LIVER DISEASE FOUNDATION

Acronym or abbreviation: CLDF

36 Great Charles Street, Birmingham, B3 3JY

Tel: 0121 212 3839
Fax: 0121 212 4300
E-mail: info@childliverdisease.org

Website:
http://www/childliverdisease.org

Enquiries:
Enquiries to: Chief Executive

Founded:
1980

Organisation type and purpose:
Registered charity (charity number 1067331).
Raise an awareness of paediatric liver disease, give
support both to children with liver disease and to
their families, promote research and provide new
facilities and trained staff.

Subject coverage:
Children's liver diseases.

Printed publications:
Leaflets
Annual Report

Access to staff:
Contact by letter, by telephone, by fax, by e-mail,
in person and via website. Appointment necessary.
Hours: Mon to Fri, 0900 to 1700

CHILDREN'S SOCIETY, THE

Formal name: Church of England Children's Society
Acronym or abbreviation: TCS

Edward Rudolf House, Margery Street, London,
WC1X 0JL

Tel: 020 7841 4400
E-mail: information@the-childrens-society.org.uk

Website:
http://www.the-childrens-society.org.uk

Founded:
1881

Organisation type and purpose:
Voluntary organisation, registered charity (charity
number 221124).

Subject coverage:
Child care; neighbourhood and community work
with the Church; advocacy; independent living;
runaways; conciliation; fundraising; voluntary
organisations.

Museum or gallery collection, archive, or library special collection:
Archive material documenting the development of the Society since it was founded in 1881
Collection of 10,000 photographic images depicting child welfare mainly at the turn of the century

Printed publications:
The Children's Society produces a range of titles covering the following subjects:
Adoption, Fostering and Care
Child Abuse and Prostitution
Children in Communities
Disability
Faltering Growth
PSE and Citizenship Resources
Poverty and Homelessness
School Exclusion and Reintegration
Young Runaways
Youth Justice
Divorce and Children (Smith R)
Hitting and Hurting – Living in a Violent Family (Pickering F)
On Small Shoulders – Learning from the Experiences of Former Young Carers (Frank J, Tatum C and Tucker S)
Order printed publications from: Publishing Department, The Children's Society
tel: 020 7837 4415, e-mail: publishing@the -childrens-society.org.uk

Publications list:
Available in print

Access to staff:
Contact by letter, by telephone, by e-mail and via website
Hours: Mon to Fri, 0930 to 1700
Special comments: Enquiries from the general public by telephone, letter or email only. No visitors.

Access to building, collection or gallery:
No access other than to staff

CHILLED FOOD ASSOCIATION

Acronym or abbreviation: CFA

PO Box 6434, Kettering, NN15 5XT

Tel: 01536 514365
Fax: 01536 515395
E-mail: cfa@chilledfood.org

Website:
http://www.chilledfood.org
CFA and membership benefits, library of information (members only).

Enquiries:
Enquiries to: Secretary-General

Founded:
1989

Organisation type and purpose:
Trade association (membership is by qualification), present number of members: 21, manufacturing industry.

Subject coverage:
Food safety, food hygiene, HACCP, technology, chilled food manufacture.

Library catalogue:
All or part available online, in-house and in print

Printed publications:
Best Practice Guidelines for the Production of Chilled Foods
Food Safety and Hygiene Training in Multicultural Environments
Guidance on the practical implementation of the EU Microbiological Criteria Regulations
Microbiological Testing and Interpretation Guidelines
Handwash Posters
Water Quality Management: Guidelines for the Chilled Food Industry
High Risk Areas Best Practice Guidelines
Pesticides Due Diligence
Packaging Hygiene Guidelines
Hygiene Design Guidelines
Microbiological Guidance for Growers

Veterinary Residues Management Guidance
Order printed publications from:
www.chilledfood.org/shop

Publications list:
Available online and in print

Access to staff:
Contact by letter, by telephone, by fax, by e-mail and via website. Appointment necessary. Access for members only.
Hours: Mon to Fri, 0900 to 1700
Special comments: Detailed information available to members only.

Access to building, collection or gallery:
No access other than to staff

Links with:
European Chilled Food Federation
website: www.ecff.net

CHILTERN SOCIETY

The White Hill Centre, White Hill, Chesham, Buckinghamshire, HP5 1AG

Tel: 01494 771250
Fax: 01494 793745
E-mail: office@chilternsociety.org.uk

Website:
http://www.chilternsociety.org.uk
Information about the Society.

Enquiries:
Enquiries to: Office Manager

Founded:
1965

Organisation type and purpose:
Membership association (membership is by subscription), present number of members: 7250, voluntary organisation, registered charity (charity number 1085163).
Local amenity society.

Subject coverage:
Conservation in the Chilterns, trees and woodlands, rivers and wetlands, rights of way, waymarking, historic works and buildings, planning, mineral resources and water supplies etc.

Library catalogue:
All or part available online, in-house and in print

Printed publications:
Chiltern News (quarterly, free to members)
The Chiltern Way & Chiltern Way Extensions
Circular Walks in Buckinghamshire
Chiltern Walks in Herts, Beds & Bucks
Chiltern Walks in Oxon and West Bucks
Treasures of the Chilterns and many more.
Over 40 books, on walks and cycle routes throughout the region
26 Chiltern Society Footpath Maps
Order printed publications from: Chiltern Society office

Electronic and video publications:
Caring for the Chilterns, describing the work of the Society (video)
The Chiltern Hills – Land of flint & beech (12.99)
St Albans – A city to inspire (video, £12.99)

Publications list:
Available online and in print

Access to staff:
Contact by letter, by telephone, by fax, by e-mail and via website. Appointment necessary.
Hours: Mon to Fri, 0900 to 1700

Affiliated to:
Civic Trust
CPRE

Founders of:
Chiltern Open Air Museum
The Chiltern Woodland Project Limited

CHINA GLASS AND GIFTWARE RETAILERS' ASSOCIATION

Acronym or abbreviation: CGGRA

PO Box 26657, London, N14 4HZ

Tel: 020 8886 8280
Fax: 020 8447 9600

Enquiries:
Enquiries to: Chief Executive

Founded:
1921

Formerly called:
The China and Glass Retailers' Association (CGRA) (year of change 1996)

Organisation type and purpose:
National organisation, trade association (membership is by subscription, qualification), present number of members: c. 80, service industry.

Subject coverage:
Retail sale of china, glass, giftware, ceramics, pottery, collectibles etc.

Printed publications:
Newsletter (6 times a year to members)

Access to staff:
Contact by letter, by telephone and by fax
Hours: Mon to Fri, 0900 to 1700

CHINA SOCIETY

16 Bridge Street, Christchurch, Dorset, BH23 1EB

Tel: 01202 482717

Enquiries:
Enquiries to: Chairman

Founded:
1906

Organisation type and purpose:
Learned society.

Subject coverage:
Generalised information only on Chinese art, history and current affairs.

Printed publications:
Booklets Publications list being revised

Access to staff:
Contact by letter and by telephone
Hours: Mon to Fri, 0900 to 2000

CHINA-BRITAIN BUSINESS COUNCIL

Acronym or abbreviation: CBBC

1 Warwick Row, London, SW1E 5ER

Tel: 020 7802 2000
Fax: 020 7802 2029

Website:
http://www.cbbc.org

Enquiries:
Enquiries to: Information Centre Manager
Direct tel: 020 7802 2014
Direct fax: 020 7802 2029
Direct e-mail: leo.liu@cbbc.org

Founded:
1998

Organisation type and purpose:
National government body, advisory body.

Subject coverage:
People's Republic of China: business and trade, economy.

Museum or gallery collection, archive, or library special collection:
Business guides, reference books, China statistical year books

Trade and statistical information:
UK-China trade statistics.

continued overleaf

Library catalogue:
All or part available in-house

Printed publications:
China-Britain Business Review (monthly, £150 annually)

Access to staff:
Contact by letter, by telephone, by fax, by e-mail and via website. Appointment necessary.
Hours: Mon to Fri, 0900 to 1700

Access to building, collection or gallery:
Prior appointment required
Hours: Mon to Fri, 0900 to 1700

CHINESE INFORMATION AND ADVICE CENTRE

Acronym or abbreviation: CIAC

1st Floor, 53 New Oxford Street, London, WC1A 1BL

Tel: 020 7692 3471
Fax: 020 7692 3476
E-mail: ciac@ciac.co.uk

Enquiries:
Enquiries to: Information Officer
Direct tel: 020 7692 3473
Direct e-mail: cheng@ciac.co.uk
Other contacts: Tel: 020 7692 3474

Founded:
1983

Organisation type and purpose:
National government body, advisory body, voluntary organisation, registered charity, training organisation.
Advice agency for Chinese community, specialising in immigration, asylum, matrimonial, employment law to Chinese Community ONLY.
Also undertakes specific project work and undertakes cases re: domestic violence issues; matrimonial law; only sees women users.

Subject coverage:
Immigration, matrimonial, employment law advice only; only sees women users re matrimonial advice.

Non-library collection catalogue:
All or part available in-house

Library catalogue:
All or part available in-house

Printed publications:
Fact sheet on immigration and asylum law in Chinese
Annual Report (available free, directly from CIAC)
Service Directory of all Chinese community centres in London (available at a cost from CIAC)

Access to staff:
Contact by letter, by telephone, by fax and by e-mail. Appointment necessary.
Hours: Mon to Fri, 0930 to 1800
Special comments: Not accessible to wheelchairs.

CHIPPENDALE SOCIETY

Temple Newsam House, Leeds, West Yorkshire, LS15 0AE

Tel: 0113 264 7321
Fax: 0113 260 2285

Enquiries:
Enquiries to: Honorary Curator

Founded:
1965

Organisation type and purpose:
Learned society (membership is by subscription), registered charity.

Subject coverage:
Life and work of Thomas Chippendale Senior and Junior, furniture, wood carving.

Museum or gallery collection, archive, or library special collection:
Furniture, manuscripts, designs

Printed publications:
Newsletter (3 times a year, members)

Access to staff:
Contact by letter
Hours: Mon to Fri, 0900 to 1700

CHIROPRACTIC PATIENTS' ASSOCIATION

Acronym or abbreviation: CPA

8 Centre One, Lysander Way, Old Sarum Park, Salisbury, Wiltshire, SP4 6BU

Tel: 01722 415027
Fax: 01722 415028
E-mail: c.p.a@dial.pipex.com

Website:
http://www.chiropatients.org.uk

Enquiries:
Enquiries to: Chairman
Other contacts: Membership Secretary

Founded:
1966

Formerly called:
British Pro Chiropractic Association; Chiropractic Advancement Association (CAA) (year of change 1996)

Organisation type and purpose:
National organisation, membership association (membership is by subscription), present number of members: 1,000, voluntary organisation, registered charity (charity number 328135), suitable for all ages.
Voluntary association of chiropractic patients which aims to ensure patient welfare, provide a patient helpline, make chiropractic treatment more easily accessible via the NHS, fund chiropractic research and education.

Subject coverage:
All aspects that relate patients to the provision of chiropractic treatment in the United Kingdom.

Printed publications:
Back Chat (magazine, free to members)
Information leaflet/Q & As (free)

Access to staff:
Contact by letter, by telephone, by fax, by e-mail and via website
Hours: Mon to Fri, 0900 to 1700

Access to building, collection or gallery:
No access other than to staff

CHOIR SCHOOLS ASSOCIATION

Acronym or abbreviation: CSA

The Minster School, Deangate, York, YO1 7JA

Tel: 01904 624900
Fax: 01904 557232

Enquiries:
Enquiries to: Administrator

Organisation type and purpose:
Professional body, registered charity (charity number 326868).
To supply information about choir schools. The Bursary Trust provides financial help to families in need of assistance.

Subject coverage:
Choir schools, information about entry, location, bursaries.

Printed publications:
Choir Schools Today (journal, annually)
Could My Child be a Chorister
List of members

Access to staff:
Contact by letter and by telephone
Hours: Mon to Fri, 0900 to 1700

Special comments: Office is open on Monday and Wednesday only during term-time.

At the same address is the:
CSA Bursary Trust

CHRIS MCALLISTER LIMITED

2 Riverside Walk, Annan, Dumfries and Galloway, DG12 6BE

Tel: 01461 205866
Fax: 01461 205838
E-mail: chris@chrismca.com

Website:
http://www.chrismca.com

Enquiries:
Enquiries to: Principal Consultant

Founded:
1985

Organisation type and purpose:
Training organisation, consultancy.

Subject coverage:
Trainer training, management training, assessor and verifier training, open learning, customer service training, advice and guidance training, team leadership training.

Information services:
Website contains useful information on e-portfolios and free downloadable resources

Special visitor services:
Delivers NVQs and SVQs anywhere in the United Kingdom (and abroad, usually by telephone)

Education services:
NVQs/SVQs in Management, Learning and Development, etc., including Assessor and Verifier training

Services for disabled people:
Telephone tutoring (as required)

Non-library collection catalogue:
All or part available online

Library catalogue:
All or part available online

Electronic and video publications:
Workbooks online as PDFs: A1.pdf and V1.pdf
Order electronic and video publications from: http://www.chrismca.com

Publications list:
Available online

Access to staff:
Contact by letter, by telephone, by fax, by e-mail, in person and via website. Appointment necessary.
Hours: Mon to Fri, 0900 to 1700

Access to building, collection or gallery:
Only by appointment

Access for disabled people:
No access

Links with:
Chartered Institute of Personnel and Development (CIPD)
tel: 020 8971 9000
Institute for Leadership and Management (ILM)
tel: 01593 251346

CHRIST CHURCH LIBRARY

Christ Church, Oxford, OX1 1DP

Tel: 01865 276169
E-mail: library@chch.ox.ac.uk

Website:
http://www.chch.ox.ac.uk/library/
General information on the library.

Enquiries:
Enquiries to: Librarian

Founded:
1546

Organisation type and purpose:
College library.

Subject coverage:
Manuscript and printed music of the 16th and 17th centuries; theology, particularly the Vulgate; theatre.

Museum or gallery collection, archive, or library special collection:
Brady Collection of theatrical prints and plays
Manuscript and printed music of 16th and 17th centuries
Medieval and Renaissance manuscripts, especially Greek
Printed books and pamphlets of 17th and 18th centuries

Non-library collection catalogue:
All or part available online, in-house and in print

Microform publications:
Microfilms of music manuscript, printed music and other manuscripts
Order microform publications from: see website www.chch.ox.ac.uk/library

Access to staff:
Contact by letter and by e-mail. Appointment necessary. Letter of introduction required.
Hours: Mon to Fri, 0900 to 1700

Part of:
University of Oxford

CHRIST'S COLLEGE LIBRARY

St Andrew Street, Cambridge, CB2 3BU

Tel: 01223 334950
Fax: 01223 339557
E-mail: library@christs.cam.ac.uk

Website:
http://www.christs.cam.ac.uk/info/library
Library Guide, admissions information, guide to the College.

Enquiries:
Enquiries to: College Librarian

Founded:
1505

Organisation type and purpose:
University library.

Subject coverage:
General academic subjects.

Museum or gallery collection, archive, or library special collection:
C. Lesingham Smith Collection of early scientific books
Collection of editions of the works of John Milton
Robertson Smith Oriental Collection
Stephen Gazelee Coptic Collection
W. H. D. Rouse Indian Collection
Wratislaw Slavonic Collection
David Stanbury Darwin Collection
Donald Dickson C. P. Snow Collection

Non-library collection catalogue:
All or part available online

Library catalogue:
All or part available online

Access to staff:
Contact by letter, by telephone, by fax and by e-mail. Appointment necessary. Access for members only. Letter of introduction required.
Hours: Mon to Fri, 0900 to 1700

Access for disabled people:
Parking provided, ramped entry, access to all public areas

CHRISTCHURCH BOROUGH COUNCIL

Civic Offices, Bridge Street, Christchurch, Dorset, BH23 1AZ

Tel: 01202 495000

Fax: 01202 482200
E-mail: post@christchurch.gov.uk

Website:
http://www.dorsetforyou.com
Council information and services, tourism, community business and transport.
http://www.christchurchtourism.info
Tourism.

Enquiries:
Enquiries to: Chief Executive
Direct tel: 01202 495126
Direct fax: 01202 482060
Direct e-mail: m.turvey@christchurch.gov.uk

Organisation type and purpose:
Local government body.

Access to staff:
Contact by letter, by telephone, by fax, by e-mail, in person and via website. Appointment necessary.
Hours: Mon to Thu, 0845 to 1715; Fri, 0845 to 1645

Access for disabled people:
Parking provided, ramped entry, toilet facilities, hearing loop, interpreting (by appointment)

CHRISTIAN AID

PO Box 100, London SE1 7RT

Tel: 020 7620 4444
E-mail: info@christian-aid.org

Website:
http://www.christian-aid.org.uk

Enquiries:
Enquiries to: Area Co-ordinator

Founded:
1945

Organisation type and purpose:
International organisation, registered charity (charity number 528003).
International development aid agency committed to working with all people to combat poverty.

Subject coverage:
Combatting poverty. Information on the 700 partners in 60 countries we work with. Campaign work on cancellation of 3rd World Debt and Trade for Life. Emergency work around the world.

Printed publications:
Resources Catalogue for Schools

Electronic and video publications:
Tapes, disks and videos available through us and publishing house

Publications list:
Available online and in print

Access to staff:
Contact by letter, by telephone, by fax, by e-mail, in person and via website
Hours: Mon to Fri, 0930 to 1615

Access for disabled people:
Level entry, access to all public areas, toilet facilities
Special comments: Lift available.

Other addresses:
Christian Aid
PO Box 100, London, SE1 7RT; tel: 020 7620 4444

Parent body:
The British Council of Churches

CHRISTIAN AID SCOTLAND

The Pentagon Centre, 36 Washington Street, Glasgow, G3 8AZ

Tel: 0141 221 7475
Fax: 0141 241 6145
E-mail: glasgow@christian-aid.org

Website:
www.christianaidscotland.org

Enquiries:
Enquiries to: Head of Christian Aid Scotland

Founded:
1955

Organisation type and purpose:
International organisation, registered charity (Scottish Charity number SC039150).

Access to staff:
Contact by letter, by telephone, by fax, by e-mail and in person. Appointment necessary.
Hours: Mon to Fri, 0900 to 1600

Also at:
Christian Aid
41 George IV Bridge, Edinburgh, EH1 1EL; tel: 0131 240 1254
Christian Aid
28 Glasgow Road, Perth, PH2 0NX; tel: 01738 643982

CHRISTIAN AID, INFORMATION RESOURCES CENTRE

PO Box 100, London, SE1 7RT

Tel: 020 7523 2414
Fax: 020 7620 0719
E-mail: irc@christian-aid.org

Website:
http://www.christian-aid.org

Enquiries:
Enquiries to: Senior Information Officer

Organisation type and purpose:
Voluntary organisation, registered charity.
An official agency of the British and Irish Churches working with local organisations in 60 countries, strengthening their efforts to eradicate poverty and increase self-reliance; also provides grants to refugees and disaster victims.

Subject coverage:
Needs of the world's poor; poverty issues; development education; emergencies, refugees and interchurch aid.

Library catalogue:
All or part available in-house

Printed publications:
Order printed publications from: Supporter Relations Department

Access to staff:
Contact by letter, by telephone, by e-mail, in person and via website. Appointment necessary.
Hours: Mon to Fri, 1000 to 1700

CHRISTIAN ALLIANCE HOUSING SERVICES LIMITED

2 Exton Street, London, SE1 8UE

Tel: 020 7593 0470
Fax: 020 7593 0478
E-mail: mail@caha.org.uk

Website:
http://www.caha.org.uk

Enquiries:
Enquiries to: Director

Organisation type and purpose:
Membership association (membership is by election or invitation), registered charity.

Subject coverage:
Residential accommodation and information.

Access to staff:
Contact by letter and by telephone
Hours: Mon to Fri, 0900 to 1700

CHRISTIAN ASSOCIATION OF BUSINESS EXECUTIVES

Acronym or abbreviation: CABE

24 Greencoat Place, London, SW1P 1BE

Tel: 020 7798 6040
Fax: 020 7798 6044

continued overleaf

Enquiries:
Enquiries to: Director

Founded:
1943

Organisation type and purpose:
Membership association, registered charity.

Access to staff:
Contact by letter
Hours: Mon to Fri, 1000 to 1700

CHRISTIAN BUSINESSMEN'S COMMITTEE (BROMLEY)

Acronym or abbreviation: CBMC

45 Tweedy Road, Bromley, Kent, BR1 3NH

Tel: 020 8289 4405
Fax: 020 8464 6033
E-mail: ted.hubbard@talk21.com

Enquiries:
Enquiries to: Secretary

Founded:
1967

Organisation type and purpose:
International organisation, membership association (membership is by election or invitation).
Religious – Christian Gospel.
A Christian organisation witnessing to business men sharing Christ with business and professional men in the market place.

Access to staff:
Contact by letter, by telephone, by fax and by e-mail
Hours: Mon to Fri, 0900 to 1700

CHRISTIAN COPYRIGHT LICENSING (EUROPE) LTD

Acronym or abbreviation: CCL

PO Box 1339, Eastbourne, East Sussex, BN21 1AD

Tel: 01323 417711
Fax: 01323 417722
E-mail: info@ccli.co.uk

Website:
http://www.ccli.com
Information on international copyright licensing and copyright education.

Enquiries:
Enquiries to: Church/School Representative

Founded:
1991

Organisation type and purpose:
International organisation.
Copyright licensing.

Subject coverage:
Hymn and worship song copyright, non-commercial licences for reproducing and photocopying text or audio/visual recordings of hymns and worship songs by churches, schools and Christian organisations.

Printed publications:
Copyright education brochure including licence application form

Access to staff:
Contact by letter, by telephone, by fax, by e-mail and via website
Hours: Mon to Fri, 0830 to 1630

Parent body:
Christian Copyright Licensing International
17201, NE Sacramento Street, Portland, OR 97230, USA

CHRISTIAN EDUCATION

1020 Bristol Road, Selly Oak, Birmingham, B29 6LB

Tel: 0121 472 4242

Fax: 0121 472 7575
E-mail: enquiries@christianeducation.org.uk

Website:
http://www.christianeducation.org.uk
Resource list, courses, online catalogue, downloads.

Enquiries:
Enquiries to: Director

Founded:
2001

Formerly called:
National Sunday School Union (NSSU), SCM in Schools (SCM) (year of change 1965); Christian Education Movement (CEM), National Christian Education Council (NCEC) (year of change 2001)

Organisation type and purpose:
National organisation, membership association (membership is by subscription), registered charity (charity number 1086990), suitable for ages: Life-long, training organisation, consultancy, research organisation, publishing house.

Subject coverage:
Religious education for all ages; ecumenism.

Printed publications:
Books, guides and leaflets supporting teachers of 5–16 year olds
Resource (termly periodical)
RE Today (termly periodical)
BJRE (termly periodical)

Electronic and video publications:
Videos for RE in secondary schools and others

Publications list:
Available in print

Access to staff:
Contact by letter, by telephone, by fax and via website
Hours: Mon to Fri, 0900 to 1700

Other addresses:
RE Today Services
1020 Bristol Road, Selly Oak, Birmingham, B29 6LB; tel: 0121 472 4242; fax: 0121 472 7575

Subsidiary body:
Professional Council for Religious Education (PCfRE)
tel: 0191 213 5227; fax: 0191 213 5227; e-mail: rachel@retoday.org.uk

CHRISTIAN ENQUIRY AGENCY

Acronym or abbreviation: CEA

27 Tavistock Square, London, WC1H 9HH

Tel: 020 7387 3659
Fax: 020 7529 8134
E-mail: enquiry@christianity.org.uk

Website:
http://www.christianity.org.uk
Information about Christian Enquiry Agency and resources for churches, opportunity to request information about the Christian faith, links to other sites.

Enquiries:
Enquiries to: Director

Founded:
1988

Organisation type and purpose:
Registered charity (charity number 297393).
To provide information about the Christian faith.

Subject coverage:
Christian faith.

Printed publications:
Christian Enquiry Agency News

Access to staff:
Contact by letter, by telephone, by fax, by e-mail and via website
Hours: Mon to Fri, 0900 to 1700
Special comments: Hours are variable but voice mail and answerphone operate.

Works in association with:
all major churches in Britain and Ireland, and many Christian organisations.

CHRISTIAN POLICE ASSOCIATION

Acronym or abbreviation: CPA

Bedford Heights , Manton Lane, Bedford, MK41 7PH

Tel: 01234 272 865
E-mail: info@cpauk.net

Website:
http://www.cpauk.net/

Enquiries:
Enquiries to: Executive Director

Organisation type and purpose:
Membership association (membership is by election or invitation), present number of members: 2000, registered charity (charity number 220482).

Access to staff:
Contact by letter, by telephone, by fax and by e-mail
Hours: Mon to Fri, 0900 to 1700

CHRISTIAN SCIENCE COMMITTEES ON PUBLICATION

9 Elysium Gate, 126 New Kings Road, London, SW6 4LZ

Tel: 020 7384 8600
Fax: 020 7371 9204
E-mail: joynesh@compub.org

Enquiries:
Enquiries to: Manager

Organisation type and purpose:
Registered charity (charity number 230940).
To provide information on Christian Science Church.

Subject coverage:
Christian Science, the writings of Mary Baker Eddy, the Bible and general information on The Church of Christ Scientist.

CHRISTIANS ABROAD

Acronym or abbreviation: Cab

The Bon Marche Centre, 241–251 Ferndale Road, London, SW9 8BJ

Tel: 08707 707990
Fax: 08707 707991
E-mail: director@cabroad.org.uk

Website:
http://www.cabroad.org.uk
http://www.wse.org.uk

Enquiries:
Enquiries to: Information Officer

Founded:
1972

Organisation type and purpose:
Voluntary organisation, registered charity (charity number 265867).
To offer opportunities for individuals with Christian commitment to work for development overseas through Christians Abroad, and debriefing sessions for review and reflection for those returning from overseas service.
To provide a consultancy for overseas recruitment and personnel management to agencies placing persons overseas in mission, and development on all matters deriving from our experience in the international movement of personnel. And as World Service Enquiry, providing information and advice about volunteering or working in the developing world. www.wse.org.uk

Subject coverage:
Work in aid, development and mission overseas; recruitment and personnel management in mission work overseas.

Printed publications:
Guide to Volunteering and Working for Development; Opportunities Abroad; The Survival Guide – A travellers e-book guide.

Publications list:
Available online and in print

Access to staff:
Contact by telephone, by e-mail and via website
Hours: Mon to Fri, 0900 to 1700

Access to building, collection or gallery:
No access other than to staff

CHRISTIE HOSPITAL & PATERSON INSTITUTE FOR CANCER RESEARCH

Medical Library, Wilmslow Road, Withington, Manchester, M20 4BX

Tel: 0161 446 3000
Fax: 0161 446 3454
E-mail: sglover@picr.man.ac.uk

Website:
http://www.christie.nhs.uk

Enquiries:
Enquiries to: Librarian
Direct tel: 0161 446 3456

Founded:
1932

Organisation type and purpose:
Research organisation.
Medical library.
Cancer.

Subject coverage:
Oncology; radiotherapy; treatment and research.

Library catalogue:
All or part available in-house

Access to staff:
Contact by telephone and by e-mail
Hours: Mon to Wed, 0900 to 1900; Thu, 0800 to 1730; Fri, 0800 to 1700; Sat, 0900 to 1300
Special comments: NHS or academic staff only.

CHURCH IN SOCIETY (THE DIOCESES OF CANTERBURY AND ROCHESTER)

Acronym or abbreviation: CIS

2–3 Bedford Place, Maidstone, Kent, ME16 8JB

Tel: 01622 755014
Fax: 01622 693531
E-mail: office@churchinsociety.org

Enquiries:
Enquiries to: Chief Executive
Direct e-mail: david@churchinsociety.org

Founded:
1893

Organisation type and purpose:
Advisory body, voluntary organisation, registered charity (charity no. 1091679), consultancy.
To advance the social mission of the Anglican Church in Kent, Bexley and Bromley.

Subject coverage:
Social action and reflective practice realting to local community and contexts, environment, world development, urban and rural issues, regeneration, community learning, community development, young people in need.

Printed publications:
Rochbury series

Publications list:
Available online and in print

Access to staff:
Contact by letter, by telephone, by fax and by e-mail
Hours: Mon to Fri, 0900 to 1700

Access to building, collection or gallery:
Prior appointment required

CHURCH MISSION SOCIETY

Acronym or abbreviation: CMS

Watlington Road, Oxford, OX4 6BZ

Tel: 01865 787552
Fax: 01865 776375
E-mail: margaret.acton@cms-uk.org

Website:
http://www.cms-uk.org

Enquiries:
Enquiries to: Records Manager

Founded:
1799

Formerly called:
Church Missionary Society

Organisation type and purpose:
Registered charity (charity number 220297).
Anglican Missionary Society.

Subject coverage:
Mission work and local church growth, particularly in Asia and Africa.

Museum or gallery collection, archive, or library special collection:
Extensive archive collection located at Birmingham University Library. Contact Special Collections, Main Library, University of Birmingham, Edgbaston, Birmingham, B15 2TT

Library catalogue:
All or part available online

Printed publications:
Catalogues for all sections of the archive collection available (various prices)
CMS Newsletter (6 times a year)
Yes (5 times a year)

Access to staff:
Appointment necessary.
Hours: Mon to Fri, 0900 to 1700

CHURCH MONUMENTS SOCIETY

Acronym or abbreviation: CMS

The Membership Secretary, 55 Bowden Park Road, Crownhill, Plymouth, PL6 5NG

E-mail: churchmonuments@aol.com

Website:
http://www.churchmonumentssociety.org

Enquiries:
Enquiries to: Honorary Secretary
Other contacts: Honorary Publicity Officer

Founded:
1979

Organisation type and purpose:
Learned society, registered charity (charity number 279597).
To promote, for the public benefit, the study, care and conservation of funerary monuments of all countries and all periods.

Subject coverage:
Art, architecture, history, costume, heraldry, lettering, geology, genealogy, iconography, epigraphy.

Printed publications:
Church Monuments (journal, annually)
Newsletter (twice a year)
Order printed publications from: Honorary Membership Secretary, Church Monuments Society, 55 Bowden Park Road, Crownhill, Plymouth, PL6 5NG; tel. 01752 773634

Access to staff:
Contact by letter, by telephone, by fax, by e-mail and via website

Also at:
Church Monuments Society
The Secretary, 10 Newton Villas, Coxhoe, Durham, DH6 4JF; tel: 0191 377 0521; e-mail: r .millerchip@btopenworld.com

CHURCH OF ENGLAND BOARD OF EDUCATION

Acronym or abbreviation: BOE

Church House, Great Smith Street, London, SW1P 3NZ

Tel: 020 7898 1501
Fax: 020 7898 1520
E-mail: janina.ainsworth@c-of-e.org.uk

Website:
http://www.cofe.anglican.org/about/education
Overview, specific links to each area of the Board's work in education.
http://www.churchschools.co.uk
Subscription service for teachers, head teachers and governors of all Church schools; resources, up-to-date information on Church school issues.
http://www.natsoc.org.uk
Collective workshop, RE centre resources, information about church schools, National Society publications.

Enquiries:
Enquiries to: General Secretary

Formerly called:
General Synod Board of Education

Organisation type and purpose:
Advisory body, voluntary organisation, suitable for ages: all.
Promote the Church's interest in education.

Subject coverage:
Church of England schools, church colleges, chaplains in colleges and universities, adult work in the Church, children's work (including Sunday schools), religious education, history of church colleges of education, human relations, training/ adult education, youth work/young people's council.

Trade and statistical information:
Data on numbers of Church of England schools – aided and controlled.

Publications list:
Available in print

Access to staff:
Contact by letter, by telephone, by fax, by e-mail and via website
Hours: Mon to Fri, 0900 to 1700

Connections with:
Church House Publishing
tel: 020 7898 1301
National Society (CofE) for Promoting Religious Education
tel: 020 7898 1518; fax: 020 7898 1493; e-mail: marie.yateman@c-of-e.org.uk

Parent body:
Archbishops' Council of the Church of England
tel: 020 7898 1000

Subsidiary body:
Lifelong Learning Team
tel: 020 7898 1514; fax: 020 7898 1520; e-mail: victoria.ekpene@c-of-e.org.uk
Schools Strategy Team
tel: 020 7898 1491; fax: 020 7898 1493; e-mail: pat .barton@c-of-e.org.uk
Training & Development Team
tel: 020 7898 1505; fax: 020 7898 0520; e-mail: janice.overington@c-of-e.org.uk

CHURCH OF ENGLAND RECORD CENTRE

Acronym or abbreviation: CERC

continued overleaf

15 Galleywall Road, South Bermondsey, London, SE16 3PB

Tel: 020 7898 1030
Fax: 020 7898 1043
E-mail: archivist@c-of-e.org.uk

Website:
http://www.cofe.anglican.org/

Enquiries:
Enquiries to: Operations Manager

Founded:
1990

Formerly called:
Church Commissioners' Archives, General Synod Archives, National Society Archives (year of change 1990)

Organisation type and purpose:
Church Administration.

Subject coverage:
Church of England; administration, buildings, education, finance, history, legislation, liturgy, ministry, mission, social responsibility.

Museum or gallery collection, archive, or library special collection:
Church Commissioners' Archives
General Synod Archives
National Society Archives

Non-library collection catalogue:
All or part available in print

Library catalogue:
All or part available online

Printed publications:
Sources for Anglican Clergy, 16th to 20th centuries
Keep or Bin – The Care of your Parish Records

Electronic and video publications:
Keep or Bin – The Care of your Parish Records
Save or Delete – Care of Diocesan Records

Access to staff:
Contact by letter, by telephone, by fax and by e-mail. Appointment necessary.
Hours: Mon to Fri, 0900 to 1700
Special comments: Reading room at Lambeth Palace Library

Access to building, collection or gallery:
Prior appointment required for reading room at Lambeth Palace Library

Access for disabled people:
Parking provided, toilet facilities

CHURCH OF JESUS CHRIST OF LATTER-DAY SAINTS

Church Offices, 751 Warwick Road, Solihull, West Midlands, B91 3DQ

Tel: 0121 712 1200

Website:
http://www.familysearch.org
Personal Ancestral File download facility.
http://www.lds.org/newsroom
Information for journalists.
http://www.mormon.org
For those wanting to know more about the Church and its teachings.
http://www.lds.org
Basic information on the Church, its history and beliefs.

Founded:
1830

Also known as:
Mormons (nickname)

Organisation type and purpose:
International organisation, membership association (membership is by qualification), present number of members: 180,000 UK and Ireland, 11,000,000 worldwide, registered charity (charity number 242451).
Church, religious organisation.

Subject coverage:
Theology, especially early Christian church, revelation; certain fields of health, especially cancer; self-sufficiency; family relationships; genealogy, especially the use of computer held genealogical records, such as the IGI (International Genealogical Index).

Printed publications:
Church News (weekly newspaper, on subscription)
Ensign (monthly magazine on subscription)
The New Era (magazine for youth, monthly, on subscription)
The Friend (magazine for children up to 12 years, monthly, on subscription)
Order printed publications from: Latter-Day Saints Distribution
399 Garrett Green Lane, Birmingham, B33 0UH, tel: 0121 785 2200

Electronic and video publications:
British Vital Records Index (CD-ROM, £13.50)
Family History Source Guide (CD-ROM, £10)
Personal Ancestral File (computer software for genealogical management, v3.0, floppy disk only 3.5 or 5.25 ins MS-DOS, £11.80)
Personal Ancestral File (computer software for genealogical management, v4.0, CD-ROM, for Windows £3.80 or free download from website)
Pedigree Resource File (CD-ROM, set of five, £19)
Order electronic and video publications from: Latter-Day Saints Distribution
399 Garrett Green Lane, Birmingham, B33 0UH, tel: 0121 785 2200

Access to staff:
Contact by letter, by telephone, by fax, by e-mail and via website. Appointment necessary.
Hours: Mon to Fri, 0900 to 1700

Access for disabled people:
Access to all public areas, toilet facilities

CHURCH OF SCOTLAND

121 George Street, Edinburgh, EH2 4YN

Tel: 0131 225 5722
Fax: 0131 220 3133
E-mail: fmacdonald@cofscotland.org.uk

Website:
http://www.churchofscotland.org.uk

Enquiries:
Enquiries to: Principal Clerk

Founded:
500 AD

Organisation type and purpose:
National church.

Subject coverage:
Church of Scotland.

Printed publications:
Life and Work (monthly)

Access to staff:
Contact by letter
Hours: Mon to Fri, 0900 to 1700

CHURCH UNION

Formal name: The Church Union
Acronym or abbreviation: CU

(may change; currently at) Faith House, 7 Tufton Street, Westminster, London, SW1P 3QN

Tel: 020 7222 6952
E-mail: secretary@churchunion.co.uk

Website:
http://www.churchunion.co.uk

Enquiries:
Enquiries to: The Secretary
Direct tel: 020 7388 3588
Other contacts: Chairman, tel: 01371 830132; Publication, tel: 01684 575893; Treasurer, tel: 01709 546441; Membership, tel: 020 7222 6952

Founded:
1859

Formerly called:
Tufton Books; Church Literature Association (publication arm of CU) (year of change 1997)

Organisation type and purpose:
Membership association (membership is by subscription), present number of members: 2000, registered charity (charity number 243535), publishing house.

Subject coverage:
The Catholic Movement within the Church of England, founded at the time of the Oxford Movement, to promote catholic faith and order, it continues this work today by providing support and encouragement to those lay people and priests who wish to see catholic faith, order, morals and spirituality maintained and upheld, and who wish to promote catholic unity. The Union is a publisher of books and tracts and has part-time staff who can advise on matters liturgical, legal and musical.

Museum or gallery collection, archive, or library special collection:
Lord Halifax's personal Library: history of the English Church Union and Anglo-Catholic congresses

Printed publications:
Church Observer (quarterly)
Modern works on liturgy and theological matters
Following published by Canterbury Press Norwich:
Order for the Eucharist (Hunwicke J, ISBN 0–85191–097–1, £6.99)
Order of Mass:
Order One: ISBN 0–8591–089–0 (per pack of 50, £22.50)
Order One: ISBN 0–8591–109–9 (per pack of 10, £4.50)
Order One: ISBN 0–8591–069–8 (singles, 50p)
Traditional: ISBN 0–8591–008–2 (per pack of 50, £22.50)
Traditional: ISBN 0–8591–174–9 (per pack of 10, £4.50)
Traditional: ISBN 0–8591–098–X (singles, 50p)
Following published by Tufton Books and CLA:
Another Look at St John's Gospel (Clutterbuck I, ISBN 0–85191–240–0, £5.95)
Baptism of Children, Order of Service (single copy/copies, ISBN 0–85191–240–0, 50p)
Baptism of Children, Order of Service (pack(s) of 10, ISBN 0–85191–241–9, £4.50)
Baptism of Children, Order of Service (pack(s) of 50, ISBN 0–85191–236–2, £22.50)
Celebration With the Sick and Dying (Pinchin T, ISBN 0–85191–270–2, £1.95)
CREDO (course book, Urwin L, ISBN 0–85191–310–5, £16.50 (out of print), book and video pack, £32.50 inc. VAT)
Parish Cards
What We Do In Church and Why (Straszak E)
Word of God for the People of God (Chadd L, ISBN 0–85191–160–9, £3.50)
Youthful Spirit (Ward P and Urwin L, ISBN 0–85191–233–8, £6.99)
Order printed publications from: Canterbury Press, St Mary's Works, St Mary Plain, Norwich, NR3 3BH, tel: 01603 612914

Electronic and video publications:
CREDO (video, Urwin L, ISBN 0–85191–310–5, £19 inc VAT)
Order electronic and video publications from: Canterbury Press

Publications list:
Available in print

Access to staff:
Contact by letter, by telephone and by e-mail. Appointment necessary.
Hours: Mon to Fri, 0900 to 1700
Special comments: Via tel only

Access to building, collection or gallery:
Prior appointment required

Also trades as:
Tufton Books

CHURCHES COMMISSION FOR RACIAL JUSTICE

Acronym or abbreviation: CCRJ

CTBI, Bastille Court, 2 Paris Garden, London, SE1 7SA

Tel: 020 7654 7241
Fax: 020 7654 7222
E-mail: ccrj@ctbi.org.uk

Website:
http://www.ctbi.org.uk/ccrj

Enquiries:
Enquiries to: Commission Secretary
Direct tel: 020 7654 7240
Direct e-mail: ccrj@ctbi.org.uk

Founded:
1992

Organisation type and purpose:
National organisation, voluntary organisation, registered charity (charity number 259688). Church Organisation.

Subject coverage:
Racial justice and community relations in Britain.

Library catalogue:
All or part available online

Printed publications:
Racial Justice Sunday Pack (2nd Sunday September)
Church and Race (3 times a year)
Occasional reports

Publications list:
Available online and in print

Access to staff:
Contact by letter, by telephone, by fax, by e-mail and via website. Appointment necessary.
Hours: Mon to Fri, 0930 to 1700

Access for disabled people:
Level entry

Affiliated to:
all community race relations bodies

CHURCHES TOGETHER IN BRITAIN AND IRELAND

Acronym or abbreviation: CTBI

3rd Floor, Bastille Court, 2 Paris Garden, London, SE1 8ND

Tel: 020 7654 7254
Fax: 020 7654 7222
E-mail: info@ctbi.org.uk

Website:
http://www.ctbi.org.uk

Enquiries:
Enquiries to: General Secretary

Organisation type and purpose:
National organisation, membership association (membership is by subscription, qualification), present number of members: 33 member churches, registered charity (charity number 259688). Fellowship of Churches in the United Kingdom and the Republic of Ireland; member churches – Protestant, Anglican, Orthodox, Roman Catholic, Pentecostal, Salvation Army, Quaker. Ecumenical.

Subject coverage:
Ecumenical cooperation: Christianity; relations with other churches and other faiths; Christian perspectives on public affairs, international affairs, race relations, mission and evangelisation, women's issues.

Printed publications:
Ecumenical studies
Reports on current issues
World Council of Churches Publications
Order printed publications from: CTBI Publications
Church House Bookshop, Great Smith Street, London, SW1P 3BN

Publications list:
Available in print

Access to staff:
Contact by letter, by telephone, by fax, by e-mail and via website. Appointment necessary.
Hours: Mon to Fri, 0900 to 1700

Access to building, collection or gallery:
Prior appointment required

Access for disabled people:
Level entry, access to all public areas, toilet facilities

Affiliated to:
Conference of European Churches
World Council of Churches

Related organisation:
Churches Together in England, Scotland, Wales
Irish Council of Churches

CHURCHES' CONSERVATION TRUST, THE

1 West Smithfield, London EC1A 9EE

Tel: 020 7213 0660
Fax: 020 7213 0678
E-mail: central@tcct.org.uk

Website:
http://www.visitchurches.org.uk
Details of all 325 churches – opening arrangements, location, short architectural description.

Enquiries:
Enquiries to: Public Relations Manager

Founded:
1969

Formerly called:
Redundant Churches Fund (year of change 1994)

Organisation type and purpose:
Statutory body, registered charity (charity number 258612).
The care and conservation of redundant churches in England.

Subject coverage:
Conservation of churches, redundant churches.

Printed publications:
County lists (free)
Guidebooks and postcards for churches under the care of The Churches Conservation Trust (available from the churches or direct)

Publications list:
Available online and in print

Access to staff:
Contact by letter, by telephone and by fax
Hours: Mon to Fri, 0900 to 1700

Access to building, collection or gallery:
No prior appointment required

CHURCHILL ARCHIVES CENTRE

Churchill College, Cambridge, CB3 0DS

Tel: 01223 336087
Fax: 01223 336135
E-mail: archives@chu.cam.ac.uk

Website:
http://www.chu.cam.ac.uk/archives
Visitor information, holdings guide.

Enquiries:
Enquiries to: Director of the Archives

Founded:
1973

Organisation type and purpose:
University department or institute.
College library and archive.

Subject coverage:
Churchill Family; diplomacy, foreign policy and international relations 1900 to date; political life and government policy 1900 to date; military and naval history 1900 to date; history of science and technology 1900 to date.

Museum or gallery collection, archive, or library special collection:
Papers of Sir Winston Churchill, together with papers of about 570 other individuals and institutions

Non-library collection catalogue:
All or part available online and in-house

Library catalogue:
All or part available in-house

Access to staff:
Contact by letter, by telephone, by fax, by e-mail and via website. Appointment necessary.
Hours: Mon to Fri, 0900 to 1700

Access to building, collection or gallery:
Prior appointment required, ID required

Access for disabled people:
Parking provided, ramped entry, toilet facilities, lift to reading rooms

CIBA SPECIALTY CHEMICALS PLC

Hawkhead Road, Paisley, Renfrewshire, PA2 7BG

Tel: 0141 887 1144
Fax: 0141 840 2283

Enquiries:
Enquiries to: Information Manager
Direct tel: 0141 887 1144 ext 5287
Direct e-mail: ailsa.morrison@cibasc.com
Other contacts: Library Assistant for general.

Formerly called:
Ciba-Geigy Pigments (year of change 1997)

Organisation type and purpose:
Manufacturing industry.

Subject coverage:
Organic pigments, colour chemistry.

Library catalogue:
All or part available in-house

Access to staff:
Contact by letter, by telephone and by e-mail.
Appointment necessary.
Hours: Mon to Fri, 0900 to 1700

Access to building, collection or gallery:
Prior appointment required

CILT, THE NATIONAL CENTRE FOR LANGUAGES

Acronym or abbreviation: CiLT

20 Bedfordbury, London, WC2N 4LB

Tel: 020 7379 5110
Fax: 020 7379 5082
E-mail: library@cilt.org.uk

Website:
http://www.nacell.org.uk
Information about language learning for under 11 year olds in the UK.
http://www.blis.org.uk
Databases of language and cultural expertise services in the field of business and employment.
http://www.cilt.org.uk
Information about the activities of CILT, CILT Cymru, the Comenius Centres, the Regional Language Networks. Links to CILT Cymru, Scottish CILT, Northern Ireland CILT, BLIS and NACELL websites.

Enquiries:
Enquiries to: Librarian

Founded:
1966

Organisation type and purpose:
Registered charity (charity number 313938).

continued overleaf

Supported by Central Government grants.

Subject coverage:
Promotion of a greater national capability in languages, including languages for employment, and to support the work of all those concerned with language teaching and learning from primary to graduate level. Research into teaching methods and learning resources in French, German, Italian, Russian, Spanish, and many other languages; English as a second language in Britain; community languages; examinations.

Museum or gallery collection, archive, or library special collection:
Books and periodicals
Teaching materials, textbooks, visual aids, software, video and audio recordings

Trade and statistical information:
Education statistics and labour market data at http://www.cilt.org.uk/statistics

Non-library collection catalogue:
All or part available online

Library catalogue:
All or part available online

Printed publications:
Methodology texts, language promotion resources, project and conference documents, downloadable free resources
Catalogue of publications (annual, over 100 titles listed)
Courses, training & events for teachers of MFL and language professionals (annotated list – 3 times a year)
Information sheets (free, see website)
Business of Language (bulletin)
Community Languages (bulletin)
Curriculum guides for community languages (5 titles forthcoming)
Early Language Learning Bulletin (3 times a year)
European Languages Portfolio (2 titles)
Higher (research and higher education bulletin – 3 times a year)
InfoTech series (5 titles)
Language Teaching (the international abstracting journal for language teachers and applied linguists, quarterly, jointly with the British Council, pub. CUP)
Languages 2006 (yearbook)
Links (language teacher training bulletin – 2 times a year)
MFL (secondary language teachers' bulletin – 3 times a year)
Netword (bulletin for further and adult education – 2 times a year)
Advanced Pathfinder series (6 titles)
Pathfinder series (also New and Classic Pathfinders – 18 titles)
Reflections on practice series (6) on professional development
Regional Language Audits (free, see website)
Resource files (5 titles)
Young Pathfinder series (13 titles for primary languages)
Order printed publications from: Central Books Ltd, 99 Wallis Road, London, E9 5LN, tel: 0845 458 9910 (mail order/enquiries) 0845 458 9911 (trade orders), fax: 0845 458 9912, e-mail: mo@centralbooks.com

Electronic and video publications:
Early Language Learning DVD
Hocus & Lotus (video, CD and other materials for teaching young children)

Publications list:
Available online and in print

Access to staff:
Contact by letter, by telephone, by fax, by e-mail and in person
Hours: Mon to Fri, 1030 to 1700
Extended opening hours during school terms: Wed, 1030 to 2000; Sat, 1000 to 1300

Affiliated to:
A network of Comenius Centres in England

CILT Cymru
tel: 029 2048 0137; fax: 029 2048 0145; e-mail: bethan.enticott@ciltcymru.org.uk; website: http://www.ciltcymru.org.uk
Northern Ireland CILT
tel: 028 9097 5955; fax: 028 9032 6571; e-mail: nicilt@qub.ac.uk; website: http://www.qub.ac.uk/edu/nicilt
Scottish CILT
tel: 01786 466290; fax: 01786 466291; e-mail: scilt@stir.ac.uk; website: http://www.scilt.stir.ac.uk/

CIMA

Formal name: Chartered Institute of Management Accountants

26 Chapter Street, London, SW1P 4NP

Tel: 020 7663 5441
Fax: 020 7663 5442

Website:
http://www.cimaglobal.com
Detailed information about the Institute, including examinations; list of members in practice; useful articles; bulletin boards for queries. Publications, courses, knowledge bank.
http://www.cimaglobal.com/main/resources/knowledge

Enquiries:
Enquiries to: Information Manager (TAS)
Direct tel: 020 8849 2259
Direct fax: 020 8849 2464
Direct e-mail: tas@cimaglobal.com

Founded:
1919

Formerly called:
Institute of Cost and Management Accountants

Organisation type and purpose:
Professional body (membership is by qualification).

Subject coverage:
Cost, financial and management accountancy; finance and financial management.

Museum or gallery collection, archive, or library special collection:
Archive of own publications from 1934
Historical collection of books relating to cost and management accounting

Library catalogue:
All or part available in-house

Printed publications:
List of Members (annually)
Management Accounting Research (in association with Academic Press)
Financial Management (11 times a year, from Journal Department)
Order printed publications from: Publishing Sales Department
tel: 020 8849 2270, fax: 020 8849 2465, e-mail: publishing-sales@cimaglobal.com

Electronic and video publications:
List of Members (annually, CD-ROM)

Publications list:
Available online

Access to staff:
Contact by letter, by telephone, by fax, by e-mail, in person and via website. Access for members only.
Hours: Mon to Fri, 1000 to 1600
Special comments: Members and bona fide researchers only.

Access to building, collection or gallery:
Prior appointment required

CIMTECH LIMITED

Acronym or abbreviation: CIMTECH

University of Hertfordshire, Innovation Centre, College Lane, Hatfield, Herts, AL10 9AB

Tel: 01707 281060
Fax: 01707 281061
E-mail: c.cimtech@herts.ac.uk

Website:
http://www.cimtech.co.uk

Enquiries:
Enquiries to: Office Manager

Founded:
1967

Formerly called:
HERTIS Information and Research, National Centre for Information Management and Technology (CIMTECH)

Organisation type and purpose:
Membership association (membership is by subscription), service industry, training organisation, consultancy, publishing house.

Subject coverage:
Image processing, electronic content, document and records management, microfilm, optical disks, CD-ROM, electronic publishing, document imaging, recognition technology, workflow management, business process re-engineering, data and document capture.

Printed publications:
Publications include the following:
Managing Information and Documents (available foc and online)

Electronic and video publications:
Information Management and Technology (online, 10 a year, subscription £80.00 per year)

Publications list:
Available online

Access to staff:
Contact by letter, by telephone, by fax, by e-mail and via website. Appointment necessary. All charged.
Hours: Mon to Thu, 0900 to 1700; Fri, 0900 to 1600

Parent body:
University of Hertfordshire

CINE GUILDS OF GREAT BRITAIN

72 Pembroke Road, London, W8 6NX

Tel: 020 7602 8319
Fax: 020 7602 8319
E-mail: cineguildsgb@btinternet.com

Enquiries:
Enquiries to: Secretary

Organisation type and purpose:
To promote the British film industry.

Subject coverage:
The British film industry.

Access to staff:
Contact by letter and by e-mail
Hours: Mon to Fri, 0900 to 1700

Access to building, collection or gallery:
No access other than to staff

CINEMA ADVERTISING ASSOCIATION LIMITED

Acronym or abbreviation: CAA

12 Golden Square, London, W1F 9JE

Tel: 020 7534 6363
Fax: 020 7534 6227

Enquiries:
Enquiries to: Secretary
Direct e-mail: sam.newsom@carltonscreen.com

Organisation type and purpose:
Trade association.

Subject coverage:
Cinema advertising medium (UK), standards of advertising practice, research.

Museum or gallery collection, archive, or library special collection:
Advertising Film Archives

Printed publications:
CAVIAR (annual research study; Cinema and Video Industry Audience Research)
Cinema Coverage and Frequency Guide (annually, free)

Access to staff:
Contact by telephone and by e-mail
Hours: Mon to Fri, 0900 to 1700

Access to building, collection or gallery:
No access other than to staff

Access for disabled people:
Access to all public areas, toilet facilities

Member of:
Advertising Association

CINEMA THEATRE ASSOCIATION

Acronym or abbreviation: CTA

44 Harrowdene Gardens, Teddington, Middlesex, TW11 0DJ

Tel: 020 8977 2608

Website:
http://www.cta-uk.org.
General information on the association's activities, including the archive and publications.

Enquiries:
Enquiries to: Honorary Secretary
Other contacts: (1) Chairman (2) Public Relations Officer (3) Archivist for (1) cinemas threatened by planning proposals (2) press releases and enquiries (3) archive

Founded:
1967

Organisation type and purpose:
Advisory body, membership association (membership is by subscription), present number of members: 1400, voluntary organisation, research organisation.
To promote interest in Britain's cinema building legacy, visit and research cinema buildings, monitor threatened cinemas of architectural importance and campaign for their protection, maintain an archive.

Subject coverage:
Cinema buildings, history, architecture, ownership, lighting, projection, stage facilities, programmes, publicity etc. (primarily in the United Kingdom).

Museum or gallery collection, archive, or library special collection:
Archive of photographs and related material
George Coles (cinema architect) photograph collection, plans and drawings
John Squires colour slide collection of cinemas
Kine Year Books (incomplete run)
Opening programmes of cinemas, photo collection, plans and drawings, and related material

Printed publications:
CTA Bulletin (6 times a year, members only)
Picture House (magazine, annually)
Over 30 books on the History of Cinemas in Britain including:
Cheshire Cinemas
Cinemas in Britain (Gray R)
Clyde Coast Picture Palaces
Halifax & surrounding area
Ribbon of Dreams, Cardiff
The Essoldo Circuit

Publications list:
Available in print

Access to staff:
Contact by letter and by telephone. Non-members charged.
Hours: Mon to Fri, 0900 to 1700

Special comments: Collections available for reference by appointment.

Access to building, collection or gallery:
Prior appointment required

CINTO

Formal name: Cleaning Industry National Training Organisation
Acronym or abbreviation: CINTO

3 Moulton Court, Anglia Way, Moulton Park, Northampton, NN3 6JA

Tel: 01604 645731
Fax: 01604 645988
E-mail: info@cleaningnto.org

Website:
http://www.cleaningnto.org
About the NTO, qualifications, advanced foundation modern apprenticeships, national standards.

Enquiries:
Enquiries to: Executive Director

Founded:
1997

Formerly called:
Cleaning and Support Services Industry Training Organisation (CSSITO); Cleaning Industry Lead Body (year of change 1997); Cleaning and Support Services National Training Organisation (CSSNTO) (year of change 2000)

Organisation type and purpose:
Training organisation.

Subject coverage:
Education and training for the cleaning and support services industry, both private and public sectors, National Standards, National Vocational Qualifications (NVQs), Scottish Vocational Qualifications (SVQs), modern apprenticeships, labour market information, skills needs, qualification structures, how to start a cleaning business.

Trade and statistical information:
Labour market information.

Printed publications:
Advanced Modern Apprenticeship Framework
National Standards for Cleaning
Foundation Modern Apprenticeship
Vocational Qualifications Information

Publications list:
Available online and in print

Access to staff:
Contact by letter, by telephone, by fax, by e-mail and via website. Appointment necessary.
Hours: Mon to Fri, 0830 to 1600

Links with:
DfES
QCA
SQA

CIRCUS SOCIETY

52 Wiltshire Road, West Harnham, Salisbury, Wiltshire, SP2 8HR

Tel: 01722 329867

Enquiries:
Enquiries to: President

Founded:
1983

Organisation type and purpose:
Membership association (membership is by subscription), voluntary organisation, research organisation.
Self-financing organisation, membership including Circus News, £13 a year; OAP and juniors under 16, £10 a year including 4 magazines.
Formed to assist circus in PR, advertising, school and media work.

Subject coverage:
Circus, past and present.

Museum or gallery collection, archive, or library special collection:
Collection of old posters, programmes and other circus associated material

Printed publications:
Circus Membership (quarterly, £13)
Circus News (magazine, quarterly, £2.75, non-members)

Access to staff:
Contact by letter and by telephone. Appointment necessary. All charged.
Hours: Mon to Fri, 1400 to 1700
Special comments: Please send stamped addressed envelope.

Assistant Secretary:
Circus Society
6 Sherwood Court, 372 London Road, Langley, Slough, Berkshire, SL3 7HX

CIRIA

Formal name: Construction Industry Research and Information Association
Acronym or abbreviation: CIRIA

Classic House, 174 – 180 Old Street, London EC1V 9BP

Tel: 020 7549 3300
Fax: 020 7253 0523
E-mail: enquiries@ciria.org

Website:
http://www.ciria.org.uk
Introduction to the Association, outline of research and information themes, details of participation routes and services. Recent publications and forthcoming events.

Enquiries:
Enquiries to: Customer Services

Founded:
1960

Organisation type and purpose:
Advisory body, professional body, membership association (membership is by subscription), research organisation, publishing house.
Providing best practice guidance for construction and the environment.

Subject coverage:
Building; structural design; construction management; materials; ground engineering; site operations; contaminated land; water engineering and environmental management; structural engineering; health and safety; quality management; information technology.

Library catalogue:
All or part available online and in print

Printed publications:
Annual Report
Reports
CIRIA News (quarterly)
A range of over 400 publications under the headings of:
Building Construction and Technology
Construction Management
Environment Management
Ground Engineering
Water Engineering

Publications list:
Available online and in print

Access to staff:
Contact by letter, by telephone, by fax, by e-mail, in person and via website
Hours: Mon to Fri, 0900 to 1700

CISION UK

Cision House, 16–22 Baltic Street West, London, EC1Y 0UL

Tel: 020 7251 7220

continued overleaf

Fax: 020 7689 1164
E-mail: info.uk@csion.com

Website:
http://uk.cision.com/

Enquiries:
Enquiries to: Information Officer

Founded:
1852

Formerly called:
Romeike Limited

Organisation type and purpose:
Media monitoring and press clipping agency.
Media monitoring and analysis.

Subject coverage:
Press clippings; media analysis; online summaries.

Access to staff:
Contact by letter, by telephone, by fax, by e-mail
and in person
Hours: Mon to Fri, 0900 to 1700

Member of:
Association of Media Evaluation Companies
(AMEC)
Fédération Internationale des Bureaux d'Extraits
de Presse (FIBEP)
International Association of Broadcast Monitors
(IABM)
Public Relations Consultants Association (PRCA)

CITB-CONSTRUCTIONSKILLS

Acronym or abbreviation: CITB

Head Office, Bircham Newton, King's Lynn,
Norfolk, PE31 6RH

Tel: 01485 577577
Fax: 01485 577684

Website:
http://www.citb.co.uk
Careers, training and publications.

Enquiries:
Enquiries to: Resource Centre
Direct tel: 01485 577682
Direct e-mail: information.centre@citb.co.uk

Founded:
1964

Organisation type and purpose:
Statutory body, registered charity (charity number
264289), training organisation.
Statutory body.
An integral part of the construction industry
concerned with craft, technicians, safety,
supervisory, management training and manpower.

Subject coverage:
Building; civil engineering and related
management; training; health and safety in the
industry.

Printed publications:
A large number of publications on:
Craft and Operative Training
Health and Safety
National and Scottish Vocational Qualifications
Prevocational Education and Equal Opportunities
Technical, Supervisory and Management Training
Order printed publications from: CITB Publications
Department
tel: 01485 577800, fax: 01485 577758

Electronic and video publications:
Computer-based training packages
Videos, particularly on safety

Access to staff:
Appointment necessary.
Hours: Mon to Fri, 0900 to 1700

CITIZENS ADVICE CYMRU

Acronym or abbreviation: CAC

Quebec House, 5–19 Cowbridge Road East,
Cardiff, CF11 9AB

Tel: 029 2037 6750
Fax: 029 2034 1541

Website:
http://www.adviceguide.org.uk

Enquiries:
Enquiries to: Office Manager

Organisation type and purpose:
Registered charity.
Advice and information service.
CAC provides central administrative support for
Citizens Advice Bureaux.

Subject coverage:
Information on services provided by, and levels of
use of, the Citizens Advice Bureaux in the South
Wales area.

Trade and statistical information:
Number and type of enquiries received and
financial grant aid achieved.

Access to staff:
Contact by letter, by telephone and by fax
Hours: Mon to Fri, 0900 to 1700

Parent body:
National Association of Citizens Advice Bureaux
Myddelton House, 115–123 Pentonville Road,
London, N1 9LZ

CITIZENS ADVICE SCOTLAND

Acronym or abbreviation: CAS

Spectrum House, 2 Powderhall Road, Edinburgh
EH7 4GB

Tel: 0131 550 1000
Fax: 0131 550 1001
E-mail: info@cas.org.uk

Website:
http://www.cas.org.uk

Enquiries:
Enquiries to: Press Officer
Other contacts: Chief Executive

Founded:
1975

Organisation type and purpose:
Membership association, voluntary organisation,
registered charity.
Policy-making body and provider of services to
Citizens Advice Bureaux in Scotland.

Subject coverage:
Citizens Advice Bureau services in Scotland and
advice centres generally; all aspects of welfare law,
Commissioners' decisions, social security,
employment, housing, consumer affairs, money
advice, Scots Law; expertise in training, volunteer
development and advice service development.

**Museum or gallery collection, archive, or library
special collection:**
Library of information related to Welfare Law

Non-library collection catalogue:
All or part available online

Library catalogue:
All or part available in-house

Printed publications:
Annual Report
Range of free information leaflets including:
CAB Information System
Getting Divorced
How can I use experience to help the Community?
Neighbour Problems
Social Policy Evidence Reports
Voicing your concerns
What's your idea of a CAB volunteer?
Working for a change

Microform publications:
CAB Information System (to members)

Electronic and video publications:
CAB Information System (CD-ROM)

Publications list:
Available online and in print

Access to staff:
Contact by letter and by telephone
Hours: Mon to Fri, 0900 to 1700

CITIZENS' BAND RADIO GOOD PUBLICITY GROUP

Hillview, Mid-Holmwood Lane, Dorking, RH5
4HD

Tel: 01306 881137
E-mail: cbrgpg@muddymail.com

Enquiries:
Enquiries to: Manager

Founded:
1997

Incorporates the former:
Communication Eleven, County Hunters DX
Group

Organisation type and purpose:
Advisory body, voluntary organisation.
Increase public awareness of the positive sides to
citizens band radio (CB Radio). Practical help and
advice on installation and use of CB radio
equipment in vehicles, homes and business
premises.

Subject coverage:
Citizens' band radio, advice on which radios are
legal and which are illegal, help with keeping a CB
station within legal limits. Specific installation
advice regarding CB in off-road vehicles, especially
Land Rovers and farm machines. Information on
specialist products available. Microphone wiring
database to stop mic compatibility problems. CB
advice for potential new users, who may be
curious as to what CB radio could do for them or
their business.

Printed publications:
4WD CB Guide (for off-road drivers, free)
Caravan CB Guide (for caravan enthusiasts, free)
CB Catalogue (free)
Farm CB Guide (for farmers, free)

Access to staff:
Contact by letter, by telephone and by e-mail.
Appointment necessary.
Hours: Mon to Fri, 0900 to 1700

Also at:
Citizens' Band Radio Good Publicity Group
PO Box 198, Reigate, Surrey, RH2 0FX

CITROËN CAR CLUB

Acronym or abbreviation: CCC

PO Box 348, Bromley, Kent, BR2 8QT

Tel: 07000 248 258
Fax: 07000 248 258
E-mail: member@citroencarclub.net

Website:
http://www.citroencarclub.org.uk
The club and its cars, membership application
form.

Enquiries:
Enquiries to: Membership Administration

Founded:
1949

Organisation type and purpose:
Membership association (membership is by
subscription), present number of members: 3000,
voluntary organisation.

Subject coverage:
Citroën cars, past and present.

**Museum or gallery collection, archive, or library
special collection:**
Comprehensive library of all back issues of
Citroënian and most English language
publications and books on Citroën

Printed publications:
Club magazine (monthly, available on
subscription)

Access to staff:
Contact by letter, by telephone, by fax, by e-mail and via website
Hours: 1000 to 1900 only
Special comments: Club membership list enquiries are not normally available, but all enquiries will be considered on merit.

CITY & GUILDS NPTC

Acronym or abbreviation: NPTC

Stoneleigh Park, Stoneleigh, Warwickshire, CV8 2LG

Tel: 024 7685 7300
Fax: 024 7669 6128
E-mail: information@nptc.org.uk

Website:
http://www.nptc.org.uk

Enquiries:
Enquiries to: Business Development Officer

Founded:
1970

Organisation type and purpose:
City & Guilds NPTC is an awarding body for the land-based industries. It is a registered charity (Charity no 272305) that seeks to 'promote competence and professionalism in the workforce of land-based and related industries by the encouragement of continous learning and the recognition of skill'. To this end it oversees a range of qualifications including Certificates of Competence, NVQs, SVQs, National Certificates, Advanced National Certificates and Diplomas.

Subject coverage:
Agriculture, horticulture, forestry, floristry, animal care, equine matters, environment and conservation, land-based machinery.

Printed publications:
Fliers and posters covering all the qualifications

Access to staff:
Contact by letter, by telephone, by fax, by e-mail and via website. Appointment necessary.
Hours: Mon to Fri, 0830 to 1700

CITY AND COUNTY OF SWANSEA LIBRARIES

Library HQ, County Hall, Oystermouth Road, Swansea, West Glamorgan, SA1 3SN

Tel: 01792 636430
Fax: 01792 636235
E-mail: swansea.libraries@swansea.gov.uk

Website:
http://www.swansea.gov.uk/culture/Libraries/LibraryIntro.htm
http://www.swansea.gov.uk/culture/libraries/locations.htm

Enquiries:
Enquiries to: Librarian

Founded:
1996

Organisation type and purpose:
Local government body, public library.

Subject coverage:
Welsh language material, culture and history of Wales, history of Swansea, Dylan Thomas.

Museum or gallery collection, archive, or library special collection:
Deffett Francis Collection
Dylan Thomas Collection
Local History Collection
Vernon Watkins Collection
Welsh Collection
Rowland Williams Collection

Non-library collection catalogue:
All or part available online and in-house

Library catalogue:
All or part available online and in-house

Microform publications:
County Library Catalogue (Com-Fiche)
Index to Cambrian Newspaper (South Wales) 1804–1870 (hardcopy and disk)

Access to staff:
Contact by letter, by telephone, by fax, by e-mail, in person and via website. Appointment necessary.
Hours: Mon to Sat, 0900 to 1700

Parent body:
City and County of Swansea
County Hall, Oystermouth Road, Swansea, SA1 3SN; tel: 01792 636000

CITY AND ISLINGTON COLLEGE

The Marlborough Building, 383 Holloway Road, London, N7 0RN

Tel: 020 7700 9333
Fax: 020 7700 4268

Website:
http://www.candi.ac.uk

Enquiries:
Enquiries to: Director of Students
Direct tel: 020 7700 9214
Other contacts: Head of Learning Resources

Formed by the amalgamation of:
City and East London College, Islington 6th Form Centre and Adult Education Service, North London College

Organisation type and purpose:
Suitable for ages: 16+.
Further education college.

Subject coverage:
Applied optics, engineering technology, access courses, GNVQ and A levels, business studies, health and leisure, ESOL, wide range of adult education courses, health and community care, wide range of IT resources, media, visual and performing arts.

Library catalogue:
All or part available online

Publications list:
Available online and in print

Access to staff:
Contact by letter, by telephone, by fax and by e-mail
Hours: Mon to Thu, 0900 to 2000; Fri, 0900 to 1700; Sat, 1100 to 1600 at Camden, Springhouse and Willen

Access to building, collection or gallery:
No access other than to staff

CITY BUSINESS LIBRARY

Acronym or abbreviation: CBL

1 Brewers' Hall Garden (off Aldermanbury Square), London, EC2V 5BX

Tel: 020 7332 1812 (enquiries)
Fax: 020 7600 1185
E-mail: cbl@cityoflondon.gov.uk

Website:
www.cityoflondon.gov.uk/citybusinesslibrary

Enquiries:
Enquiries to: Business Librarian
Direct tel: 020 7322 1841
Direct e-mail: goretti.considine@cityoflondon.gov.uk

Founded:
1970

Organisation type and purpose:
Public reference library. Printed and electronic data for individuals and for businesses of all sizes.

Subject coverage:
Management, finance, banking, insurance, employment, product, industry and country data, market research, statistics, company data.

Services for disabled people:
Induction loop. Jaws and ZoomText software for those with a visual impairment

Museum or gallery collection, archive, or library special collection:
British and overseas trade directories
Company data services (print and online databases)
Collection of United Kingdom market research reports

Trade and statistical information:
United Kingdom and some world financial statistics.

Library catalogue:
All or part available online

Printed publications:
City Business Library Guides to help visitors use various of the Library's resources
Welcome to the City Business Library (descriptive brochure)

Publications list:
Available online and in print

Access to staff:
Contact by letter, by telephone, by fax, by e-mail and in person
Hours: Mon to Fri, 0930 to 1700
Special comments: ID required for access to some materials within the library.

Access for disabled people:
Ramped entry, access to all public areas, toilet facilities

Constituent part of:
City of London library service

CITY COLLEGE BRIGHTON AND HOVE

Acronym or abbreviation: CCBH

Pelham Street, Brighton, East Sussex, BN1 4FA

Tel: 01273 667788
Fax: 01273 667748
E-mail: lrc@ccb.ac.uk

Website:
http://www.ccb.ac.uk
LRC catalogue and other online resources

Enquiries:
Enquiries to: LRC Manager
Direct tel: 01273 667733

Formerly called:
Brighton College of Technology (BCT) (year of change 2001)

Organisation type and purpose:
College of further education library.

Subject coverage:
Art and design, business, child care and education, construction, digital media and photography, ESOL, engineering – electrical, electronic, mechanical, motor vehicle, general humanities, hairdressing and beauty therapy, hospitality and catering, media and journalism, music and performing arts, science, travel and tourism

Library catalogue:
All or part available online

Access to staff:
Contact by letter, by telephone and by e-mail. Appointment necessary.
Hours: Term time: Mon to Thu, 0900 to 2000; Fri, 0900 to 1700; vacation: 0900 to 1700 (variable)

Access to building, collection or gallery:
Special comments: Visitors who wish to use the LRC should come during less busy times (after 4pm) and report to the Enquiry Desk on arrival.

CITY LITERARY INSTITUTE

Acronym or abbreviation: City Lit

Keeley Street, London, WC2B 4BA

continued overleaf

Tel: 020 7492 2600
E-mail: infoline@citylit.ac.uk

Website:
http://www.citylit.ac.uk

Enquiries:
Enquiries to: Head of Learning Centre
Direct tel: 020 7492 2666
Direct fax: lc-enquiries@citylit.ac.uk

Organisation type and purpose:
Adult education institute.

Subject coverage:
Education of deaf and partially hearing adults,
speech therapy for stammerers and hearing
impaired people.

**Museum or gallery collection, archive, or library
special collection:**
Sign language videos, CD-ROMs and books, deaf
culture and deaf awareness, aural rehabilitation,
speech therapy

Non-library collection catalogue:
All or part available online

Library catalogue:
All or part available online

Access to staff:
Contact by telephone
Hours: Term Time: Mon, 1200 to 2000; Tue to Fri,
1030 to 2000; Sat, 1200 to 1600

Access to building, collection or gallery:
No prior appointment required
Hours: Mon, 1200 to 2000; Tue to Fri, 1030 to 2000;
Sat, 1200 to 1600

CITY OF BRADFORD METROPOLITAN DISTRICT COUNCIL

City Hall, Bradford, West Yorkshire, BD1 1HY

Tel: 01274 432111
Fax: 01274 432065

Website:
http://www.bradford.gov.uk

Organisation type and purpose:
Local government body.

Subject coverage:
Local government services.

CITY OF LONDON SOLICITORS' COMPANY

Acronym or abbreviation: CLSC

4 College Hill, London, EC4R 2RB

Tel: 020 7329 2173
Fax: 020 7329 2190
E-mail: mail@citysolicitors.org.uk

Website:
http://www.citysolicitors.org.uk

Enquiries:
Enquiries to: The Clerk

Founded:
1908

Organisation type and purpose:
Membership association (membership is by
election or invitation).
City of London Livery Company.

Access to staff:
Contact by letter, by telephone, by fax, by e-mail
and via website

CITY OF SALFORD

Civic Centre, Chorley Road, Swinton, Salford,
Greater Manchester, M27 5FJ

Tel: 0161 794 4711
Fax: 0161 794 6595

Website:
http://www.salford.gov.uk

Enquiries:
Enquiries to: Public Relations Manager
Direct tel: 0161 793 3157
Direct fax: 0161 793 3234
Direct e-mail: ian.andrew@salford.gov.uk
Other contacts: Chief Executive for formal
complaints.

Organisation type and purpose:
Local government body.

Subject coverage:
Business of a local authority – metropolitan
authority – Greater Manchester. Arts and leisure,
libraries, museums, education, social services,
housing, planning issues, environmental issues.

Printed publications:
Civic Guide On Salford People (magazine)

Access to staff:
Contact by letter, by telephone, by fax, by e-mail,
in person and via website
Hours: Mon to Fri, 0830 to 1630

Access for disabled people:
Parking provided, ramped entry, access to all
public areas, toilet facilities

Includes:
Rushmoor Local History Gallery
at the same address

CITY OF SUNDERLAND

Civic Centre, Sunderland, Tyne and Wear, SR2
7DN

Tel: 0191 553 1000

Website:
http://www.sunderland.gov.uk

Enquiries:
Enquiries to: Chief Executive

Organisation type and purpose:
Local government body.

Subject coverage:
Local government services.

Access to staff:
Contact by letter, by telephone, by fax and by e-
mail. Appointment necessary.
Hours: Mon to Fri, 0900 to 1700

CITY OF WESTMINSTER ARCHIVES CENTRE

Acronym or abbreviation: COWAC

10 St Ann's Street, London, SW1P 2DE

Tel: 020 7641 5180\ Minicom no. 020 7641 4879
Fax: 020 7641 5179
E-mail: archives@westminster.gov.uk

Website:
http://www.westminster.gov.uk/archives
General information, location, opening hours,
publications for sale, talks and events, what we do.

Enquiries:
Enquiries to: Librarian
Other contacts: City Archivist, Manager for the
Business Unit Manager.

Organisation type and purpose:
Local government body, public library.
Archive.

Subject coverage:
Local studies, conservation, local history, archives,
Westminster history, Marylebone history,
Paddington history.

**Museum or gallery collection, archive, or library
special collection:**
A M Broadley Collections (Annals of the
Haymarket, and Some Social, Political and
Literary Landmarks of Bath and Piccadilly)
Artisans', Labourers' & General Dwellings
Company Limited (annual reports and accounts
1880–1956)
Francis Edwards Limited (booksellers catalogues
1938–1982)
Manuscript notes on local subjects including an 82
volume scrapbook, Inns, Taverns, Alehouses,
Coffee Houses, etc. in and around London,
compiled by D Foster c. 1900
Marylebone Gardens (over 50 songs of the 18th
century sung in the gardens, some by William
Defesch and James Hook)
The Ashbridge Collection (books, maps, prints,
watercolours and drawings relating to St
Marylebone)
The parliamentary representation of Westminster
from the 13th century to the present day
The Preston Blake Collection: books by and about
William Blake, papers, letters, periodicals,
catalogues, transparencies.
Theatre Collection (some 28,000 theatre
programmes, and playbills, news cuttings,
portraits, financial records, correspondence)
St Marylebone Housing Association
Whiteley's (catalogues for general goods, wines,
cigars, provisions etc staff magazine 1885–1958)
Books and pamphlets; rare books; newspapers and
periodicals; official local government records;
prints and photographs; census; parish registers;
wills, from 1460 onwards; maps and plans;
directories and electoral registers; business
records

Non-library collection catalogue:
All or part available online and in-house

Library catalogue:
All or part available online

Printed publications:
Guides to sources of information particularly
genealogical material
Maps from 1755 onwards
Books on the history, architecture and
development of the area including:
Regent's Park – A study of the development of the
area from 1086 to the present day (Saunders A,
£4.50 plus p&p)
St John's Wood and Maida Vale Past (Tames R,
£14.95 plus p&p)
Growth of St Marylebone and Paddington
(Whitehead J, 3rd ed., 2001, £12.95 plus p&p)
Westminster History Review (annual, vol 1 1997,
£3.99 plus p&p)
Guide to Sources for Family History held by
Westminster Archives (Cory E, 1997, £3 plus
p&p)
Tracing the History of Your House (Kenney A,
1996, £3.50 plus p&p)
Local interest publications include:
Blitz over Westminster (includes City of
Westminster Civil Defence Bomb Incident
Photographs 1940–44, Harrison R, 1990, £3.50
plus p&p)
Covent Garden Past (Richardson J, 1995, £14.95
plus p&p)
Diary of William Tayler, footman 1837 (Wise D ed,
1998, £7.50 plus p&p)
Order printed publications from: Publications Officer,
City of Westminster Archives Centre
Address as main

Microform publications:
Gillow Archive
Local Newspapers (some fifty covering various
periods)
Twentieth century Post Office London directories
Name index to St Martin-in-the-Fields Poor Law
Settlements Part 1, 1750 to 1775 (7 microfiches, £5
plus p&p)
St Marylebone Census Name Index for 1821 and
1831 (£5 each plus p&p)
Order microform publications from: St Marylebone
Census Name Index for 1821 and 1831, Published
by The Family History Shop, Norwich

Publications list:
Available online and in print

Access to staff:
Contact by letter, by telephone, by fax, by e-mail, in person and via website
Hours: Mon, Closed, Fri, Sat, 1000 to 1700; Tue to Thu, 1000 to 1900

Access to building, collection or gallery:
No prior appointment required

Access for disabled people:
Ramped entry, access to all public areas, toilet facilities
Special comments: Parking provided by prior arrangement.

CITY OF YORK & DISTRICT FAMILY HISTORY SOCIETY

The Raylor Centre, James Street, Lawrence Street, York, YO10 3DW

Tel: 01904 412204
E-mail: secretary@yorkfamilyhistory.org.uk

Website:
http://www.yorkfamilyhistory.org.uk/

Enquiries:
Enquiries to: Secretary

Founded:
1975

Organisation type and purpose:
Membership association (membership is by subscription), registered charity.

Subject coverage:
Family history.

Printed publications:
For purchase, direct only

Microform publications:
Microfiche, for purchase, direct only

Electronic and video publications:
CD-ROM, for purchase direct only

Publications list:
Available online and in print

Access to staff:
Contact by letter, by e-mail and via website

CITY OF YORK LIBRARIES

Museum Street, York, YO1 7DS

Tel: 01904 655631
Fax: 01904 611025
E-mail: reference.library@york.gov.uk

Website:
http://www.york.gov.uk
City of York Council information.
http://www.york.gov.uk/libraries

Enquiries:
Enquiries to: Head of Library Service
Direct tel: 01904 553316
Other contacts: Information Services Librarian tel: 01904 552824 reference.library@york.gov.uk.

Founded:
1891

Organisation type and purpose:
Local government body, public library.

Subject coverage:
General, York and Yorkshire.

Museum or gallery collection, archive, or library special collection:
Rowland Collection of oboe music
Sir John Marriott Memorial Library on modern European history from the French Revolution

Non-library collection catalogue:
All or part available in-house

Library catalogue:
All or part available online

Access to staff:
Contact by letter, by telephone, by fax, by e-mail and in person

Hours: Lending library: Mon, Tue, Fri, 0930 to 2000; Wed, Thu, 0930 to 1730; Sat, 0930 to 1600
Reference library: Mon, Tue, Wed, Fri, 0900 to 2000; Thu, 0900 to 1730; Sat, 0900 to 1600

Access to building, collection or gallery:
No prior appointment required

Access for disabled people:
Lift, ramped entry, access to all public areas, toilet facilities
Hours: as above

Has:
15 libraries and 1 mobile library covering the City of York Council area

Parent body:
City of York Council
tel: 01904 613161

CITY PROPERTY ASSOCIATION

Acronym or abbreviation: CPA

7th Floor, 1 Warwick Row, London, SW1E 5ER

Tel: 020 7630 1782
Fax: 020 7630 8344
E-mail: phouston@bpf.org.uk

Enquiries:
Enquiries to: Secretary

Founded:
1904

Organisation type and purpose:
Trade association.

Subject coverage:
Ownership of properties in the City of London.

Access to staff:
Contact by letter, by e-mail and in person
Hours: Tue to Thu, 0900 to 1700

CITY UNIVERSITY LONDON – DEPARTMENT OF COMPUTING

Northampton Square, London, EC1V 0HB

Tel: 020 7040 8432
Fax: 020 7040 8587

Website:
http://www.soi.city.ac.uk/doc/
Full departmental profile and details.

Enquiries:
Enquiries to: Administrator

Formerly called:
Department of Business Computing, Department of Computer Science

Organisation type and purpose:
University department or institute.

Subject coverage:
Undergraduate courses in computer science, computer science with distributed systems or AI, software engineering, business computing and information systems. Postgraduate courses in business systems analysis and design and object oriented software systems.

Publications list:
Available online

Access to staff:
Contact by letter and by e-mail. Appointment necessary.
Hours: Mon to Fri, 0900 to 1700

Access to building, collection or gallery:
Prior appointment required

Access for disabled people:
Ramped entry, access to all public areas, toilet facilities

CITY UNIVERSITY LONDON – DEPARTMENT OF LANGUAGE AND COMMUNICATION SCIENCE

Northampton Square, London, EC1V 0HB

Tel: 020 7040 8281
Fax: 020 7040 8577

Website:
http://www.city.ac.uk/lcs

Enquiries:
Enquiries to: Courses Administrator
Direct e-mail: r.fekete@city.ac.uk

Organisation type and purpose:
University department or institute.

Subject coverage:
Disorders of speech, training of speech therapists, research into disorders of speech, alternative and augmentative aids to human communication.

Museum or gallery collection, archive, or library special collection:
MSc and MPhil/PhD theses in field of disorders of human communication

Access to staff:
Contact by telephone and by e-mail
Hours: Mon to Fri, 0900 to 1700

CITY UNIVERSITY LONDON – LIBRARY

Northampton Square, London, EC1V 0HB

Tel: 020 7040 8191
Fax: 020 7040 8194
E-mail: library@city.ac.uk

Website:
http://www.city.ac.uk/library

Enquiries:
Enquiries to: Director of Information Services and Libraries
Direct tel: 020 7040 8162

Founded:
1894

Organisation type and purpose:
University library.

Subject coverage:
Cultural policy and management; banking; business; finance; language and communication science; computer science; engineering; information science; journalism; law; management; mathematics; music; optometry; property valuation; social science; nursing; midwifery.

Museum or gallery collection, archive, or library special collection:
Erna Auerbach Collection (art history)
Kipling Society Collection
Rosencweig Collection (Jewish music), now transferred to the School of Oriental and African Studies
Walter Fincham Collection (optics)

Library catalogue:
All or part available online

Printed publications:
Library information leaflets

Access to staff:
Contact by e-mail
Hours: Mon to Fri, 0900 to 1700

Access for disabled people:
Ramped entry, toilet facilities

CIVIC TRUST

17 Carlton House Terrace, London, SW1Y 5AW

Tel: 020 7930 0914
Fax: 020 7321 0180
E-mail: pride@civictrust.org.uk

Website:
http://www.civictrust.org.uk
Home page, information and publications.

continued overleaf

Enquiries:
Enquiries to: Librarian

Founded:
1957

Organisation type and purpose:
National organisation, membership association
(membership is by subscription), present number
of members: 3000 members, 60 corporate members,
voluntary organisation, registered charity (charity
number 1068759).
Working in partnership to improve the built
environment for the benefit of the community.

Subject coverage:
Urban environment, architecture, planning,
transport, conservation, regeneration, community
involvement, civic societies.

Printed publications:
Civic Focus – News from the Civic Trust (available
on subscription)
2001 Civic Trust Awards Report
A New Framework for Freight Transport (1995)
Brownfield Housing – 12 Years On (1999)
Effective Partnerships for Voluntary and
Community Groups (1999)
Effective Partnerships for Managers and Board
Managers
Investing in the High Street (1999)
Small Town Vitality: The Impact of New Housing
(2000)
Sustainable Renewal of Suburban Areas (1999)

Publications list:
Available online and in print

2nd Office:
Civic Trust Northern Office
6th Floor, The View, Gostins Building, 32–36
Hannover Street, Liverpool, L1 4LN; tel: 0151
709 1969; fax: 0151 709 2022; e-mail:
northernoffice@civictrust.org.uk

Partner organisations:
Civic Trust for Wales
3rd Floor, Empire House, Mount Stuart Square,
Cardiff, CF10 5FN; tel: 01222 484606; website:
civictrustwales.demon.co.uk
North East Civic Trust
Blackfriars, Monk Street, Newcastle upon Tyne,
NE1 4XN
Scottish Civic Trust
42 Miller Street, Glasgow, G2 1DT; tel: 0141 221
1466

CIVIL AID

Formal name: National Voluntary Civil Aid Services
Acronym or abbreviation: NVCAS

c/o Crinoids, 106 Church Road, Teddington,
Middlesex, TW11 8EY

Tel: 020 8977 2806
Fax: 020 8943 5556

Enquiries:
Enquiries to: President
Other contacts: General Secretary, tel no: 020 8942
9126

Founded:
1968

Emerged for reasons of political expediency:
Civil Defence Corps (year of change 1968)

Organisation type and purpose:
National organisation, membership association
(membership is by subscription), present number
of members: 300, voluntary organisation,
registered charity (charity number 266349),
suitable for ages: 16+, training organisation.
An autonomous, self-funded organisation which
emerged in 1968 when the Civil Defence Corps
was stood down for reasons of political
expediency. Duke of Edinburgh's Award training
organisation.
To train its members and the public in disaster
mitigation and relief, and to provide aid for any
peace-time disaster.

Subject coverage:
First aid, fire prevention and control, emergency
feeding, rescue techniques, communications, rest
centres, information centres.

Printed publications:
Newsletter

Access to staff:
Contact by letter, by telephone and by fax
Hours: Mon to Fri, 0900 to 1700

Links with:
The Institute of Civil Defence and Disaster Studies
The National Council for Civil Protection

Registered Office:
Civil Aid
Phoenix House, Greenlands Avenue, Kingsway,
Derby

CIVIL AVIATION AUTHORITY

Acronym or abbreviation: CAA

Library and Information Centre, Civil Aviation
Authority Safety Regulation Group, Aviation
House, South Area, Gatwick Airport, West Sussex,
RH6 0YR

Tel: 01293 573725
Fax: 01293 573181
E-mail: infoservices@caa.co.uk

Website:
http://www.caa.co.uk

Enquiries:
Enquiries to: Manager
Direct tel: 01293 573966
Direct e-mail: vagn.pedersen@caa.co.uk
Other contacts: Librarian for information enquiries.

Founded:
1972

Carries out the functions of the former:
Air Registration Board, Air Transport Licensing
Board

Includes the former:
Safety Regulation Group Library

Organisation type and purpose:
Statutory body. Public Authority. Aviation
regulatory body.

Subject coverage:
Civil aviation, electronics including air traffic
control, aircraft, flightcrew, airports,
telecommunications, radar etc.

**Museum or gallery collection, archive, or library
special collection:**
Aviation historical collection

Trade and statistical information:
UK airlines and airports statistics.

Library catalogue:
All or part available in-house

Publications list:
Available in print

Access to staff:
Contact by letter, by telephone, by fax, by e-mail
and in person
Hours: Mon to Fri, 0930 to 1630; 1st Wed of each
month, 1000 to 1630
Special comments: Reference use only to visitors.

Access to building, collection or gallery:
No prior appointment required

Access for disabled people:
Parking provided, level entry, access to all public
areas

CIVIL ENGINEERING
CONTRACTORS ASSOCIATION

Acronym or abbreviation: CECA

55 Tufton Street, London, SW1P 3QL

Tel: 020 7227 4621
Fax: 020 7227 4620

E-mail: enquiries@ceca.co.uk

Website:
http://www.ceca.co.uk

Enquiries:
Direct e-mail: lauraellis@ceca.co.uk

Founded:
1996

Organisation type and purpose:
Trade association.

Subject coverage:
Construction, including training and careers, legal
affairs, industrial relations, safety, economics,
statistics.

Printed publications:
Economic Reports
Contracts and associated publications
Guides, technical reports and manuals
Newsline (monthly)
Press Abstracts

Access to staff:
Contact by letter, by telephone, by fax, by e-mail
and via website
Hours: Mon to Fri, 0900 to 1730

Member of:
Construction Confederation

CIVIL SERVICE APPEAL BOARD

Acronym or abbreviation: CSAB

22 Whitehall, London, SW1A 2WH

Tel: 020 7276 3832
Fax: 020 7276 3836
E-mail: csab@cabinet-office.x.gsi.gov.uk

Website:
http://www.cabinet-office.gov.uk/civilservice/
1999/appealboard/csab.htm
CSAB Annual Reports, 1997/98 and 1998/99.
http://www.civilserviceappealboard.gov.uk

Enquiries:
Enquiries to: Secretary
Direct e-mail: keith.wright@cabinet-office.x.gsi.gov
.uk

Founded:
1971

Organisation type and purpose:
Advisory body.
An advisory non-departmental public body which
hears appeals from civil servants against: dismissal
and early retirement; part- or non-payment of the
amount of compensation paid to civil servants
dismissed on inefficiency grounds; refusal to allow
participation in political activities or forfeiture of
superannuation benefits.

Printed publications:
Civil Service Appeal Board Annual Report
(annually, free)

Access to staff:
Contact by letter, by telephone, by fax and by e-
mail
Hours: 0900 to 1700

CIVITAS: THE INSTITUTE FOR
THE STUDY OF CIVIL SOCIETY

The Mezzanine, Elizabeth House, 39 York Road,
London, SE1 7NQ

Tel: 020 7401 5470
Fax: 020 7401 5471
E-mail: robert.whelan@civitas.org.uk

Website:
http://www.civitas.org.uk

Enquiries:
Enquiries to: Deputy Director

Formerly called:
Health & Welfare Unit of the Institute of Economic
Affairs (year of change 2000)

Organisation type and purpose:
Registered charity (charity number 1085494), research organisation, publishing house.

Subject coverage:
Health, education, welfare, criminal justice, the family.

Publications list:
Available online and in print

Access to staff:
Contact by letter, by telephone, by fax, by e-mail and via website
Hours: Mon to Fri, 0900 to 1700

CLACKMANNANSHIRE COUNCIL

Greenfield, Alloa, Clackmannanshire, FK10 2AD

Tel: 01259 450000
Fax: 01259 452010
E-mail: info@clacksweb.org.uk

Website:
http://www.clacksweb.org.uk

Enquiries:
Enquiries to: Communications and Marketing Manager
Direct tel: 01259 452023
Direct fax: 01259 452117
Direct e-mail: rfry@clacks.gov.uk
Other contacts: Chief Executive

Founded:
1996

Formerly called:
Central Regional Council, Clackmannan District Council

Organisation type and purpose:
Local government body.

Subject coverage:
Scottish local government; Clackmannanshire as an inward investment area.
Schools, nurseries, adult and community education, trading standards, environmental health, roads maintenance, property maintenance and design, social work, housing, licensing, council tax.

Printed publications:
Corporate Performance Report (free)
Business Directory (for purchase)
Business Information Leaflets (free)
Clackmannanshire Area Guide (free)
Community Safety Plane (free)
Economic Development Strategy (free)
Clackmannanshire Community Plan (free)
Building Clackmannanshire: Economic
   Development Framework (free)
Order printed publications from: http://
www.clacksweb.org.uk

Publications list:
Available in print

Access to staff:
Contact by letter, by telephone, by fax, by e-mail and via website
Hours: Mon to Fri, 0900 to 1700

Access for disabled people:
Parking provided, level entry, toilet facilities

CLACKMANNANSHIRE LIBRARIES

Acronym or abbreviation: CL

Alloa Library, 26–28 Drysdale Street, Alloa, Clackmannanshire, FK10 1JL

Tel: 01259 722262
Fax: 01259 219469
E-mail: libraries@clacks.gov.uk

Website:
http://www.clacksweb.org.uk/culture/
libraryservice

Enquiries:
Enquiries to: Information Librarian and Archivist

Other contacts: Special Services Co-ordinator; Team Leader of Public Services

Founded:
1996

Formerly called:
Clackmannan District Libraries (year of change 1996); Central Region Archives Department; Central Region Schools Library Service (year of change 1997)

Organisation type and purpose:
Local government body, museum, public library. Archive service.

Subject coverage:
General, local studies, archives, schools material.

Museum or gallery collection, archive, or library special collection:
Walter Murray Local Studies Collection;
   Clackmannanshire Archives

Non-library collection catalogue:
All or part available in-house

Library catalogue:
All or part available online

Printed publications:
A range of books on local history and society
   including:
Books on Alloa and Clackmannanshire
Local Railways (2 vols)
Poems of the Maestro (3 vols) and of the Wanderer
   (3 vols)
Statistical Accounts of six areas of
   Clackmannanshire
Order printed publications from: Special Services Co-
ordinator, at the same address

Publications list:
Available online and in print

Access to staff:
Contact by letter, by telephone, by fax, by e-mail and in person

Access to building, collection or gallery:
No prior appointment required
Hours: Alloa Library: Mon, Wed, Thu, Fri, 0930 to 1900; Tue, 0930 to 1630; Sat, 0900 to 1600
Other libraries vary, all close for lunch, telephone first
Special comments: Orders for items from Archive Store (Mon to Fri only) to be lodged no later than 1700 for delivery same day.

Access for disabled people:
Level entry

Branch libraries:
Alva Community Access Point
   153 West Stirling Street, Alva; tel: 01259 760652;
   fax: 01259 760364
Clackmannan Community Access Point
   Main Street, Clackmannan; tel: 01259 721579;
   fax: 01259 212493
Dollar Community Access Point
   Dollar Civic Centre, Park Place, Dollar; tel: 01259
   743253; fax: 01259 743328
Menstrie Community Access Point
   Dumyat Leisure Centre, Main Street East,
   Menstrie; tel: 01259 769439; fax: 01259 762941
Sauchie Community Access Point
   42–48 Main Street, Sauchie; tel: 01259 721679;
   fax: 01259 218750
Tillicoultry Branch Library
   99 High Street, Tillicoultry; tel: 01259 751685
Tullibody Branch Library
   Leisure Centre, Abercromby Place, Tullibody;
   tel: 01259 218725

Parent body:
Clackmannanshire Council
   tel: 01259 450000; fax: 01259 452230

CLAN RANALD TRUST FOR SCOTLAND

Unit 35 New Street, Warsely Car Park, Edinburgh, EH8 8DW

Tel: 0131 558 9191

E-mail: clanranald@clara.net

Website:
http://www.clanranald.org
History, images, costume.

Enquiries:
Enquiries to: Chief Executive
Other contacts: Administrator

Founded:
1996

Organisation type and purpose:
Membership association (membership is by election or invitation), present number of members: 50 (charity number SCO 24881), suitable for ages: 14+.
Promotes Scottish Medieval History through education and entertainment. Constructing large motte and baille fortress in the Carronn Valley near Stirling for tourism and education.

Subject coverage:
Film, TV, combat team, period room dressing, entertainment, gala days and open events, pipers and drummers, actors, special events, walk-ons, experienced extras for film.

Library catalogue:
All or part available online

Printed publications:
Direct for free, unless commercial

Electronic and video publications:
Showcase video
Music CD-ROM

Publications list:
Available online

Access to staff:
Contact by letter, by telephone, by e-mail and via website. Appointment necessary.
Hours: Mon to Fri, 1200 to 1800

Access for disabled people:
Parking provided, level entry

Links with:
Kirkpatrick McAndrew Clan Trust
McFarlane Clan Trust
Wallace Clan Trust

CLAN TARTAN CENTRE

Formal name: Edinburgh Woollen Mills
Acronym or abbreviation: EWM

James Pringle Weavers at Leith Mills, Leith Mills, 70–74 Bangor Road, Leith, Edinburgh, EH6 5JU

Tel: 0131 553 5161
Fax: 0131 553 4415

Website:
http://www.foreverscotland.com

Enquiries:
Enquiries to: Public Relations Manager
Other contacts: Manager

Subject coverage:
Clan history, research and retail tartan and accessories, gifts, crystal, cashmere, woollens, ladies and gents fashion, designer labels, shoes, whisky shop, golf company and Scottish foods.

Printed publications:
Leaflets available on request for Corporate
   Business, Tourist and Local

Access to staff:
Contact by letter, by telephone and by fax.
Appointment necessary.
Hours: Mon to Sat, 0900 to 1730; Sun, 1000 to 1700

Access for disabled people:
Parking provided, level entry

Head Office:
Edinburgh Woollen Mill
   Waverley Mill, Langholm, Dumfriesshire, DG13
   2BR; tel: 01387 380611

CLARINET HERITAGE SOCIETY

Acronym or abbreviation: CHS

47 Hambalt Road, London, SW4 9EQ

Tel: 020 8675 3877
E-mail: chs@comhem.se; mozartsbum@aol.com

Website:
www.claamfest.org

Enquiries:
Enquiries to: Honorary Secretary

Founded:
1980

Organisation type and purpose:
International organisation, advisory body, learned
society, professional body (membership is by
subscription), training organisation, consultancy,
research organisation, publishing house.
To promote new and rare music and general
awareness for the clarinet, research, recording,
study and performance.

Subject coverage:
Discovery, publication and sound recordings of
rare, unknown music for the clarinet; history;
performance and teaching; inventions and
innovations.

**Museum or gallery collection, archive, or library
special collection:**
Book manuscript
Musical instruments and tools of a noted master
    clarinettist
Various limited music for clarinet

Printed publications:
Clarinet tutor and method
Music by Heinrich Baermann
Personal memoirs of the music business from a
    professional clarinettist
Recording: The Art of Clarinet and Piano (Stephen
    Bennett, clarinet, Joyce Riddell, piano, for sale)
Sheet music: August Henrik Winding, 3 Fantasy
    Pieces for Clarinet and Piano (for sale)

Electronic and video publications:
Cassette and CD music audio

Access to staff:
Contact by letter, by telephone and by e-mail.
Appointment necessary. Non-members charged.
Hours: Mon to Fri, 0900 to 1700

Access to building, collection or gallery:
No prior appointment required

CLASSIC KAWASAKI CLUB

Acronym or abbreviation: CKC

PO Box 528, Kings Langley, Herts WD5 5AF

Tel: 020 8737 9755
Fax: 0115 913 4223
E-mail: classkawa@aol.com

Website:
http://kawaportal.org
Reference, photographs, adverts, message board.

Enquiries:
Enquiries to: Membership Secretary
Direct tel: 07779094462
Direct e-mail: downpipe3@ntlworld.com

Founded:
1980

Formerly called:
Kawasaki Triples Club (year of change 1996)

Organisation type and purpose:
International organisation, membership
association (membership is by subscription),
present number of members: 1100, museum.

Subject coverage:
Historical reference for Kawasaki motorcycles.

**Museum or gallery collection, archive, or library
special collection:**
Technical, historical and reference data held on
    computer and hard copy

Printed publications:
Magazine (6 times a year, members)

Electronic and video publications:
Reference Guides (CD-ROM)

Access to staff:
Contact by letter, by telephone, by fax, by e-mail
and via website. Appointment necessary.
Hours: Mon to Fri, 0900 to 1700

Access to building, collection or gallery:
No prior appointment required
Special comments: Museum visits by appointment
only.

Has connections with:
Various worldwide clubs

CLASSIC SALOON CAR CLUB (GB)

Acronym or abbreviation: CSCC

15 Biddenham Turn, Garston, Hertfordshire, WD2
6PU

Tel: 01923 893518

Website:
http://www.csccgb.co.uk
Clubs rules and technical regulations with details
of present car racing activities and records of same
since 1975.

Enquiries:
Enquiries to: Registrar
Direct e-mail: robslater@csccgb.co.uk

Founded:
1975

Organisation type and purpose:
Membership association (membership is by
subscription).

Subject coverage:
Recreating the great touring car racing of the past
in the spirit of the period but to the standards of
modern motorsport, showing, racing and enjoying
historic racing touring cars.

Access to staff:
Contact by letter, by e-mail and via website
Hours: Mon to Fri, 0900 to 1700

Affiliated club:
British Automobile Racing Club
    Thruxton Circuit, Andover, Hants, SP11 8PN;
    tel: 01264 772696

Registered with Sport Governing Body:
The Motorsports Association
    Motorsports House, Riverside Park, Colnbrook,
    Berks, SL3 0HG; tel: 01753 765000; fax: 01753
    682938

CLASSICAL ASSOCIATION

Acronym or abbreviation: CA

Senate House, Malet Street, London, WC1E 7HU

Tel: 020 7862 8706
Fax: 020 7255 2297
E-mail: office@classicalassociation.org

Website:
http://www.classicalassociation.org
General information about the Association.

Enquiries:
Enquiries to: Secretary

Founded:
1904

Organisation type and purpose:
Membership association (membership is by
subscription), present number of members: 4000,
registered charity.

Subject coverage:
Classical studies generally.

Printed publications:
CA News (included in the subscription)
Classical Quarterly
Classical Review

Greece and Rome
Presidential Address (included in subscription)
Order printed publications from: The Secretary,
Classical Association
at the same address

Access to staff:
Contact by letter, by telephone, by fax and by e-
mail
Hours: Mon to Fri, 0900 to 1700

Affiliated to:
International Federation for Classical Studies
(FIEC)

CLEANING AND HYGIENE SUPPLIERS ASSOCIATION

Acronym or abbreviation: CHSA

PO Box 770, Marlow, Buckinghamshire, SL7 2SH

Tel: 01628 478273
Fax: 01628 478286
E-mail: secretary@chsa.co.uk

Website:
http://www.chsa.co.uk

Enquiries:
Enquiries to: General Secretary

Founded:
1969

Organisation type and purpose:
Trade association (membership is by subscription),
present number of members: 200.

Subject coverage:
Supply chain issues.

Access to staff:
Contact by letter, by telephone, by fax, by e-mail
and via website
Hours: Mon to Fri, 0900 to 1700

Access to building, collection or gallery:
No access other than to staff

CLEANING AND SUPPORT SERVICES ASSOCIATION

Acronym or abbreviation: CSSA

Warnford Court, 29 Throgmorton Street, London,
EC2N 2AT

Tel: 020 7920 9632
Fax: 020 7256 9360
E-mail: alarge@cleaningassoc.org

Website:
http://www.cleaningassoc.org
News and information.

Enquiries:
Enquiries to: Director General

Founded:
1967

Organisation type and purpose:
Trade association.

Subject coverage:
Site support services, industry; especially, cleaning,
hygiene, building maintenance.

Trade and statistical information:
Trade information.

Printed publications:
Membership Directory
Trade Brochures

Publications list:
Available online and in print

Access to staff:
Contact by letter, by telephone, by fax, by e-mail
and via website
Hours: Mon to Fri, 0800 to 1630

Links with:
AssetSkills
European Federation of Cleaning Industries (EFCI)

Trade Association Forum (TAF)
World Federation of Building Service Contractors
(WFBSC)

CLEAPSS

The Gardiner Building, Brunel Science Park,
Kingston Lane, Uxbridge, Middlesex, UB8 3PQ

Tel: 01895 251496
Fax: 01895 814372
E-mail: science@cleapss.org.uk

Website:
http://www.cleapss.org.uk
Information about the services offered; lists of
current publications; dates and content of
forthcoming courses; membership information;
news items.

Enquiries:
Enquiries to: Director

Founded:
1963

Formerly called:
CLEAPSE (year of change 1988)

Organisation type and purpose:
Local government body, advisory body,
membership association (membership is by
subscription), present number of members: 2000
associate members, training organisation,
consultancy.
Information service.
Members include all 180 LAs outside Scotland.
To offer guidance on practical science and
technology in schools and colleges, including
health and safety, resources, laboratories,
technicians, etc.

Subject coverage:
Secondary school and college science laboratory
resources and safety, primary science and
technology resources and safety.

Printed publications:
Mostly free but only available to members

Publications list:
Available online

Access to staff:
Contact by letter, by telephone, by fax, by e-mail
and via website. Access for members only. Non-
members charged.
Hours: Mon to Fri, 0900 to 1700

CLECKHEATON LIBRARY

Cultural Services, Kirklees Metropolitan Council,
Whitcliffe Road, Cleckheaton, West Yorkshire,
BD19 3DX

Tel: 01274 335170
Fax: 01274 335171
E-mail: cleckheaton.library@kirklees.gov.uk

Website:
http://www.kirklees.gov.uk/libraries
Library address etc, photographs, facilities,
opening hours, services.

Enquiries:
Enquiries to: Librarian

Organisation type and purpose:
Public library.

**Museum or gallery collection, archive, or library
special collection:**
Spen Valley Historical Society Collection

Non-library collection catalogue:
All or part available in-house

Library catalogue:
All or part available in-house

Access to staff:
Contact by letter, by telephone, by fax, by e-mail
and in person
Hours: Mon, 0900 to 2000; Tue and Thu, 0900 to
1930; Wed, 0900 to 1300; Fri, 0900 to 1700;
Sat, 0900 to 1600

Access for disabled people:
Parking provided, ramped entry, toilet facilities,
wheelchair lift

CLEFT LIP AND PALATE ASSOCIATION

Acronym or abbreviation: CLAPA

First Floor, Green Man Tower, 332b Goswell
Road,London EC1V 7LQ

Tel: 020 7833 4883
Fax: 020 7833 5999
E-mail: info@clapa.com

Website:
http://www.clapa.com
Feeding a baby with a cleft, news and articles,
publications, how to make contact with CLAPA,
what is the cleft lip and palate association.

Enquiries:
Enquiries to: Chief Executive
Other contacts: Feeding Co-ordinator for issues
specifically related to feeding a baby born with
cleft lip and/or palate.

Founded:
1979

Organisation type and purpose:
Registered charity (charity no. 1108160).
To offer support to families affected by cleft lip
and/or palate.

Subject coverage:
Cleft lip and/or palate.

Printed publications:
Antenatal Diagnosis of Cleft Lip and Palate
CLAPA News and Annual Report
Cleft Lip & Palate: A Guide for Sonographers
Help for Parents
Help with Feeding
How does your Palate Work?
Pharyngoplasty
Treatment of Cleft Lip and Palate – a parent's guide
  (36pp, £3)

Publications list:
Available online and in print

Access to staff:
Contact by letter, by telephone, by fax, by e-mail
and via website
Hours: Mon to Fri, 0900 to 1700

Member of:
VOCAL and Contact a Family

CLEVELAND COLLEGE OF ART AND DESIGN LIBRARY

Acronym or abbreviation: CCAD

Green Lane, Linthorpe, Middlesbrough, Cleveland,
TS5 7RJ

Tel: 01642 288000
Fax: 01642 288828

Website:
http://www.ccad.ac.uk
Course information, admission policy.

Enquiries:
Enquiries to: Learning Resource Manager
Direct tel: 01642 298732
Direct e-mail: ann.kenyon@ccad.ac.uk

Organisation type and purpose:
College of further and higher education.

Subject coverage:
Fine and applied arts and crafts, art history, design
history, history of architecture, interior design and
layout, jewellery, ceramics, textiles, graphics,
printmaking, painting, sculpture, photography
and fashion.

Library catalogue:
All or part available online

Printed publications:
Library Handbook (annually)

Access to staff:
Contact by letter, by telephone and by e-mail.
Appointment necessary.
Hours: Mon to Thu, 0900 to 1900; Fri, 0900 to 1630
Special comments: Limited access during vacation
periods.

Access for disabled people:
Ramped entry

CLEVELAND COLLEGE OF ART AND DESIGN LIBRARY – HARTLEPOOL ANNEXE

Acronym or abbreviation: CCAD

Church Square, Hartlepool, Cleveland, TS24 7EX

Tel: 01429 422000
Fax: 01429 422122

Enquiries:
Enquiries to: Librarian
Other contacts: Learning Resource Manager

Organisation type and purpose:
HE students, full and part time

Subject coverage:
Fine and applied arts and crafts, art history, design
history, history of architecture, interior design and
layout, jewellery, ceramics, textiles, printmaking
and photography.

Library catalogue:
All or part available online

Printed publications:
Library Handbook (annually)
List of periodicals, acquisitions, videos and DVDs

Access to staff:
Contact by letter and by telephone. Appointment
necessary.
Hours: Mon to Fri, 0900 to 1700

Access to building, collection or gallery:
Hours: 0900 to 1700

Access for disabled people:
Fully accessible

Parent body:
Cleveland College of Art and Design
  Green Lane, Linthorpe, Middlesbrough, TS5 7RJ;
  tel: 01642 288000; fax: 01642 288828; website:
  http://www.ccad.ac.uk

CLEVELAND, NORTH YORKS & SOUTH DURHAM FHS

1 Oxgang Close, Redcar, Cleveland, TS10 4ND

Tel: 01642 486615
Fax: 01642 486615
E-mail: pjoiner@lineone.net

Website:
http://www.wesite.lineone.net/~pjoiner/cfhs/cfhs
.html

Enquiries:
Enquiries to: General Secretary

Founded:
1980

Organisation type and purpose:
International organisation, membership
association (membership is by subscription),
present number of members: 2000, voluntary
organisation, suitable for ages: 18 to 90, research
organisation.

Subject coverage:
Family history.

Printed publications:
Journal
Monumental Inscriptions (over 250 churches and
  cemeteries)
Parish Register transcriptions
Thirsk and Helmsley areas
Various historical publications
1851 Census Indexes for North Yorkshire and
  South Durham (over 125 vols)

continued overleaf

Workhouse Census Index (18 indices)
1881 Census Index (3 booklets)

Microform publications:
Guisborough Area (HO 107 2375), 3 fiche, covers
 about 50 parishes or sub-districts including
 Danby
Parish registers, Monumental Inscriptions and
 Returns of Papists
Pickering Area (HO 107 2373), 3 fiche, covers
 Pickering and about 20 neighbouring districts
1851 Census Index for Northern Yorkshire &
 Southern Durham (in microfiche)
1851 Census Indexes Guisborough, Helmsley,
 Pickering and Thirsk Areas
1881 Census Index (in microfiche)
1881 Census Indexes South Durham
1891 Census Indexes North Riding, Yorkshire,
 South Durham
Order microform publications from: as for printed
publications

Publications Manager, Cleveland, North Yorkshire
& South Durham FHS
106 The Avenue, Nunthorpe, Middlesbrough,
Cleveland, TS7 0AH

Publications list:
Available in print

Access to staff:
Contact by letter, by fax and by e-mail
Hours: Mon to Fri, 0900 to 1700

CLIFFORD CHANCE

200 Aldersgate Street, London, EC1A 4JJ

Tel: 020 7600 1000
Fax: 020 7600 5555

Website:
http://www.cliffordchance.com
Includes list of publications.

Enquiries:
Enquiries to: Head of Information Sourcing

Founded:
1987

Formerly called:
Clifford Turn'r Coward Chance (year of change
1987)

Organisation type and purpose:
Service industry.
Law Firm.

Subject coverage:
Commercial aspects of UK, European and
international law, publications for clients and
professional contacts.

Non-library collection catalogue:
All or part available in-house

Library catalogue:
All or part available in-house

Printed publications:
Aspects of EC law and procedures
Newsletters on a range of subjects; several on
 European matters
Setting up business in (series)
Technical publications on banking, commercial,
 company, employment, environment, funds,
 insolvency, intellectual property, media,
 computer & communications, pensions &
 employee benefits, property, securities, shipping
 and tax law etc
Order printed publications from: Clifford Chance
Publications
c/o Jevons Brown, 19 Bedford Row, London, WC1R
4EB, tel: 020 7404 2917, fax: 020 7600 5555

Publications list:
Available online and in print

Access to staff:
Access for members only.
Hours: Mon to Fri, 0900 to 1730
Special comments: Publications for clients and
professional contacts.

Has:
offices worldwide

CLOTHWORKERS' COMPANY, THE

Formal name: Worshipful Company of
Clothworkers of the City of London

Clothworkers' Hall, Dunster Court, Mincing Lane,
London, EC3R 7AH

Tel: 020 7623 7041
Fax: 020 7397 0107
E-mail: enquiries@clothworkers.co.uk

Website:
http://www.clothworkers.co.uk

Founded:
1528

Organisation type and purpose:
Membership association (membership is by
election or invitation).
City of London Livery Company.

**Museum or gallery collection, archive, or library
special collection:**
Archive
Plate Collection

Non-library collection catalogue:
All or part available in-house

Library catalogue:
All or part available in-house

Publications list:
Available online

Access to staff:
Contact by letter, by telephone, by fax, by e-mail,
in person and via website. Appointment necessary.
Letter of introduction required.

Access to building, collection or gallery:
No public access

Access for disabled people:
Wheelchair access, lift access

CLUB FOR ACTS AND ACTORS

Acronym or abbreviation: CAA

20 Bedford Street, London, WC2E 9HP

Tel: 020 7836 3172
Fax: 020 7836 3172
E-mail: office@thecaa.org

Enquiries:
Enquiries to: Secretary
Other contacts: Chairman (for initiations); Treasurer
(for financial matters)

Founded:
1897

Formerly called:
Concert Artistes' Association (CAA) (year of
change early 1990s)

Organisation type and purpose:
Membership association (membership is by
subscription, election or invitation), present
number of members: 1,010 plus a few Honorary
Members, registered charity (charity number
211012).

**Museum or gallery collection, archive, or library
special collection:**
Archive Material: old members list, photographs,
 concert programmes, posters, etc.

Printed publications:
But – What Do You Do in the Winter: 100 years of
 the CAA from 1987 to 1997 (L. Parker, £9 incl.
 p&p, available direct)

Access to staff:
Contact by letter, by telephone, by fax and by e-
mail. Appointment necessary.

Hours: Mon to Fri, 0930 to 1700

Access to building, collection or gallery:
Special comments: Entry door, stairs to first floor
office.

CLUB GTI

PO Box 6506, Sutton in Ashfield, Nottinghamshire,
NG17 1NG

Tel: 07891 963823
E-mail: info@clubgti.com

Website:
http://www.clubgti.com
Information on the vehicles, events, contact details.

Enquiries:
Enquiries to: Chairman
Direct e-mail: chairman@clubgti.com

Organisation type and purpose:
International organisation, national organisation,
membership association (membership is by
subscription), present number of members: 3600.

Subject coverage:
Club GTI is a non-profit making organisation for
enthusiasts of the Volkswagen GTI and associated
models within the Volkswagen group of
companies. The club is independent of the
manufacturer, importer or dealer network.

Printed publications:
Publications available through membership

Access to staff:
Contact by letter, by telephone, by e-mail and via
website
Hours: Mon to Fri, 0900 to 1700

CLUB LOTUS

58 Malthouse Court, Dereham, Norfolk , NR20
4UA

Tel: 01362 694459 or 691144
Fax: 01362 695522
E-mail: jane@clublotus.co.uk

Website:
http://www.club-lotus.co.uk/

Enquiries:
Enquiries to: Membership Secretary
Direct e-mail: annemarie@clublotus.co.uk

Founded:
1956

Organisation type and purpose:
International organisation, membership
association (membership is by subscription),
present number of members: 10,000.
Lotus enthusiasts.

Subject coverage:
Lotus cars, technical information and all aspects.

**Museum or gallery collection, archive, or library
special collection:**
Complete book list of current titles

Access to staff:
Contact by letter, by telephone, by fax and by e-
mail. Appointment necessary.
Hours: Fri, 0900 to 1500

CLUB MARCOS INTERNATIONAL

26 Blackberry Close, Chippenham, Wiltshire, SN14
6RG

Tel: 01249 464795
E-mail: info@clubmarcos.freeserve.co.uk

Enquiries:
Enquiries to: Membership Secretary

Founded:
1986

Organisation type and purpose:
Membership association (membership is by
subscription).

Subject coverage:
The Marcos Marque.

Access to staff:
Contact by letter, by telephone, by e-mail and via website
Hours: Evenings and weekends. 24 hours answerphone

CLUB TRIUMPH

42 Greenlands Road, Staines, Middlesex, TW18 4LR

Tel: 01784 465351
Fax: 01784 465351
E-mail: enquiries@club.triumph.org.uk

Website:
http://www.club.triumph.org.uk
Club information.

Enquiries:
Enquiries to: Secretary

Founded:
1954

Organisation type and purpose:
Membership association (membership is by subscription), present number of members: 1500, voluntary organisation.
Classic car club.

Subject coverage:
Technical and other advice on Triumph cars.

Library catalogue:
All or part available in-house

Printed publications:
Directory (members only)
Newsletter (members only)
Library List (members only)
Magazine (members only)

Access to staff:
Contact by letter, by telephone, by fax, by e-mail and via website
Hours: Mon to Fri, 0900 to 1700

Public Relations Officer:
Club Triumph
1 Bure Homage Gardens, Mudeford,
Christchurch, Dorset, BH23 4DR; tel: 01425 278320; e-mail: charles.collin@ntlworld.com

CLUB TRIUMPH (EASTERN)

45 Maldon Road, Goldhanger, Maldon, Essex, CM9 8BG

Tel: 01621 788798
Fax: 01621 788798

Website:
http://clubtriumph.org
Club history, contact information, updates and reports on club activities, events calendar, links, guestbook.

Enquiries:
Enquiries to: Publicity Officer
Direct e-mail: enquiries@clubtriumph.org

Founded:
1960

Formed from:
Club Triumph Limited

Formerly called:
Triumph Sports Owners Association

Organisation type and purpose:
Membership association (membership is by subscription), voluntary organisation.
To bring together like-minded enthusiasts of the Triumph Marque and to provide technical back-up.

Subject coverage:
The Triumph motor car: the technology, enjoyment and use of all models.

Museum or gallery collection, archive, or library special collection:
Triumph motor car history
Triumph related technical information (hard copy only)

Printed publications:
Club Magazine (6 times a year, free to subscribers, back issues available for purchase £1 each plus p&p)

Access to staff:
Contact by letter, by telephone, by e-mail and via website. Appointment necessary.
Hours: 24-hour answerphone

Affiliated to:
RACMSA

CLUBS FOR YOUNG PEOPLE

Acronym or abbreviation: CYP

371 Kennington Lane, London, SE11 5QY

Tel: 020 7793 0787
Fax: 020 7820 9815
E-mail: office@clubsforyoungpeople.org.uk

Website:
http://www.clubsforyoungpeople.org.uk/
http://www.nacyp.org.uk

Enquiries:
Enquiries to: National Director
Other contacts: Director of Fundraising Officer for communications.

Founded:
1925

Formerly called:
National Association of Boys' Clubs (NABC) (year of change 2005)

Organisation type and purpose:
Membership association, present number of members: 400,000, voluntary organisation, registered charity (charity number 306065), suitable for ages: 11 to 25, training organisation. To offer young people the knowledge, understanding and help they need which will utilise their full potential as they prepare for life in society and their responsibilities as adults.

Subject coverage:
Youth leadership training; sports; creative activities; adventure opportunities, development training, youth clubs.

Printed publications:
Club Connection (magazine, quarterly, produced by NACYP, distributed to its 2500 clubs, free)
Realising Young People's Potential – Corporate Brochure
Leaders Guide – A tool for youth workers, managers and volunteers (£11.25 inc. p&p)
Working with Young People – A guide to protecting leaders and young people (£28.80 inc. p&p)

Access to staff:
Contact by letter, by fax, by e-mail and via website
Hours: Mon to Fri, 0900 to 1700

Affiliated to:
British Youth Council
National Council for Voluntary Youth Services
National Youth Agency

Has:
3000 youth clubs affiliated

CLYDEBANK LOCAL HISTORY SOCIETY

14 Birch Road, Parkhall, Clydebank, Strathclyde, G81 3NZ

Tel: 0141 562 3212

Enquiries:
Enquiries to: Secretary

Organisation type and purpose:
Voluntary organisation.

Subject coverage:
Local history of Clydebank and district.

Printed publications:
Journal (annually)

Electronic and video publications:
Video (55 minutes)

Access to staff:
Contact by letter
Hours: Mon to Fri, 0900 to 1700

Access for disabled people:
Access via ramp at side entrance in Hall Street

Links with:
Scottish Civic Trust

CMR INTERNATIONAL LIMITED

Formal name: Centre for Medicines Research International

Novellus Court, 61 South Street, Epsom, Surrey, KT18 7PX

Tel: 01372 846100
Fax: 01372 846101
E-mail: information@cmr.org

Website:
http://www.cmr.org
Description of the work of CMR International, list of publications.

Enquiries:
Enquiries to: Information Assistant

Founded:
1981

Formerly called:
Centre for Medicines Research (CMR)

Organisation type and purpose:
Membership association (membership is by subscription), present number of members: 55, consultancy, research organisation.
To collect data and conduct research into the development of medicines.

Subject coverage:
Innovation of new chemical entities, safety evaluation of medicines, international medicines regulations, research and development in the pharmaceutical industry and benchmarking.

Museum or gallery collection, archive, or library special collection:
Small collection of c. 400 books on the drug development process

Trade and statistical information:
International pharmaceutical research and development expenditure. New chemical entities reaching the world market. Development times for new medicines. Regulatory review times in major markets.

Printed publications:
Annual lectures
Newsletter
An extensive list of books and reports relating to the pharmaceutical industry dealing with R&D Expenditure, Safety Evaluation, Regulations, Socio-economics
CMR International Lecture Series
Papers in professional journals

Publications list:
Available in print

Access to staff:
Contact by letter, by e-mail and via website
Hours: Mon to Fri, 0900 to 1700

CO-OPERATIVE AND SOCIAL ENTERPRISE DEVELOPMENT AGENCY LTD

Acronym or abbreviation: CASE-DA

continued overleaf

94 New Walk, Leicester, LE1 7EA

Tel: 0116 222 5010
Fax: 0116 222 5495
E-mail: enquiries@case-da.co.uk

Website:
http://www.case-da.co.uk

Enquiries:
Enquiries to: Information Officer

Organisation type and purpose:
Voluntary organisation.
Advice, training and support to people who want to set up Social Enterprise.

Subject coverage:
Industrial and service co-operatives; how to set up and run co-operatives and social enterprises; their projects, markets, available skills and finance, legal and taxation problems, education, training, publicity.

Printed publications:
Brochure

Access to staff:
Contact by letter, by telephone, by fax, in person and via website
Hours: Mon to Fri, 0900 to 1700

CO-OPERATIVE COLLEGE

Holyoake House, Hanover Street, Manchester, M60 0AS

Tel: 0161 246 2902
Fax: 0161 246 2946
E-mail: archive@co-op.ac.uk

Website:
http://www.archive.co-op.ac.uk

Enquiries:
Enquiries to: Archivist
Direct tel: 0161 246 2925
Direct e-mail: gillian@co-op.ac.uk

Founded:
1911

Formerly called:
Co-operative College, J J Worley Memorial Library

Organisation type and purpose:
Registered charity, suitable for ages: adults, consultancy, research organisation.

Subject coverage:
Co-operation, co-operative history and co-operative society history and histories, nationally and internationally; co-operative film archive, co-operative archive, international economic development centre for alternative industrial and technological systems archive, co-operative oral history archive.

Museum or gallery collection, archive, or library special collection:
CAITS Archive
Co-operation and Owenism history collection (c. 2000 items)
Co-operative Society History
J J Worley Memorial Library
Midlands Co-operative Society Archive
Robert Owen Collection (3000 items)
George Jacob Holyoake Collection (4000 items)
National Co-operative Film Archive
Co-operative Oral History Archive
Edward Owen Greening Collection
Co-operative Women's Guild
Rochdale Equitable Pioneers Society Collection
Co-operative Party Collection
Co-operative Press Collection
Co-operative Group South East, South Midlands and Northern Region Collection
Co-operative Youth Movements

Non-library collection catalogue:
All or part available online

Printed publications:
Holdings Lists for Special Collections

Publications list:
Available in print

Access to staff:
Contact by letter, by telephone, by fax, by e-mail and via website. Appointment necessary.
Hours: Mon to Fri, 1000 to 1700

Parent body:
Co-operative Union

COBALT DEVELOPMENT INSTITUTE

Acronym or abbreviation: CDI

167 High Street, Guildford, Surrey, GU1 3AJ

Tel: 01483 578877
Fax: 01483 573873
E-mail: info@thecdi.com

Website:
http://www.thecdi.com

Enquiries:
Enquiries to: General Manager
Other contacts: Administration Manager

Founded:
1982

Formerly called:
Centre d'Information du Cobalt (CIC) (year of change 1970)

Organisation type and purpose:
Trade association (membership is by subscription). Representing the world's main cobalt producers and users; purpose is to promote cobalt and provide information on it to any interested party.

Subject coverage:
All aspects of cobalt – sources, statistics, uses, properties, extraction, environmental aspects.

Non-library collection catalogue:
All or part available in-house

Library catalogue:
All or part available in-house

Printed publications:
Cobalt Monograph Series: Superalloys, Chemicals, Catalysts, Environment, Electronics (for purchase)
Cobalt News (quarterly, free)
Cobalt Facts

Publications list:
Available online and in print

Access to staff:
Contact by letter, by telephone, by fax, by e-mail and via website. Appointment necessary.
Hours: Mon to Fri, 0900 to 1700

COCKBURN ASSOCIATION

Formal name: Cockburn Association (The Edinburgh Civic Trust)

Trunk's Close, 55 High Street, Edinburgh, EH1 1SR

Tel: 0131 557 8686
Fax: 0131 337 9387

Website:
http://www.cockburnassociation.org.uk

Founded:
1875

Organisation type and purpose:
A registered Scottish charity.

Subject coverage:
Conservation and enhancement of Edinburgh's landscape and historic and architectural heritage.

CODRINGTON LIBRARY

All Souls College, High Street, Oxford, OX1 4AL

Tel: 01865 279379
Fax: 01865 279299
E-mail: codrington.library@all-souls.ox.ac.uk

Enquiries:
Enquiries to: Librarian in Charge
Direct tel: 01865 279318

Organisation type and purpose:
College Library.

Subject coverage:
Law, history, strategic studies.

Museum or gallery collection, archive, or library special collection:
400 manuscripts including the Luttrell-Wynne Papers
British and continental early-printed books
18th century English Newspapers
Material relating to the letters of Junius
Neo-Latin and inscriptional literature

Access to staff:
Contact by letter and by e-mail. Appointment necessary. Letter of introduction required.
Hours: Term time: Mon to Fri, 0930 to 1830
Vacations: Mon to Fri, 0930 to 1630

COELIAC UK

PO Box 220, High Wycombe, Buckinghamshire, HP11 2HY

Tel: 01494 437278
Fax: 01494 474349
E-mail: admin@coeliac.co.uk

Enquiries:
Enquiries to: Chief Executive

Founded:
1968

Formerly called:
Coeliac Society of the United Kingdom, The Coeliac Society (year of change 2001)

Organisation type and purpose:
Registered charity.
To support the health, welfare and rights of coeliacs, those with Dermatitis Herpetiformis (DH). Support other medically diagnosed patients whose health and quality of life can be improved by following the dietary regime beneficial to coeliacs. To provide easily accessible written, verbal and electronic advice, information and resources to these individuals and groups. To educate the public and those in appropriate sectors of health, government, commerce and industry on the conditions and the issues. To promote and commission research into the causes, alleviation, treatment, care and cure of the coeliac and DH conditions.

Subject coverage:
General management of a gluten-free diet for those medically diagnosed as having the coeliac condition or dermatitis herpetiformis.

Printed publications:
Coeliac Handbook
Crossed Grain Magazine (2 times a year)
List of Gluten Free Manufactured Products (annually, members)
A selection of free leaflets on health and eating information
Publications for purchase include:
Gluten Free Diet booklet (£1 plus p&p)
World Travel Guide (£10 plus p&p)

Electronic and video publications:
Leaflets available to download (online)

Access to staff:
Contact by letter, by telephone, by fax and by e-mail
Hours: Mon to Fri, 0915 to 1645

COFFEE TRADE FEDERATION

Acronym or abbreviation: CTF

63A Union Street, London, SE1 1SG

Tel: 020 7403 3088
Fax: 020 7403 7730

Website:
http://www.coffeetradefederation.co.uk

Enquiries:
Enquiries to: Secretary
Direct e-mail: coffeetradefed@compuserve.com

Organisation type and purpose:
Trade association.

Subject coverage:
Coffee trade.

Printed publications:
Arbitration Rules
Brochure
Standard Contracts

Publications list:
Available online

Access to staff:
Contact by letter, by telephone, by fax and by e-mail
Hours: Mon to Fri, 1000 to 1600

COIL WINDING INTERNATIONAL MAGAZINE

Formal name: Coil Winding International & Electrical Insulation Magazine

PO Box 936, Alder Hills, Poole, Dorset, BH12 3HB

Tel: 01202 743906
Fax: 01202 736018
E-mail: coilwind@bournemouth-net.co.uk

Website:
http://www.coilwinding.co.uk

Enquiries:
Enquiries to: Editor

Founded:
1976

Organisation type and purpose:
Publishing house.

Subject coverage:
Electric motors; transformers; electromagnetic materials and components.

Printed publications:
Coil Winding International (magazine, 3 times a year)

Access to staff:
Contact by fax and by e-mail
Hours: Mon to Fri, 0900 to 1700

Access to building, collection or gallery:
Prior appointment required

COKE OVEN MANAGERS' ASSOCIATION

Acronym or abbreviation: COMA

Universal Contractors Limited, Strata Industrial Estate, Rotherham Road, Dinnington, Sheffield, South Yorkshire, S25 3RF

Tel: 01909 518778
Fax: 01909 518838
E-mail: stratag@aol.com

Website:
http://coke-oven-managers.org

Enquiries:
Enquiries to: Honorary Secretary

Founded:
1917

Organisation type and purpose:
Professional body.

Subject coverage:
Coke ovens, coking, carbonisation.

Museum or gallery collection, archive, or library special collection:
Complete set of COMA Yearbooks

Printed publications:
Coke Oven Managers' Association Bulletin (2 times a year)
Coke Oven Managers' Association Year Book (annually)

COLCHESTER BOROUGH COUNCIL

PO Box 884, Town Hall, Colchester, Essex, CO1 1FR

Tel: 01206 282222
Fax: 01206 282288

Website:
http://www.colchester.gov.uk

Enquiries:
Enquiries to: Chief Executive

Organisation type and purpose:
Local government body.

Access to staff:
Contact by letter, by telephone, by fax and in person
Hours: Mon to Fri, 0900 to 1700

COLCHESTER INSTITUTE LIBRARY

Sheepen Road, Colchester, Essex, CO3 3LL

Tel: 01206 712642
Fax: 01206 711712
E-mail: library.helpdesk@colchester.ac.uk

Website:
http://library.colchester.ac.uk

Enquiries:
Enquiries to: Head of Learning Resources and Student Services
Direct tel: 01206 712280
Direct e-mail: cilla.summers@colchester.ac.uk

Organisation type and purpose:
Suitable for ages: 16+.
College of further and higher education.

Subject coverage:
Music, art and design, catering and hospitality studies, health studies, business studies, leisure and recreation, construction, automobile and general engineering, humanities, social sciences, science, education.

Museum or gallery collection, archive, or library special collection:
Music scores, including wind band scores

Library catalogue:
All or part available online

Access to staff:
Contact by letter, by telephone, by fax, by e-mail, in person and via website. Non-members charged.
Hours: Mon to Fri, 0900 to 1700

Constituent part of:
Essex University

COLD ROLLED SECTIONS ASSOCIATION

Acronym or abbreviation: CRSA

National Metalforming Centre, 47 Birmingham Road, Birmingham, B70 6PY

Tel: 0121 601 6350
Fax: 0121 601 6373
E-mail: crsa@crsauk.com

Website:
http://www.crsauk.com

Enquiries:
Enquiries to: Secretary

Organisation type and purpose:
Trade association.

Subject coverage:
Cold roll-formed steel sections.

Printed publications:
Safe Working of Cold Roll Forming Lines
Cold Roll Forming: How it can benefit your business – A Designer's Guide

Access to staff:
Contact by telephone and by e-mail
Hours: Mon to Fri, 0900 to 1700

Connections with:
Confederation of British Metalforming (CBM) National Metalforming Centre, 47 Birmingham Road, Birmingham, B70 6PY; tel: 0121 601 6350; fax: 0121 601 6373; e-mail: info@britishmetalforming.com; website: http://www.britishmetalforming.com

COLD STORAGE AND DISTRIBUTION FEDERATION

Acronym or abbreviation: CSDF

Downmill Road, Bracknell, Berkshire, RG12 1GH

Tel: 01344 869533
Fax: 01344 869527
E-mail: dg@csdf.org.uk

Enquiries:
Enquiries to: Chief Executive

Founded:
1911

Formerly called:
National Cold Storage Federation

Organisation type and purpose:
Trade association (membership is by subscription).

Subject coverage:
All aspects of controlled storage and distribution including operations temperature, health and safety, legislative aspects, fire, construction and related food processing acts.

Printed publications:
Directory (every 2 years, £35, free to members)
Fire Risk Assessment Guide (£17)
Guide to Safety in the Use of Pallets, Pallet Converters, Palletainers and Racking (£18)
Guide to Storage and Handling of Frozen Foods (£12)
Guide to the Management and Control of Fire Risks in Temperature Controlled Structures of the Refrigerated Food Industry (£43)
Technical papers and briefs as required – apply for details

Publications list:
Available in print

Access to staff:
Contact by letter, by telephone, by fax and by e-mail. Appointment necessary.
Hours: Mon to Fri, 0900 to 1700

Affiliated to:
Refrigerated Food Industry Confederation (RFIC)

Associated European and International links:
European Cold Storage and Logistics Association (ECSLA)
European Consortium for the Responsible Application of Refrigerants
International Association of Cold Store Contractors

COLE ABBEY PRESBYTERIAN CHURCH

114 Queen Victoria Street, London, EC4V 4BA

Tel: 020 7424 5213

Website:
http://www.londonfreechurch.org.uk/
Service times, history of building.

Enquiries:
Enquiries to: Information Officer
Direct e-mail: davidtastrain@ntlworld.com

Formerly called:
Free Church of Scotland

continued overleaf

Organisation type and purpose:
Membership association (membership is by qualification), voluntary organisation, registered charity.

Subject coverage:
History and present activities of Reformed and Presbyterian Churches.

Access to staff:
Contact by letter, by telephone, by fax and via website
Hours: Mon to Fri, 0900 to 1700

Access to building, collection or gallery:
Prior appointment required

COLEG LLANDRILLO LIBRARY RESOURCE CENTRE

Llandudno Road, Rhos-on-Sea, Colwyn Bay, Conwy, LL28 4HZ

Tel: 01492 546666
Fax: 01492 543052
E-mail: info@llandrillo.ac.uk

Website:
http://www.llandrillo.ac.uk

Enquiries:
Enquiries to: Library Resource Manager
Direct tel: 01492 542342
Direct fax: 01492 548267
Direct e-mail: library1@llandrillo.ac.uk

Subject coverage:
A Level, GCSE and International Baccalaureate; business and management, further education, computer studies, special needs, hospitality management, leisure and tourism, health care and counselling, engineering, construction, motor vehicle technology, languages, art, office technology and secretarial studies.

Non-library collection catalogue:
All or part available online

Library catalogue:
All or part available online

Printed publications:
Library fact sheets (annually)

Access to staff:
Contact by letter, by telephone, by fax, by e-mail and via website. Appointment necessary. Non-members charged.
Hours: Term time: Mon, 0845 to 1745; Tue to Thu, 0845 to 2045; Fri, 0930 to 1600; Sat, 1000 to 1500
Vacations: Mon to Fri, 0845 to 1630

Branch at:
Abergele Community College
Denbigh Community College
Rhyl Community College

COLLECTIONS TRUST

Formal name: The Collections Trust

22 Hills Road, Cambridge, CB2 1JP

Tel: 01223 316 028
E-mail: office@collectionstrust.org.uk

Website:
http://www.mda.org.uk
Information and resources for cultural sector professionals.

Enquiries:
Enquiries to: Communications Manager
Other contacts: Information Officer for Assistant to Communications Manager.

Founded:
1977

Formerly called:
MDA

Organisation type and purpose:
International organisation, national government body, national organisation, registered charity. To support the management and use of collections.

Subject coverage:
Support for the cultural sector, cultural initiatives, documentation and standards work.

Printed publications:
Key texts, factsheets and pre-printed forms and registers for documenting collections.

Publications list:
Available online and in print

Access to staff:
Contact by letter, by telephone, by fax and by e-mail
Hours: Mon to Fri, 0900 to 1700

Access to building, collection or gallery:
Prior appointment required

Funded by:
The Museums, Libraries and Archives Council (in England) and the Scottish Museums Council (in Scotland)

COLLECTIONS TRUST

22 Hills Road, Cambridge, CB2 1JP

Tel: 01223 316028
Fax: 01223 364658
E-mail: office@collectionstrust.org.uk

Website:
http://www.collectionstrust.org.uk

Enquiries:
Enquiries to: Marketing Officer

Incorporates the former:
MDA (year of change 2008)

Organisation type and purpose:
Professional body, registered charity (charity number 273984).

Subject coverage:
Professional collections management and related information technology and legal issues.

Printed publications:
Publications include:
Documentation: a practical guide
SPECTRUM
Order printed publications from:
www.collectionstrust.org.uk/books

Publications list:
Available online and in print

Access to staff:
Contact by letter, by telephone, by fax, by e-mail and via website. Appointment necessary.
Hours: Mon to Fri, 0900 to 1700

Access to building, collection or gallery:
No prior appointment required

COLLEGE OF ARMS

Formal name: Corporation of the Kings, Heralds and Pursuivants of Arms; also known as Heralds' College.

Queen Victoria Street, London, EC4V 4BT

Tel: 020 7248 2762
Fax: 020 7248 6448
E-mail: enquiries@college-of-arms.gov.uk

Website:
http://www.college-of-arms.gov.uk

Enquiries:
Enquiries to: Officer in Waiting
Other contacts: Archivist for study of books or manuscripts.

Founded:
1484

Organisation type and purpose:
Advisory body, professional body (membership is by election or invitation), present number of members: 11, historic building, house or site, consultancy, research organisation.

Repository of the official registers of armorial bearings and genealogies of England, Wales, Northern Ireland and Commonwealth families. Heraldry and genealogy.

Subject coverage:
Heraldry, grants of arms, genealogy, ceremonial, precedence, changes of name.

Museum or gallery collection, archive, or library special collection:
Some of the Arundel MSS
Unique manuscript collections of heraldic and genealogical material

Non-library collection catalogue:
All or part available in-house and in print

Library catalogue:
All or part available in-house

Printed publications:
Louise Campbell and Francis Steer, A Catalogue of Manuscripts in the College of Arms: Collections vol. 1 (1988)

Access to staff:
Contact by letter, by telephone, by fax, by e-mail, in person and via website
Hours: Mon to Fri, 1000 to 1600
Special comments: Groups of visitors by appointment with Officer in Waiting.

Access to building, collection or gallery:
Prior appointment required
Hours: Mon to Fri, 1000 to 1600
Special comments: Contact Archivist, telephone 020 7236 1627

COLLEGE OF CRANIO-SACRAL THERAPY

Acronym or abbreviation: CCST

9 St Georges Mews, Primrose Hill, London, NW1 8XE

Tel: 020 7586 0148 or 7483 0120
Fax: 020 7586 9550
E-mail: info@ccst.co.uk

Website:
http://www.ccst.co.uk

Enquiries:
Enquiries to: Administrator

Founded:
1986

Organisation type and purpose:
Training organisation, research organisation. Clinic.

Subject coverage:
Cranio-sacral therapy, general health and wellbeing, physical and psychological; birth trauma, baby and child health, learning difficulties, meningitis, resolution of obscure and intractable conditions.

Printed publications:
Articles (free)
Course brochure (free)
Information leaflets (free)

Access to staff:
Contact by letter, by telephone, by fax and by e-mail
Hours: Mon to Fri, 0900 to 1800

Access to building, collection or gallery:
No prior appointment required

Also at:
Primrose Hill Natural Health Centre
9 St George's Mews, London, NW1 8XE; tel: 020 7586 0148; fax: 020 7586 9550

COLLEGE OF ESTATE MANAGEMENT

Acronym or abbreviation: CEM

Whiteknights, Reading, Berkshire, RG6 6AW

Tel: 0800 019 9697

Fax: 0118 921 4620
E-mail: courses@cem.ac.uk

Website:
http://www.cem.ac.uk

Enquiries:
Enquiries to: Admission Officer
Direct e-mail: prospectuses@cem.ac.uk

Founded:
1919

Organisation type and purpose:
Registered charity (charity number 313223), suitable for ages: 18+, research organisation.

Subject coverage:
Undergraduate, professional and postgraduate courses for the property professions, construction industry and those associated. Course subjects include estate management, arbitration, shopping centre management, property investment, building conservation, construction and real estate, project management, construction, surveying, facilities management, valuation.

Printed publications:
All Write! Effective Writing for Professional People (Bailey A, 2000)
Introduction to Civil Engineering Construction (Holmes R, 1995)
Research reports

Electronic and video publications:
No

Publications list:
Available online and in print

Access to staff:
Contact by letter, by telephone, by fax, by e-mail and via website. Appointment necessary.
Hours: Mon to Fri, 0830 to 1730

Access to building, collection or gallery:
No prior appointment required

COLLEGE OF HEALTH CARE CHAPLAINS

Acronym or abbreviation: CHCC

49 Chesterton Park, Cirencester, Gloucestershire, GL7 1XS

Tel: 01285 643660
Fax: 01285 643660
E-mail: cjw@dialin.net

Website:
http://www.leeds.ac.uk/healthcare/general/spirit/spirit.html
Research network database.
http://www.msf.org.uk
MSF home page.
http://www.healthcarechaplains.org.uk
Home page details of CHCC.

Enquiries:
Enquiries to: Registrar
Other contacts: President

Founded:
1993

Organisation type and purpose:
Trade union (membership is by subscription), present number of members: 875, training organisation, research organisation.

Subject coverage:
Pastoral care, ethics in health care, inter-faith relationships in health care.

Printed publications:
Journal (3 times a year, free to members, available to purchase to non-members)
Newsletter (4 times a year, available to members)
Occasional papers

Access to staff:
Contact by letter, by telephone, by fax and by e-mail
Hours: Mon to Fri, 0900 to 1700

Autonomous section of:
MSF

COLLEGE OF INTEGRATED CHINESE MEDICINE

Acronym or abbreviation: CICM

19 Castle Street, Reading, Berkshire, RG1 7SB

Tel: 0118 950 8880
Fax: 0118 950 8890
E-mail: info@cicm.org.uk

Website:
http://www.cicm.org.uk

Enquiries:
Enquiries to: Library Coordinator
Direct e-mail: library@cicm.org.uk

Founded:
1992

Organisation type and purpose:
Training organisation.

Subject coverage:
Training in acupuncture and Chinese herbal medicine.

Library catalogue:
All or part available in-house and in print

Access to staff:
Contact by letter, by fax, by e-mail and in person. Appointment necessary. Letter of introduction required.
Hours: Mon to Fri, 0900 to 1700

Access to building, collection or gallery:
Hours: Every Day except over Christmas and Easter, 0800 to 1700

Access for disabled people:
None to library but provision would be made for access to requested books or journals

COLLEGE OF MASONS

42 Magdalen Road, Wandsworth, London, SW18 3NP

Tel: 020 8874 8363
Fax: 020 8871 1342

Enquiries:
Enquiries to: Honorary Secretary

Founded:
1893

Organisation type and purpose:
Membership association.

Subject coverage:
Masonry and all worked materials: building, decoration, carving, lettering, sculpture, restoration, cleaning, fixings, memorials and monuments, granite, marble, slate and stone.

Access to staff:
Contact by letter, by telephone and by fax
Hours: Mon to Fri, 0900 to 1700

COLLEGE OF NORTH EAST LONDON

Acronym or abbreviation: CONEL

High Road, Tottenham, London, N15 4RU

Tel: 020 8802 3014
Fax: 020 8442 3091
E-mail: jdunster@staff.conel.ac.uk

Website:
http://www.conel.ac.uk

Enquiries:
Enquiries to: Learning Resources Team Leader
Direct tel: 020 8442 3877

Founded:
1990

Formerly called:
Haringey College, Tottenham College of Technology

Organisation type and purpose:
College of further education.

Subject coverage:
Subjects Basic Skills to A levels: accountancy; business studies; building and engineering; health care; art; design; media; hairdressing; beauty therapy; floristry; information technology; environmental health; housing; public administration; electronics; general education; sports and recreation.

Library catalogue:
All or part available in-house

Access to staff:
Contact by telephone, by e-mail and via website
Hours: Mon to Thu, 0900 to 2000; Fri 0900 to 1630; Sat, 1000 to 1600

Access to building, collection or gallery:
Prior appointment required

Access for disabled people:
Ramped entry, toilet facilities

COLLEGE OF NORTH WEST LONDON

Acronym or abbreviation: CNWL

Dudden Hill Lane, Willesden, London, NW10 2XD

Tel: 020 8208 5000
Fax: 020 8451 2718
E-mail: beatrice.mcadam@cnwl.ac.uk

Website:
http://www.cnwl.ac.uk

Enquiries:
Enquiries to: Head of Learning Resources
Direct tel: 020 8208 5145

Organisation type and purpose:
Further education.

Subject coverage:
Fashion; catering; creative and media studies; building services, plumbing, electrical and electronics engineering; construction; refrigeration; business studies; auto engineering; access provision; ESOL, EFL, modern foreign languages, interpreting, IELTS.

Museum or gallery collection, archive, or library special collection:
technical index – for construction

Trade and statistical information:
Available from website.

Library catalogue:
All or part available online

Access to staff:
Contact by letter, by telephone and by e-mail
Hours: Mon to Fri, 0900 to 1700

Also at:
College of North West London
    Wembley Park, North End Road, Middlesex, HA9 0AD
College of North West London
    Willesden Centre, Denzil Road, London, NW2 7BZ; tel: 020 8208 5050; fax: 020 8451 2718

COLLEGE OF OCCUPATIONAL THERAPISTS

106–114 Borough High Street, London, SE1 1LB

Tel: 020 7357 6480
Fax: 020 7378 1353

Enquiries:
Enquiries to: Public Relations Manager
Direct tel: 020 7450 2335
Direct fax: 020 7450 2349
Direct e-mail: david.cocke@cot.co.uk
Other contacts: Librarian for research information and booking appointments to visit COT Library.

Organisation type and purpose:
Professional body (membership is by subscription), present number of members: c. 29,000, registered charity.

continued overleaf

Subject coverage:
All aspects of occupational therapy in a variety of formats.

Museum or gallery collection, archive, or library special collection:
Archives
Code of Practice documents (for reference only)
Conferences file
Government and legal publications
Organisations file
Practice records and references

Printed publications:
Current Awareness Bulletin
Order printed publications from: Facilities Management

Electronic and video publications:
Current Research – published by the British Library (annually) from Research Register database

Publications list:
Available online and in print

Access to staff:
Contact by letter, by fax, by e-mail and via website. Appointment necessary. All charged.
Hours: Mon to Fri, 0900 to 1700

Access to building, collection or gallery:
Prior appointment required

Access for disabled people:
Level entry, toilet facilities

Parent body:
British Association of Occupational Therapists

COLLEGE OF OPTOMETRISTS

Library, The College of Optometrists, 42 Craven Street, London, WC2 5NG

Tel: 020 7839 6000
Fax: 020 7839 6800
E-mail: library@college-optometrists.org

Website:
http://www.college-optometrists.org

Enquiries:
Enquiries to: Librarian

Founded:
1901

Organisation type and purpose:
Learned society, professional body (membership is by qualification).

Subject coverage:
Anatomy and physiology of the eye, physiology and psychology of vision, vision defects and their correction, spectacles and contact lenses, geometric and visual optics, optometry and its history.

Museum or gallery collection, archive, or library special collection:
Early books on vision

Library catalogue:
All or part available online

Access to staff:
Contact by letter, by telephone, by fax, by e-mail, in person and via website. Appointment necessary. Non-members charged.
Hours: Mon to Fri, 0900 to 1300 and 1400 to 1700

Administered by:
College of Optometrists

COLLEGE OF PHARMACY PRACTICE

28 Warwick Row, Coventry, Warwickshire, CV1 1EY

Tel: 024 7622 1359
Fax: 024 7652 1110
E-mail: info@collpharm.org.uk

Website:
http://www.collpharm.org.uk

Enquiries:
Enquiries to: Chief Executive

Founded:
1981

Organisation type and purpose:
Professional body, registered charity (charity number 281771).
Membership: by subscription (Associates and Students); by qualification (Members and Fellows). Professional organisation for pharmacists to promote and maintain high standards of pharmacy practice, and continuing professional development.

Subject coverage:
Pharmacy practice in hospital, community, industry and academia, assessment methods suitable for postgraduation practice examination, professional development portfolio, professional development CPD policies, pharmaceutical services within the NHS, pharmacy practice education, training and research.

Printed publications:
Annual Report
Newsletter (quarterly)
Variety of publications from the College.

Publications list:
Available online and in print

Access to staff:
Contact by letter, by telephone, by fax, by e-mail and via website. Appointment necessary.
Hours: Mon to Thu, 0900 to 1700; Fri, 0900 to 1630

Access for disabled people:
Level entry, access to all public areas, toilet facilities

COLLEGE OF PHYTOTHERAPY (HERBAL MEDICINE)

Bucksteep Manor, Bodle Street Green, Hailsham, East Sussex, BN27 4RJ

Tel: 01323 834800
Fax: 01323 834801
E-mail: medherb@pavilion.co.uk

Website:
http://www.collegeofphytotherapy.com

Enquiries:
Enquiries to: Secretary

Founded:
1982

Formerly called:
School of Herbal Medicine

Organisation type and purpose:
Training organisation.

Subject coverage:
Herbal medicine: active constituents, actions, pharmacology, and pharmacy of drugs of botanical origin.

Printed publications:
British Journal of Phytotherapy

Access to staff:
Contact by letter, by telephone, by fax, by e-mail and via website. Appointment necessary.
Hours: Mon to Fri, 0900 to 1700

COLLEGE OF PIPING

16–24 Otago Street, Glasgow, G12 8JH

Tel: 0141 334 3587
Fax: 0141 587 6068
E-mail: info@piping.scot.net

Website:
http://www.college-of-piping.co.uk/index.html

Enquiries:
Enquiries to: Chairman
Other contacts: Principal for day to day responsibility.

Founded:
1944

Organisation type and purpose:
Voluntary organisation, museum.

Subject coverage:
Highland bagpipe and its music.

Printed publications:
Piping Times (monthly)
Tutors for piping and Piobaireachd

Access to staff:
Contact by letter, by telephone, by fax, by e-mail and in person
Hours: Mon to Fri, 0900 to 1700

Access for disabled people:
Parking provided

COLLEGE OF PSYCHIC STUDIES

Acronym or abbreviation: CPS

16 Queensberry Place, London, SW7 2EB

Tel: 020 7589 3292
Fax: 020 7589 2824
E-mail: admin@collegeofpsychicstudies.co.uk

Website:
http://www.psychic-studies.org.uk
Programme, publications, services, history, membership.

Enquiries:
Enquiries to: Administrator
Direct tel: 020 7838 4401
Other contacts: Librarian for books and research.

Founded:
1884

Formerly called:
London Spiritualist Alliance (year of change 1955); College of Psychic Science (year of change 1970)

Organisation type and purpose:
Membership association (membership is by subscription), present number of members: 2190, registered charity (charity number 212728), suitable for ages: 18+, training organisation, research organisation.
Educational charity, advice and resource centre.

Subject coverage:
Psychic research, parapsychology, occult, healing, meditation, New Age, psychic development, spiritual philosophy.

Museum or gallery collection, archive, or library special collection:
Small specialist collection of books, manuscripts, photographs and artefacts relating to psychic research and the college's history. No public access. Research by prior arrangement with the Librarian

Printed publications:
Light (journal, annually)
Programme booklet (3 times a year)
Mediumship Made Simple (Northage I, £7.99)
Journey Beyond (Northage I, £3.50)

Electronic and video publications:
Soulwork – Home Study Pack (workbook and double CD)
Psychic Development CD (Jan 2002)
Meditation CD (Jan 2002)

Publications list:
Available in print

Access to staff:
Contact by letter, by telephone, by fax, by e-mail and via website. Appointment necessary.
Hours: Mon to Fri, 1030 to 1900; Sat, 0915 to 1415
Special comments: Library for members only, no direct access to archives unless by special appointment with the Librarian.

COLLEGE OF TEACHERS

3rd Floor, 33 John Street, London, WC1N 2AT

Tel: 020 7404 2008
Fax: 020 7404 2008
E-mail: gen@cot4.freeserve.co.uk

Enquiries:
Enquiries to: Chief Executive

Founded:
1849

Formerly called:
College of Preceptors

Organisation type and purpose:
Professional body.
To make public the concerns of the teaching profession and to support the profession through its publications and qualifications.

Subject coverage:
Professional development of teachers, education, especially teacher education.

Printed publications:
Aldrich: School and Society in Victorian Britain
Course Book on methods of teaching
Education Today (termly)
Newsletter

Publications list:
Available in print

Access to staff:
Appointment necessary.
Hours: Mon to Fri, 0930 to 1700

COLLEGE OF TRADITIONAL ACUPUNCTURE, THE

Acronym or abbreviation: CTA

Haseley Manor, Hatton, Warwickshire, CV35 7LU

Tel: 01926 484158
Fax: 01926 485444
E-mail: jeanette.harper@cta-uk.net

Website:
http://www.acupuncture-coll.ac.uk
Information about: Five-element acupuncture; the college and courses offered and college events.

Enquiries:
Enquiries to: Administrator

Founded:
1960s

Formerly called:
Oriental Medical College Ltd t/a The College of Traditional Acupuncture UK (year of change 1994)

Organisation type and purpose:
Registered charity (charity number 1039702), suitable for ages: 20+.
Private college offering 3 year part-time licentiate in acupuncture for qualification as professional practitioners. Programme is fully accredited by the British Acupuncture Accreditation Board and validated as BA(Hons) by Oxford Brookes University.

Subject coverage:
Acupuncture, complementary medicine.

Access to staff:
Contact by letter, by telephone, by fax and by e-mail
Hours: Mon to Fri, 0900 to 1700

Access for disabled people:
Parking provided, ramped entry, access to all public areas, toilet facilities

COLOMBIAN EMBASSY

3 Hans Crescent, Knightsbridge, London, SW1X 0LN

Tel: 020 7589 9177
Fax: 020 7581 1829
E-mail: mail@colombianembassy.co.uk

Website:
http://www.colombiaemb.co.uk

Enquiries:
Enquiries to: Ambassador

Organisation type and purpose:
National government body.
Embassy.

Subject coverage:
Colombia, general information and economic statistics.

Printed publications:
Publications for schools

Also at:
Colombian Consulate General
3rd Floor, 15–19 Great Titchfield Street, London, W1P 7FB; tel: 020 7637 9893; fax: 020 7637 5604; e-mail: consulco@consulco.demon.co.uk

Links with:
Proexport (Trade Office)
9 Berkeley Street, London, W1X 5AD; tel: 020 7491 3535; fax: 020 7491 4295; e-mail: cici@proexport-london.co.uk

COMHAIRLE NAN EILEAN SIAR

Acronym or abbreviation: CNES

Council Offices, Sandwick Road, Stornoway, Isle of Lewis, HS1 2BW

Tel: 01851 703773
Fax: 01851 705349

Website:
http://www.w-isles.gov.uk

Enquiries:
Enquiries to: Chief Executive
Direct tel: 01851 709500
Direct fax: 01851 706022
Direct e-mail: m.burr@cne-siar.gov.uk
Other contacts: Communications Officer

Founded:
1975

Formerly called:
Western Isles Council (WIC) (year of change 1998)

Organisation type and purpose:
Local government body.

Subject coverage:
All areas of community service.

Museum or gallery collection, archive, or library special collection:
Library (open to the public)

Access to staff:
Contact by letter, by telephone, by fax, by e-mail and in person
Hours: Mon to Fri, 0900 to 1700

Access for disabled people:
Parking provided, ramped entry, level entry, access to all public areas, toilet facilities

Affiliated to:
Conference of Peripheral Maritime Regions

Council Offices:
Comhairle Nan Eilean Siar
Castlebay, Isle of Barra; tel: 01871 810431; fax: 01871 810254
Comhairle Nan Eilean Siar
Tarbert, Isle of Harris; tel: 01859 502367; fax: 01859 502283
Comhairle Nan Eilean Siar
Balivanich, Benbecula; tel: 01870 602425; fax: 01870 602332

COMIC BOOK POSTAL AUCTIONS LIMITED

Acronym or abbreviation: COMPAL

PO Box 58386, London, NW1W 9RE

Tel: 020 7424 0007
Fax: 020 7424 0008
E-mail: comicbook@compalcomics.com

Website:
http://www.compalcomics.com

Enquiries:
Enquiries to: Managing Director

Founded:
1992

Organisation type and purpose:
Publishing house.
Comic book auctions by post.

Subject coverage:
Comics.

Non-library collection catalogue:
All or part available online

Library catalogue:
All or part available online

Access to staff:
Contact by letter, by telephone, by fax and via website
Hours: Mon to Fri, 0900 to 1700

COMIC RELIEF EDUCATION DISTRIBUTION

Education House, Drywall Estate, Castle Road, Sittingbourne, Kent, ME10 3RL

Tel: 01795 437988
Fax: 01795 474871
E-mail: info@edist.co.uk

Enquiries:
Enquiries to: Information Officer

Organisation type and purpose:
Registered charity (charity number 326568).

Access to staff:
Contact by letter, by telephone, by fax and by e-mail
Hours: Mon to Fri, 0900 to 1700

Access to building, collection or gallery:
No access other than to staff

Head Office:
Comic Relief
5th Floor, 89 Albert Embankment, London, SE1 7TP

COMMEMORATIVE COLLECTORS SOCIETY

Lumless House, Gainsborough Road, Winthorpe, Newark, Nottinghamshire, NG24 2NR

Tel: 01636 671377
E-mail: commemorativecollectorssociety@hotmail.com

Website:
http://www.commemorativecollecting.co.uk

Enquiries:
Enquiries to: Honorary Secretary

Founded:
1972

Organisation type and purpose:
International organisation, membership association (membership is by subscription), present number of members: 3649, voluntary organisation, research organisation.
International society of private collectors of all types of popular commemorabilia.
To represent the interests of members, research and record/maintain archive of commemorative items and commemorative collections.

Subject coverage:
Popular/mass-produced commemorative items of any kind, in any material or medium, identification of items/events/manufacturer (if known) and historical background.

Museum or gallery collection, archive, or library special collection:
Archive of information on 12,731 different items, worldwide events, 1660–2006

continued overleaf

Commemorative Museum Trust Collection of over 5762 pieces from 1761–2006
Library of related material
Photographic Library of over 10,822 black and white photographs of popular commemorative items in any medium from 1660 to the present day. These include foreign commemoratives covering 71 countries to date

Trade and statistical information:
Market size and value for commemorative items.

Printed publications:
Members Journal
Members Newsletter
Special Reviews for major events i.e. Royal Jubilees, coronations etc

Access to staff:
Contact by letter, by telephone, by e-mail and in person. Appointment necessary.
Hours: Mon to Sun, 0900 to 1700

Access to building, collection or gallery:
Prior appointment required
Hours: 0930 to 1700

Access for disabled people:
Level entry
Hours: 0930 to 1700

COMMISSION FOR RACIAL EQUALITY

Acronym or abbreviation: CRE

Elliott House, 10–12 Allington Street, London, SW1E 5EH

Tel: 020 7828 7022\ Minicom no. 020 7932 5419
Fax: 020 7630 7605
E-mail: info@cre.gov.uk

Website:
http://www.cre.gov.uk
General information on race equality issues, texts of CRE publications, media releases, etc.

Enquiries:
Enquiries to: Information Officer
Direct tel: 020 7932 5221
Other contacts: Media Office tel no: 020 7932 5354 for media enquiries.

Founded:
1977

Formerly called:
Community Relations Commission, Race Relations Board

Organisation type and purpose:
Statutory body.

Subject coverage:
Race relations, elimination of discrimination, equality of opportunity, ethnic minorities, racial aspects of government policy on inner cities, housing, education etc.

Museum or gallery collection, archive, or library special collection:
Press cuttings on race issues from 1977 to the present day on microfilm (not indexed)

Printed publications:
Books, standards, guides, research reports, leaflets
Formal Investigation Reports
European Union and Racial Discrimination (1998)
Legal Measures to Combat Racism (1998)
Reform of the Race Relations Act (1998)
The Irish in Britain (1998)
Order printed publications from: CRE Customer Services, Stationery Office
PO Box 29, Norwich, NR3 1GN, tel: 0870 240 3697, fax: 0870 240 3698, e-mail: cre@tso.co.uk

Publications list:
Available online and in print

Access to staff:
Contact by letter, by telephone, by fax and in person. Appointment necessary.
Hours: Mon to Fri, 0900 to 1700

Access to building, collection or gallery:
Prior appointment required
Hours: Mon to Fri, 0900 to 1700
Special comments: Library is available for reference only and by appointment tel no: 020 7932 5296.

Access for disabled people:
Parking provided, toilet facilities

COMMITTEE OF SCOTTISH CLEARING BANKERS

Acronym or abbreviation: CSCB

Drumsheugh House, 38b Drumsheugh Gardens, Edinburgh, EH3 7SW

Tel: 0131 473 7770
Fax: 0131 473 7799
E-mail: info@scotbanks.co.uk

Enquiries:
Enquiries to: Operations Co-ordinator

Organisation type and purpose:
Trade association, present number of members: 4.

Subject coverage:
Most aspects of Scottish banking.

Trade and statistical information:
Aggregate statistics of Scottish clearing banks.

Access to staff:
Contact by letter, by telephone, by fax and by e-mail
Hours: Mon to Fri, 0900 to 1700

COMMITTEE ON THE ADMINISTRATION OF JUSTICE

Acronym or abbreviation: CAJ

45 Donegall Street, Belfast, BT1 2BR

Tel: 028 9096 1122
Fax: 028 9024 6706
E-mail: info@caj.org.uk

Website:
http://www.caj.org.uk

Enquiries:
Enquiries to: Office Manager

Founded:
1981

Organisation type and purpose:
Membership association, voluntary organisation, research organisation.
Civil liberties group.

Subject coverage:
Civil liberties and human rights in Northern Ireland.

Museum or gallery collection, archive, or library special collection:
Information from newspaper cuttings, legislation, conference reports, government publications, etc. on a variety of subjects including Administration of the Courts, Bill of Rights, Right to Silence, Miscarriages of Justice, Police and Policing, Equality and Criminal Justice

Printed publications:
A large number of publications including conference papers, submissions and responses

Publications list:
Available online and in print

Access to staff:
Contact by letter, by telephone, by fax and by e-mail. Appointment necessary.
Hours: Mon to Fri, 0900 to 1700

Links with:
International Federation of Human Rights
17 Passage de la Main d'Or, Paris 75011, France

COMMONWEAL COLLECTION

J B Priestley Library, University of Bradford, Richmond Road, Bradford, West Yorkshire, BD7 1DP

Tel: 01274 233404
Fax: 01274 233398
E-mail: commonweal@bradford.ac.uk

Website:
http://www.brad.ac.uk/library/services.htm
http://www.brad.ac.uk/library/services/commonweal/home.htm

Enquiries:
Enquiries to: Co-ordinator
Other contacts: Outreach Worker for questions/work about raising the profile of the library regionally and nationally.

Founded:
1958

Organisation type and purpose:
Voluntary organisation, registered charity (charity number 1053157), public library.
To provide a resource for all issues relating to non-violence and non-violent social change.
Mission Statement: The Commonweal Collection is an independent specialist library devoted to issues around non-violent social change, working to promote justice and peace. Commonweal aims to provide literature.

Subject coverage:
Theory and practice of non-violence; non-violence and peace research; Gandhi and other pacifists and political radicals; peace education; critique of war; disarmament; nuclear power and weaponry; alternative society; spirituality; ecological issues; human rights; gender issues.

Museum or gallery collection, archive, or library special collection:
Over 11,000 books and pamphlets available for loan, over 230 current alternative journals available for reference
Archival material documenting non-violent campaigns and the peace movement in Britain, including:
Collection of printed materials on Gandhi
Peace News Archives
Papers from the International Seminar on Training in Nonviolent Action
Papers from the London Office of the United Farm Workers, USA
Papers of Hugh Brock (Editor of Peace News, 1955–1964)

Library catalogue:
All or part available online

Printed publications:
Annual Report
Gandhi: A Bibliography, a complete list of the 450 books and journals held in the Commonweal Collection by and about Mohandas K Gandhi (1995, 50pp, £5 inc. p&p)
Guide to the Collections
The Commonweal Collection: a short history (Barlow S, 1996)
Travels of an International Voluntary Service Worker (Huggett D, 1996)
Bibliographies:
Citizenship and the National Curriculum
Circle Time Resources
Religious Education
Conflict Resolution and Bullying (for teachers)

Electronic and video publications:
List of videos available, may be borrowed

Access to staff:
Contact by letter, by telephone, by fax, by e-mail and in person
Hours: Term time: Mon to Thu, 0800 to 2400; Fri, 0800 to 2100; Sat, Sun, 0845 to 2100
Vacations: Mon to Fri, 0845 to 2100; Sat, Sun, 0845 to 1800

Access for disabled people:
Level entry, access to all public areas, toilet facilities
Special comments: Lifts.

Parent body:
Commonweal Trust

COMMONWEALTH ASSOCIATION OF SURVEYING AND LAND ECONOMY

Acronym or abbreviation: CASLE

University of the West of England, Faculty of Built Environment, Frenchay Campus, Coldharbour Lane, Bristol, BS16 1QY

Tel: 0117 328 3036
Fax: 0117 328 3036
E-mail: susan.spedding@uwe.ac.uk

Website:
http://www.casle.org
http://www.casle.conferences.co.uk

Enquiries:
Enquiries to: Administrator

Founded:
1969

Organisation type and purpose:
Membership association.

Subject coverage:
Education and training in surveying and land management subjects throughout the Commonwealth.

Printed publications:
Introduction to Facilities Management
Building Maintenance
CASLE Newsletter
Project Manuals on surveying topics
Survey Review Ltd – Land Surveyors Journal
 (quarterly)
Order printed publications from: Survey Review, CASLE
Room 2Q20A, Faculty of the Built Environment, University of the West of England, Bristol, BS16 1QY, tel: As main numbers

Access to staff:
Contact by letter, by telephone, by fax and by e-mail. Appointment necessary.
Hours: Mon to Fri, 0900 to 1700

COMMONWEALTH BROADCASTING ASSOCIATION

Acronym or abbreviation: CBA

17 Fleet Street, London, EC4Y 1AA

Tel: 020 7853 5550
Fax: 020 7583 5549
E-mail: cba@cba.org.uk

Website:
http://www.cba.org.uk

Enquiries:
Enquiries to: Secretary General

Founded:
1945

Organisation type and purpose:
International organisation, professional body, membership association (membership is by election or invitation), present number of members: 98 corporate members, training organisation, consultancy, research organisation. To support quality broadcasting throughout the Commonwealth.

Subject coverage:
Broadcasting in Commonwealth countries.

Printed publications:
Commonwealth Broadcaster
Commonwealth Broadcasting Directory
Order printed publications from: Postal address or email: cba@cba.org.uk

Electronic and video publications:
Commonwealth Photographic Awards (CD, available to member organisations)
Commonwealth Short Stories (CD, annually, available to member organisations)

Publications list:
Available online

Access to staff:
Contact by letter, by telephone, by fax and by e-mail
Hours: Mon to Fri, 0930 to 1730

Access to building, collection or gallery:
No access other than to staff and visitors

COMMONWEALTH EDUCATION TRUST

New Zealand House, 80 Haymarket, London, SW1Y 4TE 1

Tel: 020 7024 9822
Fax: 020 7024 9833
E-mail: information@commonwealth-institute.org

Website:
http://www.commonwealth.org.uk/

Enquiries:
Enquiries to: Head of Library Services

Founded:
1962

Formerly called:
Commonwealth Institute (year of change 2000)

Organisation type and purpose:
Registered charity (charity number 1119647). Independent educational and cultural agency working to promote learning across the many cultures of the Commonwealth.

Subject coverage:
The Commonwealth as it exists today, its 54 independent countries, its dependencies and other territories; governments, economics, life and culture, aid and development, education; arts; literature; theatre and cinema; Third World.

Museum or gallery collection, archive, or library special collection:
Commonwealth Literature Collection

Non-library collection catalogue:
All or part available online

Library catalogue:
All or part available online

Printed publications:
Annual Review
Commonwealth Curriculum Packs

Publications list:
Available online and in print

Access to staff:
Contact by letter, by telephone, by fax, by e-mail and in person
Hours: Mon to Sat, 1000 to 1600

Access to building, collection or gallery:
No access other than to staff

COMMONWEALTH FORCES HISTORY TRUST

37 Davis Road, Acton, London, W3 7SE

Tel: 020 8749 1045

Enquiries:
Enquiries to: Secretary

Founded:
1988

Organisation type and purpose:
Registered charity.

Subject coverage:
All the different units of the Defence Forces of the British Commonwealth and Empire outside the United Kingdom, from 1066 to 1946, including the American Loyalists and the Indians who fought as Allies of the King in the American Revolution and/or the War of 1812.

Museum or gallery collection, archive, or library special collection:
Books and Journals
Indices
Letters
Photographs
Tape recordings

Access to staff:
Contact by letter and by telephone. Appointment necessary.
Hours: Mon to Fri, 0900 to 1600

COMMONWEALTH FORESTRY ASSOCIATION

Acronym or abbreviation: CFA

The Crib, Dinchope, Craven Arms, Shropshire, SY7 9JJ

Tel: 01588 672868
Fax: 0870 0116645
E-mail: cfa@cfa-international.org

Website:
http://www.cfa-international.org

Enquiries:
Enquiries to: Membership Manager
Direct e-mail: jenny@cfa-international.org

Founded:
1921

Organisation type and purpose:
Professional body.

Subject coverage:
Forestry, forest products, related environmental subjects.

Museum or gallery collection, archive, or library special collection:
Commonwealth Forestry Conference Proceedings
Commonwealth Forestry Review

Printed publications:
Commonwealth Forestry Handbook (periodic)
International Forestry Review (quarterly)
The World's Forests – Rio plus 5: international initiatives towards sustainable management
The World's Forests – Rio plus 8

Access to staff:
Contact by letter, by telephone, by fax, by e-mail and via website
Hours: Mon to Fri, 0900 to 1700

Corporate member of the:
Commonwealth Professional Associations
Commonwealth Trust

COMMONWEALTH HUMAN ECOLOGY COUNCIL

Acronym or abbreviation: CHEC

Church House, Newton Road, London, W2 5LS

Tel: 020 7792 5934
Fax: 020 7792 5948
E-mail: chec@btopenworld.com

Website:
http://www.checinternational.org

Enquiries:
Enquiries to: Chief Executive
Direct tel: 020 7373 6761
Direct fax: 020 7244 7470
Other contacts: Executive Vice-Chairperson

Founded:
1969

Formerly called:
Committee on Nutrition in the Commonwealth

Organisation type and purpose:
Promotion of a human ecological approach to sustainable development, international organisation, professional body, present number of members: 220 individuals and 32 corporate, voluntary organisation, registered charity (charity number 272018), research organisation.

continued overleaf

Joint government and non-government composition.

Subject coverage:
Human ecology, Commonwealth, human settlements, poverty programmes, health education, sustainable fisheries

Non-library collection catalogue:
All or part available in-house

Library catalogue:
All or part available in-house

Printed publications:
Bibliographies, books and papers to purchase
CHEC Journal (free to members)
CHEC Points (free to all)
Conference Proceedings
Order printed publications from: from CHEC

Publications list:
Available in print

Access to staff:
Contact by letter, by telephone, by fax and by e-mail
Hours: Mon to Fri, 1030 to 1700

Access to building, collection or gallery:
By Appointment

Access for disabled people:
No access

Links with:
Commission on Sustainable Development
Economic and Social Council for Asia and the Pacific (ESCAP)
IUCN Education Commission
UN Centre for Human Settlements
UN ECOSOC
UNEP
UNESCO – Education
WHO

COMMONWEALTH JEWISH COUNCIL

Acronym or abbreviation: CJC

BCM Box 6871, London, WC1N 3XX

Tel: 020 7222 2120
Fax: 020 7222 1781
E-mail: info@cjc.org.uk

Website:
http://www.cjc.org.uk
Members, projects, contacts with the Commonwealth, about CJC, etc.

Enquiries:
Enquiries to: Administrator

Founded:
1982

Organisation type and purpose:
Registered charity (charity number 287564).
Commonwealth Jewish Trust.
CJC is the political arm of the organisation which provides the Commonwealth link between countries, high commissioners and ambassadors.

Subject coverage:
Commonwealth, Jewish communities, Judaism.

Printed publications:
Newsletter (2 times a year)

Access to staff:
Contact by letter and by e-mail
Hours: Mon to Fri, 0915 to 1745

Access to building, collection or gallery:
No access other than to staff

COMMONWEALTH LOCAL GOVERNMENT FORUM

Acronym or abbreviation: CLGF

16A Northumberland Avenue, London, WC2N 5AP

Tel: 020 7389 1490

Fax: 020 7389 1499
E-mail: lorna@clgf.org.uk

Website:
http://www.clgf.org.uk

Enquiries:
Enquiries to: PA to the Secretary General

Founded:
1995

Organisation type and purpose:
International organisation, local government body, membership association, present number of members: 160.

Subject coverage:
Local government in Commonwealth countries.

Museum or gallery collection, archive, or library special collection:
Documentation on local government in Commonwealth countries

Non-library collection catalogue:
All or part available in-house

Printed publications:
Annual Report (annually)
Bulletin (quarterly)
Reports on aspects of local government in Commonwealth Countries (available free to members)
Commonwealth Local Government Handbook

Publications list:
Available online and in print

Access to staff:
Contact by letter, by fax and by e-mail
Hours: Mon to Fri, 0900 to 1700

Access to building, collection or gallery:
Prior appointment required

COMMONWEALTH PARLIAMENTARY ASSOCIATION

Acronym or abbreviation: CPA

Suite 700, Westminster House, 7 Millbank, London, SW1P 3JA

Tel: 020 7799 1460
Fax: 020 7222 6073
E-mail: hq.sec@cpahq.org

Website:
http://www.cpahq.org
Aims of the organisation, publications, subscriptions, conference information, newsletters and latest news.

Enquiries:
Enquiries to: Secretary General

Founded:
1911

Organisation type and purpose:
International organisation, professional body (membership is by qualification), present number of members: 14,000, registered charity, training organisation, research organisation, publishing house.
To promote knowledge and education about the constitutional, legislative, economic, social and cultural systems within a parliamentary democratic framework, with particular reference to countries of the Commonwealth.

Subject coverage:
Parliaments of the Commonwealth (membership, practice and procedures etc), constitutions, standing orders, names of Commonwealth MPs, elections.

Museum or gallery collection, archive, or library special collection:
Books on parliamentary practice and procedure, the Commonwealth, Commonwealth constitutions and standing orders
PA publications, including specialist monographs

Printed publications:
The Parliamentarian (quarterly journal, annual subscription: UK £28; worldwide £36 air mail, £30 surface)

Electronic and video publications:
The Commonwealth Way (video, £10)
The Parliamentarian (on microfilm, from University Microfilms International, 300 North Zeeb Road, Ann Arbor, Michigan, USA)

Publications list:
Available online

Access to staff:
Contact by letter, by telephone, by fax, by e-mail and via website. Appointment necessary. Non-members charged.
Hours: Fri, 0900 to 1600

Access to building, collection or gallery:
Prior appointment required

Access for disabled people:
Ramped entry

Has:
branches in more than 165 national, state, provincial and territorial parliaments in the Commonwealth

COMMONWEALTH PHARMACEUTICAL ASSOCIATION

Acronym or abbreviation: CPA

1 Lambeth High Street, London, SE1 7JN

Tel: 020 7572 2364
Fax: 020 7572 2508

Website:
http://www.rpsgb.org.uk/international.html
Background and objectives of CPA.

Enquiries:
Enquiries to: Administrator

Founded:
1970

Organisation type and purpose:
Membership association (membership is by subscription), present number of members: 600.
An association of professional pharmaceutical bodies and personal members from 39 Commonwealth countries.
To establish, develop and maintain the highest possible professional standards of pharmacy throughout the Commonwealth in order to achieve better health outcomes within communities.

Subject coverage:
Pharmacy.

Access to staff:
Contact by telephone, by fax and by e-mail.
Appointment necessary.
Hours: Mon to Fri, 0900 to 1700

Access for disabled people:
Ramped entry, toilet facilities

COMMONWEALTH SCIENCE COUNCIL

Formal name: Commonwealth Science Council
Acronym or abbreviation: CSC

Marlborough House, Pall Mall, London, SW1Y 5HX

Tel: 020 7747 6220/6219
Fax: 020 7839 6174
E-mail: science@commonwealth.int

Website:
http://www.commonwealthknowledge.net

Enquiries:
Enquiries to: Information Officer
Direct tel: 020 7747 6219
Direct e-mail: t.ruredzo@commonwealth.int

Organisation type and purpose:
International organisation.
The CSC is an innovative, creative and proactive organisation that seeks to leverage the science and technology capability in the public and industry domain within the Commonwealth through networking of both knowledge and finance, using modern information technologies to facilitate the application of S&T by member countries for sustainable economic, environmental, social and cultural development.

Subject coverage:
Science and technology.

Printed publications:
Commonwealth Scientist (newsletter, quarterly)
Knowledge Networking for Development: Science and Technology for the Millennium
Paths to Prosperity – Science and technology in the Commonwealth 1999/2000
Biodiversity in Small States
Biodiversity Management Procedures Guide
Information Pack
Order printed publications from: The Publications Unit
tel: 020 7747 6342, fax: 020 7839 9081

Access to staff:
Contact by e-mail
Hours: Mon to Fri, 0900 to 1700

Access to building, collection or gallery:
Prior appointment required
Hours: Mon to Fri, 0930 to 1730

Access for disabled people:
Level entry, toilet facilities

COMMONWEALTH SECRETARIAT

Marlborough House, Pall Mall, London, SW1Y 5HX

Tel: 020 7747 6164
Fax: 020 7747 6168
E-mail: library@commonwealth.int

Website:
http://www.thecommonwealth.org
Publications, information on the Commonwealth.

Enquiries:
Enquiries to: Head of Library and Archives
Other contacts: Archivist and Records Management Officer

Founded:
1965

Organisation type and purpose:
International organisation.

Subject coverage:
Commonwealth, development, trade, agriculture, statistics, economics, technology, industry, politics, education, women and development, youth, health and science.

Museum or gallery collection, archive, or library special collection:
Collection of Commonwealth Secretariat Publications
Commonwealth Secretariat Archive, released after 30 years

Library catalogue:
All or part available in-house

Printed publications:
Publications catalogue available online
Order printed publications from: Publications Manager, Communications and Public Affairs Division, Commonwealth Secretariat; tel. 020 7747 6342; fax 020 7839 9081

Publications list:
Available online and in print

Access to staff:
Contact by letter, by telephone, by e-mail and in person. Appointment necessary.
Hours: Mon to Fri, 0915 to 1700

Access for disabled people:
Access to all public areas, toilet facilities
Special comments: Lift from ground floor.

COMMONWEALTH WAR GRAVES COMMISSION

Acronym or abbreviation: CWGC

2 Marlow Road, Maidenhead, Berkshire, SL6 7DX

Tel: 01628 634221
Fax: 01628 771208
E-mail: general.enq@cwgc.org

Website:
http://www.cwgc.org
The Debt of Honour Register, information on the task of the Commission, the worldwide commitment, country membership, commissioners, areas and agencies, publications, services and comments.

Enquiries:
Enquiries to: Enquiries Section
Direct e-mail: casualty.enq@cwgc.org
Other contacts: for casualty/cemetery enquiries.

Founded:
1917

Formerly called:
Imperial War Graves Commission (year of change 1964)

Organisation type and purpose:
International organisation.
Commemoration of members of the Forces of the Commonwealth who died in the two World Wars.

Subject coverage:
Care and maintenance in perpetuity of cemeteries and memorials of the two world wars; precise details of the burial place (or site of commemoration for those who have no known grave) of each Commonwealth casualty of those wars, as well as of civilians killed by enemy action during the Second World War.

Museum or gallery collection, archive, or library special collection:
Documents and letters relating to the history of the CWGC and its founder Sir Fabian Ware, the Commission's Architects and Commissioners. Not available for loan but may photocopy or provide information

Non-library collection catalogue:
All or part available in-house

Library catalogue:
All or part available in-house

Printed publications:
Annual Report (November)
Cemetery and Memorial registers: the dead of the two World Wars
Information Sheets on Commission's work
Michelin Maps nos. 51–53 (overprinted with Commission sites)

Electronic and video publications:
A Debt of Honour: video about the Commission's work (1996)

Publications list:
Available online and in print

Access to staff:
Contact by letter, by telephone, by fax, by e-mail and via website. Appointment necessary.
Hours: Mon to Thu, 0830 to 1700; Fri, 0830 to 1630

Access to building, collection or gallery:
Prior appointment required

Access for disabled people:
Level entry, toilet facilities

Also at:
Director United Kingdom Area
Commonwealth War Graves Commission, Jenton Road, Sydenham, Leamington Spa, Warwickshire, CV31 1XS; tel: 01926 330137; fax: 01926 339757; e-mail: ukaoffice@cwgc.org

Director, Outer Area (not Europe or the Mediterranean)
Commonwealth War Graves Commission, 2 Marlow Road, Maidenhead, Berkshire, SL6 7DX; tel: 01628 634221; fax: 01628 771643; e-mail: oaoffice@cwgc.org

COMMONWEALTH YOUTH EXCHANGE COUNCIL

Acronym or abbreviation: CYEC

7 Lion Yard, Tremadoc Road, London, SW4 7NQ

Tel: 020 7498 6151
Fax: 020 7720 5403
E-mail: mail@cyec.org.uk

Website:
http://www.cyec.org.uk

Enquiries:
Enquiries to: Chief Executive
Other contacts: Grants and Administration Officer for Youth Exchange Information Enquiries

Founded:
1970

Organisation type and purpose:
Voluntary organisation, registered charity (charity number 1086375).
National voluntary youth organisation.
Education – informal (young people's social and personal education via youth work) via international youth exchange projects.
Not able to help individuals interested in an international experience or overseas applicants.

Subject coverage:
Group youth exchanges between Britain and other Commonwealth countries for young people aged 16–25 years.

Printed publications:
Journeys Inward Journey Outward (personal record achievement for youth exchange groups)
Contact (Handbook)
Leaflets and Guidelines (free)
Crossing Frontiers (workbook for youth exchange groups)
Commonwealth (4 poster set)

Publications list:
Available in print

Access to staff:
Contact by letter, by telephone, by fax and by e-mail. Appointment necessary.
Hours: Mon to Fri, 1100 to 1800
Special comments: Send stamped addressed envelope.

Access to building, collection or gallery:
Hours: Mon to Fri, 1000 to 1700

Branch Office:
CYEC Scotland
Development Officer, 30 Wyvis Crescent, Conon Bridge, Dingwall, Highland, IV7 8BZ; tel: 01349 861110; fax: 01349 861110; e-mail: cyecscotland@btinternet.com

COMMUNICATIONS POLICY PROGRAMME

Acronym or abbreviation: CPJRU

City University, Northampton Square, London, EC1V 0HB

Tel: 020 7040 8908
Fax: 020 7040 8558
E-mail: socscipg@city.ac.uk

Website:
http://www.city.ac.uk/human/sociology
http://www.staff.city.ac.uk/p.iosifidis

Enquiries:
Enquiries to: Director
Direct e-mail: p.iosifidis@city.ac.uk

Founded:
1984

continued overleaf

Formerly called:
Communications Policy and Journalism Research
Unit, Communications Policy Centre

Organisation type and purpose:
University department or institute.

Subject coverage:
Communications Policy; New Media Technologies;
Information Society.

Access to staff:
Contact by letter, by telephone, by fax and by e-mail
Hours: Mon to Fri, 0900 to 1700

COMMUNIST PARTY OF BRITAIN

Acronym or abbreviation: CPB

BCM Box 928, London WC1N 3XX

Tel: 020 7254 8444
E-mail: office@cpgb.org.uk

Website:
http://www.cpgb.org.uk

Enquiries:
Enquiries to: Organiser

Founded:
1998

Formerly called:
Communist Party of Great Britain (CPGB) (year of
change 1991)

Organisation type and purpose:
National organisation (membership is by
subscription), present number of members: 1350.
Political party.

Printed publications:
Pamphlets:
British Road to Socialism New 7th Edition 2001
    (£2.50 inc. p&p)
Case for Trade Unions (£2.50 inc. p&p)
Women & Class (Davis M, 1999, £2.50 inc. p&p)
What We Stand For, introduction to the CPB (2001,
    £1.50 inc. p&p)
Stop the War – Terror and the New World Order
    (2001, £1.50 inc. p&p)
Books:
Fashioning a New World (Davis M, 2001, £8 inc.
    p&p)
The Communist Party of Great Britain – An
    historical analysis to 1941 (Murray A, £5 inc.
    p&p)
Communist Review (journal, quarterly, £2 inc.
    p&p)
The African Resource Wars of the 21st Century
    (Dreapir L, £1.50 inc. p&p)
The National Question (Greaves C D, 2002, £1.20
    inc. p&p)
Challenge – Journal of the Young Communist
    League (quarterly, £1.30 inc. p&p)

Publications list:
Available in print

Access to staff:
Contact by letter, by telephone, by fax and by e-mail
Hours: Mon to Fri, 0900 to 1700

Access for disabled people:
Parking provided, access to all public areas

COMMUNITIES SCOTLAND

Thistle House, 91 Haymarket Terrace, Edinburgh,
EH12 5HE

Tel: 0131 313 0044
Fax: 0131 313 2680

Website:
http://www.communitiesscotland.gov.uk
Complete picture of Scottish Homes and its
activities, including same day publication of news
releases, latest publications, etc.

Enquiries:
Enquiries to: Librarian

Direct tel: 0131 479 5016
Direct e-mail: johnstoner@communitiesscotland.gov
.uk

Founded:
2001

Formerly called:
Housing Corporation in Scotland, Scottish Special
Housing Association; Scottish Homes (year of
change 1989–2001)

Organisation type and purpose:
National government body.
The national housing agency for Scotland.

Subject coverage:
Wide-ranging information on all aspects of
housing in Scotland, including joint funding
arrangements, establishment and funding of
housing associations and housing co-operatives;
approval of landlords; urban renewal; housing
management; modernisation and rehabilitation
techniques; private developers; rural housing.

Library catalogue:
All or part available in-house

Printed publications:
Annual Report
Dozens of Newsletters on specific subjects
Home News
Research Reports
Strategic Plan

Access to staff:
Contact by letter, by telephone and by e-mail.
Appointment necessary.
Hours: Mon to Thu, 0830 to 1700; Fri, 0830 to 1630

Access to building, collection or gallery:
Prior appointment required

Access for disabled people:
Ramped entry, toilet facilities

COMMUNITY ACTION NORTHUMBERLAND

Acronym or abbreviation: CAN

Tower Buildings, 9 Oldgate, Morpeth,
Northumberland, NE61 1PY

Tel: 01670 517178
Fax: 01670 511400
E-mail: info@ca-north.org.uk

Website:
http://www.ca-north.org.uk

Enquiries:
Enquiries to: Director
Direct e-mail: davidfrancis@ca-north.org.uk

Founded:
1951

Formerly called:
Northumberland Rural Community Council; (year
of change 1974); Community Council of
Northumberland (year of change 2007)

Organisation type and purpose:
Voluntary organisation, registered charity (charity
number 224798). Community development and
voluntary sector support.

Subject coverage:
Voluntary organisations, community initiatives
and parish councils in Northumberland.
Information needed by these groups e.g. grant aid,
law, project development, working together,
further sources of help.

Printed publications:
Northumberland Community News (6 times a
    year, free)
Various guides, directories and research reports

Access to staff:
Contact by letter, by telephone, by fax, by e-mail
and in person. Appointment necessary.
Hours: Mon to Thu, 0900 to 1700; Fri, 0900 to 1630

Affiliated to:
ACRE; NAVCA
Voluntary Organisations Network North East

COMMUNITY AND DISTRICT NURSING ASSOCIATION

Acronym or abbreviation: CDNA

32–38 Uxbridge Road, Ealing, London, W5 2BS

Tel: 020 8280 5342
Fax: 020 8280 5341
E-mail: cdna@tvu.ac.uk

Website:
http://www.cdna.tvu.ac.uk

Enquiries:
Enquiries to: Chairman
Other contacts: Professional Officer for information
on professional and clinical issues.

Founded:
1971

Organisation type and purpose:
Professional body, trade union (membership is by
subscription), present number of members: 5500.

Access to staff:
Contact by letter, by telephone, by fax, by e-mail
and via website
Hours: Mon to Fri, 0900 to 1700

COMMUNITY AND YOUTH WORKERS' UNION, THE

Acronym or abbreviation: CYWU

302 The Argent Centre, 60 Frederick Street,
Birmingham, B31 3HS

Tel: 0121 233 3344
Fax: 0121 344 3345
E-mail: kerry@cywu.org.uk

Website:
http://www.cywu.org.uk

Enquiries:
Enquiries to: Administrator

Founded:
1938

Organisation type and purpose:
Trade union (membership is by subscription),
present number of members: 4500.

Subject coverage:
Community and youth work.

Printed publications:
Rapport (tabloid journal, fortnightly)
Youth Work and Community Work into the
    twenty-first Century
Planning for a Sufficient Youth Service
The Struggle for Statutory Youth Service Provision
Employment Practice and Policies in Youth and
    Community Work (£16.95, available from Russell
    House Publishing)
Health and Safety in Youth and Community Work
    – A Resource Manual
Managing Aggression and Violence – A Model for
    Youth and Community Centres of legal
    compliance, safe working practices and good
    personal safety habits for staff (1996, £19.50
    available from Pepar Publications)
Order printed publications from: CYWU

Pepar Publications
The Gatehouse, 112 Park Hill Road, Harborne,
Birmingham, B17 0HD
Russell House Publishing Limited
4 St George's House, Uplyme Road Business Park,
Lyme Regis, DT7 3LS

Publications list:
Available in print

Access to staff:
Contact by e-mail
Hours: Mon to Fri, 0900 to 1700

Affiliated to:
GFTU
TUC

COMMUNITY COMPOSTING NETWORK

Acronym or abbreviation: CCN

67 Alexandra Road, Sheffield, South Yorkshire, S2 3EE

Tel: 0114 258 0483
Fax: 0114 258 0483
E-mail: info@communitycompost.org

Website:
http://www.communitycompost.org

Enquiries:
Enquiries to: Co-ordinator

Founded:
1995

Organisation type and purpose:
National organisation, membership association (membership is by subscription), present number of members: 200, voluntary organisation. Provides advice and support to existing and 'would be' community composting projects across the UK.

Printed publications:
The Growing Heap (newsletter, 4 times a year, free to members)
Community Composting Guide (£15 members, £55, non members, incl. p&p)

Access to staff:
Contact by letter, by telephone, by fax, by e-mail and via website. Appointment necessary.
Hours: Mon to Fri, 0900 to 1700

COMMUNITY COUNCIL FOR BERKSHIRE

Acronym or abbreviation: CCB

Epping House, 55 Russell Street, Reading, Berkshire, RG1 7XG

Tel: 0118 961 2000
Fax: 0118 961 2600
E-mail: admin@ccberks.co.uk

Website:
http://www.communityberkshire.co.uk

Enquiries:
Enquiries to: PA to Chief Executive

Founded:
1973

Organisation type and purpose:
Voluntary organisation, registered charity (charity number 1056367).
To improve quality of life of local communities, and particularly of disadvantaged people in Berkshire by strengthening voluntary action and local communities.

Subject coverage:
Information on the voluntary sector in Berkshire, rural communities, advice on running a voluntary organisation, funding advice, village hall information and advice, transport, village shops, rural disadvantage, community developments, ESOL etc.

Museum or gallery collection, archive, or library special collection:
Library on voluntary sector information and rural communities

Printed publications:
Amongst many are:
Community (newsletter, free to members)
Making the Links Best Practice Guide
East Berkshire Community Transport Travel Guide

Access to staff:
Contact by letter, by telephone, by fax and by e-mail. Appointment necessary.
Hours: Mon to Fri, 0900 to 1700
Special comments: Principally to assist voluntary sector.

Access to building, collection or gallery:
Prior appointment required

Also at:
CAWB
CCB, 91a Bartholomew Street, Newbury, RG14 5DY; tel: 01635 46732

Connections with:
Community Action West Berkshire
1 Bolton Place, Newbury, RG14 1AJ

COMMUNITY COUNCIL OF DEVON

Acronym or abbreviation: CCD

School Huts, County Hall, Topsham Road, Exeter, Devon, EX2 4QB

Tel: 01392 383443
Fax: 01392 382062
E-mail: info@devonrcc.org.uk

Website:
http://www.devonrcc.org.uk
General information, reports, corporate plan, directions, links.

Enquiries:
Enquiries to: Chief Executive
Other contacts: (1) Parish Councils Officer (2) Playing Fields Officer for (1) information on Parish Councils (2) information and advice on playing fields.

Founded:
1961

Organisation type and purpose:
Voluntary organisation, registered charity (charity number 1074047).
Rural community council.

Subject coverage:
Village halls in Devon, Parish Council contacts in Devon, Charities Information Bureau, Devon Playing Fields Association, information on sources of funding, community development, parish appraisals, children's play in Devon.

Printed publications:
Annual Report
Village Green (newsletter, quarterly)

Access to staff:
Contact by letter, by telephone, by e-mail and in person
Hours: Mon to Fri, 0900 to 1700

COMMUNITY COUNCIL OF SHROPSHIRE

Acronym or abbreviation: CCS

1 College Hill, Shrewsbury, Shropshire, SY1 1LT

Tel: 01743 360641
Fax: 01743 233335
E-mail: ccs@collegehill.org.uk

Website:
http://www.collegehill.org.uk
Detailed information about the services we provide, copy of the latest issue of our quarterly newsletter, 'Buzz'.

Enquiries:
Enquiries to: Director

Founded:
1961

Organisation type and purpose:
Registered charity (charity number 218783), training organisation.

Subject coverage:
Advice for voluntary organisations, especially in rural areas, rural transport, rural housing, promotion of volunteering, funding, training, charities, parish councils.

Printed publications:
Annual Report
Information sheets on all aspects of village life, from 'Public Entertainment Licences' to 'Coping with VAT on Fuel and Power' (£1 per copy inc. p&p)

Publications list:
Available in print

Access to staff:
Contact by letter, by telephone, by fax, by e-mail and in person
Hours: Mon to Fri, 0900 to 1700

Member of:
Federation of Rural Community Councils
William House, Skipton Road, Skelton, York, YO3 6XW

COMMUNITY DEVELOPMENT FOUNDATION

Acronym or abbreviation: CDF

Unit 5, Angel Gate, 320–326 City Road, London, EC1V 2PT

Tel: 020 7833 1772
Fax: 020 7837 6584
E-mail: admin@cdf.org.uk

Website:
http://www.cdf.org.uk

Enquiries:
Enquiries to: Information and Marketing Officer
Direct e-mail: tessa.norton@cdf.org.uk

Founded:
1968

Formerly called:
Community Projects Foundation

Organisation type and purpose:
National government body, voluntary organisation, registered charity (charity number 306130), consultancy, research organisation. Promotion of community development.

Subject coverage:
Community development, community work, social policy, environment and planning, housing, health, education, social welfare, local government, economic development, employment and unemployment, voluntary sector; youth work, ethnic and racial issues, poverty, regeneration, social inclusion and capacity building.

Non-library collection catalogue:
All or part available in-house

Library catalogue:
All or part available in-house

Printed publications:
Community Currents: the Community Development Information Digest (6 times a year, £20.90 a year)
Community Groups Handbook (Pearse M and Smith J, 1990)

Electronic and video publications:
CommunityWISE (CD-ROM)

Publications list:
Available online and in print

Access to staff:
Contact by letter, by telephone, by fax, by e-mail and via website. Appointment necessary.
Hours: Mon to Fri, 0900 to 1700
Special comments: We regret we do not have wheelchair access.

Access to building, collection or gallery:
Prior appointment required

Supported by:
central and local government

COMMUNITY FIRST

Wyndhams, St Joseph's Place, Devizes, Wiltshire, SN10 1DD

Tel: 01380 722475
Fax: 01380 728476
E-mail: reception@communityfirst.org.uk

Enquiries:
Enquiries to: Director

continued overleaf

Founded:
1965

Organisation type and purpose:
Membership association (membership is by
subscription), voluntary organisation, registered
charity (charity number 288117).
Working in partnership with communities and
funders to encourage and support social, economic
and environmental initiatives in Wiltshire and
Swindon.

Subject coverage:
Rural community development, village halls,
sports clubs, children's play, parish and town
councils, funding and support for voluntary
groups, rural projects and services, rural housing,
community transport, rural policy, rural economic
development.

Printed publications:
Leaflets and other publications including:
Annual Report
Newsletter

Publications list:
Available in print

Access to staff:
Contact by letter, by telephone and by e-mail.
Appointment necessary.
Hours: Mon to Thu, 0900 to 1700; Fri, 0900 to 1600

Access for disabled people:
Parking provided, ramped entry, toilet facilities

Member of:
ACRE Network of Rural Community Councils

COMMUNITY FIRST IN HEREFORDSHIRE AND WORCESTERSHIRE

141 Church Street, Malvern, Worcestershire, WR14
2AN

Tel: 01684 573334
Fax: 01684 573367
E-mail: info@comfirst.org.uk

Website:
http://www.comfirst.org.uk
Information about the organisation's work.

Enquiries:
Enquiries to: Chief Executive Officer

Founded:
1975

Formerly called:
Rural Community Council; Community Council of
Hereford and Worcester (year of change 2001)

Organisation type and purpose:
Voluntary organisation, registered charity (charity
number 703072).
Sub-regional development agency working with
communities and voluntary organisations in
Herefordshire and Worcestershire.
Mission – To build better communities.

Subject coverage:
Rural transport initiatives, learning and skills in
the voluntary sector, information and training for
voluntary sector, community resource centres,
village halls in Herefordshire and Worcestershire;
ICT support for voluntary sector, business advice,
social enterprise support.

Printed publications:
Newsline (every other month, free to members)

Publications list:
Available in print

Access to staff:
Contact by letter, by telephone, by fax, by e-mail
and via website. Appointment necessary.
Hours: Mon to Fri, 0900 to 1700

Access to building, collection or gallery:
Prior appointment required

Access for disabled people:
Parking provided, ramped entry, toilet facilities

Other offices:
Community First – Hereford Office
  41a Bridge Street, Hereford; tel: 01432 267820

COMMUNITY FOUNDATION FOR NORTHERN IRELAND

Acronym or abbreviation: NIVT

City Link, Albert House, Belfast, BT12 4HQ

Tel: 028 9024 5927
Fax: 028 9032 9839
E-mail: info@communityfoundation.org

Enquiries:
Enquiries to: Director

Founded:
1979

Organisation type and purpose:
Registered charity (charity number XN45242).

Access to staff:
Contact by letter
Hours: Mon to Fri, 0900 to 1700

COMMUNITY FOUNDATION NETWORK

Arena House, 66–68 Pentonville Road, London, N1
9HS

Tel: 020 7713 9326
Fax: 020 7713 9327
E-mail: network@communityfoundations.org.uk

Website:
http://www.communityfoundations.org.uk

Enquiries:
Enquiries to: Director

Founded:
1991

Formerly called:
Association of Community Trusts and Foundations
(ACTAF) (year of change 1999)

Organisation type and purpose:
Membership association (membership is by
subscription), present number of members: 68,
voluntary organisation, registered charity (charity
number 1004630).
Membership is restricted to active community
foundations, although any interested body may
subscribe as an associate.
Promotion, support and development of
community foundations throughout the UK.

Subject coverage:
Community foundation development and
management.

Trade and statistical information:
Fund development and grant-making in
  community foundations in UK. Advice on the
  development of community foundations.

Library catalogue:
All or part available in-house

Printed publications:
A number of free information sheets
Occasional reports – most recent is The Price of
  Giving, Diana Leat, 2002, £10
Newsletter (3 issues a year, annual subscription
  £25)

Publications list:
Available online and in print

Access to staff:
Contact by letter, by telephone, by fax, by e-mail
and via website. Appointment necessary.
Hours: Mon to Fri, 0900 to 1700

COMMUNITY LINCS

The Old Mart, Church Lane, Sleaford, Lincolnshire,
NG34 7DF

Tel: 01529 302466

Fax: 01529 414267
E-mail: office@communitylincs.com

Website:
http://www.communitylincs.com
General information, services, etc.

Enquiries:
Enquiries to: Chief Executive's PA
Direct e-mail: teresa.palmer@communitylincs.com

Founded:
1927

Organisation type and purpose:
Voluntary organisation, registered charity (charity
number 1046569). Rural Community
Development.

Subject coverage:
Rural development in Lincolnshire.

Printed publications:
Annual Report (£1)
Grants for rural projects available from CCL (free)
Rural Links (magazine, 2 a year)

Publications list:
Available in print

Access to staff:
Contact by letter, by telephone, by fax and by e-
mail. Appointment necessary.
Hours: Mon to Fri, 0900 to 1700

Access for disabled people:
Ramped entry, access to all public areas, toilet
facilities

Affiliated to:
Federation of Rural Community Councils

Connections with:
Lincolnshire Association of Local Councils
Lincolnshire Playing Fields Association

COMMUNITY MATTERS

12–20 Baron Street, Islington, London, N1 9LL

Tel: 020 7837 7887
Fax: 020 7278 9253
E-mail: communitymatters@communitymatters.org
.uk

Enquiries:
Enquiries to: Chief Executive
Direct e-mail: d.tyler@communitymatters.org.uk
Other contacts: Performance Improvement &
Information Manager

Founded:
1945

Formerly called:
National Federation of Community Organisations
(NFCO)

Organisation type and purpose:
Membership association (membership is by
subscription), present number of members: 1500
member organisations, voluntary organisation,
registered charity (charity number 1002383),
training organisation, consultancy, research
organisation, publishing house.
To support and help develop local community
groups and associations and make sure their
interests are represented locally and nationally.

Subject coverage:
Good management of charities and community
organisations; managing community activities;
managing social contractual relations; managing
community premises, legislation affecting charities
and voluntary organisations managing buildings.

Printed publications:
Annual Report and accounts
Community (magazine, quarterly, £10 a year)
Community Start Up: How to start a community
  group and keep it going (£9.95)
How to Manage Your Money, if you have any
Information Sheets (65 titles; single copies free to
  some members)
Law Monitoring Group Bulletin (quarterly, £10 a
  year)
Managing Your Community Building

Occupying Community Premises
Organising for a Better Community

Electronic and video publications:
Model Constitution for a Community Association
(book and disc)
Occupying Community Premises (book, Dawson J,
and disc)

Publications list:
Available in print

Access to staff:
Contact by letter, by telephone, by fax and by e-mail. Appointment necessary. Non-members
charged.
Hours: Mon to Fri, 0900 to 1700

Affiliated to:
Community Sector Coalition
International Federation of Settlements
National Council for Voluntary Organisations

COMMUNITY MEDIA ASSOCIATION

Acronym or abbreviation: CMA

15 Paternoster Row, Sheffield, South Yorkshire, S1
2BX

Tel: 0114 279 5219
Fax: 0114 279 8976
E-mail: admin@commedia.org.uk

Website:
http://www.commedia.org.uk
Airflash (articles from), information sheets,
publication list, membership application form,
policy papers, project descriptions, fundraising
contacts.

Enquiries:
Enquiries to: Financial/Office Manager

Founded:
1983

Formerly called:
Community Radio Association (CRA) (year of
change 1997)

Organisation type and purpose:
National organisation, membership association
(membership is by subscription), present number
of members: 600, voluntary organisation, training
organisation, consultancy.
The CMA's primary purpose is to support the
development of local media projects for
community-based, creative and cultural
expression, community development, information
and entertainment. Media forms include
community radio, community TV, cable
broadcasting and multimedia on the internet.

Subject coverage:
Community Radio – general information on start
up, training, fundraising, consultancy, licence
application. Community media including TV, cable
and internet broadcasting.

**Museum or gallery collection, archive, or library
special collection:**
Airflash – Complete Set
Broadcast – Hard Copies Only
The Radio Magazine – Hard Copies Only

Non-library collection catalogue:
All or part available in-house and in print

Printed publications:
Airflash (magazine, quarterly)
CMA basic information pack which includes our
publications list

Publications list:
Available online and in print

Access to staff:
Contact by letter, by telephone, by fax, by e-mail
and via website. Appointment necessary.
Hours: Mon to Fri, 0930 to 1730

Access to building, collection or gallery:
Prior appointment required
Hours: Mon to Fri, 0930 to 1730

Access for disabled people:
Access to all public areas, toilet facilities

Member organisation of:
World Association of Community Radio
Broadcasters (AMARC)
705 Bourget, bureau 100, Montreal, Quebec, H2C
2M6, Canada; tel: + 1 (514) 982 0351; fax: + 1
(514) 849 7129; website: www.amarc.org

COMMUNITY MUSIC WALES

Acronym or abbreviation: CMW

2 Leckwith Place, Canton, Cardiff, CF11 6QA

Tel: 029 2038 7620
Fax: 029 2023 3022
E-mail: admin@communitymusicwales.org.uk

Website:
http://www.communitymusicwales.org.uk

Enquiries:
Enquiries to: Administrator

Founded:
1990

Organisation type and purpose:
Voluntary organisation, registered charity (charity
number 1009867), training organisation.
Concerned with developing music projects,
targeting groups of people who, through reasons
of disability or disadvantage, have little chance of
taking part in mainstream music activities.

Subject coverage:
Use of music technology in working with people
with disabilities, training for community
practitioners, role of music in working with young
people at risk.

**Museum or gallery collection, archive, or library
special collection:**
Small library of reference books

Access to staff:
Contact by letter, by telephone and by fax.
Appointment necessary.
Hours: Mon to Fri, 0900 to 1700

Access for disabled people:
Level entry, toilet facilities

COMMUNITY PRACTITIONERS AND HEALTH VISITING ASSOCIATION

Acronym or abbreviation: Amicus–CPHVA

33–37 Moreland Street, London, EC1V 8HA

Tel: 020 7505 3000
E-mail: infocphva@amicustheunion.org

Website:
http://www.amicus-cphva.org
http://www.cphvabookshop.com
Publications online

Enquiries:
Enquiries to: Information Officer
Direct tel: 020 7780 4022
Other contacts: Director

Founded:
1896

Organisation type and purpose:
National organisation, trade union, membership
association (membership is by subscription).
The CPHVA is an autonomous body of Amicus. It
is also a membership organisation giving
information on professional issues and labour
relations to members.

Subject coverage:
Health visiting, child care and development,
community care of elderly and handicapped,
health promotion, accident prevention, community
nursing, clinical effectiveness, practice nursing,
school nursing, mental health.

Information services:
Archives of the Association, available from The
Wellcome Institute, 183 Euston Road, London,
NW1 2BE

Non-library collection catalogue:
All or part available online and in-house

Library catalogue:
All or part available online and in-house

Printed publications:
Annual Report
Community Practitioner (formerly Health Visitor,
journal, monthly)
Action for Health
Action for School Health
Domestic Violence
Health Visitors, Working for Older People
Legal and Professional Issues in Child Protection
Men's Health
Postnatal Depression
Poverty and Public Health
Protecting the Child
Order printed publications from: McMillan Scott,
Garrard House, 2–6 Homesdale Road, Bromley,
Kent, BR2 2WL; tel. 020 8249 4454; fax 020 8289
7955

Publications list:
Available online and in print

Access to staff:
Contact by letter, by telephone, by fax, by e-mail,
in person and via website. Access for members
only.
Hours: Mon to Thu, 0900 to 1700; Fri, 0900 to 1600

Access to building, collection or gallery:
Prior appointment required
Hours: Mon to Thu, 0900 to 1700; Fri, 0900 to 1600
Special comments: Library and information service
for members only.

Access for disabled people:
Level entry, access to all public areas, toilet
facilities

Constituent part of:
Amicus – The Union
tel: 020 7780 4022/4023; fax: 020 7505 3030

COMMUNITY SELF BUILD AGENCY

Acronym or abbreviation: CSBA

Swale Foyer, Bridge Road, Sheerness, Kent, ME12
1RH

Tel: 01795 663 073
Fax: 01795 581 804
E-mail: info@communityselfbuildagency.org.uk

Website:
http://www.communityselfbuildagency.org.uk

Enquiries:
Enquiries to: Director

Founded:
1989

Organisation type and purpose:
National organisation.
To promote and advise on the development of
community self build housing projects for those in
housing need.

Subject coverage:
Community Self Build, where a group of local
people in housing need come together to build
homes for themselves.

Printed publications:
Basic publications available free
Other publications for sale direct

Publications list:
Available in print

Access to staff:
Contact by letter, by telephone and by e-mail.
Appointment necessary.
Hours: Mon to Fri, 0930 to 1730

COMMUNITY SERVICE VOLUNTEERS

Acronym or abbreviation: CSV

237 Pentonville Road, London, N1 9NJ

Tel: 020 7278 6601
Fax: 020 7833 0149
E-mail: information@csv.org.uk

Website:
http://www.csv.org.uk

Founded:
1962

Organisation type and purpose:
National organisation, voluntary organisation, registered charity (charity number 291222).

Subject coverage:
Volunteering and employment and media training. Volunteering for young people, older people, employees and students. Mentoring and befriending, work with young offenders, social action broadcasting, citizenship in schools, the environment, Millennium Awards, Millennium Volunteers, advice and expertise in volunteer management. Make a Difference Day – the largest single day of volunteering – is co-ordinated by CSV.

Printed publications:
Annual Review
Information leaflets and pamphlets
CSV Reports On (series); on volunteering issues

Publications list:
Available online and in print

Access to staff:
Contact by letter, by telephone, by fax, by e-mail and via website
Hours: Mon to Fri, 0900 to 1730

Access for disabled people:
Level entry, toilet facilities

COMMUNITY TRANSPORT ASSOCIATION

Acronym or abbreviation: CTA

Highbank, Halton Street, Hyde, Cheshire, SK14 2NY

Tel: 0161 351 1475
Fax: 0161 351 7221
E-mail: info@ctauk.org

Website:
http://www.ctauk.org
Information on Community Transport Association Services, events and publications.

Enquiries:
Enquiries to: Advice Service
Direct tel: 0845 130 6195

Founded:
1978

Organisation type and purpose:
National organisation, advisory body, trade association (membership is by subscription), present number of members: 1500, voluntary organisation, registered charity (charity no. 1002222), training organisation, consultancy. Representation and support services for non-profit transport sector.

Subject coverage:
All aspects of non-profit transport operations; service planning and development; accessibility and technical equipment; community development; employment and volunteering issues.

Museum or gallery collection, archive, or library special collection:
Historical records of CTA
Photograph library

Printed publications:
Community Transport Magazine (6 times a year)

A range of titles covering transport-related subjects including:
Accessible Minibuses
Community Buses – Operation of Local Bus Services by Community Groups
Community Car Schemes
Let's Get Going – An action guide for community transport in rural England
Minibus Management
Minibuses and the Law

Publications list:
Available online and in print

Access to staff:
Contact by letter, by telephone, by fax and by e-mail
Hours: Mon to Fri, 0900 to 1700

COMPANIES HOUSE

Crown Way, Cardiff, CF14 3UZ

Tel: 030 3123 4500
Fax: 029 2038 0900
E-mail: enquiries@companieshouse.gov.uk

Website:
http://www.companieshouse.gov.uk
General Companies House information, products and services, press notices, complete set of guidance notes.

Enquiries:
Enquiries to: Cardiff Contact Centre

Founded:
1844

Organisation type and purpose:
National government body. To incorporate limited companies and to maintain a register of information on them for public information.

Subject coverage:
Information on limited companies entered in the register.

Printed publications:
Companies House Annual Report
Guide to Incorporation of Companies
Guide to Public Search
Guide to Registering Foreign Companies
Guide to Sensitive Words
Guide to Winding up
The Register: Customer newsletter
Enforcement Concordat (What You Can Expect from Companies House) and How to Complain and Who to Contact
Guide for Company Directors and Secretaries

Electronic and video publications:
Companies House Direct: Remote access online system
'Its the Company you Keep': Video aimed at explaining the need for compliance under the Companies Act
Directory of current names (CD-ROM)
Directory of change of name and dissolved companies (CD-ROM)

Access to staff:
Contact by letter, by telephone, by fax, by e-mail, in person and via website. All charged.
Hours: Mon to Fri, 0900 to 1700

Also at:
Companies House
London Search Room, 21 Bloomsbury Street, London, WC1B 3XD; tel: 0870 33 33 636; fax: 029 2038 0900

Executive Agency of:
Department for Business,Enterprise and Regulatory Reform

COMPANIES HOUSE SCOTLAND

37 Castle Terrace, Edinburgh, EH1 2EB

Tel: 0870 3333636
Fax: 0131 535 5820

Website:
http://www.companieshouse.gov.uk
About Companies House, notes for guidance, products and services. Press notices. At Head Office in Cardiff.

Enquiries:
Enquiries to: Registrar
Direct tel: 0131 535 5855
Direct fax: 0131 535 5879
Direct e-mail: jhenderson@companieshouse.gov.uk

Founded:
1856

Formerly called:
Companies Registration Office (year of change 1988)

Organisation type and purpose:
National government body, statutory body. Executive agency within the Department of Trade and Industry.
To incorporate and dissolve limited companies, to examine and file documents relating to the Companies Act, to make this information available to the public.

Subject coverage:
Information on Scottish limited companies from statutory documents filed by the company directors, including financial information, details of directors, capital changes and members.

Printed publications:
A series of guidance notes (approx 20)

Microform publications:
Microfiche copies of Company records (£6.50 or £9.50 by post)

Electronic and video publications:
CH-Direct (online service)
CH-Monitor
CD-ROM
Magnetic tapes

Publications list:
Available in print

Access to staff:
Contact by letter, by telephone, by fax, by e-mail and via website. Appointment necessary.
Hours: Mon to Fri, 0900 to 1700
Special comments: Closed on Public and Bank Holidays.

Head Office:
Companies House
Crown Way, Cardiff, CF4 3UZ; tel: 0870 3333636; fax: 029 2038 0900

Other branches at:
Companies House
25 Queen Street, Leeds, LS 2TW; tel: 0113 233 8338; fax: 0113 2338335
Companies House
75 Mosley Street, Manchester, M2 2HR; tel: 0161 236 7500; fax: 0161 237 5258
Companies House
Central Library, Chamberlain Square, Birmingham, B3 3HQ; tel: 0121 233 9047; fax: 0121 233 9052
Companies House
7 West George Street, Glasgow, G2 1BQ; tel: 0141 221 5513; fax: 0141 221 3244

COMPANY OF DESIGNERS

232 Kempshott Lane, Basingstoke, Hampshire, RG22 5LR

Tel: 01256 472757
E-mail: mike-preedy@company-of-designers.co.uk

Enquiries:
Enquiries to: Managing Director

Founded:
1995

Organisation type and purpose:
Service industry, consultancy, publishing house. Design consultancy.

Design for print: books, annual reports and accounts, brochures, leaflets, promotional literature

Access to staff:
Contact by letter, by telephone and by e-mail
Hours: Mon to Fri, 0900 to 1700

Access to building, collection or gallery:
Prior appointment required

COMPANY OF SECURITY PROFESSIONALS

Formal name: Worshipful Company of Security Professionals

Willowcroft, Old Forest Road, Winnersh, Wokingham, Berkshire, RG41 1HY

Tel: 01189 794675
Fax: 01189 794675
E-mail: clerk@wcosp.org

Website:
http://www.professionalsecurity.co.uk/company

Enquiries:
Enquiries to: Clerk

Organisation type and purpose:
To promote, support and encourage standards of excellence, integrity and honourable practice in conducting the profession of security practitioners and to aid societies and other organisations connected with the security profession.

Access to staff:
Contact by letter, by telephone and by e-mail

COMPANY OF WATERMEN AND LIGHTERMEN OF THE RIVER THAMES

Acronym or abbreviation: Company of Watermen

Watermen's Hall, 16 St Mary Hill, London, EC3R 8EF

Tel: 020 7283 2373
Fax: 020 7283 0477
E-mail: admin@watermenshall.org

Website:
http://www.watermenshall.org

Enquiries:
Enquiries to: Clerk

Founded:
1555

Organisation type and purpose:
Statutory body, membership association (membership is by election or invitation), present number of members: 400, voluntary organisation, training organisation.
A working guild promoting the work of watermen and lightermen on the River Thames, training apprentices and having charitable interests.

Subject coverage:
Watermen and Lightermen of the River Thames.

Library catalogue:
All or part available in-house

Printed publications:
History of the Company (4 vols, £75)
The Life and Charities of Thomas Mann (£5.50)
Thomas Doggetts Pictur'd Book (£7)
The History of the Company Vol 5 (forthcoming, £25)
Order printed publications from: Watermen's Hall

Publications list:
Available online and in print

Access to staff:
Contact by letter, by telephone, by fax, by e-mail, in person and via website. Appointment necessary. Non-members charged.
Hours: Mon to Fri, 0900 to 1700

Access to building, collection or gallery:
By appointment
Hours: Mon to Fri, 0900 to 1700

Access for disabled people:
Accessible, lift to all floors
Special comments: Disabled access entrance at 16 St Mary-at-Hill

COMPASSIONATE FRIENDS, THE

Acronym or abbreviation: TCF

53 North Street, Bedminster, Bristol, BS3 1EN

Tel: 0845 120 3785
Fax: 0845 120 3786
E-mail: info@tcf.org.uk

Website:
http://www.tcf.org.uk

Enquiries:
Enquiries to: Helpline Worker

Founded:
1969

Organisation type and purpose:
National organisation, registered charity (charity number 1082335).
Offers support and friendship to bereaved parents and their families after the death of a child or children.

Subject coverage:
Support and friendship for bereaved parents and their families by those with a similar experience, including loss through suicide and murder.

Printed publications:
Newsletter (quarterly, available through membership scheme)
SIBBS (Support in Bereavement for Brothers and Sisters) (quarterly, newsletter)
Leaflets covering many aspects of bereavement including:
A father's grief
Grieving couples
When your adult child dies
When your child has been murdered
When your grandchild dies

Electronic and video publications:
Bereavement Services (video)

Publications list:
Available online and in print

Access to staff:
Contact by letter, by telephone, by fax, by e-mail and via website
Hours: Mon to Fri, 0900 to 1700

Subsidiary body:
Support in Bereavement for Brothers and Sisters (SIBBS)
at the same address

COMPETITION COMMISSION

Acronym or abbreviation: CC

Victoria House, Southampton Row, London, WC1B 4AD

Tel: 020 7271 0100
Fax: 020 7271 0367
E-mail: info@cc.gsi.gov.uk

Website:
http://www.competition-commission.org.uk

Enquiries:
Enquiries to: Information Centre Manager

Formerly called:
Monopolies and Mergers Commission (MMC) (year of change 1999)

Organisation type and purpose:
Statutory body.

Subject coverage:
Monopolies; mergers; industrial economics; competition policy.

Printed publications:
Information pack on the Commission

Publications list:
Available in print

Constituent part of:
Department for Business, Enterprise and Regulatory Reform (BERR)

COMPLEMENTARY THERAPISTS ASSOCIATION

PO Box 6955, Towcester, NN12 6WZ

Tel: 0845 202 2941
Fax: 0844 779 8898
E-mail: info@complementary.assoc.org.uk

Website:
www.complementary.assoc.org.uk

Enquiries:
Enquiries to: Administrator

Founded:
2003

Created by the merger of:
The International Therapists Examination Council (ITEC) and the Guild of Complementary Practitioners (GCP, which had previously merged with the Holistic Association of Reflexologists)

Organisation type and purpose:
National organisation, professional body (membership is by subscription, qualification). Member of the Parliamentary Group for Alternative & Complementary Medicine.
To maintain a national and international register of professional members, available to the general public and to other professionals.
To establish standards of professional training and qualification appropriate to the various disciplines.

Subject coverage:
Complementary medicine including aromatherapy, massage, reflexology, sports therapy, nutrition, Shiatsu, homoeopathy and Reiki.

Printed publications:
The Essential Guide to Hand and Foot Reflexology
The Theory and Practice
The Ancient Answers to Modern Ailments
Healing Points (quarterly magazine)
Reflexology: A Step-by-Step Guide
The Complete Book of Massage
Reflexology and the Intestinal Link, Chart
Reflexology and the Intestinal Link

Microform publications:
Lecture pack – Reflexology (Overhead transparencies)

Electronic and video publications:
The Timeless Art of Self healing, video

Access to staff:
Contact by letter, by telephone, by fax, by e-mail and via website
Hours: Mon to Fri, 0900 to 1700

Affiliated to:
British School of Reflexology

Member of:
British Complementary Medicine Association

COMPLIANCE INSTITUTE

107 Barkby Road, Leicester LE4 9LG

Tel: 0116 246 1316
Fax: 0116 274 2239
E-mail: hlacey.compinst@nsconnect.co.uk

Website:
http://www.complianceinstitute.co.uk/
General information

Enquiries:
Enquiries to: Secretary

Founded:
1990

continued overleaf

Formerly called:
UK Association of Compliance Officers (year of change 1997)

Organisation type and purpose:
Professional body (membership is by subscription).

Subject coverage:
Regulation – guide and assistance to Compliance staff.

Printed publications:
The Gazette (for purchase)

Access to staff:
Contact by letter
Hours: Mon to Fri, 0900 to 1700

COMPOSITES PROCESSING ASSOCIATION LIMITED, THE

Acronym or abbreviation: CPA

Sarum Lodge, St Anne's Court, Talygarn, Pontyclun, Mid Glamorgan, CF72 9HH

Tel: 01443 228867
Fax: 01443 239083
E-mail: info@composites-proc-assoc.co.uk

Website:
http://www.composites-proc-assoc.co.uk
Full directory of products and services in UK composites industry. Service and product finder. Details of all member companies. Details of National and International Standards relating to composites. Links.

Enquiries:
Enquiries to: Association Secretary

Founded:
1989

Organisation type and purpose:
Trade association, consultancy.

Subject coverage:
Raw materials, manufacturing processes, applications, research and development activity, technical exchange, international activity as related to reinforced plastic composites.

Trade and statistical information:
National and international composites industry, market statistics, market sectors, data on composite shipments worldwide.

Access to staff:
Contact by letter, by telephone, by fax, by e-mail and via website. Appointment necessary.
Hours: Mon to Fri, 0900 to 1700

Member of:
American Composites Manufacturers Association Composites Fabricators Association, 1655 North Fort Myer Drive, Suite 510, Arlington, VA22209, USA; tel: 00 1 703 525 0511; fax: 00 1 703 525 0743; e-mail: info@acmanet.org; website: www .acmanet.org

COMPUTER USERS' FORUM

Acronym or abbreviation: CUF

1 Stuart Road, Thornton Heath, Surrey, CR7 8RA

Tel: 07831 196693
E-mail: postmaster@CR78RA1uk.cix.co.uk

Enquiries:
Enquiries to: Secretary

Founded:
1980

Organisation type and purpose:
Advisory body, professional body, membership association (membership is by subscription, election or invitation), present number of members: over 5000, training organisation, consultancy, research organisation.

Subject coverage:
Expertise and knowledge in the use of computers.

Access to staff:
Contact by letter and by e-mail. All charged.
Hours: Mon to Fri, 0900 to 1700

Access to building, collection or gallery:
No access other than to staff

COMPUTING SUPPLIERS FEDERATION

Acronym or abbreviation: CSF

26–27 Brookside Business Park, Colde Meece, Stone, Staffordshire, ST15 0TZ

Tel: 01785 769090
Fax: 01785 769082
E-mail: info@csf.org.uk

Website:
http://www.csf.org.uk
Free downloads, organisational information, members-only area, case study database.

Enquiries:
Enquiries to: Managing Director

Founded:
1985

Formerly called:
Computer Graphics Suppliers Association (CGSA) (year of change 1995); Association of Visual Communicators (AVC) (year of change 1997)

Organisation type and purpose:
Trade association (membership is by subscription, qualification, election or invitation), present number of members: 200.
The CSF is a not-for-profit trade association representing specialist sectors of the IT industry.

Subject coverage:
Information management, imaging and workflow. CAD, CAM, PDM, EDM and other engineering applications, platforms and IT peripherals (including monitors, printers, workstations and storage equipment). Electronic presentations equipment (including projectors, video communications and conferencing systems).

Non-library collection catalogue:
All or part available online and in print

Printed publications:
eEngineering – Collaborating to Survive
Engineering Data across the Enterprise
Implementing Design Technology
Information Management – The Business Case
Innovation – the third dimension – using design technology to grow your business
Justifying Investing in Design Technology
Monitors Matter
New Display Technologies – making the right choice
Video Communications in the Workplace

Publications list:
Available online

Access to staff:
Contact via website
Hours: Mon to Fri, 0900 to 1700

Access for disabled people:
Parking provided, level entry, access to all public areas

CONCHOLOGICAL SOCIETY OF GREAT BRITAIN AND IRELAND

Acronym or abbreviation: CSGBI

1 Court Farm, Hillfarrance, Taunton, Somerset, TA4 1AN

Tel: 01823 461482
E-mail: c_m_gillard@compuserve.com

Website:
http://www.conchsoc.org
Publications, meetings, recording schemes, conservation, how to join, contacts, members' interests, links, news.

Enquiries:
Enquiries to: General Secretary

Founded:
1876

Organisation type and purpose:
Learned society (membership is by subscription), present number of members: 420, registered charity (charity number 208205), suitable for ages: all.
To promote the study of the Mollusca in all its aspects.

Subject coverage:
Distribution of molluscs, marine and non-marine in the United Kingdom, conservation of molluscan species and their habitats, environmental impact assessment, in general all aspects of conchology world-wide, marine, non-marine and fossil.

Museum or gallery collection, archive, or library special collection:
Distribution records
Non-marine held at NHM
Marine computerised database

Trade and statistical information:
Holds national records of non-marine and marine biogeographical distribution.

Non-library collection catalogue:
All or part available in-house and in print

Printed publications:
Atlas of the Non-Marine Mollusca of the British Isles
Conchologists Newsletter (4 a year, back numbers available)
Concordance to the Field Card for British Marine Mollusca
Journal of Conchology (2 times a year, some back numbers available)
List of Members (occasional and annual amendments)
Programme of Events (annually)
Special publications (irregular)
Packs of reprints from the Journal grouped by subject
Sea Area Atlas of the Marine Mollusca of Britain & Ireland (Seaward D R)
Order printed publications from: CSGBI, Hilliers Freith, Henley on Thames, Oxon, RG9 6PJ

Publications list:
Available in print

Access to staff:
Contact by letter, by telephone, by e-mail and via website
Hours: After 1700 weekdays and weekends
Special comments: Please note that all officers of the Society are volunteers.

Affiliated to:
Council for Nature

CONCORD MEDIA

The Rosehill Centre, 22 Hines Road, Ipswich, Suffolk, IP3 9BG

Tel: 01473 726012
Fax: 01473 274531
E-mail: sales@concordmedia.org.uk

Website:
http://www.concordmedia.org.uk
General information.

Enquiries:
Enquiries to: General Secretary

Founded:
1965

Organisation type and purpose:
Registered charity, public library.
Video and film library.

Subject coverage:
Social sciences, arts, development education, peace, counselling, medical and mental health.

Library catalogue:
All or part available online

Printed publications:
Catalogues

Electronic and video publications:
DVDs

Publications list:
Available online and in print

Access to staff:
Contact by letter, by telephone, by fax and by e-mail
Hours: Mon, Tue, Thu, Fri, 0900 to 1700; closed Wed

Access for disabled people:
Parking provided, level entry, toilet facilities

CONCRETE ADVISORY SERVICE

Acronym or abbreviation: CAS

Riverside House, 4 Meadows Business Park, Station Approach, Blackwater, Camberley, Surrey, GU17 9AB

Tel: 01276 607140
Fax: 01276 607141
E-mail: consoc@concrete.org.uk

Website:
http://www.concrete.org.uk

Organisation type and purpose:
National organisation, advisory body, membership association (membership is by subscription), consultancy.
Specialist consultancy in concrete and cementitious materials and applications.

Subject coverage:
Concrete and cementitious materials, design, construction, application, trouble-shooting.

Non-library collection catalogue:
All or part available online

Printed publications:
Purchase through www.concretebookshop.com

Publications list:
Available online and in print

Access to staff:
Contact by letter and by telephone. Access for members only. All charged.
Hours: Mon to Fri, 0900 to 1730

Parent body:
Concrete Society
    At the same address

CONCRETE PIPE ASSOCIATION

Acronym or abbreviation: CPA

Tournai Hall, Evelyn Woods Road, Aldershot Hampshire GU11 2LL

Tel: 01252 357834
Fax: 01252 357831
E-mail: lauren.fairley@corrosionprevention.org.uk

Website:
http://www.corrosionprevention.org.uk

Enquiries:
Enquiries to: Director

Founded:
1932

Organisation type and purpose:
Trade association.

Subject coverage:
Manufacture and use of precast concrete pipe products for drainage systems; foul and surface water drainage systems.

Printed publications:
Information Sheets
Technical Bulletins

Electronic and video publications:
Videos

Publications list:
Available in print

Access to staff:
Contact by letter, by telephone and by fax
Hours: Mon to Fri, 0900 to 1700
Special comments: Library for members only. Information freely available to enquirers.

Affiliated to:
British Precast Concrete Federation
International Bureau of Concrete Manufacturers
International Concrete Pipe Commission

CONCRETE REPAIR ASSOCIATION

Acronym or abbreviation: CRA

Tournai Hall, Evelyn Woods Road, Aldershot, Hampshire GU11 2LL

Tel: 01252 357835
Fax: 01252 357831
E-mail: admin@cra.org.uk

Website:
http://www.concreterepair.org.uk

Enquiries:
Enquiries to: Secretary

Founded:
1989

Organisation type and purpose:
Trade association, present number of members: 32. Represents contractors, manufacturers and consultants involved in the concrete repair industry.

Printed publications:
Directory of Members
Application of Measurement of Protective
    Coatings
Standard Method of Measurement for Concrete
    Repair
The Route to a Successful Concrete Repair

Publications list:
Available in print

Access to staff:
Contact by letter, by telephone, by fax, by e-mail and via website
Hours: Mon to Fri, 0900 to 1700

CONCRETE SOCIETY

Riverside House, 4 Meadows Business Park, Station Approach, Blackwater, Camberley, Surrey, GU17 9AB

Tel: 01276 607140
Fax: 01276 607141

Website:
www.concrete.org.uk

Enquiries:
Enquiries to: Chief Executive

Founded:
1966

Organisation type and purpose:
Learned society.

Subject coverage:
Concrete in the construction industry.

Printed publications:
Concrete (journal, monthly)
Data Sheets
Proceedings of Symposia
Technical Reports and Papers

Publications list:
Available in print

Access to staff:
Appointment necessary.
Hours: Mon to Fri, 0900 to 1700

Links with:
Glassfibre Reinforced Concrete Society

CONCRETE TILE MANUFACTURERS' ASSOCIATION

Acronym or abbreviation: CTMA

60 Charles Street, Leicester, LE1 1FB

Tel: 0116 253 6161
Fax: 0116 251 4568
E-mail: info@britishprecast.org

Enquiries:
Enquiries to: Secretary

Organisation type and purpose:
Trade association.

Subject coverage:
Precast concrete roof tiles.

Publications list:
Available online

Access to staff:
Contact by letter, by telephone, by fax and by e-mail
Hours: Mon to Fri, 0900 to 1700

Links with:
British Precast Concrete Federation

CONFED

Formal name: Confederation of Education Service Managers
Acronym or abbreviation: CONFED

The Humanities Building, University of Manchester, Oxford Road, Manchester, M13 9PL

Tel: 0161 275 8810
Fax: 0161 275 8811
E-mail: confedoffice@confed.org.uk

Website:
http://www.confed.org.uk
Outline of CONFED activities.

Enquiries:
Enquiries to: General Secretary
Other contacts: Administrator, President

Founded:
1972

Formed by the merger of:
Association of Chief Education Officers (ACEO), Society of Chief Inspectors and Advisers (SCIA), Society of Education Officers (SEO) (year of change 2002)

Organisation type and purpose:
Professional body (membership is by subscription, qualification), present number of members: 900.

Subject coverage:
Administration and management of the education service in local authorities in England and Wales.

Publications list:
Available in print

Access to staff:
Contact by letter, by telephone, by fax and by e-mail
Hours: Mon to Thu, 0900 to 1700; Fri, 0900 to 1300

CONFEDERATION OF AERIAL INDUSTRIES LIMITED

Acronym or abbreviation: CAI

Fulton House Business Centre, Fulton Road, Wembley Park, Middlesex, HA9 0TF

Tel: 020 8902 8998
Fax: 020 8903 8719
E-mail: office@cai.org.uk

Website:
http://www.cai.org.uk

Enquiries:
Enquiries to: Secretary

Founded:
1978

continued overleaf

Organisation type and purpose:
Trade association.

Subject coverage:
Aerials, satellite dishes, cables and allied equipment, manufacture, supply, installation.

Trade and statistical information:
Training for the industry.

Printed publications:
Codes of Practice for domestic aerials, door entry systems, satellite dishes and MATV/SMATV systems
Feedback
Members Directory
Year Planner

Access to staff:
Contact by letter, by telephone, by fax and by e-mail
Hours: Mon to Fri, 0900 to 1700

CONFEDERATION OF AFRICAN PROFESSIONALS (CAP) UK

Acronym or abbreviation: CAP UK

BBI Business Centre, 53 Peckham Park Road, Peckham, London SE15 6TU

E-mail: capuk@bbinitiative.com

Enquiries:
Enquiries to: Chairman/President
Direct e-mail: sunny@sunnylambe.com

Founded:
1998

Organisation type and purpose:
International organisation, national organisation, professional body, membership association (membership is by subscription, qualification, election or invitation), present number of members: 200, voluntary organisation, suitable for ages: all, consultancy, research organisation.
To provide a voice and networking opportunity for professionals of African origin.

Access to staff:
Contact by letter, by telephone, by fax and by e-mail. Appointment necessary. Letter of introduction required.
Hours: Mon to Fri, 0900 to 1700

Access to building, collection or gallery:
Prior appointment required

Access for disabled people:
Parking provided, level entry, access to all public areas, toilet facilities

CONFEDERATION OF BRITISH INDUSTRY

Formal name: Confederation of British Industry
Acronym or abbreviation: CBI

Centre Point, 103 New Oxford Street, London, WC1A 1DU

Tel: 020 7379 7400
Fax: 020 7240 0988 or 1578
E-mail: firstname.surname@cbi.org.uk

Website:
http://www.cbi.org.uk/bookshop
http://www.cbi.org.uk
Policy information, press office, events, publications, membership information.

Enquiries:
Enquiries to: Information Officer
Direct tel: 020 7395 8247
Direct e-mail: enquiry.desk@cbi.org.uk

Founded:
1965

Organisation type and purpose:
Membership association (membership is by subscription), manufacturing industry, service industry.

Representative organisation for member companies, employers organisations and trade associations.

Subject coverage:
Public policy, international, national and regional; economic situation and trends, taxation, human resources, industrial relations, conditions of employment, education and training, manufacturing, research and development, overseas affairs, commercial and company law, industrial property law, industrial effluent, energy and water resources, innovation, information society.

Trade and statistical information:
See publications.

Library catalogue:
All or part available in-house

Printed publications:
Business Voice (monthly)
Distributive Trades Survey (monthly)
Economic & Business Outlook (quarterly)
Financial Services Survey (quarterly)
Industrial Trends Survey (monthly)
Various monographs
Order printed publications from: CBI Publications tel: 020 7395 8071

Publications list:
Available online and in print

Access to staff:
Contact by letter, by telephone, by fax and by e-mail. Appointment necessary.
Hours: Mon to Fri, 0930 to 1730

CONFEDERATION OF BRITISH WOOL TEXTILES LIMITED

Acronym or abbreviation: CBWT

Textile House, Red Doles Lane, Huddersfield, HD2 1YF

Tel: 01484 346500
Fax: 01484 346501
E-mail: info@cbwt.co.uk

Website:
http://www.cbwt.co.uk

Enquiries:
Enquiries to: Administation
Direct e-mail: slawka@cbwt.co.uk

Founded:
1979

Organisation type and purpose:
Trade association (membership is by subscription), present number of members: 180.
Promotion and protection of interests of the British wool textiles industry, provision of services to member companies.

Subject coverage:
UK wool textile industry; international trade practice and technical specifications relating to the raw materials and end products.

Trade and statistical information:
Data on the British wool textile industry.

Access to staff:
Contact by fax, by e-mail and via website
Hours: Mon to Fri, 0900 to 1700

Member of:
British Apparel and Textile Confederation (BATC)
 tel: 020 7636 7788; fax: 020 7636 7515; e-mail: batc@dial.pipex.com
INTERLAINE (EEC)
 tel: + 32 2 513 06 20; fax: + 32 2 514 06 65
International Wool Textile Organization (IWTO)
 tel: + 32 2 513 06 20; fax: + 32 2 514 06 65; e-mail: info@iwto.org

CONFEDERATION OF FOREST INDUSTRIES (UK) LTD

Acronym or abbreviation: ConFor

5 Dublin Street Lane South, Edinburgh, EH1 3PX

Tel: 0131 524 8080
Fax: 0131 538 7222
E-mail: mail@confor.org.uk

Website:
http://www.confor.org.uk

Enquiries:
Enquiries to: Chief Executive

Founded:
1983

Formed from:
merged with Forestry and Timber Association (FTA), 2006; Association of Professional Foresters (APF), Timber Growers Association (TGA) (year of change 2002)

Formerly called:
Timber Growers United Kingdom Limited (year of change 1994)

Organisation type and purpose:
Trade association (membership is by subscription), present number of members: 2500.

Subject coverage:
Forestry and woodland ownership. Timber production.

Printed publications:
9 Regional Newsletters (quarterly, members only)
Timber Grower Magazine (quarterly)

Access to staff:
Contact by letter, by telephone, by fax, by e-mail and via website. Non-members charged.
Hours: Mon to Fri, 0900 to 1700

Access to building, collection or gallery:
Prior appointment required

CONFEDERATION OF INDIAN ORGANISATIONS (UK)

Acronym or abbreviation: CIO

5 Westminster Bridge Road, London, SE1 7XW

Tel: 020 7928 9889
Fax: 020 7620 4025
E-mail: headoffice@cio.org.uk

Website:
http://www.cio.org.uk

Enquiries:
Enquiries to: Chief Executive
Other contacts: Information Officer

Founded:
1975

Organisation type and purpose:
National organisation, membership association (membership is by subscription), present number of members: 150, voluntary organisation, registered charity (charity number 1075501), training organisation, research organisation.
A national South Asian umbrella organisation. Representation of the needs of South Asian community and voluntary organisations.

Subject coverage:
Information about South Asians in the UK including statistics, organisations, health issues, information resources in ethnic languages, issue-based participatory research, social policy, service provision, development of innovative models of good practice, promotion of anti-racist practices.

Library catalogue:
All or part available in-house

Printed publications:
A Cry for Change (Information Pack, Amanda Webb-Johnson, 1991, £7.50)
CIO's South Asian Mental Health Conference Report (£3.50)
Directory of Mental Health Services for South Asian Communities, 1998 (£5)
Directory of South Asian Voluntary Groups in the United Kingdom (to be published 1999)
Illness or Distress? Alternative Models of Mental Health (£3.50 plus p&p)

Mental Health Assessment and Asian Men (2001)

Publications list:
Available in print

Access to staff:
Contact by letter, by telephone and by fax.
Appointment necessary.
Hours: Mon to Fri, 0900 to 1700

Other addresses:
CIO Leicester Office
    5th Floor, Epic House, Lower Hill Street,
    Leicester, LE1 3SH; tel: 0116 225 9299; fax: 0116
    225 9298

CONFEDERATION OF PAPER INDUSTRIES

Acronym or abbreviation: CPI UK

1 Rivenhall Road, Westlea, Swindon, Wiltshire,
SN5 7BD

Tel: 01793 889600
Fax: 01793 878700
E-mail: cpi@paper.org.uk

Website:
http://www.paper.org.uk

Enquiries:
Enquiries to: Communications

Founded:
1974

Organisation type and purpose:
Advisory body, trade association (membership is
by subscription).

Subject coverage:
Paper and board industry, education, training,
health and safety, manpower, woodpulp; waste
paper, recycling, recovery, re-use of paper with
emphasis on environmental issues; history of
paper and statistics.

Trade and statistical information:
Data on the paper industry.

Printed publications:
Fact sheets on the history of paper, forestry,
    recycling, resources, packaging (free)

Electronic and video publications:
Statistics

Publications list:
Available online and in print

Access to staff:
Contact by letter, by telephone, by fax and by e-
mail. Appointment necessary.
Hours: Mon to Fri, 0900 to 1700

Access to building, collection or gallery:
No access other than to staff

Access for disabled people:
Parking provided, toilet facilities

Constituent bodies:
Association of Makers of Packaging Papers
Association of Makers of Printing and Writing
Papers
Association of Makers of Soft Tissue Papers
Corrugated Case Materials Association

Member organisation of:
Confederation of European Paper Industries
    Brussels, Belgium
Confederation of Paper Industries

CONFEDERATION OF PASSENGER TRANSPORT UK

Acronym or abbreviation: CPT

Drury House, 34–43 Russell Street, London, WC2B
5HA

Tel: 020 7240 3131
Fax: 020 7240 6565
E-mail: admin@cpt-uk.org

Website:
http://www.cpt-uk.org/

Enquiries:
Enquiries to: Public Affairs Officer
Direct e-mail: chrisnice@cpt-uk.org
Other contacts: Assistant Director Public Affairs for
media and press enquiries.

Formerly called:
Bus and Coach Council

Organisation type and purpose:
Trade association.

Subject coverage:
Public road passenger transport, bus and coach
industry, fixed track operators, technical and
operations, legal matters, statistics, informed
comment.

Printed publications:
Newsline (newsletter for members, fortnightly)

Publications list:
Available in print

Access to staff:
Contact by letter, by telephone, by fax, by e-mail
and via website. Appointment necessary.
Hours: Mon to Fri, 0900 to 1700

Subsidiary of:
Confederation of British Road Passenger Transport
Transfed

CONFEDERATION OF ROOFING CONTRACTORS LIMITED

Formal name: CRC

72 Church Road, Brightlingsea, Colchester, Essex,
CO7 0JF

Tel: 01206 306600
Fax: 01206 306200
E-mail: enquiries@corc.co.uk

Website:
http://www.corc.co.uk
List of members, benefits of membership, map of
country.

Enquiries:
Enquiries to: Membership Co-ordinator
Direct e-mail: mike@corc.co.uk

Founded:
1985

Organisation type and purpose:
Trade association (membership is by subscription),
present number of members: 580.
To protect the general public from unscrupulous
roofing contractors.

Subject coverage:
All aspects of the roofing industry.

Library catalogue:
All or part available in-house

Printed publications:
Roofing Trades Journal – The biggest circulated
    roofing magazine in Europe

Publications list:
Available in print

Access to staff:
Contact by letter, by telephone, by fax, by e-mail
and via website
Hours: Mon to Fri, 0900 to 1300 and 1400 to 1700

Access to building, collection or gallery:
Prior appointment required

Access for disabled people:
Parking provided, level entry, access to all public
areas, toilet facilities

CONFEDERATION OF SHIPBUILDING AND ENGINEERING UNIONS

Acronym or abbreviation: CSEU

140–142 Walworth Road, Walworth, London, SE17
1JW

Tel: 020 7703 2215
Fax: 020 7252 7397

Enquiries:
Enquiries to: General Secretary

Founded:
1936

Formed from:
Federation of Engineering & Shipbuilding Trades
(FESTUK) (year of change 1936)

Organisation type and purpose:
Trade union (membership is by subscription),
present number of members: 1,093,001.

Subject coverage:
Co-ordination and policy of shipbuilding and
engineering unions throughout the UK.

Access to staff:
Contact by letter, by telephone and by fax
Hours: Mon to Fri, 0900 to 1700

CONFERENCE INTERPRETERS GROUP

Acronym or abbreviation: CIG

10 Barley Mow Passage, Chiswick, London, W4
4PH

Tel: 020 8995 0801
Fax: 020 8742 1066
E-mail: cig@clara.net

Website:
http://www.cig-interpreters.com

Enquiries:
Enquiries to: Executive Secretary

Founded:
1979

Organisation type and purpose:
Service industry.
Cooperative grouping; membership restricted to
members of AIIC (Association Internationale des
Interprètes de Conférence).

Subject coverage:
Interpretation, simultaneous and consecutive.

Access to staff:
Contact by letter, by telephone and by fax
Hours: Mon to Fri, 0900 to 1700

CONGREGATIONAL LIBRARY

c/o 14 Gordon Square, London, WC1H 0AR

Tel: 020 7387 3727

Enquiries:
Enquiries to: Librarian

Founded:
1831

Organisation type and purpose:
Registered charity (charity number 260601), public
library.
Managed by Dr Williams's Library.

Subject coverage:
English religious dissent. Congregationalism.

Library catalogue:
All or part available in-house

Printed publications:
Congregational Lecture (occasional)

Publications list:
Available in print

Access to staff:
Contact by letter, by telephone and in person.
Appointment necessary.
Hours: Mon, Wed, Fri, 1000 to 1700; Tue, Thu, 1000
to 1830

continued overleaf

Parent body:
Congregational Memorial Hall Trust (1978)
Limited
  c/o Dr Williams's Library, 14 Gordon Square,
London, WC1H 0AR

CONNECT

30 St George's Road, Wimbledon, London, SW19
4BD

Tel: 020 8971 6000
Fax: 020 8971 6002
E-mail: union@connect.uk.org

Website:
http://www.connect.org.uk
http://www.connectuk.org
Services to members and updates of what is
happening on negotiations and other industry
news.

Enquiries:
Enquiries to: Researcher
Direct tel: 020 8971 6025
Direct fax: 020 8971 6026
Direct e-mail: research@connect.uk.org
Other contacts: Assistant Secretary for overseas
publications.

Formerly called:
Society of Telecom Executives (year of change
2000)

Organisation type and purpose:
Trade union (membership is by subscription),
present number of members: 18,500, service
industry.
Members are managers and professionals in the
Communications and IT industry.

Printed publications:
Various members newsletters
The Review (magazine, monthly, members)

Access to staff:
Contact by letter, by telephone and by e-mail.
Access for members only. Non-members charged.
Hours: Mon to Fri, 0900 to 1715

Access to building, collection or gallery:
No access other than to staff

Access for disabled people:
Parking provided, ramped entry, access to all
public areas, toilet facilities

Field offices at:
CONNECT
  22a Caroline Street, St Paul's Square,
Birmingham, B3 1VE; tel: 0121 236 0596 or 2637;
fax: 0121 233 2616

CONSERVATION FOUNDATION

1 Kensington Gore, London, SW7 2AR

Tel: 020 7591 3111
Fax: 020 7591 3110
E-mail: info@conservationfoundation.co.uk

Website:
http://www.conservationfoundation.co.uk

Enquiries:
Enquiries to: Executive Director

Founded:
1982

Organisation type and purpose:
International organisation, registered charity
(charity number 284656).

Subject coverage:
Initiation and management of environmental
projects.

Printed publications:
Parish Pump Newsletter
Annual Report
Healthier Profits, Business Success and the Green
  Factor
Media information pack (monthly)
What? On Earth

Access to staff:
Contact by letter, by telephone, by fax and by e-
mail
Hours: Mon to Fri, 0930 to 1730

CONSTANCE HOWARD RESOURCE AND RESEARCH CENTRE IN TEXTILES

Goldsmiths, University of London, Deptford Town
Hall Building, New Cross Road, London, SE14
6AF

Tel: 020 7717 2210
E-mail: connitex@gold.ac.uk

Website:
http://www.goldsmiths.ac.uk/constance-howard

Organisation type and purpose:
An independent centre supported by Goldsmiths
(University of London), the Arts Council, the Arts
and Humanities Research Council and other
bodies.

Subject coverage:
History of textiles since the 1940s.

**Museum or gallery collection, archive, or library
special collection:**
Textile reference library, including many books
from Eastern Europe

CONSTRUCTION CONFEDERATION

55 Tufton Street, Westminster, London, SW1P 3QL

Tel: 0870 8989 090
Fax: 0870 8989 095
E-mail: enquiries@thecc.org.uk

Website:
http://www.thecc.org.uk
http://www.constructionconfederation.co.uk

Enquiries:
Enquiries to: Press and Information
Direct tel: 020 7608 5017
Direct fax: 020 7608 5011
Direct e-mail: k.calder@thecc.org.uk

Formerly called:
Building Employers Confederation (BEC)

Organisation type and purpose:
Trade association (membership is by subscription),
present number of members: 8.

Subject coverage:
Legislation, contracts and legal services,
regulations, standards and codes of practice, safety
and training, specialist building information from
the member organisations.

Printed publications:
Publications are for member companies

Publications list:
Available in print

Access to staff:
Contact by letter, by telephone, by fax, by e-mail
and via website. Access for members only.
Hours: Mon to Fri, 0900 to 1700

Members:
British Woodworking Federation (BWF)
  tel: 020 7608 5050; fax: 020 7608 5051
Civil Engineering Contractors Association (CECA)
  tel: 020 7608 5060; fax: 020 7608 5161
Federation of Building Specialist Contractors
(FBSC)
  tel: 020 7608 5080; fax: 020 7608 5081
House Builders Federation (HBF)
  tel: 020 7608 5100; fax: 020 7608 5101
Major Contractors Group (MCG)
  tel: 020 7608 5140; fax: 020 7608 5141
National Contractors Federation (NCF)
  tel: 020 7608 5140; fax: 020 7608 5141
National Federation of Builders (NFB)
  tel: 020 7608 5150; fax: 020 7608 5151
Scottish Building (SB)
  tel: 01324 555550; fax: 01324 555551

CONSTRUCTION EMPLOYERS FEDERATION

Acronym or abbreviation: CEF

143 Malone Road, Belfast, BT9 6SU

Tel: 028 9087 7143
Fax: 028 9087 7155
E-mail: mail@cefni.co.uk

Website:
http://www.cefni.co.uk
http://www.constructionfocus.co.uk

Enquiries:
Enquiries to: Deputy Secretary
Direct e-mail: nlucas@cefni.co.uk
Other contacts: Information Officer

Founded:
1945

Formerly called:
Federation of Building and Civil Engineering
(FBCE)

Organisation type and purpose:
Advisory body, trade association (membership is
by subscription), service industry, voluntary
organisation.

Subject coverage:
Construction output data, expenditure, contract
problems.

Trade and statistical information:
State of Trade Survey.

Non-library collection catalogue:
All or part available online

Printed publications:
All current forms of building contract

Publications list:
Available in print

Access to staff:
Contact by letter. Access for members only. Letter
of introduction required.
Hours: Mon to Fri, 0900 to 1700

CONSTRUCTION EQUIPMENT ASSOCIATION

Acronym or abbreviation: CEA

Ambassador House, Brigstock Road, Thornton
Heath, Surrey, CR7 7JG

Tel: 020 8665 5727
Fax: 020 8665 6447
E-mail: cea@admin.co.uk

Website:
http://www.coneq.org.uk

Enquiries:
Enquiries to: Information Officer

Founded:
1942

Formerly called:
Federation of Manufacturers of Construction
Equipment and Cranes (FMCEC) (year of change
2000)

Organisation type and purpose:
Trade association (membership is by subscription),
present number of members: 100.
The UK trade association serving construction
equipment manufacturers, their component and
accessory suppliers and service providers.

Subject coverage:
Subjects relating to UK based manufacturers of
construction equipment, relevant components and
accessories in the UK.

Electronic and video publications:
Business Tracker (CD-ROM)

Access to staff:
Contact by letter, by telephone, by fax, by e-mail
and via website
Hours: Mon to Fri, 0900 to 1700

Member of:
Committee for European Construction Equipment (CECE)
Fédération Européenne de la Manutention (FEM)

CONSTRUCTION FIXINGS ASSOCIATION

Acronym or abbreviation: CFA

Light Trades House, 3 Melbourne Avenue, Sheffield, South Yorkshire, S10 2QJ

Tel: 0114 266 3084
Fax: 0114 267 0910
E-mail: light.trades@virgin.net

Enquiries:
Enquiries to: Secretary

Organisation type and purpose:
Trade association.

Subject coverage:
Construction fixings.

Access to staff:
Contact by letter, by telephone, by fax and by e-mail
Hours: Mon to Fri, 0900 to 1700

Affiliated to:
Federation of British Hand Tool Manufacturers

CONSTRUCTION HEALTH AND SAFETY GROUP

Acronym or abbreviation: CHSG

John Ryder Training Centre, St Ann's Road, Chertsey, Surrey, KT16 9EH

Tel: 01932 561871 or 563121
Fax: 01932 560193
E-mail: info@csh.co.uk

Website:
http://www.chsg.co.uk

Enquiries:
Enquiries to: Manager

Founded:
1953

Organisation type and purpose:
Membership association (membership is by subscription), present number of members: 430, registered charity, training organisation.

Subject coverage:
Construction safety training courses.

Access to staff:
Contact by letter, by telephone, by fax, by e-mail and via website
Hours: Mon to Fri, 0900 to 1700

CONSTRUCTION HISTORY SOCIETY

Acronym or abbreviation: CHS

c/o Library and Information Services Manager, The Chartered Institute of Building, Englemere, Kings Ride, Ascot, Berkshire, SL5 7TB

Tel: 01344 630741
Fax: 01344 630764
E-mail: secretary@constructionhistory.co.uk

Website:
http://www.constructionhistory.co.uk

Enquiries:
Enquiries to: Secretary

Founded:
1982

Formerly called:
Construction History Group (year of change 1985)

Organisation type and purpose:
Learned society (membership is by subscription), present number of members: 300, registered charity.

Subject coverage:
Construction history, construction techniques and materials, company histories, etc.

Museum or gallery collection, archive, or library special collection:
Small collections held at CIRCA
Holdings: books, periodicals, articles, archives, papers, correspondence, drawings, etc.

Printed publications:
CHS Newsletter (quarterly, free to members; on sale to others)
Construction History (annual journal, free to members; on sale to others)
The Place of Technology in Architectural History (2001, seminar papers, jtly with Society of Architectural Historians)
Proceedings of the Second International Congress on Construction History (2006, 4 vols, including index)
Order printed publications from: From the Society, as above or via website

Publications list:
Available online

Access to staff:
Contact by letter and by e-mail
Hours: Mon to Fri, 0900 to 1700

Access to building, collection or gallery:
Special comments: Archive access by appointment

Links with:
Building and Construction Industry Interest Group
Society for the History of Technology
Construction Industry Resource Centre Archive (CIRCA)
Kimmins Mill, Meadow Lane, Dudbridge, Gloucestershire, GR5 5JP
Panel for Historical Engineering Works
Institution of Civil Engineers

CONSTRUCTION INDUSTRY COMPUTING ASSOCIATION

Acronym or abbreviation: CICA

National Computing Centre, Oxford House, Oxford Road, Manchester, M1 7ED

Tel: 0161 242 2121
E-mail: michael.dean@ncc.co.uk

Website:
http://www.cica.org.uk

Enquiries:
Enquiries to: Managing Director

Founded:
1973

Organisation type and purpose:
Membership association (membership is by subscription), consultancy, research organisation. To provide impartial information and advice on the use of computers in the construction industry.

Subject coverage:
All areas of construction, including CAD, communications, management, engineering software, building services, quantity surveying; computing services, expert systems, IT strategy and standards.

Museum or gallery collection, archive, or library special collection:
Directory of software for the construction industry

Trade and statistical information:
Data on use of computers in the UK and European Construction Industry.
Data on sales of CAD systems to construction.

Printed publications:
Arup CAD Good Practice Guide
Document Management for Construction
Qualifying the Benefits of IT
The CAD Rating Guide

Publications list:
Available online and in print

Access to staff:
Contact by letter, by telephone, by e-mail and via website
Hours: Mon to Fri, 0900 to 1700

Commercial branch for consultancy and training:
CICA Services Ltd

CONSTRUCTION INDUSTRY COUNCIL

Acronym or abbreviation: CIC

26 Store Street, London, WC1E 7BT

Tel: 020 7399 7400
Fax: 020 7399 7425
E-mail: cic@cic.org.uk

Website:
http://www.cic.org.uk
General information.

Enquiries:
Direct e-mail: cic@cic.org.uk
Other contacts: Richard Biggs, Operations Director

Founded:
1988

Organisation type and purpose:
The Construction Industry Council (CIC) is the representative forum for the professional bodies, research organisations and specialist business associations in the construction industry.

Non-library collection catalogue:
All or part available in print

Printed publications:
Contact Helen Smith (hsmith@cic.org.uk) to obtain copy of list
Order printed publications from: CIC
26 Store Street, London, WC1E 7BT, tel: 020 7399 7400, fax: 020 7399 7425, e-mail: cic@cic.org.uk

Publications list:
Available online and in print

Access to staff:
Contact by letter, by telephone, by fax, by e-mail and via website. Appointment necessary.
Hours: Mon to Fri, 0900 to 1700

Access for disabled people:
lift, toilet facilities

Other address:
Construction Industry Council
26 Store Street, London, WC1E 7BT; tel: 020 7399 7400; fax: 020 7399 7425; e-mail: mail@cic.org.uk

CONSTRUCTION PLANT-HIRE ASSOCIATION

Acronym or abbreviation: CPA

52 Rochester Row, London, SW1P 1JU

Tel: 020 7630 6868
Fax: 020 7630 6765
E-mail: enquiries@c-p-a.co.uk

Website:
http://www.c-p-a.co.uk
Members services, background of CPA.

Enquiries:
Enquiries to: Director

Founded:
1941

Organisation type and purpose:
Trade association.

Subject coverage:
Construction plant-hire, health and safety, training, statistics and legal aspects.

Printed publications:
Bulletin (10 times a year, members only)
Contract forms, guidance notes and safety notes

Electronic and video publications:
List of members on disc (£100)
M Condition (CD-ROM)

continued overleaf

Publications list:
Available in print

Access to staff:
Contact by letter, by telephone and by fax
Hours: Mon to Fri, 0930 to 1700

CONSTRUCTION PRODUCTS ASSOCIATION

Acronym or abbreviation: CPA

The Building Centre, 26 Store Street, London, WC1E 7BT

Tel: 020 7323 3770
Fax: 020 7323 0307
E-mail: enquiries@constructionproducts.org.uk

Website:
http://www.constructionproducts.org.uk
Briefings, press releases/news, meetings and events, hyperlinks to members and other useful sites, industry overview and publications.

Enquiries:
Enquiries to: Director
Other contacts: Communications and External Affairs Director

Founded:
2000

Formed from the merger of:
Association of Construction Product Supplies (ACPS), Building Materials Export Group (BMEG), National Council of Building Material Producers (NCBMP)

Organisation type and purpose:
National organisation, trade association (membership is by subscription), present number of members: 60.
To demonstrate the importance of a growing and profitable construction products sector to the UK economy.

Subject coverage:
Building materials, components and fittings, industry in general; non-specialist information on availability and sources of materials; forecasts of construction industry output; statistics.

Museum or gallery collection, archive, or library special collection:
Economic, technical, wide-ranging other information on construction industry structure and organisation

Printed publications:
Construction Industry forecasts (quarterly)
Annual Report
Construction Market Trends (monthly)
Construction Product Trade Survey (4 times a year)
Weekly Notes (every Friday, members only)

Publications list:
Available online and in print

Access to staff:
Contact by letter, by telephone, by fax, by e-mail and via website. Appointment necessary. Non-members charged.
Hours: Mon to Fri, 0900 to 1700

Member of:
Confederation of British Industry (CBI)
tel: 020 7379 8001
Council of European Producers of Materials for Construction

CONSUMER COMPLAINTS SERVICE

Acronym or abbreviation: CCS

Victoria Court, 8 Dormer Place, Leamington Spa, Warwickshire, CV32 5AE

Tel: 01926 820082
Fax: 01926 431435

Website:
http://www.lawsociety.org.uk

General information about role and function of OSS.

Enquiries:
Enquiries to: Communications Officer
Direct tel: 01926 822042
Direct fax: 01926 831532
Direct e-mail: enquiries@lawsociety.org.uk

Founded:
2004

Organisation type and purpose:
Regulatory body.

Subject coverage:
Self-regulation of the solicitors' profession of England and Wales, complaints against solicitors.

Printed publications:
Free leaflets:
Can We Help?
Complaint Form
Resolution Form
Who we are, What we do
Order printed publications from: Marston Book Services
PO Box 312, Abingdon, Oxfordshire, OX14 4YH, tel: 01235 465656, fax: 01235 465660

Access to staff:
Contact by letter, by telephone and by e-mail
Hours: Mon to Fri, 0900 to 1700

Parent body:
Establishment of Law Society for England and Wales

CONSUMER CREDIT ASSOCIATION

Acronym or abbreviation: CCA

Queens House, Queens Road, Chester, Cheshire, CH1 3BQ

Tel: 01244 312044
Fax: 01244 318035
E-mail: cca@ccauk.org

Website:
http://www.ccauk.org

Enquiries:
Enquiries to: Director
Direct tel: 01244 505907
Direct fax: 01244 322528
Direct e-mail: cca@ccauk.org

Founded:
1978

Created by the merger of:
National Personal Finance Association (NPFA) and Retail Credit Federation (RCF) (year of change 1978)

Organisation type and purpose:
Trade association.
Represents over 500 companies operating in the home credit market.

Subject coverage:
Consumer credit, home credit.

Printed publications:
CCA News (quarterly)

Access to staff:
Contact by letter, by telephone, by fax and by e-mail
Hours: Mon to Fri, 0900 to 1700

CONSUMERS' ASSOCIATION

Acronym or abbreviation: CA

Head Office, 2 Marylebone Road, London, NW1 4DF

Tel: 020 7770 7400
Fax: 01992 827485
E-mail: editor@which.net or support@which.net

Website:
http://www.which.net

Enquiries:
Enquiries to: Customer Services Officer
Direct tel: 01992 589031 ext 4504

Founded:
1957

Organisation type and purpose:
Membership association (membership is by subscription), registered charity, research organisation, publishing house.
The company is Which Limited.

Subject coverage:
Consumer affairs, product testing, consumer law, standards.

Museum or gallery collection, archive, or library special collection:
Local Consumer Group magazines and Overseas Consumer magazines on microfiche

Non-library collection catalogue:
All or part available online and in print

Printed publications:
Numerous Which Guides and Books including:
Daily Consumer News
Drug and Therapeutics Bulletin
Gardening Which? (magazine, quarterly)
Good Food Guide (annually)
Good Hotel Guide
Good Pub Guide
Holiday Which? (magazine, quarterly)
Which? (magazine, monthly)
Which? Way to Health (magazine, 6 times a year)

Electronic and video publications:
Which? Online

Publications list:
Available in print

Access to staff:
Contact by letter, by telephone, by fax, by e-mail and via website
Hours: Which queries Mon to Fri, 0830 to 2000; Sat, 0900 to 1300
Which online Mon to Fri, 0830 to 2100; Sat 0900 to 1500

Connections with:
BEUC
IOCU

Links with:
Research Institute for Consumer Affairs

Other addresses:
Membership Queries
Consumers' Association, Castlemead, Gascoyne Way, Hertford, SG1 1LH

CONTACT A FAMILY

Acronym or abbreviation: CaF

209–211 City Road, London, EC1V 1JN

Tel: 020 7608 8700\ Minicom no. 020 7608 8702
Fax: 020 7608 8701
E-mail: info@cafamily.org.uk

Website:
http://www.cafamily.org.uk
CaF directory containing over 200 entries giving information on over 800 conditions affecting children. Each entry is accompanied by medical information and details of support groups.

Enquiries:
Enquiries to: Information Officers

Founded:
1979

Organisation type and purpose:
Voluntary organisation, registered charity.
Support for families who care for children with disabilities and special needs.

Subject coverage:
Children with special needs, parent carers, parents' support groups, rare conditions affecting children.

Information services:
Helpline, tel: 0808 808 3555 and textphone: 0808 808 3556

Non-library collection catalogue:
All or part available in-house

Library catalogue:
All or part available in-house

Printed publications:
Connect (magazine, quarterly)
CaF Directory of Specific Conditions & Rare
    Syndromes in Children with their Family
    Support Networks (£30)
CaF Annual Review 2000/01 (single copies free
    plus A4 sae, multiple copies 50p each)
CaF Group Action Pack (£10 plus £1 p&p)
A range of factsheets and leaflets for groups,
    individuals and professionals

Electronic and video publications:
CaF Directory (CD-ROM)

Publications list:
Available online and in print

Access to staff:
Contact by letter, by telephone, by fax, by e-mail
and via website
Hours: Mon to Fri, 0900 to 1700

Access to building, collection or gallery:
Prior appointment required

Access for disabled people:
Ramped entry, toilet facilities

CONTACT THE ELDERLY

15 Henrietta Street, Covent Garden, London,
WC2E 8QG

Tel: 020 7240 0630
Fax: 020 7379 5781
E-mail: info@contact-the-elderly.org.uk

Website:
http://www.contact-the-elderly.org.uk

Enquiries:
Enquiries to: Administration Officer

Founded:
1965

Formerly called:
CONTACT

Organisation type and purpose:
Voluntary organisation, registered charity (charity
number 244681).

Subject coverage:
Voluntary group work with frail elderly people
and the housebound, services for the elderly,
particularly to offset loneliness.

Printed publications:
Annual Report and leaflet
Contact the Elderly News

Electronic and video publications:
Videos

Access to staff:
Contact by letter, by telephone, by fax, by e-mail
and via website
Hours: Mon to Fri, 0900 to 1700

CONTEMPORARY APPLIED ARTS

2 Percy Street, London, W1P 9FA

Tel: 020 7436 2344
Fax: 020 7436 2446

Website:
http://www.caa.org.uk
Current exhibitions.

Enquiries:
Enquiries to: Press and Promotions Officer

Founded:
1948

Formerly called:
British Crafts Centre (year of change 1989)

Organisation type and purpose:
Membership association (membership is by
qualification), present number of members: 250
approx, registered charity.
Gallery.

Subject coverage:
Ceramics, glass, jewellery, furniture, textiles, wood,
metalwork.

Printed publications:
Exhibition leaflets (approx 7 times a year)

Access to staff:
Contact by letter and by telephone
Hours: Mon to Sat, 1030 to 1730
Special comments: Closed Bank Holidays and from
Christmas to early Jan.

Member of:
Federation of British Crafts Societies (FBCS)

CONTEMPORARY ART SOCIETY

Acronym or abbreviation: CAS

11–15 Emerald Street, London, WC1N 3QL

Tel: 020 7831 1243
Fax: 020 7831 1214 info@contemporaryartsociety
.org
E-mail: info@contemporaryartsociety.org

Website:
http://www.contempart.org.uk

Enquiries:
Enquiries to: Director
Direct e-mail: cas@contempart.org.uk

Founded:
1910

Organisation type and purpose:
Learned society, consultancy.

Subject coverage:
Promotion of the understanding, enjoyment and
collecting of contemporary art; acquisition of
works of contemporary art for gifts to public
museums and galleries; an extensive knowledge of
British contemporary art.

**Museum or gallery collection, archive, or library
special collection:**
Extensive data on contemporary artists
Information is held on all CAS purchases since
    1910

Access to staff:
Contact by letter, by telephone, by fax and by e-
mail. Appointment necessary.
Hours: Mon to Fri, 1000 to 1800

CONTEMPORARY GLASS SOCIETY, THE

Acronym or abbreviation: CGS

c/o Broadfield House Glass Museum, Compton
Drive, Kingswinford, West Midlands, DY6 9NS

Tel: 01603 507 737
Fax: 01603 507 737
E-mail: admin@cgs.org.uk

Website:
http://www.cgs.org.uk

Enquiries:
Enquiries to: Administrator

Founded:
1997

Formerly called:
British Artists in Glass (year of change 1997)

Organisation type and purpose:
International organisation, learned society,
professional body, membership association
(membership is by subscription), present number
of members: 350, manufacturing industry,
voluntary organisation, consultancy.

Subject coverage:
Studio glass-making, exhibitions, individuals
specialising in particular areas of glass-making,
collectors, supporters.

Library catalogue:
All or part available online and in print

Printed publications:
Journal (annually)
Newsletter

Access to staff:
Contact by letter
Hours: Mon to Fri, 0900 to 1700

CONTINYOU

Unit C1, Grovelands Court, Grovelands Estate,
Longford Road, Exhall, Coventry, Warwickshire,
CV7 9NE

Tel: 024 7658 8440
Fax: 024 7658 8441
E-mail: info.coventry@continyou.org.uk

Website:
http://www.continyou.org.uk
Information about ContinYou's work, projects,
consultancy, training, publications.
http://www.continyou.org.uk/publications
Publications list.

Enquiries:
Enquiries to: Publications Manager
Direct tel: 024 7658 8459
Direct e-mail: carolyn.sugden@continyou.org.uk

Founded:
2003

Organisation type and purpose:
Voluntary organisation, registered charity (charity
number 1097596).

Subject coverage:
Community-based learning, parental involvement
in education, extended schools, out-of-school-
hours learning, lifelong learning, family learning,
economic and community regeneration, health
improvement, promoting healthy communities.

Printed publications:
Governors' Agenda (journal)
Schools ETC (journal)
ContinYou in Action (journal)
Order printed publications from: Publications, Sales,
ContinYou
at the same address, tel: 024 7658 8470, fax: 024
7658 8441, e-mail: publications.sales@continyou
.org.uk

Publications list:
Available online and in print

Access to staff:
Contact by letter, by telephone, by fax and by e-
mail. Appointment necessary.
Hours: Mon to Thur, 0900 to 1700; Fri 0900 to 1630

CONTRACT FLOORING ASSOCIATION

Acronym or abbreviation: CFA

4c Saint Mary's Place, The Lace Market,
Nottingham, NG1 1PH

Tel: 0115 941 1126
Fax: 0115 941 2238
E-mail: info@cfa.org.uk

Website:
http://www.cfa.org.uk

Founded:
1974

Organisation type and purpose:
Trade association.

Subject coverage:
All types of floorcoverings, incl carpet, timber,
resilient.

continued overleaf

Printed publications:
Contract Flooring Journal
Guide to Contract Flooring
Members Handbook

Publications list:
Available in print

Access to staff:
Contact by letter, by telephone, by fax, by e-mail and via website
Hours: Mon to Fri, 0900 to 1700

Member of:
National Specialist Contractors Council (NSCC)

CONTROL SYSTEMS CENTRE

Acronym or abbreviation: CSC

UMIST, Department of Electrical Engineering & Electronics, PO Box 88, Manchester, M60 1QD

Tel: 0161 200 4665
Fax: 0161 200 4647
E-mail: neil@csc.umist.ac.uk

Website:
http://www.csc.umist.ac.uk

Enquiries:
Enquiries to: Head of Centre

Founded:
1966

Organisation type and purpose:
University department or institute, consultancy.
University unit within the Department of Electrical and Electronic Engineering.
Interdisciplinary research in control and systems engineering.

Subject coverage:
Control and information technology, multivariable control system design, computer-aided design, self-tuning regulators, 2-D system theory, robust control, fault detection, symbolic programming, nonlinear systems, optimisation.

Printed publications:
Control System Centre Reports
Control System Centre Book Series: a set of texts on important developments in control theory and engineering includes:
Analysis of Piecewise Linear Dynamical Systems (Pettit N, 1995)
Application of Neural Networks to Adaptive Control of Nonlinear Systems (Ng G W, 1997)
Change Detection and Input Design in Dynamical Systems (Kerestecioglu F, 1993)
Pole Assignment for Uncertain Systems (Soylemez T, 1999)
Possibility Theory with Applications to Data Analysis (Woklenhauer O, 1998)
Self Tuning Control for Two-Dimensional Processes (Heath W, 1994)
Symbolic Methods in Control System Analysis and Design (Munro N, 1999)
Order printed publications from: IEE, RSP and J Wiley

Publications list:
Available in print

Access to staff:
Contact by letter, by telephone, by fax and by e-mail
Hours: Mon to Fri, 0900 to 1700

CONVENTION OF SCOTTISH LOCAL AUTHORITIES

Acronym or abbreviation: COSLA

Rosebery House, 9 Haymarket Terrace, Edinburgh, EH12 5XZ

Tel: 0131 474 9200
Fax: 0131 474 9292
E-mail: carol@cosla.gov.uk

Website:
http://www.cosla.gov.uk

Background to COSLA, meeting dates and agendas, publications list, news releases, conference facilities.

Enquiries:
Enquiries to: Head of Media and Communications
Direct tel: 0131 474 9205
Direct e-mail: davidk@cosla.gov.uk

Founded:
1975

Organisation type and purpose:
Local government body.

Subject coverage:
Scottish local government, people, boards, and public bodies.

Printed publications:
The Directory of Scottish Local Government
Order printed publications from: COSLA Connections

Publications list:
Available online and in print

Access to staff:
Contact by letter, by telephone, by fax, by e-mail and via website
Hours: Mon to Fri, 0900 to 1700

Access to building, collection or gallery:
Main Reception
Hours: Mon to Fri, 0900 – 1700

Access for disabled people:
Yes

Also at:
COSLA
    Brussels Office, The House of Cities, Municipalities & Regions, Square de Meeus 1 , B-1000 Brussels, Belgium; tel: +32 (0)2 213 8120; fax: +32 (0)2 213 8129; e-mail: cosla@pophost.eunet.be
COSLA
    Glasgow Office, Suite 203, 69 Buchanan Street, Glasgow, G1 3HL; tel: 0141 314 3700; fax: 0141 314 3836

CONWY COUNTY BOROUGH COUNCIL

Acronym or abbreviation: CCBC

Bodlondeb, Conwy, LL32 8DU

Tel: 01492 574000
Fax: 01492 592114
E-mail: information@conwy.gov.uk

Website:
http://www.conwy.gov.uk

Enquiries:
Enquiries to: Chief Executive
Direct fax: 01492 576003
Other contacts: Corporate Information and Complaints Manager

Founded:
1996

Created by the merger of:
Colwyn Borough Council and Aberconwy Borough Council (year of change 1996)

Organisation type and purpose:
Local government body.

Subject coverage:
Information on services provided by the Authority for those who live in, work in or visit Conwy County Borough.

Information services:
Corporate Information and Complaints Service, Library and Information Services, Corporate Research and Information Unit, Marketing and Communications Unit, Tourist Information Services

Education services:
Education Services

Services for disabled people:
Physical Disability and Sensory Impairment Service

Trade and statistical information:
Local census information available, business directory, community information directory

Library catalogue:
All or part available online

Printed publications:
Numerous
Order printed publications from: Corporate Information and Complaints Service, Publications Circulation, Reception and Information Desk, Civic Offices, Colwyn Bay, LL29 8AR

Access to staff:
Contact by letter, by telephone, by fax, by e-mail, in person and via website
Hours: Mon to Thu, 0845 to 1715; Fri, 0845 to 1645

Access to building, collection or gallery:
Access is different for each council building, contact for further details

Access for disabled people:
Access is different for each council building, contact for further details

CONWY COUNTY BOROUGH COUNCIL – LIBRARY AND INFORMATION SERVICE HEADQUARTERS

Formal name: Conwy Library and Information Service
Acronym or abbreviation: CLIS

Bodlondeb, Conwy, LL32 8DU

Tel: 01492 576136
Fax: 01492 592061
E-mail: lic@conwy.gov.uk

Website:
http://www.conwy.gov.uk/library
Conwy Library and Information website
http://www.conwy.gov.uk/llyfrgell
Welsh version of Library and Information website
http://www.conwy.gov.uk
Conwy County Borough Council website.
http://talisweb.talnet.gov.uk
Online catalogue for North West Wales.

Enquiries:
Enquiries to: Prinicpal Librarian
Direct tel: 01492 576139
Direct e-mail: rhian.williams@conwy.gov.uk

Founded:
1996

Formerly a part of:
Gwynedd and Clwyd Library Services (year of change 1996)

Organisation type and purpose:
Local government body, statutory body, public library.
Information and archives service.

Subject coverage:
Local government information; Welsh history; Welsh language and literature; Welsh reference material, local information.

Museum or gallery collection, archive, or library special collection:
Alice in Wonderland Books Collection at Llandudno library
Archive access points (held at Llandudno and Colwyn Bay libraries)

Trade and statistical information:
Statistical information, e.g. population, social, etc.

Non-library collection catalogue:
All or part available online

Library catalogue:
All or part available online

Access to staff:
Contact by letter, by telephone, by fax, by e-mail and via website
Hours: Mon to Fri, 0900 to 1700
Special comments: Headquarters visitors by prior appointment only

Access to building, collection or gallery:
Hours: Opening times vary; please contact for further details

Access for disabled people:
Headquarters on second floor, with no lift

Branch libraries:
Abergele Library
  Market Street, Abergele, LL22 7BP; tel: 01745 832638; fax: 01745 823376; e-mail: llyfr.lib .abergele@conwy.gov.uk
Cerrigydrudion Library (managed from Llanrwst library)
  The Old Clinic, King Street, Cerrigydrudion, Corwen, LL21 9UB; tel: 01490 420501
Colwyn Bay Library
  Woodland Road West, Colwyn Bay, LL29 7DH; tel: 01492 532358; fax: 01492 534474; e-mail: llyfr .lib.baecolwynbay@conwy.gov.uk
Conwy Library
  Civic Hall, Castle Street, Conwy, LL32 6AY; tel: 01492 596242; fax: 01492 582359; e-mail: llyfr.lib .conwy@conwy.gov.uk
Deganwy Library (managed from Colwyn Bay library)
  Station Road, Deganwy, Conwy, LL31 9EX; tel: 01492 584705; e-mail: llyfr.lib.deganwy@conwy .gov.uk
Kinmel Bay Library (managed from Colwyn Bay library)
  Community Centre, Kendal Road, Kinmel Bay, LL18 5BT; tel: 01745 353499; e-mail: llyfr.lib .kinmel@conwy.gov.uk
Llandudno Junction Library (managed from Colwyn Bay library)
  Maes Derw, Llandudno Junction, LL31 9AL; tel: 01492 582266
Llandudno Library
  Victoria Centre, Mostyn Street, Llandudno, LL30 2RS; tel: 01492 574010 or 574020; fax: 01492 876826; e-mail: llyfr.lib.llandudno@conwy.gov .uk
Llanfairfechan Library (managed from Llanrwst library)
  Village Road, Llanfairfechan, LL33 0AA; tel: 01248 681014; e-mail: llyfr.lib.llanfairfechan@ conwy.gov.uk
Llangernyw Library (managed from Llanrwst library)
  Ysgol Bro Cernyw, Llangernyw, Abergele, LL22 8PF; tel: 01745 860413
Llanrwst Library
  Plas yn Dre, 223 Station Road, Llanrwst, LL26 0DF; tel: 01492 640043; e-mail: llyfr.lib.llanrwst@ conwy.gov.uk
Penmaenmawr Library (managed from Llanrwst library)
  Bangor Road, Penmaenmawr, LL34 6DA; tel: 01492 623619; e-mail: llyfr.lib.penmaenmawr@ conwy.gov.uk
Penrhyn Bay Library (managed from Colwyn Bay library)
  Llandudno Road, Penrhyn Bay, Llanduddno, LL30 3HN; tel: 01492 548873; e-mail: llyfr.lib .penrhyn@conwy.gov.uk

Constituent part of:
Conwy County Borough Council

COPELAND BOROUGH COUNCIL

The Copeland Centre, Catherine Street, Whitehaven, Cumbria, CA28 7SJ

Tel: 0845 095 2100
Fax: 0845 095 2140

Website:
http://www.copelandbc.gov.uk

Enquiries:
Enquiries to: General Manager
Direct tel: 01946 598320
Direct fax: 01946 598303
Direct e-mail: jstanforth@copelandbc.gov.uk

Organisation type and purpose:
Local government body.

Subject coverage:
Corporate services, education, environmental services, finance, housing, legal services, personnel services, planning development and tourism, property and technical services, roads and transportation, social services, council tax and other payments, registration of births, deaths and marriages.

Access to staff:
Contact by letter, by telephone, by fax, by e-mail and via website
Hours: Mon to Fri, 0900 to 1700

COPPER DEVELOPMENT ASSOCIATION

Acronym or abbreviation: CDA

5 Grovelands Business Centre, Boundary Way, Hemel Hempstead, HP2 7TE

Tel: 01442 275705
Fax: 01442 275716
E-mail: mail@copperdev.co.uk

Website:
http://www.copperinfo.co.uk/
http://www.cda.org.uk/
CDA publications.

Enquiries:
Enquiries to: Information Manager

Founded:
1933

Organisation type and purpose:
Advisory body, service industry, research organisation.
Non-trading organisation, sponsored by copper producers and fabricators.

Subject coverage:
Copper, its alloys and compounds, non-ferrous metals, market development and technical data.

Printed publications:
Information Sheets
Technical Notes

Electronic and video publications:
Datadiscs (8 discs for PC)
Megabytes on Copper (56 publications and 8 datadiscs on CD-ROM, £20)
Videos (8, purchase or hire)

Publications list:
Available online

Access to staff:
Contact by letter, by telephone, by fax and in person. Appointment necessary.
Hours: Mon to Fri, 0930 to 1700

COPYRIGHT LICENSING AGENCY

Acronym or abbreviation: CLA

Saffron House, 6–10 Kirby Street, London, EC1N 8TS

Fax: 020 7400 3100
E-mail: cla@cla.co.uk

Website:
http://www.cla.co.uk
Background information on copyright. Interactive questionnaire 'Do you need a photocopying licence?' Publication-specific photocopy and coursepack fees. On-line clearance for registered users.

Enquiries:
Enquiries to: PR Manager
Other contacts: Marketing Manager

Founded:
1982

Organisation type and purpose:
Service industry.
To license photocopying and scanning of extracts and clippings from copyright books, journals and magazines.

Subject coverage:
Copyright licensing, copyright, electronic copying, internet issues.

Trade and statistical information:
Photocopy fees for specific publications.

Printed publications:
Clarion (twice a year, free newsletter)
Annual Report
Various leaflets

Access to staff:
Contact by letter, by telephone and by e-mail
Hours: Mon to Fri, 0900 to 1700
Special comments: Internet online 24 hrs.

Affiliated to:
Association of Learned and Professional Society Publishers
International Federation of Reproduction Rights Organisations
Publishers Association
Publishers Licensing Society (PLS)
  37–41 Gower Street, London, WC1E 6HH; tel: 020 7299 7730; fax: 020 7299 7780; e-mail: pls@pls .org.uk
Society of Authors
Writers' Guild of Great Britain

Parent body:
Authors' Licensing and Collecting Society (ALCS)
  Marlborough Court, 14–18 Holborn, London, EC1N 2LE; tel: 020 7395 0600; fax: 020 7395 0660; e-mail: alcs@alcs.co.uk

CORBY BOROUGH COUNCIL

Deene House, New Post Office Square, Corby, Northamptonshire, NN17 1GD

Tel: 01536 402551
Fax: 01536 464640

Website:
http://www.corby.gov.uk

Enquiries:
Enquiries to: Public Relations Manager

Founded:
1993

Formerly called:
Corby District Council

Organisation type and purpose:
Local government body.

Subject coverage:
Corby Borough, services and amenities.

Access to staff:
Contact by letter, by telephone, by fax and by e-mail. Appointment necessary.
Hours: Mon to Fri, 0900 to 1700

CORD

Formal name: Christian Outreach – Relief and Development

1 New Street, Leamington Spa, Warwickshire, CV1 1HP

Tel: 01926 315301
Fax: 01926 885786
E-mail: info@cord.org.uk

Enquiries:
Enquiries to: Director

Founded:
1967

Formerly called:
Christian Outreach Project Vietnam Orphans (year of change 1999)

Organisation type and purpose:
International organisation, registered charity (charity number 1070684).
An international Christian-based relief and development organisation.

continued overleaf

Printed publications:
Compassion in Action (newsletter 6 times a year, free of charge)

Access to staff:
Contact by letter and by e-mail
Hours: Mon to Fri, 0900 to 1700

CORE

Acronym or abbreviation: Core

3 St Andrew's Place, Regent's Park, London, NW1 4LB

Tel: 020 7486 0341
Fax: 020 7224 2012
E-mail: info@corecharity.org.uk

Website:
http://www.corecharity.org.uk
Patient information, Core activities, details of research awards, newsletter

Enquiries:
Enquiries to: Administrator

Founded:
1971
Digestive Disorders Foundation

Organisation type and purpose:
Registered charity (charity no. 262762), research organisation.
Core supports research into all aspects of digestive disease.

Subject coverage:
Gastroenterology, including the physiology and pathology of the digestive system; research into causes, prevention and treatment of digestive disorders.

Printed publications:
Annual Report and Accounts, Newsletter (3 annually)
Information leaflets on common digestive disorders including: ulcers, heartburn, irritable bowel syndrome, diverticular disease, coeliac disease, indigestion, constipation, diarrhoea, gallstones, etc (free plus p&p)
Order printed publications from: Leaflets available from:, Core, 3 St Andrews Place, London, NW1 4LB

Publications list:
Available in print

Access to staff:
Contact by letter, by telephone, by fax, by e-mail and via website
Hours: Mon to Fri, 0900 to 1700
Special comments: Please send sae if requiring information.

Close association with:
British Liver Trust
Children's Liver Disease Foundation
Coeliac Society
Crohn's in Childhood Research Appeal
IA – The Ileostomy and Internal Pouch Support Group
IBS Network
National Association for Colitis and Crohn's Disease

CORK INDUSTRY FEDERATION

Acronym or abbreviation: CIF

13 Felton Lea, Sidcup, Kent, DA14 6BA

Tel: 020 8302 4801
Fax: 020 8302 4801

Website:
http://www.cork-products.co.uk
Addresses and products of all members and cork information.

Enquiries:
Enquiries to: Honorary Secretary
Other contacts: Chairman

Founded:
1969

Organisation type and purpose:
Trade association (membership is by subscription).

Subject coverage:
All aspects of cork, for domestic, decorative, industrial and architectural uses, and for use in the wine and spirit trades; advice can be given on roof drainage and insulation, material selection and design.

Museum or gallery collection, archive, or library special collection:
Details of cork products

Printed publications:
Members' Directory (annually)
Order printed publications from: Honorary Secretary, CIF

Access to staff:
Contact by letter, by telephone and by fax
Hours: Mon to Fri, 0900 to 1700

Member organisation of:
European Cork Industry Federation

CORNWALL CENTRE (KRESENN KERNOW)

Alma Place, Redruth, Cornwall, TR15 2AT

Tel: 01209 216760
Fax: 01209 210283
E-mail: cornishstudies.library@cornwall.gov.uk

Website:
http://www.cornwall.gov.uk/cornwallcentre
Library content, including newspapers list, photographic database, timeline of Cornish history.

Enquiries:
Enquiries to: Librarian

Founded:
1974

Organisation type and purpose:
Local government body, public library.
Local studies library and visitor centre.

Subject coverage:
Cornwall

Museum or gallery collection, archive, or library special collection:
Ashley Rowe Collection (general Cornish)
Hambly and Rowe Collection (general Cornish)
A. K. Hamilton Jenkin Collection (Cornish mining)
Cornish Newspapers (around 50 titles, microfilm)
Photographs (over 150,000)
Cornish Census returns
Maps
Parish Register transcriptions
Books and pamphlets about Cornwall

Library catalogue:
All or part available online

Printed publications:
Leaflets (free)
Directories
Newspapers
Parish Register transcripts

Electronic and video publications:
Microfilm of West Briton newspaper for purchase (to order)
Photographic reproductions (to order)
Cornish Newspapers (around 50 titles)

Access to staff:
Contact by letter, by telephone, by fax, by e-mail and in person
Hours: Mon to Fri, 1000 to 1800; Sat, 1000 to 1600
Special comments: Prior appointment is advisable to view microforms.

Access for disabled people:
Level entry, access to all public areas, toilet facilities

Parent body:
Cornwall County Council
Cornwall Library Service, Unit 17, Threemilestone Industrial Estate, Truro, Cornwall, TR4 9LD; tel: 01872 324316; fax: 01872 223509; e-mail: library@cornwall.gov.uk; website: http://www.cornwall.gov.uk/libraries

CORNWALL COLLEGE GROUP

Acronym or abbreviation: CCLS

Learning Services, Cornwall College, Trevenson Road, Pool, Redruth, Cornwall, TR15 3RD

Tel: 01209 616181
Fax: 01209 616184
E-mail: sue.halstead@cornwall.ac.uk

Website:
http://www.cornwall.ac.uk
General information about the College, including courses and services.

Organisation type and purpose:
Further and higher education

Subject coverage:
General.

Library catalogue:
All or part available online and in-house

Printed publications:
General Guides

Access to staff:
Access for members only. Non-members charged.
Hours: Mon to Fri, 0900 to 1630 (minimum)

Also at:
Cornwall College Newquay
Centre for Applied Zoology, Wildflower Lane, Trenance Gardens, Newquay, TR7 2LZ; tel: 01637 857930
Cornwall College Saltash
Church Road, Saltash, PL12 4AE; tel: 01752 850215
Cornwall College St Austell
Tregonissey Road, St Austell, PL25 4DJ; tel: 01726 226784
Duchy College Rosewarne
Rosewarne, Cambourne, TR14 0AB; tel: 01209 722134
Duchy College Stoke Climsland
Stoke Climsland, Callington, PL17 8PB; tel: 01579 372213
Falmouth Marine School
Killigrew Street, Falmouth, TR11 3QS; tel: 01326 310319; fax: 01326 310331

CORNWALL FAMILY HISTORY SOCIETY

Acronym or abbreviation: CFHS

5 Victoria Square, Truro, Cornwall, TR1 2RS

Tel: 01872 264044
E-mail: secretary@cornwallfhs.com

Website:
http://www.cornwallfhs.com

Enquiries:
Enquiries to: Administrator

Founded:
1976

Organisation type and purpose:
International organisation, membership association (membership is by subscription), present number of members: 5100, voluntary organisation, registered charity (charity number 288686), research organisation.
To promote interest in family history research into Cornish families.

Subject coverage:
All records concerning the tracing of Cornish family histories.

Museum or gallery collection, archive, or library special collection:
Books, documents, indexes, photographs of
    Cornish families
Much held on computer database
1837–1992 GRO index (microfiche)
1841–1901 Censuses (microfiche)

Printed publications:
Society Journal
A very large number of publications providing:
    monumental inscriptions, Pre-Civil Registration
    marriage index, Phillimore marriage index,
    1813–37 parish burial index, 1841 census index,
    1851 census index, 1861 census index, 1871
    census index, 1891 census index; the publications
    list provides details of which parishes are
    covered

Microform publications:
Directory of members' interests (microfiche,
    members only)

Publications list:
Available online and in print

Access to staff:
Contact by letter, by telephone, by e-mail, in
person and via website. Non-members charged.
Hours: Mon, 1000 to 1600; Wed to Sat, 1100 to 1500;
Tue, closed

CORNWALL LIBRARY SERVICE

Unit 17, Threemilestone Industrial Estate, Truro,
Cornwall, TR4 9LD

Tel: 01872 324316
Fax: 01872 223509
E-mail: library@cornwall.gov.uk

Website:
http://www.cornwall.gov.uk

Organisation type and purpose:
Local government body, public library.

Subject coverage:
General; metalliferous mining in Cornwall; county
local studies (at Redruth); performing arts (at St
Austell); art (at Penzance); maritime studies (at
Falmouth); law and business (at Truro).

Museum or gallery collection, archive, or library special collection:
Ashley Rowe Collection (local studies)
Cornish Methodist Historical Association (on
    deposit)
Hambley Rowe Collection (local studies)
Hamilton Jenkin Collection (local studies)
Rosewarne Collection (local studies)

Non-library collection catalogue:
All or part available online

Library catalogue:
All or part available online

Printed publications:
Subject Index

Parent body:
Cornwall County Council

CORNWALL REFERENCE AND INFORMATION LIBRARY

Union Place, Truro, Cornwall, TR1 1EP

Tel: 01872 272702; Freephone 0800 032 2345
Fax: 01872 223772
E-mail: reference.library@cornwall.gov.uk

Website:
http://www.cornwall.gov.uk/library

Enquiries:
Enquiries to: Librarian

Founded:
1896

Formerly called:
Cornwall County Reference and Information
Library

Organisation type and purpose:
Public reference library, Cornwall Centre for
Europe Direct

Subject coverage:
Law and business, European information, general
reference.

Trade and statistical information:
General statistics.

Non-library collection catalogue:
All or part available online

Library catalogue:
All or part available online

Electronic and video publications:
Community information for Cornwall (available
    online)

Access to staff:
Contact by letter, by telephone, by fax, by e-mail,
in person and via website
Hours: Mon, Tue, Thu and Fri, 0900 to 1800; Wed,
0930 to 1800; Sat, 0900 to 1600

Access for disabled people:
Parking provided, level entry, access to all public
areas

Parent body:
Chief Executive's Department
    New County Hall, Truro, Cornwall, TR1 3EW;
    tel: 01872 322000; fax: 01872 323818

CORONA WORLDWIDE

Acronym or abbreviation: CWW

Southbank House, Black Prince Road, London, SE1
7SJ

Tel: 020 7793 4020
Fax: 020 7793 4020
E-mail: corona@coronaworldwide.org

Website:
http://www.corona_worldwide.org

Enquiries:
Enquiries to: Administrative Secretary

Founded:
1950

Formerly called:
Women's Corona Society (year of change 2006)

Organisation type and purpose:
International organisation, voluntary organisation,
registered charity (charity number 204802),
suitable for ages: adults.
Notes for newcomers to over 100 countries
worldwide.
To support people going to work and live in other
countries by giving them information about living
conditions there, to welcome people coming to live
in Britain; aim is to promote friendship and
understanding around the world.

Subject coverage:
Living and working in foreign countries.

Printed publications:
Forty Years of Service (the history of the society)
Magazine (yearly, sent to members, available on
    request)
Notes for newcomers to various countries (price on
    application)

Access to staff:
Contact by letter, by telephone, by fax and by e-
mail
Hours: Tue, Thu, 0900 to 1700

Access to building, collection or gallery:
Hours: 0900 to 1700
Special comments: Security pass at reception.

CORONERS' SOCIETY OF ENGLAND AND WALES

HM Coroner's Court, The Cotton Exchange, Old
Hall Street, Liverpool, L3 9UF

Tel: 0151 233 4708

Fax: 0151 233 4710
E-mail: andre.rebello@liverpool.gov.uk

Website:
http://www.coroner.org.uk

Enquiries:
Enquiries to: Honorary Secretary

Founded:
1846

Organisation type and purpose:
Professional body (membership is by election or
invitation), present number of members: 400.
Membership restricted to coroners, deputies and
assistant deputies, and retired coroners.

Subject coverage:
Law and practice concerning coroners.

Museum or gallery collection, archive, or library special collection:
Minutes and reports 1846–

Access to staff:
Contact by letter and by e-mail
Hours: Mon to Fri, 0900 to 1700

CORPORATION OF INSURANCE, FINANCIAL AND MORTGAGE ADVISERS

Acronym or abbreviation: CIFMA

174 High Street, Guildford, Surrey, GU1 3HW

Tel: 01483 539121
Fax: 01483 301847

Enquiries:
Enquiries to: General Secretary

Founded:
1968

Formerly called:
Corporation of Mortgage Brokers (year of change
1972)

Organisation type and purpose:
Professional body, membership association
(membership is by subscription, qualification),
present number of members: c. 700.
To raise the professional standards in mortgage
broking and the associated life assurance industry
and general insurance industry.

Subject coverage:
Mortgage broking, life insurance and general
insurance.

Printed publications:
Newsletter (free to members)

Access to staff:
Contact by letter, by telephone and by fax
Hours: Mon to Fri, 0900 to 1700

CORPORATION OF LONDON RECORDS OFFICE

Acronym or abbreviation: CLRO

c/o London Metropolitan Archives, 40
Northampton Road, London, EC1R 0HB

Tel: 020 7332 3820
Fax: 020 7833 9136
E-mail: ask.lma@cityoflondon.gov.uk

Website:
http://www.cityoflondon.gov.uk/archives/lma

Enquiries:
Enquiries to: Enquiries Team

Founded:
1876

Formerly called:
City of London Record(s) Office, Guildhall
Record(s) Office

Organisation type and purpose:
Local government body.
Record office.

continued overleaf

Custody of the official archives of the Corporation of the City of London.

Subject coverage:
Archives of national as well as civic interest, reflecting the interests and activities of the Corporation, from the 11th to the 20th centuries.

Museum or gallery collection, archive, or library special collection:
Administrative records, such as: Proceedings of the Courts of Aldermen and Common Council, 15th century onwards
Financial records
Judicial records, from the civic courts and the Sessions of Gaol Delivery and Peace, 13th century onwards
Medieval compilations of City law and custom
Records of admission to the Freedom of the City
Records of the City of London Police
Rentals and deeds relating to property, some of which lay outside the City
Royal Charters 1067 onwards

Non-library collection catalogue:
All or part available online, in-house and in print

Printed publications:
A variety of histories and calendars of records are available for purchase; also some free publications available:
An Introductory Guide to the Corporation of London Records Office (out of print)
Calendar of Coroners Rolls of the City of London 1300–78 (£15)
Calendar of Early Mayor's Court Rolls 1298–1307 (out of print)
Calendar of Plea and Memoranda Rolls 1323–64, 1364–81, 1381–1412, 1413–37 (all out of print), 1437–57, 1458–82 (£15 each)
Calendar of Wills proved and enrolled in the Court of Husting, London 1258–1688
Greater London History Sources: Vol. 1 City of London (available from Guildhall Library, £14.95 hardback, £9.95 paperback)
Information Sheets (free publications)
Research Guides (free publications)
Southwark and the City (out of print)
The Fire Court, Calendar to the Decrees of the Court of Judicature on disputes as to rebuilding after the Great Fire: Vol. 1 1667–68, Vol. 2 1667–68 (£10 each)

Microform publications:
Remembrancia c.1579–1664/65 (pub. World Microfilms)
The Husting Rolls of Deeds and Wills, 1252–1485 (pub. Chadwyck-Healey, later International Imaging)
The Making of Modern London: Repertories, 1495–1692 (pub. Research Publications International)
The Whitechapel Murders Papers (pub. World Microfilms)

Publications list:
Available online and in print

Access to staff:
Contact by letter, by telephone, by fax, by e-mail, in person and via website

Access to building, collection or gallery:
Hours: Mon, Wed and Fri, 0930 to 1645; Tue and Thu, 0930 to 1930; Sat, contact for details
Special comments: Appointments required to view rare books.

Access for disabled people:
Toilet facilities

CORPORATION OF TRINITY HOUSE

Trinity House, Tower Hill, London, EC3N 4DH

Tel: 020 7481 6900
Fax: 020 7480 7662
E-mail: enquiries@this.org

Website:
http://www.trinityhouse.co.uk

Information on the history and current operations of Trinity House including profiles of all 72 lighthouses and latest news, notices to mariners.

Enquiries:
Direct e-mail: enquiries@this.org
Other contacts: Media and Communication Officer

Founded:
1514

Organisation type and purpose:
Statutory body, registered charity.
General lighthouse authority for England, Wales and Channel Islands, a deep sea pilotage authority and marine charitable organisation.

Subject coverage:
History and current operations of Trinity House.
Aids to navigation – lighthouses, light vessels, buoyage and radio navigation.

Museum or gallery collection, archive, or library special collection:
Corporations archives dating from 1660 held by Guildhall Library
Library – mainly nautical books

Printed publications:
Information pack on history and modern day activities of the Corporation (free)
Trinity House Calendar (for purchase)
Horizon (2 times a year, free)
Order printed publications from: Publications Office at the same address, tel: 020 7481 6900

Access to staff:
Contact by letter, by telephone, by fax, by e-mail and via website. Appointment necessary.
Hours: Mon to Fri, 0900 to 1700

CORPS OF COMMISSIONAIRES MANAGEMENT LIMITED

Acronym or abbreviation: The Corps

85 Cowcross Street, London, EC1M 6PF

Tel: 020 7566 0500
Fax: 020 7566 0522
E-mail: info@the-corps.co.uk

Website:
http://www.the-corps.co.uk

Enquiries:
Enquiries to: Executive Director
Other contacts: Sales and Marketing Director

Founded:
1859

Organisation type and purpose:
National organisation, present number of members: 3000, service industry.
Providers of security and facilities support services.
To help (former) members of HM's Uniformed Services find employment (worldwide).

Subject coverage:
Availability of employment using former military/ police skills.
Security – manned guarding, receptionists, patrols and key-holding, training.
Recruitment agency, international projects and consultancy.
Facilities support: mailrooms, file management, building administration and management, receptionists.

Museum or gallery collection, archive, or library special collection:
Uncatalogued collection, archive stored photographs of corps members (informal), may or may not be identifiable

Library catalogue:
All or part available in-house

Printed publications:
Directory of Services
L'Esprit (in-house staff magazine, free to staff, clients)
Our Sergeant (history of the Corps of Commissionaires, p.o.a.)

Electronic and video publications:
Corporate Video

Access to staff:
Contact by letter, by telephone and by fax.
Appointment necessary.
Hours: Mon to Fri, 0900 to 1700

Affiliations with:
Similar associations with the same name exist in Commonwealth countries – Canada and Australia

Branches at:
Corps of Commissionaires Management Limited
In 16 major UK towns, See local Yellow Pages; website: www.the-corps.co.uk

CORROSION PREVENTION ASSOCIATION

Acronym or abbreviation: CPA

Association House, 99 West Street, Farnham, Surrey, GU9 7EN

Tel: 01252 739141
Fax: 01252 739140
E-mail: cpa@associationhouse.org.uk

Website:
http://www.corrosionprevention.org.uk

Enquiries:
Enquiries to: Secretary

Founded:
1991

Formerly called:
Society for the Cathodic Protection of Re-Inforced Concrete (SCPRC) (year of change 1998)

Organisation type and purpose:
Trade association, present number of members: 22 and 8 associates.
Companies involved in the cathodic protection (including electrochemical remediation) of reinforced concrete.

Subject coverage:
Cathodic protection (including electrochemical remediation) of reinforced concrete, technology, basic principles, history and benefits.

Printed publications:
Brochure and Directory of Members (free)
Cathodic Protection of Reinforced Concrete – Status Report
Reinforced Concrete: History, Properties & Durability (monograph)
Monographs 1–7 (free and on the website)
No 8 Cathodic Protection of Steel in Concrete – Frequently Asked Questions

Publications list:
Available online and in print

Access to staff:
Contact by letter, by telephone, by fax, by e-mail and via website
Hours: Mon to Fri, 0900 to 1700

CORUS RESEARCH, DEVELOPMENT & TECHNOLOGY

Swinden Technology Centre, Library & Information Services, Moorgate, Rotherham, South Yorkshire, S60 3AR

Tel: 01709 820166
Fax: 01709 825464
E-mail: stc.library@corusgroup.com

Enquiries:
Enquiries to: Information Officer
Direct tel: 01709 825335
Direct e-mail: mike.nott@corusgroup.com

Formerly called:
British Steel plc (year of change 1999)

Organisation type and purpose:
Research organisation.

Subject coverage:
Iron and steel product applications, carbon, alloy and stainless steels, physical metallurgy, environmental sciences, welding, machinability, advanced machining, steel specifications, iron and steel roll technology, iron and steel plant.

Museum or gallery collection, archive, or library special collection:
Steel specifications and standards

Access to building, collection or gallery:
Prior appointment required

Access for disabled people:
Ramped entry

Other services:
Corus Construction Centre
Piling Advisory Service
  PO Box 1, Frodingham House, Scunthorpe, South Humberside, DN16 1BP; tel: 01724 404040
Plates Technical Advisory Centre
  PO Box 30, Motherwell, ML1 1AA; tel: 01698 266233
Stainless Steel Advisory Centre, not now part of British Steel, now Avesta
Strip Products Advisory Service
  PO Box 10, Newport, Gwent; tel: 01633 290011
Technical Hotline
  PO Box 1, Brigg Road, Scunthorpe, DN16 1BP; tel: 01724 405060
Tubes and Open Sections Structural Advisory Service
  PO Box 101, Weldon Road, Corby, Northamptonshire, NN17 1UA; tel: 01536 402121

COSMETIC, TOILETRY AND PERFUMERY ASSOCIATION LIMITED

Acronym or abbreviation: CTPA

Josaron House, 5–7 John Princes Street, London, W1G 0JN

Tel: 020 7491 8891
Fax: 020 7493 8061

Website:
http://www.ctpa.org.uk
General information about legislative controls for cosmetics, overview of CTPA and the cosmetic market. Useful contact points.

Enquiries:
Enquiries to: Company Secretary
Direct e-mail: info@ctpa.org.uk

Founded:
1945

Organisation type and purpose:
Trade association.

Subject coverage:
Cosmetic, toiletry and perfumery industry, legislation, technical information (no market information).

Information services:
Consumer Website – www.thefactsabout.co.uk

Education services:
Online Resource for Schools – www.catie.org.uk

Electronic and video publications:
The Cost of Microbes (video)

Publications list:
Available online

Access to staff:
Access for members only.
Hours: Mon to Fri, 0900 to 1700

Member organisation of:
European Association of Cosmetic Industries (COLIPA)
  Brussels

COSTUME AND TEXTILE STUDY CENTRE, CARROW HOUSE

301 King Street, Norwich, Norfolk, NR1 2TS

Tel: 01603 223870; text phone 0844 800 8011
E-mail: museums@norfolk.gov.uk

Website:
http;//www.museums.norfolk.gov.uk

Organisation type and purpose:
Study centre, with specialist facilities for students and enthusiasts.

Subject coverage:
Period costume, textiles and related material.

Access to building, collection or gallery:
In 2008 Carrow House was closed for essential building work. However, much of the Centre's collection was accessible by appointment at the Norwich Castle Study Centre

COSTUME SOCIETY OF SCOTLAND

Acronym or abbreviation: CSS

18 Grierson Crescent, Edinburgh, EH5

Tel: 0131 552 4968
E-mail: catrionasmyth@hotmail.com

Enquiries:
Enquiries to: Secretary
Direct tel: 0131 663 0967
Direct e-mail: tandd@muirpark.plus.com
Other contacts: Treasurer

Founded:
1965

Organisation type and purpose:
Membership association (membership is by subscription), present number of members: 90, suitable for ages: all.
To promote interest in all matters relating to costume and textiles.

Subject coverage:
Mourning jewellery, Scottish costume, including fisherfolks' dress. Textiles and embellishment, historical and contemporary.

Museum or gallery collection, archive, or library special collection:
Most members own some costume and books. As there are no central premises, everything is personal
Small library of books available to members

Library catalogue:
All or part available in-house

Printed publications:
Costume Society of Scotland Bulletin (A5 b/w plates, annually, £3 inc. p&p, free to members)
Mourning Jewellery – a Collector's Account (Margaret Hunter, A4, 22pp plus 3pp colour plates, £3 inc. p&p)
Order printed publications from: Treasurer, Costume Society of Scotland
28 Cameron Park, Newington, Edinburgh, EH16 5LA

Access to staff:
Contact by letter and by e-mail
Hours: Mon to Fri, 0900 to 1700

COTSWOLD DISTRICT COUNCIL

Acronym or abbreviation: CDC

Council Offices, Trinity Road, Cirencester, Gloucestershire, GL7 1PX

Tel: 01285 623000
Fax: 01285 623900

Website:
http://www.cotswold.gov.uk

Enquiries:
Enquiries to: Information Officer
Direct tel: 01285 623132
Direct e-mail: claire.mcgine@cotswold.gov.uk

Founded:
1974

Organisation type and purpose:
Local government body.

Subject coverage:
Local government, economic development, tourism, planning, housing, enabling, environmental health; conservation, landscape; arts, leisure, museums; benefits, elections, waste collection, recycling, landcharges.

Printed publications:
Cotswold News (2 times a year, free)

Access to staff:
Contact by letter, by telephone, by fax, by e-mail, in person and via website. Appointment necessary.
Hours: Mon to Fri, 0900 to 1700

Access to building, collection or gallery:
Prior appointment required

Access for disabled people:
Parking provided, ramped entry, level entry

Branch Office:
Cotswold District Council
  Moreton in Marsh, Gloucestershire; tel: 01608 650881; fax: 01608 651542

COTTAGE AND RURAL ENTERPRISES LIMITED

Acronym or abbreviation: CARE

CARE Central Office, 9 Weir Road, Kibworth, Leicestershire, LE8 0LQ

Tel: 0116 279 3225
Fax: 0116 279 6384
E-mail: jp@care-ltd.co.uk

Website:
http://www.care-ltd.co.uk
Services offered by CARE.

Enquiries:
Enquiries to: Chief Executive

Founded:
1966

Organisation type and purpose:
Voluntary organisation, registered charity (charity number 250058).
CARE is a national charity that responds creatively and innovatively to the changing needs of people with learning disabilities.

Subject coverage:
Care of adults with a learning disability in communities where they live and work.

Printed publications:
All About CARE
Principles and Policies (booklet)

Access to staff:
Contact by letter, by telephone, by fax, by e-mail and via website
Hours: Mon to Fri, 0900 to 1700

COUGAR CLUB OF AMERICA

Acronym or abbreviation: CCOA

International Office, 11 Dean Close, Partington, Manchester, M31 4BQ

Tel: 0161 775 0820
E-mail: international@cougarclub.org

Website:
http://www.cougarclub.org

Enquiries:
Enquiries to: International Manager

Founded:
1980

Organisation type and purpose:
International organisation, membership association (membership is by subscription), present number of members: 1000.

continued overleaf

Subject coverage:
Information regarding 1967 to present, Mercury Cougars i.e. options, identifications, parts availability, parts suppliers. All this information is free to members.

Printed publications:
At The Sign of the Cat (newsletter, quarterly, free to members)

Access to staff:
Contact by letter, by telephone and by e-mail
Hours: Mon to Sat, 1000 to 1900

Parent body:
Cougar Club of America
e-mail: membership@cougarclub.org

COUNCIL FOR ADVANCEMENT AND SUPPORT OF EDUCATION (EUROPE)

Acronym or abbreviation: CASE

Entrance A, Tavistock House North, Tavistock Square, London, WC1H 9HX

Tel: 020 7387 4404
Fax: 020 7387 4408
E-mail: info@eurocase.org.uk

Website:
http://www.case.org
Full information about the organisation and its activities and services.

Enquiries:
Enquiries to: Executive Director
Direct e-mail: jmotion@eurocase.org.uk

Founded:
1994

Organisation type and purpose:
International organisation, registered charity (charity number 1042724), training organisation, consultancy, research organisation, publishing house.
Dissemination of Best Practice in the advancement of education.

Subject coverage:
Educational external relations, in particular alumni relations, communications, fund raising, marketing, philanthropy, public relations, student recruitment.

Printed publications:
A large range of publications on the subject of the Council
CASE CURRENTS (10 times a year, for members)
CASE Directory of Advancement Professionals in Education

Electronic and video publications:
Audio and video cassettes on aspects of institutional advancement

Publications list:
Available in print

Access to staff:
Contact by letter, by telephone, by fax and by e-mail. Access for members only. Non-members charged.
Hours: Mon to Fri, 0900 to 1700

Connections with:
CASE
Suite 400, 11 Dupont Circle, Washington, DC, 20036–1261, USA

COUNCIL FOR ALUMINIUM IN BUILDING

Acronym or abbreviation: CAB

Bank House, Bond's Mill, Stonehouse, Gloucestershire, GL10 3RF

Tel: 01453 828851
Fax: 01453 828861
E-mail: enquiries@c-a-b.org.uk

Website:
http://www.c-a-b.org.uk

Enquiries:
Enquiries to: Chief Executive
Direct tel: 01453 828856

Founded:
1995

Incorporates the former:
Aluminium Window Association (AWA), Architectural Aluminium Association (AAA), Patent Glazing Contractors' Association (PGCA) (year of change 1995)

Organisation type and purpose:
Trade association.

Subject coverage:
Aluminium in building, patent glazing, curtain wall, aluminium windows, doors, cladding and roofing in aluminium, aluminium powder coatings, anodising, hardware, systems suppliers.

Printed publications:
Curtain Walling and Large Composite Windows, notes for guidance
Guide to Specification of Windows and Doors
Guide to the Specification of Patent Glazing Products and Services Guide
Specifying Window Performance BSI/DIN Comparison
Thermal Assessment Guide to Windows and Curtain Wall Structures

Publications list:
Available online

Access to staff:
Contact by letter, by telephone, by fax and by e-mail
Hours: Mon to Fri, 0900 to 1700

Member organisation of:
Centre for Window and Cladding Technology (CWCT)
Construction Products Association

COUNCIL FOR AWARDS IN CHILDREN'S CARE AND EDUCATION

Acronym or abbreviation: CACHE

8 Chequer Street, St Albans, Hertfordshire, AL1 3XZ

Tel: 01727 847636
Fax: 01727 867609
E-mail: info@cache.org.uk

Website:
http://www.cache.org.uk

Enquiries:
Enquiries to: Chief Executive
Other contacts: Information and Publications Officer, Marketing Officer

Founded:
1994

Formed by the merger of:
Council for Early Years Awards (CEYA), National Nursery Examination Board (NNEB), date of change, April 1994; National Association for Maternal and Child Welfare (NAMCW) (year of change 2000)

Organisation type and purpose:
Registered charity (charity number 1036232). Awarding body.
Offers courses and NVQ assessment in childcare, education and playwork.

Subject coverage:
Vocational training in child care, education and playwork; NVQs; early years workers, A&V units for assessors and verifiers.

Museum or gallery collection, archive, or library special collection:
Archive material regarding the history of the NNEB and CEYA, and the development of their awards and courses in child care and education
Pass lists of candidates who have successfully completed course and awards

Trade and statistical information:
Numbers of candidates registered as training with the Council.
Post-qualifying employment and progression.
Equal opportunities monitoring.
Numbers of study centres approved to run Council awards and which particular courses they offer.
Numbers of candidates registered for NVQ assessment.
Number of NVQ Assessment Centres approved by CACHE to offer NVQ assessment and the awards they offer.

Printed publications:
Publications on child care, education and playwork, including titles for NVQs and other awards

Electronic and video publications:
Current candidate handbooks may be downloaded from the website for planning purposes

Publications list:
Available online and in print

Access to staff:
Contact by letter, by telephone, by fax, by e-mail and via website. Appointment necessary.
Hours: Mon to Fri, 0900 to 1700

COUNCIL FOR BRITISH ARCHAEOLOGY

Acronym or abbreviation: CBA

St Mary's House, 66 Bootham, York YO30 7BZ

Tel: 01904 671417
Fax: 01904 671384
E-mail: info@britarch.ac.uk

Website:
http://www.britarch.ac.uk
Electronic information service for British archaeology, including text from British Archaeology, online database.

Enquiries:
Enquiries to: Information Officer

Founded:
1944

Organisation type and purpose:
Membership association (membership is by subscription), present number of members: 500 institutions, 10,000 individuals, voluntary organisation, registered charity (charity number 210852), research organisation, publishing house. Federation of societies, museums, universities, archaeological units and trusts.
To promote the study of Britain's historic environment, provide a forum for archaeological opinion and improve public knowledge of Britain's past.

Subject coverage:
Information on all aspects of Britain's historic environment (organisation, research in progress, conservation, legislation, management); specialises in countryside and urban archaeology, archaeology of buildings, archaeological science, nautical archaeology, archaeology in education, calendar of events and excavations.

Printed publications:
A wide variety of publications available for purchase including:
British and Irish Archaeological Bibliography (references and abstracts, 2 times a year)
British Archaeology (6 times a year)
Occasional publications including Research Reports, Practical Handbooks and publications for use in schools
Practical Handbook Series: a series of short, practical guides for both professional and independent archaeologists, historians, architects, and anyone interested in the past
The Archaeology of York (12 volumes)
Young Archaeologist (4 times a year)

Microform publications:
British and Irish Archaeological Bibliography

Publications list:
Available online and in print

Access to staff:
Contact by letter, by telephone, by fax, by e-mail, in person and via website. Appointment necessary.
Hours: Mon to Fri, 0900 to 1700

Subsidiary body for 9 to 16 year olds:
Young Archaeologists' Club

COUNCIL FOR DANCE EDUCATION AND TRAINING (UK)

Acronym or abbreviation: CDET

Old Brewer's Yard, 17–19 Neal Street, Covent Garden, London, WC2H 9UY

Tel: 020 7240 5703
Fax: 020 7240 2547
E-mail: info@cdet.org.uk

Website:
http://www.cdet.org.uk
Information on dance education and training.

Enquiries:
Enquiries to: Administrator

Founded:
1979

Organisation type and purpose:
Professional body, registered charity (charity number 277729).
Professional and representative body for dance education and training matters.

Subject coverage:
Vocational dance training, including accredited courses, sources of funding and grants, careers advice.

Museum or gallery collection, archive, or library special collection:
The first comprehensive source of information in dance training

Printed publications:
The UK Handbook of Accredited Courses in Dance and Musical Theatre
Dance Information Sheets
Code of Professional Conduct and Practice for Teachers of Dance

Access to staff:
Contact by letter, by fax and by e-mail
Hours: Mon to Fri, 0930 to 1700
Special comments: Appointment necessary.

Member of:
CDET
Conference of Professional Dance Schools

COUNCIL FOR ENVIRONMENTAL EDUCATION

Acronym or abbreviation: CEE

94 London Street, Reading, Berkshire, RG1 4SJ

Tel: 0118 950 2550
Fax: 0118 959 1955
E-mail: enquiries@cee.org.uk

Website:
http://www.cee.org.uk/
Provides a gateway to education for sustainable development in England. Includes details of the work of CEE's member organisations, resources, news and developments.

Enquiries:
Enquiries to: Information Officer

Founded:
1968

Organisation type and purpose:
CEE is an educational charity and an umbrella body for national organisations committed to environmental education and education for sustainable development in England. Founded in 1968, current membership includes 73 national organisations and 153 associates. It works to influence policy and practice and to increase the effectiveness of the environmental education movement.

Subject coverage:
Environmental Education and Education for Sustainable Development, education policy, practice and development. Promotes other organisations' courses and events on environmental and sustainable development education.

Museum or gallery collection, archive, or library special collection:
National Collection of Environmental and Sustainable Development Education Policy and Teaching Resources

Library catalogue:
All or part available in-house

Printed publications:
Annual Report (free)
CEE mail (termly – new resources, websites, events, competitions and awards for teachers and subscribers)
CEEview (quarterly – national and international activity, policy and strategy for subscribers)
Earthlines (3 times a year – information on policy, events, funding, resources and training for youth workers and subscribers)

Publications list:
Available in print

Access to staff:
Contact by letter, by telephone, by fax, by e-mail and via website. Appointment necessary.
Hours: Mon to Fri, 0900 to 1700

Affiliated to:
Department for Environment Food and Rural Affairs (DEFRA), Department for Education and Skills (DfES), Development Education Association (DEA), Heritage Lottery Fund (HLF), National Grid for Learning (NGfL)
NCVO

Council comprises:
84 member organisations

COUNCIL FOR MOSQUES

Formal name: Bradford Council for Mosques

6 Claremont, Bradford, West Yorkshire, BD7 1BQ

Tel: 01274 732479

Enquiries:
Enquiries to: Press Officer
Direct e-mail: i.ahmed@pacalis.co.uk

Founded:
1985

Organisation type and purpose:
Voluntary organisation.

Access to staff:
Contact by letter, by telephone, by e-mail and in person. Appointment necessary.
Hours: Mon to Fri, 0930 to 1900

Access for disabled people:
Ramped entry, toilet facilities

COUNCIL FOR MUSIC IN HOSPITALS, THE

Acronym or abbreviation: MiH

74 Queens Road, Hersham, Walton on Thames, Surrey, KT12 5LW

Tel: 01932 252809
Fax: 01932 252966
E-mail: info@music-in-hospitals.org.uk

Website:
http://www.music-in-hospitals.org.uk

Enquiries:
Enquiries to: Chief Executive

Founded:
1948

Organisation type and purpose:
Registered charity (charity number 1051659).

Subject coverage:
Provides live concerts (over 4000 in 2000) in hospitals, hospices, nursing homes, day centres throughout the United Kingdom. These are given by carefully selected professional musicians who are chosen not only for their high standard of musicianship but also for their ability to relate to the most confused, apathetic or ill and to involve them in the performance.

Printed publications:
Annual Report

Access to staff:
Contact by letter, by telephone, by fax and by e-mail
Hours: Mon to Fri, 0830 to 1600

Other addresses:
Scottish Branch
  10 Forth Street, Edinburgh, EH1 3LD; tel: 0131 556 5848; fax: 0131 556 0225
Welsh Office
  25 Ystrad Drive, Johnstown, Carmarthen, SA31 3PG; tel: 01267 242981; fax: 0167 242981

COUNCIL FOR REGISTERED GAS INSTALLERS, THE

Acronym or abbreviation: CORGI

1 Elmwood, Chineham Park, Crockford Lane, Basingstoke, Hampshire, RG24 8WG

Tel: 01256 372200 or 372300
Fax: 01256 708144
E-mail: enquiries@corgi-gas.co.uk

Website:
http://www.corgi-gas.com
Gas safety information, information about CORGI and its role as National Watchdog for gas safety.

Enquiries:
Enquiries to: Press Officer
Direct tel: 01256 372254
Direct e-mail: publications@corgi-gas.co.uk
Other contacts: Public Relations Manager

Founded:
1991

Formerly called:
Confederation of Registered Gas Installers (CORGI) (year of change 1991)

Organisation type and purpose:
Statutory body, present number of members: 45,000 registered installers.
National watchdog for gas safety. Registration Body.
Inspection of registered businesses, customer complaints regarding gas safety, gas safety publicity, development of nationally accredited certification scheme for individual gas fitting operatives.

Subject coverage:
The national watchdog for gas safety , providing gas safety advice for consumers, technical advice for registered installers, details of registered installers to the public.

Printed publications:
Annual Report (free)
Gas Installer Manual Domestic Series (available to purchase)
The Gas Installer Magazine (10 times a year, free to registered installers)
Order printed publications from: CORGI
Station Approach, Blackwater, Camberley, Surrey, GU17 9PD

Publications list:
Available online and in print

Access to staff:
Contact by letter, by telephone, by fax and by e-mail

continued overleaf

Hours: Mon to Thu, 0900 to 1730; Fri, 0900 to 1700

Access for disabled people:
Parking provided, ramped entry, access to all public areas, toilet facilities

COUNCIL FOR THE ADVANCEMENT OF ARAB-BRITISH UNDERSTANDING

Acronym or abbreviation: CAABU

21 Collingham Road, London, SW5 0NU

Tel: 020 7373 8414
Fax: 020 7835 2088
E-mail: caabu@caabu.org

Enquiries:
Enquiries to: Information Officer

Founded:
1967

Organisation type and purpose:
International organisation, membership association (membership is by subscription), present number of members: 900, research organisation.
Lobby, education, non-governmental. To promote understanding between peoples of Arab countries and Britain.

Subject coverage:
The Arab World, Palestine, Iraq.

Museum or gallery collection, archive, or library special collection:
Comprehensive information about all Arab countries

Trade and statistical information:
Newspaper clippings on the Middle East, information service, speakers for schools.

Printed publications:
Regular briefing papers produced on topical issues
Schools information pack (£8 including p&p)

Publications list:
Available online and in print

Access to staff:
Contact by letter, by telephone, by fax and by e-mail. Appointment necessary.
Hours: Mon to Thu, 0930 to 1730; Fri, 0930 to 1630

Access to building, collection or gallery:
Prior appointment required
Hours: Mon to Fri, 0930 to 1730

Chairs the:
European Co-ordinating Committee of Non-governmental Organisations (ECCP) on the question of Palestine

COUNCIL FOR THE HOMELESS (NI)

Acronym or abbreviation: CHNI

153 University Street, Belfast, BT7 1HR

Tel: 028 9024 6440
Fax: 028 9024 1266
E-mail: info@chni.org.uk

Website:
http://www.chni.org.uk

Enquiries:
Enquiries to: Information Officer
Other contacts: Director, Administrator

Founded:
1983

Formerly called:
Northern Ireland Council for Single Homeless

Organisation type and purpose:
Voluntary organisation, registered charity (charity number XO 544/83), training organisation.

Subject coverage:
Homelessness, housing benefits, children, finance, health, poverty, legislation, Northern Ireland housing executive, organisations and organisational development, individuals' rights, special needs, temporary accommodation, types of housing, women, young people.

Museum or gallery collection, archive, or library special collection:
Housing and Homelessness Journals
Social policy journals
Video library

Printed publications:
Accommodation, Advice and Assistance, Posters
Annual Report
Briefing papers (6 times a year)
Home-In (quarterly)
Charter for People Who are Homeless
Don't Look Away: Mental Health and Homelessness in Belfast
Rights & Responsibilities: Guidelines on the Use of Leases and Licences in Special Needs Accommodation
Room to live: Homelessness and mental health in Londonderry
Young & Homeless? Posters
The Whole Shebang (quarterly)

Access to staff:
Contact by letter, by telephone, by fax, by e-mail and in person
Hours: Mon to Fri, 0900 to 1700

Access for disabled people:
Toilet facilities

Parent body:
European Federation of National Organisations Working with the Homeless (FEANTSA)
1 Rue Defacqz, Brussels, B-1050, Belgium; tel: + 32 2 538 6669; fax: + 32 2 539 4174

COUNCIL FOR VOLUNTARY SERVICE – SOUTH LAKELAND

Acronym or abbreviation: SLCVS

Stricklandgate House, 92 Stricklandgate, Kendal, Cumbria, LA9 4PU

Tel: 01539 742627
Fax: 01539 742628
E-mail: info@slcvs.org

Enquiries:
Enquiries to: Information Officer

Organisation type and purpose:
Advisory body, membership association (membership is by election or invitation), voluntary organisation, registered charity (charity number 503635), training organisation.
Concerning voluntary organisation in South Lakeland.

Subject coverage:
Advice on voluntary organisations in South Lakeland. Advice on fundraising, recruitment, training and management of voluntary organisations. Advice on charity law. Liaison with health and social care providers.

Museum or gallery collection, archive, or library special collection:
Includes the Roger Wilson Library – all on computerised database

Printed publications:
Newsletter (monthly, to affiliated organisations)

Access to staff:
Contact by letter, by telephone, by fax, by e-mail and in person. Appointment necessary.
Hours: Mon to Fri, 0930 to 1630
Special comments: Wheelchair access to all areas.

COUNCIL FOR WORLD MISSION

Acronym or abbreviation: CWM

32–34 Great Peter Street, London, SW1P 2DB

Tel: 020 7222 4214
Fax: 020 7233 1747
E-mail: council@cwmission.org

Website:
http://www.cwmission.org

Enquiries:
Enquiries to: Communications Officer
Direct tel: 020 7227 2505
Direct fax: 020 7222 3510
Direct e-mail: kenwyn.pierce@cwmission.org

Founded:
1795

Formerly called:
London Missionary Society (year of change 1977)

Organisation type and purpose:
International organisation, registered charity.
Ecumenical organisation.
World mission (Reformed Churches and United Churches).

Subject coverage:
Christian world mission.

Museum or gallery collection, archive, or library special collection:
Archives of the former London Missionary Society

Printed publications:
Inside Out (magazine)

Publications list:
Available in print

Access to staff:
Contact by letter, by fax, by e-mail and via website. Appointment necessary.
Hours: Mon to Fri, 0900 to 1700

COUNCIL OF DISABLED PEOPLE

Formal name: Council of Disabled People – Warwickshire and Coventry
Acronym or abbreviation: CDP

Independent Options, Hillmorton Road, Rugby, Warwickshire, CV22 5AB

Tel: 01926 413334
Fax: 01926 413334

Enquiries:
Enquiries to: Director

Organisation type and purpose:
Membership association (membership is by subscription), present number of members: 150, registered charity (charity number 1028144).
Meeting the needs of disabled people.

Subject coverage:
Benefit information, resource teams.

Publications list:
Available in print

Access to staff:
Contact by letter
Hours: Mon to Fri, 0900 to 1700

Access to building, collection or gallery:
Prior appointment required

Access for disabled people:
Parking provided, level entry, access to all public areas, toilet facilities

Other addresses:
The Council of Disabled People – Warwickshire and Coventry
Fordsfield Centre, Bury Road, Leamington Spa, CV31 3HW

COUNCIL OF MORTGAGE LENDERS

Acronym or abbreviation: CML

3 Savile Row, London, W1S 3PB

Tel: 020 7437 0075
Fax: 020 7434 3791
E-mail: info@cml.org.uk

Website:
http://www.cml.org.uk

Enquiries:
Enquiries to: Information Officer

Founded:
1989

Organisation type and purpose:
Trade association.

Subject coverage:
Mortgage lending; housing market; financial services.

Printed publications:
Research Reports (occasional)

Electronic and video publications:
All publications available electronically
CML News and Views (fortnightly, electronic only)
Housing Finance (occasional, electronic only)

Publications list:
Available online and in print

Access to staff:
Contact by letter, by fax, by e-mail and via website
Hours: Mon to Fri, 0900 to 1630

Access to building, collection or gallery:
No access other than to staff

COUNCIL OF NATIONAL GOLF UNIONS

Acronym or abbreviation: CONGU

Dromin, Dunleer, Co Louth, Republic of Ireland

Tel: +353 41 686 1476
E-mail: golfinmcinere@hotmail.com

Website:
http://www.congu.com

Enquiries:
Enquiries to: Honorary Secretary

Founded:
1924

Formerly called:
British Golf Unions Joint Advisory Committee (year of change 1960)

Organisation type and purpose:
Membership association.

Subject coverage:
Golf handicaps.

Access to staff:
Contact by telephone and by e-mail
Hours: Mon to Fri, 0900 to 1700

Links with:
English Golf Union
Golfing Union of Ireland
Royal and Ancient Golf Club of St. Andrews
Scottish Golf Union
Welsh Golfing Union

COUNCIL OF SIKH GURDWARAS IN BIRMINGHAM

Acronym or abbreviation: CSGB

627 Stratford Road, Sparkhill, Birmingham, B11 4LS

Tel: 0121 773 0399
Fax: 0121 773 0699

Enquiries:
Enquiries to: General Secretary
Direct e-mail: csgb@sikh-council.demon.co.uk

Founded:
1989

Organisation type and purpose:
Membership association (membership is by election or invitation), present number of members: 13 organisations, voluntary organisation.
Consultancy on Sikh issues.

To serve and provide a collective voice for Birmingham Sikh community.

Access to staff:
Contact by letter, by telephone, by fax and by e-mail. Appointment necessary.
Hours: Mon to Fri, 1000 to 1800
Special comments: No alcohol, drugs, tobacco.

COUNCIL ON INTERNATIONAL EDUCATIONAL EXCHANGE

Acronym or abbreviation: CIEE

52 Poland Street, London, W1F 7AB

Tel: 020 7478 2020
Fax: 020 7734 7322
E-mail: info@ciee.org

Website:
http://www.councilexchanges.org.uk
Information regarding programmes, electronic publication of Update, a bi-monthly journal produced by CIEE in New York regarding international education activities. Special features include jobsearch database for finding summer jobs/internships in the USA.

Enquiries:
Enquiries to: Administrator
Direct e-mail: contact@ciee.org
Other contacts: Programme Co-ordinator for specific programme enquiries.

Founded:
1947

Formerly called:
Council Exchanges (year of change 1999)

Organisation type and purpose:
International organisation, registered charity (charity number 293969).
To arrange international educational exchanges.

Subject coverage:
Work abroad and study abroad opportunities for students and recent graduates: work abroad in USA, Canada, Australia, China and Japan; studies abroad in the USA, France, Spain, Italy and Germany.

Printed publications:
Annual Report
General Brochure
Work Abroad and Study Abroad Programme, information, brochures, application forms

Access to staff:
Contact by letter, by telephone, by fax, by e-mail and via website. Appointment necessary.
Hours: Mon to Fri, 0930 to 1730

Founder member of the:
Year Out Group

Offices in many cities worldwide including:
New York, Paris, Tokyo, Rome, Berlin and Madrid

COUNSEL AND CARE

Formal name: Counsel and Care for the Elderly

Twyman House, 16 Bonny Street, London, NW1 9PG

Tel: 020 7241 8555
Fax: 020 7267 6877
E-mail: advice@counselandcare.org.uk

Website:
http://www.counselandcare.org.uk
Information on Advice Service, training and research projects. Factsheets to download and publications list.

Enquiries:
Enquiries to: Advicework Department
Direct tel: 0845 300 7585

Founded:
1954

Formerly called:
Elderly Invalids Fund

Organisation type and purpose:
National organisation, membership association (membership is by subscription), voluntary organisation, registered charity (charity number 203429).
To provide practical help and advice to people over 60, their families and carers.

Subject coverage:
Advice for older people on welfare benefits, community care, hospital discharge, going into care and help at home. One-off grants for older people.

Printed publications:
Guides and Factsheets (39 titles, updated annually, free to individuals, but charge to organisations for full set, sae requested)
Not Only Bingo
New Appetite for Life
Your care home – is it up to standard?

Publications list:
Available online and in print

Access to staff:
Contact by letter, by telephone, by fax, by e-mail and via website. Appointment necessary.
Hours: Mon, Tue, Thu, Fri, 1000 to 1600; Wed, 1000 to 1300

Access for disabled people:
Level entry, toilet facilities

COUNTERFEITING INTELLIGENCE BUREAU

Formal name: The International Chamber of Commerce – Commercial Crime Services (CCS)
Acronym or abbreviation: CIB

Cinnabar Wharf, 26 Wapping High Street, London, E1W 1NG

Tel: 020 7423 6960
Fax: 020 7423 6961
E-mail: ccs@icc-ccs.org

Website:
http://www.icc-ccs.org/cib/overview.php

Enquiries:
Enquiries to: Director

Founded:
1985

Organisation type and purpose:
International organisation, membership association (membership is by subscription), consultancy, research organisation.

Subject coverage:
Intellectual property rights, trademarks, counterfeiting, infringements, proactive monitoring, reactive intelligence and investigations, anti-counterfeiting technology assistance.

Museum or gallery collection, archive, or library special collection:
Special reports on counterfeiting

Printed publications:
Commercial Crime International (monthly)
Confidential Bulletin (monthly to members only)
Annual Piracy Report (£15 plus p&p)
Countering Counterfeiting (guide, £50 plus p&p)
Special Reports including:
Industrial Property Protection in East Asia
China Trade – The Risk Factor

Access to staff:
Contact by letter, by telephone, by fax, by e-mail and via website. Appointment necessary.
Hours: Mon to Fri, 0900 to 1700

Access for disabled people:
Ramped entry

Specialised division of:
International Chamber of Commerce

COUNTRY LAND & BUSINESS ASSOCIATION

Acronym or abbreviation: CLA

16 Belgrave Square, London, SW1X 8PQ

Tel: 020 7235 0511
Fax: 020 7235 0528

Website:
http://www.cla.org.uk
Background information and material on Country Landowners Association policies. Contact details for head office and regional offices.

Enquiries:
Enquiries to: Public Relations Manager
Direct e-mail: richardb@cla.org.uk
Other contacts: Finance and Administration Secretary

Founded:
1907

Formerly called:
Country Landowners Association (CLA) (year of change 2000)

Organisation type and purpose:
Membership association (membership is by subscription).
Owners of rural land in England and Wales. 43 branches in England and Wales.

Subject coverage:
Legal, tax and economic aspects of rural landowning; land use, conservation, water and minerals interests.

Printed publications:
Advisory Handbooks (36 titles to date, on sale)
Country Landowner (monthly, for members)
Model forms for agreements and tenancy

Publications list:
Available in print

Access to staff:
Contact by letter. Access for members only.
Hours: Mon to Fri, 0900 to 1700

Connections with:
CBI
Confederation of European Agriculture
European Landowners Organisation
FACE
FWAG
Rural
Rural Voice
Standing Conference on Countryside Sports

Regional Office:
CLA, North West Region
Dalton Hall, Stable Yard, Burton, Carnforth, Lancashire, LA6 1NJ; tel: 01524 782209; fax: 01524 782248

COUNTRYSIDE AGENCY

John Dower House, Crescent Place, Cheltenham, Gloucestershire, GL50 3RA

Tel: 01242 521381
Fax: 01242 584270

Website:
http://www.countryside.gov.uk
About the Countryside Agency and its work. Publications list.

Enquiries:
Enquiries to: Librarian

Founded:
1999

Formed by the merger of:
Rural Industries Bureau (RIB) (year of change 1921–1968); National Parks Commission (NPC) (year of change 1949–1968); Council for Small Industries in Rural Areas (CoSIRA) (year of change 1968); Development Commission of CoSIRA (year of change 1968–1988); Countryside Commission (year of change 1968–1999); Rural Development Commission (RDC) (year of change 1988–1999)

Formerly called:
Development Commission (DC) (year of change 1909–1921)

Organisation type and purpose:
Statutory body.
The 1968 Countryside Act widened its remit to become the Countryside Commission as part of the Department of the Environment; the 1981 Wildlife and Countryside Act gave the Countryside Commission independent status as an independent grant-in-aid corporate body. The Environmental Protection Act 1990 removed the Commission's responsibilities for Wales. From 1st April 1991 these were incorporated in the newly formed Countryside Council for Wales and the Countryside Commission became responsible for England only. In April 1999, the Countryside Commission merged with the Rural Development Commission to become the Countryside Agency responsible for advising government and taking action on issues relating to the social, economic and environmental well-being of the English countryside.
To conserve and enhance England's countryside; to spread social and economic opportunity for people who live there; to help everyone, wherever they live and whatever their background, to enjoy the countryside and share in this priceless asset.
The Countryside Agency works to achieve the aims by: influencing those whose decisions affect the countryside through their expertise and research and by spreading good practice; implementing specific work programmes reflecting priorities set by Parliament, the Government and the Agency Board.

Subject coverage:
Bulk of stock is from the Countryside Commission Library and covers: conservation and enhancement of landscape beauty; provision and improvement of facilities for countryside recreation, access and rights of way, particularly national trails; planning and management of the countryside, specifically national parks, areas of outstanding natural beauty, heritage coasts. Subject coverage is being broadened to include the rural economy and rural communities.

Library catalogue:
All or part available in-house

Printed publications:
A large selection of books, leaflets, posters, reports, research documents and educational material with a reference to all aspects of the countryside, including:
Countryside Focus – Countryside Agency's Newspaper (6 times a year, free)
Eat the view: Promoting sustainable, local produce (2000, free)
Great ways to go – good practice in rural transport (2001, free)
Labour market detachment in rural England (1999)
National Trail Guides, official guide books
Not seen, not heard? Social exclusion in rural areas (2000, free)
Out in the country: where you can go and what you can do (2000 revised, free)
Rural services and social housing 1999–2000 (2001)
Towards tomorrow's countryside: A strategy for the Countryside Agency (2001, free)
Understanding the countryside: The state of the countryside 2001 (national report, free)
Order printed publications from: Countryside Agency Postal Sales (Ref: CA2)
PO Box 124, Walgrave, Northampton, NN6 0TL, tel: 01604 781848, fax: 01604 781714

Electronic and video publications:
The Character of England (CD-ROM)

Publications list:
Available online and in print

Access to staff:
Contact by letter and by telephone
Hours: Mon to Fri, 0900 to 1700
Special comments: The library closes at 1630 on Fridays.

Access to building, collection or gallery:
No access other than to staff
Special comments: Currently in temporary accommodation with no access for visitors.

Affiliated to:
Council of Europe
Federation of Nature and National Parks of Europe
International Union for the Conservation of Nature and Natural Resources (IUCNNR)

Funded by:
Department for Environment, Food and Rural Affairs

Other addresses:
Also some national functions
Dacre House, 19 Dacre Street, London, SW1H 0DH; tel: 020 7340 2900; fax: 020 7340 2911
East Midlands
18 Market Place, Bingham, Nottingham, NG13 8AP; tel: 01949 876200; fax: 01949 876222
East of England
Ortona House, 110 Hills Road, Cambridge, CB2 1LQ; tel: 01223 354462; fax: 01223 313850
North East
Cross House, Westgate Road, Newcastle upon Tyne, NE1 4XX; tel: 0191 269 1600; fax: 0191 269 1601
North West
Haweswater Road, Penrith, CA11 7EH; tel: 01768 865752; fax: 01768 890414
North West
7th Floor, Bridgewater House, Whitworth Street, Manchester, M1 6LT; tel: 0161 237 1061; fax: 0161 237 1062
South East & London
Sterling House, 7 Ashford Road, Maidstone, ME14 5BJ; tel: 01622 765222; fax: 01622 662102
South West
2nd Floor, 11–15 Dix's Field, Exeter, EX1 1QA; tel: 01392 477150; fax: 01392 477151
South West
Bridge House, Sion Place, Clifton Down, Bristol, BS8 4AS; tel: 0117 973 9966; fax: 0117 923 8086
West Midlands
Strickland House, The Lawns, Park Street, Wellington, Telford, TF1 3BX; tel: 01952 247161; fax: 01952 248700
West Midlands and Doorstep Greens National Project Team
1st Floor, Vincent House, Tindal Bridge, 92–93 Edward Street, Birmingham, B1 2RA; tel: 0121 233 9399; fax: 0121 233 9286
Yorkshire & The Humber
4th Floor, Victoria Wharf, No 4 The Embankment, Sovereign Street, Leeds, LS1 4BA; tel: 0113 246 9222; fax: 0113 246 0353

COUNTRYSIDE ALLIANCE

367 Kennington Road, London, SE11 4PT

Tel: 020 7840 9200
Fax: 020 7793 8484
E-mail: info@countryside-alliance.org

Website:
http://www.countryside-alliance.org
Wide variety of information relating to countryside issues.

Enquiries:
Enquiries to: Information Officer
Other contacts: Membership for membership queries.

Founded:
1930

Formed from:
British Field Sports Society (BFSS), Countryside Movement; Countryside Business Group (year of change 1997)

Organisation type and purpose:
Advisory body, membership association (membership is by subscription), present number of members: 85,000, suitable for ages: 10 to 18.
To champion the countryside, country sports and the rural way of life.

Subject coverage:
Rural issues – rural livelihood, businesses, lifestyles and country sports. Land management, access to the countryside and conservation.

Trade and statistical information:
Economic facts relating to country sports and countryside in general.

Printed publications:
Country Sports (magazine, quarterly)

Access to staff:
Contact by letter, by telephone, by fax, by e-mail and via website
Hours: Mon to Fri, 0900 to 1700

Regional Offices:
Countryside Alliance

COUNTRYSIDE COUNCIL FOR WALES

Acronym or abbreviation: CCW

Maes y Ffynnon, Penrhosgarnedd, Bangor, Gwynedd, LL57 2DW

Tel: 01248 385500
Fax: 01248 355782
E-mail: enquiries@ccw.gov.uk

Website:
http://www.ccw.gov.uk

Enquiries:
Enquiries to: Librarian
Other contacts: Public Relations Officer for press.

Formerly called:
Countryside Commission Wales, Nature Conservancy Council (year of change 1991)

Organisation type and purpose:
National government body.
Statutory body funded by a grant from the Welsh Assembly Government.
The Countryside Council for Wales is the government's statutory adviser on wildlife, countryside and maritime conservation matters in Wales.

Subject coverage:
Wildlife, countryside and maritime conservation matters, conservation of plants, mammals, reptiles and amphibians, promotes protection of landscape, opportunities for recreation, planning and management of the countryside.

Printed publications:
Annual Report
National Nature Reserve leaflets
Policy documents
Publications on protected areas in Wales, designated areas, special projects, species projects and habitats series (all bilingual and free of charge)

Publications list:
Available online and in print

Access to staff:
Contact by letter, by telephone, by fax, by e-mail and via website. Appointment necessary.
Hours: Mon to Fri, 0900 to 1700

Access for disabled people:
Parking provided, ramped entry, toilet facilities

Branches:
North Area Office, Countryside Council for Wales
Llys y Bont, Ffordd y Parc, Parc Menai, Bangor, Gwynedd, LL57 4BN; tel: 01248 672500; fax: 01248 679259; e-mail: s.williams@ccw.gov.uk
South and East Area Office, Countryside Council for Wales
Unit 7, Castleton Court, Fortran Road, St Mellons, Cardiff, CF3 0LT; tel: 02920 772400; fax: 02920 772412; e-mail: s.annmorgan@ccw.gov.uk
West Area Office, Countryside Council for Wales
Plas Gogerddan, Aberystwyth, Ceredigion, SY23 3EE; tel: 01970 821100; fax: 01970 828314; e-mail: i.frost@ccw.gov.uk

COUNTRYWIDE HOLIDAYS

Acronym or abbreviation: COUNTRYWIDE

Miry Lane, Wigan, Lancashire, WN3 4AG

Tel: 01942 823456
Fax: 01942 242518
E-mail: countrywidewalking@shearingsholidays.co.uk

Website:
http://www.countrywidewalking.com
Brochure reproduced.

Enquiries:
Enquiries to: Manager
Direct tel: 01942 823529
Direct fax: 01942 825034
Other contacts: (1) Marketing Manager (2) Product Manager for (1) advertising and promotion (2) new products and contracting.

Founded:
1893

Formerly called:
CHA (year of change 1992)

Organisation type and purpose:
Membership association (membership is by subscription).
Holiday company and guest house accommodation provider.

Subject coverage:
Countrywide Holidays specialises in walking and special interest holidays, including bridge, dancing, painting, photography and countryside appreciation. Holidays are offered throughout the UK to individuals, special arrangements are available for groups.

Museum or gallery collection, archive, or library special collection:
Guest House collection brochure
Historical information
Holiday brochures
Newsletters
Transparencies available for loan to journalists for promotion purposes

Printed publications:
Seasonal holiday brochures
Transparencies available for loan to journalists for promotion purposes

Access to staff:
Contact by letter, by telephone, by fax, by e-mail and via website
Hours: Mon to Sat, 0900 to 1700

COUNTY OF HEREFORDSHIRE DISTRICT COUNCIL

Acronym or abbreviation: Herefordshire Council

Brockington, 35 Hafod Road, Hereford, HR1 1SH

Tel: 01432 260000
Fax: 01432 260384

Website:
http://www.herefordshire.gov.uk

Enquiries:
Enquiries to: Chief Executive
Direct tel: 01432 260044
Direct fax: 01432 340189
Direct e-mail: npringle@herefordshire.gov.uk

Founded:
1998

Organisation type and purpose:
Local government body.

Subject coverage:
Local government services.

Access to staff:
Contact by letter, by telephone and by fax
Hours: Mon to Fri, 0900 to 1700

Access to building, collection or gallery:
No access other than to staff

COURT OF THE LORD LYON KING OF ARMS

HM New Register House, Edinburgh, EH1 3YT

Tel: 0131 556 7255
Fax: 0131 557 2148

Website:
http://www.lyon-court.com

Enquiries:
Enquiries to: Lyon Clerk

Organisation type and purpose:
Court of Law.
Court of heraldic jurisdiction.

Subject coverage:
The granting and control of heraldry in Scotland.

Museum or gallery collection, archive, or library special collection:
Heraldic, genealogical and associated library (non-lending library, not public)

Non-library collection catalogue:
All or part available in-house

Library catalogue:
All or part available in-house

Access to staff:
Contact by letter, by fax and via website.
Appointment necessary.
Hours: Mon to Fri, 1000 to 1230 and 1400 to 1600

COURTAULD INSTITUTE OF ART, BOOK LIBRARY

Somerset House, Strand, London, WC2R 0RN

Tel: 020 7848 2701
Fax: 020 7848 2887
E-mail: booklib@courtauld.ac.uk

Website:
http://www.courtauld.ac.uk

Enquiries:
Enquiries to: Book Librarian

Founded:
1933

Organisation type and purpose:
University department or institute.
Library.

Subject coverage:
Fine arts (painting, sculpture, architecture) in the Western tradition from classical antiquity to the present.

Museum or gallery collection, archive, or library special collection:
Extensive photographic collections administered separately from the Book Library

Non-library collection catalogue:
All or part available online

Library catalogue:
All or part available online and in-house

Access to staff:
Contact by letter, by telephone, by fax, by e-mail and via website. Appointment necessary.
Hours: Term time: 0930 to 2100 (last admission before 1900)
Vacations: 1030 to 1730
Special comments: A last-resort reference library.

Constituent part of:
University of London

COVENT GARDEN MARKET AUTHORITY

Acronym or abbreviation: CGMA

Covent House, New Covent Garden Market, London, SW8 5NX

Tel: 020 7720 2211
Fax: 020 7622 5307
E-mail: info@cgma.gov.uk

continued overleaf

Website:
http://www.cgma.gov.uk

Enquiries:
Enquiries to: Information Officer

Founded:
1961

Organisation type and purpose:
Statutory body.
Wholesale market operator.

Subject coverage:
Wholesaling of horticultural produce; operation of the market with over 300 market tenants including wholesalers, catering distributors, importers, hauliers and trade and official bodies.

Trade and statistical information:
Annual turnover figures for traders on New Covent Garden Market.

Printed publications:
Annual Report
Information leaflets
New Covent Garden Market (guide)
Newsletter (quarterly)

Access to staff:
Contact by telephone
Hours: Mon to Fri, 0900 to 1700

Links with:
Department for Environment, Food and Rural Affairs

COVENTRY & WARWICKSHIRE CHAMBER OF COMMERCE

Oak Tree Court, Binley Business Park, Harry Weston Road, Coventry, Warwickshire, CV3 2UN

Tel: 024 7665 4321
Fax: 024 7645 0242
E-mail: info@cw-chamber.co.uk

Website:
http://www.cw-chamber.co.uk

Enquiries:
Enquiries to: Information Officer

Founded:
2001

Formerly called:
Business Link Coventry & Warwickshire;
Coventry & Warwickshire Chamber of Commerce Training & Enterprise (year of change 2001)

Organisation type and purpose:
National government body, membership association (membership is by subscription), present number of members: 1800.
Chamber of Commerce.

Subject coverage:
Market research, export, design and innovation, information technology, manufacturing, personal business advisors, finance, start-up advice, training advice.

Museum or gallery collection, archive, or library special collection:
Reference Directories

Trade and statistical information:
Local economic assessments.

Publications list:
Available online

Access to staff:
Contact by letter, by telephone, by fax, by e-mail, in person and via website
Hours: Mon to Fri, 0900 to 1700

Access for disabled people:
Parking provided, ramped entry, access to all public areas, toilet facilities

Other addresses:
Coventry & Warwickshire Chamber of Commerce Progress House, Avenue Farm, Birmingham Road, Stratford Upon Avon, CV37 0HR

COVENTRY CITY ARCHIVES

John Sinclair House, Canal Basin, Coventry, Warwickshire, CV1 4LL

Tel: 024 7678 5164
Fax: 024 7655 1617
E-mail: info@theherbert.org

Enquiries:
Enquiries to: Archivist

Founded:
1937

Formerly called:
Coventry Record Office (CRO) (year of change 1995)

Organisation type and purpose:
Local government body.
Local government archives service.

Subject coverage:
Family history, local history of Coventry including destruction in World War II and post war reconstruction.
Local Authority Records, Coventry Borough Archives from 1182–1881, records of non-conformist churches.

Information services:
Preparing to integrate with the Local Studies service, located at the History Centre at The Herbert

Museum or gallery collection, archive, or library special collection:
Archive collections of organisations and individuals who are or have been active in Coventry from the 12th to the 20th centuries
Freemans and Apprentice Records from Coventry 1714 onwards
Cancelled vehicle registration cards to the early 1960s
Local public records, including quarter sessions, magistrates court, coroner's court and hospital records
Archive collections of individuals active in Coventry from the 12th to 20th centuries
Large collection of Architect Plans, Building Plans and Byelaws for all areas of Coventry, 1900 onwards
Collection of oral history tapes (with transcripts) covering most aspects of Coventry's recent history, especially the motor cars and allied trades
Microfilms of Church of England and Roman Catholic registers for Coventry and environs and local cemetery records
Detailed 1851 map of Coventry prepared for the local Board of Health
Plans for reconstruction of Coventry after World War II
Medieval records of the city 12th century onwards, including minutes of the Court Leet 1421 and records of Coventry's trading companies, Guilds
Records of the Blitz and post-war reconstruction of the city
Deposited and donated collections also include local and district trade union records, business records, notably Rootes (and constituent companies, e.g. Singer Motors), Armstrong-Siddley, Armstrong Whitworth, Daimler and Clarke Cluley, records of nonconformist churches, clubs, societies, schools and other local organisations
A large majority of our catalogues are computerised on the CALM database, direct customer access on site is available and also at other heritage facilities in the city
Card Indexes for Coventry Freemen (women included from 1930s), microfiche indexes of apprenticeship enrolments 1781–1841, microfiche index of Building Plans and Byelaws, card indexes for Architects plans (all of these are gradually being transferred to computer catalogue)

Non-library collection catalogue:
All or part available online and in-house

Library catalogue:
All or part available in-house

Printed publications:
Coventry at School
Coventry Celebrates 650 years of Civic Pride (1345–1995)
People to Coventry (migration and settlement from early times)
The Coventry Martyrs
Brief Guide to Records (28 leaflets)
Subject and period guides to archive holdings
Criminals, Courts and Conflict in 14th Century Coventry (A. Gooder, ed. T. Johns)

Publications list:
Available in print

Access to staff:
Contact by letter, by telephone, by fax, by e-mail and in person
Hours: Mon to Fri, 0930 to 1645
Special comments: Identification required to obtain County Archive Research Network (CARN) reader ticket.

Access to building, collection or gallery:
No prior appointment required
Special comments: Preparing to move to new premises

Access for disabled people:
Lift, access to all public areas, toilet facilities
Special comments: Minimal parking provided.

Links with:
Coventry Arts and Heritage
Herbert Art Gallery and Museum, Jordan Well, Coventry; tel: 02476 832386; fax: 02476 220171; e-mail: info@theherbert.org; website: http://www.theherbert.org

COVENTRY FAMILY HISTORY SOCIETY

Acronym or abbreviation: COVFHS

1 Barton Fields, Ecton, Northamptonshire

Tel: 01604 404777
E-mail: enquiries@covfhs.org

Website:
http://www.covfhs.org

Enquiries:
Enquiries to: General Secretary

Founded:
1994

Organisation type and purpose:
Membership association (membership is by subscription), present number of members: 450, voluntary organisation, registered charity (charity number 1070160).
To promote genealogy, family history and local history studies of Coventry, and surrounding parishes and villages.

Subject coverage:
Tracing ancestry, genealogy of local areas.

Printed publications:
Wide variety of books and leaflets, including:
Around Leamington Spa in Old Photographs (£7.95 plus 70p p&p)
Civic Heraldry of Warwickshire (£3 plus 30p p&p)
Coventry at School (£1 plus 30p p&p)
Coventry Through the Ages (£3 plus 30p p&p)
Finding out about Lady Godiva (50p plus 30p p&p)
Moments in Time (special edition, £3.50 plus 30p p&p)
Past in Warwick (£2.50 plus 30p p&p)
Plain and Fancy: ribbon weaving (50p plus 30p p&p)
Watchmaking in Coventry: History Trail (30p plus 30p p&p)
Coventry Family History Society's Publications include:
Beginner's Guide to Family History (3rd edn, £1 plus 30p p&p)
Coventry Family History Quarterly Journals (back issues £1, plus 34p p&p)
Foleshill Workhouse Punishment Book 1864–1900 (£1.50 plus 30p p&p)

Hawkesbury School 1860–1968 (£5 plus 55p p&p)
Order printed publications from: Bookshop Manager,
Coventry Family History Society, 88 Howes Lane,
Coventry, West Midlands, CV3 6PJ

Microform publications:
Coventry Apprentice Enrolment Registers 1781–
    1841 (5 vols, £2, explanatory leaflet free with first
    volume)
Death Registers of the Coventry Workhouse
    (booklet and 2 fiche, £3)
Census Index for Coventry

Publications list:
Available online and in print

Access to staff:
Contact by letter, by telephone, by e-mail and via
website. Appointment necessary. Non-members
charged.
Hours: Mon to Fri, 0900 to 1700

Links with:
Federation of Family History Societies

COVENTRY LIBRARIES AND INFORMATION SERVICES

Central Library, Smithford Way, Coventry,
Warwickshire, CV1 1FY

Tel: 024 7683 2314; 024 7683 2395 (minicom)
Fax: 024 7683 2440
E-mail: central.library@coventry.gov.uk

Enquiries:
Enquiries to: Librarian

Organisation type and purpose:
Public library.

Subject coverage:
General, industrial relations and trade union
affairs, current and historical; Coventry local
studies collection; automobile engineering; history
of automobiles (local studies, auto engineering,
auto history now at Herbert Art Gallery and
Museum)

Museum or gallery collection, archive, or library special collection:
Angela Brazil Collection (at Herbert Art Gallery
    and Museum)
Bartleet Collection on development of the bicycle
    (at Herbert Art Gallery and Museum)
Workshop Manuals Collection (at Herbert Art
    Gallery and Museum)
George Eliot Collection (at Herbert Art Gallery and
    Museum)
Tom Mann Centre for Trade Union and Labour
    Studies
Waring Brown Collection of newscuttings on
    engineering (at Herbert Art Gallery and
    Museum)

Library catalogue:
All or part available online and in-house

Printed publications:
Pamphlets, etc. on local history
Pictures of Coventry

Electronic and video publications:
OPIN (Older People's Information Network –
    website)
TALIS computer terminals

Publications list:
Available online and in print

Access to staff:
Contact by letter, by telephone, by fax, by e-mail
and in person. Appointment necessary.
Hours: Mon to Fri, 0900 to 2000; Sat, 0900 to 1630;
Sun, 1200 to 1600

Access to building, collection or gallery:
No access to non-public areas other than with staff
permission

Access for disabled people:
Access to all public areas, lifts, toilet facilities

COVENTRY UNIVERSITY

Lanchester Library, Gosford Street, Coventry,
Warwickshire, CV1 5DD

Tel: 024 7688 7688
Fax: 024 7688 7525

Website:
http://www.coventry.ac.uk
Detailed information on Coventry University
library services.

Enquiries:
Enquiries to: University Librarian

Formerly called:
Lanchester Library of Lanchester Polytechnic

Incorporates the former:
Art & Design Library (year of change 2000)

Organisation type and purpose:
University library.

Subject coverage:
Biology, building construction, business studies,
chemistry, civil engineering, communication
studies, computer science, control engineering and
systems, economics, electrical engineering,
geography and topography, health sciences,
industrial design, life sciences, linguistics,
materials science, mathematics, mechanical
engineering, microbiology, motor vehicle
engineering, operational research, physics,
physiotherapy, politics, production engineering,
social science, social work, statistics, town and
country planning, performing arts, nursing and
midwifery.
Art in general, art history , design, films and
cinema, graphic art and design, photography,
television, communication studies, computer
graphics and industrial design. (Now part of the
main collection but located on the top floor of the
library.)

Museum or gallery collection, archive, or library special collection:
Lanchester Collection (manuscripts and archives of
    Dr F W Lanchester, pioneer motor car designer
    and engineer and early theory of flight)

Library catalogue:
All or part available online

Access to staff:
Contact by letter, by telephone, by fax, in person
and via website
Hours: Termtime: Mon to Thu, 0845 to 2045; Fri,
1000 to 1715; Sat, 1000 to 1700; Sun, 1300 to 1700
Vacations, Mon to Fri, 0900 to 1700

Access for disabled people:
Parking provided, level entry, toilet facilities

CPRE

Formal name: Council for the Protection of Rural
England
Acronym or abbreviation: CPRE

Warwick House, 25 Buckingham Palace Road,
London, SW1W 0PP

Tel: 020 7976 6433
Fax: 020 7976 6373
E-mail: info@cpre.org.uk

Website:
http://www.cpre.org.uk
Information on organisation and publications,
press releases, job opportunities, resources, etc.

Enquiries:
Enquiries to: Librarian
Other contacts: Library & Information Unit for
CPRE history and archive information requests.

Founded:
1926

Formerly called:
Council for the Preservation of Rural England
(year of change 1969)

Organisation type and purpose:
Membership association (membership is by
subscription), present number of members: 49,000,
registered charity (charity number 242809),
research organisation.
Independent environment group.
Lobbying locally, Parliament, Whitehall and the EC
for countryside protection.

Subject coverage:
Improvement, protection and management of the
rural scenery and amenities of the countryside and
its towns and villages, in particular, planning,
green belts, development control, access to the
countryside, transport policies, motorways, heavy
lorries, mineral extraction, farmed landscape, land
drainage, water resources, tourism/recreation and
impact on the countryside, forestry and
woodlands, hedgerows, environmental
assessment, energy policies, rural development,
housing and urban regeneration.

Museum or gallery collection, archive, or library special collection:
CPRE documents and archives

Non-library collection catalogue:
All or part available in-house

Library catalogue:
All or part available in-house

Printed publications:
Annual Report
CPRE Voice (4 times a year)
Leaflets (free, send A4 sae)
Campaigners' Guides
Publications under the headings: campaigners'
    guides & briefings, land use change, rural
    development, planning, regional planning,
    sustainable development, housing & urban
    development, roads & transport, agriculture,
    heritage & leisure, trees & forestry, landscape
    features, water & waste, minerals, energy

Publications list:
Available in print

Access to staff:
Contact by letter, by telephone, by fax and by e-
mail. Appointment necessary.
Hours: Mon to Fri, 0930 to 1730
Special comments: Access only to bona fide
researchers on the work of CPRE.

Access to building, collection or gallery:
Prior appointment required

Has:
43 branches and district committees
    in every English county. Contact numbers
    available, from National office

CPRE LANCASHIRE

Formal name: Campaign to Protect Rural England
Lancashire Branch

Hazelwell's House, Station Road, Bamber Bridge,
Preston, PR5 6TT

Tel: 01772 627510
E-mail: ruralengland@btconnect.com

Enquiries:
Enquiries to: Company Secretary

Founded:
1933

Organisation type and purpose:
Membership association (membership is by
subscription), voluntary organisation, registered
charity (charity number 1107376).
To protect the countryside and the country towns
and villages of Lancashire and parts of Greater
Manchester and Merseyside.

Subject coverage:
Rural land use planning policy and development
control material from a wide range of sources.

continued overleaf

Museum or gallery collection, archive, or library special collection:
Library set of CPRE publications (campaigners' guides, authoritative reports and free leaflets) and can obtain stock

Printed publications:
Countrywise (newsletter, quarterly, issued to Branch members, free on request)
Occasional issue of our own leaflets (e.g. explaining Tree Preservation Orders)

Publications list:
Available online

Access to staff:
Contact by letter, by telephone, by e-mail and in person. Appointment necessary.
Hours: Mon, Tue and Thu, 0930 to 1230
Special comments: We offer no information service, only access to our collection and files.

Access for disabled people:
None in 2008

National Body:
CPRE
Warwick House, 128 Southwark St, London, SE1 0SW; tel: 020 7981 2800; e-mail: info@cpre.org.uk; website: http://www.cpre.org.uk

CPRE, THE HERTFORDSHIRE SOCIETY

Formal name: CPRE, The Hertfordshire Society
Acronym or abbreviation: CPRE Herts.

31a Church Street, Welwyn Garden City, Hertfordshire, AL6 9LW

Tel: 01438 717587
Fax: 01438 714984
E-mail: office@cpreherts.org.uk

Website:
http://www.cpreherts.org.uk

Enquiries:
Enquiries to: Executive Secretary

Founded:
1936

Formerly called:
The Hertfordshire Conservation Society (HCS) (year of change 1997)

Organisation type and purpose:
Membership association, present number of members: 1500 in Hertfordshire
47,000 nationally, voluntary organisation, registered charity (charity number 211299).
Protection of the countryside.

Subject coverage:
Protection, preservation and improvement of Hertfordshire lands, buildings and scenery; planning matters including listed buildings, green belt, roads and transport, minerals and gravel extraction, water, retail developments, agriculture; control of development; organisation of Hertfordshire's Village of the Year competition and Conservation Award Scheme.

Printed publications:
CPRE Hertfordshire Publications:
Newsletter (3 times a year)
Annual Report

Access to staff:
Contact by letter, by telephone, by fax, by e-mail and via website
Hours: Mon to Thu, 0930 to 1700; Fri, 0930 to 1430

Parent body:
Campaign to Protect Rural England (CPRE)
128 Southwark Street, London, SE1 0SW; tel: 020 7981 2800; fax: 020 7981 2899; e-mail: info@cpre.org.uk; website: http://www.cpre.org.uk

CRAFTS COUNCIL

44a Pentonville Road, Islington, London, N1 9BY

Tel: 020 7278 7700

Fax: 020 7837 6891
E-mail: admin@craftscouncil.org.uk

Website:
http://www.craftscouncil.org.uk

Enquiries:
Enquiries to: Reference Desk
Direct tel: 020 7806 2501
Direct e-mail: info@craftscouncil.org.uk

Founded:
1971

Formerly called:
Crafts Advisory Committee

Organisation type and purpose:
National organisation, registered charity (charity number 280956).
National body for the crafts.
To promote the creation and appreciation of fine crafts works.

Subject coverage:
Contemporary British craft: retail outlets, suppliers of materials, exhibitions, courses, grant aid, business practice, guilds and societies.

Museum or gallery collection, archive, or library special collection:
Colour slides, over 30,000 slides, library of contemporary work, slide loan service
Crafts Council Collection, the national collection of works by leading contemporary crafts people, available for loan to public institutions, or for study by appointment

Printed publications:
Books, catalogues, posters, postcards, information lists, exhibition catalogues, factsheets on crafts, lists of courses, careers information, opportunities overseas
Crafts Magazine (6 times a year)

Access to staff:
Contact by letter and by telephone
Hours: Tue to Sat, 1100 to 1800; Sun, 1400 to 1800; Mon, closed
Special comments: There is disabled access.

Funded by:
The Arts Council of England

CRAFTS STUDY CENTRE

University of the Creative Arts, Falkner Road, Farnham, Surrey, GU9 7DS

Tel: 01252 891450
Fax: 01252 891451
E-mail: craftscentre@ucreative.ac.uk

Website:
http://www.csc.ucreative.ac.uk

Organisation type and purpose:
A registered charity (261109) functioning as a specialist museum and a research centre of the University for the Creative Arts.

Subject coverage:
Modern calligraphy, furniture and crafts in ceramics, textiles and wood.

Museum or gallery collection, archive, or library special collection:
Supporting material includes makers' diaries, working notes and photographs dating from the 1920s

Access to building, collection or gallery:
Hours: Tue to Fri, 1000 to 1700; Sat, 1000 to 1600

Access for disabled people:
The Centre is accessible to wheelchair users

CRANFIELD PRECISION

Acronym or abbreviation: CP

Divison of Unova UK Limited, 90 Central Avenue, Wharley End, Cranfield, Bedfordshire, MK43 0JR

Tel: 01234 754222
Fax: 01234 754223

E-mail: cpsales@landis-lund.co.uk

Website:
http://www.cranfieldprecision.com
Company profile; products; services; email contacts.

Enquiries:
Enquiries to: Marketing Department

Founded:
1968

Formerly called:
Cranfield Unit for Precision Engineering (CUPE) (year of change 1987)

Organisation type and purpose:
Manufacturing industry, university department or institute, consultancy, research organisation.
OEM design, manufacture and application in machine tools.

Subject coverage:
Precision engineering, including metrology, machine design, servo system design and development, measuring systems (linear and angular), control systems. Applications in semiconductor processing and computer peripheral manufacturing, as well as in automotive, advanced optics, optoelectronics and other ultra-precision manufacturing industries.

Access to staff:
Contact by e-mail
Hours: Mon to Fri, 0830 to 1700

Parent body:
Landis Lund, Division of Unova UK Limited
tel: 01535 633211

CRANFIELD UNIVERSITY

Acronym or abbreviation: CU

Cranfield, Bedfordshire, MK43 0AL

Tel: 01234 750111
Fax: 01234 752391
E-mail: n.woodward@cranfield.ac.uk

Website:
http://www.cranfieldlibrary.cranfield.ac.uk
Library and Information Service at Cranfield Campus
http://diglib.shrivenham.cranfield.ac.uk
Defence College of Management and Technology
http://www.cranfield.ac.uk
University home page.

Enquiries:
Enquiries to: University Librarian
Direct tel: 01234 754446

Organisation type and purpose:
University library.

Subject coverage:
Aerospace engineering; electronics; mechanical engineering; advanced materials; advanced manufacturing techniques,defence science and technology, agricultural engineering; food production; land use; management, water and waste technology, biotechnology, health science, logistics, natural resources.

Museum or gallery collection, archive, or library special collection:
Aeronautical history
Aerospace Technology Reports (NASA, AGARD, AIAA, ARC)
History of ballooning (Kings Norton Library)
British Balloon Library; Kings Norton Collection.

Library catalogue:
All or part available online

Includes the:
Defence College of Management and Technology. Shrivenham
Silsoe College

CREMATION SOCIETY OF GREAT BRITAIN

Acronym or abbreviation: CSGB

Brecon House, 2nd Floor, 16–16a Albion Place, Maidstone, Kent, ME14 5DZ

Tel: 01622 688292/3
Fax: 01622 686698
E-mail: info@cremation.org.uk

Website:
http://www.cremation.org.uk

Enquiries:
Enquiries to: Secretary

Founded:
1874

Organisation type and purpose:
Advisory body, membership association, registered charity.

Subject coverage:
Cremation and its religious, legal, technical, architectural and statistical aspects; crematorium administration.

Museum or gallery collection, archive, or library special collection:
Society's records since 1874. From 1999 these have been transferred to University of Durham Library (Special Collections)

Printed publications:
Directory of Crematoria
Directory of Pet Crematoria
History of Modern Cremation in Great Britain from 1874
May Catholics Choose Cremation?
Pharos International (quarterly)
Provision for Cremation Facilities pack
What You Should Know about Cremation
What is Respectful Disposal?

Access to staff:
Contact by letter, by telephone, by fax and by e-mail
Hours: Mon to Fri, 0900 to 1700

Founder member of the:
International Cremation Federation
tel: +31 70 351 8836; fax: +31 70 351 8827; e-mail: keizer@facultatieve.com; website: www.int-crem-fed.org

CRIME CONCERN TRUST

Beaver House, 147–150 Victoria Road, Swindon, Wiltshire, SN1 3UY

Tel: 01793 863500
Fax: 01793 514654

Website:
http://www.crimeconcern.org.uk
http://www.safer-community.net

Enquiries:
Direct e-mail: info@crimeconcern.org.uk

Founded:
1988

Organisation type and purpose:
Registered charity (charity number 800735). Working with local and national partners to reduce crime and create safer communities.

Subject coverage:
Crime prevention, burglary reduction, domestic violence, racial harassment, youth crime, car crime, neighbourhood safety, drug misuse prevention, and personal safety.

Library catalogue:
All or part available online

Printed publications:
A Second Chance (1997)

Publications list:
Available online and in print

Access to staff:
Contact by letter, by telephone, by fax, by e-mail and via website
Hours: Mon to Fri, 0900 to 1715

CRIMESTOPPERS TRUST

Acronym or abbreviation: Crimestoppers

Apollo House, 66a London Road, Morden, Surrey, SM4 5BE

Tel: 020 8254 3200
Fax: 020 8254 3201
E-mail: cst@crimestoppers-uk.org

Website:
http://www.crimestoppers-uk.org
Crimestoppers Trust website with detailed information on the charity and its activities. Users can e-mail information on the website about crimes.

Enquiries:
Enquiries to: Director
Other contacts: Head of Marketing & Fundraising for any marketing or fundraising enquiries.

Founded:
1986

Formed from:
Community Action Trust (year of change 1995)

Organisation type and purpose:
Registered charity (charity number 1108687). To create an alliance to fight crime.

Subject coverage:
Crimestoppers Trust publicises the Crimestoppers Scheme and supports specific crime-fighting initiatives. To date Crimestoppers have received 320,000 anonymous phone calls leading to 30,000 arrests and the recovery of property valued at £44 million. With other offences taken into consideration, it is estimated that information given to Crimestoppers has helped to clear up almost 100,000 crimes.

Trade and statistical information:
The only UK charity dedicated to solving crimes.

Printed publications:
Publicity material is available for purchase on request

Publications list:
Available online and in print

Access to staff:
Contact by letter, by telephone, by fax, by e-mail and via website. Appointment necessary. Letter of introduction required.
Hours: Mon to Fri, 0900 to 1700

Access to building, collection or gallery:
No access other than to staff, prior appointment required

CRIMINAL BAR ASSOCIATION

Acronym or abbreviation: CBA

2–3 Cursitor Street, London, EC4A 1NE

Tel: 020 7242 1289
Fax: 020 7242 1107
E-mail: videoconference@dial.pipex.com

Website:
http://www.criminalbar.com

Enquiries:
Enquiries to: Administrator

Founded:
1969

Organisation type and purpose:
Professional body (membership is by qualification), present number of members: 2700.

Subject coverage:
Criminal procedure and practice, policy of the specialist organisation for members of the Criminal Bar, criminal justice system.

Printed publications:
CBA Newsletter

Access to staff:
Contact by letter, by fax and by e-mail
Hours: Mon to Fri, 0900 to 1700

Links with:
General Council of The Bar
3 Bedford Row, London, WC1R 4DB; tel: 020 7240 0082; fax: 020 7831 9217

CRIMINAL INJURIES COMPENSATION AUTHORITY

Tay House, 300 Bath Street, Glasgow, G2 4LN 0800 358 3601 0141 331 2287

Tel: 0800 358 3601
Fax: 0141 331 2287

Website:
http://www.cica.gov.uk

Enquiries:
Enquiries to: Media Enquiries
Direct e-mail: philip.gibson@cica.gsi.gov.uk

Formerly called:
Criminal Injuries Compensation Board

Organisation type and purpose:
National government body.
Government board.

Subject coverage:
Scheme for compensating victims of crimes of violence and persons injured while arresting an offender, or preventing an offence, or giving help to a policeman engaged in those things. Application may also be made by the widow, widower, or a close relative and dependant of a person who received fatal injuries in such circumstances, or who received injuries but died from some other cause. Traffic offences are usually excluded.

Printed publications:
Annual Report (HMSO)
Information leaflets
Text of the Scheme

CRISIS

Formal name: Crisis UK trading as Crisis

66 Commercial Street, London, E1 6LT

Tel: 0870 011 3335
Fax: 0870 011 3336
E-mail: enquiries@crisis.org.uk

Website:
http://www.crisis.org.uk
Information on the work of Crisis.

Enquiries:
Enquiries to: Marketing Executive

Founded:
1967

Formerly called:
Crisis at Christmas

Organisation type and purpose:
National organisation, voluntary organisation, registered charity (charity number 1082947). Crisis is the national charity for homeless people. We provide lasting solutions to homelessness.

Subject coverage:
Homelessness, housing, volunteering, fundraising.

Museum or gallery collection, archive, or library special collection:
Photograph library
Reports on homelessness issues

Trade and statistical information:
Statistics on homelessness and housing.

Printed publications:
A Future Foretold – New approaches to meeting the long-term needs of single homeless people
Falling Out (£6.95)
Homeless on Sea (£5)

continued overleaf

Healthy Hostels – A Guide to Promoting Health
and Well-Being Among homeless People (2001,
£7.50 plus p&p)
Homeless Truths (Crane M, 1997, £8)
Homelessness and Loneliness – The Want of
Conviviality (2001, £4.50 plus p&p)
In From the Cold (£4)
Leaving Homelessness Behind – New solutions for
a new age
Lest We Forget – Ex-servicemen and Homelessness
(2000, £7.50 plus p&p)
Prevention is Better than Cure
The Move in Experience (£6.95)
Trouble at Home – Family conflict, Young People
and Homelessness (2001, £7.50 plus p&p)
Sick to Death of Homelessness (£6.95)
Still Dying for a Home (Grenier P, 1996, £8)
Unsafe Streets – Street Homelessness and Crime
Walk on By – Begging, Street Drinking and the
Giving Age (2000, £7.50 plus p&p)
Waste Not, Want Not (Cottee P, and Webster J,
1997, £3)

Publications list:
Available online and in print

Access to staff:
Contact by letter, by telephone, by fax, by e-mail
and via website
Hours: Mon to Fri, 0930 to 1730; Sat, Sun, closed

Access to building, collection or gallery:
No access other than to staff

CROFTERS COMMISSION

4–6 Castle Wynd, Inverness, IV2 3EQ

Tel: 01463 663450
Fax: 01463 711820
E-mail: info@crofterscommission.org.uk

Website:
http://www.crofterscommission.org.uk

Enquiries:
Enquiries to: Communications Officer
Direct tel: 01463 663424
Direct e-mail: betty.mackenzie@crofterscommission
.org.uk

Founded:
1955

Organisation type and purpose:
National government body, advisory body,
statutory body.
Non-departmental government body.

Subject coverage:
Crofting regulation, community development,
rural development, agricultural grants, forestry
grants, croft house grants

Non-library collection catalogue:
All or part available online

Printed publications:
Publications available free of charge

Publications list:
Available online and in print

Access to staff:
Contact by letter, by telephone, by fax, by e-mail,
in person and via website. Appointment necessary.
Hours: Mon to Thu, 0830 to 1700; Fri, 0830 to 1630

Access for disabled people:
Fully accessible, toilet facilities

CROHN'S IN CHILDHOOD RESEARCH ASSOCIATION

Acronym or abbreviation: CICRA

Parkgate House, 356 West Barnes Lane, Motspur
Park, Surrey, KT3 6NB

Tel: 020 8949 6209
Fax: 020 8942 2044
E-mail: support@cicra.org

Website:
http://www.cicra.org

Enquiries:
Enquiries to: Charity Co-ordinator
Other contacts: Member & Support Group Liaison
for membership, fundraising and support group
activities.

Founded:
1978

Organisation type and purpose:
Membership association, present number of
members: 1500, registered charity (charity number
278212).
Free membership offered to all interested parties
including medical professionals.

Subject coverage:
Telephone advice and support for individuals and
families of children sufferering from Crohn's
Disease and Ulcerative Colitis (inflammatory
bowel disease). Literature on all aspects of
inflammatory bowel disease, especially as it affects
children and young people. Membership (free of
charge) to all relevant individuals and families,
and the medical profession. Annual meeting –
open day attended by senior medical professionals.

Printed publications:
Crohn's Disease: Ulcerative Colitis
Children with Crohn's and Colitis – A parent's
guide
Children with Crohn's and Colitis – A teacher's
guide
Children with Crohn's and Colitis – What do the
doctors mean (A-Z of terms)
Children with Crohn's and Colitis – General
information
Series of fact sheets on aspects of IBD, particularly
as it affects children
Newsletter (quarterly, members)
All the above are free of charge

Publications list:
Available in print

Access to staff:
Contact by letter, by telephone, by fax, by e-mail
and via website. Appointment necessary.
Hours: Mon to Fri, 0930 to 1730

Access to building, collection or gallery:
Prior appointment required

Access for disabled people:
Parking provided

CRONER CCH GROUP LIMITED

145 London Road, Kingston Upon Thames, Surrey,
KT2 6SR

Tel: 020 8547 3333
Fax: 020 8547 2638
E-mail: info@croner.cch.co.uk

Website:
http://www.croner.cch.co.uk
News stories, articles, questions and answers, in-
depth reports and tools, further material published
on your area of interest.

Enquiries:
Enquiries to: Customer Services Manager

Organisation type and purpose:
Publishing house.
Publishers of business information solutions.

Subject coverage:
Human resources; consumer, business and
specialist industry law; exporting, importing,
health and safety, transport; freight and haulage,
VAT and finance, IT, education, charities, care
homes, catering, health service management,
environmental management and the control of
hazardous substances.

Printed publications:
We offer loose-leaf, online, software, training,
seminar and consultancy products and services

Publications list:
Available in print

Access to staff:
Contact by letter, by telephone, by fax, by e-mail
and via website
Hours: Mon to Fri, 0830 to 1730

Part of:
Wolters Kluwer Group

CROP PROTECTION ASSOCIATION (UK) LIMITED

Acronym or abbreviation: CPA

4 Lincoln Court, Lincoln Road, Peterborough,
Cambridgeshire, PE1 2RP

Tel: 01733 349225
Fax: 01733 562523

Enquiries:
Enquiries to: Director General

Formerly called:
British Agrochemicals Association Limited (BAA)

Organisation type and purpose:
International organisation, trade association.
Represents companies who manufacture and
formulate pesticides, and distributors.

Subject coverage:
Agrochemicals, pesticides.

Printed publications:
AGCHEM (quarterly magazine)
CPA Annual Review and Handbook
Educational materials
Pesticides in Perspective (set of 9 leaflets)

Publications list:
Available in print

Access to staff:
Appointment necessary.
Hours: Mon to Fri, 0900 to 1700

Member of:
Crop Life
European Crop Protection Association (ECPA)

CROQUET ASSOCIATION

Acronym or abbreviation: CA

c/o The Cheltenham Croquet Club, Old Bath Road,
Cheltenham, GL53 7DF

Tel: 01242 242318
E-mail: caoffice@croquet.org.uk

Website:
http://www.croquet.org.uk

Enquiries:
Enquiries to: Manager

Founded:
1897

Organisation type and purpose:
Membership association (membership is by
subscription), present number of individual
members: 1,700, member clubs; 168, voluntary
organisation.
Governing body of the game.
Organises tournaments and coaching for players of
all abilities.

Subject coverage:
Croquet, handicap ratings, laws of croquet, history.

Printed publications:
Croquet (J. Solomon, £7.99 plus p&p)
Croquet Coaching Manual (£10 plus p&p)
Croquet Gazette (members only, 6 times a year)
Croquet Management (Gaunt and Wheeler £12
plus p&p)
Croquet – The Skills of the Game (B. Lamb, £7 plus
p&p)
Know the Game (£3.99 plus p&p)
Plus One on Time (D. Gaunt, £6 plus p&p)
The Full Laws and Regulations (£5 plus p&p)
Order printed publications from: Croquet
Asssociation Shop

Access to staff:
Contact by letter, by telephone, by e-mail and via website. Appointment necessary.
Hours: Mon to Thu, 0900 to 1600; Fri, 0900 to 1300

CROSS & COCKADE INTERNATIONAL

Cragg Cottage, The Cragg, Bramham, Wetherby, West Yorkshire, LS23 6QB

Tel: 01937 845320
E-mail: paulsleaman@btinternet.com
Website:
http://www.crossandcockade.com
Information on the Society and sample articles.

Enquiries:
Enquiries to: Membership Secretary
Direct tel: 01237 474703
Direct e-mail: membership.secretary@crossandcockade.com
Other contacts: Managing Editor for journal material.

Founded:
1969

Also known as:
First World War Aviation Historical Society

Formed from:
Essex Chapter Cross and Cockade

Formerly called:
Cross and Cockade Great Britain 1969

Organisation type and purpose:
International organisation, learned society (membership is by subscription), present number of members: 1400, voluntary organisation, consultancy, research organisation, publishing house.
To enable those with a common interest in any aspect of World War I aviation to share those interests, and to meet fellow enthusiasts.

Subject coverage:
Factual information about all aspects of the 1914–1918 war in the air.

Museum or gallery collection, archive, or library special collection:
Photographs and some original documents
Reference books

Printed publications:
Journal (quarterly, free to members, back numbers available, prices vary))
Seminar Papers 1995, 1997
Order printed publications from: Sales Manager, Cross and Cockade
4 Parklands, Freeland, Witney, Oxfordshire, OX29 8HX

Electronic and video publications:
Gazetteer of Northern France
Index of Journal Contents

Publications list:
Available in print

Access to staff:
Contact by letter, by telephone, by e-mail and via website. Appointment necessary. Non-members charged.
Hours: Mon to Fri, 0900 to 1700

Advertising Manager:
Cross & Cockade International
6 Cowper Road, Southgate, London, N14 5RP; tel: 020 8361 8482; e-mail: marenswilliams1@compuserve.com

Membership Secretary:
Cross & Cockade International
11 Francis Drive, Westward Ho! EX39 1XE; tel: 01237 474703; e-mail: membership.secretary@cross@cockade.com

CROSSLEY REGISTER

Willow Cottage, Lexham Road, Great Dunham, King's Lynn, Norfolk, PE32 2LS

Tel: 01328 701240
E-mail: malcolmhatfield@globalnet.co.uk
Website:
http://www.crossley-motors.org.uk

Enquiries:
Enquiries to: General Secretary
Direct e-mail: anthonycourtney@tiscali.co.uk
Other contacts: Editor

Founded:
1985

Organisation type and purpose:
Membership association (membership is by subscription), voluntary organisation.

Subject coverage:
The Crossley motor car.

Museum or gallery collection, archive, or library special collection:
Archive material on Crossley Motors Limited
Records from the company of Crossley Motors Limited

Printed publications:
Newsletter (3 times a year)

Access to staff:
Contact by letter, by telephone, by fax and by e-mail
Hours: Mon to Fri, 0900 to 1700

Access to building, collection or gallery:
Prior appointment required

Access for disabled people:
Parking provided

CROSSWORD CLUB

Coombe Farm, Awbridge, Romsey, Hampshire, SO51 0HN

Tel: 01794 524346
Fax: 01794 514988
E-mail: bh@thecrosswordclub.co.uk
Website:
http://www.thecrosswordclub.co.uk
Mainly online brochure offering information about club, including stop press items especially about latest puzzles published in Crossword and solutions of earlier puzzles.

Enquiries:
Enquiries to: Editor

Founded:
1978

Organisation type and purpose:
Membership association.

Subject coverage:
All aspects of crosswords, especially difficult examples involving gimmicks; composition; history etc.

Museum or gallery collection, archive, or library special collection:
Collections of crossword and general dictionaries
Library of books of and about crosswords

Printed publications:
Crossword (monthly, free to members)
Guide to Playfair (£1.25)
Handbook (occasional, free to members)

Access to staff:
Contact by letter, by telephone, by fax and by e-mail. Appointment necessary.
Hours: Generally 1600 to 2000 and other times on spec; 24-hour answerphone

CROWN PROSECUTION SERVICE

Acronym or abbreviation: CPS

50 Ludgate Hill, London, EC4M 7EX

Tel: 020 7273 8000
Fax: 020 7796 8651
Website:
http://www.cps.gov.uk

General information.

Enquiries:
Enquiries to: Information Officer
Direct tel: 020 7796 8023
Direct fax: 020 7796 8030
Direct e-mail: tracey.allen@cps.gsi.gov.uk

Founded:
1986

Organisation type and purpose:
National government body.

Subject coverage:
Criminal Law.

Library catalogue:
All or part available in-house

Printed publications:
Domestic Violence Policy
Domestic Violence Guidance
Prosecutions Leaflet
Introduction to CPS Leaflet
The People Leaflet
The Code for Crown Prosecutors
Witness in Court
Complaints to the CPS
CPS Area Map (Colour)
Order printed publications from: Communications Branch, CPS

Publications list:
Available online

Access to staff:
Contact by letter, by fax and by e-mail
Hours: Mon to Fri, 0900 to 1700

Access to building, collection or gallery:
No access other than to staff

Access for disabled people:
Ramped entry, level entry, access to all public areas, toilet facilities
Special comments: Parking provided in The Courtyard, 1st left turn in Old Bailey.

CROWTHER CENTRE FOR MISSION EDUCATION

Watlington Road, Oxford, OX4 6BZ

Tel: 01865 787400
Fax: 01865 776375
E-mail: info@cms-uk.org
Website:
http://www.cms-uk.org/
Online catalogue.

Enquiries:
Enquiries to: Librarian

Founded:
1987

Please select:
Partnership House Mission Studies Library

Organisation type and purpose:
Registered charity (charity number 297154).
Provides library service to the Anglican missionary societies. The Partnership House Mission Studies Library was formed in 1987 from the post-1945 library collections of CMS and the USPG. All interested in Christian Mission are welcome to use the library.

Subject coverage:
Missiology; worldwide Christian church, especially history; growth and work of Anglicanism; the ecumenical movement; other faiths; spirituality; social concerns of the church (eg race, poverty, human rights); area studies.

Museum or gallery collection, archive, or library special collection:
CMS Max Warren collection (comprises the books from the former Church Missionary Society Library which were published prior to 1946, plus copies of all CMS publications)

Non-library collection catalogue:
All or part available online

continued overleaf

Library catalogue:
All or part available online and in-house

Printed publications:
Bulletin (including JIST, journals in short – abstracting service and New Books List)

Access to staff:
Contact by letter, by telephone, by fax, by e-mail, in person and via website
Hours: Mon to Fri, 0930 to 1700
Special comments: Reference services free of charge. Loan of books (other than to missions staff) by annual subscription.

CROYDON COLLEGE LIBRARY

College Road, Fairfield, Croydon, Surrey, CR9 1DX

Tel: 020 8760 5843
E-mail: library@croydon.ac.uk

Website:
http://www.croydon.ac.uk/ipoint
Library services and catalogue access to eResources, Subject Guides

Enquiries:
Enquiries to: Librarian

Organisation type and purpose:
Suitable for ages: 16+. College of further education/ higher education.

Subject coverage:
Art and design, theatre, management, nursing, health studies, child care, social work, law, construction, business studies, education, travel and tourism, sport.

Library catalogue:
All or part available online

Access to staff:
Access for members only.
Hours: Main Campus: in term time, Mon to Thu 0800 to 2030, Fri 0800 to 1700 and Sat 1000 to 1500; vacations, Mon to Fri 0930 to 1630, occasionally closed.
Davidson Campus: term time, Mon to Fri 09:00–17:00; vacation, closed
Special comments: Library for the use of Croydon College staff and students only.

Access for disabled people:
Ramped entry, access to all public areas, toilet facilities

CROYDON LIBRARIES

Central Library, Katharine Street, Croydon, Surrey, CR9 1ET

Tel: 020 8726 6900
Fax: 020 8253 1004
E-mail: aileen.cahill@croydon.gov.uk

Website:
http://www.croydon.gov.uk/libraries
Covers all general information about the services, activities and events. Reference and information specialist areas include: business, law, information, technology, tourism, community, local and family history.

Enquiries:
Enquiries to: Assistant Director, Libraries
Direct tel: 020 8253 1001

Founded:
1888

Formerly called:
Croydon Public Library

Organisation type and purpose:
Local government body, public library.

Subject coverage:
General collection, strong in the following areas: computers, business information, European Information, law, visual arts, Croydon local history.

Information services:
Online access to encyclopedias, dictionaries, newspaper archives and business sources.

Services for disabled people:
Zoomtext on public PCs. Kurzweil reader. CCTV enlarger.

Museum or gallery collection, archive, or library special collection:
Archives
Croydon Local Studies Library
IGI complete
1881 Census Index Surrey only
Riesco Collection of Chinese Ceramics

Library catalogue:
All or part available online

Printed publications:
SWLULOP (edited by Anna Raghunanan)

Access to staff:
Contact by letter, by telephone, by fax, by e-mail, in person and via website
Hours: Main Library: Mon, 0900 to 1900; Tue, Wed and Fri, 0900 to 1800; Thu, 0930 to 1800; Sat, 0900 to 1700; Sun, 1400 to 1700

Access to building, collection or gallery:
No access other than to staff
Hours: Main Library: Mon, 0900 to 1900; Tue, Wed and Fri, 0900 to 1800; Thu, 0930 to 1800; Sat, 0900 to 1700; Sun, 1400 to 1700

Access for disabled people:
Ramped entry, access to all public areas, toilet facilities, lifts to all floors

CROYDON LOCAL HISTORY LIBRARY

Central Library, Katharine Street, Croydon, Surrey, CR9 1ET

Tel: 020 8760 5400
Fax: 020 8253 1004

Enquiries:
Enquiries to: Librarian

Organisation type and purpose:
Public library.

Subject coverage:
Local history of the Borough of Croydon and the surrounding area. By virtue of the range of the collections, local and family history of many parts of England.

Museum or gallery collection, archive, or library special collection:
IGI (microfiche)
1841–1901 Census
Maps
Large collection of volumes of English local history societies, records and transcriptions
Harleian Society volumes

Library catalogue:
All or part available in-house

Access to staff:
Contact by letter and by telephone
Hours: Mon, 0900 to 1900; Tue to Fri, 0900 to 1800; Sat, 0900 to 1700; Sun, 1400 to 1700

Access to building, collection or gallery:
No prior appointment required
Hours: Mon, 0900 to 1900; Tue to Fri, 0900 to 1800; Sat, 0900 to 1700; Sun, 1400 to 1700

Access for disabled people:
Ramped entry, access to all public areas, toilet facilities

CROYDON NATURAL HISTORY AND SCIENTIFIC SOCIETY LIMITED

Acronym or abbreviation: CNHSS

96A Brighton Road, South Croydon, Surrey, CR2 6AD

Tel: 020 8688 3593

Website:
http://www.croydononline.org/hs/cnhss/index.asp

Enquiries:
Enquiries to: Librarian
Other contacts: Membership Secretary for membership

Founded:
1870

Formed from:
Croydon Microscopical & Natural History Club (1877–1901), Croydon Microscopical Club (1870–1877)

Organisation type and purpose:
Learned society (membership is by subscription), present number of members: 360, voluntary organisation, registered charity (charity number 260739).
Research and education concerned with the geology, natural history, archaeology, local history etc of Croydon and adjoining parts of east Surrey and west Kent.

Subject coverage:
Archaeology, botany, entomology, geography, geology, industrial archaeology and history, local history, ornithology, zoology, all pertaining to the Croydon area and some parts of NE Surrey, NW Kent and adjoining London Boroughs; particularly strong in natural history, geology and industrial history, and archaeology of the extractive and transport industries.

Museum or gallery collection, archive, or library special collection:
C C Fagg Collection (early land-use surveying, regional survey, etc.)
Strong holdings relating to economic, geological, civil engineering, water supply etc
W H Bennett Collection (geological and palaeontological books and journals)

Non-library collection catalogue:
All or part available in-house

Library catalogue:
All or part available in-house

Printed publications:
Accounts of excavations
Croydon Between the Wars (2nd ed, 1993, £4.75 plus p&p)
Croydon in the 1940s and 1950s (1994, £5.25 plus p&p)
Croydon: the Story of a Hundred Years (1870–1970)
Edwardian Croydon Illustrated (2nd ed, 1990, £4.25 plus p&p)
Illustrated local history books
Victorian Croydon Illustrated (2nd ed, 1987, £3.25 plus p&p)
Various publications on the history and natural history of the area

Publications list:
Available in print

Access to staff:
Contact by letter and by telephone. Appointment necessary.
Hours: Any reasonable time

Access to building, collection or gallery:
Prior appointment required
Hours: Any mutually convenient time
Special comments: By arrangement with the librarian.

CRUISING ASSOCIATION

Acronym or abbreviation: CA

1 Northey Street, Limehouse Basin, London, E14 8BT

Tel: 020 7537 2828
Fax: 020 7537 2266
E-mail: office@cruising.org.uk

Website:
http://www.cruising.org.uk

Enquiries:
Enquiries to: General Manager

Founded:
1908

Organisation type and purpose:
Voluntary organisation.

Subject coverage:
Cruising in private sailing, auxiliary or motor yachts; pilotage, etc, worldwide.

Museum or gallery collection, archive, or library special collection:
Nautical books (said to be the largest collection in private ownership in Europe)

Non-library collection catalogue:
All or part available online

Printed publications:
Cruising Almanac
Cruising, the Journal of the Cruising Association (6 times a year)

Access to staff:
Contact by letter, by telephone, by e-mail and in person. Appointment necessary. Non-members charged.
Hours: Mon to Fri, 0930 to 1730

Access for disabled people:
Ramped entry, access to all public areas, toilet facilities

Affiliated to:
Royal Yachting Association

CRUSE BEREAVEMENT CARE

Cruse House, 126 Sheen Road, Richmond-upon-Thames, Surrey, TW9 1UR

Tel: 020 8939 9530
Fax: 020 8940 7638

Website:
http://www.crusebereavementcare.org.uk

Enquiries:
Enquiries to: Fundraising Manager
Direct tel: 020 8939 9551
Direct e-mail: deborah@crusebereavementcare.org.uk

Founded:
1959

Formerly called:
National Organisation for the Widowed and their Children

Organisation type and purpose:
National organisation, registered charity (charity number 208278).
To provide bereavement support, counselling and advice to anyone who is bereaved by death. This help also includes support groups, a monthly newsletter and a wide variety of leaflets and publications.

Subject coverage:
Welfare of bereaved people; counselling, social support and courses for counsellors.

Printed publications:
A wide range of leaflets and publications – for a mail order catalogue please send a sae
Annual Report
Bereavement Care Journal (for people dealing with the bereaved, £15 annual subscription. 3 times a year)
Books
Cruse News (£10 a year)
Leaflets and fact sheets (about 40 titles)
Packs (for educational purposes)

Publications list:
Available online and in print

Access to staff:
Contact by letter, by telephone, by fax, by e-mail and via website
Hours: Mon to Fri, 0930 to 1700

Access to building, collection or gallery:
No access other than to staff

Has:
178 branches throughout the United Kingdom and a National Helpline

CRY-SIS HELP LINE

Acronym or abbreviation: BM CRY-SIS

BM CRY-SIS, London, WC1N 3XX

Tel: 08451 228669
E-mail: info@cry-sis.org.uk

Website:
http://www.cry-sis.org.uk

Enquiries:
Enquiries to: Chairman

Founded:
1981

Also known as:
Cry-sis Support Group (year of change 1997)

Formerly called:
Serene

Organisation type and purpose:
National organisation, voluntary organisation, registered charity (charity number 295470).
Self-help and support group for families with excessively crying, sleepless and demanding babies.

Subject coverage:
Self-help and support for parents of excessively crying, sleepless and demanding babies.

Printed publications:
See publications list, available by postal application, sae please

Publications list:
Available in print

Access to staff:
Contact by letter and by telephone
Hours: Mon to Sun, 0900 to 2200
Special comments: Telephone access only and postal enquiries (sae please).

CUED SPEECH ASSOCIATION UK

9 Jawbone Hill, Dartmouth, Devon, TQ6 9RW

Tel: 01803 832784
Fax: 01803 835311
E-mail: info@cuedspeech.co.uk

Website:
http://www.cuedspeech.co.uk

Enquiries:
Enquiries to: Executive Director

Founded:
1975

Formerly called:
National Centre for Cued Speech (NCCS) (year of change 2000)

Organisation type and purpose:
National organisation, membership association (membership is by subscription, election or invitation), present number of members: 75, registered charity (charity number 279523), training organisation.
To provide information and training in Cued Speech throughout the UK.

Subject coverage:
Cued speech is a simple sound-based system which uses eight handshapes in 4 different positions in combination with the natural mouth movements of speech, to make all the sounds of spoken language clearly understandable to hearing-impaired people of all ages. It gives an exact visual representation of spoken language, at the same time as normal speech. The deaf people can 'see' spoken language in exactly the same way as hearing people hear it. Its use allows deaf children to develop their inner language, and improve literacy, lipreading and speech.

Printed publications:
Newsletter (4 times a year, free to members)
The Cued Speech Resource Book for Parents of Deaf Children (£29 inc. p&p)
Cued Speech booklet (£6 inc. p&p)
Cued Speech Explained video (£5 inc. p&p)
Wide range of information sheets (free)
Leaflet

Electronic and video publications:
Instructional tape for beginners (£15 inc p&p)

Access to staff:
Contact by letter, by telephone, by fax and by e-mail. Appointment necessary.
Hours: Mon to Fri, 0900 to 1700

Access to building, collection or gallery:
No access other than to staff

CULT INFORMATION CENTRE

Acronym or abbreviation: CIC

BCM Cults, London, WC1N 3XX

Tel: 0845 450 0868

Website:
http://www.cultinformation.org.uk
General information on cults and advice for families with a loved one in a cult. Information about books on the topic, especially 'Cults: A Practical Guide' published by Cult Information Centre.

Enquiries:
Enquiries to: General Secretary

Founded:
1987

Organisation type and purpose:
National organisation, voluntary organisation, registered charity (charity number 1012914), suitable for ages: all, training organisation, consultancy, research organisation.
Information and advice to families, ex-members, the media and researchers on cults. Gives lectures on the dangers of cults to a wide variety of audiences.

Subject coverage:
Cults.

Education services:
The cult information centres gives lectures/talks on the topic of cults to schools, professional groups, clubs, religious institutions and other community groups.

Museum or gallery collection, archive, or library special collection:
Archive of books and publicity material published relating to cults
Newscuttings
Relevant articles

Printed publications:
Cults: A Practical Guide (£4.74 inc. p&p)
Moonwebs (Freed J, £2.50 inc. p&p)
The Children of God (Davis D, £11 inc. p&p)

Electronic and video publications:
Cults (video)

Publications list:
Available online and in print

Access to staff:
Contact by letter and by telephone
Hours: Mon to Fri, 0900 to 1700

Access to building, collection or gallery:
No access other than to staff

CULTURAL HERITAGE NATIONAL TRAINING ORGANISATION

Acronym or abbreviation: CHNTO

Glyde House, Glydegate, Bradford, West Yorkshire, BD5 0UP

Tel: 01274 391056
Fax: 01274 394890

continued overleaf

E-mail: mail@chnto.co.uk

Website:
http://www.chnto.co.uk/library
Access to information about the range of CHNTO's work, including toolkits, reports, latest news, press releases, etc.

Enquiries:
Enquiries to: Communications Officer
Direct tel: 01274 391087
Direct e-mail: kathryn@chnto.co.uk

Founded:
1998

Formerly called:
Museum Training Institute (MTI) (year of change 1998)

Organisation type and purpose:
National government body, registered charity (charity number 1003074).
National training organisation.
To provide a focus for training activities and information in the museums and heritage field and to develop NVQ and SVQ standards for the sector.
To develop national occupational standards and vocational qualifications for those working in the museums, heritage and conservation sector.
To undertake research into the labour market, sector training needs and management development projects.

Subject coverage:
Careers in the museums, heritage and conservation sector, labour market information, courses information, skills development, modern apprenticeships, management development, equal opportunities, vocational qualifications and occupational standards.

Trade and statistical information:
Data on the numbers and characteristics of the heritage workforce.
Data on training needs and skills shortages in this sector.

Printed publications:
Careers booklet
NVQ and SVQ support materials
Standards of Occupational Competence
Order printed publications from: Information Assistant, Cultural Heritage National Training Organisation

Electronic and video publications:
Noticeboard (electronic bulletin)

Publications list:
Available in print

Access to staff:
Contact by letter, by telephone, by fax and by e-mail
Hours: Mon to Fri, 0900 to 1700
Special comments: Working office – not open to the public.

CUMBERLAND AND WESTMORLAND ANTIQUARIAN AND ARCHAEOLOGICAL SOCIETY

Acronym or abbreviation: CWAAS

Brantbeck, Wind Hall Road, Bowness-on-Windermere, LA23 3HX

Tel: 01539 445276
E-mail: info@cwaas.org.uk

Website:
http://www.cwaas.org.uk
Officers, publications, activities, contents of Transactions.
http://www.cumbriacad.ac.uk

Enquiries:
Enquiries to: Honorary Secretary
Other contacts: Publications, tel no: 01228 544120; Library, tel no: 01228 400300

Founded:
1866

Organisation type and purpose:
Learned society (membership is by subscription), present number of members: 850, registered charity (charity number 227786).

Subject coverage:
Archaeology and all aspects of history and customs of Cumberland and Westmorland, including genealogy, heraldry, parish registers, industrial archaeology, historic buildings etc.

Museum or gallery collection, archive, or library special collection:
Books and artefacts are held at Carlisle Museum, Tullie House, Castle Street, Carlisle, access by application to Librarian.
Library is now c/o Cumbria College of Art and Design, Brampton Road, Carlisle, Cumbria
Society's archives are held at Cumbria Record Office, The Castle, Carlisle

Non-library collection catalogue:
All or part available in-house

Library catalogue:
All or part available in-house

Printed publications:
Newsletter (3 times a year)
Medieval Carlisle (Henry Summerson 1993)
Transactions (annually, members)
Parish Registers some available back to 1927
Other volumes include:
The Building of Hadrian's Wall
The Stained Glass in the Churches of the Anglican Diocese of Carlisle
Prehistoric Habitation Sites on the Limestone Uplands of Eastern Cumbria
Additional new volumes:
The Cumbria Parishes from Bishop Gartrall's 'Notitia' 1714–1725 (1998)
The Lanercost Cartulary (1997)
The Accounts of Sir Daniel Fleming of Rydal Hall 1688–1701 (2001)
Thomas Denton: a Perambulation of Cumberland 1687–88 (2003)
The Websters of Kendal: a North-Western Architectural Dynasty (2004)
Order printed publications from: Publications Officer, Cumberland and Westmorland Antiquarian and Archaeological Society
10 Peter Street, Carlisle, Cumbria, CA3 8QP, tel: 01228 544120

Publications list:
Available in print

Access to staff:
Contact by letter, by e-mail and via website
Hours: Mon to Fri, 0900 to 1700

Access to building, collection or gallery:
No prior appointment required
Special comments: New arrangement are under discussion.

Affiliated to:
Council of British Archaeology (CBA)

Library is now at:
Cumbria Institute of the Arts
Brampton Road, Carlisle, Cumbria, CA3 9AY; tel: 01228 400300; fax: 01228 514491; website: www.cumbriacad.ac.uk

CUMBRIA ARCHIVE SERVICE – BARROW-IN-FURNESS

Cumbria Record Office & Local Studies Library, 140 Duke Street, Barrow in Furness, Cumbria, LA14 1XW

Tel: 01229 407377\ Minicom no. 01228 606336
Fax: 01229 894364
E-mail: barrow.record.office@cumbriacc.gov.uk

Website:
http://www.cumbria.gov.uk/archives
The general Cumbria Archive Service site.
http://www.cumbria.gov.uk/archives/pubs.asp
For the publications page.
http://www.a2a.pro.gov.uk/default.asp

The Access to Archives website, which includes a limited but growing number of record office catalogues.

Enquiries:
Enquiries to: Area Archivist

Founded:
1975

Formerly called:
Central Library (Local Studies), Ramsden Square, Barrow, Cumbria Record Office (Barrow) (year of change 1998)

Organisation type and purpose:
Local government body.
Record office.

Subject coverage:
General local history of Barrow-in-Furness and South West Cumbria, genealogy, iron mining and production, the Furness Railway, naval armaments production and design by Vickers Ltd, Barrow, urban growth and architecture.
Printed sources on Cumbria, chiefly the Furness area, including books, newspapers, journals; also transactions of local academic societies.

Special visitor services:
Operates a combined searchroom since Oct 1998, jointly controlled by Cumbria Archive Service and Cumbria Library Service.

Museum or gallery collection, archive, or library special collection:
Manorial records for various Furness Manors, 16th to 20th centuries
Microfilm of minute books of Furness Railway 1844–1923 and station staff registers, late 19th century
Records of the Furness Estate of the Duke of Buccleuch, c. 1820–1960
Ships armament drawings (mainly gun mountings) from Vickers Ltd, Barrow, 20th century
Early 19th century handbills, etc. from J Soulby, Ulverston and other local printers

Non-library collection catalogue:
All or part available online and in-house

Library catalogue:
All or part available online

Printed publications:
Information Sheets on: local sources for Family History, Church Registers; House History, Development of Barrow-in-Furness, Industries, Ships and Shipbuilding, Directories and Maps (first issued 1987–89, Manorial Records; Poor Relief; first issued 1989–1990, revised periodically)
The Ellen Rose Fieldhouse Collection: a catalogue of sources covering the history and dialect of the Kirkby-in-Furness area, 1992
See entry for the Carlisle office for publications available at all four offices

Microform publications:
A microfilm edition of Barrow-in-Furness Labour Party Records has been produced by Microform Academic Publishers
Order microform publications from: Microform Academic Publishers
East Ardsley, Wakefield, WF3 2AT

Publications list:
Available in print

Access to staff:
Contact by letter, by telephone, by fax, by e-mail and in person
Hours: Archives: Mon to Fri, 0930 to 1700; Sat, by appointment only, 0930 to 1600. Local Studies: Mon to Wed, Fri, 0930 to 1900; Thu, 0930 to 1700; Sat, 0930 to 1600

Access for disabled people:
Ramped entry, access to all public areas, toilet facilities

Links with:
Record Offices in Carlisle, Whitehaven and Kendal

Part of:
Cumbria (County Council) Archive Service

CUMBRIA ARCHIVE SERVICE – CARLISLE

Acronym or abbreviation: CROC

Cumbria Record Office, The Castle, Carlisle, Cumbria, CA3 8UR

Tel: 01228 227285 or 227284\ Minicom no. 01228 226336
Fax: 01228 607270 office hours only
E-mail: carlisle.record.office@cumbriacc.gov.uk

Website:
http://www.cumbria.gov.uk/archives

Enquiries:
Enquiries to: Assistant County Archivist
Direct tel: 01228 227283
Other contacts: Senior Archivist, Carlisle

Founded:
1962

Incorporates the former:
Joint Archives Committee for the Counties of Cumberland and Westmorland, and The City of Carlisle (year of change 1974)

Organisation type and purpose:
Local government body.
Record office.

Subject coverage:
History of Cumberland, Carlisle and Cumbria, history of property, mining and transport, etc., genealogy.

Museum or gallery collection, archive, or library special collection:
Archive of Catherine Marshall, suffragist and pacifist
Archive of Sir Esme Howard, diplomat

Non-library collection catalogue:
All or part available online and in-house

Printed publications:
A number of publications are available at all four of the Cumbrian Record Offices, including:
Church of England Parishes in Cumbria 1829 (1998)
Cumbrian Ancestors. Notes for Genealogical Searchers (3rd edn, 1998)
Map of Carlisle, 1745
Various subject guides available on Lonsdale estate, railways, tithes, the World Wars

Microform publications:
Original microfilm can be ordered or copies from existing film

Publications list:
Available online and in print

Access to staff:
Contact by letter, by telephone, by fax, by e-mail, in person and via website
Hours: Mon to Fri, 0900 to 1700
Special comments: CARN readers' ticket system.

Access to building, collection or gallery:
There is no car parking for visitors; please use public car park in Devonshire Walk

Access for disabled people:
Parking provided, ramped entry, toilet facilities

CUMBRIA ARCHIVE SERVICE – KENDAL

Cumbria Record Office, County Offices, Kendal, Cumbria, LA9 4RQ

Tel: 01539 773540\ Minicom no. 01228 606336
Fax: 01539 773538
E-mail: kendal.record.office@cumbriacc.gov.uk

Website:
http://www.cumbria.gov.uk/archives
Cumbria Archive Service website.

Enquiries:
Enquiries to: Archivist

Founded:
1962

Formerly called:
Westmorland Record Office (year of change 1974)

Organisation type and purpose:
Local government body.
Record office.

Subject coverage:
Records of: the historic county of Westmorland, the Cartmel area formerly in Lancashire north of the sands, Sedbergh, Garsdale and Dent area, formerly in West Riding of Yorkshire.

Museum or gallery collection, archive, or library special collection:
Records of Lady Anne Clifford of Appleby Castle (1590–1676)
Records of Sir Daniel Fleming MP of Rydal Hall (1633–1701)
Records of Thomas H Mawson (1861–1933), landscape architect of Lancaster

Non-library collection catalogue:
All or part available online and in-house

Printed publications:
Selection of books including:
Cumbrian Ancestors, notes for genealogical searchers (1998, £6.99)
The Ellen Rose Fieldhouse Collection Catalogue
Selection of maps, guides and posters including:
Church of England Parishes in Cumbria (map, 1829)
Henry Hoggarth's Plan of Kendal, 1853
John Todd's Plan of Kendal, 1787
John Wood's Plan of Kendal, 1833
Vital Statistics. The Westmorland Census of 1787 (ed Ashcroft L, £9.50 plus p&p)
See entry for the Carlisle office for publications available at all four offices

Publications list:
Available in print

Access to staff:
Contact by letter, by fax, by e-mail and in person
Hours: Mon to Fri, 0900 to 1700
Special comments: Readers' ticket required.

Access for disabled people:
Parking provided, level entry, access to all public areas, toilet facilities

Parent body:
Cumbria (County Council) Archive Service
The Castle, Carlisle

CUMBRIA CHAMBER OF COMMERCE AND INDUSTRY

The Enterprise Centre, James Street, Carlisle, Cumbria, CA2 5DA

Tel: 01228 534120
Fax: 01228 515602
E-mail: info@cumbriachamberofcommerce.co.uk

Enquiries:
Enquiries to: Chief Executive

Founded:
May 2001

Organisation type and purpose:
Membership association (membership is by subscription).

Printed publications:
Journal (two times a year)

Access to staff:
Contact by letter
Hours: Mon to Fri, 0900 to 1700

Has:
41 county groups

CUMBRIA COLLEGE OF ART AND DESIGN LIBRARY

Acronym or abbreviation: CCAD

Brampton Road, Carlisle, Cumbria, CA3 9AY

Tel: 01228 400312
Fax: 01228 514491

Website:
http://www.libraryopac.cumbriacad.ac.uk

Enquiries:
Enquiries to: Librarian
Direct e-mail: cdaniel@cumbriacad.ac.uk

Subject coverage:
Ceramics, textiles, painting, sculpture, printmaking, photography, graphic design, media studies, fashion, product design, heritage management, performing arts, archaeology, Hhstory, local history, writing.

Non-library collection catalogue:
All or part available online

Library catalogue:
All or part available online

Access to staff:
Contact by letter, by telephone and by fax. Appointment necessary.
Hours: Mon to Thu, 0845 to 2000; Fri, 0845 to 1600; Sat, 0900 to 1300

Access for disabled people:
Parking provided

Member of:
HCLRG
Northern Regional Library System and ARLIS

CUMBRIA ENVIRONMENTAL AND GEOLOGICAL SERVICES

Acronym or abbreviation: CEGS

Watch Hill, Aspatria, Wigton, Cumbria, CA7 3SB

Tel: 016973 22565
Fax: 016973 21375
E-mail: dred.cegs@bigfoot.com

Enquiries:
Enquiries to: Proprietor

Founded:
1992

Organisation type and purpose:
Consultancy.

Subject coverage:
Contaminated ground investigations and reports, environmental surveys, geotechnical site investigations and reports, geological appraisals, investigations, mapping and report writing, environmental forestry and habitat management, extensive knowledge of the farming year and farming practices in UK and overseas, knowledge of geology in relation to mine design, geomorphology, mapping and evaluation of mineral reserves, footpath surveys and risk assessments.

Access to staff:
Contact by letter, by telephone and by e-mail
Hours: Mon to Fri, 0900 to 1700

CUMBRIA RECORD OFFICE AND LOCAL STUDIES LIBRARY

Scotch Street, Whitehaven, Cumbria, CA28 7NL

Tel: 01946 506420
Fax: 01946 852919
E-mail: whitehaven.record.office@cumbriacc.gov.uk

Website:
http://www.cumbria.gov.uk/archives/whrec.asp
Guidance on finding the office, details of holdings and information relating to the educational use of the archive service and tracing a Cumbrian family history. Online catalogue of archive holdings.
http://www.a2a.org.uk

continued overleaf

Online catalogue for part of the collection

Enquiries:
Enquiries to: Archivist

Founded:
1996

Organisation type and purpose:
Local government body.

Subject coverage:
History of West Cumbria and Whitehaven.

Museum or gallery collection, archive, or library special collection:
Whitehaven Local Studies Library (formerly in the Daniel Hay Library, Whitehaven)

Non-library collection catalogue:
All or part available online and in-house

Library catalogue:
All or part available online and in-house

Printed publications:
A variety of publications to inform or entertain, relating to aspects of Cumbrian history and its archives.
Order printed publications from: See website for details.

Publications list:
Available in print

Access to staff:
Contact by letter, by telephone, by fax, by e-mail and in person

Access to building, collection or gallery:
Mon, Tue, Thu and Fri, 0930 to 1230 and 1330 to 1700; Wed, 0930 to 1230 and 1330 to 1900; alternate Sat, 0900 to 1300
Special comments: CARN readers' ticket required.

Access for disabled people:
Ramped entry, access to all public areas, toilet facilities

Constituent part of:
Cumbria Archive Service

CUMBRIA TOURISM

Windermere Road, Staveley, Cumbria, LA8 9PL

Tel: 01539 822222
Fax: 01539 825079
E-mail: info@cumbriatourism.org

Website:
http://www.golakes.co.uk

Enquiries:
Enquiries to: Chief Executive

Founded:
1974

Organisation type and purpose:
Membership association (membership is by subscription).

Subject coverage:
Tourism in Cumbria and the Lake District.

Publications list:
Available in print

Access to staff:
Contact by letter, by telephone, by fax and by e-mail
Hours: Mon to Fri, 0900 to 1700

Links with:
local authorities and commercial members
Visit Britain

CURATIVE HYPNOTHERAPY REGISTER

Acronym or abbreviation: CHR

584 Derby Road, Nottingham, NG7 2GZ

Tel: 0115 970 1233
E-mail: info@curativehypnotherapyregister.co.uk

Website:
http://www.curativehypnotherapyregister.co.uk
About hypnosis, hypnotherapy, curative hypnotherapy; information for patients; problems that can be treated; requirements/duty of members; information on the charity itself; further information sites.

Enquiries:
Enquiries to: The Directors

Founded:
1985

Organisation type and purpose:
International organisation, advisory body, professional body (membership is by subscription, qualification, election or invitation). To enhance the understanding of hypnotherapy, to provide advice/information on the subject of hypnosis/hypnotherapy; maintains a register of qualified practitioners nationwide.

Subject coverage:
Improving standards of hypnotherapy, list of qualified practitioners nationwide, information about hypnotherapy.

Printed publications:
Register of Qualified Therapists (free of charge)

Publications list:
Available online

Access to staff:
Contact by letter, by telephone, by e-mail and via website
Hours: Mon to Fri, 0900 to 1700

CUTLERY AND ALLIED TRADES RESEARCH ASSOCIATION

Acronym or abbreviation: CATRA

Henry Street, Sheffield, South Yorkshire, S3 7EQ

Tel: 0114 276 9736
Fax: 0114 272 2151
E-mail: info@catra.org

Website:
http://www.catra.org
General information about services, products and helpful advice.

Enquiries:
Enquiries to: Director of Research

Founded:
1952

Organisation type and purpose:
Consultancy, research organisation.

Subject coverage:
Corrosion, grinding, heat treatment, metal finishing, electroplating, metallography, polishes and polishing, stainless steel, silver plate, automation, robotics, quality control, quality testing, cutlery, machine knives, knives, scissors, tools, sharpening, cookware, kitchen gadgets, surgical instruments, hand tools and garden tools.

Printed publications:
Annual Report
Leaflets on the care of cutlery (for sale)
Newsletters
Technical reports (for sale)

Access to staff:
Contact by letter, by telephone, by fax, by e-mail and via website. Appointment necessary. All charged.
Hours: Mon to Fri, 0900 to 1700

Access to building, collection or gallery:
Prior appointment required

Member of:
BSI

CYCLING TIME TRIALS

Acronym or abbreviation: RTTC

77 Arlington Drive, Pennington, Leigh, Lancashire, WN7 3QP

Tel: 01942 603976
Fax: 01942 262326
E-mail: phil.heaton@cyclingtimetrials.org.uk

Website:
http://ctt.org.uk

Enquiries:
Enquiries to: National Secretary

Founded:
1937

Organisation type and purpose:
National organisation, membership association (membership is by subscription), present number of members: 1064 clubs, voluntary organisation. National governing body for cycling road time trials.

Subject coverage:
Cycle road time trials.

Printed publications:
Annual Handbook (with list of some 2000 events, £6)
Rules, Regulations, Records, Past Champions etc

Electronic and video publications:
Championship DVDs (£6)
Entry forms (disc, £2.50)

Publications list:
Available online and in print

Access to staff:
Contact by letter, by telephone, by fax, by e-mail and via website. Appointment necessary.
Hours: Mon to Fri, 0900 to 1700

Access to building, collection or gallery:
No access other than to staff

Access for disabled people:
Parking provided, ramped entry, access to all public areas, toilet facilities
Hours: Mon to Fri, 0900 to 1700

Links with:
Sports Council and the Central Council for Physical Recreation

CYCLISTS' TOURING CLUB

Acronym or abbreviation: CTC

Parklands, Railton, Road, Guildford, Surrey, GU2 9JX

Tel: 0870 873 0060
Fax: 0870 873 0064
E-mail: cycling@ctc.org.uk

Website:
http://www.ctc.org.uk

Enquiries:
Enquiries to: Public Relations Manager
Other contacts: Director

Founded:
1878

Organisation type and purpose:
Membership association.
Promotes cycling for leisure, travel and transport.

Subject coverage:
All aspects of cycling; recreational and utility cycling; technical; legal aid; cycle insurance; mail order; campaigning; information for local/central government; rights and safety of all cyclists; touring; third party insurance; publications; all ages and abilities of cyclists helped.

Museum or gallery collection, archive, or library special collection:
Cycle Archive (CTC est. 1878)

Printed publications:
Route sheets
CTC Cycle Digest (quarterly)
CTC Event Guide
Cycle Away!
CTC Handbook (annually)
Cycle Touring & Campaigning (6 times a year)
Information booklets and sheets
Tours Guide

Various research reports
CTC Cyclists Welcome

Affiliated to:
Alliance Internationale de Tourisme (AIT)
BCF
European Cycling Federation (ECF)
RTTC

CYFA

Formal name: Church Youth Fellowships
Association
Acronym or abbreviation: CYFA

CPAS, Athena Drive, Tachbrook Park, Warwick,
CV34 6NG

Tel: 01926 458458
Fax: 01926 458459
E-mail: thehub@cpas.org.uk

Website:
http://www.cpas.org.uk
Details of events and products.

Enquiries:
Enquiries to: Head
Direct tel: 01926 458438

Founded:
1930

Organisation type and purpose:
To equip, encourage, and enable churches in youth
ministry and discipleship.

Subject coverage:
Christian teaching and training for older teenagers,
training of adults for youth leadership.

Printed publications:
A range of titles under the following headings:
Youth and Children's Resources
Youth Leadership skills
Worship
Evangelism
Small Groups
Strategy and Leadership
Order printed publications from: 24 hour sales
orderline
tel: 01926 458400

Electronic and video publications:
Web-based teaching an resource materials for
leaders and youth groups

Publications list:
Available online and in print

Access to staff:
Contact by letter, by telephone, by fax, by e-mail
and via website. Appointment necessary.
Hours: Mon to Fri, 0900 to 1700

Affiliated to:
Church Pastoral Aid Society (CPAS)
at the same address

CYNGOR GWYNEDD COUNCIL

Stryd y Jêl, Shirehall Street, Caernarfon, Gwynedd,
LL55 1SH

Tel: 01286 672255
Fax: 01286 673993
E-mail: enquiries@gwynedd.gov.uk

Website:
http://www.gwynedd.gov.uk
Council services; bus timetables; library services;
tourism brochures; Gwynedd facts and figures.

Enquiries:
Enquiries to: Communications Manager
Direct tel: 01286 679310
Direct fax: 01286 679488
Direct e-mail: siongwilliams@gwynedd.gov.uk

Founded:
1996
Gwynedd County Council (year of change 1996)

Organisation type and purpose:
Local government body.

Subject coverage:
Local government services.

Library catalogue:
All or part available online

Access to staff:
Contact by letter, by telephone, by fax, by e-mail,
in person and via website. Appointment necessary.
Hours: Mon to Fri, 0900 to 1700

Other addresses:
Arfon Area Office
Penrallt, Caernarfon, Gwynedd, LL55 1BN; tel:
01286 673113; fax: 01286 672635
Dwyfor Area Office
Ffordd y Cob, Pwllheli, Gwynedd, LL53 5AA;
tel: 01758 613131; fax: 01758 613265
Meirionnydd Area Office
Cae Penarlag, Dolgellau, Gwynedd, LL40 1HL;
tel: 01341 422341; fax: 01341 423984

CYPRUS HIGH COMMISSION

93 Park Street, London, W1K 7ET

Tel: 020 7499 8272
Fax: 020 7491 0691
E-mail: cyphclondon@dial.pipex.com

Website:
http://www.cyprus.gov.cy
Official website of the Republic of Cyprus, general
information about the country of Cyprus,
information on government and independent
services, overseas and repatriated Cypriots,
business in Cyprus, news, links to other Cyprus-
related websites.
http://www.mfa.gov.cy
Website of the Cyprus Ministry of Foreign Affairs,
information on Cyprus question, Cyprus and the
European Union, foreign policy issues, also
information for overseas and repatriated Cypriots
and consular information, news.

Enquiries:
Enquiries to: Press Counsellor
Direct tel: 020 7491 8568
Direct fax: 020 7499 1346
Direct e-mail: presscounsellor@chclondon.org.uk
Other contacts: Consular General; Direct Line: 020
7569 5350 for Consular matters.

Organisation type and purpose:
National government body.
Embassy and Consulate. Diplomatic.

Subject coverage:
General information about Cyprus (press and
office information).
Consular enquiries (Consulate).

Library catalogue:
All or part available in-house

Printed publications:
Various subject publications are available free of
charge from Press and Information Office
General
Political/The Cyprus Problem
Cyprus and the European Union
Business/Economy
Others which include: Filming in Cyprus, and
Cyprus in Figures (published by the Statistical
Office of Cyprus)
Leaflets
Cyprus Tourism Organisation
University of Cyprus
Maps

Electronic and video publications:
The following are available free of charge from
Press and Information Office:
Cyprus 2000 (CD-ROM)
Cyprus History and Culture (CD-ROM)

Access to staff:
Contact by letter, by telephone, by fax and by e-
mail
Hours: Mon to Fri, 0930 to 1700
Consulate Public Hours: Mon to Fri, 0930 to 1300

Connections with:
Cyprus Tourism Organisation
17 Hanover Street, London, W1S 1YP; tel: 020
7569 8800; fax: 020 7499 4935; e-mail: ctolon@
ctolon.demon.co.uk; website: www.visitcyprus
.org.cy
Cyprus Trade Centre
3rd Floor, 29 Princes Street, London, W1R 7RG;
tel: 020 7629 6288; fax: 020 7629 5244; e-mail:
cytradecentreuk@btinternet.com

Parent body:
Ministry of Foreign Affairs of Cyprus
Dem Severis Avenue, Nicosia 1447, Cyprus; tel: +
357 22 300713; fax: + 37 7 22 665313; e-mail:
minforeign1@cytanet.com.cy; website: www.mfa
.gov.cy

CYSTIC FIBROSIS TRUST

11 London Road, Bromley, Kent, BR1 1BY

Tel: 020 8464 7211
Fax: 020 8313 0472
E-mail: enquiries@cftrust.org.uk

Website:
http://www.cftrust.org.uk

Enquiries:
Enquiries to: Chief Executive

Founded:
1964

Formerly called:
Cystic Fibrosis Research Trust

Organisation type and purpose:
Registered charity (charity number 1079049),
research organisation.
Affiliated to the International Cystic Fibrosis
(Mucoviscidosis) Association and the European
Working Group for Cystic Fibrosis.

Subject coverage:
Research into the condition, and advice in coping
with cystic fibrosis.

**Museum or gallery collection, archive, or library
special collection:**
Library of books and documents relating to cystic
fibrosis

Printed publications:
Publications include:
Annual Review
Booklets/Fact sheets
CF News
Cystic Fibrosis: the facts (£9.95, OUP 1995)
List of Research Projects

Electronic and video publications:
Audio Tapes: advice and information (available
also in Urdu and Gujerati)
Videos on Treatment and living with CF (purchase
or loan)

Publications list:
Available in print

Access to staff:
Contact by letter, by telephone, by fax, by e-mail
and via website. Appointment necessary.
Hours: Mon to Fri, 0900 to 1700

Affiliated to:
European Working Group for Cystic Fibrosis
International Cystic Fibrosis (Mucoviscidosis)
Association

Has:
local self-help groups

CYSTITIS AND OVERACTIVE
BLADDER FOUNDATION

Formal name: Cystitis and Overactive Bladder
Foundation incorporating the Interstitial Cystitis
Support Group
Acronym or abbreviation: COBFoundation

76 High Street, Stony Stratford, Buckinghamshire,
MK11 1AH

continued overleaf

Tel: 01908 569169
Fax: 01908 569169
E-mail: info@cobfoundation.org

Website:
http://www.cobfoundation.org
Full range of information.

Enquiries:
Enquiries to: Development Manager and Charity
Administrator
Direct e-mail: info@cobfoundation.org

Founded:
1994

Organisation type and purpose:
Membership association (membership is by
subscription), registered charity (charity number
1047714).
Support for those with a specific medical
condition.

Subject coverage:
Interstitial cystitis, treatments, therapies, medical
research data.

Printed publications:
Interstitial Cystitis Survival Guide
Newsletter
Series of Information Leaflets

Electronic and video publications:
Understanding and coping with Interstitial Cystitis
(video)
Understanding Interstitial Cystitis (video)

Publications list:
Available in print

Access to staff:
Contact by letter, by telephone, by fax, by e-mail
and via website
Hours: Mon to Fri, 0900 to 1700

Access for disabled people:
Special comments: Steep narrow stairs

CZECH AND SLOVAK TOURIST CENTRE

Acronym or abbreviation: CTC

16 Frognal Parade, Finchley Road, London, NW3
5HG

Tel: 020 7794 3264
Fax: 020 7794 3265
E-mail: reservations@cztc.co.uk

Website:
http://www.czech-wedding.co.uk
http://www.czechtravel.co.uk
http://www.czech-slovak-tourist.co.uk

Enquiries:
Enquiries to: Director

Founded:
1994

Formerly called:
Czech Tourist Centre

Organisation type and purpose:
National Slovak Tourist Board/Tour Operator.

Printed publications:
Photograph negatives (free hire, deposit required)

Electronic and video publications:
Videos and CD-ROMs (free hire, deposit required)

Access to staff:
Contact by letter, by telephone, by fax, by e-mail
and in person
Hours: Mon to Fri, 1000 to 1800

CZECH CENTRE

13 Harley Street, London, W1G 9QG

Tel: 020 7307 5180
Fax: 020 7323 3709
E-mail: info@czechcentre.org.uk

Website:
http://www.czechcentres.cz/london/

Enquiries:
Enquiries to: Administration and Marketing
Direct e-mail: storchova@czechcentre.org.uk

Founded:
1993

Organisation type and purpose:
International organisation.
Information centre of the Czech Republic.

Subject coverage:
Cultural information, activities, tourism, local and
foreign investment, exhibitions, trade.

Access to staff:
Contact by letter, by telephone, by fax, by e-mail
and via website
Hours: Tue, 1000 to 1900; Wed to Fri,1000 to 1800

D H LAWRENCE SOCIETY

24 Briarwood Avenue, Nottingham, NG3 6JQ

Tel: 0115 950 3008

Enquiries:
Enquiries to: Secretary

Founded:
1974

Organisation type and purpose:
Learned society (membership is by subscription),
present number of members: 200.
Study of life and works of D H Lawrence.

Subject coverage:
Life and works of D H Lawrence.

Printed publications:
D H Lawrence Society Journal (annually)
D H Lawrence Society Newsletter (2 times a year)

Access to staff:
Contact by letter and by telephone
Hours: Mon to Fri, 0900 to 1700

DACORUM BUSINESS NETWORK

Acronym or abbreviation: DBN

1–11 Bridge Street, Hemel Hempstead,
Hertfordshire, HP1 1EG

Tel: 01442 219933
Fax: 01442 219966
E-mail: info@dbn.org.uk

Enquiries:
Enquiries to: Manager

Formerly called:
Business Link Hertfordshire

Organisation type and purpose:
Local government body, advisory body, service
industry, training organisation.
To help local businesses start and grow by
providing a wide range of information and advice.

Subject coverage:
Local information, networking opportunities and
starting a business.

Access to staff:
Contact by letter, by telephone, by fax, by e-mail
and in person
Hours: Mon to Fri, 0900 to 1730

Branch office of:
Business Link Hertfordshire
St Albans, Hertfordshire

DAFFODIL SOCIETY

105 Bramcote Road, Nottingham, NG9 3GZ

Tel: 0115 925 5498
E-mail: rogerbb@lineone.net

Website:
http://www.the daffodil society .com

Enquiries:
Enquiries to: Secretary
Other contacts: Membership Secretary (tel. 01264
790745)

Founded:
1898

Organisation type and purpose:
Membership association (membership is by
subscription), societies and individual members,
voluntary organisation, registered charity (charity
number 1055817).
To encourage the cultivation of the genus
Narcissus.

Subject coverage:
Daffodils (genus Narcissus): breeding of new
cultivars; control of pest and disease; general
cultivation and exhibition.

Printed publications:
Annual Journal (February, for members)
Newsletter (July, for members)
Show Handbook (for sale)
Order printed publications from: Merchandising
Manager, The Daffodil Society, 8 Foxdalls, Birch
Green, Hertford, SG14 2LS, e-mail: baxterdaffs@
hotmail.com

Access to staff:
Contact by letter, by telephone, by e-mail and via
website

DAIRY COUNCIL, THE

Henrietta House, 17–18 Henrietta Street, Covent
Garden, London, WC2E 8QH

Tel: 020 7395 4030
Fax: 020 7240 9679
E-mail: info@dairycouncil.org.uk

Website:
http://www.milk.co.uk
Types and composition of milk, range of dairy
products, nutritional composition, history of
dairying, modern methods of production,
processing and manufacture.

Enquiries:
Enquiries to: Communications Manager

Founded:
1920

Formerly called:
The National Dairy Council (year of change 2001)

Organisation type and purpose:
Trade association.
Promotional organisation for the whole dairy
industry in Britain.

Subject coverage:
Dairy industry, milk, dairy products, nutrition,
careers in the dairy industry, market data.

**Museum or gallery collection, archive, or library
special collection:**
Foreign Dairy Industry journals
Historical exhibits
Photographic library
United Kingdom and European Community Dairy
Facts and Figures

Trade and statistical information:
Consumption data and market research on the
liquid milk market, top line data for other dairy
products.

Library catalogue:
All or part available in-house

Printed publications:
Press releases
Catalogue of education material (booklets,
factsheets, charts and posters, for Key Stage 1 to
4)
Catalogue of nutrition and health material
Consumer leaflets
Dairy Education (termly)
Dairy Mirror (quarterly)
Material for schools and teachers
UK and EC Dairy Facts and Figures

Nutrition and health education material (booklets free of charge)

Electronic and video publications:
The Dairy Channel (video, Key Stage 2, £5)
Discover Milk (CD-ROM, Key Stage 3, 4, GNVQ, £7.50)
Milk IT! (PC, Key Stage 2, £15)
Milk on the Move (video, Key Stage 1 and 2, £10)
The Meal Ticket (video, purchase not hire, £10)

Access to staff:
Contact by letter and by fax. Appointment necessary.
Hours: Mon to Fri, 0900 to 1700

Links to:
The Dairy Industry Federation (for processors)
The Milk Development Council (for farmers)

Other addresses:
Dairy Council for Northern Ireland
456 Antrim Road, Belfast, BT15 5GB; tel: 028 9077 0113

DAIRY UK

93 Baker Street, London, W1U 6QQ

Tel: 020 7486 7244
Fax: 020 7487 4734
E-mail: info@dairyuk.org

Website:
http://www.dairyuk.org/

Enquiries:
Enquiries to: Secretary
Direct tel: 020 7467 2648
Direct e-mail: sbates@dairyuk.org

Created by the merger of:
Dairy Industry Federation (DIF) and the National Dairymen's Association (NDA)

Formerly called:
Dairy Trade Federation (DTF) (year of change 1993)

Organisation type and purpose:
Trade association.
Represents the interests of United Kingdom dairy companies.

Subject coverage:
Milk and milk products.

Printed publications:
Annual Review (available for purchase)

Access to staff:
Contact by letter, by telephone, by fax and by e-mail
Hours: Mon to Fri, 0900 to 1700

Access for disabled people:
Level entry

Member of:
European Dairy Association
The Dairy Council
United Kingdom Dairy Association

DAIRY UK (NORTHERN IRELAND)

8 Ranfurly Avenue, Bangor, County Down, BT20 3SN

Tel: 028 9147 1300
Fax: 028 9147 1300
E-mail: parcher@dairyuk.org

Enquiries:
Enquiries to: Northern Ireland Director

Founded:
1995

Organisation type and purpose:
Trade association (membership is by subscription), present number of members: 9.

Subject coverage:
Dairy processing industry in Northern Ireland.

Access to staff:
Contact by letter and by e-mail

Hours: Mon to Fri, 0900 to 1700

Access to building, collection or gallery:
Prior appointment required

Access for disabled people:
Parking provided, level entry, access to all public areas, toilet facilities

DAIWA ANGLO-JAPANESE FOUNDATION

Acronym or abbreviation: DAJF

Daiwa Foundation Japan House, 13–14 Cornwall Terrace, London, NW1 4QP

Tel: 020 7486 4348
Fax: 020 7486 2914
E-mail: office@ajf.org.uk

Website:
http://www.dajf.org.uk

Enquiries:
Enquiries to: Receptionist
Direct fax: 020 7486 3049

Founded:
1988

Organisation type and purpose:
Registered charity (charity number 299955).
To support links between the UK and Japan by awarding Daiwa Scholarhips, grant-making, and a year-round programme of events.

Subject coverage:
Japan, Japanese culture and the Japanese people.

Museum or gallery collection, archive, or library special collection:
Library (open to the public)

Access to staff:
Contact by letter, by telephone, by fax, by e-mail and in person. Appointment necessary.
Hours: Mon to Fri, 0930 to 1730
Special comments: Non-commercial enquiries only.

Links with:
Daiwa Anglo-Japanese Foundation
810 TBR Building, 2–10–2 Nagata-cho, Chiyoda-Ku, Tokyo, 100–0614, Japan; tel: 00 813 5501 2980; fax: 00 813 5501 2983; e-mail: dajftkyo@qa2.50-net.ne.jp

DARTINGTON COLLEGE OF ARTS

Dartington Hall Estate, Totnes, Devon, TQ9 6EJ

Tel: 01803 862224
Fax: 01803 861666
E-mail: library@dartington.ac.uk

Website:
http://www.dartington.ac.uk
Prospectus, news.

Enquiries:
Enquiries to: Librarian
Direct tel: 01803 861651

Founded:
1961

Organisation type and purpose:
Higher education in the performing arts.

Subject coverage:
Music, theatre, visual arts, arts management, writing for performance.

Library catalogue:
All or part available online

Access to staff:
Contact by letter, by telephone, by fax, by e-mail, in person and via website. Non-members charged.
Hours: Mon to Fri, 0900 to 2100; Sat, Sun, 1330 to 1730

Access to building, collection or gallery:
No prior appointment required

Hours: Mon to Fri, 0900 to 2100; Sat, Sun, 1330 to 1730

Access for disabled people:
Level entry, toilet facilities

DARTMOOR NATIONAL PARK AUTHORITY

Acronym or abbreviation: DNP/DNPA

Parke, Bovey Tracey, Devon, TQ13 9JQ

Tel: 01626 832093
Fax: 01626 834684
E-mail: hq@dartmoor-npa.gov.uk

Website:
http://www.dartmoor-npa.gov.uk
Copy of Dartmoor Visitor and other information, links to others.

Enquiries:
Enquiries to: Chief Executive
Other contacts: Directors

Founded:
1951

Organisation type and purpose:
Local government body.
National Park Authority.

Subject coverage:
Moorland and woodland management, upland archaeology, recreation management, development control, urban and rural enhancement, listed building protection, farm conservation, species conservation, community support, information and interpretation, design techniques.

Museum or gallery collection, archive, or library special collection:
Books, photographs and slides pertaining to Dartmoor only
Taylor Collection, photographs
Parminter Collection, photographs
Minter Collection (copy archaeological excavations)
French Collection (assorted papers, photographs and artefacts)

Trade and statistical information:
Corporate Plan.

Library catalogue:
All or part available in-house

Printed publications:
A large range of books, leaflets, study pack, factsheets, maps and posters on the moor and the subjects listed
Dartmoor Visitor (newspaper, 2 per year)

Microform publications:
Planning applications, (microfilm, viewing by appointment, no sales)

Electronic and video publications:
CD: Moor Memories – Collection 1: Rabbits, whortleberries and railways. Collection 2: Lovely days. Collection 3: Blacksticks and blizzards.
Virtually Dartmoor website: A Virtual Tour of Higher Uppacott. The Moor Memories project also has an archive of over 100 oral history recordings

Publications list:
Available online and in print

Access to staff:
Contact by letter, by telephone, by fax, by e-mail, in person and via website. Appointment necessary.
Hours: Mon to Thu, 0900 to 1700; Fri, 0900 to 1630

Access to building, collection or gallery:
Prior appointment required

Access for disabled people:
Parking provided, ramped entry, toilet facilities
Special comments: Disabled access to ground floor only.

Also at:
High Moorland Visitor Centre (HMVC)
Princetown, Devon; tel: 01822 890414; e-mail: hmvc@dartmoor-npa.fsbusiness.co.uk

continued overleaf

Parent body:
Association of National Park Authorities (ANPA)

DARTMOOR PRESERVATION ASSOCIATION

Acronym or abbreviation: DPA

Duchy Hotel, Tavistock Road, Princetown, Yelverton, Devon, PL20 6QF

Tel: 01822 890646
E-mail: info@dartmoorpreservation.com

Website:
http://www.dartmoor-preservation-assoc.org.uk

Enquiries:
Enquiries to: Executive Secretary

Founded:
1883

Organisation type and purpose:
Membership association (membership is by subscription), present number of members: 2400, voluntary organisation, registered charity (charity number 215665).
Conservation and amenity interests.

Subject coverage:
All information relevant to Dartmoor.

Printed publications:
Newsletter (free to members)

Access to staff:
Contact by letter, by telephone, by e-mail and via website. Appointment necessary.
Hours: Tue and Thu, 0930 to 1430

DARTMOUTH TOURIST INFORMATION CENTRE

The Engine House, Mayors Avenue, Dartmouth, Devon, TQ6 9YY

Tel: 01803 834224
Fax: 01803 835631
E-mail: holidays@discoverdartmouth.com

Website:
http://www.discoverdartmouth.com

Enquiries:
Enquiries to: Manager

Founded:
1993

Organisation type and purpose:
Advisory body, museum, suitable for ages: 8+.

Subject coverage:
Features the Newcomen Atmospheric Engine, a preserved working steam atmospheric engine which was re-erected here in Thomas Newcomen's home town in 1963 to mark the 300th anniversary of his birth. In 1993 it was combined with a new tourist information centre.

Printed publications:
Discover Dartmouth

Access to staff:
Contact by letter, by telephone, by e-mail, in person and via website
Hours: Mon to Fri, 0930 to 1600

Access to building, collection or gallery:
No prior appointment required
Hours: Apr to Oct: Mon to Sat, 0930 to 1700; Sun, 1000 to 1400
Nov to Mar: Mon to Sat, 0930 to 1600

Access for disabled people:
Level entry, access to all public areas

DATA AND ARCHIVAL DAMAGE CONTROL CENTRE

Acronym or abbreviation: DADCC

4 Bridge Wharf, 156 Caledonian Road, London, N1 9UU

Tel: 020 7837 8215
E-mail: DADCC@netcomuk.co.uk

Website:
www.dadcc.com
Fire, flood and bomb damaged materials salavaged. Coaching and mentoring for libraries, and training

Enquiries:
Enquiries to: Managing Director
Direct tel: 07973 295155

Founded:
1986

Organisation type and purpose:
Training organisation, consultancy.
Forensic disaster management.

Subject coverage:
Salvage and restoration of books and documents damaged by fires, floods and terrorist activities; disaster planning, health and safety equipment that should be worn when entering disaster sites, training on pre-disaster planning and post-disaster recovery operations; educational literature.

Education services:
Training, talks and papers

Museum or gallery collection, archive, or library special collection:
Slide reference library in UK disaster case studies

Printed publications:
DADCC brochure online
Dockpack Information (free)
Getting it Right (free)

Access to staff:
Contact by letter, by telephone, by e-mail, in person and via website. Appointment necessary.
Hours: Mon to Fri, 0900 to 1700

Access to building, collection or gallery:
No access other than to staff

Access for disabled people:
Toilet facilities

DATA PUBLISHERS ASSOCIATION

Acronym or abbreviation: DPA

Queens House, 28 Kingsway, London, WC2B 6JR

Tel: 020 7405 0836
Fax: 020 7404 4167
E-mail: info@dpa.org.uk

Website:
http://www.dpa.org.uk

Enquiries:
Enquiries to: Marketing Co-ordinator
Direct e-mail: sarah.gooch@dpa.org.uk
Other contacts: Executive Director

Founded:
1970

Organisation type and purpose:
Trade association (membership is by subscription), present number of members: 80.
Not a directory publisher or distributor.

Subject coverage:
Directories, directory and data publishing.

Trade and statistical information:
Advertising statistics, business, salaries and benefits for directory publishing.

Printed publications:
Descriptive booklet and List of Members
Newsletter

Publications list:
Available in print

Access to staff:
Contact by letter, by telephone, by fax and by e-mail
Hours: Mon to Fri, 0900 to 1700

Access to building, collection or gallery:
No access other than to staff

Links with:
Advertising Association
Advertising Standards Board of Finance
Confederation of Information Communication Industries
Digital Content Forum
European Association of Directory and Database Publishers
Periodical Publishers Association
Publishing Skills Group

DATSUN OWNERS CLUB

40 Humber Way, Donnington, Telford, Shropshire, TF2 8LJ

Tel: 01342 321000
E-mail: adr@datsunworld.com

Website:
http://www.datsunworld.com

Enquiries:
Enquiries to: Archivist

Founded:
1993

Organisation type and purpose:
International organisation, membership association (membership is by subscription), present number of members: 300, voluntary organisation.
Preservation of Datsun cars, help with obtaining parts, bringing together owners of this marque.

Subject coverage:
History of Datsuns, technical information, whereabouts of parts or cars.

Museum or gallery collection, archive, or library special collection:
Newspaper and magazine articles
Owners' manuals
Photographs
Spare parts available for Datsun cars
Workshop manuals

Trade and statistical information:
Production numbers of Datsun cars, numbers of examples surviving.

Printed publications:
Datsun Owners Club Newsletter (4 times a year, members, annual subscription £12)

Access to staff:
Contact by letter, by telephone, by e-mail and via website. Appointment necessary.
Hours: Mon to Fri, 1000 to 1900

Archivist:
Datsun Owners Club
7 School Road, Fritton, Norwich, Norfolk, NR15 2QN; tel: 01508 499620; e-mail: nigelg@ tinyonline.co.uk

DAVID LEWIS CENTRE FOR EPILEPSY

Acronym or abbreviation: DLC

Mill Lane, Warford, Alderley Edge, Cheshire, SK9 7UD

Tel: 01565 640000
Fax: 01565 640100
E-mail: enquiries@davidlewis.org.uk

Website:
http://www.davidlewis.org.uk

Enquiries:
Enquiries to: Chief Executive

Founded:
1904

Organisation type and purpose:
Registered charity (charity number 1000392)
The David Lewis Centre provides a unique range of services for adults and children with complicated epilepsy. Services include The David Lewis School, The David Lewis College, Children's Epilepsy Outreach Assessments, Adult Social Care

Provision, Residential Behaviour Service, Adult Assessment Unit and Residential High Dependency Unit.

Subject coverage:
Epilepsy and associated disabilities, in adults and children, including behaviour problems, understanding, treatment care, stabilisation, rehabilitation, research of adults and children. Adults and children – severe epilepsy and associated problems, assessment, treatment, residential care, education, training and rehabilitation service for children and young people with acquired brain injuries.

Access to staff:
Contact by letter, by telephone, by fax and by e-mail. Appointment necessary.
Hours: Mon to Fri, 0900 to 1700

Access to building, collection or gallery:
Prior appointment required

Access for disabled people:
Ramped entry, toilet facilities

DAVID WILLIAMS PICTURE LIBRARY

Allt-na-Craobh, Old Shore Road, Connel, Argyll, PA37 1PT

Tel: 01631 710586
Fax: 01631 710586
E-mail: david@scotland-guide.co.uk

Enquiries:
Enquiries to: Proprietor

Founded:
1989

Organisation type and purpose:
Commercial picture library.

Subject coverage:
Colour photographic transparencies of Scotland, Iceland, Spain and a number of other countries, photographs of landscapes, landforms, buildings, towns and sites of historical interest.

Museum or gallery collection, archive, or library special collection:
Colour photographic transparencies of Scotland, Iceland, Spain and a number of other countries

Access to staff:
Contact by letter, by telephone, by fax and by e-mail. Appointment necessary.
Hours: ordinary business hours, also evenings and weekends

Member of:
British Association of Picture Libraries and Agencies

DAWSON BOOKS LIMITED

Foxhills House, Rushden, Northamptonshire, NN10 6DB

Tel: 01933 417500
Fax: 01933 417501

Website:
http://www.dawsonbooks.co.uk
Electronic library news.

Enquiries:
Enquiries to: Marketing Manager
Direct e-mail: marketing@dawsonbooks.co.uk

Founded:
1809

Organisation type and purpose:
International organisation, service industry, Supplier of books.

Subject coverage:
Dawson Books is a member of Dawson Holdings plc and leads the market in the use of information technology to expedite the book buying process, providing a total acquisitions package for professional librarians worldwide. Dawson sets the industry standard with its web interfaces, shelf-ready book supply and now with the delivery of eContent through dawsonera.

Printed publications:
Dawson Books Brochure of Services

Electronic and video publications:
enterBooks.com
enterProfile.com

Access to staff:
Contact by letter, by telephone, by fax and by e-mail
Hours: Mon to Thurs, 0845 to 1645, Fri 0845 to 1600

Access to building, collection or gallery:
Prior appointment required

Access for disabled people:
Parking provided, level entry, access to all public areas, toilet facilities

DAYCARE TRUST

21 St Georges Road, London, SE1 6ES

Tel: 020 7840 3350
Fax: 020 7840 3355
E-mail: info@daycaretrust.org.uk

Website:
http://www.daycaretrust.org.uk
http://www.payingforchildcare.org.uk

Enquiries:
Enquiries to: Information Officer

Founded:
1986

Formerly called:
National Childcare Campaign

Organisation type and purpose:
Voluntary organisation, registered charity (charity number 327279).

Subject coverage:
Childcare, policy and practice; family-friendly employment practices; sources of information on childcare and children's services, consultancy and training.

Trade and statistical information:
Data on childcare in the UK.

Printed publications:
Childwise
Briefing Papers
Policy Papers
Order printed publications from:
publications@daycaretrust.org.uk

Publications list:
Available online and in print

Access to staff:
Contact by letter, by telephone, by fax, by e-mail and via website. Appointment necessary.
Hours: Mon to Fri, 1000 to 1700

Access for disabled people:
Toilet facilities
Special comments: Lift entry from outside to all floors other than the kitchen.

DE MONTFORT UNIVERSITY

The Gateway, Leicester, LE1 9BH

Tel: 0116 255 1551
Fax: 0116 255 0307

Website:
http://www.library.dmu.ac.uk

Enquiries:
Enquiries to: Librarian
Direct tel: 0116 257 7165
Direct fax: 0116 257 7046

Organisation type and purpose:
University library.

Subject coverage:
Chemistry, physics, electronics, mechanical engineering, architecture, building, fashion, textiles, graphic art and design, information technology, law, public administration, economics, education, performing arts, speech and speech therapy, sport and physical education, business, health, nursing, midwifery, humanities.

Museum or gallery collection, archive, or library special collection:
HATRA Collection (former Hosiery and Allied Trades Research Association)
Hockliffe Collection of early children's books (Polhill Site)

Library catalogue:
All or part available online

Access to staff:
Contact by letter and by telephone
Hours: Varies between campuses – please consult website for full details.

Access for disabled people:
Parking provided, ramped entry, access to all public areas, toilet facilities
Special comments: Facilities may vary slightly from campus to campus.

Includes the:
Kimberlin Library
   City Campus; tel: 0116 255 1551 ext 2677
Polhill Campus Library (Bedford)
   tel: 01234 793077

Site libraries:
De Montfort University
   Polhill Campus, Polhill Avenue, Bedford, MK41 9EA; tel: 01234 793077; fax: 01234 217738
De Montfort University
   Charles Frears Campus, 266 London Road, Leicester, LE2 1RQ; tel: 0116 270 0661; fax: 0116 270 9722
De Montfort University
   Kimberlin Library, The Gateway, Leicester, LE1 9BH; tel: 0116 257 7042; fax: 0116 257 7170

DE TOMASO DRIVERS CLUB

Flint Barn, Malthouse Lane, Ashington, West Sussex, RH20 3BU

Tel: 01903 893870
Fax: 01903 893870

Enquiries:
Enquiries to: Secretary

Founded:
1982

Organisation type and purpose:
Membership association.

Subject coverage:
De Tomaso cars.

Museum or gallery collection, archive, or library special collection:
De Tomaso Books
Club Magazines

DEAFAX

No 1 Earley Gate, The University, Whiteknights Road, Reading, Berkshire, RG6 6AT

Tel: 0870 770 2461\ Minicom no. Textphone: 0870 770 2463
Fax: 0870 770 2462
E-mail: deafax@deafax.org

Website:
http://www.webcom.com/deafax/welcome.html
General information about our work, regularly updated.

Enquiries:
Enquiries to: Managing Director
Direct tel: 0870 770 2461
Direct e-mail: helen@deafax.org
Other contacts: Administrator for general enquiries.

continued overleaf

Founded:
1985

Organisation type and purpose:
International organisation, voluntary organisation, registered charity (new charity number 1095398), suitable for ages: all, training organisation, research organisation.
To deliver ICT and English literacy training and provide other support services for deaf children and adults in the UK and internationally.

Subject coverage:
Deaf issues: communications technology, training, literacy, education, support services.

Printed publications:
Information on all aspects of our work is available (free)

Electronic and video publications:
CD-ROM to teach deaf children English literacy skills (available for purchase directly)

Access to staff:
Contact by letter, by telephone, by fax and by e-mail
Hours: Mon to Fri, 0900 to 1700

Access for disabled people:
Parking provided, ramped entry, access to all public areas, toilet facilities
Special comments: Wheelchair accessible.

DEAFBLIND SCOTLAND

21 Alexandra Avenue, Lenzie, Glasgow, G66 5BG

Tel: 0141 777 6111\ Minicom no. 0141 777 6111
Fax: 0141 775 3311
E-mail: info@deafblindscotland.org.uk

Website:
http://www.deafblindscotland.org.uk
History of Deafblind Scotland, services provided, guide/communicator services, news and events.

Enquiries:
Enquiries to: Information Officer
Other contacts: Chief Executive

Founded:
1928

Organisation type and purpose:
Registered charity (charity number 802976).
To serve deafblind people and reduce their isolation through clubs, outings, holidays and provision of information; provide trained guide/communicator service where funding available, training in communication and guiding skills, awareness-raising.

Subject coverage:
Deafblind awareness, communication and guiding skills with deafblind people.

Museum or gallery collection, archive, or library special collection:
Small resource centre of books, articles, reports and publications

Printed publications:
Rainbow (magazine, quarterly)
Snippets (newspaper, fortnightly)
Also available in tape, Braille, Moon and large print formats

Electronic and video publications:
Into Touch: basic communication with deafblind people (video)
Rainbow and Snippets on tape

Access to staff:
Contact by letter, by telephone, by fax, by e-mail and via website
Hours: Mon to Fri, 0900 to 1700
Special comments: 24 hour Helpline.

DEAFBLIND UK

Acronym or abbreviation: DBUK

The National Centre for Deafblindness, John and Lucille van Geest Place, Cygnet Road, Hampton, Peterborough, PE7 8FD

Tel: 01733 358100; Free Helpline 0800 132320; Minicom 01733 358100
Fax: 01733 358356
E-mail: info@deafblind.org.uk

Website:
http://www.deafblind.org.uk

Enquiries:
Enquiries to: Information Officer
Direct e-mail: enquiries@deafblind.org.uk
Other contacts: Chief Executive

Founded:
1928

Formerly called:
National Deaf-Blind Helpers League; National Deafblind League (year of change 1996)

Organisation type and purpose:
Voluntary organisation, registered charity.
To enable those people with a dual sensory impairment to live full and active lives despite their disability. To raise awareness of deafblindness in the caring professions and amongst the wider public, to ensure sufferers' needs are met in care planning.

Subject coverage:
Activities include visiting/assessing deafblind individuals. Participation in national development/lobbying groups. Contributing to individual community care plans. Information and advice on dual sensory loss. Counselling. Training. Social activities for deafblind people, rehabilitation services, holiday flat, independent living accommodation. Linking deafblind people through magazines and newspapers in touch-based media. Free helpline accessible to deafblind people, their carers and professionals working with deafblind people.

Information services:
Information for people who have a combined sight and hearing loss, and for their families and friends.

Services for disabled people:
Volunteer befriending; interpreters; communicator guides; free helpline; case worker; formatted publications and letters; deafblind clubs; campaigning and raising awareness.

Museum or gallery collection, archive, or library special collection:
Heritage exhibition at the National Centre for Deafblindness explaining the history of combined sight and hearing loss.

Printed publications:
Information leaflets
Open Hand (quarterly, available in print, large print, Braille, Moon, cassette, CD, e-mail)
Order printed publications from: 01733 358100

Access to staff:
Contact by letter, by telephone, by fax, by e-mail and via website. Appointment necessary.
Hours: Mon to Thu, 0830 to 1700; Fri, 0830 to 1600
Free Helpline available daily, 0900 to 2130

Access for disabled people:
Level entry, toilet facilities, handrails, wheelchair and assistance dog friendly, Braille, Moon, Large Print and Audio room markings, tactile map of building.

Also at:
Deafblind UK Training and Rehabilitation Centre 18 Rainbow Court, Paston Ridings, Peterborough, Cambridgeshire, PE4 7UP; tel: 01733 325353; fax: 01733 323101

DEAFNESS RESEARCH UK

330–332 Gray's Inn Road, London, WC1X 8EE

Tel: 020 7833 1733\ Minicom no. 020 7915 1412 (text phone)
Fax: 020 7278 0404
E-mail: contact@deafnessresearch.org.uk

Website:
http://www.deafnessresearch.org.uk

Enquiries:
Enquiries to: Office Manager
Other contacts: Information Officer

Founded:
1985

Formerly called:
Defeating Deafness (year of change 2005)

Organisation type and purpose:
Voluntary organisation, registered charity.
Aims to encourage and finance research into the prevention, diagnosis, treatment and cure of hearing difficulties. It also aims to educate people about hearing problems and their treatments, offering information and advice based upon the most up-to-date evidence available.

Subject coverage:
Cochlear implants, glue ear, hearing aids, tinnitus, hyperacusis, hair cell research, genetics of hearing loss, auditory processing disorder, otosclerosis, Meniere's Disease, cholesteatoma

Printed publications:
Fact sheet on the following topics (please enclose an sae):
Cochlear Implants
Genetics and Deafness
Hair Cell Research
Glue Ear – Facts for Parents
Hyperacusis
Tinnitus
Getting a Hearing Aid on the NHS
Auditory Processing Disorder
Cholesteatoma
Trouble with your ears
In-flight ear health

Publications list:
Available in print

Access to staff:
Contact by letter, by telephone, by fax, by e-mail and via website
Hours: Office hours: Mon to Fri, 0930 to 1730
Helpline: Mon to Fri, 0900 to 1700

Parent body:
The Hearing Research Trust

DEAN FOREST RAILWAY SOCIETY

Acronym or abbreviation: DFRS

Forest Road, Lydney, Gloucestershire, GL15 4ET

Tel: 01594 843423 (information line, recorded times & dates of services)

Website:
http://www.deanforestrailway.co.uk

Enquiries:
Enquiries to: Honorary Secretary
Direct tel: 01594 845840 (shop)
Direct fax: 01594 845840
Other contacts: DFRS Membership Secretary for membership applications

Founded:
1970

Formed from:
Dean Forest Railway Preservation Society

Organisation type and purpose:
Membership association.
Members operate the Dean Forest Railway Co Ltd and Dean Forest Railfreight Ltd.

Subject coverage:
Dean Forest Railway is a predominantly steam-powered standard gauge tourist railway operating between Norchard and Lydney Junction. It is adjacent, and connected, to Railtrack. The line north of Norchard to Parkend is undergoing restoration. The railway is the sole surviving remnant of the Severn and Wye railway. The headquarters at Norchard are on the site of the

former West Gloucestershire Power Station and Norchard Colliery. Railway artefacts plus a working telephone system.

Printed publications:
Colour brochure/timetable (annual, free, please enclose an sae)
Forest Venturer (Society's magazine, £2 plus p&p, free to Society members)
Order printed publications from: Dean Forest Railway Co. Ltd
Norchard Railway Centre, at the same address, tel: 01594 845840

Electronic and video publications:
Norchard/Dean Forest Railway (video, £10.95 plus p&p, available from railway)

Access to staff:
Contact by letter. Appointment necessary.
Hours: Jan to Easter: Wed, Sat, Sun, 1000 to 1700; Easter to Oct: daily, 1000 to 1700; Nov to 1 Jan: daily, 1000 to 1500

Access to building, collection or gallery:
No prior appointment required
Hours: Library and Gift shop, Jan to Easter: Wed, Sat, Sun, 1000 to 1700; Easter to Oct: daily, 1000 to 1700; Nov to 1 Jan: daily, 1000 to 1500

Access for disabled people:
Parking provided, ramped entry, toilet facilities
Special comments: Access to shop, station etc only at Norchard.

Subsidiary companies:
Dean Forest Railway Co Ltd
95 Melville Road, Churchdown, Gloucester, GL3 2RF

DEBRA

Debra House, 13 Wellington Business Park, Dukes Ride, Crowthorne, Berkshire, RG45 6LS

Tel: 01344 771961
Fax: 01344 762661
E-mail: debra@debra.org.uk

Website:
http://www.debra.org.uk
All aspects of epidermolysis bullosa.
http://www.debra-international.org

Enquiries:
Enquiries to: Director
Direct e-mail: john.dart@debra.org.uk
Other contacts: PR and Press Officer.

Founded:
1978

Formerly called:
Dystrophic Epidermolysis Bullosa Research Association

Organisation type and purpose:
Registered charity (charity number 1084958). Funds nursing and welfare teams. Commissions research into EB (Epidermolysis Bullosa).

Subject coverage:
Epidermolysis bullosa, all types; education, self-help, care and management, counselling and research.

Library catalogue:
All or part available online

Printed publications:
Coping with Epidermolysis Bullosa
Diagnosis and Treatment (available only for professional use)
Dowling MEARA EB Simplex
Epidermolysis Bullosa: A Guide for Parents, Schools & Playgroups
Epidermolysis Bullosa: An Outline for Professionals
Epidermolysis Bullosa: Teachers' Supplement for Schools & Playgroups
Information Sheets (includes Financial Benefits, Education – Your Rights, Employment Services)
Genetics in EB
Junctional EB – Care and Management (available only for professional nursing staff)

Nutrition for Babies with EB
Play and Development in EB Children
Play and Developmental Needs of a Child with Epidermolysis Bullosa
Pregnancy and Childbirth in EB

Electronic and video publications:
Promotional video (free)

Publications list:
Available online and in print

Access to staff:
Contact by letter, by telephone, by fax, by e-mail, in person and via website
Hours: Mon to Fri, 0900 to 1700

Access for disabled people:
Access to all public areas, toilet facilities

DEBRETT'S PEERAGE LIMITED

Formal name: Debrett's Limited

18–20 Hill Rise, Richmond, Surrey, TW10 6UA

Tel: 020 8939 2250
Fax: 020 8939 2251
E-mail: people@debretts.co.uk

Website:
http://www.debretts.co.uk
Company, books and diaries, People of Today, recommendations, guide to the season, royal connections.

Enquiries:
Enquiries to: Finance and Operations Manager

Founded:
1769

Organisation type and purpose:
Publishing house.

Subject coverage:
Biographical information – general, peerage, baronetage. Etiquette and manners.

Printed publications:
Debrett's Correct Form
Debrett's Etiquette for Girls
Debrett's Manners for Men
Debrett's Guide to Entertaining
Debrett's Peerage & Baronetage (every 5 years, latest edn 2008)
Debrett's People of Today (annually, December, £120)

Electronic and video publications:
Debrett's People of Today (online, subscription)
Debrett's People of Today (CD-ROM, annually, December)

Access to staff:
Contact by letter, by e-mail and via website
Hours: Mon to Fri, 0900 to 1700
Special comments: By appointment only.

DECORATIVE ARTS SOCIETY

Formal name: The Decorative Arts Society 1850 to the Present
Acronym or abbreviation: DAS

PO Box 136, Woodbridge, Suffolk, IP12 1TG

Website:
http://www.decorativeartssociety.org.uk/

Enquiries:
Enquiries to: Honorary Secretary
Direct e-mail: links@thedecorativeartssociety.org.uk
Other contacts: Membership Secretary for membership applications, subscription rates etc.

Founded:
1975

Organisation type and purpose:
Learned society (membership is by subscription), present number of members: 650, registered charity (charity number 271838).
To encourage the study and appreciation of the Decorative Arts in Britain, Europe and America from 1850 to the present.

Subject coverage:
Decorative arts, 1850 to the present.

Printed publications:
Journal (annual, contains publications list)
Back issues of DAS Journals available for purchase through the Honorary Secretary or from Richard Dennis Publications
Index of Journals Nos 1 to 20 (pub Nov 1997)
Order printed publications from: Richard Dennis Publications, The Old Chapel
Middle Street, Shepton Beauchamp, Ilminster, Somerset, TA19 0LE

Publications list:
Available in print

Access to staff:
Contact by letter
Hours: Mon to Fri, 0900 to 1700

Membership applications:
The Decorative Arts Society
PO Box 136, Woodbridge, Suffolk, IP12 1TG

DEER COMMISSION FOR SCOTLAND

Acronym or abbreviation: DCS

Great Glen House, Leachkin Road, Inverness, IV3 8NW

Tel: 01463 725000
Fax: 01463 725048
E-mail: enquiries@deercom.com

Website:
http://www.dcs.gov.uk
Current DCS publications.

Enquiries:
Enquiries to: Communications Officer
Direct tel: 01463 725366
Other contacts: Technical Director for technical advice on deer matters in Scotland.

Founded:
1959

Formerly called:
Red Deer Commission (year of change 1996)

Organisation type and purpose:
Advisory body, statutory body (membership is by election or invitation).
Conservation body.

Subject coverage:
Conservation, control and management of wild deer in Scotland.

Printed publications:
Codes of Practice on Nightshooting and Driving Deer by Vehicle
DCS Annual Report
DCS Long Term Strategy
Rifle and Ammunition Combinations Required for the Legal Killing of Deer in Scotland
Wild Deer in Scotland: A Long Term Vision

Access to staff:
Contact by letter, by telephone, by fax and by e-mail. Appointment necessary.
Hours: Mon to Thu, 0830 to 1700; Fri, 0830 to 1630

Access for disabled people:
Ramped entry

South Scotland office at:
Deer Commission for Scotland
Alpha Centre, Unit 8, Stirling University, Innovation Park, Stirling, FK9 4NF; tel: 01786 446282; fax: 01786 446292

DEESIDE COLLEGE

Kelsterton Road, Connah's Quay, Deeside, Flintshire, CH5 4BR

Tel: 01244 831531
Fax: 01244 814305
E-mail: enquiries@deeside.ac.uk

Website:
http://www.deeside.ac.uk

continued overleaf

Enquiries:
Enquiries to: Manager
Direct tel: 01244 834516
Direct fax: 01244 834526
Direct e-mail: forresl@deeside.ac.uk

Founded:
1993

Organisation type and purpose:
College of Further Education.

Subject coverage:
All subjects including computer studies,
management and business studies.

Access to staff:
Contact by letter, by telephone, by fax, by e-mail
and via website
Hours: Term time: Mon to Thu, 0830 to 1925; Fri,
0830 to 1625
Vacations: Mon to Thu, 0830 to 1625; Fri, 0830 to
1555

Access for disabled people:
Level entry, access to all public areas

DEFENCE COLLEGE OF MANAGEMENT AND TECHNOLOGY

Acronym or abbreviation: DCMT

Cranfield University, Shrivenham, Swindon,
Wiltshire, SN6 8LA

Tel: 01793 785743
Fax: 01793 785555
E-mail: libraryenquiry.cu@defenceacademy.mod
.uk

Website:
http://www.cranfield.ac.uk/dcmt
http://diglib.shrivenham.cranfield.ac.uk
Digital Library

Enquiries:
Enquiries to: Director of Knowledge Services
Direct tel: 01793 785481

Organisation type and purpose:
University library.

Subject coverage:
Military science, military technology, computing
science, mathematics, ballistics, operational
research, statistics, defence procurement,
management, political science, social science,
international affairs, chemistry, materials science,
metallurgy, engineering design, mechanical
engineering, aeronautical engineering, military
vehicles, thermal power, control and guidance,
information technology, electromagnets, electronic
engineering, physics, electro-optics, electrical
engineering, telecommunications, electronic
warfare, command and control, guided weapons,
explosives and ammunition, weapons systems,
surveillance and target acquisition, military
management, defence administration, military
affairs, disaster management, security and
resilience, forensic science, forensic archaeology,
anthropology.

**Museum or gallery collection, archive, or library
special collection:**
Reports collection of about 50,000 items, reflects
the specialised nature of some of the campus
courses

Library catalogue:
All or part available online

Electronic and video publications:
Digital Archive
eDefence News (daily)
Inside Knowledge

Access to staff:
Contact by telephone and via website.
Appointment necessary.
Hours: Mon to Fri, 0800 to 1900; Sat, 1000 to 1500

Access for disabled people:
Parking provided, level entry

Constituent bodies:
Defence Academy

DEFENCE MANUFACTURERS ASSOCIATION OF GREAT BRITAIN

Acronym or abbreviation: DMA

Marlborough House, Headley Road, Grayshott,
Surrey, GU26 6LG

Tel: 01428 607788
Fax: 01428 604567
E-mail: enquiries@the-dma.org.uk

Website:
http://www.the-dma.org.uk
Full information on the DMA.

Enquiries:
Enquiries to: Director
Direct tel: 01428 602622
Direct fax: 01428 602628
Direct e-mail: b.salzmann@the-dma.org.uk

Founded:
1976

Organisation type and purpose:
Trade association (membership is by subscription),
present number of members: 625, manufacturing
industry, service industry.
To represent the interests of the British Defence
Industry.

Subject coverage:
Defence, police and security information.

**Museum or gallery collection, archive, or library
special collection:**
Deso publications
DMA publications
Exhibition catalogues
Foreign industry directories
Many Jane's books
Several defence periodicals
Library of Information maintained

Trade and statistical information:
Some data on the UK defence industry and Export
Markets.

Library catalogue:
All or part available in-house

Printed publications:
Draft Forms of Contract and Agency Agreement
List of EDMAG members and their Products and
Services
MOD New management strategy
Police and Security Requirements in the 90s –
Implications and Opportunities for Industry
Public Sector Purchasing Agencies
Worldwide Directory of Main Defence Contractors

Publications list:
Available in print

Access to staff:
Contact by letter, by telephone, by fax, by e-mail
and via website. Appointment necessary.
Hours: Mon to Fri, 0900 to 1700

Access to building, collection or gallery:
No prior appointment required

Affiliated to:
Association of Police and Public Security Suppliers
(APPSS)
at the same address; tel: 01428 607788; fax: 01428
602628

DEFENCE MEDICAL LIBRARY

Acronym or abbreviation: RDMC

Fort Blockhouse, Horton Block, Gosport,
Hampshire, PO12 2AB

Tel: 023 9276 5751
Fax: 023 9276 5747
E-mail: library@milmed.demon.co.uk

Enquiries:
Enquiries to: College Librarian

Direct tel: 023 9276 5899
Other contacts: Head, Defence Library Services, tel
no: 023 9276 5400

Founded:
1997

Organisation type and purpose:
National government body, training organisation,
research organisation.
Medical College.
Central medical library for the Ministry of Defence;
library for Royal Defence Medical College; linked
with the Ministry of Defence medical libraries.

Subject coverage:
Military medicine, general medicine and allied
health, primary care, nursing.

**Museum or gallery collection, archive, or library
special collection:**
Royal Army Medical Corps historical collection
(housed at Wellcome Institute)

Library catalogue:
All or part available in-house

Printed publications:
Journal of the Royal Army Medical Corps
(quarterly)

Access to staff:
Contact by letter, by telephone, by fax and by e-
mail. Access for members only.
Hours: Mon to Thu, 0800 to 1630; Fri, 0800 to 1530
Special comments: Services to Defence medical staff
and Ministry of Defence staff; to others by written
appointment only.

Access to building, collection or gallery:
Prior appointment required

Library for:
MOD Medical Services
Royal Defence Medical College

Links with:
Ministry of Defence Medical Libraries

DELIUS SOCIETY

21 Woodlands Drive, Brooklands, sale, M33 3PQ

Tel: 0161 282 3654

Enquiries:
Enquiries to: Honorary Secretary

Founded:
1962

Organisation type and purpose:
Membership association.
Society for all who appreciate Delius' music.

Subject coverage:
Life and works of the composer Frederick Delius.

Printed publications:
Delius Society Journal and Newsletter (members)

Access to staff:
Contact by letter
Hours: Mon to Fri, 0900 to 1700

Independent from, but works closely with, the:
Delius Trust

DELPHINIUM SOCIETY

Acronym or abbreviation: DS

2 The Grove, Ickenham, Uxbridge, Middlesex,
UB10 8QH

Tel: 01895 464694
Fax: 01895 235365
E-mail: roger.beauchamp@btinternet.com

Website:
http://www.delphinium-society.co.uk
http://www.delphinium.org.uk

Enquiries:
Enquiries to: Promotions and Publicity Secretary

Founded:
1928

Organisation type and purpose:
International organisation, membership
association (membership is by subscription),
present number of members: 1000.
For the study, dissemination and collection of all
information concerning the genus Delphinium and
the closely related genus Consolida. Also to study
the relationship of the genus to other members of
the family Ranunculaceae.

Subject coverage:
All aspects of the genus Delphinium and related-
genus Consolida. Scientific interest in Aconitum.

Information services:
from Promotions and Publicity Secretary

Printed publications:
Yearbook (publ in Apr/May, members only)
Bulletin (publ in Oct, annually, members only)
The Delphinium Garden
Other publications are undergoing revision

Publications list:
Available in print

Access to staff:
Contact by letter, by telephone, by fax, by e-mail
and via website

DELTA

Formal name: Deaf Education Through Listening
and Talking
Acronym or abbreviation: DELTA

The Con Powell Centre, Alfa House, Molesey
Road, Walton-on-Thames, Surrey, KT12 3PD

Tel: 0845 108 1437 / 01932 243018
E-mail: enquiries@deafeducation.org.uk

Website:
http://www.deafeducation.org.uk

Founded:
1988

Organisation type and purpose:
Voluntary organisation, registered charity (charity
number 1115603).
To guide parents and teachers in helping deaf
children to develop normal spoken language and
to live independently within the hearing society,
the practice and philosophy of the natural aural
approach to the education of deaf children.

Subject coverage:
Deaf young people, the development of
independence and communication, the attainment
levels achieved by severely and profoundly deaf
young people.

Printed publications:
Factsheets and booklets for families of deaf
children and for lay people interested in the
natural aural approach to the education of deaf
children (available on request, some free)
Chat (newsletter, twice a year)
Understanding the Natural Aural Approach:
Approaches to Communication (W. Lynas)
Parents' Guide for the Natural Aural Approach,
Vols 1 and 2 (£10 per set)

Electronic and video publications:
Sound Futures
Chattering (e-mail newsletter)
Order electronic and video publications from:
enquiries@deafeducation.org.uk

Publications list:
Available online and in print

Access to staff:
Contact by letter, by telephone and by e-mail.
Appointment necessary.
Hours: Mon to Fri, 0900 to 1700

Access to building, collection or gallery:
No access other than to staff

DELTA BIOTECHNOLOGY LIMITED

Castle Court, Castle Boulevard, Nottingham, NG7
1FD

Tel: 0115 955 3355
Fax: 0115 955 1299

Enquiries:
Enquiries to: Information Manager
Direct e-mail: alison.mitson@aventis.com

Organisation type and purpose:
Research organisation.

Subject coverage:
Recombinant technology.

Access to staff:
Contact by letter, by fax and by e-mail
Hours: Mon to Fri, 0900 to 1700

Parent body:
Aventis Behring

DENBIGHSHIRE COUNTY COUNCIL

Council Offices, Wynnstay Road, Ruthin,
Denbighshire, LL15 1YN

Tel: 01824 706000
Fax: 01824 705026

Website:
http://www.denbighshire.gov.uk
General – councillors' details, news releases,
services, what's on.

Enquiries:
Enquiries to: Public Relations Manager
Direct tel: 01824 706222
Direct fax: 01824 707446
Direct e-mail: sue.appleton@denbighshire.gov.uk

Founded:
1996

Formed from:
Clwyd County Council, Glyndwr District Council,
Rhuddlan Borough Council (year of change 1996)

Organisation type and purpose:
Local government body.

Subject coverage:
Education, social services, housing and
environment, planning, economic development,
highways, transport.

Access to staff:
Contact by telephone
Hours: Mon to Fri, 0900 to 1700

DENBIGHSHIRE HERITAGE SERVICE

46 Clwyd Street, Ruthin, Denbighshire, LL15 1HP

Tel: 01824 708223
Fax: 01824 708258

Website:
http://www.denbighshire.gov.uk

Enquiries:
Enquiries to: Curator
Direct e-mail: rose.mcmahon@denbighshire.gov.uk

Organisation type and purpose:
Local government body.
Administrative body for the libraries, museums,
art galleries and historical sites which are under
the care of Denbighshire County Council.

Subject coverage:
Administrative office for the museums and
properties in the Denbighshire area which are
under the control of the local authority. The
conservation of Denbighshire heritage.

Access to staff:
Contact by letter, by telephone, by fax, by e-mail
and via website

Parent body:
Denbighshire County Council
tel: 01824 708200; fax: 01824 708202

DENBIGHSHIRE HISTORICAL SOCIETY

1 Green Park, Erddig, Wrexham, Clwyd, LL13 7YE

Tel: 01978 353 363

Enquiries:
Enquiries to: Honorary Secretary

Founded:
1950

Organisation type and purpose:
Learned society (membership is by subscription),
present number of members: 350, registered
charity (charity number 519210).

Subject coverage:
General, social, personal and industrial history of
the former county of Denbighshire, defined by the
boundaries prior to 1974 re-organisation.

Printed publications:
Transactions (annually, £10 to non-members)

Access to staff:
Contact by letter and by telephone
Hours: Mon to Fri, 0900 to 1700

DENBIGHSHIRE RECORD OFFICE

46 Clwyd Street, Ruthin, Denbighshire, LL15 1HP

Tel: 01824 708250
Fax: 01824 708258
E-mail: archives@denbighshire.gov.uk

Website:
http://www.denbighshire.gov.uk/archives

Enquiries:
Enquiries to: Archivist
Direct tel: 01824 708285
Other contacts: County Archivist for Head of
Depository

Founded:
1972

Formerly called:
Clwyd Record Office (year of change 1996)

Organisation type and purpose:
Local government body.
Archive.
County record office holding material relating to
the pre-1974 county of Denbigh and the present
area.

Subject coverage:
Local history: former county of Clwyd, and the
historic and present county of Denbighshire.

**Museum or gallery collection, archive, or library
special collection:**
Collections relating to historic county of
Denbighshire, including quarter sessions, county
council; district councils; parish (microfilm);
schools; family and estates; census (microfilm);
newspapers (microfilm and original)

Non-library collection catalogue:
All or part available online and in-house

Publications list:
Available online and in print

Access to staff:
Contact by letter, by telephone, by fax, by e-mail
and in person
Hours: Mon to Wed, 1000 to 1645; Fri, 1000 to 1615
Special comments: Reader's ticket, prior
appointment for microfilm users.
Closed daily, 1230 to 1330.

Access for disabled people:
Parking provided, ramped entry, access to most
public areas, toilet facilities

DENTAL LABORATORIES ASSOCIATION LIMITED

Acronym or abbreviation: DLA

44–46 Wollaton Road, Beeston, Nottingham, NG9 2NR

Tel: 0115 925 4888
Fax: 0115 925 4800
E-mail: info@dla.org.uk

Website:
http://www.DLA.ORG.UK

Enquiries:
Enquiries to: Chief Executive

Founded:
1961

Organisation type and purpose:
Trade association.

Subject coverage:
Dental technology; commercial dental laboratories; Department of Health current guidelines and regulations within mechanical dentistry.

Printed publications:
Annual Report
Dental Laboratory (magazine, monthly)
Yearbook
Year Planner

Access to staff:
Contact by letter and by e-mail. Appointment necessary. Non-members charged.
Hours: Mon to Fri, 0900 to 1700

Links with:
Federation of European Dental Laboratory Owners (FEPPD)

DENTAL PRACTITIONERS' ASSOCIATION

Acronym or abbreviation: DPA

61 Harley Street, London, W1G 8QU

Tel: 020 7636 1072
Fax: 020 7636 1086
E-mail: info@UK-Dentistry.org

Website:
http://www.UK-Dentistry.org/

Enquiries:
Enquiries to: Chief Executive

Founded:
1954

Organisation type and purpose:
Professional body (membership is by subscription), present number of members: 1,200 practices, 3,000 members.
Founded in 1954 by General Dental Practitioners for GDPs. The DPA is the only organisation which exclusively promotes the interests of dentists in general practice providing support, advice and representation at all levels.

Subject coverage:
Dentistry, statistics, dental politics, dento-legal matters, business briefing, management consultancy.

Non-library collection catalogue:
All or part available online and in-house

Printed publications:
General Dental Practitioner (6 times a year)

Publications list:
Available online

Access to staff:
Contact by letter, by telephone, by fax, by e-mail and via website. Appointment necessary. Access for members only.
Hours: Mon to Fri, 1000 to 1600

Access for disabled people:
No

DENTISTS' MEDIA GROUP

Acronym or abbreviation: DMG

PO Box 15, Sindalthorpe House, Ely, Cambridgeshire, CB7 4SG

Tel: 01353 688456
Fax: 01353 688451
E-mail: soundplanltd@netscapeonline.co.uk

Enquiries:
Enquiries to: Administrator

Founded:
1996

Organisation type and purpose:
National organisation, membership association (membership is by election or invitation), present number of members: 170, voluntary organisation, training organisation, consultancy.
To encourage, and to enhance the quality of, broadcasting and writing by dentists on radio and television, local radio in particular and in the press and magazines.

Subject coverage:
The Dentists' Media Group is a source of spokespeople on all aspects of oral health.

Access to staff:
Contact by letter, by telephone, by fax and by e-mail
Hours: Mon to Fri, 0900 to 1700

Access to building, collection or gallery:
Prior appointment required

Access for disabled people:
Ramped entry

Affiliated to and at the same address as:
Association of Broadcasting Doctors (ABD)

DEPARTMENT FOR BUSINESS ENTERPRISE AND REGULATORY REFORM

Acronym or abbreviation: BERR

InfoSource, 1 Victoria Street, London, SW1H 0ET

Tel: 020 7215 5006 \ Minicom no. 020 7215 6740
E-mail: enquiries@berr.gsi.gov.uk

Website:
http://www.berr.gov.uk

Enquiries:
Enquiries to: Librarian

Founded:
2007

Created by the merger of:
part of the former Department of Trade and Industry, and the Better Regulation Executive (year of change 2007)

Formerly a part of:
Board of Trade (BoT) and Ministry of Technology and Department of Energy; Department of Trade and Industry (year of change 1983)

Organisation type and purpose:
National government body.
Government library.

Subject coverage:
Trade policy, export promotion, energy, corporate and consumer affairs, employment relations, innovation and technology, small firms, regional development and inward investment.

Museum or gallery collection, archive, or library special collection:
Archive of publications from the DTI, Department of Energy, Board of Trade, etc.

Library catalogue:
All or part available in-house

Printed publications:
Order printed publications from: BERR Publications Orderline, ADMAIL 528, London, SW1W 8YT; tel. 0845 015 0010
Or via website: http://www.berr.gov.uk/ publications/reports/index.html

Publications list:
Available online

Access to staff:
Contact by letter and by telephone. Appointment necessary.
Hours: Mon to Fri, 0900 to 1700

DEPARTMENT FOR CHILDREN, SCHOOLS AND FAMILIES – LONDON LIBRARY

Acronym or abbreviation: DCSF

Sanctuary Buildings, Great Smith Street, London, SW1P 3BT

Tel: 020 7925 5040
E-mail: enquiries.library@dcsf.gsi.gov.uk

Website:
http://www.dcsf.gov.uk/index.htm

Enquiries:
Enquiries to: Librarian

Organisation type and purpose:
National government body.

Subject coverage:
Educational theory and policy, official publications relating to the department and its predecessors, small historical collection from 19th and 20th centuries.

Library catalogue:
All or part available in-house

Publications list:
Available in print

Access to staff:
Contact by letter, by telephone, by e-mail and via website. Appointment necessary.
Hours: Mon to Fri, 0900 to 1700

Access to building, collection or gallery:
No access other than to staff

DEPARTMENT FOR CONSTITUTIONAL AFFAIRS

Acronym or abbreviation: DCA

Library, Selborne House, 54 Victoria Street, London, SW1E 6QW

Tel: 020 7210 1671
Fax: 020 7210 1617
E-mail: dca.library@dca.gsi.gov.uk

Website:
http://www.dca.gov.uk
http://courtservice.gov.uk

Enquiries:
Enquiries to: Librarian
Other contacts: Library Assistant

Organisation type and purpose:
National government body.
To run the courts, to formulate policy on legal matters, to appoint judges.

Subject coverage:
Law, administration of justice.

Library catalogue:
All or part available in-house

Printed publications:
The Department for Constitutional Affairs issues consultation papers from time to time (most free of charge from DCA Press Office)
The Court Service issues various leaflets about court proceedings (available from County Courts and Crown Courts)
Order printed publications from: DCA Press Office tel: 020 7210 8510

Access to staff:
Contact by letter, by telephone, by fax and by e-mail. Appointment necessary.
Hours: Mon to Fri, 0930 to 1700
Special comments: Generally only to other Government departments; others at the discretion of the Librarian.

Access to building, collection or gallery:
Prior appointment required

Other major libraries within the DCA are:
Law Commission Library
Supreme Court Library

DEPARTMENT FOR CULTURE, MEDIA AND SPORT

Acronym or abbreviation: DCMS

Library, Room L21, 2–4 Cockspur Street, London, SW1Y 5DH

Tel: 020 7211 6041
Fax: 020 7211 6032
E-mail: library@culture.gov.uk

Website:
http://www.lottery.culture.gov.uk
Lottery awards database.
http://www.culture.gov.uk
General information about DCMS.

Enquiries:
Enquiries to: Libraries services to DCMS staff

Founded:
1992

Formerly called:
Department of National Heritage (year of change 1997)

Organisation type and purpose:
National government body.

Subject coverage:
The arts, sport, the National Lottery, libraries, museums and galleries, broadcasting, gambling, film, press freedom and regulation, the built heritage, tourism, the creative industries, cultural property and the Government Art Collection.

Museum or gallery collection, archive, or library special collection:
On the subjects listed

Library catalogue:
All or part available online and in-house

Printed publications:
See DCMS website www.culture.gov.uk/reference_library

Publications list:
Available online

Access to staff:
Contact by letter, by telephone, by fax, by e-mail and via website. Appointment necessary.
Hours: Mon to Fri, 0900 to 1730

Access for disabled people:
Access to all public areas

DEPARTMENT FOR EDUCATION AND SKILLS – SHEFFIELD LIBRARY

Acronym or abbreviation: DfES

Moorfoot, Sheffield, South Yorkshire, S1 4PQ

Tel: 020 7925 5040
E-mail: enquiries.library@dfes.gsi.gov.uk

Website:
http://www.dfes.gov.uk
http://www.dfes.gov.uk/publications

Enquiries:
Enquiries to: Librarian

Organisation type and purpose:
National government body.

Subject coverage:
Skills, education policy, lifelong learning, management.

Library catalogue:
All or part available in-house

Access to staff:
Contact by letter, by telephone and by e-mail. Appointment necessary.

Hours: Mon to Fri, 0900 to 1700

Access to building, collection or gallery:
Special comments: Library open to public for reference only by prior appointment.

DEPARTMENT FOR ENVIRONMENT, FOOD AND RURAL AFFAIRS – INFORMATION RESOURCE CENTRE

Acronym or abbreviation: Defra

Lower Ground Floor, Ergon House, c/o Nobel House, 17 Smith Square, London, SW1P 3JR

Tel: 020 7238 6575
E-mail: defra.library@defra.gsi.gov.uk

Website:
http://www.defra.gov.uk
Publications catalogue, news releases, statistics, reports.
http://www.defra.gov.uk/corporate/publications/default.htm
Publications.

Enquiries:
Enquiries to: Librarian
Direct tel: 08459 335577 (helpdesk)
Direct fax: 020 7238 6609

Founded:
2001

Created by the merger of:
Animal Welfare and Hunting Issues from Home Office, Environment Section and Wildlife and Countryside Section of the former Department of Environment Transport and Regions (DETR), MAFF Library, Ministry of Agriculture, Fisheries and Food (MAFF) (year of change 2001)

Organisation type and purpose:
National government body, research organisation. Central Government.

Subject coverage:
Environment, conservation, countryside, sustainable development, food industry, rural issues, fisheries, water.

Non-library collection catalogue:
All or part available online, in-house and in print

Library catalogue:
All or part available in-house

Printed publications:
Reports, statistics, codes of practice
Order printed publications from: DEFRA Publications, Admail 6000, London, SW1A 2XX; tel. 0845 955 6000; e-mail defra@cambertown.com

Publications list:
Available online

Access to staff:
Appointment necessary.

Access to building, collection or gallery:
Hours: Mon to Fri, 1000 to 1600

DEPARTMENT FOR ENVIRONMENT, FOOD AND RURAL AFFAIRS – LIBRARY

Acronym or abbreviation: DEFRA

Room 15, 3 Whitehall Place, London, SW1A 2HH

Tel: 020 7270 8000
Fax: 020 7270 8419
E-mail: helpline@defra.gsi.gov.uk

Website:
http://www.defra.gov.uk/corporate/publications
Details of departmental publications
http://www.defra.gov.uk

Enquiries:
Enquiries to: Librarian
Direct tel: 020 7270 8429
Direct e-mail: kevin.jackson@defra.gsi.gov.uk

Founded:
2001

Formerly called:
Ministry of Agriculture, Fisheries & Food (MAFF) (year of change 2001)

Organisation type and purpose:
National government body.
Government departmental library.

Subject coverage:
Agriculture, fisheries, food, particularly temperate agriculture, environment, nature conservation.

Library catalogue:
All or part available in-house

Printed publications:
Full details of Departmental publications are given in HMSO Sectional Lists 1 and 23 and in DEFRA Publications Catalogue available from the website or by post
Reading lists (MAFF Library, free)
Order printed publications from: DEFRA Publications Admail 6000, London, SW1A 2XX, tel: 08459 556000, e-mail: defra@iforcegroup.com

Publications list:
Available online

Access to staff:
Contact by e-mail and via website. Appointment necessary.
Hours: Mon to Fri, 0900 to 1700

Access to building, collection or gallery:
Prior appointment required

Access for disabled people:
Toilet facilities

Also at:
Department for Environment, Food and Rural Affairs (DEFRA)
Nobel House, 17 Smith Square, London, SW1P 3JR

DEPARTMENT FOR INTERNATIONAL DEVELOPMENT

Acronym or abbreviation: DFID

Abercrombie House, Eaglesham Road, East Kilbride, Glasgow, G75 8EA

Tel: 01355 843880
Fax: 01355 843632
E-mail: library@dfid.gov.uk

Website:
http://www.dfid.gov.uk

Enquiries:
Enquiries to: Librarian
Direct tel: 020 7023 0574
Direct fax: 020 7023 0523
Direct e-mail: s-skelton@dfid.gov.uk

Formerly called:
Overseas Development Administration (ODA) (year of change 1997)

Organisation type and purpose:
National government body.
Central government library.

Subject coverage:
Social and economic development of developing countries; development aid and policy (especially for the Third World, but now also for Eastern Europe).

Access to staff:
Contact by letter, by telephone, by fax, by e-mail and via website. Appointment necessary.
Hours: Mon to Fri, 0900 to 1700

Access to building, collection or gallery:
Prior appointment required

London Office:
Department for International Development
1 Palace Street, London, SW1E 5HE; tel: 020 7023 0000; fax: 020 7023 0019

DEPARTMENT FOR WORK AND PENSIONS

Acronym or abbreviation: DWP

Information and Library Services, Room 114, Adelphi, 1–11 John Adam Street, London, WC2N 6NT

Tel: 020 7712 2500
Fax: 020 7962 8491
E-mail: library@dwp.gsi.gov.uk

Website:
http://www.dwp.gov.uk
Press releases, publications, profiles of ministers, links to DWP agency pages.

Enquiries:
Enquiries to: Librarian

Founded:
2001

Organisation type and purpose:
National government body.
Government departmental library.

Subject coverage:
Social security, social welfare (including National Insurance, industrial injuries, supplementary benefits, state and occupational pensions, family benefits); social policy, poverty, taxation, distribution of income, public administration, management; unemployment, employment.

Trade and statistical information:
UK government statistics and world-wide statistics on social security and social welfare.

Library catalogue:
All or part available in-house

Printed publications:
Journals

Access to staff:
Contact by letter, by telephone, by fax and by e-mail. Appointment necessary.
Hours: Mon to Fri, 0900 to 1700
Special comments: Library of last resort – if there is no other service for the information.

Access for disabled people:
Access to all public areas, toilet facilities

DEPARTMENT OF AGRICULTURE AND RURAL DEVELOPMENT LIBRARY

Acronym or abbreviation: DARD

Room 615, Dundonald House, Upper Newtownards Road, Belfast, BT4 3SB

Tel: 028 9052 4401
Fax: 028 9052 5546
E-mail: library@dardni.gov.uk

Website:
http://www.dardni.gov.uk
Structure of department courses, open government, agricultural information.

Enquiries:
Enquiries to: Librarian

Organisation type and purpose:
Government department.

Subject coverage:
Agriculture, fisheries, forestry and afforestation, horticulture, rural development, public administration.

Library catalogue:
All or part available online

Printed publications:
Accessions lists (regularly)

Access to staff:
Access for members only.
Hours: Mon to Fri, 0900 to 1700

DEPARTMENT OF COMPLEMENTARY THERAPIES

School of Integrated Health, University of Westminster, 115 New Cavendish Street, London, W1W 6UW

Tel: 020 7911 5000
Fax: 020 7911 5028
E-mail: course-enquiries@westminster.ac.uk

Website:
http://www.westminster.ac.uk/sih

Founded:
1983

Created by the merger of:
Centre for Community Care and Primary Health, and London School of Acupuncture and Traditional Chinese Medicine (year of change 1997)

Organisation type and purpose:
Advisory body, university department or institute, training organisation, consultancy, research organisation.

Subject coverage:
Homoeopathy, nutritional therapy, medical herbalism, remedial massage, professional entry education in traditional Chinese Medicine, acupuncture and other complementary therapies, development of research base of traditional Chinese acupuncture in the United Kingdom and other complementary therapies.

Library catalogue:
All or part available online and in-house

Printed publications:
Prospectus (by post or electronically)
Order printed publications from: Course Enquiries: course-enquiries@westminster.ac.uk, tel. 020 7911 5000

Access to staff:
Contact by letter, by telephone, by fax, by e-mail and via website
Hours: Mon to Fri, 0900 to 1700

Access to building, collection or gallery:
Prior appointment required
Hours: Mon to Fri, 0900 to 1700

Access for disabled people:
Ramped entry, toilet facilities

DEPARTMENT OF HEALTH

1W28, Quarry House, Quarry Hill, Leeds, LS2 7UE

Tel: 0113 2545080
Fax: 0113 2545084
E-mail: library.enquiries@dh.gsi.gov.uk

Website:
http://www.dh.gov.uk

Enquiries:
Enquiries to: Customer Services Librarian (Leeds)
Other contacts: Customer Services Librarian (London)

Founded:
1834

Organisation type and purpose:
National government body.
Government Department Library Service provided to all staff within the Department of Health.

Subject coverage:
Public health, health services, health services policy and management, social care policy and management, hospital buildings.

Museum or gallery collection, archive, or library special collection:
250,000 monographs
565 printed periodicals
Various databases and some e-journals

Library catalogue:
All or part available online and in-house

Printed publications:
Order printed publications from: DH Publications Order Line, PO Box 777, London, SE1 6XH, fax: 0870 1555 455, e-mail: dh@prolog.uk.com

Electronic and video publications:
DoH Thesaurus of health and social care terms
DH-Data Thesaurus (available via the DH website)
DH-Data (from DIALOG)
HMIC (from Ovid/Silver Platter)

Access to staff:
Contact by letter. Appointment necessary.
Hours: Mon to Fri, 0900 to 1700

Access to building, collection or gallery:
No access other than to staff
Special comments: Not open to the public. Written requests for access should be addressed to the Customer Services Librarian

Also at:
Chief Librarian, Department of Health Library 331B Skipton House, 80 London Road, London, SE1 6LH; tel: 020 7972 5927; fax: 020 7972 5681; e-mail: library.enquiries@dh.gsi.gov.uk; website: http://www.dh.gov.uk

DEPARTMENT OF HEALTH – LIBRARY INFORMATION SERVICES

Skipton House, 80 London Road, London, SE1 6LH

Tel: 020 7972 2000
Fax: 020 7972 1609

Website:
http://www.doh.gov.uk
General information about the Department of Health.

Enquiries:
Enquiries to: Librarian
Direct tel: 020 7972 6541
Direct fax: 020 7972 5976

Organisation type and purpose:
National government body.
Government department library.

Subject coverage:
Health and social care services, management of the National Health Service, hospitals, public health, environmental health, services for older people and those with disabilities and learning difficulties.

Museum or gallery collection, archive, or library special collection:
Collection of early Poor Law pamphlets
Government Medical Inspectors Local Reports on Public Health, 1869–1907
Local Reports to the General Board of Health, 1848–1857

Library catalogue:
All or part available in-house

Printed publications:
DH-DATA Thesaurus of Health and Social Care Terms
Order printed publications from: DH publications Orderline:
PO Box 777, London, SE1 6XH, tel: 08701 555455, fax: 01623 724524, e-mail: dh@prolog.uk.com

Microform publications:
Departmental documents, available from Chadwyck-Healey

Electronic and video publications:
DH-DATA, available through Datastar
HMIC CD-ROM (available from Ovid)

Access to staff:
Appointment necessary.
Hours: Mon to Fri, 0900 to 1700

Access to building, collection or gallery:
Prior appointment required

DEPARTMENT OF ORAL & DENTAL SCIENCE

University of Bristol Dental School, Lower Maudlin Street, Bristol, BS1 2LY

Tel: 0117 9284309
Fax: 0117 9284150
E-mail: ann.e.jones@bristol.ac.uk

Website:
http://www.deut.bris.ac.uk/research

Enquiries:
Enquiries to: Administrator

Formerly called:
Centre for Study of Oral Disease

Organisation type and purpose:
Suitable for ages: 18+.
University department, Research group of the Medical Research Council, operating within the University of Bristol Dental School with support from Wellcome Trust and Cancer Research Campaign.

Subject coverage:
Dental research including the structure, composition and histopathology of teeth; dental caries; periodontal disease; salivary gland disease; oral cancer; viruses and oral disease.

Access to staff:
Contact by letter, by telephone, by fax and by e-mail
Hours: Mon to Fri, 0830 to 1630

Access for disabled people:
Parking provided, ramped entry, toilet facilities

DEPARTMENT OF REGIONAL DEVELOPMENT

Acronym or abbreviation: DRD

Library, Room G-40, Clarence Court, 10–18 Adelaide Street, Belfast, BT2 8GB

Tel: 028 9054 1046
Fax: 028 9054 1081
E-mail: library@drdni.gov.uk

Enquiries:
Enquiries to: Librarian

Formerly called:
Department of the Environment for Northern Ireland (DOE) (year of change 2000)

Organisation type and purpose:
National government body.
There is a Core Department and two Next Steps agencies.

Subject coverage:
Planning, roads, road safety, environmental protection and conservation, local government, urban regeneration and disposal and management of the department's land and property holdings, transport, fire services, pollution, historic monuments, archaeology, water and sewerage services, building construction, public records.

Non-library collection catalogue:
All or part available online and in-house

Library catalogue:
All or part available online and in-house

Access to staff:
Access for members only.
Hours: Mon to Fri, 0900 to 1700
Special comments: Loans and personal access to civil servants only. Brief subject enquiries by letter or telephone from non-civil servants will be dealt with where possible.

Access to building, collection or gallery:
No prior appointment required

Next Steps agencies:
Roads Service
    website: http://www.roadsni.gov.uk
Water Service
    website: http://www.waterni.gov.uk

DEPARTMENT OF THE ENVIRONMENT FOR NORTHERN IRELAND

Acronym or abbreviation: MBR

Environment and Heritage Service, Monuments and Buildings Record, 5–33 Hill Street, Belfast, BT1 2LA

Tel: 028 9054 3004
Fax: 028 9054 3111
E-mail: mbr@doeni.gov.uk

Website:
http://www.ehsni.gov.uk

Enquiries:
Enquiries to: Secretary

Founded:
1992

Formerly called:
Archaeological Survey

Organisation type and purpose:
National government body.

Subject coverage:
Archaeological sites, listed buildings listings, photographic and drawings archive library, historic monuments and buildings, historic gardens, industrial archaeology, maritime archaeology.

Museum or gallery collection, archive, or library special collection:
Clokey collection (stained glass)
J S Curl photographic collection (of historic buildings)
McCutcheon archive (industrial archaeology)
McKinstry and McGeagh architectural archives
Northern Ireland sites and monuments record

Non-library collection catalogue:
All or part available in-house

Library catalogue:
All or part available in-house

Printed publications:
Carrickfergus Castle, Co Antrim
Historic Monuments of Northern Ireland

Access to staff:
Contact by letter, by telephone, by fax, by e-mail and in person
Hours: 0930 to 1300, 1400 to 1630

Access for disabled people:
Ramped entry, toilet facilities

Parent body:
Department of the Environment
    Clarence Court, Belfast, BT2 8GB; tel: 028 9054 0540

DEPARTMENT OF URBAN STUDIES

University of Glasgow, 25 Bute Gardens, Glasgow, G12 8RT

Tel: 0141 330 4190
Fax: 0141 330 4983
E-mail: e.lang@socsci.gla.ac.uk

Website:
http://www.gla.ac.uk/Inter/CHRUS/
Home page – research interests, staff etc.
http://www.gla.ac.uk/Acad/Urban/

Enquiries:
Enquiries to: Librarian
Direct tel: ext 4190
Other contacts: Resource Centre Manager

Formerly called:
Centre for Housing Research and Urban Studies (CHRUS) (year of change 1996)

Organisation type and purpose:
University department or institute, consultancy, research organisation.

Subject coverage:
Housing, urban studies.

Museum or gallery collection, archive, or library special collection:
Housing related books/reports/serials

Printed publications:
Discussion Papers (43), Occasional Papers (26), Special Publications
Studies in Housing (4)

Publications list:
Available in print

Access to staff:
Contact by telephone, by fax and by e-mail.
Appointment necessary.
Hours: Mon to Fri, 0900 to 1700

DEPAUL TRUST

1st Floor, 291–299 Borough High Street, London, SE1 1JG

Tel: 020 7939 1220
Fax: 020 7939 1221
E-mail: depaul@depaultrust.org

Website:
http://www.depaultrust.org

Enquiries:
Enquiries to: Administrator

Founded:
1989

Organisation type and purpose:
Voluntary organisation, registered charity (charity number 802384).

Subject coverage:
Depaul Trust helps young people across the UK who are homeless, vulnerable and disadvantaged, working in the very heart of local communities. It protects young people who become homeless by finding them a place to call their home. Each year it provides over 100,000 bed nights and it is open every day and night.
It prevents young people from becoming homeless by rebuilding family relationships and offering through-the-gate support to young offenders.
It provides young people with the chance to fulfil their potential in the community through education, volunteering, training and jobs.
Since Depaul Trust started in 1989, it has made a difference to over 40,000 young people.

Publications list:
Available online

Access to staff:
Contact by letter, by telephone, by fax, by e-mail and via website
Hours: Mon to Fri, 0900 to 1730

DEPRESSION ALLIANCE

35 Westminster Bridge Road, London, SE1 7JB

Tel: 020 7633 0557
Fax: 020 7633 0559
E-mail: information@depressionalliance.org

Website:
http://www.depressionalliance.org
Information on depression.

Enquiries:
Enquiries to: Office and Communications Co-ordinator

Founded:
1974

Formerly called:
Depressives Associated (year of change 1995); National Depression Campaign (year of change 2000)

Organisation type and purpose:
Membership association (membership is by subscription), present number of members: 3000, voluntary organisation, registered charity (charity number 278532).
To provide support and understanding, information, education, self-help.

continued overleaf

Subject coverage:
Depression.

Printed publications:
Free for individuals, charges for organisations and bulk orders
Leaflets on Depression, Self Help, Student Stress Pack, etc
A Single Step (magazine, quarterly)
Order printed publications from: Office Manager, Depression Alliance
As above

Electronic and video publications:
Video: Understanding Depression

Publications list:
Available online and in print

Access to staff:
Contact by letter, by telephone, by fax, by e-mail and via website
Hours: Mon to Fri, 1000 to 1700

Access to building, collection or gallery:
Prior appointment required

Other addresses:
Depression Alliance Cymru
    11 Plas Melin, Westbourne Road, Whitchurch, Cardiff, CF4 2BT; tel: 029 2069 2891; fax: 029 2052 7774
Depression Alliance Scotland
    3 Grosvenor Gardens, Edinburgh, EH12 5JU; tel: 0131 467 3050; fax: 0131 467 7701

DEPRESSION–UK

Acronym or abbreviation: D–UK

Self Help Nottingham, Ormiston House, 32–36 Pelham Street, Nottingham, NG1 2EG

E-mail: info@depressionuk.org.uk

Website:
http://www.depressionuk.org.uk

Enquiries:
Enquiries to: Honorary Secretary

Founded:
1973

Formerly called:
Depressives Anonymous (year of change 1973)

Please select:
Fellowship of Depressives Anonymous (year of change 2007)

Organisation type and purpose:
Membership association (membership is by subscription), present number of members: 700, voluntary organisation, registered charity (charity number 294482).
Encouragement and support for those with depression and those concerned for them.

Subject coverage:
Depression.

Printed publications:
Newsletter (six times a year, £2 to non-members)
Book List, Leaflets (free), Information Sheet (free)

Electronic and video publications:
Audio Tape List (free)

Publications list:
Available in print

Access to staff:
Contact by letter, by telephone and by e-mail
Hours: Mon to Fri, 0900 to 1700

DERBY CITY COUNCIL

Council House, Corporation Street, Derby, DE1 2FS

Tel: 01332 293111\ Minicom no. 01332 256666
Fax: 01322 255500
E-mail: via website

Website:
http://www.derby.gov.uk

Enquiries:
Enquiries to: Chief Executive

Organisation type and purpose:
Local government body.

Subject coverage:
All local authority services.

Access to staff:
Contact by letter, by telephone, by fax, by e-mail and in person
Hours: Mon to Thu, 0830 to 1700; Fri, 0830 to 1630

DERBY CITY LIBRARIES

Derby Local Studies Library, 25B Irongate, Derby, DE1 3GL

Tel: 01332 255393
E-mail: localstudies.library@derby.gov.uk

Website:
http://www.derby.gov.uk/libraries/about/local_studies.htm
Guide to library.

Enquiries:
Enquiries to: Librarian

Founded:
1879

Organisation type and purpose:
Public library.
Local studies library providing research facilities.

Subject coverage:
Local studies materials of all types relating to Derby and Derbyshire.

Museum or gallery collection, archive, or library special collection:
Printed materials, over 40,000 items including histories of Derby and Derbyshire, street and trade directories, poll books and registers of electors for Derby
Periodicals and newspapers dating from 1732
Maps from 1577
Illustrations and engravings including over 8500 photographs dating from 1860s to present day
Broadsheets mostly 19th century items depicting events
Family History including Census returns on microfilm for the whole of Derbyshire 1841 to 1901
IGI (microfiche) for UK
Special collections including family papers, deeds, manuscripts, business records etc

Non-library collection catalogue:
All or part available in-house

Printed publications:
General guide to collections (free)

Access to staff:
Contact by letter, by telephone, by e-mail, in person and via website
Hours: Mon, Tue, 0930 to 1900; Wed, Thu, Fri, 0930 to 1700; Sat, 0930 to 1600

Access to building, collection or gallery:
Hours: Mon, Tue, 0930 to 1900; Wed, Thu, Fri, 0930 to 1700; Sat, 0930 to 1600

Access for disabled people:
Ramped entry
Special comments: Please ring to book a parking space.

Parent body:
Derby City Council
    Derby City Libraries, Regeneration & Community, Heritage Gate, Friary Street, Derby, DE1 1QX; tel: 01332 715549; fax: 01332 716607

DERBYSHIRE AND NOTTINGHAMSHIRE CHAMBER OF COMMERCE

Acronym or abbreviation: DNCC

Canal Wharf, Chesterfield, Derbyshire, S41 7NA

Tel: 0845 601 1038
Fax: 01246 233228
E-mail: information@dncc.co.uk

Website:
http://www.dncc.co.uk

Enquiries:
Enquiries to: Information & Research Officer

Founded:
1899

Formerly called:
Derbyshire Chamber and Business Link; Nottinghamshire Chamber of Commerce and Industry (year of change 2006 and 2007)

Organisation type and purpose:
Membership association.
Chamber of Commerce.

Subject coverage:
Training, business information, business support, with emphasis on Derbyshire and Nottinghamshire. Export advice.

Information services:
Telephone and e-mail enquiry service for business

Printed publications:
InBusiness (monthly magazine, free to members).
Members' Briefing (monthly information bulletin, free to members)
Directory of Members (annually, free to members)

Electronic and video publications:
Customised databases available for purchase

Access to staff:
Contact by letter, by telephone, by fax, by e-mail and via website
Hours: Mon to Fri, 0900 to 1700
Special comments: Charges made for incurred costs and research time.

Member of:
Association of British Chambers of Commerce

DERBYSHIRE CHAMBER AND BUSINESS LINK

Commerce Centre, Canal Wharf, Chesterfield, Derbyshire, S41 7NA

Tel: 0845 601 1038
Fax: 01246 233228

Website:
http://www.derbyshire.org

Enquiries:
Enquiries to: Information and Research Officer
Direct e-mail: helen.carter@derbyshire.org

Organisation type and purpose:
Membership association (membership is by subscription).
Information and advice to small and medium sized companies in Southern Derbyshire.

Subject coverage:
General employment law information; local business information, training, business.
Business support services.

Trade and statistical information:
Local economic data particularly labour market.

Library catalogue:
All or part available in-house

Printed publications:
East Midlands Business Directory (members, free: non-members, £70)
Member's Bulletin (monthly, free)
Economic Surveys for Southern Derbyshire (quarterly)

Access to staff:
Contact by letter, by telephone, by fax, by e-mail, in person and via website. Non-members charged.
Hours: Mon to Fri, 0830 to 1730

Access to building, collection or gallery:
Prior appointment required

Access for disabled people:
Parking provided, access to all public areas, toilet facilities

Affiliated to:
Association of British Chambers of Commerce 9 Tufton Street, London, SW1P 3QB

Provider to:
Business Link Derbyshire Information Service

DERBYSHIRE COUNTY COUNCIL

Cultural and Community Services Department, County Hall, Matlock, Derbyshire, DE4 3AG

Tel: 01629 580000
Fax: 01629 585363
E-mail: derbyshire.libraries@derbyshire.gov.uk

Website:
http://www.derbyshire.gov.uk
Full catalogue.
http://www.peaklandheritage.org.uk
http://picturethepast.org.uk

Enquiries:
Enquiries to: Strategic Director of Cultural and Community Services
Other contacts: Assistant Director (for information on resources and publications)

Organisation type and purpose:
Local government body, museum, art gallery, public library.
County and Diocesan Record Office.

Subject coverage:
Derbyshire local studies; local government information; family history; lead mining.

Museum or gallery collection, archive, or library special collection:
British Cave Research Association Library (at HQ)
George Stephenson Collection of early railway history (at Chesterfield)

Non-library collection catalogue:
All or part available online and in-house

Library catalogue:
All or part available online

Printed publications:
Various publications on local history, including:
Buxton, a People's History (M. Langham, £6.99)
South Derbyshire and its People: a history (O. Hull, £10.99)
A Victorian Farmer's Diary (W. Hodkin, £6.95)
Kinder Scout, portrait of a mountain (£12.99)
Boiler Suits, Bofors and Bullets (J. Edgar, £5.99)
Trains and Trails (J. Edgar, £4.99)
Melbourne 1820–1875, a diary (J. J. Briggs, £10.99)
Free but not Easy, Autiobiography of Bas Barker of Chesterfield and his work with the Labour and Trade Union Movements (B. Barker and L. Straker, 50p)
Eleven Years Hard, or Ten Paces to the Privy: the life of a police sergeant's wife in Ilkeston and Sandiacre 1939–1950 (W. Broughton, £1)
Props, Points and Pig Iron: Life in Renishaw (J. Edgar, £5.00)
Derbyshire Detail and Character – a celebration of Derbyshire's towns and villages in pictures (B. Joyce, G. Michell and M. Williams, £12.99)
Facsimile Trade Directories: Bulmer's Chesterfield and North East Derbyshire

Electronic and video publications:
See website covering the history of the Peak District and containing a database of books and articles held in the library: www.peaklandheritage.org.uk
Picture the Past: a web-based resource containing historic images from the collections of libraries in Derby, Derbyshire, Nottingham and Nottinghamshire: www.picturethepast.org.uk

Publications list:
Available online and in print

Access to staff:
Contact by letter, by telephone, by fax, by e-mail, in person and via website

Hours: Mon to Fri, 0900 to 1700

Links with:
County local studies library at Matlock
Derbyshire County Council
Main public library at Chesterfield

DERBYSHIRE FAMILY HISTORY SOCIETY

Acronym or abbreviation: DFHS

Bridge Chapel House, St Mary's Bridge, Sowter Road, Derby, DE1 3AT

Tel: 01332 363876

Website:
http://www.dfhs.org.uk

Enquiries:
Enquiries to: Honorary Secretary

Founded:
1976

Organisation type and purpose:
Membership association (membership is by subscription), present number of members: 2000, registered charity (charity number 517162).
Family history research.

Subject coverage:
Family history in Derbyshire.

Services for disabled people:
Quarterly journal on tape for the partially sighted.

Library catalogue:
All or part available in-house and in print

Printed publications:
Journal (4 times a year)
1851 Census Books
Order printed publications from: Booksales Officer, Derbyshire Family History Society
17 Penrhyn Avenue, Littleover, Derby, DE23 6LB

Microform publications:
Memorial Inscriptions (microfiche)
Melbourne Name Index (microfiche)
1851 Census (microfiche)
1891 Census Index Fiche (microfiche)
How to trace your family tree in Derbyshire (video)
IGI
Cemetery Records
Order microform publications from: Booksales Officer

Electronic and video publications:
Journal (4 times a year, on tape for blind and partially sighted members)
1891 Census (work in progress to index the census in a computer database)
Memorial Inscriptions (work in progress to record these in a computer database)
Census Indexes 1851 and 1891 (CD-ROM)
Census Index 1861 (disketter)

Publications list:
Available online and in print

Access to staff:
Contact by letter and via website
Hours: Tue, Thu, Sat, 1000 to 1600
Special comments: Telephone 01332 363876 during these hours only.

Access to building, collection or gallery:
Hours: Tue, Thu, Sat, 1000 to 1600

Access for disabled people:
Special comments: Grade 2 listed building; please telephone to make arrangements before visiting.

Affiliated to:
Federation of Family History Societies

DERBYSHIRE GRITSTONE SHEEP BREEDERS SOCIETY

The Secretary, 5 Bridge Close, Waterfoot, Rossendale, Lancashire, BB4 9SN

Tel: 01706 228520
E-mail: info@pmcoppack.com

Website:
http://www.derbyshiregritstone.org.uk/

Enquiries:
Enquiries to: Honorary Secretary

Founded:
1906

Organisation type and purpose:
Membership association (membership is by subscription), registered charity (charity number 265539).
Support for members and to maintain/develop standard of Derbyshire Gritstone sheep.

Printed publications:
1991 brochure

Access to staff:
Contact by letter
Hours: Mon to Fri, 0900 to 1700

DERBYSHIRE RECORD OFFICE

County Hall, Matlock, Derbyshire, DE4 3AG

Tel: 01629 585959
Fax: 01629 57611
E-mail: record.office@derbyshire.gov.uk

Website:
http://www.derbyshire.gov.uk/recordoffice

Enquiries:
Enquiries to: County and Diocesan Archivist
Direct tel: 01629 585980
Direct e-mail: margaretosullivan@derbyshire.gov.uk

Organisation type and purpose:
Local government body.
County Record Office.

Subject coverage:
Archives of the County of Derbyshire, the City of Derby and the Diocese of Derby; business, industrial, diocesan, parish, family and estate, manorial, hospital, school, voluntary society and other records of Derbyshire origin

Non-library collection catalogue:
All or part available online, in-house and in print

Printed publications:
Derbyshire Record Office Guide (out of print, available online early 2009)
Annual list of archive accessions (price on application)
Parish Register Guide (dates of original parish registers and microfilm copies of registers of baptisms, banns, marriages and burials available in the Record Office, with brief administrative history of each parish/township, an introduction to parish registers and a parish map; price on application)
Archives First (a series of over 30 beginners' guides to original sources for aspects of Derbyshire's history; price on application)
Outline map of Derbyshire parishes, c.1800 (price on application)
County of Derbyshire showing parish and district boundaries c.2000 (price on application)
Order printed publications from: Derbyshire Record Office, County Hall, Matlock, DE4 3AG

Electronic and video publications:
Ordnance Survey 2nd edn 25 in:1 mile maps of Derbyshire c.1900 (on CD-ROM; £25 plus postage)
George M. Woodward: collection of 18th–19th century caricatures (on CD-ROM; price on application)
Order electronic and video publications from: Derbyshire Record Office, County Hall, Matlock, DE4 3AG

Publications list:
Available online and in print

Access to staff:
Contact by letter, by telephone, by fax, by e-mail and in person. Appointment necessary.

continued overleaf

Access to building, collection or gallery:
Hours: Mon to Fri, 0930 to 1645, one Sat per month
0900 to 1230
Special comments: Reader registration required

Parent body:
Derbyshire County Council
  Cultural and Community Services Department,
  Libraries and Heritage Division

DERBYSHIRE WILDLIFE TRUST

Acronym or abbreviation: DWT

East Mill, Bridgefoot, Belper, Derbyshire, DE56
1XH

Tel: 01773 881188
Fax: 01773 821826
E-mail: enquiries@derbyshirewt.co.uk

Website:
http://www.derbyshirewildlifetrust.org.uk
Details on the work of the trust, events,
membership, reserves and how people can get
involved.

Enquiries:
Enquiries to: Administration Assistant

Founded:
1962

Organisation type and purpose:
Voluntary organisation, registered charity (charity
number 222212).

Printed publications:
Wild Derbyshire

Publications list:
Available in print

Access to staff:
Contact by letter, by telephone, by fax, by e-mail
and via website
Hours: Mon to Thu, 0900 to 1700; Fri, 0900 to 1630

Access to building, collection or gallery:
No prior appointment required

Also at:
Countryside Centre, Derbyshire Wildlife Trust
  The Whistlestop Countryside Centre, Matlock
  Bath Railway Station, Matlock Bath, Derbyshire,
  DE4 3PT; tel: 01629 580958

DERMATITIS AND ALLIED DISEASES RESEARCH TRUST

Acronym or abbreviation: DERMATRUST

40 Queen Anne Street, London, W1G 9EL

Tel: 01604 781903
Fax: 01604 781514

Enquiries:
Enquiries to: Chairman

Founded:
1996

Organisation type and purpose:
Registered charity (charity number 1016315).
To support the care of patients with skin diseases
and to fund research into their causes and develop
new treatments.

Subject coverage:
Dermatological diseases, dermatology research.

Access to staff:
Contact by letter and by fax
Hours: Mon to Fri, 0900 to 1700

DESIGN AND ARTISTS COPYRIGHT SOCIETY

Acronym or abbreviation: DACS

33 Great Sutton Street, London, EC1V 0DX

Tel: 020 7336 8811
Fax: 020 7336 8822
E-mail: info@dacs.org.uk

Enquiries:
Enquiries to: Membership Secretary

Founded:
1983

Organisation type and purpose:
International organisation, membership
association (membership is by subscription).
DACS is the copyright and collecting society for
visual arts in the UK; acting as exclusive licensee
on behalf of its national members and as agent for
foreign artists and estates. It also actively
campaigns to create a fairer working environment
for visual creators through collective
administration and lobbying on behalf of all artists
at both national and international levels on rights-
related issues.

Printed publications:
Annual Report
Slide Collection Licensing Scheme Pack

Publications list:
Available online and in print

Access to staff:
Contact by letter, by fax and by e-mail.
Appointment necessary.
Hours: Mon to Fri, 0900 to 1800
Special comments: DACS can only act on behalf of
its members, but offers general copyright
information to all.

Access to building, collection or gallery:
No prior appointment required

DESIGN AND TECHNOLOGY ASSOCIATION

Acronym or abbreviation: DATA

16 Wellesbourne House, Walton Road,
Wellesbourne, Warwickshire, CV35 9JB

Tel: 01789 470007
Fax: 01789 841955
E-mail: DATA@data.org.uk

Website:
http://www.data.org.uk
Membership, publications, conferences, training.

Enquiries:
Enquiries to: Chief Executive

Founded:
1989

Incorporates:
National Association for Teachers of Home
Economics (NATNE), date of change, 1 April 2000

Organisation type and purpose:
Professional body (membership is by subscription),
present number of members: 4350, registered
charity (charity number 1062270), suitable for ages:
preschool to post 18, training organisation,
consultancy, research organisation.
Educational organisation of teachers and academic
institutions.
To support, develop and enhance design and
technology in all sectors of education and society.

Subject coverage:
Design and technology education.
Home economics; nutrition; childcare and
development; food and textiles; technology.

**Museum or gallery collection, archive, or library
special collection:**
Books and Resources
All issues of the ATDS journal Housecraft from
  1928 to 1982 and NATHE journal MODUS, 1928
  to present held at Hamilton House
Computerised database
Domestic science archives held at University of
  Warwick
Design and Technology Library

Printed publications:
Variety of educational books and resources,
  including:
Assessment Handbook
Teaching CAD/CAM

DATA Guidance Materials Key Stages 1, 2 and 3
DATA NEWS (newsletter, termly, free to members)
Designing (termly magazine for primary and
  secondary education)
Modus (8 times a year and 2 educational inserts; 1
  issue a year is a Resources Guide)
Primary Coordinators' File
Primary Planning into Practice
Risk Assessment in Secondary School Design and
  Technology Teaching Environments 2001

Electronic and video publications:
Electronics (educational videos)
CAD/CAM in Practice (CD)

Publications list:
Available in print

Access to staff:
Contact by letter, by telephone, by fax, by e-mail,
in person and via website
Hours: Mon to Fri, 0900 to 1700
Special comments: Library access available for
members only.

Constituent member of:
Confederation of Design and Technology
Associations
Council of Subject Teachers Associations

DESIGN HISTORY SOCIETY

Acronym or abbreviation: DHS

28 New High Street, Oxford, OX3 7AQ

Tel: 01264 353058
E-mail: webadmin@designhistorysociety.org

Website:
http://www.designhistorysociety.org
Society membership; full range of initiatives
including those aimed at students; support of
events; access to electronic discussion list.

Enquiries:
Enquiries to: Secretary

Founded:
1977

Organisation type and purpose:
Learned society (membership is by subscription),
registered charity (charity number 327326),
research organisation.

Subject coverage:
History of architecture and design, including
design of fashion and textiles; graphic design;
product design; cultural studies.

Printed publications:
Journal of Design History (quarterly)
Newsletter (quarterly)

Access to staff:
Contact by letter, by telephone, by e-mail and via
website
Hours: Mon to Fri, 0900 to 1700

DESIGNER BOOKBINDERS

6 Queen Square, London, WC1N 3AR

Tel: 01453 759063
E-mail: secretary@designerbookbinders.org.uk

Website:
http://www.designerbookbinders.org.uk

Enquiries:
Enquiries to: Secretary

Founded:
1951

Formerly called:
Guild of Contemporary Bookbinders; Hampstead
Guild of Scribes and Bookbinders (year of change
1955)

Organisation type and purpose:
Membership association, present number of
members: 600, voluntary organisation, registered
charity (charity number 282018).

Maintenance and improvement of standards of design and craft in hand bookbinding by means of exhibitions, teaching and publications.

Subject coverage:
Art of the hand-bound book, design, craftsmanship, repair and restoration.

Printed publications:
Newsletter (quarterly, for members only)
The New Bookbinder (annually, from 1981; superseded the Designer Bookbinders Review, 1973–1979)
Modern British Bookbinding (exhibition catalogue, 1985, £10)
Leighton House Exhibition (1987, £10)
DB5 (catalogue, 1987, £5)
Fine Words, Fine Books (catalogue, 1991, £10)
DB4 (illustrated directory, 1983, £5)
North American Exhibition Catalogue (2000–2001)
Order printed publications from: Designer Bookbinders Publications Limited
8 Bryn Coetmor, Bethesda, Bangor, Gwynnedd, LL57 3NL, tel: 01248 602591, fax: 01248 602591, e-mail: publications@designerbookbinders.org.uk

Publications list:
Available in print

Access to staff:
Contact by letter, by telephone, by e-mail and via website
Hours: Mon to Fri, 1800 to 2100 (answerphone 0900 to 1800)

Member of:
Federation of British Crafts Societies (FBCS)

DEUX CHEVAUX CLUB OF GREAT BRITAIN

Acronym or abbreviation: 2CVGB

PO Box 602, Crick, Northampton, NN6 7UW

E-mail: secretary@2cvgb.com

Website:
http://www.2cvgb.co.uk

Enquiries:
Enquiries to: Secretary

Founded:
1978

Organisation type and purpose:
International organisation, membership association (membership is by subscription), present number of members: 3000.

Subject coverage:
Information and parts for all Citroën A – Series vehicles.

Museum or gallery collection, archive, or library special collection:
Probably the most comprehensive archive on 'A' Series vehicles

Printed publications:
2CVGB News (monthly, £2.50)

Access to staff:
Contact by letter, by e-mail and via website
Hours: Mon to Fri, 0800 to 2200

DEVELOPMENT EDUCATION ASSOCIATION

Acronym or abbreviation: DEA

1st Floor, River House, 143–145 Farringdon Road, London EC1R 3AB

Tel: 020 7812 1282
Fax: 020 7812 1272
E-mail: dea@dea.org.uk

Website:
http://www.dea.org.uk
Main DEA website
http://www.globaldimension.org.uk
Free database of resources for school teachers interested in teaching about global issues. Managed by the DEA on behalf of DFID.

Enquiries:
Enquiries to: Communications Team

Founded:
1993

Organisation type and purpose:
Membership association (membership is by subscription), present number of members: 300, voluntary organisation, registered charity (charity number 291696), suitable for ages: all.
To promote and strengthen the development education movement in UK; to raise public awareness of global and development issues.

Subject coverage:
Provides information on availability of development education resources for researchers, youth and community workers; information and support base to development education practitioners, global perspectives in formal education (schools, higher and further education), youth work, adult and community education.

Museum or gallery collection, archive, or library special collection:
Small resource centre for internal use

Trade and statistical information:
Contact and resource information on development education sector in UK.

Printed publications:
See www.dea.org.uk/dea/publications.html for full list of publications.
Development Education Journal (3 times a year, free to members or subscribe through Trentham Books, www.trentham-books.co.uk)
Development Education News – newsletter free to members produced 10 times a year.
Order printed publications from: Contact the DEA

Publications list:
Available online and in print

Access to staff:
Contact by letter, by telephone, by fax, by e-mail and via website. Appointment necessary.
Hours: Mon to Fri, 1000 to 1700
Special comments: None

DEVON AND EXETER INSTITUTION LIBRARY

7 Cathedral Close, Exeter, Devon, EX1 1EZ

Tel: 01392 251017

Website:
http://www.lib.ex.ac.uk/search
Exeter University Library catalogue search facility.
http://www.ex.ac.uk/library/devonex.html
Description of the library.

Enquiries:
Enquiries to: Librarian in Charge
Direct e-mail: j.p.gardner@exeter.ac.uk

Founded:
1813

Organisation type and purpose:
Membership association, registered charity. Independent subscription library.

Subject coverage:
History of Exeter, Devon, Cornwall, Somerset, Dorset, 19th century periodicals, biography, history and topography.

Museum or gallery collection, archive, or library special collection:
18th and 19th century local newspapers
Early 19th century pamphlets, including medical history and locally published
South West Collection
Topographical prints and early maps

Library catalogue:
All or part available online

Printed publications:
The Devon & Exeter Institution 1813–1988 (Longridge RW, 1988, £2)

Access to staff:
Contact by letter, by telephone and by e-mail. Appointment necessary. Access for members only.
Hours: Mon to Fri, 0900 to 1700

Affiliated to:
University of Exeter

Houses the:
Devon & Cornwall Record Society
Devon Archaeological Society (as Library)
Devon Gardens Trust
Devon History Society

DEVON ARCHAEOLOGICAL SOCIETY

Acronym or abbreviation: DAS

c/o Royal Albert Memorial Museum, Queen Street, Exeter, Devon, EX4 3RX

Enquiries:
Enquiries to: Honorary Secretary
Direct e-mail: dasonline.wanadoo.co.uk

Organisation type and purpose:
Learned society, registered charity.

Subject coverage:
Archaeology of Devon, historic buildings.

Library catalogue:
All or part available in-house

Printed publications:
Devon Archaeology (occasional)
Field Guides to Archaeological Sites in Devon
Proceedings (annually)
Newsletter (for members, quarterly)

Publications list:
Available online and in print

Access to staff:
Contact by letter and by e-mail

DEVON ART SOCIETY

27 Barchington Avenue, Torquay, TQ2 8LB

Tel: 01803 310600
E-mail: lynn@drake55.fsnet.co.uk

Enquiries:
Enquiries to: Honorary Secretary
Other contacts: Chairman

Founded:
1912

Organisation type and purpose:
Membership association (membership is by qualification), present number of members: 144.

Subject coverage:
Society for professional and non-professional artists in the Torbay area. Exhibitions held twice yearly. Members meet regularly for workshops and demonstrations. Membership by selection.

Access to staff:
Contact by letter and by telephone
Hours: Mon to Fri, 0900 to 1700

DEVON CATTLE BREEDERS' SOCIETY

Acronym or abbreviation: DCBS

Wisteria Cottage, Iddesleigh, Winkeigh, Devon, EX19 8BG

Tel: 01837 810845
E-mail: lane@dcbs.fsbusiness.co.uk

Enquiries:
Enquiries to: Secretary

Founded:
1884

Formerly called:
Devon Cattle Society (year of change 2000)

continued overleaf

Organisation type and purpose:
Membership association (membership is by subscription, qualification, election or invitation), present number of members: c. 330, registered charity (charity number 248836).
Cattle breed society.
To maintain and further the breeding of the Devon breed of cattle.

Subject coverage:
The Herd books of the society which are published on an annual basis are available for reference in the reference sections of the Devon County Library Service at Barnstaple and Exeter.

Printed publications:
Davy's Devon Herd Book (annual herd book £15)
Trade Brochure (descriptive, free of charge)

Access to staff:
Contact by letter, by telephone, by fax, by e-mail and via website. Appointment necessary.
Hours: Mon to Fri, 0900 to 1700

DEVON COUNTY COUNCIL

Local Government Information Centre and Library, G53, County Hall, Topsham Road, Exeter, Devon, EX2 4QB

Tel: 01392 383206 and 01392 383444
Fax: 01392 251411
E-mail: logical@devon-cc.gov.uk

Website:
http://www.devon-cc.gov.uk

Enquiries:
Enquiries to: Information Officer

Organisation type and purpose:
Local government body.

Subject coverage:
Local government interests, information and statistics on modern Devon.

Museum or gallery collection, archive, or library special collection:
Devon County Council publications

Access to staff:
Contact by letter, by telephone, by fax, by e-mail, in person and via website
Hours: Mon to Thu, 0900 to 1700; Fri, 0900 to 1630

DEVON COUNTY FOOTBALL ASSOCIATION LIMITED

County Headquarters, Coach Road, Newton Abbot, Devon, TQ12 1EJ

Tel: 01626 332077
Fax: 01626 336814
E-mail: hq@devonfa.f9.co.uk

Enquiries:
Enquiries to: General Secretary

Subject coverage:
Association football in Devon.

DEVON LIBRARIES

Great Moor House, Bittern Road, Sowton, Exeter, EX2 7NL

Tel: 01392 384315
Fax: 01392 384316
E-mail: devlibs@devon.gov.uk

Website:
http://www.devon.gov.uk/libraries

Enquiries:
Enquiries to: Head of Libraries

Organisation type and purpose:
Local government body, public library.

Subject coverage:
General, computing, poetry, domestic pets, cinema, physics, local history, American history

Museum or gallery collection, archive, or library special collection:
Early children's books, 1692–1940; Railway Studies Collection; Westcountry Studies Library

Non-library collection catalogue:
All or part available online

Library catalogue:
All or part available online

Printed publications:
Leaflets and directories on Devon local studies

Access to staff:
Contact by letter, by telephone, by fax, by e-mail and via website
Hours: Mon to Fri, 0900 to 1700

DEVON LIBRARY SERVICES – NORTH DEVON LIBRARY AND RECORD OFFICE

Tuly Street, Barnstaple, Devon, EX31 1EL

Tel: 01271 388596
Fax: 01271 388599
E-mail: geoff.king@devon.gov.uk

Website:
http://www.devonlibrary.gov.uk

Enquiries:
Enquiries to: Manager

Formerly called:
Barnstaple Central Library (year of change 1988)

Organisation type and purpose:
Local government body, public library.

Subject coverage:
General, local and family history of North Devon, business, commercial and technical information.

Museum or gallery collection, archive, or library special collection:
Community information database

Non-library collection catalogue:
All or part available online

Library catalogue:
All or part available online

Printed publications:
Other leaflets and pamphlets are available on application to the Library

Access to staff:
Contact by letter, by telephone, by fax, by e-mail and in person. Appointment necessary.
Hours: Mon, 0930 to 1900; Tue, Fri, 0900 to 1900; Wed, 0930 to 1300; Thu, 0930 to 1700; Sat, 0930 to 1600

Access for disabled people:
Level entry, access to all public areas, toilet facilities

Accommodates the:
Devon Schools Library Service
tel: 01271 388623
North Devon Athenaeum
tel: 01271 388607
North Devon Branch of the Devon Record Office
tel: 01271 388608

Parent body:
Devon County Council, Library Services

DEVON LIBRARY SERVICES – RAILWAY STUDIES LIBRARY

Formal name: Railway Studies Collection
Acronym or abbreviation: RSC

Newton Abbot Library, Market Street, Newton Abbot, Devon, TQ12 2RJ

Tel: 01626 206422
E-mail: railway.library@devon.gov.uk

Website:
http://www.devon.gov.uk/library/catalogue

Enquiries:
Enquiries to: Librarian

Organisation type and purpose:
Local government body, public library.

Subject coverage:
All aspects of railways in United Kingdom.

Museum or gallery collection, archive, or library special collection:
Back and current issues of a very large range of railway journals and magazines, including many now discontinued, also those relating to railway modelling

Library catalogue:
All or part available online

Printed publications:
Introductory Leaflet (free)
List of Periodical Holdings (free)

Electronic and video publications:
Photographs, postcards, some ephemera

Publications list:
Available online and in print

Access to staff:
Contact by letter, by telephone, by e-mail and in person
Hours: Wed, 1000 to 1300 and 1400 to 1700; Thu, 1000 to 1300; Sat, 1000 to 1300 and 1400 to 1600
Special comments: Staffed by the Friends of the Railway Studies Collection on Saturdays.

Access for disabled people:
Toilet facilities, lift

Administered by:
Devon Library Services

DEVON RECORD OFFICE

Acronym or abbreviation: DRO

Great Moor House, Bittern Road, Sowton Industrial Estate, Exeter, EX2 7NL

Tel: 01392 384253
Fax: 01392 384256
E-mail: devrec@devon.gov.uk

Website:
http://www.devon.gov.uk/record_office.htm
General information; opening times, newsletters, etc.

Enquiries:
Enquiries to: County Archivist

Founded:
1952

Organisation type and purpose:
Local government body.
Archive office.

Subject coverage:
Mainly local political, administrative, ecclesiastical, maritime, social and economic history, including the history of towns, parishes, local institutions, farms and estates, families, houses, crime and punishment, and transport.

Museum or gallery collection, archive, or library special collection:
City of Exeter Records, and the County and City of Exeter Quarter Sessions
Devon Quarter Sessions records
Ecclesiastical records of the Diocese of Exeter
Exeter Cathedral Archives in the Cloister Library
Records of the ancient Borough of Barnstaple, in the North Devon Record Office

Printed publications:
Historical notes on Devon Schools (Bovett R, 1989, £5.00)
Map of Devon parishes (40p)
Newsletter No 1 (May 1988) and later issues published in May and November each year (free on receipt of sae)
Ship's Crew lists: a handlist of records in the Devon Record office (1987, £4.75)
Stopping the Rot: Archive Preservation Good Practice (£3.50)
Please ask for an estimate of the cost of postage and packing before sending remittance

Access to staff:
Contact by letter, by telephone, by fax, by e-mail, in person and via website
Hours: Mon to Fri, 1000 to 1800; some Saturdays, 0930 to 1230
Special comments: Charges for some postal enquiries.

NB:
West Devon Record Office became Plymouth and West Devon Record Office 1 April 1998

Parent body:
Devon County Council
County Hall, Topsham Road, Exeter; tel: 01392 382000

Subsidiary body:
North Devon Record Office
North Devon Library and Record Office, Tuly Street, Barnstaple, Devon, EX31 1EL; tel: 01271 388607; fax: 01271 388608; e-mail: ndevrec@devon.gov.uk

DEVON WILDLIFE TRUST

Acronym or abbreviation: DWT

Cricklepit Mill, Commercial Road, Exeter, Devon, EX2 4AB

Tel: 01392 279244
Fax: 01392 433221
E-mail: contactus@devonwildlifetrust.org

Website:
http://www.devonwildlifetrust.org

Enquiries:
Enquiries to: Chief Executive

Founded:
1962

Formerly called:
Devon Trust for Nature Conservation

Organisation type and purpose:
Registered charity (charity number 213224). Conservation organisation.

Subject coverage:
Wildlife conservation in Devon.

Museum or gallery collection, archive, or library special collection:
Biological Data

Printed publications:
Wild Devon (supporters' magazine, 3 times a year)

Electronic and video publications:
4 wildlife e-newsletter
Order electronic and video publications from:
contactus@devonwildlifetrust.org

Publications list:
Available online

Access to staff:
Contact by letter, by telephone, by fax and by e-mail
Hours: Mon to Fri, 0900 to 1700

Access to building, collection or gallery:
Hours: Mon to Fri, 0900 to 1700

Access for disabled people:
Hours: Mon to Fri, 0900 to 1700

Links with:
Royal Society for Nature Conservation
The Kiln, Waterside, Mather Lane, Newark, NG24 1WT; tel: 01636 677711; fax: 01636 670001

DEWSBURY COLLEGE

Halifax Road, Dewsbury, West Yorkshire, WF13 2AS

Tel: 01924 465916 ext 286
Fax: 01924 457047

Website:
http://www.dewsbury.ac.uk

Enquiries:
Enquiries to: Learning Resources Manager

Direct tel: 01924 465916 ext 240
Direct e-mail: abismillah@dewsbury.ac.uk
Other contacts: Art and Design Specialist

Formed from:
Wheelwright 6th Form Centre

Formerly called:
DABTAC (year of change 1993)

Subject coverage:
Fashion, graphics, design, media studies, surface pattern design, photography, general subjects in humanities and social studies up to A level, business studies up to HND level.

Library catalogue:
All or part available in-house

Access to staff:
Contact by letter and by e-mail
Hours: Mon to Thurs, 0850 to 2000 Fri 1000 to 1600

Access for disabled people:
Level entry, toilet facilities

Associate college of:
Huddersfield University

DFID GLOBAL SCHOOL PARTNERSHIPS

Acronym or abbreviation: DGSP

British Council Scotland, The Tun, 4 Jackson's Entry, Holyrood Road, Edinburgh, EH8 8PJ

Tel: 0131 524 5780
Fax: 0131 524 5701
E-mail: globalschools@britishcouncil.org

Website:
http://www.britishcouncil.org/globalschools.htm

Founded:
2003

Organisation type and purpose:
Registered charity.

Printed publications:
Partners in Learning: A Guide to Successful Global School Partnerships
Order printed publications from: Postal address or website

Electronic and video publications:
Partners in Learning (.pdf format)
Order electronic and video publications from: Website

Publications list:
Available in print

Access to staff:
Contact by letter, by telephone, by fax and by e-mail
Hours: Mon to Fri, 0900 to 1800

Part of:
British Council

DIABETES UK

10 Parkway, London, NW1 7AA

Tel: 020 7424 1000
Fax: 020 7424 1001
E-mail: info@diabetes.org.uk

Website:
http://www.diabetes.org.uk

Enquiries:
Enquiries to: Assistant Media Relations Officer

Founded:
1934

Formerly called:
British Diabetic Association (BDA) (year of change 2000)

Organisation type and purpose:
Advisory body, membership association (membership is by subscription), voluntary organisation, registered charity (charity number 215199), research organisation.

Helping people with diabetes and supporting diabetes research.

Subject coverage:
Diabetes and all aspects of living with diabetes.

Printed publications:
Diabetes Update (newsletter for health professionals 2 times a year)
Diabetic Medicine (journal for the medical profession 10 times a year)
Leaflets and information sheets for people living with diabetes: diet, pregnancy, exercise, travel, children and other matters
Books, reports, publicity literature covering all diabetes related subjects for healthcare professionals and those living with diabetes
Order printed publications from: Distribution Department, British Diabetic Association
PO Box 1, Portishead, Bristol, BS20 8DJ, tel: 0800 585088

Electronic and video publications:
Videos and cassettes

Publications list:
Available in print

Access to staff:
Contact by letter, by telephone, by fax, by e-mail, in person and via website
Hours: Mon to Fri, 0900 to 1700

Has:
450 branches in the UK

Regional Offices:
North West
65 Bewsey Street, Warrington, WA2 7JG; tel: 01925 653281; fax: 01925 653288
Northern & Yorkshire
Birch House, 80 East Mount, Darlington, DL1 1LE; tel: 01325 488606; fax: 01325 488816
Northern Ireland
John Gibson House, 257 Lisbon Road, Belfast, BT9 7EN; tel: 028 9066 6646; fax: 028 9066 6333
Scotland
Unit 3, 4th Floor, 34 West George Street, Glasgow, G2 1AD; tel: 0141 332 2700; fax: 0141 332 4880
Wales
The Board Room, Plas Gwynt, Sophia Close, 30 Cathedral Road, Cardiff, CF1 9TD; tel: 029 2066 8276; fax: 029 2066 8329
West Midlands
1 Eldon Court, Eldon Street, Walsall, West Midlands, WS1 2JP; tel: 01922 614500; fax: 01922 646789

DIAL UK

Formal name: Disablement Information and Advice Line

St Catherine's, Tickhill Road, Doncaster, West Yorkshire, DN4 8QN

Tel: 01302 310123\ Minicom no. 01302 310123
Fax: 01302 310404
E-mail: dialuk@aol.com

Website:
http://www.dialuk.org.uk

Enquiries:
Enquiries to: Assistant Director

Founded:
1981

Organisation type and purpose:
National organisation, advisory body, registered charity (charity number 1059530).
The national organisation for the DIAL network – 140 disability advice centres run by and for people with disabilities.
DIALs give free, independent advice on all aspects of disability over the telephone and at drop-in centres.

Subject coverage:
Help for people with disabilities. Information and advice on social, medical or economic problems of all mental, physical and sensory disablements.

continued overleaf

Access to staff:
Contact by letter and by telephone
Hours: Mon to Thu, 0900 to 1700; Fri, 0900 to 1600

DIALOG CORPORATION, THE

Oxford Office, 2 Des Roches Square, Witney, Oxford, OX28 4BE

Tel: 01993 899300
Fax: 01993 899333
E-mail: ondisc@dialog.com

Website:
http://www.dialog.com

Enquiries:
Enquiries to: Manager
Direct e-mail: mike_sullivan@dialog.com
Other contacts: Marketing Executive

Founded:
1972

Formerly called:
DIALOG, DIALOG Europe; KR OnDisc (year of change 1997)

Organisation type and purpose:
International organisation, publishing house. Providing access to online databases and publishing CD-ROMs and DVD-ROMS.

Subject coverage:
Databases on CD-ROM in science, technology, chemistry, medicine, health, biomedicine, engineering, materials, social sciences, business, law, government, economics, education, humanities, current events, newspapers and journals, indexes to book reviews, companies, and people and associations. Also web browser access to above databases (Intranet/extranet solutions).

Electronic and video publications:
About 80 CD-ROM databases including:
Aerospace Database
ASM Handbook
Business & Industry
Chemical Business News Base
Compendex Plus
EIU Business Intelligence
Encyclopedia of Physical Science and Technology
Environmental Management
Kirk Othmer Encyclopedia
Medline
Metadex
Petroleum Abstracts
Standard & Poor's Corporation
Thomas Register

Access to staff:
Contact by letter, by telephone, by fax, by e-mail and via website
Hours: Mon to Fri, 0900 to 1730

Parent body:
The Dialog Corporation

DIECASTING SOCIETY

Acronym or abbreviation: DCS

The National Metalforming Centre, 47 Birmingham Road, West Bromwich B70 6PY

Tel: 0121 601 6365
Fax: 0870 138 9714
E-mail: dcs@alfed.org.uk

Website:
http://www.dcsoc.org.uk/

Enquiries:
Enquiries to: Secretary

Founded:
1967

Organisation type and purpose:
Professional body.

Subject coverage:
Diecasting.

Access to staff:
Contact by letter, by telephone, by fax and by e-mail. Appointment necessary.
Hours: Mon to Fri, 0900 to 1700

Member of:
The Aluminium Federation

DIRECT MAIL INFORMATION SERVICE

Acronym or abbreviation: DMIS

5 Carlisle Street, London, W1D 3JX

Tel: 020 7494 0483
Fax: 020 7494 0455
E-mail: info@dmis.co.uk

Website:
http://www.dmis.co.uk
Extracts from research reports, statistics, press releases, report ordering facility.

Founded:
1991

Organisation type and purpose:
Consultancy, research organisation.
Run by HBH on behalf of the Royal Mail to provide information to assist the direct mail and marketing industry.

Subject coverage:
Direct mail statistics and research reports.

Museum or gallery collection, archive, or library special collection:
Direct mail research by DMIS and DMSB from 1982 onwards

Printed publications:
The DMIS publishes extracts from some of its reports on the direct mail industry (available free of charge)

Publications list:
Available in print

Access to staff:
Contact by letter, by telephone, by fax, by e-mail and via website
Hours: Mon to Fri, 0900 to 1700

Parent body:
HBH Partnership Limited
at the same address; tel: 020 7494 0482

DIRECT SELLING ASSOCIATION LIMITED

Acronym or abbreviation: DSA

29 Floral Street, London, WC2E 9DP

Tel: 020 7497 1234
Fax: 020 7497 3144
E-mail: info@globalnet.co.uk

Website:
http://www.dsa.org.uk

Enquiries:
Enquiries to: Director

Founded:
1965

Organisation type and purpose:
Trade association (membership is by subscription, election or invitation).
To promote high trading standards in the direct selling of consumer goods.

Subject coverage:
General industry data on direct selling of consumer groups, industry codes of practice, direct selling legislation, details of member companies.

Trade and statistical information:
Annual statistical survey of direct selling of consumer goods in UK, includes DSA members and non-members.

Printed publications:
Direct Selling
Advice leaflet, Shopping at Home (free)
Code of Business Conduct (free)
Code of Practice (free)
List of Members (free)
The Direct Selling of Consumer Goods in UK (annual survey, £20)

Access to staff:
Contact by letter, by fax, by e-mail and via website. Appointment necessary.
Hours: Mon to Fri, 0930 to 1700

Affiliated to:
Federation of European Direct Selling Associations (FEDSA)
14 Avenue de Tervueren, Brussels, B-1040, Belgium; tel: 00 32 2 736 1014; fax: 00 32 2 736 3497
World Federation of Direct Selling Associations (WFDSA)
Washington, DC, USA; tel: 00 1 202 293 5760; fax: 00 1 202 463 4569

DIRECTORS GUILD OF GREAT BRITAIN

Acronym or abbreviation: DGGB

4 Windmill Street, London, W1T 2HZ

Tel: 020 7580 9131
Fax: 020 7580 9132
E-mail: info@dggb.org

Website:
http://www.dggb.co.uk
General information and publications list.
http://www.directorstraining.org.uk
Training information.

Enquiries:
Enquiries to: Chief Executive
Direct e-mail: malcolm@dggb.co.uk

Founded:
1985

Organisation type and purpose:
Trade union (membership is by subscription), present number of members: 1250.

Subject coverage:
Directors rates, contract advice, guidance to the profession, information on contacting directors and/or other relevant organisations, organising events, masterclasses and conferences. Training website and information.

Non-library collection catalogue:
All or part available online

Printed publications:
Code of Practice for Drama and Radio
Code of Practice for TV Drama, Documentary, Film
Direct Magazine (quarterly)
Directory of Members (every 2 years)
Rate Cards for Recorded and Live Media

Electronic and video publications:
Spotlight CD-ROM (directory of members)

Access to staff:
Contact by letter, by telephone, by fax, by e-mail and via website. Appointment necessary.
Hours: 1000 to 1800

Access for disabled people:
Level entry

Member of:
Federation of European Film Directors (FERA)
Av. Everard 59-B-1190, Bruxelles
Informal European Theatre Meeting (IETM)
International Association of Audiovisual Writers and Directors (AIDAA)

DISABILITY ALLIANCE

Universal House, 88–94 Wentworth Street, London, E1 7SA

Tel: 020 7247 8776
Fax: 020 7247 8765
E-mail: office.da@dial.pipex.comWebsite: www.disabilityalliance.org

Website:
http://www.disabilityalliance.org

Enquiries:
Enquiries to: Administrator

Founded:
1974

Organisation type and purpose:
National organisation, present number of members: 380 paid member organisations, registered charity (charity number 1063115). Disability Alliance is committed to breaking the link between poverty and disability by providing information about social security benefits to disabled people, their carers and advisers through publications (like the Disability Rights Handbook (published annually in May) and Claiming Disability Living Allowance).

Subject coverage:
Social Security benefits and related services for disabled people.

Printed publications:
Including:
Disability Rights Handbook (annually)
Benefit Appeals
Benefits! Where Do I Stand?
Claiming Disability Living Allowance
Briefings, factsheets and responses on a range of subjects (available free, by post inc. large sae or downloaded via website)
Starting Out

Electronic and video publications:
Disability Rights Handbook (CD-ROM)

Publications list:
Available online and in print

Access to staff:
Contact by letter, by telephone, by fax, by e-mail and via website
Hours: Mon to Fri, 1000 to 1600
Special comments: Access for the purchase of publications only.

Access to building, collection or gallery:
Prior appointment required
Special comments: Library is only available to Disability Alliance member organisations.

Access for disabled people:
Level entry, toilet facilities

Connections with:
380 Alliance Member Organisations

DISABILITY INFORMATION SERVICES

Acronym or abbreviation: DISS

Oaklawn Road, Leatherhead, Surrey KT22 0BT

Tel: 01372 841396

Website:
DISS's services, DissBASE details and development, DISS network contact details for further information, links to disability information providers and others.

Enquiries:
Enquiries to: Manager
Direct e-mail: hue.schoenemann@diss.org.uk

Founded:
1989

Formerly called:
Disability Information Service Surrey (DISS) (year of change 2001)

Organisation type and purpose:
Voluntary organisation, registered charity (charity number 251051).
Information service.

Subject coverage:
Anything connected with disabilities, e.g. equipment, care, employment, holidays, education, social security benefits, self-help groups, recreation, transport and access.

Museum or gallery collection, archive, or library special collection:
Journal articles, leaflets, statistical materials, directories, equipment guides

Printed publications:
Directory of Further Education Opportunities (£25)
DISS Clasification Scheme (£60/£100)
Directory of Supported Employment Opportunities (£25)
DISS introductory leaflet
Disability Information Resources leaflet
DissBASE introductory leaflet
Surrey Disability News (6 times a year)

Electronic and video publications:
DissBASE over 6000 records on a national database, plus 3000 in Surrey, records relate to organisations providing services to disabled people (available for purchase)

Access to staff:
Contact by letter, by telephone, by fax, by e-mail, in person and via website. Appointment necessary.
Hours: Mon to Fri, 1000 to 1300 and 1400 to 1600
Special comments: Also textphone and typetalk.

Access for disabled people:
Parking provided, level entry, access to all public areas, toilet facilities

Parent body:
Queen Elizabeth's Foundation for Disabled People
Leatherhead Court, Leatherhead, Surrey, KT22 0BN; tel: 01372 841100; fax: 01372 844072; website: www.qefd.org

Subsidiary body:
DISS network

DISABILITY PREGNANCY AND PARENTHOOD INTERNATIONAL

Acronym or abbreviation: DPPi

The National Centre for Disabled Parents, Unit F9, 89–93 Fonthill Road, London, N4 3JH

Tel: 0800 018 4730\ Minicom no. 0800 018 9949
Fax: 020 7263 6399
E-mail: info@dppi.org.uk

Website:
http://www.dppi.org.uk

Enquiries:
Enquiries to: Administrator
Direct tel: 020 7263 3088
Direct e-mail: office@dppi.org.uk

Founded:
1993

Organisation type and purpose:
International organisation, voluntary organisation, registered charity (charity number 1070303).
To produce a quarterly journal on issues related to pregnancy, parenting and disabled people. To provide an Information Service to disabled parents, professionals and others.

Subject coverage:
Information databases related to all aspects of pregnancy and parenting for disabled people, including: condition specific, equipment, adaptations, specialist deaf parenting project, parents' rights; advocacy, local support groups.

Library catalogue:
All or part available in-house

Printed publications:
DPPI Journal (quarterly)
Extensive range of in-house publications on all aspects of disabled parenting
Order printed publications from: tel. 0800 018 4730 or via the website

Electronic and video publications:
DPPI Journal and Information Sheets (audio tape, available on request)
Extensive range of electronic publications on all aspects of disabled parenting
DVD on pregnancy and childbirth for deaf parents

Order electronic and video publications from: tel. 0800 018 4730 or online

Publications list:
Available online and in print

Access to staff:
Contact by letter, by telephone, by fax, by e-mail and via website. Appointment necessary.
Hours: Mon to Fri, 1000 to 1600

Access for disabled people:
Access to all public areas, toilet facilities

DISABILITY RIGHTS COMMISSION

Acronym or abbreviation: DRC

7th Floor, 222 Grays Inn Road, London, WC1X 8HB

Tel: 020 7211 4110\ Minicom no. 020 7211 4037
Fax: 020 7211 4141
E-mail: info@drc-gb.org/

Website:
http://www.drc-gb.org/drc/
InformationAndLegislation/page312.asp
Publications.
http://www.drc-gb.org/
Website.

Enquiries:
Enquiries to: Chief Executive
Other contacts: Chairman of the DRC

Founded:
April 2000

Organisation type and purpose:
National government body, national organisation, statutory body.
The Disability Rights Commission (DRC) is an independent body set up by Government to help secure civil rights for disabled people by advice, information, conciliation and legal enforcement.

Subject coverage:
Information, advice, conciliation and legal enforcement of the rights of disabled people.

Library catalogue:
All or part available in-house

Printed publications:
The Disability Discrimination Act 1995: A Guide for Everybody (November 1996, DL160 booklet, DL160W Welsh Language Booklet, DL162 Braille)
Code of Practice for the Elimination of Discrimination in the Field of Employment against Disabled Persons or Persons who have had a Disability (downloadable text version, available from this site)
Employing Disabled People: A Good Practice Guide for Managers and Employers (Oct 1999) (DLE7 booklet)
The Disability Discrimination Act: What Trade Organisations and Their Members Need to Know (Oct 1999, DLE10 booklet)
The Disability Discrimination Act: Education (DL100 booklet, DL100W Welsh Language booklet)
Order printed publications from: DRC Helpline Freepost MID 02164, Stratford-upon-Avon, CV37 9BR, tel: 0845 762 2633; Text Phone: 0845 762 2644, fax: 0845 777 8878, e-mail: ddahelp@stra.sitel.co.uk

Electronic and video publications:
The Disability Discrimination Act 1995: A Guide for Everybody (November 1996, DL161 audio cassette, DL166 Signed/Subtitled video, DL160D diskette, DL160WD Welsh Language disk)
Code of Practice for the Elimination of Discrimination in the Field of Employment against Disabled Persons or Persons who have had a Disability (downloadable text version, available from this site)
Employing Disabled People: A Good Practice Guide for Managers and Employers (downloadable text version, available from this site)

continued overleaf

The Disability Discrimination Act: Education
(DL100D disk, DL100W Welsh Language disk,
downloadable text version available from this
site)

Publications list:
Available online and in print

Access to staff:
Contact by letter, by telephone, by fax, by e-mail
and via website
Hours: Mon to Fri, 0900 to 1700

Access for disabled people:
Access to all public areas, toilet facilities

Initial contact should be directed to:
DRC Helpline – Open Mon to Fri, 0800 to 2000
Freepost MID 02164, Stratford-upon-Avon, CV37
9DR; tel: 0845 762 2633; fax: 0845 777 8578; Text
Phone: 0845 762 2644; e-mail: ddahelp@stra.sitel
.co.uk

Other offices:
DRC Cardiff
Units 5–6, Ty-Nant Court, Ty-Nant Road,
Morganstown, Cardiff, CF15 8LW; tel: 02920
815600; Minicom: 02920 815602; fax: 02920
815601
DRC Edinburgh
1st Floor, Riverside House, 502 Gorgie Road,
Edinburgh, EH11 3 AF; tel: 0131 444 4300;
Minicom: 0131 444 4302; fax: 0131 444 4301
DRC Manchester
2nd Floor, Arndale House, The Arndale Centre,
Manchester, M4 3AQ; tel: 0161 261 1700;
Minicom: 0161 261 1702; fax: 0161 261 1701/1800

DISABILITY SPORT ENGLAND

Acronym or abbreviation: DSE

Disability Sport Events, Belle Vue Centre, Pink
Bank Lane, Manchester, M12 5GL

Tel: 0161 953 2499
Fax: 0161 953 2420
E-mail: info@dse.org.uk

Website:
http://www.disabilitysport.org.uk

Enquiries:
Enquiries to: Marketing and Communications
Manager
Direct e-mail: sarah@dse.org.uk
Other contacts: tel no: 01325 369554 for information
re the BT/DSE swimming programme.

Founded:
1961

Formerly called:
British Sports Association for the Disabled (BSAD)

Organisation type and purpose:
Membership association (membership is by
subscription), present number of members: 80,000,
voluntary organisation, registered charity (charity
number 297035).
Provision, development and coordination of sport
for the inclusion of people with disabilities.

Subject coverage:
Sport and recreation for people with disabilities.

Printed publications:
Calendar of Event Guidelines
Information Pack wth membership
Profile Manual with Rules and Procedures

Access to staff:
Contact by letter, by telephone, by fax and by e-
mail
Hours: Mon to Fri, 1000 to 1600

Access for disabled people:
Access to all public areas

Links with:
regional branches and associations

Other address:
Disability Sport England (Water Sports)
Darlington, DL1 5QU; tel: 01325 369554

DISABILITY SPORT ENGLAND –
DARLINGTON

Acronym or abbreviation: DSE

The Dolphin Centre, The Horse Centre,
Darlington, Co Durham, DL1 5QU

Tel: 01325 369554

Enquiries:
Enquiries to: Coordinator for swimming events
Direct e-mail: patbennett@darlingtondse.freeserve
.co.uk

Founded:
1961

Organisation type and purpose:
Membership association (membership is by
subscription), present number of members: 80,000,
voluntary organisation, registered charity (charity
number 297035).

Subject coverage:
Water sports, information re the BT/DSE
swimming programme.

Access to staff:
Contact by letter, by telephone and by e-mail
Hours: Mon to Fri, 0900 to 1700

Access for disabled people:
Access to all public areas, toilet facilities

Other address:
Disability Sport England
London, N17 0DA; tel: 020 8801 4466; fax: 020
8801 6644; e-mail: info@dse.org.uk

DISABILITY SPORT ENGLAND –
WEST MIDLANDS REGION

Wyndley Lane, Sutton Coldfield, West Midlands,
B73 6ES

Tel: 0121 354 5369
Fax: 0121 355 5702

Enquiries:
Enquiries to: Administrator

Formerly called:
BSAD

Organisation type and purpose:
Voluntary organisation, registered charity (charity
number 297035).

Subject coverage:
Advice on sports opportunities for disabled
people.

Printed publications:
Information packs

Access to staff:
Contact by letter and by telephone
Hours: 24-hour answerphone

Other addresses:
Disability Sport England
Darlington, DL1 5QU; tel: 01325 369554

Parent body:
Disability Sport England
Unit 4G, 784–788 High Road, Tottenham,
London, N17 0DA; tel: 020 8801 4466; fax: 020
8801 6644

DISABLED DRIVERS INSURANCE
BUREAU

Formal name: Chartwell Insurance

292 Hale Lane, Edgware, Middlesex, HA8 8NP

Tel: 020 8958 0901 / 0900
Fax: 020 8958 3220
E-mail: info@chartwellinsurance.co.uk

Website:
http://www.chartwellinsurance.co.uk
Motor insurance for drivers with disabilities.

Enquiries:
Enquiries to: Partner
Direct tel: 020 8958 0919

Other contacts: Manager

Founded:
1965

Formed from:
Chartwell Insurance

Organisation type and purpose:
Service industry.
Insurance intermediary.

Subject coverage:
Motor car insurance for the disabled driver,
adapted vehicles i.e. vans, powerchairs, travel and
household, breakdown cover.

Printed publications:
Brochure

Access to staff:
Contact by letter, by telephone, by fax and in
person
Hours: Mon to Fri, 0900 to 1730

Access to building, collection or gallery:
Mon to Fri, 0900 to 1730

Access for disabled people:
Parking provided, ramped entry, access to all
public areas, toilet facilities

Affiliated to:
Chartwell Insurance
at the same address; tel: 020 8958 0900 or 0845
260 7051; fax: 020 8958 3220; e-mail: info@
chartwellinsurance.co.uk; website: www
.chartwellinsurance.co.uk

DISABLED LIVING FOUNDATION

Acronym or abbreviation: DLF

380–384 Harrow Road, London, W9 2HU

Tel: 020 7289 6111\ Minicom no. 0870 603 9176
Fax: 020 7266 2922
E-mail: info@dlf.org.uk

Website:
http://www.dlf.org.uk
Introduction to the work of Disabled Living
Foundation with some generalised information.
All our factsheets for downloading. Information
and advice. Discussion base, subscriber service online.

Enquiries:
Enquiries to: Information Officer
Other contacts: Director

Founded:
1970

Organisation type and purpose:
Advisory body, voluntary organisation, registered
charity (charity number 290069), training
organisation, publishing house.
Working for freedom, empowerment and choice
for disabled people and others who use equipment
or technology to enhance their independence.

Subject coverage:
The DLF works for freedom, empowerment and
choice for disabled people and others who use
equipment or technology to enhance their
independence. It runs a helpline and letter enquiry
service offering information and advice about
disability equipment, and the London Disability
Living Centre with over 600 items for people to try.
It produces a wide range of publications on
choosing and using equipment and offers a
specialist subscriber service and training for
healthcare professionals and organisations.

Printed publications:
Hamilton index, 24 Sections of detailed product
information
Fact sheets on choosing and using equipment
Other general publications on travel, gardening,
kitchen design and clothing including:
Flying High
A Garden for You
All Dressed up
A Kitchen for You

Order printed publications from: Marketing and
Publication Department, Disabled Living
Foundation
at same address

Electronic and video publications:
DLF data CD-ROM – listing over 14,000 product
records, 2000 suppliers and 1000 relevant
contacts

Publications list:
Available online and in print

Access to staff:
Contact by letter, by telephone, by fax, by e-mail
and in person. Appointment necessary.
Hours: Office: Mon to Fri, 0900 to 1700; helpline,
Mon to Fri, 1000 to 1600

Access to building, collection or gallery:
Prior appointment required
Hours: Equipment Centre: Mon to Fri, 1000 to 1600
Special comments: Prior contact will guarantee that
you see an adviser.

Access for disabled people:
Level entry, toilet facilities

Has:
40 centres in the UK

DISABLED MOTORISTS FEDERATION

Acronym or abbreviation: DMF

c/o Chester-le-Street and District CVS Volunteer
Centre, Clarence Terrace, Chester-le-Street, Co
Durham, DH3 3DQ

Tel: 0191 416 3172
Fax: 0191 416 3172
E-mail: jkillick2214@compuserve.com; jkillick2214@
yahoo.co.uk
Website:
http://www.healthworks.co.uk/daccess/D-Access/
D-Access_Factsheets/dmfgendef.html
http://www.freewebs.com/dmfed

Enquiries:
Enquiries to: Honorary Secretary
Other contacts: Vice-President

Founded:
1973

Organisation type and purpose:
National organisation, membership association
(membership is by subscription, qualification),
voluntary organisation, registered charity (charity
number 1012874).
Qualification for membership is registered
disabled or carer.
To provide information to disabled people and
their carers on matters of travel whether by road,
rail or air, including advice on suitable hotel
accommodation. To act for and on behalf of
disabled motorist clubs.

Subject coverage:
Motoring and mobility for the disabled; setting up
a local base or club for disabled drivers; vehicle
choice; overseas and UK travel; wheelchairs; home
adaptations; lifts and hoists; camping and
caravanning; route planning service and route
maps.

Information services:
Free information on travel by road, rail. air or sea
to all disabled people and their carers

Printed publications:
The Way Ahead (quarterly, free to members, £5 a
year to others)
UK Mainland River Crossings (concessions at
tunnels, bridges and ferries, free for sae)
Order printed publications from: from the Honorary
Secretary, by letter or e-mail, or see website

Access to staff:
Contact by telephone, by fax and by e-mail.
Appointment necessary.
Hours: Mon to Fri, 0900 to 1700

Also at:
Honorary Secretary
145 Knoulberry Road, Black Fell, Washington,
Tyne & Wear, NE37 1JN; tel: 0191 416 3172; fax:
0191 416 3172; e-mail: jkillick2214@yahoo.co.uk
Constituent bodies:
10 member clubs for disabled drivers throughout
Britain
website: http://www.freewebs.com/dmfed

DISABLED PHOTOGRAPHERS' SOCIETY

Acronym or abbreviation: DPS

PO Box 85, Longfield, Kent, DA3 9BA

E-mail: enquiries@disabledphotographers.co.uk
Website:
http://www.disabledphotographers.co.uk
General information and examples of members'
work.

Founded:
1968

Organisation type and purpose:
Membership association (membership is by
subscription), present number of members: 500
individuals, 55 groups, voluntary organisation,
registered charity (charity number 262866).
Encourages disabled people to take an active
interest in photography as a therapeutic and
creative pursuit primarily by collecting surplus
photographic equipment and redistributing it to
disabled users who are members of the society.

Subject coverage:
Adaptation of photographic equipment for specific
handicaps; advice on equipment and techniques;
assistance in adopting photography as a
therapeutic/leisure pursuit for disabled and
handicapped persons of all ages.

Printed publications:
Annual Exhibition
Fact Sheets
Information Sheets
Newsletter (quarterly, members)

Access to staff:
Contact by letter and by e-mail

DISFIGUREMENT GUIDANCE CENTRE/LASERFAIR

Acronym or abbreviation: DGC

PO Box 7, Cupar, Fife, KY15 4PF

Tel: 01337 870 281
Fax: 01337 870310
Website:
http://www.dgc.org.uk
Enquiries:
Enquiries to: Director
Other contacts: Publications Officer, tel no: 0133 787
0281, fax: 0133 787 0310
Founded:
1969

Organisation type and purpose:
Voluntary organisation, registered charity, research
organisation, publishing house.
UK corporate voice and centre for the disfigured,
specialist resource Skin Laser Services and
information.

Subject coverage:
All aspects of disfigurement, including treatment
developments, especially medical lasers, insurance,
compensation advice, research, family problems;
skin problems.

Non-library collection catalogue:
All or part available online and in print

Printed publications:
Publications list (please send sae)
Cosmetic-Aid: Skin Camouflage Handbook (free to
GPs on request with 50p stamp, £5 to others)

Disfigurement Newsletter (free on receipt of A4
sae)
Skinlaser Directory (annually, free to GPs on
receipt of 50p A5 sae, £5 to all others)
Full range of Companion Books on a wide range of
topics including: Acne, Social Skills, Birthmarks,
Lasers etc

Publications list:
Available in print

Access to staff:
Contact by letter, by telephone and by fax.
Appointment necessary.
Hours: Mon to Fri, 0900 to 1700
Special comments: Please send sae for information.

DIVINE INFORMATION SERVICES

PO Box 2530, Windsor, Berkshire, SL4 1WS

E-mail: informationservices@divine.com
Website:
http://www.divineinformationservices.co.uk
Main site, pdf documents on case studies and
products and contact information.

Enquiries:
Enquiries to: UK Marketing Manager

Formerly called:
RoweCom (year of change 2001)

Organisation type and purpose:
International organisation, service industry.
To provide librarians and information specialists
with a complete information solution in acting not
only as a subscription agent for both print and
electronic information resources but also in
providing librarians and information specialists
with content and information management,
content classification, search and taxonomy.

**Museum or gallery collection, archive, or library
special collection:**
Northern Light – Single Point
Print and Electronic Subscription Services

Electronic and video publications:
Content Management
Information Quest
kcentral
klibrary
kstore
New! Single Point
Virtual Library

Access to staff:
Contact by telephone, by fax and by e-mail
Hours: Mon to Fri, 0900 to 1730

Other offices:
Has 19 other offices throughout the world

DOCUMENT OPTIONS LTD

Priestley Way, Crawley, West Sussex, RH10 9NT

Tel: 01293 426677
Fax: 01293 403453
E-mail: sales@document-options.co.uk
Website:
http://www.document-options.co.uk
http://www.document-options.net
Demonstration of web document hosting.

Enquiries:
Enquiries to: Director
Founded:
1970

Organisation type and purpose:
Service industry.
Microfilming and scanning bureau.

Subject coverage:
Reprographic procedures, raster to vector
conversion, conversion of microfilm/microfiche to
digital data.

Access to staff:
Contact by telephone
Hours: Mon to Fri, 0900 to 1700

DOLMETSCH FOUNDATION INCORPORATED

27 Gilmour Gardens, Alton, Hampshire, GU34 2NR

Tel: 01420 541892

Website:
http://www.dolmetsch.com

Enquiries:
Enquiries to: Secretary

Organisation type and purpose:
Learned society.

Subject coverage:
Early music and instruments, c. 1000 to c. 1750.

Museum or gallery collection, archive, or library special collection:
File from 1929 of the annual journal, The Consort

Access to staff:
Contact by letter
Hours: Mon to Fri, 0900 to 1700

Other addresses:
Dolmetsch Foundation Incorporated
Jesses, Grayswood Road, Haslemere, Surrey, GU27 2BS

DOLMETSCH HISTORICAL DANCE SOCIETY

Acronym or abbreviation: DHDS

17 Well Lane, Stock, Ingatestone, Essex, CM4 9LT

Tel: 01277 840473
Fax: 01277 840473
E-mail: secretary@dhds.org.uk

Website:
http://www.dhds.org.uk
Publications order form; membership details; report on Summer School. Past and future events and conferences. Links to similar sites; photographs. Ability to download articles.

Enquiries:
Enquiries to: Honorary Secretary

Founded:
1970

Organisation type and purpose:
National organisation, membership association, present number of members: 120, registered charity (charity number 270896), research organisation.
To promote the practice of and research into social dance in Europe from the 15th to the 19th century.

Subject coverage:
Information on dances, dancers and dancing masters of the past; information on source material and secondary sources, including society publications; information on teachers and dance classes available; information on performing groups.

Printed publications:
Books and CDs and tapes of dances (from the 15th century onwards) produced annually for Summer School
Conference Proceedings (biennially)
Historical Dance (journal, occasionally)
Dance for Tudors and Stuarts – A resource pack for teachers (book and tape for Key Stage 2, Understanding Victorian Society through Dance)
Order printed publications from: Secretary, Dolmetsch Historical Dance Society, 17 Well Lane, Stock, ingatestone, Essex, CM4 9LT

Electronic and video publications:
Tapes and CD's of dance music
Understanding Victorian Society through Dance (CD)

Publications list:
Available online and in print

Access to staff:
Contact by letter, by telephone, by fax and by e-mail
Hours: No fixed hours.

DOMESTIC APPLIANCE SERVICE ASSOCIATION

Acronym or abbreviation: DASA

2nd Floor, 145–157 St John Street, London, EC1V 4PY

Tel: 0870 224 0343
Fax: 0870 224 0358
E-mail: dasa@dasa.org.uk

Website:
http://www.dasa.org.uk

Enquiries:
Enquiries to: Administrator
Direct e-mail: admin@dasa.org.uk

Founded:
1978

Organisation type and purpose:
Trade association (membership is by qualification), present number of members: 180, service industry. To promote quality service, efficiency and courtesy in the servicing of domestic appliances.

Subject coverage:
Promotion of good service, efficiency and courtesy to all members of the public, investigation of complaints against member firms, quality management, insurance, training.

Printed publications:
Code of Practice
Quality Criteria
Orbit Newsletter (for members)
Overview of Domestic Appliance Servicing Qualifications
Quality Assessment System

Access to staff:
Contact by letter, by telephone, by fax and by e-mail. Appointment necessary.
Hours: Mon to Fri, 0900 to 1700

Access to building, collection or gallery:
Appointment required

Member organisation of:
British Quality Foundation
tel: 020 7654 5000; fax: 020 7654 5001; e-mail: mail@quality-foundation.co.uk
Electrical and Electronics Servicing Training Council (EESTC)
tel: 020 7836 3357; fax: 020 7497 9006; e-mail: ccrouch@eeb.iie.org.uk

DOMESTIC FOWL RESEARCH

Kennerleigh, Crediton, Devon, EX17 4RS

Tel: 01363 866750
Fax: 01363 866750

Website:
http://www.goldcockerelbooks.co.uk
List and description of books.

Enquiries:
Enquiries to: Director

Founded:
1987

Organisation type and purpose:
Research organisation, publishing house.

Subject coverage:
Poultry history, poultry breeding, old breeds of hens, ducks, geese, turkeys, poultry health and small holding and countryside.

Printed publications:
Gold Cockerel series of practical books, 26 titles as at Oct 2008 including:
British Large Fowl (£8)
Chickens at Home (£7.00)
Domestic Duck and Geese in Colour (£7.50)
Modern Vermin Control (£7)

Poultry House Construction (£8.50)
Wildfowl at Home (£8)

Publications list:
Available in print

Access to staff:
Contact by letter, by telephone, by fax and by e-mail
Hours: Mon to Fri, 0900 to 1700

DOMESTIC FOWL TRUST

Station Road, Honeybourne, Evesham, Worcestershire, WR11 5QG

Tel: 01386 833083
Fax: 01386 833364
E-mail: dft@honeybourne.demon.co.uk

Website:
http://www.domesticfowltrust.co.uk

Enquiries:
Enquiries to: Director

Founded:
1975

Organisation type and purpose:
Professional body, consultancy, research organisation.

Subject coverage:
Poultry breeding, old breeds of hens, ducks, geese, turkeys; housing and management of outdoor poultry, poultry health.

Printed publications:
Mail Order Catalogue (free of charge)
Wide range of domestic poultry keeping books (available for purchase)

Access to staff:
Contact by letter, by telephone, by fax, by e-mail and in person
Hours: Mon to Sun, 1030 to 1700

Access to building, collection or gallery:
No access other than to staff
Hours: Mon to Fri, 1030 to 1700

Access for disabled people:
Parking provided, ramped entry, toilet facilities

DOMINICA HIGH COMMISSION

Formal name: High Commission for the Commonwealth of Dominica

1 Collingham Gardens, London, SW5 0HW

Tel: 020 7370 5194
Fax: 020 7373 8743
E-mail: dominicahighcom@btconnect.com

Enquiries:
Enquiries to: Secretary

Organisation type and purpose:
National government body.

Subject coverage:
Dominica, tourism, trade, consular, general information.

Access to staff:
Contact by letter, by fax and by e-mail. Appointment necessary.
Hours: Mon to Fri, 0930 to 1730

DOMINICAN REPUBLIC TOURIST BOARD

18–21 Hand Court, London, WC1V 6JF

Tel: 020 7242 7778
Fax: 020 7405 4202
E-mail: inglaterra@sectur.gov.do

Enquiries:
Enquiries to: Executive Director
Direct e-mail: dominican.rep@btconnect.com

Founded:
1996

Organisation type and purpose:
International organisation, national government body.
Promotion of tourism.

Printed publications:
Brochures, magazines etc
Order printed publications from:
inglaterra@sectur.gov.do; dominican.rep@
btconnect.com

Electronic and video publications:
inglaterra@sectur.gov.do; dominican.rep@
btconnect.com
Order electronic and video publications from:
inglaterra@sectur.gov.do; dominican.rep@
btconnect.com

Publications list:
Available online and in print

Access to staff:
Contact by letter, by telephone, by fax, by e-mail,
in person and via website
Hours: Mon to Fri, 1000 to 1700

Access to building, collection or gallery:
Mon to Fri, 1000 to 1700

Access for disabled people:
Level entry, access to public areas, no toilet
facilities

DONCASTER AND DISTRICT FAMILY HISTORY SOCIETY

Acronym or abbreviation: DDFHS

5 Breydon Avenue, Cusworth, Doncaster, South
Yorkshire, DN5 8JZ

Tel: 01302 782685
E-mail: honsecretary@doncasterfhs.co.uk
Website:
http://www.doncasterfhs.co.uk
Publications, membership form, downloads, about
the society

Enquiries:
Enquiries to: Honorary Secretary
Direct tel: 01302 7826875
Direct e-mail: honsecretary@doncasterfhs.co.uk

Founded:
1980

Formerly called:
Doncaster Family History Society (year of change
1990)

Organisation type and purpose:
Membership association (membership is by
subscription), voluntary organisation, registered
charity (charity number 516226).

Subject coverage:
Genealogy, family history.

**Museum or gallery collection, archive, or library
special collection:**
Archives (held at the Doncaster MBC Archives
Service)

Printed publications:
Publications on various topics (for sale)
The Doncaster Ancestor (4 times a year)
Order printed publications from: Doncaster and
District Family History Society
Mr K Wishart, 11 Hawthorn Terrace, New
Earswick, York, YO32 4BL

Microform publications:
Microfiche of various topics (for sale)
Order microform publications from: Doncaster and
District Family History Society
Mr K Wishart, 11 Hawthorn Terrace, New
Earswick, York, YO32 4BL

Electronic and video publications:
Various Topics (CD-ROM, for sale)
Order electronic and video publications from:
Doncaster and District Family History Society
Mr K Wishart, 11 Hawthorn Terrace, New
Earswick, York, YO32 4BL

Publications list:
Available online and in print

Access to staff:
Contact by letter, by e-mail and via website. Non-
members charged.
Hours: Mon to Fri, 0900 to 1700
Special comments: Not after 2100

Access to building, collection or gallery:
Prior appointment required
Special comments: Contact Secretary.

Access for disabled people:
Access to all public areas
Special comments: Contact Secretary.

DONCASTER ARCHIVES

Formal name: Doncaster Metropolitan Borough
Council: Library and Information Services,
Doncaster Archives

King Edward Road, Balby, Doncaster, South
Yorkshire, DN4 0NA

Tel: 01302 859811
E-mail: doncaster.archives@doncaster.gov.uk
Website:
http://www.doncaster.gov.uk/doncasterarchives
Enquiries:
Enquiries to: Principal Archivist
Founded:
1973

Formerly called:
Doncaster Archives Department

Organisation type and purpose:
Local government body.
Doncaster Archives collects, preserves and gives
public access to the documentary heritage of
Doncaster Metropolitan Borough from 1194 to the
present.

Subject coverage:
The full range of records usually to be found in a
local record office, including local government
archives, local public records, Church of England
parish records, nonconformist church records,
family and landed estate records, business
archives, political party archives, trade union
archives, voluntary society archives, local maps
and plans.

**Museum or gallery collection, archive, or library
special collection:**
Includes:
Parish Registers of 36 ancient parishes, transcribed
with surname index up to 1837 and many to later
dates

Non-library collection catalogue:
All or part available online and in-house

Library catalogue:
All or part available in-house

Printed publications:
Doncaster: A Borough and its Charters (G. H.
Martin et al, 1994, £2.50)
Guide to Doncaster Archives (2006, £5, or £7.50 by
post)
Leaflets on the department (free)
Order printed publications from: Doncaster Archives,
King Edward Road, Balby, Doncaster, South
Yorkshire, DN4 0NA

Access to staff:
Contact by letter, by telephone, by e-mail and in
person. Appointment necessary.
Hours: Mon to Fri, 0900 to 1245 and 1400 to 1645

Access to building, collection or gallery:
Special comments: Reader's ticket required

DONCASTER COLLEGE

The Hub Learning Resource Centre, Doncaster,
South Yorkshire, DN1 2RF

Tel: 01302 553553
Fax: 01302 553559

Website:
http://www.don.ac.uk
Introduction, finding information on the Internet,
Autodesk Training Centre course registration.

Enquiries:
Enquiries to: Site Librarian at The Hub
Direct tel: 01302 553745
Direct e-mail: infocentre@don.ac.uk
Other contacts: Head of Learning Resources for
responsible for all site Learning Resource Centres.

Formed by the merger of:
4 Doncaster Colleges of Technology, Art and
Design and Education

Organisation type and purpose:
College of further education.

Subject coverage:
Business studies, environmental sciences,
engineering (construction, mechanical, production,
electrical, mining and mineral), catering,
hairdressing, nursing, modern languages,
computing, education and related fields, art and
design, sociology, geography and history.

Library catalogue:
All or part available online

Access to staff:
Contact by letter. Appointment necessary. Non-
members charged.
Hours: Term time: Mon to Thu, 0845 to 2000; Fri,
0845 to 1700
Vacations: Mon to Fri, 0900 to 1230, 1330 to 1645

Other addresses:
Doncaster College
The University Centre LRC, High Melton,
Doncaster, South Yorkshire, DN5 7SZ

DONCASTER LIBRARY AND INFORMATION SERVICES

Doncaster Central Library, Waterdale, Doncaster,
South Yorkshire, DN1 3JE

Tel: 01302 734305
Fax: 01302 369749
E-mail: reference.library@doncaster.gov.uk
Website:
http://www.doncaster.gov.uk
Enquiries:
Enquiries to: Reference Librarian
Direct tel: 01302 734320
Founded:
1869

Organisation type and purpose:
Local government body, public library.

Subject coverage:
General, local studies, railways, horse racing.

Information services:
Reference and Information Service.

Education services:
Classes held in Library Premises

Services for disabled people:
Reading Aids Unit – serving the visually impaired

**Museum or gallery collection, archive, or library
special collection:**
Archives: official, ecclesiastical, family and private
records held at King Edward Road, Balby,
Doncaster, DN4 0NA, tel: 01302 859811
Local Studies Library – 1984–85 Miners' Strike
Collection
Local Studies Library – Family Album Project
Local Studies Library – Doncaster Community
Archive (CD ROM)
British Standards (online)
Britannica Online
Oxford Online

Trade and statistical information:
Mint UK online

Library catalogue:
All or part available online

continued overleaf

Printed publications:
Local Societies and Organisations
List of Rooms for Hire
List of Places of Worship
List of Speakers and Demonstrators
List of Translators
The Local Studies Library (guide to services)
Order printed publications from: Reference
Department

Access to staff:
Contact by letter, by telephone, by fax, by e-mail,
in person and via website
Hours: Mon, 0900 to 1800; Tue, 0830 to 1800; Wed
and Thu, 0830 to 2000; Fri, 0830 to 1800; Sat, 0900
to 1700

Access for disabled people:
Access to all public areas, toilet facilities

Member organisation of:
Doncaster Chamber of Commerce
European Public Information Centre
SINTO
South Yorkshire Joint Archives Service
Yorkshire and Humberside Association of Library
Services

DONKEY BREED SOCIETY

Acronym or abbreviation: DBS

The Hermitage, Pootings, Edenbridge, Kent, TN8
6SD

Tel: 01732 864414
Fax: 01732 864414
E-mail: societysecretary@donkeybreedsociaty.co.uk

Website:
http://www.donkeybreedingsociety.co.uk

Enquiries:
Enquiries to: Secretary

Founded:
1967

Organisation type and purpose:
Membership association, registered charity
(charity number 292268).
To work for the welfare of all donkeys.

Subject coverage:
The care, management and breeding of donkeys,
also their welfare, education and general activities
such as trekking, showing, driving and light
draught work.

**Museum or gallery collection, archive, or library
special collection:**
Library of limited donkey related books (for hire
by members)
Stud Book

Printed publications:
Annual Magazine (available by membership
subscription and for sale)
Information leaflets (available free to members or
for a donation to non-members)
Newsletters (available by membership
subscription)

Access to staff:
Contact by letter, by telephone and by fax
Hours: Mon to Fri, 0900 to 1700

DONKEY SANCTUARY, THE

Sidmouth, Devon, EX10 0NU

Tel: 01395 578222
Fax: 01395 579266
E-mail: enquiries@thedonkeysanctuary.com

Website:
http://www.thedonkeysanctuary.org.uk
Information on charities, Adopt a Donkey.

Enquiries:
Enquiries to: Chief Executive

Founded:
1969

Incorporates the:
International Donkey Protection Trust

Organisation type and purpose:
International organisation, registered charity
(charity number 264818).

Subject coverage:
Provision of high quality, professional advice,
training and support on donkey welfare
worldwide.

Printed publications:
The Professional Handbook of the Donkey (3rd
ed., £11.50 inc. p&p)
Newsletters, reference sheets and many other
books and posters

Electronic and video publications:
Basic Donkey Health Care (40 min video, £6.50 inc
p&p)

Publications list:
Available in print

Access to staff:
Contact by letter, by telephone, by fax, by e-mail,
in person and via website. Appointment necessary.
Hours: Mon to Fri, 0830 to 1630

Access for disabled people:
Parking provided, level entry, toilet facilities

Connections at the same address with:
The Elisabeth Svendsen Trust for Children and
Donkeys
  tel: 01395 578222; fax: 01395 579266; e-mail:
  info@elisabethsvendsentrust.org

DOROTHY L SAYERS SOCIETY

Rose Cottage, Malthouse Lane, Hurstpierpoint,
West Sussex, BN6 9JY

Tel: 01273 833444
Fax: 01273 835988
E-mail: jasmine@sayers.org.uk

Website:
http://www.sayers.org.uk/

Enquiries:
Enquiries to: Chairman
Other contacts: info@sayers.org.uk

Founded:
1976

Formerly called:
Dorothy L Sayers Historical and Literary Society

Organisation type and purpose:
Membership association (membership is by
subscription), present number of members: 500,
registered charity (charity number 272120),
suitable for ages: all.

Subject coverage:
Life, biographical details and works of Dorothy L
Sayers and the subjects in which she was involved
such as: Christian theology and apologetics,
campanology, genealogy, Dante, drama (secular
and religious), literary and theological criticism,
broadcasting, the Wimsey family, Sherlock
Holmes, detective fiction, the Detection Club,
Wimsey chronology, poetry, painting and stage
sets, locations and social references in DLS fiction.

**Museum or gallery collection, archive, or library
special collection:**
Archives include writings by DLS (articles, poetry,
speeches, letters (personal and press), reviews
and introductions and pamphlets); other
writings on DLS and her subjects, commentaries
and essays, press cuttings, certificates,
memorabilia, reviews of her plays and
biographies. Most of these items can be copied
for members only; copies of much of the work
are available at Witham County Library

Printed publications:
Archives List
Bulletin (6 times a year)
Chronology of Lord Peter Wimsey (1983)
DLS, Mystery Maker (J Brabazon, 1981)
DLS, Player of the Game (J Brabazon, 1981)

Does She Cheat? (J Morris, 1983)
Encounters with Lord Peter (Dean C ed. 1991)
Genealogy of DLS (G Lee)
Letters of Dorothy L Sayers (Reynolds B ed. 1997,
  1998, 2000)
Poetry of Dorothy L Sayers (Horne R ed. 1996)
Proceedings of Annual Seminars from 1976
Sidelights on Sayers (56 volumes, 1981 to 2008)
Studies in Sayers (Dean C ed., 1993)
Theology of DLS (P de Voil, 1983)
Tour Guides (Oxford, London, Cambridge, the
  Fens, Galloway) (1983)
Les origines du roman policier (Sayers, 2003)
The Wimsey Family (Scott-Giles & Sayers, 2007)
The Christ of the Creeds (Sayers, 2008)
Order printed publications from: Dorothy L Sayers
Society

Access to staff:
Contact by letter, by telephone, by fax, by e-mail
and via website. Appointment necessary.
Hours: Mon to Fri, 0900 to 1700

DORSET DOWN SHEEP BREEDERS ASSOCIATION

Acronym or abbreviation: DDSBA

Glaspers Land Agency Ltd, Coombe View Farm,
Branscombe, Seaton, Devon EX12 3BT

Tel: 01297 680218
Fax: 01297 680594
E-mail: glaspersltd@farmerweekly.net

Enquiries:
Enquiries to: Administrator

Founded:
1906

Organisation type and purpose:
National organisation, membership association
(membership is by subscription), present number
of members: 60, registered charity (charity number
84799).
Promotion of the breed of Dorset Down sheep.

Subject coverage:
Breeding and whereabouts of Dorset Down sheep,
and administration of the association since 1906.

**Museum or gallery collection, archive, or library
special collection:**
Flock Books, 1906 to present day

Printed publications:
Annual Flock Book (available for purchase after
  Jan each year)

Publications list:
Available in print

Access to staff:
Contact by letter, by telephone, by fax and by e-
mail
Hours: Mon to Fri, 0830 to 1700

Access to building, collection or gallery:
No prior appointment required

DORSET LIBRARY SERVICE

Headquarters, Colliton Park, Dorchester, Dorset,
DT1 1XJ

Tel: 01305 225000
Fax: 01305 224344
E-mail: dorsetlibraries@dorsetcc.gov.uk

Website:
http://www.dorsetforyou.com/libraries

Enquiries:
Enquiries to: Head of Cultural Services

Organisation type and purpose:
Local government body, public library.

Subject coverage:
General lending and reference and information
services; also specialist information on all aspects
of the County of Dorset.

Museum or gallery collection, archive, or library special collection:
Collections on T E Lawrence and Percy Westerman (Wareham Library)
Collections on Thomas Hardy, the Powys family and William Barnes, John Fowles, Sir Frederick Treves, Sylvia Townsend Warner (Dorchester Library)
Drama and Playsets Collection
Local Studies Collections (Dorset History Centre; Dorchester Library; Weymouth Library; Christchurch Library; Bridport Library)

Non-library collection catalogue:
All or part available online

Library catalogue:
All or part available online

Publications list:
Available in print

Access to staff:
Contact by letter, by telephone, by fax, by e-mail, in person and via website
Hours: Hours vary dependent on service point

Access to building, collection or gallery:
No access other than to staff

Parent body:
Dorset County Council

DORSET NATURAL HISTORY AND ARCHAEOLOGICAL SOCIETY

Dorset County Museum, High West Street, Dorchester, Dorset, DT1 1XA

Tel: 01305 262735
Fax: 01305 257180

Website:
http://www.dorsetcountymuseum.org

Enquiries:
Enquiries to: Curator

Founded:
1846

Organisation type and purpose:
Learned society, museum.
Private Library.

Subject coverage:
Dorset: local history, natural history, archaeology, social history, fine arts, geology, literature.

Museum or gallery collection, archive, or library special collection:
Dorset Archaeological Archive
Lock and Mann Hardy Collection
Mansel-Pleydell Herbarium
Photographic Collection
Sanders Hardy Collection
Sylvia Townsend Warner (author 1893–1985), manuscripts, notebooks, diaries, letters and publications
Thomas Hardy Memorial Collection
William Barnes (Dorset poet, 1801–1886) manuscripts, notebooks, letters, diaries, scrapbooks and publications

Non-library collection catalogue:
All or part available in-house

Printed publications:
Proceedings (annually)
Various publications about the geology, archaeological investigations and natural history of Dorset

Publications list:
Available in print

Access to staff:
Appointment necessary.
Hours: Mon to Fri, 1000 to 1700

DORSET RECORD OFFICE

Bridport Road, Dorchester, Dorset, DT1 1RP

Tel: 01305 250550\ Minicom no. 01305 267933 (at County Hall)

Fax: 01305 257184
E-mail: archives@dorset-cc.gov.uk

Website:
http://www.dorset-cc.gov.uk/archives
Introducing archives, contacts, news and events, opening hours, location map, our records, our friends, preservation, research service, using the service.

Enquiries:
Enquiries to: County Archivist

Founded:
1955

Organisation type and purpose:
Local government body.
Archives and record office.
The preservation of archives of Dorset and making them accessible, providing an archives service on behalf of Dorset County Council, Bournemouth Borough Council and the Borough of Poole.

Subject coverage:
Standard range of public and private archives including local government, parishes, estates, businesses, families, suitable for history, local history, family history and much else.

Museum or gallery collection, archive, or library special collection:
Standard local record office archives, documents, manuscripts, photographs, sound film
Parish registers, probate records, census records, General Register Office index (microfilm and microfiche)

Non-library collection catalogue:
All or part available in-house

Printed publications:
Free information leaflets: regulations, charter of service, location, research services, copying services, meeting room facilities, Friends of Dorset's Archives and Dorset Parish Records Preservation Project
A map of the parishes of Dorset c. 1900 (40p plus p&p)
Building Accounts of Mapperton Rectory (ed Machin R, £4 plus p&p)
Guide to the Location of the Parish Registers of Dorset (£2 plus p&p)
Guide to the Location of the Nonconformist & Roman Catholic Registers (£1.50 plus p&p)
Guide to the Transcripts held in the County Record Office (£1 plus p&p)
Farming in Dorset: Diary of James Warne, 1758; Letters of George Boswell, 1787–1805 (ed James J F & Bettey J H, £10.75 plus p&p)
List of diaries and memoirs in the Dorset Record Office (50p plus p&p)
List of documents in the Record Office relating to precautions in the county against the threat of French invasion 1797–1814 (10p plus p&p)
Puddletown: House Street and Family (ed Sinclair Williams C L, £5.75 plus p&p)
Railway Records in the Dorset Records Office (£6.95 plus p&p)
The Case Book of Sir Frances Ashley, JP Recorder of Dorchester 1614–1635 (ed Bettey J H, £6.50 plus p&p)
The Love Poems & Letters of William Barnes and Julia Miles (ed Lindgren C, £4 plus p&p)
Touching Witchcrafte and Sorcerye (ed Davies G J, £4 plus p&p)
Who's Afear'd of Family History – A guide to services in DRO (£6.95 plus p&p)
William Whiteway of Dorchester: His Diary 1618 to 1635 (£9.75 plus p&p)

Microform publications:
Microfilm available plus photocopies and microfilm printout copies are charged for

Publications list:
Available in print

Access to staff:
Contact by letter, by telephone, by fax, by e-mail and via website. Appointment necessary.
Hours: Mon, Tue, Thu, Fri, 0900 to 1700; Wed, 1000 to 1700; Sat, 0930 to 1230
Special comments: Proof of identity required.

Access for disabled people:
Level entry, toilet facilities

Other addresses:
Dorset Record Office
Archives Management Unit, County Hall, Dorchester, Dorset, DT1 1XJ; tel: 01305 225191; fax: 01305 225175

Parent bodies:
Borough of Poole
Bournemouth Borough Council
Dorset County Council

DOUGLAS PUBLIC LIBRARY

Formal name: Henry Bloom Noble Library

10/12 Victoria Street, Douglas, Isle of Man, IM1 2LH

Tel: 01624 696461
Fax: 01624 696400
E-mail: jmacartney@douglas.org.im

Enquiries:
Enquiries to: Librarian

Founded:
1886

Organisation type and purpose:
Local government body, public library.

Subject coverage:
Isle of Man: historical, social, political, economic and other aspects; cinema.

Museum or gallery collection, archive, or library special collection:
Manx Collection

Non-library collection catalogue:
All or part available in-house

Library catalogue:
All or part available in-house

Access to staff:
Contact by letter, by telephone, by fax, by e-mail and in person
Hours: Mon to Sat, 0915 to 1730

DOVE MARINE LABORATORY

Cullercoats, North Shields, Tyne and Wear, NE30 4PZ

Tel: 0191 252 4850
Fax: 0191 252 1054

Enquiries:
Enquiries to: Secretary
Direct e-mail: c.a.weiss@ncl.ac.uk

Organisation type and purpose:
Research organisation.

Subject coverage:
Marine biology; oceanography; fisheries.

Library catalogue:
All or part available in-house

Printed publications:
Reports (marine fauna of the Cullercoats district) (for sale)

Access to staff:
Contact by letter, by telephone, by fax and by e-mail
Hours: Mon to Fri, 0900 to 1700

Part of:
Department of Marine Sciences and Coastal Management
University of Newcastle upon Tyne; tel: 0191 222 6661; fax: 0191 222 7891

DOVER HARBOUR BOARD

Harbour House, Dover, Kent, CT17 9BU

Tel: 01304 240400
Fax: 01304 240465

continued overleaf

Website:
http://www.doverport.co.uk
Ferries: cars, coach, freight. Shipping: cruises, marina, cargo. Commercial: advertising, property.

Enquiries:
Enquiries to: Public Relations Officer
Direct tel: 01304 240400 ext 4801
Direct fax: 01304 241274
Direct e-mail: val.crimmin@doverport.co.uk

Founded:
1606

Also known as:
Port of Dover

Organisation type and purpose:
Statutory body.
Statutory board.

Subject coverage:
Port administration, particularly cross-channel passenger trade and roll-on roll-off traffic, cruise terminal, marina operation and fresh produce cargo facilities.

Printed publications:
All information is free of charge
Annual Report
Port Handbook
Service Brochures
Statistical Digests
Marina Guide

Access to staff:
Contact by letter, by telephone, by fax and via website
Hours: Mon to Fri, 0800 to 1800

DOWN'S HEART GROUP

Acronym or abbreviation: DHG

PO Box 4260, Dunstable, Bedfordshire, LU6 2ZT

Tel: 0845 166 8061
Fax: 0845 166 8061
E-mail: info@dhg.org.uk

Website:
http://www.dhg.org.uk
Online version of information pack plus more recent material, newsletters, conferences, etc.

Enquiries:
Enquiries to: Director
Direct e-mail: penny.green@dhg.org.uk
Other contacts: Information Officer

Founded:
1989

Organisation type and purpose:
UK national charity.

Subject coverage:
Heart defects with Down's Syndrome. Pre-natal screening for heart defects with Down's Syndrome. Bereavement.

Printed publications:
Information Pack (£5, free to families)
Newsletter (free to members)

Electronic and video publications:
Heart Problems in Children with Down's Syndrome (video, loaned free to families, £5 to purchase)

Access to staff:
Contact by letter, by telephone, by fax, by e-mail and via website. Appointment necessary.
Hours: 24-hour in emergency – contact or answerphone always available.

Access to building, collection or gallery:
Prior appointment required

Member organisation of:
Children's Heart Federation

DOWN'S SYNDROME ASSOCIATION

Acronym or abbreviation: DSA

Langdon Down Centre, 2a Langdon Park, Teddington, TW11 9PS

Tel: 0845 230 0372
Fax: 0845 230 0373
E-mail: info@downs-syndrome.org.uk

Website:
http://www.downs-syndrome.org.uk
Information about Down's Syndrome and the Association; list of publications.

Enquiries:
Enquiries to: Information Officer

Founded:
1971

Organisation type and purpose:
National organisation, membership association (membership is by subscription), present number of members: 12,000, voluntary organisation, registered charity (charity number 1061474).

Subject coverage:
Down's Syndrome: medical, educational, psychological, counselling new parents, and general aspects.

Printed publications:
Newsletter (3 times a year)
Literature List – publications of the Association and others under the headings; play and early learning, speech and language, education, behaviour, benefits, services and legal matters, health, medical and nutrition, leisure, relations and sexuality, bereavement, counselling

Electronic and video publications:
Education: Preparation for life (video)
Play and Say (video)
Down 2 Earth

Publications list:
Available in print

Access to staff:
Contact by letter, by telephone, by fax, by e-mail and via website. Appointment necessary.
Hours: Mon to Fri, 0900 to 1700

DOWN'S SYNDROME SCOTLAND

158–160 Balgreen Road, Edinburgh, EH11 3AU

Tel: 0131 313 4225
Fax: 0131 313 4285
E-mail: info@dsscotland.org.uk

Website:
http://www.dsscotland.org.uk

Enquiries:
Enquiries to: Senior Information Officer
Direct tel: 0131 313 8618
Direct e-mail: lou@dsscotland.org.uk

Founded:
1982

Formerly called:
Scottish Down's Syndrome Association (SDSA) (year of change 2001)

Organisation type and purpose:
Membership association (membership is by subscription), present number of members: 1500+, voluntary organisation, registered charity (charity number SC011012).

Subject coverage:
Down's Syndrome.

Information services:
Telephone and e-mail helplines.

Museum or gallery collection, archive, or library special collection:
Resource centre of books and DVDs available for loan

Non-library collection catalogue:
All or part available online, in-house and in print

Library catalogue:
All or part available online

Printed publications:
Annual Review
Quarterly Newsletter
Booklets: What is Down's syndrome, When a baby has Down's syndrome, Getting to know a baby with Down's syndrome, The Professionals and how they can help. Plus a range of easy read booklets for people with learning disabilites, and fact sheets.

Publications list:
Available online and in print

Access to staff:
Contact by letter, by telephone, by fax, by e-mail and via website. Appointment necessary.
Hours: Mon to Fri, 0900 to 1700

Access for disabled people:
Level entry, access to all public areas, toilet facilities

Branches in:
Ayrshire, Central, Grampian, Lothian, Tayside, West of Scotland

Sister organisation for England, Wales and Northern Ireland:
Down's Syndrome Association
Langdon Down Centre, 2a Langdon Park, Teddington, Middlesex, TW11 9PS; tel: 0845 230 0372; fax: 0845 230 0373; e-mail: info@downs -syndrome.org.uk; website: http://www.downs -syndrome.org.uk

DOZENAL SOCIETY OF GREAT BRITAIN

Acronym or abbreviation: DSGB

32 Lansdowne Crescent, Carlisle, Cumbria, CA3 9EW

Tel: 01228 596834
E-mail: dsgb@dozenalsociety.org.uk

Website:
http://www.dozenalsociety.org.uk

Enquiries:
Enquiries to: Secretary

Founded:
1958

Formerly called:
Duodecimal Society of Great Britain (year of change 1978)

Organisation type and purpose:
International organisation, learned society (membership is by subscription), present number of members: 60, research organisation.
Metrological and numbering systems past, present and future. Informed consideration of attempts to impose decimal-metric methods on areas for which they are not appropriate.
Technical and social metrologies have differing requirements and purposes. The first postulates abstract concepts which need not relate to anything but one another, to be operated on by multi-figured calculations. Social use requires human-sized units that are designated by small numbers and are in the simple proportions commonly required and instinctively employed when making comparisons of size, weight, value, etc, such as have been evolved down the ages for our convenience and understanding.
To replace base ten with base twelve.

Subject coverage:
Measurement systems and methods of numeration and arithmetic, past, present and future; principles, practical imperatives and efficiency in applied metrology and computation; historical, scientific and social metrology; derivation, relationships and purposes of basic units; application of twelve-based arithmetic; informed criticism of decimal-metric methods.

Museum or gallery collection, archive, or library special collection:
Books, papers and references on numeration, calculation and metrology

Duodecimal Bulletins of the Dozenal Society of
America since 1945
Journals of the DSGB from 1960 to date
Media cuttings over present decimalisation era
Wide bibliography of references

Non-library collection catalogue:
All or part available in-house

Library catalogue:
All or part available in-house

Printed publications:
Dozenal Journal (occasional, free to members)
Duodecimal Bulletin of the DSA
Gravity and Mass TGM, A coherent dozenal
metrology based on time

Publications list:
Available in print

Access to staff:
Contact by letter, by telephone, by e-mail and via
website. Appointment necessary.
Hours: Mon to Sun, 0900 to 2100

Links with:
British Weights and Measures Association
11 Greensleeves Avenue, Broadstone, Dorset,
BH18 8BJ; tel: 020 8922 0089; fax:
bwma@email.com; website: http://www.footrule
.org
Dozenal Society of America (DSA)
472 Village Oaks Lane, Babylon Village, NY
11702–3123, USA; tel: +1 631 669 0273; fax:
contact@dozenal.org; website: http://www
.dozenal.org

DR WILLIAMS'S LIBRARY

14 Gordon Square, London, WC1H 0AR

Tel: 020 7387 3727
Fax: 020 7388 1142
E-mail: enquiries@Dwlib.co.uk

Enquiries:
Enquiries to: Director

Founded:
1729

Organisation type and purpose:
Registered charity (charity number 214926), public
library.

Subject coverage:
Theology, ecclesiastical history (particularly early
Nonconformist history), philosophy, humanities in
general.

**Museum or gallery collection, archive, or library
special collection:**
Henry Crabb Robinson, diaries and
correspondence
New College, London, Collection
Norman Baynes Byzantine Library
Philip Doddridge Correspondence
Richard Baxter Correspondence
Roger Morrice Collection

Non-library collection catalogue:
All or part available in-house and in print

Library catalogue:
All or part available in-house

Printed publications:
Bulletin of Dr Williams's Library (annually)
Friends of Dr Williams's Library Annual Lectures,
1947-
Guide to Manuscripts in the Library (being
revised)
Library Catalogue of Accessions (1900–1950, 1951–
1960, 1961–1970, 1971–1980)
Nonconformist Congregations in Great Britain: a
list of histories (1974)

Access to staff:
Contact by letter, by telephone, by fax and by e-
mail. Appointment necessary.
Hours: Mon, Wed, Fri, 1000 to 1700; Tue, Thu, 1000
to 1830

Administers the:
Congregational Library

Parent body:
Dr Williams's Trust
14 Gordon Square, London, WC1H 0AR

DRAMA ASSOCIATION OF WALES

Acronym or abbreviation: DAW

The Old Library, Singleton Road, Splott, Cardiff,
CF24 2ET

Tel: 029 2045 2200
Fax: 029 2045 2277
E-mail: aled.daw@virgin.net

Enquiries:
Enquiries to: Administrator

Founded:
1934

Organisation type and purpose:
National organisation, advisory body, membership
association (membership is by subscription),
present number of members: 600, voluntary
organisation, registered charity (charity number
502186), public library, training organisation,
publishing house.

Subject coverage:
Information on all aspects of amateur theatre,
including funding, training, supplies of costumes,
etc., festivals, lottery funding, international
activities and contacts.

**Museum or gallery collection, archive, or library
special collection:**
Largest playscript lending library in the world
Part reference collection of former BTA
Playsets of the former British Theatre Association
(BTA) and Inner London Education Authority

Printed publications:
Dawn (newsletter, quarterly)

Publications list:
Available in print

Access to staff:
Contact by letter, by telephone, by fax, by e-mail
and in person
Hours: Mon, 1400 to 1630; Tue to Fri, 0930 to 1300
and 1400 to 1630

Links with:
CCAT
International Amateur Theatre Association (IATA)
National Association of Youth Theatres (NAYT)
Theatre Information Group (TIG)
Wales Association of the Performing Arts (WAPA)

DRAPERS' COMPANY

Formal name: Worshipful Company of Drapers

Drapers' Hall, Throgmorton Avenue, London,
EC2N 2DQ

Tel: 020 7588 5001
Fax: 020 7628 1988
E-mail: mail@thedrapers.co.uk

Website:
http://www.thedrapers.co.uk

Organisation type and purpose:
Membership association (membership is by
election or invitation).
City of London Livery Company.
To administer charitable trusts relating to relief of
need, education and almshouses, to provide
banqueting and catering services, and to fosters its
heritage and traditions of good fellowship.

Access to staff:
Contact by letter, by telephone, by fax, by e-mail
and via website

DRAUGHT PROOFING ADVISORY
ASSOCIATION LIMITED

Acronym or abbreviation: DPAA

PO Box 12, Haslemere, Surrey, GU27 3AH

Tel: 01428 654011
Fax: 01428 651401
E-mail: dpaaassociation@aol.com

Website:
http://www.dpaa-association.org.uk

Enquiries:
Enquiries to: Director

Founded:
1985

Organisation type and purpose:
Trade association (membership is by qualification).

Subject coverage:
Draught proofing.

Trade and statistical information:
Statistics on UK market for draught proofing.

Printed publications:
Advisory literature
Register of Members

Access to staff:
Contact by letter, by telephone, by fax, by e-mail
and via website
Hours: Mon to Fri, 0900 to 1700

DRIVER AND VEHICLE
LICENSING AGENCY

Royston House, 34 Upper Queen Street, Belfast,
BT1 6FA

Tel: 028 9054 2042
Fax: 028 9054 7379

Enquiries:
Enquiries to: Manager

Organisation type and purpose:
Executive Agency within the Department of the
Environment (Northern Ireland).

DRIVING INSTRUCTORS
ASSOCIATION

Acronym or abbreviation: DIA

Safety House, Beddington Farm Road, Croydon,
Surrey, CR0 4XZ

Tel: 020 8665 5151
Fax: 020 8665 5565
E-mail: driving@atlas.co.uk

Website:
http://www.driving.org

Enquiries:
Enquiries to: General Secretary

Founded:
1978

Organisation type and purpose:
Trade association (membership is by subscription),
present number of members: 10,000.

Subject coverage:
Nationwide – looking after the interests of driving
instructors and road safety educationalists.
Providing information, producing magazines and
manuals, resource material towards raising
standards of driver education, professional
qualifications including Diploma in Driving
Instruction and degree courses – BSc and BA
(Driver Education) Masters and Doctorates. Mail
order supplies and requisites – everything for
driving schools and driving instructors.

Printed publications:
Driving Instructor Magazine (alternate months)
Driving Magazine (6 times a year)
Newsletter
Resource Material for Diploma in Driving
Instruction (Dip.DI) Examinations

Access to staff:
Contact by letter, by telephone, by fax, by e-mail
and in person
Hours: Mon to Fri, 0900 to 1700

continued overleaf

Links with:
International Association of Driver Education (IVV)
  tel: 020 8660 3333; fax: 020 8665 5565; e-mail: driving@atlas.co.uk

DRIVING STANDARDS AGENCY

Acronym or abbreviation: DSA

Stanley House, 56 Talbot Street, Nottingham, NG1 5GU

Tel: 0115 901 2500
Fax: 0115 901 2940
E-mail: pressoffice@dsa.gsi.gov.uk

Website:
http://www.dsa.gov.uk

Enquiries:
Enquiries to: Customer Service Manager
Direct tel: 0115 901 2515/6
Direct fax: 0115 901 2510
Direct e-mail: customerservices@dsa.gov.uk

Founded:
1990

Organisation type and purpose:
National government body.
Government Executive Agency.
To promote road safety in Great Britain through the advancement of driving standards and by testing drivers, riders and driving instructors fairly and efficiently.

Subject coverage:
Driving standards, testing drivers, riders and driving instructors.

Trade and statistical information:
Data on pass and fail characteristics of the theory and practical driving tests.

Printed publications:
For publications see website www.dsa.gov.uk
Order printed publications from: Publications Unit, Driving Standards Agency
Paul Waller Avenue, Harrowden Lane, Cardington, Bedfordshire, MK14 3ST, tel: 01234 742297, fax: 01234 742581, e-mail: publications@dsa.gsi.gov.uk

Electronic and video publications:
For non-book media see website www.dsa.gov.uk

Publications list:
Available in print

Access to staff:
Contact by letter, by telephone, by fax, by e-mail and via website
Hours: Mon to Fri, 0800 to 1800

Access to building, collection or gallery:
Yes
Hours: Mon to Fri, 0800 to 1800

Access for disabled people:
Yes

Executive Agency of:
Department for Transport (DfT)

DRUGSCOPE

Prince Consort House, Suite 204, Second Floor, 109–111 Farringdon Road, London, EC1R 3BW

Tel: 020 7520 7550
Fax: 020 7520 7555
E-mail: info@drugscope.org.uk

Website:
http://www.drugscope.org.uk

Enquiries:
Enquiries to: Information Officer

Founded:
2000

Created by the merger of:
Institute for the Study of Drug Dependence (ISDD), Standing Conference on Drug Abuse (SCODA) (year of change 2000)

Organisation type and purpose:
Membership association (membership is by subscription), present number of members: 850, voluntary organisation, registered charity (charity number 255030), research organisation.
Centre of expertise on drugs.
To inform policy development and reduce drug-related risk by providing quality drug information, promoting effective responses to drug taking, advising on policy-making and encouraging debate.

Subject coverage:
Drug misuse; besides illegal drugs, also covers over-the-counter medicines, alcohol, presription drugs, benzodiazepines, etc. Specialist advice on local drug services and best practice information on drug treatment and care, prevention and education.

Library catalogue:
All or part available online and in-house

Printed publications:
Publications aimed at young people, drug workers, teachers and other professionals, and various publications for those providing, purchasing, or commissioning drug services or working with drug users including:
Drug Problems: Where to Get Help
Drug Notes
Substance Misuse and Pregnancy
Druglink Guide to Drugs
What Drugs Look Like (poster)
Drugs Misuse (wallchart)

Electronic and video publications:
Drug encyclopedia (CD-ROM)

Publications list:
Available online and in print

Access to staff:
Contact by letter, by telephone, by fax, by e-mail and via website. Appointment necessary. All charged.
Hours: Mon to Fri, 0900 to 1700

Access to building, collection or gallery:
By appointment

Links with:
European Monitoring Centre for Drugs and Drug Addiction (EMCDDA)
United Nations Drug Control Programme (UNDCP)

Member organisation of:
European Association of Libraries and Information Services on Alcohol and Other Drugs (ELISAD)

DRY STONE WALLING ASSOCIATION OF GREAT BRITAIN

Acronym or abbreviation: DSWA

Westmorland County Showground, Lane Farm, Crooklands, Milnthorpe, Cumbria, LA7 7NH

Tel: 01539 5679
E-mail: information@dswa.org.uk

Website:
http://www.dswa.org.uk

Enquiries:
Enquiries to: Secretary

Founded:
1968

Organisation type and purpose:
Professional body, membership association (membership is by subscription), voluntary organisation, registered charity (charity number 289678), training organisation.
To further all aspects of the craft of dry stone walling.

Subject coverage:
All aspects of the craft of dry stone walling, craft training – formal and informal, skills assessment and certification scheme.

Museum or gallery collection, archive, or library special collection:
Small collection of printed material on the craft

Printed publications:
Register of Certificated Wallers and Dykers (free with SAE)
Annual Report
Better Dry Stone Walling (Tufnell R, £1.70)
Building and Repairing Dry Stone Walls (Tufnell R, £1.70))
Building Special Features in Dry Stone (Tufnell R, £1.70)
Creating a Natural Stone Garden (Tufnell R, et al, £2)
Dry Stone Walling (Rainsford Hannay F, £5.40)
Technical publications, specification leaflets and books including:
Waller and Dyker (newsletter, 3 times a year, for members)

Electronic and video publications:
Dry Stone Country (video, £15.99 plus £1.01 p&p)
How to Build & Repair Dry Stone Walls (video, £15 plus £1.50 p&p)
Millennium Wall Project (video, £15 plus £1.50 p&p)

Publications list:
Available online and in print

Access to staff:
Contact by letter, by e-mail and via website.
Appointment necessary. Non-members charged.
Hours: Mon to Fri, 0900 to 1700
Special comments: Prior appointment only.

Has:
19 branches throughout the United Kingdom (all honorary/volunteers)

Works closely with:
Conservation Bodies
Government Agencies

DSTL KNOWLEDGE SERVICES – HEADQUARTERS

Formal name: Defence Science and Technology Laboratory
Acronym or abbreviation: Dstl

248 Building Dstl, Porton Down, Salisbury, Wiltshire, SP4 0JQ

Tel: 01980 613971
Fax: 01980 613970
E-mail: knowledge-services@dstl.gov.uk

Website:
http://www.dstl.gov.uk
Knowledge Services has own pages within Dstl site.

Founded:
2001

Organisation type and purpose:
National government body, research organisation.

Subject coverage:
Operational analysis, military policy, naval systems, general business and management, special operations, radar, electronic warfare, explosives, weapon technologies including pyrotechnics and obscurants research, countermeasures, detection, ordnance, forensics, electronic warfare, electronic detection technologies, operational research, military history, general military and defence related topics, biological sciences, chemistry, materials science, historical analysis inc history of battles, WW1 and WW2, aeronautics and space, military aviation, psychology, physiology, mathematics, statistics, biological sciences, computing and other technology areas at undergraduate / postgraduate level including signal processing, radar, lasers, acoustics and management.

Museum or gallery collection, archive, or library special collection:
Knowledge Services has over 700,000 Scientific and Technical reports, which are not publicly available, comprising:

The output from UK government-funded defence R&D and Intelligence programmes since World War ll
Scientific, technical and intelligence reports from non-UK government defence R&D programmes over the same period. 13,000 books and access to over 1000 electronic journals.

Non-library collection catalogue:
All or part available in-house

Library catalogue:
All or part available in-house

Printed publications:
Defence Reports Abstracts (monthly bulletin of reports added to stock)
DRIC Spec 1000 (standard for defence R&D reports)
Defence Technology Alerts (monthly SDI service)
Defence Newsletters

Electronic and video publications:
Defence Reports (CD-ROM)

Access to staff:
Contact by letter, by telephone, by fax, by e-mail and via website. Appointment necessary. All charged.
Hours: Mon to Thurs, 0900 to 1700, Fri 0900 to 1630

Access to building, collection or gallery:
Prior appointment required

Agency of:
Ministry of Defence (MOD)

DSTL KNOWLEDGE SERVICES – INFORMATION CENTRE

Formal name: Defence Science and Technology Laboratory
Acronym or abbreviation: Dstl

Porton Down, Salisbury, Wiltshire, SP4 0JQ

Tel: 01980 613000
Fax: 01980 613970
E-mail: knowledge-services@dstl.gov.uk

Website:
http://www.dstl.gov.uk
Website of Dstl. Knowledge Services has pages within site.

Enquiries:
Enquiries to: Team Leader
Direct tel: 01980 6134663
Direct e-mail: damey@dstl.gov.uk
Other contacts: Librarian

Formerly called:
Chemical and Biological Defence Establishment (CBDE), Chemical Defence Establishment (CDE), DERA, PLSD

Organisation type and purpose:
National government body, research organisation.

Subject coverage:
Chemical, physical and meteorological problems of defence against chemical agents; design and development of protective equipment, respirators and clothing; filters and filtration; physiological effects, toxicology and biochemistry of poisonous substances and the development of therapeutic and prophylactic procedures.

Library catalogue:
All or part available in-house

Access to staff:
Contact by letter, by telephone, by fax, by e-mail and via website. Appointment necessary.
Hours: Mon to Thu, 0900 to 1700; Fri, 0900 to 1630

Access to building, collection or gallery:
Prior appointment required

Agency of:
Ministry of Defence (MOD)

Head Office:
Dstl
Room G067 Building A2, Dstl Farnborough, Ively Road, Farnborough, GU14 0LX; tel: 01252 455838; fax: 01252 455959; e-mail: cdstewart@dstl.gov.uk
Head of Knowledge Services

DUDLEY ARCHIVES AND LOCAL HISTORY SERVICE

Acronym or abbreviation: DALHS

Mount Pleasant Street, Coseley, West Midlands, WV14 9JR

Tel: 01384 812770
Fax: 01384 812770
E-mail: archives.centre@dudley.gov.uk

Website:
http://www.dudley.gov.uk
Information relating to the services via Dudley Council's web pages and being expanded and upgraded, particularly for family history.

Enquiries:
Enquiries to: Archivist

Founded:
1947

Relocated from:
Dudley Library (year of change 1992)

Organisation type and purpose:
Local government body.

Subject coverage:
History of Dudley and the Black Country, in particular the area of the present Metropolitan Borough of Dudley.

Museum or gallery collection, archive, or library special collection:
Printed material re Dudley and the Black Country and Archives – for details see entry in 'British Archives', Foster and Sheppard, 3rd edn
The Dudley Estate Archive (the Earls of Dudley) 12th to 20th century

Non-library collection catalogue:
All or part available online and in-house

Library catalogue:
All or part available online and in-house

Printed publications:
Publication details online via website
Handlists of material, particularly for family historians
Publications relating to the history of the area – lists available

Microform publications:
Local newspapers, parish regsiters, census returns
IGI (microfiche)
GRO Indexes 1837–1960

Electronic and video publications:
Videoa, DVds, CDs, LPs, cassettes

Access to staff:
Contact by letter, by telephone, by fax, by e-mail, in person and via website
Hours: Mon, Wed, closed; Tue, Fri, 0900 to 1700; Thu, 0930 to 2100; 1st and 3rd Sat in month, 0930 to 1230
Special comments: Restricted service 1300 to 1400. CARN readers' tickets issued with two proofs of identity with name, address and signature, appointments advisable, particularly for microform material, appointments for Saturdays.

Access for disabled people:
Ramped entry, access to all public areas, toilet facilities
Special comments: On site parking on level.

Parent body:
Dudley Metropolitan Borough Council, Dudley Libraries

DUDLEY COLLEGE OF TECHNOLOGY

The Broadway, Dudley, West Midlands, DY1 4AS

Tel: 01384 363000
Fax: 01384 363311

Website:
http://www.dudleycol.ac.uk

Enquiries:
Enquiries to: Librarian
Direct tel: 01384 363353
Direct e-mail: library@dudleycol.ac.uk

Organisation type and purpose:
College of further and higher education.

Subject coverage:
Management; secretarial and office practice; work study; production control; construction; structural engineering; welding; brickwork; carpentry; joinery; electrical engineering; electronic engineering; microcomputer technology; hairdressing; beauty therapy; mechanical engineering; production engineering; motor vehicle work, local history, science, humanities.

Non-library collection catalogue:
All or part available in-house

Library catalogue:
All or part available in-house

Access to staff:
Contact by letter, by telephone and by fax. Appointment necessary.
Hours: Term time: Mon to Thu, 0900 to 2000; Fri, 0900 to 1630
Vacations: Mon to Thu, 0900 to 1700; Fri, 0900 to 1630
Special comments: Reference facilities for non-students £5 per annum; borrowing facilities for non-students £25 per annum.

Access for disabled people:
Parking provided, level entry, toilet facilities, lift access from disabled parking to ground floor library.

Subsidiary body:
International Glass Centre
tel: 01384 363067

DUDLEY PUBLIC LIBRARIES

Dudley Library, St James's Road, Dudley, West Midlands, DY1 1HR

Tel: 01384 815568 (library office)
Fax: 01384 815543
E-mail: dudley.library@dudley.gov.uk

Website:
http://www.dudley.gov.uk

Founded:
1909

Organisation type and purpose:
Local government body, public library.

Subject coverage:
Dudley and Black Country local studies

Library catalogue:
All or part available online and in-house

Access to staff:
Contact by letter, by telephone, by fax, by e-mail, in person and via website
Hours: Mon, Thu, Fri, 0900 to 1900; Tue, 0930 to 1900; Wed, Sat, 0900 to 1700; Sun, 1000 to 1400

Access for disabled people:
Disabled entrance, public lift

Branch libraries:
Brierley Hill
Halesowen
Kingswinford
Sedgley
Stourbridge

DUGDALE SOCIETY

Shakespeare Centre, Stratford-upon-Avon, Warwickshire, CV37 6QW

Tel: 01789 204016
Fax: 01789 296083
E-mail: records@shakespeare.org.uk

Website:
http://www.shakespeare.org.uk/dugdale
Details of membership and publications list.

Enquiries:
Enquiries to: Secretary

Founded:
1920

Organisation type and purpose:
Learned society, membership association (membership is by subscription), present number of members: 350, registered charity (charity number 1051033).

Subject coverage:
Warwickshire: historical records, local history and topography.

Printed publications:
Leaflet detailing the publications of the Society
Occasional Papers based on Warwickshire records
Volumes of Records of Warwickshire

Publications list:
Available online and in print

Access to staff:
Contact by letter, by telephone and by e-mail
Hours: Mon to Fri, 0930 to 1700

DUKE OF EDINBURGH'S AWARD, THE

Acronym or abbreviation: the Award

Gulliver House, Madeira Walk, Windsor, Berkshire, SL4 1EU

Tel: 01753 727400
Fax: 01753 810666
E-mail: info@theaward.org

Website:
http://www.theaward.org

Enquiries:
Enquiries to: Director
Other contacts: Communications Officer

Founded:
1956

Organisation type and purpose:
Registered charity (charity number 1072490). Voluntary programme of activities and service to others, leading to Awards which are open to all between the ages of 14 and 25; the Award Head Office is advised by national co-ordinating bodies concerned with individual activities.

Subject coverage:
Over 300 different activities from bee-keeping to ballet, first aid to farming, etc; the specialist advice and expertise of the assisting organisations is relied upon by the Award Office, especially in the field of expeditioning.

Printed publications:
Annual Report
Award Handbook
Award Journal (magazine, 3 times a year)
Expedition Guide

Access to staff:
Contact by letter, by telephone, by fax and by e-mail
Hours: Mon to Fri, 0900 to 1700

DUMFRIES & GALLOWAY LIBRARIES, INFORMATION AND ARCHIVES

33 Burns Street, Dumfries, DG1 2PS

Tel: 01387 269254

Fax: 01387 264126
E-mail: libs&i@dumgal.gov.uk

Website:
http://www.dumgal.gov.uk/lia

Enquiries:
Enquiries to: Resources Development
Other contacts: Research Officer tel no: 01387 253820 for genealogical research.

Founded:
1987

Organisation type and purpose:
Local government body.
Record office.
Preservation of, and research using, local archives.

Subject coverage:
Local and family history, civic, religious, economic and social history, architecture and genealogical studies.

Museum or gallery collection, archive, or library special collection:
Dumfries Burgh archives
Local Authority archives
Papers of local businesses, societies and families
Sanquhar Burgh archives
Stewart of Shambellie family papers
Walter Newall architectural drawings

Non-library collection catalogue:
All or part available online, in-house and in print

Printed publications:
The following publications are available for purchase:
Ancestor hunting in Dumfries Archive Centre
Court Records
Valuation, Taxation and Voting Records
Monumental Inscriptions
Census 1851 Parish Indexes
Various information sheets, source lists etc
Church records
Health records
Military records
Poor and Welfare records

Publications list:
Available in print

Access to staff:
Contact by letter, by telephone, by fax, by e-mail and in person. Appointment necessary.
Hours: Tue, Wed, Fri, 1100 to 1300 and 1400 to 1700; Thu, 1800 to 2100

Links with:
Ewart Library
Catherine Street, Dumfries, DG1 1JB; tel: 01387 253820; fax: 01387 260294; e-mail: alastairj@dumgal.gov.uk

Parent body:
Libraries, Information and Archives Service, Dumfries and Galloway Council
tel: 01387 253820; fax: 01387 260294; e-mail: alastairj@dumgal.gov.uk

DUMFRIES AND GALLOWAY COLLEGE

Acronym or abbreviation: DAGCOL

Bankend Road, Dumfries, DG1 4FD

Tel: 01387 734000
Fax: 01387 734040
E-mail: info@dumgal.ac.uk

Website:
http://www.dumgal.ac.uk

Enquiries:
Enquiries to: Learning Resource Centre Manager
Direct tel: 01387 734004
Direct e-mail: turnbullc@dumgal.ac.uk

Formerly called:
Dumfries and Galloway College of Technology

Organisation type and purpose:
Suitable for ages: 16+.
College of further and higher education.

Subject coverage:
Mechanical, electrical, electronic and motor vehicle engineering, construction and allied industries, safety, business studies, information technology, accounting, office management, art and design, computing, media/communications, hairdressing, catering, tourism, social care, education.

Library catalogue:
All or part available in-house

Access to staff:
Contact by letter, by telephone, by e-mail and via website. Non-members charged.
Hours: Mon to Thu, 0830 to 1700; Fri, 0845 to 1630

Access for disabled people:
Parking provided, ramped entry, toilet facilities

Also at:
Stranraer Campus
Lewis Street, Stranraer; tel: 01776 706633; website: http://www.dumgal.ac.uk

DUMFRIES AND GALLOWAY COUNCIL

Council Offices, English Street, Dumfries, DG1 2DD

Tel: 01387 260000
Fax: 01387 260034

Website:
http://www.dumgal.gov.uk

Enquiries:
Enquiries to: Communications Manager
Direct tel: 01387 260330
Direct fax: 01387 260334
Direct e-mail: susanbl@dumgal.gov.uk

Founded:
1996

Formerly called:
Annandale and Eskdale District Council, Dumfries and Galloway Regional Council, Nithsdale District Council, Stewartry District Council, Wigtown District Council (year of change 1996)

Organisation type and purpose:
Local government body.

Subject coverage:
All information covering Dumfries and Galloway.

Printed publications:
Annual report
Children's services plan
Community care plan
Corporate plan
Local plans
Structure plan

Access to staff:
Contact by letter, by telephone, by fax, by e-mail, in person and via website
Hours: Mon to Fri, 0900 to 1700

Access for disabled people:
Ramped entry, access to all public areas

DUMFRIES AND GALLOWAY FAMILY HISTORY SOCIETY

Acronym or abbreviation: D&GFHS

Family History Centre, 9 Glasgow Street, Dumfries, DG2 9AF

Tel: 01387 248093
E-mail: publications@dgfhs.org.uk

Website:
http://www.safhs.org.uk
All Family History Societies in the Scottish Association of Family History Societies.
http://www.dgfhs.org.uk
History and current details about the Society including membership details, publications list and order form.
http://homepages.rootsweb.com/~scottish/

Enquiries:
Enquiries to: Honorary Secretary

Founded:
1987

Organisation type and purpose:
Learned society (membership is by subscription),
present number of members: 1700, voluntary
organisation, registered charity (charity number
SC 020596), research organisation, publishing
house.
Family history research.

Subject coverage:
Genealogy, family history, local history, especially
pertaining to Dumfriesshire, Kircudbrightshire and
Wigtownshire.

**Museum or gallery collection, archive, or library
special collection:**
Wigtown Free Press newspaper indexes 1850–1920
and all these newspapers on fiche
Bank of family trees
Books, documents, manuscripts
Dumfries newspapers' indexes 1777–1930
OPRs, IGI and 1841–1901 Census records (film)

Printed publications:
Newsletter (members)
Dumfries and Galloway: some sources for local
and family history
Irregular Marriages – Annan, Dumfriesshire 1797–
1854
Irregular Marriages – Portpatrick, Wigtownshire
1759–1826
Census 1851 surname index
Census 1841 surname index
Glenluce Old and New Luce Kirkyards Memorial
Transcriptions
Portpatrick Kirkyard Memorial Transcriptions
A Scots Agricultural Glossary: Adam Gray
Stranraer Mls Vol 1 (Bridge, Thistle & Dalrymple
St & Ivy Place Burial Grounds)
Stranraer Mls Vol 2 (Sheuchan Cemetry Section 1-
Original)
Stranraer Mls Vol 3 (Sheuchan Cemetry Extension
& War Memorial)
Stoneykirk & Kirkmadrine Mls
Parish of Balmaclellan – 1792 Census
Looking back on Dalbeattie Granite Industry
Clock and Watchmakers of SW Scotland 1576–1900
1841 Census Record indexed by surname for
Wigtownshire, Kirkcudbrightshire and
Dumfriesshire
Many publications on local history

Electronic and video publications:
Digital Tours of Dumfries & Galloway (Millennium
edition)(CD-ROM, 560 Mb)(6000 images created
by Sandy Pittendreigh for D&GFHS)

Publications list:
Available online and in print

Access to staff:
Contact by letter, by telephone, by e-mail, in
person and via website. Non-members charged.
Hours: Tue to Fri; Apr to Oct, 1000 to 1600; Nov to
Mar 1100 to 1500; Sat, 1000 to 1300

Access to building, collection or gallery:
No prior appointment required

Access for disabled people:
Level entry

DUMFRIES AND GALLOWAY LIBRARIES, INFORMATION AND ARCHIVES

Ewart Library, Catherine Street, Dumfries, DG1 1JB

Tel: 01387 253820
Fax: 01387 260294
E-mail: libs&i@dumgal.gov.uk

Website:
http://www.dumgal.gov.uk/lia
Homepage of the main library website

Enquiries:
Enquiries to: Cultural Services, Libraries
Information & Archives Manager
Other contacts: Reference Librarian

Founded:
1903

Formerly called:
Dumfries and Galloway Libraries (year of change
1995)

Organisation type and purpose:
Local government body, public library.

Subject coverage:
General, local studies of Dumfries and Galloway
region; civic, religious, genealogy, architecture,
economic and social history; Lockerbie Air Disaster
at Ewart.

**Museum or gallery collection, archive, or library
special collection:**
Burns Club Collection (at Archive Centre)
Local Authority Archives
Local Studies Collection
Lockerbie Air Disaster Archive
Lord Glendyne Collection
R C Reid Manuscripts (at Ewart)

Non-library collection catalogue:
All or part available online and in-house

Library catalogue:
All or part available online and in-house

Printed publications:
A Historic Walk Through Lockerbie (£2.95)
Dumfries and Galloway Through the Lens series:
books old photographs of local scenes (30 books,
£2.50 each)
Pigot and Slater: Dumfries and Galloway 19th
Century Trade Directories (£12.50)
Robert Burns: Reflections of an Age (£7.99)
Sang 0 the Nith: poetic journey through Burns'
Country as seen through the eyes of three
generations of Dumfries poets (compiled by
Clark J, £25)
With Both Feet off the Ground: Contemporary
poetry and prose from Dumfries and Galloway
(£4.95)
Posters and maps
Order printed publications from: http://
www.dumgal.gov.uk/lia

Publications list:
Available online and in print

Access to staff:
Contact by letter, by telephone, by fax, by e-mail,
in person and via website
Hours: Ewart: Mon, to Wed, Fri, 0900 to 1930; Thu,
Sat, 0900 to 1700

Access for disabled people:
Parking provided, ramped entry, access to all
public areas, toilet facilities

Branches at:
Annan Library
Charles Street, Annan, DG12 5AG; tel: 01461
202809; fax: 01461 20280901461 202809
Castle Douglas Library
King Street, Castle Douglas, DG7 1AE; tel: 01556
502643; fax: 01556 502643
Dalbeattie Library
High Street, Dalbeattie Library, DG5 4AD; tel:
01556 610898; fax: 01556 610898
Dalry Library
Dalry, Castle Douglas, DG7 3UP; tel: 01644
430234; fax: 01644 430234
Dumfries and Galloway Archives
Archive Centre, 33 Burns Street, Dumfries, DG1
2PS; tel: 01387 269254; fax: 01387 264126
Eastriggs Library
Eastriggs Community School, Eastriggs, Annan,
DG12 6PZ; tel: 01461 40844; fax: 01461 40844
Gatehouse Library
63 High Street, Gatehouse of Fleet, DG7 2HS; tel:
01557 814646; fax: 01557 814646
Georgetown Library
Gillbrae Road, Dumfries, DG1 4EJ; tel: 01387
256059; fax: 01387 256059
Gretna Library
Richard Greenhow Centre, Central Avenue,
Gretna, DG16 5AQ; tel: 01461 338000; fax: 01461
338000

Kirkconnel Library
Greystone Avenue, Kelloholm, DG4 6RA; tel:
01659 67191; fax: 01659 67191
Kirkcudbright Library
Sheriff Court House, Kirkcudbright, DG6 4JW;
tel: 01557 331240; fax: 01557 331240
Langholm Library
Charles Street Old, Langholm, DG13 0AA; tel:
01387 380040; fax: 01387 380040
Lochmaben Library
High Street, Lochmaben, Lockerbie, DG11 1NQ;
tel: 01387 811865; fax: 01387 811865
Lochside Library
Lochside Road, Dumfries, DG2 0LW; tel: 01387
268751; fax: 01387 268751
Lochthorn Library
Lochthorn, Dumfries, DG1 1UF; tel: 01387
265780; fax: 01387 266424
Lockerbie Library
31–33 High Stree, Lockerbie, DG11 2JL; tel:
01576 203380; fax: 01576 203380
Moffat Library
Town Hall, High Street, Moffat, DG10 9HF; tel:
01683 220952; fax: 01683 220952
Newton Stewart Library
Church Street, Newton Stewart, DG8 6ER; tel:
01671 403450; fax: 01671 403450
Port William Library
Church Street, Port William, Newton Stewart,
DG8 9QL; tel: 01988 700406; fax: 01988 700406
Sanquhar Library
106 High Street, Sanquhar, DG4 6DZ; tel: 01659
50626; fax: 01659 50626
Stranraer Library
North Strand Street, Stranraer, DG9 7LD; tel:
01776 707400; fax: 01776 703565
Thornhill Library
Townhead Street, Thornhill, DG3 5NW; tel:
01848 330654; fax: 01848 330654
Whithorn Library
St John Street, Whithorn, DG8 8PF; tel: 01988
500406; fax: 01988 500406
Wigtown Library
Wigtown County Buildings, Wigtown, DG8 9JH;
tel: 01988 403329; fax: 01988 403329

DUNDEE AND TAYSIDE CHAMBER OF COMMERCE AND INDUSTRY

Chamber of Commerce Buildings, Panmure Street,
Dundee, DD1 1ED

Tel: 01382 228545
Fax: 01382 228441
E-mail: admin@dundeechamber.co.uk

Website:
http://www.dundeechamber.co.uk
Membership and service information; publications;
news and legislation briefings; electronic business
park.

Enquiries:
Enquiries to: Communications Manager
Direct e-mail: juliechristie@dundeechamber.co.uk

Organisation type and purpose:
Advisory body, trade association (membership is
by subscription).
To represent the business interests of companies in
Tayside.

Subject coverage:
Business services.

Printed publications:
Business Directory, directory and buyers guide
(250pp, annually, c. 1800, £7.50)
The Business (16pp, newspaper, 6 times a year, c.
6000 free to subscribers)

Publications list:
Available online and in print

Access to staff:
Contact by letter, by telephone, by fax, by e-mail,
in person and via website
Hours: Mon to Fri, 0900 to 1700

continued overleaf

Access to building, collection or gallery:
No prior appointment required

Access for disabled people:
Access to all public areas

DUNDEE CITY ARCHIVES

Formal name: Archive Centre of Dundee City Council

21 City Square, Dundee, DD1 3BY

Tel: 01382 434494
Fax: 01382 434666
E-mail: archives@dundeecity.gov.uk

Website:
http://www.dundeecity.gov.uk/archive/
Brief list of holdings
http://www.fdca.org.uk
Resources produced by volunteers

Enquiries:
Enquiries to: City Archivist

Founded:
1191

Formerly called:
Burgh of Dundee, County of City of Dundee (Dundee Corporation), City of Dundee District Council, Dundee City Council (year of change 1894, 1975, 1996)

Organisation type and purpose:
Local government body.

Subject coverage:
Local history from the formation of the Burgh of Dundee in 1191, shipbuilding, Port of Dundee, Customs and Excise, Presbytery records.

Non-library collection catalogue:
All or part available in-house

Printed publications:
Robert Fleming [1845–1892] and the Dundee Merchants (George A. Stout, 1999, £4.95)
Wesleyan Register of Baptisms, Dundee 1785–1898 (Grace Mann and J. G. L. Wright, 2000, £4.95)
The Kirks of Dundee Presbytery 1558–1999 (Ian McCraw, 2000, £9.99)
Dundee Motor Registrations TS1 – TS1000 (J. G. L. Wright (ed.), 2003, £4.95)
Caledon Ships (David Middleton, 2008, £9.99)
Order printed publications from: Honorary Sales Secretary, Friends of Dundee City Archive (at same address)

Access to staff:
Contact by letter, by telephone, by fax and by e-mail. Appointment necessary.
Hours: Mon to Fri, 0915 to 1300 and 1400 to 1645

Access to building, collection or gallery:
Enter by 1 Shore Terrace
Hours: Mon to Fri, 0915 to 1300 and 1400 to 1645; for local holidays check council website A–Z
Special comments: Visitor's pass will be issued at security entrance

Access for disabled people:
No lift at 1 Shore Terrace; special arrangements can be made elsewhere for those with difficulty walking.

Links with:
Friends of Dundee City Archives
c/o Dundee City Archives; website: http://www.fdca.org.uk

DUNDEE CITY COUNCIL – ARTS & HERITAGE

Leisure and Communities Department, Floor 13, Tayside House, 152 Nethergate, Dundee

Tel: 01382 433827
Fax: 01382 432252
E-mail: mcmanus.galleries@dundeecity.gov.uk

Website:
http://www.mcmanus.co.uk
http://www.dundeecity.gov.uk

Enquiries:
Enquiries to: Arts & Heritage Manager
Direct tel: 01382 432368
Direct fax: 01382 433211

Founded:
2005

Formerly called:
Dundee Art Galleries and Museums (year of change 1994); Arts and Heritage Department (year of change 2002); Leisure and Arts Department (year of change 2006)

Organisation type and purpose:
Local government body, museum, art gallery. Heritage facilities.

Subject coverage:
Tayside and North Fife region: archaeology, including sites research, history, natural sciences and environmental studies; museum education services; fine and applied art; Egyptology; astronomy; numismatics; field archaeology.

Museum or gallery collection, archive, or library special collection:
Recognised collections of fine and decorative art and whaling

Printed publications:
Ale and A'thing: the Grocer and Licensed Trade in Dundee
Art Catalogue
Fishing for the Whale
Local history books
Studies in Archaeology

Access to staff:
Contact by letter, by telephone, by fax, by e-mail, in person and via website
Hours: Mon to Fri, 0900 to 1700

Access to building, collection or gallery:
Special comments: Main Art Gallery and Museum closed for refurbishment. Scheduled to re-open in October 2009.

DUNDEE CITY COUNCIL – LIBRARIES

Leisure and Communites Department, Central Library, The Wellgate, Dundee, DD1 1DB

Tel: 01382 431500
Fax: 01382 431558
E-mail: central.library@dundeecity.gov.uk

Website:
http://www.dundeecity.gov.uk/library/
Libraries homepage.
http://libcat.dundeecity.gov.uk/cgi-bin/dundee.sh
Library catalogue.
http://www.wighton.com
Wighton database of Scottish national music.
http://www.dundeecity.gov.uk/photodb/
Photopolis – database of old Dundee photographs.

Enquiries:
Enquiries to: Head of Libraries, Information & Cultural Services
Direct tel: 01382 307462
Direct fax: 01382 307487
Direct e-mail: moira.methven@dundeecity.gov.uk
Other contacts: Manager, Central Library, for Manager of the Central Library.

Founded:
1869

Organisation type and purpose:
Local government body, public library.

Subject coverage:
General, business information, ethnic minority languages, local history, genealogy, art, music, architecture, patents, Scottish literature, open learning materials, Scottish Parliament, European information and early Scottish music.

Museum or gallery collection, archive, or library special collection:
Antiquarian Collection
British Standards
Cynicus Collection (early 20th century cartoons)

Dundee Photographic Survey 1916
Dundee Photographic Survey 1991
Lamb Collection (local history ephemera including posters, news cuttings, pamphlets, etc.)
Ower Collection (architecture)
Sir James Ivory Collection (early mathematical and scientific works)
Sturrock Collection (fine printing and binding; private press books)
Whaling Logbooks
Wighton Collection (1200 volumes of early music of UK, particularly Scottish; some unique items)
William McGonagall Collection
Wilson Collection (turn of the century photographs, mainly of Dundee)

Trade and statistical information:
The Central Library has a collection of government and inter-governmental publications, which includes such material.

Non-library collection catalogue:
All or part available online

Library catalogue:
All or part available online

Electronic and video publications:
Directory of Organisations

Access to staff:
Contact by letter, by telephone, by fax, by e-mail, in person and via website
Hours: Central Library: Mon, Tue, Thu, Fri, 0930 to 2100; Wed, 1000 to 2100; Sat, 0930 to 1700
Opening times of neighbourhood libraries vary

Access for disabled people:
Parking provided, ramped entry, level entry, access to all public areas, toilet facilities

Community libraries:
Ardler Complex
Turnberry Avenue, Dundee, DD3 3TP; tel: 01382 436442; fax: 01382 436446
Arthurstone Community Library
Arthurstone Terrace, Dundee, DD4 6RT; tel: 01382 438881; fax: 01382 438886
Blackness Community Library
225 Perth Road, Dundee, DD2 1EJ; tel: 01382 435936; fax: 01382 435942
Broughty Ferry Community Library
Queen Street, Broughty Ferry, Dundee, DD5 2HN; tel: 01382 436919; fax: 01382 436913
Charleston Community Centre and Library
60 Craigowan Road, Dundee, DD2 4NL; tel: 01382 436723; fax: 01382 436640
Coldside Community Library
150 Strathmartine Road, Dundee, DD3 7SE; tel: 01382 432849; fax: 01382 432850
Douglas Community and Library Centre
Balmoral Avenue, Dundee, DD4 8SD; tel: 01382 436944; fax: 01382 436922
Fintry Community Library
Findcastle Street, Dundee, DD4 9EW; tel: 01382 432560; fax: 01382 432559
Hub Community Centre and Library
Pitkerro Road, Dundee, DD4 8ES; tel: 01382 438648; fax: 01382 438627
Kirkton Community Centre and Library
Derwent Avenue, Dundee, DD3 0BW; tel: 01382 436453; fax: 01382 436321
Lochee Community Library
High Street, Lochee, Dundee, DD2 3AU; tel: 01382 431835; fax: 01382 431837
Menzieshill Community Centre and Library
Orleans Place, Dundee, DD2 4BH; tel: 01382 435887; fax: 01382 435888
Whitfield Library and Learning Centre
Whitfield Drive, Dundee, DD4 0DX; tel: 01382 432561; fax: 01382 432562

Parent body:
Dundee City Council
City Chambers, Dundee, DD1 3BY; tel: 01382 434000; fax: 01382 434666; e-mail: helpline@dundeecity.gov.uk

DUNDEE HERITAGE TRUST

Verdant Works, West Henderson's Wynd, Dundee, DD1 5BT

Tel: 01382 226659
Fax: 01382 225891
E-mail: info@dundeeheritage.co.uk

Website:
http://www.rrrdiscovery.com
Content of the museum exhibitions, opening hours and prices, etc., education services, special events, historical information.

Enquiries:
Enquiries to: Museums Officer

Founded:
1985

Organisation type and purpose:
Registered charity (charity number SC 002268). Museum.

Subject coverage:
Dundee's industrial history, specifically textiles (linen and jute). Textile engineering and mill architecture. RRS Discovery, polar exploration, Captain Scott and ship restoration and conservation.

Museum or gallery collection, archive, or library special collection:
Archives (not business archives), photographs and objects relating to Dundee textile industries, especially linen and jute
Archival photographs and objects relating to RRS Discovery and 1901–04 British National Antarctic Expedition under Captain Scott

Printed publications:
The Story of the Discovery (£2.50 plus p&p)
Verdant Works – The Story of Dundee and Jute (£2.50 plus p&p)
Order printed publications from: Shop Manager, Dundee Industrial Heritage Ltd
Discovery Point, Discovery Quay, Dundee, DD1 4XA, tel: 01382 309060, fax: 01382 225891, e-mail: info@dundeeheritage.co.uk

Access to staff:
Contact by letter, by telephone, by fax and by e-mail. Appointment necessary.
Hours: Mon to Fri, 0900 to 1700

Access to building, collection or gallery:
No access other than to staff
Hours: Verdant Works: April to October, Mon and Sat 1000 to 1800, Sun 1100 to 1800); November to March, Wed and Sat 1030 to 1630, Sun 1100 to 1630). Closed Mon and Tue from November to March. Closed 25 and 26 December and 1 and 2 January. Last admission is 1 hour prior to closing

Also at:
Discovery Point
Discovery Quay, Dundee, DD1 5BT; tel: 01382 309060; fax: 01382 225891; e-mail: info@dundeeheritage.co.uk

DURHAM CATHEDRAL LIBRARY

The College, Durham, DH1 3EH

Tel: 0191 386 2489
Fax: 0191 386 4267 (Chapter Office)
E-mail: library@durhamcathedral.co.uk

Website:
http://www.durhamcathedral.co.uk/library

Enquiries:
Enquiries to: Assistant Librarian

Founded:
995

Organisation type and purpose:
Cathedral library.

Subject coverage:
Durham Cathedral; manuscripts and early printed books; Durham local history; pre-1800 sacred and secular music; monasticism; Saxon and medieval monastic manuscripts.

Museum or gallery collection, archive, or library special collection:
Allan Collection of manuscripts

Collection of manuscript music books for organ and choir
Collection of over 12,000 17th- and 18th-century theses, mainly from German Universities
Falle Collection of 17th- and 18th-century printed music
Henson Collection of manuscripts
Hunter Collection of manuscripts
I. T. Ramsey Collection of manuscripts
J. B. Lightfoot Collection of manuscripts
Longstaffe Collection of manuscripts
Pre-Conquest and medieval books of the monastic house of Durham (manuscripts, c.300 vols)
Raine Collection of manuscripts
Randall Collection of manuscripts
Sir Cuthbert Sharp Collection of manuscripts

Non-library collection catalogue:
All or part available online, in-house and in print

Library catalogue:
All or part available online and in-house

Printed publications:
Guide for readers leaflet

Microform publications:
Microfilms of all medieval manuscripts available and of much manuscript and printed early music

Access to staff:
Contact by letter, by telephone, by e-mail, in person and via website. Appointment necessary. Letter of introduction required.
Hours: Mon to Fri, 0900 to 1300 and 1400 to 1700
Special comments: Closed for first two weeks of July; letter of introduction sometimes required

Parent body:
Durham Cathedral
The College, Durham, DH1 3EH; tel: 0191 386 4266; fax: 0191 386 4267; e-mail: enquiries@durhamcathedral.co.uk; website: http://www.durhamcathedral.co.uk

DURHAM COMMUNITY HERITAGE PROJECT

Formal name: Durham Community Heritage Project

Culture and Leisure, Durham County Council, County Hall, Durham, DH1 5TY

Tel: 0191 383 3016

Website:
www.durham.gov.uk/communityheritage

Enquiries:
Enquiries to: Community Heritage Officer
Direct tel: 0191 383 3016

Organisation type and purpose:
To support local County Durham communities in looking after their heritage collections and to find ways to make these collections more accessible

Access to staff:
Contact by letter, by telephone and via website

DURHAM COUNTY LOCAL HISTORY SOCIETY

Acronym or abbreviation: DCLHS

St Mary's Grove, Tudhoe, Spennymoor, DL16 6LR

Tel: 01388 816209
E-mail: johnbanham@tiscali.co.uk

Website:
http://www.durhamweb.org.uk/dclhs

Enquiries:
Enquiries to: Secretary

Founded:
1963

Organisation type and purpose:
Learned society, publishing house.

Subject coverage:
Durham, local history, mainly 15th century to present day.

Printed publications:
Journal (twice a year)
Newsletter (quarterly)
Occasional papers (irregular)

Publications list:
Available online

Access to staff:
Contact by letter and by e-mail
Hours: Mon to Fri, 0900 to 1700

DURHAM COUNTY RECORD OFFICE

Acronym or abbreviation: DCRO

County Hall, Durham, DH1 5UL

Tel: 0191 383 3253
Fax: 0191 383 4500
E-mail: record.office@durham.gov.uk

Website:
http://www.durham.gov.uk/recordoffice
Database of all catalogues, information concerning services provided, detailed lists of parish records and indexes, educational resources.

Enquiries:
Enquiries to: County Archivist
Direct tel: 0191 383 4211

Founded:
1961

Organisation type and purpose:
Local government body.
Record office.

Subject coverage:
Archives and records of the County of Durham.

Museum or gallery collection, archive, or library special collection:
Archives and records of the County of Durham held
All catalogues of these records are held in a database

Non-library collection catalogue:
All or part available online

Printed publications:
Durham Family History Gazetteer (1996)
Durham Places in the Mid-Nineteenth Century (1996)
Map of parish and chapelry boundaries circa 1800 (1983)
Streatlam and Gibside: The Bowes and Strathmore Families in County Durham (1984)
The Londonderry Papers: Catalogue of documents (1996)
Cemeteries in County Durham
Image of the Soldier
Durham Collieries
Handlists, subject guides and user guides

Publications list:
Available online and in print

Access to staff:
Contact by letter, by telephone, by fax, by e-mail, in person and via website. Appointment necessary.
Hours: Mon, Tue, Thu, 0845 to 1645; Wed, 0845 to 2000
Special comments: Fri, Sat, Sun and bank holidays closed

Access to building, collection or gallery:
Prior appointment required

Access for disabled people:
Parking provided, ramped entry, access to all public areas, toilet facilities

DURHAM HISTORICAL ENTERPRISES

3 Briardene, Margery Lane, Durham, DH1 4QU

Tel: 0191 386 1500
E-mail: dhent@dhent.fsnet.co.uk

continued overleaf

Website:
http://www.dhent.fsnet.co.uk

Enquiries:
Enquiries to: Proprietor

Founded:
1991

Organisation type and purpose:
Consultancy, research organisation, publishing house.

Subject coverage:
Durham local history, Durham family histories.

Printed publications:
Durham City 1851 Census

Access to staff:
Contact by letter, by telephone and by e-mail
Hours: Mon to Fri, 0900 to 1700

DURHAM LEARNING RESOURCES

Acronym or abbreviation: DLR

Libraries, Learning and Culture, Adult and Community Services, Sevenhills, Unit 1, Greenhills Industrial Estate, Spennymoor, Co Durham, DL16 6JB

Tel: 0191 370 6220
Fax: 01388 817099
E-mail: dlr@durham.gov.uk

Website:
http://www.durham.gov.uk/dlr

Enquiries:
Enquiries to: Manager
Direct e-mail: jeanette.stephenson@durham.gov.uk

Founded:
1991

Organisation type and purpose:
Local government body, public library.
To provide advice and information on all matters relating to the management of schools resource centres, and to provide a multimedia loans service to schools in support of the National Curriculum.

Subject coverage:
Information and advice in school resource centre management; information and training on study and library skills; knowledge of loans of museum objects, books, art and other media in support of the National Curriculum; sales of books to schools.

Non-library collection catalogue:
All or part available online

Access to staff:
Contact by letter, by telephone, by fax, by e-mail, in person and via website. Appointment necessary.
Hours: Mon to Thu, 0800 to 1730; Fri, 0800 to 1630

Access for disabled people:
Parking provided

DURHAM UNIVERSITY

Formal name: University of Durham

Mountjoy Research Centre, Stockton Road, Durham, DH1 3UR

Tel: 0191 334 4649
Fax: 0191 334 4634

Enquiries:
Enquiries to: Business Relations Manager
Direct e-mail: jonathon.lee@durham.ac.uk

Founded:
1832

Organisation type and purpose:
University department or institute, consultancy, research organisation.

Subject coverage:
All academic departments, particularly, mathematics / statistics; chemistry; physics; geological sciences; computing; business development; economics and finance; engineering;

manufacturing, environment. Particular expertise includes photonics, nanotechnology, materials, nuclear magnetic resonance, electronics.

Library catalogue:
All or part available online

DURHAM WILDLIFE TRUST

Bowlees Visitor Centre, Bowlees, Middleton in Teesdale, Co Durham, DL12 0XE

Tel: 01833 622292
Fax: 01833 622292

Enquiries:
Enquiries to: Manager
Other contacts: Education Officer tel no: 0191 548 0152

Founded:
1975

Formerly called:
Durham County Conservation Trust

Organisation type and purpose:
National organisation, membership association (membership is by subscription), service industry, voluntary organisation, registered charity (charity number 501038), suitable for ages: all.
Visitor Centre.
To highlight the natural history of Teesdale.

Subject coverage:
Wildlife and conservation in Teesdale and tourist information leaflets.

Museum or gallery collection, archive, or library special collection:
The Fitzhugh Library, previously held here, is now housed at Witham Hall in Barnard Castle

Printed publications:
The Natural History of Upper Teesdale
Durham Wildlife Trust Reserves Guide

Access to staff:
Contact by letter, by telephone and in person
Hours: 1 Apr to 31 Oct: daily, 1030 to 1700
Nov to Mar: weekends, 1030 to 1600
Special comments: Other times by prior appointment.

Access for disabled people:
Parking provided, ramped entry, level entry, access to all public areas
Special comments: Toilet facilities in main car park.

For membership details:
Rainton Meadows Site
    tel: 0191 584 3112; fax: 0191 584 3934; e-mail: durhamwt@cix.compulink.co.uk

Head Office and Visitor Centre:
Durham Wildlife Trust
    Rainton Meadows, Chilton Moor, Houghton-le-Spring, Tyne & Wear, DH4 6PU; tel: 0191 584 3112; fax: 0191 584 3934; e-mail: durhamwt@cix.compulink.co.uk

Visitor Centre at:
Low Barns
    Witton-le-Wear, Bishop Auckland, Co Durham, DL14 0AG; tel: 01388 488728; fax: 01388 488529

DVORÁK SOCIETY

The Secretary, 13 Church Lane, Knutton, Newcastle-under-Lyme, Staffordshire, ST5 6DU

E-mail: secretary@dvorak-society.org

Website:
http://www.dvorak-society.org

Enquiries:
Enquiries to: Membership Secretary
Direct tel: 01904 642407
Direct e-mail: membership@dvorak-society.org

Founded:
1974

Formerly called:
Dvorák Society of Great Britain (year of change 1986)

Organisation type and purpose:
Learned society (membership is by subscription, election or invitation), present number of members: 587, registered charity (charity number 267336), suitable for all ages.
The promotion of Czech and Slovak music.

Subject coverage:
History of Czech and Slovak music composers and musicians; contemporary Czech and Slovak music. Concert promotion, record reviews and regular listings of available recordings of Czech and Slovak music.

Museum or gallery collection, archive, or library special collection:
John Clapham Library Collection
Recorded music library

Non-library collection catalogue:
All or part available in-house

Library catalogue:
All or part available in-house

Printed publications:
Czech Music (journal, 2 times a year, £8.50 per copy)
Newsletter (quarterly, members)
Yearbook and Directory
Occasional series of specialist publications

Access to staff:
Contact by letter, by telephone, by e-mail and via website
Hours: Mon to Fri, 0900 to 1700

Access to building, collection or gallery:
No access other than to staff
Special comments: Members only

Links with:
British Czech and Slovak Association

DYLAN THOMAS SOCIETY OF GREAT BRITAIN, THE

Fernhill, 124 Chapel Street, Mumbles, Swansea, West Glamorgan, SA3 4NH

Tel: 01792 363875

Enquiries:
Enquiries to: Chair

Founded:
1977

Organisation type and purpose:
Learned society (membership is by subscription).

Subject coverage:
Life and works of Dylan Thomas.

Non-library collection catalogue:
All or part available in-house

Printed publications:
Dylan Thomas Remembered
The World I Breathe (talks and lectures to the Society)
The World Winding Home (essays)
I Sang in My Chains (essays and poems commemorating the 50th anniversary of Dylan's death, 2003)

Electronic and video publications:
Dylan Thomas Remembered (audio cassette)
Win Rees as Florence Thomas (Dylan's mother) (video)

DYNIX USERS GROUP

Acronym or abbreviation: DUG

Thompson Library, Staffordshire University, College Rd, Stoke on Trent, ST4 2XS

Tel: 01782 294755
Fax: 01782 295799
E-mail: i.haydock@staffs.ac.uk

Website:
http://www.dynixusers.org.uk

Enquiries:
Enquiries to: Honorary Secretary

Founded:
1995

Incorporates the former:
Horizon Users Group (year of change 2004)

Organisation type and purpose:
Membership association.

Subject coverage:
SirsiDynix Horizon and Dynix Classic library management system.

Access to staff:
Contact by letter, by telephone, by fax and by e-mail
Hours: Mon to Fri, 0900 to 1700

DYSLEXIA ACTION

Park House, Wick Road, Egham, Surrey, TW20 0HH

Tel: 01784 222300
Fax: 01784 222333
E-mail: info@dyslexiaaction.org.uk

Website:
http://www.dyslexiaaction.org.uk
Publications list

Enquiries:
Enquiries to: Information Officer

Founded:
1972

Organisation type and purpose:
Professional body, registered charity (charity number 268502).

Subject coverage:
Dyslexia: assessment of difficulties, teaching children and adults, teacher training, advisory service.

Non-library collection catalogue:
All or part available online

Printed publications:
As We See It (newsletter, information on dyslexia)
Leaflets and booklets including:
General Information
Developing Literacy for Study and Work (Bramley W, £38.50)
Developing Spoken Language Skills (Borwick C and Townend J, £35)
Understanding Dyslexia: a teacher's perspective (Townend J, £1.95)
Units of Sound (Bramley W)
Order printed publications from: DI Trading Limited at the same address

Publications list:
Available online and in print

Access to staff:
Contact by letter, by telephone, by e-mail and via website. Appointment necessary.
Hours: Mon to Fri, 0900 to 1700

Parent body:
Dyslexia Trust

DYSLEXIA INFORMATION CENTRE

Acronym or abbreviation: DIC

Hampton Grange, 21 Hampton Lane, Solihull, West Midlands, B91 2QJ

Tel: 0121 705 4547

Website:
http://www.dyslexiabooks.biz

Enquiries:
Enquiries to: Director
Direct e-mail: petercongdon@blueyonder.co.uk

Founded:
1978

Organisation type and purpose:
Suitable for ages: all, consultancy, publishing house.
The primary purpose of the Centre is to disseminate advice and information on the subject of specific learning difficulties/dyslexia.

Subject coverage:
Gifted children, dyslexic children and adults, left-handed children and adults.

Education services:
Assessment of children and adults suffering from dyslexia, dyspraxia, ADHD, Asperger Syndrome.

Printed publications:
Books, leaflets, teaching guides and workbooks for both children and professionals
Order printed publications from: GCIC, 21 Hampton Lane, Solihull, B91 2QJ

Publications list:
Available online and in print

Access to staff:
Contact by letter, by telephone, by e-mail, in person and via website. Appointment necessary.
Hours: Mon to Fri, 0900 to 1700

Connections with:
Gifted Children's Information Centre at the main address

DYSLEXIA SCOTLAND

Acronym or abbreviation: DS

Stirling Business Centre, Wellgreen, Stirling, FK8 2DZ

Tel: 01786 446650
Fax: 01786 471235
E-mail: info@dyslexiascotland.org.uk

Website:
http://www.dyslexiascotland.org.uk

Enquiries:
Enquiries to: Administrator
Direct e-mail: sharon@dyslexiascotland.org.uk

Founded:
1981

Organisation type and purpose:
National organisation, voluntary organisation, registered charity (charity number SCO 00951).

Subject coverage:
All aspects of dyslexia and its related difficulties.

Printed publications:
Information packs, made up to individual requirements
Leaflets
A wide range of titles on all aspects of dyslexia, educations and the family, etc

Publications list:
Available in print

Access to staff:
Contact by letter, by telephone, by fax and by e-mail. Appointment necessary.
Hours: Helpline: Mon to Fri, 1000 to 1600

Has:
a wide number of locations throughout Scotland

DYSTONIA SOCIETY

1st Floor, 89 Albert Embankment, London, SE1 7TP

Tel: 0845 458 6211
Fax: 0845 458 6311
E-mail: admin@dystonia.org.uk

Website:
http://www.dystonia.org.uk

Enquiries:
Enquiries to: Administrator
Direct tel: 0845 458 6322 (Helpline)

Direct e-mail: info@dystonia.org.uk

Founded:
1983

Organisation type and purpose:
Membership association (membership is by subscription), present number of members: 3000, registered charity (charity number 1062595).
The Dystonia Society exists to support people who are affected by any form of the neurological movement disorder known as dystonia, and their families and carers, through the promotion of awareness, research and support and information.

Subject coverage:
Neurological disorders known as the dystonias; methods of treatment and care; research to find a cure.

Information services:
Helpline, support and information for those affected by dystonia.

Services for disabled people:
Helpline, Support and Information for those affected by dystonia .

Printed publications:
Local groups newsletters (3/4 times a year, free to members)
National Newsletter (3 times a year, free to members)
Dystonia Explained
Cervical Dystonia
Blepharospasm
Botulinum Toxin Treatment
Oromandibular Dystonia
Laryngeal Dystonia
Writers Cramp
Myoclonus
Paroxysmal Dystonia
Deep Brain Stimulation
Hemifacial Spasm
Dystonia:Self Help Techniques
Dystonia – Your Questions Answered
Information pack (free to enquirers)
Various factsheets such as access to benefits, driving and dystonia etc

Electronic and video publications:
See current publications list

Publications list:
Available online and in print

Access to staff:
Contact by letter, by telephone, by fax, by e-mail, in person and via website. Appointment necessary.
Hours: Mon to Fri, 0900 to 1700; Answerphone operates at other times
Access to Helpline Mon to Fri, 1000 to 1600

Access to building, collection or gallery:
Via main reception 24 hours

Links with:
Dystonia Medical Research Foundation, USA
tel: + 1 312 755 0198; website: www.dystonia -foundation.org
Parkinson's Disease Society
tel: 020 7931 8080; fax: 020 7233 5373

E F BENSON SOCIETY

The Old Coach House, High Street, Rye, East Sussex, TN31 7JF

Tel: 01797 223114
E-mail: oakleyites@yahoo.co.uk

Website:
http://www.efbensonsociety.org
Description of the Society's activities, publications and promotions.

Enquiries:
Enquiries to: Secretary

Founded:
1985

Organisation type and purpose:
Literary society.

continued overleaf

Subject coverage:
E F Benson and the Benson Family.

Information services:
Information about the Benson family and E F Benson

Education services:
Talks and exhibitions can be arranged

Printed publications:
Publications available for purchase
Order printed publications from: The Secretary

Publications list:
Available in print

Access to staff:
Contact by letter, by telephone, by e-mail and via website. Appointment necessary. Access for members only.
Hours: Sun to Sat, 0900 to 1700

E-AMRA.COM

38 Holly Walk, Leamington Spa, Warwickshire, CV32 4LY

Tel: 01926 330935
Fax: 01926 330935
E-mail: hq@e-amra.com

Website:
http://www.e-amra.com
Membership information, hyperlink to members. Aims, scope of the association, members list, application forum and details.
http://www.amra-intl.org
AMRA(US).

Enquiries:
Enquiries to: Secretary

Founded:
1997

Formerly called:
European Automatic Meter Reading Association (Euroamra), United Kingdom Automatic Meter Recalling Association (UKAMRA) (year of change 2000)

Organisation type and purpose:
International organisation, membership association (membership is by subscription), present number of members: 74.
A European association.
Forum to address automatic meter reading issues, to foster interest, to educate and promote AMR technology, to monitor progress in technologies through seminars, to encourage communication between utilities and their customers.

Subject coverage:
Automatic meter reading technology, the collection of consumption data from customers' utility meters over telecommunications, radio, power-line and other links.

Printed publications:
Ukamra Newsletter

Publications list:
Available in print

Access to staff:
Contact by letter, by telephone, by fax, by e-mail and via website
Hours: Mon to Fri, 0900 to 1700

Links with:
AMRA(US)

E2V TECHNOLOGIES (UK) LTD

Waterhouse Lane, Chelmsford, Essex, CM1 2QU

Tel: 01245 493493 ext 3320
Fax: 01245 45341
E-mail: doug.spencer@e2v.com

Website:
http://www.e2v.com
Basic company information, product information.

Enquiries:
Enquiries to: Information Officer

Founded:
1946

Organisation type and purpose:
Manufacturing industry.

Subject coverage:
Microwave technology, CCD & CMOS sensors, magnetrons, thyratrons, spark gaps, modulators and power supplies.

Museum or gallery collection, archive, or library special collection:
Company library

Non-library collection catalogue:
All or part available in-house

Library catalogue:
All or part available in-house

Access to staff:
Contact by telephone and by e-mail. Appointment necessary.
Hours: Mon to Fri, 0800 to 1600

Access to building, collection or gallery:
Prior appointment required

Access for disabled people:
Parking provided, ramped entry

EALING LIBRARY AND INFORMATION SERVICE

Ealing Central Library, 103 Ealing Broadway Centre, London, W5 5JY

Tel: 020 8567 3656
Fax: 020 8840 2351
E-mail: collierm@ealing.gov.uk

Website:
http://www.ealing.gov.uk/leisure/libraries

Enquiries:
Enquiries to: Manager

Founded:
1965

Organisation type and purpose:
Local government body, public library.

Museum or gallery collection, archive, or library special collection:
Selborne Society Library (Gilbert White's work)

Non-library collection catalogue:
All or part available in-house

Printed publications:
Various publications on the local history of the London Borough of Ealing

Access for disabled people:
Level entry, access to all public areas

Branch libraries:
Acton, Southall, Greenford and West Ealing and seven Community Libraries

EALING, HAMMERSMITH AND WEST LONDON COLLEGE

Acronym or abbreviation: EHWLC

Learning Centre, Gliddon Road, London, W14 9BL

Tel: 0800 980 2175
Fax: 020 8741 2491

Website:
http://www.wlc.ac.uk

Enquiries:
Enquiries to: Librarian
Direct tel: 020 7565 1244

Organisation type and purpose:
College of further education.

Subject coverage:
Business studies, general education. English for speakers of other languages

Library catalogue:
All or part available online

Access to staff:
Contact by letter and by telephone
Hours: Mon to Thu, 0900 to 2030; Fri, 0900 to 1600; Sat, 1000 to 1400

Also at:
Acton and West London College
Gunnersbury Lane, Acton, London, W3 8UX; tel: 0800 980 2175
Ealing and West London College
The Green, Ealing, W5 5EW; tel: 0800 980 2175
Southall and West London College
Beaconsfield Road, Southall, Middlesex, UB1 1DP; tel: 0800 980 2175

EARLY EDUCATION

Formal name: British Association for Early Childhood Education

136 Cavell Street, London, E1 2JA

Tel: 020 7539 5400
Fax: 020 7539 5409
E-mail: office@early-education.org.uk

Website:
http://www.early-education.org.uk
Publications.

Enquiries:
Enquiries to: Chief Executive

Founded:
1923

Formerly called:
Nursery Schools Association (year of change 1974)

Organisation type and purpose:
Membership association (membership is by subscription), present number of members: 7000, voluntary organisation, registered charity (charity number 313082), suitable for ages: 0 to 8.
Promotes the right of all children to an education of the highest quality. It provides a multi-disciplinary network of support for all concerned with the education and care of young children.

Subject coverage:
Information regarding the care and early childhood education of children of up to 8 years.

Museum or gallery collection, archive, or library special collection:
Books concerning early childhood education

Library catalogue:
All or part available in-house

Printed publications:
Order printed publications from: Website

Publications list:
Available online and in print

Access to staff:
Contact by letter, by telephone, by fax and by e-mail. Appointment necessary.
Hours: Mon to Fri, 0900 to 1700

Access to building, collection or gallery:
Prior appointment required
Hours: Mon to Fri, 0900 to 1700

Access for disabled people:
Access to all public areas, toilet facilities
Special comments: Four steps to entrance and no ramp to front door.

Member of:
National Children's Bureau
National Council for Voluntary Organisations
Women's National Commission
World Organization for Early Childhood Education

EARLY ENGLISH TEXT SOCIETY

Acronym or abbreviation: EETS

Lady Margaret Hall, Oxford, OX2 6QA

Website:
http://www.eets.org.uk
General.
http://www.boydell.co.uk/eets.htm
Publications list updated monthly.

Enquiries:
Enquiries to: Executive Secretary
Direct e-mail: vincent.gillespie@ell.ox.ac.uk

Founded:
1864

Organisation type and purpose:
Learned society (membership is by subscription), present number of members: 1261.

Subject coverage:
Publications of English texts earlier than 1558; medieval studies, especially the history of English language and literature, medieval theology and sociology, medieval history.

Printed publications:
About 400 texts with at least one new one each year
Order printed publications from: for publications from 2001, Oxford University Press
Saxon Way West, Corby, Northamptonshire, NN18 9ES
for publications up to 2001, Boydell & Brewer
PO Box 9, Woodbridge, Suffolk, IP12 3DF

Publications list:
Available online and in print

Access to staff:
Contact by letter and by e-mail
Hours: Mon to Fri, 0900 to 1700

EARLY MUSIC NETWORK

Acronym or abbreviation: EMN

31 Abdale Road, London, W12 7ER

Founded:
1972

Formerly called:
Early Music Centre (EMC) (year of change 1996)

EARTH SCIENCE TEACHERS' ASSOCIATION

Acronym or abbreviation: ESTA

c/o The Geological Society, Burlington House, Piccadilly, London, W1V 0JU

Tel: 01709 300600
Fax: 01709 300601
E-mail: dawn.windley@thomroth.ac.uk

Website:
http://www.esta-uk.org

Enquiries:
Enquiries to: Chairman

Founded:
1967

Organisation type and purpose:
Membership association (membership is by subscription), present number of members: 700, voluntary organisation, registered charity (charity number 1005331).
To encourage and support the teaching of earth sciences at all levels, whether as a single subject or as part of science or geography courses.

Subject coverage:
Geology, education, earth science.

Printed publications:
Science of the Earth Packs (Key Stage 3 and Key Stage 4)
Teaching Earth Sciences (journal, quarterly)

Access to staff:
Contact by letter, by telephone, by fax, by e-mail and via website
Hours: Mon to Fri, 0900 to 1700

Also at:
Chairman, Earth Science Teachers' Association
Thomas Rotherham College, Moorgate Road, Rotherham, South Yorkshire, S60 2BE; tel: 01709 300600; fax: 01709 300601; e-mail: dawn .windley@thomroth.ac.uk

Constituent bodies:
8 Committees

EARTHKIND

Town Quay, Poole, Dorset, BH15 1HJ

Tel: 01202 682344
Fax: 01202 682366
E-mail: info@earthkind.org.uk

Website:
http://www.earthkind-uk.web

Enquiries:
Enquiries to: Administrator
Other contacts: Press and PR Officer

Founded:
1955

Formerly called:
Crusade against Cruelty to all Animals

Organisation type and purpose:
Membership association (membership is by election or invitation), voluntary organisation, registered charity (charity number 260708), suitable for ages: 4–18.
Earthkind is one of the oldest UK charities working to protect animals and the environment through humane education, campaigns and rescue. We focus on marine wildlife rescue, conservation and education.

Subject coverage:
Animal welfare, environmental issues and humane education.

Printed publications:
The Living World (magazine, quarterly)
Newslog (Earthkind's Ocean Defender ship's magazine)
Campaign updates
Annual report

Access to staff:
Contact by letter, by telephone, by fax, by e-mail and in person
Hours: Mon to Fri, 0900 to 1700

Access for disabled people:
Level entry

EAST ANGLIAN ACADEMY OF TRANSCENDENTAL MEDITATION

Acronym or abbreviation: EAATM

Old Rectory Road, Badingham, Woodbridge, Suffolk, IP13 8LA

Tel: 01728 638222
Fax: 01728 638377
E-mail: badingham_academy@compuserve.com

Enquiries:
Enquiries to: Administrator

Founded:
1978

Formerly called:
Spiritual Regeneration Movement (SRM) (year of change 1978)

Organisation type and purpose:
Registered charity (charity number 204025).
Teaching the technique of Transcendental Meditation.

Subject coverage:
Information on the technique of Transcendental Meditation and Maharishi Ayur-Veda Health System.

Printed publications:
Pamphlets and Video (free)
Books (available to purchase)

Electronic and video publications:
Various tapes, CD-ROMs, videos

Publications list:
Available in print

Access to staff:
Contact by letter, by telephone, by fax and by e-mail
Hours: Sun to Sat, 1000 to 1630

Access to building, collection or gallery:
Prior appointment required

Access for disabled people:
Parking provided, ramped entry, level entry, toilet facilities

Affiliated to:
Maharishi Foundation
National Communications Office, Beacon House, Willow Walk, Skelmersdale, Lincolnshire, WN8 6UR; tel: 08705 143733; fax: 01695 727499; e-mail: tminfo@maharishi.org.uk

EAST ASIAN HISTORY OF SCIENCE LIBRARY

8 Sylvester Road, Cambridge, CB3 9AF

Tel: 01223 311545
Fax: 01223 362703
E-mail: jm10019@cam.ac.uk

Website:
http://www.nri.org.uk/library.html
Introduction to the Library and how to access the catalogue.

Enquiries:
Enquiries to: Librarian

Founded:
1976

Organisation type and purpose:
Registered charity.
Private research institute and library.

Subject coverage:
History of traditional Chinese science, technology and medicine.

Museum or gallery collection, archive, or library special collection:
Based on personal collection of Dr Joseph Needham

Non-library collection catalogue:
All or part available online and in-house

Library catalogue:
All or part available online

Printed publications:
Science and Civilization in China (J. Needham et al, Cambridge, Cambridge University Press)

Access to staff:
Contact by letter, by telephone, by fax, by e-mail and via website. Appointment necessary.
Hours: Mon to Fri, 0900 to 1700

Access for disabled people:
Parking provided, level entry, access to all public areas, toilet facilities

EAST AYRSHIRE COUNCIL

Council Headquarters, London Road, Kilmarnock, Ayrshire, KA3 7BU

Tel: 01563 576000
Fax: 01563 576500
E-mail: the.council@east-ayrshire.gov.uk

Website:
http://www.east-ayrshire.gov.uk

Enquiries:
Enquiries to: Head of Public Relations and Marketing
Direct tel: 01563 576165
Direct fax: 01563 576525

Founded:
1996

continued overleaf

Formerly called:
Cumnock and Doon Valley District Council,
Kilmarnock and London District Council

Formerly part of:
Strathclyde Regional Council

Organisation type and purpose:
Local government body.
Public relations and marketing.

Subject coverage:
Services and amenities; corporate services,
education, environmental services, finance,
housing, legal services, personnel services,
planning development and tourism, property and
technical services, roads and transportation, social
services, council tax and other payments,
registration of births, deaths and marriages.

Access to staff:
Contact by letter, by telephone, by fax, by e-mail
and via website
Hours: Mon to Thu, 0900 to 1700; Fri, 0900 to 1600

EAST AYRSHIRE LIBRARY REGISTRATION AND INFORMATION SERVICES

Acronym or abbreviation: EALRIS

Headquarters (North), Dick Institute, 14 Elmbank
Avenue, Kilmarnock, Ayrshire, KA1 3BU

Tel: 01563 554300
Fax: 01563 554311
E-mail: libraries@east-ayrshire.gov.uk

Website:
http://www.east-ayrshire.gov.uk/comleilib
Online catalogue

Enquiries:
Enquiries to: Library, Registration and Information
Services Manager
Direct e-mail: gerald.cairns@east-ayrshire.gov.uk

Founded:
1901

Created by the merger of:
Cumnock and Doon Valley District Libraries,
Kilmarnock and Loudoun District Libraries (year
of change 1996)

Formerly called:
East Ayrshire Library and Information Services
(EALIS)

Organisation type and purpose:
Local government body, public library.

Subject coverage:
General, Robert Burns, Ayrshire history and place
names, genealogy, archaeological and historical
sites, remains and monuments in South-West
Scotland.

Museum or gallery collection, archive, or library special collection:
Braidwood Collection of incunabula and early
printed books
Hutton Collection of early printed Bibles
Papers of the Boyd Family, the Earls of Kilmarnock
Robert Burns Collection

Library catalogue:
All or part available online and in-house

Printed publications:
A range of publications on local history and places:
Greetings from Kilmarnock (F. Beattie)
Pictorial History of Newmilns (J. Mair)
Old Catrine and Sorn (R. Wilson)
The Cumnock Pottery (G. Quail)
The Ayrshire Book of Burns Lore (A. M. Boyle)

Publications list:
Available online and in print

Access to staff:
Contact by letter, by telephone, by fax, by e-mail,
in person and via website

Access to building, collection or gallery:
Hours: Mon, Tue, Thu and Fri, 0900 to 2000; Wed,
1000 to 1700; Sat, 0900 to 1700;

other libraries vary, telephone for times

Access for disabled people:
Parking provided, ramped entry, access to all
public areas, toilet facilities

Also at:
Council Offices
Library Headquarters (South), Lugar, Cumnock,
KA18 3JQ; tel: 01563 555459; e-mail: libraries@
east-ayrshire.gov.uk

Branch libraries:
Auchinleck
Community Centre, Well Road, Auchinleck,
KA18 2LA; tel: 01209 422829; e-mail: libraries@
east-ayrshire.gov.uk
Bellfield
79 Whatriggs Road, Kilmarnock, KA1 3RB; tel:
01563 534266; e-mail: libraries@east-ayrshire.gov
.uk
Catrine
A. M. Brown Institute, Catrine, KA5 6RT; tel:
01290 551717; e-mail: libraries@east-ayrshire.gov
.uk
Crosshouse
11–13 Gatehead Road, Crosshouse, KA2 0HN;
tel: 01563 573640; e-mail: libraries@east-ayrshire
.gov.uk
Cumnock
25–27 Ayr Road, Cumnock, KA18 1EB; tel: 01290
422804; e-mail: libraries@east-ayrshire.gov.uk
Dalmellington
Townhead, Dalmellington, KA6 7QZ; tel: 01292
550159; e-mail: libraries@east-ayrshire.gov.uk
Dalrymple
Barbieston Road, Dalrymple, KA6 6DZ; tel:
01292 560511; e-mail: libraries@east-ayrshire.gov
.uk
Darvel
Town Hall, West Main Street, Dravel, KA17 0AQ;
tel: 01560 322754; e-mail: libraries@east-ayrshire
.gov.uk
Drongan
Mill O'Shield Road, Drongan, KA6 7AY; tel:
01292 591718; e-mail: libraries@east-ayrshire.gov
.uk
Galston
Henrietta Street, Galston, KA4 8HQ; tel: 01563
821994; e-mail: libraries@east-ayrshire.gov.uk
Hurlford
Blair Road, Hurlford, KA1 5BN; tel: 01563
539899; e-mail: libraries@east-ayrshire.gov.uk
Kilmaurs
Irvine Road, Kilmaurs, KA3 2RJ; tel: 01563
539895; e-mail: libraries@east-ayrshire.gov.uk
Mauchline
2 The Cross, Mauchline, KA5 5DA; tel: 01290
550824; e-mail: libraries@east-ayrshire.gov.uk
Muirkirk
Burns Avenue, Muirkirk, KA18 3RQ; tel: 01290
661505; e-mail: libraries@east-ayrshire.gov.uk
New Cumnock
Community Centre, The Castle, New Cumnock,
KA18 4AH; tel: 01290 338710; e-mail: libraries@
east-ayrhire.gov.uk
Newmilns
Craigview Road, Newmilns, KA16 9DQ; tel:
01560 322890; e-mail: libraries@east-ayrshire.gov
.uk
Ochiltree
Main Street, Ochiltree, KA18 2PE; tel: 01290
700425; e-mail: libraries@east-ayrshire.gov.uk
Patna
Doonside Avenue, Patna, KA6 7LX; tel: 01292
531538; e-mail: libraries@east-ayrshire.gov.uk
Stewarton
Cunningham Institute, Stewarton, KA3 5AB; tel:
01560 484385; e-mail: libraries@east-ayrshire.gov
.uk

Constituent bodies:
District History Centre and Baird Institute
Museum
3 Lugar Street, Cumnock, KA18 1AD; tel: 01290
421701; e-mail: libraries@east-ayrshire.gov.uk

Parent body:
East Ayrshire Council (EAC)
Council HQ, London Road, Kilmarnock, KA1
5BU; tel: 01563 57600; fax: 01563 576500;
website: www.east-ayrshire.gov.uk

EAST CAMBRIDGESHIRE DISTRICT COUNCIL

Acronym or abbreviation: ECDC

The Grange, Nutholt Lane, Ely, Cambridgeshire,
CB7 4PL

Tel: 01353 665555
Fax: 01353 665240
E-mail: info@eastcambs.gov.uk

Website:
http://www.eastcambs.gov.uk

Enquiries:
Enquiries to: Chief Executive
Other contacts: Press and PR Officer for corporate
communication.

Founded:
1974

Organisation type and purpose:
Local government body.

Subject coverage:
Many subjects relating to East Cambridgeshire
district, including Ely, Soham and Littleport.
Information about projects both economic and
community based, new initiatives and all aspects
of tourism.

Non-library collection catalogue:
All or part available online

Printed publications:
ECDC (district newsletter, 2 times a year, free)

Access to staff:
Contact by letter, by telephone, by fax and by e-
mail. Appointment necessary.
Hours: Mon to Thu, 0845 to 1700; Fri, 0845 to 1630

Access for disabled people:
Level entry, toilet facilities

EAST DORSET DISTRICT COUNCIL

Acronym or abbreviation: EDDC

Council Offices, Furzehill, Wimborne, Dorset,
BH21 4HN

Tel: 01202 886201
Fax: 01202 841390

Website:
http://www.eastdorset.gov.uk/tourism
Tourism in East Dorset.
http://www.eastdorset.gov.uk
All services.

Enquiries:
Enquiries to: Public Relations Manager
Direct tel: ext 2289
Direct e-mail: chief.exec@eastdorset.gov.uk

Organisation type and purpose:
Local government body.

Subject coverage:
Local Government, elections and elected members,
electoral roll, environmental health, planning,
Council Tax and Housing Benefit, recycling and
refuse collection, tourism, local plan and grants.

Access for disabled people:
Parking provided, ramped entry, toilet facilities

EAST DUNBARTONSHIRE LIBRARIES

Library Headquarters, Wm Patrick Library, 2–4
West High Street, Kirkintilloch, Glasgow, G66 1AD

Tel: 0141 775 4501
Fax: 0141 776 0408

E-mail: libraries@eastdunbarton.gov.uk

Enquiries:
Enquiries to: Information and Lifelong Learning
Manager
Direct e-mail: elizabeth.brown@eastdunbarton.gov
.uk

Founded:
1996

Created by the merger of:
Bearsden and Milngavie District Libraries,
Strathkelvin District Libraries

Organisation type and purpose:
Local government body, public library.

Subject coverage:
General; local history of Glasgow, Stirlingshire and
Dunbartonshire.
Local information of all kinds, relating to the
Kirkintilloch area especially the communities of
Kirkintilloch, Bishopbriggs, Lenzie, Lennoxtown,
Milton-of-Campsie. Reference collection, European
PIR, Community information, Scottish Parliament
Partner Library.

**Museum or gallery collection, archive, or library
special collection:**
Archives of East Dunbartonshire Council and its
predecessor authorities, including the former
Burghs of Kirkintilloch, Milngavie, Bearsden and
Bishopbriggs, the parishes of Baldernock,
Cadder, Campsie, Kirkintilloch and New
Kilpatrick, and Strathkelvin District Council and
Bearsden and Milngavie District Council; also
deposited collections of businesses, organisations
and individuals within East Dunbartonshire,
including J. F. McEwan Transport History
Collection, Lion Foundry Co Ltd, West of
Scotland Football Club, Kirkintilloch and
Neighbourhood Friendly Funeral and Mortcloth
Society, Glasgow Garden Suburb Tenants Ltd.

Library catalogue:
All or part available in-house

Printed publications:
Local publications list (33 titles)

Publications list:
Available in print

Access to staff:
Contact by letter, by telephone, by fax, by e-mail
and in person
Hours: Mon to Fri, 0900 to 1700

Access to building, collection or gallery:
No prior appointment required
Hours: Bishopbriggs, Brookwood, Milngavie,
William Patrick Libraries: Mon to Thu, 1000 to
2000; Fri and Sat, 1000 to 1700
Lennoxtown, Lenzie, Craighead, Westerton
Libraries: Mon and Thu, 1300 to 2000; Tue, Wed
and Fri, 1000 to 1700

Access for disabled people:
Parking provided, ramped entry, level entry, access
to all public areas, toilet facilities

Branch libraries:
Bishopbriggs Library
tel: 0141 772 4513; fax: 0141 762 5363
Brookwood Library, Bearsden
166 Drymen Road, Bearsden, Glasgow, G61 3RJ;
tel: 0141 943 0121; fax: 0141 943 0200
Lennoxtown Library
tel: 01360 311436
Lenzie Library
tel: 0141 776 3021
Milngavie Library
tel: 0141 956 2776
Milton of Campsie Library
tel: 01360 311925
Westerton Library
tel: 0141 943 0780
William Patrick Library
tel: 0141 775 4524

EAST DURHAM AND HOUGHALL COMMUNITY COLLEGE

Acronym or abbreviation: EDHCC

Houghall Centre, Durham, DH1 3SG

Tel: 0191 3754710 / 3754756
Fax: 0191 3860419
E-mail: enquiry@edhcc.ac.uk

Website:
http://www.edhcc.ac.uk

Enquiries:
Enquiries to: Learning Services Manager

Founded:
June 1999

Formed by the merger of:
Durham College of Agriculture and Horticulture,
East Durham Community College (year of change
1999)

Formerly called:
Houghall College

Organisation type and purpose:
Vocational, further and higher education.

Subject coverage:
Agriculture, horticulture, equestrianism,
arboriculture, environmental management, small
animal care.

Library catalogue:
All or part available in-house

Access to staff:
Contact by letter, by telephone, by fax and by e-
mail
Hours: Mon to Thu, 0900 to 2000; Fri, 0900 to 1600

Access to building, collection or gallery:
No access other than to staff

Access for disabled people:
Parking provided, ramped entry, toilet facilities

EAST ENGLAND ARTS

Eden House, 48–49 Bateman Street, Cambridge,
CB2 1LR

Tel: 01223 454400\ Minicom no. 01223 306893
Fax: 0870 242 1271
E-mail: info@eearts.co.uk

Website:
http://www.eastenglandarts.co.uk
http://www.axisartists.org.uk

Enquiries:
Enquiries to: Helpdesk

Formed with:
Arts Council of England and the other Regional
Arts Boards (year of change 2002)

Formerly called:
Eastern Arts Board

Organisation type and purpose:
Service industry, registered charity (charity
number 1036733).
On 1st April 2002, East England Arts joined with
the Arts Council of England and the other regional
arts boards to form a single development
organisation for the arts.
East England Arts is the government arts and
culture development agency for the East of
England.

Subject coverage:
Arts funding including National Lottery, design,
dance, mime and new circus, theatre and puppetry,
literature, music, new media, visual arts,
regeneration, audience development.

Printed publications:
Annual Report
Eye (newsletter, 6 times a year)
Public Art Galleries & Studio Spaces List
Private Art Galleries List
Regional Press List
Venues List

Publications list:
Available in print

Access to staff:
Contact by letter, by telephone, by fax, by e-mail
and via website
Hours: Mon to Fri, 0900 to 1700

Access to building, collection or gallery:
Prior appointment required
Hours: Mon to Fri, 0900 to 1700

Access for disabled people:
Parking provided, ramped entry, access to all
public areas, toilet facilities. Lift/elevator access.

EAST HAMPSHIRE DISTRICT COUNCIL

Acronym or abbreviation: EHDC

Penns Place, Petersfield, Hampshire, GU31 4EX

Tel: 01730 266551; 01730 234103 (minicom)
Fax: 01730 267760
E-mail: info@easthants.gov.uk

Website:
http://www.easthants.gov.uk

Enquiries:
Enquiries to: Chief Executive

Founded:
1974

Organisation type and purpose:
Local government body.

Subject coverage:
East Hampshire demographic and environmental
information, council service information: planning,
council tax, housing, refuse collection and
recycling, benefits, tourism and leisure, grants for
community groups, animal welfare, countryside,
environmental health, business information and
advice, and local democracy.

Printed publications:
Partners Magazine

Publications list:
Available online and in print

Access to staff:
Contact by letter, by telephone, by fax, by e-mail,
in person and via website
Hours: Mon to Fri, 0900 to 1700

Access to building, collection or gallery:
No prior appointment required

Access for disabled people:
Parking provided, ramped entry

EAST HERTFORDSHIRE DISTRICT COUNCIL

Acronym or abbreviation: EHDC

Wallfields, Pegs Lane, Hertford, SG13 8EQ

Tel: 01279 655261\ Minicom no. 01279 658512
Fax: 01992 552280
E-mail: ce@ehdc.gov.uk

Website:
http://www.eastherts.gov.uk
Council services and news.

Enquiries:
Enquiries to: Public Relations Manager
Direct tel: 01279 655261 ext 449
Direct fax: 01992 505710
Other contacts: Chief Executive for complaints.

Founded:
1974

Organisation type and purpose:
Local government body.

Subject coverage:
Local government services.

Access to staff:
Contact by letter, by telephone, by fax and by e-
mail. Appointment necessary.

continued overleaf

Hours: Mon to Fri, 0830 to 1700

Other addresses:
Council Offices
The Causeway, Bishop's Stortford, Hertfordshire, CM23 2EN; tel: 01279 655261; e-mail: ce@ehdc.gov.uk

EAST HERTS ARCHAEOLOGICAL SOCIETY

Acronym or abbreviation: EHAS

11 St. Leonard's Close, Bengeo, Hertoford, Hertfordshire, SG14 3LL

Tel: 01992 423433

Enquiries:
Enquiries to: Honorary Secretary

Founded:
1898

Organisation type and purpose:
Learned society (membership is by subscription), present number of members: 100, registered charity (charity number 257254).

Subject coverage:
Archaeological, architectural information, local history in Eastern Hertfordshire.

Library catalogue:
All or part available in-house

Printed publications:
Annual Newsletter
A Century of Archaeology in East Herts
Hertfordshire Archaeology and History (published jointly with the St Albans Archaeological Society)

Access to staff:
Contact by letter and by telephone
Hours: Mon to Fri, 0900 to 1700
Special comments: Membership: adult £10, family £12 a year.

Access to building, collection or gallery:
No prior appointment required

Member of:
Council for British Archaeology
Hertfordshire Archaeological Council
Hertfordshire Archaeological Trust

EAST KENT ARCHIVES CENTRE

Acronym or abbreviation: EKAC

Enterprise Zone, Honeywood Road, Whitfield, Dover, Kent, CT16 3EH

Tel: 01304 829306
Fax: 01304 820783
E-mail: eastkentarchives@kent.gov.uk

Website:
http://www.kent.gov.uk/leisure-and-culture/archives-and-local-history/archive-centres/east-kent-archives-centre.htm

Enquiries:
Enquiries to: Manager

Founded:
2000

Formerly called:
South East Area Office, Folkestone Library (year of change 1999); Thanet Branch Archives, Ramsgate Library (year of change 1999)

Organisation type and purpose:
Local government body.
Archive service.

Subject coverage:
Archives relating to Thanet, Dover and Shepway District Council areas, except Church of England and civil registration records.

Museum or gallery collection, archive, or library special collection:
Local government, hospital, family and estate and nonconformist records

Business, schools, shipping registers

Non-library collection catalogue:
All or part available online and in-house

Access to staff:
Contact by letter, by telephone, by e-mail and in person. Appointment necessary.
Hours: Tue, Wed, Thu, 0900 to 1700

Access for disabled people:
Free parking provided, ramped entry, access to all public areas including toilet facilities

Links with:
Kent County Council

Other centre:
Centre for Kentish Studies (CKS)
Sessions House, County Hall, Maidstone, ME14 1XQ; tel: 01622 694363; e-mail: archives@kent.gov.uk

EAST LANCASHIRE CHAMBER OF INDUSTRY AND COMMERCE

Red Rose Court, Clayton Business Park, Clayton-le-Moors, Accrington, Lancashire, BB5 5JR

Tel: 01254 356400
Fax: 01254 388900
E-mail: info@chamberelancs.co.uk

Website:
http://www.chamberelancs.co.uk
http://www.chamberinternet.co.uk

Enquiries:
Enquiries to: Chief Executive

Formerly called:
Blackburn Chamber of Commerce and Industry

Organisation type and purpose:
Membership association.
Chamber of Commerce.

Subject coverage:
Export and import information; general business advice; business expansion; sources of finance and grants.

Printed publications:
Business View (6 times a year)
Newsletter (6 times a year)

EAST LOTHIAN ANTIQUARIAN AND FIELD NATURALISTS SOCIETY

Acronym or abbreviation: ELFNSoc

Inchgarth, East Links, Dunbar, East Lothian, EH42 1LT

Tel: 01368 863335
E-mail: s.bunyan@yahoo.co.uk

Website:
http://eastlothianantiquarians.org.uk/site

Enquiries:
Enquiries to: President
Other contacts: The Editor, for publications and transactions.

Founded:
1924

Organisation type and purpose:
Learned society (membership is by subscription), present number of members: c. 200, voluntary organisation. Stimulates and develops knowledge and awareness of the history and natural history of East Lothian.

Subject coverage:
East Lothian antiquities, local architecture, history and natural history, flora and fauna.

Museum or gallery collection, archive, or library special collection:
Local history books
Pictures of local interest (in the care of East Lothian Council Library and Museums Service)
Society's Transactions

Printed publications:
Dunbar Parish Church (Donaldson and Bunyan, supplement))
Society Transactions
Order printed publications from: S. A. Bunyan

Publications list:
Available in print

Access to staff:
Contact by letter, by telephone and by e-mail
Hours: Mon to Fri, 0900 to 1700
Special comments: Telephone calls may only get through to an answerphone.

EAST LOTHIAN COUNCIL

John Muir House, Haddington, East Lothian, EH41 3HA

Tel: 01620 827827
Fax: 01620 827888

Website:
http://www.eastlothian.gov.uk

Enquiries:
Enquiries to: Corporate Communications Manager
Direct tel: 01620 827655
Direct fax: 01620 827442

Founded:
1996

Formerly called:
East Lothian District Council, Lothian Regional Council

Organisation type and purpose:
Local government body.

Subject coverage:
All matters relating to local government; law and administration, policy and performance, property, personnel, finance, information technology, community services, building design direct, mechanised services, leisure and amenity services, libraries, education, social services and housing, environmental services.

Printed publications:
East Lothian Guide
Public Performance Report
A-Z of Council Services

Access to staff:
Contact by letter, by telephone, by fax and by e-mail
Hours: Mon to Thu, 0900 to 1700; Fri, 0900 to 1600

Access for disabled people:
Parking provided, level entry, toilet facilities

EAST LOTHIAN COUNCIL LIBRARY SERVICE

Library and Museum Headquarters, Dunbar Road, Haddington, East Lothian, EH41 3PJ

Tel: 01620 828200
Fax: 01620 828201
E-mail: jstevenson@eastlothian.gov.uk

Website:
http://www.eastlothian.gov.uk

Enquiries:
Enquiries to: Librarian
Other contacts: smillar@eastlothian.gov.uk (for local and family history enquiries)

Founded:
1996

Organisation type and purpose:
Local government body, public library.

Subject coverage:
General; local history and genealogy.

Museum or gallery collection, archive, or library special collection:
Library of the East Lothian Antiquarian and Field Naturalists Society, Latto Collection on Musselburgh, Gordon photograph collection.

Local history collection (at the Local History Centre, Haddington Library, Newtonport, Haddington)

Non-library collection catalogue:
All or part available online

Library catalogue:
All or part available online

Printed publications:
Guides to services

Electronic and video publications:
Haddington: A place for everything (video)
Battle of Prestonpans (video)
Another Tyne, Another Place (video)
East Lothian at War (CD-ROM)

Publications list:
Available online and in print

Access to staff:
Contact by letter, by telephone, by fax, by e-mail and in person
Hours: Mon to Fri, 0900 to 1700

Access for disabled people:
Parking provided, level entry, access to public areas, toilet facilities, except Local History Centre. Please contact 01620 823307 for details.

EAST MALLING RESEARCH

Acronym or abbreviation: EMR

New Road, East Malling, Kent, ME19 6BJ

Tel: 01732 843833
Fax: 01732 849067
E-mail: enquiries@emr.ac.uk

Website:
http://www.eastmallingresearch.com

Enquiries:
Enquiries to: Information Officer

Founded:
1913

Organisation type and purpose:
Independent company, professional body, registered charity (charity number 211581), research organisation.
Research on fruit and other perennial crops including hardy nursery stock, farm woodland and hops.

Subject coverage:
Horticulture, particularly temperate fruit culture, forestry, woody ornamentals, hops, related plant science, particularly plant physiology, plant pathology, entomology, biochemistry, IPDM, postharvest storage and quality of horticultural crops.

Museum or gallery collection, archive, or library special collection:
Cherry gene database
European apple inventory
Historical books on fruit breeding and horticulture
Index of graft transmittable diseases

Non-library collection catalogue:
All or part available in-house

Library catalogue:
All or part available in-house

Access to staff:
Contact by telephone and by e-mail. Appointment necessary.
Hours: Mon to Fri, 0900 to 1700

Access to building, collection or gallery:
Prior appointment required
Special comments: Open to members of the East Malling Research Association.

EAST MIDLANDS MUSEUMS SERVICE

Acronym or abbreviation: EmmS

Centre for Museum and Heritage Management, Nottingham Trent University, Clifton Lane, Nottingham, NG11 8NS

Tel: 0115 848 3562
Fax: 0115 848 6385
E-mail: emms@emms.org.uk

Website:
http://www.emms.org.uk

Enquiries:
Enquiries to: Executive Officer

Founded:
1981

Organisation type and purpose:
Regional museum network (membership is by subscription), present number of members: 112 (Local Authorities, independent museums, universities, national bodies and individuals), registered charity (charity number 1009683). Offers support, communication, networking, training, consultancy. Aims to enhance and improve standards in care and public use of museum collections in the East Midlands.

Subject coverage:
Museum management, organisation and practice, museum collections in the East Midlands, collections care, training and advice, Regional Emergencies and Disaster Support Service (prevention, preparedness, reaction and recovery).

Information services:
Advice and information relating to museums in the East Midlands
Regional Emergency and Disaster Support (REDS) Service.

Printed publications:
Annual Report
EmmS News (members only)

Electronic and video publications:
Emergency Manual for Historic Buildings and Collections (interactive CD-ROM, £29.50)

Publications list:
Available online

Access to staff:
Contact by letter, by telephone, by fax, by e-mail and via website. Appointment necessary.
Hours: Variable but consistent

Access to building, collection or gallery:
By appointment

EAST MIDLANDS ORAL HISTORY ARCHIVE

Acronym or abbreviation: EMOHA

Centre for Urban History, University of Leicester, LE1 7RH

Tel: 0116 252 5065
Fax: 0116 252 5769
E-mail: emoha@le.ac.uk

Website:
http://www.le.ac.uk/emoha

Organisation type and purpose:
A partnership between the University of Leicester's Centre for Urban History, Leicestershire County Council and Leicester City Museums and Library Services.

Subject coverage:
Oral history of the East Midlands (Leicestershire and Rutland).

Museum or gallery collection, archive, or library special collection:
Among the Archive's resources are the collections of the former Leicester Oral History Archive, the Mantle Archive from northwest Leicestershire, the Community History archive of Leicester City Libraries and the sound archive of BBC Radio Leicester

Access to building, collection or gallery:
The Archive is housed on the University of Leicester's satellite campus, at 1 Salisbury Road, Leicester, LE1 7QR

EAST NORTHAMPTONSHIRE COUNCIL

East Northamptonshire House, Cedar Drive, Thrapston, Kettering, Northamptonshire, NN14 4LZ

Tel: 01832 742000
Fax: 01832 734839

Website:
http://www.east-northamptonshire.gov.uk
Local government services, economic development, tourism.

Founded:
1974

Organisation type and purpose:
Local government body.

Subject coverage:
Local government services, economic development, tourism.

Access to staff:
Contact by letter and by telephone
Hours: Mon to Fri, 0900 to 1700

Other office at:
Rushden Centre (One Stop Shop)
Newton Road, Rushden, Northamptonshire, NN10 0PT; tel: 01933 412000; fax: 01933 410564

EAST OF ENGLAND TOURIST BOARD

Acronym or abbreviation: EETB

Toppesfield Hall, Hadleigh, Suffolk, IP7 5DN

Tel: 01473 822922
Fax: 01473 823063
E-mail: information@eetb.org.uk

Website:
http://www.visiteadtofengland.com

Enquiries:
Enquiries to: Managing Director

Founded:
1972

Formed from:
East Anglia Tourist Board

Formerly called:
East Anglia Tourist Board (year of change 1996)

Organisation type and purpose:
To promote the sustainable development of tourism and increase tourism expenditure in the region.

Subject coverage:
Tourism in Bedfordshire, Cambridgeshire, Essex, Hertfordshire, Norfolk and Suffolk. Information on research.

Printed publications:
Order printed publications from: Information Department

Access to staff:
Contact by letter, by telephone, by fax, by e-mail and via website
Hours: Mon to Fri, 0900 to 1700
Special comments: Closed Bank Holidays.

EAST OF LONDON FAMILY HISTORY SOCIETY

Acronym or abbreviation: EoLFHS

23 Louvaine Avenue, Wickford, Essex, SS12 0DP

E-mail: society.secretary@eolfhs.org.uk

Website:
http://www.eolfhs.org.uk

continued overleaf

Enquiries:
Enquiries to: General Secretary

Founded:
1978

Organisation type and purpose:
Membership association (membership is by subscription), present number of members: over 3000, suitable for ages: all.
Family history society.

Subject coverage:
Family history and genealogy.

Library catalogue:
All or part available in print

Printed publications:
Available from online bookstall or by post
Order printed publications from: East of London Family History Society
Bookstall Manager, 46 Brights Avenue, Rainham, Essex, RM13 9NW

Publications list:
Available online

Access to staff:
Contact by letter and by e-mail
Hours: Mon to Fri, 0900 to 1700
Special comments: Advice only provided, no research undertaken.

EAST RENFREWSHIRE COUNCIL

Council Headquarters, Eastwood Park, Giffnock, East Renfrewshire, G42 6UG

Tel: 0141 577 3000
Fax: 0141 620 0884

Enquiries:
Enquiries to: Public Relations Manager
Direct tel: 0141 577 3851
Direct fax: 0141 577 3852
Direct e-mail: RelationsP@eastrenfrewshire.gov.uk

Founded:
1996

Organisation type and purpose:
Local government body.

Subject coverage:
Local government; services and amenities; corporate services, education, environmental services, finance, housing, legal services, personnel services, planning development and tourism, property and technical services, roads and transportation, social services, council tax and other payments, registration of births, death and marriages.

Printed publications:
How to get in touch with the Council

Access to staff:
Contact by letter, by telephone, by fax and by e-mail. Appointment necessary.
Hours: Mon to Fri, 0900 to 1700

EAST RIDING ARCHIVES AND LOCAL STUDIES SERVICE

Acronym or abbreviation: Treasure House

County Hall, Beverley, East Yorkshire, HU17 9BA

Tel: 01482 392790
Fax: 01482 392791
E-mail: archives.service@eastriding.gov.uk

Website:
http://www.eastriding.gov.uk

Created by the merger of:
East Riding Archives Service and Beverley Local Studies Library (year of change 2007)

Organisation type and purpose:
Archive and Local Studies Library

Subject coverage:
East Riding of Yorkshire local history, topography and culture

Special visitor services:
Meeting rooms available for hire

Museum or gallery collection, archive, or library special collection:
Archive with collections of public, local government, church, family and estate and other local records. Local studies library with local studies books, pamphlets and journals, newspapers and directories.

Non-library collection catalogue:
All or part available online and in-house

Library catalogue:
All or part available online and in-house

Printed publications:
Guides to records, leaflets on tracing family history, house history and using the East Riding Register of Deeds
Hand Lists

Access to staff:
Contact by letter, by telephone, by fax, by e-mail and in person

Access to building, collection or gallery:
Hours: Mon, Wed, Fri, 0930 to 1700; Tue, Thu, 0930 to 2000; Sat, 0900 to 1600

Access for disabled people:
Disabled access and lift access to all public parts of building

Parent body:
East Riding of Yorkshire Council

Site address:
East Riding Archives and Local Studies Service
Treasure House, Champney Road, Beverley, HU17 9BE

EAST RIDING OF YORKSHIRE COUNCIL

Acronym or abbreviation: ERYC

County Hall, Cross Street, Beverley, East Yorkshire, HU17 9BA

Tel: 01482 887700

Website:
http://www.eastriding.gov.uk

Enquiries:
Enquiries to: Chief Executive
Direct tel: 01482 884832

Founded:
1996

Organisation type and purpose:
Local government body.

Subject coverage:
All local government services.

Museum or gallery collection, archive, or library special collection:
Archives of documents collected by Humberside County Council and former East Riding County Council and former East Riding Registry of Deeds held by the East Riding of Yorkshire Council Archives and Records Service

Access to staff:
Contact by letter, by telephone and by fax.
Appointment necessary.
Hours: Mon to Fri, 0900 to 1700

EAST STAFFORDSHIRE BOROUGH COUNCIL

Town Hall, Burton-on-Trent, Staffordshire, DE14 2EB

Tel: 01283 508000
Fax: 01283 35412
E-mail: christian.surname@eaststaffsbc.gov.uk

Website:
http://www.eaststaffsbc.gov.uk

Enquiries:
Enquiries to: Public Relations Manager

Organisation type and purpose:
Local government body.

Access to staff:
Contact by letter, by telephone, by fax, by e-mail and via website
Hours: Mon to Fri, 0800 to 1700

Access for disabled people:
Parking provided, level entry, toilet facilities

Other addresses:
East Staffordshire Borough Council
Midland Grain Warehouse, Derby Street, Burton on Trent, Staffordshire, DE14 2JJ; tel: 01283 508628; fax: 01283 508388

EAST SURREY BADGER PROTECTION SOCIETY

Acronym or abbreviation: ESBPS

PO Box 911, Warlingham, Surrey, CR6 9AF

Tel: 01883 622455
Fax: 01883 349699
E-mail: esbps@stata.com.net

Website:
http://badger-groups.org.uk/east-surrey

Enquiries:
Enquiries to: Honorary Secretary

Founded:
1979

Formerly called:
Surrey Badger Protection Society (year of change 1997)

Organisation type and purpose:
Registered charity (charity number 800270).

Subject coverage:
Badgers.

Printed publications:
Information leaflets (free)

Access to staff:
Contact by letter and by telephone
Hours: Mon to Fri, 0900 to 1700
Special comments: Also available in evenings and at weekends.

Affiliated to the:
National Federation of Badger Groups
2B Inworth Street, London, SW11 3EP

EAST SURREY FAMILY HISTORY SOCIETY

119 Keevil Drive, London, SW19 6TF

Tel: 01737 554071
E-mail: secretary@eastsurreyfhs.co.uk

Website:
http://scorpio.gold.ac.uk/genuki/sry/esfhs
List of publications, details of society and membership form.

Enquiries:
Enquiries to: Honorary Secretary

Founded:
1977

Organisation type and purpose:
International organisation, membership association (membership is by subscription), present number of members: 2000, registered charity (charity number 286659), suitable for ages: all, research organisation.

Subject coverage:
Family history (genealogy) data relating to East Surrey which includes parts of South London previously in Surrey.

Printed publications:
Introductory booklet (sent to members when they join)
Quarterly Journal (sent to members)
Census indexes for 1851, 1871 and 1891
Monumental inscriptions

Parish Registers
Record publications, Poor Law, Apprenticeships,
Settlements etc
Order printed publications from: Census Indexes and
Other Publications, East Surrey Family History
Society
4 Constance Road, Croydon, Surrey, CR0 2RS

Microform publications:
Directory of Members' Interests – 1995

Publications list:
Available online and in print

Access to staff:
Contact by letter and by e-mail
Hours: Mon to Fri, 0900 to 1700

EAST SUSSEX LIBRARY AND INFORMATION SERVICES

County Hall, Lewes, East Sussex, BN7 1SG

Tel: 01273 481870
Fax: 01273 481716
E-mail: kate.nassir-pour@eastsussex.gov.uk

Website:
http://www.eastsussex.gov.uk

Enquiries:
Enquiries to: Information Officer

Founded:
1974

Organisation type and purpose:
Local government body, public library.

Subject coverage:
Hastings, military history.

Library catalogue:
All or part available online and in-house

Access to staff:
Contact by letter, by telephone, by fax, by e-mail
and in person
Hours: Mon to Fri, 0900 to 1700

Group Headquarters at:
Hastings, Eastbourne Lewes, Bexhill and Uckfield

EAST SUSSEX RECORD OFFICE

Acronym or abbreviation: ESRO

The Maltings, Castle Precincts, Lewes, East Sussex,
BN7 1YT

Tel: 01273 482349
Fax: 01273 482341
E-mail: archives@eastsussex.gov.uk

Website:
http://www.eastsussex.gov.uk
Information leaflets, short guide to holdings
http://www.nationalarchives.gov.uk
Details of all archive repositories in England.
http://www.a2a.org.uk
Copies of lists of 90% plus of holdings

Enquiries:
Enquiries to: County Archivist

Founded:
1949

Organisation type and purpose:
Local government body.
To preserve the documentary heritage of East
Sussex, and of the Brighton and Hove Council
area, and to make its resources available to the
public for research. To act as a Diocesan Record
Office for Chichester (East Sussex Parish records).

Subject coverage:
Most aspects of the history and historical
geography of East Sussex (including Brighton and
Hove), its communities, people, public authorities
and organisations, c. 1100 to date.

**Museum or gallery collection, archive, or library
special collection:**
Archives of the usual local authority holdings
Deposited collections, including:
Battle Abbey Archives

Danny Archives
Frewen Archives
Hickstead Place Archives
Sheffield Park Archives concerning John Baker
Holroyd, 1st Earl of Sheffield, politician and
authority on commercial and agricultural topics,
late 18th century
Sussex Archaeological Society records, including
papers of the Gage family (American material)
and the Fuller family of Rosehill (West Indian
material)

Non-library collection catalogue:
All or part available online and in-house

Printed publications:
Annual Report (contains a list of accessions during
the year)
Handlist of registers of Births, Baptisms,
Marriages, Deaths and Burials (online)
Catalogues of individual archives

Microform publications:
Available for consultation in the Record office,
copies of entries provided for a fee

Publications list:
Available in print

Access to staff:
Contact by letter, by telephone, by fax, by e-mail,
in person and via website
Hours: Mon, Tue and Thu, 0845 to 1645; Wed, 0930
to 1645; Fri, 0845 to 1615; Sat, second in the month
(booking required for Sat)

Access for disabled people:
Parking provided, ramped entry
Special comments: Only one parking space but it is
bookable

EAST YORKSHIRE FAMILY HISTORY SOCIETY

Acronym or abbreviation: EYFHS

12 Carlton Drive, Aldbrough, Hull, East Yorkshire,
HU11 4SF

E-mail: secretary@eyfhs.org.uk

Website:
http://www.eyfhs.org.uk

Enquiries:
Enquiries to: Secretary

Founded:
1977

Organisation type and purpose:
Membership association (membership is by
subscription), present number of members: 1500,
registered charity (charity number 519743).

Subject coverage:
Family history in East Yorkshire.

Non-library collection catalogue:
All or part available in-house

Printed publications:
Monumental Inscriptions
Parish Register Transcripts
1851 Census of the EYFHS area (24 booklets)
1861 Census (on CD-ROM)
A3 size Maps
Order printed publications from: The Publications
Officers, East Yorkshire Family History Society
5 Curlew Close, Molescroft, Beverley, East
Yorkshire, HU17 7QN

Microform publications:
Births, Marriages and Deaths from Scarborough
Newspapers
1891 Census Scarborough Registration District

Electronic and video publications:
1891 Census Scarborough Registration District
(disc)
Births, Marriages and Deaths for the Beverley
Guardian Newspapers (disc)

Publications list:
Available online and in print

Access to staff:
Contact by letter
Hours: Mon to Fri, 0900 to 1700

Access to building, collection or gallery:
Prior appointment required

EASTERN AFRICA ASSOCIATION, THE

Acronym or abbreviation: EAA

2 Vincent Street, London, SW1P 4LD

Tel: 020 7828 5511
Fax: 020 7828 5251
E-mail: jcsmall@eaa-lon.co.uk

Website:
http://www.eaa-lon.co.uk

Enquiries:
Enquiries to: Asst Company Secretary
Direct tel: 020 7630 9493
Direct fax: 020 7828 5251
Direct e-mail: jcsmall@eaa-lon.co.uk
Other contacts: See other addresses

Founded:
1964

Formerly called:
East Africa Association (year of change 1995)

Organisation type and purpose:
Trade association (membership is by subscription),
present number of members: 270.
To support and promote investment in Eastern
Africa.

Subject coverage:
Trade and investment matters in Kenya, Uganda,
Tanzania, Ethiopia, Eritrea, Mauritius, Seychelles,
Madagascar and Rwanda

Printed publications:
Newsletter (to members only)

Access to staff:
Contact by letter, by telephone, by fax, by e-mail
and via website. Appointment necessary. Access
for members only.
Hours: Mon to Fri, 0900 to 1730

Branch Office:
The Eastern Africa Association
PO Box 41272, 5th Floor, Room 512, Jubilee Place,
Mama Ngina Street/General Kago Street,
Nairobi, Kenya; tel: 00 254 20 340341; fax: 00 254
20 214898; e-mail: info@eaa.co.ke; website: www
.eea-lon.co.uk

Local representatitve:
Resident Representative (tba)
tel: 00 256 31 224 400; e-mail: mbathink@stanbic
.com

Resident representative:
The Eastern Africa Association
Tanzania; tel: 00 255 22 245 143; e-mail: der@
kbnet.net

EASTLEIGH BOROUGH COUNCIL

Civic Offices, Leigh Road, Eastleigh, Hampshire,
SO50 9YN

Tel: 023 8068 8000
Fax: 023 8064 3952

Website:
http://www.eastleigh.gov.uk

Enquiries:
Enquiries to: Chief Executive
Other contacts: Public Relations Officer

Organisation type and purpose:
Local government body.

Subject coverage:
Local government services.

Access to staff:
Contact by letter, by telephone, by fax, by e-mail
and in person. Appointment necessary.
Hours: Mon to Thu, 0830 to 1700; Fri, 0830 to 1630

continued overleaf

Access to building, collection or gallery:
No prior appointment required

Access for disabled people:
Parking provided, ramped entry, access to all public areas, toilet facilities

EASTMAN DENTAL INSTITUTE

Formal name: Eastman Dental Institute for Oral Health Care Sciences

Eastman Dental Hospital, 256 Gray's Inn Road, London, WC1X 8LD

Tel: 020 7915 1092
Fax: 020 7915 1274
E-mail: academic@eastman.ucl.ac.uk

Website:
http://www.eastman.ucl.ac.uk

Enquiries:
Enquiries to: Admissions Officer

Formerly called:
Institute of Dental Surgery

Organisation type and purpose:
University department or institute, research organisation.
Postgraduate teaching and research.

Subject coverage:
Dentistry, dental research, dental education.

Publications list:
Available online

Access to staff:
Contact by telephone, by e-mail and via website
Hours: Mon to Fri, 0900 to 1700

Postgraduate institute affiliated to:
University College London

EC UK

Formal name: Engineering Council UK
Acronym or abbreviation: ECUK

246 High Holborn, London, WC1V 7EX 050

Tel: 020 3206 0500
Fax: 020 3206 0501
E-mail: staff@engc.org.uk

Website:
http://www.engc.org.uk
Press releases.
http://www.uk-spec.org.uk

Enquiries:
Enquiries to: Communications Manager
Direct e-mail: ehallatt@engc.org.uk

Founded:
1983

Formerly called:
The Engineering Council (year of change 2002)

Organisation type and purpose:
Regulatory authority for professional engineers and engineering technicians in the UK. Operates through 35 engineering institutions, which it licenses to assess individuals for inclusion on the ECUK register of Chartered Engineers, Incorporated Engineers and Engineering Technicians, titles that are protected by Royal Charter.

Subject coverage:
The engineering profession, education and training of Chartered Engineers, Incorporated Engineers and Engineering Technicians, continuing professional development.

Printed publications:
Annual Report, UK-SPEC (United Kingdom Standard for Professional Engineering Competence), Register News (e-bulletin), leaflets on registration.

Publications list:
Available online and in print

Access to staff:
Contact by letter, by telephone, by fax, by e-mail and via website
Hours: Mon to Fri, 0900 to 1700

Access to building, collection or gallery:
Prior appointment required

Nominated institutions:
Association of Cost Engineers
British Computer Society
British Institute of Non-Destructive Testing
Chartered Institution of Building Services Engineers
Chartered Institution of Water and Environmental Management
Energy Institute
IEE
Institute of Acoustics
Institute of Cast Metals Engineers
Institute of Healthcare Engineering & Estate Management
Institute of Highway Incorporated Engineers
Institute of Marine Engineering, Science and Technology
Institute of Materials, Minerals and Mining
Institute of Measurement and Control
Institute of Physics
Institute of Physics & Engineering in Medicine
Institute of Plumbing & Heating Engineers
Institution of Agricultural Engineers
Institution of Chemical Engineers
Institution of Civil Engineers
Institution of Electrical Engineers
Institution of Engineering Designers
Institution of Fire Engineers
Institution of Gas Engineers and Managers
Institution of Highways & Transportation
Institution of Incorporated Engineers
Institution of Lighting Engineers
Institution of Mechanical Engineers
Institution of Nuclear Engineers
Institution of Plant Engineers
Institution of Railway Signal Engineers
Institution of Structural Engineers
Institution of Water Officers
Royal Aeronautical Society
Royal Institution of Naval Architects
Society of Environmental Engineers
Society of Operations Engineers
Welding Institute

ECB ASSOCIATION OF CRICKET OFFICIALS, THE

Acronym or abbreviation: ECB ACO

The England and Wales Cricket Board, Lord's Cricket Ground, London NW8 8QZ

Tel: 020 7432 1231
E-mail: ecbaco@ecb.co.uk

Website:
http://www.acus.org.uk
Association and related cricket law, umpire and scorer details.

Enquiries:
Enquiries to: Administration Manager

Founded:
1953

Created by the merger of:
the Association of Cricket Umpires and Scorers (1953) and the ECB Officials Association (year of change 2008)

Formerly called:
Association of Cricket Umpires (ACU) (year of change 1993)

Organisation type and purpose:
International organisation, membership association (membership is by subscription, qualification), present number of members: 9500, voluntary organisation, training organisation. Examination organisation.
To improve the standard of umpiring and scoring by training, examination and example, and by any other means.

Subject coverage:
The interpretation and application of the laws of cricket.

Printed publications:
How's That? (Official journal, for members and affiliated organisations only)
Tom Smith's Cricket Umpiring and Scoring Training Manuals (purchase direct)

Electronic and video publications:
Training videos and slides (purchase through agency)

Access to staff:
Contact by letter, by telephone, by fax, by e-mail and via website
Hours: Mon to Fri, 0900 to 1700

ECCTIS LIMITED

Acronym or abbreviation: ECCTIS

Oriel House, Oriel Road, Cheltenham, Gloucestershire, GL50 1XP

Tel: 01242 252627
Fax: 01242 258600
E-mail: enquiries@ecctis.co.uk

Website:
http://www.ECCTIS.co.uk
Course Discover on-line database.

Enquiries:
Enquiries to: Marketing Manager
Direct e-mail: kitty@ecctis2000.co.uk

Founded:
1990

Formerly called:
Educational Counselling and Credit Transfer Information Service (ECCTIS)

Organisation type and purpose:
International organisation (membership is by subscription), training organisation, consultancy, research organisation, publishing house.

Subject coverage:
All award-bearing courses, from non-advanced to postgraduate level, in further and higher education throughout the UK, in colleges and universities, including standard entry requirements, course content and institutional data; non-standard entry opportunities (ie credit transfer).

Printed publications:
Newsletter (3 times a year, free)

Electronic and video publications:
DISCOURSE (CD-ROM)
ECCTIS (CD-ROM) – database of over 100,000 courses in higher and further education throughout the UK
ISCOM (CD-ROM)
KEYCLIPS (CD-ROM)
PICKUP (CD-ROM)

Publications list:
Available in print

Access to staff:
Contact via website
Hours: Mon to Fri, 0830 to 1730

Jointly owned by:
Careers Research and Advisory Centre (CRAC)
Hobsons Publishing
Times Educational Supplement

ECHO LANGUAGE SCHOOL

Acronym or abbreviation: ECHO

23 Rutland Gardens, Hove, East Sussex, BN3 5PD

Tel: 01273 202802
Fax: 01273 746464
E-mail: info@echolanguageschool.com

Website:
http://www.echolanguageschool.com
Details of courses.

Enquiries:
Enquiries to: Information Officer
Other contacts: Director of Studies

Founded:
1989

Organisation type and purpose:
Service industry, suitable for ages: 12+.
Residential language school, home tuition.

Subject coverage:
English residential language courses.

Printed publications:
Brochures

Access to staff:
Contact by letter, by telephone, by fax, by e-mail,
in person and via website
Hours: Daily, 0800 to 2000

Access to building, collection or gallery:
No prior appointment required

ECONOMIC HISTORY SOCIETY

University of Glasgow, Department of Economic
and Social History, Lilybank House, Bute Gardens,
Glasgow, G12 8RT

Tel: 0141 330 4662
Fax: 0141 330 4889
E-mail: ehsocsec@arts.gla.ac.uk

Website:
http://www.ehs.org.uk

Enquiries:
Enquiries to: Honorary Secretary
Direct tel: 0141 330 4662
Direct fax: 0141 330 4889
Direct e-mail: ehsocsec@arts.gla.ac.uk

Founded:
1926

Organisation type and purpose:
Learned society, registered charity (charity number
228494; SCO38304).
To promote the study of economic history and to
establish closer relations between students and
teachers of economic and social history.

Subject coverage:
Economic and social history.

Non-library collection catalogue:
All or part available online and in print

Printed publications:
Economic History Review (quarterly)
Refresh (no longer available, except for back issues
online)
Living Economic and Social History (essays to
mark the 75th anniversary of the Economic
History Society)

Publications list:
Available online and in print

Access to staff:
Contact by letter, by telephone, by fax and by e-mail
Hours: Mon to Fri, 0900 to 1700

ECONOMIC RESEARCH COUNCIL

Acronym or abbreviation: ERC

7 St James's Square, London, SW17 4JU

Tel: 020 7439 0271

Website:
http://www.ercouncil.org

Enquiries:
Enquiries to: Honorary Secretary

Founded:
1943

Organisation type and purpose:
Membership association, registered charity.
To promote education in economics, particularly
monetary practice.

Subject coverage:
Education in the science of economics, particularly
monetary policy; inflation, taxation, use of
resources etc.

Non-library collection catalogue:
All or part available online

Printed publications:
Britain and Overseas (quarterly)

Access to staff:
Contact by letter
Hours: Mon to Fri, 0900 to 1700

ECONOMIC RESEARCH INSTITUTE OF NORTHERN IRELAND LTD

Acronym or abbreviation: ERINI

Pearl Assurance House, 1–3 Donegall Square East,
Belfast, BT1 5HB

Tel: 028 9023 2125 or 028 261 8000
Fax: 028 9033 1250/3054
E-mail: info@niec.org.uk

Website:
http://www.niec.org.uk
Information about Council, Council Members,
Staff, publications, events and future research.
New ERINI website being developed.

Enquiries:
Enquiries to: Director
Other contacts: Administrator

Founded:
2004

Organisation type and purpose:
Economic research and policy development body.

Subject coverage:
Economics.

Printed publications:
Occasional Papers Series
Publicly Funded R&D and Economic Development
in Northern Ireland (December 1999, free)
Plus a wide variety of papers, reports and
monographs (all charged) including:
Tough Choices: Setting Health and Social Care
Priorities in Northern Ireland (April 2000)
Annual Report 2000–2001 (November 2001)
The Knowledge Driven Economy: Indicators for
Northern Ireland (April 2001)
Order printed publications from: The Administration
Group, Economic Research Institute of Northern
Ireland Ltd
tel: 028 90 232125, fax: 028 90 331250, e-mail: info@
niec.org.uk

Publications list:
Available online and in print

Access to staff:
Contact by letter, by telephone, by fax, by e-mail,
in person and via website. Appointment necessary.
Hours: Mon to Fri, 0900 to 1700

Also at:
Economic Research Institute of Northern Ireland
Ltd
  22–24 Mount Charles, Belfast, BT7 6NN

ECONOMIST INTELLIGENCE UNIT LIMITED

Acronym or abbreviation: EIU

26 Red Lion Square, London, WC1R 4HQ

Tel: 020 7576 8000
E-mail: london@eiu.com

Website:
http://www.eiu.com
http://store.eiu.com

Enquiries:
Enquiries to: Client Relations Department
Direct tel: 020 7576 8181
Direct fax: 020 7572 8476
Direct e-mail: london@eiu.com

Organisation type and purpose:
To provide country, industry and management
analysis.
To assess and forecast the political, economic and
business climates of 201 countries.
To produce intelligence on key industries.

Subject coverage:
Country specific reports – economic and political
studies; forecasts; country credit risk; commodities;
industry studies – consumer markets, energy,
rubber, travel and tourism, automotive, financial
services, food, beverages and tobacco, healthcare
and pharmaceuticals.

Trade and statistical information:
International business and economic information.

Publications list:
Available online and in print

Incorporates:
Business International Limited

Other offices:
Hong Kong
  60F Central Plaza, 18 Harbour Road, Wanchai,
  Hong Kong; tel: +852 2802 7288
New York
  The Economist Building, 111 West 57th Street,
  New York, NY 10019, USA; tel: +1 212 698 9745

Parent body:
Economist Group

EDEXCEL

One90 High Holborn, London, WC1V 7BH

Tel: 0870 240 9800
E-mail: enquiries@edexcel.org.uk

Website:
http://www.edexcel.org.uk
The Edexcel website or Edexcel On-line Services &
Resources allows customers to have access to
Edexcel's key information, resources and services
24 hours a day, 7 days a week.

Enquiries:
Enquiries to: Corporate Information Resource
Centre Manager
Direct e-mail: library@edexcel.org.uk
Other contacts: Customer Response Centre (CRC)
for information and guidance on the full range of
Edexcel programmes of study and qualifications.

Founded:
1983

Organisation type and purpose:
Body concerned with academic and vocational
qualifications in secondary and tertiary education.

Subject coverage:
The CIRC provides a 'first step' information
service for all users of Edexcel qualifications.
Guidance, contents, procedures and availability
can be given on a wide range of qualifications,
both academic and vocational, from Entry Level
right through to Professional Development
Awards.

Non-library collection catalogue:
All or part available in-house and in print

Library catalogue:
All or part available in-house

Printed publications:
A large number of course-related publications and
supporting material for all Edexcel's
qualifications including syllabuses,
specifications, guidance, past examination
papers, teacher support material and student
support material
Order printed publications from: Edexcel Publications
Adamsway, Mansfield, Nottinghamshire, NG18
4FN, tel: 01623 467467, fax: 01623 450481, e-mail:
publications@linneydirect.com

Publications list:
Available in print

continued overleaf

Access to staff:
Contact by letter, by telephone, by fax, by e-mail and via website
Hours: Mon to Fri, 0900 to 1700

EDGE HILL COLLEGE OF HIGHER EDUCATION

St Helens Road, Ormskirk, Lancashire, L39 4QP

Tel: 01695 584284
Fax: 01695 579997

Website:
http://www.ehche.ac.uk/ims
Information and media services homepage.

Enquiries:
Enquiries to: Manager
Direct e-mail: robertss@edgehill.ac.uk

Formerly called:
Edge Hill College of Further Education, Edge Hill University College

Organisation type and purpose:
University library, university department or institute.
College awards are validated by Lancaster University.

Subject coverage:
Afro-Asian studies, social science, community and race relations, drama, religious studies, English language and literature, biology, science, French, geography (human and physical), British and world history, mathematics, information technology, politics, European literature and culture, organisation and management, teacher education and educational studies, urban development, women's studies, sport studies and health.

Museum or gallery collection, archive, or library special collection:
Education Resource collection
Local history collection

Non-library collection catalogue:
All or part available online

Access to staff:
Contact by letter, by telephone, by e-mail and via website
Hours: Term time: Mon to Fri, 0845 to 2100; Sat, Sun, 1300 to 1700

Affiliated to:
University of Lancaster

EDINBURGH ASSAY OFFICE

Acronym or abbreviation: EAO

Goldsmiths' Hall, 24 Broughton Street, Edinburgh, EH1 3RH

Tel: 0131 556 1144
Fax: 0131 556 1177
E-mail: admin@assay-office.co.uk

Website:
http://www.assayofficescotland.co.uk

Enquiries:
Enquiries to: Assay Master

Organisation type and purpose:
Statutory body.
Established in accordance with the requirements of the Hallmarking Act 1973.

Subject coverage:
Assaying and hallmarking over the past 500 years of gold, silver and platinum.

Museum or gallery collection, archive, or library special collection:
Records of wares hallmarked at Edinburgh since 1799 to present day

Printed publications:
Hallmarks (booklet of the Assay Offices of GB)

Access to staff:
Contact by letter, by fax, by e-mail and in person

Hours: Mon to Fri, 0800 to 1600

Controlled by the:
Incorporation of Goldsmiths of the City of Edinburgh

EDINBURGH BIBLIOGRAPIIICAL SOCIETY

c/o National Library of Scotland, George IV Bridge, Edinburgh, EH1 1EW

Tel: 0131 623 3893
E-mail: j.marshall@nls.uk

Website:
http://www.edbibsoc.lib.ed.ac.uk

Enquiries:
Enquiries to: Treasurer
Other contacts: Honorary Treasurer of the Edinburgh Bibliographical Society.

Founded:
1890

Organisation type and purpose:
Learned society.

Subject coverage:
Bibliography (especially Scottish).

Printed publications:
Occasional publications (generally available, price and frequency variable)
Journal (annually, members only)

Publications list:
Available in print

Access to staff:
Contact by letter, by telephone and by e-mail
Hours: Mon to Fri, 0900 to 1700

EDINBURGH CENTRE FOR TROPICAL FORESTS

Acronym or abbreviation: ECTF

Pentlands Science Park, Bush Loan, Penicuik, Midlothian, EH26 0PH

Tel: 0131 440 0400
Fax: 0131 440 4141
E-mail: mail@ectf-ed.org.uk

Website:
http://www.nmw.ac.uk/ectf/
Objectives of ECTF as a whole and each of its constituent members. Consultant database.

Enquiries:
Enquiries to: Administrator

Founded:
1991

Organisation type and purpose:
Training organisation, consultancy, research organisation.
Coordinates the expertise of the members of ECTF for potential clients.

Subject coverage:
Tropical forestry, land management and sustainable development of natural resources.

Printed publications:
Rooting Cuttings of Tropical Trees (manual, Longman K A, £12.50)

Electronic and video publications:
Multiplying Tropical Trees (video, for sale)

Access to staff:
Contact by letter, by e-mail and via website
Hours: Mon to Fri, 0900 to 1700

Member organisations:
Centre for Ecology and Hydrology
  Bush Estate, Penicuik, Midlothian, EH26 0QB
Forestry Commission
  231 Corstorphine Road, Edinburgh, EH12 7AT
LTS International Limited
  Pentlands Science Park, Bush Loan, Penicuik, Midlothian, EH26 0PH

Royal Botanic Garden
  20A Inverleith Row, Edinburgh, EH3 5LR
University of Edinburgh
  Darwin Building, Mayfield Road, Edinburgh, EH9 3JU

EDINBURGH CITY LIBRARIES AND INFORMATION SERVICE

George IV Bridge, Edinburgh, EH1 1EG

Tel: 0131 242 8000
Fax: 0131 242 8009
E-mail: eclis@edinburgh.gov.uk

Website:
http://www.edinburgh.gov.uk/libraries

Enquiries:
Enquiries to: Head of Library and Information Services

Organisation type and purpose:
Local government body, public library.

Subject coverage:
Architecture, art, design and photography, business, community information, Edinburgh past and present, English literature, genealogy, government information, courses and careers, consumer information, music, dance (particularly Scottish), geography, science and technology, travel, painting, Scotland, Sir Walter Scott and R L Stevenson, Scottish Parliament.

Museum or gallery collection, archive, or library special collection:
Architectural Copy Books
British Standards (CD-ROM)
Children's Illustrated Books
Cowan Bequest (music)
Dance of Death Collection
Donald Scottish Dance Collection
Early Photography of Edinburgh and Scotland
Early Scottish Printed Music
Edinburgh Printing before 1700
Genealogy Records – Microform
General Register Office Index to Births Deaths and Marriages 1837 -1997 (microfiche)
Henry Dyer Collection of Japanese Prints
Highland Life Collection of Photographs
Individual Family Histories
James Skene Watercolours
Krishnamurti Collection
Robert Louis Stevenson Collection
Marr Collection (music/handbills)
Scottish Artists' Sketchbooks
Scottish Parliament Offficial Publications
Sir Walter Scott Collection

Trade and statistical information:
Business directories UK, government information, yearbooks and statistics.

Non-library collection catalogue:
All or part available online

Library catalogue:
All or part available online

Printed publications:
Bibliographies, booklets, calendars, postcards (list available)
Handouts; leaflets on individual service points
Notes for Exhibitors in the Fine Art Library
Welcome wallets and welcome leaflets

Electronic and video publications:
Borrow a box (Multiple CD sets)
CD-ROMs in the Central Library
CD-ROMs in the Fine Art Department

Branch libraries:
Access Services
  343 Oxgangs Road North, Edinburgh, EHB 9NE; tel: 0131 529 5683
Balerno
  1 Main Street, Edinburgh, EH14 7EQ; tel: 0131 529 5500; fax: 0131 529 5502; e-mail: balerno .library@edinburgh.gov.uk

Balgreen
173 Balgreen Road, Edinburgh, EH11 3AT; tel: 0131 529 5585; fax: 0131 529 5583; e-mail: balgreen.library@edinburgh.gov.uk

Blackhall
56 Hillhouse Road, Edinburgh, EH4 5EG; tel: 0131 529 5595; fax: 0131 336 5419; e-mail: blackhall.library@edinburgh.gov.uk

Colinton
14 Thorburn Road, Edinburgh, EH13 0BQ; tel: 0131 529 5603; fax: 0131 529 5607; e-mail: colinton.library@edinburgh.gov.uk

Corstorphine
12 Kirk Loan, Edinburgh, EH12 7HD; tel: 0131 529 5506; fax: 0131 529 5508; e-mail: costorphine .library@edinburg.gov.uk

Craigmillar
7 Niddrie Marischal Gardens, Edinburgh, EH16 4LX; tel: 0131 529 5597; fax: 0131 529 5601; e-mail: craigmillar.library@edinburgh.gov.uk

Currie
210 Lanark Road West, Edinburgh, EH14 5NN; tel: 0131 529 5609; fax: 0131 529 5613; e-mail: currie.library@edinburgh.gov.uk

Fountainbridge
137 Dundee Street, Edinburgh, EH11 1BG; tel: 0131 529 5616; fax: 0131 529 5621; website: fountainbridge.library'edinburgh.gov.uk

Gilmerton
64 Gilmerton Dykes Street, Edinburgh, EH17 8PL; tel: 0131 529 5628; fax: 0131 529 5627; e-mail: gilmerton.library@edinburgh.gov.uk

Granton
Wardieburn Terrace, Edinburgh, EH5 2DA; tel: 0131 529 5630; fax: 0131 529 5634; e-mail: granton.library@edinburgh.gov.uk

Kirkliston
Station Road, Kirkliston, Edinburgh, EH29 9BE; tel: 0131 529 5510; fax: 0131 529 5514; e-mail: kirkliston.library@edinburgh.gov.uk

Leith
28–30 Ferry Road, Edinburgh, EH6 4AE; tel: 0131 529 5517; fax: 0131 554 2720; e-mail: leith .library@edinburgh.gov.uk

McDonald Road
2 McDonald Road, Edinburgh, EH7 4LU; tel: 0131 529 5636 (also Ethnic Services tel: 0131 529 5644); fax: 0131 529 5646; e-mail: mcdonaldrd .library@edinburgh.gov.uk

Moredun
92 Moredun Park Road, Edinburgh, EH17 7HL; tel: 0131 529 5652; fax: 0131 447 5651; e-mail: moredun.library@edinburgh.gov.uk

Morningside
184 Morningside Road, Edinburgh, EH10 4PU; tel: 0131 529 5654; fax: 0131 447 4685; e-mail: morningside.library@edinburgh.gov.uk

Muirhouse
15 Pennywell Court, Edinburgh, EH4 4TZ; tel: 0131 529 5528; fax: 0131 529 5532; e-mail: muirhouse.library@edinburgh.gov.uk

Newington
17–21 Fountainhall Road, Edinburgh, EH9 2LN; tel: 0131 529 5536; fax: 0131 667 5491; e-mail: newington.library@edinburgh.gov.uk

Oxgangs
343 Oxgangs Road North, Edinburgh, EH13 9NE; tel: 0131 529 5549; fax: 0131 529 5554; e-mail: oxgangs.library@edinburgh.gov.uk

Piershill
30 Piersfield Terrace, Edinburgh, EH8 7BQ; tel: 0131 529 5685; fax: 0131 529 5685; e-mail: piershill.library@edinburgh.gov.uk

Portobello
14 Rosefield Terrace, Edinburgh, EH15 1AU; tel: 0131 529 5558; fax: 0131 669 2344; e-mail: portobello.library@edinburgh.gov.uk

Ratho
6 School Wynd, Ratho, Newbridge, Edinburgh, EH28 8TT; tel: 0131 333 5297; fax: 0131 333 5297; e-mail: ratho.library@edinburgh.gov.uk

Sighthill
6 Sighthill Wynd, Edinburgh, EH11 4BL; tel: 0131 529 5569; fax: 0131 539 5572; e-mail: sighthill.library@edinburgh.gov.uk

South Queensferry
9 Shore Road, Edinburgh, EH30 9RD; tel: 0131 529 5576; fax: 0131 529 5578; e-mail: southqueensferry.library@edinburgh.gov.uk

Stockbridge
Hamilton Place, Edinburgh, EH3 5BA; tel: 0131 529 5665; fax: 0131 529 5681; e-mail: stockbridge .library@edinburgh.gov.uk

Wester Hailes
1 West Side Plaza, Edinburgh, EH14 2ET; tel: 0131 529 5667; fax: 0131 529 5671; e-mail: westerhailes.library@edinburgh.gov.uk

Mobile Libraries:
c/o Access Services

Resource Centre (for people with disabilities):
Central Library
George IV Bridge, Edinburgh, EH1 1EG; tel: 0131 242 8136

EDINBURGH COLLEGE OF ART LIBRARY SERVICE

Acronym or abbreviation: ECA

Lauriston Place, Edinburgh, EH3 9DF

Tel: 0131 221 6180
Fax: 0131 221 6293
E-mail: library@eca.ac.uk

Website:
http://www.lib.eca.ac.uk
Access to library catalogue.

Enquiries:
Enquiries to: Principal Librarian
Other contacts: Reader Services Librarian; Technical Services Librarian

Founded:
1907

Organisation type and purpose:
University library, suitable for ages: 19 to 99, research organisation; SFC Small Specialist Institution status

Subject coverage:
Architecture; landscape architecture; painting and drawing; sculpture; applied arts (jewellery and silversmithing, glass and architectural glass); applied design (furniture and interior and product design, fashion, textiles); visual communications (graphics, photography, animation, film and TV, illustration); urban design; architectural conservation; Islamic architecture, and urbanism.

Library catalogue:
All or part available online

Access to staff:
Contact by letter, by telephone, by e-mail and in person
Hours: Term time: Mon to Thu, 0915 to 1930; Fri, 1000 to 1700; vacations: Mon to Thu, 0915 to 1630; Fri, 1000 to 1630

Access to building, collection or gallery:
Hours: Term time: Mon to Thu, 0915 to 1930; Fri, 1000 to 1700; vacations: Mon to Thu, 0915 to 1630; Fri, 1000 to 1630

EDINBURGH COLLEGE OF PARAPSYCHOLOGY

Acronym or abbreviation: ECP

2 Melville Street, Edinburgh, EH3 7NS

Tel: 0131 220 1433
Fax: 0131 220 1433
E-mail: secretary@parapsychology.org.uk

Website:
http://www.parapsychology.org.uk

Enquiries:
Enquiries to: Secretary

Founded:
1932

Formerly called:
Edinburgh Psychic College and Library (year of change 1973)

Organisation type and purpose:
Membership association (membership is by subscription), present number of members: 300, voluntary organisation, registered charity (charity number SC 000571), suitable for ages: 18+.
To help the bereaved understand that life continues after physical death, to assist enquirers in this area plus provision of education, in a non-religious context. To promote all aspects of non-religious spiritualism.

Subject coverage:
Parapsychology, mediumship, psychism, survival after death, physical phenomena, spiritualism, spiritual healing, clairvoyance, counselling.

Museum or gallery collection, archive, or library special collection:
Library of 2000 books (catalogue on computer)

Library catalogue:
All or part available in-house

Printed publications:
The Candlestick (newsletter, 3 times a year, free, direct)

Access to staff:
Contact by letter, by telephone, by fax, by e-mail and in person
Hours: Mon to Fri, 1000 to 1600

EDINBURGH DISTRICT ENGINEERING TRAINING ASSOCIATION LIMITED

Acronym or abbreviation: EDETA Ltd

Fleming House, Kinnaird Park, Edinburgh, EH15 3RD

Tel: 0131 454 4840
Fax: 0131 454 4841
E-mail: general@edeta.org.uk

Website:
http://www.edeta.org.uk
About EDETA, training services, course descriptions and dates, links to useful sites.

Enquiries:
Enquiries to: Manager

Founded:
1970

Organisation type and purpose:
National organisation, advisory body, learned society (membership is by election or invitation), service industry, registered charity, suitable for ages: 18+, training organisation.

Subject coverage:
VQ training in engineering, administration, IT, customer care, health and safety training.

Publications list:
Available online and in print

Access to staff:
Contact by letter, by telephone, by fax, by e-mail, in person and via website. Appointment necessary.
Hours: Mon to Fri, 0900 to 1700

Access for disabled people:
Parking provided, level entry, access to all public areas, toilet facilities

EDINBURGH FESTIVAL FRINGE

180 High Street, Edinburgh, EH1 1QS

Tel: 0131 226 0026\ Minicom no. 0131 220 5594
Fax: 0131 226 0016
E-mail: admin@edfringe.com

Website:
http://www.edfringe.com
Details on how to participate. Annual performance programme, background and history of organisation and public reviews of events.

continued overleaf

Enquiries:
Enquiries to: Administrator

Founded:
1947

Organisation type and purpose:
Registered charity.
Arts festival.
Promotion of the performing and visual arts in Edinburgh.

Subject coverage:
Edinburgh Festival Fringe; performance, production, marketing and technical information.
Advice and support year-round.

Printed publications:
Annual Performance Programme (postage)
FringeSafe: Technical Handbook (£5)
How to do a Show on the Fringe (£5)
How to Sell a Show on the Fringe (£5)

Access to staff:
Contact by letter, by telephone, by fax and by e-mail. Appointment necessary.
Hours: Mon to Fri, 1000 to 1800

EDINBURGH FILM FOCUS

Acronym or abbreviation: EFF

20 Forth Street, Edinburgh, EH1 3LH

Tel: 0131 622 7337
Fax: 0131 622 7338
E-mail: info@edinfilm.com

Website:
http://www.edinfilm.com
Locations brochure, production guide – directory of facilities, personnel, searchable locations library.

Enquiries:
Enquiries to: Director
Other contacts: Location Liaison

Founded:
1989

Formerly called:
Edinburgh and Lothian Screen Industries Office (ELSIO) (year of change 1997)

Organisation type and purpose:
Advisory body, service industry. Local government funded, independent. Film commission. A first point of contact for information and help on filming in Edinburgh, the Lothians and Scottish Borders.

Printed publications:
Location Brochure

Access to staff:
Contact by letter, by telephone, by fax and by e-mail. Appointment necessary.
Hours: Mon to Fri, 0900 to 1700

Access to building, collection or gallery:
By appointment
Hours: Mon to Fri, 0930 to 1700

EDINBURGH INTERNATIONAL FESTIVAL

The Hub, Castlehill, Edinburgh, EH1 2NE

Tel: 0131 473 2000\ Minicom no. Textphone: 0131 473 2098
Fax: 0131 473 2003
E-mail: info@eif.co.uk

Website:
http://www.eif.co.uk
Background and information on Edinburgh International Festival. Full programme listings and booking details.

Enquiries:
Enquiries to: Marketing Manager
Direct tel: 0131 473 2020
Direct fax: 0131 473 2002
Direct e-mail: marketing@eif.co.uk

Founded:
1947

Organisation type and purpose:
Registered charity (charity number SC 004694).
For promotion of annual arts festival.
Three-week festival presenting over 200 performances of the world's best music, opera, theatre and dance.

Subject coverage:
Performances in music, opera, dance, theatre.

Printed publications:
Edinburgh International Festival Programme (annually)
Newsletter (twice annually)
Annual Review

Access to staff:
Contact by letter, by telephone, by fax, by e-mail and via website. Appointment necessary.
Hours: Mon to Fri, 0930 to 1730

Access to building, collection or gallery:
No prior appointment required
Hours: Sun, Mon, 0930 to 1700; Tue to Sat, 0930 to 1700
Special comments: Restricted access when functions are on.

Access for disabled people:
Level entry, access to all public areas, toilet facilities

EDINBURGH INTERNATIONAL JAZZ & BLUES FESTIVAL

Formal name: Edinburgh International Jazz and Blues Festival

29 St Stephen Street, Edinburgh, EH3 5AN

Tel: 0131 225 2202
Fax: 0131 225 3321
E-mail: mikehart@edinburghjazzfestblues.com

Enquiries:
Enquiries to: Director

Founded:
1979

Organisation type and purpose:
Registered charity (charity number SCO12211).
Running an annual jazz and blues festival.

Printed publications:
Annual programme (free)

Access to staff:
Contact by letter, by telephone, by fax and by e-mail
Hours: Mon to Fri, 0900 to 1700

EDINBURGH INTERNATIONAL SCIENCE FESTIVAL

Acronym or abbreviation: EISF

4 Gayfield Place Lane, Edinburgh, EH1 3NZ

Tel: 0131 558 7666
Fax: 0131 557 9177
E-mail: eisf@scifest.co.uk

Website:
http://www.sciencefestival.co.uk
Background information on the Science Festival and full programme information.

Enquiries:
Enquiries to: Marketing Manager
Other contacts: Festival Manager

Founded:
1988

Organisation type and purpose:
Registered charity, events suitable for all ages, plus an extensive schools touring programme.
To reveal science and the excitement of discovery to the widest possible audience.

Subject coverage:
Public understanding of science. Science communication. Science shows, workshops and hands-on events.

Non-library collection catalogue:
All or part available online

Printed publications:
Information brochure
Science Festival Programme (annually, free)
Generation Science Schools Touring Programme (annually, free)

Access to staff:
Contact by letter, by telephone, by fax and by e-mail. Appointment necessary.
Hours: Mon to Fri, 0930 to 1730

Also known as:
The Science Festival

EDINBURGH MATHEMATICAL SOCIETY

Acronym or abbreviation: EMS

School of Mathematics, Edinburgh University, The King's Buildings, Mayfield Road, Edinburgh, EH9 3JZ

Tel: 0131 650 5040
Fax: 0131 650 6553
E-mail: edmathsoc@ed.ac.uk

Website:
http://www.maths.ed.ac.uk/~ems

Enquiries:
Enquiries to: Honorary Secretary

Founded:
1883

Organisation type and purpose:
Learned society.
Promotion and extension of the mathematical sciences, pure and applied, particularly in Scotland.

Subject coverage:
Pure and applied mathematics.

Printed publications:
Proceedings of the Edinburgh Mathematical Society (annual vol. in 3 parts)

EDINBURGH ROYAL CHORAL UNION

Acronym or abbreviation: ERCU

Criagroyston, Broadgate, Gullane, EH31 2DH

Tel: 01620 843299
E-mail: jane.kirk@ed.ac.uk

Website:
http://www.ercu.org.uk

Enquiries:
Enquiries to: President
Other contacts: Librarian for hire of choral music.

Founded:
1858

Organisation type and purpose:
Membership association (membership is by qualification), present number of members: 120, voluntary organisation, registered charity (charity number SC012050).
Self-governing amateur society whose objects are the study, practice and performance of music, one of Scotland's largest independent amateur choirs, promoting at least three concerts in a season, with professional orchestras and conductors.

Subject coverage:
Choral music.

Museum or gallery collection, archive, or library special collection:
Large library of choral music available for hire

Library catalogue:
All or part available online

Printed publications:
History of the Edinburgh Royal Choral Union, 1858–1983 (booklet)
Library catalogue

Publications list:
Available online

Access to staff:
Contact by letter, by telephone, by fax, by e-mail and via website
Hours: Mon to Fri, 0900 to 1700

Member of:
National Federation of Music Societies (NFMS)
7–15 Rosebery Avenue, London, EC1R 4SP; tel: 020 7841 0110; fax: 020 7841 0115; e-mail: nfms@nfms.org.uk

EDINBURGH SIR WALTER SCOTT CLUB

16/7 Albert Terrace, Edinburgh, EH10 5EA

Tel: 0131 447 6133
E-mail: murfra@btinternet.com

Website:
http://www.walterscottclub.org.uk

Enquiries:
Enquiries to: Honorary Secretary

Founded:
1894

Organisation type and purpose:
Learned society (membership is by subscription), present number of members: 350.

Subject coverage:
Life and works of Sir Walter Scott.

Museum or gallery collection, archive, or library special collection:
A few books of Scott minutes of club and council meetings
Tapes of annual dinner speeches

Printed publications:
Annual Bulletin
Occasional leaflets, with forthcoming programme of events

Access to staff:
Contact by letter, by telephone, by e-mail, in person and via website. Appointment necessary.
Hours: Mon to Fri, 0900 to 1700

Associated with:
Edinburgh University, Department of Literature

EDUCATION LAW ASSOCIATION

Acronym or abbreviation: ELAS

37 Grimston Avenue, Folkestone, Kent, CT20 2QD

Tel: 01303 211570
Fax: 01303 211570
E-mail: elassec@btinternet.com

Enquiries:
Enquiries to: Executive Secretary

Founded:
1992

Organisation type and purpose:
Professional body (membership is by subscription), present number of members: 325, registered charity (charity number 1053614), suitable for ages: all, training organisation.

Subject coverage:
Education law.

Access to staff:
Contact by letter, by telephone, by fax and by e-mail
Hours: Mon to Fri, 0900 to 1700
Special comments: No visitors, part-time staff.

EDUCATIONAL AND TELEVISION FILMS LIMITED

Acronym or abbreviation: ETV

247a Upper Street, Highbury Corner, London, N1 1RU

Tel: 020 7226 2298
Fax: 020 7226 8016
E-mail: zoe@etvltd.demon.co.uk

Website:
http://www.etvltd.demon.co.uk
Details of aspects of the collection, fully searchable database online soon.

Enquiries:
Enquiries to: Librarian

Founded:
1950

Organisation type and purpose:
Film library.

Subject coverage:
Footage of and from the history of the British Labour Movement and a wide variety of documentary and technical subjects from the former socialist countries and from the former Soviet Union, former Eastern Bloc countries, Afghanistan, China, Chile, Cuba, Korea and Vietnam, as well as a complete collection from the Spanish Civil War from the Republican side.

Museum or gallery collection, archive, or library special collection:
British Labour History films
Spanish Civil War films
A wide spectrum of international films that have a political relevance to todays news stories

Non-library collection catalogue:
All or part available in-house

Library catalogue:
All or part available in-house

Printed publications:
Catalogues available covering all aspects of the collection

Publications list:
Available in print

Access to staff:
Contact by letter, by telephone, by fax, by e-mail and via website
Hours: Mon to Fri, 0930 to 1730

Access to building, collection or gallery:
Prior appointment required
Hours: Mon to Fri, 0930 to 1730

EDUCATIONAL DISTRIBUTION SERVICE

Education House, Drywall Estate, Castle Road, Murston, Sittingbourne, Kent, ME10 3RL

Tel: 01795 427614
Fax: 01795 437988
E-mail: info@edist.co.uk

Enquiries:
Enquiries to: Managing Director

Founded:
1971

Organisation type and purpose:
International organisation, suitable for ages: all. Library and distribution service for film and video, and all resources and other goods as contracted.

Museum or gallery collection, archive, or library special collection:
GPO classic films

Printed publications:
Educational resources

Publications list:
Available in print

Access to staff:
Contact by letter, by telephone, by fax and by e-mail. Appointment necessary.
Hours: Mon to Fri, 0900 to 1700

Access to building, collection or gallery:
Prior appointment required

EDUCATIONAL GRANTS ADVISORY SERVICE

Acronym or abbreviation: EGAS

501–505 Kingsland Road, London, E8 4AU

Tel: 020 7254 6251 (Tue, Wed and Thu 1400 to 1600 only)
Fax: 020 7249 5443
E-mail: egas.enquiry@family-action.org.uk

Website:
http://www.family-action.org.uk
Information about parent organisation (Family Action) and details of services provided by EGAS.

Enquiries:
Enquiries to: Educational and Grants Manager

Founded:
1962

Parent body formerly called:
Family Welfare Association (year of change 2008)

Organisation type and purpose:
Information and grant giving service. A service provided by Family Action, registered charity number 264713.

Subject coverage:
Post-16 education in England, specialising in charitable funding.

Information services:
Guide to Student Funding, Educational Grants Search

Access to staff:
Contact by letter and by telephone
Hours: Mon to Fri, 0900 to 1700
Special comments: Telephone service only available on Tue, Wed and Thu, from 1400 to 1600

Parent body:
Family Action
501–505 Kingsland Road, London E8 4AU; tel: 020 7254 6251; fax: 020 7249 5443; e-mail: info@family-action.org.uk; website: http://www.family-action.org.uk

EDUCATIONAL INSTITUTE OF SCOTLAND

Acronym or abbreviation: EIS

46 Moray Place, Edinburgh, EH3 6BH

Tel: 0131 225 6244
Fax: 0131 220 3151
E-mail: enquiries@eis.org.uk

Website:
http://www.eis.org.uk

Enquiries:
Enquiries to: General Secretary

Organisation type and purpose:
Trade union (membership is by subscription), present number of members: 58,000.
All sectors of Scottish education.

Subject coverage:
Education and teachers in all sectors (Scotland).

Printed publications:
Scottish Educational Journal

Access to staff:
Contact by letter, by fax and by e-mail
Hours: Mon to Fri, 0900 to 1700

Affiliated to:
Trades Union Congress

EDUSERV

Queen Anne House, 11 Charlotte Street, Bath, BA1 2NE

Tel: 01225 474300
Fax: 01225 474301
E-mail: contact@eduserv.org.uk

Website:
http://www.eduserv.org.uk

continued overleaf

Founded:
1988

Organisation type and purpose:
Non-profit IT services group, aiming to realise the benefits of IT for learners and researchers at every level through services, including access and identity management; institution connections to online resources such as Athens and OpenAthens; licence negotiation and management; offers on software and data licences to the education community; web solutions and consultancy. The Foundation funds research grants, interoperability standards making, seed-funding and advice on good practice.

Subject coverage:
Access to protected online resources, web solutions and licence negotiation for software and data licences.

Access to staff:
Contact by letter, by telephone, by fax, by e-mail and via website. Appointment necessary.
Hours: Mon to Fri, 0800 to 1800

EEF – THE MANUFACTURERS' ORGANISATION

Acronym or abbreviation: EEF

Broadway House, Tothill Street, Westminster, London, SW1H 9NQ

Tel: 020 7222 7777
Fax: 020 7222 2782
E-mail: enquiries@eef-fed.org.uk

Website:
http://www.eef.org.uk
About the EEF.

Enquiries:
Enquiries to: Information Services Manager
Direct tel: 020 7654 1574
Direct e-mail: crochester@eef-fed.org.uk

Founded:
1896

Organisation type and purpose:
Trade association.
Employers' Organisation.

Subject coverage:
Representation of the engineering industry's employer interests, employee relations, personnel management, education and skills, environmental issues, health and safety, economics. (Information derived from surveys of members is not generally available.)

Non-library collection catalogue:
All or part available in-house

Library catalogue:
All or part available in-house

Printed publications:
Engineering Outlook (4 times a year, £180)
Management and Professional Engineers' Pay Survey (annually, £400)

Publications list:
Available in print

Access to staff:
Contact by letter, by telephone, by fax, by e-mail and via website. Access for members only.
Hours: Mon to Fri, 0900 to 1530

Affiliated to:
Engineering Construction Industry Association
Federation of Engineering Design Companies
Fifteen autonomous organisations, fourteen regional associations

Links with:
Engineering Council
SEMTA

Member of:
Council of European Employers of the Metal, Engineering and Technology-Based Industries

EEF YORKSHIRE AND HUMBERSIDE

Acronym or abbreviation: EEF

Fieldhead, Thorner, Leeds, West Yorkshire, LS14 3DN

Tel: 0113 289 2671
Fax: 0113 289 3170
E-mail: team@eef-yandh.org.uk

Website:
http://www.eef.org.uk

Enquiries:
Enquiries to: Director
Direct tel: 0113 289 2863

Founded:
1890

Formerly called:
Engineering and Ship Building Employers Association (Yorkshire and Humberside)

Organisation type and purpose:
Membership association.
Employers trade association.
Supports engineering and manufacturing companies.

Subject coverage:
All matters relating to the employment of people.

Printed publications:
A variety of maintained documents are available for purchase, including:
Annual Review of the Federation (free to members)
EEF Directory
EEF Employment Guide (updated 3 times a year)
Health and Safety Newsline (newsletter, 4 times a year, free to members)
Practical Risk Assessment – guidance for SMEs
Register of Environmental Regulations
Training and Development Guide

Publications list:
Available in print

Access to staff:
Contact by letter and by fax. Appointment necessary. Non-members charged.
Hours: Mon to Fri, 0900 to 1700

Affiliated to:
EEF
Tothill Street, London, SW1H 9NQ

EEMA

Formal name: European Electronic Messaging Association
Acronym or abbreviation: EEMA

Alexander House, High Street, Inkberrow, Worcester, WR7 4DT

Tel: 01386 793 028
Fax: 01386 793268
E-mail: info@eema.org

Website:
http://www.eema.org

Enquiries:
Enquiries to: Membership Director
Direct e-mail: jim.dickson@eema.org

Founded:
1987

Organisation type and purpose:
International organisation, trade association.

Subject coverage:
All aspects of electronic business including security, directory, e-commerce, XML, unified messaging, legal issues surrounding secure digital identity and trusted third party products and services, change management, e-Government and public sector, CA's and regulation authorities.

Non-library collection catalogue:
All or part available online

Printed publications:
Publications include:
Role Based Access Control

e-Business Glossary
E-mail Best Practice Document
The 16 Steps to Effective E-mail and The Nine No's of E-mail
Acceptable Computer Usage Policy
Confidentiality Issues
Practical Policies for Virus Protection
The ECAF Model
LDAP Moving Forward
Internet Personal Naming Standard

Publications list:
Available online and in print

Access to staff:
Contact by letter, by telephone, by fax and by e-mail
Hours: Mon to Fri, 0900 to 1700

Access to building, collection or gallery:
Prior appointment required

EFFECTIVE TECHNOLOGY MARKETING LIMITED

Acronym or abbreviation: ETM

PO Box 171, Grimsby, Lincolnshire, DN35 0TP

Tel: 01472 816660
Fax: 01472 816660

Website:
http://www.dataresources.co.uk
Publications and conferences.

Enquiries:
Enquiries to: Managing Director

Founded:
1987

Organisation type and purpose:
Publishing house.
Publishers distributor.

Subject coverage:
Business information, Central and Eastern Europe and the CIS, Russia.

Printed publications:
Business Information Searcher (£95)
Directory of Information & Research Specialists 2002 (1st ed., £65)
EBRD Directory Business Information Sources on Central and Eastern Europe and the CIS (£125)

Publications list:
Available in print

Access to staff:
Contact by letter, by telephone, by fax and by e-mail
Hours: Mon to Fri, 0900 to 1700

EFNARC

Acronym or abbreviation: EFNARC

EFNARC Secretary, Cobblers Cottage, Chester Road, Daresbury, Warrington, WA4 4AJ

Tel: 01925 740 581
Fax: 01925 740 581
E-mail: roland.harbron@talktalk.net

Website:
http://www.efnarc.org

Enquiries:
Enquiries to: Secretary

Founded:
March 1998

Formerly known as:
European Federation of Producers and Applicators of Specialist Products for Structures

Organisation type and purpose:
Trade association, present number of members: 15. Represents National Trade Associations and major European manufacturing companies involved in the protection and repair of concrete structures, sprayed concrete and industrial flooring.

Subject coverage:
Trade associations and major European manufacturing companies involved in the protection and repair of concrete structures, sprayed concrete and industrial flooring.

Non-library collection catalogue:
All or part available online

Printed publications:
European Specification for Sprayed Concrete (English and German editions)
Specification for Synthetic Resin Polymer-modified Cementitious Floorings for Industrial Use

Publications list:
Available online and in print

Access to staff:
Contact by letter, by telephone, by fax, by e-mail and via website
Hours: Mon to Fri, 0900 to 1700

EGG CRAFTERS GUILD OF GREAT BRITAIN

The Studio, 7 Hylton Terrace, North Shields, Tyne and Wear, NE29 0EE

Tel: 0191 258 3648
Fax: 0191 258 3648
E-mail: joanccutts@oal.com

Website:
http://www.geocities.com/eggcraftersguild
www.freewebs.com/eggcraftersguild

Enquiries:
Enquiries to: Life President/Founder

Founded:
1979

Organisation type and purpose:
International organisation, membership association (membership is by subscription, election or invitation), present number of members: 800 worldwide, voluntary organisation. Craft organisation.
Members meet at various venues to exhibit and enter competitions; many members sell their eggs, some give Guild talks to organisations.

Subject coverage:
Egg craft (painting and other art work on eggshell); exhibitions; teaching; cutting designs with electric drill. Many eggs are created in the Style of Fabergé, and all are made from real eggs.

Printed publications:
Books
Newsletter (quarterly to members only)

Access to staff:
Contact by letter, by fax and by e-mail.
Appointment necessary.
Hours: Mon to Fri, 0900 to 1600

EGYPT EXPLORATION SOCIETY

Acronym or abbreviation: EES

3 Doughty Mews, London, WC1N 2PG

Tel: 020 7242 1880
Fax: 020 7404 6118
E-mail: contact@ees.ac.uk

Website:
http://www.ees.ac.uk
About the Society and its work, history, photo galleries, library archives, fieldwork, publications, news, payment facilities.

Enquiries:
Enquiries to: Administrator
Direct tel: 020 7242 2268
Other contacts: Deputy Director

Founded:
1882

Formerly called:
The Egypt Exploration Fund (EEF) (year of change 1915)

Organisation type and purpose:
International organisation, learned society (membership is by subscription), present number of members: 3200, registered charity (charity number 212384), research organisation.

Subject coverage:
Ancient Egypt; archaeology and history of Egypt to 1900 AD.

Information services:
Library, archives, online resources.

Education services:
Publications, events.

Museum or gallery collection, archive, or library special collection:
Library of Egyptology
Archive

Non-library collection catalogue:
All or part available online

Library catalogue:
All or part available online

Printed publications:
Publications prices do not include p&p:
Egyptian Archaeology (2 times a year)
Arabic Documents from the Ottoman Period from Qasr Ibrim (Hinds M, et al, 1986, £48)
Archaeological Memoirs (intermittent)
Egyptian Archaeology, The Bulletin of the Egypt Exploration Society (2 times a year, cover price £3)
Excavation Memoirs (intermittent)
Graeco-Roman Memoirs (intermittent)
Meroitic Inscriptions, Part II (Griffith F Ll, 1912, £20)
Semna-Kumma I, The Temple of Kumma; and The Temple of Semna (Caminos R A, 1998, two-volume set, £90)
Texts from Excavations (intermittent)
The Anubieion at Saqqara I, The Settlement and the Temple Precinct (Jeffeys D G, et al, 1988, £72)
The Inscriptions of Sinai, Part II (Gardiner A H, et al, 1955, £40)
The Journal of Egyptian Archaeology (annually, £40, members £34)
The Mephite Tomb of Horemheb, Commander-in-Chief of Tutankhamun, II A Catalogue of the finds (Schneider H D, 1996, £80)
The Tomb of Tia and Tia. A Royal Monument of the Ramesside Period In The Memphite Necropolis (Martin G T, 1997, £96)
The Oxyrhynchus Papyri, Part LXVI (Gonis M, et al, 1999, £70)
The Scrolls of Bishop Timotheos (Plumley J M, 1975, £15)
Who Was Who in Egyptology, A Biographical Index from 1700 to Present Day (Bierbrier M L, 1995, £40)
Order printed publications from: Oxbow Books, 10 Hythe Bridge Street, Oxford, OX1 2EW, United Kingdom, tel: 01865 241249, fax: 01865 794449, e-mail: oxbow@oxbowbooks.com, internet: www.oxbowbooks.com

Publications list:
Available online and in print

Access to staff:
Contact by letter, by telephone, by fax, by e-mail, in person and via website. Appointment necessary. Non-members charged.
Hours: Tue to Fri, 1030 to 1630

Access to building, collection or gallery:
No prior appointment required

Links with:
Foundation for Science and Technology

EGYPTIAN STATE TOURIST OFFICE

Egyptian House, 170 Piccadilly, London, W1V 9DD

Tel: 020 7493 5283
Fax: 020 7408 0295
E-mail: egypt@freenetname.co.uk

Website:
http://www.interoz.com/Egypt
The official Ministry of Tourism website.

Enquiries:
Enquiries to: Director
Direct tel: 020 7495 6489
Other contacts: Deputy Manager

Formerly called:
Egyptian Tourist Authority (UK)

Organisation type and purpose:
National government body.
Promotion of tourism to Egypt.

Subject coverage:
Tourism, travel and transport, schedules and prices in Egypt; visa forms and information; Nile cruises; places of interest; tourist villages, destinations in Egypt. Conference and meeting facilities.

Museum or gallery collection, archive, or library special collection:
A collection of slides of Egypt
Promotional videos on the country
Posters

Printed publications:
Brochures, pictures and maps, Cairo, Luxor, Aswan, Sinai, Alexandria, Red Sea, Oasis
Press releases, statistics

Electronic and video publications:
Videos on different places

Access to staff:
Contact by letter, by telephone, by fax and by e-mail
Hours: Mon to Fri, 0930 to 1630

Links with:
Egyptian Embassy and the Egyptian Consulate tel: 020 7235 9777; fax: 020 7235 5684

Parent body:
Ministry of Tourism in Egypt tel: + 202 685 3576/9658; fax: + 202 685 4363/4788

EIL CULTURAL AND EDUCATIONAL TRAVEL

Acronym or abbreviation: EIL UK

287 Worcester Road, Malvern, Worcestershire, WR14 1AB

Tel: 01684 562577
Fax: 01684 562212
E-mail: info@eiluk.org

Website:
http://www.eiluk.org
General information.

Enquiries:
Enquiries to: Chief Executive

Founded:
1936

Formerly called:
(BAEIL)

Organisation type and purpose:
International organisation, membership association, registered charity (charity number 1070440), suitable for ages: 16+.
Non-profit making organisation. Recognised by the Economic and Social Council of the UN (ECOSOC) as category II non-governmental organisation.
Cultural and educational exchange.

Subject coverage:
Understanding between countries of the world, cross-cultural education.

Printed publications:
Newsletter (3 times a year, for members)
General organisational brochure
Outbound Programmes brochure

Access to staff:
Contact by letter, by telephone, by fax, by e-mail and via website
Hours: Mon to Fri, 0900 to 1700

continued overleaf

Affiliated to:
UNESCO, category B

ELDERLY ACCOMMODATION COUNSEL

Acronym or abbreviation: EAC

3rd Floor, 89 Albert Embankment, London, SE1 7TP

Tel: 020 7820 1343
Fax: 020 7820 3970
E-mail: enquiries@eac.org.uk

Website:
http://www.housingcare.org
Access to National Database of housing and care homes

Founded:
1985

Organisation type and purpose:
Registered charity (charity number 292552).
A national charity offering advice and information about all forms of accommodation and care for older people.

Subject coverage:
Accommodation options for older people. Elderly Accommodation Counsel (EAC) is a national charity, maintaining nation-wide databases of accommodation specifically for older people – sheltered, retirement housing to buy and to rent, extra care schemes and close care housing (sheltered accommodation where there is a care home on site), and care homes, both for personal care and for nursing. The free, independent advice line offers guidance, advice and detailed information to help older people choose and fund the support or accommodation options most suited to their needs and wishes.

Printed publications:
Accommodation options for older people (booklet)
Regional Guides on housing or on housing and care homes
Housing Options for Older People (HOOP) Toolkit
HOOP questionnaire

Access to staff:
Contact by letter, by telephone, by fax, by e-mail and via website
Hours: Mon to Fri, 0900 to 1700

Access to building, collection or gallery:
No access other than to staff

ELECTORAL REFORM INTERNATIONAL SERVICES

Formal name: Electoral Reform International Services

6 Chancel Street, London, SE1 0UU

Tel: 020 7620 3794
Fax: 020 7928 4366
E-mail: erisuk@eris.org.uk

Website:
http://www.eris.org.uk

Organisation type and purpose:
To provide support to emerging democracies for the further consolidation of democracy and good governance around the world, with a particular emphasis of the conduct of credible and transparent elections

Access to staff:
Contact by letter, by telephone, by fax, by e-mail and via website

ELECTORAL REFORM SOCIETY LIMITED

Acronym or abbreviation: ERS

6 Chancel Street, Blackfriars, London, SE1 0UU

Tel: 020 7928 1622
Fax: 020 7401 7789

E-mail: ers@reform.demon.co.uk

Website:
http://www.electoral_reform.org.uk

Enquiries:
Enquiries to: Chief Executive
Direct tel: 020 7202 8608
Direct fax: 020 7620 0829
Direct e-mail: peters@reform.demon.co.uk

Founded:
1884

Formerly called:
Proportional Representation Society from 1884 to 1959

Organisation type and purpose:
Learned society, membership association (membership is by subscription), present number of members: 1500, voluntary organisation.
Campaigning organisation.
To campaign for the introduction of proportional representation by the single transferable vote method for all elections.

Subject coverage:
All aspects of elections including electoral law and practice; voting systems, especially proportional representation; election monitoring; election campaigns; balloting in professional, trade union and other common interest organisations etc.

Museum or gallery collection, archive, or library special collection:
The Lakeman Library (formerly the Arthur McDougall Library) houses a collection of works and papers on political science, elections, election observations, voting systems, electoral reform, especially proportional representation in the United Kingdom and elsewhere. The Library is maintained by the McDougall Trust

Trade and statistical information:
Statistical information relating to elections in the UK and elsewhere.

Library catalogue:
All or part available in-house

Printed publications:
Annual Report (members)
Ballot Box (newsletter, members)
Publications include:
Ballot Secrecy (A4 58pp, £10 plus p&p)
What is STV? (leaflet, 50p plus p&p)

Publications list:
Available online and in print

Access to staff:
Contact by letter, by telephone, by fax and by e-mail. Appointment necessary.
Hours: Mon to Fri, 0930 to 1730
Special comments: Letter of introduction preferred. Charges may be made to users.

Access to building, collection or gallery:
No prior appointment required
Hours: Mon to Fri, 0930 to 1730

Access for disabled people:
Toilet facilities

Associated charity:
The McDougall Trust
tel: 020 7620 1080; fax: 020 7928 1528; e-mail: admin@mcdougall.org.uk

Consultative status with:
Economic and Social Council of the United Nations

Enquiries concerning the conduct of ballots and surveys ONLY:
Electoral Reform (Services) Ltd
The Elections Centre, 33 Clarendon Road, Hornsey, London, N8 0NW; tel: 020 8365 8909; fax: 020 8365 8587

Subsidiary body:
Electoral Reform (International Services) Ltd
tel: 020 7620 3794; fax: 020 7928 4366
Electoral Reform Ltd
tel: 020 8365 8909; fax: 020 8365 8587

ELECTRIC RAILWAY SOCIETY

Acronym or abbreviation: ERS

17 Catherine Drive, Sutton Coldfield, West Midlands, B73 6AX

Tel: 0121 354 8332
E-mail: iain@ifrew.fsnet.co.uk

Enquiries:
Enquiries to: Honorary Secretary

Founded:
1946

Organisation type and purpose:
Learned society (membership is by subscription).

Subject coverage:
History and development of electric railway and light railway services and equipment in the British Isles. Development of rail services around major cities worldwide. Development of high speed intercity passenger services worldwide.

Museum or gallery collection, archive, or library special collection:
Some material available for educational purposes
Collection of colour slides depicting tramways, electric railways, in the United Kingdom
Collection of colour slides depicting coastal ferries and pleasure steamers in British waters

Printed publications:
The Electric Railway (6 times a year, subscription £12)

Access to staff:
Contact by letter and by e-mail
Hours: Mon to Fri, 0900 to 1700

Access to building, collection or gallery:
No access other than to staff

Affiliated to:
Asociación Uruguaya Amigos del Riel
Cas Correos 857, Montevideo, Uruguay
Railway Society of Southern Africa
PO Box 12375, Jacobs, SA 4026

ELECTRICAL CONTRACTORS' ASSOCIATION

Acronym or abbreviation: ECA

ESCA House, 34 Palace Court, London, W2 4HY

Tel: 020 7313 4800
Fax: 020 7221 7344
E-mail: electricalcontractors@eca.co.uk

Website:
http://www.eca.co.uk
Background, organisation and structure.

Enquiries:
Enquiries to: Head of Marketing
Other contacts: Departmental Heads

Founded:
1901

Organisation type and purpose:
Trade association.

Subject coverage:
Electrical installation work; engineering and contracting.

Printed publications:
ECA Desk Diary
ECA Registered Electrical Contractors (annually)
Electrical Contractor (monthly)
Information Manual

Access to staff:
Contact by letter, by fax and by e-mail
Hours: Mon to Fri, 0900 to 1700

ELECTRICAL INSTALLATION EQUIPMENT MANUFACTURERS' ASSOCIATION LIMITED

Acronym or abbreviation: EIEMA

Westminster Tower, 3 Albert Embankment, London, SE1 7SL

Tel: 020 7793 3013
Fax: 020 7735 4158
E-mail: cac@beama.org.uk

Website:
http://www.eiema.org.uk

Enquiries:
Enquiries to: Director
Direct tel: 020 7793 3009
Direct e-mail: dd@eiema.demon.co.uk

Organisation type and purpose:
Trade association.

Subject coverage:
Electrical accessories; fuses; switch and fuse gear; miniature, earth leakage and moulded case circuit-breakers; distribution switchboards (cubicle and non-cubicle types); cablejoints and terminators.

Trade and statistical information:
Statistical information is strictly for members only.

Printed publications:
Guide to Busbar Trunking Systems
Guide to Fuse Link Application
Guide to 'IP' Codes for enclosures
Guide to Residual Current Devices
Guide to Switch and Fusegear Devices
Guide to the Forms of Separation
Guide to Type Tested Assemblies and Partially Type Tested Assemblies
Member and Product Guide (annually)

Access to staff:
Contact by letter, by telephone, by fax and by e-mail
Hours: Mon to Thu, 0900 to 1700; Fri, 0900 to 1545

Affiliated to:
British Electrotechnical and Allied Manufacturers Association (BEAMA)

ELECTRICITY ASSOCIATION

Acronym or abbreviation: EA

Business Information Centre, 30 Millbank, London, SW1P 4RD

Tel: 020 7963 5700
Fax: 020 7963 5959
E-mail: enquiries@electricity.org.uk

Website:
http://www.electricity.org.uk
Comprehensive site on the electricity industry in the United Kingdom with links to EA member companies, and national and international electricity organisations overseas.Various free information sheets may be downloaded.

Enquiries:
Enquiries to: Manager
Direct tel: 020 7963 5789
Direct fax: 020 7963 5870

Founded:
1990

Organisation type and purpose:
Trade association.

Subject coverage:
Structure and regulation of the electricity supply industry in the United Kingdom and Europe.

Trade and statistical information:
Statistical information on the electricity industry, annual reports and accounts of UK and overseas utilities.

Library catalogue:
All or part available in-house

Printed publications:
Electricity Industry Review (£125)
UK Electricity Supply Rates (prices on request)

Publications list:
Available online and in print

Access to staff:
Contact by e-mail. Access for members only.
Hours: Mon to Fri, 0900 to 1700
Special comments: Available to members only.

ELECTROPHYSIOLOGICAL TECHNOLOGISTS ASSOCIATION

Acronym or abbreviation: EPTA

Department of Clinical Neurophysiology, Great Ormond St Hospital, Great Ormond Street, London, WC1N 3JH

E-mail: eptasec@hotmail.com

Website:
http://www.epta.50megs.com

Enquiries:
Enquiries to: Honorary Secretary

Founded:
1949

Organisation type and purpose:
National organisation, professional body (membership is by subscription, present number of members: over 600.

Subject coverage:
Electrophysiology especially neurophysiology.

Printed publications:
Quarterly journal (annual subscription)

Access to staff:
Contact by letter and by e-mail
Hours: Mon to Fri, 0900 to 1700

Links with:
International Organisation of Societies for Electophysiology (OSET)
tel: 01785 258672

ELGAR SOCIETY, THE

The Hon Membership Secretary, 2 Marriott's Close, Haddenham, Buckinghamshire, HP17 8BT

E-mail: membership@elgar.org

Website:
http://www.elgar.org
Real Audio, extracts, biographical details, merchandise details, branches, networking, multimedia, etc.
http://www.cornucopia.org.uk
Summary catalogue.

Enquiries:
Enquiries to: Honorary Secretary
Direct tel: 01844 354096
Direct fax: 01844 350473
Direct e-mail: hon.sec@elgar.org

Founded:
1951

Merged with:
Friends of Elgar's Birthplace

Organisation type and purpose:
International organisation, learned society (membership is by subscription), present number of members: 1700 UK & world, registered charity (charity number 298062).
Trading Company formed in 2000.
To supply books, CD's, scores and other merchandise.

Subject coverage:
Sir Edward Elgar, his life and music; study, appreciation and performance of his works. Publicity for concerts, talks and lectures via website.

Museum or gallery collection, archive, or library special collection:
Scores of all Compositions
Memorabilia
Research biographies etc

Printed publications:
Elgar Society Journal (3 times a year)
Elgar Society News (3 times a year)
Order printed publications from: Elgar Editions c/o 20 High Street, Rickmansworth, Hertfordshire, WD3 1ER, or via the website

Electronic and video publications:
Elgar Choral Songs

Elgar's Interpreters on Record
King Olaf
The Black Knight
The Dream of Gerontius
The Elgar Edition
The Elgar Piano
Various CDs of choral/orchestral and piano music

Publications list:
Available online and in print

Access to staff:
Contact by letter, by telephone, by fax, by e-mail and via website
Hours: Any reasonable time

Other branches at:
Great Western Branch (Wales / Bristol)
tel: 01278 751519
Leeds (West Yorkshire)
tel: 01226 383053
London
tel: 01235 813257
North-West (Manchester)
tel: 0161 998 4404
Scotland
tel: 01383 727491
Southern (Southampton)
tel: 02392 389410
Thames Valley (Thame)
tel: 01844 212061
West Midlands (Worcester)
tel: 01684 562692

ELIZABETH FINN CARE

Acronym or abbreviation: EFC

1 Derry Street, London, W8 5HY

Tel: 020 7396 6700
Fax: 020 7396 6739
E-mail: info@elizabethfinn.org.uk

Website:
http://www.elizabethfinncare.org.uk
www.turn2us.org.uk
turn2us is a new charity offering a groundbreaking online service to help the millions of people in need in the UK. For the first time, people can access information on all benefits and grants available to them from both statutory and voluntary organisations, at no cost, through turn2us. In many cases, applications for support can be made directly from the website and we'll keep people informed by e-mail or by sending a text to their mobile phone.

Enquiries:
Enquiries to: Director of Casework
Direct e-mail: enquiries.casework@elizabethfinn.org.uk

Founded:
1897

Formerly called:
Distressed Gentlefolks Aid Association (DGAA); Homelife DGAA (year of change 1994); Elizabeth Finn Trust (year of change 2005)

Organisation type and purpose:
Voluntary organisation, registered charity (charity number 207812).
Elizabeth Finn Care is the UK's largest independent direct grant-giver dedicated specifically to helping those in poverty. As such, EFC provides support and care for people, including their immediate families, of British or Irish nationality, regardless of religious denomination, political opinion, age or place of residence.

Subject coverage:
High quality care in 12 residential and nursing homes and 10 almshouses cottages; financial support and assistance to people of all ages who live in their own homes or those requiring financial assistance toward care in other homes. The financial support we can provide includes regular allowances and one-off grants to cover specific items, such as wheelchairs, or for household repair and maintenance.

continued overleaf

Access to staff:
Contact by letter, by telephone and by fax
Hours: Mon to Fri, 0900 to 1700
Special comments: No personal callers.

ELMBRIDGE BOROUGH COUNCIL

Acronym or abbreviation: EBC

Civic Centre, High Street, Esher, Surrey, KT10 9SD

Tel: 01372 474474\ Minicom no. 01372 474219
Fax: 01372 474972
E-mail: civiccentre@elmbridge.gov.uk

Website:
http://www.elmbridge.gov.uk

Enquiries:
Enquiries to: Communications and Consultation
Officer
Direct tel: 01372 474391
Direct fax: 01372 474931
Direct e-mail: lballinger@elmbridge.gov.uk

Founded:
1974

Organisation type and purpose:
Local government body.

Subject coverage:
All aspects of Elmbridge Borough and Elmbridge
Borough Council; services, amenities, housing and
planning.

Printed publications:
A-Z of Local Services
Elmbridge Review (twice a year)
Numerous leaflets and booklets available from the
housing, planning and finance directorates

Access to staff:
Contact by letter, by telephone, by fax, by e-mail
and via website. Appointment necessary.
Hours: Mon to Fri, 0845 to 1700

Access for disabled people:
Level entry, toilet facilities

Parent body:
Surrey County Council
tel: 020 8541 8800

ELSEVIER SCIENCE BIBLIOGRAPHIC DATABASES

Customer Service Department, Linacre House
Jordan Hill, Oxford OX2 8DP

Tel: 01865 474010
Fax: 01865 474011
E-mail: directenquiries@elsevier.com

Website:
http://www.elsevier.com/
Publications catalogue.

Enquiries:
Enquiries to: Press Officer
Direct e-mail: pressoffice@elsevier.com
Other contacts: Product Manager for telephone
queries, email: a.munns@elsevier.co.uk.

Founded:
1960

Organisation type and purpose:
Publishing house.

Subject coverage:
Geology, development studies, human geography,
physical geography, textiles, fluids, civil
engineering, process engineering, ecology, physical
geography, oceanography, geomechanics.

**Museum or gallery collection, archive, or library
special collection:**
Back issues and indexes for 1966 until present

Printed publications:
The annual cumulative index is included in the last
issue of each journal:
Ecological Abstracts, ISSN 0305–196X (1838 euro)
Fluid Abstracts: Civil Engineering, ISSN 0962–7170
(1286 euro)

Fluid Abstracts: Process Engineering, ISSN 0962–
7162 (monthly, 1286 euro)
Geographical Abstracts: Human Geography, ISSN
0953–9611 (monthly, 1371 euro)
Geographical Abstracts: Physical Geography, ISSN
0954–0504 (monthly, 1800 euro)
Geological Abstracts, ISSN 0954–0512 (12 monthly,
1813 euro)
Geomechanics Abstracts, ISSN1365–1617 (6 times a
year, 531 euro)
International Development Abstracts, ISSN 0262–
0855 (6 times a year, 847 euro)
World Textile Abstracts, ISSN 0043–9118 (12
monthly, 1276 euro)
Order printed publications from: Elsevier Science,
Regional Sales Office
Customer Support Department, PO Box 211,
Amsterdam, NL-1000 AE, The Netherlands, tel: 00
31 20 485 3757, fax: 00 31 20 485 3432, e-mail: nlinfo
-f@elsevier.nl

Electronic and video publications:
FLUIDEX (on Dialog Silver Platter and EINS)
GEOBASE (on Dialog Silver Platter, OCLC and
EINS)
World Textiles (on Silver Platter, STN, Fiz-Technik
and EINS)

Publications list:
Available in print

Access to staff:
Contact by letter, by telephone, by fax, by e-mail
and via website
Hours: Mon to Fri, 0900 to 1700

Other addresses:
Elsevier Science Bibliographic Databases
Molenwerf 1, 1014 AE Amsterdam, The
Netherlands; tel: 00 31 20 485 3507; fax: 00 31 20
485 3222

Parent body:
Elsevier Science Limited
The Boulevard, Langford Lane, Kidlington,
Oxford, OX5 1GB; tel: 01865 843000; fax: 01865
843010

ELSON & ROBBINS LIMITED

Formal name: Elson and Robbins Limited
(incorporating Wade Spring)

Bennett Street, Long Eaton, Nottingham, NG10
4HL

Tel: 0115 946 3000
Fax: 0115 946 1361
E-mail: sales@elson-and-robbins.co.uk

Enquiries:
Enquiries to: Technical Director
Direct e-mail: ian@wadespring.demon.co.uk

Founded:
1926

Formerly called:
Wade Spring

Organisation type and purpose:
Manufacturing industry.

Subject coverage:
Spring cases and assemblies for upholstery and
bedding trades.

Access to staff:
Contact by letter, by telephone, by fax and by e-
mail
Hours: Mon to Fri, 0900 to 1700

Parent body:
Wade Furniture Group
Wellington Street, Long Eaton, Nottingham,
NG10 4HT

ELVA OWNERS CLUB

Acronym or abbreviation: EOC

8 Liverpool Terrace, Worthing, West Sussex, BN11
1TA

Tel: 01903 823710

Fax: 01903 823710
E-mail: roger.dunbar@elva.com

Website:
http://www.elva.com
Official Elva website.

Enquiries:
Enquiries to: Honorary Secretary

Founded:
1979

Organisation type and purpose:
Membership association (membership is by
election or invitation), present number of
members: 400.
Support for owners of Elva cars.

Subject coverage:
Information about Elva racing and sports racing
cars.

Information services:
A focal point for information relating to ELVA
Cars.

Access to staff:
Contact by letter, by telephone, by e-mail and via
website. Appointment necessary.
Hours: Mon to Fri, 0900 to 1700

EMBASSY OF DENMARK

55 Sloane Street, London, SW1X 9SR

Tel: 020 7333 0200
Fax: 020 7333 0270
E-mail: lonamb@um.dk

Website:
http://www.dk-export.com

Enquiries:
Enquiries to: Information Officer

Organisation type and purpose:
National government body.

Subject coverage:
Denmark and Danish governmental matters;
Danish commerce.

Printed publications:
Focus Denmark
Directory of Danish Subsidiaries of Danish
Companies in the UK (priced)

EMBASSY OF FINLAND

38 Chesham Place, London, SW1X 8HW

Tel: 020 7838 6200
Fax: 020 7235 3680
E-mail: sanomat.lon@formin.fi

Website:
http://www.finemb.org.uk

Enquiries:
Enquiries to: Information Officer

Organisation type and purpose:
Embassy.

Access to staff:
Contact by letter, by telephone and via website
Hours: Mon to Fri, 0830 to 1230, 1330 to 1630
Special comments: Passport and Visa Department
Open: Mon to Fri, 0900 to 1200 only; telephone
enquiries, Mon to Fri, 1400 to 1600.

EMBASSY OF HONDURAS

115 Gloucester Place, London, W1U 6JT

Tel: 020 7486 4880
Fax: 020 7486 4550
E-mail: hondurasuk@linone.net

Enquiries:
Enquiries to: Information Officer

Subject coverage:
Honduras Republic; Central America.

EMBASSY OF ICELAND

2A Hans Street, London, SW1X 0JE

Tel: 020 7259 3999
Fax: 020 7245 9649
E-mail: icemb.london@utn.stjr.is

Website:
http://www.statice.is
Statistical information. Homepage of Statistics of Iceland.
http://www.icetourist.is
Tourism in Iceland. Home page of the Tourist Board of Iceland.
http://www.iceland.org/uk
Embassy homepage.
http://www.iceland.is
Iceland Information Gateway

Enquiries:
Enquiries to: Information Officer

Organisation type and purpose:
International organisation.

Subject coverage:
Icelandic government matters, Icelandic trade.

Access to staff:
Contact by letter, by fax and by e-mail
Hours: Mon to Fri, 0930 to 1600

EMBASSY OF MONGOLIA

7 Kensington Court, London, W8 5DL

Tel: 020 7937 5238
Fax: 020 7937 1117
E-mail: office@embassyofmongolia.co.uk

Website:
http://www.embassyofmongolia.co.uk

Enquiries:
Enquiries to: Information Officer

Founded:
1969

Organisation type and purpose:
National government body.

Subject coverage:
General information about Mongolia.

Trade and statistical information:
Statistics and information about Mongolian economy.

Printed publications:
Newspaper
Press Releases

Access to staff:
Contact by letter, by telephone, by fax, by e-mail and in person. Appointment necessary.
Hours: Mon to Fri, 0900 to 1700

EMBASSY OF PERU

52 Sloane Street, London, SW1X 9SP

Tel: 020 7235 1917
Fax: 020 7235 4463
E-mail: postmaster@peruembassy-uk.com

Website:
http://www.peruembassy-uk.com
Peru general information: history, geography and politics, news, trade and investment, tourism, cultural and educational information, programmed activities in the UK and Peru.

Enquiries:
Enquiries to: Economic Advisor for trade and investment opportunities, for economic information

Organisation type and purpose:
National government body.
Diplomatic representation of Peru in the UK and Ireland.

Subject coverage:
Peruvian information.

Information services:
Trade and investment opportunities, tourism and cultural information and advice.

Education services:
Information and advice.

Trade and statistical information:
UK trade with Peru; Peruvian exports and imports; British investment in Peru; foreign investment in Peru; economic indicators for Peru; general statistical information.

Non-library collection catalogue:
All or part available in-house

Library catalogue:
All or part available in-house

Printed publications:
Opportunities (British Peruvian Chamber of Commerce publication)
Peru Exporta
Alpaca del Peru
Exportar (bilingual publication)
Tourism guides and brochures
Order printed publications from: email: postmaster@ peruembassy-uk.com

Publications list:
Available in print

Access to staff:
Contact by letter, by telephone, by fax, by e-mail, in person and via website. Appointment necessary.
Hours: Mon to Fri, 0900 to 1700

Access to building, collection or gallery:
Hours: Mon to Fri, 0900 to 1700

Links with:
Consulate General of Peru
52 Sloane Street, London, SW1X 9SP
Naval Attaché Office
5 Falstaff House, 24 Barldolph Road, Richmond, London, TW9 2LH

EMBASSY OF RWANDA

Acronym or abbreviation: AMBARWA

Uganda House, 58–59 Trafalgar Square, London, WC2N 5DS

Tel: 020 7930 2570
Fax: 020 7930 2572
E-mail: ambarwanda@compuserve.com

Website:
http://www.ambarwanda.org.uk

Enquiries:
Enquiries to: Administrator
Other contacts: First Secretary for detailed enquiries.

Founded:
1995

Organisation type and purpose:
National government body.
Embassy or Diplomatic Mission.
Consular and diplomatic relations.

Subject coverage:
Any information regarding Rwanda.

Trade and statistical information:
Trade or statistical information regarding Rwanda.

Access to staff:
Contact by letter, by telephone, by fax and by e-mail. Appointment necessary.
Hours: Mon to Fri, 0930 to 1300 and 1400 to 1730

Access for disabled people:
Level entry

EMBASSY OF SWEDEN

Press and Information, 11 Montagu Place, London, W1H 2AL

Tel: 020 7917 6400
Fax: 020 7724 4174
E-mail: ambassaden.london@foreign.ministry.se

Website:
http://www.swedenabroad.com/london

Enquiries:
Enquiries to: Information Officer

Organisation type and purpose:
Embassy.

Subject coverage:
General information on Sweden.

Access to staff:
Hours: Mon to Fri, 0900 to 1230 and 1400 to 1600

EMBASSY OF THE FEDERAL REPUBLIC OF GERMANY

23 Belgrave Square, London, SW1X 8PZ

Tel: 020 7824 1300
Fax: 020 7824 1470
E-mail: info@london.diplo.de

Website:
http://www.london.diplo.de
Services provided by the embassy, and by the information centre including life, science, economy and culture in Germany.
http://www.auswaertiges-amt.de
Information of all kinds about Germany.

Enquiries:
Enquiries to: Information Centre

Organisation type and purpose:
Government diplomatic representation.

Subject coverage:
Life, science, economy and culture in Germany.

EMBASSY OF THE REPUBLIC OF BULGARIA

186–188 Queens Gate, London, SW7 5HL

Tel: 020 7584 9433, 9400, 3144
Fax: 020 7584 4948
E-mail: bgembasy@globalnet.co.uk

Website:
http://www.bulgarianembassy.org.uk

Enquiries:
Enquiries to: Secretary
Other contacts: Trade Counsellor for trade information.

Founded:
1920

Organisation type and purpose:
National government body.
Embassy.
Diplomatic.

Access to staff:
Contact by letter and by fax. Appointment necessary.
Hours: Mon to Fri, 0900 to 1700

EMBASSY OF THE REPUBLIC OF CROATIA

21 Conway Street, London, W1T 6BN

Tel: 020 7387 2022/1640
Fax: 020 7387 0310

Enquiries:
Enquiries to: Information Officer

Organisation type and purpose:
National government body.
Diplomatic mission.

Subject coverage:
Information regarding the Republic of Croatia, the Croatian language, economic data, culture, etc.

Access to staff:
Contact by letter, by telephone, by fax and by e-mail. Appointment necessary.
Hours: Mon to Fri, 0900 to 1700
Consular Department: Mon to Thu, 1100 to 1400

EMBASSY OF THE REPUBLIC OF LITHUANIA

84 Gloucester Place, London, W1U 6AU

Tel: 020 7486 6401/6402; Consular section 020 7486 6404
Fax: 020 7486 6403
E-mail: lralon@globalnet.co.uk

Website:
http://www.users.globalnet.co.uk/~lralon

Enquiries:
Enquiries to: Head of Chancery
Other contacts: Private Secretary to the Ambassador

Organisation type and purpose:
National government body.

Subject coverage:
Lithuania.

Access to staff:
Contact by letter, by telephone, by fax and by e-mail. Appointment necessary.
Hours: Consular Section: Mon to Fri, 1000 to 1300

EMBASSY OF THE REPUBLIC OF SLOVENIA

10 Little College Street, London, SW1P 3SH

Tel: 020 7222 5400
Fax: 020 7222 5722
E-mail: vlo@mzz-dkp.gov.si

Website:
http://www.embassy-slovenia.org.uk
Information regarding Slovenia.

Enquiries:
Enquiries to: Information Officer

Founded:
1991

Organisation type and purpose:
National government body.

Subject coverage:
Slovenia and Slovene governmental matters, Slovene commerce, visa information.

Access to staff:
Contact by letter, by telephone, by fax, by e-mail and via website. Appointment necessary.
Hours: Mon to Fri, 0900 to 1700
Visas: Mon to Fri, 1000 to 1200

Access to building, collection or gallery:
Prior appointment required

Other address:
Embassy of the Republic of Slovenia
  Consular Section, 10 Cowley Street, London, SW1P

EMBASSY OF THE SLOVAK REPUBLIC

Acronym or abbreviation: Slovak Embassy

25 Kensington Palace Gardens, London, W8 4QY

Tel: 020 7313 6470
Fax: 020 7313 6481
E-mail: mail@slovakembassy.co.uk

Website:
http://www.slovakembassy.co.uk
General information, visa information, links.

Enquiries:
Enquiries to: Information Officer

Founded:
1993

Organisation type and purpose:
National government body.
Embassy.

Subject coverage:
General information on the Slovak Republic and tourist information.

Trade and statistical information:
General economy and trade information and statistics obtainable from the commercial attaché, telephone, 020 7727 3099; fax, 020 7727 3667 or via website.

Non-library collection catalogue:
All or part available in-house

Library catalogue:
All or part available in-house

Publications list:
Available online

Access to staff:
Contact by letter, by telephone, by fax and by e-mail. Appointment necessary.
Hours: General: Mon to Thu, 0900 to 1645; Fri, 0900 to 1530
Visa Department: Mon, Wed, 0900 to 1600; Tue,Thu, Fri, 0900 to 1200

Access to building, collection or gallery:
Prior appointment required
Hours: Open to Public: Mon to Thu, 0900 to 1645; Fri, 0900 to 1530
Special comments: Visa Information: tel no 020 7313 6470.

EMBASSY OF THE SYRIAN ARAB REPUBLIC

8 Belgrave Square, London, SW1X 8PH

Tel: 020 7245 9012
Fax: 020 7235 4621

Enquiries:
Enquiries to: Information Officer

Organisation type and purpose:
Diplomatic Mission.

EMBASSY OF THE UNION OF MYANMAR

19a Charles Street, London, W1J 5DX

Tel: 020 7499 4340 Option 1 Consular Section, 09001 600 306 Visa Information
Fax: 020 7493 7399
E-mail: memblondon@aol.com

Website:
http://www.myanmar.com

Enquiries:
Enquiries to: Information Officer – Consular Office
Direct tel: 020 7499 4340

Formerly called:
Embassy of the Union of Burma

Organisation type and purpose:
Diplomatic relations and consular services.

Subject coverage:
Consular, travel, investing opportunities, trade.

Printed publications:
Myanmar Visitors' Guide

Electronic and video publications:
CD-ROM on Information available for purchase from the Embassy

Access to staff:
Contact by letter, by telephone and by fax. Appointment necessary.
Hours: Mon to Fri, 0930 to 1630
Visa Section: Mon to Fri, 1000 to 1300

Access to building, collection or gallery:
Hours: Mon to Fri, 0930 to 1630
Special comments: Via Charles Street

EMBASSY OF THE UNITED ARAB EMIRATES

30 Princes Gate, London, SW7 1PT

Tel: 020 7581 1281
Fax: 020 7581 9616
E-mail: information@uaeembassyuk.net

Website:
http://www.uaeembassyuk.net

Enquiries:
Enquiries to: Information and Resources
Direct e-mail: commerce@uaeembassyuk.net

Organisation type and purpose:
National government body.
Embassy.

Subject coverage:
United Arab Emirates.

EMBROIDERERS' GUILD

Apartment 41, Hampton Court Palace, Kingston Upon Thames, Surrey, KT8 9AU

Tel: 020 8943 1229
Fax: 020 8977 9882
E-mail: administrator@embroiderersguild.com

Website:
http://www.embroiderersguild.com
Details of Young Embroiderers' Guild website; STITCH with the Embroiderers' Guild; World of Embroidery.

Enquiries:
Enquiries to: Communications and Marketing Officer
Direct tel: 020 8943 1229 ext 24
Direct e-mail: cbutterfield@embroidersguild.com
Other contacts: Curator for museum collection.

Founded:
1906

Organisation type and purpose:
Membership association (membership is by subscription), present number of members: 14,000, registered charity (charity number 234239), museum, suitable for ages: 5+, publishing house. To promote the craft of embroidery for all.

Subject coverage:
Historical and contemporary embroidery – workshops, library, bookshop and educational resources. Branches nationwide and Young Embroiderers available for children.

Museum or gallery collection, archive, or library special collection:
Collection of 11,000 pieces of historical and contemporary embroidery from the 17th century onwards; under the care of a professional Curator. Exhibitions from the collection travel to museums throughout the UK
Specialised library (by appointment)

Printed publications:
Books and booklets on all aspects of the art, techniques and history of embroidery and related techniques
Contact (newsletter, 3 times a year)
Stitch with the Embroiderers' Guild (6 times a year)
The Machine Embroidery Workbook
Embroidery Magazine (6 times a year)
The Workbook
Textile Ideas for Young Embroiderers (3 times a year)
Order printed publications from: Magazine Secretary, Embroiderers' Guild
PO Box 42B, East Molesey, Surrey, KT8 9BB, tel: 020 8943 1229 ext 28, fax: 020 8977 9882, e-mail: jjardine@embroiderersguild.com

Publications list:
Available online and in print

Access to staff:
Contact by letter, by telephone, by fax, by e-mail and via website. Appointment necessary.
Hours: Mon to Fri, 1000 to 1630
Special comments: Day pass required on arrival at Hampton Court Palace.

Access to building, collection or gallery:
No prior appointment required
Hours: Mon to Fri, 1030 to 1630

EMERSON COLLEGE

Formal name: Emerson College Trust Ltd

Forest Row, East Sussex, RH18 5JX

Tel: 01342 822238
Fax: 01342 826055
E-mail: mail@emerson.org.uk

Website:
http://www.emerson.org.uk
Home page; information on the college and all the courses.

Enquiries:
Enquiries to: Information Officer

Founded:
1962

Organisation type and purpose:
International organisation, registered charity (charity number 312101), suitable for ages: 18+ no upper limit, training organisation.
Emerson College is an international centre for adult education, training and research based on the work of Rudolf Steiner.

Subject coverage:
Steiner and Waldorf teacher training, anthroposophy and Rudolf Steiner.
Bio-dynamic, organic agriculture training.

Printed publications:
Course brochures (free)
Prospectus (free)

Access to staff:
Contact by letter, by telephone, by fax, by e-mail and via website. Appointment necessary.
Hours: Mon to Fri, 0830 to 1615; Reception is closed 1245 to 1400

Access to building, collection or gallery:
Prior appointment required
Special comments: Library is only open to current full-time students.

Access for disabled people:
Parking provided, ramped entry

Accredited by the:
British Accreditation Council (BAC)
Westminster Central Hall, Storey's Gate, London, SW1H 9NH; tel: 020 7233 3468; fax: 020 7233 3470; e-mail: info@the-bac.org

EMI MUSIC SOUND FOUNDATION

27 Wrights Lane, London, W8 5SW

Tel: 020 7795 7000
Fax: 020 7795 7296
E-mail: enquiries@emimusicsoundfoundation.com

Website:
http://www.emimusicsoundfoundation.com

Enquiries:
Enquiries to: Chief Executive

Founded:
1997

Organisation type and purpose:
Registered charity (charity number 1104027).

Subject coverage:
Improvement of people's access to music education.

Printed publications:
Annual Review

Publications list:
Available in print

Access to staff:
Contact by letter, by telephone, by fax and by e-mail
Hours: Mon to Fri, 0900 to 1730

EMIE AT NFER

Acronym or abbreviation: EMIE at NFER

NFER, The Mere, Upton Park, Slough, Berkshire, SL1 2DQ

Tel: 01753 574123
Fax: 01753 531458
E-mail: emie@nfer.ac.uk

Website:
http://www.nfer.ac.uk/emie
Includes: all EMIE publications, access to emiedirect database, links to full text of local authority documents, links to all local authority education services and other relevant sites.

Enquiries:
Enquiries to: Head of Service
Direct tel: 01753 523156
Other contacts: EMIE Information Officers

Founded:
1981

Organisation type and purpose:
Local government body, research organisation.
To provide information service and exchange on education management policy and practice for local authority staff working in or with the education service. Part of the National Foundation for Educational Research which is dedicated to providing information on education and children's service policy and practice issues for those working in or with UK local authrorities.

Subject coverage:
Information services on educational management policy and practice provided principally to local authority staff and members in England, Wales, Scotland and Northern Ireland. Not curriculum but other matters pertaining to the operation of education and children's services in the UK.

Museum or gallery collection, archive, or library special collection:
Certain categories of documentation only accessible by local authority personnel. Extensive collection of policy level documentation contributed by education and children's services authorities in England, Wales, Scotland and Northern Ireland

Trade and statistical information:
Surveys conducted on various aspects of education and children's service provision.

Printed publications:
All publications free to Local Education Authorities
Abstracts Bulletins – Synopsis and Document Digests
Regular newsletters, abstracts, bulletins, surveys and commentaries on current issues in education and children's services

Publications list:
Available online and in print

Access to staff:
Contact by letter, by telephone, by fax, by e-mail and via website. Appointment necessary.
Hours: Mon to Fri, 0915 to 1715
Special comments: Queries dealt with if resources permit but full range of services limited to local authorities and subscribers to the service

Funded by:
Education and Library Boards in Northern Ireland
Local Authorities in England, Wales, Scotland and Northern Ireland
National Foundation for Educational Research (NFER)

Housed with the:
National Foundation for Educational Research with whose researchers, and library and information services, EMIE co-operates closely

EMMS INTERNATIONAL

Acronym or abbreviation: EMMS

7 Washington Lane, Edinburgh, EH11 2HA

Tel: 0131 313 3828
Fax: 0131 313 4662
E-mail: info@emms.org

Website:
http://www.emms.org

Enquiries:
Enquiries to: Chief Executive

Founded:
1841

Formerly called:
Edinburgh Medical Missionary Society

Incorporates the former:
Emmanuel Healthcare

Organisation type and purpose:
Registered charity (charity number SC032327, company number 224402).
Medical missionary society.

Subject coverage:
History of medical missions; the Nazareth Hospital; placement of medical students for elective periods; medical missions.

Museum or gallery collection, archive, or library special collection:
Records of the Society since its foundation in 1841

Printed publications:
Annual Report
Healing Hand (3 times a year)
Prayer Focus (3 times a year)

Access to staff:
Contact by letter, by telephone, by fax and by e-mail
Hours: Mon to Fri, 0900 to 1700

Links with:
Church of Central Africa Presbyterian
Malawi
Dr Stephen Alfred
India
Emmanuel Hospital Association
India
International Nepal Fellowship

EMPICS

Formal name: EMPICS, A PA Group Photos Company

Pavilion House, 16 Castle Boulevard, Nottingham, NG7 1FC

Tel: 0115 844 7447
Fax: 0115 844 7448
E-mail: info@empics.com

Website:
http://www.empics.com

Enquiries:
Enquiries to: Sales and Marketing Director

Founded:
1867

Organisation type and purpose:
National organisation, service industry.
Picture library.

Subject coverage:
News, sport, and entertainment pictures, past and present.

Museum or gallery collection, archive, or library special collection:
PA
Empire Sport
AP
Emoics Entertainment

Non-library collection catalogue:
All or part available online

Library catalogue:
All or part available online

Electronic and video publications:
Pictures can be sent by ISDN, e-mail and by CD-ROM + FTP or downloads from website

Access to staff:
Contact by telephone, by e-mail and via website
Hours: Mon to Fri, 0900 to 1700

continued overleaf

Access to building, collection or gallery:
Prior appointment required
Hours: Mon to Fri, 0930 to 1800

Access for disabled people:
Access to all public areas, toilet facilities

EMPLOYMENT OPPORTUNITIES FOR PEOPLE WITH DISABILITIES

Acronym or abbreviation: Employment
Opportunities

Crystal Gate, 3rd Floor, 28 – 30 Worship Street,
London, EC2A 2AH

Tel: 020 7448 5420
E-mail: info@eopps.org

Website:
http://www.opportunities.org.uk
Information on Opportunities and the services
provided.

Enquiries:
Enquiries to: Administrator

Founded:
1980

Formerly called:
Opportunities for the Disabled

Organisation type and purpose:
National organisation, registered charity (charity
number 280112).
Helps people with disabilities find employment via
a network of regional centres around the country.

Subject coverage:
Disability in relation to employment.

Printed publications:
Annual Report and Accounts (May)
Information Leaflets (2)
Seetheability Booklet

Publications list:
Available online and in print

Access to staff:
Contact by letter, by telephone, by fax, by e-mail
and via website. Appointment necessary.
Hours: Mon to Fri, 0900 to 1700

Regional Centres:
Bath
  tel: 01225 461005 and minicom; fax: 01225
  461158; e-mail: eopps.diropsbath@connectfree.co
  .uk
Bristol and West
  Bristol; tel: 0117 925 5751 and minicom; fax: 0117
  925 5751; e-mail: eopps.bristol@connectfee.co.uk
East Midlands
  Leicester; tel: 0116 280 7450; minicom 7451; fax:
  0116 280 7449; e-mail: eopps.leicester@
  connectfree.co.uk
Greater London
  London; tel: 020 7580 7545 and minicom; fax: 020
  7255 3115; e-mail: eopps.grtlondon@connectfree
  .co.uk
Greater Manchester
  Manchester; tel: 0161 431 8889 and minicom; fax:
  0161 431 8889; e-mail: eopps.manchester@
  connectfree.co.uk
Merseyside and Deeside
  Wirral; tel: 0151 645 2346 and minicom; fax: 0151
  645 2346; e-mail: eopps.mersey@connectfree.co
  .uk
Newcastle and North East
  Newcastle upon Tyne; tel: 0191 232 1994 and
  minicom; fax: 0191 233 0945; e-mail: eopps
  .newcastle@connectfree.co.uk
Scotland
  Glasgow; tel: 0141 429 8429 and minicom; fax:
  0141 429 4023; e-mail: eopps.glasgow@
  connectfree.co.uk
South East Wales
  Cardiff; tel: 029 2039 4363 and minicom; fax: 029
  2039 8886; e-mail: eopps.cardiff@connectfree.co
  .uk

South Essex
  Essex; tel: 01227 201984 and minicom; fax: 01227
  202355; e-mail: eopps.brentwood@connectfree.co
  .uk
South Hampshire
  Southampton; tel: 02380 228010 and minicom;
  fax: 01329 233911; e-mail: eopps.fareham@
  connectfree.co.uk
South Yorkshire & North Midlands
  Sheffield; tel: 0114 279 5362; fax: 0114 279 7303
  and minicom; e-mail: eopps.sheffield@
  connectfree.co.uk
Surrey and East Sussex
  West Sussex; tel: 01403 262021; minicom 262031;
  fax: 01403 262021; e-mail: eopps.horsham@
  connectfree.co.uk
West Midlands
  Birmingham; tel: 0121 331 4121 and minicom;
  fax: 0121 344 4470; e-mail: eopps.birmingham@
  connectfree.co.uk

EMPLOYMENT RIGHTS ADVICE SERVICE

Acronym or abbreviation: ERAS

Low Pay Unit, 10 Dukes Road, London, WC1H
9AD

Tel: 020 7387 2911
Fax: 020 7387 2250
E-mail: enquiries@lowpayunit.org.uk

Website:
http://www.lowpayunit.org.uk

Enquiries:
Enquiries to: Director
Direct e-mail: bharti.patel@lowpayunit.org.uk
Other contacts: On-line Officer for web site.

Founded:
1974

Organisation type and purpose:
Voluntary organisation, research organisation.
Advice and campaigning body on issues related to
low pay and in-work poverty, campaigning for
better protection for the low paid.

Subject coverage:
Employment legislation and advice, information
on better employment practice.

Trade and statistical information:
Labour market data and earnings.
Poverty statistics.

Printed publications:
For purchase or free to subscribers

Publications list:
Available online and in print

Access to staff:
Contact by letter, by telephone, by fax, by e-mail
and via website
Hours: Mon to Fri, 0930 to 1730
Special comments: No disabled access.

EMPLOYMENT TRIBUNALS SERVICE

Acronym or abbreviation: ETS

The Secretary to the Tribunals, ETS/FSU, First
Floor, 100 Southgate Street, Bury St Edmunds, IP33
2AQ

Tel: 0845 795 9775; Minicom 0845 757 3722
E-mail: buryet@ets.gsi.gov.uk

Website:
http://www.employmenttribunals.gov.uk
Various tribunal information and booklets.

Enquiries:
Enquiries to: Senior Secretariat Officer

Formerly called:
Central Office of the Industrial Tribunals (COIT)

Organisation type and purpose:
National government body.

Subject coverage:
Procedures for Employment Tribunals, statistics
etc.

**Museum or gallery collection, archive, or library
special collection:**
Public registers of applications and tribunal
decisions held in Bury St Edmunds and Glasgow
for England and Wales and Scotland respectively

Non-library collection catalogue:
All or part available in-house

Printed publications:
ITL Booklets
Leaflets on employment law
Order printed publications from: DTI Orderline
tel: 0870 1502 500, fax: 0870 1502 333

Electronic and video publications:
Audio Tapes
Braille

Publications list:
Available online

Access to staff:
Contact by letter, by telephone and by fax
Hours: Mon to Fri, 0900 to 1700

Access to building, collection or gallery:
No prior appointment required
Hours: Mon to Fri, 0900 to 1700

Access for disabled people:
Ramped entry

ENABLE SCOTLAND

2nd Floor, 146 Argyle Street, Glasgow, G2 8BL

Tel: 0141 226 4541
Fax: 0141 204 4398
E-mail: enable@enable.org.uk

Website:
http://www.enable.org.uk

Enquiries:
Enquiries to: Information Service
Direct e-mail: info@enable.org.uk
Other contacts: Chief Executive

Founded:
1954

Formerly called:
Scottish Society for the Mentally Handicapped
(year of change 1993)

Organisation type and purpose:
Voluntary organisation, registered charity (charity
number SC 09024).

Subject coverage:
Law, services, employment, advocacy, education,
community care as related to people with learning
disabilities and their families.

**Museum or gallery collection, archive, or library
special collection:**
Small library

Non-library collection catalogue:
All or part available online

Library catalogue:
All or part available online and in-house

Printed publications:
Factsheets (irregular)
Newslink – ENABLE's newsletter (quarterly,
magazine)
Far beyond our Dreams – ENABLE's history
brochure (2004 free)

Electronic and video publications:
Don't Call Us Names (video)
Newslink (newsletter, quarterly, audio tape)
Lend a Hand (video)

Publications list:
Available online and in print

Access to staff:
Contact by letter, by telephone, by fax, by e-mail
and via website. Appointment necessary.
Hours: Enquiry line: Mon to Fri, 1300 to 1600

Access to building, collection or gallery:
Prior appointment required
Hours: Appointments to use the library may be made Mon to Fri, 0900 to 1600

Access for disabled people:
Toilet facilities
Special comments: Steps into building, lift, level access thereafter.

Member of:
Inclusion International

ENDANGERED DOGS DEFENCE AND RESCUE LIMITED

Acronym or abbreviation: EDDR Ltd

Post Office Box 1544, London, W7 2ZB

Tel: 0844 856 3303
E-mail: info@endangereddogs.com

Website:
http://www.endangereddogs.com
Advice on canine legislation, campaign and welfare information, current canine issues.

Enquiries:
Enquiries to: Secretary
Direct e-mail: office@endangereddogs.com

Founded:
1999

Formerly called:
Endangered Dogs Defence and Rescue (year of change 1999)

Organisation type and purpose:
Advisory body, voluntary organisation.
Advice and guidance concerning canine legislation and welfare.

Subject coverage:
Canine legislation and legal actions, canine rescue/re-homing, dogs with special needs, promoting responsible dog ownership, telephone helplines

Printed publications:
Newsletter (quarterly)

Access to staff:
Contact by letter, by telephone, by e-mail and via website
Hours: All hours

ENDAT STANDARD INDEXES LIMITED

Acronym or abbreviation: ESI

Ochil House, Springkerse Business Park, Stirling, FK7 7XE

Tel: 01786 407000
Fax: 01786 407003
E-mail: info@endat.com

Website:
http://www.endat.com
Company profile, electronic versions of printed directories.

Enquiries:
Enquiries to: Managing Director

Founded:
1989

Formerly called:
Environmental Data Research Limited (EDR), Landscape Promotions (year of change 1999)

Organisation type and purpose:
Research organisation, publishing house.

Subject coverage:
Landscape, civil engineering, horticulture, architectural landscape, products, users, local authorities, consulting engineers, facilities managers, engineers, process engineering, regulatory authorities, environmental management, water utilities, manufacturing industry, interior design.

Trade and statistical information:
Product information for designers and specifiers involved with process engineering and environmental management. Produce information for specifiers, buyers and estimators in the design and construction industry in both private and public sectors.

Printed publications:
Available in print and online:
ESI External Works (landscape design, civil engineering)
ESI Building Products (architectural design, construction)
ESI Building Services (mechanical and electrical construction)
ESI Interior Design (interior furnishings, fittings and finishes)
ESI Process Engineering (engineering, manufacturing and environmental management)

Access to staff:
Contact by letter, by telephone, by fax and by e-mail
Hours: Mon to Fri, 0900 to 1700

ENERGY INFORMATION CENTRE

Acronym or abbreviation: EIC

Rosemary House, Lanwades Business Park, Newmarket, Suffolk, CB8 7PW

Tel: 01638 751400
Fax: 01638 751801
E-mail: info@eic.co.uk

Enquiries:
Enquiries to: Membership Manager

Founded:
1975

Organisation type and purpose:
Membership association (membership is by subscription), present number of members: 650 corporate members, training organisation, consultancy, research organisation, publishing house.

Subject coverage:
Utilities market information, advice and support, covering electricity, gas, oil and water.

Trade and statistical information:
Data on the production and use of utility services; electricity, gas, oil and water.

Printed publications:
Utility Purchaser's Handbook
Centre News (6 times a year)

Access to staff:
Access for members only.
Hours: Mon to Fri, 0900 to 1730

Access to building, collection or gallery:
Prior appointment required

Access for disabled people:
Toilet facilities

Parent Company:
Metal Bulletin plc
Park House, Park Terrace, Worcester Park, Surrey, KT4 7HY

ENERGY INSTITUTE

Acronym or abbreviation: EI

61 New Cavendish Street, London, W1G 7AR

Tel: 020 7467 7100
Fax: 020 7255 1472
E-mail: info@energyinst.org

Website:
http://www.energyinst.org
Information about the EI and its publications and events, answers to frequently asked questions on the petroleum and other energy industries, careers and educational information, library information and catalogues and EI statistical services.

Enquiries:
Enquiries to: Library and Information Service Manager
Direct tel: 020 7467 7111
Direct e-mail: ccosgrove@energyinst.org
Other contacts: Information Officer

Founded:
2003

Created by the merger of:
Institute of Petroleum (founded 1913), Institute of Energy (founded 1927) (year of change Merged 2003)

Organisation type and purpose:
Membership association (membership is by subscription), present number of members: 12,000 individuals and 400 corporate, registered charity (charity number 1097899).

Subject coverage:
All forms of energy including renewables, wind, wave, electricity, nuclear, oil and gas. Especially strong on petroleum technology, petroleum geology, exploration, production, refining, transportation, physical and chemical properties of hydrocarbons, methods of analysis, petroleum products and petrochemicals, statistics, business.

Information services:
Quick queries; extended desk research; online searching; statistics service.

Education services:
Training courses.

Museum or gallery collection, archive, or library special collection:
Books dating from the mid-19th century to present day
Periodicals relating to petroleum and other energy industries dating from 1890s

Trade and statistical information:
UK petrol retailing market statistics.
UK refining statistics.
Worldwide petroleum industry statistics.

Non-library collection catalogue:
All or part available online and in-house

Library catalogue:
All or part available online and in-house

Printed publications:
Conference Proceedings
Petroleum information booklets
Petroleum Review (monthly)
Energy World (11 issues a year)
Standards and Codes of Safe Practice
Technical papers
Educational Publications, including:
Teachers Packs
A Young Person's Guide to Oil and Gas (for primary children)
Energy!
Oil and Gas: Energy for the World
Career information
Order printed publications from: Portland Customer Services, tel 01206 796351; e-mail: sales@prtland-services.com

Electronic and video publications:
IP Standard Methods for Analysis and Testing of Petroleum and Related Products and British Standards 2000 Parts, (CD-ROM) (annual publication)
Order electronic and video publications from: EI Publications available for purchase electronically. See website www.energyinst.org

Publications list:
Available online and in print

Access to staff:
Contact by letter, by telephone, by fax, by e-mail, in person and via website. Non-members charged.
Hours: Mon to Fri, 0915 to 1700
Special comments: Letter of introduction is required from students.

Access for disabled people:
Special comments: Stairs from pavement to front door.

continued overleaf

Hosts the:
Information for Energy Group (IFEG)
  tel: 020 7467 7115; e-mail: ifeg@energyinst.org

ENERGY WATCH

Formal name: Gas & Electricity Consumer Council
Acronym or abbreviation: GECC

4th Floor, Artillery House, Artillery Row, London,
SW1P 1RT

Tel: 0845 906 0708

Website:
http://www.energywatch.org.uk

Enquiries:
Enquiries to: Information Officer

Founded:
2000

Formerly called:
Electricity Consumers Council (ECC) and Gas
Consumers Council (GCC) (year of change 2000)

Organisation type and purpose:
NDPB (Non departmental public body).

Subject coverage:
Information for gas and electricity consumers.

Trade and statistical information:
Complaints statistics for UK energy firms from
consumers.

Publications list:
Available online

Access to staff:
Contact by letter, by telephone, by fax and by e-mail
Hours: Mon to Fri, 0900 to 1700

Access for disabled people:
Access to all public areas, toilet facilities

Other addresses:
energywatch, Scotland, Wales, Manchester,
Birmingham, Bournemouth, London
  tel: 0845 906 0708

ENFIELD & DISTRICT VETERAN VEHICLE TRUST

Acronym or abbreviation: EDVVT

Whitewebbs Museum, Whitewebbs Road, Enfield,
Middlesex, EN2 9HW

Tel: 020 8367 1898
Fax: 020 8363 1904
E-mail: museum@whitewebbs.fsnet.co.uk

Enquiries:
Enquiries to: Information Officer

Founded:
1979

Formerly called:
Enfield and District Veteran Vehicle Society

Organisation type and purpose:
Museum.

Subject coverage:
Vintage and classic cars, motor cycles and
commercial vehicles.

Access to staff:
Contact by letter, by telephone, by fax and by e-mail. Appointment necessary.
Hours: Tue, 1200 to 1600
Special comments: Otherwise access by
arrangement.

Access for disabled people:
Parking provided, ramped entry, toilet facilities

ENFIELD LIBRAIRES

First Stop Information, Central Library, Cecil Road,
Enfield Town, EN2 6TW

Tel: 020 8379 8341

Fax: 020 8379 8401

Website:
http://www.enfield.gov.uk/
Information on Council services and Enfield as a
location. Information on local libraries.

Organisation type and purpose:
Local government body, public library.

Subject coverage:
General; local history including material in the
museum at Forty Hall; European fiction; lingustics.

**Museum or gallery collection, archive, or library
special collection:**
European Fiction Collection
Linguistics (under the London and SE Region
  Scheme)
Local History Collection
Sound recordings of J S Bach, jazz artists BAJ to BH
  and Folk Music (Argentina, Bolivia, Chile,
  Paraguay, Uruguay) (under the Greater London
  Audio Specialising Scheme)

Access to staff:
Contact by letter, by telephone, by fax and by e-mail
Hours: Mon to Fri, 0900 to 1700
Special comments: No appointment necessary for
general libraries. Appointments are required for
local history collections and other special
collections.

ENFIELD LOCAL HISTORY UNIT

Thomas Hardy House, 39 London Road, Enfield,
EN2 6DS

Tel: 020 8379 2724
E-mail: local.history@enfield.gov.uk

Enquiries:
Enquiries to: Librarian

Founded:
1975

Organisation type and purpose:
Archive.

Subject coverage:
Local history material for Local Borough of Enfield
area.

Non-library collection catalogue:
All or part available in-house

Library catalogue:
All or part available in-house

Access to staff:
Contact by letter, by telephone, by e-mail and in
person. Appointment necessary.
Hours: Mon, Tue, Thu, Fri, 0930 to 1630

Access to building, collection or gallery:
Prior appointment required
Hours: as above

Access for disabled people:
Lift

ENGINEERING AND PHYSICAL SCIENCES RESEARCH COUNCIL

Acronym or abbreviation: EPSRC

Polaris House, North Star Avenue, Swindon,
Wiltshire, SN2 1ET

Tel: 01793 444000
E-mail: infoline@epsrc.ac.uk

Website:
http://www.epsrc.ac.uk
All matters about EPSRC.

Enquiries:
Enquiries to: Head of Media & Communications
Direct tel: 01793 444147
Direct fax: 01793 444005
Direct e-mail: lucy.brady@epsrc.ac.uk

Formerly called:
Science and Engineering Research Council, date of
change, 18 April 1994

Organisation type and purpose:
National government body.
Non-departmental governmental public body
(NDPB).
Funding agency for research and training in
engineering and the physical sciences.

Subject coverage:
General science, science policy, science and
technology, engineering science, aerospace, process
engineering and information technology.

Printed publications:
EPSRC Annual Report
Newsline

Publications list:
Available online

Access to staff:
Contact by letter, by telephone, by e-mail and via
website
Hours: Mon to Fri, 0900 to 1700

ENGINEERING EDUCATION SCHEME IN ENGLAND

Acronym or abbreviation: EES

Weltech Centre, Ridgeway, Welwyn Garden City,
Hertfordshire, AL7 2AA

Tel: 01707 393323
Fax: 01707 393133
E-mail: enquiries@eeswgc.demon.co.uk

Website:
http://www.engineering-education.org.uk

Enquiries:
Enquiries to: Director
Direct e-mail: a.ritchie@eeswgc.demon.co.uk

Founded:
1984

Organisation type and purpose:
Registered charity (charity number 1002459),
suitable for ages: year 12 students.
To encourage year 12 students into engineering.

Subject coverage:
Engineering education scheme for schools.

Printed publications:
Information File

Access to staff:
Contact by letter, by telephone and by e-mail
Hours: Mon to Fri, 0900 to 1700

Administered by:
Engineering Development Trust

Part of:
Royal Academy of Engineering's Best Programme

ENGINEERING EQUIPMENT AND MATERIALS USERS' ASSOCIATION

Acronym or abbreviation: EEMUA

10–12 Lovat Lane, London, EC3R 8DN

Tel: 020 7621 0011
Fax: 020 7621 0022
E-mail: info@eemua.org

Website:
http://www.eemua.co.uk
http://www.eemua.co.uk/pub-folder/index.htm

Enquiries:
Enquiries to: Director

Founded:
1950

Organisation type and purpose:
Industry Association.
Members are purchasers, specificiers and users of
engineering products and services in the chemical
process industries, power generation and utilities
sectors.

Aims to reduce costs and improve safety and operational effectiveness by sharing experiences and expertise, and by promotion of engineering users' interests.

Subject coverage:
Storage tanks, mechanical, electrical, instrumentation and control engineering, inspection and maintenance, quality assurance and control, health and safety at work.

Library catalogue:
All or part available online

Printed publications:
Technical handbooks

Publications list:
Available online

Access to staff:
Contact by letter, by telephone, by fax, by e-mail and via website. Appointment necessary. Access for members only.
Hours: Mon to Fri, 0900 to 1700

Administers:
Secretariat for the European Committee of User Inspectorates (ECUI)

ENGINEERING INDUSTRIES ASSOCIATION

Acronym or abbreviation: EIA

62 Bayswater Road, London, W2 3PS

Tel: 020 7298 6455
Fax: 020 7298 6456
E-mail: head.office@eia.co.uk

Website:
http://www.eia.uk

Enquiries:
Enquiries to: Director
Other contacts: Administrator (for general enquiries)

Founded:
1940

Organisation type and purpose:
Trade association.

Subject coverage:
Engineering industry; legislation, particularly health and safety and employment law; export practice; overseas missions and exhibitions.

Printed publications:
Buyers Guide and Classified Directory
Database of all members (members only)
History of the Association
Newsletter (6 times a year, members only)

Access to staff:
Contact by letter, by telephone, by fax, by e-mail and via website. Appointment necessary.
Hours: Mon to Fri, 0900 to 1700

Constituent bodies:
five regional groups

Member organisation of:
Bristol and Western Engineering Manufacturers Association (BEMA)
   tel: 0117 906 4830; fax: 0117 906 4827; e-mail: enquiries@bema.co.uk

ENGINEERING INTEGRITY SOCIETY

Acronym or abbreviation: EIS

5 Wentworth Avenue, Sheffield, South Yorkshire, S11 9QX

Tel: 0114 262 1155
Fax: 0114 262 1120
E-mail: cpinder@e-i-s.org.uk

Website:
http://www.e-i-s.org.uk
Information about the Society including conferences and seminars.

Enquiries:
Enquiries to: Secretariat Administrator

Founded:
1985

Organisation type and purpose:
Membership association (membership is by subscription), registered charity (charity number 327121).
Arrangement of courses and conferences to advance the education of persons working in the field of engineering by providing a forum for the interchange of ideas and information on engineering integrity.

Subject coverage:
Durability and fatigue; simulation; test and measurement, noise, vibration and harshness; these are the three Groups which make up the society.

Printed publications:
Engineering Integrity (journal, 2 times a year)

Access to staff:
Contact by letter, by telephone, by fax, by e-mail and via website
Hours: Mon to Fri, 0900 to 1700

ENGINEERING TRAINING COUNCIL FOR NORTHERN IRELAND

Acronym or abbreviation: ETC (NI)

Interpoint, 20–24 York Street, Belfast, BT15 1AQ

Tel: 028 9032 9878
Fax: 028 9031 0301
E-mail: info@etcni.org.uk

Website:
http://www.etcni.org.uk

Enquiries:
Enquiries to: Chief Executive

Founded:
1990

Organisation type and purpose:
Training organisation.

Subject coverage:
Industrial training, employment, qualifications, education and technical issues associated with careers and development of engineers in manufacturing industries.

Access to staff:
Contact by letter, by telephone, by e-mail and via website
Hours: Mon to Fri, 0900 to 1700

ENGLAND AND WALES CRICKET BOARD

Acronym or abbreviation: ECB

Lord's Cricket Ground, St John's Wood Road, London, NW8 8QZ

Tel: 020 7432 1200
Fax: 020 7289 5619
E-mail: @ecb.co.uk

Website:
http://lords.org
http://www.ecb.co.uk

Enquiries:
Enquiries to: Administration Manager

Founded:
1997

Formed from:
Cricket Council, National Cricket Association (NCA), Test and County Cricket Board (TCCB) (year of change 1997)

Organisation type and purpose:
Governing body for cricket at all levels in England and Wales.

Subject coverage:
Cricket: coaching, pitches (turf and non-turf), grant aid, competitions, laws of the game, insurance.

Museum or gallery collection, archive, or library special collection:
MCC Cricket Memorial Gallery (information from the Curator, MCC, Lords Cricket Ground)

Printed publications:
Constitution and Rules

Electronic and video publications:
Videos

Access to staff:
Contact by letter, by telephone, by fax and by e-mail. Appointment necessary.
Hours: Mon to Fri, 0900 to 1700

Composed of:
Marylebone Cricket Club
National Cricket Association
Test and County Cricket Board

Member of:
Sports Council

ENGLAND SQUASH

Ground Floor, Bell Vue Athletics Centre, Pink Bank Lane, Manchester, M12 5GL

Tel: 0161 231 4499
Fax: 0161 231 4231
E-mail: englandsquash@squash.uk.com

Website:
http://www.englandsquash.com

Enquiries:
Enquiries to: Chair
Other contacts: Administration Manager

Founded:
1930

Formerly called:
Squash Rackets Association (SRA) (year of change 2001)

Organisation type and purpose:
Membership association.
Governing body of squash in England.

Subject coverage:
Coach training and qualification, referee training and qualification, technical and court specification, tournament organisation, grass roots development both player and participation, membership, club and individual.

Trade and statistical information:
Some statistics held for playing numbers in UK.

Printed publications:
Squash and Fitness – The Magazine

Publications list:
Available online and in print

Access to staff:
Contact by letter and by e-mail
Hours: Mon to Fri, 0900 to 1700

Access to building, collection or gallery:
No prior appointment required

Access for disabled people:
Parking provided, level entry, toilet facilities

ENGLISH ASSOCIATION

Acronym or abbreviation: EA

University of Leicester, University Road, Leicester, LE1 7RH

Tel: 0116 252 3982
Fax: 0116 252 2301
E-mail: engassoc@le.ac.uk

Website:
http://www.le.ac.uk/engassoc/publns.html
Publications page.
http://www.le.ac.uk/engassoc/
Conferences, current contents of publications.
Student website. Current issues and debates.

continued overleaf

Enquiries:
Enquiries to: Chief Executive

Founded:
1906

Organisation type and purpose:
International organisation, learned society, professional body (membership is by subscription), present number of members: 2500, registered charity (charity number 1078935), publishing house.

Subject coverage:
English language and literature; standards of English writing and speech; educational matters relating to the teaching of English.

Museum or gallery collection, archive, or library special collection:
Own publications back to 1906

Printed publications:
Bookmarks, series of books to encourage over 16s to read more widely
English (journal, literary criticism, essays, reviews, original poetry, 3 times a year)
English 4–11 (formerly Primary English, 3 times a year)
Essays & Studies: (annually)
The English Association Newsletter (3 times a year)
The Use of English (journal, 3 times a year)
The Year's Work in Critical and Cultural Theory
The Year's Work in English Studies (annual bibliography)

Publications list:
Available online and in print

Access to staff:
Contact by letter, by telephone, by fax, by e-mail and via website
Hours: Mon to Fri, 0900 to 1700

ENGLISH BASKETBALL ASSOCIATION

Acronym or abbreviation: EBBA

c/o English Institute of Sport, Coleridge Road, Sheffield, S9 5DA

Tel: 0870 77 44 225
Fax: 0870 77 44 226
E-mail: enquiries@ebbaonline.net

Website:
http://www.englandbasketball.co.uk
General information on England Basketball, fixtures, tables, etc.

Enquiries:
Enquiries to: Chief Executive
Other contacts: General Manager

Organisation type and purpose:
Membership association (membership is by subscription), present number of members: 900 clubs; 20,000 individuals.
Governing body of sport.

Subject coverage:
Sport of basketball, coaching, officiating, playing indoor and outdoor basketball.

Printed publications:
Annual Report
A Guide to English Basketball (£4)
Attacking a Zone Defence (£5.50)
Boom Boom Boom – The Rhythm of English Basketball (£12)
Basketball Development Manual
Coaching Basketball (£5.50)
Drills Book – One (£5.50)
Drills Book – Two (£5.50)
Manual for Table Officials (£4.50)
National Competitions Handbook (£7)
Newsletter
Nike Basketball Curriculum Guide (£20)
Official Basketball Rules
Referees Manual (£7.50)
Women in Basketball (£3)

Electronic and video publications:
Basketball Skills Video (£10)

Publications list:
Available in print

Access to staff:
Contact by letter, by telephone, by fax and by e-mail. Appointment necessary.
Hours: Mon to Fri, 0900 to 1700

Affiliated to:
British Olympic Association
Central Council of Physical Recreation
International Basketball Association

ENGLISH BOWLING FEDERATION

Acronym or abbreviation: EBF

The Secretary, 14 Field Close, Worksop, Nottinghamshire, S81 0PF

Tel: 01909 474346
Fax: 01909 474346
E-mail: j.heppel@btinternet.com

Website:
http://www.fedbowls.co.uk/

Enquiries:
Enquiries to: Publicity Officer
Direct e-mail: melvin.beck@keypublishing.com

Founded:
1926

Organisation type and purpose:
National government body, membership association, present number of members: 13 County Bowling Associations.
National governing body of the sport.

Subject coverage:
Flat green bowls.

Printed publications:
Laws of the Game
Year Book

Access to staff:
Contact by letter, by telephone and by fax
Hours: Mon to Fri, 0900 to 1700

ENGLISH BRIDGE UNION LIMITED

Acronym or abbreviation: EBU

Broadfields, Bicester Road, Aylesbury, Buckinghamshire, HP19 8AZ

Tel: 01296 317200
Fax: 01296 317220
E-mail: postmaster@ebu.co.uk

Website:
http://www.ebu.co.uk

Enquiries:
Enquiries to: General Manager
Other contacts: Bridge for All helpline for students/teachers wishing to join Bridge for All education programme.

Founded:
1940

Organisation type and purpose:
Membership association (membership is by subscription), present number of members: 30,000.
National governing body for the card game of Duplicate Bridge.

Subject coverage:
Duplicate bridge in England, membership, Master Points, bridge supplies, competition entry, laws and ethics, educating and teaching, Bridge for All, overseas information.

Museum or gallery collection, archive, or library special collection:
Some archive material – books, trophies

Printed publications:
County Newsletter (to County associations)
Bridge for All – Really Easy books

English Bridge (6 times a year, free to members)
Club Newsletter (to affiliated clubs)

Electronic and video publications:
Blue Chip Bridge (CD-ROM)

Access to staff:
Contact by letter, by telephone, by fax, by e-mail, in person and via website
Hours: Mon to Fri, 0830 to 1715

Access for disabled people:
Parking provided, ramped entry, toilet facilities

Member of:
European Bridge League
World Bridge Federation

ENGLISH CHESS FEDERATION

Acronym or abbreviation: ECF

The Watch Oak, Chain Lane, Battle, East Sussex, TN33 0YD

Tel: 01424 775222
Fax: 01424 775904
E-mail: office@englishchess.org.uk

Website:
http://www.bcf.org.uk

Enquiries:
Enquiries to: Manager
Direct e-mail: cynthia@englishchess.org.uk

Founded:
1904

Formerly called:
British Chess Federation (year of change 2005)

Organisation type and purpose:
To control, direct and promote the playing of chess in England, to institute and maintain British Chess Championships, to promote national and international chess tournaments in England,

Museum or gallery collection, archive, or library special collection:
National Chess Library of 8,000 vols (housed at University Centre Hastings)

Library catalogue:
All or part available online

Printed publications:
Chess Moves (bimonthly membership magazine)

Publications list:
Available online

Access to staff:
Contact by letter, by telephone, by fax and by e-mail
Hours: Mon to Fri, 1000 to 1530 (by telephone only)

Access to building, collection or gallery:
Hours: Daily, 0900 to 1730

Access for disabled people:
Hours: Daily, 0900 to 1730

Affiliated to:
World Chess Federation (FIDE)

ENGLISH CIVIL WAR SOCIETY LIMITED

Acronym or abbreviation: ECWS

70 Hailgate, Howden, East Yorkshire, DN14 7ST

Tel: 01430 430695
Fax: 01405 430695
E-mail: press@english-civil-war-society.org

Website:
http://www.english-civil-war-society.org

Enquiries:
Enquiries to: Public Relations Manager

Founded:
1981

Formed from:
King's Army, Roundhead Association

Organisation type and purpose:
Membership association (membership is by subscription), present number of members: 2000, voluntary organisation.
Re-enactment Society specialising in period 1638–1651.

Subject coverage:
Historical re-enactment, English Civil War 1638–1651, film, television and media contacts and expertise, educational interpretation of history, living history, museum activity.

Printed publications:
Friends of the English Civil War Society (newsletter, quarterly, £5 a year)
Information leaflets (individual copies free with sae)
Soldiers' Handbook (50p)
Strife in the Kingdom; information pack on the English Civil War (£1.20)

Publications list:
Available in print

Access to staff:
Contact by letter, by telephone, by fax, by e-mail and via website
Hours: Evenings preferred

ENGLISH COLLECTIVE OF PROSTITUTES

Crossroads Women's Centre, PO Box 287, London, NW6 5QU

Tel: 020 7482 2496\ Minicom no. 020 7482 2496
Fax: 020 7209 4761
E-mail: crossroadswomenscentre@compuserve.com

Website:
http://www.prostitutescollective.net

Enquiries:
Enquiries to: Information Officer

Organisation type and purpose:
Voluntary organisation.
Pressure group.
To establish workers' rights in the sex industry, to be recognised as workers with legal, economic and civil rights. To campaign for the abolition of the prostitution laws, for the right to protection from violence, to health care, to form or join unions and for financial alternatives to prostitution.
To oppose illegal and racist enforcement of the law, and state run prostitution including toleration zones.

Subject coverage:
Prostitution laws, police legality and racism, child custody, taxes, health including HIV and AIDS, benefits.

Printed publications:
Network News
Prostitutes – Our Life
Prostitute Women and AIDS: Resisting the Virus of Repression
Some Mother's Daughter – The hidden movement of prostitute women against violence
The Hooker and the Beak

Access to staff:
Contact by letter, by telephone, by fax, by e-mail, in person and via website. Appointment necessary.
Hours: Tue and Wed, 1200 to 1600; Thu, 1700 to 1900
Telephone lines: Mon to Wed, Fri, 1000 to 1600; Thu, 1000 to 1600, 1700 to 1900

Access for disabled people:
Access to all public areas, toilet facilities

Initiated:
Legal Action for Women (LAW)
e-mail: law@crossroadswomen.net; website: http://www.allwomencount.net

Member of:
International Prostitutes Collective
website: http://www.prostitutescollectives.net
International Wages for Housework Campaign
Wages for Housework Campaign

ENGLISH CROSS-COUNTRY ASSOCIATION

Acronym or abbreviation: ECCA

22 Denham Drive, Berg Estate, Basingstoke, Hampshire, RG22 6LR

Tel: 01256 328401

Enquiries:
Enquiries to: Honorary Secretary

Founded:
1992

Organisation type and purpose:
Membership association, voluntary organisation.
National governing body, controlling body of the sport in England.
Organises and develops cross-country running.

Subject coverage:
Cross-country running.

Printed publications:
Handbook

Access to staff:
Contact by letter, by telephone and by fax
Hours: Mon to Fri, 0900 to 1700

Affiliated to:
United Kingdom Athletics

Member of:
Amateur Athletics Association of England

ENGLISH CURLING ASSOCIATION

Acronym or abbreviation: ECA

14 Donnelly Drive, Bedford, MK14 9TV

Tel: 01234 315174 (home) or 01223 372752 (business)
E-mail: jmbroons@ntlworld.com

Website:
http://www.englishcurling.org.uk

Enquiries:
Enquiries to: Secretary

Founded:
1971

Organisation type and purpose:
Membership association, present number of members: 150, suitable for ages: 13+, training organisation.
National governing body of the sport.

Subject coverage:
Sport of curling in general from beginners to world championships.

Printed publications:
Handbook (annually)

Access to staff:
Contact by letter, by telephone, by fax, by e-mail and in person. Appointment necessary.
Hours: Mon to Fri, 0900 to 1700

ENGLISH FOLK DANCE AND SONG SOCIETY

Acronym or abbreviation: EFDSS

Vaughan Williams Memorial Library, Cecil Sharp House, 2 Regent's Park Road, London, NW1 7AY

Tel: 020 7485 2206
Fax: 020 7284 0523
E-mail: library@efdss.org

Website:
http://www.efdss.org
The society details, including the library.

Enquiries:
Enquiries to: Librarian
Direct e-mail: malcolm.taylor@efdss.org

Founded:
1932

Organisation type and purpose:
Learned society (membership is by subscription), present number of members: 5000, registered charity.
To document and promote folk arts in England.

Subject coverage:
Folk music including song, dance and drama, customs involving dance and song, singing games, social history, folk tales, oral history, dialects, mainly British material but much information on other English-speaking countries, notably the USA.

Museum or gallery collection, archive, or library special collection:
BBC Archive of folk music recordings
Broadwood Collection (manuscripts, and folk song books on loan)
Butterworth Collection (manuscripts, dance and song)
Carpenter Collection (manuscripts and tapes from wax cylinders, folk song and drama)
Cecil Sharp Collection (books and manuscripts on folk song and dance)
Collection of 18th century dancing masters
Gardiner Collection (folk song)
Gilchrist Collection (folk music)
Melusine Wood (historical dance)
Percy Grainger Collection of phonograph recordings from wax cylinders (on tape)
Vaughan Williams manuscripts in the British Library (microfilm)

Non-library collection catalogue:
All or part available online and in-house

Library catalogue:
All or part available in-house

Printed publications:
Catalogue
Folk Music Journal
English Dance and Song
Library leaflets and bibliographies on aspects of folk music

Electronic and video publications:
Videos and audio cassettes and CDs

Access to staff:
Contact by letter, by telephone, by fax, by e-mail, in person and via website. Access for members only. Non-members charged.
Hours: Tues to Fri, 0930 to 1730; 1st and 3rd Sat each month, 1000 to 1600

Access to building, collection or gallery:
No access other than to staff
Hours: Tues to Fri, 0930 to 1730; 1st and 3rd Sat each month, 1000 to 1600
Special comments: Sound/audio visual collections closed 1200 to 1400 every day.

ENGLISH GARDENING SCHOOL

At The Chelsea Physic Gardens, 66 Royal Hospital Road, London, SW3 4HS

Tel: 020 7352 4347
Fax: 020 7376 3936
E-mail: egs@dircon.co.uk

Website:
http://www.englishgardeningschool.co.uk
Details of all courses and events, plus online secure booking.

Enquiries:
Enquiries to: Principal

Founded:
1984

Organisation type and purpose:
Suitable for ages: 18+, training organisation, consultancy.

Subject coverage:
Teaching a wide range of amateur and professional gardening courses; horticultural/garden design consultancy; resource for garden designers.

Publications list:
Available in print

continued overleaf

Access to staff:
Contact by letter, by telephone, by fax, by e-mail
and via website. Appointment necessary.
Hours: Mon to Fri, 0900 to 1700

ENGLISH GOLF UNION

Acronym or abbreviation: EGU

The National Golf Centre, Broadway, Woodhall
Spa, Lincolnshire, LN10 9PU

Tel: 01526 354500
Fax: 01526 354020
E-mail: info@englishgolfunion.org

Website:
http://www.englishgolfunion.org

Enquiries:
Enquiries to: Chief Executive

Founded:
1924

Organisation type and purpose:
National government body.
Governing body for the amateur game of men's
golf in England.

Subject coverage:
Amateur golf in England, handicapping, standard
scratch scores of golf courses.

Non-library collection catalogue:
All or part available online and in-house

Library catalogue:
All or part available in-house

Printed publications:
English Golf (magazine, 6 times a year)
Golfing Year (annually)
Order printed publications from: e-mail: nhayward@
englishgolfunion.org

Publications list:
Available in print

Access to staff:
Contact by letter, by fax and by e-mail
Hours: Mon to Fri, 0900 to 1700

Access to building, collection or gallery:
Prior appointment required

Access for disabled people:
Parking provided, ramped entry, toilet facilities

ENGLISH HERITAGE

Acronym or abbreviation: HBMC or EH

Fortress House, 23 Savile Row, London, W1S 2ET

Tel: 0870 333 1181 Customer Services
Fax: 01793 414926

Website:
http://www.open.gov.uk/heritage/ehehome.htm
General information.
http://www.english-heritage.org.uk
General information.

Enquiries:
Enquiries to: Customer Services Department
Other contacts: Nine Regional Education Officers at
the appropriate English Heritage Regional offices

Founded:
1984

Formerly called:
Historic Buildings and Monuments Commission
for England, Ministry of Works (MOW);
Department of the Environment (DOE) (year of
change 1983)

Organisation type and purpose:
National government body, advisory body,
statutory body, membership association
(membership is by subscription).
Heritage conservation.

Subject coverage:
The governments' official adviser on all matters
concerning the conversation of the historic
environment and the major source of public

funding for rescue archaeology, conservation areas,
and repairs to historic buildings and ancient
monuments.

**Museum or gallery collection, archive, or library
special collection:**
Historical Research Library (mainly architectural)
Listed historic buildings
Historic Plans Collection over 200,000 plans of
buildings
Mayson Beeton Collection (London social history)
Lists of scheduled monuments
Photographic library
Register of historic parks and gardens

Non-library collection catalogue:
All or part available in print

Library catalogue:
All or part available in print

Printed publications:
Annual Report and Accounts
Approximately 50 leaflets covering all aspects of
the English Heritage
Conservation Bulletin (3 times a year, free)
Archaeological Reports Series
Exploring England's Heritage Series (HMSO)
Guides to sites
Conservation Publications (various free leaflets
and priced books)
Many illustrated books on all aspects of the
resources under the care of English Heritage
including archaeology, architecture, conservation
and general publishing titles:
An Atlas of Rural Settlement in England (Roberts B
and Wrathmell S, 2000)
Food and Cooking Series (various titles)
Gatekeeper Series (various titles)
Ration Book Recipes (Corbishley G, 1990)
Region and Place (Roberts B and Wrathmell S,
2002)
Stonehenge: Mysteries of the Stones and
Landscape (Souden D, 1997)
The Albert Memorial – The Prince Consort
National Memorial, its contexts and its
conservation (Brooks C ed, 2000)
The Batsford English Heritage Series (various
titles)
Order printed publications from: Customer Services,
English Heritage
PO Box 569, Swindon, SN2 2YP, tel: 0870 333 1181

Electronic and video publications:
Videos and tapes

Publications list:
Available online and in print

Access to staff:
Contact by letter, by telephone, by fax and in
person. Appointment necessary.
Hours: Mon to Fri, 0900 to 1730

Other address:
English Heritage
Customer Services Department, PO Box 569,
Swindon, Wiltshire, SN2 5YP

Other office:
National Monuments Record Centre
Kemble Drive, Swindon, Wiltshire, SN2 2GZ; tel:
01793 414600; e-mail: nmrinfo@english-heritage
.org.uk

Parent body:
Department for Culture, Media and Sport
2–4 Cockspur Street, London, SW1Y 5DH

Regional Offices:
English Heritage (East Midlands Region)
44 Derngate, Northampton, NN1 1UH; tel: 01604
735400; fax: 01604 735401
English Heritage (East of England Region)
Brooklands, 24 Brooklands Avenue, Cambridge,
CB2 2BU; tel: 01223 582700; fax: 01223 582701
English Heritage (London Region)
23 Savile Row, London, W1S 2ET; tel: 020 7973
3000; fax: 020 7973 3000
English Heritage (North East Region)
Bessie Surtees House, 41–44 Sandhill, Newcastle
upon Tyne, NE1 3JF; tel: 0191 261 1585

English Heritage (North West Region)
Canada House, 3 Chepstow Street, Manchester,
M1 5FW; tel: 0161 242 1400
English Heritage (South East Region)
Eastgate Court, 195–205 High Street, Guildford,
Surrey, GU1 3EH; tel: 01483 252000; fax: 01483
252001
English Heritage (South West Region)
29 Queen Square, Bristol, BS1 4ND; tel: 0117 975
0700
English Heritage (West Midlands Region)
112 Colemore Row, Birmingham, B3 3AG; tel:
0121 625 6820
English Heritage (Yorkshire Region)
37 Tanner Row, York, YO1 6WP; tel: 01904
601901

ENGLISH HERITAGE – EDUCATION

3 Bunhill Row, London, EC1Y 8YZ

Tel: 020 7973 3384
Fax: 020 7973 3443
E-mail: education@english-heritage.org.uk

Website:
http://www.english-heritage.org.uk
Full details of all resources and up to-date
information about the education service and the
work of the English Heritage.
http://www.heritageeducation.org.uk

Enquiries:
Enquiries to: Head of Education

Founded:
1984

Formerly called:
Historic Buildings and Monuments Commission
for England (year of change 1984)

Organisation type and purpose:
National government body, advisory body,
statutory body, membership association
(membership is by subscription), suitable for ages:
5 to 18 (formal) and informal.
To provide an advisory and support service for
primary and secondary schools in the teaching of
history and the use of the historic environment.

Subject coverage:
The historic environment of Britain, its
preservation and use. Archaeology, architecture,
ancient monuments, conservation and listed
buildings.

Printed publications:
English Heritage advise that you contact them and
ask for a free Resources Catalogue, or visit their
website for the complete range of publications
Large selection of resources: books, posters,
computer software and videos for Key Stages 1,
2, 3, GCSE and Adult Education. Published
topics include: Local Studies, Romans, Anglo-
Saxons and Vikings, Victorian Britain, Medieval
World and Prehistory
Art and the Historic Environment (Lockey M,
£6.99)
Design and Technology and the Historic
Environment (Barnes J, £6.99)
Heritage Learning Magazine (aimed at teachers,
free)
Primary History – Guide to using historic sites for
all aspects of primary school history ((£7.99)
Teacher's Guide – History through role play
(Fairclough J, £6.99)
Free Educational Visits (how to book free
educational visits to sites, free)
Order printed publications from: English Heritage
c/o Gillards, Trident Works, Temple Cloud, Bristol,
BS39 5AZ, tel: 01761 452966, fax: 01761 453408

Electronic and video publications:
The Resources Catalogue lists all videos, CD-
ROMs, etc. Most videos are available on free loan
Teaching Primary History (video, £12.99)
Real Victorians (CD-ROM, £14.99)
The Key Stage 1 Curriculum (video, £12.99)
Video Role Up – role play with mixed ability class
(video, £12.99)

Publications list:
Available online and in print

Access to staff:
Contact by letter, by telephone, by fax and by e-mail
Hours: Mon to Fri, 0900 to 1700
Special comments: Access for visitors with disabilities should be checked with the regional office before booking a visit.

Other addresses:
English Heritage
 Customer Services Department, National Monuments Record Centre, Kemble Drive, Swindon, Wiltshire, SN2 2GZ; tel: 01793 414926

Regional addresses:
English Heritage
 Education Officer, East of England Region, 62–74 Burleigh Street, Cambridge, CB1 1DJ; tel: 01223 582715; fax: 01223 582701
English Heritage
 Education Officer, Yorkshire Region, G10, 37 Tanner Row, York, YO1 6WP; tel: 01904 601962; fax: 01904 601999
English Heritage
 Education Officer, West Midlands Region, 112 Colmore Row, Birmingham, B3 3AG; tel: 0121 625 6863; fax: 0121 625 6821
English Heritage
 Education Officer, North West Region, Canada House, 3 Chepstow Street, Manchester, M1 5FW; tel: 0161 242 1425; fax: 0161 242 1401
English Heritage
 Education Officer, East Midlands Region, 44 Derngate, Northampton, NN1 1UH; tel: 01604 735400; fax: 01604 735401
English Heritage
 Education Officer, London Region, Savile Row, London, W1S 2ET; tel: 020 7973 3485; fax: 020 7973 3470
English Heritage
 Education Officer, South West Region, 29/30 Queen Square, Bristol, BS1 4ND; tel: 0117 975 0729; fax: 0117 975 0701
English Heritage
 Education Officer, South East Region, Eastgate Court, 195–205 High Street, Guildford, GU1 3EH; tel: 01483 252000; fax: 01483 252001
English Heritage
 Education Officer, North East Region, Bessie Surtees House, 441 Sandhill, Newcastle upon Tyne, NE1 8JF; tel: 0191 269 1585; fax: 0191 261 1130

ENGLISH HERITAGE – NATIONAL MONUMENTS RECORD

Acronym or abbreviation: NMR

Kemble Drive, Swindon, Wiltshire, SN2 2GZ

Tel: 01793 414600
Fax: 01793 414606
E-mail: nmrinfo@english-heritage.org.uk

Website:
http://www.english-heritage.org.uk
Information and news about the work of the National Monuments Record (NMR) and English Heritage. Enquiry forms for remote searches of NMR archives are incorporated within the English Heritage website.
http://www.imagesof england.org.uk
Photographs of England's listed buildings at the turn of the 21st century.
http://www.pastscape.org
Information on nearly 400,000 records held in the NMR's national historic environment database.

Enquiries:
Enquiries to: Enquiry and Research Services
Other contacts: Customer Services Section

Founded:
1908

Formerly called:
Historic Buildings and Monuments Commission for England (HBMCE) (year of change 1984)

Incorporates the former:
National Archaeological Record, National Buildings Record, National Library of Air Photography; Royal Commission on the Historical Monuments of England (RCHME) (year of change 1999)

Organisation type and purpose:
National government body.
Public archive of English Heritage.

Subject coverage:
Architecture, archaeology, aerial photographs and maritime sites. The archive is of use to anyone interested in the historic built environment, local historians, researchers, archaeologists, architectural historians and environmental consultants.

Museum or gallery collection, archive, or library special collection:
Archive comprises over 10m. photographs, drawings and reports and an extensive book library specialising in architecture, archaeology and the historic environment.
Aerial photograph collection includes complete RAF post-war coverage of England, early photographs of sites such as Stonehenge and more recent Ordnance Survey and English Heritage photography.
Architectural archive includes interior and exterior photographs of buildings from the early days of photography to the present day. The National Buildings Record collection and photographs taken by Bedford Lemere, Eric De Mare, John Gay and many others are held in the NMR.
Archaeological collections include earthwork surveys, aerial photograph interpretations and photographs of historic excavations.

Trade and statistical information:
Data on archaeological sites, Scheduled Ancient Monuments and Listed Buildings.

Non-library collection catalogue:
All or part available in-house

Library catalogue:
All or part available in-house

Printed publications:
Many and varied, including:
Work
Seaside Resorts
The Birmingham Jewellery Quarter
Hillforts
Order printed publications from: http://www.english-heritageshop.org.uk

Publications list:
Available online

Access to staff:
Contact by letter, by telephone, by fax, by e-mail, in person and via website
Hours: Tue to Fri, 0930 to 1700
Special comments: Closed over Christmas and New Year (please contact for details)

Access to building, collection or gallery:
Hours: Tue to Fri, 0930 to 1700
Special comments: Limited visitor parking

Funded by:
Department of Culture, Media and Sport

Links with:
county councils and local planning departments

Parent body:
English Heritage
 1 Waterhouse Square, 138–142 Holborn, London, EC1N 2ST

ENGLISH HERITAGE (EAST MIDLANDS REGION)

44 Derngate, Northampton, NN1 1UH

Tel: 01604 735400
Fax: 01604 735401

Website:
http://www.english-heritage.org.uk

Enquiries:
Enquiries to: Marketing Executive

Organisation type and purpose:
National organisation, advisory body, membership association (membership is by subscription), suitable for ages: all.
Independent but government-sponsored body. English Heritage site administration and information service, including dates, times of opening and special events.

Subject coverage:
English Heritage East Midlands Region, administers and cares for properties and sites in Derbyshire, Northamptonshire, Rutland, Lincolnshire and Leicestershire; the conservation and preservation of the historic environment.

Access to staff:
Contact by letter, by telephone and by fax
Hours: Mon to Fri, 0900 to 1700

Heritage sites:
Ashby-de-la-Zouch Castle
 South Street, Ashby-de-la-Zouch, Leicestershire, LE6 5PR; tel: 01530 413343
Bolsover Castle
 Castle Street, Bolsover, Chesterfield, Derbyshire, S44 6PR; tel: 01246 822844; fax: 01246 241569
Gainsborough Old Hall
 Parnell Street, Gainsborough, Lincolnshire, DN21 2NB; tel: 01427 612669; fax: 01427 612779
Hardwick Old Hall
 Doe Lea, Chesterfield, Derbyshire, S44 5Ql; tel: 01246 850431
Kirby Hall
 Deene, Corby, Northamptonshire, NN17 3EN; tel: 01536 203230
Kirby Muxloe Castle
 Oakcroft Avenue, Kirby Muxloe, Leicestershire, LE9 9MD; tel: 01162 386886
Lyddington Bede House
 Blue Coat Lane, Uppingham, Rutland, LE15 9LZ, tel: 01572 822438
Medieval Bishops' Palace
 Minster Yard, Lincoln, LN2 1PU; tel: 01522 527468
Peveril Castle
 Market Place, Castleton, Derbyshire, S33 8WQ; tel: 01422 620613
Rushton Triangular Lodge
 Rushton, Kettering, Northamptonshire, NN14 1RP; tel: 01536 710761
Sibsey Trader Windmill
 Sibsey, Boston, Lincolnshire, PE22 0SY; tel: 01205 460647
Wingfield Manor
 Garner Lane, South Wingfield, Alfreton, Derbyshire, DE5 7NH; tel: 01773 832060

ENGLISH HERITAGE (EAST OF ENGLAND REGION)

Brooklands, 24 Brooklands Avenue, Cambridge, CB2 2BU

Tel: 01223 582700
Fax: 01223 582701

Website:
http://www.english-heritage.org.uk

Enquiries:
Enquiries to: Regional Marketing Executive – East of England

Organisation type and purpose:
National organisation, suitable for ages: all.
Independent but government-sponsored body. English Heritage site information service, including dates, times of opening and special events.

Subject coverage:
The conservation and preservation of the historic environment of Eastern England.

Access to staff:
Contact by letter, by telephone, by fax and by e-mail
Hours: Mon to Fri, 0900 to 1700

continued overleaf

Heritage sites:
Audley End House & Gardens
  Saffron Walden, Essex, CB11 4JF; tel: 01799
  522399
Berney Arms Windmill
  8 Manor Road, Southtown, Norfolk, NR31 0QA;
  tel: 01493 85700
Castle Acre Priory and Castle
  Stocks Green, Castle Acre, Kings Lynn, Norfolk,
  PE32 2XD; tel: 01760 755394
Castle Rising Castle
  King's Lynn, Norfolk; tel: 01553 631330
Denny Abbey & The Farmland Museum
  Near Waterbeach, Cambridge; tel: 01223 860489
Framlingham Castle
  Framlingham, Suffolk, IP8 9BT; tel: 01728 724189
Great Yarmouth Row Houses
  South Quay, Great Yarmouth, Norfolk, IP13 2RQ;
  tel: 01493 857900
Grime's Graves
  Lynford, Thetford, Norfolk, IP26 5DE; tel: 01842
  810656
Hill Hall
  Epping, Essex; tel: 01223 582700
Landguard Fort
  Felixstowe, Suffolk; tel: 01473 218245
Longthorpe Tower
  Thorpe Road, Longthorpe, Cambridgeshire, PE1
  1HA; tel: 01760 755394
Orford Castle
  Orford, Woodbridge, Suffolk; tel: 01394 450472
Saxtead Green Post Mill
  The Mill House, Saxtead Green, Suffolk, IP13
  9QQ; tel: 01728 685789
Tilbury Fort
  No 2 Office Block, The Fort, Tilbury, Essex, RM18
  7NR; tel: 01375 858489
West Park Gardens
  Silsoe, Luton, Bedfordshire, MK45 4HS; tel:
  01525 860152 (weekends only)

ENGLISH HERITAGE (LONDON REGION)

23 Savile Row, London, W1X 1AB

Tel: 020 7973 3000
Fax: 020 7937 3001

Website:
http://www.english-heritage.org.uk

Enquiries:
Enquiries to: Marketing Officer

Organisation type and purpose:
National organisation, membership association,
suitable for ages: all.
Independent but government-sponsored body.
English Heritage sites administration and
information service, including dates, times of
opening and special events.

Subject coverage:
Conservation and preservation of the historic
environment. English Heritage London Region,
administers and cares for its properties and sites in
the London area.

Education services:
Group education facilities.

Access to staff:
Contact by letter and by telephone. Appointment
necessary.
Hours: Mon to Fri, 0900 to 1700

Heritage sites:
Chapter House
  East Cloisters, Westminster Abbey, London,
  SW1P 3PE; tel: 020 7222 5897; fax: 020 7222 0960
Chiswick House
  Burlington Lane, London, W4 2RP; tel: 020 8995
  0508; fax: 020 8742 3104
Downe House
  Luxted Road, Downe, Biggin Hill, Kent, BR6 7JT;
  tel: 01689 859119; fax: 01689 862755
Eltham Palace
  Court Yard, Eltham, London, SE9 5QE; tel: 020
  8294 2548; fax: 0208 8294 2621

Jewel Tower
  Abingdon Street, Westminster, London, SW1P
  3JY; tel: 020 7222 2219; fax: 020 7222 2219
Kenwood House
  The Iveagh Bequest, Kenwood, Hampstead
  Lane, London, NW3 7JR; tel: 020 8348 1286; fax:
  020 8793 3891
Marble Hill House
  Richmond Road, Twickenham, Middlesex, TW1
  2NL; tel: 0208 892 5115; fax: 020 8607 9976
The Wernher Collection at Ranger's House
  Chesterfield Walk, Blackheath, London, SE10
  8QX; tel: 020 8853 0035; fax: 020 8853 0090
Wellington Arch
  Hyde Park Corner, London, W1J 7JZ; tel: 020
  7930 2726; fax: 020 7925 1019

ENGLISH HERITAGE (NORTH EAST REGION)

Bessie Surtees House, 41–44 Sandhill, Newcastle
upon Tyne, NE1 3JF

Tel: 0191 269 1200

Website:
http://www.english-heritage.org.uk

Enquiries:
Enquiries to: Marketing Manager

Organisation type and purpose:
National organisation, advisory body, membership
association (membership is by subscription),
suitable for ages: all. Independent but government-
sponsored body.
English Heritage site administration and
information service, including dates, times of
opening and special events.

Subject coverage:
English Heritage North East Region administers
and cares for properties and sites in
Northumberland, Tyne and Wear, County Durham
and Teesside; the conservation and preservation of
the historic environment.

Access to staff:
Contact by letter and by telephone. Appointment
necessary.
Hours: Mon to Fri, 0900 to 1700

Heritage sites:
Aydon Castle
  Corbridge, Northumberland, NE45 5PJ
Barnard Castle
  Castle House, Barnard Castle, County Durham,
  DL12 9AT
Belsay Hall, Castle and Gardens
  Belsay, Ponteland, Northumberland, NE20 0DX
Berwick Barracks
  The Parade, Berwick upon Tweed,
  Northumberland, TD15 1DF
Brinkburn Priory
  Long Framlington, Morpeth, Northumberland,
  NE65 8AR
Chesters Roman Fort and Museum
  Chollerford, Humshaugh, Hexham,
  Northumberland, NE46 4EP
Dunstanburgh Castle
  14 Queen Street, Alnwick, Northumberland,
  NE66 1RD
Etal Castle
  Etal Village, Berwick upon Tweed,
  Northumberland, TD12 4TN
Finchale Priory
  Brasside, Newton Hall, County Durham, DH1
  5SH
Hadrian's Wall Museums
Hadrian's Wall Tourism Partnership
Housesteads Roman Fort
  Haydon Bridge, Hexham, Northumberland,
  NE46 6NN
Lindisfarne Priory
  Holy Island, Berwick upon Tweed,
  Northumberland, TD15 2RX
Norham Castle
  Berwick upon Tweed, Northumberland, TD15
  2JY
Prudhoe Castle
  Prudhoe, Northumberland, NE42 6NA

Tynemouth Castle and Priory
  North Shields, Tyne and Wear, NE30 4BZ
Warkworth Castle and Hermitage
  Morpeth, Northumberland, NE66 0UJ

ENGLISH HERITAGE (NORTH WEST REGION)

Canada House, 3 Chepstow Street, Manchester, M1
5FW

Tel: 0161 242 1400

Website:
http://www.english-heritage.org.uk

Enquiries:
Enquiries to: Marketing Manager

Organisation type and purpose:
National organisation, advisory body, membership
association (membership is by subscription),
suitable for ages: all.
Independent but government-sponsored body.
English Heritage site administration and
information service, including dates, times of
opening and special events.

Subject coverage:
English Heritage North West Region administers
and cares for properties and sites in Cheshire,
Merseyside, Greater Manchester, Lancashire and
Cumbria; the conservation and preservation of the
historic environment.

Access to staff:
Contact by letter and by telephone. Appointment
necessary.
Hours: Mon to Fri, 0900 to 1700

Heritage sites:
Ambleside Roman Fort
  Ambleside, Cumbria
Beeston Castle
  Beeston, Tarporley, Cheshire, CW6 9TX
Brough Castle
  Brough, Kirby Stephen, Cumbria
Brougham Castle
  Brougham, Penrith, Cumbria, CA10 2AA
Carlisle Castle
  Carlisle, Cumbria, CA3 8UR
Furness Abbey
  Barrow-in-Furness, Cumbria, LA13 0TJ
Hadrian's Wall Museums
  The Roman Site, Corbridge, Northumberland,
  NE45 5NT
Hadrian's Wall Tourism Partnership
Lanercost Priory
  Lanercost, Brampton, Cumbria, CA8 2HQ
Stott Park Bobbin Mill
  Low Stott Park, Ulverston, Cumbria, LA12 8AX

ENGLISH HERITAGE (SOUTH EAST REGION)

Eastgate Court, 195–205 High Street, Guildford,
Surrey, GU1 3EH

Tel: 01483 252000
Fax: 01483 252001
E-mail: south-east@english-heritage.org.uk

Website:
http://www.english-heritage.org.uk/southeast

Enquiries:
Enquiries to: Marketing Assistant

Organisation type and purpose:
National organisation, advisory body, suitable for
ages: all.
Independent but government-sponsored body.
English Heritage site administration and
information service, including dates, times of
opening and special events.

Subject coverage:
English Heritage South East Region administers
and cares for properties and sites in Kent, Surrey,
Sussex, Hampshire and the Isle of Wight;
conservation and preservation of the historic
environment.

Access to staff:
Contact by letter, by telephone and by fax
Hours: Mon to Fri, 0900 to 1700

Heritage sites:
Abingdon County Hall
Oxfordshire, OX14 3HG; tel: 01235 523703
Appuldurcombe House
Wroxall, Ventnor, Isle of Wight, PO38 3EW; tel: 01983 852484; fax: 01983 840188
Battle Abbey and Battlefield
High Street, Battle, East Sussex, TN33 0AD; tel: 01424 773792
Bayham Old Abbey
Bayham, Lamberhurst, Kent, TN8 8DE; tel: 01892 890381
Bishop's Waltham Palace
Bishop's Waltham, Hampshire, SO32 1DH
Calshot Castle
Hampshire, SO4 1BR; tel: 02380 892023
Camber Castle
tel: 01797 223862
Carisbrooke Castle and Museum
Carisbrooke, Newport, Isle of Wight, PO30 6JY; tel: 01983 522107; e-mail: carismus@lineone.net
Deal Castle
Victoria Road, Deal, Kent, CT14 7BA; tel: 01304 372762
Dover Castle
The Keep, Dover, Kent, CT16 1HU; tel: 01304 211067
Down House
Luxted Road, Downe, Biggin Hill, Kent, BR6 7JT; tel: 01689 859119
Dymchurch Martello Tower
High Street, Dymchurch, Kent, CT16 1HU
Farnham Castle Keep
Castle Hill, Farnham, Surrey, GU6 0AG
Fort Brockhurst
Gunners Way, Elson, Hampshire, PO12 4DS; tel: 02392 378291
Hurst Castle
Hampshire, SO14 0TP; tel: 01590 642344
Lullingstone Roman Villa
Lullingstone Lane, Eynsford, Kent, DA4 0JA; tel: 01322 863467
Medieval Merchant's House
58 French Street, Southhampton, SO23 8NB; tel: 02380 221503
Osborne House
York Avenue, East Cowes, Isle of Wight, PO32 6JY; tel: 01983 200022; fax: 01983 281380
Pevensey Castle
Pevensey, East Sussex, BN24 5LE; tel: 01323 762604
Portchester Castle
Portchester, Hampshire, PO16 9QW; tel: 023 923 78291
Richborough Roman Fort
Sandwich, Kent, CT13 9JW
Rochester Castle
Boley Hill, Rochester, Kent, ME1 1SW; tel: 01634 402276
St Augustine's Abbey and Museum
Longport, Canterbury, Kent, CT1 1TF; tel: 01227 767345; fax: 01227 767345
Temple Manor
Strood, Rochester, Kent; tel: 01634 827980
Upnor Castle
Wainscott, Rochester, Kent; tel: 01634 718742
Walmer Castle & Gardens
Kingsdown Road, Deal, Kent, CT14 7LJ; tel: 01304 364288; fax: 01304 364826
Wolvesey Castle (Old Bishop's Palace)
College Street, Winchester, SO23 8NB
Yarmouth Castle
Quay Street, Yarmouth, Isle of Wight, PO41 0PB; tel: 01983 760678

ENGLISH HERITAGE (SOUTH WEST REGION)

Formal name: Historic Monuments & Building Commission for England
Acronym or abbreviation: HMBCE

29 Queen Square, Bristol, BS1 4ND

Tel: 0117 975 0700

Fax: 0117 975 0701
E-mail: southwest@english-heritage.org.uk

Website:
http://www.english-heritage.org.uk/southwest

Founded:
1984

Organisation type and purpose:

National organisation, advisory body, membership association (membership is by subscription), suitable for ages: all, publishing house.

English Heritage South West Region administers and cares for properties and sites in Bristol, Cornwall, Devon, Dorset, Gloucestershire, Isles of Scilly, Somerset, and Wiltshire.

Subject coverage:
The conservation and preservation of the historic environment.

Access to staff:
Contact by letter, by telephone, by fax, by e-mail and in person. Appointment necessary.
Hours: Mon to Fri, 0900 to 1700

Heritage Site:
Berry Pomeroy Castle
Totnes, Devon, TQ9 6NJ; tel: 01803 866618; e-mail: customers@english-heritage.org.uk; website: http://www.english-heritage.org.uk/berrypomeroy
Chysauster Ancient Village
Newmill, Penzance, Cornwall, TR20 8XA; tel: 07831 757934; e-mail: customers@english-heritage.org.uk; website: http://www.english-heritage.org.uk/chysauster
Cleeve Abbey
Washford, Watchet, Somerset, TA23 0PS; tel: 01984 640377; e-mail: customers@english-heritage.org.uk; website: http://www.english-heritage.org.uk/cleeve
Dartmouth Castle
Castle Road, Dartmouth, Devon, TQ6 0JN; tel: 01803 833588; e-mail: customers@english-heritage.org.uk; website: http://www.english-heritage.org.uk/dartmouth
Farleigh Hungerford Castle
Farleigh Hungerford, Bath, Somerset, BA3 6RS; tel: 01225 754026; e-mail: customers@english-heritage.org.uk; website: http://www.english-heritage.org.uk/farleighhungerford
Hailes Abbey
Winchcombe, Cheltenham, Gloucester, GL54 5PB; tel: 01242 602398; e-mail: customers@english-heritage.org.uk; website: http://www.english-heritage.org.uk/hailes
Launceston Castle
Castle Lodge, Launceston, Cornwall, PL15 7DR; tel: 01566 772365; e-mail: customers@english-heritage.org.uk; website: http://www.english-heritage.org.uk/launceston
Muchelney Abbey
Muchelney, Langport, Somerset, TA10 0DQ; tel: 01458 250664; e-mail: customers@english-heritage.org.uk; website: http://www.english-heritage.org.uk/muchelney
Okehampton Castle
Castle Lodge, Okehampton, Devon, EX20 1JB; tel: 01837 52844; e-mail: customers@english-heritage.org.uk; website: http://www.english-heritage.org.uk/okehampton
Old Sarum
Castle Road, Salisbury, Wiltshire, SP1 3SD; tel: 01722 335398; e-mail: customers@english-heritage.org.uk; website: http://www.english-heritage.org.uk/oldsarum
Old Wardour Castle
Tisbury, Salisbury, Wiltshire, SP3 6RR; tel: 01747 870487; e-mail: customers@english-heritage.org.uk; website: http://www.english-heritage.org.uk/oldwardour
Pendennis Castle
Falmouth, Cornwall, TR11 4LP; tel: 01326 316594; e-mail: customers@english-heritage.org.uk; website: http://www.english-heritage.org.uk/pendennis

Portland Castle
Castleton, Portland, Dorset, DT5 1AZ; tel: 01305 820539; e-mail: customers@english-heritage.org.uk; website: http://www.english-heritage.org.uk/portland
Restormel Castle
Lostwithiel, Cornwall, PL22 0BD; tel: 01208 872687; e-mail: customers@english-heritage.org.uk; website: http://www.english-heritage.org.uk/restormel
Sherborne Old Castle
Castleton, Dorset, 19 0SY; tel: 01935 812730; e-mail: customers@english-heritage.org.uk; website: http://www.english-heritage.org.uk/sherborne
St Mawes Castle
St Mawes, Cornwall, TR2 3AA; tel: 01326 270526; e-mail: customers@english-heritage.org.uk; website: http://www.english-heritage.org.uk/stmawes
Stonehenge
Stone Circle, Wiltshire, SP4 7DE; tel: 01980 624715 (Information line); e-mail: customers@english-heritage.org.uk; website: http://www.english-heritage.org.uk/stonehenge
Tintagel Castle
Tintagel, Cornwall, DL34 0AA; tel: 01840 770328; e-mail: customers@english-heritage.org.uk; website: http://www.english-heritage.org.uk/tintagel
Totnes Castle
Castle Street, Totnes, Devon, TQ9 5NU; tel: 01803 864406; e-mail: customers@english-heritage.org.uk; website: http://www.english-heritage.org.uk/totnes

ENGLISH HERITAGE (WEST MIDLANDS REGION)

The Axis, 10 Holliday Street, Birmingham, B1 1TG

Tel: 0121 625 6820

Website:
http://www.english-heritage.org.uk

Organisation type and purpose:
National organisation, advisory body.
Independent but government-sponsored body.
English Heritage West Midlands Region administers and cares for properties and sites in Herefordshire, Shropshire, Staffordshire, Warwickshire, West Midlands and Worcestershire.

Subject coverage:
The conservation and preservation of the historic environment.
English Heritage site administration and information service, including dates, times of opening and special events.

Access to staff:
Contact by letter, by telephone and in person
Hours: Mon to Fri, 0900 to 1700

Heritage Site:
Boscobel House and the Royal Oak
Brewood, Bishops Wood, Staffordshire, ST19 9AR
Buildwas Abbey
Ironbridge, Telford, TF8 7BW
Goodrich Castle
Goodrich, Ross on Wye, Worcestershire, HR9 6HY
Halesowen Abbey
Haughmond Abbey
Upton Magna, Uffington, Shropshire, SY4 4RW
Kenilworth Castle
Kenilworth, Warwickshire, CV8 1NE
Stokesay Castle
Craven Arms, Shropshire, SY7 9AH
Wall Roman Site (Letocetum)
Watling Street, Lichfield, Staffordshire, WS14 0AW
Wenlock Priory
Much Wenlock, Shropshire, TF13 6HS
Witley Court
Great Witley, Worcestershire, WR6 6JT
Wroxeter Roman City
Wroxeter, Shropshire, SY5 6PH

ENGLISH HERITAGE (YORKSHIRE REGION)

37 Tanner Row, York, YO1 6WP

Tel: 01904 601901

Website:
http://www.english-heritage.org.uk

Organisation type and purpose:
National organisation, advisory body.
Independent but government-sponsored body.
English Heritage Yorkshire Region administers
and cares for properties and sites in East Riding of
Yorkshire, North East Lincolnshire, North
Lincolnshire, North Yorkshire, South Yorkshire
and West Yorkshire.

Subject coverage:
The conservation and preservation of the historic
environment.
English Heritage site administration and
information service, including dates, times of
opening and special events.

Access to staff:
Contact by letter, by telephone and in person
Hours: Mon to Fri, 0900 to 1700

Heritage Site:
Aldborough Roman Site
  Main Street, Boroughbridge, Yorkshire, YO5 9EF
Brodsworth Hall and Gardens
  Brodsworth, Doncaster, South Yorkshire
Byland Abbey
  Coxwold, North Yorkshire, YO6 4BD
Clifford's Tower
  Clifford Street, York, YO11 1HY
Conisbrough Castle
Helmsley Castle
  Helmsley, North Yorkshire, YO6 5AB
Kirkham Priory
  Whitwell-on-the-Hill, North Yorkshire, YO6 7JS
Middleham Castle
  Middleham, Leyburn, North Yorkshire, DL8
  4QG
Mount Grace Priory
  Saddle Bridge, Northallerton, North Yorkshire,
  DL6 3JG
Pickering Castle
  Pickering, North Yorkshire, YO18 7AX
Richmond Castle
  Richmond, North Yorkshire, DL10 4QW
Rievaulx Abbey
  Rievaulx, Helmsley, North Yorkshire, DL10 5LB
Roche Abbey
  Maltby, Rotherham, South Yorkshire, S66 8NW
Scarborough Castle
  Castle Road, Scarborough, North Yorkshire,
  YO11 1HY
Whitby Abbey
  Whitby, North Yorkshire, YO22 4JT

ENGLISH HOCKEY

Acronym or abbreviation: EHA

The Stadium, Silbury Boulevard, Milton Keynes,
Buckinghamshire, MK9 1HA

Tel: 01908 544644
Fax: 01908 241106
E-mail: info@englishhockey.org

Website:
http://www.hockeyonline.co.uk
Official site of English Hockey, including latest
news, results, tables and links to hockey clubs in
England.

Enquiries:
Enquiries to: Marketing Director

Founded:
1886

Formerly called:
Hockey Association (HA) from 1886 to 1997; All
England Womens Hockey Association (AEWHA)
from 1895 to 1997; Mixed Hockey Association
(MHA), National Hockey Foundation (NHF) (year
of change 1997)

Organisation type and purpose:
Membership association (membership is by
subscription), present number of members: 70,000,
suitable for ages: 5 to 65.
Governing body of hockey in England.

Subject coverage:
Hockey in England, its history, past, present and
future development, English hockey in European
and world arenas; league and competition
management, coaching, umpiring and teaching,
technical information, sponsorship and
partnership, international teams, advice on all
aspects of hockey including clubs.

**Museum or gallery collection, archive, or library
special collection:**
Minute books and cash account books from the
formation of the Association in 1896
Pictorial history
Trophies, gifts, and artefacts presented by guest
  and host nations

Trade and statistical information:
Data on the market profile and on the number of
  participants in hockey, at club level split into
  regions and counties.

Printed publications:
Clothing
Coaching Packs
Handbook of English Hockey
Leaflets and posters
Rules of Hockey

Microform publications:
Coaching videos

Access to staff:
Contact by letter, by telephone, by fax, by e-mail
and via website. Appointment necessary.
Hours: Mon to Fri, 0900 to 1700

Affiliated to:
European Hockey Federation (EHF)
International Hockey Federation (FIH)

Constituent member of:
Great Britain Olympic Hockey Board

ENGLISH INDEPENDENCE PARTY

Acronym or abbreviation: EIP

27 Old Gloucester Street, London, WC1N 3XX

Tel: 020 7278 5221
E-mail: eip_enquiries@yahoo.com

Website:
www.englishindependenceparty.com
Manifesto, bibliography

Enquiries:
Enquiries to: Chairman

Founded:
1991

Formerly called:
English National Party (ENP)

Organisation type and purpose:
National organisation, membership association
(membership is by subscription), voluntary
organisation.
Political party.

Subject coverage:
English nationalism, knowledge about the English
people, UK devolution, UK politics, English
politics, nationalism, English history, culture and
language.

**Museum or gallery collection, archive, or library
special collection:**
Books related to English nationalism, etc.

Printed publications:
Manifesto
Leaflet
Progress Letters

Access to staff:
Contact by letter and by telephone. Appointment
necessary.

Hours: Mon to Fri, 1100 to 2200

Access to building, collection or gallery:
No access other than to staff

ENGLISH INDOOR BOWLING ASSOCIATION

Acronym or abbreviation: EIBA

David Cornwell House, Bowling Green, Leicester
Road, Melton Mowbray, Leicestershire, LE13 0FA

Tel: 01664 481900
Fax: 01664 482888
E-mail: enquiries@eiba.co.uk

Website:
http://www.eiba.co.uk
Full information including all national
competitions.

Enquiries:
Enquiries to: National Secretary

Founded:
1971

Organisation type and purpose:
National organisation, membership association
(membership is by subscription), present number
of members: 350 clubs.
National governing body of men's amateur level-
green, indoor bowling.

Subject coverage:
Development of facilities for indoor bowling for
men and women, details of events and
programme, player profiles.

Printed publications:
EIBA Year Book

Electronic and video publications:
Affiliated clubs' addresses

Access to staff:
Contact by letter, by telephone, by fax, by e-mail,
in person and via website. Appointment necessary.
Hours: Mon to Fri, 0900 to 1700

Affiliated to:
British Isles Indoor Bowls Council
World Indoor Bowls Council

ENGLISH LADIES GOLF ASSOCIATION

Acronym or abbreviation: ELGA

Edgbaston Golf Club, Church Road, Birmingham,
B15 3TB

Tel: 0121 456 2088
Fax: 0121 454 5542
E-mail: office@englishladiesgolf.org

Website:
http://www.englishladiesgolf.org
Information about all championships, recent news,
player profiles, information for juniors, details of
grants available.

Enquiries:
Enquiries to: Secretary

Founded:
1952

Organisation type and purpose:
Membership association (membership is by
subscription), present number of members:
135,000, voluntary organisation.
National governing body of the game, training
organisation for juniors.
Administers ladies golf in England.

Subject coverage:
Ladies golf, entry to golf clubs, queries on
handicaps and rules of golf, championship
organisation.

**Museum or gallery collection, archive, or library
special collection:**
Yearbook
Histories and Centenary Books from County
  Associations and Golf Clubs

Printed publications:
Yearbook (£4)

Access to staff:
Contact by letter, by telephone, by e-mail and via website. Appointment necessary.
Hours: Mon to Fri, 0900 to 1700

Affiliated to:
Ladies Golf Union
The Scores, St Andrews, Fife, KY16 9AT

ENGLISH NATIONAL BALLET

Markova House, 39 Jay Mews, London, SW7 2ES

Tel: 020 7581 1245
Fax: 020 7225 0827
E-mail: info@ballet.org.uk

Website:
http://www.ballet.org.uk
Includes information on ballets, dancers, current news, history of the Company, etc.

Enquiries:
Enquiries to: Assistant to Managing Director
Other contacts: Marketing Manager for general source of information about performances and other activities.

Founded:
1950

Formed from:
Festival Ballet, London Festival Ballet

Organisation type and purpose:
Membership association (membership is by subscription), registered charity (charity number 214005).
English National Ballet is a performing arts organisation. Individuals and companies can provide support and receive services/benefits by joining the Association of English National Ballet or the Council of English National Ballet or by becoming a corporate member/sponsor of the Company.

Subject coverage:
Ballet.

Museum or gallery collection, archive, or library special collection:
English National Ballet Archive includes photographs, designs, set models, music scores, press clippings and books

Printed publications:
In the Wings (magazine, free to associates with membership, minimum £8 a year)

Access to staff:
Contact by letter, by telephone, by fax and by e-mail
Hours: Mon to Fri, 1000 to 1800

Access to building, collection or gallery:
Prior appointment required
Special comments: English National Ballet Archive is available to those undertaking serious study.

ENGLISH NATIONAL OPERA

Acronym or abbreviation: ENO

London Coliseum, St Martin's Lane, London, WC2N 4ES

Tel: 020 7836 0111
Fax: 020 7836 8379

Website:
http://www.eno.org

Enquiries:
Enquiries to: Archivist
Other contacts: Operations Director or Communications Controller

Founded:
1947

Formerly called:
Sadlers Wells Opera

Organisation type and purpose:
Registered charity (charity number 257210), historic building, house or site.
Opera production in English.
Encouragement of understanding and appreciation of the dramatic art by providing, presenting, producing, organising, managing, and conducting performances of classical and educational plays, opera, ballet, films and concerts.

Subject coverage:
History and performance of opera at Sadlers Wells and The Coliseum.

Museum or gallery collection, archive, or library special collection:
Original documents relating to the history and performance of Sadlers Wells Opera and English National Opera

Access to staff:
Contact by letter and by fax
Hours: Archives: Mon to Fri, 1000 to 1800, closed at weekends

Access for disabled people:
Toilet facilities

ENGLISH PEWTER COMPANY

1 Blackmore Street, Sheffield, South Yorkshire, S4 7TZ

Tel: 0114 272 3920
Fax: 0114 276 1416
E-mail: asharp@englishpewter.co.uk

Website:
http://www.englishpewter.co.uk

Enquiries:
Enquiries to: Managing Director
Direct e-mail: sales@englishpewter.co.uk

Founded:
1977

Organisation type and purpose:
Manufacturing industry.

Subject coverage:
Pewterware.

Non-library collection catalogue:
All or part available online

Library catalogue:
All or part available online

Publications list:
Available online

Access to staff:
Contact by letter, by telephone, by fax and by e-mail. Appointment necessary.
Hours: Mon to Fri, 0900 to 1700

Access to building, collection or gallery:
Prior appointment required

Also at:
English Pewter Company
1 Blackmoor Street, Sheffield, S4 7TZ; e-mail: sales@englishpewter.co.uk

ENGLISH PLACE-NAME SOCIETY

Acronym or abbreviation: EPNS

Department of English Studies, University of Nottingham, Nottingham, NG7 2RD

Tel: 0115 951 5919
Fax: 0115 951 5924

Website:
http://www.nottingham.ac.uk/english/research/EPNS/index.html
Information provided (our purpose, publications, membership details, personnel)

Enquiries:
Enquiries to: Administrator

Founded:
1923

Organisation type and purpose:
Learned society (membership is by subscription), registered charity (charity number 257891), research organisation, publishing house.

Subject coverage:
Etymologies of English place-names, surveyed on a county basis.

Museum or gallery collection, archive, or library special collection:
English and Scandinavian onomastics
Library including the Olof von Feilitzen bequest

Library catalogue:
All or part available in-house

Printed publications:
Place-Names in Skaldic Verse
The Place-Names of West Thorney
Vocabulary of English Place-Names
Wirral and its Viking Heritage
Journal of the English Place-Name Society (issued free to members)
A Dictionary of Lincolnshire Place-Names
Annual county volume on the place-names of that county (each county takes several volumes to cover it); counties include:
Bedfordshire, Berkshire, Buckinghamshire, Cambridgeshire and the Isle of Ely, Cheshire, Cornwall, Cumberland, Derbyshire, Devon, Dorset, East Riding of Yorkshire and York, Essex, Gloucestershire, Hertfordshire, Huntingdonshire, Leicestershire, Lincolnshire, Middlesex apart from the City of London, Norfolk, North Riding of Yorkshire, Northamptonshire, Nottinghamshire, Oxfordshire, Rutland, Shropshire, Staffordshire, Surrey, Sussex, Warwickshire, West Riding of Yorkshire, Westmoreland, Wiltshire, Worcestershire

Publications list:
Available online and in print

Access to staff:
Contact by letter, by telephone and by fax.
Appointment necessary. Non-members charged.
Hours: Mon to Fri, 0900 to 1700

Affiliated to:
AHRB
Institute for Navneforskning
University of Copenhagen
Ortnamnssällskapets
University of Uppsala
Sydsvenska Ortnamnssällskapets
University of Lund

Supported by:
British Academy

ENGLISH PLAYING CARD SOCIETY

Acronym or abbreviation: EPCS

PO Box 29, North Walsham, Norfolk, NR28 9NQ

Tel: 01692 650496
Fax: 0870 127 2448
E-mail: secretary@epcs.org

Enquiries:
Enquiries to: Secretary

Founded:
1984

Organisation type and purpose:
Membership association (membership is by subscription), present number of members: 120.

Subject coverage:
All aspects of the manufacture and designs of English playing cards/card games and related subjects, including ephemera.

Printed publications:
Newsletter (3 times a year)

Access to staff:
Contact by telephone and by e-mail. Appointment necessary.
Hours: Mon to Fri, 0900 to 1700

ENGLISH RACKETBALL ASSOCIATION

50 Tredegar Road, Wilmington, Dartford, Kent, DA2 7AZ

Tel: 01322 272200
Fax: 01322 289295
E-mail: idw@kentsra.co.uk

Website:
http://www.kentracketball.co.uk

Enquiries:
Enquiries to: Secretary

Founded:
1984

Created by the merger of:
British Racketball Association (BRA) and Squash Rackets Association (SRA) (year of change 1998)

Organisation type and purpose:
Voluntary organisation.
Governing body of the sport.

Subject coverage:
Rules of racketball, coaching, tournaments, promoting racketball within Local Authority leisure centres and private squash clubs.

Access to staff:
Contact by letter, by telephone and by fax
Hours: Mon to Fri, 0900 to 1700

ENGLISH SCHOOLS' ATHLETIC ASSOCIATION

Acronym or abbreviation: ESAA

26 Newborough Green, New Malden, Surrey, KT3 5HS

Tel: 020 8949 1506
Fax: 020 8942 0943

Enquiries:
Enquiries to: Honorary Secretary

Founded:
1925

Organisation type and purpose:
Voluntary organisation.

Subject coverage:
Schools' athletics.

Printed publications:
Awards Scheme Brochure (annually, free)
History of English Schools AA 1925 to 1995 (£8.50 inc. p&p)
Handbook (annually, £3 inc. p&p)

Access to staff:
Contact by letter, by telephone and by fax
Hours: Mon to Fri, 0900 to 1700

Affiliated to:
Amateur Athletic Association of England
Central Council of Physical Recreation
National Council for School Sports
UK Athletics

ENGLISH SCHOOLS' FOOTBALL ASSOCIATION

Acronym or abbreviation: ESFA

4 Parker Court, Staffordshire Technology Park, Stafford, ST18 0WP

Tel: 01785 785970
Fax: 01785 256246
E-mail: office@esfa.co.uk

Website:
http://www.esfa.co.uk/esfa/
Competition draws and results.

Enquiries:
Enquiries to: Chief Executive

Founded:
1904

Organisation type and purpose:
Membership association, registered charity (charity number 306003).

Subject coverage:
Organisation of extra-curricular football for schools in England, regulations for schoolboy or girl footballers, competition rules.

Printed publications:
Annual Handbook (£7 plus p&p)
Annual Report
The ESFA Guide to the Teaching of Soccer in Schools (£2.95 inc. p&p)
Kicks (3 times a year, free)
Other publications available from the Football Association

Publications list:
Available in print

Access to staff:
Contact by letter, by telephone, by fax and by e-mail. Appointment necessary.
Hours: Mon to Fri, 0900 to 1700

Affiliated to:
Football Association
tel: 020 7745 4545

Has:
500 member associations

ENGLISH SHORT MAT BOWLING ASSOCIATION

Acronym or abbreviation: ESMBA

Wytheford Hall, Shawbury, Shrewsbury, Shopshire, SY4 4JJ

Tel: 01952 770218
Fax: 01952 770567

Website:
http://www.shortmatbowlsesmba.com

Enquiries:
Enquiries to: General Secretary
Other contacts: Umpires Director; Competition Secretary; Membership Secretary

Founded:
1984

Organisation type and purpose:
Membership association (membership is by subscription), present number of members: c. 27,000, voluntary organisation.
National governing body of the game in England, sports association.

Subject coverage:
The game of short mat bowls.

Printed publications:
Rule Book (£2)

Electronic and video publications:
Video (£10)

Access to staff:
Contact by letter
Hours: Daily, 0900 to 1700

ENGLISH SPEAKING BOARD (INTERNATIONAL) LIMITED

Acronym or abbreviation: ESB

26a Princes Street, Southport, Merseyside, PR8 1EQ

Tel: 01704 501730
Fax: 01704 539637
E-mail: admin@esbuk.org

Website:
http://www.esbuk.org
Full range of syllabus available plus contact information for interested organisations.

Enquiries:
Enquiries to: Chief Administration Officer

Founded:
1953

Organisation type and purpose:
International organisation, advisory body, professional body, voluntary organisation, registered charity (charity number 272565), suitable for ages: 5+, training organisation.
Examining body.

Subject coverage:
Oral education, communication, speech, English language, English teaching.

Printed publications:
Creative Oral Assessment (Burniston, 1982)
English Speaking Board: an introduction (leaflet)
Forty Years of Achievement: ESB 1953–1993
Speaking English (formerly Spoken English, 2 times a year)

Publications list:
Available in print

Access to staff:
Contact by letter, by telephone, by fax, by e-mail and via website
Hours: Mon to Fri, 0900 to 1700

Access for disabled people:
Parking provided

Affiliated to:
Australia Speech Communication Association
ESB New South Wales
New Zealand Speech Board

ENGLISH SPEAKING UNION OF THE COMMONWEALTH

Acronym or abbreviation: ESU

Page Memorial Library, Dartmouth House, 37 Charles Street, London, W1J 5ED

Tel: 020 7529 1550
Fax: 020 7495 6108
E-mail: esu@esu.org

Website:
http://www.esu.org

Enquiries:
Enquiries to: Librarian
Direct e-mail: library@esu.org

Founded:
1948

Organisation type and purpose:
International organisation, membership association (membership is by subscription), present number of members: 6104, registered charity (charity number 273136).
Promotion of international understanding; scholarships, exchange programmes, cultural events.

Subject coverage:
History, literature and culture of the United States.

Museum or gallery collection, archive, or library special collection:
ESU Archive (photographs, letters, documents)
Adlai Stevenson Memorial Collection
Main collection c. 12,000 books of US interest (history, literature, arts, social sciences)
Winifred Nerney Collection: publishers and literary figures

Access to staff:
Contact by letter, by telephone, by fax and by e-mail. Appointment necessary.
Hours: Mon to Fri, 1000 to 1700

Affiliated to:
The English Speaking Union of the United States 144 East 39th Street, New York, NY 10016, USA; tel: +1 212 818 1200; fax: +1 212 867 4177; e-mail: info@esuus.org; website: http://www.esuus.org

ENGLISH STRING ORCHESTRA LIMITED/ENGLISH SYMPHONY ORCHESTRA

Formal name: English Symphony Orchestra
Acronym or abbreviation: ESO

The Old Hop Store, Three Counties Showground, Malvern, Worcestershire, WR13 6SP

Tel: 01684 560696
Fax: 01684 560656
E-mail: info@eso.co.uk

Enquiries:
Enquiries to: Head of Finance and Administration
Other contacts: Administrator

Founded:
1980

Organisation type and purpose:
Registered charity (charity number 293345). Orchestra.

Subject coverage:
Orchestral performance and touring, music, orchestration, programme notes.
3 Youth Orchestras for grades 1–8, regular courses, bespoke concerts/programmes, indoor and outdoor. Box office services for customer events.

Electronic and video publications:
Recordings on CD and cassette by Nimbus (discography is available)

Publications list:
Available in print

Access to staff:
Contact by letter, by telephone, by fax, by e-mail and via website
Hours: Mon to Fri, 1000 to 1700

ENGLISH TABLE TENNIS ASSOCIATION

Acronym or abbreviation: ETTA

Queensbury House, Havelock Road, Hastings, East Sussex, TN34 1HF

Tel: 01424 722525
Fax: 01424 422103
E-mail: admin@etta.co.uk; vanda.jones@etta.co.uk (events)

Website:
http://www.etta.co.uk

Enquiries:
Enquiries to: National Communications Officer
Direct e-mail: richard.pettit@etta.co.uk

Founded:
1901

Formerly called:
Ping Pong Association (PPA) (year of change 1901); Table Tennis Association (year of change 1903); United Table Tennis and Ping Pong Association (UTTPPA) (year of change 1904); Table Tennis Association (TTA) (year of change 1922); English Table Tennis Association (ETTA) (year of change 1927); English Table Tennis Association Limited (year of change 2001)

Organisation type and purpose:
Governing body of the sport.

Subject coverage:
Table tennis: competition and administration; historical, technical and developmental aspects of table tennis.

Printed publications:
Official Handbook
Table Tennis News (8 times a year)

Access to staff:
Contact by letter, by telephone, by fax and by e-mail. Appointment necessary.
Hours: Mon to Fri, 0900 to 1700

Links with:
European Table Tennis Union (ETTU)
25 rue des Capucins, 1313, Luxembourg; tel: +352 223030; +352 223031; fax: +352 223060; e-mail: ettu@pt.lu
International Table Tennis Federation (ITTF)
Avenue Mon-Repos 30, Lausanne, 1005, Switzerland; tel: + 41 21 340 7090; fax: + 41 21 340 7099; e-mail: ittf@ittf.com

ENGLISH TOURING OPERA

Acronym or abbreviation: ETO

52–54 Rosebery Avenue, London, EC1R 4RP

Tel: 0207 833 2555
Fax: 0207 713 8686 admin@englishtouringopera.org.uk
E-mail: admin@englishtouringopera.org.uk

Website:
http://www.englishtouringopera.org.uk
Company background, friends, repertoire, educational work, tour venues and dates.

Enquiries:
Enquiries to: Chief Executive
Other contacts: Marketing Manager, Education Manager, Head of Development & Marketing – Fundraising

Founded:
1979

Formerly called:
Opera 80 Limited (year of change 1979–1992)

Organisation type and purpose:
Service industry, registered charity.
To take opera throughout England to venues that otherwise would receive little or no professional opera and in so doing to provide opportunities for singers in the early stages of their careers.

Subject coverage:
Opera, touring opera, opera in education and for special needs.

Access to staff:
Contact by letter, by telephone, by fax and by e-mail
Hours: Mon to Fri, 1000 to 1800

ENGLISH VOLLEYBALL ASSOCIATION

Acronym or abbreviation: EVA

27 South Road, West Bridgford, Nottinghamshire, NG2 7AG

Tel: 01509 631699
Fax: 01509 631699
E-mail: general@eng-volleyball.demon.co.uk

Enquiries:
Enquiries to: Chief Executive
Other contacts: Director

Founded:
1972

Organisation type and purpose:
Membership association (membership is by subscription), present number of members: 23,000, voluntary organisation.

Subject coverage:
Volleyball; coaching; refereeing; competitions (domestic and international); equipment recommendations, rules, qualifications, awards, beach volleyball, mini volleyball.

Printed publications:
Volleyball International Rules (£5.31)

Electronic and video publications:
Introducing Volleyball (video, £18)
Volleyball – A Movement Education (video, £18)

Publications list:
Available online and in print

Access to staff:
Contact by letter, by telephone, by fax, by e-mail and via website. Appointment necessary.
Hours: Mon to Fri, 0930 to 1630

Affiliated to:
European Volleyball Confederation
International Volleyball Federation

ENGLISH WOMEN'S INDOOR BOWLING ASSOCIATION

Acronym or abbreviation: EWIBA

3 Moulton Business Park, Scirocco Close, Northampton, NN3 6AP

Tel: 01604 494163
Fax: 01604 494434
E-mail: ewiba@btconnect.com

Website:
http://www.ewiba.com

Enquiries:
Enquiries to: Secretary

Founded:
1951

Organisation type and purpose:
Membership association (membership is by subscription), present number of members: 52,000, voluntary organisation.
Governing body of the game in England.
To administer ladies indoor bowls events, to promote the game within England and to take part in international sporting events.

Subject coverage:
Anything to do with indoor bowling for ladies within England.

Printed publications:
EWIBA Year Book (annually, £2.50)

Access to staff:
Contact by letter, by telephone, by fax and by e-mail
Hours: Mon to Fri, 0900 to 1700

Access for disabled people:
Level entry, toilet facilities

ENGLISH-SPEAKING UNION SCOTLAND

Acronym or abbreviation: ESU Scotland

23 Atholl Crescent, Edinburgh, EH3 8HQ

Tel: 0131 229 1528
Fax: 0131 229 1533
E-mail: director@esuscotland.org.uk

Website:
http://www.esuscotland.org.uk

Enquiries:
Enquiries to: Director
Other contacts: Treasurer (for financial queries)

Founded:
1918

Organisation type and purpose:
International organisation, membership association (charity number 000653). World-wide educational charity, represented in over 50 countries. Members contribute to a wide range of international and cultural events; the promotion of the awareness of current affairs; the use of the English language to create a more harmonious world. Runs international scholarships and exchanges, organises conferences and cultural events, and teaches English as a foreign language. The main providers of training and competitions in speech and debate for Scottish schools, also providing training in public speaking and presentation skills for adults.

Subject coverage:
Public speaking and debating, American studies.

Education services:
Training for schools in speech and debate. Training for adults in public speaking and presentation skills. Teaching English as a foreign language. Resources for school debate online.

Museum or gallery collection, archive, or library special collection:
American Studies Library, over 1,200 vols of North American interest, covering literature, criticism, history, politics and society

Non-library collection catalogue:
All or part available online

Library catalogue:
All or part available online

continued overleaf

Printed publications:
Newsletter (quarterly, free)

Access to staff:
Contact by letter, by telephone, by fax, by e-mail and via website. Appointment necessary.
Hours: Mon to Fri, 0900 to 1800

Links with:
English-Speaking Union of the Commonwealth Dartmouth House, 37 Charles Street, London, W1J 5ED; tel: 020 7529 1550; fax: 020 7495 6108; e-mail: esu@esu.org; website: http://www.esu .org

ENT UK

Formal name: British Association of Otorhinolaryngologists – Head and Neck Surgeons
Acronym or abbreviation: ENT UK

The Royal College of Surgeons, 35–43 Lincoln's Inn Fields, London, WC2A 3PE

Tel: 020 7404 8373
Fax: 020 7404 4200
E-mail: admin@entuk.org

Website:
http://www.entuk.org

Enquiries:
Enquiries to: Administration Manager
Direct tel: 020 7404 8373
Direct fax: 020 7404 4200
Direct e-mail: admin@entuk.org
Other contacts: Honorary Secretary

Founded:
1943

Organisation type and purpose:
Professional body (membership is by subscription, election or invitation), present number of members: 1353, registered charity (charity number 213352).
The Association (BAO-HNS) aims to promote the highest quality and standards of medical and surgical practice of the Specialty for the benefit of patients and to encourage its future advancement through education, research and audit.

Subject coverage:
Laryngology, otology, rhinology, head and neck surgery.

Publications list:
Available in print

Access to staff:
Contact by letter, by telephone, by fax and by e-mail. Appointment necessary.
Hours: Mon to Fri, 0930 to 1730
Special comments: For doctors only.

ENTERPRISE EUROPE NETWORK

Website:
http://www.enterprise-europe-network.ec.europa .eu/network_en.htm
Click on the United Kingdom in the map of Europe, or on 'the united Kingdom' in the list of countries beneath the map, to call up a list of Local Partner Organisations that have been established in the UK

Founded:
2008

Organisation type and purpose:
An initiative of the European Commission to establish a network of contact points, in the Member States of the European Union and in a number of non-EU countries, offering information and advice to companies (particularly small and medium-sized enterprises) on EU matters.

ENTERPRISE EUROPE YORKSHIRE

Bradford Design Exchange, 34 Peckover Street, Bradford, West Yorkshire, BD1 5BD

Tel: 01274 434262
Fax: 01274 432136
E-mail: info@ee-yorkshire.com

Website:
http://www.ee-yorkshire.com

Enquiries:
Enquiries to: Manager

Founded:
1990

Incorporates the former:
West Yorkshire European Information Centre (WYEIC)

Organisation type and purpose:
Member of Enterprise Europe Network
Provision of information and advice to business on EU legislation, innovation and technology transfer, and trading in Europe.

Subject coverage:
EU legislation and policies, European business information, innovation, technical standards, research and development, and the environment.

Information services:
Enquiry Service, Tenders Information Service, Alerting Service, European Partner Search Service

Museum or gallery collection, archive, or library special collection:
EC official journal prior to 1989 on microfiche
Collection of EC official documentation held

Electronic and video publications:
News from Europe
Order electronic and video publications from: via website

Access to staff:
Contact by letter, by telephone, by fax, by e-mail and via website. Appointment necessary.
Hours: Mon to Fri, 0900 to 1700

Parent body:
Bradford City Council
　Department of Regeneration

ENTRUST CARE

Clifton House, 3 St Paul's Road, Foleshill, Coventry, Warwickshire, CV6 5DE

Tel: 024 7666 5450
Fax: 024 7666 5450
E-mail: admin@entrustcare.co.uk

Website:
http://www.entrustcare.co.uk

Enquiries:
Enquiries to: General Manager

Founded:
1969
Association for Brain-Damaged Children and Young Adults (year of change 2005)

Organisation type and purpose:
Membership association (membership is by subscription), present number of members: 70, voluntary organisation, registered charity (charity number 500452).
Localised.
Respite and residential care in the Coventry area only.

Subject coverage:
Self-help group providing respite care to children and residential care to adults with learning and physical disabilities.

Printed publications:
Information Leaflet
Newsletter (2 times a year)

Access to staff:
Contact by letter, by telephone, by fax and by e-mail. Appointment necessary. Access for members only. All charged.
Hours: Mon to Fri, 0900 to 1500

Access for disabled people:
Parking provided, ramped entry

Links with:
CVS Coventry

ENVIRONMENT AGENCY – BRISTOL

Rio House, Waterside Drive, Aztec West, Almondsbury, Bristol, BS32 4UD

Tel: 01454 624400
Fax: 01454 624409
E-mail: enquiries@environment-agency.gov.uk

Website:
http://www.environment-agency.gov.uk
Contact information, state of the environment report, press releases, newsletter, Board meetings agendas & summaries, guidance notes, bathing water quality data, river habitat data, river flow data, Annual Report, environmental strategy, Corporate Plan, some consultation papers.
http://www.environment-agency.gov.uk/fish
Instant dealing of full, junior, eight-day and one-day fishing licences

Enquiries:
Enquiries to: Information & Marketing Manager
Direct tel: 0117 914 2856
Direct fax: 0117 914 2760

Founded:
1 April 1996

Formed from:
County Council Waste Regulatory Functions; London Waste Regulation Authority (year of change 1996)

Formerly called:
Her Majesty's Inspectorate of Pollution (HMIP), National Rivers Authority (NRA)

Organisation type and purpose:
National government body.
Non departmental public body.
Environmental regulation.

Subject coverage:
Water quality, water resources, conservation, water recreation, navigation, waste management, pollution control, sustainable development, environmental policy, environmental legislation, fisheries.

Museum or gallery collection, archive, or library special collection:
Principal Public Registers are:
Integrated Pollution Control (IPC) Register (industrial processes; applications, authorisations, variations, appeals, restrictions, monitoring records, enforcement and prohibition notices, revocations, convictions and appeals)
Register of Industrial Works (the 'Air Register'; industrial processes with the potential to cause air pollution)
Radioactive Substances (RAS) Register (use, accumulation and disposal of radioactive materials; applications, registrations, authorisations, variations, cancellations, enforcement and prohibition notices, convictions and appeals)
Water Quality & Pollution Control Register (discharge consent applications, decisions and appeals, changes of holder, revocations, water quality objectives, monitoring records including bathing waters, maps of freshwater limits, maps of 'controlled' coastal waters)
Water Abstraction and Impounding Register (licence applications, decisions and appeals, successions, revocations)
Maps of Waterworks (location of resource mains, water mains, discharge pipes and underground works)
Maps of Main Rivers (for each area covered by the Agency's Regional Flood Defence Committees)
Waste Management Licence Register (relating to the recovery or disposal of waste; applications, working plans, inspection reports, monitoring information, modifications, revocations, suspensions, appeals, surrenders, convictions, exemptions to licences)

Carriers and Brokers of Controlled Waste Register
(applications to carry waste)
Other Registers:
Works Discharge Register (information on owners
or occupiers of premises which abut
watercourses who have requested to be
registered in order to receive notification of
discharges caused by the Agency)
Genetically Modified Organisms Register, held on
behalf of the Department of the Environment,
Food and Rural Affairs (releases of genetically
modified organisms)
Chemical Release Inventory (releases from
processes regulated under Integrated Pollution
Control)
Special Waste Notifications (consignment notes:
disposal and location records – non-
commercially confidential, summaries of Special
Waste – when prepared by the disposal
authority)

Trade and statistical information:
Public Registers in a combination of paper and
computer files, details of water quality, consents
to discharge to water, water and effluent sample
data.

Non-library collection catalogue:
All or part available in-house

Library catalogue:
All or part available in-house

Printed publications:
Publications include:
Annual Report
Corporate Plan (annually)
Bathing Water Quality in England and Wales
Fisheries Technical Reports
Groundwater Vulnerability Map
Otters and River Habitat Management
Weather Radar and Flood Warning Services
Research and Development Outputs
Angling Guides
Order printed publications from: Free publications,
Environment Agency
Rio House, Waterside Drive, Aztec West,
Almondsbury, Bristol, BS12 4UD
Priced publications, The Stationery Office
PO Box 276, London, SW8 5DT
R&D Reports, Foundation for Water Research
Allen House, The Listons, Liston Road, Marlow,
Buckinghamshire, SL7 1FD
Regional publications, Environment Agency
Regional Offices

Publications list:
Available in print

Access to staff:
Contact by letter, by telephone, by fax, by e-mail
and via website. Appointment necessary.
Hours: Mon to Fri, 0900 to 1700

Access to building, collection or gallery:
Prior appointment required
Hours: Mon to Fri, 0900 to 1700

Access for disabled people:
Parking provided, ramped entry, toilet facilities

Libraries and Information Service:
Agency Libraries are open to the public for
reference purposes, by appointment during
working hours. They hold publications of the
former National Rivers Authority and Her
Majesty's Inspector of Pollution
Environment Agency Anglian
Kingfisher House, Goldhay Way, Orton Goldhay,
Peterborough, Cambridgeshire, PE2 5ZR; tel:
01733 371811; fax: 01733 464397
Environment Agency Head Office
Rio House, Waterside Drive, Aztec West,
Almondsbury, Bristol, BS32 4UD; tel: 01454
624400; fax: 01454 624004
Environment Agency North East Region
Tyneside House, Skinnerburn Road, Newcastle
Business Park, Newcastle upon Tyne, NE4 7AR;
tel: 0191 203 4000; fax: 0191 203 4004
Environment Agency North West
Richard Fairclough House, Knutsford Road,
Warrington, WA4 1HG; tel: 01925 653999; fax:
01925 639670

Environment Agency South West Region
Manley House, Kestrel Way, Exeter, EX2 7LQ;
tel: 01392 444000; fax: 01392 444238
Environment Agency Southern Region
Guildbourne House, Chatsworth Road,
Worthing, West Sussex, BN11 1LD; tel: 01903
832000; fax: 01903 821832
Environment Agency Thames
Kings Meadow House, Kings Meadow Road,
Reading, RG1 8DQ; tel: 0118 953 5000; fax: 0118
950 0388
Environment Agency Welsh
Rivers House/Plas-yr-Afon, St Mellons Business
Park, Fortran Road, Cardiff, CF3 0LT; tel: 029
2077 0088; fax: 029 2036 1437

Sponsoring department:
Department of the Environment, Transport and the
Regions

ENVIRONMENT AGENCY – TEWKESBURY

Area Office, Riversmeet House, Newtown
Industrial Estate, Northway Lane, Tewkesbury,
Gloucestershire, GL20 8JG

Tel: 01684 850951
Fax: 01684 293599

Website:
http://www.environment-agency.gov.uk

Enquiries:
Enquiries to: Customer Contact Team

Founded:
1996

Formerly called:
Her Majesty's Inspectorate of Pollution, National
Rivers Authority, Waste Regulation Authorities

Organisation type and purpose:
National government body, professional body.
To protect and improve the environment and
contribute towards sustainable development
through the integrated management of air, land
and water. We have specific responsibilities for
water resources, pollution prevention and control,
flood defence, fisheries, conservation, recreation
and navigation throughout England and Wales.

**Museum or gallery collection, archive, or library
special collection:**
Public Register Information

Printed publications:
Available free from the Agency or for purchase
from HMSO

Electronic and video publications:
CD-ROM and Videos, available free or for
purchase

Access to staff:
Contact by letter, by telephone and by fax
Hours: Mon to Fri, 0900 to 1700

Links with:
DEFRA
The Welsh Office

Main sponsor in the Government is:
The Department for Environment, Food & Rural
Affairs (DEFRA)

Sub-Area Office:
Environment Agency
Brooke House, Spartan Close, Tachbrook Park
Industrial Estate, Leamington Spa,
Warwickshire, CV34 6RR; tel: 01926 889474; fax:
01926 887657

ENVIRONMENTAL AWARENESS TRUST

Acronym or abbreviation: EAT

23 High Street, Wheathampstead, Hertfordshire,
AL4 8BB

Tel: 01582 834580
Fax: 01582 834547

Enquiries:
Enquiries to: Executive Director

Founded:
1990

Organisation type and purpose:
Registered charity (charity number 100042).
Prime purpose is the development of a National
Exploratorium of the Global Environment open to
members of the public of all ages.

Subject coverage:
Global environment.

Access to staff:
Contact by letter, by telephone and by fax
Hours: Mon to Fri, 0900 to 1700

ENVIRONMENTAL CAMPAIGNS

Acronym or abbreviation: ENCAMS

Elizabeth House, The Pier, Wigan, Lancashire,
WN3 4EX

Tel: 01942 612621
Fax: 01942 824778
E-mail: enquiries@encams.org

Website:
http://www.encams.org
ENCAMS – environmental campaigns – Keep
Britain Tidy, schools education programmes,
information, research.

Founded:
1961

Formerly called:
Keep Britain Tidy Group (year of change 1987);
Tidy Britain Group (year of change 2001)

Organisation type and purpose:
Voluntary organisation, Registered Charity
(Charity number 1071737), consultancy.
Independent national agency for the improvement
of the quality of local environments.

Subject coverage:
Local Environmental Quality and associated anti-
social behaviour, Cleaner Safer Greener Network,
Eco-Schools Programme, Quality Coast Award and
Blue Flag Awards.

**Museum or gallery collection, archive, or library
special collection:**
Documents, posters, printed materials, leaflets etc.

Non-library collection catalogue:
All or part available online, in-house and in print

Library catalogue:
All or part available in-house

Printed publications:
Campaigning materials
Education leaflets and packs
Information leaflets
Newsletter
Research reports and summaries

Publications list:
Available online

Access to staff:
Contact by letter, by telephone, by fax, by e-mail,
in person and via website. Access for members
only.
Hours: Mon to Fri, 0700 to 1900

Access to building, collection or gallery:
Only one Central Services Office
Hours: Mon to Fri, 0700 to 1900

Access for disabled people:
Access to all public areas, toilet facilities

ENVIRONMENTAL COMMUNICATORS' ORGANIZATION

Acronym or abbreviation: ECO Journalists

8 Hooks Cross, Watton-at-Stone, Hertford, SG14
3RY

continued overleaf

Tel: 01920 830527
Fax: 01920 830538
E-mail: alanmassam@btinternet.com

Enquiries:
Enquiries to: Chairman
Direct tel: 01920 830527
Other contacts: Press spokesman for press releases.

Founded:
1972

Organisation type and purpose:
Membership association (membership is by election or invitation).
Pressure group.
To bring a green interpretation of significant events to the attention of professional journalists and broadcasters.

Subject coverage:
Information on environmental topics provided for journalists.

Printed publications:
Countryside (bi-monthly price £1.95)
Newsletter (Occasional, 6 times a year)

Access to staff:
Contact by letter, by fax and by e-mail
Hours: Mon to Fri, 0900 to 1700

Affiliated to:
Foundation for Ethnobiology
    tel: 01992 893632; e-mail: conradgorinsky@hotmail.com

ENVIRONMENTAL HEALTH REGISTRATION BOARD

Acronym or abbreviation: EHRB

Chartered Institute of Environmental Health, Chadwick Court, 15 Hatfields, London, SE1 8DJ

Tel: 020 7928 6006
Fax: 020 7928 6953
E-mail: j.guild@cieh.org

Website:
http://www.cieh.org.uk

Enquiries:
Enquiries to: Education Officer
Direct tel: 020 7827 5842

Formerly called:
Public Health Inspectors Registration Board (PHIEB)
Environmental Health Officers Registration Board (year of change 2003)

Organisation type and purpose:
Service industry, registered charity (charity number 290350).

Subject coverage:
Registration of student and qualified environmental health officers.
Development and accreditation of courses for other environmental professional staff.

Information services:
Provides information on how to become an environmental health officer, lists accredited environmental health degree courses in the UK and accredited courses for technician qualifications such as Higher Certificate in Food Premises Inspection.

Access to staff:
Contact by letter, by telephone, by fax and by e-mail
Hours: Mon to Fri, 0900 to 1700

Administered by:
Chartered Institute of Environmental Health
    Chadwick Court, 15 Hatfields, London, SE1 8DJ; tel: 020 7928 6006

ENVIRONMENTAL INDUSTRIES COMMISSION LIMITED, THE

Acronym or abbreviation: EIC

45 Weymouth Street, London, W1G 8ND

Tel: 020 7935 1675
Fax: 020 7486 3455
E-mail: info@eic-uk.co.uk

Website:
http://www.eic-uk.co.uk
Information on current EIC activities.

Enquiries:
Enquiries to: Director

Founded:
1995

Formed from:
Association of Environmental Consultancies (AEC)

Organisation type and purpose:
National organisation, trade association (membership is by subscription), present number of members: 210.

Subject coverage:
Contact with members. Information about EIC members and in which fields they specialise.
Information about membership for potential members.

Printed publications:
Handbook of EIC's Environmental Consultancies Group Members (free)

Publications list:
Available in print

Access to staff:
Contact by telephone
Hours: Mon to Fri, 0930 to 1800

ENVIRONMENTAL INVESTIGATION AGENCY

Acronym or abbreviation: EIA

62–63 Upper Street, London, N1 0NY

Tel: 020 7354 7960
Fax: 020 7354 7961
E-mail: ukinfo@eia-international.org

Website:
http://www.eia-international.org

Enquiries:
Enquiries to: Administrator

Founded:
1984

Organisation type and purpose:
Voluntary organisation, registered charity.
Independent wildlife and environmental campaigning organisation.

Subject coverage:
Research, investigations and monitoring of illegal trade in endangered animal species and environmentally damaging commodities.
Provision of documented information on such activities to governmental authorities and the media to generate improved enforcement measures.

Printed publications:
Various publications including:
Chilling Facts About a Burning Abuse – CFC Smuggling in the European Union (£5)
Corporate Power, Corruption & Destruction of the World's Forests (£5)
The Global War Against Small Cetaceans (£5)
The Political Wilderness – India's Tiger Crisis (£5)
The Politics of Extinction – The Orangutang Crisis/ The Destruction of Indonesia's Forests (£5)

Microform publications:
Film and Photographs (for sale)

Access to staff:
Contact by letter, by telephone, by fax and by e-mail
Hours: Mon to Fri, 0930 to 1800

ENVIRONMENTAL LAW FOUNDATION

Acronym or abbreviation: ELF

Suite 309, 16 Baldwins Gardens, London, EC1N 7RJ

Tel: 020 7404 1030
Fax: 020 7404 1032
E-mail: info@elflaw.org

Website:
http://www.elflaw.org

Enquiries:
Enquiries to: Administrator
Other contacts: Director

Founded:
1992

Organisation type and purpose:
Advisory body, present number of members: 450, voluntary organisation, registered charity, research organisation.
Provides advice and assistance, refers communities to lawyers and experts to resolve environmental problems.

Subject coverage:
Environmental law; how the law can be used to resolve environmental problems, access to justice.

Museum or gallery collection, archive, or library special collection:
Case information (not available to the public)

Trade and statistical information:
Data on communities taking legal action to protect and improve the environment of the UK.

Printed publications:
Reports:
Annual Reports
ELFline (regular publication)
Environmental Risk: The Responsibilities of the Law and Science
Human Rights and the Environment
Environmental Briefings
Leaflets:
Green Issues

Publications list:
Available in print

Access to staff:
Contact by letter, by telephone, by fax and by e-mail
Hours: Mon to Fri, 1030 to 1630
Special comments: Information provided in response to specific requests only.

ENVIRONMENTAL NETWORK LIMITED

Acronym or abbreviation: ENL

The Hillocks, Tarland, Aboyne, Aberdeenshire, AB34 4TJ

Tel: 01339 881446
Fax: 01339 881618
E-mail: mail@env-net.com

Website:
http://www.env-net.com

Enquiries:
Enquiries to: Managing Director

Founded:
1993

Organisation type and purpose:
Multi-disciplinary European network organisation for R&D in sustainable development

Subject coverage:
Environmental assessment, planning and management, sustainable development, rural resource management and development; software development.

Access to staff:
Contact by letter, by telephone, by fax, by e-mail and via website. Appointment necessary.
Hours: Mon to Fri, 0900 to 1700

Other addresses:
ENL Deutschland
Fritz-von-Graevenitzstr 31, D-70839 Gerlingen;
tel: + 00 49 7156 928 383/4

ENVIRONMENTAL SERVICES ASSOCIATION

Acronym or abbreviation: ESA

154 Buckingham Palace Road, London, SW1W 9TR

Tel: 020 7824 8882
Fax: 020 7824 8753
E-mail: info@esauk.org

Website:
http://www.esauk.org
Searchable database of membership, details of
publications and press statements, ESA events and
industry legislation.
http://www.epolitix.com/forum/esa

Enquiries:
Enquiries to: Chief Executive
Other contacts: Deputy Chief Executive/Members'
Services

Founded:
1969

Formerly called:
National Association of Waste Disposal
Contractors (NAWDC) (year of change 1996)

Incorporates the former:
Energy from Waste Association (EWA) (year of
change 2001)

Organisation type and purpose:
Trade association.
ESA is the UK's sectoral trade association for waste
and secondary resource management, an industry
accounting for 0.5% GDP.

Subject coverage:
Information on integrated solutions to waste across
the full spectrum of biological, mechanical and
thermal treatment processing options, to achieve
sustainable waste management.

**Museum or gallery collection, archive, or library
special collection:**
Library containing printed products

Non-library collection catalogue:
All or part available in-house

Library catalogue:
All or part available in-house

Printed publications:
ESA Directory (A listing of waste facilities in the
UK)
Resource Management & Recovery Magazine
ESA Membership Directory
Annual Statement
Weekly Policy Bulletin

Electronic and video publications:
Virtual Tour of an Energy from Waste Plant (CD-
ROM)
Energy, Waste and the Environment (video)

Publications list:
Available online and in print

Access to staff:
Contact by letter, by telephone, by fax, by e-mail,
in person and via website. Appointment necessary.
Access for members only. All charged.
Hours: Mon to Fri, 0900 to 1700

Access to building, collection or gallery:
Prior appointment required

Access for disabled people:
Ramped entry

Member of:
European Waste Management Association (FEAD)
Avenue des Gaulois 19, Brussels, B-1040,
Belgium; tel: 00 32 2 732 3213; fax: 00 32 2 734
9592; e-mail: wg@fead.be

WAMITAB
3 The Lakes, Peterbridge House, Northampton,
NN4 7HE; tel: 01604 231950; fax: 01604 232457;
e-mail: info.admin@wamitab.org.uk

Other addresses:
Northern Ireland Environmental Services
Association (NIESA)
PO Box 21, Belfast, BT1 4WD; tel: 0870 241 3298;
e-mail: niesa@esauk.org
Scottish Environmental Services Association
(SESA)
48 Edinburgh Road, Coatbridge, Lanarkshire,
ML5 4UG; tel: 01236 437480; e-mail: sesa@esauk
.org
Welsh Environmental Services Association (WESA)
PO Box 4061, Cardiff, CF14 3YY; tel: 020 7591
3205; e-mail: wesa@esauk.org

ENVIRONMENTAL TRANSPORT ASSOCIATION

Acronym or abbreviation: ETA

ETA Services Limited, 10 Church Street,
Weybridge, Surrey, KT13 8RS

Tel: 01932 828882
Fax: 01932 829015
E-mail: eta@eta.co.uk

Website:
http://www.eta.co.uk
Details campaigns, services, factsheets.

Enquiries:
Enquiries to: Public Relations Co-ordinator
Direct e-mail: patricia.marotte@eta.co.uk

Founded:
1990

Organisation type and purpose:
National organisation, membership association
(membership is by subscription), present number
of members: 20,000, service industry.
Breakdown recovery and other insurance issues.
Motoring breakdown organisation campaigning
for greener transport.

Subject coverage:
Specialist information on transport and
environment issues.

Printed publications:
The following publications are for both ETA
members and non-members
Going Green (ETA members magazine, £5)
Car Buyer's Guide 2001 (£5)
Car Buyer's Guide 2002 (£5)
CFD Good Practice Guide (£5)
Community Tourism Guide (£9.99)
Cutting Your Car Use (£4.95)
Real Costs of Motoring (£3.50)
The Cyclists' Sourcebook (£20)

Publications list:
Available online and in print

Access to staff:
Contact by letter, by telephone, by fax, by e-mail
and via website
Hours: Mon to Fri, 0800 to 1800

Access to building, collection or gallery:
Prior appointment required

Access for disabled people:
Parking provided

Affiliated to:
European Federation for Transport and
Environment (T&E)
Boulevard de Waterloo 34, 1000 Brussels,
Belgium; tel: 00 322 502 9909; fax: 00 322 502
9908
Transport 2000 (T2000)
The Impact Centre, 12 Hoxton Street, London,
N1 6NG; tel: 020 7613 0743; fax: 020 7615 5280

ENVIROWISE

Harwell International Business Centre, Harwell,
Didcot, Oxfordshire, OX11 0QJ

Tel: 0800 585794
Fax: 0870 190 6713
E-mail: helpline@envirowise.gov.uk

Website:
http://www.envirowise.gov.uk

Enquiries:
Enquiries to: Helpline Advisor

Founded:
1994

Organisation type and purpose:
Government funded advice and information
service for business.

Subject coverage:
Waste minimisation, cleaner technology,
environment: all subjects including legislation, for
all industry and service sectors.

Printed publications:
All free to UK organisations under the following
headings including guides and case studies:
Best Practice tailored to various engineering/
manufactoring industries
Information about the Programme
Reducing Water Waste
Reducing Packaging Waste
Resource Efficiency Clubs
Reducing Solvent Use
Cleaner Technology
Information to Help Business Support
Organisations Help Businesses in the:
Printing, Foundry, Engineering, Glass, Plastics,
Paper & Board, Textiles, Metal Finishing,
Chemicals, Ceramics and Food and Drink
Industries

Electronic and video publications:
Resource Efficiency and Waste Minimisation
(guides and software)

Publications list:
Available online and in print

Access to staff:
Contact by letter, by telephone, by fax, by e-mail
and via website
Hours: Mon to Fri, 0900 to 1700
Special comments: UK only except for Web access.

Access for disabled people:
Access to all public areas, toilet facilities

EPHEMERA SOCIETY

PO Box 112, Northwood, Middlesex, HA6 2WT

Tel: 01923 829079
Fax: 01923 825207

Website:
http://www.ephemera-society.org.uk
Membership information and list of fairs.

Enquiries:
Enquiries to: Secretary

Founded:
1975

Organisation type and purpose:
Membership association.

Subject coverage:
Preservation, study and presentation of printed
and handwritten ephemera, identification, dating
and conservation, valuation and disposal of
collections of ephemera.

**Museum or gallery collection, archive, or library
special collection:**
Centre collection based on Rickards Collection
Centre for Ephemera Studies Collection based on
Rickards Collection at University of Reading

Printed publications:
The Ephemerist (quarterly, journal index and first
100 issues available to purchase)

Access to staff:
Contact by letter, by telephone and by fax
Hours: Mon to Fri, 0900 to 1700

continued overleaf

Associated with:
Foundation for Ephemera Studies

Associated with offshoot ephemera societies in:
America, Australia, Canada and Austria

Contact Centre for Ephemera Studies is the:
University of Reading

EPILEPSY ACTION

New Anstey House, Gateway Drive, Yeadon, Leeds, West Yorkshire, LS19 7XY

Tel: 0113 210 8800
Fax: 0113 391 0300
E-mail: epilepsy@epilepsy.org.uk

Website:
http://www.epilepsy.org.uk
Information on all aspects of epilepsy, children's pages, news pages, medical pages, merchandise pages.

Enquiries:
Direct tel: 0808 800 5050
Direct fax: 0808 800 5555

Founded:
1950

Organisation type and purpose:
Voluntary organisation.
Provides information and support to people with epilepsy their families and any professionals involved.

Subject coverage:
Epilepsy Action represents the interests of people with epilepsy. Services include a national information service, an epilepsy helpline, consultation to professionals, staging of conferences etc. The Association assists in the formation of local groups, funds social research and promotes a greater awareness of epilepsy among lay and professional people.

Printed publications:
Books, leaflets, pamphlets
Epilepsy Today (quarterly)
Epilepsy Professional

Electronic and video publications:
Videos available for hire from the library

Publications list:
Available in print

Access to staff:
Contact by letter, by telephone, by fax and by e-mail
Hours: Mon to Thu, 0900 to 1630; Fri, 0900 to 1600

Affiliated to:
International Bureau for Epilepsy
International League Against Epilepsy

Other addresses:
International Bureau for Epilepsy
PO Box 21, 2100, AA Heemstede, The Netherlands
Northern Ireland Office
The Old Postgraduate Medical Centre, Belfast City Hospital, Lisburn Road, Belfast, BT9 7AB; tel: 028 9089 2267

EPILEPSY RESEARCH UK

Acronym or abbreviation: ERUK

PO Box 3004, London, W4 1XT

Tel: 020 8995 4781
Fax: 020 8995 4781
E-mail: info@eruk.org.uk

Website:
http://www.epilepsyresearch.org.uk
Information about epilepsy

Enquiries:
Enquiries to: Research and Information Executive
Other contacts: Information Executive (for research enquiries)

Founded:
2007

Created by the merger of:
The Epilepsy Research Foundation and the Fund for Epilepsy (year of change 2007)

Formerly called:
British Epilepsy Research Foundation (year of change 2003)

Organisation type and purpose:
Voluntary organisation, registered charity (charity number 1100394), research organisation.
Promotes and supports basic and clinical scientific research into epilepsy throughout the United Kingdom. Independent research is supported, carried out by the best available research team.

Subject coverage:
Epilepsy.

Museum or gallery collection, archive, or library special collection:
Information available relating to epilepsy research

Printed publications:
Grant Awards
Annual Report and Accounts
General leaflets
Focus (newsletter)

Access to staff:
Contact by letter, by telephone, by fax, by e-mail and via website. Appointment necessary.
Hours: Mon to Fri, 0900 to 1700

Access to building, collection or gallery:
Prior appointment required

Member organisation of:
Association of Medical Research Charities (AMRC)
Joint Epilepsy Council (JEC)

EPILEPSY SCOTLAND

48 Govan Road, Glasgow, G51 1JL

Tel: 0141 427 4911
Fax: 0141 419 1709
E-mail: enquiries@epilepsyscotland.org.uk

Website:
http://www.epilepsyscotland.org.uk
general information on the EAS plus most of our literature.

Enquiries:
Enquiries to: Communications Manager
Direct tel: 0141 419 1701
Direct e-mail: aparker@epilepsyscotland.org.uk

Founded:
1954

Organisation type and purpose:
National organisation, membership association (membership is by subscription), present number of members: 500, voluntary organisation, registered charity (charity number SCO 00067), training organisation, consultancy.
Campaigning, lobbying and policy organisation. Network of branches and groups throughout Scotland.

Subject coverage:
Social aspects of epilepsy and associated disabilities, epilepsy in relation to employment, driving, the law, the family etc, understanding of epilepsy, support systems, professional training, community care, research and policy comment.

Printed publications:
Many publications, professional guidelines, reports and factsheets including:
Annual Report
Epilepsy News (newsletter/journal, 2 times a year)
Guidelines for Teachers
Order printed publications from: Helpline and Information Officer
e-mail: lmarley@epilepsyscotland.org.uk

Electronic and video publications:
Rectal Diazepam – Rapid Delivery: Gentle Alternative (for parents, video)
Rectal Diazepam – Rapid Delivery: Gentle Alternative (for professionals, video)
EAS video – Headwork

Publications list:
Available in print

Access to staff:
Contact by letter, by telephone, by fax, by e-mail, in person and via website. Appointment necessary.
Hours: Mon to Fri, 0900 to 1630

Access to building, collection or gallery:
Prior appointment required

Access for disabled people:
Parking provided, ramped entry, toilet facilities

Affiliated to:
International Bureau for Epilepsy
Joint Epilepsy Council of UK and Ireland

EPPING FOREST DISTRICT COUNCIL

Acronym or abbreviation: EFDC

Civic Offices, High Street, Epping, Essex, CM16 4BZ

Tel: 01992 564000
Fax: 01992 578018

Website:
http://www.eppingforestdc.gov.uk

Enquiries:
Enquiries to: Information Officer
Direct e-mail: contactus@eppingforestdc.gov.uk
Other contacts: Public Relations Manager

Founded:
1974

Organisation type and purpose:
Local government body.

Subject coverage:
All areas relating to local council matters. Most areas relating to the district.

Museum or gallery collection, archive, or library special collection:
EFDC Museum, Sun Street, EN9 1OZ

Access to staff:
Contact by letter, by telephone, by fax and by e-mail
Hours: Mon to Fri, 0900 to 1700

Access to building, collection or gallery:
Hours: Mon to Fri, 0900 to 1700

Access for disabled people:
Accessible for disabled

EPPING FOREST FIELD CENTRE

Acronym or abbreviation: FSC

Pauls Nursery Road, High Beech, Loughton, Essex, IG10 4AF

Tel: 020 8502 8500
Fax: 020 8502 8502
E-mail: enquiries.ef@field-studies-council.org

Founded:
1970

Formerly called:
Epping Forest Conservation Centre (year of change 1992)

Organisation type and purpose:
Membership association (membership is by qualification), registered charity.
Environmental education.

Subject coverage:
Environmental field work for schools at all levels. Environmental and natural history courses for adults. Out-of-school activities and environmental birthday parties.

Printed publications:
Promotional Literature
FSC Courses Brochure (annually, from head office)

Order printed publications from: FSC Publications, Preston Montford, Montford Bridge, Shrewsbury, Shropshire, SY4 1HW; tel. 01743 852140; fax 01743 852101; e-mail publications@field-studies-council .org

Publications list:
Available in print

Access to staff:
Contact by letter, by telephone, by fax and by e-mail. Appointment necessary.
Hours: Mon to Fri, 0900 to 1700
Special comments: Centre must be booked for teaching, lectures, use of library, etc.

Access to building, collection or gallery:
Prior appointment required

Access for disabled people:
Parking provided

Constituent part of:
Field Studies Council
   tel: 01743 852100; fax: 01743 852101

EQUAL OPPORTUNITIES COMMISSION

Acronym or abbreviation: EOC

Arndale House, Arndale Centre, Manchester, M4 3EQ

Tel: 0161 833 9244\ Minicom no. 0161 838 9244
Fax: 0161 838 8312
E-mail: info@eoc.org.uk

Website:
http://www.eoc.org.uk
Advice for employers and employees on sex discrimation and equal pay issues, research and statistics publications, reading lists on equal opportunities/gender issues, press releases.

Enquiries:
Enquiries to: Librarian
Direct tel: 0161 838 8343
Other contacts: Customer Contact Point for general enquiries and publications.

Founded:
1975

Organisation type and purpose:
National organisation, statutory body.
The elimination of unlawful sex and marriage discrimination, to promote equality of opportunity between men and women and to keep the Sex Discrimination (1975) and Equal Pay (1970) Acts under review.

Subject coverage:
Equal opportunity and sex discrimination (including law, education, employment, equal pay etc).

Trade and statistical information:
Statistical information on women and men available on web-site, via publications list, by application to the Research, Statistics and Information Unit.

Library catalogue:
All or part available in-house

Printed publications:
A large number of free guides on equal pay and sex equality (free, directly from EOC)

Publications list:
Available online and in print

Access to staff:
Contact by letter, by telephone, by fax, by e-mail and via website. Appointment necessary.
Hours: Mon to Fri, 0900 to 1700
Special comments: Access by arrangement only.

Other addresses:
Equal Opportunities Commission
   Windsor House, Windsor Lane, Cardiff, CF10 3GE; tel: 029 2034 3552; fax: 029 2064 1709; e-mail: wales@eoc.org.uk

Equal Opportunities Commission
   St Stephens House, 279 Bath Street, Glasgow, G2 4JL; tel: 0141 248 5833; fax: 0141 248 5834; e-mail: scotland@eoc.org.uk

EQUALITY COMMISSION FOR NORTHERN IRELAND

Acronym or abbreviation: ECNI

Equality House, 7–9 Shaftesbury Square, Belfast, BT2 7DP

Tel: 028 9089 0890
Fax: 028 9024 8687\ Textphone: 028 9050 0589
E-mail: information@equalityni.org

Website:
http://www.equalityni.org

Enquiries:
Enquiries to: Information Officer
Direct tel: 028 9050 0645

Founded:
1999

Created by the merger of:
Commission for Racial Equality for Northern Ireland, Equal Opportunities Commission for Northern Ireland, Fair Employment Commission for Northern Ireland, Northern Ireland Disability Council (year of change 1999)

Organisation type and purpose:
Statutory body.

Subject coverage:
Equality of opportunity in employment, education, goods, facilities and services; issues related to women in society.

Museum or gallery collection, archive, or library special collection:
Women in employment and in society generally, women's education, discrimination law, race issues

Library catalogue:
All or part available in-house

Printed publications:
All single copies of printed publications are available, free of charge:
Annual Report
Booklets and leaflets on equal opportunities, with regard to: sex, race, disability, fair employment, sexual orientation
Research reports on employment and education

Publications list:
Available online and in print

Access to staff:
Contact by letter, by telephone, by fax, by e-mail, in person and via website. Appointment necessary.
Hours: Mon to Fri, 0900 to 1700

Access to building, collection or gallery:
Special comments: Library is reference only

Access for disabled people:
Parking provided, level entry, access to all public areas, toilet facilities

EQUITY

Formal name: Equity

Guild House, Upper St Martins Lane, London, WC2H 9EG

Tel: 020 7379 6000
Fax: 020 7379 7001
E-mail: info@equity.org.uk

Website:
http://www.equity.org.uk

Enquiries:
Enquiries to: General Secretary
Direct fax: 020 7379 6074
Direct e-mail: info@equity.org.uk

Founded:
1930

Organisation type and purpose:
Trade union (membership by subscription).
To represent artists from across the entire spectrum of arts and entertainment, to negotiate minimum terms and conditions of employment throughout the entire world of entertainment and to endeavour to ensure these take account of social and economic changes, to lobby government and other bodies on issues of paramount importance to the membership.

Printed publications:
Equity Magazine

Access to staff:
Contact by letter, by telephone, by fax, by e-mail and via website. Access for members only.

Affitialted to:
Trades Union Congress (TUC)

ERA TECHNOLOGY LIMITED

Cleeve Road, Leatherhead, Surrey, KT22 7SA

Tel: 01372 367007
Fax: 01372 367009
E-mail: info@era.co.uk

Website:
http://www.era.co.uk
Details of ERA capabilities, conferences, publications and information services, electronic commerce service available for the purchasing of ERA publications and booking places at ERA conferences, courses and seminars.

Enquiries:
Enquiries to: Information Officer

Founded:
1920

Organisation type and purpose:
International organisation, service industry.
ERA Technology works at the leading edge of many advanced technologies and provides specialist, technology-based services including design and development, testing, assessment and expert advice. ERA has capabilities in electrical, electronic, software and communications engineering, RF microwave and radar, complex EMC, risk analysis, safety engineering, reliability and failure analysis, plant integrity, micro-electronics and materials technologies.

Subject coverage:
Electrotechnology; computing technology; electrical and electronic engineering; energy conservation; alternative energy; product design and prototype construction; new materials; testing and certification; regulatory compliance; national and international standardisation; explosion hazards; electromagnetic compatibility; servocomponents; electric motors; insulation; cables; radio frequency technology; electromechanical engineering; engineering materials; materials science; failure analysis.

Museum or gallery collection, archive, or library special collection:
Technical standards and specifications
Transactions AIEE 1923–1963

Library catalogue:
All or part available in-house

Printed publications:
Annual report and accounts
Reports List
Safety & EMC (newsletter for designers and suppliers of electrical and electronic products)
RE4view – The Recycling Electrical and Electronic Equipment Environmental Review (newsletter covering developments in the implementation of the WEEE, RoHs, and EuP directives)
Solutions@ERA (newsletter)

Publications list:
Available online and in print

Access to staff:
Contact by letter, by telephone, by fax, by e-mail and via website. Appointment necessary. Non-members charged.

continued overleaf

Hours: Mon to Fri, 0900 to 1700
Special comments: Certain services are charged for.

Access to building, collection or gallery:
Prior appointment required

ERC GROUP PLC

Acronym or abbreviation: ERC

1 Kings Court, Newmarket, Suffolk, CB8 7TG

Tel: 01638 667733
Fax: 01638 667744
E-mail: marketing@erc-world.com

Website:
http://www.erc-world.com

Enquiries:
Enquiries to: Director

Founded:
1961

Organisation type and purpose:
International organisation, service industry, consultancy, research organisation.

Subject coverage:
Food, drinks, tobacco, ophthalmics, OTC pharmaceuticals, cosmetics and toiletries, personal care, home goods. Geographical research specialisation extends to Eastern and Western Europe, Pacific Rim, Latin America, China, the USA, Middle East, India, South Africa, plus other global markets.

Printed publications:
Over 150 market research reports on the subjects listed, some by country others by manufacturer or product within the category

Electronic and video publications:
Disc, CD-ROM

Publications list:
Available online

Access to staff:
Contact by letter, by telephone, by fax, by e-mail and via website. Appointment necessary.
Hours: Mon to Fri, 0930 to 1730

Access for disabled people:
Level entry

EREWASH BOROUGH COUNCIL

Town Hall, Ilkeston, Derbyshire, DE7 5RP

Tel: 0115 907 2244\ Minicom no. 0115 949 9478
Fax: 0115 907 1121
E-mail: enquiries@erewash.gov.uk

Website:
http://www.erewash.gov.uk

Enquiries:
Enquiries to: Public Relations Manager
Direct tel: 0115 9071159

Organisation type and purpose:
Local government body.

Subject coverage:
Local government services.

Access to staff:
Contact by letter
Hours: Mon to Thu, 0830 to 1700; Fri, 0830 to 1630

Access for disabled people:
Ramped entry, access to all public areas, toilet facilities

ERGONOMICS INFORMATION ANALYSIS CENTRE

Acronym or abbreviation: EIAC

Electronic, Electrical and Computer Engineering, University of Birmingham, Edgbaston, Birmingham, B15 2TT

Tel: 0121 414 4239
Fax: 0121 414 3476

E-mail: ergo-abs@bham.ac.uk

Website:
http://www.eee.bham.ac.uk/eiac

Enquiries:
Enquiries to: Manager

Founded:
1968

Organisation type and purpose:
University department or institute.

Subject coverage:
Ergonomics, human factors, human-computer interaction.

Electronic and video publications:
Ergonomics Abstracts (online)
Order electronic and video publications from: Taylor and Francis Ltd, 4 Park Square, Milton Park, Abingdon, Oxfordshire; tel. 020 7017 6000; fax 020 7017 6336; e-mail richard.steele@tandf.co.uk

Access to staff:
Contact by letter, by telephone, by fax and by e-mail. Appointment necessary. All charged.
Hours: Mon to Fri, 0800 to 1600

Access for disabled people:
Parking provided, ramped entry, access to all public areas, toilet facilities

ERGONOMICS SOCIETY

Acronym or abbreviation: ES

Devonshire House, Devonshire Square, Loughborough, Leicestershire, LE11 3DW

Tel: 01509 234904
Fax: 01509 235666
E-mail: ergsoc@ergonomics.org.uk

Website:
http://www.ergonomics.org.uk
General information on: the society, ergonomics, society members.
http://www.ergonomics4schools.com
Information and advice for students of ergonomics in schools.

Enquiries:
Enquiries to: Honorary Secretary
Other contacts: Business Manager

Founded:
1949

Organisation type and purpose:
Professional body.

Subject coverage:
Ergonomics and human factors, work design, environmental sciences, equipment design, human and computer interaction.

Printed publications:
Applied Ergonomics (quarterly, pub Elsevier)
Behaviour and Information Technology (pub Taylor & Francis)
Ergonomics (monthly, pub Taylor & Francis)
Register of Ergonomics Consultants
Register of Professional Ergonomists
Work & Stress (quarterly, pub Taylor & Francis)

Electronic and video publications:
Register of Ergonomics Consultants
Register of Professional Ergonomists

Access to staff:
Contact by letter, by telephone, by fax and by e-mail
Hours: Mon to Fri, 0900 to 1630

Affiliated to:
International Ergonomics Association

ERIC (EDUCATION AND RESOURCES FOR IMPROVING CHILDHOOD CONTINENCE)

Acronym or abbreviation: ERIC

34 Old School House, Britannia Road, Kingswood, Bristol, BS15 8DB

Tel: 0117 960 3060 Helpline: 0845 370 8008
Fax: 0117 960 0401
E-mail: info@eric.org.uk

Website:
http://www.eric.org.uk
General information for children, parents and health professionals on bedwetting, daytime wetting, constipation and soiling.
http://www.ericshop.org.uk
http://www.trusteric.org

Enquiries:
Enquiries to: Information and Helpline Department
Other contacts: Director, for clinical issues or public relations.

Founded:
1988

Organisation type and purpose:
Subscription, registered charity (charity number 1002424).
National child health charity.
Support and information on all aspects of childhood continence including childhood bedwetting, day-time wetting and soiling.

Subject coverage:
Bedwetting (nocturnal enuresis), daytime wetting, soiling and constipation in children and young people

Printed publications:
Many titles for health professionals and parents/carers (request catalogue or visit webshop www.ericshop.org.uk for more information) including:
Bedwetting: a Guide for Parents (Dobson P, available in English, Bengali, Chinese, Hindi, Punjabi and Urdu)
Childhood Soiling: A Guide for Parents (Dobson P)
Children with Recurrent Urinary Tract Infections: A guide for families (compiled by the Kidney Unit, Nottingham City Hospital)
Day-time Wetting: A Guide for Parents (Dobson P)
ERIC Says, Quarterly Support Magazine
You and Your Alarm (Adams J)
Your Child's Alarm (Adams J)

Publications list:
Available online and in print

Access to staff:
Contact by letter, by telephone, by fax and by e-mail
Hours: Office: Mon to Fri, 0900 to 1700; Helpline: Mon to Fri, 1000 to 1600

Affiliated to:
Continence Foundation
Incontact

ESCP-EAP EUROPEAN SCHOOL OF MANAGEMENT

Formal name: Ecole Supérieure de Commerce de Paris – Ecole des Affaires de Paris
Acronym or abbreviation: ESCP-EAP

Parsifal College, 527 Finchley Road, Hampstead, London, NW3 7BG

Tel: 020 7443 8800
Fax: 020 7443 8845
E-mail: kstokes@escp-eap.net

Website:
http://www.escp-eap.net
Information about educational facilities and history of ESCP-EAP centres in London, Paris, Berlin, Madrid and Turin.

Enquiries:
Enquiries to: Business Librarian
Direct tel: 020 7443 8875

Founded:
1973

Formed by the merger of:
Ecole des Affaires de Paris (EAP) and Ecole Supérieure de Commerce de Paris (ESCP) (year of change 1999)

Organisation type and purpose:
Registered charity (charity number 293027),
suitable for ages: c. 18–30.

Subject coverage:
Management.

Library catalogue:
All or part available in-house

Access to staff:
Contact by letter, by telephone, by fax, by e-mail
and via website
Hours: Mon to Fri, 0900 to 1700
ESCP-EAP European School of Management
  Heubnerweg 6, 14059 Berlin, Germany
ESCP-EAP European School of Management
  Corso Stati Uniti 38, 10128 Turin, Italy
Other addresses:
ESCP-EAP European School of Management
  Arroyofresno 1, 28035 Madrid, Spain

Parent body:
ESCP-EAP
  79 avenue de la République, 75543 Paris Cedex
  11, France

ESDU INTERNATIONAL PLC

Formal name: Engineering Sciences Data Unit

27 Corsham Street, London, N1 6UA

Tel: 020 7490 5151
Fax: 020 7490 2701
E-mail: esdu@ihs.com

Website:
http://www.esdu.com
Full product and company information (on public
site). Product delivery via same web address for
subscribers with user name/password.

Enquiries:
Enquiries to: Sales Office Supervisor
Other contacts: Technical Director; Director of
Finance

Founded:
1940

Formerly called:
Engineering Sciences Data Unit; Royal
Aeronautical Society (RAeS) (year of change 1970)

Organisation type and purpose:
International organisation, service industry,
research organisation, publishing house.
Profit-making company but utilising large number
of committees where (250+) members give time
voluntarily.
Suppliers of validated engineering data and
software.

Subject coverage:
Acoustic fatigue; aerodynamics; composites;
dynamics; fatigue (endurance data and fracture
mechanics); fluid mechanics, internal flow; heat
transfer; metallic materials data; mechanisms;
noise; aircraft performance; physical data (in
chemical and mechanical engineering); stress and
strength; structures; transonic aerodynamics;
tribology; wind engineering; computer software.

Printed publications:
ESDU Catalogue of Validated Engineering
  Methods and Software

Electronic and video publications:
ESDU Subject Index (CD-ROM)
Supporting computer programs and computerised
  data and design procedures

Publications list:
Available online

Access to staff:
Contact by letter, by telephone, by fax, by e-mail
and via website. Appointment necessary.
Hours: Mon to Fri, 0900 to 1700

Access to building, collection or gallery:
No access other than to staff

Access for disabled people:
Level entry

Work is endorsed by the:
Institution of Chemical Engineers
Institution of Mechanical Engineers
Royal Aeronautical Society

ESPERANTO – ASOCIO DE BRITIO

Formal name: Esperanto Association of Britain
Acronym or abbreviation: EAB

Esperanto House, Station Road, Barlaston, Stoke-
on-Trent, Staffordshire, ST12 9DE

Tel: 01782 372141
E-mail: eab@esperanto-gb.org

Website:
http://www.esperanto-gb.org

Enquiries:
Enquiries to: Office Manager
Direct tel: 0845 230 1887
Other contacts: Honorary Librarian

Founded:
1976

Formerly called:
British Esperanto Association (BEA) (year of
change 1976)

Organisation type and purpose:
National organisation, membership association
(membership is by subscription), present number
of members: 700, voluntary organisation,
registered charity (charity number 272676),
suitable for all ages.
Esperanto library, book sales, courses, etc.
For the promotion of the international language,
Esperanto.

Subject coverage:
Esperanto, international language movements in
general, and related subjects.

**Museum or gallery collection, archive, or library
special collection:**
Rare publications dating from 1887

Non-library collection catalogue:
All or part available in-house

Library catalogue:
All or part available in-house

Printed publications:
Large number of both fiction and non-fiction
  publications
La Brita Esperantisto (twice a year, in Esperanto)
EAB Update (quarterly)

Electronic and video publications:
Cassettes, videos, discs and CDs

Publications list:
Available in print

Access to staff:
Contact by letter, by telephone, by fax, by e-mail
and via website. Appointment necessary.
Hours: Mon to Fri, 0900 to 1700, telephone transfer
in operation when the office is not manned

Access to building, collection or gallery:
Prior appointment required

Access for disabled people:
Parking provided, level entry, access to all public
areas

Links with:
Esperanto Teachers Association
  1 Regent Avenue, Skipton, Yorkshire, BD23 1AZ;
  tel: 01756 799912
Regional federations in the United Kingdom
World Esperanto Organisation
  Rotterdam, The Netherlands; tel: + 31 10 436
  1044; fax: + 31 10 436 1751; e-mail: uea@inter.nl
  .net

ESSENTIA GROUP, THE

Lower Ground, Skypark, 72 Finnieston Square,
Glasgow, G3 8ET

Tel: 0141 568 4000

Fax: 0141 568 4001
E-mail: info@essentiagroup.com

Enquiries:
Enquiries to: Managing Director
Other contacts: Accounts Manager, Information
Officer

Founded:
1979

Formerly called:
Network Scotland (year of change 2000)

Organisation type and purpose:
Advisory body, registered charity (charity number
SCO 02866).
Tax File Ref: CR44419/1.

Subject coverage:
Telephone counselling and information services on
predominantly health-related topics.

Access to staff:
Contact by letter, by telephone and by e-mail
Hours: Mon to Fri, 0900 to 1700 (office)

Access to building, collection or gallery:
No access other than to staff

Access for disabled people:
Access to all public areas

Connections with:
NHS Helpline
  tel: 0800 22 44 88
Sexwise
  tel: 0800 28 29 30
Smokeline
  tel: 0800 84 84 84

ESSEX ARCHAEOLOGICAL AND HISTORICAL CONGRESS

Acronym or abbreviation: Essex Congress

c/o Pauline Dalton, Hon. Secretary, Roseleigh
Epping Road, Epping, Essex, CM16 5HW

Fax: 01621 890868
E-mail: essexahc@aol.com

Enquiries:
Enquiries to: Honorary Secretary

Founded:
1964

Organisation type and purpose:
Membership association (membership is by
subscription), registered charity (charity number
27604).

Subject coverage:
Archaeology, local history and conservation of
geographical county of Essex.

Printed publications:
Essex Journal (2 times a year)

Connections with:
British Association for Local History
Council for British Archaeology
Rural Community

ESSEX COUNTY COUNCIL LIBRARIES – BASILDON LIBRARY

St Martin's Square, Basildon, Essex, SS14 1EE

Tel: 01268 288533
Fax: 01268 286326
E-mail: basildon.library@essex.gov.uk

Website:
http://askchris.essexcc.gov.uk
Book reviews/recommendations.
http://www.essexcc.gov.uk/libraries
General information on Essex Libraries.

Enquiries:
Enquiries to: Customer Service Supervisor –
Basildon
Direct tel: 0845 438438

Organisation type and purpose:
Local government body, public library.

continued overleaf

Basildon

Subject coverage:
General.

Information services:
0845 438438

Access to staff:
Contact by letter, by telephone, by fax, by e-mail, in person and via website
Hours: Mon, Fri, 0900 to 1800; Tue, 0900 to 1900; Wed, 0900 to 1800; Thu, 1000 to 1800; Sat, 0900 to 1700; Sun, 1300 to 1600

Access for disabled people:
Level entry, access to all public areas.

ESSEX COUNTY COUNCIL LIBRARIES – BRAINTREE LIBRARY

Fairfield Road, Braintree, Essex, CM7 3YL

Tel: 01376 320752
Fax: 01376 553316
E-mail: braintree.library@essexcc.gov.uk

Enquiries:
Enquiries to: District Manager – Braintree & Uttlesford

Organisation type and purpose:
Local government body, public library.

Subject coverage:
General.

Access to staff:
Contact by letter, by telephone, by fax, by e-mail and in person
Hours: Mon to Fri, 0900 to 1900; Sat, 0900 to 1700; Sun, 1300 to 1600

District library:
Braintree/Uttlesford

ESSEX COUNTY COUNCIL LIBRARIES – CHELMSFORD CENTRAL LIBRARY

PO Box 882, Market Road, Chelmsford, Essex, CM1 1LH

Tel: 01245 492758
Fax: 01245 436503
E-mail: chelmsford.library@essexcc.gov.uk

Website:
http://www.essex.gov.uk/libraries
General information on Essex Libraries.
http://askchris.essex.gov.uk
Book reviews and recommendations.

Enquiries:
Enquiries to: Group Manager – Chelmsford

Organisation type and purpose:
Local government body, public library.
District library for Chelmsford.

Subject coverage:
General, local history and studies, particularly of Chelmsford from c.1903, business, Learndirect Centre, statistics, Europe.

Library catalogue:
All or part available online

Access to staff:
Contact by letter, by telephone, by fax, by e-mail, in person and via website
Hours: Mon to Fri, 0830 to 1900; Sat, 0830 to 1730; Sun, 1230 to 1630

Access for disabled people:
Ramped entry, access to all public areas, toilet facilities
Special comments: Induction loop to counter and enquiry desks, Minicom (textphone), automatic doors.

ESSEX COUNTY COUNCIL LIBRARIES – COLCHESTER CENTRAL LIBRARY

Trinity Square, Colchester, Essex, CO1 1JB

Tel: 01206 245900
Fax: 01206 254901
E-mail: colchester.library@essex.gov.uk

Website:
http://www.essex.gov.uk/libraries
General information on Essex Libraries.
http://askchris.essexcc.gov.uk
Book reviews, recommendations.

Enquiries:
Enquiries to: Colchester Group Manager
Direct tel: 0845 603 7628
Direct e-mail: question@essex.gov.uk

Organisation type and purpose:
Local government body, public library.
District library – Colchester/Tendring District.

Subject coverage:
General, local & family history.

Museum or gallery collection, archive, or library special collection:
Castle Library (18th century subscription library)
Essex Local Studies Collection

Library catalogue:
All or part available online and in-house

Access to staff:
Contact by letter, by telephone, by fax, by e-mail and in person
Hours: Mon to Fri, 0830 to 1930; Sat, 0830 to 1700; Sun, 1230 to 1600

Access for disabled people:
Level entry, access to all public areas, toilet facilities
Special comments: Escalator to 1st floor; lift available.

ESSEX COUNTY COUNCIL LIBRARIES – EUG

County Hall, Market Road, Chelmsford, Essex CM1 1LQ

Tel: 0845 603 7628
E-mail: answers.direct@essex.gov.uk

Website:
http://www.essex.gov.uk/libraries
General information on Essex Libraries and links to other specialised online services.

Founded:
1926

Organisation type and purpose:
Local government body, public library.

Subject coverage:
General library service with 73 service points and 12 mobile libraries.

Museum or gallery collection, archive, or library special collection:
Performing Arts Service,
Business Information Service
Castle Collection example 18th century subscription library (Colchester)
Jazz archive (Loughton)
Victorian Studies Centre (Saffron Walden)

Non-library collection catalogue:
All or part available online

Library catalogue:
All or part available online

Access to staff:
Contact by letter, by telephone, by e-mail, in person and via website
Hours: Mon to Fri, 0830 to 1900; Sat 0830 to 1700; Sun 1000 to 1630

Access for disabled people:
Access to all public areas

Parent body:
Essex County Council

ESSEX COUNTY COUNCIL LIBRARIES – HARLOW LIBRARY

The High, Harlow, Essex, CM20 1HA

Tel: 01279 413772
Fax: 01279 424612
E-mail: harlow.library@essexcc.gov.uk

Website:
http://www.essexcc.gov.uk/libraries
General information on Essex Libraries.
http://www.askchris.essexcc.gov.uk
Book reviews/recommendations.

Enquiries:
Enquiries to: District Manager – Harlow/Epping

Organisation type and purpose:
Local government body, public library.
District Library – Harlow/Epping Forest District.

Subject coverage:
Essex County Council Libraries Language and Literature Librarian is based at Harlow Library, responsible for County collection of language books, audio and video courses, non-English fiction and literature stock.

Museum or gallery collection, archive, or library special collection:
International Genealogical Index (IGI UK) on microfiche
LASER joint fiction reserve (authors S-SS)

Access to staff:
Contact by letter, by telephone, by fax and in person
Hours: Mon, Tue, Thu, Fri, 0900 to 1900; Wed, 1000 to 1900; Sat, 0900 to 1700; Sun, 1300 to 1600

Access for disabled people:
Level entry, access to all public areas
Special comments: Induction loop at counter and enquiry desk.

Parent body:
Essex County Council Libraries

ESSEX COUNTY COUNCIL LIBRARIES – SAFFRON WALDEN LIBRARY

2 King Street, Saffron Walden, Essex, CB10 1ES

Tel: 01799 523178
Fax: 01799 513642
E-mail: saffronwalden.library@essex.gov.uk

Website:
http://www.essex.gov.uk

Enquiries:
Enquiries to: Librarian

Organisation type and purpose:
Local government body, public library.
Houses a Victorian studies centre based on the old Town Library Collection.

Subject coverage:
Victorian studies with special emphasis on art, literature and natural history, local studies relating to Saffron Walden and its environs.

Museum or gallery collection, archive, or library special collection:
Herts and Essex Observer (1939–2004, microfilm)
Saffron Walden Observer (1994–2004)
Saffron Walden Weekly News (1881–2004, microfilm)
Local census returns 1841, 1851, 1861, 1871, 1881, 1891 and 1901 (microfilm)
The Library of Saffron Walden Literary and Scientific Institute
Victorian Studies collection

Non-library collection catalogue:
All or part available online and in-house

Library catalogue:
All or part available online

Access to staff:
Contact by letter, by telephone, by fax, by e-mail and in person
Hours: Mon to Fri, 0900 to 1900; Sat, 0900 to 1700; Sun, 1300 to 1600

Access for disabled people:
Level entry, access to all public areas, toilet facilities

ESSEX RECORD OFFICE – CHELMSFORD

Acronym or abbreviation: ERO

Wharf Road, Chelmsford, Essex, CM2 6YT

Tel: 01245 244644
Fax: 01245 244655
E-mail: ero.enquiry@essex.gov.uk

Website:
http://www.essex.gov.uk/ero
http://www.essex.gov.uk/heritage/
Description of services offered, outline of archive holdings, publications and exhibitions, online catalogue SEAX, events calendar

Enquiries:
Enquiries to: Archive Service Manager

Founded:
1938

Incorporates the former:
Essex Record Office – Colchester (year of change 2007)

Organisation type and purpose:
Local government body.
Record office.

Subject coverage:
Topography and history of Essex, genealogy.

Special visitor services:
Conference facilities

Education services:
Heritage Education Officer

Museum or gallery collection, archive, or library special collection:
Extensive collections of local government, parish, estate and family, business and other archives relating to the county of Essex; library of Essex local history books, journals and newspapers; Essex Sound and Video Archive

Non-library collection catalogue:
All or part available online, in-house and in print

Library catalogue:
All or part available in-house

Printed publications:
Over 70 publications in print, including:
Colchester, 1815–1914 (A. J. F. Brown)
Elizabethan Life (F. G. Emmison, 5 vols)
Essex Illustrated – a county, its people and its past
Essex Quarter Sessions Order Book, 1652–1661 (ed. D. H. Allen)
Examples of English Handwriting, 1150–1750 (H. Grieve)
Foulness (J. R. Smith)
Genealogist's Guide to Essex Sources
John Horace Round (W. R. Powell)
Picture booklets (Medieval Essex, Elizabethan Essex, etc., list available)
Prosperity and Poverty – Rural Essex, 1700–1815 (A. F. J. Brown)
Reproductions of maps
Seax series of Teaching Portfolios (list available)
The Sleeper and the Shadows (H. Grieve, 2 vols)
List of new archival accessions (annual)
Order printed publications from: Address above

Microform publications:
Microfilm and microfiche of a wide variety of records can be made to order
Order microform publications from: Address above

Electronic and video publications:
Digital images of a wide variety of records can be made to order

Order electronic and video publications from: Address above

Publications list:
Available online and in print

Access to staff:
Contact by letter, by telephone, by fax, by e-mail, in person and via website
Hours: Mon, 0900 to 2030; Tue to Thu, 0900 to 1700; Fri and Sat, 0900 to 1600

Access for disabled people:
Parking provided, level entry, access to all public areas, toilet facilities

Links with:
Saffron Walden Archive Access Point
Saffron Walden Library, 2 King Street, Saffron Walden, CB10 1ES; tel: 01799 523178; e-mail: ero.saffronwalden@essex.gov.uk

ESSEX SOCIETY FOR ARCHAEOLOGY AND HISTORY

Hollytrees Museum, High Street, Colchester, Essex, CO1 1UG

Enquiries:
Enquiries to: Secretary
Direct tel: 01277 363106

Founded:
1852

Formerly called:
Essex Archaeological Society

Organisation type and purpose:
Learned society.

Subject coverage:
Essex archaeology and history.

Museum or gallery collection, archive, or library special collection:
Library is now housed at the University of Essex
17th and 18th century books (history and religion)
Archaeological journals
Brass rubbing collection (A H Brown)
Definitive collection of rubbings of Essex brasses (Christy, Porteous and Smith)
Essex Parish histories and county biography
Essex prints and photographs
Transcripts of Essex Parish Registers

Non-library collection catalogue:
All or part available in print

Library catalogue:
All or part available in print

Printed publications:
Catalogues of non-book library materials (in preparation)
Essex Archaeological News (quarterly newsletter)
Essex Archaeology and History (annual transactions)
Order printed publications from: Secretary

Access to staff:
Contact by letter. Appointment necessary.
Hours: Mon to Fri, 0900 to 1700

Affiliated to:
Council for British Archaeology
Essex Historical and Archaeological Congress

ESSO PETROLEUM COMPANY LIMITED

Esso Refinery, Fawley, Southampton, SO45 1TX

Tel: 023 8089 2511
Fax: 023 8089 6712

Enquiries:
Enquiries to: IMS Administrator
Direct tel: 023 8089 6113
Direct fax: 023 8089 6334
Direct e-mail: rob.gostt@exxonmobil.com

Organisation type and purpose:
Manufacturing industry.

Subject coverage:
Chemical engineering; combustion; corrosion; petroleum and petroleum products; oil refining; oil transport and storage; plant maintenance; pollution.

Museum or gallery collection, archive, or library special collection:
British and American industrial standards

Access to staff:
Contact by letter, by telephone, by fax and by e-mail
Hours: Mon to Fri, 0815 to 1630

Constituent part of:
ExxonMobil Corporation, USA

ESTONIAN EMBASSY

Formal name: Embassy of the Republic of Estonia

16 Hyde Park Gate, London, SW7 5DG

Tel: 020 7589 3428
Fax: 020 7589 3430
E-mail: embassy.london@estonia.gov.uk

Website:
http://www.estonia.gov.uk

Enquiries:
Enquiries to: Secretary

Formerly called:
Estonian Information Bureau (year of change 1992)

Organisation type and purpose:
National government body.
Diplomatic Mission/Embassy.

Subject coverage:
All information on Estonia: travel, economical, political, cultural, etc.

Access to staff:
Contact by letter, by telephone, by fax, by e-mail and via website
Hours: The Consular Section (for Visas): Mon, Fri, 1000 to 1300; Tue, Thu, 1300 to 1600

Access to building, collection or gallery:
Prior appointment required

ETB

Weston House, 2nd Floor, 246 High Holborn, London, WC1V 7EX

Tel: 020 3206 0400
Fax: 020 3206 0401
E-mail: info@etechb.co.uk

Website:
http://www.etechb.co.uk

Enquiries:
Enquiries to: Communications Director
Direct e-mail: ccox@etechb.co.uk

Founded:
2002

Formerly called:
Engineering and Technology Board (ETB) (year of change 2002)

Organisation type and purpose:
National organisation.
A national partnership to promote science, engineering and technology.
To ensure the supply of science, engineering and technology skills matches, and stimulates market needs.

Subject coverage:
The engineering profession, education and training, qualifications of engineers and technicians, careers advice, salary surveys, continuing education and training, career breaks for women, Young Engineers for Britain and the Environment Award for Engineers, Women Into Science and Engineers (WISE) campaign, schools and industry liaison; science, engineering and technology.

continued overleaf

Printed publications:
Annual Reports
Newsletter
Surveys, Policy Statements and Discussion
 Documents

Access to staff:
Contact by letter, by telephone, by fax, by e-mail
and via website
Hours: Mon to Fri, 0900 to 1700

ETHICAL INVESTMENT RESEARCH SERVICE

Acronym or abbreviation: EIRIS

80–84 Bondway, London, SW8 1SF

Tel: 020 7840 5700
Fax: 020 7735 5323
E-mail: ethics@eiris.org

Website:
http://www.eiris.org

Enquiries:
Enquiries to: Partnerships and Development
Manager

Founded:
1983

Organisation type and purpose:
Registered charity (charity number 1020068),
consultancy, research organisation.
Provides research on the ethical aspects of
corporate activities for ethical investors. Provides
(non-financial) information on ethical or socially
responsible investment.

Subject coverage:
Helping investors match their investments with
their ethical (incl. environmental) principles.
Providing (non-financial) information on ethical or
socially responsible investment.

Trade and statistical information:
Collated information on retail ethical funds.

Printed publications:
Does Ethical Investment Pay (download from web)
The Ethical Investor (newsletter, 4 times a year,
 and supplement, 2 times a year, annual
 subscription £15, or available online)
The following supplements are available free:
Guide to ethical banking
Guide to ethical share ownership
Guide on charities and ethical investment
Order printed publications from: EIRIS Orderline
tel: 0845 606 0324

Electronic and video publications:
All EIRIS's supplements and newsletters can be
 downloaded free from www.eiris.org
Ethical Portfolio Manager (software for
 institutional investors)

Publications list:
Available online and in print

Access to staff:
Contact by letter, by telephone, by fax, by e-mail
and via website
Hours: Mon to Fri, 0900 to 1700
Special comments: Charges for some services made
to all users. Some information available free via
website.

Member of:
Global Partners for Corporate Responsibility
Research
UK Social Investment Forum

ETON COLLEGE LIBRARY

Eton College, Windsor, Berkshire, SL4 6DB

Tel: 01753 671221
Fax: 01753 801507
E-mail: collections@etoncollege.org.uk

Founded:
1440

Organisation type and purpose:
Registered charity.
A rare book and manuscript library, maintained by
collegiate body (Provost and Fellows).
A research library.

**Museum or gallery collection, archive, or library
special collection:**
16th-century continental books
17th- and 18th-century English pamphlets (to
 c.1730)
Armenian printed books (16th–19th centuries)
Bibliography
Classical school books (15th–19th centuries)
Drawings and engravings after the antique
 (Topham Collection)
Drawings of Rome and its environs
English literature 19th and 20th centuries (Hardy,
 Browning, Swinburne, Anne Thackeray Ritchie,
 Edward Gordon Craig, Susan Hill, Moelwyn
 Merchant, Anthony Powell, Etonian authors)
Fine bindings
Incunabula
Local history collections (Eton and Windsor)
Photographic collection
Pre-Restoration English drama
Private presses
Topographical prints and drawings (mostly local)
Western and oriental manuscripts

Non-library collection catalogue:
All or part available in-house

Library catalogue:
All or part available in-house and in print

Microform publications:
Microfilms can be ordered

Access to staff:
Contact by letter, by telephone, by fax and by e-
mail. Appointment necessary.
Hours: Mon to Fri, 0930 to 1300 and 1400 to 1700

ETON FIVES ASSOCIATION

Acronym or abbreviation: EFA

3 Bourchier Close, Sevenoaks, Kent, TN13 1PD

Tel: 01732 458775
E-mail: efa@etonfives.co.uk

Website:
http://www.etonfives.co.uk
About Eton Fives, association information, courts,
historical and other articles, merchandise and
equipment, league and tournament results, clubs
and schools, picture gallery, contacts.

Enquiries:
Enquiries to: Secretary

Founded:
c. 1928

Organisation type and purpose:
National organisation, membership association
(membership is by subscription, election or
invitation), present number of members: 700 plus
50 friends.
Controlling body of the game.
To promote the playing of Eton Fives; to review
and publish the rules and laws of the game.

Subject coverage:
Eton Fives court specifications; lighting; equipment
(gloves and balls); laws of the game; court location;
court availability; archives.

**Museum or gallery collection, archive, or library
special collection:**
Archives: include books, documents, manuscripts,
 pictures, photographs and other material

Library catalogue:
All or part available online

Printed publications:
Annual Handbook
Coaching and Playing Manual

Access to staff:
Contact by letter, by telephone, by e-mail and via
website
Hours: Sun to Sat, 0800 to 2200

EUPHORBIACEAE STUDY GROUP

Acronym or abbreviation: ESG

11 Shaftesbury Avenue, Penketh, Warrington,
Cheshire, WA5 4LB

Tel: 01925 724699
Fax: 01925 791190
E-mail: 101723.3005@compuserve.com

Enquiries:
Enquiries to: Honorary Secretary

Founded:
1988

Organisation type and purpose:
International organisation (membership is by
subscription), present number of members: 200,
voluntary organisation.
The study, propagation and conservation of the
species and the exchange of information on all
aspects of cultivation etc.

Subject coverage:
Cultivation, propagation and conservation of the
Euphorbiaceae.

Printed publications:
Bulletin (3 times a year)

Publications list:
Available in print

Access to staff:
Contact by letter, by telephone, by fax and by e-
mail
Hours: Mon to Fri, 0900 to 1700

EURO INFO CENTRE – BUSINESS GATEWAY

Acronym or abbreviation: EIC

150 Broomielaw, Atlantic Quay, Glasgow, G2 8LU

Tel: 0141 228 2797
Fax: 0141 228 2327

Enquiries:
Enquiries to: Information Officer
Direct e-mail: euroinfocentre@scotent.co.uk

Organisation type and purpose:
To assist small to medium sized enterprises to
thrive in the single European market by provision
of EU information.

Subject coverage:
EU Legislation, EU programmes/initiatives, market
intelligence, public procurement, EU/UK funding
information (grants, loans, awards, etc), general
European business enquiries, business co-
operation support.

**Museum or gallery collection, archive, or library
special collection:**
Online databases and sources

Printed publications:
Business Co-operation (requests for business
 partners, agents, distributors and other forms of
 business co-operation, free)
Enquiry Service (free)
Tenders Electronic Daily (£900 a year plus VAT)
Gateway to Europe Newsletter (monthly, free)
Grantfinder – Search for grants, loans, etc for
 business (free)

Access to staff:
Contact by letter, by telephone, by fax, by e-mail
and via website
Hours: Mon to Fri, 0900 to 1700

Access to building, collection or gallery:
No access other than to staff

Access for disabled people:
Ramped entry, access to all public areas, toilet
facilities

Parent body:
Commission of The European Communities
Scottish Enterprise
 150 Broomielaw, Atlantic Quay, Glasgow, G2
 8LU

EURO INFO CENTRE NORTH WEST

Acronym or abbreviation: EICNW

No 1 Old Hall Street, Liverpool, L3 9HF

Tel: 0151 237 5005/5006
Fax: 0151 237 5000
E-mail: eic@gme.org.uk

Website:
http://www.eicnw.co.uk
Euro Info Centre North West

Enquiries:
Enquiries to: Information Manager

Founded:
1989

Organisation type and purpose:
Consultancy.
To assist small and medium sized enterprises to do business in the single market.

Subject coverage:
EC legislation, policies and programmes; information on companies, markets, trading conditions and legislation in other countries of the European Union.

Museum or gallery collection, archive, or library special collection:
Major EC official publications
Official Journal of The EC from 1990

Printed publications:
Euro Facts (fact sheets)
Euromail (alerts, breaking news)
Euro Watch (Official Journal Index)

Access to staff:
Contact by letter, by telephone, by fax, by e-mail and via website. Appointment necessary.
Hours: Mon to Fri, 0900 to 1700

Access to building, collection or gallery:
Access to businesses by appointment

Hosted by:
Greater Merseyside Enterprise Limited

Reports to:
Commission of The European Communities
DG ENTR & IND

EUROMONITOR INTERNATIONAL

60–61 Britton Street, London, EC1M 5UX

Tel: 020 7251 8024
Fax: 020 7608 3149
E-mail: info@euromonitor.com

Website:
http://www.euromonitor.com
Complete listing of market research reports, reference products and consultancy, searchable by industry, country or product.

Enquiries:
Enquiries to: Marketing Manager

Founded:
1972

Organisation type and purpose:
Professional body, consultancy, research organisation, publishing house.

Subject coverage:
International marketing information and analysis, food, drinks, tobacco, tourism, household cleaning, healthcare, cosmetics and toiletries, household goods, domestic electrical appliances, consumer electronics, leisure, automotives, catering, financial, consumer lifestyles, retailing, Europe, Eastern Europe, North and South America, Australasia, Japan and China, South East Asia.

Museum or gallery collection, archive, or library special collection:
Large in-house international library which includes directories, national statistics (Europe), trade and marketing press (Europe), company reports (international) and key data and surveys on consumer goods markets around the world

Trade and statistical information:
Data on overall and specific consumer markets to include key trends and developments, market size, sources of supply, market sectors, usership and purchasing patterns, prices and margins, brands and manufacturers, advertising, promotions and new products, retail distribution, future outlook.

Library catalogue:
All or part available in print

Printed publications:
World Directory of Business Information Libraries

Electronic and video publications:
World Consumer Markets (internet)
World Consumer Lifestyles: Data (internet)
Market Research Monitor (internet)
World Marketing Data and Statistics (internet)
World Marketing Forecasts (internet)

Publications list:
Available online and in print

Access to staff:
Contact by letter, by telephone, by fax, by e-mail and via website
Hours: Mon to Fri, 0930 to 1730

EUROPEAN ASSOCIATION FOR BRAZING AND SOLDERING

Acronym or abbreviation: EABS

5 Kent Drive, Congleton, Cheshire, CW12 1SD

Tel: 01260 271703
Fax: 01260 276729
E-mail: eabs@btconnect.com

Website:
http://www.brazingandsoldering.org
Aims and objectives, training courses available, Newsletter, technical articles, response form for technical advice.

Enquiries:
Enquiries to: Secretariat

Founded:
1970

Formerly called:
British Association for Brazing and Soldering (BABS) (year of change 2000)

Organisation type and purpose:
Training organisation.
To provide a consultancy service and technical information in the promotion of brazing and soldering technology.

Subject coverage:
Brazing (low and high temperature), soldering, diffusion bonding, adhesives, ceramics, metals, process equipment, consumables, standards.

Printed publications:
EABS Newsletter (2 or 3 times a year)

Access to staff:
Contact by letter, by telephone, by fax, by e-mail and via website. Non-members charged.
Hours: Mon to Fri, 0830 to 1630

EUROPEAN ASSOCIATION FOR PASSIVE FIRE PROTECTION

Acronym or abbreviation: EAPFP

Tournai Hall, Evelyn Woods Road, Aldershot Hampshire GU11 2LL

Tel: 01252 357836
Fax: 01252 357831
E-mail: admin@eapfp.com

Website:
http://www.eapfp.com

Enquiries:
Enquiries to: Secretary

Founded:
1988

Formerly called:
European Association for Specialist Fire Protection (EASFP)

Organisation type and purpose:
Trade association, present number of members: 7.
Corporate voice for European manufacturers and contractors involved in passive fire protection to steelwork, timber and other specialist applications.

Subject coverage:
Fire protection to steelwork, timber and other specialist fire protection applications including penetration seals and ductwork.

Printed publications:
Conference papers
EAPFP Folder (members' details and other information, free)

Publications list:
Available online and in print

Access to staff:
Contact by letter, by telephone, by fax, by e-mail and via website
Hours: Mon to Fri, 0900 to 1700

EUROPEAN ASSOCIATION OF SCIENCE EDITORS

Acronym or abbreviation: EASE

PO Box 6159, Reading, RG19 9DE

Tel: 0118 970 0322
Fax: 0118 970 0322
E-mail: secretary@ease.org.uk

Website:
http://www.ease.org.uk
Information about EASE and application form for potential members and subscribers to the journal, Editor's Bookshelf, recent copies of EASE's quarterly journal, list of conferences and meetings, job advertisements, courses offered by members, links to useful sites, how to join EASE web forum, how to join EASE, payment facility for subscriptions and handbooks

Enquiries:
Enquiries to: Secretary

Founded:
1982

Created by the merger of:
European Association of Earth Science Editors (Editerra), European Life Sciences Editors' Association (ELSE)

Organisation type and purpose:
International organisation, professional body.

Subject coverage:
Editing and copy-editing in the sciences.

Printed publications:
European Science Editing (journal for members and subscribers, quarterly, £60 to non-members)
Science Editors' Handbook (included in membership fee: new chapters issued from time to time, after editorial approval; available to non-members £35 plus p&p – see website ease.org.uk for details and price)

Access to staff:
Contact by letter, by telephone, by fax, by e-mail and via website
Hours: Mon to Fri, 0900 to 1700
Special comments: No visitors.

Links with:
International Union of Biological Sciences (IUBS)
International Union of Geological Sciences (IUGS)

EUROPEAN BANK FOR RECONSTRUCTION AND DEVELOPMENT – BUSINESS INFORMATION CENTRE

Acronym or abbreviation: EBRD

One Exchange Square, London, EC2A 2JN

continued overleaf

Tel: 020 7338 7269
Fax: 020 7338 6155
E-mail: stanojes@ebrd.com

Website:
http://www.ebrd.com
Full details of publications.

Enquiries:
Enquiries to: Senior Information Officer

Founded:
1991

Organisation type and purpose:
International organisation.
Financing the economic transition in Central and Eastern Europe and the former Soviet Union.

Subject coverage:
Business information for Central and Eastern Europe and the CIS.

Museum or gallery collection, archive, or library special collection:
Collection of books, periodicals, CD-ROMs and other documents relating to the area of Central and Eastern Europe and the CIS

Trade and statistical information:
Economic and business-related data covering the countries of Central and Eastern Europe and the CIS.

Printed publications:
EBRD Directory of business information sources on Central and Eastern Europe and the CIS (annually, £175)
Order printed publications from: ETM Ltd, PO Box 171, Grimsby, DN35 0TP; tel. 01472 816660; fax 01472 816660; e-mail sales@dataresources.co.uk

Electronic and video publications:
EBRD Directory of business information sources on Central and Eastern Europe and the CIS

Publications list:
Available online and in print

Access to staff:
Contact by letter, by fax and by e-mail.
Appointment necessary. Letter of introduction required.
Hours: Mon to Fri, 0900 to 1700

Access for disabled people:
Toilet facilities
Special comments: Access by lift in Exchange Square and access by lift to Exchange Square from Appold Street

EUROPEAN BEER CONSUMER UNION

Acronym or abbreviation: EBCU

230 Hatfield Road, St Albans, Hertfordshire, AL1 4LW

Tel: 01727 798449
Fax: 01727 867670
E-mail: ebcu@camra.org.uk

Website:
http://www.camra.org.uk

Enquiries:
Enquiries to: Communications Manager
Direct e-mail: iain.loe@camra.org.uk

Founded:
1990

Organisation type and purpose:
International organisation (membership is by subscription), present number of members: 100,000.

Subject coverage:
Beer and brewing. Legislation relating to beer, brewing, sale of alcohol. Historical information on beer and brewing.

Trade and statistical information:
Some statistical information on UK Brewing, less on the rest of Europe.

Printed publications:
Good Beer Guide (annually, pub October)
Variety of guides to pubs in the UK and parts of rest of Europe

Access to staff:
Contact by letter, by telephone and by e-mail.
Appointment necessary.
Hours: Mon to Fri, 0900 to 1700

Access for disabled people:
Parking provided, level entry

EUROPEAN CENTRE FOR MEDIUM-RANGE WEATHER FORECASTS

Acronym or abbreviation: ECMWF

Shinfield Park, Reading, Berkshire, RG2 9AX

Tel: 0118 949 9000
Fax: 0118 986 9450
E-mail: dra@ecmwf.int

Website:
http://www.ecmwf.int/
Weather information.

Enquiries:
Enquiries to: Director
Direct tel: 0118 949 9101

Founded:
1975

Organisation type and purpose:
International organisation, research organisation.

Subject coverage:
Numerical weather prediction in the medium range.

Library catalogue:
All or part available in-house

Printed publications:
Scientific work

Electronic and video publications:
Analysed fields
Observations
Meteorological data

Access to staff:
Contact by letter and by e-mail. Appointment necessary.
Hours: Mon to Fri, 0900 to 1700

Access to building, collection or gallery:
No access other than to staff

EUROPEAN CHRISTIAN MISSION

50 Billing Road, Northampton, NN1 5DH

Tel: 01604 621092
E-mail: ecm.gb@ecmi.org

Website:
http://www.ecmi.org
A large amount of information including vacancies.

Enquiries:
Enquiries to: Information Officer

Founded:
1904

Organisation type and purpose:
International organisation, voluntary organisation, registered charity.

Access to staff:
Contact by letter, by telephone, by e-mail and via website
Hours: Mon to Fri, 0900 to 1700

Access for disabled people:
Parking provided, ramped entry

EUROPEAN COMMISSION – EDINBURGH

Acronym or abbreviation: EC or EU

9 Alva Street, Edinburgh, EH2 4PH

Tel: 0131 225 2058
Fax: 0131 226 4105
E-mail: diana.hart@cec.eu.int

Website:
http://europa.eu.int
The European Union's Server.
http://www.cec.org.uk
UK Representation.
http://www.europe.org.uk
UK Resource Centres.

Enquiries:
Enquiries to: Information Officer

Founded:
1975

Formerly called:
European Economic Community (EEC)

Organisation type and purpose:
International organisation.
Representation of the EC in Scotland.

Subject coverage:
Information on the European Union.

Museum or gallery collection, archive, or library special collection:
Official Publications of the European Community

Trade and statistical information:
Eurostat.

Printed publications:
A very large number of publications including:
Documents (the COM Documents of the European Commission)
Official Journal of the EC
The European Community as a Publisher (1995) (extract from the publications catalogue)
Order printed publications from: The Stationery Office

Publications list:
Available in print

Access to staff:
Contact by letter, by telephone, by fax, by e-mail and via website. Appointment necessary.
Hours: Mon to Fri, 0900 to 1700

Access to building, collection or gallery:
Prior appointment required

EUROPEAN COMMISSION – LONDON

Formal name: The European Commission Representation in the United Kingdom

8 Storey's Gate, London, SW1P 3AT

Tel: 020 7973 1992
Fax: 020 7973 1900/10

Website:
http://europa.eu/index_en.htm
Gateway to information on the European Union policies and institutions. News, answers to key questions, institutions, policies, mailbox for comments and ideas.
http://www.europarl.org.uk/index.htm
Website of the UK office of the European Parliament.
http://ec.europa.eu/unitedkingdom/index_en.htm
Daily update of the latest developments in the EU with regard to policies and programmes, recruitment, EU-related events in the UK, publications lists, etc.

Enquiries:
Enquiries to: Public Diplomacy Unit
Direct e-mail: marguerite-marie.brenchley@ec.europa.eu

Formerly called:
Commission of the European Communities

Organisation type and purpose:
International organisation.
Representation of the European Commission.

Subject coverage:
European Community polices, legislation and documentation.

Information services:
See: http://www.europe.org.uk/info, which brings together the EU information network in the UK.

Trade and statistical information:
Eurostat publications.

Library catalogue:
All or part available in-house and in print

Printed publications:
Free publications on all aspects of EU policies: http://ec.europa.eu/unitedkingdom/information/
 publications/index_en.htm
Order printed publications from: See list of agents in the UK at http://publications.europa.eu/others/
agents/index_en.htm

Publications list:
Available online and in print

Access to staff:
Contact by letter, by telephone and by fax.
Appointment necessary.
Hours: Mon to Fri, 0900 to 1700
Special comments: The Representation in the UK is now supporting a national network of information centres (http://www.europe.org.uk/info) to whom all enquiries should be addressed. Visitors to the library may be referred to the Representation by the information centres, when they are unable to help. Visits are organised strictly by appointment.

Also at:
European Commission
 Office for Official Publications of the European Communities, 2 rue Mercier, 2985, Luxembourg; tel: 00 352 29291; e-mail: info@publications .europa.eu; website: http://publications.europa .eu/index_en.htm
European Commission
 Rue de la Loi 200, 1049, Brussels, Belgium; tel: 00 32 2 235 1111; website: http://ec.europa.eu/ index_en.htm
European Commission Office in Northern Ireland
 Windsor House, 9–15 Bedford Street, Belfast, BT2 7EG; tel: 028 9024 0708; fax: 028 9024 8241
European Commission Office in Scotland
 9 Alva Street, Edinburgh, EH2 4PH; tel: 0131 225 2058; fax: 0131 226 4105
European Commission Office in Wales / Swyddfa'r Comisiwn Ewropeaidd yng Nghymru
 2 Caspian Point / 2 Pentir Caspian, Caspian Way / Ffordd Caspian, Cardiff/Caerdydd, CF10 4QQ; tel: 029 20895020; fax: 029 20895035
European Commission Statistical Office (Eurostat)
 Bâtiment Bech, 11 Rue Alphonse Weicker, 2721, Luxembourg; tel: 00 352 43011; website: http:// epp.eurostat.ec.europa.eu/portal/page?_pageid= 1090,1&_dad=portal&_schema=PORTAL

Links with:
Members of the European Parliament (MEPs)
London Office of the EP
 2 Queen Anne's Gate , London, SW1H 9AA; tel: 020 7227 4300; e-mail: eplondon@europarl .europa.eu; website: http://www.europarl.org .uk/office/TheOfficeMain.htm

EUROPEAN COMPUTER LEASING AND TRADING ASSOCIATION

Formal name: European Computer Leasing and Trading Association
Acronym or abbreviation: ECLAT

1285 Stratford Road, Hall Green, Birmingham, B28 9AJ

Tel: 0121 778 5327
Fax: 0121 778 5924
E-mail: jgsewel@attglobal.net

Website:
http://www.eclat.net
List of members by country and details of ECLAT's conferences.
http://www.ascdi.com

List of members by country and details of ASCDI's conferences.

Enquiries:
Enquiries to: Director General

Founded:
1979

Organisation type and purpose:
Trade association (membership is by qualification, election or invitation), present number of members: 230.
Represents the interests of the computer leasing and trading industry.

Subject coverage:
Specialised knowledge on computer leasing and on purchase and sale of used computers.

Access to staff:
Contact by letter, by telephone, by fax and by e-mail. Appointment necessary. Non-members charged.
Hours: Mon to Fri, 0900 to 1730

Connections with:
Association of Service and Computer Dealers International (ASCDI)
 131 NW 1st Avenue, Derray Beach, FL 33444, USA; tel: +561 266 9016; fax: +561 266 9017; e-mail: jmarion@ix.netcom.com

EUROPEAN CONSTRUCTION INSTITUTE

Acronym or abbreviation: ECI

Loughborough University, Sir Frank Gibb Annex, Loughborough, Leicestershire, LE11 3TU

Tel: 01509 223526
Fax: 01509 260118
E-mail: eci@lboro.ac.uk

Website:
http://www.eci-online.org
ECI activities, company profiles, task forces, picture gallery, hot news, conferences/ seminars/ workshops, email addresses, publications.

Enquiries:
Enquiries to: Administrator
Direct tel: 01509 223643

Founded:
1990

Organisation type and purpose:
International organisation, membership association (membership is by subscription), research organisation.
To improve the performance of the European construction industry.

Subject coverage:
Construction in Europe.

Museum or gallery collection, archive, or library special collection:
Business Roundtable (USA) publications
Construction Industry Institute (USA) publications

Printed publications:
ECI News (3 times a year)
Taskforce papers
Construction in Europe (conference papers)
Partnering in the Public Sector
The ECI Guide to Managing Health in Construction
Over 30 publications related to the construction industry

Publications list:
Available in print

Access to staff:
Contact by letter, by telephone, by fax, by e-mail and via website. Appointment necessary.
Hours: Mon to Fri, 0900 to 1730

Has:
over 70 member companies

EUROPEAN COUNCIL OF INFORMATION ASSOCIATIONS

Acronym or abbreviation: ECIA

Aslib, Holywell Centre, 1 Phipp Street, London, EC2A 4PS

Tel: 020 7613 3031
Fax: 020 7613 5080
E-mail: ecia@aslib.com

Website:
http://www.aslib.com/ecia/index.html
ECIA VIEWS.

Enquiries:
Enquiries to: Honorary Secretary
Direct e-mail: roger.bowes@aslib.com
Other contacts: President

Founded:
1979

Formerly called:
WERTID (year of change 1992)

Organisation type and purpose:
International organisation.

Subject coverage:
Management of information.

Printed publications:
ECIA VIEWS (Newsletter)

Access to staff:
Contact by e-mail
Hours: Mon to Fri, 0900 to 1700

Members:
Associação Portuguesa para a Gestao da Informação Edificio (INCITE)
 Portugal; e-mail: incite@net.sapo.pt; website: www.incite.pt
Association Belge de Documentation, Belgische Vereniging voor Documentatie (ABD-BVD)
 Belgium; e-mail: abdbrd@abd-bvd.be; website: www.abd-bvd.be
Associazione Italiana per la Documentazione Avanzata (AIDA)
 Italy; e-mail: aida-cd@inroma.roma.it; website: www.aidaweb.it
Deutsche Gesellschaft für Informationswissenschaft und Informationspraxis (DGI)
 Germany; e-mail: zentrale@dgi-info.de; website: www.dgi-info.de
L'Association des professionnels de l'information et de la documentation (ADBS)
 France; e-mail: ADBS@adbs.fr; website: www .adbs.fr
Sociedad Española de Documentación e Información Científica (SEDIC)
 Spain; e-mail: sedic@sedic.es; website: www .sedic.es
Swedish Association for Information Specialists (TLS)
 Sweden; e-mail: kansliet@tls.se; website: www .tls.se
The Association for Information Management (ASLIB)
 UK; e-mail: ecia@aslib.com; website: www.aslib .com
Tietopalveluseura ry – Finish Society for Information Services
 Finland; e-mail: info@tietopalveluseura.fi; website: www.tietopalveluseura.fi

EUROPEAN COUNCIL OF INTERNATIONAL SCHOOLS

Formal name: European Council of International Schools
Acronym or abbreviation: ECIS

21 Lavant Street, Petersfield, Hampshire, GU32 3EL

Tel: 01730 268244
Fax: 01730 267914
E-mail: ecis@ecis.org

Website:
http://www.ecis.org

continued overleaf

Details of ECIS, links to international schools. On-line directory of international schools, job vacancies and professional development.

Enquiries:
Enquiries to: Executive, Information & Resources

Founded:
1965

Organisation type and purpose:
International organisation, membership association, present number of members: 515 schools, 400 colleges and universities, suitable for ages: 3 to 18.
Provides services to international schools worldwide including: conferences, teacher/senior administrator recruitment, school accreditation and publications.

Subject coverage:
Arranges and conducts professional meetings, publishes directories, newsletters and journals, assists member schools with finding staff, evaluates and accredits schools, conducts research and acts as a consultant, encourages the professional development of teachers and provides a link to higher education.

Printed publications:
Most Important Decision (£5 members only)
ECIS Policy Planner (£50 members only)
Sample Contracts for Heads (£5 members only)
Languages & Cultures in English-Language-Based International Schools (£17 members only)
ECIS Guide to School Evaluation & Accreditation (6th ed., £25 members only)
The 2002/3 International Schools Directory (£35)
The following three publications are available through: Sales Dept John Catt Educational Ltd, Great Glemham, Saxmundham IP17 2DH. Tel: 01728 663666 Fax:01728 663415
The ECIS Higher Education Directory 2003 (£40)
The International Schools Journal (2 times a year, £15 members)
IS, International School magazine (3 times a year, £15)

Access to staff:
Contact by letter, by telephone, by fax, by e-mail and via website
Hours: Mon to Fri, 0830 to 1700

Other offices:
European Council of International Schools PO Box 6066, 28080 Madrid, Spain; tel: +34 91 562 6722; fax: +34 91 745 1310; e-mail: ecismadrid@ecis.org
European Council of International Schools 105 Tuxford Terrace, Basking Ridge, NJ 07920, USA; tel: +1 908 903 0552; fax: +1 908 480 9381; e-mail: malyecisna@aol.com
European Council of International Schools Cumburri IEC, PO Box 367, Kilmore 3764, Victoria, Australia; tel: +61 35 781 1351; fax: +61 35 781 1151

EUROPEAN COUNCIL OF OPTOMETRY AND OPTICS

Acronym or abbreviation: ECOO

61 Southwark Street, London, SE1 0HL

Tel: 020 7928 9269
Fax: 020 7261 0228
E-mail: richardecoo@aop.org.uk

Enquiries:
Enquiries to: Secretary General

Founded:
1992

Formerly called:
GOOMAC, PEG

Organisation type and purpose:
Professional body.

Subject coverage:
Optometry, optics, eyecare, optical appliances, eye conditions and examinations, co-operation with ophthalmology.

Access to staff:
Contact by letter
Hours: Mon to Fri, 0900 to 1700

EUROPEAN DESIGN CENTRE, WALSALL COLLEGE OF ARTS AND TECHNOLOGY

St Pauls Street, Walsall, West Midlands, WS1 1XN

Tel: 01922 657000
Fax: 01922 657083
E-mail: j.pearson@walcat.ac.uk

Website:
http://www.walcat.ac.uk/

Enquiries:
Enquiries to: Library Manager
Direct tel: ext 7078

Organisation type and purpose:
training organisation.

Subject coverage:
Engineering: mechanical, production, electronic; building; business studies; catering; community care; hair and beauty; robotics, CADCAM; leisure and tourism; computing; creative arts; design; performing arts; GCSE; A levels; management; accounts and law; photography; languages; humanities; teacher training; counselling; adult education and return to learn; access to HE; motor vehicle; science; painting and decorating; interior design and soft furnishing.

Non-library collection catalogue:
All or part available online

Library catalogue:
All or part available online

Access to staff:
Contact by e-mail
Hours: Term time: Mon to Thu, 0900 to 2200; Fri, 0945 to 1630; Sat, 0930 to 1230, 1300 to 1530.
Vacations: Mon to Fri, 0900 to 1630
Special comments: There is a small charge for computer usage for non-members.

Access for disabled people:
Parking provided, ramped entry, toilet facilities

EUROPEAN DOCUMENTATION CENTRE – COVENTRY UNIVERSITY

Acronym or abbreviation: EDC

Lanchester Library, Gosford Street, Coventry, Warwickshire, CV1 5DD

Tel: 024 7688 7541
Fax: 024 7688 7525
E-mail: lbx203@coventry.ac.uk

Website:
http://www.coventry.ac.uk

Enquiries:
Enquiries to: EDC Librarian

Organisation type and purpose:
University library.

Subject coverage:
European Union.

Trade and statistical information:
Eurostats.

Library catalogue:
All or part available online

Access to staff:
Contact by letter, by telephone, by fax, by e-mail, in person and via website
Hours: Term-time: Mon to Thu, 0845 to 2045; Fri, 1000 to 1715; Sat, 1000 to 1700; Sun, 1300 to 1700
Vacations: Mon to Fri, 0900 to 1715

Access for disabled people:
Level entry, access to all public areas, toilet facilities, parking

EUROPEAN DOCUMENTATION CENTRE – DURHAM UNIVERSITY

Acronym or abbreviation: EDC

Official Publications Collection, Durham University Library, Stockton Road, Durham, DH1 3LY

Tel: 0191 334 2944
Fax: 0191 334 2971
E-mail: n.p.davies@durham.ac.uk

Website:
http://www.dur.ac.uk/library/resources/european/edc

Enquiries:
Enquiries to: European Documentation Officer

Founded:
1969

Organisation type and purpose:
University library.

Subject coverage:
European Communities legislation; preparing legislation; statistical material, background information; reports and periodicals; information on EC grants and loans; UK government publications in all fields.

Non-library collection catalogue:
All or part available online and in-house

Printed publications:
Documentation notes (occasional series)
Guide

Publications list:
Available in print

Access to staff:
Contact by letter, by telephone and by e-mail.
Appointment necessary.
Hours: Mon to Fri, 0900 to 1700 (staffed)
Special comments: For unstaffed access, see Durham University opening hours online

Access for disabled people:
Level entry, access to all public areas, toilet facilities

EUROPEAN DOCUMENTATION CENTRE – UNIVERSITY OF CAMBRIDGE

Acronym or abbreviation: EDC

Cambridge University Library, West Road, Cambridge, CB3 9DR

Tel: 01223 333138
Fax: 01223 333160
E-mail: wani000@cam.ac.uk

Enquiries:
Enquiries to: Under-Librarian

Founded:
1963

Organisation type and purpose:
University library.

Subject coverage:
All subjects.

Museum or gallery collection, archive, or library special collection:
Council of Europe publications
EU Publications
ECE publications
EFTA publications
NATO publications
Nordic Council publications
OECD publications
OSCE publications
Very many in the rest of the library

Trade and statistical information:
Worldwide collection of statistical abstracts, EC statistics, UN statistics.

Library catalogue:
All or part available online

Access to staff:
Contact by letter, by telephone, by fax and by e-mail. Appointment necessary. Letter of introduction required.
Hours: Mon to Fri, 0930 to 1845; Sat, 0930 to 1245

Access for disabled people:
Parking provided, ramped entry, access to all public areas, toilet facilities

EUROPEAN DOCUMENTATION CENTRE – UNIVERSITY OF DUNDEE

Acronym or abbreviation: EDC

Law Library, Scrymgeour Building, Park Place, Dundee, DD1 4HN

Tel: 01382 384101
Fax: 01382 381019
E-mail: e.mccubbin@dundee.ac.uk

Website:
http://www.dundee.ac.uk/edc
General information on holdings of the EDC, and classification list. Links to all EU institutions and agencies; links to related and non-EU sites.

Enquiries:
Enquiries to: Senior Assistant Librarian

Founded:
1972

Organisation type and purpose:
University library.
To promote and consolidate studies and research in European Union matters, particularly European legislation; to make the policies of the EU known to citizens.

Subject coverage:
Legislation of the European Union, via the Official Journal and websites. General information on all institutions and agencies of the EU.

Museum or gallery collection, archive, or library special collection:
Official documentation of the institutions of the European Communities, reports and studies

Non-library collection catalogue:
All or part available online

Library catalogue:
All or part available online

Access to staff:
Contact by letter, by telephone, by fax, by e-mail, in person and via website
Hours: Term time: Mon to Fri, 0900 to 2200; Sat, 1200 to 1700; Sun, 1200 to 1900
Vacations: Mon to Fri, 0900 to 1700

Access to building, collection or gallery:
No prior appointment required

Member organisation of:
European Information Association (EIA)
Central Library, St Peter's Square, Manchester, M2 5PD; tel: 0161 228 3691; fax: 0161 236 6547; e-mail: eia@manchester.gov.uk

Parent body:
University of Dundee
Perth Road, Dundee, DD1 4HN; tel: 01382 383000; fax: 01382 201604; e-mail: university@dundee.ac.uk; website: http://www.dundee.ac.uk

EUROPEAN DOCUMENTATION CENTRE – UNIVERSITY OF ESSEX

Acronym or abbreviation: EDC

Albert Sloman Library, University of Essex, PO Box 24, Colchester, Essex, CO4 3UA

Tel: 01206 873333
Fax: 01206 873598

Website:
http://libwww.essex.ac.uk/

Subject access to Internet resource; connections to other library catalogues and WWW servers; access to NISS, BUBL and a number of databases; text of various library guides.

Enquiries:
Enquiries to: EDC Librarian
Direct tel: 01206 873181
Direct fax: 01206 872289

Founded:
1976

Organisation type and purpose:
University library.

Subject coverage:
Specialised EDC, concentrating on social and economic affairs.

Trade and statistical information:
UK and EC trade statistics.

Library catalogue:
All or part available online

Access to staff:
Contact by letter, by telephone, by fax and by e-mail. Appointment necessary.
Hours: Term time: Mon to Fri, 0900 to 2000; Sat, 0900 to 1800; Sun, 1400 to 1900

Access for disabled people:
Access to all public areas, toilet facilities

EUROPEAN DOCUMENTATION CENTRES

Organisation type and purpose:
European Documentation Centres (EDCs) are set up to stimulate European awareness and the study of Europe in academic institutions. They hold copies of all documentation on the Community legislative process that has been published by the European Commission. In addition they hold preparatory documents and reports from the Commission, European Parliament and Economic and Social Committee. They do not hold stocks of documents for sale. Some produce guides and bulletins.

Contacts:
Aberdeen
Aberdeen University, Taylor Library, Dunbar Street, Aberdeen, AB9 2UE; tel: 01224 273819; fax: 01224 273819; e-mail: e.a.mackie@abdn.ac.uk
Aberystwyth
University of Wales, The Library, Hugh Owen Building, Penglais Campus, Aberystwyth, SY23 3DZ; tel: 01970 622401; fax: 01970 622404; e-mail: llis@aber.ac.uk
Ashford
Wye College, The Library, Wye, Ashford, Kent, TN25 5AH; tel: 01223 812401 ext 512; fax: 01223 813320; e-mail: w.sage@wye.ac.uk
Bath
Bath University, University Library, Claverton Down, Bath, BA2 7AY; tel: 01225 826826 ext 5594; fax: 01225 826229; e-mail: a.holbrook@bath.ac.uk
Belfast
Queen's University of Belfast, Main Library, Belfast, BT7 1LS; tel: 028 9024 5133 ext 3605; fax: 028 9032 3340; e-mail: a.mcmillan@qub.ac.uk
Birmingham
Birmingham University, Main Library, Edgbaston, Birmingham, B15 2TT; tel: 0121 414 7574 or 6570; fax: 0121 471 4691; e-mail: p.a.robinson@bham.ac.uk
Birmingham
University of Central England in Birmingham, William Kendrick Library, Perry Bar, Birmingham, B42 2SU; tel: 0121 331 5298; fax: 0121 356 2875; e-mail: linda.garratt@uce.ac.uk
Bradford
Bradford University, J B Priestley Library, Richmond Road, Bradford, West Yorkshire, BD7 1DP; tel: 01274 383402; fax: 01274 383398; e-mail: g.l.hudson@bradford.ac.uk

Brighton
University of Sussex, Library Information Services, Falmer, Brighton, East Sussex, BN1 9QL; tel: 01273 678159; fax: 01273 678441; e-mail: library@sussex.ac.uk
Bristol
Bristol University, Wills Memorial Library, Queen's Road, Bristol, BS8 1RJ; tel: 0117 928 7944; fax: 0117 925 1870; e-mail: sue.pettit@bristol.ac.uk
Cambridge
Cambridge University, University Library, West Road, Cambridge, CB3 9DR; tel: 01223 333138; fax: 01223 333160; e-mail: wan@ula.cam.ac.uk
Canterbury
University of Kent, Templeman Library, Canterbury, CT2 7NU; tel: 01227 764000 ext 3111; fax: 01227 823984; e-mail: s.h.carter@ukc.ac.uk
Cardiff
UWCC, The Guest Library, PO Box 430, Cardiff, CF1 3XT; tel: 029 2087 4262; fax: 029 2022 9340; e-mail: edc@cardiff.ac.uk and thomson@cardiff.ac.uk
Colchester
University of Essex, Albert Sloman Library, PO Box 24, Colchester, CO4 3UA; tel: 01206 873181; fax: 01206 872289; e-mail: helenb@essex.ac.uk
Coleraine
University of Ulster, The Library, Cromore Road, Coleraine, Co Londonderry, BT52 1SA; tel: 028 9132 4029; fax: 028 9132 4928; e-mail: p.j.compton@ulst.ac.uk
Coventry
University of Warwick, The Library, Gibbet Hill Road, Coventry, CV4 7AL; tel: 024 7652 3523 ext 2041; fax: 024 7652 4211; e-mail: j.bennett@warwick.ac.uk
Coventry
Coventry University, The Lanchester Library, Much Park Street, Coventry, CV1 2HF; tel: 024 7683 8295; fax: 024 7683 8686; e-mail: lbx029@coventry.ac.uk
Dundee
Dundee University, The Law Library, Perth Road, Dundee, DD1 4HN; tel: 01382 344102; fax: 01382 228669; e-mail: a.duncan@dundee.ac.uk
Durham
Durham University, The University Library, Stockton Road, Durham, DH1 3LY; tel: 0191 374 3041/3044; fax: 0191 374 7481; e-mail: r.l.caddel@durham.ac.uk
Edinburgh
Edinburgh University, Europa Library, Old College, South Bridge, Edinburgh, EH8 9YL; tel: 0131 650 2041; fax: 0131 650 6343; e-mail: kdt@festival.ed.ac.uk
Exeter
Exeter University, Law Library, Amory Building, Rennes Drive, Exeter, EX4 4RL; tel: 01392 263356; fax: 01392 263196; e-mail: p.c.overy@exeter.ac.uk
Glasgow
Glasgow University, University Library, Hillhead Street, Glasgow, G12 8QE; tel: 0141 330 6722; fax: 0141 330 4952; e-mail: gxlr30@lib.gla.ac.uk
Guildford
Surrey University, George Edwards Library, Guildford, Surrey, GU2 5XH; tel: 01483 259233; fax: 01483 259500; e-mail: s.telfer@surrey.ac.uk
Hull
Hull University, Brynmor Jones Library, Cottingham Road, Hull, HU6 7RX; tel: 01482 465941; fax: 01482 466205; e-mail: w.m.carroll@lib.hull.ac.uk or e.b.davies@lib.hull.ac.uk
Keele
Keele University, Library, Keele, Staffordshire, ST5 5BG; tel: 01782 583283; fax: 01782 711553; e-mail: b.g.finnemore@cc.keele.ac.uk
Lancaster
Lancaster University, The Library, Bailrigg, Lancaster, LA1 4YH; tel: 01524 65201; fax: 01524 63806; e-mail: m.dunne@lancaster.ac.uk
Leeds
Leeds University, Faculty of Law Library, 20 Lydon Terrace, Leeds, LS2 9JT; tel: 0113 233 5040; fax: 0113 233 5561; e-mail: j.m.porter@leeds.ac.uk

continued overleaf

Leeds
  Leeds Metropolitan University, Calverley Street,
  Leeds, LS1 3HE; tel: 0113 283 3126; fax: 0113 283
  3123; e-mail: m.message@lmu.ac.uk
Leicester
  Leicester University, Library, University Road,
  Leicester, LE1 9RH; tel: 0116 252 2044; fax: 0116
  252 2066; e-mail: arsi@leic.ac.uk
London
  London School of Economics and Political
  Science, British Library of Political and Economic
  Science, 10 Portugal Street, London, WC2A 2HD;
  tel: 020 7955 7273 or 7229; fax: 020 7955 7454; e-
  mail: f.m.shipsey@lse.ac.uk
London
  University of London, Queen Mary and
  Westfield College Library, Mile End Road,
  London, E1 4NS; tel: 020 7775 3321; fax: 020 7981
  0028; e-mail: r.d.burns@qmw.ac.uk
Loughborough
  Loughborough University, Pilkington Library,
  Loughborough, Leicestershire, LE11 3TU; tel:
  01509 222352 or 222343; fax: 01509 234806; e-
  mail: l.a.mcgarry@lut.ac.uk
Manchester
  Manchester University, John Rylands University
  Library, Oxford Road, Manchester, M13 9PP; tel:
  0161 275 3770; fax: 0161 273 7488; e-mail: h.j
  .blackhurst@man.ac.uk
Newcastle
  University of Northumbria at Newcastle, The
  City Campus Library, Ellison Place, Newcastle
  upon Tyne, NE1 8ST; tel: 0191 227 4136; fax: 0191
  2274563; e-mail: maimie.balfour@unn.ac.uk
Norwich
  University of East Anglia, University Library,
  University Plain, Norwich, Norfolk, NR4 7TJ; tel:
  01603 592412; fax: 01603 259490 (Library)
Nottingham
  Nottingham University, Hallward Library,
  Nottingham, NG7 2RD; tel: 0115 951 4579; fax:
  0115 951 4558; e-mail: susan.heaster@nottingham
  .ac.uk
Oxford
  Oxford University, Bodleian Law Library, St
  Cross Building, Oxford, OX1 3UR; tel: 01865
  271463; fax: 01865 271475; e-mail: elizabeth
  .martin@bodley.ox.ac.uk
Portsmouth
  Portsmouth University, The Frewen Library,
  Cambridge Road, Portsmouth, PO1 2ST; tel: 023
  9284 3239; fax: 023 9284 3233; e-mail: mayfield@
  libr.port.ac.uk
Reading
  Reading University, The Library, Whiteknights,
  PO Box 223, Reading, RG6 6AE; tel: 0118 931
  8782; fax: 0118 931 2335; e-mail: vlsedc@reading
  .ac.uk
Salford
  Salford University, The Library, Academic
  Information Servcies, Salford, M5 4WT; tel: 0161
  745 5846; fax: 0161 745 5888; e-mail: j.m.wilson@
  als.salford.ac.uk
Sheffield
  Sheffield Hallam University, The Library, Pond
  Street, Sheffield, S1 1WB; tel: 0114 253 2126; fax:
  0114 253 2125; e-mail: g.h.wills@shu.ac.uk
Southampton
  Southampton University, Hartley Library,
  Southampton, SO9 5NH; tel: 023 8059 3451; fax:
  023 8059 3939; e-mail: rfy@soton.ac.uk
Wolverhampton
  Wolverhampton University, Robert Scott Library,
  St Peter's Square, Wolverhampton, West
  Midlands, WV1 1RH; tel: 01902 322300; fax:
  01902 322668; e-mail: a.edwards@wlv.ac.uk

EUROPEAN FEDERATION OF FOUNDATION CONTRACTORS

Acronym or abbreviation: EFFC

Forum Court, 83 Copers Cope Road, Beckenham,
Kent, BR3 1NR

Tel: 020 8663 0948
Fax: 020 8663 0949
E-mail: effc@effc.org

Website:
http://www.effc.org

Enquiries:
Enquiries to: Secretary

Founded:
1988

Organisation type and purpose:
International organisation, trade association
(membership is by qualification), present number
of members: 17 countries, 350 companies.

Access to staff:
Contact by letter, by telephone, by fax and by e-
mail
Hours: Mon to Fri, 0900 to 1700

EUROPEAN FITTINGS MANUFACTURERS ASSOCIATION

Acronym or abbreviation: EFMA

55 Bryanston Street, London, W1H 7AJ

Tel: 020 7868 8930
Fax: 020 7868 8819
E-mail: markl@coppercouncil.org

Enquiries:
Enquiries to: Secretary

Formerly called:
European Capillary Fittings Manufacturers
Association (ECFMA)

Organisation type and purpose:
International organisation, trade association,
present number of members: 4.

Access to staff:
Contact by letter, by telephone, by fax and by e-
mail. Appointment necessary. Access for members
only.
Hours: Mon to Fri, 0900 to 1700

EUROPEAN FLEXIBLE INTERMEDIATE BULK CONTAINER ASSOCIATION

Acronym or abbreviation: EFIBCA

18 Wellesley Road, Colchester, Essex, CO3 3HF

Tel: 01206 575584
Fax: 01206 575584
E-mail: efibca@aspects.net

Website:
http://www.efibca.com

Enquiries:
Enquiries to: Director General

Founded:
1983

Organisation type and purpose:
Trade association (membership is by qualification),
present number of members: 36.

Subject coverage:
Flexible intermediate bulk containers.

Printed publications:
Safe Use of Flexible Intermediate Bulk Containers
  (FIBCs, Issue 2, 2002, £5)

Access to staff:
Contact by letter, by telephone, by fax and by e-
mail
Hours: Mon to Fri, 0900 to 1700

EUROPEAN FOODSERVICE EQUIPMENT DISTRIBUTORS ASSOCIATION

Acronym or abbreviation: EFEDA

Orbital House, 85 Croydon Road, Caterham,
Surrey, CR3 6PD

Tel: 01883 334487
Fax: 01883 334490
E-mail: efeda@admin.co.uk

Website:
http://www.efeda.org
Web page.

Enquiries:
Enquiries to: Secretary

Founded:
1990

Organisation type and purpose:
Trade association (membership is by subscription).
Organises an annual international conference
around Europe.

Subject coverage:
Standards and approvals for foodservice
equipment, directives on quality standards and
approvals, customer service and liaison between
distributors and their principals.

Printed publications:
EFEDA Guidebook for admission to the Market of
  Foodservice Equipment in the European Union
  (£40)
EFEDA Directory – list of members

Access to staff:
Contact by letter, by telephone and by fax
Hours: Mon to Fri, 0900 to 1700

Access to building, collection or gallery:
Prior appointment required

Access for disabled people:
Level entry

Affiliated to:
Allied Association of North American Association
of Food Equipment Manufacturers (NAFEM)
National Association of Food Equipment Suppliers
(Australia) (NAFES)

Liaison with:
European Federation of Catering Equipment
Manufacturers (EFCEM)
Foodservice Consultants Society International
(Europe) (FCSI)

EUROPEAN GENERAL GALVANIZERS ASSOCIATION

Acronym or abbreviation: EGGA

Maybrook House, 97 Godstone Road, Caterham,
Surrey, CR3 6RE

Tel: 01883 331277
Fax: 01883 331287
E-mail: mail@egga.com

Website:
http://www.egga.com
Newsletter and information

Enquiries:
Enquiries to: Director

Organisation type and purpose:
Trade association.

Subject coverage:
Galvanizing.

Printed publications:
Conference proceedings vols available
International Galvanizing

Access to staff:
Contact by letter, by fax and by e-mail
Hours: Mon to Fri, 0830 to 1630

EUROPEAN GUILD

Acronym or abbreviation: Euroguild

Media House, 11b High Street, Sandbach,
Cheshire, CW11 1HH

Tel: 01270 753133
Fax: 01270 753444
E-mail: europeanguild@tesco.net

Enquiries:
Enquiries to: Administrator
Direct tel: 01270 753444

Founded:
1988

Formerly called:
European Guild of Media and Marketing,
European Guild of Sales and Marketing

Organisation type and purpose:
International organisation, membership
association (membership is by subscription),
service industry, training organisation,
consultancy, research organisation.
Support to develop new projects in Europe with
PR, VT production and in rare cases sponsorship,
TV, radio, newspapers, tourism attractions, music,
art.

Subject coverage:
Radio development, applications for licence etc,
design and production of tourist attractions, voice/
over production (in-house), VT production, public
relations, tourism development.

Printed publications:
Various available on request

Electronic and video publications:
Tape, Disk, CD-ROM, Video for purchase

Access to staff:
Contact by letter, by telephone, by fax and by e-
mail. Letter of introduction required.
Hours: Mon to Fri, 0930 to 1700
Special comments: A charge of £10 per hour or 17
Euros may apply for certain assistance.

Access to building, collection or gallery:
Prior appointment required

EUROPEAN INFORMATION ASSOCIATION

Acronym or abbreviation: EIA

Central Library, St Peter's Square, Manchester, M2
5PD

Tel: 0161 228 3691
Fax: 0161 236 6547
E-mail: eia@libraries.manchester.gov.uk

Website:
http://www.eia.org.uk
Information about EIA's products and services.
Includes up-to-date news about the EU and a
currency converter.

Founded:
1980

Formerly called:
Association of European Documentation Centre
Librarians (year of change 1991)

Organisation type and purpose:
Membership association (membership is by
subscription), present number of members: 500,
registered charity (charity number 294502).
To assist information workers dealing with
European information to network, share
experience and train. To improve EU information
provision.

Subject coverage:
The European Union, its policies and legislative
process.

Publications list:
Available online and in print

Access to staff:
Contact by letter, by telephone, by fax, by e-mail
and via website. Access for members only.
Hours: Mon to Fri, 0900 to 1700
Special comments: Please phone before personal
visits.

EUROPEAN INFORMATION CENTRE, BRISTOL

Acronym or abbreviation: EIC

Bristol Chamber of Commerce, 16 Clifton Park,
Bristol, BS8 3BY

Tel: 0117 973 7373
Fax: 0117 923 8024
E-mail: eic@businesswest.co.uk

Enquiries:
Enquiries to: Manager

Organisation type and purpose:
Membership association.

Subject coverage:
European Community, Single Market legislation;
export and EC sales development; company
information, producers, suppliers distributors; EC
funding; co-operation and business opportunities.

Trade and statistical information:
EC and world trade statistics.

Access to staff:
Appointment necessary.
Hours: Mon to Fri, 0900 to 1700

Parent body:
Bristol Chamber of Commerce

EUROPEAN INFORMATION CENTRES FOR RURAL AREAS

Subject coverage:
Provide information on EU measures affecting
rural society, and encourage dialogue, partnership
and cooperation between members of rural society
and regions on common problems.

England:
Euro Info Centre
  Preston, Lancashire; tel: 01995 601207
Euro Info Centre
  Cirencester, Gloucestershire; tel: 01285 653477

Northern Ireland:
Euro Info Centre
  Clogher; tel: 028 8254 9438

Wales:
Euro Info Centre
  Llangefni, Anglesey; tel: 01248 752491
Euro Info Centre
  Carmarthen; tel: 01267 233333

EUROPEAN INSTITUTE OF GOLF COURSE ARCHITECTS

Acronym or abbreviation: EIGCA

Meadow View House, Tannery Lane, Bramley,
Surrey, GU5 0AJ

Tel: 01483 891831
Fax: 01483 891846
E-mail: info@eigca.org

Website:
http://www.eigca.org
Golf course architecture, membership services/
directory, journal.

Enquiries:
Enquiries to: Executive Officer

Founded:
2000

Formed by the merger of:
British Institute of Golf Course Architects (BIGCA),
Association Française des Architectes de Golf
(AFAG), European Society of Golf Architects
(ESGA) (year of change 2000)

Formerly called:
British Association of Golf Course Architects
(BAGCA)

Organisation type and purpose:
International organisation, advisory body,
professional body (membership is by subscription,
qualification, election or invitation), present
number of members: 133, training organisation,
consultancy.

Subject coverage:
Design of golf courses.

Non-library collection catalogue:
All or part available online

Library catalogue:
All or part available online

Printed publications:
Membership Yearbook
Information leaflets

Publications list:
Available online and in print

Access to staff:
Contact by letter, by telephone, by fax, by e-mail
and via website. Appointment necessary.
Hours: Mon to Fri, 0930 to 1430

Access to building, collection or gallery:
Prior appointment required

EUROPEAN LEAD SHEET INDUSTRY ASSOCIATION

Acronym or abbreviation: ELSIA

c/o 17a Welbeck Way, London, W1G 9YJ

Tel: 020 7499 8422
Fax: 020 7493 1555
E-mail: enq@elsia.org

Enquiries:
Enquiries to: Administrator

Founded:
1985

Organisation type and purpose:
Trade association.

Subject coverage:
Applications and specifications of rolled lead sheet
in the construction industry.

Access to staff:
Contact by letter, by telephone and by fax.
Appointment necessary.
Hours: Mon to Fri, 0900 to 1700

EUROPEAN LEISURE SOFTWARE PUBLISHERS ASSOCIATION

Acronym or abbreviation: ELSPA

Station Road, Offenham, Evesham, Worcestershire,
WR11 8JJ

Tel: 01386 830642
Fax: 01386 833871
E-mail: info@elspa.com

Website:
http://www.elspa.com

Enquiries:
Enquiries to: Deputy Director General
Direct tel: 01386 835811
Direct e-mail: michael.rawlinson@elspa.com

Organisation type and purpose:
Trade association.

Subject coverage:
Publishing and development of computer and
video games.

Trade and statistical information:
Sales data for computer and video games.

Printed publications:
European Leisure Software Yearbook (available to
  purchase)

Access to staff:
Contact by letter, by telephone, by fax and by e-
mail
Hours: Mon to Fri, 0900 to 1700

EUROPEAN LIQUID WATERPROOFING ASSOCIATION

Acronym or abbreviation: ELWA

Fields House, Gower Road, Haywards Heath, West
Sussex, RH16 4PL

Tel: 01444 417458
Fax: 01444 415616
E-mail: info@elwassociation.org.uk

continued overleaf

Website:
http://www.elwassociation.org.uk
List of members.

Enquiries:
Enquiries to: Secretary

Founded:
1979

Formerly called:
Bituminous Roof Coatings Manufacturers
Association; European Liquid Roofing Association

Organisation type and purpose:
Trade association.
Seeks to raise the level of awareness of the
technical and financial benefits of specifying liquid
waterproofing systems and to establish product
and installation standards.

Subject coverage:
Bituminous and polymer-based waterproofing
membranes, codes of practice, installation,
specification and application.

Printed publications:
Code of Practice – Liquid Waterproofing
Membranes (free of charge)

Access to staff:
Contact by letter, by telephone, by fax, by e-mail
and via website
Hours: Mon to Fri, 0900 to 1700

Affiliated to:
Flat Roofing Alliance (FRA)
Fields House, Gower Road, Haywards Heath,
West Sussex, RH16 4PL; tel: 01444 440027; fax:
01444 415616

EUROPEAN MARKETING SYSTEMS

Acronym or abbreviation: EMS

100 New Kings Road, London, SW6 4LX

Tel: 020 7736 0350
E-mail: ems@emsbase.co.uk

Website:
http://www.emsbase.co.uk

Enquiries:
Enquiries to: Managing Director

Founded:
1991

Organisation type and purpose:
Service industry, consultancy.
Database agency for corporate marketing.

Subject coverage:
Corporate data for marketing to the UK and
Europe, Central and Eastern Europe, energy and
environmental industries and financial sectors,
telecoms and IT sectors, government and EU across
Europe.

**Museum or gallery collection, archive, or library
special collection:**
News extracts on Central and Eastern Europe
(1989 to date)

Electronic and video publications:
E-LIST – 12,000 contacts involved in e-commerce
CITY LIST & OFFSHORE – 16,000 financial and
banking contacts in Europe
EASTBASE – database of 15,000 contacts trading in
or with Central and Eastern Europe
ENERGY – 8000 contacts in oil, gas, renewable,
nuclear & energy industries, carbon exchange,
NGOs & regulators
EUROBASE – companies and organisations that
are active on a national or transnational scale,
use English as a commercial language, are of a
size or standing to be essential commercial
prospects
EUROPEAN GOVERNMENT – database of over
20,000 Ministries, Embassies, EU and public
offices
TELEBASE – database of 10,000 IT/Telecoms
contacts in the commercial sector

The Green Route (EUROGREEN) – database of
29,000 organisations with an interest in
environmental issues

Publications list:
Available in print

Access to staff:
Contact by letter, by telephone, by e-mail and via
website. Appointment necessary.
Hours: Mon to Fri, 0900 to 1800 (24-hr
answerphone)

Subsidiary body:
EPIC books

EUROPEAN MOVEMENT (SCOTTISH COUNCIL)

12B Cumberland Street, South East Lane,
Edinburgh, EH3 6RU

Tel: 0131 557 9790
Fax: 0131 557 9790
E-mail: scotland@euromove.org.uk

Enquiries:
Enquiries to: National Organiser

Founded:
1990

Organisation type and purpose:
International organisation, membership
association (membership is by subscription),
present number of members: 430, voluntary
organisation.
Independent, cross-party, membership
organisation which believes in European unity and
seeks to ensure that Scotland's interests are
safeguarded and developed as Europe evolves.

Subject coverage:
The European Union, Europe, information and
activities for schools and universities. Visiting
speakers including senior European figures. Study
visits to Europe. Annual conference and dinner.
Links with other national and international
councils. Regular newsletters and information
packs.

Access to staff:
Contact by letter, by telephone, by fax and by e-
mail
Hours: Tue to Thu, 0900 to 1600

EUROPEAN ORTHODONTIC SOCIETY

Acronym or abbreviation: EOS

Flat 20, 49 Hallam Street, London, W1W 6JN

Tel: 020 7637 0367
Fax: 020 7637 0367
E-mail: eoslondon@aol.com

Enquiries:
Enquiries to: Honorary Secretary

Founded:
1907

Organisation type and purpose:
International organisation, professional body
(membership is by subscription), registered charity
(charity number 238836), training organisation,
research organisation.

Subject coverage:
Orthodontics, orthodontic services in Europe.

Printed publications:
European Journal of Orthodontics (6 times a year,
OUP)

Electronic and video publications:
Asksam list of orthodontic literature

Publications list:
Available in print

Access to staff:
Contact by letter, by telephone, by fax and by e-
mail
Hours: Mon to Fri, 0900 to 1700

EUROPEAN PARLIAMENT UK OFFICE

2 Queen Anne's Gate, London, SW1H 9AA

Tel: 020 7227 4300
Fax: 020 7227 4302
E-mail: eplondon@europarl.europa.eu

Website:
http://www.europarl.org.uk
http://www.europarl.europa.eu
EUROPARL database.

Enquiries:
Enquiries to: Librarian
Direct fax: 020 7227 4301

Organisation type and purpose:
European institution, European Parliament press
and information office.

Subject coverage:
Reports, debates and minutes of the European
Parliament, EP activities in Committee and
elsewhere, election results and systems for the EP
elections.

**Museum or gallery collection, archive, or library
special collection:**
EP reports from 1979, debates and minutes from
1973

Printed publications:
The European Parliament and Business (2003)
The Future Enlargement of the European Union
(2002)
The European Parliament and the Environment
(2002)
The European Parliament and Young People (2002)
The European Parliament and Your MEPs (2003)
EU MAP: European elections 10 June 2004 (2002)
The Eight Scottish MEPs and the European
Parliament (1999)
The Right to Petition the European Parliament

Electronic and video publications:
The European Parliament and Business (2003)
The Future Enlargement of the European Union
(2002)
The European Parliament and the Environment
(2002)
The European Parliament and Young People (2002)
The European Parliament and Your MEPs (2003)
EU MAP: European elections 10 June 2004 (2002)
The Right to Petition the European Parliament

Publications list:
Available online and in print

Access to staff:
Contact by letter, by telephone, by fax, by e-mail
and in person
Hours: Mon to Fri, 1000 to 1300, 1400 to 1730

EUROPEAN PHENOLIC FOAM ASSOCIATION

Acronym or abbreviation: EPFA

Tournai Hall, Evelyn Woods Road, Aldershot
Hampshire GU11 2LL

Tel: 01252 357837
Fax: 01252 357831
E-mail: admin@epfa.org.uk

Website:
http://www.epfa.org.uk

Enquiries:
Enquiries to: Honorary Secretary

Founded:
before 1989

Formerly called:
Phenolic Foam Manufacturers Association (PFMA)

Organisation type and purpose:
Trade association, present number of members: 8.
Members all share an interest in phenolic foam
products, either as producers or as providers of
raw materials.

Subject coverage:
Phenolic foam in insulation applications, its use based on the technical data available especially that relating to performance in fire.

Printed publications:
Several data sheets on the use of phenolic foam

Publications list:
Available online and in print

Access to staff:
Contact by letter, by telephone, by fax, by e-mail and via website
Hours: Mon to Fri, 0900 to 1700

EUROPEAN PIANO TEACHERS' ASSOCIATION, UK LIMITED

Acronym or abbreviation: EPTA UK

35 The Warren, Burgess Hill, West Sussex, RH15 0DU

Tel: 08456 581054
Fax: 08456 581054
E-mail: admin@epta-uk.org

Website:
http://www.epta-uk.org
Membership, Piano Professional, events.

Enquiries:
Enquiries to: Administrator
Other contacts: Chairman for policy matters.

Founded:
1978

Organisation type and purpose:
International organisation, membership association (membership is by election or invitation), registered charity (charity number 293698), suitable for ages: 6+.

Subject coverage:
Piano teaching and performance.

Museum or gallery collection, archive, or library special collection:
Extensive collection of audio and video tapes, books and other printed matter available for reference by members only

Printed publications:
Members' Handbook (annually, free to members, others £4 per copy)
Piano Professional (3 times a year, free to members, others £3.75 per issue)

Electronic and video publications:
Membership list (for purchase, members only)

Publications list:
Available in print

Access to staff:
Contact by letter, by telephone, by fax and by e-mail
Hours: Mon to Fri, 0900 to 1700

Access to building, collection or gallery:
Prior appointment required

Has:
31 Regional Organisers

Members reference collection:
Piano Teachers Information Centre
London College of Music, St Mary's Road, Ealing, London, W5 5RF; tel: 020 8231 2648

Parent body:
European Piano Teachers' Association
Secretary, 34 Carver Road, London, SE24 9LT; tel: 020 7274 6821; fax: 020 7737 5015

EUROPEAN POLICY FORUM LIMITED

125 Pall Mall, London, SW1Y 5EA

Tel: 020 7839 7565
Fax: 020 7839 7339
E-mail: epfltd@compuserve.com

Website:
http://www.epfltd.org

Enquiries:
Enquiries to: President

Founded:
1992

Organisation type and purpose:
Research organisation.
International research institute.

Printed publications:
For purchase only

Publications list:
Available in print

Access to staff:
Contact by letter, by telephone, by fax, by e-mail and via website. Appointment necessary.
Hours: Mon to Fri, 0900 to 1700

Access to building, collection or gallery:
No prior appointment required

EUROPEAN PUBLIC INFORMATION RELAYS

Organisation type and purpose:
Based in public libraries to provide the general public with access to information about EU policies and programmes.

England East Midlands:
Chesterfield
 tel: 01246 209292
Derby
 tel: 01332 255398
Grimsby
 tel: 01472 323600
Leicester
 tel: 0116 255 6699
Lincoln
 tel: 01522 549160
Matlock
 Derbyshire; tel: 01629 580000 ext 6578
Northampton
 tel: 01604 30404
Nottingham
 tel: 0115 941 2121
Oakham
 Rutland; tel: 01572 723654
Scarborough
 tel: 01724 860161

England Eastern:
Bedford
 tel: 01234 350931
Cambridge
 tel: 01223 712017
Chelmsford
 tel: 01245 492758
Dunstable
 tel: 01582 477073
Hatfield
 tel: 01707 281558
Ipswich
 tel: 01473 583705
King's Lynn
 tel: 01553 772568 or 761393
Luton
 tel: 01582 454580
Norwich
 Norfolk; tel: 01603 215255
Peterborough
 tel: 01733 348343

England Greater London:
Barking
 tel: 020 8517 8666
Battersea
 tel: 020 8871 7467
Bexley Heath
 tel: 020 8301 5151
Brixton
 tel: 020 7926 1067
Bromley
 Kent; tel: 020 8460 9955 ext 250
City
 tel: 020 7638 8215

Croydon
 tel: 020 8760 5400
Ealing
 tel: 020 8567 3656
Elephant & Castle
 tel: 020 7708 0516
Enfield
 tel: 020 8443 1701
Hackney
 tel: 020 8525 2576
Hammersmith
 tel: 020 8576 5053
Harringay
 tel: 020 8365 1155
Harrow
 tel: 020 8424 1055/6
Hendon
 tel: 020 8359 2883
Highbury
 tel: 020 7619 6931
Ilford
 tel: 020 8478 7145 ext 222
Kensington
 tel: 020 7937 2542
Kingston
 tel: 020 8547 6425
Lewisham
 tel: 020 8297 9430
Marylebone
 tel: 020 7641 1039
Morden
 tel: 020 8545 4089
Richmond
 tel: 020 8940 5529
Romford
 Essex; tel: 01708 772393/4
Stratford
 tel: 020 8519 6346
Sutton
 Surrey; tel: 020 8770 4785
Swiss Cottage
 London; tel: 020 7413 6527
Uxbridge
 tel: 01895 250603
Walthamstow
 tel: 020 8520 3017
Wembley
 Middlesex; tel: 020 8937 3500
Westminster
 tel: 020 7641 2034
Woolwich
 tel: 020 8312 5750

England North East:
Altrincham
 Cheshire; tel: 0161 912 5923
Ashton-under-Lyne
 tel: 0161 342 2031
Darlington
 tel: 01325 462034
Durham
 tel: 0191 383 4231
Gateshead
 Tyne & Wear; tel: 0191 477 3478
Hartlepool
 tel: 01429 272905
Middlesbrough
 tel: 01642 263364
Morpeth
 tel: 01670 512385
Newcastle upon Tyne
 tel: 0191 261 0691
North Shields
 tel: 0191 200 5424
South Shields
 tel: 0191 427 1818 ext 2133
Sunderland
 tel: 0191 514 8435

England North West:
Birkenhead
 tel: 0151 652 6106
Bolton
 Lancashire; tel: 01204 522173
Crosby
 tel: 0151 928 6487/8
Ellesmere Port
 tel: 0151 356 7606
Knowsley
 tel: 0151 443 3738

continued overleaf

Liverpool
tel: 0151 225 5435
Manchester
tel: 0161 234 1996
Oldham
tel: 0161 911 4643
Preston
Lancashire; tel: 01772 404010
Salford
tel: 0161 793 3016
Southport
tel: 0151 934 2119
St Helens
Merseyside; tel: 01744 456989/51
Stockport
tel: 0161 474 4524
Warrington
tel: 01925 442889
Wigan
tel: 01942 827619/27
Workington
Cumbria; tel: 01900 325170/77

England South East:
Aylesbury
tel: 01296 383252
Bracknell
tel: 01344 423149
Brighton
East Sussex; tel: 01273 296969
Camberley
tel: 01276 683626
Hastings
tel: 01424 716481
Maidenhead
tel: 01628 625657
Maidstone
Kent; tel: 01622 696503/511
Milton Keynes
tel: 01908 835008
Newbury
tel: 01635 40972
Newport
Isle of Wight; tel: 01983 823800
Oxford
tel: 01865 810182
Reading
Berkshire; tel: 0118 923 3234
Slough
Berkshire; tel: 01753 535166
Southampton
tel: 023 8083 2958
Worthing
Sussex; tel: 01903 212414

England South West:
Bristol
tel: 0117 929 9148
Dorchester
Dorset; tel: 01305 224448
Exeter
tel: 01392 384206
Gloucester
tel: 01452 425027
Plymouth
Devon; tel: 01752 305906
Poole
Dorset; tel: 01202 671496
Swindon
Wiltshire; tel: 01793 463240
Taunton
Somerset; tel: 01823 336354
Trowbridge
Wiltshire; tel: 01225 713727
Truro
Cornwall; tel: 01872 272702
Yate
Bristol; tel: 01454 865818

England West Midlands:
Birmingham
tel: 0121 235 4545/6
Coventry
tel: 024 7683 2325
Dudley
tel: 01384 815554/560
Kidderminster
tel: 01562 512900
Nuneaton
tel: 024 7638 4027

Shrewsbury
Shropshire; tel: 01743 255380
Solihull
tel: 0121 704 6974
Stafford
tel: 01785 278351
Stoke-on-Trent
tel: 01782 238431
Walsall
tel: 01922 653110
West Bromwich
tel: 01902 322300
Wolverhampton
tel: 01902 312026

England Yorkshire:
Barnsley
South Yorkshire; tel: 01226 773935
Beverley
tel: 01482 885081
Bradford
West Yorkshire; tel: 01274 383402
Doncaster
tel: 01302 734320
Halifax
tel: 01422 392631/2
Huddersfield
tel: 01484 221967
Hull
tel: 01482 883025
Leeds
tel: 0113 247 8282
Northallerton
North Yorkshire; tel: 01609 776202
Rotherham
tel: 01709 823614
Scarborough
North Yorkshire; tel: 01723 364285
Sheffield
tel: 0114 273 4736

Northern Ireland:
Ballymena
tel: 028 2532 3456
Ballynahinch
tel: 028 9756 6400
Belfast
tel: 028 9024 3233
Omagh
tel: 028 8224 4821
Portadown
tel: 028 3833 5247

Scotland:
Aberdeen
tel: 01224 652534
Alloa
tel: 01259 722262
Ardrossan
tel: 01294 469137
Ayr
tel: 01292 282109
Bathgate
tel: 01506 776335
Bearsden
tel: 0141 943 0121
Carrick
tel: 01292 288820
Clydebank
tel: 0141 952 1416 or 8765
Clydesdale
tel: 01555 661144
Cumbernauld
tel: 01236 725664
Cummock & Doon
tel: 01290 422111
Cupar
tel: 01334 653722 ext 111
Dumbarton
tel: 01389 763129
Dumfries
tel: 01387 253820
Dundee
tel: 01382 434336
Dunfermline
tel: 01383 723661
Dunoon
tel: 01436 679567
East Kilbride
tel: 01355 220046

Eastwood
tel: 0141 638 6511
Edinburgh
tel: 0131 225 5584
Elgin
tel: 01343 542746
Falkirk
tel: 01324 503605/08
Forfar
tel: 01307 461460
Galashiels
tel: 01896 752512
Giffnock
tel: 0141 544 4976
Glasgow
G3; tel: 0141 287 2850
Glasgow
G2; tel: 0141 621 3424
Glenrothes
tel: 01592 755866
Greenock
tel: 01475 726211
Haddington
tel: 01620 828202
Hamilton
tel: 01698 452403
Inverness
tel: 01463 235713
Kilmarnock
tel: 01563 526401
Kirkcaldy
tel: 01592 412879
Kirkintilloch
tel: 0141 776 8090
Kirkwall
Orkney; tel: 01856 873166
Lanark
tel: 01555 661144
Lerwick
Shetlands; tel: 01595 693868
Loanhead
tel: 0131 225 5584
Mephil
tel: 01333 592470
Monklands
tel: 01236 424150 or 434847
Moray
tel: 01343 544475
Motherwell
tel: 01698 251311
Oldmeldrum
tel: 01651 872707
Paisley
tel: 0141 889 2360
Perth
tel: 01738 477060
Selkirk
tel: 01750 20842
Stepps
tel: 0141 304 1800
Stirling
tel: 01786 432106
Stornoway
Lewis; tel: 01851 703064

Wales:
Barry
tel: 01446 735722
Blackwood
tel: 01495 223345
Bodlondeb
tel: 01492 860101
Bridgend
tel: 01656 767451
Caernarfon
tel: 01286 679465
Cardiff
tel: 029 2038 2116
Cwnbran
tel: 01633 867584
Ebbw Vale
tel: 01495 303069
Haverford
tel: 01473 775248
Lanelli
tel: 01554 773538
Llangefni
tel: 01248 752092

Merthyr Tydfil
  tel: 01685 723057
Mold
  tel: 01352 704400
Neath
  tel: 01639 764230
Newport
  tel: 01633 211376
Rhyl
  tel: 01745 353814
Swansea
  tel: 01792 655521
Wrexham
  tel: 01978 261932

EUROPEAN REFERENCE CENTRES

Organisation type and purpose:
The European Reference Centres (ERCs) hold collections of EC documents.

Other addresses:
Aberystwyth
  European Liaison Office, University College of Wales Aberystwyth, Laura Place, Aberystwyth, SY23 3AX; tel: 01970 622401; fax: 01970 623364
Brighton
  Brighton Central Library, Reference Library and Information Service, Church Street, Brighton, East Sussex, BN1 2UE; tel: 01273 601197; fax: 01273 695882
Chalfont St Giles
  Buckinghamshire College of Higher Education, Library, Newlands Park, Chalfont St Giles, Buckinghamshire, HP8 4AD; fax: 01494 874441
Chelmsford
  Anglia Polytechnic University, Victoria Road South, Chelmsford, Essex, CM1 1LL; tel: 01245 493131 ext 3757; fax: 01245 490935
Edinburgh
  National Library of Scotland, George IV Bridge, Edinburgh, EH1 1EW; tel: 0131 650 2041; fax: 0131 667 9780
Exmouth
  The European Reference Centre, University of Plymouth Library, Exmouth Campus, Douglas Avenue, Exmouth, Devon, EX8 2AT; tel: 01395 255352
Halifax
  Calderdale College, Francis Street, Halifax, West Yorkshire, HX1 3UZ; tel: 01422 358221 ext 2117
Hatfield
  Hertfordshire University, College Lane, Hatfield, Hertfordshire, AL10 9AD; tel: 01707 84678; fax: 01707 284670
Ipswich
  Suffolk County Reference Library, Northgate Street, Ipswich, Suffolk, IP1 3DE; tel: 01473 583705; fax: 01473 583700
London
  Thames Valley University, Ealing Campus, St Mary's Road, Ealing, London, W5 5RF; tel: 020 8231 2246; fax: 020 8231 2631
Middlesbrough
  Teesside University, Borough Road, Middlesbrough, Cleveland, TS1 3BA; tel: 01642 218123; fax: 01642 342067
Northampton
  Nene College, Boughton Green Road, Moulton Park, Northampton, NN2 7AL; tel: 01604 715000; fax: 01604 720636
Preston
  University of Central Lancashire, Library and Resources Service, St Peter's Square, Preston, Lancashire, PR1 2TQ; tel: 01772 53191/22141
Reading
  Reading University, Bulmershe Library, Woodlands Avenue, Reading, RG6 1HY; tel: 0118 931 8651
Sheffield
  Sheffield University, Crookesmoor Library, Crookesmoor Building, PO Box 598, Sheffield, S10 1FL; tel: 0114 276 8555 ext 6779; fax: 0114 275 4670
Stirling
  Stirling University, Library, Stirling, FK9 4LA; tel: 01786 467227; fax: 01786 466866

Swansea
  University College of Swansea, Natural Sciences Library, Singleton Park, Swansea, SA2 8PP; tel: 01792 205678 ext 4037
Wrexham
  European Reference Centre, North East Wales Institute of Higher Education, Information Services, Plas Coch, Mold Lane, Wrexham, Clwyd, LL11 2AW; tel: 01978 293261 or 293237; fax: 01978 293254

EUROPEAN REGIONS AIRLINE ASSOCIATION

Acronym or abbreviation: ERAA

The Baker Suite, Fairoaks Airport, Chobham, Woking, Surrey, GU24 8HX

Tel: 01276 856495
Fax: 01276 857038
E-mail: info@eraa.org

Website:
http://www.eraa.org
Background information on ERA, statistics, press releases, fleet data, presentations and briefings, publications content descriptions. Member contact details and how to join. Calendar of events, members news.

Enquiries:
Enquiries to: Corporate Communications Manager
Direct e-mail: lesley.shepherd@eraa.org
Other contacts: Director General

Founded:
1980

Formerly called:
European Regional Airline Association

Organisation type and purpose:
Trade association.
To protect and promote the interests of regional airlines throughout Europe.
To be the principal body representing the interests of organisations involved in air transport in Europe's regions.

Subject coverage:
Airlines, air safety issues, operations, maintenance, infrastructure, environmental issues, air transport policy.

Trade and statistical information:
Traffic statistics of European regional airlines and airports (ERA members only).

Printed publications:
ERA Yearbook (reference guide and contact details of members)
Performance (statistical publication, quarterly)
Regional International (newsletter, monthly)

Publications list:
Available online

Access to staff:
Contact by letter, by telephone, by fax, by e-mail and via website
Hours: Mon to Fri, 0800 to 1730

EUROPEAN RELAY CENTRES

Made up of:
European Documentation Centres
European Information Centres
European Public Information Relays
European Reference Centres

EUROPEAN RESOURCE CENTRES FOR SCHOOLS & COLLEGES

Central Bureau for Educational Visits and Exchanges, 10 Spring Gardens, London, SW1A 2BN

Tel: 020 7389 4004

Organisation type and purpose:
To provide teachers and pupils with information on Europe, and to support the development of the European dimension in the curriculum.

Museum or gallery collection, archive, or library special collection:
Extensive stocks of directories, journals, books and brochures on Europe, the EU and European issues

Printed publications:
Brochures on EU institutions, EU countries, and statistical information (free)

Contacts:
East Anglia (ACER)
  The Association of Colleges in the Eastern Region, Merlin Place, Milton Road, Cambridge, CB4 4DP; tel: 01223 424022; fax: 01223 423389
East Midlands
  Leicestershire Comenius Centre, Quorn Hall, Meynell Road, Quorn, Leicestershire, LE12 8BG; tel: 01509 416950; fax: 01509 416993
London and the Home Counties
  Kent County Council Education Department, Springfield, Maidstone, Kent, ME14 2LJ; tel: 01622 605704; fax: 01622 605704
London and the Home Counties
  Wheathampstead Education Centre (drop-in centre only), Butterfield Road, Wheathampstead, St Albans, Hertfordshire, AL4 8PY
London and the Home Counties
  Colchester Curriculum Development Centre (drop-in centre only, telephone to arrange a visit), Acacia Avenue, Greenstead, Colchester, CO4 3TQ; tel: 01206 863839
London and the Home Counties
  Central Bureau (written and telephone enquiries only), 10 Spring Gardens, London, SW1A 2BN; tel: 020 7389 4697 or 4723; fax: 020 7389 4426
London and the Home Counties (CiLT)
  Centre for Information on Language Teaching and Research, (drop-in centre only), 20 Bedfordbury, London, WC2N 4LB; tel: 020 7379 5110
North East
  European Information and Education Centre, John Smith House, 1 South View, Jarrow, NE32 5JP; tel: 0191 420 1711/428 2436; fax: 0191 489 0643
North West
  European Information Unit (drop-in centre only), Central Library, St Peter's Square, Manchester, M2 5PD
North West
  Liverpool Quality Assurance Service, Dulcie Cottages, Riverside Road, Liverpool, L19 3QN; tel: 0151 225 8110; fax: 0151 494 2846
Southern
  West Sussex County Council, Education Department, County Hall, Chichester, PO19 1RF; tel: 01243 777578; fax: 01243 777229
Southern
  International Education Office, The Hucclecote Centre, Churchdown Lane, Hucclecote, Gloucester, GL3 3QN; tel: 01452 427204 or 427270; fax: 01452 427204
Wales
  Ysgol Leithoedd Modern, School of Modern Languages, Prifysgol Cymru, Bangor, Gwynedd, LL57 2DG; tel: 01248 383874; fax: 01248 382551
Wales
  National Comenius Centre of Wales, WJEC, 245 Western Avenue, Cardiff, CF5 2YX; tel: 029 2026 5043; fax: 029 2057 6201
West Midlands
  Matthew Boulton College, 3rd Floor, Magnolia House, 73 Conybere Street, Birmingham, B12 0YL; tel: 0121 446 3400; fax: 0121 446 3401
Yorkshire & Humberside
  Elmete Professional Development Centre, Elmete Lane, Leeds, LS8 2LJ; tel: 0113 214 4072; fax: 0113 214 4069
Yorkshire & Humberside
  Hull University, Curriculum Development, Brynmor Jones Library, Cottingham Road, Hull, HU6 7RX; tel: 01482 466843; fax: 01482 466839

continued overleaf

Incorporates the:
UK Centre for European Education Partners Overseas

Parent body:
British Council

EUROPEAN SCHOOL OF OSTEOPATHY

Formal name: Osteopathic Education and Research Limited
Acronym or abbreviation: ESO

Boxley House, Boxley, Kent, ME14 3DZ

Tel: 01622 671558
Fax: 01622 662165
E-mail: library@eso.ac.uk

Website:
http://www.eso.ac.uk

Enquiries:
Enquiries to: Library Supervisor

Founded:
1973

Formerly called:
Ecole Européenne d'Ostéopathie (EEO)

Organisation type and purpose:
Registered charity.

Subject coverage:
Osteopathy and other manual and alternative medical therapies.

Library catalogue:
All or part available in-house

Access to staff:
Contact by letter, by telephone, by fax and by e-mail. Appointment necessary.
Hours: Mon to Fri, 0900 to 1700
Special comments: No loans to non-members

Also at:
European School of Osteopathy Clinic
104 Tonbridge Road, Maidstone, Kent, ME16 8SL; tel: 01622 685913; fax: 01622 661812

EUROPEAN STUDIES PROGRAMME

The Southern Education and Library Board, 3 Charlemont Place, The Mall, Armagh, BT61 9AX

Tel: 028 3751 2247
Fax: 028 3751 2285
E-mail: office@esp.dnet.co.uk

Website:
http://www.european-studies.org

Enquiries:
Enquiries to: Information Officer

Founded:
1986

Formerly called:
European Studies (Ireland and Great Britain) Project

Organisation type and purpose:
Membership association (membership is by election or invitation), present number of members: 500 schools, suitable for ages: 11 to 18. European Studies is a joint partnership between the Dept of Education NI and Dept of Education ROI promoting joint study and communication among students and teachers in 20 different jurisdictions, aiming to promote mutal understanding, awareness and tolerance in the youth of contemporary Europe.

Subject coverage:
Various units of study/topics in both the junior and senior programmes have been designed to assist students in examining not only areas of shared interest today, but also areas of conflict in the past. They are intended to broaden the student's

knowledge and understanding of their own place and their relationship to others in the Europe of today.

Publications list:
Available in print

Access to staff:
Contact by letter, by telephone, by fax, by e-mail and via website
Hours: Mon to Fri, 0900 to 1700

Access to building, collection or gallery:
Prior appointment required

Access for disabled people:
Ramped entry

EUROPEAN-ATLANTIC GROUP

Acronym or abbreviation: E-AG

4 St Paul's Way, Finchley, London, N3 2PP

Tel: 020 8632 9253
Fax: 020 8343 3532
E-mail: info@eag.org.uk

Website:
http://www.eag.org.uk

Enquiries:
Enquiries to: Director

Founded:
1954

Organisation type and purpose:
Registered charity (charity number 274898).
Provides a regular forum in the United Kingdom for informed discussion between European and Atlantic countries.
Discusses problems and possibilities for better economic, strategic and political co-operation with each other and with the rest of the world.
Disseminates authoritative information concerning the work of international organisations, such as the Council of Europe, the North Atlantic Treaty Organization, the Organisation for Economic Co-operation and Development, the European Union, the World Trade Organization and the Organization for European Security and Co-operation.

Subject coverage:
Economic, strategic and political co-operation between European and Atlantic countries, and with the rest of the world.

Printed publications:
European-Atlantic Journal
Hitler and King Boris of Bulgaria
Order printed publications from: E-AG office

Publications list:
Available online

Access to staff:
Contact by letter, by telephone, by fax and by e-mail. Appointment necessary.

EURYDICE UNIT FOR ENGLAND, WALES AND NORTHERN IRELAND

Acronym or abbreviation: Eurydice at NFER

NFER, The Mere, Upton Park, Slough, Berkshire, SL1 2DQ

Tel: 01753 637036
Fax: 01753 531458
E-mail: eurydice@nfer.ac.uk

Website:
http://www.nfer.ac.uk/eurydice

Formerly called:
Education Policy Information Centre (EPIC Europe) (year of change 1998)

Organisation type and purpose:
International organisation, research organisation.
Eurydice is part of the European Union's Lifelong Learning Programme.

Subject coverage:
Education policy throughout the European Union, EFTA/EEA states.

Printed publications:
Education in the News (current awareness bulletin)
International Review of Curriculum and Assessment Frameworks Internet Archive (INCA) (www.inca.org.uk)
Occasional briefing papers on specific policy themes, either covering the countries of the Eurydice Network or England, Wales and Northern Ireland
Factsheets
The Eurydice Network Eurybase, the European database on education systems, a series of education indicators and a range of comparative studies on education in Europe
Order printed publications from: Dissemination Unit, Eurydice Unit for England, Wales and Northern Ireland, The Mere, Upton Park, Slough, Berkshire, SL1 2DQ; online from the Eurydice European Unit (www.eurydice.org). Details of how to order printed publications are also on the website.

Access to staff:
Contact by letter, by telephone and by e-mail
Hours: Mon to Fri, 0915 to 1715
Special comments: Service restricted to national and local education policymakers.

Links with:
Eurydice European Unit (and National Units in 31 European countries)
e-mail: info@eurydice.org; website: http://www.eurydice.org

Parent body:
National Foundation for Educational Research
tel: 01753 574123; fax: 01753 691632; website: http://www.nfer.ac.uk

EVANGELICAL ALLIANCE

Acronym or abbreviation: EA

Whitefield House, 186 Kennington Park Road, London, SE11 4BT

Tel: 020 7207 2100
Fax: 020 7207 2150
E-mail: info@eauk.org

Website:
http://www.eauk.org
Information on EA projects, activities and resources. Databases of church and organisational members.

Enquiries:
Enquiries to: Information Officer
Direct tel: 020 7207 2110

Founded:
1846

Organisation type and purpose:
Membership association (membership is by subscription), present number of members: 38,000 individuals, 3,000 Churches, 700 organisations, registered charity (charity number 212325).
National para-church body representing the concerns of more than 1m. Christians from over a dozen denominations to the state, society and the wider Church.

Subject coverage:
Evangelical Christian activity in Britain.
Information on the views and beliefs of Evangelicals across the United Kingdom

Museum or gallery collection, archive, or library special collection:
19th-century documents of the Evangelical Alliance; uncatalogued collection

Printed publications:
IDEA (magazine, 6 times a year, free to members)

Publications list:
Available online and in print

Access to staff:
Contact by letter, by telephone, by fax, by e-mail and via website. Appointment necessary.
Hours: Mon to Fri, 0900 to 1700

Access to building, collection or gallery:
Please book to arrange appointmant

Access for disabled people:
Level entry, toilet facilities

Also at:
Evangelical Alliance Northern Ireland
218 York Street, Belfast, BT15 1GY; tel: 028 9029 2266; fax: 028 9029 2277; e-mail: nireland@eauk.org
Evangelical Alliance Scotland
Challenge House, 29 Canal Street, Glasgow, G4 0AD; tel: 0141 332 8700; fax: 0141 332 8704; e-mail: scotland@eauk.org
Evangelical Alliance Wales
20 High Street, Cardiff, CF10 1PT; tel: 029 2022 9822; fax: 029 2022 9741; e-mail: wales@eauk.org; cymru@eauk.org

Links with:
European Evangelical Alliance
World Evangelical Alliance

EVANGELICAL LIBRARY

Acronym or abbreviation: EL

78A Chiltern Street, London, W1U 5HB

Tel: 020 7935 6997
E-mail: stlibrary@zen.co.uk

Website:
http://www.evangelical-library.org.uk

Enquiries:
Enquiries to: Librarian
Other contacts: Treasurer (for advice on donations)

Founded:
1945

Organisation type and purpose:
Membership association (membership is by subscription), present number of members: 1,100, research organisation.
Lending, reference and research library.

Subject coverage:
Evangelical faith, hymnology, revivals, reformers, Puritans, denominational and biographical history.

Museum or gallery collection, archive, or library special collection:
Journals from 1766
Manuscripts of unpublished letters, etc.
Robinson Collection of Puritan works
Slides – Bible scene slide tours

Non-library collection catalogue:
All or part available in print

Library catalogue:
All or part available online

Printed publications:
Annual Lecture
In Writing (twice a year)
Evangelical Library Lectures are available dating from 1983, including:
A Glorious Heritage (R. Oliver, 1997)
Lex Rex, the Law and the Prince (D. Searl, 2000)
The Ecumenical Century and Evangelical Responses (H. R. Jones, 1998)
Reversal or Betrayal? Evangelicals and Socio-political Involvement (M. Tinker, 1998)
The Glory of Christ – B. B. Warfield on Jesus (C. Trueman, 2001)

Publications list:
Available in print

Access to staff:
Contact by letter, by telephone, by fax, by e-mail, in person and via website. All charged.
Hours: Mon to Sat, 1000 to 1700

Access to building, collection or gallery:
No prior appointment required

EVELYN OLDFIELD UNIT

London Voluntary Sector Resource Centre, 356 Holloway Road, London, N7 6PA

Tel: 020 7700 8213
Fax: 020 7700 8136
E-mail: administrator@evelynoldfield.co.uk

Website:
http://www.evelynoldfield.co.uk

Founded:
1994

Organisation type and purpose:
Established by a consortium of funding bodies (including the City Parochial Foundation, Thames Telethon, London Borough Grants, the Refugee Working Party and the Refugee Council) to develop specialist support for refugee organisations to enable them to tackle the pressing needs of the communities that they served.

EVENT SUPPLIER AND SERVICES ASSOCIATION

Acronym or abbreviation: ESSA

ESSA House, Uplands Business Park, Blackhorse Lane, London, E17 5QJ

Tel: 0845 122 1880
Fax: 020 8523 5204
E-mail: christine.hasler@essa.uk.com

Website:
http://www.essa.uk.com

Created by the merger of:
British Exhibition Contractors Association (BECA) and Association of Exhibition Contractors (AEC) (year of change 2008)

Organisation type and purpose:
Trade association.

Subject coverage:
Employment, legislation, health and safety, quality assurance.

Constituent member of:
CBI

EVESHAM LIBRARY

Oat Street, Evesham, Worcestershire, WR11 4PJ

Tel: 01386 442291 or 41348
Fax: 01386 765855
E-mail: eveshamlib@worcestershire.gov.uk

Enquiries:
Enquiries to: Librarian

Organisation type and purpose:
Public library.

Subject coverage:
General; local history.

Museum or gallery collection, archive, or library special collection:
Barnard Bequest (local history)

Access to staff:
Contact by letter, by telephone, by fax, by e-mail and in person. Appointment necessary.
Hours: Mon, Wed, Fri, 0930 to 1730; Tue, Thu, 0930 to 2000; Sat, 0930 to 1730

Parent body:
Worcestershire County Council Cultural Services

EVESHAM TOURIST INFORMATION AND HERITAGE CENTRE

Almonry Heritage Centre, Abbey Gate, Evesham, Worcestershire, WR11 4BG

Tel: 01386 446944
Fax: 01386 442348
E-mail: tic@almonry.ndo.co.uk

Enquiries:
Enquiries to: Tourist Information and Heritage Centre Manager

Founded:
1957

Organisation type and purpose:
Local government body, museum, suitable for ages: all.
Heritage and Tourist Information Centre.

Subject coverage:
Tourist information housed in the local heritage centre with its collection of archaeology and local history of the Evesham area, displays relating to the Battle of Evesham (1265), Evesham Abbey (701–1540) and the crafts and history of the Vale, civic regalia of the former Evesham Borough and artefacts belonging to the former Evesham Abbey. Display of Anglo-Saxon jewellery and weapons found on the site of a burial site just outside the town.

Printed publications:
A selection of books is available from the Heritage Centre, including:
Abbey and Parish Churches
Battle of Evesham
Battle of Worcester
Evesham Official Guide 2002 (every 3–4 years)
Evesham Pocket Guide and Map (every 2–3 years)
The Almonry Museum (guide to building, 1975)

Publications list:
Available in print

Access to staff:
Contact by letter, by e-mail and in person
Hours: Mon to Sat, 1000 to 1700; Sun, 1400 to 1700
Special comments: Closed Sun, Nov, Dec and Jan and for 2 weeks at Christmas and New Year.

Access for disabled people:
Level entry

Parent body:
Evesham Town Council
110–112 High Street, Evesham, Worcestershire, WR11 4EP; tel: 01386 47070; fax: 01386 423811; e-mail: fgreen@eveshamtc.ndirect.co.uk

EX-SERVICE FELLOWSHIP CENTRES

Acronym or abbreviation: EFC

8 Lower Grosvenor Place, London, SW1W 0EP

Tel: 020 7828 2468
Fax: 020 7630 6780

Enquiries:
Enquiries to: Administrator
Other contacts: Deputy Administrator

Founded:
1932

Organisation type and purpose:
Registered charity (charity number 209667).
To relieve distress among ex-service, including merchant service, men and women and their dependents.

Subject coverage:
Assistance to ex-service persons and dependents in need.

Access to staff:
Contact by letter, by telephone, by fax and in person
Hours: Mon to Fri, 0900 to 1700

Other addresses:
Hollenden House (Residential Care Home)
Buckhurst Road, Bexhill on Sea, East Sussex, TN40 1QE; tel: 01424 211017; fax: 01424 211353
New Belvedere House (Hostel for the Homeless)
Whitehorse Road, London, E1 0ND; tel: 020 7790 1474; fax: 020 7253 4997

EX-SERVICES MENTAL WELFARE SOCIETY

Acronym or abbreviation: COMBAT STRESS

Tyrwhitt House, Oaklawn Road, Leatherhead, Surrey, KT22 0BX

Tel: 01372 841600
Fax: 01372 841601
E-mail: contactus@combatstress.org.uk

Website:
http://www.combatstress.com
Treatment centres, welfare offices – their role in the society, fundraising including calendar of events, details for those wishing to donate.

Enquiries:
Enquiries to: Director Fundraising & Public Relations
Direct tel: 01372 841615
Direct fax: 01372 841601
Direct e-mail: dfpr@combatstress.org.uk

Founded:
1919

Organisation type and purpose:
Voluntary organisation, registered charity (charity number 206002).
Supports three treatment centres and welfare officers in the UK and Republic of Ireland.
The Ex-Services Mental Welfare Society, also known as Combat Stress is the only charity to specialise in helping those of all ranks of the Armed Forces and Merchant Navy who suffer from psychiatric disorders caused through or exacerbated through service.

Printed publications:
Annual Report
Combat Stress Newsletter (2 times a year)

Microform publications:
Film of the Society's work

Access to staff:
Contact by letter, by telephone, by fax, by e-mail and via website. Appointment necessary.
Hours: Mon to Fri, 0900 to 1700

Regional Offices:
Irish Office
   9–13 Waring Street, Belfast, BT1 2DW; tel: 028 9023 3894; fax: 028 9023 0329
Northern Office
   Audley Court, Audley Avenue, Newport, Shropshire, TF10 7BP; tel: 01952 825684; fax: 01952 811539
Scottish Office
   Hollybush House, Hollybush by Ayr, Ayrshire, KA6 7EA; tel: 01292 560214; fax: 01292 560871

EXEMPLAS BUSINESS INTELLIGENCE

Acronym or abbreviation: EXEMPLAS

45 Grosvenor Road, St Albans, Hertfordshire, AL1 3AW

Tel: 01727 813813
Fax: 01727 813404
E-mail: info@exemplas.com

Website:
http://www.exemplas.com

Enquiries:
Enquiries to: Information Manager

Founded:
1994

Organisation type and purpose:
Advisory body, research organisation.
Information and advice service.
Designed to improve business competitiveness through an outstanding range and quality of business information, advice and services to Hertfordshire, UK and international firms.

Subject coverage:
Business, science and technology, intellectual property, pharmaceuticals, current affairs, management and products.

Library catalogue:
All or part available in-house

Access to staff:
Contact by letter, by telephone, by fax, by e-mail and in person
Hours: Mon, Wed to Fri, 0900 to 1700; Tue, 0900 to 1600

Links with:
Hertfordshire Chamber of Commerce and Industry
Hertfordshire County Council
Hertfordshire Learning and Skills Council
University of Hertfordshire

EXERCISE, MOVEMENT AND DANCE PARTNERSHIP

Acronym or abbreviation: EMDP

1 Grove House, Foundry Lane, Horsham, West Sussex, RH13 5PL

Tel: 01403 266000
Fax: 01403 266111
E-mail: office@cmdp.org

Website:
http://www.emdp.org.uk

Enquiries:
Enquiries to: Support Administrator
Direct e-mail: sara@emdp.org

Founded:
2006

Created by the merger of:
the Keep Fit Association, the Fitness League and the Medau Society (1952)

Organisation type and purpose:
Professional body.

Subject coverage:
Medau rhythmic movement.

Printed publications:
Annual Report and Constitution
Medau Rhythmic Movement (Society handbook)
The Medau Approach to Piano Improvisation

Access to staff:
Contact by letter, by telephone, by fax and by e-mail. Access for members only.
Hours: Term time: 0930 to 1500

Links with:
Medau College
   Coburg

EXETER CATHEDRAL LIBRARY

Diocesan House, Palace Gate, Exeter, Devon, EX1 1HX

Tel: 01392 272894, Library; 01392 495954, Archives
Fax: 01392 285986
E-mail: library@exeter-cathedral.org.uk

Website:
http://www.exeter-cathedral.org.uk
Description of content and facilities.

Enquiries:
Enquiries to: Librarian
Other contacts: Assistant Librarian

Founded:
11th century

Organisation type and purpose:
Cathedral library.

Subject coverage:
Theological subjects, in early printed books, tracts etc. Early printed works on travel, law, literature, linguistics, history, local history, history of medicine, bibliography.

Museum or gallery collection, archive, or library special collection:
Cathedral archives and manuscripts
Collection of tracts (Civil War period)
Cook Collection (early foreign language material, 19th-century linguistics)
Exeter Book of Anglo-Saxon poetry c965–75
Exon Domesday 1086
Glass Collection and Exeter Medical Library (early medicine and science)
Harington Collection (theology, history, 16th to 19th century)
Manuscript books, 10th century onwards
Printed books, 15th century onwards, including a large proportion of early imprints

Non-library collection catalogue:
All or part available in-house

Library catalogue:
All or part available in-house

Printed publications:
The library and archives of Exeter Cathedral, by L J Lloyd and Audrey M Erskine, 3rd edn (Exeter 2004)

Microform publications:
Most library manuscript material available on microfilm (this does not apply to archives)

Access to staff:
Contact by letter, by telephone, by e-mail and in person
Hours: Library: Mon to Fri, 1400 to 1700
Archives: Mon to Wed, 1400 to 1700, by appointment
Special comments: Casual visitors restricted to exhibition area; browsing not permitted.

Archives jointly administered and financed by the:
Dean and Chapter of Exeter and the Devon Record Office
   Devon Record Office, Great Moor House, Bitton Road, Sowton, Exeter, EX2 7NL; tel: 01392 384253 (DRO); fax: 01392 384256 (DRO); e-mail: devrec@devon.gov.uk

Parent body:
Dean and Chapter of Exeter Cathedral
   Cathedral Office, 1 The Cloisters, Exeter, EX1 1HS; tel: 01392 255573; fax: 01392 285986; e-mail: admin@exeter-cathedral.org.uk

EXETER CENTRAL LIBRARY

Castle Street, Exeter, Devon, EX4 3PQ

Tel: 01392 384206
Fax: 01392 384208
E-mail: refdesk@devon.gov.uk

Website:
http://www.devon.gov.uk/library/
Range of services, contacts, opening hours, library catalogue, community information, local studies database.

Enquiries:
Enquiries to: Group Librarian (South and East)
Direct tel: 01392 384222

Organisation type and purpose:
Local government body, public library.
The Central Library for South and East Devon of the Devon Library & Information Services, houses the Westcountry Studies Library.

Subject coverage:
General; music and drama, West country local history, business information, careers, official publications.

Museum or gallery collection, archive, or library special collection:
British Standards
Drama Collection (play sets)
HMSO collection (selective subscription from 1975)
Pocknell Collection (early books on shorthand)
Pre-1800 Book Collection (2000 volumes)

Trade and statistical information:
Keynote market research reports, UK Business Monitors, Government trade statistics.

Library catalogue:
All or part available online

Printed publications:
Community Information Booklets

Access to staff:
Contact by letter, by telephone, by fax, by e-mail, in person and via website
Hours: Mon, Tue, Thu, Fri, 0930 to 1900; Wed 1000 to 1700; Sat 0930 to 1600; Sun 1100 to 1430

Access for disabled people:
Ramped entry, access to all public areas, toilet facilities

EXETER CHAMBER OF COMMERCE

6 Sunhill Lane, Topsham, Exeter, Devon, EX3 0BR

Tel: 01392 879595
Fax: 01392 877939
E-mail: ecc@eclipse.co.uk

Website:
http://www.exeterchamber.co.uk
http://www.exeter-chamber-of-commerce.co.uk
Full membership directory, application form, details of subscriptions, events, links to other sites of interest.

Enquiries:
Enquiries to: Administrator

Founded:
1992

Organisation type and purpose:
Trade association (membership is by subscription), present number of members: over 200.

Subject coverage:
Business information, trade and business contacts.

Printed publications:
Membership list (continually updated, £30)

Access to staff:
Contact by letter, by telephone, by fax and by e-mail. Appointment necessary.
Hours: Mon to Fri, 0900 to 1700

EXETER CITY CENTRE CONSORTIUM

PO Box 209, Exeter, Devon, EX1 1YJ

Tel: 01392 494980

Enquiries:
Enquiries to: Administrator

Founded:
1991

Organisation type and purpose:
Trade association (membership is by subscription), present number of members: 80.
To represent the interest of members; to promote Exeter City Centre by whatever means with intention of improving the prosperity of business dependent upon Exeter City Centre; to work with others for the enhancement of the city centre environment. To provide the Christmas illuminations each year. To provide and run the Storewatch Radio System.

Subject coverage:
City centre improvement.

Access to staff:
Contact by letter, by telephone and by e-mail
Hours: Mon to Fri, 0900 to 1700

EXETER CITY COUNCIL

Civic Centre, Paris Street, Exeter, Devon, EX1 1JN

Tel: 01392 277888
Fax: 01392 265265

Website:
http://www.exeter.gov.uk
All council services and city information.

Enquiries:
Enquiries to: Communications Manager
Direct tel: 01392 265319
Direct fax: 01392 265247
Direct e-mail: mandy.pearse@exeter.gov.uk

Organisation type and purpose:
Local government body.

Subject coverage:
Local government.

Printed publications:
Exeter Citizen (council newspaper, quarterly)

Access to staff:
Contact by letter, by telephone, by fax and by e-mail
Hours: Mon to Fri, 0900 to 1700

Access for disabled people:
Parking provided, ramped entry, access to all public areas, toilet facilities

EXETER HEALTH LIBRARY

Peninsula Medical School Building, Royal Devon and Exeter NHS Foundation Trust, Barrack Road, Exeter, Devon, EX2 5DW

Tel: 01392 406800
Fax: 01392 406728
E-mail: Medlib@exeter.ac.uk

Website:
http://www.exeter.ac.uk/library/eml

Enquiries:
Enquiries to: Library Manager

Organisation type and purpose:
NHS/Medical School library.

Subject coverage:
Medicine, healthcare.

Museum or gallery collection, archive, or library special collection:
Collection of pre-19th century medical books (housed in Exeter Cathedral Library)

Non-library collection catalogue:
All or part available online

Library catalogue:
All or part available online

Access to staff:
Contact by letter, by telephone, by fax, by e-mail, in person and via website. Appointment necessary.
Letter of introduction required.
Hours: Mon to Fri, 0830 to 1730

Parent body:
Royal Devon and Exeter NHS Foundation Trust Barrack Road, Exeter EX2 5DW

EXMOOR NATIONAL PARK AUTHORITY

Exmoor House, Dulverton, Somerset, TA22 9HL

Tel: 01398 323665
Fax: 01398 323150
E-mail: info@exmoor-nationalpark.gov.uk

Website:
http://www.exmoor-nationalpark.gov.uk
Information about National Park Authority and Exmoor area.

Enquiries:
Enquiries to: Head of Education and Interpretation
Other contacts: External Relations Manager for media and general enquiries

Founded:
1954

Organisation type and purpose:
Local government body, planning authority, statutory body.
Statutory purposes of the National Park are to conserve and enhance the natural beauty, wildlife and cultural heritage of the area. To promote opportunities for the understanding and enjoyment of the park's special qualities. To seek to foster the economic and social well being of the communities within the National Park without incurring significant expenditure in so doing. The Authority is also the planning authority for Exmoor.

Subject coverage:
Exmoor, its natural history, history, culture, access, recreation and tourist facilities.

Information services:
3 National Park Centres.

Education services:
Residential outdoor education centre, sleeps 40.

Services for disabled people:
Easy access trails.

Museum or gallery collection, archive, or library special collection:
Books, maps and photographs of Exmoor, including aerial photography

Printed publications:
Exmoor Visitor (newspaper, free)
National Park Management Plan
National Park Local Plan
Park Life (newspaper, free)
Various technical, educational and visitor publications
Walking Guides, General Interest
FILEXMOOR: an information pack about Exmoor National Park, written especially for students at GCSE level but of interest to anyone wanting to know more about the Park (10 Files 60p each or £6 the set in a presentation folder, plus p&p) (available on line)
QUESTEX: information about Exmoor National Park Authority, written especially for students at A level but of interest to anyone wanting to know more about management issues (6 Files 60p each plus p&p) (educational publications are downloadable from the website)
Order printed publications from: Centre Head, National Park Centre, Dulverton TA22 9EX, tel: 01398 323841

Publications list:
Available online and in print

Access to staff:
Contact by letter, by telephone, by fax, by e-mail and via website. Appointment necessary.
Hours: Mon to Thu, 0900 to 1700; Fri, 0900 to 1600

Access for disabled people:
Parking provided, ramped entry, toilet facilities, lift to committee room

Member of:
UK Association of National Park Authorities (ANPA)
126 Bute Street, Cardiff, CF10 5LE; tel: 02920 499966; e-mail: enquiries@anpa.gov.uk

National Park Centre:
ENPA
Fore Street, Dulverton, TA22 3EX; tel: 01398 323841; e-mail: npcdulverton@exmoor -nationalpark.gov.uk

EXMOOR SOCIETY

Parish Rooms, Rosemary Lane, Dulverton, Somerset, TA22 9DP

Tel: 01398 323335
Fax: 01398 323335
E-mail: exmoorsociety@yahoo.co.uk

Website:
http://www.exmoorsociety.org.uk
General information about the society, history of the society, items taken from Newsletter and Annual Report.

Enquiries:
Enquiries to: Secretary

Founded:
1959

continued overleaf

Organisation type and purpose:
Membership association (membership is by subscription), present number of members: 2200, voluntary organisation, registered charity (charity number 245761).
Conservation.

Subject coverage:
Conservation of Exmoor.

Museum or gallery collection, archive, or library special collection:
Archives from Roger Miles including:
Forestry Commission Reports
NPC Reports
Alfred Vowles Photographic Archive

Non-library collection catalogue:
All or part available in-house

Library catalogue:
All or part available in-house

Printed publications:
Annual Report
Newsletter
Exmoor Bibliography (£3.50)
Exmoor Review (annually, £3.60)
Index of Exmoor Review (£3.95)
Smuggling on Exmoor (£5, a one-off print run, copies available)

Access to staff:
Contact by letter, by telephone, by fax, by e-mail and in person
Hours: Tue to Thu, 0900 to 1600

EXMOUTH LIBRARY

40 Exeter Road, Exmouth, Devon, EX8 1PS

Tel: 01395 272677
Fax: 01395 271426
E-mail: exmouth.library@devon.gov.uk

Website:
http://www.devon.gov.uk/libraries

Enquiries:
Enquiries to: Librarian

Founded:
1946

Organisation type and purpose:
Local government body, public library.
Part of the Devon Library & Information Services.

Subject coverage:
General, Exmouth local history.

Museum or gallery collection, archive, or library special collection:
Exmouth local history

Trade and statistical information:
A selection of standard printed sources.

Library catalogue:
All or part available online

Microform publications:
Exmouth Journal (1869 to 1995)

Access to staff:
Contact by letter, by telephone and in person
Hours: Mon, Tue, Thu, Fri, 0930 to 1900; Wed, 0930 to 1300; Sat, 0930 to 1600

Access for disabled people:
Ramped entry

Parent body:
Devon County Council, Devon Library & Information Services
Great Moor House, Sowton, Exeter, EX2 7NL; tel: 01392 384315; fax: 01392 384316; e-mail: devlibs@devon.gov.uk

EXPORT CREDITS GUARANTEE DEPARTMENT

Acronym or abbreviation: ECGD

PO Box 2200, 2 Exchange Tower, Harbour Exchange Square, London, E14 9GS

Tel: 020 7512 7000
Fax: 020 7512 7649
E-mail: help@ecgd.gsi.gov.uk

Website:
http://www.ecgd.gov.uk
Information on products and services, lines of credit, country cover.

Enquiries:
Enquiries to: ECGD Help Desk
Direct tel: 020 7512 7887

Founded:
1919

Organisation type and purpose:
National government body.
Government department.
UK's official export credit agency.

Subject coverage:
Export credit insurance for UK exporters, overseas investment insurance, export finance guarantees for banks.

Printed publications:
Annual Review and Resource Accounts
Global Exporter-The Official ECGD Yearbook
ECGD News – customer newsletter (quarterly)
ECGD Customer Charter
ECGD's Business Principles
Guides to Products:
Buyer Credit Finance Guarantees
Supplier Credit Finance Guarantees
Overseas Investment Insurance
One-Stop-Shop
Credit Terms
Lines of Credit
Project Financing Scheme
Bond Insurance Policy
Export Insurance Policy
Claims and Recoveries
Recourse
Debt Conversion Scheme

Access to staff:
Contact by letter, by telephone, by fax, by e-mail and via website
Hours: Mon to Fri, 0800 to 1800

Responsible to the:
Secretary of State for Trade and Industry

EXTEND EXERCISE TRAINING LTD

Formal name: Movement to Music for the over Sixties and the Less Able of Any Age
Acronym or abbreviation: EXTEND

2 Place Farm, Wheathampstead, Hertfordshire, AL4 8SB

Tel: 01582 832760
Fax: 01582 832760
E-mail: admin@extend.org.uk

Website:
http://www.extend.org.uk

Enquiries:
Enquiries to: Extend Exercise
Other contacts: Director of Training for teacher training details.

Founded:
1976

Organisation type and purpose:
Registered charity (charity number 802498), training organisation.
Provides recreational movement to music for the over sixties and for the less able of any age.
To promoting good health and enhance the quality of life, through stimulating physical and mental health, increasing mobility and independence, improving strength, stamina, posture and coordination and to overcoming loneliness and isolation.

Subject coverage:
Recreational movement to music, recreational rehabilitation, use of music and rhythm, diet and nutrition.

Printed publications:
Leaflets (free)

Access to staff:
Contact by letter, by telephone, by fax and by e-mail. Appointment necessary. Access for members only.
Hours: Mon to Fri, 0900 to 1500

EYECARE TRUST, THE

Acronym or abbreviation: EIS

PO Box 804, Aylesbury, Buckinghamshire, HP20 9DF

Tel: 0845 129 5001
Fax: 0845 129 5001
E-mail: info@eyecaretrust.org.uk

Website:
http://www.eye-care.org.uk

Enquiries:
Enquiries to: Membership Secretary
Direct e-mail: pr@eyecaretrust.org.uk
Other contacts: Administrator

Founded:
2001

Formerly called:
Eyecare Information Bureau (ECIB), Optical Information Council (OIC); Eyecare Information Service (EIS) (year of change 2001)

Organisation type and purpose:
National organisation, advisory body, membership association (membership is by subscription), present number of members: 500, voluntary organisation, registered charity (charity number 1086146).
Public relations and promotions for the whole of optics.

Subject coverage:
All aspects of eyes and optics.

Trade and statistical information:
Statistics relating to the optical sector.

Printed publications:
Individual leaflets (free of charge to the public, bulk orders to members only)

Electronic and video publications:
CD-ROM – available to EIS 2000 members, health authority hospitals and other healthcare organisations and companies

Publications list:
Available online and in print

Access to staff:
Contact by letter, by telephone, by fax, by e-mail and via website
Hours: Mon to Fri, 1000 to 1600

Members:
Association of British Dispensing Opticians (ABDO)
Association of Contact Lens Manufacturers (ACLM)
Association of Optometrists (AOP)
British College of Optometrists (BCO)
Federation of Manufacturing Opticians (FMO)
Federation of Ophthalmic and Dispensing Opticians (FODO)

FABIAN SOCIETY

11 Dartmouth Street, London, SW1H 9BN

Tel: 020 7227 4900
Fax: 020 7976 7153
E-mail: info@fabian-society.org.uk

Website:
http://www.fabian-society.org.uk
Recent publications, events, conferences.

Enquiries:
Enquiries to: Membership Secretary
Direct e-mail: members@fabian-society.org.uk
Other contacts: Editor

Founded:
1884

Organisation type and purpose:
Membership association (membership is by subscription), present number of members: 6100, research organisation, publishing house.
Senior Think Tank for the Labour Party and the oldest socialist society affiliated to the Labour Party.

Subject coverage:
Politics, current affairs, social policy and economics.

Publications list:
Available online and in print

Access to staff:
Contact by letter, by telephone and by fax.
Appointment necessary.
Hours: Mon to Fri, 0930 to 1300 and 1400 to 1730

FACULTY OF BUILDING

Acronym or abbreviation: FOB

Central Office, 35 Hayworth Road, Sandiacre, Nottingham, NG10 5LL

Tel: 0115 949 0641
Fax: 0115 949 1664
E-mail: mail@faculty-of-building.co.uk

Website:
http://www.faculty-of-building.co.uk

Enquiries:
Enquiries to: Chief Executive

Founded:
1946

Organisation type and purpose:
Learned society.
Multi-professional society for all engaged in construction.
Construction networking.

Subject coverage:
There are 154 technical advice panels covering a very wide range of building and civil engineering, and related subjects, including acoustics, asphalt technology, bridge construction, building construction and maintenance, ceramics, contract law and procedure, demolition, district and group heating, drainage, gas engineering and technology, geodetic engineering, lift installation, materials handling, testing and purchasing, piling, quarrying, sewerage technology, timber technology.

Printed publications:
Annual Lectures Awards
Journal (2 times a year)
Newsletter (10 times a year)
Register of members
Technical papers

Access to staff:
Contact by letter, by telephone, by fax and by e-mail. Appointment necessary.
Hours: Mon to Fri, 0900 to 1730

Has:
19 regional UK branches and overseas representation

FACULTY OF CREATIVE ARTS LIBRARY, UNIVERSITY OF THE WEST OF ENGLAND, BRISTOL

Acronym or abbreviation: UWE, Bristol

Bower Ashton Campus, Kennel Lodge Road, Bristol, BS3 2JT

Tel: 0117 3284750
Fax: 0117 3284745
E-mail: library.sca@uwe.ac.uk

Website:
http://www.uwe.ac.uk/library

Enquiries:
Enquiries to: Campus/Faculty Librarian

Direct tel: 0117 3284731

Founded:
1992

Formerly called:
Bristol Polytechnic (year of change 1992)

Organisation type and purpose:
University library.

Subject coverage:
Art and design, media studies, cinema films.

Museum or gallery collection, archive, or library special collection:
Cinema films (video and DVD format)
Collection of slides
Collection of artists' books
Exhibition catalogues

Library catalogue:
All or part available online

Access to staff:
Contact by letter, by telephone, by fax and by e-mail. Appointment necessary.
Hours: Mon to Fri, 0900 to 1700

Member organisation of:
ARLIS (UK and Eire)

FACULTY OF DEAF EDUCATION AND LEARNING SUPPORT

Acronym or abbreviation: DEaLS

City Literary Institute, Keeley Street, Covent Garden, London, WC2B 4BA

Tel: 020 7492 2725; Minicom 020 7492 2746
Fax: 020 7492 2745
E-mail: deafedu@citylit.ac.uk

Website:
http://www.citylit.ac.uk/cfdp

Enquiries:
Enquiries to: Head of Centre
Other contacts: Centre Administrator and Centre Co-ordinators

Formerly called:
Central London AEI Centre for the Deaf; Centre for Deaf People and Speech Therapy (year of change 1997)

Organisation type and purpose:
Professional body, suitable for ages: 18+, training organisation.
Academic institution, formerly under the Inner London Education Authority.

Subject coverage:
Training, courses and support for deaf people and for those wishing to work with deaf people. We can provide support for deaf students in over 30 Further Education and Higher Education colleges.

Library catalogue:
All or part available in-house

Printed publications:
Prospectus
Course leaflets
Start to Sign Books
Books on wordprocessing, writing CVs

Publications list:
Available online

Access to staff:
Contact by letter, by telephone, by fax and by e-mail. Appointment necessary.
Hours: Mon to Fri, 0900 to 1800

Access to building, collection or gallery:
No prior appointment required

Access for disabled people:
Street-level entry, toilet facilities

FACULTY OF DENTAL SURGERY

Acronym or abbreviation: FDS RCSEng

Royal College of Surgeons of England, 35–43 Lincoln's Inn Fields, London, WC2A 3PN

Tel: 020 7869 6810
Fax: 020 7869 6816
E-mail: fds@rcseng.ac.uk

Website:
http://www.rcseng.ac.uk/public/fds/fds.htm

Enquiries:
Enquiries to: Executive Secretary

Founded:
1947

Organisation type and purpose:
International organisation, advisory body, professional body (membership is by subscription, qualification, election or invitation), present number of members: 4222, registered charity, training organisation.

Subject coverage:
Postgraduate dental education and training, and oral and maxillofacial surgery.

Museum or gallery collection, archive, or library special collection:
Odontological collection

Non-library collection catalogue:
All or part available in-house

Publications list:
Available online

Access to staff:
Contact by e-mail
Hours: Mon to Fri, 0900 to 1700

Access to building, collection or gallery:
Prior appointment required

Access for disabled people:
Parking provided

FACULTY OF FAMILY PLANNING AND REPRODUCTIVE HEALTH CARE

Acronym or abbreviation: FFPRHC

27 Sussex Place, Regent's Park, London, NW1 4RG

Tel: 020 7724 5681
Fax: 020 7723 5333
E-mail: journal@ffprhc.org.uk

Enquiries:
Enquiries to: Secretary

Founded:
1993

Organisation type and purpose:
Professional body (membership is by qualification), registered charity (charity number 1019969), training organisation.
Training for medical professionals (doctors).

Subject coverage:
All fields of family planning and reproductive health.

Printed publications:
Journal of Family Planning and Reproductive Health Care (quarterly)
Order printed publications from: Journal of Family Planning and Reproductive Healthcare at the main address
Subscriptions/purchasing, Professional, Managerial & Healthcare Publications Ltd., PO Box 100, Chichester, West Sussex, PO18 8HD, tel: 01243 576444, fax: 01243 576456, e-mail: admin@pmh.uk.com

Electronic and video publications:
Journal of Family Planning and Reproductive Health Care

Access to staff:
Access for members only.
Hours: Mon to Fri, 0900 to 1700

Parent body:
Royal College of Obstetricians and Gynaecologists at the same address

FAIR ISLE BIRD OBSERVATORY TRUST

Acronym or abbreviation: FIBOT

Fair Isle Bird Observatory, Fair Isle, Shetland, ZE2 9JU

Tel: 01595 760258
Fax: 01595 760258 (phone first)
E-mail: fairisle.birdobs@zetnet.co.uk

Website:
http://www.fairislebirdobs.oc.uk

Enquiries:
Enquiries to: Warden
Other contacts: Administrator for office business.

Founded:
1948

Organisation type and purpose:
Registered charity, research organisation. Ornithological research and holiday accommodation.

Subject coverage:
Seabird monitoring and migration studies at Fair Isle Bird Observatory. Accommodation for paying guests/visitors to Observatory/Isle.

Museum or gallery collection, archive, or library special collection:
Richard Richardson Library

Printed publications:
Fair Isle Bird Observatory Report
Order printed publications from: Fair Isle Bird Observatory Reports

Access to staff:
Contact by letter, by telephone, by e-mail, in person and via website
Hours: Any time, any day.

Access to building, collection or gallery:
Prior appointment required
Special comments: Open to visitors End April to End October.

FAIR ORGAN PRESERVATION SOCIETY

Acronym or abbreviation: FOPS

43 Woolmans, Fullers Slade, Milton Keynes, Buckinghamshire, MK11 2BA

Tel: 01908 263707
Fax: 01908 263707
E-mail: memsec@fops.ndirect.org

Website:
http://www.fops.org/

Enquiries:
Enquiries to: Membership Secretary

Founded:
1958

Organisation type and purpose:
Membership association (membership is by subscription), present number of members: 900 in 13 countries.
Promotion and encouragement of interest in, and the preservation of, fairground organs and mechanical musical instruments.

Subject coverage:
Fairground organs, Dutch and German street organs, Belgian dance organs.

Museum or gallery collection, archive, or library special collection:
Documentary archive held within the National Fairground Archive at Sheffield University

Printed publications:
The Key Frame (journal, quarterly, free to members, back issues for sale)
Pocket Book of Coming Events (annually, free to members)
On Display

Access to staff:
Contact by letter, by telephone, by fax, by e-mail and via website
Hours: Answerphone out of office hours

FALKIRK COLLEGE OF FURTHER AND HIGHER EDUCATION

Grangemouth Road, Falkirk, Strathclyde, FK2 9AD

Tel: 01324 403045
Fax: 01324 403046
E-mail: library@falkirkcollege.ac.uk

Enquiries:
Enquiries to: Librarian

Founded:
1963

Organisation type and purpose:
College of further education.

Subject coverage:
Automobile, electrical, electronic, mechanical, and plant engineering, construction and building, food technology, catering, health, social care, business studies, office services, leisure management, sport and recreation, computer studies, art and design, environmental management.

Library catalogue:
All or part available in-house

FALKIRK COUNCIL

Municipal Buildings, Falkirk, Strathclyde, FK1 5RS

Tel: 01324 506070
Fax: 01324 506071

Website:
http://www.falkirk.gov.uk
http://www.falkirkmuseums.org

Enquiries:
Enquiries to: Archivist
Direct e-mail: elspeth.reid@falkirk.gov.uk

Formerly called:
Central Regional Council, Falkirk District Council (year of change 1996)

Organisation type and purpose:
Local government body.

Subject coverage:
Local government administration.

FALKIRK COUNCIL – LIBRARIES AND MUSEUMS

Libraries:
Bo'ness Library
  Scotland's Close, Bo'ness, EH51 0AH; tel: 01506 778520
Bonnybridge Library
  Bridge Street, Bonnybridge, FK4 1AD; tel: 01324 503295
Denny Library
  49 Church Walk, Denny, FK6 6DF; tel: 01324 504242
Falkirk Library
  Hope Street, Falkirk, FK1 5AU; tel: 01324 503605
Grangemouth Library
  Bo'ness Road, Grangemouth, FK3 8AG; tel: 01324 504690
Larbert Library
  Main Street, Stenhousemuir, Larbert, FK5 3JX; tel: 01324 503590
Slamannan Library
  The Cross, Slamannan; tel: 01324 851373
The Information Centre
  The Steeple, High Street, Falkirk; tel: 01324 628038

Museums:
Falkirk Museum
  Callendar House, Callendar Park, Falkirk; tel: 01324 612134
Grangemouth Museum
  Victoria Library, Bo'ness Road, Grangemouth; tel: 01324 483291
Kinneil Museum
  Duchess Anne Cottages, Kinneil Estate, Bo'ness; tel: 01506 824318

FALKIRK COUNCIL ARCHIVES

Formal name: Falkirk Museums History Research Centre

Callendar House, Callendar Park, Falkirk, Strathclyde, FK1 1YR

Tel: 01324 503779
Fax: 01324 503771
E-mail: callendar.house@falkirk.gov.uk

Website:
http://www.falkirk.gov.uk/cultural/museums/archives.htm

Enquiries:
Enquiries to: Archivist
Other contacts: Museums Assistant for search room enquiries.

Founded:
1924

Organisation type and purpose:
Local government body.

Subject coverage:
Local government administration

Museum or gallery collection, archive, or library special collection:
Funds Level Finding Aid will be available via the Scottish Archives Network
Business records including: Grangemouth Dockyard, Cruikshank & Co, P&M Hurll, J Baird & Co, Grahamston Iron Co, James Ross & Co, Scottish Tar Distillers
Falkirk Herald 1845–1900 (microfilm)
Family and personal papers including: Forbes of Callendar Papers, Dewar family, Louden family, Burns family, Love Collection
Local authority records (Falkirk Burgh 1803–1975, Grangemouth Burgh 1872–1975, Bo'ness Burgh, Denny & Dunipace Burgh 1833–1975, Falkirk District 1975–1995, Stirling County District Councils 1930–1975, West Lothian County District Councils 1930–1975, Parish Councils and Parochial Boards)
Photograph collection, over 30,000 images
Records of local organisations, trade unions, professional associations
Small reference library

Non-library collection catalogue:
All or part available in-house

Access to staff:
Contact by letter, by telephone, by fax, by e-mail and in person
Hours: Mon to Fri, 1000 to 1230 and 1330 to 1700
Special comments: Closed on local public holidays.

Access to building, collection or gallery:
No prior appointment required
Hours: Mon to Sat, 1000 to 1700

Access for disabled people:
Parking provided, level entry, access to all public areas, toilet facilities

Parent body:
Falkirk Council

FALKIRK COUNCIL LIBRARY SERVICE

Victoria Buildings, Queen Street, Falkirk, FK2 7AF

Tel: 01324 506800
Fax: 01324 506801
E-mail: library.support@falkirk.gov.uk

Website:
http://www.falkirk.gov.uk/services/community/library_services/library_services.aspx

Enquiries:
Enquiries to: Principal Librarian (Support Services)
Direct tel: 01324 506804
Direct e-mail: gil.vick@falkirk.gov.uk

Founded:
1996

Organisation type and purpose:
Local government body, public library.

Subject coverage:
General, local history.

Non-library collection catalogue:
All or part available online and in-house

Library catalogue:
All or part available online and in-house

Printed publications:
Current awareness bulletin for local government
 (weekly)
The following publications are available at all
 libraries and museums:
A History of Falkirk
A series of handy guides of various historical trails
 in the district: Bo'ness Town Trail, 2,000 years of
 History: a guided trail for Kinneil Estate
Annals of a Country Parish: old days and ways in
 Bothkennar Parish (a transcript of the Kirk of
 Sessions Minutes of Bothkennar Parish 1722–41)
Bo'ness: a glimpse of the past
Bonnybridge in Bygone Days
Corsets in Stripeside (personal memoirs of the
 Denny and Dunipace area)
Edinburgh and Glasgow Union Canal (a history of
 the development of the canal)
Falkirk's Yesterdays
Grangemouth: Two Towns
Grangemouth's Modern History
Happy Valley: memories of Laurieston
Heroes Departed: Falkirk District during the First
 World War
Histories of some of the towns and villages,
 written by local authors including:
Larbert and Stenhousemuir
Maps, including Falkirk District Map, reprints of
 early Ordnance Survey Maps and street guides
Miscellaneous books and accounts
Old photographs, including:
Pits, Pints and Poverty: an account of the village of
 Standburn
Polmont and the Braes
Redding Pit Disaster: an illustrated account
Select Bibliography and Source Guide to the
 Romans in Falkirk District
Selection of local postcards/greetings cards and
 maps
Shieldhill: a glimpse of the past
Symington and the Charlotte Dundas (concise
 illustrated booklet on William Symington and
 the building of this steamship in Grangemouth)
Target – Falkirk: Falkirk District in the Second
 World War
The Dear Auld Hame: Changing Scenes in Falkirk
 District
The first and second statistical accounts giving
 descriptions of parishes in Falkirk District in the
 18th and 19th centuries
To Labour All Our Lives: Old Photographs of
 Working Lives in Falkirk District
Travelling Through Time: Transport in Falkirk
 District
Vale of Bonny: The history and the legend
Order printed publications from: Library Support,
 Victoria Buildings, Queen Street, Falkirk, FK2 7AF,
 tel: 01324 506800

Publications list:
Available online and in print

Access to staff:
Contact by letter, by telephone, by fax, by e-mail,
in person and via website
Hours: Mon to Fri, 0900 to 1700

FALKLAND ISLANDS GOVERNMENT OFFICE

Acronym or abbreviation: FIGO

Falkland House, 14 Broadway, London, SW1H
0BH

Tel: 020 7222 2542
Fax: 020 7222 2375
E-mail: rep@falklands.gov.fk

Website:
http://www.falklands.gov.fk
http://www.visitorfalklands.com
Tourism information.
Tourism information

Enquiries:
Enquiries to: Representative

Founded:
1983

Organisation type and purpose:
National government body.
To provide an information source and trade links
in the United Kingdom. Point of contact for UK
Parliament.

Subject coverage:
All aspects relating to the government,
development of trade, tourism and travel to the
Falklands. Dissemination of all information of a
general nature in connection with the Falklands.

Trade and statistical information:
General and specific information on trade to and
from the Islands.

Printed publications:
Falkland Islands... Sustaining a Secure Future (free
 brochure)
Falklands Focus (free newsheet published twice a
 year)
Tourism and Holiday Brochures (free)
Brochures and leaflets (free)
Order printed publications from: Falkland Islands
Government Office, Falkland House, 14 Broadway,
Westminster, London, SW1H 0BH

Electronic and video publications:
The Modern Falklands (free DVD)
Order electronic and video publications from: Falkland
Islands Government Office, Falkland House, 14
Broadway, Westminster, London, SW1H 0BH

Publications list:
Available in print

Access to staff:
Contact by letter, by telephone, by fax, by e-mail,
in person and via website
Hours: Mon to Fri, 0900 to 1300 and 1400 to 1730

Access to building, collection or gallery:
Prior appointment required
Hours: Mon to Fri, 0900 to 1300 and 1400 to 1730

Links with:
Falkland Islands Development Corporation
 Shackleton House, Davis Street East, Stanley,
 Falkland Islands, FIQQ 1ZZ; tel: +500 27211; fax:
 +500 27210; e-mail: sgyford@fidc.co.uk; website:
 http://www.fidc.co.fk
Falkland Islands Tourist Board
 Jetty Visitor Centre, Stanley, Falkland Islands,
 FIQQ 1ZZ; tel: +500 22215; fax: +500 22619; e-
 mail: jettyvisitorcentre@horizon.co.fk; website:
 http://www.visitorfalklands.com

Parent body:
Falkland Islands Government
 The Secretariat, Stanley, Falkland Islands, FIQQ
 1ZZ; tel: +500 27242; fax: +500 27109; e-mail:
 lbrownlee@sec.gov.fk

FAMILIES NEED FATHERS

134–146 Curtain Road, London, EC2A 3AR

Tel: 020 7613 5060
Fax: 020 7739 3410
E-mail: fnf@fnf.org.uk

Website:
http://www.fnf.org.uk

Enquiries:
Enquiries to: Secretary

Founded:
1974

Organisation type and purpose:
Membership association (membership is by
subscription), present number of members: 3000,
voluntary organisation, registered charity (charity
number 276899).
Support group, self-help society and pressure
group to change and improve the present legal
process and to eliminate unnecessary and
protracted legal conflict.
Keeping children in contact with both parents after
separation or divorce.
Promoting shared-parenting.

Printed publications:
For the Sake of the Children – FNF guide to shared
 parenting (Secker S)
Fatherhood Reclaimed (Burgess A)
Psychological Research on Fathering (Russan S)
Booklets
Leaflets

Publications list:
Available online and in print

Access to staff:
Contact by telephone, by e-mail and via website
Hours: Mon to Fri, 0900 to 1700

FAMILY AND COMMUNITY HISTORICAL RESEARCH SOCIETY

Formal name: Family and Community Historical
Research Society Limited

Unit 6, 5 West Hill, Aspley Guise, Milton Keynes,
MK17 8DW

E-mail: honsec@fachrs.org.uk

Website:
http://www.fachrs.com

Enquiries:
Enquiries to: Hon. Sec.
Direct e-mail: honsec@fachrs.org.uk

Organisation type and purpose:
Membership organisation (membership by
subscription).
Registered charity (charity number 3965865)
To promote and communicate research in family
and community history within a scholarly
framework.

Printed publications:
Journal (2 times a year)
Newsletter
Swing Unmasked (book)

Access to staff:
Contact by letter, by e-mail and via website

FAMILY FUND

Unit 4, Alpha Court, Monks Cross Drive,
Huntington, York, YO32 9WN

Tel: 01904 621115\ Minicom no. 01904 658085
Fax: 01904 652625
E-mail: info@familyfund.org.uk

Website:
http://www.familyfund.org.uk

Enquiries:
Enquiries to: Information Officer
Direct tel: 0845 130 4542

Founded:
1973

Formerly called:
Family Fund (year of change 1994)

Organisation type and purpose:
Registered charity (charity number 1053866).
To ease the stress on families who care for severely
disabled children under 16, by providing grants
related to the care of the child.

Subject coverage:
Families with disabled children.

continued overleaf

Printed publications:
After 16 – What's New? (free to young disabled
  people)
Family Fund leaflet and application form (in
  English, large print and other languages)

Publications list:
Available online and in print

Access to staff:
Contact by letter, by telephone, by fax, by e-mail
and via website
Hours: Mon to Fri, 0900 to 1700

FAMILY HISTORY SOCIETY OF CHESHIRE

Acronym or abbreviation: FHSC

Little Trees, Gawsworth Road, Gawsworth,
Macclesfield, SK11 9RA

Tel: 01625 426173
E-mail: info@fhsc.org.uk

Website:
http://www.fhsc.org.uk

Enquiries:
Enquiries to: Secretary

Founded:
1969

Organisation type and purpose:
Membership association (membership is by
subscription), present number of members: 3000,
voluntary organisation, registered charity (charity
number 515168), suitable for ages: all.
To promote interest in family history research in
Cheshire by organising monthly meetings of the 17
local groups, hosting conferences, open days, and
publishing transcriptions and indexes of local
records.

Subject coverage:
Family history in Cheshire.

**Museum or gallery collection, archive, or library
special collection:**
Over 2000 books and magazines, and exchange
  journals from other family history societies
Many films of Cheshire Parish Registers and
  Bishop's Transcripts
Microfiche of the IGI, GRO BMD 1837 to 1900
1881 Census on CD-ROM

Library catalogue:
All or part available in-house

Printed publications:
A large number of printed, microfiche and CD
  publications including:
Cheshire Ancestor (quarterly, members)
1841 Census Index Birkenhead
1841 Census Index Northwich
1851 Census Index Stockport, Macclesfield,
  Wilmslow, Runcorn, Northwich, Congleton,
  Nantwich, Chester, Wirral, Birkenhead
Order printed publications from: Family History
Society of Cheshire
91 Stretford House, Chapel Lane, Stretford,
Manchester, M32 9AY

Microform publications:
Monumental inscriptions (over 150 graveyards)
1841 Census Index Birkenhead & Tranmere
1861 Census Index Nantwich
Register transcriptions
Members Interests
Pigot's Directory of Cheshire 1830 and 1834
Order microform publications from: Family History
Society of Cheshire
9 Buckfast Close, Penketh, Warrington, Cheshire,
WA5 2NS, tel: 01925 726335

Electronic and video publications:
CDs (both own and bought in) including parish
  registers, old maps, books and various
  collections of data
Order electronic and video publications from: 5
Haydock Close, Tytherington, Macclesfield, SK10
2WG

Publications list:
Available online and in print

Access to staff:
Contact by letter, by telephone, by e-mail and via
website
Hours: Mon to Fri, 0900 to 1700

Access to building, collection or gallery:
No prior appointment required
Hours: Library: Mon to Fri, 1000 to 1600
Special comments: Library and Research Centre,
Festival Hall, Alderley Edge, Cheshire; Mon to Fri,
1000 to 1600.
Members only and joining facility.

Has Local Groups in:
Alsager, Altrincham, Bebington, Birkenhead,
Bramhall, Chester, Congleton, Crewe, Dukinfield,
Macclesfield, Nantwich, Northwich, Runcorn,
Stockton Heath, Tarporley, Wallasey, West Kirby

FAMILY SERVICE UNITS

Acronym or abbreviation: FSU

207 Old Marylebone Road, London, NW1 5QP

Tel: 020 7402 5175
Fax: 020 7724 1829
E-mail: Centraloffice@fsu.org.uk

Enquiries:
Enquiries to: Head of Fundraising and
Communications

Founded:
1948

Organisation type and purpose:
Registered charity (charity number 212114).
Network of local units.
To serve disadvantaged families in communities
which are unable to achieve their full potential
because they lack adequate resources.

Subject coverage:
Intensive counselling for children, adults and
families coping with the threat or reality of family
breakdown; specialised therapeutic work with
families where children have experienced or are at
risk of physical, emotional or sexual abuse;
playschemes, holidays, after school and
educational projects; a range of 'drop in' services
and groups where people can get together, combat
isolation and help each other; programmes
specially designed to help parents develop skills
and resources in caring for their children.

**Museum or gallery collection, archive, or library
special collection:**
Minutes and documents relating to the foundation
  and development of Pacifist Service Units (1941–
  1947) and of Family Service Units (1947 to the
  present)

Publications list:
Available in print

Access to staff:
Contact by letter
Hours: Mon to Fri, 0900 to 1700

Affiliated to:
National Council for Voluntary Childcare
Organisations

FAMILY WELFARE ASSOCIATION

Acronym or abbreviation: FWA

501–505 Kingsland Road, Dalston, London, E8
4AU

Tel: 020 7254 6251
Fax: 020 7249 5443
E-mail: fwa.headoffice@fwa.org.uk

Enquiries:
Enquiries to: Chief Executive

Founded:
1869

Formerly called:
Charity Organisation Society (year of change 1946)

Organisation type and purpose:
Registered charity, voluntary organisation (charity
number 264713).
Support for families, children and others in need.

Subject coverage:
Educational grants advice for students/potential
students, who are ineligible for statutory grants.
Information and advice to people requiring help
through various services in certain areas.

**Museum or gallery collection, archive, or library
special collection:**
Archives of Charity Organisation Society and the
  Family Welfare Association held by London
  Metropolitan Archives

Publications list:
Available in print

Access to staff:
Contact by letter
Hours: Mon to Fri, 0900 to 1700

FANY (PRVC)

Formal name: FANY (Princess Royal's Volunteer
Corps)

TA Headquarters, 95 Horseferry Rd, London,
SW1P 2DY

Tel: 020 7976 5459
Fax: 020 7630 8019
E-mail: hq@fany.org.uk

Website:
http://www.fany.org.uk
Details of the organisation, current events, history,
publications, recruitment.

Enquiries:
Enquiries to: Adjutant

Founded:
1907

Organisation type and purpose:
Voluntary organisation, suitable for women aged:
18 to 45.
To serve the country in peace and war; volunteer
Emergency Response units providing support to
the City of London and Metropolitan Police in
Major Incidents and to the British Army as
required, particularly in the protection of the
capital against terrorism.

Subject coverage:
Provides emergency response teams of women
able to cope in a variety of circumstances.

**Museum or gallery collection, archive, or library
special collection:**
Archive documents and photographs, WWI, WWII
  and to the present day

Non-library collection catalogue:
All or part available online

Access to staff:
Contact by letter, by telephone, by fax, by e-mail
and via website. Appointment necessary. Letter of
introduction required.
Hours: Mon to Thu, 0900 to 1800

Access to building, collection or gallery:
Prior appointment required

FAREHAM COLLEGE

Bishopsfield Road, Fareham, Hampshire, PO14
1NH

Tel: 01329 815200
Fax: 01329 822483

Website:
http://www.fareham.ac.uk

Enquiries:
Enquiries to: Learning Resources Centre Manager
Direct tel: 01329 815322
Direct e-mail: meg.newman@fareham.ac.uk

Founded:
1969

Organisation type and purpose:
Suitable for ages: 16+.

Subject coverage:
Full time A-level, BTEC First, BTEC National Diplomas, NVQs Levels 2 and 3.

Non-library collection catalogue:
All or part available online and in-house

Library catalogue:
All or part available online and in-house

Access to staff:
Contact by letter, by telephone, by e-mail and in person
Hours: Mon to Thu, 0830 to 1900; Fri, 0830 to 1630

Access for disabled people:
Parking provided, ramped entry, access to all public areas, toilet facilities

FARM ANIMAL WELFARE COUNCIL

Acronym or abbreviation: FAWC

Area 5a, 9 Millbank, c/o Nobel House, 17 Smith Square, London, SW1P 3JR

Tel: 020 7238 5192
Fax: 020 7238 3169
E-mail: fawcsecretariat@defra.gsi.gov.uk

Website:
http://www.fawc.org.uk
About FAWC, its membership, current work and publications.

Enquiries:
Enquiries to: Secretary
Other contacts: Assistant Secretaries

Founded:
1979

Organisation type and purpose:
Advisory body.
Advisory body to Government; membership is by Ministerial appointment.
FAWC's membership includes farmers, researchers, consumers, animal welfarists and veterinarians.
To keep under review welfare of farm animals and to advise the Government of legislative or other changes.

Subject coverage:
Farm animal welfare: studies on farm assurance schemes, cloning, broiler breeders, outdoor pigs, farmed fish, laying hens and dairy cattle have been completed. Other areas addressed include sheep, turkeys, wild boar, ostriches, broilers and transport.

Museum or gallery collection, archive, or library special collection:
Reports on all subject coverage

Printed publications:
FAWC Annual Review and all Reports
Government Animal Welfare Codes (available free from MAFF Publications)
Order printed publications from: MAFF Publications London, SE99 7TP, tel: 0645 556000

Publications list:
Available online

Access to staff:
Contact by letter, by telephone, by fax and by e-mail
Hours: Mon to Fri, 0900 to 1700

Access to building, collection or gallery:
No access other than to staff

Parent body:
Department for Environment, Food and Rural Affairs

FARM STAY (UK) LIMITED

Acronym or abbreviation: FSUK

National Agricultural Centre, Stoneleigh Park, Kenilworth, Warwickshire, CV8 2LZ

Tel: 024 7669 6909
Fax: 024 7669 6930
E-mail: admin@farmstayuk.co.uk

Website:
http://www.farmstayuk.co.uk
Comprehensive information for every member, including colour photos and interactive website with search mechanism throughout the UK.

Enquiries:
Enquiries to: Chief Executive
Other contacts: Office Manager for administrative queries, requests for information, promotional material.

Founded:
1983

Formerly called:
Farm Holiday Bureau (UK) Limited (FHB) (year of change 2000)

Organisation type and purpose:
National organisation, membership association (membership is by qualification), present number of members: 1000.
Self-funding Agricultural Cooperative. Producing a full colour brochure promoting members' businesses.

Subject coverage:
Farm-based holiday accommodation; information for farmers and customers; farm and rural tourism; tourism markets.

Printed publications:
Open Gate (newsletter, quarterly for members)
Stay On A Farm (guide to over 1000 farms, free)

Access to staff:
Contact by letter, by telephone, by fax, by e-mail and via website. Appointment necessary.
Hours: Mon to Fri, 0900 to 1700

Access to building, collection or gallery:
No prior appointment required

FARMDATA LIMITED

Westertown, Rothienorman, Inverurie, Aberdeenshire, AB51 8US

Tel: 01467 671457
Fax: 01467 671448
E-mail: sales@farmdata.co.uk

Website:
http://www.farmdata.co.uk
Full information on the company and its services.

Enquiries:
Enquiries to: Information Officer

Founded:
1978

Organisation type and purpose:
Service industry.

Access to staff:
Contact by letter, by telephone, by fax, by e-mail and via website
Hours: Mon to Fri, 0900 to 1700

FARNHAM CASTLE INTERNATIONAL BRIEFING & CONFERENCE CENTRE

Farnham Castle, Farnham, Surrey, GU9 0AG

Tel: 01252 721194
Fax: 01252 719277
E-mail: info@farnhamcastle.com

Website:
http://www.farnhamcastle.com
Latest news about the centre, full details of range of training programmes plus conference, meeting and event facilities.

Enquiries:
Enquiries to: Sales Manager

Direct tel: 01252 720418
Direct e-mail: lroberts@farnhamcastle.com
Other contacts: Client Services Administrator

Founded:
1953

Formerly called:
Centre for International Briefing (CIB) (year of change 2001)

Organisation type and purpose:
International organisation, registered charity (charity number 313648), training organisation.
Not for profit organisation offering intercultural awareness training, international assignment briefings, business briefings for people proposing to live and work overseas.

Subject coverage:
Briefings on any country, including current economics, politics, the people and their social and business culture, the business environment, social and domestic conditions, constructive and efficient conducting of verbal and non-verbal communications, agreements, discussions, negotiations; practical aspects of moving overseas; information on leisure and recreation, health, education and security. Business briefings for home-based international personnel. Intercultural workshops and repatriation programmes.

Printed publications:
Brochure about programmes

Access to staff:
Contact by letter, by telephone, by fax, by e-mail, in person and via website. Appointment necessary.
Hours: Mon to Fri, 0900 to 1700

FASHION RESEARCH CENTRE

4 Circus, Bath, BA1 2EW

Tel: 01225 477752
Fax: 01225 444793
E-mail: costume_enquiries@bathnes.gov.uk

Website:
http://www.museumofcostume.co.uk
Reference to Fashion Research Centre facilities.

Enquiries:
Enquiries to: Assistant Keeper of Collections (Costume)
Direct tel: 01225 477754
Direct e-mail: rhian_tritton@bathnes.gov.uk

Founded:
1974

Formerly called:
Costume and Fashion Research Centre

Organisation type and purpose:
Local government body.
The Centre was founded as an extension to the Museum of Costume.
To provide facilities for reference and research in the history of dress.

Subject coverage:
History of dress, particularly fashionable dress, related areas such as textiles and embroidery.

Museum or gallery collection, archive, or library special collection:
Cunnington Collection of Photographs of works of art
Fashion plates (late 18th to early 20th century)
Part of Mattli, Lachasse and Ian Thomas Archives (1940–1980s)
Part of Worth and Paquin Archive (1902–1956)
Sunday Times Fashion Archive (1957–1972)

Library catalogue:
All or part available in-house

Printed publications:
Order printed publications from: Rhian Tritton, Assistant Keeper of Collections (Costume)
Fashion Research Centre

Access to staff:
Contact by letter, by telephone, by fax, by e-mail and via website. Appointment necessary.

continued overleaf

Hours: Thu and Fri, 1000 to 1230 and 1400 to 1630
Special comments: Closed public holidays.

Links with:
Museum of Costume

Parent body:
Bath and North East Somerset Council
  Heritage Services Division

FAVERSHAM SOCIETY, THE

Fleur de Lis, 10–13 Preston Street, Faversham,
Kent, ME13 8NS

Tel: 01795 534542
Fax: 01795 533261
E-mail: ticfaversham@btconnect.com.

Website:
http://www.faversham.org/society
Full details of the centre and the society.

Enquiries:
Enquiries to: Honorary Director

Founded:
1977

Organisation type and purpose:
Membership association, present number of
members: 1000, voluntary organisation, registered
charity (charity number 250945).
The Society is run by 100% voluntary effort for the
good of the area. It is completely independent and
open to all sharing its interests.

Subject coverage:
History of Faversham area, including the port of
Faversham, and industries; family history in
Faversham area, history of explosives industry.

Special visitor services:
Networker (officer), Tourist Information Centre

**Museum or gallery collection, archive, or library
special collection:**
Museum, gallery, two libraries

Non-library collection catalogue:
All or part available in-house

Library catalogue:
All or part available in-house

Printed publications:
Faversham Papers: some 100 monographs about
  the area, including:
The History of Faversham
The Foundation of Faversham Abbey
The War Years 1939–1945 in Faversham and
  District
Faversham Stone Trail
Changing Landlords, the Annexation of the
  Maison Dieu to St John's College, Cambridge
Faversham Studies including:
Faversham and District Bibliography, Primary
  Sources (7 Volumes, Hyde P)
Faversham and District Bibliography, Secondary
  Sources (Hyde P)
Sittingbourne Papers: produced by the Faversham
  Society for the Sittingbourne Society

Electronic and video publications:
Several DVDs and CDs
Order electronic and video publications from: above
address

Publications list:
Available online and in print

Access to staff:
Contact by letter, by telephone, by fax, by e-mail,
in person and via website
Hours: Mon to Sat, 1000 to 1600; Sun, 1000 to 1300

Access to building, collection or gallery:
Hours: Mon to Sat, 1000 to 1600; Sun, 1000 to 1300

Access for disabled people:
Available over most of complex
Hours: Mon to Sat, 1000 to 1600; Sun, 1000 to 1300

Manages the:
Chart Gunpowder Mills
  Westbrook Walk, Faversham

Manages the:
Fleur de Lis Heritage Centre
  at the same address

Manages the:
Maison Dieu Museum
  Ospringe Street, Faversham

FEDERATION AGAINST COPYRIGHT THEFT LIMITED

Acronym or abbreviation: FACT

7 Victory Business Centre, Worton Road,
Isleworth, Middlesex, TW7 6DB

Tel: 020 8568 6646
Fax: 020 8560 6364
E-mail: contact@fact-uk.org.uk

Enquiries:
Enquiries to: Director General
Other contacts: Company Secretary

Founded:
1983

Organisation type and purpose:
National organisation, membership association
(membership is by subscription, election or
invitation), present number of members: 20.
Private company.

Subject coverage:
Copyright protection of motion pictures.

Access to staff:
Contact by letter and by e-mail
Hours: Mon to Fri, 0900 to 1700

Affiliated to:
Motion Picture Association

FEDERATION AGAINST SOFTWARE THEFT

Acronym or abbreviation: FAST

York House, 18 York Road, Maidenhead,
Berkshire, SL6 1SF

Tel: 01628 622121
Fax: 01628 760355
E-mail: fast@fast.org

Website:
http://www.fast.org.uk
Information on software piracy and the activities of
The Federation.

Enquiries:
Enquiries to: Public Relations Manager
Other contacts: Account Manager for membership.

Founded:
1984

Organisation type and purpose:
National organisation, advisory body, trade
association, membership association (membership
is by subscription), present number of members:
150.

Subject coverage:
Software control and management, auditing, the
law governing software copyright, forensic
examination of counterfeits, software piracy.

Printed publications:
Audit pack – Audit services contact list (free)
Computer crime – A guide for enforcement
  authorities (free)
FASTtalk (newsletter, quarterly)
Information pack (free)

Access to staff:
Contact by letter, by telephone, by fax, by e-mail
and via website
Hours: Mon to Fri, 0900 to 1700

Access to building, collection or gallery:
Prior appointment required

Access for disabled people:
Parking provided, ramped entry, level entry, toilet
facilities

FEDERATION OF BRITISH AQUATIC SOCIETIES

Acronym or abbreviation: FBAS

2 Cedar Avenue, Wickford, Essex, SS12 9DT

Tel: 01268 472095
E-mail: chris@cheswright.freeserve.co.uk

Enquiries:
Enquiries to: General Secretary

Founded:
1938

Organisation type and purpose:
Membership association (membership is by
subscription), voluntary organisation.
Central governing body for all UK aquarist clubs.

Subject coverage:
All fields of aquatics associated with fishkeeping:
coldwater, tropical, marine; the environment,
keeping, breeding and showing of fish; fish
diseases and cures.

Printed publications:
Details of Clubs around Country
Fishworld (magazine, quarterly, £5 p.a.)
Publications on all subjects given above
Order printed publications from: Merchandising
Officer, FBAS
28 The Mall, Binstead, Isle of Wight, PO33 3SF, tel:
01983 566810

Publications list:
Available in print

Access to staff:
Contact by fax
Hours: Telephone after 1800

FEDERATION OF BRITISH ARTISTS

Acronym or abbreviation: FBA

17 Carlton House Terrace, London, SW1Y 5BD

Tel: 020 7930 6844
Fax: 020 7839 7830
E-mail: press@mallgalleries.com

Website:
http://www.mallgalleries.org.uk

Enquiries:
Enquiries to: Secretary
Other contacts: Marketing and Communications
Officer

Founded:
1961

Organisation type and purpose:
Membership association (membership is by
election or invitation), present number of
members: 600, voluntary organisation, registered
charity (charity number 200048).
Federation of voluntary art societies (see list
following this entry).
The FBA promotes the visual arts in Britain and is
the umbrella organisation for nine autonomous
national art societies.

Subject coverage:
Arranging art exhibitions in the Mall Galleries,
London SW1, advice on commissioning portraits
or other art work, visual arts by contemporary
artists. Past and present society members.

**Museum or gallery collection, archive, or library
special collection:**
Catalogues of previous exhibitions

Non-library collection catalogue:
All or part available in print

Printed publications:
Catalogues of exhibitions for each art society
Newsletter (3 times a year)

Access to staff:
Contact by letter, by telephone, by fax, by e-mail
and via website
Hours: Mon to Fri, 0930 to 1730

Access to building, collection or gallery:
Prior appointment required
Hours: Mon to Fri, 0930 to 1730

Access for disabled people:
Toilet facilities
Special comments: Stair lift.

Links with:
FBA Friends Society
    contact through the FBA
Hesketh Hubbard Art Society
    contact through the FBA
Mall Galleries
    contact through the FBA
New English Art Club
    contact through the FBA
Pastel Society
    contact through the FBA
Royal Institute of Oil Painters
    contact through the FBA
Royal Institute of Painters in Watercolours
    contact through the FBA
Royal Society of British Artists
    contact through the FBA
Royal Society of Marine Artists
    contact through the FBA
Royal Society of Portrait Painters
    contact through the FBA
Society of Wildlife Artists
    contact through the FBA

FEDERATION OF BRITISH BONSAI SOCIETIES

Acronym or abbreviation: FOBBS

17 Woodland Park, Ynystawe, Swansea, West Glamorgan, SA6 5AR

Tel: 01792 845659
E-mail: ukbonsai@ntlworld.com

Website:
http://www.fobbs.co.uk
Details of clubs, events, advice, gallery.
http://uk.geocities.com/fobbs_uk

Enquiries:
Enquiries to: General Secretary

Founded:
1982

Organisation type and purpose:
Membership association (membership is by subscription), voluntary organisation, registered charity.

Subject coverage:
Bonsai and bonsai clubs, national bonsai collection, bonsai traders, bonsai events.

Museum or gallery collection, archive, or library special collection:
National Bonsai Collection at Birmingham Botanical Gardens

Printed publications:
Newsletter (once every other month)
Membership List (annual)

Access to staff:
Contact by letter, by telephone, by e-mail and via website
Hours: Any reasonable time

Affiliated to:
Friends of the National Bonsai Collection (Charitable trust); tel: 0121 378 4837; fax: 0121 311 1912

FEDERATION OF BRITISH CREMATION AUTHORITIES

Acronym or abbreviation: FBCA

41 Salisbury Road, Carshalton, Surrey, SM5 3HA

Tel: 020 8669 4521

Enquiries:
Enquiries to: Secretary

Organisation type and purpose:
Trade association.
Technical advisory service.

Subject coverage:
All matters connected with the management and operation of crematoria.

Printed publications:
Resurgam (journal, quarterly)
Technical booklets/leaflets

FEDERATION OF BRITISH ENGINEERS' TOOL MANUFACTURERS

Acronym or abbreviation: FBETM

c/o IST, Henry Street, Sheffield, S3 7EQ

Tel: 0114 278 9143
Fax: 0114 275 5573
E-mail: info@britishtools.co.uk

Website:
http://www.britishtools.co.uk

Enquiries:
Enquiries to: Secretary General

Organisation type and purpose:
Trade association.

Subject coverage:
Engineers' cutting tools industry, exhibition and export activities, publicity for the industry.

Associated with:
Federation of British Hand Tool Manufacturers

Member of:
European Cutting Tools Association (ECTA)

Members:
British Hardmetal and Engineers' Cutting Tool Association (BHELTA)
    e-mail: info@britishtools.co.uk

FEDERATION OF BRITISH HAND TOOL MANUFACTURERS

Acronym or abbreviation: FBHTM

c/o Institute of Spring Technology, Henry Street, Sheffield, S3 7EQ

Tel: 0114 278 9143
Fax: 0114 275 5573
E-mail: info@britishtools.co.uk

Website:
http://www.britishtools.co.uk

Enquiries:
Enquiries to: Association Director

Organisation type and purpose:
Trade association.

Subject coverage:
British hand tool manufacturing industry, exhibition and export activity, publicity for the industry.

Member of:
Comité Européen d'Outillage (European Hand Tool Committee) (CEO)

Members:
Construction Fixings Association
    website: www.fixingscfa.co.uk

FEDERATION OF BUILDING SPECIALIST CONTRACTORS

Acronym or abbreviation: FBSC

Unit 9 Lakeside Industrial Estate, Stanton Harcourt, Oxfordshire OX29 5SL

Tel: 01865 883557
Fax: 01865 884467
E-mail: enquiries@fbsc.org.uk

Website:
http://www.fbsc.org.uk/

Enquiries:
Enquiries to: Membership Secretary

Organisation type and purpose:
Trade association (membership is by subscription).

Subject coverage:
Details of member companies covering a wide range of specialist trades in the building industry.

Access to staff:
Contact by letter, by telephone, by fax and by e-mail
Hours: Mon to Fri, 0900 to 1700

Access to building, collection or gallery:
No prior appointment required

Member of:
Construction Confederation

FEDERATION OF CHILDREN'S BOOK GROUPS

Acronym or abbreviation: FCBG

2 Bridge Wood View, Horsforth, Leeds, West Yorkshire, LS18 5PE

Tel: 0113 2588910
E-mail: info@fcbg.org.uk

Website:
http://www.fcbg.org.uk

Enquiries:
Enquiries to: National Secretary

Founded:
1968

Organisation type and purpose:
Membership association (membership is by subscription), present number of members: 30 Book Groups, plus Individual and Professional Members, voluntary organisation, registered charity (charity number 268289).
We aim to promote enjoyment and interest in children's books and reading.

Subject coverage:
Children's booklists, book group details and locations, children's book award information, annual conference details.

Printed publications:
Various current free booklists
'Pick of the Year' booklists

Access to staff:
Contact by letter, by telephone, by e-mail and via website
Hours: Mon to Fri, 0900 to 1700

FEDERATION OF CITY FARMS AND COMMUNITY GARDENS

Acronym or abbreviation: FCFCG

The GreenHouse, Hereford Street, Bedminster, Bristol, BS3 4NA

Tel: 0117 923 1800
Fax: 0117 923 1900
E-mail: admin@farmgarden.org.uk

Website:
http://www.farmgarden.org.uk
News and events, farms and gardens in the UK, start your own, young people.

Enquiries:
Enquiries to: Director
Other contacts: Information Officer

Founded:
1980

Formerly called:
National Federation of City Farms (NFCF) (year of change 1999)

Organisation type and purpose:
Membership association (membership is by subscription), present number of members: 398 projects and affiliates, registered charity (charity number 294494).

continued overleaf

To promote community development and advance education in animal husbandry and gardening.

Subject coverage:
Farming and gardening in urban areas, legal requirements for setting up a charity or company limited by guarantee, community management of a voluntary project.

Museum or gallery collection, archive, or library special collection:
Teacher Resource Centre

Library catalogue:
All or part available in-house

Printed publications:
Various reports and information packs including:
Annual Review (free)
Community Garden Starter Pack (£6)
Compost Box
Members' newsletter (members only)
Public Newsletter (2 a year, free)

City Farm Starter Pack (£6)
Child Protection Guidelines (£2.00)
Good Practice Case Studies pack (£6)

Publications list:
Available in print

Access to staff:
Contact by letter, by fax and by e-mail.
Appointment necessary.
Hours: Mon to Fri, 0900 to 1700

Access to building, collection or gallery:
No prior appointment required

Access for disabled people:
Ramped entry, access to all public areas, toilet facilities
Hours: Mon to Fri, 0900 to 1700

Member farms and gardens:
More than 350 in the UK

Member of:
Black Environment Network
Council for Environmental Education
European Federation of City Farms
National Council for Voluntary Organisations
NCVCCO

FEDERATION OF CLOTHING DESIGNERS AND EXECUTIVES

Acronym or abbreviation: FCDE

56 Eden Park Avenue, Beckenham, Kent, BR3 3HW

Tel: 020 8650 5429
Fax: 020 8663 0073
E-mail: maggiewatts@compuserve.com

Website:
http://www.ntu.ac.uk/fas/fcde/index.htm

Enquiries:
Enquiries to: General Secretary

Founded:
1935

Formerly called:
Federation of Clothing Designers and Production Managers

Organisation type and purpose:
Trade association (membership is by election or invitation).
Improving knowledge and skills of members by technical meetings and conventions.

Subject coverage:
Technical information on clothing manufacturing in the areas of pattern technology, design, clothing and manufacturing techniques on all types of outerwear.

Access to staff:
Contact by letter, by telephone, by fax, by e-mail and via website. Non-members charged.
Hours: Mon to Fri, 0900 to 1700

Branches in:
London, Manchester, The Midlands, and Nottingham

FEDERATION OF COCOA COMMERCE LTD

Acronym or abbreviation: FCC

Cannon Bridge House, 1 Cousin Lane, London, EC4R 3XX

Tel: 020 7379 2884
Fax: 020 7379 2389
E-mail: fcc@liffe.com

Website:
http://www.cocoafederation.com
Home page.

Enquiries:
Enquiries to: Chief Executive
Direct tel: 020 7379 2882

Founded:
1929

Organisation type and purpose:
International organisation, trade association.

Subject coverage:
Cocoa trading.

Access to staff:
Contact by letter, by telephone, by fax, by e-mail and via website
Hours: Mon to Fri, 0900 to 1700

FEDERATION OF COMMUNICATION SERVICES LIMITED

Acronym or abbreviation: FCS

Burnhill Business Centre, Provident House, Burrell Row, High Street, Beckenham, Kent, BR3 1AT

Tel: 020 8249 6363
Fax: 0844 870 5927
E-mail: fcs@fcs.org.uk

Website:
http://www.fcs.org.uk

Enquiries:
Enquiries to: Chief Executive
Direct e-mail: fcs@fcs.org.uk

Founded:
1981

Organisation type and purpose:
National organisation, trade association (membership is by subscription), present number of members and associates: 360, manufacturing industry, service industry.
Mobile and telecoms services communication trade association.

Subject coverage:
Mobile communications, telecommunications, radio communications

Printed publications:
FCS Annual Report
FCS Bulletin

Access to staff:
Contact by e-mail and via website. Appointment necessary.
Hours: Mon to Fri, 0900 to 1730

Access to building, collection or gallery:
No access other than to staff

FEDERATION OF ECONOMIC DEVELOPMENT AUTHORITIES

Acronym or abbreviation: FEDA

7 Franklin's Yard, Fossgate, York, YO1 9TN

Tel: 01904 670534
Fax: 01904 670536
E-mail: feda@btconnect.com

Enquiries:
Enquiries to: Director

Founded:
1943

Organisation type and purpose:
Membership association (membership is by subscription), present number of members: local authorities in the UK.

Subject coverage:
Economic development issues in relation to impact on local authorities.

Printed publications:
FEDA (journal)

Access to staff:
Contact by letter, by telephone, by fax and by e-mail
Hours: Mon to Fri, 0930 to 1730

FEDERATION OF ENGINE RE-MANUFACTURERS

Acronym or abbreviation: FER

59 Mewstone Avenue, Wembury, Plymouth, PL9 0JT

Tel: 01752 863681
Fax: 01752 863682
E-mail: ferm@btinternet.com

Website:
http://www.fer.co.uk/

Enquiries:
Enquiries to: Director

Founded:
1938

Organisation type and purpose:
Trade association.

Subject coverage:
Re-manufacture of internal combustion engines.

Printed publications:
List of members (and associates)
Newsletter (monthly)

Access to staff:
Contact by letter
Hours: Mon to Fri, 0900 to 1700

FEDERATION OF ENGINEERING DESIGN COMPANIES LIMITED

Acronym or abbreviation: FEDC

PO Box 700, Rayleigh, Essex, SS6 7AT

Tel: 01268 772996
Fax: 01268 772996
E-mail: gthomas@fedc.org.uk

Website:
List of members, general information about FEDC, membership information, links to members and affiliated organisations.

Enquiries:
Enquiries to: General Secretary

Founded:
1956

Organisation type and purpose:
Trade association (membership is by subscription).
A voice for the industry, representing and promoting the best interests of companies and associated professions at government and trade union level.

Subject coverage:
Engineering design, technical recruitment, technical publications, information services, standards of excellence, code of practice.

Access to staff:
Contact by letter, by telephone, by fax and by e-mail
Hours: Mon to Fri, 0900 to 1700

FEDERATION OF ENVIRONMENTAL TRADE ASSOCIATIONS

Acronym or abbreviation: FETA

2 Waltham Court, Milley Lane, Hare Hatch,
Reading, Berkshire, RG10 9TH

Tel: 0118 940 3416
Fax: 0118 940 6258
E-mail: info@feta.co.uk

Website:
http://www.feta.co.uk

Enquiries:
Enquiries to: Director-General

Organisation type and purpose:
Trade association.

Subject coverage:
Building services, heating, ventilating, air
conditioning and refrigeration.

Printed publications:
Directories
Fact sheets, particularly on energy efficiency
Product, specification and services directories

Publications list:
Available online and in print

Access to staff:
Contact by letter, by telephone, by fax and by e-
mail
Hours: Mon to Thu, 0830 to 1630; Fri, 0830 to 1600

Member organisations:
British Flue and Chimney Manufacturers'
Association (BFCMA)
    same address
British Refrigeration Association (BRA)
    same address
Chilled Beam and Ceiling Association (CBCA)
    same address
Fan Manufacturers Association (FMA)
    same address
Heat Pump Association (HPA)
    same address
Heating, Ventilating and Air-Conditioning
Manufacturers' Association (HEVAC)
    same address
Hose Manufacturers' and Suppliers' Association
(HMSA)
    same address
Residential Ventilation Association (RVA)
    same address
Smoke Control Association (SCA)
    same address

FEDERATION OF FAMILY HISTORY SOCIETIES

Acronym or abbreviation: FFHS

PO Box 8857, Lutterworth, Leicestershire, LE17 9BJ

Tel: 01455 203133
E-mail: info@ffhs.org.uk

Website:
http://www.ffhs.org.uk
Latest news from the family history world, list of
member societies

Enquiries:
Enquiries to: Administrator

Founded:
1974

Organisation type and purpose:
International organisation, trade association,
membership association (membership is by
subscription), present number of members: 200,
registered charity (charity number 1038721),
suitable for all ages.

Subject coverage:
Family history, local history, genealogy, heraldry,
demography, historical research.

**Museum or gallery collection, archive, or library
special collection:**
Archive collection of member societies, not open to
public

Printed publications:
Really Useful Leaflet includes list of member
    societies

Information leaflets

Electronic and video publications:
National Burial Index (CD-ROM, £45)

Publications list:
Available online and in print

Access to staff:
Contact by letter, by telephone, by e-mail and via
website
Hours: Mon to Fri, 0900 to 1700

Access to building, collection or gallery:
No access other than to staff

FEDERATION OF HOLISTIC THERAPISTS

Acronym or abbreviation: FHT

18 Shakespeare Business Centre, Hathaway Close,
Eastleigh, Hampshire, SO50 4SR

Tel: 0844 875 2022
Fax: 023 8062 4399
E-mail: info@fht.org.uk

Website:
http://www.fht.org.uk
Membership criteria and benefits.

Enquiries:
Enquiries to: Chief Executive
Direct e-mail: steven.ridout@fht.org.uk
Other contacts: Marketing Manager for information
about International Therapist Magazine –
advertising, editorial etc.

Founded:
1962

Formerly called:
International Federation of Health and Beauty
Therapists

Organisation type and purpose:
International organisation, professional body
(membership is by qualification), present number
of members: 18,000.
Oldest and largest professional association for the
health and beauty industry. Publishers of the
International Therapist Journal.
Services to members, teachers and employers,
advisory and information service to health and
beauty employers and to the media regarding the
nature of the work, to arrange insurance and
provide a code of practice for hygiene in salons
and clinics.

Subject coverage:
Health and beauty including physical treatment
through massage, colour, sports and beauty
therapy, aromatherapy, reflexology. All aspects of
health and beauty therapy including employment.

Printed publications:
Many publications restricted to members, also:
Code of Practice for Hygiene in Beauty Salons and
    Clinics (£4.95 plus p&p)
Essential Business Guide for Therapists (updated
    yearly)
International Therapist (journal, 6 times a year)

Access to staff:
Contact by letter, by telephone, by fax, by e-mail
and via website
Hours: Mon to Fri, 0900 to 1700
Special comments: No visitors in person.

Founder member of the industry lead body:
Health and Beauty Therapy Training Board

Links with:
Association of Therapy Lecturers
Federation of Professional Sugaring
fraternal organisations in many overseas countries
Health and Beauty Employers Federation
International Council of Health, Fitness and Sports
Therapists
International Council of Holistic Therapists
International Federation of Health and Beauty
Therapists

FEDERATION OF IMAGE CONSULTANTS LIMITED

Acronym or abbreviation: TFIC

Mallory House, 27 Verulam Road, St Albans,
Hertfordshire, AL3 4DG

Tel: 0701 0701018
E-mail: info@tfic.org.uk

Website:
http://www.tfic.org.uk
History, information, training providers.

Enquiries:
Enquiries to: Information Officer

Founded:
1988

Organisation type and purpose:
International organisation, professional body
(membership is by subscription), present number
of members: 200, service industry.
To establish standards and support members of the
image profession and also provide information to
the media.

Subject coverage:
The development of personal self-esteem for
private and business people using image, colour,
style, wardrobe and presentation skills.

**Museum or gallery collection, archive, or library
special collection:**
Archive

Printed publications:
Internal Newsletter (twice a year, free to members)
Magazine (twice a year, subscription)

Access to staff:
Contact by letter, by telephone, by fax, by e-mail
and via website. Appointment necessary.
Hours: Mon to Fri, 0900 to 1700
Special comments: By appointment.

Registered address:
The Federation of Image Consultants Limited
    Mallory House, 27 Verulam Road, St Albans,
    Hertfordshire, AL3 4DG; tel: 07010 701018; fax:
    07010 701018; e-mail: info@tfic.org.uk

FEDERATION OF INDEPENDENT DETECTORISTS

Acronym or abbreviation: FID

Detector Lodge, 44 Heol Dulais, Birchgrove,
Swansea, West Glamorgan, SA7 9LT

Tel: 01792 814615
Fax: 01792 814615
E-mail: hon.sec.fid@detectorists.net

Website:
http://www.detectorists.net
http://www.newbury.net/fid
Information, photographs, free recovery service,
application form for joining, etc.

Enquiries:
Enquiries to: Honorary Secretary
Other contacts: Press and Public Relations Officer,
Ashcroft, 61 Newtown Road, Newbury, Berkshire
RG14 7BU, tel: 01635 522578

Founded:
1982

Organisation type and purpose:
International organisation, membership
association, voluntary organisation.
A lobby on behalf of the members' interests;
information service to the press, media, parliament
and local authorities.

Subject coverage:
The recreational use of metal detectors.

Printed publications:
Bulletin (quarterly, members only)
Leaflets, press releases (from time to time)

Electronic and video publications:
Internet Access (Detectorists.net, CD-ROM or
online)

continued overleaf

Access to staff:
Contact by letter, by telephone, by fax, by e-mail and via website
Hours: Mon to Fri, 0900 to 1700

Affiliated to:
Detector Information Group
Heritage 2100
Heritage for All

Member of:
Standing Conference of European Metal Detecting

FEDERATION OF IRISH SOCIETIES

Acronym or abbreviation: FIS

52 Camden Square, London, NW1 9XB

Tel: 020 7916 2725
Fax: 020 7916 2753

Enquiries:
Enquiries to: Administrator

Founded:
1973

Organisation type and purpose:
National organisation, membership association (membership is by qualification), present number of members: 100, voluntary organisation, research organisation.
Representation of the Irish community in Britain.

Subject coverage:
Information relative to the Irish Community in Britain.

Printed publications:
Alcohol and Disadvantage amongst the Irish in England, Larry Harrison and Roy Carr-Hill (£4.95 plus 80p p&p)
Developing Community Response: the Service Needs of the Irish Community in Britain, Ute Kowarzik (£4.95 plus £1 p&p)
Elderly Irish People in London: A Profile (Tilki M, £4 plus 75p p&p)
FIS Directory of Membership Organisations (voluntary organisations, £15; Statutory and commercial organisations, £40)
Index of Member Organisations (free, sae)
Irish Community Services: Meeting Diverse Needs (Kowarzik A, £4.95 plus £1 p&p)
Report of the Irish Pensioners Conference: October 1997 (£3 plus 75p p&p)
Report on the Needs of Irish Agencies: to assist Development, Seán Hutton (£4.95 plus £1 p&p)
The Health of the Irish in Britain: The Report of a Community Conference (£5 plus 75p p&p)
The Irish Community: Discrimination and the Criminal Justice System (£1 p&p)
The Irish in Britain: An Annotated Bibliography on Health and Related Issues (£5 plus 75p p&p)
Order printed publications from: Cummunity Administrative Assistant, Federation of Irish Societies
tel: 020 7916 2729, fax: 020 7916 2753

Publications list:
Available in print

Access to staff:
Contact by letter, by telephone and by fax
Hours: Mon to Fri, 0900 to 1700

FEDERATION OF LICENSED VICTUALLERS ASSOCIATIONS

Acronym or abbreviation: FLVA

128 Bradford Road, Brighouse, West Yorkshire, HD6 4AU

Tel: 01484 710534
Fax: 01483 718647
E-mail: admin@flva.fsbusiness.co.uk

Enquiries:
Enquiries to: Chief Executive

Founded:
1992

Organisation type and purpose:
Professional body, trade association.
To provide help and advice to licensed victuallers.

Subject coverage:
All aspects of the licensing trade, up-to-date legislation of employment law, health and safety, food and hygiene.

Printed publications:
Publications available free to members
Food Safety, General Food Hygiene Regulations 1995 (Guidance notes)
Helping Hand for the Licensed Trade (business plan)
Publicans Guide to the Health and Safety at Work Act

Access to staff:
Contact by letter, by telephone, by fax and by e-mail
Hours: Mon to Fri, 0900 to 1700

FEDERATION OF LONDON YOUTH CLUBS

Acronym or abbreviation: The Fed; London Youth

Bridge House, Bridge House Quay, Prestons Road, London, E14 9QA

Tel: 020 7537 2777
Fax: 020 7537 7072
E-mail: info@londonyouth.org.uk

Enquiries:
Enquiries to: Chief Executive

Founded:
1887

Formed by the merger of:
London Federation of Clubs for Young People (LFCYP), London Union of Youth Clubs (LUYC) (year of change 1999)

Formerly called:
London Federation of Boys Clubs (LFBC) (year of change 1994–1999)

Organisation type and purpose:
Voluntary organisation, registered charity (charity number 303324).
Youth work.

Subject coverage:
Youth work in London since 1887.

Access to staff:
Contact by letter, by fax and by e-mail
Hours: Mon to Fri, 0900 to 1700

Access for disabled people:
Parking provided

Other locations at:
Hindleap Warren
Wych Cross, Forest Row, East Sussex, RH18 5JS; tel: 01342 822625; fax: 01342 822913; e-mail: hindleap@londonyouth.org.uk
Woodrow High House
Cherry Tree Lane, Amersham, Buckinghamshire, HP7 0QG; tel: 01494 433531; fax: 01494 431391; e-mail: woodrow@londonyouth.org.uk

FEDERATION OF MASTER BUILDERS

Acronym or abbreviation: FMB

Gordon Fisher House, 14–15 Great James Street, London, WC1N 3DP

Tel: 020 7242 7583
Fax: 020 7404 0296

Website:
http://www.fmb.org.uk
Details about the Federation of Master Builders and pages for members only.

Enquiries:
Enquiries to: Information Officer

Founded:
1941

Organisation type and purpose:
Trade association.

Subject coverage:
Building industry; all aspects affecting the building employer; health and safety, employment law, product and manufacturer traces, contract law, EC law, technical.

Trade and statistical information:
Quarterly state of trade survey (based on response from members).

Library catalogue:
All or part available in-house

Printed publications:
Master Builder (magazine, monthly)
Regional Yearbook (available to members, local authorities and public libraries only)
Factsheets on various topics (members only)
Small Works Contract

Publications list:
Available in print

Access to staff:
Contact by letter
Hours: Mon to Fri, 0900 to 1700
Special comments: Not open to the public, no loan facilities.

Member of:
European Builders Confederation

With the:
Transport and General Workers Union formed the Building & Allied Trades Joint Industrial Council

FEDERATION OF MULTIPLE SCLEROSIS THERAPY CENTRES

Bradbury House, 155 Barkers Lane, Bedford, MK41 9RX

Tel: 01234 325781
Fax: 01234 365242
E-mail: info@ms-selfhelp.org

Website:
http://www.ms-selfhelp.org

Enquiries:
Enquiries to: Administrator
Other contacts: Chairman

Founded:
1994

Formerly called:
ARMS (Multiple Sclerosis Research) Limited

Organisation type and purpose:
Statutory body, voluntary organisation, registered charity.
70 centres provide therapy information and support to Multiple Sclerosis sufferers.

Subject coverage:
Multiple sclerosis, self-help disease management, support and information, treatment by professional therapists, support for carers of people with MS, information on MS for the general public.

Printed publications:
Diet Booklet
Information booklet
Long term results on Hyperbaric oxygen
Recipe booklet

Publications list:
Available online and in print

Access to staff:
Contact by letter, by telephone, by fax, by e-mail and via website. Appointment necessary.
Hours: Mon to Fri, 1000 to 1600

Access for disabled people:
Parking provided, ramped entry, access to all public areas, toilet facilities

FEDERATION OF OILS, SEEDS AND FATS ASSOCIATIONS LIMITED

Acronym or abbreviation: FOSFA

20 St Dunstans Hill, London, EC3R 8NQ

Tel: 020 7283 5511
Fax: 020 7623 1310
E-mail: contact@fosfa.org

Website:
http://www.fosfa.org

Enquiries:
Enquiries to: Chief Executive

Organisation type and purpose:
International organisation, trade association.

Subject coverage:
Oil seed and animal, vegetable and margarine oils and fats; HPS groundnuts; trading conditions; analysis, sampling and specification.

Access to staff:
Access for members only.
Hours: Mon to Fri, 0900 to 1700

Associated with:
National Farmers' Union
UK Agricultural Supply Trade Association

Incorporating the:
Incorporated Oil Seed Association
London Copra Association
London Oil and Tallow Trades Association
Seed, Oil, Cake and General Produce Association

Liaison with:
over 50 kindred organisations throughout the world

FEDERATION OF OPHTHALMIC AND DISPENSING OPTICIANS

Acronym or abbreviation: FODO

113 Eastbourne Mews, London, W2 6LQ

Tel: 020 7258 0240
Fax: 020 7724 1175
E-mail: optics@fodo.com

Website:
http://www.fodo.com

Enquiries:
Enquiries to: General Secretary

Founded:
1985

Formerly called:
Guild of British Dispensing Opticians (year of change 1985)

Organisation type and purpose:
Membership association (membership is by subscription), registered charity (charity number 368950).

Subject coverage:
Optical practice and dispensing, sources of optics, training, memberships.

Printed publications:
Careers leaflet for people interested in studying optics
Optics at a Glance (annually)

Access to staff:
Contact by letter and by telephone
Hours: Mon to Fri, 0900 to 1700
Special comments: By letter in the first instance.

FEDERATION OF PATIDAR ASSOCIATIONS

Patidar House, 22 London Road, Wembley, Middlesex, HA9 7EX

Tel: 020 8795 1648
Fax: 020 8795 1648
E-mail: info@patidars.org

Website:
http://www.patidars.org

Enquiries:
Enquiries to: Honorary Secretary
Other contacts: President

Founded:
November 1976

Organisation type and purpose:
Membership association (membership is by subscription), present number of members: 13 organisations, voluntary organisation, registered charity (charity number 1076284), suitable for ages: 2 to 25.
Drop-in centre for elderly; performing arts classes; yoga; youth club.

Subject coverage:
Nursery; day centre for elderly; performing arts classes (Bhart Natyam, Kathak, folk dances, music); yoga; Bollywood dance; sitar

Access to staff:
Contact by letter, by telephone and by e-mail
Hours: Mon to Fri, 1000 to 1800

Access to building, collection or gallery:
Hours: Mon to Sun, 0800 to 2200

Access for disabled people:
Hours: Mon to Fri, 1000 to 1400

FEDERATION OF PILING SPECIALISTS

Acronym or abbreviation: FPS

Forum Court, 83 Copers Cope Road, Beckenham, Kent, BR3 1NR

Tel: 020 8663 0947
Fax: 020 8663 0949
E-mail: fps@fps.org.uk

Website:
http://www.fps.org.uk

Enquiries:
Enquiries to: Executive Secretary

Organisation type and purpose:
Trade association.

Subject coverage:
Ground engineering, foundation and pile construction techniques, ground improvement

Printed publications:
Notes for Guidance on PUWER (Regulations II and Ie) in relation to Guarding and Cleaning of Augers on Piling Operations (Members, £5; non-members, £13)

Electronic and video publications:
The Application of the LOLER Regulations to Piling Rigs (available www.fps.org.uk)
Bentonite Support Fluids in Civil Engineering (available on www.fps.org.uk)

Access to staff:
Contact by letter, by telephone, by fax and by e-mail
Hours: Mon to Fri, 0900 to 1700

Member of:
European Federation of Foundation Contractors (EFFC)
Ground Forum
National Specialist Contractors Council (NSCC)

FEDERATION OF PLASTERING AND DRYWALL CONTRACTORS

Acronym or abbreviation: FPDC

1st Floor, 8–9 Ludgate Square, London, EC4M 7AS

Tel: 020 7634 9480
Fax: 020 7248 9263

Website:
http://www.fpdc.org

Enquiries:
Enquiries to: Director

Direct e-mail: estelle.stanley@fpdc.org
Other contacts: Administrator

Founded:
1942

Formerly called:
Dry Lining and Partition Association, National Federation of Plastering Contractors (year of change 1990)

Incorporates the:
London Master Plasterers Association (year of change 1997)

Organisation type and purpose:
Trade association.

Subject coverage:
Plastering and drywall construction.

Printed publications:
Specifiers Guide

Publications list:
Available online

Access to staff:
Contact by letter, by telephone and by fax
Hours: Mon to Fri, 0930 to 1715

Member of:
National Specialist Contractors Council (NSCC)
tel: 020 7608 5090; fax: 020 7608 5081

FEDERATION OF RECORDED MUSIC SOCIETIES LIMITED

Acronym or abbreviation: FRMS

FRMS Secretary, 18 Albany Road, Hartshill, Stoke-on-Trent, ST4 6BB

Tel: 01782 251460
E-mail: secretary@thefrms.co.uk

Website:
http://www.thefrms.co.uk/
All about the Federation and a growing list of affiliates' programmes.

Enquiries:
Enquiries to: Secretary

Founded:
1936

Formerly called:
National Federation of Gramophone Societies

Organisation type and purpose:
present number of members: 35 affiliated societies with members numbering 11,000, voluntary organisation.

Subject coverage:
Organisation, establishment and conduct of recorded music societies, reproducing equipment, copyright and related subjects applying to gramophone records and all forms of tape, audio matters in general.

Printed publications:
Bulletin (2 times a year)

Access to staff:
Contact by letter, by telephone and by e-mail.
Appointment necessary.
Hours: Mon to Fri, 0900 to 1700

FEDERATION OF SMALL BUSINESSES

Acronym or abbreviation: FSB

Catherine Place, London SW! 6HF

Tel: 020 7592 8100
Fax: 020 7828 5919
E-mail: press@fsb.org.uk

Website:
http://www.fsb.org.uk
Small business issues.

Enquiries:
Enquiries to: Head of Public Affairs
Direct tel: 020 7592 8112

continued overleaf

Direct e-mail: stephen.alambritis@fsb.org.uk
Other contacts: Press Office

Founded:
1974

Formerly called:
National Federation of Self-Employed and Small Businesses (year of change 1990)

Organisation type and purpose:
Trade association, membership association (membership is by subscription), present number of members: 215,000.
To represent the small business sector in the UK.

Subject coverage:
Small business issues.

Trade and statistical information:
Statistics on small businesses.

Printed publications:
First Voice (national magazine, 6 times a year, free to members)
Voice (regional magazine, 6 times a year, free to members)

Access to staff:
Contact by letter, by telephone and by e-mail. Appointment necessary. Access for members only. *Hours:* Mon to Fri, 0900 to 1700

Access to building, collection or gallery:
Prior appointment required

Links with:
ESBA – European Small Business Alliance

FEDERATION OF THE RETAIL LICENSED TRADE NORTHERN IRELAND

Acronym or abbreviation: FRLT

91 University Street, Belfast, BT7 1HP

Tel: 028 9032 7578
Fax: 028 9032 7578
E-mail: enquiries@ulsterpubs.com

Website:
http://www.ulsterpubs.com
Licensed trade information for members and public. Online details of some members.

Enquiries:
Enquiries to: Chief Executive

Founded:
1872

Organisation type and purpose:
Trade association (membership is by subscription, qualification), present number of members: 1200, training organisation.

Subject coverage:
Licensing legislation and statistics relating to Northern Ireland. Licensed trade training.

FEDERATION OF ZOOLOGICAL GARDENS OF GREAT BRITAIN AND IRELAND

Acronym or abbreviation: FZGB

Regent's Park, London, NW1 4RY

Tel: 020 7586 0230
Fax: 020 7722 4427
E-mail: fedzoo@zsl.org

Website:
http://www.zoofederation.org.uk

Enquiries:
Enquiries to: Administrator
Other contacts: Director, Conservation Co-ordinator

Founded:
1966

Formerly called:
National Federation of Zoological Gardens of Great Britain and Ireland

Organisation type and purpose:
Professional body, membership association (membership is by subscription, qualification, election or invitation), present number of members: 61, registered charity (charity number 248553).
The Federation of Zoos, the principal professional body representing the zoo community in Britain and Ireland, is a conservation, education and scientific wildlife charity dedicated to the maintenance of the world's biodiversity, the welfare of animals in zoos and the advancement of scientific knowledge.
The Federation achieves its objectives through: conservation breeding programmes and support for projects in the wild; inspiring an understanding of the natural world through environmental education; and non-invasive scientific studies of animals.

Subject coverage:
Data concerning zoos in the UK and including details of species stocked, breeding schemes, education service, conservation projects; zoo legislation; zoo standards and management; careers in zoos.

Printed publications:
Annual Report
Literature on careers in zoos
Management Guidelines for Zoo Animals (series, ten titles, prices vary)
Veterinary Guidelines for Felids (£5 members, £10 non-members)
Zoo Federation News (newsletter, 3 times a year, members and associates only)
Codes of Practice:
Notes for Inspectors (invertebrate collections, £2.75)
Euthanasia of Invertebrates (£1.75)
Hazardous Invertebrates (£4)

Electronic and video publications:
Management Guidelines for Zoo Animals (series, disc, five titles, prices vary)
Database of Browse used in Federation Zoos (CD-ROM with Microsoft Access Database and Word file with information regarding poisonous plants

Publications list:
Available in print

Access to staff:
Contact by letter, by fax, by e-mail, in person and via website. Appointment necessary. Access for members only. Non-members charged.
Hours: Mon to Fri, 0900 to 1700

Access for disabled people:
Parking provided, ramped entry, access to all public areas, toilet facilities

A member of:
European Association of Zoos and Aquaria (EAZA)
tel: + 31 20 5200 753; fax: + 31 20 5200 754; e-mail: corinne.bos@ndvzoos
World Conservation Union (IUCN)
tel: +22 999 00 01; fax: +22 999 00 02
World Zoo Organisation (IUDZG)
(The Secrtariat is currently moving from the US to the UK)

Has:
66 Member Collections (list available, £15) and 63 Associates
tel: 020 7586 0230; fax: 020 7722 4427; e-mail: fedzoo@zsl.org

Members:
Amazon World
Watery Lane, Newchurch, Isle of Wight, PO36 0LX; tel: 01983 867122; fax: 01983 868560; e-mail: amaozonworld@dialstart.net
Aquarium & Vivarium, National Museums & Galleries on Merseyside
Liverpool Museum, William Brown Street, Liverpool, L3 8EN; tel: 0151 207 0001; fax: 0151 478 4390
Banham Zoo Ltd
The Grove, Banham, Norfolk, NR16 2HE; tel: 01953 887771; fax: 01953 888445; website: http://www.banhamzoo.co.uk

Battersea Park Children's Zoo
Battersea Park, London, SW11 4NJ; tel: 020 8871 7540; fax: 020 7350 0477
Birdland
Rissington Road, Bourton-on-the-Water, Cheltenham, Gloucestershire, GL54 2BN; tel: 01451 820480; fax: 01451 822398; e-mail: sb .birdland@virgin.net
Birdworld
Holt Pound, Farnham, Surrey, GU10 4LD; tel: 01420 22140; fax: 01420 23715; website: http://www.birdworld.co.uk
Blackpool Zoo Park
East Park Drive, Stanley Park, Blackpool, Lancashire, FY3 8PP; tel: 01253 830830; fax: 01253 830800; e-mail: zookeeper@blackpool-zoo .freeserve.co.uk
Brent Lodge Park Animal Centre
Brent Lodge Park, Church Road, Hanwell, London, W7 3BP; tel: 020 8758 5019; fax: 020 8840 4244
Bristol, Clifton & West of England Zoological Society
Bristol Zoo Gardens, Clifton, Bristol, BS8 3HA; tel: 0117 974 7300; fax: 0117 973 6814; e-mail: information@bristolzoo.org.uk; website: http://www.bristolzoo.org.uk
Butterfly & Wildlife Park
Long Sutton, Spalding, Linclonshire, PE12 9LE; tel: 01406 363833; fax: 01406 363182; e-mail: butterflypark@hotmail.com
Camperdown Wildlife Centre
Camperdown Country Park, Coupar Angus Road, Dundee, DO2 4TF, and 435913 education department; tel: 01382 432661; fax: 01382 432660
Chester Zoo
North of England Zoological Society, Caughall Road, Upton-by-Chester, Cheshire, CH2 1LH; tel: 01244 380280; fax: 01244 371273; e-mail: f .jaques@chesterzoo.co.uk; website: http://www .chesterzoo.co.uk
Chestnut Centre Conservation Park
Castleton Road, Chapel-en-le-Frith, Derbyshire, SK23 0QS; tel: 01298 814099; fax: 01298 816213
City of Belfast Zoo
Antrim Road, Newtownabbey, Co Antrim, BT36 7PN; tel: 028 9077 6277; fax: 028 9037 0578; website: http://www.belfastzoo.co.uk
Colchester Zoo
Maldon Road, Stanway, Colchester, Essex, CO3 5SL; tel: 01206 331292; fax: 01206 331392; e-mail: colchester.zoo@btinternet.com; website: http://www.colchester-zoo.uk
Cotswold Wild Life Park
Burford, Oxfordshire, OX18 4JW; tel: 01993 823006; fax: 01993 823807
Curraghs Wildlife Park
Ballaugh, Isle of Man, IN7 5EA; tel: 01624 897323; fax: 01624 897327
Drusillas Zoo Park
Alfriston, East Sussex, BN26 5QS; tel: 01323 870656; fax: 01323 870846; e-mail: drusilla@ drusilla.demon.co.uk
Dublin Zoo
Zoological Society of Ireland, Phoenix Park, Dublin, 8, Republic of Ireland; tel: 00 353 1 677 1425; fax: 00 353 1 677 1660; website: http://www .dublinzoo.ie
Dudley and West Midlands Zoological Society Ltd
Dudley Zoo, 2 The Broadway, Dudley, DY1 4QB; tel: 01384 215300; fax: 01384 456048; e-mail: marketing@dudleyzoo.org.uk
Durrell Wildlife Conservation Trust
Jersey Zoo, Les Augres Manor, Trinity, Jersey, JE3 5BF; tel: 01534 860000; fax: 01534 860001; e-mail: jerseyzoo@durell.org
East Midlands Zoological Society Ltd
Twycross Zoo Park, Norton-juxta-Twycross, Atherstone, Warwickshire, CV9 3PX; tel: 01827 880250; fax: 01827 880700; e-mail: twycross.zoo@ btinternet.com
Edinburgh Zoo
Royal Zoological Society of Scotland, 134 Corstorphine Road, Edinburgh, EH12 6TS; tel: 0131 334 9171 (press 0 for operator); fax: 0131 316 4050; e-mail: amanda@edinburghzoo.org.uk; website: http://www.edinburghzoo.org.uk

Exmoor Zoological Park
  Bratton Fleming, Barnstaple, North Devon, EX31 4SG; tel: 01598 763352; fax: 01598 763352
Fota Wildlife Park
  Zoological Society of Ireland, Carrigtwohill, Co Cork, Republic of Ireland; tel: 00 353 21 812 678; fax: 00 353 21 812 744; e-mail: fota@indigo.ie
Gatwick Zoo
  Russ Hill, Charlwood, Surrey, RH6 0EG; tel: 01293 862312; fax: 01293 862550
Harewood Bird Garden
  Harewood House, Harewood, Leeds, LS17 9LQ; tel: 0113 288 6238; fax: 0113 288 6784; e-mail: birdgdn@harewood.org; website: http://www.harewood.org
Hawk Conservancy
  Weyhill, Andover, Hampshire, SP11 8DY; tel: 01264 773850; fax: 01264 773772; website: http://www.hawk-conservancy.org
Highland Wildlife Park
  Royal Zoological Society of Scotland, Kincraig, Kingussie, Inverness-shire, PH21 1NL; tel: 01540 651270; fax: 01540 651236; e-mail: wildlife@rzss.org.uk; website: http://www.kincraig.com/wildlife
Kirkleatham Owl Centre
  Kirkleatham Village, Redcar, TS10 5NW; tel: 01642 480512; fax: 01642 492790; e-mail: stan@kirk58.freeserve.co.uk; website: http://www.jillsowls.co.uk
Knowsley Safari Park
  Prescot, Merseyside, L34 4AN; tel: 0151 430 9009; fax: 0151 426 3677; website: http://www.knowsley.com
Lakeland Wildlife Oasis
  Hale, Milnthorpe, Cumbria, LA7 7BW; tel: 01539 563027; e-mail: wildlifeoasis@hotmail.com
Linton Zoological Gardens
  Hadstock Road, Linton, Cambridgeshire, CB1 6NT; tel: 01223 891308; fax: 01223 891308
London Zoo
  Zoological Gardens, Regent's Park, London, NW1 4RY, 020 7449 6551 education department; tel: 020 7722 3333; fax: 020 7586 5743; website: http://www.zsl.org
Lotherton Hall Bird Garden
  Towton Road, Near Aberford, Leeds, LS25 3EB; tel: 0113 281 3723
Manor House Wildlife and Leisure Park
  St Florence, Tenby, Dyfed, SA70 8RJ; tel: 01646 651201; fax: 01646 651201
Marwell Zoological Park
  Colden Common, Winchester, Hampshire, SO21 1JH; tel: 01962 777407; fax: 01962 777511; e-mail: marwel@marwell.org.uk
Mole Hall Wildlife Park
  Widdington, Saffron Walden, Essex, CB11 3SS; tel: 01799 540400; fax: 01799 540400; e-mail: molehall@aol.com
National Birds of Prey Centre
  Newent, Gloucestershire, GL18 1JJ; tel: 01531 821581; fax: 01531 821389; e-mail: jpj@nbpc.demon.co.uk
Newquay Zoo
  Trenance Park, Newquay, Cornwall, TR7 2LZ; tel: 01637 873342; fax: 01637 851318; e-mail: mark@newquayzoo.demon.co.uk
Owl Centre
  Muncaster Castle, Ravenglass, Cumbria, CA18 1RQ; tel: 01229 717393; fax: 01229 717107
Paignton Zoo Environmental Park
  Totness Road, Paignton, Devon, TQ4 7EU; tel: 01803 697500; fax: 01803 523457; e-mail: amy@paigntonzoo.demon.co.uk
Palacerigg Country Park
  Cumbernauld, G67 3HU; tel: 01236 720047; fax: 01236 458271; e-mail: pccreception@northlan.gw.uk
Paradise Wildlife Park
  White Stubbs Lane, Broxbourne, Hertfordshire, EN10 7QA; tel: 01992 470490; fax: 01992 440525; website: http://www.pwpark.com
Shaldon Wildlife Trust Ltd
  Ness Drive, Shaldon, Devon, TQ14 0HP; tel: 01626 872234; fax: 01626 872234; website: http://www.the-zoo.demon.co.uk

Southport Zoo and Conservation Trust
  Princes Park, Southport, Merseyside, PR8 1RX; tel: 01704 538102; fax: 01704 548102; e-mail: 100534.35@compuserve.com
Suffolk Wildlife Park
  Whites Lane, Kessingland, Lowestoft, Suffolk, NR33 7TF; tel: 01502 740291; fax: 01953 888427; website: http://www.suffolkwildlifepark.co.uk
Thrigby Hall Wildlife Gardens
  Thrigby Hall, Filby, Great Yarmouth, Norfolk, NR29 3DR; tel: 01493 369477; fax: 01493 368256
Tilgate Nature Centre
  Tilgate Park, Crawley, West Sussex, RH10 5PQ; tel: 01293 521168; fax: 01293 533981
Tropical World
  Canal Gardens, Roundhay Park, Leeds, LS8 1DF; tel: 0113 266 1850; fax: 0113 237 0077
Welsh Mountain Zoo
  Zoological Society of Wales, Colwyn Bay, Clwyd, LL28 5UY; tel: 01492 532938; fax: 01492 530498; e-mail: welshmountainzoo@enterprise.net
Whipsnade Wild Animal Park
  Zoological Society of London, Dunstable, Bedfordshire, LU6 2LF; tel: 01582 872171; fax: 01582 872649; e-mail: nick.lindsay@zsl.org; website: http://www.zsl.org
Wildfowl & Wetland Trust
  Mill Road, Arundel, West Sussex, BN18 9PB; tel: 01903 883355; fax: 01903 884834; e-mail: wwt.arundel@virgin.net; website: http://www.wwt.org.uk
Wildfowl & Wetland Trust
  District 15, Washington, Tyne & Wear, NE38 8LE; tel: 0191 416 5454; fax: 0191 416 5801; website: http://www.wwt.org.uk
Wildfowl & Wetland Trust
  Martin Mere, Fish Lane, Burscough, Ormskirk, Lancashire, L40 0TA; tel: 01704 895181; fax: 01704 892343; website: http://www.wwt.org.uk
Wildfowl & Wetland Trust
  Slimbridge, Gloucestershire, GL2 7BT; tel: 01453 890333; fax: 01453 890827; website: http://www.wwt.org.uk
Wildfowl & Wetland Trust
  Canolfan Llanelli Centre, Penclacwydd, Llwynhendy, Llanelli, Dyfed, SA14 9SH; tel: 01554 741087; website: http://www.wwt.org.uk
Wildfowl & Wetland Trust
  Castle Espie, Ballydrain Road, Comber, Co Down, BT23 6EA; tel: 028 9187 4146; fax: 028 9187 3857; website: http://www.wwt.org.uk
Woburn Safari Park
  Woburn, Bedfordshire, MK17 9QN; tel: 01525 290407; fax: 01525 290489; e-mail: WobSafari@aol.com
Yorkshire Dales Falconry and Conservation Centre
  Crows Nest, Near Giggleswick, Settle, North Yorkshire, LA2 8AS; tel: 01729 822832 Direct 01729 825164 Information; fax: 01729 825160

FEED THE MINDS

36 Causton Street, London, SW1P 4AU

Tel: 0845 121 2102
Fax: 020 7592 3939
E-mail: info@feedtheminds.org

Website:
http://www.feedtheminds.org

Enquiries:
Enquiries to: Administrator

Founded:
1964

Organisation type and purpose:
Registered charity (charity number 291333). An ecumenical Christian organisation that supports education in the world's poorest regions.

Printed publications:
Annual Report
Feed the Minds News (twice a year)

Access to staff:
Contact by letter, by telephone, by fax and by e-mail. Appointment necessary.
Hours: Mon to Fri, 0900 to 1700

Constituent bodies:
22 agencies and mission societies from Anglican, Baptist, Catholic, Methodist and Reformed backgrounds

Links with:
Council of Churches for Britain and Ireland
United Society for Christian Literature
  at the same address

Member organisation of:
Churches' Commission on Mission
World Association for Christian Communication (WACC)

FELINE ADVISORY BUREAU

Acronym or abbreviation: FAB

Taeselbury, High Street, Tisbury, Wiltshire, SP3 6LD

Tel: 01747 871872
Fax: 01747 871873
E-mail: information@fabcats.org

Website:
http://www.fabcats.org
Information on the Feline Advisory Bureau, future meetings and conferences, Feline Advisory Bureau goods, information sheets.
http://www.web.ukonline.co.uk/fab
Information on European Society of Feline Medicine.

Enquiries:
Enquiries to: Chief Executive

Founded:
1958

Organisation type and purpose:
Advisory body, membership association (membership is by subscription), present number of members: 3000, registered charity (charity number 254641), suitable for ages: adults, publishing house.
Provide information on the health and welfare of cats.

Subject coverage:
Disease, treatment, management and welfare of the feline species, particularly the domestic cat. Information on design, construction and management of boarding catteries and rescue facilities. Approved Boarding Cattery listing. Boarding Cattery Information Service: Constructing and management of boarding catteries. Advice to owners on all feline problems, behavioural or sickness, and general cat care.

Access to staff:
Contact by letter, by telephone, by fax, by e-mail and via website
Hours: Mon to Fri, 0900 to 1700

Incorporates the:
Central Fund for Feline Studies

Subsidiary body:
Boarding Cattery Information Service

Supports the:
European Society of Feline Medicine (ESFM)

FELL & ROCK CLIMBING CLUB OF THE ENGLISH LAKE DISTRICT

Acronym or abbreviation: FRCC

Library, Lancaster University Library, Bailrigg, Lancaster, LA1 4YH

Tel: 01524 65201

Enquiries:
Enquiries to: Honorary Librarian

Founded:
1907

Organisation type and purpose:
Climbing club library housed in the University Library.

continued overleaf

Subject coverage:
Fell walking and rock climbing, particularly in the English Lake District; protection of the amenities of the District; mountaineering in other parts of Great Britain, the Alps, the Himalayas, and other great ranges.

Museum or gallery collection, archive, or library special collection:
Himalayan Journal
Journals of Alpine Club, American and Canadian Alpine Clubs
Journals of FRCC, Climbers' Club, Scottish Mountaineering Club, etc

Printed publications:
Catalogue of Maps
Catalogue of the Library (2nd ed., 1987)
FRCC Guide Books (rock climbing guides to the English Lake District)

Access to staff:
Contact by letter
Hours: Mon to Fri, 0900 to 1700

FELL RUNNERS ASSOCIATION

Acronym or abbreviation: FRA

8 Leygate View, New Mills, High Peak, SK22 3FF

Tel: 01663 746476

Enquiries:
Enquiries to: General Secretary
Direct e-mail: alan.brentnall@btinternet.com

Founded:
1970

Organisation type and purpose:
National organisation, membership association (membership is by subscription), present number of members: 6500.
Governing body of the sport in England.

Subject coverage:
Fell running in the British Isles.

Printed publications:
Annual Handbook and Fixtures Calendar
The Fellrunner (magazine, 3 times a year, free of charge, available to FRA members only)

Publications list:
Available in print

Access to staff:
Contact by letter and by telephone
Hours: Mon to Fri, 0900 to 1700

FELLOWSHIP OF CHRISTIAN MOTORCYCLISTS

Acronym or abbreviation: FCM

6 St Anne's Close, Formby, Liverpool, L37 7AX

Tel: 01704 875828
E-mail: info@fcm-bikers.org.uk

Website:
http://www.fcm-bikers.org.uk
Fellowship home page, membership, information

Enquiries:
Enquiries to: Chairman

Founded:
1976

Organisation type and purpose:
Membership association (membership is by subscription), present number of members: 120.

Printed publications:
Transmission (monthly newsletter, members, and enquirers on application)

Access to staff:
Contact by letter
Hours: Mon to Fri, 0900 to 1700

FELLOWSHIP OF INDEPENDENT EVANGELICAL CHURCHES

Acronym or abbreviation: FIEC

39 The Point, Market Harborough, LE16 7QU

Tel: 01858 434540
Fax: 01858 411550
E-mail: admin@fiec.org.uk

Website:
http://www.fiec.org.uk
Resource information helpful to churches.

Enquiries:
Enquiries to: Administrator
Direct e-mail: rod@fiec.org.uk
Other contacts: Office Manager, tel: 01858 411551

Founded:
1922

Organisation type and purpose:
Advisory body, registered charity (charity number 263354).
Association of churches, ministers and Christian workers.

Subject coverage:
Church related practical issues, evangelism, pastoral care guidance.

Printed publications:
Churches Handbook
Together (magazine, 2 times a year)
FIEC Directory

Access to staff:
Contact by letter, by telephone, by fax, by e-mail and via website
Hours: Mon to Fri, 0900 to 1700

Access for disabled people:
Hours: Mon to Fri, 0900 to 1700
Special comments: Ground floor only

Affiliated to:
Affinity
PO Box 246, Bridgend, CF31 9FD; tel: 01656 646152; fax: info@affinity.org.uk; website: www.affinity.org.uk

FELLOWSHIP OF MAKERS AND RESEARCHERS OF HISTORICAL INSTRUMENTS

Acronym or abbreviation: FoMRHI

c/o Lewis Jones, London Metropolitan University, 41 Commercial Road, London, E1 1LA

E-mail: ljones@lgu.ac.uk

Website:
http://www.hrinstruments.demon.co.uk/fomrhi.html

Enquiries:
Enquiries to: Honorary Secretary

Founded:
1975

Organisation type and purpose:
Learned society (membership is by subscription).

Subject coverage:
Reconstruction of early musical instruments (from the Stone Age to about 1900, but mostly from the Middle Ages to 1800 or so), conservation and restoration of instruments of the same periods.

Printed publications:
Annual List of Members
FoMRHI Quarterly (for members)

Access to staff:
Contact by letter and by e-mail
Hours: Mon to Fri, 0900 to 1700

FELLOWSHIP OF POSTGRADUATE MEDICINE

Acronym or abbreviation: FPM

12 Chandos Street, London, W1G 9DR

Tel: 020 7636 6334
Fax: 020 7436 2535
E-mail: admin@fpm-uk.org

Website:
http://www.fpm-uk.org
Continuing Medical Education and original articles

Enquiries:
Enquiries to: Administrator

Organisation type and purpose:
Learned society (membership is by election or invitation), present number of members: c. 50, registered charity (charity number 313355).
Medical education and publishing.

Subject coverage:
Postgraduate medical education.

Access to staff:
Contact by letter and by e-mail
Hours: Tue, Wed and Thu, 1000 to 1730

FELLOWSHIP OF ST ALBAN AND ST SERGIUS

Acronym or abbreviation: FSASS

1 Canterbury Road, Oxford, OX2 6LU

Tel: 01865 552991
Fax: 01865 316700
E-mail: gensec@sobornost.org

Website:
http://www.sobornost.org

Enquiries:
Enquiries to: General Secretary
Other contacts: Treasurer for subscription enquiries.

Founded:
1928

Organisation type and purpose:
Membership association (membership is by subscription), present number of members: 1218, registered charity (charity number 245112).
To promote understanding between Western and Eastern Christian churches.

Subject coverage:
Information on the Orthodox Churches in the British Isles, information on the unity between Christians of East and West.

Museum or gallery collection, archive, or library special collection:
Small orthodoxy and theological library with emphasis on Russian Church Studies

Printed publications:
Newsletter (quarterly)
Sobornost, incorporating Eastern Churches Review (journal, 2 times a year)
Various studies supplementary to Sobornost/ECR

Microform publications:
Sobornost (available on microfiche from UMI)

Publications list:
Available online and in print

Access to staff:
Contact by letter, by telephone, by e-mail and via website
Hours: Mon to Fri, 0900 to 1300

Access to building, collection or gallery:
Prior appointment required
Special comments: Library open to members of the Fellowship.

FEMINIST LIBRARY RESOURCE AND INFORMATION CENTRE

Acronym or abbreviation: FLRIC

5 Westminster Bridge Road, London, SE1 7XW

Tel: 020 7928 7789
E-mail: feministlibrary@beeb.net

Website:
http://www.genesis.ac.uk
Archive collection description

Enquiries:
Enquiries to: Information Officer

Founded:
1975

Formerly called:
Women's Research and Resource Centre (year of change 1982)

Organisation type and purpose:
Membership association (membership is by subscription), voluntary organisation, registered charity (charity number 272410).

Subject coverage:
Women, feminism, black women, lesbians, disabled women and women's studies.

Museum or gallery collection, archive, or library special collection:
Archive material relating to second wave women's movement (WLM) 1970s
Women's Liberation Movement – Archives
Extensive journals collection from UK and around the world
10,000 books, 1500 journals, 1200 articles, 9000 pamphlets and ephemera

Library catalogue:
All or part available in-house

Printed publications:
Newsletter (quarterly)

Access to staff:
Contact by letter and by telephone. Appointment necessary.
Hours: Tue, 1100 to 2000; Wed, 1500 to 2000; Sat, 1400 to 1700

FENCING CONTRACTORS ASSOCIATION

Acronym or abbreviation: FCA

Hillside Grange, Warren Road, Trellech, Monmouth, Gwent, NP25 4PQ

Tel: 07000 560722
Fax: 01600 860614
E-mail: info@fencingcontractors.org

Website:
http://www.fencingcontractors.org

Enquiries:
Enquiries to: Chief Executive

Founded:
1942

Organisation type and purpose:
Trade association.

Subject coverage:
All types of fencing and gates including vehicle restraint systems and electric security fencing.

Museum or gallery collection, archive, or library special collection:
British Standards Parts – 1722 fences
FCA Code of Practice (PAS 48)
Publicly available specification (PAS 47) for electric fences

Printed publications:
List of members

Access to staff:
Contact by letter, by telephone, by fax and by e-mail
Hours: Mon to Fri, 0900 to 1700

Access to building, collection or gallery:
Prior appointment required
Hours: Mon to Fri, 0900 to 1700

Access for disabled people:
Parking provided, ramped entry, access to all public areas, toilet facilities

Connections with:
Association of Safety Fencing Contractors (ASFC)
  As main address
Electric Security Fencing Federation (ESFF)
  As main address

FERFA: THE RESIN FLOORING ASSOCIATION

16 Edward Road, Farnham, Surrey, GU9 8NP

Tel: 01252 714250

Website:
http://www.ferfa.org.uk

Enquiries:
Enquiries to: Secretary

Founded:
1969

Organisation type and purpose:
Trade association (membership is by subscription and election), present number of members: 85.
Represents UK manufacturers, contractors and associated companies involved in industrial resin flooring systems and surface preparation.

Subject coverage:
UK manufacturers, contractors and associated companies involved in industrial resin flooring systems and surface preparation.

Printed publications:
Publishes a range of guidance notes (many available free online)
Guide to the specification and application of synthetic resin flooring
Guide to the selection of synthetic resin flooring
Minimising slips in the workplace with the use of industrial resin floors
Osmosis in resin flooring
Anti-static flooring
Chemical resistance of resin flooring

Publications list:
Available online and in print

Access to staff:
Contact by letter, by telephone, by fax, by e-mail and via website
Hours: Mon to Fri, 0900 to 1700

Access to building, collection or gallery:
By appointment only

FERRARI OWNERS' CLUB

14 Lynn Road, Snettisham, King's Lynn, Norfolk, PE31 7PT

Tel: 01485 544500
Fax: 01485 544515
E-mail: foc.info@btinternet.com

Website:
http://www.ferrariownersclub.co.uk
General information regarding club and activities plus membership.

Enquiries:
Enquiries to: General Secretary

Founded:
1967

Organisation type and purpose:
Membership association (membership is by subscription, qualification).
To provide events, activities, information and news for Ferrari owners and enthusiasts.

Subject coverage:
Club activities including Ferrari competition, racing, sprints and hillclimb, concours events, international Ferrari events and activity, Ferrari cars old and new, technical guidance through established outlets, market trend, advertising outlets and publications.

Museum or gallery collection, archive, or library special collection:
Club library and OC register of cars

Printed publications:
Ferrari (quarterly, colour)
Ferrari News (magazine, 6 times a year, black and white)

Access to staff:
Contact by letter, by telephone and by fax
Hours: Mon to Fri, 0900 to 1700

FIBRE CEMENT MANUFACTURERS' ASSOCIATION LIMITED

Acronym or abbreviation: FCMA

ATSS House, Station Road East, Stowmarket, Suffolk, IP14 1RQ

Tel: 01449 676053
Fax: 01449 770028
E-mail: fcma@ghyllhouse.co.uk

Enquiries:
Enquiries to: Secretary General
Other contacts: Chairman

Founded:
1985

Formerly called:
Asbestos Cement Manufacturers Association

Organisation type and purpose:
Trade association.

Subject coverage:
Manufacture of fibre cement building products; technical development; health and safety, occupational training.

Access to staff:
Contact by letter, by telephone, by fax and by e-mail
Hours: Mon to Fri, 0900 to 1700

Access to building, collection or gallery:
No access other than to staff

Member of:
CBI
NFRC

FIBREOPTIC INDUSTRY ASSOCIATION

Acronym or abbreviation: FIA

The Manor House, Buntingford, Hertfordshire, SG9 9AB

Tel: 01763 273039
Fax: 01763 273255
E-mail: jane@fiasec.demon.co.uk

Website:
http://www.fia-online.org.uk
Wide ranging information on fibre optic industry and members products and services.

Enquiries:
Enquiries to: Secretary

Founded:
1990

Organisation type and purpose:
Trade association (membership is by subscription), present number of members: 200.
Technology-based trade association for the fibre optics industry.

Subject coverage:
Fibre optics, data communications, telecommunications.

Printed publications:
FIA Guide to Training
Guide to Members' Products and Services
Membership pack
Newsletter

Publications list:
Available online

Access to staff:
Contact by letter, by telephone, by fax, by e-mail and via website
Hours: Mon to Fri, 0930 to 1630

FIELD

Formal name: Foundation for International Environmental Law and Development
Acronym or abbreviation: FIELD

3 Endsleigh Street, London, WC1H 0DD

continued overleaf

Tel: 020 7872 7200
Fax: 020 7388 2826
E-mail: field@field.org.uk

Website:
http://www.field.org.uk/
Information on FIELD's four main programme
areas, RECIEL and Internships.

Enquiries:
Enquiries to: Administrator
Direct e-mail: clare.duckney@field.org.uk
Other contacts: Director for Project Co-ordinator
and fundraising.

Founded:
1989

Formerly called:
Centre for International Environment Law (CIEL)
(year of change 1989)

Organisation type and purpose:
Advisory body, registered charity (charity number
802934), training organisation, research
organisation.
To promote the progressive development of EU
and international law through research, teaching,
training and publishing.

Subject coverage:
Environmental law related to climate and energy;
trade, environment and sustainable development;
international courts and tribunals; biological
diversity and marine resources, international law
and sustainable development and EC
environmental law.

**Museum or gallery collection, archive, or library
special collection:**
Field Brochure/Folder
FIELD in Brief
RECIEL Journal

Printed publications:
Review of European Community & International
Environmental Law RECIEL (quarterly, pub.
Blackwell)
Numerous books, reports and papers include:
Principles of International Environmental Law,
Principles of Policy, Institution and Compliance
Environmental Priorities for the World Trading
System

Publications list:
Available online and in print

Access to staff:
Contact by letter, by telephone, by fax, by e-mail
and via website
Hours: Mon to Fri, 0900 to 1700

Access to building, collection or gallery:
No access other than to staff

Connections with:
IUCN
World Conservation for Nature

FIELD STUDIES COUNCIL

Acronym or abbreviation: FSC

Preston Montford, Montford Bridge, Shrewsbury,
Shropshire, SY4 1HW

Tel: 01743 852100
Fax: 01743 852101
E-mail: fsc.headoffice@field-studies-council.org

Enquiries:
Enquiries to: Chief Executive
Other contacts: Education Officer for advice,
courses, INSET.

Founded:
1943

Formerly called:
Council for the Promotion of Field Studies

Organisation type and purpose:
Membership association (membership is by
subscription), registered charity (charity number
313364), suitable for ages: 4 to adult.
Educational charity.
Environmental understanding for all.

Subject coverage:
Biology, botany, geography, ecology, environment,
environmental auditing, natural history,
photography, birds, butterfly safaris, archaeology,
walking, painting, crafts.

Printed publications:
Annual Report
Field Studies Journal (annually)
Over 500 publications, charts and studies
including:
Adult and Family Course Programmes
Discover Your National Parks (educational
resource pack, £15)
Identification guides
Synopses of the British Fauna
The Outdoor Classroom – for schools and colleges
The AIDGAP (Aids to Identification in Difficult
Groups of Animals & Plants) Project publications
Order printed publications from: Postal Sales Officer,
FSC Publications
at the same address, tel: 01743 850370

Publications list:
Available in print

Access to staff:
Contact by telephone, by fax and by e-mail.
Appointment necessary.
Hours: Mon to Fri, 0900 to 1700

FIELDEN-CEGOS LIMITED

The Towers, Towers Business Park, Wilmslow
Road, Didsbury, Manchester, M20 2FZ

Tel: 0161 445 2426
Fax: 0161 446 2051
E-mail: customerservices@fielden-cegos.co.uk

Website:
http://www.fielden-cegos.co.uk
Training courses and in-company services, access
to our international partners.

Enquiries:
Enquiries to: Course Registrar

Founded:
1949

Formerly called:
Fielden House Limited (year of change 1989)

Organisation type and purpose:
Training organisation, consultancy.
Management training centre.

Subject coverage:
Management development, supervisory training,
trainer training, health and safety, administrative/
secretarial, personnel/H.R., supply chain
management, quality management, consultancy,
sales, marketing.

Printed publications:
Courses Directory (annually)

Electronic and video publications:
Course Directory (CD-ROM, free of charge)

Access to staff:
Contact by letter, by telephone, by fax, by e-mail
and via website
Hours: Mon to Fri, 0900 to 1700

Subsidiary of:
CEGOS
France

FIELDS IN TRUST

Acronym or abbreviation: FIT

2D Woodstock Studios, 36 Woodstock Grove,
London, W12 8LE

Tel: 020 8735 3380
Fax: 020 8735 3397
E-mail: info@fieldsintrust.org

Website:
http://www.fieldsintrust.org/
http://www.npfa.co.uk/

Enquiries:
Enquiries to: Director

Founded:
1925

Formerly called:
National Playing Fields Association (NPFA) (year
of change 2007)

Organisation type and purpose:
Advisory body, membership association
(membership is by subscription), registered charity
(charity number 306070), consultancy, publishing
house.

Subject coverage:
Playing fields, their establishment, conservation
and development.

Printed publications:
Impact Absorbing Surfaces for Children's
Playgrounds
Floodlighting
Insurance and Children's Play
The New European Play Safety Standards
The NPFA Cost Guides – Play and Sport
The Six Acre Standard
Playground Management and Safety
Great Playtimes Games Kit
Playground Markings
Order printed publications from: Publications
Department, NPFA
tel: 020 7833 5360, fax: 020 7833 5365, e-mail:
publications@npfa.co.uk

Publications list:
Available online and in print

Affiliated to:
National Council for Voluntary Organisations

Also at:
Midland Sports Centre
Cromwell Lane, Coventry, CV4 8AS; tel: 024
7669 4517; fax: 024 7669 4614; e-mail: fields@npfa
.co.uk
NPFA Cymru
2 Queen Street, Cardiff, CF10 2BU; tel: 029 2035
3030; fax: 029 2035 3039; e-mail: cymru@npfa.co
.uk
NPFA Scotland
20 Queen Street, Edinburgh, EH2 1JX; tel: 0131
225 5763

FIFE COUNCIL

Fife House, North Street, Glenrothes, Fife, KY7 5LT

Tel: 01592 414141\ Minicom no. 01592 414201
Fax: 01592 414142

Enquiries:
Enquiries to: Co-ordination Assistant
Direct tel: 01592 413991
Direct fax: 01592 413939

Founded:
1 April 1996

Organisation type and purpose:
Local government body.

FIFE COUNCIL LIBRARIES &
MUSEUMS

Headquarters, East Fergus Place, Kirkcaldy, Fife,
KY1 1XT

Tel: 01592 583204
E-mail: libraries.museums@fife.gov.uk

Enquiries:
Enquiries to: Service Manager, Libraries and
Museums
Direct e-mail: libraries.museums@fife.gov.uk
Other contacts: Administration Officer

Founded:
1975

Organisation type and purpose:
Public Libraries & Museums.

With a network of 54 libraries, 10 museums, 2 heritage sites and hundreds of access points in schools, sheltered housing complexes and homes, bringing enjoyment, learning and enlightenment to all of Fife's citizens.

Subject coverage:
Libraries provide a gateway to the world of information and cultural resources, offer leisure reading and learning support on the local doorstep, open the door further with free membership, free Internet access and free requests, stock, conserve and exploit family and local history resources.
Museums collect, document, conserve and interpret objects and materials relating to Fife, encourage others to take an interest in and preserve Fife's heritage, make the objects and their history accessible, maximise the learning potential of the collections for adults and children.

Museum or gallery collection, archive, or library special collection:
Genealogical material
Local newspapers (microfilm and hard copy)
Local studies collection Fife
Natural, social & industrial artefacts and photographs relating to Fife
Art Gallery – focusing on Scottish artists

Trade and statistical information:
General trades directories.

Non-library collection catalogue:
All or part available online and in-house

Library catalogue:
All or part available online

Publications list:
Available in print

Access to staff:
Contact by letter, by telephone, by e-mail and in person
Hours: Mon to Fri, 0900 to 1700

Access to building, collection or gallery:
No prior appointment required
Hours: Hours vary between locations

Access for disabled people:
Access varies between locations

Parent body:
Fife Council
    tel: 0845 155 0000; e-mail: fife.council.fife.gov.uk; website: fifedirect.org.uk

FIFE COUNCIL LIBRARIES – EAST AREA

Library Headquarters, County Buildings, St Catherine Street, Cupar, Fife, KY15 4TA

Tel: 01334 412737
Fax: 01334 412941

Enquiries:
Enquiries to: Libraries Information Services Co-ordinator

Formerly called:
North East Fife District Libraries (year of change 1996)

Organisation type and purpose:
Local government body, public library.

Subject coverage:
Local history of East Fife area and St. Andrews, local agriculture and fisheries, genealogical records relating to North East Fife, community information.

Non-library collection catalogue:
All or part available in-house

Printed publications:
City of St Rule
Family history sources in North East Fife 1989
Fife Pictorial and Historical (A H Millar, 2 vol. reprint of 1895 original)
Local history collections in North East Fife 1989
Reminiscences of golf – St Andrews Links (maybe out of print)

The Shores of Fife (W Ballingal, reprint of 1872 edition)

Publications list:
Available in print

Access to staff:
Contact by letter, by telephone and by fax
Hours: Mon to Fri, 0900 to 1700

Parent body:
Fife Council

FIFE COUNCIL LIBRARIES – WEST FIFE AREA

Dunfermline Carnegie Library, Abbot Street, Dunfermline, Fife, KY12 7NL

Tel: 01383 312600
Fax: 01383 312608
E-mail: dunfermline.library@fife.gov.uk

Enquiries:
Enquiries to: Librarian
Direct tel: 01383 312602

Founded:
1883

Formerly called:
Dunfermline District Libraries

Organisation type and purpose:
Local government body, public library.

Subject coverage:
General, local history.

Museum or gallery collection, archive, or library special collection:
Andrew Carnegie Collection
George Reid Collection (medieval manuscripts and early printed books)
Local History Collection of books, maps, photographs, slides
Murison Burns Collection (works of Robert Burns, contains no manuscripts)

Non-library collection catalogue:
All or part available online and in-house

Library catalogue:
All or part available online and in-house

Printed publications:
Local History Publications
Murison Burns Catalogue
Various minor local interest pamphlets (eg Witchcraft in Dunfermline)

Electronic and video publications:
Audiobooks, music CD's

Publications list:
Available in print

Access to staff:
Contact by letter

Access for disabled people:
Parking provided, level entry, access to all public areas, toilet facilities

Parent body:
Fife Council, Community Services

FIFE COUNCIL MUSEUMS WEST

Acronym or abbreviation: FCMW

Museum HQ, Dunfermline Museum, Viewfield Terrace, Dunfermline, Fife, KY12 7HY

Tel: 01383 313838
Fax: 01383 313837
E-mail: lesley.botten@fife.gov.uk

Founded:
1996

Formerly called:
Dunfermline District Museum and Small Gallery (year of change 1997)

Organisation type and purpose:
Local government body, museum, suitable for ages: all.

Headquarters of Fife Council Museums West.

Subject coverage:
Local history and archaeology; 19th and 20th century luxury linen damask weaving industry history; costume; coal mining; of the west Fife area.

Museum or gallery collection, archive, or library special collection:
Comprehensive collection of machinery, designs and products from the luxury damask linen and silk industry of 19/20th century Dunfermline

Access to staff:
Contact by letter, by telephone, by fax and by e-mail. Appointment necessary.
Hours: Mon to Fri, 0900 to 1700

Access to building, collection or gallery:
Prior appointment required

Access for disabled people:
Ramped entry, level entry

Branch museums:
Dunfermline Museum
    Viewfield Terrace, Dunfermline, Fife, KY12 7HY
Inverkeithing Museum
    The Friary, Queen Street, Inverkeithing
Pittencrieff House Museum
    Pittencrieff Park, Dunfermline
St. Margaret's Cave (Dunfermline)

Parent body:
Fife Council

FIFE FAMILY HISTORY SOCIETY

Acronym or abbreviation: FFHS

Glenmoriston, Durie Street, Leven, Fife, KY8 4HF

E-mail: via website

Website:
http://www.fifefhs.org
Links to other sites and searchable databases. Publications for sale, and Society information.

Enquiries:
Enquiries to: Secretary

Founded:
1989

Organisation type and purpose:
Membership association (membership is by subscription), voluntary organisation, registered charity.

Access to staff:
Hours: Mon to Fri, 0900 to 1700

Access to building, collection or gallery:
Hours: Mon to Fri, 0900 to 1700

Chairman:
Fife Family History Society
    Hallfield, Blebo Craigs, Cupar, KY15 5UQ

FILM DISTRIBUTORS' ASSOCIATION LIMITED

22 Golden Square, London, W1F 9JW

Tel: 020 7437 4383
Fax: 020 7734 0912
E-mail: info@fda.uk.net

Website:
http://www.launchingfilms.com

Enquiries:
Enquiries to: Chief Executive

Founded:
1915

Formerly called:
Society of Film Distributors Limited (SFD) (year of change 2001)

Organisation type and purpose:
Trade association.

Subject coverage:
UK Film distribution.

continued overleaf

Electronic and video publications:
Guide to UK Film Distribution (online via website)

Publications list:
Available online

Access to staff:
Contact by letter, by telephone, by fax, by e-mail and via website
Hours: Mon to Fri, 0930 to 1730

FILMLINK

Acronym or abbreviation: FL

South Way, Leavesden, Hertfordshire, WD25 7LZ

Tel: 01923 495051
Fax: 01923 333007
E-mail: nfl@herts-filmlink.co.uk ; locations@filmlink.org

Enquiries:
Enquiries to: Centre Administrator

Founded:
1996

Formed from:
South West Herts Business Partnership (SWHBP); Herts Film Link (HFL) (year of change 1996)

Formerly called:
Business Link Hertfordshire, South West Herts Centre

Organisation type and purpose:
Advisory body.
A film and television commission office.

Subject coverage:
Filmlink is the point of contact for all film enquiries in the county. Services include location searching, location library, private and public authority liaison, production guide to the county.

Trade and statistical information:
200 location enquiries processed a month. 40 shooting days a month.

Printed publications:
Filmlink (magazine)
The Production Guide

Access to staff:
Contact by e-mail
Hours: Mon to Fri, 0800 to 1800

Access to building, collection or gallery:
No prior appointment required
Special comments: No prior appointment required for locations library.

FILTON COLLEGE LEARNING RESOURCE CENTRE

Filton Avenue, Filton, Bristol, BS34 7AT

Tel: 0117 931 2121
Fax: 0117 931 2233

Website:
http://www.filton.ac.uk

Enquiries:
Enquiries to: Learning Resources Manager
Direct e-mail: murphyc@filton-college.ac.uk

Founded:
1960

Organisation type and purpose:
Suitable for ages: 16+.
Library.

Subject coverage:
All standard A Level subjects; economics; geography; mathematics; chemistry; physics, art, photography; media studies; art and design; business and management; leisure and tourism to HND level.

Library catalogue:
All or part available in-house

Access to staff:
Contact by letter, by telephone, by fax and by e-mail

Hours: Mon to Thu, 0900 to 2000; Fri, 0900 to 1700

Access to building, collection or gallery:
Prior appointment required
Hours: Mon to Thu, 0900 to 2000; Fri, 0900 to 1700

Access for disabled people:
Parking provided, ramped entry, toilet facilities

FINANCE AND LEASING ASSOCIATION

Acronym or abbreviation: FLA

2nd Floor, Imperial House, 15–19 Kingsway, London, WC2B 6UN

Tel: 020 7836 6511
Fax: 020 7420 9655
E-mail: info@fla.org.uk

Website:
http://www.fla.org.uk

Enquiries:
Enquiries to: Head of Government Affairs
Direct tel: 020 7420 9654
Direct e-mail: edward.simpson@fla.org.uk

Founded:
1992

Formerly called:
Finance Houses Association (FHA)

Incorporates the former:
Equipment Leasing Association (ELA) (year of change 1992)

Organisation type and purpose:
Trade association

Subject coverage:
The FLA is the trade association for companies offering business finance and leasing, consumer credit and motor finance in the UK, and holds information on all of these subjects.

Trade and statistical information:
Asset finance and leasing, business finance, consumer credit, motor finance

Printed publications:
Lending Code 2006
Business Finance Code
Final demand: debt and mental health
Repaying Your Loan Early
Your Credit Decision Explained
List of Members
FLA Annual Survey of Business Finance
Free publications include:
FLA Annual Review
Code of Practice Annual Report
A Pocket Guide to Asset Finance
Key Facts 2008

Publications list:
Available online

Access to staff:
Contact by letter, by telephone, by fax and by e-mail
Hours: Mon to Fri, 0900 to 1700

Access to building, collection or gallery:
No access other than to staff

Access for disabled people:
Ramped entry

FINANCIAL OMBUDSMAN SERVICE

South Quay Plaza, 183 Marsh Wall, London, E14 9SR

Tel: 020 7964 1000
Fax: 020 7964 1001
E-mail: enquiries@financial-ombudsman.org.uk

Website:
http://www.financial-ombudsman.org.uk

Formed by the merger of:
Banking Ombudsman (BO), Building Societies Ombudsman (BSO), Insurance Ombudman Bureau (IOB), Investment Ombudsman Bureau (IOB), Office of the Investment Ombudsman (OIO)

Organisation type and purpose:
Statutory body.
Set up by law to help settle individual disputes between consumers and financial firms.

Subject coverage:
Banking, insurance, pensions, savings and investments, credit cards and store cards, loans and credit, hire purchase and pawnbroking, financial advice, stocks, shares, unit trusts and bonds.

Printed publications:
Ombudsman News (monthly newsletter)
Your Complaint and the Ombudsman leaflet
Information about the services is available in a range of languages, publications can also be produced in Braille or large print or on audiotape.

Electronic and video publications:
Annual Review
Guide for complaint handlers
Your Complaint and the Ombudsman

Publications list:
Available online and in print

Access to staff:
Contact by letter, by telephone, by fax, by e-mail and via website
Hours: Mon to Fri, 0900 to 1700

FINANCIAL SERVICES AUTHORITY, THE

Acronym or abbreviation: FSA

25 The North Colonnade, London, E14 5HS

Tel: 020 7066 1000
Fax: 020 7066 1097

Website:
http://www.fsa.gov.uk
An introduction to the FSA, the Central Register, information for investors, enforcement information, publications and press releases, investor alerts.

Enquiries:
Enquiries to: Public Enquiry Officer

Founded:
1986

Formerly called:
Securities and Investments Board (SIB), date of change, October 1997

Incorporating the former:
Building Societies Commission (BSC), Friendly Societies Commission (FSC), date of change, December 2001

Organisation type and purpose:
Statutory body.
Financial services regulation and investor protection.

Subject coverage:
Financial services regulation.

Publications list:
Available in print

Access to staff:
Contact by letter and by telephone
Hours: Mon to Fri, 0900 to 1700

FINANCIAL SERVICES COMPENSATION SCHEME

Acronym or abbreviation: FSCS

7th Floor, Lloyds Chambers, 1 Portsoken Street, London, E1 8BN

Tel: 020 7892 7300
Fax: 020 7892 7301

E-mail: enquiries@fscs.org.uk

Website:
http://www.fscs.org.uk
Full guide to the Scheme for consumers, claimants and industry.

Enquiries:
Enquiries to: Customer Services Team
Other contacts: Head of Communications for press enquiries.

Founded:
Dec 2001

Formerly called:
Deposit Protection Board (DPB), Investors Compensation Scheme (ICS), Policyholders Protection Board (PPB) (year of change 2001)

Organisation type and purpose:
Statutory body.
FSCS is a final safety net for customers of authorised financial services firms. It compensates consumers if an authorised firm is unable to pay claims against it. The Scheme covers deposits, insurance and investments.

Subject coverage:
Set up under the Financial Services and Markets Act (FSMA) 2000.

Printed publications:
Annual Report and Accounts
How to Claim
How We Can Help (consumer guide)
What to do if You're not Happy (guide to FSCS complaints' procedure)
Do's and Don'ts for Investors
Outlook (industry newsletter)

Publications list:
Available online and in print

Access to staff:
Contact by letter, by telephone, by fax and by e-mail. Appointment necessary.
Hours: Mon to Fri, 0900 to 1700

Access to building, collection or gallery:
No access other than by appointment

Access for disabled people:
Access to all public areas

Independent but accountable to:
FSA

FINANCIAL SERVICES SKILLS COUNCIL

51 Gresham Street, London, EC2V 7HQ

Tel: 020 7216 7366
Fax: 020 7216 7370
E-mail: info@fssc.org.uk

Website:
http://www.fssc.org.uk

Enquiries:
Enquiries to: Sector Support Executive
Direct e-mail: info@fsnto.org

Formerly called:
Banking Industry Training and Development Council (BITDC), BBS NTO, IRFS NTO, FS NTO

Organisation type and purpose:
Sector Skills Council.

Subject coverage:
Labour market information for the financial services sector.

Printed publications:
See website
Order printed publications from: e-mail:
www.fssc.org.uk

Electronic and video publications:
See website

Publications list:
Available online

Access to staff:
Contact by e-mail and via website

Hours: Mon to Fri, 0900 to 1700

Access to building, collection or gallery:
No access other than to staff

Access for disabled people:
Access to all public areas

FINE ART SOCIETY PLC

Acronym or abbreviation: FAS

148 New Bond Street, London, W1S 2JT

Tel: 020 7629 5116
Fax: 020 7491 9454
E-mail: art@faslondon.com

Website:
http://www.faslondon.com
Current and future exhibitions and current stock.

Enquiries:
Enquiries to: Information Officer

Founded:
1876

Organisation type and purpose:
Service industry, art gallery.
Art dealers.

Subject coverage:
Dealers in 19th and 20th century fine and contemporary arts.

Museum or gallery collection, archive, or library special collection:
Past and present exhibition catalogues held by Victoria and Albert Museum National Art Library

Printed publications:
Past and current exhibition catalogues available for sale

Access to staff:
Contact in person
Hours: Mon to Fri, 1000 to 1800; Sat, 1000 to 1300
Special comments: Closed Saturdays in August.

FINE ART TRADE GUILD

16–18 Empress Place, London, SW6 1TT

Tel: 020 7381 6616
Fax: 020 7381 2596
E-mail: info@fineart.co.uk

Website:
http://www.fineart.co.uk
Directory of members, services, publications, code of practice, etc.

Enquiries:
Enquiries to: Managing Director
Other contacts: Editor, Art Business Today for wide industry knowledge and insight.

Founded:
1910

Formerly called:
The Printsellers Association; broadened scope to become the Fine Art Trade Guild (year of change 1920)

Organisation type and purpose:
International organisation, trade association (membership is by subscription), present number of members: 1,200, service industry, manufacturing industry, publishing house.

Subject coverage:
Pictures, print publishing, limited-edition prints, picture framing industry.

Museum or gallery collection, archive, or library special collection:
Archives of limited edition prints

Printed publications:
Art Business Today (magazine, 5 times a year)
Various industry-related books
The Directory

Access to staff:
Contact by letter, by telephone, by fax, by e-mail and via website. Appointment necessary.
Hours: Mon to Fri, 0930 to 1730

Links with:
British Art Market Federation (BAMF)
10 Bury Street, London, SW1Y 6AA; tel: 020 7839 7163; fax: 020 7839 6599

FINISHING PUBLICATIONS LIMITED

105 Whitney Drive, Stevenage, Hertfordshire, SG1 4BL

Tel: 01438 745115
Fax: 01438 364536
E-mail: finpubs@compuserve.com

Website:
http://www.finishingpublications.com
http://www.surfacequery.com
Searchable database with some 130,000 technical abstracts

Enquiries:
Enquiries to: Manager

Founded:
1964

Organisation type and purpose:
Publishing house.

Subject coverage:
Surface engineering and treatment, metal finishing, electroplating, anodizing, etching, pickling, plating, printed circuit board fabrication, effluent treatment for these industries. Books relating to St Ives and its literary/artistic community

Museum or gallery collection, archive, or library special collection:
In-house Metal-Finishing Library (UK, USA, German serials, books)

Trade and statistical information:
Statistical information available from in-house database (costs, market size, etc).

Non-library collection catalogue:
All or part available online

Printed publications:
Coating and Surface Treatment Systems for Metals: A Comprehensive Guide to Selection (J. Edwards, £80)
Handbook of Effluent Treatment and Recycling for the Metal Finishing Industry (L. Hartinger, 2nd edn, £120)
History of Medicine, Surgery and Dentistry: Patent Abridgements 1620 to 1866 (facsimile)
I'll Raise the Wind Tomorrow: A Biography of Arthur Caddick (D. Calvert)
Bactericidal and Oligodynamic Action of Silver and Copper in Hygiene, Medicine and Water Treatment (Landau, et al)
Plating and Electroplating of Metals: History and Patent Abridgements, 1617 to 1866 (facsimile)
For other titles, see website

Electronic and video publications:
Cradle of Inventions (CD-ROM Database of British Patent Titles 1616–1890)
Defects in Aluminium Anodising (CD-ROM troubleshooting guide)
Defects in Plated Zinc Diecastings (CD-ROM troubleshooting guide)
Electroplating Defects and Troubleshooting (CD-ROM)
The Art of Sven Berlin (CD-ROM photo gallery)
Surface Energy and Cleanliness Testing by Wetting Methods (CD-ROM)

Publications list:
Available online

Access to staff:
Contact by letter, by telephone, by fax, by e-mail and via website. Appointment necessary.
Hours: Mon to Fri, 0900 to 1700

Access for disabled people:
Parking provided, level entry

FIRA INTERNATIONAL LTD

Formal name: Furniture Industry Research
Association
Acronym or abbreviation: FIRA

Maxwell Road, Stevenage, Hertfordshire, SG1 2EW

Tel: 01438 777700
Fax: 01438 777800
E-mail: info@fira.co.uk

Website:
http://www.fira.co.uk
FIRA activities, Industry news, Members access to
journals. List of publications available to all.

Enquiries:
Enquiries to: Technical Advisors

Organisation type and purpose:
FIRA International is acknowledged as the UK
centre of excellence for furniture research, testing,
consultancy and information who provides a suite
of products and services to a number of global
businesses.

Subject coverage:
Furniture design and manufacturing methods,
tests for furniture materials and complete items of
furniture, upholstery, standards, environmental
issues, ergonomics, flammability, fault
investigations, market research and marketing,
consultancy in product costing, factory layout etc,
machinery and material selection, statistics for the
industry.

Printed publications:
FIRA Newsletter, Members Quarterly Review,
    research and technical journals
Statistical digests/market survey reports UK and
    European furniture statistics

Publications list:
Available online

Access to staff:
Contact by letter, by telephone and by fax. Access
for members only.
Hours: Mon to Fri, 0900 to 1700

Access to building, collection or gallery:
No access other than to staff

FIRE BRIGADE SOCIETY

Acronym or abbreviation: FBS

17 Kinsbourne Way, Southampton, SO19 6HB

Website:
http://www.firebrigadesociety.freeserve.co.uk/fbs/
welcome.htm

Enquiries:
Enquiries to: General Secretary

Founded:
1963

Organisation type and purpose:
International organisation, membership
association (membership is by subscription).
Voluntary association.

Subject coverage:
Fire service, past, present and future.

Access to staff:
Contact by letter
Hours: Mon to Fri, 0900 to 1700

FIRE BRIGADES UNION

Acronym or abbreviation: FBU

Bradley House, 68 Coombe Road, Kingston upon
Thames, Surrey, KT2 7AE

Tel: 020 8541 1765
Fax: 020 8546 5187
E-mail: office@fbu.org.uk

Website:
http://www.fbu.org.uk

Enquiries:
Enquiries to: General Secretary

Founded:
1918

Organisation type and purpose:
Trade union, present number of members: 51,600.

Subject coverage:
Fire services.

Printed publications:
Journal (monthly)

Access to staff:
Contact by letter, by telephone, by e-mail and via
website
Hours: Mon to Fri, 0900 to 1700

Access to building, collection or gallery:
Prior appointment required

Affiliated to:
TUC

FIRE FIGHTING VEHICLE MANUFACTURERS ASSOCIATION

Acronym or abbreviation: FFVMA

Forbes House, Halkin Street, London, SW1X 7DS

Tel: 020 7344 9232
Fax: 020 7235 7112
E-mail: cford@smmt.co.uk

Website:
http://www.smmt.co.uk
Brief outline.

Enquiries:
Enquiries to: Director

Founded:
1972

Organisation type and purpose:
Trade association.

Subject coverage:
Legislation and standards regarding fire
appliances and associated vehicles and equipment.

Trade and statistical information:
UK Vehicle Registration Statistics.

Access to staff:
Contact by letter, by telephone, by fax and via
website. Appointment necessary.
Hours: Mon to Fri, 0900 to 1700

Affiliated to the:
Society of Motor Manufacturers & Traders (SMMT)
    tel: 020 7235 7000; fax: 020 7235 7112

FIRE INDUSTRY ASSOCIATION

Acronym or abbreviation: FIA

Thames House, 29 Thames Street, Kingston Upon
Thames, Surrey, KT1 1PH

Tel: 020 8549 5855
Fax: 020 8547 1564
E-mail: info@fia.uk.com

Website:
http://www.fia.uk.com/

Enquiries:
Enquiries to: General Manager
Other contacts: Committee Secretary

Created by the merger of:
the Fire Extinguishing Trades Association (FETA)
and the British Fire Protection Systems Association
(BFPSA)

Organisation type and purpose:
Trade association.

Subject coverage:
Development, manufacture and specialist
distribution of fire extinguishers of all types,
portable fire fighting equipment fillings.

Printed publications:
Guide to the Servicing of Portable fire
    extinguishers and hose reels (purchase)
List of Members (free)

Access to staff:
Contact by letter, by telephone and by fax
Hours: Mon to Fri, 0900 to 1700

**Affiliated to, and premises and secretarial
services shared with, the:**
Association of British Fire Trades (ABFT)
British Approvals for Fire Equipment (BAFE)
Fire Industry Confederation (FIC)

FIRE INDUSTRY CONFEDERATION

Acronym or abbreviation: FIC

Neville House, 55 Eden Street, Kingston Upon
Thames, Surrey, KT1 1BW

Tel: 020 8549 8839
Fax: 020 8547 1564

Enquiries:
Enquiries to: Secretary

Founded:
1980

Formerly called:
Fire Industry Council (FIC) (year of change 1999)

Organisation type and purpose:
Trade association.
Central council for associations within the fire
trade.

Subject coverage:
Fire protection equipment.

Publications list:
Available online and in print

Access to staff:
Contact by letter
Hours: Mon to Fri, 0900 to 1700

Access to building, collection or gallery:
No access other than to staff

Members:
Association of Specialist Fire Protection
    tel: 01252 321322; fax: 01252 333901; e-mail:
    info@associationhouse.org.uk
British Automatic Sprinkler Association
    tel: 01353 659187; fax: 01353 741628; e-mail:
    stewart-kidd@ndirect.co.uk
British Fire Protection Systems Association Limited
    tel: 020 8549 5855; fax: 020 8547 1564; e-mail:
    bfpsa@abft.org.uk
Fire Extinguishing Trades Association
    tel: 020 8549 8839; fax: 020 8541 1950; e-mail:
    feta@abft.org.uk

FIRE MARK CIRCLE

44 Kings Road, East Sheen, London, SW14 8PF

Tel: 020 8878 7123
Fax: 020 8878 7123
E-mail: saunders_mj@hotmail.com

Website:
http://www.firemarkcircle.fsnet.co.uk
Information on fire marks, on the history of fire
marks and fire insurance, information on meetings
and auctions.

Enquiries:
Enquiries to: Honorary Secretary

Founded:
1934

Organisation type and purpose:
Learned society.
For persons interested in the origin and history of
fire insurance companies, their fire marks, fire
brigades and all that pertains to the past of fire
insurance.

Subject coverage:
History of fire insurance and fire-fighting.

Printed publications:
FMC News

Publications list:
Available in print

Access to staff:
Contact by letter, by telephone, by fax, by e-mail and via website
Hours: Mon to Fri, 0900 to 1700

FIRE SERVICE COLLEGE

Acronym or abbreviation: FSC

Moreton-in-Marsh, Gloucestershire, GL56 0RH

Tel: 01608 812050
Fax: 01608 812048
E-mail: library@fireservicecollege.ac.uk

Website:
http://www.fireservicecollege.ac.uk

Enquiries:
Enquiries to: Library Manager
Direct e-mail: jmason@fireservicecollege.ac.uk
Other contacts: Customer Services for enquiries.

Organisation type and purpose:
National government body, training organisation. Government agency.
Training personnel from UK fire service and industry in fire, fire safety and related subjects.

Subject coverage:
Fire and emergency, technology, engineering, safety, operational aspects and disaster management, also related subjects and history of the Fire Service.

Museum or gallery collection, archive, or library special collection:
Archives of Fire Service History
Fire Journal from first issue
Library of over 80,000 books

Non-library collection catalogue:
All or part available online

Library catalogue:
All or part available online, in-house and in print

Access to staff:
Contact by letter, by telephone, by fax, by e-mail and via website. Appointment necessary.
Hours: Mon to Thu, 0900 to 1700; Fri, 0900 to 1400

Access to building, collection or gallery:
No public access

FIRE SERVICE PRESERVATION GROUP

Acronym or abbreviation: FSPG

50 Old Slade Lane, Iver, Buckinghamshire, SL0 9DR

Website:
http://www.f-s-p-g.org
Group and membership details.

Enquiries:
Enquiries to: Membership Secretary

Founded:
1968

Organisation type and purpose:
Membership association (membership is by subscription), present number of members: 1200.
Preservation of all types of fire appliances and equipment.

Subject coverage:
Fire appliances and equipment, equipment of the NFS and AFS, equipment dating back to the formation of the Fire Brigades, clothing spare parts, hand pumps, horse-drawn appliances and extinguishers, legislation and registration of appliances.

Museum or gallery collection, archive, or library special collection:
Library of books and reference manuals

Printed publications:
Handbook (annually, members)
Off the Run (newsletter, monthly, members)

Access to staff:
Contact by letter and via website

Hours: Mon to Fri, 0900 to 1700

Member of:
Federation of British Historic Vehicle Clubs (FBHVC)

FIRST DIVISION ASSOCIATION

Acronym or abbreviation: FDA

2 Caxton Street, London, SW1H 0QH

Tel: 020 7343 1111
Fax: 020 7343 1105
E-mail: head-office@fda.org.uk

Website:
http://www.fda.org.uk
FDA services, FDA contacts, current news, about the FDA.
http://www.fda.org.uk/members
FDA members area (restricted access).

Enquiries:
Enquiries to: General Secretary

Founded:
1919

Formerly called:
Association of First Division Civil Servants (FSA) (year of change 2001)

Organisation type and purpose:
Professional body, trade union (membership is by subscription), present number of members: 11,000.

Subject coverage:
Civil Service; modernising government; freedom of information.

Printed publications:
Public Service Magazine

Publications list:
Available online

Access to staff:
Contact by letter, by telephone, by fax, by e-mail and via website
Hours: Mon to Fri, 0900 to 1700

Access to building, collection or gallery:
Prior appointment required

Affiliated to the:
Trades Union Congress (TUC)

FIRST KEY

Oxford Chambers, Oxford Place, Leeds, West Yorkshire, LS1 3AX

Tel: 0113 244 3898
Fax: 0113 243 2541
E-mail: information@firstkeyleeds.com or admin@firstkeyleeds.com

Website:
http://www.first-key.co.uk

Enquiries:
Enquiries to: Administrator

Founded:
1984

Organisation type and purpose:
Voluntary organisation, registered charity (charity number 289552).
To improve the life chances of young people leaving public care, through training, advice, consultancy.

Subject coverage:
Young people leaving public care.

Printed publications:
Publications include:
A Study of Black Young People Leaving Care 1987
Education 'Looked After'
National Standards in Leaving Care
The Children Act 1989
The Children Act Aftercare One Year On
Training Issues for Organisations Working with Care-leavers
Whatever Next?

Publications list:
Available in print

Access to staff:
Contact by letter, by telephone, by fax and by e-mail. Appointment necessary.
Hours: Mon to Fri, 1000 to 1600

Other addresses:
First Key
    London Voluntary Sector Resource Centre, 356 Holloway Road, London, N7 6PA; tel: 020 7700 8130; fax: 020 7700 8174; e-mail: admin@firstkeylondon.com
First Key
    Room 14 Koco Building, Unit 15, The Arches, Spon End, Coventry, CV1 3JQ; tel: 02476 716259; fax: 02476 677554; e-mail: information@firstkeycoventry.com

FIRST STEPS TO FREEDOM

Acronym or abbreviation: FSTF

PO Box 476, Newquay, TR7 1WQ

Tel: 0845 120 2916
E-mail: first.steps@btconnect.com

Website:
http://www.first-steps.org

Enquiries:
Enquiries to: Secretary

Founded:
1991

Organisation type and purpose:
Membership association (membership is by subscription), present number of members: 1,400, voluntary organisation, registered charity (charity number 1006837).
To offer help, advice and support to those suffering from stress-related disorders such as phobias, panic attacks and Obsessive Compulsive Disorder

Subject coverage:
Generalised anxiety disorder (GAD), phobias, compulsive disorders
FSTF offers a confidential helpline, practical advice, telephone self-help groups, one-to-one telephone counselling and befriending, leaflets, self-help booklets and videos.

Printed publications:
Advice for carers on phobias, panic attacks and Obsessive Compulsive Disorder
Booklets on Obsessive and Compulsive Disorder, Bulimia and Panic Attacks
Fact sheets on a range of phobias

Electronic and video publications:
Audio tapes; relaxation tapes
What you really need to know about (series covering stress, depression, anxiety, etc.; videos)
Yoga (beginners, intermediate and advanced; videos)

Publications list:
Available online and in print

Access to staff:
Contact by letter, by telephone, by fax, by e-mail and via website
Hours: Helpline, daily, 1000 to 2200

Links with:
Queen Elizabeth's Hospital
    Department of Psychiatry, Welwyn Garden City, Hertfordshire

Member organisation of:
Telephone Helplines Association

FISHERIES RESEARCH SERVICES MARINE LABORATORY LIBRARY

Acronym or abbreviation: FRS

PO Box 101, 375 Victoria Road, Aberdeen, AB11 9DB

Tel: 01224 876544
Fax: 01224 295309

continued overleaf

E-mail: heaths@marlab.ac.uk

Website:
http://www.marlab.ac.uk

Enquiries:
Enquiries to: Librarian
Direct tel: 01224 295391

Organisation type and purpose:
Research organisation.
Executive Agency of the Scottish Office.

Subject coverage:
Marine biology, oceanography, fisheries, fishing
methods and gear, pollution and aquaculture,
marine ecology, fish diseases, sonar.

**Museum or gallery collection, archive, or library
special collection:**
Ogilvie Collection on diatomaceae

Non-library collection catalogue:
All or part available in-house

Library catalogue:
All or part available in-house

Printed publications:
FRS Annual Report and Accounts
Aquaculture Information Series (irregular, on sale)
Library: Weekly Contents of Recent Journals
Scottish Fisheries Information Pamphlets
Scottish Fisheries Research Reports

Publications list:
Available online

Access to staff:
Contact by letter, by telephone, by fax and by e-
mail. Appointment necessary. Non-members
charged.
Hours: Mon to Thu, 0900 to 1700; Fri, 0900 to 1630
Special comments: Charges made for photocopying.

Access for disabled people:
Toilet facilities

Branch library at the:
Freshwater Fisheries Laboratory
Pitlochry

Parent body:
Scottish Executive Environment and Rural Affairs
Department (SEERAD)

FISHERIES SOCIETY OF THE BRITISH ISLES

Acronym or abbreviation: FSBI

Martineau Johnson , No. 1 Colmore Square,
Birmingham, B4 6AA

Tel: 0870 763 1487
E-mail: membership@fsbi.org.uk

Website:
http://www.fsbi.org.uk/

Enquiries:
Enquiries to: Secretary
Direct e-mail: secretary@fsbi.org.uk

Founded:
1967

Organisation type and purpose:
Learned society.

Subject coverage:
Scientific aspects of freshwater and marine
fisheries, fish biology.

Printed publications:
Journal of Fish Biology (monthly)

Access to staff:
Contact by letter, by telephone, by fax, by e-mail
and via website
Hours: Mon to Fri, 0900 to 1700

FITNESS WALES

1B Clarke Street, Cardiff, CF5 5AL

Tel: 029 2057 5155
Fax: 029 2056 8886

E-mail: enquiries@fitnesswales.co.uk

Enquiries:
Enquiries to: Director
Other contacts: Manager for general enquiries.

Founded:
1966

Organisation type and purpose:
Training organisation.
Governing Body of Exercise and Fitness.
To promote exercise and physical fitness and to
monitor standards in the fitness sector in Wales.

Subject coverage:
Training opportunities to teach exercise and
fitness. Qualifications needed in fitness industry
(national standards). Registration of fitness
instructors. Fitness events in Wales.

Printed publications:
Diary Update
Fitness Focus

Access to staff:
Contact by letter, by telephone, by fax, by e-mail,
in person and via website
Hours: Mon to Fri, 0900 to 1700

FITZWILLIAM COLLEGE LIBRARY

Storey's Way, Cambridge, CB3 0DG

Tel: 01223 332042
Fax: 01223 477976
E-mail: library@fitz.cam.ac.uk

Website:
http://www.fitz.cam.ac.uk/library/index.jsp

Enquiries:
Enquiries to: Librarian

Founded:
1963

Organisation type and purpose:
University department or institute.
College library.

Subject coverage:
Some specialisation in international law.

Non-library collection catalogue:
All or part available online

Library catalogue:
All or part available online

Access to staff:
Contact by letter, by telephone, by fax and by e-
mail. Appointment necessary.
Hours: Mon to Fri, 0900 to 1700

FITZWILLIAM MUSEUM

Library, Trumpington Street, Cambridge, CB2 1RB

Tel: 01223 332900
Fax: 01223 332923
E-mail: fitzmuseum-enquiries@lists.cam.ac.uk

Website:
http://www.fitzmuseum.cam.ac.uk

Enquiries:
Enquiries to: Librarian
Other contacts: Keeper of Manuscripts and Printed
Books

Organisation type and purpose:
Museum, university department or institute.

Subject coverage:
The collection is valuable for its form rather than
subject coverage: illuminated manuscripts, music
manuscripts and printed music, autograph letters,
rare books of all periods, art reference works,
literary manuscripts, fine arts and antiquities.

**Museum or gallery collection, archive, or library
special collection:**
Collections include:
Most of music and some of the other manuscript
material on microfilm
Music by Patrick Hadley, MacFarren, Handel

William Hayley papers
W. S. Blunt papers

Non-library collection catalogue:
All or part available online and in print

Library catalogue:
All or part available online

Printed publications:
Biennial Report
Catalogues of the collections
Newsletter (3 times a year)

Microform publications:
Microfilm, photographs available for purchase via
Photographic Sales Officer

Access to staff:
Contact by letter, by telephone, by e-mail and in
person. Appointment necessary. Letter of
introduction required.
Hours: Tue to Fri, 1000 to 1200 and 1330 to 1630
Special comments: Access restrictions apply only to
the users of curatorial materials (i.e. manuscripts
and rare books). Introductory letter required for
use of special collections.

Access to building, collection or gallery:
No access other than to staff
Hours: Tue to Fri, 1000 to 1200 and 1330 to 1630

Parent body:
University of Cambridge

FLAG INSTITUTE

44 Middleton Road, Acomb, York, YO24 3AS

Enquiries:
Enquiries to: Editor

Founded:
1971

Organisation type and purpose:
Voluntary organisation.

Subject coverage:
Flags and related emblems both historical and
modern, with particular reference to national flags,
flag protocol and usage, flag design, the
publication of flag information in various formats,
charts and information packs.

**Museum or gallery collection, archive, or library
special collection:**
Country by country flag dossiers
Frederick Warne collection
John Sharpe Collection of flag books
Library of flag books, charts and pictures
Louis Loynes Collection of flag paintings and
drawings

Trade and statistical information:
Information on the flag trade (manufacture and
distribution) in Britain and abroad.

Printed publications:
Flagmaster (quarterly)
Pamphlets on design, protocol, terminology

Electronic and video publications:
Flag Information System includes flag images in
EPS form, available on diskette for Apple
Macintosh users

Publications list:
Available in print

Access to staff:
Contact by letter and by telephone. All charged.
Hours: Mon to Fri, 1000 to 1800

Member of:
Fédération Internationale des Associations
Vexillologiques

FLAT ROOFING ALLIANCE

Acronym or abbreviation: FRA

Fields House, Gower Road, Haywards Heath, West
Sussex, RH16 4PL

Tel: 01444 440027
Fax: 01444 415616

E-mail: info@fra.org.uk

Website:
http://www.fra.org.uk
List of members.

Enquiries:
Enquiries to: Director

Founded:
1938

Formerly called:
Felt Roofing Contractors Advisory Board (year of change 1982); Flat Roofing Contractors Advisory Board (year of change 1997)

Organisation type and purpose:
Trade association.

Subject coverage:
Flat roof design, construction and weather-proofing excluding mastic asphalt.

Printed publications:
Roofing Handbook (series of information sheets with updating service, for sale)
Directory of Members (free)
Householders Guide to Flat Roofing (free)

Publications list:
Available in print

Access to staff:
Contact by letter, by telephone, by fax and by e-mail. Appointment necessary.
Hours: Mon to Fri, 0900 to 1700

Member of:
Construction Products Asscn
National Specialist Contractors Council (NSCC)

FLINTSHIRE COUNTY COUNCIL

County Hall, Mold, Flintshire, CH7 6NB

Tel: 01352 752121
Fax: 01352 758240
E-mail: info@flintshire.gov.uk

Website:
http://www.flintshire.gov.uk

Enquiries:
Enquiries to: Corporate Communications Manager

Founded:
1996

Organisation type and purpose:
Local government body.

Access to staff:
Contact by letter, by telephone, by fax, by e-mail, in person and via website
Hours: Mon to Fri, 0830 to 1700

FLINTSHIRE HISTORICAL SOCIETY

Flintshire Record Office, The Old Rectory, Hawarden, Flintshire, CH5 3NR

Tel: 01244 532414
Fax: 01244 538344

Enquiries:
Enquiries to: Honorary Secretary
Direct tel: 01745 332220

Founded:
1911

Organisation type and purpose:
Learned society (membership is by subscription), present number of members: 324 individual, 46 corporate, registered charity (charity number 218288).

Subject coverage:
History and archaeology of the historical county of Flintshire.

Printed publications:
Journal (irregular, vols 1 to 37)
Order printed publications from: Flintshire Records Office

Publications list:
Available in print

Access to staff:
Contact by letter and by telephone. Non-members charged.
Hours: Mon to Fri, 0900 to 1700

FLINTSHIRE LIBRARY AND INFORMATION SERVICE

Library Headquarters, County Hall, Mold, Flintshire, CH7 6NW

Tel: 01352 704400
Fax: 01352 753662
E-mail: libraries@flintshire.gov.uk

Website:
http://www.flintshire.gov.uk
http://www.arthurian-collection.org
Catalogue of the Arthurian Collection.

Enquiries:
Enquiries to: Head of Libraries, Culture & Heritage

Founded:
1996

Organisation type and purpose:
Local government body, public library.

Subject coverage:
Arthurian legend, Wales and Welsh literature, general public reference service, Wales Euro Info Centre.

Museum or gallery collection, archive, or library special collection:
Arthurian Legend Collection
GRO index to births, marriages and deaths England and Wales 1837–1997 and overseas records
Local history collection

Trade and statistical information:
Data on intra and extra EC trade.

Non-library collection catalogue:
All or part available online

Library catalogue:
All or part available online

Printed publications:
Antiquarian maps and prints
Arthurian Catalogue
Bibliographies
Catalogues of the Collections
Facsimile Limited Edition Reprints of Local Study Items
Postcards

Access to staff:
Contact by letter, by telephone, by fax, by e-mail, in person and via website
Hours: Mon to Fri, 0900 to 1700; Sat, 0900 to 1230

Access for disabled people:
Parking provided, ramped entry, toilet facilities, lift

FLINTSHIRE MUSEUM SERVICE

County Hall, Mold, Flintshire, CH7 6NW

Tel: 01352 704409
Fax: 01352 753662
E-mail: museums@flintshire.gov.uk

Website:
http://www.flintshire.gov.uk

Enquiries:
Enquiries to: Principal Museums Officer
Direct e-mail: deborah.seymour@flintshire.gov.uk

Founded:
1996

Formerly called:
Clwyd County Museum Service (year of change 1996)

Organisation type and purpose:
Local government body.
Local authority museum service.

Subject coverage:
The support of local culture and history.

Museum or gallery collection, archive, or library special collection:
Flintshire historical artefacts

Non-library collection catalogue:
All or part available in-house

Access to staff:
Contact by letter, by telephone, by e-mail and via website. Appointment necessary.
Hours: Mon to Fri, 0900 to 1700

Access to building, collection or gallery:
No prior appointment required

Branch museums:
Buckley Library and Heritage Centre
The Precinct, Buckley, Flintshire, CH7 2EF; tel: 01244 549210; e-mail: museums@flintshire.gov.uk; website: http://www.flintshire.gov.uk
Mold Library and Museum
Earl Road, Mold, Flintshire, CH7 1AP; tel: 01352 754791; e-mail: museums@flintshire.gov.uk; website: http://www.flintshire.gov.uk

Links with:
Greenfield Valley Heritage Park
Greenfield, Holywell, CH8 7GH; tel: 01352 714172; e-mail: info@greenfieldvalley.com; website: http://www.greenfieldvalley.com

FLINTSHIRE RECORD OFFICE

Acronym or abbreviation: FRO

The Old Rectory, Hawarden, Flintshire, CH5 3NR

Tel: 01244 532364
Fax: 01244 538344
E-mail: archives@flintshire.gov.uk

Website:
http://www.flintshire.gov.uk

Enquiries:
Enquiries to: Principal Archivist
Direct tel: 01244 532414
Other contacts: Conservator for conservation.

Founded:
1951

Formerly called:
Flintshire Record Office from 1951 to 1974, 1996 (year of change 1951–74, 1996–present); Clwyd Record Office from 1974 to 1996 (year of change 1974–96)

Organisation type and purpose:
Local government body.
Archives, conservation, records management.

Subject coverage:
All aspects of the history of Flintshire, 12th to 20th century, official, public and deposited records for Flintshire and North East Wales.

Museum or gallery collection, archive, or library special collection:
Family papers of W. E. Gladstone

Non-library collection catalogue:
All or part available online and in-house

Library catalogue:
All or part available in-house

Printed publications:
Annual Report
Buckley in Archive Photographs
Flintshire in Archive Photographs
Guide to the Parish Records of Clwyd
Handlist of Chapel Registers (list of all records in the record office, £2.50 incl. p&p)
Handlist of the Denbighshire Quarter Sessions Records (2 vols, 1647–1971)
Handlist of the Grosvenor (Halkyn) MSS (lead and coal mining in north-east Wales, £9.70 incl. p&p)
Introductory Leaflet (free)
List of Parish Registers
Mold in Archive Photographs
Reproduction old postcards, posters, maps and prints
Sources for the Genealogist

continued overleaf

Microform publications:
Derbyshire and Flintshire census
Parish records of baptisms, marriages and burials,
and Nonconformist registers
Flintshire newspapers

Electronic and video publications:
Bygone Flintshire (CD-ROM)
Mr Gladstone (CD-ROM)

Access to staff:
Contact by letter, by telephone, by fax and by e-mail. Appointment necessary.

Access to building, collection or gallery:
Hours: Mon to Thu, 0900 to 1645; Fri, 0900 to 1615;
documents not produced between 1200 and 1330
Special comments: CARN Reader's Ticket required,
can be issued on production of proof of ID with
address and signature.

Access for disabled people:
Parking provided, level entry

Constituent part of:
Flintshire County Council
tel: 01352 752121

FLOUR ADVISORY BUREAU LIMITED

Acronym or abbreviation: FAB

21 Arlington Street, London, SW1A 1RN

Tel: 020 7493 2521
Fax: 020 7493 6785

Website:
http://www.grainchain.com
http://www.fabflour.co.uk

Enquiries:
Enquiries to: Head of Communications /
Communications Assistant
Direct e-mail: info@fabflour.co.uk

Founded:
1956

Organisation type and purpose:
Trade association.
A central source of information on matters relating
to bread and flour in the UK.

Subject coverage:
Generic information on wheat, flour and bread;
usage, recipes, educational material, nutritional
information and market trends.

Education services:
See website.

Printed publications:
Literature for schools and consumers on wheat,
flour and bread

Access to staff:
Contact by letter, by telephone, by fax, by e-mail
and via website
Hours: Mon to Fri, 0900 to 1700

Public relations arm of the:
National Association of British and Irish Millers
(NABIM)
at the same address

FLOWERS & PLANTS ASSOCIATION

Acronym or abbreviation: F&PA

266 Flower Market, New Covent Garden Market,
London, SW8 5NB

Tel: 020 7738 8044
Fax: 020 7738 8083
E-mail: press-office@flowers.org.uk

Website:
http://www.flowers.org.uk
Information on the association, flowers and plants
industry, healthy house plants, seasonal pages,
trend information, care advice.
http://www.tryflowers.org.uk

Enquiries:
Enquiries to: Chief Executive

Founded:
1984

Organisation type and purpose:
Trade association (membership is by subscription),
present number of members: 200 companies.
Promotion of fresh cut flowers and indoor pot
plants.

Subject coverage:
Commercially grown cut flowers, commercially
grown pot plants (indoor), statistical data on
market; care advice; product information; general
related topics of interest.

Trade and statistical information:
Statistics for members only.
Data on cut flower market.
Data on pot plants market.

Printed publications:
Advertising point of sale material (members only)
Booklets and leaflets on flowers and plants
Factsheets on flowers & plants
Flowers & Plants Association News (quarterly,
members)
Postcards of indoor flowers & plants
Posters of indoor flowers & plants
Trend information

Access to staff:
Contact by letter, by telephone, by fax, by e-mail
and via website. Appointment necessary. Non-
members charged.
Hours: Mon to Fri, 0900 to 1700
Special comments: Certain information is available
to members only.

FOCUS

10 Great Pulteney Street, London, W1F 9NB

Tel: 020 3214 0100
Fax: 020 3214 0126

Website:
http://www.focusnet.co.uk
Description of our services, online service is on a
separate URL and is available by subscription only.

Enquiries:
Enquiries to: Director

Founded:
1984

Still trading and formed from:
Property Intelligence Limited (year of change
2004)

Organisation type and purpose:
Service industry, research organisation.
Provides information on commercial properties
UK-wide.

Subject coverage:
Commercial properties in the UK; socioeconomic
and geo-demographic data on major UK towns, 17
million property records, 1 million deals, 900
retailers' requirements, 2.1 million occupiers, 7
town reports, planning details, auction
information, property history, rating information,
office availability, office requirements.

**Museum or gallery collection, archive, or library
special collection:**
Company prospectuses
Property journals
Property company and fund reports
Press releases

Printed publications:
Agency League Tables
Newsletter
Auction Guide Analysis
Retail Demand Report
London Office Market Report

Electronic and video publications:
FOCUS online database

Access to staff:
Contact by letter, by telephone, by fax, by e-mail
and via website. Appointment necessary. All
charged.
Hours: Mon to Fri, 0830 to 1800

Access for disabled people:
Ramped entry, toilet facilities
Special comments: Ramped Entry

Connections with:
Scottish Property Network Limited
26 New Street, Paisley, PA1 1YB; tel: 0141 561
7300; fax: 0141 561 7319; e-mail: info@
scottishproperty.co.uk

FOLKESTONE LIBRARY, MUSEUM AND SASSOON GALLERY

2 Grace Hill, Folkestone, Kent, CT20 1HD

Tel: 01303 850123\ Minicom no. 01303 240258
Fax: 01303 242907

Enquiries:
Enquiries to: Librarian
Direct tel: 01303 256710
Direct fax: 01303 256710
Direct e-mail: janet.adamson@kent.gov.uk
Other contacts: (1) Information Officer (2) Heritage
Officer for (1) reference (2) local studies.

Founded:
1888

Organisation type and purpose:
Local government body, museum, art gallery,
public library, suitable for ages: all.

Subject coverage:
General and local information, including Channel
Tunnel, local and family history.

**Museum or gallery collection, archive, or library
special collection:**
Heritage Room, historical records, maps,
photographs and newspapers for Folkestone and
the Shepway area
Bishop's Transcripts and Archdeacon's Transcripts
and Parish Registers for many parishes
(microfilm)
Census enumerator's returns for 1841–1891 for
Shepway and Capel-le-Ferne
Photographic collection
Map collection
Newspapers

Printed publications:
Creed's, Sinnock's, Pike's, Parson's and Kelly's
Directories 1871–1938 (microfiche)

Access to staff:
Contact by letter, by telephone, by fax, by e-mail
and in person
Hours: Mon, Tue, Thu, 0930 to 1800; Fri, 0930 to
1900; Sat, Wed, 0930 to 1700

Access for disabled people:
Level entry, access to all public areas, toilet
facilities

Part of:
Kent County Council, Education and Libraries
Department

FOLLY FELLOWSHIP

Acronym or abbreviation: F/F

7 Inch's Yard, Market Street, Newbury, Berkshire,
RG14 5DP

Tel: 01635 42864
E-mail: andrew@follies.fsnet.co.uk

Website:
http://www.follies.org.uk

Enquiries:
Enquiries to: Trustee
Other contacts: Membership Secretary

Founded:
1988

Organisation type and purpose:
International organisation, learned society
(membership is by subscription), registered charity
(charity number 1002646).
To protect, preserve and promote follies, grottoes
and garden buildings.

Subject coverage:
Architectural follies, grottoes and landscape
buildings in the United Kingdom and world-wide.

**Museum or gallery collection, archive, or library
special collection:**
Picture and photographic library

Printed publications:
Follies (quarterly, £3 incl. back copies from 1988)
Follies Journal (annually, £10.50)
Order printed publications from:
membership@follies.org.uk

Access to staff:
Contact by letter, by telephone, by e-mail and via
website. Appointment necessary.
Hours: Mon to Fri, 0900 to 1700

FOOD AND CHEMICAL ALLERGY
ASSOCIATION

Acronym or abbreviation: FCAA

55 Sea Lane, Ferring, West Sussex, BN12 5DY

Enquiries:
Enquiries to: Chairman and Secretary

Founded:
1976

Formerly called:
Food Allergy Association

Organisation type and purpose:
Voluntary organisation.

Subject coverage:
Information and advice relating to all forms of
allergy-induced illness; helps to discover causes of
allergies and to build up immune systems, both
essential for a return to good health; lists of doctors
working in this field and similar associations
provided on request.

Printed publications:
Understanding Allergies (available from the
Association, £2 plus medium-sized sae)
Allergies in the Under Fives: Achieving Your
Child's Potential (£7.50, p&p free)

Access to staff:
Contact by letter
Hours: Mon to Fri, 0900 to 1700
Special comments: Advice given by letter only.

FOOD AND DRINK FEDERATION

Acronym or abbreviation: FDF

6 Catherine Street, London, WC2B 5JJ

Tel: 020 7836 2460
Fax: 020 7836 0580
E-mail: generalenquiries@fdf.org.uk

Website:
http://www.fdf.org.uk
Information about FDF and the food
manufacturing industry.

Enquiries:
Enquiries to: Information Manager

Formerly called:
Food Manufacturers Federation

Organisation type and purpose:
Trade association.

Subject coverage:
UK food manufacturing industry.

Electronic and video publications:
A list of publications is available from the website

Publications list:
Available online

Access to staff:
Contact by letter, by telephone, by fax, by e-mail
and via website. Access for members only.
Hours: Mon to Fri, 0930 to 1730
Special comments: Visitors not normally permitted.

European link is the:
CIAA

Members:
Association of Cereal Food Manufacturers
British Pasta Products Association
British Starch Industry Association
Cereal Ingredient Manufacturers' Association
Frozen and Chilled Potato Processors' Association
tel: 0131 229 9415
Infant & Dietetic Foods Association
Margarine and Spreads Association
National Association of Cider Makers
Potato Processors' Association
tel: 0131 229 9415
Seasoning and Spice Association
UK Association of Manufacturers of Bakers' Yeast
UK Preserves Manufacturers' Association
UK Tea Association

FOOD COMMISSION

94 White Lion Street, London, N1 9PF

Tel: 020 7837 2250
Fax: 020 7837 1141
E-mail: enquiries@foodcomm.org.uk

Website:
http://www.foodcomm.org.uk

Enquiries:
Enquiries to: Information Officer

Founded:
1990

Formerly called:
London Food Commission (year of change 1990)

Organisation type and purpose:
Registered charity, voluntary organisation (charity
number 1000358), consultancy, research
organisation.
Consumer watchdog, campaigning for better food.

Subject coverage:
Food policy, food labelling, irradiation, claims,
nutrition and health, food composition analysis,
agriculture and the environment, pesticides,
contaminants, food adulteration, baby foods,
genetic engineering, advertising.

**Museum or gallery collection, archive, or library
special collection:**
Books, magazines and press cuttings

Printed publications:
The Food Magazine (quarterly)
The Nursery Food Book (£10.99 inc. p&p)
Healthy Eating for Babies and Children (£6.99 inc.
£1 p&p)
The Food Our Children Eat (£8.99 inc. £1 p&p)
More than Rice and Peas (£17.50 in. £2.50 p&p)
Poor Expectations – Poverty and
Undernourishment in Pregnancy (£5.50 inc. 50p
p&p)
Food Irradiation (£6.50 in. £1 p&p)
Fast Food Nation (£9.99 inc. p&p)
The Shopper's Guide to Organic Food (£8.99 inc. £1
p&p)
GM Free – A shopper's guide to genetically
modified food (£5.70 inc. p&p)
Various Photocopied Reports available from the
Food Commission

Publications list:
Available online and in print

Access to staff:
Contact by letter, by telephone and by fax.
Appointment necessary.
Hours: Mon to Fri, 1030 to 1800

Subsidiary body:
Food Additives Campaign Team
Food Commission Research Charity
Food Irradiation Campaign

FOODSERVICE CONSULTANTS
SOCIETY INTERNATIONAL

Acronym or abbreviation: FCSI

Bourne House, Horsell Park, Woking, Surrey,
GU21 4LY

Tel: 01483 761122
Fax: 01483 751991
E-mail: admin@fcsi.org.uk

Enquiries:
Enquiries to: Administrator

Founded:
1970

Formerly called:
SCHMC; Society of Catering and Hotel
Management Consultants (year of change 1996)

Organisation type and purpose:
International organisation, professional body.

Subject coverage:
Market research, design and planning facilities,
catering and hotel systems and procedures,
recruitment, equipment, human resources, all
related to hotel and catering industry.

Access to staff:
Contact by letter, by telephone, by fax and by e-
mail. Appointment necessary.
Hours: Mon to Fri, 0900 to 1700

Parent body:
Foodservices Consultants Society International
Suite 201, 304 West Liberty Street, Louisville, KY
40202 – 3068, USA; tel: 00 1 502 589 3783; fax: 00
1 502 589 3602; e-mail: fcsi@fcsi.org

FOOTBALL ASSOCIATION

Acronym or abbreviation: FA

25 Soho Square, London, W1D 4FA

Tel: 020 7745 4545
Fax: 020 7745 4546
E-mail: info@the-fa.org

Website:
http://www.fa.premier.com
Official site of the FA Carling Premiership.

Enquiries:
Enquiries to: Chief Executive

Founded:
1863

Organisation type and purpose:
Membership association.
To promote the sport of association football.

Subject coverage:
Football: coaching, competitions, refereeing and
registrations.

Printed publications:
Soccer Referee's Manual
The Winning Formula (official coaching manual)
FA Handbook
FA News (quarterly)
FA Yearbook
Laws of Association Football
Weekly Bulletin (fixtures and results)
Order printed publications from: FACA Resources
tel: 0113 279 1395, fax: 0113 231 9606

Publications list:
Available in print

Access to staff:
Contact by letter, by telephone, by fax and by e-
mail. Appointment necessary.
Hours: Mon to Fri, 0900 to 1700

Affiliated to:
FIFA
UEFA
World and European governing bodies

Has:
42,000 affiliated clubs

continued overleaf

Other address:
Football Association
62 Lancaster Mews, London, W2 3QG

FOOTBALL LICENSING AUTHORITY

Acronym or abbreviation: FLA

27 Harcourt House, 19 Cavendish Square, London, W1G 0PL

Tel: 020 7491 7191
Fax: 020 7491 1882
E-mail: fla@flaweb.org.uk

Website:
http://www.flaweb.org.uk
Statutory Remit, publications and links to relevant sites.

Enquiries:
Enquiries to: Office Manager

Founded:
1990

Organisation type and purpose:
Statutory body.
Application of Safety of Sports Ground Act 1975 amended and Football Spectators Act 1989.

Subject coverage:
Safety of sports grounds and spectators, accommodation including seating, terracing and accommodation for spectators with disabilities.

Printed publications:
Accessible Stadia
Concourses
Control Rooms

Electronic and video publications:
Publications available online at website for free download:
Annual Report
Exercise Planning
Safety Certification
Briefing / Debriefing
Contingency Planning

Access to staff:
Contact by letter, by telephone, by fax and by e-mail. Appointment necessary.
Hours: Mon to Fri, 0900 to 1700

Parent body:
Department for Culture, Media and Sport (DCMS) Sport and Recreation Division, 2–4 Cockspur Street, London, SW1Y 5DY; tel: 020 7211 6200; e-mail: enquiries@culture.gov.uk; website: www .cluture.gov.uk

FORD 400E OWNERS CLUB

1 Maltings Farm Cottages, Witham Road, White Notley, Witham, Essex, CM81 1SE

E-mail: sandy@thames400e.freeserve.co.uk

Enquiries:
Enquiries to: Membership Secretary

Founded:
1991

Organisation type and purpose:
Membership association (membership is by subscription), present number of members: 120.

Subject coverage:
Ford medium commercial vehicle range 1957–1965, 400E models.

Museum or gallery collection, archive, or library special collection:
Sales and technical literature

Printed publications:
Newsletter/Magazine (6 times a year, members only)

Access to staff:
Contact by letter and by e-mail. Appointment necessary.
Hours: Telephone: Mon and Fri only, 1900 to 2100.

FORD CORSAIR OWNERS' CLUB

Acronym or abbreviation: FCOC

4 Bexley Close, Hailsham, East Sussex, BN27 1NH

Tel: 01323 840655
E-mail: checkleylizandray@yahoo.co.uk

Website:
http://www.fordcorsair.at
Details of club and membership form.

Enquiries:
Enquiries to: Secretary

Founded:
1985

Organisation type and purpose:
Membership association (membership is by subscription), present number of members: 220.

Subject coverage:
Technical advice for Ford Corsair cars.

Access to staff:
Contact by letter, by telephone and by e-mail
Hours: Mon to Fri, 0900 to 1700; Sat and Sun, 1000 to 2000

FORD EXECUTIVE OWNERS REGISTER

3 Shanklin Road, Stonehouse Estate, Coventry, Warwickshire, CV3 4EE

Tel: 024 7651 1822

Enquiries:
Enquiries to: Information Officer

Founded:
1985

Organisation type and purpose:
Membership association (membership is by subscription).
Classic car club.

Subject coverage:
Classic Car Club, cars included are Ford Cortina 1600E, Ford Cortina 2000E, Ford Corsair 2000E, Ford Capri 3000E, Ford Escort 1300E, Ford Zodiac Executive.

Printed publications:
Free to membership

Publications list:
Available in print

Access to staff:
Contact by letter and by telephone
Hours: Mon to Fri, 0900 to 1700

FORD MADOX FORD SOCIETY

Department of English, The Open University, Walton Hall, Milton Keynes, Buckinghamshire, MK7 6AA

Tel: 01908 652472
Fax: 01908 653750
E-mail: s.j.haslam@open.ac.uk

Website:
http://www.open.ac.uk/Arts/fordmadoxford -society

Enquiries:
Enquiries to: Chair
Other contacts: Treasurer

Founded:
1996

Organisation type and purpose:
International organisation, learned society, present number of members: c.140, voluntary organisation, registered charity.
Provides information on and generates research into Ford Madox Ford. Co-ordinates conferences and publications.

Subject coverage:
Ford Madox Ford, modernism, research/ conferences

Printed publications:
Journal of FMF Studies (annually, 2002–, for purchase direct or to members)

Access to staff:
Contact by letter, by telephone, by fax and by e-mail
Hours: Any reasonable time

Access to building, collection or gallery:
No access other than to staff

Links with:
Joseph Conrad Society

FORD MK II INDEPENDENT OC INTERNATIONAL

173 Sparrow Farm Drive, Feltham, Middlesex, TW14 0DG

Tel: 020 8384 3559
Fax: 020 8890 3741

Enquiries:
Enquiries to: President

Founded:
1988

Organisation type and purpose:
Membership association, present number of members: 500.
Motor vehicle authenticator for RAC and MSA.

Subject coverage:
All aspects, and information on the Ford MKII Consul, Zephyr, Zodiac; technical advice, modification; classic car meetings and rallies, national and international.

Museum or gallery collection, archive, or library special collection:
Original parts books
Workshop manuals

Printed publications:
Newsletter (6 times a year, members)

Access to staff:
Contact by letter, by telephone and by fax
Hours: Mon to Fri, 0900 to 2100

Officially recognised by:
DVLA
   Swansea
Ford Motor Company

FORD MODEL 'T' REGISTER OF GB

3 Riverside, Strong Close, Keighley, West Yorkshire, BD21 4JP

Tel: 01535 607978
E-mail: JMA195@aol.com

Website:
http://www.t-ford.co.uk

Enquiries:
Enquiries to: Secretary

Founded:
1970

Organisation type and purpose:
Advisory body, membership association, voluntary organisation.

Subject coverage:
Register of Model T Ford vehicles, help with such and supply of parts. Magazine and events held throughout the year.

Printed publications:
Topics (magazine, quarterly, non-members £1.50)
Order printed publications from: The Secretary

Publications list:
Available in print

Access to staff:
Contact by letter, by telephone, by e-mail and via website
Hours: Mon to Fri, 1730 to 2100

FORD MOTOR COMPANY LIMITED

Eagle Way, Brentwood, Essex, CM13 3BW

Tel: 01277 253000

Enquiries:
Enquiries to: Secretary

Founded:
1928

Organisation type and purpose:
Manufacturing industry.
The principal activity in which the Company is engaged is the manufacture and sale of motor vehicles and components.

Subject coverage:
Motor vehicle manufacture; industrial engines; parts and accessories.

Access to staff:
Contact by letter
Hours: Mon to Fri, 0900 to 1700

FORECAST INTERNATIONAL/DMS INC

Templehurst House, 48 New Street, Chipping Norton, Oxfordshire, OX7 5LJ

Tel: 01608 643281
Fax: 01608 641159
E-mail: hawk@hawk.co.uk

Website:
http://www.hawk.co.uk
Internet home page: List of contents, company capabilities, news highlights, newsletters.

Enquiries:
Enquiries to: Managing Director

Founded:
1975

Organisation type and purpose:
Research organisation, publishing house.

Subject coverage:
Aircraft maintenance, budget, funding, commercial aircraft, commercial inventories, contractors, electronics, avionics, emerging technologies, gas turbines, military aircraft, military inventories, military vehicles, missiles, ordnance, munitions, power systems, space systems and satellites, component and niche market analysis.

Museum or gallery collection, archive, or library special collection:
Library containing hardcopy and CD-ROM formats for market intelligence for aerospace, defence, electronics, power systems and transportation industries

Trade and statistical information:
Production forecasts and analysis for aerospace, weapons systems, power systems, naval systems, electronic systems, US defence budget including inventories and product life cycle analysis.

Electronic and video publications:
CD-ROM/online based market intelligence services (£1595 each, £35,000 full set) covering:
Aerospace Systems Group
Geo-Political and Economic Group
Electronics Group
Weapons Systems Group
Naval Systems Group

Publications list:
Available in print

Access to staff:
Contact by telephone, by fax, by e-mail and via website
Hours: Mon to Fri, 0900 to 1700

Head office:
Forecast International/DMS
22 Commerce Road, Newtown, Connecticut, 06470, USA

FOREIGN AND COMMONWEALTH OFFICE

Acronym or abbreviation: FCO

Downing Street, London, SW1A 2AL

Tel: 020 7270 3925
Fax: 020 7270 3270
E-mail: library.historical@fco.gov.uk library
.current@fco.gov.uk

Enquiries:
Enquiries to: Librarian
Other contacts: Head of Library Enquiry Services

Formerly called:
Colonial Office (CO), Commonwealth Relations Office (CRO); Foreign Office (FO) (year of change '968)

Organisation type and purpose:
National government body.

Subject coverage:
International relations, international law, diplomacy and politics, history, administration, economics and laws of overseas countries.

Museum or gallery collection, archive, or library special collection:
Historic Collections of books of the former colonial and foreign offices
Photographic Collection mainly of Commonwealth countries and former UK Colonies
Portraits of Diplomats and Colonial Governors, places and events c. 1850 to current

Non-library collection catalogue:
All or part available in-house

Access to staff:
Contact by letter, by telephone and by e-mail. Appointment necessary.
Hours: Mon to Fri, 0900 to 1700

Access to building, collection or gallery:
Prior appointment required

Access for disabled people:
Ramped entry, toilet facilities

FOREIGN AND COMMONWEALTH OFFICE – KNOWLEDGE AND LEARNING CENTRE

Acronym or abbreviation: FCO

Room G6, Building 17, Hanslope Park, Hanslope, Milton Keynes, Buckinghamshire, MK19 7BH

Tel: 01908 515960
Fax: 01908 515943
E-mail: hanslope.library.fco@gtnet.gov.uk

Website:
http://www.fco.gov.uk
Summary of FCO services, functions, ministers, structure and main contact points, includes FCO travel advice on foreign travel.

Enquiries:
Enquiries to: Librarian
Other contacts: Librarian (London address) for non-central-government enquiries to FCO's main library in first instance.

Organisation type and purpose:
National government body.
Support and IT services for the FCO at home and abroad.

Subject coverage:
Hanslope Park Knowledge and Learning Centre is an information unit and open learning centre primarily serving FCO staff based on site. Stock is available for loan to other central government departments and agencies. Other enquirers are requested to contact the main FCO library in London, in the first instance, or consult the FCO's website, www.fco.gov.uk, for advice on foreign travel.

Non-library collection catalogue:
All or part available in-house

Printed publications:
Order printed publications from: Stationery Office Ltd (formerly HMSO)

Access to staff:
Contact by letter, by telephone and by fax. Appointment necessary.
Hours: Mon to Fri, 0830 to 1630

Access to building, collection or gallery:
Prior appointment required

Other address:
Foreign and Commonwealth Office (FCO) Library, Room E213, King Charles Street, London, SW1A 2AH; tel: 020 7270 3925; fax: 020 7270 3270/3682

FOREIGN AND COMMONWEALTH OFFICE – TRAVEL ADVICE UNIT

Acronym or abbreviation: TAU

Consular Directorate, Old Admiralty Building, Whitehall, London, SW1A 2PA

Tel: 0845 850 2829
Fax: 020 7008 0155
E-mail: consular.fco@gtnet.gov.uk

Website:
http://www.fco.gov.uk/
Travel advice notices, do's and don'ts, consular services abroad.

Enquiries:
Enquiries to: Travel Advice Clerk

Organisation type and purpose:
National government body, advisory body.

Subject coverage:
Up-to-date travel advice on threats to personal safety, arising from political unrest, lawlessness, violence, natural disasters, epidemics, anti-British demonstrations and aircraft safety, is given to help British travellers avoid trouble when overseas.

Printed publications:
Backpackers and Independent Travellers
British Consular Services Abroad (for ordering fax: 01444 246620)
Checklist for travellers
Death Overseas
Travellers' Tips
Dual Nationality
In Prison Abroad
International Child Abduction
Victims of Crime Abroad

Access to staff:
Contact by letter, by telephone, by fax and by e-mail. Appointment necessary.
Hours: Mon to Fri, 0930 to 1600

FOREIGN PRESS ASSOCIATION IN LONDON

Acronym or abbreviation: FPA

11 Carlton House Terrace, London, SW1Y 5AJ

Tel: 020 7930 0445
Fax: 020 7925 0469
E-mail: secretariat@foreign-press.org.uk

Website:
http://www.foreign-press.org.uk
Press briefings, conferences, membership information.

Enquiries:
Enquiries to: General Manager

Founded:
1888

Organisation type and purpose:
International organisation, professional body (membership is by subscription, election or invitation), present number of members: 750. Professional body/club for foreign journalists based in the UK, reciprocal temporary membership with FPA's abroad.

continued overleaf

Subject coverage:
Foreign media in the UK.

Printed publications:
List of Members (annually)
Newsletter (monthly, for members)

Access to staff:
Contact by letter, by telephone, by fax, by e-mail and in person
Hours: Mon to Fri, 0900 to 1800

FORENSIC SCIENCE SERVICE LIMITED

Acronym or abbreviation: FSS

Information Services, Forensic Science Service, 109 Lambeth Road, London, SE1 7LP

Fax: 020 7160 4651
E-mail: info.services.enquiry.desk@fss.pnn.police.uk

Website:
http://www.forensic.gov.uk
Information on the Forensic Science Service.

Enquiries:
Enquiries to: Library Services Manager

Founded:
1967

Organisation type and purpose:
Government-owned company.
Provides scientific support in the investigation of crime.

Subject coverage:
All aspects of forensic science, including serology, DNA profiling and immunology, analysis of chemicals, drugs, pesticides and trace elements, toxicology, document examination and fingerprint enhancement.
General scientific techniques applied to the analysis of small quantities of drugs, paint, glass, metals, body fluids etc; the investigation, at the scene and in the laboratory, of cases of known and suspected arson; metallurgic problems such as mechanical failures; the restoration of erased identification numbers on stolen car engines and other property; the analysis of physical evidence arising from traffic offences such as tyre examinations and the mathematical analysis of vehicle accidents; grouping systems on dried blood and body secretions; DNA profiling; high performance liquid chromatography techniques applied to drugs and lubricating oils; gas liquid chromatography for the analysis of drugs, blood-alcohol, the routine screening of drugs and extracts in toxicological analysis, hydrocarbons (petrol, paraffin, diesel etc) and other solvents; use of scanning electron microscopy for identification of very small particles; examination, analysis and identification of synthetic fibres and fibres of living origin (plant and animal); identification of bullets found at scenes, bullet and cartridge-case comparisons and the examination of firearms; examination of forged and altered documents using non-destructive techniques, such as infra-red and ultra-violet light, and the comparison of handwriting and typewriting; use of specialised photographic techniques at crime scenes and of items examined at the laboratory for the enhancement of fingerprints and other marks, blood patterns and the location of body fluids.

Museum or gallery collection, archive, or library special collection:
Analytic Data on Drugs and Chemicals
Forensic Science Bibliographic Database (FORS)
Shoeprint Collection in kind, photographs and documents
Sidelamp and Headlamp Collection
Vehicle Paint and Tyre Data

Non-library collection catalogue:
All or part available online

Library catalogue:
All or part available in-house

Printed publications:
FORSight – The Forensic Abstracts Journal (12 times a year, prices on request)
Annual Report (also available on website)
Forensic Science Thesaurus (prices on request)
Restricted Internal Research Reports
Order printed publications from: Library Services Manager
info.services.enquiry.desk@fss.pnn.police.uk

Electronic and video publications:
FORSight (current awareness bulletin)
FORS, a comprehensive online database (prices on request) on forensic science, 60,000 records from 1900 sources. Covers toxicology, firearms, fingerprints, forensic medicine, DNA profiling, etc

Access to staff:
Contact by letter, by fax, by e-mail and via website. Non-members charged.
Hours: Mon to Fri, 1000 to 1600

Laboratories at:
Chepstow, Wetherby, Chorley, Huntingdon and Birmingham

FORENSIC SCIENCE SOCIETY

Acronym or abbreviation: FSSoc

Clarke House, 18A Mount Parade, Harrogate, North Yorkshire, HG1 1BX

Tel: 01423 506068
Fax: 01423 566391
E-mail: president@forensic-science-society.org.uk

Website:
http://www.forensic-science-society.org.uk

Enquiries:
Enquiries to: Secretary

Founded:
1959

Organisation type and purpose:
Learned society (membership is by subscription), present number of members: 2300, registered charity (charity number 205992), publishing house.
To advance the study, application and standing of forensic science and to facilitate co-operation among persons interested in forensic science throughout the world.

Subject coverage:
Forensic sciences, pathology and medicine, forensic chemistry and biology, forensic serology, forensic science in connection with textiles, tyres, metallurgy, photographs and marks; forensic identification, handwriting and documents examination, explosion investigation, firearms and ballistics, aspects of alcohol.

Printed publications:
Science and Justice (quarterly)
World List of Forensic Science Laboratories, Interfaces (newsletter – quarterly)

Access to staff:
Contact via website
Hours: Mon to Fri, 0900 to 1700

FORESIGHT

28 The Paddock, Godalming, Surrey, GU7 1XD

Tel: 01483 427839
Fax: 01483 427668

Website:
http://www.foresight-preconception.org.uk

Enquiries:
Enquiries to: Chairman

Founded:
1978

Formerly called:
Foresight, The Association for the Promotion of Preconceptual Care

Organisation type and purpose:
Registered charity (charity number 279160).

Subject coverage:
Preparing couples for pregnancy.

Library catalogue:
All or part available in print

Printed publications:
Planning a Healthy Baby (Barnes B and Bradley S G)
The Hyperactive Child, what the family can do (Barnes B and Colquhoun I)
Preparation for Pregnancy: an Essential Guide (Bradley S G and Bennett N)
The Foresight Wholefood Cookbook (Jervis N and Jervis R)
Order printed publications from: Resource Centre, Foresight
Mead House, Littlemead Estate, Alfold Road, Cranleigh, Surrey, GU6 8ND, tel: 01483 548071

Publications list:
Available in print

Access to staff:
Contact by letter, by telephone, by fax and in person. Appointment necessary.
Hours: Mon to Fri, 0900 to 1700
Special comments: Organisation works almost always by letter/telephone etc.

Access to building, collection or gallery:
Prior appointment required

Access for disabled people:
Parking provided, ramped entry

FOREST

Formal name: Freedom Organisation for the Right to Enjoy Smoking Tobacco
Acronym or abbreviation: FOREST

Sheraton House, Castle Park, Cambridge, CB3 0AX

Tel: 01223 370156
E-mail: contact@forestonline.org

Website:
http://www.forestonline.org/

Enquiries:
Enquiries to: Media Enquiries
Direct tel: 07774 781840

Founded:
1979

Organisation type and purpose:
National organisation, membership association (membership is by subscription), voluntary organisation.
To promote equal rights for smokers of tobacco, and those who wish to accommodate them.

Subject coverage:
Smoking, a sensible smoking policy and different aspects of the smoking debate.

Printed publications:
A range of publications on:
Taxation and economics, rights and free choice, children, restrictions, health and environmental, tobacco smoke and the work-place
Free Choice (journal, 4 times a year)
Smoking and Its Enemies
FOREST : Smoking in the workplace : Consultancy Pack

Publications list:
Available online and in print

Access to staff:
Contact by letter, by telephone, by fax, by e-mail and via website. Appointment necessary.
Hours: Mon to Fri, 0930 to 1730

Access to building, collection or gallery:
No prior appointment required

FOREST COMMISSION

Westonbirt Arboretum, Tetbury, Gloucestershire, GL8 8QS

Tel: 01666 880220
Fax: 01666 880559

E-mail: westonbirt@forestry.gov.uk

Website:
http://www.forestry.gov.uk
http://www.fowa.org.uk

Enquiries:
Enquiries to: Curator
Other contacts: Visitor Services Manager

Founded:
1829

Organisation type and purpose:
Government Department.

Subject coverage:
Arboriculture, forestry, trees and shrubs in general.

Museum or gallery collection, archive, or library special collection:
Tree and shrub collection on computer database, over 18,000 records

Non-library collection catalogue:
All or part available in-house

Printed publications:
Westonbirt Tree Forestry

Access to staff:
Contact by letter, by telephone, by fax and by e-mail. Appointment necessary.

Access to building, collection or gallery:
Hours: Grounds and Visitor Centre: daily, 0900 to 1700

Access for disabled people:
Parking provided, ramped entry, toilet facilities, mobility scooters can be booked

Constituent part of:
Forestry Commission

FOREST HEATH DISTRICT COUNCIL

College Heath Road, Mildenhall, Suffolk, IP28 7EY

Tel: 01638 719000
Fax: 01638 716493
E-mail: info@forest-heath.gov.uk

Website:
http://www.forest-heath.gov.uk

Enquiries:
Enquiries to: Public Relations Manager

Organisation type and purpose:
Local government body.

Access to staff:
Contact by letter, by telephone, by fax, by e-mail, in person and via website
Hours: Mon to Fri, 0900 to 1700

Access for disabled people:
Parking provided, level entry, toilet facilities

FORESTRY AND TIMBER ASSOCIATION

Formal name: Association of Timber Growers and Forestry Professionals Ltd
Acronym or abbreviation: FTA

5 Dublin Street Lane South, Edinburgh, EH1 3PX

Tel: 0131 538 7111
Fax: 0131 538 7222
E-mail: info@forestryandtimber.org

Enquiries:
Enquiries to: Chief Executive

Founded:
1957

Formed from:
Ulster Timber Growers Organisation (UTGA) (year of change 2001); Association of Professional Foresters (APF), Timber Growers Association (TGA) (year of change 2002)

Organisation type and purpose:
Membership association (membership is by subscription), present number of members: 2500.

FORESTRY COMMISSION

231 Corstorphine Road, Edinburgh, EH12 7AT

Tel: 0131 334 0303
Fax: 0131 334 3047
E-mail: enquiries@forestry.gsi.gov.uk

Website:
http://www.forestry.gov.uk

Enquiries:
Enquiries to: Information Officer

Founded:
1919

Organisation type and purpose:
National government body.

Subject coverage:
Forestry.

Publications list:
Available online and in print

Access to staff:
Contact by letter, by telephone, by fax, by e-mail and in person. Appointment necessary.
Hours: Mon to Fri, 0900 to 1700

Access for disabled people:
Parking provided, ramped entry, access to all public areas, toilet facilities

Other address:
North West England Conservancy – Forestry Commission
Bassenthwiate, Cockermouth, Cumbria, CA13 9YG; tel: 017687 76616; fax: 017687 76557

FORESTRY COMMISSION – LIBRARY

Forest Research, Alice Holt Lodge, Wrecclesham, Farnham, Surrey, GU10 4LH

Tel: 01420 22255
Fax: 01420 23653
E-mail: library@forestry.gsi.gov.uk

Website:
http://www.forestry.gov.uk
Directory of addresses of Forestry Commission offices in Great Britain, background information on recreation, the forest industry, education, woodland management and forestry policy and research.

Enquiries:
Enquiries to: Librarian
Direct e-mail: research.info@forestry.gsi.gov.uk

Founded:
1919

Organisation type and purpose:
National government body, research organisation.

Subject coverage:
Forestry in temperate regions; arboriculture (information provided by the Arboricultural Advisory and Information Service)

Non-library collection catalogue:
All or part available in-house

Library catalogue:
All or part available in-house

Printed publications:
Bulletins, handbooks, field books, guidelines, information notes, practice notes, research notes, technical notes
Local Forestry Commission offices issue local trail guides and other publications
Order printed publications from: Forestry Commission Publications, PO Box 25, Wetherby, West Yorkshire, LS23 7EW; tel. 08701 214180; fax 08701 214181; e-mail forestry@capita.co.uk

Electronic and video publications:
Tree Doctor (CD-ROM, £38)

Order electronic and video publications from: Tree Health Division, Pathology Branch, Forest Research, Alice Holt Lodge, Wrecclesham, Farnham, Surrey, GU10 4LH; e-mail tree.doctor@forestry.gsi.gov.uk

Publications list:
Available online

Access to staff:
Contact by letter, by telephone, by fax and by e-mail. Appointment necessary. All charged.
Hours: Mon to Thu, 0900 to 1700; Fri, 0900 to 1630

Access for disabled people:
Level entry, toilet facilities

Also at:
Forestry Commission Public Enquiries Service
231 Corstorphine Road, Edinburgh, EH12 7AT; tel: 0131 334 0303; fax: 0131 334 3047; e-mail: enquiries@forestry.gsi.gov.uk
Public Enquiry Line
tel: 0845 FORESTS (0845 3673787)
Tree Helpline
tel: 09065 161147 (£1.50 per minute)

FORESTRY CONTRACTING ASSOCIATION

Acronym or abbreviation: FCA

Dalfling, Blairdaff, Inverurie, Aberdeenshire, AB51 5LA

Tel: 01467 651368
Fax: 01467 651595
E-mail: members@fcauk.com

Website:
http://www.fcauk.com
General background information on the Association and membership benefits.

Enquiries:
Enquiries to: Executive Director
Direct e-mail: gordon@fcauk.com
Other contacts: Membership Services

Founded:
1992

Organisation type and purpose:
Trade association.

Subject coverage:
All forestry matters; training, running a business, insurance, finance, health and safety and other legislation, wood fuel and biomass.

Printed publications:
FCA News (quarterly)
FCA Directory of Members (yearly)

Electronic and video publications:
Best Business Practice CD-ROM – Free to members

Access to staff:
Contact by letter, by telephone, by fax, by e-mail and via website. Appointment necessary.
Hours: Mon to Fri, 0900 to 1700

FORGOTTEN RACING CLUB

Acronym or abbreviation: FRC

Hillside, Holt Road, Hackney, Matlock, Derbyshire, DE4 2QD

Tel: 01629 733898

Enquiries:
Enquiries to: Membership Secretary

Founded:
1986

Formerly called:
Forgotten Era Racing Club

Organisation type and purpose:
Membership association.

Subject coverage:
Racing motorcycles predominantly from the period 1963 to 1986, their restoration and use.

continued overleaf

Printed publications:
Club magazine (6 times a year, free to members)

Access to staff:
Contact by letter and by telephone
Hours: Evenings and weekends

FORK LIFT TRUCK ASSOCIATION. THE

Manor Farm Buildings, Lasham, Alton, Hampshire, GU34 5SL

Tel: 01256 381441
Fax: 01256 381735
E-mail: mail@fork-truck.org.uk

Enquiries:
Enquiries to: Chief Executive

Founded:
1992

Formerly called:
Fork Truck Hire Association; Fork Truck Association

Organisation type and purpose:
Trade Association.

Subject coverage:
Fork lift trucks.

Non-library collection catalogue:
All or part available online

Publications list:
Available online and in print

Access to staff:
Contact by letter, by telephone, by fax and via website. Appointment necessary.
Hours: Mon to Fri, 0900 to 1700

FORTRESS STUDY GROUP

Acronym or abbreviation: FSG

6 Lanark Place, London, W9 1BS

Tel: 0020 7286 5512

Website:
http://www.fsgfort.com

Enquiries:
Enquiries to: Honorary Secretary

Founded:
1975

Organisation type and purpose:
Learned society (membership is by subscription), registered charity (charity number 288790).
To advance the education of the public in the study of all aspects of fortifications and their armaments, especially works constructed to mount or resist artillery.

Subject coverage:
Fortification since the introduction of artillery.

Printed publications:
Casemate (newsletter, 3 times a year)
Fort (journal, annually)

Access to staff:
Contact by letter, by telephone and by e-mail
Hours: Evenings

Affiliated to:
International Fortress Council

FORUM OF PRIVATE BUSINESS

Acronym or abbreviation: FPB

Ruskin Chambers, Drury Lane, Knutsford, Cheshire, WA16 6HA

Tel: 01565 634467
Fax: 0870 241 9570
E-mail: info@fpb.co.uk

Website:
http://www.fpb.org
Benefits, research, news, how to join, links.

Enquiries:
Enquiries to: Research Projects Manager
Other contacts: Media and PR Officer

Founded:
1977

Organisation type and purpose:
Business support organisation (SMEs), research organisation.
Parliamentary representative body for SMEs.

Subject coverage:
Structure and needs of UK small businesses, concerns and priorities of SME problems, financial, administrative and legal; research on specific issues, bank/SME relationships, late payment, legal identities, crime, ISO and others.

Museum or gallery collection, archive, or library special collection:
Reports, consultation responses and research on SME-related topics

Trade and statistical information:
Quarterly report on current SME issues and longitudinal survey research on specific concerns, detailed academic reports on specialised areas (banking etc).

Printed publications:
FPB Reports on Specific Issues (£75 to £500)
Press Releases (free)
Employment Guide (£175–£299; discounted rates for members)
Health & Safety Guide (£95–£205; discounted rates for members)

Access to staff:
Contact by letter, by telephone, by fax and by e-mail. Appointment necessary.
Hours: Mon to Fri, 0900 to 1730

Access to building, collection or gallery:
Prior appointment required

FOSTERING NETWORK

Acronym or abbreviation: tFN

87 Blackfriars Road, London, SE1 8HA

Tel: 020 7620 6400; Fosterline: 0800 040 7675; Infoline: 020 7261 1884
Fax: 020 7620 6401
E-mail: info@fostering.net

Website:
http://www.fostering.net

Enquiries:
Enquiries to: Information Officer
Direct tel: 020 7261 1884
Other contacts: Senior Media and Communications Officer (for media enquiries)

Founded:
1974

Formerly called:
National Foster Care Association (NFCA) (year of change 2001)

Organisation type and purpose:
Membership association (membership is by subscription), present number of members: 50,000, voluntary organisation, registered charity (charity number 280852), training organisation, consultancy, research organisation, publishing house.
To improve the quality of life for all children in foster care.

Subject coverage:
Foster care, including allowances for foster carers, dealing with difficult behaviour, dealing with allegations of abuse, after-care needs of young people, needs of foster children with disabilities, needs of teenagers in foster care.

Library catalogue:
All or part available online

Printed publications:
A large selection of books, papers and reports, including:
Booklets on aspects of being a foster carer

Foster Care (magazine, quarterly)
Leaflets on all aspects of becoming a foster carer
Research reports
Training materials
Policy guidelines
Leaving Care
Practical Guides for Carers
Order printed publications from: Central Books, 99 Wallis Road, London, E9 5LN

Electronic and video publications:
Video tapes on aspects of foster care

Publications list:
Available online and in print

Access to staff:
Contact by letter, by telephone, by fax, by e-mail, in person and via website. Appointment necessary.
Hours: Helpline: Mon to Fri, 0900 to 1700; Wed 0900 to 2000
Special comments: Preferably attend Wed, Thu and Fri, when the library and information staff are available

Access to building, collection or gallery:
By appointment with the Information Officer
Hours: Office: Mon to Thu, 0900 to 1700; Fri, 0900 to 1630

Constituent bodies:
The Fostering Network Northern Ireland
    Unit 10, 40 Montgomery Road, Belfast, BT6 9HL; tel: 028 9070 5056; fax: 028 9079 9215; e-mail: ni@fostering.net
The Fostering Network Scotland
    Ingram House, 2nd Floor, 227 Ingram Street, Glasgow, G1 1DA; tel: 0141 204 1400; fax: 0141 204 6588; e-mail: scotland@fostering.net
The Fostering Network Wales
    Suite 11, 2nd floor, Bay Chambers, West Bute Street, Cardiff, CF10 5BB; tel: 029 2044 0940; fax: 029 2044 0941; e-mail: wales@fostering.net

Member organisations:
almost all local authorities

FOUNDATION FOR ASSISTIVE TECHNOLOGY

Acronym or abbreviation: FAST

12 City Forum, 250 City Road, London, EC1V 8AF

Tel: 020 7253 3303
Fax: 020 7253 5990
E-mail: info@fastuk.org

Website:
http://www.fastuk.org
Online Database of over 700 organisations involved with research projects, research-related publications and assistive technology events, news information and links to other sites.
User Forum, a list of people who use assistive technology who are willing to participate in research and development projects.
Annual Parliamentary Report outlining assistive technology research and development funded by the government.

Enquiries:
Enquiries to: Administrator

Some services taken over from:
Disability Information Trust (DIT) (year of change 2001)

Organisation type and purpose:
National organisation, registered charity (charity number 1061636).
The Foundation for Assistive Technology (FAST) is an independent networking organisation funded by the Department of Health. We will:
- enable you to contact other people active in the Assistive Technology research and development community via our database which contains information on over 1500 organisations and individuals.
- keep you up to date and act as a signpost to useful and related information about research and development activity in Assistive Technology.

Subject coverage:
Assistive Technology.

Printed publications:
Each month FAST produces a bulletin for the AT Forum with breaking news and updates. FAST produces the annual RAPID Report on Research and Development in Assistive Technology. FAST is also commissioned by the Department of Health to produce an annual parliamentary report which provides the DoH with an overview of the outcomes of research and development funded by Government.

Access to staff:
Contact by e-mail and via website
Hours: Mon to Fri, 0900 to 1700
Special comments: Online service.

FOUNDATION FOR CREDIT COUNSELLING

Formal name: Consumer Credit Counselling Service
Acronym or abbreviation: CCCS

2 Ridgmount Street, London, WC1E 7AA

Tel: 020 7636 5214
Fax: 020 7580 0016
E-mail: mhurlston@hurlstons.com

Enquiries:
Enquiries to: Chairman
Other contacts: (1) Public Relations Officer; (2) Chief Executive Operations for (1) political, media; (2) technical.

Founded:
1993

Also:
CCCS Scotland

Organisation type and purpose:
Registered charity.

Subject coverage:
Consumer debt.

Trade and statistical information:
Data on levels of enquiries and debts.

Printed publications:
Statistical Yearbook 2005

Access to staff:
Contact by e-mail
Hours: Mon to Fri, 0900 to 1700

Access to building, collection or gallery:
No access other than to staff

Other addresses:
Customer Access
  Merrion Centre, Leeds; tel: 0800 138 1111; 0800 138 DEBT
Foundation for Credit Counselling
  Merrion Centre, Leeds; tel: 0800 138 1111; 0800 138 DEBT

FOUNDATION FOR EDUCATION AND RESEARCH IN CHILD BEARING

27 Walpole Street, London, SW3 4QS

Tel: 020 7730 2800
Fax: 020 7730 0710

Enquiries:
Enquiries to: Information Officer

Founded:
1972

Organisation type and purpose:
Registered charity (charity number 262318).

Subject coverage:
Prevention of handicaps of perinatal origin.

Printed publications:
The Prevention of Preterm Birth (Wynn M and A, £3 direct plus p&p)
The Prevention of Handicap of Perinatal Origin (Wynn, M and A, £2 direct plus p&p)

Nutrition Counselling in the Prevention of Low Birth Weight (Wynn M and A, 40p direct plus p&p)
Some Consequences of Induced Abortion to Children Born Subsequently (Wynn M and A, 60p direct plus p&p)
Prevention of Handicap of Early Pregnancy Origin: some evidence for the value of good health before conception (Wynn M and A, £5 direct plus p&p)

Access to staff:
Contact by letter, by telephone and by fax. Appointment necessary.
Hours: Mon to Fri, 0900 to 1700

FOUNDATION FOR THE STUDY OF INFANT DEATHS, THE

Acronym or abbreviation: FSID

Artillery House, 11–19 Artillery Row, London, SW1P 1RT

Tel: 020 7222 8001
Fax: 020 7222 8002
E-mail: fsid@sids.org.uk

Website:
http://www.sids.org.uk/fsid/
Information on research presently funded and previous funded work summaries.
Information available, support/in memory page, education/risk cot death, advert for project grants and research fellowships.

Enquiries:
Enquiries to: Communications Officer

Founded:
1971

Organisation type and purpose:
Voluntary organisation, registered charity (charity number 262191), research organisation.
Library holding SIDS articles and related topics.
To raise funds for research, to support families whose baby has died suddenly and unexpectedly, to disseminate information about cot death and infant health to health professionals and the general public.

Subject coverage:
Research into cot death and sudden infant death, information for bereaved families and for professionals who may have to deal with this, general information on infant health and care. The scope of FSID is all infant deaths, not just cot death.

Printed publications:
List of leaflets, booklets and books
Newsletter (twice a year)
BabyZone (free)
TravelZone (free)
Reduce the Risk of Cot Death (free)
Selected reference list of articles relevant to health education and welfare
Selected reference list of published articles on research into causes and prevention of cot deaths, management of unexpected infant death, and counselling of bereaved parents

Electronic and video publications:
Video films:
Sudden Infant Deaths: Words Can't Describe How You Feel (£20, or £30 with workbook)

Publications list:
Available in print

Access to staff:
Contact by letter, by telephone, by fax, by e-mail and via website. Appointment necessary.
Hours: Mon to Fri, 0900 to 1700

FOUNDATION FOR WOMEN'S HEALTH RESEARCH AND DEVELOPMENT

Acronym or abbreviation: FORWARD

Unit 4, 765–767 Harrow Road, London, NW10 5NY

Tel: 020 8960 4000
Fax: 020 8960 4014
E-mail: forward@forwarduk.org.uk

Website:
http://www.forward.dircon.co.uk
Introduction on FORWARD. What is FGM, etc. Publications. Other useful contacts.

Enquiries:
Enquiries to: Administrator

Founded:
1985

Organisation type and purpose:
International organisation, voluntary organisation, registered charity (charity number 292403), suitable for ages: all, consultancy, research organisation.
Leading voluntary organisation in the UK campaigning against FGM. Provision of training and education to women affected by FGM, and for health, social work, education and child protection professionals.

Subject coverage:
Minority health issues with focus on African women and children's reproductive and sexual health. Female genital mutilation (FGM) in the UK and Africa.

Printed publications:
Information pack (free on request with sae)
Islamic Ruling on Male and Female Circumcision (World Health Organisation, 1996, £3 plus p&p)
Child Protection and Female Genital Mutilation (Hedley R and Darkenoo E, £4.50 plus p&p)
A Report of the Conference on FGM – Moving Forward (£4 plus p&p)
Possessing the Secret of Joy (Walker A, £5 plus p&p)

Publications list:
Available in print

Access to staff:
Contact by letter, by telephone, by fax and by e-mail
Hours: Mon to Fri, 0900 to 1700

FOUNDRY EQUIPMENT AND SUPPLIERS ASSOCIATION

Acronym or abbreviation: FESA

Queensway House, 2 Queensway, Redhill, Surrey, RH1 1QS

Tel: 01737 768611
Fax: 01737 855469

Website:
http://www.fesa.org.uk

Enquiries:
Enquiries to: Secretary
Direct tel: 01737 855280
Direct e-mail: marywhite@uk.dmgworldmedia.com

Founded:
1925

Organisation type and purpose:
Trade association (membership is by subscription), present number of members: 34.

Access to staff:
Contact by letter
Hours: Mon to Fri, 0800 to 1300

Access to building, collection or gallery:
No access other than to staff

FOUNTAIN SOCIETY, THE

26 Binney Street, London, W1K 5BL

Tel: 020 7355 2002 ansaphone
Fax: 020 7355 2002

Website:
http://www.fountainsoc.org.uk

Enquiries:
Enquiries to: Chairman

continued overleaf

Direct tel: 01306 883874
Direct fax: 01306 883874
Direct e-mail: knowlsonpm@cix.co.uk
Other contacts: Projects Officer

Founded:
1986

Organisation type and purpose:
International organisation, membership
association (membership is by subscription),
present number of members: 320, voluntary
organisation, registered charity (charity number
292778).

Subject coverage:
Conservation and restoration of fountains of
aesthetic merit for public enjoyment, promotion of
the provision of fountains in new developments
and the restoration of cascades and waterfalls.

**Museum or gallery collection, archive, or library
special collection:**
Bibliography available to members

Printed publications:
Creating a Fountain?

Access to staff:
Contact by letter, by telephone, by fax, by e-mail
and via website
Hours: Mon to Fri, 0900 to 1700

FPA

Formal name: Family Planning Association
Acronym or abbreviation: fFPA

50 Featherstone Street, London, EC1Y 8QU

Tel: 020 7608 5240
Fax: 0845 123 2349
E-mail: library.information@fpa.org.uk

Website:
http://www.fpa.org.uk
fpa services, projects and publications. Also
information on methods of contraception, STIs,
family planning and GYN Clinics.

Enquiries:
Direct tel: 020 7923 5228

Founded:
1930

Organisation type and purpose:
Membership association (membership is by
subscription), voluntary organisation, registered
charity (charity number 250187).
To advance the sexual health and reproductive
rights and choices of all people throughout the
United Kingdom.

Subject coverage:
Family planning, contraception, sexual health,
fertility control, unplanned pregnancy, sexually
transmitted infections, sex education.

**Museum or gallery collection, archive, or library
special collection:**
Archives of the Family Planning Association,
1920–1977 (held at the Wellcome Institute for the
History of Medicine, Contemporary Medical
Archives Centre, London)

Library catalogue:
All or part available in-house

Printed publications:
Books for professionals, leaflets for consumers on
contraception and sexually transmitted
infections, booklets for young people on periods,
puberty, growing up, pregnancy and abortion
Factsheets available singly
Order printed publications from: fpa Direct
50 Featherstone Street, London, EC1Y 8QU

Electronic and video publications:
Talking to Your Kids About Sex (video)
Sex, Storks and Goosebery Bushes: Talking to
Children about Sex (video)
How Much How Soon – teaching sex in primary
schools (video)
The Fairy Godfather (video)
Challenging Homophobia (video)

Publications list:
Available in print

Access to staff:
Contact by letter, by telephone, by fax and by e-
mail. Appointment necessary.
Hours: Mon to Fri, 0900 to 1700

Access to building, collection or gallery:
Prior appointment required

Access for disabled people:
Level entry, toilet facilities

Other offices:
fpa Cymru
Greenhouse, Trevelyan Terrace, Bangor,
Gwynedd, LL57 1AX; tel: 01248 353534; fax:
01248 371138
fpa Cymru
Suite D1, Canton House, 435–451 Cowbridge
Road East, Cardiff, CF5 1JH; tel: 029 2064 4034;
fax: 029 2064 4306
fpa Northern Ireland
2nd Floor, Northern Counties Building, Custom
House Street, Derry, BT48 6AE; tel: 028 7126
0016; fax: 028 7136 1254
fpa Northern Ireland
113 University Street, Belfast, BT7 1HP; tel: 028
9032 5488; fax: 028 9031 2212
fpa Scotland
Unit 10, Firhill Business Centre, 76 Firhill Road,
Glasgow, G20 7BA; tel: 0141 576 5088; fax: 0141
576 5006

FRAGILE X SOCIETY

Rood End House, 6 Stortford Road, Great
Dunmow, Essex, CM6 1DA

Tel: 01371 875100
E-mail: info@fragilex.org.uk

Website:
http://www.fragilex.org.uk

Enquiries:
Enquiries to: National Contact
Direct fax: 01371 859915

Founded:
1990

Organisation type and purpose:
Registered charity (charity number 1003981).
To provide support, information and advice to
families whose children and adult relatives have
fragile X syndrome; offers national support and
information, telephone helplines on education
statementing, benefits and epilepsy, family-link
members, family conferences and reports, access to
latest research, free UK family membership of the
society, free attendance at Society conferences.
Fragile X shows itself in a wide range of difficulties
with learning and development delay, as well as
social, language, attentional, emotional and
behavioural problems.

Subject coverage:
Fragile X is the second most common cause of
inherited learning disabilities.

Printed publications:
What is Fragile X?
Fragile X Syndrome: An Introduction
Fragile X Syndrome: An Introduction to
Educational Needs
Issues of Diagnosis and Treatment
Titles relating to genetics, carriers and siblings
Titles relating to behavioural and cognitive
functioning, education, adolescence and
adulthood
Titles relating to treatment, health and family
experiences
Newsletter (3 times a year)

Electronic and video publications:
DVD and video

Publications list:
Available online and in print

Access to staff:
Contact by letter, by telephone, by e-mail and via
website
Hours: Mon to Fri, 0900 to 1700

FRANCIS BACON RESEARCH TRUST

Acronym or abbreviation: FBRT

Roses Farmhouse, Epwell Road, Tysoe,
Warwickshire, CV35 0TN

Tel: 01295 688185
Fax: 01295 680770
E-mail: secretary@fbrt.org.uk

Website:
http://www.fbrt.org.uk

Enquiries:
Enquiries to: Director
Direct e-mail: sarah@fbrt.org.uk

Founded:
1980

Organisation type and purpose:
International organisation, membership
association (membership is by subscription),
training organisation, consultancy, research
organisation.
Educational charity.

Subject coverage:
Study of the life and works of Sir Francis Bacon
and of all those associated with him, and to make
known and further the Great Instauration... a
world-wide scheme intended to create
understanding between peoples in which
illumined peace be acquired; ancient wisdom and
traditions, the wisdom of Shakespeare.

Printed publications:
Programme of Events (annually)
Publication Brochure (annually)
A range of books (prices vary), including:
Shakespeare Enigma
Building Paradise
Francis Bacon: Herald of New Age

Publications list:
Available in print

Access to staff:
Contact by letter, by telephone, by fax, by e-mail
and via website. Appointment necessary. Non-
members charged.
Hours: Mon to Fri, 1000 to 1700

FRANCIS BRETT YOUNG SOCIETY

Acronym or abbreviation: FBY Society

92 Gower Road, Halesowen, West Midlands, B62
9BT

Tel: 0121 422 8969

Website:
http://www.fbysociety.co.uk
Information on Society's activities.

Enquiries:
Enquiries to: Secretary

Founded:
1978

Organisation type and purpose:
Learned society (membership is by subscription),
present number of members: 210, registered
charity (charity number 1075904).
Literary society.
To provide opportunities for members to meet,
correspond, and to share the enjoyment of the
author's works.

Subject coverage:
Life and literary works of Francis Brett Young.

Printed publications:
Journal (2 times a year, for members)

FRANCIS-BARNETT OWNERS CLUB

Acronym or abbreviation: FBOC

307 Lower Hillmorton Road, Rugby, Warwickshire, CV21 4AD

Tel: 01788 544909
E-mail: mrs.eileen.lloyd@virgin.net

Website:
http://www.francis-barnett.freeserve.co.uk

Enquiries:
Enquiries to: Secretary

Founded:
1986

Organisation type and purpose:
Company limited by guarantee, registered in England and Wales, no. 4750767 (membership is by subscription), present number of members: 550. To encourage ownership, use and preservation of Francis-Barnett motorcycles.

Subject coverage:
All models of Francis Barnett motor cycles produced by that company in Coventry from 1919 until the demise of AMC (AJS, Matchless, Norton) in the late 1960s.

Museum or gallery collection, archive, or library special collection:
A library of model information manuals and spares lists for most models

Non-library collection catalogue:
All or part available in print

Library catalogue:
All or part available in print

Printed publications:
The Directory (magazine, quarterly, members only)

Access to staff:
Contact by letter
Hours: Mon to Fri, 0900 to 1700
Special comments: There are no full-time staff.

Registered office:
at the same address

FRANCO-BRITISH COUNCIL

16–18 Strutton Ground, London, SW1P 2HP

Tel: 020 7976 8380
Fax: 020 7976 8181
E-mail: fbc@cix.co.uk

Website:
http://www.francobritishcouncil.org.uk

Enquiries:
Enquiries to: Secretary General

Founded:
1972

Organisation type and purpose:
International organisation, membership association (membership is by election or invitation), registered charity.
Promoting Franco-British relations.

Printed publications:
Meeting Reports from 1992–2001, in English (£5 each) recent titles:
Transatlantic Relations (1999)
Transport Policy (1999)
Social Exclusion: Jobs for Young (2000)
Film industry: A Day in June (2000); Arts Funding (2000)
Policing (2000)
Truancy and Exclusion from School (2001)
Peacekeeping and International Crisis Management (2001)
Report: Crossing the Channel (2001)
What do we Want from Europe? (2001)
Commonwealth and Francophonie (2002)
Food and Bio-engineering (2002)

Publications list:
Available online and in print

Access to staff:
Contact by letter, by telephone, by fax and by e-mail
Hours: Tue to Thu, 0930 to 1730

FREE CHURCHES' GROUP

Acronym or abbreviation: FCG

Churches Together in England, 27 Tavistock Square, London, WC1H 9HH

Tel: 020 7539 8131
Fax: 020 7529 8134
E-mail: freechurch@cte.org.uk

Website:
http://www.cte.org.uk

Enquiries:
Enquiries to: Secretary
Direct tel: 020 7387 8413
Other contacts: Health Care Chaplaincy

Founded:
1940

Organisation type and purpose:
Voluntary organisation.
Representative body for Free Church opinion.

Subject coverage:
Free Church tradition and opinion, Free Church and ecumenical relations.

Access to staff:
Contact by letter, by telephone, by fax and by e-mail. Appointment necessary.
Hours: Mon to Fri, 0900 to 1700

Access to building, collection or gallery:
No access other than to staff

Also at:
Free Church Education Unit
27 Tavistock Square, London WC1H 9HH; tel: 020 7529 8131; fax: 020 7529 8134; e-mail: sarah.lane@cte.org.uk

Members:
Afro Westindian United Council of Churches (AWUCOC)
tel: 020 8888 9427; fax: 020 8888 2877
Baptist Union of Great Britain (BUGB)
tel: 01235 517700; fax: 01235 517715; e-mail: baptistuniongb@baptist.org.uk
Baptist Union of Wales
tel: 01792 655468; fax: 01792 469489
Congregational Federation
tel: 0115 911 1460; fax: 0115 911 1462; e-mail: michael.heaney@congregational.org.uk
Council of African and Afro-Caribbean Churches (UK) (CAAC-UK)
tel: 020 7582 4209, Work: 020 7620 4444
Countess of Huntingdon's Connexion
tel: 0118 933 2569; e-mail: brianbrendabaldwin@talk21.com
Fellowship of Churches of Christ
tel: 0121 373 7942; fax: 0121 373 7942; e-mail: hazelwilson@bigfoot.com
Free Church of England
tel: 01273 845092; fax: 01273 845092; e-mail: rtal799@aol.com
Independent Methodist Churches
tel: 01942 223526; fax: 01942 227768; e-mail: resourcecentre@imcgb.org.uk
Methodist Church
tel: 020 7486 5502; fax: 020 7467 5226; e-mail: conferenceoffice@methodistchurch.org.uk
Moravian Church
tel: 020 8883 3409/1912; fax: 020 8365 3371
New Testament Church of God
tel: 01604 643311/645944; fax: 01604 790254
Old Baptist Union
tel: 01625 422404; fax: 01625 422404
Presbyterian Church of Wales
tel: 029 2049 4913; fax: 029 2046 4293
Salvation Army
tel: 020 7367 4614; fax: 020 7367 4718; e-mail: webmajor@salvationarmy.org.uk

Undeb yr Annibynwyr Cymraeg (Union of Welsh Independents)
tel: 01792 652542/467040; fax: 01972 650647; e-mail: tyjp@tyjp.co.uk
United Reformed Church in the United Kingdom
tel: 020 7916 2020; fax: 020 7916 2021; e-mail: david.cornick@urc.org.uk
Wesleyan Reform Union
tel: 0114 272 1938; fax: 0114 272 1965; e-mail: john@wesleyan-reform.freeserve.co.uk

FREIGHT TRANSPORT ASSOCIATION LIMITED

Acronym or abbreviation: FTA

Hermes House, 157 St John's Road, Tunbridge Wells, Kent, TN4 9UZ

Tel: 01892 526171
Fax: 01892 534989
E-mail: enquiries@fta.co.uk

Website:
http://www.fta.co.uk/
General FTA information.
http://supplychain.fta.co.uk/
Series of communication platforms on logistics issues.

Enquiries:
Enquiries to: Director of Communications
Direct tel: 01892 552255
Direct fax: 01892 552323
Direct e-mail: jtanner@fta.co.uk
Other contacts: Media Relations Manager

Founded:
1889

Formerly called:
Traders Road Transport Association (year of change 1969)

Organisation type and purpose:
Trade association.

Subject coverage:
Freight transport, including transport law, costs and rates, statistics, education and training, vehicle maintenance, international transport, shipping, hazardous cargoes.

Printed publications:
Freight (magazine, monthly)
FTA Yearbook of Road Transport Law
Miscellaneous Reports

Access to staff:
Contact by letter, by telephone, by fax, by e-mail and via website
Hours: Mon to Fri, 0900 to 1700

Includes the:
British Shippers Council

FRENCH CHAMBER OF COMMERCE IN GREAT BRITAIN

Acronym or abbreviation: FCCGB

21 Dartmouth Street, Westminster, London, SW1H 0BP

Tel: 020 7304 4040
Fax: 020 7304 7034
E-mail: publications@ccfgb.co.uk

Website:
http://www.ccfgb.co.uk

Enquiries:
Enquiries to: Public Relations Manager
Direct tel: 020 7304 7017
Direct e-mail: atassi@ccfgb.co.uk

Founded:
1883

Organisation type and purpose:
Membership association (membership is by subscription), present number of members: c. 550, consultancy.
Chamber of Commerce.
Increase Franco-British trade.

continued overleaf

Subject coverage:
Publications for settling in France or Great Britain as an individual or a professional.

Museum or gallery collection, archive, or library special collection:
Databases of French companies in the UK and British companies in France, exporters/importers in the UK and France
Directories of members of the French Chamber

Printed publications:
Info (magazine)
chamber@work (newsletter)
Cross the Channel – Control your Tax
Cross Channel Transport Directory
Doing Business with France
Guide des affaires en GB
Guide pratique des Français en GB
Le registre des investissements français au Royaume-Uni
Make yourself at Home in France
Setting up a small business in France
The Franco-British Trade Directory 2001–2002 (annually)

Electronic and video publications:
List of French investments in the UK (disk, paper, labels, database)
List of members (CD-ROM, labels, book)

Publications list:
Available online and in print

Access to staff:
Contact by letter and by e-mail. Appointment necessary.
Hours: Mon to Fri, 0900 to 1700

Access to building, collection or gallery:
Prior appointment required

Access for disabled people:
Level entry

FRENCH EMBASSY – CULTURAL DEPARTMENT

23 Cromwell Road, London, SW7 2EL

Tel: 020 7073 1300
Fax: 020 7073 1320
E-mail: cultural@ambafrance.org.uk

Website:
http://www.institut_francais.org.uk/lb_about.htm

Enquiries:
Enquiries to: Cultural Counsellor

Organisation type and purpose:
Diplomatic mission.

Subject coverage:
Education in France; studies in France; teaching in France; sport exchanges; theatre; cinema; literature and publishing; music; dance; concerts and recitals; art exhibitions in France and Great Britain.

Library catalogue:
All or part available online

Printed publications:
Le Français en tête (poster)
Institut français (programme)

Electronic and video publications:
French video clips

Access to staff:
Contact by letter, by fax and by e-mail
Hours: Mon to Fri, 0900 to 1700

Other addresses:
Institut Français
17 Queensberry Place, London, SW7 2DT; tel: 020 7073 1350; fax: 020 7073 1355; e-mail: box .office@ambafrance.org.uk

FRENCH EMBASSY – SCIENCE AND TECHNOLOGY DEPARTMENT

6 Cromwell Place, London, SW7 2JN

Tel: 020 7073 1380
Fax: 020 7073 1390
E-mail: info@ambascience.co.uk

Website:
http://www.ambascience.co.uk
Online information

Enquiries:
Enquiries to: Information Officer
Other contacts: Counsellor for Science and Technology

Organisation type and purpose:
National government body.
Embassy.

Subject coverage:
French and English research in: humanities and social sciences, chemical sciences, life sciences, sciences of the Universe, physical sciences and mathematics, engineering sciences, information sciences and technology, medicine – health.

Non-library collection catalogue:
All or part available in-house

Library catalogue:
All or part available in-house

Printed publications:
A monthly review of the Press (free)
Vade-mecum of Research Funding (free)
Publications making analysis and taking stock of situations (free)

Electronic and video publications:
A monthly review of the Press (online)
Vade mecum of Research Funding (online)
Publications making analysis and taking stock of situations (online)

Publications list:
Available online and in print

Access to staff:
Contact by letter, by telephone, by fax and by e-mail
Hours: Mon to Fri, 0900 to 1730

Parent body:
Ministère des affaires étrangères et européennes (French Ministry for Foreign and European Affairs)
Paris, France

FRENCH INSTITUTE

Acronym or abbreviation: IFE

13 Randolph Crescent, Edinburgh, EH3 7TT

Tel: 0131 225 5366
Fax: 0131 220 0648
E-mail: library@ifecosse.org.uk

Website:
http://www.ifecosse.org.uk
Catalogue online.

Enquiries:
Enquiries to: Librarian

Founded:
1946

Organisation type and purpose:
International organisation, membership association (membership is by subscription).
To promote French language and culture.

Subject coverage:
French language and culture, for adults and children, contemporary France, French cinema, studies in France, documentary exhibitions.

Museum or gallery collection, archive, or library special collection:
Books: 20,000 volumes, mostly in French relating to various aspects of French life and culture
Videos and DVDs: 1100 films and documentary films with or without subtitles; 962 films of French cinema from classics to recent productions; 747 documentary films on a diversity of topics related to contemporary France

CDs and cassettes: talking books, radio interviews, classical, contemporary, popular music and jazz; 1000 CDs of popular music from traditional chanson to current trends
CD-ROMs: 200 CD-ROMs for adults and children including many games
Newspapers and magazines: 50 titles on a wide range of topics to suit everyone including daily papers
Reference: many dictionaries and encyclopaedic books; CD-ROMs including the entire searchable collection of le Monde and Libération

Non-library collection catalogue:
All or part available online and in-house

Library catalogue:
All or part available in-house

Access to staff:
Contact by letter, by telephone, by fax, by e-mail, in person and via website. Appointment necessary.
Hours: Mon to Wed, 0930 to 1300 and 1400 to 1830; Thu, 0930 to 1830; Fri, 1400 to 1830; 1st Sat of the month, 0930 to 1330

Access to building, collection or gallery:
No access other than to staff
Hours: Mon to Thu, 0930 to 1830; Fri, 1400 to 1830; 1st Sat of the month, 0930 to 1330

FRESHWATER BIOLOGICAL ASSOCIATION

Acronym or abbreviation: FBA

The Ferry House, Far Sawrey, Ambleside, Cumbria, LA22 0LP

Tel: 015394 42468
Fax: 015394 46914
E-mail: info@fba.org.uk

Website:
http://www.fba.org.uk

Enquiries:
Enquiries to: Librarian
Direct e-mail: ipettman@fba.org.uk

Founded:
1929

Organisation type and purpose:
International organisation, learned society (membership is by subscription), registered charity (charity number 214440), research organisation. The Freshwater Biological Association is an independent body that conducts research into all aspects of freshwater science, usually by awarding grants and studentships.

Subject coverage:
Limnology, freshwater biology (hydrobiology), freshwater algae, microbiology, fish, invertebrates, physics and chemistry of lakes and rivers.

Museum or gallery collection, archive, or library special collection:
Fritsch Collection of illustrations of the freshwater algae

Non-library collection catalogue:
All or part available online, in-house and in print

Library catalogue:
All or part available online, in-house and in print

Printed publications:
Annual Report
Freshwater Forum
Keys for the Identification of Freshwater Organisms
Scientific and Occasional Publications (A5 booklets)
Special Publications
Blue-Green Algae (colour poster, 12 photos plus notes, £2 plus p&p)

Microform publications:
Order microform publications from: Fritsch Collection

Electronic and video publications:
Order electronic and video publications from: see website www.freshwaterlife.org

Publications list:
Available online and in print

Access to staff:
Contact by letter, by telephone, by fax, by e-mail and via website. Appointment necessary. Non-members charged.
Hours: Mon to Fri, 0900 to 1700

FRIENDS OF ANIMALS LEAGUE

Acronym or abbreviation: FOAL

Foal Farm, Jail Lane, Biggin Hill, Kent, TN16 3AX

Tel: 01959 572386
Fax: 01959 572386
E-mail: generalmanager@foalfarm.org.uk

Website:
http://www.foalfarm.org.uk

Enquiries:
Enquiries to: General Manager

Founded:
1960

Organisation type and purpose:
Voluntary organisation, registered charity (charity number 201654).
Animal rescue and re-homing centre.

Subject coverage:
Care of sick, distressed or unwanted animals; restoring them to health; organisation and functioning of an animal sanctuary.

Printed publications:
Foal Farm News (3 times a year, posted to members, available at the centre to visitors)

Access to staff:
Contact by letter
Hours: Open every day of the week except Tuesday 1400 to 1700

Access for disabled people:
Toilet facilities

Member of:
The Association of British Dogs' and Cats' Homes

FRIENDS OF BIRZEIT UNIVERSITY

Acronym or abbreviation: FoBZU

1 Gough Square, London, EC4A 3DE

Tel: 020 7832 1340
Fax: 020 7832 1349
E-mail: fobzu@fobzu.org

Website:
http://www.fobzu.org
Information regarding relevant subjects mentioned.

Enquiries:
Enquiries to: Co-ordinator

Founded:
1978

Organisation type and purpose:
Registered charity (charity number 279026).
To support education at Birzeit University and its right to academic freedom. Birzeit University is the leading Palestinian University on the West Bank.

Subject coverage:
Palestinian higher education; human rights violations affecting university community; projects (development/education); workcamps; Arabic and Social Science courses for internationals at Birzeit University.

Printed publications:
Newsletters (2 times a year)
Occasional email reports on Palestinian higher education

Access to staff:
Contact by letter, by telephone, by fax and by e-mail. Appointment necessary.
Hours: Mon to Fri, 0930 to 1730

FRIENDS OF CATHEDRAL MUSIC

Acronym or abbreviation: FCM

27 Old Gloucester Street, London, WC1N 3XX

Tel: 0845 644 3721
E-mail: info@fcm.com.uk

Website:
http://www.fcm.org.uk
Details about the Association and its activities and publications.

Enquiries:
Enquiries to: General Secretary

Founded:
1956

Organisation type and purpose:
Membership association (membership is by subscription), present number of members: 2500, voluntary organisation, registered charity (charity number 285121).

Subject coverage:
Details and times of choral services at cathedrals and collegiate establishments in the UK.

Printed publications:
Cathedral Music (annually, free to members)
Singing in Cathedrals (published in association with the British Tourist Authority)

Access to staff:
Contact by letter and by e-mail
Hours: Mon to Fri, 0900 to 1700

FRIENDS OF CONSERVATION

Acronym or abbreviation: FOC

Kensington Charity Centre, Charles House, 375 Kensington High St, London, W14 8QH

Tel: 020 7603 5024
E-mail: focinfo@aol.com

Website:
http://www.foc-uk.com/

Enquiries:
Enquiries to: Director

Founded:
1989

Organisation type and purpose:
Registered charity (charity number 328176).
The FOC is a registered charity, with offices in the UK, USA and Kenya, which aims to protect endangered species and habitats.

Subject coverage:
Conservation education, habitat conservation, wildlife monitoring, forestry projects, community projects for local people and tourist education worldwide.

Printed publications:
Various brochures and newsletters

Access to staff:
Contact by letter and by e-mail
Hours: Mon to Fri, 0900 to 1700

FRIENDS OF ENGLISH NATIONAL OPERA

London Coliseum, St Martin's Lane, London, WC2N 4ES

Tel: 020 7845 9420
Fax: 020 7845 9272
E-mail: friends@eno.org

Enquiries:
Enquiries to: Membership Administrator
Direct tel: 020 7845 9441
Direct e-mail: rreiss@eno.org

Organisation type and purpose:
Membership association, registered charity (charity number 257210).
Supporting English National Opera.

Subject coverage:
Current activities of English National Opera.

Access to staff:
Contact by letter, by telephone, by fax and by e-mail
Hours: Mon to Fri, 1000 to 1800

FRIENDS OF REAL LANCASHIRE

1 Belvidere Park, Great Crosby, Lancashire, L23 0SP

Tel: 0151 928 2770
E-mail: csd@forl.co.uk

Website:
http://www.forl.co.uk
Information about the campaign, and information about the true identity of Lancashire.

Enquiries:
Enquiries to: Chairman
Other contacts: Membership Secretary, tel: 01539 535507, e-mail: janet.m.brooks@btinternet.com

Founded:
1992

Organisation type and purpose:
Membership association (membership is by subscription), voluntary organisation.
To promote the true identity of the traditional county of Lancashire.

Subject coverage:
The true identity of the traditional county of Lancashire.

Printed publications:
Newsletters (3 times a year, sent to members)
The Lancastrian (magazine, annually, sent to members)
OS Map of Lancashire – County Palatine of Lancaster

Access to staff:
Contact by letter, by telephone and by e-mail
Hours: Sun to Sat, 0900 to 1700, and evenings

A county group of the:
Association of British Counties

FRIENDS OF THE EARTH

26–28 Underwood Street, London, N1 7JQ

Tel: 020 7490 1555
Fax: 020 7490 0881
E-mail: info@foe.co.uk

Website:
http://www.foe.co.uk
Information about Friends of the Earth, campaign updates, your nearest local group, international news.
http://community.foe.co.uk
Information aimed at people who are campaigning locally.

Enquiries:
Enquiries to: Supporter Information Team

Founded:
1971

Organisation type and purpose:
Membership association (membership is by subscription), voluntary organisation, registered charity (charity number 281681), research organisation.
Environmental group, largely funded by subscriptions, donations and grants.

Subject coverage:
Environmental issues in general, climate change, pollution, transport, corporate accountability, biodiversity and habitats, energy, renewables, waste, recycling and packaging, resource use, sustainable development, international policy, trade, environmental justice, resources for young people and teachers.

Printed publications:
Earthmatters (magazine, three issues a year, members)

continued overleaf

A large selection of publications on the following topics: climate change, pollution, transport, corporate accountability, biodiversity and habitats, energy, renewables, waste, recycling and packaging, resource use, sustainable development, international policy, trade, environmental justice.
Order printed publications from: Publications Despatch Officer, Friends of the Earth, 56–58 Alma Street, Luton, LU1 2PH

Publications list:
Available online and in print

Access to staff:
Contact by letter, by telephone, by fax, by e-mail and via website
Hours: Mon to Fri, 0900 to 1700

Also at:
Friends of the Earth Membership Services
56–58 Alma Street, Luton, Bedfordshire, LU1 2PH; tel: 020 7490 1555; e-mail: info@foe.co.uk; website: http://www.foe.co.uk; http://community .foe.co.uk

FRIENDS OF THE LAKE DISTRICT

Acronym or abbreviation: FLD

Murley Moss, Oxenholme Road, Kendal, Cumbria, LA9 7SS

Tel: 01539 720788
Fax: 01539 730355
E-mail: info@fld.org.uk

Website:
http://www.fld.org.uk
Information on the organisation.

Enquiries:
Enquiries to: Executive Director
Direct e-mail: andrew-forsyth@fld.org.uk
Other contacts: Membership Secretary

Founded:
1934

Organisation type and purpose:
Membership association, present number of members: 7100, voluntary organisation, registered charity (charity number 11000759).
Conservation and landscape society.
To promote and organise concerted action for the protection and conservation of the landscape and natural beauty of the Lake District and the County of Cumbria.

Subject coverage:
Subjects relating to conservation and protection of landscape and natural beauty in the Lake District National Park and Cumbria, representations to planning authorities, and policies on access, tourism, development pressures, roads, transport, argiculture, forestry.

Museum or gallery collection, archive, or library special collection:
Library of books, documents and photographs (including slides)

Printed publications:
Conserving Lakeland (magazine, Summer and Winter)
Annual Report

Access to staff:
Appointment necessary.
Hours: Mon to Fri, 0900 to 1700

Affiliated to:
CPRE
128 Southwark Street, London, SE1 0SW; tel: 020 7981 2800; fax: 020 7981 2899; e-mail: info@cpre .org.uk; website: www.cpre.org.uk

Represents:
Council for the Protection of Rural England (CPRE) in Cumbria

FRIENDS OF THE NATIONAL LIBRARIES

Acronym or abbreviation: FNL

c/o Department of MSS, British Library, 96 Euston Road, London, NW1 2DB

Tel: 020 7412 7559
E-mail: secretary@fnlmail.org.uk

Enquiries:
Enquiries to: Honorary Secretary

Founded:
1931

Organisation type and purpose:
Membership association (membership is by subscription), present number of members: 723, registered charity (charity number 313020).
To give grants for the purchase of printed books, manuscripts and archives by libraries and other institutions which provide public access within the United Kingdom.

Subject coverage:
Raising of funds to save rare books and manuscripts for national and local institutions.

Printed publications:
Annual Report (members)

Access to staff:
Contact by letter, by telephone and via website
Hours: 24-hour answerphone
Special comments: Voicemail only

FRIENDS OF THE WESTERN BUDDHIST ORDER

Acronym or abbreviation: FWBO

London Buddhist Centre, 59 Roman Road, Bethnal Green, London, E2 0QU

Tel: 020 8981 1225\ Minicom no. 0845 458 4716
E-mail: info@lbc.org.uk

Website:
http://www.lbc.org.uk
Historical, doctrinal and practical introduction plus listings.

Enquiries:
Enquiries to: Communications Office Director

Founded:
1967

Organisation type and purpose:
International organisation (membership is by election or invitation), present number of members: 3000, registered charity.
Network of affiliated charities.
Religious, Buddhist, teaching Buddhism and meditation.

Subject coverage:
Buddhism, Buddhist meditation.

Printed publications:
Dharma Life Magazine; Buddhism in the West (3 times a year, £3)
Lotus Realm Magazine (3 times a year, £2)
Urthona magazine: Buddhism and the arts (3 times a year, £3)
Western Buddhist Review (Buddhism/academic occasional publication, £5.95)
Order printed publications from: Numerous titles on Buddhism, Meditation and the FWBO, Windhorse Publications
11 Park Road, Moseley, Birmingham, B13 8AB, tel: 0845 458 9514, fax: 0121 449 9191, e-mail: windhorse@compuserve.com

Electronic and video publications:
Order electronic and video publications from: Many tapes on Buddhism and Meditation, Dharmachakra Tapes
3 Coral Park, Henley Road, Cambridge, CB1 3EA, tel: 01223 516821, e-mail: enquiries@dharmachakra .com

Publications list:
Available in print

Access to staff:
Contact by letter, by telephone, by e-mail, in person and via website
Hours: Mon to Fri, 1000 to 1800

Access for disabled people:
Access to all public areas

Connections with:
30 to 40 other FWBO charities in the United Kingdom and many overseas

Press Office:
Friends of the Western Buddhist Order Communications Office, 59 Roman Road, London, E2 0QN; tel: 020 8981 8000; fax: 020 8981 5174; e-mail: communications@fwbo.org

FRISKY REGISTER

Graces Cottage, Tregagle, Monmouth, Gwent, NP25 4RZ

Tel: 01600 860420
Fax: 01600 860420

Enquiries:
Enquiries to: Registrar

Founded:
1974

Organisation type and purpose:
Membership association.
Car register.

Subject coverage:
The restoration of the Frisky car, engines, body, chassis, electrics, history, components.

Museum or gallery collection, archive, or library special collection:
Maintenance manuals
Press releases
Technical information, handbooks, engine books, article reprints

Printed publications:
General Frisky literature

Access to staff:
Contact by letter, by telephone and by fax.
Appointment necessary.
Hours: Mon to Fri, 0900 to 1700

FRONTIER: THE SOCIETY FOR ENVIRONMENTAL EXPLORATION

Acronym or abbreviation: Frontier

50–52 Rivington Street, London, EC2A 3QP

Tel: 020 7613 2422
Fax: 020 7613 2992
E-mail: info@frontier.ac.uk

Website:
http://www.frontier.ac.uk
Information about Frontier's research overseas.
Publications list. Gap year and volunteering opportunities.

Enquiries:
Enquiries to: Marketing Manager

Founded:
1989

Organisation type and purpose:
International organisation, voluntary organisation, training organisation, research organisation.
To conduct development projects and conservation research in Fiji, Nepal, Peru, Tibet, Guatemala, India, Tanzania, Madagascar, Cambodia and Nicaragua. To provide opportunities for volunteers to carry out conservation work and obtain tropical field experience.

Subject coverage:
Conservation and environmental research, development of natural resources, volunteer work abroad, teaching, community development, language courses.

Printed publications:
Information Brochure

Various Technical Reports

Publications list:
Available online and in print

Access to staff:
Contact by letter, by telephone, by fax, by e-mail and via website
Hours: Mon to Fri, 0930 to 1730
Special comments: No visits without appointment.

Branches:
Frontier-Cambodia
   PO Box 1275, General Post Office, Phlauv 13, Phnom Penh, Cambodia; tel: 00 855 23 221 163
Frontier-Madagascar
   BP413, Tulear 1 Zone Portuaire, Madagascar; tel: 00 261 20 94 430 38
Frontier-Nicaragua
   Apartado Postal no. 33, Chinandega, Nicaragua; tel: 00 505 6108723
Frontier-Tanzania
   PO Box 9473, Dar es Salaam, Tanzania; tel: 00 255 22 2780063; fax: 00 255 22 2780063; e-mail: frontier@raha.com

FRS FRESHWATER LABORATORY

Formal name: Fisheries Research Service Freshwater Laboratory
Acronym or abbreviation: FRS FL

Faskally, Pitlochry, Perthshire, PH16 5LB

Tel: 01224 294408 or 01796 472060
Fax: 01796 473523
E-mail: FL_Library@marlab.ac.uk

Website:
http://www.frs-scotland.gov.uk

Enquiries:
Enquiries to: Librarian

Founded:
1948

Organisation type and purpose:
National government body, research organisation.

Subject coverage:
Salmonid ecology, salmon fisheries, coarse fish, freshwater biology, fish biology, environmental chemistry (inorganic), fisheries science, environmental pollution, fish culture, aquaculture.

Museum or gallery collection, archive, or library special collection:
The Library is the only government research library in Great Britain which is devoted to the subject of freshwater fisheries

Trade and statistical information:
Statistical Bulletin: Scottish Salmon and Sea Trout Catches.

Library catalogue:
All or part available in-house

Printed publications:
Scottish Fisheries information pamphlets
Scottish Fisheries research reports
FRS information leaflets
Scottish Annual Fish Farms Production Survey
Scottish Annual Shellfish Farms Production Survey
Order printed publications from:
ML_Library@marlab.ac.uk

Publications list:
Available online

Access to staff:
Contact by letter, by telephone, by fax, by e-mail and via website. Appointment necessary.
Hours: Mon to Fri, 0900 to 1700

Access to building, collection or gallery:
Hours: Mon to Fri, 0900 to 1700

Constituent part of:
FRS Marine Laboratory Library
   375 Victoria Road, Aberdeen, AB11 9DB; tel: 01224 876544; fax: 01224 295309; e-mail: ML_Library@marlab.ac.uk; website: www.frs-scotland.gov.uk

FULL TIME MOTHERS

PO Box 43690, London, SE22 9WN

Tel: 020 8653 8786
Fax: 020 8761 6574
E-mail: fulltimemothers@hotmail.com

Website:
http://www.fulltimemothers.org

Enquiries:
Enquiries to: Chairman

Founded:
1990

Organisation type and purpose:
Membership association (membership is by subscription, election or invitation).
To promote understanding of the child's need for a full-time mother, enhance the status and self esteem of mothers at home, campaign for changes in the tax and benefits system and in employment policies to give women a chance to be full-time mothers.

Subject coverage:
The voice of the mother at home; information or quotes on: caring for children; mothers at home; childcare; tax and benefits relative to the family; psychology of the child; isolation and self-esteem of mothers; general motherhood; family-friendly employment policies.

Printed publications:
Newsletter (quarterly, for members)

Access to staff:
Contact by letter, by telephone and by e-mail
Hours: Mon to Fri, 0900 to 1700

Affiliated to:
Fédération des Femmes au Foyer (FEFAF)

FURNITURE HISTORY SOCIETY

Acronym or abbreviation: FHS

1 Mercedes Cottages, St John's Road, Haywards Heath, West Sussex, RH16 4EH

Tel: 01444 413845
Fax: 01444 413845
E-mail: furniturehistorysociety@hotmail.com

Website:
http://www.furniturehistorysociety.org

Enquiries:
Enquiries to: Membership Secretary
Direct e-mail: brian.austen@zen.co.uk

Founded:
1966

Organisation type and purpose:
International organisation, learned society (membership is by subscription), present number of members: 1700.
International learned society dedicated to the study and publication of research on the history of furniture and furnishings.

Subject coverage:
All aspects of the history of furniture and furnishings of all periods especially that of Europe and North America.

Printed publications:
Furniture History (journal, annually, £18 members, £30 non-members)
Newsletter (quarterly, members only)
A Bibliography of the Printed Works of the late John Forrest Hayward (£2.50 inc. p&p)
Dictionary of Edinburgh Wrights and Furniture Makers 1660–1840 (Bamford F, £20 inc. p&p)
Index to the Dictionary of English Furniture Makers 1660–1840 (Evans A, £20 inc. p&p)
Irish Furniture (ed Austen, B, £8.95)
Pictorial Dictionary of Marked London Furniture 1700–1840 (Gilbert C, £29 members, £45 non-members)
The London Furniture Trade 1700–1870 (Kirkham P, £20 inc. p&p)
The Life of the Author, Johnson T (Simon, £8.95 inc. p&p)

Directory of English Furniture Makers (Beard & Gilbert, £49 members, £75 non-members)
Makers, Dealers and Collectors – Studies in Honour of Geoffrey de Bellaigue (£24.95 inc. p&p)
Order printed publications from: Furniture History Society, or website

Publications list:
Available online and in print

Access to staff:
Contact by letter, by telephone, by fax and by e-mail. Appointment necessary.
Hours: Telephone calls acceptable 0800 to 2200, Sun to Sat

GALLOWAY CATTLE SOCIETY OF GREAT BRITAIN & IRELAND

15 New Market Street, Castle Douglas, Kirkcudbrightshire, DG7 1HY

Tel: 01556 502753
Fax: 01556 502753
E-mail: info@gallowaycattlesociety.co.uk

Enquiries:
Enquiries to: Secretary

Founded:
1877

Organisation type and purpose:
Trade association (membership is by subscription), present number of members: 450, registered charity (charity number CR 36927).
Registration and promotion of beef cattle known as Galloway. Galloway cattle are found throughout the world and, whilst they have their own societies, this society is considered the parent body by many.

Subject coverage:
History of Galloway Cattle. Pedigrees held of all registered Galloway Cattle in Britain and Ireland.

Printed publications:
Breed Journal (free to all members)

Access to staff:
Contact by letter, by telephone and by fax
Hours: Wed, Fri, 0930 to 1630

GALPIN SOCIETY

37 Townsend Drive, St. Albans, Hertfordshire, AL3 5RF

E-mail: administrator@galpinsociety.org

Website:
http://www.galpinsociety.org
Membership – how to join. Contents of journals only.

Enquiries:
Enquiries to: Administrator
Other contacts: Editor for publications & contributions to them.

Founded:
1946

Organisation type and purpose:
International organisation, learned society (membership is by subscription), present number of members: 900, registered charity (charity number 306012).
The study of development, history, construction and use of musical instruments.

Subject coverage:
History, construction, development and use of musical instruments.

Museum or gallery collection, archive, or library special collection:
The Society's archives (for members only)
Documents relating to the history of the Society (for members only)

Printed publications:
Galpin Society Journal (annually, on sale to non-members at subscription rate)

continued overleaf

Membership list (members only)
Newsletter (3 times a year, for members only)

Electronic and video publications:
Index to volumes XXI-XXV on discs

Publications list:
Available online and in print

Access to staff:
Contact by letter and by e-mail

GAMBICA ASSOCIATION LIMITED

Formal name: Association for Instrumentation, Control, Automation & Laboratory Technology

St Georges House, 195–203 Waterloo Road, London, SE1 8WB

Tel: 020 7642 8080
Fax: 020 7642 8096
E-mail: assoc@gambica.org.uk

Website:
http://www.gambica.org.uk
Includes general information on the Association including details of many of the Association groups, including hot links to member company sites. Page for ordering publications.

Enquiries:
Enquiries to: Executive Secretary
Direct tel: 020 7642 8080
Direct fax: 020 7642 8096
Direct e-mail: jgaffney@gambica.org.uk

Founded:
1915

Formerly called:
Association for the Laboratory Supply Industry (ALSI), British Instrument Control and Automation Manufacturers (BIMCAM), Control and Automation Manufacturers Association (CAMA), Scientific Instrument Manufacturers Association (SIMA); British Laboratory Ware Association (BLWA) (year of change 1991); BWLA Limited (year of change 2001)

Organisation type and purpose:
Trade association.

Subject coverage:
Instrumentation, control, automation and laboratory technology, sources of supply etc.

Printed publications:
Association Guide
Technical Guides
Technical Reports
Orgalime General Conditions and Model Forms

Publications list:
Available online

Access to staff:
Contact by letter, by fax, by e-mail and via website
Hours: Mon to Thu, 0900 to 1700; Fri, 0900 to 1530

Member of:
Association of British Health Care Industries
European Association of Optical and Scientific Instrument Manufacturers (EUROM)
ORGALIME

Secretaries of:
EROM II Optics, Lasers and Laboratory Instrumentation

GAMBLERS ANONYMOUS (UK)

Acronym or abbreviation: GA

PO Box 5382 London W1A 6SA

Tel: 020 7384 3040
E-mail: info@gamblersanonymous.org.uk

Website:
http://www.gamblersanonymous.org.uk

Enquiries:
Enquiries to: Secretary
Direct e-mail: natsec@gamblersanonymous.org.uk

Organisation type and purpose:
Voluntary organisation.
A self-help fellowship of compulsive gamblers.

Subject coverage:
Group therapy and advice on the best ways to stop gambling.

Non-library collection catalogue:
All or part available in-house

Library catalogue:
All or part available in-house

Printed publications:
Helping Agencies leaflets
Newsletter (monthly)

Access to staff:
Contact by telephone
Hours: 24-hour helpline

Links with:
GAM-ANON, for wives and/or relatives of the compulsive gambler

GAMCARE

Formal name: National Association for Gambling Care, Educational Resources and Training
Acronym or abbreviation: GAMCARE

2nd floor, 7–11 St John's Hill, Clapham Junction, London, SW11 1TR

Tel: 020 7801 7000
Fax: 020 7801 7033
E-mail: director@gamcare.org.uk

Website:
http://www.gamcare.org.uk

Enquiries:
Enquiries to: Business Administrator
Other contacts: Chairman

Founded:
1990

Formerly called:
UK Forum on Young People and Gambling (UKF) from 1990 to 1997

Organisation type and purpose:
Membership association (membership is by subscription), present number of members: 100, registered charity (charity number 1060005), suitable for ages: all.
Friends Association, National Centre for information.

Subject coverage:
Gambling, information, advice and practical help in relation to the social impact of gambling, damage done by such activities, strategies to reduce potential and actual harm to young people.

Trade and statistical information:
Statistical information on gambling, particularly in relation to the number of calls to the Helpline
Information on social impact of gambling in the UK.

Printed publications:
Books and booklets providing advice and guidance in working with problem gamblers
A Certain Bet – Exploring Gambling (£15 plus £3 p&p)
Range of leaflets addressing issues of people and gambling
Quit Compulsive Gambling (Gordon Moody, £5.99 plus 50p p&p)
Working with Young Problem Gamblers: Guidelines to Practice (£3.50 plus 30p p&p)

Electronic and video publications:
Videos

Publications list:
Available in print

Access to staff:
Contact by letter, by telephone, by fax, by e-mail and via website. Appointment necessary.
Hours: Helpline: Mon to Fri, 1000 to 2200; Sat, 1000 to 1800; Sun, 1800 to 2200

Affiliated to:
European Association for the Study of Gambling
Society for Study of Gambling
Youth Access

GAME AND WILDLIFE CONSERVATION TRUST

Acronym or abbreviation: GWCT

Fordingbridge, Hampshire, SP6 1EF

Tel: 01425 652381
Fax: 01425 655848
E-mail: info@gct.org.uk

Website:
http://www.gct.org.uk

Enquiries:
Enquiries to: Librarian
Direct tel: 01425 651019
Direct e-mail: library@gwct.org.uk

Founded:
1931

Organisation type and purpose:
Registered charity (charity number 1112023), research organisation.

Subject coverage:
Game management and conservation; habitat requirements; problems imposed by intensive farming methods on wildlife populations; predators, upland wildlife; advises government and other decision makers on wildlife policy.

Printed publications:
Annual Review
Magazine (3 times a year)
Order printed publications from: Membership Department, Game and Wildlife Conservation Trust, Burgate Manor, Fordingbridge, SP6 1EF

Access to staff:
Contact by letter, by telephone, by fax, by e-mail and via website. Appointment necessary.
Hours: Mon to Fri, 0900 to 1700

Access to building, collection or gallery:
Library facilities only
Hours: Mon to Fri, 0900 to 1700
Special comments: By appointment only

Constituent bodies:
Game and Wildlife Conservation Trust Trading Ltd

GANDHI FOUNDATION

Acronym or abbreviation: GF

21 Fleetwood Court, Madeira Road, West Byfleet, Surrey, KT14 6BE

Tel: 01932 343614
E-mail: denise.gandhifdn@phonecoop.coop

Website:
http://www.gandhifoundation.org

Enquiries:
Enquiries to: General Secretary
Other contacts: The Editor, The Gandhi Way (e-mail geomgt.paxton@virgin.net)

Founded:
1983

Organisation type and purpose:
International organisation, membership association (membership is by subscription), voluntary organisation, registered charity (charity number 292629).

Subject coverage:
The Gandhian principle of non-violence and conflict resolution through multifaith service, annual summer school, annual lectures, seminars and conferences, AGM and workshops.

Printed publications:
The Gandhi Way (quarterly)

Access to staff:
Contact by letter, by telephone, by e-mail and in person. Appointment necessary.

GARAGE EQUIPMENT ASSOCIATION LIMITED

Acronym or abbreviation: GEA

2–3 Church Walk, Daventry, Northamptonshire, NN11 4BL

Tel: 01327 312616
Fax: 01327 312606
E-mail: john@gea-ltd.demon.co.uk

Website:
http://www.gea.co.uk
Directory of members by product.

Enquiries:
Enquiries to: Administrator

Founded:
1945

Organisation type and purpose:
Trade association.

Subject coverage:
Garage equipment selection, design, layout, distribution, installation and importation.

Museum or gallery collection, archive, or library special collection:
Trade catalogues dating back to 1950s and 1960s

Printed publications:
An Introduction to Air Conditioning (£15)
Code of Practice 1996 (£13.50)
The World of Emissions (£13.50)
The World of Waveforms (£14.50)
OBD & Diagnosis After The Code (£16, update £3.50)

Publications list:
Available in print

Access to staff:
Contact by letter, by telephone, by fax, by e-mail and in person
Hours: Mon to Fri, 0830 to 1300 and 1400 to 1700

Affiliated to:
Aftermarket Association Liaison Group (AALG)

GARDEN HISTORY SOCIETY

Acronym or abbreviation: GHS

70 Cowcross Street, London, EC1M 6EJ

Tel: 020 7608 2409
Fax: 020 7490 2974
E-mail: enquiries@gardenhistorysociety.org

Website:
http://www.gardenhistorysociety.org

Enquiries:
Enquiries to: Chairman

Founded:
1965

Organisation type and purpose:
International organisation, learned society. Also statutory consultee on planning applications affecting listed historic designed landscapes. The Society's aims are to promote the study of the history of gardening, landscape gardening and horticulture in all its aspects; to promote the protection and conservation of historic parks, gardens and designed landscapes, and to promote and advise on their conservation; and to encourage the creation of new parks, gardens and designed landscapes.

Subject coverage:
Garden history, landscape design, architectural features, horticultural use of plants, conservation.

Museum or gallery collection, archive, or library special collection:
The Society's library is housed at King's Manor Library, University of York and Department of Art History, University of Bristol.

Non-library collection catalogue:
All or part available online

Library catalogue:
All or part available online

Printed publications:
Bibliography (online)
Garden History (journal, twice a year)
Newsletter (twice a year)
Order printed publications from: Back issues department

Publications list:
Available online

Access to staff:
Contact by letter, by telephone, by fax and by e-mail. Appointment necessary.
Special comments: Staff work part time

Access to building, collection or gallery:
Special comments: Appointment necessary

GARDEN INDUSTRY MANUFACTURERS ASSOCIATION (1999) LIMITED

Acronym or abbreviation: GIMA

225 Bristol Road, Edgbaston, Birmingham, B5 7UB

Tel: 0121 446 5213
Fax: 0121 446 5215
E-mail: info@gima.org.uk

Website:
http://www.gima.org.uk

Enquiries:
Enquiries to: Director
Direct tel: 01428 712513
Direct fax: 01428 712513
Direct e-mail: marshpr1@aol.com

Founded:
1999

Known as:
Garden Products Association (GPA)

Organisation type and purpose:
Trade association.

Subject coverage:
Trade specific information made available to members.

Access to staff:
Access for members only.
Hours: Mon to Fri, 0900 to 1700

Access to building, collection or gallery:
No access other than to staff

Secretariat:
British Hardware Federation (BHF)
tel: 0121 446 6688; fax: 0121 446 5215

GATESHEAD COLLEGE

Formal name: Gateshead College Library

Quarryfield Road, Baltic Business Quarter, Gateshead, Tyne and Wear, NE8 3BN

Tel: 0191 490 2306
Fax: 0191 490 2313
E-mail: louise.docherty@gateshead.ac.uk

Website:
http://www.gateshead.ac.uk

Enquiries:
Enquiries to: Customer Services Officers Learning Centres
Direct tel: 0191 490 2249
Direct e-mail: library@gateshead.ac.uk

Founded:
1956

Formerly called:
Gateshead College Learning Centre, Gateshead College Library and Resources Unit, Centre 4... Knowledge

Organisation type and purpose:
Suitable for ages: 16 to 19 and adult.
College of further education.

Subject coverage:
General subjects spread over wide range of GCSE, A-level, professional, BTEC/GNVQ and some Higher Education

Access to staff:
Contact by letter, by telephone, by fax and by e-mail. Appointment necessary. All charged.
Hours: Mon to Thu, 0845 to 2000; Fri, 1000 to 1630

Access for disabled people:
Pay and display parking provided, ramped entry, toilet facilities, internal lifts for access to floors

GATESHEAD LIBRARIES AND ARTS DEPARTMENT

Central Library, Prince Consort Road, Gateshead, Tyne and Wear, NE8 4LN

Tel: 0191 433 8400; 0191 478 2060 (minicom)
Fax: 0191 477 7454
E-mail: libraries@gateshead.gov.uk

Website:
http://www.gateshead-quays.com
Information about Music Centre Gateshead, BALTIC Centre for Contemporary Arts and other riverside developments.
http://www.gateshead.gov.uk/libraries
Library service homepage with access to OPAC, general information, weblog and Ask services, including realtime information service

Enquiries:
Enquiries to: Head of Libraries and Arts
Direct e-mail: annborthwick@gateshead.gov.uk
Other contacts: Principal Library Manager

Founded:
1885

Formerly called:
Gateshead Libraries and Arts Department

Organisation type and purpose:
Local government body, public library.

Subject coverage:
General, local, social, economic, demographic, historic studies of Gateshead, tourism, European Public Information Relay, business.

Non-library collection catalogue:
All or part available online

Library catalogue:
All or part available online

Printed publications:
Gateshead Tourist Accommodation Guide (annually)
Caedmon Live (quarterly)
Various local history publications including:
Cinemas of Gateshead
Crossing the Tyne
Making an Angel

Electronic and video publications:
Daily Talking Newspaper (free to residents in Gateshead, outside subscriptions)
ESLI – European Sign Language Interactives CD-I
Gateshead 1900 CD-I
Information tapes, transcriptions on request

Access to staff:
Contact by letter, by telephone, by fax, by e-mail and via website. Appointment necessary.
Hours: Mon, Tue, Thu and Fri, 0900 to 1900; Wed, 0900 to 1700; Sat, 0900 to 1300

Access for disabled people:
Parking provided, ramped entry, level entry, access to all public areas, toilet facilities, staff with signing skills; video-conferencing

Links with:
BALTIC: The Centre for Contemporary Art
National Network of European Relays
Newcastle-Gateshead Initiative (NGI)
Northern Grid for Learning (NGFL)
One North East
The Sage Gateshead

Parent body:
Gateshead Council

GAUGE AND TOOL MAKERS' ASSOCIATION

Acronym or abbreviation: GTMA

3 Forge House, Summerleys Road, Princes Risborough, Buckinghamshire, HP27 9DT

Tel: 01844 274222
Fax: 01844 274227
E-mail: gtma@gtma.co.uk

Website:
http://www.gtma.co.uk

Enquiries:
Enquiries to: Executive Manager
Other contacts: Business Manager for technical enquiries.

Founded:
1942

Organisation type and purpose:
Trade association.

Subject coverage:
Gauge and toolmaking, precision machining, rapid prototyping, metrology.

Printed publications:
Buyers Guide (annually)
Newletter (quarterly)
World Class Standards
Deeds of Apprenticeship
Pentamode – Code of Practice for the Plastics Industry

Access to staff:
Contact by telephone, by fax and by e-mail
Hours: Mon to Fri, 0900 to 1700

GB-RUSSIA SOCIETY, THE

Formal name: GB-Russia Society, The

24 Maida Avenue, London, W2 1ST

Website:
http://www.gbrussia.org

Enquiries:
Enquiries to: Secretary
Other contacts: Via online form at website www.gbrussia.org

Organisation type and purpose:
Registered charity (charity number 1105296)

Printed publications:
Journal (3 times a year)

Access to staff:
Contact by letter, by e-mail and via website

GEDLING BOROUGH COUNCIL

Civic Centre, Arnot Hill Park, Arnold, Nottingham, NG5 6LU

Tel: 0115 901 3901\ Minicom no. 0115 901 3935
Fax: 0115 901 3921

Enquiries:
Enquiries to: Public Relations Manager
Direct tel: 0115 901 3801
Direct fax: 0115 901 3807
Direct e-mail: carolyn.iwanowski@gedling.gov.uk

Founded:
1974

Organisation type and purpose:
Local government body.

Printed publications:
Borough Guide (free)
Business Directory (free)
Committee Reports (various, free)
Flyer (civic newspaper, free)
Planning Handbook (free)

Access to staff:
Contact by letter

Hours: Mon to Thu, 0845 to 1715; Fri, 0845 to 1645

Access for disabled people:
Parking provided, level entry, access to all public areas, toilet facilities

GEM MOTORING ASSIST

Acronym or abbreviation: GEM

Station Road, Forest Row, East Sussex, RH18 5EN

Tel: 01342 825676
Fax: 01342 824847
E-mail: info@motoringassist.com

Website:
http://www.motoringassist.com

Enquiries:
Enquiries to: Chief Executive
Direct e-mail: david.williams@motoringassist.com

Founded:
1932

Formerly called:
Company of Veteran Motorists (year of change 1983)

Organisation type and purpose:
Membership association.
Promotion of road safety, provision of motoring services to members.

Subject coverage:
Promotion of road safety, motoring law, motoring technology, motor insurance and claims.

Information services:
Advice given on Road Safety and Motoring matters

Printed publications:
Good Motoring (magazine, 4 times a year)
Various safety orientated leaflets

Publications list:
Available online

Access to staff:
Contact by letter, by telephone, by e-mail and via website. Appointment necessary.
Hours: Mon to Fri, 0900 to 1700

Access to building, collection or gallery:
By invitation only

GEMMOLOGICAL ASSOCIATION AND GEM TESTING LABORATORY OF GREAT BRITAIN

Acronym or abbreviation: GAGTL

27 Greville Street (Saffron Hill Entrance), London, EC1N 8TN

Tel: 020 7404 3334 or 020 7405 3351
Fax: 020 7404 8843
E-mail: gagtl@btinternet.com

Website:
http://www.gagtl.ac.uk/gagtl

Enquiries:
Enquiries to: Director
Other contacts: Director of Education for member of Council of Management.

Founded:
1908

Formed by the merger of:
Gem Testing Laboratory of Great Britain (1925), Gemmological Association of Great Britain (1908) (year of change 1990)

Organisation type and purpose:
Professional body, service industry, suitable for ages: 16+, training organisation, publishing house. Gemmological education, with gem testing and grading services.

Subject coverage:
Gemmology, gemstones, diamonds, pearls, gem minerals, gem materials, gem identification, gem testing methods and equipment, gemmological education.

Non-library collection catalogue:
All or part available in-house

Library catalogue:
All or part available in-house

Printed publications:
Gem and Jewellery News (joint publication with Society of Jewellery Historians, quarterly)
Journal of Gemmology (quarterly)

Access to staff:
Contact by telephone, by e-mail and via website
Hours: Mon to Fri, 0900 to 1700

Access to building, collection or gallery:
Prior appointment required

Wholly owned subsidiary:
Gemmological Instruments Limited, which sells gemmological books and instruments
tel: 020 7404 3334; fax: 020 7404 8843; e-mail: gagtl@btinternet.com

GENDER TRUST

Formal name: Gender Trust Association
Acronym or abbreviation: GT

Community Base, 113 Queens Road, Brighton, BN1 3XG

Tel: 0845 231 0505 (helpline, Mon to Fri, 1000 to 2200, Sat and Sun, 1300 to 2200)
E-mail: info@gendertrust.org.uk

Website:
http://www.gendertrust.org.uk

Enquiries:
Enquiries to: Project Manager
Direct tel: 01273 234024
Other contacts: Administrator

Founded:
1990

Organisation type and purpose:
National organisation, registered charity (charity number 1088150).
To support any adult affected by gender identity issues, throughout the United Kingdom.

Subject coverage:
Gender identity, gender dysphoria, transsexuality.

Printed publications:
GT News (quarterly, for members)
The GT Guide
Sex Reassignment Surgery: A Patient's Guide
Standards of Care for Gender Identity Disorders (6th edn)
Recommendations and Guidelines for Employees
An Employer's Guide to Transition in the Workplace (2nd edn)
Various information sheets

Publications list:
Available online and in print

Access to staff:
Contact by letter, by telephone, by e-mail and via website. Appointment necessary.
Hours: Tue to Thu, 0900 to 1700

GENERAL CONFERENCE OF THE NEW CHURCH

Swedenborg House, 20 Bloomsbury Way, London, WC1A 2TH

Tel: 020 7229 9340
Fax: 01206 302932

Enquiries:
Enquiries to: Chief Executive
Direct tel: 01206 303800
Other contacts: Treasurer for financial matters.

Founded:
1789

Organisation type and purpose:
Registered charity (charity number 253206).
Free Church organisation.

Propagation of the Christian teachings of Emanuel Swedenborg (1688–1772).

Subject coverage:
Faith and doctrines of the New Church (Swedenborgian) and the history of the organisation; life and teaching of Emanuel Swedenborg.

Museum or gallery collection, archive, or library special collection:
Archives and records of the General Conference of the New Church and individual congregations of the organisation
Works of Emanuel Swedenborg

Non-library collection catalogue:
All or part available in-house

Library catalogue:
All or part available in-house

Printed publications:
Lifeline (monthly, except Jan and Jul)
List of books published by related organisations from: New Church House, 34 John Dalton Street, Manchester M2 6LE
Outlook (quarterly)
Year Book (annually)
Order printed publications from: North of England New Church House
34 John Dalton Street, Manchester, M2 6LE, tel: 0161 834 4192

Electronic and video publications:
Some audio and video tapes are available

Publications list:
Available in print

Access to staff:
Contact by letter, by telephone and by fax. Appointment necessary.
Hours: Mon to Fri, 0900 to 1700

Chief Executive:
General Conference of the New Church
59 Campernell Close, Brightlingsea, Colchester, Essex, CO7 0PP; tel: 01206 303800; fax: 01206 303800; e-mail: michael.hindley@generalconference.org.uk

Close links with:
Swedenborg Society
20 Bloomsbury Way, London, WC1A 2TH; tel: 020 7405 7986

Organisation is made up of:
29 churches in the UK and 8 groups

Treasurer:
General Conference of the New Church
42 Hillside, Findern, Derby, DE65 6AZ; tel: 01283 702764; fax: 01283 702764; e-mail: nigel.sutton@generalconference.org.uk

GENERAL CONSUMER COUNCIL FOR NORTHERN IRELAND

Elizabeth House, 116 Holywood Road, Belfast, BT4 1NY

Tel: 028 9067 2488\ Minicom no. 028 9067 2488
Fax: 028 9065 7701
E-mail: info@consumercouncil.org.uk

Website:
http://www.consumercouncil.org.uk
Information about the Council and its work, press releases issued by the Council.
http://www.consumerline.org
Advice on consumer rights across a wide range of issues.

Enquiries:
Enquiries to: Chief Executive

Founded:
1985

Formed from:
Northern Ireland Consumer Council, Transport Users Committee (year of change 1985)

Organisation type and purpose:
Advisory body, statutory body, professional body, membership association, present number of members: 14, research organisation.
The General Consumer Council is Northern Ireland's official consumer organisation, set up by the Government in 1985.
Membership is by open competition.
To promote and safeguard the interests of consumers in Northern Ireland.

Subject coverage:
Consumer affairs generally, food, energy, electricity, coal, natural gas, transport, consumer education.

Printed publications:
Variety of leaflets and information packs on consumer affairs available online or on application to the Council, including:
Annual Report
Burning Issues – Consumers and Coal (1997)
Consumers in the Dark – Rights, Redress and Proficiency (1999)
Consumer Education Manifesto (2000)
Equality Scheme 2001
Hungry for Change (2001)
The Transport Trap (2001)
Taking Taxis (1997)
Top Tips for cutting car insurance costs (leaflet)
Transport Watchdog (2000)
What's on my Record? (leaflet)
What's Wrong with Walking? (1997)

Electronic and video publications:
Of Consuming Interest (video, 1998)

Publications list:
Available online and in print

Access to staff:
Contact by letter, by telephone, by fax, by e-mail and in person
Hours: Mon to Fri, 0900 to 1700

Access for disabled people:
Access to all public areas, toilet facilities

Affiliated to:
BEUC – the European Consumer organization

GENERAL COUNCIL AND REGISTER OF NATUROPATHS

Acronym or abbreviation: GCRN

Goswell House, 2 Goswell Road, Street, Somerset, BA16 0JG

Tel: 01458 840072
Fax: 01458 840075
E-mail: admin@naturopathy.org.uk

Website:
http://www.naturopathy.org.uk

Enquiries:
Enquiries to: Secretary

Founded:
1964

Organisation type and purpose:
Professional body (membership is by qualification).
To register suitably qualified practitioners, to enforce a code of professional conduct and maintain educational standards.

Subject coverage:
Naturopathy, natural medicine, alternative medicine, complementary medicine.

Printed publications:
Naturopathic medicine (leaflet, free for C5 sae)
Register of Practitioner Members (£2.50)

Access to staff:
Contact by letter, by telephone, by fax, by e-mail and via website
Hours: Mon to Fri, 0900 to 1700

Links with:
British Naturopathic Association

GENERAL COUNCIL OF THE BAR OF ENGLAND AND WALES

Acronym or abbreviation: Bar Council

289–293 High Holborn London WC1V 7HZ

Tel: 020 7242 0082
Fax: 020 7831 9217

Website:
http://www.barprobono.org.uk
Legal advice for charities and voluntary organisations.
http://www.barcouncil.org.uk
Work of the Bar Council.

Enquiries:
Enquiries to: Library/Registry Officer
Direct e-mail: library@barcouncil.org.uk

Founded:
1894

Formerly called:
Senate of the Inns of Court and the Bar

Organisation type and purpose:
National organisation, professional body (membership is by qualification), present number of members: 20,000.
Central governing body of the profession of the Bar of England and Wales.
Regulation of the profession and promotion of the interests of barristers.

Subject coverage:
Barristers' profession in England and Wales; official records of names and addresses of practising barristers. Provision of legal services by barristers; information on entry to the profession; recruiting information; complaints against barristers.

Printed publications:
Bar Directory
Career at the Bar
Code of Conduct for the Bar of England and Wales
Counsel (magazine, by subscription only)

Access to staff:
Contact by letter, by telephone, by fax and by e-mail
Hours: Mon to Fri, 0900 to 1700

Access to building, collection or gallery:
Prior appointment required

Access for disabled people:
Ramped entry, toilet facilities

Other departments:
Complaints Department
Northumberland House, 303/306 High Holborn, London, WC1V 7JZ
Education and Training Departments
2–3 Cursitor Street, London, EC4A 1NE; tel: 020 7440 4002 (Complaints) 020 7440 4000 (Education & Training); fax: 020 7440 4001

GENERAL DENTAL COUNCIL

Acronym or abbreviation: GDC

37 Wimpole Street, London, W1G 8DQ

Tel: 020 7887 3800 (Typetalk calls accepted)
Fax: 020 7224 3294
E-mail: information@gdc-uk.org

Website:
http://www.gdc-uk.org
Information on all aspects of the GDC's role and work. Including: searchable Dentists Register, Specialist Lists and Rolls of Dental Auxiliaries. Information for dental professionals on applying for GDC registration. Information for the public on what to do if there is a problem with a dental professional.

Founded:
1956

Organisation type and purpose:
Statutory body.

continued overleaf

The General Dental Council's purpose is to protect the public by regulating dental professionals in the UK.

Registers qualified professionals; sets standards of dental practice and conduct; assures the quality of dental education; ensures professionals keep up to date with developments in their profession; helps patients with complaints about a dental professional; and works to strengthen patient protection.

Subject coverage:
All aspects of the dental professions: regulation, registration, qualifications, education, undergraduate training and continuing professional development, specialist training in Oral Surgery, Surgical Dentistry, Endodontics, Periodontics, Prosthodontics, Restorative Dentistry, Dental Public Health, Orthodontics, Paediatric Dentistry, Oral Medicine, Oral Microbiology, Oral Pathology and Dental and Maxillofacial Radiology.

Printed publications:
All publications are also available from website
The Dentists Register (annually, available for purchase)
The Rolls of Dental Auxiliaries (dental hygienists and dental therapists, annually, available for purchase)
Specialist Lists in Distinctive Branches of Dentistry (annually, available for purchase)
Maintaining Standards
Compulsory Continuing Professional Development – what it means for you
Compulsory Continuing Professional Development – what you must do if you take time off the Dentists Register
The First Five Years – A Framework for Undergraduate Dental Education
Developing the Dental Team: Curricula Frameworks for Registrable Qualifications for Professionals Complementary to Dentistry
General Dental Council – Who we are and what we do
What to do if you have a problem with a dental professional
Regulating all Members of the dental team
GDC Gazette
GDC Annual Report and Accounts 2003

Electronic and video publications:
All publications can be downloaded from our website

Publications list:
Available online

Access to staff:
Contact by letter, by telephone, by fax, by e-mail, in person and via website
Hours: Mon to Fri, 0900 to 1700

GENERAL FEDERATION OF TRADE UNIONS

Acronym or abbreviation: GFTU

Central House, Upper Woburn Place, London, WC1H 0HY

Tel: 020 7388 0852
Fax: 020 7383 0820
E-mail: gftuhq@gftu.org.uk

Website:
http://www.gftu.org.uk

Enquiries:
Enquiries to: General Secretary

Founded:
1899

Organisation type and purpose:
Trade union.

Subject coverage:
Education and research for trade unions.

Printed publications:
Federation News

Access to staff:
Contact by letter
Hours: Mon to Fri, 0900 to 1700

GENERAL OPTICAL COUNCIL

Acronym or abbreviation: GOC

41 Harley Street, London, W1G 8DJ

Tel: 020 7580 3898
Fax: 020 7436 3525
E-mail: goc@optical.org

Website:
http://www.optical.org
Access to the Opticians Registers; overview of our work; how to make a complaint about your optician; news; GOC publications, events and consultations; careers information; hearings section with explanations of the hearings process, plus details on sanctions and outcomes from past hearings; FAQs; information for GOC registrants; legislation.

Enquiries:
Enquiries to: Registrar and Chief Executive

Founded:
1959

Organisation type and purpose:
The GOC is the regulator for the optical professions in the UK. Its purpose is to protect the public by promoting high standards of education and conduct amongst opticians. The Council currently registers around 22,000 optometrists, dispensing opticians, student opticians and optical businesses.

Subject coverage:
We hold: statutory registers of all those registered and fit to practise, train, or carry out optical business; information relating to education and training prior to registration; advice on the application of the Opticians Act 1989; information on professional conduct.

Information services:
Opticians registers – an online statutory registers of all optometrists and dispensing opticians who are registered and fit to practise in the UK.

Education services:
Careers information available.

Trade and statistical information:
Data on the number and distribution of registered opticians.

Printed publications:
Annual Report
Bulletin newsletter
Careers factsheet
Opticians Handbook
Annual Report

Electronic and video publications:
Data on registered opticians available at cost in electronic form

Publications list:
Available online

Access to staff:
Contact by letter, by telephone, by fax, by e-mail and via website. Appointment necessary.
Hours: Mon to Thur, 0900 to 1700; Fri, 0900 to 1645

Access to building, collection or gallery:
Hours: Mon to Thur, 0900 to 1700; Fri, 0900 to 1645

Access for disabled people:
Ramp available

GENERAL OSTEOPATHIC COUNCIL

Acronym or abbreviation: GOsC

Osteopathy House, 176 Tower Bridge Road, London, SE1 3LU

Tel: 020 7357 6655
Fax: 020 7357 0011
E-mail: info@osteopathy.org.uk

Website:
http://www.osteopathy.org.uk

Enquiries:
Enquiries to: Osteopathic Information Service
Direct tel: 020 7357 6655 ext 242

Founded:
1993

Organisation type and purpose:
Statutory body.
To regulate, promote and develop the profession of osteopathy.

Subject coverage:
Osteopathy.

Trade and statistical information:
Osteopathic profession.

Printed publications:
The Osteopath Magazine (apply direct for subscriptions)

Access to staff:
Contact by letter, by telephone, by fax, by e-mail and via website
Hours: Mon to Fri, 0900 to 1700

GENERAL REGISTER OFFICE (NORTHERN IRELAND)

Formal name: Northern Ireland Statistics and Research Agency
Acronym or abbreviation: NISRA

Oxford House, 49–55 Chichester Street, Belfast, BT1 4HL

Tel: 028 9025 2000
Fax: 028 9025 2044
E-mail: grostats.nisra@dfpni.gov.uk

Website:
http://www.nisra.gov.uk
General information.
http://www.groni.gov.uk

Enquiries:
Enquiries to: Assistant Registrar General
Direct tel: 028 9025 2033
Direct e-mail: annette.gilkeson@dfpni.gov.uk

Founded:
1922

Organisation type and purpose:
National government body.
Central government department.

Subject coverage:
Statistics on births, deaths, marriages, divorces and population.

Museum or gallery collection, archive, or library special collection:
Birth, death and marriage statistics from 1922
Divorce statistics from 1983

Printed publications:
Registrar General's Annual Report
Registrar General's Quarterly Returns

Access to staff:
Contact by letter, by telephone, by fax, by e-mail, in person and via website. All charged.
Hours: Mon to Fri, 0930 to 1600

Access to building, collection or gallery:
Hours: Mon to Fri, 0930 to 1700

GENERAL REGISTER OFFICE FOR SCOTLAND

Acronym or abbreviation: GROS

New Register House, Edinburgh, EH1 3YT

Tel: 0131 334 0380
Fax: 0131 314 4400
E-mail: records@gro-scotland.gsi.gov.uk

Website:
http://www.gro-scotland.gov.uk
http://www.scotlandspeople.gov.uk

Enquiries:
Enquiries to: Registrar General

Founded:
1855

Organisation type and purpose:
National government body.

Subject coverage:
Registration of births, deaths, marriages, civil partnerships, divorces, dissolution of civil partnerships, adoptions, still-births, gender-recognition, change of name in Scotland, census of population of Scotland, vital and population statistics for Scotland, law governing marriage in Scotland, NHS Central Register for Scotland.

Museum or gallery collection, archive, or library special collection:
Old parish registers of births, deaths and marriages (1553–1854)
Records of the decennial censuses of the population of Scotland (1841–1901 are open to the public)
Statutory registers of births, deaths, marriages, still-births, adoptions, civil partnerships and divorces

Trade and statistical information:
Population, census and vital events data for Scotland.

Non-library collection catalogue:
All or part available online and in-house

Library catalogue:
All or part available in-house

Printed publications:
Annual Report of the Registrar General for Scotland
Census reports
Civil Parish Maps Index
Population Estimates Scotland
Registrar General's Preliminary Return
Registrar General's Quarterly Statistics
Jock Tamson's Bairns: a history of the records of the General Register Office for Scotland (£1)

Electronic and video publications:
Small area statistics (census, CD-ROM)

Publications list:
Available online and in print

Access to staff:
Contact by letter, by telephone, by fax, by e-mail and in person. All charged.
Hours: Mon to Fri, 0900 to 1630
Special comments: Disabled persons can be accompanied by a helper.
Orders accepted by post or fax or by credit card on direct phone line: 0131 314 4411, but not by email.

Access for disabled people:
Ramped entry, toilet facilities

Also at:
General Register Office for Scotland
Ladywell House, Edinburgh, EH12 7TF; tel: 0131 334 0380; fax: 0131 314 4344; e-mail: customer@gro-scotland.gsi.gov.uk

Branches:
Census, Population Statistics, Corporate Services, Vital Events and National Health Service Central Register
Ladywell House, Corstorphine, EH12 7TF; tel: 0131 334 0380

Part of the devolved:
Scottish Administration under the Scotland Act 1998

Scottish counterpart of the:
Identity and Passport Service in England and Wales

GENERAL TEACHING COUNCIL FOR SCOTLAND

Acronym or abbreviation: GTC Scotland

Clerwood House, 96 Clermiston Road, Edinburgh, EH12 6UT

Tel: 0131 314 6000
Fax: 0131 314 6001
E-mail: gtcs@gtcs.org.uk

Website:
http://www.gtcs.org.uk
General information about the Council. Email contacts to staff members,

Enquiries:
Enquiries to: Chief Executive
Other contacts: (1) Exceptional Admissions Secretary; (2) Communications Officer for all enquiries about registration from outwith Scotland and for press enquiries and enquiries of a general nature.

Founded:
1965

Organisation type and purpose:
National organisation, advisory body, statutory body, professional body (membership is by qualification), present number of members: 83,000. Regulatory body for the teaching profession in Scotland. Registration with the Council is required for teaching in local authority and independent schools in Scotland.

Subject coverage:
Teaching in Scotland, accreditation of teacher education courses in Scotland, probationary teaching service.

Trade and statistical information:
Certain limited statistics on numbers of teachers registered with the Council, including applications under EC directive 89/48 (mutual recognition of professional qualifications).

Printed publications:
Probationer Teacher Support (separate packs for Primary/Nursery and Secondary)
The Assessment of Probationer Teachers: Guidance for Headteachers and those concerned with the management of probationers (separate packs for Primary/Nursery and Secondary)
Welcome to Teaching for First Year Probationer Teachers
Teaching Scotland (newspaper, 4 times a year)
Quadrennial Review and Accounts
Various leaflets and information packs relating to the work of the Council, including its role in supervising the support and assessment of probationer teachers (most available free of charge)

Electronic and video publications:
Various videos available for purchase

Access to staff:
Contact by letter, by telephone, by fax, by e-mail and via website. Appointment necessary.
Hours: Mon to Thu, 0900 to 1645; Fri, 0900 to 1530

Access for disabled people:
Ramped entry, access to all public areas, toilet facilities

GENERAL TEACHING COUNCIL FOR WALES

Acronym or abbreviation: GTCW

4th Floor, Southgate House, Wood Street, Cardiff, CF10 1EW

Tel: 029 2055 0350
Fax: 029 2055 0360
E-mail: information@gtcw.org.uk

Website:
http://www.gtcw.org.uk

Enquiries:
Enquiries to: Deputy Chief Executive
Direct e-mail: hayden.llewellyn@gtcw.org.uk

Founded:
2000

Organisation type and purpose:
Professional body.

Subject coverage:
Information concerning registered teachers.

Printed publications:
Annual Statistics Digest
Order printed publications from:
publications@gtcw.org.uk

Access to staff:
Contact by letter, by telephone, by fax, by e-mail, in person and via website
Hours: Mon to Fri, 0900 to 1700

Access to building, collection or gallery:
Prior appointment required

Access for disabled people:
Access to all public areas

GENETICAL SOCIETY, THE

Acronym or abbreviation: GENSOC

Roslin BioCentre, Roslin Institute, Roslin, Midlothian, EH25 9PS

Tel: 0131 527 4472
Fax: 0131 440 0434
E-mail: mail@genetics.org.uk

Website:
http://www.genetics.org.uk
Genetics Society website.
http://www.leeds.ac.uk/genetics/gensoc/gensoc.html
Meetings, contacts.

Enquiries:
Enquiries to: Executive Officer
Other contacts: Treasurer for student grant applications, meeting sponsorship/grants.

Founded:
1919

Organisation type and purpose:
Learned society (membership is by subscription), present number of members: 2000, registered charity (charity number 261062).

Subject coverage:
Genetics.

Museum or gallery collection, archive, or library special collection:
Archive material held in the John Innes Institute, Norwich

Printed publications:
Genes and Development (monthly)
Heredity (monthly)
Newsletter

Access to staff:
Contact by letter, by telephone, by fax and by e-mail
Hours: Mon to Fri, 0900 to 1700

Affiliated to:
Federation of European Genetical Societies
Institute of Biology
International Genetics Federation

GENOME DAMAGE & STABILITY CENTRE

Acronym or abbreviation: GDSC

Science Park Road, University of Sussex, Falmer, Brighton, East Sussex, BN1 9RQ

Tel: 01273 678123
Fax: 01273 678121
E-mail: qhfa1@susx.ac.uk

Website:
http://www.biols.susx.ac.uk/gdsc/

Enquiries:
Enquiries to: Director

Founded:
Oct 2001

Organisation type and purpose:
National government body, university department or institute, research organisation.

continued overleaf

Subject coverage:
The GDSC is a research centre investigating the responses of cells to genome damage and their relationship to cancer and other aspects of human disease. The purpose-built laboratories, funded by the Joint Infrastructure Fund (JIF), the Wolfson Foundation and the University, are located adjacent to the School of Life Sciences, and provide a dynamic and collaborative environment for carrying out state-of-the-art research. Much of this research is supported by the Medical Research Council via a Centre Development Grant and Programme Grants. The Centre currently houses ten research groups.

Printed publications:
Available through scientific journals

Access to staff:
Contact by letter, by telephone, by fax, by e-mail and via website. Appointment necessary.
Hours: Mon to Fri, 0900 to 1700

Access to building, collection or gallery:
Prior appointment required
Hours: Mon to Fri, 0900 to 1700

Access for disabled people:
Ramped entry, toilet facilities

Parent body:
Sussex University
tel: 01273 606755

GEOGRAPHICAL ASSOCIATION

Acronym or abbreviation: GA

160 Solly Street, Sheffield, South Yorkshire, S1 4BF

Tel: 0114 296 0088
Fax: 0114 296 7176
E-mail: info@geography.org.uk

Website:
http://www.geographyshop.org.uk
Online joining facilities and publication sales
http://www.geography.org.uk
General information and members-only access

Founded:
1893

Organisation type and purpose:
Membership association (membership is by subscription), present number of members: 7,000, voluntary organisation, registered charity (charity number 313129), publishing house.
Resource centre for the teaching of geography.

Subject coverage:
The teaching of geography, its promotion nationally and in schools.

Printed publications:
GA Magazine (incorporating GA News) (termly)
Geography (termly)
Primary Geographer (termly)
Teaching Geography (termly)
Core resources for teaching geography in all phases of education
Order printed publications from:
sales@geography.org.uk

Publications list:
Available online and in print

Access to staff:
Contact by letter, by telephone, by fax, by e-mail, in person and via website. Appointment necessary.
Hours: Mon to Fri, 0900 to 1700

GEOGRAPHY OUTDOORS

Formal name: Geography Outdoors: the centre supporting field research, exploration and outdoor learning

Royal Geographical Society (with IBG), 1 Kensington Gore, London, SW7 2AR

Tel: 020 7591 3030
Fax: 020 7591 3031
E-mail: go@rgs.org

Website:
http://www.rgs.org/go

Enquiries:
Enquiries to: Head of Expeditions and Fieldwork
Direct e-mail: s.winser@rgs.org

Founded:
1980

Formerly called:
Royal Geographical Society and Young Explorer's Trust; Expedition Advisory Centre (year of change 2006)

Organisation type and purpose:
Advisory body, registered charity, suitable for ages: university undergraduates and adult leaders and teachers, training organisation, publishing house. Information, training and advice for those planning expeditions and field research overseas.

Subject coverage:
Scientific expeditions and adventure travel overseas: planning, fieldwork, equipment, safety, medicine; logistics of operating in tropical, desert and arctic environments; environmental information, training.

Museum or gallery collection, archive, or library special collection:
Expedition reports dating back to 1965

Non-library collection catalogue:
All or part available online

Library catalogue:
All or part available in-house

Printed publications:
Expedition Planners' Handbook and Directory
Fieldwork Guides (9 titles)
Expedition Manuals
Logistics and Safety Manuals (6 titles)
Oxford Handbook of Expedition and Wilderness Medicine (2008, £28.95)
Tropical Forest Expeditions (2001, £12)
Polar Expeditions (2001, £12)
Reference books and pamphlets (6 titles)
Sources of Information for Independent and Overland Travellers (2000, £5)
Creating a University Exploration Society (1999, £2.50)

Electronic and video publications:
Joining an Expedition (annually)
Order electronic and video publications from: http://www.rgs.org/JE

Publications list:
Available online and in print

Access to staff:
Contact by letter, by telephone, by fax, by e-mail and via website. Appointment necessary.
Hours: Mon to Fri, 0900 to 1700

Access to building, collection or gallery:
Prior appointment required
Hours: Mon to Fri, 1100 to 1700

Access for disabled people:
Ramped entry, toilet facilities

Office of the:
Royal Geographical Society (with IBG)
tel: 020 7591 3000; fax: 020 7591 3001; e-mail: info@rgs.org

GEOLOGICAL CURATORS GROUP

Acronym or abbreviation: GCG

Natural History Division, National Museum of Ireland, Merrion St, Dublin 2, Republic of Ireland

Tel: +353 (0)87 122 1967
E-mail: mparkes@museum.ie

Website:
http://www.geocurator.org

Enquiries:
Enquiries to: Secretary

Founded:
1974

Organisation type and purpose:
Professional body. To improve the status of geology in museums and the standard of geological curation in general.

Subject coverage:
All aspects of geology in museums; protection/care of collections; collecting; display; conservation; history; research etc.

Printed publications:
A Directory of British Geological Museums (May 1994)
Coprolite (newsletter, 3 times a year)
Guidelines for the Curation of Geological Materials 1985
The Geological Curator (journal, 2 times a year)

Access to staff:
Contact by letter, by e-mail and via website
Hours: Mon to Fri, 0900 to 1700

Affiliated to:
Geological Society of London

GEOLOGICAL SOCIETY

Burlington House, Piccadilly, London, W1J 0BG

Tel: 020 7434 9944
Fax: 020 7439 8975
E-mail: enquiries@geolsoc.org.uk

Website:
http://www.geolsoc.org.uk

Enquiries:
Enquiries to: Science & Communications Officer
Direct fax: 020 7439 8975
Direct e-mail: ted.nield@geolsoc.org.uk
Other contacts: Librarian for bibliographical enquiries, tel no 020 7432 0999.

Founded:
1807

Incorporates the former:
Institution of Geologists

Organisation type and purpose:
Learned society, professional body (membership is by qualification, election or invitation), present number of members: 8800, registered charity (charity number 210161), publishing house.
To serve the science and profession of geology in the UK.

Subject coverage:
Geology and allied sciences.

Museum or gallery collection, archive, or library special collection:
Murchison Letters and Diaries
Rare Book Collection

Library catalogue:
All or part available online and in-house

Printed publications:
Annual Review
Geoscientist (12 times a year)
Journal of the Geological Society (6 times a year)
Memoirs
Petroleum Geoscience (4 times a year)
Quarterly Journal of Engineering Geology
Special Publications
Order printed publications from: Geological Society Publishing House
Unit 7, Brassmill Lane, Bath, Somerset, BA1 3JN, tel: 01225 445046, fax: 01225 442836, e-mail: http://bookshop.geolsoc.org.uk

Publications list:
Available online and in print

Access to staff:
Contact by letter, by fax, by e-mail and via website. Appointment necessary. Non-members charged.
Hours: Mon to Fri, 0930 to 1730
Special comments: Charges made to non-members for use of the Library and information.

Has:
23 specialist groups and joint associations

GEOLOGISTS' ASSOCIATION

Acronym or abbreviation: GA

Burlington House, Piccadilly, London, W1V 9AG

Tel: 020 7434 9298
Fax: 020 7287 0280
E-mail: geol.assoc@btinternet.com

Website:
http://www.geologist.demon.co.uk

Enquiries:
Enquiries to: Executive Secretary

Founded:
1858

Organisation type and purpose:
Learned society (membership is by election or invitation), present number of members: 2000, registered charity (charity number 233199), suitable for ages: 18+.

Subject coverage:
Geological sciences.

Printed publications:
Circular (monthly)
Proceedings (quarterly)
Geological Guides mainly districts of the UK but also places abroad such as Iceland, Jamaica and Mallorca
London Illustrated Geological Walks (two books, Robinson E, £3.95 each)

Access to staff:
Contact by letter, by telephone, by fax, by e-mail and via website
Hours: Mon to Fri, 0930 to 1600

GEORGE ELIOT FELLOWSHIP

71 Stepping Stones Road, Coventry, Warwickshire, CV5 8JT

Tel: 024 7659 2231

Enquiries:
Enquiries to: Honorary Secretary

Founded:
1930

Organisation type and purpose:
Membership association (membership is by subscription, election or invitation), present number of members: 600, voluntary organisation, registered charity (charity number 1054060). Literary society to promote interest in George Eliot.

Subject coverage:
George Eliot's life, works, family and friends.

Printed publications:
George Eliot Review (annually, £10 plus p&p)
Pitkin Guide to George Eliot (£3.50 plus p&p)
Little Sister (£1 plus p&p)
Story of the George Eliot Fellowship (£2.50 plus p&p)
Those Of Us Who Loved Her: The men in George Eliot's life (£7.50 plus p&p)
Magazine (annually)
Newsletter (quarterly)

Electronic and video publications:
Two 60 minute cassettes of readings from George Eliot's novels by Gabriel Woolf

Publications list:
Available in print

Access to staff:
Contact by letter and by telephone
Hours: Mon to Fri, 0900 to 2200

Affiliated to the:
Alliance of Literary Societies
22 Belmont Grove, Havant, Hampshire, PO9 3PU; tel: 01705 475855; fax: 01705 788842; e-mail: rosemary@sndc.demon.co.uk

Branches at:
George Eliot Fellowship
2006-13-212 Yamakuni, Yashiro-Cho, Kato-Gun, Hyogo 673-1421, Japan

George Eliot Fellowship
PO Box 10167, Springfield, MO 65808-0167, USA

GEORGE MACDONALD SOCIETY, THE

9 Medway Drive, Forest Row, East Sussex, RH18 5NU

Tel: 01342 823859
Fax: 01342 823859
E-mail: macdonald-society@britishlibrary.net

Website:
http://www.george-macdonald.com
General on MacDonald.
http://www.gmsociety.org.uk
All MacDonald Society matters.

Enquiries:
Enquiries to: Honorary Secretary
Other contacts: Membership Secretary for membership enquiries.

Founded:
1981

Organisation type and purpose:
Membership association (membership is by subscription), present number of members: 190, registered charity.
Literary society.

Subject coverage:
All matters connected with the Victorian writer, lecturer and preacher George MacDonald.

Library catalogue:
All or part available in-house

Printed publications:
North Wind (journal, annually)
Orts (newsletter, quarterly)
Order printed publications from: The George MacDonald Society, 18 Tapanhall Road Fernhill Heath, Worcester, WR3 7TR, tel: 01905 453214, fax: 01905 453214, e-mail: terryandrachel@puzzlejug.co.uk

Access to staff:
Contact by letter, by telephone, by fax and by e-mail
Hours: Any reasonable time

Other addresses:
The George MacDonald Society
The Library, King's College, Strand, London, WC2R 2LS

GEORGE PADMORE INSTITUTE

Acronym or abbreviation: GPI

76 Stroud Green Road, Finsbury Park, London, N4 3EN

Tel: 020 7272 8915
Fax: 020 7281 4662

Website:
http://www.georgepadmoreinstitute.org

Organisation type and purpose:
A registered charity (no. 1003001) offering an archive, an educational resource and a research centre.

Subject coverage:
The black community of Caribbean, African and Asian descent in Britain and continental Europe.

GEORGIAN GROUP

6 Fitzroy Square, London, W1T 5DX

Tel: 0871 750 2936
Fax: 0871 750 2937
E-mail: office@georgiangroup.org.uk

Website:
http://www.georgiangroup.org.uk
Publications list, membership information and forms, some casework reports, events and study days information.

Enquiries:
Enquiries to: Secretary

Founded:
1937

Organisation type and purpose:
Voluntary organisation, registered charity (charity number 209934).
National amenity society.

Subject coverage:
Conservation of Georgian architecture, 1700–1840; advice to owners and public authorities; uses to which such buildings can be adapted.

Non-library collection catalogue:
All or part available in-house and in print

Library catalogue:
All or part available in-house

Printed publications:
Georgian Group Guides: a series of 16 short illustrated guides on windows, doors, paint colour etc
Georgian Group Journal 1991–2001
Rescued or Ruined? (1999): Dealing with enabling development
Symposia proceedings, including Georgian Vernacular 1995
Squanderous and Lavish Profusion
The Picturesque in Late Georgian England

Publications list:
Available online and in print

Access to staff:
Contact by letter, by telephone, by fax and by e-mail
Hours: Mon to Fri, 0930 to 1730

Liaison with:
20th Century Society
English Heritage
Society for the Protection of Ancient Buildings
Victorian Society

GERMAN HISTORICAL INSTITUTE LONDON

Acronym or abbreviation: GHIL

17 Bloomsbury Square, London, WC1A 2NJ

Tel: 020 7309 2050
Fax: 020 7309 2055
E-mail: ghil@ghil.ac.uk

Website:
http://www.ghil.ac.uk

Enquiries:
Enquiries to: Librarian
Direct tel: 020 7309 2022, 2019
Direct e-mail: library@ghil.co.uk
Other contacts: Director

Founded:
1975

Organisation type and purpose:
Research organisation.
Academic institute.

Subject coverage:
German history and politics (apart from the library, the Institute's staff of German historians are experts in various periods of German and English history from the late Middle Ages onwards).

Museum or gallery collection, archive, or library special collection:
74,000 vols, including microforms
200 current periodicals on German and English history
German and English newspapers

Library catalogue:
All or part available online

Printed publications:
Annual Lectures
Bulletin (twice a year)
Vols in the English series of publications
Vols in the German series of publications

continued overleaf

Order printed publications from: For English publications: Oxford University Press, Great Clarendon Street, Oxford, OX2 6DP; tel. 01865 556767; fax 01865 556646
For German publications: Oldenbourg, Rosenheimerstrasse 145, 81671 Munich, Germany; tel. +49 8945 0510

Publications list:
Available online and in print

Access to staff:
Contact by letter, by telephone, by fax, by e-mail, in person and via website

Access to building, collection or gallery:
No prior appointment required (but check on website for short notice closures)
Hours: Mon, Tue, Wed and Fri, 1000 to 1700; Thu, 1000 to 2000
Special comments: Readers' tickets required (photograph and proof of address needed), free access, reference only.

Links with:
partners in Rome, Paris, Washington, Warsaw, Moscow, Tokyo, Beirut, Istanbul

Parent body:
Stiftung Geisteswissenschaftliche Institute im Ausland
Kronprinzenstrasse 24, 53173 Bonn, Germany; e-mail: dgia@stiftung-dgia.de; website: http://www.stiftung-dgia.de

GERMAN NATIONAL TOURIST OFFICE

Acronym or abbreviation: GNTO

PO Box 2695, London, W1A 3TN

Tel: 020 7317 0908
Fax: 020 7317 0917
E-mail: gntolon@d-z-t.com

Website:
http://www.germany-tourism.de
General and tourist information on Germany.
http://www.germany-christmas-market.org.uk
Dedicated information on German Christmas Markets.

Enquiries:
Enquiries to: Information Officer

Founded:
1951

Organisation type and purpose:
National government body.
National tourist office.
Promotion of Germany as a travel destination.

Subject coverage:
Information on travel to and within Germany, including list of tour operators, accommodation lists, tourist information, events, conferences and fairs in Germany.

Museum or gallery collection, archive, or library special collection:
Picture library (online at www.images-dzt.de)

Trade and statistical information:
Data on travel and tourism from the UK and Ireland to Germany.
Data on the German travel industry (incoming only).

Printed publications:
Printed products available through a mailing house
Approximately 500 brochures on various areas and subjects
Posters

Publications list:
Available online and in print

Access to staff:
Contact by letter, by telephone, by fax, by e-mail and via website
Hours: Mon to Fri, 0900 to 1700
Special comments: Telephone hours are 1000 to 1600. No counter service.

Access to building, collection or gallery:
No access other than to staff

Branches:
30 branch offices worldwide and representative agencies worldwide

Parent body:
Head Office (GNTB)
German National Tourist Board, Beethoven str 69, 60325 Frankfurt am Main, Germany; tel: 00 49 69 974640; fax: 00 49 69 751903; e-mail: info@d-z-t.com

GERMAN-BRITISH CHAMBER OF INDUSTRY & COMMERCE

16 Buckingham Gate, London, SW1E 6LB

Tel: 020 7976 4100
Fax: 020 7976 4101
E-mail: mail@ahk-london.co.uk

Website:
http://www.germanbritishchamber.co.uk

Enquiries:
Enquiries to: PA to Director General

Founded:
1971

Formerly called:
German Chamber of Industry & Commerce in the UK (year of change 1993)

Organisation type and purpose:
Chamber of Commerce.

Subject coverage:
Promotion of trade and investment between Germany and the United Kingdom.
Specialist Groups: membership, events, business information, legal, business partner search, marketing services, business promotion, trade fairs, VAT refund, green dot.

Publications list:
Available online and in print

Access to staff:
Contact by letter, by telephone, by fax, by e-mail, in person and via website. Appointment necessary.
Non-members charged.
Hours: Mon to Fri, 0900 to 1700

GERMANISCHER LLOYD INDUSTRIAL SERVICES (UK) LIMITED

Acronym or abbreviation: GLIS (UK)

Enterprise Court, Gapton Hall, Great Yarmouth, Norfolk, NR31 0ND

Tel: 01493 442112
Fax: 01493 444365
E-mail: glocb-great.yarmouth@gl-group.com

Website:
http://www.ocbgl.com
General details of Company divisions.

Enquiries:
Enquiries to: Company Secretary

Founded:
1976

Organisation type and purpose:
Professional body.

Subject coverage:
Verification services – i.e. oilrigs, offshore and onshore structures etc.

Printed publications:
Offshore Health and Safety
The Guide to the Law and Practice

Publications list:
Available in print

Access to staff:
Contact by letter
Hours: Mon to Fri, 0900 to 1700

Main shareholding company:
Germanischer Lloyd AG

GFK NOP

Acronym or abbreviation: GfK NOP

Ludgate House, 245 Blackfriars Road, London, SE1 9UL

Tel: 020 7890 9000
Fax: 020 7890 9001
E-mail: ukinfo@gfk.com

Website:
http://www.gfknop.co.uk

Enquiries:
Enquiries to: Chief Executive

Founded:
1957

Organisation type and purpose:
Market Research organisation.

Subject coverage:
automotive, business, consumer (including CPR, travel, new media), financial Services, healthcare, media, mystery shopping, technology, social Research, omnibus surveys.

Access to staff:
Contact by letter, by telephone, by fax, by e-mail and via website. Appointment necessary.
Hours: Mon to Fri, 0930 to 1730

Access for disabled people:
Access to all public areas

Affiliated to:
MRS, GfK Group

GIBRALTAR GOVERNMENT

Acronym or abbreviation: GIB

Arundel Great Court, 179 Strand, London, WC2R 1EH

Tel: 020 7836 0777
Fax: 020 7240 6612
E-mail: info@gibraltar.gov.uk

Website:
http://www.gibraltar.gov.uk

Enquiries:
Enquiries to: Director
Direct fax: 020 7240 6612

Formerly called:
Gibraltar Tourist Board

Organisation type and purpose:
National government body.
Information office.

Subject coverage:
Gibraltar: all subjects including political, tourism, finance, trade and industry, property, conferences, stamps, ship repair, ship registry, yacht facilities etc.

Museum or gallery collection, archive, or library special collection:
Picture library

Library catalogue:
All or part available online

Printed publications:
Gibraltar government publications (produced when required)
Main tourism brochure (annually, October)

Electronic and video publications:
Videos

Publications list:
Available online and in print

Access to staff:
Contact by letter, by telephone, by fax, by e-mail and via website
Hours: Mon to Fri, 0900 to 1700

Access to building, collection or gallery:
No prior appointment required

Access for disabled people:
Level entry

Other address:
Gibraltar Government
6 Convent Place, Gibraltar; tel: + 350 70071; fax: + 350 76396; e-mail: govscc@gibnet.gi

GIFTED CHILDREN'S INFORMATION CENTRE

Acronym or abbreviation: GCIC

Hampton Grange, 21 Hampton Lane, Solihull, West Midlands, B91 2QJ

Tel: 0121 705 4547
Fax: 0121 705 4547
E-mail: petercongdon@blueyonder.co.uk

Website:
http://www.ukselfhelp.info/giftedchildren

Enquiries:
Enquiries to: Director

Founded:
1978

Organisation type and purpose:
Advisory body, suitable for ages: all, consultancy, publishing house.

Subject coverage:
Gifted children; dyslexic children and adults; left-handed individuals; attention deficit and hyperactivity disorder; Asperger's Syndrome.

Museum or gallery collection, archive, or library special collection:
Books and guides on the above subjects

Printed publications:
Books and guides on gifted children, thinking skills, Dyslexia, ADHD and left-handed children
Computer educational software
Teaching packs for parents and teachers

Publications list:
Available in print

Access to staff:
Contact by letter, by telephone and by fax.
Appointment necessary.
Hours: 24-hour service

Connections with:
British Dyslexia Association
Dyslexia Information Centre
Dyslexia Institute
Irlen Institute
at the same address
National Association for Gifted Children (NAGC)

GILBERT AND SULLIVAN SOCIETY

7–20 Hampden Gurney Street, London, W1H 5AX

Enquiries:
Enquiries to: Honorary Secretary

Founded:
1924

Organisation type and purpose:
Membership association (membership is by subscription), registered charity (charity number 1062970).

Subject coverage:
The operas of Gilbert and Sullivan, their lives and their other works.

Museum or gallery collection, archive, or library special collection:
Society library held at the Barbican music library, London

Printed publications:
Gilbert and Sullivan News (3 times a year, free to members, on sale to non-members)

Access to staff:
Contact by letter
Hours: Mon to Fri, 0900 to 1700

Affiliated societies throughout the:
English speaking world

GILERA APPRECIATION SOCIETY

Acronym or abbreviation: GAS

Fox House, Moor Road, Langham, Colchester, Essex, CO4 5NR

Tel: 01206 272737
Fax: 01206 273064
E-mail: ged@fox-house.freeserve.co.uk

Website:
http://www.gilera.com
History of the Gilera marque, text and photographs for downloading and a search facility, links to other Gilera-related sites.

Enquiries:
Enquiries to: Information Officer

Founded:
1982

Formerly called:
Gilera Owners Club (GOC) (year of change 1987)

Organisation type and purpose:
Voluntary organisation.

Subject coverage:
History, and technical assistance on all models of the Gilera motorcycle from the earliest in 1909 until the final models in 1993; contemporary articles, road tests, manuals, sources of spare parts and relevant information appropriate to Gilera.

Museum or gallery collection, archive, or library special collection:
Sales brochures, handbooks, workshop manuals
Spare parts lists, exploded diagrams, contemporary magazine road tests, period b/w photographs

Non-library collection catalogue:
All or part available online and in-house

Library catalogue:
All or part available in-house

Printed publications:
Classic Bike
Classic Motorcycle Legends
International Classic Racer
The Classic Motorcycle

Electronic and video publications:
History of Gilera (CD-ROM)
Gilera 90th Anniversary in Arcore, Italy and Parades around Monza captured on video (VHS only)

Access to staff:
Contact by letter, by telephone, by e-mail and via website
Hours: Mon to Fri, 0900 to 2230 via telephone

Affiliated to:
Italian Motorcycle Owners Club
34 Pictor Road, Fairfield, Buxton, SK17 7TB; tel: 01298 79899

GILGAL SOCIETY, THE

PO Box 21675, London, SW16 4WY

E-mail: info@gilgalsoc.org

Website:
http://www.gilgalsoc.org
About the Gilgal Society and routes to all other pages.
http://www.gilgalsoc.org/pubs.html
List of publications.
http://www.circinfo.com
Gilgal Publications online plus links to many related pages from other information suppliers.

Enquiries:
Enquiries to: Information Officer

Founded:
1998

Organisation type and purpose:
Voluntary organisation, publishing house.
Not-for-profit publisher.
Provision of accurate, medically approved, information regarding male sexual health, with special reference to circumcision.

Subject coverage:
Male genital health with special reference to circumcision.

Printed publications:
Circumcision – An Ethnomedical Study
Circumcision – A Guide to a Decision
List of Possible Circumcisers (UK or Rest of World)
Glossary of Terms Related to Circumcision and the Genital Organs
Myths, Lies and Half-Truths about Male Circumcision
Parental Rights, Parental Duties
Questions Young People Ask About Male Circumcision
Questions Girls Ask about Male Circumcision
Principle Methods of Male Circumcision
All About Being Circumcised (for 7 – 10 year-olds)
Adult Circumcision Account
Benefits of Male Circumcision
How a Circumcision is Performed (Infants or Children or Teens/Adults)
Preparation and After-Care for Circumcision (Infant or Child or Teen/Adult)

Electronic and video publications:
Adult Circumcision (video)
Ritual and Other Circumcisions (video)

Publications list:
Available online and in print

Access to staff:
Contact by letter, by e-mail and via website.
Appointment necessary.
Hours: Daily, 0900 to 2000
Special comments: No direct access, no opening hours.

Access to building, collection or gallery:
No access other than to staff

GILLETTE ADVANCED TECHNOLOGY CENTRE UK

460 Basingstoke Road, Reading, Berkshire, RG2 0QE

Tel: 0118 987 5222
Fax: 0118 975 2822

Enquiries:
Enquiries to: Library and Information Services Manager

Formerly called:
Gillette Research & Development Laboratory (year of change 2002)

Organisation type and purpose:
Research organisation.

Subject coverage:
Shaving devices, toiletries, writing instruments.

Access to staff:
Contact by letter, by fax and by e-mail
Hours: Mon to Fri, 0800 to 1600

Access to building, collection or gallery:
No access other than to staff

Subsidiary of:
Gillette Company, USA

GIN AND VODKA ASSOCIATION

Formal name: Gin and Vodka Association of Great Britain
Acronym or abbreviation: GVA

Cross Keys House, Queen Street, Salisbury, Wiltshire, SP1 1EY

Tel: 01722 415892
Fax: 01722 415840
E-mail: gva@ginvodka.org.uk

continued overleaf

Website:
http://www.ginvodka.org.

Enquiries:
Enquiries to: Director-General

Founded:
1991

Created by the merger of:
Gin Rectifiers and Distillers Association, and
Vodka Trade Association

Organisation type and purpose:
Trade association.

Subject coverage:
Gin and vodka industries; neutral alcohol industry,
specific regulations in sector, nationally and
internationally.

Trade and statistical information:
Data on UK gin and vodka industries, data on EC
spirits industry.

Printed publications:
Annual Report

Access to staff:
Contact by fax and by e-mail
Hours: Mon to Fri, 0900 to 1700

GINGERBREAD

307 Borough High Street, London, SE1 1JH

Tel: 020 7403 9500
Fax: 020 7403 9533
E-mail: office@gingerbread.org.uk

Website:
http://www.gingerbread.org.uk

Organisation type and purpose:
National organisation, membership association,
voluntary organisation, registered charity (charity
number 282512).
To provide advice and support to lone parents and
their children.

Subject coverage:
Self-help for one-parent families.

Publications list:
Available online and in print

Access to staff:
Contact by letter, by telephone, by fax, by e-mail
and via website
Hours: Mon to Fri, 0900 to 1700
Special comments: Advice line open Mon to Fri, 1000
to 1500.

Access to building, collection or gallery:
No prior appointment required

GIRDLESTONE MEMORIAL LIBRARY

Nuffield Orthopaedic Centre, National Health
Service Trust, Headington, Oxford, OX3 7LD

Tel: 01865 738145
Fax: 01865 738147
E-mail: david.young@noc.anglox.nhs.uk

Enquiries:
Enquiries to: Librarian
Direct e-mail: library@noc.anglox.nhs.uk

Organisation type and purpose:
University department or institute.
NHS Library.

Subject coverage:
Orthopaedics, orthopaedic engineering (biomechanics), rehabilitation, rheumatology,
metabolic disease of bone, orthopaedic and trauma
nursing.

**Museum or gallery collection, archive, or library
special collection:**
Small collection of early orthopaedic texts

Non-library collection catalogue:
All or part available in-house

Library catalogue:
All or part available in-house

Printed publications:
Accessions List (annually, monthly updates, free)
Journal List (annually, free)
Library Handbook (annually, free)

Access to staff:
Contact by letter, by telephone, by fax, by e-mail
and in person. All charged.
Hours: Mon to Fri, 0800 to 1800

Access to building, collection or gallery:
24-hour card access for members

Access for disabled people:
Level entry, access to all public areas

Member organisation of:
Health Libraries Information Network
tel: 01865 221950; fax: 01865 220040

Parent body:
Oxford University
Nuffield Department of Orthopaedic Surgery
Library

GIRLGUIDING SCOTLAND

16 Coates Crescent, Edinburgh, EH3 7AH

Tel: 0131 226 4511
Fax: 0131 220 4828
E-mail: administrator@girlguiding-scot.org.uk

Enquiries:
Enquiries to: Financial Resources Manager

Founded:
1910

Formerly called:
Guide Association Scotland; The Girl Guide
Association (Scotland) (year of change 1995)

Organisation type and purpose:
Helps girls to reach their potential through
programme of activities.

Subject coverage:
Guiding in Scotland.

Access to staff:
Contact by letter, by telephone and by fax.
Appointment necessary.
Hours: Mon to Fri, 0900 to 1700

Other address:
The Guide Association Scotland
Netherurd House, Blyth Bridge, West Linton,
EH46 7AQ; tel: 01968 682208; fax: 01968 682371

GIRLGUIDING UK

17–19 Buckingham Palace Road, London, SW1W
0PT

Tel: 020 7834 6242
Fax: 020 7828 8317
E-mail: chq@girlguiding.org.uk

Website:
http://www.girlguiding.org.uk

Enquiries:
Enquiries to: Receptionist

Founded:
1910

Formerly called:
Guide Association; Girl Guides Association (year
of change 1994)

Organisation type and purpose:
Membership organisation, present number of
members: 575,000, voluntary organisation,
registered charity (charity number 306016).
Voluntary Interdenominational International
Uniformed Movement for Girls.

Subject coverage:
Guide training, outdoor pursuits, skills training,
service to community.

**Museum or gallery collection, archive, or library
special collection:**
Archives from 1910 to date
Books, documents, badges, uniforms,
photographs, exhibits

Non-library collection catalogue:
All or part available in-house

Library catalogue:
All or part available in-house

Printed publications:
Guiding Magazine
The Rainbows Annual
The Brownie Annual
Training books, handbooks, history books, activity
books for all ages, etc.
Order printed publications from: The Guide
Association, Trading Service, Atlantic Street,
Broadheath, Altrincham, Cheshire, WA14 5EQ, tel:
0161 941 2237, fax: 0161 941 6326, e-mail: tradings@
girlguiding.org.uk

Publications list:
Available in print

Access to staff:
Contact by letter, by telephone, by fax, by e-mail
and via website. Appointment necessary.
Hours: Mon to Fri, 0900 to 1700

Access to building, collection or gallery:
Prior appointment required
Hours: Archives: Mon to Fri, 1000 to 1600

Access for disabled people:
Ramped entry, access to all public areas, toilet
facilities

Links with:
Scout Association

GIRLS' BRIGADE ENGLAND AND WALES, THE

Acronym or abbreviation: GB (England and Wales)

PO Box, 129 Broadway, Didcot, Oxfordshire, OX11
8XN

Tel: 01235 510425
Fax: 01235 510429
E-mail: admin@girlsbrigadeew.org.uk

Website:
http://www.girlsbrigadeew.org.uk

Enquiries:
Enquiries to: National Director

Founded:
1965

Formerly called:
Girls' Brigade of Ireland, Girls' Guildry, Girls' Life
Brigade (year of change 1965)

Organisation type and purpose:
International organisation, membership
association, registered charity (charity number
206655).
Christian youth organisation.

Subject coverage:
Children and youth issues; Duke of Edinburgh
Award scheme; Christian teaching.

**Museum or gallery collection, archive, or library
special collection:**
History of organisation – bound copies of GB
Chronicle since 1900

Printed publications:
Annual Report
The View

Access to staff:
Contact by letter, by telephone, by fax, by e-mail,
in person and via website. Appointment necessary.
Hours: Mon to Fri, 0900 to 1700

Affiliated to:
The Girls' Brigade Ireland
The Girls' Brigade N Ireland
The Girls' Brigade Scotland

GIRLS' FRIENDLY SOCIETY

Acronym or abbreviation: GFS Platform

GFS Platform, Unit 2, Angel Gate, 326 City Road, London EC1V 2PT

Tel: 020 7837 9669
E-mail: annualreport@gfsplatform.org.uk

Website:
http://www.gfsplatform.org.uk
General.

Enquiries:
Enquiries to: Director

Founded:
1875

Formerly called:
Girls' Friendly Society and Townsend Fellowship

Organisation type and purpose:
Membership association (membership is by subscription), present number of members: 1000, voluntary organisation, registered charity (charity number 1054310).

Subject coverage:
Parish-based work with girls and women. Youth and community work with women.

Museum or gallery collection, archive, or library special collection:
Girls' Friendly Society Archives from 1875

Printed publications:
Leaflets
Newsletter (2 times a year)

Access to staff:
Contact by letter, by telephone, by fax and by e-mail. Appointment necessary.
Hours: Mon to Fri, 0900 to 1700

Member of:
Anglican Voluntary Societies Forum
National Council for Voluntary Organisations
National Council for Voluntary Youth Services

GLAMORGAN RECORD OFFICE

Glamorgan Building, King Edward VII Avenue, Cathays Park, Cardiff, CF10 3NE

Tel: 029 2078 0282
Fax: 029 2078 0284
E-mail: glamro@cardiff.ac.uk

Website:
http://www.glamro.gov.uk
Basic information, opening hours, location, main collections, leaflets, photocopying order forms, educational resources.

Enquiries:
Enquiries to: Archivist

Founded:
1939

Organisation type and purpose:
Local government body.
Serving the authorities of Bridgend, Caerphilly, Cardiff, Merthyr Tydfil, Rhondda Cynon Taff and the Vale of Glamorgan.

Subject coverage:
History of Glamorgan.

Museum or gallery collection, archive, or library special collection:
Glamorgan Quarter Sessions, Petty Sessions
Glamorgan County Council, Mid Glamorgan County Council, South Glamorgan County Council, Urban and District Councils, Boroughs
Local Boards of Health, Burial Boards, Highway Boards
Coroners, Poor Law unions, hospitals, police, vehicle licensing
Port of Cardiff Shipping Registers, crew agreements (Cardiff registered ships)
Land Tax Assessments, registers of electors, schools and education

Business and industry (including iron companies – Dowlais Iron Company, Rhymney Iron Company etc and records of the South Wales Coalfield)
Estate, families and individuals
Maps and plans
Parish records for Glamorgan parishes in the Diocese of Llandaff
Civil Parish
Nonconformist Chapels and Churches
Jewish Synagogues and individuals
Quaker records for Wales
Societies and Associations
Political
Manorial
Pictorial

Non-library collection catalogue:
All or part available in-house

Printed publications:
Books on local history
Reproduction maps, engravings, watercolours, posters, documents

Publications list:
Available online and in print

Access to staff:
Contact by letter, by telephone, by fax, by e-mail and in person. Appointment necessary.
Hours: Mon, 1300 to 1900 (1700 to 1900 by appointment only); Tue to Fri, 0930 to 1700
Special comments: Closed Bank Holidays.

GLASGOW & WEST OF SCOTLAND FAMILY HISTORY SOCIETY

Acronym or abbreviation: G&WSFHS

Unit 13, 32 Mansfield Street, Glasgow, G11 5QP

Tel: 0141 339 8303

Website:
http://www.gwsfhs.org.uk
Subscription rates, details of services and facilities.

Enquiries:
Enquiries to: Librarian
Other contacts: Publications Secretary for details of publications.

Founded:
1977

Organisation type and purpose:
Membership association (membership is by subscription), present number of members: 1750–2000, voluntary organisation, registered charity (charity number SC 010866), research organisation.
To promote the study of family history, particularly in Glasgow and the west of Scotland.

Subject coverage:
Genealogical research in Glasgow and the west of Scotland i.e. Argyll, Ayrshire, Bute, Dunbartonshire, Lanarkshire, Renfrewshire and Stirlingshire (part).

Non-library collection catalogue:
All or part available online and in-house

Library catalogue:
All or part available online and in-house

Printed publications:
See website for full list of publications

Microform publications:
1851 Census indexes for Old Monkland (microfiche, £7.50 per set, plus p&p)
Index to births and marriages in the Glasgow Herald in 1851 (fiche, £3.50 per set, plus p&p)
Index to deaths in the Glasgow Herald in 1851 (fiche, £4.50 per set, plus p&p)
1851 Census Index, Glasgow City East (12 fiche, £11 plus p&p)
1851 Census Index, Glasgow City West (11 fiche, £10 plus p&p)
1851 Census index for Renfrewshire (10 microfiches Set 1, £9; 15 microfiches Set 2, £12 plus p&p)

1851 Glasgow Herald – Index to Births, Marriages and Deaths (3 fiche, £3.50 plus p&p)

Electronic and video publications:
CD-ROM: 1851 Census Indexes for Lanarkshire, Dumbartonshire & Glasgow.
Burial indexes for Glasgow High Church & Govan

Publications list:
Available online and in print

Access to staff:
Contact by letter, by telephone and in person. Access for members only.
Hours: Tue, Sat, 1400 to 1630; Thu, 1000 to 2030
Special comments: Only members have access to the research facilities.

Access to building, collection or gallery:
No prior appointment required
Hours: Tue, Sat, 1400 to 1630; Thu, 1000 to 2030
Special comments: Members only.

Member of:
Scottish Association of Family History Societies
e-mail: longerlive@tiscali.co.uk

GLASGOW ARCHAEOLOGICAL SOCIETY

Acronym or abbreviation: GAS

Flat 1–2, 27 Kirkland Street, Glasgow, G22 6SY

Tel: 0141 287 3625
E-mail: james-mearns@yahoo.co.uk

Website:
http://www.glasarchsoc.org.uk

Enquiries:
Enquiries to: Secretary
Direct tel: 0141 945 0447 (evenings)

Founded:
1856

Organisation type and purpose:
Learned society (membership is by subscription), present number of members: 350.
Encouragement of interest and research in archaeology, especially in the West of Scotland.

Subject coverage:
Archaeology, architecture, archives.

Printed publications:
Newsletter (3 times a year)
Scottish Archaeological Journal (2 times a year)

Publications list:
Available in print

Access to staff:
Contact by letter, by telephone, by e-mail and via website
Hours: Mon to Fri, 0900 to 1700

Member of:
Council for Scottish Archaeology

GLASGOW ASSOCIATION FOR MENTAL HEALTH

Acronym or abbreviation: GAMH

St. Andrews by the Green, 33 Turnbull Street, Glasgow, G1 5PR

Tel: 0141 552 5592
E-mail: info@gamh.org.uk

Website:
http://www.gamh.org.uk
Information on GAMH and changes to services

Enquiries:
Enquiries to: Advice and Resource Centre

Founded:
1979

Organisation type and purpose:
Membership association (membership is by subscription), voluntary organisation, registered charity (charity number SCO 11684).
Advice and resource centre.

continued overleaf

Subject coverage:
Mental health in Glasgow, community-based services, befriending home support, advocacy, equalities project.

Printed publications:
Leaflets on the work of the Association and services provided

Access to staff:
Contact by letter, by telephone, by fax, by e-mail and via website. Appointment necessary.
Hours: Office 0900 to 1700, Fir, 0900 to 1630; Advice and Resource Centre Tue, Fri, 1000 to 1600

Access for disabled people:
Parking provided, level entry, toilet facilites

Citywide services:
Advice and Resource Centre
  tel: 0141 552 5592; e-mail: info@gamh.org.uk
Advocacy Matters
  tel: 0141 559 5491; e-mail: advocacy@gamh.org
  .uk
Carers Support Project
  tel: 0141 429 7593; e-mail: carers@gamh.org.uk
Homeless Support Project
  tel: 0141 554 6200; e-mail: homelesssupport@
  gamh.org.uk
Supported Living Project
  tel: 0141 429 6307; e-mail: supportedliving@
  gamh.org.uk

Services in North and East Glasgow:
Active Outreach Team
  tel: 0141 554 6200; e-mail: activeoutreach@gamh
  .org.uk
Housing Support Project – East
  tel: 0141 564 1206; e-mail: hspeast@gamh.org.uk
Housing Support Project – North
  tel: 0141 587 1018; e-mail: hspnorth@gamh.org
  .uk
North and East Community Project
  tel: 0141 558 0943; e-mail: northeast@gamh.org
  .uk
Scotia Clubhouse
  tel: 0141 556 7766; e-mail: scotiaclubhouse@gamh
  .org.uk

Services in South Glasgow:
Housing Support Project – South
  tel: 0141 433 9393; e-mail: hspsouth@gamh.org
  .uk
South Community Project
  tel: 0141 423 0408; e-mail: south@gamh.org.uk
Young Carers Southside
  tel: 0141 424 1708; e-mail: youngcarers@gamh
  .org.uk

Services in West Glasgow:
Housing Support Project – West
  tel: 0141 579 0013; e-mail: hspwest@gamh.org.uk
West Community Project
  tel: 0141 357 2570; e-mail: west@gamh.org.uk
Young Carers Riverside
  tel: 0141 424 1708; e-mail: youngcarers@gamh
  .org.uk

GLASGOW CALEDONIAN UNIVERSITY LIBRARY IN THE SALTIRE CENTRE

Formal name: Glasgow Caledonian University Library in the Saltire Centre
Acronym or abbreviation: SC

70 Cowcaddens Road, Glasgow, G4 0BA

Tel: 0141 273 1000
Fax: 0141 273 1000
E-mail: library@gcal.ac.uk

Website:
http://www.gcal.ac.uk/library/
General library information, contacts and external links.

Enquiries:
Enquiries to: Director of Learner Support
Direct tel: 0141 273 1180
Direct e-mail: t.Finnigan@gcal.ac.uk

Founded:
1992

Formed by the merger of:
Glasgow Polytechnic, Queen's College, Glasgow

Organisation type and purpose:
University library.

Subject coverage:
Biology, building and surveying, business administration, computer studies, economics, engineering, finance and accounting, health and nursing studies, law and public administration, management, mathematics, ophthalmic optics, optometry and vision science, psychology, risk and financial services, social sciences, social work, hospitality and leisure, consumer studies, physiotherapy, radiography, podiatry, nutrition, orthoptics and occupational therapy.

Museum or gallery collection, archive, or library special collection:
Norman and Janey Buchan collection (left-wing politics)
David Donald collection (left-wing politics)
Gallacher Memorial Library (left-wing politics)
Sandy Hobbs collection
George H Johannes collection (South Africa, ANC, struggle against apartheid)
William Kemp collection (left-wing politics)
John Lenihan collection
Norrie McIntosh collection (left-wing politics)
Jim Milligan collection (left-wing politics)
Queen's College collection (home economics, domestic science)
Samuel Stewart collection (left-wing politics)
Michael Scott collection (left-wing politics)
Scottish and Northern Book Distribution Centre Limited collection (alternative politics, pressure groups)

Library catalogue:
All or part available online

Printed publications:
Library Guides for students and staff and website

Publications list:
Available in print

Access to staff:
Letter of introduction required. Non-members charged.
Hours: Mon to Thu, 0830 to 2100; Fri, 0830 to 1700; Sat, Sun, 1000 to 1800

Access for disabled people:
Parking provided, access to all public areas, toilet facilities

GLASGOW CITY COUNCIL

City Chambers, George Square, Glasgow, G2 1DU

Tel: 0141 287 2000
Fax: 0141 287 5666
E-mail: pr@glasgow.gov.uk

Website:
http://www.glasgow.gov.uk

Enquiries:
Enquiries to: Public Relations Manager
Direct tel: 0141 287 0901
Direct fax: 0141 287 0904

Founded:
April 1996

Organisation type and purpose:
Local government body, statutory body.
Local government.

Subject coverage:
Local government services.

Printed publications:
Glasgow (magazine, 6 times a year)
City Insider (staff magazine, monthly)

Publications list:
Available online and in print

Access to staff:
Contact by letter, by telephone, by e-mail and via website
Hours: Mon to Fri, 0900 to 1700

GLASGOW COLLEGE OF NAUTICAL STUDIES

Library, 21 Thistle Street, Glasgow, G5 9XB

Tel: 0141 565 2582
Fax: 0141 565 2599
E-mail: resources@gcns.ac.uk

Website:
http://www.gcns.ac.uk
General college information.

Enquiries:
Enquiries to: Librarian
Direct e-mail: m.scalpello@gcns.ac.uk

Founded:
1969

Organisation type and purpose:
Suitable for ages: 16+.
Further education college.

Subject coverage:
Maritime studies, marine engineering, telecommunications, instrumentation and control, nautical science, social science, social care, computing, mathematics, sport and leisure, beauty therapy, child care, transport, aeronautical science.

Museum or gallery collection, archive, or library special collection:
Maritime History collection (print)

Non-library collection catalogue:
All or part available in-house

Printed publications:
Library Guide

Access to staff:
Contact by letter, by telephone, by fax, by e-mail, in person and via website
Hours: Term time: Mon, Tue, Thu, 0830 to 1930; Wed, 0830 to 1800; Fri, 0830 to 1700
Vacations: Mon to Fri, 0830 to 1700

Links with:
Glasgow Colleges Group (GCG)

GLASGOW COUNCIL ON ALCOHOL

Acronym or abbreviation: GCA

Seventh Floor, Newton House, 457 Sauchiehall Street, Glasgow G2 3LG

Tel: 0141 353 1800
Fax: 0141 353 1030
E-mail: email@thegca.org.uk

Website:
www.thegca.org.uk

Enquiries:
Enquiries to: Director

Founded:
1965

Organisation type and purpose:
Voluntary organisation, registered charity (charity number SCO 14501).
The aim of GCA is to reduce alcohol abuse in the community of Greater Glasgow.

Subject coverage:
Counselling, education and advice on alcohol and alcohol abuse.

Access to staff:
Contact by letter, by telephone, by fax and in person
Hours: Mon to Thu, 0900 to 2030; Fri, 0900 to 1645

Access for disabled people:
Toilet facilities

Affiliated to:
Alcohol Focus Scotland
  2nd Floor, 166 Buchanan Street, Glasgow, G1 2NH; tel: 0141 333 9677; fax: 0141 333 1606; e-mail: enquiries@alcohol-focus-scotland.org.uk

GLASGOW INTERNATIONAL JAZZ FESTIVAL

Formal name: Royal Bank Glasgow Jazz Festival
Acronym or abbreviation: GIJF

81 High Street, Glasgow, G1 1NB

Tel: 0141 552 3552
Fax: 0141 552 3592
E-mail: glasgow@jazzfest.co.uk

Website:
http://www.jazzfest.co.uk

Enquiries:
Enquiries to: Director
Direct e-mail: olive@jazzfest.co.uk

Founded:
1987

Organisation type and purpose:
Annual jazz festival organiser.
To present the best of international jazz and jazz related music.

Subject coverage:
Jazz and blues.

Museum or gallery collection, archive, or library special collection:
Photographic library
Previous festival programmes

Printed publications:
Brochure (pub in May)

Publications list:
Available online and in print

Access to staff:
Contact by letter, by telephone, by fax, by e-mail and via website
Hours: Mon to Fri, 1000 to 1700

GLASGOW LIBRARIES, INFORMATION & LEARNING

Mitchell Library, North Street, Glasgow, G3 7DN

Tel: 0141 287 2999
Fax: 0141 287 2815
E-mail: martyn.wade@cls.glasgow.gov.uk

Website:
http://www.glasgowlibraries.org
New site under construction.

Enquiries:
Enquiries to: Head of Libraries and Archives
Direct tel: 0141 287 5114
Direct fax: 0141 287 5151
Other contacts: Information Services Manager for specific remit for Mitchell Library.

Founded:
1877

Formerly called:
Glasgow City Libraries and Archives

Organisation type and purpose:
Local government body.
Public reference library.

Subject coverage:
General and business information, newspapers, philosophy, religion, social sciences, language, literature, science, technology, arts, recreation, music, history and topography, particularly Scottish, Glasgow collection.

Museum or gallery collection, archive, or library special collection:
Andrew Bain Memorial Collection (4000 vols local history)
Archives (records of the City of Glasgow)
Armour Donation (3600 vols German literature)
Bell Collection (450 pamphlets, Scottish Union)
British Standards (complete set)
Clem Edwards Donation (2000 vols Labour Movement)
Cumming Pamphlets (185 pamphlets, Scottish religion and education – 19th century)
Dante Collection (216 vols)
Donald Purchase (400 vols shorthand)

E A Reynolds Collection (711 vols Rationalist literature)
E J Thomson Collection (500 vols Scottish topography)
Forrester Pamphlets (500 pamphlets, religion – 19th century)
Gardyne Collection (1800 vols Scottish poetry)
Glasgow Collection (20,000 vols)
Gourlay Donation (1042 vols India)
Graham Collection (local history)
Henderson Purchase (2800 vols Celtic languages)
Hillhouse Purchase (300 vols draughts)
Inverclyde Donation (Inverclyde Family albums, etc.)
J H Thomson Collection (1230 vols Covenanting history)
Jenkins Donation (500 vols Spain)
Jervise Collection (1300 vols provincial poets of Scotland)
Kidson Collection (9000 vols 18th century popular music)
Lipton Collection (Sir Thomas Lipton albums, etc.)
McClelland Donation (350 vols phrenology)
Moncrieff Mitchell Collection (3000 vols and 100 prints, local history)
Moody Manners Collection (2900 vols vocal and orchestral opera scores)
Morgan Collection (6000 vols pure and applied science)
Morrison Collection (7000 vols theology)
New Church Collection (2000 vols)
North British Locomotive Company Collection (10,000 items)
Patent Specifications (5,000,000 UK, US, European)
Private Press Collection (1600 vols)
R L Stevenson Collection (200 vols)
Reid Collection (850 vols angling)
Reid Donation (134 vols Social Credit)
Russell-Fergus Collection (20 vols history of the harp)
Scottish Poetry Collection (15,000 vols including 4000 vols on Robert Burns)
Scouler Collection (2000 vols science and philosophy, 16th to 19th centuries)
Slains Castle Collection (3100 vols theology, literature, travel, 16th to 18th centuries)
Smeal Collection (117 vols anti-slavery)
Trade Unions Collection (2500 vols)
UK and Scottish Newspapers
UK patents and specifications
United Nations Collection (10,000 vols)
Wallace and Bruce Collection (310 vols)
Whitton Bequest (347 vols botany, horticulture, etc.)
William ('Crimea') Simpson Collection (103 items)
Wotherspoon Collection (41 vols Clyde steamships)

Trade and statistical information:
A wide selection of trade and statistical information, including market research reports, is available in the business information and social sciences sections.

Non-library collection catalogue:
All or part available in-house

Library catalogue:
All or part available in-house

Printed publications:
Books on the history, social and literary life of the area including:
City of the Dead – the story of Glasgow's Southern Necropolis (Hutt C, £4.99)
Glasgow Illustrated (Fairful-Smith G, £7.99)
Imagining a City, 20th Century Glasgow Writing (a catalogue, Burgess M, £3.99)
Queen's Park, Historical & Heritage Walk (Marshall I and Smith R, £2.99)
The King's Grocer. The Life of Sir Thomas Lipton (Crampsey B, £9.99)
The Seeing Eye (Oliver G, £9.99)
West of Scotland Census Returns and Old Parochial Registers (Escott A, 50p)
Order printed publications from: Stock control at the same address, tel: 0141 287 2812, fax: 0141 287 2815

Publications list:
Available in print

Access to staff:
Contact by letter, by telephone, by fax, by e-mail and in person
Hours: Mon to Thu, 0900 to 2000; Fri, Sat, 0900 to 1700
Archives: Mon to Thu, 0930 to 1645; Fri, 0930 to 1600; or by appointment

Access for disabled people:
Parking provided, toilet facilities
Special comments: Parking by prior arrangement via duty librarian.
Level entry via Kent Road.

GLASGOW METROPOLITAN COLLEGE

230 Cathedral Street, Glasgow, G1 2TG

Tel: 0141 566 1664
Fax: 0141 566 1666
E-mail: tony.donnelly@glasgowmet.ac.uk

Website:
http://www.glasgowmet.ac.uk/library
Catalogue, subject-focused guides to electronic, e-book and book collections, copyright and other guides.

Enquiries:
Enquiries to: Chief Librarian
Direct tel: 0141 566 1550

Founded:
2005

Created by the merger of:
Glasgow College of Food Technology (f. 1972) and Glasgow College of Building and Printing (year of change 2005)

Organisation type and purpose:
Further Education.

Subject coverage:
Construction, design, ESOL, commmunication and media, printing, sports science, tourism, health and safety, food technology, food science, food processing, hospitality and catering, professional cookery, travel and tourism.

Library catalogue:
All or part available online

Access to staff:
Contact by letter, by telephone, by fax, by e-mail, in person and via website. Appointment necessary. Non-members charged.
Hours: Term time: Mon to Wed, 0800 to 1930; Thu, 1000 to 1700; Fri, 0800 to 1700.
Vacation: Mon to Fri, 0900 to 1600

Access for disabled people:
Parking provided, ramped entry, access to all public areas, toilet facilities

Links with:
Glasgow Caledonian University (GCU)
Cowcaddens Road, Glasgow, G4 0BA

GLASGOW MUSEUMS

Culture & Leisure Services, 20 Trongate, Glasgow, G1 5ES

Tel: 0141 271 8310
Fax: 0141 271 8354
E-mail: museums@cls.glasgow.gov.uk

Website:
http://www.glasgowmuseums.com
Links to all the related museums and galleries

Enquiries:
Enquiries to: Director
Direct tel: 0141 287 2600
Other contacts: Marketing Officer

Founded:
1901

Formerly called:
Glasgow Museums and Art Galleries

continued overleaf

Organisation type and purpose:
Local government body, museum, art gallery, suitable for all ages.
Glasgow Museums is the corporate title for Glasgow City Council, Culture & Leisure Services, Museums Service, and administers Glasgow's 12 municipal museums and art galleries.

Subject coverage:
The subjects covered by the twelve museums of Glasgow include art, history, British history, worldwide ethnography, sociology, natural history, history of science, history of transport, religious history and content and conservation science.

Information services:
Selective dissemination services; The Open Museum Department lends objects and displays to community groups in Glasgow and Strathclyde. Glasgow Museums offers touring exhibitions to venues in UK and elsewhere. For Museum Education Department tel: 0141 276 9368.

Special visitor services:
Tape recorded guides, materials and/or activities for children.

Education services:
Group education facilities.

Trade and statistical information:
Glasgow's municipal art and design collections of over 1 million objects, a substantial proportion of which relate to the City's artistic, cultural, political and social history.

Non-library collection catalogue:
All or part available in print

Printed publications:
Variety of publications including:
Patterns of Childhood: Samplers from Glasgow Museums (£9.99)
One Million Days in China (£6.99)
Guide to the Museum of Transport (£5.99)
Guide to Provand's Lordship (£5.99)
Millet to Matisse – 19th century painting from Kelvingrove Art Gallery (£35)
Art Treasures of Kelvingrove (£7.99)
Glasgow's Spitfire (£12.99)
What Do You Want to Say? Communicating through Exhibitions – a Guide for Community Groups (free)
Annual Benchmarking Report (free)
I Knew I Was Painting for My Life – Holocaust Artworks of Marianne Grant (£5)
Glasgow's Hidden Treasure – Charles Rennie Mackintosh's Ingram Street Tearooms (£5.99)
Preview Magazine (free of charge)
Glasgow Art Gallery and Museum: The Buildings and the Collections (£6.95)
Guide to the Museum of Transport (£2.95)
The Burrell Collection: a guide (£6.95)
The People's Palace and Glasgow Green (E King, £3.99)
The St Mungo Museum of Religious Life and Art (M O'Neill, £4.99)
The Strike of the Glasgow Weavers (E King, £1.65)
Order printed publications from: Marketing Department, Culture and Leisure Services, Martyrs' School, Parson Street, Glasgow, G4 0PX

Publications list:
Available online and in print

Access to staff:
Contact by letter, by telephone, by fax and by e-mail. Appointment necessary.
Hours: Mon to Thu, Sat, 1000 to 1700; Fri, Sun, 1100 to 1700

Access to building, collection or gallery:
Prior appointment required

Access for disabled people:
Parking provided, level entry, access to all public areas, toilet facilities

Museums and Galleries:
Burrell Collection
 2060 Pollokshaws Road, Glasgow, G43 1AT; tel: 0141 287 2550; fax: 0141 287 2597

Fossil Grove
 Victoria Park, Glasgow, G14 1BN; tel: 0141 287 2000
Gallery of Modern Art (GoMA)
 Royal Exchange Square, Glasgow, G1 3AH; tel: 0141 229 1996; fax: 0141 204 5316
Glasgow Museums Resource Centre (GMRC)
 200 Woodhead Road, Nitshill, Glasgow, G53 7NN; tel: 0141 276 9300; fax: 0141 276 9305
Kelvingrove Art Gallery & Museum
 Argyle Street, Glasgow, G3 8AG; tel: 0141 287 2699; fax: 0141 287 2690
Martyrs' School (by appointment only)
 Parson Street, Glasgow, G4 0PX; tel: 0141 553 2557; fax: 0141 271 8354
McLellan Galleries (currently closed)
 270 Sauchiehall Street, Glasgow, G2 3EH; tel: 0141 565 4137; fax: 0141 565 4111
Museum of Transport
 1 Bunhouse Road, Glasgow, G3 8DP; tel: 0141 287 2720; fax: 0141 287 2692
Open Museum
 Glasgow Museums Resource Centre, 200 Woodhead Road, Nitshill, Glasgow, G53 7NN; tel: 0141 276 9368; fax: 0141 276 9305
People's Palace and Winter Gardens
 Glasgow Green, Glasgow, G40 1AT; tel: 0141 271 2951; fax: 0141 271 2960
Pollok Country Park, Pollok House (Managed by The National Trust for Scotland)
 Pollok Country Park, 2060 Pollokshaws Road, Glasgow, G43 1AT; tel: 0141 616 6410; fax: 0141 616 6521; website: www.nts.org.uk
Provand's Lordship
 3 Castle Street, Glasgow, G4 0RB; tel: 0141 552 8819; fax: 0141 552 4744
Scotland Street School Museum
 225 Scotland Street, Glasgow, G5 8QB; tel: 0141 287 0500; fax: 0141 287 0515
St Mungo Museum of Religious Life and Art
 2 Castle Street, Glasgow, G4 0RH; tel: 0141 553 2557; fax: 0141 552 4744

Parent body:
Glasgow City Council, Culture and Leisure Services
 20 Trongate, Glasgow, G1 5ES; tel: 0141 287 4350; fax: 0141 287 5558

GLASGOW PHILHARMONIC MALE VOICE CHOIR

c/o John McFarlane, 5 Chapelton Avenue, Bearsden, Glasgow, G61 2RE

Tel: 0141 586 5195
E-mail: john.mcfarlane4@ntlworld.com

Website:
http://www.glasphilmvc.org.uk

Enquiries:
Enquiries to: General Secretary

Founded:
1925

Organisation type and purpose:
Membership association (membership is by subscription), present number of members: 60.

Subject coverage:
Male voice choral singing.

Museum or gallery collection, archive, or library special collection:
Large library of male voice music, now accommodated in the Mitchell Library, Glasgow

Non-library collection catalogue:
All or part available in-house

Access to staff:
Contact by letter, by e-mail and via website
Hours: daily, before 2200

GLASGOW SCHOOL OF ART

Acronym or abbreviation: GSA

Library, 167 Renfrew Street, Glasgow, G3 6RQ

Tel: 0141 353 4500

Fax: 0141 353 4670
E-mail: c.nicholson@gsa.ac.uk

Website:
http://www.gsa.ac.uk/library
Access information, details of collections, on line catalogue.

Enquiries:
Enquiries to: Head of Learning Resources
Direct tel: 0141 353 4550
Other contacts: Archivist for extensive archives of GSA and of art and design generally.

Founded:
1845

Organisation type and purpose:
University library.
Art college library.

Subject coverage:
Fine art and design, architecture, art history.

Museum or gallery collection, archive, or library special collection:
Books, exhibition catalogues, newspaper cuttings and other documents relating to the history of the School, its staff and students
Glasgow School of Art Archives
Hill and Adamson Collection of photographic calotypes and carbon prints

Library catalogue:
All or part available online

Access to staff:
Contact by letter, by telephone and by e-mail. Non-members charged.
Hours: Term Time: Mon to Thu, 0930 to 1945; Fr, 0930 to 1645
Vacations: Mon to Fri, 0930 to 1645

Access for disabled people:
Ramped entry, toilet facilities,

GLASGOW WOMEN'S LIBRARY

Acronym or abbreviation: GWL

2nd Floor, 81 Parnie Street, Glasgow, G1 5RH

Tel: 0141 552 8345
E-mail: info@womenslibrary.org.uk

Website:
http://www.womenslibrary.org.uk

Organisation type and purpose:
A charity (no. SCO 29881) and a registered company (no. 178507), maintaining a lending library, archive collections and historical artifacts.

Subject coverage:
Women's lives, histories and achievements.

Education services:
Adult Literacy and Numeracy Project and a Black and Minority Ethnic Women's Project.

Access to building, collection or gallery:
Plans were being in made in 2008 to rehouse the Library in Glasgow's Mitchell Library

GLASSFIBRE REINFORCED CONCRETE ASSOCIATION

Acronym or abbreviation: GRCA

c/o The Concrete Society, Riverside House, 4 Meadows Business Park, Station Approach, Blackwater, Camberley, Surrey, GU17 9AB

Tel: 01276 607140
Fax: 01276 607141
E-mail: enquiries@grca.org.uk

Website:
http://www.grca.co.uk
General information on GRC, list of members, industry news, technical information.

Enquiries:
Enquiries to: Secretary
Other contacts: Director

Founded:
1975

Organisation type and purpose:
International organisation, advisory body, trade association (membership is by subscription). Technical database for GRC industry. Creation of CEN standards and representation on non-UK trade associations, relevant to the CRC (GFRC) industry.

Subject coverage:
Technical advice and sourcing of suppliers of glassfibre reinforced concrete.

Printed publications:
Codes of practice
GRC Today (free)
Manufacturing Specification
Proceedings of biennial Congresses since 1977
Register of Members
Technical information
Test Methods
Order printed publications from: The Concrete Bookshop, British Cement Association, Telford Avenue, Crowthorne, Berkshire, RG11 6YS, tel: 01344 725 704, fax: 01344 761214, e-mail: bookshop@bca.org.uk

Electronic and video publications:
CD-ROM in preparation
Video available

Publications list:
Available online and in print

Access to staff:
Contact by letter, by telephone, by fax, by e-mail and via website. Appointment necessary.
Hours: Mon to Fri, 0900 to 1700

Access to building, collection or gallery:
No prior appointment required

Other address:
Advisory Service (GRCA)
    26 Gorsey Brow, Billinge, Wigan, WN5 7NX; tel: 01744 893423; fax: 01744 892359

GLAXOSMITHKLINE

North Lonsdale Road, Ulverston, Cumbria, LA12 9DR

Tel: 01229 582261
Fax: 01229 482282

Enquiries:
Enquiries to: Technical Information Officer
Direct tel: 01229 482232
Direct fax: 01229 482257

Formerly called:
Glaxo Wellcome Operations

Organisation type and purpose:
Manufacturing industry, research organisation.

Subject coverage:
Pharmaceutical development and production.

GLAXOSMITHKLINE, RESEARCH AND DEVELOPMENT

New Frontiers Science Park (North), Third Avenue, Harlow, Essex, CM19 5AW

Tel: 01279 622000
Fax: 01279 622100

Website:
http://www.gsk.com
General GlaxoSmithKline information. No information on the library.

Enquiries:
Enquiries to: Librarian

Formerly called:
Beecham Pharmaceuticals Research Division, SmithKline Beecham Pharmaceuticals, Research and Development

Organisation type and purpose:
Research organisation.

Subject coverage:
Organic chemistry, pharmacology, neurosciences.

Non-library collection catalogue:
All or part available in-house

Library catalogue:
All or part available in-house

Access to staff:
Contact by letter and by e-mail
Hours: Mon to Fri, 0900 to 1700

Access to building, collection or gallery:
No access other than to staff
Special comments: No access to library.

Subsidiary of:
GlaxoSmithKline

GLOBAL EDUCATION MILTON KEYNES

Acronym or abbreviation: GEMK

Saxon Hall, Stantonbury Campus, Milton Keynes, Buckinghamshire, MK14 6BN

Tel: 01908 310951/324498
Fax: 01908 324401
E-mail: info@gemk.org.uk

Website:
http://www.gemk.org.uk

Enquiries:
Enquiries to: Information Officer
Other contacts: Centre Co-ordinator

Founded:
1980

Organisation type and purpose:
Charitable company (charity number 1086858; company number 4102062), training organisation. Resource Centre.
Public education in the field of sustainability, global issues and world development.

Subject coverage:
Materials for teachers and community workers on world development issues, e.g. food, water, population, India, Ghana, Tanzania, schools linking, recycling and disability, sustainable development and citizenship.

Special visitor services:
Resource Centre with loan facility for members

Education services:
Provides support for Sustainable Schools, Global Schools, Sustainable Communities and for teachers and others seeking to bring a global dimension to their work.

Museum or gallery collection, archive, or library special collection:
Everyday items from India, Ghana, Tanzania
Recycled items commonly made in Ghana and Zambia

Printed publications:
Annual Report (free)
Commonwealth Common Waste (now available online)
Challenging a Disabling World pack (for secondary schools, £12 incl. p&p)
Family Life and the 5 Rs: educational materials and slides comparing recycling in Milton Keynes and Ghana (£20 incl. p&p)

Electronic and video publications:
Compelling Learning Day Toolkit on Sustainable Communities (aimed at secondary schools)

Access to staff:
Contact by letter, by telephone and by e-mail. Appointment necessary.
Hours: Term time: Mon to Wed, afternoons
Vacations: by appointment

Links with:
Development Education Association
    River House, 143–145 Farringdon Road, London, EC1R 3AB; tel: 020 7812 1282; fax: 020 7812 1272; e-mail: dea@dea.org.uk

GLOSCAT

Formal name: Gloucestershire College of Arts and Technology
Acronym or abbreviation: GLOSCAT

Princess Elizabeth Way, Cheltenham, Gloucestershire, GL51 7SJ

Tel: 01242 532000
Fax: 01242 532196
E-mail: info@gloscat.ac.uk

Website:
http://www.gloscat.ac.uk
GLOSCAT Learning Centres – opening hours, staff, services.

Enquiries:
Enquiries to: Librarian
Direct tel: 01242 532185

Organisation type and purpose:
College of further education.

Subject coverage:
Cheltenham site: bakery, beauty therapy, business studies, caring, catering, clerical, computing, GCSEs, hairdressing, home economics, hotels, languages, leisure studies, science, secretarial, textiles, tourism.
Brunswick site: building studies, construction, design, electronic communication engineering, electronic engineering, manufacturing engineering, motor vehicles, surveying.

Library catalogue:
All or part available in-house

Access to staff:
Contact by letter, by telephone, by fax, by e-mail and via website
Hours: Mon to Fri, 0900 to 1700

Access to building, collection or gallery:
No prior appointment required
Hours: Cheltenham: term time: Mon, Wed, Thu, 0830 to 2000; Tue 0930 to 2000; Fri, 0830 to 1700
Brunswick: term time: Mon, Wed, Thu, 0830 to 2000; Tue 0930 to 2000; Fri, 0830 to 1700; Sat, 1015 to 1345
Both sites, vacations: Mon to Fri, 0900 to 1700
Special comments: Reference only.

Access for disabled people:
Level entry, access to all public areas, toilet facilities

Other site at:
GLOSCAT
    Brunswick Campus, Brunswick Road, Gloucester, GL1 1HU; tel: 01452 426530; fax: 01452 426531

GLOUCESTER CITY COUNCIL

North Warehouse, The Docks, Gloucester, GL1 2EP

Tel: 01452 522232
Fax: 01452 396140
E-mail: thecouncil@gloucester.gov.uk

Website:
http://www.gloucester.gov.uk

Enquiries:
Enquiries to: Head of Communications and Marketing
Direct tel: 01452 396133
Direct fax: 01452 396334

Organisation type and purpose:
Local government body.

Subject coverage:
Local government services.

Access to staff:
Contact by letter, by telephone, by fax, by e-mail, in person and via website. Appointment necessary.
Hours: Mon to Fri, 0830 to 1700

GLOUCESTER LIBRARY

Brunswick Road, Gloucester, GL1 1HT

continued overleaf

Tel: 01452 426979\ Minicom no. 01452 426975
Fax: 01452 521468
E-mail: localstudies@gloscc.gov.uk

Website:
http://www.gloscc.gov.uk/pubserv/gcc/clams
Gloucestershire and its heritage; individual library pages.

Enquiries:
Enquiries to: Librarian

Founded:
1900

Organisation type and purpose:
Public library.

Non-library collection catalogue:
All or part available online and in-house

Library catalogue:
All or part available in-house

Access to staff:
Contact by letter, by telephone, by fax, by e-mail, in person and via website
Hours: Mon, Tue, Thu, 1000 to 1930; Wed, Fri, 1000 to 1700; Sat, 0900 to 1300

Access for disabled people:
Access to all public areas, toilet facilities

Parent body:
Gloucestershire County Library, Arts and Museum Service
    Quayside House, Shire Hall, Gloucester, GL1 2HY

GLOUCESTERSHIRE ARCHIVES

Acronym or abbreviation: GA

Clarence Row, Alvin Street, Gloucester, GL1 3DW

Tel: 01452 425295
Fax: 01452 426378
E-mail: archives@gloucestershire.gov.uk

Website:
http://www.gloucestershire.gov.uk/archives
All archive catalogues online

Enquiries:
Enquiries to: Head of Information Management and Archives
Direct tel: 01452 425299
Other contacts: Customer Services Manager for specific historical enquiries.

Founded:
1936

Organisation type and purpose:
Local government body.
An amalgamation of the County Record Office, the Gloucester Diocesan Archives and the Gloucester City Archives; also houses the Victoria History of Gloucestershire and the Gloucester Local Studies Collection
Aims to preserve locally generated historical records of the county and all its communities dating from earliest times to the present day. The documents are kept in strong-rooms at the Record Office but ownership is retained by depositors.

Subject coverage:
Local history and topography of Gloucestershire and all its towns and parishes; biography, demography, genealogy, history of churches, landed estates, organisations, businesses, charities within the county; contribution of Gloucestershire to regional and national history.

Museum or gallery collection, archive, or library special collection:
Archives of: the diocese of Gloucester, Gloucestershire County Council and its predecessors, all District Councils and predecessor town and borough councils, City of Gloucester, boroughs of Tewkesbury and Cheltenham, also nonconformist churches, charities, schools, businesses and antiquarian collections

Many family collections including St Aldwyn, Lloyd-Baker, Bathurst, Hicks-Beach, Beaufort, Blathwayt, Codrington, Sherborne
Gloucestershire Local Studies Collection

Non-library collection catalogue:
All or part available online and in-house

Microform publications:
Microfilm of any document to order
Microfiche of parish registers for sale

Publications list:
Available online and in print

Access to staff:
Contact by letter, by telephone, by fax, by e-mail, in person and via website
Hours: Tue, Wed, Fri, 0900 to 1700; Thu, 0900 to 1830; Sat, 0900 to 1300

Access for disabled people:
Access to all public areas

Also at:
Gloucestershire Archives
    Shire Hall Record Centre, Westgate Street, Gloucester, GL1 2TG; tel: 01452 425289

Parent body:
Gloucestershire County Council
    Community and Adult Care Directorate

GLOUCESTERSHIRE COUNTY LIBRARIES AND INFORMATION

Quayside House, Shire Hall, Gloucester, GL1 2HY

Tel: 08452 305420
Fax: 01452 452042
E-mail: libraryhelp@gloucestershire.gov.uk

Website:
http://www.gloucestershire.gov.uk/libraries
http://opac.gloucestershire.gov.uk

Enquiries:
Enquiries to: Policy Development Officer: Information and Adult Learning
Direct tel: 01452 426494
Direct e-mail: pdoial@gloucestershire.gov.uk

Organisation type and purpose:
Local government body, public library.
Library headquarters, there are 39 libraries in the County.

Subject coverage:
General reference, business information, Gloucestershire local studies, Gloucestershire arts and crafts.

Information services:
Library available for reference (for conditions see Access above), on-line searching, can direct public to most appropriate library within County. Nearest is Gloucester library which holds a European and official publications collection.

Special visitor services:
Materials and/or activities for children.

Services for disabled people:
For the visually impaired; for the hearing impaired.

Museum or gallery collection, archive, or library special collection:
Art Collection
Arts – Cheltenham
Burchall English Civil War Collection
Business Information – Cheltenham
Europe Direct – Gloucester
Gloucester Collection (Historical)
Hitchings Collection of Bibles
Local Studies – Gloucester
Official Publications – Gloucester

Non-library collection catalogue:
All or part available online

Access to staff:
Contact by letter, by telephone, by fax, by e-mail and via website
Hours: Mon to Fri, 0900 to 1700

Other sites:
39 libraries

Parent body:
Gloucestershire County Council

Strategic libraries at:
Cheltenham, Cinderford, Cirencester, Gloucester, Stroud and Tewkesbury

GLOUCESTERSHIRE LOCAL HISTORY COMMITTEE

Community House, 15 College Green, Gloucester, GL1 2LZ

Tel: 01452 528491
Fax: 01452 528493
E-mail: glosrcc@grcc.org.uk

Website:
http://www.gloshistory.org.uk
Titles of articles in Gloucestershire History 1987 to date
List of Gloucestershire Local History speakers
Current local history societies' meetings

Enquiries:
Enquiries to: Secretary

Founded:
1948

Organisation type and purpose:
Voluntary organisation.

Subject coverage:
Local history and archaeology of Gloucestershire, local history and activities within Gloucestershire.

Printed publications:
Gloucestershire History (annually)
Local History Newsletter (annually, free with above)

Access to staff:
Contact by letter, by fax and by e-mail

Part of:
Gloucestershire Rural Community Council (GRCC)

GLUED LAMINATED TIMBER ASSOCIATION

Formal name: Glued Laminated Timber Association – GLULAM
Acronym or abbreviation: GLTA

Chiltern House, Stocking Lane, Hughenden Valley, High Wycombe, Buckinghamshire, HP14 4ND

Tel: 01494 565180
Fax: 01494 565487
E-mail: sales@glulam.co.uk

Website:
http://www.glulam.co.uk
Technical and pictorial information, list of members and their contact details.

Enquiries:
Enquiries to: Secretary

Founded:
1 Nov 1987

Organisation type and purpose:
Trade association (membership is by subscription), present number of members: 6.
To promote the awareness and use of glued laminated timber in the UK.

Printed publications:
Publications free, available from the secretariat

Electronic and video publications:
Publications available to download from our website

Access to staff:
Contact by letter, by telephone, by fax, by e-mail and via website
Hours: Mon to Fri, 0900 to 1700
Special comments: Visitors not normally received by secretariat.

GMB

Acronym or abbreviation: GMB

22–24 Worple Road, Wimbledon, London, SW19
4DD

Tel: 020 8947 3131
Fax: 020 8944 6552
E-mail: info@gmb.org.uk

Website:
http://www.gmb.org.uk/

Enquiries:
Enquiries to: General Secretary

Founded:
1889

Formerly called:
FTAT, National Union of Tailor and Garment
Workers (NUTGW); General & Municipal'Workers
(GMW) (year of change 1987)

Organisation type and purpose:
Trade union (membership is by subscription),
present number of members: 600,000, voluntary
organisation.

Subject coverage:
Industrial relations, collective bargaining,
employment law, occupational pensions, health
and safety at work, job education, work study.

**Museum or gallery collection, archive, or library
special collection:**
Agreements on wages and conditions of work with
companies where GMB is recognised (accessible
to public only by special arrangement)

Printed publications:
Bargaining Brief (information service to members)
Booklets, covering the above subjects (TOPICS)
Action (journal)

Publications list:
Available in print

Access to staff:
Contact by letter and by fax
Hours: Mon to Fri, 0900 to 1700

Access for disabled people:
Parking provided, ramped entry, access to all
public areas, toilet facilities

Affiliated to:
The Labour Party
Trades Union Congress

GOETHE-INSTITUT

Library, 50 Princes Gate, Exhibition Road, London,
SW7 2PH

Tel: 020 7596 4040
Fax: 020 7594 0230
E-mail: library@london.goethe.org

Website:
http://www.goethe.de
http://www.goethe.de/ins/gb/lon/inz/bib/enindex
.htm

Enquiries:
Enquiries to: Information Officer

Organisation type and purpose:
International organisation.
Cultural organisation.

Subject coverage:
Germany: general information on all aspects,
German books with some English translations
covering all fields in the arts, history, humanities
and social sciences, language, emphasis on
German literature, contemporary history, art and
language.

Library catalogue:
All or part available online and in-house

Printed publications:
Catalogue of DVD's and Videos

Access to staff:
Contact by letter, by telephone, by fax, by e-mail,
in person and via website

Hours: Mon to Thu, 1300 to 1830; Sat, 1300 to 1700

Links with:
Goethe-Institut München
Dachauer Strasse 122, München, D-80637,
Germany

GOETHE-INSTITUT, GERMAN CULTURAL INSTITUTE

3 Park Circus, Glasgow, G3 6AX

Tel: 0141 332 2555
Fax: 0141 343 1656
E-mail: library@glasgow.goethe.org

Website:
http://www.goethe.de/glasgow
Language and cultural programmes, general
library information, online catalogue.

Enquiries:
Enquiries to: Librarian
Other contacts: Language Office for language
courses in Glasgow and Germany, scholarships for
Scottish teachers of German and seminars.

Founded:
1973

Formerly called:
Goethe-Institut Inter Nationes; Goethe-Institut
(year of change 2001)

Organisation type and purpose:
International organisation.
Promotion of the German language at all levels of
education and of international cultural co-
operation, library and information service.

Subject coverage:
German language, culture and teaching.

**Museum or gallery collection, archive, or library
special collection:**
Library, books, videos, cassettes, CD-ROMs,
DVDs, CDs

Non-library collection catalogue:
All or part available online and in-house

Library catalogue:
All or part available online and in-house

Printed publications:
Calendar of events (3–4 times a year, free)
Library acquisitions lists (once or twice a year, free)
Prospectus of the language programme (2 times a
year, free)

Access to staff:
Contact by letter, by telephone, by fax, by e-mail,
in person and via website
Hours: Language Department: Mon to Thu, 1000 to
1700; Fri, 1000 to 1500
Library & Information Service: Mon, 1600 to 18.30;
Tues,Wed, 1200 to 1830; Thu, 1200 to 2030; Sat,
0930 to 1330
Special comments: A membership fee is applicable
for borrowing rights. Reference use of the library is
free.
Full: £14 annually – £7, 6 monthly.
Concession (students, unemployed, senior citizens:
£8 annually – £5, 6 monthly).
Membership for Goethe-Institut students is free.
Joint Membership for the Library of the Alliance
Française de Glasgow.

Affiliated to:
Goethe-Institut München
Dachauer Strasse 122, München, D-80637,
Germany

GOLDSMITHS

Formal name: Goldsmiths' College

Library, University of London, Lewisham Way,
New Cross, London, SE14 6NW

Tel: 020 7919 7171
Fax: 020 7919 7165
E-mail: library@gold.ac.uk

Website:
http://www.goldsmiths.ac.uk
College and departmental information.

Enquiries:
Enquiries to: Librarian
Direct tel: 020 7919 7150

Founded:
1891

Organisation type and purpose:
University library.

Subject coverage:
Anthropology, education, music, social sciences,
creative arts, humanities.

**Museum or gallery collection, archive, or library
special collection:**
A L Lloyd Collection of European and North
American Folk Music
Ewan McColl and Peggy Seeger collection
Centre for Russian Music
Serge Prokofiev Archive
Women's Art Library
LIFT video collection
Bush collection
Stevens collection

Non-library collection catalogue:
All or part available online and in-house

Library catalogue:
All or part available online

Access to staff:
Contact by letter, by telephone, by fax and by e-
mail. Appointment necessary.
Hours: Term time and Christmas and Easter
holidays: Mon to Fri, 0915 to 2045; Sat, 0930 to
1700; Sun, 1130 to 1700
Summer holidays: Mon and Wed to Fri, 0915 to
1645; Tue, 0915 to 2045; Sat, 0930 to 1700
Special comments: No access for visitors to
computers (except the library catalogue),
audiovisual collections or to electronic databases.

Access to building, collection or gallery:
No prior appointment required

Access for disabled people:
Level entry, access to all public areas, toilet
facilities

College of the:
University of London

GOLF FOUNDATION

Foundation House, The Spinney, Hoddesdon
Road, Stanstead Abbotts, Hertfordshire, SG12 8GF

Tel: 01920 876200
Fax: 01920 876211
E-mail: info@golf-foundation.org

Website:
http://www.golf-foundation.org
History of Golf Foundation; details of all
development initiatives, coaching activities and
tournaments.

Enquiries:
Enquiries to: Executive Director

Founded:
1952

Organisation type and purpose:
Registered charity (charity number 285917).
Junior Golf Development.
To promote and develop junior golf for young
people in full-time education.

Subject coverage:
Coaching and tournaments for junior
golfers.Development initiatives for grass roots
junior golf.

Printed publications:
Annual Report
Don't Be A Golf Menace (free)
Golf Rules in Brief (free)
Taking up Golf (£4.99)
Junior Golf Matters (newsletter)

continued overleaf

Publications list:
Available in print

Access to staff:
Contact by letter, by telephone, by fax and by e-mail
Hours: Mon to Fri, 0900 to 1700

GONVILLE AND CAIUS COLLEGE

Library, Cambridge, CB2 1TA

Tel: 01223 332419
E-mail: library@cai.cam.ac.uk

Website:
http://www.cai.cam.ac.uk/college/library/index
.php
History of library and details of service; all aspects of college activities covered.

Enquiries:
Enquiries to: College Librarian

Founded:
1349

Organisation type and purpose:
University library.
College library.

Subject coverage:
Music, logic, medieval literature.

Museum or gallery collection, archive, or library special collection:
15,000 early printed books
900 medieval and later manuscripts
Music manuscripts e.g. Charles Wood, Patrick Hadley
Venn manuscripts

Library catalogue:
All or part available online

Microform publications:
Microfilms of manuscripts are available for purchase by application to the Librarian.

Access to staff:
Contact by letter, by telephone, by e-mail and via website. Appointment necessary. Letter of introduction required.
Hours: Mon to Fri, 0900 to 1700

GOOD GARDENERS ASSOCIATION

Acronym or abbreviation: GGA

4 Lisle Place, Wotton-under-Edge, Gloucestershire, GL2 7AZ

Tel: 01453 520322
E-mail: info@goodgardeners.org.uk

Enquiries:
Enquiries to: Secretary General
Other contacts: Soil Scientist

Founded:
1961

Organisation type and purpose:
International organisation, membership association (membership is by subscription), voluntary organisation, registered charity (charity number 255300), suitable for ages: adults.
To teach the 'No Dig' method of growing fruit and vegetables on natural soil for the nutritional benefits that this provides in the maintenance of health worldwide.

Subject coverage:
Organics, soil fertility – nature's way, soil science, organic marketing, community supported agriculture, composting, nutrition, health from plant-orientated foods.

Printed publications:
Newsletter (quarterly)
Variety of booklets and leaflets

Publications list:
Available in print

Access to staff:
Contact by letter, by telephone and by e-mail.
Access for members only. Non-members charged.
Hours: Mon to Fri, 0900 to 1700

GOOD SCHOOLS GUIDE

Acronym or abbreviation: GSG

3 Craven Mews, London, SW11 5PW

Tel: 020 7801 0191
Fax: 0870 052 4067
E-mail: editor@goodschoolsguide.co.uk

Website:
http://www.goodschoolsguide.co.uk
The Good Schools Guide online in its entirety (for purchase), comprehensive UK educational data analysis, searches and links (free), reviewed book list (free).

Enquiries:
Enquiries to: Editor

Founded:
1985

Organisation type and purpose:
Consultancy, research organisation, publishing house.
Describes United Kingdom schools and international schools world-wide as they really are, advising parents on them. Provides information on schools and schooling over the internet and in printed form.

Subject coverage:
Primary and secondary schools in the United Kingdom, both private and state.
International schools world-wide.

Trade and statistical information:
School examination and other statistics.

Printed publications:
The Good Schools Guide (13th edn, Lucas Publications, 2008)
The Good Schools Guide – Special Educational Needs (3rd edn, Lucas Publications, 2008)
Uni in the USA (1st edn, Lucas Publications, 2005)
11+ English: A Parent's Toolkit (1st edn, Lucas Publications, 2004)
Order printed publications from:
orders@goodschoolsguide.co.uk

Electronic and video publications:
The Good Schools Guide (online)
The Good Schools Guide International (online)
Order electronic and video publications from: http://www.goodschoolsguide.co.uk

Access to staff:
Contact by letter, by telephone, by fax, by e-mail, in person and via website. Appointment necessary.
Hours: Mon to Fri, 0900 to 1700

Access for disabled people:
Access to all public areas

Administers:
The Good Schools Guide International website: http://www.gsgi.co.uk

Parent body:
Lucas Publications Ltd

GOOLE LOCAL STUDIES LIBRARY

Carlisle Street, Goole, East Riding of Yorkshire, DN14 5DS

Tel: 01405 762187
Fax: 01405 768329
E-mail: gooleref.library@eastriding.gov.uk

Enquiries:
Enquiries to: Librarian

Organisation type and purpose:
Public library.

Subject coverage:
Collections on Goole and the surrounding area, local family history resources.

Museum or gallery collection, archive, or library special collection:
2500 books covering Goole and the historic East, North and West Ridings of Yorkshire
Collections of books and 3000 photographs

Non-library collection catalogue:
All or part available online and in-house

Library catalogue:
All or part available online

Access to staff:
Contact by letter, by telephone, by fax, by e-mail and in person
Hours: Mon, Wed, 1000 to 1900; Tue, Thu, Fri, 1000 to 1700; Sat, 0900 to 1300

Access to building, collection or gallery:
No prior appointment required
Special comments: For detailed enquiries preferable to advise staff beforehand.
Prior appointment required for booking microform readers.

Access for disabled people:
Level entry
Special comments: Lift to Local Studies Library on first floor.

Parent body:
East Riding of Yorkshire Council

GORDON KEEBLE OWNERS CLUB

26 Burford Park Road, Kings Norton, Birmingham, B38 8PB

Tel: 0121 459 8700
Fax: 0121 459 9587

Enquiries:
Enquiries to: Secretary

Founded:
1970

Organisation type and purpose:
Membership association (membership is by subscription).

Subject coverage:
The Gordon Keeble car marque parts availability, location of cars.

Access to staff:
Contact by letter, by telephone and by fax.
Appointment necessary.
Hours: Mon to Fri, 0900 to 1700

GOSPORT BOROUGH COUNCIL

Town Hall, Gosport, Hampshire, PO12 1EB

Tel: 023 9258 4242
Fax: 023 9251 1279

Website:
http://www.gosport.gov.uk
Development opportunities, business pages, tourism and leisure, council services and information, events list.

Enquiries:
Enquiries to: Marketing Manager
Direct tel: 023 9254 5258
Direct fax: 023 9254 5238
Direct e-mail: econdev@gosport.gov.uk

Organisation type and purpose:
Local government body.

Subject coverage:
Local government.

Access to staff:
Contact by letter, by fax and by e-mail.
Appointment necessary.
Hours: Mon to Fri, 0900 to 1700

GOSS COLLECTORS CLUB

22 Littlebrook Gardens, Cheshunt, Hertfordshire, EN8 8QG

Tel: 0115 930 0441

E-mail: registrar@gosscollectorsclub.org

Website:
http://www.gosschina.com
Brief description of the club and its activities.

Enquiries:
Enquiries to: Registrar
Direct e-mail: auctionsecretary'gosscollectorsclub
.org
Other contacts: Auction Secretary for enquiries re
the postal auction.

Founded:
1970

Organisation type and purpose:
International organisation, membership
association (membership is by subscription).

Subject coverage:
The works of William Henry Goss, Goss china
collecting and identification, associated heraldry.

**Museum or gallery collection, archive, or library
special collection:**
Various collection of books, documents etc,
including comprehensive slide bank, held by
archivist (available to members only)

Printed publications:
The Goss Hawk Magazine (monthly, free to
members)

Access to staff:
Contact by letter, by telephone, by e-mail and via
website
Hours: Up to 2100

GOVERNING COUNCIL OF THE CAT FANCY, THE

Acronym or abbreviation: GCCF

4–6 Penel Orlieu, Bridgwater, Somerset, TA6 3PG

Tel: 01278 427575
E-mail: GCCF_CATS@compuserve.com

Website:
http://www.gccfcats.org
Information on GCCF.

Enquiries:
Enquiries to: Secretary

Founded:
1910

Organisation type and purpose:
Voluntary organisation.
Council made up of affiliated Cat Clubs.
Registration body for pedigree cats.

Subject coverage:
Pedigree cats breeds, shows and cat clubs.

**Museum or gallery collection, archive, or library
special collection:**
Cat registration records from 1910
Own records 1910 onwards

Trade and statistical information:
Analysis of cats registered.

Printed publications:
Free leaflets
Guides, stud books, lists of shows, clubs, judges etc

Publications list:
Available in print

Access to staff:
Contact by letter, by telephone, by e-mail and via
website. Appointment necessary.
Hours: Mon to Fri, 0900 to 1700

GOVERNMENT ACTUARY'S DEPARTMENT

Acronym or abbreviation: GAD

Finlaison House, 15–17 Furnival Street, London,
EC4A 1AB

Tel: 020 7211 2600
Fax: 020 7211 2650

E-mail: enquiries@gad.gov.uk

Website:
http://www.gad.gov.uk
Population projections; quinquennial review of
social security scheme; departmental contacts.

Enquiries:
Enquiries to: Director
Direct tel: 020 7211 2620
Other contacts: Directing Actuary for advice on
pensions.

Founded:
1919

Organisation type and purpose:
National government body, consultancy. Central
government department. Actuarial and financial
consultancy.

Subject coverage:
Demography (including national population
projections), survey of occupational pension
schemes, social security projection, public sector
pensions.

Printed publications:
Annual Report
Departmental Report
Occupational Pensions Schemes Survey 2000
Pension Provision in Britain (1994)
Quinquennial Review of National Insurance Fund
(1999)
Report by the Government Actuary on the drafts of
the Social Security Benefits Up-rating order 1999
and the Social Security (contributions) (Re-rating
and National Insurance Fund Payments) Order
1999
Resource Accounts
Review of Certain Contracting-out Terms (1996)
1996-based National Population Projections
2000-based Projections of Population
Order printed publications from: Publications Officer,
Government Actuary Department
tel: 020 7211 2620, fax: 020 7211 2650, e-mail:
marilyn.estrick@gad.gov.uk

Access to staff:
Contact by letter, by fax and by e-mail
Hours: Mon to Fri, 0900 to 1700

GOVERNMENT COMMUNICATIONS HEADQUARTERS

Acronym or abbreviation: GCHQ

Open Source Library and Information Services,
Room B2g, Hubble Road, Cheltenham,
Gloucestershire, GL51 0EX

Tel: 01242 221491 ext 32538
Fax: 01242 709002
E-mail: library@gchq.gsi.gov.uk

Enquiries:
Enquiries to: Librarian

Organisation type and purpose:
National government body.

Subject coverage:
Telecommunications, electronic engineering,
mathematics, computer applications,
communications security, linguistics.

Library catalogue:
All or part available in-house

Access to staff:
Contact by letter, by telephone, by fax and by e-
mail
Hours: Mon to Fri, 0900 to 1700

Access to building, collection or gallery:
No access other than to staff

GOWER PUBLISHING LIMITED

Gower House, Croft Road, Aldershot, Hampshire,
GU11 3HR

Tel: 01252 331551
Fax: 01252 344405

E-mail: info@gowerpub.com

Website:
http://www.gowerpub.com
Full online catalogue of publications, training
books and links to sister companies.

Enquiries:
Enquiries to: Customer Service Manager

Founded:
1967

Organisation type and purpose:
Publishing house. Academic, business and
professional publishing.

Subject coverage:
Business, management, personal skills, specialist
areas of business activity, information
management, training.

Printed publications:
101 Ideas to Help You be a Better Manager (£25,
pub Gower)
Dictionary of Marketing (£60, Gower Press)
Economic Bulletin (monthly, £150 a year, German
Institute for Economic Research)
European Design Guide (£45, pub. Gower)
Handbook of Food Additives: An International
Guide to 7500 Products (book and disc)
Handbook of International Credit Management
(£70, pub. Gower)
ISO 14000 and ISO 9000 – Feb 96 (£39.50, pub.
Gower)
Sources of European Economic and Business
Information (£125, pub. Gower)
World Index of Economic Forecasts (£125, pub.
Gower)
Librarianship and Information Management
publications (see publications list)
Order printed publications from: Bookpoint Limited,
Gower Publishing Direct Sales
130 Milton Park, Abingdon, Oxon, OX14 4SB, tel:
01235 827730, fax: 01235 400454, e-mail: orders@
bookpoint.co.uk

Electronic and video publications:
Gardners Chemical Synonyms and Trade Names
Electronic Handbook (£170, on CD-ROM)
Industrial Surfactants Electronic Handbook (£195,
on CD-ROM)
Plastic and Rubber Electronic Handbook (£170, on
CD-ROM)

Publications list:
Available online and in print

Access to staff:
Contact by letter, by telephone, by fax, by e-mail
and via website
Hours: Mon to Fri, 0900 to 1700

Access to building, collection or gallery:
Prior appointment required

Parent body:
Ashgate Group Publishing Limited
at the same address

Subsidiary body:
Dartmouth Press
Scolar Press
Variorum Press

GRADUATE PROSPECTS LTD

Formal name: Higher Education Careers Services
Unit
Acronym or abbreviation: HECSU

Prospects House, Booth Street East, Manchester,
M13 9EP

Tel: 0161 277 5200
Fax: 0161 277 5210
E-mail: enquiries@prospects.ac.uk

Website:
http://www.prospects.ac.uk/

Enquiries:
Enquiries to: Marketing Communications Manager

continued overleaf

Formerly called:
Central Services Unit for Graduate Careers and
Appointments Services

Subject coverage:
Graduate trends and predictions, graduate
training, graduate salaries, university output,
college output, graduate supply and demand,
postgraduate training, higher education careers
services.

Trade and statistical information:
Statistics on the graduate recruitment market.

Publications list:
Available online

Access to staff:
Contact by letter, by telephone, by fax and by e-
mail
Hours: Mon to Fri, 0900 to 1700

Access to building, collection or gallery:
No access other than to staff

Access for disabled people:
Parking provided, ramped entry, level entry, access
to all public areas, toilet facilities

Commercial subsidiary of the:
Higher Education Careers Services Unit (HECSU)

Jointly owned by:
Universities UK and the Guild HE

Publishing house for the:
Association of Graduate Careers Advisory Services
(AGCAS)

GRADUATE SCHOOL OF EUROPEAN AND INTERNATIONAL STUDIES

Acronym or abbreviation: GSEIS

University of Reading, Whiteknights, PO Box 218,
Reading, Berkshire, RG6 2AA

Tel: 0118 931 8378
Fax: 0118 975 5442
E-mail: gseis@reading.ac.uk

Website:
http://www.rdg.ac.uk/AcaDepts/ce/GSEIS/home
.html

Enquiries:
Enquiries to: Secretary

Founded:
1960

Formerly called:
GSEIS

Organisation type and purpose:
University department or institute, research
organisation.

Subject coverage:
Postgraduate teaching and training in the fields of
European and international studies, international
security studies, political theory and public ethics,
governance and international law and world order,
diplomacy.

Library catalogue:
All or part available in-house

Printed publications:
A regular series of Discussion Papers on European
and International Social Science Research and
occasional papers
Monographs, Occasional Papers, Research papers,
etc
Publicity material including the Graduate School's
Booklist
University of Reading series on Europe and
International Studies (published in association
with the Macmillan Press)

Publications list:
Available in print

Access to staff:
Contact by telephone and by e-mail

Hours: Mon to Fri, 1000 to 1600

Access for disabled people:
Ramped entry, access to all public areas

GRAHAM GREENE BIRTHPLACE TRUST

17 North Road, Berkhamsted, Hertfordshire, HP4
3DX

Tel: 01442 866694
E-mail: secretary@grahamgreenebt.org

Website:
http://www.grahamgreenebt.org
Frequent information about the Trust and its
annual festival.

Enquiries:
Enquiries to: Secretary

Founded:
1997

Organisation type and purpose:
International organisation, membership
association (membership is by subscription),
present number of members: 200, voluntary
organisation, registered charity (charity number
1064839).

Subject coverage:
Life and works of Graham Greene.

**Museum or gallery collection, archive, or library
special collection:**
Archive and Specialist Library

Library catalogue:
All or part available in print

Printed publications:
Newsletter (quarterly)
Occasional Papers (£2, £2.50 if posted)
Other publications as listed on website

Electronic and video publications:
The Voice of Graham Greene (CD-ROM, £10, incl
p&p)
Many Festival talks available on video/CD

Publications list:
Available online and in print

Access to staff:
Contact by letter, by telephone, by e-mail and via
website. Appointment necessary.
Hours: Sun to Sat, 0900 to 2100
Special comments: Answerphone out of hours.

GRAIN AND FEED TRADE ASSOCIATION

Acronym or abbreviation: GAFTA

GAFTA House, 6 Chapel Place, Rivington Street,
London, EC2A 3SH

Tel: 020 7814 9666
Fax: 020 7814 8383
E-mail: post@gafta.com

Website:
http://www.gafta.com
Membership information, list of publications,
courses, some categories of membership,
membership fees.

Enquiries:
Enquiries to: Director-General

Organisation type and purpose:
International organisation, trade association
(membership is by subscription), present number
of members: more than 1,000.

Subject coverage:
Grain, animal feedstuffs, pulses and rice, contracts,
arbitration, trade policy.

Publications list:
Available online

Access to staff:
Contact by letter, by e-mail and via website
Hours: Mon to Fri, 0900 to 1700

Access to building, collection or gallery:
Prior appointment required

Access for disabled people:
Level entry, toilet facilities

GRANTFINDER LIMITED

Enterprise House, Carlton Road, Worksop,
Nottinghamshire, S81 7QF

Tel: 01909 501200
Fax: 01909 501225
E-mail: enquiries@grantfinder.co.uk

Website:
http://www.grantfinder.co.uk
Fully searchable grantfinder database with option
to store and later retrieve project profiles. Update
and Newsflash facilities available to keep up-to-
date with new funding schemes and up-coming
deadlines.

Enquiries:
Enquiries to: Managing Director

Founded:
1985

Organisation type and purpose:
Consultancy, research organisation, publishing
house, providers of information on grants.

Subject coverage:
Information on grants, aids and incentives
available from the UK Government and European
Community to organisations in the public, private
and voluntary sectors.

Printed publications:
Grantfinder profiled publication
Grantfinder Report

Electronic and video publications:
Grantfinder

Access to staff:
Contact by e-mail and via website. All charged.
Hours: Mon to Fri, 0900 to 1730

GRAPHICAL, PAPER AND MEDIA UNION

Acronym or abbreviation: GPMU

Birmingham and West Midlands Branch, Union
House, 9 William Street North, Birmingham, B19
3QH

Tel: 0121 236 2963 or 8860
Fax: 0121 233 1731
E-mail: gpmuwestmidlands@btclick.com

Website:
http://www.gmpu.org.uk

Enquiries:
Enquiries to: Branch Secretary

Formerly called:
Birmingham Typographical Society (year of
change 1995)

Organisation type and purpose:
Trade union (membership is by subscription),
present number of members: 8000.

Subject coverage:
Information on general print, finishings, graphics,
lithography, flexography, silk screen. Electronic
and digital generations, employment legislation,
health and safety, pension information, state
benefits, welfare advice.

Access to staff:
Contact by letter, by telephone, by fax and in
person
Hours: Mon to Fri, 0900 to 1700

Affiliated to:
Graphical, Paper and Media Union
Keys House, Bromham Road, Bedford; tel: 01234
351521; fax: 01234 270580; website: www.gpmu
.org.uk

GRAY CANCER INSTITUTE

Acronym or abbreviation: GLCRT

PO Box 100, Mount Vernon Hospital, Northwood, Middlesex, HA6 2JR

Tel: 01923 828611
Fax: 01923 835210
E-mail: wardman@gci.ac.uk

Website:
http://www.gci.ac.uk

Enquiries:
Enquiries to: Deputy Director

Founded:
1955

Organisation type and purpose:
Registered charity, research organisation. Research into cancer.

Subject coverage:
Experimental cancer therapy, especially with radiation; tumour biology; tumour kinetics; tumour vasculature; radiation physics; radiation chemistry; radiation biology; neutrons; X-rays; radiation sources.

Museum or gallery collection, archive, or library special collection:
Fowler-Scott Library of books and journals related to cancer research and biological effects of radiation

Printed publications:
Papers and books published

Publications list:
Available in print

Access to staff:
Contact by letter, by telephone and by e-mail. Letter of introduction required.
Hours: Mon to Fri, 0900 to 1700

Access to building, collection or gallery:
Prior appointment required

GRAY'S INN LIBRARY

The Honourable Society of Gray's Inn, 5 South Square, Gray's Inn, London, WC1R 5ET

Tel: 020 7458 7822
Fax: 020 7458 7850
E-mail: library.information@graysinn.org.uk

Website:
http://www.graysinnlibrary.org.uk

Enquiries:
Enquiries to: Librarian

Founded:
c. 15th century

Organisation type and purpose:
Legal library

Museum or gallery collection, archive, or library special collection:
Core collection of 60,000 vols on all aspects of the the law, but specifically entertainment and sport, IT and communications law, and the law of education.
Manuscripts (medieval to 19th century)

Library catalogue:
All or part available online

Access to staff:
Contact by letter, by telephone, by fax and by e-mail. Access for members only. Letter of introduction required.

Access to building, collection or gallery:
Hours: Student and Legal terms: Mon to Fri, 0900 to 2002; holidays: see website for details
Special comments: Open to all barrister and student mems of Gray's Inn and barrister mems of all Inns of Court; other researchers by appointment with the Librarian

GRAYS CENTRAL LIBRARY

Orsett Road, Grays, Essex, RM17 5DX

Tel: 01375 413973
Fax: 01375 385504
E-mail: grays.library@thurrock.gov.uk

Website:
http://www.thurrock.gov.uk/libraries
General library details, council and community information. Electronic enquiry desk.

Enquiries:
Enquiries to: Librarian

Organisation type and purpose:
Local government body, public library.

Subject coverage:
General, local studies.

Non-library collection catalogue:
All or part available online

Library catalogue:
All or part available online

Access to staff:
Contact by letter, by telephone, by fax, by e-mail, in person and via website
Hours: Mon, Tue, Thu, 0900 to 1900; Wed, Fri, Sat, 0900 to 1700

Access to building, collection or gallery:
No access other than to staff

Access for disabled people:
Parking provided, access to all public areas, toilet facilities

Part of:
Thurrock Libraries

GREAT BRITAIN POSTCARD CLUB

34 Harper House, St James Crescent, London, SW9 7LW

Tel: 020 7771 9404

Enquiries:
Enquiries to: Executive Director

Founded:
1961

Organisation type and purpose:
Membership association.

Subject coverage:
Postcard collecting throughout the world, ephemera under 100 subjects.

Printed publications:
Postcard World (journal, 6 times a year, £10)

Access to staff:
Contact by letter
Hours: Mon to Fri, 0900 to 1700

GREAT BRITAIN RACQUETBALL FEDERATION

Acronym or abbreviation: GBRF

78 Suffolk Drive, Rendlesham, Woodbridge, Suffolk, IP12 2TP

Tel: 01394 461069
E-mail: aburrow.newman@btinternet.com

Enquiries:
Enquiries to: General Secretary

Founded:
1984

Organisation type and purpose:
National government body, membership association (membership is by subscription), voluntary organisation, suitable for ages: 8+. Promote the game of racquetball and racquetball education.

Subject coverage:
Racquetball rules, regulations, court specifications.

Access to staff:
Contact by letter and by telephone

Hours: Mon to Fri, 0900 to 1700

Affiliated to:
European Racquetball Federation
International Racquetball Federation

GREAT BRITAIN WHEELCHAIR BASKETBALL ASSOCIATION

Acronym or abbreviation: GBWBA

GBWBA Office, Suite B, Technology Centre, Epinal Way, Loughborough, Leicestershire, LE11 3GE

Tel: 01509 631671
Fax: 01509 631672
E-mail: office@gbwba.org.uk

Website:
http://www.gbwba.org.uk

Enquiries:
Enquiries to: Chief Executive
Direct e-mail: c.bethel@gbwba.org.uk ; info@gbwba.org.uk
Other contacts: League Secretary, Chairman, General Secretary

Founded:
1973

Organisation type and purpose:
Membership association (membership is by subscription), present number of members: over 700, registered charity (charity number 298045). National governing body for the sport.

Subject coverage:
All matters relating to the sport of wheelchair basketball in Great Britain.

Museum or gallery collection, archive, or library special collection:
Records of Association, member clubs, registered players and officials etc

Printed publications:
Coaching Award Manuals (Coaching Assistant Award and Coach Award)
Handbook (annual)
Information Pack
List of members and clubs
Rebound (newsletter, 2 times a year)
e-Zene (4 times a year)

Electronic and video publications:
Basic Coaching (video)
Introducing Wheelchair Basketball (video)

Publications list:
Available in print

Access to staff:
Contact by letter, by telephone, by fax, by e-mail and via website. Appointment necessary.
Hours: Mon to Fri, 0900 to 1700
Special comments: Not after 2200.

Affiliated to:
International Wheelchair Basketball Federation (IWBF)
IWBF Secretariat, 108–109 Watson Street, Winnipeg, Manitoba, Canada, R2P 2E1; tel: (204) 632 6475; e-mail: iwbfpresident@aol.com

GREAT BRITAIN-SASAKAWA FOUNDATION

Acronym or abbreviation: GBSF

Dilke House, 1 Malet Street, London, WC1E 7JN

Tel: 020 7436 9042
E-mail: gbsf@gbsf.org.uk

Website:
http://www.gbsf.org.uk

Enquiries:
Enquiries to: Chief Executive

Founded:
1984

Organisation type and purpose:
Registered charity (charity number 290766).

continued overleaf

To improve relations between the United Kingdom and Japan by promoting a deeper understanding between the peoples of both nations. Awards grants to organisations for cultural events, youth exchanges, Japanese language/studies and academic research collaboration.

Subject coverage:
Promotion of Anglo-Japanese understanding.

Publications list:
Available in print

Access to staff:
Contact by letter and by e-mail
Hours: Mon to Fri, 0900 to 1700

Also at:
Great Britain-Sasakawa Foundation
The Nippon Foundation Building 4F, 1-2-2 Akasaka, Tokyo, 107–0052, Japan; tel: +81 3 6229 5465; fax: +81 3 6229 5467; e-mail: gbsf@spf.or.jp

GREAT WESTERN SOCIETY LIMITED

Acronym or abbreviation: GWS

Didcot Railway Centre, Didcot, Oxfordshire, OX11 7NJ

Tel: 01235 817200
Fax: 01235 510621
E-mail: didrlyc@globalnet.co.uk

Website:
http://www.didcotrailwaycentre.org.uk

Enquiries:
Enquiries to: Secretary

Founded:
1961

Organisation type and purpose:
Membership association (membership is by subscription), voluntary organisation, registered charity (charity number 272616), museum.

Subject coverage:
Great Western Railway.

Non-library collection catalogue:
All or part available online and in print

Printed publications:
Didcot Railway Centre Guidebook (irregular)
Great Western Echo (quarterly, to members)

Access to staff:
Contact by letter, by telephone, by e-mail and via website
Hours: Mon to Fri, 0900 to 1700

Affiliated to:
Heritage Railway Association
Transport Trust

GREAT YARMOUTH CENTRAL LIBRARY

Tolhouse Street, Great Yarmouth, Norfolk, NR30 2SH

Tel: 01493 844551/842279
Fax: 01493 857628
E-mail: yarmouth.lib@norfolk.gov.uk

Website:
http://www.library.norfolk.gov.uk

Enquiries:
Enquiries to: Librarian

Organisation type and purpose:
Local government body, public library.

Subject coverage:
General, history and current information on Great Yarmouth and East Norfolk including newspaper cuttings; backfiles of local newspapers on microfilm, illustrations, maps etc; herring fishing, town walls and rows (narrow passageways), Dickens, Nelson, local genealogical information.

Museum or gallery collection, archive, or library special collection:
Francis Frith collection of photographs of Great Yarmouth and East Norfolk early/mid twentieth century
Herbert Tinkler MSS (early 20th century entertainments in Great Yarmouth)
W A S Wynne Collection (history of SE Norfolk and NE Suffolk)
William de Castre MSS (early 20th century writings and indexes on Great Yarmouth and Caister)
Yallop collection of glass plate negatives of Great Yarmouth Victorian/Edwardian era

Printed publications:
Family history resources available at Great Yarmouth Library
Parish Registers held at Great Yarmouth Library
The Local Studies Collection at Great Yarmouth Library

Parent body:
Norfolk Library and Information Service

Part of:
Anglian Libraries Information Exchange Scheme

GREATER GLASGOW & CLYDE VALLEY TOURIST BOARD

11 George Square, Glasgow, G2 1DY

Tel: 0141 204 4480
Fax: 0141 204 4772
E-mail: enquiries@seeglasgow.com

Website:
http://www.seeglasgow.com
Information about the Greater Glasgow & Clyde Valley area for visitors and travel trade.

Enquiries:
Enquiries to: Director
Other contacts: (i) Marketing Manager; (ii) Manager for (1) Leisure Tourism (2) Convention Bureau.

Organisation type and purpose:
Statutory body, membership association (membership is by subscription), present number of members: 700+.
Destination marketing organisation.

Subject coverage:
Information on the Greater Glasgow Clyde Valley area for visitors, i.e. accommodation information, things to see and do and assistance to tour operators and travel trade, e.g. itinerary planning.

Trade and statistical information:
Statistics relating to visitors to the Greater Glasgow & Clyde Valley Area.

Printed publications:
Accommodation Guide (free)
Essential Guide (free)
Visitor Guide (free)
Touring Route Guide (free)

Electronic and video publications:
CD-ROM of Images (for travel trade only, free)
Destination Video (for travel trade only, free)

Publications list:
Available online

Access to staff:
Contact by letter, by telephone, by fax, by e-mail, in person and via website. Appointment necessary.
Hours: Mon to Fri, 0900 to 1700
Special comments: Seasonal weekend opening for tourist information offices.

Access for disabled people:
Toilet facilities

GREATER LONDON ACTION ON DISABILITY

Acronym or abbreviation: GLAD

336 Brixton Road, London, SW9 7AA

Tel: 020 7346 5800\ Minicom no. 020 7326 4554

Fax: 020 7346 8844

Enquiries:
Enquiries to: Information Officer
Direct tel: 020 7346 5819
Other contacts: Head of Policy for information on disability equality, training and DDA training.

Formerly called:
Greater London Association of Disabled People (GLAD) (year of change 1999)

Organisation type and purpose:
Membership association (membership is by subscription, qualification), voluntary organisation, registered charity (charity number 293158), training organisation.
Centre of network of affiliated disability organisations throughout Greater London.

Subject coverage:
All non-medical disability issues such as access, aids, benefits, education, employment, holidays, housing, leisure and sport.

Printed publications:
All publications are available in large print, in Braille
BOADICEA (newsletter, 6 times a year for disabled women £4 individuals, £7 organisations)
Disability Update (current awareness bulletin and abstracting service, fortnightly, £35 voluntary organisations, £45 statutory and commercial)
London Disability News (newsletter, 10 times a year, £8 individuals, £12 organisations, also on cassette and in large print)
Who we are and what we do (leaflet free with 27p sae)
Directory of Greater London Borough Disability Organisations (2002, £25)
Self-Advocacy Training Packs
Ethnicity and Disability: Moving towards equity in service
Disabled Women and Safety

Electronic and video publications:
All publications are available on audio cassette or by e-mail

Publications list:
Available online and in print

Access to staff:
Contact by letter, by telephone, by fax and by e-mail. Appointment necessary.
Hours: Information line: Mon, Wed, Fri, 1330 to 1630

Access for disabled people:
Parking provided, ramped entry, access to all public areas, toilet facilities

Links with:
Alliance of Disability Advice and Information Providers
British Council of Disabled People
London Voluntary Service Council (LVSC)
National Council for Voluntary Organisations
National Information Forum
Rights Now!
Royal Association for Disability and Rehabilitation (RADAR)

GREATER LONDON AUTHORITY INFORMATION SERVICES

City Hall, The Queen's Walk, London, SE1 2AA

Tel: 020 7983 4455
Fax: 020 7983 4674
E-mail: isinfo@london.gov.uk

Website:
http://www.london.gov.uk

Founded:
2000

Organisation type and purpose:
Local government body, research organisation.
GLA Information Services is a specialist library and an information service for urban and social policy matters.

Subject coverage:
Planning and transport, business, the economy, labour market, education and training, health, housing and social exclusion, equalities policy, environment, culture, governance, police and community safety.

Museum or gallery collection, archive, or library special collection:
Library collection includes: more than 250,000 books, reports and journal articles (including grey literature), and 500 regular periodicals and statistical series.

Non-library collection catalogue:
All or part available in-house

Library catalogue:
All or part available in-house

Printed publications:
Culture Bulletin (monthly)
Daily Information Bulletin
Environment News (fortnightly)
Social Policy, Housing and Health Bulletin (fortnightly)
Economic and Business Bulletin (monthly)
Local Management and Finance (fortnightly)
Planning and Transport News (fortnightly)
Community Safety and Crime Bulletin (monthly)
Urban Abstracts (monthly)

Electronic and video publications:
Acompline and Urbaline database; Urbadoc

Publications list:
Available online and in print

Access to staff:
Appointment necessary. Non-members charged.
Hours: Mon to Fri, 0900 to 1730

Access for disabled people:
Lift and ramp entry, toilet facilities

GREATER LONDON FUND FOR THE BLIND

12 Whitehorse Mews, 37 Westminster Bridge Road, London, SE1 7QD

Tel: 020 7620 2066
Fax: 020 7620 2016
E-mail: info@glfb.org.uk

Website:
http://www.glfb.org.uk/

Enquiries:
Enquiries to: Information Officer

Founded:
1921

Organisation type and purpose:
Registered charity (charity number 1074958).

Subject coverage:
The visually impaired.

Access to staff:
Contact by letter, by telephone, by fax, by e-mail and in person. Appointment necessary.
Hours: Mon to Fri, 0915 to 1715

Member societies:
Clarity: Employment for Blind People
Croydon Voluntary Association for the Blind
Kingston-upon-Thames Association for the Blind
MertonVision
Metropolitan Society for the Blind
National Library for the Blind
SeeAbility
Surrey Association for Visual Impairment
Sutton Association for the Blind
The Middlesex Association for the Blind

GREATER MANCHESTER CENTRE FOR VOLUNTARY ORGANISATION

Acronym or abbreviation: GMCVO

St Thomas Centre, Ardwick Green North, Manchester, M12 6FZ

Tel: 0161 277 1000
Fax: 0161 273 8296
E-mail: gmcvo@gmcvo.org.uk

Website:
http://www.gmcvo.org.uk
GMCVO services; conference facilities; resource units on transport, access to services and rural issues; conferences and lectures; management and leadership training; consultancy; monthly news digest; bi-monthly policy briefing; print and design service.

Enquiries:
Enquiries to: Policy and Information Officer

Founded:
1975

Organisation type and purpose:
Voluntary organisation.
To strengthen the voluntary and community sector, build bridges with other sectors and influence local and national policy.

Printed publications:
Digest (monthly news round-up, £10 p.a.)
Issues (bi-monthly policy briefing, £30 p.a.)

Access to staff:
Contact by letter, by telephone, by fax, by e-mail and via website. Appointment necessary.
Hours: Phone lines open Mon to Fri, 0900 to 1700

Access for disabled people:
Ramped entry, toilet facilities

Member of:
National Association for Voluntary and Community Action
National Council for Voluntary Organisations
Voluntary Sector North West

GREATER MANCHESTER COUNTY RECORD OFFICE

Acronym or abbreviation: GMCRO

56 Marshall Street, New Cross, Manchester, M4 5FU

Tel: 0161 832 5284
Fax: 0161 839 3808
E-mail: archives@gmcro.co.uk

Website:
http://www.gmcro.co.uk

Enquiries:
Enquiries to: County Archivist

Founded:
1976

Organisation type and purpose:
Local government body.
Archive service, storage, reprographics, conservation.

Subject coverage:
Industrial and business records of Greater Manchester county, family and estate records, probate and registration indexes. Family history, public records, maps, newspapers, documentary photography archive, records of Greater Manchester County Council, societies, organisations and trade unions in Greater Manchester.

Museum or gallery collection, archive, or library special collection:
Archives relating to Greater Manchester Region from 1197 to modern day
Photographs – documentary photography archive
Photographs – Manchester Ship Canal Collection

Non-library collection catalogue:
All or part available online and in-house

Printed publications:
Printouts available from microfilm

Microform publications:
35mm microfilming of documents, maps, books and newspapers on to 35mm roll film or aperture cards

Electronic and video publications:
Video (available direct)

Access to staff:
Contact by letter, by telephone, by fax, by e-mail, in person and via website

Access to building, collection or gallery:
Hours: Mon, Tue, Thu and Fri, 0900 to 1700; Wed, 0900 to 1300; 2nd and 4th Sat, 0900 to 1200 and 1300 to 1600
Special comments: Require CARN ticket

Access for disabled people:
Access to all public areas

Parent body:
Association of Greater Manchester Authorities (AGMA)

GREATER MERSEYSIDE LEARNING AND SKILLS COUNCIL

Acronym or abbreviation: Greater Mersyside LSC

3rd Floor, Tithebarn House, Tithebarn Street, Liverpool, L2 2NZ

Tel: 0845 0194950
Fax: 0151 672 3533
E-mail: merseysideinfo@lsc.gov.uk

Website:
http://www.lsc.gov.uk

Enquiries:
Enquiries to: Information Officer

Founded:
2001

Formerly called:
Merseyside Training & Enterprise Council Limited (year of change 1991–2001)

Organisation type and purpose:
Service industry.

Subject coverage:
Labour market information.

Library catalogue:
All or part available in-house

Printed publications:
Greater Mersyside Skills Assessment

Access to staff:
Contact by letter, by telephone, by e-mail and via website
Hours: Mon to Fri, 0900 to 1700

Access to building, collection or gallery:
No access other than to staff

GREEK NATIONAL TOURISM ORGANISATION

Acronym or abbreviation: EOT / GNTO

4 Conduit Street, London, W1S 2DJ

Tel: 020 7495 9300
Fax: 020 7495 4057
E-mail: info@gnto.co.uk

Website:
http://www.visitgreece.gr
Useful information for tourists
http://www.tourist-offices.org.uk
General information on Greece and its towns and cities, historical information
http://www.antor.com/greece
Useful information for tourists
http://www.gnto.co.uk
Useful information for tourists

Enquiries:
Enquiries to: Information Officer

Organisation type and purpose:
International organisation, national government body.

continued overleaf

Subject coverage:
All forms of tourism to Greece including mainland and islands, special interest and conferences, information regarding transport, accommodation, tour operators, local festivals and cultural events.

Printed publications:
Brochures, posters, maps, general information, bus and ferry timetables, tour operator lists and special events

Microform publications:
Slides, photographs

Electronic and video publications:
Videos, CD-ROM

Access to staff:
Contact by letter, by telephone, by fax, by e-mail and in person
Hours: Mon to Thu, 0930 to 1700; Fri, 0930 to 1630

Access for disabled people:
Level entry

Parent body:
EOT
Tsocha 7, Athens, Greece; tel: +30 210 8707000; e-mail: info@gnto.gr; website: http://www .visitgreece.gr

GREEN PARTY

1a Waterlow, London, N19 5NJ

Tel: 020 7272 4474
Fax: 020 7272 6653
E-mail: office@greenparty.org.uk

Website:
http://www.greenparty.org.uk
General information about Green Party and current work.

Enquiries:
Enquiries to: Chair of the Executive
Other contacts: Head of Office

Founded:
1973

Formerly called:
People (year of change 1975); Ecology Party (year of change 1985)

Organisation type and purpose:
Political party.

Subject coverage:
Green politics, party policies.

Printed publications:
Green Activist (4 times a year, members only)
Green World: party newspaper (4 times a year, free to members)
Information booklets, briefing sheets, posters, election materials etc

Access to staff:
Contact by letter, by telephone, by e-mail and via website. Appointment necessary.
Hours: Mon to Fri, 0900 to 1700

GREENPEACE UK

Canonbury Villas, London, N1 2PN

Tel: 020 7865 8100
Fax: 020 7865 8200
E-mail: info@uk.greenpeace.org

Website:
http://www.greenpeace.org.uk
Information on campaigns, membership, press releases, photograph and video archives.

Enquiries:
Enquiries to: Information Officer

Founded:
1977

Organisation type and purpose:
International organisation.
Environmental campaigning.

Subject coverage:
Global warming, toxic waste, civil nuclear, nuclear disarmament, renewable energy, ancient forests, oceans.

Printed publications:
Briefing Sheets
Children's poster factsheets
Greenpeace Business (magazine, bi-monthly, subscription)
Connect (newsletter, subscription)
Greenpeace reports under the headings; atmosphere and energy, forests, toxins, nuclear, genetic engineering, oceans.

Electronic and video publications:
Video Lending Library:
Frontline Videos 1993–2004
Rainbow Warrior Promo

Publications list:
Available in print

Access to staff:
Contact by letter, by telephone, by fax, by e-mail and via website
Hours: Mon to Fri, 0900 to 1700

Parent body:
Greenpeace Environmental Trust at the same address

GREENWICH COMMUNITY COLLEGE LEARNING RESOURCES CENTRE

95 Plumstead Road, Plumstead, London, SE18 7DQ

Tel: 020 8488 4813
Fax: 020 8488 4899
E-mail: lib-help@gcc.ac.uk

Website:
http://www.gcc.ac.uk
Course details, open learning details.

Enquiries:
Enquiries to: Learning Resources Service Manager
Direct tel: 020 8488 4813

Formerly called:
Woolwich & Greenwich Community College Learning Resource Service; Greenwich Community College, Woolwich College (year of change 1998)

Subject coverage:
General.

Non-library collection catalogue:
All or part available online

Library catalogue:
All or part available online and in-house

Access to staff:
Contact by letter, by telephone and by fax
Hours: Mon to Fri, 0900 to 1700

Access for disabled people:
Level entry, toilet facilities, lift access

GREENWICH HERITAGE CENTRE

Artillery Square, Royal Arsenal, Woolwich, SE18 4DX

Tel: 020 8854 2452
E-mail: heritage.centre@greenwich.gov.uk

Website:
http://www.greenwich.gov.uk/greenwich/ leisureculture/historyandheritage/heritagecentre/
Guide to the heritage centre and its sources; detailed guide to family history sources.

Enquiries:
Enquiries to: Librarian

Founded:
1972

Created by the merger of:
Greenwich Borough Museum and Local History Library

Organisation type and purpose:
Local government body, public library, suitable for ages: all.

Subject coverage:
History of the London Borough of Greenwich.

Museum or gallery collection, archive, or library special collection:
Books, pamphlets, maps, illustrations, local authority archives, manuscripts, microfilms and fiche, audiotapes, and videotapes
Documents relating to the history, topography and people of Deptford, Blackheath, Greenwich, Kidbrooke, Charlton, Woolwich, Plumstead, Shooters Hill and Eltham
Martin Collection, 10,000 items relating to the history of Blackheath, Greenwich, Kidbrooke, Charlton and Lewisham
Official repository of the records of the London Borough of Greenwich and its predecessors

Non-library collection catalogue:
All or part available in-house

Library catalogue:
All or part available in-house

Printed publications:
Sugar, Spices and Human Cargo: an early Black History of Greenwich (Anim-Addo J, 1996)
Family History in Greenwich: a Guide to Sources (Reilly L, 1991)
Free for All (Watson J and Gregory W, 1993)
In the Meantime: a Book on Greenwich (Watson J and Gregory K, 1988)
Woolwich Reviewed (Watson J, 1986)

Publications list:
Available online

Access to staff:
Contact by letter, by telephone, by fax, by e-mail and in person
Hours: Tue to Sat 0900 to 1700; Sundays, Mondays and public holidays

Parent body:
Greenwich Council
tel: 020 8854 8888

GREENWICH LIBRARY AND INFORMATION SERVICE

Woolwich Reference Library, Calderwood Street, Woolwich, London, SE18 6QZ

Tel: 020 8921 5748
Fax: 020 8316 1545
E-mail: reference.library@greenwich.gov.uk

Website:
http://www.greenwich.gov.uk

Enquiries:
Enquiries to: Librarian
Direct tel: 020 8921 5749

Founded:
1965

Organisation type and purpose:
Local government body, public library.

Subject coverage:
Metropolitan Special Collection in the following fields: recreation; indoor and outdoor games and sports; dancing (excluding ballet); official books of most sports associations.

Museum or gallery collection, archive, or library special collection:
Greenwich Local History and Archives Collection (history, topography and archaeology, at the Greenwich Heritage Centre)
Metropolitan Special Collection (recreation, sports) at Library Headquarters, Plumstead Library

Non-library collection catalogue:
All or part available online

Library catalogue:
All or part available online

Printed publications:
Enquiries to Greenwich Heritage Centre

Photographic reproductions of local material (to order)

Range of local history prints, postcards and publications

Order printed publications from: Greenwich Heritage Centre, Artillery Square, Royal Arsenal, Woolwich, SE18 4DX. tel: 020 8854 2452, fax: 020 8854 2490

Access to staff:
Contact by letter, by telephone, by fax, by e-mail, in person and via website

Access to building, collection or gallery:
No prior appointment required

Constituent bodies:
Library and Information Service

Headquarters address:
Greenwich Library and Information Service
c/o Plumstead Library, High Street, Plumstead, London, SE18 1JL; tel: 020 8317 4466; fax: 020 8317 4868

Links with:
Greenwich Heritage Centre
Building 41, Royal Arsenal, Woolwich, SE18 6SP; tel: 020 8854 2452; e-mail: heritage.centre@ greenwich.gov.uk; website: http://www .greenwich.gov.uk

Parent body:
Greenwich Council, Culture and Community Services
tel: 020 8854 8888

GREEVES RIDERS ASSOCIATION

Acronym or abbreviation: GRA

4 Longshaw Close, North Wingfield, Chesterfield, Derbyshire, S42 5QR

Tel: 01246 853846

Enquiries:
Enquiries to: Membership Secretary

Founded:
1984

Organisation type and purpose:
Membership association.

Subject coverage:
Information on all Greeves motor-cycles, technical, for restoration, parts supply, clarification of models and month of manufacture.

Access to staff:
Contact by letter and by telephone
Hours: Mon to Fri, 1800 to 2100

GREGORIAN ASSOCIATION

26 The Grove, Ealing, London, W5 5LH

Tel: 020 8840 5832
Fax: 0870 055 3684
E-mail: pjsw@beaufort.demon.co.uk

Website:
http://www.beaufort.demon.co.uk/chant.htm
Activities of Gregorian Association, projects.

Enquiries:
Enquiries to: Chairman

Founded:
1870

Organisation type and purpose:
Membership association, present number of members: 100, registered charity (charity number 1003775).
Musical association.
Promotion and practice of Gregorian chant.

Subject coverage:
Singing, practice and teaching of plainsong and Gregorian chant in English and Latin.

Museum or gallery collection, archive, or library special collection:
Association's service books from the 1880s onwards

Collection of chants for daily offices and Masses in English
The Gregorian (journal)

Printed publications:
Night Prayer (£5.95)
Newsletter
The Gregorian (journal)

Access to staff:
Contact by letter, by telephone, by fax and by e-mail
Hours: Sun to Sat, 0800 to 2230

Affiliated to:
Royal School of Church Music

GREYFACE DARTMOOR SHEEP BREEDERS ASSOCIATION

Acronym or abbreviation: DSBA

The Old Rectory, Clannaborough, Crediton, Devon, EX17 6DA

Tel: 01363 85205
E-mail: greyface.dart@care4free.net

Website:
http://www.greyface-dartmoor.org.uk

Enquiries:
Enquiries to: Secretary

Founded:
1909

Organisation type and purpose:
Membership association (membership is by subscription), present number of members: 220, registered charity (charity number 266083).
Sheep Breeding Association (Greyface Dartmoor).

Subject coverage:
Sheep breeding.

Access to staff:
Contact by letter, by telephone, by fax, by e-mail and via website
Hours: Evenings preferred

GROUDLE GLEN RAILWAY

29 Hawarden Avenue, Douglas, Isle of Man, IM1 4BP

Tel: 01624 622138 (evenings only) 01624 670453 (weekends only)
E-mail: tbeard@manx.net

Enquiries:
Enquiries to: Honorary Secretary

Founded:
1982

Organisation type and purpose:
Membership association (membership is by subscription), present number of members: 700, voluntary organisation, registered charity (charity number Isle of Man No 406).
Restoration and operation of a narrow gauge railway.

Subject coverage:
Railway restoration and operation of a 2ft gauge line with steam and diesel locomotives over 3/4 mile track.

Printed publications:
Magazine (quarterly, to members)
History of the Groudle Glen Railway

Access to staff:
Contact by letter. Appointment necessary.
Special comments: No access to staff

Access for disabled people:
Special comments: Please telephone for advice before your visit

Affiliated to:
Isle of Man Steam Railway Supporters Association at the same address

GROWTH THROUGH TRAINING (GTT) LIMITED

Formal name: Growth Through Training (GTT) Ltd
Acronym or abbreviation: GTT Ltd

55 Curlew Drive, Chippenham, Wiltshire, SN14 6YG

Tel: 01249 661231
Fax: 01249 447442
E-mail: csimons@dircon.co.uk

Enquiries:
Enquiries to: Managing Director

Founded:
1985

Organisation type and purpose:
Organisational and human resource development, consultancy.
Management Development, Investors in People practitioners.

Subject coverage:
Organisational development, management development training. Investors in People consultancy, counselling at work.

Printed publications:
Effective Communication Skills for Managers (C Simons and B Naylor-Stables, Cassell Sep 1997, ISBN 0 304 331201, hardback; 0 304 33125, paperback)

Access to staff:
Contact by letter, by telephone, by fax and by e-mail. Appointment necessary.
Hours: Any reasonable time

GRUBB INSTITUTE

Formal name: Grubb Institute of Behavioural Studies Limited

Cloudesley Street, London, N1 0HU

Tel: 020 7278 8061
Fax: 020 7278 0728
E-mail: info@grubb.org.uk

Website:
http://www.grubb.org.uk

Enquiries:
Enquiries to: Executive Director

Founded:
1969

Organisation type and purpose:
Registered charity (charity number 313460), training organisation, consultancy, research organisation.

Subject coverage:
Analysis of organisation: theory, including organisational behaviour, group dynamics, systems psychology, religious behaviour; applications in the following fields: leadership and organisation of institutions, the educational process in secondary and higher education, industrial organisation and structure, management in central and local government agencies, religious institutions in society, community service and voluntary organisations, probation and after-care, prisons and penal establishments, transition from childhood to adult life, management training, group and inter-group relations, unemployment.

Printed publications:
List of published work up to 2008
Reports and Occasional Papers
Order printed publications from: Publications Secretary, e-mail: purchases@grubb.org.uk

Publications list:
Available online and in print

Access to staff:
Contact by letter, by telephone, by fax, by e-mail and via website. Appointment necessary.
Hours: Mon to Fri, 0900 to 1730

GS1 UK

10 Maltravers Street, London, WC2R 3BX

Tel: 020 7655 9000
Fax: 020 7681 2290
E-mail: info@gs1uk.org

Website:
http://www.gs1uk.org
Information to assist the understanding and use of
e-commerce, article numbering, bar coding,
electronic data interchange.

Enquiries:
Enquiries to: Chief Executive
Other contacts: Director, Business Development, for
marketing issues.

Founded:
1976

Organisation type and purpose:
Advisory body, trade association (membership is
by subscription), present number of members:
16,000 members, training organisation.
Trusted source of the best standards for business
data and the best practices for electronic
commerce.
The system provides the foundation for improved
supply chain management and electronic trading.

Subject coverage:
Best practice code for doing business electronically
across the extended enterprise. One-stop
organisation for help and advice on electronic
commerce to UK organisations. Supports and
promulgates EAN UCC standards, and electronic
commerce standards. Strong lobbying position on
behalf of 'UK plc'.

Library catalogue:
All or part available in-house

Printed publications:
The following publications are for members only:
General EAN UCC Specifications
Migration to Better Business Practice
EDIFACTS Manuals
Tradcoms (TDI) Manual
Brochures, information and advice titles for easy
reference

Electronic and video publications:
Edifacts Manuals (CD-ROM)
Producing Quality Barcodes (CD-ROM

Publications list:
Available in print

Access to staff:
Contact by letter, by fax, by e-mail and via
website
Hours: Mon to Fri, 0900 to 1700

Access to building, collection or gallery:
Prior appointment required

Access for disabled people:
Parking provided, ramped entry

Affiliated to:
International Article Numbering Association (EAN
Int)
  tel: + 32 2 2271020; fax: + 32 2 2271021

Founder member of:
EAN

GUARDIAN NEWSPAPERS LIMITED

Formal name: Guardian Media Group plc
Acronym or abbreviation: GMG

Research Department, 119 Farringdon Road,
London, EC1R 3ER

Tel: 020 7239 9772
E-mail: richard.nelsson@guardian.co.uk

Website:
http://www.guardian.co.uk

Enquiries:
Enquiries to: Information Manager

Organisation type and purpose:
Publishing house.
Media.

Subject coverage:
Content of the Observer and Guardian back to
1791, available at The British Library: Newspaper
Library.

GUILD OF AID FOR GENTLEPEOPLE

10 St Christopher's Place, London, W1U 1 HZ

Tel: 020 7935 0641
E-mail: thead@pcac.org.uk

Enquiries:
Enquiries to: Secretary

Founded:
1904

Organisation type and purpose:
National organisation, voluntary organisation,
registered charity (charity number 31/BEN).
Providing assistance to those of gentle birth and
good education.

Subject coverage:
Financial assistance to people of gentle birth and
good education that have fallen into poverty.

Printed publications:
Annual Report (free)

Access to staff:
Contact by letter and by telephone
Hours: Mon to Fri, 0930 to 1700

Access to building, collection or gallery:
No access other than to staff

Affiliated to:
Professional Classes Aid Council
  administered from the same address

GUILD OF AIR PILOTS AND AIR NAVIGATORS

Acronym or abbreviation: GAPAN

Cobham House, 9 Warwick Court, Gray's Inn,
London, WC1R 5DJ

Tel: 020 7404 4032
Fax: 020 7404 4035
E-mail: gapan@gapan.org

Website:
http://www.gapan.org

Enquiries:
Enquiries to: Clerk

Founded:
1929

Organisation type and purpose:
Professional body (membership is by subscription,
qualification, election or invitation), present
number of members: 1650, voluntary organisation,
suitable for ages: 17+.
Livery company of the City of London.
To promote air safety and aviation knowledge.

Subject coverage:
Air safety, aircrew licensing and training, technical
developments in aviation and the allocation of
flying scholarships and awards.

Access to staff:
Contact by letter, by fax, by e-mail and in person.
Appointment necessary.
Hours: Mon to Fri, 0900 to 1700

GUILD OF ALL SOULS

Acronym or abbreviation: GAS

86 Leadenhall Street, London, EC3A 3DH

Tel: 020 7621 0098
Fax: 01371 831430

Website:
http://www.guildofallsouls.org.uk

Enquiries:
Enquiries to: General Secretary

Founded:
1873

Organisation type and purpose:
Membership association (membership is by
subscription), present number of members: 1,400,
registered charity (charity number 240234).
Religious guild and patron of 40 livings.

**Museum or gallery collection, archive, or library
special collection:**
40 Advowson documents (some dating back to the
  18th century)

Access to staff:
Contact by letter, by telephone and by fax.
Appointment necessary. Access for members only.
Hours: Mon and Thu, 1030 to 1500

GUILD OF ANTIQUE DEALERS AND RESTORERS

Acronym or abbreviation: GADAR

111 Belle Vue Road, Shrewsbury, Shropshire, SY3
7NJ

Tel: 01743 271852

Enquiries:
Enquiries to: Membership Secretary
Other contacts: Chairman

Founded:
1989

Organisation type and purpose:
Advisory body, learned society, professional body,
trade association (membership is by subscription),
present number of members: 300, consultancy,
research organisation.
Advice to trade and public regarding restoration of
furniture, ceramics, glass, silver, paintings, etc.

Subject coverage:
All restoration to antiques. Information regarding
courses on restoration. Valuations for probate and
insurance.

**Museum or gallery collection, archive, or library
special collection:**
Reference books on all aspects of restoration and
  antiques

Printed publications:
Newsletter (quarterly, to members)

Access to staff:
Contact by letter, by telephone and in person
Hours: Mon and Fri, 0930 to 1700; 24-hour
answering service

Access to building, collection or gallery:
Prior appointment required

GUILD OF ARCHITECTURAL IRONMONGERS

Acronym or abbreviation: GAI

8 Stepney Green, London, E1 3JU

Tel: 020 7790 3431
Fax: 020 7790 8517
E-mail: info@gai.org.uk

Website:
http://www.gai.org.uk
Membership, standards, technical.

Enquiries:
Enquiries to: Chief Executive

Founded:
1961

Organisation type and purpose:
International organisation, trade association
(membership is by subscription), present number
of members: 400, service industry.

Subject coverage:
Architectural ironmongery and industry training.

Printed publications:
Manuals on hinges, locks, fittings etc

Publications list:
Available in print

Access to staff:
Contact by letter, by fax, by e-mail and via website
Hours: Mon to Fri, 0900 to 1700

GUILD OF BRITISH BUTLERS, ADMINISTRATORS AND PERSONAL ASSISTANTS

12 Little Bornes, Alleyn Park, Dulwich, London, SE21 8SE

Tel: 020 8670 5585
Fax: 020 8670 0055

Website:
http://www.ivorspencer.com

Enquiries:
Enquiries to: Chief Executive
Direct tel: 020 8670 5585

Founded:
1981

Organisation type and purpose:
Professional body, voluntary organisation, training organisation.

Subject coverage:
Controlling large households; banqueting; purchasing for large parties; training staff for service in hotels and private households; organisation of Royal and State banquets world-wide.

Access to staff:
Contact by letter, by telephone and by fax
Hours: Mon to Fri, 0900 to 1700

Links with:
Ivor Spencer School for Butler Administrators at the same address

GUILD OF BUILDERS AND CONTRACTORS

Crest House, 102–104 Church Road, Teddington, Middlesex, TW11 8PY

Tel: 020 8977 1105
Fax: 020 8943 3151
E-mail: info@buildersguild.co.uk

Website:
http://www.BuildersGuild.co.uk

Enquiries:
Enquiries to: Director General

Founded:
1992

Organisation type and purpose:
National organisation, trade association (membership is by subscription, election or invitation), present number of members: 1700.

Subject coverage:
Building.

Access to staff:
Contact by letter, by telephone, by fax and by e-mail
Hours: Mon to Fri, 0930 to 1600

Access to building, collection or gallery:
No access other than to staff

Access for disabled people:
Parking provided

GUILD OF CHURCH MUSICIANS

Acronym or abbreviation: GCM

Hillbrow, Godstone Road, Bletchingley, Surrey, RH1 4PJ

Tel: 01883 743168

E-mail: JohnMusicsure@orbix.co.uk

Enquiries:
Enquiries to: General Secretary

Founded:
1888

Formerly called:
Incorporated Guild of Church Musicians (IGCM) (year of change 1988)

Organisation type and purpose:
International organisation, professional body (membership is by election or invitation), present number of members: 700, registered charity, suitable for ages: all, training organisation. Examining body for Archbishop's Certificate in Church Music and Fellowship of the Guild of Church Musicians, and the Archbishop's Certificate in Public Worship.

Subject coverage:
Church music; administration of Archbishops' Certificates in Church Music and Public Worship, associate and fellowship examinations.

Non-library collection catalogue:
All or part available in print

Library catalogue:
All or part available in-house

Printed publications:
Guild Year Book
Laudate (magazine, 3 times a year)

Access to staff:
Contact by letter, by telephone, by e-mail and via website. Appointment necessary.
Hours: Mon to Fri, 0930 to 1800

Liaison with the:
Royal School of Church Music

Other addresses:
St Katharine Cree Church
86 Leadenhall Street, London, EC3; tel: 020 7283 5733

GUILD OF DISABLED HOMEWORKERS

23 Fountain Street, Nailsworth, Gloucestershire, GL6 0BL

Tel: 01453 835623
Fax: 01453 835623
E-mail: godcl@tiscali.co.uk

Enquiries:
Enquiries to: Membership Secretary

Founded:
1972

Subject coverage:
Homeworking for the disabled.

Access to staff:
Contact by letter, by telephone, by fax and by e-mail
Hours: Mon to Fri, 0930 to 1630

Access for disabled people:
Ramped entry

GUILD OF FOOD WRITERS

The Administrator, 255 Kent House Road, Beckenham, Kent, BR3 1JQ

Tel: 020 8659 0422
E-mail: guild@gfw.co.uk

Website:
http://www.gfw.co.uk

Enquiries:
Enquiries to: Administrator

Founded:
1984

Organisation type and purpose:
Professional body, membership association (membership is by subscription, election or invitation), present number of members: 350.

Publications list:
Available online

Access to staff:
Contact by letter, by telephone, by e-mail and via website
Hours: Mon to Fri, 0900 to 1700

GUILD OF FREEMEN OF THE CITY OF LONDON

PO Box 1202, Kingston upon Thames, Surrey, KT2 7XB

Tel: 020 8541 1435
Fax: 020 8541 1455
E-mail: clerk@guild-freemen-london.co.uk

Website:
http://www.guild-freemen-london.co.uk

Enquiries:
Enquiries to: The Clerk

Founded:
1908

Organisation type and purpose:
Membership association (membership is by subscription, qualification, election or invitation), present number of members: 2500.
Guild, whose Patron is The Lord Mayor of the City of London. Membership restricted to individuals having the freedom of the City of London.
To bring together Freemen of the City of London, for the purposes of Charity, Benevolence, Education and Social Activities.

Subject coverage:
History of Guild of the Freemen of the City of London and current information.

Printed publications:
History of Guild (£20)
Leaflet about Guild (free)
Annual Journal (£5)
Order printed publications from: The Clerk

Access to staff:
Contact by letter, by telephone, by fax, by e-mail and via website
Hours: Mon to Fri, 0900 to 1700

GUILD OF GLASS ENGRAVERS

Acronym or abbreviation: GGE

87 Nether Street, London, N12 7NP

Tel: 020 8446 4050
Fax: 020 8446 4050
E-mail: enquiries@gge.org.uk

Website:
http://www.gge.org.uk

Enquiries:
Enquiries to: Secretary

Founded:
1975

Organisation type and purpose:
International organisation, membership association (membership is by subscription), present number of members: 402, voluntary organisation, registered charity (charity number 1016162).

Subject coverage:
Glass engraving; methods, the copper wheel lathe, the hand-held stylus, acid etch, electrically driven hand-held drill.

Museum or gallery collection, archive, or library special collection:
Albums of photographs of Fellows' and Associate Fellows' engraved glass (available for inspection by appointment)
Books, slides, videos and films on different techniques of glass engraving

Printed publications:
Annual Report (members only)
Membership and suppliers lists (members only)

continued overleaf

Quarterly Journal (available to members of the
Guild only)

Access to staff:
Contact by letter, by telephone, by fax and by e-mail
Hours: Mon, 0930 to 1500; Tue, 0930 to 1700; Wed,
0930 to 1430

GUILD OF HANDICRAFT TRUST

Acronym or abbreviation: GofHT

6 The Old Coach, High Street, Broadway, WR12
7AY

Tel: 01386 859135/858180
E-mail: gofhtrust@ukonline.co.uk

Enquiries:
Enquiries to: Secretary

Founded:
1990

Organisation type and purpose:
Registered charity (charity number 1007696),
museum, suitable for ages: 5+.
Collections of material relating to art, craft and
design in Chipping Campden and the North
Cotswolds.
To preserve, promote and encourage an
understanding of the work of artists, craftsmen
and women, and designers of Chipping Campden
and the North Cotswolds.

Subject coverage:
Information and material relating: to C R Ashbee's
Guild of Handicraft in Chipping Campden 1902–
1919; R Welch (silversmith and product designer);
and others associated with the area e.g. Alec Miller
(woodcarver/sculptor), George Hart (silversmith)
and Paul Woodroffe (stained glass/book
illustrator). Information relating to F L Griggs, RA
(etcher/engraver) and Gordon Russell (furniture
designer and maker).

Non-library collection catalogue:
All or part available in-house

Printed publications:
A range of publications on sale at the Guild or by
post (plus p&p):
A Child in Arcadia. The Chipping Campden
boyhood of H T Osborn 1902–07 (£5)
Wilgress, J. Alec Miller: Guildsman & Sculptor in
Chipping Campden (£5)
Robert Welch: Designer-Silversmith. Catalogue of
the Retrospective Exhibition 1955–1995 (£2)
Crawford, Alan Arts and Crafts Walks in
Broadway and Chipping Campden (£8.95)

Publications list:
Available in print

Access to staff:
Contact by letter, by telephone and by e-mail.
Appointment necessary.
Hours: Any reasonable time.

GUILD OF INTERNATIONAL
BANKERS

Formal name: Guild of International Bankers

The Guild of International Bankers, 1 Bengal
Court, London, EC3V 9DD

Tel: 020 7337 1307
Fax: 020 7283 8302
E-mail: tim.woods@internationalbankers.co.uk

Website:
http://www.internationalbankers.co.uk

Enquiries:
Enquiries to: The Clerk
Direct tel: 020 7337 1307
Direct e-mail: tim.woods@internationalbankers.co
.uk

Organisation type and purpose:
Membership association (membership is by
election or invitation).
City of London Livery Company.

Access to staff:
Contact by letter, by telephone, by fax, by e-mail
and via website

GUILD OF INTERNATIONAL
PROFESSIONAL TOASTMASTERS

12 Little Bornes, Alleyn Park, Dulwich, London,
SE21 8SE

Tel: 020 8670 5585
Fax: 020 8670 0055

Website:
http://www.ivorspencer.com

Enquiries:
Enquiries to: Life President
Direct tel: 020 8670 8424

Founded:
1992

Formerly called:
Guild of Professional Toastmasters (year of change
1992)

Organisation type and purpose:
Advisory body, professional body.

Subject coverage:
Organisation of functions of all types, including
Royal events, in the UK and abroad; award of Best
Speaker of the Year.

Access to staff:
Contact by letter and by telephone
Hours: Mon to Fri, 0900 to 1700

Links with:
Guild of Professional After Dinner Speakers

GUILD OF MACE-BEARERS

C/o The Mayor's Parlour, The Town Hall,
Katharine Street, Croydon, CR9 1XW

Tel: 020 8760 5764
Fax: 020 8633 9517
E-mail: guildclerk.pa@virgin.net

Enquiries:
Enquiries to: Guild Clerk

Founded:
1933

Organisation type and purpose:
National organisation, membership association
(membership is by subscription), present number
of members: 350.

Subject coverage:
Ceremonial activities, protocol matters and advice,
toastmastering duties, chauffeuring duties.

Access to staff:
Contact by fax and by e-mail
Hours: Monday to Friday, 0900 to 1700

GUILD OF NATUROPATHIC
IRIDOLOGISTS INTERNATIONAL

Acronym or abbreviation: GNI Int

94 Grosvenor Road, London, SW1V 3LF

Tel: 020 7821 0255
Fax: 020 7821 0255
E-mail: info@gni-international.org

Website:
http://www.gni-international.org
History, mechanics and illustration on iridology.
Situations vacant, events etc. Register.

Enquiries:
Enquiries to: Vice President and Registrar
Other contacts: Managing Director, General
Secretary

Founded:
1993

Formerly called:
Holistic Health Consultancy and College (year of
change 1993); British Register of Iridologists
(MBRI) (year of change 1997); UK College of
Clinical Iridologists (year of change 1999)

Organisation type and purpose:
International organisation, advisory body,
professional body (membership is by
qualification), present number of members: 120 +
84 Licentiates + 62 Student members, training
organisation, research organisation.
Now the UK's only umbrella body for iridologists.
Affiliates 11 training colleges.

Subject coverage:
Iridology, naturopathic medicine, herbal medicine,
nutrition.

**Museum or gallery collection, archive, or library
special collection:**
Iridiagnosis (Kritzer, J Maskel MD, original
   manuscript)
Prospectuses re Accredited Training Courses
Teaching Models
EU & US Iridology Books

Trade and statistical information:
Data on recognised professional training courses,
   events and post-graduate training dates and
   venues.

Non-library collection catalogue:
All or part available in print

Library catalogue:
All or part available in-house

Printed publications:
Course Material for Holistic Health College: 19
   modules over 2 years (£150 per module)
Prospectus re training courses (send £2 in stamps)
Pupillotonia and Pupil Manifestations by Peter
   Bradbury
Register of Professionally Qualified Practitioners
Register and Information pack (send large sae)
Code of Ethics
Constitution
Newsletters (2 times a year)

Electronic and video publications:
1998 International Iridology Symposium
Videos: Aloe Vera, ME, Herbal Dispensaries
   Management (on hire only)

Publications list:
Available online and in print

Access to staff:
Contact by letter, by telephone, by fax, by e-mail
and in person. Appointment necessary. Access for
members only.
Hours: Mon to Wed, 0900 to 1700; Thu and Fri, 0800
to 1100
Special comments: Telephone Monday to
Wednesday only.

Access to building, collection or gallery:
Prior appointment required

Access for disabled people:
Access to all public areas, toilet facilities

GUILD OF ONE-NAME STUDIES

Acronym or abbreviation: GOONS

Box G, 14 Charterhouse Buildings, Goswell Road,
London, EC1M 7BA

Tel: 0800 011 2182
E-mail: guild@one-name.org

Website:
http://www.one-name.org

Enquiries:
Enquiries to: Secretary

Founded:
1979

Organisation type and purpose:
International organisation, membership association (membership is by subscription), present number of members: 2,000, registered charity (charity number 802048). Furtherance of family history.

Subject coverage:
Study of surnames.

Printed publications:
Information brochures
Journal of One-Name Studies
Register of One-Name Studies

Publications list:
Available in print

Access to staff:
Contact by letter, by telephone, by e-mail and via website
Hours: 24 hours

GUILD OF PHOTOGRAPHERS (UNITED KINGDOM)

Acronym or abbreviation: GWP

59 Fore Street, Trowbridge, Wiltshire, BA14 8ET

Tel: 01225 760088
Fax: 01225 759159
E-mail: info@gwp-uk.co.uk

Website:
http://www.gwp-uk.co.uk
Advice on choosing a wedding photographer.
Listing of qualified members.

Enquiries:
Enquiries to: Administrator

Founded:
1988

Formerly called:
Guild of Wedding Photographers UK (year of change 1999)

Organisation type and purpose:
Membership association (membership is by subscription), present number of members: 1200, service industry, suitable for ages: 18+, training organisation.
Training, qualifying and marketing services for photographers engaged in wedding and portrait photography.

Subject coverage:
Photography at weddings and other similar social functions in the UK and overseas.

Printed publications:
Big Marketing Ideas for Wedding Photographers (monthly, members only)
How to Choose Your Wedding Photographer booklet (free to members of the public)
News Sheet (monthly, members only)
Wedding Photography Today (monthly, members only)

Electronic and video publications:
Training Videos (available to members)

Publications list:
Available in print

Access to staff:
Contact by letter, by telephone, by fax, by e-mail and via website
Hours: Mon to Fri, 0900 to 1730

GUILD OF PROFESSIONAL VIDEOGRAPHERS

Acronym or abbreviation: GPV

11 Telfer Road, Coventry, Warwickshire, CV6 3DG

Tel: 024 7627 2548
Fax: 024 7627 2548
E-mail: info@professional-videographers.co.uk

Website:
http://www.professional-videographers.co.uk

Enquiries:
Enquiries to: General Secretary

Founded:
1991

Organisation type and purpose:
Advisory body, trade association (membership is by subscription, qualification), present number of members: 215, training organisation.

Subject coverage:
Information concerning copyright law. Investigations into new equipment available. Widespread international freelance videographers available for work.

Access to staff:
Contact by letter, by telephone, by fax, by e-mail, in person and via website
Hours: Mon to Fri, 0900 to 1700

GUILD OF PSYCHOTHERAPISTS, THE

47 Nelson Square, London, SE1 0QA

Tel: 020 8540 4454
E-mail: guild@psycho.org.uk

Website:
http://www.psycho.org.uk
Prospectus and events.

Enquiries:
Enquiries to: Administrator

Founded:
1974

Organisation type and purpose:
Professional body, registered charity, training organisation.

Subject coverage:
All aspects of training in psychoanalytic psychotherapy leading to UKCP registration. Referrals to psychoanalytic psychotherapists.

Printed publications:
List of Practitioners
Prospectus

Access to staff:
Contact by letter
Hours: Mon to Fri, 0900 to 1700

Member of:
UK Council for Psychotherapy Psychoanalytic and Psychodynamic Psychotherapy Section, 167–169 Great Portland Street, London, WIN 5FB; tel: 020 7436 3002; fax: 020 7436 3013; e-mail: ukcp@psychotherapy.org .uk

GUILD OF REGISTERED TOURIST GUIDES

Guild House, 52D Borough High Street, London, SE1 1XN

Tel: 020 7403 1115
Fax: 020 7378 1705
E-mail: guild@blue-badge.org.uk

Website:
http://www.visitbritain.com
http://www.blue-badge.org.uk

Enquiries:
Enquiries to: Office Manager

Founded:
1950

Formerly called:
Guild of Guide Lecturers (GGL) (year of change 1995)

Organisation type and purpose:
National organisation, advisory body, membership association (membership is by subscription, qualification), present number of members: 1800, voluntary organisation.

The Guild is the national professional association for tourist board registered guides in the United Kingdom.
It represents 1800 guides in England, Northern Ireland, Scotland, Wales, Jersey and the Isle of Man, who between them speak 38 different languages.

Subject coverage:
Tourism, guide training, organisation of tours, sources of information for tourist guides and tour operators, tourist guides, the languages spoken, special interests offered.

Printed publications:
Guide Post (newsletter, monthly)
Subscriber's Bulletin (newsletter, monthly)
The Guild Directory – Annual List of Registered Guides
The Guide's Guides

Publications list:
Available online and in print

Access to staff:
Contact by letter, by telephone, by fax, by e-mail and via website. Appointment necessary.
Hours: Mon to Fri, 0900 to 1700

Member of:
Federation of European Guides
London and Regional Tourist Boards
World Federation of Tourist Guides

GUILD OF TAXIDERMISTS

Acronym or abbreviation: GOT

Glasgow Museums Resource Centre, 200 Woodhead Road, South Nitshill, Glasgow, G53 7NN

Tel: 0141 276 9445/9311
Fax: 0141 276 9305
E-mail: duncan.ferguson@cls.glasgow.gov.uk

Enquiries:
Enquiries to: Honorary Secretary

Founded:
1976

Organisation type and purpose:
International organisation, membership association (membership is by subscription), present number of members: 210, voluntary organisation, museum, suitable for ages: all, training organisation, consultancy.

Subject coverage:
Taxidermy and natural history display work.

Museum or gallery collection, archive, or library special collection:
Photograph library plus slide collection covering many techniques

Printed publications:
Careers in taxidermy (free)
Information sheets on the purpose and work of the Guild (free)
Newsletter/journal (annually)

Access to staff:
Contact by letter, by telephone, by fax, by e-mail and in person. Appointment necessary.
Hours: Mon to Fri, 0900 to 1700

Member of:
European Taxidermy Federation at the same address

GUILD OF TRAVEL AND TOURISM

Suite 193 Temple Chambers, 3–7 Temple Avenue, London, EC4Y 0DB

Tel: 020 7583 6333
E-mail: nigel.bishop@traveltourismguild.com

Website:
http://www.traveltourismguild.com

Enquiries:
Enquiries to: Chief Executive

continued overleaf

Founded:
1994

Organisation type and purpose:
Travel industry trade association.

Printed publications:
The Travel Business

GUILDFORD BOROUGH COUNCIL

Millmead House, Millmead, Guildford, Surrey, GU2 4BB

Tel: 01483 505050
Fax: 01483 444444

Website:
http://www.guildford.gov.uk/

Enquiries:
Enquiries to: Chief Executive

Organisation type and purpose:
Local government body.

Printed publications:
About Guildford

Access to staff:
Contact by letter, by telephone, by fax, by e-mail and in person
Hours: Mon to Fri, 0900 to 1700

Access to building, collection or gallery:
Mon to Wed, 0830 to 1700; Thu, 0830 to 2000; Fri, 0830 to 1630

Access for disabled people:
Parking spaces, lift, stair-lift

Parent body:
Surrey County Council

GUILDFORD COLLEGE OF FURTHER AND HIGHER EDUCATION

Stoke Park, Guildford, Surrey, GU1 1EZ

Tel: 01483 448611
Fax: 01483 448606

Website:
http://www.guildford.ac.uk

Enquiries:
Enquiries to: Librarian
Direct e-mail: dmarshall@guildford.ac.uk

Organisation type and purpose:
Further Education College.

Subject coverage:
Health, social studies, education, mathematics, engineering, catering, management, business studies, computing, travel and tourism, geography, sport, leisure, media studies, art, graphic, printing, science, construction, humanities.

Library catalogue:
All or part available in-house

Printed publications:
Guides to the Library
List of Journals (annually)
New Additions to Stock (selective)

Access to staff:
Contact by letter, by telephone, by e-mail, in person and via website
Hours: Term time: Mon to Thu, 0830 to 2000; Fri, 0830 to 1700; Sat, 1000 to 1300

Access for disabled people:
Toilet facilities
Special comments: Lift available

GUILDFORD INSTITUTE

Ward Street, Guildford, Surrey, GU1 4LH

Tel: 01483 562142
Fax: 01483 451034
E-mail: info@guildford-institute.org.uk

Website:
www.guildford-institute.org.uk

Enquiries:
Enquiries to: Manager

Founded:
1834

Organisation type and purpose:
The Guildford Institute is registered in England and Wales as a Company limited by guarantee (Company number 6571640; registered charity number 1125031). Educational institute and library. Membership organisation (membership by subscription).

Subject coverage:
A selection of the latest fiction and non-fiction and a unique local history collection.

Museum or gallery collection, archive, or library special collection:
Library of 13,000 vols, newspapers, periodicals, local history books, ephemera, photographs, prints and drawings relating to the history, people, antiquities and topography of Guildford and the county of Surrey.
The institutional archive is held by the Surrey History Service: 130 Goldsworth Road, Woking, Surrey, GU21 1ND.

Printed publications:
Journal (2 times a year; free to members). Course booklets termly. Activities booklet distributed spring/summer/winter.

Access to staff:
Contact by letter, by telephone, by e-mail and in person. Non-members charged.
Hours: Tue to Fri, 1000 to 1500; Sat, 1000 to 1300
Special comments: Closed Mon.

GUILDHALL LIBRARY

Aldermanbury, London, EC2V 7HH

Tel: 020 7332 1868/1870 (printed books), 1839 (print room), 1863 (manuscripts)
Fax: 020 7600 3384
E-mail: printedbooks.guildhall@cityoflondon.gov.uk

Website:
http://www.cityoflondon.gov.uk/guildhalllibrary

Enquiries:
Enquiries to: Printed Books Librarian

Founded:
1820

Organisation type and purpose:
Local government body, public library.

Subject coverage:
London history, English topography, local societies, historical horology, historical technology, clockmaking, maritime history, cookery, wine trade, genealogy, parliamentary and statutory materials, business history, English law reports, history of shorthand.

Museum or gallery collection, archive, or library special collection:
Acts (public, private and local)
Antiquarian Horological Society Library
Clockmakers' Company Library
Alfred Cock Collection (Thomas More)
English Law Reports from the 17th century onwards
Fletchers' Company Library (archery)
Gardeners' Company Library
Gresham College Collection (early music)
Elizabeth David Collection (food and wine)
Institute of Masters of Wine Library
International Genealogical Index (microfiche) compiled by the Church of Jesus Christ of the Latter-Day Saints: British Isles and Ireland
International Wine and Food Society Library
Charles Lamb Society Collection
Lloyds Marine Collection
Sir Thomas More Collection
Parliamentary Papers from 1801
Public Record Office Publications
André Simon Collection (food and wine)
Stock Exchange Reports and Prospectuses c.1824–1964
Pepys Collection
Wilkes Collection (John Wilkes and 18th-century radical history)

Library catalogue:
All or part available online and in-house

Printed publications:
City of London Parish Registers
Facsimiles of Early London Maps
Greater London Parish Registers
Gresham Music Library Catalogue
City Livery Companies and Related Organisations
A Guide to Archives and Manuscripts at Guildhall Library
A Guide to Genealogical Sources in the Guildhall Library
A Guide to Lloyd's Marine Collection at Guildhall Library
A Hand List of Business Archives at Guildhall Library
A Hand List of Non-conformist, Roman Catholic, Jewish and Burial Ground Registers at Guildhall Library
Mediaeval Guildhall of London (1974)
London Buildings and Sites: A Guide for Researchers in Guildhall Library
Historic Trade Directories in Guildhall Library

Publications list:
Available in print

Access to staff:
Contact by letter, by telephone, by fax, by e-mail and in person

Access to building, collection or gallery:
No prior appointment required
Hours: Mon to Sat, 0930 to 1700; print room closed Sat

Access for disabled people:
Ramped entry, access to all public areas, toilet facilities

Parent body:
City of London Corporation

GUILDHALL SCHOOL OF MUSIC AND DRAMA

Acronym or abbreviation: GSMD

Silk Street, Barbican, London, EC2Y 8DT

Tel: 020 7382 7178
Fax: 020 7786 9378
E-mail: library@gsmd.ac.uk

Website:
http://www.gsmd.ac.uk

Enquiries:
Enquiries to: Senior Librarian
Direct tel: 020 7382 7174
Direct e-mail: keaton@gsmd.ac.uk
Other contacts: Deputy Librarian

Founded:
1880

Organisation type and purpose:
Suitable for ages: 18+ (HE).
Conservatoire of music and drama.

Subject coverage:
Music, drama.

Museum or gallery collection, archive, or library special collection:
Alkan Society Collection (material on or by Charles Alkan)
Appleby Collection of guitar music
Goossens Collection of oboe music
Harris Opera Collection
Lute Society Collection of art reproductions depicting early instruments
Merrett Collection of double bass music
Westrup Library of music and books on music

Non-library collection catalogue:
All or part available in-house

Library catalogue:
All or part available in-house

Printed publications:
Various Guides to the Library

Access to staff:
Contact by letter, by telephone, by e-mail and in person. Appointment necessary.
Hours: Mon to Fri, 0900 to 1900

Access to building, collection or gallery:
Prior appointment required

Parent body:
Corporation of London

GUN TRADE ASSOCIATION LIMITED

Acronym or abbreviation: GTA

PO Box 43, Tewkesbury, Gloucestershire, GL20 5ZE

Tel: 01684 291868
Fax: 01684 291864
E-mail: enquiries@guntradeassociation.com

Enquiries:
Enquiries to: Director
Direct e-mail: john@guntradeassociation.com

Founded:
1912

Organisation type and purpose:
Trade association.
Represents all sectors of the British sporting gun and allied trades.

Subject coverage:
The manufacture, supply and legitimate use of firearms and ammunition, the law relating to the above.

Printed publications:
Newsletter (6 times a year, members only)
Occasional publications
The Official Gun Trade Association Handbook

Access to staff:
Contact by letter, by fax and by e-mail
Hours: Mon to Fri, 0900 to 1700

Access to building, collection or gallery:
No access to building.

Member of:
British Shooting Sports Council
European Association for the Civil Commerce of Weapons
Standing Conference on Countryside Sports
World Forum on the Future of Sport Shooting Activities

GUT TRUST

Unit 5, 53 Mowbray Street, Sheffield, S3 8EN

Tel: 0114 272 3253
E-mail: info@theguttrust.org
Website:
http://www.theguttrust.org

Enquiries:
Enquiries to: Membership Officer
Direct e-mail: debbie@theguttrust.org

Founded:
1991

Formerly called:
IBS Network (year of change 2007)

Organisation type and purpose:
Membership association (membership is by subscription), voluntary organisation, registered charity (charity number 1057563).
A self-help organisation.
To inform, support and educate those with IBS.

Subject coverage:
Irritable bowel syndrome.

Museum or gallery collection, archive, or library special collection:
Art Works: entries to Living with IBS competition (2000, 2001)
Assorted books on IBS
Gut Reaction Journal (issue 1 to date)

Non-library collection catalogue:
All or part available in-house

Printed publications:
A Complete Guide to Relief from IBS (C. Dancey and S. Backhouse)
Fact Sheets (direct)
Gut Reaction (journal, quarterly, free to members, direct, back issues available)
Order printed publications from: A Complete Guide To Relief, order from IBS, Robinson Publishing, 7 Kensington Church Court, London, W8 4SP

Electronic and video publications:
Feeling Better Relaxed (CD)

Publications list:
Available online and in print

Access to staff:
Contact by letter, by telephone, by e-mail and via website
Hours: Office: Mon to Fri, 1000 to 1500
Helpline: Mon to Fri, 1800 to 2100; Sat, 1000 to 1200

Access to building, collection or gallery:
Prior appointment required

GUYANA HIGH COMMISSION

3 Palace Court, Bayswater Road, London, W2 4LP

Tel: 020 7229 7684
Fax: 020 7727 9809
E-mail: ghc.1@ic24.net

Enquiries:
Enquiries to: First Secretary

Organisation type and purpose:
National body of the Republic of Guyana.
Guyana's diplomatic representation.

Subject coverage:
Political, social, economic and cultural aspects of Guyana.

Access to staff:
Contact by letter, by telephone, by fax and by e-mail
Hours: Office Hours: Mon to Fri, 0930 to 1730
Consular Matters: Mon to Fri, 0930 to 1430

GUYS' AND ST THOMAS' POISONS UNIT, GUY'S AND ST THOMAS' NHS FOUNDATION TRUST

Acronym or abbreviation: GTPU

Wardell's Grove, Avonley Road, New Cross, London, SE14 5ER

Tel: 020 7771 5364
Fax: 020 7771 5363
E-mail: medtoxlibrary@gstt.nhs.uk

Website:
http://www.medtox.org

Organisation type and purpose:
National government body.
Poisons centre; unit of the National Health Service and part of Guy's and St Thomas' NHS Foundation Trust.

Subject coverage:
Medical toxicology, pharmacology, analytical chemistry, drug detection, therapeutic drug monitoring, addiction, drug abuse.

Information services:
Poisons information service

Library catalogue:
All or part available in-house

Access to staff:
Contact by letter, by telephone, by fax, by e-mail and via website. Appointment necessary.
Hours: Mon to Fri, 0930 to 1730

Access to building, collection or gallery:
24 hours' notice required
Hours: Mon to Fri, 0930 to 1730
Special comments: Researchers and NHS staff only

Connected with:
Guy's and St Thomas' NHS Foundation Trust
St Thomas' Hospital, Lambeth Palace Road, London, SE1 7EH; tel: 020 7188 7188; website: http://www.gstt.nhs.uk

GWE BUSINESS WEST LTD

Emlyn Square, Swindon, SN1 5BP

Tel: 01275 373373
Fax: 01275 370 706
E-mail: info@gwebusinesswest.co.uk

Website:
http://www.gwebusinesswest.co.uk
Details of a range of business support (inc training, workspace, venue hire) and Chamber of Commerce services provided by or via GWE Business West Ltd.

Enquiries:
Enquiries to: Receptionist

Founded:
2008

Created by the merger of:
Great Western Enterprise (GWE) Ltd and Business West (year of change 2008)

Organisation type and purpose:
Business support and chamber membership

Subject coverage:
Bath and Bristol Chambers of Commerce; office space to let; virtual office services; meeting room hire; conferencing facilities and venue hire; business training (courses and bespoke); mentoring; international trade advice and support; event management; networking; business advice; business workshops; business information.

Printed publications:
What's On
Business I
Update Magazine

Access to staff:
Contact via website

Branches:
Bristol Chamber of Commerce
Leigh Court, Abbey Meads, Bristol, BS8 3RA; tel: 01275 373373; website: http://www.gwebusinesswest.co.uk
Business Link (Berkshire)
The Crossbow Centre, Crossbow House, 40 Liverpool Road, Slough, Berkshire, SL1 4QZ; tel: 0845 600 9 006; website: http://www.gwebusinesswest.co.uk

Links with:
Bath Chamber of Commerce
16 Abbey Churchyard, Bath, BA1 1PB; website: http://www.gwebusinesswest.co.uk
Business Link (South West)
Leigh Court, Abbey Meads, Bristol, BS8 3RA; tel: 0845 600 9 006; website: http://www.gwebusinesswest.co.uk

GWENT LOCAL HISTORY SOCIETY

Ty Derwen, Church Road, Newport, NP19 7EJ

Tel: 01633 241564
E-mail: karen.vowles@gavowales.org.uk

Website:
http://www.gavowales.org.uk/gwent_local_history/index.htm

Enquiries:
Enquiries to: Secretary

continued overleaf

Founded:
1954

Organisation type and purpose:
Voluntary organisation.
Provides forum for local history societies within Gwent.

Subject coverage:
Gwent local history.

Printed publications:
Gwent Local History journal (2 times a year)

Access to staff:
Contact by letter, by telephone, by fax and by e-mail
Hours: Mon to Fri, 0900 to 1700

Member of:
British Association of Local History

GWENT RECORD OFFICE

Acronym or abbreviation: GRO

County Hall, Cwmbran, Newport, Gwent, NP44 2XH

Tel: 01633 644886
Fax: 01633 648382
E-mail: gwent.records@torfaen.gov.uk

Founded:
1939

Formerly called:
Monmouthshire Record Office (year of change 1974)

Organisation type and purpose:
Local government body.
County record office.

Subject coverage:
Public records; manorial and tithe records; turnpike trusts; highways boards; health and services records; estate and family records; church parochial records etc.

Museum or gallery collection, archive, or library special collection:
Archive

Non-library collection catalogue:
All or part available in-house

Printed publications:
Guides to Research (on selected subjects)

Access to staff:
Contact by letter, by telephone, by fax, by e-mail, in person and via website
Hours: Tue to Thu, 0930 to 1700; Fri, 0930 to 1600

Access for disabled people:
Hours: Tue to Thu, 0930 to 1700; Fri, 0930 to 1600

Host authority:
Torfaen County Borough Council
  Civic Centre, Pontypool, Torfaen, NP4 6YB; tel: 01495 762200; fax: 01495 755513; website: www .torfaen.gov.uk

Parent body:
Gwent Joint Records Committee

GWENT WILDLIFE TRUST

16 White Swan Court, Monmouth, Gwent, NP25 3NY

Tel: 01600 715501
Fax: 01600 715832
E-mail: gwentwildlife@cix.co.uk

Website:
http://www.wildlifetrust.org.uk

Enquiries:
Enquiries to: Chairman

Organisation type and purpose:
Membership association (membership is by subscription), present number of members: 2500, voluntary organisation.
Aims to protect and enhance wildlife sites in Gwent.

Subject coverage:
Conservation management, species protection, site protection and enhancement, ecological surveying, advice and education, trust nature reserves, Gwent wildlife.

Trade and statistical information:
Species recording, site recording.

Printed publications:
Wild about Gwent (newsletter, Jan, May and Sep)

Affiliated to:
RSNC and Wildlife Trusts Partnership

Education Centre:
Gwent Wildlife Trust
  Festival Park, Ebbw Vale, NP23 6UF; tel: 01495 305289

GWYNEDD ARCHIVES & MUSEUMS SERVICE

Victoria Dock, Caernarfon, Gwynedd

Tel: 01286 679095
Fax: 01286 679637
E-mail: archives.caernarfon@gwynedd.gov.uk

Website:
http://www.gwynedd.gov.uk/archives

Enquiries:
Enquiries to: Archivist

Organisation type and purpose:
County Record Office.

Subject coverage:
Usual county archive collection with particular strengths in the industrial (quarrying), maritime and estate records.

Education services:
Group education facilities, resources for Key Stages 1 and 2 and 3.

Non-library collection catalogue:
All or part available online and in-house

Publications list:
Available online

Access to staff:
Contact by telephone, by fax, by e-mail and in person
Hours: Closed Mon; Tue, Thu, Fri, 0930 to 1230 and 1330 to 1700; Wed, 0930 to 1230 and 1330 to 1900

Access to building, collection or gallery:
No prior appointment required
Hours: Closed Mon; open Tue, Thu, Fri, 0930 to 1230 and 1330 to 1700; Wed, 0930 to 1230 and 1330 to 1900
Special comments: CARN readers ticket required. Appointment advised for microfiche and microfilm readers

Access for disabled people:
Level entry, access to all public areas, toilet facilities

Other address:
Gwynedd Archives
  Dolgellau Area Record Office

GWYNEDD COUNTY COUNCIL

Development Directorate, Culture and Leisure, County Offices, Caernarfon, Gwynedd, LL55 1SH

Tel: 01286 672255
Fax: 01286 677347
E-mail: celf@gwynedd.gov.uk

Website:
http://www.gwynedd.gov.uk
County information, arts information, archive lists, library catalogue.

Enquiries:
Enquiries to: Assistant Director: Culture

Founded:
1996

Formerly called:
Arfon Borough Council, Dwyfor District Council, Gwynedd County Council, Meirionydd District Council (year of change 1996)

Organisation type and purpose:
Local government body, museum, art gallery, public library, suitable for ages: 4 to 18.
Archives, arts organisation.

Subject coverage:
General reference materials, local history, county archives, artefacts.

Museum or gallery collection, archive, or library special collection:
County archives collections
European Community publications
Local history collections
Maritime records, including Lloyd's Registers, Lloyd's Lists, registers, crew lists and log books
Reports, Hansard etc of Welsh Assembly
Welsh periodicals and local newspapers

Non-library collection catalogue:
All or part available online and in-house

Library catalogue:
All or part available online

Printed publications:
Maritime Wales (annually)
Series of lectures, picture books, postcards etc

Access to staff:
Contact by letter, by telephone, by fax, by e-mail and in person
Hours: Mon to Fri, 0900 to 1700; late nights to 1900
Library also Sat, 1000 to 1300

Access to building, collection or gallery:
No access other than to staff

Other addresses:
Archives and Museum Service
  County Offices, Caernarfon, Gwynedd; tel: 01286 679093; fax: 01286 679637; e-mail: archifau@gwynedd.gov.uk
County Library Headquarters
  Allt Pafiliwn, Caernarfon, Gwynedd; tel: 01286 679465; fax: 01286 671137; e-mail: llyfrgell@ gwynedd.gov.uk

GYPSUM PRODUCTS DEVELOPMENT LIMITED

Acronym or abbreviation: GPDA

PO Box 35084, London, NW1 4XE

Tel: 020 7935 8532
E-mail: admin@gpda.com

Website:
http://www.gpda.com

Enquiries:
Enquiries to: General Secretary

Founded:
1889

Organisation type and purpose:
Trade association (membership is by subscription).

Subject coverage:
Gypsum product usage (gypsum plaster, plasterboard); mainly in the fields of building and refurbishment.

Printed publications:
Publications on specific areas of gypsum product usage (irregular, free)

Publications list:
Available online

Access to staff:
Contact by letter, by telephone, by fax, by e-mail and via website
Hours: Mon to Fri, 0900 to 1700

Links with:
Construction Products Association
  tel: 020 7323 3770; fax: 020 7323 0307; e-mail: enquiries@constprod.org.uk; website: http:// www.constrprod.org.uk

Eurogypsum (European Gypsum Industry Association)
tel: +32 2 521 3890; e-mail: info@eurogypsum .org; website: http://www.eurogypsum.org

GYPSY COUNCIL, THE

Acronym or abbreviation: NGC

Greenacres Caravan Park, Common Lane, Hapsford, Frodsham, Cheshire, WA6 0JS

Tel: 01928 723138
Fax: 01928 723138

Enquiries:
Enquiries to: President

Founded:
1966

Formerly called:
National Gypsy Council (NGC)

Organisation type and purpose:
Voluntary organisation.
Membership restricted to Gypsies as defined in legislation.

Subject coverage:
Site provision for travellers, including information of site facilities, design and management; statistical information on numbers of Gypsy families in England, Wales and Scotland; existing sites and sites needed; movement of travellers; development and diversity of the travelling community in Britain; Gypsies and government policy; Gypsies and local government; Gypsy education; new age travellers, hippies.

Printed publications:
Annual Report
Gipsy Sites and Planning: an Objective Criticism of the DOE Circular 1/94 (no 2/94)
Practical Proposals for Gypsy/Traveller Law Reform (a discussion paper 1997)
Responses to government policies and documents including
Response to the Criminal Justice and Public Order Bill
Romano Drom (Gypsy News, back issues)

Publications list:
Available in print

Access to staff:
Contact by letter, by telephone and by fax
Hours: Mon to Fri, 0900 to 1700

Links with:
Romani Kris (West European Gypsy Council)

H C STARCK LIMITED

Acronym or abbreviation: HCST

UK Sales Office, Aizlewood's Mill, Nursery Street, Sheffield, S3 8GG

Tel: 0114 282 3158
E-mail: malcolm.greaves@hcstarck.com

Website:
http://www.hcstarck.com

Founded:
1969

Organisation type and purpose:
International organisation, manufacturing industry.

Subject coverage:
Refractory metals; corrosion-resistant metals e.g. tantalum, titanium, tungsten, hastelloy, zirconium, molybdenum, nickel and nickel alloys.

Printed publications:
Order printed publications from: HC Starck Inc
e-mail: Website: www.hcstarck.com

Publications list:
Available online

Access to staff:
Contact by letter, by telephone, by fax, by e-mail and via website. Appointment necessary.

Hours: Mon to Fri, 0900 to 1700

Access to building, collection or gallery:
Prior appointment required

Subsidiary of:
H C Starck Inc (HCSI)
45 Industrial Place, Newton, MA 0241–1951, USA; tel: 00 1 617 630 5800; fax: 00 1 617 630 5919; website: www.hcstarck.com

UK production site:
H C Starck Limited
1 Harris Road, Calne, Wiltshire, SN11 9PT; tel: 01249 822122; fax: 01249 823800

H G WELLS SOCIETY, THE

Acronym or abbreviation: HGWS

56 Riseholme Road, Gainsborough, Lincolnshire, DN21 1YT

E-mail: stevemclean_7@hotmail.com

Website:
http://hgwellsusa.50megs.com

Enquiries:
Enquiries to: General Secretary

Founded:
1960

Organisation type and purpose:
International organisation, learned society.
To promote and encourage an interest in, and appreciation of, the life, work and thought of H G Wells.

Subject coverage:
The life and work of Herbert George Wells (1866–1946).

Printed publications:
The Wellsian (annually)
The H G Wells Newsletter (quarterly)

Access to staff:
Contact by letter
Hours: Mon to Fri, 0900 to 1700

HABERDASHERS' COMPANY, THE

Formal name: Worshipful Company of Haberdashers

Haberdashers' Hall, 18 West Smithfield, London, EC1A 9HQ

Tel: 020 7246 9988
Fax: 020 7246 9989
E-mail: enquiries@haberdashers.co.uk

Website:
http://www.haberdashers.co.uk

Enquiries:
Enquiries to: The Clerk

Founded:
1448

Organisation type and purpose:
Membership association (membership is by election or invitation).
City of London Livery Company.

Access to staff:
Contact by letter, by telephone, by fax and by e-mail

HACKNEY ARCHIVES DEPARTMENT

43 De Beauvoir Road, London, N1 5SQ

Tel: 020 7241 2886
Fax: 020 7241 6688
E-mail: archives@hackney.gov.uk

Website:
http://www.hackney.gov.uk/ca-archives
Guide.

Enquiries:
Enquiries to: Archivist

Founded:
1965

Organisation type and purpose:
Local government body.
Record office.

Non-library collection catalogue:
All or part available online, in-house and in print

Library catalogue:
All or part available online and in-house

Publications list:
Available online and in print

Access to staff:
Contact by letter, by telephone, by fax, by e-mail and via website. Appointment necessary.
Hours: Tue, 0930 to 2000; Wed, Thu, 0930 to 1730; Fri, 0930 to 1300

Access for disabled people:
Ramped entry
Special comments: Car park is restricted to permit holders (residential and staff).

HACKNEY HORSE SOCIETY

Fallowfields, Little London, Heytesbury, Warminster, Wiltshire, BA12 0ES

Tel: 01985 840717
Fax: 01985 840616
E-mail: admin@hackney-horse.org.uk

Website:
http://www.hackney-horse.org.uk

Enquiries:
Enquiries to: Secretary General

Organisation type and purpose:
Membership association.
Breed Society.

Subject coverage:
Breeding of hackney horses and ponies.

Museum or gallery collection, archive, or library special collection:
Stud Books from 1884
Year Books from 1967

Printed publications:
Newsletter (3 times a year, members)
Stud Books (every 3 years)

Links with:
British Horse Society

HAEMOPHILIA SOCIETY

3rd Floor, Chesterfield House, 385 Euston Road, London, NW1 3AU

Tel: 020 7380 0600
Fax: 020 7387 8220
E-mail: info@haemophilia.org.uk

Website:
http://www.haemophilia.org.uk

Enquiries:
Enquiries to: Information Officer

Founded:
1950

Organisation type and purpose:
Membership association (membership is by subscription), registered charity (charity number 288260).

Subject coverage:
Haemophilia and related bleeding disorders, treatment and care, education, employment, welfare benefits, HIV, hepatitis C.

Printed publications:
HQ (4 times a year)
Essentials of Haemophilia Care
Haemophilia and Schools
Introduction to Haemophilia (4th ed.)
Living with Haemophilia (Dr P Jones)
Reports and booklets, etc
Safer Sex Guide

continued overleaf

Publications list:
Available online and in print

Access to staff:
Contact by letter, by telephone, by fax, by e-mail and via website
Hours: Mon to Fri, 0900 to 1700

Affiliated to:
European Haemophilia Consortium
World Federation of Haemophilia

HAIGH & HOCHLAND MEDICAL BOOKSHOP

Horniman House, 339–401 Oxford Road, Manchester, M13 9BL

Tel: 0161 273 6799
Fax: 0161 273 6261
E-mail: hh@couttsbookshops.com

Website:
http://www.couttsbookshops.com/hh/index.htm

Enquiries:
Enquiries to: Manager

Founded:
1952

Organisation type and purpose:
Service industry.
Library suppliers.

Subject coverage:
Academic and general books. Specialise in medical only.

Printed publications:
Catalogues & lists produced on request in specified areas (free of charge)

Access to staff:
Contact by letter, by telephone, by fax, by e-mail, in person and via website
Hours: Mon to Fri, 0900 to 1730; Sat, 1000 to 1700

Access for disabled people:
Level entry, toilet facilities

Parent body:
Coutts Library Services UK
   Headlands Business Park, Ringwood, Hampshire, BH24 3PB

HAIR AND BEAUTY INDUSTRY AUTHORITY (HABIA)

Acronym or abbreviation: HABIA

Fraser House, Nether Hall Road, Doncaster, South Yorkshire, DN7 2PH

Tel: 0845 230 6080
Fax: 01302 623171
E-mail: enquiries@habia.org

Website:
http://www.habia.org
Provides information about HABIA and training and education issues relating to Hairdressing and Beauty Therapy.
http://www.qualifications.org
http://www.salon.org.uk

Enquiries:
Enquiries to: Reception
Other contacts: Entry to the Workforce Manager for specific training, careers and education information.

Founded:
January 1997

Formed from:
Beauty Industry Authority (BIA), Hairdressing Training Board (HTB), Hairdressing Training Board Scotland

Formerly called:
Health and Beauty Therapy Training Board (HBTTB)

Organisation type and purpose:
Advisory body.
Lead body.

Subject coverage:
Hairdressing and beauty therapy.

Trade and statistical information:
Data on UK hairdressing and beauty industry.

Non-library collection catalogue:
All or part available online

Printed publications:
Extensive selection of books on all aspects of hairdressing and beauty

Publications list:
Available online and in print

Access to staff:
Contact by letter, by telephone, by fax, by e-mail and via website. Appointment necessary.
Hours: Mon to Thu, 0830 to 1700; Fri, 0830 to 1530

Access to building, collection or gallery:
No access other than to staff

Links to:
City & Guilds
   2 Giltpur Street, London, EC1A 9DD; tel: 020 7294 2468
Thomson Learning

HAIRDRESSING COUNCIL

Acronym or abbreviation: HC

30 Sydenham Road, Croydon, Surrey, CRO 2EF

Tel: 020 8760 7010
Fax: 020 8688 5372
E-mail: registrar@haircouncil.org.uk

Website:
http://www.haircouncil.org.uk

Enquiries:
Enquiries to: Registrar

Founded:
1964

Organisation type and purpose:
Statutory body.
Maintains state register of qualified hairdressers.

Subject coverage:
Hairdressing profession and industry; details of State Registered Hairdressers who are properly trained and qualified (to NVQ Hairdressing Certificate level). Details of personnel on state register; what to do in the event of a bad or unsatisfactory hairdressing experience.

Printed publications:
Hairdresser (quarterly, available to non-registered stylists at £3 plus p&p)
Handbook of Hairdressers (lists every state registered hairdresser alphabetically and by location, much useful information, £14.95 incl. p&p)

Publications list:
Available online

Access to staff:
Contact by telephone, by fax, by e-mail and via website
Hours: Mon to Fri, 0900 to 1600

Access to building, collection or gallery:
No access other than to staff

Links with:
The Guild of Hairdressers
The National Hairdressers Federation
Union of Shop Distributive and Allied Workers

Member organisations:
Association of Hairdressing Teachers in Colleges of Further Education
British Medical Association
Hairdressing Employers' Association
individuals include Members of Parliament, teachers, trichologists and other experts
Institute of Trichologists
Royal College of Physicians

HAKLUYT SOCIETY

Map Library, British Library, 96 Euston Road, London, NW1 2DB

Tel: 01428 641850
E-mail: office@hakluyt.com

Website:
http://www.hakluyt.com

Enquiries:
Enquiries to: Administrator

Founded:
1846

Organisation type and purpose:
Learned society (membership is by subscription), present number of members: 2,048, registered charity (charity number 313168).

Subject coverage:
Original narratives of important and historical voyages, travels, expeditions and other geographical records.

Non-library collection catalogue:
All or part available online

Printed publications:
Scholarly editions of records of voyages, travels and geographical material, many from the Elizabethan and Stuart periods
First Series (100 vols, 1847–1898, out of print)
Second Series (81 vols, 1899 to date, some out of print)
Third Series (15 vols, 2002 to date)
Extra Series (46 vols to date, some out of print)

Microform publications:
First Series (microfilm, from University Publications of America, UPA)
Second series (microfilm of early vols from UPA)
Extra Series (vols 1–12, microfiche from Microform Academic Publishers)

Publications list:
Available online and in print

Access to staff:
Contact by e-mail and via website

HALIFAX ANTIQUARIAN SOCIETY

Treetops, Copley Lane, Lower Skircoat Green, Halifax, HX3 0TJ

Tel: 01422 346088

Website:
www.halifaxhistory.org.uk

Enquiries:
Enquiries to: Secretary

Founded:
1900–01

Organisation type and purpose:
Learned society (membership is by subscription), present number of members: c. 300, voluntary organisation.

Subject coverage:
History of Parish of Halifax.

Museum or gallery collection, archive, or library special collection:
Books and documents re Parish of Halifax

Library catalogue:
All or part available in-house

Printed publications:
Transactions since 1901
Back Numbers to 1901 (if available, from Publications Officer)
Order printed publications from: Publications Officer, Halifax Antiquarian Society
6 Baker Fold, Raglan Street, Halifax HX1 5TX

Publications list:
Available online

Access to staff:
Contact by letter and by telephone
Hours: Mon to Fri, 0900 to 1700

HALL-CARPENTER ARCHIVES

Acronym or abbreviation: HCA

c/o Sue Donnelly, Archivist, Archives Division, Library of the London School of Economics and Political Science, 10 Portugal Street, London, WC2A 2HD

Tel: 020 7955 7223

Website:
http://www.lse.ac.uk/library/archive/gutoho/hall_carpenter_archives.htm

Organisation type and purpose:
The archive of newspaper and other cuttings is a resource for the study of gay activism in Britain since the publication of the Wolfenden Report in 1957.

Subject coverage:
Gay activism in Britain.

Museum or gallery collection, archive, or library special collection:
Collection of cuttings from newspapers and periodicals

HAMBLETON DISTRICT COUNCIL

Civic Centre, Stone Cross, Northallerton, North Yorkshire, DL6 2UU

Tel: 0845 1211 555
Fax: 01609 767228
E-mail: info@hambleton.gov.uk

Website:
http://www.hambleton.gov.uk
Information on district council services; tourism, including The World of James Herriot; leisure facilities.

Enquiries:
Enquiries to: Chief Executive
Other contacts: Press Officer for press enquiries.

Organisation type and purpose:
Local government body.

Subject coverage:
Local government services.

Access to staff:
Contact by letter, by telephone, by fax, by e-mail and in person
Hours: Mon to Fri, 0900 to 1700

Access to building, collection or gallery:
No access other than to staff
Hours: The World of James Herriott:
Mar to Oct, 1000 to 1800 (last admission 1700)
Nov to Feb, 1000 to 1700 (last admission 1600)

Access for disabled people:
Parking provided, level entry, toilet facilities

Administers:
The World of James Herriot
23 Kirkgate, Thirsk, North Yorkshire, YO7 1PL; tel: 01845 524234; fax: 01845 525333

HAMMERSMITH AND FULHAM ARCHIVES AND LOCAL HISTORY CENTRE

The Lilla Huset, 191 Talgarth Road, London, W6 8BJ

Tel: 020 8741 5159
E-mail: archives@lbhf.gov.uk

Website:
http://www.lbhf.gov.uk

Enquiries:
Enquiries to: Archivist

Founded:
1992

Organisation type and purpose:
Local government body.
Combined record office and local history library.

Subject coverage:
Local history of Hammersmith and Fulham, family history sources for Hammersmith and Fulham, records of Hammersmith and Fulham Council and its predecessors. Deposited archives of local organisations and individuals.

Museum or gallery collection, archive, or library special collection:
Special Collections:
William Morris
Kelmscott Press
A. P. Herbert
White City Exhibitions
Sir William Bull
Cecil French Bequest of pictures (British art of the late 19th and early 20th centuries, especially Sir Edward Burne-Jones)
Old Ordnance Survey Maps and other maps
Old postcards and photographs
Old local newspapers
Topographical collection of paintings and prints of the Borough
Books and pamphlets
Archives relating to the history of the Borough

Non-library collection catalogue:
All or part available in-house

Library catalogue:
All or part available in-house

Printed publications:
Books, Godfrey reproduction maps, postcards and greetings cards
Publications on the history of the area

Publications list:
Available in print

Access to staff:
Contact by letter, by telephone, by e-mail and in person

Access to building, collection or gallery:
Hours: Mon, 0930 to 1630; Tue, 0930 to 1945; Thu, 0930 to 1630; closed Wed and Fri; second and fourth Sat in month (excluding bank holiday weekends), 0930 to 1630

Access for disabled people:
Parking provided, level entry, access to all public areas, toilet facilities

Parent body:
London Borough of Hammersmith and Fulham
Hammersmith Town Hall, King Street, London, W6 9JU; tel: 020 8748 3020

HAMMERSMITH AND FULHAM LIBRARIES

Hammersmith Library, Shepherds Bush Road, London, W6 7AT

Tel: 020 8753 3813
Fax: 020 8753 3815
E-mail: info@haflibs.org.uk

Website:
http://www.lbhf.gov.uk
For information about our service.

Enquiries:
Enquiries to: Head of Library Services

Organisation type and purpose:
Local government body, public library.

Subject coverage:
English law, United Kingdom government publications, EC Public Information Relay at Hammersmith library, theology, fine art at Fulham Library.

Museum or gallery collection, archive, or library special collection:
Audio Collections: Mendelssohn, Vaughan Williams, Jazz composers HP-JEF, British poetry, Folk music of Iran, Iraq, Lebanon, Syria and Jordan
Doves Press (Archive Centre)
Early Children's Books
Special Fiction Collection: Authors CRI-DEL

Library catalogue:
All or part available online and in-house

Printed publications:
Before Windrush: the early Black presence in Hammersmith & Fulham (2000)
Hammersmith and Fulham: the twentieth century, 1999
Instant Past: old Hammersmith in pictures
Life in Fulham: old Fulham in pictures, 1984

Access to staff:
Contact by letter, by telephone, by fax and in person
Hours: Fulham and Hammersmith Libraries: Mon, Tue, Thu, 0930 to 2000; Wed, Fri, Sat, 0930 to 1700; Sun, 1315 to 1700

Branch libraries:
Askew Road Library
87–91 Askew Road, London, W12 9AS; tel: 020 8753 3863
Barons Court Library
North End Crescent, London, W14 8TG; tel: 020 8753 3888
Fulham Library
598 Fulham Road, London, SW6 5NX; tel: 020 8753 3879; fax: 020 7736 3741
Hammersmith Library
Shepherds Bush Road, London, W6 7AT; tel: 020 8753 3827; fax: 020 8753 3815
Sands End Library
The Community Centre, 59–61 Broughton Road, London, SW6 2LA; tel: 020 8753 3885
Shepherds Bush Library
7 Uxbridge Road, London, W12 8LJ; tel: 020 8753 3842; fax: 020 8740 1712

Member of:
Art Reference Libraries Information Service (ARLIS)
Association of British Theological and Philosophical Libraries
British and Irish Association of Law Librarians
Greater London Audio Specialisation Scheme
International Association of Music Libraries

Participates in:
Joint Fiction Reserve Scheme
LASER Special Collections Scheme

HAMPSHIRE AND WIGHT TRUST FOR MARITIME ARCHAEOLOGY

Acronym or abbreviation: HWTMA

Room W1/95, National Oceanography Centre, Empress Dock, Southampton, SO14 3ZH

Tel: 023 8059 3290
Fax: 023 8059 3052
E-mail: info@hwtma.org.uk

Website:
http://www.hwtma.org.uk

Organisation type and purpose:
A charitable organisation that relies on grants, donations and assistance in kind.

Subject coverage:
British maritime archaeology, with emphasis on Hampshire, the Isle of Wight and adjacent areas.

Education services:
Education and outreach programme. Educational display at the Underwater Archaeology Centre at Fort Victoria. Public lectures and talks.

HAMPSHIRE ARCHIVES AND LOCAL STUDIES

Acronym or abbreviation: HALS

Hampshire Record Office, Sussex Street, Winchester, Hampshire, SO23 8TH

Tel: 01962 846154\ Textline 0808 100 2484
Fax: 01962 878681
E-mail: enquiries.archives@hants.gov.uk

Website:
http://www.hants.gov.uk/record-office

continued overleaf

Enquiries:
Enquiries to: Archivist

Founded:
1947

Created by the merger of:
Hampshire Record Office and Hampshire Local Studies Service (year of change 2008)

Organisation type and purpose:
Local government body.

Subject coverage:
Records relating to Hampshire and Hampshire families, includes records of local government (Quarter Sessions, County Council, civil, parish, etc.), Church of England, individuals, families, businesses, societies, chapels, schools, etc.

Museum or gallery collection, archive, or library special collection:
Archives relating to Hampshire and Hampshire families
Wessex Film and Sound Archive – film, video and audio tapes from the wider Wessex region
Local Studies collection of books, pamphlets, periodicals and other printed materials

Non-library collection catalogue:
All or part available in-house

Library catalogue:
All or part available online and in-house

Printed publications:
History curriculum resource packs and videos (for schools)
Hampshire Record Series (by subscription or purchase of individual vols)
Portsmouth Record Series including: Maps of Portsmouth before 1801, Royal Charters 1194–1974 (by subscription or purchase of individual vols)
Hampshire Papers and Maps
Leaflets
Education Services Newsletter (annually)
Guides to Sources (30)

Microform publications:
Directories, will index, parish registers, Phillimore's Hampshire Marriage Registers

Electronic and video publications:
Videos for schools

Publications list:
Available online and in print

Access to staff:
Contact by letter, by telephone, by fax, by e-mail, in person and via website
Hours: Mon to Fri, 0900 to 1900; Sat, 0900 to 1600

Access for disabled people:
Parking provided, level entry, access to all public areas, toilet facilities

HAMPSHIRE COUNTY COUNCIL LIBRARY AND INFORMATION SERVICE – BASINGSTOKE LIBRARY

19–20 Westminster House, Festival Place, Basingstoke, Hampshire, RG21 7LS

Tel: 0845 603 5631
Fax: 01256 470666
E-mail: basingstoke.library@hants.gov.uk

Website:
http://libcat.hants.gov.uk
Library catalogue
http://www3.hants.gov.uk/library/reference-online.htm
For customers with Hampshire Library membership cards

Enquiries:
Enquiries to: Library Officer

Organisation type and purpose:
Local government public library

Subject coverage:
General and local history

Museum or gallery collection, archive, or library special collection:
Jane Austen Collection
Local History Collection

Trade and statistical information:
General trade directories and statistical volumes

Library catalogue:
All or part available online

Microform publications:
Local newspaper 1878–
Hants Trade Directories
Census for Basingstoke and Deane, 1891, 1901
1881 Census Index
Parish Registers
IGI 1988
IGI 1992 (Hampshire, Wiltshire and Berkshire)
Wills Index 1853–1943
GRO Index (incomplete)

Access to staff:
Contact by letter, by fax, by e-mail and in person
Hours: During normal opening hours. If specific member of staff required, please make arrangments in advance.

Access to building, collection or gallery:
Hours: Mon, Tue, Wed and Fri 0930 to 1900; Thu 0930 to 1730; Sat 0930 to 1600; Sun 1100 to 1700

Access for disabled people:
Level entry
Special comments: Lift to Library on first floor.

Links with:
Basingstoke Citizens Advice Centre same address, first floor

Parent body:
Hampshire County Council

HAMPSHIRE COUNTY COUNCIL MUSEUMS SERVICE HEADQUARTERS

Chilcomb House, Chilcomb Lane, Winchester, Hampshire, SO23 8RD

Tel: 01962 826700
Fax: 01962 869836
E-mail: musmga@hants.gov.uk

Website:
http://www.hants.gov.uk/museums/
Catalogue, whole collection, over 100,000 pages.

Enquiries:
Enquiries to: Librarian
Direct e-mail: gill.arnott@hants.gov.uk

Founded:
1944

Organisation type and purpose:
Local government body.
The headquarters service, including administration, documentation, museum library, stores, conservation workshops, photographic studio, design studio, etc.

Subject coverage:
The main subject areas are Hampshire history, archaeology, local history, social history, decorative art, ceramics, textiles, costume, toys, horology, firearms, natural science, botany, zoology, geology, conservation (museum), museology.

Museum or gallery collection, archive, or library special collection:
Archaeological site archives
Blair Collection (entomologist's notes)
Tasker Collection (steam machinery, engineering drawings, archives and plans)

Non-library collection catalogue:
All or part available online

Printed publications:
List available from the Librarian at this address

Access to staff:
Contact by letter, by telephone, by fax, by e-mail and in person. Appointment necessary.

Hours: Mon to Fri, 0900 to 1700

Access to building, collection or gallery:
Hours: Mon to Fri, 0900 to 1700

Access for disabled people:
Special comments: Access only to part of the site

Museums and related sites:
Aldershot Military Museum
Queens Avenue, Aldershot, Hampshire, GU11 2LG; tel: 01252 314598; fax: 01252 342942
Allen Gallery
Church Street, Alton, Hampshire, GU34 2BW; tel: 01420 82802
Andover Museum & Museum of the Iron Age
6 Church Close, Andover, Hampshire, SP10 1DP; tel: 01264 366283; fax: 01264 339152
Basing House
Redbridge Lane, Basing, Basingstoke, Hampshire, RG24 7HB; tel: 01256 467294; fax: 01256 326283
Bursledon Windmill
Windmill Lane, Bursledon, Southampton, SO31 8BG; tel: 023 8040 4999
Curtis Museum
High Street, Alton, Hampshire, GU34 1BA; tel: 01420 82802; fax: 01420 84227
Eastleigh Museum
25 High Street, Eastleigh, Hampshire, SO50 5LF; tel: 023 8064 3026; fax: 023 8065 3582
Flora Twort Gallery
Church Path, Petersfield, Hampshire, GU32 1HS; tel: 01730 260756
Gosport Discovery Centre (opens Spring 2005)
Walpole Road, Gosport, Hampshire, PO12 1NS; tel: 023 9258 8035; fax: 023 9250 1951
Havant Museum
56 East Street, Havant, Hampshire, PO9 1BS; tel: 023 9245 1155; fax: 023 9249 8707
Milestones: Hampshire's Living History Museum
Leisure Park, Churchill Way West, Basingstoke, Hampshire, RG21 6YR; tel: 01256 477766; fax: 01256 477784
Red House Museum
Quay Road, Christchurch, Hampshire, BH23 1BU; tel: 01202 482860; fax: 01202 481924
Rockbourne Roman Villa
Rockbourne, Fordingbridge, Hampshire, SP6 3PG; tel: 01725 518541
SEARCH
50 Clarence Road, Gosport, Hampshire, PO12 1BU; tel: 023 9250 1957; fax: 023 9250 1921
St Barbe Museum
New Street, Lymington, Hampshire, SO41 9BH; tel: 01590 676969; fax: 01590 679997
Treadgolds of Portsea Museum
1 Bishop Street, Portsmouth, Hampshire, PO1 3DA; tel: 023 9282 4745; fax: 023 9283 7310; e-mail: lawton@treadgoldm33.freeserve.co.uk
Westbury Manor Museum
84 West Street, Fareham, Hampshire, PO16 0JJ; tel: 01329 824895; fax: 01329 825917
Willis Museum
Old Town Hall, Market Place, Basingstoke, Hampshire, RG21 7QD; tel: 01256 465902; fax: 01256 471455

Parent body:
Hampshire County Council

HAMPSHIRE COUNTY LIBRARY – WINCHESTER REFERENCE LIBRARY

81 North Walls, Winchester, Hampshire, SO23 8BY

Tel: 01962 826666
Fax: 01962 856615
E-mail: winchester.reference@hants.gov.uk

Enquiries:
Enquiries to: Reference Librarian

Organisation type and purpose:
Local government body, public library.
To provide information to all who live, work and study in the county of Hampshire.

Subject coverage:
General.

Museum or gallery collection, archive, or library special collection:
ASTM Standards
British Standards (CD-ROM)
Comprehensive collection of broadsheet newspapers from 1979 onward on microfilm and CD-ROM
Official publications from 1972

Trade and statistical information:
Statistics collection including all relevant official publications (UK) and selected EC and UN publications. Trade Directories collection covering mainly the United Kingdom but with some information for overseas countries. Key British Enterprise, Equifax and Company Records Office index on CD-ROM.

Non-library collection catalogue:
All or part available online

Printed publications:
Annual index to the Hampshire Chronicle (local newspaper)

Access to staff:
Contact by letter, by telephone, by fax, by e-mail and in person
Hours: Mon to Fri, 0930 to 1900; Sat, 0930 to 1600; closed Sun

HAMPSHIRE FIELD CLUB AND ARCHAEOLOGICAL SOCIETY

Acronym or abbreviation: Hants Field Club

14 Smeeton Road, Lee On The Solent, Gosport, Hampshire, PO13 8LH

Tel: 01202 408376
E-mail: martin.goodchild@baesystems.com

Website:
http://www.fieldclub.hants.org.uk

Enquiries:
Enquiries to: General Secretary

Founded:
1885

Organisation type and purpose:
Learned society (membership is by subscription), present number of members: 611, registered charity (charity number 243773).

Subject coverage:
Archaeology, local history, natural history, industrial archaeology, geology, landscape and historical buildings of Hampshire.

Museum or gallery collection, archive, or library special collection:
Library in the Southampton University Library Archives
Photographic Collection in the Hampshire Record Office

Printed publications:
Archaeology Monographs (9 to date)
New Forest Section Annual Report
Newsletters of the Sections (2 times a year)
Proceedings of the Hampshire Field Club and Archaeological Society (Hampshire Studies) (annually)

Access to staff:
Contact by letter and by e-mail
Hours: Mon to Fri, 0900 to 1700

Member of:
Council for British Archaeology

HAMPSHIRE LIBRARY AND INFORMATION SERVICE

Library and Information Service Headquarters, 5–6 Moorside Place, Moorside Road, Winchester, SO23 7FZ

Tel: 01962 826688
Fax: 01962 856615
E-mail: library@hants.gov.uk

Website:
http://www.hants.gov.uk/library
Over 250,000 pages of information about clubs, societies, voluntary organisations, health resources, council minutes, education, business advice, leisure and tourism.

Enquiries:
Enquiries to: Acting Head of Library and Information Service

Organisation type and purpose:
Local government body, public library.

Subject coverage:
General; business information, local government information service, naval studies, railways, military history, aeronautics.

Museum or gallery collection, archive, or library special collection:
British Standards
Infocheck Register
Companies House Register
Local Studies Collections
Aeronautics Collection (Farnborough)
Military Collection (Aldershot)
Naval Collection (Gosport)
Railway Collection (Winchester)

Trade and statistical information:
Published United Kingdom, European Union and World Trade Directories, Statistical Series and Marketing Information.

Non-library collection catalogue:
All or part available online

Library catalogue:
All or part available online

Printed publications:
Various user guides to services

Access to staff:
Contact by letter, by telephone, by fax, by e-mail, in person and via website
Hours: Mon to Fri, 0900 to 1700

Access for disabled people:
Parking provided, level entry

Branch libraries:
include Basingstoke, Fareham, Farnborough and Winchester

Member organisation of:
ASLIB
EIC Consortium
European RELAY Network
Library Association

Parent body:
Hampshire County Council
tel: 01962 841841

HAMPSHIRE LIBRARY AND INFORMATION SERVICE – FARNBOROUGH

Acronym or abbreviation: HLIS

Farnborough Library, Pinehurst, Farnborough, Hampshire, GU14 7JZ

Tel: 01252 513838
Fax: 01252 511149
E-mail: CLNOREF@Hants.gov.uk

Website:
http://www.hants.gov.uk/library/

Enquiries:
Enquiries to: Information and Lifelong Learning Librarian

Organisation type and purpose:
Local government body, public library.

Subject coverage:
General; business and aviation; local studies for Farnborough area.

Museum or gallery collection, archive, or library special collection:
Aviation and aerospace
British standards (online)

Local Studies: books, maps, photographs, news cuttings, periodicals etc for Farnborough and surrounding area

Trade and statistical information:
UK and other official, unofficial statistics.
Trade and business directories.
Company reports.

Library catalogue:
All or part available online and in-house

Access to staff:
Contact by letter, by telephone, by fax, by e-mail, in person and via website
Hours: Mon, Tue, Thu, Fri, 0930 to 1900; Wed, 0930 to 1700; Sat, 0930 to 1600

Access for disabled people:
Parking provided, level entry, access to all public areas

HANNAH RESEARCH INSTITUTE

Acronym or abbreviation: HRI

Kirkhill, St Quivox, Ayr, KA6 5HL

Tel: 01292 674000
Fax: 01292 674005
E-mail: e.barbour@hannah.ac.uk

Website:
http://www.hri.sari.ac.uk

Enquiries:
Enquiries to: Librarian
Direct tel: 01292 674116

Founded:
1928

Organisation type and purpose:
Consultancy, research organisation.

Subject coverage:
Biological research, biochemistry, molecular biology, integrative biology, biological science and technology, food research, food science and technology, physical chemistry.

Printed publications:
Hannah Research Institute Yearbook (includes list of publications, annually)
Visitors Guide

Access to staff:
Contact by telephone. Appointment necessary.
Hours: Mon to Fri, 0900 to 1700

Connections with:
University of Glasgow

Funded by:
Scottish Office Agriculture, Environment and Fisheries Department

Research programme agreed in consultation with the:
Agricultural and Food Research Council
Biotechnology and Biological Sciences Research Council

HARINGEY ARCHIVE SERVICE

Bruce Castle Museum, Lordship Lane, London, N17 8NU

Tel: 020 8808 8772
Fax: 020 8808 4118
E-mail: museum.services@haringey.gov.uk

Enquiries:
Enquiries to: Local History Officer

Organisation type and purpose:
Local government body, museum.

Subject coverage:
Archives and local history of the present local authority (Borough of Haringey) and its predecessors (Tottenham, Wood Green and Hornsey).
Collections of maps, photographs, postcards, 1841 to 1891 census returns on 35mm microfilm for Tottenham, Wood Green and Hornsey, newspapers, directories.

continued overleaf

Non-library collection catalogue:
All or part available in-house

Access to staff:
Contact by letter and by telephone. Appointment necessary.
Hours: Wed to Fri, 1300 to 1645; alternate Sat, 1300 to 1645
Special comments: Appointment required.

HARINGEY LIBRARIES, ARCHIVES AND MUSEUM SERVICE

Wood Green Central Library, High Road, Wood Green, London, N22 6XD

Tel: 020 8489 2700
Fax: 020 8489 2722

Website:
http://www.haringey.gov.uk
Library news, opening hours, what's on, links, contact us.

Enquiries:
Enquiries to: Head of Library Services
Other contacts: Principal Librarian Systems and Support Services for Head of Bibliographic Computer Services.

Formerly called:
Haringey Library Services

Organisation type and purpose:
Local government body, public library.

Subject coverage:
General; instrumental recitals and the works of Telemann (under the Greater London Audio Subject Specialisation scheme GLASS).

Information services:
Enquiries desk; Online information services, printed information

Museum or gallery collection, archive, or library special collection:
Public health engineering under the LASCRA specialisation
Heath Robinson Collection (at Wood Green Library)

Non-library collection catalogue:
All or part available online

Library catalogue:
All or part available online

Printed publications:
Connections by Sylvia Caldecott
How Things Were
Lost Houses of Haringey

Access to staff:
Contact by letter, by telephone, by fax, by e-mail and in person. Appointment necessary.
Hours: Central Library: Mon to Fri, 0900 to 1900; Sat, 0900 to 1700; Sun, 1200 to 1600 (Wood Green only)
Special comments: Contact other branch libraries for information regarding opening times and disabled access facilities.

Access to building, collection or gallery:
No access other than to staff
Hours: Central Library: Mon to Fri, 0700 to 1930; Sat, 0700 to 1730; Sun, 1100 to 1630
Special comments: Staff only or by appointment before usual opening hours

Access for disabled people:
Level entry, access to all public areas, toilet facilities, lift
Hours: Central Library: Mon to Fri, 0900 to 1900; Sat, 0900 to 1700; Sun, 1200 to 1600 (Wood Green only)

Branch libraries:
Alexandra Park
   Alexandra Park Road, London, N22 7UJ; tel: 020 8883 8553
Coombes Croft
   Tottenham High Road, London; tel: 020 8348 3443

Highgate
   Shepherd's Hill, London, N6 5QT; tel: 020 8348 3443
Hornsey
   Haringey Park, London, N8 9JA; tel: 020 8489 1427
Marcus Garvey
   Tottenham Green Leisure Centre, 1 Philip Lane, London, N15 4JA; tel: 020 8489 5350
Muswell Hill
   Queens Avenue, London, N10 3PE; tel: 020 8883 6734
St Ann's
   Cissbury Road, London, N15 5PU; tel: 020 8800 4390
Stroud Green
   Quernomore Road, London, N4 4QR; tel: 020 8348 4363

Parent body:
London Borough of Haringey Education Service
   Civic Centre, High Road, Wood Green, London, N22 7UJ; tel: 020 8849 0000 (ask for Education Services)

HARLEIAN SOCIETY

College of Arms, Queen Victoria Street, London, EC4V 4BT

Tel: 020 7236 7728
Fax: 020 7248 6448
E-mail: info@harleian.co.uk

Website:
http://harleian.co.uk

Enquiries:
Enquiries to: Honorary Secretary

Founded:
1869

Organisation type and purpose:
Learned society (membership is by subscription), present number of members: 280, registered charity (charity number 253659), publishing house.

Subject coverage:
Transcribing, printing and publishing of the Heraldic Visitations of the counties of England and Wales and other unpublished manuscripts relating to genealogy, armory and heraldry in its widest sense.

Printed publications:
Over 200 publications, see website: http://harleian.co.uk

Publications list:
Available online and in print

Access to staff:
Contact by letter, by telephone, by fax and by e-mail
Hours: Mon to Fri, 0900 to 1700

HARLOW COLLEGE

Velizy Avenue, Town Centre, Harlow, Essex, CM20 3LH

Tel: 01279 868000
Fax: 01279 868260

Enquiries:
Enquiries to: College Librarian

Organisation type and purpose:
College of further education.

Subject coverage:
Education, catering, art, hairdressing, floristry, engineering, construction, journalism, social care, social sciences, business, secretarial, computing, performing arts, mathematics, sciences, leisure and community.

Library catalogue:
All or part available in-house

Printed publications:
1989 User Survey (£2)
1995 User Survey (£15)
Booklists on request

Catalogues (infrequent)
Guide to the Library (infrequent)
Subject guides (infrequent)

Access to staff:
Contact by letter and by telephone. Appointment necessary. Access for members only.
Hours: Mon to Fri, 0900 to 1700

Part of:
Essex County Library ELAN network

HARLOW DISTRICT COUNCIL

Town Hall, Harlow, Essex, CM20 1HJ

Tel: 01279 446611\ Minicom no. 01279 446026
Fax: 01279 446767
E-mail: postroom@harlow.gov.uk

Website:
http://www.harlow.gov.uk/community/info
List of community groups to join etc.
http://www.harlow.gov.uk/harlow_council/index.htm
Harlow Council.
http://www.harlow.gov.uk
Information on Harlow.

Enquiries:
Enquiries to: Chief Executive

Founded:
1974

Formerly called:
Harlow Development Corporation Commission for New Towns, Harlow District Council (year of change 1974)

Organisation type and purpose:
Local government body.
Provision of services to local people.

Subject coverage:
Social, economic, historic or local government related information specific to Harlow.

Museum or gallery collection, archive, or library special collection:
Archive held at Harlow Study Centre and the Museum of Harlow

Printed publications:
Range of printed products including:
Business Directory (£10)
Harlow Guide (free)
Harlowlife (magazine, once every other month, free)
Numerous free leaflets etc

Access to staff:
Contact by letter, by telephone, by fax, by e-mail and via website. Appointment necessary.
Hours: Mon to Fri, 0830 to 1700

Access for disabled people:
Ramped entry

Other sites:
Details available on request

HARPER ADAMS UNIVERSITY COLLEGE LIBRARY

Newport, Shropshire, TF10 8NB

Tel: 01952 820280
Fax: 01952 814783

Website:
http://www.harper-adams.ac.uk
Information about the college.

Enquiries:
Enquiries to: Library Service Manager
Direct tel: 01952 815220
Direct fax: 01952 815391
Direct e-mail: kgreaves@harper-adams.ac.uk

Founded:
1901

Organisation type and purpose:
research organisation.

Subject coverage:
Animal production (sheep, cattle, pigs, poultry), crop production (cereals, potatoes, sugar beet, grass, oilseeds), farm management; agricultural economics and policy, agricultural marketing, agricultural engineering, rural land and estate management, the environment.

Museum or gallery collection, archive, or library special collection:
18th, 19th and early 20th century agricultural books and journals
Library of the National Institute of Poultry Husbandry
Sir Edward Brown Library (18th, 19th and early 20th century poultry books)

Non-library collection catalogue:
All or part available in-house

Library catalogue:
All or part available online

Printed publications:
College Farm Guide (annually)
College Farm Report (fortnightly)
Learning Resources Guide (annually)
Silcock Fellowship for Livestock Research Reports (irregular)
Temperton Fellowship for Poultry Research Reports (irregular)

Access to staff:
Contact by letter, by telephone and in person
Hours: Term time: Mon to Fri, 0900 to 2200, Sat and Sun, 1000 to 1700
Outside Term time: Mon to Fri, 0900 to 1700
Special comments: Charges for external borrowers.

HARRIS MANCHESTER COLLEGE LIBRARY

Mansfield Road, Oxford, OX1 3TD

Tel: 01865 271016
Fax: 01865 271012
E-mail: librarian@hmc.ox.ac.uk

Website:
http://www.ox.ac.uk
Information about the College Library and the Union catalogue
http://www.hmc.ox.ac.uk
General information about the College

Enquiries:
Enquiries to: Librarian
Direct tel: 01865 281472
Other contacts: Library Assistant

Founded:
1786

Formerly called:
Manchester Academy (year of change 1786);
Manchester College (year of change 1803);
Manchester New College (year of change 1840);
Manchester College (year of change 1889); Harris Manchester College (year of change 1996)

Organisation type and purpose:
University college library.

Subject coverage:
Church history; Protestant Reformation in Europe and Great Britain (radical sects); Dissenting Church history in Britain; Socinianism in Europe and Britain; 19th-century Unitarian Church history in Great Britain and the USA.

Services for disabled people:
Through our service delivery we can make the collection accessible to all visitors

Museum or gallery collection, archive, or library special collection:
Carpenter Library of Comparative (World) Religions
Manuscripts and printed notes of lectures in Dissenting Academies
Manuscripts collections, especially letters of 19th- and 20th-century Unitarians
Old Library (pre-1800, especially Enlightenment and nonconformist authors)

Sociniana
Tract Collection (pamphlets, etc. on politics and dissent, 1500–1914)
Unitariana

Non-library collection catalogue:
All or part available online and in print

Library catalogue:
All or part available online

Printed publications:
A Catalogue of the Manuscripts of Harris Manchester College, Oxford (ed. D. Porter, the College, 1998)
Truth, Liberty, Religion: Essays Celebrating 200 Years of Manchester College (ed. B. Smith, Oxford, the College 1986, £5 plus p&p)
Order printed publications from:
librarian@hmc.ox.ac.uk

Access to staff:
Contact by letter, by telephone, by fax, by e-mail and via website. Appointment necessary. Letter of introduction required.
Hours: Mon to Fri, 0900 to 1630
Special comments: Library is also closed during College closure.
Vacations: library may be closed due to staff holidays.

Access to building, collection or gallery:
Hours: Mon to Fri, 0900 to 1630

Access for disabled people:
Ramped entry
Special comments: A reading room is available on the ground floor and staff will fetch items for individuals, e.g. parts of the old catalogue, books, periodicals, anything within reason; toilet facilities: doorway is very narrow.

Member organisation of:
Association of British Theological and Philosophical Libraries
Oxford University College
University of Oxford

HARRIS TWEED AUTHORITY

Acronym or abbreviation: HTA

6 Garden Road, Stornoway, Isle of Lewis, HS1 2QJ

Tel: 01851 702269
Fax: 01851 702600
E-mail: enquiries@harristweed.org

Website:
http://www.harristweed.org

Enquiries:
Enquiries to: Chief Executive

Founded:
1909

Organisation type and purpose:
Statutory body, trade association (membership is invitation), present number of members: 10.
Harris Tweed certification body.

Subject coverage:
Harris Tweed industry.

Education services:
information packs

Trade and statistical information:
Marketing and certification of Harris Tweed.

Printed publications:
Booklets on the manufacture, etc. of Harris Tweed

Electronic and video publications:
CD available

Access to staff:
Contact by letter, by telephone, by fax, by e-mail, in person and via website. Appointment necessary.
Hours: Mon to Thu, 0900 to 1700; Fri, 0900 to 1200

HARROW LIBRARY SERVICE

PO Box 4, Civic Centre, Harrow, Middlesex, HA1 2UU

Tel: 020 8424 1059
Fax: 020 8424 1971
E-mail: library@harrow.gov.uk

Enquiries:
Enquiries to: Interim Head of Service – Library Services
Other contacts: Principal Librarian (Reference and Information Services) 020 8424 1055/1056 for general information and local history enquiries.

Organisation type and purpose:
Local government body, public library.

Subject coverage:
General, architecture and building, civil engineering, town and country planning and the local history of Harrow and Middlesex. Also a section on family history and genealogy in general (eg IGI, 1881 Census for England and Wales on file).

Library catalogue:
All or part available online

Branch libraries:
Bob Lawrence Library
  6–8 North Parade, Mollison Way, Edgware, HA8 5QH; tel: 020 8952 4140; e-mail: boblawrence .library@harrow.gov.uk
Civic Centre Library
  Central Reference Library, Station Road, Harrow, HA1 2UU; tel: 020 8424 1055/6 (enquiries), 020 8424 1051 (renewals); e-mail: civiccentre.library@ harrow.gov.uk
Gayton Library (Central Lending Library and main music library)
  Garden House, 5 St John's Road, Harrow, Middlesex, HA1 2EE; tel: 020 8427 6012 or 8986; e-mail: gayton.library@harrow.gov.uk
Hatch End Library
  Uxbridge Road, Hatch End, HA5 4EA; tel: 020 8428 2636; e-mail: hatchend.library@harrow.gov .uk
Kenton Library
  Kenton Lane, Kenton, HA3 8UJ; tel: 020 8907 2463; e-mail: kenton.library@harrow.gov.uk
Local History Library
  e-mail: localhistory.library@harrow.gov.uk
North Harrow Library
  429–433 Pinner Road, North Harrow, HA1 4HN; tel: 020 8427 0611; e-mail: northharrow.library@ harrow.gov.uk
Pinner Library
  Marsh Road, Pinner, HA5 5NQ; tel: 020 8866 7827; e-mail: pinner.library@harrow.gov.uk
Rayners Lane Library
  Imperial Drive, Rayners Lane, HA2 7HJ; tel: 020 8866 9185; e-mail: raynerslane.library@harrow .gov.uk
Roxeth Library
  Northolt Road, South Harrow, HA2 8EQ; tel: 020 8422 0809; e-mail: roxeth.library@harrow.gov.uk
Stanmore Library
  8 Stanmore Hill, Stanmore, HA7 3BQ; tel: 020 8954 9955; e-mail: stanmore.library@harrow.gov .uk
Wealdstone Library
  Wealdstone Centre, 38–40 High Street, Wealdstone, HA3 7AE; tel: 020 8420 9333; e-mail: wealdstone.library@harrow.gov.uk

HARTLEPOOL CENTRAL LIBRARY

Reference and Information Service, 124 York Road, Hartlepool, TS26 9DE

Tel: 01429 263778
Fax: 01429 283400
E-mail: infodesk@hartlepool.gov.uk

Website:
http://www.hartlepool.gov.uk
Description of library service, library catalogues

Enquiries:
Enquiries to: Reference manager

Founded:
1895

Organisation type and purpose:
Public library.

continued overleaf

Subject coverage:
All subjects, specialist coverage: local studies, family history, local organisations database.

Museum or gallery collection, archive, or library special collection:
William Gray and Co – Ships Particulars Books 1872 to 1941
Luke Blumer and Son – Shipbuilders and Ship Repairs Accounts 1853 to 1868
Music scores
Family History Collection
Local Studies Collection
Map Collection – local area and port
Photograph Collection – local area

Library catalogue:
All or part available online and in-house

Access to staff:
Contact by letter, by telephone, by fax, by e-mail, in person and via website
Hours: Mon to Thu, 0930 to 1900; Fri to Sat, 0930 to 1700; Sun, 1130 to 1530

Access to building, collection or gallery:
No prior appointment required
Hours: Mon to Thu, 0930 to 1900; Fri to Sat, 0930 to 1700; Sun, 1130 to 1530

Access for disabled people:
Level entry, access to all public areas, toilet facilities

HARVEIAN SOCIETY OF LONDON

11 Chandos Street, Cavendish Square, London, W1M 0EB

Tel: 020 7580 1043
Fax: 020 7580 5793

Enquiries:
Enquiries to: Executive Secretary

Founded:
1831

Organisation type and purpose:
Learned society (membership is by election or invitation), present number of members: 330, registered charity.

Subject coverage:
Medicine in general, history of medicine.

Museum or gallery collection, archive, or library special collection:
Archives of Society

Access to staff:
Contact by letter and by fax
Hours: Mon to Fri, 0900 to 1700

HASTINGS REFERENCE LIBRARY

13 Claremont, Hastings, East Sussex, TN34 1HE

Tel: 01424 716481
Fax: 01424 443289
E-mail: library.hastings.ref@eastsussex.gov.uk

Website:
http://www.eastsussex.gov.uk/libraries

Enquiries:
Enquiries to: Information Services Librarian

Organisation type and purpose:
Local government body, public library.

Subject coverage:
General reference material; local studies (especially Hastings, with some Sussex).

Museum or gallery collection, archive, or library special collection:
Brassey Collection (material by, about, and relating to Thomas, 1st Earl Brassey, and his family)

Library catalogue:
All or part available online and in-house

Access to staff:
Contact by letter, by telephone, by fax, by e-mail and in person

Hours: Mon, 0930 to 1800; Tue, Thu, 0930 to 1830; Wed, 0930 to 1300; Fri, 1030 to 1830; Sat, 0930 to 1700; Sun, closed

Access for disabled people:
Access to all public areas

Parent body:
East Sussex Libraries

HAVANT BOROUGH COUNCIL

Acronym or abbreviation: HBC

Civic Offices, Civic Centre Road, Havant, Hampshire, PO9 2AX

Tel: 023 9247 4174\ Minicom no. 023 9244 6602
Fax: 023 9248 0263
E-mail: customer.services@havant.gov.uk

Website:
http://www.havant.gov.uk

Enquiries:
Enquiries to: Public Relations Manager
Direct tel: 023 9244 6420
Direct fax: 023 9244 6490

Founded:
1974

Organisation type and purpose:
Local government body.

Subject coverage:
All matters relating to local government issues within the Borough of Havant.

Printed publications:
Borough Guide
Community Strategy
Best Value Plan Summary
Council Magazine (quarterly)

Access to staff:
Contact by letter, by telephone, by fax, by e-mail and in person
Hours: Mon to Fri, 0900 to 1700

Access for disabled people:
Parking provided, level entry, access to all public areas, toilet facilities

HAVERFORDWEST PUBLIC LIBRARY

Dew Street, Haverfordwest, Pembrokeshire, SA61 1SU

Tel: 01437 765244
Fax: 01437 767092
E-mail: haverfordwestlibrary@pembrokeshire.gov.uk

Enquiries:
Enquiries to: Librarian
Direct tel: 01437 775248
Other contacts: Group Librarian, Central Services for main contacts for all County libraries.

Organisation type and purpose:
Public library.

Subject coverage:
General reference. Local studies of Pembrokeshire including: a multi-format collection relating to the people/places/events/subjects connected to the County of Pembrokeshire, past and present.

Museum or gallery collection, archive, or library special collection:
Local studies of Pembrokeshire including: a multi-format collection relating to the people/places/events/subjects connected to the County of Pembrokeshire, past and present
Francis Green Genealogical Collection covering the prominent families of Cardiganshire, Carmarthenshire and Pembrokeshire at the turn of the century

Printed publications:
The History and Antiquities of St Davids (£15.95)
Journal of Pembrokeshire Historical Society Nos 6, 7 and 8 (£5 each)

Rosemarket: A Village Beyond Wales (£2)
When the Poppies Bloom Again, Pembrokeshire and the Great War (£7.50)
Dyfed Cookery Book (£2)
Haverfordwest in Old Photographs (£7.95)
Order printed publications from: Administration Officer, Haverfordwest Public Library at the same address

Publications list:
Available in print

Access to staff:
Contact by letter, by telephone, by fax, by e-mail and in person
Hours: Mon, Wed, Thu, 0930 to 1700; Tue, Fri, 0930 to 1900; Sat 0930 to 1300

Access for disabled people:
Parking provided, toilet facilities, customer lift

Full-time Pembrokeshire Libraries:
(Central Library) Haverfordwest Library
Dew Street, Haverfordwest, SA61 1SU; tel: 01437 775244; fax: 01437 769218
Fishguard Library
High Street, Fishguard, SA65 9AR; tel: 01348 872694; fax: 01348 872694
Milford Haven Library
Hamilton Terrace, Milford Haven, SA73 3JP; tel: 01646 692897; fax: 01646 692892
Pembroke Dock Library
Water Street, Pembroke Dock, SA72 6DW; tel: 01646 686356; fax: 01646 686356
Tenby Library
Greenhill House, Tenby, SA70 7LB; tel: 01834 843934; fax: 01834 843934

Part-time Pembrokeshire Libraries:
Crymych Library
Preseli School, Crymych, SA41 3QF; tel: 01239 832092
Goodwick Library
Chestnut House, Main Street, Goodwick, SA64 0BN; tel: 01348 874838
Hakin Library
Waterloo Square, Hakin, Milford Haven, SA73 3BS; tel: 01646 690335
Narberth Library
St James Street, Narberth, SA67 7BU; tel: 01834 861781
Newport Library
Bank House, Bridge Street, Newport, SA42 0TB; tel: 01239 821169
Neyland Library
St Clements Road, Neyland, SA73 1SH; tel: 01646 600791
Pembroke Library
38 Main Street, Pembroke, SA71 4NP; tel: 01646 682973
Saundersfoot Library
Regency Hall, Saundersfoot, SA69 9NG; tel: 01834 813958
St Davids Library
City Hall, High Street, St Davids, SA62 6SD; tel: 01437 721170

HAVERGAL BRIAN SOCIETY

Acronym or abbreviation: HBS

39 Giles Coppice, Gipsy Hill, Upper Norwood, London, SE19 1XF

Tel: 020 8761 8134
E-mail: damian_rees@yahoo.com

Website:
http://www.havergalbrian.org

Enquiries:
Enquiries to: Secretary

Founded:
1974

Organisation type and purpose:
Membership association (membership is by subscription, election or invitation), present number of members: 200, registered charity (charity number 275793).

To promote public knowledge of the work of William Havergal Brian (1876–1972) and, to this end, to support and sponsor its publication, performance and recording.

Subject coverage:
Havergal Brian (1876–1972): the composer and his work.

Museum or gallery collection, archive, or library special collection:
Havergal Brian Society Archive in the University of Keele

Printed publications:
Complete Piano Works (price £11)
Havergal Brian's Gothic Symphony (Two Studies, price £10)
Havergal Brian on Music, vol. l British Music (first of six vols, 1986, published with Toccata Press; vol. 2 to be published 2008–09)
Information leaflet with Discography, Bibliography, Society's Aims and Objects
Newsletter (6 times a year, free to members)

Access to staff:
Contact by letter, by telephone, by e-mail and via website

HAVERING COLLEGE OF FURTHER AND HIGHER EDUCATION

Ardleigh Green Road, Hornchurch, Essex, RM11 2LL

Tel: 01708 455011\ Minicom no. 01708 462735
Fax: 01708 462788
E-mail: astevart@havering-college.ac.uk

Website:
http://ipac.havering-college.ac.uk

Enquiries:
Enquiries to: Head of Learning Centres
Direct tel: 01708 462831
Direct e-mail: astrande@havering-college.ac.uk
Other contacts: Library tel no: 01708 455011 ext 2040

Founded:
1948

Organisation type and purpose:
Library of a college of further and higher education.

Subject coverage:
Art; design; hairdressing; beauty therapy; graphics; media production; business studies; management; accountancy; health services administration; motor vehicle engineering; mechanical engineering; electrical engineering; electronic engineering; computer studies; robotics; humanities; mathematics; science; secretarial and office studies; social services; social work; nursery nursing; teacher education; catering, youth work.

Non-library collection catalogue:
All or part available online

Access to staff:
Contact by letter, by telephone, by fax and by e-mail
Hours: Ardleigh Green Site: Mon to Thu, 0900 to 2000; Fri, 1000 to 1700;
Quarles Site: Mon to Thu, 0900 to 1900; Fri, 0900 to 1700

Access for disabled people:
Parking provided, ramped entry, access to all public areas, toilet facilities

Annexe libraries at:
Quarles Campus
Harold Hill, Romford, Essex; tel: 01708 455011 ext 4009; e-mail: jforsyth@havering-college.ac.uk

HAWK AND OWL TRUST

Acronym or abbreviation: HOT

c/o Zoological Society of London, Regent's Park, London, NW1 4RY

Tel: 01626 334 864

Fax: 01626 334 864
E-mail: hawkandowl@aol.com

Website:
http://www.hawkandowl.org
general information on the Trust and education services at the Education Centre.

Enquiries:
Enquiries to: Chairman
Direct tel: 01761 462 017
Direct fax: 01761 462 017
Other contacts: The Hawk and Owl Trust Membership Secretary: for administration of the Trust's Adopt a Box scheme, and issues periodic reports to subscribers.

Founded:
1969

Formerly called:
The Hawk Trust

Organisation type and purpose:
Membership association (membership is by subscription), present number of members: c. 2500, voluntary organisation, registered charity (charity number 1058565), suitable for all ages, research organisation.
The conservation of birds of prey in the wild and their habitat.

Subject coverage:
Conservation of the barn owl and all birds of prey in the wild, nestboxes and habitat creation. The Law and Planning Regulations concerning birds of prey, particularly building regulations affecting barn owls.

Museum or gallery collection, archive, or library special collection:
Slide and picture library

Trade and statistical information:
Barn Owl road casualties survey.
Urban Peregrine Falcon survey.

Printed publications:
Barn Owl (Newsletter of Barn Owl Conservation Network, 2 times a year)
Boxes, Baskets and Platforms, Artificial Nest Sites for Owls and Other Birds of Prey
Peregrine (Newsletter of Hawk & Owl Trust, 2 times a year)
The Barn Owl in the British Isles, its Past, Present and Future
The Barn Owl, The Farmer's Friend, Needs a Helping Hand
Order printed publications from: Publications Officer, The Hawk and Owl Trust Publications
PO Box 530, Windlesham, GU20 6XZ, e-mail: hawkowlpub@tiscali.co.uk

Publications list:
Available in print

Access to staff:
Contact by letter, by telephone, by fax, by e-mail and via website
Hours: Mon to Fri, 0900 to 1700

Adopt a Box:
Adopt a Box
2 Mill Walk, Wheathampstead, AL4 8DT; tel: 01582 832 182; fax: 01582 832 182; e-mail: hawkandowltrust@aol.com

Education Officer:
The Hawk and Owl Trust
Exhibition and education parties at the Education Centre, Chalfont St Giles, Buckinghamshire, HP8 4AB; tel: 01494 876262; fax: 01494 876262; e-mail: hoteducation@tesco .net

Member of:
Birdlife International

Membership Secretary:
The Hawk and Owl Trust
11 St Mary's Close, Abbotskerswell, Newton Abbot, Devon, TQ12 5QF; tel: 01626 334864; fax: 01626 334864; e-mail: hawkandowl@aol.com

Other addresses:
Education Officer
c/o Chiltern Open Air Museum, Newland Park, Gorelands Lane, Chalfont St Giles, HP8 4AB; tel: 01494 876262; fax: 01494 876262; e-mail: hoteducation@tesco.net
The Hawk and Owl Trust National Conservation and Education Centre
The HOT Barn Owl Conservation Network
National Coordinator, c/o Sheepdrove Trust, Sheepdrove Organic Farm Centre, Lambourn, Berkshire, RG17 7UU; tel: 01488 674727; fax: 01488 72677

HAWTHORNS URBAN WILDLIFE CENTRE

Acronym or abbreviation: The Hawthorns

The Hawthorns, Southampton Common, Southampton, SO15 7NN

Tel: 023 8067 1921\ Minicom no. 023 8067 8079
Fax: 023 8067 6859
E-mail: lin.hand@southampton.gov.uk

Enquiries:
Enquiries to: Southampton City Council Natural Environment Manager

Founded:
1980

Organisation type and purpose:
Local government body.
Urban wildlife centre.
Urban nature conservation displays, events, education and information.

Subject coverage:
Biological records, wildlife information, urban habitat management.

Access to staff:
Contact by letter, by telephone, by fax, by e-mail and in person. Appointment necessary.
Hours: Mon to Fri, 1000 to 1700; Sat, Sun, 1200 to 1600

Access for disabled people:
Access to all public areas

Other address:
Natural Environment Unit, Southampton City Council
As main address; tel: As main numbers

Parent body:
Neighbourhoods, Southampton City Council
Civic Centre, Southampton, SO14 7LP; tel: 023 8022 3855

HAYDN SOCIETY OF GREAT BRITAIN

Heron House, Aldcliffe Mews, Lancaster, LA1 5BT

Tel: 01524 61553
Fax: 01524 61553
E-mail: d.mccaldin@lancaster.ac.uk

Website:
http://www.haydnsocietyofgb.netfirms.com

Enquiries:
Enquiries to: Director

Founded:
1979

Organisation type and purpose:
Learned society (membership is by subscription).

Subject coverage:
Music of Joseph Haydn and his contemporaries, all matters concerning Haydn performances and research.

Printed publications:
Journal (annually, ISSN 1350–1267)

Electronic and video publications:
Haydn and Schubert Masses (Meridian and Duo 89003 commercially available or direct mail from Haydn Society, CD or cassette)

continued overleaf

Haydn Nelson Mass, The Storm, Missa Brevis in F
(Meridian CDE 84393 commercially available or
from the Haydn Society)

Access to staff:
Contact by letter, by fax, by e-mail and via
website
Hours: Mon to Fri, 0900 to 1700

Links with:
similar societies world-wide

HDRA

Formal name: Henry Doubleday Research
Association
Acronym or abbreviation: HDRA

Ryton Organic Gardens, Ryton-on-Dunsmore,
Coventry, Warwickshire, CV8 3LG

Tel: 024 7630 3517
Fax: 024 7663 9229
E-mail: enquiry@hdra.org.uk

Website:
http://www.hdra.org.uk
General organic gardening.

Enquiries:
Enquiries to: Chief Executive

Founded:
1958

Organisation type and purpose:
International organisation, membership
association (membership is by subscription),
present number of members: 30,000, registered
charity (charity number 298104), suitable for ages:
all, consultancy, research organisation.
Research, education, promotion of
environmentally friendly organic gardening,
farming and food.

Subject coverage:
Organic gardening, organic horticulture, organic
farming, organic food, recycling, composting,
reafforestation, organic catering and retailing.

**Museum or gallery collection, archive, or library
special collection:**
Organic gardening and farming book collection
library and scientific papers

Trade and statistical information:
Data on organic techniques in the UK and
overseas.
Data on reafforestation tree species in developing
countries.

Printed publications:
The Organic Gardening Catalogue 2000
Organic Handbook Series
Step by Step Organic Gardening Series
The Encyclopedia of Organic Gardening
A Simple Guide to Organic Gardening
Growing Vegetables from Seed
Order printed publications from: The Organic
Gardening Catalogue – Retail, Chase Organics Ltd
River Dene Estate, Molesey Road, Hersham,
Surrey, KT12 4RG, tel: 01932 253666, fax: 01932
252707

Electronic and video publications:
An Introduction to Organic Gardening (video)

Access to staff:
Contact by letter, by telephone, by fax, by e-mail,
in person and via website
Hours: Mon to Fri, 0900 to 1700

Access for disabled people:
Parking provided, access to all public areas, toilet
facilities

Other addresses:
Yalding Organic Gardens
Benover Lane, Yalding, Maidstone, Kent, ME18
6EX; tel: 01622 814650; fax: 01622 814650

HEADMASTERS' AND HEADMISTRESSES' CONFERENCE

Acronym or abbreviation: HMC

12 The Point, Rockingham Road, Market
Harborough, Leicestershire, LE16 7QU

Tel: 01858 469 059
Fax: 01858 469 532
E-mail: hmc@hmc.org.uk

Enquiries:
Enquiries to: Secretary
Other contacts: Chairman

Founded:
1869

Formerly called:
Headmasters' Conference

Organisation type and purpose:
Professional body, trade union.

Subject coverage:
Independent education; boarding; curriculum
matters; professional development of members
and members' schools; school sport; community
service.

Printed publications:
Conference and Common Room (3 times a year)

Access to staff:
Contact by letter, by telephone and by e-mail
Hours: Mon to Fri, 0900 to 1700

HEADWAY – THE BRAIN INJURY ASSOCIATION

7 King Edward Court, King Edward Street,
Nottingham, NG1 1EW

Tel: 0115 924 0800\ Minicom no. 0115 950 7825
Fax: 0115 958 4446
E-mail: enquiries@headway.org.uk

Website:
http://www.headway.org.uk
Information and contact details for organisation
UK wide. Information on TBI; publications (full
text and priced); events and conferences; solicitors'
list.

Enquiries:
Enquiries to: Communication Officer
Direct tel: Helpline tel: 0115 924 0800 / 0808 800
2244 (freephone)

Founded:
1979

Organisation type and purpose:
National organisation, voluntary organisation,
registered charity (charity number 1025852).
Community services for people with head injuries.
We have over 112 local groups around the UK.
Over 50 run Headway House day care centres.
Contact details of local groups are available from
Central Office where we can also provide
straightforward information on many aspects of
head injury.

Subject coverage:
Head injury; traumatic brain damage and its
physical and psychological outcome; help and
support of survivors and their families.

Printed publications:
Booklets
Headway News (quarterly, members)
Leaflets
What is Head Injury
Know Someone Who Has Had a Head Injury

Microform publications:
Brain Injury: The Way Forward (video)

Publications list:
Available online and in print

Access to staff:
Contact by letter, by telephone, by fax, by e-mail
and via website
Hours: Mon to Fri, 0900 to 1700
Special comments: Helpline opening hours Mon to
Fri, 0900 to 1700.

HEALTH AND SAFETY EXECUTIVE

Acronym or abbreviation: HSE

Rose Court, 2 Southwark Bridge, London, SE1 9HS

Tel: 020 7717 6000
Fax: 020 7717 6134
E-mail: public.enquiries@hse.gov.uk

Website:
http://www.hse.gov.uk

Enquiries:
Enquiries to: Manager Site Services

Founded:
1975

Organisation type and purpose:
National government body.

Subject coverage:
Occupational health and safety policy.

Printed publications:
Order printed publications from: HSE Books, PO Box
1999
Sudbury, Suffolk, CO10 2WA, tel: 01787 881165,
fax: 01787 313995, e-mail: www.hsebooks.co.uk

Publications list:
Available in print

Access to staff:
Contact by letter, by telephone, by fax, by e-mail
and via website. Appointment necessary.
Hours: Mon to Fri, 0900 to 1700

Access for disabled people:
Level entry
Department of Transport, Local Government and
the Regions

HEALTH AND SAFETY EXECUTIVE – ELECTRICAL EQUIPMENT CERTIFICATION SERVICE

Acronym or abbreviation: EECS

Harpur Hill, Buxton, Derbyshire, SK17 9JN

Tel: 01298 28000
Fax: 01298 28244
E-mail: baseefa.info.eecs@hsl.gov.uk

Website:
http://www.baseefa.com
Information relating to services provided by EECS.
Guidance on safety in hazardous areas and
certification. List of EECS publications.

Enquiries:
Enquiries to: Director
Other contacts: Product Certification Support Team

Founded:
1926

Formerly called:
British Approvals Service for Electrical Equipment
in Flammable Atmosphere (BASEEFA) (year of
change 1987)

Organisation type and purpose:
National government body.
Government certification body, Electrical
Equipment Certification Service (EECS) of the
Health and Safety Executive.
Testing and Certification of explosion protected
electrical equipment. Safety in hazardous areas.

Subject coverage:
Explosion protection (eg flameproof, intrinsic
safety), equipment and systems for use in
hazardous areas, flammable and explosive
atmospheres, European conformity and directives,
certification, testing, quality assurance, repairs.

Printed publications:
Publications include:
BASEEFA Technical Rules (£10)
Designers Guide – Intrinsic Safety for Group II
Equipment (1994, £35)
Designers Guide – Intrinsic Safety for Mining
Equipment (P001–1993, £35)
EECS Newsletter (3 times a year, free)

Electrical Equipment Certification Service Appeals Procedure (P002–2000, free)
Quality Assurance Guide (1998, free)
Type Examination Guide (1998, free)
Verification Guide (1998, free)

Publications list:
Available online and in print

Access to staff:
Contact by letter, by telephone, by fax, by e-mail and via website. Appointment necessary.
Hours: Mon to Thu, 0900 to 1700; Fri, 0900 to 1630

Parent body:
Department of the Environment

HEALTH AND SAFETY EXECUTIVE – HEALTH AND SAFETY LABORATORY

Acronym or abbreviation: HSE

Business Development Group, Health & Safety Laboratory, Harpur Hill, Buxton, Derbyshire, SK17 9JN 01298 218000 01298 218590

Tel: 01298 218000
Fax: 01298 218590
E-mail: hslinfo@hsl.gov.uk

Website:
http://www.hsl.gov.uk/
Introduction to work, duties and publications of HSE; health and safety law; contacts, online enquiry service.

Enquiries:
Enquiries to: Information Centre Manager
Direct tel: 0114 289 2905

Founded:
1975

Organisation type and purpose:
National government body.
To ensure that risks to people's health and safety from work activities are properly controlled.

Subject coverage:
Occupational health, hygiene and safety, especially in industry including: nuclear, mines, offshore energy, factories, workshops, agriculture, construction, railways, explosives.

Museum or gallery collection, archive, or library special collection:
Historical aspects of safety in mines and factories

Printed publications:
Audiovisual catalogue (every 2 years, priced)
Publications catalogues (free)
List of organisations providing information on health and safety (free)
Video catalogue (free)
A large number of publications, some in specific series and others more general, applicable to most branches of industry and professional working environments including education, in the following groups:
Accident/Incident Reports
Annual Reports
Contract Research Reports
Guidance Notes on chemical safety, environmental hygiene, general series, medical series, and plant and machinery
Legal including Approved Codes of Practice
Methods for the Determination of Hazardous Substances, for occupational hygienists
Offshore Technology Reports
Toxicity Reviews
Order printed publications from: HSE Books
PO Box 1999, Sudbury, Suffolk, CO10 2WA, tel: 01787 881165, fax: 01787 313995, e-mail: www.hsebooks.co.uk

Electronic and video publications:
HSE Bookfinder
HSELINE (bibliographical database published commercially)
OSH-CD and OSH-OFFSHORE (pub. The Stationery Office Ltd and Silver Platter)
OSH-ROM (Silver Platter)

Publications list:
Available in print

Access to staff:
Contact by letter, by telephone, by fax, by e-mail and via website. Appointment necessary.
Hours: Mon to Fri, 0900 to 1700

Parent body:
Department of Transport, Local Government and the Regions

HEALTH AND SAFETY EXECUTIVE – INFORMATION SERVICES

Acronym or abbreviation: HSE

Caerphilly Business Park, Caerphilly, CF83 3GG

Tel: 0845 345 00 55
Fax: 0845 4089566
E-mail: hse.infoline@natbrit.com

Website:
http://www.hse.gov.uk
Information on the structure and functioning of the HSE is given together with information on the latest developments from within the HSE and the full text of HSE's free leaflets.

Enquiries:
Enquiries to: Public Enquiry Point

Organisation type and purpose:
National government body.

Subject coverage:
Occupational health and safety, particularly medical, chemical and technical information..

Printed publications:
Order printed publications from: HSE Books
PO Box 1999, Sudbury, Suffolk, CO10 2WA, tel: 01787 881165, fax: 01787 313995, e-mail: http://www.hsebooks.co.uk

Publications list:
Available online and in print

Access to staff:
Contact by letter, by telephone, by fax, by e-mail and via website
Hours: Mon to Fri, 0830 to 1700

Other address:
Health and Safety Executive

Parent body:
Department for Work and Pensions

HEALTH CARE LIBRARIES

Cairns Library, Oxford Radcliffe Hospital, Headington, Oxford, OX3 9DU

Tel: 01865 221936
Fax: 01865 221941
E-mail: library@hcl.ox.ac.uk

Website:
http://www.ouls.ox.ac.uk/hcl

Enquiries:
Enquiries to: Head of Health Care Libraries

Formerly called:
Oxford Postgraduate Medical Library (year of change 1973); Cairns Library (year of change 2002); Institute of Health Sciences Library (year of change 2002)

Organisation type and purpose:
University library.
Library of the Faculty of Clinical Medicine, University of Oxford.
Also serves as an information source for NHS staff in the Oxford Radcliffe Hospitals Trust and the Oxfordshire Primary Care Trust.

Subject coverage:
Health care including clinical medicine, nursing, physiotherapy, radiography and other paramedical subjects. Satellite libraries have specialities in cancer, diabetes, neurosciences, gerontology, public health medicine and statistics.

Library catalogue:
All or part available online

Access to staff:
Contact by letter, by telephone, by fax and by e-mail. Appointment necessary.

Access to building, collection or gallery:
No access other than to staff
Hours: 24 hours
Special comments: Members only

Access for disabled people:
Access to all public areas
Special comments: Ramped or level entry – varies on different sites.

Also at:
Knowledge Centre
University of Oxford Old Road Campus Research Building, Headington, Oxford, OX3 7DQ; tel: 01865 221936; fax: 01865 289406; e-mail: library@hcl.ox.ac.uk; website: http://www.ouls.ox.ac.uk/hcl

Links with:
University of Oxford
Wellington Square, Oxford, OX1 2JD; tel: 01865 270001

HEALTH DEVELOPMENT AGENCY

Acronym or abbreviation: HDA

Holborn Gate, 330 High Holborn, London, WC1V 7BA

Tel: 020 7430 0850
Fax: 020 7061 3390
E-mail: communications@hda-online.org.uk

Website:
http://www.hda.nhs.uk/
Health Development Agency
http://www.foodpovertyprojects.org.uk/
Food poverty projects database
http://www.hda.nhs.uk/evidence/
HDA Evidence Base
http://www.healthaction.nhs.uk/
Health Action website and knowledge management service
http://healthpromis.hda-online.org.uk/
HealthPromis database
http://www.hiagateway.org.uk/
Health Impact Assessment Gateway
http://www.quick.org.uk
Quality Information Checklist, designed for use in educational settings.
http://www.phel.gov.uk/
Public Health electronic Library
http://www.social-action.org.uk/sarp/
SARP – Provides details of the social action research projects in Nottingham and Salford, set up to find out how social interventions can contribute to the promotion of health and the reduction of inequalities.
http://www.ohn.gov.uk
Our Healthier Nation.
http://www.hda.nhs.uk/nurseeducators/
Support for Nurse Educators
http://www.wiredforhealth.gov.uk
National Healthy School Standard
http://www.welltown.gov.uk
For Key Stage 1
http://www.galaxy-h.gov.uk
For Key Stage 2
http://www.lifebytes.gov.uk
For Key Stage 3
http://www.mindbodysoul.gov.uk
For Key Stage 4

Enquiries:
Enquiries to: Director of Marketing & Communications
Direct tel: 020 7061 3110
Direct e-mail: jfrench@hda-online.org.uk

Founded:
April 2000

Formerly called:
Health Education Council (HEC); Health Education Authority (HEA) (year of change 2000)

continued overleaf

Organisation type and purpose:
Statutory body; research and review organisation; evidence-based practice;
Special Health Authority within the NHS; the HDA's functions will transfer to the National Institute for Clinical Excellence from April 2005

Subject coverage:
Accidents, alcohol, black and minority ethnic groups, breastfeeding, cancer, children, communities, coronary heart disease, diet, drugs, evaluation, evidence,
health impact assessment, health improvement, health inequalities, HIV/AIDS and sexual health, local strategic partnerships,
management and strategies, men's health, mental health, National Healthy School Standard,
health needs assessment, nutrition, obesity, older people, physical activity, pregnancy, primary care, public health,
research and review, smoking, surveys, transport, women's health, workplace health, young people

Printed publications:
Health Development Today (magazine, 6 times a year)
Health Development Agency Annual Report
Health Development Agency Delivery Plan (annual)
Health Development Agency Impact Report (annual)
HDA Catalogue which includes selected HEA titles
All HDA publications are available for download from the HDA website
Order printed publications from: Health Development Agency
PO Box 90, Wetherby, Yorkshire, LS23 7EX, tel: 0870 121 4194, fax: 0870 121 4195, e-mail: hda@twoten.press.net

Publications list:
Available online and in print

Access to staff:
Contact by letter, by telephone, by e-mail and via website. Appointment necessary.
Hours: Mon to Fri, 0900 to 1700

Access to building, collection or gallery:
No access other than to staff

Access for disabled people:
Level entry, access to all public areas

HEALTH EDUCATION BOARD FOR SCOTLAND

Acronym or abbreviation: HEBS

Woodburn House, Canaan Lane, Edinburgh, EH10 4SG

Tel: 0131 536 5500\ Minicom no. 0131 536 5593
Fax: 0131 536 5502
E-mail: library.enquiries@hebs.scot.nhs.uk

Website:
http://www.hebs.com
Website for organisation. Contains a variety of health information and information about HEBS' work.

Enquiries:
Enquiries to: Librarian
Direct tel: 0131 536 5582
Direct e-mail: margaret.forrest@hebs.scot.nhs.uk

Formerly called:
Scottish Health Education Group (SHEG) (year of change 1991)

Organisation type and purpose:
National government body.
Organisation to promote and help maintain the health of the population of Scotland through promotional and educational activities, and by offering an information and resources service.

Subject coverage:
Health education and health promotion, behavioural sciences, health statistics, sociology, smoking, addictions, alcohol misuse and abuse,

drugs, family planning, the elderly, nutrition, AIDS, cancer education, dental health education, consumer health information.

Printed publications:
A Guide to HEBS (brief introduction, free)
HEBS Annual Report (free)
Information publications to support media campaigns, e.g. alcohol, drugs, smoking, AIDS, diet and nutrition, women's health etc
Library Bulletin (6 times a year)

Electronic and video publications:
HEBS on CD-ROM (updated annually) contains a variety of databases relevant to health information
Videos (prices vary)

Access to staff:
Contact by letter, by telephone, by fax, by e-mail and in person
Hours: Mon to Thu, 0900 to 1630; Fri, 0900 to 1600

Access to building, collection or gallery:
No access other than to staff
Special comments: Library open to people resident in Scotland only.

Close links with:
Scottish Health Information Network (SHINE)

Main information service and library:
Health Promotion Library Scotland
reader enquiries, 0131 536 5593, minicom text; tel: 08459 125442; e-mail: library.enquiries@hebs.scot.nhs.uk

Parent body:
National Health Service in Scotland

HEALTH FOOD MANUFACTURERS' ASSOCIATION

Acronym or abbreviation: HFMA

63 Hampton Court Way, Thames Ditton, Surrey, KT7 0LT

Tel: 020 8398 4066
Fax: 020 8398 5402
E-mail: pviner@hfma.co.uk

Website:
http://www.hfma.co.uk

Enquiries:
Enquiries to: Director

Founded:
1965

Part of the now disbanded:
British Health Food Trade Association (year of change 1991)

Organisation type and purpose:
Trade association (membership is by subscription), present number of members: 150, manufacturing industry, consultancy.

Subject coverage:
Health foods, homoeopathic, herbal, dietetic products etc, food supplements, alternative medicines, natural beauty products, other health-related matters, import, export, labelling regulations etc.

Printed publications:
Health foods, homoeopathic, herbal, dietetic products etc

Access to staff:
Contact by letter, by telephone, by fax and by e-mail. Access for members only.
Hours: Mon to Fri, 0900 to 1700

HEALTH FOR ALL NETWORK (UK) LTD

Acronym or abbreviation: HFAN (UK)

New Century House, 52 Tithebarn Street, Liverpool, L2 2SR

Tel: 0151 231 4283
Fax: 0151 231 4209

E-mail: ukhfan@livjm.ac.uk

Website:
http://independent.livjm.ac.uk/healthforall/

Enquiries:
Enquiries to: Office Manager

Founded:
1989

Formerly called:
United Kingdom Healthy Cities Network (year of change 1991); United Kingdom Health for All Network (year of change 1995)

Organisation type and purpose:
Membership association (membership is by subscription), present number of members: 450, registered charity (charity number 1062376), suitable for ages: all, training organisation.

Subject coverage:
Information on health for all, healthy cities, work and health, public policy.

Printed publications:
Action for Health in Cities (1994, £2 plus p&p)
Annual Report
Newsletter – Network News
Our Cities Our Future
Full Resource Pack
HFA Starter Pack (M Halliday, 1993, £7 plus p&p)
Community Participation in HFA Pack (1993, £3 plus p&p)
Community Health Needs Assessment (1993, £3 plus p&p)

Publications list:
Available in print

Access to staff:
Contact by letter, by telephone, by fax and by e-mail
Hours: Mon to Fri, 0900 to 1700

HEALTH PROFESSIONS COUNCIL

Acronym or abbreviation: HPC

Park House, 184 Kennington Park Road, London, SE11 4BU

Tel: 020 7582 0866
Fax: 020 7820 9684

Website:
http://www.hpc-uk.org

Enquiries:
Enquiries to: Registrar & Chief Executive

Founded:
2002

Formerly called:
Council for Professions Supplementary to Medicine (CPSM) (year of change 2002)

Organisation type and purpose:
Statutory body.
Independently regulating 13 health professions. Protection of the public.

Subject coverage:
Matters related to courses approved for state registration of arts therapists, chiropodists, dieticians, medical laboratory scientific officers, occupational therapists, orthoptists, orthotists, prosthetists, physiotherapists and radiographers; clinical scientists; paramedics; speech and language therapists; operating department practitioners.

Museum or gallery collection, archive, or library special collection:
Registers of the professions of chiropody, dietetics, medical laboratory sciences, occupational therapy, orthoptics, physiotherapy and radiography

Trade and statistical information:
Data on numbers of professionals registered including those registered under European directives on mutual recognition of academic qualifications.

Printed publications:
Annual Register listing state-registered personnel
   in each of the professions
Annual Report
Public/Patient Leaflet
Consultation Document

Access to staff:
Contact by letter, by telephone, by fax and in
person
Hours: Mon to Fri, 0900 to 1700

Access to building, collection or gallery:
Hours: Mon to fri, 0900 to 1700

Access for disabled people:
Access to all public areas, toilet facilities
Hours: Mon to Fri, 0900 to 1700

HEALTH PROMOTION AGENCY FOR NORTHERN IRELAND

Acronym or abbreviation: HPANI

18 Ormeau Avenue, Belfast, BT2 8HS

Tel: 028 9031 1611
Fax: 028 9031 1711
E-mail: info@hpani.org.uk

Website:
http://www.healthpromotionagency.org.uk
http://www.drugsalcohol.info
Regional website, drugs and alcohol information
for health professionals.
http://mindingyourhead.info
Information to promote and increase
understanding of good mental health.
http://www.up-2-you.net
Information on health risks of drugs, alcohol and
smoking for young people aged 11–14.
http://www.breastfedbabies.org
To provide information on breastfeeding for
mothers and health professionals.

Enquiries:
Enquiries to: Finance & Administration Manager
Other contacts: Resources Manager for availability
of published resources and information

Founded:
1990

Organisation type and purpose:
Advisory body, statutory body.
Special Agency of the Department of Health, Social
Services and Public Safety.
To make health a top priority for everyone in
Northern Ireland. Summarised under the
following broad headings: policy development and
advice; research, information and analysis; public
and professional information; training and
professional development; corporate business
services.

Subject coverage:
Information on health promotion related issues,
including campaigns, research and training, topic
information on alcohol and drugs, smoking,
physical activity, nutrition and oral health, children
and young people, mental health, social health,
breastfeeding, Healthy Schools, Health Promoting
Hospitals, Health Promoting Workplaces. The
Confidential Enquiry into Maternal and Child
Health (CEMACH) aims to improve the health of
mothers, babies and children by carrying out
confidential enquiries on a nationwide basis and
widely disseminating the findings and
recommendations.

Printed publications:
A range of resources providing health promotion
   information including research reports, leaflets,
   booklets
Annual Report
Annual Research and Evaluation Reviews
Inform (newsletter, 6 times a year)

Publications list:
Available online

Access to staff:
Contact by letter, by telephone, by fax, by e-mail
and via website

Hours: Mon to Thurs, 0900 to 1700; Fri, 0900 to 1630
Special comments: Enquiries welcome from health
professionals, members of the public should
contact the central health promotion resource
service of their local Health and Social Services
Board area.

Access for disabled people:
Ramped entry, access to all public areas, toilet
facilities

HEALTH PROTECTION AGENCY

Acronym or abbreviation: HPA

Porton Down, Salisbury, Wiltshire, SP4 0JG

Tel: 01980 612711
Fax: 01980 612818
E-mail: porton.library@hpa.org.uk

Website:
http://www.hpa.org.uk

Enquiries:
Enquiries to: Librarian

Founded:
1979

Formerly called:
Centre for Applied Microbiology and Research
(year of change 2004)

Organisation type and purpose:
National government body, research organisation.
Non-departmental public body.
Public health research and production of
biopharmaceuticals.

Subject coverage:
Infectious diseases; immunology; vaccine research
and production; emergency response; molecular
biology; therapeutic products; pathogens; virology

Library catalogue:
All or part available in-house

Access to staff:
Contact by letter, by telephone, by fax and by e-
mail
Hours: Mon to Fri, 0900 to 1700

Access to building, collection or gallery:
No access other than to staff

Constituent part of:
Department of Health

HEALTH PROTECTION AGENCY – CENTRE FOR INFECTIONS

Acronym or abbreviation: HPA

61 Colindale Avenue, London, NW9 5EQ

Tel: 020 8327 7616
Fax: 020 8200 7875

Website:
http://www.hpa.org.uk

Enquiries:
Enquiries to: Library enquiries
Direct e-mail: colindale.library@hpa.org.uk

Founded:
2003

Organisation type and purpose:
National government body

Subject coverage:
Infectious diseases, medical microbiology and
virology, vaccination, microbiological aspects of
public health, microbiology of food and water.

Information services:
Reference only, by prior appointment only

Library catalogue:
All or part available online and in-house

Access to staff:
Contact by letter. Appointment necessary.
Hours: Mon to Fri, 0930 to 1700
Special comments: Prior appointment required

Access to building, collection or gallery:
Prior appointment required
Hours: Mon to Fri, 0930 to 1700

HEALTH PROTECTION AGENCY, CENTRE FOR RADIATION, CHEMICAL AND ENVIRONMENTAL HAZARDS

Acronym or abbreviation: HPA CRCE

Chilton, Didcot, Oxfordshire, OX11 0RQ

Tel: 01235 831600
Fax: 01235 833891
E-mail: david.perry@hpa.org.uk

Website:
http://www.hpa.org.uk/
Description of Health Protection Agency, its work
and publications.

Enquiries:
Enquiries to: Librarian
Direct tel: 01235 822649

Founded:
2005

Formerly called:
National Radiological Protection Board

Organisation type and purpose:
National government body, research organisation.
Government body established by statute to give
advice on health effects of radiation, chemicals.

Subject coverage:
Radiological protection, biological and medical
effects of ionising radiations, cytogenetics, health
hazards posed by chemical exposures, health
effects of non-ionising radiations; radioactivity in
consumer protection; radioactivity in the natural
environment and environmental modelling;
radioactivity in man, dosimetry; training in
radiological protection; epidemiology; medical
physics.

**Museum or gallery collection, archive, or library
special collection:**
ICRP, NCRP, ICRU, IAEA safety series, IARC
   Monographs and Scientific Publications

Library catalogue:
All or part available in-house

Printed publications:
Annual Report
Consultative Documents (occasional)
Documents of the Health Protection Agency Series
   B: Radiation, Chemical and Environmental
   Hazards (formal advice, irregular)
Information Sheets and booklets
Living with Radiation (booklet)
Technical Reports (HPA-RP series)
Chemical Hazards & Poisons Report

Electronic and video publications:
All recent publications available electronically
   (online)

Publications list:
Available online

Access to staff:
Contact by letter, by fax and by e-mail.
Appointment necessary.
Hours: Mon to Thu, 0815 to 1700; Fri, 0815 to 1600

Access to building, collection or gallery:
Prior appointment required

Access for disabled people:
Ramped entry, toilet facilities

Also at:
HPA Occupational Services
   Leeds
HPA Radiation and Environmental Monitoring
Scotland
   Glasgow

HEALTH PROTECTION AGENCY, MYCOLOGY REFERENCE LABORATORY

Acronym or abbreviation: HPA MRL

Myrtle Road, Kingsdown, Bristol, BS2 8EL

Tel: 0117 929 1326
Fax: 0117 922 6611

Enquiries:
Enquiries to: Director

Founded:
1946

Organisation type and purpose:
National government body, service industry.

Subject coverage:
Maintenance of the National Collection of Pathogenic Fungi, identification of fungi isolated from clinical sources.

Museum or gallery collection, archive, or library special collection:
National Collection of Pathogenic Fungi

Non-library collection catalogue:
All or part available online and in print

Access to staff:
Contact by letter, by telephone and by fax
Hours: Mon to Fri, 0900 to 1700

Access to building, collection or gallery:
Prior appointment required

HEALTH SCOTLAND LIBRARY

NHS Health Scotland, The Priory, Canaan Lane, Edinburgh, EH10 4SG

Tel: 0845 912 5442\ Minicom no. 0131 536 5593
Fax: 0131 536 5502
E-mail: library@health.scot.nhs.uk

Website:
http://www.healthscotland.com

Enquiries:
Enquiries to: Library Services Manager
Direct tel: 0131 536 5582
Direct e-mail: sharon.jamieson@health.scot.nhs.uk

Formerly called:
Health Promotion Library Scotland

Organisation type and purpose:
Library service for people interested in health improvement who live and/or work in Scotland.

Subject coverage:
Health improvement, health promotion and public health.

Library catalogue:
All or part available online

Printed publications:
Health Scotland publications are listed in catalogue on Internet
Library produces a bi-monthly current awareness bulletin

Publications list:
Available online

Access to staff:
Contact by letter, by telephone, by fax, by e-mail, in person and via website
Hours: Mon to Thu, 0900 to 1630; Fri, 0900 to 1600

Access to building, collection or gallery:
Hours: Mon to Thu, 0900 to 1630; Fri, 0900 to 1600

Also at:
NHS Health Scotland
Woodburn House, Canaan Lane, Edinburgh, EH10 4SG; tel: 0131 536 5500; fax: 0131 536 5501

HEALTH SERVICES MANAGEMENT CENTRE

Acronym or abbreviation: HSMC

School of Public Policy, University of Birmingham, Park House, 40 Edgbaston Park Road, Birmingham, B15 2RT

Tel: 0121 414 7060
Fax: 0121 414 7051

Website:
http://www.bham.ac.uk/hsmc/library
General information on services, access to catalogue and to list of journal holdings.

Enquiries:
Enquiries to: Librarian

Founded:
1972

Organisation type and purpose:
University department or institute, consultancy. Education and research in the field of health service management.

Subject coverage:
Health services management, quality in health services management, primary health care overseas.

Printed publications:
Discussion papers, research reports, handbook series, project reports, working papers and other publications
Order printed publications from: Maureen Alcock, Health Services Management Centre
The University of Birmingham, Park House, 40 Edgbaston Park Road, Birmingham, B15 2RT, tel: 0121 414 6210, e-mail: M.Alcock@bham.ac.uk

Publications list:
Available in print

Access to staff:
Appointment necessary.
Hours: Mon to Fri, 0900 to 1700

HEALTHLINK WORLDWIDE

56–64 Leonard Street, London, EC2A 4LT

Tel: 020 7549 0240
Fax: 020 7549 0241
E-mail: info@healthlink.org.uk

Website:
http://www.healthlink.org.uk
http://www.asksource.info

Enquiries:
Enquiries to: Information and Knowledge Manager
Direct e-mail: source@ich.ucl.ac.uk

Founded:
1977

Organisation type and purpose:
Voluntary organisation, registered charity (charity number 274260).
Non-governmental organisation.

Subject coverage:
Primary health care in developing countries, information management, information production, disability-related issues in developing countries.

Museum or gallery collection, archive, or library special collection:
Reference collection of materials on primary health care and disability in developing countries

Library catalogue:
All or part available online

Printed publications:
One-off publications including directories, 'how-to' manuals, and briefing papers
Order printed publications from: Publications Manager

Electronic and video publications:
Database available online

Publications list:
Available online and in print

Access to staff:
Contact by letter, by telephone, by fax and by e-mail. Appointment necessary. All charged.

Hours: Mon to Fri, 0900 to 1700

Access for disabled people:
Lift at entrance, toilet facilities

HEARING AID COUNCIL, THE

70 St Mary Axe, London, EC3A 8BD

Tel: 020 3102 4030
Fax: 020 3102 4476
E-mail: hac@thehearingaidcouncil.org.uk

Website:
http://www.thehearingaidcouncil.org.uk

Enquiries:
Enquiries to: Registrar

Founded:
1968

Organisation type and purpose:
Statutory body, professional body.
To regulate trade practices in the private sector of dispensing hearing aids.

Subject coverage:
Examination and registration of hearing aid dispensers.

Printed publications:
Code of Practice (free)
Regulating the Sale of Hearing Aids (free)

Access to staff:
Contact by letter, by telephone, by fax, by e-mail and via website. Appointment necessary.
Hours: Mon to Fri, 0830 to 1730

HEARING CONCERN

95 Gray's Inn Road, London, WC1X 8TX

Tel: 020 7440 9871
Fax: 020 7440 9872
E-mail: info@hearingconcern.org.uk

Website:
http://www.hearingconcern.org.uk
Factsheets, news, services, links.

Enquiries:
Enquiries to: Director

Founded:
1947

Formerly called:
British Association of the Hard of Hearing

Organisation type and purpose:
National organisation, membership association (membership is by subscription, election or invitation), present number of members: 4416, voluntary organisation, registered charity (charity number 223322).

Subject coverage:
Hearing loss, lip reading, noise, vocational and welfare matters, aids to hearing, assistive aids for the deaf, loop systems, education.

Trade and statistical information:
Numbers of Hearing Impaired people in the UK stands at 8.4 million.

Printed publications:
Hearing Concern Magazine (quarterly)
Books
Leaflets on medical matters such as tinnitus, dizziness, otosclerosis, Ménières disease
Technical leaflets on hearing and communication aids with lists of manufacturers of equipment
Choosing a Hearing Aid
Facing up to Hearing Loss in Later Life
Lipreading
You and Your Hearing Aid

Publications list:
Available online and in print

Access to staff:
Contact by letter, by telephone, by fax, by e-mail, in person and via website. Appointment necessary.
Hours: Mon to Fri, 0900 to 1700

ASLIB DIRECTORY of INFORMATION SOURCES

Access to building, collection or gallery:
Prior appointment required

Access for disabled people:
Parking provided, ramped entry, toilet facilities

Affiliated to:
Disability Alliance

HEARING DOGS FOR DEAF PEOPLE

The Grange, Wycombe Road, Saunderton, Princes Risborough, Buckinghamshire, HP27 9NS

Tel: 01844 348 100 (voice and minicom)
Fax: 01844 348 101 info@hearingdogs.org.uk
E-mail: info@hearingdogs.org.uk

Website:
http://www.hearingdogs.co.uk

Enquiries:
Enquiries to: Managing Director
Other contacts: Client Secretary for applying for a hearing dog.

Founded:
1982

Formerly called:
Hearing Dogs for the Deaf (year of change 1997)

Organisation type and purpose:
National organisation, registered charity (charity number 293358).

Subject coverage:
Hearing Dogs for Deaf People aims to offer greater independence, confidence and security to deaf people by providing dogs trained to alert them to chosen everyday sounds. Hearing dogs are free to deaf applicants.

Printed publications:
Favour (magazine)

Access to staff:
Contact by letter, by telephone, by fax, by e-mail and via website. Appointment necessary.
Hours: Mon to Fri, 0900 to 1700

Access to building, collection or gallery:
Prior appointment required

Access for disabled people:
Parking provided, ramped entry, level entry, toilet facilities

Other addresses:
Hearing Dogs for Deaf People
    29 Craigiehall Crescent, West Freelands, Erskine, Renfrewshire, PA8 7DD; tel: 0141 812 6542
Hearing Dogs for Deaf People
    12 Main Street, Crawfordsburn, Bangor, Co Down, BT19 1JE; tel: 028 9185 3669
Hearing Dogs for Deaf People
    The Beatrice Wright Training Centre, Hull Road, Cliffe, North Yorkshire, YO8 7NG
Hearing Dogs for Deaf People
    The Grange, Wycombe Road, Saunderton, Buckinghamshire, HPP27 9NS

HEART RESEARCH UK

Acronym or abbreviation: HRUK

Suite 12D, Joseph's Well, Leeds, West Yorkshire, LS3 1AB

Tel: 0113 234 7474
Fax: 0113 297 6208
E-mail: mail@heartresearch.org.uk

Website:
http://www.heartresearch.org.uk

Enquiries:
Enquiries to: National Director
Direct e-mail: info@heartresearch.org.uk
Other contacts: Grant Administrator

Founded:
1967

Formerly called:
National Heart Research Fund (year of change 2005)

Organisation type and purpose:
Registered charity (charity number 1044821), research organisation.

Subject coverage:
Prevention, treatment and cure of heart disease

Information services:
info@heartresearch.org.uk.

Education services:
lifestyle@heartresearch.org.uk.

Printed publications:
Pulse Newsletter & Healthy Heart Lifestyle Leaflets
Order printed publications from: Lifestyle Department or Richard Gledhill

Access to staff:
Contact by letter, by telephone, by fax, by e-mail and via website. Appointment necessary.
Hours: Mon to Thu, 0900 to 1700; Fri 0900 to 1600

Access for disabled people:
Parking provided

Branches:
Heart Research UK in the Midlands
    Lee House, 6a Highfield Road, Edgbaston, Birmingham, B15 3ED; tel: 0121 454 1799; fax: 0121 454 1799; e-mail: midlands@heartresearch.org.uk; website: www.heartresearch.org.uk

HEAT PUMP ASSOCIATION

Acronym or abbreviation: HPA

2 Waltham Court, Milley Lane, Hare Hatch, Reading, Berkshire, RG10 9TH

Tel: 0118 940 3416
Fax: 0118 940 6258
E-mail: info@feta.co.uk

Website:
http://www.feta.co.uk

Enquiries:
Enquiries to: Commercial Manager

Founded:
1994

Organisation type and purpose:
Trade association.

Subject coverage:
The benefits and proper use of heat pumps and heat pump technology.

Access to staff:
Contact by letter, by telephone, by fax and by e-mail
Hours: Mon to Thu, 0830 to 1630; Fri, 0830 to 1600

Member organisation of:
Federation of Environmental Trade Associations

HEAT TRANSFER & FLUID FLOW SERVICE

Acronym or abbreviation: HTFS

Hyprotech UK Ltd, Harwell International Business Centre, Gemini Building, Fermi Avenue, Didcot, Oxfordshire, OX11 0QR

Tel: 01235 448330
Fax: 01235 448350
E-mail: htfs@hyprotech.com

Website:
http://www.htfs.com
Description of products and services available.

Enquiries:
Enquiries to: Administrator

Founded:
1968

Organisation type and purpose:
International organisation, research organisation.

Subject coverage:
Heat transfer; condensation; boiling; evaporation; general fluid flow; cryogenic fluids; combustion; heat transfer in nuclear reactors, design of heat exchangers and furnaces.

Electronic and video publications:
HTFS Heatflo database (web page)

Access to staff:
Contact by fax, by e-mail and via website
Hours: Mon to Fri, 0900 to 1700

Links with:
Hyprotech Ltd
    Canada
National Engineering Laboratory

HEATHER SOCIETY

Tippitiwitchet Cottage, Hall Road, Outwell, Wisbech, Cambridgeshire, PE14 8PE

Tel: 01945 774077
Fax: 01449 711220
E-mail: admin@heathersociety.org.uk

Website:
http://www.heathersociety.org.uk
General information on heathers. Complete listing of all heathers in commerce.

Enquiries:
Enquiries to: Administrator
Other contacts: Chairman; Treasurer; Registrar

Founded:
1963

Organisation type and purpose:
International organisation, membership association (membership is by subscription), present number of members: 500, registered charity (charity number 261801).
International Registration Authority for cultivars of heathers.

Subject coverage:
Growing and propagation of heathers; nomenclature and identification; availability of individual cultivars in commerce.

Museum or gallery collection, archive, or library special collection:
Heather Society slide library (free access to members)

Printed publications:
News Bulletin (3 times a year)
Year Book
Anyone Can Grow Heathers (£2.95)
Heathers – A Guide to Designing a Heather Garden (Lambie D and B, £2.40)
Heathers of the Lizard (McClintock D, £1.75)
Recommended Heathers (£2.95)

Publications list:
Available in print

Access to staff:
Contact by letter, by telephone, by fax, by e-mail and via website
Hours: Mon to Fri, 0900 to 1700

Affiliated to:
Royal Horticultural Society

Links with:
Dutch, North American and German Heather Societies

HEATHERSLAW LIGHT RAILWAY COMPANY

Ford Forge, Heatherslaw, Etal, Cornhill on Tweed, Northumberland, TD12 4TJ

Tel: 01890 820244
Fax: 01890 820 317

Enquiries:
Enquiries to: Managing Director

Founded:
1988

continued overleaf

Organisation type and purpose:
Manufacturing industry, service industry.

Subject coverage:
Steam engine and rolling stock manufacture or repair up to 660mm, classic ironworking, small batch production.

Printed publications:
Leaflet (free, direct)
Information booklet (65p)

Access to staff:
Contact by letter, by telephone and by fax
Hours: Sun to Sat, 0900 to 1700

Subsidiary company:
Errol Hut Smithy
Letham Hill, Etal, Cornhill-on-Tweed, Northumberland; tel: 01890 820317; fax: 01890 820317

HEBRIDEAN SHEEP SOCIETY

Knox Mill, Knox Mill Lane, Harrogate, North Yorkshire, HG3 2AE

Tel: 01423 507741
E-mail: info@hebrideansheep.org.uk

Enquiries:
Enquiries to: General Secretary

Founded:
1986

Formerly called:
Hebridean Sheep Breeders' Group (year of change 1994)

Organisation type and purpose:
Membership association (membership is by subscription), present number of members: 230.
Sheep Breed Society.
Registration authority for Hebridean Sheep in UK.

Access to staff:
Contact by letter, by telephone, by fax and by e-mail
Hours: Mon to Fri, 0900 to 1700

Affiliated to:
National Sheep Association (NSA)
Sheep Centre, Malvern, Worcestershire

HELP ADVISORY CENTRE

Acronym or abbreviation: HAC

57 Portobello Road, London, W11 3DB

Tel: 020 7221 9974

Website:
http://www.helpcounselling.com

Enquiries:
Enquiries to: Administrator
Direct tel: 020 7221 7914

Founded:
1968

Organisation type and purpose:
Voluntary organisation.
Counselling centre.

Subject coverage:
Counselling, psychotherapy, communication skills, career direction, assertiveness, sexuality, life choices, life changes.

Access to staff:
Contact by letter and by telephone
Hours: Mon to Fri, 1100 to 1830

Connections with:
Virgin Co Limited
120 Campden Hill Road, London, W8 7AR

HELP THE AGED

207–221 Pentonville Road, London, N1 9UZ

Tel: 020 7278 1114
Fax: 020 7278 1116
E-mail: info@helptheaged.org.uk

Website:
http://www.helptheaged.org.uk
Information on Help the Aged and issues of concern to senior citizens.

Enquiries:
Other contacts: Policy Officer for awareness of local government policies.

Founded:
1961

Organisation type and purpose:
Voluntary organisation, registered charity (charity number 272786).
To free disadvantaged older people from poverty, isolation, and neglect.
To campaign for change in government policy, to undertake research into the needs of older people, and to provide local services in communities across the UK and overseas.

Subject coverage:
Age-related issues: demographics, welfare and disability benefits, community care, housing, residential care, health issues, home safety and security and more. Help the Aged cannot provide information on international or development issues – refer to Help Age International.

Printed publications:
Advice leaflets under the headings: financial, housing and home safety, health (free)
Other publications, some charged some free: independence of older people, transport, income and pensions, health and care, housing and homelessness, rural issues and poetry.

Electronic and video publications:
Be Strong, Be Steady (video)
Step to the Future (DVD, video)

Publications list:
Available in print

Access to staff:
Contact by letter, by telephone, by fax and by e-mail
Hours: Mon to Fri, 0900 to 1700

Access to building, collection or gallery:
No access other than to staff

Other addresses:
Help the Aged Northern Ireland
Ascot House, Shaftesbury Square, Belfast, BT2 7DB; tel: 028 9023 0666; fax: 028 9024 8183
Help the Aged Scotland
11 Granton Square, Edinburgh, EH5 1HX; tel: 0131 551 6331; fax: 0131 551 5415
Help the Aged Wales
12 Cathedral Road, Cardiff, CF11 9LJ; tel: 029 2034 6550; fax: 029 2039 0898; e-mail: infocymru@helptheaged.org.uk

Part of:
Help Age International Network which currently has 16 members

HEMEL HEMPSTEAD CENTRAL LIBRARY

Combe Street, Hemel Hempstead, Hertfordshire, HP1 1HJ

Tel: 01438 737333
Fax: 01442 404660
E-mail: hemelhempstead.library@hertscc.gov.uk

Website:
http://www.hertslib.hertscc.gov.uk
Stock catalogue for county and community information database.

Enquiries:
Enquiries to: Librarian

Organisation type and purpose:
Public library.

Library catalogue:
All or part available online

Access to staff:
Contact by letter, by telephone, by fax, by e-mail and in person

Hours: Mon, Thu, Fri, 0930 to 2000; Tue, 1030 to 2000; Wed, 0930 to 1300; Sat, 0930 to 1600
Special comments: Reference library and local statistics collection on first floor, but no lift.

Access to building, collection or gallery:
No access other than to staff
Hours: Mon, Thu, Fri, 0930 to 2000; Tue, 1030 to 2000; Wed, 0930 to 1300; Sat, 0930 to 1600

Links with:
Community Information Department
Hertfordshire County Council, County Hall, Hertford, SG13 8DE; tel: 01438 737333; fax: 01442 555614; e-mail: cidb@hertscc.gov.uk

HENLEY BUSINESS SCHOOL

Formal name: Henley Business School at the University of Reading

Greenlands, Henley-on-Thames, Oxfordshire, RG9 3AU

Tel: 01491 571454
Fax: 01491 571635
E-mail: library@henley.com

Website:
http://www.henley.reading.ac.uk

Enquiries:
Enquiries to: Librarian
Direct tel: 01491 418823
Direct fax: 01491 418896

Founded:
1945

Formerly called:
Henley Management College; Administrative Staff College

Organisation type and purpose:
Business School

Subject coverage:
Accounting, banking, business studies, currency, economics, industrial relations, management, marketing, office management and practice, operational research, personnel recruitment and management, production management and control, sales management, information management, statistics.

Museum or gallery collection, archive, or library special collection:
Papers of Colonel L. F. Urwick

Access to staff:
Contact by letter, by telephone and by e-mail.
Appointment necessary. Access for members only.
Letter of introduction required.
Hours: Mon to Fri, 0830 to 2130; Sat, 0900 to 1900; Sun, 1000 to 1800

Access to building, collection or gallery:
Special comments: Reference only

HENRY GEORGE FOUNDATION OF GT BRITAIN LIMITED

Acronym or abbreviation: Henry George Foundation

212 Piccadilly, London, W1J 9HG

Tel: 0207 377 8885
Fax: 0207 377 8885
E-mail: office@henrygeorgefoundation.org

Website:
http://www.henrygeorge.org.uk
About HGF and the progressive forum; books published; events; ideas; links.

Enquiries:
Enquiries to: Secretary

Formerly called:
Economic and Social Science Research Association (ESSRA)

Organisation type and purpose:
Membership association, present number of members: 500, registered charity (charity number 259194), suitable for ages: 18+, research organisation, publishing house.
To promote a greater understanding of ways of improving the tax system to the benefit of the whole community.

Subject coverage:
Economic theory; tax developments worldwide; history of the Georgist movement with archives; history of land tax and its implementation around the world.

Library catalogue:
All or part available in-house

Printed publications:
Land & Liberty (journal, quarterly)
Books on economics and related subjects

Publications list:
Available in print

Access to staff:
Contact by letter, by telephone, by fax, by e-mail and via website. Appointment necessary.
Hours: Mon to Fri, 0930 to 1700

Access to building, collection or gallery:
Prior appointment required

HENRY MOORE FOUNDATION

Dane Tree House, Perry Green, Much Hadham, Hertfordshire, SG10 6EE

Tel: 01279 843333
Fax: 01279 843647

Website:
http://www.henry-moore-fdn.co.uk

Founded:
1977

Organisation type and purpose:
A registered charity with the aim of advancing the education of the public by the promotion of their appreciation of the fine arts, and in particular of the works of Henry Moore.

Museum or gallery collection, archive, or library special collection:
Elmwood Library, specialising in Henry Moore studies
Henry Moore Archive
Henry Moore Image Archive of photographs recording the artist's life and works
Henry Moore Bibliography online

HENRY WATSON MUSIC LIBRARY

Central Library, St Peter's Square, Manchester, M2 5PD

Tel: 0161 234 1976
Fax: 0161 234 1961
E-mail: music@libraries.manchester.gov.uk

Website:
http://www.manchester.gov.uk/libraries/central/hwml/index.htm
Web pages.

Enquiries:
Enquiries to: Music Co-ordinator

Founded:
1899

Organisation type and purpose:
Local government body, public library.

Subject coverage:
Printed and manuscript music and the literature of music (principally classical music).

Museum or gallery collection, archive, or library special collection:
Early printed music (2000 items)
Newman Flower Collection (Handel)
Collection of orchestral and choral music (for hire)
C18 Italian manuscripts

Library catalogue:
All or part available in-house

Printed publications:
George Frideric Handel: The Newman Flower Collection in the Henry Watson Music Library (A D Walker, 1972)

Microform publications:
Microfilm available for all rare or unique items in stock

Access to staff:
Contact by letter, by telephone, by fax, by e-mail, in person and via website
Hours: Mon to Thu, 0900 to 2000; Fri to Sat, 0900 to 1700

Access to building, collection or gallery:
No prior appointment required

Access for disabled people:
Ramped entry, toilet facilities

Parent body:
Manchester City Council

HENRY WILLIAMSON SOCIETY

7 Monmouth Road, Dorchester, Dorset, DT1 2DE

Tel: 01305 264092
E-mail: zseagull@aol.com

Website:
http://www.henrywilliamson.co.uk

Enquiries:
Enquiries to: General Secretary

Founded:
1980

Organisation type and purpose:
Learned society (membership is by subscription), present number of members: 500, registered charity (charity number 288168).
To encourage interest in and a deeper understanding of the life and work of the writer, Henry Williamson.

Museum or gallery collection, archive, or library special collection:
Archive at Exeter University

Printed publications:
Publications available for purchase
Order printed publications from: Publications Manager, Henry Williamson Society
14 Nethergrove, Longstanton, Cambridge, CB4 5EL, tel: 01954 200598, e-mail: john@camnews.net

Publications list:
Available in print

Access to staff:
Contact by letter, by telephone and by e-mail
Hours: Mon to Fri, 0900 to 2000

Other addresses:
Membership Secretary
16 Doran Drive, Redhill, Surrey, RH1 6AX; e-mail: mm@misterman.freeserve.co.uk

HENSHAWS SOCIETY FOR BLIND PEOPLE

Acronym or abbreviation: hsbp

John Derby House, 88–92 Talbot Road, Old Trafford, Manchester, M16 0GS

Tel: 0161 872 1234
Fax: 0161 848 9889
E-mail: info@hsbp.co.uk

Website:
http://www.hsbp.co.uk
General information, services and events

Enquiries:
Enquiries to: Chief Executive

Founded:
1837

Organisation type and purpose:
Voluntary organisation, registered charity (charity number 221888).
Registered social landlord.

Subject coverage:
Visual impairment and related issues.

Museum or gallery collection, archive, or library special collection:
Minute books and Annual Reports of the Society since 1837
Early minute books are housed at the John Rylands' Library, Manchester

Printed publications:
Annual Report and Accounts
General factsheets
Information packs
Leaflets about the services provided

Electronic and video publications:
Sex, Eyes and Audiotape – everything you had to see to know about HIV (tape, a health education information resource for people with visual impairment)

Publications list:
Available in print

Access to staff:
Contact by letter, by telephone, by fax and by e-mail. Appointment necessary.
Hours: Mon to Fri, 0900 to 1630

Access to building, collection or gallery:
No appointment necessary but staff members may not always be available if apppointment not made in advance.

Access for disabled people:
Ramped entry, access to all public areas, toilet facilities, talking lift, loop system.

Now incorporating the:
Manchester and Salford Blind Aid Society

Other addresses:
Community Services North & West Yorkshire
50 Bond End, Knaresborough, North Yorkshire, HG5 9AL; tel: 01423 541888; fax: 01423 541889
Harrogate Community Housing
50 Bond End, Knaresborough, North Yorkshire, HG5 9AL; tel: 01423 541888; fax: 01423 541889
Henshaws Arts and Craft Centre
Bond End, Knaresborough, North Yorkshire, HG5 9AL; tel: 01423 541888; fax: 01423 541889
Henshaws College
Bogs Lane, Harrogate, North Yorkshire, HG1 4ED; tel: 01423 886451; fax: 01423 885095
Henshaws Training & Professional Development Centre
John Derby House, 88/92 Talbot Road, Old Trafford, Manchester, M16 0GS; tel: 0161 872 1234; fax: 0161 848 9889
Merseyside Resource Centre
Wellington Buildings, The Strand, Liverpool, L2 0PP; tel: 0151 227 1226; fax: 0151 236 3641
Old Trafford Resource Centre
John Derby House, 88–92 Talbot Road, Old Trafford, Manchester, M16 0GS; tel: 0161 872 1234; fax: 0161 848 9889
Patient Support Service
Manchester Royal Eye Hospital, Manchester; tel: 0161 276 5515

Works with:
Liverpool Workshops and Birkenhead Society for the Blind

HENTY SOCIETY

205 Icknield Way, Letchworth, Hertfordshire, SG6 4TT

Tel: 01462 671357
E-mail: davidwalmsley@hentysociety.org

Enquiries:
Enquiries to: Honorary Secretary

Founded:
1977

continued overleaf

Organisation type and purpose:
International organisation, learned society
(membership is by subscription), present number
of members: 171.
To further knowledge in the life and work of
George Alfred Henty (1832–1902), special
correspondent, The Standard newspaper, writer of
books for boys and young people.

Subject coverage:
19th century children's literature.

Printed publications:
Occasional lists available from Honorary Secretary

Access to staff:
Contact by letter and by telephone
Hours: Mon to Fri, 0900 to 1800
Special comments: This society is run by volunteers
from their own homes.

HER MAJESTY'S INSPECTORATE FOR EDUCATION AND TRAINING IN WALES

Acronym or abbreviation: Estyn

Anchor Court, Keen Road, Cardiff, CF24 5JW

Tel: 029 2044 6446
Fax: 029 2044 6448
E-mail: enquiries@estyn.gsi.gov.uk

Website:
http://www.estyn.gov.uk

Enquiries:
Enquiries to: Her Majesty's Chief Inspector of
Education and Training in Wales
Direct tel: 029 2044 6475
Direct fax: 029 2044 6531
Direct e-mail: chief-inspector@estyn.gsi.gov.uk
Other contacts: Communications Team

Founded:
1992

Organisation type and purpose:
National government body.
Non-ministerial government department in Wales.

Subject coverage:
Inspects quality and standards in education and
training in Wales, including: nursery schools and
settings that are maintained by, or receive funding
from, local education authorities (LEAs); primary
schools; secondary schools; special schools; pupil-
referral units; independent schools; further
education; adult community-based learning; youth
support services; LEAs; teacher education and
training; work-based learning; careers companies;
and the education, guidance and training elements
of Department for Work and Pensions-funded
training programmes.
Estyn also provides advice on quality and
standards in education and training in Wales to the
National Assembly for Wales and others, and
makes public good practice based on inspection
evidence.

Access to staff:
Contact by letter, by telephone, by fax, by e-mail
and via website. Appointment necessary.
Hours: Mon to Fri, 0900 to 1700

Access to building, collection or gallery:
Hours: Mon to Fri, 0900 to 1700

Also at:
Estyn
Broncoed House, Broncoed Business Park, Mold,
Flintshire; tel: 029 2044 6319

HERALDRY SOCIETY OF SCOTLAND

25 Craigentinny Crescent, Edinburgh, EH7 6QA

Website:
http://www.heraldry-scotland.co.uk

Enquiries:
Enquiries to: Treasurer

Founded:
1977

Organisation type and purpose:
Learned society (membership is by subscription),
present number of members: 400.

Subject coverage:
Scottish heraldry; the Heraldic Executive in
Scotland; use of heraldry in Scottish art and
architecture; Scottish heraldic families; ceremonial
in Scotland; the Order of the Thistle; the Order of
Baronets of Nova Scotia.

Printed publications:
The Double Tressure (annually)

Publications list:
Available in print

Access to staff:
Contact by letter

HERALDRY SOCIETY, THE

PO Box 32, Maidenhead, Berkshire, SL6 3FD

Tel: 0118 932 0210
Fax: 0118 932 0210
E-mail: heraldry-society@cwcom.net

Enquiries:
Enquiries to: Secretary

Founded:
1947

Organisation type and purpose:
International organisation, learned society
(membership is by subscription), present number
of members: 1000, registered charity (charity
number 241456), suitable for ages: all.
Specialist library, special facilities available to
members at Society of Antiquaries, London and
Chetham Library, Manchester.
Study of Heraldry.

Subject coverage:
Heraldry, armoury, chivalry, genealogy.

**Museum or gallery collection, archive, or library
special collection:**
Library on heraldry, for use of members only
Special facilities available to members at Society of
Antiquaries, London and Chetham Library,
Manchester.

Printed publications:
Heraldry Gazette (quarterly newsletter, members
only)
Coat of Arms (quarterly)

Publications list:
Available in print

Access to staff:
Contact by letter, by telephone, by fax and by e-
mail
Hours: Mon to Fri, 0900 to 1700
Special comments: No premises for visits.

HERB SOCIETY

Sulgrave Manor, Sulgrave, Banbury, Oxfordshire,
OX17 2SD

Tel: 01295 768899
Fax: 01295 768069
E-mail: herbs@herbsociety.org.uk

Website:
http://www.herbsociety.co.uk

Enquiries:
Enquiries to: Administrator

Founded:
1927

Organisation type and purpose:
Membership association (membership is by
subscription).

Subject coverage:
Herbs and herbal matters with emphasis on
medicinal aspects, cultivation, uses and history.

Printed publications:
Herbarium (4 times a year)
Herbs Magazine (4 times a year)

Publications list:
Available in print

Access to staff:
Contact by letter, by telephone, by fax, by e-mail,
in person and via website
Hours: Mon to Fri, 0900 to 1700

Access to building, collection or gallery:
No prior appointment required

Access for disabled people:
Parking provided, level entry, access to all public
areas, toilet facilities

HERBERT HOWELLS SOCIETY

32 Barleycroft Road, Welwyn Garden City,
Hertfordshire, AL8 6JU

Tel: 01707 335315
E-mail: andrew.millinger@virgin.net

Enquiries:
Enquiries to: Honorary Secretary

Founded:
1987

Organisation type and purpose:
Membership association (membership is by
subscription), present number of members: 200.

Subject coverage:
The Society exists to promote the performance,
publication and recording of the works of Herbert
Howells.

Access to staff:
Contact by letter, by telephone and by e-mail.
Appointment necessary.
Hours: Any reasonable time, answerphone
available

Branches:
Herbert Howells Society, North American Branch
at the same address

HEREFORD CATHEDRAL LIBRARY AND ARCHIVES

The Cathedral, Hereford, HR1 2NG

Tel: 01432 374225/6
Fax: 01432 374220
E-mail: library@herefordcathedral.org

Website:
http://www.herefordcathedral.org

Enquiries:
Enquiries to: Librarian
Other contacts: Archivist

Founded:
c. 12th century

Organisation type and purpose:
Registered charity, research organisation.
Ecclesiastical library.

Subject coverage:
Religion and theology, ecclesiastical history, history
of Hereford Cathedral, local history, rare books
and manuscripts, medieval maps ecclesiastical art
and architecture, sacred (and some secular) music,
including manuscripts of the 18th and 19th
centuries.

**Museum or gallery collection, archive, or library
special collection:**
1,500 books (manuscripts and printed) chained to
early 17th century presses
229 medieval manuscripts, from the 8th to the
early 16th centuries (microfilmed)
30,000 archives of the Dean and Chapter, dating
from the 9th to 20th centuries (some
microfilmed)
All Saints Chained Library (over 300 vols, 15th to
18th centuries, chained to early 18th century
presses)

Manuscript and printed music, 18th to 20th
  centuries (c. 350 vols)
Over 3,000 pre-1801 printed books, including 56
  incunabula, 10,000 books published post-1800 on
  subjects listed above, many borrowable

Non-library collection catalogue:
All or part available online, in-house and in print

Library catalogue:
All or part available online and in-house

Printed publications:
Catalogue of the Manuscripts of Hereford
  Cathedral Library (R. A. B. Mynors and R. M.
  Thomson, 1993)
Mappa Mundi and the Chained Library (J.
  Williams, 1999)

Microform publications:
Microfilms of the medieval manuscripts and some
  archive documents (positive copies can be
  ordered from our negatives) and some Hereford-
  related material in other collections

Access to staff:
Contact by letter, by telephone, by fax, by e-mail,
  in person and via website

Access to building, collection or gallery:
Hours: Reading Room: Tue and Thu 1000 to 1600;
  first Sat of each month 1000 to 1300; open other
  times by prior appointment

Access for disabled people:
Level entry, access to all public areas, toilet
  facilities

Parent body:
Dean and Chapter of Hereford
  tel: 01432 374200; e-mail: office@
  herefordcathedral.org; website: http://www
  .herefordcathedral.org
Hereford Mappa Mundi Trustees

HEREFORD CATTLE SOCIETY

Hereford House, 3 Offa Street, Hereford, HR1 2LL

Tel: 01432 272057
Fax: 01432 377529
E-mail: postroom@herefordcattle.org

Website:
http://www.herefordcattle.org

Enquiries:
Enquiries to: Chief Executive

Founded:
1878

Organisation type and purpose:
National organisation, membership association
  (membership is by election or invitation),
  registered charity.

Subject coverage:
Hereford cattle.

HEREFORDSHIRE COLLEGE OF TECHNOLOGY – HEREFORD CAMPUS

Folly Lane, Hereford, HR1 1LS

Tel: 01432 352235
Fax: 01432 353449
E-mail: enquiries@hct.ac.uk

Website:
http://www.hct.ac.uk/
Information on the college and the courses on offer,
  details of the student support services, what
  students feel about HCT and where they go
  afterwards.

Enquiries:
Enquiries to: Learning Resources Manager
Direct tel: 01432 365320
Direct fax: 01432 365348
Direct e-mail: woottonr@hereford-tech.ac.uk;
  wrathallc@hereford-tech.ac.uk

Founded:
1974

Formerly called:
Herefordshire Technical College (year of change
1992)

Organisation type and purpose:
Suitable for ages: post 16.
College of further and higher education.

Subject coverage:
Construction, business studies, caring, hospitality,
  tourism and leisure, engineering, farriery,
  blacksmithing, art and design, education,
  humanities, computing.

**Museum or gallery collection, archive, or library
special collection:**
FEFC Circulars and Reports
FEU information (recently changed to FEDA)
LSC Circulars and Reports

Library catalogue:
All or part available in-house

Access to staff:
Contact by letter, by telephone, by fax, by e-mail
  and in person
Hours: Mon to Thu, 0840 to 2100; Fri, 0945 to 1645

Access for disabled people:
Parking provided, ramped entry, toilet facilities

HEREFORDSHIRE COLLEGE OF TECHNOLOGY – HOLME LACY CAMPUS

Holme Lacy, Hereford, HR2 6LL

Tel: 01432 870316
Fax: 01432 870566
E-mail: enquiries@hct.ac.uk

Website:
http://www.hct.ac.uk/
College prospectus.

Enquiries:
Enquiries to: Learning Resources Manager

Founded:
1963

Formerly called:
Herefordshire College of Agriculture

Incorporates the former:
Holme Lacy College (part of the Pershore Group of
Colleges) (year of change 2007)

Organisation type and purpose:
Suitable for ages: 16+.
Land based further education.

Subject coverage:
Agriculture, horticulture, forestry, small animal
  care, equine studies, gamekeeping, floristry,
  environmental studies, sustainability, organic
  agriculture, leisure, recreation, business studies.

**Museum or gallery collection, archive, or library
special collection:**
Workman collection of forestry-related material

Non-library collection catalogue:
All or part available in-house

Library catalogue:
All or part available in-house

Access to staff:
Contact by letter, by telephone and by fax.
Appointment necessary.
Hours: Open in term time only
Special comments: Reduced hours during college
holidays as posted.

Access for disabled people:
Parking provided, ramped entry, toilet facilities
Special comments: Access to all areas of the library.

HEREFORDSHIRE FAMILY HISTORY SOCIETY

Acronym or abbreviation: HFHS

6 Birch Meadow, Gosmore Road, Clehonger,
Hereford, HR2 9RH

Tel: 01981 250974
E-mail: prosser_brian@hotmail.com

Website:
http://www.rootsweb.com/~ukhfhs
Web page for the society.

Enquiries:
Enquiries to: Secretary General

Founded:
1980

Organisation type and purpose:
Membership association (membership is by
  subscription), present number of members: 900,
  voluntary organisation, registered charity (charity
  number 517785).
Family history society with particular reference to
  Herefordshire.

Subject coverage:
General family history enquiries.

Library catalogue:
All or part available in-house

Printed publications:
Order printed publications from: Publication Officer,
  Herefordshire FHS
  79 College Road, Hereford, HR1 1ED

Publications list:
Available online and in print

Access to staff:
Contact by letter, by telephone, by e-mail and via
  website
Hours: Mon to Fri, 0900 to 1700

Access for disabled people:
Parking provided

HEREFORDSHIRE LIBRARIES

Stock Unit, Herefordshire Libraries, Shirehall,
Hereford, HR1 2HY

Tel: 01432 261570
Fax: 01432 260744
E-mail: libraries@herefordshire.gov.uk

Website:
http://www.herefordshire.gov.uk/libraries

Enquiries:
Enquiries to: Principal Libraries Officer
Direct tel: 01432 260557

Founded:
1998

Formerly called:
Hereford and Worcester County Libraries (year of
change 1998)

Organisation type and purpose:
Local government body, public library.

Subject coverage:
Local studies, particularly history of the old county
  of Hereford; apple and pear cultivation;
  cidermaking; beekeeping.

**Museum or gallery collection, archive, or library
special collection:**
Hopton Collection (local history, crosses)
Pilley Collection (local history, general and
  religious history, especially of the 19th century)
Alfred Watkins and F. C. Morgan Collections of
  photographic glass slides and negatives

Non-library collection catalogue:
All or part available in-house

Library catalogue:
All or part available online and in-house

Access to staff:
Contact by letter, by telephone, by fax and in
  person. Appointment necessary.
Hours: Mon to Fri, 0900 to 1700

Constituent bodies:
Woolhope Naturalists' Field Club

continued overleaf

Parent body:
Herefordshire Council
  Brockington, 35 Haford Road, Hereford, HR1
  1SH; tel: 01432 260044; fax: 01432 340189;
  website: http://www.herefordshire.gov.uk

HEREFORDSHIRE RECORD OFFICE

Acronym or abbreviation: HRO

Harold Street, Hereford, HR1 2QX

Tel: 01432 260750
Fax: 01432 260066
E-mail: archives@herefordshire.gov.uk

Website:
http://www.herefordshire.gov.uk/archives

Founded:
1958

Organisation type and purpose:
Local government body.
Record office.

Subject coverage:
All aspects of local and family history.

Museum or gallery collection, archive, or library special collection:
Hereford photographic survey

Printed publications:
Information leaflets about various aspects of the service (free)

Access to staff:
Contact by letter, by telephone, by fax, by e-mail, in person and via website

Access to building, collection or gallery:
Hours: Mon, 0915 to 1645; Tue to Fri, 0915 to 1645; Wed, 1000 to 1645; second Sat in each month, 0915 to 1645
Special comments: CARN Readers ticket needed for all records, ticket issued on production of identification of name and address. Searchers wishing to use microfilm readers should book in advance. Access to parish registers as well as some other heavily used material is normally only by microform.

Access for disabled people:
Special comments: Lift, automatic doors, adapted furniture, large-print and Braille leaflets

HERIOT-WATT UNIVERSITY – ARCHIVE, RECORDS MANAGEMENT AND MUSEUM SERVICE

Riccarton, Edinburgh, EH14 4AS

Tel: 0131 541 3219
Fax: 0131 451 6134
E-mail: archive@hw.ac.uk

Website:
http://www.hw.ac.uk/archive
A brief history of the University and overview of the collections.

Enquiries:
Enquiries to: Archivist

Founded:
1966

Organisation type and purpose:
Museum, university department or institute, suitable for ages: 16+.

Subject coverage:
The history of the University and its predecessor bodies.

Museum or gallery collection, archive, or library special collection:
Archives, objects and works of art recording the history of the University, its predecessor bodies and people associated with it, the history of Riccarton on which the University of Edinburgh campus is built

Also responsible for a textile archive at the Galashiels campus

Access to staff:
Contact by letter and by telephone
Hours: Mon to Fri, 0900 to 1700

Access to building, collection or gallery:
No prior appointment required

HERIOT-WATT UNIVERSITY – SCOTTISH BORDERS CAMPUS, MARTINDALE LIBRARY

Netherdale, Galashiels, Selkirkshire, TD1 3HF

Tel: 01896 892185
Fax: 01896 758965 (Campus Reception)
E-mail: servicedesk@sbc.hw.ac.uk

Website:
http://www.hw.ac.uk/sbc/library
Information service.

Enquiries:
Enquiries to: Librarian
Direct tel: 01896 892155
Direct fax: 01896 758965
Direct e-mail: p.e.c.sandison@hw.ac.uk

Founded:
1998

Formerly called:
Scottish Woollen Technical College from 1922 to 1968; Scottish College of Textiles from 1968 to 1998

Organisation type and purpose:
University department or institute.

Subject coverage:
Art, business, clothing, chemistry, computing, design, fashion, management, marketing, textiles.

Museum or gallery collection, archive, or library special collection:
The Co-operative College Collection at Heriot-Watt University, includes periodicals, books and pamphlets about the Co-operative Movement

Library catalogue:
All or part available online

Access to staff:
Contact by letter, by telephone, by e-mail, in person and via website. Appointment necessary.
Hours: Mon to Fri, 0900 to 1645

Access for disabled people:
Parking provided, ramped entry, access to all public areas, toilet facilities

Constituent part of:
Heriot-Watt University

HERIOT-WATT UNIVERSITY LIBRARY

Riccarton, Edinburgh, EH14 4AS

Tel: 0131 451 3582
Fax: 0131 451 3164
E-mail: libhelp@hw.ac.uk

Website:
http://www.hw.ac.uk/libwww/irn/irn.html
Internet Resources Newsletter (monthly).
http://www.hw.ac.uk/library
Home page and extensive pointers to relevant subject resources.

Enquiries:
Enquiries to: Librarian
Direct tel: 0131 451 3570
Direct e-mail: m.l.breaks@hw.ac.uk
Other contacts: University Archivist

Organisation type and purpose:
University library.
Also known as the Cameron Smail Library.

Subject coverage:
Librarianship and information science, history of the University, biological sciences, psychology, economics, modern European languages, building, chemical, civil, electrical, mechanical, offshore and

petroleum engineering, physics, chemistry, mathematics, statistics, electronics, computer science.

Museum or gallery collection, archive, or library special collection:
History of the University
James Watt
Sir Robert Blair MSS

Non-library collection catalogue:
All or part available online

Library catalogue:
All or part available online

Access to staff:
Contact by letter, by telephone, by fax, by e-mail, in person and via website
Hours: Mon to Fri, 0900 to 2145; Sat and Sun 1000 to 2000 (term time)

Access to building, collection or gallery:
No prior appointment required

Branch campuses:
Dubai Campus
  Dubai Academic City, PO Box 294345, Dubai, United Arab Emirates; tel: +971 4 3616999; fax: +971 4 3604800; e-mail: dubaienquiries@hw.ac .uk; website: http://www.hw.ac.uk/dubai
Scottish Borders Campus
  Netherdale, Galashiels, TD1 3HF; tel: 0131 451 2155

HERITAGE ENGINEERING

22 Carmyle Avenue, Glasgow, G32 8HJ

Tel: 0141 763 0007
Fax: 0141 763 0583
E-mail: indherco@aol.com

Enquiries:
Enquiries to: Marketing Manager

Founded:
1991

Organisation type and purpose:
Consultancy, research organisation.
Restoration of historical artifacts.

Subject coverage:
Cast and wrought iron founders; ships; trains; trams; machinery; bandstands and park furniture; architectural metal work.

Access to staff:
Contact by letter, by telephone, by fax and by e-mail. Appointment necessary.

Connected with:
The Industrial Heritage Company Limited
  tel: 0141 763 0007; fax: 0141 763 0583; e-mail: indherco@aol.com

HERITAGE LOTTERY FUND

Acronym or abbreviation: HLF

7 Holbein Place, London, SW1W 8NR

Tel: 020 7591 6000; minicom no. 020 7591 6255
Fax: 020 7591 6001
E-mail: enquire@hlf.org.uk

Website:
http://www.hlf.org.uk

Enquiries:
Enquiries to: Information Team
Direct tel: 020 7591 6042
Direct fax: 020 7591 6271

Founded:
1993

Organisation type and purpose:
Non-departmental public body. Distributes funds raised through the National Lottery. Grants are given to projects that help people to learn about, look after and celebrate heritage.

Subject coverage:
Invests in every part of heritage, including museums, parks, historic places, archaeology, natural environment and cultural traditions.

Trade and statistical information:
Statistics on grants awarded.

Electronic and video publications:
Application guidance documents
Annual reports
Order electronic and video publications from: Online

Publications list:
Available online

Access to staff:
Contact by letter, by telephone, by fax, by e-mail and via website. Appointment necessary.
Hours: Mon to Fri, 0930 to 1730

Access to building, collection or gallery:
Prior appointment required (if parking required)
Hours: Mon to Fri, 0930 to 1730

Access for disabled people:
Parking provided, ramped entry, access to all public areas, toilet facilities

Administered by:
The Trustees
National Heritage Memorial Fund; tel: 020 7591 6000; fax: 020 7591 6001; e-mail: enquire@hlf.org.uk

Also at:
Heritage Lottery Fund (HLF)
Hodge House, Guildhall Place, Cardiff, CF10 1DY; tel: 029 2034 3413; fax: 029 2034 3427; e-mail: wales@hlf.org.uk
Heritage Lottery Fund (HLF)
51–53 Adelaide Street, Belfast, BT2 8FE; tel: 028 9031 0120; fax: 028 9031 0121; e-mail: northernireland@hlf.org.uk
Heritage Lottery Fund (HLF)
28 Thistle Street, Edinburgh, EH2 1EN; tel: 0131 225 9450; fax: 0131 225 9454; e-mail: scotland@hlf.org.uk
Heritage Lottery Fund (HLF)
Terrington House, 13–15 Hills Road, Cambridge, CB2 1NL; tel: 01223 224870
Heritage Lottery Fund (HLF)
Chiltern House, St Nicholas Court, 25–27 Castle Gate, Nottingham, NG1 7AR; tel: 0115 934 9050
Heritage Lottery Fund (HLF)
St Nicholas Building, St Nicholas Street, Newcastle upon Tyne, NE1 1RF; tel: 0191 255 7570; fax: 0191 255 7571; e-mail: northeastcontact@hlf.org.uk
Heritage Lottery Fund (HLF)
9th Floor, 82 King Street, Manchester, M2 4WQ; tel: 0161 831 0850
Heritage Lottery Fund (HLF)
7 Holbein Place, London, SW1W 8NR; tel: 020 7591 6171; e-mail: southeastengland@hlf.org.uk
Heritage Lottery Fund (HLF)
Trinity Court, Southernhay East, Exeter, EX1 1PG; tel: 01392 223950; e-mail: southwest@hlf.org.uk
Heritage Lottery Fund (HLF)
Bank House, 8 Cherry Street, Birmingham, B2 5AL; tel: 0121 616 6870; e-mail: westmidlands@hlf.org.uk
Heritage Lottery Fund (HLF)
Carlton Tower, 34 St Paul's Street, Leeds, LS1 2QB; tel: 0113 388 8030; fax: 0113 388 8031; e-mail: y&hdevelopment@hlf.org.uk

HERITAGE RAILWAY ASSOCIATION

Acronym or abbreviation: HRA

10, Hurdeswell, Long Hanborough, Witney, Oxfordshire, OX29 8DH

Tel: 01993 883384
Fax: 01993 883384
E-mail: johncrane.railway@btopenworld.com

Website:
www.heritagerailways.com

Details of organisation and of many members who operate heritage railways or railway centres.

Enquiries:
Enquiries to: Press Officer
Other contacts: Managing Director

Founded:
1996

Created by the merger of:
Association of Independent Railways (AIR);
Association of Railway Preservation Societies Limited (ARPS) (year of change 1996)

Organisation type and purpose:
Advisory body, trade association (membership is by subscription), present number of members: 800, service industry, voluntary organisation, training organisation, consultancy, research organisation. National representation of preserved railways and museums.

Subject coverage:
Preserved railways, details of locomotives, rolling stock, operating and maintenance equipment, setting up and operating railway preservation organisations.

Printed publications:
Guide to Steam Trains in the British Isles (send sae)
Bi-monthly newsletters, Annual Report, Information Papers (on request)
Journal (quarterly)

Publications list:
Available in print

Access to staff:
Contact by letter, by telephone, by fax and by e-mail
Hours: Mon to Fri, 0900 to 1700
Special comments: Not by overnight fax.

Affiliated to:
International Association of Transport Museums

Managing Director:
Heritage Railway Association (HRA)
8 Ffordd Dyfrig, Tywyn, Gwynedd, LL36 9EH; tel: 01654 710344

Member organisation of:
British Incoming Tour Operators Association (BITOA)
European Federation of Museum and Tourist Railways (FEDECRAIL)
International Association of Transport and Communication Museums (IATM)
Railway Industry Training Council (RITC)
The Railway Forum

HERPES VIRUSES ASSOCIATION

Acronym or abbreviation: HVA, SPHERE

41 North Road, London, N7 9DP

Tel: helpline: 0845 123 2305; office: 020 7607 9661
Fax: on request
E-mail: marian@herpes.org.uk

Website:
http://www.herpes.org.uk
Patient-run website with clearly and sensitively written information on all aspects of herpes simplex.

Enquiries:
Enquiries to: Director
Other contacts: Administrator

Founded:
1985

Organisation type and purpose:
Registered charity.

Subject coverage:
Facial and genital herpes simplex, herpes zoster, shingles and other types of herpes viruses: research on drug trials, alternative treatments, psychological aspects of simplex.

Museum or gallery collection, archive, or library special collection:
Articles from media and medical press re herpes viruses

Non-library collection catalogue:
All or part available online

Library catalogue:
All or part available online, in-house and in print

Printed publications:
16-page booklet (£2.50, including postage)
Journal (quarterly, free to members)
Leaflets (free to members)

Electronic and video publications:
Video (£5)

Publications list:
Available online and in print

Access to staff:
Contact by letter, by e-mail and via website.
Appointment necessary.
Hours: Mon to Fri, 1000 to 2000
Special comments: Please phone helpline number not office number. Fax number available on request.

HERTFORD COLLEGE LIBRARY

Catte Street, Oxford, OX1 3BW

Tel: 01865 279400
E-mail: susan.griffin@hertford.ox.ac.uk

Enquiries:
Enquiries to: Librarian
Direct tel: 01865 279409

Organisation type and purpose:
University department or institute.
College library of the University of Oxford.

Subject coverage:
General, mainly for first degree course but with some provision for graduates; old library (16th to 18th centuries largely) in general subjects, but topography, science, theology, history and classics predominate.

Museum or gallery collection, archive, or library special collection:
Gilbert Library (geography)
Seiffert Bequest (German language and linguistics)

Non-library collection catalogue:
All or part available online and in-house

Library catalogue:
All or part available online and in-house

Access to staff:
Contact by letter, by telephone, by e-mail and in person. Appointment necessary. Letter of introduction required.
Hours: Mon to Fri, 0900 to 1530

HERTFORD REGIONAL COLLEGE

Ware Centre, Scotts Road, Ware, Hertfordshire, SG12 9JF

Tel: 01992 411400
Fax: 01992 411885
E-mail: library@hertreg.ac.uk

Website:
http://www.hrc.ac.uk
College website, general information and information on library.
http://colleges.herts.ac.uk
Library catalogue, joint one with other Hertfordshire college libraries.

Enquiries:
Enquiries to: Head of Library and Learning Services
Direct tel: 01992 411977
Direct fax: 01992 411978
Direct e-mail: library@hertreg.ac.uk

Founded:
1991

continued overleaf

Formerly called:
East Herts College, Ware College (year of change 1991)

Organisation type and purpose:
College of further education.

Subject coverage:
Child care, art and design, catering, hairdressing, beauty therapy, business studies, adult literacy, social care, computer studies, engineering, drama, media studies, leisure and tourism, information technology, special needs, management studies.

Library catalogue:
All or part available online

Access to staff:
Contact by letter, by telephone, by fax and by e-mail. Appointment necessary.
Hours: Term time: Mon to Thu, 0845 to 1930; Fri, 0845 to 1640
Vacations: Mon to Fri, 1000 to 1300 and 1400 to 1600

Access to building, collection or gallery:
No access other than to staff
Hours: Term time: Mon to Thu, 0900 to 1930; Fri, 0900 to 1640
Vacations: Mon to Fri, 1000 to 1300 and 1400 to 1600
Special comments: Reference use only for non staff or students.

Access for disabled people:
Parking provided, level entry

Other addresses:
Hertford Regional College
  Broxbourne Centre, Broxbourne, Turnford, Hertford, EN10 6AF; tel: 01992 411400; fax: 01992 411650

HERTFORDSHIRE ARCHIVES AND LOCAL STUDIES

Acronym or abbreviation: HALS

County Hall, Hertford, SG13 8EJ

Tel: 01438 737333 (customer service centre – ask for archives/local studies)
Fax: 01992 555113
E-mail: hertsdirect@hertscc.gov.uk

Website:
http://www.hertsdirect.org/hals

Founded:
1895

Formerly called:
Hertfordshire Local Studies; Hertfordshire Record Office (HRO) (year of change 1997)

Organisation type and purpose:
Local government body.
Archive, record office, local studies library.

Subject coverage:
Hertfordshire: history; family history; local history; geography; topography and environment.

Museum or gallery collection, archive, or library special collection:
Manuscripts: estate collections: Cowper of Panshanger; Lytton of Knebworth; Grimston of Gorhambury
Ebenezer Howard papers
Photographs: John Dickinson; Stingemore collection

Non-library collection catalogue:
All or part available online and in-house

Library catalogue:
All or part available online

Access to staff:
Contact by letter, by telephone, by fax, by e-mail, in person and via website

Access to building, collection or gallery:
No prior appointment required

Hours: Mon and Wed, 0900 to 1730; Tue, 1000 to 1930; Thu, 0900 to 1930; Fri, 0900 to 1700; Sat, 0900 to 1300

Access for disabled people:
Parking provided, ramped entry, access to all public areas, toilet facilities

HERTFORDSHIRE FAMILY AND POPULATION HISTORY SOCIETY

30 Blenheim Way Stevenage, Hertfordshire, SG2 8TE

E-mail: secretary@hertsfhs.org.uk

Website:
http://www.hertsfhs.org.uk

Enquiries:
Enquiries to: Honorary Secretary

Founded:
1977

Organisation type and purpose:
Membership association (membership is by subscription), present number of members: 1,000, voluntary organisation, registered charity (charity number 285008), suitable for all ages.
To further the education of family history within the ancient county of Hertfordshire.

Subject coverage:
Genealogy, family history, militia history, monumental inscription recording, hobbies, Hertfordshire.

Printed publications:
Directory of Members' Interests
Hertfordshire People (journal, quarterly, free to members, £1 plus 35p per issue)
Hertfordshire Strays: Out of Area and Late Baptisms (6 vols)
Herts People (index to surnames)
Monumental Inscriptions (68 vols to date for specific locations, a few in microfiche)
Special Publications:
Transported Beyond the Seas
Fleet Marriages of Hertfordshire People to 1754
Hertfordshire Settlement Certificates
Militia Lists, over 110 booklets listing the names of men aged between 18 and 45 in respect of liability for military service from 1757 to about 1805
Order printed publications from: Booksales Officer, Hertfordshire Family and Population History Society, 56 Dalkeith Road, Harpenden, Hertfordshire, AL5 5PW

Microform publications:
Militia Lists (113 vols to date for specific areas, microfiche and booklet)

Publications list:
Available online and in print

Access to staff:
Contact by letter, by e-mail and via website
Hours: Mon to Fri, 0900 to 1700
Special comments: Please enclose an sae or two International Reply coupons for a reply to a letter.

Access to building, collection or gallery:
Special comments: Library open for members.

Member organisation of:
Federation of Family History Societies

HERTFORDSHIRE MULTIPLE SCLEROSIS THERAPY CENTRE

Acronym or abbreviation: HMSTC

Unit 30, Campus Five, Letchworth, Hertfordshire, SG6 2JF

Tel: 01462 684214
Fax: 01462 487172
E-mail: info@hertsmstherapy.org.uk

Website:
http://www.hertsmstherapy.org.uk
Description of centre and its facilities.

Enquiries:
Enquiries to: Manager

Founded:
1983

Formerly called:
North Hertfordshire Friends of Arms (year of change 1994)

Organisation type and purpose:
Membership association (membership is by subscription), present number of members: 250, registered charity (charity number 299524).
To provide useful therapies, advice and support to people with MS in Hertfordshire.

Subject coverage:
Hyperbaric oxygen therapy, physiotherapy, yoga, aromatherapy, reflexology, counselling, dietary advice, chiropody/podiatry.

Printed publications:
Welcome pack (for prospective members, descriptive brochure)

Access to staff:
Contact by letter, by telephone, by fax, by e-mail and in person
Hours: Mon to Fri, 0900 to 1700

Access for disabled people:
Parking provided, ramped entry, toilet facilities

HERTFORDSHIRE NATURAL HISTORY SOCIETY

Acronym or abbreviation: HNHS

32 Mandeville Road, Hertford, SG13 8JQ

Tel: 01992 586150

Website:
http://www.hnhs.org

Enquiries:
Enquiries to: President
Direct e-mail: apreynolds22@hotmail.com

Founded:
1875

Organisation type and purpose:
Voluntary organisation, registered charity (charity number 218418).

Subject coverage:
Strengths at present are in botany, mammals, birds, geology, mycology, entomology, amphibians and reptiles, arachnology.

Museum or gallery collection, archive, or library special collection:
Pryor Bequest (valuable collection of rare old botanical books, held at University College under special storage conditions)

Printed publications:
Newsletter (twice a year, free to members)
Herts Naturalist Transactions have been issued regularly since 1875, currently one part is issued annually as the Bird Report and a second part of non-bird material each year when available (free to members)

Access to staff:
Contact by letter, by telephone and by e-mail
Hours: Mon to Fri, 0900 to 1700

Affiliated to:
Hertfordshire Geological Society

Includes the:
Hertfordshire Bird Club
Hertfordshire Dragonfly Group
Hertfordshire Mammal Group

HERTFORDSHIRE VISUAL ARTS FORUM

Acronym or abbreviation: HVAF

PO Box 894, St Albans, Hertfordshire AL1 9EG

E-mail: enquiries@hvaf.org.uk

Website:
http://www.hvaf.org.uk
List of members, members' gallery, press releases.

Enquiries:
Enquiries to: Public Relations Manager
Other contacts: Membership Secretary for membership.

Founded:
1990

Organisation type and purpose:
Membership association (membership is by subscription), present number of members: 250, voluntary organisation.
Develop appreciation of visual arts in Hertfordshire.

Subject coverage:
Visual arts: painting, sculpture, crafts, ceramics.

Printed publications:
Leaflet (free, direct)

Access to staff:
Contact by letter
Hours: Mon to Fri, 0900 to 1700

HESKETH OWNERS CLUB

97 Oakdale Avenue, Stanground, Peterborough, Cambridgeshire, PE2 8TE

Enquiries:
Enquiries to: Secretary

Founded:
1982

Organisation type and purpose:
International organisation, membership association (membership is by subscription), present number of members: 52.
Provide a contact point for people interested in Hesketh motorcycles.

Subject coverage:
Hesketh motorcycle, buying, selling, spares, mechanical and club services.

Museum or gallery collection, archive, or library special collection:
Large archive of material and technical information available within the club

Printed publications:
Club magazine (members)

Access to staff:
Contact by letter
Hours: Mon to Fri, 0900 to 2100

Affiliated to:
British Motorcyclists Federation

HEWLETT-PACKARD CDS

Formal name: Hewlett-Packard Customer Delivery Services
Acronym or abbreviation: HP CDS

Imperium Level 1, West Wing, Imperial Way, Reading RG2 0TD

Tel: 01189 227600
Fax: 01189 227601
E-mail: enquiries@synstar.com

Website:
http://www.synstar.com

Enquiries:
Enquiries to: Manager

Founded:
2004

Incorporates the former:
Synstar plc

Organisation type and purpose:
Service industry.

Subject coverage:
Business continuity services, computer disaster recovery, mid-range systems and PC networks, mobile recovery, business recovery, business continuity planning, services and consultancy. Business availability services: business continuity, networking, lifecycle and data management and computer services.

Trade and statistical information:
Business continuity services throughout UK and Europe.

Electronic and video publications:
Strategy – Business Continuity Planning Software

Access to staff:
Contact by letter, by telephone, by fax and by e-mail
Hours: Mon to Fri, 0900 to 1730

Subsidiary of:
Hewlett-Packard

HEWLETT-PACKARD LABORATORIES

Acronym or abbreviation: HPLB

Filton Road, Stoke Gifford, Bristol, BS34 8QZ

Fax: 0117 3128964
E-mail: bl@hplb.hpl.hp.com

Website:
http://www.hpl.hp.com/techreports/index.html
Hewlett-Packard Laboratories Technical Report Series.
http://www.uk.hpl.hp.com
Hewlett-Packard Laboratories external home page.

Enquiries:
Enquiries to: Information Services

Founded:
1984

Organisation type and purpose:
International organisation, research organisation.

Subject coverage:
Computing and telecommunications, networks and network security. Also e-services and personal appliances.

Trade and statistical information:
Hewlett Packard Laboratories Technical Report Series.

Printed publications:
Order printed publications from: Via website

Publications list:
Available online and in print

Access to staff:
Contact by letter and by e-mail
Hours: Mon to Fri, 0900 to 1700
Special comments: Services outside HPLB very limited, therefore quick reference questions only please.

HEXHAM LIBRARY

Queen's Hall, Beaumont Street, Hexham, Northumberland, NE46 3LS

Tel: 01434 652488
Fax: 01434 652474
E-mail: mmason@northumberland.gov.uk

Enquiries:
Enquiries to: Senior Librarian
Other contacts: Assistant Librarian for local history enquiries.

Formerly called:
Tynedale Area Library; West Area Library (year of change 1992); Hexham Group Library (year of change 1996); West Group Library (year of change 1998)

Organisation type and purpose:
Local government body, public library.

Subject coverage:
General, Hexham and Northumberland local history.

Museum or gallery collection, archive, or library special collection:
Brough Local Studies Collection
Census Returns (microfilm)
Electoral rolls, 1832 to 1950 (microfilm)
Local newspapers, 1864 to date (microfilm)
Parish Register transcripts
Photographs
Trades Directories

Library catalogue:
All or part available in-house

Printed publications:
Family History in Hexham Library: a guide to source material in the Brough Local Studies Collection (1996, 50p)
Border Reivers Booklist: an introduction to Hexham's Collections (1997, 30p)

Access to staff:
Contact by letter, by telephone, by fax and in person
Hours: Mon, Fri, 0930 to 1930; Tue, Wed, 0930 to 1700; Thu, closed; Sat, 0930 to 1230

Parent body:
Northumberland County Amenities Division

HEYDAY

Astral House, 1268 London Road London SW16 4ER

Tel: 0845 888 4444
E-mail: memberservices@heyday.org.uk

Website:
http://www.heyday.org.uk/
Membership benefits, campaigning activity, general news, press releases.

Enquiries:
Enquiries to: Public Relations Manager

Founded:
1988

Formerly called:
Association of Retired and Persons Over Fifty (ARP/O50) (year of change 2006)

Organisation type and purpose:
Membership association (membership is by subscription), present number of members: 107,000, suitable for ages: 50+.

Subject coverage:
Legislation affecting the retired and over 50s. Attitudes to all aspects of retirement including, finance, health, leisure and legislation as available.

Trade and statistical information:
The members of the Association provide access to a research and consumer based data collection facility.

Printed publications:
GOODTIMES, incorporating Association News (magazine, membership and news-stand)
Membership Handbook

Access to staff:
Contact by telephone, by fax, by e-mail and via website
Hours: Mon to Fri, 0930 to 1730

Also at:
Heyday
PO Box 87, Oakengates, TF3 3WT

HFT

Formal name: The Home Farm Trust
Acronym or abbreviation: HFT

Merchants House, Wapping Road, Bristol, BS1 4RW

Tel: 0117 930 2600
Fax: 0117 922 5938
E-mail: marketing@hft.org.uk

continued overleaf

Website:
http://www.hft.org.uk

Enquiries:
Enquiries to: Marketing Manager

Founded:
1962

Formerly called:
The Home Farm Trust

Organisation type and purpose:
Registered charity (charity number 313069).
Services for adults with learning disabilities.

Subject coverage:
Provision of residential and other services for
people with learning disabilities which develop
their potential and sustain their rights.

Printed publications:
Today Magazine (2 times a year, free)
Annual Report and Accounts
Christmas Catalogue
Annual Review (yearly, free)

Electronic and video publications:
Communication Training Video (£58.75)
Out and About

Access to staff:
Contact by letter, by telephone, by fax, by e-mail,
in person and via website. Appointment necessary.
Hours: Mon to Fri, 0900 to 1700

Access to building, collection or gallery:
Hours: Mon to Fri, 0900 to 1700

Access for disabled people:
Hours: Mon to Fri, 0900 to 1700

Parent body:
HFT Trading Limited
    at the same address

HI KENT

18 Brewer Street, Maidstone, Kent, ME14 1RU

Tel: 01622 691151\ Minicom no. 01622 691151
Fax: 01622 672436
E-mail: enquiries@hikent.org.uk

Website:
http://www.hikent.org.uk
Services provided by organisation and general
information on deafness.

Enquiries:
Enquiries to: Information Officer
Direct e-mail: d.lewis@hikent.org.uk

Founded:
1986

Formerly called:
Hi Kent Association (year of change 1995)

Organisation type and purpose:
Membership association (membership is by
subscription), present number of members: 72,
registered charity (charity number 1052036).
Information and resource centre for hearing
impaired.

Subject coverage:
Assistive equipment for deaf people, sign
language, deaf awareness, tinnitus.

**Museum or gallery collection, archive, or library
special collection:**
Factsheets on assistive equipment for deaf people
Information sheets on deafness
Books and videos provided by Kent County
    Council Arts and Libraries for loan in Kent only
    on deaf subjects

Non-library collection catalogue:
All or part available in-house

Library catalogue:
All or part available in-house

Printed publications:
Fact and information sheets

Access to staff:
Contact by letter, by telephone, by fax, by e-mail
and in person
Hours: Mon to Fri, 0900 to 1700

Access for disabled people:
Ramped entry, toilet facilities

Other addresses:
Hi Kent
    East Kent Centre, 46 Northgate, Canterbury,
    Kent, CT1 1BE; tel: 01227 760046; fax: 01227
    760068; e-mail: jon.lambert@kent.gov.uk
Hi Kent Medway Centre
    Audiology Unit, Medway Maritime Hospital,
    Windmill Road, Gillingham, Kent, ME7 5NY; tel:
    01634 825043; e-mail: l.dray@hikent.org.uk

Works in partnership with:
Kent County and Medway Council Social Services

HIGH COMMISSION OF THE REPUBLIC OF NAMIBIA

6 Chandos Street, London, W1G 9LU

Tel: 020 7636 6244
Fax: 020 7637 5694
E-mail: namibia-highcomm@btconnect.com

Enquiries:
Enquiries to: Information Officer
Other contacts: (1) First Secretary (2) Commercial
Counsellor (3) Tourism Attaché (4) Counsellor for
(1) educational/cultural matters (2) trade and
investment in Namibia (3) geography and history
of Namibia (4) passports/visas.

Organisation type and purpose:
National government body.

Subject coverage:
Any enquiry relating directly to Namibia, whether
political, cultural, historical, geographical or
economic; trade and investment information;
tourism and travel information; diplomatic and
consular matters, including enquiries about visa/
passports; more generalised information on Africa
and the Commonwealth.

Trade and statistical information:
Statistical documents and reports from the
    respective ministries of the Government of
    Namibia. For specific enquiries regarding trade
    and investment contact the Commerical
    Counsellor.

Access to staff:
Contact by letter, by telephone, by fax and in
person
Hours: Mon to Fri, 0900 to 1700

Parent body:
Ministry of Foreign Affairs, Information and
Broadcasting
    Government Offices (4th Floor), Robert Mugabe
    Avenue, Private Bag 13347, Windhoek, Namibia;
    tel: +26461 282 9111; fax: +26461 22 3937

HIGHBURY COLLEGE LEARNING CENTRE

Cosham, Portsmouth, Hampshire, PO6 2SA

Tel: 023 9231 3213
Fax: 023 9237 1972
E-mail: library@highbury.ac.uk

Enquiries:
Enquiries to: Librarian

Formerly called:
Highbury Technical College

Organisation type and purpose:
Suitable for ages: 16+ further education.
College of technology.

Subject coverage:
Building, hospitality and catering, business and
management studies, social welfare, leisure and
tourism, electrical and electronic engineering,
mechanical engineering.

Library catalogue:
All or part available in-house

Access to staff:
Contact by letter, by telephone, by fax, by e-mail
and in person
Hours: Term time; Mon to Thu, 0900 to 2100; Fri,
0930 to 1700
Vacations; Mon to Thu, 0900 to 1700; Fri, 0900 to
1630

Access for disabled people:
Access to all public areas

HIGHER EDUCATION FUNDING COUNCIL FOR ENGLAND

Acronym or abbreviation: HEFCE

Northavon House, Coldharbour Lane, Bristol,
BS16 1QD

Tel: 0117 931 7317
Fax: 0117 931 7203
E-mail: hefce@hefce.ac.uk

Website:
http://www.hefce.ac.uk

Enquiries:
Enquiries to: Knowledge Centre Manager
Direct tel: 0117 931 7438
Direct fax: 0117 931 7082
Direct e-mail: s.roberts@hefce.ac.uk

Founded:
1993

Created by the merger of:
Polytechnics and Colleges Funding Council
(PCFC), Universities Funding Council (UFC) (year
of change 1993)

Formerly called:
University Grants Committee (UGC) (year of
change 1988)

Organisation type and purpose:
The HEFCE is a non-departmental public body set
up under the Further and Higher Education Act
1992. Its primary role is to distribute public
funding for teaching and research and related
activities in universities and colleges in England.

Subject coverage:
Funding for higher education in England.

**Museum or gallery collection, archive, or library
special collection:**
Books and documents related to the subject of
    higher education

Library catalogue:
All or part available in-house

Printed publications:
Order printed publications from: Some publications
are available by post; all publications available via
http://www.hefce.ac.uk/pubs

Publications list:
Available online

Access to staff:
Contact by letter, by telephone, by fax, by e-mail
and via website
Hours: Mon to Fri, 0900 to 1700

Access to building, collection or gallery:
There is no public access

HIGHER EDUCATION FUNDING COUNCIL FOR WALES

Acronym or abbreviation: HEFCW

Linden Court, The Orchards, Ilex Close, Llanishen,
Cardiff, CF14 5DZ

Tel: 029 2076 1861
Fax: 029 2076 3163

Website:
http://www.elwa.ac.uk
Information on HEFCW. Copies of HEFCW
circulars, news sheets, and other publications.

Enquiries:
Enquiries to: Clerk to the Council
Direct e-mail: info@elwa.ac.uk

Founded:
1992

Organisation type and purpose:
National government body.
Non-departmental government body.
The Council is responsible for the administration of funds made available by the Welsh Assembly Government in support of the provision of higher education and the undertaking of research in higher education institutions in Wales.

Subject coverage:
Funding for higher education in Wales. Student enrolment in Wales. Council funding for research in Welsh higher education institutions.

Printed publications:
Annual Report
Corporate Plan
Operational Plan

Electronic and video publications:
Other circulars and publications available online

Publications list:
Available online and in print

Access to staff:
Contact by letter, by telephone and by e-mail
Hours: Mon to Fri, 0900 to 1700

Access to building, collection or gallery:
No access other than to staff, prior appointment required

Access for disabled people:
Parking provided, ramped entry

Parent body:
National Assembly for Wales
   Higher Education Division, Cathays Park, Cardiff, CF10 3NQ; tel: 029 2082 5111

HIGHER EDUCATION STATISTICS AGENCY

Acronym or abbreviation: HESA

95 Promenade, Cheltenham, Gloucestershire, GL50 1HZ

Tel: 01242 255577
Fax: 01242 211122
E-mail: www@hesa.ac.uk

Website:
http://www.hesa.ac.uk
Access to HOLIS (HESA on-line information system): an interactive information system allowing interrogation of datasets by users. Also details of data collected by HESA, and relevant publications.

Enquiries:
Enquiries to: Data Provision Manager

Founded:
1993

Organisation type and purpose:
Registered charity (charity number 1039709).
HESA is the official agency for the collection, analysis and dissemination of quantitative information about higher education.

Subject coverage:
Statistics of students and staff at all UK universities in six main record areas: undergraduates, postgraduates, first destinations of graduates, staff and short courses, finance.

Museum or gallery collection, archive, or library special collection:
Microfiche library of all statistical analyses produced 1972–1993 (in addition to original computerised database for same period)

Printed publications:
Higher Education Management Statistics (annually, also CD-ROM)

Reference Volume: Students in Higher Education Institutions (annually, £33 hardcopy, £35+VAT CD-ROM)
Research Datapack 1: Ethnicity (£120 hardcopy including disc)
Research Datapack 2: Entry Qualifications in HE (£120 hardcopy including disc)
Research Datapack 3: Course Results (£120 hardcopy including disc)
Research Datapack 4: First Destinations (£120 hardcopy including disc)
Research Datapack 5: Disability (£120 hardcopy including disc)
Research Datapack 6: Overseas Students (£120 hardcopy including disc)
Research Datapack 7: Regional Issues (£120 hardcopy including disc)
Research Datapack 8: Ethnicity in Higher Education (£120 hardcopy including disc)
Research Datapack 9: Academic Staff in Higher Education (£120 hardcopy including disc)
Research Datapack 10: Non-credit-bearing Courses in Higher Education (£120 hardcopy including disc)
Research Datapack 11: Ethnicity of Students 1999/2000 (£150 plus VAT, CD-ROM)

Publications list:
Available in print

Access to staff:
Contact by letter, by telephone, by fax, by e-mail and via website
Hours: Mon to Thu, 0830 to 1700; Fri, 0830 to 1600

HIGHGATE LITERARY AND SCIENTIFIC INSTITUTION

Acronym or abbreviation: HLSI

11 South Grove, Pond Square, Highgate, London, N6 6BS

Tel: 020 8340 3343
Fax: 020 8340 5632
E-mail: librarian@hlsi.net

Website:
http://www.hlsi.net

Enquiries:
Enquiries to: Librarian
Direct tel: 020 8340 3343 (option 3)

Founded:
1839

Organisation type and purpose:
Membership association (membership is by subscription), voluntary organisation. Lending library.

Subject coverage:
Literature; biography; the arts; fiction; local history.

Museum or gallery collection, archive, or library special collection:
Highgate local history and archives
John Betjeman
Samuel Taylor Coleridge
London local history

Non-library collection catalogue:
All or part available in-house

Library catalogue:
All or part available in-house

Access to staff:
Contact by letter, by telephone, by fax, by e-mail and in person. Appointment necessary.

Access to building, collection or gallery:
Hours: Tue to Fri, 1000 to 1700; Sat, 1000 to 1600
Special comments: Closed for one week at Christmas and Easter, three weeks in August.

Links with:
Association of Independent Libraries
   website: http://www.independentlibraries.co.uk

HIGHLAND FAMILY HISTORY SOCIETY

Acronym or abbreviation: HFHS

Suite 4, Third Floor, Albyn House, 37a Union Street, Inverness, IV1 1QA

E-mail: jdurham@highlandfhs.org.uk

Website:
http://www.highlandfhs.org.uk
http://www.genfair.com
Publications and membership

Enquiries:
Enquiries to: Honorary Secretary
Direct e-mail: abethune@highlandfhs.org.uk

Founded:
1981

Organisation type and purpose:
Membership association (membership is by subscription).

Subject coverage:
Genealogy, parish records, census returns, monumental inscriptions.

Printed publications:
Order printed publications from: Public Library at Farraline Park, Genfair
via http://www.genfair.com

Publications list:
Available online and in print

Access to staff:
Contact via website. Access for members only.
Hours: Tue only, 1000 to 1630

Access for disabled people:
Lift to third floor

HIGHLAND LIBRARIES

31a Harbour Road, Inverness, IV1 1UA

Tel: 01463 235713
Fax: 01463 236986
E-mail: libraries@highland.gov.uk

Enquiries:
Enquiries to: Library and Information Services Co-ordinator
Other contacts: Senior Librarian, Information Co-ordinator for reference and Information enquiries including local history.

Founded:
1975

Organisation type and purpose:
Local government body, public library.

Subject coverage:
General, specialised sections include local history, genealogy.

Museum or gallery collection, archive, or library special collection:
Held at Inverness:
Fraser Mackintosh Collection (local history, law and literature)
Gaelic Society of Inverness Library (Gaelic language and culture)
Highland Family History Society Library (extensive local history and genealogy collections)
Kirk Session Library (antiquarian interest)
Held at Wick:
John Mowat Collection (local history of Caithness and northern Scotland)

Non-library collection catalogue:
All or part available online and in-house

Library catalogue:
All or part available online and in-house

Access to staff:
Contact by letter, by telephone, by fax, by e-mail and in person. Appointment necessary.
Hours: Mon to Fri, 0800 to 1800

Access to building, collection or gallery:
No prior appointment required

continued overleaf

Access for disabled people:
Level entry

Parent body:
Highland Council
   Education, Culture and Sport Service, Inverness

HIGHLANDS & ISLANDS ENTERPRISE

Acronym or abbreviation: HIE

Cowan House, Inverness Retail & Business Park, Inverness, IV2 7GF

Tel: 01463 234171
Fax: 01463 244469
E-mail: hie.general@hient.co.uk

Website:
http://www.hie.co.uk

Enquiries:
Enquiries to: Library Officer
Direct tel: 01463 244409
Direct fax: 01463 244351
Direct e-mail: library@hient.co.uk

Founded:
1991

Organisation type and purpose:
National government body.
HIE is a government-sponsored development agency.
Economic and social development in the Highlands and Islands of Scotland.

Subject coverage:
Business information, Highlands and Islands of Scotland, regional and industrial development, training, primary industries, offshore oil and gas, fisheries, fish farming, land use, tourism, transport, community co-operatives, agriculture.

Library catalogue:
All or part available in-house

Printed publications:
Network Report & Accounts (annually)
The Brief (newsletter, once every other month)

Access to staff:
Contact by letter, by telephone, by fax, by e-mail, in person and via website. Appointment necessary. Access for members only.
Hours: Mon to Fri, 0900 to 1700

Access to building, collection or gallery:
Prior appointment required

Access for disabled people:
Parking provided, level entry, access to all public areas, toilet facilities

HILL TAYLOR DICKINSON

20–30 Irongate House, Duke's Place, London, EC3A 7HX

Tel: 020 7283 9033
Fax: 020 7283 1144
E-mail: library@htd-london.com

Enquiries:
Enquiries to: Library and Information Manager

Organisation type and purpose:
Solicitors.

Subject coverage:
Law: shipping, insurance, company and commercial, litigation, property, taxation, probate.

Member of:
British and Irish Association of Law Librarians (BIALL)

HILLCLIMB & SPRINT ASSOCIATION LIMITED

Spring Cottage, Gaydon Road, Bishops Itchington, Warwickshire, CV47 2QX

Tel: 01926 612432

Fax: 01926 612432

Enquiries:
Enquiries to: Membership Secretary
Direct tel: 01926 424609
Direct fax: 01926 424609

Founded:
1955

Organisation type and purpose:
Membership association (membership is by subscription), present number of members: 1000. Motor sport association whose members compete in speed hillclimb and sprint meetings.

Subject coverage:
Speed hillclimb and sprint car racing.

Printed publications:
Magazine (covers all aspects of the sport across the country, 6 times a year)

Access to staff:
Contact by letter, by telephone and by fax
Hours: Mon to Fri, 1800 to 2100; not weekends

HILLINGDON BOROUGH LIBRARIES

Central Library, 14–15 High Street, Uxbridge, Middlesex, UB8 1HD

Tel: 01895 250600
Fax: 01895 239794
E-mail: clibrary@lbhill.gov.uk or clibrary@hillingdon.gov.uk

Website:
http://www.hillingdon.gov.uk
London Borough of Hillingdon site includes library information pages.

Enquiries:
Enquiries to: Librarian
Direct tel: 01895 250603
Direct fax: 01895 811164

Organisation type and purpose:
Local government body, public library.

Subject coverage:
General; history of Hillingdon, Middlesex and surrounding areas.

Museum or gallery collection, archive, or library special collection:
Government Publications (SSS except for SI's)

Trade and statistical information:
All current HMSO statistical series.

Printed publications:
Local history monographs

Access to staff:
Contact by letter, by telephone, by fax, by e-mail, in person and via website
Hours: Mon to Fri, 0900 to 1700

Access to building, collection or gallery:
No access other than to staff
Hours: Mon, Tue, Thu, 0930 to 2000; Wed, 0930 to 1730; Fri, 1000 to 1730; Sat, 0930 to 1600

Access for disabled people:
Level entry, access to all public areas, toilet facilities

HILLINGDON FAMILY HISTORY SOCIETY

20 Moreland Drive, Gerrards Cross, Buckinghamshire, SL9 8BB

Tel: 01753 885602
E-mail: Gillmay@dial.pipex.com

Website:
http://www.hfhs.co.uk
Information about the Society; programme for the year; publications.
http://www.rootsweb.com/~enghfhs/
Information about the Society; programme for the year; publications.

Enquiries:
Enquiries to: Honorary Secretary

Founded:
1987

Organisation type and purpose:
Membership association (membership is by subscription).

Subject coverage:
Family history and genealogy with particular reference to the London Borough of Hillingdon.

Museum or gallery collection, archive, or library special collection:
Collection of genealogical books, journals, CD-ROMs and microforms available to members

Printed publications:
Journal (quarterly, members)

Microform publications:
Church School, Ickenham (1873–1929)
Middlesex Sessions Records (Hillingdon extracts)
Monumental Inscriptions: St Mary's, Harefield; Holy Trinity, Northwood; St Laurence, Cowley; St Martin's, West Drayton.
St Giles' parish registers
Ickenham baptisms, marriages, and burials

Publications list:
Available online and in print

Access to staff:
Contact by letter, by telephone and by e-mail
Hours: Mon to Fri, 0900 to 1700, and evenings and weekends

Member of:
Federation of Family History Societies

HILLINGDON LOCAL STUDIES, ARCHIVES AND MUSEUMS

Central Library, 1415 High Street, Uxbridge, Middlesex, UB8 1HD

Tel: 01895 250702
Fax: 01895 811164
E-mail: archives@hillingdongrid.org

Website:
http://www.hillingdon.gov.uk/libraries
Council information.

Enquiries:
Enquiries to: Local Studies and Archives Manager
Direct e-mail: ccotton@hillingdongrid.org

Formerly called:
Hillingdon Local Heritage Service; London Borough of Hillingdon Libraries (year of change 1991)

Organisation type and purpose:
Museum, public library, archives.

Subject coverage:
Local and family history of the Hillingdon area.

Museum or gallery collection, archive, or library special collection:
Challoner Collection of Uxbridge photographs
Gazette newspaper photographs 1920 to 1950
Minet Archives, deeds etc of Minet Properties in Hayes

Non-library collection catalogue:
All or part available in-house

Library catalogue:
All or part available online

Printed publications:
Hillingdon Heritage Service Items for sale include postcards of old prints of Hillingdon, notelets, brass rubbing pack, education packs, laminated photographs and books including:
Family History in Hillingdon (Hillingdon FHS, £1.50)
Ickenham and Harefield Past (Bowlt E, £14.95)
London Borough of Hillingdon: 25 years (£1)
Ruislip Past (Bowlt E, £14.95)
Uxbridge, Hillingdon & Cowley in old photographs (Pearce K R, £7.99)

Hillingdon Cultural Activities and Libraries Service has published several books and leaflets on local history and local walks of general interest including:

Gregory King's Harefield; an English village in the 1690's (Cuthbertson E, 1992, £4.90)

The Goodliest Place in Middlesex; a history of the ancient parish of Ruislip from the Domesday Book to modern times (Bowlt E, 1989, £8.50)

The History of Heathrow (Sherwood P, 2nd ed, 1993, £4.50)

Electronic and video publications:
Bygone Middlesex (video, £12.99)
Home Front (video, £12.99)

Publications list:
Available online and in print

Access to staff:
Contact by letter, by telephone, by fax, by e-mail and in person
Hours: Mon, 0930 to 2000; Tue, Wed, Thu, 1300 to 1730; Fri, 1000 to 1230 and 13.30 to 17.30; Sat, 0930 to 1200 and 1300 to 1600

Access for disabled people:
Access to all public areas, toilet facilities

HILLMAN COMMER & KARRIER CLUB

Acronym or abbreviation: HCKC

Capri House, Walton-on-Thames, Surrey, KT12 2LY

Tel: 01932 269109
Fax: 01932 269109

Enquiries:
Enquiries to: Chairman

Founded:
1989

Organisation type and purpose:
International organisation, membership association (membership is by subscription), present number of members: 1600 approx, voluntary organisation.

Subject coverage:
Hillman, Commer and Karrier and other Rootes built vehicles, mechanical and technical information, insurance, registration, restoration.

Museum or gallery collection, archive, or library special collection:
Books, manuals, technical information magazines etc relevant to Hillman, Commer, Karrier and Rootes vehicles

Library catalogue:
All or part available in-house

Printed publications:
A.R.V.O. News
H.C.K.C. News

Publications list:
Available in print

Access to staff:
Contact by letter and by fax
Hours: Mon to Fri, 0900 to 1700

Access to building, collection or gallery:
No prior appointment required

Parent body:
Association of Rootes Vehicle Owners

HINCKLEY & BOSWORTH BOROUGH COUNCIL

Council Offices, Argents Mead, Hinckley, Leicestershire, LE10 1BZ

Tel: 01455 238141
Fax: 01455 251172

Website:
http://www.hinckley-bosworth.gov.uk

Enquiries:
Enquiries to: Chief Executive

Organisation type and purpose:
Local government body.

Subject coverage:
Local government services.

Printed publications:
Councillors Guide (councillors, local services, A-Z of council services

Access to staff:
Contact by letter and by fax
Hours: Mon to Fri, 0900 to 1700

Health authority:
Leicestershire, Northamptonshire and Rutland Health Authorities

Local education authority:
Leicestershire Local Education Authority

HIRE ASSOCIATION EUROPE

Acronym or abbreviation: HAE

2 Holland Road West, Waterlinks, Birmingham, B6 4DW

Tel: 0121 380 4600
Fax: 0121 333 4109
E-mail: mail@hae.org.uk

Website:
http://www.hae.org.uk
Membership.

Enquiries:
Enquiries to: Managing Director

Founded:
1971

Organisation type and purpose:
International organisation, trade association, membership association (membership is by subscription), present number of members: 1000. Membership body for hire equipment shops.

Subject coverage:
Small plant and tool hire equipment, hire of equipment for leisure, catering, fencing and portable sanitation, training and safety supplies to the hire industry, audiovisual and powered access hire.

Trade and statistical information:
Turnover and employment statistics.

Printed publications:
Executive Hire News (magazine, 10 times a year)
Hire Standard
Safety Manuals
Technical Safety Handling leaflets

Publications list:
Available in print

Access to staff:
Contact by letter, by telephone, by fax and via website. Appointment necessary.
Hours: Mon to Fri, 0900 to 1700

Access to building, collection or gallery:
No prior appointment required
Hours: Mon to Fri, 0900 to 1700

Subsidiary body:
Executive Hire News

HISTORIC COMMERCIAL VEHICLE SOCIETY

Acronym or abbreviation: HCVS

Iden Grange, Cranbrook Road, Staplehurst, Kent, TN12 0ET

Tel: 01580 892929
Fax: 01580 893227
E-mail: hcvs@btinternet.com

Website:
http://www.hcvs.co.uk
Society details, events, magazine, insurance service.

Enquiries:
Enquiries to: Membership Secretary

Founded:
1958

Organisation type and purpose:
International organisation, national organisation, membership association (membership is by subscription), present number of members: 3500, registered charity (charity number 271123).

Subject coverage:
Historic commercial vehicles.

Library catalogue:
All or part available in-house

Access to staff:
Contact by letter, by telephone, by fax, by e-mail and via website
Hours: Mon to Fri, 0900 to 1700

Access to building, collection or gallery:
No access other than to staff
Special comments: Prior appointment required for library research (situated in Cardiff)

HISTORIC FARM BUILDINGS GROUP

Acronym or abbreviation: HFBG

c/o Museum of English Rural Life, University of Reading, PO Box 229, Whiteknights, Reading, Berkshire, RG6 6AG

Tel: 0118 931 8663
Fax: 0118 975 1264
E-mail: r.d.brigden@reading.ac.uk

Website:
http://www.chelt.ac.uk/ccru/hfbg
Information about the group, contacts and newsletter

Enquiries:
Enquiries to: Secretary

Founded:
1985

Organisation type and purpose:
Learned society.

Subject coverage:
History of old farm buildings.

Printed publications:
Annual Journal

Access to staff:
Contact by letter and by e-mail
Hours: Mon to Fri, 0900 to 1700

HISTORIC HOUSES ASSOCIATION

Acronym or abbreviation: HHA

2 Chester Street, London, SW1X 7BB

Tel: 020 7259 5688
Fax: 020 7259 5590
E-mail: info@hha.org.uk

Website:
http://www.hha.org.uk

Enquiries:
Enquiries to: Executive Secretary

Founded:
1973

Organisation type and purpose:
Membership association (membership is by subscription).

Subject coverage:
Preservation for the future of historic houses, parks, gardens and places of interest in Britain; pressure for a long-term policy based on private ownership.

Printed publications:
Historic House (HHA Journal, 4 times a year for members)
Technical manuals

continued overleaf

Yearbook (for members only)

Access to staff:
Contact by letter, by telephone, by fax, by e-mail and via website
Hours: Mon to Fri, 0900 to 1700

Access to building, collection or gallery:
Prior appointment required

Affiliated to:
European Union of Historic Houses Association

Close liaison with:
British Tourist Authority
Cadw Welsh Historic Monuments
Department of National Heritage
English Heritage
Historic Scotland
National Trust
National Trust for Scotland

HISTORIC LOTUS REGISTER

Acronym or abbreviation: HLR

Badgers Farm, Short Green, Winfarthing, Diss, Norfolk, IP22 2EE

Tel: 01953 860508

Enquiries:
Enquiries to: Honorary Secretary

Founded:
1974

Organisation type and purpose:
International organisation (membership is by subscription), present number of members: 1000, voluntary organisation.
Motor club.

Subject coverage:
Historic Lotus cars manufactured prior to 1961, preservation and research.

Museum or gallery collection, archive, or library special collection:
Lotus factory records

Printed publications:
Newsletter (quarterly)

Access to staff:
Contact by letter and by telephone
Hours: Mon to Sun 0900 to 2000

HISTORIC SCOTLAND

Acronym or abbreviation: HS

Technical Conservation Research and Education Group, Resource Centre, Longmore House, Salisbury Place, Edinburgh, EH9 1SH

Tel: 0131 668 8600
Fax: 0131 668 8699
E-mail: hs.resourcecentre@scotland.gsi.gov.uk

Website:
http://www.historic-scotland.gov.uk

Enquiries:
Enquiries to: Resource Centre Manager
Direct tel: 0131 668 8642
Direct fax: 0131 668 8669

Founded:
1991

Organisation type and purpose:
National government body, statutory body.

Subject coverage:
Information on historic buildings and monuments under the guardianship of Scottish Ministers, architecture, archaeology, conservation and the environment.

Museum or gallery collection, archive, or library special collection:
Resource Centre of 3,500 items, comprising printed and mixed media covering all aspects of built heritage – archaeology, architecture, history, conservation and related areas. This includes specialist and general journals concerning the built environment and Historic Scotland publications on specialist conservation techniques, which also include conservation of artistic works.
Separate Historic Scotland Library of 10,000 books, 2,000 reports and pamphlets, 170 periodicals, Historic Scotland guidebooks and reports
Separate photographic library of 50,000 slides of ancient monuments

Non-library collection catalogue:
All or part available online, in-house and in print

Library catalogue:
All or part available in-house

Printed publications:
A range of publications are available in the following categories:
Technical advices notes; research reports; conference proceedings and abstracts on subjects relating to the built environment and other conservation related areas.

Electronic and video publications:
CD-ROMs, DVDs, videos relating to the technical aspect of conservation

Publications list:
Available online and in print

Access to staff:
Contact by letter, by telephone, by fax, by e-mail, in person and via website. Appointment necessary.
Hours: Mon to Fri, 1000 to 1600

Access to building, collection or gallery:
Prior appointment required

Access for disabled people:
Parking provided, ramped entry, toilet facilities

Constituent part of:
Scottish Executive Education Department
tel: 0131 668 8600

HISTORIC SOCIETY OF LANCASHIRE AND CHESHIRE

Acronym or abbreviation: HSLC

Flat 4, 3 Bramhall Road, Waterloo, Liverpool, L22 3XA

Tel: 0151 920 8213
E-mail: rch2949@yahoo.co.uk

Website:
http://www.hslc.org.uk

Enquiries:
Enquiries to: Secretary

Founded:
1848

Organisation type and purpose:
Learned society (membership is by subscription), registered charity (charity number 224825).

Subject coverage:
Local history of Lancashire and Cheshire.

Museum or gallery collection, archive, or library special collection:
Society's collections held at Liverpool Record Office

Library catalogue:
All or part available online

Printed publications:
Transactions (annually, together with the Occasional Series vols, for the past 150 years)
Back numbers of the Transactions and offprints
Order printed publications from: Publications Officer, Historic Society of Lancashire and Cheshire, c/o School of History, 9 Abercromby Square, Liverpool, L69 7WZ; tel: 0151 428 4121

Publications list:
Available in print

Access to staff:
Contact by letter and by e-mail
Hours: Mon to Fri, 0900 to 1700

HISTORIC SPORTS CAR CLUB

Acronym or abbreviation: HSCC

Silverstone Circuit, Silverstone, Towcester, Northamptonshire, NN12 8TN

Tel: 01327 858400
Fax: 01327 858500
E-mail: office@hscc.org.uk

Enquiries:
Enquiries to: Executive Director

Founded:
1966

Organisation type and purpose:
International organisation, membership association (membership is by subscription), present number of members: 850.
Organiser of historic car race meetings and championships.
Appointed to coordinate European Championship for pre 1985 F1 cars by the FIA, now a major club.

Subject coverage:
History of, and information regarding, historic motor racing.

Museum or gallery collection, archive, or library special collection:
Large archive of historic motor racing books and magazines dating back to 1940s

Printed publications:
HSCC News (magazine, 6 times a year)

Access to staff:
Contact by letter, by telephone, by fax, by e-mail, in person and via website. Appointment necessary.
Hours: Mon to Fri, 0900 to 1700

Affiliated to:
RACMSA

HISTORIC VOLKSWAGEN CLUB

5 Gresley Close, Sutton Coldfield, West Midlands, B75 5HT

Tel: 0121 308 3693
E-mail: nigel.wallace@virgin.net

Website:
http://www.historicvws.org.uk

Enquiries:
Enquiries to: Membership Secretary

Founded:
1974

Organisation type and purpose:
Membership association (membership is by subscription), voluntary organisation.
Provides a focal point for owners and enthusiasts of pre-1967 (Aug) Volkswagen vehicles. Provides technical information, spares location and historical information for members and others.

Subject coverage:
Technical, historical, diary dates for gatherings of enthusiasts relating to Volkswagen products manufactured prior to August 1967.

Printed publications:
The Historic Volkswagen (4 times a year)

Access to staff:
Contact by letter, by telephone, by e-mail and via website
Hours: Mon to Fri, evenings only

HISTORICAL ASSOCIATION

Acronym or abbreviation: HA

59A Kennington Park Road, London, SE11 4JH

Tel: 020 7735 3901
Fax: 020 7582 4989
E-mail: enquiry@history.org.uk

Website:
http://www.history.org.uk

Enquiries:
Enquiries to: Membership Secretary

Founded:
1906

Organisation type and purpose:
Membership association (membership is by
subscription), registered charity (charity number
1120261).
Subject teaching association.

Subject coverage:
General information on all areas of history, history
teaching, careers in history.

**Museum or gallery collection, archive, or library
special collection:**
The following collections not open to the public:
Bound copies Annual Bulletin of Historical
Literature, 1907 to date
Bound copies of History, 1912 to date

Printed publications:
The following publications are available direct, for
purchase:
Books on Teaching History to 5 to 18 year olds
Bulletin of Historical Literature (annually)
History (3 times a year)
Short bibliographies on specific periods of history
Teaching History (4 times a year)
Primary History (3 times a year)

Publications list:
Available online and in print

Access to staff:
Contact via website
Hours: Mon to Fri, 1000 to 1700

HISTORICAL METALLURGICAL
SOCIETY LIMITED

Acronym or abbreviation: HMS

c/o The Institute of Materials, Minerals and
Mining, 1 Carlton House Terrace, London, SW1Y
5DB

Tel: 01792 233223

Website:
http://hist-met.org./ad_index.html
Archaeometallurgical datasheets.
http://hist-met.org/hmspub.htm
Publications.
http://hist-met.org/resources.html
Resources for historians.
http://hist-met.org/hm_index.html
Journal Contents.
http://hist-met.org
Membership information, journal contents,
meetings information.

Enquiries:
Enquiries to: General Secretary
Direct fax: 01792 233223
Direct e-mail: hon-sec@hist-met.org

Founded:
1979

Organisation type and purpose:
Learned society.

Subject coverage:
Metallurgical history and archaeometallurgy.

**Museum or gallery collection, archive, or library
special collection:**
A collection of miscellaneous documents relating
to metallurgical history. Includes the Charles
Blick Archive, mainly conservation of
metallurgical sites
A miscellaneous collection of largely metallurgical
books, some scarce, mostly out of date

Non-library collection catalogue:
All or part available online

Library catalogue:
All or part available online

Printed publications:
Conference Proceedings such as Boles and Smelt
Mills
Historical Metallurgy
Metals and the Sea

Order printed publications from: Publications Officer,
22 Windley Crescent, Darley Abbey, Derbyshire,
DE3 1BZ, tel: 01332 553430, e-mail: brian.read2@
ntlworld.com

Electronic and video publications:
Disk based index for Historical Metallurgy (not yet
complete)

Publications list:
Available online

Access to staff:
Contact by letter, by telephone, by fax and by e-
mail
Hours: Mon to Fri, 0900 to 2200

Affiliated to:
Institute of Materials, Minerals aand Mining

HISTORICAL MODEL RAILWAY
SOCIETY

Acronym or abbreviation: HMRS

c/o The Midland Railway Centre, Butterley Station,
Ripley, Derbyshire, DE5 3QZ

Tel: 01773 745959
Fax: 01773 745959
E-mail: studycentre-manager@hmrs.org.uk

Website:
http://www.hmrs.org.uk

Enquiries:
Enquiries to: Museum and Study Centre Manager

Founded:
1950

Organisation type and purpose:
Membership association (membership is by
subscription),
present number of members: 2500, registered
charity (charity number 273110), research
organisation.
Educational organisation.

Subject coverage:
Railways of Britain and the Commonwealth: all
aspects from their invention to the present day.

**Museum or gallery collection, archive, or library
special collection:**
Library of railway books and periodicals including
some non-published documents of railway
companies
Photographic library of over 50,000 items

Non-library collection catalogue:
All or part available online and in-house

Library catalogue:
All or part available online and in-house

Publications list:
Available online and in print

Access to staff:
Contact by letter, by fax, by e-mail and via
website
Hours: Mon to Fri, 0900 to 1700

HISTORY OF ADVERTISING
TRUST

Acronym or abbreviation: HAT

HAT House, 12 Raveningham Centre,
Raveningham, Norwich, NR14 6NU

Tel: 01508 548623
Fax: 01508 548478
E-mail: enquiries@hatads.org.uk

Website:
http://www.hatads.org.uk

Founded:
1976

Organisation type and purpose:
The HAT Archive is a registered charity (no.
276194) which seeks to collect and preserve the
UK's advertising heritage and to make it available
for research and study for all.

Subject coverage:
Advertising in the United Kingdom from the early
1800s to the present day.

Special visitor services:
Michael Cudlipp Research and Study Centre

**Museum or gallery collection, archive, or library
special collection:**
Archive of UK advertising

HISTORY OF ADVERTISING
TRUST ARCHIVE

Acronym or abbreviation: HAT Archive

HAT House, 12 Raveningham Centre,
Raveningham, Norwich, Norfolk, NR14 6NU

Tel: 01508 548623
Fax: 01508 548478
E-mail: enquiries@hatads.org.uk

Website:
http://www.hatads.org.uk

Enquiries:
Enquiries to: General Manager
Other contacts: Chief Executive; Curator

Founded:
1976

Organisation type and purpose:
Registered charity (no. 276194), educational trust
and research organisation. National archive of UK
advertising and brand communication. Aims to
rescue, collect and preserve the industry's archives
and best work and to make it available to all.

Subject coverage:
The history of advertising and brand
communications 1800-present day, including
advertising agencies; advertising controls; clubs
and organisations; corporate and retail marketing;
designers and creatives; professional interest
bodies; special collections; TV commercials (over
70,000) 1950s to present.

Information services:
Research and information service.

Special visitor services:
Study visits by appointment only

Education services:
Education services will be available in 2009

**Museum or gallery collection, archive, or library
special collection:**
Specialist library of over 6,000 books
Large collections of proofs, posters, original
artwork, market research and company records
(see website for details)

Trade and statistical information:
Over 130 advertising and marketing industry
journal titles; published industry statistics and
surveys; market research and trends; selected
titles of consumer magazines.

Non-library collection catalogue:
All or part available in-house

Library catalogue:
All or part available in-house

Printed publications:
Advertising in Britain, A History (T. A. Nevett)
British Television Advertising: The first 30 years (B.
Henry)
HAT News (quarterly newsletter)
Journal of Advertising History
HAT Annual Report and Financial Statements
Calendars, postcards, etc.
Order printed publications from:
enquiries@hatads.org.uk

Electronic and video publications:
Vintage TV commercial compilations (DVD, to
order)
Order electronic and video publications from:
enquiries@hatads.org.uk

Publications list:
Available online and in print

continued overleaf

Access to staff:
Contact by letter, by telephone, by fax, by e-mail, in person and via website. Appointment necessary. All charged.
Hours: Mon to Fri, 0900 to 1700

Access to building, collection or gallery:
Study visits by appointment only
Hours: Mon to Fri, 0900 to 1700
Special comments: Closed public holidays and weekends. UK student research visits free of charge.

Access for disabled people:
Parking provided, level entry, access to all public areas, toilet facilities

HISTORY OF EDUCATION SOCIETY

Faculty of Education, University of Winchester, Sparkford Road, Winchester, Hampshire, SO22 4NR

Tel: 01962 827125
Fax: 01962 827479
E-mail: stephanie.spencer@winchester.ac.uk

Website:
http://www.historyofeducation.org.uk
General; membership; details of society's conferences and seminars; links to other societies for history of education and related sites.

Enquiries:
Enquiries to: Secretary

Founded:
1967

Organisation type and purpose:
Learned society (membership is by subscription), present number of members: 300, registered charity (charity number 1055764).

Subject coverage:
History of education, its study and teaching.

Printed publications:
History of Education (6 times a year)
History of Education Society Bulletin (2 times a year)

Publications list:
Available in print

Access to staff:
Contact by letter, by e-mail and via website
Hours: Mon to Fri, 0900 to 1700

Member of:
International Standing Conference for the History of Education

HISTORY OF PARLIAMENT TRUST

15 Woburn Square, London, WC1H 0NS

Tel: 020 7862 8800
Fax: 020 7255 1442

Website:
http://www.ihrinfo.ac.uk
Role of history, publications, list of staff.

Enquiries:
Enquiries to: Administrator
Other contacts: Director

Founded:
1951

Organisation type and purpose:
Registered charity, research organisation.

Subject coverage:
History of Parliament.

Printed publications:
The History of Parliament: The Commons – 1386–1421 (Roskell J S et al, 4 volumes, £275)
The History of Parliament: The House of Commons – 1509–1558 (ed Bindoff S T, 3 volumes, £120)

The History of Parliament: The House of Commons – 1558–1603 (ed Hasler P W, 3 volumes, £120)
The History of Parliament: The House of Commons – 1660–1690 (ed Henning B D, 3 volumes £120)
The History of Parliament: The House of Commons – 1715–1754 (ed Sedgwick R, 2 volumes £90)
The History of Parliament: The House of Commons – 1754–1790 (eds Namier L and Brooks J, 3 volumes £120)
The History of Parliament: The House of Commons – 1790–1820 (ed Thorne R G, 5 volumes £225)
Order printed publications from: Available from, Sutton Publishing
Phoenix Mill, Far Thrupp, Stroud, Gloucestershire, GL5 2BU, tel: 01453 731114, fax: 01453 731117

Electronic and video publications:
The History of Parliament (all 23 volumes, CD-ROM, pub Cambridge University Press, 1998)

Publications list:
Available in print

Access to staff:
Contact by letter and by e-mail
Hours: Mon to Fri, 0900 to 1700

Access to building, collection or gallery:
No prior appointment required

HM CUSTOMS AND EXCISE – LIBRARY AND INFORMATION SERVICE

Formal name: Her Majesty's Custom and Excise
Acronym or abbreviation: HMC&E

New King's Beam House, 22 Upper Ground, London, SE1 9PJ

Tel: 020 7865 5668
Fax: 020 7865 5670
E-mail: libraryenquiries{NKBH}@hmce.gsi.gov.uk

Enquiries:
Enquiries to: Librarian

Organisation type and purpose:
National government body.

Subject coverage:
Indirect taxation; trade statistics; general fiscal matters; economics; revenue history, company information.

Museum or gallery collection, archive, or library special collection:
Under the terms of the Public Records Act 1958 a small selection of manuscript material is available for bona fide research into the history of commerce, sea ports, shipping, HM Customs & Excise, etc. Most records of HM Customs & Excise are in the National Archives, Kew

Non-library collection catalogue:
All or part available in-house

Library catalogue:
All or part available in-house

Printed publications:
Library accessions list

Publications list:
Available in print

Access to staff:
Contact by letter, by telephone, by fax, by e-mail and in person. Appointment necessary. Letter of introduction required.
Hours: Mon to Fri, 0900 to 1700

HM LAND REGISTRY

Acronym or abbreviation: HMLR

32 Lincoln's Inn Fields, London, WC2A 3PH

Tel: 020 7917 8888
Fax: 020 7955 0110
E-mail: enquiries.pic@landreg.gov.uk

Website:
http://www.landreg.gov.uk
Information on the works of the Land Registry. Annual Report and Accounts. Residential property price report.

Enquiries:
Enquiries to: Librarian
Direct tel: 020 7917 8888 ext 4800
Other contacts: Agency Customer Service Manager

Founded:
1862

Organisation type and purpose:
National government body.
HM Land Registry is a government executive agency and trading fund.
It aims to: maintain and develop a stable and effective land registration system throughout England and Wales; guarantee title to registered estates and interests in land; provide ready access to up-to-date and guaranteed land information.

Subject coverage:
Mapping of all the property boundaries, change of ownership of property, and land registration system in England and Wales, granting of legal title on behalf of the Crown, provides ready access to up-to-date and guaranteed information.

Trade and statistical information:
Quarterly Residential Property Price Report (published free) on property prices in England and Wales, detailing average prices and volume of sales broken down by property type, counties and London Boroughs.

Printed publications:
Annual Report
Practice advice leaflets (free)
Public relations leaflets (free)
Residential Property Price Report (quarterly, free)

Electronic and video publications:
Residential Property Price Report (on disc, £10)

Publications list:
Available in print

Access to staff:
Contact by letter, by telephone, by fax, by e-mail, in person and via website. All charged.
Hours: Mon to Fri, 0900 to 1700

Access to building, collection or gallery:
No prior appointment required

District Land Registries:
Birkenhead (Old Market) District Land Registry \
For registered land titles in Merseyside and Staffordshire and Stoke-on-Trent
Old Market House, Hamilton Street, Birkenhead, Merseyside, CH41 5FL; tel: 0151 473 1110; fax: 0151 473 0251
Birkenhead (Rosebrae) District Land Registry \ *For registered land titles in Cheshire and the London Boroughs of Kensington and Chelsea, and Hammersmith and Fulham*
Rosebrae Court, Woodside Ferry Approach, Birkenhead, Merseyside, CH41 5FL; tel: 0151 472 0666; fax: 0151 472 6789
Coventry District Land Registry \ *For registered land titles in West Midlands and Worcestershire districts of Wychavon, Bromsgrove and Redditch*
Leigh Court, Torrington Avenue, Tile Hill, Coventry, CV4 9XZ; tel: 024 7686 0860; fax: 024 7686 0021
Croydon District Land Registry \ *For registered land titles in London Boroughs of Bexley, Bromley, Merton, Croydon and Sutton*
Sunley House, Bedford Park, Croydon, CR9 3LE; tel: 020 8781 9100; fax: 020 8781 9110
Durham (Bolden House) District Land Registry \
For registered land titles in Cumbria and Surrey
Bolden House, Wheatlands Way, Pity Me, Durham, DH1 5GJ; tel: 0191 301 2345; fax: 0191 301 2300
Durham District Land Registry \ *For registered land titles in Durham, Hartlepool, Middlesbrough, Northumberland, Redcar and Cleveland, Stockton-on-Tees and Tyne & Wear*
Southfield House, Southfield Way, Durham, DH1 5TR; tel: 0191 301 3500; fax: 0191 301 0020

Gloucester District Land Registry\ *For registered land titles in Berkshire, Bristol, Gloucestershire, Oxfordshire, South Gloucestershire and Warwickshire*
Twyver House, Bruton Way, Gloucester, GL1 1DQ; tel: 01452 511111; fax: 01452 510050

Harrow District Land Registry\ *For registered land titles in Barnet, Brent, Camden, City of London, City of Westminster, Harrow, Inner & Middle Temples and Islington*
Lyon House, Lyon Road, Harrow, Middlesex, HA1 2EU; tel: 020 8235 1181; fax: 020 8862 0176

Hull District Land Registry\ *For registered land titles in Kingston upon Hull, Lincolnshire, Norfolk, North East Lincolnshire and Suffolk*
Earle House, Portland Street, Hull, Humberside, HU2 8JN; tel: 01482 223244; fax: 01482 224278

Lancashire District Land Registry\ *For registered land titles in Blackburn with Darwen, Blackpool and Lancashire*
Wrea Brook Court, Lytham Road, Warton, Preston, Lancashire, PR4 1TE; tel: 01772 836700; fax: 01772 836970

Leicester District Land Registry\ *Leicester District Land Registry\ For registered land titles in Buckinghamshire, Northamptonshire, Daventry and Leicestershire*
Westbridge Place, Leicester, LE3 5DR; tel: 0116 265 4000; fax: 0116 265 4008

Lytham District Land Registry\ *For registered land titles in Greater Manchester*
Birkenhead House, East Beach, Lytham St Annes, Lancashire, FY8 5AB; tel: 01253 840001; fax: 01253 840013

Nottingham (East) District Land Registry\ *For registered land titles in Nottinghamshire, South Yorkshire*
Robins Wood Road, Nottingham, NG8 3RQ; tel: 0115 906 5353; fax: 0115 936 0036

Nottingham (West) District Land Registry\ *For registered land titles in Derbyshire and West Yorkshire*
Chalfont Drive, Nottingham, NG8 3RN; tel: 0115 935 1166; fax: 0115 935 0038

Peterborough District Land Registry\ *For registered land titles in Bedfordshire, Cambridgeshire, Essex*
Touthill Close, City Road, Peterborough, Cambridgeshire, PE1 1XN; tel: 01733 288288; fax: 01733 280022

Plymouth District Land Registry\ *For registered land titles in Bath and North East Somerset, Cornwall, Devon, Isles of Scilly, North Somerset and Somerset*
Plumer House, Tailyour Road, Crownhill, Plymouth, PL6 5HY; tel: 01752 636000; fax: 01752 636161

Portsmouth District Land Registry\ *For registered land titles in East Sussex, Isle of Wight, West Sussex and Hampshire*
St Andrew's Court, St Michael's Road, Portsmouth, PO1 2JH; tel: 023 9276 8888; fax: 023 9276 8768

Stevenage District Land Registry\ *For registered land titles in Hertfordshire and the London Boroughs of Barking & Dagenham, Enfield, Hackney, Havering, Newham, Redbridge, Tower Hamlets and Waltham Forest*
Brickdale House, Swingate, Stevenage, Hertfordshire, SG1 1XG; tel: 01438 788888; fax: 01438 780107

Swansea District Land Registry\ *For registered land titles in Hereford & Worcester and the London Boroughs of Ealing, Hillingdon, Hounslow and Harringey*
Ty Bryn Glas, High Street, Swansea, SA1 1PW; tel: 01792 458877; fax: 01792 473236

Telford District Land Registry\ *For registered land titles in Shropshire and the London Boroughs of Greenwich, Kingston Upon Thames, Lambeth, Lewisham, Richmond Upon Thames, Southwark and Wandsworth*
Parkside Court, Hall Park Way, Telford, Shropshire, TF3 4LR; tel: 01952 290355; fax: 01952 290356

The Land Registry for Wales\ *For registered land in the principality of Wales*
Ty Cwm Tawe, Phoenix Way, Llansamlet, Swansea, SA7 9FQ; tel: 01792 355000; fax: 01792 355055

Tunbridge Wells District Land Registry\ *For registered land titles in Kent*
Forest Court, Forest Road, Tunbridge Wells, Kent, TN2 5AQ; tel: 01892 510015; fax: 01892 510032

Weymouth District Land Registry\ *For registered land titles in Dorset, Wiltshire, South Somerset and Mendip*
1 Cumberland Drive, Weymouth, Dorset, DT4 9TT; tel: 01305 363636; fax: 01305 363646

York District Land Registry\ *For registered land titles in North Yorkshire, York and East Riding of Yorkshire*
James House, James Street, York, YO1 3YZ; tel: 01904 450000; fax: 01904 450086

Parent body:
Lord Chancellor's Department

Subsidiary body:
23 District Land Registries in England and Wales

HM NAUTICAL ALMANAC OFFICE

Acronym or abbreviation: HMNAO

UK Hydrographic Office, Admiralty Way, Taunton, Somerset, TA1 2DN

Tel: 01823 337900
Fax: 01823 335396
E-mail: hmnao@ukho.gov.uk

Website:
http://www.hmnao.com
Contact information, details of publications, samples of our products, details of forthcoming astronomical events.

Enquiries:
Enquiries to: UKHO Helpdesk
Direct tel: 01823 723366
Direct fax: 01823 251816
Direct e-mail: helpdesk@ukho.gov.uk

Founded:
1831

Organisation type and purpose:
National government body, professional body.

Subject coverage:
Astronomy, navigation, land surveying using astronomy, astronomical phenomena, astronomical data, calendarial information, prayer times, first sighting of new moon, forensic astronomy, historical astronomy, astronomical software, astronomical data in various forms, e.g. camera-ready, floppy disc, e-mail and electronic.

Printed publications:
The Nautical Almanac (annually)
The Astronomical Almanac (annually)
Astronomical Phenomena (annually)
The UK Air Almanac (annually)
The Star Almanac for Land Surveyors (annually)
Rapid Sight Reduction Tables for Navigation (every five years)
NavPac and Compact Data 2006–2010 (every five years)
Planetary and Lunar Coordinates 2001–2020 (every 20 years)
Order printed publications from: UK Hydrographic Office Admiralty Brand Distributor Network: http://www.admiraltyshop.co.uk

Electronic and video publications:
The Star Almanac for Land Surveyors (annually)
NavPac and Compact Data 2006–2010 (every five years)

Publications list:
Available in print

Access to staff:
Contact by letter, by telephone, by fax, by e-mail and via website
Hours: Mon to Fri, 0800 to 1600

Links with:
Astronomical Applications Department
US Naval Observatory, 3450 Massachusetts Avenue NW, Washington, DC 20392–5420, USA; tel: +1 (202) 762 1617; fax: +1 (202) 762 1612; website: http://aa.usno.navy.mil

Parent body:
UK Hydrographic Office
Admiralty Way, Taunton, Somerset, TA1 2DN; tel: 01823 337900; 01823 251816 (helpdesk); e-mail: helpdesk@ukho.gov.uk; website: http://www.ukho.gov.uk

HOLBORN LIBRARY

32–38 Theobalds Road, London, WC1X 8PA

Tel: 020 7974 6354
Fax: 020 7974 6356

Website:
http://www.camden.gov.uk
Catalogue access via a link

Enquiries:
Enquiries to: Group Manager

Organisation type and purpose:
Local government body, public library.

Subject coverage:
General fiction and non-fiction. online databases (including Ancestry, Lexis)

Non-library collection catalogue:
All or part available online

Library catalogue:
All or part available online

Access to staff:
Contact by letter, by telephone, by fax, in person and via website
Hours: Mon, Thu, 1000 to 1900; Tue, Fri, 1000 to 1800; Wed, 1000 to 1800; Sat, 1000 to 1700

Access for disabled people:
Ramped entry, access to all public areas, toilet facilities

Parent body:
London Borough of Camden, Culture and Environment Directorate

HOLIDAY CENTRES ASSOCIATION

Acronym or abbreviation: HCA

The Coppice, Rowe Close, Bideford, Devon, EX39 5XX

Tel: 01237 421 347
Fax: 01273 421 347
E-mail: holidaycentres@aol.com

Website:
http://www.holidaycentres.com

Enquiries:
Enquiries to: Chief Executive

Founded:
1936

Formerly called:
National Association of Holiday Centres

Organisation type and purpose:
Trade association.
Represents the majority of United Kingdom holiday centres and villages.

Subject coverage:
Tourism, holiday centres and villages.

Trade and statistical information:
Data on the holiday centre sector of the tourist industry.

Printed publications:
Membership list

Access to staff:
Appointment necessary.
Hours: Mon to Fri, 0900 to 1700

HOLISTIC HEALTH COLLEGE

Acronym or abbreviation: HHC

94 Grosvenor Road, London, SW1V 3LF

Tel: 020 7834 3579
Fax: 020 7821 0255

Website:
http://www.gni-international.org
Further information.

Enquiries:
Enquiries to: General Secretary
Other contacts: Registrar

Founded:
1992

Formed from:
Holistic Health Consultancy (year of change 1983)

Formerly called:
Holistic Health Consultancy and College (year of change 1992)

Organisation type and purpose:
International organisation, training organisation, research organisation.

Subject coverage:
Iridology, herbal medicine, nutrition, naturopathy and homoeopathy.

Library catalogue:
All or part available in-house

Printed publications:
Naturopathic Iridology (course material 18 modules at £150 per module)
Intensive Iridology (course material for practitioners only, 6 modules at £110 per module plus £90 registration, total £750)
Prospectus

Electronic and video publications:
Aloe Vera and Aids (video)
Videos on ME treatments and iridiology (hire only)

Publications list:
Available in print

Access to staff:
Contact by letter and by telephone. Appointment necessary.
Hours: Mon to Wed, 0900 to 1700; Thu and Fri, 0800 to 1100

Access for disabled people:
Access to all public areas, toilet facilities

Affiliated to:
Association of Master Herbalists
  Holden Natural Health Centre, The Bield, Lewes Road, Forest Row, East Sussex, RH18 5AF; tel: 01342 826899; fax: 01342 826896; e-mail: kelly@holclinic.com
General Naturopathic Council Limited
  255 Lavender Hill, London, SW11 1JD; tel: 020 7498 9966; e-mail: maraia.harewood@btconnect.com
Guild of Naturopathic Iridologists International
  at the same address; tel: 020 7821 0255; fax: 020 7821 0255; e-mail: info@gni_international.org

Connections with:
Holistic Health Consultancy
  at the same address; tel: 020 7834 3579; fax: 020 7821 0255

Parent body:
Institute of Complementary Medicine
  PO Box 194, London, SE16 1QZ; tel: 020 7237 5165; fax: 020 7237 5175

HOLLYCOMBE STEAM AND WOODLAND GARDEN SOCIETY

Iron Hill, Midhurst Road, Liphook, Hampshire, GU30 7LP

Tel: 01428 724900
Fax: 01428 723682
E-mail: hollycombe@talk21.com

Website:
http://www.hollycombe.co.uk

Details of museum, Description of artefacts. Open days, exhibits.Up-to-date news.

Enquiries:
Enquiries to: Information Officer

Founded:
1971

Organisation type and purpose:
Membership association (membership is by subscription), present number of members: 150, voluntary organisation, registered charity, museum, suitable for ages: all.
Operates Hollycombe Steam Collection, a working steam power museum of national importance in the UK. Open to the public as advertised.

Subject coverage:
History and application of steam power to transport, agriculture, fairground, marine, industry. Shown working when open.

Printed publications:
Museum Guide Book
Publicity leaflet

Electronic and video publications:
Fairground Organ Tapes (available for purchase)

Access to staff:
Contact by letter, by telephone, by fax, by e-mail, in person and via website
Hours: Office: Mon to Fri, 0900 to 1700

Access to building, collection or gallery:
No prior appointment required
Hours: Collection open to public: Sun and Public holidays; Easter to mid Oct; daily late Jul to late Aug, 1200 to 1700
Special comments: Admission charge published. Prior appointment is required when closed to the public.

Access for disabled people:
Parking provided, level entry, toilet facilities
Special comments: Access to most areas.

HOLLYHOCK SOCIETY, ENGLAND, SCOTLAND AND WALES

5 Clarence Road, Cheltenham, Gloucestershire, GL52 2AY

Tel: 01242 2621459

Subject coverage:
Propagation and cultivation of hollyhocks.

Non-library collection catalogue:
All or part available online

HOLSTEIN UK

Acronym or abbreviation: HUK

Scotsbridge House, Scots Hill, Rickmansworth, Hertfordshire, WD3 3BB

Tel: 01923 695200
Fax: 01923 770003
E-mail: info@holstein-uk.org

Website:
http://www.holstein-uk.org
Latest sire and dam information; full ancestry records; hall of fame; press releases and news.

Enquiries:
Enquiries to: Chief Executive

Founded:
1909

Formed by the merger of:
British Holstein Society (BHS), Holstein-Friesian Society (HFS) (year of change 1999)

Formerly called:
British Friesian Cattle Society (BFCS) (year of change 1986)

Organisation type and purpose:
Membership association (membership is by subscription).

Cattle breed society.
Registration and promotion of the Holstein and Friesian breeds in the United Kingdom.

Subject coverage:
Holstein breed history and present day facts and figures related to the breeding of Holstein cows; bull proofs, cow indexes. Ancestry details, production and conformation records and genetic indexes for production and conformation for over 4 million animals.

Printed publications:
Holstein Journal (6 times a year)

Access to staff:
Contact by letter, by telephone, by fax, by e-mail and via website. Appointment necessary.
Hours: Mon to Fri, 0900 to 1700

Member of:
European Confederation of Black and White Breed Societies
World Holstein Friesian Federation

HOME ACCIDENT PREVENTION NORTHERN IRELAND

Nella House, Dargan Crescent, Belfast, BT3 9JP

Tel: 028 9050 1160
Fax: 028 9050 1164

Website:
http://www.rospa.co.uk

Enquiries:
Enquiries to: Executive Secretary

Founded:
1965

Formerly called:
Northern Ireland Home Accident Prevention Council; Northern Ireland Home Safety Council (year of change 1997)

Organisation type and purpose:
Advisory body, voluntary organisation.

Subject coverage:
Accident prevention in and around the home.

Museum or gallery collection, archive, or library special collection:
Variety of information on accidents and accident prevention

Printed publications:
ROSPA material (charges made)
Various leaflets (available free of charge)

Access to staff:
Contact by letter, by telephone, by fax, by e-mail and in person. Appointment necessary.
Hours: Closed, 1300 to 1400

Access to building, collection or gallery:
No prior appointment required

Parent body:
Royal Society for the Prevention of Accidents (ROSPA)
  tel: 028 9050 1160; fax: 028 9050 1164

HOME DECORATION RETAILERS ASSOCIATION

Acronym or abbreviation: HDRA

BHF Group, 225 Bristol Road, Edgbaston, Birmingham B5 7UB

Tel: 0121 446 6688
Fax: 0121 446 5215
E-mail: membership@bhfgroup.co.uk

Enquiries:
Enquiries to: Company Secretary

Founded:
1955

Formerly called:
Wallpaper, Paint and Wallcovering Retailers
Association (WPWRA); Wallcovering, Fabric and
Décor Retailers Association Limited (WFDRA)
(year of change 1995)

Organisation type and purpose:
Advisory body, trade association (membership is
by subscription), present number of members: 750,
publishing house.
To promote the wellbeing of the independent home
decorating specialist retailer.

Subject coverage:
Home décor trade market, decorating materials,
DIY materials, paint, wall coverings, co-ordination
of decorative materials, design, fabrics, home
furnishings.

Trade and statistical information:
Data on home décor trade products.

Printed publications:
Gold Décor Directory (annually)
Home Décor and Furnishings (magazine, 6 times a
year)

Access to staff:
Contact by letter, by telephone, by fax and by e-
mail
Hours: Mon to Fri, 0900 to 1700

Affiliated to:
Trade and Professional Alliance (TPA)

Division of:
The British Hardware Federation (BHF)

HOME OFFICE: INFORMATION AND LIBRARY SERVICES, SHARED SERVICES DIRECTORATE

Library, Lower Ground Floor, Seacole Building, 2
Marsham Street, London, SW1P 4DF

Tel: 020 7035 4041/4042
Fax: 020 7035 4022
E-mail: library@homeoffice.gsi.gov.uk

Website:
http://www.homeoffice.gov.uk

Enquiries:
Enquiries to: Librarians
Direct tel: 020 7035 4045/4014
Direct e-mail: william.mead@homeoffice.gsi.gov.uk;
martin.gilbert@homeoffice.gsi

Founded:
1782

Organisation type and purpose:
National government body.
Central government departmental library.

Subject coverage:
Social sciences, especially Parliamentary
publications; community relations; criminal law;
criminology; immigration and nationality; police;
security; drugs; citizenship.

Trade and statistical information:
The Home Office publishes a range of statistical
data such as probation statistics and statistical
bulletins. Many other statistics are published on
behalf of the Home Office by The Stationery
Office (e.g. criminal statistics).

Printed publications:
Criminal Statistics England and Wales, HM
Inspectorate of Constabulary reports, UKBA
reports, HM Inspectorate of Probation Reports
Order printed publications from: Direct
Communications Unit, 2 Marsham Street, London,
SW1P 4DF, tel: 020 7035 4848, fax: 020 7035 4745, e-
mail: public.enquiries@homeoffice.gsi.gov.uk

Access to staff:
Appointment necessary.
Hours: Mon to Thu, 0900 to 1730; Fri 0900 to 1700
Special comments: Access only for Home Office staff
and staff of other Government Agencies, by prior
appointment; no access to members of the public.

HOMEOPATHY COLLEGE, THE

Acronym or abbreviation: THC

454 Hagley Road West, Quinton, Birmingham, B68
0DL

Tel: 0121 423 1913
E-mail: admin@homoeopathytraining.co.uk

Website:
http://www.homoeopathytraining.co.uk

Enquiries:
Enquiries to: Principal
Direct e-mail: enquirer@homoeopathytraining.co.uk

Founded:
1988

Formerly called:
College of Practical Homeopathy, Midlands (year
of change 2006)

Organisation type and purpose:
Training organisation.
Training professional homeopathic practitioners.

Subject coverage:
Homeopathy.

Access to staff:
Contact by letter, by telephone, by e-mail, in
person and via website
Hours: Mon, Tue, Wed, Thu, 0930 to 1630

Access to building, collection or gallery:
Prior appointment required
Hours: Mon, Tue, Wed, Thu, 0930 to 1630

HOMERTON COLLEGE LIBRARY

Homerton College, Hills Road, Cambridge, CB2
8PH

Tel: 01223 507259
E-mail: gm10009@cam.ac.uk

Enquiries:
Enquiries to: Librarian

Organisation type and purpose:
College library

Subject coverage:
All subjects taken for the Cambridge Tripos

Museum or gallery collection, archive, or library special collection:
Children's Literature Collection

Non-library collection catalogue:
All or part available in-house

Library catalogue:
All or part available in-house

Access to staff:
Contact by letter, by telephone, by e-mail and in
person. Appointment necessary. Non-members
charged.

Access to building, collection or gallery:
Hours: Term time: Mon to Fri, 0900 to 1700
Vacations: 1000 to 1700 (please telephone first)
Special comments: Closed to general public

Constituent part of:
University of Cambridge

HOMERTON HOSPITAL NEWCOMB LIBRARY

Formal name: Homerton University Hospital NHS
Foundation Trust Newcomb Library

Homerton Row, London, E9 6SR

Tel: 020 8510 7751
Fax: 020 8510 7281
E-mail: newcomb.library@homerton.nhs.uk

Website:
http://www.homerton.nhs.uk/education/
11573611372688.html
Information re library services, opening hours,
library staff.
Links to electronic journals, databases, etc.

Enquiries:
Enquiries to: Library Manager
Direct e-mail: isabel.cantwell@homerton.nhs.uk

Formerly called:
Hackney Hospital Medical Library (year of change
1986)

Organisation type and purpose:
Multidisciplinary hospital library.

Subject coverage:
Medicine and allied subjects.

Library catalogue:
All or part available online

Printed publications:
Bibliographies of selected subjects
Journals List (annual)
Library Guide (annual)
New Books List (6 times a year)

Access to staff:
Contact by letter, by telephone, by fax, by e-mail
and via website. Appointment necessary. Letter of
introduction required.
Hours: Mon, 1100 to 2000; Tue to Fri, 0900 to 2000
Special comments: Staff availability permitting.

Links with:
London Strategic Health Authority
Nursing Union List of Journals

Member organisation of:
London Health Libraries
London Regional Library Scheme
Psychiatric Libraries Co-operative Scheme

HOMES FOR SCOTLAND

Acronym or abbreviation: SHBA

Forsyth House, 93 George Street, Edinburgh, EH2
3EJ

Tel: 0131 243 2595
Fax: 0131 243 2596
E-mail: info@homesforscotland.co.uk

Website:
http://www.homesforscotland.co.uk

Enquiries:
Enquiries to: Manager
Other contacts: Manager, Marketing and
Development

Founded:
Early 1980s

Formerly called:
Scottish Building Employers Federation (SBEF)
(year of change 1985); Scottish House-Builders
Association (SHBA) (year of change 2001)

Organisation type and purpose:
Trade association.

Subject coverage:
House building.

Trade and statistical information:
Research and produce surveys etc on house
building industry and economic factors affecting
it in Scotland.

Access to staff:
Contact by letter, by telephone, by fax and by e-
mail
Hours: Mon to Fri, 0900 to 1700

HONDA OWNERS CLUB (GB)

35 Mortimer Way, North Baddesley, Hampshire,
SO52 9NE

Website:
http://www.hoc.org.uk

Enquiries:
Enquiries to: Secretary Classic

Founded:
1961

continued overleaf

Organisation type and purpose:
Membership association (membership is by subscription), present number of members: 6000, voluntary organisation.

Subject coverage:
Honda motor cycles, insurance, discounts, help and advice.

Printed publications:
Golden Wing (magazine)
Magazine (once every two months, issued with membership)

Access to staff:
Contact by letter
Hours: Mon to Fri, 0900 to 1700

Subsidiary body:
Honda Owners Club (GB)
    Classic Section

HONG KONG TOURISM BOARD

Acronym or abbreviation: HKTB

6 Grafton Street, London, W1S 4EQ

Tel: 020 7533 7100
Fax: 020 7533 7111
E-mail: lonwwo@hktb.com

Website:
http://www.discoverhongkong.com
Tourist information on Hong Kong.

Enquiries:
Enquiries to: Regional Director

Founded:
1957

Organisation type and purpose:
National government body, statutory body, trade association (membership is by qualification), present number of members: 350.
Tourism board.
National tourist office.

Subject coverage:
Tourist information on Hong Kong.

Printed publications:
Travellers Guide to Hong Kong (free of charge)

Access to staff:
Contact by letter, by telephone, by fax, by e-mail and in person
Hours: Mon to Fri, 0930 to 1730

Location:
Hong Kong Tourism Board
    Citicorp Centre, 18 Whitfield Road, North Point, Hong Kong; tel: 00 852 2807 6543; fax: 00 852 2806 0303

HONOURABLE COMPANY OF MASTER MARINERS

HQS Wellington, Temple Stairs, Victoria Embankment, London, WC2R 2PN

Tel: 020 7836 8179
Fax: 020 7240 3082
E-mail: patricia@hcmm.org.uk

Website:
http://www.hcmm.org.uk

Enquiries:
Enquiries to: Clerk to the Company
Direct e-mail: clerk@hcmm.org.uk

Founded:
1926

Organisation type and purpose:
Professional body (membership is by qualification, election or invitation).
City of London Livery Company.

Access to staff:
Contact by letter, by telephone and by e-mail
Hours: Mon to Fri, 0900 to 1700

Access to building, collection or gallery:
No prior appointment required

HONOURABLE SOCIETY OF GRAY'S INN

8 South Square, Gray's Inn, London, WC1R 5ET

Tel: 020 7458 7800
Fax: 020 7458 7801

Enquiries:
Enquiries to: Administration Secretary

Organisation type and purpose:
Professional body.

Subject coverage:
Legal education, records, professional conduct etc (in conjunction with the Council of Legal Education and the General Council of the Bar).

Printed publications:
Graya

Access to staff:
Contact by telephone
Hours: Mon to Fri, 1000 to 1600

HONOURABLE SOCIETY OF LINCOLN'S INN

Library, Holborn, London, WC2A 3TN

Tel: 020 7242 4371
Fax: 020 7404 1864
E-mail: library@lincolnsinn.org.uk

Website:
http://www.lincolnsinn.org.uk
The Inn's homepage, includes information on the library.
http://www.lincolnsinnlibrary.org.uk
Library catalogue (for the bulk of the printed collections, but excluding some pamphlets and tracts, early continental law, superseded Commonwealth legislation).

Enquiries:
Enquiries to: Librarian

Founded:
pre 1470

Organisation type and purpose:
Professional body.
Library of an Inn of Court.

Subject coverage:
Law, including the laws of the Commonwealth countries, legal history. Genealogical information and biographical information on past members and other barristers.

Museum or gallery collection, archive, or library special collection:
Continental legal dissertations (6000 items, 17th and 18th centuries)
Manuscripts (medieval and later, including the Hale Collection)
Parliamentary Papers 1800 to date
Roman, Canon and Foreign law (15th to 19th century)
Tracts and pamphlets (15,000 items, 16th to 19th century)

Library catalogue:
All or part available online

Access to staff:
Contact by letter, by telephone, by fax and by e-mail. Appointment necessary. Letter of introduction required.
Hours: Mon to Fri, 0900 to 2000; Aug to mid-Sep, 0930 to 1800
Special comments: Current legal collection not available to the public or litigants in person. Genealogical enquiries by email or letter only.

Access for disabled people:
Level entry
Special comments: Parking by prior arrangement.

HONOURABLE SOCIETY OF THE INNER TEMPLE

The Library, Inner Temple, London, EC4Y 7DA

Tel: 020 7797 8217/8/9
Fax: 020 7583 6030
E-mail: library@innertemple.org.uk

Website:
http://www.innertemplelibrary.org.uk
Library services; history of the Inner Temple and library; Inns of Court libraries union lists; AccessToLaw (links).

Enquiries:
Enquiries to: Deputy Librarian

Founded:
1500

Organisation type and purpose:
Professional body.

Subject coverage:
Law of the United Kingdom and Commonwealth countries.

Museum or gallery collection, archive, or library special collection:
Barrington manuscripts (57 vols)
Inner Temple Records (39 vols)
Miscellaneous manuscripts (211 vols)
Mitford manuscripts (79 vols)
Petyt manuscripts (386 vols)

Non-library collection catalogue:
All or part available in print

Library catalogue:
All or part available online

Printed publications:
Catalogue of manuscripts
Guide to catalogues and indexes
Guides to Internet services & CD-ROM databases
Readers' Guide
Student Guide
Transcripts of judicial proceedings: guide to sources

Access to staff:
Contact by letter, by telephone, by fax, by e-mail and via website. Appointment necessary.
Hours: Term time: Mon to Thu, 0900 to 2000; Fri, 0900 to 1900
Vacations: Mon to Fri, 0900 to 1730
Special comments: Non-members by letter only.

Member of:
Aslib
BIALL
CILIP
NAG
UKSG

HONOURABLE SOCIETY OF THE MIDDLE TEMPLE

Library, Middle Temple Lane, London, EC4Y 9BT

Tel: 020 7427 4830
Fax: 020 7427 4831
E-mail: library@middletemple.org.uk

Website:
http://www.middletemplelibrary.org.uk

Enquiries:
Enquiries to: Keeper of the Library

Founded:
1641

Organisation type and purpose:
Learned society.
Library of an Inn of Court.

Subject coverage:
Law and legal material covering the United Kingdom, Ireland, European Communities and their member states, and the USA.

Museum or gallery collection, archive, or library special collection:
16th- and 17th-century Tracts
Archives of the Inn and its members
Phillimore Collection (legal)
Incunabula
John Donne's Library
Robert Ashley's Collection

Ecclesiastical law collection
USA law collection
Capital punishment collection

Non-library collection catalogue:
All or part available in print

Library catalogue:
All or part available online

Printed publications:
Library catalogue 1914 and 1925 supplement (out of print)
Register of Admissions to the Honourable Society of the Middle Temple, 1500–1975 (5 vols, published in 1949 and 1977)
Register of Admissions to the Honourable Society of the Middle Temple, 1976–1989 (vol. 6, out of print)
Middle Templars' Associations with America (Sir Lynden Macassey)
Middle Temple Hall, An Architectural Appreciation (Michael G. Murray)
Middle Temple Hall, Four Centuries of History (Joseph Dean, out of print)
The Middle Temple Bench Book (vol. 3, 1982–1998)
Order printed publications from: Library

Publications list:
Available in print

Access to staff:
Contact by letter, by telephone, by fax and by e-mail. Appointment necessary. Non-members charged.

Access to building, collection or gallery:
Hours: Term time: Mon to Thu, 0900 to 2000; Fri, 0900 to 1900; one Sat in every four, 1000 to 1700
Vacations: Mon to Fri, 0900 to 1730
Special comments: Open to all members of the Bar and Middle Temple students. Bone fide researchers admitted by prior appointment, at the discretion of the Librarian.

HOPE UK

25F Copperfield Street, London, SE1 0EN

Tel: 020 7928 0848
Fax: 020 7401 3477
E-mail: a.wilson@hopeuk.org

Enquiries:
Enquiries to: Executive Director

Founded:
1855

Organisation type and purpose:
National organisation, membership association (membership is by subscription), present number of members: 401, voluntary organisation, registered charity (charity number 1044475), suitable for ages: 5 to 21, training organisation. To educate children and young people, and those who work with them, about the effects of alcohol and drugs.

Subject coverage:
Hope UK is a drug education charity working from a Christian basis. Our mission is to provide accurate information which enables children and young people to consider their attitudes to alcohol and drugs. We support parents, teachers and youth leaders with quality resources, speakers and training events. Children and young people are at the centre of our work and we encourage positive peer influence and the ability to choose healthy options in the prevention of the abuse of alcohol, tobacco and other drugs.

Museum or gallery collection, archive, or library special collection:
The Liversey Collection, University of Central Lancashire, Lambeth Palace Library, London SE1 7JU

Printed publications:
Getting it Sorted (for leaders who work with 8–12's)
Focus on Drugs – a Christian perspective (1996)
How to do Drugs (practical ideas for drug prevention)

Leaflets for 8 to 12 year olds, young people and adults
Resources Guide (lists publications for sale, free)

Publications list:
Available online and in print

Access to staff:
Contact by letter, by telephone, by fax, by e-mail and via website
Hours: Mon to Fri, 0900 to 1700
Special comments: 24 hour answerphone.

Affiliated to:
All Party Parliamentary Group on Parenting
Charity Forum
Drug Education Forum
English Churches Youth Service
European Blue Cross Youth
Evangelical Alliance
Evangelical Coalition on Drugs
International Blue Cross Federation
National Centre for Volunteering
National Children's Bureau
National Council for Voluntary Organisations
National Council for Voluntary Youth Services
Parenting Forum

Connections with:
Amethyst Centre for Alcohol Concern, Reading

Other branches at:
Hope UK, Northern Ireland
Ebrington Manse, 19 Clearwater Caw, Londonderry, BT47 1BE; tel: 028 7131 1425; fax: 028 7131 1425

HORDER CENTRE

St Johns Road, Crowborough, East Sussex, TN6 1XP

Tel: 01892 665577
Fax: 01892 662142
E-mail: info@hordercentre.co.uk

Enquiries:
Enquiries to: Customer Services Manager
Direct tel: 01892 600006

Founded:
1954

Organisation type and purpose:
Service industry, registered charity (charity number 1046624).
Charitable and specialist hospital.
To offer help, advice and hospital services for people with arthritis and musculo-skeletal conditions.

Subject coverage:
Medical unit offering total comprehensive care and attention to patients with arthritis and musculo-skeletal conndition, requiring medical treatment, surgical intervention or rehabilitation, major joint reconstruction surgery.

Printed publications:
Annual Report
Information brochures

Access to staff:
Contact by letter, by telephone and by e-mail.
Appointment necessary.
Hours: Mon to Fri, 0900 to 1700

Access for disabled people:
Parking provided, ramped entry, toilet facilities

HORSES AND PONIES PROTECTION ASSOCIATION

Acronym or abbreviation: HAPPA

Taylor Building, Shores Hey Farm, Black House Lane, Briercliffe, Nr Burnley, BB10 3QU

Tel: 01282 455992
Fax: 01282 451992
E-mail: enquiries@happa.org.uk

Website:
http://www.happa.org.uk

Enquiries:
Enquiries to: General Secretary
Other contacts: Association Secretary

Founded:
1937

Organisation type and purpose:
National organisation, membership association (membership is by subscription), present number of members: 11,000, registered charity (charity number 1085211), museum.
Equine welfare.

Subject coverage:
Horse care and welfare; prosecuting horse cruelty cases; investigation of complaints re neglect and ill treatment of equines.

Printed publications:
Annual report (May)
Autumn newsletter and gift catalogue (Sep)
Leaflets on horsecare
Photographs of cruelty cases involving horses
Spring newsletter (Feb)

Access to staff:
Contact by letter, by telephone, by fax, by e-mail, in person and via website
Hours: Mon to Fri, 0900 to 1700

HORSHAM DISTRICT COUNCIL

Park House, North Street, Horsham, West Sussex, RH12 1RL

Tel: 01403 215100
Fax: 01403 262985
E-mail: contact@horsham.gov.uk

Website:
http://www.horsham.gov.uk
District Council services and information about the Horsham district.

Enquiries:
Enquiries to: Communications Manager
Direct tel: 01403 215549
Direct e-mail: richard.morris@horsham.gov.uk

Founded:
1974

Organisation type and purpose:
Local government body.

Subject coverage:
District Council services.

Printed publications:
Business directory
Council magazine (twice yearly)
Other Council publications

Electronic and video publications:
Business and Economic development (video)

Access to staff:
Contact by letter, by telephone, by fax and by e-mail
Hours: Mon to Thu, 0840 to 1720; Fri, 0840 to 1620

Access to building, collection or gallery:
No access other than to staff, no prior appointment required, prior appointment required

Access for disabled people:
Parking provided, ramped entry, level entry, access to all public areas, toilet facilities

HORTICULTURAL DEVELOPMENT COMPANY

Acronym or abbreviation: HDC

Bradbourne House, East Malling, West Malling, Kent, ME19 6DZ

Tel: 01732 848383
Fax: 01732 848498
E-mail: hdc@hdc.org.uk

Website:
http://www.hdc.org.uk

continued overleaf

Information on the HDC, Council and staff members, press releases, calendar of events, research and crop protection information (members only).

Enquiries:
Enquiries to: Communication Manager

Founded:
1986

Organisation type and purpose:
Non-Departmental Public Body.
Statutory levy body.

Subject coverage:
Horticulture.

Printed publications:
Newsletter (10 times a year)

Publications list:
Available online and in print

Access to staff:
Contact by letter, by telephone and by e-mail.
Appointment necessary.
Hours: Mon to Fri, 0900 to 1700

Sponsoring department:
Department for Environment, Food and Rural Affairs
Nobel House, 17 Smith Square, London, SW1P 3JR; tel: 020 7238 6000

HORTICULTURE RESEARCH INTERNATIONAL

Acronym or abbreviation: HRI

Wellesbourne, Warwickshire, CV35 9EF

Tel: 01789 470382
Fax: 01789 470552

Website:
http://www.hri.ac.uk

Enquiries:
Enquiries to: Business Development
Direct tel: 01789 470440
Direct fax: 01789 472069

Founded:
1990

Organisation type and purpose:
University department or institute, research organisation.
The administrative headquarters, centre for strategic science and annual crops research, research and development organisation.

Subject coverage:
Horticulture, botany, soil science, plant physiology, plant biochemistry, pesticides, weed control, entomology, plant pathology, biometrics, vegetable crops. Edible fungi, field vegetables, fruit, industrial crops, ornamentals, protected crops, tropical crops, crop production/agronomy, pest and disease control, environment, plant breeding, post-harvest technology, propagation and seed technology.

Museum or gallery collection, archive, or library special collection:
Historical books on horticulture
Vegetable gene bank

Printed publications:
Annual Report (which also lists all publications by the staff) (£15)

Access to staff:
Contact by letter, by telephone and by fax
Hours: Mon to Fri, 0900 to 1700

Affiliated to:
DEFRA

Has:
some 500 staff sited at five locations, two of which have extensive libraries

Other addresses:
Development research on field vegetables and bulbs
Willington Road, Kirton, Boston, Lincolnshire, PE20 1EJ; tel: 01205 723477; fax: 01205 722922
Development research on glasshouse crops, nursery stock, micropropagation and soft fruit
Lymington, Hampshire, SO41 0LZ; tel: 01590 673341; fax: 01590 671553
Hops research
Department of Hop Research, Wye College, Wye, Ashford, Kent, TN25 5AH; tel: 01233 812179; fax: 01233 813126
Horticultural Research International Efford
Horticultural Research International Kirton
Horticultural Research International Wye

HOSPICE INFORMATION

Formal name: Hospice Information

Help the Hospices, Hospice House, 34–44 Britannia Street, London, WC1X 9JG

Tel: 0870 903 3903 (calls charged at national rates)
Fax: 020 7278 1021
E-mail: info@hospiceinformation.info

Website:
http://www.hospiceinformation.info
Statistical information, email news bulletin, listings of educational and job opportunities, advice.

Enquiries:
Enquiries to: Information Officer

Founded:
1977

Organisation type and purpose:
International organisation, membership association (membership is by subscription), present number of members: 1000, voluntary organisation, registered charity (charity number1014851).
Hospice Information is a joint venture between St Christopher's Hospice and Help the Hospices. It is a worldwide resource for professionals and the public that encourages sharing of information and experience amongst those involved in palliative care.

Subject coverage:
Hospice and palliative care services in the UK and overseas. Care of people with advanced cancer, motor neurone disease, AIDS, research and education, nursing, medical, social work and other health professional material related to terminal and palliative care. Also pastoral care, bereavement issues and ethical aspects.

Printed publications:
Booklist (a very large number of titles)
eChoices (listing of courses and conferences, quarterly and on website)
Directory of Hospice and Palliative Care Services in the UK and Ireland (annually)
Fact sheets on Hospice Services
Hospice Information Bulletin (newsletter, quarterly)
Hospice Worldwide (directory of overseas hospices and palliative care)
Job Opportunities (listing of job vacancies, on website)
Several email newsletters on UK and international hopice and palliative care

Electronic and video publications:
Palliative Care Worldwide Links: database of palliative care practitioners and services having professional links with overseas hospices
News Bulletin (online)

Publications list:
Available online and in print

Access to staff:
Contact by letter, by telephone, by fax, by e-mail, in person and via website. Appointment necessary.
Hours: Mon to Fri, 0900 to 1700

Other address:
St Christopher's Hospice
51–59 Lawrie Park Road, London, SE26 6DZ; fax: 020 8776 9345; e-mail: info@stchristophers.org.uk

Parent body:
Help the Hospices

HOSPITAL CHAPLAINCIES COUNCIL

Acronym or abbreviation: HCC

Church House, Great Smith Street, London, SW1P 3NZ

Tel: 020 7898 1892
Fax: 020 7898 1891

Website:
http://www.nhs-chaplaincy-spiritualcare.org.uk/

Enquiries:
Enquiries to: Administrator

Organisation type and purpose:
Advisory body, training organisation.

Subject coverage:
Responsible to the General Synod of the Church of England for Anglican Hospital Chaplaincy, HCC relates to the Department of Health and NHS administration, assisting trusts in the selection, appointment and training of Healthcare Chaplains and co-operating with other Christian denominations and other faiths and traditions in promoting the highest standards of spiritual care for patients, relatives and staff.

Printed publications:
Guidelines and information leaflets for healthcare chaplains available on request
Directory of Whole-Time Hospital Chaplains & Chaplains' Assistants in the United Kingdom (£5 inc. p&p)

Publications list:
Available in print

Access to staff:
Contact by letter, by telephone, by e-mail and via website
Hours: Mon to Fri, 0930 to 1730

Close liaison with:
Department of Health

Co-operates with:
Health Care Chaplaincy Boards of the Roman Catholic Church
Hospital Chaplaincy Boards of the Free Church Federal Council

Member of:
Churches Committee for Hospital Chaplaincy

HOSPITAL CONSULTANTS AND SPECIALISTS ASSOCIATION

Acronym or abbreviation: HCSA

1 Kingsclere Road, Overton, Basingstoke, Hampshire, RG25 3JA

Tel: 01256 771777
Fax: 01256 770999
E-mail: conspec@hcsa.com

Website:
http://www.hcsa.com

Enquiries:
Enquiries to: Advisory Service Manager
Other contacts: Administrative Director.

Founded:
1945

Organisation type and purpose:
Trade union, present number of members: 3100.

Access to staff:
Contact by letter, by telephone, by fax and by e-mail. Appointment necessary.
Hours: Mon to Thu, 0900 to 1700; Fri, 0900 to 1630

Access to building, collection or gallery:
Prior appointment required

Access for disabled people:
Parking provided, ramped entry

HOSTELLING INTERNATIONAL NORTHERN IRELAND

Acronym or abbreviation: YHANI

22–32 Donegal Road, Belfast, BT12 5JN

Tel: 028 9032 4733
Fax: 028 9031 5889
E-mail: info@hini.org.uk

Website:
http://www.hini.org.uk

Enquiries:
Enquiries to: General Secretary

Founded:
1931

Organisation type and purpose:
International organisation, membership association (membership is by subscription), registered charity.
To provide budget priced accommodation for travellers.

Subject coverage:
Hostelling in Northern Ireland; knowledge, love and use of the countryside; preservation of the countryside; maintenance of rights-of-way.

Printed publications:
Accommodation Leaflet

Access to staff:
Contact by letter, by telephone and by fax
Hours: Mon to Fri, 0900 to 1700

HOTEL AND CATERING INTERNATIONAL MANAGEMENT ASSOCIATION

Acronym or abbreviation: HCIMA

191 Trinity Road, London, SW17 7HN

Tel: 020 8772 7400
Fax: 020 8772 7500
E-mail: library@hcima.org.uk

Website:
http://www.hcima.org.uk/
Homepage.

Enquiries:
Enquiries to: Director of ITS Services

Founded:
1971

Organisation type and purpose:
Professional body.
Management in all sectors of industry; examining body.

Subject coverage:
Hotels; restaurants; caterers; hospitals; school meals; staff; welfare; civic and industrial catering etc; hotel and catering industry abroad; research; tourism.

Printed publications:
HCIMA Hospitality Yearbook
Hospitality (formerly HCIMA Journal; 10 times a year)

Electronic and video publications:
WHATT (Worldwide Hospitality and Tourist Trends) (online at www.whatt.net)

Publications list:
Available in print

Access to staff:
Contact by letter, by telephone, by fax and by e-mail
Hours: Mon to Fri, 0900 to 1700
Special comments: Non-members can use the service, by appointment only, for a charge.

HOUNSLOW LIBRARY NETWORK

Acronym or abbreviation: HLN

Centre Space, 24 Treaty Centre, High Street, Hounslow, Middlesex, TW3 1ES

Tel: 020 8583 4545
Fax: 020 8583 4595

Website:
http://www.cip.org.uk

Enquiries:
Enquiries to: Strategic Library Manager (IT and Electronic Resources)
Direct tel: 020 8583 4623
Direct fax: 020 8583 4719
Other contacts: Borough Librarian

Organisation type and purpose:
Local government body, public library.

Subject coverage:
International or foreign affairs (to 1985): relations, policy, diplomacy etc; parliaments; legislative assemblies; political parties and the party systems; party organisation and tactics. Local history. Geology (from 1985).

Museum or gallery collection, archive, or library special collection:
Chiswick Press Collection (19th century)
GLASS Collection (Debussy, Wagner, Jazz)
GLASS: Greater London Audio Specialisation Scheme Collection (spoken word; American literature)
Laser Collection (international or foreign affairs 1976–1984 and geology from 1985)
Layton Collection (English historical and topographical antiquarian material, 16th to 19th centuries)

Library catalogue:
All or part available in-house

Printed publications:
Local history publications

Access to staff:
Contact by telephone, by fax and in person
Hours: Mon to Sat, 0930 to 1730

Access for disabled people:
Parking provided

Has links with:
Community Initiative Partnerships (CIP) Centrespace, Treaty Centre, High Street, Hounslow, Middlesex, TW3 1FS
Other Libraries in London Borough of Hounslow, including Chiswick Library and Feltham Library

HOUSE OF BEAULY LIMITED

Station Road, Beauly, Invernessshire, IV4 7EH

Tel: 01463 782578
Fax: 01463 782409
E-mail: info@houseofbeauly.com

Website:
http://www.houseofbeauly.com

Enquiries:
Enquiries to: Operations Manager

Founded:
1991

Organisation type and purpose:
Visitor centre, retail.

Subject coverage:
Scottish crafts, giftware and traditional textiles, marketing and retailing of crafts.

Access to staff:
Contact by letter, by telephone, by fax, by e-mail, in person and via website. Appointment necessary.
Hours: Mon to Fri, 0900 to 1700

HOUSE OF COMMONS INFORMATION OFFICE

Acronym or abbreviation: HCIO

House of Commons, Westminster, London, SW1A 2TT

Tel: 020 7219 4272
Fax: 020 7219 5839
E-mail: hcinfo@parliament.uk

Website:
http://www.parliament.uk
Enquiries on the proceedings, membership and history of the House of Commons.

Founded:
1978

Subject coverage:
All matters concerning the work, history and membership of the House of Commons and Parliamentary publications.

Printed publications:
APRILL (Access to Parliamentary Resources and Information in London Libraries)
Education Sheets and Wallcharts
House of Commons Library Documents and some 68 Factsheets on a variety of subjects including historical matters, procedures and members
Services of the HCIO (leaflet)

Publications list:
Available in print

Access to staff:
Contact by letter, by telephone, by fax and by e-mail
Hours: Mon to Thu, 0900 to 1800; Fri, 0900 to 1630

HOUSE OF LORDS INFORMATION OFFICE

House of Lords, Westminster, London, SW1A 0PW

Tel: 020 7219 3107
Fax: 020 7219 0620
E-mail: hlinfo@parliament.uk

Website:
http://www.parliament.uk
Full text of bills, Hansard and House of Lords judgments. Information on the work of the House and its membership. All Select Committee Reports.

Enquiries:
Enquiries to: Senior Information Officer

Organisation type and purpose:
National government body.
One of the Offices of the Parliament Office, House of Lords.

Subject coverage:
Composition, procedure and current activities of the House of Lords.

Museum or gallery collection, archive, or library special collection:
Collection of photographs of Members (under development)
Photographs and slides of various features of the House (the Chamber, select committees, etc)

Printed publications:
Several publications on the membership, work, attendance and history of the House (details on request) including:
The House of Lords: a brief guide and briefing papers

Electronic and video publications:
See also website

Publications list:
Available in print

Access to staff:
Contact by letter, by telephone, by fax and by e-mail
Hours: When the House of Lords is sitting: 1000 to 1800
Recess: 1000 to 1600
Special comments: Callers cannot be seen in person.

HOUSE OF LORDS LIBRARY

House of Lords, London, SW1A 0PW

continued overleaf

Tel: 020 7219 5242 or 5433
Fax: 020 7219 6396
E-mail: hllibrary@parliament.uk

Enquiries:
Enquiries to: Librarian

Founded:
1826

Organisation type and purpose:
Private library for members of the House of Lords.

Subject coverage:
All matters concerning the House of Lords, parliament, parliamentary publications, British government, administration and politics, as well as the law of England and Wales, and of Scotland.

Museum or gallery collection, archive, or library special collection:
Collections of pamphlets made by Lords Truro and Farnham in the 19th century
Lord Truro's collection of English lawbooks
Peel Tracts (c. 2000 pamphlets chiefly concerning 18th century Ireland)

Library catalogue:
All or part available in-house

Access to staff:
Contact by letter, by telephone, by fax and by e-mail
Hours: Mon to Fri, 0930 to 1730
Special comments: No facilities for personal enquiries.

HOUSEBUILDER PUBLICATIONS

Acronym or abbreviation: HBP

Housebuilder Media Ltd, Byron House, 7–9 St.James's Street, London, SW1A 1EE

Tel: 020 7960 1630 7960 1631
Fax: 020 7960 1631

Website:
http://www.house-builder.co.uk
Back issues, news online, jobs online, subscription information, etc.
http://www.hbmedia.co.uk/

Enquiries:
Enquiries to: Publishing Manager
Direct tel: 020 7608 5128
Direct e-mail: ben.roskrow@hbmedia.co.uk
Other contacts: Editor

Founded:
1955

Organisation type and purpose:
National organisation, trade association (membership is by subscription), publishing house.

Subject coverage:
New housing development, new homes marketing, housing economics, building products information.

Trade and statistical information:
UK data on new homes.

Non-library collection catalogue:
All or part available in-house

Library catalogue:
All or part available in-house

Printed publications:
On subscription if not member of HBF or NHBC

Publications list:
Available online

Access to staff:
Contact by letter, by telephone, by fax, by e-mail and via website
Hours: Mon to Fri, 0900 to 1700

Access to building, collection or gallery:
No access other than to staff

Access for disabled people:
Parking provided

Connections with:
House Builders Federation (HBF)
tel: 020 7608 5199

HOUSING CORPORATION

Maple House, 149 Tottenham Court Road, London, W1T 7BN

Tel: 0845 230 7000
Fax: 0113 233 7101
E-mail: enquiries@housingcorp.gsx.gov.uk

Website:
http://www.housingcorp.gov.uk
About the Housing Corporation, regional offices, board members, publications, circulars.

Enquiries:
Enquiries to: Head of Communications
Direct tel: 020 7393 2093
Direct fax: 020 7393 2099

Founded:
1964

Organisation type and purpose:
National government body.

Subject coverage:
The support of the social housing sector, the registration, funding, monitoring and supervising of registered social landlords, development and coordination of national policies and negotiation with central government for funds and also the development of regional strategies.

Printed publications:
Available online at website
www.housingcorp.gov.uk

Publications list:
Available online

Access to staff:
Contact by letter, by telephone, by fax, by e-mail and via website
Hours: Mon to Fri, 0900 to 1700

Regional office London:
London
Waverley House, 7–12 Noel Street, W1F 8BA

Regional office Southeast:
Croydon
Leon House, High Street, Croydon, Surrey, CR9 1UH

Regional office Southwest:
Exeter
Beaufort House. 51 New North Road, Exeter, EX4 4EP; fax: 01392 428201

Regional offices Central:
Cambridge
Westbrook Centre, Block A Suite 1, Milton Road, Cambridge, CB4 1YG
Leicester
Attenborough House, 109/119 Charles Street, Leicester, LE1 1FQ
Wolverhampton
31 Waterloo Road, Wolverhampton, WV1 4DJ

Regional offices North:
Gateshead
St George's House, Kingsway, Team Vallley, Gateshead, NE11 0NA
Leeds
1 Park Lane, Leeds, LS3 1EP
Manchester
4th Floor, One Piccadilly Gardens, Manchester, M1 1RG

HOUSING OMBUDSMAN SERVICE

Acronym or abbreviation: HOS

81 Aldwych, London, WC2B 4HN

Tel: 020 7421 3800
Fax: 020 7831 1942
E-mail: info@housing-ombudsman.org.uk

Website:
http://www.ihos.org.uk

Enquiries:
Other contacts: Deputy Ombudsman (for handling complaints); Casework Manager (for deposit disputes)

Founded:
1997

Organisation type and purpose:
National organisation, membership association (membership is by subscription), present number of members: 2,300.
To investigate complaints made by tenants against member landlords who are either RSLs or private landlords.

Subject coverage:
Housing, complaints handling, dispute resolution.

Printed publications:
Various publications available free of charge

Publications list:
Available online and in print

Access to staff:
Contact by letter, by telephone, by fax, by e-mail and via website
Hours: Mon to Fri, 0900 to 1700

Access to building, collection or gallery:
Prior appointment required

Access for disabled people:
Toilet facilities, lift.

HOUSMAN SOCIETY

80 New Road, Bromsgrove, Worcestershire, B60 2LA

Tel: 01527 874136
E-mail: info@housman-society.co.uk

Website:
http://www.housman-society.co.uk
Basic information, index of journals, book list.

Enquiries:
Enquiries to: Chairman

Founded:
1974

Organisation type and purpose:
Learned society, present number of members: 280 (charity number 1001107).
Literary Society.
Exists to promote knowledge and appreciation of the work of A E Housman. Also promotes the causes of literature and poetry in general. Sponsors an annual Housman lecture at the Hay Festival.

Subject coverage:
A E Housman and his family, his writings, poetry and life.

Museum or gallery collection, archive, or library special collection:
Books published by the society

Printed publications:
Housman Society Journal (£4)
Housman's Places (£7.99)
The Westerly Wanderer (£8.95)
Unkind to Unicorns (2nd ed, £7.50 paperback, £25 limited edition hardback)
Westminster Abbey Testimonials (£5)
Name and Nature of Poetry (£5.00)
Three Bromsgrove Poets (£7.50)

Publications list:
Available in print

Access to staff:
Contact by letter, by telephone, by e-mail and via website
Hours: Mon to Fri, 0900 to 1700

HOVERCRAFT CLUB OF GREAT BRITAIN LIMITED

Acronym or abbreviation: HCGB

PO Box 328, Bolton, Lancashire, BL6 4RR

Tel: 01204 841248
E-mail: info@hovercraft.co.uk

Website:
http://www.hovercraft.co.uk
Events, membership, sales, information.

Enquiries:
Enquiries to: Information Officer
Direct e-mail: gordon.taylor61@hotmail.com
Other contacts: Archivist for historical information

Founded:
1966

Organisation type and purpose:
Membership association, voluntary organisation,
suitable for ages: all.

Subject coverage:
Construction and use of lightweight sporting
hovercraft, history of light hovercraft
development, details of manufacturers past and
present, personalities in hovercraft.

Information services:
See website or tel for details.

Education services:
By request.

Services for disabled people:
By request.

**Museum or gallery collection, archive, or library
special collection:**
Archives include historical information on light
  hovercraft, history, development, club, people,
  manufacturers etc

Non-library collection catalogue:
All or part available in-house

Printed publications:
Cruising Hovercraft Construction Regulations (£4)
A Guide to Model Hovercraft (£6)
Hover Humour (£1.50)
Hovercraft – The Constructors Guide (£17)
Light Hovercraft (12 issues £25 annually)
National Hovercraft Competition Regulations (£4)
New Racing Driver Handbook (£4)
Racing Hovercraft Construction Regulations (£4)

Electronic and video publications:
Hovercraft Construction Regulations (CD-ROM
  £12.95, purchase direct from Information Office)
Hovercraft Video (£9.99)

Publications list:
Available online and in print

Access to staff:
Contact by letter, by telephone, by e-mail, in
person and via website. Appointment necessary.
Hours: Mon to Sat, 0900 to 1700

Access to building, collection or gallery:
No prior appointment required
Hours: By arrangement

Archivist:
Hovercraft Club of Great Britain Limited
  29 Mytton View, Clitheroe, Lancashire, BB7 5AZ;
  tel: 01200 426689; e-mail: gordon.taylor61@
  hotmail.com

HOVERCRAFT MUSEUM TRUST

Argus Gate, Daedalus site, Chark Lane, off Broom
Way, Lee-on-Solent, Gosport, Hampshire, PO13 9N

Tel: 023 9255 2090
E-mail: enquiries@hovercraft-museum.org

Website:
http://www.hovercraft-museum.org
2000 pages and pictures

Enquiries:
Enquiries to: Trustee
Direct e-mail: wjacobs@supanet.com
Other contacts: TV and Film c/o 02392 601310

Founded:
1988

Organisation type and purpose:
Learned society (membership is by subscription),
registered charity, museum, suitable for ages: all,
consultancy.

Subject coverage:
Application of the air cushion principle; hovercraft
applications in materials handling, civil
engineering and medicine; ferries, transport,
leisure, military.

**Museum or gallery collection, archive, or library
special collection:**
Early papers and books on the hovercraft principle,
  papers and proceedings, videos, photographs,
  films and slides
SRNI log book
3 Cross-Channel Hovercraft
Many early historic craft – last of types
Last SRNS and many pioneer vehicles
A collection of 40 hovercraft, and 5000 plus books,
  pictures, etc.

Non-library collection catalogue:
All or part available in-house and in print

Library catalogue:
All or part available in-house and in print

Printed publications:
Hovercraft Museum Newsletter

Electronic and video publications:
Set of 5 videos (£15 each)

Publications list:
Available online and in print

Access to staff:
Contact by letter, by telephone, by e-mail, in
person and via website
Hours: Sun to Sat, 24 hours
Special comments: To library, by appointment.

Access to building, collection or gallery:
Prior appointment required
Hours: By appointment only

Access for disabled people:
Parking provided, level entry, toilet facilities

HOVERCRAFT SEARCH AND RESCUE UK

Acronym or abbreviation: HSR-UK

2 Park Court, Pyrford Road, West Byfleet, Surrey,
KT14 6SD

Tel: 01932 340492
E-mail: info@hsr-uk.org

Website:
http://www.hsr-uk.org

Founded:
1997

Organisation type and purpose:
Registered charity (charity number 1061801).
Specialist search and rescue services.

Access to staff:
Contact by letter, by telephone and by e-mail
Hours: Mon to Fri, 0900 to 1700

HOWARD LEAGUE FOR PENAL REFORM

1 Ardleigh Road, London, N1 4HS

Tel: 020 7249 7373
Fax: 020 7249 7788
E-mail: howardleague@ukonline.co.uk

Website:
http://web.ukonline.co.uk/howard.league

Enquiries:
Enquiries to: Director

Organisation type and purpose:
Voluntary organisation, registered charity (charity
number 251926).

To promote penal reform by evidence to
government committees, working parties, public
education and campaigning.

Subject coverage:
Criminal justice, prison reform, penal history and
alternatives to prison.

Printed publications:
Annual Report
Criminal Justice Magazine (quarterly)
Good Practice Guide on Working with Young
  Offenders
The Howard Journal of Criminal Justice (quarterly)
Howard League Reports include:
Families Matter: the report of 10 community links
  workshops (1994, £8)
Suicide & Self-harm Prevention: following release

Electronic and video publications:
Video: Wake Up, Slop Out, Banged Away Again

Publications list:
Available in print

Access to staff:
Access for members only.
Hours: Mon to Fri, 0900 to 1700

HOWELL HARRIS MUSEUM

Coleg Trefeca, Brecon, Powys, LD3 0PP

Tel: 01874 711423
Fax: 01874 712212
E-mail: colegtrefeca@ebcpcw.org.uk

Website:
http://www.trefeca.org.uk/
Historical and general outline of work of the
college.
http://www.ebcpcw.org.uk
General information regarding Presbytarian
Church of Wales including Coleg Trefeca.

Enquiries:
Enquiries to: Manager

Founded:
1752

Organisation type and purpose:
Registered charity (charity number 258456),
museum, historic building, house or site, suitable
for ages: 8+.
Christian training, retreat and conference centre
and museum.

Subject coverage:
The Welsh Methodist revival by means of an
audiovisual presentation. Artefacts include the
Trefeca 'Family' period. Also features contacts with
English Methodists such as Wesley, Whitefield and
the Countess of Huntingdon.
Library on Welsh Methodist history and related
subjects, in English and Welsh, historic Grade II
listed building (1752 onwards), extensive training,
retreat and conference programme.

Information services:
Library available for reference (for conditions see
Access above)

Special visitor services:
Guided tours, materials and/or activities for
children.

Education services:
Resources for Key Stages 1 and 2, 3, 4 and Further
or Higher Education.

Services for disabled people:
For the hearing impaired; displays and/or
information at wheelchair height.

**Museum or gallery collection, archive, or library
special collection:**
Electrifying Machine. 1763
Howell Harris Preaching Chair/Pulpit. Field Pulpit.
  ca. 1741
Joseph Harris' Telescope (recorded the transit of
  Venus over sun – experiment presented to Royal
  Society) 1761
Pulpit from the Countess of Huntingdon's College,
  Trefeca

continued overleaf

Turrett clock and bell. Rose drums of Yew. 1754 added to house, restored by Barometer Shop, Leominster, 1999

Swords and guns. Brecknock Militia ('Seven Year's War', 1756)

Books published by Treveka Press 1756–1800

Non-library collection catalogue:
All or part available in-house

Library catalogue:
All or part available in-house

Printed publications:
There was a man sent A short history of Howell Harris and the Methodist revival (£1.25)
Treveka 1714–1964 (Davies G, £1.75)

Access to staff:
Contact by letter, by telephone, by fax and by e-mail. Appointment necessary.
Hours: Daily, 0900 to 1600

Access to building, collection or gallery:
Prior appointment required
Hours: Daily, 0900 to 1600
Special comments: Other times strictly by appointment only.
Dec to Feb: closed Sat, Sun.
Closed Good Friday to Easter Tuesday and Christmas.

Access for disabled people:
Parking provided, ramped entry, toilet facilities
Special comments: Access to museum area by chair lift.
Access to historic house involves one step.

Parent body:
Presbyterian Church of Wales (PCW EBC)
Tabernacle Chapel, 81 Merthyr Road, Whitchurch, Cardiff, CF14 1DD; tel: 029 2062 7465; fax: 029 2061 6188; e-mail: swyddfa.office@ebcpcw.org.uk; website: http://www.ebcpcw.org .uk

HPI LIMITED

Formal name: Hire Purchase Information Limited

Dolphin House, New Street, Salisbury, Wiltshire, SP1 2PH

Tel: 01722 422422, Consumer Service; 412888, Trade Service
Fax: 01722 412746

Website:
http://www.hpi.co.uk
Car fraud detection database.

Enquiries:
Enquiries to: Director
Direct tel: 01722 413434

Founded:
1938

Organisation type and purpose:
Service industry.
Information provider on high value mobile assets.
Business to business and consumer services.
Vehicle identity checks, written-off vehicle register, outstanding finance register and other information on used vehicles.

Subject coverage:
Information on used vehicles for motor trade, motor auctions, finance and insurance companies by subscription.
Available to consumers by credit card, Switch etc.

Printed publications:
Press material available through Harrison Sadler
Order printed publications from: Harrison Sadler
1 Bridgeman Road, Teddington, TW11 9AJ, tel: 01481 9779132

Access to staff:
Contact by telephone, by fax and by e-mail
Hours: Mon to Sat, 0800 to 2000; Sun, 1000 to 1700
Special comments: On-line information service available 24 hours.

Access for disabled people:
Access to all public areas, toilet facilities

Associate member of:
Finance and Leasing Association (FLA)
Retail Motor Industry Federation (RMIF)

HUDDERSFIELD AND DISTRICT FAMILY HISTORY SOCIETY

Acronym or abbreviation: H&D FHS

'The Root Cellar', 15 Huddersfield Road, Meltham, Holmfirth, HD9 4NJ 01484 859 229

Tel: 01484 859 229
E-mail: secretary@hdfhs.org.uk

Website:
http://www.hdfhs.org.uk

Enquiries:
Enquiries to: Research Officer
Direct e-mail: research@hdfhs.org.uk

Founded:
1987

Organisation type and purpose:
Membership association (membership is by subscription), present number of members: 1100, registered charity (charity number 702199).
Research into family history.

Subject coverage:
Family history in the metropolitan District of Kirklees including Batley, Colne Valley, Denby Dale, Dewsbury, Huddersfield, Holme Valley, Kirkburton, Meltham, Mirfield and Spen Valley.

Museum or gallery collection, archive, or library special collection:
Reference Library (borrowing facilities for UK members)
Lancashire 18611901
Yorkshire 18611901
Lincolnshire 18411901
Cheshire 18411901
Durham 18511901
1851 Census – Kirklees only
1851 for Norfolk, Devon, Warwickshire (fiche)
1881 Census England and Wales (microfiche)
1881 Census (CD-ROM)
IGI UK (microfiche)
National Probate Calendars – England and Wales 1858 to 1943 (fiche)
Soldiers Died in WWI (CD-ROM)

Printed publications:
1841 census indices for whole area covered
1851 census indices for whole area covered
Monumental Inscriptions (3 graveyards)
National Burial Indexes 1813–56 are being published in 2000
Parish Register transcriptions (16 parishes, mostly baptisms)
Order printed publications from: Librarian, Huddersfield and District Family History Society, Root Cellar, 15 Huddersfield Road, Meltham, Holmfirth, West Yorkshire, HD9 4NJ

Publications list:
Available online and in print

Access to staff:
Contact by letter, by telephone and by e-mail
Hours: Mon to Fri, 0900 to 1700

Access to building, collection or gallery:
No prior appointment required
Special comments: Tues, 1400 to 1630; Wed, 1000 to 1230 and 1400 to 1630; Thu, 1400 to 1630 and 1930 to 2200

HUDDERSFIELD CENTRAL LIBRARY

Princess Alexandra Walk, Huddersfield, West Yorkshire, HD1 2SU

Tel: 01484 221967
Fax: 01484 221974
E-mail: hudlib.reflib@kirklees.gov.uk

Website:
http://www.kirklees.gov.uk/libraries

Enquiries:
Enquiries to: Senior Reference and Information Services Librarian

Organisation type and purpose:
Local government body, public library.

Subject coverage:
Local history; modern literature in the languages of India, Pakistan and Bangladesh.

Museum or gallery collection, archive, or library special collection:
British Standards, newspaper archives, wide range of hard copy and online reference sources
Family, local authority and other archives

Non-library collection catalogue:
All or part available online and in-house

Library catalogue:
All or part available in-house

Access to staff:
Contact by letter, by telephone, by fax, by e-mail and in person

Parent body:
Kirklees Metropolitan Council

HUDSON LIBRARY

Cathedral & Abbey Church of St Alban, Sumpter Yard, St Albans, Hertfordshire, AL1 1BY

Tel: 01727 830576
Fax: 01727 850944

Enquiries:
Enquiries to: Librarian

Organisation type and purpose:
Registered charity (charity number 280566).

Subject coverage:
Comparative religion, Bible, history of Christianity, theology, philosophy, psychology, sociology, some history and literature, plus local history of Hertfordshire and Bedfordshire, particularly of St Albans City and Abbey.

Museum or gallery collection, archive, or library special collection:
Beardsmore Collection (History of Hertfordshire in book, pamphlet and ephemera)

Library catalogue:
All or part available in-house

Access to staff:
Contact by letter, by telephone and in person
Hours: Mon to Fri, 0900 to 1700

Located in:
St Alban's Abbey Chapter House

Supported by:
Diocese of St Albans and the Cathedral Council

HUGH BAIRD COLLEGE LIBRARY

Balliol Road, Bootle, Merseyside, L20 7EW

Tel: 0151 353 4409
Fax: 0151 353 4409

Website:
http://www.hughbaird.ac.uk
College prospectus including details of library and learning centre service.

Enquiries:
Enquiries to: Learning Resources Manager
Direct tel: 0151 353 4455

Organisation type and purpose:
Suitable for ages: 16+.

Subject coverage:
Art, design and display; hairdressing and beauty therapy; floristry; construction; electrical engineering; business and secretarial studies; Education; Health and Social Care;Child Care; Pre-uniform;Visual merchandising; GCSE subjects, NVQs, AVCEs, AS, A2, motor vehicle engineering.Fondation Degrees.

Library catalogue:
All or part available online and in-house

Access to staff:
Contact by letter, by telephone, by fax and via website. Appointment necessary.
Hours: Mon to Thu, 0845 to 1900; Fri, 0845 to 1600; Vacation, 0930 to 1630, 5th Floor LLC only
Special comments: Reference library only. Lending facilities to college staff and students enrolled at the College.

Access to building, collection or gallery:
ID card or visitor's pass required

HUGUENOT LIBRARY

UCL, Gower Street, London, WC1E 6BT

Tel: 020 7679 5199
E-mail: library@huguenotsociety.org.uk

Website:
http://www.huguenotsociety.org.uk/library

Enquiries:
Enquiries to: Librarian

Founded:
1885

Organisation type and purpose:
Learned society (membership is by subscription), present number of members: 1,500, registered charity.

Subject coverage:
Huguenot history, general, ecclesiastical, economic, social, art and genealogy.

Museum or gallery collection, archive, or library special collection:
Archives of the French Protestant Hospital and other manuscript material
Huguenot Pedigrees
Library of the French Hospital (La Providence)
Royal Bounty Archives

Library catalogue:
All or part available online

Printed publications:
Huguenot Families (first edn, 1999)
Newsletter
Proceedings of the Huguenot Society of Great Britain and Ireland
Quarto Series of the Huguenot Society of Great Britain and Ireland

Microform publications:
French Protestant Hospital Archives
Quarto series 1–39
Royal Bounty Archives

Electronic and video publications:
Huguenot Familes (vols 1–15)
Quarto Series (vols 1–53)
Order electronic and video publications from: See website for details.

Publications list:
Available online and in print

Access to staff:
Contact by letter, by telephone and by e-mail.
Appointment necessary. Non-members charged.
Hours: Tue and Wed, 1000 to 1600

Access to building, collection or gallery:
Tue and Wed, 1000 to 1600
Special comments: Fee of £10 per day, except for Fellows of the Huguenot Society, undergraduates, or members of UCL.

Access for disabled people:
Access during opening hours, as specified

Administered by:
Huguenot Society of Great Britain and Ireland

Also at:
French Protestant Hospital
Rochester, Kent

HULL & HUMBER CHAMBER OF COMMERCE AND INDUSTRY

34–38 Beverley Rd, Hull, HU3 1YE

Tel: 01482 324976
Fax: 01482 213962
E-mail: info@hull-humber-chamber.co.uk

Website:
http://www.hull-humber-chamber.co.uk

Enquiries:
Enquiries to: Membership and Business Manager
Direct e-mail: b.massie@hull-humber-chamber.co.uk

Organisation type and purpose:
National organisation, membership association (membership is by subscription), service industry, training organisation.

Subject coverage:
Export requirements, business information, economic surveys, training seminars.

Also at:
Hull & Humber Chamber of Commerce and Industry
Dock Offices, Cleethorpes Road, Grimsby, DN31 3LL; tel: 01472 342981; fax: 01472 349524

HULL AND HUMBER CHAMBER OF COMMERCE, INDUSTRY AND SHIPPING

34–38 Beverley Road, Hull, East Yorkshire, HU3 1YE

Tel: 01482 324976
Fax: 01482 213962
E-mail: info@hull-humber-chamber.co.uk

Enquiries:
Enquiries to: Information Officer

Founded:
1837

Organisation type and purpose:
Trade association, service industry.

Subject coverage:
Exports, including export documentation.

Printed publications:
Business Intelligence
Humber company directory
Information pack
Quarterly Economic Review

Electronic and video publications:
Who supplies what in EC countries

Access to staff:
Contact by letter, by telephone and by fax.
Appointment necessary.
Hours: Mon to Fri, 0900 to 1700

HULL CITY ARCHIVES

79 Lowgate, Kingston upon Hull, East Yorkshire, HU1 1HN

Tel: 01482 615102 or 615110
Fax: 01482 613051
E-mail: city.archives@hullcc.gov.uk

Website:
http://www.hullcc.gov.uk/portal/page?_pageid=
221,52893&_dad=portal&_schema=PORTAL
http://www.a2a.org.uk
Archive database

Enquiries:
Enquiries to: Archivist

Founded:
1968

Organisation type and purpose:
Local government body.

Hull City Archives collects, preserves and makes available records of Kingston upon Hull City Council and its predecessor bodies back to 1299, as well as collections of records relating to local businesses, societies, charities and families.

Subject coverage:
All aspects of the City of Hull from medieval times to the present day. The holdings are especially strong for the 16th to 17th centuries local government; the built environment and infrastructure (architecture and engineering); the administration of justice in the 19th and 20th centuries; the fishing industry in Hull. Important collections are held relating to maritime history of the Humber Region.

Museum or gallery collection, archive, or library special collection:
Hellyer Bros. Trawler Owners c.1890 to 1975
Hull and Goole Port Sanitary Authority
Thomas Hamling and Co, Trawler Owners c.1890 to 1980
Pease family of Hull and Hesslewood archives C17–C20
Borough of Kingston upon Hull 1299 to 1835, records of the Newlands Homes 1821–2001
Archives:
Archives of the City Council and its predecessors, 1299 to date; local courts 17th to 20th centuries, charities 13th to 19th centuries, churches 19th and 20th centuries, business 19th and 20th centuries, families 18th to 20th centuries
City of Kingston upon Hull 1835 to present

Non-library collection catalogue:
All or part available online and in-house

Library catalogue:
All or part available in-house

Printed publications:
A variety of leaflets describing topics and sources (free)
Guide to the Kingston upon Hull Record Office: Part I Records of Local Authorities whose areas or functions were taken over by the former County Borough of Kingston upon Hull (G W Oxley)

Publications list:
Available online and in print

Access to staff:
Contact by letter, by telephone, by fax, by e-mail, in person and via website. Appointment necessary.
Hours: Tue to Thu, 0900 to 1645; Fri 0900 to 1600
Special comments: Appointments are essential, closure can happen without notice.

Access to building, collection or gallery:
Tue to Thu, 0930 to 1645

Access for disabled people:
By appointment

Parent body:
Kingston upon Hull City Council
The Guildhall, Alfred Gelder Street, Kingston upon Hull, HU1 2AA; tel: 01482 300300

HULL LIBRARIES

Reference Library and Local Studies Library, Central Library, Albion Street, Hull, East Yorkshire, HU1 3TF

Tel: 01482 210055 (reference); 01482 210077 (local studies)
Fax: 01482 616858
E-mail: reference.library@hullcc.gov.uk; local.studies@hullcc.gov.uk

Website:
http://www.hullcc.gov.uk
http://prismcollect.hullcc.gov.uk
Online library catalogue

Enquiries:
Enquiries to: Specialist Librarian

Founded:
1901

continued overleaf

Organisation type and purpose:
Local government body, public library.

Subject coverage:
In Reference Library:
General coverage; family history (national resources).
In Local Studies: The study of Hull and the surrounding area – its history, geology, geography, archaeology and flora and fauna. Family history (local resources)

Museum or gallery collection, archive, or library special collection:
In Reference Library: British Standards Online, BvD MINT Company and market research, Lloyds Register of Ships 1764 to date (with gaps), Napoleon, books published 1741–1759, GRO Indexes 1837–2003 (on microfiche).
In Local Studies Library: Andrew Marvell (1621–1678); Deposited records of Forster and Andrews, organ builders of Hull, 1843–1956; Hull City Health Department photographs 1890s to 1930s; whales and whaling; William Wilberforce and slavery; Winifred Holtby (1898–1935): Correspondence, cuttings, photographs, publications, etc.

Library catalogue:
All or part available online

Access to staff:
Contact by letter, by telephone, by fax, by e-mail, in person and via website
Hours: Mon to Thu, 0930 to 2000; Fri, 0930 to 1730; Sat, 0900 to 1630

Access for disabled people:
Ramped entry, toilet facilities, lift
Special comments: Limited access to Local Studies Library at present.

HULL LOCAL STUDIES LIBRARY

First Floor, Albion Street, Hull, East Yorkshire, HU1 3TF

Tel: 01482 210077
Fax: 01482 616858
E-mail: david.smith@hullcc.gov.uk

Website:
http://www.hullcc.gov.uk

Enquiries:
Enquiries to: Senior Local Studies Librarian

Founded:
1960

Organisation type and purpose:
Local government body, public library.

Subject coverage:
Family history, the study of Kingston upon Hull and the surrounding area – its history, people, geology, geography, archaeology, flora and fauna.

Museum or gallery collection, archive, or library special collection:
Kingston upon Hull Local Studies Library special collections include:
Amy Johnson correspondence
Andrew Marvell (1621–78)
Deposited records of Forster and Andrews, organ builders of Hull, 1843–1956
Hull City Health Department photographs, 1890s to 1930s
Whales and whaling
William Wilberforce and slavery
Winifred Holtby (1898–1935) correspondence, cuttings, photographs, publications, etc.

Non-library collection catalogue:
All or part available online and in-house

Library catalogue:
All or part available in-house

Printed publications:
Hull Through the Ages: The development of Hull through maps and plans (on CDR, also includes two trade directories, a history of Hull and film footage of Amy Johnson; £15.95)

The Centenary Book of Hull (Highgate Publications (Beverley) Ltd, in conjunction with Kingston upon Hull City Libraries, 1997, £12.95, ISBN 09489 29979)
Forgotten Hull: A selection of photographs taken from the Hull Corporation Health Department Collection 1890s–1930s (G. Wilkinson and G. Watkins, Kingston Press, 1999, ISBN 1902039009, out of print)

Access to staff:
Contact by letter, by telephone, by fax, by e-mail, in person and via website

Access to building, collection or gallery:
Hours: Mon, 1730 to 2000; Tue to Thu, 0930 to 2000; Fri, 0930 to 1730; Sat, 0900 to 1630
Special comments: Hull Local Studies Library will close on 24th December 2008 to prepare the move to the History Centre, opening late summer 2009 (see website for more details)

Access for disabled people:
Ramped entry, toilet facilities; limited access

Links with:
Hull History Centre
Mason Street, Hull; website: http://www .historycentrehull.org.uk

HULTON ARCHIVE

Unique House, 21–31 Woodfield Road, London, W9 2BA

Tel: 020 7266 2662
Fax: 020 7266 3154
E-mail: info@getty-images.com

Website:
http://www.hultonarchive.com
Picture search engine, e-commerce enabled.
http://www.getty-images.com
Library history, agencies, electronic catalogue, CD-ROM data.

Enquiries:
Enquiries to: Sales Manager
Other contacts: Picture enquiries tel no: 0171 266 2662, fax: 0171 266 3154

Founded:
1947

Organisation type and purpose:
International organisation.
Commercial picture lending library.
Sale of reproduction rights for publishing, TV, and advertising, editorial, web usage, sale of prints (photographs, framed or unframed).

Subject coverage:
Over 18 million images covering all subjects from pre-history to 1980s; especially strong on social history, royalty, performing arts, sport, fashion, transport. Engravings, woodcuts, maps, etchings, cartoons etc large colour section.

Museum or gallery collection, archive, or library special collection:
Baron Collection (ballet)
Sasha Collection (theatre)
Keystone Collection
Topical Press Collection (general)
Picture Post Collection (general)
Studo Lisa Collection (royalty)
Evening Standard Collection (general)
Ernst Haas Collection
Slim Aarons Collection (personalities)
Fox Photos (general)
Central Press (general)
Weegee Collection (US crime)
Archive Photographs (general and US)

Non-library collection catalogue:
All or part available online

Printed publications:
HPC press releases
Hulton Catalogues
Seven Ages of Man (Hulton Getty catalogue)
Many books available through book sellers

Access to staff:
Contact by letter, by telephone, by fax, by e-mail and via website. Appointment necessary.
Hours: Mon to Fri, 0915 to 1800
Special comments: Fees chargeable according to usage.

Access to building, collection or gallery:
Prior appointment required
Hours: Mon to Fri, 0930 to 1730

Affiliated to:
British Association of Picture Libraries

Part of:
Getty Images
101 Bayham Street, London, NW1 0FG; tel: 020 7544 3333; fax: 020 7544 3334; e-mail: info@getty -images.com

HUMAN RIGHTS

Acronym or abbreviation: HR

Mariners Hard, High Street, Cley-next-the-Sea, Holt, Norfolk, NR25 7RX

Tel: 01263 740990
Fax: 01263 740990
E-mail: human-rights-society@ukgateway.net

Enquiries:
Enquiries to: Executive Secretary

Founded:
1971

Organisation type and purpose:
Voluntary organisation, registered charity (charity number 262328).

Subject coverage:
Alternatives to euthanasia – i.e. hospice and home care services, relief of pain in terminal illness and other help.

Printed publications:
Newsletter (Human Rights Society)
Pushing the Passing (Human Rights Society)
Reports and leaflets include:
Human Value (Human Rights Society)
The Relief of Pain (Human Rights)
No Right to Play God (Human Rights Society)
Understanding Euthanasia (Human Rights Society)

Electronic and video publications:
A Matter of Death and Life – The Future? (educational video with tutor's notes for purchase direct, Human Rights)

Publications list:
Available in print

Access to staff:
Contact by letter, by telephone, by fax and by e-mail
Hours: Variable hours

Membership body:
Human Rights Society (HRS)
at the same address

HUMANE SLAUGHTER ASSOCIATION

Formal name: Humane Slaughter Association and Council of Justice to Animals
Acronym or abbreviation: HSA

The Old School, Brewhouse Hill, Wheathampstead, Hertfordshire, AL4 8AN

Tel: 01582 831919
Fax: 01582 831414
E-mail: info@hsa.org.uk

Website:
http://www.hsa.org.uk

Enquiries:
Enquiries to: Chief Executive & Scientific Director
Other contacts: Technical Director for technical matters.

Founded:
1911

Organisation type and purpose:
Membership association (membership is by subscription), present number of members: 650, registered charity (charity number 209563), suitable for ages: adults, training organisation, research organisation.
Promotion of humane methods of slaughter and the introduction of reforms in livestock markets (including transport facilities).

Subject coverage:
Welfare of livestock (including birds) destined for slaughter. Training of vets, farmers and slaughtermen in slaughter techniques. Improvements in market facilities. Improvements in transport facilities for livestock. Training of hauliers, stockmen, market staff.

Printed publications:
Fact Sheets
Annual Newsletter
Annual Report
Technical Booklets

Electronic and video publications:
Instructional videos and CD-ROMs: educational on humane slaughter, livestock in transit, handling in markets

Publications list:
Available online and in print

Access to staff:
Contact by letter, by telephone, by fax, by e-mail and via website. Appointment necessary.
Hours: Mon to Fri, 0900 to 1600

Access to building, collection or gallery:
Prior appointment required
Hours: Mon to Fri, 0900 to 1600

HUMBER AND WOLDS RURAL COMMUNITY COUNCIL

Acronym or abbreviation: HWRCC

14 Market Place, Howden, East Yorkshire, DN14 7BJ

Tel: 01430 430904
Fax: 01430 432037
E-mail: info@hwrcc.org.uk

Website:
http://www.hwrcc.org.uk

Enquiries:
Enquiries to: Chief Executive

Founded:
1976

Organisation type and purpose:
Membership association (membership is by qualification), present number of members: approx. 1000, registered charity (charity number 505489), and company limited by guarantee (number 4606085). Administers grants and fosters community development.

Subject coverage:
Rural issues; parish and town council issues; community buildings (eg village halls).

Printed publications:
Humbrella (free)

Access to staff:
Contact by letter, by telephone, by fax and by e-mail. Appointment necessary.
Hours: Mon to Thu, 0900 to 1700; Fri, 0900 to 1630
Special comments: No disabled access but can arrange to meet visitors elsewhere.

HUMBER REGISTER, THE

175 York Road, Broadstone, Dorset, BH18 8ES

Tel: 01202 695937
E-mail: thearmans@googlemail.com

Enquiries:
Enquiries to: Registrar

Founded:
1951

Organisation type and purpose:
Membership association (membership is by subscription), present number of members: 300.

Subject coverage:
All Humber models from 1896 to 1930 plus the inlet over exhaust (i.o.e.) engined cars from 1931 and 1932.

Museum or gallery collection, archive, or library special collection:
Large library, including all known statistical information

Printed publications:
Bulletin (6 times a year, free to members)

Access to staff:
Contact by letter and by telephone
Hours: Any reasonable time.

HUNGARIAN CULTURAL CENTRE

Acronym or abbreviation: HCC

10 Maiden Lane, Covent Garden, London, WC2E 7NA

Tel: 020 7240 8448
Fax: 020 7240 4847
E-mail: culture@hungary.org.uk

Website:
http://www.hungary.org.uk

Founded:
1999

Organisation type and purpose:
Associated with Hungary's Ministry of Culture.

Subject coverage:
Hungarian culture and civilisation.

Special visitor services:
Library (open Tue and Thu 1100 to 1900).

HUNGARIAN EMBASSY

35 Eaton Place, London, SW1X 8BY

Tel: 020 7235 5218
Fax: 020 7823 1348
E-mail: office@huemblon.org.uk

Website:
http://www.huemblon.org.uk
General information on Hungary, visa and consular information, Hungarian Trade Commission, Hungarian Tourist Office, Hungary, NATO and the EU

Enquiries:
Enquiries to: Information Officer

Organisation type and purpose:
International organisation.

Printed publications:
Fact sheets on Hungary
Hungarian Quarterly
Tourist Brochures

Access to staff:
Contact by letter, by telephone, by fax and via website
Hours: Mon to Thu, 0900 to 1700; Fri, 0900 to 1400
Special comments: Consular Department is open to personal callers Mon to Fri, 0930 to 1200 only.

Other office:
The Hungarian Tourist Office
46 Eaton Place, London, SW1X 8AL; tel: 020 7823 1032; fax: 020 7823 1459
The Hungarian Trade Commission
46 Eaton Place, London, SW1X 8AL; tel: 020 7235 8767; fax: 020 7235 4319

HUNTINGDON LIFE SCIENCES

Acronym or abbreviation: HLS

Woolley Road, Alconbury, Huntingdon, Cambridgeshire, PE28 4HS

Tel: 01480 892000
Fax: 01480 892978

Website:
http://www.huntingdon.com

Enquiries:
Enquiries to: Information Officer

Organisation type and purpose:
International organisation, research organisation, consultancy.

Subject coverage:
Toxicology; environmental science; pathology; pharmacology; microbiology; cell biology; metabolic studies; analytical chemistry; veterinary science.

Library catalogue:
All or part available in-house

Access to staff:
Contact by letter, by telephone and by fax
Hours: Mon to Fri, 0900 to 1700

Access to building, collection or gallery:
No access other than to staff

HUNTINGDONSHIRE ARCHIVES

Acronym or abbreviation: HA

Grammar School Walk, Huntingdon, Cambridgeshire, PE29 3LF

Tel: 01480 375842
E-mail: hunts.archives@cambridgeshire.gov.uk

Website:
http://www.cambridgeshire.gov.uk/archives

Enquiries:
Enquiries to: Senior Archivist

Founded:
1948

Formerly called:
Huntingdonshire County Record Office (year of change 1968); County Record Office, Huntingdon (year of change 2008)

Organisation type and purpose:
Local government body.
Record office.

Subject coverage:
Local history of Huntingdonshire and to a lesser degree of the Soke of Peterborough, including genealogy and topography.

Museum or gallery collection, archive, or library special collection:
Records of the former Huntingdonshire and Soke of Peterborough County Councils. Deposited official and unofficial records relating to Huntingdonshire, including archdeaconry, parish and borough records and family and estate collections, including those of the Dukes of Manchester of Kimbolton and of the Earls of Sandwich of Hinchingbrooke, c.1200 to 20th century

Non-library collection catalogue:
All or part available online and in-house

Library catalogue:
All or part available online and in-house

Printed publications:
County Archivist's Annual Reports 1974–95
List of inclosure awards and plans (free)
Maps in the County Record Office Huntingdon (£1 plus p&p)
Summary of Sources for Genealogists (free)

Publications list:
Available in print

Access to staff:
Contact by letter, by telephone, by fax, by e-mail and in person

continued overleaf

Access to building, collection or gallery:
Hours: Tue, Wed and Thu, 0900 to 1245 and 1345 to 1715; Fri, 0900 to 1245 and 1345 to 1615; second Sat in each month, 0900 to 1200 by appointment
Special comments: CARN ticket required

Access for disabled people:
Stairlift to the first floor public search room

Parent body:
Cambridgeshire County Council, Cambridgeshire Archives and Local Studies
  Shire Hall, Castle Hill, Cambridge; tel: 01223 718131

HUNTINGDONSHIRE LOCAL HISTORY SOCIETY

3 The Lanes, Houghton, Huntingdon, Cambridgeshire, PE28 2BW

Tel: 01480 463007
E-mail: dam.coz@virgin.net

Enquiries:
Enquiries to: Honorary Secretary

Founded:
1957

Organisation type and purpose:
Voluntary organisation, registered charity (charity number 290741).
Local history society.

Subject coverage:
Local history of Huntingdonshire, vernacular architecture.

Printed publications:
Records of Huntingdonshire (annually £3.50, free to members)
Order printed publications from: Hon. Editor, Dr Philip Saunders
Deputy Country Archivist, Cambs. County Record Office, Shire hall, Castle Hill, Cambridge, CB31 0PA, e-mail: philip.saunders@cambridgeshire.gov .uk

Access to staff:
Contact by letter, by telephone and in person
Hours: Mon to Fri, 0900 to 1700, and evenings

Affiliated to:
Cambridge Local History Association

Member of:
British Association for Local History

HUNTINGDONSHIRE REGIONAL COLLEGE

California Road, Huntingdon, Cambridgeshire, PE29 1BL

Tel: 01480 379100
Fax: 01480 379127
E-mail: college@huntingdon.ac.uk

Enquiries:
Enquiries to: Librarian

Organisation type and purpose:
Suitable for ages: 16+.
Further education college.

Subject coverage:
Art, business studies, engineering, photography, general education, hairdressing, beauty therapy, care, IT.

Library catalogue:
All or part available in-house

Access to staff:
Contact by letter and by telephone
Hours: Mon to Fri, 0900 to 1700

Access to building, collection or gallery:
Prior appointment required

HUNTINGTON'S DISEASE ASSOCIATION

Acronym or abbreviation: HDA

Neurosupport Centre, Norton Street, Liverpool, L3 8LR

Tel: 0151 298 3298
Fax: 0151 298 9440
E-mail: info@hda.org.uk

Website:
http://www.hda.org.uk

Enquiries:
Enquiries to: Team Manager
Other contacts: 24 Regional care advisers around the country

Founded:
1974

Organisation type and purpose:
Membership association, present number of members: 6000, voluntary organisation, registered charity (charity number 296453).
To provide care, advice, support and education to anyone who is affected by Huntington's Disease.

Subject coverage:
Information for families, carers, and health and social service professionals, to advise and support people with Huntington's Disease.

Printed publications:
Factsheets for sufferers, carers and professionals
All about the Huntington's Disease Association
Huntington's Disease in the Family
Living with Juvenile Huntington's Disease
Physician's Guide to the Management of Huntington's Disease

Electronic and video publications:
Video

Publications list:
Available online and in print

Access to staff:
Contact by letter, by telephone and by fax
Hours: Mon to Fri, 0900 to 1630

HURLINGHAM POLO ASSOCIATION, THE

Acronym or abbreviation: HPA

Manor Farm, Little Coxwell, Faringdon, Oxfordshire, SN7 7LW

Tel: 01367 242828
Fax: 01367 242829
E-mail: enquiries@hpa-polo.co.uk

Website:
http://www.hpa-polo.co.uk
Order form for yearbooks, videos etc, general polo information and list of affiliated clubs.

Enquiries:
Enquiries to: Chief Executive

Founded:
1874

Organisation type and purpose:
National government body, membership association (membership is by subscription), present number of members: 2300, voluntary organisation.
Governing body of the game in the UK and the Commonwealth.

Subject coverage:
Polo.

Library catalogue:
All or part available in-house

Printed publications:
HPA Arena Yearbook (free to members)
HPA Yearbook (free to members)

Electronic and video publications:
Some videos available

Access to staff:
Contact by letter, by telephone, by fax, by e-mail and via website

Hours: Mon to Fri, 0900 to 1700

Access for disabled people:
Parking provided, ramped entry

HYMN SOCIETY OF GREAT BRITAIN AND IRELAND

Acronym or abbreviation: HSGBI

7 Paganel Road, Minehead, Somerset, TA24 5ET

Tel: 01643 703530
Fax: 01643 703530
E-mail: g.wrayford@breathemail.net

Website:
http://www.hymnsocgbi.org

Enquiries:
Enquiries to: Honorary Secretary

Founded:
1936

Organisation type and purpose:
Learned society (membership is by subscription), present number of members: 450.

Subject coverage:
Use of hymns in Christian worship; research in hymnology.

Printed publications:
Bulletin (quarterly)
Combined Index
Hymns and Tunes Indexed
Occasional papers

Access to staff:
Contact by letter, by telephone, by fax and by e-mail
Hours: Mon to Fri, 0900 to 1700

Member of:
Hymn Society in the United States and Canada
International Fellowship of Hymnology (IAH)

HYPERACTIVE CHILDREN'S SUPPORT GROUP

Acronym or abbreviation: HACSG

71 Whyke Lane, Chichester, West Sussex, PO19 7PD

Tel: 01243 539966
E-mail: hyperactive@hacsg.org.uk

Website:
http://www.hacsg.org.uk
Services provided, information on hyperactivity, membership application form.

Enquiries:
Enquiries to: Director

Founded:
1977

Organisation type and purpose:
Membership association, registered charity (charity number 277643).
Parent support, research & information group.

Subject coverage:
Hyperactivity in children and young people, its relationship to diet, nutrition, allergy and environment; organic brain dysfunction.

Printed publications:
Booklist
ADHD, Hyperactive Children: A Guide for Parents (£7)
A Professional Pack containing the above Handbook and a selection of articles and reprints (£10)
Doctors'/Health Visitors' Pack containing appropriate articles and reprints (£4.50)
Free introductory leaflets
Handbook (for sale separately or with membership)
Journals to members (3 times per annum)
Numerous articles and reprints for sale
Teachers' Pack containing appropriate articles and reprints (£5)

Publications list:
Available in print

Access to staff:
Contact by letter, by telephone, by e-mail and via website
Hours: Mon, thu, Fri, 1000 to 1200

Connections with:
Autism Unravelled
British Society for Nutritional Medicine
Foresight Association for Preconceptual Care
Green Network

HYPERION RECORDS LIMITED

PO Box 25, London, SE9 1AX

Tel: 020 8318 1234
Fax: 020 8263 1230
E-mail: info@hyperion-records.co.uk

Website:
http://www.hyperion-records.co.uk
Complete catalogues, distributors, biographies and photographs, etc.

Enquiries:
Enquiries to: Managing Director

Founded:
1980

Organisation type and purpose:
Publishing house.
Record company (classical CDs).

Subject coverage:
Recording and sale of classical music under the Hyperion and Helios labels.

Printed publications:
Catalogue (free)

Electronic and video publications:
Over 1000 classical CDs and some cassettes

Publications list:
Available in print

Access to staff:
Contact by letter, by telephone, by fax, by e-mail and via website
Hours: Mon to Fri, 0930 to 1730

HYPERLIPIDAEMIA EDUCATION & ATHEROSCLEROSIS RESEARCH TRUST UK

Acronym or abbreviation: H.E.A.R.T UK

7 North Road, Maidenhead, Berkshire, SL6 1PE

Tel: 01628 777046
Fax: 01628 628698
E-mail: ask@heartuk.org.uk

Website:
http://www.heartuk.org.uk

Enquiries:
Enquiries to: Nurse Advisor
Direct tel: 0845 450 5988
Other contacts: Dieticians

Founded:
2002

Formerly called:
Familial Hypercholestrolaemia, Familial Hyperlipidaemia Association

Organisation type and purpose:
Membership association (membership is by subscription, qualification), present number of members: 1300, voluntary organisation, registered charity (charity number 1003904).
To help people at high risk of coronary heart disease.

Subject coverage:
Diet, food nutrition and dietetics, lifestyle management, heart health, dietary and body/blood fats (lipids), origins of health and disease, prevention of coronary heart disease, cholesterol, familial hypercholesterolaemia, familial hyperlipidaemias.

Printed publications:
Family Heart Digest (4 times a year, £12 a year, free to members)
Booklets and leaflets on the following topics and others for a small price:
Blood Pressure
Cholesterol
Coronary Heart Disease and Familial Hyperlipidaemia
Coronary Heart Disease: a Family Problem
Family Food Guide
Healthy Eating Guide
Lipid Lowering Eating Advice
Lipids and Heart Disease: a Practical Approach
Smoking

Electronic and video publications:
Factsheets were being updated in 2008 and were to be available in downloadable format from H.E.A.R.T UK website

Publications list:
Available online and in print

Access to staff:
Contact by letter, by telephone, by fax, by e-mail and via website
Hours: Mon to Fri, 0930 to 1600

Access to building, collection or gallery:
No access other than to staff

I CAN

Formal name: I CAN
Acronym or abbreviation: I CAN

4 Dyer's Buildings, Holborn, London, EC1N 2QP

Tel: 0845 225 4071
Fax: 0845 225 4072
E-mail: ican@ican.org.uk

Website:
http://www.ican.org.uk
http://www.talkingpoint.org.uk

Enquiries:
Enquiries to: Marketing Officer
Other contacts: Chief Executive

Founded:
1888

Organisation type and purpose:
Registered charity (charity number 210031).
I CAN exists to help children communicate. Our special focus is children with a communication disability.

Subject coverage:
I CAN provides a combination of specialist therapy and education for children with the most severe and complex disabilities, information for parents and training and advice for teachers and other professionals. We also work to ensure that the needs of these children are taken into account in all children's policy and carry out research to find the best ways to support these children.

Museum or gallery collection, archive, or library special collection:
Archives (of 100 years)

Printed publications:
Information Pack (free)

Publications list:
Available in print

Access to staff:
Contact by letter, by telephone, by fax and by e-mail
Hours: Mon to Fri, 0900 to 1700

Access for disabled people:
Toilet facilities

IA – THE ILEOSTOMY AND INTERNAL POUCH SUPPORT GROUP

Acronym or abbreviation: IA

Peverill House, 1–5 Mill Road, Ballyclare, BT39 9DR

Tel: 0800 018 4724
Fax: 028 9332 4606
E-mail: info@iasupport.org

Website:
http://www.iasupport.org
General information, directory of local groups.

Enquiries:
Enquiries to: National Secretary

Founded:
1956

Organisation type and purpose:
Membership association (membership is by subscription), present number of members: 10,000, registered charity (charity number 234472).

Subject coverage:
Ileostomy: care, mutual aid, rehabilitation, equipment and skin care for those who have had their colon removed.

Printed publications:
IA Journal (quarterly)
IA Journal Omnibus Edition

Publications list:
Available in print

Access to staff:
Contact by letter, by telephone, by fax, by e-mail and via website
Hours: Mon to Fri, 0900 to 1700

Affiliated to:
International Ostomy Association, over 59 branches

IATEFL

Formal name: International Association of Teachers of English as a Foreign Language
Acronym or abbreviation: IATEFL

Darwin College, University of Kent, Canterbury, Kent, CT2 7NY

Tel: 01227 824430
Fax: 01227 824431
E-mail: generalenquiries@iatefl.org

Website:
http://www.iatefl.org

Enquiries:
Enquiries to: Executive Officer

Founded:
1967

Organisation type and purpose:
International organisation, membership association (membership is by subscription), present number of members: 4000, voluntary organisation, registered charity (charity number 1090853).

Subject coverage:
The teaching of English to those for whom it is a second language.

Publications list:
Available online and in print

Access to staff:
Contact by letter, by telephone, by fax, by e-mail and in person
Hours: Mon to Fri, 0900 to 1700

IBM UNITED KINGDOM LIMITED

Library (MP 149), Hursley Park, Winchester, Hampshire, SO21 2JN

Tel: 01962 815641
Fax: 01962 818199
E-mail: library@uk.ibm.com

Website:
http://isource.ibm.com/world/index.shtml

Enquiries:
Enquiries to: Librarian

continued overleaf

Organisation type and purpose:
Research organisation.

Subject coverage:
Data processing; computers; programming languages; computer applications; visual display units, computer software.

Museum or gallery collection, archive, or library special collection:
IBM Manuals
IBM Technical Reports
IBM History
Computing History

Library catalogue:
All or part available in-house

Access to staff:
Contact by letter, by telephone, by fax and by e-mail
Hours: Mon to Fri, 0900 to 1700

ICC – INTERNATIONAL MARITIME BUREAU

Formal name: International Chamber of Commerce – International Maritime Bureau
Acronym or abbreviation: ICC-IMB

c/o John Merrett, Arbitration Consultant, 30 Chepstow Road, London W2 5BE

Tel: 020 7838 9363
Fax: 020 7235 5447
E-mail: imb@icc-ccs.org.uk

Website:
http://www.iccwbo.org

Enquiries:
Enquiries to: Director
Other contacts: Deputy Director for piracy.

Founded:
1981

Organisation type and purpose:
International organisation (membership is by election or invitation), present number of members: 500.
The ICC-International Maritime Bureau is a specialised division of the International Chamber of Commerce. It is recognised by a special resolution of the International Maritime Organisation (IMO).

Subject coverage:
All types of maritime fraud and malpractice, piracy, investigations, cargo loss, document verification.

Non-library collection catalogue:
All or part available in-house

Library catalogue:
All or part available in-house

Printed publications:
Commercial Crime International (monthly, £95 a year)
Various books, special reports and guides
Emerging Baltic States
Enforcement Measures Against Counterfeiting & Piracy
Guide to the Prevention of Money Laundering
International Maritime Fraud
Nigerian Oil Frauds
Piracy at Sea

Publications list:
Available in print

Access to staff:
Contact by telephone, by fax, by e-mail and via website. Non-members charged.
Hours: Mon to Fri, 0900 to 1700

Access for disabled people:
Ramped entry

ICE CREAM ALLIANCE LIMITED

Acronym or abbreviation: ICA

3 Melbourne Court, Pride Park, Derby, DE24 8LZ

Tel: 01332 203333
Fax: 01332 203420
E-mail: info@ice-cream.org

Website:
http://www.ice-cream.org
Full Ice Cream Alliance web site.

Enquiries:
Enquiries to: Chief Executive
Other contacts: Administrator

Founded:
1944

Organisation type and purpose:
Trade association.

Subject coverage:
Ice cream, equipment and associated materials for manufacture and sale of the product.

Printed publications:
Ice Cream (magazine, monthly, members only, membership £110)
Code of practice for hygienic manufacture of ice cream (£3.53 inc. VAT and p&p)
Food Safety Management Manual (members: £64.62, non-members: £88.12, inc. VAT and p&p)
Guide to Safe Handling and Service of Ice Cream (£1)

Publications list:
Available online and in print

Access to staff:
Contact by letter, by telephone, by fax, by e-mail and via website. Appointment necessary.
Hours: Mon to Thu, 0830 to 1630; Fri, 0900 to 1600

Access to building, collection or gallery:
No prior appointment required

ICE ERGONOMICS LIMITED

Holywell Building, Holywell Way, Loughborough, Leicestershire, LE11 3UZ

Tel: 01509 283300
Fax: 01509 283360

Website:
http://www.ice.co.uk
Work of ICE and its sub-units.

Enquiries:
Enquiries to: Operations Director
Other contacts: Business Manager for business/financial matters.

Founded:
1970

Organisation type and purpose:
University department or institute, consultancy, research organisation.

Subject coverage:
Ergonomics in the design, development and evaluation of products, procedures, systems and environments, with application to consumer, industrial, commercial, automotive and transport areas. Special skills in occupational safety and health, accident research, and job assessment and allocation for disabled people.

Non-library collection catalogue:
All or part available in-house

Library catalogue:
All or part available in-house

Publications list:
Available in print

Access to staff:
Appointment necessary.
Hours: Mon to Fri, 0900 to 1700

Access to building, collection or gallery:
No prior appointment required

Access for disabled people:
Parking provided, level entry, access to all public areas, toilet facilities

Parent body:
Loughborough University
Ashby Road, Loughborough, Leicestershire, LE11 3TU; tel: 01509 263171

ICE HOCKEY UK

Acronym or abbreviation: IHUK

19 Heather Avenue, Rise Park, Romford, Essex, RM1 4SL

Tel: 020 8732 4505
Fax: 020 8952 9515
E-mail: ihukoffice@yahoo.co.uk

Website:
http://www.icehockeyuk.co.uk
Ice Hockey.

Enquiries:
Enquiries to: Administrator

Founded:
1936

Organisation type and purpose:
National organisation, training organisation. Governing body for ice hockey in UK and Northern Ireland.

Subject coverage:
Ice hockey.

Museum or gallery collection, archive, or library special collection:
Photographs

Access to staff:
Contact by letter, by telephone, by fax, by e-mail, in person and via website
Hours: Mon to Thu, 0900 to 1700; Fri, 0900 to 1600

Access to building, collection or gallery:
No prior appointment required

Affiliated to:
BOA
CCPR
International Ice Hockey Federation (IIHF)
Sports Council

Houses the:
English Ice Hockey Association
Northern Ireland Ice Hockey Association
Scottish Ice Hockey Association

ICON

Formal name: Institute of Conservation
Acronym or abbreviation: Icon

3rd Floor, Downstream Building, 1 London Bridge, London, SE1 9BG

Tel: 020 7785 3805
Fax: 020 7785 3806
E-mail: admin@icon.org.uk

Website:
http://www.icon.org.uk

Enquiries:
Enquiries to: Administrator

Founded:
2005

Organisation type and purpose:
International organisation, professional body, present number of members: 3,000, registered charity (charity number 1049444).

Subject coverage:
All aspects of restoration and conservation of artistic and historic works, glass, ceramics, furniture, stone, easel paintings, wall paintings, books and paper, textiles, metals, stained glass, gilding, historical interiors, natural materials and archaeological objects.

Printed publications:
Icon News (newsletter, 6 times a year, available to members)
The Conservator (annually, available to members and to purchase one year after date of publication)

The Paper Conservator (annually, available to
members and to purchase one year after date of
publication)

Access to staff:
Contact by letter, by telephone, by fax and by e-
mail
Hours: Mon to Fri, 0900 to 1300 (best time to call)

IDOX INFORMATION SERVICE

Acronym or abbreviation: PLANEX

Tontine House, 8 Gordon Street, Glasgow, G1 3PL

Tel: 0141 574 1920
Fax: 0141 248 9433
E-mail: iu@idoxplc.com

Website:
http://www.idoxplc.com

Enquiries:
Enquiries to: Information Services Manager

Founded:
1973

Formerly called:
Planning Exchange (year of change 2002)

Organisation type and purpose:
Subscription-based service, specialising in the
development and delivery of products, services
and people for information management and
knowledge sharing, for both public and private
sector clients. Information service in the fields of
economic, environmental and social development
through a database of bibliographic abstracts, a
telephone helpline and document supply.

Subject coverage:
Economic and business development,
regeneration, local government, finance and
management, education and training, community
development, the environment, housing, nature
conservation, rural and urban areas, social work,
town and country planning, regional development,
transport, leisure and tourism

**Museum or gallery collection, archive, or library
special collection:**
All Scottish planning appeal decision letters and
reports from January 1976
All Scottish local plans

Non-library collection catalogue:
All or part available online and in-house

Library catalogue:
All or part available online and in-house

Printed publications:
Scottish Planning and Environmental Law (3 times
a year)
Bulletin (weekly, part of the IDOX Information
Service)

Electronic and video publications:
New Towns Record (DVD)

Publications list:
Available online

Access to staff:
Contact by letter, by telephone, by fax, by e-mail,
in person and via website. Appointment necessary.
Non-members charged.
Hours: Mon to Fri, 0900 to 1700
Special comments: By appointment for members

IEA COAL RESEARCH

The Clean Coal Centre, Gemini House, 10–18
Putney Hill, London, SW15 6AA

Tel: 020 8780 2111
Fax: 020 8780 1746
E-mail: mail@iea-coal.org.uk

Website:
http://www.iea-coal.org.uk

Enquiries:
Enquiries to: Information Services Group Manager

Founded:
1975

Organisation type and purpose:
International organisation providing information
on coal

Subject coverage:
All aspects of coal production and use including
coal reserves and exploration, mining, preparation,
properties, processing, combustion, transport and
handling, waste management, and political, legal,
economic, environmental, health and safety
aspects.

Library catalogue:
All or part available in-house

Printed publications:
Annual Report
Newsletter (3 times a year)
Profiles (summaries of reports)
Review and assessment reports
About 200 publications on all aspects of the Coal
Industry world-wide
Order printed publications from: tel: 020 8789 0111,
fax: 020 8789 0111, e-mail: sales@iea-coal.org.uk

Electronic and video publications:
CoalPower (databases of information on over 1,850
coal-fired power stations and 5,000 individual
units and related subjects, in over 30 countries,
non-members £5,000, members £500, which
includes online access)
Coal Abstracts database (over 180,000 abstracts to
coal literature, non-members £5,000, members
£500pa; after one year non-members £3,000,
members £300, education establishments £250
(member countries))

Publications list:
Available online and in print

Access to staff:
Contact by letter, by telephone, by fax, by e-mail
and via website. Appointment necessary. All
charged.
Hours: Mon to Fri, 0900 to 1700

Links with:
International Energy Agency (IEA)
2 rue André-Pascal, Paris cedex 16, 75775, France

Member countries:
Austria, Canada, Germany, Italy, Japan, Poland,
Republic of Korea, Spain, Sweden, United
Kingdom, USA

IEEM

Formal name: Institute of Ecology and
Environmental Management
Acronym or abbreviation: IEEM

45 Southgate Street, Winchester, Hampshire, SO23
9EH

Tel: 01962 868626
Fax: 01962 868625
E-mail: enquiries@ieem.net

Website:
http://www.ieem.net
Meetings; courses; conferences; membership.

Enquiries:
Enquiries to: Executive Director

Founded:
1991

Organisation type and purpose:
Professional Body

Subject coverage:
Ecology and Environmental Management.

Library catalogue:
All or part available in-house

Printed publications:
Conference Proceedings (£21)
In Practice (quarterly) (£10 each or £30 annually)
Rooting for a Career in Ecology and
Environmental Management (free for 50p sae)
The Profession of Ecology and Ecological
Management: what you need to know (1995, £9)

Training Workshops and Events Diary (free for sae)
Guidelines on Ecological Impact Assessment 2006
(online only)

Publications list:
Available online and in print

Access to staff:
Contact by letter, by telephone, by fax and by e-
mail
Hours: Mon to Fri, 0900 to 1700
Special comments: Members only

IEPRC

Formal name: International Electronic Publishing
Research Centre Limited
Acronym or abbreviation: IEPRC

PO Box 83, Leatherhead, Surrey, KT22 7AZ

Tel: 01372 373646
Fax: 01372 379732
E-mail: admin@ieprc.org

Website:
http://www.ieprc.org
Detailed information is for members only.

Enquiries:
Enquiries to: Administrator
Direct tel: 01372 278335
Other contacts: (1) Chief Executive (2) Research
Manager (3) Company Secretary for (1) strategic
issues (2) research and development (3) finance
and administration.

Founded:
1981

Organisation type and purpose:
International organisation, membership
association (membership is by subscription,
qualification, election or invitation), present
number of members: 70 organisations, research
organisation.
Voluntary association of international multimedia
publishers and related companies.

Subject coverage:
Electronic publishing.

Trade and statistical information:
Information for members only.

Electronic and video publications:
Online/website for members only

Publications list:
Available online

Access to staff:
Contact by letter, by telephone, by fax, by e-mail
and via website. Access for members only.
Hours: Telephone is answered from 0800 to 2200,
on 01372 278335 outside usual business hours

Access to building, collection or gallery:
No access other than to staff

IFPI (INTERNATIONAL FEDERATION OF THE PHONOGRAPHIC INDUSTRY)

IFPI Secretariat, 10 Piccadilly, London, W1J 0DD

Tel: 020 7878 7900
Fax: 020 7878 7950
E-mail: info@ifpi.org

Website:
http://www.ifpi.org

Enquiries:
Enquiries to: Admin Manager
Direct e-mail: sarah.channon@ifpi.org

Founded:
1933

Organisation type and purpose:
International organisation, trade association.
Represents producers of sound recordings.

continued overleaf

Subject coverage:
Copyright in sound and video recordings,
worldwide industry turnover, estimates of piracy
of recordings.

Trade and statistical information:
Annual and half yearly sales statistics of the record
industry.

Access to staff:
Contact by fax and by e-mail
Hours: Mon to Fri, 0900 to 1730

Access to building, collection or gallery:
Prior appointment required

Consultative status with:
Council of Europe
ILO
UNESCO
WIPO

Regional bodies have relations with the:
Association of South East Asian Nations (ASEAN)
Commission of the European Communities

IFS SCHOOL OF FINANCE

6th Floor, 100 Cannon Street, London, EC4N 6EU

Tel: 020 7444 7100
Fax: 020 7444 7109
E-mail: knowledgebank@ifslearning.com

Website:
http://www.ifslearning.com
Service for members.

Enquiries:
Enquiries to: KnowledgeBank

Founded:
1879

Organisation type and purpose:
Education. A registered charity. To provide
qualifications and life long career support services
to those working within the financial services
industry and formal education to customers.

Subject coverage:
Financial services, banking, financial education for
14–19 year olds, regulatory qualifications,
accountancy, investment, economics, bank history,
financial management, risk, e-commerce, financial
technology, marketing in financial services,
monetary and financial systems, financial services
law.

Access to staff:
Contact by letter, by telephone, by fax, by e-mail
and via website

IHS

Acronym or abbreviation: IHS

Willoughby Road, Bracknell, Berkshire, RG12 8FB

Tel: 01344 328000
Fax: 01344 328008
E-mail: marketing@ihsti.com

Website:
http://uk.ihs.com
Home page and product demonstration.

Enquiries:
Enquiries to: Information Officer
Direct tel: 01344 328170

Founded:
1964

Formerly called:
Technical Indexes Ltd

Organisation type and purpose:
Manufacturing industry.
Producers and distributors of information
products on CD-ROM and online formats;
registered to ISO 9002 by BSI Quality Assurance.

Subject coverage:
Electronic engineering; process and chemical
engineering; engineering components and
materials; manufacturing and materials handling;
construction and civil engineering; standards for
construction industry; standards in health and
safety; NATO Stock Numbers; laboratory
equipment; British standards; Defence standards
and specifications; American industrial and
military standards and specifications; Canadian,
Japanese and world standards.

Printed publications:
Electronic Engineering Suppliers Guide
Engineering Design and Manufacturing Suppliers
Guide
Process Engineering Suppliers Guide

Electronic and video publications:
Construction Product Library (CD-ROM)
Engineering Product Library (CD-ROM)
Occupational Health and Safety Information
Service (CD-ROM and online)
Specify IT (online)
Construction Information Service (online)
British Standards (online)
E4 Data (online)

Publications list:
Available in print

Access to staff:
Contact by letter, by telephone, by e-mail and via
website. Appointment necessary.
Hours: Mon to Fri, 0845 to 1645

Links with:
IHS Group – Information Handling Services (IHS
Group)
Colorado, USA

Other address:
RAPIDOC – Hard Copy Supply Division
Willoughby Road, Bracknell; tel: 01344 861666;
fax: 01344 714440; e-mail: rapidoc@techindex.co
.uk

ILI

Formal name: Infonorme London Information
Acronym or abbreviation: ILI

Index House, Ascot, Berkshire, SL5 7EU

Tel: 01344 636400
Fax: 01344 291194
E-mail: databases@ili.co.uk

Website:
http://www.ili.co.uk
World standards catalogue and on-line ordering
facility plus full product description and access to
Standards Infobase, Metals Infobase, Materials
Infobase and Eurolaw.

Enquiries:
Enquiries to: Publishing Director
Direct e-mail: rboden@ili.co.uk

Founded:
1949

Organisation type and purpose:
Service industry, publishing house.
Publishing and distributing technical, legal and
regulatory databases on CD and the Internet.

Subject coverage:
Technical standards and specifications from
worldwide sources with special knowledge of US
industrial and military standards, agents and
distributors for BSI, IEEE, API, ASME, NFPA,
DoD, MoD, ASTM and numerous other standards
authorities, European law, metals and materials
databases.

**Museum or gallery collection, archive, or library
special collection:**
Over 700,000 technical specifications and
standards, including all British Standards, US
Military Standards, MOD Defence Standards,
American Standards and others

Non-library collection catalogue:
All or part available online

Printed publications:
Standards Express (newsletter, quarterly, free)

Electronic and video publications:
Eurolaw CD-ROM and web – Full text European
Union Law
Standards Infobase CD-ROM, web and intranet –
information on 700,000 national, international
and military standards.
Metals Infobase CD-ROM and web – Information
on 74,000 world metal grades
Materials Infobase CD-ROM and web. Information
on 100,000 non-metallic materials and their
suppliers.
EU Infobase CD-ROM and web, official
bibliographic database of the European
Community

Access to staff:
Contact by letter, by telephone, by fax, by e-mail
and via website. Appointment necessary.
Hours: Mon to Fri, 0830 to 1730

Other addresses:
ILI Infodisk Inc
610 Winters Avenue, Paramus, New Jersey,
07652, USA; tel: 00 1 201 986 1131; fax: 00 1 201
986 7886; e-mail: database@ili_info.com

IMAGINATE

45a George Street, Edinburgh, EH2 2HT

Tel: 0131 225 8050
Fax: 0131 225 6440
E-mail: info@imaginate.org.uk

Enquiries:
Enquiries to: Chief Executive

Founded:
1989

Organisation type and purpose:
Registered charity, suitable for ages: 3 to 14.
Largest performing arts festival for 3 to 14 year
olds in the UK.

Subject coverage:
Children's Theatre.

Printed publications:
Festival Programme

Access to staff:
Contact by letter, by telephone, by fax and by e-
mail. Appointment necessary. Letter of
introduction required.
Hours: Mon to Fri, 0900 to 1700

IMMIGRATION MANAGEMENT & BUSINESS GROUP

Acronym or abbreviation: IMB Group

75 Cannon Street, London, EC4N 5BN

Tel: 020 7556 7112
Fax: 020 7556 7001
E-mail: admin@immigration.co.uk

Website:
http://www.workpermits.com
http://www.immigration.co.uk

Enquiries:
Enquiries to: General Manager

Founded:
1985

Organisation type and purpose:
Service industry, consultancy.

Subject coverage:
All categories of UK work permit, employment
approval and fast extensions and foreign passport
endorsement.

Publications list:
Available online

Access to staff:
Contact by letter, by telephone, by fax, by e-mail
and via website. Appointment necessary.
Hours: Mon to Fri, 0830 to 1800

Access for disabled people:
Parking provided, ramped entry, toilet facilities

Connections with:
japanese-immigration.com
  Same address

IMP CLUB LIMITED

76 Star Lane, Folkestone, CT19 4QQ

Tel: 01438 741917
E-mail: membership@theimpclub.co.uk

Website:
http://www.theimpclub.co.uk

Enquiries:
Enquiries to: Chairman

Founded:
1980

Organisation type and purpose:
Membership association (membership is by
subscription).
Classic Car Club.

Subject coverage:
All Hillman Imp cars and their variants (Singer,
Sunbeam, Commer), Imp-based cars, technical
advice, history, technical services.

**Museum or gallery collection, archive, or library
special collection:**
Broad selection of technical reports and historical
  information
Comprehensive collection of photographs, sales
  literature and associated memorabilia

Non-library collection catalogue:
All or part available online and in-house

Library catalogue:
All or part available in-house

Printed publications:
Impressions (club magazine, monthly)
Several books relevant to club's interests

Access to staff:
Contact by letter, by telephone, by e-mail and via
website
Hours: Evenings and weekends

Links with:
Association of Rootes Car Clubs

IMPERIAL COLLEGE LONDON –
CENTRAL LIBRARY

Formal name: Imperial College of Science,
Technology and Medicine – Central Library

South Kensington, London, SW7 2AZ

Tel: 020 7594 8820
Fax: 020 7584 8876
E-mail: library@imperial.ac.uk

Website:
http://www.imperial.ac.uk/library

Enquiries:
Enquiries to: Helpdesk

Organisation type and purpose:
University library.

Subject coverage:
Aeronautics; biotechnology; business; chemical
engineering and chemical technology; chemistry;
civil engineering; computing; electrical and
electronic engineering; environment; earth
sciences; geology; history of science; life sciences;
materials; mathematics; mechanical engineering;
medicine; physics.

**Museum or gallery collection, archive, or library
special collection:**
Annan Collection (history of metals, mining and
  metallurgy)

Non-library collection catalogue:
All or part available online

Library catalogue:
All or part available online

Printed publications:
The following are available from Archivist:

Pictorial Histories of Imperial College, St Mary's
  Hospital Medical School
Imperial College of Science 1945: A History of the
  Future
Imperial College School of Medicine
150 Years of the Royal School of Mines

Access to staff:
Contact by letter, by telephone, by fax, by e-mail,
in person and via website. Appointment necessary.
Hours: Please check the website

Access for disabled people:
Access to all public areas, toilet facilities

Branch libraries:
Aeronautics Library
  South Kensington Campus; tel: 020 7594 5069;
  fax: 020 7584 8120; e-mail: library@imperial.ac
  .uk; aerolib@imperial.ac.uk
Charing Cross Campus Library
  Faculty of Medicine, The Reynolds Building, St
  Dunstan's Road, London, W6 8RP; tel: 020 7594
  0755; fax: 020 7594 0851; e-mail: library@imperial
  .ac.uk
Chelsea and Westminster Campus Library
  Faculty of Medicine, Fulham Road, London,
  SW10 9NH; tel: 020 8746 8107; fax: 020 8746
  8215; e-mail: library@imperial.ac.uk
Chemical Engineering and Chemical Technology
Library
  South Kensington Campus; tel: 020 7594 5598;
  fax: 020 7594 5604; e-mail: library@imperial.ac.uk
Civil and Environmental Engineering Library
  tel: 020 7594 6007; fax: 020 7225 2716; e-mail:
  library@imperial.ac.uk
Electrical and Electronic Engineering Library
  South Kensington Campus; tel: 020 7594 6182;
  fax: 020 7823 8125; e-mail: library@imperial.ac.uk
Hammersmith Campus Wellcome Library
  School of Medicine, Du Cane Road, London,
  W12 0NN; tel: 020 8383 3246; fax: 020 8383 2195;
  e-mail: library@imperial.ac.uk
Mathematics Library
  South Kensington Campus; tel: 020 7594 8542;
  fax: 020 7594 8517; e-mail: library@imperial.ac.uk
National Heart and Lung Institute Library
  School of Medicine, Royal Brompton Campus,
  Dove House Street, London, SW3 6LY; tel: 020
  7351 8150; fax: 020 7351 8117; e-mail: library@
  imperial.ac.uk; br.library@imperial.ac.uk
St Mary's Campus Library
  School of Medicine, Norfolk Place, Paddington,
  London, W2 1PG; tel: 020 7594 3692; fax: 020
  7402 3971 (mark Attn Library); e-mail: library@
  imperial.ac.uk
The Kempe Centre
  Wye Campus, High Street, Wye, Ashford, Kent,
  TN25 5AH; tel: 020 7594 2915; fax: 020 7594
  2929; e-mail: library@imperial.ac.uk
The Michael Way Library
  Silwood Park Campus, Ascot, Berkshire, SL5
  7TA; tel: 07734 078125; e-mail: library@imperial
  .ac.uk

Constituent bodies:
Lyon Playfair Library

Constituent part of:
City and Guilds College
Royal College of Science
Royal School of Mines

Shares building and some services with:
Science Museum Library
  tel: 020 7942 4242; fax: 020 7942 4243; e-mail:
  SMLinfo@sciencemuseum.org.uk

IMPERIAL COLLEGE LONDON –
WYE CAMPUS, THE KEMPE
CENTRE

Formal name: Imperial College of Science,
Technology and Medicine – Wye Campus, The
Kempe Centre

Wye, Ashford, Kent, TN25 5AH

Tel: 020 7594 2915
Fax: 020 7594 2929
E-mail: wyelibrary@imperial.ac.uk

Website:
http://www.imperial.ac.uk/library

Enquiries:
Enquiries to: Campus Library Manager

Organisation type and purpose:
University department or institute.
Faculty library.

Subject coverage:
Agriculture, horticulture and related subjects,
environmental studies, agricultural economics,
business studies, especially agribusiness, agrarian
development overseas, plant sciences and tropical
agriculture.

**Museum or gallery collection, archive, or library
special collection:**
Agriculture and horticultural books from 16th
  century onwards
Crundale Rectorial Library
Punnett Collection of books on poultry

Access to staff:
Appointment necessary.
Hours: Mon to Fri, 0900 to 1700

Access for disabled people:
Parking provided, level entry, access to all public
areas, toilet facilities

Comprises the:
Department of Agricultural Sciences of the
Imperial College of Science, Technology and
Medicine

IMPERIAL COLLEGE SCHOOL OF
MEDICINE – ST MARY'S CAMPUS
LIBRARY

Formal name: Imperial College of Science,
Technology and Medicine – St Mary's Campus
Library

Norfolk Place, Paddington, London, W2 1PG

Tel: 020 7594 3692
Fax: 020 7402 3971
E-mail: n.palmer@ic.ac.uk

Website:
http://www.lib.ic.ac.uk/depts/stindex.htm

Enquiries:
Enquiries to: Librarian

Founded:
1854

Organisation type and purpose:
University department or institute.
Medical school.

Subject coverage:
Medicine.

Access to staff:
Contact by letter. Letter of introduction required.
Non-members charged.
Hours: Term time: Mon to Fri, 0900 to 2100; Sat,
0900 to 1300
Vacations: Mon to Fri, 0900 to 1900; Sat, closed

Campus of:
Imperial College of Science, Technology and
Medicine

IMPERIAL PRESS

Pantiles, Garth Lane, Knighton, Powys, LD7 1HH

Tel: 01547 520360

Enquiries:
Enquiries to: Proprietor

Founded:
1984

Organisation type and purpose:
Publishing house.
Bookseller.

Subject coverage:
Wargaming, military history.

continued overleaf

Printed publications:
Cheshire in the Great Civil War (£1.95)
Garrisons of Shropshire in the Civil War (£6.95)
Guide to Military Museums and other places of
    military interest (once every two to three years,
    10th ed., ISBN 1–85674–035–8, £5, Aug 2001)
Liverpool During the Great Civil War (£1.95)

Publications list:
Available in print

Access to staff:
Contact by letter and by telephone
Hours: Mon to Fri, 0900 to 1700

Access to building, collection or gallery:
No access other than to staff

IMPERIAL SOCIETY OF TEACHERS OF DANCING

Acronym or abbreviation: ISTD

Imperial House, 22–26 Paul Street, London, EC2A
4QE

Tel: 020 7377 1577
Fax: 020 7247 8979
E-mail: marketing@istd.org

Website:
http://www.istd.org
Description and illustrations of various dance
faculties within society.

Enquiries:
Enquiries to: Chief Executive

Founded:
1904

Organisation type and purpose:
Professional body, present number of members:
9500, registered charity (charity number 250397),
training organisation.
Dance Examination Board.
The ISTD exists to promote knowledge of dance
and to maintain and improve teaching standards.

Subject coverage:
Ballroom dance, Latin American dance, sequence
dance, disco/freestyle/rock-n-roll dance, classical
ballet, modern theatre dance, tap dance, jazz
dance, national dance, folk dance, classical Greek
dance, South Asian dance, alternative rhythms.

**Museum or gallery collection, archive, or library
special collection:**
Library collection related to dance

Printed publications:
Dance Magazine (4 times a year, £20 or overseas,
    £26)
Examination syllabus requirements
Promotion Brochure

Publications list:
Available in print

Access to staff:
Contact by letter, by telephone, by e-mail and via
website
Hours: Mon to Fri, 0900 to 1700

IMPERIAL TOBACCO LIMITED

Acronym or abbreviation: ITL

PO Box 525, Upton Road, Southville, Bristol, BS99
1LQ

Tel: 0117 963 6636

Website:
http://www.imperial-tobacco.com

Enquiries:
Enquiries to: Data Controller
Direct tel: 0117 933 7264
Direct fax: 0117 933 7448

Founded:
1996

Organisation type and purpose:
Manufacturing industry.
Tobacco manufacturing.

Subject coverage:
Tobacco industry.

Trade and statistical information:
Tobacco trade volumes.

Library catalogue:
All or part available in-house

Access to staff:
Contact by letter
Hours: Mon to Fri, 0900 to 1700

Access to building, collection or gallery:
No access other than to staff

IMPERIAL WAR MUSEUM

Acronym or abbreviation: IWM

Department of Printed Books, Lambeth Road,
London, SE1 6HZ

Tel: 020 7416 5342
Fax: 020 7416 5246
E-mail: collections@iwm.org.uk

Website:
http://www.iwm.org.uk
Includes Collections Online catalogue and advice
pages on family history research. Historical
enquiries may be submitted to the Collections
Enquiry Service via a webform.

Enquiries:
Enquiries to: Keeper, Department of Printed Books

Founded:
1917

Organisation type and purpose:
Museum, suitable for ages: 16+.

Subject coverage:
Study of conflicts in which British and
Commonwealth forces have been engaged in the
20th century, particularly the two World Wars;
naval, military and air operations; unit records;
social, political, economic and literary aspects of
modern warfare.

**Museum or gallery collection, archive, or library
special collection:**
Over 100,000 books, 25,000 pamphlets, 8,000
    periodical titles, 45,000 maps, and other special
    or ephemera collections, etc.
British, Commonwealth, French, German and
    American unit histories
Pamphlet Collection (wartime propaganda, ration
    books and other ephemera)
United States Strategic Bombing Survey Reports
Women's Activities in the First World War

Non-library collection catalogue:
All or part available online and in-house

Library catalogue:
All or part available online and in-house

Printed publications:
Bibliographies and book lists (on some 500 topics)
Tracing Your Family History – series of guides on
    Army, Navy, RAF and Merchant Navy
A selection of facsimile reprints of official books
    and pamphlets
Order printed publications from: Mail Order, Imperial
War Museum, Duxford Air Field, Cambridge, CB2
4QR; tel. 01223 499348; fax 01223 839688; e-mail
mailorder@iwm.org.uk

Electronic and video publications:
Official History of the Great War – Military
    Operations France and Belgium 1914–1918
    MAPS (CD-ROM, from Naval and Military
    Press)
Imperial War Museum Trench Map (Great War)
    Archive (CD-ROM, from Naval and Military
    Press)
Order electronic and video publications from: Naval
and Military Press; tel. 01825 749494; e-mail order
.dept@naval-military-press.co.uk

Publications list:
Available online

Access to staff:
Contact by letter, by telephone, by fax, by e-mail
and via website. Appointment necessary.
Hours: Telephone access: Mon to Fri, 0900 to 1700

Access for disabled people:
Parking provided, ramped entry, toilet facilities
Special comments: Wheelchair-accessible study area
available during opening hours, by appointment.

Constituent bodies:
Museum Collection Division, Department of Art
    tel: 020 7416 5342; e-mail: collections@iwm.org
    .uk; website: http://collections.iwm.org.uk
Museum Collection Division, Department of
Documents
    tel: 020 7416 5221; e-mail: docs@iwm.org.uk;
    website: http://collections.iwm.org.uk
Museum Collection Division, Department of
Exhibits and Firearms
    tel: 020 7416 5342; e-mail: collections@iwm.org
    .uk; website: http://collections.iwm.org.uk
Museum Collection Division, Photograph Archive
    tel: 020 7416 5333; e-mail: photos@iwm.org.uk;
    website: http://collections.iwm.org.uk
Museum Collection Division, Sound Archive
    tel: 020 7416 5342; e-mail: collections@iwm.org
    .uk; website: http://collections.iwm.org.uk
Museum Collection Division, United Kingdom
National Inventory of War Memorials
    tel: 020 7416 5353; e-mail: memorials@iwm.org
    .uk; website: http://www.ukniwm.org.uk

IMS PRUSSIA COVE

Formal name: International Musicians Seminar,
Prussia Cove
Acronym or abbreviation: IMS

32 Grafton Square, London, SW4 0DB

Tel: 020 7720 9020
Fax: 020 7720 9033
E-mail: rosie@i-m-s.org.uk

Enquiries:
Enquiries to: Administrator

Founded:
1972

Organisation type and purpose:
International organisation, registered charity
(charity number 270204), suitable for ages: 16 to 30.
Music master classes, strings and piano for
advanced international young musicians.

Subject coverage:
Master classes/seminars provide a totally
professional atmosphere and aim to foster the
highest level of advanced study, drawing
inspiration from the mid-European tradition.

Access to staff:
Contact by letter, by telephone, by fax and by e-
mail
Hours: Mon to Fri, 0900 to 1700

INCORE, UNIVERSITY OF ULSTER

Formal name: Institute for Conflict Resolution
Acronym or abbreviation: INCORE

Aberfoyle House, Northland Road, Londonderry,
BT48 7JA

Tel: 028 7137 5500
Fax: 028 7137 5510
E-mail: incore@incore.ulst.ac.uk

Website:
http://www.incore.ulst.ac.uk
Wide variety of information on global conflict and
ethnicity, country guides, thematic guides and
academic data bank.

Enquiries:
Enquiries to: Administrator

Founded:
1991

Organisation type and purpose:
International organisation, membership association (membership is by election or invitation), present number of members: 700, university department or institute, research organisation.
Promote communication between networks of international scholars.

Subject coverage:
Ethnic and community conflict, especially in relation to education, churches, voluntary and community groups, material conditions; controlled or regulated conflict; conflict resolution; international conflict resolution.

Museum or gallery collection, archive, or library special collection:
Collection of Novels relating to the Northern Ireland Conflict
Collection of Political Ephemera Relating to the Northern Ireland Conflict

Library catalogue:
All or part available in-house

Printed publications:
From Protagonist to Pragmatist: Political Leadership in Societies in Transition (Gormley-Heenan C)
Hope and History: Study on the Management of Diversity in Northern Ireland (Leonard B)
Community Conflict Skills (Fitzduff M)
Past Imperfect: Dealing with the Past in Northern Ireland and Societies in Transition (Hamber B)
Researching Violently Divided Societies: Ethical and Methodological Issues (Edited by Smyth M and Robinson G)

Publications list:
Available online and in print

Access to staff:
Contact by letter, by telephone, by fax, by e-mail and via website. Appointment necessary.
Hours: Mon to Fri, 0900 to 1700

Access to building, collection or gallery:
No access other than to staff

Access for disabled people:
Parking provided, level entry

Collaborates with:
Initiative on Conflict Resolution and Ethnicity (INCORE)

Links with:
Conflict Archive on the Internet (CAIN)

INCORPORATED ASSOCIATION OF ORGANISTS

Acronym or abbreviation: IAO

19 The Poplars, Gosforth, Newcastle upon Tyne, NE3 4AE

Tel: 0191 285 7303
E-mail: pvc1@btinternet.com

Website:
http://www.iao.org.uk

Enquiries:
Enquiries to: Secretary General

Founded:
1913

Organisation type and purpose:
Membership association (membership is by subscription), present number of members: 6000, registered charity (charity number 269986).

Subject coverage:
Organists.

Printed publications:
Organists' Review

Access to staff:
Contact by letter, by fax and by e-mail
Hours: Mon to Fri, 0900 to 1700

INCORPORATED COUNCIL OF LAW REPORTING FOR ENGLAND AND WALES

Acronym or abbreviation: ICLR

Megarry House, 119 Chancery Lane, London, WC2A 1PP

Tel: 020 7242 6471
Fax: 020 7831 5247
E-mail: postmaster@iclr.co.uk

Website:
http://www.lawreports.co.uk
Details of publications, details of current and forthcoming cases published, student newsletter.

Enquiries:
Enquiries to: Secretary
Other contacts: Editor: fax 020 7404 1098; e-mail editorial@iclr.co.uk

Founded:
1865

Organisation type and purpose:
Professional body, registered charity (charity number 250605), publishing house.
Preparation and publication of reports of judicial decisions of the superior and appellate courts in England.

Subject coverage:
Reports (prepared by barristers) of judicial decisions of the superior and appellate courts in England.

Printed publications:
The Weekly Law Reports
The Law Reports (monthly)
The Industrial Cases Reports
The Business Law Reports
Consolidated Index (to the Law Reports, the Weekly Law Reports, the Industrial Cases Reports and other major series)
Statutes and Public General Acts

Electronic and video publications:
eLR (The Electronic Law Reports, CD-ROM)
Justis Industrial Cases (CD-ROM)
Justis Weekly Law (CD-ROM)
The Daily Law Notes (online)
Order electronic and video publications from: Justis Publishing Ltd, Grand Union House, 20 Kentish Town Road, London, NW1 9NR; tel. 020 7267 8989; fax 020 7267 1133; e-mail enquiries@justis.com

Publications list:
Available online and in print

Access to staff:
Contact by letter, by telephone, by fax, by e-mail and via website. Appointment necessary.
Hours: Mon to Fri, 0900 to 1700

Access to building, collection or gallery:
No prior appointment required
Special comments: Restricted to use of electronic search facility, for reference only

INCORPORATED FROEBEL EDUCATIONAL INSTITUTE

Acronym or abbreviation: IFEI

Templeton Priory Lane, London, SW15 5JW

Tel: 020 8878 7546
Fax: 020 8876 2753

Enquiries:
Enquiries to: Secretary

Founded:
1892

Organisation type and purpose:
University department or institute, suitable for ages: 3 to 16, research organisation.

Museum or gallery collection, archive, or library special collection:
Froebel Education Archive

Printed publications:
Functions and Seminars Brochure, Templeton House

Access to staff:
Contact by letter, by telephone and by fax. Appointment necessary.
Hours: Mon to Fri, 0900 to 1700

INCORPORATED PHONOGRAPHIC SOCIETY

Acronym or abbreviation: IPS

Bishopsgate Institute, 230 Bishopsgate, London, EC2M 4QH

Tel: 020 8684 9984
Fax: 020 8684 9984

Website:
http://www.the-ipa.org.uk

Enquiries:
Enquiries to: Administrator
Direct e-mail: jhdorrington@hotmail.com

Founded:
1872

Organisation type and purpose:
Membership association (membership is by subscription, qualification).
Examining body for shorthand and typewriting.

Subject coverage:
Pitman's shorthand (otherwise known as phonography); history of shorthand (not restricted to Pitman's); history of writing machines (mainly typewriters).

Museum or gallery collection, archive, or library special collection:
Books about and printed in Pitman shorthand; books about typewriting

Printed publications:
IPS Journal (quarterly)

Access to staff:
Contact by letter, by telephone, by fax and by e-mail
Hours: Mon to Fri, 0900 to 1700

INCORPORATED SOCIETY OF MUSICIANS

Acronym or abbreviation: ISM

10 Stratford Place, London, W1C 1AA

Tel: 020 7629 4413
Fax: 020 7408 1538
E-mail: membership@ism.org

Website:
http://www.ism.org
Membership benefits, links to members, online publications and information.

Enquiries:
Enquiries to: Chief Executive
Other contacts: Head of Professional Development (for policy development); Head of Legal and General Services (for casework)

Founded:
1882

Organisation type and purpose:
Professional body, training organisation.

Subject coverage:
Private music teachers, musicians at all stages of education, solo, ensemble and orchestral performers, composers and conductors.

Printed publications:
Yearbook
Information sheets on legal guidance, professional business advice, financial advice, ISM membership and services, professional development, professional practice, recommended minimum rates, careers information

continued overleaf

Music Journal (monthly, free to members, non-members £3)

Electronic and video publications:
Registers of Performers and Composers, Musicians in Education and Professional Private Teachers (online at www.ism.org)

Publications list:
Available online and in print

Access to staff:
Contact by letter, by telephone, by fax and by e-mail
Hours: Mon to Fri, 0930 to 1730

INDEPENDENT ASSOCIATION OF PREP SCHOOLS

Acronym or abbreviation: IAPS

11 Waterloo Place, Leamington Spa, Warwickshire, CV32 5LA

Tel: 01926 887833
Fax: 01926 888014
E-mail: iaps@iaps.org.uk

Website:
http://www.iaps.org.uk

Enquiries:
Enquiries to: Chief Executive

Founded:
1892

Organisation type and purpose:
International organisation, professional body, membership association (membership is by election or invitation).

Subject coverage:
Preparatory school education.

Printed publications:
Prep School magazine (3 times a year, poa)
Order printed publications from: Prep School, John Catt Educational Ltd, Great Glemham, Saxmundham, Suffolk, IP17 2DH; tel. 01728 663668; fax 01728 663415; e-mail enquiries@johncatt.co.uk

Access to staff:
Contact by letter, by telephone, by fax, by e-mail, in person and via website. Appointment necessary.
Hours: Mon to Fri, 0830 to 1700

Access to building, collection or gallery:
Prior appointment required

Member organisation of:
Independent Schools Council
St Vincent House, 30 Orange Street, London, WC2H 7HH; tel: 020 7766 7070; fax: 020 7766 7071; e-mail: office@isc.co.uk; website: http://www.isc.co.uk

INDEPENDENT PANEL OF ARBITRATORS

c/o Retail Motor Industry Federation, 9 North Street, Rugby, Warwickshire, CV21 2AB

Tel: 01788 538317
Fax: 01788 538326

Enquiries:
Enquiries to: Administrator

Organisation type and purpose:
To provide an alternative complaint redress mechanism for motor trade related matters.

Subject coverage:
Independent arbitration on complaints about motor vehicles.

Access to staff:
Contact by letter and by fax
Hours: Mon to Fri, 0900 to 1700

Access to building, collection or gallery:
No access other than to staff

INDEPENDENT POLICE COMPLAINTS COMMISSION

Acronym or abbreviation: IPCC

5th Floor, 90 High Holborn, London, WC1V 6BH

Tel: 08453 002 002; mincom: 020 7404 0431
Fax: 020 7404 0430
E-mail: enquiries@ipcc.gsi.gov.uk

Website:
http://www.ipcc.gov.uk

Enquiries:
Enquiries to: Chairman

Founded:
1985

Carries out the functions of the former:
Police Complaints Authority (year of change 2004)

Organisation type and purpose:
Statutory body.

Trade and statistical information:
Data on police complaints in England and Wales.

Printed publications:
PCA Annual Report to Parliament (Stationery Office, ISBN 0–10–291037–5, £15.25)
PCA 10 Police Complaints Authority – The first 10 years (HMSO, ISBN 0 11–341146–4, £4.95)
Triennial Review of the PCA 1991–4 (HMSO, ISBN 0–10–239694–9, £5.45)
Free leaflets and summary reports available on request
Custody Officer Training: investing in safety (PCA, ISBN 0–953315707–3, £3.95)
Striking a Balance: the police use of new batons (PCA, ISBN 0–9533157–1-1, £4)
Deaths in Police Custody: reducing the risks (PCA, ISBN 0–9533157–2-X, £5)
One Year On, Deaths in Police Custody: the risks reduced (PCA, ISBN 0–9533157–3-8, £5)
Order printed publications from: For charged publications: Stationery Office, PO Box 276, London, SW8 5DT, tel. 0845 7023474 (for orders), fax: 0870 600 5533, e-mail: book.orders@theso.co.uk

Publications list:
Available in print

Access to staff:
Contact by letter, by telephone, by e-mail and via website. Appointment necessary.
Hours: Complaints against police can be made at any police station or in writing to the PCA

Parent body:
Home Office
Queen Anne's Gate, London, SW1H 9AT

INDEPENDENT PUBLISHERS GUILD

Acronym or abbreviation: IPG

PO Box 93, Royston, Hertfordshire, SG8 5GH

Tel: 01763 247014
Fax: 01763 246293
E-mail: info@ipg.uk.com

Website:
http://www.ipg.uk.com

Enquiries:
Enquiries to: Executive Director

Founded:
1962

Organisation type and purpose:
Trade association (membership is by subscription), present number of members: 310.

Subject coverage:
Publishing.

Electronic and video publications:
website archive of event reports

Access to staff:
Contact by e-mail and via website. Access for members only.
Hours: Variable hours, email is fastest

INDEPENDENT SCHOOLS COUNCIL

Acronym or abbreviation: ISC

St Vincent House, 30 Orange Street, London, WC2H 7HH

Tel: 020 7766 7070
Fax: 020 7766 7071

Website:
http://www.isc.co.uk/

Enquiries:
Enquiries to: Information Officer
Direct tel: 020 7766 7067
Direct e-mail: liam.butler@isc.co.uk
Other contacts: General Administrator for all administrative matters.

Founded:
1973

Organisation type and purpose:
Considers matters of policy and administration common to its members and when required speaks collectively on their behalf. It represents its constituent members in joint discussions with the Department for Education and with other organisations.

Subject coverage:
Independent schools.

Printed publications:
Guide to Accredited Independent Schools

Access to staff:
Appointment necessary.
Hours: Mon to Fri, 0900 to 1700

Constituent associations:
Girls' Schools Association
Governing Bodies Association
Governing Bodies of Girls Schools Association
Headmasters' and Headmistresses' Conference
Incorporated Association of Preparatory Schools
Independent Schools Association Incorporated
Independent Schools Bursars' Association
Independent Schools Information Service (ISIS)
Society of Headmasters and Headmistresses of Independent Schools

INDEPENDENT SCHOOLS COUNCIL INFORMATION SERVICE

Acronym or abbreviation: ISCis

Grosvenor Gardens House, 35–37 Grosvenor Gardens, London, SW1W 0BS

Tel: 020 7798 1500
Fax: 020 7798 1501
E-mail: info@iscis.uk.net

Website:
http://www.isc.co.uk/
Information about ISCIS and its member schools.

Enquiries:
Enquiries to: Press Officer
Direct tel: 020 7766 7067
Direct e-mail: hayley.dunlop@isc.co.uk

Founded:
1972

Organisation type and purpose:
Membership association, present number of members: 1300 schools, suitable for ages: 1 to 19, consultancy.
Information service for parents, media, researchers, academics, government departments and politicians.

Subject coverage:
Independent schools in the UK, details of nearly 1300 schools, plus statistical surveys and services for the media and politicians, placement services for parents overseas who want their children educated in the UK (below university level).

Trade and statistical information:
Statistical surveys of independent schools in the UK.

Printed publications:
Annual Census
Handbooks listing member schools, National and regional, numbers of pupils, fees charged etc
Leaflets on independent education
The ISC Guide to Accredited Independent Schools

Electronic and video publications:
The ISC Guide to Accredited Independent Schools (CD-ROM, £1.50 UK, £5 EU, and £7.50 rest of world)

Publications list:
Available in print

Access to staff:
Contact by letter, by telephone, by fax, by e-mail, in person and via website
Hours: Mon to Fri, 0900 to 1700

Parent body:
Independent Schools Council (ISC)
 tel: 020 7798 1590; fax: 020 7798 1591

Sponsored by:
Governing Bodies Association
Governing Bodies of Girls Schools Association
Incorporated Association of Preparatory Schools
Independent Schools Association

INDEPENDENT WASTE PAPER PROCESSORS ASSOCIATION

Acronym or abbreviation: IWPPA

Heritage House, Vicar Lane, Daventry, NN11 4GD

Tel: 01327 703223
Fax: 01327 300612
E-mail: admin@iwppa.co.uk

Enquiries:
Enquiries to: Chief Executive

Founded:
1975

Organisation type and purpose:
Trade association.

Subject coverage:
Waste paper; disposal and recycling.

Access to staff:
Contact by letter and by e-mail
Hours: Mon to Fri, 0900 to 1700

INDEPENDENTAGE (FORMERLY THE ROYAL UNITED KINGDOM BENEFICENT ASSOCIATION)

Acronym or abbreviation: RUKBA

6 Avonmore Road, London, W14 8RL

Tel: 020 7605 4200
Fax: 020 7605 4201
E-mail: charity@independentage.org.uk

Website:
http://www.independentage.org.uk
Information on what IndependentAge does, who we help, fundraising events, our nursing and residential homes.

Enquiries:
Enquiries to: Director

Founded:
1863

Organisation type and purpose:
Membership association, registered charity (charity number 210729).

To help elderly people on very low incomes to stay in their own homes.

Subject coverage:
Care for elderly or infirm people who have devoted their personal or professional lives to others; IndependentAge maintains independence through the provision of a regular, small additional income and the practical support of over 1,000 volunteers.
RUKBA also runs three residential and nursing homes. Help may be available with care home fees.

Printed publications:
Annual Review
Information Leaflets
IndependentAge Family Matters (newsletter)

Access to staff:
Contact by letter, by telephone and by fax
Hours: Mon to Fri, 0900 to 1700

Trustees for:
Universal Beneficent Society
 at the same address

INDIA DEVELOPMENT GROUP (UK) LIMITED

Acronym or abbreviation: IDG(UK)

68 Downlands Road, Purley, Surrey, CR8 4JF

Tel: 020 8668 3161
Fax: 020 8660 8541
E-mail: idguk@clara.co.uk

Enquiries:
Enquiries to: Chief Executive
Other contacts: Administrator

Founded:
April 1970

Organisation type and purpose:
Voluntary organisation, registered charity (charity number 291167), training organisation, consultancy, research organisation.
To promote economic, social and educational development of India's rural areas where the majority of people live, to reverse drift to urban areas unable to absorb them.

Subject coverage:
Alleviation of poverty and the generation of income in the backward areas of India.
Development of appropriate technology.

Access to staff:
Contact by letter, by telephone, by fax and by e-mail
Hours: Mon to Fri, 1000 to 1500

Links with:
Schumacher Institute of Appropriate Technology
 Village Melhaur, Chinhat, Lucknow (UP), India

INDIA HOUSE LIBRARY

High Commission of India, India House, Aldwych, London, WC2B 4NA

Tel: 020 7632 3166
E-mail: info@hcilondon.net

Website:
http://www.meagor.nic.in
General information about India including newspapers.
http://www.ficci.com
Federation of Indian Chambers of Commerce and Industry
http://www.culturopedia.com
Treasure house of India's culture and heritage; art, music, dance, crafts, theatre, language and literature etc.
http://www.indiagov.nic.in
India facts
http://www.nic.in/
Information on states of India
http://www.ciionline.org.com
Confederation of Indian Industry
http://www.nic.in/ncti
National Centre for Trade Information

http://www.hci.london.net
Information on visas
http://www.mapsofindia.com/maps
Maps
http://www.commin.nic.in
Department of Commerce

Enquiries:
Enquiries to: Librarian

Founded:
ca 1925

Organisation type and purpose:
Governmental body of the Indian Ministry of External Affairs, New Delhi.

Subject coverage:
India and Indian affairs, mainly from 1950.

Museum or gallery collection, archive, or library special collection:
Indian Central Government Official Publications from 1950 to approximately 1980 mainly economic (now in the Brynmor Jones Library, University of Hull).

Trade and statistical information:
Available from the Economic Department in the High Commission.

Library catalogue:
All or part available in-house

Printed publications:
Order printed publications from: Publications Manager, Central News Agency Private Limited P-23 Connaught Circus, PO Box 374, New Delhi, 110001, India, tel: 00 91 11 3364448, fax: 00 91 11 7526036, e-mail: info@can-india.com

Electronic and video publications:
Karishma – The Wonder that is India (multi-media CD-ROM, from Delhi or the USA)
Order electronic and video publications from: CD Division, India High Commission
240 Okala Industrial Estate, Phase III, New Delhi, 110020, fax: 00 91 11 6919073
Multisynic Trends Inc
186 Laauwe Avenue, Wayne, New Jersey, 07470, USA, fax: 00 1 201 595 8281

Access to staff:
Contact by letter, by telephone and by fax
Hours: Mon to Fri, 0900 to 1700

Access to building, collection or gallery:
By appointment

INDIAN INSTITUTE READING ROOM

Bodleian Library, Broad Street, Oxford, OX1 3BG

Tel: 01865 287300
Fax: 01865 277182
E-mail: indian.institute@bodley.ox.ac.uk

Website:
http://www.ouls.ox.ac.uk/bodley/library/rooms/iirr
http://www.bodley.ox.ac.uk/oxlip
Oxford Libraries bibliographic and full text subscription databases

Enquiries:
Enquiries to: Librarian
Direct tel: 01865 277083
Direct e-mail: gillian.evison@bodley.ox.ac.uk

Organisation type and purpose:
University library.

Subject coverage:
All subjects and languages of South Asia and Tibet, excluding natural sciences; secondary material only for Afghanistan, Burma.

Museum or gallery collection, archive, or library special collection:
Malan Collection
Monier Williams Collection
Whinfield Collection

Non-library collection catalogue:
All or part available online

continued overleaf

Library catalogue:
All or part available online

Access to staff:
Contact by letter, by telephone, by fax and by e-mail. Appointment necessary.
Hours: Mon to Fri, 0900 to 1700
Special comments: See details: http://www.ouls.ox.ac.uk/bodley/services/admissions

Access for disabled people:
See details: http://www.ouls.ox.ac.uk/bodley/services/disability

Constituent part of:
Bodleian Library, University of Oxford
    Broad Street, Oxford, OX1 3BG; e-mail: reader
    .services@ouls.ox.ac.uk; website: http://www
    .ouls.ox.ac.uk/bodley/home

INDIAN MILITARY HISTORICAL SOCIETY

Acronym or abbreviation: IMHS

33 High Street, Tilbrook, Huntingdon, Cambridgeshire, PE28 0JP

Tel: 01480 860437
E-mail: imhs@mcclenaghan.waitrose.com

Enquiries:
Enquiries to: Honorary Secretary

Founded:
1983

Organisation type and purpose:
International organisation, membership association (membership is by subscription), present number of members: 230, research organisation.

Subject coverage:
History of Service units in India both before and after Independence, including details of uniforms, medals, badges, buttons and other militaria. These include: Royal Navy, British Army and Royal Air Force units which have served in India; Units of the Honourable East India Company's Army and Marine prior to 1861; the Indian Army subsequent to 1861, including the European Volunteer Corps; the Royal Indian Marine and the Royal Indian Navy; the Army of Nepal and those of the Princely States; the present day Armed Services of India, Pakistan and Bangladesh, including Frontier Corps, Paramilitary and Police Units.

Printed publications:
Four Journals each year members only (Durbar)

Access to staff:
Contact by letter and by e-mail
Hours: Mon to Fri, 0900 to 1700

INDIAN MOTORCYCLE CLUB OF GB

183 Buxton Road, Newtown, Disley, Stockport, Cheshire, SK12 2RA

Tel: 01663 747106
E-mail: indianjohn@fsmail.net

Enquiries:
Enquiries to: Membership Secretary

Founded:
1989

Organisation type and purpose:
Membership association (membership is by subscription), present number of members: 150.

Subject coverage:
Indian motorcycles manufactured in the USA between 1901 and 1953.

Museum or gallery collection, archive, or library special collection:
Part books and workshop manuals available for use by club members only

Printed publications:
Four magazines a year with interim newsletters for club members only

Access to staff:
Contact by letter. Access for members only.
Hours: Mon to Fri, 0900 to 1700

INDIVIDUAL TRAVELLERS CO LTD

Acronym or abbreviation: ITC Ltd

Spring Mill, Earby, Barnoldswick, Lancashire, BB94 0AA

Tel: 0845 604 3877
E-mail: itcpno@holidaycottagesgroup.com

Website:
http://www.individualtravellers.com/

Enquiries:
Enquiries to: Director

Founded:
1976

Organisation type and purpose:
Service industry.
Tour operator.

Subject coverage:
Self-catering in France, Italy, Spain and Portugal, New England, Sicily, Corsica, Mallorca.

Printed publications:
Brochures (available free directly or through travel agency)

Publications list:
Available online

Access to staff:
Contact by letter, by telephone, by fax, by e-mail, in person and via website
Hours: Mon to Fri, 0900 to 1730

Access to building, collection or gallery:
No prior appointment required

Links with:
Individual Travellers Spain and Portugal
    tel: 01798 869461; fax: 01798 869343; e-mail:
    spain@indiv-travellers.com
New England Country Homes
    tel: 01798 869461; fax: 01798 869343; e-mail:
    newengland@indiv-travellers.com
Vacances en Campagne
    tel: 01798 869461; fax: 01798 869343; e-mail:
    france@indiv-travellers.com
Vacanze in Italia
    tel: 01798 869461; fax: 01798 869343; e-mail:
    italy@indiv-travellers.com

INDUSTRIAL CLEANING MACHINE MANUFACTURERS' ASSOCIATION

Acronym or abbreviation: ICMMA

Westminster Tower, 3 Albert Embankment, London, SE1 7SL

Tel: 020 7793 3039
Fax: 020 7793 3003

Enquiries:
Enquiries to: Director

Founded:
1961

Organisation type and purpose:
Trade association.

Subject coverage:
Manufacture and marketing of industrial cleaning machines.

Access to staff:
Contact by letter
Hours: Mon to Fri, 0900 to 1700

Member of:
BEAMA Ltd

INDUSTRIAL DEVELOPMENT BANGOR (UWB) LIMITED

Acronym or abbreviation: IDB Ltd

University of Wales Bangor, Dean Street, Bangor, Gwynedd, LL57 1UT

Tel: 01248 382749
Fax: 01248 372105
E-mail: enquiries@idb.wales.com

Website:
http://www.idb.wales.com
General information and catalogue.

Enquiries:
Enquiries to: Managing Director
Direct tel: 01248 382748
Direct e-mail: emlyn@idb.wales.com

Founded:
1978

Organisation type and purpose:
Manufacturing industry, consultancy, research organisation.
Engineering company.
Strengthen links between industry and academia.

Subject coverage:
Design and manufacture of specialist electronic instrumentation: in particular, portable simultaneous translation systems, navigation and location by satellite, electrostatic monitors, instrumentation for nuclear and hydro-electric power generation industries.

Printed publications:
Catalogue

Publications list:
Available online and in print

Access to staff:
Appointment necessary.
Hours: Mon to Fri, 0900 to 1700

Access to building, collection or gallery:
Prior appointment required

Access for disabled people:
Parking provided, ramped entry, level entry, access to all public areas

Parent body:
University of Wales Bangor (UWB)

INDUSTRIAL INJURIES ADVISORY COUNCIL

Acronym or abbreviation: IIAC

6th Floor, The Adelphi, 1–11 John Adams Street, London, WC2N 6HT

Tel: 020 7712 2468
Fax: 020 7712 8491
E-mail: iiac@dwp.gsi.gov.uk

Website:
http://www.iiac.org.uk

Enquiries:
Enquiries to: Librarian
Other contacts: Secretary for formal questions or comment to the Council

Organisation type and purpose:
Advisory body.
IIAC is an independent body that advises the Secretary of State for Social Security on Industrial Injuries Disablement Benefit.

Subject coverage:
Industrial diseases.

Museum or gallery collection, archive, or library special collection:
No collection: library services provided by DSS Library Services

Publications list:
Available in print

INDUSTRIAL MARKETING RESEARCH ASSOCIATION

Acronym or abbreviation: IMRA

18 St Peters Steps, Brixham, Devon, TQ5 9TE

Tel: 01803 859575

Enquiries:
Enquiries to: Director General
Other contacts: Chairman

Founded:
1963

Organisation type and purpose:
Professional body (membership is by election or invitation).

Subject coverage:
Industrial market research, international marketing research.

Non-library collection catalogue:
All or part available in-house

Library catalogue:
All or part available in-house

Printed publications:
Journal of International Marketing and Marketing Research
Journal of International Selling and Sales Management
Manual of Industrial Market Research (1991)
Symposia Papers (13 titles)

Access to staff:
Contact by letter. Non-members charged.
Hours: Mon to Fri, 0900 to 1700

Access to building, collection or gallery:
No access other than to staff

Member of:
European Council for Industrial Marketing (CEMI)
Industrial Marketing Council (in the UK)
International Marketing Federation

INDUSTRIAL RELATIONS RESEARCH UNIT

Acronym or abbreviation: IRRU

Warwick Business School, University of Warwick, Coventry, CV4 7AL

Tel: 024 7652 4268
Fax: 024 7652 4184
E-mail: val.jephcott@wbs.ac.uk

Website:
http://www2.warwick.ac.uk/fac/soc/wbs/research/irru
Publications and research interests.

Enquiries:
Enquiries to: Director
Direct tel: 024 7652 4272

Founded:
1970

Organisation type and purpose:
University department or institute, research organisation.

Subject coverage:
Industrial relations.

Printed publications:
Warwick Papers in Industrial Relations (IRRU)
Warwick Studies in Industrial Relations (pub Blackwell)

Publications list:
Available online

Access to staff:
Contact by letter, by telephone, by fax, by e-mail and via website
Hours: Mon to Fri, 0900 to 1700

INDUSTRIAL ROPE ACCESS TRADE ASSOCIATION

Acronym or abbreviation: IRATA

Evelyn Woods Road, Aldershot, Hampshire, GU11 2LL

Tel: 01252 357839
Fax: 01252 357831
E-mail: info@irata.org

Website:
http://www.irata.org

Enquiries:
Enquiries to: Administrator
Direct e-mail: wendy@irata.org

Organisation type and purpose:
Trade association, present number of members: 38.
Equipment suppliers, trainers and operators involved in rope access for industrial purposes.

Subject coverage:
Equipment suppliers, trainers and operators involved in rope access for industrial purposes.

Printed publications:
Directory of IRATA Members Companies
Colour brochure on rope access
General Requirements for certification of personnel engaged in industrial rope access methods (rev 1998, £40 inc. p&p)
Guidelines on the use of rope access methods
Information sheet on LOLER
Report on Safety Record

Publications list:
Available in print

Access to staff:
Contact by letter, by e-mail and via website
Hours: Mon to Fri, 0900 to 1700

INFERTILITY NETWORK UK

Formal name: Infertility Network UK
Acronym or abbreviation: INUK

114 Lichfield Street, Walsall, West Midlands, WS1 1SZ

Tel: 08701 188088
Fax: 01424 731858

Website:
http://www.issue.co.uk
Information about ISSUE and infertility.
http://www.moretolife.co.uk
Issue initiative.

Enquiries:
Enquiries to: Chief Executive
Other contacts: Chair

Founded:
1976

Organisation type and purpose:
National organisation, membership association (membership is by subscription), present number of members: 3000, voluntary organisation, registered charity (charity number 1099960). Support group.
To help people through the infertility maze with information, counselling and support at regional and national levels.

Subject coverage:
Infertility, treatment, adoption and fostering, alternatives to childlessness, coping and living with childlessness.

Printed publications:
Factsheets
Information pack (free)
Magazine (quarterly)

Electronic and video publications:
Videos (rental or purchase)

Publications list:
Available online and in print

Access to staff:
Contact by letter, by telephone, by fax, by e-mail and via website
Hours: Mon to Fri, 0830 to 1700

Access for disabled people:
Yes

Member of the:
International Federation of Infertility Patient Associations

INFLUENCE DESIGN ASSOCIATES LTD

Influence House, 10 Moorfield Grove, Heaton Moor, Stockport, Cheshire SK4 4BQ

Tel: 0870 228 2272
Fax: 0870 228 2202
E-mail: indulge@influencedesign.com

Website:
http://www.influencedesign.com

Enquiries:
Enquiries to: Administrator
Direct e-mail: info@influencedesign.com
Other contacts: Personal Assistant

Founded:
1992

Organisation type and purpose:
Membership association (membership is by qualification), service industry, consultancy.
Design to print and production.

Library catalogue:
All or part available online

Access to staff:
Contact by letter, by fax and by e-mail
Hours: Mon to Fri, 0900 to 1700

INFONORTICS LIMITED

15 Market Place, Tetbury, Gloucestershire, GL8 8DD

Tel: 01666 505772
Fax: 01666 505774
E-mail: contact-1@infonortics.eu

Website:
http://www.infonortics.eu

Enquiries:
Enquiries to: Managing Director

Founded:
1988

Organisation type and purpose:
Conference organiser.

Subject coverage:
Information, documentation, chemical information, competitive intelligence, information technology, search engines.

Publications list:
Available online

Access to staff:
Contact by letter, by telephone, by fax, by e-mail and via website
Hours: Mon to Fri, 0900 to 1700

Access to building, collection or gallery:
No access other than to staff

INFORMATION COMMISSIONER'S OFFICE

Acronym or abbreviation: ICO

Wycliffe House, Water Lane, Wilmslow, Cheshire, SK9 5AF

Tel: 01625 545745
Fax: 01625 524510
E-mail: mail@ico.gsi.gov.uk

Website:
http://www.ico.gov.uk
The UK's independent public body set up to promote access to official information and protect personal information by promoting good practice, ruling on eligible complaints, providing information to individuals and organisations, and taking appropriate action when the law is broken.

continued overleaf

Enquiries:
Enquiries to: Marketing & Communications Officer

Founded:
1984

Organisation type and purpose:
Statutory body; non-departmental government organisation.
To enforce the Data Protection Act and the Freedom of Information Act.

Subject coverage:
Data Protection Act 1984 and its implications and application. The Freedom of Information Act 2000.

Printed publications:
All publications are free of charge
Be Open . . . Data Protection
CCTV Code of Protection
Freedom of Information – Summary
Media Briefing on the New Law
No Credit? Data Protection
Notification Exemptions and Handbook
The Data Protection Act 1998 An Introduction
(available in large print)
Using the Law to Protect Your Information (leaflet)

Electronic and video publications:
Barry's Bad Data Day (video)
Protecting the Plumstones (CD-ROM, educational)
No Credit? Data Protection (tape)
Audit Guide (CD-ROM)

Publications list:
Available online and in print

Access to staff:
Contact by letter, by telephone, by fax, by e-mail, in person and via website
Hours: Mon to Fri, 0900 to 1700

INFORMATION DIRECT

Central Library, Chamberlain Square, Birmingham, B3 3HQ

Tel: 0121 303 3333
Fax: 0121 303 1354
E-mail: information.direct@birmingham.gov.uk

Website:
http://www.birmingham.gov.uk/informationdirect
Guide to services offered by the Unit.

Enquiries:
Enquiries to: Information Officer

Founded:
1989

Organisation type and purpose:
Local government body.
Rapid response, fee-based, business research and enquiry service.

Subject coverage:
Business information, company information, market intelligence, mailing lists, company formations.

Access to staff:
Contact by letter, by telephone, by fax and by e-mail. Appointment necessary. All charged.
Hours: Mon to Fri, 0900 to 1700

Parent body:
Birmingham Library Service

INFORMATION FOR SCHOOL AND COLLEGE GOVERNORS

Acronym or abbreviation: ISCG

Avondale Park School, Sirdar Road, London, W11 4EE

Tel: 020 7229 0200
Fax: 020 7229 0651
E-mail: iscg@governors.fsnet.co.uk

Enquiries:
Enquiries to: Secretary

Founded:
1991

Organisation type and purpose:
Advisory body, research organisation.
An independent research and information service for governors.

Subject coverage:
Current concerns and needs of school and college governors.

Printed publications:
ISCG Manual for Governing Bodies and their Clerks (£10)
Helping Children to Learn (£2.50)
Investing in Ethos (£2.50)
Planning for Improvement (£5)
Parent Pack (£5)
Clerking Matters (new, free with sae)
Admissions Appeals Pack (free)
Exclusion Appeals Pack (free)
ISCG Checklists including: Governors' Visits to Schools
TGA occasional papers including:
Assessment, Recording and Reporting in Schools 1995
Inspection: A Weapon or a Tool
Reviewing the National Curriculum
ISCG Education Leaflets

Publications list:
Available in print

Access to staff:
Contact by letter, by telephone, by fax, by e-mail and via website. Appointment necessary.
Hours: Mon to Fri, 1100 to 1600
Special comments: Answerphone when office closed.

Access to building, collection or gallery:
No access other than to staff

INFORMATION ON TRANQUILLISERS AND ANTIDEPRESSANTS

Acronym or abbreviation: CITA

Cavendish House, Brighton Road, Waterloo, Merseyside, L22 5NG

Tel: 0151 474 9626
Fax: 0151 284 8324

Website:
http://www.citawithdrawal.org.uk
Information about CITA and its work together with information on tranquillisers and their effects. Details of CITA's publications.

Enquiries:
Enquiries to: Administrator

Founded:
1987

Formerly called:
Council for Involuntary Tranquilliser Addiction

Organisation type and purpose:
National organisation, advisory body, voluntary organisation, registered charity (charity number 519334), training organisation.
To provide support, counselling and GP clinics for those withdrawing from involuntary tranquilliser addiction.

Subject coverage:
Sufferers as a result of taking tranquillisers, sleeping pills or anti-depressants, benzodiazepine and tranquilliser withdrawal, anxiety management.

Printed publications:
Information Pack: includes Back to Life book, letter of protocol for GP, further information about CITA (£7.50 inc. p&p)
Information Pack: includes Back to Life book, the cassette tapes, letter of protocol for GP, some further information (£20 inc. p&p)
Alive and Kicking: personal story of addiction to tranquillisers and sleeping pills (£5.50 inc. p&p)
Back to Life: information on tranquilliser addiction and withdrawal (£4.95 inc. p&p)

Electronic and video publications:
Cassettes (£7.50 each inc p&p)

Publications list:
Available in print

Access to staff:
Contact by letter, by telephone and by fax
Hours: Mon to Fri, 1000 to 1300

INFORMATION WORLD REVIEW

Acronym or abbreviation: IWR

Incisive Media Limited, Haymarket House, 28–29 Haymarket, London, SW1Y 4RX

Website:
http://www.iwr.co.uk/
Fully searchable information and articles published by Information World Review.

Enquiries:
Enquiries to: Editor
Direct tel: 020 7316 9245
Direct e-mail: peter.williams@incisivemedia.com

Founded:
1977

Organisation type and purpose:
Business Publisher

Subject coverage:
Online information retrieval; optical publishing and storage; artificial intelligence software and tools.

Publications list:
Available in print

Access to staff:
Contact by letter, by telephone, by fax and by e-mail
Hours: Mon to Fri, 0930 to 1730

Owned by:
VNU Publishing

INFOTERRA LTD

Atlas House, 41 Wembley Road, Leicester, LE3 1UT

Tel: 0116 273 2300
Fax: 0116 273 2400
E-mail: info@infoterra-global.com

Website:
http://www.infoterra.co.uk
http://www.geostore.com
Online aerial photography and height data

Organisation type and purpose:
Geo-information products and services

Subject coverage:
Provider of geographic information products and services, including airborne and satellite data acquisition, geo-information creation, database management and outsourced hosting. Provides geospatial knowledge to companies world-wide.

Museum or gallery collection, archive, or library special collection:
Landsat and Spot satellites UK archive, a complete UK collection of photographic proof available with an image browse facility
IRS and IKONOS data
Remote Sensing Society Library

Printed publications:
Infoterra Group Brochure
Solutions for Defence and Security
Solutions for Subsidence Risk Management
Geospatial Services for Risk Management
Support for Risk Assessment
GeoStore
Solutions for Network Planning
Land Administration Services
Oil, Gas and Mineral Exploration
Global Seeps
Satellite Imagery data – Nigeria
Solutions for Flood Risk Management
Detailed Mapping of the Environment – Rapid Surveyor
Geospatial Services for Civil Engineering

Publications list:
Available online and in print

Access to staff:
Contact by telephone and by e-mail. Appointment necessary. All charged.
Hours: Mon to Fri, 0900 to 1700

Also at:
Infoterra France SAS
31 rue des Cosmonautes, 31402 Toulouse, cedex 4, France; tel: +33 562 19 55 70; fax: +33 562 19 97 81; e-mail: info@infoterra-global.com; website: http://www.infoterra-global.com
Infoterra GmbH
tel: +49 7545 8 9969; fax: +49 7545 8 5650; e-mail: info@infoterra-global.com; website: http://www .infoterra-global.com
Infoterra Hungary Kft
Soroksari ut 48, 7ep, 11.em, 1095 Budapest. Hungary; tel: +361 468 3638; fax: +361 468 3640; e-mail: info@infoterra-global.com; website: http://www.infoterra.co.uk
Infoterra Ltd
Europa House, The Crescent, Southwood, Farnborough. Hampshire. GU14 0NL; tel: 01252 362000; fax: 01252 375016; e-mail: info@infoterra -global.com; website: http://www.infoterra.co.uk

Parent body:
Astrium Limited
Anchorage Road, Portsmouth, Hampshire, PO3 5PU; website: http://www.astrium.eads.net

INLAND REVENUE LIBRARY AND INFORMATION SERVICE

1 Parliament Street, London, SW1A 2BQ

Enquiries:
Enquiries to: Librarian

Organisation type and purpose:
National government body.
Government library.

Subject coverage:
Taxation (UK), Hansard, Public General Acts.

Access to staff:
Contact by letter. Appointment necessary.

INLAND WATERWAYS ASSOCIATION

Acronym or abbreviation: IWA

PO Box 114, Rickmansworth, Hertfordshire, WD3 1ZY

Tel: 01923 711114
Fax: 01923 897000
E-mail: iwa@waterways.org.uk

Website:
http://www.waterways.org.uk/index.htm

Enquiries:
Enquiries to: Chief Executive
Direct tel: 01923 711114

Founded:
1946

Organisation type and purpose:
Membership association (membership is by subscription), present number of members: 18,000, registered charity (charity number 212342). Campaigning for the retention, restoration, conservation and development of the inland waterways for the fullest possible commercial and recreational use.

Subject coverage:
Restoration, retention and development of inland waterways in the British Isles, commercial and recreational use.

Museum or gallery collection, archive, or library special collection:
IWA John Hoap Archive, at Boat Museum, Ellesmere Port

Printed publications:
Annual Report

Wide variety of books on life afloat, decoration, waterway history and waterway travels including:
Guides, maps
Landscape with Figures (L T C Rolt)
Narrow Boat (L T C Rolt, the classic of canal books, first published 1944)
Waterways (4 times a year, free to members)

Electronic and video publications:
Various videos – specific and general
Canal Planner (Route Planning, CD-ROM for Windows 95 or 98)

Publications list:
Available in print

Access to staff:
Contact by letter and by fax
Hours: Mon to Fri, 0830 to 1630

Affiliated to:
Inland Waterways Enterprises Ltd
IWA (Sales) Ltd
Waterway Recovery Group Ltd

INMARSAT

99 City Road, London, EC1Y 1AX

Tel: 020 7728 1777
Fax: 020 7728 1142
E-mail: customer_care@inmarsat.com

Website:
http://www.inmarsat.com/
About Inmarsat, products and services, about satcoms, contacts.

Enquiries:
Enquiries to: Information Officer

Founded:
1979

Organisation type and purpose:
Mobile satellite communications operator.

Subject coverage:
Satellite communications and related areas, mobile communications (land, sea, air), engineering; electronics, international communications etc.

Non-library collection catalogue:
All or part available in-house

Publications list:
Available online

Access to staff:
Contact by letter and via website. Appointment necessary. Letter of introduction required.
Hours: Mon to Fri, 0900 to 1700

Access to building, collection or gallery:
Prior appointment required

Access for disabled people:
Level entry, toilet facilities

INNER TEMPLE LIBRARY

Formal name: Inner Temple Library

Inner Temple, London, EC4Y 7DA

Tel: 020 7797 8217
Fax: 020 7583 6030
E-mail: library@innertemple.org.uk

Website:
http://www.innertemplelibrary.org.uk

Enquiries:
Enquiries to: Librarian and Keeper of Manuscripts
Direct e-mail: mclay@innertemple.org.uk

Organisation type and purpose:
Legal library

Information services:
General Guides Database Guides

Museum or gallery collection, archive, or library special collection:
70,000 vols on law of the United Kingdom and Commonwealth

Petyt Manuscripts (386 volumes)
Barrington Manuscripts (57 vols)
Inner Temple Records (39 vols)
Mitford Collection of Legal Manuscripts (79 vols)
Miscellaneous Manuscripts (211 vols)
Inner Temple Archives (16th century to present)

Library catalogue:
All or part available online and in-house

Electronic and video publications:
Online databases, CD-ROMs

Access to staff:
Contact by letter, by telephone, by fax and by e-mail. Appointment necessary. Access for members only. Non-members charged.
Hours: Legal terms: Mon to Thu, 0900 to 0800; Fri, 0900 to 0700; Every fourth Sat in rotation with the other Inns of Court libraries, 1000 to 1700

Access to building, collection or gallery:
Open to all members of the Inner Temple and to barrister members of the other Inns of Court, not open to the general public (researcher by application to the Librarian).

INNERPEFFRAY LIBRARY

Innerpeffray by Crieff, Perthshire, PH7 3RF

Tel: 01764 652819
E-mail: info@@innerpeffraylibrary.co.uk

Website:
http://www.innerpeffraylibrary.co.uk

Enquiries:
Enquiries to: Librarian

Founded:
1680

Organisation type and purpose:
Registered charity (charity number SCO 13843), museum, research organisation.
Reference library, library museum, first lending library in Scotland.

Subject coverage:
Wide range of pre 1800 printed books, strong theological and religious content, natural history, history, agriculture, gardening, travel etc.

Museum or gallery collection, archive, or library special collection:
Accounts of Library etc
Borrowing Records from 1747 to 1968
3000 books published 1502 AD to 1800 AD
1400 volumes post 1801 AD
David Drummond Collection, 3rd Lord Maderty d.1692
Robert Hay-Drummond Collection, Archbishop of York d.1781
Visitor Books

Library catalogue:
All or part available online and in-house

Access to staff:
Contact by letter, by telephone, by e-mail, in person and via website. All charged.
Hours: Wed to Sat, 1000 to 1645; Sun, 1400 to 1600

INNOVATION NORWAY

Charles House, 5–11 Lower Regent Street, London, SW1Y 4LR

Tel: 0207 389 8800
Fax: 020 7839 6014
E-mail: london@innovationnorway.no

Website:
http://www.visitnorway.co.uk

Enquiries:
Enquiries to: Consultant
Direct e-mail: marta.dixon@innovationnorway.no

Organisation type and purpose:
National organisation.
Government foundation.

continued overleaf

Subject coverage:
Tourism in Norway; hotel accommodation, camp sites and youth hostels; timetables and local or regional area brochures; conference facilities; tour operators; ferry companies and airlines. Information is sent out on request.

Museum or gallery collection, archive, or library special collection:
Library of photographs and videos (strictly for use in travel promotion)

Access to staff:
Contact by letter, by telephone, by fax, by e-mail and via website
Hours: Mon to Fri, 0900 to 1630
Special comments: Open to trade only – not public.

Parent body:
Innovation Norway
PO Box 448, Sentrum, NO-0104, Oslo, Norway; tel: + 47 22 00 25 00; fax: + 47 22 00 25 01; e-mail: oslo@innovationnorway.no

INSITUTE FOR SPORT, PARKS AND LEISURE

Acronym or abbreviation: ISPAL

Abbey House, 1650 Arlington Business Park, Theale, Reading

Tel: 0844 418 0077
Fax: 0118 929 8001
E-mail: infocentre@ispal.org.uk

Website:
http://www.ispal.org.uk

Enquiries:
Enquiries to: Research and Resources Manager

Founded:
1983

Created by the merger of:
Institute of Leisure and Amenity Management (ILAM) and NASD (year of change 2006)

Organisation type and purpose:
Professional body.
Professional institute for sport, parks and leisure managers and aspiring managers.
To improve management in sport, parks and leisure industry and to enhance the quality of experience of those undertaking activities within these sectors.

Subject coverage:
Leisure management, sport, recreation, arts, tourism, play, countryside, parks and open spaces, local government.

Non-library collection catalogue:
All or part available online, in-house and in print

Library catalogue:
All or part available online, in-house and in print

Printed publications:
Fact sheets
Policy Position Statements
Bibliographies
Reading Lists
Current Articles Bulletin
Leisure Abstracts and Documentation Service
Order printed publications from: Research and Resources Manager

Publications list:
Available online and in print

Access to staff:
Contact by letter, by telephone, by fax, by e-mail, in person and via website. Appointment necessary. Access for members only. Non-members charged.
Hours: Mon to Fri, 0900 to 1700

Access for disabled people:
Parking provided, level entry, toilet facilities
Special comments: Please notify beforehand.

INSOLVENCY PRACTITIONERS ASSOCIATION

Acronym or abbreviation: IPA

52–54 Gracechurch Street, London, EC3V 0EH

Tel: 020 7623 5108
Fax: 020 7623 5127
E-mail: secretariat@insolvency-practitioners.org.uk

Website:
http://www.ipa.uk.com

Enquiries:
Enquiries to: Secretary

Founded:
1961

Organisation type and purpose:
Professional body.
Association of 'full-time' insolvency practitioners (Recognised Professional Body under the Insolvency Act 1986).

Subject coverage:
Insolvency.

Printed publications:
Examination Syllabus and Course Documentation
Index of Members (annually)

Access to staff:
Contact by letter
Hours: Mon to Fri, 0900 to 1700

Affiliated to:
Insol International
SPI

INSPEC

Michael Faraday House, Six Hills Way, Stevenage, Hertfordshire, SG1 2AY

Tel: 01438 313311
Fax: 01438 767339
E-mail: inspec@theiet.org

Website:
http://www.theiet.org/publications

Enquiries:
Enquiries to: Managing Director

Organisation type and purpose:
Learned society, professional body (membership is by qualification), publishing house.
Publishing, information and abstracting service; department of The Institution of Engineering and Technology.

Subject coverage:
Physics, electrical engineering, electronics, control engineering, computing, information technology and manufacturing, mechanical and production engineering.

Printed publications:
Computer and Control Abstracts (monthly)
Current Papers in Physics (twice monthly)
Electrical and Electronic Abstracts (monthly)
Key Abstracts (22 titles, monthly)
Physics Abstracts (twice monthly)
Inspec Current Awareness Services

Electronic and video publications:
INSPEC Ondisc
INSPEC Online
INSPEC Site Licences
INSPEC Data Services

Access to staff:
Contact by letter, by telephone, by fax, by e-mail and via website
Hours: Mon to Fri, 0900 to 1700

Parent body:
Institution of Engineering and Technology

INSTITUT FRANÇAIS – LA MEDIATHÈQUE

Formal name: Institut Français du Royaume Uni
Acronym or abbreviation: IFRU

17 Queensberry Place, London, SW7 2DT

Tel: 020 7073 1350
Fax: 020 7073 1363
E-mail: library@ambafrance.org.uk

Website:
http://www.institut-francais.org.uk

Enquiries:
Enquiries to: Librarian
Direct tel: 020 7073 1354
Direct e-mail: library@ambafrance.org.uk

Founded:
1910

Organisation type and purpose:
National government body (membership is by subscription), present number of members: 3500, public library.
French cultural centre.

Subject coverage:
France: humanities, mainly literature, history, geography, travel guides, but also civilisation, history, philosophy, religion, social sciences; art, bibliography and linguistics (books mostly in French; a few in English).

Museum or gallery collection, archive, or library special collection:
60,000 items (books, audio books, videos, DVDs, tapes)
French magazines and newspapers
Free French Periodicals & Special Collection about 'France Libre' and the French Resistance
Denis Saurat's archives

Non-library collection catalogue:
All or part available online and in-house

Library catalogue:
All or part available online and in-house

Printed publications:
Programme of Activities of the Institut Français du Royaume-Uni
Selected bibliographies

Electronic and video publications:
Video and Tape recordings of lectures given at the Institut (for consultation only)

Publications list:
Available in print

Access to staff:
Contact by letter, by fax, by e-mail and in person. Appointment necessary.
Hours: Tue to Fri, 1200 to 1900; Sat, 1200 to 1800
Children's Section: Tue to Sat, 1400 to 1800
Special comments: Closed 1 week at Christmas and all of August.

Access to building, collection or gallery:
No prior appointment required
Hours: 1200 to 1900

Access for disabled people:
Access available for disabled
Hours: 1200 to 1900

Other addresses:
Institut Français
Language Centre, 14 Cromwell Place, London, SW7 2JR; tel: 020 7581 2701; fax: 020 7581 0061; e-mail: language-center@ambafrance.org.uk; website: http://www.institut-francais.org.uk
Institut Français
Children's Library, 29 Harrington Road, London S.W.7; tel: 020 7073 1350; fax: 020 7073 1363; e-mail: library@ambafrance.org.uk; website: http://www.institut-francais.org.uk

INSTITUTE FOR ADVANCED STUDIES IN THE HUMANITIES

University of Edinburgh, Hope Park Square, Edinburgh, EH8 9NW

Tel: 0131 650 4671
Fax: 0131 668 2252
E-mail: iash@ed.ac.uk

Website:
http://www.iash.ed.ac.uk/
Information about the Institute, its projects and fellowships.

Enquiries:
Enquiries to: Director

Founded:
1970

Organisation type and purpose:
University department or institute.
Department of the University of Edinburgh.
To promote scholarship in the Humanities and to further inter-disciplinary enquiries, by means of research fellowships, seminars, lectures and cultural events.

Subject coverage:
All fields of the humanities very widely defined i.e. all departments of arts faculties, social sciences, theology, music and law.

Museum or gallery collection, archive, or library special collection:
Small private library available only to elected fellows of the Institute or by arrangement

Non-library collection catalogue:
All or part available online

Library catalogue:
All or part available in-house

Printed publications:
Institute Brochure
Occasional papers

Publications list:
Available in print

Access to staff:
Contact by letter, by telephone, by fax, by e-mail and via website
Hours: Mon to Fri, 0900 to 1700

Parent body:
University of Edinburgh

INSTITUTE FOR ANIMAL HEALTH – COMPTON LABORATORY

Acronym or abbreviation: IAH

Compton, Newbury, Berkshire, RG20 7NN

Tel: 01635 577256
Fax: 01635 577304
E-mail: compton.library@bbsrc.ac.uk

Website:
http://www.iah.ac.uk

Enquiries:
Enquiries to: IAH Libraries Manager

Organisation type and purpose:
Research organisation.

Subject coverage:
Diseases of economic importance in farm animals (exotic and endemic), immunology, molecular biology, veterinary science.

Museum or gallery collection, archive, or library special collection:
Specialist libraries on veterinary science

Library catalogue:
All or part available in-house

Access to staff:
Contact by letter, by telephone, by fax and by e-mail
Hours: Mon to Thu, 0900 to 1700; Fri, 0900 to 1630

Constituent part of:
Biotechnology and Biological Sciences Research Council

INSTITUTE FOR ANIMAL HEALTH – PIRBRIGHT LABORATORY

Ash Road, Pirbright, Woking, Surrey, GU24 0NF

Tel: 01483 232441

Fax: 01483 232448
E-mail: pirbright.ill@bbsrc.ac.uk

Website:
http://www.iah.bbsrc.ac.uk

Enquiries:
Enquiries to: Librarian
Direct tel: 01483 231030

Founded:
1925

Organisation type and purpose:
Research organisation.
Houses the World Reference Laboratory for Foot and Mouth Disease.
Research into infectious diseases of farm animals.

Subject coverage:
Animal virology, particularly foot and mouth disease and other viruses exotic to the United Kingdom

Museum or gallery collection, archive, or library special collection:
Collection of reprints on foot and mouth disease and other viruses
Database of 100,000 virological references

Library catalogue:
All or part available in-house

Printed publications:
Annual Report with other laboratories of the IAH

Access to staff:
Contact by letter and by e-mail. Appointment necessary.
Hours: Mon to Fri, 0800 to 1430

Parent body:
Biotechnology and Biological Sciences Research Council (BBSRC)

INSTITUTE FOR ARTS IN THERAPY AND EDUCATION

Acronym or abbreviation: IATE

2–18 Britannia Row, Islington, London, N1 8PA

Tel: 020 7704 2534
Fax: 020 7704 0171
E-mail: info@artspsychotherapy.org

Website:
http://www.artspsychotherapy.org

Enquiries:
Enquiries to: Manager
Other contacts: Administrator

Founded:
1992

Organisation type and purpose:
Training organisation.

Subject coverage:
Integrative arts psychotherapy training.

Printed publications:
Current prospective

Access to staff:
Contact by letter, by telephone, by e-mail and via website. Appointment necessary.
Hours: Mon to Fri, 0900 to 1730

Access for disabled people:
Ramped entry, toilet facilities

Full member of the:
United Kingdom Council for Psychotherapy

INSTITUTE FOR COMPLEMENTARY MEDICINE

Acronym or abbreviation: ICM

PO Box 194, London, SE16 7QZ

Tel: 020 7237 5165
Fax: 020 7237 5175
E-mail: icm@icmedicine.co.uk

Website:
http://www.icmedicine.co.uk

Enquiries:
Enquiries to: Information Officer
Other contacts: Research Director

Founded:
1982

Organisation type and purpose:
Advisory body, learned society (membership is by qualification), voluntary organisation, registered charity (charity number 326258).
To provide information on complementary medicine. To support research into complementary medicine. To develop professional standards of practice.

Subject coverage:
Complementary medicine, practitioner training and qualification, membership of the register, contacts within the field and comments on the state and range of the subject, low technology methods of health care, traditional remedies and health care methods.

Museum or gallery collection, archive, or library special collection:
A modest library

Non-library collection catalogue:
All or part available in-house

Library catalogue:
All or part available in-house

Printed publications:
Lists of schools and teaching colleges in complementary medicine
Update for practitioners

Access to staff:
Contact by letter, by telephone and by e-mail
Hours: Mon to Fri, 0930 to 1600
Special comments: Free information to public and media, fees required from commercial interests.

Access to building, collection or gallery:
Prior appointment required

Parent body:
Healing Research Trust
tel: As for ICM

INSTITUTE FOR EMPLOYMENT STUDIES

Acronym or abbreviation: IES

Mantell Building, Falmer, Brighton, East Sussex, BN1 9RF

Tel: 01273 686751
Fax: 01273 690430
E-mail: askies@employment-studies.co.uk

Website:
http://www.employment-studies.co.uk/pubs

Enquiries:
Enquiries to: Communications Manager
Direct e-mail: andy.davidson@employment-studies .co.uk

Founded:
1969

Formerly called:
Institute of Manpower Studies (year of change 1995)

Organisation type and purpose:
Research organisation.

Subject coverage:
Human resources, labour markets, public employment policy, training and skills analysis, careers, equality and diversity in employment, health and well-being at work.

Printed publications:
Annual Report
IES Reports (more than 100 titles representing the mainstream of Institute thinking and experience)
HR Insight (2 times a year)
Employment Studies (2 times a year)
Joint publishing with commercial and other publishers

continued overleaf

Order printed publications from: via http://
www.employment-studies.co.uk/pubs

Publications list:
Available online

Access to staff:
Contact by letter, by telephone, by fax, by e-mail
and via website
Hours: Mon to Fri, 0900 to 1700

Access to building, collection or gallery:
No access other than to staff

INSTITUTE FOR EUROPEAN ENVIRONMENTAL POLICY

Acronym or abbreviation: IEEP

Dean Bradley House, 52 Horseferry Road, London,
SW1P 2AG

Tel: 020 7799 2244
Fax: 020 7799 2600
E-mail: central@ieeplondon.org.uk

Website:
http://www.ieep.org.uk

Enquiries:
Enquiries to: Information Officer
Direct e-mail: cmonkhouse@ieeplondon.org.uk

Organisation type and purpose:
Voluntary organisation, registered charity (charity
number 802956), consultancy, research
organisation.
Independent body with offices in Bonn, Paris,
London, Brussels and Madrid.

Subject coverage:
EU environmental policy including, environment,
agriculture, water, air pollution, waste, chemicals,
natural resources, fisheries, transport, rural
development and strategic/horizontal issues.

Printed publications:
Manual of Environmental Policy: the EC and
Britain (Haigh N, updated 2 times a year,
available through Elsevier Science)
Various publications, see IEEP website

Publications list:
Available in print

Access to staff:
Contact by letter, by fax, by e-mail and via
website
Hours: Mon to Fri, 0900 to 1700

Brussels Office:
IEEP
18 Avenue des Gaulois, Brussels, B-1040; tel: + 32
2 732 4234/4004

INSTITUTE FOR FISCAL STUDIES

Acronym or abbreviation: IFS

7 Ridgmount Street, London, WC1E 7AE

Tel: 020 7291 4800
Fax: 020 7323 4780
E-mail: mailbox@ifs.org.uk

Website:
http://www.ifs.org.uk

Enquiries:
Enquiries to: External Relations Manager
Direct tel: 020 7291 4850

Founded:
1969

Organisation type and purpose:
Independent, non-profit making economic
research organisation.
To encourage debate and disseminate independent
information about all aspects of taxation and
government microeconomic policy. Promotes
effective economic and social policies by
understanding better their impact on individuals,
families, businesses and government finances.

Membership association (membership is by
subscription), present number of members: 1,150,
registered charity (charity number 258815).

Subject coverage:
Research in the fiscal regime, taxation (but not
individual tax matters), public economic policy,
government expenditure, local and European
activities and international development
economics.

Printed publications:
An extensive selection of publications on the
following topics: corporate behaviour, finance
and tax, econometrics, environment, Europe,
income distribution, indirect taxation and
consumer behaviour, labour supply and wage
determination, local government, pensions and
savings, personal taxation and benefits, tax law
and administration
Conference proceedings
Fiscal Studies (journal, quarterly)
Research papers
Non-technical reports
Briefing notes
Order printed publications from: mailbox@ifs.org.uk

Electronic and video publications:
Fiscal Studies (journal, articles, available free after
three years, current articles available to
subscribing academic institutions or pay-per-
view via Ingenta Journals, www.ingenta.com)
Summaries of all research and short briefing notes
(free, online)
Working papers (free, online)
Virtual Economy: an interactive teaching
simulation about the economy for A-Level and
degree students

Publications list:
Available online

Access to staff:
Contact by letter, by telephone, by fax, by e-mail
and via website. Appointment necessary.
Hours: Mon to Fri, 0930 to 1730

Access to building, collection or gallery:
Prior appointment required

Access for disabled people:
Ramped entry, access to all public areas, toilet
facilities

INSTITUTE FOR JEWISH POLICY RESEARCH

Acronym or abbreviation: JPR

79 Wimpole Street, London, W1G 9RY

Tel: 020 7935 8266
Fax: 020 7935 3252
E-mail: jpr@jpr.org.uk

Website:
http://www.jpr.org.uk
Newsletters, press releases, summaries of research
papers and Antisemitism in the World Today.
http://www.axt.org.uk

Enquiries:
Enquiries to: Director

Founded:
1941

Organisation type and purpose:
Membership association (membership is by
subscription), present number of members: 500,
registered charity (charity number 252626),
consultancy, research organisation, publishing
house.

Subject coverage:
International Jewish affairs, anti-Semitism, race
relations, civic society, human rights, neo-Nazism,
Israel (domestic issues), the Middle East, migration
and refugees, Jewish culture, history of Jewish
communities, Jewish communities in Diaspora.

Printed publications:
Recent JPR Publications:

A Community of Communities (Report of the
Commission on Representation of the Interests of
the British Jewish community, March 2000)
A guide to Jewish television: prospects and
possibilities, findings of the JPR Working Party
(July 1999)
Combating Holocaust denial through law in the
United Kingdom (Report of the J P R Law Panel,
2000)
Cultural Politics and European Jewry (Waterman
S, Feb 1999)
Developing Jewish Museums in Europe (Clark D,
Feb 1999)
Ethnic and religious questions in the 2001 UK
Census of Population: policy recommendations
(Kosmin B, Mar 1999)
French edition: Enjeux culturels et judaisme
européen (Waterman S, Février 1999)
Governance in the Jewish voluntary sector (Harris
M and Rochester C, 2001)
Grant-making trusts in the Jewish sector
(Schlesinger E, 2000)
JPR News (newsletter, 3 times a year)
Jews of the 'New South Africa'; highlights of the
1998 national survey of South African Jews,
(Kosmin B A, Goldberg J, Shain M and Bruk S,
Sep 1999)
North American Conservative Jewish teenagers'
attachment to Israel (Keysar A and Kosmin B A,
July 1999)
Patterns of Prejudice (quarterly)
The financial resources of the UK Jewish voluntary
sector (Halfpenny P and Reid M, 2000)

Electronic and video publications:
Antisemitism and Xenophobia Today
(www.axt.org.uk)

Publications list:
Available online and in print

Access to staff:
Contact by letter, by fax, by e-mail and via
website
Hours: Mon to Thu, 0930 to 1730

Access to building, collection or gallery:
No access other than to staff

INSTITUTE FOR METROPOLITAN STUDIES

Acronym or abbreviation: IMS

The Bartlett School of The Built Environment, UCL,
Gower Street, London, WC1E 8BT

Tel: 020 7243 4205
Fax: 020 7727 5268

Enquiries:
Enquiries to: Chief Executive

Organisation type and purpose:
University department or institute, consultancy,
research organisation.

Subject coverage:
Metropolitan studies with particular focus on
London.

Printed publications:
A Fresh Start for London (£15, 1992)
London In Prospect (£25, 1991)
The London Factor (£95, 1994)

Access to staff:
Contact by fax. Appointment necessary.
Hours: Mon to Fri, 0900 to 1700

Access for disabled people:
Toilet facilities

Affiliated to:
University College London

INSTITUTE FOR MIDDLE EASTERN AND ISLAMIC STUDIES

Acronym or abbreviation: IMEIS

Al Qasimi Building, Elvet Hill Road, Durham,
DH1 3TU

Tel: 0191 334 5660
Fax: 0191 334 5661
E-mail: a.ehteshami@durham.ac.uk

Website:
http://www.dur.ac.uk/~dme0www
Brief introduction to the institute.

Enquiries:
Enquiries to: Director

Founded:
early 1900s

Organisation type and purpose:
University department or institute.
Teaching and research on the Middle East.

Subject coverage:
Extensive information and documentation on all matters related to the Middle East and North Africa, Islam, including Arabic, Persian and Turkish languages, politics, economy and social science of the contemporary Middle East.

Museum or gallery collection, archive, or library special collection:
Middle East Documentation Unit (University Library)
Sudan Archive

Trade and statistical information:
Most relevant Middle East economic statistics.

Printed publications:
Economic Research Papers
Over 60 publications including:
A Bibliography of Saudi Arabia (Stevens J H and King R, 1973, £10)
The Collapse and Reconstitution of Lebanon (Najem J, 1998, £10)
The Condominium Remembered: Proceedings of the Durham Sudan Historical Records Conference 1982
The Egyptian Theatre in the Nineteenth Century (1799–1882)
Urbanisation in the Arabian Peninsula

Publications list:
Available in print

Access to staff:
Contact by letter, by telephone, by fax and by e-mail
Hours: Mon to Fri, 0900 to 1700

Access to building, collection or gallery:
Prior appointment required

Access for disabled people:
Parking provided, level entry

INSTITUTE FOR NATIONALIST AFFAIRS

Acronym or abbreviation: INA

National House, PO Box 83, Tonbridge, Kent, TN9 1YN

Tel: 01732 851259
Fax: 01732 852376
E-mail: mikeeaster@dialstart.net

Enquiries:
Enquiries to: Secretary

Founded:
1987

Organisation type and purpose:
Research organisation.

Subject coverage:
Research into fundamental matters concerning the government of the United Kingdom from the Nationalist viewpoint.

Printed publications:
Institute for Nationalist Affairs (booklet)
Occasional publications

Access to staff:
Contact by letter, by telephone and by e-mail
Hours: Mon to Fri, 0900 to 1700

INSTITUTE FOR OPTIMUM NUTRITION

Acronym or abbreviation: ION

Avalon House, 72 Lower Mortlake Road, Richmond, Surrey, TW9 2JY

Tel: 020 8614 7800
Fax: 0870 979 1133
E-mail: reception@ion.ac.uk

Website:
http://www.ion.ac.uk
About Institute for Optimum Nutrition, services ION provides, contact details for ION staff and department nutrition information.

Founded:
1984

Organisation type and purpose:
Membership association, registered charity (charity number 1013084), research organisation. Independent educational charity.

Subject coverage:
Achieving optimum nutrition and reaching the highest level of health through nutrition.
To educate both the general public and health professionals about nutrition and nutritional therapy.

Museum or gallery collection, archive, or library special collection:
Information List available on request with sae
Library of books, journals and specific research papers, nutrition and medical related (alternative and complementary medicine related)

Printed publications:
Optimum Nutrition magazine (ONM) (4 times a year)
ON Magazine (back issues available, subject to availability)
ON Magazine Reprints on previous articles available
ION Factsheet Pack
ION Directory of Nutritional Therapists

Publications list:
Available in print

Access to staff:
Contact by letter, by telephone, by fax, by e-mail and in person. All charged.
Hours: Mon to Fri, 0900 to 1700

Access to building, collection or gallery:
Prior appointment required
Hours: Mon to Fri, 1000 to 1700
Special comments: Library access to ION members and ION students only.

INSTITUTE FOR OUTDOOR LEARNING

Acronym or abbreviation: IOL

Plumpton Old Hall, Plumpton, Penrith, Cumbria, CA11 9NP

Tel: 01768 885800
Fax: 01768 885801
E-mail: institute@outdoor-learning.org

Website:
http://www.outdoor-learning.org
Membership details; insurance details; publication details; The Source, outdoor providers list.

Enquiries:
Enquiries to: Administrator

Organisation type and purpose:
National organisation, membership association (membership is by subscription), present number of members: 1400, registered charity (charity number 1085697), publishing house.
Supports, develops and promotes the achievement of learning through purposeful and planned outdoor education.

Subject coverage:
Careers and qualifications in outdoor education, safety, insurance for outdoor education, outdoor training and development; school curriculum and outdoors, access and environment, urban adventure, equal opportunities and outdoors, insurance for outdoor education.

Museum or gallery collection, archive, or library special collection:
Small library of articles and books on all aspects of outdoor learning

Printed publications:
IOL Newsletter (quarterly)
Horizons (magazine, quarterly)
Outdoor Source Book (once every two years)
Journal of Adventure Education and Outdoor Learning (annually)
Guide to Careers in the Outdoors (2 times a year)

Publications list:
Available online and in print

Access to staff:
Contact by letter, by telephone, by fax, by e-mail, in person and via website. Non-members charged.
Hours: Mon to Fri, 0900 to 1600

Access for disabled people:
Parking provided, access to all public areas, toilet facilities

INSTITUTE FOR PUBLIC POLICY RESEARCH

Acronym or abbreviation: ippr

30–32 Southampton Street, London, WC2E 7RA

Tel: 020 7470 6100
Fax: 020 7470 6111
E-mail: info@ippr.org.uk

Website:
http://www.ippr.org.uk
General information on the institute, particular information on projects and research, a publication list.

Enquiries:
Enquiries to: Information Officer

Founded:
1989

Organisation type and purpose:
Registered charity (charity number 800065).

Subject coverage:
Health and social policy, education, economy, business and public private partnerships, public and democratic involvement, citizenship and governance, the digital society.

Printed publications:
Publications available to purchase through an agency
Order printed publications from: IPPR Orders, Central Books
99 Wallis Road, London, E9 5LN, tel: 0845 458 9911, fax: 0845 458 9912, e-mail: ippr@centralbooks.com

Publications list:
Available in print

INSTITUTE FOR SOCIAL AND ECONOMIC RESEARCH

Acronym or abbreviation: ISER

University of Essex, Wivenhoe Park, Colchester, Essex, CO4 3SQ

Tel: 01206 872957
Fax: 01206 873151
E-mail: iser@essex.ac.uk

Website:
http://www.iser.essex.ac.uk/
General
http://www.iser.essex.ac.uk/pubs/index.php
Publications

continued overleaf

Enquiries:
Enquiries to: Enquiries
Direct e-mail: katet@essex.ac.uk
Other contacts: (1) Research Resources Unit
Manager (2) Communications Manager for (1)
library (2) press.

Founded:
1989

Organisation type and purpose:
Research organisation.

Subject coverage:
Household organisation, labour market, income
and wealth, housing, health, socio-economic
values, British Household Panel User Study and
longitudinal studies methodology.

**Museum or gallery collection, archive, or library
special collection:**
The Research Resource Unit (RRU) houses a
collection of survey-related documents to
support the centre's research. The collection
largely consists of 'grey literature'. Outsiders can
use the collection by prior appointment only

Non-library collection catalogue:
All or part available online

Library catalogue:
All or part available online

Printed publications:
ISER Report Series (1 paper, £15 inc. postage UK)
Occasional Paper Series (12 papers cost varies
between £3.50 and £7.50 plus postage)
Technical Paper Series (15 papers, £3.50 each inc.
postage UK)
Working Paper Series (100+ papers, £3.50 each inc.
postage UK)

Electronic and video publications:
BHPS data available from ESRC Data Archive,
University of Essex in following specifications:
floppy disk, JANET, online data access service
MIMAS (tel: 01206 872001)

Publications list:
Available online and in print

Access to staff:
Contact by letter, by telephone, by fax and by e-
mail
Hours: Mon to Fri, 0930 to 1600
Special comments: Visitors by prior appointment to
Research Resources Unit.

Access to building, collection or gallery:
Prior appointment required

Access for disabled people:
Level entry, toilet facilities

Partly funded by:
Economic and Social Science Research Council
(ESRC)

INSTITUTE FOR THE MANAGEMENT OF INFORMATION SYSTEMS

Acronym or abbreviation: IMIS

5 Kingfisher House, New Mill Road, Orpington,
Kent, BR5 3QG

Tel: 0700 00 23456
Fax: 0700 00 23023
E-mail: central@imis.org.uk

Website:
http://www.imis.org.uk

Enquiries:
Enquiries to: Chief Executive

Organisation type and purpose:
Professional body (membership is by subscription,
qualification), registered charity (charity number
291495).
Examining body.

Subject coverage:
Management of information systems and
information technology for commerce, industry
and general business.

Printed publications:
IMIS Journal (6 times a year)

Access to staff:
Contact by letter, by telephone, by fax, by e-mail
and via website. Appointment necessary.
Hours: Mon to Fri, 0900 to 1700

Connections with:
IMIS Publications Limited
at the same address

INSTITUTE FOR THE STUDY OF THE AMERICAS

Acronym or abbreviation: ISA

University of London, School of Advanced Study,
31 Tavistock Square, London, WC1H 9HA

Tel: 020 7862 8870
Fax: 020 7862 8886
E-mail: americas@sas.ac.uk

Website:
http://www.sas.ac.uk/isa

Enquiries:
Enquiries to: Information Resources Manager
Direct tel: 020 7862 8501
Direct e-mail: latam.lib@sas.ac.uk
Other contacts: Latin American Bibliographer for
librarian's absence.

Founded:
1965

Organisation type and purpose:
University department or institute.

Subject coverage:
Latin America, predominantly humanities and
social sciences.

**Museum or gallery collection, archive, or library
special collection:**
Archive collection (news sources, political party
material)
Bibliography and reference
British Union Catalogue of Latin American
(BUCLA) (author card catalogue, to 1988 closed)
Current affairs and political party ephemera (1960-
)
Nissa Torrents video collection

Non-library collection catalogue:
All or part available online and in-house

Printed publications:
Annual Report
Latin American and Caribbean Studies in the
Humanities and Social Sciences in the
Universities of the United Kingdom (1997)
Guide to Latin American and Caribbean census
material: a bibliography and union list (1990)
Latin American and Carribean library resources in
London: a guide (7th ed., 1997)
Libraries and special collections on Latin America
and the Caribbean: a directory of European
resources (1988, pub Athlone Press)
List of Booksellers dealing in Latin Americana and
Caribbeana (2nd ed., 1987)

Publications list:
Available in print

Access to staff:
Contact by letter, by telephone, by fax, by e-mail,
in person and via website. Letter of introduction
required.
Hours: Mon to Fri, 0930 to 1730
Special comments: Letter of introduction required
for undergraduate students.

Houses the editorial office of the:
Journal of Latin American Studies

Member Institute of:
University of London's School of Advanced Study

Member of:
Advisory Council on Latin American and Iberian
Information Resources (ACLAIIR)

Red Europea de Información y Documentación
sobre América Latina (REDIAL)
Seminar on the Acquisition of Latin American
Library Materials (SALALM)

INSTITUTE FOR TRANSPORT STUDIES

Acronym or abbreviation: ITS

University of Leeds, 38–40 University Road, Leeds,
West Yorkshire, LS2 9JT

Tel: 0113 233 5325
Fax: 0113 233 5334
E-mail: m.r.wardman@its.leeds.ac.uk

Website:
http://www.its.leeds.ac.uk

Enquiries:
Enquiries to: Director
Other contacts: Director of Research; Director of
Studies

Founded:
1966

Organisation type and purpose:
University department or institute, consultancy,
research organisation.

Subject coverage:
Public transport and freight economics; road safety
and accident analysis; environmental economics
and evaluation; information technology; surveys
and data capture; transport policy and appraisal;
land use and transport issues; transport demand
management; travel demand forecasting; traffic
management and control; transport network
modelling; transport operations; microsimulation
of traffic behaviour; traffic pollution monitoring
and modelling.

Printed publications:
Annual Report in Traffic Engineering and Control
(March)
Technical Note Series (lists of)
Working Paper Series (lists of)
Order printed publications from: Publications
Secretary, Institute for Transport Studies
at the same address, e-mail: akruk@its.leeds.ac.uk

Access to staff:
Contact by e-mail and via website
Hours: Mon to Fri, 0900 to 1700

Access for disabled people:
Parking provided, ramped entry, toilet facilities

Links with:
Transport Statistics Users' Group (TSUG)
Universities Transport Study Group (UTSG)

Parent body:
University of Leeds

INSTITUTE OF ACOUSTICS

Acronym or abbreviation: IOA

77A St Peter's Street, St Albans, Hertfordshire, AL1
3BN

Tel: 01727 848195
Fax: 01727 850553
E-mail: ioa@ioa.org.uk

Website:
http://www.ioa.org.uk

Enquiries:
Enquiries to: Chief Executive

Founded:
1974

Organisation type and purpose:
International organisation, learned society,
professional body (membership is by qualification,
election or invitation), present number of
members: 2600, registered charity (charity number
267026), publishing house.

Subject coverage:
Acoustics, noise, vibration, ultrasonics.

Library catalogue:
All or part available in-house and in print

Printed publications:
Acoustics Bulletin
Buyers' Guide
Members Register
Proceedings of the Institute

Publications list:
Available online and in print

Access to staff:
Contact by letter, by telephone, by fax, by e-mail, in person and via website. Appointment necessary.
Hours: Mon to Fri, 0900 to 1700

Links with:
European Acoustics Association (EAA)
International Institute of Noise Control
Engineering (I/INCE)

INSTITUTE OF ACTUARIES

Napier House, 4 Worcester Street, Oxford, OX1 2AW

Tel: 01865 268200
Fax: 01865 268211
E-mail: libraries@actuaries.org.uk

Website:
http://www.actuaries.org.uk

Enquiries:
Enquiries to: Librarian
Direct tel: 01865 268208

Founded:
1848

Organisation type and purpose:
Professional body (membership is by qualification), present number of members: 16,850.

Subject coverage:
Actuarial science, life assurance, general insurance, pensions, employee benefits, friendly societies, social security, investment, demography, mortality, probability, risk theory, histories of insurance and life assurance companies.

Museum or gallery collection, archive, or library special collection:
Small photograph collection
Small rare book and manuscript collection

Trade and statistical information:
Demographic statistics, mortality statistics.

Non-library collection catalogue:
All or part available online and in-house

Library catalogue:
All or part available online

Printed publications:
British Actuarial Journal (five a year)
Annals of Actuarial Science
Papers on actuarial subjects
The Actuary (magazine, monthly)
Annals of Actuarial Science (twice a year)
Order printed publications from: Publications Officer

Microform publications:
Actuaries' Investment Index 1928–1962

Electronic and video publications:
List of Members (annually, online only)

Publications list:
Available online and in print

Access to staff:
Contact by letter, by telephone, by fax, by e-mail and via website. Appointment necessary.

Access to building, collection or gallery:
Hours: Mon to Fri, 0900 to 1700
Special comments: Special collections are housed at Staple Inn Hall, High Holborn, London, WC1V &QJ

Access for disabled people:
Level entry, toilet facilities

Also at:
Faculty of Actuaries
   Maclaurin House, 18 Dublin Street, Edinburgh, EH1 3PP; tel: 0131 240 1311; fax: 0131 240 1313; e-mail: faculty@actuaries.org.uk
Institute of Actuaries, Staple Inn
   Staple Inn Hall, High Holborn, London, WC1V 7QJ; tel: 020 7632 2111; e-mail: libraries@actuaries.org.uk

Member organisation of:
Groupe Consultatif des Associations d'Actuaires des Pays des Communautés Européennes

INSTITUTE OF ADMINISTRATIVE MANAGEMENT

Acronym or abbreviation: IAM

6 Graphite Square, Vauxhall Walk, London, SE11 5EE

Tel: 020 7091 2600
Fax: 020 7091 2619
E-mail: info@instam.org

Website:
http://www.instam.org

Founded:
1915

Organisation type and purpose:
Established in 1915, the Institute of Administrative Management is the only professional body for both practising and aspiring Administrative Managers. Students and Members are professionals who are responsible for the management of: systems, human resources, communication, information technology, facilities, training and development, finance. The IAM supports managers (and aspiring managers) at all levels, aiming to improve both personal and organisational performance through a systematic approach to professional development.

Subject coverage:
Administrative management, office supervision, business management.

Information services:
Publications relating to the management of business.

Education services:
A wide range of professional qualifications in business management.

Printed publications:
Manager – The British Journal of Administrative Management (monthly, on annual subscription)
Study manuals
Order printed publications from: info@instam.org

Publications list:
Available online

Access to staff:
Contact by letter, by telephone, by fax, by e-mail and via website. Appointment necessary.
Hours: Mon to Fri, 0900 to 1700

INSTITUTE OF ADVANCED LEGAL STUDIES LIBRARY

Acronym or abbreviation: IALS

17 Russell Square, London, WC1B 5DR

Tel: 020 7862 5800
Fax: 020 7862 5770
E-mail: ials@sas.ac.uk

Website:
http://ials.sas.ac.uk
Information about IALS as a whole and IALS Library; access to IALS online catalogue, structured links to electronic legal research resources.

Enquiries:
Enquiries to: Library Administrative Officer
Direct tel: 020 7862 5801

Founded:
1947

Organisation type and purpose:
University department or institute.
Postgraduate legal research, other than Oriental and Eastern European law

Subject coverage:
Commonwealth Law; US Law; Western European Law; Public International Law

Museum or gallery collection, archive, or library special collection:
Commonwealth Law; US Law; Western European Law; Public International Law

Non-library collection catalogue:
All or part available online and in-house

Library catalogue:
All or part available online

Printed publications:
IALS Library, list of serials (annually)

Access to staff:
Contact by letter, by telephone, by fax, by e-mail and via website
Hours: Mon to Fri, 0900 to 2000; Sat, 1000 to 1730
Special comments: Please apply to the library for admissions leaflet and subscription rates. There are restrictions, and charges for some users.

Access for disabled people:
Toilet facilities

Member organisation of:
School of Advanced Study of the University of London
   tel: 020 7862 8659; fax: 020 7862 8657; e-mail: school@sas.ac.uk

Parent body:
University of London
   tel: 020 7862 8000

INSTITUTE OF ADVANCED MOTORISTS LIMITED

Acronym or abbreviation: IAM

IAM House, 510 Chiswick High Road, London, W4 5RG

Tel: 020 8996 9600
Fax: 020 8996 9601

Website:
http://www.iam.org.uk

Enquiries:
Enquiries to: Chief Executive

Founded:
1956

Organisation type and purpose:
Membership association (membership is by qualification), present number of members: 110,000, registered charity (charity number 249002), training organisation.
To improve road safety by raising driving standards.

Subject coverage:
Driving standards, driving techniques.

Printed publications:
Motorcycle Roadcraft (£11.99)
Passing Your Advanced Driving Test (£7.99)
Passing Your Advanced Motorcycling Test (£7.99)
Roadcraft (£13.99)

Electronic and video publications:
Advanced Driver Training (CD-ROM single user £41, multi user £103.40)
Roadcraft: An Advanced Driving Course (video, £14.99)
Safer Driving (video, £13.60)
Road Runners plus Road Skills for Life (CD-ROM, £20)
The Advanced Driving Test, Your Licence to Drive (CD-ROM, £29.99)
The Theory Test (CD-ROM, £18)
Top Rider (video, £14.49)

continued overleaf

Publications list:
Available in print

Access to staff:
Contact by letter, by telephone and by fax
Hours: Mon to Fri, 0900 to 1700

Subsidiary bodies:
IAM Fleet Training Ltd
  at the same address; tel: 0845 3108311; fax: 020 8996 9701
IAM Group Services Ltd
  at the same address

INSTITUTE OF AGRICULTURAL MANAGEMENT

Acronym or abbreviation: IAgrM

Farm Management Unit, University of Reading, PO Box 236, Reading, Berkshire, RG6 6AT

Tel: 0118 931 6578
Fax: 0118 975 6467
E-mail: iagrm@rdg.ac.uk

Website:
http://www.rdg.ac.uk/iagrm/
Full description of the Institute's activities and services.

Enquiries:
Enquiries to: Director
Direct e-mail: D.J.Ansell@reading.ac.uk

Founded:
1966

Organisation type and purpose:
Learned society, professional body (membership is by subscription), present number of members: 850, registered charity.

Subject coverage:
Business management in agriculture and associated industries; management techniques; management applications in agriculture.

Trade and statistical information:
Courses are available in Management and Supervisory Studies in agriculture and associated subjects.

Printed publications:
Agricultural Management – Reference List of Current Publications (1994, members, £1; non-members £3)
Case Studies in Agricultural & Rural Land Management (2nd ed., 1997)
Courses available in Management and Supervisory Studies (in agriculture and associated subjects, 1997)
Farm management (quarterly, free to members, otherwise on subscription)
Farm managers in 1995 (price on application)
Food – Its Production, Marketing and Consumption (1992, members £10, non-members £11.95, overseas £14)
From FMA to CMA (1993, members £3, others in UK £5, overseas £7)
Institute News (Three times a year)
Leadership & the challenge of developing rural leaders (1998)
The Manager as Farmer – Wisdom from some I have known (1996)
The Manager's Environment (1990, members £5, others in UK £8, overseas £10)

Publications list:
Available online and in print

Access to staff:
Contact by letter, by telephone, by fax, by e-mail and via website. Appointment necessary.
Hours: Mon to Fri, 0900 to 1700
Special comments: The office is manned infrequently. Answerphone at other times.

Links with:
International Farm Management Association

INSTITUTE OF AGRICULTURAL SECRETARIES AND ADMINISTRATORS

Acronym or abbreviation: IAgSA

National Agricultural Centre, Stoneleigh, Kenilworth, Warwickshire, CV8 2LZ

Tel: 024 7669 6592
Fax: 024 7641 7937
E-mail: iagsa@iagsa.co.uk

Website:
http://www.iagsa.co.uk
General.

Enquiries:
Enquiries to: General Secretary

Founded:
1967

Organisation type and purpose:
Professional body (membership is by subscription), present number of members: 900.

Subject coverage:
Agricultural secretaryship and rural business administration.

Printed publications:
Newsletter (on sale)

Access to staff:
Contact by letter, by telephone, by fax, by e-mail and via website
Hours: Mon to Fri, 0900 to 1700

INSTITUTE OF ALCOHOL STUDIES

Acronym or abbreviation: IAS

Alliance House, 12 Caxton Street, London, SW1H 0QS

Tel: 020 7222 4001
Fax: 020 7799 2510
E-mail: librarian@ias.org.uk

Website:
http://www.ias.org.uk
Current figures and statistics, including fact sheets, news bulletins and links to other sites of interest.
http://www.ias.org.uk/press.htm
IAS press digest's news service

Enquiries:
Enquiries to: Librarian

Founded:
1982

Organisation type and purpose:
National organisation, registered charity, research organisation.
A specialised reference library, which collects information on alcohol-related issues from a wide variety of sources.
To increase the knowledge of alcohol and the social and health cosequences of its misuse.

Subject coverage:
Library on alcohol-related issues with bibliographic database. Alcohol consumption and associated problems; alcohol control policies; social science research and policy studies. Historical archive of temperance-related material.

Museum or gallery collection, archive, or library special collection:
Historical (temperance) material, books, periodicals etc
Modern materials, books, scientific journals etc

Trade and statistical information:
Data and reference material on alcohol consumption and harm principally in the UK.

Library catalogue:
All or part available in-house

Printed publications:
A Great and Growing Evil: The Medical Consequences of Alcohol Abuse (Royal College of Physicians)
A Lot of Bottle (Rutherford D)

Alcohol Policy and the Public Good (Edwards G)
Alcohol Policy and the Public Good – A Guide for Action (A summary)
Alcohol Problems in the Family
Alcohol and the Young (Royal College of Physicians and British Paediatric Association, 1995)
Counterbalancing the Drinks Industry – A Eurocare Report to the European Union on Alcohol Policy
Industrial Pack (Guidelines)
UK Alcohol Alert (journal, quarterly)
The Globe (journal, quarterly)
Order printed publications from: e-mail: sales@ias.org.uk

Publications list:
Available online and in print

Access to staff:
Contact by letter, by telephone, by fax, by e-mail and via website. Appointment necessary.
Hours: Mon to Fri, 0930 to 1600
Special comments: Charges made for photocopies.

Affiliated to:
Alliance House Foundation
  at the same address; tel: 020 7222 4001
Eurocare (Alliance of alcohol problems mainly in European Union)
  tel: 01480 466766

INSTITUTE OF AMATEUR CINEMATOGRAPHERS

Acronym or abbreviation: IAC

Global House, 1 Ashley Avenue, Epsom, Surrey, KT18 5NY

Tel: 01372 822812
E-mail: admin@theiac.org.uk

Website:
http://www.theiac.org.uk
General information

Enquiries:
Enquiries to: Administrator

Founded:
1932

Organisation type and purpose:
Membership association (membership is by subscription), present number of members: 2000, voluntary organisation, registered charity (charity number 260467).

Subject coverage:
Amateur cinematography.

Museum or gallery collection, archive, or library special collection:
Archive library of amateur films

Printed publications:
Film and Video Maker (6 times a year, for members)

Access to staff:
Contact by letter, by telephone and by e-mail. Appointment necessary.
Hours: Staffed part-time only

INSTITUTE OF ANIMAL TECHNOLOGY

Acronym or abbreviation: IAT

5 South Parade, Summertown, Oxford, OX2 7JL

E-mail: iat101@btconnect.com

Website:
http://www.iat.org.uk

Enquiries:
Enquiries to: IAT Administrator
Direct e-mail: iat101@btconnect.com

Founded:
1949

Organisation type and purpose:
Professional body (membership is by qualification), present number of members: more than 2,200, voluntary organisation.
Advancing and promoting excellence in the care and welfare of animals in science.

Subject coverage:
Laboratory animal technology; animal welfare; animal husbandry; advances in new technology; transgenic technology; seminars and symposiums.

Information services:
Animal technology careers advice and opportunities

Education services:
Education and qualifications advice

Printed publications:
Animal Technology (journal, 3 times a year, for sale to non-members)
Bulletin (monthly, members only)
Membership Pack (members only)
Introduction to Animal Technology (reference handbook)
Manual of Animal Technology (reference handbook)
Career as an Animal Technologist (free guide)
Gaining Momentum (IAT brochure free)

Electronic and video publications:
With Care (a series of teaching videos)

Access to staff:
Contact by letter, by e-mail and via website
Hours: Normal working hours

INSTITUTE OF ARCHITECTURAL IRONMONGERS

Acronym or abbreviation: IAI

8 Stepney Green, London, E1 3JU

Tel: 020 7790 3431
Fax: 020 7790 8517
E-mail: info@gai.org.uk

Website:
http://www.iai.uk.com
General information.

Enquiries:
Enquiries to: General Secretary

Founded:
1970

Organisation type and purpose:
Professional body (membership is by qualification).
Parent body, the Guild of Architectural Ironmongers.

Subject coverage:
Architectural ironmongery.

Access to staff:
Contact by letter, by telephone, by fax, by e-mail and via website
Hours: Mon to Fri, 0900 to 1700

INSTITUTE OF ART AND LAW

Acronym or abbreviation: IAL

1–5 Cank Street, Leicester, LE1 5GX

Tel: 0116 253 8888
Fax: 0116 251 1666
E-mail: info@ial.uk.com

Website:
http://www.ial.uk.com

Enquiries:
Enquiries to: Administrator

Founded:
1995

Organisation type and purpose:
International organisation (membership is by subscription).

Subject coverage:
Art, law.

Printed publications:
Museums and the Holocaust (Palmer N)
Commentary on the UNESCO Convention (O'Keefe P)
Commentary on the Unidroit Convention (Prott L)
Art and Taxation: A Guide (Simmonds J)
Cultural Heritage Statutes
Cultural Rights and Wrongs
Art Treasures and War (Kowalski W)
17 Seminar Papers including:
Transacting in Art: General Issues
Title and Time in Art and Antiquity Claims
Copyright: Is your Copying Right?
Recovery of Stolen Looted Works of Art
Art, Law and the Holocaust
Beyond Reasonable Doubt? Art Crime and the Criminal Law

Publications list:
Available online and in print

Access to staff:
Contact by e-mail
Hours: Mon to Fri, 0900 to 1700

Access to building, collection or gallery:
Prior appointment required

INSTITUTE OF ASPHALT TECHNOLOGY, THE

Acronym or abbreviation: IAT

IAT Head Office, Paper Mews Place, 290 High Street, Dorking, Surrey, RH4 1QT

Tel: 01306 742792
Fax: 01306 888902
E-mail: secretary@instofasphalt.org

Website:
http://www.instofasphalt.org

Enquiries:
Enquiries to: Secretary

Founded:
1966

Organisation type and purpose:
Learned society, professional body (membership is by subscription, election or invitation), present number of members: 1650.
Furtherance of excellence in asphalt technology.

Subject coverage:
Asphalt technology, bitumen, bituminous materials.

Museum or gallery collection, archive, or library special collection:
Past journals and Year Books

Non-library collection catalogue:
All or part available in print

Library catalogue:
All or part available in-house and in print

Printed publications:
Asphalt Technology (journal, 1966 to 1991)
Asphalt Yearbook (1992 to 2005)
IAT Newsletter (1994 to 2002)
Asphalt Professional (6 times a year)

Electronic and video publications:
Sampling Bituminous Materials (video)
Hot Rolled Asphalt Production, Laying and Compaction (video)

Access to staff:
Contact by letter, by telephone, by fax, by e-mail and via website
Hours: Mon to Fri, 0900 to 1700

Has:
11 regional branches thoughout the UK and an overseas branch,
contact Head Office for details

Professional affiliate member of:
The Engineering Council

INSTITUTE OF AUCTIONEERS AND APPRAISERS IN SCOTLAND

The Rural Centre – Westmains, Ingliston, Newbridge, Midlothian, EH28 8NZ

Tel: 0131 472 4067
Fax: 0131 472 4067
E-mail: iaas@auctioneersscotland.co.uk

Enquiries:
Enquiries to: Executive Secretary
Direct e-mail: iaas@auctioneersscotland.co.uk

Founded:
1926

Organisation type and purpose:
Professional body.

Subject coverage:
Auction of livestock and chattels; urban and rural valuation; urban and rural estate agency; animal welfare; marketing; agricultural arbitration.

Printed publications:
Individual Members catalogues of sales

Access to staff:
Access for members only.
Hours: Mon to Thu, 0900 to 1300

Links with:
European Association of Livestock Markets
Livestock Auctioneers Market Committee for England and Wales

INSTITUTE OF BARRISTERS' CLERKS

Acronym or abbreviation: IBC

289–293 High Holborn, London, WC1V 7HZ

Tel: 020 7831 7144
Fax: 020 7831 7144
E-mail: admin@barristersclerks.com

Website:
http://www.barristersclerks.com
Home page, general information.

Enquiries:
Enquiries to: Administrator

Founded:
1922

Organisation type and purpose:
Membership association (membership is by subscription), present number of members: 810.

Subject coverage:
Work conditions, employment, education.

Access to staff:
Contact by letter, by telephone and by e-mail.
Appointment necessary. Non-members charged.
Hours: Mon to Fri, 0900 to 1700

Access for disabled people:
Toilet facilities
Special comments: Wheelchair access by prior arangement, lift from basement.

INSTITUTE OF BIOLOGICAL, ENVIRONMENTAL AND RURAL SCIENCES

Acronym or abbreviation: IBERS

Aberystwyth University, Gogerddan, Aberystwyth, Ceredigion, SY23 3EB

Tel: 01970 823000
Fax: 01970 828357
E-mail: tns@aber.ac.uk

Website:
http://www.aber.ac.uk/en/ibers

Enquiries:
Enquiries to: Librarian
Direct tel: 01970 823051
Other contacts: Business Manager (for external liaison and research contract enquiries)

continued overleaf

Founded:
1919

Formerly called:
IGER – Institute of Grassland and Environmental Research (year of change 2008)

Organisation type and purpose:
University research and teaching institute

Subject coverage:
Grassland, agriculture, environment, cellular and molecular biology, genetic manipulation, plant development, environmental biology, plant physiology and biochemistry, pathology, nitrogen, fixation, plant genetics, forage and cereal breeding, ecology and environmental plant science including agricultural pollution, organic farming, ruminant nutrition and forage conservation, land use including low-input legume-based technology, alternative animals and crop systems.

Museum or gallery collection, archive, or library special collection:
Antiquarian agricultural and botanical collections of books
Flora (British county and overseas), Prof. Harper reprint collection
Gene bank collections of herbage and cereal seeds, and germplasm
Herbarium flora and fauna collection
Pre-1840 books on grassland and agriculture
Works of Sir George Stapledon 1882–1960

Non-library collection catalogue:
All or part available online and in-house

Library catalogue:
All or part available online and in-house

Printed publications:
IBERS Knowledge-based Innovations (annually)
Information leaflets
Technical Advisory Report (irregular, £3)
Order printed publications from: Stapledon Library, Institute of Biological, Environmental and Rural Sciences, Aberystwyth University, Gogerddan, Aberystwyth, Ceredigion, SY23 3EB, Wales; e-mail gogstaff@aber.ac.uk

Publications list:
Available online and in print

Access to staff:
Contact by letter, by telephone, by fax, by e-mail and via website
Hours: Mon to Fri, 0900 to 1700

INSTITUTE OF BIOLOGY

Acronym or abbreviation: IOB

9 Red Lion Court, London, EC4A 3EF

Tel: 020 7936 5900
Fax: 020 7936 5901
E-mail: info@iob.org

Website:
http://www.iob.org

Enquiries:
Enquiries to: Chief Executive

Founded:
1950

Organisation type and purpose:
Professional body.

Subject coverage:
Sources of biological information; training and employment of biologists.

Printed publications:
Biologist (6 times a year)
Journal of Biological Education (quarterly)

Publications list:
Available online and in print

Access to staff:
Contact by letter, by telephone, by fax and by e-mail
Hours: Mon to Fri, 0900 to 1700

INSTITUTE OF BIOMEDICAL SCIENCE

Acronym or abbreviation: IBMS

12 Coldbath Square, London, EC1R 5HL

Tel: 020 7713 0214
Fax: 020 7436 4946

Website:
http://www.ibms.org

Enquiries:
Enquiries to: Publications Officer
Direct e-mail: ingasmith@ibms.org

Founded:
1912

Organisation type and purpose:
Professional body, present number of members: 17,500, registered charity (charity number 261926). To promote and develop biomedical science and its practitioners and to establish and maintain professional standards.

Subject coverage:
Haematology, transfusion science, medical microbiology, virology, clinical chemistry, cellular pathology, immunology, pathology, all other biomedical science disciplines, laboratory administration and management, and laboratory safety.

Printed publications:
The Biomedical Scientist (monthly)
British Journal of Biomedical Science (4 times a year)

Publications list:
Available online and in print

Access to staff:
Contact by letter, by telephone, by fax, by e-mail and via website. Non-members charged.
Hours: Mon to Fri, 0900 to 1700

Access to building, collection or gallery:
No prior appointment required

INSTITUTE OF BIOSCIENCE AND TECHNOLOGY

Cranfield University, Silsoe, Bedfordshire, MK45 4DT

Tel: 01525 863000
Fax: 01525 863001

Website:
http://www.cranfield.ac.uk/ibst
Full details of the Institute of BioScience and Technology.

Enquiries:
Enquiries to: Commercial and Marketing Director
Direct tel: 01525 863168
Direct fax: 01525 863080
Direct e-mail: l.tigwell@cranfield.ac.uk

Founded:
1981

Organisation type and purpose:
University department or institute.
Specialises in contract research, consultancy and postgraduate training, including short courses.

Subject coverage:
Biotechnology, biosensors, environmental biotechnology, food and agricultural biotechnology, analysis of pollutants, medical diagnostics, molecular biology, education in biotechnology, food spoilage, environmental monitoring, oncology, in vitro toxicity testing, advanced imaging, clinical research in in vitro diagnostic assay technology, measurement science and instrumentation, computational intelligence, bioinformatics, process monitoring and integration, systems manufacture, computational chemistry, molecularly-imprinted polymers.

Printed publications:
Publicity brochure
Research papers in national and international journals

Reports

Electronic and video publications:
Reports

Publications list:
Available in print

Access to staff:
Contact by e-mail
Hours: Mon to Fri, 0900 to 1700

Access to building, collection or gallery:
Prior appointment required

INSTITUTE OF BREWING AND DISTILLING

Acronym or abbreviation: IBD

33 Clarges Street, London, W1J 7EE

Tel: 020 7499 8144
Fax: 020 7499 1156
E-mail: enquiries@ibd.org.uk

Website:
http://www.ibd.org.uk

Enquiries:
Enquiries to: Executive Director

Founded:
1886

Organisation type and purpose:
Learned society, present number of members: 4,000, registered charity (charity number 269830).

Subject coverage:
Brewing science

Museum or gallery collection, archive, or library special collection:
Historical Brewing Science Library (brewing, distilling, malting) now held at Oxford Brookes University.

Printed publications:
The Brewer and Distiller International (monthly)
Journal of the Institute of Brewing (quarterly)
IBD Brewing and Distilling Directory (annual)
Past exam papers
General Certificate in Brewing, General Certificate in Distilling, General Certificate in Packaging – Exam Syllabus and CD-ROM of Learning Material.
Diploma in Brewing Examination Syllabus
Diploma in Distilling Examination Syllabus
Diploma in Packaging Examination Syllabus
Master Brewer Examination Syllabus
Revision material for examinations

Electronic and video publications:
General Certificate in Brewing, General Certificate in Distilling, General Certificate in Packaging – Exam Syllabus and CD-ROM of Learning Material.
Diploma in Brewing Examination Syllabus
Diploma in Distilling Examination Syllabus

Publications list:
Available online and in print

Access to staff:
Contact by letter, by telephone, by fax and by e-mail. Appointment necessary.

Access to building, collection or gallery:
Prior appointment required
Hours: Mon to Fri, 0900 to 1700; closed bank holidays, Christmas and Easter

Links with:
American Society of Brewing Chemists
Brewing, Food and Beverage Industry Suppliers Association (BFBI)
Master Brewers of America Assocation (MBAA)

INSTITUTE OF BUDDHIST STUDIES

PO Box 443, Tring, Hertfordshire, HP23 6PX

Tel: 01442 890882
Fax: 01442 822805

Enquiries:
Enquiries to: Managing Director
Direct e-mail: ts1@soas.ac.uk

Founded:
1966

Organisation type and purpose:
Learned society (membership is by election or invitation), registered charity (charity number 314166).
Promotion of Buddhist Studies.

Subject coverage:
Buddhism in Asian countries.

Printed publications:
Asceticism in Buddhism and Brahminism (£18.50)
Indo-Tibetan Studies (£25)
Tales of an Old Lama (£14.50)
The Bodhisattvapitaka (40)
The Buddhist Heritage (£20)
The Cult of the Deity Vajrakila (£21)
The Rishukyo (£27)
The Vajrabhairava Tantras (£24)
The Buddhist Forum
Buddhica Britannica

Publications list:
Available in print

Access to staff:
Contact by letter, by telephone and by fax
Hours: Mon to Fri, 0900 to 1700
Special comments: No access to public.

Access to building, collection or gallery:
No access other than to staff

INSTITUTE OF BUILDERS' MERCHANTS, THE

Acronym or abbreviation: IOBM

c/o Touchwood, 2 Oak View Rise, Harlow Wood, Mansfield, Nottinghamshire, NG18 4UT

Tel: 01623 633 228
Fax: 01623 427 693
E-mail: admin@instbm.co.uk

Website:
http://www.instbm.co.uk

Founded:
1968

Organisation type and purpose:
Professional body.

Subject coverage:
Building supplies.

Access to staff:
Contact by letter, by telephone, by fax and by e-mail
Hours: Mon to Thu, 0900 to 1300

INSTITUTE OF BUSINESS ADMINISTRATION

Acronym or abbreviation: IBA

16 Park Crescent, Trentham, London, W1B 1AH

Tel: 020 7612 7028
Fax: 020 7612 7027
E-mail: enquiries@icsa.co.uk

Website:
Membership, qualifications, courses.

Enquiries:
Enquiries to: Executive Director
Direct tel: 020 7580 4741
Other contacts: Membership Administrator for members' records held in London.

Founded:
1946

Organisation type and purpose:
International organisation, professional body (membership is by qualification, election or invitation).

Subject coverage:
Distance learning in business skills and administration, including operations, facilities, bureau resource marketing, managing change, IT and records.

Printed publications:
IBA News (journal, quarterly, £10, UK)

Publications list:
Available in print

Access to staff:
Contact by letter, by telephone, by fax, by e-mail and via website. Appointment necessary.
Hours: Mon to Fri, 0900 to 1700

Affiliated to:
Institute of Chartered Secretaries & Administrators
16 Park Crescent, London, W1N 4AH; tel: 020 7612 4741; e-mail: enquiries@icsa.co.uk

Other addresses:
Institute of Business Administration
16 Park Crescent, London, W1B 1AH; tel: 020 7580 4741; fax: 020 7612 7012

INSTITUTE OF BUSINESS ADVISERS

Acronym or abbreviation: IBA

Response House, Queen Street North, Chesterfield, Derbyshire, S41 9AB

Tel: 01246 453322
Fax: 01246 453300
E-mail: info@iba.org.uk

Website:
http://www.iba.org.uk
Help for small businesses and business advisers, general information on IBA.

Enquiries:
Enquiries to: Chief Executive
Other contacts: Membership & Communications Manager for membership and small business enquiries.

Founded:
1989

Organisation type and purpose:
Professional body (membership is by qualification, election or invitation), present number of members: 2500.

Subject coverage:
Small and medium enterprises, how to start up and run a small business, business planning, marketing, accounting, exporting, trade credit, raising finance, and all other aspects of small business growth, including related support services, business advisers, business counsellors, business mentors, business trainers and supporting staff.

Printed publications:
Series of information sheets and forms (free to £5) including:
Brief History of the Institute
Code of Conduct – for Professional Business Counsellors and Advisers
Counselling for Enterprise
Training Courses – Accredited Courses and Providers

Publications list:
Available in print

Access to staff:
Contact by letter, by telephone, by e-mail and via website. Appointment necessary.
Hours: Mon to Fri, 0900 to 1700

Professional Development and Accounts Departments:
IBA
Response House, Queen Street North, Chesterfield, S41 9AB; tel: 01246 453322; fax: 01246 453300; e-mail: info@iba.org.uk

INSTITUTE OF BUSINESS ETHICS

Acronym or abbreviation: IBE

24 Greencoat Place, London, SW1P 1BE

Tel: 020 7798 6040
Fax: 020 7798 6044
E-mail: info@ibe.org.uk

Website:
http://www.ibe.org.uk

Enquiries:
Enquiries to: Director

Founded:
1986

Organisation type and purpose:
Membership association (membership is by subscription), registered charity (charity number 1084014), training organisation, consultancy, research organisation.
To research and disseminate best practice in business.

Subject coverage:
Codes of business ethics, business and the environment, management and health of employees, education and business. Ethical aspects of information technology, the teaching of business ethics, reputation risk management, supply chain.

Printed publications:
Applying Codes of Business Ethics
Benefiting Business and the Environment (£24)
Codes of Ethics and International Business (£20)
Company Philosophies and Codes of Business Ethics
Employees' Health and Organisational Practice (£15)
Management and the Health of Employees
Priorities, Practice and Ethics in Small Firms (£20)
Risky Business – Towards best practice in managing reputation risk (£25)
What's All This About Business Ethics?
Where Did That Come From? – A study of ethical issues in the supply chain (£20)

Publications list:
Available online and in print

Access to staff:
Contact by letter, by telephone, by fax, by e-mail and via website
Hours: Mon to Fri, 0930 to 1700

Access to building, collection or gallery:
No prior appointment required

Manages the:
Humane Business Partnership

Partners of the:
The Caux Round Table

INSTITUTE OF CANCER RESEARCH

Acronym or abbreviation: ICR

15 Cotswold Road, Sutton, Surrey, SM2 5NG

Tel: 020 8643 8901
Fax: 020 7352 6283

Enquiries:
Enquiries to: Librarian
Direct tel: 020 7352 5946
Direct e-mail: fullib@icr.ac.uk

Organisation type and purpose:
Research organisation.

Subject coverage:
Oncology, cancer.

Library catalogue:
All or part available in-house

Printed publications:
Annual Report (apply secretariat)

Access to staff:
Contact by letter, by telephone, by fax and by e-mail. Appointment necessary. Access for members only.
Hours: Reference only for non-ICR staff

continued overleaf

Access to building, collection or gallery:
Prior appointment required

Affiliated to:
University of London

INSTITUTE OF CAREER GUIDANCE

Acronym or abbreviation: ICG

27A Lower High Street, Stourbridge, West Midlands, DY8 1TA

Tel: 01384 376464
Fax: 01384 440830
E-mail: hq@icg-uk.org

Website:
http://www.icg-uk.org

Enquiries:
Enquiries to: Business Development Manager
Direct tel: 01384 445631
Other contacts: Marketing Department

Founded:
1922

Organisation type and purpose:
Advisory body, professional body (membership is by subscription), present number of members: 3500.
Building principles and practice of high quality careers guidance.

Subject coverage:
All aspects of career guidance ware, including connections, careers service, information, advice and guidance partnerships, HE and FE.

Museum or gallery collection, archive, or library special collection:
Archive material on the work of Careers Service

Printed publications:
Career Guidance Today (6 times a year)
PORTICO (Appointment vacancies, fortnightly)
Personal Adviser (magazine, 6 times a year)

Access to staff:
Contact by letter, by telephone, by fax, by e-mail and via website
Hours: Mon to Fri, 0900 to 1700

INSTITUTE OF CAST METALS ENGINEERS

Acronym or abbreviation: ICME

National Metalforming Centre, 47 Birmingham Road, West Bromwich, Birmingham, B70 6HA

Tel: 0121 601 6979
Fax: 0121 601 6981
E-mail: info@icme.org.uk

Website:
http://www.icme.org.uk

Enquiries:
Enquiries to: Operations Director

Founded:
1904

Organisation type and purpose:
Professional body.

Subject coverage:
Cast metals technology, education, training.

Museum or gallery collection, archive, or library special collection:
Library available, with limited information service

Trade and statistical information:
Summary of statistics.

Printed publications:
Technical books
The Foundryman (journal, monthly)
Order printed publications from: info@icme.org.uk

Publications list:
Available online and in print

Access to staff:
Contact by letter, by telephone, by fax, by e-mail and via website. Appointment necessary.
Hours: Mon to Thu, 0900 to 1700; Fri, 0900 to 1330

Access to building, collection or gallery:
Hours: Mon to Thu, 0900 to 1700; Fri, 0900 to 1330

Access for disabled people:
Fully accessible

Links with:
International Committee of Foundry Technical Associations

INSTITUTE OF CHARTERED ACCOUNTANTS IN ENGLAND AND WALES

Acronym or abbreviation: ICAEW

Chartered Accountants' Hall, PO Box 433, Moorgate Place, London, EC2P 2BJ

Tel: 020 7920 8620
Fax: 020 7920 8621
E-mail: library@icaew.com

Website:
http://www.icaew.com/library
http://www.icaew.com

Enquiries:
Enquiries to: Head of Library and Information Services

Founded:
1880

Organisation type and purpose:
National organisation, professional body.

Subject coverage:
Accountancy, auditing, company law, taxation, management consultancy, financial management, information technology in accounting.

Museum or gallery collection, archive, or library special collection:
Files of comments on exposure drafts of accounting and auditing standards
Rare Books on book-keeping, 1494–1914

Trade and statistical information:
Accountancy research, technical releases, press releases available on website at www.icaew.co.uk.

Non-library collection catalogue:
All or part available online

Library catalogue:
All or part available online

Printed publications:
Accountancy (monthly)
Technical Releases (irregular)
Directory of ICAEW Members (annual)
Members' Handbook
Foreign Books on Book-keeping, 1494–1750: a bibliography
Historical Accounting Literature (catalogue)

Electronic and video publications:
Accountancy magazine (monthly, online via www.accountancymagazine.com)

Publications list:
Available online

Access to staff:
Contact by letter, by telephone, by fax, by e-mail, in person and via website. Letter of introduction required. Non-members charged.
Hours: Mon to Thu, 0900 to 1730; Fri, 1000 to 1730 (Closed 3 weeks during August)
Special comments: Members of the public may have access by providing a letter of introduction from a member of the ICAEW or by paying a daily fee.

Member of:
Consultative Committee of Accountancy Bodies (CCAB)

INSTITUTE OF CHARTERED ACCOUNTANTS IN IRELAND

Acronym or abbreviation: ICAI

11 Donegal Square South, Belfast, BT1 5JE

Tel: 028 9032 1600
Fax: 028 9023 0071

Website:
http://www.icai.ie
Full library catalogue (OPAC) and indexed journals (CABIN).

Enquiries:
Enquiries to: Librarian

Organisation type and purpose:
Professional body (membership is by subscription, qualification).

Subject coverage:
Taxation, accountancy, auditing.

Library catalogue:
All or part available online

Access to staff:
Access for members only. Non-members charged.
Hours: Mon to Fri, 0900 to 1700

INSTITUTE OF CHARTERED ACCOUNTANTS OF SCOTLAND

Acronym or abbreviation: ICAS

CA House, 21 Haymarket Yards, Edinburgh, EH12 5BH

Tel: 0131 347 0100
Fax: 0131 347 0105
E-mail: infoservice@icas.org.uk

Website:
http://www.icas.org.uk

Enquiries:
Enquiries to: Information Service Manager
Direct tel: 0131 347 0135
Other contacts: Information Officer

Founded:
1854

Organisation type and purpose:
National organisation, professional body (membership is by subscription, qualification), present number of members: 17,200, training organisation.

Subject coverage:
Accountancy, finance, auditing, taxation, management, company law, company accounts, company information, statutes and law reports.

Museum or gallery collection, archive, or library special collection:
Antiquarian collection on accounting and related topics, 1494–1930, now on deposit in National Library of Scotland but maintained by ICAS
Stock exchange daily official list (SEDOL) 1986 to date (microfiche)

Non-library collection catalogue:
All or part available online

Library catalogue:
All or part available online

Printed publications:
CA Magazine (monthly)
Various books, monographs and research publications
Order printed publications from: From the ICAS Research Department or ICAS website
CA Magazine from ICAS or from the CA Magazine website

Publications list:
Available online and in print

Access to staff:
Contact by letter, by telephone, by fax, by e-mail, in person and via website
Hours: Mon to Fri, 0900 to 1700

Access to building, collection or gallery:
Hours: Mon to Fri, 0900 to 1700

Special comments: Limited car parking – please book a space in advance

Access for disabled people:
Parking provided, access to all public areas

INSTITUTE OF CHARTERED FORESTERS

Acronym or abbreviation: ICF

59 George Street, Edinburgh, EH2 2JG

Tel: 0131 240 1425
Fax: 0131 240 1424
E-mail: icf@charteredforesters.org

Website:
http://www.charteredforesters.org

Enquiries:
Enquiries to: Administrative Officer
Other contacts: Executive Director (for code of ethics queries)

Founded:
1926

Organisation type and purpose:
Professional body.

Subject coverage:
Amenity planting, arboriculture, tree surveys, farm forestry, timber valuations, forest landscaping, forest management, forest pathology, forest roads planning and construction, forest investment, taxation and economics, harvesting and marketing, integrated stock and site inventory, land use appraisals, environmental assessments, nature conservation, wood-based energy, negotiations on sale and purchase of land and woodlands, poplar cultivation, sawmilling, small woods, training and education, upland forestry, urban forestry.

Printed publications:
Chartered Forester magazine
Forestry: An International Journal of Forest Research
Order printed publications from:
icf@charteredforesters.org

Publications list:
Available online and in print

Access to staff:
Contact by letter, by telephone, by fax, by e-mail and via website
Hours: Mon to Fri, 0900 to 1700

INSTITUTE OF CHARTERED SECRETARIES AND ADMINISTRATORS

Acronym or abbreviation: ICSA

16 Park Crescent, London, W1B 1AH

Tel: 020 7580 4741
Fax: 020 7323 1132
E-mail: informationcentre@icsa.co.uk

Website:
http://www.icsa.org.uk

Enquiries:
Enquiries to: Information Centre Manager
Direct tel: 020 7612 7035
Direct fax: 020 7612 7034
Other contacts: Information Officer

Founded:
1891

Organisation type and purpose:
International organisation, professional body (membership is by qualification), present number of members: 44,000, suitable for ages: 20+, training organisation, consultancy, publishing house.

Subject coverage:
Corporate governance in all sectors, English company law and company secretarial practice, charity law.

Library catalogue:
All or part available in-house

Printed publications:
Chartered Secretary (formerly Administrator, monthly)

Publications list:
Available online

Access to staff:
Contact by letter, by telephone, by fax, by e-mail and via website. Appointment necessary.

Access to building, collection or gallery:
Prior appointment required
Hours: Mon to Fri, 0930 to 1700

INSTITUTE OF CHARTERED SHIPBROKERS

Acronym or abbreviation: ICS

85 Gracechurch Street, London, EC3V 0AA

Tel: 020 7623 1111
Fax: 020 7623 8008
E-mail: info@ics.org.uk

Website:
http://ics.org.uk/

Enquiries:
Enquiries to: Director General
Direct e-mail: membership@ics.org.uk

Organisation type and purpose:
International organisation, professional body.

Subject coverage:
Ship-broking.

Printed publications:
The Shipbroker (quarterly)

Access to staff:
Contact by letter, by telephone, by e-mail and in person
Hours: Mon to Fri, 0900 to 1700

Member of:
Federation of National Associations of Shipbrokers and Agents (FONASBA)
tel: 020 7628 5559; fax: 020 7588 7836; e-mail: fonasba@ics.org.uk

INSTITUTE OF CHIROPODISTS AND PODIATRISTS

27 Wright Street, Southport, Merseyside, PR9 0TL

Tel: 01704 546141
Fax: 01704 500477
E-mail: secretary@inst-chiropodist.org.uk

Website:
http://www.inst-chiropodist.org.uk

Enquiries:
Enquiries to: General Secretary

Founded:
1955

Organisation type and purpose:
Professional body.

Subject coverage:
Foot care; training in chiropody, podiatry.

Printed publications:
Career information (supplied for sae)
Chiropody Review (6 times a year, free to members, £25 a year to others)
Footcare leaflet (£10 per 100)

Access to staff:
Contact by e-mail and via website. Appointment necessary.
Hours: Mon to Fri, 0900 to 1700

INSTITUTE OF CIVIL DEFENCE AND DISASTER STUDIES

Acronym or abbreviation: ICDDS

2 Grosvenor Gardens, Muswell Hill, London, N10 3TE

Tel: 020 8883 3555

Website:
http://www.icds.org

Enquiries:
Enquiries to: Librarian

Founded:
1938

Organisation type and purpose:
Learned society (membership is by subscription), voluntary organisation, registered charity (charity number 266522).
Educational charity.

Subject coverage:
Civil defence, civil protection, emergency planning, disaster management.

Museum or gallery collection, archive, or library special collection:
Collection on civil defence and emergency planning from 1914 to present day

Printed publications:
Journal (quarterly)
Management Congress 1988
Proceedings of the Fourth International Disaster
Study reports

Electronic and video publications:
Video: Hurricane called Camille

Publications list:
Available in print

Access to staff:
Contact by letter
Hours: Mon to Fri, 0900 to 1700

Access to building, collection or gallery:
Prior appointment required

Member of:
International Civil Defence Organization
10–12 Chemin De Surville, 1213 Petit-Lancy, Geneva, Switzerland

INSTITUTE OF CLASSICAL STUDIES LIBRARY

Acronym or abbreviation: ICS

3rd Floor, Senate House, Malet Street, London, WC1E 7HU

Tel: 020 7862 8709
Fax: 020 7862 8735
E-mail: sue.willetts@sas.ac.uk

Website:
http://icls.sas.ac.uk/library/Home.htm

Enquiries:
Enquiries to: Librarian
Direct tel: 020 7862 8710
Direct fax: 020 7862 8724
Direct e-mail: colin.annis@sas.ac.uk

Founded:
1953

Organisation type and purpose:
University department or institute.
Institute of London University and member of the University of London Research Library Services (ULRS).

Subject coverage:
All aspects of classical civilisation, including archaeology, art and architecture, language and literature, history, law, politics, religion, philosophy and science of the Minoan, Mycenaean and Hellenic world, and the Byzantine Empire; also of the early Italic and Etruscan civilisations, and of the Roman Empire to 5th century AD, including Roman Britain.

Museum or gallery collection, archive, or library special collection:
Contains 105,000 monographs and pamphlets and 19,000 bound vols of periodicals
660 current periodicals taken
Slides collection (joint library) 6,800

Library catalogue:
All or part available online

continued overleaf

Printed publications:
Bulletin of the Institute of Classical Studies, plus
  Supplements
Order printed publications from: Publications
Department, Institute of Classical Studies, at the
same address; tel. 020 7862 8700; fax 020 7862 8722;
e-mail icls.publications@sas.ac.uk

Publications list:
Available online and in print

Access to staff:
Contact by letter, by telephone, by fax, by e-mail
and in person. Access for members only.
Hours: Mon to Fri, 0930 to 1800; Sat, 1000 to 1630;
term-time, Tue, Wed and Thu, 0930 to 2000

Links with:
Society for the Promotion of Hellenic Studies
  tel: 020 7862 8730; fax: 020 7862 8731; e-mail:
  office@hellenicsociety.org.uk; website: http://
  www.hellenicsociety.org.uk
Society for the Promotion of Roman Studies
  tel: 020 7862 8727; fax: 020 7862 8728; e-mail:
  office@romansociety.org; website: http://www
  .romansociety.org

INSTITUTE OF CLERKS OF WORKS

Acronym or abbreviation: ICW

Equinox, 28 Commerce Road, Lynchwood,
Peterborough, PE2 6LR

Tel: 01733 405160
Fax: 01733 405161
E-mail: info@icwgb.co.uk

Website:
http://www.icwgb.org

Enquiries:
Enquiries to: Company Secretary

Founded:
1882

Organisation type and purpose:
Professional body.

Subject coverage:
Comprehensive and technical knowledge of the
construction process of the built environment,
particularly independent inspection of work in
process in the construction industry.

**Museum or gallery collection, archive, or library
special collection:**
Journal of the Institute of Clerks of Works from
  1883 to the present day

Printed publications:
Clerk of Works and Site Inspector Handbook (£32
  members, £39.95 non-members)
Directory of Self-Employed, Freelance and Private
  Practice Clerks of Works (annually, free)
Site Recorder: Journal of the Institute (annually,
  £34)

Access to staff:
Contact by letter, by telephone, by fax, by e-mail
and in person
Hours: Mon to Fri, 0900 to 1700

Access to building, collection or gallery:
No access other than to staff

INSTITUTE OF CLINICAL RESEARCH

Acronym or abbreviation: ICR

Institute House, Boston Drive, Bourne End,
Buckinghamshire, SL8 5YS

Tel: 0845 5210056
Fax: 01628 530641
E-mail: resources@icr-global.org

Website:
http://www.icr-global.org

Educational courses, academic courses, seminars,
conferences, publications, library and resources,
journal CRfocus, mailing and advertising
opportunities, CPD, membership

Enquiries:
Enquiries to: Head of Information Services
Direct tel: 01628 536969
Direct e-mail: hkorjonen@icr-global.org
Other contacts: General Manager

Founded:
1978

Organisation type and purpose:
Professional body, training organisation,
conference organiser, publisher

Subject coverage:
Pharmaceutical industry and clinical research.

**Museum or gallery collection, archive, or library
special collection:**
Clinical research resources only.

Non-library collection catalogue:
All or part available online, in-house and in print

Library catalogue:
All or part available online

Printed publications:
Clinical Research Focus (journal, 11 times a year)
Series of monographs and smaller publications
  (c.32 publications)
Order printed publications from: http://www.icr-
global.org

Publications list:
Available online and in print

Access to staff:
Contact by letter, by telephone, by fax, by e-mail,
in person and via website. Appointment necessary.
Access for members only. Letter of introduction
required. Non-members charged.

Access to building, collection or gallery:
No prior appointment required for members
Hours: Mon to Fri, 0800 to 1700

INSTITUTE OF COMMERCIAL MANAGEMENT

Acronym or abbreviation: ICM

The Fusee, 20A Bargates, Christchurch, Dorset,
BH23 1QL

Tel: 01202 490555
Fax: 01202 409666
E-mail: info@icm.ac.uk

Website:
http://www.icm.ac.uk

Enquiries:
Enquiries to: Chief Executive

Founded:
1979

Organisation type and purpose:
A QCA/ofqual accredited UK Examining and
Awarding body. Operating in 120 countries,
providing advisory and capacity building services
to business schools and colleges; a professional
body (membership is by qualification); present
number of full and Student Members: 210,000;
registered charity (charity number 1045370),
suitable for ages: 19+, training organisation,
consultancy, research organisation, publishing
house.
Examining body.

Subject coverage:
Business and management education, tourism,
trade and professional development.

Information services:
Industry news, by sector, from 120 countries

Education services:
The design, development of business and
management programmes from HND to degree
levels and the examination and assessment of
candidates. The design of CPD programmes for the
corporate sector

Printed publications:
A range of business and management texts

Access to staff:
Contact by letter, by telephone, by fax, by e-mail,
in person and via website

Access to building, collection or gallery:
Hours: Mon to Fri, 0900 to 1730

Access for disabled people:
Fully accessible

Links with:
a range of UK and overseas universities for HE
progression purposes for student members

INSTITUTE OF COMMONWEALTH STUDIES LIBRARY

Acronym or abbreviation: ICS

University of London, 28 Russell Square, London,
WC1B 5DS

Tel: 020 7862 8844
Fax: 020 7862 8820
E-mail: icommlib@sas.ac.uk

Website:
http://catalogue.ulrls.lon.ac.uk
Library catalogue.
http://commonwealth.sas.ac.uk/library.htm
Library homepage.
http://archives.ulrls.lon.ac.uk
Archives catalogue

Enquiries:
Enquiries to: Information Resources Manager

Founded:
1949

Organisation type and purpose:
University library, university department or
institute, research organisation.

Subject coverage:
Class, Commonwealth, culture, economics,
environment, gender, health, history, human
rights, international relations, literature, migration,
Pacific, politics, race.
Antigua and Barbuda, Australia, The Bahamas,
Bangladesh, Barbados, Belize, Botswana, Brunei
Darussalam, Cameroon, Canada, Cyprus,
Dominica, Fiji Islands, The Gambia, Ghana,
Grenada, Guyana, India, Jamaica, Kenya, Kiribati,
Lesotho, Malawi, Malaysia, Maldives, Malta,
Mauritius, Mozambique, Namibia, Nauru, New
Zealand, Nigeria, Pakistan, Papua New Guinea,
Samoa, Seychelles, Sierra Leone, Singapore,
Solomon Islands, South Africa, Sri Lanka, St Kitts
and Nevis, St Lucia, St Vincent and The
Grenadines, Swaziland, Tanzania, Tonga, Trinidad
and Tobago, Tuvalu, Uganda, Vanuatu, Zambia,
Zimbabwe.

**Museum or gallery collection, archive, or library
special collection:**
Material on the contemporary history, economics,
politics and social aspects of all Commonwealth
countries. The collections (200,000 items) include
monographs, government publications, research
papers, statistical data, census and more than
9,000 periodicals and annual publications. Over
70% of the stock is published in Commonwealth
countries
Special Collections or strengths include:
Caribbean, West Indies, including the West India
  Committee Library and minute books
Australia, New Zealand, the Pacific area, Canada
India, Pakistan, Bangladesh, Sri Lanka
African member countries
National bibliographies
Collection of more than 10,000 documents issued
  by political parties, pressure groups and trade
  unions in Commonwealth member countries

A number of important archive collections,
including the papers of Ellis Ashmead-Bartlett,
Sir Ivor Jennings, Richard Jebb and the West
India Committee. Guides to archival materials
are available
International Defence and Aid Fund newscutting
microfiche archive South Africa, 1975–90 and
Namibia, 1975–90

Trade and statistical information:
Trade statistics, census statistics.

Non-library collection catalogue:
All or part available online

Library catalogue:
All or part available online

Printed publications:
Current periodicals list
Guides and publications (in both printed and
electronic format), including:
Theses in progress in Commonwealth studies

Publications list:
Available online and in print

Access to staff:
Contact by letter, by telephone, by fax, by e-mail,
in person and via website. Letter of introduction
required. Non-members charged.

Access to building, collection or gallery:
Hours: Term time: Mon to Fri, 0930 to 1830
Vacations: Mon to Fri, 0930 to 1730
Special comments: ID required. Membership open to
all academic and academically related university
staff and postgraduates. Undergraduates admitted
free of charge.

Member organisation of:
School of Advanced Study and University of
London Research Library Services
University of London

INSTITUTE OF CONCRETE TECHNOLOGY

Acronym or abbreviation: ICT

4 Meadows Business Park, Blackwater, Camberley,
GU17 9AB

Tel: 01276 378 31
Fax: 01276 378 31
E-mail: ict@ictech.org

Website:
http://www.ictech.org
Membership, news, history, structure, contacts,
sponsors, convention, events.

Enquiries:
Enquiries to: Executive Officer

Founded:
1972

Organisation type and purpose:
Professional body.

Subject coverage:
Concrete technology.

Museum or gallery collection, archive, or library special collection:
Institute's own Convention and meeting papers
ACT reports

Non-library collection catalogue:
All or part available online

Printed publications:
Yearbook (£50, contains convention papers)

Publications list:
Available online and in print

Access to staff:
Contact by letter, by telephone, by fax and by e-mail
Hours: Mon to Thurs, 0800 to 1400
Special comments: We do not offer a technical
advisory service.

INSTITUTE OF CONFLICT MANAGEMENT

Acronym or abbreviation: ICM

840 Melton Road, Thurmaston, Leicester, LE4 8BN

Tel: 0116 260 6961
Fax: 0116 264 0141
E-mail: icm@association.org.uk

Website:
http://www.conflictmanagement.org
General information

Enquiries:
Enquiries to: Executive Secretary

Founded:
1999

Organisation type and purpose:
National organisation, advisory body, membership
association, present number of members: 200+,
service industry, age range: higher, training
organisation, research organisation.
Regulatory body, membership is by qualification
and/or by experience.

Subject coverage:
Education and training in conflict management
and other physical and non-physical intervention
skills and techniques. Prints and publishes
journals, newspapers, periodicals, books and
leaflets to advance and inform on subjects
connected with the work, theory and practices
relating to conflict management, including
statistics, scientific investigation and similar
subjects. Has established a library and other
information bureau for the use of Members and
others on all related subjects.

Printed publications:
Newsletter (quarterly)

Electronic and video publications:
Managing Work Related to Violence (CD,
published by Employment NTO)

Access to staff:
Contact by letter, by telephone, by fax, by e-mail
and via website. Appointment necessary.
Hours: Mon to Fri, 0900 to 1700

Access for disabled people:
Level entry, access to all public areas

INSTITUTE OF CONTEMPORARY ARTS

Acronym or abbreviation: ICA

12 Carlton House Terrace, London, SW1Y 5AH

Tel: 020 7930 0493
Fax: 020 7873 0051
E-mail: info@ica.org.uk

Website:
http://www.ica.org.uk
Events, listings, archive, etc.

Enquiries:
Enquiries to: Administrative Assistant
Other contacts: Education Officer for tel no: 020
7766 1423.

Founded:
1947

Organisation type and purpose:
Membership association, registered charity
(charity number 236848), art gallery, suitable for
ages: 16+.
Arts Centre.

Subject coverage:
Contemporary cultural activities, including film,
theatre, dance and music; events and exhibitions.

Museum or gallery collection, archive, or library special collection:
Pre-1990 collection at the Tate

Electronic and video publications:
1500 audio recordings of lectures
Over 200 videos of art events

Publications list:
Available in print

Access to staff:
Contact by letter, by telephone, by fax, by e-mail
and via website. Appointment necessary. Non-
members charged.
Hours: Mon to Fri, 1200 to 1930

Access to building, collection or gallery:
No prior appointment required
Hours: Mon to Fri, 1200 to 1930

Subsidiary body:
ICA Projects Ltd

INSTITUTE OF CONTEMPORARY BRITISH HISTORY

Acronym or abbreviation: ICBH

Institute of Historical Research, Senate House,
Malet Street, London, WC1E 7HU

Tel: 020 7862 8810
Fax: 020 7862 8812
E-mail: icbh@icbh.ac.uk

Website:
http://ihr.sas.ac.uk/icbh
Publications lists, conference/seminar lists, Annual
Report.

Enquiries:
Enquiries to: Administrator
Other contacts: Editor for submission of articles/
papers.

Founded:
1986

Organisation type and purpose:
Membership association (membership is by
subscription), registered charity, university
department or institute, age range: higher, research
organisation, publishing house.

Subject coverage:
British history since 1945, oral history, information
about research and scholars in these fields both in
the UK and overseas, Conservative Party in the
20th century, Labour Party in the 20th century,
current affairs (political), political economy.

Museum or gallery collection, archive, or library special collection:
The Institute library is incorporated in the
Historical Research library in the same building.

Printed publications:
Edited volumes and monographs
Modern History Review (quarterly)
13 Witness Seminar transcriptions published in
hard copy and online, including:
Britain and Europe
Development of Concord
1967 Abortion Act
Rhodesian UDI

Publications list:
Available in print

Access to staff:
Contact by letter, by telephone, by fax, by e-mail
and via website. Appointment necessary.
Hours: Mon to Fri, 0930 to 1730

Affiliated to:
Institute of Historical Research
Senate House, Malet Street, London, WC2

INSTITUTE OF CONTEMPORARY MUSIC PERFORMANCE

Acronym or abbreviation: ICMP

Foundation House, 1A Dyne Road, London, NW6
7XG

Tel: 020 7328 0222
E-mail: enquiries@guitarinstitute.co.uk

Website:
www.icmp.uk.com
http://www.guitarinstitute.co.uk

continued overleaf

Enquiries:
Enquiries to: Deputy Director

Founded:
1985

Formerly called:
Guitar Institute & Basstech

Organisation type and purpose:
Membership association (membership is by subscription), suitable for ages: all, training organisation.
Music school, accredited Institute of Thames Valley University.

Subject coverage:
Music tuition and career advice for musicians.

Printed publications:
School Prospectus (free from school)

Access to staff:
Contact by letter, by telephone, by fax, by e-mail, in person and via website. Appointment necessary.
Hours: Mon to Fri, 0900 to 1900

Access to building, collection or gallery:
No prior appointment required

Parent body:
University of East London
  Docklands Campus, University Way, London.
  E16 2RD

INSTITUTE OF COST AND EXECUTIVE ACCOUNTANTS

Acronym or abbreviation: ICEA

Akhtar House, 2 Shepherds Bush Road, London, W6 7PJ

Tel: 020 8749 7126
Fax: 020 8749 7127
E-mail: icea@enta.net

Website:
http://www.icea.enta.net

Enquiries:
Enquiries to: Secretary General
Other contacts: Membership Secretary

Founded:
1958

Organisation type and purpose:
International organisation, professional body (membership is by qualification).
Producing tomorrow's accountant.

Subject coverage:
Accountancy, executive accountancy, financial decision making, management auditing, strategic management.

Non-library collection catalogue:
All or part available online and in-house

Library catalogue:
All or part available in-house

Printed publications:
Executive Accountant (quarterly)
Newsletter

Access to staff:
Contact by letter, by telephone, by fax and by e-mail
Hours: Mon to Fri, 1000 to 1600

Member of:
European Accounting Association and Council for Education in the Commonwealth

INSTITUTE OF COUNSELLING

Acronym or abbreviation: IoC

6 Dixon Street, Glasgow, G1 4AX

Tel: 0141 204 2230
Fax: 0141 221 2841
E-mail: iofcounsel@aol.com

Website:
http://www.collegeofcounselling.com
Online course prospectus.

Enquiries:
Enquiries to: General Manager

Founded:
1985

Organisation type and purpose:
Membership association (membership is by subscription, qualification), present number of members: 600, suitable for ages: adults, training organisation.

Subject coverage:
Counselling, counselling training and bereavement.

Printed publications:
The Living Document (twice a year, members)
Open learning material

Electronic and video publications:
6 training videos (£175 for 6 videos plus manual):
Counselling in Action
Counselling in Perspective
Counselling in Depth
Counselling in Focus
Counselling in Analysis
Counselling in Role Play
Essential Skills of Counselling (series of 8 cassettes £24.95)

Publications list:
Available in print

Access to staff:
Contact by letter, by telephone, by fax, by e-mail, in person and via website. Appointment necessary.
Non-members charged.
Hours: Mon to Fri, 0900 to 1700

Also at:
Institute of Counselling
  10 High Street, Bromsgrove, B61 8HQ; tel: 01527 577803; fax: 01527 577803; e-mail: instofcoun@aol.com

INSTITUTE OF CREDIT MANAGEMENT

Acronym or abbreviation: ICM

The Water Mill, Station Road, South Luffenham, Oakham, Rutland, LE15 8NB

Tel: 01780 722900
Fax: 01780 721333
E-mail: info@icm.org.uk

Website:
http://www.icm.org.uk

Enquiries:
Enquiries to: Director General

Founded:
1939

Organisation type and purpose:
Professional body (membership is by subscription, qualification, election or invitation), present number of members: 8500, registered charity, training organisation, consultancy, research organisation.

Subject coverage:
All aspects of credit management.

Printed publications:
Credit Management (journal, monthly)
Comprehensive Credit Management Text and Reference Book Service. Books available for sale to members and non-members
Order printed publications from:
bookshop@icm.org.uk

Publications list:
Available online

Access to staff:
Contact by letter, by telephone, by fax and by e-mail. Access for members only.
Hours: Mon to Fri, 0900 to 1700

Member organisation of:
Federation of European Credit Management Associations (FECMA)

INSTITUTE OF CUSTOMER CARE

Acronym or abbreviation: IOCC

St Johns House, Chapel Lane, Westcott, Dorking, Surrey, RH4 3PJ

Tel: 01306 876210
Fax: 01306 876249

Enquiries:
Enquiries to: Membership Secretary

Founded:
1987

Organisation type and purpose:
Advisory body, membership association (membership is by subscription), training organisation, consultancy.

Subject coverage:
Customer care, total quality management, market research, complaint management, customer charters, mystery shopping, accreditation, customer satisfaction indices, quality audits, staff surveys, networking, benchmarking, training, facilities management.

Access to staff:
Contact by letter and by telephone. Non-members charged.
Hours: Mon to Fri, 0900 to 1700

INSTITUTE OF DIRECT MARKETING

Acronym or abbreviation: IDM

1 Park Road, Teddington, Middlesex, TW11 0AB

Tel: 020 8614 0274
Fax: 020 8614 0246
E-mail: enquiries@theidm.com

Website:
http://www.theidm.com
Information on membership of the IDM, direct marketing courses, the IDM Certificate and Diploma in Direct Marketing and publications available for purchase via IDM Direct. Index of published information on direct marketing.

Enquiries:
Enquiries to: Information Services Manager
Direct tel: 020 8614 0253
Direct e-mail: knowledgecentre@theidm.com

Founded:
1987

Organisation type and purpose:
Professional body (membership is by qualification), present number of members: 5000, registered charity (charity number 1001865), training organisation.

Subject coverage:
Direct marketing.

Museum or gallery collection, archive, or library special collection:
Books, journals, press cuttings, reports

Non-library collection catalogue:
All or part available online and in-house

Library catalogue:
All or part available online and in-house

Printed publications:
A large selection of books is available and includes:
The Interactive and Direct Marketing Guide, IDM, 2002 (3 vols)
Journal of Direct, Data and Digital Marketing Practice (journal, quarterly, also online)

Electronic and video publications:
Absolute Essentials (video series, IDM)

Publications list:
Available online

Access to staff:
Contact by telephone, by fax, by e-mail and via

website. Appointment necessary. Non-members charged.
Hours: Mon, Tues, 0930 to 1330; Wed, Thur, 0900 to 1600; Fri, 0900 to 1500

INSTITUTE OF DIRECTORS

Acronym or abbreviation: IoD

116 Pall Mall, London, SW1Y 5ED

Tel: 020 7839 1233
Fax: 020 7321 0145

Website:
http://www.iod.com
Description of IoD's services plus some access to press releases and information briefings.

Enquiries:
Enquiries to: Head of Information and Advsory Services
Direct tel: 020 7451 3100
Direct e-mail: businessinfo@iod.com

Founded:
1903

Organisation type and purpose:
Professional body.

Subject coverage:
Company directors, company law, boardroom practice, business, corporate governance.

Museum or gallery collection, archive, or library special collection:
Company direction collection

Trade and statistical information:
Bi-monthly business opinion survey.

Library catalogue:
All or part available online

Printed publications:
Books, policy papers and topical surveys
Director's Guide Series (23 titles)
Director (monthly)
Director's Handbook
IOD News (monthly)
Order printed publications from: Book Sales, Institute of Directors
116 Pall Mall, London, SW1Y 5ED, tel: 020 7766 8866, fax: 020 7766 8833, e-mail: pubs@iod.com

Access to staff:
Contact via website. Appointment necessary.
Hours: Mon to Fri, 0830 to 1730

Access for disabled people:
Toilet facilities

INSTITUTE OF DOMESTIC HEATING AND ENVIRONMENTAL ENGINEERS

Acronym or abbreviation: IDHEE

Unit 35A, New Forest Enterprise Centre, Chapel Lane, Totton, Southampton, SO40 9LA

Tel: 023 8066 8900
Fax: 023 8066 0888
E-mail: admin@idhee.org.uk

Website:
http://www.idhee.org.uk

Enquiries:
Enquiries to: Chairman
Direct tel: 07973 214574
Direct fax: 023 8081 4756
Direct e-mail: bill.bucknell@idhee.org.uk

Founded:
1964

Organisation type and purpose:
National organisation, professional body (membership is by subscription, qualification), present number of members: 1,026.

Subject coverage:
Domestic heating and environmental engineering.

Publications list:
Available online

Access to staff:
Contact by telephone, by e-mail and via website. Non-members charged.
Hours: Mon to Fri, 0900 to 1700

INSTITUTE OF ECONOMIC AFFAIRS

Acronym or abbreviation: IEA

2 Lord North Street, London, SW1P 3LB

Tel: 020 7799 8900
Fax: 020 7799 2137
E-mail: iea@iea.org.uk

Website:
http://www.iea.org.uk

Enquiries:
Enquiries to: Director General

Founded:
1955

Organisation type and purpose:
Registered charity (charity number CC 235 351), research organisation, publishing house.

Subject coverage:
Political economy, public choice, microeconomics.

Printed publications:
Economic Affairs (4 times a year)
Hobart Papers
IEA Readings
Occasional Papers
Research Monographs

Electronic and video publications:
Videos

Publications list:
Available online and in print

Access to staff:
Contact by letter, by telephone, by fax, by e-mail and via website
Hours: Mon to Fri, 0900 to 1700

INSTITUTE OF ECOTECHNICS

Acronym or abbreviation: IE

24 Old Gloucester Street, Holborn, London, WC1N 3AL

Tel: 020 7405 1824
Fax: 020 7405 1851
E-mail: nelson@biospheres.com

Website:
http://www.ecotechnics.edu

Enquiries:
Enquiries to: Secretary

Founded:
1972

Organisation type and purpose:
International organisation, learned society, training organisation, consultancy, research organisation. Consultant to several businesses managing demonstration projects in varied biomes internationally: Tropic Ventures Puerto Rico; Savannah Systems Pty Limited, West Australia; RV Heraclitus; Les Marroniers Conference Centre and Provençal farm, Aix-en-Provence, France; Synergia Ranch, New Mexico, USA.

Subject coverage:
Ecological management, biospheric and closed systems.

Printed publications:
Books in association with Synergetic Press (see website)
Brochure

Access to staff:
Contact by letter, by fax and by e-mail. Appointment necessary.

Hours: Mon to Fri, 0900 to 1700

Access for disabled people:
Ramped entry

INSTITUTE OF EDUCATION

Information Services, 20 Bedford Way, London, WC1H 0AL

Tel: 020 7612 6080
Fax: 020 7612 6093
E-mail: lib.enquiries@ioe.ac.uk

Website:
http://www.ioe.ac.uk/is
Catalogues, archives and special collections.

Enquiries:
Enquiries to: Library Enquiries
Other contacts: Archivist (for access to archives and special collections)

Founded:
1902

Organisation type and purpose:
University department or institute, research organisation

Subject coverage:
All aspects of education.

Museum or gallery collection, archive, or library special collection:
Largest collection on education in the United Kingdom
Assorted deposited collections and archives

Non-library collection catalogue:
All or part available online, in-house and in print

Library catalogue:
All or part available online and in-house

Printed publications:
Education libraries bulletin (1958–88)
Catalogue of the Comparative Education Library, Institute of Education (and supplement)
Catalogue of the Collection of Education of Tropical Areas

Access to staff:
Contact by letter, by telephone, by fax, by e-mail, in person and via website. Non-members charged.

Access to building, collection or gallery:
Hours: Mon to Thu, 0930 to 2000; Fri, 0930 to 1900; Sat, 0930 to 1700

Access for disabled people:
Level entry, access to all public areas, toilet facilities
Special comments: Lift from Bedford Way

INSTITUTE OF EDUCATIONAL TECHNOLOGY

Formal name: Institute of Educational Technology
Acronym or abbreviation: IET

Open University, Walton Hall, Milton Keynes, Buckinghamshire, MK7 6AA

Tel: 01908 653536
Fax: 01908 654173
E-mail: m.s.thorpe@open.ac.uk

Website:
http://iet.open.ac.uk/

Enquiries:
Enquiries to: Director
Direct tel: 01908 653136
Other contacts: Head of CITE, Head of SRC

Founded:
1970

Organisation type and purpose:
University department or institute, consultancy, research organisation.
The role of the Institute of Educational Technology is to be a centre of international excellence for the teaching, research and development of educational technology in the service of effective learning.

continued overleaf

Subject coverage:
All aspects of distance and open teaching and learning, specialist areas: course design, education and quality assessment, use of media, information technology, multimedia, disabled students.

Museum or gallery collection, archive, or library special collection:
ICDL – international database on distance education; collection of publications (including non-English)

Trade and statistical information:
National student data on media use and ownership.
National student data on vocational intentions.

Printed publications:
Masters Course Brochures MA in Open and Distance Learning

Electronic and video publications:
ICDL distance education database on CD-ROM

Publications list:
Available in print

Access to staff:
Contact by letter
Hours: Mon to Fri, 0900 to 1700

INSTITUTE OF ELECTROLYSIS, THE

27 Emerson Valley, Milton Keynes, Buckinghamshire, MK4 2AF

Tel: 01908 503161
Fax: 0870 051 3611
E-mail: institute@electrolysis.co.uk

Website:
http://www.electrolysis.co.uk
Information on hair removal, list of members.

Enquiries:
Enquiries to: Administrator

Founded:
1946

Organisation type and purpose:
International organisation, professional body (membership is by qualification), present number of members: 200.

Access to staff:
Contact by letter, by telephone and by e-mail
Hours: Mon to Fri, 0900 to 1700

INSTITUTE OF ENVIRONMENTAL MANAGEMENT & ASSESSMENT

Acronym or abbreviation: IEMA

St Nicholas House, 70 Newport, Lincoln, LN1 3DP

Tel: 01522 540069
Fax: 01522 540090
E-mail: info@iema.net

Website:
http://www.iema.net
General information on the IEMA, how to become a member, activities and new products and services.

Enquiries:
Enquiries to: Chief Executive
Other contacts: Membership Secretary for general membership enquiries.

Founded:
1990

Organisation type and purpose:
National organisation, advisory body, professional body, membership association (membership is by subscription), present number of members: 6500, training organisation, consultancy, research organisation.
To support environmental practitioners in careers by best practice advice in environmental assessment and environmental management, professional development and networking.

Subject coverage:
Sustainability and environmental management in UK industry, commerce and local government. Professional accreditation for environmental professionals; registration for environmental auditors and assessors; registration as Specialist in Land Condition (SiLC); registration for Environmental Impact Assessment (EIA); certification of training; networking and best practice; expert advice and technical support for corporate members.

Printed publications:
The following publications are available direct for purchase or via IEMA website
Best Practice (journal, 2 or 3 times a year)
EIA Guidelines – Baseline Ecological Assessment, Environmental Assessment of Road Traffic, Landscape & Visual Impact Assessment
Practitioner Journals
EIA Yearbook
The Environmentalist (journal, monthly by subscription)
Perspective (journal, participating in environmental decision-making)
Practitioner (journal, managing climate change emission)
Various environmental titles

Electronic and video publications:
Membership information, past journal articles (CD-ROM), Past Journals (CD-ROM)

Publications list:
Available online and in print

Access to staff:
Contact by letter, by telephone, by fax, by e-mail and via website. Appointment necessary.
Hours: Mon to Fri, 0900 to 1700

Access to building, collection or gallery:
Prior appointment required
Hours: Mon to Fri, 0900 to 1700
Special comments: Library available to corporate members only.

Access for disabled people:
Parking provided, toilet facilities
Special comments: Steps up to building

INSTITUTE OF EXPLOSIVES ENGINEERS

Acronym or abbreviation: IExpE

Centenary Business Centre, Hammond Close, Attleborough Fields, Nuneaton, Warwickshire, CV11 6RY

Tel: 024 7635 0846
Fax: 024 7635 0831
E-mail: info@iexpe.org

Website:
http://www.iexpe.org

Enquiries:
Enquiries to: Secretary

Founded:
1974

Organisation type and purpose:
Professional body (membership is by qualification), present number of members: 967.

Subject coverage:
Use of explosives in civil engineering (demolition, tunnelling, shaft sinking, land clearance and excavation, underwater rock breaking and excavation) and in quarries and offshore oil operations; recording and interpreting disturbances occasioned by blasting operations.

Printed publications:
Directory of Members (annually)
Explosives Engineering (quarterly)

Access to staff:
Contact by letter, by fax and by e-mail
Hours: Mon to Fri, 0815 to 1630; Fri, 0815 to 1500

INSTITUTE OF EXPORT

Acronym or abbreviation: IoE

Export House, Minerva Business Park, Lynch Wood, Peterborough, Cambridgeshire, PE2 6FT

Tel: 01733 404400
Fax: 01733 404444
E-mail: institute@export.org.uk

Website:
http://www.export.org.uk
Institute's organisation, training courses, support services to exporters, membership news, forums, newsletter.

Enquiries:
Enquiries to: Information Officer

Founded:
1935

Organisation type and purpose:
Professional body (membership is by qualification), registered charity, university department or institute, suitable for ages: Post-school and Mature, training organisation. Sets and raises standards in International Trade Management and Export Practice through professional qualifications and training.

Subject coverage:
Sources of information on all aspects of international trade and training for exporters, leading to professional qualifications.

Printed publications:
International Trade Today (10 times a year)

Electronic and video publications:
Professional Examinations

Publications list:
Available in print

Access to staff:
Contact by letter, by telephone, by fax, by e-mail and via website
Hours: Mon to Fri, 0900 to 1700

Access for disabled people:
Parking provided, level entry, toilet facilities

INSTITUTE OF FAMILY THERAPY (LONDON) LIMITED

Acronym or abbreviation: IFT

24–32 Stephenson Way, London, NW1 2HX

Tel: 020 7391 9150
Fax: 020 7391 9169
E-mail: ift@psyc.bbk.ac.uk

Website:
http://www.instituteoffamilytherapy.org.uk

Enquiries:
Enquiries to: Director
Other contacts: Senior Administrator

Founded:
1977

Organisation type and purpose:
Professional body (membership is by qualification), present number of members: 204, voluntary organisation, registered charity (charity number 284858), training organisation, consultancy.

Subject coverage:
Availability of family therapy resources across the country; advice, through appropriate professionals, on specialist subjects relating to the family, such as bereavement, divorce, child abuse, AIDS, adolescent problems, disability and many other issues.

Electronic and video publications:
Lecture video tapes
Hire of video teaching tapes

Publications list:
Available in print

Access to staff:
Contact by letter, by telephone, by fax, by e-mail
and via website
Hours: Mon to Thu, 1000 to 1800; Fri, 1000 to 1700
(some evenings)

Affiliated to:
Birkbeck College
London University
National Family Mediation

Member of:
Association of Family Therapy
European Family Therapy Association
UK Council for Psychotherapy
UK Standing Conference for Psychotherapy

INSTITUTE OF FIELD ARCHAEOLOGISTS

Acronym or abbreviation: IFA

SHES, Whiteknights, PO Box 227, Reading, RG6 6AB

Tel: 0118 931 6446
Fax: 0118 931 6448
E-mail: admin@archaeologists.net

Website:
http://www.archaeologists.net

Enquiries:
Enquiries to: Administrative Assistant

Founded:
1982

Organisation type and purpose:
Professional body, present number of members: 2,700.
To promote professional standards and ethics for conserving, managing, and understanding enjoyment of heritage.

Information services:
Jobs Information Service (JIS)

Printed publications:
Directory of Members
Jobs Information Service Bulletin
The Archaeologist (quarterly)

Publications list:
Available online and in print

Access to staff:
Contact by letter, by telephone, by fax, by e-mail
and via website
Hours: Mon to Fri, 0900 to 1730

INSTITUTE OF FINANCIAL ACCOUNTANTS

Acronym or abbreviation: IFA

Burford House, 44 London Road, Sevenoaks, Kent, TN13 1AS

Tel: 01732 458080
Fax: 01732 455848
E-mail: mail@ifa.org.uk

Website:
http://www.ifa.org.uk

Enquiries:
Enquiries to: Chief Executive

Founded:
1916

Organisation type and purpose:
Professional body.
Examining and qualifying body.

Subject coverage:
All aspects of accountancy, management, company law, data processing, information technology, taxation, economics and general administration.

Printed publications:
Financial Accountant (6 times a year)

Access to staff:
Contact by letter, by telephone, by fax, by e-mail and via website. Appointment necessary.

Hours: Mon to Thu, 0900 to 1700; Fri, 0900 to 1600

Access to building, collection or gallery:
Prior appointment required

Access for disabled people:
Parking provided

Junior body is the:
International Association of Book-Keepers

INSTITUTE OF FINANCIAL PLANNING

Acronym or abbreviation: IFP

Southgate, Whitefriars, Lewins Mead, Bristol, BS1 2NT

Tel: 0117 945 2470
Fax: 0117 929 2214
E-mail: enquiries@financialplanning.org.uk

Website:
http://www.financialplanning.org.uk

Enquiries:
Enquiries to: Chief Executive

Founded:
1986

Organisation type and purpose:
International organisation, professional body (membership is by subscription, qualification), present number of members: 1300, training organisation.
The principle aim of the Institute is to promote the understanding and recognition of the financial planning profession.

Subject coverage:
Personal financial planning and management, business planning.

Museum or gallery collection, archive, or library special collection:
Reference works

Printed publications:
List of qualified members for reference by public, press and trade
Journal (for members, back and current copies)

Electronic and video publications:
Educational tape recordings of presentations made to Institutes' past Annual Conferences (tape, available for purchase, direct)

Access to staff:
Contact by letter, by telephone, by fax, by e-mail and via website
Hours: Mon to Fri, 0915 to 1745

Member of:
International Certified Financial Planner Council

INSTITUTE OF FOOD SCIENCE AND TECHNOLOGY

Acronym or abbreviation: IFST

5 Cambridge Court, 210 Shepherds Bush Road, London, W6 7NJ

Tel: 020 7603 6316
Fax: 020 7602 9936
E-mail: info@ifst.org

Website:
http://www.ifst.org
Membership, publications, careers information, frequently asked questions, information statements.

Enquiries:
Enquiries to: Team Executive

Founded:
1964

Organisation type and purpose:
Professional body (membership is by qualification), present number of members: 2500, registered charity (charity number 264044).

Subject coverage:
Food Science and Technology.

Museum or gallery collection, archive, or library special collection:
Mounfield Collection of historic books relating to food science and technology (no public access)

Trade and statistical information:
No

Non-library collection catalogue:
All or part available in-house

Printed publications:
Development & Use of Microbiological Criteria for Foods
Food Hygiene Training: A Guide to its Responsible Management
Food Science & Technology, (quarterly, available free to members or on subscription)
Guidelines to Good Catering Practice
Guide to Food Biotechnology
International Journal of Food Science and Technology, IJFST (10 times a year subscription)
Listing of Codes of Practice applicable to Foods
Shelf Life of Foods – Guidelines for its Determination and Prediction
Food & Drink: Good Manufacturing Practice – A Guide to its Responsible Management

Publications list:
Available online and in print

Access to staff:
Contact by letter, by telephone, by fax, by e-mail and via website. Appointment necessary.
Hours: Mon to Fri, 0930 to 1300 and 1400 to 1730

Access to building, collection or gallery:
No access other than to staff

INSTITUTE OF FUNDRAISING

Park Place, 12 Lawn Lane, London, SW8 1UD

Tel: 020 7840 1000
Fax: 020 7840 1001

Website:
http://www.institute-of-fundraising.org.uk/

Enquiries:
Enquiries to: Press Team
Direct e-mail: press@institute-of-fundraising.org.uk

Founded:
1983

Formerly called:
Institute of Charity Fundraising Managers (ICFM)

Organisation type and purpose:
Professional body.

Subject coverage:
Codes of practice, training, advice and techniques for fundraisers.

Museum or gallery collection, archive, or library special collection:
Fundraising in the UK and abroad, targets including trusts and companies

Printed publications:
Various Codes of Practice and Books including:
Code of Practice on Reciprocal Mailing (£2.50)
House to House Collection (£2.50)
Schools Fundraising (£9.95)
The Complete Fundraising Handbook (£12.95)
The Scottish Code of Fundraising Practice (£10)
Fundraising on the Internet (£12.95)
Reference Manual on Payroll Giving (£2.50)

Publications list:
Available online and in print

Access to staff:
Contact by letter, by telephone and by e-mail. Appointment necessary.
Hours: Mon to Fri, 0900 to 1700

Access to building, collection or gallery:
Prior appointment required

continued overleaf

Hours: Mon to Fri, 0900 to 1700

Access for disabled people:
Ramped entry

INSTITUTE OF GROCERY DISTRIBUTION

Acronym or abbreviation: IGD

Grange Lane, Letchmore Heath, Watford, Hertfordshire, WD2 8DQ

Tel: 01923 857141
Fax: 01923 852531
E-mail: igd@igd.com

Website:
http://www.igd.com

Enquiries:
Enquiries to: Database Manager

Founded:
1909

Organisation type and purpose:
Professional body (membership is by subscription), present number of members: 500, registered charity (charity number 105680), training organisation, consultancy, research organisation.

Subject coverage:
Leading source of information and analysis on the UK and European food industry.

Printed publications:
Backhauling & Factory Gate Pricing
Category Management – Which Way Now?
Children's Food – Market Forces & Industry Responses
Consumer Watch 2002 – Consumer Attitudes to Food & Grocery Issues
Convenience Retailing 2002 – The Market Report
Driving Improvement – Business Case Studies Report
Food Consumption 2002 – The one stop guide to the food consumer
Global Retailing 2002
Grocery Wholesaling 2002 (annually)
International Retailer Profiles
Order printed publications from: Publications Department, IGD
at same address, tel: 01923 851925, fax: 01923 852531, e-mail: publications@igd.org.uk

Electronic and video publications:
All printed publications are now available electronically

Publications list:
Available in print

Access to staff:
Contact by letter, by telephone, by fax, by e-mail and via website. Appointment necessary. Non-members charged.
Hours: Mon to Fri, 0900 to 1700

Access to building, collection or gallery:
Prior appointment required

INSTITUTE OF GROUNDSMANSHIP

Acronym or abbreviation: IOG

28 Stratford Office Village, Walker Avenue, Wolverton Mill East, Milton Keynes, MK12 5TW

Tel: 01908 312511
Fax: 01908 311140
E-mail: iog@iog.org

Website:
http://www.iog.org

Enquiries:
Enquiries to: Chief Executive
Direct e-mail: marketing@iog.org

Founded:
1934

Organisation type and purpose:
Membership association, suitable for ages: 18+, training organisation, consultancy.

Subject coverage:
All matters relating to grass, or turf, in sports amenity or leisure; organiser of the largest trade exhibition for the sports amenity and landscaping industry, IOGSALTEX, held annually at the Royal Windsor Racecourse in September; consultancy service on all aspects of the turf industry.

Printed publications:
Fact Sheets on turf care problems
The Groundsman Magazine (monthly)

Access to staff:
Contact by letter, by telephone, by fax, by e-mail and via website. Appointment necessary.
Hours: Mon to Fri, 0900 to 1700

Incorporates the:
Association of Landscape Managers

Links with:
FA Technical Pitch Committee
RHS
ROSPA
Sports Council

INSTITUTE OF HEALTH PROMOTION AND EDUCATION

Acronym or abbreviation: IHPE

University Dental Hospital, Higher Cambridge Street, Manchester, M15 6FH

Tel: 0161 275 6610
Fax: 0161 275 6299
E-mail: honsec@ihpe.org.uk

Website:
http://www.ihpe.org.uk

Enquiries:
Enquiries to: Honorary Secretary

Organisation type and purpose:
Professional organisation.

Subject coverage:
Health promotion and education.

Printed publications:
International Journal of Health Promotion and Education (quarterly)

INSTITUTE OF HEALTH RECORD INFORMATION & MANAGEMENT

Acronym or abbreviation: IHRIM(UK)

IHRIM(UK) Headquarters, 141 Leander Drive, Rochdale, Lancashire, OL11 2XE

Tel: 01706 868481
Fax: 01706 868481
E-mail: ihrim@zen.co.uk

Enquiries:
Enquiries to: Chief Executive

Founded:
1948

Organisation type and purpose:
International organisation, professional body (membership is by qualification), present number of members: 1000, consultancy.

Subject coverage:
Management of health records – systems and services, health record information management.

Printed publications:
IHRIM(UK) Journal (quarterly)
Health Records Quality Handbook – A self audit tool (£35)
Understanding Medical Terminology (£5.50)

Publications list:
Available in print

Access to staff:
Contact by letter, by telephone and by fax.

Appointment necessary. Non-members charged.
Hours: Mon to Fri, 0930 to 1230

INSTITUTE OF HEALTH SCIENCES LIBRARY

Acronym or abbreviation: IHS

Old Road, Headington, Oxford, OX3 7LF

Tel: 01865 226688
Fax: 01865 226619
E-mail: library.enquiries@ihs.ox.ac.uk

Website:
http://www.library.ox.ac.uk
Oxford University libraries

Enquiries:
Enquiries to: Librarian
Direct tel: 01865 226618

Founded:
1996

Organisation type and purpose:
University library.

Subject coverage:
Health Services administration, evidence based medicine, epidemiology, primary care and public health.

Library catalogue:
All or part available online

Access to staff:
Contact by letter, by telephone, by fax and by e-mail. Non-members charged.
Hours: Mon to Fri, 0900 to 1700

Access for disabled people:
Access to all public areas, toilet facilities
Special comments: Lift to first floor

Parent body:
University of Oxford

INSTITUTE OF HEALTHCARE ENGINEERING & ESTATE MANAGEMENT

Acronym or abbreviation: IHEEM

2 Abingdon House, Cumberland Business Centre, Northumberland Road, Portsmouth, Hampshire, PO5 1DS

Tel: 023 9282 3186
Fax: 023 9281 5927
E-mail: iheem@btconnect.com

Enquiries:
Enquiries to: Librarian

Founded:
1943

Organisation type and purpose:
Learned society, professional body (membership is by qualification, election or invitation).

Subject coverage:
Hospital engineering, medical equipment, estate management relating to the healthcare sector.

Printed publications:
Journal (monthly)
Monographs and conference proceedings

Access to staff:
Contact by letter, by telephone and by fax. Non-members charged.
Hours: Mon to Fri, 0900 to 1700

Member of:
Engineering Council
International Federation of Healthcare Engineering

INSTITUTE OF HERALDIC AND GENEALOGICAL STUDIES

Acronym or abbreviation: IHGS

79–82 Northgate, Canterbury, Kent, CT1 1BA

Tel: 01227 768664

Fax: 01227 765617
E-mail: ihgs@ihgs.ac.uk

Website:
http://www.ihgs.ac.uk

Enquiries:
Enquiries to: Librarian

Founded:
1961

Organisation type and purpose:
Membership association, registered charity
(charity number 286429), research organisation.
Educational trust; training, study and research
body, supported by Professional Research
Company, Achievements Ltd.

Subject coverage:
Family history, genealogy, heraldry, foreign
heraldry, Coats of Arms, genetic diseases.

**Museum or gallery collection, archive, or library
special collection:**
Catholic Marriage Index (London and Essex)
Complete Collection of Siebmacher's
  Wappenbuchen
Armorial Indexes
Manorial and early heraldic manuscripts
Marriage Indexes not collected elsewhere
Numerous family histories and pedigrees
Pallot Marriage Index (1780–1837, mainly London)
Sources and finding aids of special significance
  including International Genealogical Index and
  other indexes on microfiche; printout services
  available
Special collections for Kent, Sussex, Hampshire,
  London and Middlesex

Non-library collection catalogue:
All or part available in-house

Library catalogue:
All or part available in-house

Printed publications:
Family History (journal)
Guide to Library
Anglo-Norman Armory (C. R. Humphery-Smith,
  1973)
Armigerous Ancestors: an essential guide and
  index to the Herald's Visitations (C. R.
  Humphery-Smith, 1997)
Hugh Revel (C. R. Humphery-Smith, 1994)
Our Family History (C. R. Humphery-Smith)

Microform publications:
Family History Journal Index (Vols 1–5 1962–67,
  microfiche)
The Protestation Returns of Kent 1641/2
  (microfiche)

Publications list:
Available in print

Access to staff:
Contact by letter, by telephone and by e-mail.
Appointment necessary. Non-members charged.
Hours: Mon to Fri, 1000 to 1630

INSTITUTE OF HIGHWAY INCORPORATED ENGINEERS

Acronym or abbreviation: IHIE

De Morgan House, 58 Russell Square, London,
WC1B 4HS

Tel: 020 7436 7487
Fax: 020 7436 7488
E-mail: information2@ihie.org.uk

Website:
http://www.ihie.org.uk

Enquiries:
Enquiries to: Secretary
Direct e-mail: secretary@ihie.org.uk

Founded:
1965

Organisation type and purpose:
Professional body, present number of members:
3,000.

Subject coverage:
Highway engineering; traffic and transportation;
highway maintenance.

Printed publications:
Transportation Professional (monthly, shared with
  Institution of Highways and Transportation)

Electronic and video publications:
IHIE Engineering Guidelines for Motorcycles
  (2005, CD-ROM)
IHIE Home Zone Design Guidelines (2002, CD-
  ROM)

Access to staff:
Contact by letter, by telephone and by e-mail.
Appointment necessary.
Hours: Mon to Fri, 0900 to 1700

Member organisation of:
Engineering Council UK

INSTITUTE OF HISTORICAL RESEARCH

Acronym or abbreviation: IHR

University of London, Senate House, Malet Street,
London, WC1E 7HU

Tel: 020 7862 8760
Fax: 020 7862 8762
E-mail: ihr.library@sas.ac.uk

Website:
http://www.history.ac.uk/library
http://www.history.ac.uk/bookshop/index.html
online publications
http://www.history.ac.uk
http://catalogue.ulrls.lon.ac.uk
Access to the library's holdings in the catalogue of
the University of London Research Library
Services (ULRLS)

Enquiries:
Enquiries to: Librarian

Founded:
1921

Organisation type and purpose:
University department or institute.
Postgraduate institute.

Subject coverage:
History of Western Europe and its expansion
overseas, c. 450 AD to the present; imperial and
colonial history; military and naval history;
diplomatic history; history of international
relations.

Library catalogue:
All or part available online

Printed publications:
Historical Research for Higher Degrees in the
  United Kingdom (annually)
Historical Research: Bulletin of the Institute of
  Historical Research (three times a year)
Teachers of History in the Universities of the
  United Kingdom (annually)
Victoria History of the Counties of England (200
  vols published, in progress)
Grants for History (annually)
Order printed publications from: Publications
Manager

Electronic and video publications:
Interviews with Historians (videos)

Publications list:
Available online and in print

Access to staff:
Contact by letter, by telephone, by e-mail and in
person. Appointment necessary.
Hours: Mon to Fri, 0900 to 2045; Sat, 0930 to 1715

INSTITUTE OF HORTICULTURE

Acronym or abbreviation: IOH

9 Red Lion Court, London, EC4A 3EF

Tel: 020 7936 5957
Fax: 020 7936 5958

E-mail: ioh@horticulture.org.uk

Website:
http://www.horticulture.org.uk

Enquiries:
Enquiries to: Administration Manager

Founded:
1984

Organisation type and purpose:
Professional body (membership is by
qualification), present number of members: 2,000.

Subject coverage:
All aspects of horticulture, education, training and
career progression in the amenity, commercial,
research and advisory sectors.

Printed publications:
Come into Horticulture (careers booklet)
Conference Proceedings: Micropropagation in
  Horticulture; Managing Gardens for Leisure and
  Profit; Growing with Plastics; Horticultural
  Exploitation of Recent Biological Developments
Courses and Training in Horticulture (for sae)
Directory of Horticultural Consultants
Landscape Plants
The Horticulturist (journal, quarterly)
Trees in the Environment: Their Biology
  Management and Control

Publications list:
Available in print

Access to staff:
Contact by letter, by telephone and by fax.
Appointment necessary.
Hours: Mon to Fri, 0900 to 1700

INSTITUTE OF INDIAN CULTURE (BHARATIYA VIDYA BHAVAN)

Formal name: Bharatiya Vidya Bhavan – Institute of
Indian Art and Culture
Acronym or abbreviation: BHAVAN

4A Castletown Road, West Kensington, London,
W14 9HQ

Tel: 020 7381 3086 or 4608
Fax: 020 7381 8758

Website:
http://www.bhavan.net
Descriptions of activities, products and facilities
available for students, members and customers.

Enquiries:
Enquiries to: Executive Director
Other contacts: Academic Director

Founded:
1972

Organisation type and purpose:
International organisation, professional body
(membership is by subscription), present number
of members: 1220, voluntary organisation,
registered charity (charity number 312879), public
library, suitable for ages: 7+, training organisation,
research organisation.
To popularise in the UK Indian Art, Archaeology,
Languages and Culture in general.

Subject coverage:
Indian philosophy, religion, languages, pilgrimage
centres, festivals, calendar dates, music, dance,
drama and all things connected with Indian art
and culture.

**Museum or gallery collection, archive, or library
special collection:**
Complete writings of Gandhi, Nehru and other
  Indian writers

Printed publications:
Books on Indian philosophy, art & culture mainly
  in English, Gujerati, Hindi and Sanskrit

Electronic and video publications:
Audio and video tapes available to purchase
  directly from us

Publications list:
Available in print

continued overleaf

Access to staff:
Contact by letter, by telephone, by fax and in person. Appointment necessary. All charged.
Hours: 0900 to 1900, seven days a week
Special comments: Wheelchair access to ground floor only.

Access to building, collection or gallery:
No prior appointment required
Hours: Mon to Fri, 0900 to 1700
Special comments: Books cannot be borrowed from Bhavani's library.

Bhavan's outreach classes at:
Alperton Community School
 Stanley Avenue, off Ealing Road, Wembley, Middlesex, HA0 4JE; tel: 020 7381 3086; fax: 020 7381 8758

Parent body and Head Office:
Bharatiya Vidya Bhavan (BHAVAN)
 Munshi Sadan, Kulapati K M Munshi Marg, Chaupatti, Mumbai, Bombay, 400 007, India; tel: 00 91 22 363 0786; fax: 00 91 22 363 0058

INSTITUTE OF INDIRECT TAXATION

Acronym or abbreviation: IIT

Suite G1, The Stables, Station Road West, Oxted, RH5 9EE

Tel: 01883 730658
Fax: 01883 717778
E-mail: enquiries@theiit.org.uk

Website:
http://www.theiit.org.uk
Conferences, membership, VAT compliance diploma, students, benefits, branches

Enquiries:
Enquiries to: Administrator
Direct e-mail: postmaster@theiit.org.uk

Founded:
1991

Organisation type and purpose:
Professional body.

Subject coverage:
Indirect taxes.

Printed publications:
Indirect TaxVoice (9 times a year, available on subscription to non-members)

Access to staff:
Contact by letter, by telephone, by fax, by e-mail and via website. Appointment necessary.
Hours: Mon to Fri, 0900 to 1700

Access to building, collection or gallery:
Mon to Fri, 0900 to 1700

Access for disabled people:
Fully accessible

INSTITUTE OF INTERNAL AUDITORS UK & IRELAND

Acronym or abbreviation: IIA UK & Ireland

13 Abbeville Mews, 88 Clapham Park Road, London, SW4 7BX

Tel: 020 7498 0101
Fax: 020 7978 2492
E-mail: info@iia.org.uk

Website:
http://www.iia.org.uk
Extensive online knowledge centre

Enquiries:
Enquiries to: Membership Services Officer

Founded:
1975

Organisation type and purpose:
Professional body (membership is by subscription), present number of members: 6000.

Subject coverage:
Corporate governance and risk management, internal control and internal auditing (general and computer).

Non-library collection catalogue:
All or part available online and in print

Library catalogue:
All or part available in-house

Printed publications:
An extensive publications list including Practice Guides, Professional Briefing Notes, IT briefing notes, Standards
Internal Auditing and Business Risks Magazine (monthly)

Publications list:
Available online and in print

Access to staff:
Contact by letter, by telephone, by fax, by e-mail and via website
Hours: Mon to Fri, 0900 to 1700

Affiliated to:
European Confederation of Institutes of Internal Auditing
Institute of Internal Auditors Incorporate, USA

INSTITUTE OF INTERNATIONAL EDUCATION IN LONDON

Acronym or abbreviation: IIEL

Charlton House, Charlton Road, Charlton, London, SE7 8RE

Tel: 020 8331 3100
Fax: 020 8331 3149
E-mail: enquiries@iiel.org.uk

Website:
http://www.iiel.org.uk

Enquiries:
Enquiries to: Course Coordinator
Direct tel: 020 7487 7678
Direct fax: 020 7487 7679
Other contacts: Publicity Coordinator

Founded:
1989

Organisation type and purpose:
International organisation, university department or institute, suitable for ages: 5+, training organisation, consultancy.
Japanese teacher training centre, EFL courses, JFL courses and consultancy on university and college entrance.

Subject coverage:
Japanese language for younger learners (mother tongue Japanese), Japanese teacher training, the study of Japanese as a foreign language, the study of English as a foreign language and entrance to British universities.

Printed publications:
Okina Chikyu (educational bulletin, quarterly)
Prospectus and course information only
Ransho (in-house newsletter)
Study of Japanese Language Teaching (bulletin, annually)

Access to staff:
Contact by letter, by telephone, by fax, by e-mail and in person. Appointment necessary.
Hours: Mon to Fri, 0900 to 1800
Special comments: Membership required.

Japan office:
ICJ
 2F Maeda Building, 2–13–2 Suido, Bunkyo-ku, Tokyo, 112–0005, Japan; tel: 00 81 3 5940 0506; fax: 00 81 3 5940 0507; e-mail: humanet@js4.so -net.ne.jp

INSTITUTE OF INTERNATIONAL LICENSING PRACTITIONERS

Acronym or abbreviation: IILP

28 Main Street, Mursley, Milton Keynes, MK17 0RT

Tel: 01296 728136
Fax: 01296 720070
E-mail: enquiries@iilp.net

Website:
http://www.iilp.net

Enquiries:
Enquiries to: The Secretariat
Direct tel: 01865 340828

Founded:
1969

Organisation type and purpose:
International organisation, professional body (membership is by qualification, election or invitation).
To provide professional licensing assistance to companies requiring technology transfer services; to set professional standards for those engaged in licensing consultancy.

Subject coverage:
Licensing, commercialising invention, technology transfer, distribution agreements, strategic alliances, joint ventures.

Printed publications:
Order printed publications from: Exploits

Access to staff:
Contact by letter, by telephone, by fax and by e-mail. Non-members charged.
Hours: Mon to Fri, 0800 to 1800

Affiliated to:
Licensing Innovation and Technology Consultants Association (LICTA)
 Let 2 Anaweg 25–27, Triesen, FL-9495, Liechtenstein; tel: +41 75 399 1000; fax: +41 75 399 1091; e-mail: enquiries@iilp.net; website: www.iilp.net

INSTITUTE OF INVENTORS

Acronym or abbreviation: IoI

19–23 Fosse Way, Ealing, London, W13 0BZ

Tel: 020 8998 3540/6372
E-mail: mikinvent@aol.com

Website:
http://www.instituteofinventors.com

Enquiries:
Enquiries to: President
Direct tel: 020 8998 6372

Founded:
1964

Organisation type and purpose:
International organisation, advisory body, professional body (membership is by subscription), present number of members: 1526, voluntary organisation, university department or institute, consultancy, research organisation.
To advise and assist inventors at all stages of their inventions, evaluation, prototypes, licence agreements, manufacture and marketing.

Subject coverage:
New inventions, invention research, invention, evaluation, exploitation, patenting, licensing, marketing and sponsorship.

Non-library collection catalogue:
All or part available online

Library catalogue:
All or part available online

Printed publications:
New Invention List (for Business Members only)

Access to staff:
Contact by telephone. Appointment necessary.
Hours: Mon to Sun, 1000 to 1800

INSTITUTE OF IRISH STUDIES

Queen's University Belfast, 8 Fitzwilliam Street, Belfast, BT9 6AW

Tel: 028 9027 3386
Fax: 028 9043 9238
E-mail: irish.studies@qub.ac.uk

Website:
http://www.qub.ac.uk/iis/
Home page, information on research, teaching, fellowship, scholarships and publications.

Enquiries:
Enquiries to: Director
Other contacts: Secretary for enquiries about courses, the work of the Institute etc.

Founded:
1965

Organisation type and purpose:
University department or institute, research organisation, publishing house.

Subject coverage:
Academic research on Ireland, primarily in the humanities.

Printed publications:
Order printed publications from: Institute of Irish Studies
at the same address, tel: 028 9027 3235, fax: 028 9043 9238, e-mail: m.mcnulty@qub.ac.uk

Publications list:
Available online and in print

Access to staff:
Contact by letter and by fax
Hours: Mon to Fri, 0900 to 1700

INSTITUTE OF ISMAILI STUDIES

Formal name: Institute of Ismaili Studies

42–44 Grosvenor Gardens, London, SW1W 0EB

Tel: 020 7881 6000
Fax: 020 7881 6040
E-mail: info@iis.ac.uk

Website:
http://www.iis.ac.uk
Information about the institite, research, lectures, seminars, study programmes and library collections

Founded:
1977

Organisation type and purpose:
Research institute, graduate studies, library.
To promote scholarship and learning of Islamic cultures and societies, historical as well as contemporary, Shi'ism in general, Isma'ilism in particular.

Subject coverage:
Islamic studies, especially Shiism and Ismailism

Museum or gallery collection, archive, or library special collection:
Library of 25,000 items, including:
Ismaili collection (in Arabic, English, French, German, Gujarati, Italian, Persian, Russian, Urdu)
Alcorani Textus Universus (Qu'ran with Latin translation)
Bibliothèque Orientale by Barthélemy Herbelot (publ. 1777–79)
The Memoirs of John Lord de Joinville
Relation du Voyage de Nasiri Khosrau
Manuscript Collection (1,000 Arabic, 300 Persian, 200 Gujarati and Khojki)
Dr Zahid Ali Collection (220 Arabic manuscripts on Ismailism)
Sherali Alidina Collection (photographs)
Amirali Mamdani Collection (slides, photographs and films)

Non-library collection catalogue:
All or part available in-house and in print

Library catalogue:
All or part available in-house

Printed publications:
Order printed publications from: Educational and research publications for specialists, the general public, adult audiences and young people.

Occasional papers, monographs, editions, translations, conference proceedings and bibliographical works, see website for details www.iis.ac.uk.

Publications list:
Available online and in print

Access to staff:
Contact by letter, by telephone, by fax, by e-mail and via website

INSTITUTE OF JEWISH STUDIES

Acronym or abbreviation: IJS

University College London, Foster Court, Gower Street, London, WC1E 6BT

Tel: 020 7679 3520
Fax: 020 7209 1026
E-mail: uclhvtm@ucl.ac.uk

Website:
http://www.ucl.ac.uk/hebrew-jewish/ijs

Organisation type and purpose:
Affiliated with University College London's Department of Hebrew and Jewish Studies, the Institute is dedicated to the promotion of all aspects of Jewish scholarship and civilisation, with the aim of reaching every section of the Jewish community and of the interested non-Jewish public, and holds public lectures, symposia, seminars and international conferences.

Subject coverage:
Jewish scholarship and civilisation.

INSTITUTE OF LARYNGOLOGY AND OTOLOGY LIBRARY

Acronym or abbreviation: ILO

Royal National Throat Nose and Ear Hospital, 330 Gray's Inn Road, London, WC1X 8EE

Tel: 020 7915 1445
E-mail: ilolib@ucl.ac.uk

Website:
http://www.ucl.ac.uk/library/ilo

Enquiries:
Enquiries to: Librarian
Direct e-mail: rnidlib@ucl.ac.uk

Founded:
1946

Organisation type and purpose:
University library.

Subject coverage:
Otorhinolaryngology, audiology, medical research, facial plastic surgery.

Museum or gallery collection, archive, or library special collection:
Historical works on otorhinolaryngology

Library catalogue:
All or part available online

Printed publications:
Annual Report in Postgraduate Prospectus of University College and Middlesex School of Medicine

Access to staff:
Contact by letter, by telephone, by e-mail, in person and via website. Appointment necessary.
Hours: Mon, Tue, 0930 to 1900; Wed to Fri, 0930 to 1730

Access for disabled people:
Arrange in advance
Special comments: No wheelchair access

Constituent part of:
Royal Free and University College Medical School
University College London Library

INSTITUTE OF LEADERSHIP & MANAGEMENT

Acronym or abbreviation: ILM

Stowe House, Netherstone, Lichfield, Staffordshire, WS13 6TJ

Tel: 01543 251346
Fax: 01543 266811
E-mail: ism@ismstowe.demon.co.uk

Website:
http://www.nebsmgt.co.uk
http://www.i-l-m.com
Under development.
http://www.ismstowe.com
Educational awards. Membership information – news and press releases. Development is on-going.

Enquiries:
Enquiries to: Information Services Manager
Direct e-mail: info@ismstowe-info.demon.co.uk

Founded:
1947

Organisation type and purpose:
Professional body (membership is by subscription, qualification), present number of members: 20,000, registered charity (charity number 248226), suitable for ages: normally 19+.
Professional institute for front line managers and supervisors.

Subject coverage:
Accreditation of management courses and NVQ/ SVQs; customer care awards, training support awards, and world class qualifications, management and training topics.

Library catalogue:
All or part available in-house

Printed publications:
ISM Mentor (3 times a year)
Modern Management (membership journal, 6 times a year, free to members)
Learning Together Guides (series) to MCI Standards level 3 (workbooks)
Progress (journal, 3 times a year, free to Centres and students)
Superseries (published by Pergamon)
See website for other items

Electronic and video publications:
See website

Access to staff:
Contact by letter, by telephone, by fax, by e-mail and via website. Appointment necessary.
Hours: Mon to Fri, 0830 to 1700

Access to building, collection or gallery:
No access other than to staff
Hours: Mon to Fri, 1000 to 1600

Access for disabled people:
Parking provided, ramped entry, toilet facilities

Second address:
Institute of Leadership & Management
1 Giltspur Street, London, EC1A 9DD; tel: 020 7294 3057; fax: 020 7294 2402; e-mail: nebsmgt@ city-and-guilds.co.uk

INSTITUTE OF LEGAL CASHIERS & ADMINISTRATORS

Acronym or abbreviation: ILCA

146–148 Eltham Hill, Eltham, London, SE9 5DX

Tel: 020 8294 2887
Fax: 020 8859 1682
E-mail: info@ilca.org.uk

Website:
http://www.ilca.org.uk
General information, course information, publications information

Enquiries:
Enquiries to: Executive Secretary
Other contacts: Editor for press information.

continued overleaf

Founded:
1978

Organisation type and purpose:
Professional body (membership is by subscription), present number of members: 2600, training organisation, research organisation, publishing house.
To promote excellence in legal finance and administration.

Subject coverage:
Legal accounting, financial control, administration, marketing, personnel management, solicitors' accounts rules, VAT, law office management, accounting for legal aid.

Printed publications:
Annual Report and Accounts
Legal Abacus (journal, 6 times a year)
Legal Software

Publications list:
Available in print

Access to staff:
Contact by letter, by telephone, by fax, by e-mail and via website. Appointment necessary.
Hours: Mon to Fri, 0900 to 1700

Access for disabled people:
Access to all public areas

Chairman:
Institute of Legal Accountants of Ireland
c/o Wellfield House, Blessington Road, Naas, County Kildare, Eire

INSTITUTE OF LEGAL EXECUTIVES

Acronym or abbreviation: ILEX

Kempston Manor, Kempston, Bedford, MK42 7AB

Tel: 01234 841000
Fax: 01234 840989
E-mail: info@ilex.org.uk

Website:
http://www.ilex.org.uk
Introduction to ILEX and how to qualify, members' news and professional issues.
http://www.legal-executive-recruitment.com
Online recruitment for Legal Executives.
http://www.ilexjournal.com
Interactive journal for members.
http://www.ilexpt.co.uk
Law for non-lawyers.
http://www.ilex-tutorial.ac.uk
Introduction to distance learning and ILEX Tutorial College.

Enquiries:
Enquiries to: Secretary General
Other contacts: Head of Communications and Public Relations for press and media enquiries, articles etc.

Founded:
1963

Organisation type and purpose:
Professional body (membership is by qualification), present number of members: 22,000.
Examining body.

Subject coverage:
Legal training services, for both lawyers and non-lawyers, law reform, distance learning.

Museum or gallery collection, archive, or library special collection:
Law Library (members only)

Printed publications:
The Legal Executive (journal, monthly)

Electronic and video publications:
The Virtual Practitioner – Develop legal skills (CD-ROM, £30 plus VAT)
Introduction to ILEX (video)
The Journal – on cassette tape for the blind (tape)

Access to staff:
Contact by letter, by telephone, by fax and by e-mail. Appointment necessary.
Hours: Mon to Fri, 0900 to 1700

Subsidiary bodies:
ILEX Paralegal Training
tel: 01234 348848; fax: 01234 266557; e-mail: ilex.pt@btconnect.com
ILEX Publishing and Advertising
tel: 01234 845721; fax: 01234 841999; e-mail: ipa@legal-executive-journal.co.uk
ILEX Tutorial College
tel: 01234 841010; fax: 01234 841373

INSTITUTE OF LICENSED TRADE STOCK AUDITORS

Acronym or abbreviation: ILTSA

7 Comely Bank Place, Edinburgh, EH4 1DT

Tel: 0131 315 2600
Fax: 0131 315 4346

Website:
http://www.iltsa.co.uk
Background information, news, stocktakers (qualified).

Enquiries:
Enquiries to: Secretary
Direct e-mail: secretary@iltsa.co.uk

Founded:
1953

Organisation type and purpose:
National organisation, professional body (membership is by qualification), present number of members: c. 400.
The only qualifying body for Stock Auditors within the licensed trade. The institute is also able to mediate in disputes concerning stocktaking and can act in an advisory capacity to any company or individual who seeks advice.

Subject coverage:
Qualified stocktakers, stocktaking, licensed trade, training, examinations, legislation affecting trade, specialist valuations.

Printed publications:
The Stock Auditor (magazine, 12 times a year)
Taking Stock (hard back copy, £15 plus £3 p&p)

Access to staff:
Contact by letter, by telephone, by fax and by e-mail
Hours: Mon to Fri, 0900 to 1700

INSTITUTE OF MAINTENANCE AND BUILDING MANAGEMENT

Acronym or abbreviation: IMBM

Keets House, 30 East Street, Farnham, Surrey, GU9 7SW

Tel: 01252 710994
Fax: 01252 737741
E-mail: imbm@btconnect.com

Enquiries:
Enquiries to: Chief Executive
Direct tel: 01252 724491
Other contacts: PA to Chief Executive

Founded:
1951

Organisation type and purpose:
Professional body (membership is by subscription, qualification).
The promotion and development of the maintenance and building management industry and the professionalism of those employed in the industry.

Subject coverage:
Building maintenance management.

Printed publications:
IMBM News (quarterly)
Institute Journal (quarterly)

Access to staff:
Contact by letter, by telephone, by fax, by e-mail and in person
Hours: Mon to Fri, 0900 to 1700

INSTITUTE OF MANAGEMENT CONSULTANCY

Acronym or abbreviation: IMC

3rd Floor, 17–18 Haywards Place, London, EC1R 0EQ

Tel: 020 7566 5220
Fax: 020 7566 5230
E-mail: consult@imc.co.uk

Website:
http://www.imc.co.uk
Full details of IMC.

Enquiries:
Enquiries to: Chief Executive

Founded:
1962

Organisation type and purpose:
Professional body.
The IMC leads the profession of management consultancy by qualifying, supporting and regulating individual management consultants and providing a forum for all management consultancy stakeholders.

Subject coverage:
Management consulting practice and careers.

Printed publications:
Annual Report 1999 (from April 2000, free)
Inside Careers Guide to Management Consultancy
Me A Management Consultant (free)
Standard Terms and Conditions of Engagement (£20)
Updat-e Newsletter
Professional Consultancy (quarterly)

Publications list:
Available in print

Access to staff:
Contact by letter, by telephone and by fax.
Appointment necessary.
Hours: Mon to Fri, 0900 to 1700

INSTITUTE OF MANAGEMENT SERVICES

Acronym or abbreviation: IMS

Brooke House, 24 Dam Street, Lichfield, Staffordshire, WS13 6AA

Tel: 01543 266909
Fax: 01543 257848
E-mail: admin@ims-stowe.fsnet.co.uk

Website:
http://www.ims-productivity.com

Enquiries:
Enquiries to: Information Officer

Founded:
1941

Organisation type and purpose:
Professional body, present number of members: 1700.

Subject coverage:
Work study; organisation and methods, business systems, work environment, motivation, information technology; quality management and control; industrial engineering, business process re-engineering.

Printed publications:
Management Services (4 times a year)
Management Services Handbook (2nd ed., 1991)
Student's Compendia
Wealth Creation – The Added Value Concept
Work Measurement

Electronic and video publications:
Activity Sampling

Clerical Work Measurement
Introducing Management Services
Method Study
Profit Improvement & Cost Reduction

Publications list:
Available in print

Access to staff:
Contact by letter, by telephone, by fax and by e-mail. Appointment necessary. Non-members charged.
Hours: Mon to Fri, 0930 to 1445

Links with:
Alliance of Manufacturing and Management Organisations (AMMO)
European Federation of Productivity Services (EFPS)
World Confederation of Productivity Science (WCPS)

INSTITUTE OF MANAGEMENT SPECIALISTS

Acronym or abbreviation: IMS

Warwick Corner, 42 Warwick Road, Kenilworth, Warwickshire, CV8 1HE

Tel: 01926 855498
Fax: 01926 513100
E-mail: info@group-ims.com

Website:
http://www.group-ims.com

Enquiries:
Enquiries to: Chairman
Other contacts: President and Founder

Founded:
1971

Organisation type and purpose:
International organisation, professional body (membership is by subscription, qualification), present number of members: 5,626, training organisation, range of professional diploma courses available.

Subject coverage:
Management (general and specialised); administration; technical and computer sciences.

Printed publications:
The Management Specialist (3 times a year)

Access to staff:
Contact by letter, by telephone, by fax, by e-mail and via website
Hours: Mon to Fri, 0900 to 1700

Links with:
Institute of Manufacturing and Professional Business and Technical Management
  at the same address
The Academy of Executives and Administrators
  at the same address
The Academy of Multi-Skills
  at the same address

INSTITUTE OF MANUFACTURING

Acronym or abbreviation: IManf

Warwick Corner, 42 Warwick Road, Kenilworth, Warwickshire, CV8 1HE

Tel: 01926 855498
Fax: 01926 513100
E-mail: info@group-ims.com

Website:
http://www.group-ims.com

Enquiries:
Enquiries to: Chairman

Founded:
1978

Organisation type and purpose:
Professional body (membership is by subscription, qualification), present number of members: 1,260, training organisation, range of professional diploma courses available.

Subject coverage:
Manufacturing; industry; management – general and specialised; technical and computer sciences; education and training.

Printed publications:
Manufacturing (annually, spring)
Manufacturing Management (annually, autumn)

Access to staff:
Contact by letter, by telephone, by fax, by e-mail and via website
Hours: Mon to Fri, 0900 to 1700

Links with:
Institute of Management Specialists and Professional Business and Technical Management
  tel: 01926 855498; fax: 01926 513100
The Academy of Executives and Administrators
  tel: 01926 855498; fax: 01926 513100
The Academy of Multi-Skills
  tel: 01926 855498; fax: 01926 513100

INSTITUTE OF MARINE ENGINEERING, SCIENCE AND TECHNOLOGY

Acronym or abbreviation: IMarEST

80 Coleman Street, London, EC2R 5BJ

Tel: 020 7382 2600
Fax: 020 7382 2670
E-mail: mic@imare.org.uk

Website:
http://www.imare.org.uk
General information on Institute of Marine Engineers, careers and jobs, events and conferences, library catalogue.

Enquiries:
Enquiries to: Manager of Information Centre
Direct tel: 020 7382 2645
Direct e-mail: dgts@imarest.org
Other contacts: Manager of Engineering, Science & Technology for technical information regarding marine engineering.

Founded:
1889

Organisation type and purpose:
Learned society, professional body (membership is by qualification), present number of members: 17,000, registered charity (charity number 212992). Promoting the maritime industries.

Subject coverage:
Marine engineering; marine electrical engineering; ocean technology, offshore engineering, naval architecture, shipping, subsea technology.

Non-library collection catalogue:
All or part available online

Printed publications:
Conference Proceedings
Marine Engineers Review (annual subscription £85, members free, 10 times a year)
Maritime IT and Electronics (annual subscription £40, 6 times a year)
The Journal of Offshore Technology (annual subscription £50, members free, 6 times a year)
Transactions Volume 113 (annual subscription £120, members £15)

Electronic and video publications:
International Directory of Maritime Consultants and Technical Services (annual, £59, available on the Web)
Marine Technology Abstracts on CD-ROM (joint venture with British Maritime Technology, available on annual subscription, available on the Web)

Publications list:
Available online and in print

Access to staff:
Contact by letter, by telephone, by fax, by e-mail, in person and via website. All charged.
Hours: Mon to Fri, 0900 to 1700

Access for disabled people:
Ramped entry

INSTITUTE OF MATERIALS, MINERALS AND MINING

Acronym or abbreviation: IOM3

1 Carlton House Terrace, London, SW1Y 5DB

Tel: 020 7451 7300
Fax: 020 7839 1702
E-mail: libraryservices@iom3.org

Website:
http://www.iom3.org/content/library-services
Information about the library services and facilities; publication list.
http://www.iom3.org

Enquiries:
Enquiries to: Information and Library Co-ordinator
Direct tel: 020 7451 7360/7324
Direct fax: 020 7451 7406
Direct e-mail: hilda.kaune@iom3.org; frances.perry@iom3.org

Founded:
1869

Organisation type and purpose:
Professional body (membership is by qualification) present number of members: 20,000. The Institute of Materials, Minerals and Mining (IOM3) is a major UK engineering institution, the activities of which encompass the whole materials cycle, from exploration and extraction, through characterisation, processing, forming, finishing and application, to product recycling and land reuse. It exists to promote and develop all aspects of materials science and engineering, geology, mining and associated technologies, mineral and petroleum engineering and extraction metallurgy, as a leading authority in the worldwide materials and mining community.

Subject coverage:
Science and technology of metals, polymers, rubbers, ceramics, composites and packaging; production and use; physics and chemistry of materials and production processes. Economic geology, mining and processing of minerals, non-ferrous extractive metallurgy.

Museum or gallery collection, archive, or library special collection:
Historical collection: antiquarian books, biographies, photographs, portraits, technical drawings, artefacts

Non-library collection catalogue:
All or part available in-house

Library catalogue:
All or part available in-house

Printed publications:
Maney Publishing for the IOM3 publishes a range of books and journals covering many aspects of materials including ceramics, polymers, ironmaking and steelmaking, materials science and technology and the minerals and mining industry
Order printed publications from: Order Processing Dept, Maney Publishing, Suite 1C, Joseph's Well, Hanover Walk, Leeds, LS3 1AB, tel: 0113 243 2800, fax: 0113 386 8178, e-mail: maney@maney.co.uk

Publications list:
Available online and in print

Access to staff:
Contact by letter, by telephone, by fax, by e-mail, in person and via website. Appointment necessary. Non-members charged.
Hours: Mon to Fri, 0930 to 1700

continued overleaf

Also at:
David West Library, Institute of Materials,
Minerals and Mining
 tel: 020 7451 7360; fax: 020 7451 7406; e-mail:
 hilda.kaune@iom3.org
Doncaster Regional Office
 Danum House, South Parade, Doncaster, DN1
 2DY; tel: 01302 320486; fax: 01302 380900
Stoke Regional Office
 Shelton House, 12 Stoke Road, Stoke-on-Trent,
 Staffordshire, ST4 2DR; tel: 01782 221700; fax:
 01782 221722

INSTITUTE OF MATHEMATICS AND ITS APPLICATIONS

Acronym or abbreviation: IMA

Catherine Richards House, 16 Nelson Street,
Southend-on-Sea, Essex, SS1 1EF

Tel: 01702 354020
Fax: 01702 354111
E-mail: post@ima.org.uk

Website:
http://www.ima.org.uk
Membership, IMA conferences, IMA publications,
event and news, mathematics website list.

Enquiries:
Enquiries to: Executive Director

Founded:
1964

Organisation type and purpose:
Professional body, registered charity (charity
number 1017777).

Subject coverage:
Mathematics, mathematical education, statistics,
applications of mathematics, operational research.

Printed publications:
Extensive range of mathematics and its
 applications books, papers, conference
 proceedings and monographs published on
 behalf of the IMA
IMA Journal of Applied Mathematics (6 times a
 year)
IMA Journal of Management Mathematics
 (quarterly)
IMA Journal of Mathematical Control and
 Information (quarterly)
Mathematical Medicine and Biology: A Journal of
 the IMA (quarterly)
IMA Journal of Numerical Analysis (quarterly)
Teaching Mathematics and its Applications: an
 International Journal of the IMA (quarterly)
Mathematics Today (6 times a year)

Publications list:
Available online and in print

Access to staff:
Contact by letter, by telephone, by fax, by e-mail
and via website
Hours: Mon to Fri, 0900 to 1700

INSTITUTE OF MEASUREMENT AND CONTROL

Acronym or abbreviation: INSTMC

87 Gower Street, London, WC1E 6AF

Tel: 020 7387 4949
Fax: 020 7388 8431
E-mail: publications@instmc.org.uk

Website:
http://www.instmc.org.uk
Institute Home Page.

Enquiries:
Enquiries to: Production Editor

Founded:
1944

Organisation type and purpose:
Learned society (membership is by qualification,
election or invitation), present number of
members: 4000, registered charity, publishing
house.
To promote for the public benefit all aspects of
measurement and control technology and its
applications.

Subject coverage:
Instrumentation, measurement, control
engineering, automation.

Library catalogue:
All or part available in-house

Printed publications:
Instrument Engineers' Yearbook
Measurement and Control (journal, 10 times a
 year)
Transactions of INSTMC (5 times a year)

Electronic and video publications:
Instrument Engineers' Yearbook (CD-ROM)

Publications list:
Available online and in print

Access to staff:
Contact by letter, by telephone, by fax, by e-mail,
in person and via website. Appointment necessary.
Hours: Mon to Fri, 0900 to 1700

Access to building, collection or gallery:
Prior appointment required
Special comments: Library is open to members only.

INSTITUTE OF METAL FINISHING

Acronym or abbreviation: IMF

Exeter House, 48 Holloway Head, Birmingham, B1
1NQ

Tel: 0121 622 7387
Fax: 0121 666 6316
E-mail: exeterhouse@instituteofmetalfinishing.org

Enquiries:
Enquiries to: Secretary

Organisation type and purpose:
Learned society.
Technical and scientific society; eight regional
branches; three technical groups.

Subject coverage:
Metal finishing and all aspects of the surface
treatment industry, metal finishing, printed
circuits, anodizing, coating, all types of metal
protection.

Printed publications:
IMformation Newsletter (6 times a year)
Reports of Working Parties
Symposia; International conference
Transactions of the Institute (6 times a year)

INSTITUTE OF NATURAL THERAPY

Acronym or abbreviation: INT

PO Box 1418, Dorchester, Dorset, DT1 1YF

Tel: 01305 267069

Website:
http://www.institute-natural-therapy.org.uk
Member list and tutors.

Enquiries:
Enquiries to: General Secretary

Founded:
1991

Organisation type and purpose:
International organisation, advisory body,
professional body (membership is by
qualification).

Subject coverage:
Hypnotherapy, healing, complementary therapies.

Access to staff:
Contact by letter and by telephone

Hours: Mon to Fri, 0900 to 1700

Patron of:
General Hypnotherapy Standards Council (GHSC)
 PO Box 204, Lymington, SO41 6WP; tel: 01590
 683770; fax: 01590 683770

INSTITUTE OF NAVAL MEDICINE

Acronym or abbreviation: INM

Alverstoke, Gosport, Hampshire, PO12 2DL

Tel: 023 9276 8101
Fax: 023 9250 4823
E-mail: lib@inm.mod.uk

Enquiries:
Enquiries to: Librarian

Organisation type and purpose:
National government body, training organisation,
research organisation.

Subject coverage:
Underwater medicine, survival medicine,
habitability, submarine environmental chemistry,
heat, cold, toxicology, nuclear medicine and
radiological protection, dosimetry, audiology and
hearing conservation, submarine medicine,
experimental physiology, occupational medicine
and hygiene, microbiology, analytical chemistry,
medical statistics, health and safety at work,
ergonomics, human factors, anthropometry,
psychology.

Library catalogue:
All or part available in-house

Printed publications:
Annual Report
Clinical Research Working Party Reports
INM Reports and Technical Memoranda
Journal of the Royal Naval Medical Service

Access to staff:
Contact by letter, by telephone, by fax and by e-
mail. Appointment necessary.
Hours: Mon to Fri, 0900 to 1700

Access to building, collection or gallery:
Prior appointment required

Access for disabled people:
Parking provided, level entry, toilet facilities

Part of:
Ministry of Defence, Medical Directorate (Naval)

INSTITUTE OF NAVAL MEDICINE – HISTORIC COLLECTIONS LIBRARY

Acronym or abbreviation: INM

Alverstoke, Gosport, Hampshire, PO12 2DL

Tel: 023 0276 8238
Fax: 023 9250 4823
E-mail: cat1@inm.mod.uk

Website:
http://www.rnreference.mod.uk/09/inm/inmintro
.htm

Enquiries:
Enquiries to: Historic Collections Librarian

Founded:
2001

Organisation type and purpose:
National government body.

Subject coverage:
Naval history; history of medicine; history of naval
medicine; natural history (small proportion); early
printed books (small proportion).

**Museum or gallery collection, archive, or library
special collection:**
Works of James Lind
Dr Robert McKinnal bequest
Dr Leonard Gillespie bequest
Navy List
Health of the Navy

Archive material (incomplete) from former staff of
RNHs Haslar and Plymouth; some photographs
Small collection of papers relating to William J.
Maillard, VC (1863–1903), holder of the only
Royal Naval Medical Service Victoria Cross

Non-library collection catalogue:
All or part available in-house

Library catalogue:
All or part available in-house

Access to staff:
Contact by letter, by telephone, by fax and by e-
mail. Appointment necessary.
Hours: Mon to Fri, 0930 to 1730

Access to building, collection or gallery:
Prior appointment required
Hours: Mon to Fri, 0930 to 1730
Special comments: Visitors must call at main gate on
arrival.

Access for disabled people:
Parking provided
Special comments: Level entry to main building but
steps with rails to collections. Arrangements can be
made to view items elsewhere on site.

Parent body:
Admiralty Library
Naval Historical Branch, PP 20, Main Road, HM
Naval Base, Portsmouth, PO1 3LU; tel: 02392
725297; e-mail: cnsnhbal@a.dii.mod.uk

INSTITUTE OF OCCUPATIONAL MEDICINE

Acronym or abbreviation: IOM

Research Avenue North, Riccarton, Edinburgh,
EH14 4AP

Tel: 0870 850 5131
Fax: 0870 850 5132
E-mail: info@iom-world.org

Website:
http://www.iom-world.org

Enquiries:
Enquiries to: Information Officer

Founded:
1969

Organisation type and purpose:
International organisation, service industry,
registered charity, consultancy, research
organisation.

Subject coverage:
Health, hygiene and safety at work; occupational
and environmental health, hygiene and
epidemiology; ergonomics; hearing loss;
respiratory diseases; asbestos; asbestosis; silica;
pneumoconiosis; personal protective equipment.

Printed publications:
Booklets on COSHH and Noise
IOM Research Reports
Research Papers

Publications list:
Available in print

Access to staff:
Contact by letter, by telephone, by fax and by e-
mail. Appointment necessary.
Hours: Mon to Fri, 0900 to 1700

INSTITUTE OF OPERATIONS MANAGEMENT

Acronym or abbreviation: IOM

CILT(UK), Earlstrees Court, Earlstrees Road,
Corby, Northamptonshire, NN17 4AX

Tel: 01536 740105
Fax: 01536 740101
E-mail: info@iomnet.org.uk

Website:
http://www.iomnet.org.uk
On-line Index to Control, access to IOM Alert.

Enquiries:
Enquiries to: Membership Enquiries
Direct e-mail: members@iomnet.org.uk

Founded:
1969

Organisation type and purpose:
Professional body.
Professional institute for operations and
production managers.

Subject coverage:
Production management and control; inventory
management; stock control; logistics; supply chain
management; materials management; business
process re-engineering; advanced planning and
scheduling; ERP; MRPII; learn manufacturing;
Just-in-Time (JIT).

**Museum or gallery collection, archive, or library
special collection:**
Library of specialised technical books and journals
on all aspects of operations management
particularly production and inventory control

Library catalogue:
All or part available in-house

Printed publications:
IOM Link (electronic newsletter)
Control (8 issues, free to members, sold to non-
members)

Electronic and video publications:
ROME Programme: An internet/CD-ROM distance
learning programme, utilising a virtual factory
coupled with an interactive handbook (ca. 550
pages)

Publications list:
Available online and in print

Access to staff:
Contact by letter, by telephone, by fax, by e-mail
and via website. Appointment necessary. Non-
members charged.
Hours: Mon to Thu, 0900 to 1700; Fri, 0900 to 1600
Special comments: Members only may borrow from
library.

Access for disabled people:
Parking provided, level entry, access to all public
areas, toilet facilities
Hours: Mon to Thu, 0900 to 1700; Fri, 0900 to 1600

INSTITUTE OF OPTOMETRY, THE

56 Newington Causeway, London, SE1 6DS

Tel: 020 7407 4183
Fax: 020 7403 8007
E-mail: admin@ioo.org.uk

Website:
http://www.ioo.org.uk
Details of clinics run, courses and staff.

Enquiries:
Enquiries to: Director of Administration

Founded:
1922

Organisation type and purpose:
Registered charity (charity number 207965).

Subject coverage:
Optometric examination and prescription/
treatment for patients, continuing education and
training for optometrists, optometric research.

Access to staff:
Contact by letter, by telephone, by fax and by e-
mail
Hours: Mon to Thu, 0900 to 2100; Fri, 0900 to 1700

INSTITUTE OF PAPER CONSERVATION

Acronym or abbreviation: IPC

Leigh Lodge, Leigh, Worcester, WR6 5LB

Tel: 01886 832323
Fax: 01886 833688

E-mail: information@ipc.org.uk

Website:
http://www.ipc.org.uk

Enquiries:
Enquiries to: Executive Secretary
Other contacts: Membership Secretary for
membership.

Founded:
1976

Organisation type and purpose:
International organisation, professional body
(membership is by subscription, qualification),
present number of members: 1400, registered
charity (charity number 280888), training
organisation, publishing house.
Care and repair of artefacts on paper.

Subject coverage:
Training in paper conservation, all types of paper-
related materials including books, textiles, globes,
wallpaper, archives, maps, works of art,
photographs, manuscripts, frames, parchment.
Collection care, conservation surveys, disaster
planning, storage and preservation.

**Museum or gallery collection, archive, or library
special collection:**
Specialist library at 1 Grove Cottage, St Cross
Road, Oxford OX1 3TX

Trade and statistical information:
Data on conservation profession.
Register of accredited book and paper
conservators.

Non-library collection catalogue:
All or part available in print

Library catalogue:
All or part available in print

Printed publications:
Conference Papers
Paper Conservator (annually, vols 1–26 1976–2002,
£15 each, £25 non-members)
The Care and Repair of Paper Artefacts (leaflet)
Defaced (leaflet)
Guidelines for Conservation Framing (leaflet)

Publications list:
Available online and in print

Access to staff:
Contact by letter, by telephone, by fax and by e-
mail
Hours: Mon to Fri, 0915 to 1715

INSTITUTE OF PARALEGAL TRAINING, THE

The Mill, Climping Street, Climping,
Littlehampton, West Sussex, BN17 5RN

Tel: 01903 714276
Fax: 01903 713710
E-mail: amanda@ibberson.fsbusiness.co.uk

Enquiries:
Enquiries to: Secretary General

Founded:
1976

Organisation type and purpose:
International organisation, professional body
(membership is by qualification, election or
invitation), service industry, training organisation.

Access to staff:
Contact by letter, by telephone, by fax and by e-
mail
Hours: Mon to Fri, 0900 to 1700

INSTITUTE OF PATENTEES AND INVENTORS

Acronym or abbreviation: IPI

PO Box 39296, London, SE3 7WH

Tel: 0871 226 2091
Fax: 020 8293 5920

continued overleaf

E-mail: ipi@invent.org.uk

Website:
http://www.invent.org.uk/
Information on Institute, membership, etc.

Enquiries:
Enquiries to: Secretary

Founded:
1919

Organisation type and purpose:
National organisation, advisory body, professional
body, membership association (membership is by
subscription), present number of members: 700.
A non-profit organisation offering its members
advice and guidance on all aspects of inventing
from idea conception to innovation and
development.

Subject coverage:
National and international patents, registered
designs, trade-marks, copyright, the furtherance,
protection and exploitation of inventions through
to industrial innovation.

Printed publications:
Future and the Inventor (newsletter, quarterly, free
to members)
General information pack including publications
list of a selection of books available to help the
lone inventor (various prices, discounts to
members, available free on request)

Publications list:
Available in print

Access to staff:
Contact by letter, by telephone, by fax, by e-mail
and via website
Hours: Mon to Fri, 1000 to 1700

INSTITUTE OF PAYROLL AND PENSIONS MANAGEMENT

Acronym or abbreviation: IPPM

Shelly House, Farmhouse Way, Monkspath,
Solihull, West Midlands, B90 4EH

Tel: 0121 712 1000
Fax: 0121 712 1001
E-mail: ippm@ippm.org

Website:
http://www.ippm.org

Enquiries:
Enquiries to: Marketing Department

Founded:
1985

Organisation type and purpose:
Professional body (membership is by subscription),
present number of members: 4500, training
organisation, consultancy.

Subject coverage:
Payroll administration, law, education and
qualifications (MSc, NVQ3 and NVQ5), and
pensions administration.

Museum or gallery collection, archive, or library special collection:
Pensions books, leaflets, payroll

Printed publications:
Pay Advice (12 times a year, free to members)

Publications list:
Available in print

Access to staff:
Contact by telephone, by e-mail and via website
Hours: Mon to Fri, 0900 to 1700

Access to building, collection or gallery:
No access other than to staff

INSTITUTE OF PHYSICS

Acronym or abbreviation: IoP

76–78 Portland Place, London, W1B 1NT

Tel: 020 7470 4800

Fax: 020 7470 4848
E-mail: physics@iop.org

Website:
http://www.iop.org/bo.html
Catalogue of books and other publications.
http://www.iop.org
General news about the institute, its membership
and its publishing products.

Enquiries:
Enquiries to: Public Affairs Manager
Direct e-mail: dianne.stilwell@iop.org
Other contacts: Public Affairs

Founded:
1874

Organisation type and purpose:
Learned society, professional body, publishing
house.
To promote a knowledge of and education in pure
and applied physics.

Subject coverage:
Aspects of physics, pure and applied, in education,
industry, the public sector and the media.

Printed publications:
Books, magazines and journals
Order printed publications from: Institute of Physics
Publishing

Electronic and video publications:
A range of electronic products

Publications list:
Available online and in print

Access to staff:
Contact by letter, by telephone, by fax, by e-mail
and via website
Hours: Mon to Fri, 0900 to 1700

Access for disabled people:
Ramped entry, toilet facilities

Member of:
European Optical Society
European Physical Society

Subsidiary body:
Institute of Physics Publishing
Dirac House, Temple Back, Bristol, BS1 6BE; tel:
0117 929 7481; fax: 0117 929 4318; e-mail:
custserv@iop.org

INSTITUTE OF PHYSICS AND ENGINEERING IN MEDICINE

Acronym or abbreviation: IPEM

Fairmount House, 230 Tadcaster Road, York, YO24
1ES

Tel: 01904 610821
Fax: 01904 612279
E-mail: office@ipem.ac.uk

Website:
http://www.ipem.ac.uk
IPEM membership, scientific meetings,
publications, training schemes and general
information.

Enquiries:
Enquiries to: General Secretary

Founded:
1995

Organisation type and purpose:
Professional body (membership is by qualification,
election or invitation), registered charity (charity
number 1047999), training organisation,
publishing house.

Subject coverage:
Physical science as applied to medicine, including
radiation protection, radiotherapy, diagnostic
radiology, nuclear magnetic resonance, nuclear
medicine, ultrasonics, lasers, rehabilitation
engineering, physiological measurement,
bioengineering, non-ionising radiation.

Printed publications:
Physiological Measurement (4 times a year)

Medical Engineering and Physics (8 times a year)
Physics in Medicine and Biology (journal,
fortnightly)
Scientific and Conference Reports

Publications list:
Available online and in print

Access to staff:
Contact by telephone and by fax. Non-members
charged.
Hours: Mon to Thu, 0900 to 1700: Fri, 0900 to 1600

Access to building, collection or gallery:
No prior appointment required

INSTITUTE OF PHYSICS PUBLISHING

Acronym or abbreviation: IOP Publishing

Dirac House, Temple Back, Bristol, BS1 6BE

Tel: 0117 929 7481
Fax: 0117 929 4318
E-mail: custserv@iop.org

Website:
http://www.journals.iop.org
Publication list for journals. All journals full text.
Many other services such as access to abstracts and
multimedia functionality.

Enquiries:
Enquiries to: Managing Director
Direct tel: 0117 930 1144
Direct fax: 0117 920 0775
Direct e-mail: jerry.cowhig@iop.org

Founded:
1874

Organisation type and purpose:
International organisation, learned society,
professional body (membership is by subscription,
qualification, election or invitation), present
number of members: 37,000, registered charity,
publishing house.
The Institute, which has its origins in the Physical
Society established in 1874, is one of the world's
leading publishers in physics and related subjects.
Journals go back to 1874 and include several world
leaders in their respective fields.
Dissemination of knowledge and education in
physics.

Subject coverage:
Physics.

Non-library collection catalogue:
All or part available online

Printed publications:
Journals published in the fields of: Astronomy,
Astrophysics, Geophysics; Atomic, Molecular
and Plasma Physics; Condensed Matter,
Materials Science and Semiconductor Physics;
Electronics and Electrical Engineering;
Engineering and Technology; Mathematics,
Mathematical Physics and Computer Science;
Measurement Science, Technology/Sensors and
Smart Materials; Medical Physics and Biomedical
Engineering; Nuclear and High Energy Physics;
Optics and Quantum Optics
Journals relating to: Applied Mathematics and
Mathematical Physics; Applied Physics; Atomic,
Molecular and Optical Physics; Computer
Science and Information Processing; Condensed
Matter and Materials Science; Measurement
Science and Sensors; Medical Physics; Nuclear
Physics and Particle Physics; Physics Education;
Plasma Physics; Optics

Microform publications:
All journals also available in microfiche form

Electronic and video publications:
All journals also available in electronic format (see
Web site)

Publications list:
Available online and in print

Access to staff:
Contact by letter, by telephone, by fax, by e-mail and via website
Hours: Mon to Fri, 0900 to 1700

Access for disabled people:
Ramped entry, access to all public areas, toilet facilities

INSTITUTE OF PLUMBING AND HEATING ENGINEERING

Acronym or abbreviation: IPHE

64 Station Lane, Hornchurch, Essex, RM12 6NB

Tel: 01708 472791
Fax: 01708 448987
E-mail: info@iphe.org.uk

Website:
http://www.iphe.org.uk

Enquiries:
Enquiries to: Editor of Plumbing & Heating Engineering Magazine
Direct tel: 01708 463114
Direct e-mail: carolc@iphe.org.uk

Founded:
1906

Organisation type and purpose:
Professional body (membership is by qualification), present number of members: 12,000, registered charity (charity number 278169), suitable for ages: 18 to 60.
To improve the standards of plumbing in the public interest.

Subject coverage:
Plumbing, heating and allied subjects, names of registered plumbers.

Printed publications:
Plumbing Engineering Services Design Guide (reprinted 2002)
Business Directory of Registered Plumbers
P&HE Magazine (6 times a year)

Electronic and video publications:
Business Directory of Registered Plumbers (CD-ROM)
Annual Directory

Access to staff:
Contact by letter, by telephone, by fax, by e-mail and via website. Appointment necessary.
Hours: Mon to Fri, 0900 to 1700

INSTITUTE OF POLYMER TECHNOLOGY AND MATERIALS ENGINEERING

Acronym or abbreviation: IPTME

Loughborough University, Loughborough, Leicestershire, LE11 3TU

Tel: 01509 223331
Fax: 01509 223949
E-mail: iptme@lboro.ac.uk

Website:
http://www.lboro.ac.uk/departments/IPTME
Departmental overview, programmes, research groups, academic staff listing, staff room and telephone numbers. ISST, short courses and conferences, opportunities.

Enquiries:
Enquiries to: Director
Direct tel: 01509 223330
Direct e-mail: j.binner@lboro.ac.uk

Founded:
1967

Organisation type and purpose:
University department or institute.
Postgraduate education, research and consultancy.
Loughborough Materials Characterisation Centre.

Subject coverage:
Polymers; metals; ceramics; materials characterisation centre with advanced thermal method units; Institute of Surface Science and Technology; electron microscope unit; X-ray unit.

Printed publications:
MSc Programmes leaflets
Research brochure
Short course list
Undergraduate programmes brochure

Publications list:
Available in print

Access to staff:
Contact by letter, by telephone, by fax, by e-mail and via website
Hours: Mon to Fri, 0900 to 1700

Connections with:
Institute of Surface Science and Technology (ISST)
Address as IPTME; tel: 01509 223387; fax: 01509 234225; e-mail: lmcc@lboro.ac.uk

INSTITUTE OF PRACTITIONERS IN ADVERTISING

Acronym or abbreviation: IPA

44 Belgrave Square, London, SW1X 8QS

Tel: 020 7235 7020
Fax: 020 7245 9904
E-mail: info@ipa.co.uk

Website:
http://www.ipa.co.uk
General information, events and publications.

Enquiries:
Enquiries to: Head of Information Systems

Founded:
1917

Organisation type and purpose:
Professional body, trade association (membership is by subscription).

Subject coverage:
Advertising including European and international advertising, marketing, media, public relations, all aspects of communication, and related fields.

Printed publications:
Publications available on the website

Publications list:
Available online and in print

Access to staff:
Contact by letter, by telephone, by fax and by e-mail. Access for members only.
Hours: Mon to Fri, 0900 to 1700
Special comments: IPA members only.

Access for disabled people:
Access to all public areas, toilet facilities

Member of:
Advertising Association
European Association of Communication Agencies (EACA)

INSTITUTE OF PROFESSIONAL INVESTIGATORS LIMITED

Acronym or abbreviation: IPI

Runnymede Malthouse, off Hummer Road, Egham, Surrey, TW20 9BD

Tel: 0870 330 8622
Fax: 0870 330 8612
E-mail: admin@ipi.org.uk

Website:
http://www.ipi.org.uk
Courses available, directory of members in private practice, benefits of membership.

Enquiries:
Enquiries to: Secretary General

Founded:
1976

Organisation type and purpose:
Professional body.

Subject coverage:
Investigation services and practice; further education within the profession.

Printed publications:
Directory of Members in Private Practice
Instructional leaflets on subjects relating to investigations practice

Access to staff:
Contact by letter, by telephone, by fax and by e-mail
Hours: Mon to Fri, 1000 to 1600

Access to building, collection or gallery:
No access other than to staff

INSTITUTE OF PROFESSIONAL WILLWRITERS

Acronym or abbreviation: IPW

Trinity Point, New Road, Halesowen, B63 3HY

Tel: 08456 442042
Fax: 08456 442043
E-mail: office@ipw.org.uk

Website:
http://www.ipw.org.uk

Enquiries:
Enquiries to: Office Manager
Other contacts: Chairman for public relations.

Founded:
1991

Organisation type and purpose:
Professional body (membership is by qualification), present number of members: 500, suitable for ages: 18+, training organisation.

Subject coverage:
All aspects of wills and their writing, current members local to enquirer, membership requirements.

Education services:
Willwriting courses

Printed publications:
Code of Practice for Willwriting Profession (free, 2008)
Journal (12 times a year for members and interested persons)
Inheritance Matters (quarterly journal)
Order printed publications from: IPW Accounts

Access to staff:
Contact by letter, by telephone, by fax, by e-mail, in person and via website. Appointment necessary.
Hours: Mon to Fri, 0900 to 1700

INSTITUTE OF PSYCHIATRY

De Crespigny Park, Denmark Hill, London, SE5 8AF

Tel: 020 7848 0204
Fax: 020 7848 0209
E-mail: iop.library@iop.kcl.ac.uk

Website:
http://www.iop.kcl.ac.uk/iopweb/departments/home/default.aspx?locator=12

Enquiries:
Enquiries to: Librarian

Organisation type and purpose:
University department or institute.

Subject coverage:
Psychiatry, psychology, neurology and neuroscience, psychopharmacology, genetics and genomics.

Museum or gallery collection, archive, or library special collection:
Guttmann-Maclay Collection of psychotic art
Henry Maudsley Collection of historic books in psychiatry

continued overleaf

Mayer-Gross Collection of historic texts in
European psychiatry

Non-library collection catalogue:
All or part available online

Library catalogue:
All or part available in-house

Printed publications:
Maudsley Monographs series
Maudsley Discussion papers (11 titles)

Publications list:
Available in print

Access to staff:
Contact by letter, by telephone, by e-mail and via
website. Appointment necessary. Non-members
charged.
Hours: Mon to Fri, 0900 to 2000; Term time: Sat,
1000 to 1700; Summer vacation: Sat, 1000 to 1500.

Parent body:
King's College London

INSTITUTE OF PSYCHO-ANALYSIS

Formal name: British Psychoanalytical Society
Acronym or abbreviation: BPAS

112A-114 Shirland Road, London, W9 2EQ

Tel: 020 7563 5000
Fax: 020 7563 5001
E-mail: bpasadmin@compuserve.com

Website:
http://www.psychoanalysis.org.uk

Enquiries:
Enquiries to: Institute Manager

Founded:
1919

Organisation type and purpose:
Professional body (membership is by
qualification), present number of members: 510,
registered charity (charity number 212330),
training organisation.
The training organisation for Psychoanalysis in
Britain, also treats patients in The London Clinic of
Psychoanalysis at the same addess.

Subject coverage:
Psycho-analysis.

**Museum or gallery collection, archive, or library
special collection:**
Archives

Library catalogue:
All or part available in-house

Printed publications:
International Journal of Psycho-analysis

Electronic and video publications:
PEP CD-ROM

Access to staff:
Contact by letter, by telephone, by fax, by e-mail
and in person. Non-members charged.
Hours: Mon to Fri, 0930 to 1730

Access to building, collection or gallery:
No prior appointment required
Hours: Mon to Thu, 1200 to 2100; Fri to Sun, closed
Special comments: Archives, apply to the Honorary
Archivist for access. Public membership of the
library is available.

Access for disabled people:
Ramped entry, toilet facilities

Member of:
International Psycho-Analytical Association

INSTITUTE OF PSYCHOANALYSIS

112A Shirland Road, Maida Vale, London, W9 2EQ

Tel: Switchboard: 020 7563 5000; Library: 020 7563
5008
Fax: 020 7563 5001
E-mail: library@iopa.org.uk

Website:
http://www.psychoanalysis.org.uk

Enquiries:
Enquiries to: Librarian
Other contacts: Assistant Librarian

Founded:
1913

Organisation type and purpose:
Professional body (membership is by
qualification), present number of members: 510,
registered charity (charity number 212330),
training organisation, research organisation,
publishing house.

Subject coverage:
Psychoanalysis

**Museum or gallery collection, archive, or library
special collection:**
Archives of the British Psychoanalytical Society

Non-library collection catalogue:
All or part available in-house

Library catalogue:
All or part available in-house

Printed publications:
Archives of the British Psychoanalytical Society

Electronic and video publications:
PEP (CD-ROM)

Access to staff:
Contact by letter, by telephone, by fax, by e-mail,
in person and via website. Appointment necessary.
Non-members charged.
Hours: Mon to Thu, 1230 to 2030; Fri, 1030 to 1700
Special comments: Please contact before visiting

Access to building, collection or gallery:
No prior appointment required
Hours: Mon to Thu, 0930 to 2030; Fri, 0930 to 1700
Special comments: Library: public membership of
the Library by the day or week for a fee
Archives: access by application to the Honorary
Archivist

Access for disabled people:
Parking provided, level entry

Constituent part of:
The Institute of Psychoanalysis
at the same address; tel: 020 7563 5000; fax: 020
7563 5001; e-mail: editor@psychoanalysis.org.uk;
website: http://www.psychoanalysis.org.uk

INSTITUTE OF PSYCHOSEXUAL MEDICINE

Acronym or abbreviation: IPM

12 Chandos Street, Cavendish Square, London,
W1G 9DR

Tel: 020 7580 0631
Fax: 020 7580 0631
E-mail: ipm@telinco.co.uk

Enquiries:
Enquiries to: Administrator
Other contacts: Referrals Secretary

Founded:
1974

Organisation type and purpose:
National organisation, professional body
(membership is by subscription), present number
of members: 450, registered charity (charity
number 298172), university department or
institute, training organisation.
Referral service.
Refers members of the public to psychosexual
doctors.

Subject coverage:
Training for doctors in the field of psychosexual
medicine (sexual difficulties and related marital or
psychosomatic problems); training over 2 years for
Diploma from Institute of Psychosexual Medicine
and at 4 years for membership of Institute of
Psychosexual Medicine.

Trade and statistical information:
List of doctors qualified in the field of
psychosexual medicine and able to receive
referrals through our referrals secretary.

Printed publications:
Institute of Psychosexual Medicine Journal
available to total membership of IPM three times
a year

Publications list:
Available online and in print

Access to staff:
Contact by letter, by telephone, by fax, by e-mail
and via website
Hours: Mon to Fri, 0900 to 1700
Special comments: Answerphone also. Prefer sae
from those wanting list of doctors.

INSTITUTE OF PSYCHOSYNTHESIS

65A Watford Way, London, NW4 3AQ

Tel: 020 8202 4525
Fax: 020 8202 6166
E-mail: institute@psychosynthesis.org

Website:
http://www.psychosynthesis.org
Information on training and booklist for training.

Enquiries:
Enquiries to: Administration

Founded:
1973

Organisation type and purpose:
Membership association, training organisation.
Psychology, coaching, counselling and
psychotherapy training, low cost clinic open to
members of the public.

Subject coverage:
Psychotherapy and counselling, coaching,
psychology.

Printed publications:
Some books available to purchase, contact direct
for pricing

Publications list:
Available online

Access to staff:
Contact by letter, by telephone, by e-mail and via
website. Appointment necessary.
Hours: Mon to Fri, 1000 to 1700
Special comments: Appointments for the clinic are
made in advance.

Access to building, collection or gallery:
Prior appointment required
Hours: Mon to Fri, 0700 to 2100

Access for disabled people:
There is a staircase

Member of:
British Association for Counselling and
Psychotherapy (BACP)
European Association for Pyschotherapy
European Mentoring and Coaching Council
United Kingdom Council for Psychotherapy
(UKCP)

INSTITUTE OF PUBLIC LOSS ASSESSORS

Acronym or abbreviation: IPLA

Coughtry House, 112–116 Broad Street, Chesham,
Bucks, HP5 3ED

Tel: 01494 793370
E-mail: jdturberville@tiscali.co.uk

Enquiries:
Enquiries to: General Secretary

Founded:
1963

Organisation type and purpose:
Professional body.
To represent the interests of professional loss assessors in their dealings with their clients.

Subject coverage:
Loss assessment, preparation, submission and negotiation of all types of statutory and insurance claims on behalf of the public and corporate bodies.

Printed publications:
List of members (in return for A5 sae)

Access to staff:
Contact by letter and by telephone
Hours: Mon to Fri, 0900 to 1700

INSTITUTE OF PUBLIC RIGHTS OF WAY MANAGEMENT LIMITED

Acronym or abbreviation: IPROW

PO Box 78, Skipton, North Yorkshire, BD23 4UP

Tel: 07000 782318
Fax: 07000 782318
E-mail: iprow@iprow.co.uk

Website:
http://www.iprow.co.uk

Enquiries:
Enquiries to: Executive Officer

Founded:
1986

Organisation type and purpose:
Professional body.

Subject coverage:
Public rights of way, outdoor access management.

Printed publications:
Waymark (magazine)

Publications list:
Available in print

Access to staff:
Contact by letter, by e-mail and via website
Hours: Mon to Fri, 0900 to 1700

Access to building, collection or gallery:
No access

INSTITUTE OF PYRAMIDOLOGY

Acronym or abbreviation: IOP

108 Broad Street, Chesham, Buckinghamshire, HP5 3ED

Tel: 01494 771774
E-mail: 101234.1734@compuserve.com

Enquiries:
Enquiries to: Director

Founded:
1940

Organisation type and purpose:
International organisation, membership association (membership is by subscription), voluntary organisation, research organisation.

Subject coverage:
Pyramidology: study of the Great Pyramid of Egypt; books on pyramidology.

Printed publications:
Pyramid Quarterly

Access to staff:
Contact by letter, by telephone and by e-mail
Hours: Mon to Fri, 0900 to 1700

INSTITUTE OF QUALIFIED PROFESSIONAL SECRETARIES LIMITED

Acronym or abbreviation: IQPS

Suite 464, 24–28 St Leonards Road, Windsor, Berkshire, SL4 3BB

Tel: 0844 8000 182
Fax: 01753 775798
E-mail: office@iqps.org

Website:
http://www.iqps.org

Enquiries:
Enquiries to: General Administrator

Founded:
1957

Organisation type and purpose:
Professional body.
To provide guidance and advice on all aspects of secretarial work, facilitate and encourage training and continuing professional development, raise professional standards, liaise with the media, government, business and the educational community.

Subject coverage:
Professional development and training of secretaries.

Printed publications:
Career Secretary (journal, quarterly)

Access to staff:
Contact by letter, by telephone, by fax and by e-mail. Appointment necessary.
Hours: Mon to Fri, 0900 to 1300

Access to building, collection or gallery:
Prior appointment required

Has a:
network of branches

INSTITUTE OF QUARRYING

7 Regent Street, Nottingham, NG1 5BS

Tel: 0115 941 1315
Fax: 0115 948 4035
E-mail: mail@quarrying.org

Website:
http://www.quarrying.org

Enquiries:
Enquiries to: Information Officer
Other contacts: Secretary

Founded:
1917

Organisation type and purpose:
Professional body (membership is by qualification), present number of members: 6000, registered charity.

Subject coverage:
Quarrying.

Printed publications:
Technical Handbooks include:
Sand and Gravel Production (Littler A, £25)
Sand and Gravel Planning & Restoration (Littler A, £22.50)
Crushing and Screening (Rothery K, £25)
Use of Explosives in Quarrying (White T E & Robinson P, £22.50)
A Dictionary of Quarrying Terms (Sheppard R P, £22.50)
Safety and Legislation (Darlow E C, £25)

Access to staff:
Contact by letter, by telephone, by fax and by e-mail
Hours: Mon to Fri, 0900 to 1700

INSTITUTE OF RACE RELATIONS

Acronym or abbreviation: IRR

2–6 Leeke Street, London, WC1X 9HS

Tel: 020 7837 0041
Fax: 020 7278 0623
E-mail: info@irr.org.uk

Website:
http://www.irr.org.uk

Founded:
1958

Organisation type and purpose:
Registered charity (charity number 223989), research organisation.
Educational charity.

Subject coverage:
Race and minority group relations; racism; imperialism; Third World issues.

Library catalogue:
All or part available in-house

Printed publications:
Annual Report
European Race Bulletin (ed. Fekete, quarterly, £7.50)
Race and Class (quarterly, £7)
Broadsheet on racism in Britain
Educational pamphlets
European Race Audit Bulletin
Race Relations Abstracts
Order printed publications from: IRR

Electronic and video publications:
HomeBeats: Struggles for Racial Justice (CD-ROM)

Publications list:
Available in print

Access to staff:
Contact by telephone and by e-mail. Appointment necessary.
Hours: Mon to Thu, 1000 to 1300 and 1400 to 1700 (hours may be restricted)
Special comments: Access at librarian's discretion.

INSTITUTE OF REFRACTORIES ENGINEERS

Formal name: Institute of Refractories Engineers
Acronym or abbreviation: IRE

General Secretary and Treasurer, Joan Royd Cottage, Penistone, Sheffield, S36 9DA

Tel: 01226 762578
Fax: 01226 762673
E-mail: secretary@ireng.org

Website:
http://ireng.org/
All activities of Institute, developments in refractories engineering and contacts with other professional institutes.

Enquiries:
Enquiries to: General Secretary
Direct e-mail: alanhey@ireng.org
Other contacts: Treasurer

Founded:
1961

Organisation type and purpose:
Learned society (membership is by qualification, election or invitation), present number of members: 1500.

Subject coverage:
Refractories – manufacture and use, research and development, education and training.

Printed publications:
Guide to Good Practice for Installation of Monolithics
The Refractories Engineer (6 times a year)

Publications list:
Available in print

Access to staff:
Contact by letter, by telephone, by fax, by e-mail and via website
Hours: Mon to Fri, 0900 to 1700

INSTITUTE OF REFRIGERATION

Acronym or abbreviation: IOR

Kelvin House, 76 Mill Lane, Carshalton, Surrey, SM5 2JR

Tel: 020 8647 7033
Fax: 020 8773 0165
E-mail: ior@ior.org.uk

continued overleaf

Website:
http://www.ior.org.uk

Enquiries:
Enquiries to: Secretary

Founded:
1899

Organisation type and purpose:
Learned society (membership is by subscription).

Subject coverage:
Refrigeration and air conditioning.

Museum or gallery collection, archive, or library special collection:
Reference library at Cambridge Refrigeration Technology

Non-library collection catalogue:
All or part available online

Publications list:
Available online

Access to staff:
Contact by letter, by telephone, by fax, by e-mail and via website. Appointment necessary.
Hours: Mon to Fri, 0900 to 1700

Links with:
Cambridge Refrigeration Technology

INSTITUTE OF REVENUES, RATING AND VALUATION

Acronym or abbreviation: IRRV

41 Doughty Street, London, WC1N 2LF

Tel: 020 7831 3505
Fax: 020 7831 2048
E-mail: enquiries@irrv.org.uk

Website:
http://www.irrv.org.uk
Background information on the Institute.

Founded:
1882

Organisation type and purpose:
Local government body, professional body.

Subject coverage:
Local taxation and property valuation issues including: Council Tax (Council Tax benefits, banding, enforcement), housing benefits, non-domestic rates.

Printed publications:
Details of magazines, guides and books available at website www.irrv.org.uk
Order printed publications from: Communications Manager

Electronic and video publications:
Note: all prices excl. VAT:
Benefit Legislation Infobase (£300, updates £195)
Council Tax Legislation Infobase (£300, updates £195)
NNDR Legislation Infobase (£300, updates £195)
Rating Cases Infobase (£300, updates £195)

Publications list:
Available online and in print

Access to staff:
Contact by letter, by fax and by e-mail.
Appointment necessary.
Hours: Mon to Fri, 0900 to 1700

Access to building, collection or gallery:
Prior appointment required

Represents:
over 6000 local authority revenues and benefits officers
private valuers and officers from appellate bodies

INSTITUTE OF RISK MANAGEMENT

Acronym or abbreviation: IRM

Lloyds Avenue House, 6 Lloyds Avenue, London, EC3N 3AX

Tel: 020 7709 9808
Fax: 020 7709 0716
E-mail: enquiries@irmgt.co.uk

Website:
http://www.theIRM.org

Enquiries:
Enquiries to: Executive Director
Other contacts: Examinations Officer, Membership Officer

Founded:
1986

Organisation type and purpose:
International organisation, advisory body, professional body (membership is by subscription, qualification), present number of members: 1700, research organisation.
To provide a diploma in risk management.

Subject coverage:
Business organisation and finance, occupational health and safety, public sector, finance, physical risk, liability exposures, contingency and disaster, risk analysis, business organisation and finance, local authority risk management, health sector.

Printed publications:
Annual Report
Inform (journal, 6 times a year)
Reading List
The Risk Management Series (books)

Electronic and video publications:
Introduction to Risk Management (video, VHS version, £99 plus VAT; NTSC, version £150 plus VAT)

Publications list:
Available in print

Access to staff:
Contact by letter, by telephone, by fax and by e-mail. Appointment necessary.
Hours: Mon to Fri, 0900 to 1700

INSTITUTE OF ROAD SAFETY OFFICERS

Acronym or abbreviation: IRSO

Pin Point, 1–2 Rosslyn Crescent, Harrow, Middlesex, HA1 2SB

Tel: 0870 010 4442
Fax: 0870 333 7772
E-mail: irso@dbda.co.uk

Website:
http://www.irso.org.uk

Enquiries:
Enquiries to: Executive Secretary
Direct tel: 01202 262051
Direct fax: 01202 262091
Direct e-mail: k.saunders@poole.gov.uk
Other contacts: National Secretary

Founded:
1971

Organisation type and purpose:
Professional body (membership is by subscription), training organisation.
Mainly local government officers.

Subject coverage:
Road safety; education, training and publicity, engineering and enforcement.

Trade and statistical information:
Accident statistics.

Printed publications:
Inroads (quarterly)

Access to staff:
Contact by letter, by telephone and by fax.
Appointment necessary.
Hours: Mon to Fri, 0900 to 1700

Access to building, collection or gallery:
No access other than to staff

INSTITUTE OF ROOFING

Acronym or abbreviation: IoR

24 Weymouth Street, London, W1N 3FA

Tel: 020 7436 0103
Fax: 020 7637 5215

Website:
http://www.instituteofroofing.org.uk

Enquiries:
Enquiries to: Director
Direct fax: 020 7636 1287
Direct e-mail: info@instituteofroofing.org.uk

Founded:
1980

Organisation type and purpose:
Professional body (membership is by qualification).

Subject coverage:
Education within the roofing industry.

Access to staff:
Contact by letter, by telephone, by fax, by e-mail and via website
Hours: Tue, Wed, Thu, 1000 to 1500

Access to building, collection or gallery:
Prior appointment required

INSTITUTE OF SALES PROMOTION

Acronym or abbreviation: ISP

Arena House, 66–68 Pentonville Road, London, N1 9HS

Tel: 020 7837 5340
Fax: 020 7837 5326
E-mail: enquiries@isp.org.uk

Website:
http://www.isp.org.uk

Enquiries:
Enquiries to: Chief Executive Officer

Founded:
1933

Organisation type and purpose:
Trade association.

Subject coverage:
Promotional marketing.

Access to staff:
Contact by letter, by telephone, by fax, by e-mail and via website
Hours: Mon to Fri, 0900 to 1700

Access to building, collection or gallery:
Prior appointment required
Hours: Mon to Fri, 0900 to 1700

INSTITUTE OF SOUND AND VIBRATION RESEARCH

Acronym or abbreviation: ISVR

The University, Southampton, SO17 1BJ

Tel: 023 8059 2294
Fax: 023 8059 3190
E-mail: mzs@isvr.soton.ac.uk

Website:
http://www.isvr.soton.ac.uk

Enquiries:
Enquiries to: Director

Founded:
1963

Organisation type and purpose:
University department or institute, consultancy, research organisation.

Subject coverage:
Acoustics; structural dynamics; audiology; fluid dynamics; signal processing; active control; subjective acoustics; human response to vibration; automotive engineering; instrumentation; random

process analysis; human response to noise and vibration; hearing conservation; urban planning and noise; vibration engineering and control; machinery noise and vibration, signal processing etc.

Museum or gallery collection, archive, or library special collection:
Literature on the human response to vibration

Non-library collection catalogue:
All or part available online

Printed publications:
Annual Report (listings and summary of research projects, staff publications)

Publications list:
Available online and in print

Access to staff:
Contact by letter, by telephone, by fax and by e-mail
Hours: Mon to Fri, 0900 to 1700

Access to building, collection or gallery:
Prior appointment required

Access for disabled people:
Parking provided, ramped entry, toilet facilities

Associated with:
ISVR Consultancy Service
tel: 01703 582162; e-mail: djfiis@isvr.soton.ac.uk

INSTITUTE OF SPORT AND RECREATION MANAGEMENT

Acronym or abbreviation: ISRM

Sir John Beckwith Centre for Sport, Loughborough University, Loughborough, Leicestershire, LE11 3TU

Tel: 01509 226474
Fax: 01509 226475
E-mail: ralphriley@isrm.co.uk

Website:
http://www.isrm.co.uk
ISRM courses, media releases, ISRM information service, publications, recreation magazine, ISRM vacancy service.

Enquiries:
Enquiries to: Chief Executive

Founded:
1921

Organisation type and purpose:
Membership association (membership is by qualification), present number of members: 2300, registered charity (charity number 250902). Educational Charity.
National professional body for sport and recreation facility management and operation.

Subject coverage:
Management and operation of public baths and recreation facilities, education and training.

Printed publications:
ISRM Conference Papers
ISRM Publications leaflet, listing Publications/Posters/Codes of Practice for Management and Operation
Recreation (magazine, 10 times a year)
Energy Conservation in Sports Centres and Swimming Pools
Guidance Documents for Risk Assessment
ISRM Integrated Management System
The Operation of Giant Waterslides
The Safe Use and Operation of Bouncy Castles

Electronic and video publications:
Training Videos

Publications list:
Available online and in print

Access to staff:
Contact by letter, by telephone, by fax and by e-mail
Hours: Mon to Fri, 0830 to 1630

INSTITUTE OF SPORTS AND EXERCISE MEDICINE

Acronym or abbreviation: ISEM

30 Devonshire Street, London, W1G 6PU

Tel: 020 7288 5310
E-mail: d.patterson@ucl.ac.uk

Website:
http://www.fsem.co.uk

Enquiries:
Enquiries to: Secretary

Founded:
1965

Organisation type and purpose:
Learned society, professional body, registered charity (charity number 313301).
To encourage postgraduate medical research, teaching and treatment in all aspects of sports medicine.

Subject coverage:
Sports and Exercise Medicine.

Access to staff:
Contact by letter, by fax and by e-mail
Hours: Mon to Fri, 0900 to 1700
Special comments: No access – co-ordinating centre only.

Access to building, collection or gallery:
No access other than to staff

INSTITUTE OF SPORTS SPONSORSHIP

Acronym or abbreviation: ISS

Warwick House, 25–27 Buckingham Palace Road, London, SW1W 0PP

Tel: 020 7233 7747
Fax: 020 7828 7099
E-mail: info@sportsmatch.co.uk

Website:
http://www.sports-sponsorship.co.uk

Enquiries:
Enquiries to: Director

Founded:
1985

Organisation type and purpose:
Professional body (membership is by subscription). National association of commercial companies sponsoring sport.

Subject coverage:
Sports sponsorship.

Printed publications:
Code of Conduct – Best practice for sponsors (free)
ISS Corporate Brochure – History, operations and membership benefits of ISS (free)
Sports Sponsorship Source – Bibliography of current research and other information for sponsors (free)
Playing the Game (booklet explaining sponsorship, free)
Sponsorship Guide – Introduction for smaller company/organisation (£5.99 inc. p&p)
Legal Checklist – Legal requirements in starting/running sponsorships (£10 inc. p&p)
Model Contract – Detailed draft contract for sport and sponsor (£50 inc. p&p)
Making Sponsorship a Success – A Sponsorship Manual (£28.50 inc. p&p)

Publications list:
Available in print

Access to staff:
Contact by letter, by telephone, by fax and by e-mail
Hours: Mon to Fri, 0900 to 1700

INSTITUTE OF SPRING TECHNOLOGY LIMITED

Acronym or abbreviation: IST

Henry Street, Sheffield, South Yorkshire, S3 7EQ

Tel: 0114 276 0771
Fax: 0114 252 7997
E-mail: ist@ist.org.uk

Website:
http://www.ist.org.uk

Enquiries:
Enquiries to: Information Manager
Direct tel: 0114 252 7982
Direct e-mail: mom@ist.org.uk

Founded:
1945

Formerly called:
Spring Research and Manufacturers' Association (SRAMA) (year of change 1997)

Organisation type and purpose:
Trade association (membership is by subscription), present number of members: 300, research organisation.

Subject coverage:
Spring technology; design study and investigation of failures in springs and materials; technical, contract, testing and inspection services including SEM facilities; training; relevant British and foreign standards.

Information services:
Technical information on all aspects of spring technology – free to members, chargeable to non-members

Education services:
Training Courses on all aspects of spring technology – including tailored in-house

Printed publications:
Facilities and Services leaflets
Directory of British Spring Manufacturers (occasional)
Membership Directory
Newsletter (quarterly)
Research Reports and Index thereto
Spring Design Guides

Electronic and video publications:
Spring design and validation software
Spring Material Selector (CD-ROM)

Publications list:
Available in print

Access to staff:
Contact by letter, by telephone, by fax and by e-mail. Appointment necessary. Non-members charged.
Hours: Mon to Thu, 0800 to 1630; Fri, 0800 to 1500

INSTITUTE OF SWIMMING POOL ENGINEERS LIMITED

Acronym or abbreviation: ISPE

PO Box 3083, Norwich NR6 7YL

Tel: 01603 499959
Fax: 01603 499959

Enquiries:
Enquiries to: General Secretary

Founded:
1978

Organisation type and purpose:
Professional body (membership is by qualification, election or invitation), present number of members: 850, training organisation, publishing house.
Membership also by direct application.
Professional membership, education and training to those in the swimming pool industry.

Subject coverage:
All aspects of engineering related to swimming pools.

Printed publications:
Home Study Course – filtration, construction, water chemistry and pool heating
ISPE Magazine (4 times a year, free to members)

continued overleaf

Update (Swimming Pool Industry Directory and
Specifier, £25 plus p&p)
Quick reference guide (£10 plus p&p)
Market Survey (£15 plus p&p)
Technical papers include the following plus 16
other titles:
Disinfection Fundamentals (Turk J, Marks C and
Reid R, £9 plus p&p)
Modern Pool Water Testing Technology (Shute G,
£13 plus £2 p&p)
Water Treatment for Pool Operators (Lamb J, £10
plus p&p)

Publications list:
Available in print

Access to staff:
Contact by letter, by telephone, by fax and by e-
mail
Hours: Mon to Fri, 0900 to 1700

INSTITUTE OF THE MOTOR INDUSTRY

Acronym or abbreviation: IMI

Fanshaws, Brickendon, Hertford, SG13 8PQ

Tel: 01992 511521
Fax: 01992 511548
E-mail: imi@motor.org.uk

Website:
http://www.motor.org.uk
Training and education programmes; details of
membership of IMI; book list; Institute news,
publications.

Enquiries:
Enquiries to: Director of Marketing
Direct e-mail: nigelb@motor.org.uk
Other contacts: Dirctor of Communications

Founded:
1920

Organisation type and purpose:
International organisation, professional body,
present number of members: 26,000.

Subject coverage:
Professional guidance for individuals in the retail
motor industry, including information on training
and education and qualifications in all sectors.

Printed publications:
Motor Industry Management (magazine, 10 times
a year, UK subscription £35)
Text Books, including:
Engines, Electronics and Related Systems (3rd ed,
2001)
Maintenance and Repair of Road Vehicles (3rd ed,
2001)
Transmission, Chassis and Related Systems (2001)
Vehicle Maintenance Service Replacement (2001)
Motor Trade Administration and Organisation
Motor Trade Management and Finance
Motor Trade Law

Electronic and video publications:
Autodata on CD-ROM

Publications list:
Available in print

Access to staff:
Contact by letter, by telephone, by fax, by e-mail
and via website
Hours: Mon to Fri, 0900 to 1700

Access to building, collection or gallery:
Prior appointment required
Hours: Mon to Fri, 0900 to 1700

INSTITUTE OF TRADE MARK ATTORNEYS

Acronym or abbreviation: ITMA

Canterbury House, 2–6 Sydenham Road, Croydon,
Surrey, CR0 9XE

Tel: 020 8686 2052
Fax: 020 8680 5723

E-mail: tm@itma.org.uk

Website:
http://www.itma.org.uk
Brochures, careers leaflets, fact sheets and
membership list.

Enquiries:
Enquiries to: Secretary
Other contacts: Public Relations Manager for press
enquiries, presentations.

Founded:
1934

Organisation type and purpose:
Professional body (membership is by subscription,
election or invitation), present number of
members: 1500.

Subject coverage:
Trade marks and allied matters.

Printed publications:
Brochures and careers leaflets
Information Circular (members only)
Membership list
Newsletter (monthly, members only)
Register of Trade Mark Agents
Fact sheets

Access to staff:
Contact by letter, by telephone, by fax and by e-
mail
Hours: Mon to Fri, 0900 to 1700

INSTITUTE OF TRANSLATION AND INTERPRETING (ITI)

Acronym or abbreviation: ITI

Fortuna House, South Fifth Street, Milton Keynes,
Buckinghamshire, MK9 2EU

Tel: 01908 325250
Fax: 01908 325259
E-mail: info@iti.org.uk

Website:
http://www.iti.org.uk
Organisation description and activities. Online
Directory of Members. Events Calendar.

Enquiries:
Enquiries to: Office Administrator

Founded:
1986

Organisation type and purpose:
Professional body (membership is by
qualification), present number of members: c. 3000,
training organisation.

Subject coverage:
Translation and Interpreting.

Printed publications:
ITI Bulletin (6 times a year)

Electronic and video publications:
Directory of Members

Publications list:
Available in print

Access to staff:
Contact by letter, by telephone, by fax and by e-
mail. Appointment necessary.
Hours: Mon to Fri, 0900 to 1730

Access to building, collection or gallery:
No access other than to staff

Full member of:
Fédération Internationale des Traducteurs (FIT)
63 Rue La Fontaine, F-75016, Paris, France

INSTITUTE OF TRANSPORT ADMINISTRATION

Acronym or abbreviation: IoTA

The Old Studio, 25 Greenfield Road, Westoning,
Bedfordshire, MK45 5JD

Tel: 01525 634940
Fax: 01525 750016

E-mail: director@iota.org.uk

Website:
http://www.iota.org.uk
Home page

Enquiries:
Enquiries to: Director

Founded:
1944

Organisation type and purpose:
Professional body, present number of members:
25,000.

Subject coverage:
Transport management and operations.

Printed publications:
Guides to Careers and Membership (free for
schools)
Transport Management (journal, 6 times a year,
free to members, others on subscription)

Access to staff:
Contact by letter, by telephone, by fax and by e-
mail. Appointment necessary.
Hours: Mon to Fri, 0900 to 1600

INSTITUTE OF TRAVEL AND TOURISM

Acronym or abbreviation: ITT

PO Box 217, Ware, Hertfordshire, SG12 8WY

Tel: 0870 770 7960
Fax: 0870 770 7961
E-mail: admin@itt.co.uk

Website:
http://www.itt.co.uk

Enquiries:
Enquiries to: Chairman

Founded:
1956

Organisation type and purpose:
Professional body (membership is by
qualification), present number of members: 3200.

Subject coverage:
Education and training in the travel and tourism
industry.

Printed publications:
Careers Pack
ITT Bulletin (quarterly)
Year Book (annually)

Access to staff:
Contact by letter, by telephone, by fax and by e-
mail. Appointment necessary.
Hours: Mon to Fri, 0900 to 1730

Access for disabled people:
Level entry, toilet facilities

INSTITUTE OF VEHICLE ENGINEERS

Acronym or abbreviation: IVehE

31 Redstone Farm Road, Birmingham, B28 9NU

Tel: 0121 778 4354
Fax: 0121 702 2615
E-mail: info@ivehe.org

Website:
http://www.ivehe.org

Enquiries:
Enquiries to: Executive Director
Direct e-mail: james@ivehe.org

Founded:
1881

Organisation type and purpose:
Professional body.

Subject coverage:
Manufacturing section of the vehicle industry,
original equipment.

Museum or gallery collection, archive, or library special collection:
Library of books on historic automobiles and carriages

Printed publications:
Vehicle Technology (journal, 4 times a year)

Access to staff:
Contact by letter, by telephone, by fax, by e-mail and via website
Hours: Mon to Fri, 0900 to 1700

Access to building, collection or gallery:
No access other than to staff, prior appointment required

INSTITUTE OF VITREOUS ENAMELLERS

Acronym or abbreviation: IVE

39 Sweetbriar Way, Heath Hayes, Cannock, Staffs, WS12 2UST

Tel: 01543 450596
Fax: 08700 941237
E-mail: info@ive.org.uk

Website:
http://www.ive.org.uk/

Enquiries:
Enquiries to: Secretary General

Founded:
1934

Incorporates:
the Vitreous Enamel Association (VEA, founded in 1956 as the Vitreous Enamel Development Council; name changed in 1995)

Please select:

Organisation type and purpose:
Trade association.
Represent the vitreous enamel industry by presentations to the public, industry and education also control the cleaner scheme – approval of cleaners for vitreous enamel.

Subject coverage:
Nature and uses of vitreous enamel finishes.

Printed publications:
How to Clean Vitreous Enamel
List of cleaning products for use on vitreous enamel
Vitreous Enamel – A Performance Guide (1984, for sale)

Electronic and video publications:
Videos: Part 1 for architects, designers and engineers; parts 2 and 3 for domestic use (1991, for purchase)

Access to staff:
Contact by letter, by telephone, by fax and by e-mail. Appointment necessary.
Hours: Mon to Fri, 0900 to 1700

Access to building, collection or gallery:
No prior appointment required

Affiliated to:
British Cookware Manufacturers Association

Parent body:
The Institute of Vitreous Enamel (IVE)

INSTITUTE OF WOMEN'S HEALTH

Acronym or abbreviation: IWH

PO Box 9010, Leicester, LE1 8BX

Tel: 0116 255 2100
E-mail: instituteofwomenshealth@yahoo.co.uk / info@iwhealth.co.uk

Website:
http://www.iwhealth.co.uk

Enquiries:
Enquiries to: Trustee

Founded:
1999

Organisation type and purpose:
Registered charity (charity number 1065037/0), suitable for ages: Adults, training organisation.
To provide information and education on subject of menopause and related issues so that women feel able to make informed health choices.

Subject coverage:
Menopause; osteoporosis; other gynaecological issues.
Management Therapies: hormone replacement therapy, lifestyle aspects, complementary therapy.

Museum or gallery collection, archive, or library special collection:
Textbooks, leaflets, videos, audio tapes, journals on subject areas covered

Non-library collection catalogue:
All or part available in-house

Printed publications:
Leaflets on subject areas (individually free, in bulk 10/50 leaflets charge)

Access to staff:
Contact by letter, by telephone, by e-mail and in person. Appointment necessary.
Hours: Wed, Thu, 1000 to 1400

Access for disabled people:
Parking provided, level entry, toilet facilities

INSTITUTE OF WOOD SCIENCE

Acronym or abbreviation: IWSc

3rd Floor D, Carpenters' Hall, 1 Throgmorton Avenue, London, EC2N 2BY

Tel: 0207 256 2700
Fax: 0207 256 2701
E-mail: info@iwsc.org.uk

Website:
http://www.iwsc.org.uk

Enquiries:
Enquiries to: Director

Founded:
1955

Organisation type and purpose:
Professional body (membership is by qualification, election or invitation, present number of members: 1,400, registered charity (charity number 800626).

Subject coverage:
The study of timber and wood-based materials.

Printed publications:
Biannual publication £80 for two issues
Institute of Wood Science Journal
Refereed papers
Wood Focus (magazine, twice a year, £35 for 2 issues)

Access to staff:
Contact by letter, by telephone, by fax and by e-mail
Hours: Mon to Fri, 0900 to 1700

INSTITUTION OF AGRICULTURAL ENGINEERS

Acronym or abbreviation: IAgrE

Barton Road, Silsoe, Bedford, MK45 4FH

Tel: 01525 861096
Fax: 01525 861660
E-mail: secretary@iagre.org

Website:
http://www.iagre.org

Enquiries:
Enquiries to: Chief Executive
Direct e-mail: crw@iagre.org

Founded:
1938

Organisation type and purpose:
Professional body.

Subject coverage:
Agricultural engineering; agricultural machinery; agriculture, horticulture, forest engineering; engineering for amenity areas; engineering for food storage and handling; food process engineering; environmental engineering; renewable energy.

Printed publications:
Landwards (IAgrE journal, 4 times a year, £52 a year)

Microform publications:
Conference proceedings, The Agricultural Engineer including the former Soil and Water (microfiche)

Electronic and video publications:
AgEng 2000 (CD-ROM)
Forest Engineering Group Symposia 1989–2000 (CD-ROM)

Access to staff:
Contact by letter, by telephone, by fax, by e-mail and in person
Hours: Mon to Fri, 0900 to 1700

Affiliated to:
Engineering Council (UK)

Links with:
European Society of Agricultural Engineers

INSTITUTION OF ANALYSTS AND PROGRAMMERS

Acronym or abbreviation: IAP

Charles House, 36 Culmington Road, London, W13 9NH

Tel: 020 8567 2118
Fax: 020 8567 4379
E-mail: dg@iap.org.uk

Website:
http://www.iap.org.uk/iapdg

Enquiries:
Enquiries to: Secretary

Founded:
1981

Organisation type and purpose:
Professional body.
The Institution is Britain's leading specialised professional organisation for computer programmers and systems analysts.

Subject coverage:
Advice on matters relating to training and career development in the IT industry.

Printed publications:
Register of Consultants (a booklet listing qualified and experienced computer programmers and/or analysts who have passed the Institute's selection procedures)

Electronic and video publications:
Register of Consultants (disc)

Access to staff:
Contact by telephone and by e-mail
Hours: Mon to Fri, 0900 to 1700

INSTITUTION OF BRITISH ENGINEERS

Acronym or abbreviation: IBE

Clifford Hill Court, Clifford Chambers, Stratford-upon-Avon, Warwickshire, CV37 8AA

Tel: 01789 298739
Fax: 01789 267060
E-mail: info@britishengineers.com

Website:
Published papers

Enquiries:
Enquiries to: Vice-President
Direct e-mail: bob.ganguly@yahoo.ca

continued overleaf

Founded:
1928

Organisation type and purpose:
Learned society, suitable for ages: 16+, training organisation.
Registering and certifying organisation for four engineering qualifications.

Subject coverage:
The promotion of all aspects of engineering: IT electronic, electrical, mechanical, civil, automative, aerospace, rail, design, chemical, nuclear, marine, oil and gas, sales, bilingual engineers.

Access to staff:
Contact by letter, by telephone, by fax, by e-mail and via website
Hours: Mon to Fri, 0900 to 1700

Close links with:
Engineering Industries Association

INSTITUTION OF CIVIL ENGINEERING SURVEYORS

Acronym or abbreviation: ICES

Dominion House, Sibson Road, Sale, Cheshire, M33 7PP

Tel: 0161 972 3100
Fax: 0161 942 3118
E-mail: ices@ices.org.uk

Website:
http://www.ices.org.uk
General information with reference to civil engineering surveying, routes to membership, information about ICES.

Enquiries:
Enquiries to: Administrator

Founded:
1972

Organisation type and purpose:
Advisory body, professional body (membership is by qualification, election or invitation), present number of members: 4,000, registered charity, suitable for ages: 18+.
Qualifying body for engineering and quantity surveyors involved with civil engineering.

Subject coverage:
Construction, commercial management including: quantity surveying, project management, estimating, construction law, construction economics, planning, procurement engineering.
Geospacial Engineering surveying including: land surveying, engineering surveying, hydrographic surveying, remote sensing, cartography, geographical information systems, photogrammetry.

Printed publications:
Civil Engineering Surveyor (journal, monthly, free to members)
Information literature free to schools, employers, students etc
Various technical publications

Publications list:
Available in print

Access to staff:
Contact by letter, by telephone, by fax, by e-mail and via website
Hours: Mon to Fri, 0830 to 1700

Access for disabled people:
Parking provided, access to all public areas, toilet facilities

Associated institution of the:
Institution of Civil Engineers

Member of:
Construction Industry Council
International Federation of Surveyors
Survey and Mapping Alliance

Wholly owned marketing and publications company is:
SURCO Limited

INSTITUTION OF CIVIL ENGINEERS

Acronym or abbreviation: ICE

1 Great George Street, Westminster, London, SW1P 3AA

Tel: 020 7222 7722
Fax: 020 7976 7610
E-mail: library@ice.org.uk

Website:
http://www.ice.org.uk

Enquiries:
Enquiries to: Head Knowledge Transfer
Direct tel: 020 7665 2252
Other contacts: Archivist for access for archives.

Founded:
1818

Organisation type and purpose:
Learned society.
Qualifying body.

Subject coverage:
Civil engineering and related theoretical and applied sciences; civil engineering, building, construction; concrete, iron, steel and timber in structures; geotechnical engineering; public health engineering; hydrology and hydraulics; municipal engineering; history of technology; transport, environment.

Museum or gallery collection, archive, or library special collection:
18th and 19th century pamphlets
Archives of Council of Engineering Institutions
Archives of Institution of Civil Engineers
Archives of Institution of Municipal Engineers
Archives of Smeatonian Society
B L Vulliamy Horological Library
Films, videos and photographic collections
Gibb Collection
J G James Collection
Mackenzie Collection
MSS of Telford, Smeaton, the Rennies, Brunel and other early civil engineers

Non-library collection catalogue:
All or part available online, in-house and in print

Library catalogue:
All or part available online

Printed publications:
Advances in Cement Research (quarterly)
Conference publications
Geotechnique (quarterly)
Ground Engineering (monthly)
Magazine of Concrete Research
NEC International (monthly)
New Civil Engineer (weekly)
Nuclear Energy (6 times a year)
Offshore Engineer (monthly)
Proceedings (10 parts, quarterly)
Key facts pamphlets (annual, free of charge)

Electronic and video publications:
Audio visual catalogue (£2)

Publications list:
Available online and in print

Access to staff:
Contact by letter, by telephone, by fax, by e-mail, in person and via website. Appointment necessary. Access for members only. Letter of introduction required. Non-members charged.
Hours: Mon to Fri, 0915 to 1730
Special comments: Charges made to all users for certain services.

Houses the:
British Dam Society
British Geotechnical Association
British Hydrological Society
British Tunnelling Society
Central Dredging Association – British Section
European Council of Civil Engineers
International Association for Hydraulic Research – British Section
International Commission on Irrigation and Drainage – British Section (ICID)

International Navigation Association – British Section (PIANC)
Nuclear Institute
Offshore Engineering Society
Railway Civil Engineers Association
Society for Earthquake and Civil Engineering Dynamics (SECED)
Transport Planning Society
Wind Engineering Society

INSTITUTION OF DIESEL AND GAS TURBINE ENGINEERS

Acronym or abbreviation: IDGTE

Bedford Heights, Manton Lane, Bedford, MK41 7PH

Tel: 01234 214340
Fax: 01234 355493
E-mail: enquiries@idgte.org

Website:
http://www.idgte.org/

Enquiries:
Enquiries to: Secretary

Founded:
1913

Organisation type and purpose:
International organisation, learned society (membership is by subscription, qualification), present number of members: 700.
The institution is devoted to the advancement of diesel and gas engines, gas turbines and related products and technology.

Subject coverage:
Diesel engines and gas turbines.

Printed publications:
Technical papers (6 times a year, for members; on sale to non-members)

Electronic and video publications:
Annual Working Cost and Operational Report (available on disk, for sale to members and non-members)

Publications list:
Available in print

Access to staff:
Contact by letter, by telephone, by fax, by e-mail and via website
Hours: Mon to Fri, 0900 to 1700

Access to building, collection or gallery:
Prior appointment required

INSTITUTION OF ENGINEERING AND TECHNOLOGY

Acronym or abbreviation: IET

Savoy Place, London, WC2R 0BL

Tel: 020 7240 5461
Fax: 020 7240 8467
E-mail: libdesk@theiet.org

Website:
http://www.theiet.org
The IET; publishing; news; education and careers; events; membership; engineering policy; communities; research.
http://www.theiet.org/archives
History of IET, online catalogue, biographies, online exhibitions
http://www.theiet.org/publishing
Publications catalogue, online journals, books, etc.
http://www.theiet.org/library
Library service, including access to the catalogue and virtual library

Enquiries:
Enquiries to: Librarian
Direct tel: 020 7344 5461
Direct fax: 020 7344 8467
Direct e-mail: jcoupland@theiet.org
Other contacts: Archivist

Founded:
1871

Created by the merger of:
Institution of Electrical Engineers (IEE) and
Institution of Incorporated Engineers (IIE) (year of
change 2006)

Organisation type and purpose:
International organisation, learned society
(membership is by subscription, qualification),
present number of members: 150,000, registered
charity (charity number 211014), publishing house.
Qualifying body.

Subject coverage:
Electrical, electronic and control engineering,
computer science, information technology,
manufacturing, engineering, telecommunications.

Information services:
Technical and business research service

**Museum or gallery collection, archive, or library
special collection:**
Silvanus Thompson Memorial Collection (rare
books and manuscripts)
Sir Francis Ronalds Collection (19th-century rare
books and manuscripts on electricity)

Trade and statistical information:
Small collection of market reports

Non-library collection catalogue:
All or part available online

Library catalogue:
All or part available online

Printed publications:
A large range of books, abstract publications,
journals, symposia proceedings, etc. (see also
INSPEC), including:
Books (some 150 current titles; about 20 new titles
a year)
Electronics Letters (fortnightly)
Power Engineering Journal (6 times a year)
Proceedings of the IEE (10 bi-monthly parts)
Ships Regulations
Wiring Regulations
Order printed publications from: Publications Sales,
IET, PO Box 96, Stevenage, Hertfordshire, SG1
2SD; tel. 01438 767328; fax 01438 742792; e-mail
sales@theiet.org

Electronic and video publications:
CD-ROMs, online services, tape services

Publications list:
Available online and in print

Access to staff:
Contact by letter, by telephone, by fax, by e-mail,
in person and via website. Non-members charged.
Hours: Mon to Fri, 0900 to 1700

Access to building, collection or gallery:
No prior appointment required
Hours: Mon to Fri, 0900 to 1700

Access for disabled people:
Ramped entry, toilet facilities

Also at:
IET
Michael Faraday House, Six Hills Way,
Stevenage, Hertfordshire, SG1 2AY; tel: 01438
313311; fax: 01438 313465; e-mail: postmaster@
theiet.org; website: http://www.theiet.org

Parent body:
Inspec
Michael Faraday House, Stevenage, SG1 2AY;
tel: 01438 767540; fax: 01438 742840; e-mail:
inspec@theiet.org; website: http://www.theiet
.org/inspec

INSTITUTION OF ENGINEERING DESIGNERS

Acronym or abbreviation: IED

Courtleigh, Westbury Leigh, Westbury, Wiltshire,
BA13 3TA

Tel: 01373 822801

Fax: 01373 858085
E-mail: ied@ied.org.uk

Enquiries:
Enquiries to: Secretary

Founded:
1945

Organisation type and purpose:
Professional body (membership is by qualification,
election or invitation), present number of
members: 5300, registered charity (charity number
269879).

Subject coverage:
Engineering design, engineering drawing, design,
design education.

Printed publications:
Conference proceedings, etc
Engineering Designer (6 times a year)
Guide to Engineering Design Courses in the UK

Access to staff:
Contact by letter, by telephone, by fax, by e-mail
and via website
Hours: Mon to Fri, 0900 to 1700

Nominated body of the:
Engineering Council
tel: 020 7240 7891

INSTITUTION OF ENVIRONMENTAL SCIENCES

Acronym or abbreviation: IES

PO Box 16, Bourne, Lincolnshire, PE10 9FB

Tel: 01778 394846
Fax: 01778 394846
E-mail: ies-uk@breathemail.net

Website:
http://www.greenchannel.com/ies

Enquiries:
Enquiries to: Honorary Secretary

Founded:
1971

Organisation type and purpose:
Professional body.

Subject coverage:
Environmental science including ecology,
pollution, public health, urban problems, genetic
effects, climatic effects, effects of technology and
transport.

Printed publications:
Environmental Careers Handbook (£9.95)
Environmental Scientist (6 times a year, £4 per
copy)
IES leaflet (free)
Monographs (occasional)
Proceedings (2 times a year)

Access to staff:
Contact by letter and by e-mail
Hours: Mon to Fri, 0900 to 1700

INSTITUTION OF FIRE ENGINEERS

Acronym or abbreviation: IFE

London Road, Moreton-in-Marsh, Gloucestershire,
GL56 0RH

Tel: 01608 812 580
Fax: 01608 812 581
E-mail: info@ife.org.uk

Website:
http://www.ife.org.uk
General information, and publications

Enquiries:
Enquiries to: Membership Officer
Direct e-mail: gill.haynes@ife.org.uk

Organisation type and purpose:
Professional body (membership is by subscription).

Subject coverage:
Fire engineering.

Printed publications:
Fire Prevention and Fire Engineers Journal
(monthly)

Access to staff:
Contact by letter, by telephone, by fax, by e-mail
and via website. Appointment necessary.
Hours: Mon to Fri, 0900 to 1700

Part of:
Federation of British Fire Organisations

INSTITUTION OF GAS ENGINEERS AND MANAGERS

Formal name: International Institution of Gas
Engineers and Managers
Acronym or abbreviation: IGEM

Charnwood Wing, Holywell Park, Ashby Road,
Loughborough, Leicestershire, LE11 3GH

Tel: 01509 282728
Fax: 01509 283110
E-mail: general@igem.org.uk

Website:
http://www.igem.org.uk
General information on IGEM plus specific
information on publications, membership, journal,
library, etc.

Enquiries:
Enquiries to: Librarian
Direct tel: 020 7927 9917
Direct e-mail: anita@igem.org.uk

Founded:
1863

Organisation type and purpose:
Professional body, registered charity (charity
number 214011).

Subject coverage:
Gas engineering, manufacture, transmission and
distribution, gas utilisation, natural gas, LNG, gas
by-products, gas industry administration and
personnel, gas industry history.

Library catalogue:
All or part available in-house

Printed publications:
Communications Series – technical publications
subjects include: transmission and distribution
practice, safety recommendations, gas
measurement, utilisation procedures, gas
legislation guidance
International Gas Engineering and Management
(10 times a year)
Recommendations for Transmission, Distribution,
Safety, Measurement and Environmental Practice

Publications list:
Available online and in print

Access to staff:
Contact by letter, by telephone, by fax, by e-mail
and via website. Appointment necessary. Non-
members charged.
Hours: Mon to Fri, 0900 to 1700

Member organisation of:
Engineering Council
International Gas Union

INSTITUTION OF HIGHWAYS AND TRANSPORTATION

Acronym or abbreviation: IHT

6 Endsleigh Street, London, WC1H 0DZ

Tel: 020 7387 2525
Fax: 020 7387 2808
E-mail: iht@iht.org

Website:
http://www.iht.org
IHT activities, staff contacts, publications.

continued overleaf

Enquiries:
Enquiries to: Chief Executive
Other contacts: Director of Technical Affairs for technical enquiries.

Founded:
1930

Organisation type and purpose:
Learned society, registered charity (charity number 267321).

Subject coverage:
Highways and transportation infrastructure, planning and design for: roads, traffic, light rail, safety, disabled access, environment.

Printed publications:
IHT Guidelines including – Transport in the Urban Environment (1997, £49)
Guidelines – Safety Audit of Highways (1996, £15)
Alan Brant Seminar Papers 1995, 1996, 1997, 1998 and 1999 (£10 each)
Cycle Audit and Cycle Review (1998, £25 UK)
Highways and Transportation (monthly, free to members or on subscription)
Operational Management of the Highway Network (1997, £10)
Planning for Public Transport in Development (1999)
Rural Safety Management (1999, £25)

Electronic and video publications:
Guidelines – Transport in the Urban Environment (CD-ROM, 1997, £49)
Code of Pracice for Highways Maintenance (CD-ROM, £85 UK)
The Environmental Management of Highways (CD-ROM, 2001, £45 UK)
Providing for Journey on Foot (CD-ROM, £29 UK)
Rural Safety Management (CD-ROM, £25 UK)

Publications list:
Available in print

Access to staff:
Contact by letter, by telephone, by fax, by e-mail and via website. Appointment necessary.
Hours: Mon to Fri, 0930 to 1700
Special comments: Access difficult for those with mobility handicaps.

Access to building, collection or gallery:
No prior appointment required
Hours: Library: Mon to Fri, 0930 to 1700
Special comments: Not open if meeting in library.

Close professional cooperation with the:
Institute of Highways Incorporated Engineers (IHIE)

INSTITUTION OF LIGHTING ENGINEERS

Acronym or abbreviation: ILE

Lennox House, 9 Lawford Road, Rugby, Warwickshire, CV21 2DZ

Tel: 01788 576492
Fax: 01788 540145
E-mail: info@ile.co.uk

Website:
http://www.ile.co.uk
Regional information, technical reports, events, contacts, news, jobs.

Enquiries:
Enquiries to: Chief Executive
Other contacts: Technical Services Manager for technical advice.

Founded:
1924

Organisation type and purpose:
National organisation, professional body (membership is by qualification), present number of members: 2075, registered charity (charity number 268547), suitable for ages: all, training organisation, research organisation, publishing house.
To promote excellence in lighting.

Subject coverage:
All aspects of lighting, particularly exterior including street, sports, flood, emergency, tunnel lighting.

Museum or gallery collection, archive, or library special collection:
Small library

Library catalogue:
All or part available in-house

Printed publications:
Guidance Notes for the Reduction of Light Pollution (1997)
Lighting Journal (6 times a year, free to members)
Technical reports
A Practical Guide to the Procurement of Street Lighting Projects through the Private Finance Initiative (1999)
Lighting and Crime (1999)
A Guide for Crime and Disorder Reduction through a Public Lighting Strategy (1999)
Appraising the use of Remote Monitoring and Switching Technology in Street Lighting Services (1999)

Electronic and video publications:
Lighting Video
Brightness of Illuminated Advertisements (CD-ROM)

Publications list:
Available online and in print

Access to staff:
Contact by letter, by telephone, by fax, by e-mail and via website. Appointment necessary. Non-members charged.
Hours: Mon to Fri, 0900 to 1700

Access to building, collection or gallery:
Prior appointment required

Nominated body of the:
Engineering Council

INSTITUTION OF MECHANICAL ENGINEERS

Acronym or abbreviation: IMechE

1 Birdcage Walk, Westminster, London, SW1H 9JJ

Tel: 020 7222 7899; 020 7973 1274 (information and library service)
Fax: 020 7222 4557
E-mail: library@imeche.org

Website:
http://www.imeche.org

Enquiries:
Enquiries to: Manager
Direct fax: 020 7222 8762
Other contacts: Archivist (for access to archives)

Founded:
1847

Organisation type and purpose:
Professional body (membership is by subscription, qualification), registered charity (charity number 206882).
To create a natural home for all involved in mechanical engineering science that commands high regard in the community, whose members' expert views are sought on all important, relevant issues, and to membership of which every mechanical engineer aspires.

Subject coverage:
Mechanical engineering and related fields: tribology, solid mechanics and machine systems, energy, materials, manufacturing technology and design, combustion engines, environmental engineering, offshore engineering, pressurised systems, aerospace and automotive engineering, maritime engineering, power engineering, railway engineering.

Museum or gallery collection, archive, or library special collection:
Archives of: Institution of Mechanical Engineers, Institution of Locomotive Engineers, Institution of Automobile Engineers
Manuscripts of: George Stephenson and Robert Stephenson; James Nasmyth; David Joy; FW Lanchester; Christopher Hinton; Joseph Whitworth; Livesey, Henderson and Company; many others
Library contains technical papers dating back to 1847
ESDU Data Sheets
More than 200 professional and trade journals, over 122,000 vols of books, some of which date back to the foundation of the Institution
American Society of Automotive Engineers, SAE, pre-prints

Non-library collection catalogue:
All or part available online and in-house

Library catalogue:
All or part available online

Printed publications:
International Journal of Engine Research (6 a year)
Automotive Engineer (11 a year)
Journal of Strain Analysis for Engineering Design (8 a year)
List of Current Periodicals (ILS)
Proceedings of the Institution (separate papers, 14 parts as follows)
Part A Journal of Power and Energy (8 a year)
Part B Journal of Engineering Manufacture (12 a year)
Part C Journal of Mechanical Engineering Science (monthly)
Part D Journal of Automobile Engineering (monthly)
Part E Journal of Process Mechanical Engineering (quarterly)
Part F Journal of Rail and Rapid Transit (quarterly)
Part G Journal of Aerospace Engineering (6 a year)
Part H Journal of Engineering in Medicine (8 a year)
Part I Journal of Systems and Control Engineering (8 a year)
Part J Journal of Engineering Tribology (8 a year)
Part K Journal of Multi-body Dynamics (quarterly)
Part L Journal of Materials: Design and Applications (quarterly)
Part M Journal of Maritime Environment (quarterly)
Part N Journal of Nanoengineering and Nanotechnology (quarterly)
Part O Journal of Risk and Reliability (twice a year)
Professional Engineering (twice a month)
Order printed publications from: Professional Engineering Publishing, 1 Birdcage Walk, London, SW1H 9JJ

Electronic and video publications:
Full text of current journal proceedings available online for members only

Publications list:
Available online and in print

Access to staff:
Contact by letter, by telephone, by fax, by e-mail, in person and via website. Appointment necessary.

Access to building, collection or gallery:
No prior appointment required
Hours: Mon to Fri, 0915 to 1730
Special comments: Loans available to members only. Some services charged.

Access for disabled people:
Access to all public areas, toilet facilities
Special comments: Lift

INSTITUTION OF NUCLEAR ENGINEERS

Acronym or abbreviation: INucE

Allan House, 1 Penerley Road, London, SE6 2LQ

Tel: 020 8698 1500 or 4750
Fax: 020 8695 6409

E-mail: inuce@lineone.net

Website:
http://www.inuce.co.uk
General, conferences and seminars, application for membership.

Enquiries:
Enquiries to: General Secretary
Other contacts: President

Founded:
1959

Organisation type and purpose:
Learned society, professional body.

Subject coverage:
Peaceful aspects of nuclear technology; nuclear engineering in relation to other disciplines, electronic/nuclear, mechanical/nuclear, nuclear physics, nuclear mathematics.

Printed publications:
Nuclear Engineer (6 times a year)

Microform publications:
Microfiche
Order microform publications from: UMI, Bell and Howell Co
300 N Zeeb Road, Ann Arbor, MI 48106–1346, USA

Publications list:
Available in print

Access to staff:
Contact by letter, by telephone, by fax, by e-mail and via website. Appointment necessary.
Hours: Mon to Fri, 0830 to 1700

Affiliated to:
The Engineering Council

Member society of the:
European Nuclear Society

INSTITUTION OF OCCUPATIONAL SAFETY AND HEALTH

Acronym or abbreviation: IOSH

The Grange, Highfield Drive, Wigston, Leicestershire, LE18 1NN

Tel: 0116 257 3100
Fax: 0116 257 3101
E-mail: enquiries@iosh.co.uk

Website:
http://www.iosh.co.uk
Information about IOSH; magazine style update feature; chat forum for occupational safety and health professionals; abstracts; technical information.

Enquiries:
Enquiries to: Media Officer

Founded:
1945

Organisation type and purpose:
Learned society, professional body (membership is by qualification), present number of members: 29,500, registered charity (charity number 210981), training organisation, publishing house.

Subject coverage:
Occupational safety, health and hygiene; training; legislation; environmental management.

Printed publications:
Policy and Practice in Health and Safety (twice a year)
The Safety and Health Practitioner (monthly, published by CMP Information)
Principles of Health and Safety at Work (7th UK edn)
Principles of Health and Safety at Work (Int'l edn)
Protect Your People and Your Business: the Practical One-stop Health and Safety Toolkit
Questioning Performance: the Director's Essential Guide to Health, Safety and the Environment
Health and Safety: Risk Management
Health and Safety: Hazardous Agents

Essentials of Environmental Management
Workplace Ergonomics

Publications list:
Available in print

Access to staff:
Contact by letter, by telephone, by fax, by e-mail, in person and via website
Hours: Mon to Fri, 0900 to 1700

IOSH has:
regional branches in the UK and Ireland and a number of special interest groups

INSTITUTION OF STRUCTURAL ENGINEERS

Acronym or abbreviation: IStructE

11 Upper Belgrave Street, London, SW1X 8BH

Tel: 020 7235 4535
Fax: 020 7235 4294
E-mail: mail@istructe.org

Website:
http://www.istructe.org

Enquiries:
Enquiries to: Manager, Library and Information Services
Direct tel: 020 7201 9105
Direct fax: 020 7201 9118
Direct e-mail: library@istructe.org

Founded:
1908

Formerly called:
Concrete Institute (year of change 1922)

Organisation type and purpose:
Learned society.

Subject coverage:
Structural engineering, defined as the science and art of designing and making with economy and elegance, buildings, bridges, frames and other similar structures so that they can safely resist the forces to which they may be subjected.

Information services:
Library service for IStructE members

Library catalogue:
All or part available online

Printed publications:
The Structural Engineer (23 times a year)
Structural use of glass in buildings (1999)
Temporary demountable structures: guidance on procurement, design and use (2nd edn, 1999)
Subsidence of low-rise buildings (2nd edn, 2000)
Inspection of underwater structures (2001)
Guidance for the use of computers for engineering design calculations (2002)
Design recommendations for multi-storey and underground car parks (2002)
Safety in tall buildings and other buildings of large occupancy (2002)
Manual for the design of reinforced concrete building structures (2nd edn, 2002)
Introduction to the fire safety engineering of structures (2003)
Expert evidence: a guide for expert witnesses and their clients (2nd edn, 2003)
Design and construction of deep basements including cut-and-cover structures (2004)
Manual for the design of plain masonry in building structures (2nd edn, 2005)
Standard method of detailing structural concrete: a manual for best practice (3rd edn, 2006)
Manual for the design of concrete building structures to Eurocode 2 (2006)
Temporary demountable structures: guidance on procurement, design and use (2007)
Guide to the advanced fire safety engineering of structures (2007)
The operation and maintenance of bridges access gantries and runways (2nd edn, 2007)
Manual for the design of timber building structures to Eurocode 5 (2007)
Manual for the design of plain masonry in building structures to Eurocode 6 (2008)

Guide to surveys and inspections of buildings and associated structures (2008)
Manual for the design of steelwork building structures (3rd edn, 2008)
Order printed publications from: Publications Department, at the same address

Publications list:
Available online and in print

Access to staff:
Contact by letter, by telephone, by fax, by e-mail, in person and via website. Access for members only.
Hours: Mon to Fri, 0930 to 1730
Special comments: Prior appointment required for non-members

Access to building, collection or gallery:
Prior appointment required for non-members
Hours: Mon to Fri, 0930 to 1730

Access for disabled people:
Ramp available

Constituent bodies:
Standing Committee on Structural Safety (SCOSS)

Member organisation of:
Construction Industry Council
EC (UK)

INSTOCK FOOTWEAR SUPPLIERS ASSOCIATION

Acronym or abbreviation: IFSA

Marlow House, Churchill Way, Fleckney, Leicester, LE8 8UD

Tel: 0116 240 3232
Fax: 0116 240 2762

Enquiries:
Enquiries to: Information Officer

Organisation type and purpose:
National organisation, trade association, membership association (membership is by subscription), present number of members: 8.

Subject coverage:
Footwear wholesaling in the UK.

Access to staff:
Contact by letter, by telephone and by fax
Hours: Mon to Fri, 0900 to 1700

Access to building, collection or gallery:
No access other than to staff

Affiliated to:
Federation of Wholesale and Industrial Distributors and the Footwear Distributors

INSULATED RENDER AND CLADDING ASSOCIATION

Acronym or abbreviation: INCA

PO Box 12, Haslemere, Surrey, GU27 3AH

Tel: 01428 654011
Fax: 01428 651401
E-mail: incaassociation@aol.com

Website:
http://www.inca-ltd.org.uk

Enquiries:
Enquiries to: Information Officer

Founded:
1983

Organisation type and purpose:
Advisory body, trade association (membership is by qualification), present number of members: 60.

Subject coverage:
Insulated render and cladding for solid or defective walled housing/buildings.

Trade and statistical information:
UK insulated render and cladding market sales figures.

continued overleaf

Printed publications:
Advisory literature
Insulated Render and Cladding: Specifiers and
   Property Owners' Briefing (free)
The Industry Insurance Guarantee Scheme (free)
Members List incorporating Register of Installers
   (free)
Register of Systems (free)
Code of Practice for Approved Applicators (free)
Code of Practice for Approved Systems (free)

Publications list:
Available online

Access to staff:
Contact by letter, by telephone, by fax, by e-mail
and via website
Hours: Mon to Fri, 0900 to 1700

INSULATION AND ENVIRONMENTAL TRAINING TRUST LIMITED

Acronym or abbreviation: IETTL

TICA House, Allington Way, Yarm Road Business
Park, Darlington, Co Durham, DL1 4QB

Tel: 01325 466704
Fax: 01325 487691
E-mail: enquiries@tica-acad.co.uk

Enquiries:
Enquiries to: Director

Organisation type and purpose:
Registered charity, training organisation.

Subject coverage:
Industry training in insulation and asbestos
removal.

Access to staff:
Contact by letter, by fax and by e-mail
Hours: Mon to Thu, 0830 to 1700; Fri, 0830 to 1530

Access to building, collection or gallery:
Prior appointment required

Access for disabled people:
Parking provided

Affiliated to:
Insulation & Environmental Training Agency
(IETA)
   tel: 01325 466704; fax: 01325 487691; e-mail:
   enquiries@tica-acad.co.uk
Thermal Insulation Contractors Association (TICA)
   tel: 01325 466704; fax: 01325 487691; e-mail:
   enquiries@tica-acad.co.uk

INSURANCE INSTITUTE OF LONDON

Acronym or abbreviation: IIL

5th Floor, 20 Aldermanbury, London, EC2V 7HY

Tel: 020 7600 1343
Fax: 020 7600 6857
E-mail: iil.london@cii.co.uk

Website:
http://www.iilondon.co.uk

Founded:
1907

Organisation type and purpose:
Professional body.
To raise the professional knowledge of those
working in insurance in the London Market.

Subject coverage:
Insurance industry.

Printed publications:
The New London Journal
London Institute Centenary Souvenir Booklet
Research Studies including:
208B – Construction Insurance (December 1999)
228 – Professional Indemnity Insurance
   (September 2001)
234 – Directors' and Officers' Liability Insurance
   (May 1999)

237 – Insuring Industrial and Process Machinery
   (May 2000)
240 – Marine Insurance in the Former Soviet Union
   (July 1999)
244 – Developments in Excess of Loss Reinsurance
   (May 2000)
253 – Run-off Management and Commutations in
   Practise (December 2006)
254 – Insurance of Revenue for Projects under
   Construction (September 2003)
258 – War Risks and Terrorism (October 2007)
249 – Business Continuity (December 2007)

Publications list:
Available online and in print

Access to staff:
Contact by letter, by telephone, by fax and by e-
mail. Appointment necessary.
Hours: Mon to Thu, 0900 to 1700; Fri, 0900 to 1645

Parent body:
Chartered Insurance Institute
   at the same address

INTER FAITH NETWORK FOR THE UK

8A Lower Grosvenor Place, London, SW1W 0EN

Tel: 020 7931 7766
Fax: 020 7931 7722
E-mail: ifnet@interfaith.org.uk

Website:
http://www.interfaith.org.uk
General information, online publications, annual
reviews.

Enquiries:
Enquiries to: Director

Founded:
1987

Organisation type and purpose:
Voluntary organisation, registered charity (charity
number 1068934).

Subject coverage:
Information and contacts for Britain's faith
communities at national and local level; advice and
information on inter faith matters.

Printed publications:
Inter Faith Update (newsletter, 3 times a year)
Building Good Relations with People of Different
   Faiths and Beliefs
Connect: Different Faiths Shared Values
Inter Faith Organisations in the UK: A Directory
Local Inter Faith Activity in the UK: A Survey
The Quest for Common Values
The Local Inter Faith Guide

Publications list:
Available online and in print

Access to staff:
Contact by letter, by telephone, by fax, by e-mail
and via website. Appointment necessary.
Hours: Mon to Fri, 0930 to 1730

Access to building, collection or gallery:
Prior appointment required

INTER-CREDIT INTERNATIONAL

Formal name: Inter-Credit International Ltd

4th Floor, South Point House, 321 Chase Road,
Southgate, London, N14 6JT

Tel: 020 8482 4444
Fax: 020 8482 4455
E-mail: collection@intercred.com

Website:
http://www.intercred.com/

Enquiries:
Enquiries to: Managing Director

Founded:
1971

Organisation type and purpose:
Service industry.
National and international debt recovery agency
and credit reference agency.

Subject coverage:
Credit scoring.

INTERCONTINENTAL CHURCH SOCIETY

Acronym or abbreviation: ICS

1 Athena Drive, Tachbrook Park, Warwick, CV34
6NL

Tel: 01926 430347
Fax: 01926 888092
E-mail: enquiries@ics-uk.org

Website:
http://www.ics-uk.org

Enquiries:
Enquiries to: Communications Manager

Founded:
1823

Organisation type and purpose:
Membership association (membership is by
subscription), present number of members: 830,
voluntary organisation, registered charity (charity
number 1072584).
ICS, an evangelical Anglican mission society,
supports the ministry of English-speaking,
international congregations in several continents,
ministers to holidaymakers in Europe and the
Mediterranean.

Subject coverage:
English-language church services abroad.

Printed publications:
Directory of English-speaking Churches Abroad
   (1999, £3.75)
ICS News (4 times a year, 1999 £20 suggested
   combined minimum donation with ICS Prayer
   Diary)
ICS Prayer Diary (4 times a year, 1999 £20
   suggested combined minimum donation with
   ICS News)

Access to staff:
Contact by letter, by telephone, by fax, by e-mail
and via website
Hours: Mon to Fri, 0930 to 1700

Access to building, collection or gallery:
No access other than to staff

Access for disabled people:
Level entry

Links with:
Partnership for World Mission (PWM)
   157 Waterloo Road, London, SE1 8AX; tel: 020
   7928 8681

INTERMEDIATE TECHNOLOGY DEVELOPMENT GROUP LIMITED

Acronym or abbreviation: ITDG

The Schumacher Centre for Technology and
Development, Bourton Hall, Bourton on
Dunsmore, Rugby, Warwickshire, CV23 9QZ

Tel: 01926 634400
Fax: 01926 634401
E-mail: itdg@itdg.org.uk

Website:
http://www.itdg.org

Enquiries:
Enquiries to: Information Officer
Direct e-mail: carolr@itdg.org.uk

Founded:
1966

Organisation type and purpose:
International organisation, registered charity
(charity number 247257).

An international development agency working at the cutting edge of sustainable community development through country offices in Africa, Asia and South America.
To build the technical skills of poor people in developing countries, enabling them to improve the quality of their lives and that of future generations.

Subject coverage:
Appropriate technology, low-cost and small-scale manufacturing processes suitable for the developing countries, in agriculture, water supply and sanitation, building materials and construction, energy, transport, food production, food processing, mining and small industries.

Museum or gallery collection, archive, or library special collection:
Books on appropriate technologies and grey literature

Printed publications:
Books on all aspects of the work of the group
Annual Report
Small World (magazine)
Waterlines (quarterly)
Order printed publications from: IT Publications 103–105 Southampton Row, London, WC1B 4HH, tel: 020 7436 9761, fax: 020 7436 2013, e-mail: itpubs@itpubs.org.uk

Publications list:
Available in print

Access to staff:
Contact by letter, by telephone, by fax, by e-mail and via website. Appointment necessary.
Hours: Mon to Fri, 0900 to 1700

INTERNATIONAL ACCOUNTING STANDARDS BOARD

Acronym or abbreviation: IASB

1st Floor, 30 Cannon Street, London, EC4M 6XH

Tel: 020 7246 6410
Fax: 020 7246 6411
E-mail: iasb@iasb.org.uk

Website:
http://www.iasb.org.uk
Details of the organisation, structure, aims and publications.

Enquiries:
Enquiries to: Secretary General
Other contacts: Publications Director

Founded:
1973

Organisation type and purpose:
Accountancy regulatory body.
To formulate international accounting standards and to promote their use worldwide.

Subject coverage:
International accounting standards.

Printed publications:
IASC's Annual review (for purchase)
IASC Update (for purchase)
IASC Insight (quarterly newsletter, all three on subscription £120)
International Accounting Standards (for purchase)
Exposure Drafts of proposed International Accounting Standards (for purchase)
Hedge Accounting (£10)
Order printed publications from: Publications Department, IASB
tel: 020 7427 5927, fax: 020 7353 0562

Electronic and video publications:
International Accounting Standards (CD-ROM)

Publications list:
Available online and in print

Access to staff:
Contact by letter and by telephone
Hours: Mon to Fri, 0900 to 1700

Special comments: Access for members only.

Access to building, collection or gallery:
No access other than to staff

INTERNATIONAL ACUPUNCTURE ASSOCIATION OF PHYSICAL THERAPISTS

Acronym or abbreviation: IAAPT

Hilltop, Benjamin Road, High Wycombe, Buckinghamshire, HP13 6SR

Tel: 01494 451295
Fax: 01494 451295
E-mail: merianmum@hotmail.com

Enquiries:
Enquiries to: UK Representative
Direct e-mail: merianmum@hotmail.com

Founded:
1991

Organisation type and purpose:
Professional body.

Subject coverage:
Acupuncture and physiotherapy.

Printed publications:
Meridian Worldwide – in-house newsletter

Access to staff:
Contact by letter and by fax
Hours: Unrestricted

Affiliated to:
World Confederation for Physical Therapy (WCPT)

Links with:
Acupuncture Association of Chartered Physiotherapists (AACP)

INTERNATIONAL AESTHETICIENNES

International Beauty Therapy Examination Board, Bache Hall, Bache Hall Estate, Chester, Cheshire, CH2 1BR

Tel: 01244 376539
Fax: 01244 373571
E-mail: info@iabeauty.com

Website:
http://www.iabeauty.com

Enquiries:
Enquiries to: Secretary

Founded:
1979

Organisation type and purpose:
International organisation, professional body (membership is by subscription, qualification).

Subject coverage:
Beauty, body and electrolysis, examinations, Membership with or without insurance.

Electronic and video publications:
Open Learning
Training videos and syllabus for purchase

Access to staff:
Contact by letter, by telephone, by fax and by e-mail
Hours: Sat, 0900 to 1700

INTERNATIONAL AFRICAN INSTITUTE

Acronym or abbreviation: IAI

SOAS, Thornhaugh Street, Russell Square, London, WC1H 0XG

Tel: 020 7898 4429
Fax: 020 7898 4410
E-mail: iai@soas.ac.uk

Website:
http://www.internationalafricaninstitute.org

Enquiries:
Enquiries to: Secretary

Founded:
1926

Organisation type and purpose:
International organisation, learned society (membership is by election or invitation), present number of members: 27, registered charity (charity number 1084798), research organisation, publishing house.
The International African Institute has been the foremost international association engaged in encouraging the study of African society and disseminating the results of research. Its prime objective is to facilitate communication between scholars within the continent and Africans throughout the world on issues that are of direct relevance to the peoples of this region. It achieves this objective through its publication programme, seminars, African and non-African scholars; and projects which are concerned with the infrastructure for learning and research in Africa.

Subject coverage:
Communications between scholars in Africa and elsewhere, African societies and cultures.

Printed publications:
Africa (quarterly)
Africa Bibliography (annually)
African Issues (series, published with James Currey Publishers)
Classics in African Anthropology (published with James Currey Publishers)
International Africa (library series published with Edinburgh University press)
Readings in African Arguments (series, published with Zed Books)
Order printed publications from: Edinburgh University Press
22 George Square, Edinburgh, EH8 9LF
James Currey Publisher
73 Botley Road, Oxford, OX2 0BS

Publications list:
Available online and in print

Access to staff:
Contact by e-mail
Hours: Mon to Fri, 0900 to 1700

INTERNATIONAL ALUMINIUM INSTITUTE

Acronym or abbreviation: IAI

New Zealand House, Haymarket, London, SW1Y 4TE

Tel: 020 7930 0528
Fax: 020 7321 0183
E-mail: iai@world-aluminium.org

Website:
http://www.world-aluminium.org

Enquiries:
Enquiries to: Secretary General

Founded:
1972

Organisation type and purpose:
International organisation, trade association, membership association (membership is by qualification), present number of members: 22. International association of the primary aluminium industry.

Subject coverage:
Aluminium industry; aluminium products; energy requirements; statistics, developments; environmental health and safety.

Trade and statistical information:
Information and statistics are available on the website.

Publications list:
Available online

continued overleaf

Access to staff:
Contact by letter, by telephone, by fax and by e-mail
Hours: Mon to Fri, 0900 to 1700

INTERNATIONAL ARTIST MANAGERS' ASSOCIATION

Acronym or abbreviation: IAMA

23 Garrick Street, Covent Garden, London, WC2E 9BN

Tel: 020 7379 7336
Fax: 020 7379 7338
E-mail: info@iamaworld.com

Website:
http://www.iamaworld.com
Publications.

Enquiries:
Enquiries to: Chief Executive

Founded:
1954

Organisation type and purpose:
International organisation, membership association (membership is by election or invitation), present number of members: 230.

Subject coverage:
Artist management, concert promotion (classical music).

Printed publications:
Directory of Artists (online)
Quarterly Newsletter (free to members)

Publications list:
Available online and in print

Access to staff:
Contact by letter, by telephone, by fax, by e-mail and via website
Hours: Mon to Fri, 0930 to 1730

INTERNATIONAL ASSOCIATION OF BOOK-KEEPERS

Acronym or abbreviation: IAB

Burford House, 44 London Road, Sevenoaks, Kent, TN13 1AS

Tel: 01732 458080
Fax: 01732 455848
E-mail: mail@iab.org.uk

Website:
http://www.ifa.org.uk
http://www.iab.org.uk
Membership information, course syllabus, etc.

Enquiries:
Enquiries to: Chief Executive

Founded:
1973

Organisation type and purpose:
Professional body.
Examining body.

Subject coverage:
All aspects of book-keeping and accountancy.

Printed publications:
Financial Accountant (6 times a year)
International Book-keeper (6 times a year)

Access to staff:
Contact by letter, by telephone, by fax, by e-mail and via website. Appointment necessary.
Hours: Mon to Fri, 0900 to 1700

Parent body:
Institute of Financial Accountants
Burford House, 44 London Road, Sevenoaks, Kent, TN13 1AS; tel: 01732 458080; fax: 01732 455848; e-mail: mail@ifa.org.uk

INTERNATIONAL ASSOCIATION OF CLASSIFICATION SOCIETIES

Acronym or abbreviation: IACS

6th Floor, 36 Broadway, London, SW1H 0BH

Tel: 020 7976 0660
Fax: 020 7808 1100
E-mail: permsec@iacs.org.uk

Website:
http://www.iacs.org.uk
General information on classification, IACS and its Members, publications lists and downloadable publications.

Enquiries:
Enquiries to: Permanent Secretary
Other contacts: Principal Technical Officer for technical enquiries.

Founded:
1992

Organisation type and purpose:
International organisation, membership association (membership is by qualification), present number of members: 10 members, 2 associates, voluntary organisation, registered charity, research organisation.
Trade association representing the world's 10 largest classification societies.

Subject coverage:
Ship classification; vessel surveys; vessel repairs; vessel hull and essential engineering systems; international maritime conventions and regulations; safety at sea; prevention of marine pollution.

Trade and statistical information:
IACS member societies classify the hull and essential engineering systems of over 90% of the world's merchant fleet by tonnage on behalf of well over 100 sovereign states worldwide.

Printed publications:
Bulk Carriers: Guidelines for Survey Assessment and Repair of Hull Structures (£22 inc. p&p)
Guidelines for the Inspection and Maintenance of Double Hull Tanker Structures (£35 plus p&p)
IACS Brochure, free
IACS Unified Requirements (£250 plus p&p)

Electronic and video publications:
IACS Unified Requirements (CD-ROM, £250 plus p&p)

Publications list:
Available online

Access to staff:
Contact by letter, by telephone, by fax, by e-mail and via website. Appointment necessary.
Hours: Mon to Fri, 0900 to 1700

Access to building, collection or gallery:
Prior appointment required

Access for disabled people:
Level entry

Associate members:
Indian Register of Shipping
Mumbai, India; tel: 00 91 22 2570 3627; fax: 00 91 22 2570 3611; e-mail: ho@irclass.org

Full Members:
American Bureau of Shipping
ABS Plaza, 16855 Northchase Drive, Houston, TX 77060, USA; tel: 00 1 281–877–6000; fax: 00 1 281–877–6001; e-mail: abs-worldhq@eagle.org
Bureau Veritas
Paris, France; tel: 00 33 1 42 91 52 91; fax: 00 33 1 42 91 52 93; e-mail: veristarinfo@bureauveritas.com
China Classification Society
Beijing, China; tel: 00 86 10 5811 2288; fax: 00 86 10 5811 2811; e-mail: ccs@ccs.org.cn
Det Norske Veritas
Hovik, Norway; tel: 00 47 67 57 99 00; fax: 00 47 67 57 99 11; e-mail: iacs@dnv.com
Germanischer Lloyd
Hamburg, Germany; tel: 00 49 40 36 14 90; fax: 00 49 40 36 14 9200; e-mail: headoffice@gl-group.com

Korean Register of Shipping
Taejon, Korea; tel: 00 82 42 869 9114; fax: 00 82 42 862 6011; e-mail: krsiacs@krs.co.kr
Lloyd's Register of Shipping
London; tel: 00 44 20 7709 9166; fax: 00 44 20 7488 4796; e-mail: lloydsreg@lr.org
Nippon Kaiji Kyokai
Tokyo, Japan; tel: 00 81 3 3230 1201; fax: 00 81 3 3230 3524; e-mail: xad@classnk.or.jp
Register of Shipping (Russia)
St Petersburg, Russia; tel: 00 7 812 312 3569; fax: 00 7 812 312 3569; e-mail: 004@rs-head.spb.ru
Registro Italiano Navale
Genova, Italy; tel: 00 39 010 53 851; fax: 00 39 010 59 1877; e-mail: info@rina.org

Links with:
European Association of Classification Societies (EURACS)

Other address:
IACS QSCS OPS
Suite 2, Orchard House, 51–67 Commercial Road, Southampton, SO15 1GG; tel: 023 8021 1369; fax: 023 8023 7653; e-mail: qscs.ops@iacs.org.uk

INTERNATIONAL ASSOCIATION OF HYDROGEOLOGISTS

Acronym or abbreviation: IAH

PO Box 9, Kenilworth, Warwickshire, CV8 1JG

Tel: 01926 450677
Fax: 01926 856561
E-mail: iah@iah.org

Website:
http://www.iah.org
Information on the Association publications, information on hydrogeology.

Enquiries:
Enquiries to: Secretary General

Founded:
1956

Organisation type and purpose:
International organisation, professional body (membership is by subscription), present number of members: 3500.

Subject coverage:
Hydrogeology, groundwater, role in developing countries.

Printed publications:
Hydrogeology (journal, pub Springer Verlag)
International Contributions to Hydrogeology (book series, pub Balkerna, Rotterdam)

Electronic and video publications:
Newsletter (online)

Publications list:
Available online

Access to staff:
Contact by letter, by fax, by e-mail and via website
Hours: Irregular

Affiliated to:
International Union of Geological Sciences

INTERNATIONAL ASSOCIATION OF INSTITUTES OF NAVIGATION

Acronym or abbreviation: IAIN

Royal Institute of Navigation, 1 Kensington Gore, London, SW7 2AT

Tel: 020 7591 3130
Fax: 020 7591 3131
E-mail: prentpage@aol.com

Website:
http://www.rin.org.uk/iain/frame1.htm

Enquiries:
Enquiries to: Secretary General
Direct tel: 01444 232405
Direct fax: 01444 232405

Organisation type and purpose:
International organisation.
Coordinating and consulting body of 19 national institutes of navigation throughout the world.

Subject coverage:
Navigation by land, sea, air and in space.

Printed publications:
Newsletter

Electronic and video publications:
Newsletter available via website

Access to staff:
Contact by letter, by fax, by e-mail and via website
Hours: Mon to Fri, 0900 to 1700

Members are the institutes of navigation of:
Arab States, Argentine, Austria, Australia, Czech Republic, China, France, Germany, Italy, Japan, Korea, Netherlands, Nordic States, Poland, Russia, Spain, Switzerland, UK, USA
Phone, Fax, Email Nos on IAIN website (www.rin.org.uk/iain/frame1.htm)

INTERNATIONAL ASSOCIATION OF MUSIC LIBRARIES, ARCHIVE AND DOCUMENTATION CENTRES (UNITED KINGDOM BRANCH)

Acronym or abbreviation: IAML (UK & Irl)

Website:
http://www.iaml-uk-irl.org

Founded:
1953

Organisation type and purpose:
International organisation, professional body (membership is by subscription, election or invitation), present number of members: 295.
Voluntary association in liaison with the Chartered Institute of Library Information Professionals. Promotes music libraries and supports anyone working in music libraries or related fields.

Subject coverage:
Music bibliography and librarianship.

Museum or gallery collection, archive, or library special collection:
A collection of books and magazines about music librarianship is held at the Department of Music, University of Oxford

Library catalogue:
All or part available online and in print

Printed publications:
BRIO (journal, 2 times a year)
British Union Catalogue of Music Periodicals (BUCOMP2)
First Stop for Music (2001)
Working with Music in Libraries
Library and Information Plan for Music (1993)
Newsletter (2 times a year)
The Availability of Printed Music in Great Britain (1988)
Music Sets Survey (1997)
Access to Music (2003)
Concert Programmes in the UK and Ireland (2003)
Order printed publications from: Publications Officer, IAML (UK & Irl), County Library Headquarters, Walton Street, Aylesbury, Buckinghamshire, HP20 1UU, tel: 01296 382266, fax: 01296 382274, e-mail: mroll@buckscc.gov.uk

Publications list:
Available online

Access to staff:
Contact by letter, by telephone, by fax, by e-mail and in person. Appointment necessary.
Hours: Mon to Fri, 0900 to 1700

Links with:
Chartered Institute of Library and Information Professionals

INTERNATIONAL ASSOCIATION OF TOUR MANAGERS

Acronym or abbreviation: IATM

397 Walworth Road, London, SE17 2AW

Tel: 020 7703 9154
Fax: 020 7703 0358
E-mail: iatm@iatm.co.uk

Website:
http://www.iatm.co.uk

Enquiries:
Enquiries to: General Manager

Founded:
1962

Organisation type and purpose:
Trade association, membership association (membership is by subscription).

Subject coverage:
Tour management.

Printed publications:
IATM Newsletter

Access to staff:
Contact by letter, by telephone, by fax, by e-mail and via website
Hours: Mon to Fri, 0900 to 1430

Access to building, collection or gallery:
No access other than to staff

INTERNATIONAL AUTISTIC RESEARCH ORGANISATION – AUTISM RESEARCH LIMITED

Acronym or abbreviation: IARO

49 Orchard Avenue, Shirley, Croydon, Surrey, CR0 7NE

Tel: 020 8777 0095
Fax: 020 8776 2362
E-mail: iaro@autismresearch.wanadoo.co.uk

Website:
http://www.iaro.org.uk

Enquiries:
Enquiries to: Director
Other contacts: Secretary

Founded:
1981

Organisation type and purpose:
International organisation, membership association (membership is by subscription), present number of members: 300+, voluntary organisation, registered charity (charity number 802391), research organisation.
Information body.
To encourage research into autism and to disseminate the useful results of such research. Information provision and awareness-raising of scientific research into autism.

Subject coverage:
Information in autism and the latest research.

Education services:
Medical research only.

Printed publications:
Newsletter
An Essential Facts Leaflet for Carers, Persons with Autism and Professionals (free)
Research papers (nominal fee)
Asperger's Syndrome Symptoms (10p)
Asperger's Language, Cognition, Behaviour (10p)
Genetic Information (80p)

Publications list:
Available in print

Access to staff:
Contact by letter, by telephone, by fax and by e-mail
Hours: Mon to Fri, 0900 to 1700
Special comments: By appointment only.
Charges made to non-members for printed matters.

Access to building, collection or gallery:
Prior appointment required

Access for disabled people:
Special comments: No wheelchair access.

Networking:
Autism Research Review International
4182 Adams Avenue, San Diego, CA 92116, USA; tel: (619) 281 7165; fax: (619) 563 6840; website: www.AutismResearchInstitue.com
Autism Society of America
7910 Woodmont Avenue, Suite 300, Bethesda, Maryland 20814–3067, USA; tel: (301) 657 0881; fax: (301) 657 0869; website: www.autism-society .org
Autistik (Autism Society of the Czech Republic)
Estonia Autistic Society
Tartu EE2400, Estonia
Indiana Research Centre, Indiana University, Indiana Institute on Disability Community, Indiana's Centre for Excellence on Disability
2853 East Tenth Street, Bloomington, IN 74708–2696, USA; tel: (812) 855 6508; fax: (812) 855 9630; e-mail: cbow-man@indianna.edu

INTERNATIONAL BEE RESEARCH ASSOCIATION

Acronym or abbreviation: IBRA

16 North Road, Cardiff, CF10 3DY

Tel: 029 2037 2409
Fax: 056 0113 5640
E-mail: mail@ibra.org.uk

Website:
http://www.ibra.org.uk

Enquiries:
Enquiries to: Director
Direct e-mail: joneshr@ibra.org.uk
Other contacts: Development Manager

Founded:
1949

Organisation type and purpose:
International organisation, learned society, membership association (membership is by subscription), present number of members: 395, registered charity (charity number 209222), museum, consultancy, publishing house.
Library; Research Data Collection.
The world information service for bee science and beekeeping.

Subject coverage:
Apiculture; bees (all species, but especially honeybees); substances used by bees; plants foraged by bees; bee products and their uses; pollination by bees and other insects; pests and diseases of bees; history of beekeeping; beekeeping development programmes in the Third World.

Museum or gallery collection, archive, or library special collection:
Apis Library, Morland, Manley and Essinger Collections
Eva Crane Library (over 40,000 publications)
Historical and Contemporary Beekeeping Material
Picture Collection

Non-library collection catalogue:
All or part available in-house and in print

Library catalogue:
All or part available in-house

Printed publications:
A selected list:
Anatomy and Dissection of the Honeybee (1994)
Beeswax and Propolis for Pleasure and Profit (1997)
Bee World Index 1919–49
Bibliography of Tropical Apiculture (1978)
British Bee Books: a Bibliography 1500–1976
Bumble Bees for Pleasure and Profit (1995)
Dictionary of Beekeeping Terms with Allied Scientific Terms (in several vols, each multilingual)
Garden Plants Valuable to Bees

continued overleaf

Habitat Management for Wild Bees and Wasps
(1998)
Honey and Healing (2001)
Journal of Apicultural Research incorporating Bee
World (quarterly, from 1962)
The New Varroa Handbook (2007)
The Rock Art of Honey Hunters (2001)
Varroa Fight The Mite (1996)
Form and Function in the Honey Bee (2003)
Bibliography of Commonwealth Apiculture (2005)
Making a Beeline (2003)
Eva Crane – Bee Scientist (2008)
Field Notes on Queen Rearing (2008)
Buzz Extra (newsletter/magazine, quarterly from
2003)
Order printed publications from: IBRA Bookshop, 16
North Road, Cardiff, CF10 3DY, or via http://
www.ibra.org.uk/shop

Microform publications:
Index to Apicultural Abstracts 1950–83 (on
microfiche)

Electronic and video publications:
Available on CD:
Apicultural Abstracts, various year ranges and
topics
Journal of Apicultural Research, various themes
spanning the last 10 years.
The IBRA Historical Collection – an Overview
(2005)
The IBRA Collection – Protective Clothing for
Beekeepers (2006)
The IBRA Historical Collection – Skeps and Skep-
making accessories (2007)
Order electronic and video publications from: IBRA
Bookshop, 16 North Road, Cardiff, CF10 3DY, or
via http://www.ibra.org.uk/shop

Publications list:
Available online and in print

Access to staff:
Contact by letter, by telephone, by fax, by e-mail,
in person and via website. Appointment necessary.
Non-members charged.
Hours: Mon to Fri, 1000 to 1600

Access to building, collection or gallery:
Contact before visiting
Hours: Mon to Fri, 1000 to 1600

Access for disabled people:
Limited access (stairs, no lift, parking difficult), but
most information offered online or by telephone.

Links with:
International Union for Biological Sciences
Bat 442, Université Paris Sud 11, 91 405 Orsay
Cedex, France; tel: +33 1 69155027; e-mail:
secretariat@iubs.org; website: http://www.iubs
.org
National Library of Wales
Aberystwyth; tel: 01970 632 800; fax: 01790 615
709; website: http://www.llgc.org.uk

INTERNATIONAL BIBLE STUDENTS ASSOCIATION

Watch Tower House, The Ridgeway, London, NW7
1RN

Tel: 020 8906 2211
Fax: 020 8371 0051

Website:
http://www.watchtower.org
http://www.jw-media.org

Enquiries:
Enquiries to: Public Relations Manager
Direct e-mail: opi@wtbts.org.uk

Founded:
1914

Organisation type and purpose:
International organisation, membership
association (membership is by qualification),
present number of members: Britain: 127,206,
worldwide: 6,613,829, voluntary organisation,
registered charity (charity number IBSA: 216647;
Watch Tower: 1077961), publishing house.

To promote understanding of the Bible and its
message. Bible based educational work.

Subject coverage:
Comprehensive Bible education (free).

Printed publications:
Awake! (monthly)
The Watchtower (semi-monthly)
See official website for other publications

Electronic and video publications:
Jehovah's Witnesses, The Organization Behind The
Name (video)
The Bible A Book of Fact and Prophecy, Parts 1 to 3
(video)
Others available, contact for details

Publications list:
Available online and in print

Access to staff:
Contact by letter and by telephone
Hours: Mon to Fri, 0800 to 1200 and 1300 to 1700

Connections with:
Watch Tower Bible and Tract Society of
Pennsylvania
25 Columbia Heights, Brooklyn, NY 11201, USA;
tel: 00 1 718 560 5000

INTERNATIONAL BIOGRAPHICAL CENTRE

Acronym or abbreviation: IBC

Melrose Press Limited, St Thomas Place, Ely,
Cambridgeshire, CB7 4GG

Tel: 01353 646600
Fax: 01353 646601
E-mail: tradesales@melrosapress.co.uk

Website:
http://www.melrosepress.co.uk
Publication schedule and title information.

Enquiries:
Enquiries to: Chief Executive

Organisation type and purpose:
Publishing house.

Subject coverage:
Publishers of biographical reference books in areas
such as music, literature, medicine, the arts in
general.

Printed publications:
Dictionary of International Biography (31st ed.,
2004, £160))
The World Who's Who of Women (14th ed., 1997,
£135)
Who's Who in Asia and the Pacific Nations (4th
ed., 1999, £95)

Publications list:
Available in print

Access to staff:
Contact by letter, by telephone, by fax and by e-
mail
Hours: Mon to Fri, 0900 to 1700

INTERNATIONAL BOATBUILDING TRAINING COLLEGE

Acronym or abbreviation: IBTC

Sea Lake Road, Oulton Broad, Lowestoft, Suffolk,
NR32 3LQ

Tel: 01502 569663
Fax: 01502 500661
E-mail: ibtc@globalnet.co.uk

Website:
http://www.htk.co.uk/ibtc

Enquiries:
Enquiries to: Managing Director
Other contacts: Course Secretary for general.

Founded:
1974

Organisation type and purpose:
Service industry, training organisation.
Provision of practical training in boatbuilding
skills.

Subject coverage:
Boatbuilding, boatyard and marine management.

Access to staff:
Contact by letter, by telephone, by fax, by e-mail
and via website. Appointment necessary.
Hours: Mon to Fri, 0830 to 1630

Access for disabled people:
Parking provided, ramped entry, toilet facilities

Parent body:
Broadblue Limited
At the same address

INTERNATIONAL CAMELLIA SOCIETY

UK Region, 41 Galveston Road, London, SW15
2RZ

Tel: 020 8870 6884
Fax: 020 8874 4633
E-mail: patricia_short@btconncct.com

Website:
http://www.camellia-ics.org
International Camellia Society – a variety of
information, articles, etc.

Enquiries:
Enquiries to: Honorary Secretary

Organisation type and purpose:
International organisation, membership
association (membership is by subscription).

Subject coverage:
History, nomenclature, cultivation, propagation,
exhibition and arrangement of camellias; trial
grounds (2 in England, 1 in Scotland, 1 in N
Ireland).

Printed publications:
International Journal (annually, free to members)
UK Region Newsletter (2 times a year, free to
members)

Access to staff:
Contact by letter, by telephone, by fax and by e-
mail
Hours: Mon to Fri, 0900 to 1700

INTERNATIONAL CENTRE FOR CONSERVATION EDUCATION

Acronym or abbreviation: ICCE

Brocklebank House, Butts Lane, Woodmancote,
Cheltenham, Gloucestershire, GL52 9QH

Tel: 01242 674839
Fax: 01242 674839
E-mail: icce@brocklebank.plus.com

Website:
http://www.icce.org.uk

Enquiries:
Enquiries to: Executive Director
Direct e-mail: enquiries@icce.org.uk

Founded:
1984

Organisation type and purpose:
International organisation, registered charity
(charity number 289468), consultancy, publishing
house. Environmental education. To promote
greater understanding of global environmental
issues and sustainable development.

Subject coverage:
Environmental education and development of
resources for all levels.

**Museum or gallery collection, archive, or library
special collection:**
Books, games and packs
Environmental photolibrary

Printed publications:
Primary education resource material
Secondary education resource material

Microform publications:
Slide packs (to purchase)

Electronic and video publications:
CD-ROMs
Photo library/Imagebank
Videos

Publications list:
Available online and in print

Access to staff:
Contact by letter, by telephone and by e-mail
Hours: Mon to Fri, 0900 to 1700

INTERNATIONAL CENTRE FOR DISTANCE LEARNING

Formal name: International Centre for Distance Learning
Acronym or abbreviation: ICDL

Open University, Library and Learning Resource Centre, Walton Hall, Milton Keynes, Buckinghamshire, MK7 6AA

Tel: 01908 659001
Fax: 01908 653571
E-mail: lib-help@open.ac.uk

Website:
http://lcdlit.open.ac.uk

Founded:
1983

Organisation type and purpose:
University department or institute.
Documentation Centre.
Documentation centre specialising in distance education across the world.

Subject coverage:
Distance education encompassing all disciplines and all education levels.

Museum or gallery collection, archive, or library special collection:
Approximately 15,000 printed items; books, journals, conference papers, research reports, dissertations and other types of literature, all relating to the theory and practice of distance education
Distance education library

Non-library collection catalogue:
All or part available online

Library catalogue:
All or part available online and in-house

Access to staff:
Contact by e-mail and via website
Hours: Mon, Wed, 0830 to 2100; Tue, Thu, 0830 to 2100; Fri, 0830 1700; Sat, 0900 to 1700

Access to building, collection or gallery:
No access other than to staff

Access for disabled people:
Parking provided, level entry, toilet facilities

Parent body:
Open University

INTERNATIONAL CENTRE FOR PROTECTED LANDSCAPES

Acronym or abbreviation: ICPL

8E, Cefn Llan Science Park, Aberystwyth, Ceredigion, SY23 3AH

Tel: 01970 622620
Fax: 01970 622619
E-mail: icpl@protected-landscapes.org

Website:
http://www.protected-landscapes.org

Enquiries:
Enquiries to: Executive Director

Founded:
1991

Organisation type and purpose:
Training organisation, consultancy, research organisation.
To promote the concept of integrated conservation and development especially in relation to protected areas, through professional training, higher education, research and consultancy.

Subject coverage:
Protected areas and landscapes, integrated conservation and development.

Library catalogue:
All or part available in-house

Publications list:
Available in print

Access to staff:
Contact by letter, by telephone, by fax, by e-mail and via website. Appointment necessary.
Hours: Mon to Fri, 0900 to 1700

Access to building, collection or gallery:
Prior appointment required

Access for disabled people:
Parking provided, ramped entry, access to all public areas, toilet facilities

Member of:
The World Conservation Union (IUCN)

INTERNATIONAL CENTRE FOR RESEARCH IN ACCOUNTING

Acronym or abbreviation: ICRA

The Management School, University of Lancaster, Lancaster, LA1 4YX

Tel: 01524 593632
Fax: 01524 847321
E-mail: p.pope@lancaster.ac.uk

Enquiries:
Enquiries to: Director

Founded:
1971

Organisation type and purpose:
Registered charity (charity number 501487), research organisation.

Subject coverage:
Accountancy, particularly the financial reporting practices of companies and their regulation and standard-setting processes, corporate governance, derivative products.

Printed publications:
ICRA Occasional Paper Series

Electronic and video publications:
Corporate governance and board quality databases

Access to staff:
Contact by letter, by telephone, by fax and by e-mail
Hours: Mon to Fri, 0900 to 1700

Links with:
Lancaster University

INTERNATIONAL CENTRE FOR TECHNICAL RESEARCH LIMITED

Acronym or abbreviation: ICTR

Unit 1A Crusader House, 249–289 Cricklewood Broadway, London, NW2 6NX

Tel: 020 8450 8383
Fax: 020 8452 3366
E-mail: info@reictr.com

Enquiries:
Enquiries to: Chairman
Other contacts: Director

Founded:
1981

Organisation type and purpose:
International organisation, university department or institute, consultancy.

Subject coverage:
A non-profit-making organisation aimed at the transfer of technology to third world countries via consultancy, education and conferences.

Access to staff:
Contact by letter, by fax and by e-mail
Hours: Mon to Fri, 0900 to 1700

Access for disabled people:
Ramped entry, level entry, access to all public areas

INTERNATIONAL CHAMBER OF COMMERCE (UNITED KINGDOM)

Acronym or abbreviation: ICC UK

14–15 Belgrave Square, London, SW1X 8PS

Tel: 020 7823 2811
Fax: 020 7235 5447
E-mail: richardbate@iccorg.co.uk

Website:
http://www.iccuk.net

Enquiries:
Enquiries to: Director

Founded:
1920

Organisation type and purpose:
International organisation, membership association (membership is by subscription), present number of members: 350.

Printed publications:
A range of publications on arbitration and settlement of disputes, banking practice, commerce and transport, marketing and advertising
Reference works, reports and studies

Publications list:
Available in print

Access to staff:
Contact by letter, by telephone, by fax and by e-mail. Appointment necessary.
Hours: Mon to Fri, 0900 to 1700

INTERNATIONAL CHAMBER OF SHIPPING

Acronym or abbreviation: ICS

Carthusian Court, 12 Carthusian Street, London, EC1M 6EZ

Tel: 020 7417 8844
Fax: 020 7417 8877
E-mail: ics@marisec.org

Website:
http://www.marisec.org
ISC home page
http://www.marisec.org/pubs
Publication list

Enquiries:
Enquiries to: Secretary General

Founded:
1921

Organisation type and purpose:
International organisation, trade association, membership association, publishing house.

Subject coverage:
International shipping, safe ship operations e.g. tanker safety, helicopter and ship operations, prevention of drug trafficking.

Printed publications:
Model Ballast Management Plan (2nd ed 2000)
On Board Training Record Books
Personal Training and Service Record Books
Order printed publications from: Marisec Publications at the same address, e-mail: publications@marisec.org

continued overleaf

Publications list:
Available online and in print

Access to staff:
Contact by letter, by telephone, by fax and by e-mail
Hours: Mon to Fri, 0900 to 1700

Has consultative status with the:
International Maritime Organization
Various inter-governmental organisations

Members are the:
General Council of British Shipping
National shipowners' associations in 34 countries

INTERNATIONAL CHILDCARE TRUST

Acronym or abbreviation: ICT

Development House, 56–64 Leonard Street,
London EC2A 4LT

Tel: 020 7065 0970
Fax: 020 7065 0971
E-mail: info@ict-uk.org

Website:
http://www.ict-uk.org

Enquiries:
Enquiries to: President

Founded:
1982

Organisation type and purpose:
International organisation, registered charity.
To assist impoverished/distressed children and families.

Subject coverage:
Street kids, women's groups, training, environment, and health, all abroad. The Trust rarely funds other projects.

Electronic and video publications:
CD-ROM available

Access to staff:
Contact by letter, by telephone, by fax and by e-mail
Hours: Mon to Fri, 0900 to 1700

Has links with:
BOND
CSC
EC NGO Network

INTERNATIONAL CLEMATIS SOCIETY

Acronym or abbreviation: ICIS

3 Cuthberts Close, Waltham Cross, Hertfordshire,
EN7 5RB

Tel: 01992 636524
E-mail: clematis@clematisinternational.com

Website:
http://www.clematisinternational.com

Enquiries:
Enquiries to: Secretary

Founded:
1984

Organisation type and purpose:
International organisation, membership association (membership is by subscription), present number of members: 275.

Subject coverage:
Clematis, cultivation and propagation.

Printed publications:
Clematis International (annually)
Newsletter (twice a year)

Access to staff:
Contact by letter, by telephone, by e-mail and via website
Hours: Mon to Fri, 0900 to 1700

INTERNATIONAL COCOA ORGANISATION

Acronym or abbreviation: ICCO

Commonwealth House, 1–19 New Oxford Street,
London, WC1A 1NU

Tel: +44 (0)20 7400 5050
Fax: +44 (0)20 7421 5500
E-mail: info@icco.org

Website:
http://www.icco.org

Enquiries:
Enquiries to: Information Officer
Direct e-mail: library@icco.org

Founded:
1973

Organisation type and purpose:
International organisation.
Intergovernmental organisation.

Subject coverage:
Cocoa, economics, production and processing.

Trade and statistical information:
Statistics: production and consumption.

Printed publications:
Annual Report
Bulletin of Cocoa Statistics (quarterly)
ICCO World Cocoa Directory
Cocoa and Chocolate in Brazil
Cocoa Consumption in the Russian Federation
Country studies of Cocoa Production and Cocoa Consumption (irregular)

Publications list:
Available online and in print

Access to staff:
Contact by letter, by telephone, by fax, by e-mail and via website. Appointment necessary.
Hours: Library: 0900 to 1700 by appointment

Affiliated to:
UNCTAD

INTERNATIONAL COLLEGES OF ISLAMIC SCIENCES

Acronym or abbreviation: ICIS

Unit 1A Crusader House, 249–289 Cricklewood
Broadway, London, NW2 6NX

Tel: 020 8450 8383
Fax: 020 8452 3366
E-mail: Registrar@IslamicColleges.com

Enquiries:
Enquiries to: Chairman
Other contacts: Registrar

Founded:
1990

Organisation type and purpose:
International organisation, registered charity (charity number 802651), university department or institute.
Education.

Subject coverage:
Islamic higher education.

Printed publications:
Islamic University Journal (quarterly, annual subscription £40)

Publications list:
Available in print

Access to staff:
Contact by letter, by telephone and by fax
Hours: Mon to Fri, 1000 to 1730

Parent body:
International Centre for Technical Research
tel: 020 8450 8383; fax: 020 8452 3366

INTERNATIONAL COMMISSION ON ZOOLOGICAL NOMENCLATURE

Acronym or abbreviation: ICZN

The Natural History Museum, Cromwell Road,
London, SW7 5BD

Tel: 020 7942 5653
E-mail: iczn@nhm.ac.uk

Website:
http://www.iczn.org

Enquiries:
Enquiries to: Scientific Administrator
Other contacts: Executive Secretary

Founded:
1895

Organisation type and purpose:
International organisation (membership is by election or invitation), present number of members: 28.
International Commission for the furtherance of stability and universality in the nomenclature of animals.

Subject coverage:
Zoological nomenclature, maintenance and interpretation of the International Code of Zoological Nomenclature, rulings on particular problems.

Printed publications:
Bulletin of Zoological Nomenclature (journal, quarterly)
Towards Stability in the Names of Animals (1995)
International Code of Zoological Nomenclature (4th edn, 1999)
Official lists and indexes of names and works in zoology (1987)
Official lists and indexes of names and works in zoology – Supplement 1986–2001

Access to staff:
Contact by letter and by e-mail
Hours: Mon to Fri, 0900 to 1700

Links with:
International Union of Biological Sciences

INTERNATIONAL COMMITTEE FOR THE CONSERVATION OF THE INDUSTRIAL HERITAGE

Acronym or abbreviation: TICCIH

Chygarth, 5 Beacon Terrace, Camborne, Cornwall,
TR14 7BU

Tel: 01209 612142
Fax: 01209 612142
E-mail: stuartbsmith@chygarth.co.uk

Website:
http://www.mnactec.com/ticcih
http://www.ticcih.org

Enquiries:
Enquiries to: Secretary

Founded:
1978

Organisation type and purpose:
International organisation, membership association (membership is by subscription), present number of members: 500, registered charity (charity number 1079809).
To promote the preservation, interpretation of industrial sites throught the world.

Subject coverage:
International co-operation in the preservation, conservation, investigation, documentation, research and presentation of industrial heritage, promotion of education in these matters. This includes the physical remains of the industrial past, such as landscapes, sites, structures, plant, equipment, products and other fixtures and fittings, as well as the documentation, consisting of both verbal and graphic material, and memories and opinions of the people involved.

Printed publications:
Bulletin (quarterly)

Publications list:
Available in print

Access to staff:
Contact by letter, by telephone, by fax, by e-mail and via website
Hours: Mon to Fri, 0900 to 1700

Links with:
ICOMOS
tel: +33 145 67 6770; fax: +33 145 66 0622; e-mail: secretariat@icomos.org
National representatives and correspondents in 49 countries

INTERNATIONAL COUNCIL FOR SELF-ESTEEM

Acronym or abbreviation: ICSE

5 Ferry Path, Cambridge, CB4 1HB

Tel: 01223 365351
Fax: 01223 365351
E-mail: esteemhere@aol.com

Website:
http://www.murraywhite-selfesteem.co.uk

Enquiries:
Enquiries to: UK Representative

Founded:
1990

Organisation type and purpose:
International organisation, learned society, present number of countries in membership: 70
To promote concept of self-esteem and its significance; facilitates the co-ordination of self-esteem activities throughout the world.

Subject coverage:
Self-esteem in homes, schools and organisations, behaviour issues.

Printed publications:
Details of workshops and talks: a range of photocopiable resources and CD-ROMs
Magic Circles: Self-esteem for Everyone through Circle Time (Murray White, Sage Publications, London, 2009, £25)
Raising Self-Esteem, 50 Activities (Murray White, Pearson, Cambridge, £26)
Picture This for Families (Murray White, Sage Publications, London)

Publications list:
Available online and in print

Access to staff:
Contact by letter, by telephone, by e-mail, in person and via website. Appointment necessary.
Hours: Mon to Fri, 0900 to 1700

INTERNATIONAL COUNCIL OF TANNERS

Acronym or abbreviation: ICT

Leather Trade House, Kings Park Road, Moulton Park, Northampton, NN3 6JD

Tel: 01604 679999
Fax: 01604 679998
E-mail: sec@tannerscouncil.org

Website:
http://www.tannerscouncilict.org

Enquiries:
Enquiries to: Secretary
Direct tel: 01604 679917

Founded:
1926

Organisation type and purpose:
International organisation.

Subject coverage:
Leather production and related activities.

Trade and statistical information:
Surveys of production and relevant information eg environmental regulations normally restricted to members.

Printed publications:
International Glossary of Leather Terms

Access to staff:
Contact by letter, by fax and by e-mail
Hours: Mon to Fri, 0900 to 1700

INTERNATIONAL COUNCIL ON MONUMENTS AND SITES UK

Acronym or abbreviation: ICOMOS-UK

70 Cowcross Street, London, EC1M 6EJ

Tel: 020 7566 0031
Fax: 020 7566 0045
E-mail: admin@icomos-uk.org

Website:
http://www.icomos.org/uk/

Enquiries:
Enquiries to: The Secretary

Founded:
1965

Organisation type and purpose:
International organisation, advisory body, membership association (membership is by subscription), present number of members: 250, voluntary organisation, registered charity (charity number 1057254).

Subject coverage:
Preservation and management of monuments and historic sites.

Printed publications:
Publications List available on request

Publications list:
Available online and in print

Access to staff:
Contact by letter and by fax
Hours: Irregular, dependent on part-time staff

Links with:
ICOMOS International Secretariat
49–51 rue de la Fédération, 75015 Paris, France

INTERNATIONAL CRAFT AND HOBBY FAIR LIMITED

Acronym or abbreviation: ICHF Ltd

Dominic House, Seaton Road, Christchurch, Dorset, BH23 5HW

Tel: 01425 272711
Fax: 01425 279369
E-mail: info@ichf.co.uk

Website:
http://www.ichf.co.uk

Enquiries:
Enquiries to: Manager

Founded:
1976

Organisation type and purpose:
Service industry.
Exhibition Organisers.

Subject coverage:
Crafts and hobbies, design and technology, needlecraft.

Printed publications:
Lists of UK exhibitions

Access to staff:
Contact by letter, by telephone, by fax, by e-mail and via website
Hours: Mon to Fri, 0900 to 1700
Special comments: All listings, addresses and exhibiting companies are held solely for ICHF use only.

INTERNATIONAL CREMATION FEDERATION

Acronym or abbreviation: ICF

Van Stolkweg 29A, 2585 JN, The Hague, The Netherlands

Tel: +31 70 351 8836
Fax: +31 70 351 8827
E-mail: keizer@facultatieve.com

Website:
http://www.int-ciem-fed.org

Enquiries:
Enquiries to: Secretary-General

Founded:
1937

Organisation type and purpose:
International organisation, advisory body, registered charity.
The provision of a central, international, source of help, advice and information to all those interested or involved in any aspect of cremation.

Subject coverage:
All aspects of cremation.

Trade and statistical information:
International cremation statistics, cremation figures and details of cremation societies throughout the world.

Printed publications:
Pharos International (journal, quarterly, for sale)

Access to staff:
Contact by letter, by telephone, by fax and by e-mail
Hours: Mon to Fri, 0900 to 1700

INTERNATIONAL DANCE TEACHERS' ASSOCIATION

Acronym or abbreviation: IDTA

International House, 76 Bennett Road, Brighton, East Sussex, BN2 5JL

Tel: 01273 685652
Fax: 01273 674388
E-mail: info@idta.co.uk

Website:
http://www.idta.co.uk

Enquiries:
Enquiries to: General Secretary
Other contacts: Administration Officer

Founded:
1903

Organisation type and purpose:
International organisation, professional body (membership is by qualification), present number of members: 6000, service industry, suitable for ages: all.
Awarding body.

Subject coverage:
Dance (social and theatre); statistics related to dance; amateur tests in dance.

Museum or gallery collection, archive, or library special collection:
History of Dance

Printed publications:
Dance Teacher (monthly)
Dancing Year Book (£15)
Freestyle (£10)
Rock 'n' Roll (£10)
Technique of Ballroom Dancing (£16 inc. p&p)
Technique of Latin Dancing (£17 inc. p&p)
Technique of Theatre Dance (£17 including binder)
The Story of British Popular Dancing (£11 inc. p&p)
Order printed publications from: IDTA Sales Ltd – International Sales
at the same address, tel: 01273 608583

Electronic and video publications:
Ballroom Dancing (video)
Freestyle, Latin and Salsa (video, for sale)

continued overleaf

Various Dance Music (CD-ROM)
Various Dance Videos
Various Theatre Dance Subjects (CD-ROM)
Various Theatre Dance Subjects (video)

Publications list:
Available online and in print

Access to staff:
Contact by letter, by fax, by e-mail and via
website
Hours: Mon to Fri, 0900 to 1700

Access to building, collection or gallery:
No access other than to staff

Affiliated to:
British Council of Ballroom Dancing
Central Council of Physical Recreation

Member of:
Council for Dance Education and Training
Stage Dance Council International
    13 Braemar Road, Fallowfield, Manchester, M14
    6PQ

INTERNATIONAL FEDERATION FOR MODERN LANGUAGES AND LITERATURES

Formal name: Fédération Internationale des
Langues et Littératures Modernes
Acronym or abbreviation: FILLM

Institutionen för kultur- och medievetenskaper,
Umeå University, 901 87 Umeå, Sweden

Tel: +46 090 786 5797
Fax: +46 090 786 7845
E-mail: anders.pettersson@littvet.umu.se

Website:
http://www.fillm.ulg.ac.be

Enquiries:
Enquiries to: Secretary-General

Founded:
1928

Organisation type and purpose:
International organisation, membership
association.
A federation of 19 international learned societies in
the field of modern languages and literatures
under the auspices of UNESCO.

Subject coverage:
Modern languages and literatures.

Access to staff:
Contact by letter, by fax and by e-mail.
Appointment necessary.
Hours: Mon to Fri, 0900 to 1700

Access to building, collection or gallery:
No prior appointment required

INTERNATIONAL FEDERATION OF ACTORS

Acronym or abbreviation: FIA

Guild House, Upper St Martin's Lane, London,
WC2H 9EG

Tel: 020 7379 0900
Fax: 020 7379 8260
E-mail: office@fia-actors.com

Website:
http://www.fia-actors.com

Enquiries:
Enquiries to: General Secretary

Founded:
1952

Organisation type and purpose:
Trade union.
Representation of 100 performers' unions in 75
countries.

Subject coverage:
FIA provides four main services to member
unions: representation at the various international
organisations as an accredited non-governmental
organisation; defence of the artistic freedom of
performers; union development; information
exchange.

Printed publications:
FIA Focus (2–3 times a year)

Access to staff:
Contact by letter, by telephone, by fax and by e-
mail. Appointment necessary.
Hours: Mon to Fri, 0900 to 1700

INTERNATIONAL FEDERATION OF AROMATHERAPISTS

Acronym or abbreviation: IFA

7B Walpole Court, Ealing Green, Ealing, London
W5 5ED

Tel: 020 8567 2243
Fax: 020 8840 9288
E-mail: office@ifaroma.org

Website:
http://www.ifaroma.org/

Enquiries:
Enquiries to: Public Relations Manager
Direct e-mail: office@ifarom.org
Other contacts: Chairperson

Founded:
1985

Organisation type and purpose:
International organisation, professional body,
registered charity (charity number 327290).
Registration of courses.

Subject coverage:
Aromatherapy, aromatherapy training, registered
courses.

**Museum or gallery collection, archive, or library
special collection:**
Aromatherapy books
Lists of members and courses

Printed publications:
Aromatherapy Times (quarterly, £15 UK, £18
    Europe)
Directory of Members Registered with IFA (£2.50)
Directory of Training Courses Registered with IFA
    (£2.50)

Access to staff:
Contact by letter, by telephone and by fax
Hours: Mon to Fri, 0900 to 1700
Special comments: Charges for some services.

Affiliated to:
ICM
    Unit 15, Tavern Quay, Commercial Centre, Rope
    Street, London, SE16 1TX

Member of:
Aromatherapy Organisations Council
    PO Box 19834, London, SE25 6LB

INTERNATIONAL FEDERATION OF BUSINESS AND PROFESSIONAL WOMEN

Acronym or abbreviation: IFBPW

PO Box 568, Horsham, West Sussex, RH13 9ZP

Tel: 01403 739343
Fax: 01403 734432
E-mail: members@bpwintl.com

Website:
http://www.bpwintl.com
Background / history, international executive and
contacts, headquarters and director contact details,
diary dates of future activities, membership
enquiries and general information.

Enquiries:
Enquiries to: Director
Other contacts: International President

Founded:
1930

Organisation type and purpose:
International organisation, membership
association (membership is by subscription),
present number of members: 38,000, voluntary
organisation, registered charity.
International non-governmental organisation.
Promote the status of women.

Subject coverage:
Business and professional women and all issues
relating to achieving equal status for women in
political, economic and civil spheres of society.

Printed publications:
Newsletter (monthly)
Biography of Founder
First part history of IFBPW plus a variety of other
    publications
Part II of History of BPW International (IFBPW)

Publications list:
Available in print

Access to staff:
Contact by letter, by telephone, by fax, by e-mail,
in person and via website. Appointment necessary.
Hours: Mon to Fri, 0900 to 1700

Subsidiary regional groups:
Africa
Asia and Pacific
Europe
Latin America and Spanish-speaking West Indies
North America and non-Spanish-speaking West
Indies

INTERNATIONAL FEDERATION OF GYNAECOLOGY AND OBSTETRICS

Acronym or abbreviation: FIGO

70 Wimpole Street, London, W1G 8AX

Tel: 020 7224 3270
Fax: 020 7935 0736
E-mail: figo@figo.org

Website:
http://www.figo.org

Enquiries:
Enquiries to: Secretariat
Other contacts: Secretary General

Founded:
1954

Organisation type and purpose:
International organisation, membership
association (membership is by subscription),
present number of members: 103 national societies.
Non-governmental organisation.

Subject coverage:
Obstetrics and gynaecology.

Printed publications:
International Journal of Gynaecology and
    Obstetrics (monthly, on subscription)
Newsletter (members only)
Report on Gynaecological Cancer

Publications list:
Available online

Access to staff:
Contact by letter, by telephone, by fax, by e-mail,
in person and via website
Hours: Mon to Fri, 0900 to 1700

Cooperation with:
19 non-governmental organisations involved in
women and children's health

Incorporated in Geneva, its title is the:
Fédération Internationale de Gynécologie et
d'Obstétrique

INTERNATIONAL FEDERATION OF INSPECTION AGENCIES

Formal name: International Federation of Inspection Agencies Limited
Acronym or abbreviation: IFIA

22 Great Tower Street, London, EC3R 5HE

Tel: 020 7283 1001 / 020 7280 3200
Fax: 020 7626 4416
E-mail: webmaster@ifia-federation.org

Enquiries:
Enquiries to: Director General

Founded:
1982

Organisation type and purpose:
Trade association.

INTERNATIONAL FEDERATION OF PROFESSIONAL AROMATHERAPISTS

Acronym or abbreviation: IFPA

82 Ashby Road, Hinckley, Leicestershire, LE10 1SN

Tel: 01455 637987
Fax: 01455 890956
E-mail: admin@ifparoma.org

Website:
http://www.ifparoma.org

Enquiries:
Enquiries to: Administrator
Other contacts: Membership Secretary for membership enquiries.

Founded:
2002

Organisation type and purpose:
International organisation, professional body, membership association (membership is by subscription, qualification, present number of members: 2061, registered charity (charity number 1091325).

Subject coverage:
Aromatherapy, qualified therapists, educational standards.

Printed publications:
In Essence (journal, quarterly)

Access to staff:
Contact by letter, by telephone, by fax, by e-mail and via website
Hours: Mon to Fri, 0900 to 1700

Access for disabled people:
Parking provided, level entry, toilet facilities

Subsidiary body:
48 accredited schools throughout the UK and overseas

INTERNATIONAL FERTILISER SOCIETY

PO Box 4, York, YO32 5YS

Tel: 01904 492700
Fax: 01904 492700
E-mail: secretary@fertiliser-society.org

Website:
http://www.fertiliser-society.org

Enquiries:
Enquiries to: Secretary

Founded:
1947

Organisation type and purpose:
International organisation, learned society, professional body.

Subject coverage:
Scientific, technical, economic and environmental aspects of the production, marketing, distribution, use and application of fertilisers and crop nutrients.

Museum or gallery collection, archive, or library special collection:
Complete proceedings of the Society 1947 (foundation) to date (approx 600)
Complete set of papers written by Dr George Cooke FRS

Library catalogue:
All or part available online

Printed publications:
Proceedings of the Society (irregular, £12.50)

Publications list:
Available online

Access to staff:
Contact by letter, by telephone, by fax, by e-mail and via website
Hours: Mon to Fri, 0900 to 1700

INTERNATIONAL FINE ART & ANTIQUE DEALERS SHOW

Acronym or abbreviation: IFAADS

31 Old Burlington Street, London, W1S 3AS

Tel: 020 7734 5491
Fax: 020 7494 4604
E-mail: info@haughton.com

Website:
http://www.haughton.com

Enquiries:
Enquiries to: Public Relations Manager
Direct e-mail: s.harcourt-webster@houghton.com

Founded:
1989

Organisation type and purpose:
International organisation.
Antique fair.

Subject coverage:
Art and antiques from all periods and countries, including pictures, sculpture, furniture, ceramics, jewellery, silver, manuscripts, textiles, ethnographica.

Museum or gallery collection, archive, or library special collection:
Catalogues of All Our Fairs

Printed publications:
Catalogues for International Ceramics Fair and Seminar (hardback) and New York international fairs (softback)

Access to staff:
Contact by letter, by telephone, by fax and by e-mail
Hours: Mon to Fri, 1000 to 1800

Access for disabled people:
Yes

Includes the:
International Ceramics Fair & Seminar
Park Lane Hotel, Piccadilly, London, W1; tel: 020 7734 5491; fax: 020 7494 4604; e-mail: info@ haughton.com

Parent body:
Haughton International Fairs
31 Old Burlington Street, London, W1S 3AS; tel: 020 7734 5491; fax: 020 7494 4604; e-mail: info@ haughton.com; website: www.haughton.com

INTERNATIONAL FOOD INFORMATION SERVICE

Acronym or abbreviation: IFIS

Lane End House, Shinfield Road, Shinfield, Reading, Berkshire, RG2 9BB

Tel: 0118 988 3895
Fax: 0118 988 5065
E-mail: ifis@ifis.org

Website:
http://www.ifis.org

Information on IFIS products and services; hot topics of interest to food scientists; latest IFIS news re product developments; links to IFIS World Wide Web products.

Enquiries:
Enquiries to: General Manager
Other contacts: Head of Sales and Marketing for general enquiries.

Founded:
1968

Organisation type and purpose:
International organisation, service industry, registered charity (charity number 1068176), publishing house.
International cooperative organisation.
Information products and services to the food science, food technology and human nutrition sectors.

Subject coverage:
Food science, food technology and human nutrition – all aspects including biotechnology, food safety and toxicology, food psychology, sensory analysis, novel foods, economics, all commodities (meat, fish etc), standards and patents relating to food, legislation, engineering and packaging.

Printed publications:
Food Info (newsletter, free)
Food Science and Technology Abstracts (FSTA) (monthly)
Food Science and Technology Abstracts (FSTA) Thesaurus (2000)
FSTA in print (monthly, annual subscription)
Serial Publications Scanned for FSTA (free)

Electronic and video publications:
FSTA via SilverPlatter Information
Food Science Alerts on the World Wide Web
FSTA via Ovid Technologies
FSTA Intranet Solution
FSTA Specialist Search Services
Online via: Datastar/DIALOG/DIMDI/ Questel.Orbit/STN

Access to staff:
Contact by letter, by telephone, by fax, by e-mail and via website. Appointment necessary.
Hours: Mon to Fri, 0900 to 1700

Research and education arm:
IFIS Gmbh
Deutsche Landwirtschafts-Gesellschaft, Eschborner Landstrasse 122, Frankfurt am Main, D-60489, Germany; tel: 00 49 69 24788 308; fax: 00 49 69 24788 115

Sponsored by:
CAB International
Centrum voor Landbouwpublikaties en Landbouwdocumentatie (PUDOC) Netherlands
Deutsche Landwirtschafts-Gesellschaft Germany
Institute of Food Technologists (IFT) USA

INTERNATIONAL FRIENDSHIP LEAGUE, BRITISH SECTION

Acronym or abbreviation: IFL

Head Office, 3 Creswick Road, Acton, London, W3 9HE

Website:
http://www.ifl-peacehaven.co.uk

Enquiries:
Enquiries to: Chairman

Founded:
1931

Organisation type and purpose:
Membership association (membership is by subscription), voluntary organisation.

continued overleaf

Subject coverage:
International friendship and understanding by services of home hospitality, pen friends, entertaining and helping overseas visitors.

Printed publications:
Friendship News

Access to staff:
Contact by letter
Hours: Mon to Fri, 0900 to 1700
Special comments: By letter only, except in connection with the Guest House.

Affiliated to:
United Nations Association

Includes the:
IFL Pen Friend Service (Overseas)
    3 Creswick Road, Acton, London, W3 9HE
International Guest House
    Peace Haven, 3 Creswick Road, Acton, London, London, W3 9HE; tel: 020 8752 0055; fax: 020 8752 0066; e-mail: ifl-peacehaven@tiscali.co.uk

Parent body:
IFL Head Office
    3 Creswick Road, Acton, London, W3 9HE

INTERNATIONAL FUND FOR ANIMAL WELFARE

Acronym or abbreviation: IFAW

87–90 Albert Embankment, London, SE1 7UD

Tel: 020 7587 6700
Fax: 020 7587 6720

Website:
http://www.ifaw.org
Information on the IFAW and its work.

Enquiries:
Enquiries to: Public Relations Manager
Direct tel: 020 7587 6708
Direct fax: 020 7587 6718
Direct e-mail: lkey@ifaw.org

Founded:
1969

Organisation type and purpose:
International organisation, present number of members: 2 million worldwide.
Conservation organisation.

Subject coverage:
Animal welfare, conservation.

Museum or gallery collection, archive, or library special collection:
Picture and video library
Digital picture library

Printed publications:
Animal Update (quarterly, free)
Report: Is the fox a pest? (£5)
Report: How will a ban on hunting affect the
    British fox population? (£5)
Annual Report

Electronic and video publications:
Video of the IFAW's campaigning work
Digital photo library

Access to staff:
Contact by letter, by telephone, by fax, by e-mail and via website
Hours: Mon to Fri, 0900 to 1730

Access to building, collection or gallery:
Prior appointment required

Parent body:
IFAW
    International headquarters, 411 Main Street, Yarmouth Port, MA 02675, USA; tel: 00 1 508 744 2076; fax: 00 1 508 744 2079

INTERNATIONAL GLACIOLOGICAL SOCIETY

Acronym or abbreviation: IGS

Scott Polar Research Institute, Lensfield Road, Cambridge, CB2 1ER

Tel: 01223 355974
Fax: 01223 354931
E-mail: igsoc@igsoc.org

Website:
http://www.igsoc.org

Enquiries:
Enquiries to: Secretary-General
Other contacts: Assistant to Secretary-General (for subscriptions)

Founded:
1936

Organisation type and purpose:
International organisation, learned society (membership is by subscription), present number of members: 900, registered charity (charity number 231043).
To facilitate communication and information exchange between all individuals having a scientific, practical or general interest in any aspect of snow and ice.

Subject coverage:
Glaciology, cryosphere, atmospheric ice, avalanches, chemistry of ice and snow, floating ice, glacial geology, glaciers, ground ice, ice, ice and climate, ice cores, icebergs, permafrost, physics of ice and snow, sea ice, snow, Antarctica, Greenland.

Museum or gallery collection, archive, or library special collection:
Book, documents and manuscripts on various aspects of glaciology

Printed publications:
Journal of Glaciology
Annals of Glaciology
Books
Ice (news bulletin)

Publications list:
Available online and in print

Access to staff:
Contact by letter, by telephone, by fax and by e-mail. Appointment necessary.
Hours: Mon to Fri, 0830 to 1630

INTERNATIONAL GLAUCOMA ASSOCIATION

Acronym or abbreviation: IGA

Woodcote House, 15 Highpoint Business Village, Henwood, Ashford, Kent, TN24 8DH

Tel: 01233 648164
Fax: 01233 648179
E-mail: info@iga.org.uk

Website:
http://www.glaucoma-association.com

Enquiries:
Enquiries to: Awareness Project Co-ordinator
Direct tel: 01233 648169
Direct e-mail: s.zerbib@iga.org.uk
Other contacts: CEO

Founded:
1974

Organisation type and purpose:
International organisation (membership is by subscription), present number of members: 6,000, registered charity (charity number 274681).

Subject coverage:
Glaucoma, its diagnosis, treatment and research. Public awareness.

Information services:
Sightline (tel. 01233 648170), Mon to Fri, 0930 to 1700

Trade and statistical information:
Glaucoma prevalence information, high risk categories and groups.

Non-library collection catalogue:
All or part available online

Printed publications:
Newsletter (for members, quarterly)
Booklets:
Glaucoma: A Guide
Glaucoma: A Greater Understanding
Glaucoma in Babies and Children
Ocular Hypertension Guide
Dry Eye Syndrome: A Guide
Numerous specialised pamphlets relating to aspects of glaucoma

Publications list:
Available online and in print

Access to staff:
Contact by letter, by telephone, by fax, by e-mail and via website. Appointment necessary.
Hours: Mon to Fri, 0930 to 1700

Access to building, collection or gallery:
Prior appointment required

Links with:
International Agency for the Prevention of Blindness

INTERNATIONAL GRAINS COUNCIL

Acronym or abbreviation: IGC

One Canada Square, Canary Wharf, London, E14 5AE

Tel: 020 7513 1122
Fax: 020 7513 0630
E-mail: igc-fac@igc.org.uk

Website:
http://www.igc.org.uk

Enquiries:
Enquiries to: Executive Director

Founded:
1949

Organisation type and purpose:
International organisation, present number of members: 26 governments including the European Community. Intergovernmental commodity organisation, administers the Grains Trade Convention of the International Grains Agreement 1995 and provides administrative services for the Food Aid Convention of the IGA.
To further international cooperation in trade in grains, to promote the expansion of grains trade, to contribute to the stability of the international grain market, and to enhance food security.

Subject coverage:
Statistics and general information on wheat and coarse grains, market developments; long-term and short-term outlook for world grain economy, grain production, use, consumption, stocks, trade and prices; review of national grain policies and their effects; grain handling and transportation, including ocean freight rates; international co-operation and wheat agreements, food aid shipments.

Trade and statistical information:
Details of international trade in wheat, wheat flour and coarse grains, excepting Intra-EC.

Non-library collection catalogue:
All or part available online

Printed publications:
Grain Market Report (11 times a year), weekly Grain Market Indicators
Report of the Council (annually)
Report on Food Aid Shipments (annually)
Wheat and coarse grains shipments (annually)
World Grain Statistics (annually) (this and all titles are for sale)

Publications list:
Available online and in print

Access to staff:
Contact by letter, by fax and by e-mail.
Appointment necessary. Non-members charged.
Hours: Mon to Fri, 0900 to 1730

INTERNATIONAL GRAPHOLOGY ASSOCIATION

Acronym or abbreviation: IGA

Stonedge, Dunkerton, Bath, BA2 8AS

Tel: 01761 437809
Fax: 01761 432572
E-mail: ljw@graphology.org.uk

Website:
http://www.graphology.org.uk
Information about graphology, analyses, research, etc.

Enquiries:
Enquiries to: Director

Founded:
1983

Organisation type and purpose:
Professional body, suitable for ages: adults, consultancy, research organisation.
International professional society.
Provision of training and examination in graphology. Undertaking research.

Subject coverage:
Graphology; handwriting; analysis for personality assessment.

Museum or gallery collection, archive, or library special collection:
Handwriting samples

Printed publications:
Journal (quarterly, free to members or by subscription to non-members)
Books, monographs and combined papers on graphology including:
Personality in Handwriting
Graphologists Dictionary
Evaluation Guide

Publications list:
Available in print

Access to staff:
Contact by letter, by telephone, by fax, by e-mail, in person and via website. Appointment necessary.
Hours: Mon to Fri, 0900 to 1700

INTERNATIONAL GUILD, BUTLER ADMINISTRATORS AND PERSONAL ASSISTANTS

12 Little Bornes, Alleyn Park, Dulwich, London, SE21 8SE

Tel: 020 8670 5585
Fax: 020 8670 8424

Website:
http://www.ivorspencer.com

Enquiries:
Enquiries to: Chief Executive

Founded:
1981

Organisation type and purpose:
Professional body.

Subject coverage:
Butler administrators and personal assistants.

Access to staff:
Contact by letter, by telephone, by fax, by e-mail and via website
Hours: Mon to Fri, 0900 to 1700

INTERNATIONAL HEALTH AND BEAUTY COUNCIL

Acronym or abbreviation: IHBC

3rd Floor, Eastleigh House, Market Street, Eastleigh, Hampshire, SO50 9FD

Tel: 023 8068 4500
Fax: 023 8065 1493
E-mail: info@vtct.org.uk

Website:
http://www.vtct.org.uk

Enquiries:
Enquiries to: Information Officer
Other contacts: Head of Quality Assurance for training centres as opposed to individual enquiries.

Founded:
1962

Organisation type and purpose:
International organisation.
Awarding body – service sector (beauty therapy).

Subject coverage:
All aspects of health and beauty, qualification and training.

Education services:
Courses are provided at more than 400 centres in the UK, mostly Colleges of Further Education.

Museum or gallery collection, archive, or library special collection:
Photographs of treatments

Printed publications:
List of centres providing training in health and beauty therapy, also available on our website

Access to staff:
Contact by letter
Hours: Mon to Fri, 0900 to 1700
Special comments: No visitors in person.

Affiliated to:
Action for Lifelong Learning Limited
  tel: 01243 842064; fax: 01243 842489; e-mail: info@vtct.org.uk
Vocational Awards International Limited
  tel: 01243 842064; fax: 01243 842489; e-mail: info@vtct.org.uk

Subsidiary of:
Vocational Training Charitable Trust (VTCT)
  tel: 023 8068 4500; fax: 023 8065 1493; e-mail: info@vtct.org.uk

INTERNATIONAL HOSPITAL FEDERATION

Acronym or abbreviation: IHF

46–48 Grosvenor Gardens, London, SW1W 0EB

Tel: 020 7881 9222
Fax: 020 7881 9223
E-mail: 101662.1262@compuserve.com

Website:
http://www.hospitalmanagement.net

Enquiries:
Enquiries to: Director General

Organisation type and purpose:
International organisation, voluntary organisation.
Dependent non-governmental association.

Subject coverage:
Planning and management of hospitals and health services.

Printed publications:
Hospital International Newsletter (quarterly)
Hospital Management International (yearbook)
New World Health (year book)
Occasional books and papers
World Hospitals and Health Services (3 times per annum)

Access to staff:
Contact by letter, by telephone, by fax, by e-mail and via website
Hours: Mon to Fri, 0900 to 1700

Collaboration with:
Kings Fund Library

Official liaison with the:
International Council of Nurses
World Health Organization
World Medical Association

INTERNATIONAL HOUSE

Acronym or abbreviation: IH

106 Piccadilly, London, W1V 9FL

Tel: 020 7518 6900
Fax: 020 7518 6941
E-mail: info@ihlondon.co.uk

Website:
http://www.international-house.org
http://www.ihlondon.com

Enquiries:
Enquiries to: Director

Founded:
1953

Organisation type and purpose:
Professional body, training organisation.

Access to staff:
Contact by letter, by telephone, by fax, by e-mail, in person and via website. Appointment necessary.
Hours: Mon to Fri, 0900 to 1700

INTERNATIONAL IMMIGRATION ADVISORY SERVICES

65 Kingsway, Manchester, M19 2LL

Tel: 0161 224 1973
Fax: 0161 224 4449
E-mail: intias@hotmail.com

Enquiries:
Enquiries to: Principal
Direct tel: 07785 541375

Founded:
1991

Organisation type and purpose:
Consultancy.

Subject coverage:
International immigration, nationality and law.

Access to staff:
Contact by letter, by telephone, by fax and by e-mail. Appointment necessary. All charged.
Hours: Mon to Fri, 0900 to 1730; Sat, 1030 to 1400

Access to building, collection or gallery:
No prior appointment required

Access for disabled people:
Level entry, toilet facilities

INTERNATIONAL INSTITUTE FOR CONSERVATION OF HISTORIC AND ARTISTIC WORKS

Acronym or abbreviation: IIC

6 Buckingham Street, London, WC2N 6BA

Tel: 020 7839 5975
Fax: 020 7976 1564
E-mail: iic@iiconservation.org

Website:
http://www.iiconservation.org
Membership, publications, congress.

Enquiries:
Enquiries to: Executive Secretary

Founded:
1950

Organisation type and purpose:
International organisation, membership association, registered charity (charity number 209677).

Subject coverage:
Conservation of heritage.

Printed publications:
Archaeological Conservation and its Consequences (Preprints of the IIC Copenhagen Congress 1996, members £20, non-members £40)
Case Studies in the Conservation of Stone and Wall Paintings (Preprints of the IIC Bologna Congress 1986, members £20, non-members £40)

continued overleaf

Conservation of Far Eastern Art (Preprints of the IIC Kyoto Congress 1988, members £20, non-members £40)

Conservation of the Iberian and Latin American Cultural Heritage (Preprints of the IIC Madrid Congress 1992, members £20, non-members £40)

Painting Techniques: History, Materials and Studio Practice (Contributions to the IIC Dublin Congress 1998, members £25, non-members £40)

Preventive Conservation: Practice, Theory & Research (Preprints of the IIC Ottawa Congress 1992, members £20, non-members £40)

Tradition and Innovation: Advances in Conservation (Contributions to the IIC Melbourne Congress 2000, members £25, non-members £40)

Works of Art on Paper, Books, Documents and Photographs: Techniques and Conservation (Contributions to the IIC Baltimore Congress 2002, members £25.00, non-members £40.00)

Modern Art: New Museums (Contributions to the IIC Bilbao Congress 2004, members £25, non-members £40)

The Object in Context: Crossing Conservation Boundaries (Contributions to the IIC Munich Congress 2006, members £25, non-members £40)

Conservation and Access (Contributions to the IIC London Congress 2008, members £25, non-members £40)

News in Conservation (prices and availability on application)

Reviews in Conservation (prices and availability on application)

Studies in Conservation (prices and availability on application)

Publications list:
Available online and in print

Access to staff:
Contact by letter, by telephone, by fax, by e-mail and via website. Access for members only.

INTERNATIONAL INSTITUTE FOR ENVIRONMENT AND DEVELOPMENT

Acronym or abbreviation: IIED

3 Endsleigh Street, London, WC1H 0DD

Tel: 020 7388 2117
Fax: 020 7388 2826
E-mail: iied@iied.org

Website:
http://www.iied.org
General information, publication list, participation database,

Enquiries:
Enquiries to: Information Officer
Direct e-mail: info@iied.org

Founded:
1971

Organisation type and purpose:
Registered charity (charity number 800066), research organisation.
Promotion of sustainable patterns of world development.

Subject coverage:
Natural resources, human settlements, governance, climate change, sustainable markets

Non-library collection catalogue:
All or part available online

Printed publications:
Annual Report
Drylands – Haramata (quarterly newsletter in English and French)
Environment and Urbanisation (journal, twice a year)
Environmental Economics – Discussion Paper Series
Participatory Learning and Action Notes
List of publications available on web site

Electronic and video publications:
For details of DVDs and CD-ROMs see website www.iied.org

Publications list:
Available online and in print

Access to staff:
Contact by letter, by telephone, by fax and by e-mail
Hours: Mon to Fri, 0900 to 1700

Also at:
International Institute for Environment and Development
  4 Hanover Street, Edinburgh, EH2 2EN; tel: 0131 624 7040

INTERNATIONAL INSTITUTE FOR STRATEGIC STUDIES

Acronym or abbreviation: IISS

13–15 Arundel Street, London, WC2R 3DX

Tel: 020 7379 7676
Fax: 020 7836 3108
E-mail: iiss@iiss.org

Website:
http://www.iiss.org

Enquiries:
Enquiries to: Librarian
Direct tel: 020 7395 9122
Direct e-mail: library@iiss.org

Founded:
1958

Organisation type and purpose:
International organisation, membership association (membership is by subscription), research organisation.

Subject coverage:
Nuclear issues; arms control, agreements, negotiations and possibilities; regional security issues (world-wide); Armed Forces of the World; current conflict situations; non-military aspects of national security (economic, demography, scarce resources, environment, etc.).

Museum or gallery collection, archive, or library special collection:
Subject files from 1958

Trade and statistical information:
Data on holdings of weapons (by system) for all countries of the world.

Non-library collection catalogue:
All or part available online

Library catalogue:
All or part available online and in-house

Printed publications:
Adelphi Papers (Monograph Series, approximately 8 a year)
Strategic Survey – Annual retrospective of the year's political and military trends (annually)
Survival (6 a year, subscription student rate)
The Military Balance – Inventory of the world's armed forces (annually)
Order printed publications from: Journals Customer Services, Taylor and Francis, Cheriton House, North Way, Andover, Hampshire, SP10 5BE; tel: 020 7017 5544; fax: 020 7017 4760; e-mail: journals .orders@tandf.co.uk or book.orders@routledge.co .uk

Electronic and video publications:
Russian Regional Perspectives online
Strategic Comments (10)

Publications list:
Available online and in print

Access to staff:
Contact by letter, by telephone, by fax, by e-mail, in person and via website. Non-members charged.

Access to building, collection or gallery:
No prior appointment required
Hours: Institute: Mon to Fri, 0900 to 1700
Library: Mon to Fri, 1000 to 1700

INTERNATIONAL INSTITUTE OF COMMUNICATIONS

Acronym or abbreviation: IIC

3rd Floor, Westcott House, 35 Portland Place, London, W1B 1AE

Tel: 020 7323 9622
Fax: 020 7323 9623
E-mail: enquiries@iicom.org

Website:
http://www.iicom.org

Enquiries:
Enquiries to: Director

Founded:
1968

Organisation type and purpose:
Membership association.
Global forum for communications.

Subject coverage:
Communications; copyright; all aspects of telecommunication; all aspects of broadcasting, radio, television, multimedia; satellite communications; development in its political, social, cultural, economic spheres; regulatory side of above topics/subjects.

Museum or gallery collection, archive, or library special collection:
Regulatory and legislative materials eg acts, statutes, bills etc on broadcasting and telecommunications, principally in Europe but increasingly outside Europe

Trade and statistical information:
Telecom voice traffic flows, television flows.

Printed publications:
Intermedia (journal, 6 times a year, £150 p.a.)

Publications list:
Available in print

Access to staff:
Appointment necessary.
Hours: Mon to Fri, 0900 to 1700

INTERNATIONAL INSTITUTE OF HEALTH AND HOLISTIC THERAPIES

Acronym or abbreviation: IIHHT

VTCT, 3rd Floor, Eastleigh House, Upper Market Street, Eastleigh, Hampshire, SO50 9FD

Tel: 023 8068 4500
Fax: 023 8065 1493
E-mail: info@vtct.org.uk

Website:
http://www.vtct.org.uk

Enquiries:
Enquiries to: Information Officer
Direct e-mail: recordsoffice@vtct.org.uk
Other contacts: Head of Quality Assurance for training centres as opposed to individual enquiries.

Founded:
1962

Organisation type and purpose:
International organisation. International education organisation. Provides qualifications in holistic, health, fitness and complementary therapies.

Subject coverage:
Body massage, aromatherapy, reflexology.

Education services:
Courses are provided at Centres across the UK, primarily in Colleges of Further Education.

Printed publications:
List of centres providing courses for qualifications in the above fields (free) also available on our website

Access to staff:
Contact by letter
Hours: Mon to Fri, 0900 to 1700
Special comments: No visitors in person.

Affiliated to:
Action for Lifelong Learning Limited
tel: 01243 842064; fax: 01243 842489; e-mail: info@vtct.org.uk
Vocational Awards International Limited
tel: 01243 842064; fax: 01243 842489; e-mail: info@vtct.org.uk

Subsidiary of:
Vocational Training Charitable Trust (VTCT)
tel: 023 8668 4500; fax: 023 8064 1493; e-mail: info@vtct.org.uk

INTERNATIONAL INSTITUTE OF RISK AND SAFETY MANAGEMENT

Acronym or abbreviation: IIRSM

70 Chancellors Road, London, W6 9RS

Tel: 020 8600 5536/7/8/9
Fax: 020 8741 1349
E-mail: enquiries@iirsm.org

Website:
http://www.iirsm.org

Enquiries:
Enquiries to: Organising Secretary

Founded:
1975

Organisation type and purpose:
International organisation, professional body (membership is by qualification), registered charity (charity number 269326).
The institute's main objective is to advance public education in accident prevention and occupational health in industry.

Subject coverage:
General safety; safety management; principles of risk management; international organisations.

Printed publications:
Health & Safety Managers Newsletter: Includes listing of professional vacancies (11 times a year, free to members)
IIRSM Update (as and when required)
Safety Management Magazine of British Safety Council (11 times a year)
Safety Management, by Tony Corfield, IIRSM/ISM (1988)

Access to staff:
Contact by letter, by telephone, by fax, by e-mail and via website. Access for members only.
Hours: Mon to Fri, 0900 to 1700

Affiliated to:
British Safety Council
tel: 020 8741 1231; fax: 020 8741 4555

INTERNATIONAL INSTITUTE OF SECURITY

Acronym or abbreviation: IISec

Suite 8, The Business Centre, 57 Torquay Road, Paignton, Devon, TQ3 3DT

Tel: 01803 663275
Fax: 01803 663251
E-mail: iisec@btconnect.com

Website:
http://www.iisec.co.uk

Enquiries:
Enquiries to: Company Secretary

Founded:
1968

Organisation type and purpose:
International organisation, professional body (membership is by qualification), present number of members: 650, suitable for ages: 18+, training organisation.
Academic Body.
Examining body.

Subject coverage:
The study of security management.

Museum or gallery collection, archive, or library special collection:
12,000 to 15,000 theses on matters relating to security management

Access to staff:
Contact by letter, by telephone, by fax and by e-mail
Hours: Mon to Fri, 0900 to 1700

INTERNATIONAL INSTITUTE OF SPORTS THERAPY

Acronym or abbreviation: IIST

VTCT, 3rd Floor, Eastleigh House, Upper Market Street, Eastleigh, Hampshire, SO50 9FD

Tel: 023 8068 4500
Fax: 023 8065 1493
E-mail: info@vtct.org.uk

Website:
http://www.vtct.org.uk

Enquiries:
Enquiries to: Information Officer
Direct e-mail: recordsoffice@vtct.org.uk
Other contacts: Head of Quality Assurance for training centres as opposed to individual enquiries.

Founded:
1962

Organisation type and purpose:
International organisation.
Provision of qualifications in fitness and sport therapies.

Subject coverage:
All aspects of health, fitness and sports therapy and especially centres providing training in these subjects. Largest Awarding Body in this sector, courses are provided across the UK, primarily in Colleges of Further Education.

Museum or gallery collection, archive, or library special collection:
Photographs of treatments

Printed publications:
List of approved centres providing above qualification in the above fields (free) also on the website

Access to staff:
Contact by letter
Hours: Mon to Fri, 0900 to 1700
Special comments: No visitors in person.

Affiliated to:
Action for Lifelong Learning Limited
tel: 01243 842064; fax: 01243 842489; e-mail: info@vtct.org.uk
Vocational Awards International Limited
tel: 01243 842064; fax: 01243 842489; e-mail: info@vtct.org.uk

Susidiary of:
Vocational Training Charitable Trust (VTCT)
tel: 023 8068 4500; fax: 023 8065 1493; e-mail: info@vtct.org.uk

INTERNATIONAL INSULATION CONTRACTORS ORGANISATION

Acronym or abbreviation: IICO

Tournai Hall, Evelyn Woods Road, Aldershot, Hampshire, GU11 2LL

E-mail: timsa@associationhouse.org.uk

Website:
http://www.associationhouse.org.uk

Enquiries:
Enquiries to: Secretary

Founded:
1980

Organisation type and purpose:
International organisation, trade association, present number of members: 21.

Comprises contracting companies engaged in international industrial insulation projects, drawn from many countries throughout the world.

Subject coverage:
Contact between international contracting companies involved in thermal, fire and acoustic insulation.

Printed publications:
Standard Method of Measurement

Publications list:
Available in print

Access to staff:
Contact by letter, by telephone, by fax, by e-mail and via website
Hours: Mon to Fri, 0900 to 1700

INTERNATIONAL INTELLIGENCE ON CULTURE

Acronym or abbreviation: IIC

4 Baden Place, Crosby Row, London, SE1 1YW

Tel: 020 7403 6454
Fax: 020 7403 2009

Enquiries:
Enquiries to: Information Officer
Direct tel: 020 7403 7001

Founded:
1994

Organisation type and purpose:
Independent company specialising in cultural policy analysis and intelligence; consultancy; research; project management; training; and advisory and information services with an international cultural dimension.
To provide a comprehensive range of services and respond to the needs of the international cultural sector.

Subject coverage:
Policy intelligence, consultancy, research, project management, training, information and advice services for the international cultural sector.

Printed publications:
Arts Networking Europe
On the Road – the start up guide to touring the arts in Europe (1995)
To Travel, Hopefully! A guide to travel grant opportunities (rev 1998)
Order printed publications from: Library and Publications, Arts Council of England
4 Great Peter Street, London, SW1P 3NQ, tel: 020 7973 6931, fax: 020 7973 6590, e-mail: enquiries@artscouncil.org.uk

Publications list:
Available in print

Access to staff:
Contact by letter, by telephone, by fax and by e-mail
Hours: Mon to Fri, 0930 to 1730; please call to check opening times of enquiry service, which are subject to change
Special comments: Offices are not open for drop-in services.

Funded by:
Irish Arts Council

Links with:
Arts Council of Scotland
Arts Council of Wales
British Film Institute
Crafts Council
Cultural Information and Research Centres Liaison in Europe (CIRCLE)
Museum and Galleries Commission

INTERNATIONAL INTERFAITH CENTRE

Acronym or abbreviation: IIC

PO Box 750, Oxford OX3 3BR

continued overleaf

Tel: 01865 202745
Fax: 01865 202746
E-mail: iic@interfaith-centre.org

Website:
http://www.interfaith-centre.org
Homepage: information about the IIC and other relevant interfaith contacts and resources.

Enquiries:
Enquiries to: Director

Founded:
1993

Organisation type and purpose:
International organisation, registered charity, consultancy, research organisation.
To facilitate interreligious encounter and dialogue.

Subject coverage:
Religion, interreligious issues, interfaith issues, projects, conferences, contacts and research, courses, videos.

Museum or gallery collection, archive, or library special collection:
Interfaith and religious journals from around the world

Printed publications:
IIC newsletter
Conference papers
Also: see website for further details of publications

Electronic and video publications:
Faith and Interfaith Video Series, interviews with various people from different faiths, countries, cultures (video, £10 each plus p&p)

Access to staff:
Contact by letter, by telephone, by fax, by e-mail, in person and via website
Hours: By appointment only (phone)

INTERNATIONAL LABOUR ORGANISATION

Acronym or abbreviation: ILO

International Labour Office, Millbank Tower, 21–24 Millbank, London, SW1P 4QP

Tel: 020 7828 6401
Fax: 020 7233 5925
E-mail: london@ilo.org

Website:
http://www.ilo.org/london

Enquiries:
Enquiries to: Manager, Publications/Information Unit

Founded:
1919

Organisation type and purpose:
International organisation.
The UN specialised agency concerned with work and employment issues.

Subject coverage:
International labour standards; labour statistics; management; workers' education; women and work; industrial relations; migrant labour; labour administration; employment and conditions of work; labour legislation; human rights; freedom of association; training, retraining and rehabilitation; safety and health.

Museum or gallery collection, archive, or library special collection:
All ILO publications and documents since its establishment in 1919

Printed publications:
CIS Abstracts (8 times a year, on safety and health)
ILO Catalogue of Safety Publications
Projects currently in progress (continuously)

Publications list:
Available online and in print

Access to staff:
Contact by letter, by telephone, by fax and by e-mail. Appointment necessary.

Hours: Mon to Fri, 1000 to 1300 and 1400 to 1630

Head Office:
International Labour Office
Geneva 22, CH 211, Switzerland; tel: + 41 22 799 6111; fax: + 41 22 799 8577; e-mail: communication@ilo.org; website: http://www.ilo.org

Works with:
International Centre for Occupational Safety and Health (CIS)

INTERNATIONAL LANGUAGE (IDO) SOCIETY OF GREAT BRITAIN

Acronym or abbreviation: ILSGB

24 Nunn Street, Leek, Staffordshire, ST13 8EA

Tel: 01538 381491

Website:
http://www.users.aol.com/idolinguo

Enquiries:
Enquiries to: Honorary Secretary

Founded:
1913

Organisation type and purpose:
Membership association.

Subject coverage:
The international language IDO.

Printed publications:
Various books in and about the language

Publications list:
Available in print

Access to staff:
Contact by letter and by telephone
Hours: Mon to Fri, 0900 to 1700

Affiliated to:
International Uniono por la Lingo Internaciona at the same address

INTERNATIONAL LASER CLASS ASSOCIATION

PO Box 26, Falmouth, Cornwall, TR11 3TN

Tel: 01326 315064
Fax: 01326 318968
E-mail: office@laserinternational.org

Website:
http://www.laserinternational.org

Enquiries:
Enquiries to: Executive Secretary

Organisation type and purpose:
International organisation.

Subject coverage:
Sailing laser class boats.

Access to staff:
Contact by e-mail and via website
Hours: Mon to Fri, 0900 to 1730

INTERNATIONAL LAW ASSOCIATION

Acronym or abbreviation: ILA

Charles Clore House, 17 Russell Square, London, WC1B 5DR

Tel: 020 7323 2978
Fax: 020 7323 3580
E-mail: info@ila-hq.org

Website:
http://www.ila-hq.org
Full homepage: history, activities, branches, committees, newsletters, etc.

Enquiries:
Enquiries to: Secretary

Founded:
1873

Organisation type and purpose:
International organisation, learned society (membership is by subscription, election or invitation), registered charity (charity number 249637).

Subject coverage:
Space law, international monetary law, maritime neutrality, international human rights law and practice, water resources law, coastal state jurisdiction over marine pollution, international commercial arbitration, legal aspects of sustainable development, refugee procedures, legal aspects of inter-country adoption and protection of the family, the formation of customary international law, international securities regulation, cultural heritage law, international law in national courts, regional economic development law, arms control and disarmament law, feminism and international law, extradition and human rights, international civil and commercial litigation, international trade law, Islamic law and international law, internally displaced persons, aspects of the law of state succession, diplomatic protection of persons and property, accountability of international organisations.

Publications list:
Available in print

Access to staff:
Contact by letter, by telephone, by fax and by e-mail. Appointment necessary.
Hours: Mon to Thu, 0900 to 1700

Has:
50 branches world-wide

INTERNATIONAL LEAD AND ZINC STUDY GROUP

Acronym or abbreviation: ILZSG

2 King Street, London, SW1Y 6QL

Tel: 020 7484 3300
Fax: 020 7930 4635
E-mail: root@ilzsg.org

Website:
http://www.ilzsg.org

Enquiries:
Enquiries to: Information Officer

Founded:
1959

Organisation type and purpose:
International organisation, research organisation.

Subject coverage:
Lead and zinc.

Trade and statistical information:
International trade and world situation in lead and zinc, including movements of stocks and prices.

Printed publications:
Lead and Zinc Statistics – Monthly Bulletin
Lead and Zinc New Mine and Smelter Projects
Various reports and conference proceedings including:
Principal Uses of Lead and Zinc
Recycling Lead and Zinc into the 21st Century (2 vols, July 1995)
World Directory: Lead and Zinc Mines and Primary Metallurgical Works (5th ed., July 1994)
World Directory: Primary and Secondary Lead Plants (1997)
World Directory: Primary and Secondary Zinc Plants (1997)

Publications list:
Available in print

Access to staff:
Contact by letter and via website
Hours: Mon to Fri, 0900 to 1700

Founded in 1959 by the:
United Nations

INTERNATIONAL LEAGUE FOR THE PROTECTION OF HORSES

Acronym or abbreviation: ILPH

Anne Colvin House, Snetterton, Norfolk, NR16 2LR

Tel: 01953 498682
Fax: 01953 498373
E-mail: ilph@ilph.org

Website:
http://www.ilph.org

Enquiries:
Enquiries to: Communications Manager
Direct tel: 0870 366 6955
Direct fax: 0870 904 1927
Direct e-mail: phils@ilph.org

Founded:
1927

Organisation type and purpose:
International organisation, registered charity (charity number 206658).
Equine welfare organisation.
Working for a world where the horse is used but never abused.

Subject coverage:
Equine care and management; transportation of equines for slaughter – overseas; recovery and rehabilitation of equines – UK; NGO training on saddlery, farriery, horse management and nutrition in developing countries.

Printed publications:
Mail Order catalogue
Newsletter (quarterly)
Individual leaflets on each of the 4 UK Equine recovery and rehabilitation centres
Order printed publications from: Communications Manager

Electronic and video publications:
Used But Never Abused – The work of the ILPH in the 21st century (Video and CD-ROM, each £4.95, to purchase direct)

Access to staff:
Contact by letter, by telephone, by fax, by e-mail, in person and via website. Appointment necessary.
Hours: Mon to Fri, 0900 to 1700

Collaboration with other major equine organisations eg:
Animal Health Trust
    Newmarket, Suffolk
International Equestrian Federation, Lausanne, Switzerland (FEI)
Liverpool University
    Department of Veterinary Clinical Science and Animal Husbandry
Royal (Dick) School of Veterinary Studies, University of Edinburgh

INTERNATIONAL MARINE CONTRACTORS ASSOCIATION

Acronym or abbreviation: IMCA

5 Lower Belgrave Street, London, SW1W 0NR

Tel: 020 7824 5520
Fax: 020 7824 5521
E-mail: imca@imca-int.com

Website:
http://www.imca-int.com

Enquiries:
Enquiries to: Chief Executive

Founded:
1995

Organisation type and purpose:
International organisation, trade association (membership is by subscription), present number of members: 530, service industry.

Subject coverage:
Offshore, marine and underwater engineering companies

Printed publications:
Wide variety of publications (prices vary):
AODC documents
Complete collection of all AODC, IMCA (excluding Marine Division) and DMAC Guidance Notes and Codes of Practice
Diving Medical Advisory Committee (DMAC) documents
DPVOA and IMCA Marine Division documents
IMCA Diving Division documents
IMCA ROV Division documents
Log books
Pocket safety cards and safety posters
Careers material
Order printed publications from: via website

Electronic and video publications:
Various CDs and DVDs

Publications list:
Available online and in print

Access to staff:
Contact by letter, by telephone, by fax, by e-mail, in person and via website. Appointment necessary.
Hours: Mon to Fri, 0900 to 1700

Access to building, collection or gallery:
No prior appointment required

INTERNATIONAL MARITIME ORGANIZATION

Acronym or abbreviation: IMO

4 Albert Embankment, London, SE1 7SR

Tel: 020 7735 7611
Fax: 020 7587 3210
E-mail: info@imo.org

Website:
http://www.imo.org

Enquiries:
Enquiries to: Head, Public Information Services
Direct tel: 020 7587 3153

Founded:
1959

Organisation type and purpose:
International organisation.
To promote safety and security at sea and to prevent pollution of the sea from ships.

Subject coverage:
Prevention of marine pollution, safety at sea, security, IMO conventions, technical co-operation

Museum or gallery collection, archive, or library special collection:
Maritime Knowledge Centre: houses a complete collection of IMO publications, IMO meetings documents in English, French and Spanish (some reports in Russian, Chinese and Arabic)
UN documents related to the maritime world

Trade and statistical information:
Casualty statistics, marine pollution, maritime transport, safety of life at sea

Non-library collection catalogue:
All or part available online

Library catalogue:
All or part available online

Printed publications:
IMO Library Acquisitions List (quarterly)
IMO Library Current Awareness Bulletin (fortnightly)
IMO News (quarterly)
International Shipping and World Trade – Facts and Figures
Available free to bona fide organisations
Order printed publications from: Publishing Services

Electronic and video publications:
International Maritime Dangerous Goods Code (IMDG Code, CD-ROM and diskettes, for sale)
IMO VEGA database (for identification of applicable IMO requirements, CD-ROM, for sale)
See Catalogue, video on IMO
Order electronic and video publications from: Publishing Services

Publications list:
Available online and in print

Access to staff:
Contact by letter, by telephone, by fax, by e-mail and via website. Appointment necessary.
Hours: Mon to Fri, 0900 to 1700
Special comments: closed for Christmas

Access to building, collection or gallery:
Prior appointment required

Access for disabled people:
Toilet facilities

Parent body:
United Nations

INTERNATIONAL MOHAIR ASSOCIATION

Acronym or abbreviation: IMA

10–12 The Grove, Ilkley, West Yorkshire, LS29 9EG

Tel: 01943 817149
Fax: 01943 817150
E-mail: info@int-mohair.com

Website:
http://www.int-mohair.com
Members lists, care and properties of mohair, the angora goat, sales information, promotional items, links, forum, what's new, contact.

Enquiries:
Enquiries to: Manager

Founded:
1974

Organisation type and purpose:
Trade association.
To promote, advance and protect the interests of its members and their manufactured mohair products.

Subject coverage:
Mohair.

Printed publications:
Mohair – A Review of Its Properties, Processing and Applications (Dr Lawrence Hunter, programme manager at the CSIR, Port Elizabeth, South Africa, £50 plus p&p)

Access to staff:
Contact by letter, by telephone, by fax, by e-mail and via website. Appointment necessary.
Hours: Mon to Thu, 0930 to 1230

INTERNATIONAL NETWORK FOR THE AVAILABILITY OF SCIENTIFIC PUBLICATIONS

Acronym or abbreviation: INASP

58 St. Aldates, Oxford, OX1 1ST

Tel: 01865 249909
Fax: 01865 251060
E-mail: inasp@inasp.info

Website:
http://www.inasp.info
Newsletters, leaflets, programme information. Full text electronic publishing, reader and other reference markers and guidebooks.

Enquiries:
Enquiries to: Director

Founded:
1992

Organisation type and purpose:
International organisation.
Charity.
INASP is a programme of the International Council for Science (ICSU). It aims to improve worldwide access to information.

Subject coverage:
Information about research publication and access, information about library and book development in developing and transitional countries.

continued overleaf

Printed publications:
Newsletter (3 times a year)

Electronic and video publications:
Newsletter (3 times a year)
Directories
Monographs

Publications list:
Available online

Access to staff:
Contact by letter, by telephone, by fax, by e-mail and via website. Appointment necessary.
Hours: Mon to Fri, 0900 to 1700

INTERNATIONAL OIL POLLUTION COMPENSATION FUNDS

Acronym or abbreviation: IOPC Funds

Portland House, Bressenden Place, London, SW1E 5PN

Tel: 020 7592 7100
Fax: 020 7592 7111
E-mail: info@iopcfund.org

Website:
http://www.iopcfund.org

Enquiries:
Enquiries to: Information Officer

Founded:
1978

Organisation type and purpose:
International organisation.
The International Oil Pollution Compensation Funds are two intergovernmental organisations which provide compensation for oil pollution damage resulting from spills of persistent oil from tankers.

Subject coverage:
Oil pollution compensation.

Publications list:
Available online

Access to staff:
Contact by letter, by telephone, by fax, by e-mail and via website. Appointment necessary.
Hours: Mon to Fri, 0900 to 1730

Access to building, collection or gallery:
Prior appointment required

Access for disabled people:
Access to all public areas

INTERNATIONAL ORDER OF KABBALISTS

Acronym or abbreviation: IOK

6 Oakwood, 62 King Charles Road, Surbiton, Surrey, KT5 8QR

Fax: 020 8390 5604
E-mail: iokoffice@yahoo.com

Website:
http://www.internationalorderofkabbalists.com

Enquiries:
Enquiries to: Secretary

Founded:
1969

Organisation type and purpose:
Membership association (membership is by subscription).

Subject coverage:
The Kabbalah, related occult and esoteric subjects.

Printed publications:
Aromatics in Ritual and Therapeutics (J. Sturzaker)
Gemstones and their Occult Powers (J. Sturzaker)
Kabbalistic Aphorisms (J. Sturzaker)
Meaning, Dangers and Purpose of Ritual (M. Defries)
The Twelve Rays (J. Sturzaker)

Colour and Kabbalah (J. Sturzaker and D. L. Sturzaker)
A Practical Guide to Symbolism (J. Sturzaker)
Booklets and study papers

Publications list:
Available online and in print

Access to staff:
Contact by letter, by fax, by e-mail and via website
Hours: Mon to Fri, 0900 to 1700

INTERNATIONAL OTTER SURVIVAL FUND

Acronym or abbreviation: IOSF

7 Black Park, Broadford, Isle of Skye, IU49 9DE

Tel: 01471 822487
Fax: 01471 822487
E-mail: iosf@otter.org

Website:
http://www.otter.org
General description.

Enquiries:
Enquiries to: Director
Direct e-mail: iosf2@aol.com

Founded:
1988

Organisation type and purpose:
Registered charity (charity number SC003875).
Wildlife conservation.

Subject coverage:
Otter ecology and conservation, wildlife, wild animal care and treatment.

Information services:
By email.

Library catalogue:
All or part available online and in print

Printed publications:
Otter News
Otters in Britain
Otter Journal, 2007
Otter Road Mortalities

Electronic and video publications:
Videos for sale

Publications list:
Available online and in print

Access to staff:
Contact by letter, by telephone, by fax, by e-mail and via website. Appointment necessary.
Hours: Mon to Fri, 0900 to 1700

Access to building, collection or gallery:
Prior appointment required

Access for disabled people:
Parking provided

INTERNATIONAL PEN

9–10 Charterhouse Buildings, Goswell Road, London, EC1M 7AT

Tel: 020 7253 4308
Fax: 020 7253 5711
E-mail: intpen@dircon.co.uk

Website:
http://www.oneworld.org/internatpen

Enquiries:
Enquiries to: Administrative Secretary
Direct e-mail: penasst@dircon.co.uk
Other contacts: Administrative Assistant for subscriptions, general information.

Founded:
1921

Organisation type and purpose:
International organisation, professional body, voluntary organisation, registered charity (charity number 1010627).

Non-governmental organisation.
PEN originally stood for Poets, Essayists, Novelists, but now membership is open to all writers.

Subject coverage:
Literature as common currency between nations; freedom of expression and free press; origins and history of International PEN; positions of banned, imprisoned or otherwise mistreated writers.

Printed publications:
Pen International (magazine, 2 times a year, £8 or $13 a year)

Access to staff:
Contact by letter, by telephone, by fax and by e-mail
Hours: Mon to Fri, 1030 to 1800

Access to building, collection or gallery:
No access other than to staff

In consultative relation with:
UNESCO

Other addresses:
132 centres in 95 countries throughout the world including:
English Centre
152–156 Kentish Town Road, London, NW1 9QB; tel: 020 7267 9444
International PEN
International PEN
International PEN
Scottish Centre
c/o Greenleaf Editorial, 126 West Princess Street, Glasgow, G4 9DB
Welsh Centre
80 Plymouth Road, Gwynneth Street, Penarth, CF64 5DL

INTERNATIONAL PESTICIDE APPLICATION RESEARCH CENTRE

Acronym or abbreviation: IPARC

Imperial College at Silwood Park, Sunninghill, Ascot, Berkshire, SL5 7PY

Tel: 020 7594 2234
Fax: 020 7594 2450
E-mail: g.matthews@ic.ac.uk

Website:
http://www.bio.ic.ac.uk/staff/gamat/matthews.htm

Enquiries:
Enquiries to: Information Officer

Organisation type and purpose:
University department or institute, consultancy, research organisation.

Subject coverage:
Pest management – particularly equipment needed for effective and safe application of pesticides.

Museum or gallery collection, archive, or library special collection:
Collection of pesticide application equipment with emphasis on that which is manually carried or operated

INTERNATIONAL PHONETIC ASSOCIATION

Acronym or abbreviation: IPA

Centre for Language & Communication Studies, Arts Building, Trinity College, Dublin, Dublin 2, Republic of Ireland

Tel: 00 353 1 608 1348
Fax: 00 353 1 677 2694
E-mail: anichsid@tcd.ie

Website:
http://www.arts.gla.ac.uk/IPA/ipa.html

Enquiries:
Enquiries to: Treasurer

Founded:
1886

Organisation type and purpose:
International organisation, learned society
(membership is by subscription), present number
of members: 900.

Subject coverage:
Phonetics and phonology; the International
Phonetic Alphabet.

Printed publications:
Available to purchase, direct

Access to staff:
Contact by letter, by telephone, by fax, by e-mail
and via website
Hours: Mon to Fri, 0900 to 1700

INTERNATIONAL POWERED ACCESS FEDERATION LIMITED

Acronym or abbreviation: IPAF

Bridge End Business Park, Milnthorpe, LA7 7RH

Tel: 015395 62444
Fax: 015395 64686
E-mail: info@ipaf.org

Website:
http://www.ipaf.org
Services available from IPAF, industry news,
details of IPAF approved training scheme and
location of training centres.

Enquiries:
Enquiries to: Managing Director

Founded:
1983

Organisation type and purpose:
International organisation, trade association
(membership is by subscription), training
organisation.
To represent the interests of the mobile elevating
work platform industry on an international basis.

Subject coverage:
Powered access equipment.

**Museum or gallery collection, archive, or library
special collection:**
British, EC, US, Canadian Standards for powered
access equipment (on mobile elevated) work
platforms

Printed publications:
IPAF Guide to Mast Climbing Work Platforms
Mobile Elevating Work Platform Operators Safety
Guide

Access to staff:
Contact by letter, by telephone, by fax, by e-mail
and via website. Appointment necessary. Non-
members charged.
Hours: Mon to Fri, 0900 to 1700

INTERNATIONAL PRIMATE PROTECTION LEAGUE (UK)

Acronym or abbreviation: IPPL

166 Gilmore Road, London, SE13 5AE

Tel: 020 8297 2129
Fax: 020 8297 2099
E-mail: enquiries@ippl-uk.org

Website:
http://www.ippl-uk.org

Enquiries:
Enquiries to: Conservation and Welfare Officer

Founded:
1976

Subject coverage:
Protection of primates.

Printed publications:
Monkey Tales (newsletter, 3 times a year)

Access to staff:
Contact by letter, by telephone, by e-mail and via
website. Appointment necessary. Letter of
introduction required.

Hours: Mon to Fri, 0900 to 1700

Access to building, collection or gallery:
Prior appointment required

INTERNATIONAL PSYCHOANALYTICAL ASSOCIATION

Acronym or abbreviation: IPA

Broomhills, Woodside Lane, London, N12 8UD

Tel: 020 8446 8324
Fax: 020 8445 4729
E-mail: ipa@ipa.org.uk

Website:
http://www.ipa.org.uk

Enquiries:
Enquiries to: Membership Secretary

Founded:
1908

Organisation type and purpose:
Professional body, membership association
(membership is by subscription), present number
of members: 12,000

Subject coverage:
Psychoanalysis.

Access to staff:
Contact by e-mail
Hours: Mon to Fri, 0900 to 1700

INTERNATIONAL RECORDS MANAGEMENT TRUST

Formal name: International Records Management
Trust

Haines House, 6th floor, 21 John Street, London,
WC1N 2BP

Tel: 020 7831 4101
Fax: 020 7831 6303
E-mail: info@irmt.org

Website:
http://www.irmt.org

Enquiries:
Enquiries to: Director
Direct e-mail: athurston@irmt.org

Founded:
1989

Organisation type and purpose:
To develop new strategies for managing public
sector records, through consultancy, education and
research.
Registered charity (charity number 3477376).

Subject coverage:
Archives, records management, conservation

Access to staff:
Contact by letter, by telephone, by fax, by e-mail
and via website

INTERNATIONAL SAFETY COUNCIL

21 Tilton Road, Borough Green, Sevenoaks, Kent,
TN15 8RS

Tel: 01732 886581
E-mail: smitht@nsc.org

Website:
http://www.nsc.org
Safety information; environmental health.

Enquiries:
Enquiries to: Executive Director

Founded:
1913

Organisation type and purpose:
International organisation.
Non-profitmaking public service organisation
holding consulting status with the United Nations.

Subject coverage:
Health and Safety: occupational, home and
community, public, transportation.

Trade and statistical information:
Worldwide accident statistics.

Non-library collection catalogue:
All or part available online

Printed publications:
A variety of subject areas is covered by the large
selection of published material, and includes:
Accident investigation (6 publications)
Confined Spaces (6 books)
Environmental (5 books)
Ergonomics (over 30 publications)
Integrated Safety Programs for facilitators,
managers and participants (4 programmes)
Job Safety Analysis (training programme, poster
and booklet)
Machine Safety (manuals, booklets and posters)
Material Handling (20 books and manuals)
Professional Resources (magazines, posters, books,
technical references and manuals)
Training Agency Manuals

Publications list:
Available online and in print

Access to staff:
Contact by letter, by telephone, by e-mail and via
website. Appointment necessary.
Hours: Mon to Fri, 0900 to 1700

Also at:
International Safety Council
1121 Spring Lake Drive, Itasca, Illinois, USA; tel:
00 1 630 285 1121; fax: 00 1 630 285 1613; e-mail:
smitht@nsc.org; website: www.nsc.org

Parent body:
National Safety Council (USA)
1121 Spring Lake Drive, Itasca, Illinois, USA; tel:
00 1 708 285 1121; fax: 00 1 708 285 1613

INTERNATIONAL SCHOOL OF LONDON

Acronym or abbreviation: ISL

139 Gunnersbury Avenue, London, W3 8LG

Tel: 020 8992 5823
Fax: 020 8993 7012
E-mail: mail@islondon.com

Website:
http://www.islondon.com

Enquiries:
Enquiries to: Development Officer

Founded:
1972

Organisation type and purpose:
Education

Subject coverage:
Primary and secondary education; international
baccalaureate; ESL, intensive English; home
languages taught.

Access to staff:
Contact by letter, by telephone, by fax, by e-mail
and via website
Hours: Mon to Fri, 0800 to 1800

Access to building, collection or gallery:
Prior appointment required
Hours: Mon to Fri, 0800 to 1700

INTERNATIONAL SEISMOLOGICAL CENTRE

Acronym or abbreviation: ISC

Pipers Lane, Thatcham, Newbury, Berkshire, RG19
4NS

Tel: 01635 861022
Fax: 01635 872351
E-mail: admin@isc.ac.uk

continued overleaf

Website:
http://www.isc.ac.uk

Enquiries:
Enquiries to: Director
Other contacts: Administration Officer for publication sales.

Founded:
1964

Organisation type and purpose:
International organisation, consultancy, research organisation.
Collection, collation, analysis and publication of world earthquake data.

Subject coverage:
Seismology; world earthquakes.

Museum or gallery collection, archive, or library special collection:
Complete sets of seismological journals and other historical published matter

Printed publications:
Bibliography of Seismology (2 times a year, now discontinued)
Bulletin of ISC (monthly, 2 years in arrears of event)
Felt and Damaging Earthquakes, 1976–90 (annually, now discontinued)
Information brochure
Regional Catalogues of Earthquakes (2 times a year, 2 years in arrears)

Electronic and video publications:
The following Bulletins of ISC, are on CD-ROM for purchase
Bulletin of ISC 1964 to 1977
Bulletin of ISC 1978 to 1985
Bulletin of ISC 1986 to 1991
Bulletin of ISC 1992 to 1993
Bulletin of ISC 1994 to 1995
Bulletin of ISC 1996
Bulletin of ISC 1997
Bulletin of ISC 1998
Bulletin of ISC 1999

Access to staff:
Contact by e-mail
Hours: Mon to Fri, 0900 to 1700

Links with:
UNESCO
  Paris, France
WMO
  Geneva

INTERNATIONAL SHAKESPEARE ASSOCIATION

Acronym or abbreviation: ISA

Shakespeare Centre, Henley Street, Stratford-upon-Avon, Warwickshire, CV37 6QW

Tel: 01789 201840
Fax: 01789 294911
E-mail: isa@shakespeare.org.uk

Website:
http://www.shakespeare.org.uk
Under 'Education'.

Enquiries:
Enquiries to: Executive Secretary

Founded:
1974

Organisation type and purpose:
International organisation, learned society (membership is by subscription), present number of members: 600.

Subject coverage:
Shakespearean research, publication, translation and performance, initiation and planning of international Shakespeare congresses.

Museum or gallery collection, archive, or library special collection:
Archive of the International Shakespeare Association and books donated to it are deposited in the Shakespeare Centre Library at the same address

Printed publications:
Newsletter (annual)
Occasional papers
Proceedings of the ISA Congresses (every 5 years)

Publications list:
Available in print

Access to staff:
Contact by letter, by telephone, by fax and by e-mail
Hours: Mon to Fri, 0900 to 1700

INTERNATIONAL SHEEP DOG SOCIETY, THE

Acronym or abbreviation: ISDS

Clifton House, 4a Goldington Road, Bedford, MK40 3NF

Tel: 01234 352672
Fax: 01234 348214
E-mail: office@isds.org.uk

Website:
http://www.isds.org.uk
Information about the Society, general information and articles about sheepdog trialling and Border Collies, and details of UK trials and results.

Enquiries:
Enquiries to: Chief Executive

Founded:
1906

Organisation type and purpose:
Membership association (membership is by subscription), present number of members: 5000, registered charity (charity number 209009).
To maintain a breed register (Stud Book) for working sheepdogs as represented by the Border Collie, organise the major UK National and World Sheepdog trials, and provide a range of member services.

Subject coverage:
Sheepdog trialling in the UK.

Museum or gallery collection, archive, or library special collection:
Breed records for ISDS registered dogs

Printed publications:
Stud Books from 1985 (for purchase)
Newsletters (issued to members)
Introductory material available to enquirers

Access to staff:
Contact by letter, by telephone, by fax and by e-mail. Access for members only.
Hours: Mon to Fri, 0900 to 1700

Access to building, collection or gallery:
No access other than to staff

INTERNATIONAL SOCIETY FOR SOIL MECHANICS AND GEOTECHNICAL ENGINEERING

Acronym or abbreviation: ISSMGE

City University, Northampton Square, London, EC1V 0HB

Tel: 020 7040 8154
Fax: 020 7040 8832
E-mail: secretariat@issmge.org

Website:
http://www.issmge.org

Enquiries:
Enquiries to: Secretary General

Organisation type and purpose:
International organisation, professional body.

Subject coverage:
Soil mechanics, foundation engineering, geotechnical engineering, environmental geotechnics.

Printed publications:
Conference Proceedings
Lexicon
Report on Penetration Testing
Report on Pile Testing

INTERNATIONAL SOCIETY FOR TRENCHLESS TECHNOLOGY

Acronym or abbreviation: ISTT

15 Belgrave Square, London, SW1X 8PS

Tel: 020 850 9119
Fax: 020 850 7447
E-mail: info@istt.co.uk

Website:
http://www.istt.com
Inter-active site giving full details of the Society's activities.

Enquiries:
Enquiries to: Executive Secretary
Other contacts: Membership Secretary for alternative contact.

Founded:
1986

Organisation type and purpose:
International 'not for profit' professional organisation, membership is by subscription, present number of members: 3500, registered charity (charity number 295274).
ISTT aims to promote and increase the use of trenchless technology worldwide. Trenchless technology is for the installation and maintenance of underground utility services with minimum surface excavation. Trenchless technology has been accepted by the United Nations Environment Programme
(UNEP) as an Environmentally Sound Technology for supporting its sustainability initiatives

Subject coverage:
Information on the various types of trenchless technology for the installation, renovation and repair of pipeline systems under ground in order to minimise excavation and environmental damage.

Trade and statistical information:
World data on the use of trenchless technology and advice on the latest techniques.

Library catalogue:
All or part available online

Printed publications:
Trenchless Technology Research (once every 4 months, pub Elsevier Oxford)
Trenchless Technology International (bi-monthly, Benjamin Media, USA)

Electronic and video publications:
Trenchless Technology Database (CD-ROM, purchase, direct)

Publications list:
Available online

Access to staff:
Contact by letter, by fax, by e-mail, in person and via website
Hours: Mon to Fri, 0900 to 1700

Access to building, collection or gallery:
Belgrave Square is the registered address only. The staff are home based using the internet. For contact use Fax or Email

INTERNATIONAL STAR REGISTRY

Acronym or abbreviation: ISR

23–28 Penn Street, London, N1 5DL

Tel: 020 7684 4444
Fax: 020 7684 4443

E-mail: orion@starregistry.co.uk

Website:
http://www.international-star-registry.org
Information on how to name a star.

Enquiries:
Enquiries to: Public Relations Manager

Founded:
1991

Organisation type and purpose:
International organisation, service industry.
Name a star service. Naming a star in the heavens as a gift idea.

Subject coverage:
Astronomy, naming stars in the heavens.

Museum or gallery collection, archive, or library special collection:
Your Place in the Cosmos, volumes I to V
Register of International Star Registry star names worldwide, 1979–1999

Printed publications:
Package of commemorative documents issued when a star is named
Information packs (free)

Access to staff:
Contact by letter, by telephone, by fax, by e-mail and via website
Hours: Mon to Fri, 0900 to 1700

Access to building, collection or gallery:
Prior appointment required

Has:
16 offices worldwide

INTERNATIONAL STEEL TRADE ASSOCIATION

Acronym or abbreviation: ISTA

Broadway House, Tothill Street, Westminster, London, SW1H 9NQ

Tel: 020 7799 2662
Fax: 020 7799 2468
E-mail: hbailey@steeltrade.co.uk

Website:
http://www.steeltrade.co.uk

Enquiries:
Enquiries to: Director

Organisation type and purpose:
Trade association.

Subject coverage:
International iron and steel trade.

Access to staff:
Access for members only.
Hours: Mon to Fri, 0900 to 1700

INTERNATIONAL STUDENTS HOUSE

Acronym or abbreviation: ISH

1 Park Crescent, Regent's Park, London, W1B 1SH

Tel: 020 7631 8300
Fax: 020 7631 8315
E-mail: general@ish.org.uk

Website:
http://www.ish.org.uk

Enquiries:
Enquiries to: Executive Director
Direct tel: 020 7631 8301
Direct fax: 020 7631 8307
Direct e-mail: p.anwyl@ish.org.uk

Founded:
1965

Organisation type and purpose:
Registered charity (charity number 313512).
To provide housing and social facilities for overseas students.

Subject coverage:
Welfare advice service for overseas students.

Printed publications:
The International Students A-Z Guide to London
The International Students A-Z Guide to Scotland

Access to staff:
Contact by letter, by telephone, by fax, by e-mail and via website. Appointment necessary.
Hours: 24-hour access

Access for disabled people:
Parking provided, level entry, toilet facilities

INTERNATIONAL SUGAR ORGANIZATION

Acronym or abbreviation: ISO

1 Canada Square, Canary Wharf, Docklands, London, E14 5AA

Tel: 020 7513 1144
Fax: 020 7513 1146
E-mail: exdir@isosugar.org

Website:
http://www.isosugar.org
Details of publications.

Enquiries:
Enquiries to: Executive Director
Direct e-mail: info@isosugar.org

Founded:
1937

Organisation type and purpose:
International organisation.

Subject coverage:
Statistics on production, consumption, exports and imports of sugar in all countries of the world.

Printed publications:
MECAS Series, including:
MECAS (07)18 Outlook for the White Sugar Premium after the EU Sugar Reform
MECAS (07)17 Government Biofuels Policy and Sugar Crops: Outlook to 2015
MECAS (07)16 Import Dynamics and World Sugar Prices
Proceedings of Previous ISO seminars and workshops
Full list at http://www.isosugar.org/publications.htm
Order printed publications from: Publications division, tel: 020 7715 9436, e-mail: publications@isosugar.org, or website

Electronic and video publications:
CD: 2007: International Conference – Egypt – Proceedings (£175)
CD: 2005: International Conference – Egypt – Proceedings (£150)

Publications list:
Available online and in print

Access to staff:
Contact by letter, by telephone, by fax and by e-mail
Hours: Mon to Fri, 0930 to 1730

Access to building, collection or gallery:
Prior appointment required

The agreement (ISA) is under the auspices of:
UNCTAD
Geneva

INTERNATIONAL SUPPORT VESSEL OWNERS ASSOCIATION

Acronym or abbreviation: ISOA

12 Carthusian Street, London, EC1M 6EZ

Tel: 020 7417 8844
Fax: 020 7417 8877
E-mail: isoa@marisec.org

Enquiries:
Enquiries to: Assistant Secretary

Founded:
1985

Organisation type and purpose:
Shipping association.
Common forum for discussion of issues specific to the offshore industry, in particular international support vessel owners.

Access to staff:
Contact by letter, by telephone, by fax and by e-mail
Hours: Mon to Fri, 0900 to 1700

INTERNATIONAL SWAMINARAYAN SATSANG ORGANISATION

Acronym or abbreviation: ISSO

ISSO Central Office, 72 Colmer Road, Streatham, London, SW16 5JS

Tel: 020 8830 0771
Fax: 020 8830 0804
E-mail: info@swaminarayan.info

Website:
http://www.isso-europe.org
The Swaminarayan Sampraday explained with details of branches.

Enquiries:
Enquiries to: General Secretary

Founded:
1990

Organisation type and purpose:
International organisation, learned society, registered charity.
Religious Hindu organisation specialising in the Swaminarayan Faith/Sect.

Subject coverage:
Information from authentic sources on the Swaminarayan Sect of Hinduism.

Museum or gallery collection, archive, or library special collection:
References available through published and unpublished documents on the way of life in Gujarat, India about 200 years ago

Printed publications:
Large choice of publications in English, Gujarati, Hindi
Order printed publications from: International Swaminarayan Satsang Organisation
e-mail: central@issa.org.uk

Electronic and video publications:
Exploring Shikshapatri – Understanding God's word via a multimedia CD-ROM
Inauguration of Temples – The Vedic Way (video, for purchase)
Swaminarayan Nagar – The Swaminarayan Way (video, for purchase)

Access to staff:
Contact by letter, by fax and by e-mail.
Appointment necessary.
Hours: Mon to Fri, 0900 to 1700

Associate temple:
Swaminarayan Temples
37 Forradsgatan, Mariestad, S-54235, Sweden; tel: 00 46 501 12473; e-mail: sweden@isso.org.uk

Parent body:
Shree Swaminarayan Temple
Kalupur Ahmedabad, Gujarat, 380 001, India; tel: 00 91 79 213 6818; fax: 00 91 79 745 2145; e-mail: info@swaminarayan.info

Swaminarayan Temples in:
Leicester
139–141 Loughborough Road, Leicester, LE4 5LQ; tel: 0116 2666 210; fax: 0116 2666 210; e-mail: leicester@isso.org.uk
London
72 Colmer Road, London, SW16 5SZ; tel: 020 8679 8050; e-mail: streatham@isso.org.uk

INTERNATIONAL TABLE TENNIS FEDERATION

Acronym or abbreviation: ITTF

Chemin de la Roche 11, Renens/Lausanne, 1020, Switzerland

Tel: 00 41 21 340 70 90
Fax: 00 41 21 340 70 99
E-mail: ittf@ittf.com

Website:
http://www.ittf.com
Competition results, ranking lists, approved equipment list, rules, archives, museum, press releases.

Enquiries:
Enquiries to: Executive Director

Founded:
1926

Organisation type and purpose:
International organisation.
Governing body of the sport.

Subject coverage:
Table tennis.

Printed publications:
ITTF Directory
ITTF Handbook
ITTF Handbook for Match Officials
ITTF Rules Booklet
Table Tennis Illustrated (6 times a year)
ITTF News

Publications list:
Available online and in print

Access to staff:
Contact by letter, by telephone, by fax, by e-mail and via website. Appointment necessary.
Hours: Mon to Fri, 0900 to 1700

Access to building, collection or gallery:
Prior appointment required

Access for disabled people:
Access to all public areas

Other offices:
ITTF
1125 Colonel by Drive, Ontario, K1S 5R1, Canada; tel: 00 1 613 7332468; fax: 00 1 613 7334603; e-mail: ittf@ittf.com
Marketing Division & President's Office,

INTERNATIONAL TANKER OWNERS POLLUTION FEDERATION LIMITED

Acronym or abbreviation: ITOPF

1 Oliver's Yard, 55 City Road, London, EC1Y 1HQ

Tel: 020 7566 6999
Fax: 020 7566 6950
E-mail: central@itopf.com

Website:
http://www.itopf.com
Information about ITOPF's history, staffing, technical services and publications, plus general information on tanker spills (including statistics), clean up techniques, compensation arrangements, etc.

Enquiries:
Enquiries to: Information Officer
Direct e-mail: deborah.ansell@itopf.com

Founded:
1968

Organisation type and purpose:
International organisation, membership association.
ITOPF offers a broad range of technical and information services in the field of oil spill response, damage assessment, claims analysis and contingency planning, to its tanker owner members, their oil pollution insurers and other groups worldwide.

Subject coverage:
Regulations and insurance aspects of oil spills from tankers; organisation and contingency planning for oil spill clean-up; clean-up equipment and techniques; environmental effects of marine oil pollution; environmental planning.

Museum or gallery collection, archive, or library special collection:
Trade literature covering all types of oil spill clean-up equipment
Books, journal articles, conference papers on oil pollution from tankers and related topics

Library catalogue:
All or part available in-house

Printed publications:
Annual Review
Handbook
Ocean Orbit – annual newsletter (free)
Response to Marine Oil Spills (also available in French, Spanish, Japanese and Korean) 1987
Technical Information Papers (12 titles)

Publications list:
Available in print

Access to staff:
Contact by letter, by telephone, by fax, by e-mail and via website. Appointment necessary.
Hours: Mon to Fri, 0900 to 1700

INTERNATIONAL TEA COMMITTEE LIMITED

Acronym or abbreviation: ITC

1 Carlton House Terrace, London, SW1Y 5DB 020 7839 5090

Tel: 020 7839 5090
E-mail: info@inttea.com

Website:
http://www.inttea.com/

Enquiries:
Enquiries to: Executive Assistant
Direct e-mail: rumi.ali@inteacom.globalnet.co.uk

Organisation type and purpose:
Membership association.
Statistical secretariat for tea throughout the world.

Subject coverage:
Tea statistics for producing, consuming countries; acreage; world auction prices; imports, exports, consumption, supply and absorption.

Trade and statistical information:
Statistics for tea going back over 60 years.

Printed publications:
Annual Bulletin of Statistics
Monthly Statistical Summary
World Tea Statistics 1910–1990

Access to staff:
Contact by letter, by telephone, by fax, by e-mail and via website
Hours: Mon to Fri, 0830 to 1630

INTERNATIONAL THEATRE INSTITUTE LIMITED

Acronym or abbreviation: ITI

ITI @ Goldsmiths College, University of London, Lewisham Way, New Cross, London, SE14 6NW

Tel: 020 7919 7276
Fax: 020 7919 7277
E-mail: iti@gold.ac.uk

Website:
http://iti.gold.ac.uk

Enquiries:
Enquiries to: Administrator

Founded:
1948

Organisation type and purpose:
International organisation, membership association (membership is by subscription), registered charity (charity number 295092). Non-governmental organisation under the auspices of UNESCO. To facilitate networking and exchange of information, produce events and play an active role in promoting cultural exchange.

Subject coverage:
Theatre, dance and music theatre. Facilitates international contacts, research and networking in the performing arts. (Members may also approach any of the 95 centres worldwide.)

Museum or gallery collection, archive, or library special collection:
Archive containing performing arts books, journals, directories, scripts, reviews and funding information from around the world

Printed publications:
Transcripts of seminars and conferences
Information bulletin (quarterly, free to members)
International Theatre Institute books and directories

Publications list:
Available in print

Access to staff:
Contact by letter, by telephone, by fax and by e-mail. Appointment necessary. Access for members only.
Hours: Mon to Fri, 0930 to 1730
Special comments: Open 2 days per week.

Access to building, collection or gallery:
No prior appointment required

Has:
95 national centres around the world

Secretariat of the:
ITI
Paris

Works in liaison with:
AICT (critics)
AITA (amateur theatre)
ASSITEJ (young people's theatre)
FIA (actors federation)
FIRT (arts research)
OISTAT (scenographers and technicians)
SIBMAS (libraries and museums)
UNIMA (puppeteers)

INTERNATIONAL THERAPY EXAMINATION COUNCIL

Acronym or abbreviation: ITEC

4 Heathfield Terrace, London, W4 4JE

Tel: 020 8994 4141
Fax: 020 8994 7880
E-mail: info@itecworld.co.uk

Website:
http://www.itecworld.co.uk
Range of pages on qualifications; colleges registered; how to get information; books and teaching materials.

Enquiries:
Enquiries to: Director

Founded:
1973

Organisation type and purpose:
International awarding body for therapy qualifications.
Provides a syllabus and examinations for professional vocational qualifications in beauty, complementary and sports therapies.

Subject coverage:
ITEC provide an independent examination system for the beauty, therapy, health, sport and leisure industries, and complementary therapies.

Printed publications:
ITEC News Bulletin
ITEC Registration Pack
ITEC Syllabus

Publications list:
Available online and in print

Access to staff:
Contact by letter, by telephone, by fax and by e-mail. Appointment necessary.
Hours: Mon to Fri, 0900 to 1700

Parent body:
ITEC Professionals
at the same address; tel: 020 8994 7856; fax: 020 8994 7880; e-mail: professionals@itecworld.co.uk

INTERNATIONAL TRANSPORT WORKERS' FEDERATION

Acronym or abbreviation: ITF

4960 Borough Road, London, SE1 1DR

Tel: 020 7403 2733
Fax: 020 7357 7871
E-mail: mail@itf.org.uk

Website:
http://www.itfglobal.org

Enquiries:
Enquiries to: General Secretary
Direct tel: 020 7940 9257
Direct fax: 020 7407 0319
Direct e-mail: hawke_jenny@itf.org.uk

Founded:
1896

Organisation type and purpose:
Trade union.
International trade union federation.
Provides a wide range of support and advice for its affiliated unions.

Subject coverage:
Transport industry and trade unionism.

Museum or gallery collection, archive, or library special collection:
19th and 20th century trade union history (held by Warwick University)

Library catalogue:
All or part available in-house

Printed publications:
About the ITF (leaflet, 2001, available in many languages)
Globalising Solidarity Manual (2002)
Women Transporting the World (2002)
Human Rights are Workers' Rights (2002)
Transport International (quarterly, from mid 2000)
Various other current subject publications which include: Education, Women, Seafarers/Fisheries, Agreements, Ports, Railways/Road and Urban Transport, Civil Aviation

Electronic and video publications:
Some of the following videos are available in other languages:
A Seafarer's Tale (video, 2000)
Flags for Sale (video, 1998)
Global Mariner (video, 2000)
The Voyage of the Global Mariner (4 videos, 2000/2001)
Life at Sea (CD-ROM, 1999)

Publications list:
Available in print

Access to staff:
Contact by letter and by e-mail. Appointment necessary.
Hours: Mon to Fri, 0900 to 1700

Access to building, collection or gallery:
Prior appointment required

Access for disabled people:
Ramped entry

INTERNATIONAL TREE FOUNDATION

Acronym or abbreviation: ITF

Sandy Lane, Crawley Down, Crawley, West Sussex, RH10 4HS

Tel: 0870 774 4269
Fax: 01342 718282
E-mail: info@internationaltreefoundation.org

Website:
http://www.internationaltreefoundation.org

Enquiries:
Enquiries to: Information Officer

Founded:
1924

Organisation type and purpose:
Membership association (membership is by subscription), present number of members: 3000, registered charity (charity number 1106269).
To protect and plant trees worldwide.

Subject coverage:
Tree planting, tree care, arboriculture.

Printed publications:
Trees (journal, annually)
Trees are News (newsletter, 2 times a year)

Access to staff:
Contact by letter, by telephone, by fax, by e-mail, in person and via website
Hours: Mon to Fri, 0900 to 1700

INTERNATIONAL UNDERWRITING ASSOCIATION

Formal name: International Underwriting Association of London
Acronym or abbreviation: IUA

London Underwriting Centre, 3 Minster Court, Mincing Lane, London, EC3R 7DD

Tel: 020 7617 4444
Fax: 020 7617 4440
E-mail: info@iua.co.uk

Website:
http://www.lirma.co.uk
General background and Association news.
http://www.iua.co.uk
An interactive website including information about the IUA London Market, membership, current projects, press updates, events, contact details and downloadable publications.

Enquiries:
Enquiries to: Chief Executive
Direct tel: 020 7617 4446
Other contacts: Press & PR Manager for general enquiries.

Founded:
1998

Organisation type and purpose:
Trade association.
For ordinary members, central accounting and processing of insurance and reinsurance contracts, also central settlement of claims. Representation and research provision.

Subject coverage:
International insurance, reinsurance; reinsurance statistics; earthquake studies, bodily injury awards trends, regulation, claims, marine insurance and reinsurance, aviation, eRisks and industry clauses.

Museum or gallery collection, archive, or library special collection:
Master copy of all publications and information relevant to members held

Trade and statistical information:
Reports of information meetings and seminars, annual membership statistics, earthquakes hazard atlas, reports of forum meetings, marine statistics, eLondon company market statistics, UK Bodily Injury Studies.

Printed publications:
Annual Report and Accounts
EMU – What it means to the London Market
Earthquake studies (irregular)
IUA Digest (for members only)
IUMI Marine & Casualty Statistics
Information bulletins (hardcopies and on disk)
Reinsurance Statistics

Summary of Indirect Taxation on Insurance Contracts in Europe
Risk Today
The London Insurance Market
UK Bodily Injury Awards Study 1 & 2
The Rating of Pro-rata Treaties
World @ Risk
Weather Studies
Order printed publications from: Publications Distribution Manager, IUA
3 Minster Court, Mincing Lane, London, EC3R 7DD, tel: 020 7617 5443, fax: 020 7617 9440, e-mail: anthony.dickinson@iua.co.uk

Electronic and video publications:
Competition Act (CD-ROM)
eRisk – The New Frontier (CD-ROM)
FSA's Impact on Senior Management (CD-ROM)
Reinsurance Clauses (CD-ROM)

Publications list:
Available in print

Access to staff:
Contact by letter, by telephone, by fax, by e-mail and via website
Hours: Mon to Fri, 0900 to 1700

Access to building, collection or gallery:
Prior appointment required

Access for disabled people:
Ramped entry, access to all public areas, toilet facilities

INTERNATIONAL VISUAL COMMUNICATION ASSOCIATION

Acronym or abbreviation: IVCA

19 Pepper Street, Glengall Bridge, Docklands, London, E14 9RP

Tel: 020 7512 0571
Fax: 020 7512 0591
E-mail: info@ivca.org

Website:
http://www.ivca.org

Enquiries:
Enquiries to: Information Officer

Founded:
1988/89

Organisation type and purpose:
International organisation, advisory body, trade association.
Provides collective voice for the business communication industry, and products and services to benefit membership.

Subject coverage:
Business communications, industry and products, film and video.

Trade and statistical information:
Data on the UK business communications industry.

Printed publications:
A Guide to Copyright
Commissioning a Programme
IVCA Business Media Handbook
IVCA Update (newsletter, monthly)
The Case Study Booklet

Publications list:
Available online

Access to staff:
Contact by letter, by telephone, by e-mail and via website
Hours: Mon to Fri, 0930 to 1730

Access to building, collection or gallery:
Prior appointment required

Parent body:
Independent Television Association Limited (ITVA)

INTERNATIONAL VOLUNTARY SERVICE

Acronym or abbreviation: IVS

7 Upper Bow, Edinburgh, EH1 2JN

Tel: 0131 226 6722
Fax: 0131 226 6723
E-mail: scotland@ivs-gb.org.uk

Website:
http://www.ivs-gb.org.uk

Enquiries:
Enquiries to: Scottish Co-ordinator

Founded:
1931

Organisation type and purpose:
International organisation, voluntary organisation, registered charity.

Subject coverage:
Opportunities for short-term voluntary work throughout Britain and the world.

Printed publications:
Annual Listing
International Voluntary Service
Short-term projects

Publications list:
Available online

Access to staff:
Contact by letter, by telephone, by fax, by e-mail, in person and via website
Hours: Mon- Fri, 0900 to 1700

IVS is the British branch of:
Service Civil International (SCI)
A worldwide movement

Member bodies:
IVS
Castlehill House, 21 Otley Road, Leeds, LS6 3AA
IVS
Old Hall, East Bergholt, Colchester, Essex, CO7 6TQ

Parent body:
Service Civil International (SCI)

INTERNATIONAL VOLUNTARY SERVICE (NORTH)

Acronym or abbreviation: IVS

Castlehill House, 21 Otley Road, Leeds, West Yorkshire, LS6 3AA

Tel: 0113 230 4600
Fax: 0113 230 4610
E-mail: ivsgbn@ivsgbn.demon.co.uk

Website:
http://www.ivsgbn.demon.co.uk

Enquiries:
Enquiries to: Regional Co-ordinator
Other contacts: National Fundraiser

Founded:
1931

Organisation type and purpose:
International organisation, national organisation, voluntary organisation, registered charity (charity number 275424).
To promote peace, justice and international understanding through voluntary work.

Subject coverage:
Information on over 700 international work camps, on opportunities for short and medium term volunteering for British volunteers in Europe, North America, CIS, North Africa, Japan and Australia.

Printed publications:
Information Leaflets
Interactions (newsletter, quarterly)
Workcamp Listing (annually, published April)

Access to staff:
Contact by letter and by e-mail
Hours: Mon to Fri, 0900 to 1700

Other addresses:
IVS – Scotland
7 Upper Bow, Edinburgh, EH1 2JN; tel: 0131 226 6722; fax: 0131 226 6723; e-mail: ivsgbscot@ivsgbscot.demon.co.uk
IVS – South
Old Hall, East Bergholt, Colchester, CO7 6TQ; tel: 01206 298215; fax: 01206 299043; e-mail: ivsgbsouth@ivsgbsouth.demon.co.uk

Parent body:
Service Civil International (SCI)

INTERNATIONAL WATER ASSOCIATION

Acronym or abbreviation: IWA

12 Alliance House, Caxton Street, London, SW1H 0QS

Tel: 020 7654 5500
Fax: 020 7654 5555
E-mail: water@iwahq.org.uk

Website:
http://www.iwahq.org.uk
Membership, conferences, publications and specialist technical groups.

Enquiries:
Enquiries to: Executive Director

Founded:
1965

Organisation type and purpose:
International organisation, professional body, membership association (membership is by subscription), registered charity (charity number 1076690).
Exchange of information between those engaged in water supply.

Subject coverage:
Wastewater treatment processes, water reuse, impact of pollutants on water bodies. Water suppliers national and worldwide.

Non-library collection catalogue:
All or part available online

Printed publications:
Advances in Water Pollution Control (book series containing proceedings of conferences, etc.)
Scientific and Technical Reports
Water Quality International (magazine, 6 times a year)
Water Research (journal, monthly, original research papers)
Water Science and Technology (journal, 24 times a year, proceedings of conferences, etc.)
Yearbook and Directory of Members

Publications list:
Available in print

Access to staff:
Contact by letter and by e-mail
Hours: Mon to Fri, 0900 to 1700

Access to building, collection or gallery:
Prior appointment required

Affiliated to:
World Health Organisation

Non-governmental organisation of:
The United Nations

INTERNATIONAL WHALING COMMISSION

Acronym or abbreviation: IWC

The Red House, 135 Station Road, Impington, Cambridge, CB24 9NP

Tel: 01223 233971
Fax: 01223 232876
E-mail: secretariat@iwcoffice.org

Website:
http://www.iwcoffice.org

Enquiries:
Enquiries to: Editor

Founded:
1946

Organisation type and purpose:
International organisation, membership association, present number of members: 81 member nations.
Conservation of whales and regulation of whaling.

Subject coverage:
Whales, whaling, population, biology, resource management, ecosystem management, genetics, statistical surveys, whale catch and sightings database.

Non-library collection catalogue:
All or part available in print

Printed publications:
Annual Reports, Journal of Cetacean Research and Management, Special Issues (all available, priced)
Basic Documents (convention, schedule)
Free information leaflets
Journal of Cetacean Research and Management
Special Issues on various whaling topics
Order printed publications from: PA to the Secretary, IWC

Electronic and video publications:
Published and unpublished scientific documents on bibliographical database

Publications list:
Available online and in print

Access to staff:
Contact by letter, by telephone, by fax, by e-mail and via website. Appointment necessary.
Hours: Mon to Fri, 0900 to 1700
Special comments: Dependent upon availability of staff.

Access to building, collection or gallery:
Prior appointment required
Hours: Mon to Fri, 0900 to 1700

Access for disabled people:
Parking provided, ramped entry
Special comments: Level access on ground floor.

INTERNATIONAL WILDLIFE COALITION TRUST

Acronym or abbreviation: IWCT

141A High Street, Edenbridge, Kent, TN8 5AX

Tel: 01732 866955
Fax: 01732 966995
E-mail: iwcuk@iwcmail.demon.co.uk

Website:
http://www.iwc.org

Enquiries:
Enquiries to: Director

Founded:
1987

Organisation type and purpose:
International organisation, voluntary organisation, registered charity (charity number 1035381).

Publications list:
Available online and in print

Access to staff:
Contact by letter, by telephone, by fax, by e-mail, in person and via website. Appointment necessary.
Hours: Mon to Fri, 0900 to 1700

Access to building, collection or gallery:
Prior appointment required

INTERNATIONAL WINE & FOOD SOCIETY

Acronym or abbreviation: IWFS

9 Fitzmaurice Place, Berkeley Square, London, W1J 5JD

Tel: 020 7495 4191
Fax: 020 7495 4172
E-mail: sec@iwfs.org

Enquiries:
Enquiries to: Executive Director
Other contacts: Membership Administrator

Founded:
1933

Organisation type and purpose:
International organisation, membership association (membership is by subscription), present number of members: 7500. Educational and social.

Subject coverage:
Every aspect of wine and cookery, gastronomy.

Museum or gallery collection, archive, or library special collection:
Library is situated in Guildhall Public Library, City of London

Printed publications:
Monographs Series
Quarterly Newsletters of European, North American and Asian Pacific Membership

Publications list:
Available in print

Access to staff:
Contact by letter, by telephone, by fax and by e-mail. Appointment necessary. Non-members charged.
Hours: Mon to Fri, 1000 to 1630
Special comments: Membership card required.

Also:
140 local branches worldwide

INTERNATIONAL YOUTH FOUNDATION OF GREAT BRITAIN

Acronym or abbreviation: IYF

6a Pont Street, London, SW1X 9EL

Tel: 020 7235 7671
Fax: 020 7235 7370
E-mail: info@euyo.org.uk

Website:
http://www.euyo.org.uk

Enquiries:
Enquiries to: Secretary General

Founded:
1978

Organisation type and purpose:
International organisation, registered charity (charity number 281420).

Subject coverage:
Youth orchestras, choirs, ballet, opera, folk and youth bands, formation and development of national youth orchestras, music and education in the European Union.

Printed publications:
Annual brochure and programme

Access to staff:
Contact by letter, by telephone, by fax and by e-mail
Hours: Mon to Fri, 0930 to 1730

Under its auspices is the:
European Union Youth Orchestra (EUYO) at the same address; tel: 020 7235 7671; fax: 020 7235 7370; e-mail: info@euyo.org.uk

INTERNATIONAL ZEN ASSOCIATION (UNITED KINGDOM)

Acronym or abbreviation: IZAUK

91–93 Gloucester Road, Bristol, BS7 8AT

Tel: 0117 942 4347

Website:
http://www.izauk.org

Enquiries:
Enquiries to: Information Officer

Founded:
1986

Organisation type and purpose:
Registered charity (charity number 296285). Spiritual and religious practice.

Subject coverage:
Soto Zen Buddhism.

Printed publications:
Book list (available on request)
Leaflet (available on request)

Access to staff:
Contact by letter, by telephone, by e-mail and in person
Hours: By arrangement

Branches:
10 subsidiary groups in the United Kingdom, in Bristol, Manchester, London, Leeds, Norwich, Oxford, Bournemouth and Cwmbran

Member organisation of:
Association Zen Internationale
175 rue de Tolbiac, Paris, 75013, France

INTERPAVE, THE PRECAST CONCRETE PAVING AND KERB ASSOCIATION

60 Charles Street, Leicester, LE1 1FB

Tel: 0116 253 6161
Fax: 0116 251 4568
E-mail: info@paving.org.uk

Website:
http://www.paving.org.uk

Enquiries:
Enquiries to: Secretary

Organisation type and purpose:
Trade association.

Subject coverage:
Precast concrete paving flags, block paving and kerbs.

Printed publications:
Literature Pack (free)
The Structural Design of Heavy Duty Pavements for Ports and Other Industries

Access to staff:
Contact by letter, by telephone, by fax and by e-mail. Appointment necessary.
Hours: Mon to Fri, 0900 to 1700

Member organisation of:
British Precast Concrete Federation

INVENSYS APV

23 Gatwick Road, Crawley, West Sussex, RH10 9JB

Tel: 01293 527777
Fax: 01293 552640

Website:
http://www.apv.co.uk

Enquiries:
Enquiries to: Marketing Manager
Direct tel: 01293 574380

Founded:
1910

Organisation type and purpose:
International organisation. Company.
Provision of components, process engineering, automation and service to the food, drink, pharmaceutical and healthcare industries.

Subject coverage:
Design, production, installation and technical know-how of food, liquid food and pharmaceutical engineering processes. Provision of automation solutions to the above industries.

Access to staff:
Contact by letter, by telephone and by fax. Appointment necessary.
Hours: Mon to Fri, 0900 to 1700

Access for disabled people:
Ramped entry

Parent body:
Invensys plc
Invensys House, Carlisle Place, London, SW1P 1BX; tel: 020 7834 3848; fax: 020 7834 3879

INVERCLYDE LIBRARIES

Central Library, Clyde Square, Greenock, Renfrewshire, PA15 1NA

Tel: 01475 712323
Fax: 01475 712339
E-mail: library.central@inverclyde.gov.uk

Website:
http://www.inverclyde.gov.uk/Libraries

Enquiries:
Enquiries to: Librarian

Organisation type and purpose:
Local government body, public library.

Subject coverage:
General, local history.

Museum or gallery collection, archive, or library special collection:
Watt Library (local history, 18th and 19th century publications)

Library catalogue:
All or part available online and in-house

Access to staff:
Contact by letter, by telephone, by fax, by e-mail and in person
Hours: Mon, Tue, Thu, 0930 to 1900; Fri, 0930 to 1700; Wed, 0930 to 1300; Sat, 1000 to 1300

INVESTMENT MANAGEMENT ASSOCIATION

Acronym or abbreviation: IMA

65 Kingsway, London, WC2B 6TD

Tel: 020 7831 0898
Fax: 020 7831 9975
E-mail: ima@investmentuk.org

Website:
http://www.investmentuk.org

Enquiries:
Enquiries to: Head of Communications

Founded:
1959

Created by the merger of:
Association of Unit Trusts and Investment Funds (AUTIF) and Fund Managers Association (FMA) (year of change 2002)

Formerly called:
Unit Trust Association

Organisation type and purpose:
Trade association (membership is by subscription) for asset management companies. Affiliate membership for service providers to asset management companies.

Subject coverage:
Unit trusts, open-ended investment companies (OEICs), ISAs, investment, saving, pensions, markets.

Museum or gallery collection, archive, or library special collection:
Historical statistics

continued overleaf

Trade and statistical information:
UK data on asset management, unit trusts OEIC and ISA sales data.

Printed publications:
Introducing Investment (booklet)
Introducing IMA (corporate brochure)
Factsheets, including:
Ethical Investment Funds
Investing in ISAs
Monthly Savings
Investment Funds and Tax
IMA Pocket Guide
Child Trust Fund
Enabling Choice in Retirement
Annual Asset Management in the UK Survey

Publications list:
Available online and in print

Access to staff:
Contact by letter, by telephone and by e-mail
Hours: Mon to Fri, 0900 to 1700

Access to building, collection or gallery:
No access other than to staff

IOP: THE PACKAGING SOCIETY

Acronym or abbreviation: IOP

Springfield House, Springfield Business Park, Grantham, Lincolnshire, NO31 7BG

Tel: 01476 514590
Fax: 01476 514591
E-mail: iop@pi2.org.uk

Website:
http://www.iop.co.uk
Full range of Institute of Packaging's products and services.

Enquiries:
Enquiries to: Head of Education, Training & Development
Direct tel: 01664 502150
Direct e-mail: gordon-stewart@iop.co.uk

Founded:
1947

Organisation type and purpose:
Professional body, present number of members: 3500, registered charity (charity number 295762), consultancy, publishing house.
Supports courses at Brunel and Loughborough Universities.
To promote packaging and provide education and training in packaging technology.

Subject coverage:
Packaging technology, packaging and the environment, legislation, packaging education and qualification, packaging publications, overseas contacts and exhibitions.

Museum or gallery collection, archive, or library special collection:
Reference library dedicated to packaging, packaging technology and related topics. Includes British Standards, periodicals and technical conference papers in addition to text books

Trade and statistical information:
Details of overseas trade exhibitions related to packaging and grants available to firms.

Printed publications:
Fundamentals of Packaging Technology
Packaging – The Facts (schools)

Electronic and video publications:
Open This End (video for schools)

Access to staff:
Contact by letter, by telephone, by fax, by e-mail and via website. Appointment necessary.
Hours: Mon to Fri, 0900 to 1700
Special comments: Three steps up to front door.

Secretariat for the:
Packaging Federation
at the same address

Pressure Sensitive Manufacturers Association
at the same address

IP3

Formal name: Institute of Paper, Printing and Publishing

Runnymede Malthouse, off Hummer Road, Egham, Surrey, TW20 9BD

Tel: 0870 330 8625
Fax: 0870 330 8615
E-mail: info@ip3.org.uk

Website:
http://www.ip3.org.uk/

Enquiries:
Enquiries to: Information Officer

Founded:
2004

Created by the merger of:

Organisation type and purpose:
Professional body.

Printed publications:
Annual Lecture Booklet (free to members)
Calculations Booklet (£6 inc. p&p, to non-members)
Manual of Paper Trading (£44.50 inc. p&p, to non-members)
Paper Today (member magazine, quarterly, free to members)
Paper Samples Book (£25 inc. p&p, to non-members)
Yearly Prospectus (free)

Access to staff:
Contact by telephone, by fax and by e-mail
Hours: Mon to Fri, 0900 to 1700

IPSEA

Formal name: Independent Panel for Special Education Advice
Acronym or abbreviation: IPSEA

6 Carlow Mews, Woodbridge, Suffolk, IP12 1EA

Tel: 01394 3877411 \ helpline: 0800 0184016
Fax: 01394 380518
E-mail: ipsea.info@

Website:
http://www.ipsea.org.uk

Enquiries:
Enquiries to: Administrator
Direct tel: 01394 384711
Direct fax: 01394 446577

Organisation type and purpose:
Voluntary organisation.

Subject coverage:
IPSEA offers free and independent advice and support to parents of children with special educational needs including, free advice on LEAs' legal duties towards children with SEN, free home visits where necessary, free support and possible representation for those parents appealing to the Special Educational Needs Tribunal, and free second opinions on a child's needs and the provision required to meet those needs.

Printed publications:
Sent Ahead – a parents guide to the Special Educational Needs Tribunal
Taking Action – your child's right to special educational provision

Publications list:
Available in print

Access to building, collection or gallery:
No prior appointment required

IPSOS MORI

Formal name: Ipsos MORI
Acronym or abbreviation: MORI

79–81 Borough Road, London, SE1 1FY

Tel: 020 7347 3000
Fax: 020 7347 3800

Website:
http://www.mori.com/pubinfo/articles.htm

Enquiries:
Enquiries to: Marketing Executive
Direct e-mail: patricia.ifejika@mori.com
Other contacts: Head of Communications Department

Founded:
October 2005

Organisation type and purpose:
International organisation, research organisation. Full market research agency.

Subject coverage:
Specialist knowledge of over 40 specialist business areas, including financial, corporate image, employee, leisure and tourism and social research.

Printed publications:
Publication list available on-line or via the marketing department. All free of charge
Order printed publications from: Marketing Department

Electronic and video publications:
Corporate video available free of charge

Publications list:
Available online

Access to staff:
Contact by telephone and by e-mail
Hours: Mon to Fri, 0830 to 1800

Other addresses:
Ipsos MORI
Kings House, Kymberley Road, Harrow, HA1 1PT; tel: 020 8861 8000; fax: 020 8861 5515

IPSWICH INSTITUTE

Reading Room and Library, 15 Tavern Street, Ipswich, Suffolk, IP1 3AA

Tel: 01473 253992
E-mail: library@ipswichinstitute.org.uk

Enquiries:
Enquiries to: Executive Secretary

Founded:
1824

Organisation type and purpose:
Membership association (membership is by subscription), present number of members: 2400, registered charity (charity number 304772). Private subscription library with reading room having 9000 books.
To advance the education of the inhabitants of Ipswich and neighbourhood.

Subject coverage:
Fiction and non-fiction books, talking tapes, newspapers, magazines.

Access to staff:
Contact by letter, by telephone and by e-mail. Appointment necessary.
Hours: Mon to Fri, 0900 to 1700; Sat, 0900 to 1600

Access to building, collection or gallery:
No prior appointment required
Special comments: Membership organisation – one visit acceptable prior ro membership.

Also at:
Ipswich Institute
13 Tower Street, Ipswich, Suffolk, IP1 3PG; tel: 01473 253992

Member of:
Association of Independent Libraries
Leeds Library, 18 Commercial Street, Leeds, LS1 6AL; website: www.independentlibraries.co.uk

IQEA LIMITED

Formal name: Improving the Quality of Education for All

Sycamores, Holebottom Road, Todmorden, Lancashire, OL14 8DD

Tel: 01706 839274
Fax: 01706 839274
E-mail: admin@iqea.com

Website:
http://www.iqea.com
Background information on the project and current details of research being undertaken.

Enquiries:
Enquiries to: Managing Director
Direct tel: 07920 449247
Other contacts: IQEA Co-ordinator for details about schools involved in the project

Founded:
2002

Organisation type and purpose:
International organisation, advisory body, learned society (membership is by election or invitation), present number of members: 100 schools, university department or institute, suitable for ages: primary and secondary, training organisation, consultancy, research organisation. School Improvement Network.
To support school improvement efforts locally, nationally and internationally. The key purpose is to enhance the quality of student learning and achievement.

Subject coverage:
The quality of education in primary and secondary schools.

Library catalogue:
All or part available in-house and in print

Printed publications:
Many papers in professional publications

Access to staff:
Contact by letter, by telephone, by fax, by e-mail, in person and via website. Appointment necessary. Non-members charged.
Hours: Mon to Fri, 0900 to 1700

Access to building, collection or gallery:
No public access

IQEA LIMITED – CAMBRIDGE

Formal name: Improving the Quality of Education for All Limited
Acronym or abbreviation: IQEA Ltd

c/o 29 Cavendish Avenue, Cambridge, CB1 7UP

Tel: 01223 514849
Fax: 01223 575116
E-mail: j.f.beresford@ntlword.com

Website:
http://www.iqea.net
General education.

Enquiries:
Enquiries to: Research Officer

Founded:
1991

Organisation type and purpose:
International organisation, membership association (membership is by subscription), present number of members: 150 schools, suitable for ages: Primary and secondary, training organisation, consultancy, research organisation. School improvement network.

Subject coverage:
Education, especially school improvement.

Printed publications:
Creating the Conditions for Classroom Improvement (Hopkins D et al)
Creating the Conditions for School Improvement (Ainscow M et al, 2000)
Creating the Conditions for Teaching and Learning (Hopkins D et al)

Creating Winning Classrooms (Hook P and Vass A)
Collecting Information for School Improvement (Beresford J)
Improving the Quality of Education for All: Progress and Change (Hopkins D et al, 1996)
Quality in Schools: Developing a Model for School Improvement (West M, in press)
Variety of papers prepared for educational conferences including BERA, ECER and ICSEI
Variety of papers prepared for educational journals including Reading, Managing Schools Today, The Curriculum Journal, TES, Education and School Organisation

Publications list:
Available in print

Access to staff:
Contact by letter, by telephone, by fax, by e-mail, in person and via website. Non-members charged.
Hours: Mon to Fri, 0900 to 1700

IRAN SOCIETY

2 Belgrave Square, London, SW1X 8PJ

Tel: 020 7235 5122
Fax: 020 7259 6771
E-mail: info@iransociety.org

Website:
http://www.iransociety.org

Enquiries:
Enquiries to: Honorary Secretary

Organisation type and purpose:
Membership association (membership is by subscription, election or invitation), present number of members: 350, voluntary organisation (charity number 248678).
Promotes the study of Iran, its peoples and culture and particularly aims to advance education through the study of language, literature, art, history, religion, antiquities, usages, institutions and customs of Iran.

Subject coverage:
Iran (excluding contemporary politics).

Access to staff:
Contact by letter, by telephone, by fax, by e-mail and via website
Hours: Wed to Fri, 0930 to 1700

IRISH COUNCIL OF CHURCHES & THE IRISH INTER-CHURCH MEETING

Acronym or abbreviation: ICC & IICM

48 Elmwood Avenue, Belfast, BT9 6AZ

Tel: 028 9066 3145
Fax: 028 9066 4160
E-mail: info@irishchuches

Website:
http://www.irishchurches.org
Resources, news, photos, links.

Enquiries:
Enquiries to: Administrator

Founded:
1922

Organisation type and purpose:
National organisation, registered charity (charity number XN 48617).
Church body.

Subject coverage:
Information on Irish ecumenism.

Publications list:
Available online and in print

Access to staff:
Contact by letter, by telephone, by fax, by e-mail and in person
Hours: Mon to Fri, 0900 to 1700

IRISH FOOTBALL ASSOCIATION

Acronym or abbreviation: IFA

20 Windsor Ave, Belfast BT9 6EG

Tel: 02890 669458
E-mail: info@irishfa.com

Website:
http://www.irishfa.com/
News, results, fixtures for all Irish league clubs and competitions, updated tables, weekly newsletter, interactive section.

Enquiries:
Enquiries to: General Secretary
Other contacts: President

Founded:
1880

Merged with:
the Irish Football League (IFL, founded 1890) (year of change 2003)

Organisation type and purpose:
Sporting body.

Subject coverage:
Soccer in Northern Ireland, Irish league clubs.

Access to staff:
Contact by letter, by telephone, by fax and by e-mail
Hours: Mon to Fri, 0900 to 1700

IRISH LINEN GUILD

c/o Riverside Factory, Victoria Street, Lurgan, Craigavon, County Armagh BT67 9DU

E-mail: info@irishlinen.co.uk

Website:
http://www.irishlinen.co.uk
Information on all aspects of the Irish Linen Industry.

Enquiries:
Enquiries to: Director

Founded:
1928

Organisation type and purpose:
Professional body, membership association (membership is by qualification), present number of members: 35.
Promotion of Irish linen.

Subject coverage:
History and production of Irish linen, sourcing Irish linen products including yarn, fabric and household textiles.

Printed publications:
Education Packs: teachers (£10), students (£7.50), pupils (£2.50)
Apparel Weavers Company Directory (free)
History Book (£4.50)
Brochure (£1 plus vat)

Electronic and video publications:
Video (£12 plus vat)

Publications list:
Available in print

Access to staff:
Contact by letter, by telephone, by fax, by e-mail, in person and via website
Hours: Mon to Fri, 0900 to 1700

IRISH SEA FORUM

Acronym or abbreviation: ISF

Oceanography Laboratories, The University of Liverpool, Liverpool, L69 3BX

Tel: 0151 794 4089
Fax: 0151 794 4099
E-mail: d.f.shaw@liv.ac.uk

Website:
http://www.liv.ac.uk/

continued overleaf

Enquiries:
Enquiries to: Director
Other contacts: Administrative Officer for all information about Irish Sea Forum.

Founded:
1992

Organisation type and purpose:
Membership association (membership is by subscription), present number of members: 95, voluntary organisation.
Non-profit making organisation operating within the University of Liverpool; liaison with industry and commerce, voluntary and statutory organisations, and educational establishments on all shores of the Irish Sea, individual membership welcomed from those wishing to support the purpose of the Forum.
To bring together those who are interested in the enhancement of the environmental health of the Irish Sea and its coastal features and estuaries, and the sustainable development of its resources.

Subject coverage:
All aspects of environmental management pertaining to the Irish Sea.

Printed publications:
Irish Sea Forum, Seminar Series (available from Irish Sea Forum, Administrator, 3 times a year)
Irish Sea Group reports (1990) vols 1–4

Publications list:
Available in print

Access to staff:
Contact by letter, by telephone, by fax, by e-mail and via website. Appointment necessary.
Hours: Mon to Fri, 0900 to 1700

Access to building, collection or gallery:
No prior appointment required

IRISH TEXTS SOCIETY

Acronym or abbreviation: ITS

Royal Bank of Scotland, Drummonds Branch, 49 Charing Cross, Admiralty Arch, London, SW1A 2DX

Website:
http://www.ucc.ie/locus/ITS.html

Enquiries:
Enquiries to: Secretary
Direct e-mail: shuttonseanfile@aol.com
Other contacts: Honorary Treasurer; email burnsfarm@iol.ie for book orders, membership queries/ applications.

Founded:
1898

Organisation type and purpose:
Learned society (membership is by subscription), publishing house.

Subject coverage:
Irish language, history; texts and translations; poetry and prose.

Museum or gallery collection, archive, or library special collection:
The archives of the Society are in the Library of University College Cork, Ireland

Printed publications:
57 titles; new volume approximately each year; subsidiary publications series, proceedings of annual ITS/UCC Seminar
A guide to the archives is contained in Pádraig ó Riain Ed. Irish Texts Society: The First Hundred Years (ITS, 1998)
ITS Newsletter (members only)

Publications list:
Available in print

Access to staff:
Contact by letter and by e-mail
Hours: Mon to Fri, 0900 to 1700

Connections with:
ITS/UCC Seminar (annually)
  website: www.ucc.ie/locus/its.html

IRM UK STRATEGIC IT TRAINING LIMITED

Acronym or abbreviation: IRM UK

Bishops Walk House, 19–23 High Street, Pinner, Middlesex, HA5 5PJ

Tel: 020 8866 8366
Fax: 020 8866 7966
E-mail: customerservice@irmuk.co.uk

Website:
http://www.irmuk.co.uk

Enquiries:
Enquiries to: Managing Director
Direct e-mail: jeremy.hall@irmuk.co.uk

Founded:
1999

Organisation type and purpose:
Service industry, training organisation.

Subject coverage:
Seminars and conferences on business process management, enterprise architecture, data management, software development, value driven IT, mastering the requirements process, project management, information quality.

Printed publications:
Conference Documentations are as follows, plus p&p per copy £10 UK, £20 Europe or £30 rest of the world:
Europe's Most Authoritative Data Management and Information Quality Conferences 2001, 2002, 2003, 2004(£300 a year on CD)
Harnessing E-Business to Empower the 21st Century Energy Company (£200)
Enterprise Architecture Conference Europe 2001, 2002, 2003, 2004 (£250 a year on CD)
Global Business Process Forum 2004 (£300 on CD)

Access to staff:
Contact by letter, by telephone, by fax, by e-mail and via website. Appointment necessary.
Hours: Mon to Fri, 0900 to 1700

Access to building, collection or gallery:
No access other than to staff

Access for disabled people:
Access to all public areas

IRONBRIDGE GORGE MUSEUM TRUST

Acronym or abbreviation: Ironbridge Gorge Museums

Coach Road, Coalbrookdale, Telford, Shropshire, TF8 7DQ

Tel: 01952 433522
Fax: 01952 433204
E-mail: info@ironbridge.org.uk

Website:
http://www.ironbridge.org.uk

Enquiries:
Enquiries to: Head of Marketing
Direct e-mail: marketing@ironbridge.org.uk

Founded:
1967

Organisation type and purpose:
Registered charity (charity number 503717-R), museum, suitable for ages: 5+.

Subject coverage:
A series of museums and monuments which capture the stories of Britain's Industrial Revolution. Ten museums covering six square miles of East Shropshire coalfields.

Information services:
Library available for reference (for conditions see Access above). Educational and school visits, tel: 01952 433970 or e-mail:
education@ironbridge.org.uk. Group visits: telephone , or e-mail: visits@ironbridge.org.uk.

Special visitor services:
Guided tours, materials and/or activities for children.

Education services:
Group education facilities, resources for Key Stages 1 and 2, 3, 4 and Further or Higher Education.

Services for disabled people:
For the visually impaired; for the hearing impaired; displays and/or information at wheelchair height.

Museum or gallery collection, archive, or library special collection:
Collection on the life and works of Thomas Telford
Elton Collection (paintings, prints, book, pamphlets and memorabilia relating to the history of the Industrial Revolution)

Non-library collection catalogue:
All or part available online, in-house and in print

Library catalogue:
All or part available online

Printed publications:
Educational publications
Site specific guidebooks available to purchase
Souvenir Guide which covers all main sites
Various books which cover site subject matter, available on request
Order printed publications from: Mail Order Department

Electronic and video publications:
Souvenir Video

Access to staff:
Contact by letter, by fax and by e-mail
Hours: Mon to Fri, 0900 to 1700

Access for disabled people:
Parking provided, ramped entry, toilet facilities
Special comments: Sites vary, access guides available on request.

Historic Site:
Blists Hill Victorian Town
Broseley Pipeworks
Coalport China Museum
Enginuity
Ironbridge Gorge Museum Trust
Jackfield Tile Museum
Museum of Iron
Museum of the Gorge
Tar Tunnel
The Darby Houses
The Iron Bridge and Tollhouse
The Merrythought Teddy Bear Shop and Museum

Links with:
Association for Industrial Archaeology

Maintains the:
Blists Hill Open Air Museum
Broseley Pipeworks Museum
Coalbrookdale Museum of Iron and Furnace
Coalport China Museum
Jackfield Tile Museum
Long Warehouse which houses the Ironbridge Institute and the Museum library and archives
Museum of the Gorge

Manages:
Ironbridge Institute

Secretariat of the:
Association for Industrial Archaeology (AIA)

IRONBRIDGE GORGE MUSEUM TRUST – MUSEUM LIBRARY

Coach Road, Coalbrookdale, Telford, Shropshire, TF8 7DQ

Tel: 01952 432141
Fax: 01952 432237
E-mail: library@ironbridge.org.uk

Website:
http://www.ironbridge.org.uk

Enquiries:
Enquiries to: Librarian and Information Officer

Founded:
1968

Organisation type and purpose:
Registered charity, suitable for ages: 16+.
Private library. Courses at the Library run from Birmingham University.

Subject coverage:
Industrial history, particularly East Shropshire Coalfield; history of technology; museology.

Education services:
Group education facilities, resources for Further or Higher Education.

Non-library collection catalogue:
All or part available in-house

Library catalogue:
All or part available in-house

Access to staff:
Contact by letter, by telephone, by fax and by e-mail. Appointment necessary.
Hours: Mon to Fri, 0900 to 1700

Access to building, collection or gallery:
Prior appointment required
Hours: Mon to Fri, 0930 to 1700

Access for disabled people:
Toilet facilities
Special comments: Many stairs, access to ground floor only and not to library itself. Staff happy to assist disabled users, please telephone for information.

Links with:
Birmingham University

IRONBRIDGE INSTITUTE

Ironbridge Gorge Museum Trust, Coalbrook, Telford, Shropshire, TF8 7DX

Tel: 01952 432751
Fax: 01952 435937
E-mail: j.p.fletcher@bham.ac.uk

Website:
http://www.ironbridge.bham.ac.uk

Enquiries:
Enquiries to: Administrator

Founded:
1980

Organisation type and purpose:
University department or institute.
Postgraduate training and professional development.

Subject coverage:
All aspects of the industrial past, industrial archaeology, management of heritage resources (museums, historic buildings, townscapes and the natural environment).

Museum or gallery collection, archive, or library special collection:
Elton Collection
Telford Collection

Access to staff:
Contact by letter, by telephone, by fax, by e-mail and in person
Hours: Mon to Fri, 0900 to 1700

Managed jointly by the:
Institute of Archaeology and Antiquity
    The University of Birmingham
Ironbridge Gorge Museum Trust

ISBA

Formal name: ISBA – The Voice of British Advertisers

Langham House, 1B Portland Place, London, W1B 1PN

Tel: 020 7291 9020
Fax: 020 7291 9030
E-mail: answers@isba.org.uk

Website:
http://www.isba.org.uk
All information about ISBA, our activities and services.

Enquiries:
Enquiries to: Director of Marketing Services
Other contacts: Director of Membership Development

Founded:
1900

Organisation type and purpose:
Membership association (membership is by subscription), present number of members: over 310 companies.
Non-profit making organisation representing advertisers to the Government, media, agencies and other organisations.
ISBA acts as a catalyst encouraging advertisers to join forces, debate and take action on any issue affecting market communications.

Subject coverage:
Advertising in the UK and overseas; voluntary controls; legislation: terms and conditions of business in all advertising media; public relations; direct marketing; sales promotion.

Printed publications:
Annual Report
Best Practice Guides, codes, research reports, etc
British Advertisers – Advancing the Nation's Prosperity (2001 Update)
Glossary of Advertising Media Terms (1996 Update)
Guide to Sponsorship Evaluation (1998)
Parliamentary Guide to Advertising (2000)
The Internet – A Practical Guide for Marketers (1999)

Publications list:
Available in print

Access to staff:
Contact by letter, by fax, by e-mail and via website
Hours: Mon to Fri, 0900 to 1730

Associated with:
Advertising Association (AA)
World Federation of Advertising and the Advertisers (WFA)

ISI (EUROPE, MIDDLE-EAST AND AFRICA)

Formal name: Institute for Scientific Information
Acronym or abbreviation: ISI

Thomson Reuters, 77 Hatton Garden, London, EC1N 8JS

Tel: 020 7433 4000
Fax: 020 7433 4001

Website:
http://scientific.thomson.com/isi/
Latest news, corporate information.
http://www.isinet.com/emea
Support and training materials in English, German, Spanish

Enquiries:
Enquiries to: Press Office
Direct tel: 0207 433 4691
Direct e-mail: eoin.bedford@thomsonreuters.com

Founded:
1958 (USA)

Organisation type and purpose:
Service industry, research organisation.

Subject coverage:
Produces multidisciplinary and scientific information tools for the international research community. ISI's databases link the researcher to the world's scholarly literature through its indexes of bibliographic information and cited references. Areas covered include all areas of pure and applied sciences, social sciences, arts and humanities.

Printed publications:
Arts and Humanities Citation Index (twice yearly and annually, 5 year cumulations)
Biotechnology Citation Index
Chemistry Citation Index
Current Contents (weekly, 7 editions: Life Sciences; Agriculture, Biology & Environmental Sciences; Engineering, Computing & Technology; Arts & Humanities; Clinical Medicine; Physical, Chemical & Earth Sciences; Social & Behavioural Sciences)
Index to Scientific and Technical Proceedings (monthly and annual cumulations)
Index to Scientific Book Contents
Index to Scientific Reviews
Index to Social Sciences and Humanities Proceedings
Materials Science Citation Index
Neuroscience Citation Index
Science Citation Index (6 times a year and annual, 5-year and 10-year cumulations))
Social Sciences Citation Index (2 times a year and annual, 5-year and 10-year cumulations)

Microform publications:
Journal Citation Reports

Electronic and video publications:
BIOSIS Previews
CAB Abstracts
Current Contents Connect
Derwent Innovations Index
Journal Citation Reports
Web of Knowledge
Web of Science (3 indexes – SCIE, SSCI and AHCI)

Publications list:
Available online and in print

Access to staff:
Contact by letter, by telephone, by fax, by e-mail and via website
Hours: Mon to Fri, 0900 to 1730

Access to building, collection or gallery:
Prior appointment required

Access for disabled people:
Toilet facilities

Other addresses for ISI:
ISI (Australia & New Zealand) (ISI)
    100 Harris Street, Pyrmont, NSW 2009, Australia; tel: +61 (2) 8587 7948; fax: +61 (2) 8587 7848; e-mail: asiainfo@isinet.com
ISI (Japan) (ISI)
    Thomson Corporation KK, Palaceside Building 5F, 1–1-1 Hitotsubashi, Chiyoda-ku, Tokyo, 100–0003, Japan; tel: +81 3 5218 6530; fax: +81 3 5218 6536; e-mail: jpinfo@isinet.com (inquiries)
ISI (North America, Latin America and Caribbean) (ISI)
    3501 Market Street, Philadelphia, PA 19104, USA; tel: +1 215 386 0100; fax: +1 215 386 2911; e-mail: sales@isinet.com
ISI (People's Republic of China) (ISI)
    Room 1291/1292 Pana Tower, #128 Zhi Chun Road, Hai Dan District, Beijing, 100086, PR China; tel: +86 10 8261 1504; fax: +86 10 6257 8045; e-mail: chinainfo@isinet.com
ISI (Republic of Korea) (ISI)
    10FL Daenong Building, 33–1 Mapo-dong, Mapo-ku, Seoul, 121–708, Republic of Korea; tel: +82 2 711 3412; fax: +82 2 711 3520; e-mail: koreainfo@isinet.com
ISI (South/South East Asia, Hong Kong & Taiwan) (ISI)
    6 Battery Road #29–03, Standard Chartered Bank Building, Singapore, 049909; tel: +65 6879 4118; fax: +65 6223 2634; e-mail: asiainfo@isinet.com (inquiries)

Subsidiary of:
ISI
    3501 Market Street, Philadelphia, PA 19104, USA; tel: +1 215 386 0100; fax: +1 215 386 2911; e-mail: sales@isinet.com

ISLAMIC CULTURAL CENTRE

London Central Mosque, 146 Park Road, London, NW8 7RG

Tel: 020 7724 3363
Fax: 020 7724 0493
E-mail: islamic200@aol.com

Website:
http://www.islamicculturalcentre.co.uk

Enquiries:
Enquiries to: Director-General

Founded:
1977

Organisation type and purpose:
Place of worship and for cultural activities. Information point for the religion of Islam, facility provider for Muslim community and advice to government, local authorities, statutory bodies and voluntary organisations.

Subject coverage:
Islam, religion, culture, history (modern and ancient), Arabic language, art and heritage.

Museum or gallery collection, archive, or library special collection:
Numerous books, documents in Arabic, Urdu, Farsi etc on the religion of Islam, history, culture etc

Printed publications:
Books and pamphlets
Islamic Quarterly (academic journal)
Bookshop leased to private company

Electronic and video publications:
Cassette and CDs of the Holy Quran (available for purchase)

Access to staff:
Contact by letter, by telephone, by fax, by e-mail and in person. Appointment necessary.
Hours: Mon to Fri, 0900 to 1700
Special comments: No filming or press interviews without prior arrangement.

Access to building, collection or gallery:
No prior appointment required
Special comments: Prior appointment required for media.

Access for disabled people:
Parking provided, ramped entry, level entry, access to all public areas, toilet facilities

ISLAND HISTORY TRUST

Dockland Settlement, 197 East Ferry Road, London, E14 3BA

Tel: 020 7987 6041
E-mail: eve@islandhistory.org.uk

Website:
http://www.islandhistory.org.uk

Organisation type and purpose:
A community history project dedicated to recording and preserving the history of London's Isle of Dogs.

Subject coverage:
History of the Isle of Dogs.

Museum or gallery collection, archive, or library special collection:
Local photographs

Printed publications:
Island History News (newsletter)

Access to building, collection or gallery:
Hours: Tue, Wed and first Sun of the month 1330 to 1630; at other times by appointment

ISLE OF AXHOLME FAMILY HISTORY SOCIETY

Acronym or abbreviation: IofAFHS

Colywell, 43 Commonside, Westwoodside, Nr Doncaster, DN9 2AR

Tel: 01427 752692
E-mail: secretary@axholme-fhs.org.uk

Website:
http://lwww.axholme-fhs.org.uk
Information about the society.

Enquiries:
Enquiries to: Honorary Secretary
Other contacts: Vice Chairman; webmaster@axholme-fhs.org.uk

Founded:
1988

Organisation type and purpose:
Membership association (membership is by subscription), present number of members: 261, voluntary organisation, research organisation. To assist people with an ancestry or an interest in the 12 parishes of the Isle of Axholme.

Subject coverage:
Family history in the 12 Lincolnshire parishes, west of the River Trent: i.e. the Isle of Axholme.

Museum or gallery collection, archive, or library special collection:
Transcriptions of Parish Registers, Census Returns
Local historical matters in booklets, CD-ROMs and floppy disks pertaining to the Isle of Axholme

Library catalogue:
All or part available in-house

Printed publications:
Monumental Inscriptions (16 churches and cemeteries)
Parishes Registers (separate volumes, 51 for baptisms, 45 for marriages and 46 for burials)
Bishop's Transcripts for Luddington, Keadby with Althorpe
Census 1851–1901 all parishes, 1871–1891 Crowle
The Isle of Axholme before Vermuyden (Thirsk J)
The Crowle Poor Law Rate Book 1857
Order printed publications from: J Oliver, 17B West End Road, Epworth, Doncaster, DN9 1LA

Electronic and video publications:
Marriage Indexes (disc) for Amcotts, Belton, Epworth, Crowle, Haxey, Keadby with Althorpe, Luddington, Owston Ferry, Wroot, West Butterwick and Eastoft
Crowle Churchwarden's Accounts 1790–1812 (CD-ROM)
Order electronic and video publications from: Isle of Axholme Family History Society, Alberma, Luddington Road, Garthorpe, Isle of Axhome, Lincolnshire, DN17 4RU, e-mail: interests@axholme-fhs.org.uk

Publications list:
Available online and in print

Access to staff:
Contact by letter, by telephone, by e-mail and via website
Hours: Anytime 1000 to 2200

Access to building, collection or gallery:
4th Thu in month, except August and December
Hours: 0700 to 2100

ISLE OF MAN CIVIL REGISTRY

The Registries, Deemsters Walk, Bucks Road, Douglas, Isle of Man, IM1 3AR, Isle of Man

Tel: 01624 687039
Fax: 01624 685237
E-mail: civil@registry.gov.im

Enquiries:
Enquiries to: Registrar

Organisation type and purpose:
Manx government body.

Subject coverage:
Isle of Man Records of birth, death and marriage registrations, parish records of baptisms, marriages and burials pre-1878 (Church of England).

Printed publications:
Chief Registrar's Annual Report (contains a wide range of population statistics)

Access to staff:
Contact by letter, by telephone, by fax, by e-mail and in person
Hours: Mon to Fri, 0900 to 1300 and 1400 to 1700

Access to building, collection or gallery:
No prior appointment required

Access for disabled people:
Parking provided, level entry, access to all public areas, toilet facilities

ISLE OF MAN DEPARTMENT OF TOURISM AND LEISURE

Sea Terminal Buildings, Douglas, Isle of Man, IM1 2RG, Isle of Man

Tel: 01624 686801
Fax: 01624 686800
E-mail: tourism@gov.im

Website:
http://www.visitisleofman.com

Enquiries:
Enquiries to: Tourist Information Manager
Direct tel: 01624 686851
Direct fax: 01624 627443
Direct e-mail: june.collister@dtl.gov.im

Organisation type and purpose:
National government body.
Promotion of tourism and leisure.

Subject coverage:
Promotion of tourism in the Isle of Man.

Printed publications:
Isle of Man Holiday Guide
Various free tourist leaflets; saleable publications list on request

Publications list:
Available online and in print

Access to staff:
Contact by letter, by telephone, by fax, by e-mail and in person
Hours: Winter: Mon to Fri, 0915 to 1700
Summer: Daily, 0915 to 1900

Access for disabled people:
Parking provided, level entry, toilet facilities

ISLE OF MAN PUBLIC RECORD OFFICE

Acronym or abbreviation: IOMPRO

Unit 3, Spring Valley Industrial Estate, Braddan, Douglas, Isle of Man, IM2 2QR, Isle of Man

Tel: 01624 613383
Fax: 01624 613384
E-mail: public.records@registry.gov.im

Website:
http://www.gov.im/deptindex/reginfo.html
General information.

Enquiries:
Enquiries to: Public Records Officer

Founded:
1992

Organisation type and purpose:
National government body, statutory body.
Record office.

Subject coverage:
History of public administration in the Isle of Man.

Museum or gallery collection, archive, or library special collection:
Records of the Isle of Man Government and other public bodies, particularly 20th century

Access to staff:
Contact by letter, by telephone, by fax and by e-mail. Appointment necessary.
Hours: Mon to Fri, 0900 to 1700

Parent body:
Isle of Man Government
General Registry

ISLE OF MAN TRANSPORT

Banks Circus, Douglas, Isle of Man, IM1 5PT

Tel: 01624 663366
Fax: 01624 663637
E-mail: businfo@bus-rail.gov.im

Enquiries:
Enquiries to: Director

Founded:
1873

Organisation type and purpose:
National government body, service industry.
Government transport undertaking bus and rail,
public transport operator.

Subject coverage:
Public transport on the Isle of Man: railway, bus,
tram network and workshops.

Printed publications:
Railway leaflets and transport timetables (free)

Access to staff:
Contact by letter, by telephone, by fax and by e-
mail
Hours: Mon to Fri, 0900 to 1700

Access to building, collection or gallery:
No access other than to staff

Access for disabled people:
Toilet facilities

Connections with:
Isle of Man Government
    Department of Tourism & Leisure, Sea Terminal,
    Douglas, Isle of Man

Constituent bodies:
Isle of Man Bus Service
Isle of Man Railway
Manx Electric Railway
Snaefell Mountain Railway

ISLE OF WIGHT ARCHAEOLOGY AND HISTORIC ENVIRONMENT SERVICE

County Archaeological Centre, 61 Clatterford
Road, Carisbrooke, Newport, Isle of Wight, PO30
1NZ

Tel: 01983 823810

Website:
http://www.iwight.com/living_here/planning/
archaeology

Organisation type and purpose:
A local government body which advises
individuals, organisations and the local planning
authority on managing, preserving and
understanding archaeological remains on the Isle
of Wight.

Subject coverage:
Archaeology and history of the Isle of Wight.

**Museum or gallery collection, archive, or library
special collection:**
Sites and Monuments Record (SMR), a
computerised database cataloguing
archaeological information, complemented by
documentary archives and historic maps, aerial
photographs and an archaeological library;
access is by prior appointment only

ISLE OF WIGHT CHAMBER OF COMMERCE AND INDUSTRY

Acronym or abbreviation: IWCOC

Mill Court, Furrlongs, Newport, Isle of Wight,
PO30 2AA

Tel: 01983 520777
Fax: 01983 554555

Website:
http://www.iwchamber.co.uk
Island business magazine online, internet directory
of Island businesses, general business information.

Enquiries:
Enquiries to: Membership & Marketing Officer
Direct tel: 01983 554539

Founded:
1910

Organisation type and purpose:
Membership association.

Subject coverage:
A chamber of commerce for Isle of Wight
businesses, business advice and support, export
documentation service.

**Museum or gallery collection, archive, or library
special collection:**
All relevant business support books, Croner etc

Printed publications:
Island Business (magazine, 6 times a year)
Membership Directory

Access to staff:
Contact by letter and by e-mail
Hours: Mon to Fri, 0900 to 1700

Access to building, collection or gallery:
Prior appointment required

Access for disabled people:
Parking provided

ISLE OF WIGHT COLLEGE

Medina Way, Newport, Isle of Wight, PO30 5TA

Tel: 01983 526631
Fax: 01983 521707
E-mail: library@iwcollege.ac.uk

Website:
http://www.iwcollege.ac.uk
Basic information about the learning resources
centre

Enquiries:
Enquiries to: Learning Resources Manager
Direct tel: 01983 535201
Direct e-mail: fidelma.washington@iwcollege.ac.uk
Other contacts: Library Coordinator: bev.vaughan@
iwcollege.ac.uk

Founded:
1954

Subject coverage:
Horticulture, health and community studies, crafts,
education, computer studies, engineering,
construction, business studies, management, office
skills, adult education, travel and tourism, local
history, composites, marine engineering, fitness,
fashion, performing arts, animal care, A-levels in
hospitality and catering.

Non-library collection catalogue:
All or part available online

Library catalogue:
All or part available online

Access to staff:
Contact by letter, by telephone, by e-mail and via
website. Appointment necessary. Access for
members only.
Hours: Term-time: Mon to Thu 0855 to 2000; Fri
1000 to 1700; Sat 1000 to 1500. Vacations: Mon to
Fri, 0900 to 1700
Special comments: Use of learning resources centre
for reference only unless college student. IT
facilities available only to College students and
staff.

Access for disabled people:
Lift

Associate college of:
Portsmouth University

ISLE OF WIGHT LIBRARIES – REFERENCE LIBRARY

Lord Louis Library, Orchard Street, Newport, Isle
of Wight, PO30 1LL

Tel: 01983 823800

Fax: 01983 825972
E-mail: reflib@postmaster.co.uk

Enquiries:
Enquiries to: Reference Librarian

Organisation type and purpose:
Local government body, public library.

Subject coverage:
General, Isle of Wight and related areas, local
history, maritime history, local geology and
archaeology, European Information Relay, family
history.

**Museum or gallery collection, archive, or library
special collection:**
Isle of Wight local collection
Maritime collection

Library catalogue:
All or part available in-house

Printed publications:
Local Clubs and Societies List

Access to staff:
Contact by letter, by telephone, by fax, by e-mail
and in person
Hours: Mon to Wed and Fri, 0930 to 1730; Thu, 1000
to 2000; Sat, 0900 to 1700; Sun, 1000 to 1600

Access for disabled people:
Ramped entry, level entry, access to all public areas

Links with:
County Library Headquarters
    Parkhurst Road, Newport, Isle of Wight, PO30
    5TX; tel: 01983 825717; fax: 01983 528047

ISLE OF WIGHT LIBRARY SERVICE

Library Headquarters, 5 Mariners Way, Somerton
Industrial Estate, Cowes, Isle of Wight, PO31 8PD

Tel: 01983 203880

Website:
http://www.iwight.gov.uk/thelibrary
Library service website, transactional based.

Enquiries:
Enquiries to: Head of Libraries and Information
Services

Founded:
1904

Organisation type and purpose:
Local government body, public library, suitable for
ages: all.

Subject coverage:
General, Isle of Wight and related areas.

**Museum or gallery collection, archive, or library
special collection:**
Isle of Wight, music scores, maritime history

Non-library collection catalogue:
All or part available in-house

Access to staff:
Contact by letter, by telephone, by fax, by e-mail
and in person
Hours: Mon to Fri, 0900 to 1700

Access to building, collection or gallery:
Prior appointment required

Access for disabled people:
Ramped entry, access to all public areas

ISLE OF WIGHT RECORD OFFICE

26 Hillside, Newport, Isle of Wight, PO30 2EB

Tel: 01983 823820/823821
Fax: 01983 823820
E-mail: record.office@iow.gov.uk

Website:
http://www.iwight.com/library/record_office
Basic information about range of records held by
office.
http://www.a2a.pro.gov.uk

continued overleaf

National database comprising online catalogues (some of which relate to Isle of Wight).

Enquiries:
Enquiries to: County Archivist

Founded:
1961

Organisation type and purpose:
Local government body.
To preserve archives relating to Isle of Wight and make them available to the public for research purposes.

Subject coverage:
Local history and genealogy relating to Isle of Wight.

Museum or gallery collection, archive, or library special collection:
Numerous including:
Records of parish churches, nonconformist churches, estates, businesses, local government, schools, hospitals
Census returns, newspapers, copy wills, photographs and maps

Non-library collection catalogue:
All or part available online and in-house

Access to staff:
Contact by letter, by telephone, by fax, by e-mail, in person and via website
Hours: Mon, 0930 to 1225 and 1300 to 1700; Tue to Fri, 0900 to 1225 and 1300 to 1700
Special comments: Appointment necessary to view material held on microfilm/fiche.

Access for disabled people:
Parking provided
Special comments: Telephone Record Office to reserve a parking space. Access to building is possible for wheelchairs, but assistance required.

ISLES OF SCILLY WILDLIFE TRUST

Acronym or abbreviation: IOSWT

Carn Thomas, St Mary's, Isles of Scilly, TR21 0PT

Tel: 01720 422153
Fax: 01720 422153
E-mail: enquiries@ios-wildlifetrust.org.uk

Website:
http://www.ios-wildlifetrust.org.uk

Founded:
1986

Formerly called:
Isles of Scilly Environmental Trust (year of change 2001)

Organisation type and purpose:
Membership association (membership is by subscription), registered charity (charity number 293512), conservation.

Subject coverage:
Wildlife habitat management, satellite environmental records centre, visitor centre.

Printed publications:
Leaflets
Membership magazine (joint with Cornwall Wildlife Trust)
Order printed publications from: via the office or the website

Publications list:
Available online and in print

Access to staff:
Contact by letter, by telephone, by fax, by e-mail and in person. Appointment necessary.
Hours: Mon, Tue and Fri, 1000 to 1600; by appointment for other times

Links with:
The Wildlife Trust (UK Office)
The Kiln, Waterside, Mather Road, Newark, Nottinghamshire, NG24 1WT; tel: 01636 677711; fax: 01636 670001

ISLINGTON ARCHAEOLOGY AND HISTORY SOCIETY

Formal name: Islington Archaeology and History Society

8 Wynyatt Street, EC1V 7HU

Tel: 020 7833 1541

Website:
http://www.iahs.org.uk

Founded:
1975

Organisation type and purpose:
Membership association (membership by subscription).
To arrange lectures, visits and courses in relation to the archaeology and history of the London Borough of Islington.
To publish work on the archaeology and history of the Borough.
To cooperate with local government bodies and other agencies in matters of planning and development within the Borough in order to record and protect Islington's sites which are of archaeological and historical importance.

Printed publications:
Newsletter (4 times per year)

Access to staff:
Contact by letter and by telephone

ISLINGTON LIBRARY AND HERITAGE SERVICES

Central Library, 2 Fieldway Crescent, Islington, London, N5 1PF

Tel: 020 7527 6900
Fax: 020 7527 6902
E-mail: library.informationunit@islington.gov.uk

Website:
http://www.islington.gov.uk/Education/LocalHistory
http://www.islington.gov.uk/libraries
Library services, opening hours, local history, learning centres, and the Islington Museum, plus links to the library catalogue and online Directory of Local Services.

Enquiries:
Enquiries to: Information Manager
Direct tel: 020 7527 6922
Direct fax: 020 7527 6926
Direct e-mail: john.smith@islington.gov.uk
Other contacts: Central Reference Librarian (tel. 020 7527 6931)

Organisation type and purpose:
Local government body, public library service.

Subject coverage:
General, local community information, photography and local history of Islington.

Information services:
Online local information directory, online resources – general and business, European Information, Reference and Information library.

Services for disabled people:
Adaptive hardware and software in all branches but especially at Central Reference Library.

Museum or gallery collection, archive, or library special collection:
Local History Archive
Joe Orton Book Jacket Collection
Local history archives
Sadlers Wells Collection (at Finsbury library)
Sickert Collection

Trade and statistical information:
General collection of trade directories and statistical information.

Library catalogue:
All or part available online

Printed publications:
Local information fact sheets, e.g. halls for hire, community groups, etc.

Guide to the local history collections
Local history publications and reprints including books, postcards, maps and prints
Subject booklists
Order printed publications from: Central Reference Library, at the same address, tel: 020 7527 6931, fax: 020 7527 6939, e-mail: centralref.library@islington.gov.uk

Publications list:
Available in print

Access to staff:
Contact by letter, by telephone, by fax, by e-mail, in person and via website. Appointment necessary.

Access for disabled people:
All buildings fully accessible

Branch libraries:
Archway Library
Hamlyn House, Highgate Hill, London, N19 5PH; tel: 020 7527 7820; e-mail: archway.library@islington.gov.uk
Finsbury Library
245 St. John Street, London, EC1V 4NB; tel: 020 7527 7960; e-mail: finsbury.library@islington.gov.uk
John Barnes Library
275 Camden Road, London, N7 0JN; tel: 020 7527 7900; e-mail: johnbarnes.library@islington.gov.uk
Lewis Carroll Children's Library
180 Copenhagen Street, London, N1 0ST; tel: 020 7527 7936; e-mail: lewiscarroll.library@islington.gov.uk
Mildmay Library
21–23 Mildmay Park, London, N1 4NA; tel: 020 7527 7880; e-mail: mildmay.library@islington.gov.uk
N4 Library
26 Blackstock Road, London, N4 2DW; tel: 020 7527 7800; e-mail: n4.library@islington.gov.uk
North Library
Manor Gardens, London, N7 6JX; tel: 020 7527 7840; e-mail: north.library@islington.gov.uk
South Library
115–117 Essex Road, London, N1 2SL; tel: 020 7527 7860; e-mail: south.library@islington.gov.uk
West Library
Bridgeman Road, London, N1 1BD; tel: 020 7527 7920; e-mail: west.library@islington.gov.uk

Branch museums:
Islington Museum
245 St John Street, London, EC1V 4NB; tel: 020 7527 3235; e-mail: islington.museum@islington.gov.uk

Branches:
First Steps Learning Centre
Central Library, 2 Fieldway Crescent, London, N5 1PF; tel: 020 7527 7002; e-mail: sineadgannon@isonline.org
Islington Computer Skills Centre
Finsbury Library, 245 St. John Street, London, EC1V 4NB; tel: 020 7713 6593; e-mail: info@icskills.co.uk
Islington Local History Centre
Finsbury Library, 245 St. John Street, London, EC1V 4NB; tel: 020 7527 7988; e-mail: local.history@islington.gov.uk

ISO/BIZZARRINI CLUB

47 St Margarets Road, Twickenham, Middlesex, TW1 2LL

Tel: 020 8891 6663
E-mail: iso.bizz@tesco.net

Website:
http://www.burstow0.demon.co.uk

Enquiries:
Enquiries to: Secretary

Founded:
1988

Organisation type and purpose:
Membership association.

Subject coverage:
All aspects (spares, technical and encouragement) of owning and maintaining an ISO or Bizzarrini car.

Access to staff:
Contact by letter, by telephone and by e-mail
Hours: Mon to Fri, 0900 to 1700

ISRAEL GOVERNMENT TOURIST OFFICE

Acronym or abbreviation: IGTO

UK House, 180 Oxford Street, London, W1D 1NN

Tel: 020 7299 1111
Fax: 020 7299 1112
E-mail: info@igto.co.uk

Website:
http://www.thinkisrael.com

Enquiries:
Enquiries to: Office Manager and PA
Direct tel: 020 7299 1100

Organisation type and purpose:
National government body.
National government tourist office.
To advertise, sell and promote Israel as a destination for winter sun holidays, pilgrimages, vacations, birdwatching, hiking, etc.

Subject coverage:
Holidays in Israel, pilgrimages and Holy Land tours, hotel lists, traveller information, trade information and Israel events.

Museum or gallery collection, archive, or library special collection:
Feature article library
Photograph and slide library (CD-ROM)
Video library (DVD)

Trade and statistical information:
Data on number of visitors to Israel from United Kingdom and world-wide.
Statistics and data on different type of visitors ie how many arrive as pilgrims, birdwatchers, holiday, etc.

Printed publications:
All promotional literature is free and available, including maps, posters, videos, slide and window displays

Access to staff:
Contact by letter, by telephone, by fax and by e-mail
Special comments: By appointment only

Parent body:
Israel Ministry of Tourism
    Jerusalem

ISRAELI EMBASSY

2 Palace Green, London, W8 4QB

Tel: 020 7957 9500
Fax: 020 7957 9555
E-mail: info-sec@london.mfa.gov.il

Website:
http://london.mfa.gov.il

Enquiries:
Enquiries to: Information Officer

Organisation type and purpose:
National government body.

Access to staff:
Contact by letter, by telephone, by fax and by e-mail
Hours: Mon to Thu, 0900 to 1800; Fri, 0900 to 1400

Also at:
Israeli Embassy
    15a Old Court Place, London, W8 4PL

ISSB LIMITED

Formal name: Iron and Steel Statistics Bureau

Acronym or abbreviation: ISSB

1 Carlton House Terrace, London, SW1Y 5DB

Tel: 020 7343 3900
Fax: 020 7343 3901
E-mail: info@issb.co.uk

Website:
http://www.issb.co.uk
Various.

Organisation type and purpose:
To provide statistical information on the steel industry and trade in steel and related products including raw materials.

Subject coverage:
International steel statistics.

Trade and statistical information:
World data on steel production.

Printed publications:
UK Iron and Steel Industry: Annual Statistics (£175)
International Steel Statistics Country Books 2001 (£190 per country, £2600 for complete series)
World Steel Exports – All Qualities 2001 (£650)
World Steel Statistics Monthly (£950)

Access to staff:
Contact by letter, by telephone, by fax, by e-mail and via website. All charged.
Hours: Mon to Fri, 0900 to 1700

Subsidiary company of:
UK Steel Association
    Broadway House, Tothill Street, London, SW1H 9NQ; tel: 020 7222 7777; fax: 020 7222 3531; e-mail: enquiries@uksteel.org.uk

ITALIAN CULTURAL INSTITUTE

39 Belgrave Square, London, SW1X 8NX

Tel: 020 7235 1461
Fax: 020 7235 4618
E-mail: icilondon@esteri.it

Website:
http://www.bibliowin.it/iic/ICLN/
For the library catalogue online.
http://www.italcultur.org.uk

Enquiries:
Enquiries to: Information Officer
Direct tel: 020 7396 4406

Founded:
1950

Organisation type and purpose:
National government body, membership association (membership is by subscription), present number of members: 539
Also has life and honorary members.
The cultural office of the Italian Embassy.
To promote Italian culture in the United Kingdom.

Subject coverage:
General and language studies in Italy; education in Italy; bursaries; music and arts; exhibitions; study qualifications; Italy and events of Italian interest.

Museum or gallery collection, archive, or library special collection:
Dante Collection
Italian contemporary fiction and poetry
Good collection of videos especially Italian Cinema

Library catalogue:
All or part available online

Printed publications:
Annual Leaflet on Bursaries in Italy
Bulletin of Events of Italian Interest in London

Access to staff:
Contact by letter, by telephone, by fax, by e-mail, in person and via website
Hours: Mon to Fri, 1000 to 1300 and 1400 to 1700

ITDG PUBLISHING

Bourton Hall, Bourton-on-Dunsmore, Rugby, CU23 9QZ

Tel: 01926 634501
Fax: 01926 634502
E-mail: info@itpubs.org.uk

Website:
http://www.itdgpublishing.org.uk
Information on publishing company.
http://www.developmentbookshop.com
Thousands of development titles from many publishers. Comprehensive site.

Organisation type and purpose:
Publishing house.

Subject coverage:
Development technology for developing world, water and sanitation, development and disaster relief, food security.

Library catalogue:
All or part available in-house

Publications list:
Available in print

Access to staff:
Contact by letter and by fax
Hours: Mon to Fri, 0830 to 1730

Access to building, collection or gallery:
Prior appointment required

Access for disabled people:
Level entry

ITRI INNOVATION LTD

Unit 3, Curo Park, Frogmore, St. Albans, Hertfordshire, AL2 2DD

Tel: 01727 875544
Fax: 01727 871341
E-mail: info@itri.co.uk

Website:
http://www.lead-free.org
Lead-free soldering – news, events, technical information, etc.
http://www.itri-innovation.com
Tin and its uses, facilities, Member information, etc.

Enquiries:
Enquiries to: Information Officer
Direct e-mail: jeremy.pearce@itri.co.uk; tony.wallace@itri.co.uk

Founded:
1932

Formerly called:
Tin Technology Ltd (year of change 2008)

Organisation type and purpose:
Membership association (membership is by subscription), present number of members: 75, research organisation.

Subject coverage:
Tin and its alloys and compounds, and their applications, solder and soldering, tin and tin alloy plating, pewter, bearing metals, whitemetals, tin in cast iron, organo-tins and other tin chemicals, fire retardants, non-toxic ammunition, lead-free wheel weights.

Museum or gallery collection, archive, or library special collection:
40,000 published papers on tin from 1932 – on microfiche

Trade and statistical information:
Tin – production information and statistics.

Non-library collection catalogue:
All or part available online and in-house

Electronic and video publications:
Technical publications on tin technology (CD-ROM and online)

Publications list:
Available in print

continued overleaf

Access to staff:
Contact by letter, by telephone, by fax, by e-mail and via website. Appointment necessary. Non-members charged.
Hours: Mon to Fri, 0900 to 1645

Access to building, collection or gallery:
Prior appointment required

Access for disabled people:
Parking provided, ramped entry, toilet facilities
ITRI Ltd
   Unit 3, Curo Park, Frogmore, St Albans, Hertfordshire, AL2 2DD

IVY BOOKS

351 Woodstock Road, Oxford, OX1 3JB

Tel: 01865 310987 or 515962
Fax: 01865 310987

Enquiries:
Enquiries to: Honorary Secretary
Other contacts: Manager

Founded:
1995

Organisation type and purpose:
Learned society, professional body, publishing house.
The publication of learned journals, biographies, letters.

Subject coverage:
Books and journals relating to the 19th century. John Ruskin (1819–1910), artist and art historian, architecture, economics organiser.

Library catalogue:
All or part available in print

Printed publications:
Byron's Love Letters to the Hon Augusta Leigh
   (Dec 1999, £25)
The Love Letters of John Keats (£23.50)
The Ruskin Gazette (£10, free to members)
Ruskin Recalled (£35)

Access to staff:
Contact by letter, by telephone and by fax. All charged.
Hours: Mon to Fri, 0900 to 1700

Access to building, collection or gallery:
No access other than to staff

IWO

Formal name: Institution of Water Officers
Acronym or abbreviation: IWO

4 Carlton Court, Team Valley, Gateshead, Tyne and Wear, NE11 0AZ

Tel: 0191 422 0088
Fax: 0191 422 0087
E-mail: info@iwo.org.uk

Website:
http://www.iwo.org.uk

Enquiries:
Enquiries to: Chief Executive
Direct e-mail: lynn@iwo.org.uk

Founded:
1945

Organisation type and purpose:
Membership association (membership is by subscription), present number of members: 1700.

Subject coverage:
Water industry.

Printed publications:
IWO Journal (journal, quarterly, free to members, £30 annual subscription in UK; £50 annual subscription overseas)

Access to staff:
Contact by letter, by telephone, by fax, by e-mail and via website. Appointment necessary.
Hours: Mon to Fri, 0900 to 1700

J S PUBLICATIONS

PO Box 505, Newmarket, Suffolk, CB8 7TF

Tel: 01638 561590
Fax: 01638 560924
E-mail: ukrew@jspubs.com

Website:
http://www.jspubs.com

Enquiries:
Enquiries to: Customer Services Manager

Founded:
1988

Organisation type and purpose:
Publishing house.

Subject coverage:
Publishers of the UK Register of Expert Witnesses, the UK's largest and longest established database of vetted expert witnesses. Recognised by the UK legal profession and various Government bodies, the Register provides a listing of individuals who are both expert in their own field and qualified to give expert evidence in court and write expert reports connected with litigation. Also available is a full range of support services for both instructing solicitors (eg assistance in locating a specific expert) and experts themselves (newsletters/factsheets/helpline).

Printed publications:
UK Register of Expert Witnesses (including electronic version, annually, £106 plus VAT)

Electronic and video publications:
UK Register of Expert Witnesses (on disc and CD-ROM, available free to registered users of printed product)

Access to staff:
Contact by letter, by telephone, by fax, by e-mail and via website
Hours: Mon to Fri, 0900 to 1700

JACOB SHEEP SOCIETY

14 Mortimer Road, Kenilworth, Warwickshire, CV8 1FR

Tel: 01923 855393
Fax: 01923 855393
E-mail: valhunt@jacobsheep.freeserve.co.uk

Enquiries:
Enquiries to: Secretary

Founded:
1979

Organisation type and purpose:
Membership association (membership is by subscription), present number of members: 763, registered charity.
Sheep Breed Society.

Access to staff:
Contact by letter, by telephone and by e-mail
Hours: Mon to Fri, 0930 to 1500

Links with:
National Sheep Association (NSA)
   Malvern, Worcestershire

JAGUAR ENTHUSIASTS' CLUB

Acronym or abbreviation: JEC

Abbeywood Office Park, Emma Chris Way, Filton, Bristol, BS34 7JU

Tel: 01179 698186
Fax: 01179 791863
E-mail: jechq@btopenworld.com

Website:
http://www.jec.org.uk
Full information on the club and its activities.

Enquiries:
Enquiries to: General Manager
Direct e-mail: graham.searle@btinternet.com

Founded:
1984

Organisation type and purpose:
Membership association.
To maintain and promote interest in Jaguar Cars.

Subject coverage:
History of Jaguar cars, technical information, insurance, specialist tools, parts, rallies and shows, books and accessories, specialist guide.

Printed publications:
Magazine (monthly, members)

Access to staff:
Contact by letter, by telephone, by fax, by e-mail, in person and via website
Hours: Mon to Fri, 0800 to 1700

JAMAICA TRADE COMMISSION

Formal name: Jamaica Promotions Corporation
Acronym or abbreviation: JAMPRO

1 Prince Consort Road, London, SW7 2BZ

Tel: 020 7584 8894
Fax: 020 7823 9886
E-mail: jamprouk@investjamaica.com

Website:
http://www.investjamaica.com

Enquiries:
Enquiries to: Trade Commissioner

Organisation type and purpose:
International organisation, national government body, manufacturing industry, service industry. Investment; trade; promotion.

Subject coverage:
Trade and investment information in Jamaica.

Access to staff:
Contact by letter, by telephone, by fax, by e-mail and via website. Appointment necessary.
Hours: Mon to Fri, 0930 to 1700

JANE AUSTEN SOCIETY

9 Nicola Close, South Croydon, Surrey, CR2 6NA

Tel: 020 8680 1216

Website:
http://www.janeaustensociety.org.uk
History of the Society, publications, regional groups in the UK, subscriptions, education, biography.

Enquiries:
Enquiries to: Honorary Secretary

Founded:
1940

Organisation type and purpose:
Learned society (membership is by subscription), present number of members: 1700 UK, 350 overseas, registered charity (charity number 1040613).

Subject coverage:
Life and works of Jane Austen, the Austen family, English literature, Georgian history and female novelists of the 18th and 19th century.

Museum or gallery collection, archive, or library special collection:
Collection of documents, books and memorabilia held at Jane Austen's house and museum at Chawton, Hampshire. Telephone or fax 01420 83626

Publications list:
Available online and in print

Access to staff:
Contact by letter, by telephone, by fax and by e-mail
Hours: Mon to Fri, 0900 to 1700

Has:
10 branches in the UK and overseas societies in Australia, Canada, the USA, and Japan

JANE'S INFORMATION GROUP

Acronym or abbreviation: Jane's

Sentinel House, 163 Brighton Road, Coulsdon, Surrey, CR5 2YH

Tel: 020 8700 3700
Fax: 020 8763 1006

Website:
http://www.janes.com/
Company and product details. Subscriptions to specific products.
http://catalogue.janes.com
Full online list of publications.

Enquiries:
Enquiries to: PR Manager
Direct tel: 020 8700 3745
Direct e-mail: amanda.castle@janes.com

Founded:
1898

Organisation type and purpose:
International organisation, publishing house.
Publishers of defence, transport and law enforcement information to governments, militaries, businesses and universities worldwide.

Subject coverage:
Technical specifications, quantities, details of manufacturers and users of defence, aerospace and law enforcement, terrorism and security as well as transportation equipment; geopolitical and strategic information. Also analysis and consulting services are offered in all mentioned areas.

Museum or gallery collection, archive, or library special collection:
Back numbers of Jane's Yearbooks

Non-library collection catalogue:
All or part available online and in print

Printed publications:
Online services, magazines, directories, yearbooks (over 40 titles)
Jane's International Defence Review
Jane's Airport Review
Jane's Defence Weekly
Jane's Intelligence Review
Jane's Police Review
Jane's Intelligence Digest
Jane's Islamic Affairs Analyst
Jane's Terrorism and Security Monitor
Jane's Foreign Report

Microform publications:
Jane's Fighting Ships
Jane's All the World's Aircraft
Jane's World Railways

Electronic and video publications:
All products are available via CD-ROM, Internet (online), in html. Some email services

Publications list:
Available online and in print

Access to staff:
Contact by letter, by telephone, by fax, by e-mail and via website. Appointment necessary. All charged.
Hours: Mon to Fri, 0900 to 1700

Access to building, collection or gallery:
Prior appointment required

Access for disabled people:
Parking provided, level entry, access to all public areas, toilet facilities

Parent body:
The Woodbridge Company Limited

JANSSEN-CILAG LIMITED

PO Box 79, Saunderton, High Wycombe, Buckinghamshire, HP14 4HJ

Tel: 01494 567444
Fax: 01494 567445
E-mail: medinfo@janssen-cilag.co.uk

Website:
http://www.janssen-cilag.co.uk
General and specific information on Company's product portfolio.

Enquiries:
Enquiries to: Information Officer

Organisation type and purpose:
Trade association, research organisation.

Subject coverage:
Pharmaceutical medicine: gastroenterology, antifungals, anaesthesia, drug safety, psychiatry, pain, neurology.

Part of:
Johnson and Johnson

JAPAN 21

Swire House, 59 Buckingham Gate, London, SW1E 6AJ

Tel: 020 7630 8696
Fax: 020 7931 8453
E-mail: info@japan21.org.uk

Website:
http://www.japan21.org.uk

Enquiries:
Enquiries to: Information Officer

Founded:
2003

Organisation type and purpose:
Advisory body, registered charity (charity number 1019046), consultancy.
To support and encourage Japan-related educational and grassroots activity.

Printed publications:
Japan in Focus (newsletter, free to mailing list)
Japan: A geography resource pack for secondary schools (£3)
Ready Steady Nihon-Go! 10-lesson Japanese language course for Keystage 2

Access to staff:
Contact by letter, by telephone, by fax, by e-mail and via website. Appointment necessary.
Hours: Mon to Fri, 0900 to 1700

JAPAN FOUNDATION

Formal name: Kokusai Koryu Kikin (in Japanese)

Russell Square House, 10–12 Russell Square, London, WC1B 5EH

Tel: 020 7436 6695
Fax: 020 7323 4888
E-mail: info@jpf.org.uk

Enquiries:
Enquiries to: Assistant Programme Officer

Founded:
1972

Organisation type and purpose:
Promotion of Japanese culture overseas through various grant programmes.

Subject coverage:
Japanese culture, enquiries may be referred to the appropriate organisations.

Museum or gallery collection, archive, or library special collection:
Reference books

Printed publications:
Japan Foundation News (Japanese)
Japan Foundation Newsletter
Japan Foundation Japanese Language Centre News

Access to staff:
Contact by letter, by telephone, by fax, by e-mail and in person. Appointment necessary.
Hours: Mon to Fri, 0930 to 1730

Parent body:
Japan Foundation (Kokusai Koryu Kikin)
Ark Mori Building, 1 12 32 Akasaka, Minato-ku, Tokyo, 107, Japan

JAPAN NATIONAL TOURIST ORGANIZATION

Acronym or abbreviation: JNTO

Heathcoat House, 20 Savile Row, London, W1S 3PR

Tel: 020 7734 9638
Fax: 020 7734 4290
E-mail: info@jnto.co.uk

Website:
http://www.jnto.go.jp
Japan travel updates, news, regional tourism information, maps, festivals and events, budget travel tips, accommodation directories.

Enquiries:
Enquiries to: Public Relations Manager
Other contacts: Deputy Director

Founded:
1953

Organisation type and purpose:
National government body.
Tourist office.
Promoting Japan as a business and leisure travel destination. Offering information and advice to people planning to visit Japan.

Subject coverage:
All areas of travel to and within Japan including transport (rail, air, ferry, bus), accommodation, attractions, resorts, places to visit, package holidays and tours, travelling on a budget, food, shopping, climate etc; festivals, events, conventions, conferences and exhibitions in Japan, conference and convention facilities; other information.

Museum or gallery collection, archive, or library special collection:
Films, videos and slides

Trade and statistical information:
Statistics on number of visitors to Japan (by country and purpose of visit) and on number of Japanese overseas travellers.

Non-library collection catalogue:
All or part available in-house

Printed publications:
Range of tourist information pamphlets, accommodation guides and maps available free of charge
Japan: Your Guide
Travel Manual (updated annually, for agents and tour operators)

Publications list:
Available in print

Access to staff:
Contact by telephone, by fax, by e-mail and in person
Hours: Mon to Fri, 0930 to 1730
Special comments: Closed on some Japanese National Holidays.

Links with:
Asia Travel Marketing Association
Association of National Tourist Office Representatives
Pacific Asia Travel Association

Parent body:
Japan National Tourist Organization
2–10–1 Yuraku-cho, Chiyoda-ku, Tokyo, 100, Japan

JAPAN SOCIETY OF THE UK

Formal name: Japan Society of the UK

Swire House, 59 Buckingham Gate, London, SW1E 1AJ

continued overleaf

Tel: 020 7828 6330
Fax: 020 7828 6331
E-mail: info@japansociety.org.uk

Website:
http://www.japansociety.org.uk/

Enquiries:
Enquiries to: Office Director
Direct e-mail: sec@japansociety.org.uk

Founded:
1891

Organisation type and purpose:
Membership organisation and information service.
To enhance Anglo-Japanese relations with the aim
of providing a better mutual understanding of the
cultures, societies and businesses of Japan and the
United Kingdom.
Registered charity (charity number 1063952)

Subject coverage:
Anglo-Japanese relations

**Museum or gallery collection, archive, or library
special collection:**
Library of 6,000 vols

Library catalogue:
All or part available online

Access to staff:
Contact by letter, by telephone, by fax, by e-mail
and via website. Appointment necessary.

Access to building, collection or gallery:
Special comments: Library: Wed, 1400 to 1700; Fri,
1200 to 1500

JAPANESE CHAMBER OF COMMERCE AND INDUSTRY IN THE UNITED KINGDOM

Acronym or abbreviation: JCCI

5th Floor, Salisbury House, 29 Finsbury Circus,
London, EC2M 5QQ

Tel: 020 7628 0069
Fax: 020 7374 2280
E-mail: chamber@jcci.org.uk

Website:
http://www.jcci.org.uk

Enquiries:
Enquiries to: Manager (Research and PR)

Founded:
1959

Organisation type and purpose:
Trade association (membership is by subscription).
Chamber of Commerce for Japanese companies in
the United Kingdom.

Subject coverage:
Japanese commercial interests in the United
Kingdom; United Kingdom trade with Japan.

**Museum or gallery collection, archive, or library
special collection:**
Collection of directories on Japanese business and
trade

Printed publications:
Leaflets on trade with Japan

Access to staff:
Contact by letter, by telephone, by fax and by e-
mail. Appointment necessary.
Hours: Mon to Fri, 0930 to 1230 and 1330 to 1730

Access to building, collection or gallery:
Prior appointment required

JAPANESE CONSULATE-GENERAL

2 Melville Crescent, Edinburgh, EH3 7HW

Tel: 0131 225 4777
Fax: 0131 225 4828

Website:
http://www.edinburgh.uk.emb-japan.go.jp

Enquiries:
Enquiries to: Consul-General

Founded:
1991

Organisation type and purpose:
Diplomatic Mission.

Subject coverage:
Information relating to Japan (information section),
passports, visas, etc. (consular section).

Printed publications:
Selected publications on various aspects of
Japanese life (available from Information Section)

Access to staff:
Contact by letter, by telephone and by fax.
Appointment necessary.
Hours: Mon to Fri, 0930 to 1300 and 1430 to 1730

Parent body:
Ministry for Foreign Affairs
Tokyo, Japan

JAPANESE EMBASSY

Acronym or abbreviation: JICC

Japan Information and Cultural Centre, 101–104
Piccadilly, London, W1V 9FN

Tel: 020 7465 6500
Fax: 020 7465 6546
E-mail: info@embjapan.org.uk

Website:
http://www.embjapan.org.uk

Enquiries:
Enquiries to: Information Officer

Organisation type and purpose:
National government body.

Subject coverage:
All cultural aspects of Japan, lists of specialised
companies or organisations for specific requests.

**Museum or gallery collection, archive, or library
special collection:**
Small library (no appointment necessary, open to
the public, Mon to Fri, 0930 to 1245 and 1430 to
1700)
Slide, video and artefact collections for schools and
organisation (apply in writing, free of charge)

Trade and statistical information:
Basic statistics on culture, population and
economy.

Printed publications:
Varied depending on availability (no charge)

Access to staff:
Contact by letter, by telephone, by fax, by e-mail
and via website. Appointment necessary.
Hours: Mon to Fri, 0930 to 1300 and 1430 to 1700
Special comments: Slides, videos etc only to
organisations not individuals; does not provide
tourist information.

JENNIFER TRUST FOR SPINAL MUSCULAR ATROPHY

Acronym or abbreviation: JTSMA

Elta House, Birmingham Road, Stratford-upon-
Avon, Warwickshire, CV37 0AQ

Tel: 0870 774 3651
Fax: 0870 774 3652
E-mail: Jennifer@jtsma.org.uk

Website:
http://www.jtsma.org.uk

Enquiries:
Enquiries to: Information Officer

Founded:
1985

Organisation type and purpose:
National organisation, membership association
(membership is by subscription), present number
of members: 1500, voluntary organisation,
registered charity (charity number 327669),
research organisation.
Subscription is free.
The Jennifer Trust is a support group offering
information, advice and friendship to those
affected or involved with spinal muscular atrophy.

Subject coverage:
Information and advice on issues relating to living
with spinal muscular atrophy.

Library catalogue:
All or part available in print

Printed publications:
Newsletter (quarterly)
Information sheets available free of charge to
families and adults with the condition
JTSMA General Information Leaflet
Severe SMA Information Booklet, Type II, Type III,
Adult onset
My First Book on SMA (aimed at 3–7 year olds)
JTSMA Library Book List
JTSMA Toy Library

Publications list:
Available online and in print

Access to staff:
Contact by letter, by telephone, by fax, by e-mail
and via website
Hours: Mon to Fri, 0900 to 1700

JEROME K JEROME SOCIETY

Acronym or abbreviation: JKJ Society

Tony Gray, Fraser Wood, Mayo & Pinson, 15
Lichfield Street, Walsall, West Midlands, WS1 1TS

Tel: 01922 627077
Fax: 01922 721065
E-mail: tonygray@jkj.demon.co.uk

Website:
http://www.jeromekjerome.com

Enquiries:
Enquiries to: Honorary Secretary
Direct tel: 07801 788532

Founded:
1984

Organisation type and purpose:
Learned society (membership is by subscription),
present number of members: 150, registered
charity (charity number 517057).
To stimulate interest in Jerome's works. Access to
the author's birthplace in Belsize House, Bradford
St, Walsall.

Subject coverage:
Life and works of Jerome Klapka Jerome (1859–
1927) novelist and playwright.

Printed publications:
Idle Thoughts (magazine, 2 times a year)

Access to staff:
Contact by letter, by fax and by e-mail
Hours: Mon to Fri, 0900 to 1700

Access to building, collection or gallery:
By prior appointment with Yvette Fletcher, tel:
09122 633214
Hours: Mon to Fri, 0900 to 1700, subject to prior
appointment

JERSEY ARCHIVE

Clarence Road, St Helier, Jersey, JE2 4JY, Channel
Islands

Tel: 01534 833300
Fax: 01534 833301
E-mail: archives@jerseyheritagetrust.org

Website:
http://www.jerseyheritagetrust.org
General introduction to our services. Online
searchable catalogue of all holdings.

Founded:
1993

Organisation type and purpose:
Archive or Record Office.

Subject coverage:
The written history of Jersey.

Museum or gallery collection, archive, or library special collection:
The Jersey Archive collects and preserves the records of the States of Jersey, States Committees and Departments, The Royal Court, The Lieutenant Governor, parishes, churches, businesses, societies and individuals relating to the Island.

Non-library collection catalogue:
All or part available online and in-house

Printed publications:
A Glossary for the Historian of Jersey (Aubin C N, 1997, £9.95)

Access to staff:
Contact by letter, by telephone, by fax, by e-mail and in person
Hours: Tue to Thur, 0900 to 1700; last Thur of the month, 0900 to 1900

Access to building, collection or gallery:
No prior appointment required

Access for disabled people:
Parking provided, level entry, toilet facilities
Special comments: Hearing Loop; Lift to Reading Rooms.

Connections with:
Jersey Heritage Trust
Jersey Museum, The Weighbridge, St Helier, Jersey, JE2 3NF, Channel Islands; tel: 01534 633300; fax: 01534 633301

JERSEY LIBRARY

Halkett Place, St Helier, Jersey, JE2 4WH, Channel Islands

Tel: 01534 448700
Fax: 01534 448730
E-mail: je.library@gov.je

Website:
http://www.gov.je/library

Enquiries:
Enquiries to: Chief Librarian

Founded:
1743

Organisation type and purpose:
Public library.

Subject coverage:
Channel Islands bibliography and history, geography, archaeology, particularly the Bailiwick of Jersey.

Museum or gallery collection, archive, or library special collection:
17th- and 18th-century belles lettres and religion
Falle Collection

Library catalogue:
All or part available online and in-house

Access to staff:
Contact by letter, by telephone, by fax, by e-mail and in person
Hours: Mon and Wed to Fri, 0930 to 1730; Tue, 0930 to 1930; Sat, 0930 to 1600

Access for disabled people:
Level entry, access to all public areas, toilet facilities

JERSEY TOURISM

Liberation Square, St Helier, Jersey, JE1 1BB, Channel Islands

Tel: 01534 500700
Fax: 01534 500899
E-mail: info@jersey.com

Organisation type and purpose:
National government body.

Subject coverage:
Jersey.

Publications list:
Available online

Access to staff:
Contact by e-mail
Hours: Mon to Fri, 0900 to 1700

Access for disabled people:
Ramped entry

JESUS COLLEGE OLD LIBRARY

Jesus College, Cambridge, CB5 8BL

Tel: 01223 339405
Fax: 01223 339407

Website:
http://www.jesus.cam.ac.uk
Introduction to Old Library.

Enquiries:
Enquiries to: Keeper, or Assistant, of the Old Library
Direct fax: 01223 339427
Direct e-mail: sch1000@hermes.cam.ac.uk
Other contacts: archives@jesus.cam.ac.uk

Founded:
c.1500

Organisation type and purpose:
College library, of Cambridge University.

Subject coverage:
Subjects directly related to University studies prior to 1850, especially theology, classics, mathematics, law.

Museum or gallery collection, archive, or library special collection:
Medieval manuscripts
Military Books of the 17th century
Part of the Library of T R Malthus (1766–1834)

Non-library collection catalogue:
All or part available in print

Library catalogue:
All or part available in-house

Access to staff:
Contact by letter and by fax. Appointment necessary. Letter of introduction required.
Hours: Mon to Fri, 1000 to 1700

Access to building, collection or gallery:
Prior appointment required

JETRO LONDON

Formal name: Japan External Trade Organisation
Acronym or abbreviation: JETRO

Japan Trade Centre, MidCity Place, 71 High Holborn, London, WC1V 6AL

Tel: 020 7421 8300
Fax: 020 7421 0009
E-mail: ldnresearch@jetro.go.jp

Website:
http://www.jetro.go.jp/uk/
Details of JETRO London's activities.
http://www.jetro.go.jp
Head Office, Tokyo.

Enquiries:
Enquiries to: Information Officer

Founded:
1958

Organisation type and purpose:
International organisation.
Japanese government related trade promotion organisation.

Subject coverage:
Promotion of trade between Japan and the UK.

Trade and statistical information:
Statistics related to Japan.

Library catalogue:
All or part available in-house

Printed publications:
Access to Japan's Import Market: 35 different product reports
Focus Japan (periodical, monthly)
JETRO Marketing Series
Directory for Doing Business in Japan
Directory of Japanese-Affiliated Companies in Asia (with CD-ROM)
Directory of Japanese-Affiliated Companies in USA and Canada
Directory of Japanese-Affiliated Companies in the EU (with CD-ROM)
A Guide to Investment in Japan
Human Resource Management Guidebook
Japan Trade Directory (annually, with CD-ROM)
Japanese Lifestyles
New Technology Japan (monthly
Setting up Enterprises in Japan
Specifications and Standards for Food, Food Additives etc under the Food Sanitation Law
Numerous publications (many free) providing information to companies wishing to export to, and/or set up in, the Japanese market
Order printed publications from: Japan External Trade Organisation
2–5 Toranomon 2-chome, Minato-ku, Tokyo, 105–8466, Japan, tel: +81 3 3582 5511, fax: +81 3 3587 0219
OCS Tokyo (door-to-door delivery service)
2–9 Shibaura, Minato-ku, Tokyo, 108–8701, Japan, tel: +81 3 5476 8131, fax: +81 3 3453 8091
Public Relations Department (for advice first)
JETRO London, tel: 020 7470 4700, fax: 020 7491 7570

Electronic and video publications:
Video catalogue

Publications list:
Available online and in print

Access to staff:
Contact by letter and by fax. Appointment necessary.
Hours: Mon to Fri, 0930 to 1230 and 1330 to 1730
Special comments: If contacting by fax, give full address as we reply by letter.

Access to building, collection or gallery:
Prior appointment required
Hours: Mon to Fri, 0930 to 1230 and 1400 to 1630

Funded by:
Ministry of Economy Trade and Industry, Japan

JEWEL & ESK COLLEGE

Acronym or abbreviation: JEC

Edinburgh Campus, 24 Milton Road East, Edinburgh, EH15 2PP

Tel: 0131 344 7000
Fax: 0131 344 7001
E-mail: pmccafferty@jec.ac.uk

Website:
http://www.jec.ac.uk
College web entry of course and college information.

Enquiries:
Enquiries to: Marketing Officer
Direct tel: 0131 344 7199
Direct e-mail: marketing@jec.ac.uk

Founded:
1987

Formerly called:
Jewel & Esk Valley College (year of change 2007)

Organisation type and purpose:
Local government body, suitable for ages: 12+, training organisation.
Further Education College.

continued overleaf

Subject coverage:
Business and management studies, office systems and administration, hairdressing and hospitality, caring studies, video production studies, educational support, computing and music, general education, mathematics and science, electronic engineering, electrical engineering, building, manufacturing, plant and instrumentation, sport and leisure, safety and first aid.

Information services:
tel: 0131 344 7152

Special visitor services:
tel: 0131 344 7405

Education services:
tel: 0131 344 7166

Services for disabled people:
tel: 0131 344 7405

Non-library collection catalogue:
All or part available online, in-house and in print

Library catalogue:
All or part available online and in-house

Printed publications:
College Prospectus (annually)

Electronic and video publications:
College promotional video 8 mins
Food hygiene and handling 35 mins (REHIS approved)
Both available direct from college, or food video also through REHIS, can be supplied in any format
College Prospectus (CD-ROM)

Publications list:
Available online and in print

Access to staff:
Contact by letter, by telephone, by fax, by e-mail, in person and via website
Hours: Mon to Fri, 0830 to 1630

Access to building, collection or gallery:
No prior appointment required
Hours: Edinburgh Campus: Mon, Fri, 0845 to 1630, Tue, Wed, Thu, 0845 to 1930
Midlothian Campus: Mon to Fri, 0845 to 1630

Access for disabled people:
Parking provided, ramped entry, level entry, access to all public areas, toilet facilities

Also at:
Jewel & Esk College
Midlothian Campus, 46 Dalhousie Road, Dalkeith, Midlothian, EH22 3FR; tel: 0131 344 7000; e-mail: info@jevc.ac.uk

Parent body:
Lothian Region Department of Education

JEWELLERY DISTRIBUTORS' ASSOCIATION

Acronym or abbreviation: JDA

Federation House, 10 Vyse Street, Birmingham, B18 6LT

Tel: 0121 237 1100
Fax: 0121 236 3921
E-mail: secretariat@jda.org.uk

Website:
http://www.jda.org.uk

Enquiries:
Enquiries to: Manager

Founded:
1947

Organisation type and purpose:
Trade association (membership is by subscription). The Jewellery Distributors Association is the national trade body for distributors and wholesalers of precious and fashion jewellery.

Subject coverage:
Product – fashion and precious jewellery.

Publications list:
Available in print

Access to staff:
Contact by letter, by telephone, by fax, by e-mail and in person
Hours: Mon to Fri, 0900 to 1700

Access for disabled people:
Parking provided, ramped entry, level entry, access to all public areas, toilet facilities
Special comments: Lift.

Parent body:
British Jewellery and Giftware Federation Limited at the same address; tel: 0121 236 2657; fax: 0121 236 3921

JEWISH BLIND AND DISABLED

Acronym or abbreviation: JBD

35 Langstone Way, London, NW7 1GT

Tel: 020 8371 6611
Fax: 020 8371 4225
E-mail: info@jbd.org

Website:
http://www.jbd.org

Founded:
1969

Organisation type and purpose:
National organisation, voluntary organisation, registered charity (charity number 259480).

Subject coverage:
Welfare services, particularly sheltered housing, for Jewish blind or disabled people, couples or families.

Printed publications:
Newsletter
Diary
Appeal Leaflets
Braille Cards
Moon Cards

Access to staff:
Contact by letter, by telephone, by fax, by e-mail and via website
Hours: Mon to Thu, 0905 to 1730; Fri, 0905 to 1400

Access for disabled people:
Parking provided, ramped entry, level entry, access to all public areas, toilet facilities

JEWISH CARE

Stuart Young House, 221 Golders Green Road, London, NW11 9DQ

Tel: 020 8922 2000\ Minicom no. 020 8922 2233
Fax: 020 8922 1998
E-mail: info@jcare.org

Enquiries:
Enquiries to: Reception
Direct tel: 020 8922 2000
Direct fax: 020 8922 1998

Founded:
1990

Organisation type and purpose:
Voluntary organisation, registered charity (charity number 802559).
Voluntary association.
Provides a wide range of social services for the Jewish Community living in Greater London and the South East.

Subject coverage:
Information on all Jewish Care Resource Centres including: residential homes, day centres, social services, home care, specialist services, including services for people who are mentally ill, physically disabled, visually impaired, as well as Holocaust survivors and refugees.

Museum or gallery collection, archive, or library special collection:
Archive material on Jewish Welfare Board and Jewish Blind Society dating back to 1819 held at University of Southampton

Printed publications:
Annual Report (since 1859)
Careline (in-house magazine)
Information pack
Volunteer News

Access to staff:
Contact by letter
Hours: Mon to Fri, 0900 to 1730

Access to building, collection or gallery:
Prior appointment required

Access for disabled people:
Level entry, toilet facilities

Affiliated to:
Central Council for Jewish Social Service

Trustees for:
Relief of the Jewish Poor Registered

JEWISH EAST END CELEBRATION SOCIETY

Acronym or abbreviation: JEECS

PO Box 57317, London, E1 3WG

E-mail: enquiries@jeecs.org.uk

Website:
http://www.jeecs.org.uk

Organisation type and purpose:
A registered charity (no. 1107714), with membership by subscription, which focuses on Jewish life and culture in the East End of London, documenting past Jewish life and preserving the area's Jewish heritage, and reinvigorating and supporting current Jewish life through education, events, publications and good relations with other cultures represented in the area.

Subject coverage:
Jewish life and culture in the East End of London.

Printed publications:
Newsletter

JEWISH EDUCATION BUREAU

Acronym or abbreviation: JEB

8 Westcombe Avenue, Leeds, West Yorkshire, LS8 2BS

Tel: 0870 800 8532
Fax: 0844 873 1046
E-mail: jeb@jewisheducationbureau.co.uk

Website:
http://www.jewisheducationbureau.co.uk
Resources, workshops, local Jewish history.

Enquiries:
Enquiries to: Director
Direct tel: 0870 730 0532

Founded:
1974

Organisation type and purpose:
Consultancy.
Promotes the study of Judaism as a world religion in British schools and colleges through religious education, multicultural education and the humanities.

Subject coverage:
Judaism; anti-Semitism, especially the Holocaust; Israel.

Education services:
Visits to schools and colleges. Arranges visits to synagogues

Printed publications:
Large number of books and leaflets including:
Dictionary of 1,000 Jewish Proverbs
Ecology and the Jewish Spirit

Explorer's Guide to Judaism
Illustrated History of the Jewish People (2,500
  years, £25)
Jewish Ceremonial Designs
Judaism: A Religion of Deeds and Ideas
The Jewish Contribution to the 20th Century (short
  biography of 1,000 people, £20)
The Jewish Home (festivals, life-cycle, home
  observances, £9.95)

Electronic and video publications:
CD-ROMs, cassettes and videos
Learning About the Holocaust (CD-ROM, £19.99)

Publications list:
Available in print

Access to staff:
Appointment necessary.
Hours: Mon to Fri, 0900 to 1700

Links with:
Consultation of Northern Religious Education
Centres
Professional Council for Religious Education

JEWISH HISTORICAL SOCIETY OF ENGLAND

Acronym or abbreviation: JHSE

33 Seymour Place, London, W1H 5AP

Tel: 020 7723 5852
Fax: 020 7723 5852
E-mail: info@jhse.org

Website:
http://www.jhse.org

Enquiries:
Enquiries to: Administrator
Other contacts: Board of Deputies of British Jews for
general Jewish queries.

Founded:
1893

Organisation type and purpose:
International organisation, learned society
(membership is by subscription), present number
of members: 720, registered charity (charity
number 217331).

Subject coverage:
Anglo-Jewish history.

**Museum or gallery collection, archive, or library
special collection:**
Library is the Mocatta Library which is now the
  University College London, Jewish Studies
  Library

Printed publications:
List of Works (some 42 titles)
Miscellanies (13 parts)
Transactions (40 vols)

Access to staff:
Contact by letter, by telephone, by fax and by e-
mail. Appointment necessary.
Hours: Answerphone service
Special comments: 15 hours weekly, on various days

Links with:
Anglo-Jewish Archives

JEWISH MARRIAGE COUNCIL

Acronym or abbreviation: JMC

23 Ravenshurst Avenue, London, NW4 4EE

Tel: 020 8203 6311
Fax: 020 8203 8727
E-mail: info@jmc-uk.org

Enquiries:
Enquiries to: Director

Founded:
1946

Organisation type and purpose:
National organisation, voluntary organisation,
registered charity (charity number 1078723).

Recognised by the Lord Chancellor's Department,
Office of the Chief Rabbi and local authorities.

Subject coverage:
Marriage preparation, guidance and counselling;
family and individual counselling, divorce
counselling, marriage bureau and divorce advisory
service, mediation service.

Printed publications:
Annual Report (copies available free of charge)

Publications list:
Available in print

Access to staff:
Contact by letter, by telephone, by fax and by e-
mail
Hours: Mon to Fri, 0935 to 1730
Special comments: Closes at 1400 on Fridays in
winter.

Access for disabled people:
Ramped entry

Branch office:
Jewish Marriage Council (JMC)
  Nicky Alliance Centre, 85 Middleton Road,
  Manchester, M8 4JY; tel: 0161 740 5764

JEWISH MUSIC INSTITUTE

Acronym or abbreviation: JMI

SOAS, University of London, PO Box 232, Harrow,
Middlesex, HA1 2NN

Tel: 020 8909 2445
Fax: 020 8909 1030
E-mail: jewishmusic@jmi.org.uk

Website:
http://www.jmi.org.uk

Founded:
1983

Organisation type and purpose:
An independent, non-religious arts organisation
with charitable status, based at the University of
London's School of Oriental and African Studies
(SOAS) and working closely with the School's
Department of Music and the SOAS library. The
institute documents, preserves and teaches all
aspects of the Jewish musical heritage, and
presents that heritage to the public, supporting
university courses and running workshops,
summer schools, regular classes and outreach
projects. Aims to provide an international focus for
study and musicianship through such initiatives as
the International Forum for Suppressed Music, the
International Forum for Yiddish Culture and the
Forum for the Promotion of Arab–Jewish Dialogue
through Music.

Subject coverage:
All aspects of the Jewish musical heritage,
including liturgical, classical, ethnic and folk music
and music suppressed by the Nazi and Soviet
regimes.

Education services:
Summer schools, regular classes and outreach
projects.

**Museum or gallery collection, archive, or library
special collection:**
Library of recordings, books, manuscripts and
  scores in all genres of Jewish music, dating from
  the Middle Ages to the present

JOCKEY CLUB

151 Shaftesbury Avenue, London, WC2H 8AL

Tel: 020 7189 3800
Fax: 020 7189 3801
E-mail: info@thejockeyclub.co.uk

Website:
http://www.thejockeyclub.co.uk

Enquiries:
Enquiries to: Public Relations Officer

Founded:
1752

Organisation type and purpose:
National organisation (membership is by election
or invitation).
Regulatory body for horseracing in Great Britain.
To set and maintain standards for racing, to
support the British Horseracing Board in
administering and developing the best interests of
horseracing and breeding.

Subject coverage:
Safety and welfare of horse and rider, licensing
individuals and racecourses, and compiling and
applying rules of racing.

Access to staff:
Contact by letter, by telephone, by fax and by e-
mail
Hours: Mon to Fri, 0900 to 1700

JODRELL BANK OBSERVATORY

Jodrell Bank, Lower Withington, Macclesfield,
Cheshire, SK11 9DL

Tel: 01477 571321
Fax: 01477 571618

Website:
http://www.jb.man.ac.uk
Information on research activities.

Enquiries:
Enquiries to: Public Relations Manager

Founded:
1957

Organisation type and purpose:
University department or institute, research
organisation.

Subject coverage:
Astronomy; radio astronomy techniques, radio
telescope design and control, low noise receive-
systems, long and short baseline interferometry;
signal processing and computing techniques;
galactic structure; hydrogen line observations;
radio sources and source surveys and
identifications; pulsars; radio stars; active galactic
nuclei; radio galaxies; quasars; cosmic microwave
background.

Access to staff:
Contact by letter
Hours: Mon to Fri, 0900 to 1700

Part of:
Department of Physics and Astronomy, University
of Manchester

JOHANN STRAUSS SOCIETY OF GREAT BRITAIN

12 Bishams Court, Church Hill, Caterham, Surrey,
CR3 6SE

Tel: 01883 349681
E-mail: strauss-soc@johann-strauss.org.uk

Enquiries:
Enquiries to: Honorary Secretary

Founded:
1964

Organisation type and purpose:
Learned society (membership is by subscription),
present number of members: 550, voluntary
organisation.
Musical appreciation society.

Subject coverage:
History of the Strauss Family and their music,
performance and recording of lesser-known works
of the Strauss Family and their Viennese
contemporaries.

Printed publications:
Newsletter (6 times a year, members)
Vienna Music (journal, twice yearly)

Access to staff:
Contact by letter and by telephone

continued overleaf

Hours: Mon to Fri, 0900 to 1700

Affiliated to other:
Johann Strauss Societies in Vienna, France, Germany, Italy, Japan, Poland, Southern Africa, Sweden, Australia, Romania, Czech Republic and Slovak Republic

JOHN BUCHAN SOCIETY

Acronym or abbreviation: JBSoc

The Toft, 37 Waterloo Road, Lanark, ML11 7QH

Tel: 01555 662103
E-mail: glennismac2000@yahoo.co.uk

Website:
http://www.johnbuchansociety.co.uk

Enquiries:
Enquiries to: Honorary Secretary

Founded:
1979

Organisation type and purpose:
Learned society, voluntary organisation.
To promote a wider understanding and appreciation of the life and works of John Buchan and to support the John Buchan Centre at Broughton, near Peebles.

Non-library collection catalogue:
All or part available in-house

Printed publications:
Journal (2 times a year)
Newsletter twice yearly

Access to staff:
Contact by letter, by telephone and by e-mail.
Access for members only.
Hours: Mon to Fri, 0900 to 1700

JOHN CABOT CITY TECHNOLOGY COLLEGE

Formal name: John Cabot City Technology College Bristol Trust
Acronym or abbreviation: John Cabot CTC

Woodside Road, Kingswood, South Gloucestershire, BS15 8BD

Tel: 0117 976 3000
Fax: 0117 976 0630
E-mail: info@cabot.ac.uk

Website:
http://www.cabot.ac.uk
Full description of college operation and multiple hot links.

Enquiries:
Enquiries to: Principal

Founded:
1993

Organisation type and purpose:
Suitable for ages: 11 to 19.
Independent state maintained secondary school.

Subject coverage:
Specialist education in maths, science and technology.

Printed publications:
Annual prospectus

Access to staff:
Contact by letter
Hours: Hire of facilities out of hours

JOHN CLARE SOCIETY

9 The Chase, Ely, Cambridgeshire, CB6 3DR

Tel: 01353 668438 (evenings)

Website:
http://vzone.virgin.net/linda.curry/jclare
For information about the John Clare Society.
http://human.ntu.ac.uk/clare.html

Bibliography, chronology, selection of articles related to Clare and current information on Clare events.
http://www.johnclare.org.uk
General information, book sales, membership information, events and useful links

Enquiries:
Enquiries to: Honorary Secretary
Other contacts: Chairman for website, e-mail, linked to university.

Founded:
1981

Organisation type and purpose:
International organisation, learned society (membership is by subscription), present number of members: 650, voluntary organisation.

Subject coverage:
Promoting the study of the life and works of John Clare, poet (1793–1864).

Museum or gallery collection, archive, or library special collection:
None owned by the Society but note:
Manuscripts and books (at Northampton Central Reference Library)
Manuscripts (the largest collection at Peterborough Museum)

Printed publications:
A Descriptive Catalogue of the John Clare Collection on Peterborough Museum and Art Gallery
John Clare, Flower Poems (ed Kovesi S)
Cumulative Index of Journals 1982–2001
For John Clare: an anthology of verse (selected and edited by John Lucas)
John Clare – Love Poems (ed Kovesi S)
John Clare, the Northamptonshire Poet (ed Carr)
John Clare, The Poet and the Place (Moyse P, contact peter.moyse@amserve.com)
The John Clare Society Journal (annually)
The John Clare Society Newsletter (quarterly)
The Life and Times of John Clare

Publications list:
Available online and in print

Access to staff:
Contact by letter and by telephone
Hours: Mon to Fri, 0900 to 1700
Special comments: Enquiries by letter enclosing sae please.

Autonomous affiliate:
John Clare Society of North America
Executive Director, Department of English, University of Maryland, Baltimore County, Baltimore, MD21250, USA; tel: 00 1 410 455 2164

Member of:
The Alliance of Literary Societies
Hon. Secretary, 71 Stepping Stones Road, Coventry, CV5 8JT

JOHN FROST NEWSPAPERS

Formal name: John Frost Newspapers Limited

22B Rosemary Avenue, Enfield, Middlesex, EN2 0SS

Tel: 020 8366 1392/0946
Fax: 020 8366 1379
E-mail: andrew@johnfrostnewspapers.com

Website:
http://www.johnfrostnewspapers.co.uk
Summary of holdings.
http://www.johnfrostnewspapers.com

Enquiries:
Enquiries to: Archivist

Founded:
1965

Organisation type and purpose:
Research organisation.
In depth files on crime, royalty, war, politics, pop.

Subject coverage:
UK and overseas newspapers reporting outstanding events since 1640 – political, economy, royalty, disasters. crime, sport, war etc.

Museum or gallery collection, archive, or library special collection:
100,000 press cuttings reporting historic and outstanding events 1640 to present day
80,000 newspapers: British and overseas

Printed publications:
Pamphlet available on request

Publications list:
Available online and in print

Access to staff:
Contact by letter, by telephone and by fax.
Appointment necessary.
Hours: Mon to Fri, 0900 to 1700

Access to building, collection or gallery:
Prior appointment required

Access for disabled people:
Toilet facilities

Other address:
John Frost Newspapers
8 Monks Avenue, New Barnet, Hertfordshire, EN5 1DB; tel: 020 8440 3159

JOHN INNES CENTRE AND SAINSBURY LABORATORY

Acronym or abbreviation: JIC

Norwich Research Park, Colney, Norwich, Norfolk, NR4 7UH

Tel: 01603 450000
Fax: 01603 450045

Website:
http://www.jic.bbsrc.ac.uk
John Innes Centre homepage.

Enquiries:
Enquiries to: Librarian
Direct e-mail: jic.library@bbsrc.ac.uk
Other contacts: Archivist for Historical Collections Librarian.

Founded:
1994

Organisation type and purpose:
Registered charity (charity number 223852), research organisation.

Subject coverage:
Mostly at postgraduate level and above, currently includes classical botany, horticulture, crop plants, plant breeding, classical and molecular plant genetics, plant genome mapping, plant biochemistry, physiology and cell biology, plant virology and pathology and plant biotechnology. In addition, we hold material on microbial genetics (notably Streptomyces and Rhizobium), nitrogen fixation and enzymology, bioinorganic chemistry, history of genetics, history of plant sciences.

Museum or gallery collection, archive, or library special collection:
Cyril Darlington Library
History of Genetics Library
John Innes reprint collection and archives
John Innes Trustees' collection of rare botanical books
William Bateson Library and letters

Non-library collection catalogue:
All or part available online and in print

Library catalogue:
All or part available in-house

Printed publications:
Annual Report
Proceedings: John Innes Symposia

Access to staff:
Contact by telephone and by e-mail. Appointment necessary. Non-members charged.
Hours: Mon to Fri, 0900 to 1700

Access to building, collection or gallery:
Prior appointment required

Grant-aided by:
Biotechnology and Biological Sciences Research
Council (BBSRC)

JOHN INNES MANUFACTURERS ASSOCIATION

Acronym or abbreviation: JIMA

PO Box 8, Department M14/A, Harrogate, North
Yorkshire, HG2 8XB

Tel: 01423 879208
Fax: 01423 870025
E-mail: info@johninnes.info

Website:
http://www.johninnes.info

Enquiries:
Enquiries to: Secretary and PR Officer

Founded:
1977

Organisation type and purpose:
Trade association.

Subject coverage:
Loam-based potting mixes and related growing
media for both amateur gardening and
professional growers in the United Kingdom.

Printed publications:
Benefits of Loam-Based Composts (leaflet, free)
18 Technical data and information sheets series
(free) including
TDS1 The History of John Innes Composts
TDS2 Formulation of John Innes Composts
TDS4 Grades and Application of JI Composts
TDS5 Storage of John Innes Composts
TDS6 How to Use John Innes Composts
TDS7 What Compost Do I Use? – That is the
question!
TDS10 Registered Manufacturers of John Innes
TDS16 John Innes for Planters, Tubs and Window
Boxes
TDS14 John Innes Ericaceous Compost
TDS17 JIMA Quality Control Specifications

Publications list:
Available online and in print

Access to staff:
Contact by letter, by telephone, by fax and by e-
mail. Appointment necessary.
Hours: Mon to Fri, 0900 to 1800

JOHN LEWIS PARTNERSHIP

171 Victoria Street, London, SW1E 5NN

Tel: 020 7828 1000

Website:
http://www.waitrose.com
Transactional ISP information site – Waitrose
supermarkets.
http://www.johnlewis.com
Transactional information site – John Lewis
department stores.
http://www.johnlewispartnership.co.uk
Corporate site – John Lewis Partnership.

Enquiries:
Enquiries to: Head of Business Information
Direct tel: 020 7592 6219
Direct fax: 020 7592 6294
Direct e-mail: business_information@johnlewis.co
.uk

Organisation type and purpose:
Service industry.
Retail business run on co-operative principles.

Subject coverage:
Retailing; industrial democracy.

Trade and statistical information:
Weekly trading figures for John Lewis plc are
published in The Gazette of the John Lewis
Partnership and on the corporate website.

Library catalogue:
All or part available in-house

Access to staff:
Appointment necessary.
Hours: Mon to Fri, 0900 to 1730

Access to building, collection or gallery:
Prior appointment required

JOHN MEADE FALKNER SOCIETY

Acronym or abbreviation: JMF Soc

Greenmantle, Main Street, Kings Newton,
Melbourne, Derbyshire, DE73 8BX

Tel: 01332 865315
E-mail: nebuly@hotmail.co.uk

Enquiries:
Enquiries to: Honorary Secretary

Founded:
1999

Organisation type and purpose:
Learned society (membership is by subscription),
present number of members: 45, voluntary
organisation.
To promote the appreciation and study of John
Meade Falkner's life, times and works.

Library catalogue:
All or part available in-house

Printed publications:
Journal (annually)
Newsletters
Order printed publications from: Honorary Secretary

Access to staff:
Contact by letter, by telephone, by e-mail and via
website
Hours: Mon to Fri, 0900 to 1700

JOHN RYLANDS UNIVERSITY LIBRARY OF MANCHESTER

Acronym or abbreviation: JRULM

Oxford Road, Manchester, M13 9PP

Tel: 0161 275 3738
Fax: 0161 273 7488
E-mail: libtalk@man.ac.uk

Website:
http://rylibweb.man.ac.uk/
General Library information and access to the
catalogue of the John Rylands University Library
as well as other external information collections.

Enquiries:
Enquiries to: Administrator
Direct tel: 0161 275 3760
Direct e-mail: peter.wadsworth@man.ac.uk
Other contacts: Subject and Information Services
enquiries tel no: 0161 275 3751; publications
enquiries tel no: 0161 275 3749

Founded:
1851

Organisation type and purpose:
University library.

Subject coverage:
American studies, ancient history, archaeology,
architecture, astronomy, audiology, biological
sciences, Celtic studies, chemistry, classical studies,
computer science, dentistry, drama, earth sciences,
education, engineering, English, European studies,
French, geography, German, health services
administration, history, history of art, history of
science and medicine, Italian, law, linguistics,
materials science, mathematics, medicine,
metallurgy, Middle Eastern studies, military
studies, music, nursing, palaeontology, pharmacy,
philosophy, physics, planning and landscape,
polymer science, Portuguese, psychotherapy, radio
astronomy, religious studies, Russian, Spanish,
theology.

**Museum or gallery collection, archive, or library
special collection:**
Anti-Slavery (Raymond English Collection; H G
Wilson Pamphlet Collection)
Architecture (Archives of the Manchester Society
of Architects; Archives of the Society of
Architectural Historians of GB)
British Standards
Celtic Studies (Strachan Celtic Books; Katharine
Tynan Collection)
Childrens' Literature (Alison Uttley Books and
Papers; Vera Southgate Booth Collection;
Marmion Collection)
Church and Society (Audenshaw Collection;
William Temple Collection)
Dante Collection
Drama. See Theatre and Drama
Early Printed Books (Spencer, Aldine, Christie and
Bullock Collections)
Education for Special Needs (Deaf Education
Collection; Hester Adrian Collection; Hilliard
Collection)
English Historians (Papers of E A Freeman, James
Tait and T F Tout)
English Literature (George Bellairs, Elizabeth
Gaskell, L P Hartley, Howard Spring and Thrale-
Piozzi MSS)
Esperanto Collection
European Communities Collection (European
Documentation Centre)
Family Muniments (Bagshawe, Bromley-
Davenport, Cornwall-Legh, Ducie, Dunham
Massey, Legh of Lyme, Tabley and Warburton)
French Studies (Victor Hugo Correspondence;
Mazarinades Pamphlets; French Revolution
Collection; Alexandre Dumas, père, collection)
Geography (Manchester Geographical Society
Collection; Map Collection)
German Studies (Peter Huchel Collection)
Health and Safety Collection
History of Astronomy (Archives of Zdenek Kopal,
Bernard Lovell; Jodrell Bank Collection)
History of Chemistry (Papers of John Dalton and H
E Roscoe; Partington Collection)
History of Medicine (Manchester Medical Society
Collection)
Industrial and Commercial History (Archives of
Bolton Cotton Spinners, Thomas Botfield and
Co., McConnel and Kennedy, Oldham Textile
Employers and Owen Owens)
Journalism (Guardian Archives; Papers of W P
Crozier, Alastair Hetherington, P J Monkhouse
and C P Scott; Newspaper Collection)
Judaica (Moses Gaster Collection including
Genizah Fragments; Haskalah and Marmorstein
Collections)
Local History (Cheshire, Lancashire and
Derbyshire Family Muniment Collections)
Manchester Museum Collection
Manchester University Archives
Military Studies (Clinton, Auchinleck and Dorman
O'Gowan Papers; World War I Collection)
NASA and NIST Deposit Library
Near Eastern Book and MSS Collections (especially
Arabic and Persian)
Nonconformity (Methodist Archives;
Congregational College, Northern Baptist
College and Unitarian College Collections;
Papers of T W Manson and Thomas Raffles)
Official Publications (British and International
Organisations)
Oriental Book and MSS Collections
Papyri (Arabic, Coptic, Greek, Hieratic and
Hieroglyphic)
Philosophy (Papers of Samuel Alexander and
Robert Adamson)
Political Economy (W S Jevons Papers)
Political Parties (Labour Party Newscuttings and
Pamphlets)
Pre-Raphaelites (Papers of Holman Hunt and John
Ruskin)
Private Press Books (eg Kelmscott)
Russian History (eg Alexis Aladin Papers)
Spectral and Technical Data Collection
Sport (Brockbank Cricket Collection)
Suffragette Collections

continued overleaf

Theatre and Drama (Papers of Basil Dean, Stephen Joseph, C E Montague and A N Monkhouse; G L Brook, Annie Horniman and Allardyce Nicoll Collections)

Transport (eg Kenneth Brown and T J Edmondson Railway Collections)

United Nations Deposit Library

Western Medieval MSS (especially Latin, English and French)

Printed publications:
Publications: for sale
Bulletin of the John Rylands University Library of Manchester, including off-prints and indexes (list available)
Catalogues of certain special collections: manuscript and printed book collections
Commercial microfilm and facsimile publications (listed in Publications in Print 1993, pp. 68–71)
Exhibition catalogues
John Rylands Research Institute Prospectus
Research Guides
Slides: Treasures from the John Rylands University Library

Created in its present form by the merger of the:
Manchester University Library and the John Rylands Library

Provides headquarters for the:
John Rylands Research Institute
Manchester Bibliographical Society
Manchester Medical Society

JOHNSON MATTHEY TECHNOLOGY CENTRE

Acronym or abbreviation: JMTC

Blounts Court, Sonning Common, Reading, Berkshire, RG4 9NH

Tel: 0118 924 2000
Fax: 0118 924 2254

Website:
http://www.matthey.com
General, divisional and product information for Johnson Matthey.

Founded:
1817

Organisation type and purpose:
Manufacturing industry, research organisation. Serving the Catalysts and Chemicals, and Precious Metals Divisions of Johnson Matthey plc.

Subject coverage:
Platinum group metals; gold; base metals; inorganic chemistry; materials science; catalysis; pollution control; fuel cells; electrochemistry

Museum or gallery collection, archive, or library special collection:
London Collection (books c. 1850 to early 1900s on history of London)

Printed publications:
Platinum (annually)
Platinum Metals Review (quarterly)

Access to staff:
Contact by telephone and by fax
Hours: Mon to Fri, 0900 to 1700

JOINT ASSOCIATION OF CLASSICAL TEACHERS

Acronym or abbreviation: JACT

Senate House, Malet Street, London, WC1E 7HU

Tel: 020 7862 8719
Fax: 020 7255 2297
E-mail: office@jact.org

Website:
http://www.jact.org
General information about JACT.

Enquiries:
Enquiries to: Administrator

Founded:
1961

Organisation type and purpose:
Professional body, registered charity (charity number 313165).

Subject coverage:
Teaching of Classics (Greek, Latin, classical civilisation and ancient history) at all levels; bibliographic and teaching aids.

Printed publications:
Journal of Classics Teaching (3 times a year)
Omnibus (2 times a year)

Microform publications:
Filmstrips

Access to staff:
Contact by letter, by telephone, by fax, by e-mail and in person. Appointment necessary.
Hours: Tues to Fri, 1000 to 1700

JOINT COUNCIL FOR GENERAL QUALIFICATIONS

Devas Street, Manchester, M15 6EX

Tel: 0161 958 3737
Fax: 0161 958 3745
E-mail: jointcouncil@jcgg.org.uk

Enquiries:
Enquiries to: Servicing Officer

Organisation type and purpose:
Membership association (membership is by election or invitation), suitable for ages: 11 to 19.

Printed publications:
GCE, VCE, GCSE and GNVQ: Regulations and Guidance Relating to Candidates with Particular Requirements, 1 September 2001 to 31 August 2002
GCE, VCE, GCSE and GNVQ: Instructions for the Conduct of Examinations, 1 September 2001 to 31 August 2002
Order printed publications from: See list of Member Awarding Bodies

Publications list:
Available in print

Access to staff:
Contact by letter, by fax and by e-mail
Hours: Mon to Fri, 0900 to 1700

Member Awarding Bodies:
Assessment and Qualifications Alliance (AEB/SEG)
Stag Hill House, Guildford, Surrey, GU2 5XJ; tel: 01483 506506
Edexcel
Stewart House, 32 Russell Square, London, WC1B 5DN; tel: 0870 240 9800
Northern Ireland Council for the Curriculum Examinations and Assessment
29 Clarendon Raod, Belfast, BT1 3BG; tel: 01232 261200
OCR
Syndicate Buildings, 1 Hills Road, Cambridge, CB1 2EU; tel: 01223 553998
The Assessment and Qualifications Alliance (NEAB)
Devas Street, Manchester, M15 6EX; tel: 0161 953 1180
Welsh Joint Education Committee
245 Western Avenue, Cardiff, CF5 2YX; tel: 02920 265000

JOINT COUNCIL FOR LANDSCAPE INDUSTRIES

Acronym or abbreviation: JCLI

c/o The Landscape Institute, 6/8 Barnard Mews, London, SW11 1QU

Tel: 020 7350 5200
Fax: 020 7350 5201
E-mail: mail@l-i.org.uk

Enquiries:
Enquiries to: Secretary

Other contacts: Committee Services Officer

Organisation type and purpose:
National organisation.
Umbrella body for the landscape industry.

Subject coverage:
Co-ordinates views of member organisations and represents those members in all matters of common interest and concerns at all levels, including Local and National Government and internationally represents British Landscape interests and promotes and encourages greater public interest.

Printed publications:
Order printed publications from: The Landscape Institute

Publications list:
Available in print

Access to staff:
Contact by letter, by telephone, by fax and by e-mail
Hours: Mon to Fri, 0900 to 1700

Connections with:
Arboricultural Association (AA)
British Association of Landscape Industries (BALI)
Horticultural Trades Association (HTA)
Institute of Leisure and Amenity Management (ILAM)
Landscape Institute (LI)
National Farmers Union (NFU)

JOINT COUNCIL FOR THE WELFARE OF IMMIGRANTS

Acronym or abbreviation: JCWI

115 Old Street, London, EC1V 9RT

Tel: 020 7251 8708
Fax: 020 7251 8707
E-mail: info@jcwi.org.uk

Website:
http://www.jcwi.org.uk

Enquiries:
Enquiries to: Chief Executive
Direct e-mail: habib@jcwi.org.uk
Other contacts: Training Officer for training.

Founded:
1967

Organisation type and purpose:
Membership association (membership is by subscription), present number of members: 1000, voluntary organisation, training organisation, campaign organisation, publishing house.
1000 affiliated organisations and individuals; mainly black and ethnic minority organisations, advice agencies, community relations councils, local authorities, solicitors.
Immigration Law advice and training agency.

Subject coverage:
Immigration, nationality and refugee law and practice.

Printed publications:
JCWI Bulletin (quarterly)
A small number of books, leaflets and briefings including:
JCWI Immigration Nationality & Refuge Law Handbook (2002)

Publications list:
Available online and in print

Access to staff:
Contact by letter, by telephone, by fax and by e-mail. Appointment necessary.
Hours: Mon to Fri, 0900 to 1700

Access for disabled people:
Ramped entry, toilet facilities

JOINT EDUCATIONAL TRUST

Acronym or abbreviation: JET

6–8 Fenchurch Buildings, London, EC3M 5HT

Tel: 020 3217 1100
Fax: 020 3217 1110
E-mail: admin@jetcharity.org

Website:
www.jetcharity.org

Enquiries:
Enquiries to: Director

Founded:
1971

Organisation type and purpose:
Registered charity (charity number 313218), suitable for ages: 7 to 13.

Subject coverage:
Suitable schools for vulnerable children with needs.

Printed publications:
Order printed publications from: free from JET

Access to staff:
Contact by letter, by telephone and by e-mail
Hours: Mon to Fri, 0900 to 1700

Access to building, collection or gallery:
No access other than to staff

Access for disabled people:
Access to all public areas, toilet facilities

JOINT INDUSTRY BOARD FOR THE ELECTRICAL CONTRACTING INDUSTRY

Acronym or abbreviation: JIB

Kingswood House, 47–51 Sidcup Hill, Sidcup, Kent, DA14 6HP

Tel: 020 8302 0031
Fax: 020 8309 1103

Website:
http://www.jib.org.uk
Including the Handbook.

Enquiries:
Enquiries to: Chief Executive

Founded:
1968

Organisation type and purpose:
Membership association (membership is by qualification), present number of members: 27,000. Implements national wage agreement and working rules in the electrical contracting industry.

Subject coverage:
Wage rates and terms and conditions of employment for hourly paid employees in the electrical contracting industry.

Printed publications:
Health and Safety Handbook (£4)
Handbook (annual, £5)

Electronic and video publications:
Electronic version of the Handbook can be downloaded from the web site

Access to staff:
Contact by letter
Hours: Mon to Fri, 0900 to 1700

JOINT LIBRARY OF THE HELLENIC AND ROMAN SOCIETIES

3rd Floor, Senate House, Malet Street, London, WC1E 7HU

Tel: 020 7862 8709
Fax: 020 7862 8735

Website:
http://icls.sas.ac.uk/library/Home.htm

Enquiries:
Enquiries to: Librarian
Direct tel: 020 7862 8710
Direct fax: 020 7862 8724
Direct e-mail: colin.annis@sas.ac.uk

Founded:
1950

Organisation type and purpose:
Private Library combined with Institute of Classical Studies Library.

Subject coverage:
All aspects of classical civilisation, including archaeology, art and architecture, language and literature, history, law, politics, religion, philosophy and science relating to the Minoan, Mycenaean, Ancient Greek and early Byzantine World; also to early Italic and Etruscan civilisations, and to the Roman World from the beginning to the 5th century AD (including Roman Britain).

Museum or gallery collection, archive, or library special collection:
106,000 monographs and pamphlets
18,900 bound volumes of periodicals
6800 slides
660 current periodicals taken

Library catalogue:
All or part available online

Printed publications:
Britannia (available to members as part of the subscription; available for purchase to non-members)
Journal of Hellenic Studies (available to members as part of the subscription; available for purchase to non-members)
Journal of Roman Studies (available to members as part of the subscription; available for purchase to non-members)
Order printed publications from: Secretary, Hellenic Society, at the same address, tel: 020 7862 8730, fax: 020 7862 8731, e-mail: office@hellenicsociety.org.uk
Secretary, Roman Society, at the same address, tel: 020 7862 8727, fax: 020 7862 8728, e-mail: office@romansociety.org

Publications list:
Available online and in print

Access to staff:
Contact by letter, by telephone, by fax, by e-mail and in person. Access for members only.
Hours: Mon to Fri, 0930 to 1800
Term time: Tue, Wed and Thu, 0930 to 2000; Sat, 1000 to 1630; closed Sat during August

Combined with:
Institute of Classical Studies Library (ICS)

JOINT NATURE CONSERVATION COMMITTEE

Acronym or abbreviation: JNCC

Monkstone House, City Road, Peterborough, Cambridgeshire, PE1 1JY

Tel: 01733 562626
Fax: 01733 555948
E-mail: communications@jncc.gov.uk

Website:
http://www.jncc.gov.uk
Work of JNCC, news and information, online catalogue and the list of available JNCC reports, together with forthcoming publications, online publications such as the Annual Report and Corporate Plan.

Founded:
1991

Organisation type and purpose:
Advisory body.
Responsible to the UK Government for research and advice on nature conservation at both UK and international levels, on behalf of the Countryside Council for Wales, Natural England, Scottish Natural Heritage, and the Council for Nature Conservation and the Countryside (Northern Ireland); the Committee also includes independent members.

Subject coverage:
Nature conservation

Printed publications:
Corporate Plans
Wide variety of books on birds, coasts, earth science, habitat, herpetofauna, invertebrates, land use, mammals, marine life, plants and pollution.
Annual Reports from 1991 onwards
Order printed publications from: NHBS, 2–3 Wills Road, Totnes, Devon, TQ9 5XN, tel: 01803 865913, fax: 01803 865280, e-mail: nhbs@nhbs.co.uk

Publications list:
Available online and in print

Access to staff:
Contact by letter, by telephone, by fax, by e-mail and via website. Appointment necessary.
Hours: Mon to Thu, 0830 to 1700; Fri, 0830 to 1630

Also at:
JNCC (Aberdeen Office)
Dunnet House, 7 Thistle Place, Aberdeen, AB10 1UZ; tel: 01224 655704; fax: 01224 621488; e-mail: communications@jncc.gov.uk; website: http://www.jncc.gov.uk

JOINT SERVICES COMMAND & STAFF COLLEGE LIBRARY

Acronym or abbreviation: JSCSC

Faringdon Road, Watchfield, Shrivenham, Wiltshire, SN6 8TS

Tel: 01793 788234
Fax: 01793 788281
E-mail: dsdinfo.jscsc@defenceacademy.mod.uk

Enquiries:
Enquiries to: Librarian
Direct tel: 01793 788000
Direct e-mail: chobson.jscsc@da.mod.uk

Founded:
1997

Organisation type and purpose:
National government body.
Central government establishment.
Military staff training college.

Subject coverage:
Air power, aviation (military), modern warfare, historical warfare, defence policy and studies, NATO, Warsaw Pact countries, international affairs, communications skills, management techniques, Armed Forces, sea power, Royal Navy, navies, land warfare, British Army, armies and Royal Air Force.

Library catalogue:
All or part available online and in-house

Access to staff:
Contact by letter, by telephone, by fax and by e-mail. Appointment necessary.
Hours: Mon to Fri, 0800 to 1800

Access to building, collection or gallery:
Prior appointment required
Hours: Mon to Fri, 0800 to 1800

Access for disabled people:
Access to all public areas

Parent body:
Ministry of Defence

JONES LANG LASALLE

22 Hanover Square, London, W1A 2BN

Tel: 020 7493 6040
Fax: 020 7399 5818

Website:
http://www.joneslanglasalle.co.uk

Enquiries:
Enquiries to: Information Manager
Direct e-mail: infodesk@en.jll.com

Founded:
1999

continued overleaf

Organisation type and purpose:
Consultancy.

Subject coverage:
Real estate.

Printed publications:
Central London Market Report (4 times a year)
Office Service Charges (annually)
Property Index (quarterly)

Publications list:
Available online and in print

Access to staff:
Contact by letter and by e-mail
Hours: Mon to Fri, 0900 to 1730

Access to building, collection or gallery:
No access other than to staff

JORDAN INFORMATION BUREAU

Acronym or abbreviation: JIB

6 Upper Phillimore Gardens, London, W8 7HB

Tel: 020 7937 9499
Fax: 020 7937 6741
E-mail: info@jiblondon.com

Website:
http://www.jordanembassyuk.gov.jo
Tourism, economic, news, contacts, general
information, weekly publications.

Enquiries:
Enquiries to: Director
Other contacts: Information Officer

Founded:
1992

Organisation type and purpose:
Part of Diplomatic Mission.
Press, media and information section.

Subject coverage:
General information about Jordan, history, politics,
economy, culture, social life, and the Middle East
Peace process.

**Museum or gallery collection, archive, or library
special collection:**
Library containing information on Jordan and the
Middle East

Printed publications:
General information on Jordan

Electronic and video publications:
Some video information (available for loan only)
CD-ROM on Jordan

Access to staff:
Contact by letter, by telephone, by fax, by e-mail
and via website
Hours: Mon to Fri, 0900 to 1600

Access to building, collection or gallery:
No prior appointment required

Connections with:
Embassy of The Hashemite Kingdom of Jordan
6 Upper Phillimore Gardens, London, W8 7HB

JORDANS LIMITED

21 St Thomas Street, Bristol, BS1 6JS

Tel: 0117 923 0600
Fax: 0117 923 0063
E-mail: businessinformation@jordans.co.uk

Website:
http://www.jordans.co.uk

Enquiries:
Enquiries to: Customer Service Administrator
Direct tel: 0117 918 1283
Direct e-mail: denise_sebastian@jordans.co.uk
Other contacts: Customer Services Administrator
for purchase of data, or for quotations.

Founded:
1898

Organisation type and purpose:
Registration agents, law agents.
Business information provider.
Publishing house, printers and stationers.

Subject coverage:
Company financial information including
information for marketing, credit checking,
performance analysis, status reports, money-
laundering report, official filings at Companies
House.

Trade and statistical information:
Industry sector reports: financial analysis of
companies by industry region, size, growth etc.

Printed publications:
Financial Reports
Top 10,000 privately owned companies

Electronic and video publications:
Amadeus: financial database of top 200,000
European companies on CD/DVD-ROM and
internet
A wide variety of reports on disc
FAME (Financial Analysis Made Easy) Database
on CD/DVD-ROM and internet (2.5m UK and
Irish cos)
Jordan Company Database of 2,000 plcs holding
more than 0.15% shares
Shareholder Information on disc
Jordanwatch for financial profiles and image-link
(online)
KYC (Know Your Client) money-laundering data
(online)

Publications list:
Available online and in print

Access to staff:
Contact by letter, by telephone, by fax, by e-mail,
in person and via website. Appointment necessary.
Hours: Mon to Fri, 0900 to 1700

Other addresses:
Jordans Limited
20–22 Bedford Row, London, WC1R 4JS; tel: 020
7400 3333; fax: 020 7400 3366
Jordans Limited
44 Whitchurch Road, Cardiff, CF4 3UQ; tel: 029
2037 1901; fax: 029 2038 2342
Oswalds
24 Great King Street, Edinburgh, EH3 6QN; tel:
0131 557 6966; fax: 0131 556 2917

Parent body:
West of England Trust Limited
21 St Thames Street, Bristol, BS1 6JS

JOSEPH ROWNTREE FOUNDATION

Acronym or abbreviation: JRF

The Homestead, 40 Water End, York, YO30 6WP

Tel: 01904 629241
Fax: 01904 620072
E-mail: info@jrf.org.uk

Website:
http://www.jrf.org.uk
Corporate information, summaries of research
supported by the Foundation in the form of
'Findings', from 1998: list of current research
supported by the Foundation.

Enquiries:
Enquiries to: Library Administrator
Direct tel: ext 243
Direct e-mail: janet.mccullough@jrf.org.uk

Organisation type and purpose:
Research organisation.
Housing Association.

Subject coverage:
Housing research; social policy; social care;
poverty; drugs and alcohol; housing associations;
New Earswick (model village); Rowntree family
history.

Printed publications:
Over 500 books and reports published since 1989
including:

Death in Britain: How Local Mortality Rates Have
Changed: 1950s–1990s
Findings (reports of projects)
Report of the Independent Working Group on
Drug Consumption Rooms
Meeting Part M and designing lifetime homes
Monitoring poverty and social exclusion: 2005
Poverty and Social Exclusion in Britain
Search (2 or 3 times a year)
People in Low-Paid Informal Work: Need not
Greed
'Planned' Teenage Pregnancy: Views and
Experiences of Young People from Poor and
Disadvantaged Backgrounds
Order printed publications from: York Publishing
Services, 64 Hallfield Road, Layerthorpe, York,
YO3 7XQ; tel. 01904 430033; fax 01904 430868

Publications list:
Available online and in print

Access to staff:
Contact by letter, by telephone, by fax and by e-
mail. Appointment necessary.
Hours: Mon to Fri, 0900 to 1230 and 1400 to 1700

Access to building, collection or gallery:
Prior appointment required

JOSEPHINE BUTLER SOCIETY

Acronym or abbreviation: JBS

4 The Hedges, Maidstone, Kent, ME14 2JW

Tel: 01622 679630

Website:
http://www.jbs.webeden.co.uk

Enquiries:
Enquiries to: Honorary Correspondence Secretary

Founded:
1869

Organisation type and purpose:
Membership association (membership is by
subscription), present number of members: 90,
voluntary organisation.

Subject coverage:
Objects: to promote a high and equal standard of
morality and sexual responsibility for men and
women in public opinion, law and practice. To
secure the abolition of state regulation of
prostitution internationally and prevent all forms
of exploitation of prostitutes by third parties. To
examine existing and proposed legislation on all
matters connected with prostitution, and to
promote social, legal and administrative reform,
the law as it affects prostitutes and related subjects
e.g. kerb crawling, sexual offences etc. Combating
the traffic in persons (known in the past as the
White Slave Trade).

**Museum or gallery collection, archive, or library
special collection:**
Main JBS collection is held at the Women's Library,
London; smaller collection at the Durham
University Library, Durham

Library catalogue:
All or part available online

Printed publications:
News and Views (magazine, annually)
Occasional papers

Access to staff:
Contact by letter and by telephone
Hours: Mon to Fri, 0900 to 1700

Links with:
Anti-Slavery Society
tel: 020 7924 9555; fax: 020 7738 4110; e-mail:
antislavery@gn.apc.orb
Church Army
tel: 020 8318 1226
Church of England Board for Social Responsibility
tel: 020 7222 9011
Council for Voluntary Services

Fawcett Society
tel: 020 7628 4441; fax: 020 7628 2865; e-mail:
fawcett@gn.apc.org; website: http://www.gn.apc
.org/fawcett
Human Rights Network
International Abolitionist Federation
France; e-mail: b.amont@libertysurf.fr
International Alliance of Women
tel: 612 6568 6239 (Australia)
International Council of Women
tel: 00 331 47 42 19 40; fax: 00 331 42 66 26 23
(France); e-mail: icw_cif@wanadoo.fr
Minority Rights Group
tel: 020 7978 9498
Mothers Union
tel: 020 7222 5533
National Council of Women of Great Britain
tel: 020 7354 2395; fax: 020 7354 9214; website:
http://www.cerbernet.co.uk/ncwgb/
Salvation Army
tel: 020 7332 0022; fax: 020 7236 6272
Wellclose Trust
tel: 01823 325 632

JOSIAH WEDGWOOD & SONS LIMITED

Barlaston, Stoke-on-Trent, Staffordshire, ST12 9ES

Tel: 01782 204141
Fax: 01782 204666

Website:
http://www.wedgwood.co.uk
Company history, product information, visitor
centre, events, company magazine, gift ideas.

Enquiries:
Enquiries to: Public Relations Manager
Direct tel: 01782 282516
Direct fax: 01782 204433
Direct e-mail: andrew.stanistreet@wedgwood.com

Founded:
1759

Organisation type and purpose:
Manufacturing industry, museum.

Subject coverage:
Manufacturing processes of fine bone china and
earthenware, company history from 1759.

Museum or gallery collection, archive, or library special collection:
Museum of ceramics and manuscripts

Access to staff:
Contact by letter, by fax and by e-mail
Hours: Mon to Fri, 0900 to 1700

JOZEF PILSUDSKI INSTITUTE OF RESEARCH LIMITED

Science Institute, 238–240 King Street, London, W6 0RF

Tel: 020 8748 6197
Fax: 020 8748 6197
E-mail: instytut@pilsudski.org.uk

Enquiries:
Enquiries to: General Secretary
Direct tel: 020 8579 3823

Founded:
1947

Organisation type and purpose:
Learned society (membership is by election or
invitation), present number of members: 140,
registered charity, museum, research organisation.
Reference library.
Historical research into the recent history of Poland
in relation to work and deeds of Jozef Pilsudski.

Subject coverage:
The Struggle for Polish independence before and
during World War I, political and military events
during the years of independence 1918–1939 and
organisation of Polish State.

Museum or gallery collection, archive, or library special collection:
Archives of documents, manuscripts and
photographs (mostly in Polish)
Militaria Library related to recent history of Poland
before 2nd World War
Museum of personal objects of Marshal Pilsudski

Non-library collection catalogue:
All or part available in-house

Library catalogue:
All or part available in-house

Printed publications:
Over 40 publications in Polish includes the
following:
Jozef Pilsudski – Korespondencja 1914–1917 (£10)
Niepodleglosc 17 volumes (for sale)

Publications list:
Available in print

Access to staff:
Contact by letter, by telephone, by fax, by e-mail
and in person
Hours: Tue and Thu, 1000 to 1700; or by
appointment

Access for disabled people:
Ramped entry

JUDGE INSTITUTE OF MANAGEMENT

University of Cambridge, Trumpington Street,
Cambridge, CB2 1AG

Tel: 01223 339700
Fax: 01223 339701
E-mail: enquiries@jims.cam.ac.uk

Website:
http://www.jims.cam.ac.uk
Information about the institute and links to
research and workshop papers.

Enquiries:
Enquiries to: Communications Manager
Direct tel: 01223 388608
Direct fax: 01223 766920
Direct e-mail: press-publicity@jims.cam.ac.uk

Founded:
1990

Organisation type and purpose:
University Business School.

Subject coverage:
Management studies, Business and Management.

Trade and statistical information:
Market and Company Information.

Non-library collection catalogue:
All or part available online

Library catalogue:
All or part available online

Printed publications:
Working Papers
Order printed publications from: Publications
Secretary
As main address

Electronic and video publications:
Working Papers – current year

Publications list:
Available online and in print

Access to staff:
Contact by letter, by telephone, by fax, by e-mail
and via website
Hours: Mon to Fri, 0900 to 1700

Access to building, collection or gallery:
No access other than to staff

Access for disabled people:
Parking provided, level entry, access to all public
areas, toilet facilities

Links with:
Cambridge Business Research Centre (CBRC)
Cambridge Entrepreneurship Centre

CMI
Management Studies Group
Department of Engineering, University of
Cambridge
Massachusetts Institute of Technology (MIT)

JUNIOR CHAMBER OF COMMERCE FOR LONDON

Formal name: Junior Chamber of Commerce for
London also known as London Jaycees
Acronym or abbreviation: JCCL

33 Queen Street, London, EC4R 1AP

Tel: 020 7203 1951

Website:
http://www.juniorchamberlondon.org.uk

Enquiries:
Enquiries to: Membership Secretary
Direct e-mail: sam@thane.demon.co.uk

Founded:
1953

Organisation type and purpose:
International organisation (membership is by
election or invitation), present number of
members: 120, voluntary organisation, suitable for
ages: 18 to 40, training organisation.
Part of a worldwide organisation dedicated to
developing the business and managerial skills of
the future business leaders of our communities.

Subject coverage:
Concentrates on 5 areas of opportunities;
International, business networking, community
projects, leadership development and management
opportunities.

Access to staff:
Contact by letter, by telephone and by e-mail
Hours: Mon to Fri, preferably evenings

Affiliated to:
British Junior Chamber, which is affiliated to Junior
Chamber International

Head Office:
British Junior Chamber (BJC)
12 Regent Place, Rugby, Warwickshire, CV21
2PM; tel: 01788 572795; fax: 01788 542091; e-
mail: 1007633171@compuserve.com

JUPITER OWNERS AUTO CLUB

Acronym or abbreviation: JOAC

Rivermead, Hoarwithy, Hereford, HR2 6QS

Tel: 01432 840347
Fax: 01432 840347
E-mail: ed@jowettjupiter.co.uk

Website:
http://www.jowettjupiter.co.uk

Enquiries:
Enquiries to: Membership Secretary
Direct tel: 01273 843457

Founded:
1962

Organisation type and purpose:
Membership association (membership is by
subscription), present number of members: 220.
Club for owners of Jowett Jupiter Cars 1950–54.

Subject coverage:
About 900 Jowett Jupiters were built from 1950 to
1954 – many still survive and we aim to keep these
interesting and rare collectible cars on the road and
restored.

Access to staff:
Contact by letter, by e-mail and via website
Hours: Mon to Fri, 0900 to 1700

JUSTICE

59 Carter Lane, London, EC4V 5AQ

Tel: 020 7329 5100

continued overleaf

Fax: 020 7329 5055
E-mail: admin@justice.org.uk

Website:
http://www.justice.org.uk
Overview of Justice's work, news of legal events
and issues, copies of briefings and information on
reports.

Enquiries:
Enquiries to: Director
Other contacts: Legal Officer

Founded:
1957

Organisation type and purpose:
Membership association (membership is by
subscription), present number of members: 2000,
voluntary organisation, registered charity (charity
number 1058580).
An international non-governmental organisation
concerned with promoting observance of the Rule
of Law, law reform and the legal protection of
Human Rights.

Subject coverage:
Law reform, rule of law, access to justice, human
rights in UK and EU.

**Museum or gallery collection, archive, or library
special collection:**
Archive material 1990-.
ICJ reports
Justice reports and memoranda

Printed publications:
Justice Bulletin (Spring, Summer and Autumn, free
to members)
Reports on criminal law, civil and family law,
administrative and public laws and the legal aid
system
Criminal Justice Reform Briefings

Publications list:
Available in print

Access to staff:
Contact by letter
Hours: Mon to Fri, 0930 to 1730

British Section of the:
International Commission of Jurists
Geneva

JUSTICE FOR ALL VACCINE-DAMAGED CHILDREN

Acronym or abbreviation: JVDC

Erin's Cottage, Fussell's Buildings, Whiteway
Road, Bristol, BS5 7QY

Tel: 0117 955 7818

Enquiries:
Enquiries to: Secretary
Other contacts: Justice and Basic Support for MMR
vaccine damage.

Founded:
1981

Organisation type and purpose:
Voluntary organisation.
To ensure the safer manufacture of vaccines, that
all medical personnel are aware of the Vaccine
Damage Payments Act (1979), that all adverse
reactions are reported to the Committee on Safety
of Medicines.

Subject coverage:
Compensation for vaccine-damaged children.

Access to staff:
Contact by telephone
Hours: Mon to Sun, 0900 to 2100 telephone only

Also at:
Justice for all Vaccine-Damaged Children
99 Hendris Road, Kirkcaldy, Fife, KY2 5DB

Other vaccine damage groups:
Justice, Awareness, Basic Support (JABS)
1 Gawsworth Road, Golbourne, Warrington,
Cheshire, WA3 3RF; tel: 01942 713565

The Informed Parent
PO Box 870, Harrow, Middlesex; tel: 020 861
1022
Victims of Vaccination Support Group
27 Malcolm Grove, Rednal, Birmingham, BH5
9BS; tel: 0121 2437759

JUVENILE DIABETES RESEARCH FOUNDATION

Acronym or abbreviation: JDRF

19 Angel Gate, City Road, London, EC1V 2PT

Tel: 020 7713 2030
Fax: 020 7713 2031
E-mail: info@jdrf.org.uk

Website:
http://www.jdrf.org.uk

Enquiries:
Enquiries to: Director of Communications

Founded:
1986

Organisation type and purpose:
National organisation, registered charity (charity
number 295716).
To find a cure for diabetes through the support of
research. To provide information about the
progress of research.

Access to staff:
Contact by letter, by telephone, by fax, by e-mail
and via website
Hours: Mon to Fri, 0900 to 1730
Special comments: 3rd floor – lift access.

Access to building, collection or gallery:
Prior appointment required

Affiliated to:
The Juvenile Diabetes Foundation International
120 Wall Street, New York, USA; website: www
.jdrf.org

Regional offices:
JDRF Merseyside
Suite 146 1st Floor, 9 Slater Street, Liverpool, L1
4BW; tel: 0151 709 5533
JDRF South West
32–34 Hotwell Road, Hotwells, Bristol, BS8 4UD;
tel: 0117 9452491
JDRF West Midlands
Suite 32 Fifth Floor, Queensgate, 121 Suffolk
Street, Queensway, Birmingham, B1 1LX; tel:
0121 685 7102

JVC PROFESSIONAL EUROPE LIMITED

Acronym or abbreviation: JVC

JVC House, JVC Business Park, 12 Priestley Way,
London, NW2 7BA

Tel: 020 8208 6200
Fax: 020 8208 6260
E-mail: sales@jvcpro.co.uk

Website:
http://www.jvcproeurope.com
Main products sold by model number, product
specification, user application.

Enquiries:
Enquiries to: Sales Manager

Founded:
1988

Organisation type and purpose:
Manufacturing industry.
UK marketing and distribution of JVC professional
products.

Subject coverage:
Professional video equipment, CD-ROM library
systems, Ethernet compatible interoffice IR
communications, closed circuit television, video/
data projection.

Access to staff:
Contact by letter, by telephone, by fax and by e-
mail
Hours: Mon to Fri, 0900 to 1700

Access for disabled people:
Ramped entry, toilet facilities

KAOLIN AND BALL CLAY ASSOCIATION

Acronym or abbreviation: KABCA

Par Moor Centre, Par Moor, Par, Cornwall, PL24
2SQ

Tel: 01726 811328
Fax: 01726 811200

Website:
http://www.kabca.org/

Enquiries:
Enquiries to: Secretary
Direct e-mail: george.muskett@imerys.com

Organisation type and purpose:
Trade association (membership is by election or
invitation), present number of members: 3 member
companies.
The Kaolin and Ball Clay Association is a
representative of the china and ball clay industry. It
studies matters ranging from commercial
legislation and environmental issues to
employment, planning and technical issues.

Subject coverage:
Production and sale of china and ball clay.

Trade and statistical information:
Information service provided to external solicitors
in planning searches associated with house
purchase, land development etc.

Access to staff:
Contact by letter, by telephone and by fax
Hours: Tue, Thu, 0900 to 1730

Members of:
Goonvean Ltd
tel: 01726 822381
IMERYS Minerals Limited
tel: 01726 818000
WBB Minerals Limited
tel: 01626 322331

KAPUSTIN SOCIETY, THE

9 Burnside Close, Twickenham, Middlesex, TW1
1ET

Tel: 020 8287 5518
Fax: 020 8287 5518
E-mail: KapustinSoc@blueyonder.co.uk

Website:
http://www.trg.ed.ac.uk

Enquiries:
Enquiries to: Secretary

Founded:
2002

Organisation type and purpose:
Learned society, membership association
(membership is by subscription).

Subject coverage:
Music of Nikolai Kapustin (1937-).

Printed publications:
Photocopies of most solo piano and some chamber
music scores
Projected Bulletin

Access to staff:
Contact by letter, by telephone, by fax and by e-
mail. Appointment necessary.
Hours: Mon to Fri, 0900 to 1700

Access to building, collection or gallery:
Prior appointment required

Access for disabled people:
Parking provided, level entry, toilet facilities

KARMANN GHIA OWNERS' CLUB (GB)

13 Hilltop Road, Toms Lane, Kings Langley, Hertfordshire, WD4 8NS

Tel: 01923 263658
E-mail: john@jfigg.freeserve.co.uk

Enquiries:
Enquiries to: General Secretary

Founded:
1982

Organisation type and purpose:
National organisation.

Subject coverage:
Karmann Ghia motorcars, sale of cars, insurance benefits, club events, national related events, international events, specialist services.

Museum or gallery collection, archive, or library special collection:
History of the manufacture of the car
Service and repair data

Access to staff:
Contact by letter, by telephone and by e-mail
Hours: Mon to Fri, 0900 to 1700

KATE SHARPLEY LIBRARY

Acronym or abbreviation: KSL

BM Hurricane, London, WC1N 3XX

E-mail: info@katesharpleylibrary.net

Website:
http://www.katesharpleylibrary.net
Introduction. Online version of bulletin, details of publications, wants list, book reviews and online documents

Enquiries:
Enquiries to: Information Officer

Founded:
1979

Organisation type and purpose:
Voluntary organisation, research organisation, publishing house.
To research and publish materials on anarchist history especially in areas that have been ignored or misrepresented by academic experts.

Subject coverage:
Anarchism; anarcho-syndicalism; council communism; Labour Movement; Libertarian socialism; revolutionary industrial unionism (Industrial Workers of the World); situationism; Spanish Civil War and Resistance; Syndicalism.

Museum or gallery collection, archive, or library special collection:
The Library covers Anarchist, Syndicalist, Libertarian Socialist, Situationist and Council Communist books, pamphlets and periodicals in all languages
Various archive collections including Albert Meltzer papers (Anarchism)

Non-library collection catalogue:
All or part available in-house

Library catalogue:
All or part available in-house

Printed publications:
Please send an sae for up to date list
KSL Bulletin of the Kate Sharpley Library (quarterly)
The Anarchist resistance to Franco, Biographical notes (£2)
British Syndicalism: Pages from Labour History (Brown T, £1)
Mayday and Anarchism (2004, £3)
Prisoners and Partisans: Italian Anarchists in the struggle against Fascism (1999, £3)
Revolutionary activism: The Spanish Resistance in context (Alberola O, Millán A, Zambrana J, £3)
Unknown Heroes : Biographies of Anarchist Resistance Fighters (2005, £3)
The Walsall Anarchists (£1)

With The Poor People Of The Earth : A Biography Of Doctor John Creaghe of Sheffield & Buenos Aires (2004, £3)
Yiddish Anarchist Bibliography (1998, £7.50)

Publications list:
Available online and in print

Access to staff:
Contact by letter, by e-mail and via website. Appointment necessary.

Other address:
Kate Sharpley Library (KSL)
PMB 820, 242S Channing Way, Berkeley, California, CA 94704, USA

KEELE UNIVERSITY LIBRARY

Keele, Staffordshire, ST5 5BG

Tel: 01782 733535
Fax: 01782 734502
E-mail: libhelp@keele.ac.uk

Website:
http://www.keele.ac.uk/depts/li

Founded:
1949

Organisation type and purpose:
University Library.

Subject coverage:
American studies; English; history; music; philosophy; economics; history; education; biological sciences; pharmacology; management; chemistry; communication and neuroscience; computer science; geology; mathematics; physics; medicine; geography; international relations; industrial relations; law; politics; criminology; social gerontology; psychology; social policy; social work; physiology; sociology; social anthropology.

Museum or gallery collection, archive, or library special collection:
Arnold Bennett Collection
Sneyd Papers (Sneyd family of Keele Hall 1600 onwards)
Spode Papers

Trade and statistical information:
European Documentation Centre

Printed publications:
Guides and leaflets regularly updated

Access to staff:
Contact by letter, by telephone, by fax and by e-mail
Hours: Term time: Mon to Fri, 0850 to 2200; Sat, 0930 to 2200; Sun, 1000 to 2200
Vacations: please enquire

Access for disabled people:
Accessible, via entrance on ground floor

Member organisation of:
SCONUL Access
Society of College, National and University Libraries

KEIGHLEY & DISTRICT FHS

2 The Hallows, Shann Park, Keighley, West Yorkshire, BD20 6HY

Tel: 01535 672144
E-mail: suedaynes@hotmail.co.uk

Website:
http://www.kdfhs.org

Enquiries:
Enquiries to: Honorary Secretary
Other contacts: Administration and Programme Secretary

Founded:
1986

Organisation type and purpose:
Membership association (membership is by subscription), present number of members: 300, voluntary organisation.
To exchange information, ideas regarding individual family histories. Discuss research problems.

Subject coverage:
Family history in the Keighley and District Area which includes: Bingley to the East, West to Kildwick, Skipton and the Aire Valley, and the villages of the Worth Valley, Haworth, Oakworth, Oxenhope etc.

Non-library collection catalogue:
All or part available in-house

Library catalogue:
All or part available in-house

Printed publications:
An extensive list of monumental inscriptions, parish registers and transcripts is given online
Order printed publications from: Publications Secretary, 13 King Edward Street, Sutton in Craven, Keighley, West Yorkshire, BD20 7ET, e-mail: a.thorley171@btinternet.com

Publications list:
Available online and in print

Access to staff:
Contact by letter, by e-mail and via website. Appointment necessary. Access for members only.
Hours: Mon to Fri, 0900 to 1700

Access to building, collection or gallery:
at Keighley Public Library, Local Studies Library on 1st floor
Hours: Mon to Fri, 0900 to 1900; Sat, 0900 to 1700
Special comments: Access to Society's reference library for members only on sight of membership card.

Access for disabled people:
Use Albert Street entrance and lift to 1st floor
Hours: Mon to Fri, 0900 to 1900; Sat, 0900 to 1700

Links with:
Federation of Family History Societies
Artillery House, 15 Byron Street, Manchester M3 4PF; e-mail: admin@ffhs.org.uk

Membership Secretary:
Keighley & District FHS
3 Walton Street, Skipton, North Yorkshire, BD23 2QX; website: sjp03tiscali.co.uk

KELVEDON HATCH SECRET BUNKER

Brentwood, Essex, CM14 5TL

Tel: 01277 364883
Fax: 01277 365260
E-mail: bunker@sapar.demon.co.uk

Website:
http://www.japar.demon.co.uk

Enquiries:
Enquiries to: Managing Director

Founded:
1994

Organisation type and purpose:
Nuclear bunker.

Subject coverage:
Cold War bunker built in 1952 for government.

Access to staff:
Contact by letter, by fax, by e-mail and via website
Hours: Mar to Oct, Mon to Fri, 1000 to 1600; Sat and Sun, 1000 to 1700
Nov to Feb, Thu to Sun, 1000 to 1600
Special comments: Charge for admission.

Access for disabled people:
Parking provided, toilet facilities
Special comments: Limited entry.

KENNEL CLUB

Formal name: The Kennel Club

1–5 Clarges Street, Piccadilly, London, W1J 8AB

Tel: 0870 606 6750
Fax: 020 7518 1058

Website:
www.thekennelclub.org.uk/library
Library services, catalogue.
www.dogimages.org.uk
Photo library.
www.thekennelclub.org.uk/gallery
Art collection.

Enquiries:
Enquiries to: Library and Collections Manager
Direct tel: 020 7518 1009
Direct fax: 020 7518 1045
Direct e-mail: library@thekennelclub.org.uk

Founded:
1873

Organisation type and purpose:
Membership association (membership is by
election or invitation), present number of
members: 750.
To promote in every way the general improvement
of dogs.

Subject coverage:
Dogs: choice, care, training, breeding, health,
welfare, showing, obedience, agility, walking and
field trials, pedigree dog registration.

**Museum or gallery collection, archive, or library
special collection:**
Books, archive, photographs, artwork, ephemera
etc

Library catalogue:
All or part available in-house

Printed publications:
Guides to Showing and Judging
Kennel Club Breed Records Supplement
(quarterly)
Kennel Club Stud Book (annually)
Kennel Club Yearbook
Kennel Gazette (monthly)
Rescue Directory
The Kennel Club's Illustrated Breed Standards
Treasures of The Kennel Club

Electronic and video publications:
Footage of Crufts and Discover Dogs available for
purchase

Access to staff:
Contact by letter, by telephone, by e-mail and via
website
Hours: Mon to Fri, 0930 to 1630

Access to building, collection or gallery:
Prior appointment required
Hours: Library: Mon to Fri, 0930 to 1630

KENSINGTON AND CHELSEA (ROYAL BOROUGH) LIBRARY

Formal name: Royal Borough of Kensington and
Chelsea
Acronym or abbreviation: RBKC

Central Library, Phillimore Walk, London, W8 7RX

Tel: 020 7937 3010
Fax: 020 7361 2976
E-mail: information.services@rbkc.gov.uk

Website:
http://www.rbkc.gov.uk/general/default.asp?/
libraries/zone=service

Enquiries:
Enquiries to: Head of Library Service
Other contacts: Head of Service

Founded:
1965

Organisation type and purpose:
Local government body, public library.

Subject coverage:
General, biography and genealogy, customs and
folklore, language.

**Museum or gallery collection, archive, or library
special collection:**
Kensington and Chelsea local history and current
information
Records of the Chelsea Arts Club 1890–1974

Non-library collection catalogue:
All or part available in-house

Library catalogue:
All or part available online and in-house

Printed publications:
Historic Chelsea in Maps
Historic Kensington in Maps
Kensington and Chelsea Street Names
St Mary Abbots Church Registers; marriage entries
1676–1775
Kensington and Chelsea in old Photographs
(Barbara Denny and Carolyn Starren, £7.99)

Publications list:
Available in print

Access to staff:
Contact by letter, by telephone, by fax, by e-mail,
in person and via website
Hours: Mon, Tue, Thu, Fri, 0930 to 2000; Wed, Sat,
0930 to 1700

KENT AND EAST SUSSEX RAILWAY

Acronym or abbreviation: K&ESR

Tenterden Town Station, Tenterden, Kent, TN30
6HE

Tel: 01580 765155
Fax: 01580 765654
E-mail: enquiries@kesr.org.uk

Website:
http://www.kesr.org.uk

Enquiries:
Enquiries to: Commercial Manager
Other contacts: Bookings and Administration
Secretaries for general information and bookings.

Founded:
1971

Organisation type and purpose:
Voluntary organisation, registered charity.
Preserved steam railway operating between
Tenterden, Kent and Bodiam, East Sussex.

Access to staff:
Contact by letter, by telephone, by fax and by e-
mail
Hours: Mon to Fri, 0900 to 1700
Special comments: Trains run approximately 190
days per year – please telephone for timetable
details.

Access for disabled people:
Parking provided, ramped entry, level entry, toilet
facilities

KENT ARCHAEOLOGICAL SOCIETY

Acronym or abbreviation: KAS

The Museum, St Faith's Street, Maidstone, Kent,
ME14 1LH

E-mail: secretary@kentarchaeology.org.uk

Website:
http://www.kentarchaeology.org.uk

Enquiries:
Enquiries to: Librarian
Direct tel: 01795 472218
Direct fax: 01795 472218
Direct e-mail: dr.fh.panton@grove-end-tunstall
.fsnet.co.uk
Other contacts: Hon Gen Sec, email secretary@
kentarchaeology.org.uk

Founded:
1857

Organisation type and purpose:
Learned society, present number of members: c.
1300, voluntary organisation, registered charity
(charity number 2243382), suitable for ages: all,
training organisation, research organisation,
publishing house.
To promote the study and publication of
archaeology and history in all their branches,
especially within the ancient county of Kent.
Library open (on request to Hon. Librarian) to
bona fide non-members, lectures, training.

Subject coverage:
Fieldwork; vernacular architecture, historic
buildings and churches; Place names; visual
records; local history.

**Museum or gallery collection, archive, or library
special collection:**
Extensive collections on history etc, Kent, runs of
County, National (UK) and overseas (Western
Europe) publications on archaeological,
genealogical, numismatic, place names,
ecclesiastical records etc; manuscript material
held by Kent County Council Archives, Centre
for Kentish Studies

Non-library collection catalogue:
All or part available online

Library catalogue:
All or part available online and in-house

Printed publications:
Archaeologia Cantiana (one or more volumes
annually)
Newsletter (quarterly)
Research and records volumes
Order printed publications from: Assistant Secretary,
Ashton Lodge
Church Road, Lyminge, Folkestone, Kent, CT18
8JA, tel: 01303 862368, e-mail: history.research@
btinternet.com

Publications list:
Available in print

Access to staff:
Contact by letter, by telephone and by e-mail.
Appointment necessary. Letter of introduction
required.
Hours: Members: Mon to Sat, 1000 to 1630; Sun,
1100 to 1600 (other times by appointment) on
production of membership card and signing of
visitors book. For Non-members by appointment
with Hon. Librarian.

KENT COUNTY COUNCIL LIBRARIES AND ARCHIVES

Acronym or abbreviation: KCC Libraries and Archive

County Central Library, Springfield, Maidstone,
Kent, ME14 2LH

Tel: 01622 696511
Fax: 01622 696494
E-mail: libraries@kent.gov.uk

Website:
http://www.kent.gov.uk/libraries

Enquiries:
Enquiries to: Information Services Team
Direct tel: 01622 696438
Direct fax: 01622 696445
Direct e-mail: libraries.informationservices@kent
.gov.uk

Organisation type and purpose:
Public library

**Museum or gallery collection, archive, or library
special collection:**
Wide range of online databases
Canterbury Cathedral and City, archives
Centre for Kentish Studies, archives
East Kent Archives

Library catalogue:
All or part available online and in-house

Publications list:
Available online

Access to staff:
Contact by letter, by telephone, by fax, by e-mail, in person and via website

Access to building, collection or gallery:
Hours: Mon to Fri, 0900 to 1800; Sat, 0900 to 1700; check branch libraries online

Branch libraries:
Ashford Library
    Church Road, Ashford, TN23 1QX; tel: 01233 620649; fax: 01233 620295
Canterbury Library
    18 High Street, Canterbury, CT1 2JF; tel: 01227 463608; fax: 01227 768338
Dartford Library
    Central Park, Dartford; tel: 01322 221133; fax: 01322 278271
Dover Discovery Centre
    Market Square, Dover, CT16 1PH; tel: 01304 204241; fax: 01304 225914
Folkestone Library
    2 Grace Hill, Folkestone, CT20 1HD; tel: 01303 850123; fax: 01303 242907
Gravesend Library
    Windmill Street, Gravesend, DA12 1BE; tel: 01474 352758; fax: 01474 320284
Margate Library
    Thanet Gateway, Cecil Square, Margate, CT9 1RE; tel: 01843 223626; fax: 01843 293015
Sevenoaks Library
    Buckhurst Lane, Sevenoaks, TN13 1LQ; tel: 01732 453118; fax: 01732 742682
Sittingbourne Library
    Central Avenue, Sittingbourne, ME10 4AH; tel: 01795 476545; fax: 01795 428376
Tonbridge Library
    Avebury Avenue, Tonbridge, TN9 1TG; tel: 01732 352754; fax: 01732 358300
Tunbridge Wells Library
    Mount Pleasant Road, Tunbridge Wells, TN1 1NS; tel: 01892 522352; fax: 01892 514657

Member organisation of:
Association of Local Government Information Services
Chartered Institute of Librarians and Information Professionals (CILIP)
European Public Information Centre Network (EPIC)
International Association of Music Librarian
Kent Information and Libraries Network

KENT FAMILY HISTORY SOCIETY

Acronym or abbreviation: KFHS

Bullockstone Farm, Bullockstone Road, Herne Bay, Kent, CT6 7NL

Tel: 01227 363030
E-mail: kristn@globalnet.co.uk

Website:
http://www.kfhs.org.uk
Details of the society, recent publications with prices and ordering information.

Enquiries:
Enquiries to: Secretary

Founded:
1974

Organisation type and purpose:
International organisation, membership association (membership is by subscription), present number of members: 3500, voluntary organisation.
To promote interest in family history research in Kent.

Subject coverage:
Family history in Kent, including the diocese of Canterbury and part of the Rochester diocese.

Library catalogue:
All or part available in-house

Microform publications:
Approximately 2000 microfiche publications including:
New Members' Interest Directory up to December 2001
Complete Listing of Microfiche Publications, November 2001
Order microform publications from: Kent Family History Society
41 The Street, Kennington, Ashford, Kent, TN24 9HD

Electronic and video publications:
Some publications online

Publications list:
Available in print

Access to staff:
Contact by letter, by e-mail and via website. Non-members charged.
Hours: Mon to Fri, 0900 to 1700

KENT INSTITUTE OF ART AND DESIGN AT MAIDSTONE

Acronym or abbreviation: KIAD

Oakwood Park, Oakwood Road, Maidstone, Kent, ME16 8AG

Tel: 01622 757286
Fax: 01622 621100
E-mail: librarymaid@kiad.ac.uk

Website:
http://www.kiad.ac.uk
Prospectus, student and staff work, exhibition information etc, library catalogue.

Enquiries:
Enquiries to: Head of Library and Learning Resources
Direct e-mail: vcrane@kiad.ac.uk

Founded:
1988

Organisation type and purpose:
Suitable for ages: 18+.
College of higher and further education.
Art, design and architecture education.

Subject coverage:
Fine art, architecture, fashion design, interior design, graphic design, film and video, photography, jewellery and precious metalwork, ceramics, illustration.

Museum or gallery collection, archive, or library special collection:
Early printed books and books from private presses
Slide Collection

Library catalogue:
All or part available online

Access to staff:
Contact by letter. Appointment necessary. Letter of introduction required.
Hours: Mon to Fri, 0900 to 1900

Location:
Kent Institute of Art and Design
    New Dover Road, Canterbury, Kent, CT1 3AN; tel: 01227 769371; fax: 01227 817500; e-mail: librarycant@kiad.ac.uk
Kent Institute of Art and Design
    Fort Pitt, Rochester, Kent, ME1 1DZ; tel: 01634 830022; fax: 01634 820300; e-mail: libraryroch@kiad.ac.uk

KENT WILDLIFE TRUST

Tyland Barn, Sandling, Maidstone, Kent, ME14 3BD

Tel: 01622 662012
Fax: 01622 671390
E-mail: kentwildlife@cix.co.uk

Website:
http://www.kentwildlife.org.uk

Describes Kent Wildlife Trust, its work and how people can help.

Enquiries:
Enquiries to: Director

Founded:
1958

Organisation type and purpose:
Membership association (membership is by subscription), present number of members: 13,000, registered charity (charity number 239992).
One of 46 county wildlife trusts.
To secure a better future for the native wildlife of Kent.

Subject coverage:
Wildlife conservation in Kent.

Printed publications:
Please enquire

Access to staff:
Contact by letter, by telephone, by fax and by e-mail
Hours: Mon to Fri, 0900 to 1700

Parent body:
The Wildlife Trust

KERRIER DISTRICT COUNCIL

Dolcoath Avenue, Camborne, Cornwall, TR14 8SX

Tel: 01209 614000
Fax: 01209 614491
E-mail: kerrierdc@kerrier.gov.uk

Enquiries:
Enquiries to: Chief Executive
Other contacts: Marketing & Public Relations Officer for press/media enquiries.

Organisation type and purpose:
Local government body.

Subject coverage:
Local government services.

Printed publications:
A-Z of Council Services
Various departmental publications including:
Holiday Guide
Planning and Building Control Handbook
Civic Magazine
Kerrier Coast to Coast
Annual Performance (update)
Best Value Performance Plan
Order printed publications from: Marketing & Public Relations Officer, Kerrier District Council at the same address, tel: 01209 614000, fax: 01209 614494, e-mail: marketing@kerrier,gov,uk

Access to staff:
Contact by letter, by telephone, by fax and by e-mail
Hours: Mon to Fri, 0900 to 1700

Access to building, collection or gallery:
Prior appointment required
Hours: 0845 to 1715
Special comments: No prior appointment required for Revenues and Benefits

Access for disabled people:
Parking provided, level entry, toilet facilities

KESTON INSTITUTE

PO Box 752, Oxford, OX1 9QF

Tel: 01865 792929
Fax: 01865 240042
E-mail: admin@keston.org.uk

Website:
http://www.keston.org.uk/

Enquiries:
Enquiries to: Director

Founded:
1970

continued overleaf

Organisation type and purpose:
Registered charity (charity number 314103),
research organisation.

Subject coverage:
Keston promotes religious freedom and studies
religious affairs in the postcommunist and
communist world. With staff and correspondents
throughout its area including Moscow and Central
Asia, and a unique archive/library, Keston's quality
and objectivity is acknowledged worldwide by
believers, scholars, governments, and the
international news media. Keston's funding is
solely dependent upon charitable donations.

Printed publications:
Frontier (6 times a year, £12 per annum)
Religion, State and Society (quarterly, £45 per
annum)

Electronic and video publications:
Keston News Service (e-mail, £30 per annum)
Keston News Service Summary (weekly, email,
free of charge)

Publications list:
Available in print

Access to staff:
Contact by letter, by telephone, by fax, by e-mail
and via website. Appointment necessary. All
charged.
Hours: Mon to Fri, 0900 to 1700

KETTERING BOROUGH COUNCIL

Municipal Offices, Bowling Green Road, Kettering,
Northamptonshire, NN15 7QX

Tel: 01536 410333
Fax: 01536 532424
E-mail: customerservices@kettering.gov.uk

Website:
http://www.kettering.gov.uk
Community information, democratic information,
leisure information, business information.

Organisation type and purpose:
Local government body.

Subject coverage:
Information on the Borough of Kettering.

Education services:
via Northamptonshire County Council, tel: 01604
236236.

Services for disabled people:
via Northamptonshire County Council, tel: 01604
236236.

Printed publications:
Various information leaflets

Publications list:
Available online and in print

Access to staff:
Contact by letter, by telephone, by fax, by e-mail,
in person and via website. Appointment necessary.
Hours: Mon to Fri, 0830 to 1730; Sat, 0900 to 1300

Access for disabled people:
Parking provided, toilet facilities
Special comments: Access to all public areas

KEYGRAPHICA

Acronym or abbreviation: Keygraphica

PO Box 1381, Rugby, Warwickshire, CV21 2ZF

Tel: 01788 536389
Fax: 01788 550152
E-mail: keygraphica@assocnbureau.demon.co.uk

Enquiries:
Enquiries to: Secretary

Organisation type and purpose:
Trade association.

Subject coverage:
Artwork; photographic facilities; toolmaking;
anodising; etching; plating; litho and screen
printing; paint spraying; laminating; press work;
die cutting; stamping-embossing; casting; machine
engraving; injection moulding; standards.

KIDDERMINSTER LIBRARY

Market Street, Kidderminster, Worcestershire,
DY10 1AD

Tel: 01562 824500
Fax: 01562 512907
E-mail: kidderminsterlib@worcestershire.gov.uk

Website:
http://www.worcestershire.gov.uk/homepage.htm
County internet providing information on national
and local government, local clubs and community
groups, tourism, leisure and cultural activities.

Enquiries:
Enquiries to: Information Officer

Founded:
1855

Organisation type and purpose:
International organisation, membership
association (membership is by subscription), public
library, consultancy, research organisation.

Subject coverage:
General, including music; local studies on
Kidderminster and nearer parts of Salop in
particular, Worcestershire and Shropshire in
general; carpets and textiles.

**Museum or gallery collection, archive, or library
special collection:**
Carpet and Textile Collection
Local History Collection (Worcestershire and
Salop)

Non-library collection catalogue:
All or part available online

Printed publications:
Carpet and Textile Collection List (irregular)
Current Events (monthly)
Library guides and booklists and guides to the
Local Collection
Local Societies List (2 times a year)

Access to staff:
Contact by letter, by telephone, by fax, by e-mail,
in person and via website
Hours: Mon, Fri, 0930 to 1730; Tue,Wed, Thu, 0930
to 2000; Sat 0930 to 1730

Access for disabled people:
Access to all public areas, toilet facilities

Library of the:
Worcestershire County Libraries

KIDS

6 Aztec Row, Berners Road, London, N1 0PW

Tel: 020 7359 3635
Fax: 020 7359 3520
E-mail: enquiries@kids.org.uk

Website:
http://www.kids.org.uk

Enquiries:
Enquiries to: Information Officer

Founded:
1970

Formerly called:
Kids Active, HAPA

Organisation type and purpose:
Membership association, registered charity
(charity number 275936).
Working with disabled children, young people and
their families.

Subject coverage:
KIDS is the leading national voice for the policy
and practice of inclusive play. This is undertaken
by promoting inclusive play nationwide via
training, consultancy and publications, and by
providing play opportunities on seven adventure
playgrounds in London. KIDS works with disabled
children and their families. KIDS works in
partnership with parents to provide services which
aim to meet the full range of children's needs,
including educational, social, developmental and
emotional. These services include early years
education, play and leisure facilities, family
support, and advice.

Printed publications:
Newsletter (2 times a year)

Microform publications:
Photographs, slides

Publications list:
Available online and in print

KIDSCAPE

2 Grosvenor Gardens, London, SW1W 0DH

Tel: 020 7730 3300
Fax: 020 7730 7081
E-mail: contact@kidscape.org.uk

Website:
http://www.kidscape.org.uk
Child safety information, books available, updated
information and conference details.

Enquiries:
Enquiries to: Director

Founded:
1984

Organisation type and purpose:
Registered charity (charity number 326864),
training organisation, research organisation.

Subject coverage:
Child protection, anti-bullying.

Printed publications:
Booklets & leaflets (one copy available with sae
and 6 loose first class stamps)
Books
Posters

Electronic and video publications:
Videos for purchase about child protection and
bullying

Publications list:
Available online and in print

Access to staff:
Contact by letter, by telephone, by fax, by e-mail,
in person and via website. Appointment necessary.
Hours: Mon, Tue, 1000 to 2000; Wed to Fri, 1000 to
1600

KILVERT SOCIETY

The Secretary, Seend Park Farm,
Semington,Trowbridge, Wiltshire, BA14 7LH

E-mail: via website

Website:
http://www.communigate.co.uk/here/
kilvertsociety
Information on the Revd Francis Kilvert and The
Kilvert Society.

Enquiries:
Enquiries to: Honorary Secretary
Other contacts: Membership Secretary for enquiries
from prospective new members.

Founded:
1948

Organisation type and purpose:
Learned society (membership is by subscription),
present number of members: 646, voluntary
organisation.

To foster an interest in the Reverend Francis Kilvert, his work, his diary, and the countryside he loved.

Subject coverage:
Rev Francis Kilvert and his Diary.

Non-library collection catalogue:
All or part available in-house

Printed publications:
Kilvert's Kathleen Mavoureen (Farmery E and Taylor R B, £3)
Francis Kilvert (Lockwood D, 1990, £6.60)
Journal (3 times a year)
The Bevan-Dew Extracts
Order printed publications from: Publications Officer, Kilvert Society Publications, Tregothnan, Pentrosfa Crescent, Llandrindod Wells, Powys, LD1 5NW, tel: 01597 822062

Access to staff:
Contact by letter and by telephone
Hours: Mon to Fri, 0900 to 1700
Special comments: No personal callers.

Access to building, collection or gallery:
No prior appointment required

Other addresses:
Kilvert Society
25 Prospect Road, Abergavenny,
Monmouthshire, NP7 5DU; tel: 01873 857520
Membership Secretary

KING'S COLLEGE LIBRARY

King's College, Cambridge, CB2 1ST

Tel: 01223 331232
Fax: 01223 331891
E-mail: library@kings.cam.ac.uk

Website:
http://library.kings.cam.ac.uk

Enquiries:
Enquiries to: Librarian
Direct tel: 01223 331337
Other contacts: Archivist for modern manuscripts and college archives only; Rowe Music Librarian for the music collection.

Organisation type and purpose:
University department or institute.

Subject coverage:
Academic subjects, incorporating a music library.

Museum or gallery collection, archive, or library special collection:
English books printed before 1800
Incunabula
Keynes Library (English literature, including 17th century plays; manuscripts by and concerning Isaac Newton; works of a number of authors important in the history of thought. The Newton Manuscripts are available on microfilm in the University Library; modern Literary Papers in the fields of 20th century art, literature and economics including Rupert Brooke, E.M. Forster, T.S. Eliot and members of the Bloomsbury group. Papers of Economists (J.M. Keynes, J.M. Robinson, Richard Kahn, Nicholas Kaldor))
College's own administrative records, 11th – 21st centuries.
Rowe Music Library (collected works and scores; strong in 18th century music, especially Handel)

Non-library collection catalogue:
All or part available online, in-house and in print

Library catalogue:
All or part available online and in-house

Access to staff:
Contact by letter, by telephone, by fax, by e-mail, in person and via website. Appointment necessary. Access for members only. Letter of introduction required.
Hours: Mon to Fri, 0900 to 1730

KING'S COLLEGE LONDON – INFORMATION SERVICES CENTRE AT WESTON EDUCATION CENTRE

Cutcombe Road, London, SE5 9RJ

Tel: 020 7848 5541/2
Fax: 020 7848 5550
E-mail: janet.hopcroft@kcl.ac.uk

Website:
http://www.kcl.ac.uk/iss/library/denmark.html

Enquiries:
Enquiries to: Information Services Centre Manager
Direct tel: 020 7848 5554

Organisation type and purpose:
University library, NHS Trust

Subject coverage:
Clinical medicine and dentistry, health services, biomedical sciences.

Museum or gallery collection, archive, or library special collection:
Historical texts

Library catalogue
All or part available online

Access to staff:
Contact by letter, by telephone, by fax and by e-mail. Appointment necessary. Access for members only.
Hours: Mon to Fri, 0830 to 2100; Sat, 0930 to 1730; Sun, 1100 to 1900

Parent body:
King's College London
Strand, London, WC2R 2LS

KING'S COLLEGE LONDON – MAUGHAN LIBRARY AND INFORMATION SERVICES CENTRE

Chancery Lane, London, WC2R 1LR

Tel: 020 7848 2424
Fax: 020 7848 2277
E-mail: issenquiry@kcl.ac.uk

Website:
http://www.kcl.ac.uk/iss

Enquiries:
Enquiries to: Site Services Manager
Direct e-mail: vivien.robertson@kcl.ac.uk

Founded:
1829

Organisation type and purpose:
University library.

Subject coverage:
American studies, Australian studies, Byzantine and modern Greek, classics, cultural and creative industries, digital culture and technology, English, European studies, film studies, French, geography, German, history, linguistics, music, philosophy, Portuguese and Brazilian studies, Spanish and Spanish-American studies, theology and religious studies, war studies, law (including the Institute of Taxation's Tony Arnold Library), medical ethics, computer science, engineering, mathematics and physics

Museum or gallery collection, archive, or library special collection:
Adam Collection (20th-century poetry, Romanian and French literature)
Box Collection (Hebrew and Old Testament studies)
Carnegie Collection of British Music (early 20th-century British music)
Cohn Collection (German and Swiss Law)
De Beer Collection (works on or about Charles Darwin)
Early Science Collection (science and technology mainly 1800–1915)

Foreign and Commonwealth Office Historical Collection (European diplomatic history, British colonial history, voyages and travels, international law and relations)
Glaessner Collection (history of the German Democratic Republic)
Guy's Hospital Medical School Historical Collection (medicine pre-1900)
Guy's Hospital Physical Society Collection (science and pre-1900 medicine)
H. G. Adler Collection (history of the Holocaust)
Hamilton Collection (military history and poetry)
Institute for the Study and Treatment of Delinquency Collection (the causes of crime and the punishment, treatment and rehabilitation of offenders)
Institute of Psychiatry Historical Collection (psychology and psychiatry)
Kantorowicz Collection (German literature and Juadaica)
King's College School of Medicine and Dentistry (pre-1900 medicine)
Marsden Collection (philology, early Bibles, voyages and travels)
Maurice Collection (19th-century military history)
Mottram Collection (English and American literature)
Rainbow Collection (liturgical music)
Rare Books Collection (mostly pre-1801 items in a wide range of subjects, including, science, classics, travel, theology, Portuguese studies, Greece and the eastern Mediterranean)
Ratcliff Collection (liturgy and church history)
Relton Collection (ecclesiastical history and Christian dogmatic theology)
Ruggles Gates Collection (genetics, eugenics, botany)
Skeat and Furnivall Collection (Old and Middle English, Elizabethan literature, linguistics, philology)
St Thomas's Hospital Historical Medical Collection (medicine)
Stebbing Collection (marine zoology)
Wheatstone Collection (physics, telegraphy)

Non-library collection catalogue:
All or part available online and in-house

Library catalogue:
All or part available online

Access to staff:
Contact by letter, by telephone, by fax and by e-mail. Non-members charged.
Hours: Term time: Mon to Fri, 0830 to 2030; Sat, 0930 to 1730; Sun, 1100 to 1900; check website for vacation opening hours

Access to building, collection or gallery:
Hours: Term time: Mon to Fri, 0830 to 2200; Sat, 0930 to 1730; Sun, 1100 to 1900; check website for vacation opening hours

Access for disabled people:
Ramps to entrance, lifts provide access to most of building, induction loops at service desks

Constituent part of:
University of London

KING'S COLLEGE LONDON – NEW HUNT'S HOUSE INFORMATION SERVICES CENTRE

Guy's Campus, London, SE1 1UL

Tel: 020 7848 6740
Fax: 020 7848 6743
E-mail: andrew.baster@kcl.ac.uk

Website:
http://www.kcl.ac.uk

Enquiries:
Enquiries to: Manager

Founded:
1903

Organisation type and purpose:
University library.

continued overleaf

Subject coverage:
Medical and related sciences, medical librarianship and information work, dental science, history of medicine.

Museum or gallery collection, archive, or library special collection:
Historical collection of printed books
Books by Guy's Men 19th and 20th Centuries

Library catalogue:
All or part available online

Printed publications:
Readers' Guides

Access to staff:
Contact by letter, by telephone, by fax and by e-mail. Appointment necessary.
Hours: Term time: Mon to Fri, 0900 to 2045, Sat, 0900 to 1645
Vacations: Mon to Fri, 0900 to 1900

Member of:
South Thames Regional Library and Information Service

Other addresses:
King's College London
    Warner Dental Library

Parent body:
University of London

KING'S COLLEGE LONDON – ST THOMAS' HOSPITAL MEDICAL LIBRARY

Acronym or abbreviation: KCL

Lambeth Palace Road, London, SE1 7EH

Tel: 020 7188 3740
Fax: 020 7401 3932
E-mail: thomdesk@kcl.ac.uk

Website:
http://www.kcl.ac.uk/iss

Enquiries:
Enquiries to: NHS Information Specialist
Direct tel: 020 7188 3744
Direct e-mail: sarah.lawson@kcl.ac.uk

Founded:
1903

Organisation type and purpose:
University library, NHS Trust.

Subject coverage:
Medicine, health care, history of medicine.

Museum or gallery collection, archive, or library special collection:
History of St Thomas' Hospital
Printed books and manuscripts on medicine and related sciences

Library catalogue:
All or part available online

Access to staff:
Contact by letter, by telephone, by fax and by e-mail. Appointment necessary.
Hours: Term time: Mon to Fri, 0900 to 2100 (reference use only from 1900);
Vacations: 0900 to 1700

Access for disabled people:
Special comments: By appointment during opening hours; please contact thomdesk@kcl.ac.uk; limited access to all floors

Member of:
South Thames Regional Library and Information Service
    website: www.londonlinks.ac.uk

Parent body:
University of London
    Senate House, Malet Street, London, WC1E 7HU; tel: 020 7862 8000; website: www.lon.ac.uk

KING'S COLLEGE LONDON – STAMFORD STREET INFORMATION SERVICES CENTRE

Acronym or abbreviation: KCL

Franklin-Wilkins Building, 150 Stamford Street, London, SE1 8WA

Tel: 020 7848 4498
Fax: 020 7848 4290
E-mail: peter.walsh@kcl.ac.uk

Website:
http://www.kcl.ac.uk

Enquiries:
Enquiries to: Manager

Founded:
1829

Organisation type and purpose:
University library.

Subject coverage:
Education, life sciences, management, nutrition, nursing, pharmacy.

Museum or gallery collection, archive, or library special collection:
Listed under the Strand Campus entry

Library catalogue:
All or part available online

Access to staff:
Contact by letter and by telephone
Hours: Mon to Fri, 0900 to 2100; Sat, 0930 to 1730

Also at:
Director of Library Services (no library at this address)
    King's College London, London, WC2R 2LS; tel: 020 7848 2139; fax: 020 7848 1777; website: http://www.kcl.ac.uk/depsta/iss/servicesindex.html
Information Services Centre
    New Hunt's House, Guys Hospital, St Thomas Street, London, SE1 9RT; tel: 020 7848 6600; fax: 020 7848 6743; website: http://www.kcl.ac.uk/depsta/iss/sites/guys/topguys.html
Information Services Centre
    Franklin-Wilkins Building, 150 Stamford Street, London, SE1 9NN; tel: 020 7848 4378; website: http://www.kcl.ac.uk/depsta/iss/sites/waterloo/topwaterloo.html
King's College London
    Strand, London, WC2R 2LS
Library and Information Services Centre
    Chancery Lane, London, WC2A 1LR; tel: 020 7848 2424; fax: 020 7848 2277; website: http://www.kcl.ac.uk/depsta/iss/sites/chancery/index.html
Medical Library
    Weston Education Centre, Cutcombe Road, London, SE5 9JP; tel: 020 7848 5541; fax: 020 7848 5550; website: http://www.kcl.ac.uk/depsta/iss/sites/denmarkhill/topdenmarkhill.ht
Medical Library
    St Thomas' Hospital, Lambeth Palace Road, London, SE1 7EH; tel: 020 7928 9292 ext 2367; fax: 020 7401 3932; website: http://www.kcl.ac.uk/depsta/iss/sites/stthomas/topthomas.html

KING'S FUND

11–13 Cavendish Square, London, W1G 0AN

Tel: 020 7307 2400
Fax: 020 7307 2801

Website:
http://www.kingsfund.org.uk

Enquiries:
Enquiries to: Chief Executive
Other contacts: Director of Corporate Affairs

Founded:
1897

Organisation type and purpose:
Registered charity (charity number 207401), training organisation, research organisation.

To promote good health in London to reduce inequalities in health, promote the benefits of diversity, to involve the public in health policymaking and to break down boundaries between organisations working for health.

Subject coverage:
Health care (not clinical medicine), grant making, training and education, social care and policy and public health.

Museum or gallery collection, archive, or library special collection:
Health Services library; reports and journals in health and social care

Printed publications:
Reports of Studies dealing with subjects such as; acute care, carers, community care, ethics and consensus, health and race, health services management, inequalities in health, learning difficulties, London, medical education, medical technology, mental health, nursing, patient choice, physical disability, primary health care, user view and surveys
Order printed publications from: King's Fund Bookshop
at the same address, tel: 020 7307 2591, e-mail: bookshop@kingsfund.org.uk

Publications list:
Available online and in print

Access to staff:
Contact by letter, by telephone and in person
Hours: Mon to Fri, 0900 to 1700

Access to building, collection or gallery:
No prior appointment required

Access for disabled people:
Parking provided, level entry, access to all public areas, toilet facilities

KING'S FUND INFORMATION AND LIBRARY SERVICE

Formal name: King Edward's Hospital Fund for London

11–13 Cavendish Square, London, W1G 0AN

Tel: 020 7307 2568
Fax: 020 7307 2805
E-mail: library@kingsfund.org.uk

Website:
http://www.kingsfund.org.uk
The site provides the latest information about King's Fund work projects, publications and research findings. It explains how to apply for a Fund grant, or to attend one of the Fund's education and leadership development programmes. It has an extensive links section.

Enquiries:
Enquiries to: Librarian

Founded:
1897

Organisation type and purpose:
Registered charity.
To improve the health of, and health care for, Londoners.

Subject coverage:
Health care policy, social care policy, planning, organisation and management; hospital and community-based health services in the UK.

Museum or gallery collection, archive, or library special collection:
350 current serial titles
30,000 items including grey literature
Collection of NHS Policy Reports (earliest 1897)
Department of Health Circulars
King's Fund Publications
WHO – Regional Office for Europe Publications

Non-library collection catalogue:
All or part available online and in-house

Library catalogue:
All or part available online and in print

Printed publications:
Library Guide (available free)
Reading lists on popular topics (available free on the web)
Current journals list (available free in paper and on the web)

Electronic and video publications:
HMIC (online and CD-ROM) comprising databases of the King's Fund Library and the Department of Health
Current Awareness Bulletin (every 2 weeks, by email, subscription service)
News alert on health policy issues (twice-weekly, by email, free)

Publications list:
Available online and in print

Access to staff:
Contact by letter, by telephone, by fax, by e-mail, in person and via website
Hours: Mon, Tue, Thu, Fri, 0930 to 1730; Wed, 1100 to 1730; Sat, 0930 to 1700.

Access for disabled people:
Level entry, access to all public areas, toilet facilities

KING'S LYNN LIBRARY

London Road, King's Lynn, Norfolk, PE30 5EZ

Tel: 01553 772568 or 761393
Fax: 01553 769832
E-mail: kings.lynn.lib@norfolk.gov.uk

Website:
http://www.library.norfolk.gov.uk
Norfolk electronic library, library catalogue, information about services provided by Norfolk Libraries, local information.

Enquiries:
Enquiries to: Manager
Other contacts: Community Librarian

Founded:
1904

Organisation type and purpose:
Local government body, public library.

Subject coverage:
General, history of King's Lynn and West Norfolk.

Museum or gallery collection, archive, or library special collection:
St Margaret's Library Collection (founded 1631)
St Nicholas' Library Collection (founded 1617)
Stanley Library Collection (founded 1854)
Medical, historical, religious and travel works of 15th to 19th centuries

Non-library collection catalogue:
All or part available in-house

Library catalogue:
All or part available online

Access to staff:
Contact by letter, by telephone, by fax, by e-mail and in person
Hours: Mon to Fri, 0900 to 1700

Access for disabled people:
Ramped entry

Parent body:
Norfolk County Council Library and Information Service

KINGSTON LIBRARIES

Kingston Library, Fairfield Road, Kingston upon Thames, Surrey, KT1 2PS

Tel: 020 8547 6400
Fax: 020 8547 6401

Website:
http://www.kingston.gov.uk/Enjoying/Libraries/default.htm
Library catalogue, community information, opening hours, library services, online reference.

Enquiries:
Enquiries to: Head of Library Services
Direct tel: 020 8547 6413
Direct fax: 020 8547 6426
Direct e-mail: jo.gloyn@rbk.kingston.gov.uk
Other contacts: Information Librarian

Founded:
1902

Organisation type and purpose:
Local government body, public library.

Subject coverage:
General, English literature, fine arts, statistics, non-HMSO and HMSO government publications.

Library catalogue:
All or part available online

Access to staff:
Contact by letter, by telephone, by fax and by e-mail. Appointment necessary.
Hours: Mon, 0930 to 1900; Tue and Fri, 0930 to 1730; Wed, closed; Thu, 0930 to 2000; Sat, 0900 to 1730

Access for disabled people:
Ramped entry, access to all public areas

Parent body:
Royal Borough of Kingston upon Thames

KINGSTON UNIVERSITY

Information Services, Penrhyn Road, Kingston Upon Thames, Surrey, KT1 2EE

Tel: 020 8547 2000
Fax: 020 8417 2111
E-mail: library@kingston.ac.uk

Website:
http://www.kingston.ac.uk/library
Addresses, opening hours, subject coverage, catalogues.

Enquiries:
Enquiries to: Director of Information Services

Organisation type and purpose:
University library.

Subject coverage:
Business, law, chemistry, pharmacy, life sciences, mathematics, computer science, surveying, civil, mechanical, production and aeronautical engineering, geography, geology, art and design, architecture, performing art, social sciences, economics, history, English, education, healthcare studies.

Museum or gallery collection, archive, or library special collection:
Iris Murdoch Collections, Vane Ivanovic Library, Sheridan Morley Theatre Collection

Non-library collection catalogue:
All or part available online

Library catalogue:
All or part available online

Printed publications:
Library guides

Access to staff:
Contact by letter, by telephone, by e-mail, in person and via website
Hours: Mon to Fri, 0900 to 1700
Special comments: Please see website for full details.

Access to building, collection or gallery:
Special comments: Visitors are advised to carry identification.

KINGSTON UPON HULL CITY LIBRARIES

Hull Central Library, Albion Street, Hull, East Yorkshire, HU1 3TF

Tel: 01482 210055/66/223344
Fax: 01482 616858
E-mail: rosemary.reed@hullcc.gov.uk

Website:
http://www.hullcc.gov.uk
General information on the library departments, Council, local interest, libraries and museums, business.

Enquiries:
Enquiries to: Librarian
Direct e-mail: reference.library@hullcc.gov.uk

Founded:
1996

Organisation type and purpose:
Local government body, public library.

Subject coverage:
General, food technology, fish and fishing industry, paint and organic chemicals, edible oils, ports, pharmaceuticals, building industry, business information, reference enquiries, local information for Kingston upon Hull, family history, slavery, literature, arts, religion.

Museum or gallery collection, archive, or library special collection:
Andrew Marvell
British Standards (CD-ROM)
Civil War
Corporation Health Department photographs
Forster and Andrews Organ Builders
IGI (microfiche)
Lloyds Registers (1760 to present day)
Napoleon
Nonconformist religions during the reign of Charles I
Regimental histories
Slavery
Substantial range of international directories, indexes and standards
Whaling
William Wilberforce
Winifred Holtby Collection

Trade and statistical information:
Range of statistical information, European Public Information Centre (EPIC), market research info.

Non-library collection catalogue:
All or part available in-house

Library catalogue:
All or part available online

Printed publications:
Forgotten Hull (Wilkinson G and Watkins G, £12.75)
Dan Billany (Reeves V A and Showan V, £6.95)
Lost Pubs of Hull (Wilkinson G and Gibson P, £12.75)
Town and Gun (Howes A and Foreman M, £9.95)
Wilberforce & Hull (Deverell L and Watkins G)
Order printed publications from: Kingston Press at the same address, tel: 01482 616814, fax: 01482 616827, e-mail: steve@hullcc.demon.co.uk

Publications list:
Available online and in print

Access to staff:
Contact by letter, by telephone, by fax, by e-mail, in person and via website
Hours: Mon to Thu, 0930 to 2000; Fri 0930 to 1730; Sat 0900 to 1630

Access to building, collection or gallery:
Hours: Mon to Thu, 0930 to 2000; Fri 0930 to 1730; Sat 0900 to 1630

Access for disabled people:
Ramped entry, toilet facilities
Special comments: Limited access to some departments: Local Studies Library, Music and Multimedia Library.

Has:
1 central, 16 branch libraries

KIPLING SOCIETY

6 Clifton Road, London, W9 1SS

Tel: 020 7286 0194
Fax: 020 7286 0194
E-mail: jane@keskar.fsworld.co.uk

continued overleaf

Website:
http://www.kipling.org.uk

Enquiries:
Enquiries to: Honorary Secretary
Other contacts: Honorary Librarian for the library

Founded:
1927

Organisation type and purpose:
Learned society (membership is by subscription), registered charity (charity number 2758885).

Subject coverage:
Life, works and associations of Rudyard Kipling 1865–1936.

Museum or gallery collection, archive, or library special collection:
Library of books on and by R Kipling

Library catalogue:
All or part available in-house

Printed publications:
The Kipling Journal (quarterly, from 1927 onwards)

Access to staff:
Contact by letter, by telephone, by fax, by e-mail and via website
Hours: Mon to Fri, 0900 to 1700
Special comments: Library open to members only, by appointment.

Access to building, collection or gallery:
No prior appointment required

Library housed at:
City University
  Northampton Square, London; tel: 020 7359 2464

Representative in:
USA and Australia

KIRKLEES COLLEGE – HUDDERSFIELD CENTRE

Acronym or abbreviation: KC

Library, New North Road, Huddersfield, West Yorkshire, HD1 5NN

Tel: 01484 536521
Fax: 01484 511885
E-mail: library@kirkleescollege.ac.uk

Website:
http://www.huddcoll.ac.uk

Enquiries:
Enquiries to: Librarian
Direct e-mail: libraryenquiries@kirkleescollege.ac.uk

Created by the merger of:
Huddersfield Technical College and Dewsbury College (year of change 2008)

Subject coverage:
Business studies, catering, engineering, science, construction, computing, music, social work, leisure and recreation, motor vehicle technology, education and training, art and design, hairdressing, animal care sciences.

Library catalogue:
All or part available online and in-house

Electronic and video publications:
CD-ROMs, videos, DVDs, Shibboleth access to databases, journals

Access to staff:
Contact by letter, by telephone, by fax, by e-mail and in person. Appointment necessary.
Hours: Mon to Thu, 0845 to 2000; Fri, 0845 to 1600

Access for disabled people:
Parking provided, level entry, access to all public areas, toilet facilities
Special comments: Lifts for disabled

KIRKLEES METROPOLITAN BOROUGH COUNCIL

Cultural Services Headquarters, Red Doles Lane, Huddersfield, West Yorkshire, HD2 1YF

Tel: 01484 226300
Fax: 01484 226342
E-mail: jonathan.drake@kirkleesmc.gov.uk

Website:
http://www.kirkleesmc.gov.uk

Enquiries:
Enquiries to: Head of Service
Other contacts: (1) Assistant Head of Service (2) Assistant Head of Service for (1) libraries and information service (2) community history, arts and town halls.

Organisation type and purpose:
Local government body, museum, art gallery, public library.

Subject coverage:
Local government services.

Library catalogue:
All or part available in-house

Printed publications:
Publications include:
Happy Inspiration: the story of Castle Hill and its Tower (Bywater H)
Heritage of Huddersfield (Schofield I)
History of the Huddersfield Fire Brigade (Smith C)
Huddersfield: A Most Handsom Town (Haigh E A H)
Oakwell Hall
Three in a Bed: memories of a Dewsbury lass (Braybrook I)
Order printed publications from: Bibliographical Services, at the same address, tel: 01484 226374, fax: 01484 226342, e-mail: julie.peel@kirkleesmc.gov.uk

Publications list:
Available in print

Access to staff:
Contact by letter, by telephone, by fax, by e-mail, in person and via website
Hours: Mon to Fri, 0900 to 1700

KITE SOCIETY OF GREAT BRITAIN

Acronym or abbreviation: KSGB

PO Box 2274, Great Horkesley, Colchester, Essex, CO6 4AY

Tel: 01206 271489
Fax: 01206 271489
E-mail: info@thekitesociety.org.uk

Website:
http://www.thekitesociety.org.uk

Enquiries:
Enquiries to: General Secretary

Founded:
1979

Organisation type and purpose:
Membership association.

Subject coverage:
Kite design, kite groups, kite events, kite shops, kite-flying.

Printed publications:
Kite Design Booklets
Kite Material Suppliers Booklet
Kitefliers Handbook
The Kiteflier (newsletter, quarterly)

Access to staff:
Contact by letter, by telephone, by fax and by e-mail
Hours: Mon to Fri, 0900 to 1700

Has:
most local kite groups as affiliates

KNITTING & CROCHET GUILD OF GREAT BRITAIN

PO Box 4421, Kidderminster, Worcestershire, DY11 6YW

Website:
http://www.knitting-and-crochet-guild.org.uk

Organisation type and purpose:
A registered national educational charity (no. 01113468).

Subject coverage:
Knitting and crochet.

Museum or gallery collection, archive, or library special collection:
Library of books, periodicals and patterns
Collection of garments, samples, domestic knitting machines, yarns, tools and ephemera from the past two hundred years

KNITTING INDUSTRIES' FEDERATION

Acronym or abbreviation: KIF

12 Beaumanor Road, Leicester, LE1 5XY

Tel: 0116 266 3332
Fax: 0116 266 3335
E-mail: directorate@knitfed.co.uk

Enquiries:
Enquiries to: Director

Founded:
1942

Organisation type and purpose:
Trade association (membership is by subscription), present number of members: 300, manufacturing industry.

Subject coverage:
Industrial relations, trade policy, government lobbying, environment, health and safety statistics.

Trade and statistical information:
Knitstats – comprehensive summary of knitting industry statistics.

Printed publications:
Industry Analysis 1993 to 1997 (£75)
Knitstats (£50)

Access to staff:
Contact by letter, by telephone, by fax and by e-mail. Appointment necessary. Non-members charged.
Hours: Mon to Fri, 0900 to 1700

Access to building, collection or gallery:
No prior appointment required

A sector of the:
British Clothing Industry Association Limited

KNOWSLEY LIBRARY SERVICE

Huyton Library, Civic Way, Huyton, Knowsley, Merseyside, L36 9GD

Tel: 0151 443 3738
Fax: 0151 443 3739
E-mail: huyton.reference.library.dlcs@knowsley.gov.uk

Website:
http://history.knowsley.gov.uk
Local history of Knowsley Borough and its townships including text, images, maps, town trails, audio clips etc.
http://www.knowsley.gov.uk
Information on Knowsley Metropolitan Borough Council, including libraries.

Enquiries:
Enquiries to: Information Services Manager

Organisation type and purpose:
Local government body, public library.

Subject coverage:
General and local history.

Museum or gallery collection, archive, or library special collection:
Local history of Knowsley Metropolitan Borough

Library catalogue:
All or part available in-house

Printed publications:
Archive Photography Series – Huyton with Roby
Archive Photography Series – Kirkby and Knowsley
Huyton and Roby: A History of The Townships
Inns of Prescot and Whiston
Tracing your Family History in the Knowsley Area at Huyton Library
Whiston: A Young Person's Guide

Publications list:
Available in print

Access to staff:
Contact by letter, by telephone, by fax, by e-mail, in person and via website
Hours: Mon to Fri, 0915 to 1900; Sat, 1000 to 1600; Sun, 1200 to 1600

Access for disabled people:
Parking provided, ramped entry, level entry, access to all public areas, toilet facilities

KODAK EUROPEAN RESEARCH

332 Science Park, Cambridge, CB4 0WN

Tel: 01223 228010
Fax: 01223 426202
E-mail: gb-cambridge-enquiries@kodak.com

Website:
http://www.kodak.com

Founded:
2006

Organisation type and purpose:
Manufacturing industry.

Subject coverage:
Photographic science and technology; related disciplines in science and technology.

Museum or gallery collection, archive, or library special collection:
Archive of books on photographic processes
Biographies of early photographic scientists

Printed publications:
Instructional and promotional material for users

Access to staff:
Appointment necessary.
Hours: Mon to Fri, 0900 to 1700

KODÁLY INSTITUTE OF BRITAIN

Acronym or abbreviation: KIB

Queen's Gate School, 133 Queen's Gate, London, SW7 5LE

Tel: 020 7823 7371 or 020 7589 3056
Fax: 020 7584 7691

Enquiries:
Enquiries to: Administrator
Other contacts: Director

Founded:
1994

Organisation type and purpose:
International organisation, professional body (membership is by subscription), present number of members: 150, training organisation.
Music education/training for adults using the Kodály concept.

Subject coverage:
Principles and practice of the Kodály concept.

Printed publications:
The Kodály Way to Music, Book 1 by Cecilia Vajda (book for purchase)
The Kodály Way to Music, Book 2 by Cecilia Vajda (book for purchase)

Electronic and video publications:
Early Childhood Music Education (video for hire)
Musicianship Training at Key Stage 2 (video for hire)
Musicianship Training at Key Stage 3 (video, for purchase)
Series of five Musicianship Training (cassettes, for purchase)
Sing and Play – The Kodály Way (cassette for purchase)
The Kodály Concept (video for purchase)

Publications list:
Available in print

Access to staff:
Contact by letter, by telephone and by fax.
Appointment necessary.
Hours: Mon to Sun, 0900 to 2200

Parent body:
International Kodály Society
Budapest, Hungary

Subsidiary:
Liszt Academy of Music
Budapest

KOREA NATIONAL TOURISM ORGANIZATION

Acronym or abbreviation: KNTO

3rd Floor, New Zealand House, Haymarket, London, SW1Y 4TE

Tel: 020 7321 2535
Fax: 020 7321 0876
E-mail: london@mail.knto.or.kr

Website:
http://www.tour2korea.com

Enquiries:
Enquiries to: Director
Other contacts: Marketing Manager

Founded:
1960

Organisation type and purpose:
National government body.
Tourist office.
To promote travel and tourism to South Korea.

Subject coverage:
Tourism in Korea.

Printed publications:
Available free, directly – generally

Publications list:
Available online

Access to staff:
Contact by letter, by telephone, by fax, by e-mail, in person and via website. Appointment necessary.
Access for members only.
Hours: Mon to Fri, 0900 to 1700

Access to building, collection or gallery:
Hours: Mon to Fri, 0900 to 1700

Access for disabled people:
Access to all public areas

Has:
over 50 overseas branches

KPMG

Acronym or abbreviation: KPMG

20 Farringdon Street, London, EC4A 4PP

Tel: 020 7311 1000
Fax: 020 7311 3311

Enquiries:
Enquiries to: Tax Librarian
Direct tel: 020 7311 3970
Direct fax: 020 7311 3886
Direct e-mail: john.ridgley@kpmg.co.uk

Organisation type and purpose:
Accounting and management consultancy.

Subject coverage:
Accountancy; auditing; company law; corporate finance; taxation; management in many countries and various industries.

Non-library collection catalogue:
All or part available in-house

Access to staff:
Contact by telephone, by fax and by e-mail.
Appointment necessary. Access for members only.
Hours: Mon to Fri, 0930 to 1730

Access to building, collection or gallery:
No prior appointment required

LA LECHE LEAGUE (GREAT BRITAIN)

Acronym or abbreviation: LLLGB

PO Box 29, West Bridgford, Nottingham, NG2 7NP

Tel: 0845 456 1866\ 0115 981 5599
Fax: 0845 4561877\ 0115 981 5597
E-mail: lllgb@wsds.co.uk

Website:
http://www.laleche.org.uk
About the organisation and its services.
http://www.lllbooks.org.uk
Publications and how to order them.

Enquiries:
Enquiries to: Administrator

Founded:
1973

Organisation type and purpose:
Membership association (membership is by subscription), present number of members: 1000, registered charity (charity number 283771).
To provide information, help and support to mothers wanting to breastfeed.

Subject coverage:
Breastfeeding.

Non-library collection catalogue:
All or part available online and in print

Printed publications:
The Womanly Art of Breastfeeding (6th ed, 465pp, £14.99)
Breastfeeding Your Premature Baby (Gotsch G, 56pp, £6.99)
Books and leaflets on breastfeeding and family life including:
The Breastfeeding Answer Book (Mohrbacher N and Stock J, 2nd ed, 608pp, £48)
Order printed publications from: LLL Books Ltd
PO Box 29, West Bridgford, Nottingham, NG2 7NP

Publications list:
Available online and in print

Access to staff:
Contact by letter and by telephone
Hours: 24-hour helpline
Office admin: Mon to Fri, 0900 to 1800

Access to building, collection or gallery:
No access other than to staff

Other address:
LLLGB
Administrative Office, PO Box 29, West Bridgford, Nottingham, NG2 7NP; tel: 0115 945 5772

LABAN CENTRE LONDON

Formal name: Laban Centre for Movement and Dance Limited

14–18 Creekside, Deptford, London, SE8 3DZ

Tel: 020 8692 4070 ext 120
Fax: 020 8694 8749
E-mail: library@laban.co.uk

Website:
http://www.laban.co.uk

Enquiries:
Enquiries to: Librarian

continued overleaf

Organisation type and purpose:
Registered charity (charity number 801973),
suitable for ages: 18+.

Subject coverage:
Practical and academic education in dance and
movement, all kinds of dance: ballet,
contemporary, social, theatre, community, dance
therapy and related subjects e.g. anatomy, music,
psychology, scenography, dance notation, Rudolf
Laban, dance medicine, Pilates, European Tanz
theatre.

**Museum or gallery collection, archive, or library
special collection:**
Grey Literature
Laban Collection (Laban's work in Germany, 1920–
    1930s) – microfiche
Other printed and audio visual materials
Peter Williams Collection (books, photographs,
    manuscripts etc, 1930–1995)
Peter Brinson Collection (sociology, education,
    working archive of 'Ballet for All')
Shirley Wynn Collection (historical dance,
    notation)

Non-library collection catalogue:
All or part available in-house

Library catalogue:
All or part available in-house

Printed publications:
Book List – see website
Dance Theatre Journal (4 times a year)

Publications list:
Available online

Access to staff:
Contact by letter, by telephone, by fax, by e-mail,
in person and via website. Appointment necessary.
Non-members charged.
Hours: Term time: Mon, Wed & Thu, 0900 to 2000;
Tue, 0900 to 1930; Fri, 0900 to 1700; Sat, 1030 to
1430
Vacations: Mon to Fri, 0900 to 1700

LABAN GUILD FOR MOVEMENT AND DANCE

5/24 Westcote Road, Reading, Berkshire, RG30 2DE

Tel: 0118 961 6903

Enquiries:
Enquiries to: Secretary

Founded:
1946

Organisation type and purpose:
International organisation, membership
association (membership is by subscription),
present number of members: 400, registered
charity, voluntary organisation (charity number
266435).
To promote and advance the study of Laban based
movement and dance.

Subject coverage:
We are an organisation which provides a resource
for its members within which they can experience
teaching, development, exchange of information
and a sense of identity. We promote the
development of movement as an art form, the
study of human movement, particularly
recognising the contribution made by the late
Rudolf Laban.

Printed publications:
Magazine (quarterly)

Access to staff:
Contact by letter
Hours: Mon to Fri, 0900 to 1700

LABORATORY ANIMAL SCIENCE ASSOCIATION

Acronym or abbreviation: LASA

PO Box 3993, Tamworth, Staffordshire, B78 3QU

Tel: 01827 259130

Fax: 01827 259188
E-mail: lasa@globalnet.co.uk

Website:
http://www.lasa.co.uk

Enquiries:
Enquiries to: Secretary

Organisation type and purpose:
Learned society (membership is by subscription).
Advancement of care, welfare and use of animals
and replacement where appropriate.

Subject coverage:
Animal welfare, refinement in animal studies,
alternatives to animal use, education, training in
laboratory animal science, laboratory animal
health, regulatory controls over uses of laboratory
animals, laboratory animal genetics, laboratory
animal nutrition, toxicology tests, management of
laboratory animal units.

Printed publications:
Newsletter (quarterly, members only)
Laboratory Animals (quarterly)

Publications list:
Available in print

Access to staff:
Contact by letter, by telephone, by fax and by e-
mail
Hours: Mon to Fri, 0900 to 1700

Affiliated to:
Federation of European Laboratory Animal
Science Associations (FELASA)

LABOUR PARTY

Eldon House, Regent Centre, Newcastle Upon
Tyne, NE3 3PW

Tel: 08705 900 200

Website:
http://www.labour.org.uk/

Organisation type and purpose:
Internal resource centre of a political party.

Subject coverage:
Social sciences, especially politics, labour history.

**Museum or gallery collection, archive, or library
special collection:**
Archives of the Labour Party held at National
    Museum of Labour History, 103 Princess Street,
    Manchester M1 6DD, Tel no: 0161 228 7212

Access to staff:
Contact by letter, by telephone, by fax and by e-
mail
Hours: No access

LABOUR RELATIONS AGENCY

Acronym or abbreviation: LRA

Head Office, 2–8 Gordon Street, Belfast, BT1 2LG

Tel: 028 9032 1442\ Minicom no. 028 9023 8411
Fax: 028 9033 0827
E-mail: info@lra.org.uk

Website:
http://www.lra.org.uk

Enquiries:
Enquiries to: Director
Other contacts: (1) Director (Corporate Services) (2)
Director (Advisory Services) (3) Director
(Conciliation and Arbitration)

Founded:
1976

Organisation type and purpose:
Statutory body.
Provides mediation, arbitration, conciliation and
advisory services to employers, trade unions etc
and issues codes of practice on employment
relations matters.

Subject coverage:
Joint consultative and negotiating machinery,
employment relations legislation, internal relations
and communications, grievance, disciplinary,
dismissal and redundancy procedures, trade union
recognition, terms and conditions of employment,
recruitment, selection and induction, payment
systems and job evaluation, manpower planning,
labour turnover and absenteeism, employment
relations research, training, maternity provisions
and legislation, equality legislation.

Printed publications:
Annual Reports
Codes of Practice; Research Reports; Advisory
    Guides
Information Notes Series covering various
    employment relations topics
Review of Employment Topics (peer-reviewed
    journal 1993 to 1997)

Publications list:
Available online and in print

Access to staff:
Contact by letter, by telephone, by fax, by e-mail
and in person. Appointment necessary.
Hours: Mon to Fri, 0900 to 1700

Access to building, collection or gallery:
No prior appointment required

Access for disabled people:
Ramped entry, level entry, access to all public
areas, toilet facilities
Special comments: Parking provided at head office.

Regional Office:
Labour Relations Agency
    1–3 Guildhall Street, Londonderry, BT48 6BJ; tel:
    028 7126 9639; fax: 028 7126 7729; e-mail: lra@
    dnet.co.uk

LACE GUILD

Formal name: The Lace Guild

The Hollies, 53 Audnam, Stourbridge, West
Midlands, DY8 4AE

Tel: 01384 390739
Fax: 01384 444415
E-mail: hollies@laceguild.org

Website:
http://www.laceguild.demon.co.uk
Home page with links to: About the Guild; Craft of
Lace; Lace magazine; events; publications;
suppliers.

Enquiries:
Enquiries to: Secretary
Other contacts: Headquarters staff for availability
on a daily basis

Founded:
1976

Organisation type and purpose:
International organisation, national organisation,
membership association (membership is by
subscription), present number of members: 5000
approx, voluntary organisation, registered charity
(charity number 274397), museum, suitable for
ages: all.
Registered museum no RD 1950.
The role of The Lace Guild is to promote
understanding and appreciation of all aspects of
lace and lacemaking.

Subject coverage:
All aspects of lace including: history (social and
technical); making of all English and most
European bobbin, needle and craft laces;
equipment and materials; publications; exhibitions;
courses.

**Museum or gallery collection, archive, or library
special collection:**
Collections of lace and lace related artefacts,
    including patterns, tools, materials, sample
    books

Comprehensive library of books, magazines (from around the world), photographs, documents and study folios covering every aspect of lace

Non-library collection catalogue:
All or part available in-house

Library catalogue:
All or part available in print

Printed publications:
Information leaflets
Instruction books
Magazine and Newsletter (quarterly, members)
Patterns and Pattern books
Young Lacemakers Magazine

Publications list:
Available online and in print

Access to staff:
Contact by letter, by telephone, by fax, by e-mail and via website. Appointment necessary.
Hours: Mon to Fri, 0900 to 1600

Access to building, collection or gallery:
Prior appointment required

LADIES EUROPEAN TOUR

Acronym or abbreviation: LET

The Old Hall, Dorchester Way, Macclesfield, Cheshire, SK10 2LQ

Tel: 01625 611444
Fax: 01625 610406
E-mail: mail@ladieseuropeantour.com

Website:
http://www.ladieseuropeantour.com
Profile of players, information on tournaments, results and money list, press releases.

Enquiries:
Enquiries to: Executive Director

Founded:
1988

Organisation type and purpose:
Professional Sports Body.

Subject coverage:
Women's professional golf.

Printed publications:
Yearly Tour Guide listing top players with profiles

Access to staff:
Contact by letter, by fax, by e-mail and via website. Appointment necessary.
Hours: Mon to Fri, 0900 to 1700

LADIES' GOLF UNION

Acronym or abbreviation: LGU

The Scores, St Andrews, Fife, KY16 9AT

Tel: 01334 475811
Fax: 01334 472818
E-mail: info@lgu.org

Website:
http://www.lgu.org

Enquiries:
Enquiries to: CEO

Founded:
1893

Organisation type and purpose:
Membership association.

Subject coverage:
Ladies' amateur golf from 1893.

Museum or gallery collection, archive, or library special collection:
Photograph albums 1893–1929
Records of British ladies' golf since 1893

Printed publications:
Handbook (annually, February)
eNews

Access to staff:
Contact by letter, by telephone, by fax, by e-mail and via website
Hours: Mon to Fri, 0900 to 1700

LAKE DISTRICT NATIONAL PARK AUTHORITY

Acronym or abbreviation: LDNPA

Murley Moss Business Park, Oxenholme Road, Kendal, Cumbria, LA9 7RL

Tel: 01539 724555\ Minicom no. 01539 731263
Fax: 01593 740822
E-mail: hq@lake-district.gov.uk

Website:
http://www.lake-district.gov.uk

Enquiries:
Enquiries to: Communications Manager
Direct tel: 01539 792683
Direct fax: 01539 740822
Direct e-mail: mick.casey@lake-district.gov.uk

Founded:
1951

Organisation type and purpose:
Local government body, membership association (membership is by election or invitation), present number of members: 26, service industry.
To conserve and enhance natural beauty, wildlife and cultural heritage of the National Park, promote opportunities for understanding and enjoyment of its special qualities, seeking to foster economic and social well-being of its local communities.

Subject coverage:
Information on the National Park: access, conservation, landscape, historic sites, buildings etc, farming, mining and quarrying, traffic and parking, tourism. Local community, control of development.

Printed publications:
Lake District National Park Management Plan (£10 plus p&p)
Lake District National Park Local Plan (£16.50 plus p&p)
Cumbria and Lake District Joint Structure Plan (£10 plus p&p)
Other specific area management plans
Repairing Upland Path Erosion (£19.95 plus p&p)
The Caravan and Tent Guide (99p plus p&p)

Publications list:
Available online and in print

Access to staff:
Contact by letter, by telephone, by fax, by e-mail and via website. Appointment necessary.
Hours: Mon to Thu, 0900 to 1700; Fri, 0900 to 1645

Access for disabled people:
Parking provided, level entry, toilet facilities

Member of:
Association of National Park Authorities (ANPA)
Ponsford House, Moretonhampstead, Newton Abbot, Devon, TQ13 8NL; tel: 01647 440245
Federation of Nature and National Parks of Europe

LAKELAND DIALECT SOCIETY

Acronym or abbreviation: LDS

Gale View, Main Street, Shap, Penrith, Cumbria, CA10 3NH

Tel: 01931 716386
E-mail: lakespeak@aol.com

Website:
http://www.lakelanddialectsociety.org

Enquiries:
Enquiries to: Honorary Secretary
Other contacts: Vice President and Editor, tel: 01931 715359

Founded:
1939

Access to staff:
Contact by letter, by telephone, by fax, by e-mail and via website
Hours: Mon to Fri, 0900 to 1700

Organisation type and purpose:
Membership association (membership is by subscription), present number of members: 300, voluntary organisation.

Subject coverage:
The Cumbrian dialect in general, its origins and its use today.

Museum or gallery collection, archive, or library special collection:
Small collection of Cumbrian dialect literature, minute books and papers of the Society (held in Carlisle Library, Globe Lane, Carlisle). May be viewed by arrangement

Printed publications:
Annual Journal (free to members and on sale to the general public, £1.50)
Lakeland Treasury – the works of Lance Porter (£5.50)

Electronic and video publications:
Lakeland Gems 73 minutes of stories, poems and songs in dialect (CD, £11.50, audio tape, £5.50 inc p&p)

Access to staff:
Contact by letter, by telephone, by e-mail, in person and via website
Hours: Mon to Fri, 0900 to 1800
Special comments: Evenings after 1945 hours.

Access to building, collection or gallery:
No prior appointment required

Internal links with:
Cumberland Women's Institute
Yorkshire Dialect Society
Librarian, School of English, University of Leeds, Leeds, LS2 9JT

LAKELAND HORTICULTURAL SOCIETY

Acronym or abbreviation: LHS

Holehird Gardens, Patterdale Road, Windermere, Cumbria, LA23 1NP

Tel: 01539 446008

Website:
http://www.holehirdgardens.org.uk

Enquiries:
Enquiries to: Honorary Secretary

Founded:
1969

Organisation type and purpose:
Membership association (membership is by subscription), present number of members: 1600, registered charity (charity number 259847).
The purpose of the organisation is to promote and develop the science, practice and art of horticulture with particular reference to Lakeland conditions. The 10 acre garden is maintained entirely by volunteers and supported entirely by members' subscriptions and voluntary contributions.

Subject coverage:
To promote and develop the science, practice and art of horticulture, with special reference to Lakeland conditions, within this area to promote and facilitate co-operation between all horticultural organisations and to serve the interests of all horticulturists.

Museum or gallery collection, archive, or library special collection:
Three national plant collections; hydrangea, astilbe, polystichum ferns

Printed publications:
The Lakeland Gardener (Journal of the Society, published Spring and Autumn, free to all members and available from the Secretary or Reception, £1 each)

Access to staff:
Contact by letter
Hours: Mon to Fri, 0900 to 1700

continued overleaf

Affiliated to:
Royal Horticultural Society (RHS)

LAMBETH ARCHIVES DEPARTMENT

Minet Library, 52 Knatchbull Road, London, SE5 9QY

Tel: 020 7926 6076
Fax: 020 7926 6080

Enquiries:
Enquiries to: Archivist

Organisation type and purpose:
Local government body, public library.
Record office.
To preserve and make accessible the records of the London Borough of Lambeth, its predecessors, and the records of Lambeth people and places.

Subject coverage:
Records of the London Borough of Lambeth and its predecessors; deposited records of local Lambeth organisations; local history and topography of Lambeth and the old county of Surrey; manorial records; estate records; business records.

Museum or gallery collection, archive, or library special collection:
Crystal Palace Collection (books, programmes, cuttings)
South London Theatres Collection (playbills and programmes)
Surrey Collection
Vauxhall Gardens Collection (playbills, cuttings, songbooks, manuscripts)
Woolley Collection of Doulton and other stoneware

Printed publications:
Born & Bred – Tracing your Lambeth family history
Clapham
Guide to Lambeth Archives
Lambeth Stoneware
Lambeth's Open Spaces
Short Guide to the Surrey Collection
St Luke, West Norwood, 1825–1975
Story of Norwood

Publications list:
Available in print

Access to staff:
Contact by letter, by telephone, by fax, by e-mail and in person. Appointment necessary.
Hours: Mon to Fri, 0900 to 1700

Access for disabled people:
Ramped entry

Parent body:
London Borough of Lambeth

LAMBETH PALACE LIBRARY

London, SE1 7JU

Tel: 020 7898 1400
Fax: 020 7928 7932
E-mail: lpl.staff@lpl.c-of-e.org.uk

Website:
http://www.lambethpalacelibrary.org
Conditions of access, hours of opening, etc; holdings guide; research guides; catalogue of printed books online; reprographics; Friends of the Library.

Enquiries:
Enquiries to: Librarian

Founded:
1610

Organisation type and purpose:
Academic Research Library.

Subject coverage:
Ecclesiastical history, particularly of the Church of England; general history; palaeography; early printing; art history; American colonial history; bibliography; genealogy; topography.

Museum or gallery collection, archive, or library special collection:
Archives of the Province of Canterbury, including marriage allegations, wills, Court of Arches, etc
Incunables (200)
Manuscripts from 9th century to present (4000)
Papers of the Archbishops of Canterbury from the 16th century
Papers of the Bishops of London, including extensive collections concerning colonial America and the West Indies from the 17th century
Papers of the Commonwealth, Earls of Shrewsbury, Anthony Bacon, George Carew (Earl of Totnes), Commissioners for Building 50 New Churches (Queen Anne Churches)
Papers of societies etc, within the Church of England, Anglo-Continental Society, Christian Faith Society, Church of England Temperance Society, Church Union, Clergy Orphan Corporation, Confraternity of the Blessed Sacrament etc
Papers of statesmen and bishops, Gladstone, Selborne, Bishops G K A Bell, A C Headlam, E J Palmer, C Wordsworth etc
Printed books collection (approximately 200,000 items)
Prints collection (church topography and portraits)
Records of Lambeth Conferences, from 1867
Records of the Incorporated Church Building Society (19th and 20th centuries, 16,000 originals and database)
Registers of foreign churches, Basra, Khartoum, Shanghai, Shantung
Registers of the Archbishops of Canterbury, from 13th century
Sion College collection (manuscripts and printed books pre 1850)
STC Titles (3500)

Non-library collection catalogue:
All or part available online, in-house and in print

Library catalogue:
All or part available in-house

Printed publications:
Annual Report
List of catalogues of some of the Collections (leaflet, available from the Lambeth Palace Library)

Microform publications:
Filming facilities for some material (for purchase directly)
Some material commercially available through publishing house. Please enquire

Publications list:
Available in print

Access to staff:
Contact by letter, by telephone, by fax and in person. Letter of introduction required.
Hours: Mon to Fri, 1000 to 1700
Special comments: Closed for 10 days at Christmas and Easter.

Access for disabled people:
Parking, bathroom facilities, ramp, hearing induction loop.

Funded by:
Church Commissioners for England (Church of England)

LAMBRETTA CLUB GB

Acronym or abbreviation: LCGB

8 Trent Close, Rainhill, Prescot, Merseyside, L35 9LD

Tel: 0151 426 9839
Fax: 0151 426 9839
E-mail: lcgb2@blueyonder.co.uk

Website:
http://www.lcgb.co.uk

Enquiries:
Enquiries to: General Secretary
Direct tel: 07966 265588 (Mobile)

Founded:
1953

Organisation type and purpose:
International organisation, membership association.
To further the interests of Lambretta enthusiasts worldwide.

Subject coverage:
Everything for the Lambretta enthusiast from shows, events, competition, technical information, DVLA approved for registration problems.

Museum or gallery collection, archive, or library special collection:
Various books and manuals relevant to Lambretta

Printed publications:
Club magazine (free to members)
We also sell a wide range of products bearing the club's logo

Electronic and video publications:
Various Lambretta videos and DVD's

Access to staff:
Contact by letter, by telephone, by fax and by e-mail
Hours: Mon to Fri, 0930 to 1730
Special comments: Contact by fax 0930 to 1730, mark for the attention of Kev Walsh.

LANARK LIBRARY

Lindsay Institute, 16 Hope Street, Lanark, ML11 7LZ

Tel: 01555 661144
E-mail: lanark.ref@library.s-lanark.org.uk

Website:
http://www.southlanarkshire.gov.uk
General information regarding public library service.

Enquiries:
Enquiries to: Reference Library Supervisor

Organisation type and purpose:
Local government body, public library.

Subject coverage:
Reference and local history.

Museum or gallery collection, archive, or library special collection:
William Smellie Collection (mainly 18th-century midwifery, obstetrics, gynaecology)
Robert Owen Collection (co-operative movement, New Lanark)
Coalburn Collection (330 images of a coal mining village c. 1880–1930)
Poster Collection (200 posters of local events, including circuses, visiting shows, sports and civic functions)

Library catalogue:
All or part available in-house

Access to staff:
Contact by letter, by telephone, by e-mail and in person
Hours: Mon, 0915 to 1930; Tue and Thu, 0915 to 2000; Wed and Sat, 0915 to 1700; Fri, 0930 to 1930

Access to building, collection or gallery:
Public access during opening hours

Access for disabled people:
To ground and second floors only. No disabled access to upper-floor IT suite. However, Internet access is also available on second floor.

LANCASHIRE AND CHESHIRE ANTIQUARIAN SOCIETY

Acronym or abbreviation: LCAS

59 Malmesbury Road, Cheadle Hulme, Cheadle, Cheshire, SK8 7QL

Tel: 0161 439 7202
E-mail: morrisgarratt@sky.com

Website:
http://www.landcas.org.uk

Enquiries:
Enquiries to: Honorary Secretary

Founded:
1883

Organisation type and purpose:
Learned society (membership is by subscription), present number of members: 320, suitable for all ages

Subject coverage:
Interests are broad, encompassing national and local events and all historical aspects of the life and topography of the region. Current fields of study include archaeology, both traditional and industrial; architecture and the arts; social and economic history, particularly religious and educational developments; the history of trade, trades and transport; and the history of institutions and local government.

Museum or gallery collection, archive, or library special collection:
Library books, chiefly relating to the north-west of England, (c.1,600 vols)

Library catalogue:
All or part available in print

Printed publications:
Transactions (almost annually since 1883; 103 vols to date)
Offprints of many papers in the Transactions are available separately

Publications list:
Available online

Access to staff:
Contact by letter, by telephone, by e-mail and via website
Hours: Mon to Fri, 0930 to 1630 (Portico Library)

Access to building, collection or gallery:
No access other than to staff
Special comments: Library housed in Manchester Central Library. Members may request library tickets.

Also at:
c/o Portico Library
    57 Mosley Street, Manchester, M2 3HY; tel: 0161 236 6785
Honorary Membership Secretary (subscriptions)
    3 Syddal Crescent, Bramhall, Stockport

LANCASHIRE COUNTY LIBRARY

Harris Library, Reference and Information Service, Harris Library, Market Square, Preston, Lancashire, PR1 2PP

Tel: 01772 532668/9
Fax: 01772 555527
E-mail: harris.reference@lcl.lancscc.gov.uk

Website:
http://www.lancashire.gov.uk/libraries
Home page with general information on the library service.

Enquiries:
Enquiries to: Reference Librarian

Founded:
1879

Organisation type and purpose:
Local government body, public library.

Subject coverage:
Business information, commerce, standards, general information in social studies and humanities fields, genealogy, market research reports, European Community information.

Museum or gallery collection, archive, or library special collection:
Dr. Shepherd Library of mostly 18th and 19th century books of medical, general and historical interest
Francis Thompson Collection (poetry)
Local Studies – Lancashire
Spencer Collection of Children's Books
Stocks Massey Music Library (Burnley Central Library)

Trade and statistical information:
Annual data on international trade. Standard UK statistical series.

Non-library collection catalogue:
All or part available online

Library catalogue:
All or part available online

Printed publications:
Family History in Preston

Access to staff:
Contact by letter, by telephone, by fax, by e-mail and in person
Hours: Mon, Wed, Fri, 0930 to 1930; Tue, Thu, Sat, 0930 to 1700; Sun, 1100 to 1600

Access for disabled people:
Ramped entry
Special comments: Lift.

Parent body:
Lancashire County Council

LANCASHIRE COUNTY MUSEUM SERVICE

Stanley Street, Preston, Lancashire, PR1 4YP

Tel: 01772 634061
Fax: 01772 534079
E-mail: museum.enquiries@mus.lancscc.gov.uk

Website:
http://www.lancsmuseums.gov.uk

Enquiries:
Enquiries to: Marketing Assistant

Founded:
1983

Organisation type and purpose:
Local government body, suitable for ages: all. Administrative body for the local government museums.

Subject coverage:
The subjects covered by the museums of Lancashire include: military history, local history, social history, maritime history, textile machinery, art, fine art, childhood collections, geology, natural science and conservation.

Access to staff:
Contact by letter, by telephone, by fax, by e-mail and via website
Hours: Mon to Fri, 0900 to 1700

Access for disabled people:
Ramped entry, access to all public areas, toilet facilities

Museums, Galleries or Historic Sites:
Fleetwood Museum
    Queens Terrace, Fleetwood, Lancashire, FY7 6BT; tel: 01253 876621; fax: 01253 878088; e-mail: fleetwood.museum@mus.lancscc.gov.uk
Gawthorpe Hall
    Padiham, Nr Burnley, BB12 8UA; tel: 01282 771004; fax: 01282 770178; e-mail: gawthorpe.hall@mus.lancscc.gov.uk
Helmshore Mills Textile Museum
    Holcombe Road, Helmshore, Rossendale, Lancashire, BB4 4NP; tel: 01706 226459; fax: 01706 218554; e-mail: helmshore.museum@mus.lancscc.gov.uk
Judges' Lodgings
    Church Street, Lancaster, LA1 1YS; tel: 01524 32808; e-mail: judges.lodgings@mus.lancscc.gov.uk

Lancaster Castle
    Shire Hall, Castle Parade, Lancaster, LA1 1YJ; tel: 01524 64998; fax: 01524 847914
Lancaster City Museum
    Market Square, Lancaster, LA1 1HT; tel: 01524 64637; fax: 01524 841692; e-mail: lancaster.citymuseum@mus.lancscc.gov.uk
Lancaster Cottage Museum
    15 Castle Hill, Lancaster, LA1 1HT; tel: 01524 64637; fax: 01524 841692
Lancaster Maritime Museum
    Custom House, St. George's Quay, Lancaster, LA1 1RB; tel: 01524 382264; fax: 01524 841692
Museum of Lancashire
    Stanley Street, Preston, PR1 4YP; tel: 01772 534075; fax: 01772 534079
Queen Street Mill
    Harle Skye, Burnley, Lancashire, BB10 2HX; tel: 01282 412555; fax: 01282 430220; e-mail: queenstreet.mill@mus.lancscc.gov.uk
Rossendale Museum
    Whitaker Park, Rawtenstall, Rossendale, BB4 6RE; tel: 01706 244682; fax: 01706 250037; e-mail: rossendalemuseum@btconnect.com
Turton Tower
    Chapeltown Road, Turton, Nr Bolton, Lancashire, BL7 0HG; tel: 01204 852203; fax: 01204 853759; e-mail: turton.tower@mus.lancscc.gov.uk

Parent body:
Lancashire County Council
    County Hall, Preston, Lancashire

LANCASHIRE RECORD OFFICE

Acronym or abbreviation: LRO

Bow Lane, Preston, Lancashire, PR1 2RE

Tel: 01772 533039
Fax: 01772 533050
E-mail: record.office@ed.lancscc.gov.uk

Website:
http://www.a2a.org.uk
Some catalogues available.
http://www.archives.lancashire.gov.uk

Enquiries:
Enquiries to: County Archivist

Founded:
1940

Organisation type and purpose:
Local government body.
County Record Office.
Providing archive services to Lancashire, Blackburn with Darwen and Blackpool.

Subject coverage:
Historical primary source material relating to all aspects of life and society in Lancashire 12th century to present day.

Museum or gallery collection, archive, or library special collection:
Lancashire Local Studies Library
8 miles of archives, too extensive to specify
For listings see Guide to Lancashire Record Office and Guide to Lancashire Record Office, a Supplement 1977–1989

Non-library collection catalogue:
All or part available online and in-house

Library catalogue:
All or part available online and in-house

Printed publications:
Guide to Lancashire Record Office 1940–1976 (£3.00 plus p&p)
Guide to Lancashire Record Office, A supplement 1977–1989 (£3.00 plus p&p)
Note: both publications can be bought together for £5.00 plus p&p

Microform publications:
Copy material can be purchased in certain instances

continued overleaf

Electronic and video publications:
Finding Folk: A Handlist of Genealogical Sources (online)

Publications list:
Available online and in print

Access to staff:
Contact by letter, by telephone, by fax, by e-mail, in person and via website
Hours: Mon, Wed, Fri, 0900 to 1700; Tue, 0900 to 2030; Thu, 1000 to 1700
Open 2nd Saturday of each month (except holiday weekends), 1000 to 1600
Special comments: County Archives Research Network (CARN) ticket required (can be issued on production of an acceptable ID).

Access to building, collection or gallery:
No access other than to staff

Access for disabled people:
Parking provided, access to all public areas, toilet facilities
Special comments: Disabled persons' lift.

Provide archive services for unitary councils:
Blackpool Council and Blackburn with Darwen Council

LANCASHIRE TEACHING HOSPITALS NHS FOUNDATION TRUST

Library and Information Service, Royal Preston Hospital, Sharoe Green Lane, Preston, Lancashire, PR2 9HT

Tel: 01772 522763
Fax: 01772 523491
E-mail: mandy.beaumont@lthtr.nhs.uk

Website:
www.lancsteachinghospitals.nhs.uk

Enquiries:
Enquiries to: Knowledge and Library Services Manager
Direct e-mail: libraryRPH@lthtr.nhs.uk

Organisation type and purpose:
National government body.
Health library.
Multiprofessional library.

Subject coverage:
Medicine, health sciences, NHS management, nursing, general practice.

Library catalogue:
All or part available in-house

Printed publications:
A-Z Guide to the Library (subject guide)
Clinical Librarian Service
Guide to the Library (pamphlet)
Journal Holdings (booklet)
Library Bulletin

Publications list:
Available online

Access to staff:
Contact by letter, by telephone, by fax, by e-mail, in person and via website. Appointment necessary.
All charged.
Hours: Wed, Fri, 0900 to 1700; Mon, Tue, Thu, 0900 to 1900

Member of:
British Medical Association (BMA)
Library and Information Health Network Northwest (LIHNN)
Royal College of Surgeons

LANCASHIRE YOUTH ASSOCIATION

Acronym or abbreviation: LYA

10 Fishergate Hill, Preston, Lancashire, PR1 8JB

Tel: 01772 556127
Fax: 01772 251334
E-mail: mail@lya.org.uk

Website:
http://www.lya.org.uk

Enquiries:
Enquiries to: Director

Founded:
1923

Organisation type and purpose:
Membership association, present number of members: 107 youth groups and clubs, voluntary organisation, registered charity (charity number 518147), suitable for ages: year 12 students, training organisation.
Youth service.

Subject coverage:
Personal and social development of young people including those who have disabilities, support and advice to youth groups/clubs, links with other voluntary youth organisations, links with local government youth and community services.

Printed publications:
Annual Report
Grassroots (newsletter, for members)

Access to staff:
Contact by letter, by telephone, by fax, by e-mail and via website. Appointment necessary.
Hours: Mon to Fri, 0930 to 1630

Affiliated to:
British Confederation of Youth Clubs
European Federation of Youth Clubs
Irish Confederation of Youth Clubs
UK Youth
  11 Bride Street, London, EC4A 4AS

LANCASTER CENTRAL LIBRARY

Market Street, Lancaster, LA1 1HY

Tel: 01524 580700
Fax: 01524 580709
E-mail: lancaster.library@lancscc.gov.uk

Website:
http://www.lancashire.gov.uk/libraries/
librarydetails/libsearch1.asp?name=Lancaster

Enquiries:
Enquiries to: Librarian
Other contacts: District Manager; Community History Manager

Founded:
1932

Organisation type and purpose:
Public library.

Subject coverage:
General, local history.

Information services:
Information Desk, Quick Reference, Online Reference Library.

Education services:
Heritage Centre (local, community and family history).

Trade and statistical information:
via the Online Reference Library accessible to library members.

Non-library collection catalogue:
All or part available online

Library catalogue:
All or part available online

Access to staff:
Contact by letter, by telephone, by fax, by e-mail, in person and via website
Hours: Mon to Wed and Fri, 0930 to 1700; Thu, 0930 to 1900; Sat, 0930 to 1600

LANCASTER CITY COUNCIL

Town Hall, Lancaster, LA1 1PJ

Tel: 01524 582000\ Minicom no. 01524 582175
Fax: 01524 582161
E-mail: customerservices@lancaster.gov.uk

Website:
http://www.lancaster.gov.uk/
Information about the area; council services; useful links.

Enquiries:
Enquiries to: Chief Executive

Founded:
1974

Organisation type and purpose:
Local government body.

Subject coverage:
Public and local information about services available within the Lancaster district.

Museum or gallery collection, archive, or library special collection:
Various public records relating to the Lancaster district

Printed publications:
Information leaflets and brochures
Public documents including the electoral register and committee agenda minutes

Access to staff:
Contact by letter, by telephone, by fax, by e-mail, in person and via website
Hours: Mon to Fri, 0845 to 1715

LANCASTER CITY MUSEUMS

Market Square, Lancaster, LA1 1HT

Tel: 01524 64637
Fax: 01524 841692
E-mail: lancaster.citymuseum@mus.lancsoc.gov.uk

Website:
http://www.lancsmuseum.gov.uk
Brief history, opening hours, brief details of collections.

Founded:
1923

Organisation type and purpose:
Local government body, museum, suitable for ages: 5+.

Subject coverage:
King's Own Royal Regiment, maritime history, archaeology, local history, social history, costume, numismatics, fine art, decorative art, transport, military history.

Information services:
Guided tours on request.

Special visitor services:
Guided tours, materials and/or activities for children.

Education services:
Group education facilities, resources for Key Stages 1 and 2, 3, 4 and Further or Higher Education.

Services for disabled people:
For the visually impaired; displays and/or information at wheelchair height.

Museum or gallery collection, archive, or library special collection:
Archive and library relating to the King's Own Royal Regiment (Lancaster) (inc important MSS)

Printed publications:
Exhibition lists (annually)
Local history publications (21 titles), irregular additions, for sale
Museum guidebooks (2) for sale
Subject leaflets (12, irregular additions, for sale)

Access to staff:
Contact by letter, by telephone, by fax, by e-mail, in person and via website. Appointment necessary.
Hours: Mon to Sat, 1000 to 1700
Special comments: Prior appointment required.

Access to building, collection or gallery:
No prior appointment required
Hours: Mon to Sat, 1000 to 1700
Special comments: Closed Christmas and New Year.

Access for disabled people:
Ramped entry, access to all public areas

Comprises 3 local Government Museums and a trustee museum:
King's Own Regimental Museum

Museum sites:
City Museum
  same address
Cottage Museum
  15 Castle Hill, Lancaster
Lancaster Maritime Museum
  St George's Quay, Lancaster, LA1 1RB; tel: 01524 64637; fax: 01524 841692; e-mail: awhite@lancaster.gov.uk

Parent body:
Lancaster City Council
  at the same address

Supported by:
Friends of Lancaster City Museum
  at the same address

LANCASTER UNIVERSITY LIBRARY

Bailrigg, Lancaster, LA1 4YH

Tel: 01524 592536
Fax: 01524 63806 or 65719
E-mail: library@lancaster.ac.uk

Website:
http://www.libweb.lancs.ac.uk
Library home page.
http://cat.lib.lancs.ac.uk
Library catalogue.

Enquiries:
Enquiries to: Librarian
Direct e-mail: j.whiteside@lancaster.ac.uk

Founded:
1963

Organisation type and purpose:
University library.

Subject coverage:
Usual fields of university study, (excluding medicine), science and technology, social sciences, business studies, humanities.

Museum or gallery collection, archive, or library special collection:
Beetham Vestry Library
Burnley Grammar School Collection (rare books, 17th and 18th centuries)
Business Histories
European Documentation Centre
Ford Railway Collection
Headlam-Morley Religious pamphlets
Jack Hylton Archive
Legal History Collection
Library of the Fell and Rock Climbing Club of the English Lake District
Patten Second World War Pamphlet Collection
Preston Library (Cartmel Priory)
Quaker Collection
Redlich Collection (music)
Socialist Collection

Trade and statistical information:
Numerous holdings, including government publications, to support the teaching and research of the Economics Department and Management School.

Library catalogue:
All or part available online

Printed publications:
Numerous library guides covering most library subject areas, functions and services

Access to staff:
Contact by letter, by telephone, by fax, by e-mail and in person. Non-members charged.
Hours: Term time: Mon, Tue, Thu, Fri, 0845 to 2200; Wed, 0930 to 2200; Sat, 1000 to 1700; Sun, 1400 to 1900 (except exam periods, 1200 to 1900)

Vacations: Mon, Tue, Thu, 0845 to 2200, Wed, 0930 to 2200, Fri, 0845 to 1700, Sat, 1000 to 1700; Sun, closed
Special comments: Term time: Reference services only Sun 1400 to 1900.
Vacation: Reference services only Sat, 1300 to 1700.

Parent body:
Lancaster University
  Bailrigg, Lancaster, LA1 4YW; tel: 01524 65201; fax: 01524 846243

LANDCRAB OWNERS CLUB INTERNATIONAL LIMITED

Acronym or abbreviation: LOCI

5 Rolston Avenue, Huntington, York, YO31 9JD

Tel: 01904 620125 (evenings only)

Website:
http://www.landcrab.net

Enquiries:
Enquiries to: Chairman
Other contacts: Spares Secretary, Historian

Founded:
1988

Organisation type and purpose:
Membership association (membership is by subscription), voluntary organisation.

Subject coverage:
Austin Morris Wolseley 1800 and 2200s, from 1964 to 1975 (ADO 17): advice; spares; interest and exhibitions of these vehicles.

Non-library collection catalogue:
All or part available in-house

Library catalogue:
All or part available in-house

Printed publications:
Club magazine

Access to staff:
Contact by letter and by telephone
Hours: Telephone: evenings only

Has:
Local groups

Member of:
Federation of British Historic Vehicle Clubs (FBHVC)
  PO Box 2506, Henfield, West Sussex; tel: 01273 495051

LANDLIFE

National Wildflower Centre, Court Hey Park, Liverpool, L16 3NA

Tel: 0151 737 1819
Fax: 0151 737 1820
E-mail: info@landlife.org.uk

Website:
http://www.landlife.org.uk
Charitable activities, trading activities, National Wildflower Centre.

Enquiries:
Enquiries to: Administrator
Other contacts: Chief Executive

Founded:
1975

Organisation type and purpose:
National organisation, voluntary organisation, registered charity (charity number 290510).
Landlife is a charity taking action for a better environment by creating new opportunities for wildlife and encouraging people to enjoy them.

Subject coverage:
Wildflower landscaping and gardening, creative conservation consultancy service, environmental advice for community groups and schools, derelict land reclamation techniques and research, sales of wildflower seed, plants and publications.

Library catalogue:
All or part available online and in print

Printed publications:
Annual Report
Newsletter (members)
Wildflower seed and plant catalogue (free, gardeners and trade)
Wildflowers Work, creative conservation techniques (£12.50)
How to make Wildflower Habit Gardens (16pp full colour, £2)

Publications list:
Available online and in print

Access to staff:
Contact by letter, by telephone, by fax and by e-mail. Appointment necessary.
Hours: Mon to Fri, 0900 to 1700

Access for disabled people:
Parking provided, ramped entry, toilet facilities

Links with:
National Wildflower Centre
  (Landlife's Millennium project); tel: 0151 737 1819; fax: 0151 737 1820; e-mail: info@nwc.org.uk
UK MAB Urban Forum
Urban Wildlife Partnership
Wildlife Trusts

Trading subsidiary:
Landlife Wildflowers Limited
  tel: 0151 737 1819; fax: 0151 737 1820; e-mail: info@wildflower.org.uk

LANDMARK INFORMATION GROUP

7 Abbey Court, Eagle Way, Sowton, Exeter, Devon, EX2 7HY

Tel: 01392 441700
Fax: 01392 441709

Website:
http://www.landmark-information.co.uk
Company site.
http://www.promap.co.uk
http://www.home-envirosearch.com
Product information.
http://www.old-maps.co.uk
First edition Ordnance Survey maps.

Enquiries:
Enquiries to: Customer Services

Founded:
1995

Organisation type and purpose:
Service industry.
Suppliers of environmental risk information, current and historical mapping.

Subject coverage:
Environmental risk management, digital mapping, contaminated land, previous land use, current land use.

Museum or gallery collection, archive, or library special collection:
Digital historical maps (with OS)
Environmental information database

Printed publications:
Envirocheck
Envirosearch Commercial
Envirosearch Residential
Promap
Sitecheck
Site Search

Electronic and video publications:
Envirocheck
Promap Envirosearch

Access to staff:
Contact by letter, by telephone, by fax, by e-mail and via website
Hours: Mon to Fri, 0900 to 1700

Access to building, collection or gallery:
No access other than to staff

continued overleaf

Hours: Mon to Fri, 0900 to 1700

Access for disabled people:
Level entry, toilet facilities

Other address:
Landmark Information Group
   3rd Floor, Challanger House, 42 Adler Street,
   London, E1 1EE; tel: 020 7958 4999; fax: 020 7958
   4981; e-mail: mailbox@landmark-information.co
   .uk
Prodat Systems plc
   Northpoint House, Highlands Lane, Henley on
   Thames, Oxon, RG9 4PR; tel: 01491 413030; fax:
   01491 413031; e-mail: sales@promap.co.uk

Parent body:
Daily Mail and General Trust Group (DMGT)
   Northcliffe House, 2 Derry Street, Kensington,
   London, W8 5TT

LANDMARK TRUST

Shottesbrooke, Maidenhead, Berkshire, SL6 3SW

Tel: 01628 825920
Fax: 01628 825417

Website:
http://www.landmarktrust.org.uk

Enquiries:
Enquiries to: Public Relations Manager

Founded:
1965

Organisation type and purpose:
Registered charity in England and Wales 243312
and Scotland SC039205.
Building preservation charity.

Subject coverage:
Restoration of historic buildings for self-catering
holidays all year round.

**Museum or gallery collection, archive, or library
special collection:**
A picture library of all Landmarks.

Printed publications:
Handbook (approximately once every two years)
Legacy leaflets and brochures (occasional)
Newsletter (2 times a year)
Price List (annually)

Access to staff:
Contact by letter
Hours: Mon to Fri, 0900 to 1700

LANDS TRIBUNAL FOR SCOTLAND

Acronym or abbreviation: LTS

George House, 126 George Street, Edinburgh, EH2
4HH

Tel: 0131 271 4350
Fax: 0131 271 4399
E-mail: mailbox@lands-tribunal-scotland.org.uk

Website:
http://www.lands-tribunal-scotland.org.uk

Enquiries:
Enquiries to: Clerk to the Tribunal
Other contacts: Depute Clerk

Founded:
1971

Organisation type and purpose:
Judicial body.
Various jurisdictions relating to valuation of land
in Scotland.

Subject coverage:
Discharge and variation of title conditions;
determination of disputed compensation (eg
following compulsory purchase); disputed
valuations for tax purposes (eg assessment for
ratings); appeals against Keeper of the Registers of
Scotland and disputes arising from Tenants' Rights
legislation in relation to tenants' right to buy.

Access to staff:
Contact by letter, by telephone, by fax, by e-mail
and in person
Hours: Mon to Thu, 0900 to 1700; Fri, 0900 to 1600

Access to building, collection or gallery:
Hours: as above

Access for disabled people:
Hours: as above

LANDSCAPE INSTITUTE

Acronym or abbreviation: LI

33 Great Portland Street, London

Tel: 020 7299 4500
Fax: 020 7299 4501
E-mail: mail@l-i.org.uk

Website:
http://www.l-i.org.uk

Enquiries:
Enquiries to: Director General
Other contacts: Reference library service, tel: 020
7299 4502

Founded:
1929

Organisation type and purpose:
Professional body.
To promote the highest standard of professional
service in the application of the arts and sciences of
landscape architecture, management and science.

Subject coverage:
Landscape design, management, conservation or
restoration.

Printed publications:
Directory of Registered Landscape Practices
   (annually)
Landscape (12 times a year)
A range of titles covering all aspects of landscape
   architecture

Publications list:
Available online

Access to staff:
Contact by letter, by telephone, by fax and by e-
mail
Hours: Mon to Fri, 0900 to 1700

Access to building, collection or gallery:
No prior appointment required
Hours: Library: Mon-Fri, 0900 to 1700

Member of:
Construction Industry Council
International Federation of Landscape Architects
(IFLA)
World Conservation Union (IUCN)

LANDSCAPE RESEARCH GROUP LTD

Acronym or abbreviation: LRG

PO Box 1482, Oxford, OX4 9DN

E-mail: admin@landscaperesearch.org

Website:
http://www.landscaperesearch.org.uk

Enquiries:
Enquiries to: Administrator

Founded:
1967

Organisation type and purpose:
International organisation, learned society
(membership is by subscription), voluntary
organisation, registered charity (charity number
287610).

Subject coverage:
Landscape: aesthetics, design, management,
conservation, perception, assessment, planning;
landscape and the arts; landscape, literature and
ecology.

Printed publications:
Conference Reports (for purchase directly)
Landscape Research (journal, quarterly, for
   purchase directly or via publishing house)
Landscape Research Extra (newsletter, 3 a year, for
   purchase directly)

Access to staff:
Contact by letter and by e-mail
Hours: Mon to Fri, 0900 to 1700

LANGHOLM LIBRARY

The Library Buildings, High Street, Langholm,
Dumfries & Galloway, DG13 0DJ

Enquiries:
Enquiries to: Chairman

Founded:
1800

Organisation type and purpose:
Voluntary organisation, registered charity (charity
number SCO 11403).

Library catalogue:
All or part available in-house

Access to staff:
Contact by letter. Appointment necessary.
Hours: Tue, Fri, 1000 to 1200; Thu, 1900 to 2100

LANGTON MATRAVERS LOCAL HISTORY AND PRESERVATION SOCIETY

Acronym or abbreviation: LMLHPS

Barton, The Hyde, Langton Matravers, Swanage,
Dorset, BH19 3HE

Tel: 01929 423168

Website:
http://www.langtonia.org.uk

Enquiries:
Enquiries to: Membership Secretary
Direct tel: 01929 421481
Direct e-mail: localhistory@langtonia.org.uk
Other contacts: Publicity Officer, tel: 01929 422218

Founded:
1971

Organisation type and purpose:
Learned society (membership is by subscription),
registered charity (charity number 272407),
museum.
To research and publish local history.

Subject coverage:
Local history, family history, local industries.

**Museum or gallery collection, archive, or library
special collection:**
Genealogical charts, transcripts of parish registers,
   memorial inscriptions, national census returns
   etc
Local history library

Non-library collection catalogue:
All or part available in-house

Library catalogue:
All or part available in-house

Publications list:
Available online and in print

Access to staff:
Contact by letter, by telephone, by e-mail, in
person and via website
Hours: Mon to Fri, 0900 to 1700

Access to building, collection or gallery:
No prior appointment required
Hours: Apr 1 to Sept 30: Mon to Sat, 1000 to 1200
and 1400 to 1600
Special comments: Or by appointment.

Access for disabled people:
Parking provided, level entry, access to all public
areas

Parent body for:
Langton Matravers Museum
  at the same address

LARGS AND NORTH AYRSHIRE FAMILY HISTORY SOCIETY

c/o Bogriggs Cottage, Carlung, West Kilbride, Ayrshire, KA23 9PS

Tel: 01294 823690

Website:
http://www.lnafhs.freeyellow.com

Enquiries:
Enquiries to: General Secretary

Founded:
1988

Organisation type and purpose:
Membership association, present number of members: 140.
Family history society.

Subject coverage:
Advice in family history research sources.

Library catalogue:
All or part available in-house

Access to staff:
Contact by letter and by telephone
Hours: Mon to Fri, 0900 to 1700

LATIN MASS SOCIETY

11–13 Macklin Street, London, WC2B 5NH

Tel: 020 7404 7284
Fax: 020 7831 5585
E-mail: thelatinmasssociety@snmail.co.uk

Website:
http://www.latin_mass_society.org

Enquiries:
Enquiries to: Secretary

Founded:
1965

Organisation type and purpose:
Learned society, registered charity.

Subject coverage:
Preservation and restoration of the Tridentine Rite of Mass in the Catholic Church, liturgy of Latin Mass.
Restoration of the church's treasury of liturgical music, esp. Gregorian chant.

Printed publications:
Newsletter (quarterly, for members)
The Plain Man's Guide to the Traditional Rite of Holy Mass
Simplicissimus: a New Approach to Learning the Latin of the Traditional Roman Missal
ORDO (annually)

Access to staff:
Contact by letter, by telephone, by fax, by e-mail, in person and via website
Hours: Mon to Fri, 0930 to 1700

Access to building, collection or gallery:
Hours: Mon to Fri, 0930 to 1700
Special comments: Entryphone only.

Access for disabled people:
Lift

Affiliated to:
Una Voce International
  44 Queensway, Shotley Bridge, Consett, Co. Durham, DH8 0RZ

LAUTERPACHT CENTRE FOR INTERNATIONAL LAW

Acronym or abbreviation: LCIL

5 Cranmer Road, Cambridge, CB3 9BL

Tel: 01223 335358

Fax: 01223 300406
E-mail: admin@rcil.cam.ac.ul

Website:
http://lcil.law.cam.ac.uk

Enquiries:
Enquiries to: Administrator

Founded:
1983

Organisation type and purpose:
University department or institute.

Subject coverage:
Public international law.

Printed publications:
Order printed publications from: Cambridge University Press
Edinburgh Building, Shaftesbury Road, Cambridge, CB2 2RU

Publications list:
Available online

Access to staff:
Contact by letter, by e-mail and via website
Hours: Mon to Fri, 0900 to 1700

Access to building, collection or gallery:
No prior appointment required

LAVENDER LINE LIMITED

Isfield Station, Isfield, Uckfield, East Sussex, TN22 5XB

Tel: 01825 750515

Website:
http://www.lavender-line.co.uk
General and specific information about the Line, facilities available and special events

Enquiries:
Enquiries to: Secretary

Founded:
1992

Organisation type and purpose:
Registered charity (charity number 1010085), museum.

Subject coverage:
Preservation and running a railway.

Museum or gallery collection, archive, or library special collection:
Steam engines, steam crane, main line and industrial diesel locomotives, some running and some in the course of restoration and repair

Non-library collection catalogue:
All or part available online

Access to staff:
Contact by letter, by telephone and in person
Hours: Mon to Fri, 0900 to 1700

Access for disabled people:
Parking provided, ramped entry
Special comments: Not suitable for the severely disabled

LAW CENTRES FEDERATION

Acronym or abbreviation: LCF

293–299 Kentish Town Road, London, NW5 2TJ

Tel: 020 7428 4400
Fax: 020 7428 4401
E-mail: info@lawcentres.org.uk

Website:
http://www.lawcentres.org.uk

Enquiries:
Enquiries to: Office Manager

Founded:
1978

Organisation type and purpose:
Voluntary organisation.

Representative body for the national network of Law Centres.

Subject coverage:
Information about Law Centres generally, how they originated, what they do, how to set one up, how to develop existing services; their place in the provision of legal services; whereabouts of Law Centres and the areas of legal advice in which they specialise.

Printed publications:
Legal and Advice Services – A Pathway out of Social Exclusion
LCF 2007 Annual Report
Law Centres Federation – Promoting Access to Justice
Law Centres – Providing Access to Justice
What is a Law Centre?
Access to Justice Series 1999:
History and Funding of Law Centres
A New Deal for Social Justice
Law Centres and Local Government
Law Centres in the Community
Law Centres – A Quality Service
Law Centres in the Digital Age
Law Centres – Working Together
Working for a Law Centre
List of Law Centres

Access to staff:
Contact by letter, by telephone, by fax, by e-mail and via website
Hours: Mon to Fri, 1000 to 1700

Branches:
Avon and Bristol Law Centre
  2 Moon Street, Bristol, BS2 8QE; tel: 0117 924 8662; fax: 0117 924 8020; e-mail: mail@ablc .demon.co.uk
Barnet Law Service (Law Centre)
  9 Bell Lane, London, NW4 2BP; tel: 020 8203 4141; fax: 020 8203 8042; e-mail: info@barnetlaw .co.uk; website: http://www.barnetlaw.co.uk
Battersea Law Centre (part of South-West London Law Centres)
  14 York Road, London, SW11 3QA; tel: 020 7228 9462; fax: 020 7978 5348; e-mail: solicitors@ battersealawcentre.fsnet.co.uk
Bradford Law Centre
  31 Manor Row, Bradford, West Yorkshire, BD1 4PX; tel: 01274 306617; fax: 01274 390939; e-mail: enquiries@bradfordlawcentre.co.uk
Brent Community Law Centre
  389 High Road, Willesden, London, NW10 2JR; tel: 020 8451 1122; fax: 020 8830 2462; e-mail: brentlaw@brentlaw.org.uk
Bury Law Centre
  19 Knowsley Street, Bury, BL9 0ST; tel: 0161 272 0666; fax: 0161 272 0011; e-mail: info@ burylawcentre.co.uk
Cambridge House Law Centre
  137 Camberwell Road, Camberwell, London, SE5 0HF; tel: 020 7358 7000; fax: 020 7703 2903; e-mail: lawcentre@ch1889.org
Camden Community Law Centre
  2 Prince of Wales Road, London, NW5 3LG; tel: 020 7284 6510; fax: 020 7267 6218; e-mail: admin@cclc.org.uk; website: http://www.cclc.org .uk
Cardiff Law Centre
  41–42 Clifton Street, Cardiff, CF24 1LS; tel: 029 2049 8117; fax: 029 2049 7118; e-mail: cardiff .lawcentre@dial.pipex.com
Carlisle Law Centre
  8 Spencer Street, Carlisle, CA1 1BG; tel: 01228 515129; fax: 01228 515819; e-mail: reception@ comlaw.co.uk; website: http://www .communitylaw.org.uk
Central London Law Centre
  19 Whitcombe Street, London, WC2H 7HA; tel: 020 7839 2998; fax: 020 7839 6158; website: http:// www.londonlawcentre.org.uk
Chesterfield Law Centre
  44 Park Road, Chesterfield, Derbyshire, S40 1XZ; tel: 01246 550674; fax: 01246 551069; e-mail: chesterfieldlawcentre@dial.pipex.com; website: http://www.chesterfieldlawcentre.org.uk

continued overleaf

Coventry Law Centre
The Bridge, Broadgate, Coventry, CV1 1NG; tel: 024 7622 3053; fax: 024 7622 8551; e-mail: enquiries@covlaw.org.uk; website: http://www .covlaw.org.uk

Devon Law Centre
Virginia House, 40 Looe Street, Plymouth, Devon, PL4 0EB; tel: 01752 519 794; fax: 01752 267 939; e-mail: information@devonlawcentre .org.uk; website: http://www.devonlawcentre .org.uk

Enfield Law Centre
38 Market Square (1st Floor), Edmonton Green, Edmonton, London, N9 0TZ; tel: 020 8807 8888; fax: 020 8807 8844; e-mail: info@enfieldlawcentre .co.uk; website: http://www.enfieldlawcentre.org .uk

Gloucester Law Centre
75–81 Eastgate Street, Gloucester, GL1 1PN; tel: 01452 423492; fax: 01452 387594; e-mail: admin@ gloucesterlawcentre.co.uk; website: http://www .gloucesterlawcentre.co.uk

Greenwich Community Law Centre
187 Trafalgar Road, London, SE10 9EQ; tel: 020 8853 2550; fax: 020 8858 5253; e-mail: info@gclc .co.uk

Hackney Community Law Centre
8 Lower Clapton Road, London, E5 0PD; tel: 020 8985 8364; fax: 020 8533 2018; e-mail: info@hclc .org.uk

Hammersmith and Fulham Law Centre
142–144 King Street, London, W6 0QU; tel: 020 8741 4021; fax: 020 8741 1450; e-mail: hflaw@ hflaw.ogr.uk

Harehills and Chapletown Law Centre
263 Roundhay Road, Leeds, LS8 4HS; tel: 0113 249 1100; fax: 0113 235 1185; e-mail: admin@ leedslawcentre.org.uk

Haringey Law Centre
Ground Floor, 7 Holcombe Road, Tottenham, London, N17 9AA; tel: 020 8808 5354; fax: 020 8801 1516; e-mail: tottenhamlawcentre@tiscali.co .uk

Hillingdon Law Centre
12 Harold Avenue, Hayes, Middlesex, UB3 4QW; tel: 020 8561 9400; fax: 020 8756 0837; e-mail: info@hillingdonlawcentre.co.uk; website: http:// www.hillingdonlaw.org.uk

Hounslow Law Centre
51 Lampton Road, Hounslow, Middlesex, TW3 1JG; tel: 020 8570 9505; fax: 020 8572 0730; e-mail: info@hounslowlawcentre.org.uk; website: http://www.hounslowlawcentre.org.uk

Islington Law Centre
161 Hornsey Road, London, N7 6DU; tel: 020 7607 2461; fax: 020 7700 0072; e-mail: info@ islingtonlaw.org.uk; website: http://www .islingtonlaw.org.uk

Kirklees Law Centre
Units 11–12, Empire House, Wakefield Old Road, Dewsbury, West Yorkshire, WF12 8DJ; tel: 01924 439829; fax: 01924 868140; e-mail: info@ kirkleeslc.org.uk

Lambeth Law Centre
Unit 4, The Co-op Centre, 11 Mowll Street, London, SW9 6BG; tel: 020 7840 2000; fax: 020 7820 8303; e-mail: admin@lambethlawcentre.org

Law Centre (Northern Ireland)
Western Area Office, 9 Clarendon Street, Londonderry, BT48 7EP; tel: 028 7126 2433; fax: 028 7126 2343; e-mail: admin.derry@ lawcentreniwest.org; website: http://www .lawcentreniwest.org

Law Centre (Northern Ireland)
124 Donegall Street, Belfast, BT1 2GY; tel: 028 9024 4401; fax: 028 9023 6340; e-mail: admin .belfast@lawcentreni.org; website: http://www .lawcentreni.org

Luton Law Centre
6th Floor, Cresta House, Alma Street, Luton, Bedfordshire, LU1 2PL; tel: 01582 481000; fax: 01582 482581; e-mail: admin@lutonlawcentre.org .uk

Newcastle Law Centre
1st floor, 1 Charlotte Square, Newcastle Upon Tyne, NE1 4XF; tel: 0191 230 4777; fax: 0191 233 0295; e-mail: info@newcastlelawcentre.co.uk

North Kensington Law Centre
74 Golborne Road, London, W10 5PS; tel: 020 8969 7473; fax: 020 8968 0934; e-mail: info@nklc .co.uk; website: http://www.nklc.co.uk

North Manchester Law Centre
Harpurhey District Centre, off Rochdale Road, Harpurhey, Manchester, M9 4DH; tel: 0161 205 5040; fax: 0161 205 8654; e-mail: info@nmlc.org .uk; website: http://www.nmlc.org.uk

Nottingham Law Centre
119 Radford Road, Nottingham, NG7 5DU; tel: 0115 978 7813; fax: 0115 979 2969; e-mail: nottlawcent@btconnect.com

Oldham Law Centre
First Floor, Archway House, Bridge Street, Oldham, OL1 1ED; tel: 0161 627 0925; fax: 0161 620 3411; e-mail: admin@oldhamlawcentre.org

Paddington Law Centre
439 Harrow Road, London, W10 4RE; tel: 020 8960 3155; fax: 020 8968 0417; e-mail: paddingtonlaw@btconnect.com

Plumstead Community Law Centre
105 Plumstead High Street, London, SE18 1SB; tel: 020 8855 9817; fax: 020 8316 7903; e-mail: info@pclc.org.uk

Rochdale Law Centre
Smith Street, Rochdale, OL16 1HE; tel: 01706 657766; fax: 01706 346588; e-mail: info@ rochdalelawcentre.org.uk; website: http://www .rochdalelawcentre.org.uk

Saltley and Nechells Law Centre
2 Alum Rock Road, Saltley, Birmingham, B8 1JB; tel: 0121 328 2307; fax: 0121 327 7486; e-mail: snlc@btconnect.com

Sheffield Law Centre
1st Floor, Waverley House, 10 Joiner Street, Sheffield, S3 8GW; tel: 0114 273 1501; fax: 0114 273 7778; e-mail: post@slc.org.uk; website: http:// www.slc.org.uk

South Manchester Law Centre
584 Stockport Road, Manchester, M13 0RQ; tel: 0161 225 5111; fax: 0161 225 0210; e-mail: admin@smlc.org.uk; website: http://www.smlc .org.uk

Southwark Law Centre
Hanover Park House, 14–16 Hanover Park, Peckham, London, SE15 5HS; tel: 020 7732 2008; fax: 020 7732 2034; e-mail: general@ southwarklawcentre.org.uk

Springfield Law Centre
Springfield Hospital, Glenburnie Road, London, SW17 7DJ; tel: 020 8767 6884; fax: 020 8767 6996; e-mail: info@springfieldlawcentre.org.uk

Streetwise Community Law Centre
1–3 Anerley Station Road, Penge, London, SE20 8PY; tel: 020 8778 5854; fax: 020 8776 9392

Thamesmead Law Centre
4 Cross Street, Erith, Kent, DA8 1AB; tel: 020 8311 0555; fax: 01322 331 073; e-mail: advice@ tmlc.org.uk; website: http://www.tmlc.org.uk

Tower Hamlets Law Centre
214 Whitechapel Road, London, E1 1BG; tel: 020 7247 8998; fax: 020 7247 9424; e-mail: info@thlc .co.uk

Vauxhall Law and Information Centre
Vauxhall Training and Enterprise Centre, Silvester Street, Liverpool, L5 8SE; tel: 0151 482 2001; fax: 0151 207 4948

Wandsworth and Merton Law Centre (part of the South-West London Law Centres)
101a Tooting High Street, London, SW17 0SU; tel: 020 8767 2777; fax: 020 8767 2711; e-mail: info@swllc.org.uk

Warrington Law Centre
The Boultings, Winwick Street, Warrington, Cheshire, WA2 7TT; tel: 01925 258360; fax: 01925 637668; e-mail: admin@warringtonlawcentre .com

Wiltshire Law Centre
Temple House, 115–118 Commercial Road, Swindon, Wiltshire, SN1 5PL; tel: 01793 486926; fax: 01793 432193; e-mail: info@wiltslawcentre.co .uk; website: http://www.wiltslawcentre.org.uk

Wythenshawe Law Centre
260 Brownley Road, Wythenshawe, Manchester, M22 5EB; tel: 0161 498 0905/6; fax: 0161 498 0750; e-mail: info@wlawcentre.co.uk

Links with:
Scottish Association of Law Centres
c/o Drumchapel Law and Money Advice Centre, Unit 28, 42 Dalsetter Avenue, Drumchapel, Glasgow, G15 8TE; tel: 0141 944 0507/0281; fax: 0141 944 7605; e-mail: law@dlmac.fsnet

Member organisation of:
Advice Services Alliance
12th Floor, New London Bridge House, 25 London Bridge Street, London, SE1 9SG; tel: 020 7378 6428; fax: 020 7407 6822; e-mail: info@asauk .org.uk; website: http://www.asauk.org.uk

Member organisations:
AIRE – Advice on Individual Rights in Europe
Third Floor, 17 Red Lion Square, London, WC1R 4QH; tel: 020 7831 3850; fax: 020 7404 7760

Castlemilk Law and Money Advice Centre
30–32 Dougrie Drive, Castlemilk, Glasgow, G45 9AD; tel: 0141 634 0313; fax: 0141 634 8727; e-mail: castlemilk@lawcentre.1.freeserve.co.uk

Disability Law Service
Ground Floor, 39–45 Cavell Street, London, E1 2BP; tel: 020 7791 9800 (Minicom 020 7791 9801); fax: 020 7791 9802; e-mail: advice@dls.org.uk

Earth Rights
Little Orchard, School Lane, Mole Hill Green, Takeley, Essex, CM22 69J; tel: 07071 2255011; e-mail: earthright@gn.apc.org

Free Legal Advice Centre (Ireland)
13 Lower Dorset Street, Dublin 1, Ireland; tel: +353 1874 5690; fax: +353 1874 5320

Greater Manchester Immigration Aid Unit
1 Delaunays Road, Crumpsall Green, Manchester, M8 4QS; tel: 0161 740 7722; fax: 0161 740 5172

Mary Ward Legal Centre
26–27 Boswell Street, London, WC1N 3JZ; tel: 020 7831 7079; fax: 020 7831 5431; e-mail: enquiries@marywardlegal.org.uk

LAW COMMISSION

Conquest House, 37–38 John Street, Theobalds Road, London, WC1N 2BQ

Tel: 020 7453 1220
Fax: 020 7453 1297
E-mail: chief.executive@lawcommission.gsi.gov.uk

Website:
http://www.lawcom.gov.uk
Contains the most recent reports and CPs.

Enquiries:
Enquiries to: Librarian
Direct tel: 020 7453 1241
Direct fax: 020 7453 1296
Direct e-mail: library@lawcommission.gsi.gov.uk
Other contacts: Chief Executive

Founded:
1965

Organisation type and purpose:
Statutory body.
Law reform body for England & Wales.

Subject coverage:
Law, programmes of the Law Commission.

Library catalogue:
All or part available in-house

Printed publications:
Annual Report (includes outline of yearly progress and list of publications)
Law under Review: list of law reform projects (on website)
Programmes of Law Reform (3 issues)
Reports and Consultation Papers on law reform proposals
Reports on proposals for the consolidation or repeal of statute law
Order printed publications from: The Stationery Office

Publications list:
Available online

Access to staff:
Contact by telephone and by e-mail

Hours: Open to the staff of the Commission 24 hours a day
Special comments: No public access.

Parent body:
Department for Constitutional Affairs

LAW SOCIETY LIBRARY

113 Chancery Lane, London, WC2A 1PL

Tel: 0870 606 2511; 020 7320 5972
Fax: 020 7831 1687
E-mail: library@lawsociety.org.uk

Website:
http://www.lawsociety.org.uk/library
http://www.lawsociety.org.uk/libraryonline

Founded:
1825

Organisation type and purpose:
Professional body.
Professional society for solicitors in England and Wales.

Subject coverage:
Law: UK including England, Scotland, Wales, Northern Ireland; Eire; and European Union; Channel Islands; Isle of Man.

Information services:
The library runs a document delivery service.

Museum or gallery collection, archive, or library special collection:
Over 43,000 vols of material dating back to the 13th century, comprising practitioner textbooks (current and previous edns), public legislation (up-to-date and historical), private and local legislation, law reports, parliamentary material, journals and legal encyclopaedias (current and previous edns).
Historical collections (trials, legal history, history of solicitors' profession, archives)
Mendham Collection of religious books (on loan to Canterbury Cathedral Library)
Parliamentary papers, 1801 onwards (on microfiche)

Non-library collection catalogue:
All or part available in print

Library catalogue:
All or part available online

Printed publications:
Publishes over 100 titles
Order printed publications from: http://www.lawsociety.org.uk/bookshop

Publications list:
Available online

Access to staff:
Contact by letter, by telephone, by fax, by e-mail, in person and via website. Access for members only.
Hours: Mon to Thu, 0900 to 1800; Fri, 0900 to 1700

Access for disabled people:
Access to library via lift; equipped for sight-impaired members to use computers.

LAW SOCIETY OF NORTHERN IRELAND

Acronym or abbreviation: LSNI

The Law Society House, 98 Victoria Street, Belfast, BT1 3JZ

Tel: 028 9023 1614
Fax: 028 9031 1323
E-mail: info@lawsoc-ni.org

Website:
http://www.lawsoc-ni.org

Enquiries:
Enquiries to: Head of Library and Information Services
Direct e-mail: heather.semple@lawsoc-ni.org

Organisation type and purpose:
Professional body.

Subject coverage:
Education and regulation of solicitors in Northern Ireland; various services available for solicitors in Northern Ireland; any matter concerning the conduct of solicitors in Northern Ireland.

Library catalogue:
All or part available online

Printed publications:
Leaflets on services provided by Solicitors
The Writ (journal of the LSNI, monthly)
Miscellaneous other publications

Publications list:
Available in print

Access to staff:
Contact by letter, by telephone, by fax and by e-mail. Access for members only.
Hours: Mon to Fri, 0900 to 1700
Special comments: Members' only library – other users by appointment.

Access for disabled people:
Toilet facilities

Affiliated to:
CCBE
International Bar Association

LAW SOCIETY OF SCOTLAND

26 Drumsheugh Gardens, Edinburgh, EH3 7YR

Tel: 0131 226 7411
Fax: 0131 225 2934
E-mail: lawscot@lawscot.org.uk

Website:
http://www.lawscot.org.uk
Information on a wide range of law-related subjects for the benefit of the public and the profession such as Scots law, solicitors and firms in Scotland, professional practice information and Society news.

Enquiries:
Enquiries to: Director, Corporate Communications (for media enquiries)

Founded:
1949

Organisation type and purpose:
Statutory body, professional body (membership is by qualification), present number of members: 8600, service industry.
The promotion of the interests of the solicitor's profession in Scotland and the interests of the public in relation to that profession.

Subject coverage:
Information to solicitors re council and committee work. Information to public re solicitors in Scotland. Information on international law, law reform, practice management, legal education, seminars, and referral to solicitors in Scotland. Information on Scots Law, legal history and legal topics to the public.

Printed publications:
Journal of the Law Society of Scotland (monthly, £84 per annum)
Scottish Civil Law Reports (£180 per annum) from 1st November 2006.
Scottish Criminal Case Reports (£180 per annum) from 1st November 2006.
Leaflets (free)

Access to staff:
Contact by letter, by telephone, by fax, by e-mail and via website
Hours: Fri, 0900 to 1630

Access to building, collection or gallery:
Prior appointment required

Brussels Office:
Law Society of Scotland
142–144 Avenue de Tervuren, 1150 Brussels, Belgium; tel: 00 32 2 743 8585; fax: 00 32 2 743 8586; e-mail: brussels@lawsociety.org.uk

Links with:
various Scottish faculties of solicitors and bar associations, new lawyers associations and commercial organisations

LAWN TENNIS ASSOCIATION

Acronym or abbreviation: LTA

Queen's Club, West Kensington, London, W14 9EG

Tel: 020 7381 7000
Fax: 020 7381 5965

Website:
http://www.LTA.org.uk

Enquiries:
Enquiries to: Information Officer
Direct tel: 020 7381 7111
Direct fax: 020 7381 3773
Other contacts: Chief Executive

Organisation type and purpose:
Membership association.
Governing body of the game of lawn tennis in Great Britain.

Subject coverage:
Tennis: rules and equipment, coaching, affiliated clubs, championships.

Museum or gallery collection, archive, or library special collection:
Tennis magazines and journals

Printed publications:
ACE (formerly Serve and Volley, monthly)
Coach to Coach
Events and Tournaments (annually)
Official Handbook (annually)
Schools Tennis

Access to staff:
Contact by letter, by telephone, by fax, by e-mail and in person
Hours: Mon to Fri, 0915 to 1715

Member of:
International Tennis Federation
Lawn Tennis Association

LAWRENCE BATLEY CENTRE FOR THE NATIONAL ARTS EDUCATION ARCHIVE (TRUST)

Acronym or abbreviation: NAEA

Special Collections, University of Leeds, Bretton Hall Campus, West Bretton, Wakefield, West Yorkshire, WF4 4LG

Tel: 01924 830261
Fax: 01924 832077
E-mail: s.kielty@bretton.ac.uk

Website:
http://naea.bretton.ac.uk

Enquiries:
Enquiries to: Curator

Founded:
1987

Organisation type and purpose:
Registered charity (charity number 519437), museum, art gallery, research organisation. Education archive.

Subject coverage:
Visual and performing arts education.

Museum or gallery collection, archive, or library special collection:
97 catalogued collections, and others not yet catalogued, of complex and extensive material tracing the development of art education in the UK, includes papers; letters; paintings; drawings; games; puzzles; video and film; photography etc including:
A E Halliwell Collection (graphic design)
Franz Cizek Collection (children's art)

continued overleaf

Independent Television Commission Collection
(videos of ITV Schools Programmes 1960–1992,
ITV and Channel 4 Adult Education Programmes
1962–1992)
Nicolai Legat Collection (ballet)
Richard Hamilton (student artwork)
Royal Opera House Covent Garden (Education)
Collection
Victor Pasmore (student artwork)

Non-library collection catalogue:
All or part available online

Library catalogue:
All or part available online

Printed publications:
Leaflet (on-line catalogue and web information)

Access to staff:
Contact by letter, by telephone, by fax, by e-mail
and via website. Appointment necessary.
Hours: Mon to Thu, 0900 to 1700; Fri, 0900 to 1630
Special comments: Closed Weekends and Bank
Holidays.

Access to building, collection or gallery:
No prior appointment required
Hours: Prior appointment required for Collections:
Mon to Thu, 0900 to 1700; Fri, 0900 to 1630

Access for disabled people:
Level entry, access to all public areas, toilet
facilities

LCIA

Formal name: London Court of International
Arbitration
Acronym or abbreviation: LCIA

70 Fleet Street, London, EC4Y 1EU

Tel: 020 7936 7007
Fax: 020 7936 7008
E-mail: lcia@lcia.org

Website:
http://www.lcia.org
LCIA arbitration rules and schedule of costs, LCIA
mediation procedure, mediation schedule of fees
and expenses, introductory brochure, membership
leaflet and details of forthcoming events.

Enquiries:
Enquiries to: Registrar
Other contacts: Manager – Membership &
Conferences for membership or conference
enquiries.

Founded:
1892

Organisation type and purpose:
The expert and cost-effective administration of
arbitration and ADR worldwide, under LCIA and
other rules and procedures.

Subject coverage:
International commercial dispute resolution.

Printed publications:
Arbitration International and LCIA Newsletter
LCIA Arbitration Rules and Schedule of Costs (free
of charge)
LCIA Mediation Procedure and Schedule of Fees
and Expenses (free of charge)
LCIA Introductory Brochure (free of charge)
LCIA Membership/Services Leaflet (free of charge)

Access to staff:
Contact by letter, by telephone, by fax, by e-mail
and via website. Appointment necessary.
Hours: Mon to Fri, 0900 to 1700

Access to building, collection or gallery:
No access other than to staff
Hours: Mon to Fri, 1000 to 1700
Special comments: No smoking or eating in the
library.

LE VELO CLUB LIMITED

74 Warwick Avenue, Quorn, Loughborough,
Leicestershire, LE12 8HE

Tel: 01509 554230
E-mail: davidfbod@yahoo.co.uk

Website:
http://www.leveloclub.org.uk

Enquiries:
Enquiries to: Honorary Secretary

Founded:
1983

Organisation type and purpose:
Membership association (membership is by
subscription), present number of members: 1,300.
To promote enjoyment, riding and restoration of
LE, Valiant, Vogue and Viceroy motorcycles.

Subject coverage:
Technical and historical information on LE Velo
motorcycle and its derivatives.

**Museum or gallery collection, archive, or library
special collection:**
Extensive collection of original drawings (now on
CD-ROM)

Non-library collection catalogue:
All or part available online

Printed publications:
Magazine (6 times a year, members)

Access to staff:
Contact by letter, by e-mail and via website
Hours: Mon to Fri, 0900 to 1700

LEA CASTLE CENTRE LIBRARY

North Warwickshire Primary Care NHS Trust, Lea
Castle Centre, Wolverley, Kidderminster,
Worcestershire, DY10 3PP

Tel: 01562 850461
Fax: 01562 859010
E-mail: janette.hill@nhs.net

Enquiries:
Enquiries to: Librarian

Organisation type and purpose:
Medical Library, NHS Trust.
Centre for people with learning disabilities.

Subject coverage:
Psychiatry, learning disabilities, mental health
nursing.

Library catalogue:
All or part available in-house

Access to staff:
Contact by letter, by telephone, by fax and by e-
mail. Access for members only.
Hours: Mon, Thu, Fri, 1300 to 1700; Tue, Wed, 0900
to 1700

LEA-FRANCIS OWNERS' CLUB

Acronym or abbreviation: LFOC

French's, Long Wittenham, Abingdon,
Oxfordshire, OX14 4QQ

Tel: 01865 407515

Website:
http://www.lfoc.org
Club officers and services listed; events notified;
cars for sale advertised.

Enquiries:
Enquiries to: General Secretary
Direct e-mail: secretary@lfoc.org
Other contacts: Membership Secretary for
applications to join.

Founded:
1953

Organisation type and purpose:
International organisation, membership
association (membership is by subscription),
present number of members: 340.
Factory records and histories of individual
vehicles, technical details and information on the
repair and maintenance of most models.

Preservation and use of Lea-Francis vehicles.

Subject coverage:
History of all Lea-Francis products, production
history, racing history, as well as history of
individual vehicles, technical information on all
models.

**Museum or gallery collection, archive, or library
special collection:**
Catalogues, information sheets, brochures and
other sales literature issued by Lea-Francis Cars
Technical literature and handbooks for most
models

Printed publications:
The LeaFlet (magazine, 6 times a year, free to
members)
Lea-Francis Owners' Club Jubilee Book 2003

Electronic and video publications:
Video of 1995 Centenary Rally

Access to staff:
Contact by letter, by telephone, by e-mail and via
website
Hours: Mon to Sun, 0900 to 2200

Access to building, collection or gallery:
No access other than to staff

LEAD DEVELOPMENT ASSOCIATION INTERNATIONAL

Acronym or abbreviation: LDAI

17a Welbeck Way, London, W1G 9YJ

Tel: 020 7499 8422
Fax: 020 7493 1555
E-mail: enq@ldaint.org

Website:
http://www.ldaint.org

Enquiries:
Enquiries to: Director

Founded:
1946

Organisation type and purpose:
Trade association.

Subject coverage:
Building, batteries, coatings, environment, health
and safety, extraction, refining and production,
noise insulation, economics and statistics.

Printed publications:
Technical leaflets, brochures, books

Electronic and video publications:
Videos

Publications list:
Available online and in print

Access to staff:
Contact by letter, by telephone, by fax and by e-
mail
Hours: Mon to Fri, 0930 to 1715

LEAD SHEET ASSOCIATION

Acronym or abbreviation: LSA

Unit 10, Archers Park, Branbridges Road, East
Peckham, Tonbridge, Kent, TN12 5HP

Tel: 01622 872432
Fax: 01622 871649
E-mail: leadsa@globalnet.co.uk

Website:
http://www.leadsheetassociation.org.uk
Outline of LSA services.

Enquiries:
Enquiries to: Administrator
Other contacts: Company Secretary

Founded:
1926

Organisation type and purpose:
Trade association (membership is by subscription, election or invitation), manufacturing industry, training organisation, consultancy.

Subject coverage:
Technical advice and training on the specification and use of rolled lead sheet in the construction industry.

Museum or gallery collection, archive, or library special collection:
All relevant industry publications

Trade and statistical information:
Confidential industry statistics not for general release.

Printed publications:
Rolled Lead Sheet: The Complete Manual

Publications list:
Available online and in print

Access to staff:
Contact by letter, by telephone, by fax, by e-mail and via website. Appointment necessary.
Hours: Mon to Fri, 0900 to 1700

LEAD SMELTERS AND REFINERS ASSOCIATION

Acronym or abbreviation: LSRA

c/o 17a Welbeck Way, London, W1G 9YJ

Tel: 020 7499 8422
Fax: 020 7493 1555
E-mail: enq@ldaint.org

Enquiries:
Enquiries to: General Secretary

Organisation type and purpose:
Trade association.

Subject coverage:
Smelting and refining of lead.

Trade and statistical information:
Confidential – not generally available.

Access to staff:
Contact by letter, by telephone and by fax
Hours: Mon to Fri, 0900 to 1700

LEADHILLS AND WANLOCKHEAD RAILWAY

The Station, Leadhills, Lanarkshire, ML12 6XP

Tel: 01555 662963
E-mail: secretary@leadhillsrailway.co.uk

Website:
http://www.leadhillsrailway.co.uk

Enquiries:
Enquiries to: Secretary
Other contacts: Publicist (e-mail: davidwinpenny@hotmail.com)

Founded:
1983

Organisation type and purpose:
Membership association (membership is by subscription), voluntary organisation.

Subject coverage:
Railway preservation.

Special visitor services:
Train service Sat and Sun during May to Sept

Education services:
Museum in shop

Non-library collection catalogue:
All or part available online

Printed publications:
The Leadhills and Wanlockhead Light Railway (the original branch line, 1901–38, 64pp illustrated, £5)
Leaflet about industrial heritage available

Access to staff:
Contact by letter, by telephone, by e-mail and via website. Appointment necessary.
Hours: Mon to Fri, 0900 to 1700

Access to building, collection or gallery:
Hours: Sat and Sun, 1000 to 1700

Access for disabled people:
Access to building, but restricted access on train

LEAGUE AGAINST CRUEL SPORTS LIMITED

Acronym or abbreviation: LACS

83–87 Union Street, London, SE1 1SG

Tel: 020 7403 6155
Fax: 020 7403 4532

Website:
http://www.league.uk.com
Information about the campaign to ban hunting.

Enquiries:
Enquiries to: Information Officer
Other contacts: PA to Chief Executive

Founded:
1924

Organisation type and purpose:
National organisation, membership association (membership is by subscription), voluntary organisation.
Company.
To campaign to end cruel sports and to protect threatened animals.

Subject coverage:
Hunting of wild animals with dogs, hare coursing, shooting, wildlife protection and conservation.

Trade and statistical information:
Information on hunted animals and on cruel sports.

Printed publications:
Wildlife Guardian (quarterly, free to members)
A Brush with Conscience
Care for the Wild
Draghunting – A family sport
Falconry in Britain
How to Make a Wildlife Garden
Rearing Pheasants for Shoots
Uncivil Liberties
The Red Fox: Friend or Foe?
The Tradition of Staghunting on Exmoor & the Quantocks
Wildlife Protection

Publications list:
Available online and in print

Access to staff:
Contact by letter, by telephone, by fax and by e-mail
Hours: Mon to Fri, 0900 to 1700

LEAGUE FOR THE EXCHANGE OF COMMONWEALTH TEACHERS

Acronym or abbreviation: LECT

Commonwealth House, 7 Lion Yard, Tremadoc Road, London, SW4 7NQ

Tel: 0870 770 2636
Fax: 0870 770 2637
E-mail: info@lect.org.uk

Website:
http://www.lect.org.uk

Enquiries:
Enquiries to: Director
Direct e-mail: anna.tomlinson@lect.org.uk

Founded:
1901

Organisation type and purpose:
International organisation, membership association, present number of members: 2500, registered charity.

Subject coverage:
Education in the Commonwealth including information about international professional D+V for teachers.

Electronic and video publications:
Newsletter (email)
Library of research reports on overseas visits undertaken (via website)

Access to staff:
Contact by letter, by telephone, by fax, by e-mail, in person and via website
Hours: Mon to Fri, 0900 to 1700

LEARNING & SKILLS COUNCIL LONDON NORTH

Acronym or abbreviation: LSC London North

Dunmayne House, 1 Fox Lane, Palmers Green, London, N13 4AB

Tel: 0845 019 4158
Fax: 020 8882 5931

Enquiries:
Enquiries to: Customer Services

Founded:
1991

Organisation type and purpose:
Statutory body, training organisation.
Organisation and strategic funding of post-16 education (excluding higher education) in London North area.

Subject coverage:
Information available for youth programmes, adult training and initiatives, business services, information for employers/employees. Special projects including equal opportunities policies, special needs provision, childcare, capacity building for voluntary sector, and other ongoing projects.

Printed publications:
Social and Economic Assessment
Skills and Employer Survey Reports
Needs Analysis

Publications list:
Available in print

Access to staff:
Contact by letter, by telephone, by fax and in person
Hours: Mon to Fri, 0900 to 1700

Access to building, collection or gallery:
No access other than to staff

Access for disabled people:
Parking provided, level entry, access to all public areas, toilet facilities

LEARNING AND SKILLS COUNCIL – COVENTRY

Acronym or abbreviation: LSC

Cheylesmore House, Quinton Road, Coventry, Warwickshire, CV1 2WT

Tel: 0845 019 4170
Fax: 024 7682 3675
E-mail: info@lsc.gov.uk

Website:
http://www.lsc.gov.uk

Enquiries:
Enquiries to: Head of Information Services
Direct e-mail: knowledge@lsc.gov.uk

Founded:
2001

Organisation type and purpose:
National government body.
The Learning and Skills Council has taken over most of the functions of FEFC and TECs since April 2001.

continued overleaf

Subject coverage:
Further and vocational education in England, especially funding arrangements, quality, student numbers and policy, post-16 education and training, work-based learning and skills.

Library catalogue:
All or part available in-house

Publications list:
Available online

Access to staff:
Contact by letter, by telephone, by fax, by e-mail and via website. Appointment necessary.
Hours: Mon to Thu, 0900 to 1700; Fri, 0900 to 1600

Access to building, collection or gallery:
Prior appointment required

Branches:
nine regional LSCs

Parent body:
Department for Innovation, Universities and Skills

LEARNING AND SKILLS COUNCIL FOR KENT AND MEDWAY

Acronym or abbreviation: LSC or LSCKM

26 Kings Hill Avenue, Kings Hill, West Malling, Kent, ME19 4AE

Tel: 0845 019 4152
Fax: 01732 876917
E-mail: informationline@lsc.gov.uk

Website:
http://www.lsc.gov.uk/kentandmedway

Enquiries:
Enquiries to: Information Officer

Founded:
2001

Organisation type and purpose:
Service industry, training organisation.
Learning and Business Link.

Subject coverage:
Education and training funding, private training companies, FE colleges, adult and community education initiatives, workforce development, investors in people, business and education partnerships.

Printed publications:
Annual Report
Strategic Plan
Training Provider Directory

Electronic and video publications:
Employer (CD-ROM)

Access to staff:
Contact by letter, by telephone, by fax, by e-mail and via website
Hours: Mon to Fri, 0830 to 1730

Access for disabled people:
Parking provided, level entry, access to all public areas, toilet facilities

LEARNING AND SKILLS COUNCIL SOUTH EAST

Princes House, 53 Queens Road, Brighton, BN1 3XB

Tel: 01273 783555
Fax: 01273 783507
E-mail: info@lsc.gov.uk

Website:
http://www.lsc.gov.uk/regions/SouthEast/

Enquiries:
Enquiries to: Marketing and PR Manager
Direct tel: 01329 228502

Founded:
2001

Organisation type and purpose:
Local government body, service industry.
Comprises five local Councils.
Post-16 learning and education.

Subject coverage:
Support for post-16 and education.

Trade and statistical information:
Labour and market economic information for Hampshire.

Access to staff:
Contact by letter, by telephone and by fax
Hours: Mon to Fri, 0900 to 1700

LEARNING AND SKILLS COUNCIL THAMES VALLEY

Acronym or abbreviation: LSC

LSC South East, Pacific House, Imperial Way, Reading, RG2 0FT

Tel: 0845 019 4147
Fax: 0118 908 2109
E-mail: SE-ESFCo-financing@lsc.gov.uk

Website:
http://www.lsc.gov.uk
Information about our mission, what we do, contact details, publications.

Enquiries:
Enquiries to: Regional ESF Administrator
Direct tel: 01273 783614

Founded:
2001

Organisation type and purpose:
National government body, national organisation, service industry, training organisation.
To plan and fund all post-16 training and education, except higher education.
To raise participation and attainment through high quality education and training which puts learners first.

Subject coverage:
Investors in people, training, National Vocational Qualification, local labour market, workforce development, modern apprenticeship, Foundation Apprenticeship, adult learning, schools, college, 6th forms, ESF funding, management development.

Museum or gallery collection, archive, or library special collection:
Various business and grants databases

Printed publications:
Investors in People
Modern Apprenticeships
Strategic Plan 2002–2005
Workforce Development

Access to staff:
Contact by letter, by telephone, by fax, by e-mail and via website
Hours: Mon to Fri, 0900 to 1700

Access to building, collection or gallery:
No access other than to staff

Access for disabled people:
Parking provided, ramped entry, toilet facilities

Funded by:
Central Government

National Office:
Learning and Skills Council
Cheylesmore house, Quinton Road, Coventry, CV1 2WT; tel: 024 7670 3241; fax: 024 7686 3100; e-mail: nationalinfo@lsc.gov.uk

LEARNING AND SKILLS DEVELOPMENT NETWORK

Acronym or abbreviation: LSN

Fifth Floor, Holborn Centre, 120 Holborn, London, EC1N 2AD

Tel: 0845 071 0800

E-mail: enquiries@lsneducation.org.uk

Website:
http://www.lsneducation.org.uk/
http://www.lsda.org.uk

Enquiries:
Enquiries to: Information Officer
Other contacts: Communications Managerr, tel no: 020 7840 5360 for press and PR.

Founded:
1995

Formerly a part of:
the Learning and Skills Development Agency (year of change 2006)

Organisation type and purpose:
National development agency, educational organisation.
Research for the further education sector.

Subject coverage:
Information for education managers on aspects of post-16 further education which relate to: developing competence, curriculum and staff management, curriculum planning and management, equal opportunities, flexible learning, provision for adults, new technologies, European links, governors, quality issues, key skills, professional development, vocational learning and research for the post-16 sector.

Non-library collection catalogue:
All or part available in-house

Printed publications:
Briefing (newsletter)
A wide range of reports, papers, bulletins, books and other publications

Publications list:
Available online and in print

Access to staff:
Contact by letter, by telephone, by fax, by e-mail and via website. Appointment necessary.
Hours: Mon to Fri, 0900 to 1700

Access to building, collection or gallery:
Prior appointment required

LEARNING AND TEACHING SCOTLAND

Acronym or abbreviation: LTS

The Optima, 58 Robertson Street, Glasgow, G2 8DU

Tel: 0141 2825000
Fax: 0141 2825050
E-mail: enquiries@ltscotland.org.uk

Website:
http://www.ltscotland.org.uk

Enquiries:
Enquiries to: Senior Communications and Information Officer
Direct e-mail: t.wallace@ltscotland.org.uk

Founded:
2000

Organisation type and purpose:
Executive non-departmental public body sponsored by Scottish Government, Learning and Teaching Scotland is the main organisation for the development and support of the Scottish curriculum, combining expertise in the curriculum 0–18 with advice on the use of ICT in education.

Subject coverage:
LTS is responsible for leading and supporting improvement in the delivery of education for children and young people; working closely with a wide range of partner organisations to share interesting innovative practice; providing advice, support, resources and staff development, which can enhance the quality of learning and teaching; playing a key role in all major developments in Scottish education; moving education forward in partnership with key stakeholders.

Library catalogue:
All or part available in-house

Printed publications:
Over 200 publications on aspects of education and subjects in the curriculum
Annual review
Order printed publications from: Learning and Teaching Scotland, Distribution Centre, 7 Tom Johnston Road, West Pitkerro, Dundee, DD4 8XD

Publications list:
Available online

Access to staff:
Contact by letter, by telephone, by fax, by e-mail, in person and via website. Appointment necessary.
Hours: Mon to Fri, 0845 to 1645

Funded by:
Scottish Government

LEARNING CENTRE LIBRARY

Walsall Hospitals NHS Trust, Manor Hospital, Moat Road, Walsall, West Midlands, WS2 9PS

Tel: 01922 656628
Fax: 01922 656220
E-mail: kaljinder.dhanda@walsallhospitals.nhs.uk

Enquiries:
Enquiries to: Librarian

Founded:
1970

Organisation type and purpose:
NHS hospital library.

Subject coverage:
Medical information.

Information services:
Multi-disciplinary collection of medical and healthcare textbooks covering undergraduate and postgraduate. Split across two sites.

Special visitor services:
All staff and students on placement or working for Walsall Hospitals NHS Trust and Walsall Teaching Primary Care Trust, including members of other Base libraries. Reference only to non-members.

Non-library collection catalogue:
All or part available online

Library catalogue:
All or part available online

Access to staff:
Access for members only. Non-members charged.
Hours: Mon to Fri, 0900 to 1700

Access for disabled people:
Ground floor access.

LEARNING ON SCREEN

Enquiries:
Enquiries to: Administrator

Founded:
1968

Organisation type and purpose:
International organisation, trade association (membership is by subscription), present number of members: 150, registered charity (charity number 325081-R).
Members are concerned with the production and use of materials for learning and training. They include broadcasters, producers, universities, colleges and schools.

Subject coverage:
Uses of screen-based media in education and training, selection of video equipment for education and training, production of material for education and training, research into the effectiveness of screen-based material for learning and training, television in distance learning.

Printed publications:
Screen Seen (magazine, quarterly)

Access to staff:
Contact by letter, by telephone, by e-mail and via website. Appointment necessary.
Hours: Mon to Fri, 0830 to 1600

Recognised by the:
Department for Education and Employment
Scottish Education Department
Welsh Education Office

LEARNING THROUGH LANDSCAPES

Acronym or abbreviation: LTL

Third Floor, Southside Offices, The Law Courts, Winchester, Hampshire, SO23 9DL

Tel: 01962 846258
Fax: 01962 869099
E-mail: schoolgrounds-uk@ltl.org.uk

Website:
http://www.ltl.org.uk
Projects, membership, benefits of becoming members, publications list.

Enquiries:
Enquiries to: Information Officer

Founded:
1990

Organisation type and purpose:
Registered charity.
To improve the quality of school grounds.

Subject coverage:
School grounds.

Museum or gallery collection, archive, or library special collection:
Around 1000 documents on school grounds projects and associated organisations

Library catalogue:
All or part available in-house

Printed publications:
A Guide to the Management and Maintenance of School Grounds (£10.95)
Developing School Grounds Toolkit (video, management guide and photocopiable material)
The Challenge of an Urban School Site (£10.95)
In the School Grounds Series (KS1 and KS2):
Arts in the School Grounds (£8.99)
English in the School Grounds (£7.95)
Geography in the School Grounds (£8.99)
Mathematics in the School Grounds (£7.95)
Science in the School Grounds (£7.95)
Trees in the School Grounds (£6.95)
Order printed publications from: Southgate Publishers Limited
The Square, Sandford, Crediton, Devon, EX17 4LW, tel: 01363 776888, fax: 01363 776889

Electronic and video publications:
3 videos available for purchase
Seating in the School Grounds (CD-ROM)

Publications list:
Available in print

Access to staff:
Contact by letter, by telephone, by fax, by e-mail and via website. Appointment necessary.
Hours: Mon to Fri, 0900 to 1700
Special comments: Charges for some services.

LEATHER CONSERVATION CENTRE

University College Campus, Boughton Green Road, Moulton Park, Northampton, NN2 7AN

Tel: 01604 719766
Fax: 01604 719649
E-mail: lcc@northampton.ac.uk

Website:
http://www.leatherconservation.org

Enquiries:
Enquiries to: Head of Conservation

Founded:
1978

Organisation type and purpose:
Registered charity (charity number 276485).

Subject coverage:
Conservation and analysis of historical leather, history of leather manufacture.

Museum or gallery collection, archive, or library special collection:
Reference collection of leather types

Printed publications:
Conservation of Leathercraft and Related Objects (ICOM, 1992, £15)
Oils and Lubricants Used on Leather (£5)
Fungicides Used on Leather (£5)
Leather Conservation – A Current Survey (£5)
Leather Manufacture in the post Medieval Period (Museum of Leathercraft, 1981, £4)
Leather Manufacture Through the Ages (EMIAC, 1983, £5)

Publications list:
Available online and in print

Access to staff:
Contact by letter, by telephone and by fax
Hours: Mon to Fri, 0900 to 1700

Associate member of:
British Leather Confederation

Institutional member of:
Historic Houses Association

LEATHERHEAD FOOD INTERNATIONAL

Acronym or abbreviation: LFI

Randalls Road, Leatherhead, Surrey, KT22 7RY

Tel: 01372 376761
Fax: 01372 386228
E-mail: help@lfra.co.uk

Website:
http://www.leatherheadfood.com/lfi

Enquiries:
Enquiries to: Business Manager, Library and Electronic Information
Direct tel: 01372 822279
Direct fax: 01372 822268
Direct e-mail: library@lfra.co.uk

Organisation type and purpose:
Scientific and information services for the international food industry

Subject coverage:
Food science and technology, nutrition, sensory analysis, analytical chemistry, food microbiology, food hygiene, food toxicology.

Printed publications:
Majority of publications are confidential to members
Market Reports
Food Legislation Surveys
Literature Surveys
Research Reports
Scientific and Technical Surveys
Technical Circulars
Order printed publications from: http://www.leatherheadfood.com/lfi/submenu.asp?section=11§ionname=Bookshop

Electronic and video publications:
FoodlineWeb Science database (food science and technology)
FoodlineWeb Market database (market and product intelligence)
FoodlineWeb Legal database (additives legislation)
FoodlineWeb News database (food industry news)
Global Food Markets (reports on international food markets and trends)
Regulatory Manuals (UK, EU and International)
Order electronic and video publications from: http://services.leatherheadfood.com/foodline/subscribe.aspx

continued overleaf

Publications list:
Available online

Access to staff:
Contact by letter, by telephone, by fax, by e-mail, in person and via website. Access for members only. Non-members charged.
Hours: Mon to Fri, 0830 to 1730
Special comments: Non-members at the discretion of the Librarian.

LEBANESE EMBASSY

21 Kensington Palace Gardens, London, W8 4QN

Tel: 020 7229 7265
Fax: 020 7243 1699
E-mail: emb.leb@btinternet.com

Enquiries:
Enquiries to: Ambassador's Secretary

Organisation type and purpose:
National government body.
Embassy.
The issue of visas and passports, and actions as power of attorney (Consular Section).

Subject coverage:
Lebanon; its economy and tourism.

Printed publications:
Lebanon – 59 Years of Independence

Access to staff:
Contact by letter, by telephone, by fax and in person. Appointment necessary.
Hours: Mon to Fri, 0900 to 1530

Parent body:
Ministry for Foreign Affairs
   Beirut, Lebanon

LEBRECHT MUSIC AND ARTS PHOTO LIBRARY

3 Bolton Road, London, NW8 0RJ

Tel: 020 7625 5341
Fax: 020 7625 5341
E-mail: pictures@lebrecht.co.uk

Website:
http://www.lebrecht.co.uk

Enquiries:
Enquiries to: Director

Founded:
1992

Organisation type and purpose:
Consultancy, research organisation.
Picture library.
Supply of arts and music pictures to commercial clients from the world's largest specialist music archive and with access to over 8m. arts pictures.

Subject coverage:
Opera, choirs, music scores, concert halls, composers, instruments, musicians, singers, authors, theatre, monuments of famous composers and arts (politics, history, visual arts, literature).

Museum or gallery collection, archive, or library special collection:
Alan Bush Foundation
Kurt Weill Foundation
Martinu Archives
Royal Academy of Music Collection of Images

Non-library collection catalogue:
All or part available online, in-house and in print

Library catalogue:
All or part available online and in-house

Publications list:
Available online

Access to staff:
Contact by letter, by telephone, by fax, by e-mail and via website. Appointment necessary.
Hours: Mon to Fri, 0900 to 1730

LEEDS (SOUTH) METHODIST CIRCUIT OFFICE

Trinity House, Lodge Lane, Leeds, West Yorkshire, LS11 6LR

Tel: 0113 271 6641
E-mail: lsmc@dial.pipex.com

Enquiries:
Enquiries to: Superintendent Minister
Other contacts: Circuit Minister

Founded:
18th Century

Organisation type and purpose:
Voluntary organisation.
Church organisation.

Subject coverage:
Methodist Churches in South Leeds.

Access to staff:
Contact by letter, by telephone and by e-mail
Hours: Mon to Fri, 0900 to 1700

LEEDS CITY LIBRARIES – BUSINESS AND PATENT INFORMATION SERVICES

Acronym or abbreviation: BAPIS

Central Library, Calverley Street, Leeds, LS1 3AB

Tel: 0113 247 8266
Fax: 0113 247 8268
E-mail: piu@leeds.gov.uk

Website:
http://www.businessandpatents.org

Enquiries:
Enquiries to: Manager
Other contacts: Librarian

Organisation type and purpose:
Local government body, public library.

Subject coverage:
All aspects of business, commerce, statistics, company information, market research, job-seeking, trademarks, patents.

Museum or gallery collection, archive, or library special collection:
British Standards
Company Information
D & B KBE
MINT, FAME
KeyNote Market research
Mintel Market Research
Trade Marks
Patent information
Leeds Inventors Group

Library catalogue:
All or part available online and in-house

Printed publications:
Information handouts and its services
Separate sheets on company information, mailing lists
Top 700 companies in Leeds

Access to staff:
Contact by letter, by telephone, by fax, by e-mail, in person and via website
Hours: Mon to Fri, 0900 to 1700; Sat, 1000 to 1300

Access to building, collection or gallery:
Hours: Mon to Wed, 0900 to 2000; Thu and Fri, 0900 to 1700; Sat, 1000 to 1700; Sun, 1300 to 1700

Access for disabled people:
Ramped entry, toilet facilities, lift

LEEDS COLLEGE OF TECHNOLOGY

Acronym or abbreviation: LCOT

Cookridge Street, Leeds, West Yorkshire, LS2 8BL

Tel: 0113 297 6300\ Minicom no. 0113 297 6470
Fax: 0113 297 6301

Enquiries:
Enquiries to: Librarian
Direct tel: 0113 297 6353
Direct e-mail: library@leeds-lcot.ac.uk

Organisation type and purpose:
Suitable for ages: 16+.
Further education college.

Subject coverage:
Engineering, manufacturing, computing, business, media studies, health and social care.

Library catalogue:
All or part available online

Access to staff:
Contact by letter, by telephone, by fax, by e-mail and in person
Hours: Mon to Thu, 0830 to 2030; Fri, 0830 to 1630
Special comments: Letter of introduction required for non LCOT students.

Access for disabled people:
Ramped entry, access to all public areas, toilet facilities
Special comments: Above disabled facilities for Central Site only.

Also at:
Leeds College of Technology
   East Street, Leeds, LS2 8PH; tel: 0113 297 7272; fax: 0113 297 7273
Leeds College of Technology
   Westland Road, Leeds, LS11 5SB; tel: 0113 297 9400; fax: 0113 297 9401

LEEDS INDUSTRIAL MUSEUM

Armley Mills, Canal Road, Armley, Leeds, West Yorkshire, LS12 2QF

Tel: 0113 263 7861
Fax: 0113 224 4365
E-mail: armley.mills@leeds.gov.uk

Website:
http://www.leeds.gov.uk
Web page covering areas of collections.
http://www.leeds.gov.uk/tourinfo/attract/museums/armley/index.html
Armley Mills homepage.
http://www.leeds.gov.uk/tourinfo/events/lmg_arm.html
Events listings.

Enquiries:
Enquiries to: Curator

Founded:
1982

Organisation type and purpose:
Local government body, professional body, museum.
Museum holding information on Leeds' industrial history.

Subject coverage:
Leeds industrial history, printing, photography, cinematography, engineering, textiles, ready made clothing, locomotive building, cranes, transport (road rollers etc).

Information services:
Library available for reference (for conditions see Access above); Library available for reference by appointment.

Special visitor services:
Materials and/or activities for children.

Museum or gallery collection, archive, or library special collection:
Working exhibits include:
1904 Spinning Mule
Ploughing engine, mill engine, steam locomotive
1920s cinema
Archives of photographs/documents relating to Leeds Industries

Printed publications:
Guide Book
Building Sights (Beesley I, commissioned by Museum)

Access to staff:
Contact by letter, by telephone, by fax, by e-mail, in person and via website. Appointment necessary.
Hours: Mon, by appointment only, 0900 to 1700; Tue to Fri, 0900 to 1700

Access for disabled people:
Parking provided, ramped entry, toilet facilities
Special comments: Access to most areas; touch trail; lift to all floors.

Owned by:
Director of Museums and Galleries
  Leeds City Council, Leisure Services Department, Museums & Galleries Division, Leeds Town Hall, Leeds, West Yorkshire

LEEDS LIBRARY AND INFORMATION SERVICES

Central Library, Municipal Buildings, Calverley Street, Leeds, West Yorkshire, LS1 3AB

Tel: 0113 247 6016
Fax: 0113 247 4222
E-mail: enquiry.express@leeds.gov.uk

Website:
http://www.leeds.gov.uk
Council services, tourist information, business and economic information, FE colleges, libraries, local history, and the Leeds photographic archive.

Enquiries:
Enquiries to: Manager
Direct tel: 0113 247 6016
Direct fax: 0113 247 4222

Organisation type and purpose:
Local government body, public library.

Subject coverage:
Business and company information, patents information, local history (Leeds and Yorkshire) also general information service covering all other subjects; separate Art and Music Libraries. Research Library.

Museum or gallery collection, archive, or library special collection:
Art Library:
Gillow Archives (business archives of Gillow Furniture Company)
Kitson Collection (early English watercolours and Rembrandt etchings
Leeds pottery (including Pattern Books)
Sanderson Collection (19th century fashion plates and periodicals)
Music Library:
Scores and cassettes, compact discs
Taphouse Collection (17th and 18th century music and books on music)
Business and Research Library:
British Standards
Gascoigne Collection (military and naval history)
Gott Bequest (early gardening books)
HMSO publications
Leeds Philatelic Society Library
Local History Collection (Leeds and Yorkshire)
Extensive archive of Leeds Theatre materials including posters, indexed by actor, theatre, play, author, etc
Porton Collection (Judaica)
Private press and early printed books
Yorkshire Ramblers Club Library (mountaineering, speleology)

Non-library collection catalogue:
All or part available in-house

Library catalogue:
All or part available in-house

Access to staff:
Contact by letter, by telephone, by fax and by e-mail
Hours: Mon, Tue, Wed, 0900 to 2000; Thu, 0930 to 1730; Sat, 1000 to 1700; Sun, 1200 to 1600

Access for disabled people:
Level entry, toilet facilities

LEEDS LIBRARY, THE

18 Commercial Street, Leeds, LS1 6AL

Tel: 0113 2453071
Fax: 0113 2451191
E-mail: enquiries@theleedslibrary.org.uk

Website:
http://www.theleedslibrary.org.uk

Enquiries:
Enquiries to: Librarian

Founded:
1768

Organisation type and purpose:
Subscription library (Company no. 5577905; Charity no. 1114386).

Museum or gallery collection, archive, or library special collection:
Library of 135,000 items
Civil War pamphlets
Reformation Tracts

Printed publications:
The Dial (newsletter, occasional)

Access to staff:
Contact by letter, by telephone, by fax, by e-mail and via website. Appointment necessary. Letter of introduction required.
Hours: Mon to Fri, 0900 to 1700

LEEDS MEDICAL INFORMATION

Acronym or abbreviation: LMI

University of Leeds, Leeds, West Yorkshire, LS2 9JT

Tel: 0113 343 5552
Fax: 0113 343 5568
E-mail: lmi@leeds.ac.uk

Website:
http://www.leeds.ac.uk/lmi/
http://www.leeds.ac.uk/lmi/publications.html
List of all publications which can then be accessed from this page.

Enquiries:
Enquiries to: Manager
Direct tel: 0113 343 4381
Direct e-mail: n.v.king@leeds.ac.uk

Founded:
1974

Organisation type and purpose:
University library.
Academic publishing unit and information consultancy; based at the University of Leeds.

Subject coverage:
Clinical cancer (oncology), cancer; palliative care

Printed publications:
Mitomycin-C Update (quarterly)
Progress in Palliative Care (6 times a year)

Access to staff:
Contact by letter, by telephone, by fax and by e-mail
Hours: Mon to Fri, 0900 to 1700

Parent body:
University of Leeds

LEEDS METROPOLITAN UNIVERSITY

Learning Centre, Leslie Silver Building, City Campus, Leeds, West Yorkshire, LS1 3HE

Tel: 0113 283 5956
Fax: 0113 283 6779
E-mail: p.payne@lmu.ac.uk

Website:
http://www.lmu.ac.uk/lis/lss
Guide to Learning Centres; subject guides, documentation, frequently asked questions, access to electronic services.

Enquiries:
Enquiries to: Head of Learning Support Services
Direct tel: 0113 283 5966
Direct e-mail: p.payne@lmu.ac.uk
Other contacts: Administration Assistant (Recruitment) for recruitment.

Organisation type and purpose:
University learning support services.

Subject coverage:
European Union – single market; accounting and finance; art, design, film and photography; business studies, management, law; health and science; hospitality management; engineering; social sciences; computing and information systems; education; European languages; human movement, leisure and tourism; architecture; landscape design; construction; quantity surveying; civil engineering; environmental health; urban development; library and information studies.

Museum or gallery collection, archive, or library special collection:
Collection of the West Yorkshire Society of Architects
European Documentation Centre

Trade and statistical information:
European information via Mid Yorkshire European Information Centre.

Non-library collection catalogue:
All or part available online

Library catalogue:
All or part available online

Printed publications:
Quote, unquote: The Harvard Style of Referencing Published Material (Learning and Information Services, 2nd ed., May 2001, £5, cheque with order)

Access to staff:
Contact by letter, by telephone, by fax, by e-mail and in person. Non-members charged.
Hours: Term time: Mon to Thu, 0845 to 2245; Fri, 0845 to 1845; Sat, 1000 to 1545; Sun, 1000 to 1745
Special comments: Mid-Yorkshire European Information Centre from 0845 to 1700. Restrictions on accessing CD-ROM and Internet services apply. Charges made for borrowing.

Other addresses:
Harrogate College
Learning Centre
  Hornbeam Park, Harrogate, HG2 8QT; tel: 0113 283 2600 ext 8282; e-mail: a.sargeant@lmu.ac.uk
Learning Centre
  James Graham Building, Beckett Park, Leeds, LS6 3QS; tel: 0113 283 7467; fax: 0113 283 3211; e-mail: n.thompson@lmu.ac.uk
Leeds Metropolitan University

LEEK GROWERS' ASSOCIATION

133 Eastgate, Louth, Lincolnshire, LN11 9QG

Tel: 01507 602427
Fax: 01507 607165
E-mail: crop.association@pvga.co.uk

Website:
http://www.british-leeks.co.uk

Enquiries:
Enquiries to: Membership Secretary

Founded:
1980s

Organisation type and purpose:
National organisation, trade association.

Subject coverage:
Leeks.

LEGAL ACTION GROUP

Acronym or abbreviation: LAG

242 Pentonville Road, London, N1 9UN

continued overleaf

Tel: 020 7833 2931
Fax: 020 7837 6094
E-mail: lag@lag.org.uk

Website:
http://www.lag.org.uk
Policy, comment, publications and training courses.

Enquiries:
Enquiries to: Director

Founded:
1972

Organisation type and purpose:
Voluntary organisation, registered charity (charity number 265703).
Solicitors, barristers, advisers, academics, students and others, concerned to improve legal services to the community.

Subject coverage:
Legal services, legal profession, social welfare, law, penal affairs and crime.

Printed publications:
Legal Action (monthly magazine)
Community Care Law reports (quarterly)
Books include:
Employment Law (T. Lewis, 2007, £30)
Defending Suspects at Police Stations (E. Cape with J. Luqmani, 2006, £52)
Support for Asylum-Seekers (S. Willman et al, 2004, £19.50)

Publications list:
Available in print

Access to staff:
Contact via website. Appointment necessary.
Hours: Mon to Fri, 1000 to 1700

Constituent part of:
LAG Education and Service Trust Limited

LEGAL SERVICES OMBUDSMAN

3rd Floor, Sunlight House, Quay Street, Manchester, M3 3JZ

Tel: 0161 839 7262 / Lo-call 0845 601 0794
Fax: 0161 832 5446
E-mail: lso@olso.gsi.gov.uk

Website:
http://www.olso.org

Enquiries:
Enquiries to: Information Officer

Founded:
1990

Subject coverage:
Deals with complaints about the behaviour and quality of service of solicitors if the Solicitors Complaints Bureau has failed to provide satisfaction.

Printed publications:
Annual reports, leaflets.

Access to staff:
Contact by letter, by telephone, by fax and by e-mail
Hours: Mon to Fri, 0900 to 1630

Access to building, collection or gallery:
No prior appointment required

Access for disabled people:
Level entry

LEICESTER CENTRAL LEARNING AND INFORMATION LIBRARY

Bishop Street, Leicester, LE1 6AA

Tel: 0116 299 5401
Fax: 0116 299 5444
E-mail: central.reference@leicester.gov.uk

Website:
http://www.leicester.gov.uk

Enquiries:
Enquiries to: Manager
Direct tel: 0116 299 5413
Direct e-mail: sally.mitchell@leicester.gov.uk
Other contacts: Duty Officer

Founded:
1905

Formerly called:
Reference and Information Library (year of change 2007)

Organisation type and purpose:
Public library.

Subject coverage:
Business information, Public and General Acts dating back to 1650, statistics, government publications, local group and societies database for Leicestershire; Leicester maps, local history, health, arts and law.

Museum or gallery collection, archive, or library special collection:
19th-century periodicals: hardcopy, excellent collection
Burchnall film collection
Stretton railway collection

Non-library collection catalogue:
All or part available in-house

Library catalogue:
All or part available online

Access to staff:
Contact by letter, by telephone, by fax, by e-mail, in person and via website
Hours: Mon to Thu, 0930 to 1900; Fri, 0900 to 1700; Sat, 0900 to 1600

Access to building, collection or gallery:
No access other than to staff

Access for disabled people:
Fully accessible

LEICESTER CENTRAL LENDING LIBRARY

54 Belvoir Street, Leicester, LE1 6QG

Tel: 0116 299 5402
Fax: 0116 299 5434
E-mail: artsl203@leicester.gov.uk

Enquiries:
Enquiries to: Manager

Organisation type and purpose:
Public library.

Access to staff:
Contact by letter, by telephone, by fax, by e-mail and in person
Hours: Mon to Thu, 0930 to 1900; Fri, 0930 to 1700; Sat, 0900 to 1600

Access to building, collection or gallery:
No prior appointment required

Access for disabled people:
Ramped entry

LEICESTER CITY COUNCIL

New Walk Centre, Welford Place, Leicester, LE1 6ZG

Tel: 0116 254 9922
Fax: 0116 254 5531

Website:
http://www.demontforthall.co.uk
http://www.leicester.gov.uk
http://www.leicestermuseums.ac.uk
http://www.leicesterspark.co.uk
http://www.leicester-env-city.org.uk

Enquiries:
Enquiries to: Chief Executive

Organisation type and purpose:
Local government body.

LEICESTER LONGWOOL SHEEP BREEDERS ASSOCIATION

Acronym or abbreviation: LLSBA

Driffield Agricultural Society, The Showground, Kelley Thorpe, Driffield, East Yorkshire, YO25 9DN

Tel: 01377 257494
Fax: 01377 257464
E-mail: office@driffieldshow.co.uk

Website:
http://www.stockmaster.co.uk
Breeds of livestock with contact details.

Enquiries:
Enquiries to: Secretary

Founded:
1883

Organisation type and purpose:
Membership association (membership is by subscription), present number of members: 81. Breed society.

Printed publications:
Flock Book (purchase to non-members)

Publications list:
Available online

Access to staff:
Contact by letter, by telephone, by fax, by e-mail and in person
Hours: Mon to Fri, 0900 to 1700

Connected with:
National Sheep Association (NSA)
Rare Breeds Survival Trust (RBST)

LEICESTERSHIRE ARCHAEOLOGICAL AND HISTORICAL SOCIETY

Acronym or abbreviation: LAHS

The Guildhall, Leicester, LE1 5FQ

Tel: 0116 270 3031
E-mail: alan@dovedale2.demon.co.uk

Website:
http://www.leicester.ac.uk/archaeology/lahs/lahs.html

Enquiries:
Enquiries to: Honorary Secretary
Direct e-mail: alan@dovedale2.demon.co.uk

Founded:
1855

Organisation type and purpose:
International organisation, national organisation, learned society (membership is by subscription), registered charity.

Subject coverage:
Archaeology; local history; Leicestershire vernacular architecture; history of Leicester and Leicestershire.

Museum or gallery collection, archive, or library special collection:
Local History and Archaeology Library

Library catalogue:
All or part available in-house

Printed publications:
Leicestershire Historian (annually)
Transactions of the Society (annually)
Newsletter (2 times a year)

Access to staff:
Contact by letter and by e-mail
Hours: Mon to Fri, 0900 to 1700

LEICESTERSHIRE CHAMBER OF COMMERCE

Acronym or abbreviation: LCCI

Charnwood Court, 5b New Walk, Leicester, LE1 6TE

Tel: 0116 247 1800
Fax: 0116 247 0430
E-mail: leics@chamberofcommerce.co.uk

Website:
http://www.chamberofcommerce.co.uk

Enquiries:
Enquiries to: Chief Executive

Founded:
1860

Organisation type and purpose:
Membership association (membership is by
subscription), present number of members: 1,500,
manufacturing industry, service industry.

Subject coverage:
International trade services, training, general
employment information, business networking
events.

Access to staff:
Contact by letter, by telephone, by fax, by e-mail
and via website. Appointment necessary. Access
for members only.
Hours: Mon to Fri, 0900 to 1700

Access to building, collection or gallery:
Prior appointment required

LEICESTERSHIRE COUNTY COUNCIL

Acronym or abbreviation: LLIS

Libraries & Information Service, County Hall,
Glenfield, Leicester, LE3 8SS

Tel: 0116 265 7372
Fax: 0116 265 7370
E-mail: poldroyd@leics.gov.uk

Website:
http://www.leics.gov.uk/libraries

Enquiries:
Enquiries to: Chief Librarian
Other contacts: Head of Library Services for
Education for Library Services for Education/
Schools.

Organisation type and purpose:
Local government body, statutory body, public
library.

Subject coverage:
General; Leicestershire.

**Museum or gallery collection, archive, or library
special collection:**
Hunting Collection at Melton Mowbray Library

Library catalogue:
All or part available online

Printed publications:
Local History Material
Order printed publications from: Publicity and
Promotions Officer, Leicestershire Libraries and
Information Service
County Hall, tel: 0116 265 7386, fax: 0116 265 7370

Publications list:
Available in print

Access to staff:
Contact by letter, by telephone, by fax, by e-mail,
in person and via website
Hours: Mon to Fri, 0900 to 1700

Other addresses:
Library Services for Education
   929–931 Loughborough Road, Rothley, Leicester,
   LE7 7NH; tel: 0116 267 8000; fax: 0116 267 8039;
   e-mail: gwillars@leics.gov.uk

LEICESTERSHIRE LIBRARY SERVICES

Acronym or abbreviation: LLS

County Hall, Glenfield, Leicester, LE3 8SS

Tel: 0116 305 7378
Fax: 0116 305 7370

Website:
http://www.leics.gov.uk/libraries

Enquiries:
Enquiries to: Head of Library Services
Direct e-mail: mbellamy@leics.gov.uk
Other contacts: Information Development Librarian.

Organisation type and purpose:
Local government body, statutory body, public
library.

Subject coverage:
General, Leicestershire.

**Museum or gallery collection, archive, or library
special collection:**
Hunting collection at Melton Mowbray library

Library catalogue:
All or part available online

Printed publications:
Local history material

Publications list:
Available in print

Access to staff:
Contact by letter, by telephone, by fax, by e-mail,
in person and via website
Hours: Mon to Fri, 0900 to 1700

Parent body:
Leicestershire County Council

LEICESTERSHIRE MUSEUMS SERVICE

County Hall, Glenfield, Leicester, LE3 8RA

Tel: 0116 265 6783
Fax: 0116 264 5820
E-mail: museums@leics.gov.uk

Website:
http://www.leics.gov.uk/museums

Enquiries:
Enquiries to: Director

Organisation type and purpose:
Local government body, museum.
Headquarters of Leicestershire Museums.

Subject coverage:
Coal mining

**Museum or gallery collection, archive, or library
special collection:**
Library of coal-mining at Snibston Museum,
   Coalville

Non-library collection catalogue:
All or part available in-house

Access to staff:
Contact by letter, by telephone, by fax, by e-mail,
in person and via website. Appointment necessary.
Hours: Mon to Fri, 0900 to 1630

Access to building, collection or gallery:
Prior appointment required

Access for disabled people:
Parking provided, toilet facilities

LEISURE DATABASE COMPANY, THE

33 Bedford Street, Covent Garden, London, WC2E
9EJ

Tel: 020 7379 3197
Fax: 020 7379 0898

Website:
http://www.theleisuredatabase.com
Company services.

Enquiries:
Enquiries to: Managing Director
Direct tel: 020 7395 6171
Other contacts: Director, Sales and Subscriptions for
sales enquiries.

Founded:
1981

Organisation type and purpose:
Research organisation.
Commercial information company.
Providing the country's leading database of sports,
health and fitness provision.

Subject coverage:
Sports provision, health and fitness.

Trade and statistical information:
Sport facilities charges in London.
Data on Leisure Facility Management: UK-wide.
Data on health and fitness clubs: UK-wide.
Data on public sector sports provision: UK-wide.

Printed publications:
State of the Health & Fitness Industry (annually)
Sports Facility Charges in the London Boroughs

Electronic and video publications:
Private Health Clubs UK Dataset
Local Authority Sports Venues

Publications list:
Available in print

Access to staff:
Contact by letter, by telephone, by fax and by e-
mail
Hours: Mon to Fri, 0900 to 1800

LEISURE, CULTURE AND LIFELONG LEARNING

Libraries and Heritage Central Library, Lichfield
Street, Walsall, West Midlands, WS1 1TR

Tel: 01922 653110
Fax: 01922 654013
E-mail: librarycentref@walsall.gov.uk

Website:
http://www.walsall.gov.uk/libraries

Enquiries:
Enquiries to: Information Officer

Founded:
1906

Organisation type and purpose:
Local government body, public library.

Subject coverage:
Tourist information, clubs and societies relating to
Walsall, business information, council information,
European information.

**Museum or gallery collection, archive, or library
special collection:**
Guardian 1990– , KBE–Current, Social Trends,
   Times 1990– (CD-ROMs)

Non-library collection catalogue:
All or part available online

Library catalogue:
All or part available online

Printed publications:
Local Organisations Directory
How to contact your Walsall Councillor
Periodical catalogue
Tourist information for Walsall
Walsall information guides – listing clubs, societies
   and local organisations in Walsall

Access to staff:
Contact by letter, by telephone, by fax, by e-mail
and in person
Hours: Mon to Fri, 0900 to 1700

Member organisation of:
Black Country Libraries in Partnership

LEO BAECK COLLEGE

Acronym or abbreviation: LBC

Sternberg Centre for Judaism, 80 East End Road,
London, N3 2SY

Tel: 020 8349 5600
Fax: 020 8349 5619
E-mail: info@lbc.ac.uk

continued overleaf

Website:
http://www.lbc.ac.uk

Enquiries:
Enquiries to: Director of Finance and
Administration
Direct e-mail: stephen.ross@lbc.ac.uk

Founded:
1956

Organisation type and purpose:
International organisation, registered charity
(charity number 209777), suitable for ages:
postgraduate.
Rabbinic training and Jewish college.

Subject coverage:
Jewish studies.

Education services:
Rabbinic studies, Jewish Adult learning, GCSE
exams, Lectures, Shiurim, MA and Advanced
Diploma courses, Early Years courses in Jewish
education

**Museum or gallery collection, archive, or library
special collection:**
Library: 30,000 books, pamphlets, etc.

Library catalogue:
All or part available online

Printed publications:
Annual diary
A selection of Jewish Educational material
Book Series
European Judaism (learned journal, twice yearly)
Shalom Batsheva (a girl's life during the war; price
£4.50)

Electronic and video publications:
Jewish Heritage Video (intermediate age, lower
secondary, four videos for £15)
The Western Wall Video (Jerusalem, the city of
three great faiths; price £7.50)

Publications list:
Available online and in print

Access to staff:
Appointment necessary.
Hours: Mon to Fri, 0900 to 1700

LEONARD CHESHIRE

Head Office, 66 South Lambeth Road, London,
SW8 1RL

Tel: 020 3242 0200
Fax: 020 3242 0250
E-mail: info@lcdisability.org

Website:
http://www.leonard-cheshire.org
Information on Leonard Cheshire's services and
activities.

Enquiries:
Enquiries to: Information Resources Officer

Founded:
1948

Organisation type and purpose:
Voluntary organisation.
To provide choice and opportunity to people with
disabilities, emphasising the right of the individual
to decide how he or she wants to live.

Subject coverage:
Operating in 55 countries worldwide. It promotes
the care, general well-being and rehabilitation of
people with physical and learning disabilities. In
the UK the Foundation comprises 85 Cheshire
Homes offering a range of care services, including
full-time residential care, respite and day care and
short-stay holiday breaks. Some of these also offer
accommodation for full or semi-independent living
with all the advantages of separate housing
combined with 24 hour help close at hand if
needed. In addition, there are a growing number of
Care at Home Services (37 in 1993) which provide
personal care and undertake day to day tasks for
people with disabilities in their own homes.

**Museum or gallery collection, archive, or library
special collection:**
Personal Collection of Founder, Group Captain
Leonard Cheshire VC, available in hardcopy,
microform; also audiovisual and photographs
available
Administrative Archive of organisations he
founded: Leonard Cheshire, Ryder-Cheshire and
World Memorial Fund

Non-library collection catalogue:
All or part available in-house

Printed publications:
Variety of leaflets and reports (free)
International Services Directory
Leonard Cheshire Service Directory
The Hidden World (Cheshire L)
Still the Candle Burns (Beslievre J)
Rydale Pilgrimage (52 prints of Yorkshire churches
with personal impressions, history and
architecture, Goodall D)

Electronic and video publications:
Enabling Ordinary Lives (video, free plus £3.95 for
p&p)
Database of services available

Publications list:
Available in print

Access to staff:
Contact by letter, by telephone, by fax, by e-mail
and via website
Hours: Mon to Fri, 0900 to 1700

Access to building, collection or gallery:
Prior appointment required

Access for disabled people:
Parking provided, level entry, access to all public
areas, toilet facilities

LEONARD CHESHIRE DISABILITY ARCHIVE

Leonard Cheshire Disability Archive Centre,
Newlands House, Main Street, Netherseal, DE12
8DA

Tel: 01283 763951
Fax: 01283 763951
E-mail: archive@lcdisability.org

Website:
http://www.lcdisability.org/?lid=21
http://www.leonard-cheshire.org

Enquiries:
Enquiries to: Honorary Secretary
Other contacts: Archivist

Founded:
1948

Organisation type and purpose:
International organisation, voluntary organisation,
registered charity (charity number 218186).
The archive of The Leonard Cheshire Foundation.
The parent body The Leonard Cheshire
Foundation offers services to people with
disabilities.

Subject coverage:
Leonard Cheshire (the man), Group Captain Lord
Cheshire of Woodhall, VC OM DSO DFC.
Leonard Cheshire Foundation's work; Ryder-
Cheshire Foundation's work; services for people
with disabilities provided by these organisations.

Non-library collection catalogue:
All or part available in-house

Printed publications:
Order printed publications from: National
Information Officer, Leonard Cheshire
30 Millbank, London, SW1P 4QD, tel: 020 7802
8200

Electronic and video publications:
Enabling Ordinary Lives – details, aims and scope
of Leonard Cheshire – Outlines products and
services (CD-ROM and tape)

Access to staff:
Contact by letter, by telephone and by fax.
Appointment necessary.
Hours: Mon to Fri, 0900 to 1700
Special comments: Some material on restricted
access.

Access to building, collection or gallery:
No prior appointment required

Other address:
Leonard Cheshire Disability
66 South Lambeth Road, London, SW8 1RL; tel:
020 3242 0200; fax: 020 3242 0250

LEPROSY MISSION INTERNATIONAL, THE

Acronym or abbreviation: TLM

80 Windmill Road, Brentford, Middlesex, TW8
0QH

Tel: 020 8326 6767
Fax: 020 8326 6777
E-mail: friends@tlmint.org

Website:
http://www.leprosymission.org
Information on organisation and the disease of
leprosy; national office contacts.

Enquiries:
Enquiries to: Communications Officer
Direct e-mail: fionac@hmint.org

Founded:
1874

Organisation type and purpose:
International organisation, voluntary organisation,
registered charity.
To minister in the name of Jesus Christ to people
affected by leprosy.

Subject coverage:
Leprosy (Hansen's disease), historical, medical,
current field work.

**Museum or gallery collection, archive, or library
special collection:**
Library of Leprosy-related books
Archive photographs dating from 1890s to present
TLM's annual reports (dating back to early 1900s)

Printed publications:
Annual Report and other magazines and
information packs for general public
Books sold through TLM Trading Catalogue

Publications list:
Available in print

Access to staff:
Contact via website. Appointment necessary.
Hours: Mon to Fri, 0900 to 1700

Access for disabled people:
Parking provided, ramped entry, level entry, access
to all public areas, toilet facilities

Member of:
Global Connections
International Federation of Anti-Leprosy
Associations (ILEP)
234 Blythe Road, London, W14 0HJ

Other addresses:
Leprosy Mission England and Wales (includes The
Channel Islands and The Isle of Man)
Goldhay Way, Orton Goldhay, Peterborough,
Cambridgeshire, PE2 5GZ; tel: 01733 370505; fax:
01733 404880; e-mail: post@tlmew.org.uk;
website: www.leprosymission.org.uk
Leprosy Mission Northern Ireland
Lagan House, 2A Queens Road, Lisburn, BT27
4TZ; tel: 028 9038 1842; e-mail: info@tlm-ni.org;
website: www.tlm-ni.org
Leprosy Mission Scotland
Suite 2, Earlsgate Lodge, Livilands Lane, Stirling,
FK8 2BG; tel: 01786 449266; e-mail: office@
tlmscotland.org.uk; website: www.tlmscotland
.org.uk

LESOTHO HIGH COMMISSION

7 Chesham Place, London, SW1X 8HN

Tel: 020 7235 5686
Fax: 020 7235 5023
E-mail: lhc@lesotholondon.org.uk

Website:
http://www.lesotholondon.org.uk

Enquiries:
Enquiries to: First Secretary
Other contacts: First Secretary, Information Officer

Founded:
1966

Organisation type and purpose:
International organisation, national government body.
Diplomatic mission.

Subject coverage:
Lesotho.

Access to staff:
Contact by letter, by telephone, by fax, by e-mail and via website. Appointment necessary.
Hours: Mon to Fri, 0900 to 1245 and 1400 to 1600

Access to building, collection or gallery:
No access other than to staff

LEUKAEMIA CARE SOCIETY

2 Shrubbery Avenue, Worcester, WR1 1QH

Tel: 01905 330003 or Care Line: 0800 1696680
Fax: 01905 330090
E-mail: enquiries@leukaemiacare.org.uk

Website:
http://www.leukaemiacare.org.uk

Enquiries:
Enquiries to: Network Operations Manager

Founded:
1967

Organisation type and purpose:
Voluntary organisation, registered charity (charity number 259483).

Subject coverage:
Information about leukaemia and allied blood disorders, friendship, support and practical help for sufferers and their relatives, caravan holidays, limited financial assistance.

Printed publications:
Brochure and leaflets (free)
Newsletter (free, 2 times a year)

Access to staff:
Contact by letter, by telephone, by fax, by e-mail and via website. Appointment necessary.
Hours: 0900 to 1630
Special comments: Telephone diversion outside office hours.

LEUKAEMIA RESEARCH

Acronym or abbreviation: LRF

43 Great Ormond Street, London, WC1N 3JJ

Tel: 020 7405 0101
Fax: 020 7405 3139
E-mail: info@lrf.org.uk

Website:
http://www.lrf.org.uk

Enquiries:
Enquiries to: Information Officer

Founded:
1960

Organisation type and purpose:
National organisation, voluntary organisation, registered charity (charity number 216032), research organisation.
Improving treatment, finding cures and causes of leukaemia, lymphoma, myeloma, myelodysplasia, myeloproliferative disorders and aplastic anaemia.

Subject coverage:
Leukaemia, acute leukaemia in children, coping with childhood leukaemia, acute lymphoblastic leukaemia, acute myeloid leukaemia, chronic myeloid leukaemia, bone marrow and stem cell transplantation, the lymphomas, multiple myeloma, myelodysplastic syndromes, aplastic anaemia, dictionary of leukaemia and related diseases, chronic lymphocytic leukaemia, less common disorders related to leukaemia, myeloproliferature disorders.

Printed publications:
Abstracts of Research Workshops
Annual Guest Lectures
Annual Review
Booklets and leaflets on each of the several types of leukaemia, lymphoma, myeloma and related conditions (free)
Newsletters
Proceedings of International Symposia

Publications list:
Available online and in print

Access to staff:
Contact by letter, by telephone, by fax, by e-mail, in person and via website
Hours: Mon to Fri, 0930 to 1645

Member organisation of:
UK Co-ordinating Committee for Cancer Research

LEUKAEMIA RESEARCH UNIT

Centre for Adult Leukaemia, Hammersmith Hospital/Imperial College, Du Cane Road, London, W12 0NN

Tel: 020 8383 3238
Fax: 020 8740 9679

Enquiries:
Enquiries to: Chairman

Founded:
1988

Organisation type and purpose:
Professional body, university department or institute.

Subject coverage:
Leukaemia.

Printed publications:
Order printed publications from: Chairman, Department of Haematology
Imperial College School of Medicine, Hammersmith Hospital, Du Cane Road, London, W12 0NN

LEWIS CARROLL SOCIETY

Acronym or abbreviation: LCS

69 Cromwell Road, Hertford, SG13 7DP

E-mail: alanwhite@tesco.net

Enquiries:
Enquiries to: Secretary

Founded:
1969

Organisation type and purpose:
International organisation, learned society (membership is by subscription), present number of members: 400, registered charity (charity number 266239), suitable for all ages: .

Subject coverage:
Charles Dodgson: life and works (Lewis Carroll).

Printed publications:
Bandersnatch (newsletter, quarterly)
Lewis Carroll Review (reviewing journal, occasional)
The Carrollian (replaces Jaberwocky, journal, quarterly)
Order printed publications from: The Lewis Carroll Society
Yew Tree Cottage, Parks Road, Clifford, Hereford, HR3 5HQ

Publications list:
Available online and in print

Access to staff:
Contact by letter, by e-mail and via website
Hours: Mon to Fri, 0900 to 1700

Links with:
Lewis Carroll Society of North America

LEWISHAM LOCAL HISTORY AND ARCHIVES CENTRE

Lewisham Library, 199–201 Lewisham High Street, London, SE13 6LG

Tel: 020 8297 0682
Fax: 020 8297 1169
E-mail: local.studies@lewisham.gov.uk

Website:
http://www.lewisham.gov.uk

Enquiries:
Enquiries to: Archivist

Founded:
1960

Organisation type and purpose:
Local government body, public library.
Archives.
Archive and local studies service for the London Borough of Lewisham.

Subject coverage:
London Borough of Lewisham; history and current information.

Museum or gallery collection, archive, or library special collection:
Archives of the Borough and predecessor authorities, and of organisations within the Borough
Local studies material relating to the Borough
Small museum collection

Non-library collection catalogue:
All or part available online and in-house

Publications list:
Available online and in print

Access to staff:
Contact by letter, by telephone, by fax, by e-mail and in person
Hours: Mon, 1000 to 1700; Fri, 0900 to 1700; Tue and Thu, 0900 to 2000; Sat, 0900 to 1700
Special comments: Appointments advised

Access for disabled people:
Access to all public areas

Parent body:
London Borough of Lewisham
London, SE6

LEWISHAM REFERENCE LIBRARY

199–201 Lewisham High Street, London, SE13 6LG

Tel: 020 8297 9430
Fax: 020 8297 1169
E-mail: reference.library@lewisham.gov.uk

Website:
http://www.lewisham.gov.uk
Information about Lewisham as a local authority.

Enquiries:
Enquiries to: Librarian

Organisation type and purpose:
Local government body, public library.

Subject coverage:
Arts, humanities and social sciences, specialist holding at Library Service Bookstore, Hither Green Lane, London SE13 6TJ: biology.

Library catalogue:
All or part available in-house

Access to staff:
Contact by telephone, by e-mail and in person
Hours: Wed, Fri and Sat, 0900 to 1700; Mon, Tue, Thu, 0900 to 2000; Sun, 1300 to 1600

continued overleaf

Access for disabled people:
Parking provided, level entry, access to all public areas, toilet facilities

Member of:
South East Area Libraries Information Service

Official:
European Public Information Centre (EPIC)

LGC

Formal name: LGC

Queens Road, Teddington, Middlesex, TW11 0LY

Tel: 020 8943 7000
Fax: 020 8943 2767
E-mail: info@lgc.co.uk

Website:
http://www.lgc.co.uk

Enquiries:
Enquiries to: Client Services

Organisation type and purpose:
International organisation, statutory body, service industry, training organisation, consultancy, research organisation.

Subject coverage:
Analytical chemistry, methods of analysis: wines, soft drinks, spirits, beer, sugar composites, foods, pesticide formulations and residues, drug analysis, radionuclides in water, water analysis, environmental analysis and advice, contaminated land analysis, background information on a wide variety of products, including plastics, chemicals, hydrocarbon and essential oils, safety and health, analytical quality control and certified reference materials, lifesciences (DNA services) and analytical molecular biology.

Library catalogue:
All or part available in-house

Printed publications:
Annual Report
Corporate Brochure
Annual Review of the Government Chemist

Publications list:
Available in print

Access to staff:
Contact by letter, by telephone, by fax and by e-mail
Hours: Mon to Fri, 0900 to 1730

Access to building, collection or gallery:
No access other than to staff

LIBERAL DEMOCRATS

4 Cowley Street, London, SW1P 3NB

Tel: 020 7222 7999
Fax: 020 7799 2170
E-mail: libdems@cix.co.uk

Website:
http://www.libdems.org.uk

Enquiries:
Enquiries to: Information Officer
Direct tel: 020 7227 1385

Organisation type and purpose:
Membership association (membership is by subscription), present number of members: 90,000. Political party.

Subject coverage:
Party policy, party structure and organisation, party history.

Museum or gallery collection, archive, or library special collection:
Liberal Party archive held at London School of Economics and Political Science Library, Houghton Street, London WC2A 2AE
SDP archive held at Albert Sloman Library, University of Essex

Printed publications:
Handbook and Directory

Liberal Democrat News (weekly, on subscription)
Policy papers, policy briefings, annual report
Order printed publications from: Liberal Democrat Publications
4 Cowley Street, London, SW1P 3NB, tel: 020 7222 7999, fax: 020 7799 2170, e-mail: ld-membservs@cix .co.uk

Publications list:
Available in print

Access to staff:
Contact by letter, by telephone, by fax, by e-mail and via website
Hours: Mon to Fri, 0930 to 1730

Full member of the:
Federation of European Liberal Democrat and Reform Parties (ELDR)
Building Leo (D2), 55C rue Wiertz, Brussels, B-1047, Belgium; tel: + 322 284 3169; fax: + 322 231 1907
Liberal International (LI)
1 Whitehall Place, London, SW1A 2HE; tel: 020 7839 5905; fax: 020 7925 2685; e-mail: worldlib@ cix.co.uk

Other addresses:
Liberal Democrats, Wales
Bay View House, 102 Bute Street, Cardiff, CF1 6AD; tel: 029 2031 3400; fax: 029 2031 3401; e-mail: ldwales@cix.co.uk
Scottish Liberal Democrats
4 Clifton Terrace, Edinburgh, EH12 5DR; tel: 0131 337 2314; fax: 0131 337 3566; e-mail: scotlibdem@cix.co.uk; website: www .scotlibdems.org.uk

LIBERAL INTERNATIONAL

Acronym or abbreviation: LI

1 Whitehall Place, London, SW1A 2HD

Tel: 020 7839 5905
Fax: 020 7925 2685
E-mail: all@liberal-international.org

Website:
http://www.liberal-international.org
The official homepage of more than 83 liberal parties and youth organisations worldwide.

Enquiries:
Enquiries to: Secretary General
Other contacts: (1) Programme Officer (2) Political Assistant for (1) specific information about member parties (2) specific information about member parties and general information.

Founded:
1947

Organisation type and purpose:
International organisation.
A global network of Liberals as well as the world union of Liberal parties. It acts as a platform and political meeting point and represents its member parties. The main goal of the organisation is the promotion of Liberal values.

Subject coverage:
International liberalism, human rights, democratisation, tolerance, freedom and an economy based on market principles.

Museum or gallery collection, archive, or library special collection:
Basic documents on liberal ideology

Printed publications:
A Sense of Liberty: The History of Liberal International
Giovanni Malagodi
Liberalism in the World (annual)
London Aerogramme (6 times a year)
Reports and brochures
The Local Politics Toolbox
Various Leaflets

Access to staff:
Contact by letter, by telephone, by fax, by e-mail and via website. Access for members only.

Hours: Mon to Fri, 0900 to 1700

Access to building, collection or gallery:
No access other than to staff

LIBERAL JUDAISM

The Montagu Centre, 21 Maple Street, London, W1T 4BE

Tel: 020 7580 1663
Fax: 020 7631 9838
E-mail: montagu@liberaljudaism.org

Website:
http://www.liberaljudaism.org

Enquiries:
Enquiries to: Office Manager
Direct tel: 020 7631 9822
Direct e-mail: s.o'dwyer@liberaljudaism.org

Founded:
1902

Organisation type and purpose:
International organisation, membership association (membership is by subscription), present number of members: over 9000, voluntary organisation, registered charity (charity number 236590), publishing house.
National organisation of synagogues.

Subject coverage:
Progressive Judaism in Great Britain, education, Liberal Judaism.

Printed publications:
Books and prayer books
From Belsen to Buckingham Palace (Oppenheimer P)
Judaism for Today
On Being Jewish (Neuberger J)
The Illuminated Haggadah
The People's Bible
Liberal Judaism: A Judaism for the 21st Century
Liberal Judaism: The First 100 Years
Order printed publications from: Liberal Judaism at the same address, e-mail: books@liberaljudaism .org

Electronic and video publications:
How to do Seder (tape and booklet)
This is Liberal Judaism (CD-Rom)

Publications list:
Available online and in print

Access to staff:
Contact by letter, by fax, by e-mail and in person
Hours: Mon to Thu, 0900 to 1700; Fri, 0900 to 1500

Access to building, collection or gallery:
No access other than to staff

Affiliated to:
World Union for Progressive Judaism

LIBERTARIAN ALLIANCE

Acronym or abbreviation: LA

25 Chapter Chambers, Esterbrook Street, London, SW1P 4NN

Tel: 020 7821 5502
Fax: 020 7834 2031
E-mail: admin@libertarian.co.uk

Website:
http://www.libertarian.co.uk

Enquiries:
Enquiries to: Director

Founded:
1965

Organisation type and purpose:
Voluntary organisation, publishing house.
Political organisation, radical pro-free market and civil libertarian group.

Subject coverage:
Libertarian issues, civil and economic liberties, free market economics, data base on scholars, scholarship and organisations in these areas.

Museum or gallery collection, archive, or library special collection:
Photographs of leading contemporary and historical Libertarian and Classical Liberal scholars and writers

Printed publications:
Free Life (journal, quarterly)
Libertarian News (irregular)
Tanstaafl Times (2 times a month)
Irregular notes, guides, and other publications covering:
Political notes
Philosophical notes
Legal notes
Cultural notes
Historial notes
Sociological notes
Foreigh Policy Perspectives
Libertarian Fictions etc

Publications list:
Available online and in print

Access to staff:
Contact by letter, by telephone, by fax and by e-mail. Appointment necessary.
Hours: Mon to Fri, 0900 to 1700

Affiliated to:
International Society for Individual Liberty
Libertarian International
Liberty: The National Council for Civil Liberties

Subsidiary body:
British Association of Libertarian Feminists

LIBERTY

Formal name: National Council for Civil Liberties

21 Tabard Street, Borough, London, SE1 4LA

Tel: 020 7403 3888
Fax: 020 7407 5354
E-mail: info@liberty-human-rights.org.uk

Website:
http://www.liberty-human-rights.org.uk
Campaigns and lobbying; human rights test cases; policy; events and legal training; lawyers for liberty.

Enquiries:
Enquiries to: Information Officer

Founded:
1934

Organisation type and purpose:
National organisation, membership association (membership is by subscription), present number of members: 7000.
Commissions and publishes research, and runs the Civil Liberties Library.

Subject coverage:
Civil liberties, especially administration of justice, children's rights, women's rights and sex discrimination, race discrimination, discrimination against homosexuals, police powers, official secrecy and freedom of information, privacy; Bill of Rights; human rights, prisoners' rights, academic freedom, securing services, Northern Ireland, public order, policing, criminal justice.

Museum or gallery collection, archive, or library special collection:
Collection of publications since the foundation in 1934

Library catalogue:
All or part available in-house

Printed publications:
Civil Liberty (newsletter, quarterly)
Judging Inequality (book)
Bibliography of Civil Liberties Teaching Material
Bibliographies from the database
Annual Report, covering current research and education projects

Publications list:
Available in print

Access to staff:
Contact by letter. Appointment necessary. All charged.
Hours: Mon to Fri, 1000 to 1300 and 1400 to 1730

Affiliated to:
International League for Human Rights

Charitable arm is the:
Civil Liberties Trust

Established by members of, and shares premises with, the:
National Council of Civil Liberties

LIBRARY AND MUSEUM OF FREEMASONRY, THE

Formal name: Library and Museum Charitable Trust of the United Grand Lodge

Freemasons' Hall, Great Queen Street, London, WC2B 5AZ

Tel: 020 7395 9251
Fax: 020 7404 7418
E-mail: libmus@ugle.org.uk

Website:
http://www.freemasonry.london.museum

Enquiries:
Enquiries to: Director
Other contacts: Librarian for research queries.

Founded:
1996

Organisation type and purpose:
Professional body, registered charity (charity number 1058497), museum.
Research library.

Subject coverage:
Freemasonry, historical record and information, extensive library and artefact collection.

Non-library collection catalogue:
All or part available in-house

Library catalogue:
All or part available in-house

Access to staff:
Contact by letter, by telephone, by fax and in person. All charged.
Hours: Mon to Fri, 1000 to 1700

LIBRARY CAMPAIGN

22 Upper Woburn Place, London, WC1H 0TB

Tel: 0845 450 5946
Fax: 0845 450 5946
E-mail: librarycam@aol.com

Website:
http://www.librarycampaign.com

Enquiries:
Enquiries to: Secretary

Founded:
1984

Organisation type and purpose:
Registered Charity (England and Wales no. 1102634). National organisation, advisory body, membership association (membership is by subscription), present number of members: 600, voluntary organisation.
Charitable aims: to advance the lifelong education of the public by the promotion, support, assistance and improvement of libraries, and through the activities of friends and user groups. To be the national voice of users of Library Services through our network of local groups. To co-ordinate a network of Friends of Library Groups.

Subject coverage:
Information on local user groups for libraries, where they are and how to start a group.

Printed publications:
Handbook for Library Freinds and User Groups
The Library Campaigner (journal, 2–3 a year)
Various leaflets

Access to staff:
Contact by letter, by telephone and by e-mail
Special comments: 24-hour answerphone. The Campaign is run by volunteers

Member organisations:
Has approximately 40 local organisations

LIBRARY OF AVALON

Acronym or abbreviation: LOA

Rear Courtyard, Above 2–4 High Street, Glastonbury, Somerset, BA6 9DU

Tel: 01458 832759
E-mail: librarian@libraryofavalon.org.uk

Website:
http://www.libraryofavalon.org.uk
Book catalogue, general information.

Enquiries:
Enquiries to: Honorary Secretary
Other contacts: Events Co-ordinator for Library of Avalon annual short story and poetry competition

Founded:
1988

Organisation type and purpose:
Membership association (membership is by subscription), present number of members: 109, voluntary organisation, registered charity (charity number 1065014).

Subject coverage:
Arthurian and related subjects; earth mysteries; history and archaeology; alternative and complementary medicine; psychology, personal development, social psychology; astrology; occult and esoteric thought and studies, including magical practice and theory; mythology; comparative religion including paganism; eastern religion and philosophy; Glastonbury.

Museum or gallery collection, archive, or library special collection:
A selection of magazines on paganism and earth mysteries (reference only)
Book catalogue held on database (title, author and publisher details only, no text)
Wessex research group collection
Willem Koppejan collection
Rilko collection

Non-library collection catalogue:
All or part available online and in-house

Library catalogue:
All or part available in-house

Publications list:
Available online

Access to staff:
Contact by letter, by telephone, by e-mail, in person and via website
Hours: Mon, Wed, Thu, 1330 to 1630; Tue, 1100 to 16.30; Fri, 1200 to 1700; Sat, 1200 to 1600; Sun (most; tel. to check), 1200 to 1500
Special comments: Specialist library open to the public with reading room, but only members may take publications out of the building.

Access to building, collection or gallery:
Hours: as above

Access for disabled people:
Ramped entry

LIBRARY OF JAPANESE SCIENCE AND TECHNOLOGY

Acronym or abbreviation: LJST

Special Collections, Robinson Library, Back Jesmond Road West, Newcastle upon Tyne, NE2 4HQ

Tel: 0191 222 7662
E-mail: marion.burn@ncl.ac.uk

Website:
http://www.ncl.ac.uk/library/

continued overleaf

Enquiries:
Enquiries to: Education Officer – Special Collections
Direct tel: 0191 222 3516
Direct e-mail: sara.bird@ncl.ac.uk

Founded:
1961

Organisation type and purpose:
Voluntary organisation, research organisation.
Independent non-profit library; collections are
housed in the Porter Building, University of
Newcastle upon Tyne.
To improve the supply and use of Japanese
scientific, technical and industrial publications in
the UK.

Subject coverage:
Japanese science, technology, industry and
business in its broadest sense; material in social
and economic sciences also held where this is
relevant to industry and business, material is held
in both English and Japanese.

Information services:
Current awareness, literature searching (charged
services) on a contract basis

**Museum or gallery collection, archive, or library
special collection:**
3800 current Japanese serials with special strengths
   in government and prefectural publications
Annual reports and profiles of Japanese companies
Japanese business histories, Nen-Shi, Sha-Shi etc
University journals
Some material on microfiche, microfilm and CD-
   ROM

Trade and statistical information:
Production and trade statistical publications
   related to Japanese industry, business etc.
Company statistics, production, sales etc.

Non-library collection catalogue:
All or part available in-house

Library catalogue:
All or part available in-house

Printed publications:
Library Bulletin (irregular, selected mailing list)
List of Annual Reports, Profiles available in library
   (chargeable)

Microform publications:
English language versions of Japanese official
   publications

Access to staff:
Contact by letter, by telephone and by fax.
Appointment necessary.
Hours: Mon to Fri, 0900 to 1700

Access to building, collection or gallery:
Prior appointment required

LIBRARY RESEARCH AGENCY

Burberry, Devon Road, Salcombe, Devon, TQ8 8HJ

Tel: 01548 842769
Fax: 01548 842536

Enquiries:
Enquiries to: Managing Director

Founded:
1983

Organisation type and purpose:
Public library, university library, university
department or institute, research organisation.

Subject coverage:
Research in French, German, Russian, Serbo-Croat,
Bulgarian languages, from major libraries,
cryptology, cryptanalysis.

Access to staff:
Contact by letter, by telephone and by fax
Hours: Mon to Fri, 0900 to 1700

LIBRARY, MEDICAL EDUCATION CENTRE

Queen's Hospital, Burton Hospitals NHS Trust,
Belvedere Road, Burton-on-Trent, Staffordshire,
DE13 0RB

Tel: 01283 511511 ext 2104
Fax: 01283 593174
E-mail: library.bur@burtonh-tr.wmids.nhs.uk

Enquiries:
Enquiries to: Library Manager

Founded:
1973

Organisation type and purpose:
NHS Medical Library.

Subject coverage:
Medicine, general aspects and specialities
including nursing.

Library catalogue:
All or part available in-house

Access to staff:
Contact by letter, by telephone, by fax, by e-mail
and in person. Appointment necessary. Non-
members charged.
Hours: Mon to Wed, 0900 to 1900; Thu, 0900 to
1700; Fri, 0900 to 1630

LICHFIELD DISTRICT COUNCIL

District Council House, Frog Lane, Lichfield,
Staffordshire, WS13 6YU

Tel: 01543 308000\ Minicom no. 01543 308078
Fax: 01543 309899
E-mail: enquiries@lichfielddc.gov.uk

Enquiries:
Enquiries to: Chief Executive

Founded:
1974

Organisation type and purpose:
Local government body.

Subject coverage:
All functions of the local authority; planning,
economic development, leisure and environmental
health.

Access to staff:
Contact by letter, by telephone and by fax.
Appointment necessary.
Hours: Mon to Fri, 0845 to 1715

Access for disabled people:
Parking provided, ramped entry, toilet facilities

LICHFIELD RECORD OFFICE

Acronym or abbreviation: LRO

The Friary, Lichfield, Staffordshire, WS13 6QG

Tel: 01543 510720
Fax: 01543 510716
E-mail: lichfield.record.office@staffordshire.gov.uk

Website:
http://www.staffordshire.gov.uk/archives/lich.htm

Enquiries:
Enquiries to: Area Archivist

Founded:
1959

Organisation type and purpose:
Local government body. To preserve and make
available archives of the diocese of Lichfield and
archives created in, and/or relating to, the city of
Lichfield and the town of Burton upon Trent and
their surrounding areas.

Subject coverage:
Ecclesiastical, social, economic and political history
of the diocese and City of Lichfield and of Burton
upon Trent; genealogy.

Non-library collection catalogue:
All or part available online, in-house and in print

Printed publications:
Directly for purchase

Publications list:
Available online and in print

Access to staff:
Contact by letter, by telephone, by fax, by e-mail
and in person. Appointment necessary.

Access to building, collection or gallery:
Hours: Mon, Tue, Wed and Fri, 0930 to 1700; Thu,
1130 to 1900; second Sat of each month, 0930 to
1230
Special comments: Some records closed for 30 or
more years from latest date.

Branches:
Staffordshire Record Office
   Eastgate Street, Stafford; tel: 01785 278379; e-
   mail: staffordshire.record.office@staffordshire
   .gov.uk
Stoke on Trent Archives
   tel: 01782 238420; e-mail: stoke.archives@stoke
   .gov.uk

Parent body:
Staffordshire and Stoke on Trent Archive Service

LIDDELL HART CENTRE FOR MILITARY ARCHIVES

Acronym or abbreviation: LHCMA

King's College London, Strand, London, WC2R
2LS

Tel: 020 7848 2015
Fax: 020 7848 2760
E-mail: archives.web@kcl.ac.uk

Website:
http://www.kcl.ac.uk/iss/archives
Summary guides to all collections, detailed
catalogues of main collections.

Enquiries:
Enquiries to: Director of Archives and Information
Management

Founded:
1964

Subject coverage:
Archive repository for the papers of senior defence
personnel, authors and commentators on
international security and defence policy, with the
scope of the holdings ranging from high-level
defence policy and strategic planning, to the
command of individual units in the field in almost
every major campaign in which British troops have
fought from 1900 to present day. Additional
material on the history of science and journalism,
and the study of racial interaction and colonial
administration.

**Museum or gallery collection, archive, or library
special collection:**
The Centre holds the papers of over 700 senior
   defence personnel, including:
Sir Basil Liddell Hart (1895–1970)
FM Lord Alanbrooke (1883–1993)
FM Lord Allenby (1861–1936)
ACM Sir Robert Brooke-Popham (1878–1953)
Sir Arthur Bryant (1899–1985)
Sir Frank Cooper (1922–2002)
Maj-Gen. J. F. C. Fuller (1878–1966)
Gen. Sir Ian Hamilton (1853–1947)
Gen. Lord Ismay (1887–1965)
Gen. Sir Richard O'Connor (1889–1981)
FM Lord Milne (1866–1948)
FM Sir Archibald Montgomery-Massingberd
   (1871–1947)
FM Sir William Robertson (1860–1933)
Gen. Sir Hugh Stockwell (1903–1986)
Television documentary archives include:
The Nuclear Age (1989)
The Death of Yugoslavia (1995)
The Washington Version (1992) (Gulf War)
The Fall of the Wall (1994)

Non-library collection catalogue:
All or part available online

Access to staff:
Contact by letter, by telephone, by fax, by e-mail and via website. Appointment necessary. Letter of introduction required.
Hours: Mon to Fri, 0930 to 1730

Access for disabled people:
Level entry, toilet facilities

LIFE

LIFE House, 1 Mill Street, Leamington Spa, Warwickshire, CV31 1ES

Tel: 01926 421587
Fax: 01926 336497
E-mail: info@lifecharity.org.uk

Website:
http://www.lifecharity.org.uk

Enquiries:
Enquiries to: Trustee
Other contacts: Research Officer

Founded:
1970

Organisation type and purpose:
Voluntary organisation, registered charity. Opposed to all direct abortion and offering free practical help to women with unplanned pregnancies. Counselling before and after abortion. Accommodation for homeless pregnant women.

Subject coverage:
Abortion, pregnancy, birth, counselling after abortion, housing single mothers, infertility, fertility control, infertility treatment, school talks and study days.

Printed publications:
A wide range of leaflets about different aspects of abortion and 'Life' issues
LIFE News (journal, four times a year)

Electronic and video publications:
Life in the Millennium
Life, what it does and why
Whose choice is it anyway? (video, £15)

Access to staff:
Contact by letter, by telephone, by fax, by e-mail and via website
Hours: Mon to Fri, 0900 to 1700

LIFE EDUCATION CENTRES

Acronym or abbreviation: LEC

1st Floor, 53–56 Great Sutton Street, London, EC1V 0DG

Tel: 020 7490 3210
Fax: 020 7490 3610
E-mail: lec@life-education.demon.co.uk

Website:
http://www.lec.org
Information on LEC.

Enquiries:
Enquiries to: Director of Research

Founded:
1979

Organisation type and purpose:
Registered charity (charity number 800727), suitable for ages: 3 to 15, training organisation, publishing house.
Drug prevention charity for children, schools and families.

Subject coverage:
Drug prevention (theory, research), drug information (effects etc), evaluation of drug prevention programmes.

Museum or gallery collection, archive, or library special collection:
Drug prevention and research: books, reports, journals, newspaper clippings

Trade and statistical information:
Statistical information on drug use (especially youth).
Data on prevention programme effects (especially LEC).

Printed publications:
Being Yourself: A Teenage Pregnancy Prevention Pack
Body System Posters
Day of the Dinosaur: introduction for 9–12 year olds to HIV studies
Harold the Giraffe Activity Books, Songbook and Cassette
How to Talk to Your Child About Drugs: The Life Education Parents' Guide
Taking Care; An HIV/AIDS Pack for Teaching 10–12 year olds
Order printed publications from: Publications Manager, Life Education Centres at the same address

Electronic and video publications:
Ozone (CD-ROM)
You Make the Difference (LEC's Video guide for parents and carers)
Harold's Greatest Hits (cassette)

Publications list:
Available in print

Access to staff:
Contact by letter, by telephone and by fax
Hours: Mon to Fri, 0900 to 1700

Parent body:
Life Education International (LEI)

LIFETIME MANAGEMENT OF MATERIALS ADVISORY SERVICE

Acronym or abbreviation: LMM

National Physical Laboratory, Hampton Road, Teddington, Middlesex, TW11 0LW

Tel: 020 8943 6142
E-mail: lmm@npl.co.uk

Website:
http://www.npl.co.uk/npl/lmmt/aqueous/about_ncs.html

Enquiries:
Enquiries to: Executive Secretary
Direct tel: 020 8943 6179

Founded:
1975

Formerly called:
National Corrosion Service (year of change 2007)

Organisation type and purpose:
Advisory body, consultancy, research organisation. The United Kingdom's gateway to corrosion, materials expertise and advice.

Subject coverage:
Corrosion control and prevention; design and selection of materials; coating systems; cathodic protection; environmental factors; failure analysis and investigations.

Printed publications:
Avoidance of Corrosion in Plumbing Systems (free)
Guide to Stress Corrosion Cracking
Guide to Bimetallic Corrosion
Corrosion in Pumps and Valves
Checklist for Corrosion Control
Protection of Structural Steelwork

Publications list:
Available online and in print

Access to staff:
Contact by letter, by telephone, by fax, by e-mail and via website. Appointment necessary.
Hours: Mon to Fri, 0900 to 1700

Constituent part of:
Serco Group plc
Serco House, 16 Bartley Wood Business Park, Hook, Hants, RG27 9UY

LIFT AND ESCALATOR INDUSTRY ASSOCIATION

Acronym or abbreviation: LEIA

33–34 Devonshire Street, London, W1G 6PY

Tel: 020 7935 3013
Fax: 020 7935 3321
E-mail: enquiries@leia.co.uk

Enquiries:
Enquiries to: Director

Founded:
1997

Organisation type and purpose:
Trade association, present number of members: c. 150.

Subject coverage:
Lifts, escalators, passenger conveyors, safety, design and standardisation.

Access to staff:
Contact by letter, by telephone and by fax
Hours: Mon to Fri, 0900 to 1700

Member of:
Specialist Engineering Contractors Group

LIFTING EQUIPMENT ENGINEERS ASSOCIATION

Acronym or abbreviation: LEEA

3, Osprey Court, Kingfisher Way, Hinchingbrooke Business Park, Huntingdon, Cambridgeshire, PE29 6FN

Tel: 01480 432801
Fax: 01480 436314
E-mail: mail@leea.co.uk

Website:
http://www.leea.co.uk
About the LEEA, What's new, membership list, publications, benefits of membership, how to join the LEEA, member information (password).

Enquiries:
Enquiries to: Chief Executive

Founded:
1944

Organisation type and purpose:
Trade association.

Subject coverage:
Lifting equipment.

Library catalogue:
All or part available online and in-house

Printed publications:
Code of Practice for the Safe Use of Lifting Equipment (2006 ed., £135)
Lifting Equipment – A User's Pocket Guide (£8)
Lifting Engineers Handbook (£20)
Hand Chain Blocks and Lever Hoists in the ofshore Environment (£15)
Membership List (2 times a year, free)
Newsletter

Publications list:
Available online and in print

Access to staff:
Contact by letter, by telephone, by fax and by e-mail. Appointment necessary. Access for members only.
Hours: Mon to Fri, 0830 to 1700

LIGHTING ASSOCIATION

Stafford Park 7, Telford, Shropshire, TF3 3BQ

Tel: 01952 290905
Fax: 01952 290906
E-mail: enquiries@lightingassociation.com

Website:
http://www.lightingassociation.com
Wide range of information available covering membership and services.

continued overleaf

Enquiries:
Enquiries to: PR & Marketing Manager

Founded:
1939

Organisation type and purpose:
Trade Association.

Subject coverage:
Product and lighting company sourcing, technical information, regulations, lighting manufacture, distribution and assembly.

Printed publications:
Buyers Guide (annually)
Diary (with member companies)
President's Report (annually)

Access to staff:
Contact by letter, by telephone, by fax, by e-mail and via website. Appointment necessary.
Hours: Mon to Fri, 0900 to 1700

Links with:
Association of Exhibition Organisers (AEO)

LINACRE COLLEGE LIBRARY

St Cross Road, Oxford, OX1 3JA

Tel: 01865 271650
Fax: 01865 271668
E-mail: library@linacre.oc.ac.uk

Website:
http://www.linacre.ox.ac.uk/Linacre/it-library/linacre-college-library

Enquiries:
Enquiries to: Assistant Librarian
Direct tel: 01865 271661

Founded:
1962

Organisation type and purpose:
University library.

Subject coverage:
Small coverage in all disciplines.

Museum or gallery collection, archive, or library special collection:
Ryle Collection (early 20th-century philosophy in England)

Library catalogue:
All or part available online

Access to staff:
Contact by e-mail
Hours: Mon to Fri, 0900 to 1700

Access to building, collection or gallery:
No prior appointment required
Special comments: Access is restricted to members of Linacre College.

Access for disabled people:
Toilet facilities

Constituent part of:
University of Oxford

LINCOLN CATHEDRAL LIBRARY

Minster Yard, Lincoln, LN2 1PX

Tel: 01522 561640
Fax: 01522 561641
E-mail: librarian@lincolncathedral.com

Website:
http://www.lincolncathedral.com

Enquiries:
Enquiries to: Librarian

Founded:
1092

Organisation type and purpose:
Cathedral library.

Subject coverage:
Early printed books (especially 17th century); cathedrals (especially Lincoln); ecclesiastical history and architecture; liturgy.

Museum or gallery collection, archive, or library special collection:
3,000 17th-century pamphlets and Broadsides
E. J. Willson Collection (architectural drawings)
John Wilson Library (17th- and 18th-century theological works)
Medieval manuscripts
19th-century Religious Tracts
Pre-1800 printed books
Post-medieval manuscripts

Non-library collection catalogue:
All or part available online

Printed publications:
Library publications are issued through Lincoln Cathedral Publications
Pamphlets about the history, architecture and art of the Cathedral

Publications list:
Available in print

Access to staff:
Contact by letter. Appointment necessary. Letter of introduction required.
Hours: Mon, Tue, 1000 to 1230 and 1400 to 1600

Access to building, collection or gallery:
No access other than to staff
Hours: Exhibition open April to October: Mon to Fri, 1300 to 1500; Sat, 1100 to 1500; closed Sun

Links with:
Lincoln Record Society
  Lincoln Cathedral Library, Minster Yard, Lincoln, LN2 1PX; tel: 01522 561640; e-mail: secretary@ lincoln-record-society.org.uk; website: http:// www.lincoln-record-society.org.uk

LINCOLN CITY COUNCIL

City Hall, Beaumont Fee, Lincoln, LN1 1DB

Tel: 01522 881188
Fax: 01522 521736

Website:
http://www.lincoln-info.org.uk

Enquiries:
Enquiries to: Policy Officer
Direct tel: 01522 873384
Direct e-mail: nicola.desforges@lincoln.gov.uk

Organisation type and purpose:
Local government body.

Subject coverage:
Local government services.

Access to staff:
Contact by letter, by telephone, by fax and by e-mail
Hours: Mon to Fri, 0900 to 1700

LINCOLN COLLEGE LIBRARY

Lincoln College, Turl Street, Oxford, OX1 3DR

Tel: 01865 279831

Enquiries:
Enquiries to: Librarian
Direct e-mail: library@lincoln.oxford.ac.uk

Founded:
1427

Organisation type and purpose:
University department or institute.

Subject coverage:
General.

Museum or gallery collection, archive, or library special collection:
Old Senior Library of rare books and College Archives

Access to staff:
Contact by letter and by e-mail. Access for members only.
Hours: Mon to Fri, 0900 to 1700

Constituent part of:
University of Oxford

LINCOLN LONGWOOL SHEEP BREEDERS ASSOCIATION

Lincolnshire Showground, Grange-de-Lings, Lincoln, LN2 2NA

Tel: 01522 511395
Fax: 01552 520345
E-mail: lincolnlongwool@lineone.net

Enquiries:
Enquiries to: Secretary
Direct tel: 01522 730033

Organisation type and purpose:
Membership association (membership is by subscription), present number of members: 90 approx, registered charity (charity number 215539).

Subject coverage:
Lincoln longwool sheep.

Access to staff:
Contact by letter, by telephone, by fax and by e-mail
Hours: Mon to Fri, 0900 to 1700

LINCOLN RECORD SOCIETY

Acronym or abbreviation: LRS

Lincoln Cathedral Library, Minster Yard, Lincoln, LN2 1PX

Tel: 01522 561640
Fax: 01522 561641

Enquiries:
Enquiries to: Honorary Secretary

Founded:
1910

Organisation type and purpose:
Learned society.

Subject coverage:
History of the ancient county and diocese of Lincoln.

Printed publications:
Annual Report
Some 89 record texts relating to the ancient county and diocese of Lincoln (issued either annually or bi-annually, free to subscribers and available for purchase by non-members)

Publications list:
Available in print

Access to staff:
Contact by letter
Hours: Mon to Fri, 0900 to 1700

Connections with:
Society for Lincolnshire History and Archaeology

LINCOLN RED CATTLE SOCIETY

Showground, Grange-de-Lings, Lincoln, LN2 2NA

Tel: 01522 511395
Fax: 01522 520345
E-mail: info@lincolnredcattlesociety.co.uk

Website:
http://www.lincolnredcattlesociety.co.uk

Enquiries:
Enquiries to: Secretary

Founded:
1896

Organisation type and purpose:
Membership association (membership is by subscription), present number of members: 120 approx, registered charity (charity number 215662).

Access to staff:
Contact by letter, by telephone and by fax
Hours: Mon to Fri, 0900 to 1700

LINCOLN'S INN LIBRARY

Formal name: Lincoln's Inn Library

The Honourable Society of Lincoln's Inn, The Treasury Office, Lincoln's Inn, London, WC2A 3TL

Tel: 020 7242 4371
Fax: 020 7404 1864
E-mail: library@lincolnsinn.org.uk

Website:
http://www.lincolnsinn.org.uk/lib_gen.asp

Enquiries:
Enquiries to: Librarian
Direct tel: 020 7693 5160
Direct e-mail: librarian@lincolnsinn.org.uk

Founded:
c. 15th century

Organisation type and purpose:
Legal library

Museum or gallery collection, archive, or library special collection:
150,000 vols of English law, Commonwealth law and Parliamentary papers
Hale Manuscripts
Black Books (Inn records, 1422 to present))

Non-library collection catalogue:
All or part available in print

Library catalogue:
All or part available online

Access to staff:
Contact by letter, by telephone, by fax, by e-mail and via website. Appointment necessary. Access for members only.
Hours: Normal: Mon to Fri, 0900 to 2000; Every fourth Sat, by rotation with other Inns of Court libraries, 1000 to 1700
Aug to mid-Sept: Mon to Fri, 0930 to 1800

Access to building, collection or gallery:
Open to all members of the Inn and all barristers with chambers in the Inn and their pupils. Barristers who are not members and have chambers elsewhere are welcome to use the Library for material not held by their own Inn, but may not borrow. Solicitors may use the library as last resort only. Other researchers by appointment.

LINCOLN-ZEPHYR OWNERS CLUB

22 New North Road, Hainault, Ilford, Essex, IG6 2XG

Tel: 020 8500 4039

Website:
http://www.lzoc.org
Membership details, information on Lincoln-Zephyrs.

Enquiries:
Enquiries to: Information Officer

Founded:
1968

Subject coverage:
Lincoln-Zephyr cars.

Access to staff:
Contact by letter and by telephone
Hours: Mon to Fri, 0900 to 1700

LINCOLNSHIRE ARCHIVES

Acronym or abbreviation: LA

St Rumbold Street, Lincoln, LN2 5AB

Tel: 01522 782040 (search room bookings), 526204 (enquiries)
Fax: 01522 530047
E-mail: lincolnshire_archive@lincolnshire.gov.uk

Website:
http://www.lincolnshire.gov.uk/archives
Information about Lincolnshire Archives and services; list of convicts transported to Australia 1788–1840 (with document references).

Enquiries:
Enquiries to: Site Coordinator

Founded:
1948

Organisation type and purpose:
Local government body.
Record office.

Subject coverage:
History of the historical County and the ancient Diocese of Lincoln; rights of way; boundary delineation; family history; local and village history; school and university projects; leisure and general interest, research, educational research, official and legal enquiries.

Museum or gallery collection, archive, or library special collection:
Business records
Ecclesiastical records
Estate and family records
Foster Library (local history, national, historical and archaeological journals)
Local authority and public records

Non-library collection catalogue:
All or part available online and in-house

Library catalogue:
All or part available online and in-house

Microform publications:
All deposited Lincoln Diocese Parish Registers on microfilm and fiche

Publications list:
Available online and in print

Access to staff:
Contact by letter, by telephone, by fax, by e-mail, in person and via website. Appointment necessary.
Hours: Tue to Sat, 1000 to 1600; Mon, closed
Special comments: Reader Ticket (apply in person).

Access for disabled people:
Parking provided, level entry, access to all public areas, toilet facilities

Incorporated within the service is the:
Lincoln Diocesan Record Office

Parent body:
Lincolnshire County Council

LINCOLNSHIRE LIBRARY SERVICE

Education and Cultural Services Directorate, County Offices, Newland, Lincoln LN1 1YL

Tel: 01522 553207
Fax: 01522 552811/20
E-mail: library.support@lincolnshire.gov.uk

Website:
http://www.lincolnshire.gov.uk
County council information, community information, database 20,000 screens includes 'What's On', health advice, education.

Enquiries:
Enquiries to: Head of Libraries, Sport and Support Services
Other contacts: Support Services Manager

Founded:
1974

Organisation type and purpose:
Local government body, public library

Subject coverage:
General, music and drama, education, local government and management, agriculture, foreign languages, medicine, Tennyson, literature, local studies.

Museum or gallery collection, archive, or library special collection:
Abell Collection (local studies, 90 scrapbooks) at Central Library, Lincoln
Armitage Collection (drainage of the county) at Central Library, Lincoln
Banks Collection (Sir Joseph Banks collection of letters, manuscripts and drawings on Lincolnshire and Lincolnshire churches) at Central Library, Lincoln
Binnal Collection (Louth and Lincolnshire) at Louth Library
Exley Collection (Lincolnshire) at Central Library, Lincoln
Goulding Collection (Lincolnshire and Louth) at Louth Library
Lincolnshire illustrations index
Medical Library at Lincoln County Hospital
Medical Library at Pilgrim Hospital, Boston
Newcombe Library (17th and early 18th century theology, philosophy and history) at Grantham Library
Newton Collection (material by and about Sir Isaac Newton) at Lincoln Central and Grantham Libraries
Pye Collection (Grimsby and Cleethorpes district) at Central Library, Lincoln
Ross Collection (Lord Monson's collection on Lincoln and Lincolnshire villages) at Central Library, Lincoln
Tennyson Research Collection
Wheeler Collection (drainage of the Fens and the building of the port of Boston) at Boston Library
CD's, videos, tapes

Non-library collection catalogue:
All or part available online

Library catalogue:
All or part available online

Publications list:
Available in print

Access to staff:
Contact by letter, by telephone, by fax, by e-mail and via website. Appointment necessary.
Hours: Mon to Fri, 0900 to 1700

Access for disabled people:
Level entry

Includes the:
Tennyson Research Centre

Parent body:
Lincolnshire County Council
County Offices, Newland, Lincoln

LINCOLNSHIRE TOURIST GUIDES ASSOCIATION

Winterbourne, Church Lane, Tathwell, Louth, Lincolnshire, LN11 9SR

Tel: 01507 604717
E-mail: jrbh@btinternet.com

Enquiries:
Enquiries to: Booking Officer

Founded:
1985

Subject coverage:
Guided walks and tours, talks on all aspects of Lincolnshire's heritage.

Access to staff:
Contact by letter, by telephone and by e-mail
Hours: Mon to Fri, 0900 to 1700

LINDE MATERIAL HANDLING (UK) LTD

Kingsclere Road, Basingstoke, Hampshire, RG21 6XJ

Tel: 01256 342000
Fax: 01256 342923
E-mail: enquiries@linde-mh.co.uk

Website:
http://www.linde-mh.co.uk/

Enquiries:
Enquiries to: Public Relations Officer

Founded:
1943

continued overleaf

Formerly called:
Lansing Linde Limited (year of change 2003)

Organisation type and purpose:
Manufacturing industry.

Subject coverage:
Materials handling using industrial trucks, including freight, warehousing, high density storage; fork truck operation and maintenance; rental and leasing.

Printed publications:
Technical data sheets and catalogues

Access to staff:
Contact by letter, by telephone and by fax
Hours: Mon to Fri, 0900 to 1700

Access to building, collection or gallery:
No prior appointment required

LINEN HALL LIBRARY

17 Donegall Square North, Belfast, BT1 5GB

Tel: 028 9032 1707
Fax: 028 9043 8586
E-mail: info@linenhall.com

Website:
http://www.linenhall.com
Guide to library collections, online catalogue, information of events, details of publications, membership and gift shop.

Enquiries:
Enquiries to: Librarian

Founded:
1788

Organisation type and purpose:
Registered charity.
Independent subscription library.

Subject coverage:
Irish (especially Ulster) local history and biography, Irish bibliography, Irish genealogy, Belfast printed books, political literature and general subjects.

Museum or gallery collection, archive, or library special collection:
Belfast printed book collection
Genealogical collection
Irish newspaper and periodical collection
Irish postcard collection
Kennedy collection of Ulster poetry
Northern Ireland political collection
Theatre and Performing Arts Archive

Non-library collection catalogue:
All or part available online

Library catalogue:
All or part available online and in-house

Printed publications:
The Library publishes a selection of books and prints linked to the collections and of Irish interest

Microform publications:
Northern Ireland political literature on microfiche; phase 1 periodicals 1966–1989

Electronic and video publications:
Troubled Images (CD-ROM)

Publications list:
Available online and in print

Access to staff:
Contact by letter, by telephone, by fax, by e-mail, in person and via website
Hours: Mon to Fri, 0930 to 1730; Sat, 0930 to 1300

Access to building, collection or gallery:
No prior appointment required

Access for disabled people:
Access to all public areas, toilet facilities

LINK CENTRE FOR DEAFENED PEOPLE

Acronym or abbreviation: LINK

19 Hartfield Road, Eastbourne, East Sussex, BN21 2AR

Tel: 01323 638230\ Minicom no. 01323 739998
Fax: 01323 642968
E-mail: info@linkdp.org

Website:
http://www.linkdp.org

Enquiries:
Enquiries to: Helpdesk

Founded:
1972

Organisation type and purpose:
Voluntary organisation, registered charity.
Rehabilitation for deafened adults.

Subject coverage:
Care and welfare of adults with severe or total irreversible deafness or severe progressive deafness not compensated by hearing aids, sudden deafness, speech conservation, speech-reading, lipreading, counselling, rehabilitation, advice and help to family or companion of the sufferer, self-management of deafness, psychosocial rehabilitation.

Publications list:
Available online and in print

Access to staff:
Contact by letter, by telephone, by fax and by e-mail. Appointment necessary.
Hours: Mon to Fri, 0900 to 1700

Access for disabled people:
Ramped entry, access to all public areas, toilet facilities
Special comments: Loop available.

LINKINDIA

41A The Downs, London, SW20 8HG

Tel: 020 8944 6933
E-mail: library@linkpicturelibrary.com

Website:
http://www.linkpicturelibrary.com

Enquiries:
Enquiries to: Librarian
Other contacts: Proprietor

Founded:
1982

Organisation type and purpose:
Commercial picture library.

Subject coverage:
Photographic collections covering many aspects of India. Also able to source images and professional photographers in India.

Information services:
Specialist image collection from and about India

Library catalogue:
All or part available in-house

Access to staff:
Contact by letter, by telephone, by e-mail and via website. Appointment necessary.
Hours: Mon to Fri, 0900 to 1700

Access to building, collection or gallery:
Appointment required
Hours: Mon to Fri, 0900 to 1730

Links with:
Dinodia Picture Library
website: http://www.dinodia.com

LINNEAN SOCIETY OF LONDON

Burlington House, Piccadilly, London, W1J 0BF

Tel: 020 7434 4479
Fax: 020 7287 9364

E-mail: lynda@linnean.org

Website:
http://www.linnean.org

Enquiries:
Enquiries to: Librarian
Other contacts: Assistant Librarian (for IT queries)

Founded:
1788

Organisation type and purpose:
Learned society (membership is by election or invitation), present number of members: 3,000, registered charity.
Promote taxonomy in all its branches.

Subject coverage:
Anthropology; natural history; evolutionary biology; botany; zoology; taxonomy; history of science.

Museum or gallery collection, archive, or library special collection:
Correspondence and manuscripts of 18th- and 19th-century naturalists
J. E. Smith Collection
J. Insch Tea Library
Linnaean Collection

Non-library collection catalogue:
All or part available online

Library catalogue:
All or part available online

Printed publications:
Biological Journal (monthly)
Botanical Journal (monthly)
Catalogue of Manuscripts, parts I to IV
Symposia
Synopses of British Fauna
Zoological Journal (monthly)
Order printed publications from: Office Manager

Publications list:
Available online and in print

Access to staff:
Contact by letter, by telephone, by fax and by e-mail. Appointment necessary.
Hours: Mon to Fri, 1000 to 1700
Special comments: Letter of introduction required for manuscript access only.

Access to building, collection or gallery:
No prior appointment required

Links with:
Institute of Biology
International Association of Plant Taxonomists

LIST AND INDEX SOCIETY

Acronym or abbreviation: L&I

The National Archives, Kew, Richmond-upon-Thames, Surrey, TW9 4DU

Tel: 020 8876 3444
Fax: 020 8392 5286
E-mail: listandindexsociety@nationalarchives.gov.uk

Enquiries:
Enquiries to: Secretary

Founded:
1965

Organisation type and purpose:
Learned society (membership is by subscription).

Subject coverage:
To publish and provide Public Record Office search room lists and indexes, coverage – public records from 13th to 20th centuries.

Printed publications:
Typed catalogue of the society's publications is available on request

Publications list:
Available in print

Access to staff:
Contact by letter, by fax and by e-mail
Hours: Mon to Fri, 0900 to 1700

Affiliated to:
Public Record Office

LISTENING BOOKS

12 Lant Street, London, SE1 1QH

Tel: 020 7407 9417
Fax: 020 7403 1377
E-mail: info@listening-books.org.uk

Website:
http://www.listening-books.org.uk

Enquiries:
Enquiries to: Membership Services Officer

Founded:
1977

Organisation type and purpose:
Membership association (membership is by subscription), present number of members: 3111, voluntary organisation, registered charity (charity number 264221).

Subject coverage:
A postal audiobook library service for people who cannot read or hold a book in the usual way, due to illness, disability or special education needs.

Library catalogue:
All or part available online and in print

Printed publications:
Annual Report
Newsletter and leaflet

Electronic and video publications:
All on tape – not reproducible on standard tape recorders and players

Publications list:
Available in print

Access to staff:
Contact by letter, by telephone, by fax, by e-mail and via website
Hours: Mon to Fri, 0900 to 1700

Access to building, collection or gallery:
Prior appointment required

LISTER INSTITUTE OF PREVENTIVE MEDICINE

PO Box 1083, Bushey, Hertfordshire, WD23 9AG

Tel: 01923 801886
Fax: 01923 801886
E-mail: secretary@lister-institute.org.uk

Website:
http://www.lister-institute.org.uk
History of the Institute and details of the Fellowship scheme. Research examples included.

Enquiries:
Enquiries to: Secretary

Founded:
1891

Organisation type and purpose:
Registered charity (charity number 206271). Promoting biomedical excellence in the UK through the support of research projects with implications for preventive medicine.

Subject coverage:
Biomedical research in the UK within research institutions.

Printed publications:
Lister Institute of Preventive Medicine – A concise history

Access to staff:
Contact by letter, by telephone, by fax, by e-mail and via website
Hours: Mon to Fri, 0930 to 1700

Access to building, collection or gallery:
No access other than to staff

LISU

Loughborough University, Loughborough, Leicestershire, LE11 3TU

Tel: 01509 635680
Fax: 01509 635699
E-mail: lisu@lboro.ac.uk

Website:
http://www.lboro.ac.uk/departments/dis/lisu

Enquiries:
Enquiries to: Director

Formerly called:
Library and Information Statistics Unit (year of change 2004)

Organisation type and purpose:
Library and information statistics unit. Research organisation, publishing house, consultancy.

Subject coverage:
Regular publication of average prices of academic books in the United Kingdom and the USA. Surveys and statistics of public, academic, special and school librarians and information centres in the United Kingdom and Europe.

Printed publications:
LISU Annual Library Statistics: featuring a 10-year trend analysis
Public Library Materials Fund and Budget Survey (annually)
A Survey of Library Services to schools and children in the UK
Average Prices of British Academic Books (twice a year)
Average Prices of USA Academic Books (twice a year)
Occasional papers
Who else writes like? A readers' guide to fiction
Who next? A children's guide to fiction

Electronic and video publications:
LAMPOST (Libraries, Archives, Museums, Publishing Online Statistics Tables (online)

Publications list:
Available online and in print

Access to staff:
Contact by letter, by telephone, by fax, by e-mail and via website. Appointment necessary.
Hours: Mon to Fri, 0900 to 1700

Constituent part of:
Loughborough University
Department of Information Science

LISZT SOCIETY, THE

9 Burnside Close, Twickenham, Middlesex, TW1 1ET

Tel: 020 8287 5518
Fax: 020 8287 5518
E-mail: LisztSoc@blueyonder.co.uk

Enquiries:
Enquiries to: Secretary

Founded:
1950

Organisation type and purpose:
Learned society.
To encourage, and promote enjoyment in and appreciation of the music of Liszt, to draw attention to live performances or recordings, to encourage research into his compositions and life and the exchange of views and information about them.

Subject coverage:
Music of Franz (Ferenc) Liszt, 1811–1886: his life, times, influence and contemporaries.

Printed publications:
Journal (annually)
Music scores
Newsletters (quarterly)
Order printed publications from: Hardie Press (for scores)
details from the Society

Access to staff:
Contact by letter, by telephone, by fax and by e-mail. Appointment necessary.
Hours: Mon to Sun, 0800 to 2200

Access to building, collection or gallery:
Prior appointment required

Access for disabled people:
Parking provided, level entry, toilet facilities

Connections with:
Liszt Societies Worldwide

LITERARY & PHILOSOPHICAL SOCIETY OF NEWCASTLE UPON TYNE

23 Westgate Road, Newcastle upon Tyne, NE1 1SE

Tel: 0191 232 0192
Fax: 0191 261 4494
E-mail: library@litandphil.org.uk

Website:
http://www.litandphil.org.uk

Enquiries:
Enquiries to: Librarian

Founded:
1793

Organisation type and purpose:
Learned society (membership is by subscription), present number of members: 1200, registered charity (charity number 528069). Private subscription library.

Subject coverage:
The humanities with older scientific and technological material of particular importance to the region, plus local collections relating to Northumberland and Durham, 19th century periodicals.

Museum or gallery collection, archive, or library special collection:
Joseph Crawhall collection
Douglas W Dickenson collection for the history of the Northern Architectural Association
Manuscripts and other documents recording the history of the Society
Northern Arts manuscript collection
Pamphlets and tracts from 19th century onwards
Rosner collection of books, periodicals and reports on Town Planning
Wesley Historical Society collection relating to Methodism in the North East
Range of 19th century periodicals

Printed publications:
Annual Reports
Occasional publications of notable lectures
Literary and Philosophical Society Bicentenary Lecture 1993 (Philipson J, £15 plus £1.50 p&p)
The History of the Literary and Philosophical Society of Newcastle upon Tyne vol. II 1896–1989 (£15 plus £1.50 p&p)
Sir Joseph Wilson Swan FRS (Chirnside RC, 75p)
Reverend William Turner: dissent and reform in Georgian Newcastle upon Tyne (Harbottle S T L, Northern Universities Press, £20; £17.50 to non-members)

Access to staff:
Contact by letter, by telephone, by fax, by e-mail and in person. Appointment necessary.
Hours: Mon to Fri, 0930 to 1900; Tue, 0930 to 2000; Sat, 0930 to 1300

LITTLE ROYALTY

2 Ninehams Gardens, Caterham, Surrey, CR3 5LP

Tel: 020 8660 3738

Enquiries:
Enquiries to: Manager

Founded:
1997

continued overleaf

Organisation type and purpose:
Service industry.

Subject coverage:
Restoration of soft toys damaged by owners and time, in as authentic a manner possible. Also completion of unfinished needlework projects including cross stitch kits, tapestries and dress-making projects.

Access to staff:
Contact by letter and by telephone
Hours: Mon to Fri, 0900 to 1700
Special comments: Please send an sae for price list.

LIVERPOOL & SW LANCASHIRE FAMILY HISTORY SOCIETY

Acronym or abbreviation: L&SWLFHS

6 Kirkmore Road, Liverpool, L18 4QN

E-mail: patchwork34@waitrose.com

Website:
http://www.liverpool-genealogy.org.uk
Outline of the society, contact addresses, publications.

Enquiries:
Enquiries to: General Secretary

Founded:
1976

Organisation type and purpose:
Learned society (membership is by subscription), present number of members: 2050, registered charity (charity number 512908).
To provide educational facilities for the study of family history in the area, to transcribe, index, and wherever possible publish relevant material, and to provide links with other similar societies.

Subject coverage:
Family history and genealogy in the area of the ancient County of Lancashire known as the Hundred of West Derby.

Printed publications:
Wide range of books concerning Lancashire, Leigh, Liverpool, St Helens, Warrington and Wigan areas
The Liverpool Historian (journal, quarterly)
1851 Census of Liverpool Inner Districts (34 vols)
1851 Census of Liverpool Outer Districts (over 30 vols)
Order printed publications from: Publications Officer, Liverpool & SW Lancashire Family History Society 9 Manor Road, Lymm, Cheshire, WA13 0AY, tel: 01925 755469, e-mail: joe.griffiths@lineone.net

Microform publications:
Wide range of microfiche register transcriptions and census indexes

Electronic and video publications:
1851 Census of Liverpool index (CD-ROM)

Publications list:
Available online and in print

Access to staff:
Contact by letter
Hours: Mon to Fri, 0900 to 1700

Local groups covering:
Liverpool, Leigh & District, Southport
Widnes, Skelmersdale & Upholland, Warrington

LIVERPOOL ASSOCIATION OF DISABLED PEOPLE

Acronym or abbreviation: LAD

Lime Court Centre, Upper Baker Street, Liverpool, L6 1NB

Tel: 0151 263 8366\ Minicom no. 0151 260 3187
Fax: 0151 263 1855
E-mail: ladisabled@freenetname.co.uk

Website:
http://www.ladisabled.co.uk

Enquiries:
Enquiries to: Manager

Founded:
1966

Organisation type and purpose:
Advisory body, membership association (membership is by subscription), voluntary organisation.

Subject coverage:
Campaigns for civil and welfare rights of disabled people.

Printed publications:
Contact (magazine)

Access to staff:
Contact by letter, by telephone, by fax and by e-mail. Appointment necessary.
Hours: Mon to Thu, 0900 to 1700; Fri, 0900 to 1630

Access for disabled people:
Parking provided, level entry, access to all public areas, toilet facilities

Member of:
BCODP
FIAC

LIVERPOOL CHAMBER OF COMMERCE AND INDUSTRY

Number One, Old Hall Street, Liverpool, L3 9HG

Tel: 0151 227 1234
Fax: 0151 236 0121
E-mail: chamber@liverpoolchamber.org.uk

Website:
http://www.liverpoolchamber.org.uk
Description of facilities and services.

Enquiries:
Enquiries to: Infopool Agent
Direct tel: 0845 145 1115
Direct fax: 0845 145 1116
Direct e-mail: infopool@liverpoolchamber.org.uk

Founded:
1850

Organisation type and purpose:
Membership association.
Delivering accredited services for members and other businesses which improve their profit and increase their efficiency. Providing opportunities for contact and trade between members. Representing members' needs and views at local, national and international levels. Work in partnership with other organisations to improve the prosperity of the region.

Subject coverage:
Mailing lists, company information, financial information, product sourcing, market research, grant searches, employment law, pay statistics, local economic surveys, international trade, trade missions (inward and outward), international market awareness events, European funding schemes, transnational links, Ordnance Survey (large and small scale mapping), The Stationery Office, British Standards, Health and Safety Agency, original research.

Museum or gallery collection, archive, or library special collection:
Reference library, over 700 directories, electronic sources

Printed publications:
Directory of Members (annually, free to members)
Export Matters (10 times a year, not Aug or Dec, free)
Liverpool Packet (6 times a year, free to members)
Greater Merseyside Quarterly Economic Survey (available at www.merseysidebusinessservey.org.uk, free)
North West Chambers of Commerce Directory (includes Liverpool Chamber of Commerce members, annually, free to members)

Access to staff:
Contact by letter, by telephone, by fax, by e-mail, in person and via website
Hours: Mon to Fri, 0900 to 1700

Access for disabled people:
Ramped entry, access to all public areas, toilet facilities

LIVERPOOL CHARITY AND VOLUNTARY SERVICES

Acronym or abbreviation: LCVS

14 Castle Street, Liverpool, L2 0NJ

Tel: 0151 236 7728
Fax: 0151 258 1153
E-mail: info@lcvs.org.uk

Website:
http://www.lcvs.org.uk

Enquiries:
Enquiries to: Chief Executive

Founded:
1909

Organisation type and purpose:
Professional body, voluntary organisation, registered charity (charity number 223485).

Subject coverage:
The information and advisory service is for and about the voluntary sector, and includes charity law, charity registration, sources of funding, management, the workings of government, local, central and European.

Museum or gallery collection, archive, or library special collection:
Small library of information relating to voluntary organisations and charities archive material

Printed publications:
Liverpool Link (news magazine, 10 times a year)
Take it From Here – A Handbook of Social Services on Merseyside (annual directory)
Merseyside Directory of Grant Making Trusts (once every 2 years)
Liverpool Community Network Newsletter (6 times a year)

Publications list:
Available in print

Access to staff:
Contact by letter, by telephone, by fax, by e-mail and via website
Hours: Mon to Fri, 0900 to 1700

LIVERPOOL HOPE UNIVERSITY

Hope Park, Liverpool, L16 9JD

Tel: 0151 291 3000
Fax: 0151 291 2037
E-mail: taylorl@hope.ac.uk

Website:
http://www.hope.ac.uk/library

Enquiries:
Enquiries to: Director of Library, Learning and Information Services
Direct tel: 0151 251 3528
Other contacts: Deputy Director of LLIS

Founded:
1844

Formerly called:
Liverpool Hope University College; Liverpool Institue of Higher Education (LIHE)

Organisation type and purpose:
Suitable for ages: 18+.

Subject coverage:
Information technology; media; creative and performing arts; psychology; theology; sociology; social work; physical education; business and management; law; politics; art; music; literature;

geography; tourism; education; history; children's fiction; science; environmental science; sport; drama.

Museum or gallery collection, archive, or library special collection:
Gradwell Collection, theology
Picton Collection, theology
National Ex-Church of England Society, religious education
Professor Andrew F. Walls African-Asian Christianity Collection
Archbishop Stuart Blanch (1918–94)

Library catalogue:
All or part available online

Access to staff:
Contact by letter, by telephone, by fax and by e-mail. Appointment necessary.
Hours: Term time: Mon, Thu, 0900 to 1915; Fri, 0900 to 1645; Sun, 1400 to 1645 (see website for details)

Access to building, collection or gallery:
Special comments: University ID card or signing in required

Access for disabled people:
Parking provided, level entry, access to all public areas, toilet facilities

LIVERPOOL INSTITUTE FOR PERFORMING ARTS

Acronym or abbreviation: LIPA

Mount Street, Liverpool, L1 9HF

Tel: 0151 330 3000
Fax: 0151 330 3131
E-mail: k.odonoghue@lipa.ac.uk

Website:
http://www.lipa.ac.uk

Enquiries:
Enquiries to: Director of Information Services and Technical Support
Direct tel: 0151 330 3250

Founded:
1990

Organisation type and purpose:
Membership association, present number of members: 620, university library, suitable for ages: 18+.
Degree-awarding body, Liverpool John Moores University.

Subject coverage:
Performing arts, sound technology, performance design, acting, dance, music, enterprise management, community arts.

Library catalogue:
All or part available in-house

Access to staff:
Contact by letter, by telephone, by fax, by e-mail and via website. Appointment necessary.
Hours: Mon to Fri, 0900 to 1700

LIVERPOOL JOHN MOORES UNIVERSITY – AVRIL ROBARTS LEARNING RESOURCE CENTRE

Acronym or abbreviation: LJMU

79 Tithebarn Street, Liverpool, L2 2ER

Tel: 0151 231 4022
Fax: 0151 231 4479

Website:
http://www.ljmu.ac.uk/lea
For all the University Learning Resource Centres.
http://www.ljmu.ac.uk/lea/avril
Information on Avril Robarts Learning Resource Centre including opening hours.

Enquiries:
Enquiries to: Principal Information Officer (Operations)
Direct e-mail: c.haddock@ljmu.ac.uk

Organisation type and purpose:
University department or institute.
Learning resource centre.

Subject coverage:
Sciences, engineering, health and applied social sciences.

Library catalogue:
All or part available online

Printed publications:
Numerous publications including guides to the service, course materials, fact sheets, subject literature guides and user guides

Publications list:
Available online and in print

Access to staff:
Contact by letter, by fax and by e-mail
Hours: Mon to Thu, 0900 to 2100; Fri, 0930 to 1700; Sat, Sun, 1000 to 1600

Access for disabled people:
Disabled access available

LIVERPOOL JOHN MOORES UNIVERSITY – LEARNING AND INFORMATION SERVICES

Acronym or abbreviation: LJMU

Aldham Robarts Learning Resource Centre, Mount Pleasant Campus, Maryland Street, Liverpool, L3 5UZ

Tel: 0151 231 3544
Fax: 0151 231 3113
E-mail: m.melling@ljmu.ac.uk

Website:
http://www.ljmu.ac.uk/lea

Enquiries:
Enquiries to: Director of Learning and Information Services

Organisation type and purpose:
University Library.

Subject coverage:
Art and design; fashion; business; management; law; civil, mechanical, electrical and electronic engineering; surveying; architecture; natural sciences; health; humanities; social sciences; sport and recreation; librarianship; computing; home economics; languages; education; social work.

Museum or gallery collection, archive, or library special collection:
Everyman Theatre Archive
Frankie Vaughan Collection of Scores and Parts
Jon Savage Punk Collection
Liddle Hart Collection on Fashion
Stafford Beer Collection
Cold War Collection
Barry Miles Archive

Library catalogue:
All or part available online

Printed publications:
Catalogue of the Liddle Hart Collection
Union List of Legal Materials held in Liverpool, 1985

Publications list:
Available in print

Access to staff:
Contact by letter, by telephone, by fax, by e-mail and via website. Appointment necessary. Non-members charged.
Hours: Mon to Fri, 0900 to 1700

LIVERPOOL LIBRARIES AND INFORMATION SERVICES

Formal name: City of Liverpool Libraries and Information Services (Dept)

Central Library, William Brown Street, Liverpool, L3 8EW

Tel: 0151 233 5835/36\ Minicom no. 0151 233 5850

Fax: 0151 233 5886
E-mail: refbt.central.library@liverpool.gov.uk

Website:
http://www.liverpool.gov.uk/libraries
Description of services.

Enquiries:
Enquiries to: Head of Libraries and Information Services
Direct tel: 0151 233 6346
Direct fax: 0151 233 6399
Other contacts: Team Leader, Services to Business for main contact for business information services.

Founded:
1852

Organisation type and purpose:
Local government body, public library.
Reorganised into three departments; information services, lending services, record office and family history services.

Subject coverage:
All subject fields are covered, including: arts and recreation; government; law, economics, transport, business information, statistics; librarianship; religion, philosophy, sociology and education; language, literature, history and topography; local studies; science and technology, including computers, health and safety, medicine, engineering, patents and standards, publications of British Government and International organisations.

Museum or gallery collection, archive, or library special collection:
British Government publications
Carl Rosa Opera Collection
Earl of Derby Papers
Complete set of BSI
Parish Registers and other church records
European Union documents
H F Hornby bequest and other rare book collections consisting of c. 12,000 manuscripts, finely printed and illustrated books and fine bindings; c. 8000 etchings, engravings and woodcuts; c. 75,000 bookplates
Historical Collection of Childrens' books
Liverpool City Council Archives and a wide range of deposited archives
Merseyside County Council, Merseyside Development Corporation and joint authority archives
Melly Papers
Moore Papers
Norris Papers
Patent specifications, including Patent Co-operation Treaty, European, US and GB (on CD-ROM)
Roscoe Papers
UN and WHO collection
Walter Crane Collection

Trade and statistical information:
Wide range of official and commercial statistical publications, including UK government, EU, UN, Mintel and Keynote market research reports.

Non-library collection catalogue:
All or part available in-house

Library catalogue:
All or part available in-house

Publications list:
Available in print

Access to staff:
Contact by letter, by telephone, by fax, by e-mail and in person
Hours: Mon to Thu, 0900 to 1800; Fri, 0900 to 1800; Sat, 0900 to 1700; Sun, 1200 to 1600

Access for disabled people:
Parking provided, ramped entry, toilet facilities
Special comments: IT equipment and software available for disabled customers – Contact services to Disabled People Unit, 0151 233 5865

continued overleaf

Parent body of:
LADSIRLAC
tel: 0151 233 5825; fax: 0151 233 5886; e-mail: stb
.central.library@liverpool.gov.uk
Liverpool Record Office and Family History
Service
tel: 0151 233 5817; fax: 0151 233 5886; e-mail:
recoffice.central.library@liverpool.gov.uk

LIVERPOOL MEDICAL INSTITUTION

Acronym or abbreviation: LMI

114 Mount Pleasant, Liverpool, L3 5SR

Tel: 0151 709 9125
Fax: 0151 707 2810
E-mail: library@lmi.org.uk

Website:
http://www.lmi.org.uk

Enquiries:
Enquiries to: Librarian

Founded:
1779

Organisation type and purpose:
Learned society (membership is by election or
invitation), present number of members: 1200,
registered charity (charity number 210112).

Subject coverage:
History of medicine.

**Museum or gallery collection, archive, or library
special collection:**
Historical Collection of medical books

Non-library collection catalogue:
All or part available in-house and in print

Library catalogue:
All or part available in-house

Printed publications:
Catalogue of Books in the Liverpool Medical
Institution Library to the end of the Nineteenth
Century,1968
History of the Liverpool Medical Institution (J A
Shepherd, 1979)

Access to staff:
Contact by letter, by telephone, by fax, by e-mail
and via website. Appointment necessary. Access
for members only. Letter of introduction required.
Non-members charged.
Hours: Mon to Fri, 0930 to 1730

Access to building, collection or gallery:
Prior appointment required

Access for disabled people:
Parking provided, ramped entry, level entry, access
to all public areas, toilet facilities

LIVERPOOL RECORD OFFICE AND LOCAL HISTORY SERVICE

Central Library, William Brown Street, Liverpool,
L3 8EW

Tel: 0151 233 5817/5811
Fax: 0151 233 5886 (for central library)
E-mail: recoffice.central.library@liverpool.gov.uk

Website:
http://www.liverpool.gov.uk
Brief details of the service under libraries.
http://www.liverpool.gov.uk/archives
Archives catalogue, images, publications,
information leaflets

Enquiries:
Enquiries to: Manager

Founded:
1850

Organisation type and purpose:
Local government body, public library.

Subject coverage:
Local history, family history, primarily City of
Liverpool, but some more general material for
Merseyside and Lancashire and Cheshire.

**Museum or gallery collection, archive, or library
special collection:**
Archives and local studies materials on all aspects
of the City's history

Non-library collection catalogue:
All or part available online and in-house

Library catalogue:
All or part available online and in-house

Printed publications:
Handlists:
Church of England Parish Registers and Records
(rev Sep 1999)
Roman Catholic Parish Records
Cemetery and Burial Records
Non-Conformist Churches
Maps:
Map of Church of England Parishes
Plan of Liverpool (Eyes J, June 1765)
Map of Liverpool (Tallis J, 1851)
Liverpool in 1859 (Isaac J R)
Leaflets:
Liverpool Record Office, Local Studies and Family
History Service, general information
Merseyside Record Office, general guide
Liverpool Record Office Information Leaflets:
series of guides to sources

Electronic and video publications:
Archive photographs with archive film footage
(CD-ROM)

Publications list:
Available online and in print

Access to staff:
Contact by letter, by telephone, by fax, by e-mail,
in person and via website. Appointment necessary.
Hours: Mon to Fri, 0900 to 1800; Sat, 0900 to 1700,
Sun, 1000 to 1600
Special comments: Annual closure, 3rd and 4th
weeks of June.

Access for disabled people:
Ramped entry, toilet facilities

LIVERPOOL SCHOOL OF TROPICAL MEDICINE

Pembroke Place, Liverpool, L3 5QA

Tel: 0151 708 9393
Fax: 0151 708 8733
E-mail: robbinsv@liverpool.ac.uk

Enquiries:
Enquiries to: Director
Other contacts: (1) Librarian (2) Secretary LATH for
(1) library and publications (2) Liverpool
Associates in Tropical Health Limited.

Founded:
1898

Organisation type and purpose:
Registered charity (charity number 222655),
university department or institute, research
organisation.

Subject coverage:
Human health in tropical and developing
countries; tropical community health; management
in primary health care; health information systems,
health education and promotion; clinical tropical
medicine; tropical paediatrics and child health;
maternal health; parasitology, medical
entomology; immunology and molecular biology
as applied to tropical medicine; veterinary
parasitology; epidemiology and statistics.

**Museum or gallery collection, archive, or library
special collection:**
Archive collection on all aspects of the School's
history
Dawes Parasitology Collection
Library of some 40,000 volumes

Reference collections of trypanosomes of man and
animals
Rodent malaria parasites and Leishmania

Printed publications:
Annals of Tropical Medicine and Parasitology (6
times a year)
Annals of Tropical Paediatrics (quarterly)
Annual Report
Prospectus

Publications list:
Available in print

Access to staff:
Contact by letter, by telephone, by fax, by e-mail
and via website. Appointment necessary.
Hours: Mon to Fri, 0900 to 1700

Affiliated to:
University of Liverpool

Subsidiary body:
Liverpool Associates in Tropical Health (LATH)

LIVING STREETS

Acronym or abbreviation: PA

3rd Floor, 31–33 Bondway, London, SW8 1SJ

Tel: 020 7820 1010
Fax: 020 7820 8208
E-mail: info@pedestrians.org.uk

Website:
http://www.pedestrians.org.uk

Enquiries:
Enquiries to: Director

Founded:
1929

Organisation type and purpose:
National organisation, membership association
(membership is by subscription), present number
of members: 1400, voluntary organisation,
registered charity (charity number 206006),
suitable for ages: all.
Living Streets is a national charity working to
create streets and public spaces that people on foot
can use and enjoy.

Subject coverage:
Statistical, legal, parliamentary, local government,
town planning, highway and traffic engineering,
and medical aspects of walking with special regard
for its safety and convenience.

**Museum or gallery collection, archive, or library
special collection:**
Association archives

Printed publications:
Walk (members magazine, 3 times per annum)
Annual Report
Living Streets – Action Manifesto (free of charge)
Schools Resource Pack
The School Run: Blessing or Blight?
Taking the Stategy Step
Walk to School (leaflet)

Publications list:
Available online and in print

Access to staff:
Contact by letter, by telephone, by fax, by e-mail
and via website
Hours: Mon to Fri, 0930 to 1730

Affiliated to:
Federation of Europe Pedestrians Associations
International Federation of Pedestrians

Local contacts:
Countrywide

LLANELLI LIBRARY

Vaughan Street, Llanelli, Carmarthenshire, SA15
3AS

Tel: 01554 773538
Fax: 01554 750125
E-mail: libraries@carmarthenshire.gov.uk

Enquiries:
Enquiries to: Manager

Founded:
1860

Organisation type and purpose:
Local government body, public library.

Subject coverage:
General

Museum or gallery collection, archive, or library special collection:
1800 coal mine plans
Collection of manuscripts
Theodore Nichol Collection

Non-library collection catalogue:
All or part available in-house

Library catalogue:
All or part available online and in-house

Printed publications:
Local history publications

Publications list:
Available online and in print

Access to staff:
Contact by letter, by telephone, by fax and in person
Hours: Mon to Fri, 0900 to 1700

Access to building, collection or gallery:
No access other than to staff

Access for disabled people:
Ramped entry, access to all public areas, toilet facilities
Special comments: Lift to first floor.

LLANGEFNI LIBRARY

Lon y Felin, Llangefni, Anglesey, LL77 7RT

Tel: 01248 752908
Fax: 01248 752999
E-mail: jrtlh@ynysmon.gov.uk

Website:
http://www.ynysmon.gov.uk
Isle of Anglesey County Council corporate web-site.

Enquiries:
Enquiries to: Manager

Founded:
1996

Organisation type and purpose:
Local government body, public library.

Subject coverage:
Local history, the Isle of Anglesey.

Museum or gallery collection, archive, or library special collection:
Local studies collection – Isle of Anglesey

Non-library collection catalogue:
All or part available in-house

Library catalogue:
All or part available online

Access to staff:
Contact by letter, by telephone, by fax, by e-mail and in person
Hours: Mon to Fri, 0900 to 1700

Access to building, collection or gallery:
No prior appointment required

Access for disabled people:
Parking provided, level entry, access to all public areas, toilet facilities

Parent body:
Isle of Anglesey County Council
Library, Information and Archives Services

LLOYD'S MOTOR UNDERWRITERS ASSOCIATION

Acronym or abbreviation: LMUA

Irongate House, Duke's Place, London, EC3A 7LQ

Tel: 020 7626 7235 or 7006
Fax: 020 7929 1224
E-mail: lmua@lloyds.com

Enquiries:
Enquiries to: Chief Executive

Founded:
1931

Organisation type and purpose:
Trade association.

Subject coverage:
Motor insurance.

Access to staff:
Contact by letter, by telephone and by fax
Hours: Mon to Fri, 0930 to 1700

LLOYD'S REGISTER OF SHIPPING

71 Fenchurch Street, London, EC3M 4BS

Tel: 020 7709 9166
Fax: 020 7488 4796

Website:
http://www.lr.org
Details of organisation.

Enquiries:
Enquiries to: Information Officer & Archivist
Direct tel: 020 7423 2077
Direct fax: 020 7423 2039

Founded:
1760

Organisation type and purpose:
International organisation, advisory body, statutory body, service industry, training organisation, consultancy, research organisation, publishing house.
Classification Society and Independent Inspection Agency.

Subject coverage:
Ships: classification, specification and advisory service, international conventions, Register Book (full details of all known merchant ships of the world over 100 tons), statistics, technical records; offshore services: certification and classification in connection with steel and concrete, submersibles and underwater habitats, welding, linepipe etc; land-based industry: nuclear power stations, thermal and hydro-electric power stations, oil refineries and chemical plants, freight containers, and general engineering; other services include yachts, cargo gear, docks etc; instrumentation; refrigeration and cold stores; mass-produced machinery; computer services; offshore rigs.

Museum or gallery collection, archive, or library special collection:
Complete set of the Lloyd's Register Statistical Tables from 1878
Complete set of the Lloyd's Register of Ships from 1764
Complete set of the Lloyd's Register of Yachts from 1878 to 1980
Complete set of the Lloyd's Register Casualty Return 1890 to date

Trade and statistical information:
Shipping statistics 1878 to date.
Casualty (shipping) information from 1890 to date.
Shipping Information (Specific Ships) 1764 to date.
Shipowners 1876 to date.
Yachts 1904 to 1980.
Shipbuilders 1886 to date.

Non-library collection catalogue:
All or part available in-house

Library catalogue:
All or part available in-house

Printed publications:
Register of International Ship Managers (3 times a year)
Register of International Shipowning Groups (3 times a year)

Register of Offshore Units, Submersibles and Underwater Systems (annually)
Register of Ships (vols 3, annually, plus weekly supplements)
Rules and Regulations for the Classification of Ships
Rules and Regulations for the Classification of Yachts and Small Craft
Rules for Inland Waterway Ships
Shipyard Orders Weekly Report (weekly)
The List of Shipowners Managers and Managing Agents (annually)
The Maritime Guide (annually)
World Casualty Statistics (annually)
World Fleet Statistics (annually)
World Shipbuilding Statistics (quarterly)
Order printed publications from: Lloyd's Register Fairplay Ltd
Lombard House, 3 Princess Way, Redhill, RH1 1UP, tel: 01737 379000, fax: 01737 379001

Electronic and video publications:
Electronic shipping information available on CD-ROM
The Ultimate Guide to Ships (CD-ROM)
Rules and Regulations for the classification of ships (CD-ROM)

Publications list:
Available online

Access to staff:
Contact by letter, by telephone, by fax and in person. Appointment necessary. All charged.
Hours: Mon to Fri, 0930 to 1200 and 1300 to 1630
Special comments: Closed on public holidays and between Christmas and New Year.

Access for disabled people:
Access to all public areas, toilet facilities
Special comments: Entry to building by lift, prior notice appreciated but not necessary.

LOCAL AUTHORITIES COORDINATORS OF REGULATORY SERVICES

Acronym or abbreviation: LACORS

Local Government House, Smith Square, London, SW1P 3HZ

Tel: 020 7665 3888
Fax: 020 7665 3887
E-mail: info@lacors.gov.uk

Website:
http://www.lacors.gov.uk
General information on organisation. Detailed information by subscription (details on web)

Enquiries:
Enquiries to: Executive Director

Founded:
1978

Organisation type and purpose:
Local government statutory body.

Subject coverage:
Food, trading standards, health and safety, animal health and welfare, environmental protection, private-sector housing, licensing and gambling

Publications list:
Available in print

Access to staff:
Contact by letter, by telephone, by fax, by e-mail and via website
Hours: Mon to Fri, 0900 to 1700

Access to building, collection or gallery:
Prior appointment required

Access for disabled people:
Ramped entry

LOCAL AUTHORITY ACTION FOR SOUTHERN AFRICA

Acronym or abbreviation: LAACTSA

continued overleaf

c/o Glasgow City Council, DRS, 229 George Street, Glasgow, G1 1QU

Tel: 0141 287 8665
Fax: 0141 287 9958
E-mail: john.mcfadden@drs.glasgow.gov.uk

Enquiries:
Enquiries to: Membership Secretary

Founded:
1995

Organisation type and purpose:
Local government body, advisory body, membership association (membership is by subscription), present number of members: 60 UK Councils, training organisation, consultancy, research organisation.
Supporting development and democracy in post-apartheid South Africa.

Subject coverage:
Local government in Southern Africa (South Africa and other countries within SADC – Angola, Mozambique, Zambia, Zimbabwe, Tanzania, DRC, Lesotho, Namibia, Swaziland, Botswana, Malawi, Seychelles and Mauritius). British local government links with Southern Africa.

Printed publications:
2001 Special Report

Access to staff:
Contact by letter, by fax and by e-mail
Hours: Wed to Fri, 1000 to 1800

Sister organisation:
Action for Southern Africa (ACTSA)
231 Vauxhall Bridge Road, London, SW1V 1EH; tel: 020 3263 2001; fax: 020 7931 9398; e-mail: info@actsa.org

Special interest group of:
Local Government Association LGA (LGIB)

LOCAL AUTHORITY CATERERS ASSOCIATION

Acronym or abbreviation: LACA

Bourne House, Horsell Park, Woking, Surrey, GU21 4LY

Tel: 01483 766777
Fax: 01483 751991
E-mail: admin@laca.co.uk

Enquiries:
Enquiries to: Administrator

Founded:
1991

Organisation type and purpose:
Professional body.
Providers of catering services and supplies to education, social services, leisure and civil catering.

Subject coverage:
Catering with local authorities, including education, welfare, civic, leisure; development of school meals services.

Trade and statistical information:
Data on uptake of school meals.
Data on volume of purchasers in local authority catering.

Printed publications:
Handbook (annually)
List of Information on Provision of Services
List of Members
Newsletter (quarterly)
Survey of School Meals

Access to staff:
Contact by letter, by telephone, by fax and by e-mail
Hours: Mon to Fri, 0900 to 1700

LOCAL GOVERNMENT ASSOCIATION

Acronym or abbreviation: LGA

Local Government House, Smith Square, London, SW1P 3HZ

Tel: 020 7664 3131
Fax: 020 7664 3030
E-mail: info@lga.gov.uk

Website:
http://www.lga.gov.uk

Enquiries:
Enquiries to: Information Officer

Founded:
1997

Organisation type and purpose:
Local government body.
The national voice for local authorities in England and Wales. It speaks for over 480 local authorities representing 50 million people.

Subject coverage:
Local government in England and Wales, policy including finance, education, libraries, economic development, social services, transport, leisure, housing, tourism, contracts, environment, personnel, police, fire, consumer protection, health etc.

Museum or gallery collection, archive, or library special collection:
Policy and structure issues; review team; finance; economic development, tourism and leisure; legal and parliamentary; planning, transport, environment and housing

Library catalogue:
All or part available in-house

Printed publications:
Checklist of circulars (weekly, members only)
First (weekly)
Information Digest (irregular)
LGA yearbook (annually)
Library Bulletin
Other publications available on the following topics: best value, development, drugs, education, environment, equal opportunities, finance, highways, housing, leisure and tourism, management, planning, police, quality, social services, surveys and research and transport
Order printed publications from: LG Connect, Publication Sales
Local Government House, Smith Square, London, SW1P 3HZ, tel: 020 7664 3131

Publications list:
Available online

Access to staff:
Contact by letter, by telephone, by fax and by e-mail
Hours: Mon to Fri, 0900 to 1700

Access to building, collection or gallery:
No prior appointment required

Autonomous Welsh arm replaces the:
Assembly of Welsh Counties
Committee of Welsh Districts

LOCAL GOVERNMENT BOUNDARY COMMISSION FOR SCOTLAND

3 Drumsheugh Gardens, Edinburgh, EH3 7QJ

Tel: 0131 538 7510
Fax: 0131 538 7511
E-mail: secretariat@scottishboundaries.gov.uk

Website:
http://www.lgbc-scotland.gov.uk
Information on the boundaries of local government areas in Scotland and their electoral wards, and on reviews of those boundaries.

Enquiries:
Enquiries to: Secretary

Founded:
1973

Organisation type and purpose:
Statutory body. Advisory non-departmental public body, constituted under the Local Government (Scotland) Act 1973, reporting to the Scottish Government.

Subject coverage:
Local government boundaries.

Printed publications:
Reports on electoral and administrative area reviews
Order printed publications from: The Secretary

Electronic and video publications:
Reports available from website as PDF files

Publications list:
Available online

Access to staff:
Contact by letter, by telephone, by fax, by e-mail and via website
Hours: Mon to Fri, 0900 to 1700

LOCAL GOVERNMENT BOUNDARY COMMISSION FOR WALES

Acronym or abbreviation: LGBCW

1st Floor, Caradog House, 1–6 St Andrews Place, Cardiff, CF10 3BE

Tel: 029 2039 5031
Fax: 029 2039 5250
E-mail: lgbc@lgbc-wales.gov.uk

Website:
http://www.lbgc-wales.gov.uk

Enquiries:
Enquiries to: Secretary

Founded:
1972

Organisation type and purpose:
National government body.
A statutory body which reviews local government electoral and boundary arrangements in Wales.

Subject coverage:
The work of the LGBCW involving local government electoral and boundary reviews on Wales since 1972.

Museum or gallery collection, archive, or library special collection:
All reports published and related working files and maps

Printed publications:
Reports (free, distributed to local authorities and other interested parties on publication, members of the public may write for copies or call by appointment)

Publications list:
Available online and in print

Access to staff:
Contact by letter, by telephone, by fax and by e-mail. Appointment necessary.
Hours: Mon to Fri, 0800 to 1630

Parent body:
National Assembly for Wales
Cathays Park, Cardiff, CF10 3NQ

LOCAL GOVERNMENT INTERNATIONAL BUREAU

Acronym or abbreviation: LGIB

Local Government House, Smith Square, London, SW1P 3HZ

Tel: 020 7664 3100
Fax: 020 7664 3128
E-mail: enquiries@lgib.gov.uk

Website:
http://www.lgib.gov.uk

Information about LGIB; information about UK delegation to Committee of the Regions; on-line database of European Information Service 1997-; access to European Twinning market.

Enquiries:
Enquiries to: Public Relations Manager
Direct tel: 020 7664 3112
Other contacts: Twinnings Officer for information about town twinning and local authority international links.

Founded:
1988

Organisation type and purpose:
International organisation, local government body, national organisation, professional body (membership is by qualification), present number of members: 500.
European and International Affairs Unit of the Local Government Association and Welsh Local Government Association. LGIB also represents Northern Ireland Local Government Association. Funded from the local government revenue support grant.

Subject coverage:
European policy and legislation as it affects UK local government, European information of interest to local government, details of international representation by UK local government, projects and funding, development cooperation, information on international linking (eg town twinning).

Museum or gallery collection, archive, or library special collection:
Committee of the Regions papers
EU legislation and policy

Library catalogue:
All or part available online

Printed publications:
Publications include:
Special Reports on Committee of the Regions, EU Budget, Brussels Offices, International local government links
European Information Service (EIS, 10 times a year) 2001–02 subscription £290 a year, discount for UK local authorities (£145)
Leaflet on the Work of the Bureau
Linking News (5 times a year)

Electronic and video publications:
EIS Online – access to 5 year archive of European Information Service, available as part of EIS subscription

Publications list:
Available online and in print

Access to staff:
Contact by letter, by telephone, by fax, by e-mail and via website
Hours: Mon to Fri, 0900 to 1700
Special comments: No visitors as no library facilities.

British member of the:
Council of European Municipalities and Regions (CEMR)
International Union of Local Authorities (IULA)

Other addresses:
Brussels Office
Rue d'Arlon 22, 1050 Brussels, Belgium; tel: 00 32 2 502 3680; fax: 00 32 2 502 4035; e-mail: brussels .office@lgib.org

Parent body:
Local Government Association

LOCAL GOVERNMENT OMBUDSMAN

Formal name: Commission for Local Adminstration in England

10th Floor, Millbank Tower, Millbank, London, SW1P 4QP

Tel: 020 7217 4620
Fax: 020 7217 4621
E-mail: enquiries@lgo.org.uk

Website:
http://www.lgo.org.uk
Most publications, including digest of cases; guidance notes; leaflet on how to complain; plus origins and functions of the organisation; recent summaries of investigation reports; and recent customer satisfaction survey reports.

Enquiries:
Enquiries to: Secretary

Founded:
1974

Organisation type and purpose:
Statutory body.

Subject coverage:
Local Government Ombudsmen investigate complaints of injustice arising from maladministration by local authorities and certain other bodies. The objective is to secure, where appropriate, satisfactory redress for complainants and better administration for the authorities. The Ombudsmen have the power to examine files of local authorities and to interview officers and members. The authority must consider an Ombudsman's report and recommendations and notify him/her of the action it intends to take.

Museum or gallery collection, archive, or library special collection:
All investigation reports

Library catalogue:
All or part available in-house

Printed publications:
Complaint about the council? How to complain to the Local Government Ombudsman (in 10 languages, large print, Braille and tape free)
Annual Report (free up to 10 copies)
Digest of cases for 1996, 1997, 1998, 1999, 2000, 2001, 2002/03, 2003/04, 2004/05 (free up to 5 copies)
Guidance on good practice a series of 3 titles (free up to 5 copies)
Order printed publications from: Administrative Assistant, Local Government Ombudsman at the same address, tel: 020 7217 4683, fax: 020 7217 4621, e-mail: t.davey@lgo.org.uk

Publications list:
Available online and in print

Access to staff:
Contact by letter, by telephone, by fax and by e-mail. Appointment necessary.
Hours: Mon to Fri, 0900 to 1700
Special comments: Personal callers by appointment only.

Access to building, collection or gallery:
No prior appointment required
Hours: Mon to Fri, 0900 to 1700

Access for disabled people:
Ramped entry, toilet facilities

Other addresses:
Local Government Ombudsman
The Oaks No. 2, Westwood Way, Westwood Business Park, Coventry, CV4 8JB; tel: 024 7682 0000; fax: 024 7682 0001
Local Government Ombudsman
Beverley House, 17 Shipton Road, York, YO30 5FZ; tel: 01904 380200; fax: 01904 380269

LOCAL GOVERNMENT REFORM SOCIETY

Acronym or abbreviation: LGRS

14 Princes Avenue, Bognor Regis, West Sussex, PO21 2DY

Tel: 01243 863726

Enquiries:
Enquiries to: General Secretary
Other contacts: Information Officer

Founded:
1960

Organisation type and purpose:
International organisation, voluntary organisation. Non-profit-making organisation.
Radical reform of local government to guarantee real democratic and public trustee basis.

Subject coverage:
History of local government and its reform, private bills relating to local government, corruption in local government, maladministration, reform of individual authorities, rating reform and use of the local referendum.

Printed publications:
Newsletter
Research Papers
Seminar Study Reports

Access to staff:
Contact by letter
Hours: Mon to Fri, 0900 to 1700

LOCAL STUDIES CENTRE

Central Library, Northumberland Square, North Shields, Tyne and Wear, NE30 1QA

Tel: 0191 200 5424
Fax: 0191 200 6118
E-mail: local.studies@northtyneside.gov.uk

Website:
http://www.northtyneside.gov.uk/libraries/index .htm

Enquiries:
Enquiries to: Librarian

Founded:
1974

Organisation type and purpose:
Local government body.
Archive.

Subject coverage:
Contains printed sources dealing with people and organisations in or from the present North Tyneside Borough, past, present and future. There is also a collection of local photographs.

Museum or gallery collection, archive, or library special collection:
Theatre Royal, North Shields, playbills, 1820s
Shields Daily News 1864–

Non-library collection catalogue:
All or part available online and in-house

Library catalogue:
All or part available online, in-house and in print

Publications list:
Available online

Access to staff:
Contact by letter, by telephone, by fax, by e-mail and in person

Access for disabled people:
Level entry, access to all public areas, toilet facilities
Special comments: Wheelchair available.

Links with:
North Tyneside Council

LONDON 21 SUSTAINABILITY NETWORK

Unit LS2, The Kensington Charity Centre, Fourth Floor, Charles House, 375 Kensington High Street, W14 8QH

Tel: 020 7471 6795
Fax: 020 7471 6796
E-mail: office@london21.org

Website:
http://www.london21.org
Community projects in London.

Enquiries:
Enquiries to: Coordinator
Direct e-mail: vinciane.rycroft@london21.org

continued overleaf

Founded:
1998

Organisation type and purpose:
Voluntary organisation.
Network.
To promote, support and network community-based action for a greener, healthier London; to engage communities and individuals with local sustainability issues.

Subject coverage:
Information on organisations and projects regarding sustainability and Agenda 21 in Greater London and community initiatives. Channels for policy formation and information exchange.

Access to staff:
Contact by letter, by telephone and by e-mail.
Access for members only.
Hours: Monday to Fri, 0930 to 1700

LONDON ACADEMY OF DRESSMAKING AND DESIGN

Acronym or abbreviation: LADD

18 Dobree Avenue, Willesden, London, NW10 2AE

Tel: 020 8451 7174
Fax: 020 8459 7927
E-mail: info@londonacademy.com

Website:
http://www.londonacademy.com

Enquiries:
Enquiries to: Principal Designer

Founded:
1969

Organisation type and purpose:
School of dressmaking and designing.

Subject coverage:
Advance designing in ladies' and children's wear, bridal wear, fashion drawing, draping, bead and silk embroidery, grading, soft furnishing, millinery, swim wear and lace appliqué; senior diploma, basic and advanced diploma, basic foundation diploma.

Printed publications:
Prospectus

Access to staff:
Contact by letter, by telephone, by fax, by e-mail, in person and via website. Appointment necessary.
Hours: Mon to Fri, 0900 to 1700

LONDON ACADEMY OF PERFORMING ARTS

Acronym or abbreviation: LAPA

Saint Matthew's Church, Saint Petersburgh Place, Bayswater, London, W2 4LA

Tel: 020 7727 0220
Fax: 020 7727 0330
E-mail: admin@lapadrama.com

Enquiries:
Enquiries to: Administrator

Founded:
1981

Organisation type and purpose:
Registered charity (charity number 1045796), suitable for ages: 21+, training organisation.
To train young people to work as actors.

Subject coverage:
Working in theatre, film, TV, radio, on stage drama, music, dance, creative movement, fencing, stage combat, English, history, costume, masks and mime, singing, voice techniques.

Trade and statistical information:
We generally know about student cost of living in London.

Printed publications:
Prospectus

Publications list:
Available in print

Access to staff:
Contact by letter, by telephone, by fax, by e-mail and via website. Appointment necessary.
Hours: Mon to Fri, 0900 to 1700
Special comments: Occasional access to church building restricted by church functions.

Access to building, collection or gallery:
No access other than to staff
Special comments: Not generally open.

LONDON ADVICE SERVICES ALLIANCE

Acronym or abbreviation: LASA

Universal House, 88 Wentworth Street, London, E1 7SA

Tel: 020 7377 2748
Fax: 020 7247 4725
E-mail: info@lasa.org.uk

Website:
http://www.lasa.org.uk
http://www.rightsnet.org.uk
Welfare rights information for advice workers.
http://www.multikulti.org.uk
Information on debt, housing, immigration and asylum, employment, education, health, welfare benefits and racism in 12 community languages.

Founded:
1984

Organisation type and purpose:
Voluntary organisation, registered charity, training organisation, consultancy, research organisation.

Subject coverage:
Research and consultancy into advice service provision and development; training to advice workers on welfare rights; IT consultancy and advice to voluntary sector. Website services, case management software and representation services.

Printed publications:
Review (on subscription, £19 voluntary sector, £24 others)
Computanews (free to download)
Computanews Factsheets including:
Buying IT (£5)
Managing IT (£5)
Networks (£5)
Project Management (free)

Electronic and video publications:
AIMS, Enquiry Recording and Case Management (software)
rightsnet.org.uk – information on welfare benefits

Publications list:
Available online and in print

Access to staff:
Contact by letter, by telephone, by fax, by e-mail and via website
Hours: Mon to Fri, 0930 to 1730
Special comments: Charges for major undertakings such as consultancies and research.

Access to building, collection or gallery:
Mon to Fri, 0900 to 1700

LONDON AND MIDDLESEX ARCHAEOLOGICAL SOCIETY

Acronym or abbreviation: LAMAS

Museum of London, London Wall, London, EC2Y 5HN

Tel: 020 7600 3699
Fax: 020 7600 1058
E-mail: jkeily@museumoflondon.org.uk

Website:
http://www.lamas.org.uk

Enquiries:
Enquiries to: Secretary
Direct tel: 020 7814 5734

Founded:
1855

Organisation type and purpose:
Membership association (membership is by subscription), present number of members: 658, voluntary organisation, registered charity (charity number 267552).
To further the study of archaeology, local history and the historic buildings of the London area and to publish the results of such research; to encourage public interest in those areas and so promote preservation of historic buildings, ancient monuments and other remains of historic or archaeological interest.

Subject coverage:
History and archaeology of London and the London area; preservation of historic buildings in this area.

Museum or gallery collection, archive, or library special collection:
Books and periodicals

Library catalogue:
All or part available in-house

Printed publications:
Newsletter (quarterly)
Special Papers (occasional)
Transactions (annually)

Publications list:
Available online

Access to staff:
Contact by letter, by telephone, by e-mail and via website
Hours: Mon to Fri, 0900 to 1700

Access to building, collection or gallery:
Prior appointment required
Special comments: Members only

Links with:
about 50 local societies in London

Member organisation of:
Council for British Archaeology

LONDON ASSOCIATION OF PRIMAL PSYCHOTHERAPISTS

Acronym or abbreviation: LAPP

West Hill House, 6 Swains Lane, London, N6 6QU

Tel: 020 7267 9616 / 020 7482 4212
Fax: 020 7485 7957
E-mail: info@lapp.org

Website:
http://www.lapp.org

Enquiries:
Enquiries to: General Secretary

Founded:
1990

Organisation type and purpose:
Professional body (membership is by qualification, election or invitation), present number of members: 55, voluntary organisation.

Subject coverage:
Psychotherapy.

Access to staff:
Contact by letter, by telephone, by fax, by e-mail and via website. Appointment necessary. Non-members charged.
Hours: Mon to Fri, 0900 to 1900; Sat

Affiliated to:
The United Kingdom Council for Psychotherapy (UKCP)
tel: 020 7436 3002

LONDON BAPTIST ASSOCIATION

Acronym or abbreviation: LBA

235 Shaftesbury Avenue, London, WC2H 8EP

Tel: 020 7692 5592

Fax: 020 7692 5593
E-mail: lbaoffice@londonbaptist.org.uk

Website:
http://www.londonbaptist.org.uk

Enquiries:
Enquiries to: Secretary

Founded:
1865

Organisation type and purpose:
Membership association (membership is by election or invitation), registered charity.

Subject coverage:
Baptist churches in Greater London.

Museum or gallery collection, archive, or library special collection:
Records of statistics, ministers, locations of Baptist Churches in Greater London, 1865 onwards

Printed publications:
Annual Directory

Access to staff:
Contact by letter, by fax and by e-mail
Hours: Mon to Fri, 0900 to 1700

Affiliated to:
Baptist Union of Great Britain

LONDON BEREAVEMENT NETWORK

Acronym or abbreviation: LBN

356 Holloway Road, London, N7 6PA

Tel: 020 7700 8134
Fax: 020 7700 8146
E-mail: info@bereavement.org.uk

Website:
http://www.bereavement.org.uk

Enquiries:
Enquiries to: Director
Other contacts: Chairperson

Founded:
1993

Organisation type and purpose:
Membership association (membership is by qualification), present number of members: 115, voluntary organisation, registered charity (charity number 1077215).
Membership is by subscription and qualification. To refer bereaved members of the public in the Greater London area on to their local bereavement support service. To offer training, information and support to staff and volunteers of members services.

Subject coverage:
Bereavement, bereavement counselling and the training of volunteer counsellors.

Museum or gallery collection, archive, or library special collection:
A reference library of journals and periodicals on bereavement and voluntary sector. Issues available to staff and volunteers of member services only
Small lending library of books, videos and audio tapes
Small library of books, periodicals, tapes and videos on bereavement counselling available to members

Printed publications:
Annual Report
Leaflet

Access to staff:
Contact by letter, by telephone, by fax, by e-mail and via website
Hours: Mon to Fri, 0900 to 1700
Special comments: Answerphone outside office hours.

Umbrella body for the:
bereavement support services across London

LONDON BEREAVEMENT RELIEF SOCIETY

175 Tower Bridge Road, London, SE1 2AH

Tel: 020 7407 7585
Fax: 020 7403 6711

Enquiries:
Enquiries to: Information Officer

Founded:
1823

Organisation type and purpose:
Registered charity (charity number 208260).

Subject coverage:
Financial relief in relation to bereavement.

Printed publications:
Annual Report
Leaflet about the Society

Access to staff:
Contact by letter
Hours: Mon to Fri, 0900 to 1700

LONDON BOROUGH OF BARKING AND DAGENHAM

Civic Centre, Dagenham, Essex, RM10 7BN

Tel: 020 8592 4500\ Minicom no. 020 8227 2685
Fax: 020 8595 3758
E-mail: jbufton@barking-dagenham.gov.uk

Website:
http://www.barking-dagenham.gov.uk

Enquiries:
Enquiries to: Chief Executive

Organisation type and purpose:
Local government body.

Subject coverage:
Council.

Access to staff:
Contact by letter, by telephone, by fax, by e-mail and via website
Hours: Mon to Fri, 0900 to 1700

Access for disabled people:
Parking provided, ramped entry

LONDON BOROUGH OF BARNET ARCHIVES AND LOCAL STUDIES CENTRE

80 Daws Lane, Mill Hill, London, NW7 4SL

Tel: 020 8959 6657
E-mail: library.archives@barnet.gov.uk

Website:
http://www.earl.org.uk/familia
Genealogical sources.
http://www.hmc.gov.uk
Deposited lists, RHMC.
http://www.barnet.gov.uk/localstudies

Enquiries:
Enquiries to: Local Studies Manager

Founded:
1965

Organisation type and purpose:
Local government body, public library.

Subject coverage:
All aspects of local study for the area of the London Borough of Barnet.
Records of predecessor authorities.

Non-library collection catalogue:
All or part available online and in-house

Access to staff:
Contact by letter, by telephone, by e-mail, in person and via website. Appointment necessary.
Hours: Tue, Wed, Fri, 0930 to 1630; Thu, 1300 to 1900

LONDON BOROUGH OF BEXLEY CENTRAL LIBRARY AND LOCAL STUDIES

Townley Rd, Bexleyheath, DA6 7HJ

Tel: 020 8303 7777
Fax: 020 8304 7058
E-mail: libraries@bexley.gov.uk

Website:
http://www.bexley.gov.uk/service/publications.html
Publications list.
http://elibrary.bexley.gov.uk/rooms

Enquiries:
Enquiries to: Head of Libraries & Cultural Services

Founded:
1899

Organisation type and purpose:
Local government body, public library.

Subject coverage:
Public library and museums service. Local collections.

Museum or gallery collection, archive, or library special collection:
Local studies collections

Non-library collection catalogue:
All or part available online

Library catalogue:
All or part available online

Printed publications:
A range of local history titles including:
Bexley Deneholes (Le Gear R F)
Family History in Bexley (Reilly L)
Hall Place (Shaw J C M and Scott. M)
Medieval Bexley (Du Boulay F R H)
Story of Barnehurst (Thomas E O)
Order printed publications from: Bexley Local Studies and Archives Centre
Hall Place, Bourne Road, Bexley, DA5 1PQ, tel: 01322 526574

Publications list:
Available online and in print

Access to staff:
Contact by letter, by telephone, by fax, by e-mail and in person. Appointment necessary.
Hours: Dependent on service

Access for disabled people:
Access to all public areas

Other addresses:
12 Branch Libraries
Please consult website
Central Library
Townley Road, Bexleyheath, Kent, DA6 7HJ; tel: 020 8301 1066; fax: 020 8303 9052; e-mail: libraries.els@bexley.gov.uk

LONDON BOROUGH OF CAMDEN

Camden Town Hall, Judd Street, London, WC1H 9JE

Tel: 020 7278 4444
Fax: 020 7974 3210
E-mail: info@camden.gov.uk

Website:
http://cindex.camden.gov.uk
http://www.camden.gov.uk

Enquiries:
Enquiries to: Chief Executive

Organisation type and purpose:
Local government body.

Subject coverage:
Camden Council services and referral to other local services.

Library catalogue:
All or part available online

Printed publications:
Annual Report

continued overleaf

A-Z of Council Services
Camden Citizen (newspaper, monthly, free)

Access to staff:
Contact by letter, by telephone, by fax, in person and via website
Hours: Mon to Fri, 0900 to 1700

Other address:
Camden Information Services
Crowndale Centre, 218 Eversholt Street, London, NW1 1BD; tel: 020 7974 1656; fax: 020 7974 1566; e-mail: cameninformationservices@camden.gov.uk

LONDON BOROUGH OF CAMDEN – LEISURE AND COMMUNITY SERVICES DEPARTMENT

Crowndale Centre, 216–218 Eversholt Street, London, NW1 1DE

Tel: 020 7974 4001
Fax: 020 7974 1615

Enquiries:
Enquiries to: Librarian
Direct e-mail: david.jones@camden.gov.uk

Founded:
1965

Organisation type and purpose:
Public library.

Subject coverage:
General public library service, philosophy and psychology.

Museum or gallery collection, archive, or library special collection:
Kate Greenaway collection of early children's books
Special collections on philosophy and psychology

Non-library collection catalogue:
All or part available online and in-house

Library catalogue:
All or part available online

Publications list:
Available online

Access to staff:
Contact by letter, by telephone, by fax, by e-mail, in person and via website
Hours: Mon to Fri, 0900 to 1700

Access to building, collection or gallery:
No access other than to staff
Hours: Central Reference Library: Mon, Thu, 1000 to 1900; Tue, Wed, Fri, 1000 to 1800; Sat, 1000 to 1700

Access for disabled people:
Level entry, toilet facilities

Also at:
Central Reference Library
Swiss Cottage, 88 Avenue Road, London, NW3 3HA; tel: 020 7974 6522; fax: 020 7974 6505

LONDON BOROUGH OF ENFIELD – CENTRAL LIBRARY

Cecil Road, Enfield, Middlesex, EN2 6TW

Tel: 020 8379 8366\ Minicom no. 020 8379 8343
Fax: 020 8379 8401
E-mail: central.library@enfieldgov.uk

Website:
http://www.enfield.gov.uk

Enquiries:
Enquiries to: Librarian
Direct tel: 020 8379 8391
Direct fax: 020 8379 8401
Direct e-mail: central.reference.library@enfield.gov.uk
Other contacts: Local History Librarian 020 8379 2724; Music Librarian 020 8379 8392

Founded:
1908

Organisation type and purpose:
Local government body, public library.

Subject coverage:
Linguistics collection (regional specialisation); local history.

Non-library collection catalogue:
All or part available online

Library catalogue:
All or part available online and in-house

Access to staff:
Contact by letter, by telephone, by fax, by e-mail, in person and via website
Hours: Central Library: Mon, Tue, Thu & Sat, 0900 to 2000; Wed, 0900 to 1700; Fri, 0900 to 1730. Please check for all other libraries

Access for disabled people:
Ramped entry

Branch libraries:
Bowes Road Library
Bowes Road, London, N11 1BD; tel: 020 8379 1707; fax: 020 8368 6025; e-mail: bowesroadlibrary@yahoo.co.uk
Bullsmoor Library
Kempe Road, Enfield, Middlesex, EN1 1QS; tel: 020 8379 1723; fax: 01992 788761; e-mail: bullsmoore.library@enfield.gov.uk
Bush Hill Park Library
Agricola Place, Enfield, Middlesex, EN1 1DW; tel: 020 8379 1709; fax: 020 8367 2213; e-mail: bush.hill.library@enfield.gov.uk
Enfield Highway Library
258 Hertford Road, Enfield, Middlesex, EN3 5BN; tel: 020 8379 1710; fax: 020 8443 5034; e-mail: enfield.highway.library@enfield.gov.uk
Oakwood Library
185–187 Bramley Road, Enfield, Middlesex, N14 4XA; tel: 020 8379 1711; fax: 020 8367 4715; e-mail: oakwood.library@enfield.gov.uk
Ponders End Library
College Court, High Street, Enfield, Middlesex, EN3 4EY; tel: 020 8379 1712; fax: 020 8443 5035; e-mail: ponders.end.library@enfield.gov.uk
Weir Hall Library
Millfield Arts Complex, Silver Street, Edmonton, London, N18 1PJ; tel: 020 8379 1717; fax: 020 8807 3193; e-mail: weir.hall.library@enfield.gov.uk
Winchmore Hill Library
Greens Lane, Winchmore Hill, London, N21 3AP; tel: 020 8379 1718; fax: 020 8364 1060; e-mail: winchmore.hill.library@enfield.gov.uk

Main libraries:
Edmonton Green Library
36–44 South Mall, Edmonton, London, N9 0TN; tel: 020 8379 2600; fax: 020 8379 2615; e-mail: edmonton.green.library@enfield.gov.uk
Ordnance Road Library
645 Hertford Road, Enfield, Middlesex, EN3 6ND; tel: 020 8379 1725/6; fax: 01992 788763; e-mail: ordnance.road.library@enfield.gov.uk
Palmers Green Library
Broomfield Lane, Palmers Green, London, N13 4EY; tel: 020 8379 2711; fax: 020 8379 2712; e-mail: palmers.green.library@enfield.gov.uk
Ridge Avenue Library
Ridge Avenue, Winchmore Hill, London, N21 2RH; tel: 020 8379 1714/5; fax: 020 8364 1352; e-mail: ridge.avenue.library@enfield.gov.uk
Southgate Circus Library
High Street, Southgate, London, N14 6BP; tel: 020 8350 1124; fax: 020 8886 3669; e-mail: southgate.circus.library@enfield.gov.uk

LONDON BOROUGH OF HAVERING LIBRARY SERVICE

Central Library, St Edwards Way, Romford, Essex, RM1 3AR

Tel: 01708 432393
Fax: 01708 432391
E-mail: informationservices.library@havering.gov.uk

Website:
http://www.havering.gov.uk

Enquiries:
Enquiries to: Information Services Manager
Other contacts: Borough Library Manager

Founded:
1965

Organisation type and purpose:
Local government body, public library.

Subject coverage:
General reference material, central government publications, European information, local history.

Museum or gallery collection, archive, or library special collection:
Local studies

Non-library collection catalogue:
All or part available online, in-house and in print

Library catalogue:
All or part available online and in print

Printed publications:
Making of Emerson Park (£4.95)
Hornchurch and the New Zealand connection (£5)
A history of Havering-Atte-Bower (£5.95)
A short history of Stubbers (£2.95)
Childhood memories of Hornchurch (£1.50)
From country to cockney (£4.95)
History of Queen's Theatre, Hornchurch (£2.95)
Victoria County History, Romford and Hornchurch (£4.50)

Publications list:
Available in print

Access to staff:
Contact by letter, by telephone, by fax and by e-mail. Appointment necessary.
Hours: Mon, 1000 to 2000; Tue to Fri, 0900 to 2000; Sat, 0900 to 1600

Parent body:
London Borough of Havering
(Romford) Town Hall, Romford, Essex, RM1 3BD; tel: 01708 434343

LONDON BOROUGH OF HOUNSLOW

Acronym or abbreviation: LBH

The Civic Centre, Lampton Road, Hounslow, Middlesex, TW3 4DN

Tel: 020 8583 2000
Fax: 020 8583 2598
E-mail: information.ced@hounslow.gov.uk

Website:
http://www.lbhounslow.gov.uk

Enquiries:
Enquiries to: Customer Services Manager
Direct tel: 020 8583 2590
Direct fax: 020 8583 2592

Founded:
1965

Organisation type and purpose:
Local government body.

Subject coverage:
Council information, council tax, refuge, planning, environmental education, leisure services, housing, councillors, groups, societies, organisations, charities and advice-givers.

Access to staff:
Contact by letter, by telephone, by fax, by e-mail, in person and via website. Appointment necessary.
Hours: Mon to Thu, 0845 to 1700; Fri, 0845 to 1645

Access for disabled people:
Parking provided, ramped entry, access to all public areas, toilet facilities

LONDON BOROUGH OF LEWISHAM

Lewisham Town Hall, Catford, London, SE6 4RU

Tel: 020 8695 6000
Fax: 020 8314 5659

Website:
http://www.lewisham.gov.uk

Enquiries:
Enquiries to: Chief Executive
Direct e-mail: barry.quirk@lewisham.gov.uk

Organisation type and purpose:
Local government body.

Subject coverage:
Local government services.

Access to staff:
Contact by letter, by telephone, by fax, by e-mail
and in person
Hours: Mon to Fri, 0900 to 1700

Access to building, collection or gallery:
No prior appointment required

Access for disabled people:
Parking provided, ramped entry, level entry, access
to all public areas, toilet facilities

LONDON BOROUGH OF LEWISHAM – LIBRARY SERVICE

1st Floor, Town Hall Chambers, Rushey Green,
Catford, London, SE6 4RU

Tel: 020 8314 8024
Fax: 020 8314 3229

Enquiries:
Enquiries to: Librarian

Organisation type and purpose:
Local government body, public library.

Subject coverage:
General, local studies.

Non-library collection catalogue:
All or part available in-house

Access to staff:
Contact by letter, by telephone, by fax and in
person
Hours: Varies from library to library

Libraries at:
Blackheath Village Library
3–4 Blackheath Grove, London, SE3 0DD; tel:
020 8852 5309
Catford Library
Laurence House, Catford, London, SE6 4RU; tel:
020 8314 6399; fax: 020 8314 1110
Crofton Park Library
Brockley Road, London, SE4 2AF; tel: 020 8692
1683
Downham Library
Moorside Road, Downham, London, BR1 5EP;
tel: 020 8698 1475
Forest Hill Library
Dartmouth Road, London, SE23 3HZ; tel: 020
8699 2065; fax: 020 8699 8296
Grove Park Library
Somertrees Avenue, London, SE12 0BX; tel: 020
8857 5794
Lewisham Library
199–201 Lewisham High Street, London, SE13
6LG, minicom 8369; tel: 020 8297 9677; fax: 020
8297 1169
Lewisham Reference Library
199–201 Lewisham High Street, London, SE13
6LG; tel: 020 8297 9430; fax: 020 8297 1169
Local Studies Centre
199–201 Lewisham High Street, London, SE13
6LG; tel: 020 8297 0682; fax: 020 8297 1169
Manor House Library
Old Road, Lee, London, SE13 5SY; tel: 020 8852
0357
New Cross Library
283/5 New Cross Road, London, SE14 6AS; tel:
020 8694 2534
Sydenham Library
Sydenham Road, London, SE26 5SE; tel: 020
8778 7563

Torridon Road Library
Torridon Road, Catford, London, SE6 1RQ; tel:
020 8698 1590
Wavelengths Library
Griffin Street, Deptford, London, SE8 4RJ; tel:
020 8694 2535; fax: 020 8694 9652

LONDON BOROUGH OF TOWER HAMLETS

Mulberry Place, 5 Clove Crescent, London, E14
2BG

Tel: 020 7364 5000
Fax: 020 7364 4296

Website:
http://www.towerhamlets.gov.uk/

Enquiries:
Enquiries to: Press Office

Organisation type and purpose:
Local government body.

LONDON BUDDHIST CENTRE

Acronym or abbreviation: LBC

51 Roman Road, Bethnal Green, London, E2 0HU

Tel: 0845 458 4716
Fax: 0871 433 5995
E-mail: info@lbc.org.uk

Website:
http://www.lbc.org.uk
http://www.londonbuddhistcentre.com

Enquiries:
Enquiries to: Centre Director
Other contacts: Assistant Centre Director

Founded:
1978

Organisation type and purpose:
International organisation, voluntary organisation,
registered charity.
Religious Centre.

Subject coverage:
Buddhism, the Western Buddhist Order;
meditation, yoga, Tai Chi, acupuncture, alternative
health, Alexander Technique, osteopathy,
reflexology, shiatsu, homoeopathy, naturopathy,
nutritional therapy, medical herbalism, massage,
kinesiology, hypnotherapy, polarity therapy, reiki,
counselling and psychotherapy.

**Museum or gallery collection, archive, or library
special collection:**
Book, video and audio-tape library

Printed publications:
A concise history of Buddhism
Introducing Buddhism
Newsletter
Change Your Mind
Many other books on Buddhism
Order printed publications from: Books, Windhorse
Publications, 11 Park Road, Birmingham, B13 8AB,
tel: 0121 449 9997, e-mail: shantavira@compuserve
.com

Electronic and video publications:
Clear Vision (series of videos)
Dharmachakra Tapes and CD-ROMs
Order electronic and video publications from: Audio
Artefacts, Dharmachakra, 3 Coral Park, Henley
Road, Cambridge, CB1 3EA, tel: 01223 516821, e-
mail: orders@dharmachakra.freeserve.co.uk
Visual Artefacts, Clearvision Trust, 16–20 Turner
Street, Northern Quarter, Manchester, M4 1DZ, tel:
0161 839 9579, fax: 0161 839 4815, e-mail:
clearvision@clear-vision.org

Publications list:
Available in print

Access to staff:
Contact by letter, by telephone, by fax, by e-mail,
in person and via website. Appointment necessary.
Hours: Mon to Fri, 1000 to 1700

Access to building, collection or gallery:
No prior appointment required
Hours: Mon to Fri, 1000 to 1700

Centre of the:
Friends of the Western Buddhist Order (FWBO)
30 Chantry Road, Birmingham, B13 8AL; tel:
0121 449 3700; fax: 0121 449 3780; e-mail:
communications@fwbo.org; website: http://
www.fwbo.org/

Has:
22 public centres in UK and retreat centres and
smaller groups, also centres abroad

LONDON BUDDHIST VIHARA

Dharmapala Building, The Avenue, Chiswick,
London, W4 1UD

Tel: 020 8995 9493
Fax: 020 8994 8130
E-mail: london.vihara@virgin.net

Website:
http://www.londonbuddhistvihara.org

Enquiries:
Enquiries to: Secretary
Other contacts: Head Monk

Founded:
1926

Organisation type and purpose:
Voluntary organisation.
Religious institution.
To spread knowledge of Buddhism.

Subject coverage:
General Buddhism, specialising in the Theravada
tradition; teaching of Pali and Sinhala languages
(the latter to GCSE); meditation.

**Museum or gallery collection, archive, or library
special collection:**
Buddhist scriptures written in Pali language on Ola
leaves (palm leaves)
Reference Library (over 3500 titles) of books in
English, Pali, Sinhalese, Burmese and many
European languages

Library catalogue:
All or part available in-house

Printed publications:
Information sheets
Samadhi (magazine, quarterly)
Newsletter

Access to staff:
Contact by letter, by telephone, by fax, by e-mail
and in person
Hours: 0900 to 2100, seven days a week

Access to building, collection or gallery:
No access other than to staff

Access for disabled people:
Ramped entry, access to all public areas, toilet
facilities

Managers:
Maha Bodhi Society of Sri Lanka

Owned by:
Anagarika Dharmapala Trust (Sri Lanka)

LONDON BUSINESS SCHOOL

Acronym or abbreviation: LBS

Sussex Place, Regent's Park, London, NW1 4SA

Tel: 020 7262 5050
Fax: 020 7724 7875

Website:
http://www.london.edu/library/
London Business School library catalogue
including details of working papers and
accessions.

Enquiries:
Enquiries to: Librarian
Other contacts: Information Service Manager for
enquiries about fee-based business research.

continued overleaf

Organisation type and purpose:
University department or institute.

Subject coverage:
Management and business management;
education; international business; marketing;
market data; production; finance; company
financial data; accounting; economics and
economic forecasting; industries; operational
research; statistics; computers and data processing;
Europe.

**Museum or gallery collection, archive, or library
special collection:**
Corporate Library: annual reports of about 8000
British, European, North American, and Asian
Pacific companies
Market Research Reports

Library catalogue:
All or part available online

Printed publications:
Serials Holdings lists (twice a year, £15)
London Classification of Business Studies
Thesaurus (revised ed. Feb 1998)

Access to staff:
Non-members charged.
Hours: Mon to Fri, 0900 to 1700

Access for disabled people:
Level entry, toilet facilities

Affiliated to:
University of London

Other addresses:
London Business School Information Service (Fee
based)
tel: 020 7723 3404; fax: 020 7706 1897; e-mail:
infoserve@london.edu

LONDON CENTRE FOR FASHION STUDIES

Acronym or abbreviation: LCFS

Bradley Close, 8 White Lion Street, Islington,
London, N1 9PF

Tel: 020 7713 1991
Fax: 020 7713 1997
E-mail: learnf@shion.demon.co.uk

Website:
http://www.fashionstudies.co.uk
http://www.fashion.studies.com
Details of full and part time courses.

Enquiries:
Enquiries to: Director

Founded:
1991

Organisation type and purpose:
University department or institute, suitable for
ages: 18+, training organisation, consultancy,
publishing house.
Independent fashion school.

Subject coverage:
Fashion: pattern technology, pattern grading
techniques, grading and dress modelling, fashion
business, marketing, merchandising, production,
teacher training – fashion teachers.

Printed publications:
Grading for the Fashion Industry
Pattern Cutting and Making Up
Pattern Cutting and Making Up for Outerwear
Fashions
The Art of Dress Modelling

Electronic and video publications:
The Art of Dress Modelling (video, series 1 and 2)
The Art of Jacket Pattern Cutting (video, series 3)

Publications list:
Available in print

Access to staff:
Contact by letter, by telephone, by fax, by e-mail,
in person and via website
Hours: Open some evenings

In partnership with:
Middlesex University

LONDON CENTRE FOR PSYCHOTHERAPY

Acronym or abbreviation: LCP

32 Leighton Road, London, NW5 2QE

Tel: 020 7482 2002
Fax: 020 7482 4222

Website:
http://www.lcp-psychotherapy.org.uk

Enquiries:
Enquiries to: Chairman

Founded:
1973

Organisation type and purpose:
Professional body (membership is by subscription,
qualification), present number of members: 200,
registered charity (charity number 267244),
training organisation.

Subject coverage:
Psychotherapy.

Access to staff:
Contact by letter, by telephone, by e-mail and via
website
Hours: Mon to Fri, 1000 to 1600

Access to building, collection or gallery:
Prior appointment required

LONDON CHAMBER OF COMMERCE AND INDUSTRY

Acronym or abbreviation: LCCI

33 Queen Street, London, EC4R 1AP

Tel: 020 7248 4444
Fax: 020 7489 0391
E-mail: lc@londonchamber.co.uk

Website:
http://www.londonchamber.co.uk
Outline of services offered. Details of events and
press releases.

Enquiries:
Enquiries to: Information Officer
Direct e-mail: info@londonchamber.co.uk

Founded:
1881

Organisation type and purpose:
Membership association (membership is by
subscription), present number of members: 3500.
To help London businesses succeed by promoting
their interests and expanding their opportunities as
members of a worldwide business network.

Subject coverage:
Business information in the broadest sense,
company information, market information,
economic and financial data, suppliers of goods
and services, occupational; Euro Information
Centre, European legislation.

Trade and statistical information:
Activities on the London Economy. European
statistics.

Printed publications:
Annual Review of the London Economy
(subscribers only)
Directory of Members (free to members)
Quarterly Economic Report and Survey
(subscribers only)

Access to staff:
Contact by letter, by telephone, by fax, by e-mail,
in person and via website. Non-members charged.
Hours: Mon to Fri, 0900 to 1730

Access to building, collection or gallery:
No prior appointment required for members
Hours: Mon to Fri, 0900 to 1730

Special comments: Access free to members only; no
access to non-members.

Access for disabled people:
Level entry, toilet facilities

LONDON CHAMBER OF COMMERCE AND INDUSTRY EXAMINATIONS BOARD

Acronym or abbreviation: LCCIEB

Athena House, 112 Station Road, Sidcup, Kent,
DA15 7BJ

Tel: 020 8302 0261
Fax: 020 8302 4169
E-mail: custserv@lccieb.org.uk

Website:
http://www.lccieb.com

Enquiries:
Enquiries to: General Manager – Sales and
Marketing

Founded:
1887

Organisation type and purpose:
International organisation, registered charity.
Examinations board and business related NVQ
awarding body.

Subject coverage:
LCCIEB offers a wide range of qualifications both
timetabled and on demand. English and
International Languages, Information Technology,
Secretarial and Business Administration, Customer
Service and Marketing, Finance, Travel and
Tourism and a wide range of business-related
NVQs.

Publications list:
Available online and in print

Access to staff:
Contact by letter, by telephone, by fax, by e-mail
and via website
Hours: Mon to Fri, 0900 to 1700

Access to building, collection or gallery:
No access other than to staff

LONDON CHAMBER PLAYERS

Acronym or abbreviation: LCP

PO Box 84, London, NW11 8AL

Tel: 020 8455 6799
Fax: 020 8455 6799
E-mail: london-players@excite.com

Enquiries:
Enquiries to: Director
Direct fax: 020 8455 6799

Founded:
1979

Organisation type and purpose:
Registered charity, suitable for ages: children,
adults
Musical performances.

Subject coverage:
Music, music education

Access to staff:
Contact by letter, by telephone, by fax and by e-
mail. Appointment necessary.
Hours: Mon to Fri, 0930 to 1730

Access to building, collection or gallery:
Prior appointment required

LONDON CLEARING HOUSE LIMITED, THE

Acronym or abbreviation: LCH

Aldgate House, 33 Aldgate High Street, London,
EC3N 1EA

Tel: 020 7426 7000

Fax: 020 7426 7001

Website:
http://www.lch.com

Enquiries:
Enquiries to: Corporate Communications Director
Direct tel: 020 7426 7234
Direct fax: 020 7426 7665
Direct e-mail: matchm@lch.co.uk

Founded:
1888

Organisation type and purpose:
International organisation, present number of members: 116, service industry.
To clear contracts traded on London's major exchanges. Clearing house for LCH Repoclear – Interbank trades in European Government Repos; Clearing house for LCH Swapclear – Interbank interest rate swaps. Clearing house for LCH Equity Clear – equities traded on the London Stock Exchange's SETS system.

Subject coverage:
Risk management, clearing, settlement.

Printed publications:
Market Protection (free)
Rules, Regulations and Procedures (free, available on-line)
Understanding London Span (free, available on-line)
Order printed publications from: Member Liaison Department
at the same address

Publications list:
Available in print

Access to staff:
Contact by telephone, by fax, by e-mail and via website
Hours: Mon to Fri, 0930 to 1730

LONDON COLLEGE OF COMMUNICATION

Acronym or abbreviation: LCP

Library and Learning Resources, Elephant and Castle, London, SE1 6SB

Tel: 020 7514 6638
Fax: 020 7514 6597
E-mail: s.mahurter@lcp.linst.ac.uk

Website:
http://www.arts.ac.uk/library

Enquiries:
Enquiries to: Head of Library and Learning Resources
Other contacts: Reader Services Librarian for access to library and learning resources.

Organisation type and purpose:
University department or institute.

Subject coverage:
Art and design; fine art; graphic design; marketing and management; printing and publishing; retail; travel and tourism; topography; visual merchandising; film and video; journalism; media; photography.

Museum or gallery collection, archive, or library special collection:
Calendars
Ephemera
Posters
Printing Historical Collection – The Art of the Western Book
Script Collection – The History and the Development of Published and Unpublished Scripts
Slides
Videos

Library catalogue:
All or part available online

Printed publications:
Information guides in major subject areas
Prospectus

Access to staff:
Contact by letter. Appointment necessary. Letter of introduction required.
Hours: Mon to Thu, 0930 to 2015; Fri, 0930 to 1745; Sat, 1000 to 1545
Vacation opening times please telephone to confirm

Part of:
University of the Arts London

LONDON COLLEGE OF FASHION LIBRARY

20 John Princes Street, London, W1G 0BJ

Tel: 020 7514 7453/7455
Fax: 020 7514 7580

Website:
http://www.linst.ac.uk/library

Enquiries:
Enquiries to: Chief Librarian
Direct tel: 020 7514 7518

Subject coverage:
Fashion, design, clothing manufacture, embroidery, hairdressing, beauty therapy, costume history, textile history, footwear and accessories.

Museum or gallery collection, archive, or library special collection:
Clothing Institute Special Collection on historic tailoring
Fashion Photographs
Hairdressers Journal (bound volumes 1882 to the present; unique in the world)
History of Costume Collection

Access to staff:
Appointment necessary.
Hours: Mon to Thu, 0930 to 2015; Fri, 1000 to 1715

Constituent college of the:
London Institute

Other address:
Cordwainers at The London College of Fashion 182 Mare Street, London, E8 3RE

LONDON COLLEGE OF MASSAGE

Acronym or abbreviation: LCM

16 Bramley Court, Wickham Street, Kent, DA16 3DG

Tel: 020 3259 0000
E-mail: training@londoncollegeofmassage.co.uk

Website:
http://www.massagelondon.com

Enquiries:
Enquiries to: Director

Founded:
1987

Organisation type and purpose:
Training organisation.
Clinic.

Subject coverage:
Massage training and treatments; complementary health; anatomy and physiology; remedial and sports massage and other related postgraduate courses.

Museum or gallery collection, archive, or library special collection:
Dissertations relating to massage therapy

Printed publications:
Home Health Massage (Kavanagh W, pub Hamlyn)
The massage manual (Fiona Harrold, pub Headline)

Electronic and video publications:
Basic Massage (Pickwick video PV2256)

Publications list:
Available in print

Access to staff:
Contact by letter, by telephone, by fax and by e-mail. Appointment necessary.
Hours: Mon to Fri, 1100 to 1900

Affiliated to:
British Complementary Medicine Association
9 Soar Lane, Leicester, LE3 5DE; tel: 0116 242 5406; fax: 0116 242 5496
British Massage Therapy Council
17 Rymers Lane, Oxford, OX4 3JU; tel: 01865 774123; fax: 01865 774123
Institute of Complementary Medicine
PO Box 194, London, SE16 1QZ; tel: 020 7237 5165; fax: 020 7237 5175

LONDON COLLEGE OF OSTEOPATHIC MEDICINE/ OSTEOPATHIC ASSOCIATION CLINIC

Acronym or abbreviation: LCOM

8–10 Boston Place, London, NW1 6QH

Tel: 020 7262 1128
Fax: 020 7723 7492

Enquiries:
Enquiries to: Administrator

Founded:
1946

Organisation type and purpose:
Registered charity (charity number 209713), suitable for ages: post-graduates, training organisation.
Postgraduate college training (qualified doctors only) in Osteopathy, charity clinic for osteopathic patients.

Printed publications:
Directory of members

Access to staff:
Contact by letter, by telephone and by fax. Appointment necessary.
Hours: Mon to Fri, 0930 to 1645

LONDON COLLEGE OF TRADITIONAL ACUPUNCTURE AND ORIENTAL MEDICINE

Acronym or abbreviation: LCTA

60 Ballards Lane, Finchley, London, N3 2BUAZ

Tel: 020 8371 0820
Fax: 020 8371 0830
E-mail: college@lcta.com

Website:
http://www.lcta.com
Course information.

Enquiries:
Enquiries to: Course Administrator

Founded:
1992

Organisation type and purpose:
Training organisation.

Subject coverage:
Professional training in acupuncture, oriental herbal medicine, tui na massage, nutrition and medical qi gong.

Printed publications:
Prospectus (free)
Dragons Tale (newsletter)

Access to staff:
Contact by letter, by telephone, by fax, by e-mail and via website. Appointment necessary.
Hours: Mon to Sun, 0900 to 1730

LONDON CYCLO-CROSS ASSOCIATION

Acronym or abbreviation: LCCA

25 Lenham Road, Platt Heath, Kent, ME17 2NY

continued overleaf

Tel: 01622 850533
E-mail: MondSBarry@aol.com

Website:
http://www.britishcycling.org.uk

Enquiries:
Enquiries to: General Secretary
Direct tel: 020 8662 3963

Organisation type and purpose:
Voluntary organisation.
Cyclo-cross racing.

Subject coverage:
Sport, cycling, mountain biking, competition,
cyclo-cross.

Access to staff:
Contact by letter, by telephone, by e-mail and via
website
Hours: Mon to Fri, 0900 to 1700

Parent body:
British Cycling
Stuart Street, Manchester, M11 4DQ; tel: 0870
871 2000; fax: 0870 871 2001; e-mail: cyclo-cross@
britishcycling.org.uk; website: www
.britishcycling.org.uk

LONDON DISTRICT SURVEYORS ASSOCIATION

Acronym or abbreviation: LDSA

c/o Building Control Officer, London Borough of
Merton, Merton Civic Centre, London Road,
Morden, Surrey, SM4 5DX

Tel: 020 8545 3121
Fax: 020 8543 6085
E-mail: trevor.mcintosh@merton.gov.uk

Website:
http://www.londonbuildingcontrol.org/
Contacts, history, publications, regulations,
frequently asked questions

Enquiries:
Enquiries to: Honorary Secretary

Founded:
1987

Organisation type and purpose:
Professional body (membership is by election or
invitation), present number of members: 33.
An organisation of the Heads of the Building
Control service in all the 32 London Boroughs and
the City of London.
To further the profession and be a vehicle for
achieving uniformity; to collate and disseminate
information and to cooperate with similar bodies;
to promote training and continuing professional
development; to petition, confer with and promote
deputations to government and other public or
professional bodies; to guide the building control
offices in London with up-to-date, expert advice to
achieve uniformity of interpretation and operation
of the Building Regulations.

Subject coverage:
Commitees include those dealing with the
following subjects: electrical and mechanical;
career development and training; management
and legislation; publications and seminars; safety
at sports grounds; fire safety and means of escape;
licensing; technical and foundations; LANTAC;
and marketing. IT working Party and benchmark
forum.

**Museum or gallery collection, archive, or library
special collection:**
Minutes of general meetings, policy decisions,
questions and information

Printed publications:
National Directory of Development Services –
Listing Local Authorities & Contact Names
(1997)
Level of Service – Recommended Level of Service
for the Building Control Function (1999)
Enforcement Procedures – Building Regulations
Practical Guidance (1995)

Risk Assessment – Management of Health & Safety
at Work
Technical Standards for Places of Entertainment
(2001)
Model National Standard Conditions for Places of
Entertainment (2002)
Fire Safety Guides (2 documents, 1990–1997)
Safety of Sports Grounds (8 documents, 1990–
1999)
Foundations No 1 – Guidance Notes for the Design
of Bored Straight Shafted Piles in London Clay
(2000)
Order printed publications from: LDSA Publications
PO Box 266, Bromley, Kent, BR2 9ZN, tel: 07958
496044, fax: 020 8460 4313, e-mail: ldsa@goldserve
.net

Electronic and video publications:
Some publications are available on disc

Publications list:
Available online and in print

Access to staff:
Contact by letter, by e-mail and via website
Hours: Mon to Fri, 0900 to 1700

A region of the:
District Surveyors Association (of England &
Wales) (DSA)
c/o LABC Services, 137 Lupus Street, London,
SW1V 3HE; tel: 020 7607 6495; fax: 020 7607
6495; e-mail: ggriesbach@thedsa.co.uk

Liaison with bodies such as:
London Fire and Emergency Planning Authority
(LFEPA)
8 Albert Embankment, London, SE1 7SD; tel: 020
7587 2000; e-mail: info@london-fire.gov.uk

LONDON DOUGLAS MOTOR CYCLE CLUB LIMITED

Acronym or abbreviation: LDMCC

48 Standish Avenue, Stoke Lodge, Patchway,
Bristol, BS34 6AG

Tel: 01454 898185

Website:
http://www.douglasmotorcycles.co.uk
Club history, activities and contact address, online
application form.

Enquiries:
Enquiries to: Membership Secretary
Direct e-mail: via website

Founded:
1928

Organisation type and purpose:
Membership association (membership is by
subscription), present number of members: 1100.

Subject coverage:
Douglas motor cycles manufactured at
Kingswood, Bristol 1907–1957; spares service for
pre-war and post-war machines; marque specialist
providing technical information on most models; a
register of all Douglas machines known to the club
throughout the world providing a source of
information for identification and dating; machine
transfers and badges.

**Museum or gallery collection, archive, or library
special collection:**
Archive of technical information

Printed publications:
The New Conrod (magazine, 6 times a year, club
members only)

Access to staff:
Contact by letter
Hours: Mon to Fri, 0900 to 1700

Affiliated to:
Auto Cycle Union under title of 'LDMCC' as 'Non-
Territorial Club'

LONDON ELECTRONICS COLLEGE

Acronym or abbreviation: LEC

20 Penywern Road, London, SW5 9SU

Tel: 020 7373 8721
Fax: 020 7244 8733
E-mail: contact@lec.org.uk

Website:
http://www.lec.org.uk

Enquiries:
Enquiries to: Principal

Founded:
1892

Organisation type and purpose:
Independent further and higher education.

Subject coverage:
Electronics, TV and video, telecommunications,
microprocessors, software, IT, computer systems,
networks.

Access to staff:
Appointment necessary.
Hours: Mon to Fri, 0900 to 1700

LONDON FERTILITY CENTRE

Acronym or abbreviation: LFC

Lozens House, 112a Harley Street, London, W1G
7JH

Tel: 020 7224 0707
Fax: 020 7224 3102
E-mail: info@lfc.org.uk

Website:
http://www.lfc.org.uk
Information on LFC and treatments offered.

Enquiries:
Enquiries to: Information Officer
Other contacts: Centre Manager.

Founded:
1990

Organisation type and purpose:
Assisted conception, IVF and gynaecology

Subject coverage:
Gynaecology and fertility.

Printed publications:
The following available free, direct:
Information Packs
Patient Information Leaflets
Price Lists

Access to staff:
Contact by letter, by telephone, by fax, by e-mail
and via website
Hours: Mon to Fri, 0900 to 1730; Sat, Sun, 0900 to
1600

Access for disabled people:
Ramped entry, toilet facilities

LONDON FIRE AND EMERGENCY PLANNING AUTHORITY

Acronym or abbreviation: LFEPA

Room 520, Hampton House, 20 Albert
Embankment, London, SE1 7SD

Tel: 020 7587 2000
Fax: 020 7587 6086
E-mail: libraryservices@london-fire.gov.uk

Website:
http://www.london-fire.gov.uk

Enquiries:
Enquiries to: Library Information Resources Centre
Manager
Direct tel: 020 7587 6340

Founded:
1983

Organisation type and purpose:
Local government body.
Responsible for running London Fire Brigade and providing emergency planning in London.

Subject coverage:
Fire protection, fire fighting, fire prevention, chemical hazards, history of fire fighting, emergencies.

Access to staff:
Contact by letter, by telephone, by fax and via website. Appointment necessary.
Hours: Mon to Fri, 9000 to 1700

Also known as:
London Fire Brigade

Member of:
Fire Information Group, an information exchange co-operative in the fire and loss prevention field

LONDON GREEN BELT COUNCIL

13 Oakleigh Park Avenue, Chislehurst, Kent, BR7 5PB

Tel: 020 8467 5346

Enquiries:
Enquiries to: Honorary Secretary

Founded:
1954

Organisation type and purpose:
Membership association (membership is by subscription), voluntary organisation.

Subject coverage:
Green Belts, and particularly the Metropolitan Green Belt.

Access to staff:
Contact by letter and by telephone
Hours: All hours with answerphone

Membership includes:
Amenity societies
Council for the Preservation of Rural England
Cyclists' Touring Club
Open Spaces Society
Ramblers Association

LONDON GYMNASTICS FEDERATION

Acronym or abbreviation: LGF

4 Victoria Road, Chingford, London, E4 6BZ

Tel: 020 8529 1142
Fax: 020 8529 1142
E-mail: lgf@longym.freeserve.co.uk

Website:
http://www.longym.freeserve.co.uk
General information plus links to find further information.

Enquiries:
Enquiries to: General Secretary

Organisation type and purpose:
Membership association (membership is by subscription), present number of members: 65 clubs, 11,000 members, voluntary organisation. Governing body of the sport for London.

Subject coverage:
Gymnastics, pre-school, boys, girls, adults, special needs, competitive and recreational, all information regarding gymnastic clubs in the Greater London area, gymnastic coaching courses, gymnastic competitions and events.

Printed publications:
Regional newsletter (6 times a year, £10 a year)

Access to staff:
Contact by telephone, by fax, by e-mail and via website
Hours: Mon to Fri, 0900 to 1700

Parent body:
British Gymnastics Association (BG)
 tel: 01952 820330

LONDON HAZARDS CENTRE

Acronym or abbreviation: LHC

Hampstead Town Hall Centre, 213 Haverstock Hill, London, NW3 4QP

Tel: 020 7794 5999
Fax: 020 7794 4702
E-mail: mail@lhc.org.uk

Website:
http://www.lhc.org.uk
Bibliographic and full-text databases for subscribers and affiliates.

Enquiries:
Enquiries to: The Advice Worker
Other contacts: Information Officer

Founded:
1984

Organisation type and purpose:
Advisory body, membership association (membership is by subscription), voluntary organisation, registered charity (charity number 1981088), training organisation, consultancy, research organisation, publishing house.
Work with tenants associations and workplace safety representatives.

Subject coverage:
Work-related ill health, occupational health and safety law, health and safety in the workplace and the community.

Printed publications:
Chemical Hazards Handbook 1999 (£15 plus p&p)
Factsheets (contact the Centre for current list)
Fluorescent Lighting: A health hazard overhead (£5 plus p&p)
Hard Labour: Stress, ill-health and hazardous employment practices (1994, £6.95 plus p&p)
Practical handbooks on health and safety in the workplace and community, including:
RSI Hazards Handbook (1996, £12 plus p&p)
Sick Building Syndrome – causes, effects and control (1990, £4.50 plus p&p)
The Asbestos Hazards Handbook (1995, £12 plus p&p)
The Daily Hazard (newspaper, members)
VDU Work and the Hazards to Health (1993, £6.50 plus p&p)

Publications list:
Available online and in print

Access to staff:
Contact by letter, by telephone, by fax, by e-mail and via website
Hours: Mon, Tue, Thu, Fri, 1000 to 1200 and 1400 to 1700
Special comments: Charges to professional organisations, solicitors, media, etc. Free service only to Londoners.

Access to building, collection or gallery:
No prior appointment required

Connections with:
London Hazards Centre Trust Ltd
 at the same address

LONDON INSTITUTE FOR CONTEMPORARY CHRISTIANITY

Acronym or abbreviation: LICC

St Peters Church, Vere Street, London, W1G 0DQ

Tel: 020 7399 9555
Fax: 020 7399 9556
E-mail: mail@licc.org.uk

Website:
http://www.licc.org.uk
Work of LICC, articles, publications, events, courses.

Enquiries:
Enquiries to: Executive Director
Other contacts: Director of Operations for operational and administrative

Founded:
1982

Organisation type and purpose:
Registered charity (charity number 286102), public library, suitable for ages: all, training organisation. Christian adult education.

Subject coverage:
The relevance and application of the Bible and the Christian faith in today's world, application of biblical teaching to contemporary issues and everyday life.

Museum or gallery collection, archive, or library special collection:
Specialist theological library

Library catalogue:
All or part available in-house

Printed publications:
Magazines (quarterly, free to applicants)
Workwise (electronic magazine)
Email newsletter on Biblical reflection and contemporary culture (2 times per week)

Electronic and video publications:
Audio tapes of lectures (available for sale)
Catalogue available on request

Access to staff:
Contact by letter, by telephone, by fax, by e-mail and in person
Hours: Mon to Fri, 0900 to 1700

LONDON INVESTMENT BANKING ASSOCIATION

Acronym or abbreviation: LIBA

6 Frederick's Place, London, EC2R 8BT

Tel: 020 7796 3606
Fax: 020 7796 4345
E-mail: liba@liba.org.uk

Website:
http://www.liba.org.uk

Enquiries:
Enquiries to: Secretary

Organisation type and purpose:
Trade association (membership is by subscription).

Subject coverage:
Investment banking and securities industry in the United Kingdom including corporate finance, asset management and securities trading, and the regulation thereof.

Museum or gallery collection, archive, or library special collection:
Book of Prospectuses, June 1939 to August 1984
Issuing House Year Book from 1939 to 1987
Prospectuses on UK companies to 6 June 1939 Times (later Extel)

Printed publications:
Annual Report

Access to staff:
Contact by letter and by e-mail
Hours: Mon to Fri, 0930 to 1730

Access to building, collection or gallery:
No access other than to staff

LONDON IRISH CENTRE

52 Camden Square, London, NW1 9XB

Tel: 020 7916 2222
Fax: 020 7916 2638
E-mail: info@irishcentre.org

Website:
http://www.irishcentre.org

Enquiries:
Enquiries to: Director

Founded:
1954

Organisation type and purpose:
Advisory body, voluntary organisation, registered charity (charity number 221172), training organisation, research organisation.

continued overleaf

Subject coverage:
Welfare, culture and social events.

Information services:
Advice and support; social and cultural activities.

Education services:
Various classes.

Access to staff:
Contact by letter, by telephone, by fax, by e-mail, in person and via website
Hours: Mon to Fri, 0900 to 1700

Access to building, collection or gallery:
Hours: 0900 to 2200

Access for disabled people:
Lift assistance

LONDON JEWISH CULTURAL CENTRE

Ivy House, 94–96 North End Road, London, NW11 7SX

Tel: 020 8457 5000
E-mail: admin@ljcc.org.uk

Website:
http://www.ljcc.org.uk

Organisation type and purpose:
A registered charity (no. 1081014) and company limited by guarantee (no. 3811133), funded by donors, benefactors and supporters and by income generated from courses and events.

Subject coverage:
Jewish history, life and learning, languages, current affairs, music, literature, art and film.

Education services:
Day and evening courses in Jewish history, life and learning, languages, current affairs, music, literature, art and film, and outreach courses to the wider community. Holocaust and Anti-racism Education Department.

Museum or gallery collection, archive, or library special collection:
Archive of Jewish-related feature and
documentary film

LONDON LESBIAN AND GAY SWITCHBOARD

Acronym or abbreviation: LLGS

PO Box 7324, London, N1 9QS

Tel: Helpline 020 7837 7324\ Minicom no. 020 7689 8501
Fax: 020 7837 7300
E-mail: admin@llgs.org.uk

Website:
http://www.llgs.org.uk
Information on the organisation

Enquiries:
Enquiries to: Administrator
Direct tel: 020 7837 6768

Founded:
1974

Organisation type and purpose:
Voluntary organisation, registered charity (charity number 296193).
To provide information and advice to lesbians and gay men.

Subject coverage:
Sexual health, legal advice and information, for all callers around lesbian, gay, bisexual and transgender issues (LGBT).

Publications list:
Available online and in print

Access to staff:
Contact by letter, by telephone, by e-mail and via website
Hours: 0930 to 1800

Special comments: General public should use the 24 hour Helpline telephone number.

Access to building, collection or gallery:
No access other than to staff and volunteers

Links with:
Telephone Helplines Association (THA)

LONDON LIBRARY

14 St James's Square, London, SW1Y 4LG

Tel: 020 7930 7705
Fax: 020 7766 4766
E-mail: membership@londonlibrary.co.uk

Website:
http://www.londonlibrary.co.uk

Enquiries:
Enquiries to: Librarian

Founded:
1841

Organisation type and purpose:
Membership association (membership is by subscription), present number of members: 8000, registered charity (charity number 312175). Independent subscription library (lending and reference).

Subject coverage:
Extensive collection of books and periodicals in English and all major European languages within the arts and humanities with particular strengths in literature, history and related subjects. Good representation of fine and applied art, architecture, bibliography, philosophy, religion, topography and travel, with some coverage of the social sciences.

Museum or gallery collection, archive, or library special collection:
Heron-Allen Collection (on Omar Khayyam)
Higginson Collection (books on hunting and field
sports)

Non-library collection catalogue:
All or part available online

Access to staff:
Contact by letter, by telephone, by fax, by e-mail and via website. Appointment necessary. Access for members only. Letter of introduction required. All charged.
Hours: Mon to Wed, 0930 to 1930; Thu to Sat, 0930 to 1730

LONDON LIBRARY & INFORMATION DEVELOPMENT UNIT

Acronym or abbreviation: LLIDU

20 Guildford Street, London, WC1N 1DZ

Tel: 020 7692 3389
Fax: 020 7692 3393
E-mail: ldnlidu@llidu.ac.uk

Website:
http://www.londonlinks.ac.uk
Supports access to electronic information for librarians and healthcare professionals.

Enquiries:
Enquiries to: Head of Unit
Other contacts: Unit Co-ordinator

Founded:
April 2001

Organisation type and purpose:
NHS health care library information network; 50 library service points offering a range of services. The Unit is a strategic and advisory body working closely with Workforce Development Confederations and other stakeholders and professional colleagues to co-ordinate and develop library and information services for all NHS staff in line with national policy guidance.

Subject coverage:
Strategic advice on library and information services to support NHS staff.

Electronic and video publications:
Union List of Serials and Regional Documents
Database (CD-ROM)

Publications list:
Available online

Access to staff:
Contact by telephone, by fax, by e-mail and via website
Hours: Mon to Fri, 0900 to 1700

Access to building, collection or gallery:
Prior appointment required

Affiliated to:
London Department of Postgraduate Medical & Dental Education
NHS London Region

LONDON MARATHON

Formal name: The Flora London Marathon

PO Box 1234, London, SE1 8RZ

Tel: 020 7620 4117
Fax: 020 7620 4208

Website:
http://www.london-marathon.co.uk

Enquiries:
Enquiries to: Administrator

Organisation type and purpose:
Registered charity (charity number 283813). Organisation of sporting events.

Access to staff:
Contact by letter, by telephone and by fax
Hours: Mon to Fri, 0900 to 1700

Access to building, collection or gallery:
No access other than to staff

LONDON MATHEMATICAL SOCIETY

Acronym or abbreviation: LMS

De Morgan House, 57–58 Russell Square, London, WC1B 4HS

Tel: 020 7637 3686
Fax: 020 7323 3655
E-mail: lms@lms.ac.uk

Website:
http://www.lms.ac.uk

Enquiries:
Enquiries to: Executive Secretary

Founded:
1865

Organisation type and purpose:
Learned society.

Subject coverage:
Mathematics.

Museum or gallery collection, archive, or library special collection:
Photographs of academic mathematicians from
1865 onwards to the present

Printed publications:
Publications direct through a publishing house
Order printed publications from: Oxford University Press

Electronic and video publications:
via our website

Publications list:
Available online and in print

Access to staff:
Contact by letter, by telephone, by fax and by e-mail
Hours: Mon to Fri, 0930 to 1700

Access to building, collection or gallery:
Prior appointment required

LONDON MEDIEVAL SOCIETY

Acronym or abbreviation: LMS

The Colloquia Secretary, 3 Rothwell Street,
London, NW1 8YH

Tel: 020 7722 1040
E-mail: gopa.roy.robertson@gmail.com

Website:
http://www.the-lms.org/

Enquiries:
Enquiries to: Membership Secretary
Direct e-mail: c.lay@qmul.ac.uk

Founded:
1946

Organisation type and purpose:
Learned society (membership is by subscription),
present number of members: 200, voluntary
organisation.

Subject coverage:
Literature and language relating to the medieval
European vernaculars and to medieval Latin.
Historical and cultural context of medieval Europe.

Printed publications:
Annual Newsletter
Contacts Directory
Occasional catalogue of medieval research projects
in London

Access to staff:
Contact by letter, by telephone and by e-mail
Hours: Mon to Fri, 0900 to 1700

LONDON MENNONITE CENTRE

Formal name: London Mennonite Centre

14 Shepherds Hill, Highgate, London N6 5AQ

Tel: 020 8340 8775
Fax: 020 8341 6807
E-mail: lmc@menno.org.uk
previous

Website:
http://www.menno.org.uk

Organisation type and purpose:
To embody Mennonite and Anabaptist ideas and
insights within the wider church and cultivate
Christian discipleship as a whole way of life.

Subject coverage:
Mennonites, Anabaptism and Christianity.

**Museum or gallery collection, archive, or library
special collection:**
Library of Anabaptism, Mennonite history and
theology, Radical Reformation, Amish and
Hutterites.

Access to staff:
Contact by letter, by telephone, by fax, by e-mail,
in person and via website
Hours: Mon to Fri, 0900 to 1700

LONDON METROPOLITAN ARCHIVES

Acronym or abbreviation: LMA

40 Northampton Road, London, EC1R 0HB

Tel: 020 7332 3820
Fax: 020 7833 9136
E-mail: ask.lma@cityoflondon.gov.uk

Website:
http://www.cityoflondon.gov.uk/archives/lma
A guide to the holdings and access information.

Enquiries:
Enquiries to: Assistant Director (Heritage)

Founded:
1965

Organisation type and purpose:
Local government body.
Record office.

Subject coverage:
London County Council, Greater London Council,
Metropolitan Board of Works, Middlesex County
Council, London local government, education,
health, topography, the built environment,
philanthropy, transport, parish and diocesan
administration, history of medicine, City of
London Corporation.

**Museum or gallery collection, archive, or library
special collection:**
79 kilometres of archives including:
Local government
Ecclesiastical
Health
Family
Business
Manorial and other records
Prints and drawings (over 40,000 items) including:
Harben Bequest
John Burns Collection
Hanslip Fletcher Studio Collection
110,000 printed monographs
London Directories (from 1744)
London local government publications and
minutes
350,000 photographs forming a visual record of the
history and topography of London, from the late
19th century to the 1980s, schools, housing,
transport, parks, bridge, public buildings,
private and historic buildings and houses, street
scenes, including:
Whiffin Collection
Olney Collection
Morris Collection
Over 10,000 maps and plans
Archives of the Family Welfare Association
Books and pamphlets of the Charity Organisation
Society to 1946
London Library of John Burns (19th-century LCC
Councillor)
London Topographical Library
London Vestry and District Board Reports 1855–
1900
Minute books of the Charity Organisation Society
to 1946
Microfilmed archives on charities from 1869

Non-library collection catalogue:
All or part available online and in-house

Library catalogue:
All or part available in-house

Printed publications:
Information leaflets on the holdings (free with sae)
We Think You Ought to Go (£5)

Publications list:
Available in print

Access to staff:
Contact by letter, by telephone, by fax, by e-mail,
in person and via website
Hours: Mon, Wed, Fri, 0930 to 1645; Tue, Thu, 0930
to 1930; selected Sat, please enquire for details

Parent body:
City of London
Guildhall, PO Box 270, London, EC2P 2EJ; tel:
020 7606 3030

LONDON METROPOLITAN POLYMER CENTRE

Acronym or abbreviation: LMPC

London Metropolitan University, Holloway Road,
London, N7 8DB

Tel: 020 7133 2248
Fax: 020 7133 2184
E-mail: polymers@londonmet.ac.uk

Website:
http://www.londonmet.ac.uk/polymers
Information on the London Metropolitan
University including the London Metropolitan
Polymer Centre.

Enquiries:
Enquiries to: Business Development Manager
Direct tel: 020 7133 2189

Direct e-mail: alison.green@londonmet.ac.uk
Other contacts: Adam Bradley for information on
short courses and training.

Founded:
1896

Organisation type and purpose:
University department or institute, training
organisation, consultancy, research organisation.
short courses, distance learning programmes.
To provide education, training, consultancy and
research for the UK and International Polymer and
allied industries.

Subject coverage:
Polymer materials and composites, polymer
processing, mould and die design, injection
moulding, extrusion, blown film, blow moulding,
thermo vacuum forming, materials testing and
characterisation, industrial studies, training,
education, short courses, distance learning
programmes, consultancy, research.

Trade and statistical information:
Information on polymer materials and processing.

Printed publications:
Information booklets
Distance Learning Programmes
Order printed publications from: Business
Development Manager

Electronic and video publications:
Distance Learning Programmes

Publications list:
Available online and in print

Access to staff:
Contact by letter, by telephone, by fax, by e-mail
and via website. Appointment necessary.
Hours: Mon to Fri, 0900 to 1700
Special comments: Voice Mail active out of hours.

Access for disabled people:
Ramped entry, toilet facilities

LONDON METROPOLITAN UNIVERSITY

31 Jewry Street, London, EC3N 2EY

Tel: 020 7423 0000

Website:
http://www.londonmet.ac.uk/library

Enquiries:
Enquiries to: Help Desk at any of the sites who will
refer on if necessary

Founded:
1896

Organisation type and purpose:
Suitable for ages: 18+.

Subject coverage:
Business, environment, social studies, science,
computing, engineering, humanities, teaching.
Art and design: cabinet making, design studies,
design for disability, fine arts, furniture design,
production and history, interior design, jewellery,
media studies, musical instrument technology,
photography, silversmithing.
Management, accountancy, economics, financial
services, law, shipping and transport, civil
aviation, computing and information systems,
psychology.

**Museum or gallery collection, archive, or library
special collection:**
European Documentation Centre
TUC Library Collections
Workers Educational Association Archive

Library catalogue:
All or part available online

Access to staff:
Contact by letter and by telephone
Hours: Mon to Fri, 0900 to 1700

continued overleaf

Other addresses:
London Metropolitan University
  Commercial Road ILRC, 41–71 Commercial
  Road, London, E1 1LA; tel: 020 7320 1863; fax:
  020 7320 1862
London Metropolitan University
  Moorgate Library, 84 Moorgate, London, EC2M
  6SQ; tel: 020 7320 1561; fax: 020 7320 1565
London Metropolitan University
  City Campus, Calcutta House Library, Old
  Castle Street, London, E1 7NT; tel: 020 7320 1000;
  fax: 020 7320 1177
London Metropolitan University
  Ladbroke House Library, Highbury Grove,
  London, N5 2AD; tel: 020 7133 5149; fax: 020
  7133 5100
London Metropolitan University
  Holloway Road Learning Centre, 236–250
  Holloway Road, London, N7 6PP; tel: 020 7133
  2442; fax: 020 7133 2066

LONDON NARROW BOAT ASSOCIATION

Acronym or abbreviation: LNBA

Battlebridge Moorings, Rear of Battlebridge Court,
Wharfdale Road, London, N1 9UY

Tel: 07970 799 032

Enquiries:
Enquiries to: Secretary

Founded:
1978

Organisation type and purpose:
Membership association (membership is by
election or invitation), voluntary organisation.
Waterways campaigning.

Subject coverage:
Moorings in London area.

Access to staff:
Contact by letter
Hours: Mon to Fri, 0900 to 1700

Members of:
Aylesbury Canal Society (ACS)
  Canal Basin, Walton Street, Aylesbury, HP21
  7QG
Inland Waterways Association (IWA)
  PO Box 114, Rickmansworth, WD3 1WP

LONDON NATURAL HISTORY SOCIETY

Acronym or abbreviation: LNHS

21 Green Way, Frinton-on-Sea, Essex, CO13 9AL

Tel: 01255 674678
Fax: 01255 674678

Website:
http://www.users.globalnet.co.uk~lnhsweb

Enquiries:
Enquiries to: Secretary

Founded:
1858

Organisation type and purpose:
Learned society (membership is by subscription).

Subject coverage:
Natural history of the London area, research and
identification of species, observation and
conservation, botany, ecology, entomology,
geology, ornithology.

**Museum or gallery collection, archive, or library
special collection:**
Library is housed at Imperial College of Science,
  Technology and Medicine, Central Libraries

Printed publications:
Books on breeding birds, flora and butterflies of
  the London area
London Bird Report (annually)
London Naturalist (annually)
Newsletters (for members, 6 times a year)

Access to staff:
Contact by letter
Hours: Mon to Fri, 0900 to 1700

LONDON PLAYING FIELDS FOUNDATION

Acronym or abbreviation: LPFF

73 Collier Street, London, N1 9BE

Tel: 0845 0262292
E-mail: enquiries@lpff.org.uk

Website:
http://www.lpff.org.uk
All about the LPFF

Enquiries:
Enquiries to: Chief Executive
Direct e-mail: cgw@lpff.org.uk
Other contacts: Operations Director

Founded:
1890

Organisation type and purpose:
Registered charity, voluntary organisation (charity
number 302925).
The main charity for the provision, protection and
promotion of playing fields in Greater London.

Subject coverage:
Managing sports facilities within the Greater
London area, including football, cricket, rugby,
hockey and tennis, for the use of local
communities, especially the young, the elderly, the
disabled and the disadvantaged.

Printed publications:
Annual Report
Newsletter (2 a year)
Centenary history 1890–1990

Access to staff:
Contact by letter, by telephone, by fax, by e-mail
and via website. Appointment necessary.
Hours: Mon to Fri, 0900 to 1730

LONDON RAPE CRISIS CENTRE

Formal name: Rape Counselling and Research
Project
Acronym or abbreviation: LRCC

PO Box 69, London, WC1X 9NJ

Tel: 020 7916 5466
Fax: 020 7916 5519
E-mail: contact@londonrapecrisis.co.uk

Enquiries:
Enquiries to: Director
Other contacts: Development Worker

Founded:
1976

Organisation type and purpose:
Advisory body, membership association
(membership is by subscription), present number
of members: 50, voluntary organisation, registered
charity (charity number 1047437), training
organisation, research organisation.
To counsel women and girl survivors of rape/
sexual violence.

Subject coverage:
Sexual violence, health, law.

Printed publications:
Annual Report
Booklist
Fact Sheets/Newsletter
Sexual Violence: The Reality for Women (book, 3rd
  ed, £7.99)

Publications list:
Available in print

Access to staff:
Contact by letter, by telephone, by fax and by e-
mail

Hours: Mon, Wed, Fri, 0900 to 1700; Tue, Thu, 1000
to 1900
Special comments: Counselling line: Mon to Fri, 1800
to 2200; Sat, Sun, 1000 to 2200.

LONDON RECORD SOCIETY

PO Box 300, Hertford, SG13 9EF

Fax: 020 7862 8793
E-mail: londonrecordsoc@btinternet.com

Website:
http://www.londonrecordsociety.org.uk
General information and list of publications.

Enquiries:
Enquiries to: Honorary Secretary
Other contacts: Honorary Editor for book proposals

Founded:
1964

Organisation type and purpose:
Learned society, registered charity.
Publishing society.
To publish editions of primary sources for London
history.

Subject coverage:
Primary sources and archives on the history of
London.

Printed publications:
Cartulary of Holy Trinity, Aldgate (1971)
London Viewers and their certificates, 1508–1588
  (1989)
Chamber accounts of the 16th century (1984)
Church in London, 1375–1392 (1977)
Commissions for building 50 new churches (1986)
Committees for Repeal of the Test and Corporation
  minutes, 1786–1790, 1827–1828 (1978, out of
  print)
Joshua Johnson's Letterbook, 1771–4 (1979)
Justice in 18th Century Hackney (1991)
Letters of John Paige, London Merchant, 1648–58
  (1984)
London and Middlesex Chantry Certificate, 1548
  (1980)
London and Middlesex Published Records (1970,
  out of print)
London Assize of Nuisance, 1301–1401: a calendar
  (1973)
London Bridge: selected accounts, 1381–1547
  (1995)
London Consistory Court Wills, 1492–1547 (1967)
London Consistory Court Depositions, 1586–1611
  (1997)
London debating societies, 1776–1799 (1994)
London Eyre of 1244 (1970) now o/p
London Eyre of 1276 (1976)
London Inhabitants within the Walls, 1695 (1966)
London Politics, 1713–1713 (1981)
London Pollbooks, 1713 (1981)
London Possessory Assizes: a calendar (1965)
London Radicalism, 1830–1843 (1970)
London Viewers and their certificates 1508–1588
  (1989)
Port and Trade of Early Elizabethan London (1972)
Records of St Andrew Hubbard, 1454–1560 (1999)
Register of the Fraternity of the Trinity and SS.
  Fabian and Sebastian in the Church of St Botolph
  (1982)
Richard Hutton's complaints book (1987)
Scriveners Company Common Paper, 1357–1628;
  continuation to 1678 (1968, out of print)
Settlement and bastardy examinations of St Luke,
  Chelsea, 1730–66 (1999)
Spanish Company (1973, out of print)
Survey of documentary sources for property
  holding in London before the Great Fire (1985)
The overseas trade of London, 1480–1481 (1990)
Trinity House of Deptford: transactions, 1609–35
  (1983)
Two Calvinistic Methodist Chapels, 1743–1811
  (1975)
Two Tudor subsidy assessment rolls, 1541 and 1582
  (1993)
Westminster Abbey charters, 1066 to c. 1214 (1988)
Selected Letters of William Freeman (2002)

Checklist of Unpublished Diaries by Londoners
and Visitors (2003)
The English Fur Trade in the Later Middle Ages
(2nd ed, 2003)
The Bede Roll of the Parish Clerks' Company (2
vols, 2004)
The Estate and Household Accounts of William
Worsley, Dean of St Paul's Cathedral, 1479–97
(2004)
A Woman in Wartime London: the Diary of
Kathleen Tipper, 1941–45 (2006)
Prisoners' Letters to the Bank of England, 1781–
1827 (2007)
The Apprenticeship of a Mountaineer: Edward
Whymper's London Diary 1855–59 (2008)
Some vols can be viewed via the British History
Online website

Publications list:
Available online and in print

Access to staff:
Contact by letter, by e-mail and via website.
Appointment necessary.
Hours: Mon to Fri, 0900 to 1700

LONDON RETAIL MEAT TRADERS LIMITED

Acronym or abbreviation: LRMTA

Gate 27, Central Markets, Smithfield, London,
EC1A 9EB

Tel: 020 8248 0732
Fax: 020 8329 1463

Enquiries:
Enquiries to: Secretary

Founded:
1926

Organisation type and purpose:
National organisation, trade association
(membership is by election or invitation), present
number of members: 350, service industry.

Subject coverage:
Meat retailing, small scale meat processing,
training.

Access to staff:
Contact by letter, by telephone and by fax
Hours: Mon to Thu, 0800 to 1500

Affiliated to:
National Federation of Meat & Food Traders
Tunbridge Wells, Kent, TN1 1YW; tel: 01892
541412; fax: 01892 535462; e-mail: INFO@
NFMFT.co.uk

Members include:
local butchers associations

LONDON SCHOOL OF HYGIENE AND TROPICAL MEDICINE

Acronym or abbreviation: LSHTM

Keppel Street, London, WC1E 7HT

Tel: 020 7927 2276
Fax: 020 7927 2273
E-mail: library@lshtm.ac.uk

Website:
http://www.lshtm.ac.uk/as/library/libintro.htm

Founded:
1899

Organisation type and purpose:
University department or institute.
Postgraduate medical school.

Subject coverage:
Environmental health, epidemiology, human
nutrition, medical microbiology, entomology,
parasitology, medical statistics, population studies
and demography, tropical medicine, public health,
health policy, the health of developing countries
and international health.

**Museum or gallery collection, archive, or library
special collection:**
Historical collection (books on public health and
tropical medicine)
Manson Collection (papers of Sir Patrick Manson)
Reece Collection (on vaccination)
Ross Archives (papers of Sir Ronald Ross)

Non-library collection catalogue:
All or part available online

Library catalogue:
All or part available online and in print

Printed publications:
Annual Report
Health Policy and Planning (quarterly, pub. OUP)
Tropical Medicine and International Health (6
times a year, pub. Blackwell's)

Access to staff:
Contact by letter, by telephone, by e-mail and via
website
Hours: Mon to Fri, 0930 to 1730

Access for disabled people:
Ramped entry, toilet facilities

Parent body:
University of London

LONDON SCHOOL OF JOURNALISM LIMITED

Acronym or abbreviation: LSJ

126 Shirland Road, London, W9 2BT

Tel: 020 7289 7777
Fax: 020 7432 8141
E-mail: info@lsjournalism.com

Website:
http://www.home-study.com
Details of all courses and terms etc.
http://www.lsj.org
Details of all courses and terms, etc.

Enquiries:
Enquiries to: Administrator
Direct tel: 020 7432 8140
Direct fax: 020 7432 8140
Direct e-mail: enquiries@lsjournalism.com
Other contacts: Director of Studies for tutorial
course information.

Founded:
1921

Organisation type and purpose:
Training organisation. Training by distance
learning. Postgraduate attendance courses.

Subject coverage:
Training for news journalism, freelance writing
and creative writing, both by distance learning and
by attendance classes.

Printed publications:
General Prospectus (free, available on request)

Access to staff:
Contact by letter, by telephone, by fax, by e-mail
and via website. Appointment necessary.
Hours: Mon to Fri, 1000 to 1630
Special comments: Times may vary, telephone in
advance.

Member of:
(OLF) (ABCC)
Association of British Correspondence Colleges
(OLF) (ABCC) (ODLQC)
Open and Distance Learning Quality Council

LONDON SCHOOL OF PUBLISHING

Acronym or abbreviation: LSP

David Game House, 69 Notting Hill Gate, London,
W11 3JS

Tel: 020 7221 3399
Fax: 020 7243 1730
E-mail: lsp@easynet.co.uk

Website:
http://www.publishing-school.co.uk
Training programmes and courses.

Enquiries:
Enquiries to: Administrator
Other contacts: Courses Co-ordinator

Founded:
1983

Organisation type and purpose:
Training organisation.
Training courses that run in the evening on a part
time basis. Courses run in Feb, Oct and May –
some day courses available.
To provide training courses and programmes for
graduates who wish to enter the publishing
industry, as well as for those who are in the early
stages of their publishing careers, or those who
wish to change career paths.

Subject coverage:
Training in: editing (book and magazine), feature
writing, picture research, Quark Xpress,
Photoshop, HTML, Dreamweaver.

Printed publications:
Prospectuses (detailing training programmes)

Publications list:
Available online and in print

Access to staff:
Contact by telephone and by e-mail
Hours: Mon to Fri, 0930 to 1830
Special comments: No weekend access.

Access for disabled people:
Access to all public areas

Connections with:
National Union of Journalists (NUJ)

LONDON SCHOOL OF THEOLOGY

Acronym or abbreviation: LSt

Green Lane, Northwood, Middlesex, HA6 2UW

Tel: 01923 456190
Fax: 01923 456001
E-mail: library@lst.ac.uk

Website:
http://www.lst.ac.uk
Information on the college and its courses;
Christian
comment on current issues; book and film reviews
by faculty members.

Enquiries:
Enquiries to: Librarian
Direct tel: 01923 456192
Direct e-mail: a.linfield@lst.ac.uk
Other contacts: Library Administrator for routine
enquiries.

Founded:
1943

Organisation type and purpose:
Suitable for ages: 18+.
To prepare students for Christian ministry and to
further the academic
study and research of theology.

Subject coverage:
Theology, predominant emphasis is on Christian
theology but also Islamics collection in process of
ongoing development.

**Museum or gallery collection, archive, or library
special collection:**
Papers of Dr Donald Guthrie (not yet catalogued or
otherwise organised)

Library catalogue:
All or part available online and in-house

Access to staff:
Contact by letter, by telephone, by fax, by e-mail,
in person and via website. Appointment necessary.
Non-members charged.
Hours: Mon to Fri, 0900 to 1700

continued overleaf

Special comments: If at all possible visitors are encouraged to visit during vacations as space in the library is in heavy demand during term time.

Associated college of:
Brunel University

Subsidiary body:
Centre for Islamic Studies
LST Postgraduate School of Theology

LONDON SOCIETY

Mortimer Wheeler House, 46 Eagle Wharf Road, London, N1 7ED

Tel: 020 7253 9400
E-mail: info@londonsociety.org.uk

Website:
http://www.londonsociety.org.uk

Enquiries:
Enquiries to: Administrator

Founded:
1912

Organisation type and purpose:
National organisation, membership association (membership is by subscription), registered charity (charity number 206270).
Advancing the practical improvement and artistic development of London.

Subject coverage:
Ancient and modern London, history, architecture and planning, improvement and enhancement of London by the efforts of its citizens, the environment, visits to places of interest within Greater London.

Museum or gallery collection, archive, or library special collection:
Library; 3000 books, 100 maps, housed in the Museum of London (Mortimer Wheeler House)

Library catalogue:
All or part available online

Printed publications:
Journal (twice a year, free to members)

Access to staff:
Contact by letter and by telephone. Appointment necessary.
Hours: Mon to Fri, 0900 to 1700

Links with:
Civic Trust
Europa Nostra
Green Belt Council

LONDON SOUTH BANK UNIVERSITY – ENGINEERING, SCIENCE AND THE BUILT ENVIRONMENT

103 Borough Road, London, SE1 OAA

Tel: 020 7815 8320
Fax: 020 7815 8366

Website:
http://www.lsbu.ac.uk/esbe/
Library guide, helpsheets, catalogue, staff contacts.

Enquiries:
Enquiries to: Faculty Administrative Officer
Direct e-mail: teidyk@lsbu.ac.uk
Other contacts: Information Advisers

Organisation type and purpose:
University library, university department or institute.

Subject coverage:
Architecture; town planning; built environment law; land and building economics; estate management; construction; civil engineering.

Museum or gallery collection, archive, or library special collection:
Reference collection on architectural theory, history, practice and related crafts and technology, 17th-20th centuries (particularly strong 1717–1759 and 1880–1920)

Library catalogue:
All or part available online

Access to staff:
Contact by letter, by telephone and by fax
Hours: Term time: Mon, Tue, Thu, 0830 to 2100; Wed, Fri, 0830 to 1900
Vacations: 0900 to 1700
Special comments: Non-members must apply for reference facilities in writing.

Access to building, collection or gallery:
No prior appointment required
Special comments: In term time, unless a member of the M25 Group. In vacation, any university students may have reference access on production of current ID card.

Access for disabled people:
Toilet facilities
Special comments: Main floor of library accessible by lift, gallery level by arrangement.

LONDON SOUTH BANK UNIVERSITY – LIBRARY

103 Borough Road, London, SE1 OAA

Tel: 020 7815 6607
Fax: 020 7261 1865
E-mail: postmaster@vax.sbu.ac.uk

Website:
http://www.sbu.ac.uk/lioa

Enquiries:
Enquiries to: Director of Learning Information Services
Direct tel: 020 7815 6601
Direct fax: 020 7815 6699
Direct e-mail: john.akeroyd@sbu.ac.uk

Organisation type and purpose:
University library.

Subject coverage:
Business studies; accountancy; management; finance; public sector studies; chemical engineering; electrical engineering; electronics; mathematics and computing; mechanical and production engineering; environmental engineering; bakery; building technology, practice and management; civil and structural engineering; transportation; land economics; multi-environment; architecture; law; humanities; nursing; health services; occupational hygiene; sociology; biotechnology; social policy; education; town planning.

Museum or gallery collection, archive, or library special collection:
Architectural books 1717–1740, 1790–1830, 1880–1920
Building manuals, directories and patents 1750 to date

Printed publications:
Annual Report

Access to staff:
Contact by letter. Appointment necessary. Letter of introduction required.
Hours: Mon to Fri, 0900 to 2100

LONDON SOUTH BANK UNIVERSITY – LITC

Acronym or abbreviation: LITC

103 Borough Road, London, SE1 OAA

Tel: 020 7815 7872
Fax: 020 7815 7050
E-mail: litc@sbu.ac.uk

Website:
http://www.sbu.ac.uk/litc

All services and publications from LITC, reports on research projects, press release database, industry news database, resources of interest to LIS IT practitioners and researchers.

Enquiries:
Enquiries to: Associate Director
Direct tel: 020 7815 7058
Direct e-mail: coxam@sbu.ac.uk
Other contacts: Administrator for general enquiries, information, publications.

Founded:
1982

Organisation type and purpose:
University department or institute, consultancy, research organisation.

Subject coverage:
Library management, library automation, electronic publishing, on-demand printing and publishing, document formats, information retrieval, library networking and communications, CD-ROM networking, internet solutions, copyright, management technologies, library research publishing, metadata, online and e-learning.

Printed publications:
Guide to Library Systems for Schools, (2 times a year)
Library and Information Briefings (60 titles, 10 a year, £7 each)
Vine (4 times a year)
Communications software for online searching (Introductory Pack £15)
Information retrieval software for MS-DOS and Windows (Introductory Pack £15)
Library housekeeping systems for MS-DOS and Windows (Introductory Pack £15)
Library systems for schools (Introductory Pack £15)
CD-ROM: a practical guide for information professionals (1990, £20)
CD-ROM networking in practice (£20)
LIBSYS.UK: a directory of library systems in the United Kingdom (1995, £35)
LITC Reports on specific topics concerning practical aspects of library automation
LITC Report No. 1 – Planning and implementing an automated library system (£15)
LITC Report No. 2 – Guide to choosing an automated library system (£15)
LITC Report No. 3 – Evaluating library systems at a demonstration (£15)
LITC Report No. 4 – Retrospective conversion and sources of bibliographic record supply (£15)
LITC Report No. 5 – Document encoding formats for on-demand publishing (£20)
LITC Report No. 6 – World-Wide Web in Libraries (£20)
LITC Report No. 7 – Z39.50 and SR (£20)
LITC Report No. 8 – Electronic Copyright Management Systems (£20)
LITC Report No. 9 – Decision Support Systems in Libraries (£20)
LITC Report No. 10 – Document Management Systems for Learning Resources (£20)
LITC Report No. 11 – News and Alerting Services on the Internet (£20)
LITC Report No. 12 – Library Systems Migration: technical and management considerations
LITC Report No. 13 – Managing Access to Electronic Resources
Digital Books? On-demand printing and publishing (£20)
Web Publishing: Introduction to HTML (2nd ed., 1998)
Order printed publications from: Horizon Logistics Area D, AWD Future, Boscombe Road, Dunstable, LU5 4SE, tel: 01582 501070, fax: 01582 501067, e-mail: trade@horizon-logistics.com

Publications list:
Available online and in print

Access to staff:
Contact by letter, by telephone, by fax, by e-mail and via website
Hours: Mon to Fri, 0900 to 1700

Access to building, collection or gallery:
Prior appointment required

Access for disabled people:
Access to all public areas

Unit of the:
Department of Learning and Information Services (LIS)
tel: 020 7815 6602; fax: 020 7815 6699

LONDON SPORTS FORUM FOR DISABLED PEOPLE

Acronym or abbreviation: LSF

Unit 2B07, London South Bank University, Technopark, 90 London Road, London, SE1 6LN

Tel: 020 7717 1699
E-mail: info@londonsportsforum.org.uk

Website:
http://www.londonsportsforum.org.uk

Enquiries:
Enquiries to: Marketing and Communications Manager
Direct tel: 020 7717 1699
Direct e-mail: ruth@londonsportsforum.org.uk

Founded:
1981

Organisation type and purpose:
Membership association (membership is by subscription, election or invitation), voluntary organisation, registered charity (charity number 1055683), suitable for ages: all, training organisation.
To develop sporting and recreational opportunities for all disabled people including those with learning disabilities, physical impairments, visual impairments and deaf people.

Subject coverage:
Sporting and recreational activities for disabled people, training programmes, equipment.

Museum or gallery collection, archive, or library special collection:
Books and magazines relevant to sport and/or disabled people

Printed publications:
Events Calendar
SportsForum (newsletter, twice a year, free)

Electronic and video publications:
Information available on disc, cassette in braille and other languages upon request (free of charge)

Publications list:
Available online

Access to staff:
Contact by letter, by telephone, by fax, by e-mail and via website. Appointment necessary.
Hours: Mon to Fri, 0900 to 1700

Access for disabled people:
Parking provided, ramped entry, toilet facilities

LONDON SUBTERRANEAN SURVEY ASSOCIATION

Acronym or abbreviation: LSSA

98 Cambridge Gardens, London, W10 6HS

Tel: 020 8968 1360
E-mail: wolstan-dixie@hotmail.co.uk

Enquiries:
Enquiries to: Secretary

Founded:
1968

Organisation type and purpose:
Learned society (membership is by election or invitation).

Subject coverage:
Man-made or used underground space or constructions in London and their effect on surface development.

Museum or gallery collection, archive, or library special collection:
Books, maps, pamphlets, grey literature, press cuttings, videos, photographs, illustrations

Access to staff:
Contact by letter, by telephone and by e-mail. Non-members charged.
Hours: Mon to Fri, 1000 to 1800

Links with:
Subterranea Britannica

LONDON SYMPHONY ORCHESTRA LIMITED

Acronym or abbreviation: LSO

Barbican Centre, London, EC2Y 8DS

Tel: 020 7588 1116
Fax: 020 7374 0127
E-mail: admin@lso.co.uk

Website:
http://www.lso.co.uk
Book tickets for concerts, order LSO Live CDs, artist features and interviews, news and information

Enquiries:
Enquiries to: Head of Marketing
Direct fax: 020 7638 4578

Founded:
1904

Organisation type and purpose:
International organisation, registered charity (charity number 232391).
Orchestra, arts organisation.

Subject coverage:
Orchestra, music, classical music, arts.

Museum or gallery collection, archive, or library special collection:
LSO Archives, photographs, publicity material including programmes

Printed publications:
LSO News
The LSO at 90 (Stewart A)
Leaflet; LSO Education – Projects for Primary Schools, Secondary Schools, Special Needs; daytime concerts for schools and families
Living Music: The London Symphony Orchestra Magazine (free to members)
Season brochures; Spring, Summer and Autumn

Electronic and video publications:
LSO Live, the LSO's own record label, plus classical recordings for major record companies and film sound tracks

Publications list:
Available in print

Access to staff:
Contact by letter, by telephone, by fax, by e-mail and via website. Appointment necessary.
Hours: Mon to Fri, 0930 to 1800

Other address:
LSO St Luke's
UBS & LSO Music Education Centre, 161 Old Street, London, EC1V 9NJ; tel: 020 7588 1116; fax: 020 7384 0127; e-mail: swales@lso.co.uk

LONDON TANKER BROKERS' PANEL LIMITED

Acronym or abbreviation: LTBP

Copenhagen House, 5–10 Bury Street, London, EC3A 5AT

Tel: 020 7456 6600
Fax: 020 7456 6601
E-mail: ltbp@worldscale.co.uk

Website:
http://www.ltbp.co.uk

Enquiries:
Enquiries to: Managing Director

Founded:
1953

Organisation type and purpose:
Consultancy.

Subject coverage:
Oil tanker freight rates, AFRA (average freight rate assessment), time charter rates, assessment of freight consideration for tankers.

Museum or gallery collection, archive, or library special collection:
Tanker freight rates

Printed publications:
Monthly statistics (on subscription only)

Publications list:
Available in print

Access to staff:
Contact by letter, by telephone, by fax and by e-mail. Appointment necessary.
Hours: Mon to Fri, 0900 to 1700

LONDON THAMES GATEWAY FORUM OF VOLUNTARY AND COMMUNITY ORGANISATIONS

Acronym or abbreviation: LTGF

The Brady Centre, 192 Hanbury Street, London, E1 5HU

Tel: 020 7377 1822
Fax: 020 7247 5637
E-mail: mail@ltgf.co.uk

Website:
Under development.

Enquiries:
Enquiries to: Information Officer
Other contacts: Director, Regeneration for planning and regeneration.

Founded:
1975

Organisation type and purpose:
Membership association (membership is by qualification), present number of members: 506, voluntary organisation.

Subject coverage:
Geography, sociology and politics of urban change in the London Thames Gateway area and the inner city generally, environment, regeneration issues.

Non-library collection catalogue:
All or part available in-house

Library catalogue:
All or part available in-house

Printed publications:
Amongst many are:
Docklands Forum Annual Review
Docklands Forum – 20th Anniversary Publication
Conservation in Dockland – Old buildings in a changing environment (Calvocoressi P, 1990, £1.50)
Docklands Redevelopment – A Moral Dimension (Bishop of Stepney, £5)
Heliports (1997, £7.50)
Housing and the Regeneration of Docklands (£4)
Proposed Exhibition Centre in the Royal Victoria Dock (1997, £4)
Urban Clearway (1997, £5)
Urban Regeneration. Partnerships for Success (1997, £3.50)
Breaking Barriers & Bridging the Gap, Achieving Social Inclusion (1999)
Your Plan Your Future, Getting to grips with your UDP and Its Review (1999)
A Community Vision for the Thames Gateway London (1999)

continued overleaf

Urban Sustainable Development, The Policy
Context and Use of Indicators, in Developing
and Assessing Initiatives (1999)
London Thames Gateway Forum Annual Report
Newsletters 2000-
Membership Survey Report 2001

Publications list:
Available online and in print

Access to staff:
Contact by letter, by telephone, by fax and by e-
mail. Appointment necessary.
Hours: Mon to Fri, 1000 to 1800

Access to building, collection or gallery:
No access other than to staff, prior appointment
required
Hours: Mon to Fri, 1000 to 1800

Access for disabled people:
Parking provided, ramped entry, toilet facilities
Special comments: Need to pre-check for parking
space.

LONDON THEOLOGICAL SEMINARY

Acronym or abbreviation: LTS

104 Hendon Lane, London, N3 3SQ

Tel: 020 8346 7587
E-mail: admin@ltslondon.org

Website:
http://www.ltslondon.org

Enquiries:
Enquiries to: Administrator

Founded:
1977

Organisation type and purpose:
Registered charity. Training for Christian ministry.

Subject coverage:
Theology.

**Museum or gallery collection, archive, or library
special collection:**
Dr Martyn Lloyd-Jones' Library

Library catalogue:
All or part available in-house

Access to staff:
Contact by letter and by e-mail
Hours: Mon to Fri, 0900 to 1700

LONDON TOPOGRAPHICAL SOCIETY

Acronym or abbreviation: LTS

36 Old Deer Park Gardens, Richmond-upon-
Thames, Surrey, TW9 2TL

Tel: 020 8940 5419
E-mail: patfrazer@yahoo.co.uk

Website:
http://www.topsoc.org

Enquiries:
Enquiries to: Honorary Secretary

Founded:
1880

Organisation type and purpose:
Learned society (membership is by subscription),
present number of members: 1,100.
To publish material relating to the study of London
topography.

Subject coverage:
London topography, maps, prints and views.

Printed publications:
Annual publications (books, maps, views – free to
members; available for purchase by non-
members)
London Topographical Record (journal every 5
years – free to members; available for purchase
by non-members)

Newsletters (twice a year; free to members)
Order printed publications from: Honorary Treasurer,
Flat 13, 13 Tavistock Place, London, WC1H 9SH

Publications list:
Available online and in print

Access to staff:
Contact by letter and by e-mail
Hours: No access.

LONDON TOURIST BOARD AND CONVENTION BUREAU

Acronym or abbreviation: LTB

1 Warwick Row, London, SW1E 5ER

Tel: 020 7932 2000
Fax: 020 7932 0222

Website:
http://www.visitlondon.co.uk
London information: accommodation, attractions,
events, restaurants, shopping.

Enquiries:
Enquiries to: Information Services Manager

Organisation type and purpose:
Membership association (membership is by
subscription), present number of members: 1300.
Regional Tourist Board.

Subject coverage:
Events in London, places of interest, location,
history and opening hours, ceremonies,
restaurants, hotels, shops and general amenities in
London, other facets of London life, conferences
and exhibitions which have been or are to be, held
in London.

Trade and statistical information:
Recent Trends in Tourism – Visits to London (free)
London Attractions with over half a million visits
(free)
Overseas Visits to the United Kingdom (free)
London Tourism Statistics (for sale)
Survey among overseas Visitors to London (for
sale)
Business Confidence Monitor (for sale).

Printed publications:
Budget Accommodation for Travellers
Capital Breaks (free)
Convention and Exhibition London
Events in London (6 times a year)
Information leaflets on attractions, accommodation
(free)
Travel Trade London (free)

Publications list:
Available in print

Access to staff:
Contact by letter and by fax. Appointment
necessary.
Hours: Mon to Fri, 0900 to 1700

Liaison with:
British Tourist Authority
English Tourism Council
London Boroughs

LONDON TRAVELWATCH

Formal name: London Transport Users' Committee

6 Middle Street, London, EC1A 7JA

Tel: 020 7505 9000
Fax: 020 7505 9003
E-mail: info@londontravelwatch.org.uk

Website:
http://www.londontravelwatch.org.uk

Enquiries:
Enquiries to: Chief Executive
Direct e-mail: enquiries@londontravelwatch.org.uk
Other contacts: Casework Team

Founded:
2000

Organisation type and purpose:
National government body, advisory body,
statutory body, membership association, present
number of members: 21.
Statutory consumer watchdog.
Acts as an appeals body considering suggestions
and complaints concerning the service.
To represent the interests of transport provided,
procured or licensed by Transport for London,
Heathrow Express, Eurostar and the national
railways in and around London.

Subject coverage:
Matters relating to public transport in and around
London; problems faced by people using public
transport in and around London.

**Museum or gallery collection, archive, or library
special collection:**
An extensive library of transport related material
The Cullen inquiry into the Ladbroke Grove Rail
crash (transcript)
The Uff inquiry into the Southall Rail crash
(transcript)
The Fennell inquiry into the Kings Cross Fire
(transcript)
The Hidden inquiry into the Clapham Junction
Rail crash (transcript)

Trade and statistical information:
Data on users' comments, complaints and
suggestions.

Publications list:
Available online

Access to staff:
Contact by letter, by telephone, by fax, by e-mail
and in person. Appointment necessary.
Hours: Mon to Fri, 0900 to 1700

Access for disabled people:
Wheelchair access, hearing loop

LONDON UNDERGROUND RAILWAY SOCIETY

Acronym or abbreviation: LURS

54 Brinkley Road, Worcester Park, Surrey, KT4 8JF

Tel: 020 8330 1855

Website:
http://www.lurs.org.uk
General information about the Society.

Enquiries:
Enquiries to: Secretary

Founded:
1961

Organisation type and purpose:
Membership association (membership is by
subscription), present number of members: 900,
voluntary organisation.

Subject coverage:
All aspects of London's underground railways,
past, present and future.

**Museum or gallery collection, archive, or library
special collection:**
Cartographic Collection
Chandos Papers
Photographic Collection
Sound and Vision Collection

Printed publications:
Specialised books published by the Society are
now out of print. Books written about the
Underground, many written by members, are
now published by commercial houses
specialising in public transport subjects
Underground News (monthly)

Access to staff:
Contact by letter
Hours: Mon to Fri, any reasonable time

ASLIB DIRECTORY of INFORMATION SOURCES

LONDON VIDEO TRADE ASSOCIATION

314 Walworth Road, London, SE17 2NA

Tel: 020 7703 3081
Fax: 020 7703 3081

Enquiries:
Enquiries to: Secretary

Founded:
1982

Organisation type and purpose:
Trade association (membership is by qualification), present number of members: 44.
Help and advice to video shops.

Subject coverage:
Video trade.

Access to staff:
Contact by letter, by telephone, by fax and in person
Hours: Mon to Fri, 1030 to 1800

Access for disabled people:
Ramped entry

LONDON VOLUNTARY SERVICE COUNCIL

Acronym or abbreviation: LVSC

356 Holloway Road, London, N7 6PA

Tel: 020 7700 8107
Fax: 020 7700 8108
E-mail: library@lvsc.org.uk

Website:
http://www.lvsc.org.uk

Enquiries:
Enquiries to: Resource Officer
Direct tel: 020 7700 8192

Organisation type and purpose:
Voluntary organisation, registered charity (charity number 276886).

Subject coverage:
Social policy affecting London's voluntary sector, organisational support for London's voluntary sector, information on London's voluntary sector.

Museum or gallery collection, archive, or library special collection:
Over 5000 items related to London's voluntary and community sector including general information and organisational development information.
Access to Funderfinder by appointment.

Library catalogue:
All or part available in-house

Printed publications:
Publications include (prices inc. p&p):
Avoiding the wastepaper basket (1996)
Just about Managing – effective management for voluntary organisations and community groups
Voluntary But Not Amateur – a guide to the law for voluntary organisations and community groups
Voluntary Voice (subscription, voluntary organisations 1–5 staff £18, voluntary organisations 6+ staff £21, individuals £30, other organisations £30)
LVSC's Annual Report

Publications list:
Available in print

Access to staff:
Contact by letter, by telephone, by fax, by e-mail and in person
Hours: Varies for different services

LONDON WILDLIFE TRUST

Skyline House, 200 Union Street, London, SE1 0LX

Tel: 020 7261 0447
Fax: 020 7261 0538
E-mail: enquiries@wildlondon.org.uk

Website:
http://www.wildlondon.org.uk

Enquiries:
Enquiries to: Education Co-ordinator

Founded:
1981

Organisation type and purpose:
Membership association (membership is by subscription), registered charity (charity number 283895).
The London Wildlife Trust fights to sustain and enhance London's wildlife habitats to create a city richer in wildlife.

Subject coverage:
Wildlife, urban wildlife, site protection and management, environmental education and training.

Museum or gallery collection, archive, or library special collection:
Environmental education publications

Printed publications:
Create a School Wildlife Garden
Enviroscope
Gardening for Wildlife
Literally Wild: Wildlife Text for Literacy Hour
RiverWATCH
The Cycle of Wood
The Habitat Pack
The Wildlife Action Pack
Wildlife Facts Leaflets
Wild Seasons

Publications list:
Available in print

Access to staff:
Contact by letter, by telephone, by fax, by e-mail and via website. Appointment necessary.
Hours: Mon to Fri, 0930 to 1730

Access to building, collection or gallery:
No prior appointment required

Affiliated to:
Wildlife Watch

Manages:
57 sites across London

Part of:
Wildlife Trusts

LONG DISTANCE WALKERS' ASSOCIATION LIMITED

Acronym or abbreviation: LDWA

Bank House, High Street, Wrotham, Sevenoaks, Kent, TN15 7AE

Tel: 01732 883705
E-mail: secretary@ldwa.org.uk

Website:
http://www.ldwa.org.uk

Enquiries:
Enquiries to: General Secretary
Other contacts: Long Distance Path Information Officer for information about long distance paths and routes.

Founded:
1972

Organisation type and purpose:
Membership association (membership is by subscription), present number of members: 6500, voluntary organisation.
Recognised governing body.
To further the interests of those who enjoy long distance walking.

Subject coverage:
Long distance walking, paths and trails.

Museum or gallery collection, archive, or library special collection:
Details of over 600 walks and trails etc are held

Printed publications:
Details of Walks/Trails

Guidelines for Walking Events (£1.50)
Long Distance Walkers Handbook (7th ed., £12.99)
Strider (journal, 3 times a year, free to members)
Order printed publications from: Merchandising Officer, Long Distance Walkers Association
2 Sandy Lane, Beeston, Nottinghamshire, NG9 3GS, tel: 0115 922 1849

Access to staff:
Contact by letter, by telephone and by e-mail
Hours: Mon to Fri, 0900 to 2200

Affiliated to:
European Ramblers Association
Ramblers Association
Scottish Rights of Way Society
Sports Council

LOTTERIES COUNCIL

2 Regan Road, Moira, Swadlincote, Derbyshire, DE12 6DS

Tel: 01925 710880
Fax: 01925 710880
E-mail: judith@lotteriescouncil.co.uk

Website:
http://www.lotteriescouncil.co.uk

Enquiries:
Enquiries to: Secretary
Other contacts: Executive Officer

Founded:
1979

Organisation type and purpose:
Trade association, present number of members: 145.

Subject coverage:
Management of lotteries; accounting procedures; requirements under the Lotteries and Amusements Act 1976, and the National Lotteries Act 1993, etc.; history of lotteries in the UK; lottery regulations.

Printed publications:
Annual Conference Report and Annual General Meeting
Code of Conduct booklet
Lottery Magazine (quarterly)
The Acts Combined (brings together in one booklet the Laws on Lotteries to Date)

Access to staff:
Contact by letter, by telephone, by fax and by e-mail
Hours: Mon to Fri, 0900 to 1700

Other addresses:
Executive Officer
21 Bristow Close, Great Sankey, Warrington, WA5 8EU; tel: 01925 710880; fax: 01925 710880

LOTUS SEVEN CLUB

Formal name: Lotus Seven Club of Great Britain

PO Box 777, Haywards Heath, West Sussex, RH16 2YA

Tel: 07000 572582
Fax: 07000 572582
E-mail: memsec@lotus7club.co.uk

Website:
http://www.lotus7club.co.uk

Enquiries:
Enquiries to: Membership Secretary

Founded:
1985

Organisation type and purpose:
International organisation, membership association, present number of members: 3000.

Subject coverage:
Lotus Seven from 1957 to 1973 and the Caterham Seven from 1973 to date.

Museum or gallery collection, archive, or library special collection:
Video lending library (members only)

739

continued overleaf

Original Lotus Seven Specifications

Printed publications:
Low Flying (magazine, monthly, free to members)

Access to staff:
Contact by letter, by telephone, by fax, by e-mail and via website
Hours: Mon to Fri, 0900 to 1700

LOUGHBOROUGH UNIVERSITY – DEPARTMENT OF INFORMATION SCIENCE

Acronym or abbreviation: DIS

Epinal Way, Loughborough, Leicestershire, LE11 3TU

Tel: 01509 223051
Fax: 01509 223053
E-mail: dis@lboro.ac.uk

Website:
http://www.lboro.ac.uk/departments/dis

Enquiries:
Enquiries to: Head of Department
Direct tel: 01509 223065

Founded:
1972

Organisation type and purpose:
University department or institute.

Subject coverage:
Exploitation of business information; database design and development; marketing library and information services; development of expert systems for library and information services; archives and records management; conservation of materials; communications and information networks; intellectual property law; distance learning in library and information education; information skills; cataloguing and bibliographic control of materials; library planning, information, dissemination, strategic planning, electronic document delivery, electronic journals/publishing.

Museum or gallery collection, archive, or library special collection:
Mary Ward Collection of children's literature
Parish Libraries of Ashby de la Zouch and Loughborough (on deposit)

Trade and statistical information:
A range of statistical and related data as accumulated through various research projects and studies (including that of LISU).

Non-library collection catalogue:
All or part available in-house

Printed publications:
Prospectuses on departmental activities – teaching, research and consultancy

Access to staff:
Contact by letter, by telephone, by fax and by e-mail. Appointment necessary.
Hours: Mon to Fri, 0900 to 1700

Access for disabled people:
Parking provided, ramped entry, access to all public areas, toilet facilities

Constituent bodies:
Higher Education Academy Information and Computer Science Study Centre
tel: 01509 635708; fax: 01509 223053; e-mail: a.s .mcnab@lboro.ac.uk
Library and Information Statistics Unit (LISU)
tel: 01509 635680; fax: 01509 635699; e-mail: c .creaser@lboro.ac.uk

LOUGHBOROUGH UNIVERSITY – UNIVERSITY LIBRARY

Loughborough, Leicestershire, LE11 3TU

Tel: 01509 222360
Fax: 01509 223993
E-mail: library@lboro.ac.uk

Website:
http://www.lboro.ac.uk/library

Enquiries:
Enquiries to: Service Development Manager
Direct tel: 01509 222355
Direct e-mail: j.g.walton@lboro.ac.uk

Organisation type and purpose:
University library.

Subject coverage:
Art; business studies; design and technology; economics; English and drama; European studies; geography; human sciences; information studies; management; social sciences; chemical engineering; chemistry; civil engineering; computer studies; electrical and electronic engineering; human biology; ergonomics; materials technology; mathematics; mechanical engineering; physics; transport technology; manufacturing engineering; sports science

Non-library collection catalogue:
All or part available online

Library catalogue:
All or part available online

Access for disabled people:
Parking provided, level entry, access to all public areas, toilet facilities

Links with:
LISU

LOUTH NATURALISTS' ANTIQUARIAN AND LITERARY SOCIETY

Acronym or abbreviation: LNALS

The Museum, 4 Broadbank, Louth, Lincolnshire, LN11 0EQ

Tel: 01507 601211
E-mail: louthmuseum@btconnect.com

Website:
http://www.louth.org.uk

Enquiries:
Enquiries to: Manager

Founded:
1884

Organisation type and purpose:
Learned society (membership is by subscription), present number of members: 205, registered charity (charity number 504370), museum, publishing house.

Subject coverage:
Local history relating to Louth and district.

Museum or gallery collection, archive, or library special collection:
Architectural Drawings of James Fowler, FRIBA, 1828–92, architect of Louth
Paintings by Peter DeWint
Works of Thomas Wilkinson Wallis, 1821–1903, internationally known woodcarver
Louth-made flat-weave carpets
Brick making
1920 Louth flood interpretation
domestic and commercial bygones

Printed publications:
The Louth Flood
William Brown and the Louth Panorama
The Story of Hubbards Hills
The Lincolnshire Rising 1536
Tales of a Lincolnshire Parson
Upon the Parish Rate (Workhouse history)
Louth House of Correction (Prison history)
Recollections of a Lincolnshire Miller
Lincolnshire Stuff (Wool industry-based fiction)
Order printed publications from: Louth Museum, 4 Broadbank, Louth, LN11 0EQ; tel. 01507 601211

Access to staff:
Contact by letter, by telephone, by e-mail and in person. Appointment necessary. Non-members charged.

Access to building, collection or gallery:
No prior appointment required
Hours: April to October: Tue to Sat, 1000 to 1600

Access for disabled people:
Fully accessible

Member organisation of:
Lincoln Record Society
Society for Lincolnshire History and Archaeology

LP GAS ASSOCIATION

Acronym or abbreviation: LPGA

Unit 14, Bow Court, Fletchworth Gate, Burnsall Road, Coventry, CV5 6SP

Tel: 02476 672108
E-mail: mail@lpga.co.uk

Website:
http://www.lpga.co.uk

Enquiries:
Enquiries to: Director General

Founded:
1970

Organisation type and purpose:
Professional body, trade association (membership is by subscription), present number of members: 180.

Subject coverage:
Liquefied petroleum gas, safety, standards, distribution, storage, handling and utilisation, LPG cylinders, hoses, vessels and systems.

Museum or gallery collection, archive, or library special collection:
Codes of practice for the LP Gas Industry

Printed publications:
Codes of Practice (30 titles)
Guides

Publications list:
Available online and in print

Access to staff:
Contact by letter, by telephone, by fax, by e-mail and via website
Hours: Mon to Thu, 0830 to 1700; Fri, 0830 to 1630

Member of:
Association Européen des Gas de Petrole Lingfiés (AEGPL)

LUBRICANTS UK LIMITED

Castrol Technology Centre, Whitchurch Hill, Pangbourne, Reading, Berkshire, RG8 7QR

Tel: 0118 984 3311
Fax: 0118 976 5536
E-mail: toomeym@castrol.com

Website:
http://www.castrol.com
Castrol's home page. Information about our automotive, marine and industrial lubricants range, the origins of synthetic and mineral oils, company history, information about Castrol's sponsorship.

Enquiries:
Enquiries to: Librarian
Direct tel: 01189 765396 or 765229

Founded:
1899

Organisation type and purpose:
Research organisation.
Research and development on lubricants, greases, antifreeze, hydraulic fluids etc.

Subject coverage:
Lubrication, tribology, greases, antifreeze, hydraulic fluids.

Library catalogue:
All or part available in-house

Access to staff:
Contact by letter, by telephone, by fax and by e-mail. Appointment necessary.
Hours: Mon to Fri, 0900 to 1700

Parent body:
BP plc
Britannic House, 1 Finsbury Circus, London, EC2M 7BA

LUPUS UK

St James House, Eastern Road, Romford, Essex, RM1 3NH

Tel: 01708 731251
Fax: 01708 731252
E-mail: headoffice@lupusuk.org.uk

Website:
http://www.lupusuk.org.uk

Enquiries:
Enquiries to: Administrator
Other contacts: Director

Founded:
1990

Organisation type and purpose:
Registered charity.
Fund-raising for medical research into cure and treatment for lupus; publicity and information.

Subject coverage:
Systemic lupus erythematosus, its nature, treatment and research; support for sufferers from the disease.

Printed publications:
Factsheets (free with sae)
Living with Lupus (£8)
Lupus: a guide for patients (£3)
Lupus in Children and Young People (£3)
The Lupus Book (£13.50)
Understanding Lupus (£10.50)
Posters and leaflets

Electronic and video publications:
Living with Lupus (video, £8)

Publications list:
Available in print

Access to staff:
Contact by letter, by telephone, by fax, by e-mail and in person
Hours: Mon to Fri, 0900 to 1700

LUTON CENTRAL LIBRARY

St Georges Square, Luton, Bedfordshire, LU1 2NG

Tel: 01582 547418
Fax: 01582 547461
E-mail: referencelibrary@lutonculture.com

Website:
http://www.lutonlibraries.co.uk

Enquiries:
Enquiries to: Director of Libraries
Direct tel: 01582 547422
Direct e-mail: jean.george@lutonculture.com
Other contacts: Central Library Manager (for administration of building and services); Principal Librarian (for information services, adult/young people services)

Organisation type and purpose:
Charitable trust, public library.

Subject coverage:
General, and the history of Luton.

Museum or gallery collection, archive, or library special collection:
Workshop manual collection
Local studies collection, focusing on Luton

Non-library collection catalogue:
All or part available in-house

Library catalogue:
All or part available online

Printed publications:
Luton: collection of old photographs, by Mark Stubbs
Luton Local Studies material

Electronic and video publications:
Luton Celebrates: 50 years of history (video)

Access to staff:
Contact by letter, by telephone, by fax, by e-mail and in person
Hours: Mon, 1100 to 1900; Tue to Thu, 0900 to 1900; Fri, 0900 to 1700; Sat, 0930 to 1600; Sun, 1400 to 1700

Branch libraries:
Leagrave Library
Marsh Road, Luton, Bedfordshire, LU3 2NL; tel: 01582 556650; fax: 01582 556651
Lewsey Library
Landrace Road, Luton, Bedfordshire, LU4 0SW; tel: 01582 696094; fax: 01582 696094
Marsh Farm Library
Purley Centre, Luton, Bedfordshire, LU3 3SR; tel: 01582 574803; fax: 01582 574803
Stopsley Library
Hitchin Road, Luton, Bedfordshire, LU2 7UG; tel: 01582 706368; fax: 01582 706368
Sundon Park Library
Hill Rise, Luton, Bedfordshire, LU3 3EE; tel: 01582 574573; fax: 01582 574573
Wigmore Library
Wigmore Lane, Luton, Bedfordshire, LU3 8DJ; tel: 01582 706340; fax: 01582 706340

Member organisation of:
European Public Information Relay

Parent body:
Luton Cultural Services Trust
LCST HQ, 4th floor, Luton Central Library, St Georges Square, Luton, LU1 2NG; tel: 01582 547470; fax: 01582 547461; website: http://www.lutonculture.com

LUTYENS TRUST

Goddards, Abinger Common, Dorking, Surrey, RH5 6JH

Tel: 01306 730487

Website:
http://www.lutyenstrust.org.uk

Enquiries:
Enquiries to: Honorary Secretary

Founded:
1984

Organisation type and purpose:
Learned society (membership is by subscription), present number of members: 350, registered charity (charity number 326776).
The Lutyens' Trust is an educational charity which acts as a source of information and help on the care and maintenance of the works of Sir Edwin Lutyens.
To protect the spirit and substance of the work of Sir Edwin Lutyens OM.

Subject coverage:
Historical and technical information on the buildings designed by Edwin Lutyens between 1889–1944.

Museum or gallery collection, archive, or library special collection:
Goddards, a Lutyens house. Though still owned by the Lutyens Trust it is managed by the Landmark Trust

Printed publications:
Newsletter

Access to staff:
Appointment necessary.
Hours: Mon to Fri, 0900 to 1700
Special comments: Open Wednesday afternoon between April and September, appointments to be made with The Landmark Trust.

Access to building, collection or gallery:
Prior appointment required

Goddards transferred to the:
Landmark Trust

LUXEMBOURG EMBASSY

Formal name: Ambassade du Grand-Duché de Luxembourg à Londres

27 Wilton Crescent, London, SW1X 8SD

Tel: 020 7235 6961
Fax: 020 7235 9734

Enquiries:
Enquiries to: Counsellor
Direct e-mail: londres.amb@mae.etat.lu

Organisation type and purpose:
Embassy/Consulate.

Subject coverage:
Luxembourg: its history, political system, geography, economy, taxation, statistics, cultural life, education, commerce.

Museum or gallery collection, archive, or library special collection:
Memorials (Journal Officiel du Grand-Duché de Luxembourg), 3 series A, B and C covering laws, regulations and administration, company information

Access to staff:
Contact by letter and by e-mail. Appointment necessary.
Hours: Mon to Fri, 0900 to 1700

LUXEMBOURG TOURIST OFFICE

Sicilian House, Sicilian Avenue, London, WC1 1QH

Tel: 020 7434 2800
E-mail: tourism@luxembourg.co.uk

Website:
http://www.luxembourg.co.uk

Enquiries:
Enquiries to: Director

Founded:
1954

Organisation type and purpose:
National government body.

Subject coverage:
Luxembourg (the country and city).

Trade and statistical information:
General statistics on Luxembourg.

Printed publications:
Available free of charge (return sae appreciated):
Camping guides
General brochures and maps
Hotel lists

Electronic and video publications:
Pictures, photographs (CD-ROM and online)

Access to staff:
Contact by letter, by telephone, by fax, by e-mail, in person and via website
Hours: Mon to Fri, 1000 to 1700

Access to building, collection or gallery:
Hours: Mon to Fri, 1000 to 1700

Access for disabled people:
Level entry
Special comments: Lift.

LYMPHOMA ASSOCIATION

Acronym or abbreviation: LA

PO Box 386, Aylesbury, Buckinghamshire, HP20 2GA

Tel: 01296 619400
Fax: 01296 619400
E-mail: information@lymphomas.org.uk

Website:
http://www.lymphomas.org.uk

continued overleaf

Details of Association's services and how to contact the Helpline.

Enquiries:
Enquiries to: Chief Executive
Direct tel: 0808 808 5555 (Helpline)

Founded:
1986

Organisation type and purpose:
Advisory body, membership association (membership is by subscription), present number of members: 1800 (charity number 1068395), training organisation.
Provides information and emotional support for patients with Hodgkin Lymphoma and non-Hodgkin Lymphoma and their families.

Subject coverage:
Lymphomas, Hodgkin Lymphoma, non-Hodgkin Lymphoma, diagnosis, treatment, chemotherapy, radiotherapy, coping with disease and treatment, local support groups, patient-to-patient links, buddy links.

Museum or gallery collection, archive, or library special collection:
DVDs, CDs, loan collection

Printed publications:
Comprehensive literature available (free)

Electronic and video publications:
Hodgkin Lymphoma and its Treatment (DVD, for loan)
Understanding Non Hodgkin Lymphoma (video, for loan)

Publications list:
Available online and in print

Access to staff:
Contact by letter, by telephone and by fax
Hours: Mon to Thu, 0900 to 1800; Fri, 0900 to 1700

MAARA

Formal name: Midlands Asthma and Allergy Research Association

No. 1 Mill, The Wharf, Shardlow, Derby, DE72 2GH

Tel: 01332 799600
E-mail: enquiries@maara.org

Website:
http://www.maara.org
Medical website gives extensive help and information on asthma and allergy and also gives detailed information on the services, charity and supports.

Enquiries:
Enquiries to: General Manager

Founded:
1968

Organisation type and purpose:
Rregistered charity (charity number 257131). Concerned with funding research into asthma and other allergies, runs an information service and is renowned for aerobiological research.
Main aim is to fund research into the cause and treatment of asthma and allergy.

Subject coverage:
Information on asthma and other allergic conditions, aerobiology, patient education, pollen and spore levels, pollen forecasts, anaphylaxis.

Trade and statistical information:
Aerobiological data.

Printed publications:
Leaflets on allergic conditions
MAARA Newsletter (annually)
Aerobiology research publications

Publications list:
Available online

Access to staff:
Contact by letter, by telephone, by fax, by e-mail, in person and via website. Appointment necessary.

Hours: Mon to Fri, 0900 to 1630

Branch:
MAARA
PO Box 1057, Leicester, LE2 3GZ; tel: 0116 270 7557; fax: 0116 270 9338; e-mail: eva.day@virgin.net

MACAULAY LAND USE RESEARCH INSTITUTE

Acronym or abbreviation: Macaulay Institute

Craigiebuckler, Aberdeen, AB15 8QH

Tel: 01224 395000
Fax: 01224 395010
E-mail: l.robertson@macaulay.ac.uk

Website:
http://www.macaulay.ac.uk

Enquiries:
Enquiries to: Librarian
Direct e-mail: library@macaulay.ac.uk

Founded:
1987

Organisation type and purpose:
Research organisation.

Subject coverage:
Soil science; crop suitability; land use; hill farming; plant physiology; peat and forest soils; forestry; environmental conservation and pollution; land reclamation; drainage; water research.

Library catalogue:
All or part available in-house

Printed publications:
Annual Report
Land capability for agriculture maps
Land use maps
Soil maps
Soil Survey of Scotland (HMSO, Edinburgh; in continuation) consists of monographs and soil maps

Publications list:
Available in print

Access to staff:
Contact by letter, by telephone, by fax and by e-mail. Appointment necessary.
Hours: Mon to Thu, 0900 to 1700; Fri, 0900 to 1600

Access to building, collection or gallery:
Prior appointment required

Access for disabled people:
Parking provided, level entry, access to all public areas, toilet facilities

Grant administered by the:
Scottish Executive (SERAD)

State-aided institute of the:
Agricultural and Food Research Council

MACCLESFIELD BOROUGH COUNCIL

Town Hall, Macclesfield, Cheshire, SK10 1AH

Tel: 01625 500500\ Minicom no. 01625 500321
Fax: 01625 504203

Website:
http://www.macclesfield.gov.uk
Economic profile, tourism, general information about the borough.

Enquiries:
Enquiries to: Public Relations Manager
Direct tel: 01625 504165
Direct fax: 01625 504155

Founded:
1974

Organisation type and purpose:
Local government body.

Subject coverage:
Services and amenities of the local borough council.

Access to staff:
Contact by letter, by telephone, by fax and by e-mail. Appointment necessary.
Hours: Mon to Thu, 0845 to 1700; Fri, 0845 to 1630

Access for disabled people:
Parking provided, ramped entry, toilet facilities

MACECORP LIMITED

Acronym or abbreviation: AIIT

Somers House, 1 Somers Road, Reigate, Surrey, RH2 9DU

Tel: 01737 224427
Fax: 01737 224428
E-mail: mcl@aiit.demon.co.uk

Website:
http://www.aiit.com/
Information on the company, its products and services, including multiclient studies, databases and newsletters.

Enquiries:
Enquiries to: Managing Director
Other contacts: Senior Consultant for Research Head.

Founded:
1985

Organisation type and purpose:
International organisation, advisory body, professional body, consultancy, research organisation.
IT and telecommunications management consultancy.

Subject coverage:
IT, telecommunications, market research, business strategy, market positioning, IT budgeting, and resourcing, partnership search, product/vendor/objective analyses, support and training in product launch, information services, temporary experts.

Trade and statistical information:
European telecommunications spend statistics, voice resale markets in Europe, key European and International IT activities.

Printed publications:
Market Analyzer newsletter (monthly)
Topics of the Month

Publications list:
Available in print

Access to staff:
Contact by letter, by telephone, by fax, by e-mail and via website. Appointment necessary.
Hours: Mon to Fri, 0900 to 1800

Access to building, collection or gallery:
Prior appointment required

Associates in:
France, Germany, Ireland, Italy, Netherlands, Belgium, Spain, Sweden and USA

MACHINE TOOL TECHNOLOGIES ASSOCIATION

Acronym or abbreviation: MTTA

62 Bayswater Road, London, W2 3PS

Tel: 020 7298 6413
E-mail: mtta@mtta.co.uk

Website:
http://www.mtta.org.uk

Enquiries:
Enquiries to: Marketing Manager
Direct e-mail: bromige@mtta.co.uk

Founded:
1919

Organisation type and purpose:
Trade association.
Representing metalcutting and metal forming manufacturers.

Subject coverage:
Information supplied on: statistics, education and training, technical assistance ie: CE marks, standards. public relations, relevant exhibitions in the United Kingdom and abroad, trade missions, distributor and agent information, market sector reports, meetings, presentations, publications, industry representation.

Trade and statistical information:
A full range of data on machine tool users and suppliers.

Printed publications:
British Machine Tools and Equipment (annually, free of charge)
Electrical Equipment of Machine Tools
Machine Tool Enterprise (quarterly, free)
Machine Tool Statistics (annually, for sale)
Safety Codes of Practice for Machine Tools and Robots
Standards and booklets

Electronic and video publications:
Manufacturers (CD-ROM)
Importers (CD-ROM)

Publications list:
Available in print

Access to staff:
Contact by letter, by telephone, by fax, by e-mail and via website. Non-members charged.
Hours: Mon to Fri, 0900 to 1700

Access to building, collection or gallery:
No access other than to staff
Special comments: Prior appointment required for access to library.

MACMILLAN CANCER RELIEF

39 Albert Embankment, London, SE1 7UQ

Tel: 020 7340 7840\ Minicom no. 0808 808 0121
Fax: 020 7840 7841
E-mail: cancerline@macmillan.org.uk

Website:
http://www.macmillan.org.uk

Enquiries:
Enquiries to: Corporate Communications Assistant
Direct tel: 020 7840 7817
Direct e-mail: oplummer@macmillan.org.uk

Founded:
1911

Organisation type and purpose:
Voluntary organisation, registered charity (charity number 261017).
Helps to provide expert care and practical and emotional support for people living with cancer, including families, friends and carers. In order to achieve this it raises funds for specialist Macmillan nurses and doctors, builds vitally needed treatment centres, provides grants for patients with financial difficulties, offers training and resources to cancer self-help and support groups, and provides a range of information locally and nationally.

Subject coverage:
General information on help for cancer patients, applications for financial grants accepted from health professionals on behalf of cancer patients, domiciliary nursing care for cancer patients.

Museum or gallery collection, archive, or library special collection:
Cancer information

Printed publications:
Help is There (details of over 40 cancer support and care charities in the UK)
The Cancer Guide
Information leaflets about Macmillan Cancer Relief's Services:
All About Macmillan
Macmillan Nurses
Macmillan Information Services
Macmillan Patient Grants
Macmillan Doctors

Information leaflets:
Common Breast Problems
Breast Cancer: How to Help Yourself
Gynaecological Cancers: How to Help Yourself
Staying Well: Gynaecological Health
No Time to Draw Breath: What Every Smoker Should Know
Breathing Easier

Microform publications:
A Presentation on Macmillan Cancer Relief (slide set describing the service)

Publications list:
Available online and in print

Access to staff:
Contact by letter, by telephone, by fax, by e-mail and via website
Hours: Mon to Fri, 0930 to 1930

Affiliated to:
BACUP
Breast Cancer Care
British Colostomy Association
CancerLink
National Association of Laryngectomee Clubs

MACULAR DISEASE SOCIETY

Acronym or abbreviation: MDS

PO Box 1870, Andover, Hampshire, SP10 9AD

Tel: 01264 350551
Fax: 01264 350558
E-mail: info@maculardisease.org

Website:
http://www.maculardisease.org

Enquiries:
Enquiries to: Information
Direct tel: helpline: 0845 241 2041

Founded:
1987

Subject coverage:
Macular disease, sight impairment, low vision aids, emotional support.

Museum or gallery collection, archive, or library special collection:
Information material (booklets, pamphlets etc, free on request via helpline)

Trade and statistical information:
Data on sight impairment.

Printed publications:
Side View (4 times a year, large print and audiotape)
Digest annually
Booklets (various)

Access to staff:
Contact by letter, by telephone, by fax and by e-mail
Hours: Mon to Fri, 0900 to 1700

Access to building, collection or gallery:
No access other than to staff

MADE-UP TEXTILES ASSOCIATION LIMITED

Acronym or abbreviation: MUTA

42 Heath Street, Tamworth, Staffordshire, B79 7JH

Tel: 01827 52337
Fax: 01827 310827
E-mail: associations@compuserve.com

Website:
http://www.muta.org.uk

Enquiries:
Enquiries to: Administrator

Founded:
1919

Organisation type and purpose:
Trade association.

Subject coverage:
The making-up industry of heavy industrial textiles into marquees, tarpaulins, covers, sails, tents etc.

Printed publications:
Industrial Textiles (trade magazine, quarterly)
Members Trade Directory

Publications list:
Available online

Access to staff:
Contact by letter, by telephone, by fax, by e-mail and via website
Hours: Mon to Fri, 0900 to 1700

MAG (UK)

Formal name: Motorcycle Action Group

PO Box 750, Rugby, Warwickshire, CV21 3ZR

Tel: 0870 444 8448
Fax: 0870 444 8449
E-mail: mag-hq@mag-uk.org

Website:
http://www.mag-uk.org
Main information

Enquiries:
Enquiries to: Chief Executive
Direct e-mail: henry@mag9.demon.co.uk
Other contacts: Press Officer for all political/ technical matters, all media and PR matters.

Founded:
1973

Organisation type and purpose:
National organisation, membership association (membership is by subscription), present number of members: 20,000, voluntary organisation, consultancy, research organisation, publishing house.
Representative lobby group for motorcyclists ie user group, service organisation, multiple member benefits.

Subject coverage:
Motorcycle user related information.

Museum or gallery collection, archive, or library special collection:
Motorcycle related archive, mostly hard copy, PC indexed

Trade and statistical information:
Some statistical source data from outside bodies; government etc.

Non-library collection catalogue:
All or part available online and in print

Library catalogue:
All or part available online and in print

Printed publications:
Streetbiker (newspaper, 56/64 A3 format pages, 6 times a year, free to members direct, on request to non-members £1.60)
Network (12 times a year to groups)

Access to staff:
Contact by letter, by telephone, by fax, by e-mail and via website. Access for members only. Non-members charged.
Hours: Mon to Fri, 0900 to 1700

Access to building, collection or gallery:
Prior appointment required

Affiliated to:
Federation of European Motorcyclists Associations (FEMA)
Rue Des Champs 62, Brussels, B-1040, Belgium; tel: +32 2 736 9407; fax: +32 2 736 9401; e-mail: fema-ridersrights@compuserve.com

MAGDALEN COLLEGE

Library and Archives, Oxford, OX1 4AU

Tel: 01865 276045
Fax: 01865 276057

continued overleaf

E-mail: library@magd.ox.ac.uk

Website:
http://www.magd.ox.ac.uk/college_life/
libraries_and_archives.shtml

Enquiries:
Enquiries to: Librarian
Other contacts: Archivist, tel: 01865 276088 for
archives queries

Founded:
1458

Organisation type and purpose:
College library and archives.

Subject coverage:
All taught subjects; college-related archives.

**Museum or gallery collection, archive, or library
special collection:**
Gibbard Bequest 1608 (medical books)
Goodyer Bequest 1664 (botanical books)
Throckmorton Bequest 1626 (continental books)

Non-library collection catalogue:
All or part available in-house

Library catalogue:
All or part available online

Printed publications:
Magdalen College Occasional Papers (series)
Magdalen Poets (2000), Hidden Magdalen (2008),
 History of Magdalen College (2008) (books)
Order printed publications from: Home Bursar's
Office, Magdalen College, Oxford OX1 4AU

Publications list:
Available online

Access to staff:
Contact by letter, by telephone, by e-mail and via
website. Appointment necessary.
Hours: Mon to Fri, 0900 to 1700

Access to building, collection or gallery:
Members only, or by appointment

MAGDALENE COLLEGE

Pepys Library, Cambridge, CB3 0AG

Tel: 01223 332115
Fax: 01223 332187
E-mail: pepyslibrary@magd.cam.ac.uk

Enquiries:
Enquiries to: Pepys Librarian
Direct e-mail: pepyslibrary@magd.cam.ac.uk

Founded:
1703

Organisation type and purpose:
Private library with restricted public access.

Subject coverage:
General, pre-1703, nautical, musical, literary,
ballads, prints, calligraphy, medieval manuscripts.

**Museum or gallery collection, archive, or library
special collection:**
Personal library of the diarist and Secretary of the
 Admiralty, Samuel Pepys (1633–1703), preserved
 in its original presses, closed on his death, and
 bequeathed by him to his old college

Library catalogue:
All or part available in print

Printed publications:
Catalogue (Latham R C ed., 16 vols, 1980–1994,
 pub. Boydell & Brewer, Woodbridge)
The Pepys Library (booklet, for sale in library)

Access to staff:
Contact by letter, by fax and by e-mail.
Appointment necessary. Letter of introduction
required.
Hours: Term time: 1130 to 1230 and 1430 to 1530
from beginning of Easter term to the end of
August; only 1430 to 1530 in Michaelmas and Lent
terms

Special comments: Accredited scholars with specific
enquiries only by pre-arrangement. The library
may be viewed during opening hours by visitors.

Access for disabled people:
Special comments: Please ask at the Porter's Lodge

MAGIC CIRCLE, THE

Centre for the Magic Arts, 12 Stephenson Way,
London, NW1 2HD

Tel: 020 7387 2222
Fax: 020 7387 5114
E-mail: prattmsm@hotmail.com

Website:
http://www.themagiccircle.co.uk
General information about the Magic Circle.

Enquiries:
Enquiries to: Secretary
Direct tel: 01707 654971
Direct fax: 01707 654971

Founded:
1905

Organisation type and purpose:
Membership association (membership is by
subscription, qualification, election or invitation),
present number of members: 1400.

Subject coverage:
Art of magic, magical inventions and
presentations.

Access to staff:
Contact by letter, by telephone and by fax
Hours: Mon to Fri, 0900 to 1700

MAGIC LANTERN SOCIETY

Acronym or abbreviation: MLS

South Park, Galphay Road, Kirkby Malzeard,
Ripon, North Yorkshire, HG4 3RX

Tel: 01765 658485
Fax: 01765 658485
E-mail: lmh.smith@magiclanternsocy.demon.co.uk

Website:
http://www.magiclantern.org.uk
All information about the Society.

Enquiries:
Enquiries to: Honorary Secretary

Founded:
1976

Organisation type and purpose:
Learned society (membership is by subscription),
present number of members: 400.

Subject coverage:
All aspects of pre-cinema optical entertainment.

Printed publications:
Journal
Short-run, high quality books occasionally
 published
Newsletter (quarterly)

Publications list:
Available in print

Access to staff:
Contact by letter, by telephone, by fax, by e-mail
and via website
Hours: Mon to Fri, 0900 to 1700

MAGISTRATES' ASSOCIATION

Acronym or abbreviation: MA

28 Fitzroy Square, London, W1T 6DD

Tel: 020 7387 2353
Fax: 020 7383 4020
E-mail: communications@magistrates-association
.org.uk

Website:
http://www.magistrates-association.org.uk

The Magistrates' Association – the voice of the
magistracy – representing, informing, consulting,
training and supporting the magistracy in England
and Wales. Providing advice and information
about magistrates and magistrates' courts.

Enquiries:
Enquiries to: Chief Executive
Other contacts: Communications Manager for
media and public relation enquiries, information
enquiries.

Founded:
1920

Organisation type and purpose:
Membership association.
To advise and represent magistrates in England
and Wales.

Subject coverage:
All matters of relevance to the lay magistracy.

**Museum or gallery collection, archive, or library
special collection:**
A small library of law books relating to
 magistrates' courts and the magistracy

Library catalogue:
All or part available in-house

Printed publications:
Annual Report
Journal (monthly)
Sentencing Guidelines

Access to staff:
Contact by letter, by telephone, by fax, by e-mail
and via website. Appointment necessary.
Hours: Mon to Fri, 0915 to 1700

Access to building, collection or gallery:
Prior appointment required

MAHARISHI FOUNDATION

Beacon House, Willow Walk, Woodley Park,
Skelmersdale, Lancs, WN8 6UR

Tel: 01695 728847
E-mail: reception@maharishi-european-sidhaland
.org.uk

Website:
http://www.maharishi.co.uk

Enquiries:
Enquiries to: Administrator
Direct tel: 020 7937 3353
Direct fax: 020 7376 9625

Founded:
1975

Organisation type and purpose:
Registered charity (charity number 270157).
Educational charity.
To advance the education of the public by
establishing, conducting and maintaining an
institution of higher education; and by offering
such courses of instruction to the public as will
promote the mental and creative development of
the individual.

Subject coverage:
Transcendental meditation, Maharishi's Vedic
Science, Maharishi's Vedic approach to health,
Maharishi's integrated system of education,
Maharishi Ayur Veda, Maharishi Jyotish,
Maharishi Sthapatya Ved, Maharishi Gandharva
Ved.

Printed publications:
The Cosmic Computer (£20)
Perfect Blood Pressure Naturally (2001, £6.99)
Bhagavad Gita (paperback, £12.99)
Science of Being (paperback, £16)
Transcendental Meditation (Roth R, £12)
The TM Book (Denniston D, £11)
The Crime Vaccine (£15)
Neurophysiology of Enlightenment (£13)
Enlightened Management (£11)
Success from Within (£11)
Growing Up Enlightened (£13)
Self-Recovery: Treating Addictions (£24)
Key to Kingdom of Heaven (£4.95)

Order printed publications from: Maharishi Ayur-Veda Products, FREEPOST 5128, Skelmersdale, Lancashire, WN8 6BR, tel: 01695 51015, fax: 01695 50517

Electronic and video publications:
Maharishi Ayurveda Introductory Video (£5)
Bhagavad Gita (audio book, £60)
Science of Being (audio book, £70)
Maharishi at Lake Louise (video, £50)
A Promise for the Family of Man (video, £48)
Maharishi on Government (video, £38)
Maharishi's Lecture at the Harvard Law Forum (video, £38)
Maharishi on Education (video, £38)
Maharishi at the Royal Albert Hall (video, £48)
Maharishi Sthapatya Veda – Architecture in Harmony with Natural Law (video 30mins, £22)
The Physics of Flying (£39)
Is Consciousness the Unified Field? (£39)

Publications list:
Available online and in print

Access to staff:
Contact by letter, by telephone, by fax, by e-mail and via website
Hours: Mon to Fri, 1000 to 1700

Affiliated to:
Maharishi University of Natural Law at the same address

National Enquiry Office:
Beacon House
    Woodley Park, Skelmersdale, Lancashire, WN8 6UR; tel: 01695 51213

MAIDENHEAD LIBRARY

St Ives Road, Maidenhead, Berkshire, SL6 1QU

Tel: 01628 796969
Fax: 01628 796971
E-mail: maidenhead.library@rbwm.gov.uk

Website:
http://www.rbwm.gov.uk

Enquiries:
Enquiries to: Librarian

Organisation type and purpose:
Local government body, registered charity, public library.

Library catalogue:
All or part available online

Access to staff:
Contact by letter, by telephone, by fax, by e-mail, in person and via website
Hours: Mon and Wed, 0930 to 1700; Tue and Thu, 0930 to 2000; Fri, 0930 to 1900; Sat, 0930 to 1600

Access for disabled people:
Ramped entry, access to all public areas, toilet facilities
Special comments: Parking opposite in the road, unreserved.

Parent body:
Royal Borough of Windsor and Maidenhead

MAIDSTONE & TUNBRIDGE WELLS NHS TRUST

Acronym or abbreviation: MTW

The Library, Kent & Sussex Hospital, Mount Ephraim, Tunbridge Wells, Kent, TN4 8AT

Tel: 01892 632384
Fax: 01892 531975
E-mail: gm.e.mtw-tr.library@nhs.net

Enquiries:
Enquiries to: Library & Information Services Manager
Direct tel: ext 2384
Other contacts: Site Librarian

Founded:
1974

Organisation type and purpose:
Education (NHS).

Subject coverage:
General surgery, otolaryngology, general practice, general medicine, trauma and orthopaedics.

Non-library collection catalogue:
All or part available online

Access to staff:
Appointment necessary. Non-members charged.
Hours: Mon to Fri, 0900 to 1700

Access to building, collection or gallery:
Prior appointment required

Access for disabled people:
Level entry, access to all public areas, toilet facilities

Member of:
Health Libraries Network

MAIDSTONE BOROUGH COUNCIL

5–11 London Road, Maidstone, Kent, ME16 8HR

Tel: 01622 602000
Fax: 01622 692246
E-mail: customercare@maidstone.gov.uk

Website:
http://www.maidstone.gov.uk

Enquiries:
Enquiries to: Chief Executive

Founded:
1974

Organisation type and purpose:
Local government body.

Subject coverage:
Local government services.

Publications list:
Available online and in print

Access to staff:
Contact by letter, by telephone, by fax, by e-mail, in person and via website
Hours: Mon to Thu, 0830 to 1700; Fri, 0830 to 1630

Access for disabled people:
Parking provided, level entry, toilet facilities

MAIL ORDER TRADERS' ASSOCIATION

Acronym or abbreviation: MOTA

PO Box 342, Southport, Merseyside, PR8 2XB

Tel: 01704 563787
Fax: 01704 551247
E-mail: ukmota@aol.com

Enquiries:
Enquiries to: Director

Organisation type and purpose:
Trade association.

Subject coverage:
General information regarding the home shopping/catalogue mail order trade.

Trade and statistical information:
Collated statistical figures relating to the catalogue mail order trade.

Access to staff:
Contact by letter, by telephone, by fax and by e-mail
Hours: Mon to Fri, 0900 to 1700

MAJOR CONTRACTORS GROUP

Acronym or abbreviation: MCG

55 Tufton Street, London, SW1P 3QL

Tel: 020 7227 4505
Fax: 020 7227 4506
E-mail: enquiries@mcg.org.uk

Website:
http://www.mcg.org.uk/

Enquiries:
Enquiries to: Director

Founded:
July 1996

Organisation type and purpose:
Trade association (membership is by election or invitation), present number of members: 23.

Subject coverage:
Construction industry.

Access to staff:
Contact by letter and by e-mail
Hours: Mon to Fri, 0900 to 1700

Member of:
Construction Confederation

MAKING MUSIC

Formal name: National Federation of Music Societies
Acronym or abbreviation: NFMS

2–4 Great Eastern Street, London, EC2A 3NW

Tel: 020 7422 8280
Fax: 020 7422 8299
E-mail: info@makingmusic.org.uk

Website:
http://www.makingmusic.org.uk

Enquiries:
Enquiries to: Communications Manager
Direct e-mail: sarah.robinson@makingmusic.org.uk

Founded:
1935

Organisation type and purpose:
Membership association (membership is by subscription), present number of members: 2,650, registered charity (charity number 249219), training organisation, research organisation. Making Music provides members with services and information to aid them in their voluntary activities.

Subject coverage:
Forming and running amateur music groups in the voluntary sector e.g. choirs, orchestras, music clubs, steel bands, jazz groups, classical Indian etc.

Non-library collection catalogue:
All or part available online and in print

Printed publications:
Highnotes (3 times a year)
Information sheets and How to Guides available in print

Electronic and video publications:
Information sheets and How to Guides available online
iNotes and regional e-bulletins
Repertoire service
Music Exchange service

Access to staff:
Contact by letter, by telephone, by fax, by e-mail and via website
Hours: Mon to Fri, 1000 to 1800

Affiliated to:
Association of British Orchestras
Incorporated Society of Musicians
Music Education Council (MEC)
National Campaign for the Arts
National Music Council of Great Britain
Voluntary Arts Network
World Federation of Amateur Orchestras

MALACOLOGICAL SOCIETY OF LONDON

Acronym or abbreviation: The Malsoc

Central Science Laboratory, Sand Hutton, York YO10 4JW

Tel: 01904 462 349

continued overleaf

E-mail: vasiliki@flari.fsnet.co.uk

Website:
http://www.malacsoc.org.uk/index.html

Enquiries:
Enquiries to: Honorary Secretary

Founded:
1893

Organisation type and purpose:
Learned society.

Subject coverage:
Molluscan biology, applied malacology, zoology, marine biology, snail culture, slugs and snails in agriculture, ecology, biochemistry, parasitology.

Printed publications:
The Malacologist (newsletter, twice a year)
Journal of Molluscan Studies (quarterly, pub. OUP)
Supplements to the Journal (17 titles to date of which numbers 6–17 are currently available)
Order printed publications from: Oxford University Press
Great Clarendon Street, Oxford, OX2 6DP, tel: 01865 267907, e-mail: jnlorders@oup.co.uk

Access to staff:
Contact by letter, by fax and by e-mail
Hours: Mon to Fri, 0900 to 1700

MALAYSIAN INDUSTRIAL DEVELOPMENT AUTHORITY

Acronym or abbreviation: MIDA

17 Curzon Street, London, W1J 5HR

Tel: 020 7493 0616
Fax: 020 7493 8804
E-mail: midalon@btconnect.com

Website:
http://www.mida.gov.my
Investment opportunities in Malaysia's manufacturing sector.

Enquiries:
Enquiries to: Director

Founded:
1967

Organisation type and purpose:
National government body.
Malaysian Government body.
Promotes inward investment into Malaysia's manufacturing sector.

Subject coverage:
Investment opportunities in Malaysia's manufacturing sector.

Printed publications:
Malaysia Your Profit Centre in Asia
Investment in the Manufacturing Sector: Policies, Incentives and Facilities
The Cost of Doing Business in Malaysia
The Functions of MIDA
Why Malaysia
Map of Malaysia

Publications list:
Available in print

Access to staff:
Contact by letter, by telephone, by fax, by e-mail and in person
Hours: Mon to Fri, 0900 to 1700

Headquarters:
Malaysian Industrial Development Authority (MIDA)
Plaza Sentral, Jalan Stesen Sentral 5, KL Sentral, 50470 Kuala Lumpur, Malaysia; tel: +60 3 2267 3633; fax: +60 3 2274 7970; e-mail: promotion@mida.gov.my

MALONE SOCIETY

c/o Dr C. Richardson, School of English, University of Kent, Canterbury, CT2 7NX

Tel: 01227 824656

E-mail: c.t.richardson@kent.ac.uk

Website:
http://ies.sas.ac.uk/malone/index.htm

Enquiries:
Enquiries to: Orders Secretary

Founded:
1906

Organisation type and purpose:
International organisation, learned society (membership is by subscription), present number of members: 650, registered charity (charity number 1027048).
To make accessible materials for the study of English drama up to 1642 by editing and publishing dramatic texts and related documents.

Subject coverage:
English drama up to 1642.

Printed publications:
Over 150 books published, most still in print. Available via annual subscription (£15 or equivalent), or (recent titles) from Oxford University Press, or (older titles) by direct application
Order printed publications from: Orders Secretary at the same address

Publications list:
Available online

Access to staff:
Contact by letter, by telephone and by e-mail
Hours: Mon to Fri, 0900 to 1700

Access to building, collection or gallery:
No access other than to staff

MALTA TOURIST OFFICE

Malta House, 36–38 Piccadilly, London, W1J 0LD

Tel: 020 7292 4900
Fax: 020 7734 1880
E-mail: office.uk@visitmalta.com

Website:
http://www.visitmalta.com

Enquiries:
Enquiries to: Director
Direct e-mail: john.montague@visitmalta.com

Organisation type and purpose:
National government body.
Tourist office.

Subject coverage:
General tourist information.

Trade and statistical information:
Number of tourists to Malta.
Percentage of countries visiting Malta.

Library catalogue:
All or part available in-house

Printed publications:
Malta brochure, brochures on Valleta, Mdina, Gozo, hotel guides
Religion historic sites, events

Electronic and video publications:
Videos on Malta

Access to staff:
Contact by letter, by telephone, by fax, by e-mail, in person and via website. Appointment necessary.
Hours: Mon to Fri, 0900 to 1700

Access for disabled people:
Level entry

Parent body:
Malta Tourism Authority
Merchants Str, Valletta, Malta; tel: 00 356 2122 4444; fax: 00 356 2122 0401; e-mail: info@visitmalta.com

MALTSTERS ASSOCIATION OF GREAT BRITAIN

Acronym or abbreviation: MAGB

31B Castlegate, Newark, Nottinghamshire, NG24 1AZ

Tel: 01636 700781
Fax: 01636 701836
E-mail: info@ukmalt.com

Website:
http://www.malt.info.com
http://www.ukmalt.com

Enquiries:
Enquiries to: Executive Director

Founded:
1827

Organisation type and purpose:
Trade association.

Subject coverage:
Malting.

Access to staff:
Contact by letter, by telephone and by fax
Hours: Mon to Fri, 0900 to 1700

MALVERN LIBRARY

Graham Road, Malvern, Worcestershire, WR14 2HU

Tel: 01684 561223
Fax: 01684 892999
E-mail: malvernlib@worcestershire.gov.uk

Website:
http://www.worcestershire.gov.uk
County-wide information service web site (includes information on all County Council services with links to many useful web sites).

Founded:
1905

Organisation type and purpose:
Local government body, public library.

Subject coverage:
General, local history of Malvern.

Museum or gallery collection, archive, or library special collection:
Local Studies Collection, including a substantial collection of illustrations

Non-library collection catalogue:
All or part available in-house

Library catalogue:
All or part available online

Access to staff:
Contact by letter, by telephone, by fax, by e-mail and in person. Appointment necessary.
Hours: Mon, Fri, 0900 to 1730; Tue to Thu, 0900 to 2000; Sat, 0900 to 1730; Sun, closed

Access to building, collection or gallery:
No prior appointment required
Hours: Mon, Fri, 0900 to 1730; Tue to Thu, 0900 to 2000; Sat, 0900 to 1730
Special comments: Sun, closed. Closed on Bank holidays, Good Friday and over Christmas.

Access for disabled people:
Parking provided, ramped entry

Constituent part of:
Worcestershire County Council
County Hall, Spetchley Road, Worcester, WR5 2NP; tel: 01905 763763; fax: 01905 766244; e-mail: kkirk@worcestershire.gov.uk

MAMMAL SOCIETY

3 The Carronades, New Road, Southampton, SO14 0AA

Tel: 0238 023 7874
Fax: 0238 063 4726
E-mail: enquiries@mammal.org.uk

Website:
http://www.mammal.org.uk

Enquiries:
Enquiries to: Office Manager

Founded:
1954

Organisation type and purpose:
Membership association (membership is by subscription), present number of members: 2,000, voluntary organisation, registered charity (charity number 278918).
To protect British mammals, halt the decline of threatened species and advise on all issues affecting British mammals.

Subject coverage:
British mammals, their biology, conservation, ecology, management, distribution and status, and methods of study.

Printed publications:
Books, guides and occasional publications including:
Mammals of the British Isles, Handbook 4th Edn
A Review of British Mammals (latest population estimates and review of their conservation status, 1995, £16.40)
British Mammal Fact Sheet Series
Mammal News (newsletter)
Mammal Review (journal, quarterly, free to members)
Mammalaction News (for teenagers)

Publications list:
Available online

Access to staff:
Contact by letter, by telephone, by fax, by e-mail and via website
Hours: Mon to Fri, 0900 to 1700

Access to building, collection or gallery:
No access other than to staff

Member organisation of:
IUCN

MAN B&W DIESEL LIMITED, PAXMAN

Paxman Works, PO Box 8, Colchester, Essex, CO1 2HW

Tel: 01206 795151
Fax: 01206 797869
E-mail: mike-johnson@manbwltd.com

Enquiries:
Enquiries to: Information Officer
Direct tel: 01206 875508
Direct e-mail: mike.johnson@alstom.ind.com

Founded:
1865

Organisation type and purpose:
Trade association.

Subject coverage:
General engineering, diesel engines, design and manufacture.

Library catalogue:
All or part available in-house

Access to staff:
Contact by letter, by telephone, by fax and by e-mail. Appointment necessary. Letter of introduction required.
Hours: Mon to Thu, 0900 to 1700; Fri, 0900 to 1600

MANAGEMENT CONSULTANCIES ASSOCIATION

Acronym or abbreviation: MCA

49 Whitehall, London, SW1A 2BX

Tel: 020 7321 3990
Fax: 020 7321 3991
E-mail: mca@mca.org.uk

Website:
http://www.mca.org.uk

Enquiries:
Enquiries to: Deputy Director
Direct tel: 020 7321 3993
Direct e-mail: sarah.taylor@mca.org.uk

Founded:
1956

Organisation type and purpose:
Trade association (membership is by qualification), present number of members: 39.

Subject coverage:
Management consulting, selection of management consultants, statistics relating to members' earnings, career guidance, case studies, journal and reports on management issues.

Trade and statistical information:
Members' earnings broken down by type or consultancy work performed and industry.

Printed publications:
Annual Report
Careers in Management Consulting
Statement of Best Practice
MCA Journal
MCA Think Tank Reports

Access to staff:
Contact by letter, by telephone, by fax, by e-mail and via website. Appointment necessary.
Hours: Mon to Fri, 0900 to 1700

Access to building, collection or gallery:
Prior appointment required

Member of:
Federation of European Management Consultancies Associations
3/4/5 Avenue des Arts, Brussels, B-1210, Belgium; tel: +32 2 250 0650; fax: +32 2 250 0651; e-mail: feaco@feaco.org

MANCHESTER AND LANCASHIRE FAMILY HISTORY SOCIETY

Acronym or abbreviation: M&LFHS

Clayton House, 59 Piccadilly, Manchester, M1 2AQ

Tel: 0161 236 9750
Fax: 0161 237 3812
E-mail: office@mlfhs.org.uk

Website:
http://www.mlfhs.org.uk
General information about the Society. Mail order book list and order form. Membership details and application form.

Enquiries:
Enquiries to: General Secretary

Founded:
1964

Organisation type and purpose:
Membership association (membership is by subscription), present number of members: 4000, registered charity (charity number 515599).

Subject coverage:
Genealogy, heraldry and local history.

Library catalogue:
All or part available in-house

Printed publications:
1851 Census Indexes (59 volumes)
Irish in 1861 Census
Publications of the Bolton & District Branch

Microform publications:
Unfilmed 1851 Census Transcripts
Oldham Area Burial Transcripts
Indexes to Army Deserters

Electronic and video publications:
Scots in E & W 1851 Census (CD-ROM)
Manchester City Battalions Book of Honour (CD-ROM)

Publications list:
Available online and in print

Access to staff:
Contact by letter, by telephone, by fax, by e-mail, in person and via website
Hours: Mon, Fri, 1015 to 1300; Tue, Thu, 1015 to 1600

Subsidiary:
Anglo Scottish Branch
Bolton & District Branch
Irish Ancestry Branch
Oldham & District Branch

MANCHESTER ARCHIVES AND LOCAL STUDIES

Acronym or abbreviation: MALS

Central Library, St Peter's Square, Manchester, M2 5PD

Tel: 0161 234 1979/1980
Fax: 0161 234 1927
E-mail: archiveslocalstudies@manchester.gov.uk

Website:
http://www.manchester.gov.uk/libraries/arls/archives.htm
Archive information.
http://www.images.manchester.gov.uk
Print Collection address.
http://www.manchester.gov.uk/libraries/arls
Main address.

Enquiries:
Enquiries to: Archives & Local Studies Officer
Direct tel: 0161 234 1960
Direct e-mail: r.bond@manchester.gov.uk

Founded:
1991

Organisation type and purpose:
Local government body, public library.
Archive and local studies service for City of Manchester.

Subject coverage:
Political, economic, religious, educational and historical development of Manchester and the region.

Museum or gallery collection, archive, or library special collection:
Archives (approx. 10,000 linear feet) of churches, businesses and local government
Broadside Collection (6576 items)
Map Collection (approximately 13,000 OS and other maps and plans)
Miscellaneous Collection (ephemera and three-dimensional objects)
Print Collection (approx. 145,000 items, prints, photographs, postcards etc) of which 77,000 available in digital form
Microform collections:
Census Returns (Manchester 1841–1901)
Directories of Manchester, 1772–1969
Local Newspapers from early 18th century
Parish Registers (large collection, Manchester, Cheshire and Lancashire)

Non-library collection catalogue:
All or part available online, in-house and in print

Library catalogue:
All or part available online and in-house

Printed publications:
Municipal Palace: a bibliography on the construction and opening of Manchester Town Hall, 1877 (1977)
Peterloo 1819: a portfolio of contemporary documents (1975)
Peterloo: a bibliography (1969)
Manchester Wartime Memories (2006) (book, CD)
Selection of reproduction maps, 1800–1876
Selection of reproduction posters, mainly 18th century
Various information sheets

Microform publications:
Women's Suffrage Collection (30 Microfilms, available from Adam Matthew Publications, 8 Oxford Street, Marlborough, Wilts, SN8 1AP)
Parish Register – subject to permission (microfilm, details on archives section of website)

Access to staff:
Contact by letter, by telephone, by fax, by e-mail, in person and via website

continued overleaf

Hours: Mon to Thu, 0900 to 2000; Fri and Sat, 0900 to 1700; archives only available Mon to Thu, 0900 to 1600
Special comments: Archives may need to be booked in advance.

Access for disabled people:
Parking nearby, ramped entry, access to all public areas, toilet facilities

Parent body:
Manchester City Council
 Town Hall, Manchester, M60 2LA; tel: 0161 234 5000; website: www.manchester.gov.uk

MANCHESTER ARTS LIBRARY

Central Library, St Peter's Square, Manchester, M2 5PD

Tel: 0161 234 1974
Fax: 0161 234 1961
E-mail: arts@libraries.manchester.gov.uk

Website:
http://www.manchester.gov.uk/libraries

Enquiries:
Enquiries to: Arts Coordinator

Founded:
1852

Organisation type and purpose:
Local government body, public library.

Subject coverage:
Art and design in general, costume and fashion, town planning, architecture, decorative arts, antiques, interiors, textiles, ceramics, sculpture, drawing and painting, graphics, photography, cinema, radio and TV, theatre, dance, sport and recreation.

Museum or gallery collection, archive, or library special collection:
18th and 19th century sales catalogues
Local Theatre Material Collection (estimated 30,000 items, from mid-18th century to present day)
News Chronicle Photograph Collection (52 boxes, mainly 1940–60 costume accessories)
Many important 19th century periodicals. Videos and DVDs of classic films.

Access to staff:
Contact by letter, by telephone, by fax, by e-mail, in person and via website
Hours: Mon to Thu, 1000 to 2000; Fri, Sat, 1000 to 1700

Access for disabled people:
Ramped entry, lift, toilet facilities
Special comments: Limited parking; access to most areas; staff will assist with access to lifts etc as required.

MANCHESTER BUSINESS SCHOOL

Acronym or abbreviation: MBS

Booth Street West, Manchester, M15 6PB

Tel: 0161 275 6507
Fax: 0161 275 6505
E-mail: kkirby@man-mbs.ac.uk

Website:
http://www.mbs.ac.uk

Enquiries:
Enquiries to: Information and Services Manager
Direct tel: 0161 275 6499
Other contacts: Head of Business Information Service for an information brokerage to companies on a fee paying basis.

Founded:
1965

Organisation type and purpose:
University department or institute.

Subject coverage:
Management science and education, marketing, production, finance, personnel management, economics, operations research, accounting, computing, statistics, business and companies information, market data.

Museum or gallery collection, archive, or library special collection:
Business and management journals, both printed and electronic
20,000 books

Trade and statistical information:
Collection of UK and other official statistics – OECD, European Union, UN, ILO.
Also various trade association statutes.

Printed publications:
Research Reports
Working Papers

Access to staff:
Contact by letter, by telephone, by fax and by e-mail. Non-members charged.
Hours: Term time: Mon to Fri, 0830 to 2030; Sat, 0930 to 1700
Vacations: Mon to Fri, 1000 to 1700
Special comments: The library is open to members of MBS and post-graduates and staff of other Manchester Universities. Researchers from other universities may use the library for reference purposes, by arrangement. All other users are charged an access fee.

Faculty of:
Business Administration, University of Manchester, but separately funded

Member of:
Manchester Federal School of Business and Management

MANCHESTER CENTRAL LIBRARY

St Peter's Square, Manchester, M2 5PD

Tel: 0161 234 1900\ Minicom no. 0161 234 1984
Fax: 0161 234 1963

Organisation type and purpose:
Public library.

MANCHESTER CENTRAL LIBRARY – SOCIAL SCIENCES LIBRARY

St Peters Square, Manchester, M2 5PD

Tel: 0161 234 1983/4\ Minicom no. 0161 234 1983/4
Fax: 0161 234 1927
E-mail: socsci@libraries.manchester.gov.uk

Website:
http://www.manchester.gov.uk/libraries
Information about the Central Library and district libraries.

Enquiries:
Enquiries to: Librarian

Founded:
1852

Organisation type and purpose:
Public library.

Subject coverage:
Bibliography, philosophy, religion, social sciences, home economics, archaeology, geography, history, biography within subject areas indicated.

Museum or gallery collection, archive, or library special collection:
18th and 19th century pamphlets
National Newspapers (on microfilm)
Parish Registers and related genealogical material
Parliamentary papers
Private Press books

Access to staff:
Contact by letter, by telephone, by fax, by e-mail, in person and via website

Hours: Mon to Thu, 1000 to 2000; Fri and Sat, 1000 to 1700

Access for disabled people:
Ramped entry

MANCHESTER CENTRE FOR REGIONAL HISTORY

Acronym or abbreviation: MCRH

Department of History and Economic History, Manchester Metropolitan University, Room 103, Geoffrey Manton Building, Rosamond Street West, Manchester, M15 6LL

Tel: 0161 247 6491
E-mail: c.horner@mmu.ac.uk

Website:
http://www.mcrh.mmu.ac.uk

Founded:
1998

Organisation type and purpose:
Research centre of Manchester Metropolitan University.

Subject coverage:
History of Manchester and the northwest of England.

Printed publications:
Manchester Region History Review (journal)

MANCHESTER CITY GALLERIES

Mosley Street, Manchester, M2 3JL

Tel: 0161 235 8888 \ Minicom no. 0161 235 8893
Fax: 0161 235 8899
E-mail: cityart@mcrl.poptel.org.uk

Website:
http://www.cityartgalleries.org.uk

Enquiries:
Enquiries to: Administration

Founded:
1882

Organisation type and purpose:
Local government body, art gallery, historic building, house or site, suitable for ages: all. Administrative body for the Manchester City Art Galleries and Museums.

Subject coverage:
Fine and decorative art from antiquity to present day; costume, picture, decorative art, and costume restoration.

Special visitor services:
Guided tours, tape recorded guides, materials and/or activities for children.

Education services:
Group education facilities, resources for Key Stages 1 and 2, 3, 4 and Further or Higher Education.

Museum or gallery collection, archive, or library special collection:
20th century British Paintings
Assheton-Bennett Collection of English silver and 17th century Dutch painting
Old Masters
Pre-Raphaelites
Thomas Greg Collection of English pottery

Non-library collection catalogue:
All or part available online, in-house and in print

Printed publications:
Concise Catalogue of British Paintings (2 vols)
Foreign Paintings
Large selection of printed items eg posters, prints, postcards, greetings cards etc
Other catalogues of temporary exhibitions
Pre-Raphaelite Paintings

Access to staff:
Contact by letter, by telephone and via website.
Appointment necessary.
Hours: Mon to Fri, 0900 to 1700

Galleries and historic houses:
Gallery of Costume
  Platt Hall, Wilmslow Road, Rusholme,
  Manchester, M14 5LL; tel: 0161 224 5217; fax:
  0161 256 3278
Heaton Hall
  Heaton Park, Prestwich, Manchester, M25 5SW;
  tel: 0161 773 1231
Manchester Art Gallery
  Mosley Street, Manchester, M2 3JL; tel: 0161 235
  8888; fax: 0161 235 8899
Queen's Park Conservation Studio
  Queen's Park, Rochdale Road, Harpurhey,
  Manchester, M9 5SH; tel: 0161 205 2645; fax:
  0161 205 6164
Wythenshawe Hall
  Wythenshaw Park, Northenden, Manchester,
  M23 0AB; tel: 0161 998 2331

Parent body:
Manchester City Council
  website: www.manchester.gov.uk

MANCHESTER GEOGRAPHICAL SOCIETY

Acronym or abbreviation: MGS

Friends' Meeting House, 6 Mount Street,
Manchester, M2 5NS

E-mail: paulhindle@talktalk.net

Website:
http://www.mangeogsoc.org.uk

Enquiries:
Enquiries to: Honorary Secretary

Founded:
1884

Organisation type and purpose:
Learned society (membership is by subscription),
present number of members: 120, registered
charity (charity number 222037), research
organisation, publishing house.
To encourage the study of geography at all levels.

Subject coverage:
Geography.

**Museum or gallery collection, archive, or library
special collection:**
Library – held by John Rylands University Library
  of Manchester

Library catalogue:
All or part available online and in print

Printed publications:
Library catalogue
Manchester Geographer (annually) now replaced
  by:
North West Geography (2 times a year)

Electronic and video publications:
Order electronic and video publications from: see
website www.mangeogsoc.org.uk/nwgeog.htm

Publications list:
Available online

Access to staff:
Contact by e-mail and via website
Hours: Tue, 1000 to 1230

MANCHESTER LANGUAGE AND LITERATURE LIBRARY

Central Library, St Peter's Square, Manchester, M2
5PD

Tel: 0161 234 1972
Fax: 0161 234 1963
E-mail: lang_lit@libraries.manchester.gov.uk

Website:
http://www.manchester.gov.uk/libraries/central/
langlit/index.htm
General guide to department e-resources.

Enquiries:
Enquiries to: Librarian

Founded:
1852

Organisation type and purpose:
Local government body, public library.

Subject coverage:
Language; literature; folklore.

**Museum or gallery collection, archive, or library
special collection:**
Alexander Ireland Collection (works by or relating
  to Charles and Mary Lamb, William Hazlitt,
  Leigh Hunt, Thomas and Jane Carlyle, Ralph W
  Emerson)
Bellot Chinese Collection
Brontë Collection
Coleridge Collection
de Quincey Collection
Elizabeth Gaskell Collection
Foreign library (lending collection of literature in
  28 languages)
Index of local translators
James L Hodson Collection
Language courses on tape for loan (72 languages)
Literature and criticism on cassette
Manchester Ballad and Chapbook Collections
Videos of literary interest

Non-library collection catalogue:
All or part available in-house

Access to staff:
Contact by letter, by telephone, by fax, by e-mail
and in person
Hours: Mon to Thu, 0900 to 2000; Fri, 0900 to 1700;
Sat, 0900 to 1700

MANCHESTER LAW LIBRARY

Formal name: Manchester Incorporated Law
Library Society
Acronym or abbreviation: MILLS

14 Kennedy Street, Manchester, M2 4BY

Tel: 0161 236 6312
Fax: 0161 236 6119
E-mail: librarian@manchester-law-library.co.uk

Website:
http://www.manchester-law-library.co.uk

Enquiries:
Enquiries to: Librarian

Founded:
1820

Organisation type and purpose:
Membership association.
Subscription Library for practising barristers,
solicitors and in-house lawyers.

Subject coverage:
All aspects of law likely to be of interest to
practising lawyers.

**Museum or gallery collection, archive, or library
special collection:**
nominate reports and local and personal acts from
  1837

Library catalogue:
All or part available in-house

Access to staff:
Contact by letter, by telephone, by fax, by e-mail
and in person. Access for members only. All
charged.

Access to building, collection or gallery:
Hours: Mon to Fri, 0900 to 1700
Special comments: members only

MANCHESTER METROPOLITAN UNIVERSITY – DEPARTMENT OF INFORMATION AND COMMUNICATIONS

Geoffrey Manton Building, Rosamond Street West,
off Oxford Road, Manchester, M15 6LL

Fax: 0161 247 6351
E-mail: infcomms-hums@mmu.ac.uk

Website:
http://www.hlss.mmu.ac.uk/infocomms/
Course details, research information, contact
details.

Enquiries:
Enquiries to: Executive assistant, HLSS

Organisation type and purpose:
University department or institute.

Subject coverage:
Library and information education and research.

Access to staff:
Contact by letter, by telephone, by fax, by e-mail
and via website. Appointment necessary.
Hours: Mon to Fri, 0900 to 1700

Access for disabled people:
Parking provided, level entry, access to all public
areas, toilet facilities

MANCHESTER METROPOLITAN UNIVERSITY – UNIVERSITY LIBRARY

All Saints Building, Grosvenor Square, Oxford
Road, Manchester, M15 6BH

Tel: 0161 247 3096
Fax: 0161 247 6349
E-mail: lib-website@mmu.ac.uk

Website:
http://www.mmu.ac.uk/services/library
Information about services, access to catalogue and
to other Web resources.

Enquiries:
Enquiries to: Librarian
Direct e-mail: c.harris@mmu.ac.uk

Founded:
1992

Organisation type and purpose:
University library.

Subject coverage:
Art and design; business studies; clothing
technology; education; finance and accounting;
health sciences; home economics; hotel and
catering studies; humanities; languages; law;
librarianship; management; media studies; music;
psychology; science; social science; speech
pathology; sports science and technology.

**Museum or gallery collection, archive, or library
special collection:**
Artists Archives, including Barnet Freedman,
  Rigby Graham, Paul Hogarth
Book Design Collection (12,000 items including
  1000 artists' books)
Children's Book Collection (3000 items, 19th and
  20th century books and periodicals)
Cotton Collection (history of 20th century cotton
  trade)
Historical collection of books on cookery and
  household management from the 17th to mid-
  20th century
Laura Seddon Collection of Victorian and
  Edwardian greeting cards
Local Studies (3000 items)
Manchester Society of Architects' Library (books
  on 18th and 19th century architecture)
Morten-Dandy Collection (19th century children's
  fiction, textbooks, readers and picture books)
Nonesuch Press (250 items)
Sir Harry Page Collection of Victorian Ephemera

Library catalogue:
All or part available online

Printed publications:
Illustrated Exhibition Catalogues mostly related to
  the Library's Book Design collection

Access to staff:
Contact by letter, by e-mail and via website.
Appointment necessary.
Hours: Mon to Fri, 0900 to 1630

MANIPULATION ASSOCIATION OF CHARTERED PHYSIOTHERAPISTS

Formal name: Manipulation Association of Chartered Physiotherapists
Acronym or abbreviation: MACP

Chartered Society of Physiotherapy, 14 Bedford Row, London, WC1R 4ED

Tel: 020 7306 6666
Fax: 020 7306 6611
E-mail: macp_admin@btinternet.com

Website:
http://www.macp-online.co.uk
Details of organisation, benefits of membership, directory of members, guidance papers, touch-note.

Enquiries:
Enquiries to: Administrator
Direct tel: 01992 589380

Founded:
1967

Organisation type and purpose:
Professional body (membership is by qualification), present number of members: 850, training organisation.
To maintain and further develop clinical excellence in neuro-musculoskeletal physiotherapy which will be of benefit to the current and future needs of both the profession and the general public.

Subject coverage:
Physiotherapy, manual therapy, manipulation, neuro-musculoskeletal physiotherapy.

Printed publications:
Touchnote (free to subscribing members)
Manual Therapy (4 times a year, pub Churchill Livingstone)
Order printed publications from: Manual Therapy, Churchill Livingstone Marketing
Robert Stevenson House, 1–3 Baxter's Place, Leith Walk, Edinburgh, EH1 3AF, tel: 0800 801 405

Publications list:
Available online

Access to staff:
Contact by letter, by telephone, by fax, by e-mail and via website
Hours: Mon to Fri, 0900 to 1700

Group within the:
Chartered Society of Physiotherapy
14 Bedford Row, London, WC1R 4ED; tel: 020 7366 6666; fax: 020 7306 6611

MANORIAL SOCIETY OF GREAT BRITAIN

Acronym or abbreviation: MSGB

104 Kennington Road, London, SE11 6RE

Tel: 020 7735 6633
Fax: 020 7582 7022
E-mail: manorial@msgb.co.uk

Website:
http://www.msgb.co.uk
Website with information on the Society and sales. Titles in upcoming auctions.

Enquiries:
Enquiries to: Chairman
Direct tel: 020 7582 1588

Founded:
1906

Organisation type and purpose:
International organisation, learned society (membership is by election or invitation), research organisation, publishing house.

Subject coverage:
Holders and addresses of feudal titles; legal research into title; holders and addresses of British peerage and baronetage; publishers; conference and exhibitions (all historical) organisers.

Museum or gallery collection, archive, or library special collection:
Historical, topographical and genealogical library
Paper file on 4500 manors and feudal baronies. Not available to general public

Trade and statistical information:
Sale price of titles (2006) ranges from £6000 to £40,000: 80% UK, most of rest US and Canada.

Publications list:
Available in print

Access to staff:
Contact by letter, by telephone, by fax and by e-mail. Appointment necessary.
Hours: Mon to Fri, 1000 to 1700
Special comments: No members of the public except by appointment

Access to building, collection or gallery:
Prior appointment required

Affiliated to:
English Manor Register Ltd
Institute of Constitutional research
Manorial Auctioneers Limited
  tel: 020 7582 1588; fax: 020 7582 7022; e-mail: msgb@manor.net
Smith's Peerage Limited
  tel: 020 7793 0063; fax: 020 7582 7022; e-mail: msgb@manor.net

MANX NATIONAL HERITAGE LIBRARY

Acronym or abbreviation: MNH

Manx Museum and National Trust, Kingswood Grove, Douglas, Isle of Man, IM1 3LY, Isle of Man

Tel: 01624 648000
Fax: 01624 648001
E-mail: enquiries@mnh.gov.im

Website:
http://www.gov.im/mnh

Enquiries:
Enquiries to: Librarian-Archivist

Founded:
1886

Organisation type and purpose:
National government body, registered charity (charity number 603), museum, art gallery, public library, research organisation.
National reference library and archives of the Isle of Man.

Subject coverage:
Manx studies, particularly history, archaeology, folklore, natural history and art, all aspects of Manx heritage, politics, international relations, economy, peoples, music etc, 12th century to present.

Special visitor services:
Film theatre, restaurant, galleries.

Museum or gallery collection, archive, or library special collection:
Family Papers of the Derby and Atholl Families, relating to their Lordship of the Isle of Man
Manx Government Records, 1417 to the present

Printed publications:
Bibliography of the literature of the Isle of Man, vol. I 1933, vol. II 1939
Guides and handbooks
Guides to branch museums
History of the Isle of Man
Journal of the Manx Museum
Order printed publications from: Website

Electronic and video publications:
See website

Publications list:
Available in print

Access to staff:
Contact by letter, by telephone, by fax, by e-mail and in person
Hours: Mon to Sat, 1000 to 1700

Access to building, collection or gallery:
No access other than to staff
Hours: Mon to Sat, 1000 to 1700

Access for disabled people:
Disabled access available
Hours: Mon to Sat, 1000 to 1700

MAPLE SOCIETY

The Membership Secretary, 12 Rustens Manor Road, Wymondham, Norfolk, NR18 0NH

Enquiries:
Enquiries to: Membership Secretary
Other contacts: Chairman for technical information.

Founded:
1991

Organisation type and purpose:
International organisation, membership association (membership is by subscription), present number of members: 152.
To dispense information on and facilitate the study of Maples.

Subject coverage:
Cultivation and after care, indentification, historical information of Maple species and 'Japanese Maples'.

Printed publications:
The Newsletter (quarterly, to members, free; otherwise by subscription)

Access to staff:
Contact by letter and by telephone

MARENDAZ SPECIAL CAR REGISTER

c/o 107 Old Bath Road, Cheltenham, Gloucestershire, GL53 7DA

Enquiries:
Enquiries to: Registrar

Founded:
1971

Organisation type and purpose:
Register.

Subject coverage:
Marendaz Special cars, technical information, historical data, photographs.

Access to staff:
Contact by letter

MARGARINE AND SPREADS ASSOCIATION

Acronym or abbreviation: MSA

6 Catherine Street, London, WC2B 5JJ

Tel: 020 7836 2460
Fax: 020 7379 5735
E-mail: jhowarth@fdf.org.uk

Website:
http://www.margarine.org.uk
History, chemistry, manufacturing, nutrition and health and uses of margarine and spreads

Enquiries:
Enquiries to: Secretary General
Direct tel: 020 7420 7121 (direct)

Founded:
1966

Organisation type and purpose:
Trade association (membership is by subscription, qualification, election or invitation), present number of members: 9, manufacturing industry.

Subject coverage:
The UK margarine and spread industry, including the history and chemistry of margarine and spreads and how they are manufactured. Nutrition

and health information relating to the role played by fats in the diet. Specialist area: all legislation pertaining to food.

Trade and statistical information:
Production statistics and value.

Printed publications:
Brochure – Lifting the lid, spreading the word, raising the standards

Access to staff:
Contact by letter, by telephone, by fax, by e-mail and via website. Appointment necessary.
Hours: Mon to Fri, 0930 to 1730

Links with:
International Federation of Margarine Associations (IFMA)
International Margarine Association of the countries of Europe (IMACE)

Member of:
The Food and Drink Federation

MARGERY KEMPE SOCIETY, THE

1 Auckland Road, London, SW11 1EW

Tel: 020 7924 5868

Enquiries:
Enquiries to: Honorary Treasurer

Founded:
1999

Organisation type and purpose:
National organisation, learned society (membership is by subscription), present number of members: 15.
To encourage and facilitate study of Margery Kempe, late medieval female piety.

Subject coverage:
Margery Kempe.

Printed publications:
Newsletter (members only)
Bibliography (members only)

Access to staff:
Contact by letter
Hours: Mon to Fri, 0900 to 1700

MARIA MONTESSORI TRAINING ORGANISATION

Acronym or abbreviation: MMTO

26 Lyndhurst Gardens, London, NW3 5NW

Tel: 020 7435 3646
Fax: 020 7431 8096
E-mail: info@mariamontessori.org

Website:
http://www.montessori-ami.org

Founded:
1952

Organisation type and purpose:
Registered charity (charity number 313087)
Training adults to work with children using the Montessori approach to education.
Also runs 5 Montessori schools in London.

Subject coverage:
Institute which trains people in the Montessori approach to education, specialising in children under six years old (AMI International Diploma on completion).

Printed publications:
Training Course Prospectus

Access to staff:
Contact by letter, by telephone, by fax and by e-mail. Appointment necessary.
Hours: Mon to Fri, 0900 to 1600

Links with:
Association Montessori Internationale (AMI)
Koninginneweg 161, 1075 CN Amsterdam, The Netherlands; tel: +31 206 798932; fax: +31 206 767341; e-mail: ami@xs4all.nl; website: http://www.montessori-ami.org

MARINE CONSERVATION SOCIETY

Acronym or abbreviation: MCS

9 Gloucester Road, Ross-on-Wye, Herefordshire, HR9 5BU

Tel: 01989 566017
Fax: 01989 567815
E-mail: info@mcsuk.org

Website:
http://www.mcsuk.org
http://www.goodbeachguide.co.uk
http://www.adoptabeach.org.uk

Enquiries:
Enquiries to: Communications Officer

Founded:
1983

Organisation type and purpose:
Professional body, membership association (membership is by subscription), registered charity (charity number 1004005).
The UK's national charity for the protection of the marine environment and its wildlife.

Subject coverage:
Water quality, coastal zone management, marine debris, fisheries, marine wildlife, toxins in the marine environment, coral reefs.

Museum or gallery collection, archive, or library special collection:
Marine environment and marine wildlife photographic library
Transparencies available for use under licence and fee

Trade and statistical information:
Annual Beachwatch Report (sources and quantity of UK beach litter).
Good Beach Guide (Recommended UK beaches where bathing water quality is considered safe to use).

Library catalogue:
All or part available in-house

Printed publications:
The Good Fish Guide Marine Conservation Magazine
Beachwatch Report
Information Packs on: Coral Reef Conservation; Marine Species; Marine Habitats; Pollution; Sea Empress
Marine Conservation – The UK Action Guide
No Take Zones – A Realistic Tool for Fisheries Management
School Curriculum Packs
The Good Beach Guide
The Species Directory (British Isles and Surrounding Areas)

Publications list:
Available online and in print

Access to staff:
Contact by letter, by telephone, by fax, by e-mail and via website
Hours: Mon to Fri, 0900 to 1700

Access to building, collection or gallery:
No prior appointment required
Special comments: Members only.

Also at:
Marine Conservation Society
3 Coates Place, Edinburgh, EH3 7AA; tel: 0131 226 6360; fax: 0131 226 2391; e-mail: mcs.scotland@care4free.net

MARINE ENGINE AND EQUIPMENT MANUFACTURERS ASSOCIATION

Acronym or abbreviation: MEEMA

56 Braycourt Avenue, Walton-on-Thames, Surrey, KT12 2BA

Tel: 01932 224910
Fax: 01932 224910

E-mail: bcbaali@aol.com

Website:
http://www.bmif.co.uk

Enquiries:
Enquiries to: Secretary

Founded:
1960

Organisation type and purpose:
Trade association, present number of members: 75.

Subject coverage:
For UK companies within the British Marine Industries Federation who have a common interest in the manufacture or distribution and retail sales of marine engines and related equipment, including personal watercraft.

Access to staff:
Contact by letter, by telephone, by fax and by e-mail
Hours: Mon to Fri, 0900 to 1700

Affiliated to:
British Marine Industries Federation
tel: 01784 473377; fax: 01784 439678; e-mail: bmif@bmif.co.uk

MARINE LEISURE ASSOCIATION

Acronym or abbreviation: MLA

General Secretary, Marine Leisure Association, Burrwood, 24 Peterscroft Avenue, Southampton, SO40 7AB

Tel: 023 8029 3822
Fax: 023 8029 3888
E-mail: info@marineleisure.co.uk

Website:
http://www.marineleisure.co.uk

Enquiries:
Enquiries to: General Secretary

Founded:
1964

Formerly called:
Association of Bonded Sailing Companies, National Federation of Sea Schools, Yacht Charter Assocation (year of change 2005)

Organisation type and purpose:
Trade association for training, charter and holidays. Formed to offer the general public better protection, guidance and advice. A Group Association within the BMF (British Marine Federation), representing MLA Members' views within the BMF Council. All members are expected to abide by both the MLA Code of Conduct and the BMF Code of Practice. Has representation on various National Committees to safeguard interests of Members and the general public.

Subject coverage:
Marine leisure industry.

Trade and statistical information:
Statistics on the marine leisure industry including participation, economic benefits, labour market assessment, tourism and industry assessment.

Printed publications:
MLA Bareboat Charter Agreement, MLA Skippered Charter Agreement and MLA Management Charter Agreement available for sale; a discounted price is available for multiple purchases
Annual membership brochure containing a full A-Z membership listing together with guidance information on training, charter and holidays worldwide

Access to staff:
Contact by letter, by telephone, by fax, by e-mail and via website. Appointment necessary.
Hours: Mon to Fri, 0900 to 1700

continued overleaf

Parent body:
British Marine Federation (BMF)
tel: 01784 473377; fax: 01784 439678; e-mail:
info@britishmarine.co.uk; website: http://www
.britishmarine.co.uk

MARINE SOCIETY, THE

202 Lambeth Road, London, SE1 7JW

Tel: 020 7261 9535
Fax: 020 7401 2537
E-mail: enq@marine-society.org

Website:
http://www.marine-society.org
Details of services and activities.

Enquiries:
Enquiries to: Director

Founded:
1756

Organisation type and purpose:
Voluntary organisation, registered charity (charity
number 313013), training organisation.
Education, training and welfare of seafarers.

Subject coverage:
Merchant Navy, Royal Navy, careers at sea,
seafaring.

**Museum or gallery collection, archive, or library
special collection:**
All above Records held at National Maritime
Museum
British Ship Adoption Society (from 1936)
Incorporated Thames Nautical Training College
(from 1862)
Marine Society Records (from 1756)
Seafarers Education Service (from 1919)

Printed publications:
General Publications on the Society (free)
Schools posters and Project material on Marine
subjects (price on application)
The Seafarer (quarterly, £10 p.a.)

Access to staff:
Contact by letter, by telephone, by fax, by e-mail,
in person and via website
Hours: Mon to Fri, 0900 to 1700

Access to building, collection or gallery:
Prior appointment required

Access for disabled people:
Parking provided, ramped entry

MARITIME AND COASTGUARD
AGENCY

Acronym or abbreviation: MCA

Spring Place, 105 Commercial Road, Southampton,
SO15 1EG

Tel: 023 8032 9100\ 0870 600 6505 (Infoline)
Fax: 023 8032 9122
E-mail: infoline@mcga.gov.uk

Website:
http://www.mcga.gov.uk
Work of MCA, publications, flagging-in, contact
list, contingency plan.

Enquiries:
Enquiries to: Publications Manager
Direct tel: 023 8032 9401
Direct e-mail: mca_mic@mcga.gov.uk

Founded:
1998

Organisation type and purpose:
National Government Agency.

Subject coverage:
Civil maritime search and rescue, maritime safety,
major oil spillages and other hazardous substances
at sea from ships, civil maritime emergencies,
safety advice and assistance to local authorities,
and port and harbour authorities, merchant
shipping, carriage by sea of dangerous goods,
hovercraft and high speed craft legislation, safety

of navigation and related topics, ownership of
items found in or on the shores of the sea or any
tidal water.

Trade and statistical information:
National and international fleet and accident
statistics.

Printed publications:
Codes of Practice (available from TSO)
Consolidated List of M Notices (available from
TSO, £120)
MSN, MGN & MIN – Mail Marketing (Scotland)
Also available on MCA website

Access to staff:
Contact by letter, by telephone, by fax, by e-mail
and via website. Appointment necessary.
Hours: Mon to Fri, 0900 to 1700

Access for disabled people:
Level entry, toilet facilities

Executive Agency of:
Department of Transport

Other addresses:
Branches throughout the UK

MARITIME INFORMATION
ASSOCIATION

Acronym or abbreviation: MIA

The Marine Society, 202 Lambeth Road, London,
SE1 7JW

Website:
http://www.maritime-information.org

Enquiries:
Enquiries to: Honorary Secretary

Founded:
1977

Organisation type and purpose:
Professional body (membership is by subscription).
Forum for those active in maritime information,
with regular visits, an annual conference and
opportunities to network.

Subject coverage:
Marine technology; shipping; shipbuilding; marine
engineering and telecommunications; maritime
law and economics; maritime history; ports; cargo
handling; fisheries; offshore activities (not marine
biology or life sciences).

Printed publications:
List of Members (for members only)
Marine Information: a guide to libraries and
sources of information in the UK (4th ed., 2004,
£25)

Access to staff:
Contact by fax

MARKET RESEARCH SOCIETY

Acronym or abbreviation: MRS

15 Northburgh Street, London, EC1V 0JR

Tel: 020 7490 4911
Fax: 020 7490 0608
E-mail: info@mrs.org.uk

Website:
http://www.mrs.org.uk
Information on MRS, including training,
qualifications, products and events.

Founded:
1946

Organisation type and purpose:
Professional body.

Subject coverage:
Methodology of market research; market research
industry.

Non-library collection catalogue:
All or part available online and in-house

Library catalogue:
All or part available online and in-house

Printed publications:
International Journal of Market Research
MRS Conference Proceedings
Occupation Groupings: A Job Directory
Research (monthly)
Research Buyer's Guide
Range of guidelines on market research

Electronic and video publications:
Research Buyer's Guide
Order electronic and video publications from: http://
www.rbg.org.uk

Publications list:
Available online

Access to staff:
Contact by letter, by telephone, by fax, by e-mail
and via website. Access for members only.
Hours: Mon to Fri, 1000 to 1700

MARKETING GUILD, THE

Regency House, Westminster Place, York Business
Park, York, YO26 6RW

Tel: 01904 520820
Fax: 01904 520899
E-mail: help@marketing-guild.com

Website:
http://www.marketing-guild.com
Marketing ideas and free sample reports.

Enquiries:
Enquiries to: Managing Director

Founded:
1986

Organisation type and purpose:
Professional body (membership is by subscription),
present number of members: 1400, service
industry.
Marketing ideas and support for professional and
service businesses.

Subject coverage:
Marketing and sales information, ideas and
strategies.

Printed publications:
Strategic Marketing (newsletter)
Marketing Insider
Marketing in Action

Electronic and video publications:
Encyclopaedia of marketing strategies with
support manuals (Argosy CD software)
Audio cassettes and training

Publications list:
Available online and in print

Access to staff:
Contact by letter, by telephone and by e-mail.
Non-members charged.
Hours: Mon to Fri, 0900 to 1700

Connected with and at the same address as the:
Internet Marketing Guild

MARKS AND CLERK

Sussex House, 83–85 Mosley Street, Manchester,
M2 3LG

Tel: 0161 236 2275
Fax: 0161 236 5846
E-mail: manchester@marks-clerk.com

Website:
http://www.marks-clerk.com
Details of UK and International offices, history of
the firm, information service on all aspects of
intellectual property.

Enquiries:
Enquiries to: Information Manager
Direct tel: 0161 233 5803

Founded:
1887

Organisation type and purpose:
Service industry.

Professional firm of patent and trade mark agents.

Subject coverage:
Patents; trade marks; designs; copyright; licensing; intellectual property; technology licensing, litigation.

Access to staff:
Contact by letter, by telephone, by fax and by e-mail. Appointment necessary.
Hours: Mon to Fri, 0900 to 1700

MARLOWE SOCIETY, THE

The Secretary, Address: 27, Melbourne Court, Randolph Avenue, London, W9 1BJ

E-mail: valerie.colin-russ@marlowe-society.org

Website:
http://www.marlowe-society.org
Society news, membership details, meetings and events, Marlowe's life, education, works, reference books

Enquiries:
Enquiries to: Membership Secretary

Founded:
1955

Organisation type and purpose:
International organisation, learned society (membership is by subscription), present number of members: 140, registered charity (charity number 1075418).
To promote interest and research into Christopher Marlowe, Elizabethan poet/dramatist.

Subject coverage:
Christopher Marlowe's life and works; his associates; his contribution to the growth of secular drama; life in the Tudor period; contemporary dramatists, particularly those influenced by Marlowe. A memorial in Poets Corner, Westminster Abbey 2002.

Non-library collection catalogue:
All or part available online

Library catalogue:
All or part available online

Printed publications:
Newsletter (periodically; free to members)
Occasional booklets

Publications list:
Available online

Access to staff:
Contact by letter, by telephone, by fax, by e-mail and via website. Appointment necessary.
Hours: Mon to Fri, 0900 to 1700

MARTIN CENTRE FOR ARCHITECTURAL AND URBAN STUDIES

University of Cambridge, Department of Architecture, 6 Chaucer Road, Cambridge, CB2 2EB

Tel: 01223 331700
Fax: 01223 331701

Website:
http://www.arct.cam.uc.uk/

Enquiries:
Enquiries to: Publications Officer

Founded:
1967

Organisation type and purpose:
University department or institute, research organisation.

Subject coverage:
Environmental design, architectural acoustics, energy conservation, Third World planning and construction technology, building in earthquake areas, computer-aided design.

Museum or gallery collection, archive, or library special collection:
British New Towns collection

Printed publications:
Annual Report
Occasional reports and working papers

Access to staff:
Contact by letter, by telephone and by fax
Hours: Mon to Fri, 0900 to 1700

Within the:
Cambridge University Department of Architecture

MARX MEMORIAL LIBRARY

37A Clerkenwell Green, London, EC1R 0DU

Tel: 020 7253 1485
Fax: 020 7251 6039
E-mail: info@marx-memorial-library.org

Website:
http://www.marx-memorial-library.org

Enquiries:
Enquiries to: Librarian

Founded:
1933

Organisation type and purpose:
National organisation, membership association (membership is by subscription), registered charity (charity number 270309), historic building, house or site.
Independent subscription library.
To provide materials for the study of Marxism, socialism and history of working class movements.

Subject coverage:
Marxist classics, philosophy, economics, political theory, labour and trade union history, social conditions and movements, early socialist thought (radical, chartist, etc.), international working class movement), socialist countries, Spanish Civil War, US Labor Movement, peace.

Museum or gallery collection, archive, or library special collection:
BSP and SDF pamphlets
Daily Worker and Morning Star (bound vols)
General Strike
International Brigade – Spanish Civil War (International Brigade Archive)
J. D. Bernal Peace Movement Library (books and documents from the libraries of Prof. J. D. Bernal and Ivor Montagu)
James Klugman Collection (books, pamphlets and tracts mainly of the Chartist and early British Labour Movement, and ceramics)
John Williamson American Labour History Collection
May Day
Photograph library
Spanish War and International Brigade Collection
US labour and socialist history 1920–70s

Printed publications:
Bulletin (2 times a year)
Spanish War and International Brigade catalogue (3 vols)

Microform publications:
BSP and SDF Pamphlets, Daily Worker 1938–1941
Inprecorr to be read on site
International Brigade Memorial Archive (Collection up to 1986, available from Mindata Ltd Bath)

Electronic and video publications:
Videos of Library lectures
Videos and CD-ROM of library history, present and future

Access to staff:
Contact by letter, by telephone, by fax, by e-mail and in person. Appointment necessary. Access for members only.
Hours: Mon to Thu, 1300 to 1800 (visitors 1300 to 1400, or by appointment)

Access for disabled people:
Ramped entry
Special comments: Access to ground floor. Books brought to desk on ground floor for readers unable to reach first floor reading room.

MARY ROSE TRUST

Acronym or abbreviation: PORMR

College Road, HM Naval Base, Portsmouth, Hampshire, PO1 3LX

Tel: 023 9275 0521
Fax: 023 9287 0588
E-mail: mail@maryrose.org

Website:
http://www.maryrose.org

Founded:
1979

Organisation type and purpose:
Museum, research organisation, tourist attraction.
Registered Charity Number 277503; Registered Company Number 1415654 England; VAT Registration Number GB 339 0628 49.
Designated as an Outstanding Collection and MLA Accredited Museum.
Objectives: to find, record, excavate, raise, bring ashore, preserve, publish, report on and display for all time in Portsmouth the Mary Rose. To establish, equip and maintain a museum or museums in Portsmouth to house the Mary Rose and related or associated material. To promote and develop interest, research and knowledge relating to the Mary Rose and all matters relating to the underwater cultural heritage. All for the education and benefit of the nation.

Subject coverage:
Henry VIII's warship Mary Rose, launched in 1511, social and maritime history of the Tudor period, evolution of the wooden ship in the late medieval period, conservation and care of material excavated from wet sites, archaeology and underwater technology.

Museum or gallery collection, archive, or library special collection:
The Mary Rose (the only recovered 16th-century warship) together with the excavated military, domestic and personal artefacts, ecofacts and human remains.
Excavation archive.
Photographic library for hire.

Non-library collection catalogue:
All or part available online

Printed publications:
The Archaeology of the Mary Rose (vols 1–5)
Annual Reports
Leaflets and fact sheets
Firstwatch

Electronic and video publications:
Video for hire

Publications list:
Available online

Access to staff:
Contact by letter, by telephone, by e-mail and via website. Appointment necessary.
Hours: Mon to Fri, 1000 to 1700
Special comments: The Trust is located in an operational Naval Base. MoD security restrictions may apply.

Constituent bodies:
Mary Rose Society and Mary Rose Information Group
c/o The Mary Rose Trust, College Road, HM Naval Base, Portsmouth, Hampshire, PO1 3LX; tel: 023 9275 0521; fax: 023 9287 0588; e-mail: mail@maryrose.org

MASTER CARVERS' ASSOCIATION

Unit 20, 21 Wren Street, London, WC1X 0HF

continued overleaf

Tel: 020 7278 8759
Fax: 020 7278 8759
E-mail: info@mastercarvers.co.uk

Website:
http://www.mastercarvers.co.uk/

Enquiries:
Enquiries to: Honorary Secretary

Founded:
1897

Organisation type and purpose:
Trade association.
Promotion and protection of the interests of stone carving, woodcarving and modelling generally, and of the members of the association in particular.

Subject coverage:
Wood and stone carving; architectural furniture, restoration, ecclesiastical, heraldic, conservation, apprenticeship; rates of wages and conditions of service; modelling.

Printed publications:
List of Members and their specialist crafts

Access to staff:
Contact by letter, by telephone, by fax and by e-mail. Appointment necessary.
Hours: Mon to Fri, 0900 to 1700

MASTER LOCKSMITHS ASSOCIATION

Acronym or abbreviation: MLA

5D Great Central Way, Woodford Halse, Daventry, Northamptonshire, NN11 3PZ

Tel: 01327 262255
Fax: 01327 262539
E-mail: enquiries@locksmiths.co.uk

Website:
http://www.locksmiths.co.uk/

Enquiries:
Enquiries to: Chief Executive Officer

Founded:
1958

Organisation type and purpose:
Advisory body, professional body, trade association, training organisation, consultancy.

Subject coverage:
Physical security, mechanical security, locks, safes, vehicle security, access systems, training, consultancy, expert witness, product testing, keycutting, bolts.

Museum or gallery collection, archive, or library special collection:
Collection of books on locksmithing – reference purposes and for use by members only

Printed publications:
Keyways (magazine, 6 times a year, members)
Lists of Trade Division Members

Access to staff:
Contact by letter, by telephone, by fax and by e-mail. Appointment necessary. Letter of introduction required.
Hours: Mon to Fri, 0830 to 1700

Affiliated to:
Associated Locksmiths of Ireland

Affiliated to:
Associated Locksmiths of America
European Locksmiths Federation

Subsidiary body:
British Locksmiths Institute
MLA Trade Division

MASTER PHOTOGRAPHERS ASSOCIATION OF GREAT BRITAIN

Acronym or abbreviation: MPA

Hallmark House, 1 Chancery Lane, Darlington, Co Durham, DL1 5QP

Tel: 01325 356555
Fax: 01325 357813
E-mail: mpa@mpauk.com

Website:
http://www.mpauk.com

Enquiries:
Enquiries to: Chief Executive

Founded:
1952

Organisation type and purpose:
Trade association.

Subject coverage:
Association for full-time professional photographers.

Access to staff:
Contact by letter, by telephone, by fax, by e-mail and via website
Hours: Mon to Fri, 0900 to 1700

MASTERFOODS EDUCATION CENTRE

Acronym or abbreviation: MEC

4 Bedford Square, London, WC1B 3RA

Tel: 020 7255 1100
Fax: 020 7631 0602

Website:
http://www.pet-educationresources.co.uk
Free worksheets to download for teaching literacy, numeracy, science and PSHE & Citizenship for Key Stages 1 and 2. Pets are the theme of the resources.

Enquiries:
Enquiries to: Public Relations Manager
Direct e-mail: mec@uk.grayling.com

Founded:
1971

Organisation type and purpose:
Suitable for ages: 4 to 11.

Subject coverage:
Resource material for schools about pets and responsible pet ownership; putting pets onto the National Curriculum in schools – applicable to Key Stages 1 and 2.

Printed publications:
Packs, posters, stories, leaflets

Publications list:
Available online and in print

Access to staff:
Contact by letter, by telephone, by fax and by e-mail
Hours: Mon to Fri, 0900 to 1700

MASTERS OF DEERHOUNDS ASSOCIATION

Acronym or abbreviation: MDHA

Bilboa House, Dulverton, Somerset, TA22 9DW

Tel: 01398 323475

Enquiries:
Enquiries to: Honorary Secretary

Founded:
1951

Organisation type and purpose:
Membership association.
Governing body of packs of hounds hunting wild deer in Great Britain.

Subject coverage:
Conservation and control of the last remaining sizeable herd of red deer in England, hunting wild deer with recognised packs of hounds.

Printed publications:
Pamphlets relevant to deer hunting (available on request)

Access to staff:
Contact by letter and by telephone
Hours: Mon to Fri, 0900 to 1700

MASTIC ASPHALT COUNCIL

Acronym or abbreviation: MAC

PO Box 77, Hastings, East Sussex, TN35 4WL

Tel: 01424 814400
Fax: 01424 814446
E-mail: masphaltco@aol.com

Website:
http://www.masticasphaltcouncil.co.uk

Enquiries:
Enquiries to: Director

Founded:
1948

Organisation type and purpose:
Trade association.

Subject coverage:
Information on the use of Mastic Asphalt with member lists and insurance backed guarantees.

Museum or gallery collection, archive, or library special collection:
Technical guide on the application of mastic asphalt. Information regarding codes of practice and British Standards

Publications list:
Available in print

Access to staff:
Contact by letter, by telephone, by fax, by e-mail and via website. Appointment necessary.
Hours: Mon to Fri, 0900 to 1700

Access to building, collection or gallery:
Prior appointment required

Member of:
National Specialist Contractors Council (NSCC)

MATERIALS HANDLING ENGINEERS ASSOCIATION

Acronym or abbreviation: MHEA

2B Hills Lane, Ely, Cambridgeshire, CB6 1AY

Tel: 01353 666298
Fax: 01353 666298
E-mail: pw@mhea.co.uk

Website:
http://www.mhea.co.uk

Enquiries:
Enquiries to: Secretary
Other contacts: Chairman of Technical Committee for technical or publications.

Founded:
1938

Organisation type and purpose:
Trade association.

Subject coverage:
The UK Centre for technical and commercial excellence regarding the manufacture and use of bulk and continuous materials handling equipment.

Printed publications:
Guide to the Design of Transfer Chutes & Chute Linings (2002)
Recommended Practice for Troughed Belt Conveyors (available for purchase)

Publications list:
Available in print

Access to staff:
Contact by letter, by telephone, by fax, by e-mail and via website
Special comments: Charges to non-members if justified.

Access to building, collection or gallery:
No access other than to staff

MATHEMATICAL ASSOCIATION

Acronym or abbreviation: MA

259 London Road, Leicester, LE2 3BE

Tel: 0116 221 0013
Fax: 0116 212 2835
E-mail: office@m-a.org.uk

Website:
http://www.m-a.org.uk

Enquiries:
Enquiries to: Senior Administrator
Direct e-mail: senioradministrator@m-a.org.uk

Founded:
1871

Organisation type and purpose:
Membership association (membership is by subscription), registered charity (charity number 313281).
To support and improve the teaching of mathematics.

Subject coverage:
Mathematics and the teaching of mathematics.

Museum or gallery collection, archive, or library special collection:
Library housed in Leicester University Library

Library catalogue:
All or part available in-house

Printed publications:
Books, reports covering infant years to 6th form for pupils and teachers including:
Mathematical Gazette (termly)
Mathematics in School (5 times a year)
Mathematical Pie (termly)
Primary Mathematics (termly)
Equals (termly)
Symmetry Plus+ (termly)
The MA News (termly)

Publications list:
Available online and in print

Access to staff:
Contact by letter, by telephone, by fax, by e-mail, in person and via website
Hours: Mon to Fri, 0900 to 1700

Access to building, collection or gallery:
No prior appointment required

Affiliated to:
JMC

MATHEMATICS RESEARCH CENTRE

Acronym or abbreviation: MRC

University of Warwick, Coventry, Warwickshire, CV4 7AL

Tel: 024 7652 8317
Fax: 024 7652 3548
E-mail: mrc@maths.warwick.ac.uk

Website:
http://www.maths.warwick.ac.uk/research

Enquiries:
Enquiries to: Secretary

Founded:
1968

Organisation type and purpose:
University department or institute, research organisation.
Symposium and conference organisation in mathematics.

Subject coverage:
Mathematics.

Access to staff:
Contact by e-mail. Appointment necessary.
Hours: Mon to Fri, 0900 to 1600

Associated with:
Mathematics Department, University of Warwick

MATRA ENTHUSIASTS' CLUB UK

Acronym or abbreviation: MEC

6 Woodlands Court, Woodlands Road, Harrow, Middlesex, HA1 2RU

Tel: 020 8861 1035
E-mail: roy@matraclub.org.uk

Website:
http://www.matraclub.org.uk/

Enquiries:
Enquiries to: Secretary
Direct tel: 01892 652964

Founded:
1983

Organisation type and purpose:
International organisation, membership association (membership is by subscription), present number of members: 150.

Subject coverage:
Technical and historical information Matra cars from 1964 to present day, including DJet, M530, Bagheera, Rancho, Murena, Espace.

Museum or gallery collection, archive, or library special collection:
Most books and magazines in English and French about Matra automobiles or containing road tests or reports of its products

Printed publications:
Newsletter (6 times a year, members)

Access to staff:
Contact by telephone, by fax, by e-mail and via website
Hours: Telephone 1800 to 2200

Connections with:
French, Belgian and other European clubs and the North American Matra Register

MCC

Formal name: Marylebone Cricket Club
Acronym or abbreviation: MCC

Library, Lord's Cricket Ground, St John's Wood, London, NW8 8QN

Tel: 0207 616 8559
Fax: 0207 616 8659
E-mail: mcclibrary@mcc.org.uk

Website:
http://www.lords.org/history/mcc-library

Enquiries:
Enquiries to: Collections Assistant

Founded:
1787

Organisation type and purpose:
Membership association (membership is by election or invitation), historic building, house or site.
Private Cricket Club.

Subject coverage:
History of cricket, modern cricket, scores and statistics, real tennis, some other sports, history of Lord's and the MCC.

Museum or gallery collection, archive, or library special collection:
Early cricket books and bats
Sir George Allen scrapbooks

Non-library collection catalogue:
All or part available in-house

Library catalogue:
All or part available in-house

Access to staff:
Contact by letter, by telephone, by e-mail and via website. Appointment necessary.
Hours: Mon to Thu, 1000 to 1700; Fri, 1000 to 1600
Special comments: Open Sat and Sun by arrangement on cricket days.

Access to building, collection or gallery:
Prior appointment required

MCDOUGALL TRUST

Formal name: Arthur McDougall Fund

6 Chancel Street, London, SE1 0UX

Tel: 020 7620 1080
Fax: 020 7928 1528
E-mail: admin@mcdougall.org.uk

Website:
http://www.mcdougall.org.uk

Enquiries:
Enquiries to: Executive Secretary
Other contacts: Chairman (for formal correspondence)

Founded:
1948

Organisation type and purpose:
Voluntary organisation, registered charity (charity number 212151), research organisation, publishing house.
To advance study and knowledge of economic and political science, especially electoral science and methods of election and government of representative organisations of all kinds.

Subject coverage:
All aspects of elections including electoral law and practice, voting systems, electoral reform, proportional representation, election monitoring, election campaigns, balloting in organisations of all kinds, representation and democracy, political science, suffrage.

Museum or gallery collection, archive, or library special collection:
2,500 books and 2,500 pamphlets
Early pamphlets on PR in Britain, USA, Australia, including Charles Dodgson
Papers of Lord Courtney of Penwith and Dr J. F. S. Ross
Pamphlets donated by H. R. Droop
Extensive press cuttings and other printed material from mid-19th century on electoral reform, proportional representation, suffrage and related issues
Reports on various recent international election observation missions

Trade and statistical information:
Electoral statistics relating to elections in the United Kingdom and elsewhere.

Non-library collection catalogue:
All or part available in-house

Library catalogue:
All or part available in-house

Printed publications:
Annual Report
Representation: Journal of Representative Democracy (ISSN: 0034–4893)
Twelve Democracies: Electoral Systems in the European Community (Enid Lakeman, out-of-print)
Comparative Electoral Systems (Robert A. Newland)
Order printed publications from: Executive Secretary, McDougall Trust

Access to staff:
Contact by letter, by telephone, by fax and by e-mail. Appointment necessary. Letter of introduction required.
Hours: Mon to Fri, 0930 to 1730

Access for disabled people:
Toilet facilities

Constituent bodies:
Lakeman Library for Electoral Studies
tel: 020 7620 1080; fax: 020 7928 1528; website: http://www.mcdougall.org.uk

Links with:
Electoral Reform Society
tel: 020 7928 1622

MCTIMONEY CHIROPRACTIC ASSOCIATION

Acronym or abbreviation: MCA

Crowmarsh Gifford, Wallingford, Oxfordshire, OX10 8DJ

Tel: 01491 829211
Fax: 01491 829492
E-mail: admin@mctimoney-chiropractic.org

Website:
http://www.mctimoney-chiropractic.org
Information on chiropractic treatment and practitioner location.

Enquiries:
Enquiries to: Administrator
Other contacts: Secretary

Founded:
1979

Organisation type and purpose:
Professional body, voluntary organisation, training organisation, research organisation.

Subject coverage:
McTimoney Chiropractic, education, training and information.

Trade and statistical information:
Membership and subject information data.

Printed publications:
Practitioner Directory
Human Chiropractic LFLT
Animal Chiropractic LFLT
Inhouse Magazine

Access to staff:
Contact by letter, by telephone, by fax and by e-mail. Appointment necessary. Non-members charged.
Hours: Mon to Fri, 0900 to 1700

MDC EVALUATIONS

Unit 4, Greenways Business Park, Bellinger Close, Chippenham, Wiltshire, SN15 1BN

Tel: 01249 467272
Fax: 01249 467273
E-mail: enquiry@mdcevaluations.co.uk

Website:
http://www.mdcevaluations.co.uk
Information on UK dairy industry. PTAs, statistics, bull/cow lists, publications.

Enquiries:
Enquiries to: PA to Technical Director

Founded:
2002

Subject coverage:
Predicted transmitting abilities for dairy bulls and cows in UK.
Genetic trends in UK dairy industry.
Industry statistics (UK dairy industry).
Technical information on UK evaluation system for dairy bulls and cows.

Trade and statistical information:
Statistics on UK dairy industry.

Non-library collection catalogue:
All or part available online

Printed publications:
Breed Books
Fact Sheets
Statistics Books
Technical Bulletin
Various publications free of charge, direct or website

Publications list:
Available online

Access to staff:
Contact by letter, by telephone, by fax, by e-mail and via website
Hours: Mon to Fri, 0900 to 1700

MDF THE BIPOLAR ORGANISATION

Acronym or abbreviation: MDF

Castle Works, 21 St Georges Road, London, SE1 6ES

Tel: 08456 340540
Fax: 020 7793 2639
E-mail: mdf@mdf.org.uk

Website:
http://www.mdf.org.uk
Books, factsheets.

Enquiries:
Enquiries to: Administrator

Founded:
1984

Organisation type and purpose:
National organisation, membership association (membership is by subscription), present number of members: 4000, voluntary organisation, registered charity (charity number 293340).

Subject coverage:
Mental health, manic depression, self-help group support, drug treatment, self-management.

Non-library collection catalogue:
All or part available online and in print

Library catalogue:
All or part available online

Printed publications:
Information pack (free)
Leaflets, factsheets, books
Pendulum (journal, quarterly)

Publications list:
Available in print

Access to staff:
Contact by letter, by telephone, by fax, by e-mail and via website
Hours: Mon to Fri, 0900 to 1700

ME ASSOCIATION

Formal name: Myalgic Encephalopathy Association
Acronym or abbreviation: MEA

7 Apollo Office Court, Radclive Road, Gawcott, Buckinghamshire, MK18 4DF

Tel: 01280 818968
E-mail: meconnect@meassociation.org.uk

Website:
http://www.meassociation.org.uk

Enquiries:
Enquiries to: Publicity and Fundraising Manager
Direct tel: 01406 370293
Direct e-mail: tbritton02@yahoo.com

Founded:
1976

Organisation type and purpose:
Registered Charity Number 801279. The MEA is a campaigning national charity that provides information and support to an estimated 240,000 people in the United Kingdom with ME/Chronic Fatigue Syndrome, their families and carers. This is provided through a quarterly magazine, literature, education and training. We also run ME Connect, the United Kingdom's premier helpline for people with ME/CFS. The charity supports research into the physical nature and cause of ME via The MEA Ramsay Research Fund

Subject coverage:
Myalgic encephalopathy (ME) – information, support, education and training.

Information services:
Telephone helpline open daily, 1000 to 1200, 1400 to 1600, 1900 to 2100: 0870 444 1836

Non-library collection catalogue:
All or part available online and in print

Library catalogue:
All or part available online and in print

Printed publications:
ME Essential magazine (quarterly, to members)
Extensive list of leaflets (available online)
Order printed publications from: Buckinghamshire office; tel. 01280 818968; e-mail meconnect@ meassociation.org.uk

Publications list:
Available online and in print

Access to staff:
Contact by letter, by telephone, by e-mail, in person and via website
Hours: Mon to Fri, 0930 to 1630

Also at:
The ME Association Publicity and Fundraising 60 Broadgate, Weston, Spalding, PE12 6HY; tel: 01406 370293; e-mail: tbritton02@yahoo.com

MECHANICAL-COPYRIGHT PROTECTION SOCIETY LIMITED

Acronym or abbreviation: MCPS

(Central London Office), Copyright House, 29–33 Berners Street, London, W1T 3AB

Tel: 020 7580 5544
Fax: 020 7306 4455
E-mail: info@mcps.co.uk

Website:
http://www.mcps.co.uk

Enquiries:
Enquiries to: Corporate Communications

Founded:
1924

Organisation type and purpose:
Membership association (membership is by subscription).
MCPS licenses the recording of its composer and publisher members copyright musical works in many different formats.

Subject coverage:
Music copyright and royalties; licensing of music recorded into any format; collection and distribution of mechanical royalties.

Printed publications:
Annual Report
For The Record
On the Right Track

Access to staff:
Contact by letter, by telephone, by fax, by e-mail and via website. Appointment necessary.
Hours: Mon to Fri, 0900 to 1700

Access for disabled people:
Ramped entry

Links with:
British Music Rights
Performing Right Society Limited

Parent body:
Music Publishers' Association

Streatham Office:
Mechanical-Copyright Protection Society Limited Elgar House, 41 Streatham High Road, London, SW16 1ER; tel: 020 8664 4400; fax: 020 8769 8792

MÉDECINS SANS FRONTIÈRES

Acronym or abbreviation: MSF

67–74 Saffron Hill, London, EC1N 8QX

Tel: 020 7404 6600
Fax: 020 7404 4466
E-mail: office@london.msf.org

Website:
http://www.msf.org

Enquiries:
Enquiries to: Public Information Administrator
Direct tel: 020 7404 6600
Other contacts: (1) Fundraising Administrator (2) Recruitment Assistant for (1) donation enquiries (2) recuitment enquiries.

Founded:
1971

Organisation type and purpose:
International organisation, voluntary organisation, registered charity (charity number 1026588).
To provide medical emergency relief to victims of disaster worldwide.

Subject coverage:
Humanitarian and medical aid, emergency relief.

Printed publications:
Dispatches (newsletter, quarterly, free)
International Activity Report (annually)
Order printed publications from: Médecins Sans Frontières
8 Rue Saint Sabin, Paris Cedex 11, 75544, France, tel: 00 33 1 40 21 29 29, fax: 00 33 1 48 06 68 68, e-mail: office@paris.msf.org

Access to staff:
Contact by letter, by telephone, by fax, by e-mail and via website. Appointment necessary.
Hours: Mon to Fri, 0900 to 1800
Special comments: No wheelchair access.

International office:
Médecins Sans Frontières
39 Rue de la Tourelle, Brussels, B-1040, Belgium; tel: 00 32 2 280 18 81; fax: 00 32 2 280 01 73

MEDIATION RESOURCE CENTRE

6 Cheston Street, Carrickfergus, Co Antrim, BT38 7BH

Tel: 028 9335 0377
Fax: 028 9335 0455
E-mail: davidmccombe@mrc6.fsnet.co.uk

Enquiries:
Enquiries to: Manager

Founded:
1997

Subject coverage:
Mediation, conflict resolution.

Printed publications:
The Other View (magazine, quarterly)

Access to staff:
Contact by letter, by telephone, by fax and by e-mail
Hours: Mon to Fri, 0800 to 1500

MEDIATION UK

Alexander House, Telephone Avenue, Bristol, BS1 4BS

Tel: 0117 904 6661
Fax: 0117 904 3331
E-mail: enquiry@mediationuk.org.uk

Website:
http://www.mediation.org.uk
Basic information, publications and conferences, training opportunities, services list, information about mediation.

Enquiries:
Enquiries to: Director

Founded:
1984

Organisation type and purpose:
National organisation, membership association (membership is by subscription), present number of members: 503, registered charity (charity number 1019275).
Network of projects, organisations and individuals interested in mediation and constructive conflict resolution; umbrella organisation for mediation schemes in the UK.
Mediation UK is a national charity which represents and promotes mediation within local communities. It has a membership of 170 registered services throughout the UK which offer mediation to parties in dispute. The majority of these services are free to the user, and a national helpline exists to direct the public to their nearest

mediation service. Services specialise in one or more areas including neighbour disputes, school bullying, and victim/offender mediation.
Mediation UK also supports mediation within the workplace, and sectors like the health service. Mediation UK is actively involved in encouraging the establishment of new mediation services around the country, as well as ensuring mediation services adhere to quality standards and guidelines.

Subject coverage:
Mediation and constructive conflict resolution, including neighbour disputes and community mediation; victim/offender mediation; conflict resolution and mediation in schools; other conflict resolution projects; training in mediation and conflict resolution skills.

Printed publications:
Annual Report
Information sheets, occasional papers
Introductory Leaflet
Mediation (magazine, for sale)
Training Manual in Community Mediation Skills
Conflict Resolution Peer Mediation in Schools – A Directory of Services and Training
The Rough Guide to Restorative Justice and the Crime & Disorder Act
Mediation Works
Victor/Offender Mediation Pack

Electronic and video publications:
Some printed material available in fully accessible formats

Publications list:
Available in print

Access to staff:
Contact by letter, by telephone, by fax, by e-mail and via website. Appointment necessary.
Hours: Mon to Fri, 0900 to 1700

Also at:
Mediation Wales
1 The Spa Centre, Station Crescent, Llandrindod Wells, Powys, LD1 5BB; tel: 01597 829100

MEDIAWATCH-UK

3 Willow House, Kennington Road, Ashford, Kent, TN24 0NR

Tel: 01233 633936
Fax: 01233 633836
E-mail: info@mediawatchuk.org

Website:
http://www.mediawatchuk.org

Enquiries:
Enquiries to: Director

Founded:
1965

Organisation type and purpose:
National organisation, membership association (membership is by subscription), voluntary organisation.
Campaigning for good media standards and effective reform of the law on obscenity.

Subject coverage:
Mass media, broadcasting, programme standards, obscene publications.

Printed publications:
Brochure (free on request)
mediawatch-uk newsbrief (3 times a year, formerly The Viewer and Listener)

Access to staff:
Contact by letter, by telephone, by fax, by e-mail and in person. Appointment necessary.
Hours: Mon to Fri, 0900 to 1700

MEDICAL ADVISORY SERVICE

Acronym or abbreviation: MAS

PO Box 3087, London, W4 4ZP

Tel: 020 8994 9874 (general medical)

Website:
http://www.medicaladvisoryservice.org.uk

Enquiries:
Enquiries to: Director
Direct tel: 020 8995 8503 (admin. only)
Direct fax: 020 8995 3275 (admin. only)

Founded:
1986

Organisation type and purpose:
Registered charity (charity number 295953).

Subject coverage:
General medical helpline to the public.

Printed publications:
Newsletter (quarterly, yearly membership)
A Guide to a good night's sleep (included in a general sleep information pack)
Order printed publications from: Medical Advisory Service
PO Box 3087, London, W4 4ZP

Publications list:
Available in print

Access to staff:
Contact by letter and by telephone
Hours: Mon to Fri, 1800 to 2000

Links with:
Sleep Matters
PO Box 3087, London, W4 4ZP; tel: 020 8994 9874

MEDICAL ADVISORY SERVICES FOR TRAVELLERS ABROAD

Acronym or abbreviation: MASTA

29 Harley Street, London, W1G 9QR

Tel: 09068 224100 Travellers Healthline
Fax: 020 7323 5843
E-mail: rattewell@masta.org

Website:
http://www.masta.org
Travel health information.

Enquiries:
Enquiries to: Medical Director

Founded:
1984

Organisation type and purpose:
Advisory body, professional body, service industry, training organisation, research organisation.

Subject coverage:
Health risks for travellers abroad; information is maintained on 230 countries, and 84 conditions and diseases that affect travellers in varying living conditions. Healthcare items catalogue for travellers.

Printed publications:
Health briefs sent by 1st class post for any journey requested via Travellers Healthline 09068 224100
Order printed publications from: Travellers Healthline
tel: 09068 224100

Publications list:
Available in print

Access to staff:
Contact by telephone, by e-mail and via website
Hours: 24-hour helpline

Associated with:
Boots Travel Clinics
MASTA Travel Clinics

Sales and Marketing & Technical:
MASTA
Moorfield Road, Yeadon, Leeds, LS19 7BN; tel: 01132 387500

MEDICAL COUNCIL ON ALCOHOL, THE

Acronym or abbreviation: MCA

continued overleaf

4 St Andrew's Place, Regent's Park, London, NW1
4LB

Tel: 020 7487 4445
Fax: 020 7935 4479
E-mail: mca@medicouncilalcol.demon.co.uk

Website:
http://www.medicouncilalcol.demon.co.uk

Enquiries:
Enquiries to: Administrative Secretary

Founded:
1967

Organisation type and purpose:
Professional body (membership is by subscription),
present number of members: 370, voluntary
organisation, registered charity (charity number
265242).
Devoted to improving medical understanding of
alcohol-related problems, their prevention and
treatment.

Subject coverage:
Alcohol and alcoholism: medical aspects and
facilities for dealing with the problem.

**Museum or gallery collection, archive, or library
special collection:**
Information on alcohol in relation to health
including education of medical students on
alcohol

Trade and statistical information:
Morbidity and mortality statistics.

Printed publications:
Alcohol Abuse Detection (leaflet)
Alcohol and Alcoholism (journal, 6 times a year)
Alcohol and Health Handbook for Nurses,
Midwives and Health Visitors
Alcoholism (newsletter for general practitioners, 6
times a year)
Drinking Diary
Handbook: Alcohol and Health
Hazardous Drinking Handbook for General
Practitioners
Problem Drinking at Work Notes for the
Occupational Physician
Taking Care of Alcohol Issues at Work (for small
businesses)
You, Your Patients and Alcohol (for 1st year
medical students)

Publications list:
Available in print

Access to staff:
Contact by letter, by telephone, by fax and by e-
mail. Appointment necessary.
Hours: Mon to Fri, 0930 to 1630

MEDICAL DEFENCE UNION LIMITED

Acronym or abbreviation: MDU

230 Blackfriars Road, London, SE1 8PJ

Tel: 020 7202 1500
Fax: 020 7202 1666

Website:
http://www.the-mdu.com

Enquiries:
Enquiries to: Librarian
Direct tel: 020 7202 1788
Direct fax: 020 7202 1671
Direct e-mail: morgandj@the-mdu.com

Founded:
1885

Organisation type and purpose:
Membership association (membership is by
subscription), service industry.

Subject coverage:
Medical negligence, litigation, ethics.

Non-library collection catalogue:
All or part available online

Access to staff:
Access for members only.
Hours: Mon to Wed, 1030 to 1730

Access to building, collection or gallery:
Prior appointment required

Access for disabled people:
Parking provided

MEDICAL FOUNDATION FOR THE CARE OF VICTIMS OF TORTURE

111 Isledon Road, London, N7 7JW

Tel: 020 7697 7777
Fax: 020 7697 7799
E-mail: info@torturecare.org.uk

Website:
http://www.torturecare.org.uk

Enquiries:
Enquiries to: Information Officer

Founded:
1986

Organisation type and purpose:
Registered charity (charity number 1000340).
The Medical Foundation aims to provide survivors
of torture in the UK with medical treatment,
practical assistance and psychotherapeutic
support, document evidence of torture, provide
training for health professionals working with
torture survivors, educate the public and decision-
makers about torture and its consequences, ensure
that Britain honours its international obligations
towards asylum-seekers and refugees.

Subject coverage:
Medical foundation providing survivors of torture
in the UK with medical treatment, social assistance
and psychotherapeutic support, documentation of
evidence of torture, education of the public and
decision-makers about torture and its
consequences.

**Museum or gallery collection, archive, or library
special collection:**
Library

Non-library collection catalogue:
All or part available in-house and in print

Library catalogue:
All or part available in-house

Printed publications:
Evidence of torture: A study of Pakistani torture
survivors coming to the UK (Salinsky M, 2001,
£3)
Guidelines for the examination of survivors of
torture, (Forrest D and Hutton F, 2nd ed, 2000,
£3)
Caught in middle: A study of Tamil torture
survivors coming to the UK from Sri Lanka
(2000, £3)
Lives under threat: A study of Sikhs coming to the
UK from Punjab (Forrest D, Salinsky M, Verity
Smith S, Carroll S, 2nd ed, 1999, £3)
Staying alive by accident: torture survivors from
Turkey in the UK (Salinsky M, Miller C, 1999, £3)
Zaire: A torture State (Porta C, 1998, £5)
Rape as a Method of Torture: Peel M (2004, £18 inc.
p&p)
Mental Health Services in Kosovo, Bolderson H
and Simpson K (2004, £5)
Right First Time? Home Office Asylum
Interviewing and Reasons for Refusal Letters,
Smith E (2004, £5)
Every Morning, Just Like Coffee: Torture in
Cameroon, Ball O (2002, £3)
Extensive selection of papers written by Medical
Foundation Staff
All publications are charged to cover the costs of
production and postage

Publications list:
Available online and in print

Access to staff:
Contact by letter and by telephone
Hours: Mon to Fri, 0900 to 1830

Access to building, collection or gallery:
Prior appointment required
Hours: Mon to Fri, 1000 to 1700

Access for disabled people:
Ramped entry, lift, toilet facilities

MEDICAL INDEMNITY REGISTER

Acronym or abbreviation: MIR

PO Box 44375, London, SW19 8WA

Tel: 020 8739 0066
Fax: 020 8739 0077
E-mail: malpractice@btconnect.com

Website:
http://www.medicalindemnity.com
Medical malpractice insurance, PL + EL insurance,
D&O cover

Enquiries:
Enquiries to: Registrar

Founded:
1990

Organisation type and purpose:
Advisory body, medical malpractice insurance for
individuals and companies, present number of
members: 2000, also a training organisation.

Subject coverage:
Pre-hospital life support (PHLS), medical
malpractice and public liability insurance.

Education services:
First Aid and EMT training.

Non-library collection catalogue:
All or part available online

Printed publications:
M.I.R. News (quarterly)

Publications list:
Available online and in print

Access to staff:
Contact by letter, by fax, by e-mail and via
website. Non-members charged.
Hours: Mon to Fri, 0900 to 1700

Access to building, collection or gallery:
No access other than to staff

MEDICAL PRACTITIONERS UNION

Acronym or abbreviation: MPU

33–37 Moreland Street, London, EC1V 8HA

Tel: 020 7505 3000
Fax: 020 7505 3200
E-mail: carol.english@unitetheunion.com

Enquiries:
Enquiries to: National Secretary
Direct tel: 020 7780 4061

Founded:
1914

Organisation type and purpose:
Trade union.

Subject coverage:
Medico-politics; National Health Service,
industrial relations, equal opportunities.

Printed publications:
MPU Newsletter
Salaried Service, Threat or Opportunity?
The Future of Primary Care

Publications list:
Available in print

Access to staff:
Contact by letter and by e-mail
Hours: Mon to Fri, 0900 to 1700

Access to building, collection or gallery:
No access other than to staff

Access for disabled people:
Level entry

Section of:
Unite
  tel: 020 7505 3000

MEDICAL PROTECTION SOCIETY

Acronym or abbreviation: MPS

Granary Wharf House, Leeds, LS11 5PY

Tel: 0845 605 4000
Fax: 0113 241 0500
E-mail: info@mps.org.uk

Website:
http://www.mps.org.uk
About the Medical Protection Society; contact
information; medico-legal advice; publications;
case reports, risk management.

Enquiries:
Enquiries to: Librarian
Direct tel: 0113 241 0615
Direct e-mail: tony.albrow@mps.org.uk

Founded:
1892

Organisation type and purpose:
International organisation, advisory body,
professional body (membership is by subscription),
service industry.
A mutual society of doctors, dentists and other
healthcare professionals. It is a source for its
members of medico-legal advice, legal
representation and indemnity for clinical
negligence cases.

Subject coverage:
Medico-legal matters.

Printed publications:
Journal 'Casebook'(4 times a year, UK and various
  overseas editions)
Publications free to members and freely available
  on website; £2.50 to non-members:
Consent
Keeping Medical Records
Writing Reports and Giving Evidence in Court
Common Problems: Managing the Risks in
  Hospital Practice
Common Problems: Managing the Risks in
  General Practice

Publications list:
Available in print

Access to staff:
Contact by letter, by telephone, by fax, by e-mail
and via website. Appointment necessary.
Hours: Mon to Fri, 0900 to 1700

Access for disabled people:
Access to all public areas, toilet facilities

Other addresses:
Medical Protection Society
  33 Cavendish Square, London, W1G 0PS; tel:
  0845 605 4000; fax: 020 7399 1401; e-mail: info@
  mps.org.uk

MEDICAL RESEARCH COUNCIL – CANCER DIVISION, MRC CLINICAL TRIALS UNIT

Acronym or abbreviation: MRC CTU

222 Euston Road, London, NW1 2DA

Tel: 020 7670 4700
Fax: 020 7670 4818
E-mail: contact@ctu.mrc.ac.uk

Website:
http://www.ctu.mrc.ac.uk
Information about the office, current trials, news,
methodology, meta-analysis, IT, UK register of
trials, links.

Enquiries:
Enquiries to: Information Officer
Direct tel: 020 7670 4737
Direct e-mail: rs@ctu.mrc.ac.uk

Founded:
1977

Organisation type and purpose:
Membership association, present number of
members: 80, research organisation.
The conduct of multi-centre clinical trials in the
treatment of HIV, cancer, and associated research.

Subject coverage:
To design, conduct and analyse clinical trials in
cancer in most solid tumour sites, mainly on behalf
of the MRC.
To undertake teaching, supervisory, editorial and
refereeing work.
The Cancer Division is a member of the editorial
boards of various journals including the British
Medical Journal, British Cancer Journal, Clinical
Oncology etc.
The Cancer Division is the UK editorial office for
the journal Statistics in Medicine.

Printed publications:
Various publications are available, listed in the
  Annual Report

Publications list:
Available online and in print

Access to staff:
Contact by letter, by fax, by e-mail and via
website. Appointment necessary.
Hours: Mon to Fri, 0900 to 1700

Parent body:
Medical Research Council
  Head Office, 20 Park Crescent, London, W1N
  4AL; tel: 020 7636 5422

MEDICAL RESEARCH COUNCIL – COGNITION AND BRAIN SCIENCES UNIT

Acronym or abbreviation: MRC-CBU

15 Chaucer Road, Cambridge, CB2 2EF

Tel: 01223 355294
Fax: 01223 359062

Website:
http://www.mrc-cbu.cam.ac.uk
Staff and research details.

Enquiries:
Enquiries to: Secretary

Founded:
1944

Organisation type and purpose:
Research organisation.

Subject coverage:
Fundamental human psychological functions in
domains such as attention, memory, language and
emotion. Clinical implications for patient therapy
and rehabilitation.

Library catalogue:
All or part available in-house

Printed publications:
Annual list of articles with abstracts, submitted to
  journals

Publications list:
Available online and in print

Access to staff:
Contact by letter and by e-mail. Appointment
necessary.
Hours: Mon to Fri, 0900 to 1700

Access to building, collection or gallery:
No access other than to staff

Access for disabled people:
Parking provided, ramped entry, toilet facilities

MEDICAL RESEARCH COUNCIL – HARWELL

Harwell, Didcot, Oxfordshire, OX11 0RD

Tel: 01235 841000 ext 1121

Fax: 01235 841200
E-mail: m.bulman@har.mrc.ac.uk

Website:
http://www.har.mrc.ac.uk/initial.html

Enquiries:
Enquiries to: Librarian

Organisation type and purpose:
Research organisation.

Subject coverage:
Mammalian genetics, particularly mouse genetics.

Library catalogue:
All or part available online

Access to staff:
Contact by telephone and by e-mail. Appointment
necessary.
Hours: Mon to Fri, 0900 to 1700

MEDICAL SOCIETY OF LONDON

11 Chandos Street, London, W1M 0EB

Tel: 020 7580 1043
Fax: 020 7580 5793

Enquiries:
Enquiries to: Registrar

Founded:
1773

Organisation type and purpose:
Learned society (membership is by election or
invitation), registered charity.

Subject coverage:
Medicine and the history of medicine.

Printed publications:
Transactions of the Medical Society of London

Access to staff:
Contact by letter. Appointment necessary.
Hours: Mon to Fri, 0900 to 1700

MEDICAL WOMEN'S FEDERATION

Acronym or abbreviation: MWF

Tavistock House North, Tavistock Square, London,
WC1H 9HX

Tel: 020 7387 7765
Fax: 020 7388 9216
E-mail: admin.mwf@btconnect.com

Website:
http://www.medicalwomensfederation.org.uk

Enquiries:
Enquiries to: Honorary Secretary

Founded:
1917

Organisation type and purpose:
Membership association (membership is by
subscription), present number of members: c.1,500,
voluntary organisation, registered charity (charity
number 261820).

Subject coverage:
Careers for women doctors working on a full- or
part-time basis.

**Museum or gallery collection, archive, or library
special collection:**
Archives on history of women in medicine (now on
  permanent loan to the Wellcome Institute on the
  History of Medicine)

Printed publications:
Medical Woman (newsletter)

Access to staff:
Contact by letter, by telephone, by fax, by e-mail
and via website
Hours: Mon to Fri, 0900 to 1700

Access to building, collection or gallery:
Prior appointment required

Links with:
Medical Womens' International Association

MEDICINES AND HEALTHCARE PRODUCTS REGULATORY AGENCY

Acronym or abbreviation: MHRA

Information Centre, 10th Floor, Market Towers, 1 Nine Elms Lane, London, SW8 5NQ

Tel: 020 7084 2000
Fax: 020 7084 2353
E-mail: info@mhra.gsi.gov.uk

Website:
http://www.mhra.gov.uk
MHRA home page describing the organisation and giving contact names and numbers.

Enquiries:
Enquiries to: Central Enquiry Point, Information Centre

Founded:
1989

Created by the merger of:
Medicines Control Agency (MCA) and Medical Devices Agency (MDA) (year of change 2003)

Organisation type and purpose:
National government body, statutory body. Executive Agency of the Department of Health. Regulatory body for human medicines and devices in the UK.

Subject coverage:
Safeguarding public health by ensuring that medicines and medical devices work, and are acceptably safe.

Museum or gallery collection, archive, or library special collection:
British National Formulary 1947 to date
British Pharmaceutical Codex 1923 to date
British Pharmacopoeia 1898 to date
Data Sheet Compendiums 1974 to date

Non-library collection catalogue:
All or part available online

Library catalogue:
All or part available online

Publications list:
Available online

Access to staff:
Contact by letter, by telephone, by fax and by e-mail
Hours: Mon to Fri, 0900 to 1700
Special comments: A private information centre serving MHRA staff, only open to researchers as a last resort.

Executive agency of:
Department of Health

MEDIEVAL SETTLEMENT RESEARCH GROUP

Acronym or abbreviation: MSRG

c/o Dr Neil Christie, School of Archaeology and Ancient History, University of Leicester, Leicester, LE1 7RH

Tel: 0116 252 2617
Fax: 0116 252 5005
E-mail: njc10@leicester.ac.uk

Website:
http://www.britarch.ac.uk/msrg
Introduction to the Group, forthcoming events, list of publications, grants and prizes, contact details, policy statement.

Enquiries:
Enquiries to: Honorary Secretary
Other contacts: (1) Treasurer (2) Editor (3) President for (1) membership (2) publications

Founded:
1986

Organisation type and purpose:
Learned society (membership is by subscription), registered charity (charity number 801634), research organisation.

To advance knowledge of rural settlements of all kinds, particularly those of the 5th to 16th centuries.

Subject coverage:
Medieval manors and moats; English, Welsh and some Continental rural settlement studies, especially for the 5th to 16th centuries.

Museum or gallery collection, archive, or library special collection:
The Library is held as part of the Marc Fitch Library, The University of Leicester – for information contact Prof. C. Dyer, School of English Local History, The University of Leicester
The former MVRG sites archive is held on the MSRG's behalf by the National Monuments Record in Swindon (English Heritage). Archive has a computerised index

Printed publications:
Annual Report (free to members)
Bibliography of Moated Sites
Index to Volumes 1 to 10 of Annual Report (1997)
Policy Statement on Medieval Rural Settlements (1996)
Seasonal Settlement (1995)
Order printed publications from: Annual Report

Publications list:
Available online and in print

Access to staff:
Contact by letter, by telephone, by fax and by e-mail. Appointment necessary.
Hours: Mon to Fri, 0900 to 1700

Affiliated to:
Council for British Archaeology (CBA)
St Mary's House, 66 Bootham, York, YO30 7BZ; tel: 01904 671417; fax: 01904 671384; e-mail: archaeology@csi.com; website: www.britarch.ac.uk
Society for Medieval Archaeology (SMA)
website: www.socmedarch.org

MEDITERRANEAN ASSOCIATION TO SAVE THE SEA TURTLES

Acronym or abbreviation: MEDASSET

c/o 24 Park Towers, 2 Brick Street, London, W1J 7DD

Tel: 020 7629 0654
Fax: 020 7629 0654
E-mail: medasset@medasset.org

Website:
http://www.medasset.org
http://www.euroturtle.org

Enquiries:
Enquiries to: Executive Director

Founded:
1988

Organisation type and purpose:
International organisation (membership is by subscription), present number of 'friends': UK 80, Greece 300, voluntary organisation, UK registered charity (charity number 1077649), research and conservation organisation.
Non-governmental organisation.
Organisation working exclusively on the conservation of sea turtles throughout the Mediterranean Sea.

Museum or gallery collection, archive, or library special collection:
Videos, CDs, slides, newspaper cuttings
Holds an extensive list of related publications, technical reports, papers, etc.

Non-library collection catalogue:
All or part available online and in-house

Library catalogue:
All or part available in-house

Printed publications:
Posters, several leaflets and brochures relevant to sea turtle conservation (free)

Publications list:
Available online and in print

Access to staff:
Contact by letter, by telephone, by fax and by e-mail. Appointment necessary.
Hours: Mon to Fri, 0900 to 1700
Special comments: Telephone first for access hours.

Also at:
MEDASSET Greece
1(c) Licavitou Street, Athens 10672, Greece; tel: +30 210 3613572; +30 210 3640389; fax: +30 210 3613572; e-mail: medasset@medasset.gr; medasset@hol.gr; website: http://www.medasset.gr

MEDITERRANEAN GARDEN SOCIETY

Acronym or abbreviation: MGS

Hall Farm, Sidbury, Bridgnorth, Shropshire, WV16 6PY

Tel: 01746 718547
Fax: 01746 718707
E-mail: freda@fredacox.freeserve.co.uk

Website:
http://www.mediterraneangardensociety.org
Garden/plant information, details/history of society, membership details, articles, photographs, etc.

Enquiries:
Enquiries to: Chairman

Founded:
1995

Organisation type and purpose:
International organisation, membership association (membership is by subscription), present number of members: 1050, voluntary organisation.
To promote understanding and interest in Mediterranean plants and gardening and water-wise gardening.

Subject coverage:
The society provides a forum for members on any related Mediterranean garden/plant topics.

Printed publications:
Journal (quarterly, available free to members or £5 per copy to non-members, subscription £20 per annum UK)

Other addresses:
MGS
Sparoza, PO Box 14, 190 02 Peania, Greece

MEDWAY ARCHIVES AND LOCAL STUDIES CENTRE

Acronym or abbreviation: MALSC

Civic Centre, Strood, Rochester, Kent, ME2 4AU

Tel: 01634 732714/332238
Fax: 01634 297060
E-mail: archives@medway.gov.uk

Website:
http://cityark.medway.gov.uk
Piece-level database of archives stock organised in folders, sub-folders and flat html files according to provenance and structure of collections, comprising descriptions of documents. Imagebase of selected collections. Imagebase of parish records.
http://libcat.medway.gov.uk/cgi-bin/vps2_viewpoint.sh
Library catalogue

Enquiries:
Enquiries to: Borough Archivist

Direct tel: 01634 332238
Direct e-mail: archives@medway.gov.uk
Other contacts: Local Studies Librarians for local studies stock.

Founded:
1990

Organisation type and purpose:
Local government body, public library (reference only).
Archives.

Subject coverage:
Archives: Rochester City Council, Rochester upon Medway City Council, Hoo Rural District Council, Chatham Borough Council, Rochester City Council, Gillingham Borough Council, Strood Rural District Council, parish councils for north west Kent, state school and school board records (Medway Council area), Rochester Cathedral, Hawkins' Hospital (Chatham), Rochester Dickens' Fellowship, Watts' Charity (Rochester), St. Bartholomew's Hospital (Rochester/Chatham), Foord Almshouses (Rochester), Earls of Darnley of Cobham Hall, Best family of Boxley and Chatham, Winget Ltd. (Strood), Blaw Knox Ltd. (Rochester), Dove, Phillips and Pett Ltd. (Strood and Rochester), Rogers, Stevens and Chance (Chatham), Winch and Winch (Chatham), Church of England parishes (Rochester Archdeaconry area), Methodist Church Medway Towns Circuit, Chatham Memorial Synagogue (Rochester), Unitarian Church (Chatham), Congregational Church (Clover Street, Chatham), Medway Conservancy Board, Medway Navigation Company, Port of Rochester shipping registers and crew lists, Medway and Swale Dock Labour Board, Rochester Book Society, Rochester and District Natural History Society, Dickens' Country Protection Society, Old Roffensian Society (Rochester), City of Rochester Society, King's School (Rochester), Sir Joseph Williamson's Mathematical School (Rochester); local studies: Dickens' collection, naval collection, local history, Medway Council area and Kent topography, Kent periodicals, census, IGI, GRO Index, public access computers, CDRoms, OS maps, electoral registers, telephone and street directories, local area newspapers and parish register index fiche.

Museum or gallery collection, archive, or library special collection:
Dickens collection
IGI
Naval collection
Usual local authority archive stock

Trade and statistical information:
Census.

Non-library collection catalogue:
All or part available online

Library catalogue:
All or part available online and in-house

Printed publications:
Local Military Ancestors (£2.50)
Subject Guide to Archives (£2.50)
Archive and Local Studies Leaflets (free)

Microform publications:
Films and Microfiche by arrangement

Electronic and video publications:
Public access computers, People's Network, Ancestry, 1901 Census online (tokens for sale)

Access to staff:
Contact by letter, by telephone, by fax, by e-mail, in person and via website. Appointment necessary.
Hours: Mon, Thu, Fri, 0900 to 1700; Tue, 0900 to 1800; Sat, 0900 to 1600
Special comments: CARN reader's ticket for archives.

Access for disabled people:
Parking provided, level entry, wheelchair access to all public areas, toilet facilities, loop system, screen reader software, evac chair

Parent body:
Medway Council
    Directorate of Community Services; tel: 01634 306000; fax: 01634 732848

MEDWAY CHAMBER OF COMMERCE

Medway Business Point, Stirling House, Sunderland Quay, Medway City Estate, Rochester, Kent, ME2 4HN

Tel: 01634 311411
Fax: 01634 311440
E-mail: chamber@medway.co.uk

Enquiries:
Enquiries to: Information Officer

Founded:
1891

Organisation type and purpose:
Membership association (membership is by subscription), present number of members: 450, service industry.

Subject coverage:
Business services.

Access to staff:
Contact by telephone, by e-mail and in person
Hours: Mon to Fri, 0900 to 1700

Access to building, collection or gallery:
No prior appointment required

Access for disabled people:
Ramped entry, toilet facilities

MEDWAY COUNCIL

Medway Libraries, c/o Chatham Library, Gun Wharf, Dock Road, Chatham, Kent, ME4 4TX

Tel: 01634 337799
Fax: 01634 337800
E-mail: chatham.library@medway.gov.uk

Website:
http://www.medway.gov.uk/libraries
http://libcat.medway.gov.uk

Enquiries:
Enquiries to: Librarian

Founded:
1998

Organisation type and purpose:
Local government body, public library.

Subject coverage:
Business information, European information, Community Legal Service Quality Mark, UK Online Centre, Archives, Local Studies

Library catalogue:
All or part available online

Access to staff:
Contact by letter, by telephone, by fax, by e-mail and in person
Hours: Mon, Wed and Fri, 0900 to 1800; Tue, 1000 to 1900; Thu, 0900 to 1900; Sat, 0900 to 1700

Access to building, collection or gallery:
No prior appointment required

Also at:
Medway Archives and Local Studies Centre
    Clocktower Building, Civic Centre, Strood, ME2 4AU; tel: 01634 332714; fax: 01634 297060; e-mail: local.studies@medway.gov.uk; website: http://cityarc.medway.gov.uk

Member organisation of:
Community Legal Service Quality Mark
European Information Association
European Public Information Centres
UK Online Centre

MEDWAY LIBRARY, INFORMATION & MUSEUM SERVICE

Civic Centre, Strood, Rochester, Kent, ME2 4AU

Tel: 01634 306000

Website:
http://cityark.medway.gov.uk
Archives database.
http://libcat.medway.gov.uk
Library catalogue.

Enquiries:
Enquiries to: Librarian
Direct tel: 01634 843589
Direct fax: 01634 827976
Direct e-mail: gill.butler@medway.gov.uk
Other contacts: Reference, Archives, Local Studies Manager for reference, local studies and archives.

Founded:
1998

Organisation type and purpose:
Local government body, public library.

Subject coverage:
Local studies and archives, business information.

Museum or gallery collection, archive, or library special collection:
See Leaflets

Non-library collection catalogue:
All or part available online

Library catalogue:
All or part available online

Printed publications:
Order printed publications from: Chatham Reference Library
Riverside, Chatham, Kent, ME4 4SN, e-mail: chatham.library@medway.gov.uk

Access to staff:
Contact by letter, by telephone, by fax, by e-mail, in person and via website
Hours: Various

Other address:
Chatham Library
    Riverside, Chatham, Kent, ME4 4SN; tel: 01634 843589; fax: 01634 827976; e-mail: chatham .library@medway.gov.uk
Medway Archives and Local Studies Centre
    Clocktower Building, Civic Centre, Strood, ME2 4AU; tel: 01634 332714
Medway Library Information and Museum Service, Education and Leisure
    Civic Centre, Strood, Kent, ME2 4AU; tel: 01634 306000; fax: 01634 332756

MEET A MUM ASSOCIATION

Acronym or abbreviation: MAMA

National MAMA Office, 7 Southcourt Road, Linslade, Leighton Buzzard, Beds LU7 2QF

Tel: 0845 120 6162
E-mail: meet_a_mum.assoc@btinternet.com

Website:
http://www.mama.co.uk/

Enquiries:
Enquiries to: Manager
Other contacts: Helpline Administrator for listing details.

Founded:
1979

Organisation type and purpose:
National organisation, membership association (membership is by subscription), registered charity (charity number 283271).
National charity.

Subject coverage:
Support for mums or mums-to-be with post-natal depression or a feeling of isolation.

Non-library collection catalogue:
All or part available in-house

continued overleaf

Printed publications:
Publications are available, for a small fee, on related subjects including:
Postnatal illness
The effects of a new baby on the family
Difficulties faced by women following childbirth
How to support a women with PNI
Plus leaflets and factsheets for mothers on panic attacks, relaxation techniques and notes for carers (free)

Publications list:
Available online and in print

Access to staff:
Contact by letter, by telephone, by e-mail and via website
Hours: Mon to Fri, 1000 to 1530

Access to building, collection or gallery:
No prior appointment required

Has:
over 35 local groups throughout the UK

MELTON BOROUGH COUNCIL

Council Offices, Nottingham Road, Melton Mowbray, Leicestershire, LE13 0UL

Tel: 01664 502502
Fax: 01664 410283

Website:
http://www.melton.gov.uk

Enquiries:
Enquiries to: Public Relations Manager
Direct tel: 01664 502385
Direct e-mail: jpagett@melton.gov.uk

Organisation type and purpose:
Local government body.

Access to staff:
Contact by letter, by telephone and by fax
Hours: Mon to Fri, 0900 to 1700

MEN OF THE STONES

Acronym or abbreviation: MOS

Beech Croft, Weston-under-Lizard, Shifnal, Shropshire, TF11 8JT

Tel: 01952 850269
Fax: 01952 850269
E-mail: mltebbutt@lineone.net

Enquiries:
Enquiries to: Chairman
Direct tel: 07980 63118 (mobile)
Other contacts: Honorary Secretary

Founded:
1947

Organisation type and purpose:
Learned society, membership association (membership is by subscription), present number of members: 465, registered charity (charity number 229497).
A society advocating the use of stone and other natural and local building materials, for encouraging craftsmanship and preserving good architectural qualities.

Subject coverage:
Architecture and good buildings of all periods; conservation, preservation, repair; use and re-use of stone and other natural and local materials; constructional arts and crafts of architecture, including stone masonry, sculpture, carving; gilding; pargetting, wrought iron and cast lead work, stone roof slating.

Printed publications:
Annual Report (members only)
Yearbook and Directory (free to members, £5 others)

Access to staff:
Contact by letter, by telephone and by e-mail
Hours: Mon to Fri, 0900 to 1700

Affiliated to:
Ancient Monuments Society
English Heritage (West Midlands Region) tel: 0121 625 6820
Georgian Group
Society for the Protection of Ancient Buildings

Links with:
Collyweston Stone Slaters Trust
Orton Trust Stonemasonry Training Centre

MENINGITIS RESEARCH FOUNDATION

Midland Way, Thornbury, Bristol, BS35 2BS

Tel: 01454 281811
Fax: 01454 281094
E-mail: info@meningitis.org

Website:
http://www.meningitis.org

Enquiries:
Enquiries to: Head of Communications and Campaigns
Direct e-mail: harpinderc@meningitis.org

Founded:
1989

Organisation type and purpose:
Registered charity (charity number 1091105).

Subject coverage:
Meningitis Research Foundation funds vital scientific research into the prevention, detection and treatment of meningitis and septicaemia – the blood poisoning form of the disease. Raises awareness of the diseases, and offers support through in-depth information and befriending to those affected.

Museum or gallery collection, archive, or library special collection:
General Public – Symptoms Literature
Health Professionals – Diagnosis guidelines and treatment protocols, and photo library

Library catalogue:
All or part available online

Printed publications:
Various publications available free of charge (however, Meningitis Reasearch Foundation is a registered charity and welcomes donations to help to continue vital work)

Electronic and video publications:
Awareness (video)
Symptoms Information (tapes)

Publications list:
Available online and in print

Access to staff:
Contact by letter, by telephone, by fax and by e-mail
Hours: Mon to Fri, 0900 to 1700; 24-hour Helpline: 0808 800 3344

Access for disabled people:
Parking provided, toilet facilities

Other addresses:
Meningitis Research Foundation
63 Lower Gardiner Street, Dublin 1, Republic of Ireland; tel: +353 1 819 6931; fax: +353 1 819 6931; e-mail: meningitis@iol.ie
Meningitis Research Foundation
133 Gilmore Place, Edinburgh, EH3 9PP; tel: 0131 228 3322; fax: 0131 221 0300; e-mail: info@ scotland-meningitis.org.uk
Meningitis Research Foundation
71 Botanic Avenue, Belfast, BT7 1JL; tel: 028 9032 1283; fax: 028 9032 1284; e-mail: info@meningitis -ni.org

MENTAL HEALTH FOUNDATION

Acronym or abbreviation: MHF

9th Floor, Sea Containers House, 20 Upper Ground, London, SE1 9QB

Tel: 020 7803 1101
Fax: 020 7803 1111
E-mail: mhf@mhf.org.uk

Website:
http://www.mentalhealth.org.uk
Home page, frames based website.

Enquiries:
Enquiries to: Head of Information
Direct tel: 020 7802 0315
Direct e-mail: press@mhf.org.uk

Founded:
1949

Organisation type and purpose:
Registered charity (charity number 801130).
Mental Health Foundation incorporating the Foundation for People with Learning Disabilities, is the leading UK charity working in mental health and learning disabilities.
With pioneering research and community projects we aim to improve the support available for people with mental health problems and people with learning disabilities.

Subject coverage:
Mental health, learning disabilities, mental illness, depression, anxiety, dementia, manic depression, schizophrenia, stress therapy, psychiatry, psychology, user movement, attention deficit, conduct disorder, eating disorder.

Printed publications:
The Mental Health Foundation has a comprehensive booklist including:
Because You Care (Dr K Hinchliffe and Dr G Livingstone, 1994, free for A5 sae, bulk orders 50p per booklet)
Challenging Behaviour – What We Want to Know (Sep 1995, £7)
Chinese Mental Health Issues in Britain: Perspectives form the Chinese Mental Health Association (1997, £9)
Citizens Advice Bureaux Service for People with Mental Health Problems
Creating Community Care: Report of the Mental Health Foundation Inquiry into Community Care for People with Severe Mental Illness (Sep 1994, £9.50)
Don't Forget Us. Services for Children with Learning Disabilities and Severe Challenging Behaviour (1997, £12)
Healing Minds (Wallcraft J, July 1998, £12)
Helping You Cope: A Guide to Starting and Stopping Tranquillisers and Sleeping Tablets (1994, free for A5 sae, bulk orders 40p per booklet)
Knowing Our Own Minds (Faulkner A, Feb 1997, £15)
Legal Issues Arising for the Care, Control and Safety of Children with Learning Disabilities who also Present Severe Challenging Behaviour (Professor C Low, June 1994)
Mental Health Care: A Guide for Housing Workers (June 1995, £7)
Nowhere Else to Go (Fleischmann P and Wigmore J, July 2000, £9.99)
Strategies for Living: The Research Report (Mar 2000, £22.50)
The Fundamental Facts: All the Latest Facts and Figures on Mental Illness (Bird L, Feb 1999, £15)
Too Many for the Road (1996, £10)

Electronic and video publications:
Restoring the Balance – a self-help CD-ROM designed for people with mild to moderate anxiety and depression
Peer Support (video)

Publications list:
Available online and in print

Access to staff:
Contact by letter, by telephone, by fax, by e-mail and via website
Hours: Mon to Fri, 0900 to 1700 plus Dial & Listen Service

Other address:
Mental Health Foundation – Scotland Office
24 St George's Square, Glasgow, G2 1EG; tel:
0141 572 0125; fax: 0141 572 0246; e-mail:
scotland@mhf.org .uk

MENTAL HEALTH MEDIA

Acronym or abbreviation: MHM

The Resource Centre, 356 Holloway Road, London,
N7 6PA

Tel: 020 7700 8171
Fax: 020 7686 0959

Website:
http://www.mhmedia.com

Enquiries:
Enquiries to: Director
Direct tel: 020 7700 8131

Founded:
1983

Organisation type and purpose:
Voluntary organisation, registered charity (charity
number 286467), training organisation,
consultancy, research organisation.
A charity working with the media, statutory and
voluntary organisations and service users to break
down the stigma of mental distress.

Subject coverage:
Mental health and distress, wellbeing, stress and
stress management, ability and disability,
community care, coping with bereavement,
cultural identity and racism, women and well-
being, counselling and psychotherapy, learning
difficulties, sexuality, child abuse, advocacy,
housing, video production and working with the
media.

Electronic and video publications:
Behind the Behaviour
Behind the Symptoms
Friends & Family
Insight in Mind
Mannki Baat
Myths about Madness
Testimony
Working Partners
What Women Want
Open Up Anti-Discrimination Toolkit: Challenging
Discrimination in Everyday Life
Fired Up

Publications list:
Available in print

Access to staff:
Contact by letter, by telephone, by fax and by e-
mail. Appointment necessary.
Hours: Mon to Fri, 0900 to 1800

MENTAL WELFARE COMMISSION FOR SCOTLAND

Acronym or abbreviation: MWC

K Floor, Argyle House, 3 Lady Lawson Street,
Edinburgh, EH3 9SH

Tel: 0131 222 6111
Fax: 0131 222 6112
E-mail: enquiries@mwcscot.org.uk

Website:
http://www.mwcscot.org.uk

Enquiries:
Enquiries to: Communications Manager

Founded:
1960

Organisation type and purpose:
Statutory body.

Subject coverage:
Mental welfare.

Museum or gallery collection, archive, or library special collection:
Mental Health Law
Reports and Grey Literature (relating to Mental
Health)
Small collection of reference books and some
journal titles

Library catalogue:
All or part available in-house

Printed publications:
Annual reports
Inquiry reports
Good Practice Evidence

Publications list:
Available online

Access to staff:
Contact by letter, by telephone, by fax, by e-mail
and via website
Hours: Mon to Fri, 0900 to 1700

Access to building, collection or gallery:
Prior appointment required

Access for disabled people:
Access to all public areas

MENZIES CENTRE FOR AUSTRALIAN STUDIES

Acronym or abbreviation: MCAS

King's College London, The Australia Centre,
Strand, London, WC2B 4LG

Tel: 020 7240 0220
Fax: 020 7240 8292
E-mail: menzies.centre@kcl.ac.uk

Website:
http://www.kcl.ac.uk/menzies

Enquiries:
Enquiries to: Secretary

Founded:
1982

Organisation type and purpose:
University department or institute.

Subject coverage:
Australian tertiary education; Australian literature,
poetry and drama; international relations, history,
politics, art, film ; Australian scholarships and
fellowships administered by MCAS.

Museum or gallery collection, archive, or library special collection:
Australia House Library (old Australian High
Commission Library)
Files of Britain-Australia Bicentennial Committee

Non-library collection catalogue:
All or part available online

Printed publications:
Conference papers (3 titles in hard copy)
Newsletter (termly, free, all available in hard copy
and on web)
Special lectures (21 titles available on web, 12 in
hard copy)
London Papers and Working papers of seminars
(17 titles in print, 88 available on web; variable
number produced each year)

Publications list:
Available online and in print

Access to staff:
Contact by letter, by telephone, by fax and by e-
mail. Appointment necessary.
Hours: Mon to Fri, 1000 to 1700
Special comments: Secretarial staff answer telephone
enquiries; academic staff available for comment
and research advice on Australian subjects. Access
to Australia House library collection with
permission from MCAS.

Access to building, collection or gallery:
Prior appointment required

Funded by:
Sir Robert Menzies Memorial Foundation
(Australia)
The Australian Government

Housed within the:
King's College London, University of London

MERCEDES-BENZ CLUB LIMITED

18 Viga Road, Winchmore Hill, London, N21 1HJ

Tel: 07071 818868

Website:
http://www.mercedes-benzownersclub.co.uk

Enquiries:
Enquiries to: Director and Membership Secretary
Direct e-mail: vharris@mercedes-benzownersclub
.co.uk

Founded:
1952

Organisation type and purpose:
Membership association (membership is by
subscription), present number of members: 8000.

Subject coverage:
Mercedes-Benz cars.

Museum or gallery collection, archive, or library special collection:
Library of books and documents covering
Mercedes-Benz cars from 1884 to the present

Printed publications:
Gazette (monthly, members only)

Access to staff:
Contact by e-mail and via website
Hours: Mon to Fri, 0900 to 1700

MERCHANT TAYLORS' COMPANY

Formal name: Guild of Merchant Taylors of the
Fraternity of St John Baptist in the City of London

Merchant Taylors' Hall, 30 Threadneedle Street,
London, EC2R 8JB

Tel: 020 7450 4440
Fax: 020 7450 4499
E-mail: livery@merchant-taylors.co.uk

Website:
http://www.merchant-taylors.co.uk

Founded:
1327

Organisation type and purpose:
Membership association (membership is by
election or invitation).
City of London Livery Company.

Access to staff:
Contact by letter, by telephone, by fax, by e-mail
and via website

MERCK, SHARP AND DOHME RESEARCH LABORATORIES

Acronym or abbreviation: MSDRL

Hertford Road, Hoddesdon, Hertfordshire, EN11
9BU

Tel: 01992 467272
Fax: 01992 451075
E-mail: externalaffairs_uk@merck.com

Website:
http://www.msd-uk.com/
Website for the site.
http://www.merck.com
Website for Global Company.

Enquiries:
Enquiries to: Literature Resources Associate
Direct tel: 01279 440131
Direct fax: 01279 440667

Founded:
1983

continued overleaf

Organisation type and purpose:
International organisation.
Research division of multinational pharmaceutical company.

Subject coverage:
Medicinal and organic chemistry; diseases of central nervous system; pharmacology; biochemistry.

Non-library collection catalogue:
All or part available in-house

Library catalogue:
All or part available in-house

Printed publications:
Merck Index
Merck Manual
Order printed publications from: Public Affairs Department, Merck and Co Inc
Whitehouse Station, New Jersey, 08889–0100, USA, tel: 00 1 908 423 1000

Access to staff:
Contact by letter and by e-mail
Hours: Mon to Fri, 0900 to 1700
Special comments: Not open to the public.

Links with:
Merck & Co Inc
Whitehouse Station, One Merck Drive, PO Box 100, Whitehouse Station, NJ 08889–0100, USA

MERIONETH HISTORICAL AND RECORD SOCIETY

Acronym or abbreviation: MHS

Area Record Office, Cae Penarlag, Dolgellau, Gwynedd, LL40 2YB

Tel: 01341 422341 ext 4442/4444

Enquiries:
Enquiries to: Secretary

Founded:
1939

Organisation type and purpose:
Learned society (membership is by subscription), present number of members: 318, voluntary organisation.

Subject coverage:
History, geography and literature of Merioneth.

Printed publications:
Annual journal
History of Merioneth Vol II 'The Middle Ages'

MERRIST WOOD CAMPUS

Worplesdon, Guildford, Surrey, GU3 3PE

Tel: 01483 884000
Fax: 01483 884001
E-mail: mwinfo@guildford.ac.uk

Website:
http://www.guildford.ac.uk
Home page, details of courses, new, special events.

Enquiries:
Enquiries to: Learner Services
Direct tel: 01483 884040

Founded:
1945

Organisation type and purpose:
Suitable for ages: 16+.
College of the land-based industries.

Subject coverage:
Arboriculture, horticulture, countryside, practical habitat management, small-scale farming, plant production, garden design, landscape construction, equine studies, animal care, greenkeeping and sports turf management, professional floristry, golf studies, bespoke training, public services

Printed publications:
Prospectus and course details available on request

Access to staff:
Contact by letter, by telephone, by fax, by e-mail, in person and via website
Hours: Mon to Fri, 0900 to 1700

MERSEY TELEVISION GROUP, THE

Formal name: Mersey Television Independent Television Company
Acronym or abbreviation: Mersey Television

Campus Manor, Childwall Abbey Road, Liverpool, L16 0JP

Tel: 0151 722 9122
Fax: 0151 722 6839
E-mail: admin@merseytv.com

Website:
http://www.merseytv.com
http://www.connect.org.uk/brookside
Brookside.
http://www.connect.org.uk/eastenders
Eastenders.
http://www.andover.org.uk/shaun/emmerdale.htm
Emmerdale.
http://www.brookside.com
http://www.hollyoaks.com

Enquiries:
Enquiries to: Administrator

Founded:
1982

Organisation type and purpose:
Television production company.

Subject coverage:
Television programmes and production.

Access to staff:
Contact by letter
Hours: Mon to Fri, 0900 to 1700

Access to building, collection or gallery:
No access other than to staff
Special comments: This area is a closed site.

MERSEYSIDE INDUSTRIAL HERITAGE SOCIETY

Acronym or abbreviation: MIHS

Merseyside Maritime Museum, Albert Dock, Liverpool, L3 4AQ

Tel: 0151 478 4402
Fax: 0151 478 4590

Enquiries:
Enquiries to: Secretary

Founded:
1964

Organisation type and purpose:
Learned society.

Subject coverage:
Industrial archaeology and history, particularly of Merseyside; history of public services, docks, railways, canals, manufacturing industries, buildings, trades, chemical industry, transport, power generation, mining and quarrying.

Museum or gallery collection, archive, or library special collection:
Site Record Cards (held by Merseyside Archaeological Service, tel: 0151 478 4258)

Printed publications:
Bulletin (monthly)
Occasional publications
A Guide to Merseyside's Industrial Past

Publications list:
Available in print

Works closely with:
Merseyside Maritime Museum (part of National Museums and Galleries on Merseyside)
Albert Dock, Liverpool, L3 4AQ; tel: 0151 207 0001

MERSEYSIDE RECORD OFFICE

Central Library, William Brown Street, Liverpool, L3 8EW

Tel: 0151 233 5817 / 5811
Fax: 0151 233 5886 (for Central Library)
E-mail: recoffice.central.library@liverpool.gov.uk

Enquiries:
Enquiries to: Archivist

Founded:
1974

Organisation type and purpose:
Local government body.
Record office.

Subject coverage:
Merseyside County Council, residuary body and joint authority records; Liverpool, Southport and Wirral coroners; some hospital records; some Nonconformist church records; some business records; social agencies e.g. League of Welldoers.

Non-library collection catalogue:
All or part available in-house

Printed publications:
Brief general information leaflet (free)
Education on Merseyside: a guide to sources, 1992 (£2 plus p&p)
Public Health on Merseyside: a guide to sources, 1991 (£2 plus p&p)
Transport on Merseyside: a guide to sources, 1994 (£2 plus p&p)

Access to staff:
Contact by letter, by fax, by e-mail and in person
Hours: Mon to Fri, 0900 to 1800; Sat, 0900 to 1700; Sun, 1200 to 1600
Annual closure 3rd and 4th weeks in June
Special comments: Search fee for written enquiries requiring research.
Proof of identity required including address.

Access for disabled people:
Ramped entry, toilet facilities

MERTHYR TYDFIL COUNTY BOROUGH COUNCIL

Acronym or abbreviation: MTCBC

Civic Centre, Castle Street, Merthyr Tydfil, Mid Glamorgan, CF47 8AN

Tel: 01685 725000
Fax: 01685 722146
E-mail: customer.care@merthyr.gov.uk

Website:
http://www.merthyr.gov.uk

Enquiries:
Enquiries to: Public Relations Manager
Direct tel: 01685 725166
Direct fax: 01685 374397
Direct e-mail: public.relations@merthyr.gov.uk

Founded:
1996

Organisation type and purpose:
Local government body.

Subject coverage:
Local government, education, social services, community services, technical services, local government finance.

Library catalogue:
All or part available online, in-house and in print

Publications list:
Available online and in print

Access to staff:
Contact by letter, by telephone, by fax, by e-mail and via website. Appointment necessary.
Hours: Mon to Thu, 0830 to 1700; Fri, 0830 to 1630

MERTHYR TYDFIL PUBLIC LIBRARIES

Central Library, High Street, Merthyr Tydfil, Mid Glamorgan, CF47 8AF

Tel: 01685 723057
Fax: 01685 370690
E-mail: library.services@merthyr.gov.uk

Enquiries:
Enquiries to: Librarian

Founded:
1935

Organisation type and purpose:
Local government body, public library.

Subject coverage:
Local history collection, the borough of Merthyr Tydfil, 19th century iron and steel industry, coal mining in South Wales, Quakerism, Aberfan and the 1966 disaster.

Museum or gallery collection, archive, or library special collection:
Aberfan Tribunal Report
Photographic collection – Borough of Merthyr Tydfil
Welsh ballads

Non-library collection catalogue:
All or part available online and in print

Library catalogue:
All or part available online and in-house

Printed publications:
Local history booklets illustrated with old photographs
Books on local history including:
History of the Hamlet of Gellideg
Merthyr Boat Boy (Thomas C et al, £7.50)
The Dowlais Ironworks
The Merthyr Tydfil and District Naturalists' Society – Historic Taf Valleys (vols 2 & 3, £6 each)
The Merthyr Tydfil Historical Society – Merthyr Historian vols 5 to 12

Electronic and video publications:
Oral History video recordings – available directly

Publications list:
Available in print

Access to staff:
Contact by letter, by telephone, by fax, by e-mail and in person
Hours: Mon, Fri, 0900 to 1800; Tue, 0900 to 1900; Wed, Thurs, 0900 to 1730

Access to building, collection or gallery:
No access other than to staff

Access for disabled people:
Ramped entry

MERTON COLLEGE LIBRARY

Merton College, Oxford, OX1 4JD

Tel: 01865 276380
Fax: 01865 276361
E-mail: library@admin.merton.ox.ac.uk

Website:
http://www.lib.ox.ac.uk/libraries/libcats.html
Bibliographic records of current holdings and of pre-1800 imprints

Enquiries:
Enquiries to: Librarian

Founded:
1264

Organisation type and purpose:
University department or institute.

Subject coverage:
General, no special fields.

Museum or gallery collection, archive, or library special collection:
Max Beerbohm Collection
F H Bradley Collection

Brenchley Collection of printed materials by T S Eliot
Medieval manuscripts
Merton College Archives
Merton Blackwell Collection of archival material relating to Sir Basil Blackwell and Blackwells booksellers and publishers

Non-library collection catalogue:
All or part available online and in-house

Library catalogue:
All or part available online and in-house

Access to staff:
Contact by letter, by telephone, by fax and by e-mail. Appointment necessary.
Hours: Mon to Fri, 0900 to 1700

Access to building, collection or gallery:
Prior appointment required

College library of the:
University of Oxford

MERTON LIBRARIES AND HERITAGE SERVICES

2nd Floor, Apollo House, 66a London Road, Morden, Surrey, SM4 5BE

Tel: 020 8545 3783
Fax: 020 8545 3237
E-mail: ingrid.lackajis@merton.gov.uk

Website:
http://www.merton.gov.uk
Information about Merton.
http://www.merton.gov.uk/libraries
Libraries in Merton.

Enquiries:
Enquiries to: Head of Library and Heritage Services
Direct tel: 020 8545 3770
Direct e-mail: library.enquiries@merton.gov.uk

Organisation type and purpose:
Local government body, museum, public library.

Subject coverage:
General and local studies: at Morden Library, William Morris, Horatio Nelson, Wimbledon Library. Business and European information: at Morden Library, Merton Local Studies Centre.

Museum or gallery collection, archive, or library special collection:
The following are all in Local Studies Centre:
Carters Tested Seeds Collection at Morden
Simpson Papers at Morden
Tom Francis Picture Collection (transparencies) at Morden

Non-library collection catalogue:
All or part available online and in-house

Library catalogue:
All or part available online and in-house

Printed publications:
Local history publications

Access to staff:
Contact by letter, by telephone, by fax, by e-mail and in person. Appointment necessary.
Hours: Variable hours – please contact for details

Access to building, collection or gallery:
Appointment required

Parent body:
London Borough of Merton, Community and Housing Department
Merton Civic Centre, London Road, Morden, Surrey, SM4 5DX; website: www.merton.gov.uk

MESEMB STUDY GROUP

Formal name: Mesembryanthemum Study Group
Acronym or abbreviation: MSG

Brenfield, Bolney Road, Ansty, West Sussex, RH17 5AW

Tel: 01444 441193
Fax: 01444 454061
E-mail: msg@cactus-mall.com

Website:
http://www.mesemb.org/index.html
Sample bulletin pages, membership information, links, index of bulletin information.

Enquiries:
Enquiries to: Honorary Secretary

Founded:
1985

Organisation type and purpose:
International organisation, membership association (membership is by subscription).

Subject coverage:
Study of plants of the family mesembryanthemaceae.

Printed publications:
MESEMB Study Group Bulletin (quarterly, ISSN 0955 8276)

Publications list:
Available in print

Access to staff:
Contact by letter, by telephone, by fax, by e-mail and via website. Appointment necessary.
Hours: Mon to Fri, 0900 to 1700

Access to building, collection or gallery:
Prior appointment required

Access for disabled people:
Level entry

MESSERSCHMITT OWNERS CLUB

Acronym or abbreviation: MOC

169 Coulsdon Road, Coulsdon, Surrey, CR5 1EG

Tel: 01527 61826
E-mail: andrew.woolley@fmrservices.co.uk

Website:
http://www.messerschmitt.co.uk
Kabinews on-line.

Enquiries:
Enquiries to: General Secretary

Founded:
1956

Organisation type and purpose:
Membership association.

Subject coverage:
Preservation of Messerschmitt/Fend vehicles and historic technical data relating to their design, specific vehicle information, given chassis numbers etc.

Museum or gallery collection, archive, or library special collection:
Refer to Messerschmitt Foundation of Great Britain, 0121 744 2615

Printed publications:
Kabinews (magazine, monthly)

Access to staff:
Contact by letter and by e-mail
Hours: Mon to Fri, 0900 to 1700

Affiliated to:
Messerschmitt Club Deutschland eV

MET OFFICE – EDINBURGH

Saughton House, Broomhouse Drive, Edinburgh, EH11 3XQ

Tel: 0131 528 7319
Fax: 0131 244 8389
E-mail: hazel.clement@metoffice.com

Website:
http://www.metoffice.gov.uk

Enquiries:
Enquiries to: Superintendent

Founded:
1855

continued overleaf

Organisation type and purpose:
National government body.
Public record office.

Subject coverage:
Meteorology, climatology.

Museum or gallery collection, archive, or library special collection:
Weather Records for Scotland

Non-library collection catalogue:
All or part available in-house

Access to staff:
Contact by letter, by telephone, by fax and by e-mail. Appointment necessary.
Hours: Mon to Fri, 0930 to 1600

Access for disabled people:
Yes
Hours: Mon to Fri, 0930 to 1600

Library is a branch of:
National Met Library
  Met Office, FitzRoy Road, Exeter, Devon, EX1 3PB; tel: 0870 900 0100; fax: 0870 900 5050; e-mail: enquiries@metoffice.gov.uk

MET OFFICE – EXETER

FitzRoy Road, Exeter, Devon, EX1 3PB

Tel: 01392 885680
Fax: 01392 885681
E-mail: enquiries@metoffice.gov.uk

Website:
http://www.metoffice.com

Enquiries:
Enquiries to: Press Officer
Direct tel: 01392 886655
Direct e-mail: pressoffice@metoffice.gov.uk
Other contacts: Library Information Officer tel: 01344 854841/856694; Archive Manager tel: 01344 855960

Founded:
1854

Organisation type and purpose:
National government body.
Government Agency (Trading Fund).
The UK's National Met Service providing advice on the world's weather and natural environment to private and public sector customers.

Subject coverage:
Meteorology, climatology and most aspects of atmospheric and related sciences, application and meteorological information to weather-sensitive activities and planning, fundamental research in meteorology and professional training.

Museum or gallery collection, archive, or library special collection:
Original weather records (4.5 km of shelves) archived under the terms of the Public Records Act
Rare and historical books and pamphlets on meteorology and climatology held in conjunction with the Royal Meteorological Society

Printed publications:
Annual Report and Accounts
Commercial Publications (market sector/product specific)
HMSO Sectional List No. 37
Marine Observer (quarterly)
Records Act
Science & Technical Review
Scientific Papers and other Reports

Access to staff:
Contact by telephone
Hours: By telephone to Customer Centre – 24 hours
Special comments: National Meteorological Library and Archives open to the general public.

Access for disabled people:
Parking provided, ramped entry, toilet facilities

Trading arm of the:
Ministry of Defence

METAL PACKAGING MANUFACTURERS ASSOCIATION

Acronym or abbreviation: MPMA

The Stables, Tintagel Farm, Sandhurst Road, Wokingham, Berkshire, RG40 3JD

Tel: 01189 788433
Fax: 01189 788433
E-mail: enquiries@mpma.org.uk

Website:
http://www.mpma.org.uk
List of members and products manufactured. Information on how cans are made. Statistics and press information.

Enquiries:
Enquiries to: Director

Founded:
1977

Organisation type and purpose:
Trade association.

Subject coverage:
Metal packaging; cans, tins, and other containers and closures; statistics of the industry.

Trade and statistical information:
UK statistics.

Printed publications:
Best in Metal Awards Brochure (free)

Access to staff:
Contact by e-mail
Hours: Mon to Fri, 0900 to 1700

Access to building, collection or gallery:
No access other than to staff

METALFORMING MACHINERY MAKERS ASSOCIATION LIMITED

Acronym or abbreviation: MMMA

The Cottage, Down End, Hook Norton, Oxfordshire, OX15 5LW

Tel: 01608 737129
Fax: 01295 253333
E-mail: enquiries@mmma.org.uk

Website:
http://www.mmma.org.uk
Details on Association and its services, member pages, member products and services.

Enquiries:
Enquiries to: Secretary

Founded:
1949

Organisation type and purpose:
Trade association.

Subject coverage:
Metal forming machinery trade.

Printed publications:
Handbook (free)

Access to staff:
Contact by letter, by telephone, by fax and by e-mail
Hours: Mon to Fri, 0900 to 1700

Member of:
METCOM

METALS INDUSTRY SKILLS & PERFORMANCE LIMITED

5–6 Meadowcourt, Amos Road, Sheffield, South Yorkshire, S9 1BX

Tel: 0114 244 6833
Fax: 0114 256 2855
E-mail: enquiries@metskill.co.uk

Website:
http://www.metskill.co.uk

Enquiries:
Enquiries to: Director, Marketing and Communications
Direct e-mail: d.vinall@metskill.co.uk

Founded:
1990

Organisation type and purpose:
Membership association (membership is by subscription), present number of members: 90 companies, training organisation, consultancy. To raise the profile, quality and effectiveness of training, to contribute to the competitive success of the UK steel industry, to influence the training field.

Subject coverage:
All types of education, training, qualifications and skills for the steel and metals industries.

Trade and statistical information:
An analysis of steel industry skills.
Workforce Development Plan.

Electronic and video publications:
Steel Industry Modern Apprenticeship (video)
Steel Industry NVQs (video)
Steel Industry Production NVQs (CD-ROM)

Publications list:
Available in print

Access to staff:
Contact by letter, by telephone, by fax, by e-mail and via website. Appointment necessary.
Hours: Mon to Fri, 0900 to 1700

Access to building, collection or gallery:
Prior appointment required

Access for disabled people:
Parking provided, level entry, toilet facilities

Also at:
Metals Industry Skills and Performance Limited
Suite 15, Vision Point, Vaughan Trading Estate, Sedgely Road East, Tipton, West Midlands, DY4 7UJ; tel: 0121 521 5511/5512/5513; fax: 0121 521 5510; e-mail: enquiries@metskill.co.uk

Has a division:
Metals Industry Competitive Enterprise (MICE)
e-mail: enquiries@metalsindustry.co.uk

Parent body:
UK Steel Association

METAMORPHIC ASSOCIATION

Acronym or abbreviation: MA

PO Box 32368, London, SW17 8YB

Tel: 0870 770 7984
Fax: 020 8672 5951
E-mail: metamorphicassoc@aol.com

Website:
http://www.metamorphicassociation.org.uk
Listing of events such as workshops, exhibitions and open days. Lists of practitioners and teachers, UK and international. Materials that can be ordered from the Association including books, videos etc. General information.

Enquiries:
Enquiries to: Director

Founded:
1979

Organisation type and purpose:
Membership association (membership is by qualification), present number of members: 500+, registered charity (charity number 326525), training organisation.

Subject coverage:
Teaching and practice of the Metamorphic Technique for self-healing and personal growth.

Printed publications:
Information Pack
Metamorphosis: Journal of the Metamorphic Association
The Metamorphic Technique – Principles and Practice (book)

Electronic and video publications:
Video and audio cassette

Publications list:
Available online and in print

Access to staff:
Contact by letter, by telephone, by fax, by e-mail and in person. Appointment necessary.
Hours: Mon to Fri, 0930 to 1730

METANOIA INSTITUTE

13 North Common Road, Ealing, London, W5 2QB

Tel: 020 8579 2505
Fax: 020 8832 3070
E-mail: info@metanoia.ac.uk

Website:
http://www.metanoia.ac.uk

Enquiries:
Enquiries to: General Manager

Founded:
1994

Organisation type and purpose:
Membership association (membership is by subscription), present number of members: 1000, registered charity (charity number 1050175), suitable for ages: adults, training organisation. Training in counselling, psychotherapy and counselling psychology – part-time.

Subject coverage:
Training in counselling, psychotherapy and counselling psychology with optional academic awards validated by Middlesex University at BA, MSc, Masters, Doctorate level.

Library catalogue:
All or part available in-house

Printed publications:
Newsletter (quarterly for members)

Access to staff:
Contact by letter, by telephone, by fax, by e-mail, in person and via website
Hours: Mon to Fri, 0900 to 1700
Special comments: Training at weekends 0930 to 1730.

Access to building, collection or gallery:
No prior appointment required
Hours: Mon to Fri, 0900 to 1700
Special comments: Trainees only at weekends.

Access for disabled people:
Ramped entry, toilet facilities

METEOROLOGICAL OFFICE

Weather Centres/Climate Offices:
Aberdeen Weather Centre
  Lime Street, Aberdeen, AB11 5FJ; tel: 01224 210574; fax: 01224 210575
Belfast Climate Offices
  32 College Street, Belfast, BT1 6BQ; tel: 028 9032 8457; fax: 028 9032 8457
Belfast Weather Centre
  Meteorological Office, Belfast International Airport, Belfast, BT29 4AB; tel: 028 9442 2339; fax: 028 9445 4091
Birmingham Weather Centre
  2040 The Crescent, Birmingham Business Park, Birmingham, B37 7YE; tel: 0121 717 0575; fax: 0121 717 0577
Bristol Weather Centre
  8th Floor, The Gaunt's House, Denmark Street, Bristol, BS1 5DH; tel: 0117 927 9298; fax: 0117 927 9060
Cardiff Weather Centre
  Southgate House, Wood Street, Cardiff, CF1 1EW; tel: 029 2039 7020; fax: 029 2039 0435
Glasgow Weather Centre
  Wallace House, 220 St Vincent Street, Glasgow, G2 5QD; tel: 0141 248 3451; fax: 0141 303 0101
Leeds Weather Centre
  Oak House, Park Lane, Leeds, LS3 1EL; tel: 0113 245 1990; fax: 0113 2457760

London Weather Centre
  127 Clerkenwell Road, London, EC1R 5DB; tel: 020 7242 3663; fax: 020 7404 4314
Manchester Weather Centre
  Applicon House, Exchange Street, Stockport, Cheshire, SK3 0ER; tel: 0161 477 1060; fax: 0161 476 0714
Newcastle Weather Centre
  Portman House, Portland Road, Newcastle upon Tyne, NE2 1AQ; tel: 0191 232 3808; fax: 0191 261 4965
Norwich Weather Centre
  Rouen House, Rouen Road, Norwich, Norfolk, NR1 1RB; tel: 01603 660779; fax: 01603 623531
Scottish Climate Office
  Wallace House, 220 St Vincent Street, Glasgow, G2 5QD; tel: 0141 303 0110; fax: 0141 303 0101
Southampton Weather Centre
  160 High Street, Southampton, SO14 2BT; tel: 023 8022 8844; fax: 023 8022 8846

METHODIST ARCHIVES AND RESEARCH CENTRE

Acronym or abbreviation: JRULM

John Rylands University Library of Manchester, Deansgate, Manchester, M3 3EH

Tel: 0161 834 5343 or 6765
Fax: 0161 834 5574
E-mail: peter.nockles@man.ac.uk

Website:
http://rylibweb.man.ac.uk/data1/dg/text/method.html
General information, listings, collections, guides, including some content of publication guides, e.g., to special collections, and catalogues, manuscript and picture gallery, on-line exhibitions, Methodist internet links.

Enquiries:
Enquiries to: Methodist Librarian

Organisation type and purpose:
University library.

Subject coverage:
Methodist church archives, Methodist history, women's studies, family history, chapel history, popular religion, social history, Methodist theology, Wesley family.

Museum or gallery collection, archive, or library special collection:
Books, letters, diaries, printed works of John Wesley
Collection of Class Tickets and Circuit Plans
Diaries (some 80 volumes, of prominent Methodists)
General pamphlet literature, 1562–1933 (6000 items)
Letters of Methodist Ministers (50,000 items)
Pamphlet literature of the Methodist Movement (600 items)
Percy Collection (nucleus of a collection of hymn books, some 3000)
Papers of John and Mary Fletcher, 43 boxes of manuscripts

Printed publications:
Newsletter
Bulletin of the JRULM

Publications list:
Available in print

Access to staff:
Contact by letter, by telephone, by fax, by e-mail and via website. Appointment necessary.
Hours: Mon to Fri, 1000 to 1730; Sat, 1000 to 1300
Special comments: E-mail or letter are preferred.

METHODIST MISSIONARY SOCIETY

Acronym or abbreviation: MMS

Methodist Church House, 25 Marylebone Road, London, NW1 5JR

Tel: 020 7486 5502
Fax: 020 7467 3761
E-mail: helpdesk@methodistchurch.org.uk

Enquiries:
Enquiries to: Archivist
Direct tel: 020 7467 5166

Founded:
1818

Organisation type and purpose:
Registered charity (charity number Exception Order No 180/1996).

Subject coverage:
Missionary work overseas since 1786.

Museum or gallery collection, archive, or library special collection:
Records of British Methodist Missionary Work (including photographs) from late 18th century to 1945, world-wide cover and on microfiche
Later accessions continue to be made available, 19th century publications held with archives

Printed publications:
Detailed inventories in typescript of a large part of the Archives
Guide to the Archives (available free, from the publisher, to those who intend to order parts of the Archives on microfiche)

Microform publications:
Microfiche for purchase through publishing house

Access to staff:
Contact by letter. Letter of introduction required.
Hours: Mon to Thu, 0900 to 1700

Archives are held at the:
Special Collections Reading Room
  The Library, School of Oriental and African Studies, Thornhaugh Street, Russell Square, London, WC1H 0XG; tel: 020 7691 3347

METROPOLITAN BOROUGH OF BURY

Acronym or abbreviation: Bury Metro

Town Hall, Knowsley Street, Bury, Lancashire, BL9 0SW

Tel: 0161 253 5000
Fax: 0161 253 5079
E-mail: b.hargreaves@bury.gov.uk

Website:
http://www.bury.gov.uk
A to Z of services, list and details of all councillors, facts and figures on Bury Metro.

Enquiries:
Enquiries to: Information Officer

Founded:
1974

Organisation type and purpose:
Local government body (membership is by election or invitation), present number of members: 51.

Subject coverage:
Local government services.

Publications list:
Available in print

Access to staff:
Contact by letter, by telephone, by fax, by e-mail and via website. Appointment necessary.
Hours: Mon to Fri, 0900 to 1700

Access for disabled people:
Parking provided, ramped entry, level entry, access to all public areas, toilet facilities

METROPOLITAN BOROUGH OF DONCASTER

Acronym or abbreviation: DMBC

2 Priory Place, Doncaster, South Yorkshire, DN1 1BN

Tel: 01302 734444

continued overleaf

Fax: 01302 734040

Website:
http://www.doncaster.gov.uk
Community website and information relating to
Council, its services and councillors.

Enquiries:
Enquiries to: Chief Executive
Other contacts: Press and Public Relations Manager
for media, public relations.

Founded:
1974

Organisation type and purpose:
Local government body.

Subject coverage:
Doncaster Borough, local authority matters.

Access to staff:
Contact by letter, by telephone, by fax and by e-
mail
Hours: Mon to Fri, 0900 to 1700

Access to building, collection or gallery:
No prior appointment required

METROPOLITAN BOROUGH OF
KNOWSLEY

Municipal Buildings, Archway Road, Huyton,
Merseyside, L36 9YU

Tel: 0151 489 6000
Fax: 0151 443 3507
E-mail: knowsley@connect.org.uk

Website:
http://www.knowsley.gov.uk
general information and services.

Enquiries:
Enquiries to: Chief Executive
Direct tel: 0151 443 3772
Direct fax: 0151 443 3030
Direct e-mail: steve.gallagher@knowsley.gov.uk

Founded:
1974

Organisation type and purpose:
Local government body.

Subject coverage:
Local government services.

Printed publications:
Borough Guide
Knowsley Street Atlas
Who's Who in Knowsley

Electronic and video publications:
Bubble reef (CD-ROM)
Community Information Programme (CD-ROM)
Invest in Knowsley (CD-ROM)
Knowsley Wood (CD-ROM)
Lifeskills (CD-ROM)
Pixel (CD-ROM)

Access to staff:
Contact by letter, by telephone, by fax, by e-mail
and via website
Hours: Mon to Fri, 0900 to 1700

Access to building, collection or gallery:
No access other than to staff

Access for disabled people:
Parking provided, level entry, toilet facilities

METROPOLITAN BOROUGH OF
WIGAN

Acronym or abbreviation: Wigan Council

Town Hall, PO Box 36, Library Street, Wigan,
Lancashire, WN1 1NN

Tel: 01942 244991
Fax: 01942 827451

Website:
http://www.wiganmbc.gov.uk
A to Z of services, internal telephone directory,
press releases, and description of Council, etc.

Enquiries:
Enquiries to: Chief Executive
Direct tel: 01942 827001

Founded:
1246

Organisation type and purpose:
Local government body.

Subject coverage:
Local government services, all aspects of the lives
of 310,000 citizens from architects to gravediggers.

Trade and statistical information:
Census details and demographic analyses,
employment figures and resource procurement
advice.

Non-library collection catalogue:
All or part available in-house

Library catalogue:
All or part available in-house

Printed publications:
The A to Z of Council Services
Wigan Borough Guide
Introducing Wigan Council
Wigan Town Trail
Leigh Town Trail

Publications list:
Available in print

Access to staff:
Contact by letter, by telephone, by fax, by e-mail
and in person
Hours: Mon to Fri, 0900 to 1700

Access to building, collection or gallery:
No access other than to staff

Access for disabled people:
Ramped entry, access to all public areas, toilet
facilities

METROPOLITAN POLICE
ECONOMIC SPECIALIST CRIME
OCU

Acronym or abbreviation: MPS Specialist Crime OCU

67–73 Buckingham Gate, London, SW1E 6BE

Tel: 020 7230 1212
Fax: 020 7230 1133

Enquiries:
Enquiries to: Grade 9
Direct tel: 020 7230 1220
Direct e-mail: fraud.alert@met.police.uk

Organisation type and purpose:
National government body.

Access to staff:
Contact by letter
Hours: Mon to Fri, 0900 to 1700

METROPOLITAN SOCIETY FOR
THE BLIND

Acronym or abbreviation: MSB

Lantern House, 102 Bermondsey Street, London,
SE1 3UB

Tel: 020 7403 6184
Fax: 020 7234 0708
E-mail: enquiries@msb.gb.com

Enquiries:
Enquiries to: Secretary

Founded:
1834

Subject coverage:
The MSB assists blind and partially sighted
residents of 12 Inner London Boroughs and the
City of London.

Access to staff:
Contact by letter, by telephone, by fax and by e-
mail

Hours: Mon to Fri, 0930 to 1600

Access for disabled people:
Level entry, access to all public areas, toilet
facilities

MG OCTAGON CAR CLUB

Unit 1–3, Parchfields Farm, Trent Valley, Rugeley,
Staffordshire, WS15 3HB

Tel: 01889 574666
Fax: 01889 574555
E-mail: harry@mgoctagoncarclub.com

Website:
http://www.mgoctagoncarclub.com

Enquiries:
Enquiries to: Secretary

Founded:
1969

Organisation type and purpose:
International organisation, membership
association (membership is by subscription).
Caters for Pre-56 MG's only.

Subject coverage:
Pre-1956 MG parts, literature and publications,
advise and assistance, valuations.

**Museum or gallery collection, archive, or library
special collection:**
Chassis files, workshop manuals, parts lists, hand
books

Printed publications:
Bulletin (monthly)

Publications list:
Available online and in print

Access to staff:
Contact by letter, by telephone, by fax, by e-mail
and via website. Appointment necessary.
Hours: Mon to Fri, 0900 to 2200

MG OWNERS' CLUB

Octagon House, 1 Over Road, Swavesey,
Cambridgeshire, CB24 4QZ

Tel: 01954 231125
Fax: 01954 232106
E-mail: mginfo@mgownersclub.co.uk

Website:
http://www.mgownersclub.co.uk
Forthcoming events, technical archive, online
regalia sales, world-wide contacts, membership,
classified cars and spares adverts, race
championship news.

Enquiries:
Enquiries to: Secretary

Founded:
1973

Organisation type and purpose:
Membership association (membership is by
subscription), present number of members: 32,000.
To assist all owners of MG sports cars.

Subject coverage:
MG sports cars.

Trade and statistical information:
Full technical information service available, by
written enquiry, fax or telephone for all MG
models 1920s to present.
Full range of spares available on mail order,
competitive insurance rates.

Printed publications:
Enjoying MG (magazine, monthly on subscription)

Access to staff:
Contact by letter, by telephone, by fax, by e-mail,
in person and via website
Hours: Mon to Fri, 0900 to 1730; Sat, 1000 to 1300

Access for disabled people:
Parking provided, ramped entry, toilet facilities

MG OWNERS' CLUB (NORTHERN IRELAND)

Acronym or abbreviation: MGOC(NI)

17 Meadowlands, Newtownabbey, Co Antrim, BT37 0VL

Tel: 028 9086 2807
E-mail: samone@btinternet.com

Website:
http://www.mgocni.btinternet.co.uk

Enquiries:
Enquiries to: Secretary

Founded:
1981

Organisation type and purpose:
Membership association.

Subject coverage:
The MG car in Northern Ireland.

Access to staff:
Contact by letter and by e-mail
Hours: Mon to Fri, 0900 to 1700

Affiliated to:
MGOC, Swavesey

MI-21 WORLD METAL INDEX

Acronym or abbreviation: MI-21 WMI

Sheffield Libraries, Archives and Information, Central Library, Surrey Street, Sheffield, South Yorkshire, S1 1XZ

Tel: 0114 273 4714 and 0114 273 4744
Fax: 0114 275 7405
E-mail: wmi@sheffield.gov.uk

Website:
http://www.sheffield.gov.uk/worldmetalindex
http://www.mi-21.com

Enquiries:
Enquiries to: Information Services Officer

Organisation type and purpose:
Local government body.
Information service.

Subject coverage:
The World Metal Index is the key to a unique collection of standards and specifications, trade literature and technical journals on both ferrous and non-ferrous metals. Over 200,000 individual metal grades are included, both current and historical. Together with Namtec and TWI, MI-21 World Metal Idex provides in-depth information and technical support services. 20,000 datasheets currently available online by subscription. Access to remaining 180,000 as well as additonal resources and services of WMI is by telephone, fax and e-mail.
24-hour access to search the database by grade name, trade name, chemical and mechanical properties.
Information on metal properties, heat treatment, working, fabrication, welding, machining, corrosion, fatigue, creep and rupture properties.

Information services:
Metals identification service; metals information service

Museum or gallery collection, archive, or library special collection:
National standards and specifications: BS, BSEN, BSENISIO, ASTM, AMS, DIN, AFNOR, UNI; emerging producer nations' standards, e.g. China

Trade and statistical information:
Trade literature collection from metal producers and suppliers.

Access to staff:
Contact by letter, by telephone, by fax, by e-mail and via website. Appointment necessary. All charged.
Hours: Mon to Fri, 0930 to 1630

Links with:
National Metals Technology Centre (Namtec)
Swinden House, Moorgate Road, Rotherham, South Yorkshire, S60 3AR; tel: 01709 724990; fax: 01709 724999; e-mail: info@namtec.co.uk; website: http://www.namtec.co.uk

MID BEDFORDSHIRE DISTRICT COUNCIL

The Limes, 12 Dunstable Street, Ampthill, Bedfordshire, MK45 2JT

Tel: 01525 402051
Fax: 01525 406288

Website:
http://www.midbeds.gov.uk

Enquiries:
Direct e-mail: mark.nustwitt@midbeds.gov.uk

Founded:
1974

Organisation type and purpose:
Local government body.

Subject coverage:
The working of Mid Bedfordshire District Council, community services – leisure and tourism, grants, environmental services, environmental health, dog wardens, planning, building control, economic development, job search, revenues and benefits.

Museum or gallery collection, archive, or library special collection:
Planning Applications

Access to staff:
Contact by letter, by telephone, by fax, by e-mail, in person and via website. Appointment necessary.
Hours: Ampthill: Mon to Thu, 0900 to 1645; Fri, 0900 to 1545

Access for disabled people:
Parking provided, ramped entry, access to all public areas, toilet facilities
Special comments: Access for disabled refers to Ampthill.

Other addresses:
Mid Bedfordshire District Council
23 London Road, Biggleswade, SG18 8ER; tel: 01767 313137; fax: 01767 316717

MID DEVON DISTRICT COUNCIL

The Great House, 1 St Peter Street, Tiverton, Devon, EX16 6NY

Tel: 01884 255255\ Minicom no. 01884 255294
Fax: 01884 258852
E-mail: corps@middevon.gov.uk

Enquiries:
Enquiries to: Public Relations Co-ordinator

Organisation type and purpose:
Local government body.

Subject coverage:
Provision of local services ranging from planning to recycling.

Publications list:
Available in print

Access to staff:
Contact by letter, by telephone, by fax, by e-mail and in person
Hours: Mon to Thu, 0900 to 1700; Fri, 0900 to 1630

MID SUFFOLK DISTRICT COUNCIL

Council Offices, 131 High Street, Needham Market, Suffolk, IP6 8DL

Tel: 01449 720711\ Minicom no. 01140 727120
Fax: 01449 721946

Website:
http://www.mid-suffolk-dc.gov.uk

Enquiries:
Enquiries to: Publicity and Information Officer
Direct tel: 01449 727193
Direct fax: 01449 727187
Direct e-mail: elizabeth.woolnough@midsuffolk.co.uk

Organisation type and purpose:
Local government body.

Access to staff:
Contact by letter, by telephone and by fax
Hours: Mon to Fri, 0900 to 1700

MIDDLE EAST CENTRE LIBRARY AND ARCHIVES

Acronym or abbreviation: MEC

St Antony's College, Woodstock Road, Oxford, OX2 6JF

Tel: 01865 284700
Fax: 01865 311475
E-mail: mastan.ebtehaj@sant.ox.ac.uk

Website:
http://www.sant.ox.ac.uk/areastudies/middle-east.shtml
The Centre's web page with links to the library and archives.

Enquiries:
Enquiries to: Librarian
Direct tel: 01865 284764
Other contacts: Archivist, tel 01865 284706, email debbie.usher@sant.ox.ac.uk

Organisation type and purpose:
University department or institute.
Regional centre of postgraduate college of Oxford University.

Subject coverage:
Modern history, politics, international affairs and economics of the Middle East.

Museum or gallery collection, archive, or library special collection:
Papers of many Middle East diplomats

Access to staff:
Contact by letter, by fax and by e-mail.
Appointment necessary. Access for members only. Letter of introduction required.
Hours: Mon to Fri, 0930 to 1245 and 1345 to 1715

Includes the:
Middle East Centre
tel: 01865 284764

MIDDLE EAST LIBRARIES COMMITTEE (UK)

Acronym or abbreviation: MELCOM(UK)

The Library, School of Oriental and African Studies, University of London, Thornhaugh Street, Russell Square, London, WC1H 0XG

Tel: 020 7898 4152
Fax: 020 7436 3844
E-mail: lis-middleeast@mailbase.ac.uk

Website:
http://www.ex.ac.uk/melcom/

Enquiries:
Enquiries to: Secretary
Direct tel: 020 7323 6099
Direct e-mail: pc7@soas.ac.uk

Founded:
1967

Organisation type and purpose:
Voluntary organisation, university department or institute.
Libraries having substantial Middle East collections, and of individuals in the UK concerned with collecting, organising and making available materials on the Middle East.

continued overleaf

Subject coverage:
Middle Eastern studies from the rise of Islam to the present; Islamic studies; Arabic, Persian and Turkish studies.

Museum or gallery collection, archive, or library special collection:
Collections are held by most of the member libraries; notable are those of Cambridge University Library; Middle East Centre, St Antony's College Oxford; Durham University Library; British Library Oriental Collections; London University School of Oriental and African Studies Library; John Rylands University Library of Manchester; Exeter University Library and The Bodleian Library, Oxford Documents are held by the Documentation Unit, Centre for Middle Eastern and Islamic Studies, University of Durham and the Documentation Unit, Centre for Arab Gulf Studies, University of Exeter; Selly Oak Colleges Library, Birmingham; Edinburgh University Library

Printed publications:
Arab Islamic Bibliography, 1977
Arabic Biographical Dictionaries, 1987
Bibliographical Guide to Iran, 1982
Books From the Arab World: a guide to selection and acquisition, 1988
Collections in British Libraries on Middle Eastern and Islamic Studies, 1982
Introductory Guide To Middle Eastern and Islamic Bibliography, 1990
Middle East and Islam: a bibliographical introduction, (1979 and Supplement, 1977–83, 1986)
Middle East Materials in United Kingdom and Irish Libraries: a directory, 1982
Middle Eastern photographic collections in the United Kingdom, 1989
Official Publications on the Middle East: a selective guide to the statistical sources, 1985
Periodicals in Turkish and Turkic Languages: a union list of holdings in UK Libraries, 1993
The Intifada: a bibliography of books and articles 1987–1992, 1993
Union Catalogue of Arabic Serials and Newspapers in British Libraries, 1977
Union Catalogue of Persian Serials and Newspapers in British Libraries, 1985
Order printed publications from: Joppa Books Limited
68 High Road, Byfleet, Surrey, KT14 7QL, tel: 01932 336777, fax: 01932 348881, e-mail: joppa@dial.pipex.com

Publications list:
Available online

Access to staff:
Contact by e-mail
Hours: Mon to Fri, 0900 to 1700

Affiliated to:
British Society for Middle Eastern Studies

MIDDLE TEMPLE LIBRARY

Middle Temple Lane, London, EC4Y 9BT

Tel: 020 7427 4830
Fax: 020 7427 4831
E-mail: library@middletemple.org.uk

Website:
http://www.middletemplelibrary.org.uk

Enquiries:
Enquiries to: Keeper of the Library

Founded:
1641

Organisation type and purpose:
Legal library

Subject coverage:
Law

Museum or gallery collection, archive, or library special collection:
150,000 vols of mainly English law
Law Reports

Government publications
Ecclesiastical Collection
Rare Books Collection
EU Collection
American Collection
Capital Punishment Collection
Middle Temple Archive (administrative, financial, membership and property records of the Inn since 1501)

Library catalogue:
All or part available online

Access to staff:
Contact by letter, by telephone, by fax and by e-mail. Appointment necessary. Access for members only. Non-members charged.
Hours: Term time: Mon to Thu, 0900 to 2000; Fri, 0900 to 1900; every fourth Sat in rotation with the other Inns of Court Libraries, 1000 to 1700

Access to building, collection or gallery:
Private library for use by members of the four Inns of Court. Enquiries under special circumstances from non-members, for whom access is strictly by appointment. Visits for research by appointment only.
Hours: Term time: Mon to Thu, 0900 to 2000; Fri, 0900 to 1900. Vacation time: Mon to Fri, 0900 to 1730

Access for disabled people:
Wheelchair ramp at library entrance; lift between floors.

MIDDLESBROUGH LIBRARIES AND INFORMATION

Central Library, Victoria Square, Middlesbrough, TS1 2AY

Tel: 01642 729001
Fax: 01642 729954
E-mail: reference_library@middlesbrough.gov.uk

Website:
http://www.middlesbrough.gov.uk
Middlesbrough Borough Council website. Information on all departments, including the public library service.

Enquiries:
Enquiries to: Central Reference Librarian

Organisation type and purpose:
Local government body, public library.

Subject coverage:
All areas covered, local history of Cleveland County, North Yorkshire and South Durham; archives department.

Museum or gallery collection, archive, or library special collection:
Dickie Collection (maritime subjects)
William Kelly Collection (mostly theological works and Bibles)
All major national newspapers published in England from 1990 to 1996 on CD-ROM
North Eastern Daily Gazette, Middlesbrough, 1869 to present (microfilm); Times, 1785 to present, many other local and national newspapers

Non-library collection catalogue:
All or part available in-house

Library catalogue:
All or part available online

Printed publications:
Leaflets on the Library's services

Access to staff:
Contact by letter, by telephone, by fax, by e-mail and in person. Appointment necessary.
Hours: Mon, Tue, Thu, 0930 to 1900; Wed, Fri, Sat, 0930 to 1700

Comprises:
12 libraries

Connected to other:
local organisations with business information resources

Member of:
North East Museums, Libraries and Archives (NEMLAC)

MIDDLESEX UNIVERSITY

Learning Resources, The Sheppard Library, The Burroughs, London, NW4 4BT

Tel: 020 8411 5234
Fax: 020 8362 5163
E-mail: via website

Website:
http://www.lr.mdx.ac.uk/
Front page to various library services including the catalogue.

Enquiries:
Enquiries to: Director of Learning Resources and University Librarian

Founded:
1973

Organisation type and purpose:
University library.

Subject coverage:
Accountancy and finance; business; mathematics; business studies; management; marketing; economics; computing science; product design; geography; pollution; art and design; interior design; humanities; law; sociology and social policy; social work; psychology; criminology; architecture and interior design; education; performance arts (music, dance, drama); computer graphics; flood hazard research; hotel catering and tourism management; psychology; robotics; transport planning and management; teacher training; education; nursing; health studies.

Museum or gallery collection, archive, or library special collection:
Runnymede Trust Library
Black Theatre Forum Archive
Bernie Grant Archive
Hall-Carpenter Archive (jointly held with BLPES), a national lesbian and gay archive, 40,000 items of press cuttings

Non-library collection catalogue:
All or part available online

Library catalogue:
All or part available online

Access to staff:
Contact by letter, by telephone, by fax, by e-mail and via website. Appointment necessary. Letter of introduction required. Non-members charged.
Hours: Hours vary (term time only) by campus, within: Mon to Thu, 0900 to 2000; Fri, 0900 to 1800; Sat, 1100 to 1700

Access to building, collection or gallery:
Hours: Mon to Thu, 0830 to 2200; Fri, 0830 to 2000; Sat, 1100 to 1700

Access for disabled people:
Parking provided
Special comments: Access arrangements vary at each campus.

Campuses at:
Archway
  10 Highgate Hill, London, N19 5ND
Cat Hill
  Barnet, Hertfordshire, EN4 8HT; tel: 020 8411 5042
Hendon
  The Burroughs, London, NW4 4BT
Trent Park
  Bramley Road, London, N14 4YZ

MIDLAND RAILWAY CENTRE

Butterley Station, Ripley, Derbyshire, DE5 3QZ

Tel: 01773 747674
Fax: 01773 570721
E-mail: information@midlandrailwaycentre.co.uk

Enquiries:
Enquiries to: Manager

Founded:
1969

Organisation type and purpose:
Membership association (membership is by subscription), present number of members: 1200, voluntary organisation, registered charity (charity number 502278), museum, training organisation.

Subject coverage:
Railway history, demonstration signal box, Victorian railwayman's church. 3.5 mile heritage railway, Golden Valley Light Railway (2ft gauge), Butterly Park Miniature Railway (3.5 and 5 in gauges), model railways.

Museum or gallery collection, archive, or library special collection:
Archive of railway books, records and photography
Collection of railway equipment, mainly Midland Railway, its predecessors and successors
Princess Royal Class Locomotive Trust Depot
Midland Diesel Group collection of main line diesel power
Stationary Power Gallery

Printed publications:
The Wyvern (quarterly magazine)
Guide
Stockbook

Access to staff:
Contact by letter, by telephone and by fax. Appointment necessary.
Hours: Mon to Fri, 0900 to 1700

Access to building, collection or gallery:
Prior appointment required
Hours: Static display: daily, 1000 to 1615
Closed Christmas Day

Access for disabled people:
Parking provided, toilet facilities

Affiliated to:
Midland Railway Enterprises plc
Midland Railway Trust

MIDLANDS AGRICULTURAL INFORMATION GROUP

Acronym or abbreviation: MidAIG

Warwickshire College, Moreton Morrell Centre, Moreton Morrell, Warwick, CV35 9BL

Tel: 01926 318278
Fax: 01926 318300

Enquiries:
Enquiries to: Membership Secretary
Direct e-mail: librarymm@warksccl.ac.uk

Founded:
1982

Organisation type and purpose:
Voluntary organisation.
An informal group of information services personnel who meet annually with an informal network to assist each other professionally – interlibrary co-operation.

Subject coverage:
Generally land-based industries: agriculture, horticulture, conservation of natural resources, food science and applied biology, equine industry, small animal care, arboriculture, construction, greenkeeping.

Access to staff:
Contact by letter, by telephone, by fax and by e-mail. Appointment necessary.
Hours: Mon to Thu, 0830 to 2200; Fri, 0830 to 1700; Sat, 1000 to 1600
Vacations: Mon to Fri, 0915 to 1645

Access to building, collection or gallery:
Prior appointment required

Access for disabled people:
Level entry, access to all public areas, toilet facilities

Members are:
Librarians and information professionals and other staff in libraries and information services with an agricultural/land-based industry related subject area or interest

MIDLANDS CLUB CRICKET CONFERENCE

Acronym or abbreviation: MCCC

65 Tilesford Close, Monkspath, Solihull, West Midlands, B90 4YF

Tel: 0121 744 6746; 07890 739489
E-mail: murray.ali@gmail.com

Website:
http://www.mccc.co.uk

Enquiries:
Enquiries to: Honorary Secretary

Founded:
1947

Organisation type and purpose:
Membership association, voluntary organisation.

Subject coverage:
All matters relating to cricket.

Printed publications:
Newsletter (quarterly, free to members, for sale to non-members)
Year book (free to members, for sale to non-members)

Access to staff:
Contact by letter, by telephone, by e-mail and via website
Hours: Mon to Fri, 0900 to 2100

MIDLOTHIAN COUNCIL

Midlothian House, Buccleuch Street, Dalkeith, Midlothian, EH22 1DN

Tel: 0131 270 7500\ Minicom no. 0131 271 3610
Fax: 0131 271 3050

Website:
http://www.midlothian.gov.uk
Information on Midlothian Council and links to related websites.
http://www.earl.org.uk/partners/midlothian/index.html
Information on libraries only.

Enquiries:
Enquiries to: Communication Manager
Direct tel: 0131 271 3425
Direct fax: 0131 271 3536
Direct e-mail: Susan.Whiteford@midlothian.gov.uk

Founded:
1996

Organisation type and purpose:
Local government body.

Subject coverage:
Information about council services available to the people of Midlothian, and how to access them.

Library catalogue:
All or part available in-house

Printed publications:
Midlothian News (free to all householders in Midlothian)
Business News (free to Midlothian business community)

Publications list:
Available online

Access to staff:
Contact by letter, by e-mail and via website
Hours: Mon to Fri, 0930 to 1530

Access to building, collection or gallery:
No prior appointment required

MIDLOTHIAN COUNCIL LIBRARY SERVICES

Library Headquarters, 2 Clerk Street, Loanhead, Midlothian, EH20 9DR

Tel: 0131 271 3980
Fax: 0131 440 4635
E-mail: library.hq@midlothian.gov.uk

Website:
http://www.midlothian.gov.uk/library

Enquiries:
Enquiries to: Library Services Manager
Direct tel: 0131 271 3970
Direct e-mail: alan.reid@midlothian.gov.uk

Founded:
1996

Organisation type and purpose:
Local government body, public library.

Subject coverage:
General, local history of Midlothian.

Museum or gallery collection, archive, or library special collection:
Black Collection (Penicuik historical interest)
Midlothian Council Archive

Library catalogue:
All or part available online

Printed publications:
The Dalkeith Tolbooth and Market Cross (D R Smith, £5)
Publications on local subjects include:
Early Railways of the Lothians (Worling M J, £3.95)
From Rosewell to the Rhondda (£2.95)
Mauricewood Disaster (Donaldson A B, £2.95)
Midlothian Gravestones (Donaldson I, £6.95)
Music of Midlothian (booklet and cassette)
The Prisoners at Penicuik – French and Other Prisoners of War 1803–1814 (MacDougall I, £3.95)
New Statistical Account of Midlothian (3 volumes)
Parish of Cockpen (Mitchell P, £1.80)
The Origins of Street Names in Dalkeith (Williamson M G, £6.99)

Electronic and video publications:
Newtongrange Silver Band Play Variations (CD and cassette)
Music of Midlothian (cassette)
The Midlothian 2000 CD-ROM (CD-ROM, £15)
Scottish Brewers Silver Band, Newtongrange (CD and cassette)

Publications list:
Available online and in print

Access to staff:
Contact by letter, by telephone, by fax, by e-mail and via website. Appointment necessary.
Hours: Mon to Thu, 0900 to 1700; Fri, 0900 to 1545
Special comments: Opening hours vary, contact individual branch.

Access for disabled people:
Parking provided, ramped entry, toilet facilities

Branch libraries:
Bonnyrigg Library
  3 Polton Street, Bonnyrigg, Midlothian, EH19 3HB; tel: 0131 663 6762; fax: 0131 654 9019; e-mail: bonnyrigg.library@midlothian.gov.uk
Dalkeith Library
  White Hart Street, Dalkeith, Midlothian, EH22 1AE; tel: 0131 663 2083; fax: 0131 654 9029; e-mail: dalkeith.library@midlothian.gov.uk
Danderhall Library
  1a Campview, Danderhall, Midlothian, EH22 1QD; tel: 0131 663 9293; e-mail: danderhall.library@midlothian.gov.uk
Gorebridge Library
  98 Hunterfield Road, Gorebridge, Midlothian, EH23 4TT; tel: 01875 820630; fax: 01875 823657; e-mail: gorebridge.library@midlothian.gov.uk
Loanhead Library
  George Avenue, Loanhead, Midlothian, EH20 9HD; tel: 0131 440 0824; e-mail: loanhead.library@midlothian.gov.uk

continued overleaf

Local Studies Library
2 Clerk Street, Loanhead, Midlothian, EH20 9DR; tel: 0131 271 3976; fax: 0131 440 4635; e-mail: local.studies@midlothian.gov.uk

Mayfield Library
Stone Avenue, Mayfield, Dalkeith, Midlothian, EH22 5PB; tel: 0131 663 2126; e-mail: mayfield.library@midlothian.gov.uk

Newtongrange Library
St David's, Newtongrange, Midlothian, EH22 4LG; tel: 0131 663 1816; fax: 0131 654 1990; e-mail: newtongrange.library@midlothian.gov.uk

Penicuik Library
Bellman's Road, Penicuik, Midlothian, EH26 0AB; tel: 01968 672340; fax: 01968 679968; e-mail: penicuik.library@midlothian.gov.uk

Roslin Library
9 Main Street, Roslin, Midlothian, EH25 9LD; tel: 0131 448 2781; e-mail: roslin.library@midlothian.gov.uk

Woodburn Library
(Dalkeith Leisure Centre), 6 Woodburn Road, Dalkeith, Midlothian, EH22 2AR; tel: 0131 654 4323; e-mail: woodburn.library@midlothian.gov.uk

Parent body:
Midlothian Council
Midlothian House, Buccleuch Street, Dalkeith, Midlothian, EH22 1DJ; tel: 0131 270 7500; fax: 0131 271 3050; e-mail: enquiries@midlothian.gov.uk

MIGRAINE ACTION ASSOCIATION

Acronym or abbreviation: MAA

27 East Street, Leicester, LE1 6NB

Tel: 0116 275 8317
Fax: 0116 254 2023
E-mail: info@migraine.org.uk

Website:
http://www.migraine.org.uk

Enquiries:
Enquiries to: Director

Founded:
1958

Organisation type and purpose:
Membership association (membership is by subscription), present number of members: 12,000, registered charity (charity number 207783), suitable for ages: all.
To encourage and support research into all aspects of migraine.

Subject coverage:
All aspects of migraine and associated headaches, information re drugs and treatments, encouragement, reassurance and understanding for sufferers.

Printed publications:
Migraine Action News (4 times a year)
Managing Your Migraine
Migraine – We Can Help
Migraine in Children
Migraine News Letter (3 times a year)

Publications list:
Available online

Access to staff:
Contact by letter, by telephone, by fax, by e-mail and via website. Appointment necessary.
Hours: Mon to Fri, 0900 to 1700

Access to building, collection or gallery:
Prior appointment required
Hours: Mon to Fri, 0900 to 1700

Access for disabled people:
Parking provided, ramped entry, toilet facilities

MIGRAINE TRUST, THE

Formal name: William Morrise Society and Kemscott Fellowship

55–56 Russell Square, London, WC1B 4HP

Tel: 020 7436 1336
Fax: 020 7436 2880

Website:
http://www.migrainetrust.org
Advice, lists of publications, how to support us, volunteering, current events, archive of press releases.

Enquiries:
Enquiries to: Director
Direct tel: 020 7831 4818
Direct fax: 020 7831 5174
Direct e-mail: info@migrainetrust.org
Other contacts: (1) Helpline and Support Services Manager; (2) Communications Officer for (1) first point of contact for migraine sufferers; (2) press enquiries.

Founded:
1965

Organisation type and purpose:
International organisation, voluntary organisation, registered charity (charity number 244250), suitable for ages: all, research organisation.
It funds and promotes research into migraine and related headaches, improving its diagnosis and treatment; holds international migraine symposia, helps sufferers, funds clinics.

Subject coverage:
The Migraine Trust is a medical research and patient support charity with over 40,000 members. Committed to supporting sufferers and their families by providing information and advice on managing migraine and raising awareness of migraine as a significant health problem.

Printed publications:
List of research projects available from the Trust
All About Drugs
Migraine News (quarterly) and other literature including:
Finding Your Trigger Factors
Migraine and Sleep
Migraine in Childhood
Taking Control of Your Migraine
Understanding Migraine
Women and Migraine

Publications list:
Available online and in print

Access to staff:
Contact by letter, by telephone, by fax, by e-mail and via website
Hours: Answerphone before 0900 and after 1700

MIGRANTS RESOURCE CENTRE

24 Churton Street, London, SW1V 2LP

Tel: 020 7834 2505

Website:
http://www.migrantsresourcecentre.org.uk

Organisation type and purpose:
The Centre works with migrants and refugees from all over the world, providing assistance and advice and helping to enable full participation in British society.

Information services:
Online Centre.
Legal Advice Team at: Derry House, Penfold Street, London, NW8 8HJ; tel: 0845 241 0961

MILITARY HERALDRY SOCIETY

The Cloth Insignia Research and Collectors Society, Windyridge, 27 Sandbrook, Ketley, Telford, Shropshire, TF1 5BB

Tel: 01952 270221

Website:
http://www.militaryheraldrysociety.co.uk

Enquiries:
Enquiries to: Publicity Officer
Direct tel: 01952 270221

Direct e-mail: billbowbagins@hotmail.com

Founded:
1951

Organisation type and purpose:
International organisation, membership association (membership is by subscription), present number of members: 320, research organisation.
Collecting.

Subject coverage:
Research and study of military cloth insignia (formation signs, shoulder titles, regimental and unit flashes, skill-at-arms and similar cloth items).

Printed publications:
Formation Sign (journal, quarterly)

Access to staff:
Contact by letter, by telephone and by e-mail

MILITARY VEHICLE TRUST

Acronym or abbreviation: MVT

General Secretary, Meadowhead Cottage, Beaumaris Avenue, Blackburn, Lancashire, BB2 4TP

Tel: 01254 202253
E-mail: gensec@mvt.org.uk

Website:
http://www.mvt.org.uk

Enquiries:
Enquiries to: Membership Secretary
Direct tel: 0845 475 1941
Direct e-mail: membershipsec@mvt.org.uk

Founded:
1968

Organisation type and purpose:
Membership association, registered charity.
Contact with owners of all ex-military vehicles to share information and give advice on preservation, and to provide details of club activities. Vehicle verification service. Shop. Monitoring of new legislation to ensure continuing use of preserved vehicles.

Subject coverage:
Preservation and restoration of historic military vehicles.

Museum or gallery collection, archive, or library special collection:
Vehicle manual library (for the use of members)

Printed publications:
Windscreen (magazine, quarterly, for members)
Green Sheet (newsletter, 6 a year, for members)

Access to staff:
Contact by letter
Hours: daytime, evenings and weekends up to 2100

MILTON KEYNES & NORTH BUCKS CHAMBER OF COMMERCE

Acronym or abbreviation: MKCOC

World Trade Center @ The Hub, 9 Rillaton Walk, Central Milton Keynes, MK9 2FZ

Tel: 01908 259000
Fax: 01908 246799
E-mail: enquiry@mk-chamber.co.uk

Website:
http://www.mk-chamber.co.uk
Information about the organisation.

Enquiries:
Enquiries to: Information Services Manager
Direct tel: 01908 259433

Founded:
1995

Organisation type and purpose:
Membership association (membership is by subscription), present number of members: over 1400.
Business Link brings together a wide range of support services for growing businesses in Milton Keynes. Part of a national network it is committed to improving the competitiveness of UK Industry and Commerce.

Subject coverage:
International trade, Europe desk, business information (local, UK and worldwide).

Museum or gallery collection, archive, or library special collection:
Business and trade directories, reference books
CD-ROM and online databases

Trade and statistical information:
International trade department covers export and import worldwide.
Milton Keynes and North Bucks Economic survey.

Printed publications:
Opportunity

Access to staff:
Contact by letter, by telephone, by fax and by e-mail. Appointment necessary. All charged.
Hours: Mon to Fri, 0900 to 1700

Access to building, collection or gallery:
Prior appointment required

Affiliated to:
Association of British Chambers of Commerce
Business Link

Parent body:
Milton Keynes and North Buckinghamshire
Chamber of Commerce

MILTON KEYNES COLLEGE LEARNING RESOURCES CENTRE

Chaffron Way Campus, Woughton Campus West, Leadenhall West, Milton Keynes, Buckinghamshire, MK6 5LP

Tel: 01908 684444\ Minicom no. 01908 684401
Fax: 01908 684399

Enquiries:
Enquiries to: Learning Resources Manager
Direct tel: 01908 684429

Organisation type and purpose:
Suitable for ages: 16+.

Subject coverage:
Business, administrative, secretarial subjects, social care; non-advanced engineering (electrical, electronic, mechanical, motor vehicle), hospitality and catering, beauty therapy, sport and leisure and general education, art and design.

Library catalogue:
All or part available in-house

Access to staff:
Contact by letter, by telephone, by fax and in person
Hours: Term time: Mon to Thu; 0900 to 2000; Fri, 1000 to 1600
Vacations: hours will differ

Other addresses:
Bletchley Centre
Sherwood Drive, Bletchley, Milton Keynes, Buckinghamshire, MK3 6DR; tel: 01908 684444; fax: 01908 684199

MILTON KEYNES COUNCIL

Acronym or abbreviation: MKC

Civic Offices, 1 Saxon Gate East, Milton Keynes, Buckinghamshire, MK9 3HG

Tel: 01908 691691\ Minicom no. 01908 252727
Fax: 01908 252456

Enquiries:
Enquiries to: Public Relations Manager

Founded:
1997

Organisation type and purpose:
Local government body.

Subject coverage:
Local government services.

MILTON KEYNES LEARNING CITY LIBRARIES NETWORK

Open University Library, Walton Hall, Milton Keynes, Buckinghamshire, MK7 6AA

Tel: 01908 653254
Fax: 01908 653571

Website:
http://www.mkweb.co.uk/mk-libraries-network
http://www.mkinspire.org.uk

Enquiries:
Enquiries to: Chairman
Direct e-mail: n.whitsed@open.ac.uk
Other contacts: Secretary

Founded:
2004

Formerly called:
Beds & Bucks Information Plan (BBi)

Organisation type and purpose:
Collaboration of local libraries.
To facilitate and encourage the use of all major libraries in the Milton Keynes area by everyone who lives, works, or studies in Milton Keynes

Subject coverage:
Education, health, co-operative training.

Non-library collection catalogue:
All or part available online

Library catalogue:
All or part available online

Electronic and video publications:
Electronic products all web-based

Publications list:
Available online

Access to staff:
Contact by letter, by telephone, by fax, by e-mail and via website. Appointment necessary.

MIND (THE MENTAL HEALTH CHARITY)

Formal name: National Association for Mental Health

Granta House, 15–19 Broadway, Stratford, London, E15 4BQ

Tel: 020 8519 2122
Fax: 020 8522 1725
E-mail: contact@mind.org.uk

Website:
http://www.mind.org.uk

Enquiries:
Enquiries to: Administrator
Direct tel: 020 8215 2235
Direct fax: 020 8215 2468
Direct e-mail: k.field@mind.org.uk

Founded:
1945

Organisation type and purpose:
Membership association (membership is by subscription), voluntary organisation, registered charity (charity number 219830).

Subject coverage:
Mental health, mental illness, the mental health services, service provision, especially community care, rights of service recipients, legislation, treatments, sources of therapy, voluntary associations, housing, women; employment.

Non-library collection catalogue:
All or part available online, in-house and in print

Library catalogue:
All or part available in-house

Printed publications:
Benefits and Employment (7 titles)
Care in the Community (13 titles)
Drugs and Treatment (20 titles)
Fact sheets, reading lists, books, reports
Making Sense Series (6 titles)
Openmind Magazine (6 times a year)

Publications list:
Available online and in print

Access to staff:
Contact by letter, by telephone, by fax, by e-mail and via website. Appointment necessary.
Hours: Mon to Fri, 0915 to 1715

Access to building, collection or gallery:
No prior appointment required

Branch at:
Mind Cymru
3rd Floor, Quebec House, Castlebridge Road East, Castlebridge, Cardiff, CF11 9AB; tel: 029 2039 5123

MINERAL INDUSTRY RESEARCH ORGANISATION

Acronym or abbreviation: MIRO

Concorde House, Trinity Park, Solihull, Birmingham, West Midlands, B37 7UQ

Tel: 0121 635 5225
Fax: 0121 635 5226
E-mail: mail@miro.co.uk

Website:
http://www.miro.co.uk

Enquiries:
Enquiries to: Administrator

Founded:
1972

Organisation type and purpose:
Membership association (membership is by subscription), present number of members: 70, consultancy, research organisation.
To organise collaborative research projects.

Subject coverage:
Geosciences, mineral exploration; mining, mineral processing, metal refining, recycling and environmental issues.

Museum or gallery collection, archive, or library special collection:
The Stan Nelmes Collection – a collection of books, journals and reports of interest to those in the metallurgical industry dating from 1903 to 1990, 66 titles in total

Non-library collection catalogue:
All or part available online and in print

Library catalogue:
All or part available online and in print

Printed publications:
Publications include:
Quarry Reclamation
Mixing and Dewatering in the Mineral Industry
TRAWMAR (Targeted Research Action on Waste Minimisation and Recycling) (2000)
Technical Review Series including:
Pressure Hydrometallurgy – A Review
REMINDER (A Review and Evaluation of Minerals Industry Databases of Environmental References)
Treatment Options for Waste Products from Metallurgical Operations
The use of Micro Organisms in the Minerals and Metals Industries (Vol 1 1991, Vol 2 1995, Vol 3 2000)
Order printed publications from: Administrator, MIRO

Electronic and video publications:
A Technical Framework for Mine Closure Planning (CD-ROM)

continued overleaf

Impurity Control and Removal in Extractive
  Metallurgy (CD-ROM)
SOLVEX solvent extraction database (disk)
The use of Micro Organisms in the Minerals and
  Metals Industries (Vols 2 and 3) (CD-ROM)
Pressure Hydrometallurgy: A Review (CD-ROM)
TRAWMAR (Targeted Research Action on Waste
  Minimisation and Recycling) Workshop
  Proceedings, 1998, 1999, 2000 (CD-ROM)

Publications list:
Available online and in print

Access to staff:
Contact by letter, by telephone, by fax, by e-mail
and via website
Hours: Mon to Fri, 0900 to 1700

Access to building, collection or gallery:
Prior appointment required

Access for disabled people:
Ramped entry, access to all public areas, toilet
facilities

Member of:
Association of Independent Research and
Technology Organisations (AIRTO)
Mining Association of the United Kingdom

MINERALOGICAL SOCIETY OF GREAT BRITAIN AND IRELAND

Acronym or abbreviation: MinSoc

41 Queen's Gate, London, SW7 5HR

Tel: 020 7584 7516
Fax: 020 7823 8021
E-mail: info@minersoc.org

Website:
http://www.minersoc.org.uk
Membership, publications, events, conferences,
special interest groups, shop, education.

Enquiries:
Enquiries to: Executive Secretary

Founded:
1876

Organisation type and purpose:
National organisation, learned society, registered
charity (charity number 233706), publishing house.

Subject coverage:
Mineralogy, petrology, geochemistry,
crystallography and environmental science.

Library catalogue:
All or part available online

Printed publications:
Elements (6 times a year)
Clay Minerals (quarterly)
Mineralogical Magazine (bi-monthly)

Electronic and video publications:
Clay Minerals
Mineralogical Magazine (available online)
MINABS (online)

Publications list:
Available online and in print

Access to staff:
Contact by letter, by telephone, by fax, by e-mail
and via website. Appointment necessary.
Hours: Mon to Fri, 0900 to 1700

Access to building, collection or gallery:
Prior appointment required
Hours: Mon to Fri 0900 to 1700
Special comments: Library housed at Kingston
University.

MINERALS ENGINEERING SOCIETY

Acronym or abbreviation: MES

2 Ryton Close, Blyth, Worksop, Nottinghamshire,
S81 8DN

Tel: 01909 591940

Fax: 01909 591940
E-mail: hon.sec.mes@lineone.net

Enquiries:
Enquiries to: Honorary Secretary

Founded:
1958

Organisation type and purpose:
Learned society.

Subject coverage:
Minerals engineering; mineral processing; coal
preparation.

Printed publications:
MQR Magazine (10 times a year)
Minerals Engineering Handbook
Symposia Handbooks

Access to staff:
Contact by letter, by telephone, by fax and by e-
mail
Hours: Mon to Fri, 0700 to 2200

MINI MARCOS OWNERS CLUB

Acronym or abbreviation: MMOC

28 Meadow Road, Claines, Worcester, WR3 7PP

Tel: 01905 458533
E-mail: info@minimarcos.org.uk

Website:
http://www.minimarcos.org.uk

Enquiries:
Enquiries to: Secretary

Founded:
1977

Organisation type and purpose:
International organisation, membership
association (membership is by subscription).

Subject coverage:
History and development of Mini Marcos and Mini
Jem cars, history of Kingfisher Sprint cars.

Printed publications:
Club Magazine (including back issues)
Club Technical Manual
Order printed publications from: Publications Officer,
Mini Marcos Owners Club, 16 Townfield, Kidford,
Billingshurst, West Sussex, RH14 0LZ

Publications list:
Available online

Access to staff:
Contact by letter, by telephone, by e-mail and via
website
Hours: Evenings and weekends

Links with:
RACMSA

MINI OWNERS CLUB

Formal name: National Mini Owners Club

15 Birchwood Road, Boley Park, Lichfield,
Staffordshire, WS14 9UN

Tel: 01543 257956
Fax: 01543 257956
E-mail: nmoc@yahoo.com

Website:
http://www.miniownersclub.co.uk
Club information and other Mini related
information.

Enquiries:
Enquiries to: Secretary

Founded:
1979

Organisation type and purpose:
Membership association (membership is by
subscription).

Subject coverage:
Mini cars, technical advice.

Access to staff:
Contact by letter, by telephone, by fax, by e-mail
and via website
Hours: Mon to Sun, 0900 to 2100

MINIATURE AFV ASSOCIATION

Formal name: Miniature Armoured Fighting
Vehicles Association
Acronym or abbreviation: MAFVA

45 Balmoral Drive, Holmes Chapel, Cheshire, CW4
7JQ

Tel: 01477 535373
Fax: 01477 535892
E-mail: mafvahq@aol.com

Website:
http://www.mafva.net

Enquiries:
Enquiries to: Honorary Secretary

Founded:
1965

Organisation type and purpose:
International organisation, membership
association (membership is by subscription),
present number of members: 7,500, voluntary
organisation.
Collection and dissemination of information on
military vehicles and equipment.

Subject coverage:
Armoured fighting vehicles and other military
equipment, arms, materials and accoutrements
from the World War I to date; scale models and
information, markings, colour schemes, badges
and insignia.

**Museum or gallery collection, archive, or library
special collection:**
Collection of military insignia (particularly cloth)
  of the British Army, British Indian Army and
  Army Cadet Force, 1914 to date: quantity several
  thousand
Vehicle markings and colour schemes

Non-library collection catalogue:
All or part available in-house

Printed publications:
Branch newsletters (Dragon, etc.)
Tankette (6 a year)
Order printed publications from: Honorary Secretary

Electronic and video publications:
Index of Tankette Magazine Vol. 1 to 34 (floppy
  disk £1)

Publications list:
Available online and in print

Access to staff:
Contact by letter, by telephone, by fax, by e-mail
and via website. Appointment necessary. Non-
members charged.
Hours: Daily

Access to building, collection or gallery:
No prior appointment required

MINISTRY OF DEFENCE – TECHNICAL INFORMATION CENTRE ROYAL ENGINEERS

Acronym or abbreviation: TICRE

Chetwynd Barracks, Chilwell, Nottingham, NG9
5HA

Tel: 0115 957 2310
Fax: 0115 957 2294

Enquiries:
Enquiries to: Librarian
Direct tel: 0115 957 2309

Founded:
1979

Organisation type and purpose:
National government centre, of the Ministry of
Defence.

To provide technical information for the Corps of Royal Engineers.

Subject coverage:
Civil, mechanical and electrical engineering, construction, fortifications.

Library catalogue:
All or part available in-house

Printed publications:
In-house publications only

Access to staff:
Contact by letter, by telephone and by fax. Appointment necessary.
Hours: Mon to Thu, 0800 to 1630; Fri, 0800 to 1600

Access to building, collection or gallery:
Prior appointment required
Hours: Mon to Thu, 0800 to 1630; Fri, 0800 to 1600

MINISTRY OF DEFENCE INFORMATION AND LIBRARY SERVICE – GLASGOW

Acronym or abbreviation: MOD

Room 1410, Kentigern House, 65 Brown Street, Glasgow, G2 8EX

Tel: 0141 224 2500
Fax: 0141 224 2257

Enquiries:
Enquiries to: Librarian
Direct tel: 0141 224 2501

Organisation type and purpose:
National government body.
Central government department.

Subject coverage:
Defence policy, armed forces, public administration, management, computing and information science, health and safety, standards, military science and engineering.

Museum or gallery collection, archive, or library special collection:
Full set of British standards on CD-ROM

Library catalogue:
All or part available in-house

Access to staff:
Appointment necessary.
Hours: Mon to Fri, 0900 to 1700

Branch of the:
Ministry of Defence Information and Library Service, Whitehall Library

MINISTRY OF DEFENCE INFORMATION AND LIBRARY SERVICE – WHITEHALL INFORMATION AND LIBRARY CENTRE

Acronym or abbreviation: MOD

Ground Floor, Zone D, Main Building, Whitehall, London, SW1A 2HB

Tel: 020 7218 4445
Fax: 020 7218 5413
E-mail: info-svcslibrary-office@mod.uk

Website:
http://www.mod.uk
About defence: MOD, United Kingdom armed services, defence issues related to the United Kingdom, links to related organisations and to useful sites.

Organisation type and purpose:
National government body.

Subject coverage:
Defence policy, organisation, strategy and technology; politics, government and international relations; management; company and commercial; computers; public administration.

Library catalogue:
All or part available in-house

Access to staff:
Contact by letter. Appointment necessary.
Hours: Mon to Fri, 0830 to 1630
Special comments: Charges made to all visitors.

MINTEL INTERNATIONAL GROUP

18–19 Long Lane, London, EC1A 9PL

Tel: 020 7606 4533
Fax: 020 7606 5932

Website:
http://www.cior.com
List of publications and services, contents pages, prices, ordering information.

Enquiries:
Enquiries to: Director

Founded:
1972

Organisation type and purpose:
Research organisation.
Global information provider.

Subject coverage:
Retailing, retailers, retail trade and retail topics in the UK and Europe, retailers based elsewhere but with a presence in the European market, global cross border activity.

Museum or gallery collection, archive, or library special collection:
Specialist retailing library and files (including historical information)
Extensive files on individual retail companies and operations, UK, Europe especially
Retail sector information
Retail statistical data

Trade and statistical information:
Retail trade data by country, by sector, data on cross-border retailing and retailers.

Printed publications:
Retail Reports and Database Service on over 30 topics, many sectors and on the UK, Europe and US
Consumer Product Market Surveys across Europe, Providing: market size, market shares, consumption patterns, distribution (£150)
European Retail Statistics – 17 Countries (£195)

Electronic and video publications:
Euro-RETAILNET (online database, 3000 company profiles, updated daily, from £1500)

Publications list:
Available in print

Access to staff:
Contact by letter, by telephone, by fax and in person
Hours: Mon to Fri, 0900 to 1730

Other locations:
Chicago; Frankfurt; Sydney; Belfast; Los Angeles

MINTEL INTERNATIONAL GROUP LIMITED

18–19 Long Lane, London, EC1A 9HE

Tel: 020 7606 4533
Fax: 020 7606 5932
E-mail: enquiries@mintel.com

Website:
http://www.mintel.com

Enquiries:
Enquiries to: Head of Marketing
Direct e-mail: stevec@mintel.com

Founded:
1972

Organisation type and purpose:
Research organisation.
Consumer research publisher.

Subject coverage:
Pan-European studies, FMCG (fast moving consumer goods) markets, food and drink, retail industry, leisure industry, personal finance industry, new products, company profiles, consumer research, life styles, business to business, Irish, industrial.

Trade and statistical information:
Comprehensive market data on all UK consumer, European and Industrial markets.

Printed publications:
European intelligence
Finance intelligence (annually)
Industrial intelligence
Irish intelligence
Leisure intelligence (annually)
Market intelligence (annually)
Retail intelligence (annually)
Special Reports (annually)
US Consumer Research

Publications list:
Available in print

Access to staff:
Contact by telephone, by e-mail and via website
Hours: Mon to Fri, 0900 to 1700

Affiliated to:
Chartered Institute of Marketing

MIRA LIMITED

Formal name: Motor Industry Research Association
Acronym or abbreviation: MIRA

Watling Street, Nuneaton, Warwickshire, CV10 0TU

Tel: 024 7635 5000
Fax: 024 7635 5355
E-mail: enquiries@mira.co.uk

Website:
http://www.mira.co.uk/aic
General information about MIRA as well as access to MIRA databases.

Enquiries:
Enquiries to: Information Officer
Direct tel: 024 7635 5275
Direct fax: 024 7635 5036

Founded:
1946

Organisation type and purpose:
Consultancy, research organisation.

Subject coverage:
Automobile engineering; problems applicable to motor vehicles including noise, vibration, comfort, safety and air pollution.

Trade and statistical information:
World data on automotive industry.

Printed publications:
Automobile Abstracts (monthly)
Automotive Business Index (weekly)
Bibliographies and information searches

Publications list:
Available online and in print

Access to staff:
Contact by e-mail and via website. Appointment necessary. Non-members charged.
Hours: Mon to Fri, 0900 to 1600

European agent for the:
Japan Society of Automotive Engineers Review

MISCARRIAGE ASSOCIATION, THE

c/o Clayton Hospital, Northgate, Wakefield, West Yorkshire, WF1 3JS

Tel: 01924 200799
Fax: 01924 298834
E-mail: info@miscarriageassociation.org.uk

continued overleaf

Website:
http://www.miscarriageassociation.org.uk

Enquiries:
Enquiries to: Administrator

Founded:
1982

Organisation type and purpose:
Registered charity (charity number 1076829).
Has a network of over 200 volunteer telephone contacts and 50 support groups in the UK.
To provide support and information for all on the subject of pregnancy loss.

Subject coverage:
Management and understanding of miscarriage in hospitals and the community.

Printed publications:
Basic Information Pack
We are sorry you have had a miscarriage (introductory leaflet)
Blighted Ovum
Ectopic Pregnancy
About the Cervical Stitch
Miscarriage: Guidelines for good practice

Publications list:
Available online and in print

Access to staff:
Contact by letter, by telephone, by fax, by e-mail and via website
Hours: Mon to Fri, 0900 to 1600

MISSING PEOPLE

PO Box 28908, London, SW14 7ZU

Tel: 0500 700 700; 020 8392 4590 (administration)
Fax: 020 8878 7752
E-mail: enquiries@missingpeople.org.uk

Website:
http://www.missingpeople.org.uk

Enquiries:
Enquiries to: Information Officer
Direct e-mail: amy.belcher@missingpeople.org.uk

Founded:
1994

Organisation type and purpose:
Registered charity (charity number 1020419).
Missing People is the United Kingdom's only charity that works with young runaways, missing and unidentified people, their families and others who care for them. As well as actively searching for missing people and supporting those who are trying to find them, the charity offers three other services: Runaway Helpline 0808 800 7070 for young runaways; Message Home 0800 700 740 for missing adults; and Identification Helpline resolves cases of unidentified people.

Subject coverage:
Missing people

Trade and statistical information:
Data on missing people

Printed publications:
General information leaflets: Missing People, Runaway Helpline, Message Home and Identification
Newsletter
Order printed publications from:
amy.belcher@missingpeople.org.uk

Access to staff:
Contact by letter, by telephone, by fax, by e-mail and via website
Hours: 24-hour service

MISSION AVIATION FELLOWSHIP (UK)

Acronym or abbreviation: MAF (UK)

Castle House, Castle Hill Avenue, Folkestone, Kent, CT20 2TN

Tel: 0845 8509505

Fax: 01303 852800
E-mail: supporter.relations@maf-uk.org

Enquiries:
Enquiries to: Chief Executive

Founded:
1947

Organisation type and purpose:
International organisation, registered charity (charity number 1064598).
Providing aviation and technical support to church, mission and relief agencies in the developing world.

Subject coverage:
Speakers and presentations of the work on Mission Aviation Fellowship are available on request.

Printed publications:
MAF News (magazine, quarterly, available on request free of charge)

Electronic and video publications:
Videos of operational work overseas available for purchase

Access to staff:
Contact by letter, by telephone, by fax and by e-mail. Appointment necessary.
Hours: Mon to Fri, 0900 to 1700

Branch Office:
Mission Aviation Fellowship
29 Canal Street, Glasgow, G4 0AD; tel: 0141 332 5222; fax: 0141 332 5222; e-mail: maf-scot.off@maf-uk.org

Member of:
Evangelical Alliance
Global Connections

MISSION TO SEAFARERS, THE

St Michael Paternoster Royal, College Hill, London, EC4R 2RL

Tel: 020 7248 5202
Fax: 020 7248 4761
E-mail: general@missiontoseafarers.org

Website:
http://www.missiontoseafarers.org
Information about where we work and what we do.

Enquiries:
Enquiries to: Public Relations Officer

Organisation type and purpose:
Voluntary organisation, registered charity (charity number 212432).
The Mission to Seafarers, a world mission agency of the Anglican church, cares for the welfare of seafarers of all nationalities and faiths in ports around the world.

Subject coverage:
Seafarers' conditions and welfare.

Museum or gallery collection, archive, or library special collection:
Selected archive material of The Mission to Seafarers and activities

Printed publications:
The Sea (newspaper for seafarers, every other month issued via centres and mailing list, subscription £1.50 per annum, 6 issues)
Flying Angel News (newspaper, three time a year for members/supporters, subscription £2 per annum, 3 issues)

Access to staff:
Contact by letter, by telephone, by fax, by e-mail and via website. Appointment necessary.
Hours: Mon to Fri, 0900 to 1700

Access to building, collection or gallery:
Prior appointment required

Members of:
International Christian Maritime Association (ICMA)
Herald House, 15 Lambs Passage, London EC1Y 8TQ, UK; tel: 020 7256 9216; fax: 020 7256 9217; e-mail: icma.secgen@btconnect.com; website: www.icma.as

MISSIONARY INSTITUTE LONDON

Acronym or abbreviation: MIL

Holcombe House, The Ridgeway, London, NW7 4HY

Tel: 020 8906 1893
Fax: 020 8906 4937
E-mail: mil@mdx.ac.uk

Enquiries:
Enquiries to: Librarian
Other contacts: Secretary for enquiries about courses.

Founded:
1969

Organisation type and purpose:
Registered charity (charity number 269713), university department or institute.

Subject coverage:
Theology, missiology, church history, social anthropology.

Library catalogue:
All or part available in-house

Access to staff:
Contact by letter, by fax and by e-mail
Hours: Mon to Fri, 0900 to 1700

Access to building, collection or gallery:
Prior appointment required
Hours: Mon to Fri, 0900 to 1700
Special comments: No loans to non-registered students.

Access for disabled people:
Parking provided, level entry

MKI CORTINA OWNERS CLUB

The Membership Secretary, 51 Studley Rise, Trowbridge, BA14 0PD

Tel: 01225 763888
E-mail: info@mk1cortina.com

Website:
http://www.mk1cortina.com
History of club, application form, bulletin board – cars for sale, spares, online order form.

Enquiries:
Enquiries to: Membership Secretary
Direct e-mail: alison-membership@blueyonder.co.uk

Founded:
1982

Organisation type and purpose:
Membership association (membership is by subscription), present number of members: 1100, voluntary organisation.
Car club.

Subject coverage:
Ford Cortina MKI car events, spares sourcing, legislation, insurance.

Printed publications:
Newsletter (members)

Publications list:
Available in print

Access to staff:
Contact by letter, by telephone, by fax, by e-mail and via website
Hours: Mon to Fri, 1800 to 2130

MOBILISE

Formal name: Mobilise Organisation

National Headquarters, Ashwellthorpe, Norwich, Norfolk, NR16 1EX

Tel: 01508 489449
Fax: 01508 488173
E-mail: enquiries@mobilise.info

Website:
http://www.mobilise.info

Enquiries:
Enquiries to: Information Officer

Founded:
2005

Created by the merger of:
Disabled Drivers' Association and Disabled Drivers' Motor Club (year of change 2005)

Organisation type and purpose:
Membership, campaigning charity (membership is by subscription, qualification), present number of members: 20,000, voluntary organisation, registered charity (charity number 1111826). To help disabled people on mobility issues.

Subject coverage:
Mobility benefits and queries, assessment centres, licensing problems, car/vehicle insurance for disabled people, car acquisition and adaptation, holidays, ferry concessions, legislation on transport and parking.

Museum or gallery collection, archive, or library special collection:
Archive of Magic Carpet magazines (bound vols) dating back to foundation in 1948, which form a valuable historical resource.

Printed publications:
A range of leaflets: VAT relief on motor vehicles adapted for disabled people, Blue Badge, Parking in London, Returing to driving, Ferry concessions, Toll concessions, Guide to mobility vehicles. Leaflets are free to members, £10 for all leaflets to non-members.

Access to staff:
Contact by letter, by telephone, by fax, by e-mail, in person and via website
Hours: Mon to Fri, 0900 to 1700
Special comments: Answerphone outside office hours.

Access for disabled people:
Parking provided, level entry, access to all public areas, toilet facilities

Branches:
30 local groups

MOBILITY ADVICE AND VEHICLE INFORMATION SERVICE

Acronym or abbreviation: MAVIS

Website:
http://www.dft.gov.uk/access/MAVIS
Information on mobility issues for disabled and elderly people.
http://www.mobility-centres.org.uk

Enquiries:
Enquiries to: Manager

Founded:
1985

Organisation type and purpose:
National government body, advisory body. Driving advice and assessment services.

Subject coverage:
Advice on adaptations, driving assessments, access assessments for disabled and older motorists

Information services:
Free information on all aspects of personal private transport

Museum or gallery collection, archive, or library special collection:
Information held on all aspects of mobility for disabled motorists

Printed publications:
Fact sheets including:
How to return to driving
Choosing a car
Fitting of hand controls
Leaflets including:
Advice to older drivers
Blue badge scheme

Publications list:
Available online and in print

Access to staff:
Contact by letter, by telephone, by fax and by e-mail. Appointment necessary.
Hours: Mon to Fri, 0830 to 1700

Access for disabled people:
Parking provided, ramped entry, access to all public areas, toilet facilities

Forum of Mobility Centres:
Cornwall Mobility centre
Tehidy House, Royal Cornwall Hospital, Truro, Cornwall, TR1 3LJ; tel: 01872 254920; fax: 01872 254921
Derby Regional Mobility Centre
Kingsway Hospital, Kingsway, Derby, DE22 3LZ; tel: 01332 371929; fax: 01332 382377; e-mail: info@derbyregionalmobilitycentre.co.uk; website: www.derbyregionalmobilitycentre.co.uk
Edinburgh Driving Assessment Centre
Astley Ainslie Hospital, 133 Grange Loan, Edinburgh, EH9 2HL; tel: 0131 537 9192; fax: 0131 537 9193
Kilverstone Mobility Centre
2 Napier Place, Thetford, Norfolk, IP24 3RL; tel: 01842 753029; fax: 01842 755950; e-mail: mail@kmacmobil.org.uk; website: www.kmacmobil.org.uk
Mobility Advice and Vehicle Information Service (MAVIS)
O Wing, Macadam Avenue, Old Wokingham Road, Crowthorne, Berkshire, RG45 6XD; tel: 01344 661000; fax: 01344 661066; e-mail: mavis@dft.gsi.gov.uk; website: www.dft.gov.uk/access/MAVIS
Mobility Centre
Regional Rehabilitation Centre, Hunters Road, Newcastle Upon Tyne, NE 4NR; tel: 0191 219 5694; fax: 0191 219 5665; website: www.nap.nhs.uk/snre/index.html
North Wales Drivers' Assessment Centre
Glan Clwyd Hospital, Rhuddlan Road, Bodelwyddan, Denbighshire, LL18 5UJ; tel: 01745 584858; fax: 01745 582762; e-mail: alexbarr@btconnect.com
Northern Ireland Mobility Centre
Disability Action, Portside Business Park, 189 Airport Road West, Belfast, BT3 9ED; tel: 028 9029 7880; fax: 028 9029 7881; e-mail: mobilitycentre@disabilityaction.org; website: www.disabilityaction.org
Oxford Driving Assessment Centre
Mary Marlborough Lodge, Windmill Road, Headington, Oxford, OX3 7LD; tel: 01865 227600; fax: 01865 227294; e-mail: oxford.mobilityservice@noc.anglox.nhs.uk
Queen Elizabeth's Foundation Mobility Centre
Damson Way, Fountain Drive, Carshalton, Surrey, SM5 4NR; tel: 020 8770 1151; fax: 020 8770 1211; e-mail: info@mobility-qe.org; website: www.qefd.org/mobilitycentre
South Wales Disabled Drivers' Assessment Centres
Rookwood Hospital, Fairwater Road, Llandaff, Cardiff, CF5 2YN; tel: 029 2055 5130; fax: 029 2055 5130; e-mail: WDDAC@btconnect.com
The Mobility Service of the Disabled Living Centre (West of England)
The Vassall Centre, Gill Avenue, Fishponds, Bristol, BS16 2QQ; tel: 0117 965 9353; fax: 0117 965 3652; e-mail: mobserve@dlcbristol.org

William Merritt Disabled Living Centre
St Mary's Hospital, Green Hill Road, Armley, Leeds, LS12 3QE; tel: 0113 305 5288; fax: 0113 231 9291; e-mail: wmmobilityservices@cwcom.net
Wrightington Mobility Centre
Wrightington Hospital, Hall Lane, Appley Bridge, Wigan, Lancashire, WN6 9EP; tel: 01257 256409; fax: 01257 253409; e-mail: mobility.centre@alwpct.nhs.uk

Other Mobility Centres:
Clatterbridge Driving Assessment Centre for the Disabled
Wirral Limb Centre, Clatterbridge Hospital, Bebington, Wirral, CH63 4JY; tel: 0151 604 7439; fax: 0151 604 7438
Hertfordshire Action on Disability
The Woodside Centre, Welwyn Garden City, Herts, AL7 4DD; tel: 01707 324 581; fax: 01707 371 297; e-mail: driving@hadnet.org.uk; website: www.hadnet.org.uk
Maidstone and Tunbridge Wells NHS Trust Car Mobility Advice Centre
Preston Hall Hospital, Larkfield Ward, Aylsford, Kent, ME20 7NJ; tel: 01622 225684; fax: 01622 225685; e-mail: janice.stannard@nhs.net
Mid Staffordshire Driving Assessment Service
Cannock Chase Hospital, Brunswick Road, Cannock, Staffs, WS11 2XY; tel: 01543 576411; fax: 01543 576555
Mobility Freedon
20 Fowey Avenue, Torquay, Devon, TQ2 7RE; tel: 01803 616661/01626 353942
Mobility Information Service
Unit B1 Greenwood Court, Cartmel Drive, Shrewsbury, SY1 3TB; tel: 01743 463063; fax: 01743 463065; e-mail: mis@nmcuk.freeserve.co.uk
Motoring Advice, Assessment and Tuition Service (MAATS)
Blackheath Drive, Clontarf, Dublin 3; tel: 00 3531 8338241; fax: 00 3531 8333873

MOBILITY INFORMATION SERVICE – SHREWSBURY

Acronym or abbreviation: MIS

Unit B1, Greenwood Court, Cartmel Drive, Shrewsbury, Shropshire, SY1 3TB

Tel: 01743 463072
Fax: 01743 463065
E-mail: mis@nmcuk.freeserve.co.uk

Website:
http://www.mis.org.uk

Enquiries:
Enquiries to: Chief Officer

Founded:
1979

Organisation type and purpose:
Advisory body, voluntary organisation, registered charity (charity number 1085593). Accredited Assessment Centre.

Subject coverage:
Mobility for disabled persons, disabled driver assessment and tuition, wheelchair and powered pavement vehicle assessment, advice on allowances, vehicle adaptations, product development and evaluation, passenger-carrying vehicles, adaptations, discounts on vehicles, disabled driver adaptations, motability, insurance, international travel for disabled persons.

Trade and statistical information:
Trade publications held on products of vehicle manufacturers and manual and powered wheelchairs, DSS Benefits available to disabled persons.

Printed publications:
Adaptations for the Disabled Driver (£1.25)
Disabled Driver Pack (£5)
Driving After a Stroke (£1)
Driving with Spina Bifida (free)
Road Tests (various)
Wheelchair Information Pack

continued overleaf

Access to staff:
Contact by letter, by telephone, by fax, by e-mail, in person and via website
Hours: Mon to Fri, 1000 to 1700

Access for disabled people:
Parking provided, level entry, access to all public areas, toilet facilities

Affiliated to:
Disabled Motorists Federation

Associate member of:
European Mobility Group
Mobility International

MOBILITY INFORMATION SERVICE – TELFORD

20 Burton Close, Dawley, Telford, TF4 2BX

Tel: 01743 340269
E-mail: mis@nmcuk.freeserve.co.uk

Website:
http://www.mis.org.uk

Enquiries:
Enquiries to: Chief Officer
Other contacts: Information Officer for general information on mobility matters.

Founded:
1979

Organisation type and purpose:
International organisation, voluntary organisation, registered charity (charity number 1085593). Provides mobility information to disabled people in order to help them attain independence.

Subject coverage:
Information on all aspects of mobility.

Museum or gallery collection, archive, or library special collection:
Hamilton Index
Handynet database
Rehadat

Non-library collection catalogue:
All or part available online and in-house

Printed publications:
Adaptions for the Disabled Driver: definitive listing of driver adaptions and specialist suppliers (£3.95 inc. p&p)
The Disabled Passenger (£3.95 inc. p&p)

Publications list:
Available online and in print

Access to staff:
Contact by letter, by telephone, by e-mail and via website
Hours: Tue, Fri, 1030 to 1530

Access for disabled people:
No public access

Links with:
Camping for the Disabled

MOD ADMIRALTY LIBRARY

Naval Historical Branch, No. 24 Store, PP 20, Main Road, HM Naval Base, Portsmouth, PO1 3LU

Tel: 02392 725297
Fax: 02392 724003
E-mail: cnsnhbal@a.dii.mod.uk

Founded:
1809

Organisation type and purpose:
National government body.
Historical Library.

Subject coverage:
History of the Royal Navy, with particular reference to administration, policy, doctrine, operations, strategy, tactics, hydrography, naval aviation, signalling and gunnery.

Museum or gallery collection, archive, or library special collection:
Approximately 160,000 vols and 100,000 pamphlets, in process of being catalogued. Catalogue of manuscripts and some printed charts searchable on Royal Naval Museum website. Historical collections of the Royal Naval Medical Services held at the Institute of Naval Medicine.

Library catalogue:
All or part available online, in-house and in print

Printed publications:
The following out-of-print catalogues will in due course be replaced by an online database:
Admiralty Library. Subject Catalogue of Printed Books, Part 1. Historical Section (London HMSO, 1912)
Admiralty Library. Subject Catalogue of Printed Books, Part 2. Law Section (London HMSO, 1915)
Catalogue of the Naval Library, Ministry of Defence, London (5 vols, Boston, MA, G. K. Hall, 1967)

Access to staff:
Contact by letter, by telephone, by fax, by e-mail and in person. Appointment necessary.
Hours: Mon to Thu, 1000 to 1700

Access to building, collection or gallery:
Appointment necessary
Hours: Mon to Thu, 1000 to 1700

Access for disabled people:
Access to all public areas, toilet facilities. Reserved parking space adjacent to building

Branches:
Admiralty Library, Portsmouth
No. 12 Store, PP64, Semaphore Tower Road, HM Naval Base, Portsmouth, PO1 JNH; tel: 023 9272 3795; fax: 023 9272 3942; e-mail: library@ royalnavalmuseum.org; website: http://www .royalnavalmuseum.org
Historical Library
Institute of Naval Medicine, Crescent Road, Alverstoke, Gosport, Hampshire, PO12 2DL; tel: 023 9276 8238; fax: 023 9250 4823; e-mail: cat1@ inm.mod.uk; website: http://www.royalnavy .mod.uk/server/show/nav.5724

Constituent part of:
Naval Historical Branch (NHB)
No. 24 Store, PP 20, Main Road, HM Naval Base, Portsmouth PO1 3LU; tel: 02392 725300; fax: 02392 724003

MODEL YACHTING ASSOCIATION

Acronym or abbreviation: MYA

Five Oaks, Church Lane, Oakley, Bedfordshire, MK43 7RU

Tel: 01234 822408
E-mail: m.clifton@easynet.co.uk

Website:
http://www.radiosailing.org.uk
Racing calendar; results; clubs; general information; links.

Enquiries:
Enquiries to: Information Officer
Direct tel: 01789 751800
Direct e-mail: graham.reeves@virgin.net

Founded:
1911

Organisation type and purpose:
Membership association.
National sporting authority.

Subject coverage:
Competitive sailing of wind-powered models; design, construction, operation of model yachts; locations of affiliated clubs; history of the sport.

Museum or gallery collection, archive, or library special collection:
Comprehensive reference library of printed books and magazines since 1879

Minutes and other administrative records of the MYA since 1931

Printed publications:
Acquaints (individual members and affiliated clubs, 4 times a year)
Rating Rules for Model Yachts
Year Book

Publications list:
Available in print

Access to staff:
Contact by letter, by telephone and by e-mail
Hours: Mon to Fri, 0900 to 2100

Associated with:
Central Council for Physical Recreation
International Sailing Federation (Radio Sailing Division) (ISAF/RSD)
Royal Yachting Association

MODERN CHURCHPEOPLE'S UNION

Acronym or abbreviation: MCU

MCU Office, 9 Westward View, Liverpool, Merseyside, L17 7EE

Tel: 0845 345 1909/ 0151 726 9730
E-mail: office@modchurchunion.org

Website:
http://www.modchurchunion.org

Enquiries:
Enquiries to: General Secretary

Founded:
1898

Organisation type and purpose:
Learned society (membership is by subscription), present number of members: 700, voluntary organisation, registered charity (charity number 281573).

Subject coverage:
Church affairs, especially Church of England; theology; philosophy of religion; ethics.

Printed publications:
Modern Believing (4 times a year)
The Contemporary Challenge of Modernist Theology
The New Liberalism: Faith for the Third Millennium
Hastings Rashdall: Bibliography of the Published Writings

Publications list:
Available in print

Access to staff:
Contact by letter, by telephone, by e-mail and via website. Appointment necessary.
Hours: Mon to Fri, 0900 to 1500

MODERN HUMANITIES RESEARCH ASSOCIATION

Acronym or abbreviation: MHRA

Department of European Studies and Modern Languages, University of Bath, Bath, BA2 7AY

Tel: 01225 826826 ext 5404
Fax: 01225 826099
E-mail: mail@mhra.org.uk

Website:
http://www.mhra.org.uk
Publications and activities.

Enquiries:
Enquiries to: Honorary Secretary

Founded:
1918

Organisation type and purpose:
International organisation, learned society, registered charity.

Subject coverage:
Modern and medieval languages and literatures, including English.

Printed publications:
Annual Bibliography of English Language and
    Literature
Austrian Studies
MHRA Annual Bulletin
MHRA Bibliographies
MHRA Critical Texts
MHRA Style Guide
MHRA Texts and Dissertations
Modern Language Review (quarterly)
Oxford German Studies (jointly with Maney
    Publishing)
Portuguese Studies (biannual)
Publications of the MHRA
Slavonic and East European Review (quarterly)
Year's Work in Modern Language Studies
Yearbook of English Studies (biannual)

Electronic and video publications:
Annual Bibliography of English Language and
    Literature (online)

Publications list:
Available online and in print

Access to staff:
Contact by letter, by telephone and by e-mail.
Appointment necessary.
Hours: Mon to Fri, 0900 to 1700

MODERN PENTATHLON ASSOCIATION OF GREAT BRITAIN, THE

Acronym or abbreviation: MPAGB

Norwood House, University of Bath, Claverton
Down, Bath, BA2 7AY

Tel: 01225 386808
Fax: 01225 386995
E-mail: admin@mpagb.org.uk

Website:
http://www.mpagb.org.uk
About association, athletes, clubs calendar, links
with other sports and federations.

Enquiries:
Enquiries to: Administration Officer

Founded:
1948

Organisation type and purpose:
Membership association (membership is by
subscription), present number of members: 1500,
voluntary organisation.
Governing body and co-ordinating authority.

Subject coverage:
Modern pentathlon – compilation of five sports:
fencing, swimming, shooting, running and riding;
biathlon, triathlon, tetrathlon, pentathlon,
coaching, events.

Printed publications:
Broadsheet (3 times a year, members)
Modern Pentathlon Rule Book (£5.50 plus p&p)

Access to staff:
Contact by letter, by telephone, by fax, by e-mail
and via website
Hours: Mon to Fri, 0900 to 1700

MOLE VALLEY DISTRICT COUNCIL

Pippbrook, Dorking, Surrey, RH4 1SJ

Tel: 01306 885001\ Minicom no. 01372 819094
Fax: 01306 876821
E-mail: information@molevalley.gov.uk

Website:
http://www.molevalley.gov.uk

Enquiries:
Enquiries to: Communications Officer
Direct tel: 01306 879113

Other contacts: communications@molevalley.gov.uk
Founded:
1974

Organisation type and purpose:
Local government body.

Subject coverage:
Local authority services, Mole Valley district
including the main towns of Dorking and
Leatherhead.

Trade and statistical information:
Data on area and population.

Printed publications:
Mole Valley District Guide – A guide to towns and
    countryside around Dorking and Leatherhead
Mole Valley street map
Various information leaflets relating to Mole Valley
    services and amenities
Walking in Mole Valley (series of 20)

Access to staff:
Contact by letter, by telephone, by fax, by e-mail
and in person
Hours: Mon to Fri, 0830 to 1700; helpline open
same hours

Parent body:
Surrey County Council
    County Hall, Penrhyn Road, Kingston upon
    Thames, KT1 2DN; tel: 020 8541 8800; fax: 020
    8541 9005

MONEYFACTS PUBLICATIONS

Formal name: Moneyfacts Group plc

Moneyfacts House, 66–70 Thorpe Road, Norwich,
Norfolk, NR1 1BJ

Tel: 01603 476476
Fax: 01603 476477
E-mail: enquiries@moneyfacts.co.uk

Enquiries:
Enquiries to: Librarian

Founded:
1988

Organisation type and purpose:
Research organisation, publishing house.

Subject coverage:
Mortgage, savings, pensions, investments, and
business finance information.

Trade and statistical information:
UK mortgage, savings and investment rates,
    offshore mortgage and savings rates, business
    finance data, data on life, pensions and unit trust
    products.

Printed publications:
Business Moneyfacts: Guide to Business Finance
    (monthly, £87.50 annual subscription)
Life & Pensions Moneyfacts (monthly, £88.50,
    annual subscription)
Moneyfacts: Guide to Savings and Mortgage Rates
    (monthly, £89.50 annual subscription)

Publications list:
Available in print

Access to staff:
Contact by letter, by telephone and by fax. All
charged.
Hours: Mon to Fri, 0900 to 1700

Access for disabled people:
Parking provided, ramped entry

MONMOUTHSHIRE COUNTY COUNCIL

County Hall, Croesyceiliog, Cwmbran, Gwent,
NP44 2XH

Tel: 01633 644644
Fax: 01633 644666

Website:
http://www.monmouthshire.gov.uk

Enquiries:
Enquiries to: Communication Officer
Direct tel: 01633 644402
Direct e-mail: paulaskyrme@monmouthshire.gov
.uk

Founded:
1996

Organisation type and purpose:
Local government body.

Subject coverage:
Local government services, background to
Monmouthshire.

**Museum or gallery collection, archive, or library
special collection:**
The former Gwent County Record Office and
    Archives hold all records and collections

Printed publications:
Order printed publications from: Community Spirit
(residents' newspaper)

Access to staff:
Contact by letter, by telephone, by fax and by e-
mail. Appointment necessary.
Hours: Fri, 0900 to 1600

Access to building, collection or gallery:
By appointment

Access for disabled people:
Parking provided, level entry, toilet facilities

MONMOUTHSHIRE LIBRARIES AND INFORMATION SERVICE

Acronym or abbreviation: MLIS

County Hall, 5th Floor, Cwmbran, Gwent, NP44
2XH

Tel: 01633 644551
Fax: 01633 644545
E-mail: infocentre@monmouthshire.gov.uk

Website:
http://www.monmouthshire.gov.uk/leisure/
libraries
http://libraries.monmouthshire.gov.uk
Community information database.

Enquiries:
Enquiries to: Principal Librarian

Founded:
1996

Organisation type and purpose:
Local government body, public library.

Subject coverage:
Local studies, historical Monmouthshire, advice
and self-help information.

**Museum or gallery collection, archive, or library
special collection:**
Chepstow Collection (material pertaining to
    Chepstow, donated by the Chepstow Society in
    1952 and housed in Chepstow Library)

Trade and statistical information:
Welsh Assembly Government collection at
    Chepstow.

Non-library collection catalogue:
All or part available online

Library catalogue:
All or part available online

Publications list:
Available in print

Access to staff:
Contact by letter, by telephone, by fax, by e-mail,
in person and via website

Access to building, collection or gallery:
Hours: Hours vary from site to site

Access for disabled people:
Ramped entry

continued overleaf

Branch libraries:
Abergavenny Library
 Baker Street, Abergavenny, NP7 5BD; tel: 01873
 735980; fax: 01873 735985; e-mail:
 abergavennylibrary@monmouthshire.gov.uk
Caldicot Library
 Woodstock Way, Caldicot, NP26 4DB; tel: 01291
 426425; fax: 01291 426426; e-mail:
 caldicotlibrary@monmouthshire.gov.uk
Chepstow Library and Information Centre
 Manor Way, Chepstow, NP16 5HZ; tel: 01291
 635730; fax: 01291 635736; e-mail:
 chepstowlibrary@monmouthshire.gov.uk
Gilwern Library
 Village Hall, Crickhowell Road, Gilwern, NP7
 0DE; tel: 01873 833055; fax: 01873 833055; e-mail:
 gilwernlibrary@monmouthshire.gov.uk
Monmouth Library
 Rolls Hall, Whitecross Street, Monmouth, NP25
 3BY; tel: 01600 775215; fax: 01600 775218; e-mail:
 monmouthlibrary@monmouthshire.gov.uk
Usk Library
 18A Maryport Street, Usk, NP15 1AE; tel: 01291
 674925; fax: 01291 674924; e-mail: usklibrary@
 monmouthshire.gov.uk

Parent body:
Monmouthshire County Council
 tel: 01633 644644; fax: 01633 644545

MONTESSORI SOCIETY AMI (UK), THE

26 Lyndhurst Gardens, London, NW3 5NW

Tel: 020 7435 7874
Fax: 020 7431 8096
E-mail: montessorisociety@fsmail.net

Website:
http://www.montessori-uk.org

Enquiries:
Enquiries to: Honorary Secretary

Founded:
1935

Organisation type and purpose:
National organisation, professional body,
membership association (membership is by
subscription), present number of members: 300,
voluntary organisation.
To spread the ideas of child development and
philosophy set out by Dr Maria Montessori to
parents and others concerned with children.

Subject coverage:
Montessori system of education, child
development, location of Montessori schools,
training, training courses recognised by AMI,
apparatus, supply information, Montessori
literature.

Printed publications:
Book list containing publications by and about
 Maria Montessori
Introducing Montessori
The Montessori Direction (newsletter)
The Montessori Review (magazine)

Electronic and video publications:
Montessori in Action: Learning for Life (video)

Publications list:
Available in print

Access to staff:
Contact by letter, by telephone, by fax and by e-
mail. Appointment necessary. Letter of
introduction required.
Hours: Mon to Fri, 0900 to 1700

Affiliated to:
Association Montessori Internationale (AMI)
 tel: + 31 20 679 8932; fax: + 31 20 676 7341; e-mail:
 ami@xs4all.nl; website: http://www.montessori
 -ami.org

MONUMENTAL BRASS SOCIETY

Society of Antiquaries, Burlington House,
Piccadilly, London, W1J 0BE

Tel: 01206 337239
Fax: 01206 861852
E-mail: martinstuchfield@btconnect.com

Website:
http://www.mbs-brasses.co.uk

Founded:
1887

Organisation type and purpose:
Learned society.

Subject coverage:
Preservation of monumental brasses, indents of
lost brasses and incised slabs.

Printed publications:
Bulletin (3 times a year)
Portfolio (occasional, 5 or 6 plates of brasses and
 incised slabs)
Transactions (annually)

Access to staff:
Contact by letter, by fax and by e-mail
Hours: Mon to Fri, 0900 to 1700

MOOR GREEN

Formal name: Moor Green (Brain Injury
Rehabilitation Centre)
Acronym or abbreviation: Moor Green

Moseley Hall Hospital, Alcester Road, Moseley,
Birmingham, B13 8JL

Tel: 0121 442 3400
Fax: 0121 442 3420
E-mail: Liz.wright@sbcht.wmids.nhs.uk

Enquiries:
Enquiries to: Clinical Manager

Founded:
1967

Organisation type and purpose:
National Health Service.
To provide out-patient rehabilitation following
brain injury. Assessment for services and
equipment etc. To provide information, advice,
counselling, loan equipment and special services.

Subject coverage:
Rehabilitation of people who have suffered head
injuries (middle to late stage treatment).

**Museum or gallery collection, archive, or library
special collection:**
Literature on Brain injury

Printed publications:
Moor Green leaflets

Access to staff:
Contact by letter, by telephone and by fax.
Appointment necessary.
Hours: Mon to Fri, 0900 to 1700

Links with:
West Midlands Rehabilitation Centre
 Oak Tree Lane, Selly Oak, Birmingham, B29 6JA

MORAVIAN CHURCH IN GREAT BRITAIN

Moravian Church House, 5–7 Muswell Hill,
London, N10 3TJ

Tel: 020 8883 3409
Fax: 020 8365 3371
E-mail: moravianchurchhouse@btinternet.com

Website:
http://www.moravian.org.uk

Enquiries:
Enquiries to: General Secretary
Other contacts: Archivist for visits to the archives
and library.

Founded:
1457

Organisation type and purpose:
International organisation, present number of
members: 2000, voluntary organisation, registered
charity.
Christian church.
To worship God and spread the gospel.

Subject coverage:
History, doctrine and practices of the Moravian
Church in the UK and overseas.

**Museum or gallery collection, archive, or library
special collection:**
Manuscript diaries and letters from the 18th and
 19th centuries relating to the growth and work of
 the Church, especially in West Indies and
 Labrador
Numerous letters from John Wesley to Moravian
 leaders

Printed publications:
Various hymn and prayer books
Over 40 publications including:
Baptism and Confirmation certificates
Church Order of the Unitas Fratrum
Customs and Practices of the Moravian Church
History of the Moravian Church
Moravian Mission in Labrador

Publications list:
Available online and in print

Access to staff:
Contact by letter, by telephone and by e-mail.
Appointment necessary.
Hours: Mon to Fri, 0930 to 1700

MORAY COUNCIL DEPARTMENT OF EDUCATIONAL SERVICES

Council Offices, High Street, Elgin, Moray, IV30
1BX

Tel: 01343 543451
Fax: 01343 563478
E-mail: campbea@moray.gov.uk

Website:
http://www.moray.gov.uk

Enquiries:
Enquiries to: Library and Museums Manager
Direct tel: 01343 563398
Other contacts: Principal Librarian

Organisation type and purpose:
Local government body, public library.

Subject coverage:
General, local history of Moray, Nairn and
Banffshire, family history.

**Museum or gallery collection, archive, or library
special collection:**
Archives of preceding and current local authorities
Falconer Papers
Local history collection
Local newspapers on microfilm
Microfilm records of births, marriages and deaths
 and early census returns
Wittet and Doig Collection of 10,000 architectural
 plans, 1828–1900

Non-library collection catalogue:
All or part available online

Library catalogue:
All or part available online

Printed publications:
A Flannel Sark an Vik (1999)
Churches of Moray (1981)
Elgin Past and Present (1980, revised 1995)
Laich O'Moray Past and Present (1985)
Tar Atween Yer Taes (1999)
The Lintie O'Moray (facsimile of 1984 edn)
Order printed publications from: Principal Librarian
(Central Services), Elgin Library, Cooper Park,
Elgin, Morayshire, IV30 1BX, tel: 01343 562607, fax:
01343 562630, e-mail: elgin.library@moray.gov.uk

Publications list:
Available online

Access to staff:
Contact by letter, by telephone, by fax, by e-mail and in person
Hours: Mon to Fri, 0845 to 1700

Member organisation of:
European Information Relay
Scottish Library and Information Council

MORAY COUNCIL LOCAL HERITAGE SERVICE

Old East End School, Institution Road, Elgin, Moray, IV30 1RP

Tel: 01343 569011
E-mail: heritage@moray.gov.uk

Website:
http://www.moray.org/heritage/roots.html
http://www.moray.org/heritage/index.html

Enquiries:
Enquiries to: Local Heritage Officer

Founded:
1996

Organisation type and purpose:
Local government body, research organisation.

Subject coverage:
Sources relating to Moray including archives, books, maps, newspapers and genealogical records.

Education services:
Resources for Further or Higher Education.

Non-library collection catalogue:
All or part available in-house

Library catalogue:
All or part available in-house

Access to staff:
Contact by letter, by telephone, by e-mail, in person and via website

Access to building, collection or gallery:
No prior appointment required
Hours: Mon, Wed, Thu, Fri, 1000 to 1700; Tue, 1000 to 2000; Sat, 1000 to 1200

Access for disabled people:
Access to all public areas

MORDEN LIBRARY

Merton Civic Centre, London Road, Morden, Surrey, SM4 5DX

Tel: 020 8545 4040\ Minicom no. 020 8946 1136
Fax: 020 8545 4037
E-mail: morden.library@merton.gov.uk

Enquiries:
Enquiries to: Library and Service Manager
Direct tel: 020 8545 3775
Direct e-mail: di.reynolds@merton.gov.uk

Founded:
1960

Organisation type and purpose:
Local government body, public library.

Subject coverage:
General, local history covering the area of Merton London Borough and its predecessor authorities.

Museum or gallery collection, archive, or library special collection:
Collection of Catalogues etc from Carters Tested Seeds
Lord Nelson
Simpson Papers
Tom Francis Collection of photographic negatives
William Morris, books, pictures and other material

Non-library collection catalogue:
All or part available in-house

Library catalogue:
All or part available in-house

Printed publications:
Various local history publications including:

Paradise Merton: the story of Nelson and the Hamiltons at Merton Place (Philip Rathbone, £2.50)
William Morris at Merton (David Saxby, £3.95)

Publications list:
Available in print

Access to staff:
Contact by letter, by telephone, by fax, by e-mail and in person
Hours: Mon, Tues, Thurs, Fri, 0930 to 1900; Wed, 0930 to 1300; Sat, 0930 to 1700

Access to building, collection or gallery:
No prior appointment required

Access for disabled people:
Parking provided, level entry, access to all public areas, toilet facilities

Also at the same address:
Merton Local Studies Centre
tel: 020 8545 3239

Parent body and at the same address:
London Borough of Merton, Merton Library Service

MOREDUN RESEARCH INSTITUTE

International Research Centre, Pentlands Science Park, Bush Loan, Penicuik, Midlothian, EH26 0PZ

Tel: 0131 445 5111
Fax: 0131 445 6235
E-mail: library@mri.sari.ac.uk

Website:
http://www.mri.sari.ac.uk

Enquiries:
Enquiries to: Librarian

Founded:
1920

Organisation type and purpose:
Research organisation.

Subject coverage:
Veterinary aspects of bacteriology, microbiology, pathology, molecular biology, parasitology, immunology, virology, especially relating to ruminants and particularly sheep.

Non-library collection catalogue:
All or part available in-house

Library catalogue:
All or part available in-house

Printed publications:
Annual List of Papers by Institute Staff
Annual Report

Access to staff:
Contact by telephone and by e-mail. Appointment necessary.
Hours: Mon to Fri, 0850 to 1715

Access to building, collection or gallery:
Prior appointment required

Access for disabled people:
Level entry

Funded by:
Scottish Executive Environment and Rural Affairs Department

Links with:
BBSRC

Parent body:
Moredun Foundation

MORLEY COLLEGE

Formal name: Morley College (1993) Limited

61 Westminster Bridge Road, London, SE1 7HT

Tel: 020 7928 8501
Fax: 020 7928 4074
E-mail: enquiries@morleycollege.ac.uk

Website:
http://www.morleycollege.ac.uk

Enquiries:
Enquiries to: Library Manager
Direct tel: 020 7450 9229

Organisation type and purpose:
Registered charity.
Adult education.

Subject coverage:
Music, art, languages (self tuition courses), social studies, literature, theatre, exercise and health, self tuition wordprocessing, spreadsheets etc, courses, multimedia.

Access to staff:
Contact by letter, by telephone, by e-mail and in person. Appointment necessary. Access for members only.
Hours: Term time: Mon to Thu, 1100 to 2000; Fri, 1100 to 1900

MOROCCAN NATIONAL TOURIST OFFICE

Formal name: Moroccan National Tourist Office
Acronym or abbreviation: MNTO

205 Regent Street, London, W1B 4HB

Tel: 020 7437 0073
Fax: 020 7734 8172
E-mail: mnto@btconnect.com

Website:
http://www.tourism-in-morocco.com

Enquiries:
Enquiries to: Director
Other contacts: Information Officer for information relevant to tourism in Morocco.

Founded:
1916

Organisation type and purpose:
National government body.
Morocco's official tourist representation, under the jurisdiction of the Moroccan Tourism Ministry. The main objective of the MNTO is to promote Morocco abroad as a distinctive destination choice for tourism.

Subject coverage:
Tourist information and advice for Morocco.

Museum or gallery collection, archive, or library special collection:
Maps
Posters
Slides (are kept in our office library)

Trade and statistical information:
Information is obtainable from the Moroccan Embassy on 020 7581 5001, contact the Economic Attaché.

Printed publications:
List of contacts for tour operators and travel agents
Tourist literature (free of charge, direct)
Promotional material in brochures, guides and posters

Electronic and video publications:
Documentaries on video
Various Hotel Properties in Morocco (Video and CD-ROM)

Publications list:
Available in print

Access to staff:
Contact by letter, by telephone, by fax, by e-mail and in person. Appointment necessary.
Hours: Mon to Fri, 0900 to 1730

Parent body:
Moroccan National Tourist Office, Rabat, Morocco
31 Angle Rue Oued Fès Avenue, Al Abtal-Agdal-Rabat, Morocco; tel: 00 2123 7 681531/32/33; fax: 00 2123 7 777437 or 681527; e-mail: visitmorocco@onmt.org.ma

MORRAB LIBRARY

Morrab House, Morrab Gardens, Penzance, Cornwall, TR18 4DA

Tel: 01736 364474

Website:
http://www.morrablibrary.co.uk

Enquiries:
Enquiries to: Librarian
Other contacts: Chairman (for committee decisions)

Founded:
1818

Organisation type and purpose:
Membership association (membership is by subscription).
Independent library.

Subject coverage:
General: all subjects, particularly history, English literature, theology, art. Special collections; Cornish collections; archival holdings, mostly Cornish; photographic archive (West Cornwall).

Museum or gallery collection, archive, or library special collection:
Stock of 50,000 books
Dawson Collection: Napoleana, Peers of the Realm
Photographic archive
Borlase manuscripts

Non-library collection catalogue:
All or part available in-house

Library catalogue:
All or part available in-house

Access to staff:
Contact by letter, by telephone, by e-mail and in person. Appointment necessary. Non-members charged.
Hours: Tue to Fri, 1000 to 1600; Sat, 1000 to 1300
Special comments: Appointment necessary for archives.

MORRIS COWLEY & OXFORD OWNERS CLUB

Acronym or abbreviation: MCOC

202 Chantry Gardens, Southwick, Trowbridge, Wiltshire, BA14 9QX

Tel: 01225 766800

Enquiries:
Enquiries to: Secretary

Founded:
1979

Organisation type and purpose:
Membership association (membership is by subscription).
To supply parts to classic vehicle owners, clubs etc.

Subject coverage:
General information which appertains to the Morris Cowley, Oxford and Isis range of vehicles (built 1954–60); spares availability, costing and cars for sale. Also information/membership for owners of Hindustan Ambassadors.

Printed publications:
The Cowley News (magazine, quarterly, members)

Access to staff:
Contact by letter, by telephone and in person
Hours: Mon to Fri, 0900 to 2100, and weekends

MORRIS FEDERATION

Acronym or abbreviation: MF

Corner Cottage, 2 Lower Street, Sproughton, Ipswich, IP8 3AA

Tel: 01473 742334
E-mail: archive@morrisfed.org

Website:
http://www.morrisfed.org

Enquiries:
Enquiries to: Archive Officer

Founded:
1975

Organisation type and purpose:
Membership association (membership is by subscription), present number of members: 350, voluntary organisation.
To promote Morris Dancing.

Subject coverage:
Morris dancing, sword dancing, mumming.

Museum or gallery collection, archive, or library special collection:
Archive of Morris material

Non-library collection catalogue:
All or part available in-house

Library catalogue:
All or part available in-house

Printed publications:
Information Leaflet (on request)
Newsletter (quarterly)

Publications list:
Available in print

Access to staff:
Contact by letter, by telephone and by e-mail.
Appointment necessary. Access for members only.
All charged.
Hours: Tue to Sun, 0900 to 2000

Access to building, collection or gallery:
Prior appointment required

Also at:
FeeLock (CMF Secretary)
28 Fairstone Close, Hastings, Sussex, TN35 5EZ; tel: 01424 436052; e-mail: sec@morrisfed.org

Related organisation:
English Folk Dance & Song Society
tel: 020 7485 2206; fax: 020 7284 0534
Morris Ring
Open Morris

MORRIS MARINA OWNERS CLUB AND MORRIS ITAL REGISTER

39 Portley Road, Dawley, Telford, Shropshire, TF4 3JW

Tel: 01952 504900
E-mail: ajmmarina@aol.com

Enquiries:
Enquiries to: General Secretary
Other contacts: Life President, Chairman

Founded:
1985

Organisation type and purpose:
Membership association (membership is by subscription), present number of members: 450.

Subject coverage:
Morris Marina and Morris Ital, saloon, coupe, estate, van, pickup, caravanette and motor caravan versions marketed and produced worldwide.

Museum or gallery collection, archive, or library special collection:
Information collected and held by members, brochures, workshop manuals, road test reports, press release information

Printed publications:
Marina Matters (magazine, quarterly)

Access to staff:
Contact by letter, by telephone and by e-mail
Hours: Mon to Fri, 0900 to 1700

MORRIS MARINA/ITAL DRIVERS' CLUB

Acronym or abbreviation: MIDC

12 Nithsdale Road, Liverpool, L15 5AX

Enquiries:
Enquiries to: Membership Secretary

Founded:
1984

Formerly called:
Morris Marina Owners' Club (year of change 1986)

Organisation type and purpose:
International organisation, membership association (membership is by subscription), present number of members: 5.
To assist owners and enthusiasts of Morris Marina and Ital cars and their derivatives to restore, maintain, preserve and operate the cars.

Subject coverage:
Maintenance, preservation and restoration of Morris Marina and Ital cars; historical and production information on Morris Marina and Ital cars.

Museum or gallery collection, archive, or library special collection:
Technical reference library; workshop manuals, parts lists, magazine articles etc, register

Printed publications:
Last of The Line (newsletter, 6 times a year)
Something for Everyone, 3 vols
Alternative Parts Numbers List
Order printed publications from: J G Lawson at above address

Electronic and video publications:
Something for Everyone (120,000 word book available on disk)

Publications list:
Available in print

Access to staff:
Contact by letter. Appointment necessary. Access for members only.
Hours: Mon to Fri, 0900 to 1700

Connections with:
Marina/Ital Specialist Workshop
44 Sanderson's Croft, Leigh, Lancashire, WN7 2BA
North American Marina Owner's Registry
1107 Angel Drive, Alexander, Arkansas, 72002–7015, U.S.A.
Scandinavian Marina Club
Eftevaag, Kristiansand, N-7639, Norway
Sun-Tor Register
35 Walkerith Road, Morton, Gainsborough, Lincolnshire, DN21 3DA

MORRIS MINOR OWNERS CLUB LIMITED

8 Castings Road, Sir Francis Ley Industrial Estate, Derby, DE23 8YL

Tel: 01332 291675
Fax: 01332 290661
E-mail: andrew.booth@morrisminoroc.co.uk

Website:
http://www.morrisminoroc.co.uk
Club information.

Enquiries:
Enquiries to: Membership Administrator
Other contacts: Magazine Editor for magazine entries.

Founded:
1976

Organisation type and purpose:
Membership association (membership is by subscription), present number of members: 13,500.

Subject coverage:
General information on all Morris Minor cars manufactured between 1948 and 1971.

Printed publications:
Magazine (6 times a year, members)

Access to staff:
Contact by letter, by telephone, by fax, by e-mail and via website
Hours: Mon to Fri, 0900 to 1700. 24-hour answerphone

MORTAR INDUSTRY ASSOCIATION

Acronym or abbreviation: MIA

156 Buckingham Palace Road, London, SW1W 9TR

Tel: 020 7730 8194
Fax: 020 7730 4355
E-mail: james@qpa.org

Website:
http://www.mortar.org.uk
Datasheets for download, general information.

Enquiries:
Enquiries to: Secretary

Founded:
1971

Organisation type and purpose:
Trade association.
To promote the use of all factory made mortars, to further this it maintains an interest in and actively promotes masonry construction in the wider sense.

Subject coverage:
Factory made mortars for constructing brickwork, blockwork and stonework, external render, internal plaster and paving mortar.

Printed publications:
Data sheets (various topics)
Benefits (brochure)

Electronic and video publications:
Video

Publications list:
Available in print

Access to staff:
Contact by letter, by telephone, by fax, by e-mail and via website
Hours: Mon to Fri, 0900 to 1700

Founder member of:
Masonry Society

Parent body:
Quarry Products Association (QPA)
at the same address

MOTABILITY

Warwick House, Roydon Road, Harlow, Essex, CM19 5PX

Tel: 0845 456 4566
Fax: 01279 632000

Website:
http://www.motability.co.uk
A step by step guide to the Motability scheme.

Enquiries:
Enquiries to: Customer Helpline

Founded:
1977

Organisation type and purpose:
Registered charity, charity number 299745.
The Motability Scheme is the UK's leading car scheme for disabled people providing affordable, convenient, trouble-free motoring to 430,000 disabled customers and their families. Powered wheelchairs and scooters can also be financed using the scheme. Motability also provides financial assistance to customers who would otherwise be unable to afford the mobility solution they need.

Subject coverage:
Cars and powered wheelchairs, for recipients of the higher rate mobility component of DLA (Disability Living Allowance), or the war pensioners' mobility supplement.

Printed publications:
Leaflets and brochures
Lifestyle (magazine)

Electronic and video publications:
DVDs

Access to staff:
Contact by letter, by telephone and by fax
Hours: Mon to Fri, 0845 to 1715

Access for disabled people:
Parking provided, access to all public areas, toilet facilities

MOTHERS' UNION

Acronym or abbreviation: MU

Mary Sumner House, 24 Tufton Street, London, SW1P 3RB

Tel: 020 7222 5533
Fax: 020 7227–9736
E-mail: marketing@themothersunion.org

Website:
http://www.themothersunion.org

Enquiries:
Enquiries to: Head of Marketing

Founded:
1876

Organisation type and purpose:
International organisation, voluntary organisation, registered charity.
To strengthen and preserve marriage and Christian family life.

Subject coverage:
Family and marriage-related subjects, role and status of women overseas, law reform, the media, prayer and spirituality.

Museum or gallery collection, archive, or library special collection:
Committee and administrative archives, founder's correspondence
Set of MU periodicals

Library catalogue:
All or part available online

Printed publications:
Books, leaflets, prayers and services

Publications list:
Available online and in print

Access to staff:
Contact by letter, by telephone, by fax, by e-mail, in person and via website
Hours: Mon to Fri, 0900 to 1800

Links with:
66 dioceses in the British Isles and 27 Provinces of the Anglican Communion world-wide

MOTO GUZZI CLUB GB

Acronym or abbreviation: MGCGB

Mole Cottage, 26 The Crescent, The Wells, Epsom, Surrey, KT18 7LL

Tel: 01372 724681
Fax: 01372 724681

Website:
http://www.motoguzzigb.com

Enquiries:
Enquiries to: General Secretary

Founded:
1976

Organisation type and purpose:
Membership association (membership is by subscription), present number of members: 3000.

Subject coverage:
All aspects of Moto Guzzi motorcycle ownership; discounts, technical advice, local club branches, social events, continental touring, factory visits, deals on insurance and valuation service, DVLA approved for marque requests.

Printed publications:
Gambalunga (magazine, 6 times a year)

Access to staff:
Contact by letter, by telephone and by fax
Hours: Mon to Fri, 1800 to 2000

Parent body:
British Motorcycle Federation

MOTOR CARAVANNERS' CLUB LIMITED

22 Evelyn Close, Twickenham, Middlesex, TW2 7BN

Tel: 020 8893 3883
Fax: 020 8893 8324
E-mail: info@motorcaravanners.eu

Website:
http://www.motorcaravanners.eu
Details of club membership and club activities.
Diary of club events.

Enquiries:
Enquiries to: Executive Secretary

Founded:
1962

Organisation type and purpose:
Membership association (membership is by subscription), present number of members: 11,500.

Subject coverage:
Motor caravans, DIY conversions, UK touring, European touring, technical information.

Printed publications:
Only to Club members

Publications list:
Available in print

Access to staff:
Contact by letter, by telephone, by fax, by e-mail and via website
Hours: Mon to Thu, 0900 to 1700; Fri, 0900 to 1400

Member of:
The Federation Internationale de Camping and Caravanning (FICC)

MOTOR CYCLE INDUSTRY ASSOCIATION LIMITED

Acronym or abbreviation: MCI

Starley House, Eaton Road, Coventry, Warwickshire, CV1 2FH

Tel: 08700 70 6242
Fax: 08700 70 3291
E-mail: motorcycling@mcia.co.uk

Website:
http://www.mcia.co.uk
Corporate website.

Enquiries:
Enquiries to: Marketing Manager
Direct tel: 0870 330 7813
Direct fax: 0870 070 3292
Direct e-mail: john@motorcycleshow.co.uk

Founded:
1910

Organisation type and purpose:
Trade association.

Subject coverage:
Structure of the UK motor cycle industry, manufacture, technical and legislative information, imports, accessories, market statistics.

continued overleaf

Trade and statistical information:
Data on import and export production, vehicles in use and registrations by type and capacity of mopeds and motorcycles.

Printed publications:
Annual Report
Bespoke Industry Statistics
Members List
Statistics Digest (monthly)
Various Industry Publications

Publications list:
Available in print

Access to staff:
Contact by letter, by fax and by e-mail
Hours: Mon to Fri, 0900 to 1700

Subsidiary and at the same address is:
Motorcycle Industry Exhibitions (MCIE)

MOTOR CYCLING CLUB LIMITED

Acronym or abbreviation: MCC

20 Old Shipyard Centre, West Bay, Bridport, Dorset, DT6 4HG

Tel: 01308 420706
E-mail: johnaley@portwrinkle.fsnet.co.uk

Website:
http://www.themotorcyclingclub.org.uk

Enquiries:
Enquiries to: Secretary General

Founded:
1901

Organisation type and purpose:
Membership association (membership is by subscription), present number of members: 1050.
Motor club.
Organisation of motoring events, particularly classic trials for motorcycles and cars.

Access to staff:
Contact by letter, by telephone, by e-mail and via website
Hours: Day or Evening
Special comments: No personal callers.

MOTOR INSURANCE REPAIR RESEARCH CENTRE

Acronym or abbreviation: MIRRC/Thatcham

Colthrop Way, Thatcham, Berkshire, RG19 4NR

Tel: 01635 868855
Fax: 01635 871346
E-mail: enquiries@thatcham.org

Website:
http://www.NCSR.co.uk
Security web site
http://www.thatcham-orangepages.info
Crash repair directory (October 2002)
http://www.ncwr.co.uk
head restraint ratings
http://www.thatcham.org
Main Thatcham web site

Enquiries:
Enquiries to: Public Relations Manager
Direct tel: 01635 294829
Direct fax: 01635 861862
Direct e-mail: lesley@thatcham.org
Other contacts: Research and Operations Director for research or engineering enquiry.

Founded:
1969

Organisation type and purpose:
Training organisation, consultancy, research organisation, publishing house.
Sponsored by Motor Insurance Companies and Lloyds Syndicates.

Subject coverage:
Vehicle body repair, cost control and standards improvement.

Printed publications:
Available on subscription:
Paint Cost Guide
Repair booklets
Special Reports
Thatcham Newsletters
Order printed publications from: Subscriptions Department, MIRRC/Thatcham
Colthrop Way, Thatcham, Berkshire, RG19 4NR

Microform publications:
Many video recordings on repair techniques and crash testing (for purchase)

Electronic and video publications:
General Thatcham Introduction (CD-ROM)
eScribe – Crash repair methods & terms
TPA – Parts Price Analysis
TPG – Summary Parts Prices
TPS – Parts Prices
TTS – Repair Times
TVIS – Vehicle Identification (CD-ROM)

Access to staff:
Contact by letter, by telephone, by fax, by e-mail and via website. Appointment necessary.
Hours: Mon to Thu, 0830 to 1630; Fri, 0830 to 1545

Access for disabled people:
Parking provided, toilet facilities

Sponsored by:
Lloyds Syndicates
Motor insurance companies

MOTOR INSURERS' BUREAU

Acronym or abbreviation: MIB

Linford Wood House, 6–12 Capital Drive, Milton Keynes, Buckinghamshire, MK14 6XT

Tel: 01908 830001
Fax: 01908 671660
E-mail: enquiries@mib.org.uk

Enquiries:
Enquiries to: Finance Director

Founded:
1946

Organisation type and purpose:
International organisation, membership association (membership is by qualification).
To compensate victims of uninsured/untraceable drivers. United Kingdom's green card bureau.

Subject coverage:
Green card matters. Compensation from uninsured and untraced accidents.

Access to staff:
Contact by letter, by telephone and by fax
Hours: Mon to Fri, 0900 to 1700

MOTOR NEURONE DISEASE ASSOCIATION

Acronym or abbreviation: MND Association

PO Box 246, Northampton, NN1 2PR

Tel: 01604 250505
Fax: 01604 624726
E-mail: enquiries@mndassociation.org

Website:
http://www.mndassociation.org

Enquiries:
Enquiries to: Information Services Coordinator

Founded:
1979

Organisation type and purpose:
Voluntary organisation, registered charity.

Subject coverage:
Management, research and symptoms of motor neurone disease; care of patients, including information, compiled by professionals, for medical and paramedical staff; equipment, including loan service.

Museum or gallery collection, archive, or library special collection:
Unpublished reports on Motor Neurone Disease

Printed publications:
Annual Review
Basic and specific leaflets (available upon request)
Leaflets for professional use
Thumb Print (magazine, quarterly)

Publications list:
Available in print

Access to staff:
Contact by letter, by telephone, by fax, by e-mail and via website
Hours: Mon to Fri, 0900 to 1700

Member and Secretariat of:
International Alliance of ALS/MND Associations

Member of:
Association of Medical Research Charities
Neurological Alliance

MOTOR SPORTS ASSOCIATION, THE

Formal name: The Royal Automobile Club Motor Sports Association Limited
Acronym or abbreviation: MSA

Motor Sports House, Riverside Park, Colnbrook, Slough, Berkshire, SL3 0HG

Tel: 01753 765000
Fax: 01753 682938
E-mail: msa_mail@compuserve.com

Website:
http://www.msauk.org
Website ordering of publications.

Enquiries:
Enquiries to: Communications Manager
Other contacts: Corporate Executive for media, PR etc.

Organisation type and purpose:
Statutory body.
Governing body of motor car sport in Great Britain and Northern Ireland.

Subject coverage:
Motor car sport, racing, rallying, autotests and trials, grasstrack, historic cars, karting, technical and medical administration, safety; fire precautions.

Printed publications:
MSA Kart Book (£3 a year)
FIA Yearbook of Automobile Sport (£50 a year)
FIA Yearbook of Karting Sport (£22 a year)
Motor Sport Club News (monthly £40 a year)
MSA Motor Sports Directory (£3 a year)
Motorsports Now! (newsletter, quarterly £40 a year)
MSA Officials' Yearbook (£5 a year)
MSA Yearbook (including regulations, £20 a year)
MSA Go Motorsport (£3 a year)
Order printed publications from: Data Base Controller

Electronic and video publications:
Kart Yearbook (CD-ROM, £25)
MSA Yearbook (CD-ROM)
MSA Officials Yearbook (CD-ROM)

Publications list:
Available online and in print

Access to staff:
Contact via website. Appointment necessary.
Hours: Mon to Fri, 0900 to 1730

Access for disabled people:
Access to all public areas, toilet facilities

Has:
17 regional associations

MOUNT SAINT BERNARD ABBEY LIBRARY

Coalville, Leicestershire, LE67 5UL

Tel: 01530 832298 or 832022
Fax: 01530 814608
E-mail: mountsaintbernard@btinternet.com

Enquiries:
Enquiries to: Librarian

Founded:
1835

Organisation type and purpose:
Registered charity (charity number 211004).

Subject coverage:
All aspects of theology, specialising in monasticism and patrology.

Museum or gallery collection, archive, or library special collection:
Recusant literature from the 16th-17th centuries
Two 12th century manuscripts

Access to staff:
Contact by letter, by telephone, by fax and by e-mail
Hours: Mon to Fri, 0900 to 1700

Access to building, collection or gallery:
No access other than to staff, prior appointment required

MOUNTAIN LEADER TRAINING SCOTLAND

Acronym or abbreviation: MLTS

Glenmore, Aviemore, Inverness-shire, PH22 1QU

Tel: 01479 861248
Fax: 01479 861249
E-mail: smltb@aol.com

Website:
http://www.mltscotland.org
Course dates; registration forms; Winter Mountain Leader Award documentation.

Enquiries:
Enquiries to: Executive Secretary

Founded:
1964

Scottish Mountain Leader Training Board Formed from:
Scottish Sports Council

Organisation type and purpose:
National government body, training organisation.

Subject coverage:
All aspects of training and assessment of those involved in leading groups hill walking, mountaineering and climbing in the United Kingdom.

Access to staff:
Contact by letter, by telephone, by fax, by e-mail and in person. Appointment necessary.
Hours: Mon to Fri, 0900 to 1700

MOUNTAIN RESCUE COUNCIL

Acronym or abbreviation: MRC

69 Werneth Road, Glossop, Derbyshire, SK13 6NF

Tel: 01457 869506
Fax: 01457 869506

Enquiries:
Enquiries to: Honorary Secretary

Founded:
1930

Organisation type and purpose:
Voluntary organisation (charity number 222596). Representative body dealing with mountain rescue in England and Wales.

Subject coverage:
Search and rescue of people in mountainous or wild places; assistance to statutory bodies with off-road incidents.

Printed publications:
History of the Mountain Rescue Committee

Mountain and Cave Rescue (handbook, annually)

Microform publications:
Mountain Rescue films (distributed by National Audio-Visual Aids Library)

Access to staff:
Contact by letter and by telephone
Hours: Mon to Fri, 0900 to 1700

Some support from the:
Department of Health and Social Security
Home Office

MOVEMENT FOR REFORM JUDAISM

Sternberg Centre for Judaism, 80 East End Road, Finchley, London, N3 2SY

Tel: 020 8349 5640
Fax: 020 8349 5699
E-mail: admin@reformjudaism.org.uk

Website:
http://www.reformjudaism.org.uk

Enquiries:
Enquiries to: Public Relations Manager
Direct tel: 020 8349 5689

Organisation type and purpose:
Registered charity (charity number 250060).
Religious body.

Subject coverage:
All matters relating to the practices of Reform Judaism.

Museum or gallery collection, archive, or library special collection:
Leo Baeck College Rabbinical seminary and library

Printed publications:
Annual Report
Manna Journal (quarterly, £15 a year)

Access to staff:
Contact by letter, by telephone, by fax, by e-mail and via website. Appointment necessary.
Hours: Mon to Thu, 0930 to 1700; Fri, 0930 to 1500, excluding Jewish Holy Days

Access for disabled people:
Parking provided, toilet facilities

Links with:
42 synagogues throughout the United Kingdom

MOWLEM (JOHN MOWLEM & COMPANY PLC)

White Lion Court, Swan Street, Isleworth, Middlesex, TW7 6RN

Tel: 020 8568 9111
Fax: 020 8758 1252
E-mail: info@mowlem.co.uk

Website:
http://www.mowlem.com

Enquiries:
Enquiries to: Group Marketing Manager
Direct tel: 020 8957 7243
Direct e-mail: raymond.reed@mowlem.com

Founded:
1822

Organisation type and purpose:
International organisation.

Subject coverage:
Construction and project management, civil engineering, soil mechanics, groundworks, property development, scaffolding and associated services, building services, building maintenance and restoration, materials testing, facilities management, process engineering.

Printed publications:
Annual Report
Catalogues

Access to staff:
Contact by e-mail

Hours: Mon to Fri, 0900 to 1700

Main offices:
Bracknell, Bath, Leeds

MRC

Formal name: Medical Research Council
Acronym or abbreviation: MRC

Head Office, 20 Park Crescent, London, W1B 1AL

Tel: 020 7636 5422
Fax: 020 7436 6179
E-mail: corporate@headoffice.mrc.ac.uk

Website:
http://www.mrc.ac.uk/
List of research establishments, detailed information about current research supported by MRC, research support schemes, research career opportunities, schools programme, research and the public, commercial ventures, latest MRC research news.

Enquiries:
Enquiries to: Information Officer
Direct e-mail: corporate@headoffice.mrc.ac.uk

Founded:
1913

Organisation type and purpose:
Research organisation.
To promote the balanced development of medical and related biological research and to advance knowledge that will lead to the maintenance and improvement of human health.

Subject coverage:
Medical and scientific research. Cannot give personal medical advice.

Printed publications:
Annual Report (annually, autumn)
Ethics Series
Field Reviews
Research in Focus (issues of topical interest eg cancer, ageing, stem cell therapy)
MRC/NIAS GCSE Worksheets
MRC Research Updates 1995–1999
Strategic Plan (annually, late spring)

Electronic and video publications:
Most publications available directly on website

Publications list:
Available in print

Access to staff:
Contact by letter, by telephone, by fax, by e-mail and via website
Hours: Mon to Fri, 0900 to 1700

MRC COLLABORATIVE CENTRE FOR HUMAN NUTRITION RESEARCH

Acronym or abbreviation: MRC HNR

Elsie Widdowson Laboratory, Fulbourn Road, Cambridge, CB1 9NL

Tel: 01223 426356
Fax: 01223 437515
E-mail: susan.jones@mrc-hnr.cam.ac.uk

Website:
http://www.mrc-hnr.cam.ac.uk
Mission statement, nutrition communication/ consultancy, seminars, details of research publications, library information.

Enquiries:
Enquiries to: Librarian
Direct tel: 01223 437519

Founded:
1998

Incorporates the former:
MRC Dunn Nutrition Unit (year of change 1998)

Organisation type and purpose:
Advisory body, research organisation.
Collaborative centre.

continued overleaf

Subject coverage:
HNR is a Medical Research Council collaborative centre to advance knowledge of the relationships between human nutrition and health by providing a national centre of excellence for the measurement and interpretation of biochemical, functional and dietary indications of nutritional status and health.

Museum or gallery collection, archive, or library special collection:
Library of nutrition publications
Archival material

Trade and statistical information:
Nutrition information.

Non-library collection catalogue:
All or part available in-house

Library catalogue:
All or part available in-house

Publications list:
Available online

Access to staff:
Contact by letter, by telephone, by fax, by e-mail and via website. Appointment necessary.
Hours: Mon to Fri, 1030 to 1330 and 1400 to 1530

Access to building, collection or gallery:
Special comments: Reference only

Access for disabled people:
Parking provided, level entry, access to all public areas, toilet facilities

Links with:
Addenbrooke's Hospital
Cambridge; tel: 01223 245151; website: http://www.addenbrookes.org.uk
University of Cambridge
tel: 01223 337733; website: http://www.cam.ac.uk

Parent body:
Medical Research Council
20 Park Crescent, London, W1B 1AL; tel: 020 7636 5422; fax: 020 7436 6179; website: http://www.mrc.ac.uk

MRC HUMAN GENETICS UNIT

Formal name: Medical Research Council Human Genetics Unit
Acronym or abbreviation: MRC HGU

Crewe Road, Edinburgh, EH4 2XU

Tel: 0131 332 2471
Fax: 0131 467 8456
E-mail: library@hgu.mrc.ac.uk or siobhan.marron@hgu.mrc.ac.uk

Website:
http://www.hgu.mrc.ac.uk/
Home page.

Enquiries:
Enquiries to: Librarian
Direct tel: 0131 467 8420

Founded:
1913

Organisation type and purpose:
Research Organisation.

Subject coverage:
Human genetics; cancer genetics; population genetics; gene therapy; molecular biology, mouse genetics developmental biology; molecular cytogenetics; chromosome structure; yeast molecular genetics; bioinformatics.

Museum or gallery collection, archive, or library special collection:
MRC Human Genetics Unit reprints by unit staff, 1948 to the present

Non-library collection catalogue:
All or part available in-house

Library catalogue:
All or part available in-house

Printed publications:
Annual Report of the Library (free)

Journals Holdings of the Unit (free)
Publications List of staff papers (annually)

Publications list:
Available in print

Access to staff:
Contact by letter, by telephone, by fax, by e-mail and in person. Appointment necessary.
Hours: Mon to Fri, 0845 to 1645

MRC INSTITUTE OF HEARING RESEARCH

University Park, University of Nottingham, Nottingham, NG7 2RD

Tel: 0115 922 3431
Fax: 0115 951 8503
E-mail: @ihr.mrc.ac.uk

Website:
http://www.ihr.mrc.ac.uk
Epidemiology and public health.

Enquiries:
Enquiries to: Information Officer
Direct e-mail: Enquiries@ihr.mrc.ac.uk
Other contacts: Unit Manager

Founded:
1977

Organisation type and purpose:
Research organisation.

Subject coverage:
Auditory Processessing Disorder, hereditary deafness, neural representation of complex sounds, assessment of cochlear function in humans, auditory perception, hearing disability, rehabilitation and benefit from hearing aids, cochlear implants, service delivery and rehabilitation, clinical studies of tinnitus, epidemiological and public health aspects of hearing disorders, causes, consequences and management of middle ear disease.

Printed publications:
Annual Report
List of Journals held in Library
Publication Report listed under eight themes: hereditary deafness; auditory neurophysiology; peripheral auditory function in humans; central auditory function; hearing disability; rehabilitation and benefit from hearing aids; cochlear implantation; epidemiology and public health; causes, consequences and treatment of middle-ear disease
A variety of well-specified clinical procedures and test procedures plus equipment or software to support their use

Electronic and video publications:
Toy Test illustrates administration of the McCormick Toy Discrimination Toy Test (video)
Glue Ear (video)
CD-ROMs that include test materials.

Publications list:
Available online

Access to staff:
Contact by letter, by fax, by e-mail and via website
Hours: Mon to Fri, 0900 to 1700

Parent body:
Medical Research Council
tel: 020 7636 5422; fax: 020 7436 6179; e-mail: @headoffice.mrc.ac.uk

MS TRUST

Formal name: Multiple Sclerosis Trust

Spirella Building, Bridge Road, Letchworth Garden City, Hertfordshire, SG6 4ET

Tel: 01462 476700
Fax: 01462 476710
E-mail: info@mstrust.org.uk

Website:
http://www.mstrust.org.uk

Information on all aspects of the MS Trust's work, information, education, research, fundraising, campaigns.

Founded:
1993

Formerly called:
MS Research Trust (year of change 2001)

Organisation type and purpose:
Charity working with and for the 85,000 people in the United Kingdom with multiple sclerosis (MS), to enable them to live their lives to the full. Provides information, education for health professionals, research into better management of MS, support for anyone affected by MS

Subject coverage:
Multiple sclerosis: information on all aspects of the disease, especially the management of symptoms.

Information services:
Information for anyone affected by multiple sclerosis, either personally or professionally. Publications, newsletters and personal enquiry service.

Education services:
Education courses for health and social care professionals working with people with MS.

Printed publications:
Wide range of publications – see http://www.mstrust.org.uk/publications
Order printed publications from: tel. 01462 476700; e-mail: info@mstrust.org.uk; online via http://www.mstrust.org.uk/publications, or by post

Electronic and video publications:
MS Together (DVD for recently diagnosed)
Move It For MS (DVD of exercises, £1)
Order electronic and video publications from: tel. 01462 476700; e-mail: info@mstrust.org.uk; online via http://www.mstrust.org.uk/publications, or by post

Publications list:
Available online and in print

Access to staff:
Contact by letter, by telephone, by fax, by e-mail and via website
Hours: Mon to Fri, 0900 to 1700; answerphone outside office hours

Access to building, collection or gallery:
No access other than to staff

MSI MARKETING RESEARCH FOR INDUSTRY

Acronym or abbreviation: MSI

Viscount House, River Lane, Saltney, Chester, Cheshire, CH4 8RH

Tel: 01244 681186
Fax: 01244 681457
E-mail: enquiries@msi-marketingresearch.co.uk

Enquiries:
Enquiries to: Managing Director
Other contacts: Sales and Marketing Co-ordinator for marketing purposes.

Founded:
1980

Organisation type and purpose:
Consultancy, research organisation.

Subject coverage:
Market research across wide range of sectors; principally covering non-consumer markets such as industrial, engineering and construction markets.

Printed publications:
Market Research Reports (over 150 titles, list available) under the headings: Construction & Building Products, Distribution, Engineering Components, Electrical Components & Telecommunications, Environmental, Service Markets, Packaging & Paper, Metals & Metalworking Industry, Transportation &

Infrastructure, Utilities & Process Industries, Security & Heating, Healthcare, Industrial Services, Marketing Presentations
Marketing Surveys Index (10 times a year)

Electronic and video publications:
MSI reports available online

Publications list:
Available in print

Access to staff:
Contact by letter, by telephone, by fax and by e-mail. Appointment necessary.
Hours: Mon to Fri, 0900 to 1700

MULLARD SPACE SCIENCE LABORATORY

Acronym or abbreviation: MSSL

Department of Space and Climate Physics, University College London, Holmbury St Mary, Dorking, Surrey, RH5 6NT

Tel: 01483 274111
Fax: 01483 278312

Website:
http://www.mssl.ucl.ac.uk/

Enquiries:
Enquiries to: Director

Organisation type and purpose:
University department or institute, research organisation.

Subject coverage:
X-ray astronomy; solar X-ray studies; magnetospheric studies; earth remote sensing for climate and geodetic studies.

Publications list:
Available online and in print

Also at:
Department of Space and Climate Physics University College London, Gower Street, London, WC1E 6BT; tel: 020 7679 2000

MULTI-FAITH CENTRE

Acronym or abbreviation: MFC

University of Derby, Kedleston Road, Derby, DE22 1GB

Tel: 01332 591285
E-mail: mfc@derby.ac.uk

Website:
http://www.multifaithcentre.org

Enquiries:
Enquiries to: Director

Founded:
1999

Organisation type and purpose:
Registered charity (charity number 1087140), university department or institute, research organisation. Information on world religious traditions and commitments, and inter-faith and multi-faith initiatives.

Subject coverage:
Religious organisations in the United Kingdom, religions, statistics, demographics, inter-faith relations.

Museum or gallery collection, archive, or library special collection:
Collection of questionnaires underlying the publication: Religions in the UK: A multi-faith directory
Directories of many UK religious organisations
Ephemera from many religious organisations

Trade and statistical information:
Data on religious organisations in the UK, data on religious statistics.

Non-library collection catalogue:
All or part available in-house

Library catalogue:
All or part available in-house

Printed publications:
Religions in the UK: Directory (2007 edn: £30.00 incl. p&p)
Order printed publications from: available from the Multi-Faith Centre at the University of Derby

Access to staff:
Contact by letter, by telephone, by e-mail and via website. Appointment necessary.
Hours: Mon to Fri, 0900 to 1700

Access to building, collection or gallery:
Prior appointment required

MULTIPLE BIRTHS FOUNDATION

Acronym or abbreviation: MBF

Hammersmith House – Level 4, Queen Charlotte's & Chelsea Hospital, Du Cane Road, London, W12 0HS

Tel: 020 8383 3519
Fax: 020 8383 3041
E-mail: mbf@imperial.nhs.uk

Website:
http://www.multiplebirths.org.uk

Enquiries:
Enquiries to: Administrator

Founded:
1988

Organisation type and purpose:
Registered charity (charity number 1094546). To offer professional support for families with multiple births as well as advice and training to medical, educational and other professionals involved in their care.

Subject coverage:
Multiple births.

Museum or gallery collection, archive, or library special collection:
Library and resource centre of books, journals, articles and videos relating to multiple births

Printed publications:
Are They Identical? Zygosity Determination
Feeding Twins, Triplets and More
Preparing for Twins and Triplets (E Bryan, 1996, £2.50)
Guidelines for Professionals (Bryan E, Denton J and Hallett F):
Bereavement
Facts about Multiple Births
Infertility New Choices – New Dilemmas
Multiple Pregnancy
Twins & Multiple Births
Twins, Triplets and More

Publications list:
Available online and in print

Access to staff:
Contact by letter, by telephone and by e-mail
Hours: Mon to Fri, 0900 to 1700

MULTIPLE SCLEROSIS INTERNATIONAL FEDERATION

Acronym or abbreviation: MSIF

3rd Floor, Skyline House, 200 Union Street, London, SE1 0LX

Tel: 020 7620 1911
Fax: 020 7620 1922
E-mail: info@msif.org

Website:
http://www.msif.org
World of multiple sclerosis.

Enquiries:
Enquiries to: Chief Executive

Founded:
1967

Organisation type and purpose:
International organisation, membership association (membership is by subscription, qualification, election or invitation), present number of members: 42 autonomous national member societies, voluntary organisation, registered charity.
Coordinating the work of National MS societies world-wide.

Subject coverage:
The full integration of people with MS, international development, coordination and furthering of the work of national MS societies worldwide, scientific research and educational information relating to MS; development of existing societies.

Printed publications:
Making Connections (annual review, free)
MS Management (twice a year, free)
MS Research in progress (£10 plus p&p)
Multiple Sclerosis – A Guide to Treatment and Therapies (£9 plus p&p, every 2 years)

Publications list:
Available in print

Access to staff:
Contact by letter, by telephone, by fax, by e-mail and via website. Appointment necessary.
Hours: Mon to Fri, 0930 to 1730

Access for disabled people:
Parking provided, ramped entry, access to all public areas, toilet facilities

Members:
42 National MS Societies

MULTIPLE SCLEROSIS RESOURCE CENTRE

Acronym or abbreviation: MSRC

7 Peartree Business Centre, Peartree Road, Stanway, Colchester, Essex, CO3 0JN

Tel: 01206 505444
Fax: 01206 505449
E-mail: themsrc@yahoo.com

Website:
http://www.msrc.co.uk
Comprehensive site for anyone affected by Multiple Sclerosis.

Enquiries:
Enquiries to: Office Manager
Direct tel: 01206 505453
Direct fax: 01206 505449
Direct e-mail: info@msrc.co.uk
Other contacts: Counsellors for counselling – 24 Hr Telephone Counselling 0800 783 0518.

Founded:
1993

Subject coverage:
Offers support to those affected by MS, information helpline, support counselling, referal to other agencies, publications.

Printed publications:
New Pathways, magazine, once every other month)
All 21 Leaflets (available free, direct)
The Multiple Sclerosis Resource Centre A-Z Guide to Complementary Therapies (Graham J and Pulling F, 2000, £12.50)
Eating & MS – Information & Recipes (£6.95)
Emotional Reactions to MS (Revised 1994, £4)
Multiple Sclerosis Pregnancy & Parenthood (Graham J, 1996, £7.75)

Publications list:
Available in print

Access to staff:
Contact by letter, by telephone, by fax, by e-mail, in person and via website. Appointment necessary.
Hours: Mon to Fri, 0900 to 1700

Access for disabled people:
Parking provided, ramped entry

MULTIPLE SCLEROSIS SOCIETY

Formal name: Multiple Sclerosis Society of Great Britain and Northern Ireland
Acronym or abbreviation: MSS

MS National Centre, 372 Edgware Road, Cricklewood, London, NW2 6ND

Tel: 020 8438 0700
Fax: 020 8438 0701
E-mail: info@mssociety.org.uk

Website:
http://www.mssociety.org.uk
Extensive website including details of current activities / services / publications, and access to online library database which includes many full text publications aimed at a lay audience.

Enquiries:
Enquiries to: Information Officer
Direct tel: 020 8438 0799
Direct e-mail: infoteam@mssociety.org.uk
Other contacts: Information Officers

Founded:
1953

Organisation type and purpose:
The Society is a registered charity (charity number 207495) which offers support to all those affected by MS. To this end it funds MS research, runs respite care centres, provides information, grants (financial assistance), education and training on MS. It produces numerous publications on MS and runs a freephone specialist Helpline.

Subject coverage:
Research into the cause and cure of multiple sclerosis, issues relating to all those affected by multiple sclerosis.

Information services:
Enquiry line and library.

Services for disabled people:
Services available.

Museum or gallery collection, archive, or library special collection:
Oliver Ball Library

Library catalogue:
All or part available online

Printed publications:
Publications (free of charge, donations are welcome) include:
What is MS? (booklet)
Just diagnosed (booklet)
MS Essentials – 28 booklets on all aspects of MS
MS Matters (magazine, six times a year)
Standards of Healthcare for People with MS
Order printed publications from: http://www.mssociety.org.uk/publications

Electronic and video publications:
Video (for loan only)

Publications list:
Available online and in print

Access to staff:
Contact by letter, by telephone, by fax, by e-mail, in person and via website
Hours: Mon to Fri, 0900 to 1700

Access to building, collection or gallery:
No prior appointment required
Hours: Mon to Fri, 0900 to 1700

Access for disabled people:
Parking provided, ramped entry, toilet facilities
Hours: Mon to Fri, 0900 to 1700

Affiliated to:
Multiple Sclerosis International Federation (MSIF)

Branches:
Multiple Sclerosis Society in Scotland
Ratho Park, 88 Glasgow Road, Ratho Station, Newbridge, EH28 8PP; tel: 0131 335 4050; fax: 0131 335 4051; e-mail: enquiries@mssocietyscotland.org.uk; website: http://www.mssocietyscotland.org.uk

Multiple Sclerosis Society Northern Ireland
34 Annadale Avenue, Belfast, BT7 3JJ; tel: 028 9080 2802; e-mail: info@mssocietyni.co.uk; website: http://www.mssocietyni.co.uk
Multiple Sclerosis Society Wales / Cymru
Temple Court, Cathedral Road, Cardiff, CF11 9HA; tel: 029 2078 6676; fax: 029 2078 6677; c mail: mscymruwales@mssociety.org.uk; website: http://www.mssociety.org.uk/wales

MURRAY EDWARDS COLLEGE

Rosemary Murray Library, Huntingdon Road, Cambridge, CB3 0DF

Tel: 01223 762202
Fax: 01223 763110
E-mail: library@newhall.cam.ac.uk

Website:
http://www.newhall.cam.ac.uk/facilities/library

Enquiries:
Enquiries to: Librarian

Founded:
1954

Formerly called:
New Hall (year of change 2008)

Organisation type and purpose:
College library.

Subject coverage:
All Tripos subjects and those of the special collections.

Museum or gallery collection, archive, or library special collection:
Bequests of Eleonora Duse, Elizabeth Rawson, Classics and Ancient History, and Dorothy Gabe French
Women's studies

Library catalogue:
All or part available in-house

Printed publications:
Women's Art at New Hall (catalogue)
New Hall 1954–1972: The making of a college

Access to staff:
Appointment necessary. Access for members only.
Hours: Mon to Fri, 0900 to 1700

Access for disabled people:
Level entry, toilet facilities

Parent body:
University of Cambridge

MUSCULAR DYSTROPHY CAMPAIGN

Acronym or abbreviation: MDC

61 Southwark Street, London, SE1 0HL

Tel: 020 7803 4800 020 7401 3495 info@muscular-dystrophy.org
Fax: 020 7803 4800 020 7401 3495
E-mail: info@muscular-dystrophy.org

Website:
http://www.muscular-dystrophy.org
Information on neuromuscular disorders and the Group.

Enquiries:
Enquiries to: Information Officer

Founded:
1959

Organisation type and purpose:
Voluntary organisation, registered charity (charity number 205395).
Medical research.
Support and care.

Subject coverage:
Neuromuscular conditions, muscular dystrophy, aids and equipment, research.

Printed publications:
Annual Report

Annual Review
Target MD (4 times a year)

Publications list:
Available in print

Access to staff:
Contact by letter, by telephone and by fax
Hours: Mon to Fri, 0900 to 1700

Member of:
European Alliance of Neuromuscular Disorders Associations (EADMA)

MUSEUM IN DOCKLANDS

Docklands Library and Archives, No 1 Warehouse, West India Quay, Hertsmere Road, London, E14 4AL

Tel: 020 7001 9800
Fax: 020 7001 9801
E-mail: info@museumindocklands.org.uk

Enquiries:
Direct tel: 020 7001 9825

Founded:
1984

Organisation type and purpose:
Museum, historic building, house or site, suitable for ages: 5+.

Subject coverage:
The history and development of the Port of London from 1770 to date, including the current regeneration of London's Docklands, the enclosed docks and riverside wharves, the docks and river, cargo handling, dock trades, dock police, dock equipment, labour history of the docks, tools and equipment used in the docks.

Museum or gallery collection, archive, or library special collection:
20,000 photographs of docks and river
British Ports Authority archive covering the port transport industry nationally from 1911–1975
Coal Meter's Society archive c. 1750 to c. 1980
Data on the registered dock labour force in London (1950–1988)
Data on the trade of the port of London (1800 to the present)
Docklands Forum archive 1975–1995
Historic films of docks 1921–1970
Port of London Authority records 1909 to date (historic records only ie non-operational)
Records of the Corporation of London River Thames Committee (1770–1857) and the Thames Conservators (1857–1909)
The surviving business records of the private dock companies operating on the Thames (1799–1909)

Trade and statistical information:
Data on the trade of the Port of London (1800 to the present).
Data on the registered dock labour force in London 1950–1988.

Non-library collection catalogue:
All or part available in-house

Library catalogue:
All or part available in-house

Printed publications:
Dockland Life: historic and social history 1860–1970 (for sale)
Gateway to the East (for sale)
Liquid History: the first 50 years of the PLA (for sale)

Electronic and video publications:
City of Ships (1938) video (for sale)
Waters of Time (1951) video (for sale)

Access to staff:
Contact by letter, by telephone, by fax and by e-mail. Appointment necessary.
Hours: Mon to Fri, 1030 to 1630

Access for disabled people:
Parking provided, ramped entry, access to all public areas, toilet facilities
Special comments: Dedicated disabled persons lift

Funded jointly by:
Corporation of London (COL)
Department for Culture, Media and Sport (DCMS)

Museum:
Museum in Docklands
At same address

Parent body:
Museum of London
150 London Wall; tel: 020 7600 3699

MUSEUM OF ADVERTISING & PACKAGING

Albert Warehouse, The Docks, Gloucester, GL1 2EH

Tel: 01452 302309

Website:
http://www.themuseum.co.uk

Enquiries:
Enquiries to: Curator

Founded:
1984

Organisation type and purpose:
Museum.

Subject coverage:
Advertising, packaging and social history 1850 to present.

Museum or gallery collection, archive, or library special collection:
Television commercial programmes
The Robert Opie Collection (300,000 items relating to the history of the consumer society)

MUSEUM OF ENGLISH RURAL LIFE

Acronym or abbreviation: MERL

University of Reading, Redlands Road, Reading, RG1 5EX

Tel: 0118 378 8660
Fax: 0118 378 5632
E-mail: merl@reading.ac.uk

Website:
http://www.reading.ac.uk/merl
Museum website and online catalogue.

Enquiries:
Enquiries to: Librarian
Other contacts: Archivist for archive and photographic enquiries.

Founded:
1951

Organisation type and purpose:
Museum, university department or institute, research organisation.

Subject coverage:
Agricultural and rural history including history of agricultural engineering, and food manufacturing and processing industries, agricultural societies, history of environmental organisations, rural industries, farm implements, craft tools, machines, domestic equipment; agricultural museology.

Museum or gallery collection, archive, or library special collection:
Book collections:
NIRD and Milk Marketing Board Collection (Dairying); Nuptown House and Fussell Collections (pre-1850 agriculture and agricultural history); Edgar Thomas Collection (agricultural research papers)
Archive collections:
Records of agricultural engineering, processing and seed production firms; records of agricultural co-operatives and organisations; records of countryside and rural affairs organisations; farm records collection; records relating to crafts and rural industires; agricultural research papers
Photographic collections:

Local collections; press collections (including 'Farmers Weekly' and 'Farmer and Stockbreeder' Archives); countryside and environment collections; farm machinery and engineering collections; film and video collections

Trade and statistical information:
Agricultural statistics.
Food consumption and expenditure statistics.

Non-library collection catalogue:
All or part available online and in-house

Library catalogue:
All or part available online

Access to staff:
Contact by letter, by telephone, by fax, by e-mail, in person and via website. Appointment necessary.
Hours: Mon to Fri, 0900 to 1700

Access to building, collection or gallery:
Hours: Museum: Tue to Fri, 0900 to 1700; Sat and Sun, 1400 to 1630
Reading Room, for access to library and archives: Mon to Fri, 0900 to 1700

Parent body:
University of Reading

MUSEUM OF THE HISTORY OF EDUCATION

Leeds University, Parkinson Court, Leeds, West Yorkshire, LS2 9JT

Tel: 0113 233 4665/4545
Fax: 0113 233 4529

Website:
http://education.leeds.ac.uk/edu/inted/museum.htm

Enquiries:
Enquiries to: Curator

Founded:
1951

Organisation type and purpose:
Museum.
University collection and centre for research and publication.

Subject coverage:
History of education and educational administration.

Museum or gallery collection, archive, or library special collection:
Board of Education files 1939–1945
Educational artefacts
Library of the history of education
Pupil exercise books
West Riding County Council Education Committee Minutes 1904–1974 and other documents

Printed publications:
Catalogue 1980
Educational Administration and History Monographs (list available from the Museum)
Journal of Educational Administration and History (2 times a year)

Access to staff:
Contact by letter and by telephone. Appointment necessary.
Hours: Mon, Wed, Fri, 1330 to 1630; Thu, 1330 to 1630; Tue closed

Access to building, collection or gallery:
Prior appointment required
Special comments: The museum is closed for staff and public holidays and when in use by students. Prior booking of visits advised.

Access for disabled people:
Ramped entry

MUSEUMS ASSOCIATION

Acronym or abbreviation: MA

24 Calvin Street, London, E1 6NW

Tel: 020 7426 6970

Fax: 020 7426 6961
E-mail: info@museumsassociation.org

Website:
http://www.museumsassociation.org

Enquiries:
Enquiries to: Information Officer

Founded:
1889

Organisation type and purpose:
Professional body, registered charity (charity number 313024).

Subject coverage:
Museums, particularly professional matters and training.

Printed publications:
Museum Practice (3 times a year)
Museums Journal (monthly)
Museums Yearbook

Publications list:
Available in print

Access to staff:
Contact by letter, by telephone, by fax, by e-mail and via website
Hours: Mon to Fri, 0900 to 1700

MUSEUMS, LIBRARIES AND ARCHIVES COUNCIL

Formal name: Museums, Libraries and Archives Council
Acronym or abbreviation: MLA

Victoria House, Southampton Row, London, WC1B 4EA

Tel: 020 7273 1444
Fax: 020 7273 1404
E-mail: info@mla.gov.uk

Website:
http://www.mla.gov.uk

Founded:
2000

Organisation type and purpose:
To connect people and change lives through museums, libraries and archives; to increase and sustain participation; to put museums, libraries and archives at the heart of national, regional and local life; to establish a world class and sustainable sector and put it on the best footing for the future; to lead sector strategy and policy development.

Subject coverage:
Museums, libraries and archives

Access to staff:
Contact by letter, by telephone, by fax, by e-mail and via website

Regional agencies:
MLA East Midlands, MLA East of England, MLA London, MLA North East, MLA North West, MLA South East, MLA South West, MLA West Midlands, MLA Yorkshire

MUSEUMS, LIBRARIES AND ARCHIVES SOUTH EAST

Acronym or abbreviation: MLA South East

Headquarters, 15 City Business Centre, Hyde Street, Winchester, Hampshire, SO23 7TA

Tel: 01962 858844
Fax: 01962 878439
E-mail: info@mlasoutheast.org.uk

Website:
http://www.semlac.org.uk
General information and publications.

Organisation type and purpose:
Registered charity (charity number 1086030).

Subject coverage:
A regional development agency for the museum, library and archive sector in the South East.

continued overleaf

Printed publications:
Library Case Studies
Framework for the Future (online)

Other location:
MLA South East (Chatham Office)
The Garden Room, Historic Dockyard, Chatham, Kent, ME4 4TE; tel: 01634 405031
MLA South East (Reading Office)
Reading Central Library, Abbey Square, Reading, Berkshire, RG1 3BQ; tel: 0118 958 9197
MLA South East (Suusex Office)
Univercity of Sussex Library, Falmer, Brighton, BN1 9QL; tel: 01273 873494

MUSEUMS, LIBRARIES AND ARCHIVES YORKSHIRE

Acronym or abbreviation: MLA Yorkshire

MLA Yorkshire, Ground Floor, Marshall Court, 1 Marshall Street, Leeds, LS11 9YP

Tel: 0113 394 4840
Fax: 0113 243 9872
E-mail: info@mlayorkshire.org.uk

Website:
http://www.mlayorkshire.org.uk

Enquiries:
Enquiries to: Information Officer

Formerly called:
Yorkshire Museums, Libraries & Archives Council; Yorkshire Museums Council

Organisation type and purpose:
Regional Development Agency for museums, libraries and archives
One of eight regional agencies in the MLA Partnership and the Museums, Libraries and Archives Council (MLA)

Subject coverage:
The provision of a co-operative service for associated regional organisations, including local authority and independent charitable trust museums, libraries and archives.

MUSHROOM GROWERS' ASSOCIATION

Acronym or abbreviation: MGA

2 St Paul's Street, Stamford, Lincolnshire, PE9 2BE

Tel: 01780 766888
Fax: 01780 766558
E-mail: carolyn@snowcapmushrooms.co.uk

Enquiries:
Enquiries to: Secretary to the Association

Founded:
1945

Organisation type and purpose:
Trade association (membership is by subscription).

Subject coverage:
Mushroom cultivation.

Printed publications:
Mushroom Journal (monthly)

Access to staff:
Contact by letter
Hours: Mon to Fri, 0900 to 1700

Specialist branch of the:
National Farmers' Union

MUSIC EDUCATION COUNCIL

Acronym or abbreviation: MEC

54 Elm Road, Hale, Altrincham, Cheshire, WA15 9QP

Tel: 0161 928 3085
Fax: 0161 929 9648
E-mail: ahassan@easynet.co.uk

Website:
http://www.mec.org.uk

Information about MEC, current work and projects, members and links.

Enquiries:
Enquiries to: Professional Officer

Organisation type and purpose:
Membership association (membership is by subscription), present number of members: 168 corporate, 70 individual, registered charity (charity number 270004).
Umbrella body for music education and training.

Subject coverage:
Music education.

Printed publications:
Newsletter (6 times a year)

Access to staff:
Contact by letter, by telephone, by fax and by e-mail
Hours: Mon to Fri, 0900 to 1700

Acts as UK's representative body on:
International Society for Music Education

MUSIC MASTERS' AND MISTRESSES' ASSOCIATION

Acronym or abbreviation: MMA

Wayfaring, Smithers Lane, East Peckham, Tonbridge, Kent, TN12 5HT

Tel: 01622 871576
Fax: 01622 871576
E-mail: mma.admin@ntlworld.com

Enquiries:
Enquiries to: Administrator

Organisation type and purpose:
Membership association.

Subject coverage:
Teaching of music in schools.

Printed publications:
Directory of Members
Journal (3 times a year, members)
Music Awards at Independent Senior Schools (annual guide to music scholarships)

Access to staff:
Contact by letter, by telephone, by fax and by e-mail
Hours: Mon to Fri, 0900 to 1700

MUSICAL BOX SOCIETY OF GREAT BRITAIN

Acronym or abbreviation: MBSGB

PO Box 373, Welwyn, AL6 0WY

E-mail: mail@mbsgb.org.uk

Website:
http://www.mbsgb.org.uk
General information about the Society and how to join.

Enquiries:
Enquiries to: Secretary

Founded:
1962

Organisation type and purpose:
International organisation, membership association (membership is by subscription), voluntary organisation.
Collectors, museums, restorers.
To promote the preservation, restoration and enjoyment of mechanical music.

Subject coverage:
Mechanical music, technical details, history, restoration and repair, dealers and auctioneers, authors.

Museum or gallery collection, archive, or library special collection:
Society Archives

Printed publications:
Books and booklets

Music Box (quarterly, members)
Tune Sheet Book
The Organette Book

Publications list:
Available in print

Access to staff:
Contact by letter, by e-mail and via website
Hours: Mon to Fri, 0900 to 1700

MUSICIANS' UNION

Acronym or abbreviation: MU

60–62 Clapham Road, London, SW9 0JJ

Tel: 020 7582 5566
Fax: 020 7582 9805
E-mail: info@musiciansunion.org.uk

Website:
http://www.musiciansunion.org.uk

Enquiries:
Enquiries to: Deputy General Secretary

Founded:
1893

Organisation type and purpose:
Trade union (membership is by subscription), present number of members: 31,000.

Subject coverage:
Music, rates for musicians, contract advice.

Printed publications:
Musician (quarterly)

Access to staff:
Contact by letter, by fax and via website
Hours: 1000 to 1730

Access to building, collection or gallery:
Prior appointment required

Also at:
Musicians' Union
40 Canal Street, Manchester, M1 3WD; tel: 0161 236 1764; fax: 0161 236 0159
Musicians' Union
11 Sandyford Place, Glasgow, G3 7NB; tel: 0141 248 3723; fax: 0141 204 3510
Musicians' Union
Benson House, Lombard Street, Birmingham, B12 0QN; tel: 0121 622 3870; fax: 0121 622 5361
Musicians' Union
131 St Georges Road, Bristol, BS1 5UW; tel: 0117 926 5438; fax: 0117 925 3729

MUSLIM EDUCATIONAL TRUST

Acronym or abbreviation: MET

130 Stroud Green Road, London, N4 3RZ

Tel: 020 7272 8502
Fax: 020 7281 3457
E-mail: info@muslim-ed-trust.org.uk

Website:
http://www.muslim-ed-trust.org.uk

Enquiries:
Enquiries to: Director
Other contacts: Assistant Director and Sales Manager.

Founded:
1966

Organisation type and purpose:
Registered charity (charity number 313192), suitable for ages: 4 to 18, publishing house.
Educational charity.

Subject coverage:
Muslim, Islamic education in a non-Muslim country; religious education for Muslim children; Islamic studies.

Printed publications:
British Muslims and Schools (Sarwar G, 1994, £2.50)
Islam: a brief guide (Sarwar G, 15th ed., 2003, free)
Islam: Beliefs and Teachings (Sarwar G, 7th ed., 2003, £6.50 inc. p&p)

Islam for Younger People (Sarwar G, 4th ed., 2003, £3 inc. p&p)
Issues in Islamic Education: a collection of twelve essays (1996, £3.75 inc. p&p)
Posters (A2, colour, laminated, £2 inc. p&p)
Parents and Children in Islam
5 Basic Duties of Islam
3 Most Sacred Places of Islam
How to make Wudu and How to Perform Salah
Prophets of Allah
Islamic Manners
Reflect (magazine for young Muslims, 3 times a year)
Sex Education – The Muslim Perspective (Sarwar G, 4th ed., 2004, £3.75 inc. p&p)
The beginner's Book of Salah (Sarwar G, 6th ed. £3 inc. p&p)
What does Islam say? (Hewitt I, 4th ed., 2004, £3.75 inc. p&p)

Publications list:
Available online and in print

Access to staff:
Contact by letter, by telephone and by fax. Appointment necessary.
Hours: Mon to Fri, 0900 to 1700

Affiliated to:
Religious Education Council of UK and Eire
CEM, Royal Buildings, Victoria Street, Derby, DE1 1GW; tel: 01332 296655; fax: 01332 343253

MUSLIM WOMEN'S WELFARE ASSOCIATION

425 Lea Bridge Road, London, E10 7EA

Tel: 020 8539 7478
Fax: 020 8539 7478

Enquiries:
Enquiries to: Co-ordinator

Founded:
1983

Access to staff:
Contact by letter, by telephone, by fax and in person
Hours: Mon to Fri, 1000 to 1530

Access to building, collection or gallery:
No access other than to staff

Access for disabled people:
Level entry

MUSLIM WORLD LEAGUE

46 Goodge Street, London, W1T 4LU

Tel: 020 7636 7568
Fax: 020 7637 5034
E-mail: mwl@webstar.com.uk

Enquiries:
Enquiries to: Deputy Director

Founded:
1982

Organisation type and purpose:
International organisation, registered charity (charity number 290098).
To help the community in educational, cultural and religious matters.

Subject coverage:
Information about the problems, rights, duties etc concerning the Muslim Community in UK and Eire.

Library catalogue:
All or part available in-house

Access to staff:
Contact by letter, by telephone, by fax, by e-mail and in person. Appointment necessary. Letter of introduction required.
Hours: Mon to Fri, 1030 to 1600

Access to building, collection or gallery:
No prior appointment required

Links with:
Muslim World League (MWL)
PO Box 537, Makkah, Saudi Arabia; tel: 00 9662 560 0919; fax: 00 9662 560 1267/560 1319; e-mail: mul@aol.com
Supreme Council of Mosques
Makkah, Saudi Arabia

MVRA LIMITED

Glenfield Business Park, Philips Road, Blackburn, Lancashire, BB1 5QH

Tel: 0870 458 3051
Fax: 0870 458 3149
E-mail: info@mvra.com

Website:
http://www.mvra.com

Enquiries:
Enquiries to: Managing Director
Direct e-mail: enquiry@mvra.com
Other contacts: Membership Services Manager for membership.

Founded:
1988

Subject coverage:
Motor industry, accident management, quality repairers, quality body and mechanical garages/repairers.

Trade and statistical information:
Data covering all aspects of the motor industry.

Access to staff:
Contact by letter, by telephone and by e-mail
Hours: Closed Bank Holidays

Access to building, collection or gallery:
Mon to Fri, 0900 to 1700

Access for disabled people:
Parking provided, toilet facilities

MYCOBACTERIUM REFERENCE UNIT

Acronym or abbreviation: MRU

Public Health Laboratory, King's College Hospital (Dulwich), East Dulwich Grove, London, SE22 8QF

Tel: 020 8693 1312
Fax: 020 8346 6477

Website:
http://www.phls.co.uk

Enquiries:
Enquiries to: Director

Organisation type and purpose:
National government body, research organisation.

Subject coverage:
Laboratory diagnosis of tuberculosis and other mycobacterial diseases in man and animals; identification and sensitivity testing of mycobacteria; advice on treatment of such diseases. Basic research into host pathogen interactions and the epidemiology of mycobacterial diseases.

Access to staff:
Contact by letter and by fax
Hours: Mon to Fri, 0900 to 1715

Links to:
Public Health Laboratory Service (PHLS)
61 Colindale Avenue, London, NW9

MYCOLOGY REFERENCE CENTRE

Department of Microbiology, University of Leeds, Leeds, West Yorkshire, LS2 9JT

Tel: 0113 233 5600/1
Fax: 0113 233 5640

Website:
http://www.leeds.ac.uk/mbiology/res/mycol/mrl.htm
Services, research, interests.

Enquiries:
Enquiries to: Clinical Scientist

Organisation type and purpose:
Diagnostic medical laboratory.

Subject coverage:
Diseases of man and animals caused by infection with fungi; allergy to fungi; examination of cultures; tissue section; serological and molecular tests; antifungal assays.

Access to staff:
Contact by letter, by telephone and by fax. All charged.
Hours: Mon to Fri, 0900 to 1700
Special comments: Posting of samples subject to Royal Mail regulations.

Parent bodies:
Leeds Teaching Hospitals NHS Trust
Leeds, LS1 3EX
University of Leeds
Leeds, LS2 9JT

NACELL

Formal name: National Advisory Centre on Early Language Learning
Acronym or abbreviation: NACELL

c/o CILT, the National Centre for Languages, 20 Bedfordbury, London, WC2N 4LB

Tel: 020 7379 5101
Fax: 020 7379 5082
E-mail: nacell@cilt.org.uk

Website:
http://www.nacell.org.uk

Enquiries:
Enquiries to: Information Officer

Organisation type and purpose:
NACELL is a Department for Education and Skills Initiative to promote and develop the provision and quality of Modern Foreign Language learning in the Primary sector.
NACELL is coordinated by CILT, the National Centre for Languages. National organisation, registered charity (charity number 313938), public library, university department or institute, suitable for ages: all.

Subject coverage:
Early language learning, primary languages, teaching foreign languages to young children (under 11s).

Non-library collection catalogue:
All or part available online and in-house

Library catalogue:
All or part available online and in-house

Printed publications:
Order printed publications from: Central Books Ltd 99 Wallis Road, London, E9 5LN, tel: 0845 4589910, e-mail: mo@centralbooks.com

Publications list:
Available online and in print

Access to staff:
Contact by letter, by telephone, by fax, by e-mail, in person and via website
Hours: Term time, Mon, Tue, Thu, Fri, 1030 to 1700; Wed, 1030 to 2000; Sat, 1000 to 1300:
Vacations, Mon to Fri, 1030 to 1700

Access to building, collection or gallery:
No prior appointment required
Hours: Term time, Mon, Tue, Thu, Fri, 1030 to 1700; Wed, 1030 to 2000; Sat, 1000 to 1300:
Vacations, Mon to Fri, 1030 to 1700

Access for disabled people:
Toilet facilities

Parent body:
CILT, the National Centre for Languages at the same address

NACRO, THE CRIME REDUCTION CHARITY

Formal name: Nacro

159 Clapham Road, London, SW9 0PU

Tel: 020 7840 6464
Fax: 020 7840 6420
E-mail: helpline@nacro.org.uk

Website:
http://www.nacro.org.uk

Enquiries:
Enquiries to: Resettlement Helpline Officer

Founded:
1966

Organisation type and purpose:
To reduce crime by giving disadvantaged people – offenders and those at risk of offending – a positive stake in society. Provides direct services (education and employment, housing, youth projects, advice), and consultancy and training services. Runs a resettlement helpline to give advice and information to ex-offenders, their family and friends and others around issues such as housing and employment.

Subject coverage:
Resettlement services for ex-offenders, Rehabilitation of Offenders Act 1974, special needs housing, employment, training, education, youth crime, crime and criminal justice (especially prisons), mentally disordered offenders, community safety, race and criminal justice.

Printed publications:
Wide range of reports, practical guides, leaflets and briefing papers on the subjects listed

Publications list:
Available online

Access to staff:
Contact by letter, by telephone, by fax and by e-mail
Hours: Mon to Fri, 0900 to 1700

NAFAS

Formal name: National Association of Flower Arrangement Societies
Acronym or abbreviation: NAFAS

Osborne House, 12 Devonshire Square, London, EC2M 4TE

Tel: 020 7247 5567
Fax: 020 7247 7232
E-mail: flowers@nafas.org.uk

Website:
http://www.nafas.org.uk
Events, courses and publications.

Enquiries:
Enquiries to: Administrator

Founded:
1959

Organisation type and purpose:
Membership association, present number of members: 100,000, registered charity (charity number 289038), suitable for ages: 8+.
Education charity.
To promote the art and teaching of flower arranging.

Subject coverage:
Flower arranging.

Library catalogue:
All or part available in-house

Printed publications:
The Flower Arranger (magazine)
Instruction leaflets

Publications list:
Available in print

Access to staff:
Contact by letter, by telephone, by fax, by e-mail and via website. Appointment necessary.
Hours: Mon to Fri, 0900 to 1700

Access to building, collection or gallery:
Prior appointment required

Affiliated to:
Royal Horticultural Society

NAMIBIA HIGH COMMISSION

Formal name: High Commission for the Republic of Namibia

6 Chandos Place, London, W1G 9LU

Tel: 020 7636 6244
Fax: 020 7687 5694
E-mail: namibia-highcomm@btconnect.com

Website:
http://www.namibhc.demon.co.uk/invest

Enquiries:
Enquiries to: Information Officer
Other contacts: (1) First Secretary; (2) Commercial Attaché; (3) Tourism Attaché for (1) Consular matters; (2) trade enquiries; (3) tourism enquiries.

Organisation type and purpose:
National government body, national organisation. Protocol and bilateral relations between Namibia and the UK, consular enquiries (visas, work permits, passports). Tourism departments, political, economic, trade and educational links between Namibia and the UK.

Subject coverage:
General enquiries regarding geography, wildlife and environment of Namibia; Namibian cultures and customs; economic and political affairs; education and other matters. Contact names and addresses of individuals and organisations in Namibia can be provided.

Museum or gallery collection, archive, or library special collection:
Outside Namibia, the most comprehensive collection of materials relating to Namibian History and Culture is held at: Namibia Resource Centre, Basler Afrika Bibliographien, PO Box 2037, CH-4001, Basel, Switzerland

Trade and statistical information:
The Commercial Attaché (from the Ministry of Trade) can answer most enquiries, and help establish commercial relationships with Namibian Companies.

Printed publications:
A variety of printed material is available from the Commercial Attaché
For tourist information and brochures contact the Tourist Office

Access to staff:
Contact by letter, by telephone, by fax, by e-mail, in person and via website. Appointment necessary.
Hours: Mon to Fri, 0900 to 1700

Connections with:
Namibia Tourist Office
At the same address; tel: 020 7636 2924; fax: 020 7636 2969; e-mail: info@namibiatourism.co.uk

NAPIER UNIVERSITY – LEARNING INFORMATION SERVICES

Craiglockhart Campus, Edinburgh, EH14 1DJ

Tel: 0131 455 4269
Fax: 0131 455 4276

Website:
http://nulis.napier.ac.uk
http://www.napier.ac.uk

Enquiries:
Enquiries to: Director of Learning Information Services
Direct tel: 0131 455 4270
Direct e-mail: c.pinder@napier.ac.uk

Organisation type and purpose:
University library.

Subject coverage:
Communication arts; design and media arts; law; psychology and sociology; music; built environment; computing; engineering; health and life sciences; accounting and economics; management; marketing and tourism; mathematics and statistics.

Museum or gallery collection, archive, or library special collection:
Edward Clark Collection on printing and book production
War poets' collection, material relating to Wilfred Owen, Siegfried Sassoon and war poetry generally.

Non-library collection catalogue:
All or part available online

Library catalogue:
All or part available online

Printed publications:
General guides to services and collections
Guides to finding information
Subject guides

Access to staff:
Contact by letter, by telephone and by e-mail. Non-members charged.
Hours: Term time: Mon to Thu, 0845 to 2100; Sat and Sun, 1000 to 1600

NAPIER UNIVERSITY – MELROSE CAMPUS LIBRARY

Education Centre, Borders General Hospital, Melrose, Roxburghshire, TD6 9BD

Tel: 01896 827620 \ Minicom no. 01896 661630
Fax: 01896 823869

Enquiries:
Enquiries to: Information Services Adviser
Direct tel: 01896 827620
Direct e-mail: ml.mitchell@napier.ac.uk
Other contacts: Campus Library Manager (e-mail: v.smith@napier.ac.uk)

Founded:
1974

Organisation type and purpose:
University library also serving NHS
NHS Library.

Subject coverage:
Nursing, primary care, medicine, psychiatry, public health, psychology, complementary therapies, social work, child care, NHS management.

Non-library collection catalogue:
All or part available online

Library catalogue:
All or part available online

Access to staff:
Contact by letter, by telephone, by fax, by e-mail and in person. Non-members charged.
Hours: Mon to Thu, 0900 to 2100; Fri, 0900 to 1700

Access to building, collection or gallery:
No prior appointment required

Access for disabled people:
Level entry, toilet facilities

Also at:
Napier University Learning Information Services (NULIS)
Craiglockhart Campus, Edinburgh, EH14 1DJ

Links with:
NHS Borders
Newstead, Melrose

NAPLIB

Acronym or abbreviation: NAPLIB

c/o RCAHMS, John Sinclair House, Edinburgh, EH8 9NX

Tel: 0131 662 1456

Fax: 0131 662 1477
E-mail: kevin.mclaren@rcahms.gov.uk

Website:
http://www.naplib.org
NAPLIB's aims, membership, publications,
activities.

Enquiries:
Enquiries to: Honorary Secretary

Founded:
1989

Organisation type and purpose:
National organisation, advisory body, professional
body, membership association (membership is by
subscription), present number of members: 75,
voluntary organisation, suitable for ages: all,
publishing house.
An independent organisation promoting the use
and preservation of aerial photography. Sponsor
membership £100 a year; individual membership
£10 a year; library membership £30 a year; affiliate
membership (student, unsalaried, retired) £5 a
year.
To increase public awareness of the existence of the
photographs, and facilitate access to them.

Subject coverage:
Aerial photography: coverage, storage and
archiving, indexing.

Printed publications:
Directory of Aerial Photographic Collections in the
United Kingdom (1993, 2nd ed., 1998, £10 inc.
p&p)
The Guide to the Care and Storage of Photographs
(Wilson D, 1997, £5 inc. p&p)
NAPLIB Flyer (quarterly from 1990)
Order printed publications from: NAPLIB
c/o National Monuments Record, Great Western
Village, Kemble Drive, Swindon, SN2 2GZ, tel:
01793 41447, fax: 01793 414848, e-mail: sharon
.bishop@rchme.co.uk

Publications list:
Available online and in print

Access to staff:
Contact by letter, by telephone, by fax, by e-mail
and via website
Hours: Mon to Fri, 0900 to 1700

NAPO

Formal name: National Association of Probation
Officers
Acronym or abbreviation: Napo

4 Chivalry Road, Battersea, London, SW11 1HT

Tel: 020 7223 4887
Fax: 020 7223 3503
E-mail: info@napo.org.uk

Website:
http://www.napo.org.uk

Enquiries:
Enquiries to: HR & Office Manager
Direct e-mail: kwaldrone@napo.org.uk

Founded:
1912

Organisation type and purpose:
Professional body, trade union, present number of
members: 9500.
Trade union and professional association for
Family Court and probation staff.

Subject coverage:
Probation Service, criminal justice system, Family
Court Service.

Printed publications:
Napo News (monthly)
Probation Journal (quarterly)

Access to staff:
Contact by letter, by telephone, by fax, by e-mail
and via website. Appointment necessary.
Hours: Mon to Fri, 0900 to 1700

Access to building, collection or gallery:
Prior appointment required

NAPOLEONIC SOCIETY

Formal name: Napoleonic Society of Great Britain

157 Vicarage Road, Leyton, London, E10 5DU

Tel: 020 8539 3876
Fax: 020 8539 3876
E-mail: keys@fsmail.net

Enquiries:
Enquiries to: Secretary

Founded:
1969

Organisation type and purpose:
Learned society.

Subject coverage:
Napoleon. French and Napoleonic history 1769–
1945.

Non-library collection catalogue:
All or part available in-house

Library catalogue:
All or part available in-house

Printed publications:
Napoleon (occasional bulletin)

Access to staff:
Contact by letter, by telephone, by fax and by e-
mail. Appointment necessary.
Hours: Mon to Sat, 1100 to 1900

Access for disabled people:
Limited access

NASO

Formal name: National Adult School Organisation

Riverton, 370 Humberstone Road, Leicester, LE5
0SA

Tel: 0116 253 8333
Fax: 0116 253 8333
E-mail: gensec@naso.org.uk

Enquiries:
Enquiries to: General Secretary

Founded:
1899

Organisation type and purpose:
Membership association (membership is by
subscription), present number of members: 1194,
voluntary organisation, registered charity (charity
number 227844), suitable for ages: 50+, publishing
house.

Subject coverage:
Informal education through friendship and
discussion groups, items relating to history of the
organisation. Provision of printed materials to aid
training and discussions.

**Museum or gallery collection, archive, or library
special collection:**
Annual reports and histories and biographies
relating to Adult Schools' role in education
Complete sets of Study Handbooks (1911 to
present)
Memorabilia (photographs, trophies and
documents) relating to NASO history
One and All, with supplement (1891 to present)

Printed publications:
Annual Study Handbook
Information leaflets
One & All (magazine, 6 times a year)
Training Papers

Access to staff:
Contact by letter, by telephone, by fax, by e-mail
and in person
Hours: By telephone, any time (answerphone); in
person, by appointment, 7 days a week, including
evenings

Affiliated regions:
Lancs and Cheshire
74 Mooreway, Rainhill Stoops, Prescot,
Merseyside, L35 6PD; tel: 0151 426 2505

Leicestershire
56 Meadow Gardens, Leicester, LE2 6QL; tel:
0116 291 9552
Midland
17 Mytton Road, Bournville, Birmingham, B30
1SL; tel: 0121 475 7933
North East
4 Bywell Gardens, Lobley Hill, Gateshead, Tyne
and Wear, NE11 0AY

Directly affiliated groups:
Bristol
6 Park Road, Keynsham, Bristol, BS31 1BS; tel:
0117 942 3852
Ewell
1 Jedwill, 44a Kingston Road, Ewell, Surrey,
KT17 2AB; tel: 020 8393 2133
Huddersfield
256 Quarmby Road, Quarmby, Huddersfield,
HD3 4FA; tel: 01484 657761; e-mail: honsec@
yasu.org.uk
Morley Sunday
18 Marshall Crescent, Morley, Leeds, LS27 0HB;
tel: 0113 253 0902
Rayners Lane
41 Sutton Close, Old Eastcote, Pinner, Middlesex,
HA5 2JX; tel: 01895 630010
Shrewsbury
85 Tudor Road, Shrewsbury, Shropshire; tel:
01743 351888

Linked organisations:
Hassocks
54 Stonepound Road, Hassocks, West Sussex,
BN6 8PR; tel: 01273 844051
Morley Monday
29 Pawson Street, Morley, Leeds, LS27 0QB; tel:
0113 253 2609
Northamptonshire
2 Northampton Road, Blisworth,
Northamptonshire, NN7 3DN; tel: 01604 858252
Yorkshire
256 Quarmby Road, Quarmby, Huddersfield,
HD3 4FA; tel: 01484 657761

NASPCS

Formal name: National Advisory Service for Parents
of Children with a Stoma
Acronym or abbreviation: NASPCS

51 Anderson Drive, Valley View Park, Darvel,
Ayrshire, KA17 0DE

Tel: 01560 322024
E-mail: john@stoma.freeserve.co.uk

Enquiries:
Enquiries to: Chairman

Founded:
1986

Organisation type and purpose:
National organisation, membership association,
present number of members: 650 families,
voluntary organisation, registered charity (charity
number 327922).
National advisory service for parents of
incontinent children and children with a stoma.
Membership is free.
To provide a contact and information service for
parents, on the practical day-to-day management
of a child with either a colostomy, ileostomy or
urostomy.

Subject coverage:
Bladder and bowel incontinence, ileostomy,
urostomy, colostomy, Hirschsprung's disease,
imperforate anus, cloacal exstrophy, exompholus,
prune belly syndrome, Vater syndrome, ectopia
vesicae, colonic/intestinal neuronal dysplasia and
gastroschisis.

Printed publications:
My Child Has Hirschsprung's Disease (free)
Beating Sneaky Poo (free)
Our Special Children – A practical guide to stoma
care in babies and young children (free)
Newsletter (quarterly)
8 information sheets (free)
ACE Procedure – A guide for nurses (free)

continued overleaf

My Child Has An Imperforate Anus (free)
Breaking the Taboo – Support leaflet of young
  people (free)

Publications list:
Available in print

Access to staff:
Contact by letter, by telephone and by e-mail
Hours: Mon to Fri, 0900 to 1700

Access to building, collection or gallery:
No access other than to staff

Members of:
International Ostomy Association

Membership Secretary:
NASPCS
  Maran Bank, Main Street, Glenfarg, Tayside, PH2
  9NT; tel: 01577 830661

Northern Ireland Representative:
NASPCS
  11 Earlford Heights, Doagh Road,
  Newtownabbey, Belfast, BT36 8WZ; tel: 01232
  837972

NATIONAL 39/45 MILITARY VEHICLE GROUP

9 Cordelia Way, Rugby, Warwickshire, CV22 6JU

Tel: 01788 812250

Enquiries:
Enquiries to: Treasurer

Founded:
1972

Organisation type and purpose:
Membership association, voluntary organisation,
research organisation.

Subject coverage:
Restoration of World War II Allied and Axis
military vehicles and equipment, uniforms,
memoirs, archives; film advice and vehicle supply;
vehicle date verification.

Museum or gallery collection, archive, or library special collection:
Archive photographs and drawings of airborne
  vehicle modifications
British and American military vehicle numbers

Printed publications:
Club Magazine (quarterly)

Access to staff:
Contact by letter and by telephone
Hours: Telephone after 1800

NATIONAL ACCESS & SCAFFOLDING CONFEDERATION

Acronym or abbreviation: NASC

4th Floor, 12 Bridewell Place, London EC4V 6AP

Tel: 020 7822 7400
Fax: 020 7822 7401
E-mail: enquiries@nasc.org.uk

Website:
http://www.nasc.org.uk

Enquiries:
Enquiries to: Director

Founded:
1943

Organisation type and purpose:
Trade association.

Subject coverage:
All aspects of scaffolding; technical information,
safety, suppliers and contractors.

Printed publications:
Yearbook
Technical and safety guidance notes

Publications list:
Available in print

Access to staff:
Contact by letter, by telephone and by fax
Hours: Mon to Fri, 0900 to 1700

Member of:
National Specialist Contractors Council (NSCC)

NATIONAL ACQUISITIONS GROUP

Acronym or abbreviation: NAG

12–14 King Street, Wakefield, WF1 2SQ

Tel: 01924 383010
Fax: 01924 383010
E-mail: nag1@btconnect.com

Website:
http://www.nag.org.uk

Enquiries:
Enquiries to: Administrator

Founded:
1986

Organisation type and purpose:
Professional body, membership association
(membership is by subscription), present number
of members: 481.
Bringing together those concerned in library
acquisitions, publishers, booksellers, system
suppliers and librarians (public, academic, special,
etc.).

Subject coverage:
Library acquisitions and collections management
in the United Kingdom and the Republic of
Ireland, technological developments, producers,
suppliers and libraries.

Printed publications:
Taking Stock (journal, twice a year)
The Tender Guide (2005)
Guidelines to Servicing – Part 1: Books
Value to Libraries of Special Services
Public Library Stock Management
Order printed publications from: same address

Electronic and video publications:
NAG News, Servicing Guidelines, Supply
  Specification, Directory of Acquisitions
  Librarians 2008
Order electronic and video publications from: As part
of membership benefits or from the Group

Publications list:
Available online and in print

Access to staff:
Contact by letter, by telephone, by fax, by e-mail
and via website

Access to building, collection or gallery:
Hours: Mon to Fri, 0900 to 1700

Access for disabled people:
Special comments: Steep stairs in old building

Links with:
CILIP
  7 Ridgmount Street, London, WC1E 7AE; tel: 020
  7255 0500; website: http://www.cilip.org.uk

NATIONAL AIDS TRUST

Acronym or abbreviation: NAT

New City Cloisters, 196 Old Street, London, EC1V
9FR

Tel: 020 7814 6767
Fax: 020 7216 0111
E-mail: info@nat.org.uk

Website:
http://www.nat.org.uk
Work of the organisation.
http://www.worldaidsday.org
World Aids Day.

Enquiries:
Enquiries to: Senior Communications Manager
Direct tel: 020 7814 6730
Other contacts: Deputy Director

Founded:
1988

Organisation type and purpose:
National organisation, voluntary organisation,
registered charity (charity number 297977).
The National Aids Trust (NAT) aims to: promote a
wider understanding of HIV and AIDS; develop
and support initiatives to prevent the spread of
HIV; improve the quality of life for people affected
by HIV and AIDS.

Subject coverage:
Policy; World Aids Day; employers' initiatives;
special projects.

Museum or gallery collection, archive, or library special collection:
Art of Awareness Collection: 100 framed images
  created depicting AIDS awareness, various
  media

Library catalogue:
All or part available in-house

Printed publications:
Available free and for purchase, direct

Electronic and video publications:
Specific videos available direct

Publications list:
Available online and in print

Access to staff:
Contact by letter, by telephone, by fax, by e-mail
and via website. Appointment necessary.
Hours: Mon to Fri, 0900 to 1700

Access to building, collection or gallery:
No prior appointment required

NATIONAL ANIMAL WELFARE TRUST

Acronym or abbreviation: NAWT

Tyler's Way, Watford By-pass, Watford,
Hertfordshire, WD25 8WT

Tel: 020 8950 0177
Fax: 020 8420 4454
E-mail: watford@nawt.org.uk

Website:
http://www.nawt.org.uk

Enquiries:
Enquiries to: Chief Executive

Founded:
1971

Organisation type and purpose:
Registered charity, voluntary organisation (charity
number 1090499).
Rescue and rehoming of unwanted animals.

Subject coverage:
Animal rescue and rehoming.

Printed publications:
NAWT Centre leaflets
NAWT News (2 times a year)

Access to staff:
Contact by letter, by telephone, by fax, by e-mail,
in person and via website
Hours: Administration: Mon to Fri, 0900 to 1700;
Rescue Centres: Watford, 1100 to 1500; Langport
(Somerset), 1100 to 1530; Cornwall, 1300 to 1600;
Berkshire, 1100 to 1600

Access for disabled people:
Parking provided, ramped entry, access to all
public areas, toilet facilities

Other addresses:
National Animal Welfare Trust
  Heaven's Gate Farm, West Henley, Langport,
  Somerset, TA10 9BE; tel: 01458 252656; fax:
  01458 253806
National Animal Welfare Trust
  Trindledown Farm, Wantage Lane, Great
  Shefford, Newbury, Berkshire, RG17 7DQ; tel:
  01488 638584; fax: 01488 638141

National Animal Welfare Trust
Wheal Alfred Farm, Wheal Alfred Road, Hayle,
Cornwall, TR27 5JT; tel: 01736 756005

NATIONAL ANKYLOSING SPONDYLITIS SOCIETY

Acronym or abbreviation: NASS

Unit 0.2, One Victoria Villas, Richmond upon
Thames, Surrey, TW9 2GW

Tel: 020 8948 9117
E-mail: admin@nass.co.uk

Website:
http://www.nass.co.uk
Guidebook for patients, forum, members section,
newsletters, charity news, fundraising news, shop

Enquiries:
Enquiries to: Administrator

Founded:
1976

Organisation type and purpose:
Registered charity (charity number 272258). NASS
is a membership charity which gives information
and support to people with ankylosing spondylitis.
Has about 100 branches in the United Kingdom.

Subject coverage:
Ankylosing spondylitis.

Printed publications:
Guidebook for Patients (free)
Newsletter (twice yearly)
Car Driving with Ankylosing Spondylitis

Electronic and video publications:
Exercise (DVD)

Publications list:
Available online and in print

Access to staff:
Contact by letter, by telephone, by e-mail and via
website
Hours: Mon to Fri, 0930 to 1730

Access to building, collection or gallery:
No public access

Links with:
Ankylosing Spondylitis International Federation
at the same address

NATIONAL ANTI-HUNT CAMPAIGN

Acronym or abbreviation: NAHC

PO Box 66, Stevenage, SG1 2TR

Tel: 01442 240246
Fax: By arrangement
E-mail: nahc@nahc.freeserve.co.uk

Website:
http://www.liberation-mag.org.uk/nahc.htm

Enquiries:
Enquiries to: Information Officer

Founded:
1992

Organisation type and purpose:
Membership association (membership is by
subscription), voluntary organisation.
Peaceful legal campaigning against all hunting
with dogs.

Subject coverage:
All areas relating to hunting with hounds, legal
problems with hunt trespass etc.

Printed publications:
Free leaflets and factsheets are available on all
aspects of hunting

Access to staff:
Contact by letter, by telephone, by fax and by e-
mail
Hours: Mon to Fri, 0900 to 1700

NATIONAL ARCHIVES

Formal name: The National Archives
Acronym or abbreviation: TNA

Kew, Richmond, Surrey, TW9 4DU

Tel: 020 8876 3444 \ Minicom no. 020 8392 9198
E-mail: http://www.nationalarchives.gov.uk/
contact/form

Website:
http://www.nationalarchives.gov.uk
Information about The National Archives, access to
online catalogues and digitised public records,
online bookshop, ordering copies of records, and
contact information. Website includes global
search facility, for searches across a number of
different catalogues. Also includes access to Your
Archives, a wiki, where users can contribute
knowledge of archival sources.
http://www.nationalarchives.gov.uk/catalogue
Catalogue descriptions of over 10 million
documents held by The National Archives.

Founded:
1838

Created by the merger of:
Public Record Office (PRO) and Historical
Manuscripts Commission (HMC); (The Office of
Public Sector Information was incorporated in
2006) (year of change 2004)

Organisation type and purpose:
National government body. Government
department and executive agency under the
Secretary of State for Justice.
National Archive Office.

Subject coverage:
As the official archive for England, Wales and the
central UK government, The National Archives
holds records ranging from parchment and paper
scrolls through to digital files and archived
websites. Increasingly, these records are being put
online, making them universally accessible. The
collection covers the British Isles, the territories
that formed the British Empire and the countries of
the Commonwealth.
The National Archives is at the heart of
information policy, setting standards and
supporting innovation in information and records
management across the UK, providing advice on
opening up and encouraging the re-use of public
sector information. Through its efforts in
promoting best practice in information
management, it looks to ensure the survival of
today's information for the future.

Education services:
http://www.nationalarchives.gov.uk/teachers

**Museum or gallery collection, archive, or library
special collection:**
The collections are too numerous to specify
(documents number many millions, and
currently cover 100 miles of shelving)
Famous documents include the Domesday Book,
Shakespeare's will, the Log of HMS Victory,
World Wars documents

Non-library collection catalogue:
All or part available online

Library catalogue:
All or part available online

Printed publications:
Research guides available free of charge on website
Many published sources available including:
First World War Army Service Records
Army Records: a guide for family historians
Census: the expert guide
Naval Records for Genealogists
Tracing Your Ancestors

Publications list:
Available online and in print

Access to staff:
Contact by letter, by telephone, by fax, by e-mail,
in person and via website
Hours: Mon, Fri, 0900 to 1700; Tue, Thu, 0900 to
1900; Wed, 1000 to 1700; Sat, 0930 to 1700

Access to building, collection or gallery:
Access during open hours. A reader's ticket is
required for access to orginal documents. A ticket
can be obtained free of charge by bringing proof of
identity and proof of address. A list of suitable
identification documents is on the website at:
http://www.nationalarchives.gov.uk/registration
Hours: Mon, Fri, 0900 to 1700; Tue, Thu, 0900 to
1900; Wed, 1000 to 1700; Sat, 0930 to 1700

Access for disabled people:
Parking provided, level entry, access to all public
areas, toilet facilities
For more information see website: http://
www.nationalarchives.gov.uk/visit/
disabled.htm?source=ddmenu_visit7

NATIONAL ARCHIVES – CHANCERY LANE

Acronym or abbreviation: NA

Quality House, Quality Court, Chancery Lane,
London, WC2A 1HP

Tel: 020 7242 1198
Fax: 020 7831 3550
E-mail: nra@hmc.gov.uk

Website:
http://www.hmc.gov.uk/
General information on the HMC and its activities;
HMC information sheets for researchers; the
Indexes to the National Register of Archives, part
of the Manorial Documents Register; the thematic
digests of Accessions to Repositories, ARCHON –
Archival Resources Online information gateway;
Archives in Focus site providing introductory
guide to archives and their use for lifelong
learning.

Enquiries:
Enquiries to: Secretary

Founded:
1869

Organisation type and purpose:
National government body, advisory body.
To provide information and advice about the
location, nature and care of manuscript sources for
British history.

Subject coverage:
Nature and whereabouts in the United Kingdom of
papers, manuscript collections and archives of
value for the study of British history, outside the
public records; care and disposal of such records,
advice on conservation and storage, associated
published finding aids to historical manuscripts
throughout the world.

**Museum or gallery collection, archive, or library
special collection:**
The National Register of Archives (NRA) includes
over 43,000 lists of archives held by record
offices, libraries, museums, universities,
businesses, other public and private
organisations and individuals.
Manorial Documents Register and other finding
aids
Published finding aids to historical manuscripts
throughout the world which are of importance to
British history
The Commission does not hold collections of
manuscripts

Printed publications:
Annual Review 2000–2001 (2001, pub HMSO, £6)
Archive Buildings in the United Kingdom 1977–
1992 (pub. HMSO, £17.95)
Guides to Sources for British History
Archives at the Millennium: the Twenty-eighth
Report (1999, £9.50)
Prime Ministers' Papers (papers of nineteenth
century statesmen)
Record Repositories in Great Britain (11th ed.,
1999, £4.99)
Other titles listed in publications leaflet and on
website

Publications list:
Available online and in print

continued overleaf

Access to staff:
Contact by letter, by fax, by e-mail, in person and via website
Hours: Mon to Fri, 0930 to 1700

Access to building, collection or gallery:
No prior appointment required
Hours: Mon to Fri, 0930 to 1700

Moving towards the end of 2003 to:
National Archives
Ruskin Avenue, Kew, Richmond-upon-Thames, Surrey, TW9 4DU

NATIONAL ARCHIVES OF SCOTLAND

Acronym or abbreviation: NAS

HM General Register House, 2 Princes Street, Edinburgh, EH1 3YY

Tel: 0131 535 1314
Fax: 0131 535 1360
E-mail: enquiries@nas.gov.uk

Website:
http://www.nas.gov.uk

Enquiries:
Enquiries to: Keeper of the Records of Scotland

Founded:
1789

Organisation type and purpose:
National government body, statutory body.
Record office and archive.
Repository for the public and legal records of Scotland, accepts many local and private archives for which it is felt to be the most suitable repository.

Subject coverage:
Scottish affairs, history, topography, law, genealogy.

Museum or gallery collection, archive, or library special collection:
Administrative records of pre-Union Scotland, registers of central and local courts of law, public registers of property rights and legal documents, local and church records and private archives (computerised database for some)
Records of Scottish parliament and government departments, nationalised industries, maps and plans, and business records

Non-library collection catalogue:
All or part available online, in-house and in print

Library catalogue:
All or part available online and in-house

Printed publications:
A Proper Repository: the building of General Register House
The Guide to the National Archives of Scotland
Tracing Your Scottish Ancestors: The Official Guide
Tracing Scottish Local History
Leaflet on the records (free)

Electronic and video publications:
Scottish Archives for Schools (CD-ROMs)

Publications list:
Available online and in print

Access to staff:
Contact by letter, by telephone, by fax, by e-mail and in person
Hours: Mon to Fri, 0900 to 1700

Access for disabled people:
For wheelchair users and people with mobility impairments disabled
parking is available within the car park off West Register Street. Note this parking is
limited and it is recommended an appointment is made. Access to the building can be made
via either a ramp or disabled lift adjacent to the car park. Disabled toilet facilities are available on all floors.

NATIONAL ART LIBRARY

Acronym or abbreviation: NAL

Victoria and Albert Museum, Cromwell Road, South Kensington, London, SW7 2RL

Tel: 020 7942 2400
Fax: 020 7942 2394 or 2401
E-mail: nal.enquiries@vam.ac.uk

Website:
http://www.vam.ac.uk/nal
Information on services, holdings, events and current news.

Enquiries:
Enquiries to: Deputy Keeper
Direct tel: 020 7942 2562
Direct e-mail: j.meriton@vam.ac.uk
Other contacts: Head of Access, email: m.flynn@vam.ac.uk

Founded:
1837

Organisation type and purpose:
National organisation, art gallery, historic building, house or site.
National Art Library, open to the public, research library.

Subject coverage:
Architecture, fine and applied art and design of all periods and western countries, as well as Indian, Islamic and Far Eastern; prints, drawings, paintings; modern art; design; sculpture; metalwork; book production and the art of the book (bindings, illustration, fine printing); history of art; crafts; history of printing; history of costume; private presses; photography; artists' books; comics; children's books; calligraphy; manuscript illumination; heraldry; interior design; furniture and woodwork; ceramics and glass; textiles and dress; museums and museology; Beatrix Potter; Natalia Goncharova; Mikhail Larionov.

Museum or gallery collection, archive, or library special collection:
The General Collection contains: 1,000,000 books, 2000 current periodical titles, 9000 closed periodical titles, 60,000 exhibition catalogues, 300 illuminated manuscripts, 50,000 sales catalogues, 20,000 information files, literature from international exhibitions
Archives, artists' books, letters and manifestos, books using innovative technology or structure, books with notable dustjackets, calligraphy, children's books, comics and graphic novels, documentary manuscripts, early printed books, ephemera and jobbing printing, fine and noteworthy bindings and printing, illuminated manuscripts, modern book and magazine design, typography, writing and lettering books
Artists' Books
Exhibition Catalogues
Sales Catalogues
Trade Literature
The Special Collections are varied and include:
19th century Periodicals
Clements Collection of armorial bindings
Cole Collection: diaries, notebooks, correspondence and books of Sir Henry Cole
Forster Collection: English literature and history 16th to 19th centuries (including manuscripts of Charles Dickens)
Dyce Collection: literature and theatre, Britain and Europe 16th to 19th centuries
Harrod Collection: 19th century illustrated books
Hole Bequest: 17th and 18th century literature
Hutton Bequest: works on fencing, swordsmanship, weapons and self-defence
Jobbing Printing Collection: material from the 1920s, 1930s and 1960s
Jones Collection: literature and works relating to art and manufacturing
Osbert Lancaster Collection: comic art, humour
Larionov Collection: work by Larionov and Goncharova, theatre and opera in Europe (especially Russia and France)
Liberty and Company Printed Catalogues Collection

Linder Bequest and Collection: Beatrix Potter drawings, watercolours, manuscripts and letters (held at Blythe House)
Guy Little Bequest: children's books
Mediaeval Manuscripts
Osman-Gidal Collection: photojournalism
Pinto Bequest: directories relating to London and the provinces
Piot Collection: fairs and festivals
Queen Mary's Collection of children's books (held at Blythe House)
Rakoff Collection: comics and graphic novels
Ranier Collection (held at Blythe House)
Weale Collection: part of the working library of W H James Weale, Keeper of the National Art Library, 1890–1899

Library catalogue:
All or part available online

Printed publications:
Following publications describe parts of the Library's Special Collections:
Beatrix Potter: the V & A collection (A S Hobbs and J I Whalley, 1985)
Bookbindings (Harthan J P, 3rd ed., 1985)
Bookbindings and rubbings of bindings in the National Art Library, South Kensington Museum, (W H Weale, 1894–1898, 2 volumes)
Fine Illustrations in Western European Printed Books (T M MacRobert, 1969)
From Manet to Hockney: modern artists illustrated books (C Hogben and R Watson, 1985)
From the 1890s to the 1980s: fashion periodicals (1988)
Islamic Bookbindings in the Victoria and Albert Museum (D Haldane, 1983)
Series of booklets on modern British private presses
The History of the Illustrated Book (Harthan J P, 1981)
The Universal Penman: a survey of western calligraphy from the Roman period (Whalley J I, 1980)

Publications list:
Available online

Access to staff:
Contact by letter, by telephone, by fax, by e-mail, in person and via website
Hours: Tue, Wed, Thu, Sat, 1000 to 1730; Fri, 1000 to 1830
Special comments: Closed Bank Hol weekends, Christmas to New Year and two weeks' annual stocktaking in Aug.
All users must register after showing means of identification, access with readers' tickets only; visitors by prior appointment for reserved materials.

Access to building, collection or gallery:
No prior appointment required
Hours: Sun to Sat, 1000 to 1745; Fri, 1000 to 2200 (selected galleries remain open after 1800)
Special comments: Closed 24, 25 & 26 Dec

Access for disabled people:
Parking provided, ramped entry, toilet facilities
Special comments: 4 parking bays for vehicles with stickers for disabled people, next to the Exhibition Road entrance.

Parent body:
Victoria and Albert Museum

Subsidiary body:
Archive of Art and Design
23 Blythe Road, London, W14 0QF; tel: 020 7603 1514; fax: 020 7602 0980; e-mail: archive@vam.ac.uk; website: http://www.vam.ac.uk/resources/archives

NATIONAL ASSEMBLY FOR WALES

Library, New Crown Building, Cathays Park, Cardiff, CF10 3NQ

Tel: 029 2082 5449 or 823683
Fax: 029 2082 5508

Website:
http://www.wales.gov.uk

Enquiries:
Enquiries to: Librarian
Direct tel: 029 2082 3362

Founded:
1999

Organisation type and purpose:
National government body.

Subject coverage:
Local government; housing; education; health and social services; public finance and administration; law; libraries and museums; agriculture; economic planning; land use; transport and highways; tourism; ancient monuments; national parks; water; environment.

Trade and statistical information:
Welsh statistics.

Library catalogue:
All or part available in-house

Printed publications:
Many titles including:
Current Information Bulletins (7 titles)
Digest of Welsh Historical Statistics
Digest of Welsh Statistics
Health Statistics, Wales
List of Welsh Official Publications (monthly and annually)
Statistics of Education and Training in Wales

Publications list:
Available online

Access to staff:
Appointment necessary.
Hours: Mon to Fri, 0900 to 1700

NATIONAL ASSOCIATION FOR CHILDREN OF ALCOHOLICS

Acronym or abbreviation: NACOA

PO Box 64, Fishponds, Bristol, BS16 2UH

Tel: 0117 924 8005; 0800 358 3456 (helpline)
Fax: 0117 942 2928
E-mail: helpline@nacoa.org.uk

Website:
http://www.nacoa.org.uk

Enquiries:
Enquiries to: Administrator
Other contacts: Chief Executive

Founded:
1990

Organisation type and purpose:
Advisory body, membership association, registered charity (charity number 1009143), research organisation.
To raise the public consciousness to the needs of children of alcoholics, educate professionals as to their specific needs, provide advice, information and fellowship and promote research.

Subject coverage:
Information and advice on children of alcoholics for professionals and client group; other resources available, suggested reading.

Printed publications:
Leaflets for children of alcoholics and professionals (free), including:
Information for Children of Alcoholics
Some Mums and Dads Drink Too Much or Use Drugs (and poster)
A Guide for Schools: Children of Alcoholics in the Classroom
If a child of an alcoholic or addict comes to you
If you think someone in your family drinks too much or uses drugs
NACOA Annual Report
NACOA News
Suggested Reading List

Publications list:
Available online and in print

Access to staff:
Contact by letter, by telephone, by fax and by e-mail
Hours: Administration: Mon to Fri, 1000 to 1600
Helpline: Mon, Fri, 1000 to 1900; Tues, Wed, Thu, 1000 to 2100; Sat, 1000 to 1500

NATIONAL ASSOCIATION FOR COLITIS AND CROHN'S DISEASE

Acronym or abbreviation: NACC

4 Beaumont House, Sutton Road, St Albans, Hertfordshire, AL1 5HH

Tel: 01727 830038 (admin); 844296 (information)
Fax: 01727 862550
E-mail: nacc@nacc.org.uk

Website:
http://www.nacc.org.uk
Information about Colitis and Crohn's, and about the organisation. Contact details for overseas organisations.

Enquiries:
Enquiries to: Director
Direct tel: 01727 734479
Other contacts: PA to Director

Founded:
1979

Organisation type and purpose:
Membership association (membership is by subscription), present number of members: 28,000, voluntary organisation (charity number 282732).

Subject coverage:
Inflammatory bowel diseases, colitis, Crohn's disease, support of sufferers and their families.

Printed publications:
Newsletters, booklets, etc. (members)
Some information sheets available to non-members

Electronic and video publications:
Talkabout Colitis (video, Linkward Productions)
Talkabout Crohn's Disease (video, Linkward Productions)

Access to staff:
Contact by letter, by telephone, by fax, by e-mail and via website
Hours: Mon to Fri, 0900 to 1700

Has:
65 area groups in the UK

NATIONAL ASSOCIATION FOR ENVIRONMENTAL EDUCATION (UK)

Acronym or abbreviation: NAEE (UK)

University of Wolverhampton, Walsall Campus, Gorway Road, Walsall, West Midlands, WS1 3BD

Tel: 01922 631200
E-mail: info@naee.org.uk

Website:
http://www.naee.org.uk

Enquiries:
Enquiries to: Honorary General Secretary
Direct tel: 01922 631200
Direct e-mail: info@naee.org.uk
Other contacts: The Office Administrator for general enquiries.

Founded:
1968

Organisation type and purpose:
Membership association (membership is by subscription), registered charity, suitable for ages: all, early years to university.
Offer guidance and assistance in the delivery of environmental education for sustainable development within the formal education sector.

Subject coverage:
Environmental education in schools.

Printed publications:
Environmental Education (journal, 3 times a year)
Occasional Papers
Practical Guides
Resource Pack

Publications list:
Available in print

Access to staff:
Contact by letter, by telephone, by e-mail, in person and via website. Appointment necessary.
Hours: Thu

Access to building, collection or gallery:
Prior appointment required
Special comments: Please telephone for details.

Access for disabled people:
Parking provided

Associated with:
Environmental Education Advisers Association
Field Studies Council

NATIONAL ASSOCIATION FOR GIFTED CHILDREN

Acronym or abbreviation: NAGC

Suite 14, Challenger House, Sherwood Drive, Bletchley, Milton Keynes, Buckinghamshire, MK3 6DP

Tel: 0870 7703217
Fax: 0870 7703219
E-mail: amazingchildren@nagcbritain.org.uk

Website:
http://www.nagcbritain.org.uk
Information in identification, support and education of gifted and able children.

Enquiries:
Enquiries to: Director
Direct e-mail: kenbore@nagcbritain.org.uk
Other contacts: Education Consultants

Founded:
1965

Organisation type and purpose:
National organisation, membership association (membership is by subscription), present number of members: 2500, voluntary organisation, registered charity (charity number 313182), suitable for ages: 0 to 20, training organisation, consultancy, research organisation, publishing house.
To support gifted children, their families and schools concerned with their education and welfare.

Subject coverage:
Identification of gifted children, education of gifted children, local branches and helpful contacts (where available).

Museum or gallery collection, archive, or library special collection:
Books on gifted children and their needs

Printed publications:
Help with Bright Children
Intelligence
Newsletter
The Social, Educational and Emotional Needs of Gifted Children

Publications list:
Available in print

Access to staff:
Contact by letter, by telephone, by fax, by e-mail, in person and via website. Appointment necessary. All charged.
Hours: Helpline: Mon, Wed, Thu, Fri, 0930 to 1430
Visitors: Mon to Fri, 0900 to 1630
Special comments: Charges made for training and consultancy, free access to Helpline.

Access to building, collection or gallery:
Prior appointment required

Access for disabled people:
Access to all public areas

continued overleaf

Member of:
National Children's Bureau
Telephone Helplines Association

NATIONAL ASSOCIATION FOR LITERATURE DEVELOPMENT

Acronym or abbreviation: NALD

PO Box 49657, London, N8 7YZ

E-mail: director@nald.org

Website:
http://www.nald.org

Enquiries:
Enquiries to: Co-ordinator

Organisation type and purpose:
National organisation, membership association
(membership is by subscription), present number
of members: 144.

Subject coverage:
Networking and professional development
information for literature development sector.

Electronic and video publications:
E-Newsletter (fortnightly to members)

Publications list:
Available online

Access to staff:
Contact by letter, by telephone, by e-mail, in
person and via website
Hours: Mon to Fri, 0900 to 1700

Access to building, collection or gallery:
No access other than to staff

NATIONAL ASSOCIATION FOR PASTORAL CARE IN EDUCATION

Acronym or abbreviation: NAPCE

c/o Institute of Education, University of Warwick,
Coventry, Warwickshire, CV4 7AL

Tel: 024 7652 3810
Fax: 024 7652 4110
E-mail: base@napce.org.uk

Website:
http://www.napce.org.uk
About NAPCE: People, purpose, role etc; journal
information; on-line purchase and membership;
publication; conference, workshop information;
useful links: pastoral, training, education general.

Enquiries:
Enquiries to: Base Administrator
Other contacts: Chairman for press contact.

Founded:
1982

Organisation type and purpose:
International organisation, membership
association (membership is by subscription),
present number of members: 1500, registered
charity (charity number 291295), training
organisation, research organisation, publishing
house.

Subject coverage:
Pastoral care in schools and colleges, personal-
social education, effective learning.

**Museum or gallery collection, archive, or library
special collection:**
Small collection of materials on bullying

Printed publications:
Journal of Pastoral Care in Education
Broadsheets on topical issues:
Children and Bereavement, Death and Loss: what
    can the school do?
Developing Effective Links with Parents
From Head of Year to Year Curriculum
    Coordinator?
Governors and Pastoral Care
Improving School Behaviour
Learning about Learning
PSE and the Whole Curriculum

Quality Review in Pastoral Care
Reducing School Bullying: What Works?
Refugee children in school
Staff development Resources:
Reclaiming Pastoral Care
Targeting Strategies
The Value of Pastoral Care & PSE?
Tutor Review
Tutoring for Learning
Whole-School PSE: Policy and Practice

Microform publications:
Journal of Pastoral Care in Education (Blackwell)

Electronic and video publications:
Staff Development Resources (on disk)

Publications list:
Available online and in print

Access to staff:
Contact by letter, by telephone, by fax, by e-mail
and via website. Appointment necessary.
Hours: Mon to Fri, 0900 to 1330

Chairman:
National Association for Pastoral Care in
Education

NATIONAL ASSOCIATION FOR PATIENT PARTICIPATION

Acronym or abbreviation: N.A.P.P.

10 Rosegarth Avenue, Aston, Sheffield, S26 2DD

Tel: 0114 2874035
Fax: 0114 2874035
E-mail: enquire@napp.org.uk

Website:
http://www.napp.org.uk
General information about patient and public
involvement in health. Pointers to more specific
information.

Enquiries:
Enquiries to: Hon Secretary

Founded:
1977

Organisation type and purpose:
National organisation, membership association
(membership is by subscription), voluntary
organisation, registered charity (charity number
292157).
Promotes patient participation in primary health
care at local GPs surgeries, health centres.
Promotes and supports patient's participation in
their own primary health care with their GPs
through a network of regional representatives.
N.A.P.P. is the patient's participation voice at
meetings and conferences organised by NHS and
health organisations.

Subject coverage:
Practical advice, guidance and information to
affiliated patients groups who are located in local
surgeries. Experienced help provided in setting up
patients' groups and network potential via
affiliation.

Printed publications:
Members' Handbook for affiliated patients' groups
Newsletter (quarterly)
Information Pack for those interested in forming a
    group

Publications list:
Available in print

Access to staff:
Contact by letter, by telephone, by fax, by e-mail
and via website
Hours: 24 hours (answerphone)
Special comments: Volunteers work from home.

Regular contact with:
BMA Events
Kings Fund Conferences
NCVO Affiliation
Patient Liaison Committee of the Royal College of
General Practitioners

Representation on:
Doctor Patient Partnership
UK Patients' Forum

NATIONAL ASSOCIATION FOR PREMENSTRUAL SYNDROME

Acronym or abbreviation: NAPS

41 Old Road, East Peckham, Kent TN12 5AP

Tel: 0870 777 2178
E-mail: contact@pms.org.uk

Website:
http://www.pms.org.uk

Enquiries:
Enquiries to: Chief Executive

Founded:
1984

Organisation type and purpose:
Advisory body, membership association
(membership is by subscription), voluntary
organisation, registered charity (charity number
289901), research organisation.

Subject coverage:
Premenstrual syndrome, postnatal depression and
tension.

**Museum or gallery collection, archive, or library
special collection:**
Bibliographical research database available to
    professional members

Printed publications:
Understanding PMS
Information Pack
N.A.P.S. News
Premenstrual Syndrome – A Clinical Review

Publications list:
Available online and in print

Access to staff:
Contact by letter, by telephone, by e-mail and via
website
Hours: 24-hour information line

NATIONAL ASSOCIATION FOR PRIMARY EDUCATION

Acronym or abbreviation: NAPE

Nape National Office, Moulton College, Moulton,
Northampton, NN3 7RR

Tel: 01604 647646
Fax: 01604 647660
E-mail: nationaloffice@nape.org.uk

Website:
http://www.nape.org.uk
Information about NAPE and its activities.

Enquiries:
Enquiries to: Honorary Secretary
Direct tel: 01865 890281
Other contacts: Press & Information Officer for
comments on policy and educational news

Founded:
1980

Organisation type and purpose:
International organisation, national organisation,
advisory body, membership association
(membership is by subscription, election or
invitation), present number of members: 200,000
covered by group membership, voluntary
organisation, registered charity (charity number
289645), suitable for ages: birth to 13, training
organisation, consultancy, research organisation.
To promote high quality education for every child
from birth to 13 years.

Subject coverage:
Primary education, funding of schools, class sizes,
current issues in education as they arise e.g.
OfSTED inspections, teacher stress/morale,
inclusion, home/school partnership, workload,
teacher shortage, classroom assistant issues.

Printed publications:
NAPE Publications include:
Newsbrief
The Numbers Game (Alexander P, £2.25)
Current Home and School Council publications
In His Own Words (Schiller C, £5.95)
New Childhood (journal, 2 times a year, free to members)
Shining in the Sun (poems by children from NAPE Poetry competition 1995)
Why am I Starting School? (Backbone Productions)
Home and School Council Publications include:
Children Can Enjoy Writing Stories (Taylor G, £2)
Choosing and Using Books for Children (Inglis J, £1.50)
Parents & Reading (Tibertius S, £2)
Spelling: a Visual Approach (Cripps C and Bushell R, £2)

Electronic and video publications:
Starting School (video, Marks & Spencer)

Publications list:
Available in print

Access to staff:
Contact by letter, by telephone, by fax, by e-mail and via website. Appointment necessary.
Hours: Mon to Fri, 0900 to 1330
Special comments: School terms only.

NATIONAL ASSOCIATION FOR SPECIAL EDUCATIONAL NEEDS, THE

Acronym or abbreviation: NASEN

NASEN House, 4–5 Amber Business Village, Amber Close, Amington, Tamworth, Staffordshire, B77 4RP

Tel: 01827 311500
Fax: 01827 313005
E-mail: welcome@nasen.org.uk

Website:
http://www.nasen.org.uk
Information on publications, courses, journals, membership, consultation documents, press releases, policy gathering forum.

Enquiries:
Enquiries to: Honorary General Secretary

Founded:
1992

Organisation type and purpose:
National organisation, membership association (membership is by subscription), present number of members: 11,200, service industry, voluntary organisation, registered charity (charity number 1007023), suitable for ages: mainly KS1, KS2 and KS3, training organisation, research organisation, publishing house.
NASEN aims to promote the education, training, advancement and development of all those with special educational needs.

Subject coverage:
Development of children and young people with special educational needs, education, welfare, treatment, rehabilitation, equal opportunities.

Printed publications:
British Journal of Special Education (journal, quarterly)
Behaviour series
Language development
Literacy handbooks
Mathematics handbooks
Other handbooks
Special! (magazine, termly)
Staff development series
Support for Learning (journal, quarterly)
Teachers and Parents: Together for Reading

Electronic and video publications:
CD-ROM for purchase through NASEN

Publications list:
Available online and in print

Access to staff:
Contact by letter, by telephone, by fax, by e-mail, in person and via website. Appointment necessary.
Hours: Mon to Fri, 0900 to 1700

Access to building, collection or gallery:
Prior appointment required

Access for disabled people:
Parking provided, ramped entry, toilet facilities

NATIONAL ASSOCIATION FOR THE RELIEF OF PAGET'S DISEASE

Acronym or abbreviation: NARPD

323 Manchester Road, Walkden, Worsley, Manchester, M28 3HH

Tel: 0161 799 4646
Fax: 0161 799 6511
E-mail: director@paget.org.uk

Website:
http://www.paget.org.uk

Enquiries:
Enquiries to: Director

Founded:
1973

Organisation type and purpose:
Membership association (membership is by subscription), present number of members: 2400, registered charity (charity number 266071). To offer information and support for those suffering from Paget's Disease. To raise awareness of the disease to the medical profession and the public at large. To encourage and assist research.

Subject coverage:
Information on research into the cause, prevention, treatment and cure of Paget's Disease of the bone, and support for sufferers and their families.

Printed publications:
General Information for patients suffering from Paget's Disease of Bone (free)
Paget's Disease of Bone – Its Nature and Management (A Guide for Patients) (free)
The Treatment of Paget's Disease of Bone (free)
Newsletter (quarterly, members)

Publications list:
Available in print

Access to staff:
Contact by letter, by telephone, by fax, by e-mail and via website. Appointment necessary.
Hours: Mon to Fri, 0900 to 1700

Access to building, collection or gallery:
Prior appointment required

Access for disabled people:
Parking provided

Links with:
Paget's Disease Foundation of America
Paget's Disease Support Group New Zealand

NATIONAL ASSOCIATION FOR THE TEACHING OF ENGLISH

Acronym or abbreviation: NATE

50 Broadfield Road, Sheffield, South Yorkshire, S8 0XJ

Tel: 0114 255 5419
Fax: 0114 255 5296
E-mail: info@nate.org.uk

Website:
http://www.nate.org.uk

Enquiries:
Enquiries to: Director
Direct tel: 0114 255 5170

Founded:
1963

Organisation type and purpose:
Membership association (membership is by subscription), present number of members: 5500, suitable for ages: 5 to 21, publishing house.

Subject coverage:
Teaching of English through all age ranges; English language and literature.

Printed publications:
English in Education (journal)
NATE News (newsletter)
English Drama Media (magazine)
Pamphlets etc

Publications list:
Available online and in print

Access to staff:
Contact by letter, by telephone, by fax and by e-mail. Appointment necessary.
Hours: Mon to Fri, 0845 to 1630

Affiliated to:
International Federation for the Teaching of English

Is organised by:
14 Regions in the UK

Member of:
College of Teachers

NATIONAL ASSOCIATION FOR VOLUNTARY AND COMMUNITY ACTION

Acronym or abbreviation: NAVCA

The Tower, 2 Furnival Square, Sheffield, South Yorkshire, S1 4QL

Tel: 0114 278 6636
Fax: 0114 278 7004
E-mail: navca@navca.org.uk

Website:
http://www.navca.org.uk

Enquiries:
Enquiries to: Policy and Communications Officer

Founded:
1991

Formerly called:
National Association of Councils for Voluntary Service

Organisation type and purpose:
National organisation, membership association (membership is by qualification). National voice of local third sector infrastructure in England. Members work with 164,000 local third sector groups and organisations that provide community services, regenerate neighbourhoods, promote volunteering and tackle discrimination in partnership with local public bodies.

Subject coverage:
Information on management of voluntary organisations, contacts in local infrastructure organisations and councils for voluntary service, setting up and managing voluntary organisations.

Printed publications:
See website http://www.navca.org.uk/publications

Publications list:
Available online and in print

Access to staff:
Contact by letter, by telephone, by fax and by e-mail. Appointment necessary.
Hours: Mon to Fri, 0900 to 1700

Access to building, collection or gallery:
Prior appointment required

Access for disabled people:
Access to all public areas, toilet facilities

Member of:
National Council for Voluntary Organisations (NCVO)
Volunteering England

continued overleaf

Subsidiary bodies:
364 local third sector infrastructure organisations
in England

NATIONAL ASSOCIATION OF ADULT PLACEMENT SERVICES

Acronym or abbreviation: NAAPS

72 Rodney Street, Liverpool, L1 9AF

Tel: 0151 709 1200
Fax: 0151 709 7144

Enquiries:
Enquiries to: Co-ordinator

Founded:
1992

Organisation type and purpose:
National organisation, membership association
(membership is by subscription), present number
of members: 1500+, voluntary organisation,
registered charity (charity number 1019231).
To promote and develop adult placement services
as a resource within the community.

Subject coverage:
Adult placement.

Access to staff:
Contact by letter, by telephone and by fax
Hours: Mon to Fri, 0900 to 1700

NATIONAL ASSOCIATION OF AGRICULTURAL CONTRACTORS

Acronym or abbreviation: NAAC

Samuelson House, 62 Forder Way, Hampton,
Peterborough, PE7 8JB

Tel: 0845 644 8750
Fax: 01733 352806
E-mail: jill.hewitt@naac.co.uk

Website:
http://www.naac.co.uk

Enquiries:
Enquiries to: Chief Executive

Founded:
1893

Organisation type and purpose:
Trade association.

Subject coverage:
Contract services to agriculture and allied land-
based industries including crop protection and
spraying, whole farm and whole crop contracting,
vegetation control, mobile seed cleaning and
processing, cultivating and harvesting of all UK
crops.

Printed publications:
NAAC Newsletter (members)
Contracting Bulletin

Access to staff:
Contact by letter, by telephone, by fax, by e-mail
and via website
Hours: Mon to Fri, 0900 to 1700

NATIONAL ASSOCIATION OF BANK & INSURANCE CUSTOMERS

Acronym or abbreviation: NABIC

PO Box 15, Caldicot, Newport, Gwent, NP26 5YD

Tel: 0845 123 5002
Fax: 0845 123 5002
E-mail: webmaster@lemonaid.net

Website:
http://www.lemonaid.net
Information, advice and general background to
NABIC and its activities.

Enquiries:
Enquiries to: Information Officer

Other contacts: Chief Executive for press comment,
member query or complaint.

Founded:
1991

Organisation type and purpose:
International organisation, membership
association (membership is by subscription),
present number of members: 25,000, training
organisation, consultancy, research organisation.
To protect and promote the interests of private and
commercial users of bank and insurance services
through information, education and mediation
processes. To build a detailed database of
procedures and abuses.

Subject coverage:
Banking, insurance, legal representation, customer
complaints, recalculation of bank statements to
find errors, business planning services, business
planning software and customer service standards.

**Museum or gallery collection, archive, or library
special collection:**
Database of queries and complaints and standard
responses

Trade and statistical information:
Data on the frequency and type of bank and
insurance disputes.

Printed publications:
Adhoc reports on technical matters
Banking Charter
Datasheets on a variety of topics (free to members)
Occasional newsletter (free to members)

Electronic and video publications:
Business Planning Software

Access to staff:
Contact by letter, by telephone, by fax, by e-mail
and via website
Hours: Mon to Fri, 0900 to 1700

Links with:
ADICAE
    Spain
ADOSBEF
    Italy
AFUB
    France
AIC
    USA
CONSUMENT and GELDZAKEN
    Holland
European Union of Financial Service Users
    contact via NABIC

NATIONAL ASSOCIATION OF BRITISH MARKET AUTHORITIES

Acronym or abbreviation: NABMA

13 Moor Road, Wigan, Lancashire, WN5 8DN

Tel: 01942 203797
Fax: 01942 205885
E-mail: nabma@nabma.com

Website:
http://www.nabma.com
List of member authorities, news and events for
public, members only secured area for members of
this Association.

Enquiries:
Enquiries to: General Secretary

Founded:
1919

Organisation type and purpose:
Local government body, membership association.

Subject coverage:
Organisation and operation by local authorities of
markets of all kinds including open retail markets,
market halls, wholesale fruit, vegetable, flower,
fish and meat markets; livestock markets; public
abattoirs, and pleasure fairs.

Printed publications:
Annual Conference Report including conference
    papers

Rules

Access to staff:
Contact by letter, by telephone and by fax
Hours: Mon to Fri, 0900 to 1700

Member of:
European Association of Livestock Markets
World Union of Wholesale Markets

NATIONAL ASSOCIATION OF CHILD CONTACT CENTRES

Acronym or abbreviation: NACCC

Minerva House, Spaniel Row, Nottingham, NG1
6EP

Tel: 0845 4500280
Fax: 0845 4500420
E-mail: contact@naccc.org.uk

Website:
http://www.naccc.org.uk

Enquiries:
Enquiries to: Administrator
Other contacts: Chief Executive for matters of policy
as opposed to administration.

Organisation type and purpose:
Registered charity (charity number 1003868).
To promote safe child contact within a national
framework of 325 Child Contact Centres

Subject coverage:
Neutral meeting places where children of
separated families can spend time with one or both
parents, and sometimes other family members, in a
safe and comfortable environment when there is
no viable alternative.

Printed publications:
General information leaflet
Ben's Story, An Introduction to Child Contact
    Centres (for children £2.50)
Lily's Story, An Introduction to Child Contact
    Centres for the Very Young (£2.50)
NACCC Manual (available only to members)
NACCC Directory of Member Centres, includes
    referral details, opening times etc (available only
    to members)

Electronic and video publications:
NACCC Training Video (£30 non-members
    outright purchase, £10 members outright
    purchase, £5 members only 2 week hire charge)

Publications list:
Available online

NATIONAL ASSOCIATION OF CHIMNEY SWEEPS

Acronym or abbreviation: NACS

Unit 15, Emerald Way, Stone Business Park, Stone,
Staffordshire, ST15 0SR

Tel: 01785 811732
Fax: 01785 811712
E-mail: nacs@chimneyworks.co.uk

Website:
http://www.nacs.org.uk

Enquiries:
Enquiries to: Administrator

Founded:
1982

Organisation type and purpose:
Trade association.

Subject coverage:
Chimney sweeping and chimneys in general.

Library catalogue:
All or part available in-house

Printed publications:
Code of practice
Chimney Journal (trade magazine, Apr, Aug, Dec)
Heat your Home Safely (leaflet)
List of members

Access to staff:
Contact by letter, by telephone, by fax and by e-mail
Hours: Mon to Fri, 0800 to 1600

Access to building, collection or gallery:
Prior appointment required

Access for disabled people:
Parking provided, level entry

Links with:
HETAS
    tel: 01242 513747; fax: 01242 513747; e-mail: billk@albionmillshouse.freeserve.co.uk
NACE
    tel: 01773 599095; fax: 01773 599195; e-mail: info@nace.org.uk
NFA
    tel: 0121 200 2100; fax: 0121 200 1306

Member of:
European Federation of Chimney Sweeps (ESCHFO)
    tel: 00 49 2241 340713; fax: 00 49 2241 340710; e-mail: ziv-kelz-quadt@schornsteinfeger.de

NATIONAL ASSOCIATION OF CHOIRS

Acronym or abbreviation: NAC

Fig Tree House, 9 The Green, Glinton, Peterborough, Cambridgeshire, PE6 7JN

Tel: 01733 252464
Fax: 01733 252464
E-mail: gensecnac@gensecnac.force9.co.uk

Website:
http://www.ukchoirsassoc.co.uk
Details of all member choirs, officers, services provided, links to supppliers, etc.

Enquiries:
Enquiries to: General Secretary

Founded:
1920

Organisation type and purpose:
Voluntary organisation.

Subject coverage:
Study and performance of choral music, choral societies and choirs.

Printed publications:
News and Views (newsletter, quarterly)
Year Book

Publications list:
Available in print

Access to staff:
Contact by letter, by telephone, by fax, by e-mail and via website
Hours: Any day up to 2200

Affiliated to:
British Federation of Music Festivals

Member of:
British Federation of Youth Choirs
National Choral Advisory Body

NATIONAL ASSOCIATION OF CITIZENS ADVICE BUREAUX

Acronym or abbreviation: NACAB

Myddelton House, 115–123 Pentonville Road, London, N1 9LZ

Tel: 020 7833 2181 (Admin only)
Fax: 020 7833 4371 (Admin only)

Website:
http://www.nacab.org.uk
To find your nearest CAB.
http://www.adviceguide.org.uk
For CAB information online.

Enquiries:
Enquiries to: Communications Assistant

Founded:
1939

Organisation type and purpose:
National organisation, advisory body, voluntary organisation, registered charity.
To provide information and advice on any topic.

Subject coverage:
Debt and consumer, social security, employment, housing, property and land, family and personal, administration of justice, taxes and duties, local information, health, national and international travel, transport and holidays, education, immigration and nationality, communication and leisure.

Printed publications:
Annual Report
CAB News (annually)
Evidence Papers (list available)

Access for disabled people:
Parking provided, level entry, access to all public areas, toilet facilities
Special comments: Myddleton House only.

Affiliated to:
Advice Services Alliance
National Council for Voluntary Organisations

Has:
approximately 1300 CABs throughout the country

Links with:
Citizens Advice Scotland

NATIONAL ASSOCIATION OF CLINICAL TUTORS

Acronym or abbreviation: NACT

1 Wimpole Street, London, W1G 0AE

Tel: 020 7629 4000
Fax: 020 7629 4000
E-mail: office@nact.org.uk

Website:
http://www.nact.org.uk

Enquiries:
Enquiries to: Chairman

Organisation type and purpose:
Professional body.

Subject coverage:
Postgraduate medical training; career counselling in medicine; educational techniques related to medicine.

Printed publications:
Directory of Postgraduate Medical Centres
Training Pack for Clinical Tutors

Access to staff:
Contact by letter, by telephone, by fax and by e-mail. Appointment necessary. Access for members only.
Hours: Mon to Fri, 0900 to 1700

Access for disabled people:
Level entry, toilet facilities

NATIONAL ASSOCIATION OF CYCLE TRADERS LIMITED

Acronym or abbreviation: ACT

31a High Street, Tunbridge Wells, Kent, TN1 1XN

Tel: 01892 526081
Fax: 01892 544278
E-mail: act@act-bicycles.com

Website:
http://www.act-bicycles.com

Enquiries:
Enquiries to: Information Officer

Founded:
1920

Organisation type and purpose:
Trade association.

Subject coverage:
Cycle safety and standards, cycle mechanics accreditation scheme, cycle retailing, technical information.

Printed publications:
Newsletter (quarterly, members)

Access to staff:
Contact by letter, by e-mail and via website
Hours: Mon to Fri, 0900 to 1700

NATIONAL ASSOCIATION OF DEAFENED PEOPLE

Acronym or abbreviation: NADP

PO Box 50, Amersham, Buckinghamshire, HP6 6XB

Tel: 0845 055 9663
Fax: 01305 262591
E-mail: enquiries@nadp.org.uk

Website:
http://www.nadp.org.uk

Enquiries:
Enquiries to: Honorary Secretary

Founded:
1984

Organisation type and purpose:
Membership association (membership is by subscription), present number of members: 300, voluntary organisation, registered charity (charity number 294922).
To provide a network of information and support for deafened people.

Subject coverage:
Increasing public awareness of the needs and problems of deafened people; the promotion of an improvement in the rehabilitation, education, training, re-training and employment opportunities available for deafened people.

Printed publications:
Deaf People Can (employment handbook, £2.50 plus 50p p&p)
Introduction to Cochlear Implants (2nd edn, £2.50 plus 50p p&p)
Network (newsletter, quarterly, members only)

Publications list:
Available online and in print

Access to staff:
Contact by letter, by fax, by e-mail and via website

Access to building, collection or gallery:
No access to office

NATIONAL ASSOCIATION OF DECORATIVE & FINE ARTS SOCIETIES

Acronym or abbreviation: NADFAS

NADFAS House, 8 Guilford Street, London, WC1N 1DT

Tel: 020 7430 0730
Fax: 020 7242 0686
E-mail: enquiries@nadfas.org.uk

Website:
http://www.nadfas.org.uk

Enquiries:
Enquiries to: PA to Chairman & Chief Executive

Founded:
May 1968

Organisation type and purpose:
International organisation, membership association (membership is by subscription), present number of members: 88,000, registered charity (charity number 263487), art gallery.
Arts educational charity.

continued overleaf

Volunteer-led cultivation, appreciation and study of the decorative and fine arts, and giving aid to the preservation of national artistic heritage for the benefit of the general public.

Subject coverage:
Decorative and fine arts. NADFAS is an arts educational organisation based on leisure interests rather than careers. It consists of member societies that meet on a monthly basis for lectures, and organises visits to places of historic interest and museums. In addition members carry out voluntary work in museums, historic houses and churches.

Printed publications:
NADFAS News (magazine, 2 times a year)
Inside Churches (£9.95 or £6.67 to trade)
Order printed publications from: Manager, NADFAS Enterprises
at the same address

Access to staff:
Contact by letter, by telephone and by e-mail
Hours: Mon to Fri, 0930 to 1730

Access to building, collection or gallery:
No prior appointment required

Has:
320 societies in the UK, 22 in Australia and 9 in Europe

Head Office:
National Association of Decorative & Fine Arts Societies (NADFAS)
at the same address

NATIONAL ASSOCIATION OF EDUCATIONAL INSPECTORS, ADVISERS AND CONSULTANTS

Acronym or abbreviation: NAEIAC

Woolley Hall, Woolley, Wakefield, West Yorkshire, WF4 2JR

Tel: 01226 383428
Fax: 01226 383427
E-mail: naeiac@gemsoft.co.uk

Website:
http://www.naeiac.co.uk
Membership information, services provided.

Enquiries:
Enquiries to: General Secretary

Founded:
1918

Organisation type and purpose:
National organisation, professional body, trade union (membership is by subscription).

Subject coverage:
Education from pre-school to higher education: curriculum, management, inspection and advice.

Printed publications:
Briefing
Business Register Directory
Information Bulletin

Access to staff:
Contact by letter, by telephone, by fax, by e-mail and via website
Hours: Mon to Thu, 0830 to 1700; Fri, 0830 to 1630

Representation on:
Soulbury Committee

NATIONAL ASSOCIATION OF FARRIERS, BLACKSMITHS AND AGRICULTURAL ENGINEERS

Acronym or abbreviation: NAFBAE

Avenue B, 10th Street, National Agricultural Centre, Stoneleigh, Kenilworth, Warwickshire, CV8 2LG

Tel: 02476 696595
Fax: 02476 696708
E-mail: nafbaehq@nafbae.org.uk

Enquiries:
Enquiries to: Membership Secretary
Other contacts: National Organiser

Founded:
1904

Organisation type and purpose:
National organisation, trade association (membership is by subscription).

Access to staff:
Contact by letter, by telephone, by fax and by e-mail. Access for members only.
Hours: Mon to Fri, 0900 to 1700

Access to building, collection or gallery:
No prior appointment required

NATIONAL ASSOCIATION OF FUNERAL DIRECTORS

Acronym or abbreviation: NAFD

618 Warwick Road, Solihull, West Midlands, B91 1AA

Tel: 0845 230 1343
Fax: 0121 711 1351
E-mail: info@nafd.org.uk

Website:
http://nafd.org.uk

Enquiries:
Enquiries to: Chief Executive Officer

Founded:
1905

Organisation type and purpose:
Trade association, present number of members: 3272.

Subject coverage:
All aspects of the funeral profession.

Printed publications:
Careers in the Funeral Service
Code of Practice
Independent Chairman's Report of the Disciplinary Committee
Funeral Arbitration Scheme

Access to staff:
Contact by letter, by telephone, by fax, by e-mail, in person and via website
Hours: Mon to Fri, 0900 to 1700

Access to building, collection or gallery:
No prior appointment required

Access for disabled people:
Parking provided

NATIONAL ASSOCIATION OF GOLDSMITHS OF GREAT BRITAIN AND IRELAND

Acronym or abbreviation: NAG

78a Luke Street, London, EC2A 4XG

Tel: 020 7613 4445
Fax: 020 7613 4450
E-mail: nag@jewellers-online.org

Website:
http://www.jewellers-online.org

Enquiries:
Enquiries to: Information Manager
Direct e-mail: information@jewellers-online.org

Founded:
1894

Organisation type and purpose:
Trade association (membership is by subscription, election or invitation), present number of members: 1200 companies, training organisation, consultancy, publishing house.
To provide services, support, education and information to best encourage professionalism in the retail jewellery industry.

Subject coverage:
All aspects of the jewellery industry; history, materials, gems, gold, silver, retail, valuations.

Information services:
Available

Education services:
Available

Printed publications:
The Jeweller Magazine
Order printed publications from: NAG switchboard

Publications list:
Available in print

Access to staff:
Contact by letter, by fax and by e-mail
Hours: Mon to Fri, 0900 to 1700

NATIONAL ASSOCIATION OF HEALTH WORKERS FOR TRAVELLERS

Acronym or abbreviation: NAHWT

Balsall Heath Health Centre, 43 Edward Road, Balsall Heath, Birmingham, B12 9LB

Tel: 0121 446 2300
Fax: 0121 446 5936
E-mail: joanne.davis@hobtpct.nhs.uk

Enquiries:
Enquiries to: Secretary

Founded:
1992

Subject coverage:
Health care relating to Travellers and Gypsies in Britain.

Access to staff:
Contact by letter, by fax and by e-mail
Hours: Mon to Wed, 0900 to 1700

Access to building, collection or gallery:
No access other than to staff

Links with:
Community Practioners and Health Visitors Association
40 Bermondsey Street, London, SE1 3UD; tel: 020 7939 7000; fax: 020 7403 2976

NATIONAL ASSOCIATION OF HOSPITAL & COMMUNITY FRIENDS

Acronym or abbreviation: NAHCF

Fairfax House, Causton Road, Colchester, Essex, CO1 1RJ

Tel: 01206 761227
Fax: 01206 560244
E-mail: info@hc-friends.org.uk

Website:
http://www.hc-friends.org.uk
General information on organisation and services. Currently being updated to include 'members only' area.

Enquiries:
Enquiries to: Chief Executive
Other contacts: Communications Officer for external inquiries contact (general).

Founded:
1949

Organisation type and purpose:
National organisation, membership association (membership is by subscription), present number of members: over 800, voluntary organisation, registered charity (charity number 210391).

Subject coverage:
Volunteering in the health sector. Legal, financial and general advice relating to running Friends' charities in hospital or the community.

Museum or gallery collection, archive, or library special collection:
Archive information available relating to the history of the National Association of Hospital and Community Friends

Non-library collection catalogue:
All or part available in-house

Printed publications:
Hospital and Community Friend (quarterly journal, free to members, annual subscription £12)
Safer Volunteer Recruitment – a Guide for Charities and Voluntary Groups (£14.99 plus £3.50 p&p)

Publications list:
Available in print

Access to staff:
Contact by letter, by telephone, by fax, by e-mail, in person and via website. Appointment necessary.
Hours: Mon to Fri, 0900 to 1700

Access to building, collection or gallery:
Prior appointment required

Access for disabled people:
Parking provided, ramped entry, access to all public areas, toilet facilities

Has:
800 independent affiliated health and social care charities ie Hospital and Community Friends

NATIONAL ASSOCIATION OF INDEPENDENT TRAVEL AGENTS

Acronym or abbreviation: NAITA

79–80 Margaret Street, London, W1W 8TA

Tel: 020 7323 3408
Fax: 020 7323 5189
E-mail: naita@advantage4travel.com

Website:
http://www.advantage4travel.com

Enquiries:
Enquiries to: Manager
Direct e-mail: debbiew@advantage4travel.com
Other contacts: Membership Co-ordinator for membership enquiries.

Founded:
1978

Organisation type and purpose:
National organisation, trade association (membership is by subscription), present number of members: 904.
Commercial and Marketing Consortia (Travel). To enhance, from a commercial and marketing viewpoint, the business and professionalism of our members (independent travel agents in the UK) and help maximise their profitability.

Subject coverage:
Travel trade consortia for independent travel agents in the UK, offering commercial and marketing support, to include signage, window decals, hanging banners, late availability board, tactical campaigns, monthly magazine and supplier-led promotions, together with a professional sales development team offering expert advice and support to all members.

Access to staff:
Contact by letter, by telephone, by fax, by e-mail and via website. Appointment necessary.
Hours: Mon to Fri, 0830 to 1800

Trading as:
Advantage Travel Centres
38 Anderston Quay, Glasgow, G3 8BX; tel: 0141 248 3466; fax: 0141 248 5170; e-mail: glasgow@advantage4travel.com

NATIONAL ASSOCIATION OF LADIES' CIRCLES

Formal name: National Association of Ladies' Circles of Great Britain and Ireland

Acronym or abbreviation: NALC

Marchesi House, 4 Embassy Drive, Edgbaston, Birmingham, B15 1TP

Tel: 0121 456 0304
E-mail: headquarters@ladies-circle.org.uk

Website:
http://www.ladies-circle.org.uk

Enquiries:
Enquiries to: Association Secretary

Founded:
1936

Organisation type and purpose:
National organisation, membership association (membership is by subscription), present number of members: 6500, voluntary organisation.

Subject coverage:
Charities, fund-raising, community service, women's issues, family issues.

Printed publications:
The Circler (twice a year, April and September, free to members)

Access to staff:
Contact by letter, by telephone, by fax, by e-mail and via website
Hours: Mon to Fri, 0900 to 1700

Affiliated to:
Ladies Circle International
    at the same address

NATIONAL ASSOCIATION OF LARYNGECTOMEE CLUBS

Acronym or abbreviation: NALC

Lower Ground Floor, 152 Buckingham Palace Road, London, SW1W 9TR

Tel: 020 7730 8585
Fax: 020 7730 8584
E-mail: info@laryngectomy.org.uk

Website:
http://www.laryngectomy.org.uk/

Enquiries:
Enquiries to: General Secretary

Founded:
1976

Organisation type and purpose:
National organisation, membership association, present number of members: 97 clubs with 5000, voluntary organisation, registered charity (charity number 273635).
National Association with clubs situated throughout the UK for those who have undergone a laryngectomy operation, their family and friends.

Subject coverage:
Rehabilitation of laryngectomee patients, availability of speech aids and medical supplies.

Printed publications:
NALC pamphlet
NATO Alphabet, pocket card
Professional Care, pack of 3 leaflets
Living with A Laryngectomy, pack of 4 leaflets
Emergency card
Information pamphlet
Clan (newsletter, quarterly)
Work of the Association (pamphlet)
Stoma care pamphlet
Resources pamphlet
Resuscitation pamphlet
NALC Handbook

Electronic and video publications:
LIFE, Laryngectomy Information for First aid and Emergency Treatment (video)
Talking it Through (video)
Nursing and Laryngectomee Care (video)

Publications list:
Available in print

Access to staff:
Contact by letter, by telephone and by fax.
Appointment necessary.
Hours: Mon to Thu, 0900 to 1630; Fri, 0900 to 1600

Links with:
Macmillan Cancer Relief
national associations in various countries

NATIONAL ASSOCIATION OF LICENSED PARALEGALS

Acronym or abbreviation: NAPL

9 Unity Street, Bristol, BS1 5HH

Tel: 0117 927 7077
Fax: 0117 929 3887
E-mail: legalnapl@aol.com

Enquiries:
Enquiries to: General Secretary
Direct tel: 0117 927 7077
Direct fax: 01208 863195
Direct e-mail: info@nationalparalegals.com

Founded:
1987

Organisation type and purpose:
Regulatory and professional body, suitable for ages: 18+. Educational, training and career development organisation.

Subject coverage:
Career guidance for paralegals, qualifications by examination and otherwise for paralegals and legal secretaries, training for career progression, seminars, workshops and courses on legal subjects.

Printed publications:
Distance learning packs
Information Pack
Newsletter (quarterly)

Access to staff:
Contact by letter, by telephone, by fax, by e-mail and via website
Hours: Mon to Fri, 0900 to 1700

Access to building, collection or gallery:
Prior appointment required

Other addresses:
National Association of Paralegals
    Vocational Training Office, Suite 401, No 302 Regent Street, London, W1R 6HH; tel: 020 7625 5211; fax: 020 7681 0354

Subsidiary body:
Institute of Legal Secretaries and PAs
    at the same address

NATIONAL ASSOCIATION OF LOCAL COUNCILS

Acronym or abbreviation: NALC

109 Great Russell Street, London, WC1B 3LD

Tel: 020 7637 1865
Fax: 020 7436 7451
E-mail: nalc@nalc.gov.uk

Website:
http://www.nalc.gov.uk

Enquiries:
Enquiries to: Deputy Chief Executive

Founded:
1947

Organisation type and purpose:
Local government body, membership association.

Subject coverage:
Any matter to do with small scale local government, particularly rural, legal and financial.

Museum or gallery collection, archive, or library special collection:
A complete law library

Printed publications:
Booklets and leaflets (32 titles, some free)
Conduct of Parish Meetings

continued overleaf

Local Council Review (quarterly)
Powers and Constitution of Local Councils
Standing Orders and Chairmanship

Access to staff:
Contact by letter, by fax and by e-mail.
Appointment necessary.
Hours: Mon to Fri, 0900 to 1700

Access to building, collection or gallery:
No access other than to staff

NATIONAL ASSOCIATION OF MASTER BAKERS

Acronym or abbreviation: NAMB

21 Baldock Street, Ware, Hertfordshire, SG12 9DH

Tel: 01920 468061
Fax: 01920 461632
E-mail: namb@masterbakers.co.uk

Website:
http://www.masterbakers.co.uk

Enquiries:
Enquiries to: Chief Executive

Founded:
1887

Organisation type and purpose:
Trade association.

Subject coverage:
Bread, flour and confectionery.

Museum or gallery collection, archive, or library special collection:
Copies of Bakers' Review from 1887 to present day

Printed publications:
Bakers' Review (monthly)
Handbook and Buyers Guide (annually)

NATIONAL ASSOCIATION OF MASTER LETTER CARVERS

Acronym or abbreviation: NAMLC

c/o NAMM, Castle Mews, Rugby, CV21 2XL

Tel: 01788 542264
Fax: 01788 542276
E-mail: enquiries@namm.org.uk

Enquiries:
Enquiries to: Honorary Secretary

Founded:
1920

Organisation type and purpose:
Trade association, present number of members: 50,
consultancy.
Publication of list of members. Setting
recommended prices.

Subject coverage:
Hand-carved lettering in stone and wood,
memorials, monuments etc.

Museum or gallery collection, archive, or library special collection:
History of Association
Minutes since 1920

Printed publications:
Introduction to the Association

Access to staff:
Contact by letter and by telephone
Hours: Mon to Fri, 0900 to 1700

NATIONAL ASSOCIATION OF MEMORIAL MASONS

Acronym or abbreviation: NAMM

1 Castle Mews, Rugby, CU21 2XL

Tel: 01788 542264
Fax: 01788 542276
E-mail: enquiries@namm.org.uk

Website:
http://www.namm.org.uk

Enquiries:
Enquiries to: National Executive Officer

Founded:
1907

Organisation type and purpose:
Trade association (membership is by subscription).

Subject coverage:
All matters relating to natural stone memorials,
standards in the trade, training.

Printed publications:
Choosing a Memorial
List of Members
Newsletter
Code of Working Practice
Order printed publications from: National
Association of Memorial Masons
as above

Access to staff:
Contact by letter, by telephone, by fax and by e-
mail
Hours: Mon to Fri, 0900 to 1700

Associate member of:
Confederation of Burial Authorities
Council of British Funeral Services
EURO-ROC
International Monument Federation

NATIONAL ASSOCIATION OF MINING HISTORY ORGANISATIONS

Acronym or abbreviation: NAMHO

Peak District Mining Museum, The Pavilion,
Matlock Bath, Derbyshire, DE4 3NR

Tel: 01629 583834

Website:
http://www.namho.org

Enquiries:
Enquiries to: Honorary Secretary

Founded:
1979

Organisation type and purpose:
National organisation, learned society
(membership is by election or invitation), present
number of members: 75, voluntary organisation,
registered charity (charity number 297301).
Representative body for mining history.

Subject coverage:
Mining history; past and present mining in the UK;
access policy and legislation thereon; conservation
and display of artefacts; production of codes of
practice on research techniques.

Printed publications:
Archival Research
Codes of Practice (free on receipt of sae)
Exploration (leaders)
Exploration (novices)
Guidelines for the Leisure Use of Mines
Mineral collection
Mining Heritage Guide
Removal of Artefacts

Access to staff:
Contact by letter and by telephone
Hours: Mon to Fri, 0900 to 1700
Special comments: SAE required for reply.

Member of:
National Caving Association
Momomark House, 27 Old Gloucester Street,
London, WC1N 3XX

NATIONAL ASSOCIATION OF MUSIC EDUCATORS

Acronym or abbreviation: NAME

Gordon Lodge, Snitterton Road, Matlock,
Derbyshire, DE4 3LZ

Tel: 01629 760791
Fax: 01629 760791
E-mail: musiceducation@name.org.uk

Website:
http://www.name.org.uk

Enquiries:
Enquiries to: Administrator

Founded:
1996

Organisation type and purpose:
Company limited by guarantee, registered charity.

Subject coverage:
Music education.

Printed publications:
Information Bulletins (£1.50)
Composing in the Classroom (£7)
Rites of Passage (£11)
Ideas In Music Out (£8)
Bluebirds and Crows (£8)
Ways into Music (£11)
No Need for Words (£11)
Music and the Power of Partnerships (£11)
Order printed publications from: Administrator,
NAME
at same address

Publications list:
Available online and in print

Access to staff:
Contact by letter, by telephone, by fax, by e-mail
and via website
Hours: Mon to Fri, 0900 to 1700

NATIONAL ASSOCIATION OF PENSION FUNDS

Acronym or abbreviation: NAPF

NIOC House, 4 Victoria Street, London, SW1H
0NX

Tel: 020 7808 1300
Fax: 020 7222 7585
E-mail: jane.dawson@napf.co.uk

Website:
http://www.napf.co.uk
Full details of the NAPF Press Office, including
releases, speeches, articles, publications and other
services.

Enquiries:
Enquiries to: Public Relations Manager
Other contacts: Press Officer

Founded:
1923

Organisation type and purpose:
Trade association.

Subject coverage:
All aspects of occupational pensions, both benefits
and investments.

Printed publications:
Policy Watch (monthly)
NAPF News (4 times a year)
Leaflets and other pensions material
NAPF Annual Survey of Occupational Pension
    Schemes (£120 members, £160 non-members)
Series of guides, leaflets and handbooks for
    pension funds and others in the pensions
    industry

Electronic and video publications:
Interactive introduction to the NAPF (CD-ROM,
free)

Publications list:
Available online and in print

Access to staff:
Contact by letter, by telephone, by fax, by e-mail
and via website. Appointment necessary.
Hours: Mon to Fri, 0915 to 1715

NATIONAL ASSOCIATION OF POULTRY SUPPLIERS

1 Belgrove, Tunbridge Wells, Kent, TN1 1YW

Tel: 01892 541412
Fax: 01892 535462
E-mail: naps@nfmft.co.uk

Enquiries:
Enquiries to: Secretary
Direct e-mail: graham@nfmft.co.uk

Organisation type and purpose:
National organisation, trade association
(membership is by subscription).

Subject coverage:
All aspects of wholesale poultry trade.

Access to staff:
Contact by letter, by telephone and by fax
Hours: Mon to Fri, 0900 to 1700

NATIONAL ASSOCIATION OF PRISON VISITORS

Acronym or abbreviation: NAPV

29 Kimbolton Road, Bedford, MK40 2PB

Tel: 01234 359763
Fax: 01234 359763

Enquiries:
Enquiries to: General Secretary

Founded:
1924

Organisation type and purpose:
National organisation, membership association
(membership is by subscription), present number
of members: 1400, voluntary organisation, suitable
for ages: 21 to 70.

Subject coverage:
Concern and friendship for, and visits to, people in
prison.

Printed publications:
Newsletter (2 times a year)

Access to staff:
Contact by letter, by telephone and by fax
Hours: Mon to Fri, 0900 to 1700

NATIONAL ASSOCIATION OF PUBLIC GOLF COURSES

Acronym or abbreviation: NAPGC

12 Newton Close, Redditch, Worcestershire, B98
7YR

Tel: 01527 542106
Fax: 01527 455320
E-mail: eddiemitchell@blueyonder.co.uk

Website:
http://www.napgc.org.uk

Enquiries:
Enquiries to: Secretary

Founded:
1927

Organisation type and purpose:
Voluntary organisation.
Specially for the cohesion of golf clubs formed on
public golf courses.

Subject coverage:
Golf club and course management authority
integration, national golf tournaments for public
course clubs.

Printed publications:
Year Book

Links with:
English Golf Union
Royal & Ancient Golf Club of St Andrews

NATIONAL ASSOCIATION OF ROUND TABLES OF GREAT BRITAIN AND IRELAND

Acronym or abbreviation: RTBI

Marchesi House, 4 Embassy Drive, Edgbaston,
Birmingham, B15 1TP

Tel: 0121 456 4402
Fax: 0121 456 4185
E-mail: hq@roundtable.org.uk

Website:
http://www.roundtable.org.uk/
Home page.

Enquiries:
Enquiries to: General Secretary

Founded:
1927

Organisation type and purpose:
Membership association (membership is by
election or invitation), present number of
members: 10,000.
Fellowship.

Subject coverage:
Community service, normally within local Table
area.

Access to staff:
Contact by letter, by telephone, by fax and by e-
mail
Hours: Mon to Fri, 0900 to 1700

Access for disabled people:
Access to all public areas

NATIONAL ASSOCIATION OF SCHOOLMASTERS AND UNION OF WOMEN TEACHERS

Acronym or abbreviation: NASUWT

Northern Ireland Centre, Ben Madigan House,
Edgewater Office Park, Edgewater Road, Belfast,
BT3 9JQ

Tel: 028 9078 4480
Fax: 028 9078 4489
E-mail: rc-nireland@mail.nasuwt.org.uk

Website:
http://www.northern-ireland.nasuwt.org.uk
Professional and trade union information.

Enquiries:
Enquiries to: Regional Organiser (Northern Ireland)

Founded:
1962

Organisation type and purpose:
National organisation, trade union (membership is
by subscription), present number of members:
11,100 in NI.

Subject coverage:
All matters pertaining to school teachers.

Non-library collection catalogue:
All or part available online and in print

Library catalogue:
All or part available online and in print

Printed publications:
Teaching Today
Platform

Access to staff:
Contact by letter, by telephone, by fax, by e-mail
and via website
Hours: Mon to Fri, 0830 to 1730

Access to building, collection or gallery:
Prior appointment required
Hours: Mon to Fri, 0830 to 1730

Access for disabled people:
Parking provided, access to all public areas, toilet
facilities

Parent body:
National Association of Schoolmasters and Union
of Women Teachers
Rose Hill, Rednal, Birmingham, B45 8RS; tel:
0121 453 6150; fax: 0121 457 6208/9; e-mail:
nasuwt@mail.nasuwt.org.uk

NATIONAL ASSOCIATION OF SCHOOLMASTERS AND UNION OF WOMEN TEACHERS – HILLSCOURT EDUCATION CENTRE

Acronym or abbreviation: NASUWT

Rose Hill, Rednal, Birmingham, B45 8RS

Tel: 0121 453 6150
Fax: 0121 457 6208/9
E-mail: nasuwt@mail.nasuwt.org.uk

Website:
http://www.teachersunion.org.uk

Enquiries:
Enquiries to: General Secretary

Founded:
1919/1965

Organisation type and purpose:
Professional body, trade union, present number of
members: 250,000.

Subject coverage:
Salaries, superannuation and conditions of service
of UK teachers; education in the UK; primary and
secondary school education; teacher training and
education.

Printed publications:
Pamphlets (no catalogue is available, free to
members)
Teaching Today (free to members)
Various information updates

Access to staff:
Contact by letter, by telephone, by fax, by e-mail
and via website. Appointment necessary. Access
for members only.
Hours: Mon to Fri, 0830 to 1730

Affiliated to:
Education International
European Trade Union Committee for Education
Federation of Professional Workers
Irish Congress of Trade Unions
National Foundation for Educational Research
Scottish Trades Union Congress
Trades Union Congress
Welsh Trades Union Congress

Headquarters address:
NASUWT
5 King Street, London, WC2E 8HN; tel: 020 7420
9670; fax: 020 7420 9679

NATIONAL ASSOCIATION OF SELF EMPLOYED

Acronym or abbreviation: NAS

Lynch House, 91 Mansfield Road, Nottingham,
NG1 3FN

Tel: 0115 947 5046
Fax: 0115 950 9139
E-mail: nas@n-a-s.org.uk

Website:
http://www.nase.org/

Enquiries:
Enquiries to: General Secretary
Other contacts: Northern Ireland Regional Secretary
for persons interested in membership in Northern
Ireland.

Founded:
1942

Organisation type and purpose:
Trade association, membership association
(membership is by subscription).

continued overleaf

Non-profit making association to support and advise the self-employed section of the business world. Representation of the interest of the self employed.

Subject coverage:
The self-employed including employment law, health and safety at work, self-assessment, late or no payment for goods and work, local and national government legislation.

Printed publications:
Magazine (2 times a year to members)

Access to staff:
Contact by letter, by telephone, by fax and by e-mail. Appointment necessary.
Hours: Mon to Thu, 0900 to 1700; Fri, 0900 to 1600

Access to building, collection or gallery:
Prior appointment required

NATIONAL ASSOCIATION OF SESSIONAL GPS

Acronym or abbreviation: NASGP

PO Box 188, Chichester, West Sussex, PO19 2FP

Fax: 01243 536428
E-mail: info@nanp.org.uk

Website:
http://www.nasgp.org.uk

Enquiries:
Enquiries to: Chief Executive

Founded:
1997

Organisation type and purpose:
National organisation, membership association (membership is by subscription), present number of members: 2500, voluntary organisation. Independent voluntary organisation of non-principal general practitioners, such as locums and assistants, who work in the NHS, to improve status and welfare of its members.

Subject coverage:
Non-principal general practitioners in the NHS.

Publications list:
Available online

Access to staff:
Contact by letter, by fax, by e-mail and via website
Hours: Mon to Fri, 0900 to 1700

NATIONAL ASSOCIATION OF SHOPFITTERS

Acronym or abbreviation: NAS

NAS House, 411 Limpsfield Road, The Green, Warlingham, Surrey, CR6 9HA

Tel: 01883 624961
Fax: 01883 626841
E-mail: nas@clara.net

Website:
http://www.shopfitters.org
Members list, membership benefits, general information.

Enquiries:
Enquiries to: Director

Founded:
1919

Organisation type and purpose:
Trade association.

Subject coverage:
Shopfitting.

Printed publications:
Annual Report and Directory
Guide to Controlling Risks to Health in the Shopfitting Industry
Shopfitters' Guide to CDM Regulations
ShopSpec (annually, pub Nexus Media Limited)
Code of Practice on Safe Erection of Hoardings etc

Publications list:
Available online and in print

Access to staff:
Contact by letter, by telephone, by fax, by e-mail and via website
Hours: Mon to Fri, 0900 to 1700

Affiliated to:
International Shopfitters Organisation

Houses the:
Automatic Door Suppliers Association

NATIONAL ASSOCIATION OF STEEL STOCKHOLDERS

Acronym or abbreviation: NASS

First Floor, The Citadel, 190 Corporation Street, Birmingham, B4 6QD

Tel: 0121 200 2288
Fax: 0121 236 7444
E-mail: info@nass.org.uk

Website:
http://www.nass.org.uk

Enquiries:
Enquiries to: Director-General

Founded:
1928

Organisation type and purpose:
Trade association.

Subject coverage:
United Kingdom steel stockists and suppliers.

Printed publications:
Annual Report
List of Members
NASS News
Safety Guidelines (£100)
Steel and its Distribution (£10)
Safe Delivery and Unloading of Steel Products
Order printed publications from: info@nass.org.uk

Electronic and video publications:
Industry Video (£150)
Safe Delivery and Unloading of Steel Products (downloadable)
Order electronic and video publications from: info@nass.org.uk

Access to staff:
Contact by letter, by telephone, by fax, by e-mail and via website
Hours: Mon to Fri, 0900 to 1700

NATIONAL ASSOCIATION OF SWIMMING CLUBS FOR THE HANDICAPPED

Acronym or abbreviation: NASCH

The Willows, Mayles Lane, Wickham, Hampshire, PO17 5ND

Tel: 01329 833689

Enquiries:
Enquiries to: Administrator

Organisation type and purpose:
Membership association (membership is by subscription), present number of members: 101, registered charity (charity number 247772).

Subject coverage:
Swimming for the handicapped, including swimming aids, hoists and other equipment, tuition, formation of clubs, insurance, and the Distance Award (incentive) scheme.

Printed publications:
Classification Systems in Competitive Swimming Facilities
Forming a Club
Free booklets
Lifting and Handling
Medical Considerations
Register of Swimming Clubs and Organised Swimming Sessions for Handicapped People (twice a year, for sale)
Swimming and Epilepsy
Teaching Disabled People to Swim (series of 2 booklets)

NATIONAL ASSOCIATION OF TEACHERS OF DANCING

Acronym or abbreviation: NATD

Bateman House, 44–47 The Broadway, Thatcham, Newbury, Berkshire, RG19 3HP

Tel: 01635 868888
Fax: 01635 872301
E-mail: info@natd.org.uk

Website:
http://www.natd.org.uk

Enquiries:
Enquiries to: General Secretary

Founded:
1906

Organisation type and purpose:
Membership association (membership is by subscription), training organisation.

Subject coverage:
Dance teaching.

Access to staff:
Contact by letter, by telephone, by fax, by e-mail and via website
Hours: Mon to Fri, 0830 to 1600

Access to building, collection or gallery:
No access other than to staff

NATIONAL ASSOCIATION OF THE LAUNDERETTE INDUSTRY LIMITED

Acronym or abbreviation: NALI

146 Welling Way, Welling, Kent, DA16 2RS

Tel: 020 8856 9798
Fax: 020 8856 9394

Enquiries:
Enquiries to: Secretary

Organisation type and purpose:
Trade association.

Subject coverage:
Launderettes and coin-operated dry cleaners.

Printed publications:
Launderette and Cleaning World (quarterly, members only)
What Every Launderette Owner Should Know (£5.50 inc. p&p)

Access to staff:
Contact by letter, by telephone and by fax
Hours: Mon to Fri, 0900 to 1700

NATIONAL ASSOCIATION OF TOOL DEALERS

Acronym or abbreviation: NATD

225 Bristol Road, Edgbaston, Birmingham, B5 7UB

Tel: 0121 446 6688
Fax: 0121 446 5215
E-mail: natd@bhfgroup.demon.co.uk

Enquiries:
Enquiries to: Managing Director

Founded:
1899

Organisation type and purpose:
Trade association.
Representation of members interests to government and others.

Subject coverage:
Hand and power tools.

Printed publications:
Hardware Today

Member of:
BHF Group

NATIONAL ASSOCIATION OF TOY AND LEISURE LIBRARIES

Acronym or abbreviation: NATLL

68 Churchway, London, NW1 1LT

Tel: 020 7255 4600
Fax: 020 7255 4602
E-mail: admin@playmatters.co.uk

Website:
http://www.natll.org.uk

Enquiries:
Enquiries to: Helpline
Direct tel: 020 7255 4616
Direct e-mail: helpline@playmatters.co.uk

Founded:
1967

Organisation type and purpose:
National organisation, membership association (membership is by subscription), present number of members: 1,000 toy libraries, 30 leisure libraries; voluntary organisation, registered charity (charity number in England and Wales 270291 and in Scotland SCO39458), suitable for ages: Toy Library: 0 to 12, usually extended for children with special needs, training organisation.
The national body for toy and leisure libraries throughout the United Kingdom. Toy libraries lend good quality, carefully chosen toys to all families with young children, including children with special needs. They offer a befriending, supportive service to parents and carers.
NATLL offers help, advice, information and support for people setting up and running toy and leisure libraries; sells a range of publications on the topic of toys and play; organises training courses for the voluntary and statutory sectors. Also offers Quality Assurance Scheme 'Quality Play Matters' to member toy libraries. Contract with the Department for Children, Schools and Families to deliver services under Every Child Matters. Also contracts with the Scottish Executive and the Welsh Assembly.

Subject coverage:
Toy libraries; leisure libraries; toys and play, particularly for children with special needs; Extended Schools Games Club Project: recreational activities for people with additional needs.

Education services:
Extended Schools Games Club Project

Services for disabled people:
Toy libraries offer loan of specialist toys and equipment, and support to families of children with special needs.

Printed publications:
Play Matters Magazine (formerly ARK; journal, quarterly for members)
Books and leaflets include:
Good Toy Guide (annually)
Guide to Choosing and Using Musical Instruments (2001)
Nuts and Bolts: Setting up a Toy Library (2003)
Nytiau a Boltau (Welsh version of Nuts and Bolts)
Play Matters for Adults Too (1999)
More Playsense Activity Cards
Quality PlayMatters Workbook
The really useful guide to involving volunteers
Toy Care
Starting Out
Special Needs Supplies (2000)
Starting a Toy Library in School (1999)
Switch into Action (2000)
Toys and Play in Child Development (1995)
Games Pack for Extended Schools
Order printed publications from: Via website; mail order from HQ

Electronic and video publications:
Learning to Share (video with training facilitator's pack, 1995)
Play Helps Video
Order electronic and video publications from: Via website; mail order from HQ

Publications list:
Available online and in print

Access to staff:
Contact by letter, by telephone, by fax, by e-mail and via website. Appointment necessary.
Hours: Mon to Fri, 0900 to 1700
Special comments: Please send A4 sae

Access to building, collection or gallery:
Prior appointment required

Access for disabled people:
Level entry to ground floor only, access to rest of building difficult.

Also at:
National Association of Toy and Leisure Libraries Gilmerton Community Centre, 4 Drum Street, Edinburgh, EH17 8QG; tel: 0131 664 2746; fax: 0131 664 2753; e-mail: natll.scotland@playmatters.co.uk
Re-create (Cardiff Play Resources Centre) Ely Bridge Industrial Estate, Wroughton Place, Cardiff, CF5 4AB; tel: 02920 566333; fax: 02920 566399; e-mail: natll.wales@playmatters.co.uk

Constituent bodies:
ACTIVE

Member organisation of:
NCVCCO
NCVO
VOLCUF

NATIONAL ASSOCIATION OF WIDOWS

Acronym or abbreviation: NAW

48 Queens Road, Coventry, Warwickshire, CV1 3EH

Tel: 024 7663 4848
E-mail: info@nawidows.co.uk

Website:
http://www.nawidows.co.uk
The website is being updated and is currently a holding site.

Enquiries:
Enquiries to: Administrator

Founded:
1971

Organisation type and purpose:
National organisation (membership is by subscription), present number of members: 3000, voluntary organisation, registered charity (charity number 1096896).
Run by widows for widows; providing friendship and support with local branches throughout the country; Head Quarters membership is also available for widows who have no local contact.

Printed publications:
Newsletter (2 times a year)
Information Sheets (free) include:
Widowed mothers and their children
Disability Support
Solo Holidays
Social activities and volunteering
Helpful Books

Access to staff:
Contact by letter, by telephone and by e-mail
Hours: Mon , Tues, Thu, Fri, 0900 to 1600

Access to building, collection or gallery:
No prior appointment required

Access for disabled people:
Lift

NATIONAL ASSOCIATION OF WOMEN PHARMACISTS

Acronym or abbreviation: NAWP

c/o The Royal Pharmaceutical Society of Great Britain, 1 Lambeth High Street, London, SE1 7JN

E-mail: enquiries@nawp.org.uk

Website:
http://www.nawp.org.uk

Enquiries:
Enquiries to: Honorary Secretary
Direct tel: 01296 712568
Direct e-mail: renatainglis@hotmail.com

Founded:
1905

Organisation type and purpose:
Professional body (membership is by subscription, qualification), present number of members: 300.

Subject coverage:
Pharmacy, academic, hospital, community, industrial; returners, continuing education.

Museum or gallery collection, archive, or library special collection:
Early records and newsletters held in the Archives of the Royal Pharmaceutical Society of Great Britain

Printed publications:
Newsletter (3 times a year, members)

Access to staff:
Contact by telephone, by e-mail and via website
Hours: 24-hour access

Links with:
Royal Pharmaceutical Society of Great Britain 1 Lambeth High Street, Lambeth, London, SE1 7JN

Member organisation of:
Standing Conference of Women Returners Network
Standing Conference of Women's Organisations

NATIONAL ASSOCIATION OF WOMEN'S CLUBS

Acronym or abbreviation: NAWC

5 Vernon Rise, Kings Cross Road, London, WC1X 9EP

Tel: 020 7837 1434
Fax: 020 7713 0727

Enquiries:
Enquiries to: Administrator
Other contacts: National Secretary

Founded:
1935

Organisation type and purpose:
Registered charity, voluntary organisation (charity number 273397).
To advance education and recreation or leisure time occupation for women in the interests of social welfare.

Subject coverage:
Assistance in running or opening new clubs for women to provide education and recreation.

Museum or gallery collection, archive, or library special collection:
Minutes of meetings, photographs

Printed publications:
Annual Report
Education, Friendship and Fun – a History of NAWC
Newsletters (members)

Access to staff:
Contact by letter, by telephone and by fax
Hours: Mon to Fri, 0930 to 1630

Affiliated to:
National Council of Women of Great Britain

continued overleaf

Member of:
Women's National Commission

NATIONAL ASSOCIATION OF YOUTH ORCHESTRAS

Acronym or abbreviation: NAYO

Central Hall, West Tollcross, Edinburgh, EH3 9BP

Tel: 0131 221 1927
Fax: 0131 229 2921
E-mail: admin@nayo.org.uk

Website:
http://www.nayo.org.uk
General information on NAYO.

Enquiries:
Enquiries to: General Manager
Other contacts: Administrator

Founded:
1961

Organisation type and purpose:
Voluntary organisation, registered charity (charity number 281493).
To represent youth orchestras throughout the UK and to foster their development.

Subject coverage:
Youth orchestral work: training, performance repertoire, organisation and maintenance, touring, international exchanges, courses; Edinburgh and Glasgow Festivals of British Youth Orchestras; European Youth Music Week, Allianz Cornhill Musical Insurance Youth Orchestra Awards, Allianz Cornhill Musical Insurance Conducting Prize/Seminar.

Museum or gallery collection, archive, or library special collection:
Marion Semple Weir Library of Chamber Music

Library catalogue:
All or part available online, in-house and in print

Printed publications:
Full Orchestra (newsletter, 3 times a year)
General leaflet (annually)
Leaflet from European Youth Music Week
Directory of Youth and Student Orchestras
Child Protection Guidelines

Access to staff:
Contact by letter, by telephone, by fax, by e-mail and via website. Appointment necessary.
Hours: Mon to Fri, 0900 to 1700

Access to building, collection or gallery:
Prior appointment required

Affiliated to:
Association of British Orchestras
Edinburgh Festival Fringe
European Association of Youth Orchestras
Incorporated Society of Musicians
Music Education Council
Voluntary Arts Network

NATIONAL ASSOCIATION OF YOUTH THEATRES

Acronym or abbreviation: NAYT

The Arts Centre, Vane Terrace, Darlington, Co Durham, DL3 7AX

Tel: 01325 363330
Fax: 01325 363313
E-mail: nayt@btconnect.com

Website:
http://www.nayt.org.uk

Enquiries:
Enquiries to: Management Assistant

Founded:
1982

Organisation type and purpose:
National organisation, advisory body, present number of registered groups: 846, voluntary organisation, registered charity (charity number 1046042).

Subject coverage:
Youth theatre provision, practice and location in the United Kingdom, public and national support.

Printed publications:
Information Bulletin (bi-monthly)

Access to staff:
Contact by letter, by telephone and by e-mail.
Appointment necessary.
Hours: Mon to Fri, 0900 to 1700

Access to building, collection or gallery:
Prior appointment required

Funded by:
Arts Council of Great Britain (additional funds)
Department for Education and Employment

NATIONAL AUDIT OFFICE

Acronym or abbreviation: NAO

157–197 Buckingham Palace Road, London, SW1W 9SP

Tel: 020 7798 7000
Fax: 020 7798 7894
E-mail: enquiries@nao.gsi.gov.uk

Website:
http://www.nao.org.uk

Enquiries:
Enquiries to: Library Enquiries Desk
Direct tel: 020 7798 7264

Organisation type and purpose:
Statutory body.
Audit of centrally funded bodies and government departments.

Subject coverage:
Value for Money and Financial Audit Reports (relating to
centrally funded bodies and government departments).

Information services:
Regularly updated press notices, corporate information, full text of reports 1999/2000 parliamentary session to present (all online)

Printed publications:
Annual Report

Access to staff:
Contact by letter, by telephone and by fax.
Appointment necessary.
Hours: Mon to Fri, 0900 to 1700

Access to building, collection or gallery:
Prior appointment required

NATIONAL AURICULA & PRIMULA SOCIETY (SOUTHERN)

67 Warnham Court Road, Carshalton Beeches, Surrey, SM5 3ND

E-mail: info@auricula.org.uk

Website:
http://www.southernauriculaprimula.org

Enquiries:
Enquiries to: Honorary Secretary

Founded:
1876

Organisation type and purpose:
Learned society (membership is by subscription).

Subject coverage:
Breeding and cultivation of auriculas, primroses, polyanthus, and all primula species and hybrids, their exhibition and history.

Printed publications:
Newsletter
Year Book

Access to staff:
Contact by letter
Hours: Mon to Fri, 0900 to 1700

Affiliated to:
Royal Horticultural Society

Has a:
Midland and West Section
Northern Section

NATIONAL AUTISTIC SOCIETY

Acronym or abbreviation: NAS

393 City Road, London, EC1V 1NG

Tel: 020 7833 2299; 0845 070 4004 (autism helpline)
Fax: 020 7833 9666
E-mail: nas@nas.org.uk

Website:
http://www.autism.org.uk

Founded:
1962

Organisation type and purpose:
National organisation, membership association (membership is by subscription), present number of members: 15,000, voluntary organisation, registered charity (charity number 269425).

Subject coverage:
Autism; The Autism Helpline provides impartial and confidential information, advice and support for people with an autistic spectrum disorder, their families and professionals.

Museum or gallery collection, archive, or library special collection:
Library of books, journals, videos
Database of 21,000 records at www.autism.org.uk/autismdata

Non-library collection catalogue:
All or part available online

Library catalogue:
All or part available online

Printed publications:
Communication (journal, quarterly, members)
Numerous publications on all aspects of autism and Asperger syndrome.
Order printed publications from: Central Books Ltd, 99 Wallis Road, London, E9 5LN; tel. 0845 458 9911; fax 0845 458 9912; e-mail nas@centralbooks.com

Electronic and video publications:
Videos
Autism Update (via login on website, 6 times a year, £14.99)
Titles in Autism (via login on website, 6 times a year, £14.99)

Publications list:
Available online and in print

Access to staff:
Contact by letter, by telephone, by fax, by e-mail and via website
Hours: Mon to Fri, 0930 to 1700

Access to building, collection or gallery:
Prior appointment required
Hours: Mon to Fri, 1000 to 1600

Access for disabled people:
Parking provided, ramped entry, toilet facilities

NATIONAL AUTOCYCLE AND CYCLEMOTOR CLUB LTD

Acronym or abbreviation: NACC

7 St. Nicholas Road, Copmanthorpe, York, YO23 3UX

Tel: 01904 704373
E-mail: info@thebuzzingclub.co.uk

Website:
http:// www.thebuzzingclub.co.uk

Founded:
1981

Organisation type and purpose:
International organisation, membership association (membership is by subscription), present number of members: 1,800. Library covering machines for which the club caters. Aims to promote interest, restoration and use of all autocycles, cyclemotors and mopeds under 100cc.

Subject coverage:
Restoration and preservation of autocycles, cyclemotors and mopeds under 100cc marque enthusiasts, help and advice, library, transfers, etc. Certified machine dating. Authorised by the DVLA to approve V.765 applications for the retention or original registration marks and age-related registration numbers.

Museum or gallery collection, archive, or library special collection:
Parts lists, manuals, road tests, sales cats, etc.

Non-library collection catalogue:
All or part available in-house

Library catalogue:
All or part available in-house

Printed publications:
Buzzing (magazine, 6 times a year, free to members)
Fact and advice sheets
Library booklet of literature held

Publications list:
Available in print

Access to staff:
Contact by letter, by telephone, by e-mail and via website
Hours: 0900 to 2100
Special comments: By telephone, e-mail or letter to the Chairman; please enclose sae for reply.

Access to building, collection or gallery:
No access other than to staff

NATIONAL BED FEDERATION

Acronym or abbreviation: NBF

High Corn Mill, Chapel Hill, Skipton, North Yorkshire, BD23 1NL

Tel: 0845 055 6406
Fax: 0845 055 6407
E-mail: info@bedfed.org.uk

Website:
http://www.bedfed.org.uk

Enquiries:
Enquiries to: Administrator
Other contacts: PR Consultant for media and consumer enquiries

Founded:
1912

Organisation type and purpose:
Trade association (membership is by subscription), present number of members: 72, manufacturing industry.
To represent UK manufacturers of beds and mattresses and their suppliers.

Subject coverage:
Beds and mattresses in the UK market.

Printed publications:
Consumer leaflets (free):
The Good-night Guide for Children
The Sleep Good Feel Good Guide
The Bed Buyers Guide
Back In Bed – A bed guide for people with back problems

Publications list:
Available online

Access to staff:
Contact by letter, by telephone, by fax, by e-mail and via website
Hours: Mon to Fri, 0900 to 1700

NATIONAL BEEF ASSOCIATION

Acronym or abbreviation: NBA

Mart Centre, Tyne Green, Hexham, NE46 3SG

Tel: 01434 601005
Fax: 01434 601008
E-mail: info@nationalbeefassociation.com

Website:
http://www.nationalbeefassociation.com/

Enquiries:
Enquiries to: General Secretary

Founded:
1998

Organisation type and purpose:
Trade association (membership is by subscription), present number of members: 3000, voluntary organisation.
Umbrella organisation to help the cattle industry.

Access to staff:
Contact by letter, by telephone and by e-mail
Hours: Mon to Fri, 0900 to 1700

NATIONAL BENEVOLENT INSTITUTION

Acronym or abbreviation: NBI

Peter Hervé House, Eccles Court, Tetbury, Gloucestershire, GL8 8EH

Tel: 01666 505500
Fax: 01666 503111
E-mail: nbi@btinternet.com

Website:
http://www.nbicharity.com

Enquiries:
Enquiries to: Chief Executive

Founded:
1812

Organisation type and purpose:
Registered charity 212450.
Financial assistance for the elderly in need. Residential nursing home in Tetbury, Gloucestershire. Self-contained flats in Old Windsor.

Subject coverage:
Geriatrics.

Access to staff:
Contact by letter, by telephone, by fax, by e-mail and in person. Appointment necessary.
Hours: Mon to Fri, 0900 to 1600

NATIONAL BIRDS OF PREY CENTRE

Acronym or abbreviation: NBPC

Great Boulsdon, Newent, Gloucestershire, GL18 1JJ

Tel: 0870 9901992
Fax: 01531 821389
E-mail: jpj@nbpc.demon.co.uk

Website:
http://www.nbpc.co.uk/
All information on the Centre, courses, membership.

Enquiries:
Enquiries to: Business Administrator

Founded:
1967

Organisation type and purpose:
Membership association, suitable for ages: all, research organisation.
Conservation through education, captive breeding and research.

Subject coverage:
Information on birds of prey and owls, hunting with them, welfare and management, captive breeding, education on them, research projects.

Education services:
Group education facilities.

Printed publications:
Amazing Birds of Prey (Parry-Jones J, pub. Dorling Kindersley)
The Really Useful Owl Guide (Parry-Jones J, pub. TFH Kingdom)
Eye Witness Eagle (Parry-Jones J, pub. Dorling Kindersley)
Falconry-care, Captive Breeding & Conservation (Parry-Jones J, pub. David & Charles)
Training Birds of Prey (Parry-Jones J, pub. David & Charles)
Understanding Owls (Parry-Jones J, pub. David & Charles)

Electronic and video publications:
Videos on falconry, owls, captive breeding

Access to staff:
Contact by letter, by telephone and by e-mail
Hours: Open to public 7 days, Feb to Nov

Access for disabled people:
Parking provided, ramped entry, level entry, access to all public areas, toilet facilities

Has:
200 International connections

NATIONAL BLOOD AUTHORITY

Acronym or abbreviation: NBA

Oak House, Reeds Crescent, Watford, Hertfordshire, WD24 4QN

Tel: 01923 486800
Fax: 01923 486801

Website:
http://www.blood.co.uk
NBS web site.

Enquiries:
Enquiries to: Head of Corporate Communications
Direct tel: 0113 214 8734
Direct fax: 0113 214 8736
Direct e-mail: jim.moir@nbs.nhs.uk

Organisation type and purpose:
National government body.
Part of the National Health Service.
Control of collection, processing and distribution of blood and blood products in England.

Subject coverage:
Collection, processing, testing and distribution of blood products in England from voluntary unpaid donors.

Access to staff:
Contact by letter. Appointment necessary.
Hours: Mon to Fri, 0900 to 1700

Links with:
Northern Ireland Blood Transfusion Service
Scottish National Blood Transfusion Service
Welsh Blood Service

National Blood Service Centres:
NBS Birmingham Blood
    Vincent Drive, Edgbaston, Birmingham, B15 2DG; tel: 0121 253 4000; fax: 0121 253 4005
NBS Brentwood
    Crescent Drive, Brentwood, Essex, CM15 8DP; tel: 01277 306000; fax: 01227 306132
NBS Bristol
    Southmead Road, Bristol, BS10 5ND; tel: 0117 991 2000; fax: 0117 991 2002
NBS Cambridge
    Long Road, Cambridge, CB2 2PT; tel: 01223 548000; fax: 01223 548114
NBS Lancaster
    Royal Lancaster Infirmary, Ashton Road, Lancaster, LA1 4GT; tel: 01524 306250; fax: 01524 306273
NBS Leeds
    Bridle Path, Leeds, LS15 7TW; tel: 0113 214 8600; fax: 0113 214 8737
NBS Liverpool
    West Derby Street, Liverpool, L7 8TW; tel: 0151 551 8800; fax: 0151 551 8896

continued overleaf

NBS Manchester
 Plymouth Grove, Manchester, M13 9LL; tel: 0161
 251 4200; fax: 0161 251 4331
NBS Newcastle
 Holland Drive, Newcastle upon Tyne, NE2 4NQ;
 tel: 0191 219 4400; fax: 0191 219 4505
NBS North London
 Colindale Avenue, London, NW9 5BG; tel: 020
 8258 2700; fax: 020 8258 2970
NBS Oxford
 John Radcliffe Hospital, Headington, Oxford,
 OX3 9DU; tel: 01865 447900; fax: 01865 447915
NBS Plymouth
 Derriford Hospital, Derriford Road, Plymouth,
 PL6 8DH; tel: 01752 617815; fax: 01752 617806
NBS Sheffield
 Longley Lane, Sheffield, S5 7JN; tel: 0114 203
 4800; fax: 0114 203 4911
NBS South Thames
 75 Cranmer Terrace, London, SW17 0RB; tel: 020
 8258 8300; fax: 020 8258 8453
NBS Southampton
 Coxford Road, Southampton, SO16 5AF; tel: 023
 8029 6700; fax: 023 8029 6760

Other addresses:
Bio Products Laboratory
 Dagger Lane, Elstree, Hertfordshire, WD6 3BX;
 tel: 020 8258 2200; fax: 020 8258 2601

NATIONAL BOTANIC GARDEN OF WALES, THE

Acronym or abbreviation: NBGW

Llanarthne, Carmarthenshire, SA32 8HG

Tel: 01558 668768
Fax: 01558 668933
E-mail: reception@gardenofwales.org.uk

Website:
http://www.gardenofwales.org.uk
Garden guide, news and events information,
pricing and opening hours, directions.

Enquiries:
Enquiries to: Executive Director for Development

Founded:
2000

Organisation type and purpose:
International organisation, registered charity
(charity number 1036354), research organisation.

Subject coverage:
Botanic garden.

Access to staff:
Contact by letter, by telephone, by fax and by e-
mail
Hours: Summer, Mon to Sun, 1000 to 1800
Winter, Mon to Sun, 1000 to 1630

Access for disabled people:
Parking provided, level entry, access to all public
areas, toilet facilities

NATIONAL CAMPAIGN FOR FIREWORK SAFETY

Acronym or abbreviation: NCFS

118 Long Acre, London, WC2E 9PA

Tel: 020 7836 6703
Fax: 020 7836 6703

Website:
http://www.cgsystems.co.uk/ncfs
http://www.firework.co.uk/ncfp
CG Systems.

Enquiries:
Enquiries to: Director

Founded:
1969

Organisation type and purpose:
International organisation, national organisation,
membership association (membership is by
subscription), present number of members:
370,000, voluntary organisation, registered charity,
research organisation.
To amend the 1875 and 1976 firework laws; to
introduce legislation restricting fireworks to
holders of licences over 18 for properly organised
firework displays and a national training scheme.
To promote history and education on the subject.

Subject coverage:
International firework legislation, history of
fireworks, education and technical training, films
and documentaries.

Trade and statistical information:
Firework accident statistics.

Non-library collection catalogue:
All or part available in-house

Library catalogue:
All or part available online and in print

Printed publications:
Information sheets (£1)
Reports (£5)

Microform publications:
Safety films

Access to staff:
Contact by letter, by telephone, by fax and by e-
mail. Appointment necessary. Non-members
charged.
Hours: Mon to Fri, 0900 to 1800
Special comments: Not weekends except 15 October
to 10 November.

Access to building, collection or gallery:
No access other than to staff, prior appointment
required

Links with:
Age Concern
Cats Protection League
CBI
Fire Brigades Union
Institute of Trading Standards Offices
London Fire & Civil Defence Authority
National Canine Defence League
National Federation of Retirement Pensioners
Royal College of Nursing
The RSPCA
TUC
UK Noise Association (UKNA)

Other addresses:
NCFS Manchester
 19 Plummer Avenue, Cholton, Manchester, M21
 2FU
NCFS Northumberland
 53 Longstone Close, Bradwell, Northumberland,
 NE67 5BS

NATIONAL CAMPAIGN FOR NURSERY EDUCATION

Formal name: The National Campaign for Real
Nursery Education
Acronym or abbreviation: NCNE

Membership Secretary, Tachbrook Nursery School,
Aylesford Street, London, SW1V 3RN

E-mail: ncrne@yahoo.co.uk

Website:
http://www.ncne.co.uk/

Enquiries:
Enquiries to: Membership Secretary
Direct e-mail: head.tachbrook.westminster@lgfl.net

Founded:
1965

Organisation type and purpose:
Membership association (membership is by
subscription), service industry, suitable for ages: 3
to 5.
Campaign Group.

To campaign for the expansion of state-funded
nursery education, and to defend existing
provision.

Subject coverage:
Necessity of education for two years before
statutory school age, extension and protection of
the provision of education.

Printed publications:
Defending and Promoting State Nursery
 Education
Four Year Olds in Reception Classes
Newsletters and papers on current issues
 concerned with nursery education
The Importance of the Local Education Authority
 Nursery School
When Should Your Child Start School?
What is Nursery Education?

Access to staff:
Contact by letter
Hours: Mon to Fri, 0900 to 1700

NATIONAL CARAVAN COUNCIL LIMITED

Acronym or abbreviation: NCC

Catherine House, Victoria Road, Aldershot,
Hampshire, GU11 1SS

Tel: 01252 318251
Fax: 01252 322596
E-mail: info@nationalcaravan.co.uk

Website:
http://www.nationalcaravan.co.uk
List of NCC members, products and services
provided.

Enquiries:
Enquiries to: Director General

Founded:
1939

Organisation type and purpose:
Trade association (membership is by subscription),
present number of members: 500.
Representative body.

Subject coverage:
Centre of information on all aspects of the caravan
industry providing an advisory service on
technical legislation, regulation and commercial
matters.

Non-library collection catalogue:
All or part available online

Printed publications:
Annual Report
The Business (quarterly magazine)
Various other NCC industry and consumer
 publications

Access to staff:
Contact by letter, by telephone, by fax, by e-mail
and via website. Access for members only. Letter
of introduction required.
Hours: Mon to Fri, 0900 to 1700

NATIONAL CARE ASSOCIATION

Acronym or abbreviation: NCHA

45–49 Leather Lane, London, EC1N 7TJ

Tel: 020 7831 7090
Fax: 020 7831 7040
E-mail: info@nca.gb.com

Website:
http://www.nca.gb.com

Enquiries:
Enquiries to: Chief Executive

Founded:
1981

Organisation type and purpose:
Trade association.

Subject coverage:
Community care, social security, residential care, nursing home care.

Publications list:
Available in print

Access to staff:
Contact by letter, by telephone, by fax and by e-mail. Appointment necessary.
Hours: Mon to Fri, 0900 to 1700

Access to building, collection or gallery:
Prior appointment required

Access for disabled people:
Access to all public areas

Subsidiary body:
National Care Homes Association Commercial Limited

NATIONAL CATALOGUING UNIT FOR THE ARCHIVES OF CONTEMPORARY SCIENTISTS

Acronym or abbreviation: NCUACS

University of Bath, Claverton Down, Bath, BA2 7AY

Tel: 01225 383522
Fax: 01225 386229
E-mail: lispbh@bath.ac.uk

Website:
http://www.bath.ac.uk/ncuacs
Information about the role of the NCUACS and work completed.

Enquiries:
Enquiries to: Director

Founded:
1973

Carries out the functions of the former:
Contemporary Scientific Archives Centre (year of change 1987)

Organisation type and purpose:
Research organisation.
Locating, cataloguing and finding places of permanent deposit for the manuscript papers of eminent contemporary British scientists and engineers.

Subject coverage:
Professional and personal papers and correspondence of distinguished UK scientists and engineers deceased since c. 1950; scientific source material; cataloguing such material.

Printed publications:
Catalogues of complete collections (lists of catalogues available)
Progress Reports (2 times a year)

Publications list:
Available online

Access to staff:
Contact by letter and by e-mail
Hours: Mon to Fri, 0900 to 1700

Access to building, collection or gallery:
No access other than to staff

NATIONAL CENTRE FOR EARLY MUSIC

Acronym or abbreviation: NCEM

St Margaret's Church, Walmgate, York, YO1 9TL

Tel: 01904 658338
Fax: 01904 612631
E-mail: info@ncem.co.uk

Website:
http://www.ncem.co.uk

Organisation type and purpose:
Administered by the York Early Music Foundation, registered charity no. 1068331, certificate of incorporation 3499629. Offers conference and

recording facilities and performances of early music. Hosts the York Early Music Festival and the Beverley and East Riding Early Music Festival.

Education services:
Year-round community and education programme.

Access for disabled people:
The Centre is flat-floored throughout, making it accessible for wheelchair users. There are two designated disabled parking places in the adjacent car park, an entrance ramp and disabled toilet facilities

NATIONAL CENTRE FOR EATING DISORDERS

Acronym or abbreviation: NcfeD

54 New Road, Esher, Surrey, KT10 9NU

Tel: 0845 838 2040
Fax: 01372 469550
E-mail: ncfed@btclick.com

Website:
http://www.eating-disorders.org.uk
About the organisation, treatments and training.

Enquiries:
Enquiries to: Information Officer
Direct fax: 01372 469550

Founded:
1984

Organisation type and purpose:
Professional body, training organisation, consultancy.
Treatment service for eating disorders and weight problems. Training for counselling skills in eating disorders.

Subject coverage:
Compulsive or binge eating, bulimia nervosa, anorexia, obesity, slimming pill abuse, body image problems and therapies for eating problems.

Printed publications:
Factsheets available on all aspects of eating disorders
A contemporary assessment of Bulimia Nervosa
A contemporary assessment of Anorexia Nervosa
Does Eating Rule Your Life

Publications list:
Available online and in print

Access to staff:
Contact by letter, by telephone, by e-mail and via website. Appointment necessary.
Hours: Mon to Fri, 0900 to 1700

Access to building, collection or gallery:
Prior appointment required

Affiliated to:
up to 60 individual therapists nationwide receiving referrals from head office

NATIONAL CENTRE FOR ENGLISH CULTURAL TRADITION

Acronym or abbreviation: NATCECT

University of Sheffield, Sheffield, South Yorkshire, S10 2TN

Tel: 0114 222 0196
E-mail: j.c.beal@shef.ac.uk

Website:
http://www.shef.ac.uk/english/natcect/
Overview of unit, services and facilities.

Enquiries:
Enquiries to: Director
Other contacts: Archivist

Founded:
1964

Organisation type and purpose:
Museum, university department or institute, consultancy, research organisation.

National repository for material on all aspects of English tradition and language. Teaching and research in these subject areas.

Subject coverage:
English language and linguistics; English cultural tradition; folklore; folk music; dialectology; sociolinguistics; onomastics; local and oral history; Canadian studies (especially language and folklore); social and economic history (especially of Sheffield area); ethnology; culture; traditional drama and narrative; iconography; heritage interpretation.

Museum or gallery collection, archive, or library special collection:
Atlas Linguarum Europae
Charlotte Norman (well-dressing traditions)
E Wagner (films, slides)
English Dialect Lexicon database
Hudlestone (Yorkshire songs and folklore)
Library and archive material on all topics above
Richard Blakeborough (custom and belief: Yorkshire)
Russell Wortley (traditional music, dance and drama)
Survey of English Dialects
Survey of Yorkshire Dialects

Non-library collection catalogue:
All or part available in-house

Library catalogue:
All or part available online and in-house

Microform publications:
English Regional Dialects (audiotape)

Publications list:
Available online and in print

Access to staff:
Contact by letter, by telephone, by fax, by e-mail and via website. Appointment necessary.
Hours: Mon to Fri, 0900 to 1700

Links with:
Institute for Folklore Studies
  Canada
Institute for Folklore Studies
  UK
Memorial University of Newfoundland

NATIONAL CENTRE FOR SOCIAL RESEARCH

35 Northampton Square, London, EC1V 0AX

Tel: 020 7250 1866
Fax: 020 7250 1524
E-mail: info@natcen.ac.uk

Website:
http://www.natcen.ac.uk
Information about the Centre's research and publications.

Enquiries:
Enquiries to: Information Officer
Direct e-mail: s.johnson@natcen.ac.uk

Founded:
1969

Organisation type and purpose:
Registered charity, research organisation.

Subject coverage:
Social research, especially social policy surveys and survey methodology.

Printed publications:
National Centre publications covering the following subjects:
Crime and Socio-Legal Studies
Education and Lifetime Learning
Ethnic Minority Research
Health
Labour Market Studies
Methodology
Political and Electoral Behaviour
Social Attitudes
Social Security

continued overleaf

Publications list:
Available online

Access to staff:
Contact by letter, by telephone, by fax and by e-mail
Hours: Mon to Fri, 0900 to 1700

Access to building, collection or gallery:
No access other than to staff
Special comments: Only to consult the National Centre Publications.

NATIONAL CENTRE FOR TRAINING AND EDUCATION IN PROSTHETICS AND ORTHOTICS

Acronym or abbreviation: NCTEPO

Curran Building, 131 St James' Road, Glasgow, G4 0LS

Tel: 0141 548 3814
Fax: 0141 552 1283
E-mail: h.smart@strath.ac.uk

Website:
http://www.recal.org.uk
Description of all RECAL products and services. Subscription access to RECAL Bibliographical Database.

Enquiries:
Enquiries to: Information Officer
Direct tel: 0141 548 3814
Direct fax: 0141 552 1283
Direct e-mail: h.smart@strath.ac.uk

Founded:
1978

Organisation type and purpose:
University department or institute.
University of Strathclyde Centre, having an internationally used library and information service.

Subject coverage:
Prosthetics and orthotics, related physical medicine and rehabilitation engineering.

Non-library collection catalogue:
All or part available online

Printed publications:
RECAL Current Awareness
RECAL Bibliographic Database
RECAL Thesaurus

Electronic and video publications:
RECAL Bibliographic Database (CD-ROM and on-line)

Access to staff:
Contact by letter, by telephone, by fax and by e-mail. Appointment necessary.
Hours: Mon to Fri, 0900 to 1700

Access to building, collection or gallery:
No prior appointment required

Parent body:
University of Strathclyde
   tel: 0141 552 4400

NATIONAL CENTRE FOR YOUNG PEOPLE WITH EPILEPSY

Acronym or abbreviation: NCYPE

St Piers Lane, Lingfield, Surrey, RH7 6PW

Tel: 01342 832243
Fax: 01342 834639
E-mail: info@ncype.org.uk

Website:
http://www.ncype.org.uk
General information about the NCYPE.
Information about services including education, treatment, assessment, rehabilitation and care.

Enquiries:
Enquiries to: Marketing Development Officer
Direct tel: 01342 832243 ext. 432
Direct fax: 01342 834639

Direct e-mail: mbaillie@ncype.org.uk
Other contacts: Admissions Co-ordinator for further information about admission to the NCYPE

Founded:
1898

Organisation type and purpose:
National organisation, voluntary organisation, registered charity (charity number 311877), suitable for ages: 5 to 25.
The NCYPE provides education, treatment, assessment, rehabilitation and care to young people with epilepsy and other complex neurological disorders in partnership with Great Ormond Street Hospital for Children NHS Trust. It provides residential medical care and education for children and young people with epilepsy and other complex special needs.

Subject coverage:
The NCYPE is the major provider of specialised services for young people with epilepsy in the UK. Multidisciplinary team-working between many different experts, medical consultants, teachers, nurses, therapists, psychologists, carers and skilled support staff support the many different needs of students and help each individual achieve their true potential.

Printed publications:
Leaflets and brochures
Research project information may be made available
Order printed publications from: Marketing Development Officer, NCYPE: tel: 01342 832243

Access to staff:
Contact by letter, by telephone, by fax, by e-mail and via website. Appointment necessary. Letter of introduction required.
Hours: Mon to Fri, 0830 to 1700

Access to building, collection or gallery:
Prior appointment required

Access for disabled people:
Parking provided, toilet facilities

Member of:
Association of National Specialist Colleges
Joint Epilepsy Council for Great Britain and Ireland
National Association of Independent and Non-maintained Special Schools
National Association of Special Schools

Partnership with:
Great Ormond Street Hospital for Children NHS Trust

NATIONAL CHEMICAL EMERGENCY CENTRE

Acronym or abbreviation: NCEC

AEA Technology, B329 Harwell, Didcot, Oxfordshire, OX11 0QJ

Tel: 0870 190 6621
Fax: 0870 190 6614
E-mail: ncec@aeat.com

Website:
http://www.aeat-env.com/ncec/index.html
Information on products and services.
http://www.the-ncec.com

Enquiries:
Enquiries to: Manager
Direct tel: 0870 190 6621

Founded:
1973

Organisation type and purpose:
National centre operating within AEA Technology as a commercial company.

Subject coverage:
Chemicals, hazards, emergency action, spillage, fire, health and safety, international transport of dangerous goods, legislation, general chemical information systems.

Museum or gallery collection, archive, or library special collection:
Chemical Safety Datasheet Collection

Printed publications:
Hazchem scale cards (available for purchase, direct)

Electronic and video publications:
Computerised databank CHEMDATA on emergency response information available in languages other than English and supplied for downloading onto end users computers on an annual subscription basis
CSE – CD-ROM linking dangerous goods list, approved supply list and workplace exposure limits
Multilingual Tremcard Software

Access to staff:
Contact by letter, by fax, by e-mail and via website
Hours: Mon to Fri, 0800 to 1630
Special comments: 24 hour emergency information service provided to public emergency services and industry.

NATIONAL CHILDREN'S BUREAU

Acronym or abbreviation: NCB

8 Wakley Street, Islington, London, EC1V 7QE

Tel: 020 7843 6000
Fax: 020 7843 6007
E-mail: library@ncb.org.uk

Website:
http://www.ncb.org.uk

Enquiries:
Enquiries to: Head of Library and Information Service
Direct tel: 020 7843 6008
Direct fax: 020 7843 6007

Founded:
1963

Organisation type and purpose:
Registered charity (charity number 2633796).

Subject coverage:
Children and young people including children in care, children's services, child protection, adolescence, children's rights and participation, crime and youth justice, disability and special educational needs, drug education, PSHE and sex education, HIV/AIDS, family law, family and parenting, child health, child psychology, poverty and social exclusion, early childhood, play.

Library catalogue:
All or part available online

Printed publications:
NCB produce a wide range of books, journals and newsletters (publications lists available)
ChildData Abstracts (monthly)
Children in the News (weekly)
Children & Young People Now (weekly, members)
Childstats (quarterly digest of statistics)
Highlights (8 times a year)
Lists of research projects
Reviews of literature and research

Electronic and video publications:
ChildData (Web)

Publications list:
Available online and in print

Access to staff:
Contact by telephone, by e-mail, in person and via website. Appointment necessary. Non-members charged.
Hours: Mon to Fri, 1000 to 1700
Special comments: Enquiry line: 1000 to 1200 and 1400 to 1600.

Access for disabled people:
Parking provided, level entry, toilet facilities
Special comments: Parking available on request.

Bureau established under its aegis the:
Council for Disabled Children
tel: 020 7843 6334; fax: 020 7278 9512

Working in partnership with:
Children in Scotland
tel: 0131 228 8484
Children in Wales
tel: 029 2034 2434

NATIONAL CHILDREN'S CENTRE

Brian Jackson House, New North Parade,
Huddersfield, West Yorkshire, HD1 5JP

Tel: 01484 519988
Fax: 01484 435150
E-mail: nfo@nccuk.org.uk

Enquiries:
Enquiries to: Chief Executive

Founded:
1975

Organisation type and purpose:
Registered charity.

Subject coverage:
Child care, education, families from overseas,
training young people, addressing offending,
school truancy, homeless families, family support,
parent training.

Museum or gallery collection, archive, or library special collection:
Brian Jackson archive, contains manuscripts,
printed works on social and political history,
child care issues and educational issues

Printed publications:
1st Age Brochure
Annual Reports
Future Parenthood Paper
Reports on 4 National Conferences on the Chinese
Community in Great Britain

Access to staff:
Contact by letter, by telephone and by fax
Hours: Mon to Fri, 0900 to 1700

Access for disabled people:
Ramped entry, level entry, access to all public
areas, toilet facilities

NATIONAL CHRYSANTHEMUM SOCIETY

Acronym or abbreviation: NCS

c/o Mr. Peter Fraser, 317 Plessey Road, Blyth,
Northumberland, NE24 3L J

Tel: 01670 353580
E-mail: peter@fpeter.fsnet.co.uk

Website:
http://www.ncsuk.info/index.htm

Enquiries:
Enquiries to: Membership Secretary

Founded:
1846

Organisation type and purpose:
International organisation, advisory body,
membership association (membership is by
subscription), present number of members: 4000,
voluntary organisation, registered charity (charity
number 248484), suitable for ages: 10+,
consultancy.
British registry office for chrysanthemums.
To promote the growing of chrysanthemums.

Subject coverage:
Chrysanthemum cultivation, pest and disease
control, literature.

Printed publications:
List (some 12 titles) available from the Society
including:
Bulletin (spring and autumn, free to members, £3
each)
Manual (regular update, £14.95)
Year Book (free to members, £5 others)

Other specialised publications

Electronic and video publications:
Videos

Publications list:
Available in print

Access to staff:
Contact by letter, by telephone, by fax and in
person
Hours: Mon to Fri, 0900 to 1700

Access to building, collection or gallery:
Prior appointment required

Access for disabled people:
Access to all public areas, toilet facilities

Affiliated to:
Royal Horticultural Society

Has:
6 regional groups, South, West, Midland, North,
Welsh, Scottish, access via main office

NATIONAL CHURCHES TRUST

31 Newbury Street, London, EC1A 7HU

Tel: 020 7600 6090
Fax: 020 7796 2442
E-mail: info@historicchurches.org.uk

Website:
http://www.nationalchurchestrust.org
Information for donors and grant applicants.

Enquiries:
Enquiries to: Chief Executive
Direct e-mail: info@nationalchurchestrust.org
Other contacts: Grants Manager for applications for
funding

Founded:
1953

Formerly called:
Historic Churches Preservation Trust (year of
change 2007)

Organisation type and purpose:
National organisation, registered charity (charity
number 1119845).
A charity which offers financial assistance to
Christian churches of any recognised
denomination for essential fabric repairs.

Subject coverage:
Churches, chapels and meeting houses in the UK.

Printed publications:
Annual Review
Historic Churches (review)

Access to staff:
Contact by letter, by telephone, by fax and by e-
mail
Hours: Mon to Fri, 0930 to 1730

Access to building, collection or gallery:
No access other than to staff

NATIONAL CO-OPERATIVE ARCHIVE

Co-operative College, Holyoake House, Hanover
Street, Manchester, M60 0AS

Tel: 0161 246 2925
Fax: 0161 246 2946
E-mail: archive@co-op.ac.uk

Website:
http://archive.co-op.ac.uk/
National Co-operative Archive at the Co-operative
College, information, bibliographies etc

Enquiries:
Enquiries to: Archivist
Direct e-mail: gillian@co-op.ac.uk

Founded:
1869

Formerly called:
Co-operative Union Archive (year of change 2000);
Co-operative College Archive (year of change
2000)

Subject coverage:
History of the British co-operative movement;
contemporary co-operative developments and
issues;
overseas co-operative movements; history of the
labour movement in Britain; co-operative leaders
and social reformers; Co-operation; co-operative
history nationally and internationally; co-operative
society history and histories; co-operative film
archive; co-operative archive;
international economic development; centre for
alternative industrial and technological systems
archive; co-operative oral history archive.

Museum or gallery collection, archive, or library special collection:
Christian Socialists, books, pamphlets and
periodicals
Co-operative Society histories and rule books
Co-operative Society pamphlets, 1830 to date
MS Collection of E O Greening correspondence
and documents (11,000 items)
MS Collection of G J Holyoake correspondence and
documents, 1835–1903 (4000 items)
MS Collection of Robert Owen correspondence and
documents, 1820 onwards (3000 items)
Rare 19th century books, newspapers and
periodicals on co-operation and social reform
CAITS Archive
Midlands Co-operative Society Archive
Co-operative Group South East, South Midlands
and Northern Region Co-operative Archive
Co-operative Youth Movements
National Co-operative Film Archive
Co-operative Oral History Archive
Periodicals

Non-library collection catalogue:
All or part available online, in-house and in print

Printed publications:
Holdings lists for special collections
Co-operative Commemorative Plateware
Co-operative Congress Special Papers
Co-operative Education
Co-operative Party
Co-operative Periodicals
Co-operative Plays and Sketches
Co-operative Production
Co-operative Society Histories
Co-operative Society Rules
Co-operative Women's Guild
Co-operative Youth
Dividend & Check Systems
Edward Owen Greening
Edward Vansittart Neale
George Jacob Holyoake
Historical Periodicals
National Co-operative Film Archive
National Co-operative Oral History Archive
National Guild of Co-operators
Philatelic Collection
Robert Owen
Rochdale Pioneers

Access to staff:
Contact by letter, by telephone, by fax and by e-
mail. Appointment necessary.
Hours: Mon to Fri, 1000 to 1645

Access to building, collection or gallery:
Hours: Mon to Fri, 1000 to 1700
Special comments: By appointment.

Governing body:
Co-operative Heritage Trust

Member of:
Co-operatives UK
Euro-co-op
International Cooperative Alliance

NATIONAL COLLECTION OF TYPE CULTURES

Acronym or abbreviation: NCTC

continued overleaf

Health Protection Agency Centre for Infections, 61 Colindale Avenue, London, NW9 5EQ

Tel: 0870 084 2000
Fax: 020 8205 7483
E-mail: nctc@hpa.org.uk

Website:
http://www.hpa.org/nctc
Information on NCTC and its parent organisation.

Enquiries:
Enquiries to: Head of NCTC

Founded:
1920

Organisation type and purpose:
Research organisation.
Maintaining and supplying cultures of authenticated bacteria of medical/veterinary interest.

Subject coverage:
Microbiology, especially medical/veterinary; reference strains of bacteria for particular usage (taxonomic), antibiotic assay, teaching, controls for bacteriological tests; freeze-drying; mycoplasmas; plasmid-bearing strains; availability of cultures in other culture collections (UK and abroad).

Museum or gallery collection, archive, or library special collection:
Early works on bacteriology etc

Non-library collection catalogue:
All or part available online

Printed publications:
Catalogue of the NCTC (PHLS) (8th ed., 1994)

Access to staff:
Contact by letter, by telephone, by fax, by e-mail and via website
Hours: Mon to Fri, 0900 to 1700

Access to building, collection or gallery:
Prior appointment required

Access for disabled people:
Parking provided, ramped entry, level entry, access to all public areas, toilet facilities

Associated with:
European Culture Collection Organisation
UK Federation for Culture Collections
World Federation for Culture Collections

European Resource Centre for:
Plasmids

Member of:
United Kingdom National Culture Collection (UKNCC)

Parent body:
Public Health Laboratory Service (PHLS)

NATIONAL COLLEGE OF HYPNOSIS AND PSYCHOTHERAPY

Acronym or abbreviation: NCHP

PO Box 5779, Loughborough, LE12 5ZF

Tel: 01509 881477
E-mail: enquiries@nchp.org.uk

Website:
http://www.hypnotherapyuk.net

Enquiries:
Enquiries to: Administrator

Founded:
1977

Organisation type and purpose:
Hypno-psychotherapy training.

Subject coverage:
Hypno-psychotherapy.

Access to staff:
Contact by letter, by telephone, by fax, by e-mail, in person and via website. Appointment necessary.
Hours: Mon to Fri, 0900 to 1700

Access to building, collection or gallery:
Prior appointment required

Access for disabled people:
Level entry

Connections with:
UK Council for Psychotherapy (UKCP)
2nd Floor, Edward House, 2 Wakley Street, London, EC1V 7LT; tel: 0870 167 2131; website: http://www.psychotherapy.org.uk

NATIONAL COMPUTING CENTRE LIMITED

Formal name: National Computing Centre
Acronym or abbreviation: NCC

Oxford House, Oxford Road, Manchester, M1 7ED

Tel: 0161 228 6333
Fax: 0161 242 2499
E-mail: info@ncc.co.uk

Website:
http://www.ncc.co.uk
Generally on products and services, but also specific information for members.

Enquiries:
Enquiries to: Marketing Manager
Direct tel: 0161 242 2146
Direct e-mail: Michael.Dean@ncc.co.uk
Other contacts: IT Manager/Director

Founded:
1966

Organisation type and purpose:
National organisation, membership association (membership is by subscription), present number of members: 1300, research organisation.
Promotes the most effective use of IT.

Subject coverage:
IT: all aspects of computing in UK and internationally.

Non-library collection catalogue:
All or part available online

Printed publications:
IT User Survey
Salary and Staff Issues in IT Survey (annually)
Security Breaches Survey

Electronic and video publications:
Centrelink
Filetab

Publications list:
Available online and in print

Access to staff:
Contact by letter, by telephone, by fax, by e-mail and via website. Appointment necessary. Non-members charged.
Hours: Mon to Fri, 0900 to 1700

Access to building, collection or gallery:
Prior appointment required

Access for disabled people:
Access to all public areas

NATIONAL CONSUMER CREDIT FEDERATION

Acronym or abbreviation: NCCF

98–100 Holme Lane, Sheffield, South Yorkshire, S6 4JW

Tel: 0114 234 8101
Fax: 0114 234 5459
E-mail: nccf@talk21.com

Enquiries:
Enquiries to: General Secretary

Founded:
1927

Organisation type and purpose:
Trade association (membership is by subscription).

Subject coverage:
Consumer credit.

Printed publications:
Code of Practice
Newsletter

Access to staff:
Contact by letter, by telephone and by fax
Hours: Mon to Fri, 0930 to 1630

NATIONAL CONSUMER FEDERATION

Acronym or abbreviation: NCF

24 Hurst House, Penton Rise, London, WC1X 9ED

Tel: 020 7837 8545
Fax: 020 7837 8545
E-mail: secretary@ncf.info

Website:
http://www.ncf.info.uk

Enquiries:
Enquiries to: Honorary Secretary

Founded:
2001

Organisation type and purpose:
Voluntary organisation.
Co-ordinates the activities of local consumer groups and represents the views of consumers to government and business.

Subject coverage:
Consumer affairs, consumer law, food.

Printed publications:
Consumer News (quarterly, on subscription)

Electronic and video publications:
Newsheet (monthly, online)

Access to staff:
Contact by letter, by telephone, by fax, by e-mail and via website. Non-members charged.
Hours: Mon to Fri, 0900 to 1200; outside office hours by e-mail

NATIONAL CORRESPONDENCE CHESS CLUB

81 Surrey Street, Norwich, NR1 3PG

Tel: 01603 491199
E-mail: simoncarer@aol.com

Enquiries:
Enquiries to: Chairman

Founded:
1932

Organisation type and purpose:
National organisation (membership is by subscription).
Postal Chess Club.

Subject coverage:
Correspondence chess.

Access to staff:
Contact by letter and by e-mail
Hours: Any reasonable time.

Affiliated to:
British Postal Chess Federation
e-mail: norman.king2@virgin.net

NATIONAL COUNCIL FOR DRAMA TRAINING

Acronym or abbreviation: NCDT

5 Tavistock Place, London, WC1H 9SS

Tel: 020 7387 3650
Fax: 020 7681 4733
E-mail: ncdt@lineone.net

Website:
http://www.ncdt.co.uk

Enquiries:
Enquiries to: Executive Secretary

Founded:
1976

Organisation type and purpose:
National government body, professional body, registered charity.
Accreditation body maintaining standards at professional drama schools.

Subject coverage:
List of courses in professional, vocational actor and stage management training accredited by the NCDT.

Non-library collection catalogue:
All or part available online

Printed publications:
List of accredited courses in the UK

Publications list:
Available online and in print

Access to staff:
Contact by letter, by telephone, by fax, by e-mail and via website
Hours: Mon to Fri, 0930 to 1730

Access to building, collection or gallery:
No access other than to staff

Members of the organisation are:
BBC
British Actors Equity
Channel 4
Conference of Drama Schools
Society of London Theatre
Theatre Management Association

NATIONAL COUNCIL FOR SCHOOL SPORTS

Acronym or abbreviation: NCSS

c/o RFU National Centre for Schools and Youth, Castlecroft Stadium, Castlecroft Road, Wolverhampton, West Midlands, WV3 8NA

Tel: 01902 380302
Fax: 01902 380311
E-mail: castlecroftschools@rfu.com

Enquiries:
Enquiries to: Honorary Secretary

Founded:
1948

Organisation type and purpose:
Membership association (membership is by subscription, election or invitation), present number of members: 31, voluntary organisation.
To co-ordinate the work of the National School's Sports Associations. To represent the views of members to government departments, National Sports Associations, local education authorities and wherever else necessary.

Subject coverage:
Schools sports organisations – governing and regional bodies details of activities staged with participation and spectator figures, general details and participation in sports in schools, coaching development plans for sports. International schools activities.
Sports activities of children (5 to 18 years), administration of school sport at national and local level, formation of new associations in sports where none exists.

Printed publications:
National Council for Schools' Sports Handbook (annually)
Information leaflets and other documents
Official Journal (6 times a year)

Access to staff:
Contact by letter and by e-mail
Hours: Mon to Fri, 0900 to 1700

Executive Officer:
National Council for School Sports
95 Boxley Drive, West Bridgford, Nottinghamshire, NG2 7GN; tel: 0115 923 1229; e-mail: schoolsport@ntlworld.com

NATIONAL COUNCIL FOR THE CONSERVATION OF PLANTS AND GARDENS

Acronym or abbreviation: NCCPG

12 Home Farm, Loseley Park, Guildford, Surrey, GU3 1HS

Tel: 01483 447540
Fax: 01483 458933
E-mail: info@nccpg.org.uk

Website:
http://www.nccpg.com

Enquiries:
Enquiries to: Plant Conservation Officer
Other contacts: Executive Officer

Founded:
1978

Organisation type and purpose:
National organisation overseeing the conservation of plants in cultivation
through the National Plant Collections scheme; supported by members and area groups; registered charity (charity number 1004009).

Subject coverage:
Matters relating to organisation of NCCPG, the National Collection Scheme,
conservation of plants in cultivation and general conservation information.

Museum or gallery collection, archive, or library special collection:
The NCCPG co-ordinates the 650 collections registered under its National Collections Scheme (50,000 plants held in the collections)

Non-library collection catalogue:
All or part available online

Printed publications:
National Plant Collections Directory 2009 (£6.50 incl. p&p)
Plant Heritage (journal for members)
Booklets are available on:
Cistus, Dianthus, Kalmia, Lathyrus, Lonicera, Origanum, Polemonium, Russell Lupins, Vireya Rhododendrons, Viburnum, Yuccas, Garden Plants of Leicestershire and Rutland

Publications list:
Available online and in print

Access to staff:
Contact by letter, by telephone, by fax, by e-mail and via website. Appointment necessary.
Hours: Mon to Fri, 0900 to 1700

Access to building, collection or gallery:
Ground floor

Access for disabled people:
Fully accessible

Links with:
all the major horticultural bodies in Great Britain
over 40 county-based groups throughout Great Britain

NATIONAL COUNCIL FOR THE DIVORCED AND SEPARATED

Acronym or abbreviation: NCDS

National Secretary, c/o 101 Anson Road, Southtown, Great Yarmouth, Norfolk, NR31 0EG

Tel: 07041 478120
E-mail: info@ncds.org.uk

Enquiries:
Enquiries to: Honorary Secretary

Organisation type and purpose:
Membership association (membership is by qualification), present number of members: 10,000, voluntary organisation.
A means of meeting people in, or who have been in, a situation similar to their own, giving opportunity for a social life again.

Subject coverage:
All aspects relating to separation and divorcee.

Printed publications:
NCDS News (quarterly)

Access to staff:
Contact by letter, by telephone, by e-mail and via website
Hours: Mon to Sat, 0900 to 2000

Has:
6 Regional Clubs and several non-regional branches

NATIONAL COUNCIL FOR THE TRAINING OF JOURNALISTS

Acronym or abbreviation: NCTJ

The New Granary, Station Road, Newport, Saffron Walden, Essex, CB11 3PL

Tel: 01799 544014
Fax: 01799 544015
E-mail: info@nctj.com

Website:
http://www.nctj.com
Careers advice, etc. Details of courses, colleges, etc.

Enquiries:
Enquiries to: Chief Executive
Direct e-mail: rob@nctj.com

Founded:
1951

Organisation type and purpose:
National organisation, advisory body, learned society, registered charity (charity number 1026685), training organisation.
Training and examining organisation.
To advance the education and training of trainee journalists and press photographers.

Subject coverage:
Careers and training in journalism, at college/ university, by distance learning.

Trade and statistical information:
UK newspaper industry's own training scheme for journalists.

Printed publications:
Books, tapes and examination papers, including:
Distance learning courses
Journalists' Guide to Common Medicines (£7.50)
Journalists' Introduction to Courts and Lawyers (£7.50)
Journalist Training and Assessment (NCTJ Handbook)
Essential Law for Journalists (Walter Greenwood and Tom Welsh, 14th ed., £14.95)
NCTJ News (6 times a year)

Electronic and video publications:
So You Want to be a Journalist? (careers training video £16.99)

Publications list:
Available online and in print

Access to staff:
Contact by letter, by telephone, by fax, by e-mail and via website. Appointment necessary.
Hours: Mon to Fri, 0900 to 1700

Access for disabled people:
Parking provided, access to all public areas

There are 5 constituent bodies, the:
Chartered Institute of Journalists
tel: 020 7252 1187; fax: 020 7252 2302
National Union of Journalists
tel: 020 7278 7916; fax: 020 7837 8143
Newspaper Society
tel: 020 7636 7014; fax: 020 7631 5119

continued overleaf

Scottish Newspaper Publishers Association
tel: 0131 220 4353; fax: 0131 220 4344
Society of Editors
tel: 01223 304080; fax: 01223 304090

Wholly owned trading company is:
NCTJ Training Ltd
tel: 01279 430009; fax: 01279 438008; e-mail:
info@nctj.com

NATIONAL COUNCIL FOR VOLUNTARY ORGANISATIONS

Acronym or abbreviation: NCVO

Regent's Wharf, 8 All Saints Street, London, N1
9RL

Tel: 020 7713 6161\ Minicom no. 0800 0188111
Fax: 020 7713 6300
E-mail: ncvo@ncvo-vol.org.uk

Website:
http://www.ncvo-vol.org.uk/main/about/info/
publications/html
Publications listing
http://www.ncvo-vol.org.uk
General information

Enquiries:
Enquiries to: Information Officer

Founded:
1919

Organisation type and purpose:
Membership association (membership is by
subscription, qualification, present number of
members: 2100 voluntary organisations, voluntary
organisation, registered charity (charity number
225922).
NCVO champions the cause of voluntary
organisations and works to increase their
effectiveness.

Subject coverage:
Voluntary organisations and their response to
current social issues; resources for voluntary
organisations; interests and independence of such
organisations; current legislation; government
funding and its efficient use; trustee and
governance issues; relationship of sector with
business and public sectors, rural aspects.

Trade and statistical information:
Data on voluntary sector issues eg: size of sector,
profiling of areas of work.

Printed publications:
Voluntary Sector Magazine (10 times a year)
Publications and Events Catalogue
The Voluntary Agencies Directory (annually, 2002,
£30)
The Voluntary Sector Almanac 2000
A range of guides and handbooks including:
Dealing With Disputes in Voluntary
Organisations:An Introduction (Laurance L and
Radford A, £5)
Directory of NCVO-Approved Consultants 2001–
2002 (Moran F ed, £10)
Managing Risk! Guidelines for medium-sized
organisations (Clark C, £15)
The Good Employment Guide for the Voluntary
Sector (Dyson J, 2nd ed, 1999, £30)
Order printed publications from: NCVO, Hamilton
House Mailings
Earlstrees Court, Earlstrees Road, Corby,
Northamptonshire, NN17 4AX, tel: 01536 399016,
fax: 01536 399012, e-mail: hhmailings@aol.com

Publications list:
Available online and in print

Access to staff:
Contact by letter, by telephone, by fax, by e-mail
and via website
Hours: Mon to Fri, 0900 to 1700
Special comments: Charges to some non-members.

Access for disabled people:
Level entry, toilet facilities

NATIONAL COUNCIL FOR VOLUNTARY YOUTH SERVICES

Acronym or abbreviation: NCVYS

3rd Floor, Lancaster House, 33 Islington High
Street, London, N1 9LH

Tel: 020 7278 1041
Fax: 020 7833 2491
E-mail: mail@ncvys.org.uk

Website:
http://www.ncvys.org.uk
Description of the organisation, news,
publications, work areas, etc.

Enquiries:
Enquiries to: Communication Officer
Direct tel: 020 7253 1010

Founded:
1936

Organisation type and purpose:
National organisation, membership association
(membership is by subscription), present number
of members: 144, voluntary organisation,
registered charity (charity number 281632).
Representing about 160 National Voluntary Youth
Organisations and Local and Regional Councils for
Voluntary Youth Services. Provides support
information and representation to a national
network of youth organisations.

Subject coverage:
Voluntary youth services and social issues
affecting young people; child protection; equal
opportunities, diversity, youth participation.

Printed publications:
In The Service of Youth: A History of NCVYS
(book, £7.50, free to members)
Out of Harm's Way: A Survey of Child Protection
Policy and Practice in National Voluntary Youth
Organisations (Smith D R, 1999, £7.50 statutory/
commercial, £4.50 voluntary, £3.50 members)
The NCVYS Voluntary Youth Sector Infrastructure
Project (Wright L and Jeffs L, 1999, £7.50
statutory/commercial, £4.50 voluntary, £3.50
members)
Annual Directory
Network (magazine, quarterly, free to members or
£20 a year)
NCVYS Facts Sheet: a concise guide to NCVYS and
its purpose

Publications list:
Available online and in print

Access to staff:
Contact by letter, by telephone, by fax, by e-mail
and via website. Appointment necessary. Non-
members charged.
Hours: Mon to Fri, 0900 to 1700

NATIONAL COUNCIL OF PAKISTANI ORGANISATIONS (UK)

Acronym or abbreviation: NCOPO

103 Wexham Close, Luton, Bedfordshire, LU3 3TX

Tel: 01582 598394
Fax: 01582 618335
E-mail: mshafikhan@hotmail.com

Enquiries:
Enquiries to: Chairman

Founded:
1982

Organisation type and purpose:
National organisation, advisory body, learned
society (membership is by qualification), voluntary
organisation, consultancy.
To guide and support organisations and
individuals as and when needed for their
development in the community in every respect of
their life. Also to help in social, welfare and
cultural development, legal matters, and
encourage integration of Pakistani community into
the host community.

Subject coverage:
All aspects of Pakistan as a country and Pakistani
culture in general.

Access to staff:
Contact by letter, by telephone and by fax
Hours: Any reasonable time

Access to building, collection or gallery:
Prior appointment required

NATIONAL COUNCIL OF VOLUNTARY CHILD CARE ORGANISATIONS

Acronym or abbreviation: NCVCCO

Unit 25 Angel Gate, City Road, London, EC1V 2PT

Tel: 020 7833 3319
Fax: 020 7833 8637
E-mail: office@ncvcco.org

Website:
http://www.ncvcco.org/

Enquiries:
Enquiries to: Information Officer
Direct e-mail: ian@ncvcco.org

Founded:
1942

Organisation type and purpose:
Membership association (membership is by
subscription), present number of members: 110,
voluntary organisation, registered charity (charity
number 1044239).
To assist the work of English child care charities.

Subject coverage:
Child care particularly in the voluntary sector;
residential care of children, day care of children,
family support within communities, fostering and
adoption, funding for voluntary child care groups,
European initiatives including child care and
funding.

**Museum or gallery collection, archive, or library
special collection:**
Small library on child care and the voluntary sector
(for members' use only)

Printed publications:
Magnet (bulletin, monthly)
Outlook (journal, quarterly)

Publications list:
Available in print

Access to staff:
Contact by letter, by telephone, by fax and by e-
mail
Hours: Mon to Fri, 0900 to 1700

Access to building, collection or gallery:
Prior appointment required

Member of:
European Forum for Child Welfare
International Forum for Child Welfare

NATIONAL COUNCIL OF WOMEN OF GREAT BRITAIN

Acronym or abbreviation: NCW

36 Danbury Street, London, N1 8JU

Tel: 020 7354 2395
Fax: 01325 367378
E-mail: ncwgb@danburystreet.freeserve.co.uk

Enquiries:
Enquiries to: President

Founded:
1895

Organisation type and purpose:
National organisation, membership association
(membership is by subscription), present number
of members: 1000 plus 70 affiliated societies,
voluntary organisation, registered charity.

To improve the quality of life for all, and to encourage the effective participation of women in the life of the nation.

Subject coverage:
Arts, consumer affairs, education, health, housing, international affairs, mass media, scientific development, social welfare, status and employment of women and transport.

Museum or gallery collection, archive, or library special collection:
Minutes of Meetings 1890 to date, working papers etc
NCW archives
Publications and reports produced by NCW

Printed publications:
New News (newsletter, 4 times a year)
Many reports on matters of concern and women's issues
Responses to government consultation papers (published quarterly)
Securing Our Future, Women and Economics of Later Life

Publications list:
Available online and in print

Access to staff:
Contact by letter, by telephone and by e-mail
Hours: Mon to Fri, 0900 to 1700

Access to building, collection or gallery:
No prior appointment required
Special comments: Pre 1980 archive deposited with London Record Office.

Access for disabled people:
Level entry

Has:
70 affiliated organisations

Member of:
International Council of Women

NATIONAL COUNCIL ON ARCHIVES

Acronym or abbreviation: NCA

Ruskin Avenue, Kew, Richmond upon Thames, Surrey, TW9 4DU

E-mail: nca@nationalarchives.gov.uk

Website:
http://www.ncaonline.org.uk

Founded:
1988

Organisation type and purpose:
A membership organisation, registered charity (charity no. 1088088) and company limited by guarantee (company no. 4124338). Aims to bring together the major bodies and organisations, including service providers, users, depositors and policy makers across the UK, concerned with archives and their use; to develop consensus on matters of mutual concern; and to provide an authoritative common voice for the archival community.

Subject coverage:
Archives.

NATIONAL DAY NURSERIES ASSOCIATION

Acronym or abbreviation: NDNA

Oak House, Woodvale Road, Brighouse, West Yorkshire, HD6 4AB

Tel: 0870 774 4244
Fax: 0870 774 4243
E-mail: info@ndna.org.uk

Website:
http://www.ndna.org.uk
Home page.
http://www.ndna.org.uk/publications
Publications listing.

Enquiries:
Enquiries to: Membership Officer

Founded:
1991

Organisation type and purpose:
Membership association (membership is by subscription), present number of members: 2300, registered charity (charity number 1078275). A national childcare charity that is dedicated to the provision, support and promotion of high quality care and education for all children in the early years.

Subject coverage:
Advice, support and training to help nurseries deliver quality early years education and care.

Printed publications:
Starting a Day Nursery (£25)
Policy and Procedures Pack (£100, £50 NDNA members)
Nutrition, Serving Food & Oral Health (£10)
Recruitment and Selection Pack (£100, £50 NDNA members)
NDNA Nursery Cookbook (£10)
Working in a Day Nursery video (£10)

Publications list:
Available online and in print

Access to staff:
Contact by letter, by telephone, by fax and by e-mail. Appointment necessary.
Hours: Mon to Fri, 0900 to 1700

NATIONAL DEAF CHILDREN'S SOCIETY

Acronym or abbreviation: NDCS

15 Dufferin Street, London, EC1Y 8UR

Tel: helpline 0808 800 8880 (also minicom)
Fax: 020 7251 5020
E-mail: helpline@ndcs.org.uk

Website:
http://www.ndcs.org.uk

Founded:
1944

Organisation type and purpose:
National organisation, membership association, present number of members: 10,000, voluntary organisation, registered charity (charity number 1016532).
Membership subscription for professionals, free to parents of deaf children.
An organisation of parents, carers and families which exists to enable deaf children and young people to maximise their skills and abilities, and which works to facilitate this process by every possible means.

Subject coverage:
Childhood deafness, audiology, technology for deaf children, benefits for deaf children, education and communication.

Museum or gallery collection, archive, or library special collection:
Journals
Reference collection of books on deafness

Printed publications:
Fact sheets and guides on:
Audiology and Health
General Information
State Benefits and Disability Living Allowance
Information in Community Languages
Education
Technology
Youth Service
Careers
Further Education
Family Information Pack (introducing the NDCS to parents of newly diagnosed children, free to parents of young deaf people)
Guide to Services
NDCS Reports – various

NDCS Magazine (quarterly magazine, incorporates Bulletin (technology magazine), free to parents and members)

Publications list:
Available online and in print

Access to staff:
Contact by letter, by telephone, by fax and by e-mail. Appointment necessary.
Hours: Mon to Fri, 0830 to 1700
Special comments: Helpline: Mon to Fri, 0930 to 1700

Access to building, collection or gallery:
Prior appointment required

Access for disabled people:
Level entry, access to all public areas, toilet facilities
Special comments: Loop system in meeting room.

Also at:
NDCS Northern Ireland
Wilton House, 5 College Square North, Belfast, BT1 6AR; tel: 028 9031 3170 (voice and text); fax: 028 9031 3170
NDCS Scotland
293 Central Chambers, 93 Hope Street, Glasgow, G2 6LD; tel: 0141 248 4457 (voice and text); fax: 0141 248 2597
NDCS Wales
Room 2, 1st Floor, 43 Charles Street, Cardiff, CF10 2GB; tel: 029 2037 3474 (voice and fax); fax: 029 2038 4277

Branches:
120 local deaf children's societies

Links with:
National Association for Special Educational Needs (NASEN)
National Children's Bureau

Member organisation of:
American Society for Deaf Children
Deaf Accord
UK Council on Deafness
Voluntary Council for Disabled Children

NATIONAL DEBTLINE

Acronym or abbreviation: NDL

Tricorn House, 51–53 Hagley Road, Edgbaston, Birmingham, B16 8TP

Tel: 0808 808 4000
Fax: 0121 410 6230
E-mail: advice@nationaldebtline.co.uk

Website:
http://www.nationaldebtline.co.uk

Enquiries:
Direct tel: 0121 410 6251/2

Founded:
1987

Organisation type and purpose:
Voluntary organisation, registered charity (charity number 1099506).
Telephone helpline for debt.

Subject coverage:
National telephone helpline for people with debt problems; covers all aspects of dealing with debt issues eg: repossession, magistrates court, county court and high court procedures, negotiations with creditors, bankruptcy, consumer credit, benefits and income maximisation.

Museum or gallery collection, archive, or library special collection:
Library of relevant publications to money advice work including some legislation and case reports, books and periodicals

Library catalogue:
All or part available in-house

Printed publications:
Self help packs, including:
Dealing with your debts (£5)
Dealing with your Debts: Scotland
Fact sheets (24)(£2 each, £15 per set, Scotland)

continued overleaf

Fact sheets (34)(£2, or £40 per set, England & Wales)
Free to callers in debt. Charges made to agencies
Order printed publications from: National Debtline

Publications list:
Available online and in print

Access to staff:
Contact by letter, by telephone, by fax, by e-mail and via website
Hours: Mon to Fri, 0900 to 2100; Sat, 0930 to 1300
Special comments: 24 hour voicemail service.

A project of:
Money Advice Trust

NATIONAL DEPOSIT FRIENDLY SOCIETY LIMITED

Acronym or abbreviation: NDFS

4–5 Worcester Road, Clifton, Bristol, BS8 3JL

Tel: 0117 973 9003
Fax: 0117 974 1367
E-mail: @nationaldeposit.co.uk

Website:
http://www.nationaldeposit.co.uk
Products and services.

Enquiries:
Enquiries to: Information Officer

Founded:
1868

Organisation type and purpose:
National organisation, service industry.
Friendly Society – provision of life assurance, investments, sickness, accident and medical insurance for members.

Access to staff:
Contact by letter and by e-mail
Hours: Mon to Fri, 0900 to 1700

Access to building, collection or gallery:
Prior appointment required

NATIONAL DISABILITY ARTS FORUM

Acronym or abbreviation: NDAF

Website:
http://www.ndaf.org
Information about disability arts.

Enquiries:
Enquiries to: Director

Founded:
1990

Organisation type and purpose:
National organisation, membership association, registered charity.

Subject coverage:
Disability arts, arts and disability.

Museum or gallery collection, archive, or library special collection:
Disability Arts Database, UK and Europe; UK Arts Access Database

Printed publications:
e-Newsletter (weekly, free)

Publications list:
Available online

Access to staff:
Contact by letter, by telephone, by fax, by e-mail and in person. Appointment necessary.
Hours: Mon to Fri, 0900 to 1700

Access to building, collection or gallery:
No access other than to staff

Also at:
National Disability Arts Forum

NATIONAL DOG TATTOO REGISTER

PO Box 5720, Harwich, Essex, CO12 3SY

Tel: 01255 552455
Fax: 01255 552412

Subject coverage:
Identification of individual dogs by marking with tattoo. Register of marked dogs makes tracing of individual dogs possible.

Access to staff:
Contact by letter, by telephone and by fax
Hours: Access seven days a week

NATIONAL EARLY MUSIC ASSOCIATION

Acronym or abbreviation: NEMA

137 Preston Road, Wembley, HA9 8NW

Tel: 020 8904 1076
Fax: 020 8723 7787
E-mail: mark@nema-uk.org

Website:
http://www.nema-uk.org

Enquiries:
Enquiries to: Administrator
Direct e-mail: mark@nema-uk.org

Founded:
1981

Organisation type and purpose:
International organisation, membership association (membership is by subscription), present number of members: 350, voluntary organisation, registered charity (charity number 297300).

Subject coverage:
Mediaeval, renaissance, baroque music; singing; dance; instrument makers; early music in education; amateur and professional music making; societies concerned with early music and dance; promotion of conferences and workshops.

Printed publications:
Early Music Yearbook, incorporates directory of instrument makers and players (annually)
Magazine (twice a year)
Early Music Performer

Publications list:
Available online

Access to staff:
Contact by letter, by telephone, by fax and by e-mail
Hours: Mon to Fri, 0900 to 1700

NATIONAL ECZEMA SOCIETY

Hill House, Highgate Hill, London, N19 5NA

Tel: 020 7281 3553 (Business only)\ 0800 0891122 (Helpline)
Fax: 020 7281 6395
E-mail: helpline@eczema.org

Website:
http://www.eczema.org
Information and events.

Enquiries:
Enquiries to: Information and Education Manager
Other contacts: Helpline for advice, 0800 to 2000.

Founded:
1975

Organisation type and purpose:
Registered charity (charity number 1009671).
To help those affected by eczema to make informed choices through information, advice and support. Campaign to raise awareness and understanding of eczema. To run continuous research programme to gather the facts about eczema and its treatment. To provide education and training to spread awareness amongst the medical profession and general public. Organises fundraising to support the work of the charity.

Subject coverage:
Management and care of eczema; details of research into eczema treatments and advice on products suitable for people with eczema, information on complementary therapy treatments.

Non-library collection catalogue:
All or part available in print

Library catalogue:
All or part available in-house

Printed publications:
Range of booklets and information sheets, some free, others charged at approximately £4.50 each
Exchange – Our Members Journal (quarterly, free to members, £5 to non-members)

Publications list:
Available online and in print

Access to staff:
Contact by letter, by telephone, by fax, by e-mail and via website
Hours: Mon to Fri, 0800 to 2000

Access to building, collection or gallery:
No access other than to staff

NATIONAL EDUCATIONAL VIDEO LIBRARY

Acronym or abbreviation: NEVL

Arfon House, Bontnewydd, Caernarfon, Gwynedd, LL54 7UN

Tel: 01286 676001
Fax: 01286 676001
E-mail: tryfannevl@aol.com

Website:
Being reconstructed and will contain the catalogue list of library.

Enquiries:
Enquiries to: Manager

Founded:
1997

Organisation type and purpose:
International organisation, professional body, suitable for ages: Keystage 1 to 4 and Further Education.
Sale of films, video and multimedia kits; film to video transfer.

Subject coverage:
Educational and training material available on history, geography, business studies, technology, sport science, biology, mathematics, home economics, arts and crafts, social studies and teacher education.

Library catalogue:
All or part available in-house

Publications list:
Available in print

Access to staff:
Contact by letter, by telephone and by fax
Hours: Mon to Fri, 0900 to 1700

Parent body:
Tryfan Audio Visual Services (TAVS)
tel: 01286 676001; e-mail: tryfanav@aol.com

NATIONAL ELECTRONIC AND VIDEO ARCHIVE OF THE CRAFTS

Acronym or abbreviation: NEVAC

University of the West of England – Bristol, School of Creative Arts, Bower Ashton Campus, Kennel Lodge Road, off Clanage Road, Bristol, BS3 2JT

Tel: 0117 328 4746
E-mail: matthew.partington@uwe.ac.uk

Website:
http://www.media.uwe.ac.uk/nevac

Organisation type and purpose:
Aims to gather and digitise interviews with people engaged in crafts.

Subject coverage:
Crafts and craftsmen.

NATIONAL ENDOMETRIOSIS SOCIETY

Suite 50, Westminster Palace Gardens, 1–7 Artillery Row, London, SW1P 1RR

Tel: 020 7222 2781
Fax: 020 7222 2786
E-mail: nes@endo.org.uk

Website:
http://www.endo.org.uk
General information about endometriosis and about the Society.

Enquiries:
Enquiries to: Chief Executive
Other contacts: Office Manager

Founded:
1981

Organisation type and purpose:
Membership association (membership is by subscription), present number of members: 2600, voluntary organisation, registered charity (charity number 1035810).

Subject coverage:
Endometriosis, support for sufferers.

Printed publications:
Please contact the Sociey for a full list of publications

Publications list:
Available in print

Access to staff:
Contact by letter, by telephone, by fax and in person
Hours: Mon to Fri, 0900 to 1700
Special comments: Helpline, some mornings, most evenings, some afternoons

NATIONAL ENERGY ACTION

Acronym or abbreviation: NEA

St Andrew's House, 90–92 Pilgrim Street, Newcastle upon Tyne, NE1 6SG

Tel: 0191 261 5677
Fax: 0191 261 6496
E-mail: info@nea.org.uk

Website:
http://www.nea.org.uk

Enquiries:
Enquiries to: Library Manager

Founded:
1981

Organisation type and purpose:
Registered charity (charity number 290511).
To develop policies and practices to tackle the heating and insulation problems of low-income households through improvements in energy efficiency.

Subject coverage:
Fuel poverty, energy efficiency.

Printed publications:
Energy Action (journal, quarterly)
Demonstration Project Reports
Policy Reports
Training, educational and technical publications
Good Practice Briefings
Publications for school children, nursery to Key Stage 4

Publications list:
Available in print

Access to staff:
Contact by letter, by telephone, by fax and by e-mail. Appointment necessary.
Hours: Mon to Thu, 0930 to 1630; Fri, 0930 to 1600

NATIONAL ENERGY FOUNDATION

Acronym or abbreviation: NEF

Davy Avenue, Knowlhill, Milton Keynes, Buckinghamshire, MK5 8NG

Tel: 01908 665555
E-mail: nef@natenergy.org.uk

Website:
http://www.natenergy.org.uk
Energy efficiency (mainly domestic).
http://www.greenergy.org.uk
Renewable energy.
http://www.powered.org.uk
Renewable energy kits for schools.
http://www.solar-schools.org.uk
Schools' renewable energy advice, visits.

Enquiries:
Enquiries to: Deputy Director
Other contacts: Manager, NEF Renewables for information about Renewable Energy.

Founded:
1988

Organisation type and purpose:
National organisation (membership is by election or invitation), registered charity (charity number 298951).
Encouraging the sustainable use of energy.

Subject coverage:
Energy efficiency, renewable energy.

Printed publications:
Leaflets on Renewable Energy and Energy Efficiency (available free of charge)

Electronic and video publications:
Understanding Energy (CD-ROM, available through publishing house, Anglia Multimedia)

Access to staff:
Contact by letter, by telephone, by e-mail and via website. Appointment necessary.
Hours: Mon to Fri, 0900 to 1700

Access to building, collection or gallery:
Prior appointment required

Access for disabled people:
Level entry, access to all public areas, toilet facilities

NATIONAL EQUINE DEFENCE LEAGUE

Oaktree Farm, Wetheral Shields, Wetheral, Carlisle, Cumbria, CA4 8JA

Tel: 01228 560082
Fax: 01228 560985

Enquiries:
Enquiries to: Organising Secretary

Founded:
1909

Organisation type and purpose:
Membership association (membership is by subscription), voluntary organisation, registered charity (charity number 280700).

Subject coverage:
Animal welfare matters.

Printed publications:
Annual Report
Many leaflets dealing with several aspects of welfare

Publications list:
Available in print

Access to staff:
Contact by letter, by telephone, by fax and in person
Hours: Mon to Sat, 0930 to 1730

Access for disabled people:
Parking provided, ramped entry, toilet facilities

NATIONAL EXAMINATION BOARD IN OCCUPATIONAL SAFETY AND HEALTH

Acronym or abbreviation: NEBOSH

Dominus Way, Meridian Business Park, Leicester, LE19 1QW

Tel: 0116 263 4700
Fax: 0116 282 4000
E-mail: info@nebosh.org.uk

Website:
http://www.nebosh.org.uk

Enquiries:
Enquiries to: Information Officer

Founded:
1979

Organisation type and purpose:
Examination board.

Subject coverage:
The NEBOSH National General Certificate in Occupational Health and Safety.
The NEBOSH National Diploma in Occupational Health and Safety.
The NEBOSH Specialist Diploma in Environmental Management.
The NEBOSH National Certificate in Construction Safety and Health.
The NEBOSH International General Certificate in Occupational Safety and Health.
The NEBOSH Certificate in Fire Safety and Risk Management.

Printed publications:
NEBOSH National Diploma Series:
Past Examination Question Papers for the NEBOSH National Diploma (£2.50 per unit)
Examiners Reports for the NEBOSH National Diploma (£8.50 each)
NEBOSH Specialist Diploma in Environmental Management:
Syllabus for the NEBOSH Specialist Diploma (£13)
Past Examination Question Papers (£2.50 each)
Examiners Reports (£6 each)
Guide to the NEBOSH National General Certificate (£12)
Plus numerous other publications

Publications list:
Available online and in print

Access to staff:
Contact by letter, by telephone, by fax, by e-mail and via website
Hours: Mon to Fri, 0900 to 1700

Access for disabled people:
Parking provided, level entry, toilet facilities

NATIONAL EXHIBITORS ASSOCIATION

Acronym or abbreviation: NEA

29a Market Square, Biggleswade, Bedfordshire, SG18 8AQ

Tel: 01767 316255
Fax: 01767 316430

Enquiries:
Enquiries to: Information Officer

Founded:
1988

Organisation type and purpose:
Trade association.

continued overleaf

Access to staff:
Contact by letter, by telephone and by fax
Hours: Mon to Fri, 0900 to 1700

NATIONAL EXTENSION COLLEGE TRUST LIMITED

Acronym or abbreviation: NEC

Michael Young Centre, Purbeck Road, Cambridge, CB2 2HN

Tel: 01223 400200
Fax: 01223 400399
E-mail: info@nec.ac.uk

Website:
http://www.nec.ac.uk
The latest information on distance learning courses and open learning services for all areas of education and training.
http://www.nec.ac.uk/resources
NEC's online catalogue.

Enquiries:
Enquiries to: Customer Relations Manager
Other contacts: Executive Assistant for records.

Founded:
1963

Organisation type and purpose:
Registered charity (charity number 311454), suitable for ages: all.
Providers of open and distance learning materials.

Subject coverage:
Open learning resources for the following areas; A level, GCSE, LGCSE, language and communications skills, learning and study skills, numeracy and literacy skills, IT user skills, foreign language skills, NVQs in accounting and administration, marketing, vocational and professional skills, training, IT and office skills, small business development, voluntary work, care and childcare NVQs, caring and health, counselling and guidance, staff development, resource development, leisure and general interest. Home Study courses in the following areas: GCSE, LGCSE and A Level, book-keeping and accounting, marketing, management and professional skills, personal development, business skills, sports management, office skills, creative writing, childcare and early years, counselling, art history.

Printed publications:
Guide to Courses (GCSE, A Level, etc.)
NEC Catalogue
A wide range of titles covering:
Key Skills
Vocational and Professional Training
General Education
Care and Early Years Training
Management

Electronic and video publications:
Key Skills Collection CD-ROM

Publications list:
Available online and in print

Access to staff:
Contact by letter, by fax and by e-mail
Hours: Mon to Fri, 0900 to 1700

Access to building, collection or gallery:
No access other than to staff

Access for disabled people:
Parking provided, toilet facilities

NATIONAL EYE RESEARCH CENTRE

Acronym or abbreviation: NERC

Bristol Eye Hospital, Lower Maudlin Street, Bristol, BS1 2LX

Tel: 0117 929 0024
Fax: 0117 925 1421
E-mail: nerc-charity@bris.ac.uk

Website:
http://www.nerc.co.uk
Description of the charity, details from annual report including accounts.

Enquiries:
Enquiries to: Director

Founded:
1986

Organisation type and purpose:
Registered charity (charity number 294087), research organisation.
Research into eye diseases and eye disabilities, and the prevention of blindness.

Subject coverage:
Research projects being funded into the causes and treatment of eye disease and disabilities of the eye, and the prevention of blindness.

Printed publications:
Annual Report

Access to staff:
Contact by letter, by telephone, by fax and by e-mail. Appointment necessary.
Hours: Mon to Fri, 0900 to 1700

Other addresses:
National Eye Research Centre (Yorkshire) (NERC(Y))
   Eye Department, Leeds General Infirmary, Leeds, LS2 9NS; tel: 0113 292 2837; fax: 0113 292 2837; e-mail: nercy.lgi@leedsth.nhs.uk

Subsidary body:
Corneal Support Group
Rotary Eye Bank Campaign

NATIONAL FAMILY MEDIATION

Acronym or abbreviation: NFM

4 Barnfield Hill, Exeter, Devon, EX1 1SR

Tel: 01392 271610
Fax: 01392 271945
E-mail: general@nfm.org.uk

Website:
http://www.nfm.org.uk

Enquiries:
Enquiries to: Administrator
Direct fax: 020 7838 5994
Other contacts: Communications Manager (for press enquiries)

Founded:
1991

Organisation type and purpose:
Registered charity (charity number 1074796).
A service with over 50 branches throughout the United Kingdom.

Subject coverage:
Provision of assistance to separating or divorcing parents in making joint decisions regarding children, finance and property, family mediation, separation and divorce.

Printed publications:
Annual Report

Access to staff:
Contact by letter, by telephone, by e-mail and via website
Hours: Mon to Fri, 0900 to 1630

Branches:
African-Caribbean Family Mediation Service (Lambeth, Lewisham, Wandsworth, Southwark)
   2–4 St John's Crescent, Brixton, London, SW9 7LZ; tel: 020 7737 2366; fax: 020 7733 0637; e-mail: donna@acfms.org
Berkshire FMS (Reading, Newbury and Wokingham)
   Third Floor, 160–163 Friar Street, Reading, RG1 1HE; tel: 0118 957 1159; fax: 0118 958 4755; e-mail: roger@berksfm.fsnet.co.uk

Birmingham and District FMS (Birmingham, Solihull, Walsall)
   First Floor, Coleridge Chambers, 177 Corporation Street, Birmingham, B4 6RG; tel: 0121 233 1999; fax: 0121 233 3399; e-mail: bdfm@netcomuk.co.uk
Boys and Girls Welfare Society Mediation Services (Cheshire)
   Goss Chambers, Goss Street, Chester, CH1 2BG; tel: 01244 400658; fax: 01244 343751; e-mail: cms.bgws@virgin.net
Bristol FMS (Avon and South Gloucestershire)
   25 Hobbs Lane, Bristol, BS1 5ED; tel: 0117 929 2002; fax: 0117 929 9312; e-mail: mediation@bfmbristol.co.uk
Cambridge and District FMS (Cambridge, Huntingdon and surrounding areas)
   Essex House, 71 Regent Street, Cambridge, CB2 1AB; tel: 01223 576308; fax: 01223 576309; e-mail: contact@cfadc.freeserve.co.uk
Central Middlesex Family Mediation (Harrow, Ealing, Hillingdon, Brent)
   Civic Centre Complex, Station Road, Harrow, London, HA1 2HX; tel: 020 8427 2076; fax: 020 8861 3471; e-mail: familymediation@ukf.net
Chiltern FMS (Amersham, Watford, Aylesbury)
   1 King George V Road, Amersham, Buckinghamshire, HP6 5TT; tel: 01494 732782; fax: 01494 732782
Cleveland FMS (Cleveland and neighbouring areas)
   St Mary's Centre, 82–90 Corporation Road, Middlesbrough, Cleveland, TS1 2RW; tel: 01642 222967; fax: 01642 210782; e-mail: clevelandfms@compuserve.com
Coventry and Warwickshire FMS
   Suite 11, Koco Building, The Arches, Spon End, Coventry, CV1 3QJ; tel: 024 7671 7109; fax: 024 7671 7119; e-mail: cw.fms@virgin.net
Cumbria FMS
   Stricklandgate House, 92 Stricklandgate, Kendal, LA9 4PU; tel: 01539 733705; fax: 01539 733705; e-mail: nwcfms@mail.nch.org.uk
Derbyshire FMS
   NCH Action for Children, 32a Newbold Road, Chesterfield, North Derbyshire, S41 7PH; tel: 01246 277422; fax: 01246 277363; e-mail: mddfmp@mail.nch.org.uk
Durham and Darlington Family Mediation (County Durham and Darlington)
   First Floor, 72–76 North Road, Durham City, DH1 4SQ; tel: 0191 386 5418; fax: 0191 386 3057; e-mail: nedadfm@mail.nch.org.uk
Exeter and District FMS (Exeter and East Devon)
   49 Polsloe Road, Exeter, EX1 2DT; tel: 01392 410529; e-mail: nfmexeter@eurobell.co.uk
Eye to Eye Mediation (Inner London Probation Area)
   NCH Action for Children, 231 Camberwell New Road, London, SE5 0TH; tel: 020 7701 1114 or 703 2532; fax: 020 7703 6129; e-mail: inetem@mail.nch.org.uk
Family Mediation (Hull) (Kingston upon Hull, East Yorkshire, North and North-East Lincolnshire)
   34 Bishop Lane, Hull, HU1 1PA; tel: 01482 329740; fax: 01482 323991; e-mail: dorothy@familymediation.karoo.uk
Family Mediation (North Wiltshire) (West and North Wiltshire, parts of Berkshire, Gloucestershire, Oxon)
   34 Milton Road, Swindon, Wiltshire, SN1 5JA; tel: 01793 527285; fax: 01793 420532; e-mail: admin@familymediation.fsnet.co.uk
Family Mediation Centre (Greater Manchester)
   21 Knowsley Street, Bury, Lancashire, BL9 0ST; tel: 0161 797 9910; fax: 0161 763 9311; e-mail: nwfmsgm@mail.nch.org.uk
Family Mediation Service (North West Yorkshire) (Harrogate, Craven and Richmondshire, Hambleton)
   13 Dragon Parade, Harrogate, North Yorkshire, HG1 5BZ; tel: 01423 525156; fax: 01423 520983; e-mail: fmsnwy@lineonline.net

Family Mediation Service (Northumberland and Tyneside FMS) (Newcastle, Gateshead, North Tyneside, Northumberland)
NCH, MEA House, Ellison Place, Newcastle upon Tyne, NE1 8XS; tel: 0191 261 9212; fax: 0191 233 0634; e-mail: nenatfms@mail.nch.org.uk

Family Mediation Service Cardiff
42 Cardiff Street, Cardiff, CF10 2GE; tel: 029 2022 9692; fax: 029 2039 9505

Gloucestershire Family Mediation
PO Box 95, Gloucester, GL1 3YG; tel: 01452 411843; fax: 01452 418441; e-mail: gfm@mediation.fsbusiness.co.uk

Gwent Mediation Service
NCH, 66 Lower Dock Street, Newport, NP20 1EF; tel: 01633 263 065; fax: 01633 222743; e-mail: wagms@mail.nch.org.uk

Hampshire FMS (Hampshire and Isle of Wight)
58d High Street, Cosham, Portsmouth, PO6 3AG; tel: 023 9243 3388; fax: 023 9243 3358; e-mail: admin@hantsmed.org.uk

Herefordshire FMS (Herefordshire and surrounding area)
Second Floor, Berrows Business Centre, Hereford, HR1 2HE; tel: 01432 264087/277996; fax: 01432 351993; e-mail: herefordshire@familymediation.fslife.co.uk

Hertfordshire and Essex FMS (West Essex and parts of Hertfordshire)
Sewell House, 349 The Hides, Harlow, Essex, CM20 3QY; tel: 01279 426749; fax: 01279 426749; e-mail: hefms@dial.pipex.com

Hertfordshire FMS
62–72 Victoria Street, St Albans, Hertfordshire, AL1 3XH; tel: 01727 839300; fax: 01727 839123; e-mail: admin@hertsfms.fsnet.co.uk

Jersey Family Mediation
2 Charles House, Charles Street, St Helier, Jersey, JE2 4SF; tel: 01534 734980; fax: 01534 619945; e-mail: relate.jersey@jerseymail.co.uk

Kent FMS
6 Park Road, Sittingbourne, Kent, ME10 1DR; tel: 01795 429689; fax: 01795 476949; e-mail: familymediation.kent@virgin.net

Lancashire FMS
19 Ribblesdale Place, Preston, Lancashire, PR1 3NA; tel: 01772 204248; fax: 01772 204246; e-mail: mediation@lfms.net

Lincolnshire FMS
Claxten House, 62 Clasketgate, Lincoln, LN2 1JZ; tel: 01522 575700; fax: 01522 575700; e-mail: lfms@lincs-ln2.freeserve.co.uk

Mediation in Divorce (South West London)
13 Rosslyn Road, East Twickenham, London, TW1 2AR; tel: 020 8891 6860; fax: 020 8891 3107; e-mail: admin@mediationindivorce.co.uk

Merseyside FMS
5a Swiss Road, Liverpool, L6 3AT; tel: 0151 260 9155; fax: 0151 260 0548; e-mail: mediation@pss.org.uk

Milton Keynes Family Mediation (Milton Keynes, North Buckinghamshire, North Hertfordshire and Bedfordshire)
City Counselling Centre, 320 Saxon Gate West, Central Milton Keynes, Buckinghamshire, MK9 2ES; tel: 01908 231293; fax: 01908 690211; e-mail: familymediationmk@talk21.com

Norfolk FMS
Charing Cross Centre, 17–19 St John Maddermarket, Norwich, Norfolk, NR2 1DL; tel: 01603 620 588; fax: 01603 620 588; e-mail: norfolk.fammed@lineone.net

North Devon FMS
The Castle Centre, Castle Street, Barnstaple, Devon, EX31 1DR; tel: 01270 321888; fax: 01271 321888; e-mail: ndfms@lineone.net

North London FMS (Barnet, Haringey, Hertsmere and Enfield)
267 Ballards Lane, Finchley, London, N12 8NR; tel: 020 8343 9899; fax: 020 8445 6603; e-mail: nlmed@email.com

North Staffordshire FMS (Stafford, Stoke and North Staffordshire)
Winton House, Stoke Road, Stoke-on-Trent, Staffordshire, ST4 2RN; tel: 0845 602 0301/01782 416111; fax: 01782 416444; e-mail: nsfms@hotmail.com

Northamptonshire FMS
49 York Road, First Floor, Northampton, NN1 5QJ; tel: 01604 636651; fax: 01604 637313; e-mail: familymediation@excite.co.uk

Northern Ireland Family Mediation Service
76 Dublin Road, Belfast, BT2 7HP; tel: 028 9032 2914; fax: 028 9315 298

Nottinghamshire Children and Families Mediation Service (FAME)
3 Pelham Court, Pelham Road, Nottingham, NG5 1AP; tel: 0115 985 8855; fax: 0115 962 3606; e-mail: mj@famenottingham.fsbusiness.co.uk

Oxfordshire FMS
First Floor, 125 London Road, Headington, Oxford, OX3 9HZ; tel: 01865 741781; fax: 01865 744393; e-mail: oxmedserv@aol.com

Peterborough and District FMS
61 Broadway, Peterborough, Cambridgeshire, PE1 1SY; tel: 01733 347353; fax: 01733 347353; e-mail: pfms@tinyonline.co.uk

Plymouth Mediation (Plymouth and District)
St Peter's Centre, 18 Harwell Street, Plymouth, PL1 5BA; tel: 01752 312121; fax: 01752 312123; e-mail: plymed@dial.pipex.com

Salisbury and District FMS (Salisbury, South Wiltshire, North Dorset, North West Hampshire)
24b St Edmund's Church Street, Salisbury, Wiltshire, SP1 1EF; tel: 01722 332936; fax: 01722 332936; e-mail: fms@southwilts.nda.co.uk

Scarborough and District FMS
1 Westbourne Grove, Scarborough, North Yorkshire, YO11 2DJ; tel: 01723 507775; fax: 01723 507775; e-mail: manager@sdfms.fsnet.co.uk

Shropshire Family Mediation
65 Withywood Drive, Malinslee, Telford, Shropshire, TF3 2HU; tel: 01952 520091; fax: 01952 520092; e-mail: shropshire.mediation1@virgin.net

Somerset FMS
The Myrtle Tree, 34 Bridge Street, Taunton, Somerset, TA1 1UD; tel: 01823 352013; fax: 01823 352013; e-mail: mary@relate-somerset.org.uk

South Essex FMS
29 Harcourt Avenue, Southend-on-Sea, Essex, SS2 6HT; tel: 01702 436466; fax: 01702 431173; e-mail: mediation.southessexrelate@virgin.net

South Staffordshire FMS (South Staffordshire, Cannock, Lichfield, Tamworth)
33 Park Road, Cannock, Staffordshire, WS11 1JN; tel: 01543 572600; fax: 01543 579390; e-mail: ssfmscannock@hotmail.com

South Yorkshire FMS
Queen's Building, 55 Queen Street, Sheffield, S1 2DX; tel: 0114 275 2227; fax: 0114 275 3996; e-mail: user@syfm.fsnet.co.uk

South-East London Family Mediation Bureau (Bexley, Bromley, Croydon and Surrounding areas)
5 Upper Park Road, Bromley, Kent, BR1 3HN; tel: 020 8460 4606; fax: 020 8466 6572; e-mail: info@familymediationlondon.org.uk

Sunderland and South Tyneside FMS (Sunderland, Washington, Houghton-le-Spring, South Shields, Jarrow)
54 John Street, Sunderland, Tyne and Wear, SR1 1QH; tel: 0191 514 3849; fax: 0191 514 2481; e-mail: sastfms@aol.com

Surrey FMS
316 High Street, Dorking, Surrey, RH4 1QX; tel: 01306 741777; fax: 01306 741383; e-mail: surreyfms@cs.com

Sussex FMS (East and West Sussex)
Garton House, 22 Stanford Avenue, Brighton, East Sussex, BN1 6DD; tel: 01273 550563; fax: 01273 555412; e-mail: sxfms@supanet.com

Thames Valley FMS (South Buckinghamshire, East Berkshire, High Wycombe, Slough, Windsor and Bracknell)
Windsor Magistrates Court, Side Entrance, Alma Road, Windsor, Berkshire, SL4 3HD; tel: 01753 830770; fax: 01753 830770; e-mail: thames@valleyfm.fsnet.co.uk

The FMS-Institute of Family Therapy (Central London and North West)
24–32 Stephenson Way, London, NW1 2HX; tel: 020 7391 9150; fax: 020 7391 9169; e-mail: ift@psyc.bbk.ac.uk

West Yorkshire FMS (Bradford, Wakefield, Dewsbury, Halifax, Huddersfield, Leeds)
31 Manor Road, Bradford, West Yorkshire, BD1 4PS; tel: 01274 732768 or 0845 419403; fax: 01274 730115; e-mail: wyfamilymed@netscapeonline.co.uk

Worcestershire FMS
14 Castle Street Street, Worcester, WR1 3ZB; tel: 01905 610925; fax: 01905 619526; e-mail: worcester@familymediation.fsbusiness.co.uk

York FMS (York, Selby, parts of Ryedale and Hambleton)
The Old Coach House, Grange Garth, York, YO10 4BS; tel: 01904 646068; fax: 01904 646068; e-mail: yorkfms@care4free.net

Links with:
Dorset Relate
8 Maumbury Road, Dorchester, Dorset, DT1 1QW; tel: 01305 751781; fax: 01305 751781; e-mail: general@dorsetfamilymediation.co.uk

Leicester Relate
83 Aylestone Road, Leicester, LE2 7LL; tel: 0116 254 1149

North East London FMS (Ilford, Romford, Barking and Dagenham)
Relate Office, Althorne Way, Dagenham, Essex, RM10 7AY; tel: 020 8593 6827; fax: 020 8593 8111; e-mail: nel_mediation@talk21.com

North Wales FMS (Colwyn Bay, Rhyl, Bangor)
Eryl Wen, Eryl Place, Llandudno, LL30 2TX; tel: 01492 870876; fax: 01492 870846

NATIONAL FARMERS' UNION

Acronym or abbreviation: NFU

Agriculture House, Stoneleigh Park, Stoneleigh, Warwickshire, CV8 2TZ

Tel: 024 7685 8500
Fax: 024 7685 8501
E-mail: nfu@nfu.org.uk

Website:
http://www.nfu.org.uk

Enquiries:
Enquiries to: Press Officer
Direct tel: 020 7331 7295
Direct fax: 020 7331 7370
Direct e-mail: sharon.hockley@nfu.org.uk
Other contacts: Director General; President for general management; 'politics'.

Founded:
1908

Organisation type and purpose:
Trade association (membership is by subscription), present number of members: 135,000.
Representing farmers and growers in England and Wales.
To provide farmers and growers with professional and technical services.

Subject coverage:
Policy, economic, legal and other material relating to agriculture, horticulture, land use, agricultural trade and statistics, livestock and crop production.

Museum or gallery collection, archive, or library special collection:
British Farmer, NFU Magazine, NFU Business NFU yearbooks since 1910

Trade and statistical information:
UK Agricultural (June census) statistics from 1866.
Agricultural statistics from 1940.
Household food consumption survey from 1940.

Printed publications:
Annual Report
National and Regional NFU journals available on subscription

Publications list:
Available online

Access to staff:
Contact by letter, by telephone, by fax and by e-mail. Appointment necessary. Non-members charged.

continued overleaf

Hours: Archives held in out of town store, 48 hours notice needed for retrieval

Access to building, collection or gallery:
No access other than to staff

Affiliated to:
CBI
European Federation of Farmers' Organisations (COPA)
International Chamber of Commerce (ICC)
International Federation of Agricultural Producers (IFPA)

Has:
8 regional offices, HQ outstations and approximately 400 local branches

NATIONAL FEDERATION OF 18 PLUS GROUPS OF GB

Acronym or abbreviation: 18 PLUS

8–10 Church Street Chamber, Church Street, Newent, Gloucestershire, GL18 1PP

Tel: 01531 821210
Fax: 01531 821474
E-mail: office@18plus.org.uk

Website:
http://www.18plus.org.uk
History of 18 Plus, 18 Plus group programmes, links to member group pages, other email contacts.

Enquiries:
Enquiries to: Administrator
Other contacts: Honorary General Secretary

Founded:
1941

Organisation type and purpose:
Membership association (membership is by subscription), present number of members: 1200, voluntary organisation, suitable for ages: 18 to 35, training organisation.
A social activities organisation for young adults wishing to make friends and take part in a wide range of activities.

Subject coverage:
Social group, personal development training and a variety of activities.

Printed publications:
Information pack for membership enquiries (free of charge on receipt of name and postal address)

Access to staff:
Contact by letter, by telephone, by fax, by e-mail and via website
Hours: 24-hour answerphone

NATIONAL FEDERATION OF ANGLERS

Acronym or abbreviation: NFA

Halliday House, Egginton Junction, Hilton, Derbyshire, DE65 6GU

Tel: 01283 734735
Fax: 01283 734799
E-mail: office@nfahq.freeserve.co.uk

Enquiries:
Enquiries to: Administration Manager

Founded:
1903

Organisation type and purpose:
Voluntary organisation.
Governing body of coarse angling.

Subject coverage:
Fisheries and fishing; coarse fishing; problems of pollution, water abstraction and land drainage, fishery protection; research; competitions, sponsored events.

Printed publications:
NFA Booklet
NFA Codes
NFA Rules and Constitution

Access to staff:
Contact by letter and by e-mail
Hours: Mon to Fri, 0900 to 1700

Member of:
Confédération Internationale de la Pêche Sportive (CIPS)

NATIONAL FEDERATION OF BUILDERS

55 Tufton Street, London, SW1P 3QL

Tel: 0870 8989 091
Fax: 0870 8989 096

Website:
http://builders.org.uk/

Enquiries:
Direct e-mail: paul.smith@citypress.co.uk

Organisation type and purpose:
Trade association.

Subject coverage:
Building companies.

Member of:
Construction Confederation

NATIONAL FEDERATION OF DEMOLITION CONTRACTORS LIMITED

Acronym or abbreviation: NFDC LTD

Resurgam House, 1a New Road, The Causeway, Staines, Middlesex, TW18 3DH

Tel: 01784 456799
Fax: 01784 461118
E-mail: info@demolition-nfdc.com

Website:
http://www.demolition-nfdc.com
List of members and federation officers.

Enquiries:
Enquiries to: National Secretary

Founded:
1941

Organisation type and purpose:
Trade association.

Subject coverage:
General demolition, demolition of mass and reinforced concrete structures, chimney demolition, dangerous structures, machinery dismantling, shoring, site clearance and excavation, demolition by licensed explosives engineers, asbestos stripping and disposal, thermic boring, plant hire, supplies of hardcore, sale of reclaimed building materials.

Printed publications:
Demolition and Dismantling (journal, quarterly)
List of Members
NFDC Yearbook
The First Fifty Years (history of the federation 1941–91)

Electronic and video publications:
Voice of the Industry (video)

Access to staff:
Contact by letter, by telephone, by fax, by e-mail and via website. Appointment necessary.
Hours: Mon to Fri, 0900 to 1700

Access for disabled people:
Parking provided

Founder member of:
European Demolition Association
tel: + 31 30 259 8330; fax: + 31 30 259 8600; e-mail: eda@eda-demolition.com

NATIONAL FEDERATION OF FISH FRIERS LIMITED

Acronym or abbreviation: NFFF

New Federation House, 4 Greenwood Mount, Meanwood, Leeds, West Yorkshire, LS6 4LQ

Tel: 0113 230 7044
Fax: 0113 230 7010
E-mail: mail@federationoffishfriers.co.uk

Enquiries:
Enquiries to: Review Manager
Direct tel: 0113 230 7009

Founded:
1913

Organisation type and purpose:
Trade association, present number of members: 2500, training organisation.
Looks after the interests of fish friers throughout the United Kingdom.

Subject coverage:
Covers interests of the members of the fish frying trade; fish, potatoes and other cooking ingredients, frying and refrigeration equipment, health and safety issues.

Printed publications:
Fish Friers Review (journal, to members, annual subscription £41.52)

Access to staff:
Contact by letter, by telephone, by fax, by e-mail and via website. Appointment necessary.
Hours: Mon to Fri, 0900 to 1630

NATIONAL FEDERATION OF MEAT AND FOOD TRADERS, THE

Acronym or abbreviation: NFMFT

1 Belgrove, Tunbridge Wells, Kent, TN1 1YW

Tel: 01892 541412
Fax: 01892 535462
E-mail: info@nfmft.co.uk

Enquiries:
Enquiries to: Chief Executive

Founded:
1888

Organisation type and purpose:
Trade association.

Subject coverage:
Represents the interests of member independent retail butchers in England and Wales.

Printed publications:
Food Trader (journal, monthly)
Essential Business Guide (annual guide to regulations)

Access to staff:
Contact by letter, by telephone, by fax and by e-mail. Appointment necessary. Access for members only. Letter of introduction required.
Hours: Mon to Fri, 0900 to 1715

NATIONAL FEDERATION OF RETIREMENT PENSIONS ASSOCIATIONS

Acronym or abbreviation: NFORPA

Thwaites House, Railway Road, Blackburn, Lancashire, BB1 5AX

Tel: 01254 52606
Fax: 01254 52606

Enquiries:
Enquiries to: General Secretary

Founded:
1940

Organisation type and purpose:
Membership association.

Subject coverage:
Retirement pensions, supplementary pensions and allowances, National Health Service Acts, rent and rates rebates, other interests of pensioners.

Printed publications:
Pensioners' Voice (9 times a year)

Access to staff:
Contact by letter
Hours: Mon to Fri, 0930 to 1600

NATIONAL FEDERATION OF ROOFING CONTRACTORS LIMITED

Acronym or abbreviation: NFRC

24 Weymouth Street, London, W1G 7LX

Tel: 020 7436 0387
Fax: 020 7637 5215
E-mail: info@nfrc.co.uk

Website:
http://www.nfrc.co.uk
Product matrix by category of all NFRC associate members with a keyword selector.
Product and service matrices search for roofers by area and discipline.

Enquiries:
Enquiries to: Secretary
Other contacts: (1) Membership Secretary (2) Public Relations Executive for (2) media, publications information.

Founded:
1893

Organisation type and purpose:
Trade association.

Subject coverage:
Technical roofing information, insurance schemes, education and training in roofing, product and application standards, health and safety.

Printed publications:
Householders Guide to Flat Roofing
NFRC Directory
Roofing & Cladding in Windy Conditions
Safety Passport
Technical Bulletins
UPDATE (magazine, monthly)

Electronic and video publications:
The NFRC Guide to Quality Roofing (disk)

Publications list:
Available online and in print

Access to staff:
Contact by letter, by telephone, by fax, by e-mail and via website. Appointment necessary.
Hours: Mon to Fri, 0900 to 1700

Member of:
National Specialist Contractors Council (NSCC) Carthisian Court, 12 Carthisian Street, London, EC1M 6EZ; tel: 0870 429 6351; fax: 0870 429 6352

NATIONAL FEDERATION OF SUBPOSTMASTERS

Acronym or abbreviation: NFSP

Evelyn House, 22 Windlesham Gardens, Shoreham-by-Sea, West Sussex, BN43 5AZ

Tel: 01273 452324
Fax: 01273 465403
E-mail: nfsp@subpostmasters.org.uk

Website:
http://www.subpostmasters.org.uk

Enquiries:
Enquiries to: Information Officer

Founded:
1897

Organisation type and purpose:
National organisation, trade association, trade union (membership is by subscription), present number of members: 14,000.
Certificated independent trade union recognised by The Post Office to represent subpostmasters.

Subject coverage:
Post office management.

Access to staff:
Contact by letter and by telephone
Hours: Mon to Fri, 0900 to 1700

Access to building, collection or gallery:
No access other than to staff

NATIONAL FEDERATION OF TERRAZZO MARBLE & MOSAIC SPECIALISTS

Acronym or abbreviation: NFTMMS

PO Box 2843, London, W1A 5PG

Tel: 0845 609 0050
Fax: 0845 607 8610
E-mail: dslade@nftmms.org

Website:
http://www.nftmms.org
Details of activities and services, list of members.

Enquiries:
Enquiries to: Secretary

Founded:
1933

Organisation type and purpose:
Trade association (membership is by election or invitation), present number of members: 40.

Subject coverage:
Technical advice on the laying of terrazzo, mosaic and marble; granite; limestone; investigation of complaints; inspection and reports on work, application etc.

Printed publications:
Members list
Technical specifications to complement British Standards
General Federation Brochure

Access to staff:
Contact by letter, by telephone, by fax and by e-mail
Hours: Mon to Fri, 0900 to 1700

NATIONAL FEDERATION OF THE BLIND OF THE UNITED KINGDOM

Acronym or abbreviation: NFBUK

Sir John Wilson House, 215 Kirkgate, Wakefield, West Yorkshire, WF1 1JG

Tel: 01924 291313
Fax: 01924 200244
E-mail: nfbuk@nfbuk.org

Website:
http://www.nfbuk.org

Enquiries:
Enquiries to: Honorary General Secretary
Other contacts: Public Relations Officer for information.

Founded:
1947

Organisation type and purpose:
Membership association (membership is by subscription), present number of members: 2000, registered charity, voluntary organisation (charity number 236629).
Campaigning organisation.

Subject coverage:
The real needs of the blind and partially-sighted from their perspective e.g. a safer environment, obstructions in pavements, and the particular needs of the deafblind.

Printed publications:
Publications are available both free and for purchase
Information is also available in print and braille

Electronic and video publications:
2 videos are available for purchase
Information is also available on tape and disk

Publications list:
Available in print

Access to staff:
Contact by letter, by telephone, by fax and by e-mail
Hours: Mon, Tue, Thu, Fri, 0900 to 1600; Wed, closed

NATIONAL FEDERATION OF WOMEN'S INSTITUTES

Acronym or abbreviation: NFWI

104 New Kings Road, Fulham, London, SW6 4LY

Tel: 020 7371 9300
Fax: 020 7736 3652
E-mail: gensec@nfwi.org.uk

Website:
http://www.thewi.org.uk

Enquiries:
Enquiries to: General Secretary

Founded:
1915

Organisation type and purpose:
Membership association (membership is by subscription), present number of members: 205,000, voluntary organisation, registered charity.

Subject coverage:
Rural affairs, current and public affairs, particularly on environment and issues of concern to women, health, social welfare, employment, standards of life, home economics, music and drama, education, crafts, sport.

Museum or gallery collection, archive, or library special collection:
The Women's Library, Old Castle Street, London E1

Printed publications:
Annual Report
WI Life (magazine, 8 times a year)
WI Books (various titles)

Publications list:
Available in print

Access to staff:
Contact by letter, by telephone, by fax, by e-mail and via website
Hours: Mon to Fri, 0900 to 1700

Access for disabled people:
None

Also at:
Denman College
Marcham, Abingdon, Oxfordshire, OX13 6NW; tel: 01865 391991; fax: 01865 391966; e-mail: info@denman.org.uk
NFWI Wales Office (NFWI)
19–21 Cathedral Road, Cardiff, CF1 9LJ; tel: 02920 221712; fax: 02920 387236

NATIONAL FEDERATION OF WOMEN'S INSTITUTES – WALES

Acronym or abbreviation: NFWI-Wales

19 Cathedral Road, Cardiff, CF11 9HA

Tel: 029 2022 1712
Fax: 029 2038 7236
E-mail: walesoffice@nfwi-wales.org.uk

Website:
http://www.womens-institute.org.uk

Enquiries:
Enquiries to: Head of Wales Office
Other contacts: Administrative/Public Affairs Officer for preliminary enquiries.

Founded:
1915

continued overleaf

Organisation type and purpose:
Membership association (membership is by subscription), present number of members: 20,000, voluntary organisation, registered charity (charity number 803793), suitable for ages: 16+.
The National Federation of Women's Institutes offers opportunities for all women to enjoy friendship, to learn, to widen their horizons, and together to influence local, national and international affairs.

Non-library collection catalogue:
All or part available online

Publications list:
Available in print

Access to staff:
Contact by letter, by telephone and by e-mail
Hours: Mon to Fri, 0900 to 1700

There are:
13 Federation offices throughout Wales

NATIONAL FILM AND TELEVISION SCHOOL

Acronym or abbreviation: NFTS

Beaconsfield Studios, Station Road, Beaconsfield, Buckinghamshire, HP9 1LG

Tel: 01494 671234
Fax: 01494 674042
E-mail: info@nfts.co.uk

Website:
http://www.nfts.co.uk

Enquiries:
Enquiries to: Registrar
Direct tel: 01494 731425

Founded:
1971

Organisation type and purpose:
National organisation, suitable for ages: Post-graduate, training organisation.

Subject coverage:
Information about MA and Diploma courses in directing (animation, documentary or fiction), cinematography, composing for film and television, digital post-production, editing, producing, producing and directing television entertainment, production design, production management, screenwriting, script development, SFX/VFX, sound post-production, sound recording

Printed publications:
Prospectus (free, from Registry)
Order printed publications from: Registry

Electronic and video publications:
Prospectus (free, online)

Access to staff:
Contact by letter, by telephone, by fax, by e-mail and via website. Appointment necessary.
Hours: Mon to Fri, 0930 to 1730

Access for disabled people:
Parking provided, level entry, toilet facilities
Special comments: Most areas accessible. Special arrangements can be made for individual requirements, preferably give advance notice

Links with:
ShortCourses@NFTS
at Beaconsfield Studios; tel: 01494 677903; fax: 01494 678708; e-mail: shortcourses@nfts.co.uk; website: http://www.nfts.co.uk

NATIONAL FILM BOARD OF CANADA

Acronym or abbreviation: NFB

Canada House, Trafalgar Square, London, SW1Y 5BJ

Tel: 020 7258 6480
Fax: 020 7258 6532
E-mail: london@nfb.ca

Website:
http://www.nfb.ca
About the NFB and its productions.

Enquiries:
Enquiries to: Sales Representative
Direct tel: 020 7258 6482
Direct e-mail: s.swan@nfb.ca

Founded:
1939

Organisation type and purpose:
Film production and distribution.

Subject coverage:
Film and video production and distribution.

Museum or gallery collection, archive, or library special collection:
Collection of 17,000 titles, mainly documentaries and animation (includes educational programmes)

Printed publications:
NFB Annual Report
NFB Productions

Electronic and video publications:
Videos available for purchase through NFB London office or through its UK distributors

Access to staff:
Contact by letter, by telephone, by fax, by e-mail and via website
Hours: Mon to Fri, 1000 to 1800

NATIONAL FILM THEATRE

Acronym or abbreviation: NFT

South Bank Centre, Belvedere Road, Waterloo, London, SE1 8XT

Tel: 020 7928 3535
Fax: 020 7815 1419
E-mail: nft@bfi.org.uk

Website:
http://www.bfi.org.uk/nft50
http://www.bfi.org.uk/nft

Enquiries:
Enquiries to: Press and Marketing Department

Founded:
1952

Organisation type and purpose:
Cinema.

Subject coverage:
Film and video information related to its own screening.

Printed publications:
NFT 50: A celebration of 50 years of the National Film Theatre researched and written by Allen Eyles (£5)

Electronic and video publications:
Education resource materials (for purchase, from the museum's education department)

Access to staff:
Contact by letter, by telephone, by fax, by e-mail and via website
Hours: Mon to Fri, 1000 to 1800

Access for disabled people:
Parking provided, level entry, toilet facilities

Parent body:
British Film Institute
21 Stephen Street, London, W1P 1PL

NATIONAL FIREPLACE ASSOCIATION

Acronym or abbreviation: NFA

PO Box 583, High Wycombe, HP15 6XT

Tel: 0121 288 0050
Fax: 0870 130 6747
E-mail: enquiry@nfa.org.uk

Website:
http://www.nfa.org.uk
One page description of services, publications available and listings of members in categories.

Enquiries:
Enquiries to: Director
Other contacts: Public Relations Officer for all public relations enquiries.

Founded:
1970

Organisation type and purpose:
Trade association.
Promotional body for the fire and fireplace industry. Promotion to the end user.

Subject coverage:
Fireplaces, open fires, stoves, roomheaters and fuels (solid fuel, gas, natural and LPG).

Printed publications:
10 Technical Information Leaflets (£3 each or £36 for the set):
Air Supply for open flued fires (covers solid fuel and gas)
Chimney Problems and how to cure them
Coal and Log Effect Gas Fires
Fireplace Safety, Maintenance and Chimney Sweeping
Fireplaces, their construction and installation
Fireplace Fixing Instructions (£1 inc. p&p)
Fuels for your fire (covers solid fuels, wood, natural gas, LPG)
Lining old chimneys
Masonry Chimneys, their design and construction
Open Fires for coal and wood
Stoves and Roomheaters for solid fuel and wood
The Fireplace Yearbook (£4 inc. p&p)

Publications list:
Available online and in print

Access to staff:
Contact by letter, by telephone, by fax, by e-mail and via website
Hours: Mon to Fri, 0900 to 1700

Member of:
METCOM

Other addresses:
Fire (PR) Service
PO Box 583, Holmer Green, High Wycombe, Buckinghamshire, HP15 6XT; tel: 01494 711430; fax: 0870 130 6747; e-mail: PeterHealy@ fireplacepr.force9.co.uk

NATIONAL FOREST COMPANY

Enterprise Glade, Bath Yard, Bath Lane, Swadlincote, Derbyshire, DE12 6BD

Tel: 01283 551211
Fax: 01283 552844
E-mail: enquiries@nationalforest.org

Website:
http://www.nationalforest.org
Full information on the National Forest

Founded:
1995

Organisation type and purpose:
Government funded company.
Creating a new multipurpose forest in the Midlands (Leicestershire, Derbyshire, Staffordshire).

Subject coverage:
Grants for woodland creation, forestry investment and sponsorship opportunities in the National Forest.

Printed publications:
Newsletter (2 times a year)
Visitor Guide
Food Guide
Walks and Site Guides

Publications list:
Available online and in print

Access to staff:
Contact by letter and by e-mail
Hours: Mon to Fri, 0900 to 1700

NATIONAL FOUNDATION FOR EDUCATIONAL RESEARCH

Chestnut House, Tawe Business Village, Phoenix Way, Enterprise Park, Llansamlet, Swansea, West Glamorgan, SA7 9LA

Tel: 01792 459800
Fax: 01792 797815
E-mail: scya@nfer.ac.uk

Website:
http://www.nfer.ac.uk

Enquiries:
Enquiries to: Information Officer
Other contacts: Head of NFER Welsh Unit

Founded:
1946

Organisation type and purpose:
Registered charity (charity number 313392), suitable for ages: 3 to 100, research organisation. Education research – independent charity. NFER conducts independent and objective research through external sponsors and customers. Through its own resources conducts evaluations and surveys and develops tests and assessment materials. NFER Welsh unit at Swansea also specialises in Welsh language research.

Subject coverage:
Education and training.

Access to staff:
Contact by letter, by telephone and by fax
Hours: Mon to Fri, 0900 to 1700

Access for disabled people:
Parking provided

Main office:
National Foundation for Educational Research (NFER)
   The Mere, Upton Park, Slough, SL1 2DQ; tel: 01753 574123

NATIONAL FOX WELFARE SOCIETY

Acronym or abbreviation: NFWS

135 Higham Road, Rushden, Northamptonshire, NN10 6DS

Tel: 01933 411996
Fax: 01933 397324
E-mail: natfox@ntlworld.com

Website:
http://www.nfws.org.uk/
http://www.mange.org.uk
Information on the occurrence and treatment of sarcoptic mange.

Enquiries:
Enquiries to: Any Co-ordinator

Founded:
1993

Organisation type and purpose:
National organisation, membership association (membership is by subscription), voluntary organisation.
Animal welfare society providing advice and practical assistance on all fox-related issues.

Subject coverage:
All fox-related subjects, behaviour, rescue, advice, help with treatment for injuries and/or mange.

Printed publications:
Information pack available on request (A4 sae with 44p stamp)
Vulpine Observer (members only, £12 per annum)
Foxwatching – in the Shadow of the Fox (£7.99 plus 75p p&p)
Urban Foxes (£9.99 plus £1 p&p)
Unearthing the Urban Fox (£4.95 plus 50p p&p)

Publications list:
Available in print

Access to staff:
Contact by letter, by telephone, by e-mail and via website
Hours: Mon to Fri, 1000 to 1800
Special comments: 24 hours, 365 days a year for emergencies.

Access to building, collection or gallery:
No access other than to staff

NATIONAL GALLERIES OF SCOTLAND

Press and Information Department, Dean Gallery Lodge, Belford Road, Edinburgh, EH4 3DS

Tel: 0131 624 6200
Fax: 0131 343 3250

Website:
http://www.nationalgalleries.org

Enquiries:
Enquiries to: Press and Information Assistant
Direct tel: 0131 624 6332
Direct e-mail: pressinfo@nationalgalleries.org

Founded:
1859

Organisation type and purpose:
Art gallery.

Subject coverage:
Provision of information on the National Gallery of Scotland, Scottish National Gallery of Modern Art, Scottish National Portrait Gallery and Dean Gallery.

Printed publications:
Order printed publications from: Publications Department, National Galleries of Scotland, Dean Gallery, Belford Road, Edinburgh, EH4 3DS, tel: 0131 624 6256/6259/6261, fax: 0131 315 2963, e-mail: publications@nationalgalleries.org

Publications list:
Available online and in print

Access to staff:
Contact by letter, by telephone and by e-mail
Hours: Mon to Sun, 1000 to 1700

Access to building, collection or gallery:
No prior appointment required
Hours: Mon to Sun, 1000 to 1700

Access for disabled people:
Access to all public areas, toilet facilities

Also at:
Duff House
   Banff, Banffshire, AB45 2SX; tel: 01261 818181; fax: 01261 818181; e-mail: duff.house@aberdeenshire.gov.uk; website: http://www.duffhouse.com
National Gallery of Scotland
   The Mound, Edinburgh, EH2 2EL; tel: 0131 624 6200; fax: 0131 220 0917; e-mail: nginfo@nationalgalleries.org; website: http://www.nationalgalleries.org
Paxton House
   Berwick-upon-Tweed, Berwickshire, TD15 1SZ; tel: 01289 386291; fax: 01289 386660; e-mail: info@paxtonhouse.com; website: http://www.paxtonhouse.co.uk
Scottish National Gallery of Modern Art
   75 Belford Road, Edinburgh, EH4 3DR; tel: 0131 624 6200; fax: 0131 343 2802; e-mail: gmainfo@nationalgalleries.org; website: http://www.nationalgalleries.org
Scottish National Portrait Gallery
   1 Queen Street, Edinburgh, EH2 1JD; tel: 0131 624 6200; fax: 0131 558 3691; e-mail: pginfo@nationalgalleries.org; website: http://www.nationalgalleries.org
The Dean Gallery
   73 Belford Road, Edinburgh, EH4 3DS; tel: 0131 624 6200; fax: 0131 343 2802; e-mail: deaninfo@nationalgalleries.org; website: http://www.nationalgalleries.org

NATIONAL GALLERY

Technical Library, Scientific Department, Trafalgar Square, London, WC2N 5DN

Tel: 020 7747 2400 ext 2829
Fax: 020 7839 3897

Website:
http://www.nationalgallery.org.uk

Enquiries:
Enquiries to: Technical Librarian
Direct tel: 020 7747 2829

Founded:
1950

Organisation type and purpose:
National government body, museum, art gallery, research organisation.
Art museum departmental library. Non-Governmental Departmental Body.

Subject coverage:
Materials, techniques and history of painting, particularly of European easel painting from c. 1300 to 1900, scientific examination of works of art, climate control for works of art, safe exhibition and storage conditions.

Museum or gallery collection, archive, or library special collection:
Eastlake Collection of early books and manuscripts on materials and techniques of painting, and other arts and crafts (part)

Printed publications:
National Gallery Technical Bulletin (£19.95, published by the National Gallery with contributions from the Scientific and Conservation Departments, annually)
Order printed publications from: National Gallery Company Limited
St Vincent House, 30 Orange Street, London, WC2H 7HH, tel: 020 7281 9080

Publications list:
Available online and in print

Access to staff:
Contact by letter, by telephone and by fax
Hours: Mon to Fri, 0930 to 1730
Special comments: No enquiries in person.

Access to building, collection or gallery:
National Gallery hours, dailiy, 1000 to 1800 except Wed, 1000 to 2100

Access for disabled people:
Lift
Hours: Mon to Fri, 1000 to 1730

NATIONAL GAS ARCHIVE, THE

Unit 1, Europa Court, Europa Boulevard, Warrington, WA5 7TN

Tel: 01925 425740
Fax: 01925 425748
E-mail: archive@uk.ngrid.com

Website:
http://www.gasarchive.org
History of gas industry, scope of collections, facilities.

Enquiries:
Enquiries to: Archivist

Founded:
1995

Organisation type and purpose:
National organisation.

Subject coverage:
Gas history, technical and engineering history, chemical industry.

Non-library collection catalogue:
All or part available online, in-house and in print

Library catalogue:
All or part available in-house

continued overleaf

Access to staff:
Contact by letter, by telephone, by fax, by e-mail and via website. Appointment necessary.
Hours: Mon to Fri, 0900 to 1700

Access to building, collection or gallery:
Prior appointment required

Access for disabled people:
Parking provided, level entry, toilet facilities

Connections with:
National Grid

NATIONAL GERBIL SOCIETY

Acronym or abbreviation: NGS

373 Lynmouth Avenue, Morden, Surrey, SM4 4RY

Tel: 020 8241 8942
Fax: 0870 1600 845
E-mail: jackie@gerbils.co.uk

Website:
http://www.gerbils.co.uk
A broad range of information relating to the society, the care of gerbils and jirds, information of general interest relating to gerbils and jirds.

Enquiries:
Enquiries to: Honorary Secretary

Founded:
1970

Organisation type and purpose:
National organisation, membership association (membership is by subscription), present number of members: 80, suitable for ages: all.
To promote the keeping of gerbils and jirds as exhibition animals and as pets, and to promote education about gerbils and how to keep them.

Subject coverage:
Information on the keeping and healthcare etc of all species of gerbils and jirds.

Printed publications:
Newsletter (quarterly, members only)
Yearbook (members only)

Access to staff:
Contact by letter, by telephone and by e-mail
Hours: Telephone only, Mon to Fri, 1800 to 2200

NATIONAL GOVERNORS' ASSOCIATION

Acronym or abbreviation: NGA

2nd Floor, SBQ1, 29 Smallbrook Queensway, Birmingham, B5 4HG

Tel: 0121 643 5787
Fax: 0121 633 7141
E-mail: governorhq@nga.org.uk

Website:
http://www.nga.org.uk/
Information about National Governors' Association, its activities, conferences, members etc. Consultation documents and responses forum.

Enquiries:
Enquiries to: Administrator

Founded:
2006

Created by the merger of:
the National Governors' Council (NGC) and the National Association of School Governors (NASG)

Organisation type and purpose:
National organisation, membership association (membership is by qualification), voluntary organisation, registered charity (charity number 1070331), suitable for ages: nursery to 18.
The national voice for school governing bodies, members are local associations of governing bodies.
Promoting the education and welfare of our children and the high standards of our schools through the effectiveness of governing bodies.

Subject coverage:
Matters relating to school governance.

Printed publications:
Trigger packs for new governors

Access to staff:
Contact by letter, by telephone, by fax, by e-mail and via website
Hours: Mon to Fri, 0900 to 1700

NATIONAL GROUP ON HOMEWORKING

Acronym or abbreviation: NGH

Unit 26, 30–38 Dock Street, Leeds, West Yorkshire, LS10 1JF

Tel: 0113 245 4273
Fax: 0113 246 5616
E-mail: admin@ngh.org.uk

Website:
http://www.ngh.org.uk

Enquiries:
Enquiries to: Administration
Other contacts: Advice Worker for employment rights advice relating to homeworking.

Founded:
1984

Organisation type and purpose:
Membership association (membership is by subscription), voluntary organisation, consultancy, research organisation.
This is the only national organisation in the UK working on issues related to homeworking.
Campaigning and lobbying organisation, relating specifically to industrial homeworkers/outworkers in the UK.

Subject coverage:
Homeworking, outworking and related issues.

Information services:
Available, tel: 0800 174095

Museum or gallery collection, archive, or library special collection:
Books on homeworking, other research information, photographs of homeworkers

Trade and statistical information:
Rates of pay and conditions of homeworkers in the United Kingdom, research, reports and other information.

Printed publications:
Briefing Papers (free)
Homework employment guides and information leaflets (free)
Reports
Bibliography of publications on homeworking

Publications list:
Available online and in print

Access to staff:
Contact by letter, by telephone, by fax, by e-mail and via website. Appointment necessary.
Hours: Mon to Fri, 0930 to 1700

Part of:
European and international network on homeworking

NATIONAL HAIRDRESSERS' FEDERATION

Acronym or abbreviation: NHF

One Abbey Court, Fraser Road, Priory Business Park, Bedford, MK44 3WH

Tel: 0845 345 6500
Fax: 01234 838875
E-mail: enquiries@nhf.info

Enquiries:
Enquiries to: General Secretary

Founded:
1942

Organisation type and purpose:
National organisation, trade association (membership is by subscription), present number of members: 7500, service industry.
Advance, defend, promote, protect and represent the interests of hairdressing salon owners in every possible way.

Subject coverage:
Matters affecting hairdressers' employment, independent contractors in salons, management of hairdressing business.

Printed publications:
Chain Renting in Hairdressing Salons
Independent Contractor Agreements
Headline News (6 times a year)
Setting Up Your Own Salon

Access to staff:
Contact by letter, by telephone, by fax and by e-mail. Appointment necessary.
Hours: Mon to Fri, 0900 to 1700

Access to building, collection or gallery:
No access other than to staff

Affiliated to:
Coiffure Europe
Godierserf 400 Huizen, PO Box 212, Huizen, 1270 AE Huizen, The Netherlands; tel: 00 31 35 525 9200; fax: 00 31 35 526 3786
Organisation Mondiale de la Coiffure
1–3 Place de la Bourse, F75082, Paris, Cedex 02, France; tel: 00 33 1 42 61 59 09; fax: 00 33 1 42 61 66 83; e-mail: omcoif@wanadoo.fr

NATIONAL HAMSTER COUNCIL

Acronym or abbreviation: NHC

PO Box 4, Llandovery, SA20 0ZH

Tel: 01550 720127
E-mail: peter@towyvale.com

Website:
http://www.hamsters-uk.org
Information on hamster keeping, details of NHC affiliated clubs, details of forthcoming shows.

Enquiries:
Enquiries to: Secretary
Direct tel: 01793 764450
Direct e-mail: rosiehams@yahoo.co.uk

Founded:
1949

Organisation type and purpose:
Membership association.
Governing body of the hamster fancy in the UK.
Represents the interests of all concerned with the keeping, exhibiting and/or breeding of all species of hamsters.

Subject coverage:
Hamsters.

Access to staff:
Contact by letter, by telephone, by e-mail and via website
Hours: Mon to Fri, 0900 to 1700

NATIONAL HEART FORUM

Acronym or abbreviation: NHF

Tavistock House South, Tavistock Square, London, WC1H 9LG

Tel: 020 7383 7638
Fax: 020 7387 2799
E-mail: nhf-post@heartforum.org.uk

Website:
http://www.heartforum.org.uk

Enquiries:
Enquiries to: Administrative Co-ordinator
Direct e-mail: dan.french@heartforum.org.uk
Other contacts: Deputy Chief Executive (for press, media, general)

Founded:
1989

Formerly called:
National Forum for the Prevention of Coronary
Heart Disease

Organisation type and purpose:
Membership association (membership is by
election or invitation), present number of
members: 50 organisations, registered charity
(charity number 803286).

Subject coverage:
Influencing the prevention of heart disease and
associated chronic diseases

Information services:
Free weekly e-news briefing service by
subscription: e-mail briefings@heartforum.org.uk

Printed publications:
Annual Review (free)
At Least Five a Day: Strategies to increase
  vegetable and fruit consumption (£19.99)
Looking to the Future: Making coronary heart
  disease an epidemic of the past (£22.50)
Physical activity: An agenda for action (£5)
Preventing coronary heart disease: The role of
  antioxidants, vegetables and fruit (£19.99)
Preventing coronary heart disease in primary care:
  The way forward (£7.95)
Social Inequalities in CHD (£19.95)
Order printed publications from: Enquire at NHF
office for availability

Publications list:
Available in print

Access to staff:
Contact by letter, by telephone, by fax, by e-mail
and via website. Appointment necessary.
Hours: Mon to Fri, 0900 to 1730

Access to building, collection or gallery:
Appointment required

NATIONAL HERITAGE LIBRARY

313–315 Caledonian Road, London, N1 1DR

Tel: 020 7609 9639

Enquiries:
Enquiries to: Director

Founded:
1971

Organisation type and purpose:
Membership association (membership is by
subscription), suitable for ages: all.
A vast, comprehensive educational reference
collection covering every aspect of what there is to
see throughout the landscape and culture of the
British Isles.

Subject coverage:
Everything there is to see throughout the
landscape and culture of the British Isles: every
kind of arts, cultural, environmental, historical and
sporting site. Every facet of past and present social
history, including: education, social welfare, public
buildings, commerce, transport and travel,
industry both past and present, alternative
technology, religions, farming, historical buildings.

**Museum or gallery collection, archive, or library
special collection:**
Books and maps, and extensive fieldwork research
and photographic recording by the Founder-
Director since the 1960s including over 120,000
photographs in colour, recording a vast range of
sites, including many unique photographs of
buildings important in their country's social
history that have since been demolished

Non-library collection catalogue:
All or part available in-house

Library catalogue:
All or part available in-house

Printed publications:
Fieldguides covering the other countries and
  regions of the British Isles
Fieldguide to Wales
Fieldguide to Ireland

Access to staff:
Contact by letter. Appointment necessary.
Hours: Open by prior appointment

Access to building, collection or gallery:
Prior appointment required

Access for disabled people:
Parking provided, level entry

NATIONAL HERITAGE
MEMORIAL FUND

Acronym or abbreviation: NHMF

7 Holbein Place, London, SW1W 8NR

Tel: 020 7591 6000
Fax: 020 7591 6001
E-mail: enquire@hlf.org.uk

Website:
http://www.hlf.org.uk

Enquiries:
Enquiries to: Information Officer
Direct tel: 020 7591 6042/3/5

Founded:
1980

Organisation type and purpose:
Non-departmental public body.

Printed publications:
Application pack

Publications list:
Available online and in print

Access to staff:
Contact by letter, by telephone, by fax, by e-mail
and via website. Appointment necessary.
Hours: Mon to Fri, 0900 to 1730

Access to building, collection or gallery:
Prior appointment required
Hours: 0930 to 1730

Access for disabled people:
Parking provided, ramped entry, access to all
public areas, toilet facilities

NATIONAL HOME
IMPROVEMENT COUNCIL

Acronym or abbreviation: NHIC

Carlyle House, 235 Vauxhall Bridge Road, London,
SW1V 1EJ

Tel: 020 7828 8230
Fax: 020 7828 0667
E-mail: info@nhic.org.uk

Website:
http://www.nhic.org.uk

Enquiries:
Enquiries to: Director

Founded:
1975

Organisation type and purpose:
Advisory body, trade association, research
organisation, consultancy.

Subject coverage:
Condition of housing stock, market research on
home improvement, attitude research to home
improvement.

Library catalogue:
All or part available online

Access to staff:
Contact by letter, by telephone, by fax and by e-
mail
Hours: Mon to Fri, 0900 to 1700

Established the:
NHIC Educational Trust in 1980 to further its aims

NATIONAL HOSPITAL
DEVELOPMENT FOUNDATION

Formal name: The National Hospital for Neurology
and Neurosurgery Development Foundation

National Hospital, PO Box 123, Queen Square,
London, WC1N 3BG

Tel: 020 7829 8724
Fax: 020 7676 2068
E-mail: theresa.dauncey@uclh.nhs.uk

Enquiries:
Enquiries to: Director

Founded:
1984

Organisation type and purpose:
Registered charity (charity number 290173).

Subject coverage:
Neurology and neurosurgery.

Access to staff:
Contact by letter, by telephone, by fax, by e-mail
and via website
Hours: Mon to Fri, 0900 to 1700

NATIONAL HOUSEWIVES
ASSOCIATION

Acronym or abbreviation: NHA

30 Tollgate, Bretton, Peterborough,
Cambridgeshire, PE3 9XA

Tel: 01733 333138

Enquiries:
Enquiries to: Chairman

Founded:
1973

Organisation type and purpose:
National organisation, voluntary organisation.
Aims to put forward the voice of the housewife on
matters that are of concern to them. Campaigning
for Elderly Residential Homes not to be closed.

Subject coverage:
Consumer affairs.

Printed publications:
Newsletter to members
Special Reports as required

Access to staff:
Contact by letter and by telephone
Hours: Mon to Fri, 0900 to 1700

Links with:
Consumers in European Community Group (This
is being taken over by NCC)
London Food Commission
Ministry of Agriculture, Fisheries and Food
National Consumer Council
Potato Marketing Board
Soil Association
Womens Farming Union

NATIONAL HOUSING
FEDERATION

Acronym or abbreviation: NHF

Lion Court, 25 Procter Street, London WC1V 6NY

Tel: 020 7067 1010
Fax: 020 7067 1011

Website:
http://www.housing.org.uk

Enquiries:
Enquiries to: Communications Officer
Direct e-mail: NickF@housing.org.uk

Founded:
1935

Organisation type and purpose:
Voluntary organisation.
Central representative body for social housing
providers in England.

continued overleaf

Subject coverage:
Housing associations, research and training.

Printed publications:
Directory of Members
Training brochure
A large range of publications on social housing including:
Equality in housing: a code of practice
Maintenance and the Law: a guide for housing associations
Neighbourhood renewal funding streams 2002: at a glance guide
Race equality: a framework for review and action
Countdown to rent restructuring: seven steps to implementation
A question-and-answer guide for tenants: the future of housing association rents

Publications list:
Available online and in print

East Midlands Office:
National Housing Federation
2A High Street, Wellingborough, Northampton, NN8 4HR; tel: 01933 440191; fax: 01933 224499

North West Region:
National Housing Federation
City Point, 701 Chester Road, Stretford, Manchester, M32 0RW; tel: 0161 848 8132; fax: 0161 858 8134

South East Region:
National Housing Federation
3rd Floor, Phoenix Building, 32 West Street, Brighton, East Sussex, BN1 2RT; tel: 01273 777445; fax: 01273 721807

NATIONAL INFORMATION FORUM

33 Highshore Road, London, SE15 5AF

Tel: 020 7708 5943

Website:
http://www.nif.org.uk

Enquiries:
Enquiries to: Director

Founded:
1981

Organisation type and purpose:
Advisory body, membership association (membership is by election or invitation), voluntary organisation, registered charity (charity number 1099335).
Encourages provision of information to disabled people and others seriously disadvantaged by lack of information.

Subject coverage:
Provision of information to disabled people and carers and others disadvantaged by lack of information, particularly asylum seekers and refugees and care leavers.

Information services:
Via website

Printed publications:
Alf Morris (biography)
Order printed publications from: Postal address

Publications list:
Available in print

Access to staff:
Contact by letter and by telephone
Hours: Mon to Fri, 0900 to 1700
Special comments: Staff cannot respond to individual problems.

Access to building, collection or gallery:
No public access

NATIONAL INSTITUTE FOR BIOLOGICAL STANDARDS AND CONTROL

Acronym or abbreviation: NIBSC

Blanche Lane, South Mimms, Potters Bar, Hertfordshire, EN6 3QG

Tel: 01707 641000
Fax: 01707 646845
E-mail: library@nibsc.ac.uk

Website:
http://www.nibsc.ac.uk

Enquiries:
Enquiries to: Information Services Manager
Direct e-mail: abrewer@nibsc.ac.uk

Organisation type and purpose:
Research organisation.
National control and standardisation laboratory for biologicals used in medicine; operates as one of eight European control authorities for testing of biologicals.

Subject coverage:
Standardisation and control of antisera, bacterial and viral vaccines, blood products, enzymes and hormones, AIDS, biochemistry, chemistry, haematology, endocrinology, microbiology, immunobiology, virology, electronmicroscopy.

Museum or gallery collection, archive, or library special collection:
Publications on biological standards

Library catalogue:
All or part available online

Printed publications:
Annual Report
Catalogue of Biological Standards and Reference Materials
Corporate Plan
Processing Biological Reference Materials

Access to staff:
Appointment necessary.
Hours: Mon to Fri, 0900 to 1700

Funded by:
Department of Health

NATIONAL INSTITUTE FOR CAREERS EDUCATION AND COUNSELLING

Acronym or abbreviation: NICEC

Sheraton House, Castle Park, Cambridge, CB3 0AX

Tel: 01223 460277
Fax: 01223 311708
E-mail: nicec@crac.org.uk

Website:
http://www.crac.org.uk/nicec

Enquiries:
Enquiries to: Chair

Founded:
1975

Organisation type and purpose:
Registered charity (charity number 313164), consultancy, research organisation.
Careers.
To develop theory, enhance practice and inform policy in the field of careers.

Subject coverage:
Theory, policy and practice in careers guidance and career development.

Museum or gallery collection, archive, or library special collection:
CRAC/NICEC library is now held at the Library, University of London Institute of Education, 20 Bedford Way, London WC1H 0AL and at the Library, University of Derby, Kedleston Road, Derby DE22 1GB

Library catalogue:
All or part available online

Printed publications:
NICEC Journal (3 times a year, subscription £27, international £40)
NICEC Project Reports
CRAC/NICEC Conference Briefings (free with sae)

NICEC Briefings (free with sae)
NICEC Research Reports Consult online catalogue

Publications list:
Available online and in print

Access to staff:
Contact by letter, by telephone, by fax and by e-mail
Hours: Mon to Fri, 0900 to 1700

Access to building, collection or gallery:
Prior appointment required

Sponsored by:
Careers Research and Advisory Centre (CRAC)

NATIONAL INSTITUTE FOR MEDICAL RESEARCH

Formal name: MRC National Institute for Medical Research
Acronym or abbreviation: NIMR

The Ridgeway, Mill Hill, London, NW7 1AA

Tel: 020 8816 2228
Fax: 020 8816 2230
E-mail: library@nimr.mrc.ac.uk

Website:
http://www.nimr.mrc.ac.uk
Summaries of research activities of each division, publications, library services, essays on biomedical topics

Enquiries:
Enquiries to: Librarian

Founded:
1913

Organisation type and purpose:
Research organisation.
Research Council Institute.
To undertake a broad spectrum of basic medical research.

Subject coverage:
Molecular biology, biochemistry, parasitology, virology, neuroscience, embryology, immunology, cell biology, developmental biology, basic biomedical sciences, structural biology, bioinformatics.

Museum or gallery collection, archive, or library special collection:
NIMR Archives
MRC Publications

Library catalogue:
All or part available online

Printed publications:
Influenza Bibliography
Mill Hill Essays
Research Opportunities

Access to staff:
Contact by letter, by telephone and by e-mail.
Appointment necessary. Access for members only.
Letter of introduction required.
Hours: Mon to Fri, 0900 to 1700

Access to building, collection or gallery:
Prior appointment required
Special comments: Intending visitors should write, requesting permission from the Institute Director.

Constituent part of:
Medical Research Council (MRC)
20 Park Crescent, London; tel: 020 7636 5422; fax: 020 7436 6179

NATIONAL INSTITUTE OF ADULT CONTINUING EDUCATION (ENGLAND AND WALES)

Acronym or abbreviation: NIACE

21 De Montfort Street, Leicester, LE1 7GE

Tel: 0116 204 4200
Fax: 0116 285 4514
E-mail: information@niace.org.uk

Website:
http://www.niace.org.uk
Information on National Institute of Adult
Continuing Education publications and
conferences, etc.

Enquiries:
Enquiries to: Librarian
Direct tel: 0116 204 4208
Direct e-mail: helenb@niace.org.uk

Organisation type and purpose:
National organisation, voluntary organisation,
registered charity (charity number 2603322),
suitable for ages: 19+, consultancy.

Subject coverage:
Adult and continuing education, community
education, education for the disadvantaged, the
unemployed and the elderly.

**Museum or gallery collection, archive, or library
special collection:**
Collection of local education authority policy
documents

Library catalogue:
All or part available in-house

Printed publications:
Journal of Access and Credit Studies (journal, twice
a year)
Marking Time: The NIACE survey on adult
participation in learning 1999 (Tuckett A, Sargant
N)
Adults Learning (journal, 10 times a year)
Studies in the Education of Adults (journal, twice a
year)
Adult Learning Yearbook 2001–2002

Publications list:
Available online and in print

Access to staff:
Contact by letter, by telephone, by e-mail and via
website
Hours: Mon to Fri, 0900 to 1700

Access to building, collection or gallery:
Prior appointment required
Hours: Mon-Fri 0900- 1700

Access for disabled people:
Level entry, toilet facilities
Special comments: Lift to library on third floor

Associated body:
Basic Skills Agency

Welsh office:
NIACE Dysgu Cymru
35 Cathedral Road, Cardiff, CF11 9HB; tel: 029
2037 0900; fax: 029 2037 0909; e-mail: enquiries@
niacedc.org.uk

NATIONAL INSTITUTE OF APPLIED POLAROLOGY RESEARCH

Acronym or abbreviation: NIAPR

6 Beechvale, Hillview Road, Woking, Surrey, GU22
7NS

Enquiries:
Enquiries to: Director of Research

Founded:
1938

Organisation type and purpose:
Advisory body, research organisation.

Subject coverage:
Applied research in polarology.

Printed publications:
Reprints of research papers, following journal
publication

Access to staff:
Contact by letter
Hours: Mon to Fri, 0900 to 1700

Associated with:
British Polarographic Research Institute
Institute of Pure Polarology Research

National Centre for Polarological and
Polarographic Operational Research
Polarographic Society
UK Polarosciences Research Establishment
Department of Pure and Applied Polarology

Parent body:
British Polarological Research Society (BPRS)
6 Beechvale, Hillview Road, Woking, Surrey,
GU22 7NS

NATIONAL INSTITUTE OF CARPET AND FLOORLAYERS

Acronym or abbreviation: NICF

4c St Mary's Place, The Lace Market, Nottingham,
NG1 1PH

Tel: 0115 958 3077
Fax: 0115 941 2238
E-mail: info@nicfltd.org.uk

Website:
http://www.nicfltd.org.uk

Founded:
1979

Organisation type and purpose:
Trade association.

Subject coverage:
Carpets of all types, carpet fitting, resilient
floorcoverings, wood, laminate.

**Museum or gallery collection, archive, or library
special collection:**
Carpet manufacturers, their products and types

Access to staff:
Contact by letter, by telephone, by fax, by e-mail
and via website
Hours: Mon to Fri, 0900 to 1700

NATIONAL INSTITUTE OF CONDUCTIVE EDUCATION

Acronym or abbreviation: NICE

Cannon Hill House, 14 Russell Road, Moseley,
Birmingham, B13 8RD

Tel: 0121 449 1569
Fax: 0121 449 1611
E-mail: foundation@conductive-education.org.uk

Website:
http://www.conductive-education.org.uk

Enquiries:
Enquiries to: Librarian

Founded:
1986

Organisation type and purpose:
Membership association (membership is by
subscription), registered charity (charity number
295873).

Subject coverage:
Conductive education, Hungary, special
educational needs, Parkinson's disease, cerebal
palsy, stroke, head injury, disability issues.

**Museum or gallery collection, archive, or library
special collection:**
Conductive Education – all aspects and all media

Non-library collection catalogue:
All or part available in-house

Printed publications:
Recent Advances in Conductive Education
(journal, 2 times a year)
The Conductor (magazine, quarterly)
Adult Conductive Education (Brown M and
Mikula Toth A, pub Stanley Thornes Publishing,
£18.50 plus £1.28 (p&p)
A Different Outlook (Read J, £5 plus £1.25 p&p)
Conductive Education 1987–1992: the transitional
years (Read J, £6.95 plus £1.10 p&p)
Dina: A Mother Practices Conductive Education
(English Edition, Akos K and M, £11.95 plus
£1.10 p&p)

Last year in Jerusalem (Sutton A, £5 plus £1.25
p&p)
Memoirs of the Beginning of Conductive Pedagogy
and András Peto (Forrai J, £10.95 plus £1.39 p&p)
Maria Hari on Conductive Pedagogy (Maguire, G.
and Sutton, A. £10 plus £1.00 p&p)
Looking Back and Looking Forwards (Maguire, G.
and Nanton, R. £10 plus £1.00 p&p)
Order printed publications from: Librarian

Publications list:
Available online and in print

Access to staff:
Contact by letter, by telephone, by fax, by e-mail,
in person and via website. Appointment necessary.
Non-members charged.
Hours: Mon to Fri, 0900 to 1700

Access for disabled people:
Parking provided, level entry, access to all public
areas, toilet facilities

NATIONAL INSTITUTE OF ECONOMIC AND SOCIAL RESEARCH

Acronym or abbreviation: NIESR

2 Dean Trench Street, Smith Square, London, SW1P
3HE

Tel: 020 7222 7665
Fax: 020 7654 1900
E-mail: library@niesr.ac.uk

Website:
http://www.niesr.ac.uk
Staff and publications information, latest quarterly
review overview, discussion papers in full text.

Enquiries:
Enquiries to: Librarian
Direct tel: 020 7654 1907
Other contacts: Communications Officer (for press/
publication enquiries)

Founded:
1938

Organisation type and purpose:
Research organisation.

Subject coverage:
Economic conditions in the United Kingdom and
the world; economic forecasting; education and
training.

Information services:
For NIESR research staff only

**Museum or gallery collection, archive, or library
special collection:**
Runs of international and foreign statistics difficult
to find elsewhere

Library catalogue:
All or part available in-house

Printed publications:
Annual Report
Monographs, various series
National Institute Economic Review (quarterly)

Publications list:
Available online

Access to staff:
Contact by e-mail. Appointment necessary. Letter
of introduction required.
Hours: Mon to Fri, 0930 to 1730

NATIONAL INSTITUTE OF MEDICAL HERBALISTS LIMITED

Acronym or abbreviation: NIMH

Elm House, 54 Mary Arches Street, Exeter, Devon,
EX4 3BA

Tel: 01392 426022
Fax: 01392 498963
E-mail: info@nimh.org.uk

Website:
http://www.nimh.org.uk

continued overleaf

Enquiries:
Enquiries to: Information Officer

Founded:
1864

Organisation type and purpose:
Professional body, training organisation, research organisation.

Subject coverage:
Herbs, use of herbs in treatment of disease, how medical herbalists work, training in medical herbalism, pharmacology of plant medicines.

Printed publications:
European Journal of Herbal Medicine
Caring Profession (leaflet)
Register of Practitioners (annually, send sae)

Access to staff:
Contact by letter, by telephone, by fax and by e-mail
Hours: Mon, Fri, 1000 to 1700; Tue, Wed, Thu, 0930 to 1530

NATIONAL INSULATION ASSOCIATION LIMITED

Acronym or abbreviation: NIA

2 Vimy Court, Vimy Road, Leighton Buzzard, Beds, LU7 1FG

Tel: 08451 636363
Fax: 01525 854918
E-mail: info@nationalinsulationassociation.org.uk

Website:
http://www.nationalinsulationassociation.org.uk/

Enquiries:
Enquiries to: Press Officer (Evolution PR Ltd)
Direct e-mail: nia@evolution-pr.co.uk

Founded:
1975

Organisation type and purpose:
Trade association (membership is by subscription), present number of members: 130.

Subject coverage:
Cavity wall insulation; loft insulation; draught proofing; insulated thermal linings

Trade and statistical information:
United Kingdom injected cavity wall insulation market.

Printed publications:
Advisory literature (free)
Register of members

Access to staff:
Contact by letter, by telephone, by fax, by e-mail and via website
Hours: Mon to Fri, 0900 to 1700

NATIONAL JOINT COUNCIL FOR THE MOTOR VEHICLE RETAIL AND REPAIR INDUSTRY

Acronym or abbreviation: NJCMVR&RI

201 Great Portland Street, London, W1W 5AB

Tel: 01788 538309
Fax: 01788 538335

Enquiries:
Enquiries to: Secretary
Direct tel: 01892 664353
Direct e-mail: coryton@supanet.com
Other contacts: Joint Secretary representing the trade unions interests.

Founded:
1943

Organisation type and purpose:
Membership association (membership is by qualification), service industry.
Negotiating and dispute resolving body.

Subject coverage:
Terms and conditions of employment in the industry.

Printed publications:
NJC Handbook
NJC Resolution
Order printed publications from: Business Stationery, Retail Motor Industry Federation
Unit C, Brewery Industrial Estate, Wenlock Road, London, N1 7TA, tel: 020 7307 3429, fax: 020 7490 4197

Access to staff:
Contact by letter, by telephone and by fax
Hours: Mon to Fri, 0900 to 1700

NATIONAL KIDNEY FEDERATION

6 Stanley Street, Worksop, Nottinghamshire, S81 7HX

Tel: 01909 487795
Fax: 01909 481723
E-mail: nkf@kidney.org.uk

Website:
http://www.kidney.org.uk

Enquiries:
Enquiries to: Chairman
Other contacts: Chief Executive

Founded:
1978

Organisation type and purpose:
National organisation, membership association (membership is by subscription), present number of members: 18,000, voluntary organisation, registered charity (charity number 278616).

Subject coverage:
Care of persons suffering from kidney failure – medical, social and psychological aspects, treatment options, availability of renal services, issues in transplantation, representation of patients' interests to government.

Library catalogue:
All or part available in-house and in print

Printed publications:
Adult Polycystic Kidney Disease
Anaemia in Kidney Failure
Introduction to Haemodialysis
Introduction to Peritoneal Dialysis
Newsletter (quarterly)
Role of the National Kidney Federation
Sexual Relationships in Kidney Failure
Skin Care in Renal Transplant Patients

Publications list:
Available online and in print

Access to staff:
Contact by letter, by telephone, by fax, by e-mail, in person and via website
Hours: Mon to Fri, 0900 to 1700

Affiliated to:
CEAPIR
European Kidney Federation (CEAPIR)

NATIONAL LANDLORDS' ASSOCIATION

Acronym or abbreviation: NLA

22–26 Albert Embankment, London, SE1 7TS

Tel: 0870 241 0471
Fax: 0871 247 7535
E-mail: mail@landlords.org.uk

Website:
http://www.landlords.org.uk/
Information for the landlord of residential property.

Enquiries:
Enquiries to: Office Manager

Founded:
1973

Organisation type and purpose:
Trade association (membership is by subscription), voluntary organisation.
To protect and promote the interests of the individual private landlord of residential property.

Subject coverage:
Landlord and tenant matters, residential property, the 1988 and 1996 Housing Acts and 1977 Rent Act.

Printed publications:
Journal
The UK Landlord
Various information sheets for members

Access to staff:
Contact by letter, by telephone and via website.
Access for members only. All charged.
Hours: Mon to Fri, 0900 to 1700

NATIONAL LIBRARY OF SCOTLAND

George IV Bridge, Edinburgh, EH1 1EW

Tel: 0131 623 3700
Fax: 0131 623 3701
E-mail: enquiries@nls.uk

Website:
http://www.nls.uk
http://www.nls.ac.uk/catalogues/index.html
Library catalogue and other online resources.

Enquiries:
Enquiries to: Head of Reference Services
Other contacts: Director of Special Collections for access to manuscript, rare book, music and map collections.

Founded:
1682

Organisation type and purpose:
National government body.
British legal deposit library since 1710.
To acquire, preserve and make available the printed and manuscript record of Scotland's culture.

Subject coverage:
The national reference collection in Scotland of printed material in English and for the humanities; all European and Western languages. The foreign scientific periodicals of the Royal Society of Edinburgh were recently taken over to complement British scientific periodicals received by legal deposit. Extensive coverage of printed materials of Scottish relevance. Manuscript collection relates mainly to Scottish history and literature and activities of Scots, at home and abroad.
Map Library: extensive collection of current and recent atlases and maps of all areas; large historical collection, especially maps of Scotland.
Music collection: classical music of all periods, historical Scottish collection, popular music received by legal deposit.

Museum or gallery collection, archive, or library special collection:
Astorga Collection (Hispanic)
Balfour Collection (Handel)
Birkbeck Collection (printing and typography)
Blaikie Collection (Jacobite movement)
Blair Collection (Scottish Gaelic and Celtic)
Blairs Collection (theology)
British Architectural Library of unpublished manuscripts in microform
Bute Collection (English plays)
Campbell of Islay (Scottish Gaelic and Celtic)
Christie's Pictorial Archive in microform
Combe Collection (phrenology)
Cowan Collection (theology)
Crawford Collection (German theses and programmata)
Early Scottish Book Collections (Rosebery, Lauriston Castle, Ferguson)
Dieterichs Collection (early German theses and programmata)
Dowden Collection (theology)

Early English Newspapers in microform
Ferguson Collection (early Scottish books)
Glen Collection (Scottish music)
Graham Brown Collection (Alps and
  mountaineering)
Gray Collection (theology)
Haxton Collection (theology)
Hew Morison Collection (Scottish Gaelic and
  Celtic)
Hopkinson Collections (Berlioz and Verdi)
Incunabula Collection
Ingli's Collection (Scottish music)
Jolly Collection (theology)
Labour History Collection
Lauriston Castle Collection (early Scottish books)
Lloyd Collection (Alps and mountaineering)
Lyle Collection (ships and shipping)
Macadam Collection (baking and confectionery)
McCurdy Collection (Leonardo da Vinci)
McDonald Collection (colour slides of town
  planning)
Maclure Collection (French Revolution)
Maitland Thomson (English plays)
Marischal Collection (Scottish maps)
Murdoch Henderson Collection (Scottish music)
Newman Collection (road-books)
Ossian Collection
Protestant Institute Collection (theology)
Rosebery Collection (early Scottish books)
Tait Collection (civil engineering)
Thomason Tracts Collection in microform
Thorkelin Collection (Scandinavian and Icelandic)
Townley Collection (7500 postcards on early 20th
  century topography and railways)
Warden Collection (Arctic and Antarctic
  exploration)

Non-library collection catalogue:
All or part available online and in print

Library catalogue:
All or part available online

Printed publications:
Annual Report
Catalogue of Manuscripts vols 1–8
Catalogues of exhibitions

Microform publications:
Catalogue of Manuscripts vol. 1 on microfiche

Publications list:
Available online

Access to staff:
Contact by letter, by fax, by e-mail, in person and
via website
Hours: Main Reading Room: Mon, Tue, Thu, Fri,
0930 to 2030; Wed, 1000 to 2030; Sat, 0930 to 1300
Map Library: Mon, Tue, Thu, Fri, 0930 to 1700;
Wed, 1000 to 1700; Sat, 0930 to 1300
Special comments: Certain restrictions apply to
undergraduate and school students.

Other addresses:
Map Library
  33 Salisbury Place, Edinburgh, EH9 1SL; tel: 0131
  226 4531
National Library of Scotland Inter-Library Services
  33 Salisbury Place, Edinburgh, EH9 1SL; tel: 0131
  226 4531

NATIONAL LIBRARY OF WALES

Llyfrgell Genedlaethol Cymru, Aberystwyth,
Ceredigion, SY23 3BU

Tel: 01970 632800
Fax: 01970 615709
E-mail: holi@llgc.org.uk

Website:
http://www.llgc.org.uk
Extensive details of services and collections, virtual
exhibitions and some access to databases.

Enquiries:
Enquiries to: Librarian
Direct tel: 01970 632805
Direct fax: 01970 632886
Direct e-mail: mdn@llgc.org.uk

Founded:
1907

Organisation type and purpose:
National government body.
Entitled to privileges under the Copyright Acts.

Subject coverage:
General reference material, specialising in printed,
manuscript and graphic material relating to Wales
and other Celtic countries.

**Museum or gallery collection, archive, or library
special collection:**
Archives of Welsh Churches
Arthuriana
Bourdillon Collection of medieval French romance
Court of Great Sessions records
Egyptology Collection
Estate records
Geoff Charles Photographic Collection
Gregynog and other private presses
H I Bell Collection on papyrology
Howell Lloyd Davies Collection of dictionaries and
  grammars
Papers of eminent Welsh scholars and literary
  figures
Political papers of Lloyd George, Clement Davies,
  Desmond Donnelly, James Griffiths, etc
Pre-1858 Welsh ecclesiastical probate records
Sidney Hartland Collection of ethnology and
  folklore
Sir John Williams Collection
Thomas Stanford Collections of incunabula
  including Euclid
Tithe maps relating to Wales

Printed publications:
A Bibliography of Wales
Handlist of Manuscripts in the National Library of
  Wales
National Library of Wales Journal
Order printed publications from: Marketing
Department, The National Library of Wales
at the same address, tel: 01970 632858, fax: 01970
615709

Publications list:
Available online and in print

Access to staff:
Contact by letter, by telephone, by fax, by e-mail
and in person
Hours: Mon to Fri, 0930 to 1800; Sat, 0930 to 1700
Special comments: Closed Bank holidays. Closed
first full week in Oct.

NATIONAL LIFE STORIES

Acronym or abbreviation: NLS

British Library Sound Archive, 96 Euston Road,
London, NW1 2DB

Tel: 020 7412 7404
Fax: 020 7412 7441
E-mail: nsa-nlsc@bl.uk

Website:
http://www.bl.uk/nsa
Information about Sound Archive, including oral
history collections and National Life Story
Collection and publications.
http://www.cadensa.bl.uk
Catalogue of all Sound Archive collections,
including oral history and National Life Story
collections.

Enquiries:
Enquiries to: Administrator
Other contacts: Oral History Curator

Founded:
1987

Organisation type and purpose:
Registered charity (charity number 327571),
research organisation.
Collecting and archiving oral histories.

Subject coverage:
Oral history.

**Museum or gallery collection, archive, or library
special collection:**
C409 City Lives
C410 Living Memory of the Jewish Community
C466 Artists' Lives
C467 Architects' Lives
C468 Fawcett Collection
C532 Lives in Steel
C736 Legal Lives
C821 Food From Source to Sale Point
C872 Book Trade Lives
C960 Crafts' Lives
C963 Lives in the Oil Industry
C1007 An Oral History of the Post Office
C1015 Oral History of Wolff Olins
C1029 Down to Earth: An Oral History of British
  Horticulture
C1173 Oral History of British Theatre Design
C1276 Authors' Lives
C1316 The Legacy of the English Stage Company

Non-library collection catalogue:
All or part available online

Library catalogue:
All or part available online

Printed publications:
City Lives (C. Courtney and P. Thompson,
Methuen)
Voices of the Holocaust Education Pack (booklet
  and tapes)
Order printed publications from: British Library
bookshop; tel. 020 7412 7735

Electronic and video publications:
Lives in Steel (CD-ROM and tape)

Access to staff:
Contact by letter, by telephone, by fax and by e-
mail. Appointment necessary.
Hours: Mon to Fri, 0900 to 1700

Access for disabled people:
Ramped entry, access to all public areas, toilet
facilities
Special comments: Parking spaces for disabled
people are in Midland Road.

NATIONAL LITERACY TRUST

Acronym or abbreviation: NLT

68 South Lambeth Road, London, SW8 1RL

Tel: 020 7587 1842
Fax: 020 7587 1411
E-mail: contact@literacytrust.org.uk

Website:
http://www.literacytrust.org.uk

Founded:
1993

Organisation type and purpose:
Voluntary organisation, registered charity.
Raise literacy standards and encourage more
reading and writing for pleasure.

Subject coverage:
Literacy news and initiatives; policy summaries
and responses; research summaries

Printed publications:
Support materials for professionals
Order printed publications from: via website

Electronic and video publications:
Research papers and policy responses (online)

Publications list:
Available online

Access to staff:
Contact by letter, by telephone, by fax, by e-mail
and via website
Hours: Mon to Fri, 0900 to 1700

Constituent bodies:
Reading Champions
  website: http://www.readingchampions.org.uk
Reading Connects
  website: http://www.readingconnects.org.uk
Reading is Fundamental, UK
  website: http://www.rif.org.uk

continued overleaf

Reading the Game
    website: http://www.readingthegame.org.uk
Talk To Your Baby
    website: http://www.talktoyourbaby.org.uk

NATIONAL LOTTERY COMMISSION

Acronym or abbreviation: NLC

101 Wigmore Street, London, W1U 1QU

Tel: 020 7016 3400
Fax: 020 7016 3401
E-mail: publicaffairs@natlotcomm.gov.uk

Website:
http://www.natlotcomm.gov.uk

Enquiries:
Enquiries to: Head of Communications
Direct e-mail: s.hanratty@natlotcomm.gov.uk

Founded:
1993

Formerly called:
Oflot (year of change 1999)

Organisation type and purpose:
National government body.
Non-departmental public body (NDPB).
Regulator of the National Lottery.

Subject coverage:
The National Lottery, Regulation, Gambling

Trade and statistical information:
Quarterly Lottery Sales Data, and Quarterly
    returns to good causes

Printed publications:
Annual Report, Operator Performance reports
Order printed publications from:
publicaffairs@natlotcomm.gov.uk

Electronic and video publications:
Research into under-16s lottery play, internet use
    and gambling behaviours. Research into
    women's gambling behaviours, and randomness
    of draw-based games.
Order electronic and video publications from:
www.natlotcomm.gov.uk; publicaffairs@
natlotcomm.gov.uk

Access to staff:
Contact by letter, by telephone, by fax, by e-mail,
in person and via website. Appointment necessary.
Hours: Mon to Fri, 0900 to 1700

Access for disabled people:
Access to all public areas, toilet facilities

Parent body:
DCMS
    2–4 Cockspur Street, London, SW1Y 5DH; tel:
    020 7211 6200; fax: 020 7211 6201; e-mail:
    enquiries@culture.gov.uk; website: http://www
    .culture.gov.uk

NATIONAL MARKET TRADERS' FEDERATION

Acronym or abbreviation: NMTF

Hampton House, Hawshaw Lane, Hoyland,
Barnsley, South Yorkshire, S74 0HA

Tel: 01226 749021
Fax: 01226 740329
E-mail: enquiries@nmtf.co.uk

Website:
http://www.nmtf.co.uk

Enquiries:
Enquiries to: Chief Executive Officer

Founded:
1899

Organisation type and purpose:
National organisation, trade association
(membership is by subscription), present number
of members: 34,000.

Subject coverage:
Retail markets in the UK; market law.

**Museum or gallery collection, archive, or library
special collection:**
Documents of the Royal Commission on Market
    Rights and Tolls (1891)

Printed publications:
Federation Newsletter (Fed News) (6 times a year,
    members)

Access to staff:
Contact by letter, by telephone, by fax, by e-mail
and via website
Hours: Mon to Fri, 0900 to 1700

Access to building, collection or gallery:
Hours: Mon to Fri, 0900 to 1700

Access for disabled people:
Parking provided, ramped entry, toilet facilities
Hours: Mon to Fri, 0900 to 1700

Affiliated to:
Retail Markets Alliance (RMA)
World Union of Wholesale Markets (WUWM)

NATIONAL MEDIATION CENTRE

Acronym or abbreviation: NMC

23 St James Gardens, Swansea, West Glamorgan,
SA1 6DY

Tel: 01792 469626
Fax: 01792 650642
E-mail: mediation@dispute.co.uk

Enquiries:
Enquiries to: Chief Executive

Founded:
1995

Organisation type and purpose:
International organisation, national organisation,
professional body, service industry, training
organisation.
Provider of mediation service.

Subject coverage:
Dispute resolution, mediation.

Access to staff:
Contact by letter, by telephone, by fax and by e-
mail
Hours: Mon to Fri, 0900 to 1700

NATIONAL MEMORIAL ARBORETUM

Acronym or abbreviation: NMA

Croxall Road, Alrewas, Burton-on-Trent,
Staffordshire, DE13 7AR

Tel: 01283 792333
Fax: 01283 792034
E-mail: info@thenma.org.uk

Website:
http://www.thenma.org.uk

Enquiries:
Enquiries to: Development Manager

Founded:
2001

Organisation type and purpose:
National organisation, registered charity (charity
number 1043992).

Subject coverage:
Tree planting, tree collections, Armed Service
contacts, educational visits, conference and events
facilities.

Special visitor services:
Group visits welcomed by prior arrangement

Education services:
School visits welcomed by prior arrangement

**Museum or gallery collection, archive, or library
special collection:**
FEPOW Memorial Building

Printed publications:
Guidebook, map, walks leaflets
Order printed publications from: tel. 01283 792333

Access to staff:
Contact by letter, by telephone, by fax, by e-mail,
in person and via website. Appointment necessary.
Hours: Daily, 0900 to 1700

Access to building, collection or gallery:
Hours: Daily, 0900 to 1700; closed Christmas Day

Access for disabled people:
Parking provided, level entry, toilet facilities

Constituent part of:
The Royal British Legion
    48 Pall Mall, London, SW1Y 5JY; tel: 020 7973
    7207

NATIONAL METEOROLOGICAL LIBRARY AND ARCHIVE

Acronym or abbreviation: Met Office Library

Fitzroy Road, Exeter, EX1 3PB

Tel: 01392 884841
Fax: 01392 885681
E-mail: metlib@metoffice.gov.uk

Website:
http://www.metoffice.com/corporate/library/index
.html

Enquiries:
Enquiries to: Information Officer
Other contacts: Archive Manager (tel. 01392 360987,
metarc@metoffice.gov.uk)

Founded:
1870

Organisation type and purpose:
National government body, learned society, public
library.
Specialist meterological records and publications.
To provide public access to official meterological
records and the comprehensive meterological
library.

Subject coverage:
Meteorology, climatology and most aspects of
atmospheric and related sciences; original weather
reports; summaries and published books, articles
and pamphlets; approximately 3m. items, from
16th century to date.

**Museum or gallery collection, archive, or library
special collection:**
Library and archive collections of the
    Meteorological Office; books, documents and
    photographs
Original weather records archived under the terms
    of Public Records Act
Rare and historical books and pamphlets on
    meteorology and climatology held in conjunction
    with the Royal Meteorological Society

Non-library collection catalogue:
All or part available online

Library catalogue:
All or part available online and in-house

Microform publications:
Microfiche available to read

Publications list:
Available online

Access to staff:
Contact by letter, by telephone, by fax and by e-
mail. Appointment necessary.

Access to building, collection or gallery:
Hours: Mon to Fri, 0830 to 1630 (archive, 1000 to
1800); closed bank holidays

Access for disabled people:
Ramped entry, toilet facilities

Constituent part of:
Met Office, Ministry of Defence
    tel: 0870 900 0100; e-mail: enquiries@metoffice
    .gov.uk; website: http://www.metoffice.gov.uk

NATIONAL MUSEUM OF SCIENCE AND INDUSTRY

Constituent bodies:
National Museum of Photography, Film and Television
National Railway Museum
Science Museum
Science Museum Library

NATIONAL MUSEUM WALES

Acronym or abbreviation: NMGC/NMGW

Library, Cathays Park, Cardiff, CF10 3NP

Tel: 029 2057 3202
Fax: 029 2057 3216
E-mail: library@museumwales.ac.uk

Website:
http://www.nmgw.ac.uk
For the museum as a whole.

Enquiries:
Enquiries to: Librarian
Direct fax: 029 2037 3216

Founded:
1907

Organisation type and purpose:
National government body, museum, art gallery.

Subject coverage:
Archaeology; art; botany; geology; industrial archaeology; zoology; museum science; architecture; private press; in particular, the special interests of Wales in those subjects.

Museum or gallery collection, archive, or library special collection:
Library of the Cambrian Archaeological Association
Library of the Cardiff Naturalists Society
Tomlin Collection (conchology)
Vaynor Collection (astronomy, travels)
Willoughby Gardner Collection (early books on natural history)

Non-library collection catalogue:
All or part available online, in-house and in print

Library catalogue:
All or part available in-house

Printed publications:
What's On (quarterly listing of events)
Annual Report, Premier (newsletter)
Publications on Museum collections and related topics

Publications list:
Available in print

Access to staff:
Contact by letter, by telephone, by fax, by e-mail and via website. Appointment necessary.
Hours: Tue to Fri, 1000 to 1700

Access for disabled people:
Parking provided, ramped entry, toilet facilities

Parent body:
National Museums & Galleries of Wales

Set up by Royal Charter and funded through the:
National Assembly for Wales

NATIONAL MUSEUMS AND GALLERIES OF WALES

Constituent parts:
Big Pit National Mining Museum of Wales
Blaenafon, Torfaen, NP4 9XP; tel: 01495 790311; fax: 01495 792618; e-mail: bigpit@nmgw.ac.uk
Museum of the Welsh Woollen Industry
Museum of Welsh Life
St Fagans, Cardiff, CF5 6XB; tel: 029 2057 3500; fax: 029 2057 3490
National Museum & Gallery Cardiff
Cathays Park, Cardiff, CF1 3NP; tel: 029 2039 7951; fax: 029 2037 3219

Roman Legionary Museum
High Street, Caerleon, NP6 1AE; tel: 01633 423134; fax: 01633 422869
Segontium Roman Museum
Beddgelert Road, Caernarfon, Gwynedd, LL55 2LN; tel: 01286 675625; fax: 01286 678416
Turner House Gallery
Plymouth Road, Penarth, South Glamorgan, CF64 3DM; tel: 029 2070 8870
Welsh Industrial and Maritime Museum
Welsh Slate Museum
Gilfach Ddu, Llanberis, Gwynedd, LL55 4TY; tel: 01286 870630; fax: 01286 871906

NATIONAL MUSEUMS OF SCOTLAND

Acronym or abbreviation: NMS

Chambers Street, Edinburgh, EH1 1JF

Tel: 0131 247 4137, library enquiries; 4219, museum enquiries
Fax: 0131 247 4819, general; 4311, library
E-mail: info@nms.ac.uk

Website:
http://www.nms.ac.uk
General site for the National Museums of Scotland, including details of current exhibitions, collections and departments of the constituent museums. Includes details of the library collections, services and access arrangements.

Enquiries:
Enquiries to: Librarian
Direct tel: 0131 247 4042
Direct fax: 0131 220 4819
Other contacts: (1) Librarian (2) PR & Marketing Assistant for (1) specific enquiries.

Organisation type and purpose:
Registered charity (charity number SC 011130), museum.
Non-departmental public body – NDPB.

Subject coverage:
Decorative arts; archaeology; ethnography; history, especially Scottish; geology; zoology; history of science and technology; museology and museum conservation; military history, especially of the Scottish regiments.

The Museum of Scotland tells for the first time the history of Scotland – its land, its people, and their achievements – through the incomparable national collections. The collections include that started by the Society of Antiquaries in 1781 and continued in the former Museum of Antiquities.

Information services:
Library available for reference (for conditions see Access above), on-line searching, CD-ROM based services, bibliography compilation, selective dissemination services

Special visitor services:
Guided tours.

Education services:
Group education facilities, resources for Key Stages 1 and 2, 3, 4 and Further or Higher Education.

Services for disabled people:
For the visually impaired; for the hearing impaired.

Museum or gallery collection, archive, or library special collection:
J A Harvie-Brown manuscripts, library and reprint collections (natural history)
Society of Antiquaries of Scotland manuscripts and archives
The Duke of Cumberland's Papers (microfilm)
W S Bruce manuscripts (natural history)
William Jardine manuscripts (natural history)
Book stock: 80,000 on arts, 30,000 on science, 800 current periodicals

Non-library collection catalogue:
All or part available in-house

Library catalogue:
All or part available in-house

Printed publications:
Guides to permanent and temporary exhibitions
Highlight (leaflet, free)
National Museums of Scotland Annual Reports
Collections in Context (Waterson C D)
Going to Church (MacLean C)
Going on Holiday (Simpson E)
Going to School (Withrington D)
No Ordinary Journey – John Rae, Arctic Explorer 1813–1893 (Bunyan I, Calder J et al)
Robert Burns, Farmer (Sprott G)
Scotland's Weather (ed Martin A)
Scottish Endings: Writings on Death (ed Martin A)
The Scots in Sickness and Health (Burnett J)
The Scottish Home (ed Carruthers A)
The Story of the Scottish Soldier 1600–1914 – Bonny Fighters (Calder J)
The Thistle at War: Scotland's Battles (ed McCorry H)
Treasure Islands – A Robert Louis Stevenson Anthology (ed Calder J)
Photographs Series:
Bairns – Scottish Children in Photographs (McGregor I)
Into the Foreground – Scottish Women in Photographs (Leneman L)
To See Oursels – Rural Scotland in Old Photographs (Kidd D I)
Order printed publications from: NMS Publishing
Royal Museum, Chambers Street, Edinburgh, EH1 1JF, tel: 0131 247 4026, fax: 0131 247 4012, e-mail: publishing@nms.ac.uk

Electronic and video publications:
Investigating the Lewis Chess Pieces (CD-ROM)

Publications list:
Available online and in print

Access to staff:
Contact by letter, by telephone, by fax, by e-mail and via website. Appointment necessary.
Hours: Royal Museum Library: Mon to Fri, 1000 to 1300 and 1400 to 1700
National War Museum of Scotland Library: Mon to Fri, 1000 to 1230 and 1400 to 1700

Access for disabled people:
Access to all public areas, toilet facilities
Special comments: Level entry at the Museum of Scotland

Constituent museums:
Museum of Flight
East Fortune Airfield, East Lothian; tel: 01620 880308; fax: 01620 880355; e-mail: info@nms.ac.uk
Museum of Scottish Country Life
Wester Kittochside, East Kilbride, G76 9HR; tel: 01355 224181; fax: 01355 571290; e-mail: info@nms.ac.uk
National War Museum of Scotland
Edinburgh Castle, Edinburgh, EH1 2NG; tel: 0131 225 7534; fax: 0131 225 3848; e-mail: library@nms.ac.uk
Royal Museum & Museum of Scotland
Chambers Street, Edinburgh, EH1 1JF; tel: 0131 247 4219/4422; fax: 0131 220 4819; e-mail: info@nms.ac.uk or library@nms.ac.uk
Shambellie House
New Abbey, Dumfriesshire; tel: 01387 850375; fax: 01387 850461; e-mail: info@nms.ac.uk

The library also includes the collection of the former:
Museum of Antiquities Library

The library is on two sites:
National War Museum of Scotland
Edinburgh Castle
Royal Museum of Scotland
Chambers Street

NATIONAL MUSIC AND DISABILITY INFORMATION SERVICE

Acronym or abbreviation: NMDIS

continued overleaf

7 Tavern Street, Stowmarket, Suffolk, IP14 1PJ

Tel: 01449 673990
Fax: 01449 673994
E-mail: info@soundsense.org

Website:
http://www.soundsense.org

Enquiries:
Enquiries to: NMDIS Officer

Founded:
1978

Organisation type and purpose:
Advisory body, membership association, registered charity (charity number 1080918). To provide information and advice on music and disability.

Subject coverage:
Music and disability and anything connected with these areas. Information covers music for any purpose, in education, therapy, performance, recreation, leisure, rehabilitation, palliative care etc.

Museum or gallery collection, archive, or library special collection:
Resource centre holds textbooks, journals, articles, music, videos and cassettes on music and disability

Printed publications:
A range of titles in the following categories:
Careers information
Music and disability
All about community music
SoundSense events and conference reports
SoundSense response and evidence papers
One-handed Scores
Funding
Music on the (and where to find it) (1998, £17.95)
Music for Nursery and Young Children (1993, £3.60)

Publications list:
Available online and in print

Access to staff:
Contact by letter, by telephone, by fax, by e-mail and via website
Hours: Mon to Fri, 0900 to 1700

Access to building, collection or gallery:
Prior appointment required

Access for disabled people:
Parking provided
Special comments: Please advise and we will do utmost to provide access.

NATIONAL MUSIC COUNCIL

Acronym or abbreviation: NMC

60–62 Clapham Road, London, SW9 0JJ

Tel: 0870 909 2621
Fax: 0870 706 5329
E-mail: info@nationalmusiccouncil.org.uk

Website:
http://www.nationalmusiccouncil.org.uk

Enquiries:
Enquiries to: Administrator

Founded:
1953

Organisation type and purpose:
Membership association (membership is by subscription), present number of members: 33, registered charity (charity number 239178). National forum.

Subject coverage:
Music; the encouragement of development of all British musical activities. Issues facing those working in music in the United Kingdom.

Printed publications:
A Sound Performance – the economic value of music to the United Kingdom (out of print)

Electronic and video publications:
Annual Report 2006–07 (online)
Counting the Notes – the economic value of music to the United Kingdom (online)
Sounding out the Future – post education and training in the UK music industry (online)

Publications list:
Available online

Access to staff:
Contact by letter, by telephone, by fax and by e-mail. Appointment necessary.
Hours: Mon to Fri, 0900 to 1700

NATIONAL NEIGHBOURHOOD WATCH ASSOCIATION

Acronym or abbreviation: NNWA

Schomberg House, 80–82 Pall Mall, London, SW1Y 5HF

Tel: 020 7772 3348
Fax: 020 7662 3513
E-mail: info@neighbourhoodwatch.net

Website:
http://www.neighbourhoodwatch.net

Enquiries:
Enquiries to: Director General
Direct e-mail: john.howell@dia.pipex.com

Founded:
1982

Organisation type and purpose:
Registered charity (charity number 1049584).

Subject coverage:
Establishment and best practice of Neighbourhood Watch, community safety and crime prevention in relation to Neighbourhood Watch activities.

Printed publications:
Annual Review
Factsheets on particular topics
Information pack
National Directory of Neighbourhood Watch contacts (police only)
National Neighbourhood Watch Association Newspaper (NNWA News)

Publications list:
Available online

Access to staff:
Contact by letter, by telephone, by fax, by e-mail and via website. Appointment necessary. Letter of introduction required.
Hours: Mon to Fri, 0900 to 1700

Access to building, collection or gallery:
Prior appointment required

Access for disabled people:
Level entry

NATIONAL NEWPIN

Sutherland House, 35 Sutherland Square, Walworth, London, SE17 3EE

Tel: 020 7358 5900
Fax: 020 7701 2660
E-mail: nationalnewpin@talk21.com

Website:
http://www.newpin.org.uk

Enquiries:
Enquiries to: Information Officer

Founded:
1982

Organisation type and purpose:
International organisation, voluntary organisation, registered charity (charity number 1022931). To help parents with children under 6.

Subject coverage:
Helps parents under stress break the cyclical effect of destructive family behaviour. Through a network of local centres, expectant mothers, parents, carers and children are offered a unique

opportunity to achieve positive changes in their lives and relationships based on respect, support, equality and empathy. The work focuses on alleviating maternal depression and other mental distress.

Access to staff:
Contact by letter, by telephone, by fax, by e-mail, in person and via website. Appointment necessary.
Hours: Mon to Fri, 0900 to 1700

Centres at:
Chesterfield NEWPIN
    10 & 11 The Villas, Walton Hospital, Chesterfield, Derbyshire, S40 3HN; tel: 01246 552867; fax: 01246 558747
Deptford NEWPIN
    Deptford Mission, 1 Creek Road, Deptford, London, SE8 3BT; tel: 020 8694 6052; e-mail: centre@deptfordnewpin.freeserve.co.uk
Feltham NEWPIN
    Hunter House, Highfields Road, Highfields Estate, Feltham, Middlesex, TW13 4DL; tel: 020 8893 1716; fax: 020 8893 1377
Foyle NEWPIN
    18–19 Jasmine Court, Waterside, Derry, BT47 2DZ; tel: 0150 434 4477; fax: 0150 434 4477; e-mail: foyle.newpin@virgin.net
Greenwich and Lewisham NEWPIN
    1–4 Bissextile House, Bliss Crescent, Lewisham, London, SE13 7RH, tel: 020 8694 0201; fax: 020 8694 0201
Hoxton NEWPIN
    St John's Centre, 85 Pitfield Street, London, N1 6NP; tel: 020 7739 9196; e-mail: centre@ hoxtonnewpin.freeserve.co.uk
Newham NEWPIN
    Mayflower Centre, Vincent Street, Canning Town, London, E16 1LZ; tel: 020 7473 6688; fax: 020 7473 6688
NEWPIN
    10–12 Rathmullan Drive, Rathcoole, Newtonabbey, BT37 9NF; tel: 028 9086 6622; fax: 028 9086 6722; e-mail: centre@rathcodenewpin .freeserve.co.uk
NEWPIN
    160 Wincobank Avenue, Sheffield, S5 6BB; tel: 0114 256 1533
St Paul's NEWPIN
    St Paul's Centre, Rossmore Road, London, NW1 6NJ; tel: 020 7724 6765
Sutton NEWPIN
    204 Thornton Road, St Helier Estate, Carshalton, Surrey, SM5 1NF; tel: 020 8646 8604
Tower Hamlets NEWPIN
    Bancroft Green, Hadleigh Close, London, E1 4LH; tel: 020 7423 9656
Walworth NEWPIN
    35 Sutherland Square, London, SE17 3EE; tel: 020 7703 5271
Wandsworth NEWPIN
    Patmore Centre, Patmore Street, London, SW8 4JD; tel: 020 7622 2750; fax: 020 7622 7338

NATIONAL NUCLEAR LABORATORY

Information Retrieval Service (IRS), B709, Springfields Works, Salwick, Preston, Lancashire, PR4 0XJ

Tel: 01772 764884
Fax: 01772 762385
E-mail: louise.collins@nnl.co.uk

Enquiries:
Enquiries to: Information Officer

Formerly called:
AEA Technology, Northern Research Laboratories

Organisation type and purpose:
Research organisation.
Government.

Subject coverage:
Nuclear fuel technology; industrial research.

Library catalogue:
All or part available online and in-house

Publications list:
Available in print

Access to staff:
Contact by letter, by telephone, by fax and by e-mail
Hours: Mon to Fri, 0900 to 1700

NATIONAL OCEANOGRAPHIC LIBRARY

Acronym or abbreviation: NOCS

National Oceanography Centre, University of Southampton Waterfront Campus, European Way, Southampton, SO14 3ZH

Tel: 023 8059 6111
Fax: 023 8059 6115
E-mail: nol@noc.soton.ac.uk

Website:
http://www.soton.ac.uk/library/about/nol

Enquiries:
Enquiries to: Head of Information Services
Direct e-mail: mias@noc.soton.ac.uk

Founded:
1995

Organisation type and purpose:
University department or institute, consultancy, research organisation.

Subject coverage:
Ocean and earth sciences: marine chemistry, biology, geology, geophysics and physics, ocean engineering, associated ocean instrumentation for deep oceans and shallow seas, air-sea interaction, waves, currents, sea levels, coastal oceanography, water mass dynamics,
seabed topography, sediment mobility, deep ocean, biological organisms etc., terrestrial geology, palaeontology

Museum or gallery collection, archive, or library special collection:
Discovery Collection, British Marine Science Archives

Non-library collection catalogue:
All or part available online

Library catalogue:
All or part available online

Printed publications:
Annual Report
Reports Series

Electronic and video publications:
Marine, Freshwater and Oceanographic Resources (CD-ROM/Internet)

Publications list:
Available online and in print

Access to staff:
Contact by letter, by telephone, by fax, by e-mail and via website. Appointment necessary. Non-members charged.
Hours: Mon to Fri, 0900 to 1700

Access to building, collection or gallery:
Prior appointment required

Access for disabled people:
Access to all public areas

Parent bodies (joint):
Natural Environment Research Council; and University of Southampton

NATIONAL OFFICE ANIMAL HEALTH (NOAH)

Acronym or abbreviation: NOAH

3 Crossfield Chambers, Gladbeck Way, Enfield, Middlesex, EN2 7HF

Tel: 020 8367 3131
Fax: 020 8363 1155
E-mail: noah@noah.co.uk

Website:
http://www.noah.co.uk

Enquiries:
Enquiries to: Communications Manager

Founded:
1986

Organisation type and purpose:
National organisation, trade association (membership is by subscription).
NOAH represents the UK animal medicine industry: its aim is to promote the benefits of safe, effective, quality medicines for the health and welfare of all animals.

Subject coverage:
Animal medicines and issues relating to the animal medicine industry. The production of healthy food from healthy animals and the role of animal medicines (including antibiotics, vaccines, antiparasite products). Medicines for companion animals. How animal medicines are approved, and their use controlled. The Code of Practice for the Promotion of Animal Medicines.

Trade and statistical information:
Summary data on the animal medicine market in the UK (ex-manufacturers' prices).

Printed publications:
NOAH Compendium of Data Sheets for Animal Medicines (published anually)
Animal Medicine Record Book (in conjunction with Animal Health Distributors' Association)
Poisoning in Veterinary Practice

Electronic and video publications:
Online version of the NOAH Compendium of Data Sheets for Animal Medicines at www.noahcompendium.co.uk;
NOAH News (electronic newsletter for NOAH members only)

Publications list:
Available online and in print

Access to staff:
Contact by letter, by fax, by e-mail and via website
Hours: Mon to Fri, 0900 to 1700
Special comments: Electronic contact preferred.

Access to building, collection or gallery:
No access other than to staff

Associated body of:
Pet Health Council (PHC)
website: www.pethealthcouncil.co.uk

Member of:
Animal Medicines Training Regulatory Authority (AMTRA)
website: www.amtra.org.uk
IFAH (International Federation for Animal Health)
website: www.ifahsec.org
Pet Advisory Committee (PAC)
website: www.petadvisory.org.uk
Responsible Use of Medicines in Agriculture Alliance (RUMA)
website: www.ruma.org.uk

Trustee of:
National Pet Week
website: www.nationalpetweek.org.uk

NATIONAL OPERATIC AND DRAMATIC ASSOCIATION

Acronym or abbreviation: NODA

58–60 Lincoln Road, Peterborough, PE1 2RZ

Tel: 0870 770 2480
Fax: 0870 770 2490
E-mail: info@noda.org.uk

Website:
http://www.noda.org.uk

Enquiries:
Enquiries to: Chief Executive

Founded:
1899

Organisation type and purpose:
Membership association (membership is by subscription), present number of members: 2500 societies, 3000 individuals, registered charity (charity number 254640).
Servicing amateur theatre societies.

Subject coverage:
Pantomime agency; sales of sheet music; rehearsal material for plays; musicals, operettas, operas and pantomimes at discounts to members; insurance for amateur theatre, help and advice.

Museum or gallery collection, archive, or library special collection:
Collection of vocal scores (some first editions)
Rehearsal material at discounts to members
Sheet music

Printed publications:
Area bulletins
NODA National News (quarterly)
NODA Pantomimes and reference books

Publications list:
Available online

Access to staff:
Contact by letter, by telephone, by fax, by e-mail and via website. Appointment necessary.
Hours: Mon to Fri, 0900 to 1700
Special comments: Non-members by special arrangement.

Access to building, collection or gallery:
Prior appointment required

NATIONAL ORGANISATION OF ASIAN BUSINESSES

Acronym or abbreviation: NOAB

East End House, Kenrick Way, West Bromwich, West Midlands, B71 4EA

Tel: 0121 553 1999
Fax: 0121 525 6565
E-mail: tonydeep@eastendfoods.co.uk

Enquiries:
Enquiries to: Manager

Founded:
1993

Organisation type and purpose:
Voluntary organisation.

Subject coverage:
Representation of the interests of Asian businesses at a national level.

Access to staff:
Contact by letter, by telephone, by fax and by e-mail
Hours: Mon to Fri, 0900 to 1700

Access for disabled people:
Parking provided, ramped entry, toilet facilities

NATIONAL OSTEOPOROSIS SOCIETY

Camerton, Bath, BA2 0PJ

Tel: 01761 471771 (Switchboard) \ 0845 450 0230 (Helpline)
Fax: 01761 471104
E-mail: info@nos.org.uk

Website:
http://www.nos.org.uk

Enquiries:
Enquiries to: Information Centre

Founded:
1986

Organisation type and purpose:
Membership association (membership is by subscription), voluntary organisation, registered charity (charity number 1102712 in England and Wales and SC 039755 in Scotland).

continued overleaf

Subject coverage:
Information on treatment and prevention of osteoporosis for the general public and the medical professions, hormone replacement therapy (HRT), the menopause.

Printed publications:
Series of booklets and information sheets
Order printed publications from: Information Centre

Publications list:
Available online and in print

Access to staff:
Contact by letter, by telephone, by fax, by e-mail, in person and via website. Appointment necessary.
Hours: Mon to Fri, 1000 to 1600; Helpline: Mon to Fri, 0900 to 1700

Access to building, collection or gallery:
Prior appointment required

Access for disabled people:
Parking provided, level entry, toilet facilities

Affiliated to:
Association of Medical Research Charities
European Foundation for Osteoporosis
Long-term Medical Conditions Alliance
National Council of Women of Great Britain

NATIONAL OUTDOOR EVENTS ASSOCIATION

Acronym or abbreviation: NOEA

7 Hamilton Way, Wallington, Surrey, SM6 9NJ

Tel: 020 8669 8121
Fax: 020 8647 1128
E-mail: secretary@noea.org.uk

Website:
http://www.noea.org.uk
General information.

Enquiries:
Enquiries to: General Secretary

Founded:
1979

Organisation type and purpose:
Trade association.

Subject coverage:
General and technical information on the world of outdoor events for clients and suppliers, basic standards and codes of practice, hazards and risk assessment, statutory requirements.

Printed publications:
NOEA Code of practice for outdoor events (£20, revised addendum, £5)
NOEA Yearbook

Publications list:
Available in print

Access to staff:
Contact by letter, by telephone, by fax and by e-mail
Hours: Mon to Fri, 0900 to 1700

Access to building, collection or gallery:
No access other than to staff

Access for disabled people:
Level entry

NATIONAL PARK HOMES COUNCIL

Acronym or abbreviation: NPHC

Catherine House, Victoria Road, Aldershot, Hampshire, GU11 1SS

Tel: 01252 336092
Fax: 01252 322596
E-mail: info@nationalcaravan.co.uk

Website:
http://www.theparkhome.net
List of members, products and services provided.

Enquiries:
Enquiries to: Director General

Founded:
1983

Organisation type and purpose:
Membership association (membership is by subscription), present number of members: 150. Representative body for residential park homes industry, manufacturers, park operators and specialist products and services suppliers.

Subject coverage:
Centre of information on all aspects of the park homes industry.
Gold Shield Ten Year Warranty Scheme.
Quality Award Scheme.

Publications list:
Available in print

Access to staff:
Contact by letter, by telephone, by fax, by e-mail and via website
Hours: Mon to Fri, 0900 to 1700

NATIONAL PEST TECHNICIANS ASSOCIATION

Acronym or abbreviation: NPTA

NPTA House, Hall Lane, Kinoulton, Nottingham, NG12 3EF

Tel: 01949 81133
Fax: 01949 823905
E-mail: officenpta@aol.com

Website:
http://www.npta.org.uk

Enquiries:
Enquiries to: Administrator

Founded:
1993

Organisation type and purpose:
Professional body.

Subject coverage:
Pest control.

Printed publications:
Today's Technician (quarterly, free to members)

Publications list:
Available online and in print

Access to staff:
Contact by letter, by telephone, by fax, by e-mail and via website. Appointment necessary.
Hours: Mon to Fri, 0900 to 1700

NATIONAL PHARMACY ASSOCIATION

Acronym or abbreviation: NPA

Mallinson House, 38–42 St Peter's Street, St Albans, Hertfordshire, AL1 3NP

Tel: 01727 832161
Fax: 01727 840858
E-mail: npa@npa.co.uk

Website:
http://www.npa.co.uk

Enquiries:
Enquiries to: Information Operations Manager
Direct tel: 01727 858687 (ext. 3207)
Direct fax: 01727 795902
Direct e-mail: s.garner@npa.co.uk

Founded:
1921

Organisation type and purpose:
Trade association.

Subject coverage:
Community pharmacy; prescription and other medicines.

Museum or gallery collection, archive, or library special collection:
Foreign pharmacopoeias

Printed publications:
Annual Report
Information leaflets
In Touch magazine (monthly)

Access to staff:
Contact by letter, by telephone, by fax and by e-mail. Access for members only. Non-members charged.
Hours: Mon to Fri, 0900 to 1800; Sat, 0900 to 1300

NATIONAL PHILATELIC SOCIETY

Acronym or abbreviation: NPS

c/o The British Postal Museum & Archive, Freeling House, Phoenix Place, London WC1X 0DL

Tel: 020 7239 2571
E-mail: nps@ukphilately.org.uk/nps

Website:
http://ukphilately.org.uk/

Enquiries:
Enquiries to: General Secretary
Direct e-mail: nps@ukphilately.org.uk

Founded:
1899

Organisation type and purpose:
International organisation, membership association (membership is by subscription), present number of members: 4700, philatelic library, suitable for ages: 14+, publishing house. Non-profit-making society.

Subject coverage:
Philately, postal history, stamp collecting and related hobby material.

Museum or gallery collection, archive, or library special collection:
Collection of forged stamps
Library of philatelic and postal history works, philatelic journals
Reference collection of philatelic archive material

Library catalogue:
All or part available online and in-house

Printed publications:
Stamp Lover (6 times a year, £2 per issue)

Access to staff:
Contact by letter and by telephone
Hours: Tue, Wed, Thu, 1100 to 1615 and second Sat in each month

Access to building, collection or gallery:
No prior appointment required
Hours: Tue, Wed, Thu, 1100 to 1615 and second Sat in each month

NATIONAL PHYSICAL LABORATORY

Acronym or abbreviation: NPL

Queens Road, Teddington, Middlesex, TW11 0LW

Tel: 020 8977 3222
Fax: 020 8943 6458
E-mail: enquiry@npl.co.uk

Website:
http://www.npl.co.uk
About NPL, measurement advice, units of measurement, news and events, services, getting together, scientific centres, vacancies.

Enquiries:
Enquiries to: National Physical Laboratory Helpline
Direct tel: 020 8943 6880

Founded:
1900

Organisation type and purpose:
National organisation, consultancy, research organisation.
UK national standards laboratory.
Development of highly accurate measurement techniques and their application for industry and government.

Subject coverage:
National and international standards, physics and engineering, including electrical and optical standards and standards of radioactivity and measurement of ionizing radiations, physical acoustics and noise, application of computers and information technology, engineering materials, environmental metrology, measurement and calibration, research and development, knowledge transfer.

Printed publications:
Annual Review
Points of Contact (information on the work of NPL's specialist teams with their contact details, also details of clubs and training services)
Specialist books and booklets (HMSO)
Technical reports and memoranda

Access to staff:
Contact by letter, by telephone, by fax, by e-mail and via website
Hours: Mon to Fri, 0900 to 1700

Operated on behalf of the:
Department of Trade and Industry by NPL Management Limited
a wholly owned subsidiary of Serco Group plc

NATIONAL PIERS SOCIETY

Acronym or abbreviation: NPS

4 Tyrrell Road, South Benfleet, Essex, SS7 5DH

Tel: 01268 757291
Fax: 020 7483 1902
E-mail: pjredditch@msn.com

Website:
http://www.piers.co.uk

Enquiries:
Enquiries to: Honorary Secretary
Other contacts: Chairman

Founded:
1976

Organisation type and purpose:
Learned society (membership is by subscription), voluntary organisation, research organisation.

Subject coverage:
Piers: construction, history, uses, development, architecture, maintenance, grant-aid, assessment and surveying, construction materials, design, engineering, shipping associations, attractions (eg theatres); pier tramways and railways.

Museum or gallery collection, archive, or library special collection:
Copies of most books covering piers, their construction and history; various documents, information files, photographs, drawings and souvenirs

Printed publications:
Piers (journal, quarterly to members)
Reports (irregularly)
Order printed publications from: Piers Information Bureau
3 Withburn Close, Upton, Wirral, L49 6QH, tel: 0151 606 0595

Publications list:
Available in print

Access to staff:
Contact by letter, by telephone, by fax and by e-mail
Hours: Mon to Fri, 0900 to 1700

Links with:
British Association of Leisure Parks, Piers and Attractions
Paddle Steamer Preservation Society

NATIONAL PIGEON ASSOCIATION

Acronym or abbreviation: NPA

Bridge Villa, Main Street, Pollington, Goole, East Yorkshire, DN14 0DW

Tel: 01405 869516
Fax: 01405 869516
E-mail: tracey@edwardspm.fsnet.co.uk

Website:
http://www.zyworld.com/NPA/index.htm
Secretary, activities, costs, dovecote package, found pigeons, breed clubs, championship shows.

Enquiries:
Enquiries to: Secretary

Organisation type and purpose:
Membership association (membership is by subscription), present number of members: 856, voluntary organisation.
For breeding and exhibition of fancy pigeons.

Subject coverage:
Feeding, rearing, management and exhibition of fancy pigeons in general, with advice on sources of further information. Contacts supplied for specialist breed clubs.

Printed publications:
Dovecote Designs and Package (price on request)
Feathered World (magazine, Winckley Publishing, Preston for poultry and fancy pigeons)
Instruction booklet for beginners
Send stamp with request

Electronic and video publications:
An Introduction to Fancy Pigeons (video, £12.50, £14 inc p&p from Secretary or Feathered World)

Access to staff:
Contact by letter and by telephone
Hours: Mon to Fri, 0900 to 1700

Access to building, collection or gallery:
No access other than to staff

Rings and lost birds:
The Ring Distributor
Bridge Villa, Main Street, Pollington, Goole, DN14 0DW; tel: 01405 869516

NATIONAL POISONS INFORMATION SERVICE (CARDIFF CENTRE)

Acronym or abbreviation: NPIS

Gwenwyn Ward, Llandough Hospital, Penarth, Cardiff, CF64 2XX

Tel: 029 2071 5013
Fax: 029 2070 4357
E-mail: poison.information@cardiffandvale.wales.nhs.uk

Enquiries:
Enquiries to: Manager

Founded:
1963

Organisation type and purpose:
Welsh Office service.
Advice on poisonings by all routes, to medical personnel only.

Subject coverage:
Specialist information on all types of poisoning, clinical toxicology; pharmacology.

Publications list:
Available in print

Access to staff:
Contact by letter, by telephone, by fax and by e-mail
Hours: 24-hour service, 365 days a year
Special comments: Not a public access service.

Part of:
National Poisons Information Service

NATIONAL POISONS INFORMATION SERVICE, EDINBURGH CENTRE

Acronym or abbreviation: NPIS Edinburgh / SPIB

Scottish Poisons Information Bureau, Royal Infirmary, Edinburgh, EH16 4SA

Tel: 0131 242 1383
Fax: 0131 242 1387
E-mail: spib@luht.scot.nhs.uk

Website:
http://www.toxbase.org
http://www.show.scot.nhs.uk/spib

Enquiries:
Enquiries to: Manager
Other contacts: Information Officer

Founded:
1963

Organisation type and purpose:
Advisory body.
Poisons information for medical professionals.

Subject coverage:
Toxicology, poisons information, chemicals.

Information services:
Clinical toxicology management advice for registered NHS users

Access to staff:
Contact by letter, by telephone, by fax, by e-mail and via website
Hours: Mon to Fri, 0800 to 2000
Special comments: Medical profession only.

NATIONAL POLICE LIBRARY

Formal name: National Policing Improvement Agency
Acronym or abbreviation: NPIA

NPIA, Bramshill, Hook, Hampshire, RG27 0JW

Tel: 01256 602650
Fax: 01256 602285
E-mail: library@npia.pnn.police.uk

Website:
http://www.npia.police.uk

Enquiries:
Enquiries to: Chief Librarian
Direct tel: 01256 602227

Founded:
1948

Formerly called:
National Police Training (year of change 1993); Centrex (year of change 2007)

Organisation type and purpose:
NPIA provides and supports a range of products and services that underpins its commitment to improving policing priorities in: personal development and HR; systems and IT services; science and forensics; operational policing services; programmes for improvement and research; identification resources and databases

Subject coverage:
Police-related subjects, criminal justice, management.

Museum or gallery collection, archive, or library special collection:
Annual Report of HM Inspectors of Constabulary, 1858 to date
Police and Constabulary Almanac, 1858 to date
Police Journal, 1928 to date
Police Review, 1893 to date

Library catalogue:
All or part available online and in-house

Printed publications:
Monthly list of additions to stock (electronic format only)

Access to staff:
Contact by letter, by telephone, by fax, by e-mail, in person and via website. Appointment necessary. Letter of introduction required. Non-members charged.
Hours: Mon to Thu, 0830 to 1700; Fri, 0830 to 1600

Access for disabled people:
Restricted access

continued overleaf

Parent body:
National Policing Improvement Agency
tel: 01256 602100

NATIONAL PONY SOCIETY

Acronym or abbreviation: NPS

Willingdon House, 102 High Street, Alton,
Hampshire, GU34 1EN

Tel: 01420 88333
Fax: 01420 80599

Enquiries:
Enquiries to: Secretary

Founded:
1893

Organisation type and purpose:
Membership association.

Subject coverage:
Training for stud assistant's qualification, British
Riding Pony Stud Book registration, native breeds,
showing competitions, sales, welfare of ponies,
training of judges.

Printed publications:
National Pony Society Review (annually)
Stud Book and Register of Riding Ponies

Representation on:
Association of British Equine Societies
British Show Pony Society
Councils of the British Horse Society
Joint Measurement Board
NASTA
National Equine Welfare Council

NATIONAL PORTAGE ASSOCIATION

Acronym or abbreviation: NPA

Kings Court, 17 School Road, Hall Green,
Birmingham, B28 8JG

Tel: 0121 244 1807
Fax: 0121 244 1801
E-mail: npa@portageuk.freeserve.co.uk

Website:
http://www.portage.org.uk

Enquiries:
Enquiries to: Administrator

Founded:
1976

Organisation type and purpose:
Voluntary organisation, registered charity (charity
number 1087865).
Educational organisation, company limited by
guarantee no. 4165317.

Subject coverage:
Support for families caring for children with
special needs by promoting and supporting
portage educational home visiting services.

Printed publications:
Code of Practice and Ethics
Delivering Portage in Multi Cultural Britain (£2
members)
NPA Leaflet
Leaflets are also available in Urdu, Bengali and
Punjabi
Staff Safety

Publications list:
Available online and in print

Access to staff:
Contact by letter, by telephone, by fax, by e-mail
and via website
Hours: Office hours

NATIONAL PORTRAIT GALLERY

Acronym or abbreviation: NPG

Heinz Archive and Library, St Martin's Place,
London, WC2H 0HE

Tel: 020 7306 0055
Fax: 020 7306 0056 (general); 020 7306 0058
(development/press)
E-mail: archives@npg.org.uk

Website:
http://www.npg.org.uk

Enquiries:
Enquiries to: Head of Archive and Library
Direct e-mail: archiveenquiry@npg.org.uk

Founded:
1856

Organisation type and purpose:
National government body, art gallery, suitable for
all ages.
Archive and library.
Founded in 1856 to collect the likenesses of famous
British men and women, and constitutes a unique
record of the men and women who created (and
are still creating) the history and culture of the
nation. Paintings from the collection on display in
locations around the country.

Subject coverage:
British portraits and portrait artists, 1400s to
present day.

Information services:
Library available for reference (for conditions see
Access above); Consultation service, Wed, 1400 to
1700.

**Museum or gallery collection, archive, or library
special collection:**
Unparalleled collection of British portraiture.
Reference collection of portrait engravings.
Collection of approximately 600,000 reproductions
of painted and photographic portraits, arranged
in separate 'sitter' and 'artist' files; extensive
index to portraits reproduced or cited in
publications.
Collection of artists' sitter books, account books,
papers, and research papers relating to portrait
artists.
Gallery acquisition, conservation and institutional
records.

Non-library collection catalogue:
All or part available online, in-house and in print

Library catalogue:
All or part available online and in-house

Printed publications:
Annual reports
Complete Illustrated Catalogue (2004)
Early Georgian Portraits (HMSO, 1977)
Early Victorian Portraits (HMSO, 1974)
Mid-Georgian Portraits (2004)
National Portrait Gallery: an architectural history
(2000)
National Portrait Gallery: an illustrated guide
(revised edn, 2000)
National Portrait Gallery Collection (1988)
Regency Portraits (1985)
Tudor and Jacobean Portraits (HMSO, 1969),
(National Portrait Gallery, 1997)
Various: exhibitions catalogues
Various: thematic monographs

Microform publications:
Scharf notebooks

Publications list:
Available online and in print

Access to staff:
Contact by letter, by telephone and by e-mail.
Appointment necessary.

Access to building, collection or gallery:
Hours: Archive and Library: Tue to Fri, 1000 to
1700
Special comments: Access to Archive and Library by
appointment only.

Access for disabled people:
Ramped entry, toilet facilities

Also at:
Beningbrough Hall
Beningbrough, York, North Yorkshire, YO30
1DD; tel: 01904 472027; website: http://www
.nationaltrust.org.uk/main/w
-beningbroughhallandgardens
Bodelwyddan Castle
Bodelwyddan, Rhyl, Denbighshire, LL18 5YA;
tel: 01745 584060; fax: 01745 584563; website:
http://www.bodelwyddan-castle.co.uk
Gawthorpe Hall
Padiham, nr Burnley, Lancashire, BB12 8UA; tel:
01282 771004; website: http://www.nationaltrust
.org.uk/main/w-gawthorpehall
Montacute House
Montacute, Somerset, TA15 6XP; tel: 01935
823289; website: http://www.nationaltrust.org
.uk/main/w-vh/w-visits/w-findaplace/w
-montacute

NATIONAL PORTRAITURE ASSOCIATION

59–60 Fitzjames Avenue, London, W14 0RR

Tel: 020 7602 0892
Fax: 020 7602 6705
E-mail: enquiries@natportrait.com

Website:
http://www.natportrait.com
Provides client – selection galleries of artists' work
with special facilities for transmission of overseas
portraits.

Enquiries:
Enquiries to: Director

Founded:
1971

Organisation type and purpose:
International organisation, membership
association.
Organisation for the undertaking of portrait
commissions.

Subject coverage:
Portrait commissions; portraitists.

Access to staff:
Contact by letter, by telephone, by fax, by e-mail
and via website. Appointment necessary.
Hours: Mon to Fri, 0900 to 1700

NATIONAL REGISTER OF PERSONAL TRAINERS

Acronym or abbreviation: NRPT

16 Borough High Street, London, SE1 9QG

Tel: 0870 200 6010
Fax: 020 7407 9225
E-mail: info@nrpt.co.uk

Website:
http://www.nrpt.co.uk
Details on trainers, training companies and why a
personal trainer could be good for you.

Enquiries:
Enquiries to: Managing Director
Direct tel: 020 7407 9223
Direct e-mail: will@nrpt.co.uk

Founded:
1992

Organisation type and purpose:
National organisation, membership association
(membership is by subscription), service industry.

Subject coverage:
Personal fitness trainers across the UK, information
about personal training and personal training
companies.

Access to staff:
Contact by letter, by telephone and by fax. All
charged.
Hours: Mon to Fri, 0900 to 1700

Access to building, collection or gallery:
Prior appointment required

NATIONAL REGISTER OF WARRANTED BUILDERS

Acronym or abbreviation: NRWB

4 Brooklands Avenue, Cambridge, CB2 2BB

Tel: 01223 508407
Fax: 01223 300848
E-mail: registrar@fmb.org.uk

Website:
http://www.fmb.org.uk

Enquiries:
Enquiries to: Registrar

Founded:
1980

Organisation type and purpose:
Trade association (membership is by subscription, qualification), present number of members: 3000.

Access to staff:
Contact by letter and by e-mail
Hours: Mon to Fri, 0900 to 1700

Links to:
Federation of Master Builders (FMB)
14–15 Great James Street, London, WC1N 3DP

NATIONAL RIFLE ASSOCIATION/ NATIONAL SHOOTING CENTRE LIMITED

Acronym or abbreviation: NRA

Bisley Camp, Brookwood, Woking, Surrey, GU24 0PB

Tel: 01483 797777
Fax: 01483 797285
E-mail: info@nra.org.uk

Website:
http://www.nra.org.uk

Enquiries:
Enquiries to: Chief Executive
Direct tel: ext 126
Direct e-mail: elaine.buttle@nra.org.uk
Other contacts: Membership Secretary for membership enquiries.

Founded:
1860

Organisation type and purpose:
International organisation, membership association (membership is by subscription), present number of members: 5500, registered charity, suitable for ages: all.
Governing body of full-bore rifle and pistol shooting in the UK. Central body for affiliated schools and 1000 shooting clubs and associations.

Subject coverage:
Full-bore rifle and pistol shooting, marksmanship, rules and regulations in competition shooting, construction of new ranges.

Museum or gallery collection, archive, or library special collection:
Archives since the Association's foundation in 1860
Museum of historic fire arms and memorabilia

Printed publications:
NRA Journal (quarterly)
NRA Rifle and Pistol Coaching Notes
NRA Rules of Full-bore Shooting (annually)

Access to staff:
Contact by letter, by telephone, by fax and by e-mail
Hours: Mon to Fri, 0900 to 1700

Member of:
British Shooting Sports Council
Great Britain Target Shooting Federation

NATIONAL RIVERS AUTHORITY

Acronym or abbreviation: NRA

Regional Offices:
Anglian Region
  Kingfisher Home, Goldhay Way, Orton Goldhay, Peterborough, Cambridgeshire, PE2 0ZE; tel: 01733 371811; fax: 01733 231840
North West Region
  PO Box 432, Warrington, WA4 1HH
North West Region
  Richard Fairclough House, Knutsford Road, Warrington, WA4 1HG; tel: 01925 53999; fax: 01925 415961
North West Region
  Road Three, Winsford Industrial Estate, Winsford, CW7 3SL
North West Region
  Abbotsfield Road, Reginald Road Industrial Estate, St Helens, WA9 4HU
North West Region
  Chertsey Hill, London Road, Carlisle, CA1 2QX
North West Region
  Holme Road, Bamber Hill, Preston, PR5 6BP
Northumbria & Yorkshire Region
  Eldon House, Regent Centre, Gosforth, Newcastle upon Tyne, NE3 3UB; tel: 0191 213 0266 or 284 5069
Northumbria & Yorkshire Region
  21 Park Square South, Leeds, LS1 2QG; tel: 0113 244 0191; fax: 0113 246 1889
Severn Trent Region
  Sapphire East, 550 Streetsbrook Road, Solihull, Birmingham, B91 9QT; tel: 0121 711 2324; fax: 0121 711 5824
Severn Trent Region
  PO Box 299, Shrewsbury, Shropshire, SY3 8WD
Severn Trent Region, Upper Severn Area
  Hafren House, Welshpool Road, Shelton, Shrewsbury, Shropshire, SY3 8BB
South Western Region
  Manley House, Kestrel Way, Exeter, EX2 7LQ; tel: 01392 444000; fax: 01392 444238
South Western Region, Bridgewater Office
  Rivers House, East Quay, Bridgwater, Somerset, TA6 4YS; tel: 01278 457333; fax: 01278 452985
Southern Region
  Portfield Depot, Oving Road, Chichester, PO20 6AG
Southern Region
  Guildbourne House, Chatsworth Road, Worthing, West Sussex, BN11 1LD; tel: 01903 820692; fax: 01903 821832
Southern Region
  Southern Region Laboratory, 4 The Meadows, Waterberry Drive, Waterlooville, PO7 7XX
Southern Region
  20 Manners View, Newport, Isle of Wight, PO30 5FA
Southern Region
  Ladymead, Guildford, GU1 1BZ
Thames Region
  Isis House, Howbery Park, Wallingford, Oxfordshire, OX10 8BD
Thames Region
  3rd Floor, Kings Meadow House, Kings Meadow Road, Reading, RG1 8DG; tel: 0118 953 5000; fax: 0118 950 0388
Welsh Region
  Rivers House, St Mellons Business Park, St Mellons, Cardiff, CF3 0LT; tel: 029 2077 0088; fax: 029 2079 8555

NATIONAL ROLLER HOCKEY ASSOCIATION OF ENGLAND LTD

Acronym or abbreviation: NRHA

82 Greenfield Road, Farnham, Surrey, GU9 8TQ

Tel: 07702 503383
Fax: 01252 723635
E-mail: gail-whattingham@tinyonline.co.uk

Website:
http://www.nrha.co.uk

Enquiries:
Enquiries to: Public Relations Manager
Other contacts: General Secretary; Archive Historian

Founded:
1912

Organisation type and purpose:
Statutory body, membership association, present number of members: 1,500.
Governing body of the sport.

Subject coverage:
Club addresses, organisation of taster courses; help with development and coaching, courses on coaching for all coaches and referees to international standard.

Non-library collection catalogue:
All or part available in print

Printed publications:
ABC of Roller Hockey
Basic Roller Hockey
Coaching manuals
Roller Hockey (newsletter, quarterly)
Roller Hockey Goalkeeping
The Early Years of English Roller Hockey 1884– 1914 (R. Pout)

Electronic and video publications:
Videos

Access to staff:
Contact by letter, by telephone, by fax, by e-mail and via website
Hours: Mon to Fri, 0900 to 1700

Links with:
British Skater Hockey Association
European Committee of Roller Skating (CERS)
International Federation of Roller Skating (FIRS)
National Skating Association
Sport England

Member organisation of:
Central Council of Physical Recreation

NATIONAL ROUNDERS ASSOCIATION

Acronym or abbreviation: NRA

55 Westland Gardens, Sheffield, South Yorkshire, S20 8ES

Tel: 01142 480357
E-mail: nra@tooda.demon.co.uk

Website:
http://www.nra-rounders.co.uk
Covers all areas of rounders, awards, coaching, etc.

Enquiries:
Enquiries to: Administrator
Other contacts: Office Manager; Development Officer for details of all publications and prices; development issues.

Founded:
1943

Organisation type and purpose:
Membership association (membership is by subscription), voluntary organisation.
National governing body of the sport of rounders.

Subject coverage:
Affiliations; coaching awards; umpiring awards; school skills awards; competitions; rules; national league; centres for excellence; international opportunities; how to set up a league; equipment safety policy; advice on all matters relating to the sport.

Museum or gallery collection, archive, or library special collection:
Rounders' photographs
Past publications

Printed publications:
1st Post, 2nd Post, 3rd Post (newsheet)
4th Post (magazine includes Annual Report)
Rules and Hints to Umpires (£4)
GCSE Lesson Plans and Award Scheme (£6.590
Small Sided Games (£5)
Information Pack (£5)
Teachers' Handbook Skills Award (£3.50)

continued overleaf

Publications list:
Available online and in print

Access to staff:
Contact by letter, by telephone, by fax and by e-mail
Hours: Mon to Thu, 0900 to 1500
Special comments: Telephone answering service available at other times.

Access to building, collection or gallery:
No access other than to staff

Links with:
Central Council for Physical Recreation (CCPR)
National Council for School Sports
Sport England
Sportscoach UK
Women's Sports Foundation

NATIONAL SCHIZOPHRENIA FELLOWSHIP (SCOTLAND)

Acronym or abbreviation: NSF(S)

Claremont House, 130 East Claremont Street, Edinburgh, EH7 4LB

Tel: 0131 557 8969
Fax: 0131 557 8968
E-mail: info@nsfscot.org.uk

Website:
http://www.nsfscot.org.uk
Information on schizophrenia and the work of NSF(Scotland).

Enquiries:
Enquiries to: Information Officer

Founded:
1984

Organisation type and purpose:
Membership association (membership is by subscription), present number of members: 500, voluntary organisation, registered charity (charity number SCO 13649).

Subject coverage:
Mental illness, particularly schizophrenia.

Library catalogue:
All or part available in-house

Printed publications:
see website for details

Publications list:
Available online and in print

Access to staff:
Contact by letter, by telephone, by fax, by e-mail and in person
Hours: Mon to Fri, 0900 to 1700

Access for disabled people:
Level entry, access to all public areas

NATIONAL SCHOOLS SEVENS

Acronym or abbreviation: NSS

PO Box 52, East Peckham, Tonbridge, Kent, TN12 5ZP

Tel: 01622 871170
Fax: 01622 873426
E-mail: ns7s@btinternet.com

Website:
http://www.armyns7.co.uk
Format, draw, accommodation list, all relevant information for forthcoming tournaments.

Enquiries:
Enquiries to: Tournament Organisers

Founded:
1939

Organisation type and purpose:
National organisation.
Rugby Union Tournament for schools.
To provide a first class Rugby Union Tournament for Schools aged 13 to 18.

Subject coverage:
Seven-a-side rugby union in schools.

Printed publications:
Tournament Programme (available from Tournament Organisers from 1st March, annually)

Access to staff:
Contact by letter, by telephone, by fax, by e-mail and via website
Hours: Sun to Sat, 0900 to 1700

Access for disabled people:
Toilet facilities

NATIONAL SCREEN AND SOUND ARCHIVE OF WALES

Acronym or abbreviation: NSSAW

The National Library of Wales, Aberystwyth, SY23 3BU

Tel: 01970 632828
Fax: 01970 632544
E-mail: agssc@llgc.org.uk

Website:
http://screenandsound.llgc.org.uk

Founded:
2001

Subject coverage:
Films, television programmes, videos, sound recordings and music relating to Wales and the Welsh.

Special visitor services:
Viewing and listening services.

Museum or gallery collection, archive, or library special collection:
Incorporates the collections of:
Wales Film and Television Archive
National Library of Wales' Sound and Moving Image collection

Access to building, collection or gallery:
Hours: Mon to Fri, 1000 to 1700

NATIONAL SECULAR SOCIETY

Acronym or abbreviation: NSS

25 Red Lion Square, London, WC1R 4RL

Tel: 020 7404 3126
Fax: 0870 762 8971
E-mail: enquiries@secularism.org.uk

Website:
http://www.secularism.org.uk

Enquiries:
Enquiries to: Administrator

Founded:
1866

Organisation type and purpose:
Campaigning organisation (membership is by subscription), voluntary organisation.

Subject coverage:
Secular humanism; atheism; civil liberties; rational education; freethought history.

Museum or gallery collection, archive, or library special collection:
C Bradlaugh MP – papers at Bishopsgate Library, Liverpool Street, London EC2

Library catalogue:
All or part available in-house

Printed publications:
Bulletin (3 times a year)
Annual Report
Newsline (weekly email newsletter)

Access to staff:
Contact by letter, by telephone, by e-mail and via website. Appointment necessary.
Hours: Mon to Fri, 0900 to 1700

Access to building, collection or gallery:
Prior appointment required

Affiliates of:
Abortion Rights; Amnesty International; European Humanist Federation; International Humanist and Ethical Union; Liberty; Network for Peace.
International Humanist and Ethical Union

NATIONAL SHEEP ASSOCIATION

Acronym or abbreviation: NSA

The Sheep Centre, Malvern, Worcestershire, WR13 6PH

Tel: 01684 892661
Fax: 01684 892663
E-mail: enquiries@nationalsheep.org.uk

Enquiries:
Enquiries to: Chief Executive

Founded:
1892

Organisation type and purpose:
Membership association (membership is by subscription), present number of members: 12,000, registered charity (charity number 249255).
Agricultural Organisation.
Representative body for sheep farmers.

Subject coverage:
Sheep and the UK sheep industry.

Printed publications:
British Sheep Book (every 3/4 years, breeds of sheep found in Britain including imported breeds)
Sheep Farmer (6 times a year, members only)

Access to staff:
Contact by letter. Appointment necessary.
Hours: Mon to Fri, 0900 to 1700

NATIONAL SMALL-BORE RIFLE ASSOCIATION

Acronym or abbreviation: NSRA

Lord Roberts Centre, Bisley Camp, Brookwood, Woking, Surrey, GU24 0NP

Tel: 01483 485500
Fax: 01483 476392
E-mail: info@nsra.co.uk

Website:
http://www.nsra.co.uk

Enquiries:
Enquiries to: Information Officer
Direct tel: 01483 485505
Direct e-mail: jpage@nsra.co.uk

Founded:
1901

Organisation type and purpose:
Membership association (membership is by subscription), present number of members: 15,500, voluntary organisation, registered charity (charity number 215468).
Governing body for small-bore rifle and pistol shooting, and air rifle and air pistol shooting, and match crossbow shooting.

Subject coverage:
Rifle, pistol small-bore target shooting; air rifle, air gun (.177 calibre) target shooting; match crossbow shooting; range construction, firearms legislation, sale of ammunition, guns and equipment to members.

Printed publications:
Rifleman (quarterly)
Firearm Law
Gun Law
NSRA Rules
Successful Pistol Shooting
Successful Rifle Shooting

Electronic and video publications:
Videos on shooting air rifles, pistol and small-bore rifles

Publications list:
Available in print

Access to staff:
Contact by letter, by telephone, by fax, by e-mail and in person. Access for members only.
Hours: Mon to Fri, 0900 to 1700

Access to building, collection or gallery:
No prior appointment required

Member of:
British Olympic Association
British Shooting Sports Council
Great Britain Target Shooting Federation
International Shooting Sport Federation

NATIONAL SOCIETY FOR CLEAN AIR AND ENVIRONMENTAL PROTECTION

Acronym or abbreviation: NSCA

44 Grand Parade, Brighton, East Sussex, BN2 9QA

Tel: 01273 878770
Fax: 01273 606626
E-mail: info@nsca.org.uk

Website:
http://www.nsca.org.uk
NSCA information.

Enquiries:
Enquiries to: Project Manager

Founded:
1899

Organisation type and purpose:
National organisation, membership association (membership is by subscription), present number of members: 1300, registered charity (charity number 221026).
The Society is a non-governmental, non-political organisation. NSCA brings together pollution expertise from industry, local and central government, technical, academic and institutional bodies.
Objectives are to secure environmental improvement by promoting clean air through the reduction of air pollution, noise and other contaminants while having due regard for other aspects of the environment.

Subject coverage:
Air pollution, noise, water and land pollution, policy and legislation.

Museum or gallery collection, archive, or library special collection:
Archive Collection on Air Pollution and Environment

Printed publications:
Books, information leaflets, factsheets, reports and schools resources
NSCA Yearbook
NSCA Pollution Handbook Annual
Teaching Resources

Publications list:
Available online and in print

Access to staff:
Contact by letter, by telephone, by fax, by e-mail and via website. Appointment necessary.
Hours: Mon to Fri, 0900 to 1700

Access to building, collection or gallery:
Prior appointment required

Affiliated to and provides the secretariat for:
International Union of Air Pollution Prevention Associations (IUAPPA)
at the same address; tel: 01273 878772; fax: 01273 606626; e-mail: iuappa@nsca.org.uk

NATIONAL SOCIETY FOR EDUCATION IN ART AND DESIGN

Acronym or abbreviation: NSEAD

The Gatehouse, Corsham Court, Corsham, Wiltshire, SN13 0BZ

Tel: 01249 714825
Fax: 01249 716138
E-mail: johnsteers@nsead.org

Website:
http://www.nsead.org

Enquiries:
Enquiries to: General Secretary

Founded:
1888

Organisation type and purpose:
Learned society, trade union (membership is by subscription), present number of members: 2000, publishing house.

Subject coverage:
Art and design in education across all education sectors; careers in art and design; international and national contacts in field of art and design education.

Trade and statistical information:
Data on art education development throughout the world via the International Society for Education in Art.

Printed publications:
A Guide to Courses and Careers in Art, Craft and Design
A range of some 80 books from Key Stage 1 to Research
Start Primary Magazine
International Journal of Art and Design Education (3 times a year)
NSEAD Newsletter (6 times a year)

Publications list:
Available online and in print

Access to staff:
Contact by letter, by telephone, by fax, by e-mail and via website. Appointment necessary.
Hours: Mon to Fri, 0900 to 1700

Member of:
International Society for Education in Art

NATIONAL SOCIETY FOR EPILEPSY

Acronym or abbreviation: NSE

Chesham Lane, Chalfont St Peter, Buckinghamshire, SL9 0RJ

Tel: 01494 601300\ 01494 601400 (Helpline)
Fax: 01494 871927

Website:
http://www.e-epilepsy.org.uk
Professional website, collection of articles
http://www.epilepsynse.org.uk
Copies of leaflets and fact sheets.

Enquiries:
Enquiries to: Information Officer
Direct tel: 01494 601392
Direct fax: 01494 601337

Founded:
1892

Organisation type and purpose:
National organisation (membership is by subscription), voluntary organisation, registered charity (charity number 206186), training organisation, research organisation.
To provide long-term and respite residential care for adults with epilepsy, to research into, and provide assessment and treatment services for, adults with epilepsy, to raise public awareness and understanding, to provide information, training and other support to people with epilepsy and their carers.

Subject coverage:
Epilepsy; help for people with epilepsy, residential homes, treatment, care and rehabilitation, research, diagnosis, support and management.

Non-library collection catalogue:
All or part available online

Printed publications:
Epilepsy information card and wallet (1 copy free, thereafter 20p each)
Epilepsy (2002, donation in the region of £8 to cover costs)
Fact sheets and leaflets (5 copies free, thereafter 10p for each factsheet and 20p each leaflet, please send large sae and 50p stamp)

Electronic and video publications:
DVD Packs:
Administration of Rectal Diazepam: training package for professionals (£10) and an information DVD for parents/carers (£8)
Putting You in the Picture: video for people with epilepsy and their families (£14.99)
Epilectic Seizures – a 35 min video explaining functions of brain and showing genuine seizures (£60)
About Epilepsy – information pack for adults with mild to moderate learning disabilities (9 booklets, £2.50)
Urdu information pack – contains audio tapes and leaflets for people who have Urdu as their first language (£15 plus £3 p&p)

Publications list:
Available online and in print

Access to staff:
Contact by letter and by telephone
Hours: Mon to Fri, 0900 to 1700
Special comments: Helpline open Mon to Fri, 1000 to 1600.

Access for disabled people:
Level entry, access to all public areas, toilet facilities

Affiliated to:
National Hospital of Neurology and Neurosurgery

NATIONAL SOCIETY FOR PHENYLKETONURIA

Formal name: National Society for Phenylketonuria (United Kingdom)
Acronym or abbreviation: NSPKU

PO Box 26642, London, N14 4ZF

Tel: 020 8364 3010
Fax: 0845 004 8341
E-mail: info@nspku.org

Website:
http://www.nspku.org
Information about phenylketonuria and the work of NSPKU. Online copies of many of the Society's leaflets and booklets.

Enquiries:
Enquiries to: Administrator
Direct tel: 020 8364 3010

Founded:
1973

Organisation type and purpose:
Registered charity (charity number 273670).

Subject coverage:
Help and advice for people with PKU, their families and carers.

Printed publications:
Dietary booklets (£1.50 to £2)
Leaflets and booklets for PKUs, their families, teachers, GPs and employers (small charge)
News and Views (magazine, quarterly, £1)

Publications list:
Available online and in print

Access to staff:
Contact by letter, by telephone and by e-mail
Hours: 24 hours

NATIONAL SOCIETY FOR RESEARCH INTO ALLERGY

Acronym or abbreviation: NSRA

2 Armadale Close, Hollycroft, Hinckley, Leicestershire, LE10 0SZ

Tel: 01455 250715
Fax: 01455 250715
E-mail: eunicerose@talktalk.net

Website:
http://all-allergy.org

Enquiries:
Enquiries to: Honorary Secretary
Other contacts: Honorary Vice-Chairperson (tel. 01455 291294)

Founded:
1980

Organisation type and purpose:
Advisory body, membership association (membership is by subscription), voluntary organisation, registered charity (charity number 32608).
Aims to see allergy and intolerance accepted and for there to be adequate, effective and safe treatment within the NHS. To assist and impart information to GPs, hospital doctors, and members of other caring and teaching professions, as well as sufferers.

Subject coverage:
Eczema, asthma, urticaria, hyperactivity, irritable bowel syndrome, Crohn's disease, migraine, arthritis, air-born allergy, ME, post-viral syndrome, PIMS and any other allergy or sensitivity, determination of allergy, medically backed diets, substitute foods, hyperventilation, criminal behaviour, thyroid problems.

Printed publications:
Allergy and Intolerance in Babies and Small Children (£2)
Anaphylaxis information leaflet (£1)
Crime Busting (£1)
Enzyme Potentiated Desensitisation (£1)
Enzyme Potentiated Desensitisation: Rules for people having this form of treatment (£5)
Hyperactivity (booklet, £2)
Hyperventilation (booklet, £2)
Is It Something you Ate?: allergy exclusion diets that really work (£5, free to members)
List of research projects
Reaction (magazine, 3 times a year, members)
Recipe Book (£5, free to members)

Publications list:
Available in print

Access to staff:
Contact by letter, by telephone, by e-mail and in person. Appointment necessary.
Hours: Mon to Fri, 0900 to 1700

NATIONAL SOCIETY OF ALLIED AND INDEPENDENT FUNERAL DIRECTORS, THE

Acronym or abbreviation: SAIF

SAIF Business Centre, 3 Bullfields, Sawbridgeworth, Hertfordshire, CM21 9DB

Tel: 0845 230 6777
Fax: 01279 726300
E-mail: info@saif.org.uk

Website:
http://www.saif.org.uk
Membership listing and information about the society.

Enquiries:
Enquiries to: Administration Manager
Direct e-mail: linda@saif.org.uk
Other contacts: Commercial Manager for membership and professional enquiries.

Founded:
1989

Organisation type and purpose:
Trade association (membership is by subscription), present number of members: 750.

Subject coverage:
All aspects of the UK funeral service.

Access to staff:
Contact by letter, by telephone, by fax and by e-mail
Hours: Mon to Fri, 0900 to 1700

NATIONAL SOCIETY OF ALLOTMENT AND LEISURE GARDENERS LIMITED

Acronym or abbreviation: NSALG

O'Dell House, Hunters Road, Corby, Northamptonshire, NN17 5JE

Tel: 01536 266576
Fax: 01536 264509
E-mail: natsoc@nsalg.org.uk

Enquiries:
Enquiries to: General Secretary

Founded:
1930

Organisation type and purpose:
Membership association (membership is by subscription), present number of members: 80,000, voluntary organisation.
National representative body.
Represents the interests of allotment holders.

Subject coverage:
Horticulture and gardening; interpretation of allotments legislation; environmental planning and development; preparation of leases and tenancy agreements.

Trade and statistical information:
Allotment survey.

Printed publications:
Allotment and Leisure Gardeners (quarterly, members free)

Access to staff:
Contact by letter, by telephone and by fax
Hours: Mon to Fri, 0900 to 1700

Affiliated to:
International League of Leisure Gardens

NATIONAL SOCIETY OF MASTER THATCHERS

Acronym or abbreviation: NSMT

20 The Laurels, Tetsworth, Thame, Oxfordshire, OX9 7BH

Tel: 01844 281568
Fax: 01844 281568
E-mail: nsmt@bigfoot.com

Website:
http://www.nsmt.hypermart.net

Enquiries:
Enquiries to: Secretary

Founded:
1963

Organisation type and purpose:
Trade association (membership is by qualification), present number of members: 80, voluntary organisation.

Subject coverage:
Thatching.

Printed publications:
How to select your thatched roof
The NSMT: its aims its functions

Access to staff:
Contact by letter and by e-mail
Hours: Evenings and weekends

NATIONAL SOCIETY'S RELIGIOUS EDUCATION CENTRE

Formal name: National Society (Church of England) for Promoting Religious Education
Acronym or abbreviation: NSREC

Church House, Great Smith Street, London, SW1P 3NZ

Tel: 020 7898 1495 or 1518
Fax: 020 7898 1493
E-mail: julia.jones@natsoc.c-of-e.org.uk

Website:
http://www.dspace.dial.pipex.com/nsrec
http://www.natsoc.org.uk

Enquiries:
Enquiries to: Information Officer

Founded:
1811

Organisation type and purpose:
Voluntary organisation, registered charity (charity number 313070).

Subject coverage:
Religious education, spiritual development.

Library catalogue:
All or part available in-house

Printed publications:
Order printed publications from: The National Society Church House, Great Smith Street, London, SW1P 3NZ, tel: 020 7898 1518, fax: 020 7898 1493

Publications list:
Available online and in print

Access to staff:
Contact by letter, by telephone, by fax, by e-mail and via website. Appointment necessary.
Hours: Mon to Fri, 0930 to 1630
Special comments: Closed bank holidays, Ascension Day, Maundy Thursday, and Christmas to New Year.

NATIONAL SOIL RESOURCES INSTITUTE

Acronym or abbreviation: SSLRC

Cranfield University, Silsoe, Bedfordshire, MK45 4DT

Tel: 01525 863242
Fax: 01525 863253
E-mail: nsridata@cranfield.ac.uk

Website:
http://www.silsoe.cranfield.ac.uk/nsri
General capability information. Downloadable details of the datasets avaliable

Enquiries:
Enquiries to: Development Manager
Direct tel: 01525 863263
Direct e-mail: d.thompson@cranfield.ac.uk

Founded:
2001

Organisation type and purpose:
Consultancy, research organisation.

Subject coverage:
Soils and land use, crop suitability, suitability of land for a wide range of uses, chemical and physical properties of soils, environmental risk assessment and pollution control.

Non-library collection catalogue:
All or part available in-house and in print

Printed publications:
Soil books and maps; national, by region and local, large and small scale
Technical and research reports
Order printed publications from: Publications Officer, National Soil Resources Institute
at the same address, tel: 01525 863242, fax: 01525 863253, e-mail: e.m.paynter@cranfield.ac.uk

Electronic and video publications:
Digital versions of the 1:250,000 scale National Soil
  Map plus soil proerty data sets
NSI Profile, NSI Site and NSI Elements; data at
  each intersect on a 5-kilometre grid across
  England and Wales
Soil type interpretation
Software

Publications list:
Available online and in print

Access to staff:
Contact by letter, by telephone, by fax, by e-mail
and via website. Appointment necessary.
Hours: Mon to Fri, 0900 to 1700

Access to building, collection or gallery:
Prior appointment required

Access for disabled people:
Level entry, toilet facilities

Other addresses:
National Soil Resources Institute
  NSRI, North Wyke, Okehampton, Devon, EX20
  2SB; tel: 01837 89188; fax: 01837 82139
National Soil Resources Institute
  NSRI, The Innovation Centre, York Science Park,
  Heslington, York, YO10 5DG; tel: 01904 435220;
  fax: 01904 435221
National Soil Resources Institute
  NSRI, Cambria House, 29, Newport Road,
  Cardiff, CF24 0TP; tel: 07775 865701

Parent body:
Cranfield University

NATIONAL SPECIALIST CONTRACTORS COUNCIL

Acronym or abbreviation: NSCC

Carthusian Court, 12, Carthusian Street, London,
EC1M 6EZ

Tel: 0870 429 6351
Fax: 0870 429 6352
E-mail: enquiries@nscc.org.uk

Website:
http://www.nscc.org.uk/index2.htm

Enquiries:
Enquiries to: Director

Founded:
1994

Organisation type and purpose:
Trade association.
Umbrella association representing the interests of
trade associations in the construction industry.

Subject coverage:
Contractors and sub-contractors in the specialist
sector and trade sector of construction.

Access to staff:
Contact by letter, by telephone and by fax
Hours: Mon to Fri, 0900 to 1700

Has:
28 member organisations

NATIONAL SPIRITUAL ASSEMBLY OF THE BAHA'IS OF THE UNITED KINGDOM

27 Rutland Gate, London, SW7 1PD

Tel: 020 7584 2566
Fax: 020 7584 9402
E-mail: secretariat@bahai.org.uk

Website:
http://www.bahai.org.uk
UK Baha'i community and local Baha'i
communities. Information about Baha'i Faith,
statements on a range of issues, links to local and
international sites.
http://www.onecountry.org
Social and Economic Development issues.

Enquiries:
Enquiries to: National Public Information Officer

Direct tel: 020 7590 8785
Direct e-mail: opi@bahai.org.uk
Other contacts: Information Officer

Founded:
1923

Organisation type and purpose:
Membership association, present number of
members: 6000 believers, voluntary organisation,
registered charity (charity number 250851).
Religious charity.

Subject coverage:
The Baha'i Faith – its history, teachings, national
and international standing; its relationship to
United Nations (ECOSOC, UNICEF, UNEP, WHO,
Human Rights Commission, UNESCO).

**Museum or gallery collection, archive, or library
special collection:**
Afnan Trust Library (by appointment only)
National Reference Library

Printed publications:
A wide range of titles on all aspects of Baha'i
  teachings and life available
Order printed publications from: Baha'i Books UK
5 Station Approach, Oakham, Leicestershire, LE15
6QW, tel: 01572 722780, fax: 01572 724280, e-mail:
bpt.sales@bahai.org.uk

Publications list:
Available in print

Access to staff:
Contact by telephone, by fax, by e-mail and via
website. Appointment necessary.
Hours: Mon to Fri, 0930 to 1700

Access to building, collection or gallery:
Prior appointment required
Hours: Mon to Fri, 0930 to 1700

Access for disabled people:
Toilet facilities

NATIONAL SPORTS MEDICINE INSTITUTE OF THE UK

Acronym or abbreviation: NSMI

32 Devonshire Street, London, W1G 6PX

Tel: 020 7908 3636
Fax: 020 7908 3635
E-mail: enquiry@nsmi.org.uk

Enquiries:
Enquiries to: Chief Executive
Direct tel: 020 7908 3637
Direct e-mail: francesca.wood@nsmi.org.uk
Other contacts: Library and Information Officer

Founded:
1986

Organisation type and purpose:
Registered charity, suitable for ages: 18+, training
organisation, research organisation.
Serves as the national focus and forum for all those
interested in or concerned with sport and exercise
medicine. The Institute also promotes good
medical practice in sports injury prevention,
treatment and rehabilitation. It aims to encourage
optimum levels of safety and care in order to
enhance the ability of those engaged in exercise
and sport from grass roots to international levels
throughout the UK.

Subject coverage:
Sports and exercise medicine and sciences,
including exercise physiology, nutrition, injury
prevention and rehabilitation, biomechanics, sport
psychology and the use of performance-enhancing
substances, health and fitness, disease; sport and
exercise medicine for children, women and
disabled.

**Museum or gallery collection, archive, or library
special collection:**
Core reference collection on sport and exercise
  medicine
Over 150 journals

Publications: Sports Medicine and Sports Science
  Journals in the library.

Library catalogue:
All or part available online and in print

Printed publications:
SMART (monthly)
SMART Plus
SMART: Drugs in Sport (6 times a year, £16)
SMART Health & Fitness (6 times a year, £16)
SMART Nutrition (6 times a year, £16)
SMART Physiotherapy (6 times a year, £16)
Sportscare news (quarterly)

Electronic and video publications:
SMART database (CD-ROM)
SMART Online (annual)

Publications list:
Available online and in print

Access to staff:
Contact by letter, by telephone, by fax, by e-mail
and in person. All charged.
Hours: Mon, Tue, Thu, Fri, 0900 to 1700; Wed, 0900
to 1800

Funded by:
Sports England
UK Sport

NATIONAL STOOLBALL ASSOCIATION

Acronym or abbreviation: NSA

53 Kings Road, Horsham, West Sussex, RH13 5PP

Tel: 01403 252419
E-mail: kr.price@homecall.co.uk

Website:
http://www.stoolball.co.uk
History of stoolball, rules of the game, mini
stoolball, pitch dimensions, newsletter, what's on.

Enquiries:
Enquiries to: Honorary Secretary
Other contacts: (1) Insurance Officer tel no 01293
772469 or leddy@tiscali.co.uk (2) Sales Officer tel
no 01403 252419 or kr.price@homecall.co.uk for (1)
personal accident and public liability (2) stoolball
equipment.

Founded:
1979

Organisation type and purpose:
Advisory body, voluntary organisation.
Governing body of stoolball.

Subject coverage:
All enquiries about stoolball.

**Museum or gallery collection, archive, or library
special collection:**
Archive records from 1880–1950 held at Barbican
  Museum, Lewes, Sussex; appointment needed
  for inspection

Electronic and video publications:
DVD, Let's Play Stoolball (£20.50)
Coaching Pack (2 DVDs) (£24.95)
Order electronic and video publications from:
Honorary Secretary

Publications list:
Available online and in print

Access to staff:
Contact by letter, by telephone, by e-mail and via
website
Hours: Any reasonable time, answerphone
available

Access to building, collection or gallery:
Prior appointment required

Access for disabled people:
Parking provided

NATIONAL SWEET PEA SOCIETY

Acronym or abbreviation: NSPS

continued overleaf

8 Wolseley Road, Parkstone, Poole, Dorset, BH12 2DP

Tel: 01202 734088
E-mail: bg.bulstrode@btinternet.com

Website:
http://www.sweetpea.org.uk

Enquiries:
Enquiries to: Secretary

Founded:
1900

Organisation type and purpose:
Membership association, registered charity.

Subject coverage:
Breeding, cultivation, development of lathyrus odoratus (sweet pea) and other lathyrus species; exhibiting and garden decoration.

Museum or gallery collection, archive, or library special collection:
All publications, since the formation of the Society in 1901

Printed publications:
Yearbook
Enjoy Sweet Peas (handbook)
Spring and Autumn Bulletins

Access to staff:
Contact by letter and by telephone. Access for members only.
Hours: Mon to Fri, 0900 to 1700

Affiliated to:
Royal Horticultural Society

NATIONAL SYMPHONY ORCHESTRA

Formal name: National Symphony Orchestra of London
Acronym or abbreviation: NSO

177 John Ruskin Street, London, SE5 0PQ

Tel: 020 7703 3148
Fax: 020 7703 5334
E-mail: enquiries@nso.co.uk

Website:
http://www.nso.co.uk
History of the NSO, personnel, current activities.

Enquiries:
Enquiries to: Artistic Director

Founded:
1940

Organisation type and purpose:
Symphony Orchestra.

Subject coverage:
Music, arts, entertainment.

Electronic and video publications:
Wide range of CD-ROMs available from major record shops

Access to staff:
Contact by letter, by telephone, by e-mail and in person
Hours: Mon to Fri, 0900 to 1700

NATIONAL TAXI ASSOCIATION

Acronym or abbreviation: NTA

5 Clifton Hill, Brighton, East Sussex, BN1 3HL

Tel: 01273 729403
Fax: 01273 728122
E-mail: enquiries@brighton-streamline.co.uk

Website:
http://www.brighton-streamline.co.uk

Enquiries:
Enquiries to: Administrator

Founded:
1967

Organisation type and purpose:
National organisation, trade association (membership is by subscription).

Subject coverage:
Taxi cabs.

Access to staff:
Contact by letter and by e-mail
Hours: Mon to Fri, 0900 to 1700

NATIONAL THEATRE

Acronym or abbreviation: NT

Upper Ground, London, SE1 9PX

Tel: 020 7452 3000 box office; 020 7452 3333 stage door/admin\ Minicom no. 020 7452 3009
Fax: 020 7452 3030 box office

Website:
http://www.nationaltheatre.org.uk
Information about current and forthcoming productions and general information on the National.

Enquiries:
Enquiries to: Information Officer
Direct tel: 020 7452 3400

Founded:
1963

Organisation type and purpose:
Registered charity (charity number 224223).
The National Theatre is central to the creative life of the country. In its three theatres on the South Bank in London, it presents an eclectic mix of new plays and classics, with seven or eight productions in repertory at any one time. It aims constantly to re-energise the great traditions of the British stage and to expand the horizons of audiences and artists alike. It aspires to reflect in its repertoire the diversity of the culture. At its Studio, the National offers a space for research and development of the NT's stages and the theatre as a whole. Through the NT Education Department, tomorrow's audiences are addressed. Through an extensive programme of Platform performances, backstage tours, foyer music, exhibitions, and free outdoor entertainment it recognises that the theatre does not begin and end with the rise and fall of the curtain. And by touring, the National shares its work with audiences in the UK and abroad.

Subject coverage:
World drama; free exhibitions and live music; platform performances and events; education and community outreach work; theatre backstage tours; bookshop; bars and restaurants.

Non-library collection catalogue:
All or part available online

Printed publications:
Platform papers
Programmes
Books
Collections of Transcripts
Leaflets
Supporters & Education Newsletter
Order printed publications from: National Theatre Bookshop
At the address above, tel: 020 7452 3456, e-mail: bookshop@nationaltheatre.org.uk

Access to staff:
Contact by letter, by telephone and by fax
Hours: Foyers: Mon to Sat, 1000 to 2300; Box Office: Mon to Sat, 1000 to 2000

Access for disabled people:
Parking provided, ramped entry, access to all public areas, toilet facilities
Special comments: Audio-described and sign language interpreted performances.

NATIONAL TORTOISE CLUB OF GREAT BRITAIN & TORTOISE HELPLINE

2 Laith Close, Cookridge, Leeds, West Yorkshire, LS16 6LE

Tel: 0113 267 7587

Enquiries:
Enquiries to: Chairman

Founded:
1970

Organisation type and purpose:
International organisation, advisory body, membership association, voluntary organisation, consultancy.
Advisory service UK and Europe; funded entirely by Founders.
Permanent sanctuary to any tortoise, on request, free.

Subject coverage:
All aspects of the needs of tortoises and box tortoises (often incorrectly called turtles) throughout the year; health and sickness, diet, hibernation, breeding, care and well-being of all species.

Information services:
Helpline.

Printed publications:
Care sheet by experts (at small cost)

Access to staff:
Contact by letter and by telephone
Hours: Mon to Fri, 0900 to 1700
Special comments: Enclose an sae for reply, donations appreciated. If messages left on answerphone no calls back made without assurance that reversed charges will be accepted.

NATIONAL TRACTION ENGINE TRUST

Acronym or abbreviation: NTET

153 Micklefield Road, High Wycombe, Buckinghamshire, HP13 7HA

Tel: 01494 521727
Fax: 01494 521727
E-mail: suejackson@themutual.net

Enquiries:
Enquiries to: Secretary General

Founded:
1954

Organisation type and purpose:
Membership association (membership is by subscription), voluntary organisation, registered charity.
Most local steam groups with similar aims are affiliated.

Subject coverage:
History of engines and their manufacturers, as well as up-to-date information as to repairs, spares and information about traction engine rallies each year, for organisers and the general public, preservation and operation of steam driven traction engines.

Printed publications:
Steaming (quarterly, free to members)

Access to staff:
Contact by letter, by telephone, by fax and by e-mail
Hours: Mon to Fri, 0900 to 1700

NATIONAL TROLLEYBUS ASSOCIATION

Acronym or abbreviation: NTA

24 Heath Farm Road, Ferndown, Dorset, BH22 8JW

Website:
http://www.trolleybus.co.uk/nta

Enquiries:
Enquiries to: Editor
Direct e-mail: carl.isgar@lineone.net
Other contacts: editor.tm@btinternet.com

Founded:
1963

Organisation type and purpose:
Membership association.
To produce publications relating to trolleybuses and to preserve trolleybuses (five of which are currently owned).

Subject coverage:
Description of present day trolleybus operation, new vehicle developments, system histories, comprehensive worldwide trolleybus news with maps and illustrations.

Museum or gallery collection, archive, or library special collection:
H Brearley, photographic collection
R F Mack, photographic collection

Trade and statistical information:
Statistics on all aspects of trolleybuses and trolleybus systems.
Information on new vehicles, technical developments etc.

Printed publications:
Trolleybus Magazine (6 times a year)

Access to staff:
Contact by letter and by e-mail
Hours: Mon to Fri, 0900 to 1700

Affiliated to:
Trolleybus Museum Company Ltd

Membership enquiries:
National Trolleybus Association
2 St John's Close. Claines, Worcester, WR3 7PT

Subsidiary for publication sales:
Autumn Reach
The Close, St Ives, Ringwood, BH24 2PE

NATIONAL TRUST

Formal name: National Trust for Places of Historic Interest or Natural Beauty
Acronym or abbreviation: NT

36 Queen Anne's Gate, London, SW1H 9AS

Tel: 020 7222 9251
Fax: 020 7222 5097
E-mail: enquiries@thenationaltrust.org.uk

Website:
http://www.nationaltrust.org.uk
Includes a section dedicated to providing online access to information about their holdings, which include buildings, collections, libraries and archives

Enquiries:
Enquiries to: Director General
Other contacts: Customer Care Manager for general enquiries.

Founded:
1895

Organisation type and purpose:
National organisation, membership association (membership is by subscription), present number of members: 2.9 million, voluntary organisation, registered charity (charity number 205846), museum, historic building, house or site, suitable for ages: all, research organisation, publishing house.
Membership is the principal means by which the NT is supported, but access to its services is not restricted to members.
The National Trust preserves places of historic interest or natural beauty for all to enjoy, now and forever.

Subject coverage:
Conservation of buildings and land of historic interest or natural beauty held in perpetuity for the nation, inalienably. History of the National Trust. Visitor management, sustainability, policy issues etc.

Museum or gallery collection, archive, or library special collection:
Details may be found in the Trust's handbook and on the website
Some country houses contain antiquarian libraries for which the central catalogue is still in the development stage. All these collections are managed and accessed by different arrangements, many of which are local to the property itself

Printed publications:
Magazine (3 times a year, members)
Properties List (every 5 years)
National Trust Handbook (annually)
Books related to the properties eg architecture and horticulture, and cooking and children's stories (sold in National Trust Shops and good bookshops)
Guide books to practically every property open to the public (available at the properties or from Reception at 36 Queen Anne's Gate)
The Lake District: a resource book for teachers
Books for children include:
The Investigating Series: 12 titles connected to Key Stages 2 and 3 of the National Curriculum
The Mud Pack Series, conservation in England, Wales and Northern Ireland
See website for complete list

Electronic and video publications:
National Trust British Countryside (CD-ROM, from Anglia Multimedia, tel 01603 615151, £29.99)
Timeline: Trust houses brought to life

Publications list:
Available online and in print

Access to staff:
Contact by letter, by telephone, by fax, by e-mail, in person and via website
Hours: Mon to Fri, 0900 to 1700

Other addresses:
Learning Community and Volunteering Office
Rowan House, Kembrey Park, Swindon, Wiltshire, SN2 6UG; tel: 0870 609 5383
National Trust Conservation Directorate
33 Sheep Street, Cirencester, Gloucestershire, CL7 1RQ; tel: 0870 609 5382
National Trust Enterprises
The Stable Block, Heywood House, Westbury, Wiltshire, BA13 4NA; tel: 0870 609 5381
National Trust for Scotland
Wemyss House, 28 Charlotte Square, Edinburgh, EH2 4ET; tel: 0131 243 9300
National Trust Office for Northern Ireland
Rowallane House, Saintfield, Ballynahinch, Co Down, BT24 7LH; tel: 028 9751 0721; fax: 028 9751 1242
National Trust Office for Wales
Trinity Square, Llandudno, LL30 2DE; tel: 01492 860123; fax: 01492 860233
National Trust Theatre Projects
The National Trust, Sutton House, 2 & 4 Homerton High Street, Hackney, London, E9 6JQ; tel: 020 8986 0242
The National Trust Membership Department
PO Box 39, Bromley, Kent, BR1 3XL; tel: 020 8466 6824

Regional Offices:
National Trust, Devon & Cornwall
Killerton House, Broadclyst, Exeter, Devon, EX5 3LE; tel: 01392 881691; fax: 01392 881954
National Trust, Devon & Cornwall
Lanhydrock, Bodmin, Cornwall, PL30 4DE; tel: 01208 74281; fax: 01208 77887
National Trust, East Anglia (Bedfordshire, Cambridgeshire, Essex, part of Hertfordshire, Norfolk & Suffolk)
The Dairy House, Ickworth, Suffolk, IP29 5QE; tel: 0870 609 5388; fax: 01284 736066

National Trust, East Midlands (Derbyshire, Leicestershire, S Lincolnshire, Northamptonshire, Nottinghamshire & Rutland)
Clumber Park Stableyard, Worksop, Nottinghamshire, S80 3BE; tel: 01909 486411; fax: 01909 486377
National Trust, North West (Cheshire, Cumbria, Greater Manchester & Lancashire, Merseyside)
The Hollens, Grasmere, LA22 9QZ; tel: 0870 609 5391; fax: 015394 35353
National Trust, South East (East Sussex, Kent, Surrey & West Sussex)
Polesden Lacey, Dorking, Surrey, RH5 6BD; tel: 01372 453401; fax: 01372 452023
National Trust, Thames & Solent (Berkshire, Buckinghamshire, Hampshire, part of Hertfordshire, Isle of Wight, Greater London & Oxfordshire)
Hughenden Manor, High Wycombe, Buckinghamshire, HP14 4LA; tel: 01494 528051; fax: 01494 463310
National Trust, Wessex (Bristol/Bath, Dorset, Gloucestershire, Somerset & Wiltshire)
Eastleigh Court, Bishopstrow, Warminster, Wiltshire, BA12 9HW; tel: 01985 843600; fax: 01985 843624
National Trust, West Midlands (Birmingham, Hereford, Shropshire, Staffordshire, Warwickshire & Worcestershire)
Attingham Park, Shrewsbury, Shropshire, SY4 4TP; tel: 01743 708100; fax: 01743 708150
National Trust, Yorkshire & North East (Co Durham, Newcastle & Tyneside, Northumberland)
Scots' Gap, Morpeth, Northumberland, NE61 4EG; tel: 01670 774691; fax: 01670 774317
National Trust, Yorkshire & North East (Yorkshire, Teesside & N Lincolnshire)
Goddards, 27 Tadcaster Road, York, YO24 1GG; tel: 01904 702021; fax: 01904 771970

NATIONAL TRUST (DEVON & CORNWALL REGIONAL OFFICES) – BODMIN

Formal name: National Trust for Places of Historic Interest or Natural Beauty
Acronym or abbreviation: NT

Lanhydrock, Bodmin, Cornwall, PL30 4DE

Tel: 01208 74281
Fax: 01208 77887
E-mail: enquiries@thenationaltrust.org.uk

Website:
http://www.nationaltrust.org.uk
Information about the National Trust properties, opening times and facilities, special events, educational information.

Enquiries:
Enquiries to: Customer Service Manager

Founded:
1895

Organisation type and purpose:
National organisation, independently owned, membership association (membership is by subscription), registered charity (charity number 205846), historic building, house or site, suitable for ages: all.

Subject coverage:
Administration and management of Trust sites in the region.
The preservation and upkeep of places of historic interest and natural beauty in Cornwall.

Publications list:
Available online and in print

Links with:
Trevithick Trust
Trevithick Road, Pool, Redruth, Cornwall, TR15 3NP; tel: 01209 210900; e-mail: info@ trevithicktrust.com

National Trust Sites:
Antony House
Torpoint, Plymouth, PL11 2QA; tel: 01752 812191

continued overleaf

Cornish Mines & Engines
   Trevithick Road, Pool, Redruth, Cornwall, TR15 3NP; tel: 01209 210900
Cotehele House
   St. Dominick, Saltash, Cornwall, PL30 5AD; tel: 01579 351346; e-mail: cctlce@smtp.ntrust.org.uk
Godolphin Estate
   Lizard Countryside Office, Helston, Cornwall; tel: 01326 562882
Lanhydrock House
   Cornwall; tel: 01208 73320; e-mail: clhlan@smtp.ntrust.org.uk
Lawrence House Museum
   9 Castle Street, Launceston, Cornwall, PL15 8BA; tel: 01566 773277
Levant Steam Engine
   Trewellard, Pendeen, St Just, Cornwall; tel: 01736 786156
St Michael's Mount
   Marazion, Penzance, Cornwall, TR17 0EF; tel: 01736 710507 / 710233; e-mail: godolphin@manor-office.co.uk
Tintagel Old Post Office
   Fore Street, Tintagel, Cornwall, PL34 0DB; tel: 01840 770024
Trerice Manor House
   Kestle Mill, Newquay, Cornwall, TR8 4PG; tel: 01637 875404

NATIONAL TRUST (DEVON & CORNWALL REGIONAL OFFICES) – EXETER

Formal name: National Trust for Places of Historic Interest or Natural Beauty
Acronym or abbreviation: NT

Killerton House, Broadclyst, Exeter, Devon, EX5 3LE

Tel: 01392 881691
Fax: 01392 881954
E-mail: enquiries@thenationaltrust.org.uk

Website:
http://www.nationaltrust.org.uk
Information about the National Trust properties, opening times and facilities, special events, educational information, and publications.

Enquiries:
Enquiries to: Service Supporter Manager

Founded:
1895

Organisation type and purpose:
National organisation, independently owned, membership association (membership is by subscription), registered charity (charity number 205846), historic building, house or site, suitable for ages: Life long.
Administration and management of Trust sites in Devon.

Subject coverage:
The preservation and upkeep of places of historic interest and natural beauty in Devon.

Non-library collection catalogue:
All or part available in-house

Library catalogue:
All or part available in-house

Publications list:
Available online and in print

Access to staff:
Contact by letter, by telephone, by fax, by e-mail, in person and via website
Hours: Sun to Sat, 0900 to 1700

Access to building, collection or gallery:
Hours: Generally 1100 to 1700, but please check before visit

National Trust sites:
A La Ronde
   Summer Lane, Exmouth, Devon, EX8 5BD; tel: 01395 265514
Arlington Court
   Arlington, Barnstaple, Devon, EX31 4LP; tel: 01271 850296; fax: 01271 850711

Bradley House
   Totnes Road, Newton Abbot, Devon, TQ12 6BN; tel: 01626 354513
Buckland Abbey
   Yelverton, Devon, PL20 6EY; tel: 01822 853607; fax: 01822 855448
Castle Drogo
   Drewsteignton, Exeter, Devon, EX6 6PB; tel: 01647 433306; fax: 01647 433186
Clyston Mill
   Killerton, Broadclyst, Exeter, Devon, EX5 3EW; tel: 01392 462425
Coleton Fishacre House
   Coleton, Brownstone Road, Kingswear, Dartmouth, Devon, TQ6 0EQ; tel: 01803 752466
Compton Castle
   Marldon, Paignton, Devon, TQ3 1TA; tel: 01803 875740
Finch Foundary Museum of Rural Industry
   Sticklepath, Okehampton, Devon, EX20 2NW; tel: 01837 840046
Killerton House
   Broadclyst, Exeter, Devon, EX5 3LE; tel: 01392 881345
Knightshayes Court
   Bolham, Tiverton, Devon, EX16 7RQ; tel: 01884 254665
Loughwood Meeting House
   Dalwood, Axminster, Devon, EX13 7DU; tel: 01392 881691; fax: 01392 881954
Marker's Cottage
   Killerton, Broadclyst, Exeter, Devon, EX5 3HR; tel: 01392 461546
Newhall Equestrian Centre
   Killerton, Broadclyst, Exeter, Devon, EX5 3LW; tel: 01392 462453
Old Bakery, Manor Mill and Forge
   Branscombe, Seaton, Devon, EX12 3DB; tel: 01297 680333
Overbeck's Museum and Gardens
   Sharpitor, Salcombe, Devon, 01548 842893; tel: 01548 842893
Saltram House
   Plympton, Plymouth, Devon, PL7 1UH; tel: 01752 333500; fax: 01752 336474
Shute Barton
   Shute, Axminster, Devon, EX13 7PT; tel: 01297 34692
Watersmeet House
   Watersmeet Road, Lynmouth, Devon, EX35 6NT; tel: 01598 753348

NATIONAL TRUST (EAST MIDLANDS REGIONAL OFFICE)

Formal name: National Trust for Places of Historic Interest or Natural Beauty
Acronym or abbreviation: NT

Clumber Park Stableyard, Worksop, Nottinghamshire, S80 3BE

Tel: 01909 486411
Fax: 01909 486377
E-mail: enquiries@thenationaltrust.org.uk

Website:
http://www.nationaltrust.org.uk
Information about the National Trust properties, opening times and facilities, special events, educational information, and publications.

Enquiries:
Enquiries to: Customer Service Manager

Founded:
1895

Organisation type and purpose:
National organisation, independently owned, membership association (membership is by subscription), registered charity (charity number 205846), historic building, house or site, suitable for ages: Life long.
Administration and management of Trust sites in the East Midlands.

Subject coverage:
The preservation and upkeep of places of historic interest and natural beauty in Derbyshire, Leicestershire, South Lincolnshire, Northamptonshire, Nottinghamshire and Rutland.

Publications list:
Available online and in print

Access to staff:
Contact by letter, by telephone, by fax, by e-mail, in person and via website
Hours: Mon to Fri, 0900 to 1700

National Trust sites:
Belton House
   Belton, Grantham, Lincolnshire, NG32 2LS; tel: 01476 566116; e-mail: belton@smpt.ntrust.org.uk
Calke Abbey
   Ticknall, Derbyshire; tel: 01332 863822; e-mail: ecbxxx@smpt.ntrust.org.uk
Canons Ashby House
   Canons Ashby, Daventry, Northamptonshire, NN1 6SD; tel: 01327 860044; fax: 01327 860168; e-mail: canonsashby@ntrust.org.uk
Grantham House
   Castle Gate, Grantham, Lincolnshire, NG31 6SS; tel: 01909 486411 (Regional Office)
Gunby Hall
   Gunby, Spilsby, Lincolnshire, PE23 5SS; tel: 01909 486411 (Regional Office)
Hardwick Hall
   Doe Lea, Chesterfield, Derbyshire, S44 5QJ; tel: 01246 850430
Kedleston Hall
   Kedleston, Derby, DE22 5JH; tel: 01332 842191; fax: 01332 841972; e-mail: kedlestonhall@ntrust.org.uk
Lyveden New Bield
   Oundle, Peterborough, Northamptonshire, PE8 5AT; tel: 01832 205358; e-mail: lyvedennewbield@ntrust.org.uk
Mr Straws House
   7 Blyth Grove, Worksop, Nottinghamshire, S81 0JG; tel: 01909 482380; e-mail: estxxx@smtp.ntrust.org.uk
Museum of Childhood
   Sudbury Hall, Sudbury, Ashbourne, Derbyshire, DE6 5HT; tel: 01283 585305
Priest's House
   39 Church Street, Easton on the Hill, Stamford, Northamptonshire, PE9 3LL; tel: 01909 486411 (Regional Office)
Stainsby Mill
   c/o Hardwick Hall, Doe Lea, Chesterfield, Derbyshire, S44 5QJ; tel: 01246 850430; e-mail: ehwxxx@smtr.ntrust.org.uk
Staunton Harold Church
   Staunton Harold, Ashby-de-la-Zouch, Leicestershire; tel: 01332 863822; fax: 01332 865272; e-mail: stauntonharold@ntrust.org.uk
Sudbury Hall
   Sudbury, Ashbourne, Derbyshire, DE6 5HT; tel: 01283 585305
Tattershall Castle
   Tattershall, Lincoln, LN4 4LR; tel: 01526 342543; e-mail: tattershallcastle@ntrust.org.uk
The Workhouse
   Upton Road, Southwell, Nottinghamshire, NG25 0PT; tel: 01636 817250
Whitegates Cottage
   Gunby Hall Estate, Mill Lane, Bratoft, Spilsby, Lincolnshire; tel: 01909 486411 (Regional Office)
Woolsthorpe Manor
   23 Newton Way, Woolsthorp-by-Colsterworth, Grantham, Lincolnshire, NG33 5NR; tel: 01476 860338

NATIONAL TRUST (EAST OF ENGLAND REGIONAL OFFICE)

Formal name: National Trust for Places of Historic Interest or Natural Beauty
Acronym or abbreviation: NT

Westley Bottom, Bury St Edmunds, Suffolk, IP33 3WD

Tel: 01284 747500
Fax: 01284 747506

E-mail: enquiries@thenationaltrust.org.uk

Website:
http://www.nationaltrust.org.uk
Information about the National Trust properties, opening times and facilities, special events, educational information, and publications.

Enquiries:
Enquiries to: Customer Service Manager

Founded:
1895

Organisation type and purpose:
National organisation, independently owned, membership association (membership is by subscription), registered charity (charity number 205846), historic building, house or site, suitable for ages: Life long.
Administration and management of Trust sites in East Anglia.

Subject coverage:
The preservation and upkeep of places of historic interest and natural beauty in Bedfordshire, Cambridgeshire, Essex, part of Hertfordshire, Norfolk and Suffolk.

Publications list:
Available online and in print

Access to staff:
Contact by letter, by telephone, by fax, by e-mail, in person and via website
Hours: Mon to Fri, 0900 to 1700

National Trust sites:
Anglesey Abbey, Gardens and Lode Mill
  Quy Road, Nr Lode, Cambridge, CB5 9EJ; tel: 01223 811200; e-mail: aayusr@ntrust.org.uk
Blickling Hall
  Blickling, Norwich, Norfolk, NR11 6NF; tel: 01263 738030; e-mail: blickling@ntrust.org.uk
Bourne Mill
  Bourne Road, Colchester, Essex, CO2 8RT; tel: 01206 572422
Coggeshall Grange Barn
  Grange Hill, Coggeshall, Colchester, Essex, CO6 1RE; tel: 01376 562226
Elizabethan House Museum
  4 South Quay, Great Yarmouth, Norfolk, NR30 2QH; tel: 01493 855746; fax: 01493 745459
Felbrigg Hall
  Felbrigg, Norwich, Norfolk, NR11 8PR; tel: 01263 837444; e-mail: afgusr@smtp.ntrust.org.uk
Guildhall of Corpus Christi
  Market Place, Sudbury, Suffolk, CO10 9QZ; tel: 01787 247646; e-mail: almjtg@smtp.ntrust.org.uk
Horsey Windpump
  Horsey, Great Yarmouth, Norfolk, NR29 4EF; tel: 01493 393904 (on open days); e-mail: horsey@ntrust.org.uk
Houghton Mill
  Houghton, Huntingdon, Cambridgeshire, PE28 2EZ; tel: 01480 301494
Ickworth House, Park & Garden
  Horringer, Bury St Edmunds, Suffolk, IP29 5QE; tel: 01284 735270
Melford Hall
  Long Melford, Sudbury, Suffolk, CO10 9AA; tel: 01787 880286; e-mail: amdklx@smtp.ntrust.org.uk
Oxburgh Hall
  Oxborough, Kings Lynn, Nofolk, PE33 9PS; tel: 01366 328258; fax: 01366 328066; e-mail: aohusr@smtp.ntrust.org.uk
Paycocke's
  West Street, Coggeshall, Colchester, Essex, CO6 1NS; tel: 01376 561305
Peckover House
  North Brink, Wisbech, Cambridgeshire, PE13 1JR; tel: 01945 583463; e-mail: aprigix@smtp.ntrust.org.uk
Ramsey Abbey Gatehouse
  Abbey School, Ramsey, Huntingdon, Cambridgeshire, PE17 1DH; tel: 0870 609 5388
Shaw's Corner
  Ayot St Lawrence, Welwyn Garden City, Hertfordshire, AL6 9BX; tel: 01438 820307; e-mail: shawscorner@ntrust.org.uk

Suffolk Horse Museum
  The Market Hill, Woodbridge, Suffolk, IP12 4LP; tel: 01394 380643
Sutton Hoo
  Woodbridge, Suffolk; tel: 01394 389700
Theatre Royal
  Westgate Street, Bury St Edmunds, Suffolk, IP33 1QR; tel: 01284 769505
Wimpole Hall
  Arrington, Royston, Hertfordshire, SG8 0BW; tel: 01223 207257; fax: 01223 207383; e-mail: aweusr@smtp.org.uk

NATIONAL TRUST (NORTH WEST REGIONAL OFFICE)

Formal name: National Trust for Places of Historic Interest or Natural Beauty
Acronym or abbreviation: NT

The Hollens, Grasmere, Cumbria, LA22 9QZ

Tel: 015394 35599
Fax: 015394 35353
E-mail: enquiries@thenationaltrust.org.uk

Website:
http://www.nationaltrust.org.uk

Enquiries:
Enquiries to: Customer Service Manager

Founded:
1895

Organisation type and purpose:
National organisation, independently owned, membership association (membership is by subscription), registered charity (charity number 205846), historic building, house or site, suitable for ages: life-long.
Administration and management of Trust sites in the North West region.

Subject coverage:
The preservation and upkeep of places of historic interest and natural beauty in Cheshire, Cumbria, Greater Manchester and Lancashire, Merseyside.

Publications list:
Available online and in print

Access to staff:
Contact by letter, by telephone, by fax, by e-mail, in person and via website
Hours: Mon to Fri, 0900 to 1700

National Trust sites:
20 Forthlin Road
  Liverpool, L24 1YP; tel: 0151 427 7231 (bookings); e-mail: 20forthlinroad@ntrust.org.uk
Beatrix Potter Gallery
  Main Street, Hawkshead, Ambleside, Cumbria, LA22 0NS; tel: 015394 36355; fax: 015394 36187; e-mail: beatrixpottergallery@ntrust.org.uk
Cartmel Gatehouse Heritage Centre
  Cavendish Street, Cartmel, Grange-over-Sands, Cumbria, LA11 6QA; tel: 015395 36874; fax: 015395 36636; e-mail: cartmelpriory@ntrust.org.uk
Dunham Massey
  Altrincham, Greater Manchester, Cheshire, WA14 4SJ; tel: 0161 941 1025; fax: 0161 929 7508; e-mail: dunhammassey@ntrust.org.uk
Gawthorpe Hall
  Padiham, Burnley, Lancashire, BB12 8UA; tel: 01282 771004; fax: 01282 770178; e-mail: gawthorpehall@ntrust.org.uk
Hill Top
  Near Sawrey, Ambleside, Cumbria, LA22 0LF; tel: 015394 36269; fax: 015394 36188; e-mail: hilltop@ntrust.ofg.uk
Little Moreton Hall
  Congleton, Cheshire, CW12 4SD; tel: 01260 272018; e-mail: littlemoretonhall@ntrust.org.uk
Lyme Park
  Disley, Stockport, Cheshire, SK12 2NX; tel: 01663 762023; fax: 01663 765035; e-mail: lymepark@ntrust.org.uk

Nether Alderley Mill
  Congleton Road, Nether Alderley, Macclesfield, Cheshire, SK10 4TW; tel: 01625 584412; e-mail: netheralderleymill@ntrust.org.uk
Quarry Bank Mill and Styal Estate
  Quarry Bank Road, Styal, Wilmslow, Cheshire, SK9 4LA; tel: 01625 527468; fax: 01625 539267; e-mail: quarrybankmill@ntrust.org.uk
Rufford Old Hall
  Rufford, Ormskirk, Lancashire, L40 1SG; tel: 01704 821254; fax: 01704 821254; e-mail: ruffordhall@ntrust.org.uk
Sizergh Castle and Garden
  Sizergh, Kendal, Cumbria, LA8 8AE; tel: 01539 560070; fax: 015395 61621; e-mail: ntrust@sizerghcastle.fsnet.co.uk
Speke Hall
  The Walk, Liverpool, L24 1XD; tel: 0151 427 7231; fax: 0151 427 9860; e-mail: spekehall@ntrust.org.uk
Tatton Park
  Knutsford, Cheshire, WA16 6QN; tel: 01625 534400; fax: 01625 534403; e-mail: tatton@cheshire.gov.uk
Townend
  Troutbeck, Windermere, Cumbria, LA23 1LB; tel: 01539 432628; e-mail: townend@ntrust.org.uk
Wordsworth House
  Main Street, Cockermouth, Cumbria, CA13 9RX; tel: 01900 824805; fax: 01900 824805; e-mail: wordsworthhouse@ntrust.org.uk

NATIONAL TRUST (SOUTH EAST REGIONAL OFFICE)

Formal name: National Trust for Places of Historic Interest or Natural Beauty
Acronym or abbreviation: NT

Polesden Lacey, Dorking, Surrey, RH5 6BD

Tel: 01372 453401
Fax: 01372 452023
E-mail: enquiries@thenationaltrust.org.uk

Website:
http://www.nationaltrust.org.uk
Information about the National Trust properties, opening times and facilities, special events, educational information, and publications.

Enquiries:
Enquiries to: Customer Service Manager

Founded:
1895

Organisation type and purpose:
National organisation, independently owned, membership association (membership is by subscription), registered charity (charity number 205846), historic building, house or site, suitable for ages: Life long.
Administration and management of Trust sites in the South East region.

Subject coverage:
The preservation and upkeep of Trust properties of historic interest and natural beauty in East Sussex, Kent, Surrey and West Sussex.

Publications list:
Available online and in print

Access to staff:
Contact by letter, by telephone, by fax, by e-mail, in person and via website
Hours: Mon to Fri, 0900 to 1700

National Trust sites:
Alfriston Clergy House
  The Tye, Alfriston, Polegate, East Sussex, BN26 5TL; tel: 01323 870001; fax: 01323 871318; e-mail: alfriston@nationaltrust.org.uk
Bateman's
  Bateman's Lane, Burwash, Etchingham, East Sussex, TN19 7DS; tel: 01435 882302; fax: 01435 882811; e-mail: batemans@nationaltrust.org.uk
Bodiam Castle
  Bodiam, Robertsbridge, East Sussex, TN32 5UA; tel: 01580 830436; fax: 01580 830398; e-mail: bodiamcastle@nationaltrust.org.uk

continued overleaf

Chartwell
Mapleton Road, Westerham, Kent, TN16 1PS; tel: 01732 868381; fax: 01732 868193; e-mail: chartwell@nationaltrust.org.uk

Clandon Park
West Clandon, Guildford, Surrey, GU4 7RQ; tel: 01483 222482; fax: 01483 223479; e-mail: clandonpark@nationaltrust.org.uk

Claremont Landscape Garden
Portsmouth Road, Esher, Surrey, KT10 9JG; tel: 01372 467806; e-mail: claremont@nationaltrust.org.uk

Emmetts Garden
Ide Hill, Sevenoaks, Kent, TN14 6AY; tel: 01732 751509; e-mail: emmetts@nationaltrust.org.uk

Hatchlands Park
East Clandon, Guildford, Surrey, GU4 7RT; tel: 01483 222482; fax: 01483 223176; e-mail: hatchlands@nationatrust.org.uk

Ightham Mote
Ivy Hatch, Sevenoaks, Kent, TN15 0NT; tel: 01732 810378; fax: 01732 811029; e-mail: ighthammote@nationaltrust.org.uk

Knole
Sevenoaks, Kent, TN15 0RP; tel: 01732 462100; fax: 01732 465528; e-mail: knole@nationaltrust.org.uk

Lamb House
West Street, Rye, East Sussex, TN31 7ES; e-mail: lambhouse@nationaltrust.org.uk

Monk's House
Rodmell, Lewes, East Sussex, BN7 3HF; e-mail: monkshouse@nationaltrust.org.uk

Nymans
Handcross, nr Haywards Heath, West Sussex, RH17 6EB; tel: 01444 405250; e-mail: nymans@nationaltrust.org.uk

Oakhurst Cottage
Hambledon, Godalming, Surrey, GU8 4HF; e-mail: oakhurstcottage@nationaltrust.org.uk

Petworth House
Church Street, Petworth, West Sussex, GU28 0AE; tel: 01798 342207; fax: 01798 342963; e-mail: petworth@nationaltrust.org.uk

Polesden Lacey
Great Bookham, Dorking, Surrey, RH5 6BD; tel: 01372 452048; fax: 01372 452023; e-mail: polesdenlacey@nationaltrust.org.uk

Quebec House
Quebec Square, Westerham, Kent, TN16 1TD

River Wey & Godalming Navigations and Dapdune Wharf
Dapdune Wharf, Wharf Road, Guildford, Surrey, GU1 4RR; tel: 01483 561389; fax: 01483 531667; e-mail: riverwey@nationaltrust.org.uk

Scotney Castle Garden and Estate
Lamberhurst, Tunbridge Wells, Kent, TN3 8JN; tel: 01892 893868; fax: 01892 890110; e-mail: scotneycastle@nationaltrust.org.uk

Shalford Mill
Shalford, Guildford, Surrey, GU4 8BS; tel: 01483 561389; e-mail: shalfordmill@nationaltrust.org.uk

Sheffield Park Garden
Sheffield Park, East Sussex, TN22 3QX; tel: 01825 790231; e-mail: sheffieldpark@nationaltrust.org.uk

Sissinghurst Castle Garden
Sissinghurst, Cranbrook, Kent, TN17 2AB; tel: 01580 710700; fax: 01580 710702; e-mail: sissinghurst@nationaltrust.org.uk

Smallhythe Place
Smallhythe, Tenterden, Kent, TN30 7NG; tel: 01580 762334; fax: 01580 762334; e-mail: smallhytheplace@nationaltrust.org.uk

South Foreland Lighthouse
The Front, St Margaret's Bay, Dover, Kent, CT15 6HP; tel: 01304 852463; fax: 01304 215484; e-mail: southforeland@nationaltrust.org.uk

Standen
West Hoathly Road, East Grinstead, West Sussex, RH19 4NE; tel: 01342 323029; fax: 01342 316424; e-mail: standen@nationaltrust.org.uk

Uppark House
South Harting, Petersfield, GU31 5QR; tel: 01730 825415; fax: 01730 825873; e-mail: uppark@nationaltrust.org.uk

Wakehurst Place
Ardingly, Haywards Heath, West Sussex, RH17 6TN; tel: 01444 894066; fax: 01444 894069; e-mail: wakehurst@kew.org

Winkworth Arboretum
Hascombe Road, Godalming, Surrey, GU8 4AD; tel: 01483 208477; e-mail: winkwortharboretum@nationaltrust.org.uk

NATIONAL TRUST (THAMES AND SOLENT REGIONAL OFFICE)

Formal name: National Trust for Places of Historic Interest or Natural Beauty
Acronym or abbreviation: NT

Hughenden Manor, High Wycombe, Buckinghamshire, HP14 4LA

Tel: 01494 755500
Fax: 01494 463310
E-mail: enquiries@thenationaltrust.org.uk

Website:
http://www.nationaltrust.org.uk

Enquiries:
Enquiries to: Marketing and Supporter Development Manager
Direct tel: 01494 755550

Founded:
1895

Organisation type and purpose:
National organisation, independently owned, membership association (membership is by subscription), registered charity (charity number 205846), historic building, house or site, suitable for ages: life-long.
Administration and management of Trust sites in the Thames and Solent region.

Subject coverage:
The preservation and upkeep of places of historic interest and natural beauty in Berkshire, Buckinghamshire, Hampshire, part of Hertfordshire, Isle of Wight, Greater London and Oxfordshire.

Publications list:
Available online and in print

Access to staff:
Contact by letter, by telephone, by fax, by e-mail, in person and via website
Hours: Mon to Fri, 0900 to 1700

National Trust sites:
2 Willow Road
2 Willow Road, Hampstead, London, NW3 1TH; tel: 020 7435 6166; e-mail: 2willowroad@nationaltrust.org.uk

Basildon Park
Lower Basildon, Reading, Berkshire, RG8 9NR; tel: 0118 984 3040; e-mail: basildonpark@nationaltrust.org.uk

Boarstall Tower
Boarstall, Aylesbury, Buckinghamshire, HP18 9UX; tel: 01844 239339

Buscot Old Parsonage
Buscot, Faringdon, Oxfordshire, SN7 8DQ; tel: 01793 7622209; e-mail: buscot@nationaltrust.org.uk

Buscot Park
Buscot, Faringdon, Oxfordshire, SN7 8BU; tel: 01367 240786; fax: 01367 241794; e-mail: estbuscot@aol.com

Carlyle's House
24 Cheyne Row, Chelsea, London, SW3 5HL; tel: 020 7352 7087; fax: 020 7352 5108; e-mail: carlyleshouse@nationaltrust.org.uk

Claydon House
Middle Claydon, Near Buckingham, Buckinghamshire, MK18 2EY; tel: 01296 730349; fax: 01296 738511; e-mail: claydon@nationaltrust.org.uk

Cliveden
Taplow, Maidenhead, Buckinghamshire, SL6 0JA; tel: 01628 605069; fax: 01628 669461; e-mail: cliveden@nationaltrust.org.uk

Eastbury Manor House
Eastbury Square, Barking, IG11 9SN; tel: 020 8724 1002; fax: 020 8724 1003; e-mail: eastburyhouse@lbbd.gov.uk

Fenton House
Windmill Hill, Hampstead, London, NW3 6RT; tel: 020 7435 3471; e-mail: fentonhouse@nationaltrust.org.uk

Greys Court
Rotherfield Greys, Henley-on-Thames, Oxfordshire, RG9 4PG; tel: 01491 628529; fax: 01491 628935; e-mail: greyscourt@nationaltrust.org.uk

Hinton Ampner
Bramdean, Arlesford, Hampshire, SO24 0LA; tel: 01962 771305; fax: 01962 793101; e-mail: hintonampner@nationaltrust.org.uk

Hughenden Manor Estate
Hughenden Valley, High Wycombe, Buckinghamshire, HP14 4LA; tel: 01494 755573; fax: 01494 474284; e-mail: hughenden@nationaltrust.org.uk

Long Crendon Court House
Long Crendon, Aylesbury, Buckinghamshire, HP18 9AN; tel: 01494 528051; fax: 01280 822850

Mottisfont Abbey
Mottisfont, Romsey, Hampshire, SO51 0LP; tel: 01794 340757; fax: 01794 341492; e-mail: mottisfontabbey@nationaltrust.org.uk

Needles Old Battery
West Highdown, Totland, Isle of Wight, PO39 0JH; tel: 01983 754772

Old Town Hall, Newtown
Newtown, Newport, Isle of Wight, PO30 4PA; tel: 01983 531785

Rainham Hall
The Broadway, Rainham, Essex, RM13 9YN; tel: 020 7447 6605

Sandham Memorial Chapel
Harts Lane, Burghclere, Newbury, Hampshire, RG20 9JT; tel: 01635 278394; fax: 01635 278394; e-mail: sandham@nationaltrust.org.uk

Sutton House
2/4 Homerton High Street, Hackney, London, E9 6JQ; tel: 020 8986 2264; e-mail: suttonhouse@nationaltrust.org.uk

The Vyne
Sherborne St John, Basingstoke, Hampshire, RG24 9HL; tel: 01256 883858; fax: 01256 881720; e-mail: thevyne@nationaltrust.org.uk

Waddesdon Manor
Waddesdon, Aylesbury, Buckinghamshire, HP18 0JH; tel: 01296 653226; fax: 01296 653212; e-mail: waddesonmanor@nationaltrust.org.uk

West Wycombe Park
West Wycombe, Buckinghamshire, HP14 3AJ; tel: 01494 513569

NATIONAL TRUST (WESSEX REGIONAL OFFICE)

Formal name: National Trust for Places of Historic Interest or Natural Beauty
Acronym or abbreviation: NT

Bishopstrow, Warminster, Wiltshire, BA12 9HW

Tel: 01985 843600
Fax: 01985 843624
E-mail: enquiries@thenationaltrust.org.uk

Website:
http://www.nationaltrust.org.uk
Information about the National Trust properties, opening times and facilities, special events, educational information, and publications.

Enquiries:
Enquiries to: Customer Service Manager

Founded:
1895

Organisation type and purpose:
National organisation, independently owned, membership association (membership is by subscription), registered charity (charity number 205846), historic building, house or site, suitable for ages: Life long.
Administration and management of Trust sites in the Wessex region.

Subject coverage:
The preservation and upkeep of places of historic interest and natural beauty in Bristol/Bath, Dorset, Gloucestershire, Somerset and Wiltshire.

Publications list:
Available online and in print

Access to staff:
Contact by letter, by telephone, by fax, by e-mail, in person and via website
Hours: Mon to Fri, 0900 to 1700

National Trust sites:
Avebury
Barn Gallery, High Street, Avebury, Marlborough, Wiltshire, SN8 1RF; tel: 01672 539494; e-mail: avebury@ntrust.org.uk
Barrington Court
Barrington, Ilminster, Somerset, TA19 0NQ; tel: 01460 241938; fax: 01460 241938; e-mail: barringtoncourt@ntrust.org.uk
Bath Assembly Rooms
Bennett Street, Bath, BA1 2QH; tel: 01225 477789
Chedworth Roman Villa
Yanworth, Cheltenham, Gloucestershire, GL54 3LJ; tel: 01242 890256
Clevedon Court
Tickenham Road, Clevedon, Somerset, BS21 6QU; tel: 01275 872257
Coleridge Cottage
35 Lime Street, Nether Stowey, Bridgwater, Somerset, TA5 1NQ; tel: 01278 732662
Corfe Castle
West Street, Corfe Castle, Wareham, Dorset, BH20 5EZ; tel: 01929 481294
Dunster Castle
Dunster, Minehead, Somerset, TA24 6SL; tel: 01643 821314; fax: 01643 823000; e-mail: wdugen@smtp.ntrust.org.uk
Dyrham Park
Dyrham, Chippenham, SN14 8ER; tel: 01179 372501; e-mail: dyrhampark@ntrust.org.uk
Great Chalfield Manor
Melksham, Wiltshire, SN12 8NJ; tel: 01225 782239; fax: 01225 783379
Hardy's Cottage
Higher Bockhampton, Dorchester, Dorset, DT2 8QL; tel: 01305 262366
Horton Court
Horton, Chipping Sodbury, Bristol, BS17 6QR; tel: 01249 730141
King John's Hunting Lodge
Axbridge, Somerset, BS26 2AP; tel: 01934 732012
Kingston Lacy
Wimbourne, Dorset, BH21 4EA; tel: 01202 883402
Kingston Lacy
Wimbourne, Dorset, BH21 4EA; tel: 01202 883402; fax: 01202 882402
Lacock Abbey and Fox Talbot Museum
Lacock, Chippenham, Wiltshire, SN15 2LG; tel: 01249 730227
Little Clarendon House
Dinton, Salisbury, Wiltshire, SP3 5DZ; tel: 01985 843600 (Regional Office)
Lodge Park House
Aldsworth, Cheltenham, Gloucestershire, GL54 3PP; tel: 01450 844130; fax: 01451 844131; e-mail: lodgepark@ntrust.org.uk
Lytes Cary Manor
nr Charlton Mackrell, Somerton, Somerset, TA11 7HU; tel: 01985 224471; e-mail: lytescarymanor@ntrust.org.uk
Max Gate
Alington Avenue, Dorchester, Dorset, DT1 2AA; tel: 01305 262538; fax: 01305 250978
Mompesson House
The Close, Salisbury, Wiltshire, SP1 2EL; tel: 01722 335659; fax: 01722 321559; e-mail: mompessonhouse@ntrust.org.uk
Montacute House
Montacute, Somerset, TA15 6XP; tel: 01935 823289; e-mail: montacute@ntrust.org.uk
Newark Park
Ozleworth, Wotton under Edge, Gloucestershire, GL12 7PZ; tel: 01453 842644
Philipps House and Ditton Park
Ditton, Salisbury, Wiltshire, SP3 5HH; tel: 01985 843600 (Regional Office)

Snowshill Manor
Snowshill, Broadway, Gloucestershire, WR12 7JU; tel: 01386 852410; fax: 01386 852410; e-mail: snowshillmanor@ntrust.org.uk
Stonehenge Down
Amesbury, Salisbury, Wiltshire, SP4 7DE; tel: 01980 624715 (Infoline)
Stourhead House
Stourton, Warminster, Wiltshire, BA12 6QD; tel: 01747 841152
Westwood Manor
Westwood, Bradford on Avon, Wiltshire, BA15 2AF; tel: 01225 863374
White Mill
Sturminster Marshall, Wimborne, Dorset, BH21 4BX; tel: 01258 858051

NATIONAL TRUST (WEST MIDLANDS REGIONAL OFFICE)

Formal name: National Trust for Places of Historic Interest or Natural Beauty
Acronym or abbreviation: NT

Attingham Park, Shrewsbury, Shropshire, SY4 4TP

Tel: 01743 708100
Fax: 01743 708150
E-mail: enquiries@thenationaltrust.org.uk

Website:
http://www.nationaltrust.org.uk
Information about the National Trust properties, opening times and facilities, special events, educational information, and publications.

Enquiries:
Enquiries to: Customer Service Manager

Founded:
1895

Organisation type and purpose:
National organisation, independently owned, membership association (membership is by subscription), registered charity (charity number 205846), historic building, house or site, suitable for ages: Life long.
Administration and management of Trust sites in the West Midlands.

Subject coverage:
The preservation and upkeep of Trust properties of historic interest and natural beauty in Birmingham, Herefordshire, Shropshire, Staffordshire, Warwickshire and Worcestershire.

Publications list:
Available online and in print

Access to staff:
Contact by letter, by telephone, by e-mail, in person and via website
Hours: Mon to Fri, 0900 to 1700

National Trust sites:
Attingham Hall
Attingham Park, Shrewsbury, Shropshire, SY4 4TP; tel: 01743 709203; fax: 01743 708175; e-mail: attingham@nationaltrust.org.uk
Baddesley Clinton Hall
Rising Lane, Baddesley Clinton Village, Knowle, Solihull, West Midlands, B93 0DQ; tel: 01564 783294; fax: 01564 782706; e-mail: baddesleyclinton@nationaltrust.org.uk
Benthall Hall
Broseley, Shropshire, TF12 5RX; tel: 01952 882159; e-mail: benthall@nationaltrust.org.uk
Berrington Hall
Leominster, Herefordshire, HR6 0DW; tel: 01568 615721; fax: 01568 613263; e-mail: berrington@.nationaltrust.org.uk
Brockhampton House and Estate
Bringsty, Worcester, WR6 5TB; tel: 01885 482077; e-mail: brockhampton@nationaltrust.org.uk
Charlecote Park
Warwick, CV35 9ER; tel: 01789 470277; fax: 01789 470544; e-mail: charlecotepark@nationaltrust.org.uk
Croft Castle & Parkland
Leominster, Herefordshire, HR6 9PW; tel: 01568 780246; e-mail: croftcastle@nationaltrust.org.uk

Dudmaston Hall
Quatt, Bridgnorth, Shropshire, WV15 6QN; tel: 01746 780866 (Dudmaston Estate); fax: 01746 780744; e-mail: dudmaston@nationaltrust.org.uk
Farnborough Hall
Banbury, OX17 1DU; tel: 01295 690002; e-mail: farnboroughhall@nationaltrust.org.uk
Greyfriars
Friar Street, Worcester, WR1 2LZ; tel: 01905 23571; e-mail: greyfriars@nationaltrust.org.uk
Hanbury Hall
School Road, Hanbury, Droitwich, Worcestershire, WR9 7EA; tel: 01527 821214; fax: 01527 821251; e-mail: hanburyhall@nationaltrust.org.uk
Morville Hall
Morville, Bridgnorth, Shropshire, WV16 5NB; tel: 01743 708100 (Regional Office); e-mail: morvillehall@nationaltrust.org.uk
Moseley Old Hall
Moseley Old Hall Lane, Fordhouses, Wolverhampton, West Midlands, WV10 7HY; tel: 01902 782808; e-mail: moseleyoldhall@nationaltrust.org.uk
Packwood House
Lapworth, Solihull, West Midlands, B94 6AT; tel: 01564 783294; fax: 01564 782706; e-mail: packwood@nationaltrust.org.uk
Sunnycroft
200 Holyhead Road, Wellington, Telford, Shropshire, TF1 2DR; tel: 01952 242884; e-mail: sunnycroft@nationaltrust.org.uk
Upton House & Gardens
Near Banbury, Oxfordshire, OX15 6HT; tel: 01295 670266; e-mail: uptonhouse@nationaltrust.org.uk
Wall Roman Site (Letocetum)
Wall, Lichfield, Staffordshire, WS14 0AW; tel: 01543 480768; e-mail: letocetum@nationaltrust.org.uk
Wightwick Manor
Wightwick Bank, Wolverhampton, West Midlands, WV6 8EE; tel: 01902 761108 (Infoline); fax: 01902 764663; e-mail: wightwickmanor@nationaltrust.org.uk
Wilderhope Manor
Longville, Much Wenlock, Shropshire, TF13 6EG; tel: 01694 771363; e-mail: wilderhopemanor@nationaltrust.org.uk

NATIONAL TRUST (YORKSHIRE & NORTH EAST REGIONAL OFFICES) – MORPETH

Formal name: National Trust for Places of Historic Interest or Natural Beauty
Acronym or abbreviation: NT

Scots' Gap, Morpeth, Northumberland, NE61 4EG

Tel: 01670 774691
Fax: 01670 774317
E-mail: enquiries@thenationaltrust.org.uk

Website:
http://www.nationaltrust.org.uk
Information about the National Trust properties, opening times and facilities, special events, educational information, and publications.

Enquiries:
Enquiries to: Communications Marketing Manager
Direct tel: 07500 993500
Direct e-mail: eve.jackson@nationaltrust.org.uk

Founded:
1895

Organisation type and purpose:
National organisation, independently owned, membership association (membership is by subscription), registered charity (charity number 205846), historic building, house or site, suitable for ages: Life long.
Administration and management of Trust sites in the North East.

Subject coverage:
The preservation and upkeep of Trust properties of historic interest and natural beauty in Co Durham, Newcastle and Tyneside, Northumberland.

continued overleaf

Publications list:
Available online and in print

Access to staff:
Contact by letter, by telephone, by e-mail, in person and via website
Hours: Mon to Fri, 0900 to 1700

Access to building, collection or gallery:
Hours: Mon to Fri, 0900 to 1700

National Trust sites:
Cherryburn
    Station Bank, Mickley, Stocksfield, Northumberland, NE43 7DD; tel: 01661 843276; e-mail: cherryburn@nationaltrust.org.uk
Cragside House
    Rothbury, Morpeth, Northumberland, NE65 7PX; tel: 01669 620333; fax: 01669 620066; e-mail: cragside@nationaltrust.org.uk
Dunstanburgh Castle
    Craster, Alnwick, Northumberland; tel: 01665 576211
George Stephenson's Birthplace
    Street House, Wylam, Newcastle upon Tyne, Northumberland, NE41 8BP; tel: 01661 853457; fax: 01670 774317
Gibside
    nr Rowlands Gill, Burnopfield, Newcastle upon Tyne, Tyne & Wear, NE16 6BG; tel: 01207 542255; fax: 01207 542255; e-mail: gibside@nationaltrust.org.uk
Hadrian's Wall & Housesteads Roman Fort
    Bardon Mill, Hexham, Northumberland, NE47 6NN; tel: 01434 344363 (EH Custodian)
Lindisfarne Castle
    Holy Island, Berwick-upon-Tweed, Northumberland, TD15 2SH; tel: 01289 389244; fax: 01289 389349; e-mail: lindisfarne@nationaltrust.org.uk
Ormesby Hall
    Ormesby, Middlesbrough, Cleveland, TS7 9AS; tel: 01642 324188; fax: 01642 300937; e-mail: ormesbyhall@nationaltrust.org.uk
Souter Lighthouse
    Coast Road, Whitburn, Sunderland, Tyne and Wear, SR6 7NH; tel: 0191 529 3161; Infoline tel: 01670 773966; fax: 0191 529 0902; e-mail: souter@nationaltrust.org.uk
Wallington
    Cambo, Morpeth, Northumberland, NE6 4AR; tel: 01670 773967 (Infoline); fax: 01670 774420; e-mail: wallington@nationaltrust.org.uk
Washington Old Hall
    The Avenue, District 4, Washington Village, Washington, Tyne and Wear, NE38 7LE; tel: 0191 416 6879; fax: 0191 416 2065; e-mail: washington.oldhall@nationaltrust.org.uk

NATIONAL TRUST (YORKSHIRE & NORTH EAST REGIONAL OFFICES) – YORK

Formal name: National Trust for Places of Historic Interest or Natural Beauty
Acronym or abbreviation: NT

Goddards, 27 Tadcaster Road, York, YO24 1GG

Tel: 01904 702021
Fax: 01904 771970
E-mail: enquiries@thenationaltrust.org.uk

Website:
http://www.nationaltrust.org.uk
Information about the National Trust properties, opening times and facilities, special events, educational information, and publications.

Enquiries:
Enquiries to: Marketing & Supporter Development Manager
Direct e-mail: yne.customerservice@nationaltrust.org.uk

Founded:
1895

Organisation type and purpose:
National organisation, independently owned, membership association (membership is by subscription), registered charity (charity number 205846), historic building, house or site, suitable for ages: Life long.
Administration and management of Trust sites in Yorkshire & the North East.

Subject coverage:
The preservation and upkeep of Trust properties of historic interest and natural beauty in Yorkshire, Teesside and North Lincolnshire.

Publications list:
Available online and in print

Access to staff:
Contact by letter, by telephone, by fax, by e-mail, in person and via website
Hours: Mon to Fri, 0900 to 1700

National Trust sites:
Beningbrough Hall
    Beningbrough, York, YO30 1DD; tel: 01904 472027; fax: 01904 470002; e-mail: beningbrough@nationaltrust.org.uk
East Riddlesden Hall
    Bradford Road, Keighley, West Yorkshire, BD20 5EL; tel: 01535 607075; fax: 01535 691462; e-mail: eastriddlesden@nationaltrust.org.uk
Fountains Abbey & Studley Royal
    Fountains, Ripon, North Yorkshire, HG4 3DY; tel: 01765 608888; fax: 01765 601002; e-mail: fountainsenquiries@nationaltrust.org.uk
Mount Grace Priory
    Osmotherley, Northallerton, North Yorkshire, DL6 3JG; tel: 01609 883494
Nostell Priory
    Doncaster Road, Wakefield, West Yorkshire, WF4 1QE; tel: 01924 863892; fax: 01924 866846; e-mail: nostellpriory@nationaltrust.org.uk
Nunnington Hall
    Nunnington, York, YO62 5UY; tel: 01439 748283; fax: 01439 748284; e-mail: nunningtonhall@nationaltrust.org.uk
Treasurer's House
    Minster Yard, Chapter House Street, York, YO1 7JL; tel: 01904 624247; fax: 01904 647372; e-mail: treasurershouse@nationaltrust.org.uk
Yorkshire Coast
    Old Coastguard Station, The Dock, Robin Hood's Bay, Whitby, North Yorkshire, YO22 4SJ; tel: 01947 885900; e-mail: yorkshirecoast@nationaltrust.org.uk

NATIONAL TRUST FOR SCOTLAND

Acronym or abbreviation: NTS

28 Charlotte Square, Edinburgh, EH2 4ET

Tel: 0131 243 9300
Fax: 0131 243 9301
E-mail: information@nts.org.uk

Website:
http://www.nts.org.uk
Information about the National Trust for Scotland properties, opening times and facilities, special events, educational information, and publications.

Enquiries:
Enquiries to: Archivist
Direct tel: 0131 243 9524
Direct e-mail: cbain@nts.org.uk

Founded:
1931

Organisation type and purpose:
Independently owned, membership association (membership is by subscription), registered charity (charity number SCO07410), suitable for ages: all.
Conservation of sites which have significance for the natural or built heritage of Scotland.

Subject coverage:
Practical aspects of conserving and making available to the public, with information and visitor services, country houses, small buildings, gardens, battlefields, and countryside and all places of natural beauty or historic or architectural interest in Scotland.

Museum or gallery collection, archive, or library special collection:
Archives of the National Trust for Scotland (1931-current) and some collections of family papers associated with some of our properties
A small reference library

Non-library collection catalogue:
All or part available in-house

Library catalogue:
All or part available in-house

Printed publications:
Annual Report
Architecture and Interiors
Corporate Brochure
Corporate Plan
Educational publications relating to the properties
Guidebooks, brochures and leaflets to Trust properties
Heritage Scotland (magazine, quarterly)
Resource packs
Scotland's Gardens Scheme Handbook 1999

Publications list:
Available in print

Access to staff:
Contact by letter, by telephone, by fax and by e-mail
Hours: Mon to Fri, 0930 to 1630
Special comments: Limited disabled access.

Other locations:
National Trust for Scotland (North America)
    One Boston Place, Fifth Floor, Boston, MA 02108, USA; tel: 00 1 617 619 3631; e-mail: nationaltrustforscotland@mediaone.net
National Trust for Scotland London (Office)
    19 Cockspur Street, London, SW1Y 5BL; tel: 020 7321 5765; fax: 020 7389 0758

Regional Offices:
Highlands and Islands Regional Office (North)
    Balnain House, 40 Huntly Street, Inverness, IV3 5HR; tel: 01463 232034; fax: 01463 732620
Highlands and Islands Regional Office (South)
    Lochvoil House, Dunuraran Road, Oban, PA34 4NE; tel: 01631 570000; fax: 01631 570011
National Trust for Scotland (North-East Region)
    The Stables, Castle Fraser, Sauchen, Inverurie, Aberdeenshire, AB51 7LD; tel: 01463 232034; fax: 01463 732620
National Trust for Scotland (South Region)
    Northgate House, 32 Northgate, Peebles, EH45 8RS; tel: 01721 722502; fax: 01721 726000
National Trust for Scotland (West Region)
    Greenbank House, Flenders Road, Clarkston, Glasgow, G76 8RB; tel: 0141 616 2266; fax: 0141 616 0550

NATIONAL TRUST FOR SCOTLAND (NORTH-EAST REGION)

Acronym or abbreviation: NTS

The Stables, Castle Fraser, Sauchen, Inverurie, Aberdeenshire, AB51 7LD

Tel: 01330 833225
Fax: 01330 833666

Website:
http://www.nts.org.uk

Enquiries:
Enquiries to: Public Affairs Manager
Direct tel: 01330 833559
Direct e-mail: glovie@nts.org.uk

Founded:
1931

Organisation type and purpose:
National organisation, independently owned, membership association (membership is by subscription), registered charity (charity number SCO 07410), suitable for ages: all.
Administration and management of Trust sites in Perthshire, Angus, Aberdeen & Grampian.

Subject coverage:
Heritage, conservation and environmental projects.

Publications list:
Available in print

Access to staff:
Contact by letter, by telephone and by fax
Hours: Mon to Fri, 0900 to 1700

National Trust for Scotland sites:
Angus Folk Museum
 Kirkwynd, Glamis, Forfar, Angus, DD8 1RT; tel: 01307 840288
Barry Water Mill
 Barry, Carnoustie, Angus, DD7 7RJ; tel: 01241 856761
Castle Fraser
 Sauchen, Inverurie, Aberdeenshire, AB51 7LD; tel: 01330 833463; fax: 01330 833819
Craigievar Castle
 Alford, Aberdeenshire, AB33 8JF; tel: 013398 83635; fax: 013398 83280
Crathes Castle, Garden & Estate
 Banchory, Aberdeenshire, AB31 5QJ; tel: 01330 844525; fax: 01330 844797; e-mail: crathes@nts.org.uk
Drum Castle, Garden & Estate
 Drumoak, Banchory, Aberdeenshire, AB31 5EY; tel: 01330 811204; fax: 01330 811962; e-mail: drum-castle@nts.org.uk
Dunkeld
 Ell Shop, The Cross, Dunkeld, Perthshire, PH8 0AN; tel: 01350 727460; e-mail: dunkeld@nts.org.uk
Dunkeld and The Hermitage
 Dunkeld, Perthshire; tel: 01350 728641 (Ranger Office); fax: tel/fax 01796 473233 (Killiecrankie Visitor Centre)
Finavon Doocot
 Finavon, Angus
Fyvie Castle
 Fyvie, Turriff, Aberdeenshire, AB53 8JS; tel: 01651 891266; fax: 01651 891107
Haddo House
 Ellon, Aberdeenshire, AB41 7EQ; tel: 01651 851440; fax: 01651 851888; e-mail: haddo@nts.org.uk
House of Dun
 Montrose, Angus, DD10 9LQ; tel: 01674 810264; fax: 01674 810722; e-mail: houseofdun@nts.org.uk
J M Barrie's Birthplace
 9 Brechin Road, Kirriemuir, Angus, DD8 4BX; tel: 01575 572646
Killiecrankie Visitor Centre
 Pitlochry, Perth & Kinross, PH16 5LG; tel: 01796 473233; e-mail: killiecrankie@nts.org.uk
Leith Hall, Garden & Estate
 Huntly, Aberdeenshire, AB54 4NQ; tel: 01464 831216; fax: 01464 831594; e-mail: leithhall@nts.org.uk
Museum of Farming Life
 Pitmedden Garden, Ellon, Aberdeenshire, AB41 0PD; tel: 01651 842352; fax: 01651 843 188; e-mail: sburgess@nts.org.uk
Pitmedden Garden
 Ellon, Aberdeenshire, AB41 7PD; tel: 01651 842352; fax: 01651 843188

Parent body:
National Trust for Scotland
 28 Charlotte Square, Edinburgh, EH2 4ET; tel: 0131 243 9300; fax: 0131 243 9301; e-mail: information@nts.org.uk

NATIONAL TRUST FOR SCOTLAND (SOUTH REGION)

Acronym or abbreviation: NTS

Northgate House, 32 Northgate, Peebles, Borders, EH45 8RS

Tel: 01721 722502
Fax: 01721 726000
E-mail: information@nts.org.uk

Website:
http://www.nts.org.uk
Information about the National Trust for Scotland properties, opening times and facilities, special events, educational information, and publications.

Enquiries:
Enquiries to: Director

Founded:
1931

Organisation type and purpose:
Independently owned, membership association (membership is by subscription), registered charity (charity number SCO 07410), suitable for ages: all.

Subject coverage:
Specific information on its own properties and sites also conservation, environmental issues and heritage.
Administration and management of Trust sites in Dumfries and Galloway, Scottish Borders, Edinburgh and The Lothians, and Fife.

Trade and statistical information:
Tourist, visitor attractions, building conservation.

Access to staff:
Contact by letter, by telephone, by fax and by e-mail. Appointment necessary.
Hours: Mon to Fri 0900 to 1700

National Trust for Scotland sites:
Balmerino Abbey
 Balmerino, Fife
Broughton House
 12 High Street, Kirkcudbright, Dumfries & Galloway, DG6 4JX; tel: 01557 330437; e-mail: broughtonhouse@nts.org.uk
Caiy Stane
 Caiystane View, Edinburgh
Falkland Palace
 Falkland, Cupar, Fife, KY15 7BU; tel: 01337 857397; fax: 01337 857980; e-mail: falklandpalace@nts.org.uk
Georgian House
 7 Charlotte Square, Edinburgh, EH2 4DR; tel: 0131 226 3318; e-mail: thegeorgianhouse@nts.org.uk
Gladstone's Land
 477B Lawnmarket, Edinburgh, EH1 2NT; tel: 0131 226 5856; fax: 0131 226 4851
Hill of Tarvit Mansion House & Gardens
 Cupar, Fife, KY15 5PB; tel: 01334 653127
House of the Binns
 Linlithgow, West Lothian, EH49 7NA; tel: 01506 834255; e-mail: houseofthebinns@nts.org.uk
Kellie Castle and Garden
 Pittenweem, Anstruther, Fife, KY10 2RF; tel: 01333 720271; fax: 01333 720326
Newhailes
 Newhailes Road, Musselburgh, East Lothian, EH21 6RY; tel: 0131 665 1546
No 28 Charlotte Square
 Edinburgh, EH2 4ET; tel: 0131 243 9300; fax: 0131 243 9339
Preston Mill and Phantassie Doocot
 East Linton, East Lothian, EH40 3DS; tel: 01620 860426
Robert Smail's Printing Works
 7–9 High Street, Inverleithen, Borders, EH44 6HA; tel: 01896 830206; e-mail: smails@nts.org.uk
Royal Burgh of Culross
 Culross, Fife, KY12 8JH; tel: 01383 880359; fax: 01383 882675
Threave
 Castle Douglas, Dumfries & Galloway, DG7 1RX; tel: 01556 502575; fax: 01556 502683; e-mail: threave@nts.org.uk

Parent body:
National Trust for Scotland
 Wemyss House, 28 Charlotte Square, Edinburgh, EH2 4ET; tel: 0131 243 9300; fax: 0131 243 9301; e-mail: information@nts.org.uk

NATIONAL TRUST FOR SCOTLAND (WEST REGION)

Acronym or abbreviation: NTS

Greenbank House, Flenders Road, Clarkston, Glasgow, G76 8RB

Tel: 0141 616 2266
Fax: 0141 616 0550
E-mail: kcarr@nts.org.uk

Website:
http://www.nts.org.uk

Enquiries:
Enquiries to: Public Relations Officer
Other contacts: Regional Director (for policy)

Founded:
1931

Organisation type and purpose:
National organisation, membership association, present number of members: 246,000, voluntary organisation, registered charity (charity number SCO 07410), suitable for ages: all.

Subject coverage:
Specific information on the properties, also conservation and environmental issues, particularly in this region of Scotland.
Administration and management of Trust sites in Ayrshire and Arran, Greater Glasgow and Clyde Valley and Cental Scotland.

Museum or gallery collection, archive, or library special collection:
Many collections appropriate to individual properties (details on request)

Trade and statistical information:
Tourist, visitor attractions, building conservation.

Printed publications:
Full colour guide books to many properties
NTS Annual Report (free)
NTS Guide to Over 100 Properties
NTS Handbook
Publications under the following headings:
Architecture and Interiors
Birthplaces, Industrial and Social History
Garden Books, Guides and leaflets
Maps and Charts
Mountains, Islands and Countryside
Walks and Trails

Electronic and video publications:
Wide variety of films, slides and videos for sale and hire, including:
A Sampling of Scotland
Britain: Kingdom of the Sea
Countryside in Trust (slides and notes)
Fair Isle – The Happy Island
Gardens in Trust (slides and notes)
House of Dun ... no more handsome and convenient a house of the bigness in all the ancient Kingdom
Scotland a Heritage
Scotland in Trust (slides and notes)
St Kilda Story
The Tenement House, Glasgow
The Work of the Weavers

Publications list:
Available in print

Access to staff:
Contact by letter, by telephone, by fax, by e-mail and via website
Hours: Mon to Fri, 0900 to 1700

National Trust for Scotland sites:
Alloa Tower
 Alloa Park, Alloa, FK10 1PP; tel: 01259 211701; fax: 01259 218744
Bannockburn Heritage Centre
 Glasgow Road, Bannockburn, Stirling, FK7 0LJ; tel: 01786 812664; fax: 01786 810892
Batchelors' Club
 Sandgate Street, Tarbolton, South Ayrshire, KA5 5RB; tel: 01292 541940
Black Hill
 Lanark, South Lanarkshire

continued overleaf

Brodick Castle Garden and Country Park
Brodick, Isle of Arran; tel: 01770 302202; fax: 01770 302312; e-mail: brodick@nts.org.uk
Culzean Castle and Country Park
Maybole, South Ayrshire, KA19 8LE; tel: 01655 884455; fax: 01655 884503; e-mail: culzean@nts.org.uk
David Livingstone Centre
165 Station Road, Glasgow, South Lanarkshire, G72 9BT; tel: 01698 8231140; fax: 01698 821424
Holmwood House
61–63 Netherlee Road, Cathcart, Glasgow, G44 3YG; tel: 0141 637 2129; fax: 0141 637 2129; e-mail: holmwood@nts.org.uk
Hutchesons' Hall
158 Ingram Street, Glasgow, G1 1EJ; tel: 0141 552 8391; fax: 0141552 7031; e-mail: hutchesonshall@nts.org.uk
Menstrie Castle
Castle Street, Menstrie, Clackmannanshire
Moirlanich Longhouse
Near Killin, Stirling
Museum of Scottish Country Life
Wester Kittochside, East Kilbride, G76 9HR; tel: 01355 224181; fax: 01355 571290
Pollok House
Pollok Country Park, 2060 Pollokshaws Road, Glasgow, G43 1AT; tel: 0141 616 6410; fax: 0141 616 6521; e-mail: pollokhouse@nts.org.uk
Souter Johnnie's Cottage
Main Road, Kirkoswald, Ayrshire, KA19 8HY; tel: 01655 760603
Tenement House
145 Buccleuch Street, Garnethill, Glasgow, G3 6QN; tel: 0141 333 0183; e-mail: tenementhouse@nts.org.uk
The Hill House
Upper Colquhoun Street, Helensburgh, G849AJ; tel: 01436 673900; fax: 01436 674685
The Pineapple
North of Airth, Falkirk; tel: 01324 831137
Weaver's Cottage
Shuttle Street, The Cross, Kilbarchan, Renfrewshire, PA10 2JG; tel: 01505 705588

Parent body:
National Trust for Scotland
Wemyss House, 28 Charlotte Square, Edinburgh, EH2 4ET; tel: 0131 243 9300; fax: 0131 243 9301; e-mail: information@nts.org.uk

NATIONAL TRUST FOR SCOTLAND HIGHLANDS AND ISLANDS OFFICE (NORTH)

Acronym or abbreviation: NTS

Balnain House, 40 Huntly Street, Inverness, IV3 5HR

Tel: 01463 232034
E-mail: information@nts.org.uk

Website:
http://www.nts.org.uk

Enquiries:
Enquiries to: Director

Organisation type and purpose:
Independently owned, membership association (membership is by subscription), voluntary organisation, registered charity, suitable for ages: all.

Subject coverage:
Specific information on its own properties and sites also conservation, environmental issues and heritage.
Administration and management of Trust sites in Ross-shire, Inverness, Nairn, Moray and The Black Isle, and Northern Islands.

National Trust for Scotland sites:
Balmacara Estate
Lochalsh House (NTS), Balmacara, Kyle, Ross-shire, IV40 8DN; tel: 01599 566359; e-mail: balmacara@nts.org.uk
Boath Doocot
Auldearn, Nairn, Moray

Brodie Castle
Brodie, Forres, Moray, IV36 2TE; tel: 01309 641371; fax: 01309 641600; e-mail: brodiecastle@nts.org.uk
Culloden Moor Visitors Centre
Culloden Moor, Inverness, Highland, IV2 5EU; tel: 01463 790607; fax: 01463 794294; e-mail: rmackenzie@nts.org.uk
Strome Castle
Ross-shire

Parent body:
National Trust for Scotland

NATIONAL TRUST FOR SCOTLAND HIGHLANDS AND ISLANDS OFFICE (SOUTH)

Acronym or abbreviation: NTS

Lochviol House, Dunaran Road, Oban, Argyll, PA34 4NE

Tel: 01631 570000
Fax: 01631 570011
E-mail: information@nts.org.uk

Website:
http://www.nts.org.uk
Information about the National Trust for Scotland properties, opening times and facilities, special events, educational information, and publications.

Enquiries:
Enquiries to: Director

Organisation type and purpose:
Registered charity (charity number SCO 07410), suitable for ages: all.
Administration and management of Trust sites in Argyll & Lochaber and West Coast Islands.

Subject coverage:
Heritage, conservation and environmental projects. Administration and management of Trust sites in Argyll and Lochaber, and West Coast Islands.

Access to staff:
Contact by letter, by telephone, by fax and by e-mail. Appointment necessary.
Hours: Mon to Fri, 0900 to 1700

National Trust for Scotland sites:
Glencoe and Dalness
The National Trust for Scotland Visitor Centre, Glencoe, Argyll, PH49 4LA; tel: 01855 811729; fax: 01855 811772; e-mail: glencoe@nts.org.uk
Glenfinnan Monument
National Trust for Scotland Information Centre, Glenfinnan, Highland, PH37 4LT; tel: 01397 722250; e-mail: glenfinnan@nts.org.uk

Parent body:
National Trust for Scotland
28 Charlotte Square, Edinburgh, EH2 4ET; tel: 0131 243 9300; fax: 0131 243 9301; e-mail: information@nts.org.uk

NATIONAL TRUST OFFICE FOR NORTHERN IRELAND

Rowallane House, Saintfield, Ballynahinch, Co Down, BT24 7LH

Tel: 020 9751 0721
Fax: 028 9751 1242

Website:
http://www.ntni.org.uk

Enquiries:
Enquiries to: Manager

Organisation type and purpose:
National organisation, membership association (membership is by subscription), registered charity (charity number 205846), suitable for ages: all.
The preservation and upkeep of places of historic interest or natural beauty.

Subject coverage:
The conservation of places of historic interest or natural beauty in Northern Ireland.

Access to staff:
Contact by letter, by telephone, by fax and by e-mail
Hours: Mon to Fri, 0900 to 1700

Other Trust sites:
Ardress House
64 Ardress Road, Portadown, Co Armagh, BT62 1SQ; tel: 028 3885 1236; fax: 028 3885 1236; e-mail: ardress@nationaltrust.org.uk
Castle Coole
Enniskillen, Co Fermanagh, BT74 6JY; tel: 028 6632 2690; fax: 028 6632 5665; e-mail: castlecoole@nationaltrust.org.uk
Castle Ward
Strangford, Downpatrick, Co Down, BT30 7LS; tel: 028 4488 1204; fax: 028 4488 1729; e-mail: castleward@nationaltrust.org.uk
Derrymore House
Bessbrook, Newry, Co Armagh, BT35 7EF; tel: 028 3083 8361; e-mail: derrymore@nationaltrust.org.uk
Florence Court
Enniskillen, Co Fermanagh, BT92 1DB; tel: 028 6634 8249; fax: 028 6634 8873; e-mail: florencecourt@nationaltrust.org.uk
Gray's Printing Press
49 Main Street, Strabane, Co Tyrone, BT82 8AU; tel: 028 7188 0055; fax: 028 7188 0055
Hezlett House
107 Sea Road, Castlerock, Coleraine, Co Londonderry, BT51 4TW; tel: 028 7084 8567; fax: 028 2073 1582; e-mail: hezletthouse@nationaltrust.org.uk
Mount Stewart House, Garden and Temple of the Winds
Newtownards, Co Down, BT22 2AD; tel: 028 4278 8387; fax: 028 4278 8569; e-mail: mountstewart@nationaltrust.org.uk
Patterson's Spade Mill
Templepatrick, Co Antrim, BT39 0AP; tel: 028 9443 3619; fax: 028 9443 9713; e-mail: patterson@nationaltrust.org.uk
Rowallane Garden
Saintfield, Ballynahinch, Co Down, BT24 7LH; tel: 028 9751 0131; fax: 028 9751 1242; e-mail: rowallane@nationaltrust.org.uk
Springhill
20 Springhill Road, Moneymore, Magherafelt, Co Londonderry, BT45 7NQ; tel: 028 8674 8210; fax: 028 8674 8210; e-mail: springhill@nationaltrust.org.uk
The Argory
Moy, Dungannon, Co Tyrone, BT71 6NA; tel: 028 8778 4753; fax: 028 8778 9598; e-mail: argory@nationaltrust.org.uk
Wellbrook Beetling Mill
20 Wellbrook Street, Corkhill, Cookstown, Co Tyrone, BT80 9RY; tel: 028 8674 8210/8675 1735; fax: 028 8675 1735; e-mail: wellbrook@nationaltrust.org.uk

NATIONAL TRUST OFFICE FOR WALES

Acronym or abbreviation: NT

Trinity Square, Llandudno, LL30 2DE

Tel: 01492 860123
Fax: 01492 860233
E-mail: ntwales@nt.org.uk

Website:
http://www.nt.org.uk

Enquiries:
Enquiries to: Marketing Manager

Organisation type and purpose:
National organisation, independently owned, membership association (membership is by subscription), registered charity (charity number 205846), suitable for ages: all.
The preservation and upkeep of places of historic interest or natural beauty.

Subject coverage:
Places of Historic Interest or Natural Beauty.

Access to staff:
Contact by letter, by telephone, by fax, by e-mail and via website
Hours: Mon to Fri, 0900 to 1700

Other Trust sites:
Aberconwy House
    Castle Street, Conwy, Gwynedd, LL32 8AY; tel: 01492 592246
Aberdulais Falls and Turbine House
    Aberdulais, Neath, West Glamorgan, SA10 8EU; tel: 01639 636674; e-mail: gaberd@smtp.ntrust .org
Chirk Castle
    Chirk, Wrexham, Clwyd, LL14 5AF; tel: 01691 777701; e-mail: gcwmsn@smtp.ntrust.org.uk
Conwy Suspension Bridge
    Conwy, Gwynedd, LL32 8LD; tel: 01492 573282
Dinefwr
    Llandeilo, SA19 6RT; tel: 01558 825912; e-mail: gdrcsh@smtp.ntrust.org.uk
Dolaucothi Gold Mines
    Pumsaint, Llanwrda, Carmarthenshire, SA19 8US; tel: 01558 650177; e-mail: gdoest@smtp .ntrust.org.uk
Erddig Hall
    Wrexham, Clwyd, LL13 0YT; tel: 01978 355314 (info 01978 315151); e-mail: geroff@smtp.ntrust .org.uk
Llanerchaeron
    Aberaeron, Ceredigion, SA48 8DG; tel: 01545 570200; e-mail: glnest@smtp.ntrust.org.uk
Penrhyn Castle
    Bangor, Gwynedd, LL57 4HN; tel: 01248 353084; fax: 01248 371281
Plas Newydd
    Llanfairpwll, Anglesey, Gwynedd, LL61 6DQ; tel: 01248 714795; e-mail: ppnmsn@smtp.ntrust .org.uk
Plas Yn Rhiw
    Rhiw, Pwllheli, Gwynedd, LL53 8AB; tel: 01758 780219; e-mail: gprmet@smtp.ntrust.org.uk
Powis Castle & Garden
    Welshpool, Powys, SY21 8RF; tel: 01938 551920; e-mail: ppcmsn@smtp.ntrust.org.uk
Tudor Merchant's House
    Quay Hill, Tenby, Pembrokeshire, SA70 7BX; tel: 01834 842279
Ty Mawr Wybrnant
    Penmachno, Betws-y-Coed, Conwy, LL25 0HJ; tel: 01690 760213
Ty'n-Y-Coed Uchaf
    Penmachno, Betws-y-Coed, Conwy, LL24 0PS; tel: 01690 760229

NATIONAL TRUST THEATRE

Sutton House, 2–4 Homerton High Street, Hackney, London, E9 6JQ

Tel: 020 8986 0242
Fax: 020 8985 2343
E-mail: theatre@nationaltrust.org.uk

Website:
http://www.nationaltrust.org.uk/learning

Enquiries:
Enquiries to: Administrator

Founded:
1977

Organisation type and purpose:
Registered charity (charity number 205846), suitable for ages: all.

Museum or gallery collection, archive, or library special collection:
Stage Costumes – mainly Tudor and Victorian

Printed publications:
The War Child – WW2 drama resource book (available for purchase)

Access to staff:
Contact by letter, by telephone, by fax and by e-mail. Appointment necessary.
Hours: Mon to Fri, 0930 to 1730

Access to building, collection or gallery:
Prior appointment required

Access for disabled people:
Toilet facilities
Hours: Mon to Frid, 0930 to 1730
Special comments: No lift to upper floors

Other address:
The National Trust Learning
    Rowan, Kembrey Park, Swindon, SN2 6UG

NATIONAL TYRE DISTRIBUTORS ASSOCIATION

Acronym or abbreviation: NTDA

Elsinore House, Buckingham Street, Aylesbury, Buckinghamshire, HP20 2NQ

Tel: 0870 9000 600
Fax: 0870 9000 610
E-mail: info@ntda.co.uk

Website:
http://www.ntda.co.uk

Enquiries:
Enquiries to: Director

Founded:
1936

Organisation type and purpose:
Trade association.

Subject coverage:
Tyres, the tyre industry and fast fit products in the United Kingdom.

Trade and statistical information:
Market Monitor (monthly).

Printed publications:
COSHH Manual (£10)
Directory of Members & Yearbook (£25)
Health and Safety Policy Manual (£30)
Technical Manual (£30)
The UK Tyre Market Report 2001 (£175)

Access to staff:
Contact by letter, by fax and by e-mail
Hours: Mon to Fri, 0900 to 1700

NATIONAL UNION OF KNITWEAR, FOOTWEAR AND APPAREL TRADES

Acronym or abbreviation: KFAT

55 New Walk, Leicester, LE1 7EB

Tel: 0116 255 6703
Fax: 0116 254 4406
E-mail: headoffice@kfat.org.uk

Website:
http://www.kfat.org.uk
Membership, policy and press statements.

Enquiries:
Enquiries to: General Secretary
Other contacts: (1) Research and Press Officer (2) Deputy General Secretary for (1) press enquiries (2) general enquiries.

Founded:
1991

Organisation type and purpose:
Trade union, present number of members: 30,000.

Subject coverage:
Industrial relations issues for the knitwear, footwear, leather, hosiery, and apparel industries.

Printed publications:
KFAT News (3 times a year)

Access to staff:
Contact by letter and by e-mail
Hours: Mon to Fri, 0900 to 1700

Access to building, collection or gallery:
No prior appointment required

Affiliated to:
General Federation of Trade Unions
International Textile Garment and Leather Workers Federation

Labour Party
Trades Union Congress

NATIONAL UNION OF RESIDENTS ASSOCIATIONS

Acronym or abbreviation: NURA

20 Park Drive, Romford, Essex, RM1 4LH

Tel: 01708 749119
Fax: 01708 736213
E-mail: info@ian-henry.com

Enquiries:
Enquiries to: Chairman

Founded:
1927

Organisation type and purpose:
Voluntary organisation.
Co-ordinating body of ratepayers, residents and kindred.

Subject coverage:
Interests of ratepayers; economical local government administration, finance, transport and public utilities; non-party politics in local government.

Printed publications:
A Simple Guide to Planning Applications (£5.25 plus 50p postage)

Access to staff:
Contact by letter, by telephone, by fax and by e-mail
Hours: Sat, Sun, 0900 to 1900

Access to building, collection or gallery:
No access other than to staff

NATIONAL UNION OF STUDENTS

Formal name: National Union of Students
Acronym or abbreviation: NUS

2nd Floor, Centro 3, Mandela Street, London, NW1 0DY

Tel: 0871 221 8221
Fax: 0871 221 8222
E-mail: nusuk@nus.org.uk

Website:
http://www.nusonline.co.uk

Enquiries:
Enquiries to: National Secretary

Founded:
1922

Organisation type and purpose:
National organisation, membership association (membership is by subscription, qualification), present number of members: 650, voluntary organisation, training organisation, research organisation, publishing house.
To represent the interests of students' unions and students in the United Kingdom.

Subject coverage:
All aspects of student and students' union life.

Printed publications:
NUS Directory

Publications list:
Available online and in print

Access to staff:
Contact by letter, by telephone, by fax, by e-mail and via website. Appointment necessary. Non-members charged.
Hours: Mon to Fri, 0900 to 1700
Special comments: Parking by advance notice.

Access for disabled people:
Ramped entry, toilet facilities
Special comments: Parking provided by appointment.

NATIONAL UNION OF TEACHERS

Acronym or abbreviation: NUT

Hamilton House, Mabledon Place, London, WC1H
9BD

Tel: 020 7388 6191
Fax: 020 7387 8458

Website:
http://www.teachers.org.uk
Union policy documents, consultation documents
e.g., user comments on recent Government White
and Green papers and consultative papers.
Teachers' salary scales and conditions of service,
health and safety, regional map and addresses of
Union regional offices, membership application
forms, Union newsletters e.g., NUT News.

Enquiries:
Enquiries to: Information Officer
Direct tel: 020 7380 4713
Direct e-mail: j.friedlander@nut.org.uk

Founded:
1870

Organisation type and purpose:
Trade union (membership is by subscription),
present number of members: 314,174.

Subject coverage:
Education.

**Museum or gallery collection, archive, or library
special collection:**
Archives now at Modern Records Centre, Warwick
    University, Coventry CV4 7AL, tel: 01203 524219
Government publications since 1816
NUT Annual Reports, 1871 to the present
Schoolmaster (now the Teacher), No. 1 (January
    1872-)
Union publications since its inception in 1870

Non-library collection catalogue:
All or part available online and in print

Printed publications:
Pamphlets are available from Despatch, Education,
    Membership and Communications Departments

Access to staff:
Contact by letter, by telephone, by fax and by e-
mail. Appointment necessary.
Hours: Mon to Fri, 0900 to 1700
Special comments: Quick reference enquiries, and
access to NUT documentation only for members
and others.

Access to building, collection or gallery:
No prior appointment required

Affiliated to:
Trades Union Congress
    tel: 020 7636 4030; fax: 020 7636 0632; e-mail:
    info@tuc.org.uk

NATIONAL VINTAGE TRACTOR AND ENGINE CLUB

Acronym or abbreviation: NVT&EC

Farview, 93 Church Road, Bickerstaffe, Ormskirk,
Lancashire, L39 0EB

Tel: 01695 722219
Fax: 01695 722219
E-mail: noone@nowhere.com

Website:
http://www.nvtec.co.uk

Enquiries:
Enquiries to: Honorary Secretary

Founded:
1965

Organisation type and purpose:
Membership association (membership is by
subscription), present number of members: 5800.

Subject coverage:
History of agricultural vehicles, machines, hand
tools and all associated equipment.

**Museum or gallery collection, archive, or library
special collection:**
Workshop manuals and sales literature

Printed publications:
Vaporising (magazine, quarterly, members only)

Access to staff:
Contact by letter, by telephone, by fax and by e-
mail
Hours: Mon to Fri, 0900 to 2200

Affiliated to:
National Traction Engine Trust

Archivist:
National Vintage Tractor and Engine Club
    Waylode, Tetbury Road, Old Sodbury, Bristol,
    BS17 6RJ; tel: 01454 313305

Has:
33 groups of NVTEC throughout England and
Wales with another 25 separate clubs affiliated

NATIONAL WAITING LIST HELPLINE

Acronym or abbreviation: NWLH

St Margaret's House, 21 Old Ford Road, London,
E2 9PL

Tel: 020 8983 1133
Fax: 020 8983 1553

Enquiries:
Enquiries to: Information Manager
Direct tel: 020 8983 1225
Direct e-mail: info@collegeofhealth.org.uk

Founded:
1991

Organisation type and purpose:
Advisory body, registered charity.

Subject coverage:
Waiting lists for patients waiting for NHS
treatment or surgery.

Trade and statistical information:
Data on the length of waiting lists in England by
    hospital and surgical speciality.

Electronic and video publications:
Licence available for website access

Access to staff:
Contact by telephone
Hours: Mon, Thu, 1100 to 1900; Fri, 1100 to 1700

Access to building, collection or gallery:
No access other than to staff

Parent body:
College of Health

NATIONAL WATER SPORTS TRAINING CENTRE

Isle of Cumbrae, Millport, Ayrshire, KA28 0HQ

Tel: 01475 530757
Fax: 01475 530013
E-mail: cumbraecentre@sportscotland.org.uk

Website:
http://www.nationalcentrecumbrae.org.uk
Brochure.

Enquiries:
Enquiries to: Principal

Founded:
1974

Organisation type and purpose:
National government body, advisory body,
registered charity, training organisation.

Subject coverage:
Specialist knowledge of all watersports: all aspects
of sailing, kayaking and sub-aqua.

Printed publications:
Brochure

Access to staff:
Contact by letter, by telephone, by fax and in
person. Appointment necessary.
Hours: Any reasonable time

Managed by:
SportScotland

NATIONAL WEIGHTS AND MEASURES LABORATORY

Acronym or abbreviation: NWML

Stanton Avenue, Teddington, Middlesex, TW11
0JZ

Tel: 020 8943 7272
Fax: 020 8943 7270
E-mail: info@nwml.gov.uk

Website:
http://www.nwml.gov.uk

Enquiries:
Enquiries to: General Receptionist
Other contacts: Heads of Units, Measuring
Instruments Certification Unit, Metrology and
Quality Unit, Legal Metrology Policy Unit,
Business Support

Founded:
1987

Organisation type and purpose:
National government body.
Executive Agency.

Subject coverage:
Legal metrology in the United Kingdom;
examination and approval of new weighing and
measuring equipment to be used for trade,
calibration, testing and certification, training.

Printed publications:
Annual Reports and Accounts
NWML Now! (twice a year)
Information leaflets and notes for guidance

Electronic and video publications:
MID Certificates, UK National Certificates, NAWI
    and EEC Certificates for Type Approval of
    instruments (online)

Publications list:
Available in print

Access to staff:
Contact by letter, by telephone, by fax, by e-mail
and via website. Appointment necessary.
Hours: Mon to Fri, 0900 to 1700

Links with:
International Organisation of Legal Metrology
    tel: 020 8943 7274
OIML Publications, Bureau International de
Métrologie Légale (BIML)
    11 rue Turgot, Paris 75009, France; tel: +33 1 48 78
    12 82; fax: +33 1 42 82 17 27

Parent body:
Department for Innovation, Universities and Skills
    Kinsgate House, 66–74 Victoria Street, London,
    SW1E 6SW; tel: 020 7215 5555; e-mail: info@dius
    .gsi.gov.uk; website: http://www.dius.gov.uk

NATIONAL WILDFLOWER CENTRE

Court Hey Park, Roby Road, Liverpool, L16 3NA

Tel: 0151 738 1913
E-mail: info@nwc.org.uk

Website:
http://www.wildflower.co.uk

Founded:
2001

Organisation type and purpose:
A registered charity (no. 1078314). Visitor centre
set in Victorian Court Hey Park.

Subject coverage:
Wild flowers.

Education services:
Educational facilities.

NATIONAL WOMEN'S REGISTER

Acronym or abbreviation: NWR

3A Vulcan House, Vulcan Road North, Norwich, Norfolk, NR6 6AQ

Tel: 01603 406767
Fax: 01603 407003
E-mail: office@nwr.org.uk

Website:
http://www.nwr.org.uk

Enquiries:
Enquiries to: Administrator
Direct tel: 01442 391556
Direct fax: 01442 401657
Direct e-mail: dodkins@ntlworld.com
Other contacts: Marketing Co-ordinator for publicity.

Founded:
1960

Organisation type and purpose:
Membership association (membership is by subscription), registered charity (charity number 295198).

Subject coverage:
Charity for women only, to make new friends, explore new interests, lively conversation and informal discussion.

Museum or gallery collection, archive, or library special collection:
NWR archive held at Fawcett Library

Printed publications:
Newsletter (2 times a year, members)
Magazine (2 times a year, members)

Access to staff:
Contact by letter, by telephone, by fax, by e-mail and via website
Hours: Mon, Tue, Thu, 0930 to 1615; Wed, 0900 to 1430

Branches:
national organisations in Australia, Netherlands, South Africa and Zimbabwe
subsidiary groups in Europe

NATIONAL YOUTH AGENCY

Eastgate House, 19–23 Humberstone Road, Leicester, LE5 3GJ

Tel: 0116 242 7350
Fax: 0116 242 7444
E-mail: nya@nya.org.uk

Website:
http://www.youthinformation.com
Information toolkit for use by young people.
http://www.nya.org.uk
Information on the work of NYA.

Enquiries:
Enquiries to: Information Officer
Direct tel: 0116 285 3792
Direct fax: 0116 285 3775
Direct e-mail: dutydesk@nya.org.uk

Organisation type and purpose:
Registered charity (charity number 1035804).
Specified public body.
A resource agency in informal social education.

Subject coverage:
The work of the youth service statutory and voluntary, major issues affecting the lives of young people, the curriculum for informal social and health education, education and training initiatives, community involvement and participation, counselling and information for young people, training in youth work.

Museum or gallery collection, archive, or library special collection:
Archive material on intermediate treatment

Archive material on the Youth Service
Educational kits and games
Videos

Non-library collection catalogue:
All or part available online

Printed publications:
Youth Policy Update (10 times a year)
Shabaab (newsletter, 3 times a year)
Young People Now (monthly)
Youth Action (3 times a year)
Youth and Policy (4 times a year)
Library Catalogue
Resources for Youth Work, including:
Have You Ever? – handbook of resource activities for detached youth workers
Louder Than Words – youth work and learning for sustainable development
Carnegie Young People Initiative series, including:
Citizenship and Community
Family Formation
Independent Living: income and housing
Posters
Order printed publications from: Sales Department
tel: 0116 285 3709, fax: 0116 285 3777, e-mail: sales@nya.org.uk

Electronic and video publications:
Tolerance in diversity: a video documentary

Publications list:
Available online and in print

Access to staff:
Contact by letter, by telephone, by e-mail and via website. Appointment necessary.
Hours: Mon to Thu, 0900 to 1730; Fri, 0900 to 1700

Access for disabled people:
Level entry, toilet facilities
Special comments: Disabled lift into NYA library available.

Funded by:
Department for Education and Skills
Local Government Association

Funded in part by the:
Home Office
   Active Community Unit

NATIONAL YOUTH JAZZ ORCHESTRA OF GREAT BRITAIN

Acronym or abbreviation: NYJO

11 Victor Road, Harrow, Middlesex, HA2 6PT

Tel: 020 8863 2717
Fax: 020 8863 8685
E-mail: bill.ashton@virgin.net

Website:
http://www.classical-artists.com/nyjo
Aims, date sheet (concerts), recordings, how to contact.

Enquiries:
Enquiries to: Musical Director

Founded:
1965

Organisation type and purpose:
National organisation, membership association (membership is by qualification, election or invitation), registered charity (charity number 274578), suitable for ages: up to 25.
Provides an opportunity for gifted young musicians to meet together and play big band jazz to a very high standard. Enables young musicians to gain experience of working to professional standards in major concert venues.

Subject coverage:
All aspects of the National Youth Jazz Orchestra of Great Britain. Becoming a participating musician, obtaining recordings, concert dates, becoming a friend.

Printed publications:
News from NYJO (magazine, quarterly, £10 voluntary donation, includes catalogue of recordings on CD, cassette, vinyl and videos)

Access to staff:
Contact by letter, by telephone, by fax, by e-mail and via website
Hours: Mon to Fri, 0900 to 1700
Special comments: No callers in person.

Access to building, collection or gallery:
No access other than to staff

NATIONAL YOUTH ORCHESTRAS OF SCOTLAND

Acronym or abbreviation: NYOS

13 Somerset Place, Glasgow, G3 7JT

Tel: 0141 332 8311
Fax: 0141 332 3915
E-mail: info@nyos.co.uk

Website:
http://www.nyos.co.uk

Enquiries:
Enquiries to: Chief Executive

Founded:
1979

Organisation type and purpose:
Membership association (membership is by subscription), present number of members: 360, suitable for ages: 8 to 28.
Classical and Jazz orchestras.
To provide top class education and performance experience.

Subject coverage:
Orchestral training, development of youth musicians in Scotland, orchestral music, chamber music, jazz music, professional tuition.

Electronic and video publications:
CD NYOS001 (The National Youth Orchestra of Scotland)
CD NYOS002 (Camerata Scotland)
CD NYOS003 (Camerata Scotland)
CD NYOS004 (The National Youth Orchestra of Scotland)
CD NYOS005 (The National Youth Jazz Orchestra of Scotland)
CD NYOS006 (The National Youth Orchestra of Scotland)

Access to staff:
Contact by letter, by telephone, by fax and by e-mail
Hours: Mon to Fri, 0930 to 1730

Member of:
Association of British Orchestras
European Federation of National Youth Orchestras
National Association of Youth Orchestras
National Federation of Music Societies
World Federation of Amateur Orchestras

Subsidiary body:
Camerata Scotland (NYOS Chamber Orchestra)
National Children's Orchestra of Scotland
National Youth Jazz Orchestra of Scotland
National Youth Orchestra of Scotland
NYOS Futures
NYOS Strings

NATIONAL YOUTH THEATRE OF GREAT BRITAIN

Acronym or abbreviation: NYT

443 Holloway Road, London, N7 6LW

Tel: 020 7281 3863
Fax: 020 7281 8246
E-mail: info@nyt.org.uk

Enquiries:
Enquiries to: General Manager
Other contacts: Development Manager for sponsorship and donations.

Founded:
1956

continued overleaf

Organisation type and purpose:
Voluntary organisation, registered charity (charity number 306075), suitable for ages: 13 to 21.

Access to staff:
Contact by letter, by telephone, by fax, by e-mail and via website
Hours: Mon to Fri, 1000 to 1800

Access for disabled people:
Parking provided, level entry, access to all public areas, toilet facilities

NATURAL DEATH CENTRE

12A Blackstock Mews, London, N4 2BT

Tel: 0871 288 2098
Fax: 020 7354 3831
E-mail: contact@naturaldeath.org.uk

Website:
http://www.naturaldeath.org.uk
Online access to Natural Death Handbook, Before and After, Creative Endings, Sooner or Later books, discussions of death and dying, bereavement, alternative funerals etc, woodland burial grounds, mail order coffins, good undertakers, etc.

Enquiries:
Enquiries to: Director

Founded:
1991

Organisation type and purpose:
Voluntary organisation, registered charity, research organisation, publishing house.

Subject coverage:
Death, dying, cardboard coffins, cheap coffins, shrouds, helpful undertakers, crematoria, funeral suppliers, funeral directors, befriending network for those with critical illness, green burial grounds, green, or family-organised funerals.

Printed publications:
Natural Death Handbook (£5.50 inc. p&p)
How to Organise an Inexpensive funeral e-mail (£10)
Set of forms: Living Will; Advance Funeral Wishes; Death Plan (for £7 donation)
Sooner or Later
Progressive Endings
After Life
Ways to Go Naturally

Electronic and video publications:
Publications available as pdfs

Access to staff:
Contact by letter, by telephone, by fax and by e-mail. Appointment necessary.
Hours: Mon to Fri, 1100 to 1400

Also at the same address:
Association of Natural Burial Grounds

Links with:
Befriending Network

NATURAL ENGLAND

Northminster House, Northminster, Peterborough, PE1 1UA

Tel: 01733 455094
Fax: 01733 568834
E-mail: library@naturalengland.org.uk

Website:
http://www.naturalengland.org.uk

Enquiries:
Enquiries to: Information and Library Services

Founded:
2006

Created by the merger of:
English Nature, the landscape, access and recreation elements of the Countryside Agency, and the environmental land management functions of the Rural Development Service (year of change 2006)

Organisation type and purpose:
Advisory body, statutory body.
Natural England aims to conserve and enhance the natural environment, for its intrinsic value, the wellbeing and enjoyment of people and the economic prosperity that it brings.

Subject coverage:
Natural England has been charged with the responsibility to ensure that England's unique natural environment including its land, flora and fauna, freshwater and marine environments, geology and soils are protected and improved. Also has responsibility for helping people enjoy, understand and access the natural environment.

Printed publications:
Wide range of printed materials (browse the publications catalogue online)

Publications list:
Available online and in print

Access to staff:
Contact by letter, by telephone, by fax, by e-mail, in person and via website
Hours: Mon to Thu, 0830 to 1700; Fri, 0830 to 1630

Access to building, collection or gallery:
Prior appointment required
Hours: Mon to Thu, 0830 to 1700; Fri, 0830 to 1630

Access for disabled people:
Ramped entry

Headquarters address:
Natural England
1 East Parade, Sheffield, S1 2ET; tel: 0114 241 8920; fax: 0114 241 8921; e-mail: enquiries@ naturalengland.org.uk; website: http://www .naturalengland.org.uk

NATURAL ENVIRONMENT RESEARCH COUNCIL

Acronym or abbreviation: NERC

Polaris House, North Star Avenue, Swindon, Wiltshire, SN2 1EU

Tel: 01793 411500
Fax: 01793 411501
E-mail: requests@nerc.ac.uk

Website:
http://www.nerc.ac.uk
NERC Home page includes the NERC mission, environmental issues, NERC contacts, funding routes, training and careers.

Enquiries:
Enquiries to: Information Officer

Founded:
1965

Organisation type and purpose:
Research organisation.
The Natural Environment Research Council (NERC) is the leading body in the UK for research, survey, monitoring and training in the environmental sciences. NERC funds research in universities and in its own centres, surveys and units.

Subject coverage:
Science policy, science and technology, natural environment.

Printed publications:
NERC Annual Report
Planet Earth (quarterly journal)

Publications list:
Available online

Access to staff:
Contact by letter, by telephone, by fax and by e-mail
Hours: Mon to Fri, 0900 to 1700

Centre for Coastal and Marine Science, incorporating the following institutes:
Dunstaffnage Marine Laboratory
PO Box 3, Oban, Argyll, PA34 4AD; tel: 01631 562244; fax: 01631 565518
Plymouth Marine Laboratory
Prospect Place, Plymouth, PL1 3DH; tel: 01752 633100; fax: 01752 633101
Proudman Oceanographic Laboratory
Bidston, Birkenhead, L43 7RA; tel: 0151 653 8633; fax: 0151 653 6269

Centre for Ecology & Hydrology, incorporating the following institutes:
Institute of Freshwater Ecology
The Ferry House, Far Sawrey, Ambleside, Cumbria, LA22 0LP; tel: 01539 442468; fax: 01539 446914
Institute of Hydrology
Maclean Building, Crowmarsh Gifford, Wallingford, Oxfordshire, OX10 8BB; tel: 01491 838800; fax: 01491 692424
Institute of Terrestrial Ecology
Monks Wood, Abbots Ripton, Huntingdon, PE28 2LS; tel: 01487 773381; fax: 01487 773467
Institute of Virology and Environmental Microbiology
Mansfield Road, Oxford, OX1 3SR; tel: 01865 281630; fax: 01865 281696

NERC Centres and Surveys:
British Antarctic Survey
High Cross, Madingley Road, Cambridge, CB3 0ET; tel: 01223 221400; fax: 01223 362616
British Geological Survey
Kingsley Dunham Centre, Keyworth, Nottingham, NG12 5GG; tel: 0115 936 3100; fax: 0115 936 3200
Southampton Oceanography Centre
(a joint venture between NERC and the University of Southampton), Empress Dock, Southampton, SO14 3ZH; tel: 023 8059 6666; fax: 023 8059 6032

NATURAL HISTORY MUSEUM

Acronym or abbreviation: NHM

Cromwell Road, London, SW7 5BD

Tel: 020 7942 5000
Fax: 020 7942 5559
E-mail: library@nhm.ac.uk

Website:
http://www.nhm.ac.uk/info/library/index.html
Description of each library, including the Museum Archives, with contact details: provides access to the library catalogue via telnet; link to main museum home page; lists admissions, opening hours and services provided in the library.
http://www.nhm.ac.uk
Main museum home page.

Enquiries:
Enquiries to: Librarian
Other contacts: Specialist Library and Information Services, see below

Founded:
1881

Organisation type and purpose:
International organisation, national government body, museum, public library, suitable for ages: all, training organisation, research organisation.

Subject coverage:
Botany; biodiversity; entomology; geography, expeditions and travel; mineralogy; museum techniques; oceanography; ornithology; palaeontology; parasitology; physical anthropology; tropical medicine; zoology; environmental studies.

Information services:
Library available for reference (for conditions see Access above), online searching, CD-ROM based services, bibliography compilation, selective dissemination services. Helpline available, tel: 020 7942 5011 information line; Field study tours Study days for teachers and museum professionals

Special visitor services:
Guided tours, tape recorded guides, materials and/
or activities for children.

Education services:
Group education facilities, resources for Key
Stages 1 and 2, 3 and Further or Higher Education.

Services for disabled people:
Displays and/or information at wheelchair height.

**Museum or gallery collection, archive, or library
special collection:**
Albert Gunther (zoology)
Day Library (natural history dealers)
John Murray (oceanography)
Joseph Banks (natural history, note-books etc from
    Cook's first voyage around the world)
Linnaeus Collection (binomial nomenclature
    system in classification; works on plants and
    animals)
Richard Owen (anatomy)
Robert Brown (botany, including material from the
    Australian expedition 1801–1805)
Sloane (natural history and collection of curiosities
    and artefacts of c. 1753. Sloane's collection was
    the foundation of the British Museum)
Sowerby (natural history, especially botany; the
    family were artists and publishers)
Sydney Parkinson (natural history; drawings)
Tweeddale Library (zoology)
Walsingham (entomology)
Walter Rothschild (zoology)

Library catalogue:
All or part available online

Printed publications:
A large number of publications on the above
subjects including:
Bulletin of the Natural History Museum: Botany
    series, Entomology series, Geology series,
    Zoology series
Catalogue of the Books and Manuscripts, Maps
    and Drawings in the British Museum (Natural
    History)
Catalogue of the Works of Linnaeus
List of Serials of the Natural History Museum
Monographs, handbooks, guide books including:
Coral Fish (Pitkin L)
Crystals (2nd ed, Cressey G and Mercer I F)
From the Beginning (Edwards K and Rosen B)
Gold (Herrington R J et al)
Lichens (Purvis W et al)
Nature's Connections – An Exploration of Natural
    History (McGirr N)
Snakes (Stafford P)
The Deep Sea (Rice T)
Volcanoes (2nd ed, van Rose S and Mercer I F)

Publications list:
Available online and in print

Access to staff:
Contact by letter, by telephone, by fax, by e-mail
and via website. Appointment necessary.
Hours: Mon to Fri, 1000 to 1630

Access for disabled people:
Access to all public areas, toilet facilities

Other libraries:
Botany Library
    tel: 020 79425685; e-mail: botlib@nhm.ac.uk
Earth Sciences Library
    tel: 020 7942 5476; e-mail: earthscilib@nhm.ac.uk
Entomology Library
    tel: 020 7942 5751; e-mail: entlib@nhm.ac.uk
General and Zoology Libraries
    tel: 020 7942 5460; e-mail: genlib@nhm.ac.uk
Ornithological and Rothschild Libraries
    Akeman Street, Tring, Hertfordshire, HP23 6AP;
    tel: 020 7942 6158; fax: 020 7942 6150; e-mail:
    ornlib@nhm.ac.uk
Zoological Museum Library
    Tring, Hertfordshire; tel: 020 7942 6159

NATURAL HISTORY SOCIETY OF NORTHUMBRIA

Acronym or abbreviation: NHSN

Hancock Museum, Barras Bridge, Newcastle upon
Tyne, NE2 4PT

Tel: 0191 232 6386
Fax: 0191 232 2177
E-mail: nhsn@ncl.ac.uk

Website:
http://www.nhsn.ncl.ac.uk

Enquiries:
Enquiries to: Secretary

Founded:
1829

Organisation type and purpose:
Advisory body, learned society (membership is by
subscription), present number of members: 850,
voluntary organisation, registered charity,
museum, publishing house.

Subject coverage:
Natural history of Northumbria, with particular
reference to geology, ornithology, entomology,
mammalia and botany; also Farne Islands.

**Museum or gallery collection, archive, or library
special collection:**
Bewick Collection (water colour drawings)
Collection of early natural history books from late
    18th to 19th century

Printed publications:
Farne Island Bird Report (annually, free to
    members; on sale to general public)
Flora of Northumberland
Bulletin (3 times a year, to members)
Transactions of Natural History Society of
    Northumbria (annually, free to members; on sale
    to general public)
The following are published as part of the
    Transactions, but on sale to general public:
Red Data Book for Northumberland
Robson's Geology of North East England

Publications list:
Available in print

Access to staff:
Contact by letter, by telephone, by fax, by e-mail
and in person
Hours: Mon to Fri, 1000 to 1300
Special comments: Use of library by members only,
or by prior appointment.

Access to building, collection or gallery:
No prior appointment required

NATURAL SCIENCES COLLECTIONS ASSOCIATION

Acronym or abbreviation: NatSCA

Natural History Museum, Cromwell Road,
London, SW7 5BD

Tel: 020 7942 5196
E-mail: pab@nhm.ac.uk

Website:
http://www.nhm.ac.uk/hosted_sites/natSCA

Enquiries:
Enquiries to: Chair

Founded:
2003

Incorporates the former:
Biology Curators Group (year of change 1975);
Natural Sciences Conservation Group (year of
change 1995)

Organisation type and purpose:
National organisation, advisory body, professional
body, membership association (membership is by
subscription), voluntary organisation.
To promote: the care, knowledge and use of
natural sciences collections and their conservation;
and museum-based, natural sciences-related
activities.

Subject coverage:
The acquisition, long-term care and use of natural
sciences collections. The propagation of natural
sciences information to a wide range of users, and
the promotion of natural sciences .

Trade and statistical information:
Nature, content and possible use of museum-based
    natural sciences collections, as well as many non-
    museum-based collections.

Printed publications:
NatSCA News

Publications list:
Available online

Access to staff:
Contact by letter, by telephone, by e-mail, in
person and via website. Appointment necessary.
Hours: Mon to Fri, 0900 to 1700

NATURE IN ART TRUST

Wallsworth Hall, Main A38, Twigworth,
Gloucester, GL2 9PA

Tel: 01452 731422
Fax: 01452 730937
E-mail: ninart@globalnet.co.uk

Website:
http://www.nature-in-art.org.uk
Current special exhibitions/courses/artist in
residence. Group/school visit details and booking
forms. Overview of the collection, events listing,
contacts, email facility.

Enquiries:
Enquiries to: Director

Founded:
1982

Organisation type and purpose:
Registered charity (charity number 1000553),
museum, art gallery.
Registered with the Museum and Galleries
Commission No 935.

Subject coverage:
All aspects of art inspired by nature, through the
ages; the use of art in environmental and
conservation education, and contacts with
contemporary artists from the UK and abroad.

**Museum or gallery collection, archive, or library
special collection:**
The Trust owns and manages Nature in Art, the
    world's first museum dedicated exclusively to art
    inspired by nature, it includes:
Work of any media of international stature, scope
    and appeal
Work spanning 1500 years collected from over 60
    countries
Small library containing slide collection and
    reference collection

Printed publications:
Nature in Art Magazine (quarterly, free to
    members)
Nature in Art – 300 years of Wildlife Paintings (£35
    or £14.96 paper-backed)

Access to staff:
Contact by letter, by telephone, by fax, by e-mail
and via website. Appointment necessary.
Hours: Tue to Sun, 1000 to 1700; closed Mon, and
December 24/25/26

Access to building, collection or gallery:
No prior appointment required
Special comments: Appointment required for the
library, but not for the gallery etc.

Access for disabled people:
Parking provided, ramped entry, access to all
public areas, toilet facilities

Affiliated to:
Area Museums Council for the South West
Gloucestershire Museums Group
Museums Association
Natur and Kunst (Germany)

NATURIST FOUNDATION

Sheepcote Lane, Orpington, Kent, BR5 4ET

Tel: 01689 871200
E-mail: natfound@hotmail.co.uk

Website:
http://www.naturistfoundation.org

Enquiries:
Enquiries to: General Secretary
Other contacts: Trustees

Founded:
1948

Organisation type and purpose:
Registered charity, voluntary organisation (charity number 271420).

Subject coverage:
Naturist recreational facilities locally and throughout the United Kingdom

Access to staff:
Contact by letter, by telephone, by e-mail and via website
Hours: Mon, Thu, Fri, Sat and Sun, 0930 to 1700

Links with:
Central Council for British Naturism
International Naturist Federation

Member organisation of:
ASA
Kent County Playing Fields Association
RLSS

NAUTICAL INSTITUTE

202 Lambeth Road, London, SE1 7LQ

Tel: 020 7928 1351
Fax: 020 7401 2817
E-mail: pubs@nautinst.org

Website:
http://www.nautinst.org
Information on the Institute, its books and publications.

Enquiries:
Enquiries to: Chief Executive
Direct e-mail: sec@nautinst.org

Founded:
1972

Organisation type and purpose:
Professional body, registered charity (charity number 1002462).
To promote high standards of competence at sea and in the management of maritime operations

Subject coverage:
Navigation, seamanship, maritime operations.

Printed publications:
Books on (seagoing) Command, Work of the Harbour Master, Work of the Nautical Surveyor; pilotage; management of safety
Conference Proceedings
Monographs on various aspects of nautical science
Seaways (members' journal, monthly)

Electronic and video publications:
CD-ROMs for selected publications

Publications list:
Available online and in print

Access to staff:
Contact by letter, by telephone, by fax, by e-mail and via website. Appointment necessary.
Hours: Mon to Fri, 0900 to 1700

Access to building, collection or gallery:
No access other than to staff

NAVY RECORDS SOCIETY

Acronym or abbreviation: NRS

Pangbourne College, Pangbourne, Berkshire, RG8 8LA

E-mail: robin.brodhurst@pangcoll.co.uk

Website:
http://navyrecordssociety.com

Enquiries:
Enquiries to: Honorary Secretary
Other contacts: Membership Secretary

Founded:
1893

Organisation type and purpose:
International organisation, learned society (membership is by subscription), present number of members: 825, registered charity (charity number 210836).
Publication of naval texts.

Subject coverage:
Naval history of Britain, as recorded in documents and published in some 150 volumes since 1893; the series includes the papers of famous naval commanders as well as statesmen and administrators of the Royal Navy; virtually every campaign in which the Navy has fought from the 15th century is covered; other subjects are: naval administration, shipbuilding and victualling, manning the fleet, everyday life at sea, naval songs, health of seamen, signals, fighting instructions, maritime law and piracy, naval brigades, Naval Air Service.

Printed publications:
Over 150 titles, including:
British Naval Documents 1204–1960 (ed. J. B. Hattendorf, et al)
Naval Administration, 1715–1750 (D. A. Baugh)
The Navy of the Lancastrian Kings: Accounts and Inventories of William Soper, Keeper of the King's Ships 1422–1427 (S. Rose)
The Royal Navy in the Mediterranean, 1915–1918 (ed. P. G. Halpern)
State Papers relating to the Defeat of the Spanish Armada, Anno 1588 (2 vols)
The Battle of the Atlantic and Signals Intelligence: U-boat Situations and Trends, 1941–1945 (ed. D. Syrett)
The Cunningham Papers: Vol I The Mediterranean Fleet, 1939–1942 (ed. M. Simpson)
The Channel Fleet and the Blockade of Brest, 1793–1801 (ed. R. A. Morriss)
The Submarine Service, 1900–1918 (ed. N. Lambert)

Publications list:
Available in print

Access to staff:
Contact by letter
Hours: Mon to Fri, 0900 to 1700

NCDL

Formal name: National Canine Defence League

17 Wakley Street, London, EC1V 7RQ

Tel: 020 7837 0006
Fax: 020 7833 2701
E-mail: info@ncdl.org.uk

Website:
http://www.ncdl.org.uk
General information on the Charity and it's services – access to factsheets which can be downloaded/printed.

Enquiries:
Enquiries to: Information Officer
Direct tel: 020 7833 7657
Direct e-mail: victoria.horsley@ncdl.org.uk

Founded:
1891

Organisation type and purpose:
Voluntary organisation, registered charity (charity number 227523).
To protect and defend all dogs, rehabilitation and re-homing of stray and abandoned dogs, no healthy dog is ever destroyed.

Subject coverage:
Dog legislation, welfare and control, in particular rescue and care of stray dogs.

Museum or gallery collection, archive, or library special collection:
Annual Reports from the start of the League in 1897, old photos

Printed publications:
Annual Report
Newsletter (3 times a year)
Information leaflets and factsheets including:
Basic dog training
How to be a good dog owner
Routine Healthcare
The History of the NCDL
The NCDL Ruff Guide to Behaviour Problems
Which Puppy (a guide on how to buy a puppy)

Publications list:
Available in print

Access to staff:
Contact by letter, by telephone, by fax, by e-mail and via website. Appointment necessary.
Hours: Mon to Fri, 0900 to 1645

Member of:
Association of British Dogs and Cats Homes (ABDCH)
The Secretary, ABDCH, Battersea Dogs Home, 4 Battersea Park Road, London, SW8 4AA

Rehoming Centres at:
NCDL Ballymena
Fairview, 60 Teeshan Road, Ballymena, Co Antrim, BT43 5PN; tel: 028 2565 2977; fax: 028 2565 8463
NCDL Bridgend
Tondu Road, Bridgend, Mid Glamorgan, CF31 4LH; tel: 01656 652771; fax: 01656 647495
NCDL Canterbury
Radfall Road, Chestfield, Whitstable, Kent, CT5 3ER; tel: 01227 792505; fax: 01227 793988
NCDL Darlington
Hill House Farm, Sadberge, Co Durham, DL2 1SL; tel: 01325 333114; fax: 01325 333048
NCDL Dumfries
Dovecotewell, Glencaple, Dumfriesshire, DG1 4RH; tel: 01387 770346; fax: 01387 770242
NCDL Evesham
89 Pitcher's Hill, Wickhamford, Evesham, Worcestershire, WR11 6RT; tel: 01386 830613; fax: 01386 832617
NCDL Ilfracombe
Hazeldene, West Down, Ilfracombe, Devon, EX34 8NU; tel: 01271 812709; fax: 01271 814098
NCDL Kenilworth
Honiley, Kenilworth, Warwickshire, CV8 1NP; tel: 01926 484398; fax: 01926 484196
NCDL Leeds
Eccup Lane, Adel, Leeds, LS16 8AL; tel: 0113 261 3194; fax: 0113 230 0886
NCDL Merseyside
Whiston Lane, Huyton, Liverpool, L36 6HP; tel: 0151 480 0660; fax: 0151 480 6176
NCDL Newbury
Plumb's Farm, Hamstead Marshall, Newbury, Berkshire, RG20 0HR; tel: 01488 658391; fax: 01488 657211
NCDL Roden
Roden Lane Farm, Roden, Telford, Shropshire, TF6 6BP; tel: 01952 770225; fax: 01952 770416
NCDL Salisbury
45 Amesbury Road, Newton Tony, Wiltshire, SP4 0HW; tel: 01980 629 634; fax: 01980 629 706
NCDL Shoreham
Brighton Road, Shoreham-by-Sea, West Sussex, BN43 5LT; tel: 01273 452576; fax: 01273 440856
NCDL Snetterton
North Farm Kennels (Snetterton), North End Road, Snetterton, Norfolk, NR16 2LD; tel: 01953 498377; fax: 01953 498325
NCDL West Calder
Bentyhead, Hartwood Road, West Calder, West Lothian, EH55 8LE; tel: 01506 873459; fax: 01506 873275

NCS COLOUR CENTRE

71 Ancastle Green, Henley-on-Thames, Oxfordshire, RG9 1TS

Tel: 01491 411717

Fax: 01491 411231
E-mail: info@ncscolour.co.uk

Website:
http://www.ncscolour.co.uk
Explanation of the NCS System. Details of products and services, Free online RIBA CPD seminars, Case studies, FAQs, Glossary. Links to Worldwide NCS Colour Centres.

Enquiries:
Enquiries to: Customer Services
Direct tel: 01491 411717
Direct fax: 01491 411231
Direct e-mail: sales@ncscolour.co.uk

Founded:
1997

Organisation type and purpose:
Service industry, training organisation, consultancy.
To advise on use of and supply Natural Colour System standards in manufacturing, architecture and design.

Subject coverage:
Use of the NCS (Natural Colour System) in manufacturing, architecture and design.

Non-library collection catalogue:
All or part available online

Library catalogue:
All or part available online

Printed publications:
NCS Atlas (£290)
NCS Educational Material (various)
NCS Colour Index (£135) NCS Colour Atlas (£323)
Order printed publications from: http://www.ncscolour.co.uk

Electronic and video publications:
NCS Measurement programme (computer software for PC)
NCS Palette (CD-ROM for Mac and PC)
NCS Palette ArchiCAD (CD-ROM for Mac and PC)
NCS Palette AutoCAD (CD-ROM for PC)

Publications list:
Available online and in print

Access to staff:
Contact by letter, by telephone, by fax, by e-mail and via website. Appointment necessary.
Hours: Mon to Fri, 0900 to 1700

Parent body:
Scandinavian Colour Institute AB
PO Box 49022, SE-100, 28, Stockholm, Sweden

NCT

Alexandra House, Oldham Terrace, London, W3 6NH

Tel: 0300 330 0770 (enquiry line); 0844 243 6000 extn 2315 (library)
Fax: 0844 243 6001
E-mail: library@nct.org.uk

Website:
http://www.nct.org.uk
http://www.nctshop.co.uk
NCT Shop

Enquiries:
Enquiries to: Information Officer and Librarian

Founded:
1956

Formerly called:
National Childbirth Trust

Organisation type and purpose:
Membership association (membership is by subscription), registered charity (charity number 801395).
To offer information and support in pregnancy, childbirth and early parenthood. We aim to give every parent the chance to make informed choices.

Subject coverage:
Pregnancy, childbirth, first year of parenthood, maternity care, breastfeeding, homebirth, caesarean.

Museum or gallery collection, archive, or library special collection:
Archive of NCT materials and other relevant materials – books, videos, films, slides.

Non-library collection catalogue:
All or part available in-house

Library catalogue:
All or part available online and in-house

Printed publications:
Wide variety of books and booklets, information sheets
Order printed publications from: NCT Shop, 239 Shawbridge Street, Glasgow, G43 1QN, tel: 0845 8100 100, fax: 0845 8100 120, e-mail: contactus@nctshop.co.uk

Electronic and video publications:
DVDs and CDs
Order electronic and video publications from: NCT Shop

Publications list:
Available online and in print

Access to staff:
Contact by letter, by telephone, by fax and by e-mail. Appointment necessary. Letter of introduction required. Non-members charged.
Hours: Mon to Fri, 0900 to 1700
Special comments: Library and information service is mainly for use of members.

Access for disabled people:
Parking provided
Special comments: Restricted wheelchair access to library.

Branches:
across the United Kingdom

NEATH PORT TALBOT COUNTY BOROUGH COUNCIL

Civic Centre, Port Talbot, West Glamorgan, SA13 1PJ

Tel: 01639 763333
Fax: 01639 763444

Website:
http://www.neath-porttalbot.gov.uk
guide to county borough and council information.

Enquiries:
Enquiries to: Chief Executive
Direct tel: 01639 763308
Direct fax: 01639 763751
Direct e-mail: d.merchant@neath-porttalbot.gov.uk

Founded:
1996

Organisation type and purpose:
Local government body.

Access to staff:
Contact by letter, by telephone and by fax.
Appointment necessary.
Hours: Mon to Fri, 0900 to 1700

Also at:
Civic Centre Neath
Neath; tel: 01639 763333; fax: 01639 764666

NEIL MUNRO SOCIETY, THE

8 Briar Road, Kirkintilloch, Glasgow, G66 3SA

Tel: 0141 776 4280
Fax: 0141 776 4280
E-mail: brian@bdosborne.fsnet.co.uk

Website:
http://www.neilmunro.co.uk

Enquiries:
Enquiries to: Secretary

Founded:
1996

Organisation type and purpose:
Learned society (membership is by subscription), present number of members: 180, voluntary organisation.

Subject coverage:
Life and work of Neil Munro (1863–1930) Scottish novelist, poet, critic and journalist.

Museum or gallery collection, archive, or library special collection:
Archival Collection of books, MSS relating to Neil Munro held by Royal College of Physicians and Surgeons of Glasgow on behalf of Society.

Non-library collection catalogue:
All or part available online

Printed publications:
Paragraph (magazine, 2 times a year, supplied as part of membership package)

Access to staff:
Contact by letter, by telephone, by e-mail and via website
Hours: Mon to Fri, 0900 to 1700

Access to building, collection or gallery:
Prior appointment required
Hours: Mon to Fri, 0900 to 1700
Special comments: Archive held by Royal College of Physicians and Surgeons of Glasgow.

NEL

Formal name: National Engineering Laboratory
Acronym or abbreviation: NEL

East Kilbride, Glasgow, G75 0QU

Tel: 01355 220222
Fax: 01355 272999
E-mail: info@nel.uk

Website:
http://www.nel.uk
National Engineering Laboratory services and activities.

Enquiries:
Enquiries to: Information Officer

Founded:
1947

Organisation type and purpose:
Service industry, consultancy, research organisation.

Subject coverage:
Fluid power engineering, heat exchangers, heat transfer, offshore engineering, physical properties of liquids and gases, pumps, software, structural analysis and testing, turbo machinery, control of noise and vibration in machinery.

Printed publications:
Conference and Symposia Proceedings (for sale, apply to Events Co-ordinator)

Access to staff:
Contact by letter, by fax, by e-mail and via website
Hours: Mon to Fri, 0900 to 1700

Business of the:
TÜV Suddeutschland Group

NERINE AND AMARYLLID SOCIETY

Acronym or abbreviation: NAAS

2 The Grove, Ickenham, Uxbridge, Middlesex, UB10 8QH

Tel: 01895 464694
Fax: 0870 0529321
E-mail: roger.beauchamp@btinternet.com

Website:
http://www.nerine.org.uk

continued overleaf

Enquiries:
Enquiries to: Secretary

Founded:
1997

Organisation type and purpose:
National organisation, membership association (membership is by subscription), present number of members: 140.
For the study, dissemination and collection of all information concerning all genera within the family Amaryllidaceae and closely associated families.

Subject coverage:
All aspects of all genera in the family Amaryllidaceae.

Printed publications:
Journal (three times a year)

Publications list:
Available in print

Access to staff:
Contact by letter, by telephone, by fax and by e-mail

NESCOT LEARNING RESOURCES CENTRE

Reigate Road, Ewell, Epsom, Surrey, KT17 3DS

Tel: 020 8394 3055
Fax: 020 8394 3030
E-mail: ghodge@nescot.ac.uk

Website:
http://lrc.nescot.ac.uk
Is the home page of the Learning Resources Unit, providing online access to the catalogue, databases, electronic journals and subject guides.

Enquiries:
Enquiries to: Library Services Manager

Founded:
1954

Subject coverage:
Biology, building and construction, health and social care, business and computing, art, design, photography, performing arts.

Library catalogue:
All or part available online

Access to staff:
Contact by letter, by telephone, by fax, by e-mail and in person
Hours: Term time: Mon to Thu, 0830 to 2000; Fri, 0830 to 1700
Vacations: Mon to Fri, 0900 to 1700 (unless otherwise stated)

Access to building, collection or gallery:
No prior appointment required
Hours: Advance notification preferred.

Access for disabled people:
Parking provided, ramped entry, access to all public areas, toilet facilities

NETHERLANDS – BRITISH CHAMBER OF COMMERCE

307–308 High Holborn, London, WC1V 7LS

Tel: 020 7405 1358
Fax: 020 7405 1689
E-mail: nbcc@btinternet.com

Website:
http://www.nbcc.co.uk

Enquiries:
Enquiries to: Manager
Direct fax: 020 7831 4831

Founded:
1891

Organisation type and purpose:
International organisation, advisory body, membership association (membership is by subscription), present number of members: 300, consultancy.
Chamber of Commerce.
To provide information on Anglo-Dutch trade.

Subject coverage:
Anglo-Dutch trade.

Printed publications:
See publications list

Electronic and video publications:
Information supplied on request

Publications list:
Available online and in print

Access to staff:
Contact by letter, by telephone, by fax, by e-mail, in person and via website. Appointment necessary. Non-members charged.
Hours: Mon to Fri, 0900 to 1700

Other addresses:
Netherlands – British Chamber of Commerce
   NZ Voorburgwal 328L, 1012 RW, Amsterdam, The Netherlands; tel: + 31 20 421 7040; fax: + 31 20 421 7003; e-mail: nbccnl@btinternet.com

NETWORK 81

1–7 Woodfield Terrace, Chapel Hill, Stansted, Essex, CM24 8AJ

Tel: 0845 074 4055
Fax: 0845 077 4057
E-mail: network81@btconnect.com

Website:
http://www.network81.org

Enquiries:
Enquiries to: Administrator
Other contacts: National Development Manager

Founded:
1986

Organisation type and purpose:
Voluntary organisation, registered charity (charity number 1061950).

Subject coverage:
Help, support and advice for parents of children with special educational needs through the assessment and statementing process; 1996 Education Act, Part IV, code of practice.

Printed publications:
Parents Guide (£8.50)

Publications list:
Available online

Access to staff:
Contact by letter, by telephone, by fax, by e-mail and via website
Hours: Mon to Fri, 0900 to 1500
Special comments: Helpline: 1000 to 1300.

NEUROFIBROMATOSIS ASSOCIATION

Quayside House, 38 High Street, Kingston on Thames, KT1 1HL

Tel: 020 8439 1234
Fax: 020 8439 1200
E-mail: nfa@zetnet.co.uk

Website:
http://www.nfauk.org.uk

Enquiries:
Enquiries to: General Secretary
Other contacts: Helpline: 0845 602 4173 (Mon, Thu, 0900 to 1600; Tue, 0900 to 1200)

Founded:
1982

Organisation type and purpose:
Membership association (membership is by subscription), present number of members: 2300, registered charity (charity number 1078790).
To provide help and support to those affected, their families & friends.

Subject coverage:
Information on neurofibromatosis for GPs and health visitors, patients and carers, public; access to consultants via medical advisory board; data for researchers (subject to ethical controls); information on learning difficulties in Nf.

Printed publications:
Annual Report
Newsletter (3 times a year)
Introduction booklet (free)
Fact sheets (free)

Electronic and video publications:
Neurofibromatosis
Order electronic and video publications from: see website

Publications list:
Available online

Access to staff:
Contact by letter, by telephone, by fax and by e-mail
Hours: Mon to Fri, 0900 to 1700

Connections with:
Genetic Interest Group (GIG)
International Neurofibromatosis Association
LMCA Neurological Alliance

NEW ALLIANCE

PO Box 13199, London, SW6 6ZU

Tel: 020 7386 1837
E-mail: info@newalliance.org.uk

Website:
http://www.newalliance.org.uk/contact.htm
http://www.newalliance.org.uk
Home page.
http://www.newalliance.org.uk/fasti.htm
Fast index, site map.

Enquiries:
Enquiries to: Campaign Manager
Other contacts: Treasurer for donations, legacies.

Founded:
1997

Organisation type and purpose:
Learned society, voluntary organisation, consultancy, research organisation, publishing house.
Campaigning group.
Educating business and the public about the alternatives to European Union membership.

Subject coverage:
European Union, defence, policing, criminal justice and legal issues, constitution, taxation, business legislation, employment policy, regional policy, the Euro, economic and monetary union, environment, motoring, agriculture, ID cards, referendum issues, BBC coverage, public consultations, metrication.

Non-library collection catalogue:
All or part available online, in-house and in print

Printed publications:
Animal welfare
Newsletters (sent to registered supporters)
Fact sheets on European Union topics:
Alternatives to EU membership
Defence
Policing
Taxation
Business legislation
Employment policy
Regional policy
The Euro
Economic and monetary union
Environment
Motoring
Agriculture
ID Cards

Referendum Legislation
The Treaty of Nice
BBC Coverage
Metrication
Constitution
Criminal Justice & Legal Issues

Electronic and video publications:
Fast Index online via website
Can be supplied via electronic and paper media to
schools and recognised research institutions

Publications list:
Available online

Access to staff:
Contact by letter, by telephone, by e-mail and via
website
Hours: Mon to Sun, 0900 to 2100

Access to building, collection or gallery:
No access other than to staff

Affiliated organisation:
National Referendum Campaign

Affiliated to:
Statewatch

NEW COLLEGE LIBRARY

Holywell Street, Oxford, OX1 3BN

Tel: 01865 279580
Fax: 01865 279590
E-mail: library@new.ox.ac.uk

Website:
http://www.new.ox.ac.uk/The_Library

Enquiries:
Enquiries to: Librarian
Direct e-mail: naomi.vanloo@new.ox.ac.uk

Founded:
1379

Organisation type and purpose:
University college library.

Subject coverage:
Subjects studied by undergraduates in the
University of Oxford; the subjects covered by the
special collections listed.

**Museum or gallery collection, archive, or library
special collection:**
Archives collection since the foundation of the
College
Medieval manuscripts
Early printed books
Papers of Lord Milner (Bodley deposit)
Seton-Watson Collection (Eastern Europe)

Library catalogue:
All or part available online and in-house

Printed publications:
New College Oxford 1379–1979 (J. Buxton and P.
Williams, OUP, 1979)
Archives of New College Oxford (F. W. Steer,
Phillimore, 1974)

Microform publications:
Microfilms of medieval manuscripts

Access to staff:
Contact by letter, by telephone and by e-mail.
Appointment necessary. Access for members only.
Letter of introduction required.
Hours: Mon to Fri, 0900 to 1700

Access to building, collection or gallery:
Hours: Mon to Fri, 0930 to 1245 and 1415 to 1645

Constituent part of:
University of Oxford

NEW ENGLISH ART CLUB

Acronym or abbreviation: NEAC

17 Carlton Terrace, London, SW1Y 5BD

Tel: 020 7930 6844
Fax: 020 7930 7830
E-mail: press@mallgalleries.com

Website:
http://www.mallgalleries.org.uk

Enquiries:
Enquiries to: Secretary
Other contacts: Marketing and Communications
Officer

Founded:
1885

Organisation type and purpose:
Membership association (membership is by
election or invitation), present number of
members: 84, registered charity (charity number
295780).
To foster and promote the art of draftsmanship and
observation.

Printed publications:
NEAC catalogues available during the annual
exhibition.

Access to staff:
Contact by letter, by telephone, by fax and by e-
mail. Appointment necessary.
Hours: Mon to Fri, 0930 to 1730

Access to building, collection or gallery:
No access other than to staff

Access for disabled people:
Toilet facilities
Special comments: Stair lift

Links with:
Federation of British Artists
17 Carlton House Terrace, London, SW17 5BD;
tel: 020 7930 6844; fax: 020 7839 7830

NEW FOREST PONY BREEDING
AND CATTLE SOCIETY

Acronym or abbreviation: NFPB & CS

The Corner House, Ringwood Road, Brausgoe,
Hampshire, BH23 8AA

Tel: 01425 672775
Fax: 01425 672775
E-mail: info@newforestpony.com

Website:
http://newforestpony.com

Enquiries:
Enquiries to: Curator

Founded:
1938

Organisation type and purpose:
Membership association (membership is by
subscription), present number of members: 1200,
registered charity (charity number 1064746).
Breed society.
Conserve and promote New Forest ponies.

Subject coverage:
New Forest ponies.

**Museum or gallery collection, archive, or library
special collection:**
Stud book back numbers

Printed publications:
A Celebration of New Forest Ponies (available
from office, £14.95 plus £2 p&p)
Leaflet
Newsletter (2 times a year)
Stud Book (annually)

Access to staff:
Contact by letter, by telephone, by fax and by e-
mail. Appointment necessary.
Hours: Telephone: 0830 to 0930 and evenings

Chairman:
New Forest Pony Breeding and Cattle Society
Randalls Farm, Burley Street, Ringwood,
Hampshire; tel: 01425 402459; e-mail:
forestpony@enterprise.net

Daughter New Forest Pony Societies in the:
Netherlands, France, Belgium, Sweden, Finland,
Germany, N America and Australia

Member of:
National Pony Society

NEW IMPERIAL OWNERS'
ASSOCIATION

Acronym or abbreviation: NIOA

Lyndhurst House, Victoria Road, Hayling Island,
Hampshire, PO11 0LU

Tel: 023 9246 9098
Fax: 023 9246 9098
E-mail: info@newimperial.co.uk

Website:
http://www.newimperial.co.uk

Enquiries:
Enquiries to: Honorary Secretary

Founded:
1987

Organisation type and purpose:
International organisation, membership
association (membership is by subscription),
present number of members: 285.
Historic motorcycle club.

Subject coverage:
Information about New Imperial motor cycles
manufactured in Birmingham between 1901 and
1939.

Printed publications:
New Imperial News (quarterly, free, members
only)

Access to staff:
Contact by letter, by telephone, by fax and by e-
mail. Appointment necessary.
Hours: Daily, 0900 to 2200

Links with:
Federation of British Historic Vehicle Clubs
tel: 01865 400845; fax: 01865 400845; e-mail:
secretary@fbhvc.co.uk

NEW INTERNATIONALIST

Acronym or abbreviation: NI

55 Rectory Road, Oxford, OX4 1BW

Tel: 01865 811400
Fax: 01865 793152
E-mail: ni@newint.org

Website:
http://www.newint.org

Enquiries:
Enquiries to: Administrator

Founded:
1972

Organisation type and purpose:
Publishing house.

Subject coverage:
Global political and social stories.

Printed publications:
New Internationalist (magazine, 11 issues a year,
£32.85 a year)

Access to staff:
Contact by letter and by e-mail
Hours: Mon to Fri, 0930 to 1730

NEW PRODUCERS ALLIANCE

Acronym or abbreviation: NPA

9 Bourlet Close, London, W1W 1PB

Tel: 020 7580 2480
Fax: 020 7580 2484
E-mail: queries@npa.org.uk

Website:
http://www.npa.org.uk
Information on the film industry and NPA
activities and special additional online section
restricted to members.

continued overleaf

Enquiries:
Enquiries to: Administrator

Founded:
1993

Organisation type and purpose:
National organisation, membership association (membership is by subscription), present number of members: c. 1000, registered charity (charity number 1059200), training organisation. Training and information for film makers.

Subject coverage:
Film production, development and distribution.

Museum or gallery collection, archive, or library special collection:
Reference books and magazines relating to the film industry

Non-library collection catalogue:
All or part available online

Publications list:
Available online

Access to staff:
Contact by letter, by telephone, by fax, by e-mail and via website. Appointment necessary.
Hours: Mon to Fri, 0900 to 1700

NEW ZEALAND HIGH COMMISSION

New Zealand House, 80 Haymarket, London, SW1Y 4TQ

Tel: 020 7930 8422
Fax: 020 7839 4580
E-mail: aboutnz@newzealandhc.org.uk

Website:
http://www.nzembassy.com/uk
General information for New Zealanders in the United Kingdom and Republic of Ireland.

Organisation type and purpose:
New Zealand Government Representative.

Subject coverage:
Limited general information e.g. not on immigration; research and development in government, industry, universities, institutes and associations.

Access to staff:
Contact by letter, by telephone, by fax, by e-mail and via website
Hours: Mon to Fri, 0900 to 1700

Access to building, collection or gallery:
Prior appointment required

Access for disabled people:
Ramped entry

Parent body:
Ministry of Foreign Affairs and Trade
   Private Bag 18–901, Wellington, New Zealand

NEW ZEALAND IMMIGRATION SERVICE

Mezzanine Floor, New Zealand House, 80 Haymarket, London, SW1Y 4TE

Tel: 0906 9100 100
Fax: 020 7973 0370

Website:
http://www.immigration.govt.nz

Organisation type and purpose:
International organisation.

Subject coverage:
Emigration to New Zealand.

Access to building, collection or gallery:
No prior appointment required
Hours: Mon to Fri, 1000 to 1545

NEWBURY CENTRAL LIBRARY

Newbury Library, The Wharf, Newbury, Berkshire, RG14 5AU

Tel: 01635 519900
Fax: 01635 519906
E-mail: newburylibrary@westberks.gov.uk

Website:
http://www.westberks.gov.uk/libraries

Enquiries:
Enquiries to: Librarian

Organisation type and purpose:
Local government body, public library.

Subject coverage:
General public library material, Newbury and West Berkshire local history.

Library catalogue:
All or part available online

Access to staff:
Contact by letter, by telephone, by fax, by e-mail, in person and via website
Hours: Mon, Tue, Thu, 0900 to 1900; Wed, Fri, 0900 to 1700; Sat, 0930 to 1600

Access for disabled people:
Level entry, access to all public areas, toilet facilities

NEWBURY LIBRARY

The Wharf, Newbury, Berkshire, RG14 5AU

Tel: 01635 519900
Fax: 01635 519906
E-mail: newburylibrary@westberks.gov.uk

Website:
http://www.westberks.gov.uk/libraries

Organisation type and purpose:
Public library.

Subject coverage:
General.

Museum or gallery collection, archive, or library special collection:
West Berkshire Local History Collection

Library catalogue:
All or part available online

Access to staff:
Contact by letter, by telephone, by fax, by e-mail, in person and via website
Hours: Mon, Tue, Thu, 0900 to 1900; Wed, Fri, 0900 to 1700; Sat, 0930 to 1600

Access to building, collection or gallery:
Mon, Tue, Thu, 0900 to 1900; Wed, Fri, 0900 to 1700; Sat, 0930 to 1600

Access for disabled people:
Access to all public areas, toilet facilities

Parent body:
West Berkshire District Council
   Council Offices, Market Street, Newbury, RG14 5LD; tel: 01635 42400; fax: 01635 519392; website: http://www.westberks.gov.uk

NEWCASTLE COLLEGE LIBRARY SERVICES

Rye Hill Campus, Scotswood Road, Newcastle upon Tyne, NE4 7SA

Tel: 0191 200 4020
Fax: 0191 200 4100
E-mail: thelibrary@ncl-coll.ac.uk

Website:
http://ncl-coll.ac.uk
General information relating to Newcastle College.

Enquiries:
Enquiries to: Head of Library Services
Direct tel: 0191 200 4017

Subject coverage:
Engineering, construction, art and design, food industries, computing, business studies, information technology, music, performing arts, humanities, science, hotel and catering management, leisure, childcare, social welfare, training/education, local studies.

Museum or gallery collection, archive, or library special collection:
Local collection

Library catalogue:
All or part available online

Printed publications:
Prospectus

Access to staff:
Contact by letter, by telephone, by fax and by e-mail. Appointment necessary.
Hours: Mon to Fri, 0900 to 1700

NEWCASTLE LIBRARIES AND INFORMATION SERVICE

Acronym or abbreviation: NLIS

City Library, PO Box 88, Newcastle upon Tyne, NE99 1DX

Tel: 0191 277 4100 (from June 2009)
Fax: 0191 277 4137
E-mail: tony.durcan@newcastle.gov.uk

Enquiries:
Enquiries to: Head of Culture, Libraries and Lifelong Learning
Other contacts: City Libraries' Manager

Founded:
1880

Organisation type and purpose:
Local government body, public library.

Subject coverage:
Local studies – city and region; general reference collections; genealogy, local and national; patents; business information; community information.

Museum or gallery collection, archive, or library special collection:
Auty-Hastings Collection of glass plate negatives and prints, 1890–1920 (local scenes)
British Standards – Full Set (CD-ROM)
British, European, American and PCT Patent specifications
C. P. Taylor Collection (playwrights' manuscripts)
Clark Music Library (concert programmes, theatre playbills, c.1880–1920, with indexes in the care of the Local History Librarian)
Gibsone's Conches (over 20,000 watercolour paintings of Conch shells bought for the City in 1889)
Local studies illustrations collection c.70,000 items
Newspapers 1707 to date
Northern Playwrights Collection
Patents collection (UK, Europe, USA, Japan)
Seymour Bell Collection (plans and charts of the sea)
Thomas Bewick Collection (the 18th-century engraver's books and blocks, Pease Bequest)
Thomlinson Collection (16th- to 18th-century books)
Tyneside Unidentified Flying Objects Society Collection

Non-library collection catalogue:
All or part available in-house

Library catalogue:
All or part available online

Printed publications:
A large range of books on local history

Publications list:
Available in print

Access to staff:
Contact by letter, by telephone, by fax, by e-mail, in person and via website
Hours: Mon, Thu, 0900 to 2000; Tue, Wed, Fri, Sat, 0900 to 1700

Access for disabled people:
Ramped entry, toilet facilities
Special comments: Automatic doors at main entrance.

Member organisation of:
local co-operatives

Parent body:
City of Newcastle Upon Tyne, Chief Executive's Office Directorate

NEWCASTLE UNIVERSITY

Robinson Library, Back Jesmond Road West, Newcastle upon Tyne, NE2 4HQ

Tel: 0191 222 7662
Fax: 0191 222 6235
E-mail: lib-readerservices@newcastle.ac.uk

Website:
http://www.ncl.ac.uk/library

Enquiries:
Enquiries to: Librarian
Direct tel: 0191 222 7674
Direct e-mail: t.w.graham@newcastle.ac.uk
Other contacts: Special Collections Librarian (tel. 0191 222 7671)

Founded:
1963

Organisation type and purpose:
University library.

Subject coverage:
Accounting and finance, management, economics, geography, politics, sociology and anthropology, architecture, planning, English (literature and linguistics), fine art, modern languages, music, archaeology, classics, history, religious studies, museum studies, medicine, dentistry, speech, psychology, education, law, agriculture and biological sciences (including marine), chemical engineering, civil engineering, electrical engineering, marine technology, mechanical materials and manufacturing engineering, chemistry, physics, statistics, computing science, geomatics, mathematics (applied, pure and engineering).

Museum or gallery collection, archive, or library special collection:
Collections include:
Barry MacSweeney Papers (poetry)
Catherine Cookson Collection
Chapbooks and Broadsides (many of these chapbooks are available on microfilm)
C. V. Stanford Collection (musical manuscripts)
Gertrude Bell Collection (history and archaeology of the Middle East)
Lady Plowden Papers (education)
Library of Japanese science and technology
Merz Collection (mathematics and philosophy)
Pybus Collection (medical history)
Robert White Collection (English literature, Border history and Antiquities)
Robinson Collection (multilingual rare books covering exploration, literature and music)
Runciman Papers (early 20th-century politics)
Shefton Collection (Greek archaeology)
Sid Chaplin Papers (literature)
Trevelyan Papers (19th- and 20th-century arts, literature and politics)
UK Government publications
Victorian Collection (literature)
Wallis Collection (mathematics)

Non-library collection catalogue:
All or part available online

Access to staff:
Contact by letter, by telephone, by fax, by e-mail and in person. Appointment necessary. Non-members charged.
Hours: Term time: Mon to Thu, 0900 to 2200; Fri, 0900 to 2100; Sat, 0900 to 1630; Sun, 1100 to 1730
Vacations: variable, see website or telephone

Access for disabled people:
Parking provided, level entry, toilet facilities

NEWMAN COLLEGE

Library, Genners Lane, Bartley Green, Birmingham, B32 3NT

Tel: 0121 476 1181
Fax: 0121 476 1196
E-mail: library@newman.ac.uk

Website:
http://www.newman.ac.uk

Enquiries:
Enquiries to: Librarian

Founded:
1968

Organisation type and purpose:
College of higher education.

Subject coverage:
Art in general, English language, English literature, geography, history, Islamics, physical education, sports science, religious education, theology, West Midlands history, education in general.

Museum or gallery collection, archive, or library special collection:
Cardinal John Henry Newman (books)
West Midlands history – books, pamphlets, photographs

Access to staff:
Contact by letter, by telephone, by fax, by e-mail and via website
Hours: Mon, Tue, Thu, 0845 to 2000; Wed, 0945 to 2000; Fri, 0845 to 2000; Sat, 1000 to 1500

Validated by:
Coventry University

NEWPORT AND GWENT CHAMBER OF COMMERCE AND INDUSTRY

Acronym or abbreviation: ngb2b

Unit 30, The Orion Suite, Enterprise Way, Newport, Gwent, NP20 2AQ

Tel: 01633 222664
Fax: 01633 222301
E-mail: info@ngb2b.org.uk

Website:
http://www.ngb2b.co.uk
Activities and services of organisations, benefits to business

Enquiries:
Enquiries to: International Trade Manager
Direct e-mail: jennifer@ngb2b.org.uk

Founded:
1867

Organisation type and purpose:
Membership association (membership is by election or invitation).

Subject coverage:
Material sourcing, financial references, EC legislation, national legislation, export documentation, certificates of origin, VAT legislation, local affairs, available grants via Welsh Office, local developments, infogrants, inforules, training courses.Information and product sourcing, training and seminars, exporting, certificates of origin, networking, commercial services, databases, newsletters, marketing services, credit checks, Chambersign, representation.

Museum or gallery collection, archive, or library special collection:
HMSO Customs and Tariffs
Local business directories
Overseas national directories
Parliamentary and EC year books
Croner's Reference Books (various titles)

Printed publications:
Newsletter (6 times a year, all local businesses and subscribers)
Business in Wales (monthly)
South Wales Business Directory (annually)

Publications list:
Available in print

Access to staff:
Contact by letter, by telephone, by fax, by e-mail, in person and via website
Hours: Mon to Fri, 0900 to 1200, 1300 to 1700

Access to building, collection or gallery:
Prior appointment required

Access for disabled people:
Parking provided, toilet facilities

Affiliated organisations:
Chepstow Chamber of Commerce & Tourism
Gwent Business Women's Network
Monmouth District Chamber of Commerce
Newport Business Club
Newport Chamber of Trade
Royal Forest of Dean Business and Professional Club

NEWPORT CITY COUNCIL

Civic Centre, Newport, Gwent, NP20 4UR

Tel: 01633 656656
Fax: 01633 232537

Website:
http://www.newport.gov.uk

Enquiries:
Enquiries to: Managing Director

Founded:
1996

Organisation type and purpose:
Local government body.

Subject coverage:
Newport.

Trade and statistical information:
Newport inward investment.

Printed publications:
Community Plan (annual, free)
Economic Development Annual Report (free)

Access to staff:
Contact by letter, by telephone and by fax. Appointment necessary.
Hours: Mon to Fri, 0830 to 1630

NEWPORT COMMUNITY LEARNING AND LIBRARIES

Central Library, John Frost Square, Newport, Gwent, NP20 1PA

Tel: 01633 656656
Fax: 01633 414705
E-mail: central.library@newport.gov.uk

Website:
http://www.newport.gov.uk/libraries

Enquiries:
Enquiries to: Librarian

Organisation type and purpose:
Public library.

Subject coverage:
Local history; local Chartism, general reference, family history.

Museum or gallery collection, archive, or library special collection:
Arthur Machen Collection (local author)
Haines Collection (local history)
Phillips Collection (mainly private press books and the arts)
Mrs Delany's Letters (local history)

Non-library collection catalogue:
All or part available online and in-house

Library catalogue:
All or part available online

Access to staff:
Contact by letter, by telephone, by fax, by e-mail and in person

continued overleaf

Hours: Mon to Thu, 0900 to 1800; Fri, 0900 to 1800; Sat, 0900 to 1700

Access for disabled people:
Level entry, toilet facilities
Special comments: Wheelchair available, hearing loops

Parent body:
Continuing Learning and Leisure
  Newport County City Council

NEWQUEST (HERALD & TIMES) LTD

Formal name: Scottish Media Group Newspapers

200 Renfield Street, Glasgow, G2 3QB

Tel: 0141 302 7000
Fax: 0141 302 7383
E-mail: ian.watson@glasgow.newsquest.co.uk

Enquiries:
Enquiries to: Information Officer
Direct e-mail: newslib@glasgow.newsquest.co.uk

Founded:
1783

Organisation type and purpose:
Service industry, publishing house.
Newspaper publisher.

Subject coverage:
Current affairs, sport, arts.

Museum or gallery collection, archive, or library special collection:
Extensive Photo Collection (c. 5 million)

Printed publications:
The (Glasgow) Herald
Sunday Standard (ceased 1983)
Sunday Herald
Evening Times

Microform publications:
All titles available on Microfilm

Electronic and video publications:
Herald and Sunday Herald (CD-ROM)

Publications list:
Available online

Access to staff:
Contact by letter, by fax and by e-mail.
Appointment necessary. All charged.
Hours: Mon to Fri, 0900 to 1700

Access to building, collection or gallery:
Prior appointment required

Access for disabled people:
Parking provided, level entry, toilet facilities

NEWS INTERNATIONAL NEWSPAPERS LIMITED

Information Services, 1 Viginia Street, London, E98 1ES

Tel: 020 7782 6000
E-mail: info@newsint.co.uk

Website:
http://www.newsinternational.co.uk/

Enquiries:
Enquiries to: Information Services Manager
Direct tel: 020 7782 6398
Direct fax: 020 7782 3650

Organisation type and purpose:
Newspaper publishing.

Access to staff:
Contact by letter. Appointment necessary. Non-members charged.
Hours: Mon to Fri, 0900 to 1700

Access to building, collection or gallery:
Prior appointment required

Access for disabled people:
Ramped entry, toilet facilities

Subsidiary of:
News Corporation
  website: www.newscorp.com

NEWSPAPER PUBLISHERS ASSOCIATION LIMITED

Acronym or abbreviation: NPA

8th Floor, St Andrew's House, 18–20 St Andrew Street, London, EC4A 3AY

Tel: 020 7636 7014
Fax: 020 7631 5119
E-mail: lynne_anderson@newspapersoc.org.uk

Enquiries:
Direct tel: 020 7931 3806
Direct e-mail: Guy.Black@telegraph.co.uk

Founded:
1906

Organisation type and purpose:
Trade association.
National newspapers.

Subject coverage:
Distribution, advertising, marketing, newsprint.

Access to staff:
Appointment necessary.
Hours: Mon to Fri, 0900 to 1700

NEWSPAPER SOCIETY, THE

Acronym or abbreviation: NS

Bloomsbury House, 74–77 Great Russell Street, London, WC1B 3DA

Tel: 020 7636 7014
Fax: 020 7631 5119
E-mail: ns@newspapersoc.org.uk

Website:
http://www.newspapersoc.org.uk/new-reports/publications/a-zpublications.html
Publications
http://www.newspapersoc.org.uk.
Facts and figures about the regional press, case studies/research, circulation/readership figures, links/planning aids.

Enquiries:
Enquiries to: Communications Executive
Direct fax: 020 7580 7167
Direct e-mail: lisa_mccarthy@newspapersoc.org.uk

Founded:
1836

Organisation type and purpose:
Trade association (membership is by subscription, qualification), present number of members: 327.
Represents the regional and local press in the UK.

Subject coverage:
All information relating to Britain's regional press: including training, technical, industrial relations, legal and government matters, advertising sales and distribution, free newspapers, research, editorial readership, newspapers in education, press regulation and promotion.

Electronic and video publications:
A wide variety of publications available online, including:
Ad Control News
Barcoding and the Regional Press 2000 (pdf)
Consumers Choice IV Pocket Book 2000
Focus on ... regional newspapers and retailing terms 2000 (pdf)
Headlines
Intelligence News
NS News
Parliamentary & European Brief
Production Journal
Regional Press Fact Book – Sep 2001 (pdf)
Renaissance of Regional Nations 2000
Reporting Restrictions in the Crown Court (2000)
Reporting Restrictions in the Magistrates Court 2001
UK Automotive Industry 1999

UK Property Market

Publications list:
Available online

Access to staff:
Contact by letter, by fax and by e-mail
Hours: Mon to Fri, 0900 to 1700

Member of:
European Newspaper Publishers' Association
International Federation of Newspaper Publishers
Newspaper Conference

NEWSROOM, GUARDIAN AND OBSERVER ARCHIVE AND VISITOR CENTRE

60 Farringdon Road, London, EC1R 3GA

Tel: 020 7886 9898
Fax: 020 7490 8359
E-mail: newsroom@guardian.co.uk

Website:
http://www.guardian.co.uk/newsroom

Enquiries:
Enquiries to: Centre Administrator

Organisation type and purpose:
To preserve and promote the histories and values of the Guardian, The Observer and Guardian Unlimited through archive, education and exhibitions.

Subject coverage:
Newspapers

Museum or gallery collection, archive, or library special collection:
Individual collections (correspondence, diaries, notebooks, original sketches and photographs):
Jane Bown (Observer photographer)
WP Crozier (editor of the Guardian 1932–44)
Richard Fry (financial editor of the Guardian 1939–65)
Jean Stead (home news editor 1969–78 and reporter)
Donald Trelford (editor of the Observer 1975–93)
Corporate records:
The Guardian Archive (1968 to present)
The Observer Archive (1917 to present)
Newspaper holdings:
Guardian Weekly (1920–1949, 1972-current)
Guardian Commercial (1920–1939)
Observer magazine (1964–1994)
Bound volumes of the original newspapers are held but for preservation reasons surrogates are used where available.

Electronic and video publications:
Order electronic and video publications from:
Guardian (14 July 1984 to present)
Observer (3 January 1993 to present)

Access to staff:
Contact by letter, by telephone, by fax, by e-mail, in person and via website
Hours: Mon to Fri, 1000 to 1700

NEXUS INSTITUTE

119 University Street, Belfast, BT7 1HP

Tel: 028 9032 6803
Fax: 028 9032 5623
E-mail: info@nexusinstitute.org

Website:
http://www.nexusinstitute.org
Information on organisation, training, jobs, services.

Enquiries:
Enquiries to: Manager

Founded:
1984

Organisation type and purpose:
Voluntary organisation, registered charity (charity number XN 46002), training organisation.
Counselling.

For adult survivors of sexual abuse.

Subject coverage:
Field of sexual abuse, counselling of sexual abuse survivors, counsellor training.

Printed publications:
Annual Report (available free with postage paid)
Book of Survivor Poems (£2)

Access to staff:
Contact by letter, by telephone and by e-mail. Appointment necessary. All charged.
Hours: Mon to Thu, 0900 to 1700; Fri, 0900 to 1600
Special comments: Evening appointments available by arrangement.

Other branches:
Nexus Institute
    38 Clarendon Street, Londonderry, BT48 7ET
Nexus Institute
    6 Portmore Street, Portadown, BT62 3NG
Nexus Institute
    104 Irvinestown Road, Enniskillen, BT74 6DN

NFU SCOTLAND

Acronym or abbreviation: NFUS

Rural Centre, West Mains, Ingliston, Newbridge, Midlothian, EH28 8LT

Tel: 0131 472 4000
Fax: 0131 472 4010
E-mail: webmaster@nfus.org.uk

Website:
http://www.nfus.org.uk

Enquiries:
Enquiries to: Chief Executive

Founded:
1913

Organisation type and purpose:
Professional body (membership is by subscription), voluntary organisation.
Represents the political interests of the Scottish agricultural, horticultural and crofting industries and acts as a professional association for Scottish farmers, growers and crofters.

Subject coverage:
Cereals, fish farming, horticulture, legal, labour and technology matters, livestock, milk, potatoes, poultry, publicity, animal health and welfare, crofting, pigs, environment, landlord/tenant, parliamentary.

Printed publications:
The Scottish Farming Leader (house magazine,
    circulation 12,000, 12 times a year)
Variety of other booklets (irregular)

Access to staff:
Contact by letter and by fax
Hours: Mon to Fri, 0900 to 1700

NGS PICTURE LIBRARY

Formal name: National Galleries of Scotland Picture Library

National Galleries of Scotland, Dean Gallery, 73 Belford Road, Edinburgh, EH4 3DS

Tel: 0131 624 6258; 0131 624 6260
Fax: 0131 623 7135
E-mail: picture.library@nationalgalleries.org

Website:
http://www.nationalgalleries.org

Organisation type and purpose:
National organisation, art gallery, public library.

Subject coverage:
Brings together the works in all the collections of the National Galleries of Scotland including photographs and slides. Material depicting the work of artists from the Renaissance to the present day, including the major painters, and a wide variety of subjects, media and styles.

Non-library collection catalogue:
All or part available in-house and in print

Publications list:
Available online and in print

Access to staff:
Contact by letter, by telephone, by fax, by e-mail and via website. Appointment necessary.
Hours: Mon to Fri, 0900 to 1700

Access to building, collection or gallery:
No prior appointment required
Hours: Daily, 1000 to 1700; Thu to 1900
Special comments: Closed 25, 26 December; open 1 January, 1200 to 1700

Access for disabled people:
Access to all public areas, toilet facilities

Parent body:
National Galleries of Scotland
    Belford Road, Edinbrugh, EH4 3DR; tel: 0131 624 6200; fax: 0131 623 7126; e-mail: enquiries@ nationalgalleries.org

NGS: GARDENS OPEN FOR CHARITY

Formal name: National Gardens Scheme
Acronym or abbreviation: NGS

Hatchlands Park, East Clandon, Guildford, Surrey, GU4 7RT

Tel: 01483 211535
Fax: 01483 211537
E-mail: ngs@ngs.org.uk

Website:
http://www.ngs.org.uk
Ordering publications.

Enquiries:
Enquiries to: Marketing Communications Manager
Direct tel: 01483 213900
Direct e-mail: cmorley@ngs.org.uk

Founded:
1927

Organisation type and purpose:
Voluntary organisation, registered charity (charity number 1112664).

Subject coverage:
Approximately 3,500 mainly privately owned gardens in Engaland and Wales are opened to the public on behalf of the NGS each year, in order to raise money for good causes.

Printed publications:
The Yellow Book 2007 (£8.99 inc. p&p)
Order printed publications from: Website

Publications list:
Available online

Access to staff:
Contact by letter, by telephone, by fax, by e-mail and via website
Hours: Mon to Fri, 0900 to 1700

Fund-raising body for:
additional charities nominated by Owners
County Nursing Associations
Crossroads
Gardeners Royal Benevolent Society
Help the Hospices
Macmillan Cancer Support
Marie Curie Cancer Care
National Trust Careership Scheme
Queens Nursing Institute
Royal Gardeners' Orphan Fund

NHBC

Formal name: National House Building Council
Acronym or abbreviation: NHBC

Buildmark House, Chiltern Avenue, Amersham, Buckinghamshire, HP6 5AP

Tel: 0870 2414302
Fax: 01494 735201
E-mail: mediaenquiries@nhbc.co.uk

Website:
http://www.nhbc.co.uk

Register of builders, building new homes, building your own home, consultancy services, press, site map, factsheets, statistics.

Enquiries:
Enquiries to: Head of Corporate Communications
Direct tel: 01494 735262
Other contacts: Media Manager for company information.

Founded:
1936

Organisation type and purpose:
National organisation, professional body, present number of members: 17,000 registered builders. Independent standard-setting body for the UK house-building industry.
A non-profit distributing company limited by guarantee, aim to improve standards of new homes in the UK, benchmark best practice and work with builders to raise standards and protect homeowners.

Subject coverage:
NHBC sets standards for the building of new homes in the UK. It raises standards by providing new home warranty and insurance services for home buyers, setting construction standards for new homes and inspecting at key stages, registering builders and being a service provider of Health and Safety, training and engineering services.

Trade and statistical information:
New house-building statistics eg UK new home
    starts and completions, UK average daily sales,
    new home prices.

Printed publications:
Publications available free and also for purchase
NHBC Rules
Guide to your New Home
Solo for Self Build Guide

Publications list:
Available in print

Access to staff:
Contact by letter, by telephone and by e-mail. Appointment necessary.
Hours: Mon to Fri, 0900 to 1730

Access to building, collection or gallery:
Prior appointment required
Hours: Mon to Fri, 0900 to 1730

Access for disabled people:
Parking provided, level entry

Other offices based in:
Belfast, Edinburgh, Droitwich, London, Milton Keynes and York
    Addresses available on website pages

NHS EDUCATION FOR SCOTLAND

22 Queen Street, Edinburgh, EH2 1JX

Tel: 0131 226 7371
Fax: 0131 225 9970
E-mail: enquiries@nes.scot.nhs.uk

Website:
http://www.nes.scot.nhs.uk

Enquiries:
Direct tel: 0131 220 8603
Other contacts: Corporate Services Manager

Founded:
2002

Organisation type and purpose:
National government body, statutory body, training organisation.
Oversight of postgraduate education of doctors, dentists, clinical psychologists, midwives, nurses, and allied health professions.

Subject coverage:
Postgraduate medical and dental education in Scotland.

continued overleaf

Access to staff:
Contact by letter, by telephone and by e-mail
Hours: Mon to Fri, 0900 to 1730

Access for disabled people:
Level entry, toilet facilities

Accountable to the:
Scottish Executive

NHS ESTATES, INFORMATION CENTRE

Department of Health, 1 Trevelyan Square, Boar Lane, Leeds, West Yorkshire, LS1 6AE

Tel: 0113 254 7070
Fax: 0113 254 7167
E-mail: nhs.estates@doh.gov.uk

Website:
http://www.nhsestates.gov.uk/
publications_guidance/index.asp

Enquiries:
Enquiries to: Information Officer

Organisation type and purpose:
National government body.
To enable optimum use of the estates for better healthcare.

Subject coverage:
Health estate management, Health buildings and facilities design, Health technical advice on building components, access to Department of Health Library database, fire and safety design – Health buildings, estate policy advice Health estate.

Museum or gallery collection, archive, or library special collection:
Archival Health buildings directorate publications
Collection of audiovisual material – slides, photographs of hospital building projects (various stages)
Very old departmental circulars and letters

Non-library collection catalogue:
All or part available in-house

Library catalogue:
All or part available in-house

Printed publications:
Various HMSO and NHS Estates publications include:
Design and Briefing: General, Health Building Notes (HBN)
Operational: Firecode, Health Guidance Notes (HGN), Health Technical Memoranda (HTM), Model Engineering Specifications (MES)
Strategic: Commissioning, Concode, Energy, Water & Waste, Environment, Estatecode, Estate Strategy, Facilities Management, Miscellaneous
NHS Estates Policy and Initiatives & General Quarterly Briefing
Order printed publications from: HMSO, PO Box 276 London, SW8 5DT, tel: 0870 600 5522, fax: 0870 600 5533

Electronic and video publications:
Building Better Healthcare 2 (CD-ROM)

Publications list:
Available online and in print

Access to staff:
Contact by telephone, by e-mail and via website. Appointment necessary.
Hours: Mon to Thu, 0830 to 1730; Fri, 0830 to 1700

Access for disabled people:
Ramped entry, access to all public areas, toilet facilities
Special comments: Parking provided upon request.

Parent body:
Department of Health

NIAB

Formal name: National Institute of Agricultural Botany

Acronym or abbreviation: NIAB

Huntingdon Road, Cambridge, CB3 0LE

Tel: 01223 342200
Fax: 01223 277602
E-mail: info@niab.com

Website:
http://www.niab.com
Guide to NIAB services.

Founded:
1919

Organisation type and purpose:
Membership association (membership is by subscription), present number of members: 2500, registered charity, research organisation.

Subject coverage:
Variety testing of most agricultural and horticultural crops (except fruit), choice of variety, seed certification, seed testing procedures, botanical description of varieties, plant pathology, plant science research.

Museum or gallery collection, archive, or library special collection:
Seed catalogues (1900-)

Printed publications:
The following publications available for purchase
Biennial Report
Seed identification
Pocket Guides to Crop Varieties
Plant Genetic Resources (journal, 3 times a year)

Publications list:
Available online and in print

Access to staff:
Contact by letter, by telephone, by e-mail, in person and via website. Appointment necessary. Access for members only. Non-members charged.
Hours: Mon to Thu, 0900 to 1700; Fri, 0900 to 1645
Special comments: Association members only.

Access to building, collection or gallery:
No prior appointment required

Access for disabled people:
Ramped entry, toilet facilities

Includes the:
Official Seed Testing Station for England and Wales
at the same address

NICKEL INSTITUTE

Acronym or abbreviation: NI

The Holloway, Alvechurch, Birmingham, B48 7QB

Tel: 01527 584777
Fax: 01527 585562
E-mail: birmingham@nickelinstitute.org

Website:
http://www.nickelinstitute.org
All publications available.

Enquiries:
Enquiries to: European Director
Other contacts: Technical Director

Founded:
1957

Organisation type and purpose:
International organisation, present number of members: 15 industrial members, consultancy. Market development organisation, offering expert advice in the form of published information and discussion with consultants.
To support, sustain and defend worldwide use of nickel and its alloys.

Subject coverage:
Oil and gas industry, marine offshore industry, electroplating and electroforming, welding, casting and foundry, chemical, environmental, all as applied to nickel and its alloys (especially stainless steel).

Museum or gallery collection, archive, or library special collection:
Computer databases
Technical publications on nickel and its alloys
Videos

Non-library collection catalogue:
All or part available online

Library catalogue:
All or part available online

Printed publications:
Nickel (3 times a year)
Technical information and advice to anyone concerned with nickel and its alloys – designers, specifiers, engineers, architects, manufacturers etc (almost 1000 publications in catalogue, all free)

Electronic and video publications:
Fresh Approaches to Mold Steel Selection (video)
Stainless Steel: The Effective Solution (video)

Publications list:
Available online and in print

Access to staff:
Contact by letter, by telephone, by fax, by e-mail and in person. Appointment necessary.
Hours: Mon to Fri, 0900 to 1700
Special comments: By prior appointment

Access for disabled people:
Special comments: By prior appointment

Has:
offices in 8 countries

Head office:
NI
55 University Avenue, Suite 1801, Toronto, Ontario, M5T 2H7, canada; tel: +1 416 591 7999; fax: +1 416 591 7987; e-mail: ni_toronto@ nickelinstitute.org; website: www.nickelinstitute .org

NIELSEN BOOK

3rd Floor, Midas House, 62 Goldsworth Road, Woking, Surrey, GU21 6LQ

Tel: 01483 712200
Fax: 01483 712201
E-mail: libraries.book@nielsen.com

Website:
http://www.nielsenbook.co.uk
A company profile, plus details of BookData's full range of library services.

Enquiries:
Enquiries to: Head of Data Sales – Libraries
Direct tel: 07764 357391
Direct e-mail: paul.dibble@nielsen.com
Other contacts: Library Executive

Founded:
2002

Formerly called:
Book Data, Whitaker Information Services, First Edition (year of change 2002)

Organisation type and purpose:
Data partner for the book industry, playing a pivotal role within the industry and offering a comprehensive source of bibliographic data and associated services in the United Kingdom. Working with publishers large and small, data is collected from 60,000 publishers in over 70 countries. Over 7.5m. titles are held and millions of changes are made annually to ensure that the most timely, accurate and comprehensive data is available.

Subject coverage:
Bibliographic data, acquisitions, search and discovery, cataloguing, ordering and promotion.

Printed publications:
Directory of UK and Irish Book Publishers (in association with the Booksellers' Association)

Electronic and video publications:
A range of services for libraries and library
 suppliers world-wide:
BookData Online
BookData MARC and Multimedia (data feed of
 MARC records)
BookScan for Libraries
Range of Disc services
BookNet EDI
Catalogue Enrichment

Publications list:
Available online

Access to staff:
Contact by letter, by telephone, by fax, by e-mail,
in person and via website. Appointment necessary.
Access for members only.
Hours: Mon to Fri, 0900 to 1700

Access to building, collection or gallery:
Prior appointment required

Access for disabled people:
Parking provided, disabled lift, toilet facilities

NIGERIAN HIGH COMMISSION

Nigeria House, 9 Northumberland Avenue,
London, WC2N 5BX

Tel: 020 7839 1244
Fax: 020 7839 8746

Website:
http://www.nigeriahighcommissionuk.com

Enquiries:
Enquiries to: Librarian
Direct tel: ext 279 or 303
Other contacts: Head of Chancery for official
government statements.

Founded:
1960

Organisation type and purpose:
National government body.

Subject coverage:
Federal government of Nigeria matters e.g. history,
economics, laws etc.
Tourist information.

Library catalogue:
All or part available in-house

Printed publications:
The Nigerian (newsletter, published in-house)

Access to staff:
Contact by letter, by telephone and by fax.
Appointment necessary.
Hours: Library: Mon to Fri, 1000 to 1700
Offices: Mon to Fri, 0900 to 1700

Access to building, collection or gallery:
Prior appointment required

Consular Section:
Nigerian High Commission
 56–57 Fleet Street, London, EC4; tel: 020 7353
 3776

NIPPA – THE EARLY YEARS ASSOCIATION

Acronym or abbreviation: NIPPA

6c Wildflower Way, Belfast, BT12 6TA

Tel: 028 9066 2825
Fax: 028 9038 1270
E-mail: mail@nippa.org

Website:
http://www.nippa.org

Enquiries:
Enquiries to: Information Officer

Founded:
1965

Organisation type and purpose:
Membership association (membership is by
subscription), present number of members: c. 900,
voluntary organisation, registered charity, suitable
for ages: up to 12, training organisation.

Subject coverage:
Information about early childhood, care and
education.

Library catalogue:
All or part available online

Printed publications:
Publications for purchase, direct

Publications list:
Available online and in print

Access to staff:
Contact by telephone, by e-mail, in person and via
website
Hours: Mon to Fri, 0900 to 1700

Access for disabled people:
Parking provided, level entry, access to all public
areas, toilet facilities

NISSAN INSTITUTE OF JAPANESE STUDIES

University of Oxford, 27 Winchester Road, Oxford,
OX2 6NA

Tel: 01865 274570
Fax: 01865 274574
E-mail: secretary@nissan.ox.ac.uk

Website:
http://www.nissan.ox.ac.uk
Basic information about the Nissan Institute.

Enquiries:
Enquiries to: Secretary

Founded:
1981

Organisation type and purpose:
University institute.
To promote the study of modern and
contemporary Japan within the University of
Oxford.

Subject coverage:
The modern history, politics, economy,
international relations, society and education
systems of Japan.

**Museum or gallery collection, archive, or library
special collection:**
See Bodleian Japanese Library (separate institution
 from the Nissan Institute)

Printed publications:
Nissan Institute Occasional Papers (35 papers
 published, 1986–2004; enquiries to the Secretary,
 Nissan Institute)
Nissan Institute/Routledge Japanese Studies Series.
 (66 titles published 1986–2006; available through
 bookshops)

Access to staff:
Contact by letter, by fax, by e-mail and via
website
Hours: Mon to Fri, 0900 to 1230 and 1400 to 1645
Special comments: Primarily university access.

Access for disabled people:
Ramped entry
Special comments: Lift

Parent body:
University of Oxford

NMPH

Formal name: National Missing Persons Helpline
Acronym or abbreviation: NMPH

PO Box 28908, London, SW14 7ZU

Tel: 020 8392 4590
Fax: 020 8878 7752
E-mail: admin@missingpersons.org

Website:
http://www.missingpersons.org
Newsletter, leaflets, posters, etc.

Enquiries:
Enquiries to: Information Officer
Other contacts: Co-founders for senior management

Founded:
1992

Organisation type and purpose:
National organisation, registered charity (charity
number 1020419).
A national and confidential Freephone helpline 24
hours a day, 7 days a week.
The charity is dedicated to helping missing
persons, their families and those who care for
them.

Subject coverage:
Missing persons.

Trade and statistical information:
Data on vulnerable and non-vulnerable missing
 people.
Computer software for 'ageing' photographs of
 people missing many years.

Printed publications:
Newsletter (quarterly)
General information leaflets

Access to staff:
Contact by letter, by telephone, by e-mail and via
website
Hours: 24-hour service

Other address:
Message Home
 at the same address; tel: 020 8392 4550; fax: 020
 8878 7752

NO PANIC

Formal name: National Organisation for Phobias,
Anxiety Neurosis Information and Care

93 Brands Farm Way, Randlay, Telford, Shropshire,
TF3 2JQ

Tel: 01952 590005
Fax: 01952 270962
E-mail: ceo@nopanic.org.uk

Website:
http://www.nopanic.org.uk

Enquiries:
Enquiries to: Chief Executive

Founded:
1991

Organisation type and purpose:
International organisation, membership
association (membership is by subscription),
present number of members: 2,500, voluntary
organisation, registered charity (charity number
1018184).
The relief and rehabilitation of people suffering
from anxiety disorders.

Subject coverage:
Sufferers and carers of anxiety disorders caused by
panic attacks, phobias, obsessive/compulsive
disorders and tranquilliser withdrawal.

Library catalogue:
All or part available online and in print

Printed publications:
Leaflets on a variety of anxieties and phobias,
 including general anxiety disorder, panic,
 darkness, dogs, cats, crane flies, bees, birds,
 spiders, driving, weather and injections
Newsletter (6 a year, members only)
Any Question – The most asked questions about
 phobias (K. Sell, £4.90)
Counselling – How to help others (K. Sell, £3.50)
Helpful Hints for Phobics (G. Marsden, £2)
Me and My Phobia – How sufferers tackled their
 phobias (K. Sell, £6.60)
No Panic – A practical guide to managing panic
 and phobia (K. Gournay, £9.50)

continued overleaf

O.C.D. Carers' Questions Answered – All you
want to know about O.C.D. (K. Sell, £2.30)
Stress Management – A guide to coping with stress
(K. Gournay, £6.95)
To Thine Own Self Be True (S. Holmes, £6.95)

Electronic and video publications:
Agoraphobia and Panic (video)
Muscle Relaxation (cassette)
New Horizons, Agoraphobia Recovery (cassette)
New Horizons, Carers Support (cassette)
New Horizons, Obsessive/Compulsive Disorder
(cassette)
New Horizons, Panic Attacks/Anxiety (cassette)
Obsessive/Compulsive Disorder (video)
Social Phobia (video)
Vomit (video)
Weather Sound Effects (cassette)

Publications list:
Available online and in print

Access to staff:
Contact by letter, by telephone and by fax.
Appointment necessary.
Hours: Mon to Fri, 0900 to 1700

NOISE ABATEMENT SOCIETY

Acronym or abbreviation: NAS

44 Grand Parade, Brighton, East Sussex, BN2 9QA

Tel: 01273 682223
Fax: 01273 682223
E-mail: nas@noiseabatementsociety.fsnet.co.uk

Website:
http://www.noiseabatementsociety.com

Enquiries:
Enquiries to: Director

Founded:
1959

Organisation type and purpose:
National organisation, membership association
(membership is by subscription), voluntary
organisation, registered charity (charity number
272040), research organisation.
To reduce noise from all sources.

Subject coverage:
Noise abatement in all fields.

Printed publications:
Newsletter

Access to staff:
Contact by letter, by telephone, by fax, by e-mail,
in person and via website. Appointment necessary.
Access for members only.
Hours: Mon to Fri, 0900 to 1600

Access to building, collection or gallery:
No access other than to staff

Affiliated to:
International Association Against Noise

NORCAP

Formal name: National Organisation for
Counselling Adoptees and Parents
Acronym or abbreviation: NORCAP

112 Church Road, Wheatley, Oxfordshire, OX33
1LU

Tel: 01865 875000
Fax: 01865 875686
E-mail: enquiries@norcap.org

Enquiries:
Enquiries to: Administrator

Founded:
1982

Organisation type and purpose:
Membership association (membership is by
subscription), present number of members: 6000,
voluntary organisation, registered charity (charity
number 1063428).

Subject coverage:
Advice on searching for those within the adoption
triangle. Contact the Registrar. Research service
and intermediary service.

**Museum or gallery collection, archive, or library
special collection:**
Avaiable to members of NORCAP only, microfiche
of births, marriages and deaths for England and
Wales 1904–1999

Printed publications:
Searching Guide available for purchase

Access to staff:
Contact by letter, by telephone, by fax, by e-mail
and via website. Appointment necessary.
Hours: Mon to Fri, 1000 to 1300 and 1330 to 1500

Access to building, collection or gallery:
Prior appointment required

Access for disabled people:
Level entry, access to all public areas

NORDOFF-ROBBINS MUSIC
THERAPY CENTRE

2 Lissenden Gardens, London, NW5 1PQ

Tel: 020 7267 4496
Fax: 020 7267 4369
E-mail: admin@nordoff-robbins.org.uk

Website:
http://www.nordoff-robbins.org.uk
Description of music therapy, information re clinic
referrals, training requirements and course content,
information about conferences and open days.

Enquiries:
Enquiries to: Administrator

Organisation type and purpose:
Professional body, registered charity, training
organisation.
Music therapy clinic, music therapy training
degree course, research department.

Subject coverage:
Music therapy and related fields.

**Museum or gallery collection, archive, or library
special collection:**
Library of books and some tapes

Library catalogue:
All or part available in-house

Printed publications:
Brochure, Newsletter

Access to staff:
Appointment necessary.
Hours: Mon to Fri, 0900 to 1700

Access to building, collection or gallery:
Prior appointment required
Hours: Mon to Fri, 0900 to 1630; Sat, 0900 to 1500
Special comments: Telephone before coming. Library
for reference only.

Access for disabled people:
Ramped entry, toilet facilities

NORFOLK & NORWICH
MILLENNIUM LIBRARY

The Forum, Millennium Plain, Norwich, Norfolk,
NR2 1AW

Tel: 01603 774774
Fax: 01603 774705
E-mail: millennium.lib@norfolk.gov.uk

Website:
http://www.library.norfolk.gov.uk
Summary of services provided by the Norfolk
Library and Information Service, with links to
pages giving more information on some of them.
http://icon.norfolk.gov.uk
Database of local organisations (Icon).

Enquiries:
Enquiries to: Area Librarian

Organisation type and purpose:
Local government body, public library.

Subject coverage:
History of Norfolk and Norwich; history of 2nd
Air Division, 8th US Army Air Force, 1942–1945;
USA travel and culture; general subjects.

**Museum or gallery collection, archive, or library
special collection:**
American Memorial Library (US life and history)
Bosworth Harcourt and Buck bequests (theatrical,
literary and historical)
Colman and Rye Collections of Local History
(seriously affected by the fire of 1994)
Norwich City Library, 1608 (incunabula, theology
and general literature)
Photographic collections by G C Davies, T D
Eaton, P H Emerson, Payne Jennings
Publications of the Public Record Office, Historical
Manuscripts Commission
Family history resources on microfilm and
microfiche include Indexes to Births Marriages
and Deaths (national), Probate Indexes (national)
and Census returns and name indexes (local)
British Standards online
Market research, business information,
newspapers etc online
Database of local organisations (Icon) available in
library and via the internet

Non-library collection catalogue:
All or part available online

Library catalogue:
All or part available online

Access to staff:
Contact by letter, by telephone, by fax, by e-mail
and in person
Hours: Mon to Fri, 0900 to 1700

Access for disabled people:
Parking provided, ramped entry, access to all
public areas, toilet facilities

Member of:
Anglian Libraries Information Exchange Scheme
(ANGLES)

Parent body:
Norfolk Library and Information Service
tel: 01603 222048; fax: 01603 222422

NORFOLK & NORWICH NOVI
SAD ASSOCIATION, THE

Acronym or abbreviation: NNNSA

Glebelands, Star Lane, Rockland St Mary,
Norwich, Norfolk, NR14 7BX

Tel: 01508 480262
Fax: 01508 480262
E-mail: peter@beckleyp.freeserve.co.uk

Enquiries:
Enquiries to: Honorary Secretary

Founded:
1985

Organisation type and purpose:
National organisation, membership association
(membership is by subscription).

Subject coverage:
Promoting informal links between people and
organisations in the City of Norwich and the
County of Norfolk, and those in the municipality
of Novi Sad, Serbia; supports the official twinning
between the City of Norwich and the City of Novi
Sad.

**Museum or gallery collection, archive, or library
special collection:**
Archive material relating to the twinning links
between the cities of Norwich and Novi Sad

Printed publications:
Newsletter (3 or 4 times a year)

Access to staff:
Contact by letter, by telephone, by fax and by e-
mail
Hours: Mon to Fri, 0900 to 1700

Links with:
City Council Novi Sad
Norfolk County Council
Norwich City Council

NORFOLK AND NORWICH ARCHAEOLOGICAL SOCIETY

Acronym or abbreviation: NNAS

64 The Close, Norwich, NR1 4DH

Tel: 01603 891437

Website:
http://www.nnas.info

Enquiries:
Enquiries to: Librarian

Founded:
1846

Organisation type and purpose:
Learned society (membership is by subscription), present number of members: 400, registered charity (charity number 311116).

Subject coverage:
Archaeology, history, architecture and antiquities of the county of Norfolk.

Museum or gallery collection, archive, or library special collection:
On loan to Norfolk Record Office, County Hall, Norwich:
King Collection of drawings and watercolours of East Anglian specimens of stained and painted glass
Transcripts of Norfolk Parish Registers

Library catalogue:
All or part available in-house

Printed publications:
Newsletter (2 times a year)
Norfolk Archaeology (annually)

Access to staff:
Contact by letter and by telephone. Appointment necessary. Access for members only.
Hours: Mon to Fri, 0900 to 1700

Access to building, collection or gallery:
By appointment

NORFOLK ASSOCIATION OF VILLAGE HALLS

Acronym or abbreviation: NAVH

20 Market Place, Hingham, Norwich, Norfolk, NR9 4AF

Tel: 01953 851408
Fax: 01953 850695
E-mail: nrcc@norfolkrcc.org.uk

Enquiries:
Enquiries to: Secretary

Founded:
1984

Organisation type and purpose:
Membership association (membership is by subscription), present number of members: 310, voluntary organisation, registered charity (charity number 1053152).

Subject coverage:
Management of village halls and community centres, training for committee members, sources of funds and charity law.

Access to staff:
Contact by letter, by telephone, by fax and by e-mail. Appointment necessary. Access for members only.
Hours: Mon to Fri, 0900 to 1700

Access to building, collection or gallery:
Prior appointment required

NORFOLK CHURCH TRUST LIMITED

Acronym or abbreviation: NCT

9 The Old Church, St Matthews Road, Norwich, Norfolk, NR1 1SP

Tel: 01603 767576
Fax: 01986 798776

Website:
http://www.norfolk-churches.co.uk
General information about the Trust.

Enquiries:
Enquiries to: Chief Executive

Founded:
1976

Organisation type and purpose:
Membership association (membership is by subscription, election or invitation), present number of members: 1200, voluntary organisation, registered charity (charity number 271176), consultancy.
To ensure Christian Churches remain open as places of worship in Norfolk and the Diocese of Norwich

Subject coverage:
General state of repair, restoration and maintenance of the churches in Norfolk.

Printed publications:
Treasure for the Future: A Celebration of the Norfolk Churches Trust 1976–2001 (ed Roberts C)
Sculptured Monuments in Norfolk Churches (Spencer N)
The Brasses of Norfolk Churches (Greenwood R and Norris M)

Access to staff:
Contact by letter, by telephone and by fax

Access to building, collection or gallery:
Prior appointment required

NORFOLK COUNTY ASSOCIATION OF PARISH & TOWN COUNCILS

Acronym or abbreviation: NCAPTC

North Wing, County Hall, Norwich, Norfolk, NR1 2UF

Tel: 01603 664869
Fax: 01603 664871
E-mail: enquiries@ncaptc.gov.uk

Enquiries:
Enquiries to: Executive Officer

Founded:
1941

Publications list:
Available in print

Access to staff:
Contact by letter, by telephone, by fax and by e-mail. Access for members only.
Hours: Mon to Fri, 0900 to 1700

Affiliated to:
National Association of Local Councils (NALC)

NORFOLK COUNTY COUNCIL LIBRARY AND INFORMATION SERVICE

County Hall, Martineau Lane, Norwich, Norfolk, NR1 2UA

Tel: 0844 800 8020
Fax: 01603 222422
E-mail: libraries@norfolk.gov.uk

Website:
http://www.norfolk.gov.uk
Key contact details and general information about range of services and locations offered by Norfolk Library and Information Service.

Enquiries:
Enquiries to: Head of Library and Information Service

Founded:
1974

Organisation type and purpose:
Local government body, public library.
Headquarters and administration centre, no library at this address.

Subject coverage:
General.

Museum or gallery collection, archive, or library special collection:
Norwich: Colman and Rye local studies collection
King's Lynn: St Margaret's Parish collection
Thetford: Duleep Singh collection
Thetford: Thomas Paine collection

Non-library collection catalogue:
All or part available online and in-house

Library catalogue:
All or part available online

Access to staff:
Contact by letter, by telephone, by fax and by e-mail. Appointment necessary.
Hours: Mon to Fri, 0900 to 1700

Access to building, collection or gallery:
No prior appointment required

Main libraries:
Great Yarmouth Library
Tollhouse Street, Great Yarmouth, Norfolk, NR30 2SH; tel: 01943 844551; fax: 01943 857628; e-mail: yarmouth.lib@norfolk.gov.uk
King's Lynn Library
London Road, King's Lynn, Norfolk, PE30 5EZ; tel: 01553 772568; fax: 01553 769832; e-mail: kings.lynn.lib@norfolk.gov.uk
Norfolk & Norwich Millennium Library
The Forum, Millennium Plain, Norwich, Norfolk, NR2 1AW; tel: 01603 774774; fax: 01603 774705; e-mail: millennium.lib@norfolk.gov.uk
Thetford Library
Raymond Street, Thetford, Norfolk, IP24 2EA; tel: 01842 752048; fax: 01842 750125; e-mail: thetford.lib@norfolk.gov.uk

NORFOLK COUNTY PETANQUE ASSOCIATION

Acronym or abbreviation: NCPA

26 Sun Lane, Norwich, NR3 3NF

Tel: 01603 419897

Enquiries:
Enquiries to: Secretary
Direct e-mail: normanguest.petanque@lineone.net

Organisation type and purpose:
Membership association (membership is by subscription), present number of members: 235 (in Norfolk only).
A sporting association.
To promote and foster the game of Pétanque in Norfolk.
To promote and organise Pétanque competitions.

Subject coverage:
The rules of Pétanque and method of play; how to construct, and dimensions of, a playing surface.

Access to staff:
Contact by letter, by telephone and by e-mail
Hours: Mon to Fri, 0900 to 1700

NORFOLK FAMILY HISTORY SOCIETY

Kirby Hall, 70 St Giles Street, Norwich, Norfolk, NR2 1LS

Tel: 01603 763718
E-mail: nfhs@paston.co.uk

Website:
http://www.norfolkfhs.org.uk

continued overleaf

Enquiries:
Enquiries to: Company Secretary

Founded:
1968

Organisation type and purpose:
Membership association (membership is by subscription), present number of members: 4000, registered charity (charity number 1055410).

Non-library collection catalogue:
All or part available online

Publications list:
Available online and in print

Access to staff:
Contact by letter and in person
Hours: Tue, Thu, Sun, 1000 to 1300; Wed, 1000 to 1600
Special comments: Donations invited from visiting non-members.

Access to building, collection or gallery:
No prior appointment required

Access for disabled people:
Parking provided, ramped entry, toilet facilities

NORFOLK RECORD OFFICE

The Archive Centre, Martineau Lane, Norwich, Norfolk, NR1 2DQ

Tel: 01603 222599
Fax: 01603 761885
E-mail: norfrec@norfolk.gov.uk

Website:
http://archives.norfolk.gov.uk
Access information, facilities, publications, price list, brief information resources for popular subjects of research, summary guide, online catalogues.

Enquiries:
Enquiries to: County Archivist

Founded:
1963

Organisation type and purpose:
Local government body.
County Record Office.

Subject coverage:
Norfolk Record Office holdings.

Museum or gallery collection, archive, or library special collection:
Archives for the County of Norfolk and Diocese of Norwich, 11th to 21st centuries

Non-library collection catalogue:
All or part available online, in-house and in print

Printed publications:
A Guide to the Records of Norwich Cathedral (F. Meeres, 1998, £6.95 plus p&p)
Norfolk Parish Map: showing the locations of parishes (50p plus p&p)
50 free information leaflets, including guides to sources

Microform publications:
Duplicates of many of the Norfolk Record Office's holdings on film and fiche, including some parish registers, can be purchased

Publications list:
Available online and in print

Access to staff:
Contact by letter, by telephone, by fax, by e-mail, in person and via website. Appointment necessary.

Access to building, collection or gallery:
Hours: Mon, Wed, Thu and Fri, 0900 to 1700; Tue, 0930 to 1700; Sat, 0900 to 1200. Closed bank holidays and Sat before Easter, and spring and summer bank holidays; closed for two weeks in late Nov and early Dec for stocktaking.
Special comments: County Archive Research Network reader's ticket required for access to original manuscripts.

NORFOLK YOUTH MUSIC TRUST

Wahnfried, 4 Church Close, Buxton, Norwich, Norfolk, NR10 5ER

Tel: 01603 279742
E-mail: info@norfolk-youth-music-trust.org.uk

Website:
http://norfolk-youth-music-trust.org.uk

Enquiries:
Enquiries to: Chairman / Secretary

Founded:
2001

Formerly called:
Music at Saint George's (year of change 2001)

Organisation type and purpose:
Voluntary organisation, registered charity (charity number 1043945).
To promote, encourage, maintain, develop and improve public education in, and appreciation of, the art and science of music in all its aspects within the county of Norfolk. The trust also aims to help the development of highly-talented Norfolk-based young musicians to pursue careers as professionals by offering grants and occasional public-performing opportunities.

Subject coverage:
Annual round of grants available to under-30s engaged in studies to become professional musicians.

Museum or gallery collection, archive, or library special collection:
Norfolk 'Icon'

Trade and statistical information:
Database in Local Studies Library, Norwich

Non-library collection catalogue:
All or part available in-house and in print

Printed publications:
The Music Makers 1977–2001 (132pp, 2001, ISBN 1–903923–00-X, £8.50)
I'll Take You Where the Music's Playing (Hosgood I, 2005, £9.95)
Order printed publications from: Postal address

Electronic and video publications:
WPCD1 and WPCD2 The Last Day 3 Feb 2001 (2 CD Set, £10 per set)
WPCD3 and WPCD4 The Last Day 3 Feb 2001 (2 CD Set, £10 per set)

Publications list:
Available in print

Access to staff:
Contact by letter, by telephone, by e-mail and via website. Appointment necessary.
Hours: Mon to Fri, 0900 to 1700

Access for disabled people:
Full access for public concerts
Hours: Concert performance times only

NORSKE VERITAS

Acronym or abbreviation: DNV

Palace House, 3 Cathedral Street, London, SE1 9DE

Tel: 020 7357 6080
Fax: 020 7716 6736

Website:
http://www.dnv.com/maritime/publicationlist/index.asp
Publication list.
http://www.dnv.com

Enquiries:
Enquiries to: Information Scientist
Direct tel: 020 7716 6583
Direct fax: 020 7716 6730

Founded:
1864

Organisation type and purpose:
Service industry, training organisation, consultancy.

Provides consulting, engineering, verification, certification and training services.

Subject coverage:
Industrial safety, offshore oil and gas, chemical industries, risk assessment, safety management, environmental management, quality management, marine transport, reliability assessment, loss prevention, environmental assessment, environmental risk, safety assessment.

Museum or gallery collection, archive, or library special collection:
Books, reports, documents, periodicals, legislation, standards, codes, guidelines

Non-library collection catalogue:
All or part available in-house

Library catalogue:
All or part available in-house

Printed publications:
Various publications available for purchase, direct
Rules for Classification
Standards for Certification
Insurance Plans
Offshore Standards
Order printed publications from: For international orders, Distribution Department
Det Norske Veritas, Norwegian Office, e-mail: distribution@dnv.com
Information Scientist, Det Norske Veritas Aberdeen Office

Electronic and video publications:
Some publications available online, free of charge, and available for purchase, direct

Publications list:
Available online and in print

Access to staff:
Contact by letter, by telephone and by fax
Hours: Mon to Fri, 0900 to 1700

Access to building, collection or gallery:
No access other than to staff

Access for disabled people:
Level entry, access to all public areas

Other offices:
Det Norske Veritas (DNV)
Cromarty House, 67–72 Regent Quay, Aberdeen, AB11 5AR; tel: 01224 335000; fax: 01244 593311

Parent body:
Det Norske Veritas, Norway (DNV)
Veritasveien 1, 1322 Høvik, Norway; tel: +47 67 57 99 00; fax: +47 67 57 99 11; website: http://www.dnv.com

NORTH AYRSHIRE LIBRARY AND INFORMATION SERVICE

39–41 Princes Street, Ardrossan, Ayrshire, KA22 8BT

Tel: 01294 469137
Fax: 01294 604236
E-mail: libraryhq@north-ayrshire.gov.uk

Website:
http://www.north-ayrshire.gov.uk

Enquiries:
Enquiries to: Library and Information Service Manager
Direct tel: 01294 212716
Direct fax: 01294 222509
Direct e-mail: asutton@north-ayrshire.gov.uk
Other contacts: Library Operations Manager

Founded:
1996

Organisation type and purpose:
Local government body, public library and education resource service.

Subject coverage:
Local history and archives relating to Cunninghame, North Ayrshire, Burghs in that area, the islands of Arran and Millport.

Museum or gallery collection, archive, or library special collection:
Alexander Wood Memorial Library (local and Scottish books)

Non-library collection catalogue:
All or part available in-house

Library catalogue:
All or part available online

Printed publications:
The Scottish Co-operative Movement (40p)
Ardrossan Castle
Cunninghame Maps
Town Trails: Ardrossan, Saltcoats and Stevenston
North Ayrshire Street Guides
Other leaflets of local history including:
Ardeer and the Nobel Heritage (£5)
Auchenbarvie Colliery: An early history (£1)
History of the Ancient Society of Archers (25p)
Irvine Carter's Society (£3)
Things that befel in Ayrshire (£4.50)

Publications list:
Available in print

Access to staff:
Contact by letter, by telephone, by fax, by e-mail, in person and via website. Appointment necessary.
Hours: Mon to Thu, 0900 to 1645; Fri, 0900 to 1630

Access to building, collection or gallery:
No prior appointment required
Hours: Mon to Thu, 0900 to 1645; Fri, 0900 to 1630

Access for disabled people:
Parking provided, ramped entry, toilet facilities

NORTH CORNWALL DISTRICT COUNCIL

Acronym or abbreviation: NCDC

Higher Trenant Road, Wadebridge, Cornwall, PL27 6TW

Tel: 01208 893333
Fax: 01208 893232
E-mail: public.relations@ncdc.gov.uk

Website:
http://www.ncdc.gov.uk

Enquiries:
Enquiries to: Information Officer
Direct tel: 01208 893318

Founded:
1974

Organisation type and purpose:
Local government body.

Access to staff:
Contact by letter, by fax and via website
Hours: Mon to Thu, 0845 to 1700; Fri, 0845 to 1630

Access for disabled people:
Parking provided, ramped entry, toilet facilities

NORTH COUNTRY CHEVIOT SHEEP SOCIETY

16 St Vincent Road, Tain, Ross-shire, IV19 1JR

Tel: 01862 894014
Fax: 01862 894014
E-mail: wm@nc-cheviot.co.uk

Website:
http://www.nc-cheviot.co.uk

Enquiries:
Enquiries to: Secretary

Founded:
1945

Organisation type and purpose:
Membership association (membership is by subscription), present number of members: 400, registered charity (charity number SCO 12265). To promote the North Country Cheviot sheep breed.

Subject coverage:
Information on the sustainability of North Country Cheviot sheep in different environments and for different breeding/crossing programmes.

Printed publications:
Annual Flock Book

Publications list:
Available in print

Access to staff:
Contact by letter, by telephone, by fax, by e-mail, in person and via website. Appointment necessary.
Hours: Mon to Fri, 0900 to 1700

NORTH DEVON BRITISH MOTORCYCLE OWNERS CLUB

Acronym or abbreviation: NDBMOC

32 Merrythorn Road, Fremington, Barnstaple, Devon, EX31 3AL

Tel: 01271 379170
E-mail: andylin@andbmocl.freeserve.co.uk

Website:
http://www.ndbmoc.freeserve.co.uk
Details of club, entry forms.

Enquiries:
Enquiries to: Secretary

Founded:
1978

Organisation type and purpose:
Membership association (membership is by subscription), present number of members: 120, suitable for ages: 18+.

Subject coverage:
Post-war British motorcycles, mechanical and electrical advice for most popular models: AMC, Ariel, BSA Norton, Triumph, Vincent.

Printed publications:
Magazine (spring and autumn)

Access to staff:
Contact by letter and by telephone
Hours: Any reasonable time after 1800

Access for disabled people:
Ramped entry, access to all public areas, toilet facilities

NORTH DEVON COLLEGE

Old Sticklepath Hill, Barnstaple, Devon, EX31 2BQ

Tel: 01271 338170 (main library line)
Fax: 01271 388121
E-mail: library@ndevon.ac.uk

Website:
http://www.nedevon.ac.uk
Main college website.

Enquiries:
Enquiries to: Learning Resources Manager
Direct tel: 01271 388018
Other contacts: Learning Resources Team Leader and Librarian

Organisation type and purpose:
Suitable for ages: mainly 16 to 19.
College of further education.

Subject coverage:
Academic subjects and some local material.

Non-library collection catalogue:
All or part available online

Library catalogue:
All or part available online

Access to staff:
Contact by letter, by telephone, by fax and by e-mail
Hours: Term time: Mon to Wed, 0830 to 1900; Thu, Fri, 0830 to 1630
Vacations: Mon to Fri, 0900 to 1300

Access for disabled people:
Parking provided, access to all public areas, toilet facilities

NORTH DEVON LOCAL STUDIES CENTRE

Library and Record Office, Tuly Street, Barnstaple, Devon, EX31 1EL

Tel: 01271 388607

Enquiries:
Enquiries to: Librarian
Other contacts: (1) Archivist (2) Curator for (1) documents (2) photographs.

Founded:
1988

Organisation type and purpose:
Local government body, public library, suitable for ages: school and adult.

Subject coverage:
Local, house and family history.

Access to staff:
Contact by letter and in person
Hours: Mon, Tue, Thu, Fri, 0930 to 1700; Wed, 0930 to 1300; Sat, 0930 to 1400

Other addresses:
West Country Studies Library
Castle Street, Exeter; tel: 01392 384216

Parent body:
Devon County Council
Topsham Road, Exeter

NORTH DEVON RECORD OFFICE

Acronym or abbreviation: NDRO

North Devon Library and Record Office, Tuly Street, Barnstaple, Devon, EX31 1EL

Tel: 01271 388608
Fax: 01271 388608
E-mail: ndevrec@devon.gov.uk

Website:
http://www.devon.gov.uk/record_office.htm
Introduction to holdings, opening times, access requirements, some lists of records.

Enquiries:
Enquiries to: Archivist

Founded:
1988

Organisation type and purpose:
Local government body.

Subject coverage:
Archives for North Devon area.

Museum or gallery collection, archive, or library special collection:
Records of local authorities, Devon County Council; North Devon and Torridge District Councils and their predecessors, the urban and rural district councils; the borough councils of Barnstaple, Bideford, Great Torrington and South Molton; parish councils
Public records, shipping registers, Quarter sessions, Petty Sessional Division records, local hospitals and coroner
Poor Law Union and Public Assistance Institution records
Taw and Torridge Fishery Board records
Education records
Ecclesiastical records for the Archdeaconry of Barnstaple, including parish registers and records
Records of nonconformist denominations (including the Bible Christian branch of the Methodist Church founded in North Devon)
Collections of estate records and private papers
Records of local solicitors; businesses; clubs and societies; charities and trusts
Parish registers, electoral registers, wills and land tax assessments (microfilm or microfiche)

continued overleaf

Non-library collection catalogue:
All or part available online

Access to staff:
Contact by letter, by telephone, by e-mail and in person. Appointment necessary.

Access for disabled people:
Level entry, access to all public areas, toilet facilities

NORTH EAST CHAMBER OF COMMERCE, TRADE & INDUSTRY

Acronym or abbreviation: NECC

Aykley Heads Business Centre, Aykley Heads, Durham, DH1 5TS

Tel: 0191 386 1133
Fax: 0191 386 1144
E-mail: info@necc.co.uk

Website:
http://www.ne-cc.co.uk
Site includes practical advice and information for business in the North East of England. All Chamber members are on the site in the Directory section to allow searches for North East companies in particular business sectors.

Enquiries:
Enquiries to: Information Services Manager

Founded:
1995

Organisation type and purpose:
Membership association (membership is by subscription), present number of members: 5500, service industry, training organisation.
Chamber of commerce.
Business services and representation of members.

Subject coverage:
All aspects of business information with specific reference to commerce and industry in the North East.

Printed publications:
Contact (business magazine, monthly)
North East Regional Business Directory (annually)

Electronic and video publications:
prEview (members only, monthly)

Access to staff:
Contact by letter, by telephone, by fax, by e-mail, in person and via website. Appointment necessary.
Access for members only. Non-members charged.
Hours: Mon to Fri, 0900 to 1700

Member of:
Association of British Chambers of Commerce

Partner in the 5 offices of:
Business Link (North East)

NORTH EAST DERBYSHIRE DISTRICT COUNCIL

Council House, Saltergate, Chesterfield, Derbyshire, S40 1LF

Tel: 01246 231111
Fax: 01246 550213
E-mail: jill.ward@ne-derbyshire.gov.uk

Website:
http://www.ne-derbyshire.gov.uk

Enquiries:
Enquiries to: Head of Strategic Support

Founded:
1974

Organisation type and purpose:
Local government body.

Subject coverage:
Local government services.

Printed publications:
NED News (civic newspaper, 5 times a year)

Access to staff:
Contact by letter, by telephone, by fax, by e-mail and via website
Hours: Mon to Fri, 0900 to 1700

NORTH EAST LINCOLNSHIRE ARCHIVES

Town Hall, Town Hall Square, Grimsby, Lincolnshire, DN31 1HX

Tel: 01472 323585
Fax: 01472 323582
E-mail: john.wilson@nelincs.gov.uk

Website:
http://www.nelincs.gov.uk/leisure/archives

Enquiries:
Enquiries to: Archivist

Founded:
1951

Formerly called:
Grimsby Borough Archives Office (year of change 1974); South Humberside Area Archives Office (year of change 1996)

Organisation type and purpose:
Local government body.

Subject coverage:
Archives for local authorities in North East Lincolnshire and North Lincolnshire including Grimsby Borough (1201–1996), local boards of health, rural sanitary authorities, urban sanitary authorities, burial boards, school boards, education committees (and over 100 schools), rural district councils, urban district councils (1894–1974), borough councils (1974–1996), parish councils, registers of Grimsby ships (1824–1925), register of Grimsby fishing apprentices (1879–1937) Grimsby fishing vessel crew lists (1864–1914), manorial records, public records.
The office is not a Diocesan Record Office. For original church records etc. see Lincolnshire Archives, Lincoln.

Museum or gallery collection, archive, or library special collection:
Archives collected by the North Lincolnshire Museum, Scunthorpe
Local and Personal Acts, Private Acts (of Parliament, 1889–1966)
Parish registers of the eleven northern Deaneries of the Diocese of Lincoln (microfiche, appointment required to consult)

Non-library collection catalogue:
All or part available online

Printed publications:
Guidance leaflets

Publications list:
Available in print

Access to staff:
Contact by letter, by telephone, by fax and by e-mail. Appointment necessary.
Hours: Mon to Thu, 0930 to 1230 and 1300 to 1600

Access to building, collection or gallery:
Prior appointment required

Access for disabled people:
Ramped entry, access to all public areas
Special comments: Toilet access

NORTH EAST LINCOLNSHIRE LIBRARY SERVICE

Formal name: North East Lincolnshire Council Public Library Service

Central Library, Town Hall Square, Grimsby, Lincolnshire, DN31 1HG

Tel: 01472 323600
Fax: 01472 323634
E-mail: lib@nelincs.gov.uk

Website:
http://www.nelincs.gov.uk/libraries

Enquiries:
Enquiries to: Head of Cultural Services
Direct tel: 01472 323611
Direct fax: 01472 323618
Direct e-mail: steve.hipkins@nelincs.gov.uk
Other contacts: Principal Librarian (Strategy and Support, tel. 01472 323612)

Founded:
1996

Organisation type and purpose:
Public library.

Subject coverage:
General, local history, family history.

Museum or gallery collection, archive, or library special collection:
Business and company information
Local history collection (Grimsby, Cleethorpes and surrounding area)
Skelton Collection (posters and handbills of local printers), Ruhleben collection WWI

Trade and statistical information:
UK markets.

Non-library collection catalogue:
All or part available online

Library catalogue:
All or part available online and in-house

Access to staff:
Contact by letter, by telephone, by fax, by e-mail, in person and via website
Hours: Mon to Fri, 0830 to 1930; Sat, 0900 to 1600; Sun, 1000 to 1600

Branches:
one central and 10 branch libraries

Parent body:
North East Lincolnshire Council

NORTH EAST OF SCOTLAND DOUBLE BASS SOCIETY

343 Holburn Street, Aberdeen, AB10 7FQ

Tel: 01224 590521

Enquiries:
Enquiries to: Honorary Secretary

Founded:
1996

Organisation type and purpose:
Voluntary organisation.
To promote the enjoyment of, listening to and playing of the double bass repertoire.

Subject coverage:
History of the double bass in North East Scotland.

Access to staff:
Contact by letter
Hours: Mon to Fri, 0900 to 1700

NORTH EAST WALES INSTITUTE OF HIGHER EDUCATION

Acronym or abbreviation: NEWI

Library, Postal Point 22L, Plas Coch, Mold Road, Wrexham, Clwyd, LL11 2AW

Tel: 01978 293250
Fax: 01978 293435
E-mail: p.jeorrett@newi.ac.uk

Website:
http://www.newi.ac.uk/library/index.htm
Information about NEWI and information and student services.

Enquiries:
Enquiries to: User Services Manager

Founded:
1975

Organisation type and purpose:
University library, suitable for ages: 18+

Subject coverage:
Chemistry, physics, environmental sciences, engineering, education, art and design, nursing, social work, management, computing.

Library catalogue:
All or part available online

Access to staff:
Contact by letter, by telephone, by fax, by e-mail and in person
Hours: Term time: Mon to Thu, 0845 to 2100; Fri, 0845 to 1700; Sat, 1000 to 1700

Access for disabled people:
Parking provided, level entry, toilet facilities

NORTH EAST WORCESTERSHIRE COLLEGE

Acronym or abbreviation: NEW College

Learning Resources Centre, Blackwood Road, Bromsgrove, Worcestershire, B60 1PQ

Tel: 01527 570020
Fax: 01527 572900

Enquiries:
Enquiries to: Head of Department, Learning Services
Direct tel: 01527 572517
Direct fax: 01527 572560
Direct e-mail: cduncan@ne-worcs.ac.uk

Founded:
1988

Organisation type and purpose:
Suitable for ages: 16+.
College of further education.

Subject coverage:
Business, management, law, art and design, media studies, music, hospitality and catering, community care, social work, secretarial studies, travel and tourism, engineering, beauty, nursery nursing, sixth form studies.

Access to staff:
Contact by letter. Appointment necessary. Letter of introduction required.
Hours: Mon to Thu, 0830 to 2000; Fri, 0830 to 1630
Special comments: Access to registered staff and students by arrangement.

Other addresses:
North East Worcestershire College
  Peakman Street, Redditch, B98 8DW; tel: 01527 570020

NORTH EASTERN EDUCATION AND LIBRARY BOARD

Acronym or abbreviation: NEELB/NELS

Library Headquarters, Demesne Avenue, Ballymena, Co Antrim, BT43 7BG

Tel: 028 2566 4100
Fax: 028 2563 2038
E-mail: info.neelb@ni-libraries.net

Website:
http://www.ni-libraries.net

Enquiries:
Enquiries to: Librarian

Organisation type and purpose:
Northern Ireland Government body.
Public and schools library.

Subject coverage:
North Eastern local studies plus all public and schools library subjects.
Community Services Unit.

Non-library collection catalogue:
All or part available online

Library catalogue:
All or part available online

Printed publications:
Library Charter

Access to staff:
Contact by letter, by telephone, by fax, by e-mail, in person and via website
Hours: Mon to Fri, 0900 to 1700
Special comments: Branch libraries have late night and Sat opening.

Access to building, collection or gallery:
No prior appointment required

Access for disabled people:
Ramped entry, access to all public areas, toilet facilities

NORTH HAMPSHIRE CHAMBER OF COMMERCE AND INDUSTRY

Acronym or abbreviation: NHCCI

Winchester Business Centre, 10 Parchment Street, Winchester, Hampshire, SO23 8AT

Tel: 01962 841000
Fax: 01962 870423
E-mail: info@nhcci.co.uk

Website:
http://www.nhcci.co.uk/

Enquiries:
Enquiries to: Secretary

Founded:
1918

Subject coverage:
Business information and support.

Printed publications:
Monthly Business Bulletin (free to members)
List of chamber members
List of Winchester businesses

Access to staff:
Contact by letter, by telephone, by fax and in person
Hours: Mon to Fri, 0900 to 1700

Business Helpline:
Hampshire Training and Enterprise Council Limited
  25 Thackeray Mall, Fareham, PO16 0PQ; tel: 0800 373833

Member of:
Hampshire Chambers of Commerce

Other addresses:
North
  Blackwater Valley Enterprise Trust, Princes Gardens, Aldershot, GU11 1BJ; tel: 0800 132301
South East
  South East Hampshire Chamber of Commerce and Industry, 27 Guildhall Walk, Portsmouth, PO1 2RP; tel: 0800 132302
South West
  Southampton Chamber of Commerce and Industry, 53 Bugle Street, Southampton, SO14 2LF; tel: 0800 132303

Other local offices at:
Basingstoke Chamber of Commerce (BCC)
  Business Support Centre, Deanes Building, London Road, Basingstoke, RG21 7YP; tel: 01256 352275; fax: 01256 479391
North East Hampshire
  Civic Offices, Harlington Way, Fleet, GU51 4AE; tel: 01252 811470; fax: 01252 812096
Winchester
  Abbey Mill, Colebrook Street, Winchester, SO23 9LH; tel: 01962 841000; fax: 01962 870423

NORTH HERTFORDSHIRE DISTRICT COUNCIL

Acronym or abbreviation: NHDC

Council Offices, Gernon Road, Letchworth, Hertfordshire, SG6 3JF

Tel: 01462 474000
Fax: 01462 474227

Website:
http://www.north-herts.gov.uk

Organisation type and purpose:
Local government body.

Subject coverage:
Housing advice, leisure, community development, planning, building control, environmental health, health and safety, community grants, community safety, economic development, noise and environmental pollution, electoral services, council tax/housing benefits, local government finance.

Museum or gallery collection, archive, or library special collection:
Hitchin and Letchworth museums

Printed publications:
Outlook (residents magazine)
A–Z of Services
Best Value Performance Plan
Comments, Compliments, Complaints (booklet)
Sustainable Community Strategy
Corporate Plan

Access to staff:
Contact by letter, by telephone, by fax, by e-mail and in person
Hours: Mon to Fri, 0900 to 1700

Access to building, collection or gallery:
Hours: Mon to Fri, 0900 to 1700

Access for disabled people:
Fully accessible

Also at:
Finance and Regulatory Services
  Town Lodge, Gernon Road, Letchworth, Hertfordshire, SG6 3HN

NORTH HERTS & DISTRICT CITIZENS ADVICE BUREAU

The Town Hall, Melbourn Street, Royston, Hertfordshire, SG8 7DA

Tel: 01763 238020
Fax: 01763 238017
E-mail: bureau@roystoncab.cabnet.org.uk

Enquiries:
Enquiries to: Manager
Direct tel: 01763 238017

Organisation type and purpose:
Voluntary organisation, registered charity (charity number 1086489).

Access to staff:
Contact by letter, by fax and by e-mail
Hours: Mon to Fri, 1000 to 1300

NORTH HIGHLAND ARCHIVE

Acronym or abbreviation: NHA

Wick Library, Sinclair Terrace, Wick, Caithness, KW1 5AB

Tel: 01955 606432
Fax: 01955 603000
E-mail: north.highlandarchive@highland.gov.uk

Website:
http://www.highland.gov.uk/educ/publicservices/archivedetails/northarchive.htm

Enquiries:
Enquiries to: Archivist

Founded:
1995

Organisation type and purpose:
Local government body, public library.
Local archive and record office.

Subject coverage:
Maritime history, poor relief, council administration, police activity, education, planning (building development). Less significant: WWII, archaeology, trade, estates and agriculture, nursing, church activity.

continued overleaf

Museum or gallery collection, archive, or library special collection:
Local and family history sources including census/ OPR microfilms, maps, valuations rolls, school records, council and parochial board records, and private collections of major local significance such as Wick Harbour Trust
A number of smaller private collections come from local businesses or major landowning professional families

Non-library collection catalogue:
All or part available online and in-house

Library catalogue:
All or part available in-house

Printed publications:
Beyond the Registers: family history from archives and ephemera (£1.50)
Guide to the Highland Council Archive (£7)
Guide to printed sources at the North Highland Archive (£2.50)
Leaflet, newsletter and numerous information sheets (free)

Access to staff:
Contact by letter, by telephone, by fax, by e-mail and in person
Hours: Mon, Thu, Fri, 1000 to 1300 and 1400 to 1730; Tue, 1000 to 1300 and 1400 to 2000; Wed, 1000 to 1300
Special comments: May be advisable to book in the summer months to ensure access to microfilm readers.

Access to building, collection or gallery:
No access other than to staff

Access for disabled people:
On request

Parent body:
Highland Council Archive, Inverness

NORTH KESTEVEN DISTRICT COUNCIL

Acronym or abbreviation: NKDC

Council Offices, Kesteven Street, Sleaford, Lincolnshire, NG34 7EF

Tel: 01529 414155
Fax: 01529 413956
E-mail: info@n-kesteven.gov.uk

Website:
http://www.n-kesteven.gov.uk

Enquiries:
Enquiries to: Press and Publications Officer
Direct tel: ext 2467
Direct e-mail: julie_wetton@n.kesteven.gov.uk

Organisation type and purpose:
Local government body, advisory body, statutory body, service industry, training organisation, consultancy, research organisation.

Subject coverage:
Environmental health, planning, council tax, business rates, housing benefits.

Access to staff:
Contact by letter, by telephone, by fax, by e-mail and via website
Hours: Mon to Thu, 0830 to 1700; Fri, 0830 to 1630

Access to building, collection or gallery:
No access other than to staff

Access for disabled people:
Parking provided, ramped entry, toilet facilities

NORTH LANARKSHIRE COUNCIL

PO Box 14, Civic Centre, Motherwell, North Lanarkshire, ML1 1TW

Tel: 01698 302222
Fax: 01698 275125

Website:
http://www.northlan.gov.uk/your+council

Enquiries:
Enquiries to: Chief Executive

Founded:
1996

Organisation type and purpose:
Local government body.

Subject coverage:
Local government affairs.

NORTH LANARKSHIRE COUNCIL – EDUCATION RESOURCE SERVICE

Acronym or abbreviation: ERS

Department of Education, 8 Kildonan Street, Coatbridge, Lanarkshire, ML5 3LP

Tel: 01236 434377
Fax: 01236 436224
E-mail: ERSMail@northlan.gov.uk

Website:
http://www.northlan.gov.uk

Enquiries:
Enquiries to: Principal Librarian

Founded:
1996

Organisation type and purpose:
Local government body, suitable for ages: 3 to 18.
School library service.
To provide advice, support and resources to all educational establishments in North Lanarkshire.

Subject coverage:
Educational resources: nursery, primary, special and secondary schools.

Museum or gallery collection, archive, or library special collection:
Artefacts and staff development
Pre 5 years Multimedia collections
5 to 14 years Multimedia collections
Support for Learning

Access to staff:
Contact by letter, by telephone, by fax and by e-mail. Appointment necessary.
Hours: Mon to Thu, 0845 to 1645; Fri, 0845 to 1615
Special comments: Resources available to the general public for reference only.

Affiliated to:
Education Department
Municipal Buildings, Kildonan Street, Coatbridge, ML5 3BT; tel: 01236 812222; fax: 01236 812247

NORTH LANARKSHIRE COUNCIL – INFORMATION SECTION

Formal name: North Lanarkshire Libraries and Information Service

Motherwell Library, 35 Hamilton Road, Motherwell, North Lanarkshire, ML1 3BZ

Tel: 01698 332628
Fax: 01698 332625

Website:
http://www.northlan.gov.uk
home page

Enquiries:
Enquiries to: Libraries & Information Manager
Direct tel: 0141 304 1843
Direct e-mail: foxj@northlan.gov.uk

Founded:
1904

Organisation type and purpose:
Local government body, public library.

Subject coverage:
General subjects.

Museum or gallery collection, archive, or library special collection:
Chinese collection of books and magazines for children and adults
Gaelic collection of books and magazines for children and adults
Urdu collection of books and magazines for children and adults

Printed publications:
Local history publications
Order printed publications from: North Lanarkshire Libraries and Information Service, Motherwell Library
tel: 01698 332628

Access to staff:
Contact by letter, by telephone, by fax and via website
Hours: Mon, Tue, Thu, Fri, 0900 to 1930; Wed, 0900 to 1200, lending library, 0900 to 1730 Information library, Sat, 0900 to 1600

Access to building, collection or gallery:
No prior appointment required

Access for disabled people:
Ramped entry, toilet facilities
Special comments: Ramp/lift to ground floor, lift to first floor

Other locations:
24 branches and 6 mobile vans

Parent body:
North Lanarkshire Council

NORTH LANARKSHIRE COUNCIL ARCHIVES

10 Kelvin Road, Lenziemill, Cumbernauld, North Lanarkshire, G67 2BA

Tel: 01236 737114
Fax: 01236 781762
E-mail: museums@northlan.gov.uk

Enquiries:
Enquiries to: Archivist

Founded:
1996

Organisation type and purpose:
Local government body.
Local authority archive.

Subject coverage:
We hold archives of: landed estates; local firms and individuals; clubs and societies; historical miscellany; prior local authorities.

Non-library collection catalogue:
All or part available online and in-house

Library catalogue:
All or part available in-house

Access to staff:
Contact by letter, by telephone, by fax and by e-mail. Appointment necessary.
Hours: Mon to Fri, 0930 to 1630

Access to building, collection or gallery:
Prior appointment required

Links with:
North Lanarkshire Community Services
Head of Museums and Heritage, Museums and Heritage Section, Buchanan Tower, Stepps, Glasgow; tel: 0141 304 1800

NORTH LINCOLNSHIRE COUNCIL

Pittwood House, Ashby Road, Scunthorpe, Lincolnshire, DN16 1AB

Tel: 01724 296296\ Minicom no. 01724 296294
Fax: 01724 296079

Website:
http://www.northlincs.gov.uk

Enquiries:
Enquiries to: Library and Information Services Manager
Direct tel: 01724 297869

Museum or gallery collection, archive, or library special collection:
Library of indexes and other references for North West Kent and South East London area. Held on Microfiche or printed form

Non-library collection catalogue:
All or part available in-house

Library catalogue:
All or part available in-house

Printed publications:
Journal (quarterly, members)
All publications available from the Society are listed with current price and p&p in the journal and on website, these include:
Parish Register transcriptions, monumental inscriptions, indexes to records in Bromley Journal & West Kent Herald, Census indexes
Order printed publications from: NWKFHS 141 Princes Road, Dartford, DA1 3HJ

Microform publications:
Microfiche publications for sale

Electronic and video publications:
Details will be advertised on the website when CD-ROM available

Publications list:
Available online and in print

Access to staff:
Contact by letter, by e-mail and via website
Hours: None

Branches at:
Bromley, Dartford, Sevenoaks, Orpington (Computer)

Member of:
Federation of Family History Societies (FFHS)

Membership Secretary:
North West Kent Family History Society 6 Windermere Road, Bexleyheath, Kent, DA7 6PW

NORTH WEST LEICESTERSHIRE DISTRICT COUNCIL

Acronym or abbreviation: NWLDC

Council Offices, Coalville, Leicester, LE67 3FJ

Tel: 01530 454545
Fax: 01530 454546
E-mail: info@nwleicestershire.gov.uk

Website:
http://www.nwleics.gov.uk
Community information, tourist information, economic development/inward investment, the National Forest.

Enquiries:
Enquiries to: Chief Executive

Founded:
1973

Organisation type and purpose:
Local government body.

Subject coverage:
Local government services.

Printed publications include:
Business Information
District Guide
Street Maps
Tourist Information

Access to staff:
Contact by letter, by telephone, by fax, by e-mail
and in person
Hours: Mon to Fri, 0900 to 1700

Access for disabled people:
Parking provided, level entry, toilet facilities

NORTH WEST LONDON HOSPITALS NHS TRUST

John Squire Medical Library, Watford Road, Harrow, Middlesex, HA1 3UJ

Tel: 020 8869 3322 (enquiries)
Fax: 020 8869 3332
E-mail: jslib@clara.net

Website:
http://www.jslib.clara.net

Enquiries:
Enquiries to: Head Librarian

Organisation type and purpose:
Hospital.

Subject coverage:
Clinical, medical and complementary basic sciences, nursing and health service management.

Library catalogue:
All or part available online

Printed publications:
Handlist of current journals (annually)
Library Bulletin (monthly)

Access to staff:
Contact in person
Hours: Mon to Fri, 0900 to 1800

Access to building, collection or gallery:
No prior appointment required
Hours: Mon to Fri, 0900 to 1800
Special comments: Must have bona fide need to access library resources.

Funded by:
Brent, Kensington, Chelsea & Westminster Mental Health NHS Trust
Harrow Primary Care Trust
London Deanery
North West London Hospitals NHS Trust

NORTH WEST SOUND ARCHIVE

c/o The County Archivist, 56 Marshall Street, New Cross, Manchester, M4 5FU

Tel: 0161 832 5284
E-mail: nwsa@ed.lancscc.gov.uk

Website:
http://www.gmcro.co.uk/other/NWSA/nwsa.htm

Founded:
1979

Organisation type and purpose:
Collection located at the Greater Manchester County Record Office. Aims to provide source material for reminiscence therapy, local history, actors, the education sector, journalists and researchers.

Subject coverage:
Sound recordings relating to life in the northwest of England.

Education services:
Education packs for schools.

Museum or gallery collection, archive, or library special collection:
Collection includes:
50,000 recordings from BBC Radio Manchester
2.5 tonnes of 78-rpm gramophone records
Survey of English dialect

NORTH WILTSHIRE DISTRICT COUNCIL

Acronym or abbreviation: NWDC

Monkton Park, Chippenham, Wiltshire, SN15 1ER

Tel: 01249 706111
Fax: 01249 443158

Website:
http://www.northwilts.gov.uk

Enquiries:
Enquiries to: Public Relations Manager
Direct tel: 01249 706618

Direct fax: 01249 654999
Direct e-mail: plangcaster@northwilts.gov.uk
Other contacts: Chief Executive

Founded:
1974

Organisation type and purpose:
Local government body.

Subject coverage:
Services and amenities of the District Council.

Printed publications:
Annual reviews
District and town guides
Economic development plans
Forward strategy

Access to staff:
Contact by letter, by telephone and by fax
Hours: Mon to Thu, 0900 to 1700; Fri, 0900 to 1630

NORTH YORK MOORS NATIONAL PARK AUTHORITY

The Old Vicarage, Bondgate, Helmsley, North Yorkshire, YO62 5BP

Tel: 01439 770657
Fax: 01439 770691
E-mail: info@northyorkmoors-npa.gov.uk

Website:
http://www.moors.uk.net
Tourist information, education, events, plans and policies, press releases, publications, detailed information and work of the Authority.

Enquiries:
Enquiries to: Information Officer

Founded:
1952

Organisation type and purpose:
Local government body.
National Park administration.
To conserve and enhance the natural beauty, wildlife and cultural heritage of the area, and to promote opportunities for the understanding and enjoyment of the special qualities of the area by the public.

Subject coverage:
North York Moors: history, geography, archaeology, agriculture, ecology, planning, tourism, travel.

Printed publications:
Annual Report
Local history books
Plans and reports
The North York Moors Landscape Heritage
Walks and trail guides
Wild Plants and their Habitats in the North York Moors

Publications list:
Available online and in print

Access to staff:
Contact by letter, by telephone, by fax and by e-mail. Appointment necessary.
Hours: Mon to Thu, 0830 to 1700; Fri, 0830 to 1630

Access for disabled people:
Parking provided, level entry, toilet facilities

Member of:
Association of National Park Authorities

NORTH YORKSHIRE COUNTY COUNCIL, LIBRARY AND INFORMATION CENTRE

Victoria Avenue, Harrogate, North Yorkshire, HG1 1EG

Tel: 01423 720300
Fax: 01423 523158
E-mail: harrogate.library@northyorks.gov.uk

Website:
http://www.northyorks.gov.uk/libraries

Direct fax: 01724 296343
Direct e-mail: customerservice@northlincs.gov.uk

Founded:
1996

Organisation type and purpose:
Local government body.
Created as a unitary council following abolition of the County of Humberside.
Unitary council responsible for all local government services, including 82 schools, 25,500 pupils and a gross budget (annual) of £315m.

Subject coverage:
Local government.

Library catalogue:
All or part available online

Access to staff:
Contact by letter, by telephone, by fax, by e-mail and in person
Hours: Mon to Thu, 0830 to 1700; Fri, 0830 to 1630

Access to building, collection or gallery:
No prior appointment required

Access for disabled people:
Parking provided, ramped entry, access to all public areas, toilet facilities

NORTH LINCOLNSHIRE LIBRARIES AND INFORMATION SERVICES

North Lincolnshire Central Library, Carlton Street, Scunthorpe, Lincolnshire, DN15 6TX

Tel: 01724 860161
Fax: 01724 860161
E-mail: library.enquiries@northlincs.gov.uk

Website:
http://www.northlincs.gov.uk/library

Enquiries:
Enquiries to: Library and Information Services Manager

Founded:
1996

Organisation type and purpose:
Local government body, statutory body, service industry, public library.

Subject coverage:
General, steel industry, Wesley family, Asian languages.

Museum or gallery collection, archive, or library special collection:
Asian Language Collection

Non-library collection catalogue:
All or part available in-house

Library catalogue:
All or part available in-house

Access to staff:
Contact by letter and by telephone. Appointment necessary. Non-members charged.
Hours: Library: to be arranged.

Branches:
14 libraries and two mobile libraries

Parent body:
North Lincolnshire Council

NORTH NORFOLK DISTRICT COUNCIL

Holt Road, Cromer, Norfolk, NR27 9EL

Tel: 01263 513811
Fax: 01263 515042
E-mail: districtcouncil@north-norfolk.gov.uk

Website:
http://www.north-norfolk.gov.uk

Enquiries:
Enquiries to: Communications Manager
Direct tel: 01263 516344

Direct e-mail: media@north-norfolk.gov.uk

Organisation type and purpose:
Local government body.

Subject coverage:
Local government.

Museum or gallery collection, archive, or library special collection:
Library of photographs of North Norfolk

Printed publications:
Brochures, booklets and leaflets available giving tourism, business and other district information

Access to building, collection or gallery:
No prior appointment required

NORTH OF ENGLAND INSTITUTE OF MINING AND MECHANICAL ENGINEERS

Neville Hall, Westgate Road, Newcastle upon Tyne, NE1 1SE

Tel: 0191 232 2201
Fax: 0191 232 2201
E-mail: imm@skynow.net

Enquiries:
Enquiries to: Administrator
Other contacts: Honorary Secretary for qualification queries.

Founded:
1852

Organisation type and purpose:
Learned society, professional body (membership is by subscription), present number of members: 480, registered charity (charity number 220208).

Subject coverage:
Mining and allied subjects: history and technology.

Museum or gallery collection, archive, or library special collection:
A large number of MSS and other collections

Non-library collection catalogue:
All or part available in-house

Library catalogue:
All or part available in-house

Access to staff:
Contact by letter and by telephone. Appointment necessary. Non-members charged.
Hours: Library: to be arranged.

NORTH OF ENGLAND MULE SHEEP ASSOCIATION

Acronym or abbreviation: NEMSA

Eslaforde, Wear View, Frosterley, Bishop Auckland, Co Durham, DL13 2RB

Tel: 01388 527411
Fax: 01388 526728

Website:
http://www.nemsa.co.uk

Enquiries:
Enquiries to: Secretary
Direct e-mail: info@nemsa.co.uk

Founded:
1980

Organisation type and purpose:
Membership association (membership is by subscription), present number of members: 1024, registered charity.
Breed society, promotional body.

Subject coverage:
The North of England Mule is the top commercial breeding sheep for prime lamb production.

Printed publications:
Mule News (annually)
Sales booklet (annually)
Order printed publications from: http://www.nemsa.co.uk

Electronic and video publications:
Mule Views (video)

Publications list:
Available online

Access to staff:
Contact by letter, by telephone, by fax and by e-mail
Hours: Mon to Fri, 0900 to 1700

NORTH OF ENGLAND ZOOLOGICAL SOCIETY

Formal name: North of England Zoological Society
Acronym or abbreviation: NEZS

Chester Zoo, Caughall Road, Upton by Chester, Chester, Cheshire, CH2 1LH

Tel: 01244 380280
Fax: 01244 371273
E-mail: marketing@chesterzoo.co.uk

Website:
http://www.chesterzoo.org

Enquiries:
Enquiries to: Director

Founded:
1934

Organisation type and purpose:
International organisation, membership association (membership is by subscription), present number of members: 17,000 plus, registered charity (charity number 306077), suitable for ages: all.

Subject coverage:
Zoological.

Library catalogue:
All or part available in-house

Printed publications:
Chester Zoo Life (magazine, quarterly for members)

Electronic and video publications:
Zoo (CD-ROM and videos, also via website or on site shop)

Access to staff:
Contact by letter and by e-mail
Hours: Mon to Fri, 0900 to 1200

Access to building, collection or gallery:
No prior appointment required
Special comments: Access to library, Mon to Fri, 1200 to 1500

Access for disabled people:
Parking provided, ramped entry, toilet facilities
Special comments: Electric scooters and chairs for hire, tactile maps.

Member of:
European Association of Zoos and Aquaria (EAZA)
Federation of Zoological Gardens of Great Britain and Ireland
World Association of Zoos and Aquariums (WAZA)

NORTH SOMERSET COUNCIL

Town Hall, Weston-Super-Mare, Somerset, BS23 1UJ

Tel: 01934 888888
Fax: 01934 888822
E-mail: customer.services@n-somerset.gov.uk

Website:
http://www.n-somerset.gov.uk

Enquiries:
Enquiries to: Marketing and Communications Manager
Direct tel: 01275 888728
Direct e-mail: vanessa.setterington@n-somerset.gov.uk

Founded:
1996

continued overleaf

Organisation type and purpose:
Local government body.

Subject coverage:
Local government services.

NORTH STAFFORDSHIRE CHAMBER OF COMMERCE AND INDUSTRY

Commerce House, Festival Park, Stoke-on-Trent, Staffordshire, ST1 5BE

Tel: 01782 202241
Fax: 01782 274394
E-mail: business@northstaffs.chamber.co.uk

Website:
http://www.northstaffs.chamber.co.uk
Directory of members, diary of activities.

Enquiries:
Enquiries to: Information Services Manager

Founded:
1949

Organisation type and purpose:
Membership association (membership is by subscription), present number of members: 1054. Chamber of Commerce.

Subject coverage:
Business information and advice; importing and exporting advice and documentation; training; translations; UK and international credit checking; trade missions; UK and overseas marketing and sourcing information.

Trade and statistical information:
Product information on the ceramic industry. Trade in North Staffordshire.

Printed publications:
Business Bulletin (free to members)
Focus (business journal, 6 times a year)
North Staffordshire and South Cheshire Industrial and Commercial Directory (annually)
Overseas Bulletin (free to members)

Publications list:
Available online

Access to staff:
Contact by letter, by telephone and by fax. Non-members charged.
Hours: Mon to Fri, 0900 to 1700

Member of:
Association of British Chambers of Commerce

Partner in:
Business Link Staffordshire

NORTH TANDRIDGE LOCAL HISTORY CENTRE

Caterham Valley Library, Stafford Road, Caterham, Surrey, CR3 6JG

Tel: 08456 009009
Fax: 01883 330872
E-mail: libraries@surreycc.gov.uk

Website:
http://www.surreycc.gov.uk/northtandridgelocalhistory

Organisation type and purpose:
A partnership between Surrey Libraries, Surrey History Centre, the Bourne Society, East Surrey Museum and East Surrey Family History Society.

Subject coverage:
Local and family history of the parishes of Caterham, Chaldon, Chelsham, Farleigh, Godstone, Tatsfield, Titsey, Warlingham, Whyteleafe and Woldingham.

Access to building, collection or gallery:
Hours: 1st Tue of the month, 1400 to 1600; 2nd and 4th Sats of the month, 1000 to 1200

NORTH TRAFFORD COLLEGE LIBRARY

Talbot Road, Stretford, Manchester, M32 0XH

Tel: 0161 886 7012
Fax: 0161 872 7921

Enquiries:
Enquiries to: Senior Librarian
Direct e-mail: jim.temple@ntc.ac.uk

Organisation type and purpose:
College of further education.

Subject coverage:
Gas engineering; chemical process engineering; automotive engineering; mechanical, electrical, electronic engineering; computing; business studies; childcare; building services; CAD; health care; music; science; community studies; social care; basic skills; ESOL; business studies; accounting; teacher training; information technology.

Library catalogue:
All or part available in-house

Access to staff:
Access for members only.
Hours: Mon, Thu, 0845 to 1900; Tues, Wed, Fri, 0845 to 1700

NORTH TYNESIDE LIBRARIES

Central Library, Northumberland Square, North Shields, Tyne and Wear, NE30 1QU

Tel: 0191 200 5424
Fax: 0191 200 6118
E-mail: central@ntlib.demon.co.uk

Website:
http://www.northtyneside.gov.uk/libraries

Enquiries:
Enquiries to: Libraries and Information Manager

Founded:
1870

Organisation type and purpose:
Local government body, public library.

Subject coverage:
General and local studies.

Museum or gallery collection, archive, or library special collection:
Edington collection of prints and engravings (7000 items, Northumberland and Tyne and Wear)
British Standards in microform

Printed publications:
And Then We Moved to Royal Quays
Blyth & Tyne Handbook
Cuddling, Ripyard – Shipyard Muddling (The poems of Jack Davitt)
Full Steam Ahead for Tynemouth Station (published in conjunction with Friends of Tynemouth Station)
How Long Did the Ponies Live?
Lambert's Handbook to Tynemouth and the Blyth and Tyne Railway (facsimile of c. 1865 ed)
Last of the Hunters
North Shields (Hollerton E, local studies librarian)
North Shields: second selection
Richardson History of Wallsend (fascimile ed, published in conjunction with Newcastle City Libraries)
Shipyard muddling
Swans of the Tyne (Swan Hunter ships)
Tynemouth in Old Picture Postcards (Hollerton E, local studies librarian)
Wallsend Pit Disaster
Where the Wall Ends
Whitley Bay Historic Trails 1 & 2
Order printed publications from: Publications Department, Wallsend Library
Ferndale Avenue, Wallsend, NE26 7NB, tel: 0191 200 6968, fax: 0191 200 6967

Access to staff:
Contact by letter, by telephone, by fax, by e-mail and in person

Hours: Central Library: Mon and Fri, 0930 to 1730; Tue and Thu, 0930 to 1900; Sat, 0930 to 1700, Wed, 0930 to 1230.
Times vary for other libraries

Other addresses:
Battle Hill Library
Berwick Drive, Battle Hill, Wallsend, Tyne & Wear, NE28 9EF; tel: 0191 200 6976
Coast Road Library
25 Coast Road, North Shields, NE29 7PG; tel: 0191 200 5857
Cullercoats Library
St George's Road, Cullercoats, North Shields, NE30 3JY; tel: 0191 200 8537
Fordley Library
Fern Drive, Dudley, Northumberland, NE23 7AG; tel: 0191 200 8014
Forest Hall Library
Whitfield Road, Forest Hall, Newcastle, NE12 0LJ; tel: 0191 200 7839
Howdon Library
Churchill Street, Howdon, Wallsend, Tyne & Wear, NE28 7TG; tel: 0191 200 6979
Killingworth Library
White Swan Centre, Citadel East, Killingworth, Newcastle, NE12 6SS; tel: 0191 200 8266
Longbenton Library
Black Friars Way, Longbenton, Newcastle, NE12 8SY; tel: 0191 200 7865
Monkseaton Library
Woodleigh Avenue, Monkseaton, Whitley Bay, NE25 8ET; tel: 0191 200 8538
Shiremoor Library
Stanton Road, Shiremoor, Newcastle upon Tyne, NE27 0PW; tel: 0191 200 8539
Tynemouth Library
Front Street, Tynemouth, North Shields, NE30 4DZ; tel: 0191 200 5856
Wallsend Library
Ferndale Avenue, Wallsend, Tyne & Wear, NE28 7NB; tel: 0191 200 6968; fax: 0191 200 6967
Whitley Bay Library
Park Road, Whitley Bay, NE26 1EJ; tel: 0191 200 8500; fax: 0191 200 8536
Wideopen Library
Canterbury Way, Wideopen, Newcastle, NE13 6JJ; tel: 0191 200 7900

Parent body:
North Tyneside Council

NORTH WALES TOURISM

Acronym or abbreviation: NWT

77 Conway Road, Colwyn Bay, Conwy, LL29 7LN

Tel: 01492 531731
Fax: 01492 530059
E-mail: croeso@nwt.co.uk

Website:
http://www.nwt.co.uk
Descriptive information on North Wales, where to visit, where to stay, where to eat and events.

Enquiries:
Enquiries to: Manager
Other contacts: Visitor Services Manager for management and operation of tourist information centre.

Founded:
1991

Organisation type and purpose:
Advisory body, membership association (membership is by subscription), service industry. Private company. Affiliated local government body. Part statutory body.
To promote North Wales as a holiday destination and provide aftercare services through Tourist Information Centres.

Subject coverage:
North Wales tourist attractions, mountains, Snowdonia National park, stately homes, castles, Isle of Anglesey, sailing, golf, pony trekking, cycling and walking. All areas of North Wales and its activities.

Printed publications:
Brochures on marketing areas of North Wales, accommodation and attractions information

Publications list:
Available in print

Access to staff:
Contact by letter, by telephone, by fax, by e-mail and via website
Hours: Mon to Fri, 0900 to 1700

Parent body:
Wales Tourist Board
Brunel House, 2 Fitzallan Road, Cardiff, C72 1UY; tel: 029 2049 9909; fax: 029 2048 5031

Tourist Information Centres:
Bangor
Town Hall, Ffordd Deiniol, Bangor, LL57 7RE; tel: 01248 352786; fax: 01248 362701; e-mail: bangor.tic@gwynedd.gov.uk
Betws-y-Coed
tel: 01690 710426
Caernarfon
Oriel Pendeitsh, Castle Street, Caernarfon, LL55 1SE; tel: 01286 672232; fax: 01285 678209; e-mail: caernarfon.tic@gwynedd.gov.uk
Colwyn Bay
Imperial Building, Princes Drive, Colwyn Bay, LL29 8LF; tel: 01492 530478; fax: 01492 534789; e-mail: colwynbay.tic@virgin.net
Conwy
Conwy Castle Visitor Centre, Conwy, LL32 8LD; tel: 01492 592248; fax: 01492 573545; e-mail: conwy.tic@virgin.net
Holyhead
Stena Line, Terminal 1, Holyhead, LL65 1DQ; tel: 01407 762622; fax: 01407 761462; e-mail: holyhead.tic@virgin.net
Llanberis
41a High Street, Llanberis, LL55 4EH; tel: 01286 870765; fax: 01286 871924; e-mail: llanberis.tic@gwynedd.gov.uk
Llandudno
1–2 Chapel Street, Llandudno, LL30 2YU; tel: 01492 876413; fax: 01492 872722; e-mail: llandudno.tic@virgin.net
Llanfaipwllgwyngyll
Station Site, Llanfaipwllgwyngyll, LL61 5UJ; tel: 01248 713177; fax: 01248 715711; e-mail: llanfaipwll.tic@virgin.net
Llangollen
Town Hall, Castle Street, Llangollen, LL20 5PD; tel: 01978 860828; fax: 01978 861563; e-mail: llangollen.tic@virgin.net
Mold
Library, Museum and Gallery, Earl Road, Mold, CH7 1AP; tel: 01352 759331; fax: 01352 759331; e-mail: mold.tic@virgin.net
Porthmadog
Y Ganolfan, High Street, Porthmadog, LL49 9LP; tel: 01766 512981; fax: 01766 515312; e-mail: porthmadog.tic@gwynedd.gov.uk
Prestatyn
Offa's Dyke Centre, Central Beach, Prestatyn, LL19 7EY; tel: 01745 889092
Pwllheli
Min-y-Don, Station Square, Pwllheli, Gwynedd, LL53 6HE; fax: 01758 701651; e-mail: pwllheli.tic@gwynedd.gov.uk
Rhyl
Children's Village, The Promenade, Rhyl, Denbighshire, LL18 1HZ; tel: 01745 355068; fax: 01745 342255; e-mail: rhyl.tic@denbighshire.gov.uk
Ruthin
Ruthin Craft Centre, Park Road, Ruthin; tel: 01824 703992; fax: 01824 703992
Wrexham
tel: 01978 292015

NORTH WARWICKSHIRE BOROUGH COUNCIL

The Council House, South Street, Atherstone, Warwickshire, CV9 1BD

Tel: 01827 715341
Fax: 01827 719130

E-mail: customerservices@northwarks.gov.uk

Website:
http://www.northwarks.gov.uk
Information on North Warwickshire iand Borough Council services.

Enquiries:
Enquiries to: Chief Executive

Founded:
1974

Organisation type and purpose:
Local government body.

Printed publications:
Best Value Performance Plan
Guide to North Warwickshire
North Talk (residents newsletter, 2 times a year)
North Warwickshire Commercial Property Guide
Tourism leaflet and Accommodation list

Access to staff:
Contact by letter, by telephone, by fax, by e-mail, in person and via website. Appointment necessary. Access for members only.
Hours: Mon to Fri, 0850 to 1715

NORTH WEST EMPLOYERS

Formal name: North Western Local Authorities' Employers' Organisation
Acronym or abbreviation: NWEO

6th Floor, Delphian House, Riverside, New Bailey Street, Manchester, M3 5AP

Tel: 0161 834 9362
Fax: 0161 831 7268
E-mail: mail@nweo.org.uk

Website:
http://www.nweo.org.uk

Enquiries:
Enquiries to: Human Resources Adviser
Other contacts: Learning and Development; Member Development; Human Resources; Local Government

Founded:
1920

Organisation type and purpose:
Local government body, advisory body, training organisation, consultancy.

Subject coverage:
Training, conditions of service, industrial relations, personnel, management.

Printed publications:
see website: http://www.nweo.org.uk

Access to staff:
Contact by letter, by telephone and by e-mail. Appointment necessary.
Hours: Mon to Fri, 0845 to 1645

NORTH WEST FILM ARCHIVE

Acronym or abbreviation: NWFA

Manchester Metropolitan University, Minshull House, 47–49 Chorlton Street, Manchester, M1 3EU

Tel: 0161 247 3097
Fax: 0161 247 3098
E-mail: n.w.filmarchive@mmu.ac.uk

Website:
http://www.nwfa.mmu.ac.uk
General information on the Archive's collection, access services, what's new etc. Online searchable film and video database.

Enquiries:
Enquiries to: Collection Assistant

Founded:
1977

Organisation type and purpose:
University department/ institute.
Public film archive.

Rescuing and ensuring the survival of moving images about the North West of England for the education and enjoyment of the region's people, both today and in the future.

Subject coverage:
North West of England (Greater Manchester, Lancashire, Cheshire, Merseyside, Cumbria): mid-1890s to the present; working life and leisure, traditions, industry, two World Wars, healthcare, housing, transport, professional and amateur material on all gauges.

Museum or gallery collection, archive, or library special collection:
Collection of over 31,500 items dating from pioneer days of film in mid-1890s to contemporary video productions, all relating to life in the North West of England. It includes cinema newsreels, documentaries, advertising and promotional material, educational and travel films, home movies, corporate videos and regional television programmes
Complementary collections of photographs, taped interviews and original documentation relating to North West's film and cinema industries

Non-library collection catalogue:
All or part available online and in-house

Printed publications:
General leaflet on NWFA (free)
The Picture House: a photographic album of North West film and cinema (1988, £6.95)

Electronic and video publications:
A North West Journey: buses, trams and trolleybuses 1927–1935 (video, £19.50)
Manchester Ship Canal Centenary Video (£12.99)
Moving Memories, series of video cassette compilations from 1990 (£14.99)
Primary and Secondary school National Curriculum video resource packs (prices vary)

Publications list:
Available online

Access to staff:
Contact by letter, by telephone, by fax, by e-mail and in person. Appointment necessary.
Hours: Mon to Fri, 0900 to 1700

Access for disabled people:
Parking provided, ramped entry, access to all public areas, toilet facilities

Parent body:
Manchester Metropolitan University Library Service

NORTH WEST KENT FAMILY HISTORY SOCIETY

Acronym or abbreviation: NWKFHS

11 Cliftonville Avenue, Cliftonville, Kent,

E-mail: chairman@nwkfhs.org.uk

Website:
http://www.nwkfhs.org.uk
Details of all aspects of the Society colour photographs of parishes cr churches.

Enquiries:
Enquiries to: Chairman

Founded:
1978

Organisation type and
International organisa
association (memb
present number
charity (charit
To further th
and famil

Subjec
Fami
East
co
Bri

Direct fax: 01724 296343
Direct e-mail: customerservice@northlincs.gov.uk

Founded:
1996

Organisation type and purpose:
Local government body.
Created as a unitary council following abolition of the County of Humberside.
Unitary council responsible for all local government services, including 82 schools, 25,500 pupils and a gross budget (annual) of £315m.

Subject coverage:
Local government.

Library catalogue:
All or part available online

Access to staff:
Contact by letter, by telephone, by fax, by e-mail and in person
Hours: Mon to Thu, 0830 to 1700; Fri, 0830 to 1630

Access to building, collection or gallery:
No prior appointment required

Access for disabled people:
Parking provided, ramped entry, access to all public areas, toilet facilities

NORTH LINCOLNSHIRE LIBRARIES AND INFORMATION SERVICES

North Lincolnshire Central Library, Carlton Street, Scunthorpe, Lincolnshire, DN15 6TX

Tel: 01724 860161
Fax: 01724 860161
E-mail: library.enquiries@northlincs.gov.uk

Website:
http://www.northlincs.gov.uk/library

Enquiries:
Enquiries to: Library and Information Services Manager

Founded:
1996

Organisation type and purpose:
Local government body, statutory body, service industry, public library.

Subject coverage:
General, steel industry, Wesley family, Asian languages.

Museum or gallery collection, archive, or library special collection:
Asian Language Collection

Non-library collection catalogue:
All or part available in-house

Library catalogue:
All or part available in-house

Access to staff:
Contact by letter, by telephone, by fax, by e-mail, in person and via website
Hours: Mon, Wed, 0900 to 1900; Tue, Thu, Fri, 0900 to 1700; Sat, 0900 to 1630

Branches:
14 libraries and two mobile libraries

Parent body:
North Lincolnshire Council

NORTH NORFOLK DISTRICT COUNCIL

Holt Road, Cromer, Norfolk, NR27 9EL

Tel: 01263 513811
Fax: 01263 515042
E-mail: districtcouncil@north-norfolk.gov.uk

Website:
http://www.north-norfolk.gov.uk

Enquiries:
Enquiries to: Communications Manager
Direct tel: 01263 516344

Direct e-mail: media@north-norfolk.gov.uk

Organisation type and purpose:
Local government body.

Subject coverage:
Local government.

Museum or gallery collection, archive, or library special collection:
Library of photographs of North Norfolk

Printed publications:
Brochures, booklets and leaflets available giving tourism, business and other district information

Access to building, collection or gallery:
No prior appointment required

NORTH OF ENGLAND INSTITUTE OF MINING AND MECHANICAL ENGINEERS

Neville Hall, Westgate Road, Newcastle upon Tyne, NE1 1SE

Tel: 0191 232 2201
Fax: 0191 232 2201
E-mail: imm@skynow.net

Enquiries:
Enquiries to: Administrator
Other contacts: Honorary Secretary for qualification queries.

Founded:
1852

Organisation type and purpose:
Learned society, professional body (membership is by subscription), present number of members: 480, registered charity (charity number 220208).

Subject coverage:
Mining and allied subjects: history and technology.

Museum or gallery collection, archive, or library special collection:
A large number of MSS and other collections

Non-library collection catalogue:
All or part available in-house

Library catalogue:
All or part available in-house

Access to staff:
Contact by letter and by telephone. Appointment necessary. Non-members charged.
Hours: Library: to be arranged.

NORTH OF ENGLAND MULE SHEEP ASSOCIATION

Acronym or abbreviation: NEMSA

Eslaforde, Wear View, Frosterley, Bishop Auckland, Co Durham, DL13 2RB

Tel: 01388 527411
Fax: 01388 526728

Website:
http://www.nemsa.co.uk

Enquiries:
Enquiries to: Secretary
Direct e-mail: info@nemsa.co.uk

Founded:
1980

Organisation type and purpose:
Membership association (membership is by subscription), present number of members: 1024, registered charity.
Breed society, promotional body.

Subject coverage:
The North of England Mule is the top commercial breeding sheep for prime lamb production.

Printed publications:
Mule News (annually)
Sales booklet (annually)
Order printed publications from: http://www.nemsa.co.uk

Electronic and video publications:
Mule Views (video)

Publications list:
Available online

Access to staff:
Contact by letter, by telephone, by fax and by e-mail
Hours: Mon to Fri, 0900 to 1700

NORTH OF ENGLAND ZOOLOGICAL SOCIETY

Formal name: North of England Zoological Society
Acronym or abbreviation: NEZS

Chester Zoo, Caughall Road, Upton by Chester, Chester, Cheshire, CH2 1LH

Tel: 01244 380280
Fax: 01244 371273
E-mail: marketing@chesterzoo.co.uk

Website:
http://www.chesterzoo.org

Enquiries:
Enquiries to: Director

Founded:
1934

Organisation type and purpose:
International organisation, membership association (membership is by subscription), present number of members: 17,000 plus, registered charity (charity number 306077), suitable for ages: all.

Subject coverage:
Zoological.

Library catalogue:
All or part available in-house

Printed publications:
Chester Zoo Life (magazine, quarterly for members)

Electronic and video publications:
Zoo (CD-ROM and videos, also via website or on site shop)

Access to staff:
Contact by letter and by e-mail
Hours: Mon to Fri, 0900 to 1200

Access to building, collection or gallery:
No prior appointment required
Special comments: Access to library, Mon to Fri, 1200 to 1500

Access for disabled people:
Parking provided, ramped entry, toilet facilities
Special comments: Electric scooters and chairs for hire, tactile maps.

Member of:
European Association of Zoos and Aquaria (EAZA)
Federation of Zoological Gardens of Great Britain and Ireland
World Association of Zoos and Aquariums (WAZA)

NORTH SOMERSET COUNCIL

Town Hall, Weston-Super-Mare, Somerset, BS23 1UJ

Tel: 01934 888888
Fax: 01934 888822
E-mail: customer.services@n-somerset.gov.uk

Website:
http://www.n-somerset.gov.uk

Enquiries:
Enquiries to: Marketing and Communications Manager
Direct tel: 01275 888728
Direct e-mail: vanessa.setterington@n-somerset.gov.uk

Founded:
1996

continued overleaf

Organisation type and purpose:
Local government body.

Subject coverage:
Local government services.

NORTH STAFFORDSHIRE CHAMBER OF COMMERCE AND INDUSTRY

Commerce House, Festival Park, Stoke-on-Trent, Staffordshire, ST1 5BE

Tel: 01782 202241
Fax: 01782 274394
E-mail: business@northstaffs.chamber.co.uk

Website:
http://www.northstaffs.chamber.co.uk
Directory of members, diary of activities.

Enquiries:
Enquiries to: Information Services Manager

Founded:
1949

Organisation type and purpose:
Membership association (membership is by subscription), present number of members: 1054. Chamber of Commerce.

Subject coverage:
Business information and advice; importing and exporting advice and documentation; training; translations; UK and international credit checking; trade missions; UK and overseas marketing and sourcing information.

Trade and statistical information:
Product information on the ceramic industry. Trade in North Staffordshire.

Printed publications:
Business Bulletin (free to members)
Focus (business journal, 6 times a year)
North Staffordshire and South Cheshire Industrial and Commercial Directory (annually)
Overseas Bulletin (free to members)

Publications list:
Available online

Access to staff:
Contact by letter, by telephone and by fax. Non-members charged.
Hours: Mon to Fri, 0900 to 1700

Member of:
Association of British Chambers of Commerce

Partner in:
Business Link Staffordshire

NORTH TANDRIDGE LOCAL HISTORY CENTRE

Caterham Valley Library, Stafford Road, Caterham, Surrey, CR3 6JG

Tel: 08456 009009
Fax: 01883 330872
E-mail: libraries@surreycc.gov.uk

Website:
http://www.surreycc.gov.uk/
northtandridgelocalhistory

Organisation type and purpose:
A partnership between Surrey Libraries, Surrey History Centre, the Bourne Society, East Surrey Museum and East Surrey Family History Society.

Subject coverage:
Local and family history of the parishes of Caterham, Chaldon, Chelsham, Farleigh, Godstone, Tatsfield, Titsey, Warlingham, Whyteleafe and Woldingham.

Access to building, collection or gallery:
Hours: 1st Tue of the month, 1400 to 1600; 2nd and 4th Sats of the month, 1000 to 1200

NORTH TRAFFORD COLLEGE LIBRARY

Talbot Road, Stretford, Manchester, M32 0XH

Tel: 0161 886 7012
Fax: 0161 872 7921

Enquiries:
Enquiries to: Senior Librarian
Direct e-mail: jim.temple@ntc.ac.uk

Organisation type and purpose:
College of further education.

Subject coverage:
Gas engineering; chemical process engineering; automotive engineering; mechanical, electrical, electronic engineering; computing; business studies; childcare; building services; CAD; health care; music; science; community studies; social care; basic skills; ESOL; business studies; accounting; teacher training; information technology.

Library catalogue:
All or part available in-house

Access to staff:
Access for members only.
Hours: Mon, Thu, 0845 to 1900; Tues, Wed, Fri, 0845 to 1700

NORTH TYNESIDE LIBRARIES

Central Library, Northumberland Square, North Shields, Tyne and Wear, NE30 1QU

Tel: 0191 200 5424
Fax: 0191 200 6118
E-mail: central@ntlib.demon.co.uk

Website:
http://www.northtyneside.gov.uk/libraries

Enquiries:
Enquiries to: Libraries and Information Manager

Founded:
1870

Organisation type and purpose:
Local government body, public library.

Subject coverage:
General and local studies.

Museum or gallery collection, archive, or library special collection:
Edington collection of prints and engravings (7000 items, Northumberland and Tyne and Wear)
British Standards in microform

Printed publications:
And Then We Moved to Royal Quays
Blyth & Tyne Handbook
Cuddling, Ripyard – Shipyard Muddling (The poems of Jack Davitt)
Full Steam Ahead for Tynemouth Station (published in conjunction with Friends of Tynemouth Station)
How Long Did the Ponies Live?
Lambert's Handbook to Tynemouth and the Blyth and Tyne Railway (facsimile of c. 1865 ed)
Last of the Hunters
North Shields (Hollerton E, local studies librarian)
North Shields: second selection
Richardson History of Wallsend (fascimile ed, published in conjunction with Newcastle City Libraries)
Shipyard muddling
Swans of the Tyne (Swan Hunter ships)
Tynemouth in Old Picture Postcards (Hollerton E, local studies librarian)
Wallsend Pit Disaster
Where the Wall Ends
Whitley Bay Historic Trails 1 & 2
Order printed publications from: Publications Department, Wallsend Library
Ferndale Avenue, Wallsend, NE26 7NB, tel: 0191 200 6968, fax: 0191 200 6967

Access to staff:
Contact by letter, by telephone, by fax, by e-mail and in person

Hours: Central Library: Mon and Fri, 0930 to 1730; Tue and Thu, 0930 to 1900; Sat, 0930 to 1700, Wed, 0930 to 1230.
Times vary for other libraries

Other addresses:
Battle Hill Library
Berwick Drive, Battle Hill, Wallsend, Tyne & Wear, NE28 9EF; tel: 0191 200 6976
Coast Road Library
25 Coast Road, North Shields, NE29 7PG; tel: 0191 200 5857
Cullercoats Library
St George's Road, Cullercoats, North Shields, NE30 3JY; tel: 0191 200 8537
Fordley Library
Fern Drive, Dudley, Northumberland, NE23 7AG; tel: 0191 200 8014
Forest Hall Library
Whitfield Road, Forest Hall, Newcastle, NE12 0LJ; tel: 0191 200 7839
Howdon Library
Churchill Street, Howdon, Wallsend, Tyne & Wear, NE28 7TG; tel: 0191 200 6979
Killingworth Library
White Swan Centre, Citadel East, Killingworth, Newcastle, NE12 6SS; tel: 0191 200 8266
Longbenton Library
Black Friars Way, Longbenton, Newcastle, NE12 8SY; tel: 0191 200 7865
Monkseaton Library
Woodleigh Avenue, Monkseaton, Whitley Bay, NE25 8ET; tel: 0191 200 8538
Shiremoor Library
Stanton Road, Shiremoor, Newcastle upon Tyne, NE27 0PW; tel: 0191 200 8539
Tynemouth Library
Front Street, Tynemouth, North Shields, NE30 4DZ; tel: 0191 200 5856
Wallsend Library
Ferndale Avenue, Wallsend, Tyne & Wear, NE28 7NB; tel: 0191 200 6968; fax: 0191 200 6967
Whitley Bay Library
Park Road, Whitley Bay, NE26 1EJ; tel: 0191 200 8500; fax: 0191 200 8536
Wideopen Library
Canterbury Way, Wideopen, Newcastle, NE13 6JJ; tel: 0191 200 7900

Parent body:
North Tyneside Council

NORTH WALES TOURISM

Acronym or abbreviation: NWT

77 Conway Road, Colwyn Bay, Conwy, LL29 7LN

Tel: 01492 531731
Fax: 01492 530059
E-mail: croeso@nwt.co.uk

Website:
http://www.nwt.co.uk
Descriptive information on North Wales, where to visit, where to stay, where to eat and events.

Enquiries:
Enquiries to: Manager
Other contacts: Visitor Services Manager for management and operation of tourist information centre.

Founded:
1991

Organisation type and purpose:
Advisory body, membership association (membership is by subscription), service industry. Private company. Affiliated local government body. Part statutory body.
To promote North Wales as a holiday destination and provide aftercare services through Tourist Information Centres.

Subject coverage:
North Wales tourist attractions, mountains, Snowdonia National park, stately homes, castles, Isle of Anglesey, sailing, golf, pony trekking, cycling and walking. All areas of North Wales and its activities.

Printed publications:
Brochures on marketing areas of North Wales, accommodation and attractions information

Publications list:
Available in print

Access to staff:
Contact by letter, by telephone, by fax, by e-mail and via website
Hours: Mon to Fri, 0900 to 1700

Parent body:
Wales Tourist Board
Brunel House, 2 Fitzallan Road, Cardiff, C72 1UY; tel: 029 2049 9909; fax: 029 2048 5031

Tourist Information Centres:
Bangor
Town Hall, Ffordd Deiniol, Bangor, LL57 7RE; tel: 01248 352786; fax: 01248 362701; e-mail: bangor.tic@gwynedd.gov.uk
Betws-y-Coed
tel: 01690 710426
Caernarfon
Oriel Pendeitsh, Castle Street, Caernarfon, LL55 1SE; tel: 01286 672232; fax: 01285 678209; e-mail: caernarfon.tic@gwynedd.gov.uk
Colwyn Bay
Imperial Building, Princes Drive, Colwyn Bay, LL29 8LF; tel: 01492 530478; fax: 01492 534789; e-mail: colwynbay.tic@virgin.net
Conwy
Conwy Castle Visitor Centre, Conwy, LL32 8LD; tel: 01492 592248; fax: 01492 573545; e-mail: conwy.tic@virgin.net
Holyhead
Stena Line, Terminal 1, Holyhead, LL65 1DQ; tel: 01407 762622; fax: 01407 761462; e-mail: holyhead.tic@virgin.net
Llanberis
41a High Street, Llanberis, LL55 4EH; tel: 01286 870765; fax: 01286 871924; e-mail: llanberis.tic@gwynedd.gov.uk
Llandudno
1–2 Chapel Street, Llandudno, LL30 2YU; tel: 01492 876413; fax: 01492 872722; e-mail: llandudno.tic@virgin.net
Llanfaipwllgwyngyll
Station Site, Llanfaipwllgwyngyll, LL61 5UJ; tel: 01248 713177; fax: 01248 715711; e-mail: llanfaipwll.tic@virgin.net
Llangollen
Town Hall, Castle Street, Llangollen, LL20 5PD; tel: 01978 860828; fax: 01978 861563; e-mail: llangollen.tic@virgin.net
Mold
Library, Museum and Gallery, Earl Road, Mold, CH7 1AP; tel: 01352 759331; fax: 01352 759331; e-mail: mold.tic@virgin.net
Porthmadog
Y Ganolfan, High Street, Porthmadog, LL49 9LP; tel: 01766 512981; fax: 01766 515312; e-mail: porthmadog.tic@gwynedd.gov.uk
Prestatyn
Offa's Dyke Centre, Central Beach, Prestatyn, LL19 7EY; tel: 01745 889092
Pwllheli
Min-y-Don, Station Square, Pwllheli, Gwynedd, LL53 6HE; fax: 01758 701651; e-mail: pwllheli.tic@gwynedd.gov.uk
Rhyl
Children's Village, The Promenade, Rhyl, Denbighshire, LL18 1HZ; tel: 01745 355068; fax: 01745 342255; e-mail: rhyl.tic@denbighshire.gov.uk
Ruthin
Ruthin Craft Centre, Park Road, Ruthin; tel: 01824 703992; fax: 01824 703992
Wrexham
tel: 01978 292015

NORTH WARWICKSHIRE BOROUGH COUNCIL

The Council House, South Street, Atherstone, Warwickshire, CV9 1BD

Tel: 01827 715341
Fax: 01827 719130

E-mail: customerservices@northwarks.gov.uk

Website:
http://www.northwarks.gov.uk
Information on North Warwickshire iand Borough Council services.

Enquiries:
Enquiries to: Chief Executive

Founded:
1974

Organisation type and purpose:
Local government body.

Printed publications:
Best Value Performance Plan
Guide to North Warwickshire
North Talk (residents newsletter, 2 times a year)
North Warwickshire Commercial Property Guide
Tourism leaflet and Accommodation list

Access to staff:
Contact by letter, by telephone, by fax, by e-mail, in person and via website. Appointment necessary. Access for members only.
Hours: Mon to Fri, 0850 to 1715

NORTH WEST EMPLOYERS

Formal name: North Western Local Authorities' Employers' Organisation
Acronym or abbreviation: NWEO

6th Floor, Delphian House, Riverside, New Bailey Street, Manchester, M3 5AP

Tel: 0161 834 9362
Fax: 0161 831 7268
E-mail: mail@nweo.org.uk

Website:
http://www.nweo.org.uk

Enquiries:
Enquiries to: Human Resources Adviser
Other contacts: Learning and Development; Member Development; Human Resources; Local Government

Founded:
1920

Organisation type and purpose:
Local government body, advisory body, training organisation, consultancy.

Subject coverage:
Training, conditions of service, industrial relations, personnel, management.

Printed publications:
see website: http://www.nweo.org.uk

Access to staff:
Contact by letter, by telephone and by e-mail. Appointment necessary.
Hours: Mon to Fri, 0845 to 1645

NORTH WEST FILM ARCHIVE

Acronym or abbreviation: NWFA

Manchester Metropolitan University, Minshull House, 47–49 Chorlton Street, Manchester, M1 3EU

Tel: 0161 247 3097
Fax: 0161 247 3098
E-mail: n.w.filmarchive@mmu.ac.uk

Website:
http://www.nwfa.mmu.ac.uk
General information on the Archive's collection, access services, what's new etc. Online searchable film and video database.

Enquiries:
Enquiries to: Collection Assistant

Founded:
1977

Organisation type and purpose:
University department/ institute.
Public film archive.

Rescuing and ensuring the survival of moving images about the North West of England for the education and enjoyment of the region's people, both today and in the future.

Subject coverage:
North West of England (Greater Manchester, Lancashire, Cheshire, Merseyside, Cumbria): mid-1890s to the present; working life and leisure, traditions, industry, two World Wars, healthcare, housing, transport, professional and amateur material on all gauges.

Museum or gallery collection, archive, or library special collection:
Collection of over 31,500 items dating from pioneer days of film in mid-1890s to contemporary video productions, all relating to life in the North West of England. It includes cinema newsreels, documentaries, advertising and promotional material, educational and travel films, home movies, corporate videos and regional television programmes
Complementary collections of photographs, taped interviews and original documentation relating to North West's film and cinema industries

Non-library collection catalogue:
All or part available online and in-house

Printed publications:
General leaflet on NWFA (free)
The Picture House: a photographic album of North West film and cinema (1988, £6.95)

Electronic and video publications:
A North West Journey: buses, trams and trolleybuses 1927–1935 (video, £19.50)
Manchester Ship Canal Centenary Video (£12.99)
Moving Memories, series of video cassette compilations from 1990 (£14.99)
Primary and Secondary school National Curriculum video resource packs (prices vary)

Publications list:
Available online

Access to staff:
Contact by letter, by telephone, by fax, by e-mail and in person. Appointment necessary.
Hours: Mon to Fri, 0900 to 1700

Access for disabled people:
Parking provided, ramped entry, access to all public areas, toilet facilities

Parent body:
Manchester Metropolitan University Library Service

NORTH WEST KENT FAMILY HISTORY SOCIETY

Acronym or abbreviation: NWKFHS

11 Cliftonville Avenue, Cliftonville, Kent, CT9 2AJ

E-mail: chairman@nwkfhs.org.uk

Website:
http://www.nwkfhs.org.uk
Details of all aspects of the Society. Details and colour photographs of parishes covered and their churches.

Enquiries:
Enquiries to: Chairman

Founded:
1978

Organisation type and purpose:
International organisation, membership association (membership is by subscription), present number of members: 2000, registered charity (charity number 282627R).
To further the education and research in genealogy and family history.

Subject coverage:
Family history in North West Kent and the South East area of London once part of the ancient county of Kent including Dartford, Sevenoaks, Bromley, Bexley.

continued overleaf

Museum or gallery collection, archive, or library special collection:
Library of indexes and other references for North West Kent and South East London area. Held on Microfiche or printed form

Non-library collection catalogue:
All or part available in-house

Library catalogue:
All or part available in-house

Printed publications:
Journal (quarterly, members)
All publications available from the Society are listed with current price and p&p in the journal and on website, these include:
Parish Register transcriptions, monumental inscriptions, indexes to records in Bromley Journal & West Kent Herald, Census indexes
Order printed publications from: NWKFHS
141 Princes Road, Dartford, DA1 3HJ

Microform publications:
Microfiche publications for sale

Electronic and video publications:
Details will be advertised on the website when CD-ROM available

Publications list:
Available online and in print

Access to staff:
Contact by letter, by e-mail and via website
Hours: None

Branches at:
Bromley, Dartford, Sevenoaks, Orpington (Computer)

Member of:
Federation of Family History Societies (FFHS)

Membership Secretary:
North West Kent Family History Society
6 Windermere Road, Bexleyheath, Kent, DA7 6PW

NORTH WEST LEICESTERSHIRE DISTRICT COUNCIL

Acronym or abbreviation: NWLDC

Council Offices, Coalville, Leicester, LE67 3FJ

Tel: 01530 454545
Fax: 01530 454546
E-mail: info@nwleicestershire.gov.uk

Website:
http://www.nwleics.gov.uk
Community information, tourist information, economic development/inward investment, the National Forest.

Enquiries:
Enquiries to: Chief Executive

Founded:
1973

Organisation type and purpose:
Local government body.

Subject coverage:
Local government services.

Printed publications:
Free publications include:
Business Information
District Guide
Street Maps
Tourist Information

Access to staff:
Contact by letter, by telephone, by fax, by e-mail and in person
Hours: Mon to Fri, 0900 to 1700

Access for disabled people:
Parking provided, level entry, toilet facilities

NORTH WEST LONDON HOSPITALS NHS TRUST

John Squire Medical Library, Watford Road, Harrow, Middlesex, HA1 3UJ

Tel: 020 8869 3322 (enquiries)
Fax: 020 8869 3332
E-mail: jslib@clara.net

Website:
http://www.jslib.clara.net

Enquiries:
Enquiries to: Head Librarian

Organisation type and purpose:
Hospital.

Subject coverage:
Clinical, medical and complementary basic sciences, nursing and health service management.

Library catalogue:
All or part available online

Printed publications:
Handlist of current journals (annually)
Library Bulletin (monthly)

Access to staff:
Contact in person
Hours: Mon to Fri, 0900 to 1800

Access to building, collection or gallery:
No prior appointment required
Hours: Mon to Fri, 0900 to 1800
Special comments: Must have bona fide need to access library resources.

Funded by:
Brent, Kensington, Chelsea & Westminster Mental Health NHS Trust
Harrow Primary Care Trust
London Deanery
North West London Hospitals NHS Trust

NORTH WEST SOUND ARCHIVE

c/o The County Archivist, 56 Marshall Street, New Cross, Manchester, M4 5FU

Tel: 0161 832 5284
E-mail: nwsa@ed.lancscc.gov.uk

Website:
http://www.gmcro.co.uk/other/NWSA/nwsa.htm

Founded:
1979

Organisation type and purpose:
Collection located at the Greater Manchester County Record Office. Aims to provide source material for reminiscence therapy, local history, actors, the education sector, journalists and researchers.

Subject coverage:
Sound recordings relating to life in the northwest of England.

Education services:
Education packs for schools.

Museum or gallery collection, archive, or library special collection:
Collection includes:
50,000 recordings from BBC Radio Manchester
2.5 tonnes of 78-rpm gramophone records
Survey of English dialect

NORTH WILTSHIRE DISTRICT COUNCIL

Acronym or abbreviation: NWDC

Monkton Park, Chippenham, Wiltshire, SN15 1ER

Tel: 01249 706111
Fax: 01249 443158

Website:
http://www.northwilts.gov.uk

Enquiries:
Enquiries to: Public Relations Manager
Direct tel: 01249 706618

Direct fax: 01249 654999
Direct e-mail: plangcaster@northwilts.gov.uk
Other contacts: Chief Executive

Founded:
1974

Organisation type and purpose:
Local government body.

Subject coverage:
Services and amenities of the District Council.

Printed publications:
Annual reviews
District and town guides
Economic development plans
Forward strategy

Access to staff:
Contact by letter, by telephone and by fax
Hours: Mon to Thu, 0900 to 1700; Fri, 0900 to 1630

NORTH YORK MOORS NATIONAL PARK AUTHORITY

The Old Vicarage, Bondgate, Helmsley, North Yorkshire, YO62 5BP

Tel: 01439 770657
Fax: 01439 770691
E-mail: info@northyorkmoors-npa.gov.uk

Website:
http://www.moors.uk.net
Tourist information, education, events, plans and policies, press releases, publications, detailed information and work of the Authority.

Enquiries:
Enquiries to: Information Officer

Founded:
1952

Organisation type and purpose:
Local government body.
National Park administration.
To conserve and enhance the natural beauty, wildlife and cultural heritage of the area, and to promote opportunities for the understanding and enjoyment of the special qualities of the area by the public.

Subject coverage:
North York Moors: history, geography, archaeology, agriculture, ecology, planning, tourism, travel.

Printed publications:
Annual Report
Local history books
Plans and reports
The North York Moors Landscape Heritage
Walks and trail guides
Wild Plants and their Habitats in the North York Moors

Publications list:
Available online and in print

Access to staff:
Contact by letter, by telephone, by fax and by e-mail. Appointment necessary.
Hours: Mon to Thu, 0830 to 1700; Fri, 0830 to 1630

Access for disabled people:
Parking provided, level entry, toilet facilities

Member of:
Association of National Park Authorities

NORTH YORKSHIRE COUNTY COUNCIL, LIBRARY AND INFORMATION CENTRE

Victoria Avenue, Harrogate, North Yorkshire, HG1 1EG

Tel: 01423 720300
Fax: 01423 523158
E-mail: harrogate.library@northyorks.gov.uk

Website:
http://www.northyorks.gov.uk/libraries

General information about North Yorkshire County Library, service details, library opening times and locations.

Enquiries:
Enquiries to: Community and Information Officer

Founded:
1887

Organisation type and purpose:
Local government body, public library.

Subject coverage:
General, family history.

Museum or gallery collection, archive, or library special collection:
Illustrated 19th and 20th century English books
Mineral waters: books and pamphlets from 1572, with particular reference to Harrogate from 1626

Parent body:
North Yorkshire County Council, Library and Information Centre
21 Grammar School Lane, Northallerton, DL6 1DF; tel: 01609 767800; fax: 01609 780793

NORTH YORKSHIRE COUNTY COUNCIL, LIBRARY AND INFORMATION SERVICES

21 Grammar School Lane, Northallerton, North Yorkshire, DL6 1DF

Tel: 01609 767800
Fax: 01609 780793
E-mail: libraries@northyorks.gov.uk

Website:
http://www.northyorks.gov.uk/libraries/

Enquiries:
Enquiries to: Assistant Director (Business and Community Services)

Founded:
1974

Organisation type and purpose:
Local government body, public library.

Subject coverage:
General.

Museum or gallery collection, archive, or library special collection:
Bertram Unne Photograph Collection of Yorkshire landscape, people and buildings 1945–1975
Editions of some 210 titles from private presses (at Stokesley)
Illustrated 19th and 20th century English books (at Harrogate)
Mineral waters: books and pamphlets from 1572 with particular reference to Harrogate from 1626 (at Harrogate)
North Yorkshire Census Returns: 1841, 1851, 1861, 1871, 1881 held at local core libraries
Petyt Collection of material on 17th century history and theology (at Skipton)

Non-library collection catalogue:
All or part available in-house

Library catalogue:
All or part available in-house

Department of the:
North Yorkshire County Council

Has:
45 libraries and 12 mobile libraries in the region

NORTH YORKSHIRE COUNTY RECORD OFFICE

Acronym or abbreviation: NYCRO

Malpas Road, Northallerton, North Yorkshire, DL7 8TB

Tel: 01609 777585

Enquiries:
Enquiries to: Archives Development Manager

Organisation type and purpose:
Local government body.
Record office.

Subject coverage:
Manuscript sources relating to North Yorkshire, including historical and geographical subjects.

Printed publications:
Guide no. 1: calendars, transcripts and microfilms in the record office (1992 ed.)
Guide no. 2: parish registers, census returns, land tax assessments, tithe apportionments, enclosure awards in the record office
Guide no. 3: maps and plans – list of North Yorkshire and North Riding maps and plans in the record office
Guide no. 4: enclosure awards in the record office (a detailed list)
Guide no. 5: North Yorkshire parish registers – including dates and whereabouts of parish registers, transcripts, microfilm
Guide no. 6: North Yorkshire gazetteer of townships and parishes
Guide no. 7: list of non-conformist and chapel registers, and of monumental inscriptions in the record office
Guide no. 8: North Yorkshire and North Riding railway plans
Guide no. 9: Mining plans
Guide no. 10: List of architectural plans in the North Yorkshire County Record Office
Histories of places, people, families and organisations within North Yorkshire, as books, reports, surveys and journals; lists of holdings of parish registers, maps, plans etc

Access for disabled people:
Parking provided, level entry, toilet facilities

Parent body:
North Yorkshire County Council

NORTH-EAST CLUB FOR PRE-WAR AUSTINS

Acronym or abbreviation: NECPWA

6 College View, Monkwray, Whitehaven, Cumbria

Tel: 01946 67640
E-mail: john@johnandcarolyn.freeserve.co.uk

Website:
http://www.necpwa.demon.co.uk

Enquiries:
Enquiries to: Honorary Secretary

Founded:
1966

Organisation type and purpose:
Membership association.
Restoration and regular use of historic motor vehicles.

Subject coverage:
The restoration and usage of historic motor vehicles. Members own many different makes of vehicles both pre- and post-war.

Museum or gallery collection, archive, or library special collection:
Club library of obsolete magazines, handbooks, manuals etc

Printed publications:
Newsletter (monthly, members only)

Access to staff:
Contact by letter
Hours: Mon to Fri, 0900 to 1700

NORTHAMPTON BOROUGH COUNCIL

The Guildhall, St Giles Square, Northampton, NN1 1DE

Tel: 01604 838383\ Minicom: 01604 838970
Fax: 01604 838729
E-mail: publicrelations@northampton.gov.uk

Website:
http://www.northampton.gov.uk
Unforgettable Northampton, a visitors guide.

Enquiries:
Enquiries to: Public Relations Manager
Direct tel: 01604 238726
Direct fax: 01604 238780

Organisation type and purpose:
Local government body.

Subject coverage:
Normal range of council subjects, housing, environmental health, planning, highways, council tax, cleansing.

Printed publications:
Bibliographies
Promotional literature on Northampton and its expansion

Access to staff:
Contact by letter, by telephone, by fax and by e-mail. Appointment necessary.
Hours: Mon to Fri, 0900 to 1700

Access for disabled people:
Access to all public areas

Community Services Directorate:
Northampton Borough Council
Westbridge Depot, St James Mill Road, Northampton, NN5 5JW

Development and Environment Directorate:
Northampton Borough Council
Cliftonville House, Bedford Road, Northampton, NN4 7NR

NORTHAMPTONSHIRE INSPECTION AND ADVISORY SERVICE

Acronym or abbreviation: NIAS

PO Box 216, John Dryden House, 8–10 The Lakes, Northampton, NN4 7DD

Tel: 01604 236242
Fax: 01604 236240
E-mail: nias@northamptonshire.gov.uk

Enquiries:
Enquiries to: Chief Education Adviser
Direct e-mail: eadams@northamptonshire.gov.uk

Founded:
1995

Organisation type and purpose:
Local government body, suitable for ages: nursery and 4 to 18, training organisation, consultancy, publishing house.
To provide educational consultancy and training, school inspection and curriculum resources.

Subject coverage:
Specialising in educational consultancy, training, school inspection, curriculum resources.

Printed publications:
NIAS includes in its services the production of a wide range of curriculum products including:
Activity Booklets for KS1 and KS2
Book Study Guides
Picture Packs for KS1 and KS2
Schemes of Work
Science Activities Boxes
Order printed publications from: NIAS Products, Training and Sales
Spencer Centre, Lewis Road, Northampton, NN5 7BJ, tel: 01604 587441, fax: 01604 757799

Electronic and video publications:
Picture Packs for KS2 on CD-ROM (£10)

Publications list:
Available in print

Access to staff:
Contact by letter, by telephone, by fax and by e-mail. Appointment necessary.
Hours: Mon to Fri, 0900 to 1700

Access for disabled people:
Parking provided, level entry, toilet facilities

continued overleaf

Administrative Centres:
NIAS Computer/Audio Visual Centre
  Covington Street, Northampton, NN15JU; tel:
  01604 24190
NIAS Inspection Services
  Cliftonville Middle School, Cliftonville Road,
  Northampton, NN1 5BW; tel: 01604 259876; e-
  mail: niasclif@easymail.rmplc.co.uk
NIAS TPS
  Spencer Centre, Lewis Road, Northampton, NN5
  7BJ; tel: 01604 758758; e-mail: spencer@rtcnias
  .rmplc.co.uk

Professional development centres:
Corby PDC
  Firdale, Cottingham Road, Corby,
  Northamptonshire, NN17 1TD; tel: 01536
  266833; e-mail: corby.north@easymail.rmplc.co
  .uk
Northampton PDC
  Barry Road, Northampton, NN1 5JS; tel: 01604
  30815; e-mail: northampton.north@easymail
  .rmplc.co.uk
Wellingborough PDC
  86 Stanley Road, Wellingborough,
  Northamptonshire, NN8 1DY; tel: 01933 225104;
  e-mail: welling.north@easymail.rmplc.co.uk

NORTHAMPTONSHIRE LIBRARIES AND INFORMATION SERVICE

Acronym or abbreviation: NLIS

PO Box 216, John Dryden House, 8–10 The Lakes,
Northampton, NN4 7DD

Tel: 01604 236236
Fax: 01604 237937
E-mail: nlis@northamptonshire.gov.uk

Website:
http://www.northamptonshire.gov.uk
Public information service including
Northamptonshire, local democracy, people and
places, local facilities, community organisations
and groups.

Organisation type and purpose:
Local government body, public library.

**Museum or gallery collection, archive, or library
special collection:**
Beeby Thompson Collection (geology)
Charles Bradlaugh Collection (local MP, 19th
  century)
H. E. Bates Collection
John Clare Collection (poems, MSs, etc. of local
  poet)
Leather and Footwear Collection
Philip Doddridge Collection (collection of a local
  minister, 18th century; nonconformist church
  history)
Sir Henry Dryden Collection (architectural
  drawings)

Non-library collection catalogue:
All or part available online

Library catalogue:
All or part available online

Printed publications:
Range of greetings cards showing local scenes
Catalogues of some of the special collections
Local history publishing programme of maps,
  prints, books
Waterways of Northamptonshire (D. Blagrove)
Steaming into Northamptonshire (R. Coleman and
  J. Rajczonek, eds)
Philip Doddridge of Northampton (M. Deacon)
The Life and Times of H. E. Bates (P. Eads)
The Life and Times of John Clare (D. Powell)
The Life and Times of J. L. Carr (B. Rogers)

Publications list:
Available online and in print

Access to staff:
Contact by letter, by telephone, by fax, by e-mail
and via website
Hours: Please contact Enquiries

Branches:
in Northampton, Weston Favell, Corby, Kettering,
Wellingborough, Rushden, Daventry, Towcester,
and 28 others

Parent body:
Northamptonshire County Council

NORTHAMPTONSHIRE LIBRARIES AND INFORMATION SERVICE – DAVENTRY LIBRARY

Acronym or abbreviation: NLIS

North Street, Daventry, Northamptonshire, NN11
4GH

Tel: 01327 703130
Fax: 01327 300501
E-mail: davlib@northamptonshire.gov.uk

Enquiries:
Enquiries to: Librarian

Organisation type and purpose:
Local government body, public library.

Subject coverage:
General; local information and local history.

Non-library collection catalogue:
All or part available online, in-house and in print

Library catalogue:
All or part available online

Publications list:
Available in print

Access to staff:
Contact by letter, by telephone, by fax, by e-mail
and in person. Appointment necessary.
Hours: Mon, Thu, Fri, 0900 to 1800; Tue, 0900 to
1900; Wed, 0900 to 1230; Sat, 0930 to 1600

Access for disabled people:
Parking provided, ramped entry, level entry, access
to all public areas, toilet facilities

Parent body:
Northamptonshire Libraries & Information Service
(NLIS)
  tel: 01604 236236; fax: 01604 237937; e-mail: nlis@
  northamptonshire.gov.uk

NORTHAMPTONSHIRE RECORD OFFICE

Acronym or abbreviation: NRO

Wootton Hall Park, Northampton, NN4 8BQ

Tel: 01604 762129
Fax: 01604 767562
E-mail: archivist@northamptonshire.gov.uk

Website:
http://www.northamptonshire.gov.uk
Information leaflet.
Redevelopment in progress.
http://www.a2a.pr.gov.uk
Catalogue for part of the collections.

Enquiries:
Enquiries to: County Archivist

Founded:
1920

Organisation type and purpose:
Local government body.
Record office and archives repository.

Subject coverage:
A great variety of records in different formats are
preserved: charters, court rolls, deeds, parish and
non-conformist registers, maps, letters, diaries,
accounts, minute books, wills, photographs and
films. They include the official, judicial and
administrative records of the county and other
local government authorities, records of the
diocese of Peterborough covering
Northamptonshire, the Soke of Peterborough and
Rutland, probate records for the same area as well
as records of local families and estates, business
and professional firms and societies.

Education services:
Contact Heritage Education Officer.

**Museum or gallery collection, archive, or library
special collection:**
Houses the Library of the Northamptonshire
  Antiquarian Society and other donated specialist
  libraries
Includes records of the former Soke of
  Peterborough

Non-library collection catalogue:
All or part available online

Printed publications:
Information Leaflet for House Historians
General Information Leaflet
Information Leaflet for Genealogists

Microform publications:
Parish Registers for the Diocese of Peterborough
  (microfiche)

Access to staff:
Contact by letter, by telephone, by fax, by e-mail
and in person
Hours: Tue to Wed, 0900 to 1645; Thu, 0900 to 1945;
Fri, 0900 to 1615; 2 Sats each month, 0900 to 12.15

Access to building, collection or gallery:
No prior appointment required

Access for disabled people:
Parking provided, level entry, toilet facilities

Parent body:
Northamptonshire County Council (NCC)

NORTHAMPTONSHIRE RECORD SOCIETY

Wootton Hall Park, Northampton, NN4 8BQ

Tel: 01604 762297

Website:
http://www.northamptonshirerecordsociety.org
.uk/

Enquiries:
Enquiries to: Secretary

Founded:
1920

Organisation type and purpose:
Learned society (membership is by subscription),
registered charity (charity number 204597).
Historical research of all aspects of the ancient
County of Northamptonshire.

Subject coverage:
Local history of Northamptonshire in all its forms.

**Museum or gallery collection, archive, or library
special collection:**
Extensive library, members only, others on request,
  but not for removal from the premises

Library catalogue:
All or part available in-house

Printed publications:
Annual Report
Northamptonshire Past and Present (journal,
  annual, prices vary)
Northamptonshire history series (letters, papers,
  documents etc, but not transcripts of parish
  registers, every 2 years)
Hardbacked volumes (about every 2 years)
Order printed publications from: Secretary

Publications list:
Available in print

Access to staff:
Contact by letter, by telephone and in person.
Access for members only.
Hours: Wed and Thu only, 1000 to 1200 and 1330 to
1630
Special comments: Access to the library normally
Wed and Thu, 1030 to 1630, non-members by prior
appointment.

Access to building, collection or gallery:
No prior appointment required
Hours: Wed and Thu only, 1000 to 1200 and 1330 to 1630

NORTHBROOK COLLEGE, SUSSEX

Littlehampton Road, Worthing, West Sussex, BN12 6NU

Tel: 01903 606060
Fax: 01903 606007

Enquiries:
Enquiries to: Head of Library Services

Organisation type and purpose:
College of further and higher education.

Subject coverage:
Broad range of curriculum topics in further and higher education.

Access to staff:
Contact by letter
Hours: Mon to Fri, 0900 to 1700

Liaison with:
LASER
West Sussex County Library

Member of:
Circle of Sussex College Librarians (COSCOL)
Surrey and Sussex Libraries in Cooperation (SASLIC)

NORTHERN ARC LIMITED

Acronym or abbreviation: NA

Great Western Business Centre, Emlyn Square, Swindon, Wiltshire, SN1 5BP

Tel: 0845 600 9966
E-mail: info@businesslinksw.co.uk

Website:
http://www.businesslinksw.co.uk

Enquiries:
Enquiries to: Information Officer
Direct e-mail: sarah.harris@businesslinksw.co.uk

Founded:
1995

Formerly called:
Business Link Berkshire and Wiltshire (year of change 2007)

Organisation type and purpose:
Training organisation, consultancy.
Single point of contact for local businesses to access advice, information, training and finance.

Subject coverage:
Business advice, business start-up advice, training for business, property information, innovation advice, information on exporting, market intelligence, economic and demographic information for Wiltshire and Berkshire; local business information including company information, market intelligence and funding searches.

Publications list:
Available in print

Access to staff:
Contact by letter, by telephone, by fax, by e-mail, in person and via website
Hours: Mon to Fri, 0900 to 1700
Special comments: Charges made for most services.

Access to building, collection or gallery:
Prior appointment required

Access for disabled people:
Parking provided, ramped entry

Parent body:
GWEBusiness West Ltd
  Great Western Business Centre, Emlyn Square, Swindon, SN1 5BP; tel: 01793 428320; fax: 01793 428345; e-mail: tony.horn@gwebusinesswest.co.uk; website: http://www.gwebusinesswest.co.uk

NORTHERN HAMSTER CLUB

Acronym or abbreviation: NHC

Club Secretary, 1 Richard Avenue, Smithies, Barnsley. S71 1UZ

Tel: 01226 218439
E-mail: enquiries@northernhamsterclub.co.uk

Website:
http://www.northernhamsterclub.com/

Enquiries:
Enquiries to: Membership Secretary

Founded:
1947

Organisation type and purpose:
Membership association (membership is by subscription), present number of members: 90, voluntary organisation, suitable for ages: all.
Promote the keeping, exhibition and breeding of all species of hamster.

Subject coverage:
Keeping, breeding and exhibition of all species of hamster.

Printed publications:
Journal (monthly, free to members, membership fee £10 a year includes £1.50 registration fee, annual renewal £8.50 a year, printed by the National Hamster Council)
Information sheets (free on request, sae required)

Access to staff:
Contact by letter, by telephone, by e-mail and via website
Hours: Mon to Sun, 0900 to 2100

Affiliated to:
National Hamster Council
  PO Box 154, Rotherham, S66 0FL

NORTHERN IRELAND ADVISORY COMMITTEE ON TELECOMMUNICATIONS

Acronym or abbreviation: NIACT

Northern Ireland Chamber of Commerce & Industry, 22 Great Victoria Street, Belfast, BT2 7BA

Tel: 028 9024 4113
Fax: 028 9024 7024
E-mail: niact@acts.org.uk

Website:
http://www.acts.org.uk/niact/default.htm

Enquiries:
Enquiries to: Manager

Founded:
1984

Organisation type and purpose:
Local government body, advisory body.
Northern Ireland representative of Oftel (the UK telecoms regulator).

Subject coverage:
NIACT is the Northern Ireland representative for Oftel – the UK telecommunications regulator. We represent NI consumers on all issues of telecommunications. We publicise issues of concern to NI consumers.

Printed publications:
Annual Report

Electronic and video publications:
Publications list available online

Publications list:
Available online and in print

Access to staff:
Contact by letter, by telephone and by e-mail
Hours: Mon to Thu, 0900 to 1700; Fri, 0900 to 1600

Access for disabled people:
Level entry

NORTHERN IRELAND AGRICULTURAL PRODUCERS' ASSOCIATION

15 Molesworth Street, Cookstown, Co Tyrone, BT80 8NX

Tel: 028 8676 5700
Fax: 028 8675 8598
E-mail: niapa@hotmail.com

Enquiries:
Enquiries to: Information Officer

Founded:
1974

Organisation type and purpose:
Advisory body, membership association (membership is by subscription).
To assist farmers. Farmers representative group, provide farm insurance.

Access to staff:
Contact by letter, by telephone, by fax, by e-mail and in person
Hours: Mon to Fri, 0900 to 1700

NORTHERN IRELAND ASSEMBLY LIBRARY

Parliament Buildings, Stormont, Belfast, BT4 3XX

Tel: 028 9052 1250
Fax: 028 9052 1922
E-mail: issuedesk.library@niassembly.gov.uk

Enquiries:
Enquiries to: Librarian (Resource Team)
Direct e-mail: george.woodman@niassembly.gov.uk

Founded:
1921

Organisation type and purpose:
National government body.
Government library.
To serve staff and members of Northern Ireland Assembly; to act as reference library for Northern Ireland Government Departments.

Subject coverage:
Northern Ireland Parliamentary and Assembly papers, debates and legislation, since 1921; Westminster Parliament Sessional and House of Lords papers and debates; Northern Ireland Departmental papers; Northern Ireland history, politics and government; Irish history; statute law and constitutional law.

Museum or gallery collection, archive, or library special collection:
18th- and 19th-century travel books relating to Ireland
Back runs of Belfast newspapers, Irish Times and Times extending back to at least 1921
Complete set of Hansard dating back to the 1830s
Complete sets of Northern Ireland legislation and very large collection of official publications
Statutes, journals and votes of pre-1800 Irish Parliament

Non-library collection catalogue:
All or part available in-house

Library catalogue:
All or part available in-house

Access to staff:
Contact by letter, by telephone, by fax and by e-mail
Hours: Mon to Fri, 0900 to 1700
Special comments: Access normally limited to members and staff of the NI Assembly and staff of the NI Government Departments.

Access to building, collection or gallery:
Prior appointment required
Hours: Mon to Fri, 0900 to 1700 and when Northern Ireland Assembly is sitting (closes 30 minutes after House rises)

Access for disabled people:
Parking provided, ramped entry, toilet facilities

NORTHERN IRELAND ASSOCIATION OF CITIZENS ADVICE BUREAUX

Acronym or abbreviation: NIACAB

11 Upper Crescent, Belfast, BT7 1NT

Tel: 028 9023 1120
Fax: 028 9023 6522

Website:
http://www.niacab.org
Information on the regional services provided by
CAB, job opportunities, publications, news about
CAB and developments within the organisation,
FAQs, press releases, weekly employment rights
columns and bureaux locations, opening times.

Enquiries:
Enquiries to: Senior Information Officer

Founded:
1974

Organisation type and purpose:
Voluntary organisation, registered charity (charity
number 85136).
To develop networks with other agencies to ensure
that individuals do not suffer through ignorance of
either their rights or of the services available to
them, or through an inability to explain their needs
effectively.

Subject coverage:
General information for CAB workers in Northern
Ireland; social policy background information
based on evidence from CABx.

**Museum or gallery collection, archive, or library
special collection:**
Northern Ireland statutes and statutory rules

Printed publications:
Annual Report
A Debt Handbook for Advisors in Northern
   Ireland (£6 inc. p&p)
Basic Questions About Divorce (£2.50 inc. p&p)
CAB Appeals Guide (£19.50 inc. p&p)
Self Help Guides to Claiming Disability Living
   Allowance and AA
The World of Work Redefined (£4 inc. p&p)
Women and Citizenship by Ruth Lister (£2.50 inc.
   p&p)

Access to staff:
Contact by letter and by telephone
Hours: Mon to Fri, 0900 to 1700

Subsidiary bureaux throughout:
Northern Ireland

NORTHERN IRELAND ATHLETIC FEDERATION

Acronym or abbreviation: NIAF

Athletics House, Old Coach Road, Belfast, BT9 5PR

Tel: 028 9060 2707
Fax: 028 9030 9939
E-mail: info@niathletics.org

Enquiries:
Enquiries to: Administrator

Founded:
1989

Organisation type and purpose:
Governing body of athletics in Northern Ireland.

Subject coverage:
Amateur athletics.

Access to staff:
Contact by letter and by e-mail
Hours: Mon to Fri, 0900 to 1700

Affiliated to:
UK Athletics

NORTHERN IRELAND BANKERS' ASSOCIATION

Acronym or abbreviation: NIBA

Stokes House, 17–25 College Square East, Belfast,
BT1 6DE

Tel: 028 9032 7551
Fax: 028 9033 1449
E-mail: sharon@niba.demon.co.uk

Enquiries:
Enquiries to: Secretary

Founded:
1949

Organisation type and purpose:
Trade association.

Subject coverage:
Banking in Northern Ireland.

Access to staff:
Contact by letter
Hours: Mon to Fri, 0900 to 1700

NORTHERN IRELAND CHILDMINDING ASSOCIATION

Acronym or abbreviation: NICMA

16–18 Mill Street, Newtownards, Co Down, BT23
4LU

Tel: 028 9181 1015
Fax: 028 9182 0921
E-mail: bridget.nodder@nicma.org

Website:
http://www.nicma.org

Enquiries:
Enquiries to: Director

Founded:
1984

Organisation type and purpose:
Membership association (membership is by
subscription, election or invitation), present
number of members: 2500, voluntary organisation,
registered charity (charity number XO 549),
training organisation.
Child care organisation.
To promote the development of children by
providing quality home-based care within
registered settings.

Subject coverage:
All aspects of child care provision.

Printed publications:
Annual Report
Publications include:
Accident and Medication Record Book (to enable
   childminders to fulfil the legal requirements of
   record keeping)
Children Come First
Child Protection – Policy and Procedures (a good
   practice guide for registered childminders)
Negotiating with Parents (a guide for childminders
   and parents when setting fees and drawing up
   contracts)

Publications list:
Available online and in print

Access to staff:
Contact by letter, by telephone, by fax, by e-mail,
in person and via website. Appointment necessary.
Hours: Mon to Fri, 0900 to 1700

Access for disabled people:
Level entry, toilet facilities

NORTHERN IRELAND COMMUNITY RELATIONS COUNCIL

Acronym or abbreviation: CRC

6 Murray Street, Belfast, BT1 6DN

Tel: 028 9022 7500
Fax: 028 9022 7551
E-mail: info@nicrc.org.uk

Website:
http://www.nicrc.org.uk

Enquiries:
Enquiries to: Information Officer

Founded:
1990

Organisation type and purpose:
Advisory body, voluntary organisation, registered
charity (charity number XR 16701), consultancy,
publishing house.

Subject coverage:
Northern Ireland, peace, conflict resolution,
community relations and cultural diversity.

**Museum or gallery collection, archive, or library
special collection:**
Reference library

Library catalogue:
All or part available in-house

Printed publications:
Annual Report, Shared Space (research journal)
   and others, see website
Order printed publications from: Resource Centre
Manager, Community Relations Council, 6 Murray
Street, Belfast, BT1 6DN, e-mail: as above

Publications list:
Available online

Access to staff:
Contact by letter, by telephone, by fax, by e-mail,
in person and via website. Appointment necessary.
Hours: Information Centre: Mon to Thu, 0900 to
1700; Fri, 0900 to 1630

Access to building, collection or gallery:
No prior appointment required

Access for disabled people:
Ramped entry, toilet facilities
Special comments: Elevator to 1st floor. Toilet
facilities on ground floor.

NORTHERN IRELAND COUNCIL FOR VOLUNTARY ACTION

Acronym or abbreviation: NICVA

61 Duncairn Gardens, Belfast, BT15 2GB

Tel: 028 9087 7777\ Minicom no. 028 9087 7776
Fax: 028 9087 7799
E-mail: info@nicva.org

Website:
http://www.nicva.org
http://www.communityni.org
http://www.grant-tracker.org

Enquiries:
Enquiries to: Information Officer
Other contacts: Member Services Manager

Founded:
1938

Organisation type and purpose:
Membership association (membership is by
subscription), present number of members: over
1000, voluntary organisation, registered charity
(charity number XN 47024), training organisation,
research organisation.
Umbrella body for voluntary and community
groups.

Subject coverage:
Social policy, social action, voluntary action,
community development, funding information,
research, charity advice

**Museum or gallery collection, archive, or library
special collection:**
Library (book, grey literature) of more than 5000
   items
Journals and periodicals

Trade and statistical information:
Data on the economic contribution and structure of
   the voluntary and community sector in Northern
   Ireland.

Library catalogue:
All or part available in-house

Printed publications:
State of the Sector IV – Northern Ireland Voluntary
Sector Almanac 2006, SCOPE – social affairs
magazine, NICVA News, eNews

Electronic and video publications:
Grant Tracker (online subscription)

Publications list:
Available online and in print

Access to staff:
Contact by letter, by telephone, by fax, by e-mail
and via website. Appointment necessary.
Hours: Mon to Thu, 0900 to 1700; Fri, 0900 to 1630
Special comments: Some charges made.

Access to building, collection or gallery:
Prior appointment required
Special comments: Prior appointment required for
the library.

Access for disabled people:
Parking provided, ramped entry, level entry, access
to all public areas, toilet facilities

NORTHERN IRELAND
ENVIRONMENT AGENCY

Acronym or abbreviation: NIEA

Klondyke Building, Cromac Avenue, Lower
Ormeau Road, Belfast, BT7 2JA

Tel: 028 9056 9230
Fax: 028 9056 9264
E-mail: nieainfo@doeni.gov.uk

Website:
http://www.ni-environment.gov.uk

Enquiries:
Other contacts: Director of Water Quality, Director
of Natural Heritage, Director of Built Heritage (for
specific research)

Formerly called:
Environment and Heritage Service (year of change
2008)

Organisation type and purpose:
National government body.

Subject coverage:
Built Heritage, Natural Heritage, Environmental
Protection.

Printed publications:
Downloadable online
Order printed publications from: at the same address

Access to staff:
Contact by letter, by telephone, by fax and by e-
mail. Appointment necessary.

Access to building, collection or gallery:
Hours: Mon to Fri, 0900 to 1700

Also at:
Northern Ireland Environment Agency
Water Management Unit, 7 Antrim Road,
Lisburn; tel: 028 9262 3100; e-mail: waterinfo@
doeni.gov.uk
Northern Ireland Environment Agency
Built Heritage, Waterman House, 5–33 Hill
Street, Belfast, BT1 2LA; tel: 028 9023 5000; fax:
028 9054 3111; e-mail: bh@doeni.gov.uk

NORTHERN IRELAND
ENVIRONMENT LINK

Acronym or abbreviation: NIEL

89 Loopland Drive, Belfast, BT6 9DW

Tel: 028 9045 5770
Fax: 028 9094 2151
E-mail: info@nienvironmentlink.org

Website:
http://www.nienvironmentlink.org

Enquiries:
Enquiries to: Director
Other contacts: Communications and Membership
Officer

Founded:
1990

Organisation type and purpose:
Membership association (membership is by
subscription), present number of members: 109,
voluntary organisation, registered charity (charity
number XR 19598).
Umbrella and networking body for voluntary
environmental groups.

Subject coverage:
Environmental issues, conservation, pollution and
countryside management, sustainable
development, waste management, biodiversity,
environmental education. Policy and policy
development.

**Museum or gallery collection, archive, or library
special collection:**
Library of recent government and NGO
publications

Library catalogue:
All or part available in-house

Printed publications:
Case Studies of Environmental Projects
Directory of Environmental Organisations in
Northern Ireland
Environmental Briefing Notes
Environmental Factsheets (3 a year)
Environmental Strategy (out of print)
Lines from the Environmental Educational Forum
(6 times a year)
NIEL News (monthly newsletter)
Policy Priorities for Northern Ireland's
Environment – The Way Ahead

Publications list:
Available online

Access to staff:
Contact by letter, by telephone, by fax, by e-mail,
in person and via website. Appointment necessary.
Hours: Mon to Fri, 0900 to 1700

NORTHERN IRELAND
FEDERATION OF CLUBS

1 Sultan Square, Belfast, BT12 4SU

Tel: 028 9029 5134
Fax: 028 9023 3286
E-mail: info@nifederationofclubs.com

Website:
http://www.nifederationofclubs.com/

Enquiries:
Enquiries to: Executive Secretary
Direct e-mail: info@nifederationofclubs.com

Founded:
1983

Organisation type and purpose:
Advisory body, trade union (membership is by
subscription), present number of members: 301,
service industry, voluntary organisation,
consultancy, research organisation.

Subject coverage:
Information on the N Ireland Registration of Clubs
Order and Accounts Regulations 1996. Private
member clubs, management, contracts of
employment for persons employed in registered
clubs, and general advice.

Printed publications:
Club Review (magazine, 10 times a year, free to
members)
Order printed publications from: Media Marketing
B1.01 Portview Trade Centre, Belfast, BT4 1RX, tel:
028 9045 9864, fax: 028 9045 9034

Access to staff:
Contact by letter, by telephone, by fax, by e-mail
and via website. Appointment necessary.
Hours: Mon to Fri, 0900 to 1700

Access to building, collection or gallery:
Prior appointment required

Access for disabled people:
Access to all public areas, toilet facilities

NORTHERN IRELAND HEALTH
AND SOCIAL SERVICES LIBRARY

Queen's University Medical Library, Mulhouse
Building, Mulhouse Road, Belfast, BT12 6DP

Tel: 028 9063 2504
Fax: 028 9063 5038
E-mail: med.office@qub.ac.uk

Enquiries:
Enquiries to: Information Officer

Founded:
1954

Organisation type and purpose:
University department or institute.
University medical and regional health service
library.

Subject coverage:
Medicine, dentistry, nursing, paramedical subjects,
health organisation and social services.

**Museum or gallery collection, archive, or library
special collection:**
Samuel Simms Collection on the history of
medicine and other historical works
Works by Northern Ireland doctors

Non-library collection catalogue:
All or part available online

Library catalogue:
All or part available online

Access to building, collection or gallery:
No access other than to staff

NORTHERN IRELAND HERITAGE
GARDENS COMMITTEE

Acronym or abbreviation: NIHGC

PO Box 252, Belfast, BT9 6GY

Tel: 028 9066 8817
Fax: 028 9066 6506
E-mail: belindajupp@lineone.net

Enquiries:
Enquiries to: Secretary

Founded:
1980

Organisation type and purpose:
Learned society, voluntary organisation.
Committee is by invitation.
Lobbying body, disseminators of information.

Subject coverage:
Conservation, preservation and research in historic
parks, gardens, plants and demesnes in Ireland.

Printed publications:
Glory of Donard (Nelson E C, 1993)
Daisy Hill Nursery, Newry. A history of 'The Most
Interesting Nursery Probably in the World'
(Nelson EC, 1998)
Northern Gardens; Gardens & Parks of
Outstanding Historic Interest in Northern
Ireland (1982)
Heritage Gardens Inventory (Jupp B, 1992)

Publications list:
Available in print

Access to staff:
Contact by letter, by telephone, by fax and by e-
mail
Hours: Mon to Fri, 0900 to 1700

NORTHERN IRELAND LOCAL
GOVERNMENT ASSOCIATION

Acronym or abbreviation: NILGA

123 York Street, Belfast, BT15 1AB

Tel: 028 9024 9286
Fax: 028 9023 3328

Enquiries:
Enquiries to: Chief Executive

continued overleaf

Founded:
2001

Organisation type and purpose:
Local government body.
An organisation representing the interests of local government in Northern Ireland.

Subject coverage:
The functions and responsibilities of District Councils in Northern Ireland.

Printed publications:
The Councillors' Handbook (Revised ed. 1994, £10)

Access to staff:
Contact by letter and by fax
Hours: Mon to Fri, 0900 to 1700

Member of:
Local Government International Bureau
tel: 020 7664 3100

Representing the British section of:
CEMR
IULA

NORTHERN IRELAND MASTER PLUMBERS' ASSOCIATION

Acronym or abbreviation: NIMPA

38 Hill Street, Belfast, BT1 2LB

Tel: 028 9032 1731
Fax: 028 9024 7521
E-mail: info@crawfordsedgwick.co.uk

Enquiries:
Enquiries to: Secretary

Founded:
1931

Organisation type and purpose:
Trade association.

Subject coverage:
Plumbing and mechanical services.

Access to staff:
Contact by letter, by telephone and by fax
Hours: Mon to Fri, 0900 to 1700

Member of:
Scottish & Northern Ireland Plumbing Employers' Federation
2 Walker Street, Edinburgh, EH3 7LB; tel: 0131 225 2255; fax: 0131 226 7638; e-mail: info@snipef .org; website: http://www.snipef.org

NORTHERN IRELAND OMBUDSMAN

Formal name: Assembly Ombudsman for Northern Ireland/Northern Ireland Commissioner for Complaints

Progressive House, 33 Wellington Place, Belfast, BT1 6HN

Tel: 028 9023 3821 / 0800 343424 freephone
Fax: 028 9023 4912
E-mail: ombudsman@ni-ombudsman.org.uk

Website:
http://www.ni-ombudsman.org.uk
General information about the role of the Ombudsman.

Enquiries:
Enquiries to: Office Manager

Founded:
1969

Organisation type and purpose:
Statutory body.
Ombudsman.

Subject coverage:
Complaints from people who claim to have suffered injustice because of maladministration by government departments and public bodies in Northern Ireland.

Printed publications:
2 explanatory leaflets available free on request

Annual Report available for purchase from HMSO

Publications list:
Available online

Access to staff:
Contact by letter, by telephone, by fax, by e-mail, in person and via website. Appointment necessary.
Hours: Personal callers: Mon to Fri, 0930 to 1600

Access for disabled people:
Level entry, access to all public areas, toilet facilities

NORTHERN IRELAND OPTOMETRIC SOCIETY

Acronym or abbreviation: NIOS

PO Box 28, Dromore, County Down, BT25 1YH, Northern Ireland

Tel: 028 8224 2137
Fax: 028 8224 9330
E-mail: lizgillespie.nios@btopenworld.com

Website:
http://www.nios.org

Enquiries:
Enquiries to: Secretary

Founded:
1952

Organisation type and purpose:
Professional body (membership is by subscription).

Subject coverage:
The NIOS represents the profession of optometry in Northern Ireland. The core activity of the society is to promote high standards of primary eye care, and to enhance further education and learning.

Trade and statistical information:
Data on number of optometrists resident or practising in Northern Ireland.

Access to staff:
Contact by letter
Hours: Mon to Fri, 0900 to 1700

NORTHERN IRELAND POSTAL CHESS ASSOCIATION

27 Cherry Valley Gardens, Belfast, BT5 6PQ

Tel: 028 9059 1142
E-mail: david.blair4@ntlworld.com

Website:
http://www.chessmail.com

Enquiries:
Enquiries to: Honorary Secretary & Treasurer

Founded:
1985

Organisation type and purpose:
Membership association (membership is by subscription).
To organise and play correspondence chess nationally and internationally.

Subject coverage:
Correspondence chess.

Library catalogue:
All or part available online

Electronic and video publications:
Chessmail (CD-ROM, available)
Order electronic and video publications from: Editor, Chessmail
e-mail: editor@chessmail.com

Publications list:
Available online and in print

Access to staff:
Contact by letter and by e-mail
Hours: Mon to Fri, 1700 to 1900; Sat, Sun, 0900 to 1700
Special comments: No phone Mon to Fri, 0900 to 1700.

Affiliated to:
British Postal Chess Federation

NORTHERN IRELAND TEXTILES & APPAREL ASSOCIATION

c/o Riverside Factory, Victoria Street, Lurgan, Craigavon, County Armagh BT67 9DU

Tel: 028 3831 1399
Fax: 028 3832 1816
E-mail: info@nita.co.uk

Enquiries:
Enquiries to: Director

Organisation type and purpose:
Trade association (membership is by subscription), present number of members: 50.

Subject coverage:
Textiles and apparel.

Access to staff:
Contact by letter, by telephone, by fax, by e-mail and in person. Appointment necessary.
Hours: Mon to Fri, 0900 to 1700

Access for disabled people:
Parking provided, level entry, toilet facilities
Special comments: Access to ground floor only.

Member of:
British Apparel and Textile Confederation (BATC)
5 Portland Place, London, W1B 1PW; tel: 020 7636 7788; fax: 020 7636 7515; e-mail: batc@dial .pipex.com

NORTHERN IRELAND TOURIST BOARD

Acronym or abbreviation: NITB

St Anne's Court, 59 North Street, Belfast, BT1 1NB

Tel: 028 9023 1221
Fax: 028 9024 0960
E-mail: info@nitb.com

Website:
http://www.ni-tourism.com
http://www.nitb.com

Enquiries:
Enquiries to: Information Officer
Direct e-mail: lking@nitb.com
Other contacts: (1) Research and Information Librarian (2) Photographic Librarian for (1) reports etc (2) film and transparencies.

Founded:
1948

Organisation type and purpose:
Local government body, statutory body.
National tourist board.

Subject coverage:
Northern Ireland tourism facts and figures, accommodation, transport and sightseeing information, activities and events.

Museum or gallery collection, archive, or library special collection:
Photographic library, 30,000 transparencies for loan and hire, plus videos and slides
Research library (5000 titles) NI and UK tourism statistics, market research, planning, environment, annual reports etc
TIC – booklets, brochures, maps – leaflets on particular places or subjects, some free

Printed publications:
Annual Report (£5)
Booklets, brochures and maps (24 titles, most free)
Illustrated leaflets on particular places (16 titles, free)
Information bulletins on particular subjects (20 titles, free)
Research reports
The Best of Northern Ireland

Access to staff:
Contact by letter, by telephone, by fax, by e-mail, in person and via website. Appointment necessary.

Hours: Mon to Fri, 0900 to 1700
Research Library: Tue, Thu, 0900 to 1700; Wed, 0900 to 1500

NORTHERN IRELAND TRANSPLANT ASSOCIATION

Acronym or abbreviation: NITA

51 Circular Road, Belfast, BT4 2GA

Tel: 028 9076 1394
E-mail: nitransplants@email.com

Website:
http://www.nita.org.uk
Overall view, many personal stories of transplants.

Enquiries:
Enquiries to: Information Officer
Other contacts: Chairman

Founded:
October 1991

Organisation type and purpose:
Membership association (membership is by election or invitation), present number of members: 160, registered charity (charity number XO 19630).
To advise and support those involved with organ transplants, including donor families, and to supply relevant information. To encourage registration of donors and the carrying of organ donor cards.

Subject coverage:
Organ transplantation and donors.

Printed publications:
General leaflets explaining the transplant and donor card programme
Leaflets on personal stories of people who have had transplants
Specialised leaflets on each type of transplant (heart, liver, lung etc)

Electronic and video publications:
Video on various aspects of organ transplantation, lent free to individuals

Access to staff:
Contact by letter, by telephone, by e-mail and via website
Hours: 24-hour telephone answering

NORTHERN IRELAND, WESTERN EDUCATION AND LIBRARY BOARD

Library Headquarters, 1 Spillars Place, Omagh, Co Tyrone, BT78 1HG

Tel: 028 8224 4821
Fax: 028 8224 6716

Website:
http://www.ni-libraries.net

Enquiries:
Enquiries to: Librarian

Organisation type and purpose:
Local government body, statutory body (membership is by election or invitation), present number of members: 21, public library.
Public Library Service; District Libraries at Londonderry, Omagh, Co Tyrone and Enniskillen/County Fermanagh, Limavady and Strabane. Some material for consultation only.

Subject coverage:
Humanities, history, local history, education, business, fine arts and bibliographical.

Museum or gallery collection, archive, or library special collection:
William Carleton Collection
Nawn Collection (local and Irish history)
Local and Irish history
Material on Ireland; Art; Bibliophily
Irish Joint Fiction Reserve (authors A, F and I)

Trade and statistical information:
Regulatory, economic, financial, technical and marketing material.

Non-library collection catalogue:
All or part available online and in-house

Library catalogue:
All or part available online and in print

Printed publications:
Public Service Current Awareness Bulletins

Access to staff:
Contact by letter, by telephone, by fax, by e-mail, in person and via website. Appointment necessary.
Hours: Library HQ and Divisional HQs, Mon to Fri, 0900 to 1715
Branch libraries vary, all are open Tue pm, Fri, and Sat 1000 to 1300; telephone for more precise details

North West Divisional Library:
Northern Ireland, Western Education and Library Board
35 Foyle Street, Londonderry, BT48 6AL; tel: 028 7127 2300; fax: 028 7126 9084

Other libraries:
Castlederg Library
1a Hospital Road, Castlederg, BT81 7BU; tel: 028 8167 1419; fax: 028 8167 9048; e-mail: castlederg.library@ni-libraries.net
Central Library
35 Foyle Street, Londonderry, BT48 6AL; tel: 028 7126 6888; fax: 028 7126 9084
Creggan Library
59 Central Drive, Creggan Estate, Londonderry, BT48 9QH; tel: 028 7126 6168; fax: 028 7130 8939; e-mail: creggan.library@ni-libraries.net
Dungiven Library
74 Main Street, Dungiven, Co Londonderry, BT47 4LD; tel: 028 7174 1475; e-mail: dungiven.library@ni-libraries.net
Enniskillen Library
Halls Lane, Enniskillen, BT74 7DR; tel: 028 6632 2886; fax: 028 8632 4685; e-mail: enniskillen.library@ni-libraries.net
Fintona Library
112–114 Main Street, Fintona, BT78 2BY; tel: 028 8284 1774; fax: 028 8284 1774; e-mail: fintona.library@ni-libraries.net
Irvinestown Library
Main Street, Irvinestown, Co Fermanagh, BT94 1GT; tel: 028 6862 1383; fax: 028 6862 1383; e-mail: irvinestown.library@ni-libraries.net
Limavady Library
5 Connell Street, Limavady, Co Londonderry, BT49 0EA; tel: 028 7776 2540; fax: 028 7772 2006; e-mail: limavady.library@ni-libraries.net
Lisnaskea Library
Drumhaw, Lisnaskea, Co Fermanagh, BT92 0FC; tel: 028 6772 1222; fax: 028 6772 1222; e-mail: lisnaskea.library@ni-libraries.net
Newtownstewart Library
Main Street, Newtownstewart, BT87 4AA; tel: 028 8266 1245; fax: 028 8266 1245; e-mail: newtonstewart.library@ni-libraries.net
Omagh Library
1 Spillars Place, Omagh, BT78 1HL; tel: 028 8224 4821; fax: 028 8224 6722; e-mail: omagh.library@ni-libraries.net
Shantallow Library
92 Racecourse Road, Shantallow, Co Londonderry, BT4 8DA; tel: 028 7135 4185; fax: 028 7135 4122; e-mail: shantallow.library@ni-libraries.net
Sion Mills Library
Church Square, Sion Mills, BT78 9HA; tel: 028 8265 8513; fax: 028 8265 8513; e-mail: sionmills.library@ni-libraries.net
Strabane Library
1 Railway Road, Strabane, BT82 8AN; tel: 028 7188 3686; fax: 028 7138 2745; e-mail: strabane.library@ni-libraries.net
Strathfoyle Library
Claragh Crescent, Strathfoyle, Co Londonderry, BT47 7HQ; tel: 028 7186 0385; fax: 028 7186 0385; e-mail: strathfoyle.library@ni-libraries.net
Waterside Library
23 Glendermott Road, Waterside, Londonderry, BT47 1BG; tel: 028 7134 2963; fax: 028 7131 8283; e-mail: waterside.library@ni-libraries.net

South West Divisional Library:
Northern Ireland, Western Education and Library Board
Halls Lane, Enniskillen, BT74 7DR; tel: 028 6632 2886; fax: 028 6632 4685; e-mail: enniskillen.library@ni-libraries.net

NORTHERN MINE RESEARCH SOCIETY

Acronym or abbreviation: NMRS

Winshaw Barn, Chapel-le-Dale, Ingleton, Yorkshire, LA6 3AT

Tel: 01524 241851
E-mail: sbassham@nildram.co.uk

Website:
http://www.nmrs.co.uk

Enquiries:
Enquiries to: General Enquiries / Publication Sales
Other contacts: Editor, for publishing enquiries; Recorder, for historical requests.

Founded:
1960

Organisation type and purpose:
Learned society (membership is by subscription), present number of members: 400, registered charity (charity number 326704), suitable for ages: 18+, research organisation, publishing house. Researching all aspects of the history of Britain's extractive (mining and quarrying) industries.

Subject coverage:
British mining history, mining technology, past and present mining of minerals in UK, some aspects of University field work.

Museum or gallery collection, archive, or library special collection:
Documents, maps and plans relating to British mines
Indexes of mining sites
Mining history books

Trade and statistical information:
Historical data on the production of materials in Britain.

Non-library collection catalogue:
All or part available online and in-house

Library catalogue:
All or part available in-house

Printed publications:
Four Newsletters for members
Individual Survey Series 1966–1974
Memoirs, 1964–2006
Transactions, 1960–1964
British Mining, 1976-to date (see website)

Publications list:
Available online and in print

Access to staff:
Contact by letter and by e-mail
Hours: Recorder only, by appointment.

Access to building, collection or gallery:
Recorder only, by appointment

Access for disabled people:
Recorder only

Member of:
Association for Industrial Archaeology
Council for British Archaeology Group 4
National Association of Mining History Organisations

NORTHERN REGION FILM AND TELEVISION ARCHIVE

Acronym or abbreviation: NRFTA

School of Arts and Media, University of Teesside, Middlesborough, Tees Valley, TS1 3BA

Tel: 01642 384022
E-mail: enquiries@nrfta.org.uk

continued overleaf

Website:
http://www.nrfta.org.uk

Founded:
1998

Organisation type and purpose:
Public-sector moving image archive serving County Durham, Cumbria, Northumberland, Tees Valley, and Tyne and Wear.

Subject coverage:
Film and television in County Durham, Cumbria, Northumberland, Tees Valley, and Tyne and Wear.

Museum or gallery collection, archive, or library special collection:
important collections include:
BBC Look North collection
Tyne Tees Television collection
Border Television collection
Turners' Film Unit collection
Tyne and Wear Archives Service (TWAS) collection

NORTHUMBERLAND COLLECTIONS SERVICE

Woodhorn Experience, Northumberland Museums and Archives, Queen Elizabeth II Country Park, Ashington, Northumberland, NE63 9YF

Tel: 01670 528080
Fax: 01670 514815
E-mail: collections@woodhorn.org.uk

Website:
www.northumberland.gov.uk/collections/

Enquiries:
Enquiries to: Senior Archivist

Organisation type and purpose:
Local government body.
Archive service.

Subject coverage:
Historic records relating to the county of Northumberland.
Incorporates Northumberland County Archive Service (formerly Northumberland Record Office), Northumberland County Council's Local Studies Collection, and Northumberland County Council's Modern Records Service

Non-library collection catalogue:
All or part available in-house

Printed publications:
Leaflets
Introduction to Record Offices

Publications list:
Available in print

Access to staff:
Contact by letter, by telephone, by fax, by e-mail and in person

Constituent bodies:
Berwick Record Office
Council Offices, Wallace Green, Berwick upon Tweed, Northumberland, TD15 1ED; tel: 01259 330044 ext 230

NORTHUMBERLAND COLLEGE

College Road, Ashington, Northumberland, NE63 9RG

Tel: 01670 814200 ext 240
Fax: 01670 841201
E-mail: fiona.middlemist@northland.ac.uk

Website:
http://www.northland.ac.uk
Description of college; services and courses provided.

Enquiries:
Enquiries to: Librarian

Organisation type and purpose:
Suitable for ages: 16+.
College of further education.

Subject coverage:
General; particular strengths: sociology and social welfare, tourism, electrical and electronic engineering, business and management studies, European Community. Land-based industries: horticulture, aboriculture, conservation, agriculture, animal husbandry, equine studies, small animals.

Library catalogue:
All or part available in-house

Printed publications:
Leaflets including services to staff, services to students, CD-ROMS in stock (free)
Programme area subject guides (free)

Access to staff:
Contact by letter, by telephone, by fax and by e-mail. Appointment necessary.
Hours: Term time: Mon, Tue, Thu, 0900 to 2000; Fri, 0900 to 1630; Wed, 0900 to 1900
Vacations: Mon to Thu, 0900 to 1630; Fri, 0900 to 1600

Access for disabled people:
Parking provided, ramped entry, access to all public areas, toilet facilities

Other location:
Northumberland College At Kirkley Hall
Kirkley Hall, Ponteland, NE20 0AQ; tel: 01670 814200 ext 519; e-mail: malcolm.large@northland.ac.uk

NORTHUMBERLAND COUNTY LIBRARY – COUNTY CENTRAL LIBRARY

Beechfield, Morpeth, Northumberland, NE61 1TA

Tel: 01670 533000
E-mail: libraries@northumberland.gov.uk

Website:
http://www.northumberlandlibraries.com

Enquiries:
Enquiries to: Service Development Manager
Direct tel: 01670 534508
Direct e-mail: infohelp@northumberland.gov.uk

Founded:
1926

Organisation type and purpose:
Public library.

Subject coverage:
General, modern poetry, cinema, Northumberland.

Museum or gallery collection, archive, or library special collection:
Film and cinema
Modern poetry
Northern Poetry Library
Northumberland

Library catalogue:
All or part available online

Printed publications:
A range of books on aspects of the county's history including:
A Howky Gan Te Parliament (A biography of Thomas Burt MP 1837–1922, £1.50)
A Northumbrian Methodist Childhood (£5.95)
England's Border County: A history of Northumberland County Council 1889–1989 (J. M. Taylor, £8.95)
Walks around the old grain ports of Northumberland: Alnmouth, Seahouses and Berwick (T. Barrow, ed., £3.95)

Publications list:
Available in print

Access to staff:
Contact by letter, by telephone, by fax, by e-mail, in person and via website
Hours: Mon to Fri, 0900 to 1930; Sat, 0930 to 1230

Access to building, collection or gallery:
Mon, Tue, Wed, Fri, 0900 to 1930; Sat, 0930 to 1230

Parent body:
Northumberland County Council

NORTHUMBERLAND COUNTY LIBRARY – HEXHAM

Queen's Hall, Beaumont Street, Hexham, Northumberland, NE46 3LS

Tel: 01434 652488
Fax: 01434 652490
E-mail: hexhamlibrary@northumberland.gov.uk

Enquiries:
Enquiries to: Librarian

Organisation type and purpose:
Public library.

Museum or gallery collection, archive, or library special collection:
Census returns, parish registers, newspapers all on microfilm
International Genealogical Index (on microfilm)
The Brough Collection: Local History Sources

Non-library collection catalogue:
All or part available in print

Library catalogue:
All or part available online

Printed publications:
Local Studies: resources for family and local historians in the Brough Local Studies Collection, 4th edn

Access to staff:
Contact by letter, by telephone, by fax, by e-mail and in person
Hours: Mon to Wed, 0930 to 1700; Fri, 0930 to 1930; Sat, 0930 to 1230

Access for disabled people:
Level entry

NORTHUMBERLAND RECORD OFFICE

Melton Park, North Gosforth, Newcastle upon Tyne, NE3 5QX

Tel: 0191 236 2680
Fax: 0191 217 0905
E-mail: archives@northumberland.gov.uk

Website:
http://www.a2a.pro.gov.uk
Many NRO catalogues available on-line.
http://www.swinhope.myby.co.uk/nro/

Enquiries:
Enquiries to: Senior Archivist
Northumberland Record Office

Organisation type and purpose:
Local government body.
Archive service.

Subject coverage:
Historic records relating to the County of Northumberland.

Museum or gallery collection, archive, or library special collection:
Main map collection for the county including enclosure awards, deposited plans, estate maps, tithe awards, ordnance survey maps
Main photographic collection for the county
Family and estate papers
Manorial
Business
Records of the Society of Antiquaries of Newcastle upon Tyne
Records of the North of England Institute of Mining and Mechanical Engineers
Private small collections

Non-library collection catalogue:
All or part available online

Printed publications:
Many guidance leaflets including:
Anglican Parish Registers
Civil Cemetery Records

Enclosure Awards in the Northumberland Record
  Office
Family History Resources for North
  Northumberland
Historic Census Returns for Northumberland
  1841–1891
Historic Maps and Plans
Methodist Registers
Presbyterian and Congregational Registers
Roman Catholic Parish Registers
Trade Directories

Microform publications:
A large number of microfiche copies and
  transcriptions of censuses, registers, monumental
  inscriptions, names in wills, school records,
  directories

Publications list:
Available in print

Access to staff:
Contact by letter, by telephone, by fax and in
person
Hours: Wed, 0930 to 1300, 1400 to 2000; Thu, Fri,
0930 to 1300, 1400 to 1700

Access to building, collection or gallery:
No prior appointment required

Access for disabled people:
Parking provided

Branch office:
Berwick Record Office
  Council Offices, Wallace Green, Berwick upon
  Tweed, Northumberland, TD15 1ED; tel: 01259
  330044 ext 230; fax: 01289 330540; e-mail:
  archives@berwickc.demon.co.uk
Morpeth Records Centre
  The Kylins, Loansdean, Morpeth,
  Northumberland, NE61 2EQ; tel: 01670 504084;
  fax: 01670 514815

NORTHUMBRIA UNIVERSITY – EUROPEAN DOCUMENTATION CENTRE

City Campus Library, Ellison Place, Newcastle
upon Tyne, NE1 8ST

Tel: 0191 243 7704
Fax: 0191 227 4563
E-mail: maimie.balfour@northumbria.ac.uk

Website:
http://www.northumbria.ac.uk/edc

Enquiries:
Enquiries to: Information Specialist

Founded:
1974

Organisation type and purpose:
University library.
To provide a service of EU information in the
northern region of the United Kingdom to all staff
and students internally and in Higher or Further
Education institutions, and external clients.

Subject coverage:
EU legislation, EU policy, EU statistics, official
publications, etc., including information officially
published by all the EC institutions.

**Museum or gallery collection, archive, or library
special collection:**
EU information deposited by the Commission of
the EC

Non-library collection catalogue:
All or part available online

Access to staff:
Contact by letter, by telephone, by fax and by e-
mail. Appointment necessary.
Hours: http://www.northumbria.ac.uk/edc

NORTHUMBRIA UNIVERSITY – UNIVERSITY LIBRARY

Ellison Place, Newcastle upon Tyne, NE1 8ST

Tel: 0191 227 4125
Fax: 0191 227 4563
E-mail: ask4help@northumbria.ac.uk

Website:
http://www.northumbria.ac.uk/sd/central/library
http://librarycat.northumbria.ac.uk/TalisPrism
Web OPAC

Enquiries:
Enquiries to: Director of Library and Learning
Services
Direct tel: 0191 227 4126
Direct e-mail: jane.core@northumbria.ac.uk

Formerly called:
Newcastle Polytechnic (year of change 1992)

Organisation type and purpose:
University Library.

Subject coverage:
Art and design, economics, education, English
literature, geography, government, history, law,
librarianship and information science, modern
languages, nursing, philosophy, politics,
psychology, religion, social welfare, sociology,
accountancy, building, business, chemistry, civil
engineering, electrical and electronic engineering,
industrial design, management, marketing,
materials science, mathematics, mechanical
engineering, statistics, surveying, computing,
physics.

**Museum or gallery collection, archive, or library
special collection:**
Thompson Newspaper Archive
Visual Art UK Archives

Library catalogue:
All or part available online

Printed publications:
Guides to the literature of particular subjects
Research reports
University prospectuses, handbooks, etc.

Access to staff:
Contact by letter, by telephone, by e-mail, in
person and via website
Hours: Term time: Mon to Thu, 0900 to 2100; Fri,
0900 to 1900; Sat, 0930 to 1700; Sun, 1100 to 1700

Access to building, collection or gallery:
Visitors welcome; Northumbria members and
subscribers smartcard to University.
Hours: Term time: 24-hour opening, daily;
vacations: daily, 0800 to 2400
Special comments: Visitors require proof of identity,
incl. photo. No entry without a smartcard outside
staff-supervised hours

Access for disabled people:
Ramped entry, access to all public areas, toilet
facilities

NORTHUMBRIAN PIPERS' SOCIETY

Acronym or abbreviation: NPS

Park House, Lynemouth, Morpeth,
Northumberland, NE61 5XQ

Tel: 01670 860215
E-mail: secretary@northumbrianpipers.org.uk

Website:
http://www.northumbrianpipers.org.uk

Enquiries:
Enquiries to: Honorary Secretary

Founded:
1928

Organisation type and purpose:
Unincorporated Association: voluntary society to
support the playing, making and music of the
Northumbrian pipes

Subject coverage:
Making of the Northumbrian smallpipes and
related technical matters; pipe makers, pipe
players and availability of music and recordings,
materials, etc.; meetings of pipers within and
outside Northumberland.

**Museum or gallery collection, archive, or library
special collection:**
W. A. Cocks Collection of Pipes and Manuscripts,
  held in the Morpeth Chantry Bagpipe Museum

Printed publications:
Magazine (annually)
Members' handbook
Newsletter (quarterly, for members)
Books as listed online
Order printed publications from:
booksales@northumbrianpipers.org.uk

Publications list:
Available in print

Access to staff:
Contact by letter, by telephone, by e-mail, in
person and via website
Hours: By e-mail or phone, any reasonable time.
In person by appointment

Also at:
Morpeth Chantry Bagpipe Museum
  tel: 01670 500717; e-mail: anne.moore@
  castlemorpeth.gov.uk

NORTHWEST DEVELOPMENT AGENCY

Acronym or abbreviation: NWDA

PO Box 37, Renaissance House, Centre Park,
Warrington, Cheshire, WA1 1XB

Tel: 01925 400100
Fax: 01925 400400
E-mail: information@nwda.co.uk

Website:
http://www.nwda.co.uk
Activities, addresses and reports.

Enquiries:
Enquiries to: Director of Marketing

Founded:
1999

Organisation type and purpose:
Local government body, advisory body,
membership association, consultancy.
Regional Development Agency for North West
England with remit of economic and social
development of the region through business
support, inward investment and regeneration.

Subject coverage:
Inward investment into North West England,
economic development of North West England,
regeneration of North West England, and business
support to North West England.

Printed publications:
Annual Report
Brochures on North West England

Electronic and video publications:
Press Releases
Regional Strategy for North West England

Publications list:
Available online

Access to staff:
Contact by letter, by telephone, by fax, by e-mail
and via website. Appointment necessary. Non-
members charged.
Hours: Mon to Fri, 0830 to 1730

Access to building, collection or gallery:
Prior appointment required

Access for disabled people:
Parking provided, level entry, toilet facilities

Links with:
English Partnerships (EP)
  New Town House, Buttermarket Street,
  Warrington, WA1 2LF; tel: 01925 644744

887

continued overleaf

Invest in Britain Bureau (IBB)
 1 Victoria Street, London; tel: 020 7215 5000
North West Regional Assembly
 4th Floor, Loops Business Centre, 11 Dorning
 Street, Wigan, WN1 1HE; tel: 01942 737915

NORTON OWNERS CLUB

Acronym or abbreviation: NOC

Clifton House, 4a Goldington Road, Bedford,
MK40 3NF

Tel: 01234 352672
E-mail: secretary@nortonownersclub.org

Website:
http://www.noc.co.uk

Enquiries:
Enquiries to: Secretary

Founded:
1959

Organisation type and purpose:
International organisation, membership
association (membership is by subscription),
present number of members: 5,000, voluntary
organisation.
To promote an interest in Norton Motorcycles.

Subject coverage:
Technical, historical, model, type information on
Norton Motorcycles.

Non-library collection catalogue:
All or part available in-house

Library catalogue:
All or part available in-house

Printed publications:
Roadholder (magazine, 6 times a year, to
 members)

Electronic and video publications:
Engine and Gearbox Strip (videos / DVD)

Publications list:
Available online and in print

Access to staff:
Contact by letter, by telephone and by e-mail
Hours: Mon to Fri, 0900 to 1700

Access to building, collection or gallery:
No access

NORWEGIAN TRADE COUNCIL

Formal name: Royal Norwegian Embassy, Trade
and Technology Office

Charles House, 5–11 Regent Street, London, SW1Y
4LR

Tel: 020 7389 8800
Fax: 020 7973 0189
E-mail: london@ntc.no

Website:
http://www.ntclondon.com

Enquiries:
Enquiries to: Information Officer

Organisation type and purpose:
National government body.

Subject coverage:
Companies in Norway, export products,
Norwegian companies in UK and Ireland.

**Museum or gallery collection, archive, or library
special collection:**
Norway export brochures

Non-library collection catalogue:
All or part available in-house

Library catalogue:
All or part available in-house

Printed publications:
Publications are free of charge
Norway Export Brochures on:

Aerospace, automotive, building products and
services, space, environmental technology,
fishing gear, furniture, road and traffic
technology, health care, software and multimedia
products, oil and gas technology, defence
products, pleasure boats, power generation,
ships gear, underground facilities, production
technology, giftware, seafood, rock engineering,
concrete and road technology, Norwegian
brands, Norwegian design, aquaculture
technology and equipment

Access to staff:
Contact by letter, by telephone, by fax, by e-mail
and via website
Hours: Mon to Fri, 0900 to 1700

Access to building, collection or gallery:
No access other than to staff

Access for disabled people:
Level entry

NORWICH CITY COLLEGE OF FURTHER EDUCATION

Library, Ipswich Road, Norwich, Norfolk, NR2 2LJ

Tel: 01603 773224
Fax: 01603 760326
E-mail: lrc@ccn.ac.uk

Website:
http://heritage.ccn.ac.uk

Enquiries:
Enquiries to: Learning Resources Manager
Direct tel: 01603 773114

Organisation type and purpose:
College library.

Subject coverage:
Business management, hospitality industry,
science, construction, electrical and mechanical
engineering.

Non-library collection catalogue:
All or part available in-house

Library catalogue:
All or part available online

Printed publications:
Information sheets
Library Guide (annually)

Access for disabled people:
Parking provided, access to all public areas, toilet
facilities

NORWICH CITY COUNCIL

City Hall, Norwich, Norfolk, NR2 1NH

Tel: 01603 622233\ Minicom no. 01603 212059
Fax: 01603 213000

Website:
http://www.norwich.gov.uk

Enquiries:
Enquiries to: Public Relations Manager

Organisation type and purpose:
Local government body.

Access to staff:
Contact by letter, by telephone, by fax and in
person. Appointment necessary.
Hours: Mon to Fri, 0900 to 1700

NORWICH PUPPET THEATRE

Formal name: Norwich Puppet Theatre Trust Ltd
Acronym or abbreviation: NPT

St James's, Whitefriars, Norwich, Norfolk, NR3
1TN

Tel: 01603 615564
Fax: 01603 617578
E-mail: info@puppettheatre.co.uk

Website:
http://www.puppettheatre.co.uk

Enquiries:
Enquiries to: Manager
Other contacts: Marketing Co-ordinator

Founded:
1978

Organisation type and purpose:
Registered charity (charity number 271041).
Theatre.
Puppet theatre with 20-year archive of own
puppets, access to some written references.

Subject coverage:
Puppetry and puppet theatre.

**Museum or gallery collection, archive, or library
special collection:**
Puppets from the last 20 years

Access to staff:
Contact by letter, by telephone, by fax, by e-mail
and in person. Appointment necessary.
Hours: Mon to Fri, 0930 to 1630

Access to building, collection or gallery:
Mon to Fri, performance Sat
Hours: Mon to Fri, 0930 to 1630; other times by
appointment

Access for disabled people:
Level entry, access to all public areas, toilet
facilities

NOTTINGHAM BUSINESS CENTRES

Lenton Boulevard, Nottingham, NG7 2BY

Tel: 0115 955 2107/0115 915 9245
Fax: 0115 955 2108
E-mail: info@nottinghambusinesscentres.co.uk

Website:
http://www.nbtg.co.uk
Information about accommodation available at
each business centre, services provided on site and
full list of companies currently licensing offices and
or workshops.

Enquiries:
Enquiries to: Service Manager

Organisation type and purpose:
Local government body, service industry.
Commercial property provider and business
support.
Provide managed workspace (offices and
workshops) for start-up and expanding small
businesses in Nottingham City area.

Subject coverage:
Commercial property, licensed business
accommodation, managed workspace, business
centres, support for start-up businesses, support
for expanding small businesses, availability of
business premises in Nottingham.

Trade and statistical information:
Data on the cost of business premises.
Data on support available for small businesses in
Nottingham.

Printed publications:
Brochure (available free, by contacting main
 switchboard)

Access to staff:
Contact by letter, by telephone and by fax.
Appointment necessary.
Hours: Mon to Fri, 0830 to 1700

Links with:
Nottingham City Council
 Design & Property Services, Severns House,
 Middle Pavement, Nottingham, NG1 7BW; tel:
 0115 915 5555; fax: 0115 915 8307

Satellite Offices:
Ashforth Business Centre
 Ashforth Street, St Ann's, Nottingham, NG3 4BG;
 tel: 0115 955 2017/0115 915 9245; fax: 0115 955
 2108

Bulwell Business Centre
Sellers Wood Drive, Bulwell, Nottingham, NG6 8GN; tel: 0115 955 2107 (main switchboard); fax: 0115 955 2108
Helston Drive Business Centre

NOTTINGHAM CITY COUNCIL

Corporate Affairs, The Guildhall, Burton Street, Nottingham, NG1 4BT

Tel: 0115 915 5555

Website:
http://www.nottinghamcity.gov.uk

Enquiries:
Enquiries to: Head of Corporate Affairs
Direct tel: 0115 915 4725
Direct fax: 0115 915 4434
Direct e-mail: marie.mcglinchey@nottinghamcity .gov.uk
Other contacts: City Information Centre for Tourist Information Centre, council services.

Founded:
1996

Organisation type and purpose:
Local government body.

Subject coverage:
The City of Nottingham and its council; media relations; corporate marketing; civic affairs.

Printed publications:
The Arrow (Civic newspaper)

Publications list:
Available in print

Access to staff:
Contact by letter, by telephone, by fax, in person and via website
Hours: Mon to Fri, 0900 to 1700

Access for disabled people:
Parking provided, ramped entry, level entry, toilet facilities

Subsidiary body:
City Information Centre
Smithy Row, Nottingham; tel: 0115 915 5330

NOTTINGHAM CITY LIBRARY

Angel Row, Nottingham, NG1 6HP

Tel: 0115 915 2828\ Minicom no. 0115 915 2847
Fax: 0115 915 2840
E-mail: enquiryline@nottinghamcity.gov.uk

Website:
http://www.nottinghamcity.gov.uk/libraries

Enquiries:
Enquiries to: Librarian
Direct tel: 0115 915 2842

Founded:
1868

Organisation type and purpose:
Local government body, public library.

Subject coverage:
Information service offered by five subject libraries: arts, business, leisure, local studies, music.

Museum or gallery collection, archive, or library special collection:
British Standards (CD-ROM)
Byron Collection
D. H. Lawrence Collection
Local Printing Collection
Robin Hood Collection
UK street maps

Library catalogue:
All or part available online

Access to staff:
Contact by letter, by telephone, by fax, by e-mail, in person and via website
Hours: Mon to Fri, 0900 to 1900; Sat, 0900 to 1300

Access for disabled people:
Ramped entry, access to all public areas, toilet facilities

Links with:
Nottinghamshire County Library
Trent Bridge House, Fox Road, West Bridgford, Nottingham, NG2 6BJ; tel: 0115 982 3823; fax: 0115 977 2428

NOTTINGHAM TRENT UNIVERSITY

Libraries and Learning Resources, Boots Library, Goldsmith Street, Nottingham, NG1 5LS

Tel: 0115 848 6434
Fax: 0115 848 4485
E-mail: libweb@ntu.ac.uk

Website:
http://www.ntu.ac.uk/llr
http://opac.ntu.ac.uk
Library online catalogue

Enquiries:
Enquiries to: Administrative Services Manager
Direct tel: 0115 8482775
Direct e-mail: helen.bran@ntu.ac.uk

Organisation type and purpose:
University library.

Subject coverage:
Art and design, humanities, business, law, education, science and technology, social sciences, animal, rural and environmental sciences, architecture, design and the built environment.

Museum or gallery collection, archive, or library special collection:
Lace collection

Trade and statistical information:
Statistics collection (United Kingdom and EC).

Printed publications:
RAM Bulletin (robotics and advanced manufacturing)

Electronic and video publications:
RAM-PC (robotics and advanced manufacturing)

Access to staff:
Contact by letter, by telephone, by fax, by e-mail and in person. Non-members charged.

Access to building, collection or gallery:
Hours: Term time: Mon to Fri, 0830 to 2100; Sat, 0900 to 1700; Sun, 1400 to 1900. Vacations: Mon to Fri, 0830 to 1700; Sat, 1000 to 1400 (closed Sat during August). IT resources rooms open 24 hours.

Also at:
Brackenhurst Campus Library
Nottingham Trent University, Nottingham Road, Southwell, NG25 0QF; tel: 01636 8175249
Clifton Campus Library
Nottingham Trent University, Clifton Lane, Nottingham, NG11 8NS; tel: 0115 848 6612; fax: 0115 848 6304

NOTTINGHAMSHIRE ARCHIVES

County House, Castle Meadow Road, Nottingham, NG2 1AG

Tel: 0115 958 1634 and 950 4524
Fax: 0115 941 3997
E-mail: archives@nottscc.gov.uk

Website:
http://www.nottscc.gov.uk/libraries/archives
General introduction to services.

Enquiries:
Enquiries to: Archivist

Organisation type and purpose:
Local government body.

Subject coverage:
Archives of Nottinghamshire County and Nottingham City, also the Southwell Diocesan Record Office.

Museum or gallery collection, archive, or library special collection:
Local authority records, including County, District and Parish Councils
Public records, including courts and hospitals
Ecclesiastical records, including parish and non-conformist
Family and estate
Business
Societies and organisations

Non-library collection catalogue:
All or part available online and in-house

Library catalogue:
All or part available in-house

Microform publications:
Nottinghamshire Parish Registers upto 1950
Probate records
Electoral registers
Burial registers
Census returns
GRO index, 1837–1965

Publications list:
Available in print

Access to staff:
Contact by letter, by telephone, by fax, by e-mail, in person and via website
Hours: Mon, Wed to Fri, 0900 to 1645; Tue, 0900 to 1915; Sat, 0900 to 1245
Special comments: CARN Readers Ticket required to consult original archives (but not books or microfiche).

Access for disabled people:
Parking provided, level entry, toilet facilities
Special comments: Please ring to book parking space.

NOTTINGHAMSHIRE FAMILY HISTORY SOCIETY

Acronym or abbreviation: NFHS

The Secretary, 9 The R. W. S. Homes, 22 Chestnut Grove, Mapperly Park, Nottingham NG3 5AE

Website:
http://www.nottsfhs.org.uk
Surname lists, membership details, publications, computer searches, Society information.

Enquiries:
Enquiries to: Secretary

Founded:
1971

Organisation type and purpose:
Membership association (membership is by subscription), present number of members: 1800, registered charity (charity number 515898), research organisation.

Subject coverage:
Family history in Nottinghamshire.

Printed publications:
Journal (includes a quarterly update of the publications)
The Records Series (books on a variety of topics such as: rate books, banns registers, alehouse recognisances, Methodist ministers and lay officers etc)
Yesterday's Nottingham (a series of books with old postcards of the various areas with a short piece of information about the picture. The cards are mainly from the turn of the century.)
Order printed publications from: Notts FHS
10 Sherwin Walk, St Anns, Nottingham, NG3 1AH

Microform publications:
1841 Census Nottinghamshire – the complete census transcript has been put on to computer, the index is available on microfiche)
Census Surname Indexes (pre 1841, 1841, 1851, 1861, 1871, 1881, 1891, microfiche)
Marriages Index (Parishes in Phillimore, microfiche)
Marriages Index (Parishes not in Phillimore, microfiche)

continued overleaf

Members' Interests (annually, April 1998, 2 fiche £1
plus 45p p&p)
Nottinghamshire 1813–1837 Marriage Index
(microfiche)
Monumental Inscriptions (a large number of
churches, chapels, cemeteries and burial
grounds, microfiche)
Nottinghamshire Marriages Indexes from
beginning of registers up to 1900 (over 30
parishes, male and female surname indexes both
in alphabetical and chronological order
(microfiche)
Surname Indexes to Nottinghamshire Baptisms
(microfiche)

Electronic and video publications:
CD-ROM versions of some microform products

Publications list:
Available online and in print

Access to staff:
Contact by letter, by e-mail and via website
Hours: Mon to Fri, 0900 to 2100

NOTTINGHAMSHIRE LIBRARIES, ARCHIVES & INFORMATION

Nottinghamshire County Council, Culture &
Community, 4th Floor, County Hall, West
Bridgford, Nottingham, NG2 7QP

Tel: 0115 977 4401
Fax: 0115 977 2807
E-mail: cslibraries@nottscc.gov.uk

Website:
http://www.nottscc.gov.uk/libraries/
County Library services and sites, Education
Library service, Archives service, links to other
sites.

Enquiries:
Enquiries to: Librarian
Direct e-mail: david.lathrope@nottscc.gov.uk
Other contacts: Assistant Director (Libraries,
Archives & Information)

Founded:
1998

Organisation type and purpose:
Local government body, public library.

Subject coverage:
General, local archives.

Non-library collection catalogue:
All or part available online

Library catalogue:
All or part available online and in-house

Printed publications:
Amongst many are:
Lost Houses of Nottinghamshire (£5.99)
Timber-Frame Buildings of Nottinghamshire
(£3.99)
Victorian Lady's Diary 1838–1842 (£5.95)
Viewing the Lifeless Body, A Coroner and his
inquests held In Nottinghamshire Public Houses
during the Nineteenth Century 1828–1866 (£7.95)
Discovering Civil War in Nottinghamshire (£2.95)
Muniment Evidences & Writing, The History of
Archives in Notts (£1)
Newark Civil War & Seigeworks (£3.99)
Newark the Bounty of Beer (£3.99)
Nottinghamshire Country Houses: Past and
Present (£3.95)
Park for All Seasons: History of Wollaton Park
(£3.95)
Robin Hood Country: The County Guide to
Nottinghamshire (£2.95)
Robin Hood and the Lords of Wellow (£4.99)

Publications list:
Available online and in print

Access to staff:
Contact by letter, by telephone, by fax, by e-mail
and in person
Hours: Public Libraries, Core Times: Mon to Fri,
0930 to 1700; Sat, 0900 to 1300

Special comments: County Library Headquarters
Sections at 4th Floor, County Hall, West Bridgford,
Nottingham NG2 7QP, Mon to Fri, 0830 to 1630;
not available on Saturdays.

**County Library Headquarters – Education
Library Service:**
Nottinghamshire County Council
Glaisdale Parkway, Nottingham, NG8 4GP; tel:
0115 985 4200; fax: 0115 928 6400; e-mail: carole
.brittan@nottscc.gov.uk

Other libraries:
Arnold Library
Front Street, Arnold, Nottingham, NG5 7EE; tel:
0115 920 2247; fax: 0115 967 3378; e-mail: Arnold
.library@nottscc.gov.uk
Beeston Library
Foster Avenue, Beeston, Nottingham, NG9 1AE;
tel: 0115 925 5168; fax: 0115 922 0841; e-mail:
beeston.library@nottscc.gov.uk
Mansfield Library
Four Seasons Centre, Westgate, Mansfield,
Nottinghamshire, NG18 1NH; tel: 01623 627591;
fax: 01623 629276; e-mail: Mansfield.library@
nottscc.gov.uk
Newark Library
Beaumond Gardens, Baldertongate, Newark on
Trent, Nottinghamshire, NG24 1UW; tel: 01636
703966; fax: 01636 610045; e-mail: Newark
.library@nottscc.gov.uk
Nottinghamshire Archives
County House, Castle Meadow Road,
Nottingham, NG2 1AG; tel: 0115 950 4524; fax:
0115 941 3997
Retford Library
Churchgate, Retford, Nottinghamshire, DN22
6PE; tel: 01777 708724; fax: 01777 710020

NOTTINGHAMSHIRE LOCAL HISTORY ASSOCIATION

Acronym or abbreviation: NLHA

6 Cornwall Road, Retford, DN22 6SH

Tel: 01777 702475

Enquiries:
Enquiries to: Honorary Secretary
Direct tel: 01623 870515
Other contacts: Membership Secretary for
membership.

Founded:
1960

Organisation type and purpose:
Membership association (membership is by
subscription), present number of members: 250,
voluntary organisation.
Support to history societies, educational institutes,
individuals.

Subject coverage:
Local history of Nottinghamshire.

Printed publications:
Nottinghamshire Historian (2 times a year)
Occasional works on Nottinghamshire local
history
Order printed publications from: The Editor, NLHA
The Notts Historian
30 Repton Road, West Bridgford, Nottinghamshire,
NG2 7EJ, tel: 0115 923 3901

Access to staff:
Contact by letter and by telephone
Hours: Mon to Fri, 0900 to 1700

NSPCC

Formal name: National Society for the Prevention of
Cruelty to Children
Acronym or abbreviation: NSPCC

Weston House, 42 Curtain Road, London, EC2A
3NH

Tel: 020 7825 2500\ (24 hour child protection
helpline: 0808 800 5000)
Fax: 020 7825 2525
E-mail: info@nspcc.org.uk

Website:
http://www.nspcc.org.uk/inform
Free, online, specialised child protection resource
for practitioners, researchers, trainers, policymakers and other professionals working to protect
children.
http://www.nspcc.org.uk
NSPCC homepage

Enquiries:
Enquiries to: NSPCC and ChildLine Public Enquiry
Point
Direct tel: 020 7825 2775
Direct fax: 020 7825 2763
Direct e-mail: info@nspcc.org.uk
Other contacts: Records Manager

Founded:
1884

Organisation type and purpose:
Voluntary organisation, registered charity (charity
number 216401).
Child protection agency.

Subject coverage:
Child protection; child abuse; neglect; domestic
violence; child welfare; family therapy; social
work; prevention; statistics; child development;
positive parenting.

**Museum or gallery collection, archive, or library
special collection:**
Archives and historical material on the NSPCC
dating back to 1884

Library catalogue:
All or part available online

Printed publications:
Annual Report
Full publications list available from Publications
Sales, tel: 020 7825 7422, or see website.
Order printed publications from: NSPCC Publications
tel: 020 7825 7422

Publications list:
Available online and in print

Access to staff:
Contact by letter, by telephone, by e-mail and via
website. Appointment necessary.
Hours: Mon to Fri, 0900 to 1700
Special comments: Library suitable for child
protection practitioners and researchers by
appointment only. Restricted access to some of the
archives.

Access for disabled people:
Parking provided, level entry, toilet facilities

NSU OWNERS CLUB

Acronym or abbreviation: NSUOC

Nutleigh, Rabies Heath Road, Bletchingley, Surrey,
RH1 4LX

Tel: 01883 744431
Fax: 01883 742437
E-mail: nsuoc@btinternet.com

Website:
http://www.nsuoc.co.uk

Enquiries:
Enquiries to: General Secretary

Founded:
1961

Organisation type and purpose:
International organisation, membership
association (membership is by subscription),
present number of members: 170.

Subject coverage:
Technical advice on NSU cars, contact address UK
and overseas, sources of new and used parts.

**Museum or gallery collection, archive, or library
special collection:**
Collection of cards, posters, sales brochures,
videos, photographs
Repair books, parts books for most models

Trade and statistical information:
Product market values.

Printed publications:
Magazine (quarterly)

Access to staff:
Contact by letter, by telephone and by fax.
Appointment necessary.
Hours: Up to 2130

Affiliated to:
NSU Gmbh
Postfach 1144, Neckarsulm, D-7107, Germany

NSU RO80 CLUB GB

Round Barn, Entwistle, Bolton, Lancashire

Tel: 01204 852425

Enquiries:
Enquiries to: Membership Secretary

Founded:
1980

Organisation type and purpose:
Membership association (membership is by
subscription), present number of members: 100.
Club association.

Subject coverage:
NSU, Wankel engine motor car.

Printed publications:
Newsletter (4 times a year, £20)

Publications list:
Available in print

Access to staff:
Contact by letter and by telephone
Hours: Mon to Fri, 0800 to 2130

Access to building, collection or gallery:
No access other than to staff

NUCLEAR INDUSTRY ASSOCIATION

Acronym or abbreviation: NIA

First Floor, Whitehall House, 41 Whitehall,
London, SW1A 2BY

Tel: 020 7766 6640
Fax: 020 7839 4695
E-mail: info@niauk.org

Website:
http://www.niauk.org

Enquiries:
Enquiries to: Chief Executive
Other contacts: Information Officer for information
requests on nuclear power.

Organisation type and purpose:
NIA was established in the early 1960s; it is the
trade association and information and
representative body for the British civil nuclear
industry; it represents over 80 companies including
the operators of the nuclear power stations, those
engaged in decommissioning, waste management,
nuclear liabilities management and all aspects of
the nuclear fuel cycle, nuclear equipment
suppliers, engineering and construction firms;
nuclear research organisations; and legal, financial
and consultancy companies.

Subject coverage:
Nuclear power and its connection with: the
environment, UK business, energy costs, pollution
and waste, energy strategies, nuclear reactors, DTI
and parliament, safety.

Printed publications:
Industry Link (single copies, free)
Nuclear Business Directory (£25)

Access to staff:
Contact by letter, by telephone, by fax, by e-mail
and via website. Appointment necessary.
Hours: Mon to Fri, 0900 to 1700

NUFFIELD COLLEGE LIBRARY

New Road, Oxford, OX1 1NF

Tel: 01865 278550
Fax: 01865 278621
E-mail: library-enquiries@nuffield.ox.ac.uk

Website:
http://www.nuffield.ox.ac.uk/library

Enquiries:
Enquiries to: Librarian
Direct e-mail: librarian@nuffield.ox.ac.uk

Founded:
1937

Organisation type and purpose:
Library of a college of the University of Oxford

Subject coverage:
Social sciences (economics, politics, sociology).

**Museum or gallery collection, archive, or library
special collection:**
G. D. H. Cole Collection
Modern manuscripts (political, social, economic)
William Cobbett Collection
Lord Cherwell Archives

Non-library collection catalogue:
All or part available online

Library catalogue:
All or part available online

Access to staff:
Contact by letter, by telephone, by fax, by e-mail,
in person and via website. Appointment necessary.
Hours: Mon to Fri, 0930 to 1730
Special comments: No information service outside
the University, except for Archives.

NUFFIELD COUNCIL ON BIOETHICS

Acronym or abbreviation: NCOB

28 Bedford Square, London, WC1B 3JS

Tel: 020 7681 9619
Fax: 020 7637 1712
E-mail: bioethics@nuffieldfoundation.org

Website:
http://www.nuffieldfoundation.org/bioethics

Enquiries:
Enquiries to: Director

Founded:
1991

Organisation type and purpose:
Voluntary organisation.
Voluntary council.

Subject coverage:
Ethical questions raised by recent advances in
biological and medical research, home and abroad.

**Museum or gallery collection, archive, or library
special collection:**
Material on bioethics abroad
Press cuttings on bioethics in the UK

Printed publications:
The following publications are available for
purchase, direct:
Animal-to-human transplants: the ethics of
xenotransplantation
Discussion paper on the ethics of clinical research
in developing countries (free)
Genetically Modified Crops: the ethical and social
issues
Genetic Screening: Ethical Issues (out of print)
Human Tissue: Ethical and Legal Issues
Mental Disorders and Genetics: the ethical context
Stem Cell Therapy: the ethical issues (discussion
paper, free)

Publications list:
Available online

Access to staff:
Contact by letter, by fax and by e-mail
Hours: Mon to Fri, 0900 to 1700

Appointed by the:
Trustees of the Nuffield Foundation

NURSING AND MIDWIFERY COUNCIL

Acronym or abbreviation: NMC

23 Portland Place, London, W1B 1PZ

Tel: 020 7637 7181
Fax: 020 7436 2924
E-mail: communications@nmc-uk.org

Website:
http://www.nmc-uk.org

Enquiries:
Enquiries to: Communications Manager

Founded:
2002

Organisation type and purpose:
Registered charity in England (charity number
1091434) and Scotland (charity number SC038362).
Statutory regulatory body.
To safeguard the health and wellbeing of the public
by continually regulating, reviewing and
promoting nursing and midwifery standards.
Aims to uphold the reputation of the professions in
the eyes of the public, government, other
healthcare organisations, and nurses and
midwives themselves.

Subject coverage:
Issues relating to the Council's statutory
responsibilities regarding registration, pre-
registration and post-registration education;
professional conduct of all nurses and midwives
on the Council's register in the United Kingdom.

Printed publications:
An NMC guide for students of nursing and
midwifery
Complaints about unfitness to practise: A guide for
members of the public (also in Welsh)
Good health and good character: Guidance for
students and registrants
Guidance for Continuing Professional
Development for Nurse and Midwife Prescribers
Guidelines for records and record keeping
(currently under review)
Modern supervision in action: a practical guide for
midwives
How to complain about a nurse or midwife (in
Arabic, Bengali, Chinese, Greek, Gujarati, Hindi,
Punjabi, Somali, Turkish, Urdu, Vietnamese
translations)
How to complain about a nurse or midwife in
England
How to complain about a nurse or midwife in
Northern Ireland
How to complain about a nurse or midwife in
Scotland
How to complain about a nurse or midwife in
Wales
Midwives rules and standards
NMC Fitness to practise annual reports
Registering as a nurse or midwife in the United
Kingdom
Reporting lack of competence: A guide for
employers and managers (also in Welsh)
Reporting unfitness to practise: A guide for
employers and managers (also in Welsh)
Standards for medicines management
Standards for the preparation and practice of
supervisors of midwives
Standards for the supervised practice of midwives
Standards of proficiency for nurse and midwife
prescribers
Standards of proficiency for pre-registration
midwifery education (also in Welsh)
Standards of proficiency for pre-registration
nursing education (also in Welsh)
Standards of proficiency for pre-registration
specialist community public health nursing
education (in Welsh)
Standards of proficiency for specialist community
public health nurses
Standards to support learning and assessment in
practice

continued overleaf

The Code: Standards of conduct, performance and
ethics for nurses and midwives (also in Welsh)
The PREP handbook
What to expect from a nurse or midwife who can
prescribe drugs
Order printed publications from: http://nmc-
uk.linney.com/orderpage1.aspx

Publications list:
Available online and in print

Access to staff:
Contact by letter, by telephone, by fax, by e-mail,
in person and via website
Hours: Mon to Fri, 0800 to 1700

Access to building, collection or gallery:
Prior appointment usually required

Access for disabled people:
Ramped entry, toilet facilities

NUTRICIA LIMITED

New Market Avenue, Whitehorse Business Park,
Trowbridge, Wiltshire, BA14 0XQ

Tel: 01225 711677
Fax: 01225 711972

Enquiries:
Enquiries to: Librarian
Direct tel: ext 1731
Direct e-mail: bwilliams@nutricia.co.uk

Organisation type and purpose:
Manufacturing industry.

Subject coverage:
Infant nutrition, general nutrition, food technology
and milk technology.

**Museum or gallery collection, archive, or library
special collection:**
Infant feeding bottles dating back to the early 18th
century

Library catalogue:
All or part available in-house

Printed publications:
Medical information sheets
Product data cards
Teaching aids and films on infant nutrition

Publications list:
Available in print

Access to staff:
Contact by letter and by e-mail
Hours: Tue to Thu, 0900 to 1600

Access to building, collection or gallery:
No access other than to staff

Access for disabled people:
Parking provided, toilet facilities

Subsidiary of:
Nutricia Limited

NUTRITION SOCIETY

Acronym or abbreviation: Nut Soc

Unit 10, Cambridge Court, 210 Shepherds Bush
Road, London, W6 7NJ

Tel: 020 7602 0228
Fax: 020 7602 1756
E-mail: info_officer@nutsoc.org.uk

Website:
http://www.nutritionsociety.org

Enquiries:
Enquiries to: Cheif Executive
Direct e-mail: office@nutsoc.org.uk

Founded:
1941

Organisation type and purpose:
Learned society, registered charity (charity number
272071).

Subject coverage:
Nutrition.

Printed publications:
British Journal of Nutrition
Nutrition Research Reviews
Proceedings of the Nutrition Society
Public Health Nutrition

Publications list:
Available online and in print

Access to staff:
Contact by letter, by telephone, by fax, by e-mail
and via website
Hours: Mon to Fri, 0900 to 1700

Headquarters address:
Nutrition Society
10 Cambridge Court, 210 Shepherds Bush Road,
London, W6 7NJ; tel: 020 7602 0228; fax: 020
7602 1756

OAKLANDS COLLEGE

Smallford Campus, Hatfield Road, St Albans,
Hertfordshire, AL4 0JA

Tel: 01727 737700
Fax: 01727 737752
E-mail: gill.hall@oaklands.ac.uk

Website:
http://colleges.herts.ac.uk
Library catalogue
http://www.oaklands.ac.uk

Enquiries:
Enquiries to: Learning Resources Supervisor
Direct tel: 01727 737716/7

Founded:
1921

Organisation type and purpose:
College learning resources centre.

Subject coverage:
Science and husbandry of British agriculture,
horticulture, floristry, equine studies and small
animal care.

Non-library collection catalogue:
All or part available online

Library catalogue:
All or part available online

Access to staff:
Contact by letter, by telephone, by fax and by e-
mail
Hours: Term time: Mon to Thu, 0900 to 2000; Fri,
0900 to 1600
Vacations: Mon to Thu, 0900 to 1700; Fri, 0900 to
1630

Other sites at:
Oakland College
St Albans City Campus; tel: 01727 737000; fax:
01727 737010
Oakland College
Borehamwood Campus; tel: 01727 737400; fax:
01727 737440
Oakland College
Welwyn Garden City Campus, Welwyn Garden
City; tel: 01707 737500; fax: 01707 737544

OBJECT MANAGEMENT GROUP

Acronym or abbreviation: OMG

Eric Leach Marketing, Sinclair House, The Avenue,
West Ealing, London, W13 8NT

Tel: 020 8758 7587
Fax: 020 8758 7517
E-mail: eric_leach@compuserve.com

Website:
http://www.omg.org
General Information, SIGS and Task Forces,
Membership Information, Technical Document
Listings. Publication list and sales.

Enquiries:
Enquiries to: UK Representative

Founded:
1989

Organisation type and purpose:
Membership association (membership is by
subscription), present number of members: 760.
It is a not-for-profit consortium that produces and
maintains computer industry specifications; eg
CORBA and UML, for interoperable enterprise
applications.

Subject coverage:
The Common Object Request Broker Architecture
(CORBA); object technology; component
technology; Unified Modelling Language (UML);
Modes Driven Architecture (MDA); Meta object
Facility (MOF); Common Warehouse Metamodel
(CWM).

Trade and statistical information:
World data on CORBA and object and component
technology.

Publications list:
Available online

Access to staff:
Contact by letter, by telephone, by fax, by e-mail
and via website
Hours: Mon to Fri, 0930 to 1700

OMG Headquarters:
OMG
First Needham Place, 250 First Avenue, Suite 201,
Needham, MA 02194, USA; tel: 00 1 781 444
0404; fax: 00 1 781 444 0320

OCCUPATIONAL AND
ENVIRONMENTAL DISEASES
ASSOCIATION

Acronym or abbreviation: OEDA

PO Box 26, Enfield, Middlesex, EN1 2NT

Tel: 020 8360 6413

Website:
http://www.oeda.demon.co.uk

Enquiries:
Enquiries to: Director
Direct fax: 020 8360 6413

Founded:
1978

Organisation type and purpose:
Voluntary organisation, registered charity (charity
number 1031036), consultancy, asbestos research
organisation and information resource.
Advice on prevention and information to help
those affected by asbestos.

Subject coverage:
Asbestos-related illnesses including asbestosis,
mesothelioma, pneumoconiosis, pleural plaques,
and asbestos-related lung cancer

**Museum or gallery collection, archive, or library
special collection:**
Early papers on asbestos

Printed publications:
Information Notes
Newsletters
Asbestos Facts
Asbestos Fibres in Lung Tissue (£10)
Asbestos: To Challenge Fibre Counts (£10)
Report to IIAC (£10)

Publications list:
Available in print

Access to staff:
Contact by letter. Appointment necessary.
Hours: Mon to Fri, 0930 to 1700

Access to building, collection or gallery:
Prior appointment required

Access for disabled people:
Special comments: All communications by letter or
phone

OCKENDEN INTERNATIONAL

PO Box 1275, Woking, Surrey GU22 2FT

Tel: 01483 772012
Fax: 01483 750774
E-mail: oi@ockenden.org.uk

Website:
http://www.ockenden.org.uk
General programme.

Enquiries:
Enquiries to: Head of Policy
Direct e-mail: graham.wood@ockenden.org .uk

Founded:
1951

Organisation type and purpose:
International organisation, registered charity
(charity number 1053720).
Assistance to refugees.

Subject coverage:
Support to refugees and displaced people,
primarily overseas but also through reception
services and residential care in the United
Kingdom.

**Museum or gallery collection, archive, or library
special collection:**
Annual Reports of Ockenden Venture's work from
the early 1960s

Printed publications:
Annual Report and Quarterly Newsletter

Electronic and video publications:
Introduction to Ockendon (video)

Access to staff:
Contact by letter, by fax and by e-mail
Hours: Mon to Fri, 0900 to 1730

Access for disabled people:
Parking provided, level entry, toilet facilities

Member agency of the:
British Aid to Afghanistan Group
British Refugee Council
International Consortium for Refugees in Iran

OFCOM

Riverside House, 2a Southwark Bridge Road,
London, SE1 9HA

Tel: 020 7981 3000
Fax: 020 7981 3333

Website:
http://www.ofcom.org.uk
http://www.ofcom.org.uk/consumer_guides/
Comprehensive consumer guides on all aspects of
radio, television, telecommunications and wireless
services.

Enquiries:
Enquiries to: Ofcom Contact Centre
Direct tel: 0845 456 3000\ Textphone: 0845 456 6006
Direct fax: 0845 456 3333
Direct e-mail: contact@ofcom.org.uk

Founded:
2003

Combined from:
Broadcasting Standards Commission, Independent
Television Commission, Oftel, Radio Authority,
Radiocommunications Agency

Organisation type and purpose:
Communications regulator
Responsible for: complaints handling (including
telecommunications, broadcasting content and TV
/ radio interference); general enquiries or queries
regarding licensing spectrum (including fees),
broadcasting or telecommunications; business
radio licensing authorisations; publication requests

Printed publications:
Publications that were created by the original five
regulators will continue to be issued, in some
cases even after the end of 2003. These
publications should be deemed to be Ofcom
approved until such time as they are either
withdrawn or superseded by new Ofcom
publications.

Publications list:
Available online

Access to staff:
Contact by telephone, by fax and by e-mail

OFFA'S DYKE ASSOCIATION

Acronym or abbreviation: ODA

West Street, Knighton, Powys, LD7 1EN

Tel: 01547 528753
E-mail: oda@offasdyke.demon.co.uk

Website:
http://www.offasdyke.demon.co.uk

Enquiries:
Enquiries to: Centre Manager

Founded:
1969

Organisation type and purpose:
Membership association, registered charity
(charity number 503821).
Official tourist information centre.

Subject coverage:
Offa's Dyke as walking route (facilities and
accommodation for walkers), history of Offa and
the Dyke, history of Knighton as tourist centre,
Welsh Border environmental and planning issues.

**Museum or gallery collection, archive, or library
special collection:**
Frank Noble library of books etc on Offa's Dyke
and Welsh Border History

Printed publications:
Newsletter (3 times a year, free to members)
Publications list of numerous titles as well as
charts, maps etc
Strip maps of the Offa's Dyke Path
The ODA Book of Offa's Dyke Path
Where to Stay and Public Transport Guide to Offa's
Dyke Path (revised annually)
Wye Valley Walk
Circular Walks from the Offa's Dyke Path
OD Path South (2007)
OD Path North (2008)
Severn Way

Electronic and video publications:
Tape concerning general information relating to
Association, Dyke and Path can be made
available for sale

Publications list:
Available online and in print

Access to staff:
Contact by letter, by telephone, by fax, by e-mail,
in person and via website
Hours: Easter to end October: daily, 1000 to 1700
End of October to Easter: Mon, Wed, Fri, Sat, 1000
to 1600; Tue, Thu, 1000 to 1700

Access for disabled people:
Parking provided, level entry, access to all public
areas, toilet facilities

Connections with:
Countryside Commission
Countryside Council for Wales
Powys County Council
Wales Tourist Board
Youth Hostels Association

OFFENDER'S TAG ASSOCIATION

Acronym or abbreviation: OTA

128 Kensington Church Street, London, W8 4BH

Tel: 020 7221 7166
Fax: 020 7792 9288
E-mail: ota@stacey-international.co.uk

Website:
http://www.offenderstag.co.uk

Enquiries:
Enquiries to: Director

Founded:
1982

Organisation type and purpose:
Independent organisation.
To promote use of electronic tagging to reduce
offending

Subject coverage:
Penal affairs, electronic monitoring of offenders.

Printed publications:
Publications list available online

Publications list:
Available online and in print

Access to staff:
Contact by letter, by fax and by e-mail
Hours: Mon to Fri, 0900 to 1700

Access to building, collection or gallery:
No prior appointment required

OFFICE FOR NATIONAL STATISTICS

Acronym or abbreviation: ONS

Government Buildings, Cardiff Road, Newport,
NP10 8XG

Tel: 0845 6013034\ Minicom no. 01633 812399
Fax: 01633 652747
E-mail: info@ons.gov.uk

Website:
http://www.statistics.gov.uk

Founded:
1996

Organisation type and purpose:
Government department and agency for the
collection and publication of UK industrial and
economic and social statistics, reports to United
Kingdom Statistics Authority.

Subject coverage:
Statistics on national income, finance, balance of
payments, household expenditure; social statistics;
regional statistics

Trade and statistical information:
Statistics on: manufacturing of specific products,
selected service industries, invisible trade, gross
national product, balance of payments, price
indices, social and regional trends, census and
demographic data, social surveys and social
historical data.

Printed publications:
Annual Abstract of Statistics
Britain: An official handbook
Economic and Labour Market Review
Family Spending
Monthly Digest (with annual supplement)
National Income and Expenditure 'Blue Book'
(annual)
Population Trends (quarterly)
Regional Trends (annual)
Social Trends (annual)
UK Balance of Payments 'Pink Book' (annual)
UK National Accounts
Health Statistics Quarterly
Health in England 1998: Investigating the links
between social inequalities and health costs
Order printed publications from: Palgrave Macmillan
for all ONS Publications

Electronic and video publications:
25 years of Social Trends
Health of Adult Britain
Index to British Place Names
Mortality 1900 to date
PACSTAT

Publications list:
Available online and in print

Access to staff:
Contact by letter, by telephone, by fax, by e-mail
and in person. Appointment necessary.
Hours: Mon to Fri, 0900 to 1700

continued overleaf

Access for disabled people:
Ramped entry; toilet facilities

Also at:
Office for National Statistics
Segensworth Road, Titchfield, Fareham,
Hampshire, PO15 5RR; tel: 0845 601 3034; e-mail: info@ons.gov.uk

OFFICE FOR NATIONAL STATISTICS LIBRARY (LONDON)

Acronym or abbreviation: ONS

1 Drummond Gate, London, SW1V 2QQ

Tel: 0845 6013034\ Minicom no. 01633 812399
Fax: 01633 652747
E-mail: info@statistics.gov.uk

Website:
http://www.statistics.gov.uk
General website address for ONS, descriptions of ONS publications.

Enquiries:
Enquiries to: Librarian

Founded:
1996

Organisation type and purpose:
National government body.

Subject coverage:
Demography, epidemiology, vital registration e.g. births, deaths and marriages, survey methodology, census, economic and financial data, business data, data from the government's statistical service.

Museum or gallery collection, archive, or library special collection:
All published census data from 1801 onwards
Demographic and health statistics 1837 onwards
Government social survey reports 1941 onwards
International statistics, e.g. UN, WHO

Publications list:
Available online

Access to staff:
Contact by letter, by telephone, by fax, by e-mail and in person
Hours: Mon to Fri, 0900 to 1700

Access to building, collection or gallery:
No prior appointment required
Hours: Mon to Fri, 0900 to 1700

Access for disabled people:
Ramped entry, toilet facilities

Branch library:
Segensworth Road
Titchfield, Fareham, Hampshire, PO15 5RR

Other addresses:
Office for National Statistics Library (Newport)
Government Buildings, Cardiff Road, Newport,
Gwent, NP9 1XG; tel: 0845 6013034

OFFICE OF COMMUNICATIONS

Acronym or abbreviation: OFCOM

Riverside House, 2a Southwark Bridge Road,
London SE1 9HA

Tel: 020 7981 3000
Fax: 020 7981 3333

Enquiries:
Enquiries to: Information Officer
Direct e-mail: ofcomnews@ofcom.org.uk

Founded:
1984

Formerly called:
Office of Telecommunications (OFTEL)

Organisation type and purpose:
National government body.
Non-ministerial government department.

Subject coverage:
Telecommunications, information technology, consumer affairs and competition policy.

Museum or gallery collection, archive, or library special collection:
Public register of licences, approved apparatus and approved maintainers of the apparatus (visitors by prior appointment)

Library catalogue:
All or part available in-house

Printed publications:
Annual Reports (available from The Stationery Office only)
Consumer Guides including:
Choosing a telephone company, 2001
Economic Working Papers
How to complain about your telephone service, 2001
Your rights as a telephone user, 2001
What is Oftel? 2001
OFTEL Information Notes and Statements
OFTEL News (quarterly)
Statistical Notes
Technical Publications
Variety of publications including those on:
Telecommunication for Disabled and Elderly People
Statements & Consultative documents
Determinations
Numbering, including: Access Codes for Directory Enquiries Services (2002)
Licensing

Publications list:
Available online and in print

Access to staff:
Contact by letter, by telephone, by fax, by e-mail and via website. Appointment necessary.
Hours: Mon to Fri, 0930 to 1200 and 1400 to 1600
Special comments: Access only allowed by prior appointment.

Parent body:
Department of Trade and Industry – for Library Service

OFFICE OF FAIR TRADING

Acronym or abbreviation: OFT

Fleetbank House, 2–6 Salisbury Square, London,
EC4Y 8JX

Tel: 020 7211 8000
Fax: 020 7211 8800
E-mail: enquiries@oft.gov.uk

Website:
http://www.oft.gov.uk
Summaries of recent reports, consumer information, publications list.

Enquiries:
Enquiries to: Publicity Officer

Founded:
1973

Organisation type and purpose:
National government body.

Subject coverage:
Consumer affairs, consumer credit (including trader guidance), competition policy, monopolies, mergers, restrictive trade practices, anti-competitive practices, estate agency.

Museum or gallery collection, archive, or library special collection:
Consumer Credit Licences public register
Estate Agents Act public register
Restrictive Trading Agreements public register

Non-library collection catalogue:
All or part available online

Printed publications:
Annual Report
Wide range of leaflets, booklets, posters; videos covering consumer topics, competition policy, trader guidance on consumer credit (available free of charge)

Publications list:
Available online and in print

Access to staff:
Contact by letter, by telephone, by fax, by e-mail and via website
Hours: Mon to Fri, 0900 to 1700

Access to building, collection or gallery:
Prior appointment required
Special comments: Access only to public registers by appointment.

Common service ties exist with the:
Department of Trade and Industry

Parliamentary responsibility lies with the:
Secretary of State for Trade and Industry

OFFICE OF GAS AND ELECTRICITY MARKETS

Acronym or abbreviation: Ofgem

9 Millbank, London, SW1P 3GE

Tel: 020 7901 7000
Fax: 020 7901 7066
E-mail: library@ofgem.gov.uk

Website:
http://www.ofgem.gov.uk

Enquiries:
Enquiries to: Librarian
Direct tel: 020 7901 7003
Direct e-mail: keith.smith@ofgem.gov.uk

Founded:
1999

Organisation type and purpose:
National government body, advisory body, statutory body.
Regulatory body.
Independent Government watchdog for the gas and electricity industry.

Subject coverage:
Regulation of the gas and electricity industry.

Museum or gallery collection, archive, or library special collection:
Various journals on the gas, electricity and utility industry

Library catalogue:
All or part available in-house

Printed publications:
Publications include:
Consultation documents and general reports (free)
Order printed publications from: Office of Gas and Electricity Markets, 9 Millbank, London, SW1P 3GE, e-mail: distribution@ofgem.gov.uk

Publications list:
Available online and in print

Access to staff:
Contact by telephone and by e-mail
Hours: Mon to Fri, 1000 to 1630
Special comments: Visitors by appointment only, 24 hours' notice required.

Access to building, collection or gallery:
Prior appointment required
Hours: Library: Mon to Fri, 1400 to 1630

Access for disabled people:
Access to all public areas, toilet facilities

OFFICE OF GOVERNMENT COMMERCE

Acronym or abbreviation: OGC

Rosebery Court, St Andrews Business Park,
Norwich, Norfolk, NR7 0HS

Tel: 0845 000 4999
Fax: 01603 704817

OFFICE OF HEALTH ECONOMICS

Acronym or abbreviation: OHE

12 Whitehall, London, SW1A 2DY

Tel: 020 7930 9203
Fax: 020 7747 1419

Website:
http://www.ohe.org
Mostly publications information.

Enquiries:
Enquiries to: Business Manager
Direct tel: 020 7930 9203 ext 1464
Direct e-mail: myork@ohe.org
Other contacts: (1) Associate Director (2) Secretary
for (1) work of the OHE (2) OHE publications.

Founded:
1962

Organisation type and purpose:
Consultancy, research organisation, publishing
house.

Subject coverage:
Economics of the pharmaceutical industry,
healthcare, health technology, assessment,
biotechnology industry and related public policy
issues.

Trade and statistical information:
Compendium of Health Statistics, providing
statistical data on health and healthcare in the
UK and comparative data with economically
developed nations.
Health Economics Evaluation Database (HEED)
containing approximately 23,500 economic
evaluations, carefully selected for use by health
economists.

Printed publications:
Compendium of Health Statistics
OHE information sheets and briefings
Monographs and briefings on subject areas listed

Electronic and video publications:
HEED – Health Economics Evaluation Database –
available from OHE/IFPMA Database Limited,
phone and fax as for OHE. Monthly CD-ROM
Compendium of Health Statistics (CD-ROM)
Internet version due to be launched 2002

Publications list:
Available online and in print

Access to staff:
Contact by letter, by telephone, by fax, by e-mail
and via website
Hours: Mon to Fri, 0900 to 1700

Access to building, collection or gallery:
Prior appointment required

Access for disabled people:
Ramped entry

Funded by:
Association of the British Pharmaceutical Industry
12 Whitehall, London, SW1A 2DY; tel: 020 7930
3477; fax: 020 7747 1411; e-mail: abpi@abpi.org
.uk

OFFICE OF MANPOWER ECONOMICS

Acronym or abbreviation: OME

6th Floor, Kingsgate House, 66–74 Victoria Street,
London, SW1E 6SW

Tel: 020 7215 8252
Fax: 020 7215 4445

Website:
http://www.ome.uk.com
Information on the Independent Pay Review
Bodies including the Police Negotiating and
Advisory Boards.

Enquiries:
Enquiries to: Information Officer

Founded:
1971

Organisation type and purpose:
Secretariat to the Independent Pay Review Bodies
and Police Boards

Access to staff:
Contact by letter and by telephone
Hours: Mon to Fri, 0900 to 1700

Access for disabled people:
Toilet facilities

OFFICE OF THE CHIEF RABBI

Formal name: Office of the Chief Rabbi of the
United Hebrew Congregations of the
Commonwealth

Adler House, 735 High Road, London, N12 0US

Tel: 020 8343 6301
Fax: 020 8343 6310
E-mail: info@chiefrabbi.org

Website:
http://www.chiefrabbi.org

Enquiries:
Enquiries to: Chief Executive
Other contacts: Director of Communications for
media.

Founded:
1700

Organisation type and purpose:
Religious institution.

Subject coverage:
Judaism.

**Museum or gallery collection, archive, or library
special collection:**
Anglo-Jewish historical archives

Printed publications:
Radical Then, Radial Now – Letter in the Scroll
(American ed., 2001, Harper Collins London)
Celebrating Life (2000, Harper Collins London)
New Revised Edition: Politics of Hope (Vintage,
2000)
Morals and Markets – Institute of Economic Affairs
London 1999 (pamphlet, issued by Institute of
Economic Affairs)
The Politics of Hope (1997, Jonathan Cape,
London)
Christian-Jewish Dialogue (Fry H, Sacks J, 1996,
University of Exeter Press)

Publications list:
Available online and in print

Access to staff:
Contact by letter, by telephone, by fax, by e-mail
and via website. Appointment necessary.
Hours: Mon to Fri, 0900 to 1700

Access to building, collection or gallery:
Prior appointment required

Houses the:
Chief Rabbinate of the British Commonwealth

Other addresses:
Court of The Chief Rabbi

OFFICE OF THE DEPUTY PRIME MINISTER AND DEPARTMENT FOR TRANSPORT

Acronym or abbreviation: ODPM

Library and Information Centre, Ashdown House,
123 Victoria Street, London, SW1E 6DE

Tel: 020 7944 3039
Fax: 020 7944 6098

Website:
http://www.dft.gov.uk
Department for Transport web site
http://www.odpm.gov.uk
Office for the Deputy Prime Minister web site

Enquiries:
Enquiries to: Assistant Librarian
Direct e-mail: enquiryodpm@odpm.gsi.gov.uk

Founded:
2002

Organisation type and purpose:
National government body.

Subject coverage:
Provides an internal service to policy divisions of
the Office for the Deputy Prime Minister and
Department for Transport. Subject areas cover
devolution and the regions, housing,
homelessness, urban policy, planning, local and
regional government, neighbourhood renewal,
social exclusion, rent assessment panels and fire
services. For DfT: railways and aviation, transport
strategy, roads, local transport, maritime.

Non-library collection catalogue:
All or part available in-house

Library catalogue:
All or part available in-house

Printed publications:
Order printed publications from: DETR Free
Literature
PO Box 236, Wetherby, West Yorkshire, LS23 7NB,
tel: 0870 1226 236, fax: 0870 1226 237
Publications Sales Centre
Unit 21, Goldthorpe Industrial Estate, Goldthorpe,
Rotherham, S63 9BL, tel: 01709 891318, fax: 01709
881673

Publications list:
Available online

Access to staff:
Contact by letter, by telephone, by fax, by e-mail
and via website. Appointment necessary.
Hours: Mon to Fri, 0900 to 1700

OFFICE OF THE PARLIAMENTARY AND HEALTH SERVICE OMBUDSMAN

Acronym or abbreviation: PHSO

Millbank Tower, Millbank, London, SW1P 4QP

Tel: 0845 015 4033
Fax: 020 7217 4000
E-mail: phso.enquiries@ombudsman.org.uk

Website:
http://www.ombudsman.org.uk

Enquiries:
Enquiries to: Information Manager
Direct tel: 020 7217 4102/4104
Direct fax: 020 7217 4295
Direct e-mail: library@ombudsman.gsi.gov.uk

Founded:
1967

Organisation type and purpose:
Statutory body.
Investigation of complaints by members of the
public who have suffered injustice through
maladministration by government departments or
certain public bodies, or the National Health
Service.

Subject coverage:
Ombudsman schemes.

Printed publications:
See list online, or leaflet available

Access to staff:
Contact by letter, by telephone, by fax, by e-mail
and via website
Hours: Mon to Fri, 0900 to 1700

Access to building, collection or gallery:
No prior appointment required

OFFICE OF THE REPRESENTATIVE OF NOVI SAD

Acronym or abbreviation: ORNS

Glebelands, Star Lane, Rockland St Mary,
Norwich, Norfolk, NR14 7BX

Tel: 01508 480262
Fax: 01508 480262
E-mail: orns@lineone.net

continued overleaf

Enquiries:
Enquiries to: Appointed Representative

Founded:
1999

Organisation type and purpose:
To represent the city of Novi Sad in Great Britain and elsewhere.

Subject coverage:
Information on Novi Sad and its environs, information for businesses, assistance in making commercial contacts.

Access to staff:
Contact by letter, by telephone, by fax and by e-mail
Hours: Mon to Fri, 0900 to 1700

Links with:
British Embassy
  Belgrade
Serbian Embassy
  London

OFFICE OF TIBET

Tibet House, 1 Culworth Street, London, NW8 7AF

Tel: 020 7722 5378
Fax: 020 7722 0362
E-mail: info@tibet.com

Website:
http://www.tibet.com
Information on Tibet including on the Central Tibetan Administration of His Holiness the Dalai Lama.

Enquiries:
Enquiries to: Secretary/Press & Information Officer

Founded:
1981

Organisation type and purpose:
To represent the Central Tibetan Administration of His Holiness the Dalai Lama based in Dharamsala, India. The Office of Tibet based in London is the official agency of His Holiness the Dalai Lama for the UK, Northern Europe, the Baltic States and Poland.

Subject coverage:
Information on Tibet and Tibetan affairs including the Central Tibetan Administration of His Holiness the Dalai Lama.

Museum or gallery collection, archive, or library special collection:
Small information library on Tibet and Tibetan affairs.

Publications list:
Available in print

Access to staff:
Contact by letter, by telephone, by fax, by e-mail and via website. Appointment necessary.
Hours: Mon to Fri, 0900 to 1700

Parent body:
Central Tibetan Administration of H H the Dalai Lama
  Dharamsala, India; tel: +91 1892 222457; fax: +91 1892 224957; e-mail: diir@gov.tibet.net; website: http://www.tibet.net

OFFICE OF WATER SERVICES

Acronym or abbreviation: OFWAT

Centre City Tower, 7 Hill Street, Birmingham, B5 4UA

Tel: 0121 625 1300\ Minicom no. 0121 625 1422
Fax: 0121 625 1400
E-mail: enquiries@ofwat.gsi.gov.uk

Website:
http://www.ofwat.gov.uk

Enquiries:
Enquiries to: Librarian & Information Services Manager

Direct tel: 0121 625 1361
Direct fax: 0121 625 1362

Founded:
1989

Organisation type and purpose:
National government body.
Central government department.
Economic regulator for the water industry.

Subject coverage:
Water industry; economic regulation, privatisation, consumer protection.

Museum or gallery collection, archive, or library special collection:
Director General's register

Printed publications:
Annual Report
Customer issues (some free)
Documents on charging for water and water metering (some free)
Reports, guidelines, consultation, occasional and research papers, reviews
Variety of information notes and leaflets (free)

Electronic and video publications:
July Return 1996 (CD-ROM)
July Return 1997 (CD-ROM)
July Return 1998 (CD-ROM)
July Return 1999 (CD-ROM)
July Return 2000 (CD-ROM)
Special agreements register (disc)

Publications list:
Available online and in print

Access to staff:
Contact by letter, by telephone, by fax, by e-mail and via website. Appointment necessary.
Hours: Mon to Fri, 0930 to 1630

Access to building, collection or gallery:
Prior appointment required
Hours: Mon to Fri, 0930 to 1630

Has:
10 Customer Service Committees and Regulates 24 companies

OFFICE OF WATER SERVICES – COMPANIES REGULATED BY OFWAT

Water and Sewerage Companies Regulated by OFWAT:
Anglian Water Services Limited
  Henderson House, Lancaster Way, Huntingdon, Cambridgeshire, PE29 6XQ; tel: 01480 323000; fax: 01480 323115; website: www.anglianwater.co.uk
Dwr Cymru Cyfyngedig (Welsh Water)
  Pentwyn Road, Nelson, Treharris, Mid Glamorgan, CF46 6LY; tel: 01443 452300; fax: 01443 452323; website: http://www.dwrcymru.co.uk
Northumbrian Water Limited
  Abbey Road, Pity Me, Durham, DH1 5FJ; tel: 0191 383 2222; fax: 0191 384 1920; website: http://www.nwl.co.uk/
Severn Trent Water Limited
  2297 Coventry Road, Sheldon, Birmingham, B26 3PU; tel: 0121 722 4000; fax: 0121 722 4800; website: http://www.stwater.co.uk
South West Water Limited
  Peninsular House, Rydon Lane, Exeter, EX2 7HR; tel: 01392 446688; fax: 01392 434966; website: http://www.south-west-water.co.uk
Southern Water Services Limited
  Southern House, Yeoman Road, Worthing, Sussex, BN13 3NX; tel: 01903 264444; fax: 01903 262185; website: http://www.southernwater.co.uk
Thames Water Utilities Limited
  Clearwater Court, Vastern Road, Reading, Berkshire, RG1 8DB; tel: 0118 373 8000; fax: 0118 373 8500; website: http://www.thames-water.com

United Utilities Water plc
  Dawson House, Great Sankey, Warrington, WA5 3LW; tel: 01925 234000; fax: 01925 233360; website: http://www.unitedutilities.com/
Wessex Water Services Limited
  Claverton Down Road, Claverton, Bath, BA2 7WW; tel: 01225 526000; fax: 01225 526000; website: http://www.wessexwater.co.uk
Yorkshire Water Services Limited
  Western House, Western Way, Bradford, BD6 2LZ; tel: 01274 691111; fax: 01274 604764; website: http://www.yorkshirewater.com/

Water only Companies Regulated by OFWAT:
Albion Water (Shotton) Limited
  Ground floor Riverview House, Beavor Lane, Hammersmith, London, W6 9AR; tel: 020 8748 9991; fax: 020 8741 6060; website: http://www.enviro-logic.com/
Bournemouth and West Hampshire Water plc
  George Jessel House, Francis Avenue, Bournemouth, BH11 8NB; tel: 01202 591111; fax: 01202 597022; website: http://www.bwhwater.co.uk
Bristol Water plc
  PO Box 218, Bridgwater Road, Bristol, BS99 7AU; tel: 0117 966 5881; fax: 0117 963 4576
Cambridge Water Company pls
  41 Rustat Road, Cambridge, CB1 3QS; tel: 01223 403000; fax: 01223 214052; website: http://www.cambridge-water.co.uk/
Cholderton and District Water Company Limited
  Estate House, Cholderton, Salisbury, Wiltshire, SP4 0DR; tel: 01980 629203; fax: 01980 629307
Dee Valley Water plc
  Packsaddle, Wrexham Road, Rhostyllen, Wrexham, Clwyd, LL14 7EH; tel: 01978 846946; fax: 01978 846888
Essex and Sufflok Water (Now part of Northumbrian Water Limited)
  Hall Street, Chelmsford, Essex, CM2 0HH; tel: 01245 491234; fax: 01245 212345; website: http://www.eswater.co.uk
Folkestone and Dover Water Services Limited
  Cherry Garden Lane, Folkestone, Kent, CT19 4QB; tel: 01303 298800; fax: 01303 276712; website: http://www.fdws.co.uk
Hartlepool Water plc
  3 Lancaster Road, Hartlepool, TS24 8LW; tel: 01429 868555; fax: 01429 858000
Mid Kent Water plc
  PO Box45, High Street, Snodland, Kent, ME6 5AH; tel: 01634 240313; fax: 01634 242764; website: http://www.midkent.co.uk
Portsmouth Water plc
  PO Box 8, West Street, Havant, Hampshire, PO9 1LG; tel: 023 9249 9888; fax: 023 9245 3632; website: http://www.portsmouthwater.co.uk
South East Water plc
  3 Church Road, Haywards Heath, West Sussex, RH16 3NY; tel: 01444 448200; fax: 01444 413200; website: http://www.southeastwater.co.uk/
South Staffordshire Water plc
  Green Lane, Walsall, West Midlands, WS2 7PD; tel: 01922 638282; fax: 01922 723631; website: http://www.south-staffs-water.co.uk/
Sutton and East Surrey Water plc
  London Road, Redhill, Surrey, RH1 1LJ; tel: 01737 772000; fax: 01737 766807; website: http://www.waterplc.com
Tendring Hundred Water Services
  Mill Hill, Manningtree, Essex, CO11 2AZ; tel: 01206 399200; fax: 01206 399210; website: http://www.thws.co.uk
Three Valleys Water plc
  PO Box 48, Bishop's Rise, Hatfield, Hertfordshire, AL10 9HL; tel: 01707 268111; fax: 01707 277333; website: http://www.3valleys.co.uk

OFFICERS' ASSOCIATION

48 Pall Mall, London, SW1Y 5JY

Tel: 020 7930 0125
Fax: 020 7930 9053

Enquiries:
Enquiries to: Assistant General Secretary
Direct tel: 020 7389 5203

Direct e-mail: ags@oaed.org.uk

Founded:
1920

Organisation type and purpose:
Voluntary organisation, registered charity (charity number 201321).
Services charity.
To relieve distress amongst ex-officers, their widows and dependants. To aid and promote their interests.

Subject coverage:
Resettlement and employment, advice on homes for the elderly, financial assistance to relieve distress, provision of residential home accommodation.

Access to staff:
Contact by letter, by telephone, by fax and by e-mail
Hours: Mon to Fri, 0900 to 1700

Connections with:
Royal British Legion, Officers Benevolent Department

OFFSHORE ENGINEERING INFORMATION SERVICE

Heriot-Watt University, Edinburgh, EH14 4AS

Tel: 0131 451 3579
Fax: 0131 451 3164
E-mail: oeis@hw.ac.uk

Website:
http://www.eevl.ac.uk/offshore/
Subscription service for enquiry answering and search services, alerting services and the Petroleum and Offshore Engineering Bulletin containing calendar and bibliographic information.

Enquiries:
Enquiries to: Senior Information Scientist

Founded:
1974

Organisation type and purpose:
Membership association (membership is by subscription), registered charity, university department or institute, consultancy, research organisation.

Subject coverage:
Petroleum and offshore engineering, marine technology, petroleum and marine environmental protection, offshore health and safety.

Printed publications:
Information Bulletin (monthly)
Marine Technology Microthesaurus

Electronic and video publications:
Information Bulletin (monthly, by email)

Access to staff:
Contact by letter and by e-mail. Appointment necessary. All charged.
Hours: Mon to Fri, 0900 to 1700

Parent body:
Heriot-Watt University Library

OFFSHORE SUPPORT VESSEL ISSUES COMMITTEE

Chamber of Shipping, Carthusian Court, 12 Carthusian Street, London, EC1M 6EZ

Tel: 020 7417 2819
Fax: 020 7600 1534
E-mail: robert.ashdown@british.shipping.org

Website:
http://www.british-shipping.org/

Enquiries:
Enquiries to: Secretary

Organisation type and purpose:
Trade association.
Represents the owners and operators of UK based Offshore Support Vessels (OSV's).

Subject coverage:
Offshore support vessels serving oil and gas installations.

Access to staff:
Contact by letter and by e-mail
Hours: Mon to Fri, 0900 to 1700

One of the Committees of the:
Chamber of Shipping

OIL AND COLOUR CHEMISTS ASSOCIATION

Acronym or abbreviation: OCCA

Priory House, 967 Harrow Road, Wembley, Middlesex, HA0 2SF

Tel: 020 8908 1086
Fax: 020 8908 1219
E-mail: gensec@occa.org.uk

Website:
http://www.surfex2010.net
http://surfacecoatingsonline.net

Enquiries:
Enquiries to: General Secretary
Direct e-mail: enquiries@occa.org.uk
Other contacts: Assistant General Secretary

Founded:
1917

Organisation type and purpose:
Learned society, professional body (membership is by qualification), registered charity, training organisation.

Subject coverage:
Raw materials, plant, equipment and services for the paint, ink, resins, varnishes, drying oils, lacquers, adhesives, and treated fabrics industries; organic surface coatings in general.

Library catalogue:
All or part available online and in print

Printed publications:
Colour Photography: Past Present and Future
Physical Chemical Aspects of Pigment Application
Pigments: structures and synthetic properties
Student Monograph Series (8 titles to date)
Surface Coatings International (6 issues a year)
Journal of Coatings Technology and Research (4 issues a year)
UK Surface Coatings Handbook (annually)

Electronic and video publications:
UK Surface Coatings Handbook

Publications list:
Available online and in print

Access to staff:
Contact by letter, by telephone, by fax, by e-mail and via website
Hours: Mon to Fri, 0900 to 1700

Access to building, collection or gallery:
No access other than to staff

OLDHAM COLLEGE

Rochdale Road, Oldham, Lancashire, OL9 6AA

Tel: 0161 624 5214
Fax: 0161 785 4234
E-mail: info@oldham.ac.uk

Website:
http://www.oldham.ac.uk/
Prospectus, general college information, employment opportunities.

Enquiries:
Enquiries to: Librarian

Organisation type and purpose:
Suitable for ages: 16+.

Subject coverage:
Mechanical, electrical, electronic and production engineering; building; business studies; mathematics; computing; catering; performing arts.

Access to staff:
Contact by telephone, by fax, by e-mail and via website
Hours: Mon to Fri, 0900 to 1700

Access to building, collection or gallery:
No prior appointment required

Access for disabled people:
Level entry

OLDHAM LIBRARIES

Union Street, Oldham, Lancashire, OL1 1DN

Tel: 0161 911 4634/4645 general; 4643 Reference Library
Fax: 0161 911 4630
E-mail: els.reference.lib@oldham.gov.uk

Website:
http://www.oldham.gov.uk
Oldham Council web page.

Enquiries:
Enquiries to: Principal Libraries Officer
Direct tel: 0161 911 4632
Direct e-mail: els.richard.lib@oldham.gov.uk

Organisation type and purpose:
Local government body, public library.

Subject coverage:
General.

Museum or gallery collection, archive, or library special collection:
British Standards on microfiche
Cobbett Collection (books by and about William Cobbett, 1762–1835)

Publications list:
Available in print

Access to staff:
Contact by letter, by telephone, by fax, by e-mail, in person and via website
Hours: Mon, Wed, Thu, 0930 to 1900; Tue, Fri, 9300 to 1700; Sat, 0930 to 1600

Access for disabled people:
Ramped entry, access to all public areas, toilet facilities

OLDHAM LOCAL STUDIES AND ARCHIVES

84 Union Street, Oldham, Lancashire, OL1 1DN

Tel: 0161 911 4654\ Minicom no. 0161 911 4654
Fax: 0161 911 4654
E-mail: archives@oldham.gov.uk or local.studies@oldham.gov.uk

Website:
http://www.oldham.gov.uk/local_studies
Handouts.

Enquiries:
Enquiries to: Local Studies Officer
Direct tel: 0161 911 4655
Other contacts: Archives Officer for use of archives.

Founded:
1885

Organisation type and purpose:
Local government body, public library.

Subject coverage:
History of Oldham, records of predecessor authorities, Oldham County Borough, Urban Districts of Chadderton, Crompton, Failsworth, Lees, Royton, Saddleworth, Springhead and Uppermill.

Museum or gallery collection, archive, or library special collection:
Butterworth MSS including press reports 1829 to 1843, notes for Baines History of Lancashire (1836)
Census returns (microfilm)
Extensive record of local Co-operative Society and textile trade unions
Higson antiquarian collection

continued overleaf

Newspapers including the Oldham Chronicle 1854 to date, Oldham Standard 1859–1946 (microfilm)
Oldham Walton Archive (collection of material about Sir William Walton)
Oral history
Parish Registers (microfilm)
Personal papers of Dame Sarah and Marjory Lees of Werneth Park including suffragette material
Rowbottom Diaries: daily events in Oldham 1787–1829
Books, pamphlets, maps, press cuttings
20,000 photographs of Oldham's past

Non-library collection catalogue:
All or part available in-house

Printed publications:
Illustrated books on local history including:
Oldham Brave Oldham: An illustrated history of Oldham
Cotton Mills of Oldham
Looking Back at series (Lees, Crompton, Royton)
The Wild Flowers of Oldham

Microform publications:
Butterworth Manuscripts

Publications list:
Available in print

Access to staff:
Contact by letter, by telephone, by e-mail and in person
Hours: Mon, Thu, 1000 to 1900; Tue, 1000 to 1400; Wed, Fri, 1000 to 1700; Sat, 1000 to 1600

Access for disabled people:
Ramped entry, toilet facilities

OMBUDSMAN FOR ESTATE AGENTS

Acronym or abbreviation: OEA

Beckett House, 4 Bridge Street, Salisbury, Wiltshire, SP1 2LX

Tel: 01722 333306
Fax: 01722 332296
E-mail: admin@oea.co.uk

Website:
http://www.oea.co.uk

Enquiries:
Enquiries to: Ombudsman

Founded:
1998

Organisation type and purpose:
Membership association (membership is by subscription, qualification), present number of members: 583, service industry.

Subject coverage:
Disputes between member agencies and actual or potential buyers or sellers of residential property in the UK.

Printed publications:
Annual Report
Code of Practice (available in member agency offices)
Consumer Guide (available in member agency offices)
Information Package

Electronic and video publications:
Printed products available on website

Access to staff:
Contact by letter, by telephone, by fax, by e-mail and via website
Hours: Mon to Fri, 0900 to 1700

OMNIBUS SOCIETY

Acronym or abbreviation: OS

185 Southlands Road, Bromley, Kent, BR2 9QZ

Tel: 020 8460 0576

Website:
http://www.omnibussoc.org

Enquiries:
Enquiries to: Secretary

Founded:
1929

Organisation type and purpose:
Voluntary organisation, registered charity (charity number 1048887).
Independent society.
To study every aspect of the history and development of road passenger transport.

Subject coverage:
Public road passenger transport mainly UK but to a lesser extent abroad, traffic, engineering and methods of operation of buses, coaches, trams and trolleybuses, current and historical.

Museum or gallery collection, archive, or library special collection:
The society has a large collection of timetables, fare tables, directories, tickets and other items, many dating back 60 to 70 years

Printed publications:
Area Bulletins
Historical Bulletins
Omnibus Magazine (6 times a year)

Access to staff:
Contact by letter
Hours: Mon to Fri, 0900 to 1700

ONE NORTHEAST

Stella House, Goldcrest Way, Newburn Riverside, Newcastle Upon Tyne, NE15 8NY

Tel: 0191 229 6200
Fax: 0191 229 6201
E-mail: info@onenortheast.co.uk

Website:
http://www.onenortheast.co.uk
Home page – description of the organisation and its activities.

Enquiries:
Enquiries to: Resource Manager, Business Information Resource

Organisation type and purpose:
Regional development agency.

Subject coverage:
Economic, business and industrial information on the North of England, environment, investment, technologies, statistical data.

Non-library collection catalogue:
All or part available online and in print

Library catalogue:
All or part available online

Printed publications:
Annual Report

Access to staff:
Contact by letter, by telephone, by fax, by e-mail and via website. Appointment necessary.
Hours: Mon to Fri, 0900 to 1700

Access for disabled people:
Ramped entry, access to all public areas, toilet facilities

ONE PARENT FAMILIES / GINGERBREAD

Formal name: National Council for One Parent Families

255 Kentish Town Road, London, NW5 2LX

Tel: 020 7428 5400
Fax: 020 7482 4851
E-mail: info@oneparentfamilies.org.uk

Website:
http://www.oneparentfamilies.org.uk

Enquiries:
Enquiries to: Administrator

Founded:
1918

Created by the merger of:
One Parent Families, and Gingerbread (year of change 2007)

Organisation type and purpose:
Voluntary organisation, registered charity (charity number 230750).
Campaigning and lobbying organisation.

Subject coverage:
One-parent families with reference to poverty, social security, welfare rights, housing and homelessness, equality of women, family law, divorce, pregnancy and parenthood, child care.

Printed publications:
Annual Report (£5.25)
Publications (free to single parents) include:
Getting it right: benefits and tax (£4.50)
Children: legal rights and responsibilities of parents not living together (£4.25)
Holidays (£3.50)
Maintenance and the Child Support Agency (£4.25)
Returning to Work: A Guide for Lone Parents (£4.75)
Troubleshooting childcare for lone parents (£1.50)
Other publications charged to all:
Lone Parents into Employment: A Practical Guide (£15)

Publications list:
Available online and in print

Access to staff:
Contact by letter and by telephone
Hours: Mon to Fri, 0900 to 1700

Access to building, collection or gallery:
No access other than to staff

ONE PARENT FAMILIES SCOTLAND

Acronym or abbreviation: OPFS

13 Gayfield Square, Edinburgh, EH1 3NX

Tel: 0131 556 3899 or 4563\ Helpline 0808 801 0323
Fax: 0131 557 7899
E-mail: info@opfs.org.uk

Website:
http://www.opfs.org.uk

Enquiries:
Enquiries to: Information Officer

Founded:
1945

Organisation type and purpose:
Membership association (membership is by subscription), present number of members: 400, voluntary organisation, registered charity (charity number SCO 06403).
Equivalent of the National Council for One Parent Families in Scotland but not affiliated to them.
Advice and support to lone parents in Scotland.

Subject coverage:
One-parent families, all organisations working for one-parent families, children, divorce and separation, conciliation, health, housing, holidays, childcare, poverty, maintenance, social security/ tax, rights issues, statistics, women's issues.

Museum or gallery collection, archive, or library special collection:
Library of books, leaflets and press cuttings

Printed publications:
Lone Parent Rights Guide Annual (£5)
Sitter/Flexicare Service Directory (2005)
Family Support Organisations Directory (£10)

Publications list:
Available in print

Access to staff:
Contact by letter, by telephone, by fax, by e-mail and via website. Appointment necessary.
Hours: Mon to Fri, 0930 to 1630

Works in association with:
One Plus, One Parent Families Strathclyde
39 Hope Street, Glasgow, G2 6AE; tel: 0141 248 3488

ONE PLUS ONE

Formal name: One Plus One Marriage and Partnership Research

1 Benjamin Street, London, EC1M 5QG

Tel: 020 7553 9530
Fax: 020 7553 9550
E-mail: info@oneplusone.org.uk

Website:
http://www.oneplusone.org.uk

Enquiries:
Enquiries to: Information Officer
Other contacts: Communications Co-ordinator for press enquiries.

Founded:
1971

Organisation type and purpose:
Registered charity (charity number 1087994), research organisation.
To conduct research into all aspects of marriage and partnership, and to put research findings into use in initiatives such as training programmes.

Subject coverage:
All aspects of marriage, divorce and relationships, including both statistics, research reports, international and historical trends.

Information services:
Online resources for academics, students, researchers and practitioners involved in the field of family and relationships.

Museum or gallery collection, archive, or library special collection:
Marriage manuals of historic interest.
Information on One plus One research and projects

Library catalogue:
All or part available in-house

Printed publications:
Growing together of drifting apart? Children with disabilities and their parents' relationship (F. Glenn, available online)
Informing unmarried parents about their legal rights at birth registration (R. Panades, R. Corney, C. Ayles, J. Reynolds, F. Hovsepian, available online)
Fragile Families and Child Wellbeing (One Plus One, available online)
How helping works: Towards a shared model of process (One Plus One, Parentline Plus and The Centre for Parent and Child Support, available online)
Marital Breakdown and the Health of the Nation (F. McAllister, ed., £5)
Not in Front of the Children? (J. Reynolds, ed., £9.99)
One plus One Information Sheets (available free online)
The Relationship Revolution (D. Dormer, £9)

Publications list:
Available online

Access to staff:
Contact by e-mail and via website. Appointment necessary. Non-members charged.
Hours: Mon to Fri, 1000 to 1600

Access to building, collection or gallery:
Prior appointment required.
Hours: Library; Mon to Fri, 1000 to 1600.
Special comments: Library available by appointment only.

Access for disabled people:
Access to all public areas.

ONLINE DATA SERVICES

Acronym or abbreviation: ODS

74 Chancery Lane, London, WC2A 1AA

Tel: 020 7404 2100
Fax: 020 7404 8600
E-mail: theapexgroup@netscapeonline.co.uk

Enquiries:
Enquiries to: Managing Director

Founded:
1998

Organisation type and purpose:
Consultancy, research organisation.
Business and Information Publisher.

Subject coverage:
Market intelligence reports on business, retailing, leisure, consumer and retail markets. Bespoke market and business analysis.

Trade and statistical information:
Market intelligence on wide variety of UK markets.
Special projects on Europe/World by request.

Printed publications:
List of all publications free of charge, by fax, post or email

Publications list:
Available in print

Access to staff:
Contact by letter, by telephone and by fax
Hours: Mon to Fri, 0900 to 1700

Access to building, collection or gallery:
No access other than to staff

Parent body:
The Apex Group
at the same address

OPEN AND DISTANCE LEARNING QUALITY COUNCIL

Acronym or abbreviation: ODLQC

16 Park Crescent, London, W1B 1AH

Tel: 020 7612 7090
Fax: 020 7612 7092
E-mail: info@odlqc.org.uk

Website:
http://www.odlqc.org.uk

Enquiries:
Enquiries to: Chief Executive

Founded:
1969

Organisation type and purpose:
Registered charity (charity number 325125).
Independent body, formed with the co-operation of the Secretary of State for Education and Science. Accrediting body and advisory service for Open and Distance Learning.

Subject coverage:
Education, training and tuition, open and distance learning methods and activities, standards and improvement, new techniques, assessment, quality control and accreditation.

Printed publications:
Buyer's Guide to Distance Learning and information booklet listing accredited organisations and courses offered (single copies free, possible postal charge for multiple copies)

Access to staff:
Contact by letter, by telephone, by fax, by e-mail and via website
Hours: Mon to Fri, 0900 to 1700

OPEN COLLEGE NETWORK LONDON REGION

Acronym or abbreviation: OCNLR

Unit 15, Angel Gate, 326 City Road, London, EC1V 2SF

Tel: 020 7278 5511
Fax: 020 7833 8289
E-mail: enquiries@ocnlr.org.uk

Website:
www.ocnlr.org.uk

Enquiries:
Enquiries to: Chief Executive

Organisation type and purpose:
Awarding body.

Access to staff:
Contact by letter, by telephone, by fax and by e-mail
Hours: Mon to Fri, 0900 to 1700

OPEN COLLEGE OF THE ARTS

Acronym or abbreviation: OCA

Unit 1B, Redbrook Business Park, Wilthorpe Road, Barnsley, South Yorkshire, S75 1JN

Tel: 0800 731 2116
Fax: 01226 730838
E-mail: enquiries@oca-uk.com

Website:
http://www.oca-uk.com
Comprehensive guide to all courses.

Enquiries:
Enquiries to: Academic Services

Founded:
1987

Organisation type and purpose:
Registered charity (charity number 327446), suitable for ages: 16+.
Distance learning.

Subject coverage:
Art and design, painting, drawing, textiles, sculpture, garden design, interior design, music, calligraphy, creative writing, water colour, printmaking, art history, photography.

Printed publications:
Guide to Courses
Showcase newsletter
Order printed publications from: OCA

Access to staff:
Contact by letter, by telephone, by fax, by e-mail and via website
Hours: Office: Mon to Thu, 0900 to 1700; Fri, 0900 to 1600

Links with:
Buckinghamshire New University

OPEN SPACES SOCIETY

Formal name: Commons, Open Spaces and Footpaths Preservation Society
Acronym or abbreviation: OSS

25a Bell Street, Henley-on-Thames, Oxfordshire, RG9 2BA

Tel: 01491 573535
E-mail: hq@oss.org.uk

Website:
http://www.oss.org.uk

Enquiries:
Enquiries to: General Secretary

Founded:
1865

Organisation type and purpose:
Learned society, professional body (membership is by subscription), present number of members: 2,600, voluntary organisation, registered charity (charity number 214753).

Subject coverage:
Public rights of way, protection of common land, village greens, open spaces, public paths, public access to the countryside.

Museum or gallery collection, archive, or library special collection:
Reports of the Society's work since 1868

Printed publications:
Information sheets

continued overleaf

Open Space (magazine, 3 times a year)
Our Common Land: law and history of commons
and village greens
Getting Greens Registered: a guide to law and
procedure for town or village greens

Publications list:
Available online and in print

Access to staff:
Contact by letter, by telephone and by e-mail.
Access for members only.
Hours: Mon to Fri, 0930 to 1730

OPEN UNIVERSITY

Acronym or abbreviation: OUCEM

Centre for Education in Medicine, Walton Hall,
Crowther 208, Milton Keynes, Buckinghamshire,
MK7 6AA

Tel: 01908 653776
Fax: 01908 659374
E-mail: oucem@open.ac.uk

Website:
http://iet.open.ac.uk/oucem/

Enquiries:
Enquiries to: Personal Assistant

Organisation type and purpose:
University department or institute, suitable for
ages: professional, training organisation,
consultancy, research organisation, publishing
house.
Postgraduate medical education.

Subject coverage:
Postgraduate and continuing medical education.

Printed publications:
An Evaluation Kit for Education in General
Practice (£17 plus p&p)
The Place of Research in Medical Training (£15.80
plus p&p)
Career Choice, Development and Change in
Medicine (£12.50 plus p&p)
Good Assessment Guide (£19.95)
Making Medical Audit Effective (£12.50 plus p&p)
Approaches to Experimental Learning, Course
Delivery and Validation in Medicine (£6 plus
p&p)
The Effectiveness in Continuing Professional
Development (£8 plus p&p)
PEAKit: Postgraduate Educational Audit Kit (£22
plus p&p)
Pre-Registration House Officer Placements in
General Practice (£15 plus p&p)
Evaluation of the Reforms to Higher Specialist
Training (£25 plus p&p)
Good CPD Guide – A Practical guide to Managed
CPD (£19.95 plus p&p)

Electronic and video publications:
Evaluation of the Reforms to Higher Specialist
Training 1996–1999 (CD-ROM, £25 plus p&p)

Publications list:
Available online and in print

Access to staff:
Contact by letter, by telephone, by fax, by e-mail
and via website. Appointment necessary.
Hours: Mon to Fri, 0830 to 1700

Access for disabled people:
Parking provided, ramped entry, access to all
public areas, toilet facilities

Link with:
Open University (IET)
Institute of Educational Technology, Milton
Keynes, MK7 6AA; tel: 01908 274066; fax: 01908
654173; e-mail: iet-queries@open.ac.uk

OPEN UNIVERSITY LIBRARY AND LEARNING RESOURCES CENTRE

Acronym or abbreviation: OU

Walton Hall, Milton Keynes, Buckinghamshire,
MK7 6AA

Tel: 01908 653138
Fax: 01908 653571
E-mail: lib-help@open.ac.uk

Website:
http://library.open.ac.uk
Information about the library, contacts, services to
students and staff; online resources; access to
OPAC; library news.

Enquiries:
Enquiries to: Director of Library Services
Direct tel: 01908 653254
Direct e-mail: N.Whitsed@open.ac.uk

Founded:
1969

Organisation type and purpose:
University library.

Subject coverage:
Modern languages, arts, mathematics, computing,
science, social sciences, technology, education,
environmental sciences, educational research,
management, vocational qualifications, health and
social welfare, law

**Museum or gallery collection, archive, or library
special collection:**
Open University distance teaching materials,
including television and radio programmes,
illustrations and photographs relating to OU
work; Fauvel history of mathematics collection
held for the British Association for the History of
Mathematics; Jennie Lee papers (archive); Betty
Boothroyd papers (archive); Walter Perry (first
OU vice-chancellor) papers (archive)

Non-library collection catalogue:
All or part available online

Library catalogue:
All or part available online

Access to staff:
Contact by letter, by telephone, by fax, by e-mail,
in person and via website
Hours: Mon, Wed, 0830 to 1930; Tue, Thu, 0830 to
2100; Fri, 0830 to 1700; Sat 0900 to 1700

Access for disabled people:
Parking provided, access to all public areas, toilet
facilities

OPEN UNIVERSITY PRESS

Acronym or abbreviation: Open UP

McGraw-Hill House, Shoppenhangers Road,
Maidenhead, Berkshire, SL6 2QL

Tel: 01628 502500
Fax: 01628 770224
E-mail: enquiries@openup.co.uk

Website:
http://www.openup.co.uk
Details of books published.

Enquiries:
Enquiries to: Marketing Manager

Organisation type and purpose:
Publishing house.

Subject coverage:
Education, Higher Education, Health and Social
Welfare, Sociology, Politics, Psychology,
Counselling, Management, Criminology, and
Media, Film and Cultural Studies.

Printed publications:
New Books March – August
New Books September – February
Subject Catalogues
Order printed publications from: Open University
Press, McGraw-Hill House, Shoppenhangers Road,
Maidenhead, SL6 2QL

Publications list:
Available in print

Access to staff:
Contact by letter, by telephone, by fax, by e-mail
and via website. Appointment necessary.
Hours: Mon to Fri, 0900 to 1700

OPERATIONAL RESEARCH SOCIETY

Acronym or abbreviation: ORSOC

Seymour House, 12 Edward Street, Birmingham,
B1 2RX

Tel: 0121 233 9300
Fax: 0121 233 0321
E-mail: email@orsoc.org.uk

Website:
http://www.theorsociety.com

Enquiries:
Enquiries to: General Secretary

Founded:
1954

Organisation type and purpose:
Learned society, professional body (membership is
by subscription), present number of members: 3000
(charity number 313713), training organisation,
research organisation, publishing house.
Conference organisation. Careers information
provider.

Subject coverage:
Operational research, management science.

**Museum or gallery collection, archive, or library
special collection:**
The Society has a library based at Brunel
University Library, Uxbridge

Trade and statistical information:
Salaries in operational research.

Printed publications:
European Journal of Information Systems (6 times
a year, members £8)
Journal of the Operational Research Society
(monthly, £8 to members, non-members £880)
Monograph Series
OR Insight (quarterly £60, members free)
OR Newsletter (monthly, members only)
Knowledge Management Research and Practice (4
times a year, non-members £212, members £8)
Journal of Simulation

Access to staff:
Contact by letter, by telephone, by fax, by e-mail
and via website. Appointment necessary.
Hours: Mon to Fri, 0830 to 1630

Member of:
International Federation of Operational Research
Societies (IFORS)

The Society's Library is housed at the:
Brunel University Library

OPTICAL CONSUMER COMPLAINTS SERVICE

Acronym or abbreviation: OCCS

PO Box 219, Petersfield, GU32 9BY

Tel: 0844 800 5071
Fax: 01730 265058
E-mail: postbox@opticalcomplaints.co.uk

Website:
http://www.opticalcomplaints.co.uk

Enquiries:
Enquiries to: Administrator

Founded:
1993

Organisation type and purpose:
Advisory body.
Provides mediation in disputes between patients
and registered opticians relating to goods or
services supplied by opticians.

Subject coverage:
Availability of professional advisers, optical
matters, such as eye examination results,
prescriptions, dispensing, spectacles, frames,
lenses and contact lenses; resolution of complaints
by negotiation; communication between
practitioners and customers.

Printed publications:
Advice Leaflet
Annual Report

Access to staff:
Contact by letter, by telephone, by fax, by e-mail and via website
Hours: Mon to Fri, 0900 to 1700

Access to building, collection or gallery:
Not open to visitors

ORAL HISTORY SOCIETY

c/o Department of History, University of Essex, Wivenhoe Park, Colchester, Essex, CO4 3SQ

Tel: 01206 873333
Fax: 01206 873410
E-mail: rob.perks@bl.uk

Website:
http://www.oralhistory.org.uk

Enquiries:
Enquiries to: Secretary
Direct tel: 020 7412 7405
Direct fax: 020 7412 7441
Other contacts: Editor

Founded:
1969

Organisation type and purpose:
International organisation, national organisation, advisory body, learned society (membership is by subscription), present number of members: c.1,000, voluntary organisation, registered charity (charity number 288805), training organisation, publishing house.
Regular exchange of information with US oral history organisations and other major fields of oral history activity world-wide.

Subject coverage:
Oral history, life-story research, reminiscence therapy, local history, sound recording and archiving, interviewing skills, women's history, ethnic community history, sociology and social studies.

Museum or gallery collection, archive, or library special collection:
Central oral history database at the British Library Sound Archive
Informed access to oral history collections throughout Great Britain

Printed publications:
Oral History (journal, twice a year)
Oral History in Schools, (booklet for sale)
Remembering in Groups, (booklet for sale)
Talking About the Past: Oral History (booklet for sale)
Various free publicity leaflets

Publications list:
Available in print

Access to staff:
Contact by letter, by telephone, by fax and by e-mail
Hours: Mon to Fri, 1000 to 1800

Administers:
Oral History Society Regional Network
local membership through local representatives

Links with:
British Library Sound Archive
History Workshop Movement

ORCHESTRA OF ST JOHN'S

Acronym or abbreviation: OSJ

The White House, Eltham College, Grove Park Road, London, SE9 4QF

Tel: 020 8857 8579
Fax: 020 8857 9340
E-mail: info@osj.org.uk

Enquiries:
Enquiries to: Assistant to the Chief Executive

Other contacts: (1) Marketing Manager; (2) Concerts Director for (1) Promotional/Marketing; (2) Concerts, Engagements.

Founded:
1967

Organisation type and purpose:
Service industry, registered charity (charity number 289106), suitable for ages: all.
Orchestra (performing arts).
Education, concerts, activities.

Subject coverage:
Orchestral music.

Printed publications:
Quarterly Magazine, available direct

Electronic and video publications:
CD-ROMs for purchase available direct

Access to staff:
Contact by telephone and by e-mail
Hours: Mon to Fri, 0930 to 1730

Connections with:
Choir of the Orchestra of St John's (COSJ)

ORCHID SOCIETY OF GREAT BRITAIN

Acronym or abbreviation: OSGB

c/o 16 The Rise, Amersham, Buckinghamshire, HP7 9AG

Tel: 01494 434730
E-mail: annerutter@dsl.pipex.com

Website:
http://www.orchid-society-gb.org.uk

Enquiries:
Enquiries to: Honorary Secretary

Founded:
1951

Organisation type and purpose:
Membership association (membership is by subscription), present number of members: 1100, voluntary organisation, registered charity (charity number 261273).

Subject coverage:
Growing, conservation and identification of orchids.

Museum or gallery collection, archive, or library special collection:
Books, many out of print
Library of 35mm slides of orchids

Printed publications:
Quarterly journal (members only)

Access to staff:
Contact by letter, by telephone and by e-mail
Hours: Mon to Sun, 0900 to 1700
Special comments: Stamped addressed envelope required for reply.

Affiliated to:
American Orchid Society
Royal Horticultural Society

ORDERS AND MEDALS RESEARCH SOCIETY

Acronym or abbreviation: OMRS

PO Box 1904, Southam, Warwickshire, CV47 2ZX

Tel: 01295 690009
E-mail: gensec@omrs.org.uk

Website:
http://www.omrs.org.uk
Basic information on the Society.

Enquiries:
Enquiries to: General Secretary

Founded:
1942

Organisation type and purpose:
Learned society (membership is by subscription, election or invitation), present number of members: 2750.

Subject coverage:
British Orders, decorations and medals, foreign Orders etc, to a lesser extent, history, provenance and description.

Printed publications:
Journal (quarterly)
Miscellany of Honour (occasional)

Access to staff:
Contact by letter
Hours: Mon to Fri, 0900 to 1700

Also at:
Orders and Medals Research Society
PO Box 248, Snettisham, Kings Lynn, PE31 7TA

ORDNANCE SURVEY

Acronym or abbreviation: OS

Romsey Road, Maybush, Southampton, SO16 4GU

Tel: 023 8079 5000
Fax: 023 8079 2615
E-mail: customerservice@ordnancesurvey.co.uk

Website:
http://www.ordnancesurvey.co.uk
Catalogues, information papers. Location of UK towns.
http://www.ordsvy.gov.uk/products/Landranger/lrmsearch.cfm

Enquiries:
Enquiries to: Customer Service Advisor
Direct tel: 08456 050505
Direct fax: 023 8079 2615
Other contacts: Librarian, tel no: 023 8079 2334 for bibliographic enquiries.

Founded:
1791

Organisation type and purpose:
National government body.
Government agency; national mapping organisation.

Subject coverage:
Survey and mapping of Great Britain, geodesy, surveying, photogrammetry, remote sensing, cartography, GIS.

Museum or gallery collection, archive, or library special collection:
Archive collection of OS maps
Aerial photographs
Books and other published material on relevant subjects
Collection of overseas maps and survey data (former directorate of overseas surveys library)

Library catalogue:
All or part available in-house

Printed publications:
Administrative maps
Archaeological and historical maps
Educational materials
Map catalogues
Services leaflets
Small and large scale maps
Order printed publications from: Sales are through agents, a list is available

Electronic and video publications:
Digital map data

Publications list:
Available online and in print

Access to staff:
Contact by letter, by telephone, by fax, by e-mail and via website
Hours: Mon to Fri, 0830 to 1730
Special comments: Charges made for some services.

Access to building, collection or gallery:
No prior appointment required
Hours: Library: 0930 to 1530
Map Library: 0800 to 1600

continued overleaf

Exhibition Centre: 0900 to 1700
Special comments: A charge is made for access to the
Map Library.

ORDNANCE SURVEY OF NORTHERN IRELAND

Acronym or abbreviation: OSNI

Colby House, Stranmillis Court, Belfast, BT9 5BJ

Tel: 028 9025 5755
Fax: 028 9025 5700
E-mail: osni@osni.gov.uk

Website:
http://www.osni.gov.uk

Founded:
1791

Organisation type and purpose:
National government body.
To supply mapping and geographical information
for Northern Ireland.

**Museum or gallery collection, archive, or library
special collection:**
Archive of aerial photographs
Archive of large scale and small scale maps, street
maps and atlases
Digital topographical archive

Printed publications:
Administrative Maps
Atlases and Guides
Discoverer Series: cover Northern Ireland Scale
1:50,000
Holiday Map Sheet 1 – Northern Ireland Scale
1:250,000
Large scale maps of Northern Ireland
Outdoor pursuit Maps

Electronic and video publications:
Colour Raster Data for 1:50,000 and 1:250,000
mapping
Vector and raster data from the topographical
archive

Publications list:
Available online and in print

Access to staff:
Contact by letter, by telephone, by fax, by e-mail,
in person and via website
Hours: Mon to Fri, 0900 to 1700

Access for disabled people:
Parking provided, ramped entry, toilet facilities

ORFF SOCIETY (UK)

7 Rothesay Avenue, Richmond-upon-Thames,
Surrey, TW10 5EB

Tel: 020 8876 1944
Fax: 020 8876 1944
E-mail: orffsocuk@btconnect.com

Website:
http://www.orff.org.uk
Aims of the Orff approach, information about
current teachers' workshops, Enquiry form for
joining the Society.

Enquiries:
Enquiries to: Honorary Secretary

Founded:
1964

Organisation type and purpose:
Professional body (membership is by subscription),
present number of members: 157, suitable for ages:
all, training organisation.
To promote the experience and understanding of
Carl Orff's approach to music education; a creative
way of teaching music to groups using voices in
speech/singing, movement/dance and all
percussion in the early stages.

Subject coverage:
Information, both specific and related to the Orff
approach to music education, as applied to all
types of schooling including special education.

**Museum or gallery collection, archive, or library
special collection:**
A wide range of books and articles (some in
German) on the subject of Orff-Schulwerk (the
international name of the Orff approach to music
education) by British and American authors

Printed publications:
Orff Times (magazine for members, Feb, Jun, Oct)

Access to staff:
Contact by letter, by telephone, by fax, by e-mail
and via website
Hours: Mon to Sun, 0900 to 1900

Access to building, collection or gallery:
Prior appointment required
Hours: By arrangement

ORGANIC FOOD FEDERATION

Acronym or abbreviation: OFF

31 Turbine Way, EcoTech Business Park, Swaffham,
Norfolk, PE37 7XD

Tel: 01760 720444
Fax: 01760 720790
E-mail: info@orgfoodfed.com

Enquiries:
Enquiries to: Executive Secretary

Founded:
1986

Organisation type and purpose:
International organisation, membership
association (membership is by qualification),
present number of members: 350.
Certification body.
To provide certification to producers, processors,
importers and retailers of organic food.

Subject coverage:
The Federation provides inspection, certification
and registration of organic foods. Represents
members' interests in communicating with
government and European institutions.

Access to staff:
Contact by letter, by telephone, by fax and by e-
mail
Hours: Mon to Fri, 0900 to 1700

Connections with:
Defra
Nobel House, 17 Smith Square, London, SW1P
3JR; tel: 020 7238 5605

ORGANISATION OF BLIND AFRICAN CARIBBEANS

Acronym or abbreviation: OBAC

Gloucester House, 8 Camberwell New Road,
London, SE5 0TA

Tel: 020 7735 3400
Fax: 020 7582 8334
E-mail: orgblindafricarib@ukonline.co.uk

Website:
http://www.obac.org.uk
OBAC service provisions, annual reports,
newsletter and membership form.

Enquiries:
Enquiries to: Director

Founded:
1988

Organisation type and purpose:
Voluntary organisation, registered charity (charity
number 1042756), training organisation.
OBAC provides information, advice and support
on a range of issues such as: welfare rights,
housing, immigration, training, education,
employment issues, counselling, aids and
adaptation for visually impaired people.

Subject coverage:
Welfare rights, housing, immigration, training,
education, employment issues, counselling, aids
and adaptation for visually impaired people.

Printed publications:
OBAC (newsletter, bi-monthly)
The Voice Newspaper (weekly)
The New African Magazine (monthly)

Electronic and video publications:
Tapes and disks are available (free, direct)

Access to staff:
Contact by letter, by telephone, by fax, by e-mail
and in person
Hours: Mon to Fri, 0930 to 1730
Special comments: Full disabled access.

Access for disabled people:
Ramped entry, toilet facilities
Special comments: Chairlift.

ORGANON LABORATORIES LIMITED

Cambridge Science Park, Milton Road, Cambridge,
CB4 0FL

Tel: 01223 432700
Fax: 01223 424368

Website:
http://www.organon.com

Enquiries:
Enquiries to: Medical Information Officer
Direct tel: 01223 432756

Founded:
1935

Organisation type and purpose:
Manufacturing industry.
Pharmaceutical manufacturing company.

Subject coverage:
Clinical pharmacology; contraception; hormone
replacement therapy (HRT), (CNS) depression.

Access to staff:
Contact by letter, by telephone and by fax
Hours: Mon to Fri, 0900 to 1700

Access to building, collection or gallery:
No access other than to staff

Access for disabled people:
Parking provided

Parent body:
AKZO

ORIEL COLLEGE LIBRARY

Oxford, OX1 4EW

Tel: 01865 276558
E-mail: library@oriel.ox.ac.uk

Enquiries:
Enquiries to: Librarian

Founded:
1326

Organisation type and purpose:
University department or institute.
Library of a college of Oxford University.

Subject coverage:
General, matters relating to old members of the
college, Oxford Movement.

**Museum or gallery collection, archive, or library
special collection:**
Orielensia – books by or about old members
Tractarian and Oxford Movement Collection

Access to staff:
Appointment necessary.
Hours: Mon to Fri, 0930 to 1700

Access to building, collection or gallery:
Appointment must be made before entry is
allowed

ORKNEY LIBRARY AND ARCHIVE

44 Junction Road, Kirkwall, Orkney, KW15 1AG

Tel: 01856 873166

Fax: 01856 875260
E-mail: general.enquiries@orkneylibrary.org.uk

Website:
http://www.orkneylibrary.org.uk/

Enquiries:
Enquiries to: Librarian
Other contacts: Principal Archivist

Founded:
1683

Organisation type and purpose:
Local government body, public library.

Subject coverage:
Orkney.

Museum or gallery collection, archive, or library special collection:
Archives – Church Records, Local Authority – Orkney, Customs and Excise, Sheriff Court, Earldom Estate, private papers, business archive
Orkney Room collection – books, pamphlets
Photographic archive (40,000 negatives)
Sound Archive (2000 tapes)

Access to staff:
Contact by letter, by telephone, by fax, by e-mail and in person
Hours: Mon to Fri, 0900 to 2000; Sat, 0900 to 1700

Access for disabled people:
Ramped entry, toilet facilities

ORKNEY TOURIST BOARD

6 Broad Street, Kirkwall, Orkney, KW15 1NX

Tel: 01856 872856/872001
Fax: 01856 875056
E-mail: info@otb.ossian.net

Website:
http://www.orkney.com
Community, tourism and product information.

Enquiries:
Enquiries to: Chief Executive

Organisation type and purpose:
Statutory body (membership is by subscription), present number of members: 320.
Local area Tourist Board.

Subject coverage:
Tourism in Orkney.

Trade and statistical information:
Tourism in Orkney.

Printed publications:
Annual brochure

Electronic and video publications:
Tourism promotional video

Access to staff:
Contact by letter, by fax and via website.
Appointment necessary.
Hours: Mon to Fri, 0900 to 1700

ORTON TRUST

PO Box 34, Rothwell, Kettering, Northamptonshire, NN14 6XP

Tel: 01536 761303 (Courses Director home telephone)
E-mail: info@ortontrust.org.uk

Website:
http://www.ortontrust.org.uk

Enquiries:
Enquiries to: Courses Director

Founded:
1968

Organisation type and purpose:
Registered charity (charity number 304232), training organisation.

Subject coverage:
Traditional stonemasonry skills, restoration and conservation of historic buildings, stone sculpture and lettering.

Access to staff:
Contact by letter, by telephone, by e-mail and via website
Hours: Mon to Fri, 0900 to 1700

OSCAR WILDE SOCIETY, THE

The Membership Secretary, Kambah, Harcourt Hill, Oxford, OX2 9AS

E-mail: cressida.battersby@virgin.net

Website:
http://www.oscarwildesociety.co.uk/

Enquiries:
Enquiries to: Deputy Chair.
Direct e-mail: michael.seeney@btinternet.com

Founded:
1992

Organisation type and purpose:
Membership association (membership is by subscription).
Literary society.
Literary society devoted to the appreciation of Oscar Wilde, promoting knowledge and study of his life, personality and works.

Subject coverage:
Oscar Wilde.

Access to staff:
Contact by letter, by telephone and by e-mail
Hours: Mon to Fri, 0900 to 1700

OUTDOOR INDUSTRIES ASSOCIATION

Acronym or abbreviation: COLA

Morritt House, 58 Station Approach, South Ruislip, Middlesex, HA4 6SA

Tel: 020 8842 1111
Fax: 020 8842 0090
E-mail: info@go-outdoors.org.uk

Website:
http://www.go-outdoors.org.uk

Enquiries:
Enquiries to: Administration Officer
Other contacts: Director, Financial Controller; Marketing Director

Founded:
1961

Organisation type and purpose:
Trade association.
The Outdoor Industries Association is the UK's leading trade body for manufacturers, suppliers and retailers of outdoor clothing and equipment.

Subject coverage:
Clothing, equipment and accessories for camping, outdoor leisure, climbing, mountaineering, walking, hiking and canoeing, manufacturers' trade names and retailers.

Printed publications:
Go Outdoors Bulletin
Consumer Care Guides
Membership Directory

Access to staff:
Contact by letter, by telephone, by fax and by e-mail
Hours: Mon to Fri, 0900 to 1700

OUTSELL, INC

25 Floral Street, London, WC2E 9DS

Tel: 020 8090 6590
E-mail: info@outsellinc.com

Website:
http://www.outsellinc.com

Enquiries:
Enquiries to: Research and Consultancy Director

Founded:
1985

Incorporates the former:
Electronic Publishing Services (year of change 2008)

Organisation type and purpose:
Consultancy, market research, publishing house.

Subject coverage:
All aspects of the publishing industry and electronic publishing, including online.

Museum or gallery collection, archive, or library special collection:
Library of documents and publications on electronic information products and services

Trade and statistical information:
Data on electronic information services, especially statistics on UK, EU and North American services.

Electronic and video publications:
Data available via website (some available free, most only available to subscribers)

Publications list:
Available online

Access to staff:
Contact by letter, by telephone and by e-mail.
Appointment necessary. All charged.
Hours: Mon to Fri, 0930 to 1730

Access to building, collection or gallery:
Prior appointment required

OUTSIDERS

Formal name: The Outsiders Trust

BCM Box Lovely, London, WC1N 3XX

Tel: 020 7354 8291
E-mail: office@outsiders.org.uk

Website:
http://www.spod-uk.org

Enquiries:
Enquiries to: Co-ordinator
Direct e-mail: trust@outsiders.org.uk

Founded:
1972

Formerly called:
The Association to Aid the Personal and Sexual Relationships of People with a Disability (SPOD)

Organisation type and purpose:
Registered charity (charity number 290482).
To assist the sexual and personal relationships of people with disabilities.

Subject coverage:
Sexual problems of the disabled, counselling, education, workshops.

Printed publications:
Advisory leaflets and resource lists
Quarterly Information Bulletin to members

Publications list:
Available online and in print

Access to staff:
Contact by letter, by telephone, by fax and by e-mail
Hours: Mon to Thu, 1000 to 1600

Access to building, collection or gallery:
Prior appointment required
Hours: Mon to Thu, 1000 to 1600

Access for disabled people:
Ramped entry, toilet facilities

OUTWARD BOUND TRUST

Hackthorpe Hall, Hackthorpe, Penrith, Cumbria, CA10 2HX

continued overleaf

Tel: 01931 740000
Fax: 01931 740001
E-mail: enquiries@outwoodbound.org.uk

Website:
http://www.theoutwardboundtrust.org.uk
Centre and course information.

Enquiries:
Enquiries to: Administrator

Founded:
1941

Organisation type and purpose:
Registered charity (charity number 313645),
training organisation.
Educational charity.

Subject coverage:
Outdoor education; development training, safety
in the outdoors, professional development,
personal development.

Printed publications:
Course brochure (annually, free)
Specialist interest leaflets (regularly, courses for
    managers, women, people with a disability)
Order printed publications from: Sales Director, The
Outward Bound Trust
Watermillock, Penrith, Cumbria, CA11 0JL, tel:
017684 85017

Electronic and video publications:
CD-ROM and videos

Access to staff:
Contact by letter, by telephone, by fax, by e-mail
and via website
Hours: Mon to Fri, 0900 to 1730

Also at:
Outward Bound Professional
    Eskdale Green, Holmrook, Cumbria, CA19 1TE;
    tel: 01946 723281
Outward Bound Scotland
    Loch Eil, Fort William, Inverness-shire, PH33
    7NN; tel: 01397 772866
Outward Bound Ullswater
    Penrith, Cumbria, CA11 0JL; tel: 08705 134227
Outward Bound Wales
    Aberdovey, Gwynedd, LL35 0RA; tel: 01654
    767464

OVERSEAS ADOPTION HELPLINE

64–66 High Street, Barnet, Hertfordshire, EN5 5SJ

Tel: 0870 516 8742 Helpline
Fax: 0208 440 5675
E-mail: info@oah.org.uk

Website:
http://www.oah.org.uk

Enquiries:
Enquiries to: Director
Direct tel: 020 8449 2562

Founded:
1997

Organisation type and purpose:
Registered charity (charity number 1067313).
Provides information and advice to inter-country
adopters, inter-country adopted people and their
families and also for professionals involved in
inter-country adoption.

Subject coverage:
Inter-country adoption.

Printed publications:
General Introductory Pack
Regional Summaries
16 Country Information Booklets

Publications list:
Available online and in print

Access to staff:
Contact by telephone and by e-mail
Hours: Mon to Fri, 0900 to 1300 and 1400 to 1700

OVERSEAS DEVELOPMENT INSTITUTE

Acronym or abbreviation: ODI

111 Westminster Bridge Road, London, SE1 7JD

Tel: 020 7922 0300
Fax: 020 7922 0399
E-mail: odi@odi.org.uk

Website:
http://www.odi.org.uk
Institutional descriptions, full text of free
publications, research in progress, publications list,
annual report.

Enquiries:
Enquiries to: Publications Officer

Founded:
1960

Organisation type and purpose:
Registered charity (charity number 228248),
research organisation.
ODI is Britain's leading independent think-tank on
international development and humanitarian
issues.
ODI's mission is to inspire and inform policy and
practice which lead to the reduction of poverty, the
alleviation of suffering and the achievement of
sustainable livelihood in developing countries.

Subject coverage:
Overseas development, aid, development policy,
trade adjustment, finance, food aid, food security,
disasters, environment, agriculture, extension,
pastoralism, irrigation, water resources, rural
forestry.

**Museum or gallery collection, archive, or library
special collection:**
Grey literature collection of the Rural Resources
    Management Group

Non-library collection catalogue:
All or part available online and in-house

Library catalogue:
All or part available in-house

Printed publications:
Annual Report
Briefing Papers
Development policy review (quarterly)
Disasters, Journal of Disaster Studies and
    Management (quarterly)
Economic Crisis in Developing Countries
Index to development literature (6 times a year)
Monetary Policy in Developing Countries
ODI working papers

Publications list:
Available in print

Access to staff:
Contact by letter, by telephone, by fax, by e-mail
and in person
Hours: Mon to Fri, 0930 to 1700
Special comments: In person, Mon to Thu, 1000 to
1700 only.

Access to building, collection or gallery:
No prior appointment required

Affiliated to:
European Association of Development Institutes
(EADI)
Information for Development Coordinating
Committee (IDCC)

Houses the:
Agricultural Administration Unit

Subsidiary body:
Agricultural Research and Extension Network
Humanitarian Policy Group
Humanitarian Practice Network
Pastoral Development Network
Rural Development Forestry Network
Water Resources Group

OVERSEAS SERVICE PENSIONERS' ASSOCIATION

Acronym or abbreviation: OSPA

138 High Street, Tonbridge, Kent, TN9 1AX

Tel: 01732 363836
Fax: 01732 365070
E-mail: mail@ospa.org.uk

Website:
http://www.ospa.org.uk

Enquiries:
Enquiries to: Secretary

Founded:
1960

Organisation type and purpose:
Membership association (membership is by
qualification), present number of members: c. 5000.
To represent, safeguard and promote the interests
of members in all matters relating to or affecting
Overseas Service pensions, and to promote
understanding of all aspects of the former Colonial
Service/HMOCS in British colonial rule and
development.

Subject coverage:
Matters relating directly or indirectly to Service
pensions of former members of the Colonial
Service and HM Overseas Civil Service; general
interest in past British administration and
development in former and present colonial
territories.

Printed publications:
The Overseas Pensioner, biannual official
    membership journal
Order printed publications from: The Secretary,
OSPA, 138 High Street, Tonbridge, Kent TN9 1AX

Access to staff:
Contact by letter, by telephone, by fax and by e-
mail. Appointment necessary.
Hours: Mon to Thu, 0900 to 1630

OXFORD BROOKES UNIVERSITY – HARCOURT HILL LIBRARY

Harcourt Hill Campus, Oxford, OX2 9AT

Tel: 01865 488222 or 488319 (Wesley Centre)
Fax: 01865 488224
E-mail: library@brookes.ac.uk

Website:
http://www.brookes.ac.uk/library
http://catalogue.brookes.ac.uk
Library catalogue

Enquiries:
Enquiries to: Head of Learning Resources

Organisation type and purpose:
University library.

Subject coverage:
Education, theology, human development,
communication, sport and performing arts

**Museum or gallery collection, archive, or library
special collection:**
Wesley Historical Society library and archives
Westminster College archives
Art collections such as the Methodist Collection of
    Modern Christian Art and works by James
    Smetham
Archives of Bletchley Park College and Lady
    Spencer Churchill College

Library catalogue:
All or part available online

Access to staff:
Contact by letter, by telephone, by fax, by e-mail
and via website
Hours: Term time: Mon to Thu, 0845 to 2100; Fri,
0845 to 1800; Sat, Sun, 1200 to 1800. Vacations:
Mon to Fri, 0845 to 1700

OXFORD BROOKES UNIVERSITY – HEADINGTON LIBRARY

Headington Campus, Gipsy Lane, Headington,
Oxford, OX3 0BP

Tel: 01865 483156

Fax: 01865 483998
E-mail: library@brookes.ac.uk

Website:
http://www.brookes.ac.uk/library
http://catalogue.brookes.ac.uk
Library catalogue.

Enquiries:
Enquiries to: Director of Learning Resources and
University Librarian

Organisation type and purpose:
University library.

Subject coverage:
Architectural planning and estate management,
social sciences, education, management and
business studies, humanities, arts, languages,
construction, sciences, catering and tourism,
publishing, nursing, theology.

**Museum or gallery collection, archive, or library
special collection:**
Andre Deutsch Collection (the published output of
Andre Deutsch Ltd and Allan Wingate as well as
titles from Deutsch's own personal library)
Books that Shaped the Century (a collection of
books published in the 20th century deemed by
the advisory board of LOGOS to have
'significantly influenced the way people thought
and acted, and thus influenced the course of
history for better or worse')
Dorset House Archive (the history of the first
School of Occupational Therapy in the United
Kingdom, the Casson family and the wider
history of Occupational Therapy education in
Britain from 1930 to 1980)
Fuller Collection (books, pamphlets, journals and
cuttings on catering, cookery and gastronomy)
Harold Fullard Collection of Atlases
Jane Grigson Collection (books and pamphlets on
cookery and gastronomy)
Local Collection (books and pamphlets on Oxford
and Oxfordshire)
Medical Sciences Video Archive (biographical
interviews with leading medical scientists)
National Brewing Library (a unique English-
language collection relating to brewing, other
alcoholic beverages and dependent trades)
Oxfordshire Society of Architects Collection (books
and journals about architecture and construction,
on permanent loan from the local branch of the
Royal Institute of British Architects)
Publishing in Africa Collection (materials relating
to publishing and the book trade in Africa)

Library catalogue:
All or part available online

Printed publications:
Library guides
Subject journal lists
Wide range of specialist handouts on library
services

Access to staff:
Contact by letter, by telephone, by fax, by e-mail
and via website
Hours: Term time: Mon to Thu, 0900 to 2200; Fri,
0900 to 2000; Sat, Sun, 1000 to 1600. Vacations:
Mon to Fri, 0900 to 1700

OXFORD BROOKES UNIVERSITY –
WHEATLEY LIBRARY

Wheatley Campus, Oxford, OX33 1HX

Tel: 01865 485869
Fax: 01865 485750
E-mail: library@brookes.ac.uk

Website:
http://www.brookes.ac.uk/library
http://catalogue.brookes.ac.uk
Library catalogue.

Enquiries:
Enquiries to: Head of Learning Resources

Founded:
1948

Organisation type and purpose:
University library.

Subject coverage:
Business, management, economics, computing,
mathematics and engineering

Library catalogue:
All or part available online

Access to staff:
Contact by letter, by telephone, by fax, by e-mail
and via website
Hours: Term time: Mon to Thu, 0900 to 2100; Fri,
0900 to 1800; Sat, Sun, 1000 to 1600. Vacations:
Mon to Fri, 0900 to 1700

OXFORD BUSINESS COLLEGE

Acronym or abbreviation: OBC

65 George St, Oxford, OX1 2BQ

Tel: 01865 791908
Fax: 01865 245059
E-mail: enquiries@oxfordbusinesscollege.co.uk

Website:
http://www.oxfordbusinesscollege.co.uk

Enquiries:
Enquiries to: Principal

Founded:
1985

Organisation type and purpose:
Suitable for ages: 17+, training organisation.

Subject coverage:
Marketing, business, management and law;
English language, secretarial studies, computing,
cookery.

Printed publications:
Prospectus

Access to staff:
Contact by letter, by telephone and by fax
Hours: Mon to Fri, 0900 to 1730

OXFORD CENTRE FOR HEBREW
AND JEWISH STUDIES

Yarnton Manor, Church Lane, Yarnton, Oxford,
OX5 1PY

Tel: 01865 377946
Fax: 01865 375079
E-mail: enquiries@uchjs.ac.uk

Website:
http://associnst.ox.ac.uk/ochjs

Enquiries:
Enquiries to: President
Other contacts: Librarian for library information,
email: muller.library@ochjs.ac.uk

Founded:
1972

Organisation type and purpose:
Registered charity (charity number 309720),
university department or institute, suitable for
ages: post-graduate.

Subject coverage:
Hebrew and Jewish studies.

**Museum or gallery collection, archive, or library
special collection:**
The Centre's Leopold Muller Memorial Library
holds a wide range of collections, for more
information contact the Librarian

Non-library collection catalogue:
All or part available in-house

Library catalogue:
All or part available in-house

Printed publications:
Herbert S Frankel: An Economist's Testimony
(autobiography, 1992, £25)

Journal of Jewish Studies (2 issues a year, £48
institution subscription, £32 institutions
subscription, £18 student subscription, £18 single
issue)
Occasional Papers (most are from lectures at the
centre)
Publications of The Yarnton Trust (£2.50)
Israel Studies (2 issues a year, copies available from
Indiana University Press)
Annual Report (free)
A Bibliography of Publications 1972–1986, 1987
(free)
Newsletter from the Centre (free)
The Kressel Collection (1981, free)
Order printed publications from: For Israel Studies,
Journals Division
Indiana University Press, 601 N Morton Street,
Bloomington, IN 47404, USA
Other titles, Oxford Centre for Hebrew and Jewish
Studies

Publications list:
Available in print

Access to staff:
Contact by letter, by telephone, by fax and by e-
mail. Appointment necessary.
Hours: Mon to Fri, 0900 to 1700

Access to building, collection or gallery:
No prior appointment required

OXFORD CENTRE FOR ISLAMIC
STUDIES

George Street, Oxford, OX1 2AR

Tel: 01865 278730
Fax: 01865 248942
E-mail: islamic.studies@oxcis.ac.uk

Website:
http://www.oxcis.ac.uk

Enquiries:
Enquiries to: Enquiry Line

Subject coverage:
Islam.

Access to staff:
Contact by letter, by telephone, by fax, by e-mail
and via website
Hours: Mon to Fri, 0900 to 1700

OXFORD CITY COUNCIL

St Aldate's Chambers, St Aldate's, Oxford, OX1
1DS

Tel: 01865 249811
Fax: 01865 252338

Website:
http://www.oxford.gov.uk
Web edition of 'The City' newspaper, information
from Oxford City Council.

Enquiries:
Enquiries to: Chief Executive

Organisation type and purpose:
Local government body.

Printed publications:
The City (newspaper, 3 times a year, available free
on request)
Various corporate publications, leaflets etc

Access to staff:
Contact by letter, by telephone, by fax and in
person
Hours: Mon to Fri, 0900 to 1700

OXFORD DOWN SHEEP
BREEDERS ASSOCIATION

Hillfields Lodge, Lighthorne, Warwickshire

Tel: 01926 650098
E-mail: cqlfroehlich@hotmail.com

Enquiries:
Enquiries to: Secretary

continued overleaf

Founded:
1889

Organisation type and purpose:
Sheep breed society.

Subject coverage:
Oxford Down sheep.

Access to staff:
Contact by letter, by telephone and by e-mail
Hours: Mon to Fri, 0900 to 1700

OXFORD EDUCATIONAL RESOURCES LIMITED

Acronym or abbreviation: OER

PO Box 106, The Barn, Kidlington, Oxfordshire, OX5 1HY

Tel: 01865 842552
Fax: 01865 842551
E-mail: sales@oer.co.uk

Website:
http://www.oer.co.uk

Enquiries:
Enquiries to: Managing Director

Founded:
1978

Organisation type and purpose:
Training organisation.
Publishing and distribution of non-book material.

Subject coverage:
Training material for medicine, health and biology.

Publications list:
Available in print

Access to staff:
Contact by fax and by e-mail
Hours: Mon to Fri, 0900 to 1700

OXFORD INFORMATION CENTRE

Acronym or abbreviation: Oxford TIC

15–16 Broad Street, Oxford, OX1 3AS

Tel: 01865 726871
Fax: 01865 240261
E-mail: tic@oxford.gov.uk

Website:
http://www.visitoxford.org

Enquiries:
Enquiries to: Information Officer

Organisation type and purpose:
Local government body.
Tourist Information Centre.
To assist local people and visitors to make the most of the time they spend in Oxford and the surrounding area.

Subject coverage:
Tourist information including: guided walking tours, maps, guides and accommodation, reservations (B&B), local information.

Non-library collection catalogue:
All or part available online

Printed publications:
Staying in Oxford (£1)
University City of Oxford (In French, German, Russian, Spanish, Italian and Japanese, £3.50 plus p&p each)
Welcome to Oxford (including map)(£1.30)

Electronic and video publications:
Various videos

Publications list:
Available online and in print

Access to staff:
Contact by letter, by telephone, by fax, by e-mail and in person
Hours: Mon to Sat, 0930 to 1700; Sun and Public Holidays, 1000 to 1600

Access for disabled people:
Level entry

Parent body:
Oxford City Council

OXFORD INSTITUTE OF RETAIL MANAGEMENT

Acronym or abbreviation: OXIRM

Said Business School, University of Oxford, Egrove Park, Oxford, Oxfordshire, OX1 5NY

Tel: 01865 422500
Fax: 01865 422501
E-mail: oxirmenquiries@sbs.ox.ac.uk

Website:
http://www.sbs.ox.ac.uk/oxirm

Enquiries:
Enquiries to: Research Director

Founded:
1985

Organisation type and purpose:
University department or institute, research organisation.

Subject coverage:
Retail management.

Museum or gallery collection, archive, or library special collection:
Research papers, reports, directories, etc.

Printed publications:
The Retail Digest (quarterly)
Factors Affecting the Structure and Pattern of Retailing in London
Assessing the Productivity of the UK Retail Sector
Retail Strategy: The View from the Bridge
Internationalisation in Retailing: The Global Performance Perspective
Customer Loyalty Schemes in Retailing Across Europe
Home Shopping
Own Brands in Food Retailing Across Europe
Retailing in the Nordic Countries
Information from Retailers – Individual Customer Information

Publications list:
Available online and in print

Access to staff:
Contact by letter, by telephone, by fax and by e-mail. Appointment necessary. Letter of introduction required.
Hours: Mon to Fri, 0900 to 1700

Access to building, collection or gallery:
Special comments: Academic status.

OXFORD PRESERVATION TRUST

Acronym or abbreviation: OPT

10 Turn Again Lane, St Ebbes, Oxford, OX1 1QL

Tel: 01865 242918
Fax: 01865 251022
E-mail: info@oxfordpreservation.org.uk

Enquiries:
Enquiries to: Director

Founded:
1927

Organisation type and purpose:
Membership association (membership is by subscription), present number of members: 1000, registered charity (charity number 203043).
Charitable trust.
Area of concern, Oxford and its Green Belt setting.

Subject coverage:
Conservation in Oxford and its Green Belt.

Museum or gallery collection, archive, or library special collection:
Archives accessed through Trust Office

Printed publications:
Annual Report
Newsletter (2 times a year)
Occasional Studies (available in the Local Studies Library and the Bodleian Library)

Access to staff:
Contact by letter, by telephone, by fax and by e-mail. Appointment necessary.
Hours: Mon to Fri, 0900 to 1600

Connections with:
Civic Trust
Europa Nostra

OXFORDSHIRE COUNTY COUNCIL

Acronym or abbreviation: OCC

Cultural Services, Central Library, Westgate, Oxford, OX1 1DJ

Tel: 01865 815549
Fax: 01865 721694
E-mail: oxfordcentral.library@oxfordshire.gov.uk

Website:
http://www.oxfordshire.gov.uk
http://www.libcat.oxfordshire.gov.uk
Oxfordshire County Council Library Catalogue

Enquiries:
Enquiries to: Head of Cultural Services
Direct tel: 01865 810191
Direct fax: 01865 810187
Other contacts: County Reference and Information Librarian

Organisation type and purpose:
Local government body, public library.

Subject coverage:
Logic, New Testament, international relations, women, costumes, gypsies, customs and folklore, inland waterways, nuclear physics, hydraulic engineering, woodworking, India, Indian religions (Buddhism, etc.), indoor games and amusements, genealogy, heraldry and family history, local studies in Oxfordshire, internal-combustion engines, motor vehicle engineering, cleaning and dyeing, accountancy, rubber technology, business information.

Non-library collection catalogue:
All or part available online

Library catalogue:
All or part available online

Access to staff:
Contact by letter, by telephone, by fax, by e-mail and in person
Hours: Contact for details

Links with:
European Information Association
European Public Information Centres (Network)
South-Western Regional Library System

OXFORDSHIRE FAMILY HISTORY SOCIETY

Acronym or abbreviation: OFHS

19 Mavor Close, Woodstock, Oxford, OX20 1YL

Website:
http://www.ofhs.org.uk
Family history information.

Enquiries:
Enquiries to: Honorary Secretary
Direct tel: 01993 812258
Other contacts: Membership Secretary

Founded:
1976

Organisation type and purpose:
Membership association (membership is by subscription), present number of members: 1300, registered charity (charity number 275891).

Subject coverage:
Family history.

Museum or gallery collection, archive, or library special collection:
Library

Printed publications:
Several family history publications
Order printed publications from: Oxfordshire Family History Society
Windmill Place, Windmill Road, Minchinhampton, Stroud, Gloucestershire, GL6 9EE, tel: 01453 881446, e-mail: HKearsey@aol.com

Microform publications:
Parish registers, marriage index, census index

Publications list:
Available in print

Access to staff:
Contact by letter
Hours: Mon to Fri, 0900 to 1700
Special comments: No office.

OXFORDSHIRE RECORD OFFICE

Acronym or abbreviation: ORO

St Luke's Church, Temple Road, Cowley, Oxford, OX4 2EX

Tel: 01865 398200
Fax: 01865 398201
E-mail: archives@oxfordshire.gov.uk

Website:
http://www.oxfordshire.uk/records/index.htm
Guide to Oxfordshire Record Office.

Enquiries:
Enquiries to: County Archivist

Founded:
1935

Organisation type and purpose:
Local government body, professional body.
Record office.

Subject coverage:
Records of Oxfordshire.

Museum or gallery collection, archive, or library special collection:
Quarter Sessions, local government, diocesan and parish, private

Non-library collection catalogue:
All or part available online and in-house

Publications list:
Available in print

Access to staff:
Contact by letter, by telephone, by fax, by e-mail and in person
Hours: Wed to Sat, 0900 to 1700

Access for disabled people:
Parking provided, ramped entry, access to all public areas, toilet facilities

OXFORDSHIRE RECORD SOCIETY

Bodleian Library, Oxford, OX1 3BG

Tel: 01865 277164
E-mail: srt@bodley.ox.ac.uk

Enquiries:
Enquiries to: Secretary

Founded:
1919

Organisation type and purpose:
Learned society.
Exists to publish editions of Oxfordshire local history texts.

Subject coverage:
Oxfordshire local history.

Access to staff:
Contact by letter and by e-mail
Hours: Mon to Fri, 0900 to 1700

OXFORDSHIRE RURAL COMMUNITY COUNCIL

Acronym or abbreviation: ORCC

Jericho Farm, Worton, Near Cassington, Witney, Oxfordshire, OX29 4SZ

Tel: 01865 883488
Fax: 01865 883191
E-mail: oxonrcc@ruralnet.org.uk

Enquiries:
Enquiries to: Chief Executive

Founded:
1920

Organisation type and purpose:
Voluntary organisation, registered charity (charity number 900560).

Subject coverage:
Oxfordshire Rural Community Council (ORCC) supports, promotes and develops local voluntary action and rural services (including shops and rural transport). Offers information on a wide range of local voluntary organisations, community and self-help groups. Provides information and advises village hall management committees and advises on sources of grants for community projects. Also provides parish councils with advice and guidance in partnership with the Oxfordshire Association of Local Councils and the Oxfordshire Playing Fields Association. (All three organisations based at Jericho Farm).

Printed publications:
The following are available free or for purchase upon request
Advice leaflets for community hall committees
Annual Reports
Community Transport in Oxfordshire (Directories)
ORCC News (newsletter, quarterly, for members)
Various publications available for parish councils and community shops

Access to staff:
Contact by letter, by telephone, by fax and by e-mail. Appointment necessary.
Hours: Mon to Fri, 0900 to 1700

Access to building, collection or gallery:
Prior appointment required

Houses the:
Oxfordshire Association of Local Councils
tel: 01865 883488; fax: 01865 883191; e-mail: oalc@ruralnet.org.uk
Oxfordshire Playing Fields Association
tel: 01865 883488; fax: 01865 883191; e-mail: oxonrcc@ruralnet.org.uk

OXFORDSHIRE STUDIES

Central Library, Westgate, Oxford, OX1 1DJ

Tel: 01865 815749
Fax: 01865 810187
E-mail: oxfordshire.studies@oxfordshire.gov.uk

Website:
http://www.oxfordshire.gov.uk/oxfordshirestudies
Information about the service and collections, access to online catalogues and images, order forms

Enquiries:
Enquiries to: Local Studies Manager

Founded:
1991

Organisation type and purpose:
Local government body, museum, public library.
Local studies and family history resource centre for Oxfordshire.

Subject coverage:
Oxfordshire local studies, local history and archaeology, family history, maps, photographs and oral history.

Museum or gallery collection, archive, or library special collection:
Indexes and databases

Oxfordshire printed materials, microforms, digital resources
Photographs and audiotapes
Catalogues

Non-library collection catalogue:
All or part available online and in-house

Library catalogue:
All or part available online and in-house

Access to staff:
Contact by letter, by telephone, by fax, by e-mail and in person. Appointment necessary.
Special comments: Booking advisable for access to microfilms and computers, appointments may be necessary for specialist advice.

Access to building, collection or gallery:
Hours: Tue, Thu, Fri, Sat 0900 to 1700; Mon, Wed, Sun closed.

Access for disabled people:
Access to all public areas

Parent body:
Oxfordshire County Council

P & O GROUP

Formal name: The Peninsular and Oriental Steam Navigation Company

16 Palace Street, London, SW1E 5JQ

Tel: 020 7901 4000
Fax: 020 7901 4015
E-mail: communications@pogroup.com

Website:
http://www.pogroup.com

Founded:
1837

Organisation type and purpose:
Service industry.

Subject coverage:
Shipping, present day and historical (since c. 1830), other transport and logistics (present day), constituent companies, history and current operations of P & O constituent companies.

Access to staff:
Contact by letter, by telephone, by fax, by e-mail, in person and via website. Appointment necessary.
Hours: Mon to Fri, 0900 to 1700

Access to building, collection or gallery:
Prior appointment required

Access for disabled people:
Ramped entry, access to all public areas, toilet facilities

PACKAGING AND INDUSTRIAL FILMS ASSOCIATION

Acronym or abbreviation: PIFA

3rd Floor, Gothic House, Barker Gate, Nottingham, NG7 7GR

Tel: 0115 959 8389
Fax: 0115 959 9326
E-mail: pifa@pifa.co.uk

Website:
http://www.pifa.co.uk
General information and publications

Enquiries:
Enquiries to: Chief Executive
Other contacts: PR Principal for exhibitions, press releases, presentations and essential media contacts.

Founded:
1957

Organisation type and purpose:
National organisation, trade association (membership is by subscription).
To communicate with Government, Government Agencies, Ministers and MP's on all issues affecting the competitiveness, environmental performance

continued overleaf

and operation of the industry. To provide factual and scientific information to universities, schools, local authorities and other social groups.

Subject coverage:
Production and conversion of plastics films used in healthcare, agriculture, packaging, building construction, commerce and industry. Issues include competitiveness, the environment, safety, trade matters, processes, products and applications, education and public awareness.

Trade and statistical information:
Detailed production/consumption, import/export and related statistics maintained.

Non-library collection catalogue:
All or part available online and in print

Printed publications:
Environmental statements
PIFA product standards – numbers 1 to 11 (for sale)
Technical Reports, Briefings and application leaflets including:
A Responsible Approach to the Environmental Challenge
A Statement of Environmental Policy
Meeting the Environmental Challenge

Publications list:
Available online and in print

Access to staff:
Contact by letter, by telephone, by fax, by e-mail and via website. Appointment necessary.
Hours: Mon to Fri, 0900 to 1700

Access to building, collection or gallery:
No prior appointment required

Access for disabled people:
Parking provided, toilet facilities

Affiliated to:
British Plastics Federation

Member of:
C of C
CBI
Plasteurofilm
Polymer NTO

PADDLE STEAMER PRESERVATION SOCIETY

Acronym or abbreviation: PSPS

17 Stockfield Close, Hazlemere, High Wycombe, Buckinghamshire, HP15 7LA

Tel: 01494 812979

Enquiries:
Enquiries to: Secretary

Founded:
1959

Organisation type and purpose:
Membership association (membership is by subscription), present number of members: 4000, voluntary organisation.
Education of the public in the appreciation of paddle steamers and their preservation.

Subject coverage:
Paddle steamers of Britain and Europe.

Museum or gallery collection, archive, or library special collection:
Library of Paddle Steamer photographs and books

Printed publications:
Paddle Wheels (quarterly)

Access to staff:
Contact by letter
Hours: Mon to Fri, 0900 to 1700

Affiliated to:
Transport Trust

PAGAN FEDERATION

Acronym or abbreviation: PF

BM Box 7097, London, WC1N 3XX

Tel: 01209 831850
Fax: 01209 831519
E-mail: secretary@paganfed.demon.co.uk

Website:
http://www.paganfed.demon.co.uk
Information pack, Hallowe'en information, articles from Pagan Dawn, events and conferences.
Introduction to Paganism, regional contact details.

Enquiries:
Enquiries to: Secretary
Other contacts: Media Officer for immediate coverage of breaking news.

Founded:
1971

Organisation type and purpose:
Membership association (membership is by subscription), present number of members: 4500, voluntary organisation.
To inform the public about Paganism and to support Pagans in the practice of their religion.

Subject coverage:
Nature, spirituality, goddess worship, Wicca (the old religion of witchcraft), Druidism, Shamanism, Pagan folklore and belief, contemporary Pagan ritual practices, religious and legal rights, defamation of Pagans, concerns about ritual child abuse, Pagan ethics, inter-faith dialogue, worship of traditional European deities.

Museum or gallery collection, archive, or library special collection:
Cuttings collection – stories on Pagan-related subjects
Extensive collection of Pagan and esoteric magazines, back issues and current issues

Library catalogue:
All or part available in-house

Printed publications:
Pagan Federation Information Pack (£2.50)
Pagan Dawn (magazine, quarterly, £12, £15 overseas, a year)
Witchcraft Information (£2.50)
Northern Tradition Information Pack (£2.50)
Druidry Information Pack (1998, £2.50)
We Emerge – the origins & history of the Pagan Federation (£6)

Publications list:
Available in print

Access to staff:
Contact by letter and by e-mail
Hours: Mon to Fri, 0900 to 1700

Access to building, collection or gallery:
No access other than to staff

PAIN RESEARCH INSTITUTE

Acronym or abbreviation: PRI

Clinical Sciences Centre for Research and Education, University Hospital Aintree, Lower Lane, Liverpool, L9 7AL

Tel: 0151 529 5820
Fax: 0151 529 5821
E-mail: secretary@painrelieffoundation.org.uk

Website:
http://www.painrelieffoundation.org.uk

Enquiries:
Enquiries to: Information and education services
Direct tel: 0151 529 5838
Direct e-mail: mm27@liv.ac.uk

Founded:
1979

Organisation type and purpose:
Registered charity, research organisation.

Subject coverage:
All chronic pain conditions, causes, treatment.

Information services:
Patient/public information leaflets about chronic pain

Education services:
Postgraduate education courses for health professionals

Printed publications:
Leaflets about chronic pain conditions
News Bulletins
Order printed publications from: Pain Relief Foundation

Publications list:
Available online

Access to staff:
Contact by letter, by telephone, by fax, by e-mail and via website
Hours: Mon to Fri, 0900 to 1700

Access to building, collection or gallery:
No access other than to staff

Links with:
Pain Relief Foundation

PAIN SOCIETY

9 Bedford Square, London, WC1B 3RE

Tel: 020 7631 8870
Fax: 020 7323 2015
E mail: info@painsociety.org

Website:
http://www.painsociety.org

Enquiries:
Enquiries to: Honorary Secretary

Founded:
1967

Organisation type and purpose:
Professional body.

Subject coverage:
Pain research and management, education, organisation of pain clinics.

Printed publications:
Desirable Criteria for Pain Management Programmes (£4)
Information for Patients (free)
Lists of pain clinics in any county (free)

Access to staff:
Contact by letter, by telephone, by fax, by e-mail and via website
Hours: Mon to Fri, 0930 to 1730
Special comments: Letters preferred, no personal callers.

Access to building, collection or gallery:
No access other than to staff

British Chapter of the:
International Association for the Study of Pain

PAINT RESEARCH ASSOCIATION

Acronym or abbreviation: PRA

PRA Coatings Technology Centre, 14 Castle Mews, High Street, Hampton, Middlesex, TW12 2NP

Tel: 020 8487 0800
Fax: 020 8487 0801
E-mail: library@pra.org.uk

Website:
http://www.pra.org.uk
Details of the organisation, including research projects, information about training courses, conferences, technical services and contact details of staff.
http://www.pra-world.com/

Enquiries:
Enquiries to: Librarian
Direct e-mail: c.haworth@pra.org.uk

Founded:
1926

Organisation type and purpose:
Research organisation.

Subject coverage:
Paint science and technology; corrosion; deterioration and biodeterioration of materials; pigments; oils; resins; polymers; paint application; health hazards and toxicology; industrial hazards and anti-pollution legislation; organic and inorganic chemistry; analytical chemistry; anti-fouling technology; spectroscopy; rheology; colour science and colorimetry; paint testing; powder coatings; microbiology; building materials; standards, specifications, reports and patents.

Trade and statistical information:
Available in Coatings COMET.

Non-library collection catalogue:
All or part available online

Library catalogue:
All or part available in-house

Printed publications:
Annual Review
Coatings COMET (Companies Markets Economic Trends)
CORE (Coatings, Regulations and the Environment)
Emulsion Polymer Technologies (current literature and patent alerting review)
Paint Titles (220 titles; weekly, current awareness service)
Polymer Curing Technologies
RADnews
SHE Alert (Safety, Health and the Environment)
Waterborne and High-solids Coatings (bulletin, monthly)
World Surface Coatings Abstracts (WSCA) (monthly, with SDI Service)

Electronic and video publications:
Almost all publications are available in electronic formats
SHE Alert (Safety, Health and the Environment, PC disk)
WSCA (quarterly, CD-ROM)

Publications list:
Available online and in print

Access to staff:
Contact by letter, by telephone, by fax, by e-mail and via website. Non-members charged.
Hours: Mon to Fri, 0900 to 1700

Access to building, collection or gallery:
No prior appointment required

Access for disabled people:
Parking provided, level entry, toilet facilities

PAINTING AND DECORATING ASSOCIATION

Acronym or abbreviation: PDA

32 Coton Road, Nuneaton, Warwickshire, CV11 5TW

Tel: 024 7635 3776
Fax: 024 7635 4513
E-mail: info@paintingdecoratingassociation.co.uk

Website:
http://www.paintingdecoratingassociation.co.uk
Complete profile of association.

Enquiries:
Enquiries to: Chief Executive

Founded:
2002

Created by the merger of:
British Decorators Association and Painting and Decorating Federation (year of change 2002)

Organisation type and purpose:
Trade association.

Subject coverage:
All matters relating to the decorating industry, arbitration, insurance, training and education, employment legislation.

Printed publications:
British Decorator (6 times a year, free to members)

Reference Handbook (annually)

Access to staff:
Contact by letter, by telephone, by fax, by e-mail and via website. Appointment necessary. Non-members charged.
Hours: Mon to Fri, 0900 to 1700

Access to building, collection or gallery:
Prior appointment required

Access for disabled people:
Parking provided, level entry, access to all public areas

Member of:
National Specialist Contractors Council (NSCC) tel: 0870 429 6351

PAINTING AND DECORATING FEDERATION

Acronym or abbreviation: PDF

32 Coton Road, Nuneaton, Warwickshire CV11 5TW

Tel: 02476 353776
Fax: 02476 354513
E-mail: info@paintingdecoratingassociation.co.uk

Website:
http://www.paintingdecoratingassociation.co.uk/

Enquiries:
Enquiries to: Executive Administrator

Founded:
1942

Organisation type and purpose:
Trade association.

Subject coverage:
Painting and decorating.

Printed publications:
Specifiers Guide – incorporating a directory of members
Health and Safety in Painting
Order printed publications from: The Health & Safety in Painting publication is available from, CIP on tel: 0121 722 8200

Access to staff:
Contact by letter, by telephone, by fax, by e-mail and via website
Hours: Mon to Fri, 0930 to 1715

Member of:
National Specialist Contractors Council (NSCC) tel: 020 7608 5090; fax: 020 7608 5081

PALAEOECOLOGY CENTRE

Queen's University of Belfast, Belfast, BT7 1NN

Tel: 028 9033 5141
Fax: 028 9031 5779
E-mail: g.johnson@qub.ac.uk

Website:
http://www.qub.ac.uk/arcpal
About the School of Archaeology and Palaeoecology at Queen's University, Belfast.

Enquiries:
Enquiries to: Secretary

Founded:
1970

Organisation type and purpose:
University department or institute.

Subject coverage:
Palaeoecology.

Access to staff:
Contact by letter, by telephone and by e-mail
Hours: Mon to Fri, 0915 to 1315

PALAEONTOGRAPHICAL SOCIETY

Department of Palaeontology, Natural History Museum, Cromwell Road, London, SW7 5BD

Tel: 020 7942 5712
E-mail: S.Long@nhm.ac.uk

Website:
http://www.nhm.ac.uk/hosted_sites/palsoc
General information on the Society, its governing council, membership and publications.

Enquiries:
Enquiries to: Honorary Secretary

Founded:
1847

Organisation type and purpose:
Learned society.
To figure and describe British fossils by publishing monographs restricted geographically, stratigraphically and palaeontologically.

Subject coverage:
British fossils; study of geology in relation to fossils, particularly by publications upon them.

Printed publications:
Monographs of British fossils
An annual volume published, consisting of a number of complete or part monographs, each enclosed in its own cover
Order printed publications from: Marketing Manager, Palaeontographical Society
27 The Crescent, Maidenhead, Berkshire, SL6 6AA

Publications list:
Available in print

Access to staff:
Contact by letter and by e-mail
Hours: Mon to Fri, 1000 to 1600

PALAEONTOLOGICAL ASSOCIATION

Department of Earth Sciences, University of Durham, South Road, Durham, DH1 3LE

Tel: 0191 334 2320
Fax: 0191 334 2301
E-mail: secretary@palass.org

Website:
http://www.palass.org
Newsletter, list of publications, lists of meetings, general information.

Enquiries:
Enquiries to: Secretary
Other contacts: Executive Officer for membership enquiries; publication orders.

Founded:
1957

Organisation type and purpose:
Learned society.

Subject coverage:
Palaeontology.

Printed publications:
Field Guides to Fossils (series)
Palaeontology (6 times a year)
Special Papers on Palaeontology (1 or 2 times a year, over 40 available)
Order printed publications from: Executive Officer

Publications list:
Available online and in print

Access to staff:
Contact by letter, by telephone, by fax and by e-mail. Appointment necessary.
Hours: Mon to Fri, 0900 to 1700

Other address:
Palaeontological Association
Executive Officer, Institute of Geography and Earth Sciences, University of Wales Aberystwyth, Aberystwyth, Ceredigion, SY23 3BD; tel: 01970 627107; fax: 01970 627107; e-mail: palass@palass.org

PANAMANIAN EMBASSY

40 Hertford Street, London, W1J 7SH

continued overleaf

Tel: 020 7493 4646
Fax: 020 7493 4333
E-mail: emb.pan@lineone.net

Website:
http://www.panamainfo.com
Tourism.
http://www.presidencia.gob.pa/gobierno.html
Political.
http://www.panamatours.com
Tourism.

Enquiries:
Enquiries to: Counsellor

Organisation type and purpose:
International organisation.

Subject coverage:
Education; economy; culture; politics; historical and geographical information about Panama, tourism etc.

Printed publications:
Press Release

Access to staff:
Contact by letter, by fax and by e-mail
Hours: Mon to Fri, 1030 to 1630

PANHARD ET LEVASSOR CLUB GB

La Dyna, 11 Arterial Avenue, Rainham, Essex, RM13 9PD

Tel: 01708 524425

Website:
http://www.panhardclub.co.uk

Enquiries:
Enquiries to: Vice President/Membership Secretary

Organisation type and purpose:
Membership association (membership is by subscription), present number of members: 75.

Subject coverage:
Deals mainly with the 1950s and 1960s cars but information can be obtained about any Panhard Levassor cars.

Access to staff:
Contact by letter and by telephone
Hours: Mon to Fri, 0900 to 2100

PANOS LONDON

Formal name: Panos Institute London

9 White Lion Street, London, N1 9PD

Tel: 020 7278 1111
Fax: 020 7278 0345
E-mail: info@panos.org.uk

Website:
http://www.panos.org.uk
Development and environment information, feature articles and briefings.

Enquiries:
Enquiries to: External Relations Assistant
Direct tel: 020 7239 7609

Founded:
1986

Organisation type and purpose:
Panos works to provide the world's poorest people with access to information on issues that affect them, and to make their voices heard on decisions that relate to their lives.

Subject coverage:
Environment, HIV/AIDS, communication for development, technology issues, oral testimony, globalisation and trade, research communication.

Library catalogue:
All or part available online

Printed publications:
Reports
Books
Media Briefings (£5 each or from website)

Photograph Library – commercial notes
Voices from the Mountain – oral testimony series (8 to date)

Publications list:
Available online

Access to staff:
Contact by letter, by telephone, by fax, by e-mail and via website. Appointment necessary. All charged.
Hours: Mon to Fri, 0930 to 1730

Parent body to:
Panos Picture Library
1 Chappel Court, Borough High Street, London, SE1 1HH; tel: 020 7234 0010

Sister organisations:
Worldwide including Asia, Africa, America and the Caribbean

PANOS PICTURE LIBRARY

1 Honduras Street, London, EC1Y 0TH

Tel: 020 7253 1424
Fax: 020 7253 2752
E-mail: pics@panos.co.uk

Website:
http://www.panos.co.uk

Enquiries:
Enquiries to: Archive Manager
Direct e-mail: zoe@panos.co.uk

Subject coverage:
Third world issues.

Parent body:
Panos Institute
9 White Lion Street, London, N1 9PD; tel: 020 7278 1111

PANTHER ENTHUSIASTS CLUB UK

91 Fleet Road, Farnborough, Hampshire, GU14 9RE

Tel: 01252 540217
Fax: 01252 540217
E-mail: george@pantherclub.co.uk

Website:
http://www.pantherclub.co.uk

Enquiries:
Enquiries to: Secretary

Founded:
1998

Organisation type and purpose:
Membership association (membership is by subscription), present number of members: 450.

Subject coverage:
Panther cars.

Access to staff:
Contact by letter, by telephone and by fax
Hours: Mon to Fri, 0900 to 1700

PAPER INDUSTRY TECHNICAL ASSOCIATION

Acronym or abbreviation: PITA

5 Frecheville Court, Bury, Lancashire, BL9 0UF

Tel: 0161 764 5858
Fax: 0161 764 5353
E-mail: info@pita.co.uk

Website:
http://www.pita.co.uk
General information and news of forthcoming events.

Enquiries:
Enquiries to: Chief Executive
Other contacts: Operations Executive for membership enquiries.

Founded:
1920

Organisation type and purpose:
Professional body (membership is by subscription), present number of members: 1700.

Subject coverage:
Papermaking technology, coating technology, finishing, environmental issues.

Museum or gallery collection, archive, or library special collection:
Complete set of Paper Technology formerly Paper Technology and Industry
Conference proceedings for all association events and many others

Non-library collection catalogue:
All or part available online, in-house and in print

Printed publications:
Conference Reports
Numerous reports and Seminar publications
Paper and Board Manufacture
Paper Science & Paper Manufacture (Peel Dr J)
Paper Technology (10 times a year, £100 a year plus p&p)
The Essential Guide to Aqueous Coating of Paper and Board

Electronic and video publications:
How Paper is Made (TAPPI, 3 CD-ROMs)

Publications list:
Available online and in print

Access to staff:
Contact by letter, by telephone, by fax and by e-mail. Appointment necessary.
Hours: Mon to Fri, 0900 to 1730

Access for disabled people:
Parking provided

PAPER MAKERS ALLIED TRADES ASSOCIATION

Acronym or abbreviation: PMATA

24 Beatrice Road, Worsley, Manchester, M28 2TN

Tel: 0161 794 5734
Fax: 0161 793 0827

Enquiries:
Enquiries to: Honorary Secretary

Founded:
1931

Organisation type and purpose:
Trade association (membership is by subscription), manufacturing industry.
Fostering good relations between the paper industry and its suppliers.

Subject coverage:
Paper industry, chemicals and supplies.

PAPERS PAST

Chapel Row, Truro, Cornwall TR1 2EA

Tel: 01872 261220
Fax: 01872 261220

Website:
http://www.paperspast.co.uk/
Service and product description and order form.

Enquiries:
Enquiries to: Archivist

Founded:
1981

Organisation type and purpose:
Mail order birthday/anniversary newspaper supplier.

Subject coverage:
Archive newspapers. Early 19th century to early 21st century.

Museum or gallery collection, archive, or library special collection:
Newspapers

Printed publications:
Original issues of 19th and 20th century newspapers

Access to staff:
Contact by letter, by telephone and by fax
Hours: Mon to Sun, 0900 to 1900

Access to building, collection or gallery:
No access other than to staff

PARENTLINE PLUS

Acronym or abbreviation: PLP

520 Highgate Studios, 53–79 Highgate Road, Kentish Town, London, NW5 1TL

Tel: 0808 800 2222\ Minicom no. 0800 783 6783
Fax: 020 7284 5501
E-mail: parentsupport@parentlineplus.org.uk

Website:
http://www.parentlineplus.org.uk

Enquiries:
Enquiries to: Chief Executive

Founded:
1983

Organisation type and purpose:
Voluntary organisation, registered charity (charity number 1077722).
Provision of advice, support and information, research and training, represents issues to government, encourages informed media coverage.

Subject coverage:
Any parenting issue; stepfamilies, stepparents, stepmothering, stepchildren, shared parenting, post-divorce, remarriage, re-partnering, teenagers and bullying.

Printed publications:
Publications on a variety of family issues including:
Books for children and young people
Divorce, Separation and New Families (12 publications)
Finance
Guides for parents
Helping Children Learn Series (5 leaflets)
Parenting
Resources for Professionals
Stepfamilies
Sexual Health

Electronic and video publications:
Videos for parents and teenagers

Publications list:
Available in print

Access to staff:
Contact by letter, by telephone, by fax, by e-mail and via website
Hours: Mon to Fri, 0900 to 1700

Branches:
Parentline Plus
  Gloucestershire; tel: 01453 768160
Parentline Plus
  Nottingham; tel: 0115 841 0432
Parentline Plus
  Wirral; tel: 0151 201 7876
Parentline Plus
  Croydon; tel: 020 8689 2252
Parentline Plus
  Hadleigh, Essex; tel: 01702 554782
Parentline Plus
  East Midlands; tel: 01780 480893
Parentline Plus
  Hampshire; tel: 0238 061 9826
Parentline Plus
  Hertfordshire; tel: 01707 270696
Parentline Plus
  North East; tel: 01780 480893

PARENTS FOR CHILDREN

3 Angel Gate, 326 City Road, London, EC1V 2PT

Tel: 020 7520 2880
E-mail: info@parentsforchildren.org.uk

Website:
http://www.parentsforchildren.org.uk/

Enquiries:
Enquiries to: Chief Executive
Other contacts: Fostering Development Co-ordinator for foster parents for children.

Founded:
1976

Organisation type and purpose:
Voluntary organisation, registered charity.
Adoption agency. Specialises in family-finding for children with very special needs.

Subject coverage:
Adoption and long-term fostering of disturbed and disabled children; post-placement and post-adoption support.

Printed publications:
Annual Report

Access to staff:
Contact by letter and by telephone
Hours: Mon to Fri, 0900 to 1700

Also at the same address:
Foster Parents for Children
  tel: 020 7359 7530; fax: 020 7226 7840

PARENTS FOR INCLUSION

Acronym or abbreviation: Pi

Unit 1, Winchester House, Kennington Park Business Centre, Cranmer Road, London, SW9 6EJ

Tel: 020 7735 7735
Fax: 020 7735 3828
E-mail: info@parentsforinclusion.org

Website:
http://www.parentsforinclusion.org

Enquiries:
Enquiries to: Managing Director

Founded:
1984

Organisation type and purpose:
Membership association (membership is by subscription), present number of members: 200, voluntary organisation, registered charity.
To promote inclusive education of special needs children. Parents helping parents so that their disabled children can learn, make friends and have a voice in ordinary school and throughout life.
Aims to help parents whose children are said to have special educational needs to get the support their children need in mainstream schools.

Subject coverage:
Disability, inclusive education and training for parents and young people.

Printed publications:
Action for Inclusion (£7 inc. p&p)
Breaking of Relationships (£2.50 inc. p&p)
Disability Equality in the Classroom: A Human Rights Issue (£15)
Parents and Partnership (£2.50 inc. p&p)
The Inclusion Papers: Strategies To Make Inclusion Work (£8.50)

Electronic and video publications:
Altogether Better (video, £7.50 inc p&p)
Audiotapes
Including All Children (video, £10 plus £1 p&p, £5 to parents)

Publications list:
Available in print

Access to staff:
Contact by letter, by telephone, by fax and by e-mail. Appointment necessary.
Hours: Mon to Fri, 0900 to 1700

Special comments: Advice line: Tue, Wed, Thu, 1000 to 1200 and 1300 to 1500.

Access for disabled people:
Parking provided, ramped entry, access to all public areas, toilet facilities

PARKES LIBRARY

The Hartley Library, University of Southampton, Highfield, Southampton, SO17 1BJ

Tel: 023 8059 2721 or 8059 3335
Fax: 023 8059 5451
E-mail: library@soton.ac.uk; archives@soton.ac.uk

Website:
http://www.soton.ac.uk/library/resources/collections/parkes/index.html
http://www-lib.soton.ac.uk
University library catalogue, including the Parkes Library.
http://www.southampton.ac.uk/archives/cataloguedatabases/guideintro.html
Guide to archive collections.

Enquiries:
Enquiries to: Librarian

Organisation type and purpose:
University library.
Library collection within the Southampton University Library; devoted to relations between Jewish and non-Jewish communities.

Subject coverage:
History of Jewish communities; Zionism and Palestine; Middle Eastern history and Israel; Jewish society, religion and ethics; Jewish-Christian relations; anti-Semitism.

Museum or gallery collection, archive, or library special collection:
Manuscript collections covering all aspects of Anglo-Jewry and its origins, relating to national and international organisations and to individuals within the Jewish community

Library catalogue:
All or part available online

Printed publications:
Guide to the Archive and Manuscript Collections of the Hartley Library, University of Southampton
Parkes Library Lectures
Parkes Library Pamphlets (series)
Sources for Research (Special Collections Division, Hartley Library, University of Southampton)
USL Archive lists, catalogues and guides series

Access to staff:
Contact by letter, by telephone, by fax, by e-mail and in person
Hours: Mon to Fri, 0930 to 1700

PARKINSON'S DISEASE SOCIETY OF THE UNITED KINGDOM

Acronym or abbreviation: PDS

215 Vauxhall Bridge Road, London, SW1V 1EJ

Tel: 020 7931 8080 \ Helpline: 0808 800 0303
Fax: 020 7233 9908
E-mail: enquiries@parkinsons.org.uk

Website:
http://www.parkinsons.org.uk

Enquiries:
Enquiries to: PR Administrator
Direct tel: 020 7932 1323
Direct e-mail: atebb@parkinsons.org.uk

Founded:
1969

Organisation type and purpose:
National organisation, membership association (membership is by subscription), present number of members: 30,000, voluntary organisation, registered charity (charity number 258197), research organisation.

continued overleaf

Subject coverage:
Parkinson's disease: information and advice for sufferers and carers; support also to general practitioners, ancillary para-medical personnel and other healthcare professionals.

Printed publications:
Magazine (4 times a year)
Living With Parkinson's Disease
Parkinson's at your Fingertips (£11.95)
Variety of information for professionals
Variety of information for patients, families and carers

Electronic and video publications:
Keeping Moving: an exercise programme for people with Parkinson's (£18.00)

Publications list:
Available in print

Access to staff:
Contact by letter, by telephone, by fax and by e-mail. Appointment necessary.
Hours: Mon to Fri, 0800 to 1730
Special comments: Helpline, Mon to Fri, 0930 to 1730.

Access to building, collection or gallery:
Prior appointment required

Branches:
Scotland
   Forsythe House, Lommond Court, Castle Business Park, Stirling, FK9 4TU; tel: 01786 433811; fax: 01786 431811; e-mail: pds.scotland@parkinsons.org.uk; website: www.parkinsons.org.uk

Has:
over 300 branches

Member of:
European Parkinson's Disease Association

PARLIAMENTARY ADVISORY COUNCIL FOR TRANSPORT SAFETY

Acronym or abbreviation: PACTS

St Thomas' Hospital, Governors Hall, Block 5 South Wing, Lambeth Palace Road, London, SE1 7EH

Tel: 020 7922 8112
Fax: 020 7401 8740
E-mail: admin@pacts.org.uk

Website:
http://www.pacts.org.uk
Publications list

Enquiries:
Enquiries to: Administrator

Founded:
1982

Organisation type and purpose:
Membership association (membership is by subscription), present number of members: 250, voluntary organisation, registered charity (charity number 1068607), research organisation. Parliamentary advisory body (transport safety).

Subject coverage:
Road, rail and air transport safety. PACTS advises parliamentarians on issues of transport safety based on research solutions.

Printed publications:
PACTS' Publications (£10 to £20)

Publications list:
Available online

Access to staff:
Contact by telephone and by e-mail
Hours: Mon to Fri, 0900 to 1700

Founder member of:
European Transport Safety Council (ETSC)
   Rue du Cornet 34, Brussels, B-1040, Belgium

PARLIAMENTARY AND HEALTH SERVICE OMBUDSMAN

Formal name: Office of the Parliamentary Commissioner for Administration and the Health Service Commissioners

Millbank Tower, Millbank, London, SW1P 4QP

Tel: 020 7217 4000
Fax: 020 7217 4940
E-mail: lrc@ombudsman.org.uk

Website:
http://www.ombudsman.org.uk

Enquiries:
Enquiries to: Information Officer
Direct tel: 020 7217 4104

Founded:
1967

Organisation type and purpose:
National organisation.

Subject coverage:
Ombudsman issues.

Printed publications:
Order printed publications from: For purchase via the Stationery Office

Access to staff:
Contact by letter, by telephone, by fax and by e-mail
Hours: Mon to Fri, 0900 to 1700

PARLIAMENTARY AND SCIENTIFIC COMMITTEE

48 Westminster Palace Gardens, Artillery Row, London, SW1P 1RR

Tel: 020 7222 7085
Fax: 020 7222 5355

Enquiries:
Enquiries to: Secretary

Founded:
1939

Organisation type and purpose:
Membership association (membership is by subscription).

Subject coverage:
Parliament and science.

Printed publications:
Science in Parliament (the journal of the Parliamentary and Scientific Committee)

Access to staff:
Contact by letter, by telephone and by fax
Hours: Mon to Fri, 1000 to 1800

PARLIAMENTARY ARCHIVES

Acronym or abbreviation: HLRO

House of Lords Record Office, London, SW1A 0PW

Tel: 020 7219 3074
Fax: 020 7219 2570
E-mail: hlro@parliament.uk

Website:
http://www.parliament.uk/archives
Index-A-Archives for general information including records held, details of location and access, list of publications in print, on-line exhibitions
http://www.portcullis.parliament.uk catalogue of collections

Enquiries:
Enquiries to: Clerk of The Records

Founded:
1946

Organisation type and purpose:
One of the Offices of Parliament.
To preserve and make available the archives of Parliament.

Subject coverage:
History of both Houses of Parliament, history of the Palace of Westminster; the Private Bill Records contain a great deal of information about local history e.g. local government, railways, roads, canals, electricity, gas and water works; political history from the special collections; legal and contemporary issues. Sources for genealogists include certain legislation, Private Bill evidence, Protestation Returns of 1642 and other Lords papers.

Museum or gallery collection, archive, or library special collection:
records of the House of Lords from 1497 and of the House of Commons from 1547, Papers of 1st Viscount Samuel, Lord Beaverbrook, Lloyd George, Bonar Law and others

Trade and statistical information:
Published Parliamentary reports.
Evidence given to select committees.

Non-library collection catalogue:
All or part available online and in-house

Library catalogue:
All or part available online and in-house

Printed publications:
Calendar of the Manuscripts of the House of Lords, volumes I-XII (new series) 1693–1718 (HMSO)
Guide to the Records of Parliament (Bond M F, 1971, pub HMSO)
Annual Review (TSO)
House of Lords Record Office Memoranda including:
Witnesses Before Parliament (1997)
House of Lords Record Office Occasional Publications including:
A Handlist of the Braye Manuscripts in the House of Lords Record Office (HMSO, 1993)
Catalogue of the Beaverbrook Papers in the House of Lords Record Office: Canadian and Business Papers (TSO, 1997)

Microform publications:
Parliamentary Papers (pub Proquest)
Main papers (Harvester)
Minutes, Committee Books etc (pub Adam Matthew Publications)

Publications list:
Available online and in print

Access to staff:
Contact by letter, by telephone, by fax, by e-mail and via website. Appointment necessary.
Hours: Mon, Wed to Fri, 0930 to 1700; Tue, 0930 to 2000, booking one week in advance only when Parliament is in session

Access for disabled people:
Toilet facilities
Special comments: Parking by special arrangement, access by lift.

PARLIAMENTARY MONITORING SERVICES

Acronym or abbreviation: PMS

19 Douglas Street, London, SW1P 4PA

Tel: 020 7233 8283
Fax: 020 7821 9352
E-mail: lionel.zetter@parliamentary-monitoring.co.uk

Website:
http://www.politicalwizard.co.uk

Enquiries:
Enquiries to: Managing Director

Founded:
1978

Organisation type and purpose:
Research organisation, publishing house.
We are an independent commercial political research, news and publishing company.

Subject coverage:
Politics: local, national and European Union, legislation, issues and personalities.

Printed publications:
European Public Affairs Directory 1998 (annually, £69)
Legitimate Lobbying (£9)
PMS Guide to Pressure Groups (3rd ed., £17.50)
PMS Parliament Companion (quarterly, £11 per issue, £33 annual subscription)
PMS Update Bulletin (approximately 40 issues a year, £75 annual subscription)
Parliamentary Bulletin for Local Government Executives (weekly, £75 annual subscription)

Electronic and video publications:
Online databases with biographical details on MPs, peers, MEPs and civil servants
PMS Biographical Guide to the Civil Service
PMS Biographical Guide to the House of Commons
PMS Biographical Guide to the House of Lords
PMS Biographical Guides (the three online £900 annual subscription)

Publications list:
Available in print

Access to staff:
Contact by letter, by telephone, by fax and by e-mail. Appointment necessary.
Hours: Mon to Fri, 0900 to 1730

Access to building, collection or gallery:
No prior appointment required

Subsidiary body:
PMS Publications Limited

PARTIALLY SIGHTED SOCIETY

Acronym or abbreviation: PSS

PO Box 322, Doncaster, South Yorkshire, DN1 2XA

Tel: 01302 323132
Fax: 01302 368998
E-mail: info@partsight.org.uk

Enquiries:
Enquiries to: Information Officer

Founded:
1973

Organisation type and purpose:
Membership association, voluntary organisation, registered charity (charity number 254052).
Helping the visually impaired make best use of their remaining sight.

Subject coverage:
Education, employment, mobility, daily living, leisure, aids and adaptations in relation to living with partial sight.

Printed publications:
Crossword Books
Good News for the Partially Sighted
Large print crossword book
Light for Low Vision
Mail Order Brochure for daily living aids
Oculus (large print magazine, 4 times a year)

Publications list:
Available in print

Access to staff:
Contact by letter, by telephone, by fax, by e-mail and via website. Appointment necessary.
Hours: Mon to Fri, 0900 to 1700

PARTICLE PHYSICS AND ASTRONOMY RESEARCH COUNCIL

Acronym or abbreviation: PPARC

Polaris House, North Star Avenue, Swindon, Wiltshire, SN2 1SZ

Tel: 01793 442000
Fax: 01793 442002
E-mail: pr_pus@pparc.ac.uk

Website:
http://www.pparc.ac.uk
News in particle physics and astronomy. Directory of contacts. Details of PPARC awards.

Enquiries:
Enquiries to: Librarian
Other contacts: Press Officer

Organisation type and purpose:
Research organisation.
State aided organisation.
One of the seven research councils. PPARC directs and co-ordinates the funding of United Kingdom research into the physics of the Universe.

Subject coverage:
Astronomy, planetary science, particle physics, science policy.

Printed publications:
Leaflets for schools and the general public about particle physics and astronomy
Order printed publications from: Strategic Planning & Communications, Particle Physics and Astronomy Research Council
at the same address

Access to staff:
Contact by letter, by telephone, by fax, by e-mail and via website
Hours: Mon to Fri, 0900 to 1700

Laboratories:
Royal Observatory (Edinburgh)
Royal Observatory (Greenwich)

PARTNERSHIP FOR THEOLOGICAL EDUCATION

Formal name: Luther King House Library
Acronym or abbreviation: PTE

Luther King House, Brighton Grove, Rusholme, Manchester, M14 5JP

Tel: 0161 249 2514
Fax: 0161 248 9201
E-mail: library@lkh.co.uk

Website:
http://www.lutherkinghouse.org.uk
http://www.lkhlibrarycatalogue.org.uk
Online catalogue

Enquiries:
Enquiries to: Learning Resources Tutor
Other contacts: Learning Resources Assistant

Founded:
1988

Formerly called:
Manchester Christian Institute (year of change 1992); Northern Federation for Training in Ministry (year of change 2000)

Organisation type and purpose:
Registered charity, university department or institute.
Theological college.

Subject coverage:
Theology; Free Church and general ecclesiastical history; ministry; Bible commentaries; worship; social sciences; biography; history; philosophy; ethics; missiology; spirituality; pastoral theology; ecumenism; comparative religion; community studies.

Museum or gallery collection, archive, or library special collection:
Collections housed in the John Rylands Library, Manchester
Hobill Collection and Primitive Methodist Material
Northern (Congregational College) Collection
Rawdon Collection of historical Baptist material, mostly from 18th and 19th centuries (Northern Baptist College Deposit)
Unitarian College Collection (McLachlan Library) Unitarian and Nonconformist history, Socinianism

Non-library collection catalogue:
All or part available online

Library catalogue:
All or part available online

Access to staff:
Contact by letter, by telephone, by fax, by e-mail, in person and via website. Appointment necessary. Non-members charged.
Hours: Mon to Fri, 0900 to 1700

Access for disabled people:
Parking provided, ramped entry, toilet facilities

Constituent bodies:
Hartley Victoria College
Luther King House Open College
Northern Baptist College
Northern College (United Reformed and Congregational)
Unitarian College

Links with:
William Temple Foundation
at the same address

Recognised by the:
Department of Religions and Theology of the University of Manchester
Department of Theology and Religious Studies of the University of Chester

PASSENGER SHIPPING ASSOCIATION

Acronym or abbreviation: PSA

1st Floor, 41–42 Eastcastle Street, London, W1W 8DW

Tel: 020 7436 2449
Fax: 020 7636 9206
E-mail: h.tapping@psa-psara.org

Website:
http://www.ferryinformationservice.co.uk
http://www.cruiseinformationservice.co.uk

Enquiries:
Enquiries to: Director
Other contacts: Administrator

Organisation type and purpose:
Membership association (membership is by subscription).

Subject coverage:
Passenger shipping.

Access to staff:
Contact by e-mail
Hours: Mon to Fri, 0900 to 1700

Access to building, collection or gallery:
No access other than to staff, prior appointment required

PASSIVE FIRE PROTECTION FEDERATION

Acronym or abbreviation: PFPF

Tournai Hall, Evelyn Woods Road, Aldershot Hampshire GU11 2LL

Tel: 01252 357841
Fax: 01252 357831
E-mail: admin@pfpf.org

Website:
http://pfpf.org/

Enquiries:
Enquiries to: Secretary

Organisation type and purpose:
Trade association, present number of members: 16.
Federation of trade associations, test houses, certification and government bodies involved in passive fire protection.

Subject coverage:
Trade associations, test houses, certification and government bodies involved in passive fire protection.

continued overleaf

Access to staff:
Contact by letter, by telephone, by fax, by e-mail
and via website
Hours: Mon to Fri, 0900 to 1700

PASTEL SOCIETY

Acronym or abbreviation: PS

17 Carlton House Terrace, London, SW1Y 5BD

Tel: 020 7930 6844
Fax: 020 7839 7830
E-mail: press@mallgalleries.com

Website:
http://www.thepastelsociety.org.uk
http://www.mallgalleries.org.uk
FBA and Mall Galleries information

Enquiries:
Enquiries to: Secretary
Other contacts: Marketing and Communications
Officer

Founded:
1898

Organisation type and purpose:
Membership association (membership is by
election or invitation), present number of
members: 68, voluntary organisation, registered
charity (charity number 200048).
To foster and promote the art of pastel painting.

Subject coverage:
Pastel art.

**Museum or gallery collection, archive, or library
special collection:**
Examples of pastel artists' work on slides, photos
and some original pastel paintings

Printed publications:
Annual Exhibition Catalogue
Books on Pastel Painting on sale during annual
exhibition

Access to staff:
Contact by letter, by telephone, by fax, by e-mail
and via website. Appointment necessary.
Hours: Mon to Fri, 0930 to 1730

Access to building, collection or gallery:
No access other than to staff, prior appointment
required
Hours: Mon to Fri, 0930 to 1730

Access for disabled people:
Toilet facilities
Special comments: Stairlift.

Links with:
Federation of British Artists (FBA)
at the same address

PATENT OFFICE

Cardiff Road, Newport, South Wales, NP10 8QQ

Tel: 01633 814000, Operator; 0845 9500505, Central
Enquiry Unit (local rate)\ Minicom no. 0645 222
250 (local rate)
Fax: 01633 814444
E-mail: enquiries@patent.gov.uk

Website:
http://www.patent.gov.uk
Advice and information regarding patents,
designs, trade and service marks and copyright,
including a search engine for Patents.

Enquiries:
Enquiries to: Information Officer
Direct fax: 01633 813600

Founded:
1852

Organisation type and purpose:
National government body.
Executive agency of the Department of Trade and
Industry.

Subject coverage:
All areas of Intellectual Property incorporating:
Patents, Designs, Trade marks and Copyright.

Printed publications:
An Introduction to the Services of the Patent Office
and Trade Marks and Design Registries
Design Registration
How to prepare a UK Patent application
Managing Intellectual Property
Official Journal (Patents)
Patent Abstracts
Patent Protection
Registering a Trademark
Trade Mark Journal
What is Intellectual Property
Your Software and How to Protect it

Electronic and video publications:
Managing Intellectual Property
UK Patent applications on CD-ROM available for
sale

Access to staff:
Contact by letter, by telephone, by fax, by e-mail,
in person and via website
Hours: Mon to Fri, 0900 to 1700

Access to building, collection or gallery:
No prior appointment required
Special comments: Trade Mark Searches in Newport
require an appointment.

Other addresses:
The Patent Office
Harmsworth House, 13–15 Bouverie Street,
London, EC4Y 8DP; tel: 020 7596 6518; e-mail:
enquiries@patent.gov.uk

PATHOLOGICAL SOCIETY OF GREAT BRITAIN AND IRELAND

2 Carlton House Terrace, London, SW1Y 5AF

Tel: 020 7976 1260
Fax: 020 7976 1267
E-mail: admin@pathsoc.org.uk

Website:
http://www.pathsoc.org.uk

Enquiries:
Enquiries to: Administrator

Founded:
1906

Organisation type and purpose:
Learned society (membership is by election or
invitation), present number of members: 1500
(charity number 214702).
Research communication for the continuing
education of pathologists.

Subject coverage:
Pathology.

Printed publications:
Journal of Pathology (monthly)

Access to staff:
Contact by letter, by telephone, by fax and by e-
mail
Hours: Mon to Fri, 0900 to 1730

PATTERN, MODEL AND MOULDMAKERS ASSOCIATION

Acronym or abbreviation: PMMMA

c/o Eur. Ing. Andrew Turner, National
Metalforming Centre, 47 Birmingham Road, West
Bromwich, West Midlands, B70 6PY

Tel: 0121 601 6976
Fax: 01544 340332
E-mail: andrew@pmmma.co.uk

Website:
http://www.pmmma.co.uk

Organisation type and purpose:
Trade association.

Subject coverage:
Pattern-making, industrial patterns and moulds.

Access to staff:
Contact by letter, by telephone and by fax

PCET PUBLISHING

27 Kirchen Road, London, W13 0UD

Tel: 020 8567 9206 or 5343
Fax: 020 8566 5120
E-mail: info@pcet.co.uk

Website:
http://www.pcet.co.uk
Sample of charts from subject leaflets and
information about teaching, guides, money savers,
photocopiable activity books, catalogue requests.

Enquiries:
Enquiries to: Managing Director
Direct e-mail: Director@pcet.co.uk

Founded:
1964

Organisation type and purpose:
Publishing house.
Non-profit making publisher of educational visual
aids.

Subject coverage:
Educational visual aids in all areas of the National
Curriculum, except modern languages.

Printed publications:
Mail order catalogue (annually, with additional
supplements)
Titles cover a wide range of subjects including:
Art
Geography
History
Religion
The 20th Century
Mathematics
Music
Sciences
English

Publications list:
Available in print

Access to staff:
Contact by letter, by telephone, by fax, by e-mail
and via website. Appointment necessary.
Hours: Mon to Fri, 0900 to 1700

PDSA

Acronym or abbreviation: PDSA

Whitechapel Way, Priorslee, Telford, Shropshire,
TF2 9PQ

Tel: 01952 290999
Fax: 01952 291035
E-mail: pr@pdsa.org.uk

Website:
http://www.pdsa.org.uk
PDSA veterinary services, pet care advice, PDSA
news and fundraising opportunities.

Enquiries:
Enquiries to: Public Relations Manager

Founded:
1917

Organisation type and purpose:
Registered charity (charity number 208217).
The PDSA provides free veterinary treatment to
sick and injured pets whose owners qualify for
help, by receiving either Housing Benefit or
Council Tax Benefit, and live within an area served
by a PDSA PetAid hospital or PetAid practice.

Subject coverage:
Veterinary and associated social and educational
subjects (eg pet care).

Printed publications:
General information leaflets
Pet Care Leaflets

Publications list:
Available in print

Access to staff:
Contact by letter, by telephone, by fax, by e-mail and via website
Hours: Mon to Fri, 0900 to 1700

PEAK DISTRICT NATIONAL PARK AUTHORITY

Acronym or abbreviation: PDNPA

National Park Office, Aldern House, Baslow Road, Bakewell, Derbyshire, DE45 1AE

Tel: 01629 816200
Fax: 01629 816310
E-mail: customer.service@peakdistrict.gov.uk

Website:
http://www.peakdistrict.gov.uk

Enquiries:
Enquiries to: Head of Communications (for media enquiries)
Direct tel: 01629 816356
Direct e-mail: john.fern@peakdistrict.gov.uk

Founded:
1951

Organisation type and purpose:
Local government body, advisory body, statutory body, training organisation, publishing house.

Subject coverage:
The Peak District National Park, conservation of the National Park environment, integrated rural development, moorland erosion, recreation, and restoration; general information on the history, geology, agriculture, wildlife, and recreation opportunities, rural public transport, environmental education and training.

Printed publications:
Annual Report
National Park Management Plan
Planning publications and official reports
Parklife (2 times a year)
Peak District National Park Cycle Routes

Publications list:
Available in print

Access to staff:
Contact by letter, by telephone, by e-mail and via website. Appointment necessary.
Hours: Mon to Fri, 0845 to 1700

Access to building, collection or gallery:
Prior appointment required

Access for disabled people:
Parking provided, ramped entry, toilet facilities

PEEBLES AREA LIBRARY

Chambers Institution, High Street, Peebles, Borders, EH45 8AG

Tel: 01721 720123
Fax: 01721 724424
E-mail: libpeebles@scotborders.gov.uk

Enquiries:
Enquiries to: Area Librarian
Direct e-mail: ptaylor@scotborders.gov.uk

Founded:
1859

Organisation type and purpose:
Local government body, public library.

Subject coverage:
General, Peeblesshire local history, John Buchan material.

Library catalogue:
All or part available in-house

Access to staff:
Contact by letter, by telephone, by fax, by e-mail and in person
Hours: Mon, Wed and Fri, 0930 to 1700; Tue and Thu, 0930 to 1900; Sat, 0900 to 1230

Access for disabled people:
Lift to Library area on first floor, only

Parent body:
Scottish Borders Library Service
St Marys Hill, Selkirk, TD7 5EW; tel: 01750 20842; fax: 01750 22875

PEMBROKE COLLEGE

McGowin Library, Oxford, OX1 1DW

Tel: 01865 276409
Fax: 01865 276418

Website:
http://www.pmb.ox.ac.uk

Enquiries:
Enquiries to: Librarian/Archivist
Direct e-mail: library@pmb.ox.ac.uk

Founded:
1624

Organisation type and purpose:
College library.

Subject coverage:
Aristotle, Samuel Johnson, College history.

Museum or gallery collection, archive, or library special collection:
Archive of Pembroke College
Aristotle (Chandler Collection)
Samuel Johnson

Access to staff:
Contact by letter, by telephone, by fax, by e-mail and via website. Appointment necessary. Letter of introduction required.
Hours: Mon to Fri, 0900 to 1700

PEMBROKESHIRE COAST NATIONAL PARK AUTHORITY

Acronym or abbreviation: PCNPA

Llanion Park, Pembroke Dock, Pembrokeshire, SA72 6DY

Tel: 0845 345 7275
Fax: 01646 689076
E-mail: info@pembrokeshirecoast.org.uk

Website:
http://www.pcnpa.org.uk

Enquiries:
Enquiries to: Switchboard

Founded:
1952

Organisation type and purpose:
Local government body, advisory body, statutory body, present number of members: 18
National Park Authority and Local Planning Authority.
Conservation of landscape, wildlife and culture of the National Park; promotion of the enjoyment and understanding of the Park's special qualities; foster the social and economic well-being of the local community.

Subject coverage:
Conservation, National Parks, recreation, countryside access, interpretation, education, local information, communities, cultural heritage, wildlife, planning.

Museum or gallery collection, archive, or library special collection:
Local maps and aerial photographs
Planning Records
Teachers' Resources

Trade and statistical information:
Statistics on the National Park (as available).

Printed publications:
Children's Leaflets
Guides to walks in the National Park
Guides for the Coast Path Walker
Subject guides including wild flowers and beaches
Safety information
Access information (including disabled, etc.)
Easy Access Routes

Order printed publications from: Tenby Information Centre Manager, Pembrokeshire Coast National Park Authority, Ruabon House, South Parade, Tenby, SA70 7DL

Electronic and video publications:
Pembrokeshire Coast Long Distance Path video
Carew Castle Education Pack (includes video)

Publications list:
Available online and in print

Access to staff:
Contact by letter, by telephone, by fax, by e-mail, in person and via website
Hours: Headquarters: Mon to Thu, 0900 to 1700; Fri, 0900 to 1630

Access for disabled people:
Parking provided, ramped entry, wheelchair lifts and toilet facilities

Branches:
Carew Castle and Tidal Mill
Carew, Pembrokeshire, SA70 8SL; tel: 01646 651782; fax: 01646 651782; e-mail: enquiries@carewcastle.com
Castell Henllys Iron Age Fort
Meline, Crymych, Pembrokeshire, SA41 3UT; tel: 01239 891319; fax: 01239 891319; e-mail: enquiries@castellhenllys.com
Cilrhedyn Woodland Centre
Llanychaer, Fishguard, Pembrokeshire, SA65 9TN; tel: 01348 881441; fax: 01348 881713
Landscape Gallery and National Park Information Centre, Oriel y Parc
The Grove, St Davids, Pembrokeshire, SA62 6NW; tel: 01437 725087; fax: 01437 720099; e-mail: enquiries@stdavids.pembrokeshirecoast.org.uk
National Park Information Centre (all year)
Ruabon House, South Parade, Tenby, SA70 7DL; tel: 01834 845040; fax: 01834 840871; e-mail: contact.centre@pembrokeshire.gov.uk
National Park Information Centre (Seasonal)
Bank Cottages, Long Street, Newport, SA42 0TN; tel: 01239 820912; fax: 01239 820912

Links with:
Parc Naturel Regional d'Armorique
15 place aux Foires, BP 27, 29590, Le Faou, France; tel: +33 2 98 81 90 08; fax: +33 2 98 81 90 09

PEMBROKESHIRE COUNTY COUNCIL

County Hall, Haverfordwest, Pembrokeshire, SA61 1TP

Tel: 01437 764551
Fax: 01437 775303
E-mail: enquiries@pembrokeshire.gov.uk

Website:
http://www.pembrokeshire.gov.uk
Tourism and Inward Investment. General information re Pembrokeshire and Pembrokeshire County Council.

Enquiries:
Enquiries to: Head of Marketing Communications
Direct tel: 01437 775850
Direct e-mail: david.thomas@pembrokeshire.gov.uk

Founded:
April 1996

Organisation type and purpose:
Local government body.

Subject coverage:
All local government services.

Museum or gallery collection, archive, or library special collection:
County archives department, county libraries and county museums

Printed publications:
Community Newspaper (2 times a year, free)
Holiday Brochure for Pembrokeshire (free)
Various other publications and leaflets on services provided and policy documents

continued overleaf

Access to staff:
Contact by letter, by telephone, by fax, by e-mail, in person and via website. Appointment necessary.
Hours: Mon to Fri, 0900 to 1700

Access for disabled people:
Parking provided, level entry, toilet facilities

PEMBROKESHIRE RECORD OFFICE

The Castle, Haverfordwest, Pembrokeshire, SA61 2EF

Tel: 01437 763707
Fax: 01437 768539
E-mail: record.office@pembrokeshire.gov.uk

Website:
http://www.pembrokeshire.gov.uk
Brief description of service, with opening hours.

Enquiries:
Enquiries to: Archivist

Founded:
1963

Organisation type and purpose:
Local government body.
Local authority record office.

Subject coverage:
The history of Pembrokeshire.

Museum or gallery collection, archive, or library special collection:
Pembrokeshire historical material, mainly manuscript collections

Non-library collection catalogue:
All or part available in-house

Library catalogue:
All or part available in-house

Publications list:
Available in print

Access to staff:
Contact by letter, by telephone, by fax, by e-mail and in person
Hours: Mon to Thu, 0900 to 1645; Fri, 0900 to 1615

Access to building, collection or gallery:
No access other than to staff
Hours: Mon to Thu, 0900 to 1645; Fri, 0900 to 1615
Special comments: 1st Mon in the month, 1000 to 1645
1st Sat in the month except bank holiday weekends, 0930 to 1230

Access for disabled people:
Parking provided, ramped entry, access to all public areas, toilet facilities

PENGUIN COLLECTORS' SOCIETY

Acronym or abbreviation: PCS

c/o 31 Myddelton Square, London, EC1R 1YB

Tel: 020 7278 8064
E-mail: tresurer@penguincollectorssociety.org

Website:
http://www.penguincollectorssociety.com
Details of society, membership application form, illustrations and descriptions of publications.

Enquiries:
Enquiries to: Secretary

Founded:
1974

Organisation type and purpose:
Charity (membership is by subscription), present number of members: c. 400.
Study, research, and publishing on 20th-century books, especially those published by Penguin Books Limited.

Subject coverage:
Penguin Books, their history and publications.

Printed publications:
Journal and monographs

Publications list:
Available in print

Access to staff:
Contact by letter and by e-mail

PENNINE WAY ASSOCIATION

Acronym or abbreviation: PWA

29 Springfield Park Avenue, Chelmsford, Essex, CM2 6EL

Tel: 01245 256772
E-mail: penninewayassociation@hotmail.com

Website:
http://www.penninewayassociation.co.uk

Enquiries:
Enquiries to: Chairman
Direct e-mail: penninewayassociation@hotmail.com

Founded:
1971

Formerly called:
Pennine Way Council (year of change 1992)

Organisation type and purpose:
Membership association (membership is by subscription), present number of members: 360, voluntary organisation, registered charity (charity number 511519).

Subject coverage:
To secure the protection of the Pennine Way, to provide information about the Way to the public, to educate users of the Way and its environs in a proper respect for the countryside, and to provide a forum in which different interests connected with the Way and its use can discuss problems of mutual concern.

Printed publications:
Pennine Way woven badge
PW Memento (£3.00 incl. postage)
Pennine Way Accommodation and Camping Guide (2008/09 downloadable from the PWA website)
Walkers' factsheet (send sae)

Access to staff:
Contact by letter, by telephone, by e-mail and via website
Hours: Answerphone

PENSIONS ADVISORY SERVICE LTD, THE

Acronym or abbreviation: TPAS

11 Belgrave Road, London, SW1V 1RB

Tel: 0845 6012923
Fax: 020 7233 8016
E-mail: enquiries@pensionsadvisoryservice.org.uk

Website:
http://www.pensionsadvisoryservice.org.uk
Casework reports, leaflets.

Founded:
1983

Organisation type and purpose:
Advisory body, voluntary organisation.
To provide help and advice on various pension problems, helps to resolve any difficulties encountered with the trustees or administrators of pension schemes.

Subject coverage:
Occupational and personal pensions and state pensions.

Printed publications:
Getting Information About Your Pension (free)
Ill-Health Retirement (free)
Information (free)
Pension Dispute Procedures (free)
Personal Pension Problems (free)
Transferring a Pension to another Scheme (free)

What are AVC's? (free)
Where Is My Pension? (free)
Winding Up a Pension Scheme (free)
Women and Pensions (free)

Publications list:
Available in print

Access to staff:
Contact by letter, by telephone, by fax and by e-mail
Hours: Mon to Fri, 0900 to 1700

PENSIONS MANAGEMENT INSTITUTE

Acronym or abbreviation: PMI

PMI House, 4–10 Artillery Lane, London, E1 7LS

Tel: 020 7247 1452
Fax: 020 7365 0603
E-mail: enquiries@pensions-pmi.org.uk

Website:
http://www.pensions-pmi.org.uk

Enquiries:
Enquiries to: Secretary General

Founded:
1976

Organisation type and purpose:
Professional body (membership is by subscription), present number of members: 4500.
Qualifying institute for the Trustee Certificate of Basic Pensions Knowledge and Diploma in International Employee Benefits and the awarding body for 2 S/NVQs in Pensions Administration.

Subject coverage:
Pension schemes, administration and management; pensioners.

Printed publications:
Annual Handbook
Annual Yearbook
Glossary of Pension Terms
Newsletter (monthly)
Pensions and Divorce (1991)
Research Papers
Technical News (quarterly)
Tuition material

Access to staff:
Contact by letter, by telephone, by fax, by e-mail and via website
Hours: Mon to Fri, 0900 to 1700

PENSIONS OMBUDSMAN

6th Floor, 11 Belgrave Road, London, SW1V 1RB

Tel: 020 7834 9144
Fax: 020 7821 0065

Enquiries:
Enquiries to: Administrator
Direct e-mail: michael.lydon@pensions -ombudsman.org.uk
Other contacts: Press Officer for press enquiries.

Founded:
1990

Organisation type and purpose:
Independent statutory body.

Subject coverage:
In cases where a complaint or dispute cannot be resolved, normally after the intervention of OPAS, an application can be made to the Pensions Ombudsman for an adjudication. The Ombudsman can investigate and determine any complaint or dispute of fact or law involving the management of occupational and personal pension schemes. The services of the Ombudsman are available to scheme members, and prospective members of schemes, as well as to (in some circumstances) employers, trustees or managers.

Printed publications:
The Pensions Ombudsman – What he can do (available free, direct)

The Pensions Ombudsman – Annual Report
(Stationery Office, charged)

Access to staff:
Contact by letter, by telephone, by fax and by e-mail
Hours: Mon to Fri, 0900 to 1700
Special comments: No personal callers.

PENSIONS REGULATOR, THE

Napier House, Trafalgar Palce, Brighton, East Sussex, BN1 4DW

Tel: 0870 606 3636
Fax: 0870 241 1144
E-mail: customersupport@thepensionsregulator.gov.uk

Website:
http://www.thepensionsregulator.gov.uk
http://www.trusteetoolkit.co.uk

Enquiries:
Enquiries to: Customer Support

Founded:
2005

Organisation type and purpose:
Statutory body.

Publications list:
Available online and in print

Access to staff:
Contact by letter, by telephone, by e-mail and via website
Hours: Mon to Fri, 0900 to 1730

PENWITH DISTRICT COUNCIL

Council Offices, St Clare, Penzance, Cornwall, TR18 3QW

Tel: 01736 362341
Fax: 01736 336595

Website:
http://www.penwith.gov.uk

Organisation type and purpose:
Local government body.

PEOPLE & PLANET

51 Union Street, Oxford, OX4 1JP

Tel: 01865 245678
Fax: 01865 791927
E-mail: people@peopleandplanet.org

Website:
http://peopleandplanet.org
People & Planet UK students taking action on world poverty, human rights and the environment.

Enquiries:
Enquiries to: Administrator

Founded:
1969

Organisation type and purpose:
Student action on world poverty, human rights and the environment.

Subject coverage:
Global poverty, human rights and the environment, campaigning and education with UK students.

Printed publications:
Variety of leaflets, posters, information packs etc

Access to staff:
Hours: Mon to Fri, 1000 to 1600

PERFECT INFORMATION

Acronym or abbreviation: PI

35 Chiswell Street, London, EC1Y 4SE

Tel: 020 7892 4200
Fax: 020 7892 4201

E-mail: research@perfectinfo.com

Website:
http://www.perfectinfo.com

Enquiries:
Enquiries to: Director

Founded:
1990

Organisation type and purpose:
Service industry.

Subject coverage:
All compliance documentation released by UK listed companies including: directors shareholdings, board changes, changes in substantial shareholdings, results, bids, acquisitions, report and accounts, circulars to shareholders, all available on-line in original form with an archive back to 1982.

Museum or gallery collection, archive, or library special collection:
All UK Company Reports and accounts
EDGAR SEC filings and International Bonds
Entire London Stock Exchange microfiche collection back to 1982
European and Asian Company Annual Reports
RNS Announcements
UK Company Circulars

Electronic and video publications:
Occasional bureau-based facility can be provided, call for details
Online service can be accessed via ISDN link, fax or dedicated Kilostream link

Access to staff:
Contact by letter, by telephone, by fax, by e-mail and via website. All charged.
Hours: Mon to Fri, 0900 to 1730

Connections with:
Centaur Communications
50 Poland Street, London, W1F 7AX

Other address:
Perfect Information Inc (PI)
245 Park Avenue, 39th Floor, New York, NY 10167, USA; tel: 1 212 792 4350; fax: 1 212 792 4307

PERFORMING RIGHT SOCIETY LIMITED

Acronym or abbreviation: PRS

29–33 Berners Street, London, W1T 3AB

Tel: 020 7580 5544
Fax: 020 7306 4550
E-mail: press@mcps-prs-alliance.co.uk

Website:
http://www.prs.co.uk

Enquiries:
Enquiries to: Chief Executive

Founded:
1914

Organisation type and purpose:
Membership association (membership is by subscription).
To license the public performance, broadcast and cable transmission of its composer and publisher members' copyright.

Subject coverage:
Music copyright and royalties; public performance; broadcasting; collection and distribution of performance royalties.

Printed publications:
M (magazine)
PRS Handbook
PRS Yearbook

Access to staff:
Contact by letter, by telephone, by fax, by e-mail and via website. Appointment necessary.
Hours: Mon to Fri, 0900 to 1700

Access for disabled people:
Ramped entry

Affiliated to:
similar performing right organisations, throughout the world

Links with:
British Music Rights
Mechanical Copyright Protection Society Limited

PERMANENT WAY INSTITUTION

Acronym or abbreviation: PWI

11 Caraway Place, Meir Park, Stoke-On-Trent, Staffordshire, ST3 7FE

Tel: 01782 397880
Fax: 01782 397546
E-mail: pwi.bjn@virgin.net

Website:
http://www.permanentwayinstithtion.com

Enquiries:
Enquiries to: Secretary

Founded:
1884

Organisation type and purpose:
Learned society (membership is by subscription), present number of members: 3,800 British Isles, 1,500 rest of world.

Subject coverage:
Railway permanent-way engineering (a branch of civil engineering): design, construction and maintenance.

Non-library collection catalogue:
All or part available online

Library catalogue:
All or part available online and in-house

Printed publications:
British Railway Track – Design Construction and Maintenance (7th edn in 12 seperate vols; vols 1, part 3, vol. 4, 5 and 9 available), (6th edn, 1993, £30.00)
History of the PWI – the first 100 Years, 1884–1984 (£10 incl. p&p)
Light Rail Supplement, Tracks to the Cities (£10 incl. p&p)
The Evolution of Permanent Way (£5.00 incl. p&p)
Order printed publications from: Secretary, Permanent Way Institution

Publications list:
Available online and in print

Access to staff:
Contact by letter, by telephone, by fax and by e-mail
Hours: Mon to Fri, 0900 to 1630

Has:
19 sections in UK, 1 for all Ireland, 5 overseas

Links with:
Union of European Railway Engineer Associations
Verband Deutscher Eisenbahn Ingenieure (VDEI) Germany

Member organisation of:
Union of European Railway Engineer Associations (UEEIV)

PERSONAL FINANCE SOCIETY

Acronym or abbreviation: PFS

42–48 High Road, South Woodford, London, E18 2JP

Tel: 020 8530 0852
Fax: 020 8530 3052
E-mail: customer.serv@thepfs.org

Website:
http://www.thepfs.org/

Enquiries:
Enquiries to: Press and PR Co-ordinator
Direct e-mail: alex.thompson@cii.co.uk

continued overleaf

Founded:
2004

Created by the merger of:
The Society of Financial Advisers and the Life Insurance Association (1972)

Organisation type and purpose:
Professional body (membership is by subscription), present number of members: 25,000.

Subject coverage:
Life assurance; pensions; unit linked products; financial services;
professional education, ethics and standards.

Printed publications:
Prospect (magazine, monthly, for members, £3.50 to non-members or by subscription on application)

Access to staff:
Contact by letter, by telephone, by fax, by e-mail and via website. Appointment necessary.
Hours: Mon to Fri, 0900 to 1700

Associated with:
Chartered Insurance Institute (London)
LIA Ireland
Dublin
National Association of Life Underwriters
Washington, DC, USA

Network of:
35 regions in UK and Ireland

PERSONAL SAFETY MANUFACTURERS ASSOCIATION

Acronym or abbreviation: PSMA

Tamesis House, 35 St Philip's Avenue, Worcester Park, Surrey, KT4 8JS

Tel: 020 8330 6446
Fax: 020 8330 7447
E-mail: psma@tamgroup.co.uk

Enquiries:
Enquiries to: General Secretary

Founded:
1998

Organisation type and purpose:
Trade association.

Subject coverage:
Production and marketing of industrial protective and safety equipment within the PSE Directive of the EC.

Printed publications:
C/E Market Product Directory (free on written application enclosing an A5 sae with first class stamp)

Access to staff:
Contact by e-mail
Hours: Mon to Fri, 0900 to 1700

Access to building, collection or gallery:
Prior appointment required

Affiliated to:
British Safety Industry Federation (BSIF)
St Asaph Business Park, St Asaph, Denbighshire, LL17 0LJ; tel: 01745 585600; fax: 01745 585800; e-mail: info@bsif.co.uk; website: www.bsif.co.uk

PERTH AND KINROSS COUNCIL

2 High Street, Perth, Tayside, PH1 5PH

Tel: 01738 475000
Fax: 01738 475710
E-mail: enquiries@pkc.gov.uk

Website:
http://www.pkc.gov.uk

Enquiries:
Enquiries to: Research and Consultation Assistant
Direct tel: 01738 475084
Direct fax: 01738 475010
Direct e-mail: tbrunton@pkc.gov.uk

Founded:
1996

Organisation type and purpose:
Local government body.

Subject coverage:
Information on the council, tourism, socio-economic property, education, roads, planning, leisure and cultural services, social work, law and administration, environmental health, Europe social policy, finance, human resources, housing.

Access to staff:
Contact by letter
Hours: Mon to Fri, 0900 to 1700

Access for disabled people:
Ramped entry, toilet facilities

PERTH AND KINROSS LIBRARIES

A K Bell Library, York Place, Perth, Perthshire, PH2 8EP

Tel: 01738 444949\ Minicom no. 01738 620114 (textphone)
Fax: 01738 477010
E-mail: library@pkc.gov.uk

Website:
http://www.pkc.gov.uk/library

Enquiries:
Enquiries to: Head of Libraries and Archives
Direct e-mail: mmoir@pkc.gov.uk

Founded:
1996

Organisation type and purpose:
Local government body, public library.

Subject coverage:
General, local history, local archives, Scots language.

Museum or gallery collection, archive, or library special collection:
Atholl Collection (17th and 18th century Scottish folk and dance music)
District archives
Local history
McIntosh Collection (17th century ecclesiastical and general works)
William Soutar Collection (poetry and Scottish literature)

Non-library collection catalogue:
All or part available in print

Printed publications:
A selection of books of particular local interest, including:
A Vision of Perth (Muro D, 2001)
Alert: the War Years in Perth (1989)
Along the A6, The Great North Road (MacDonald A, 2001)
Heritage of Perth (Findlay Dr W H, 1996)
Life in the Atholl Glens (Kerr J, 1993, £9.95)
The Easy Trip (Knaggs B, 2001)
The Story of Errol Station (Beech J, 1993, £2.95)

Publications list:
Available online and in print

Access to staff:
Contact by letter, by telephone, by fax, by e-mail, in person and via website. Appointment necessary.
Hours: Mon, Wed, 0930 to 1700; Tue, Thu, 0930 to 2000; Fri, 0900 to 1700; Sat, 0930 to 1600

Access for disabled people:
Parking provided, level entry, access to all public areas, toilet facilities

Part of:
Perth and Kinross Council
2 High Street, Perth; tel: 01738 475000; fax: 01738 475710; website: pkc.gov.uk

PERTHES ASSOCIATION

PO Box 773, Guildford, GU1 1XN

Tel: 01483 306637 (helpline); 534431 (admin)
E-mail: info@perthes.org.uk

Website:
http://www.perthes.org.uk

Enquiries:
Enquiries to: Secretary

Founded:
1976

Organisation type and purpose:
National organisation, membership association (membership is by subscription), present number of members: 803 full, 2,000 part members, voluntary organisation, registered charity (charity number 326161), suitable for all ages.

Subject coverage:
Help advice and support to sufferers of Perthes Disease of the hip, all forms of osteochondritis and MED (multiple epiphyseal dysplasia), in both children and adults; medical information, financial advice (benefits), housing, education, special equipment and clothing, counselling.

Printed publications:
Factsheet (free)
Newsletter (quarterly, members)
Layman's Guide to Osteochondritis
Perthes Association Handbook
How to care for your Child in an Immobilising Hip Spica Plaster
Order printed publications from: Secretary, at the same address

Access to staff:
Contact by letter, by telephone, by e-mail and via website. Non-members charged.
Hours: Mon to Fri, 0900 to 1700

Links with:
Contact a Family
Long Term Medical Conditions Alliance
NCVO
RADAR

PERTHSHIRE TOURIST BOARD

Acronym or abbreviation: PTB

Administrative Headquarters, Lower City Mills, West Mill Street, Perth, Tayside, PH1 5QP

Tel: 01738 627958/9
Fax: 01738 630416
E-mail: info@perthshire.co.uk

Website:
http://www.perthshire.co.uk/
General information on Perthshire: attractions, events, activities and accommodation.
Visit the 'contact us' section for a list of publications.

Enquiries:
Enquiries to: Chief Executive
Other contacts: Head of Marketing; Head of Visitor Services

Organisation type and purpose:
Statutory body, membership association (membership is by subscription), present number of members: 1300.
Non-governmental public body, area tourist board. To position Perthshire as a world-class destination, where visitor expectations are exceeded through product quality, delivery of service and unique destination characteristics, in such a manner that Perthshire's maximum potential for long-term economic and social prosperity is realised through a sustainable tourism industry.

Subject coverage:
Information on all matters pertaining to tourism in Perthshire, 2000 square miles in Central Scotland, accommodation, visitor attractions, sporting and recreational facilities, events and entertainments.

Trade and statistical information:
Data on the volume and value of tourism in Perthshire. Research and statistical information. Marketing advice to Tourist Board members.

Printed publications:
Activity Days Brochure (free)
Angling in Tayside (£5)
An invitation to brief introduction to the eight
  areas of Perthshire (8 leaflets, free)
Explore Perthshire (free)
A range of factsheets and publications on local
  walks
Cycling and Mountain Biking in Perthshire (free)
Factsheet for Visitors with Disabilities (free)
Perthshire Conference Brochure (free)
Perthshire: The Essential Guide (£1.50, inc. p&p)
Perthshire Where to Stay Guide (free)
Perthshire Map (£4.30)
Perthshire, Angus and Fife Walks (£10.95)
Perthshire Big Tree Country (free)
Selected Cycle Routes (£1.80)
Snowsports and Winter Activities (free)

Electronic and video publications:
CD-ROM of Perthshire images for use by the press
  and members of Perthshire Tourist Board

Publications list:
Available online and in print

Access to staff:
Contact by letter, by telephone, by fax, by e-mail,
in person and via website
Hours: Mon to Fri, 0900 to 1700
Special comments: Administrative Headquarters is
open office hours; tourist information centres open
longer, particularly during tourist season.

Tourist Information Centres:
Aberfeldy (open all year)
  The Square, Aberfeldy, Perthshire, PH15 2DD;
  tel: 01887 820276; fax: 01887 829495; e-mail:
  aberfeldytic@perthshire.co.uk
Auchterarder (open all year)
  90 High Street, Auchterarder, Perthshire, PH3
  1BJ; tel: 01764 663450; fax: 01764 664235; e-mail:
  auchterardertic@perthshire.co.uk
Blairgowrie (open all year)
  26 Wellmeadow, Blairgowrie, Perthshire, PH10
  6AS, Ski-line 875800; tel: 01250 872960; fax:
  01250 873701; e-mail: blairgowrietic@perthshire
  .co.uk
Crieff (open all year)
  High Street, Crieff, Perthshire, PH7 3HU; tel:
  01764 652578; fax: 01764 655422; e-mail:
  criefftic@perthshire.co.uk
Dunkeld (open all year)
  The Cross, Dunkeld, Perthshire, PH8 0AN; tel:
  01350 727688; fax: 01350 727688; e-mail:
  dunkeldtic@perthshire.co.uk
Kinross (open all year)
  Heart of Scotland Visitor Centre, adjacent to
  service area, Junction 6, M90, Kinross, Perthshire,
  KY13 7NQ; tel: 01577 863680; Activity line: 01577
  861186; fax: 01577 863370; e-mail: kinrosstic@
  perthshire.co.uk
Perth (open all year)
  Lower City Mills, West Mill Street, Perth, PH1
  5QP; tel: 01738 450600; fax: 01738 444863; e-mail:
  perthtic@perthshire.co.uk
Pitlochry (open all year)
  22 Atholl Road, Pitlochry, Perthshire, PH16 5BX;
  tel: 01796 472215 or 472751; fax: 01796 474046; e-
  mail: pitlochrytic@perthshire.co.uk

PET CARE TRUST

Acronym or abbreviation: PCT

Bedford Business Centre, 170 Mile Road, Bedford,
MK42 9TW

Tel: 01234 273933
Fax: 01234 273550
E-mail: info@petcare.org.uk

Website:
http://www.petcare.org.uk
Material about the Trust, its member services and
training opportunities.

Enquiries:
Enquiries to: Operations Manager
Direct e-mail: stephen@petcare.org.uk

Founded:
1986

Organisation type and purpose:
National organisation, professional body, trade
association (membership is by subscription),
present number of members: 1506, service
industry, voluntary organisation, registered charity
(charity number 1052488), suitable for ages: all,
training organisation.
To promote high standards of training in the
industry; to promote responsible pet ownership.

Subject coverage:
Training information and information on pet care
and related legislation.

Trade and statistical information:
Data on pet care industry, market and population.

Printed publications:
Training manuals and video material
Pet Care Trust – Review (newsletter, once every
  other month)
UK Pet Trade Year book and Buyers Guide
  (updated annually)

Access to staff:
Contact by letter, by telephone, by fax and by e-
mail. Appointment necessary.
Hours: Mon to Fri, 0830 to 1700

Access to building, collection or gallery:
Prior appointment required

Access for disabled people:
Parking provided, level entry, toilet facilities

Subsidiary body:
British Dog Groomers Association
  tel: 01234 273933; fax: 01234 273550; e-mail: pat@
  petcare.org.uk

PET FOOD MANUFACTURERS' ASSOCIATION LIMITED

Acronym or abbreviation: PFMA

20 Bedford Street, Covent Garden, London, WC2E
9HP

Tel: 020 7379 9009
Fax: 020 7379 8008
E-mail: info@pfma.org.uk

Website:
http://www.pfma.com
Information on the prepared pet food industry in
the UK. Also general background on keeping and
feeding of pets, information on related charities
and organisations.

Enquiries:
Enquiries to: Administration Secretary

Founded:
1971

Organisation type and purpose:
Trade association.

Subject coverage:
General information relating to the UK prepared
pet food industry, pet related issues and interests.

Trade and statistical information:
Data on UK prepared pet food market.
Data on UK dog and cat populations.

Access to staff:
Contact by letter, by telephone, by fax and by e-
mail
Hours: Mon to Fri, 0900 to 1700

Access to building, collection or gallery:
No access other than to staff

Member of:
FEDIAF
  Avenue Louise 89, Brussels, B-1050, Belgium

PETERBOROUGH CENTRAL LIBRARY AND THEATRE

Broadway, Peterborough, Cambridgeshire, PE1
1RX

Tel: 01733 742700
Fax: 01733 555277
E-mail: libraries@peterborough.gov.uk

Website:
http://www.peterborough.gov.uk/council/libraries

Enquiries:
Enquiries to: Enquiry Services Manager
Direct tel: 01733 742715
Direct e-mail: louise.bennett@peterborough.gov.uk
Other contacts: (1) Local Studies Librarian (2)
Learning Centre Manager for (1) Special collection:
Peterborough.

Organisation type and purpose:
Local government body, public library.
Central reference library for the Greater
Peterborough area.

Subject coverage:
General, history and study of Peterborough and its
area, business information, environmental
information, open learning and training materials
and information (the Learning Centre), European
Union information (European Public Information
Centre).

**Museum or gallery collection, archive, or library
special collection:**
John Clare Collection
Local history collection

Non-library collection catalogue:
All or part available online and in-house

Access to staff:
Contact by letter, by telephone, by fax, by e-mail
and in person
Hours: Mon, Fri, Sat, 0930 to 1700; Tue, Wed, Thu,
0930 to 1900

Access to building, collection or gallery:
No prior appointment required

Access for disabled people:
Parking provided, level entry, access to all public
areas, toilet facilities

Parent body:
Peterborough City Council

PETERBOROUGH REGIONAL COLLEGE LEARNING RESOURCES AND LIBRARY CENTRE

Park Crescent, Peterborough, Cambridgeshire, PE1
4DZ

Tel: 01733 762137
Fax: 01733 767986

Website:
http://www.peterborough.ac.uk
College website.

Enquiries:
Enquiries to: Learning Resources and Library
Centre Manager

Organisation type and purpose:
College of further and higher education.

Subject coverage:
Accounting; electrical engineering; mechanical
engineering; building construction; chemistry;
physics; mathematics; biology; psychology;
sociology; economics; geography; geology; English
literature; management; catering; media; history;
sport; computing.

Library catalogue:
All or part available in-house

Access to staff:
Appointment necessary.
Hours: Term time: Mon to Wed, 0845 to 1945; Thu,
0845 to 2015; Fri, 0845 to 1630; Sat, 0930 to 1230

Access for disabled people:
Parking provided, level entry, toilet facilities

PETERBOROUGH ROYAL FOXHOUND SHOW SOCIETY

East of England Showground, Peterborough, Cambridgeshire, PE2 6XE

Tel: 01733 234451
Fax: 01733 370038
E-mail: andrew@eastofengland.org.uk

Enquiries:
Enquiries to: Secretary

Founded:
1878

Organisation type and purpose:
Foxhound show society.

Subject coverage:
Foxhounds; breeding and showing.

Museum or gallery collection, archive, or library special collection:
Handwritten record books listing winners in each of the above classes, over the years

PETROL RETAILERS ASSOCIATION

Acronym or abbreviation: PRA

201 Great Portland Street, London, W1W 5AB

Tel: 020 7307 3593
Fax: 020 7307 3592
E-mail: pra@rmif.co.uk

Website:
http://www.rmif.co.uk

Enquiries:
Enquiries to: Secretary

Founded:
1913

Subject coverage:
Petrol retailing.

Member of the:
Retail Motor Industry Federation

Other addresses:
Petrol Retailers Association
  107a Shore Road, Belfast, BT15 3BB; tel: 028 9037 0137; fax: 028 9037 0706

PETROLEUM OPEN LEARNING

Acronym or abbreviation: OPITO

Minerva House, Bruntland Road, Portlethan, Aberdeen, AB12 4QL

Tel: 01224 787800
Fax: 01224 787830
E-mail: richard.bain@opito.net

Website:
http://www.petroleumopenlearning.com

Enquiries:
Enquiries to: Marketing Advisor
Direct tel: 01224 787813
Direct e-mail: corinnam@opito.co.uk

Founded:
1988

Organisation type and purpose:
Advisory body, training organisation.
The national training organisation for oil and gas extraction.

Subject coverage:
Oil and gas well technology, petroleum processing technology, health and safety.

Printed publications:
Books and modules for Open learning, include:
Oil and Gas Well Technology Series (3 Modules)
Petroleum Processing Technology Series (10 Modules)

Publications list:
Available online and in print

Access to staff:
Contact by letter, by telephone, by fax, by e-mail, in person and via website. Appointment necessary.
Hours: Mon to Fri, 0900 to 1700

Access for disabled people:
Parking provided, ramped entry, level entry, access to all public areas, toilet facilities

Parent body:
Cogent SSC Ltd
  Minerva House, Bruntland Road, Portlethen, Aberdeen, AB12 4QL; tel: 01224 787800; fax: 01224 787830; website: www.cogentplus.co.uk

PEWTER SOCIETY

37 Hurst Lane, Bollington, Cheshire, SK10 5LT

E-mail: secretary@pewtersociety.org

Website:
http://www.pewtersociety.org

Enquiries:
Enquiries to: Secretary

Founded:
1918

Organisation type and purpose:
Learned society, present number of members: 250, voluntary organisation.

Subject coverage:
Antique pewter – its history, manufacture and social context. Identification, conservation and information about specific pewterers.

Museum or gallery collection, archive, or library special collection:
The library holds all British and many foreign books published on pewter and many papers on pewter and pewter-related topics

Library catalogue:
All or part available online and in-house

Printed publications:
Journal of Pewter Society (twice a year, members only but available in some libraries)
Newsletter (twice a year, members only)
Occasional special publications, which are available to non-members, such as:
Irish Pewter (1995)
The Richard Neate Touch Plate (1996)
Books on European Pewter Marks (1999)
Five Centuries of Base Metal Spoons (reprinted 1999)
Pewterers of London 1600–1900 (2001)
English Candlesticks of the Second Half of the 17th Century (2004)
The Records of the York Company of Pewterers (2004)

Electronic and video publications:
Database of British Pewterers and their Marks (online, members only)

Publications list:
Available online

Access to staff:
Contact by letter, by e-mail and via website
Special comments: No access

Access to building, collection or gallery:
No access

PHARMACEUTICAL SOCIETY OF NORTHERN IRELAND

Acronym or abbreviation: PSNI

73 University Street, Belfast, BT7 1HL

Tel: 028 9023 1163
Fax: 028 9043 9919
E-mail: chief.executive@psni.org.uk

Enquiries:
Enquiries to: Chief Executive Secretary & Registrar
Other contacts: Secretary

Founded:
1925

Organisation type and purpose:
Statutory body, professional body (membership is by qualification), present number of members: 1700, service industry.
Registration authority for pharmacists and pharmacies in Northern Ireland.

Subject coverage:
Pharmaceutical matters.

Access to staff:
Contact by letter, by telephone, by fax and by e-mail
Hours: Mon to Fri, 0900 to 1700

PHILADELPHIA ASSOCIATION

Acronym or abbreviation: PA

4 Marty's Yard, 17 Hampstead High Street, London, NW3 1QW

Tel: 020 7794 2652
Fax: 020 7794 2652
E-mail: paoffice@globalnet.co.uk

Enquiries:
Enquiries to: Administrator

Founded:
1965

Organisation type and purpose:
Registered charity.
Charity in the field of mental health.

Subject coverage:
Training in phenomenology and psychoanalytic psychotherapy, residential therapeutic communities, psychotherapy referrals.

Library catalogue:
All or part available in-house

Printed publications:
Information on training and psychotherapy
Thresholds between Philosophy and Psychoanalysis (book)

Access to staff:
Contact by letter, by telephone and by fax.
Appointment necessary.
Hours: Mon, 1330 to 1730; Tue, Thu, Fri, 1630 to 2030

Access to building, collection or gallery:
No access other than to staff

PHILATELIC TRADERS SOCIETY LIMITED

Acronym or abbreviation: PTS

PO Box 371, Fleet, Hampshire, GU52 6ZX

Tel: 01252 628006
Fax: 01252 684674
E-mail: info@philatelic-traders-society.co.uk

Website:
http://www.philatelic-traders-society.co.uk
Information on the Society; list of dealers; information on Stampex Exhibitions

Enquiries:
Enquiries to: General Secretary

Founded:
1949

Organisation type and purpose:
Trade association.

Subject coverage:
Philatelic trade; support for stamp collecting as a hobby; organisers of the two national stamp exhibitions, Spring Stampex and Autumn Stampex.

Printed publications:
Membership Directory (available for purchase)
PTS News (6 times a year, members only)

Access to staff:
Contact by letter, by telephone, by fax, by e-mail and in person. Appointment necessary.
Hours: Mon to Thu, 1000 to 1700; Fri, 1000 to 1300

Constituent bodies:
Stampex Ltd
  tel: 01252 628006; fax: 01252 684674

PHILIPPINE EMBASSY

9a Palace Green, London, W8 4QE

Tel: 020 7937 1600
Fax: 020 7937 2925
E-mail: embassy@philemb.demon.co.uk

Website:
http://www.microtron.net/philemb/index.shtml
Information on Philippines. Philippine Embassy
Services, news, visa, passport application forms
(downloadable).

Enquiries:
Enquiries to: H E The Ambassador
Direct e-mail: embassy@philemb.co.uk
Other contacts: Information Officer

Organisation type and purpose:
International organisation.

Subject coverage:
The Philippines: Consular matters.

Printed publications:
Information bulletin (limited list of recipients)

Access to staff:
Contact by letter, by telephone, by fax, by e-mail,
in person and via website. Appointment necessary.
Hours: Mon to Fri, 0900 to 1700
Special comments: Closed during Philippine
holidays.

Access to building, collection or gallery:
No prior appointment required
Hours: Mon to Fri, 0900 to 1700

Other addresses:
Office of the Tourism Attaché
  146 Cromwell Road, London, SW7 4EF; tel: 020
  7835 1100; fax: 020 7835 1926; e-mail: Tourism@
  pdot.co.uk
Philippine Department of Trade
  1A Cumberland House, Kensington Court,
  London, W8; tel: 020 7937 7998 1898; fax: 020
  7937 2747; e-mail: dtilondon@aol.com

PHILIPS RESEARCH LABORATORIES

Cross Oak Lane, Redhill, Surrey, RH1 5HA

Tel: 01293 815000
Fax: 01293 815500

Enquiries:
Enquiries to: Librarian
Direct tel: 01293 815432

Founded:
1945

Organisation type and purpose:
Research organisation.

Subject coverage:
Computer science and technology, electronic
engineering, electronics, radar, solid state physics,
mobile communications, television, compact disc
technology, interactive media.

Library catalogue:
All or part available in-house

Access to building, collection or gallery:
No access other than to staff

Part of:
Philips Electronics UK

PHILOLOGICAL SOCIETY

School of Oriental and African Studies, University
of London, Thornhaugh Street, Russell Square,
London, WC1H 0XG

Tel: 020 7898 4653
Fax: 020 7898 4399
E-mail: secretary@philsoc.org.uk

Website:
http://www.philsoc.org.uk

Enquiries:
Enquiries to: Honorary Secretary

Founded:
1841

Organisation type and purpose:
Learned society (membership is by election or
invitation), present number of members: 700,
registered charity (charity number 1014370).
To investigate and promote the study and
knowledge of the structure, affinities, and history
of language.

Subject coverage:
Linguistics; philology.

Printed publications:
Transactions (3 a year)
Occasional special publications including:
On Early English Pronunciation (A. J. Ellis, Part V
  1889, £5 plus p&p)
Phonology as Functional Phonetics (A. Martinet,
  1949, reprint 1975, £3 plus p&p)
The Dialect of Pusey (Wiltshire) (J. Kjederqvist,
  1903, £1 plus p&p)
The Pronunciation of English in Cannock,
  Staffordshire (C. D. Heath, 1980, £9 plus p&p)
Order printed publications from: for Transactions,
Blackwell Publishers Journals, PO Box 805, 108
Cowley Road, Oxford, OX4 1FH

Publications list:
Available in print

Access to staff:
Contact by letter, by fax and by e-mail
Hours: Mon to Fri, 0900 to 1700

PHONOGRAPHIC PERFORMANCE LIMITED

Acronym or abbreviation: PPL

1 Upper James Street, London, W1F 9DE

Tel: 020 7534 1000
Fax: 020 7534 1111

Enquiries:
Enquiries to: Public Relations Manager

Founded:
1934

Organisation type and purpose:
Membership association.
Established by the UK record companies as a non-
profit company to license the broadcast and public
performance of their sound recordings.
Copyright licensing body.

Subject coverage:
Copyright relating to public performance and
broadcasting of commercial sound recordings,
including records, tapes and re-recordings, in the
United Kingdom, on behalf of the British record
industry.

Printed publications:
Copyright Protection (information sheet, 1996,
  free)
Annual Report
Newsletter (quarterly, free)

Publications list:
Available in print

Access to staff:
Contact by letter, by telephone and by fax
Hours: Mon to Fri, 0930 to 1730

Links with:
BPI
IFPI

PHOTO MARKETING ASSOCIATION INTERNATIONAL (UK) LIMITED

Acronym or abbreviation: PMA

Wisteria House, 28 Fulling Mill Lane, Welwyn,
Hertfordshire, AL6 9NS

Tel: 0870 240 4542
Fax: 01438 716572
E-mail: pmauk@pmai.org

Website:
http://www.pmai.org

Enquiries:
Enquiries to: Director of UK operations
Other contacts: Administration Manager

Founded:
1923

Organisation type and purpose:
International organisation, trade association
(membership is by subscription), consultancy.
To expand the photographic industry and to make
its members more profitable.

Subject coverage:
Photographic industry trends – worldwide,
consumer research, the photo, video and digital
industries, retailers, minilabs, wholesale photo
finishers, camera repairers, school photographs.

Trade and statistical information:
Industry trends report – annual statistics on the
  photo industry.

Printed publications:
Business resources catalogue
Mini Lab Information Package
Promote Your Image and Build Your Business
Who's Who in Photographic Management: A
  membership, product and service directory

Microform publications:
Photographic Colour Prints

Electronic and video publications:
Mini Lab Training Series (video)
Photofinishing Training Series (video)

Access to staff:
Contact by letter, by telephone, by fax, by e-mail
and via website. Appointment necessary. Non-
members charged.
Hours: Mon to Fri, 0930 to 1730

Affiliated to:
Photo Marketing Association International
  3000 Picture Place, Jackson, Michigan, 49201,
  USA

Subsidiary body:
APL Services Limited

PHOTOGRAPHIC WASTE MANAGEMENT ASSOCIATION

Acronym or abbreviation: PWMA

Ambassador House, Brigstock Road, Thornton
Heath, Surrey, CR7 7JG

Tel: 020 8665 5395
Fax: 020 8665 6447
E-mail: pwma@admin.co.uk

Enquiries:
Enquiries to: Secretary

Founded:
1993

Organisation type and purpose:
Trade association.

Subject coverage:
Photographic waste management.

Printed publications:
Services Guide and List of Members

Access to staff:
Contact by letter
Hours: Mon to Fri, 0900 to 1700

Member of:
British Imaging and Photographic Association

PHYSICAL PROPERTIES DATA SERVICE

Acronym or abbreviation: PPDS

TUV NEL Ltd, Scottish Enterprise Technology Park, East Kilbride, South Lanarkshire, G75 0QU

Tel: 01355 272527
Fax: 01355 272265
E-mail: ppds@tuvnel.com

Website:
http://www.ppds.co.uk
http://www.nelfood.com
Database of physical properties of foods.

Enquiries:
Enquiries to: Manager
Direct tel: 01355 593775
Direct e-mail: ajohns@tuvnel.com

Organisation type and purpose:
Service industry, training organisation, consultancy, research organisation.

Subject coverage:
Constant, thermodynamic and transport properties for over 1,500 organic compounds; vapour liquid equilibrium package containing seven different methods and nine different calculations; data for petroleum fractions and steam; liquid properties for 22 aqueous solutions and 97 commercial heat transfer fluids.

Printed publications:
Newsletter (also available online, free)
Product factsheets

Electronic and video publications:
PPDS Software Package (for calculation of physical properties of pure fluids and their mixtures including equilibria)
http://www.netfood.com (database of properties of foods)

Access to staff:
Contact by letter, by telephone, by fax, by e-mail and via website
Hours: Mon to Fri, 0900 to 1700

Access to building, collection or gallery:
No access other than to staff

PHYSIO FIRST

Formal name: Organisation of Chartered Physiotherapists in Private Practice

Cedar House, Bell Plantation, Watling Street, Towcester, Northamptonshire, NN12 6GX

Tel: 01327 354441
Fax: 01327 354476
E-mail: towcester@physiofirst.org.uk

Website:
http://www.physiofirst.org.uk

Enquiries:
Enquiries to: General Secretary

Founded:
1951

Organisation type and purpose:
Professional body (membership is by subscription, qualification), present number of members: 3800. Represents private practitioners, provides members with education, information and legal advice, to ensure patients of high professional standards.

Subject coverage:
Back care, neck care; sports injury treatments, arthritic conditions, neurological stress, chest complaints.

Printed publications:
Directory of members (annually)
In Touch (quarterly)

Publications list:
Available in print

Access to staff:
Contact by letter, by telephone, by fax and by e-mail

Hours: Mon to Fri, 0900 to 1700

Occupational Group of:
Chartered Society of Physiotherapy

PHYSIOLOGICAL SOCIETY, THE

PO Box 11319, London, WC1X 8WP

Tel: 020 7269 5710
Fax: 020 7269 5720
E-mail: admin@physoc.org

Website:
http://www.physoc.org
Publications, meetings, news, special interest groups, grants, membership, vacancies, contacts.

Enquiries:
Enquiries to: Chief Executive

Founded:
1876

Organisation type and purpose:
Learned society (membership is by election or invitation), registered charity (charity number 211585).

Subject coverage:
Physiological and cognate biomedical sciences; special interest groups on autonomic function, blood-brain barrier, cardiovascular control, comparative and invertebrate neuroscience, cellular neurophysiology, comparative physiology, developmental physiology, epithelia and membrane transport, gastrointestinal tract, heart and cardiac muscle, history of physiology, human physiology, higher sensory functions, ionic channels, microvascular and endothelial physiology, muscle contraction, neuroendocrinology, placental and perinatal physiology, renal physiology, respiratory physiology, sensorimotor control, smooth muscle, somatosensory physiology; physiology as a career.

Museum or gallery collection, archive, or library special collection:
Archives (held at Wellcome Institute for the History of Medicine)
Video and film collection

Printed publications:
Genes and Function, in conjunction with the Genetical Society
Undergraduate booklet on the use of animals in medical experiments (free)
Physiology News (in-house magazine)
Journal of Experimental Physiology (6 times a year)
Journal of Physiology (24 issues a year plus 6 proceedings volumes and index)
Monographs, guides, careers information
Physiology: education and career (careers booklet, free)

Access to staff:
Contact by letter, by telephone, by fax, by e-mail and via website. Appointment necessary.
Hours: Mon to Fri, 0900 to 1700

Access to building, collection or gallery:
Prior appointment required

Accredited society of the:
Foundation for Science and Technology

Affiliated to:
Biosciences Foundation
Institute of Biology

Supports the:
International Union of Physiological Sciences (Munich)

PIANOFORTE TUNERS ASSOCIATION

Acronym or abbreviation: PTA

10 Reculver Road, Herne Bay, Kent, CT6 6LD

Tel: 01227 368808
Fax: 01227 368808

E-mail: secretary@pianotuner.org.uk

Website:
http://www.pianotuner.org.uk

Enquiries:
Enquiries to: Secretary

Founded:
1913

Organisation type and purpose:
Professional body, advisory body.

Subject coverage:
Pianoforte tuning, training facilities, entry into the industry.

Printed publications:
Information leaflet
Sound Advice – Your Piano Your Questions Answered
Sound Advice – Buying a Piano

Access to staff:
Contact by letter, by telephone and by fax
Hours: Including evenings

PILKINGTON GROUP LTD

Pilkington Technology Centre, Hall Lane, Lathom, Ormskirk, Lancashire, L40 5UF

Tel: 01695 50000
Fax: 01695 54366
E-mail: kevin.green@pilkington.com

Enquiries:
Enquiries to: Information Manager
Direct tel: 01695 54231

Founded:
1826

Organisation type and purpose:
Manufacturing industry.

Subject coverage:
Fundamental research in flat glass, applied research leading to improvements in the manufacturing of glass and related materials, development of new processes and products in flat glass, pressed and moulded glass, optical, ophthalmic and other special glasses, surface-treated glass.

Museum or gallery collection, archive, or library special collection:
Comprehensive collection of books on glass

Library catalogue:
All or part available in-house

Access to staff:
Contact by letter, by telephone, by fax and by e-mail. Appointment necessary.
Hours: Mon to Fri, 0900 to 1700
Special comments: By appointment only.

Access to building, collection or gallery:
By appointment only.

PIPER SPORTS AND RACING CAR CLUB

Acronym or abbreviation: Piper Club

PO Box 55, Bourne, Lincolnshire, PE10 9FX

E-mail: contact@thepiperclub.org.uk

Website:
http://www.thepiperclub.org.uk

Enquiries:
Enquiries to: Secretary

Founded:
1977

Organisation type and purpose:
Membership association, present number of members: 45.

Subject coverage:
Piper cars.

Printed publications:
Newsletter

Access to staff:
Contact by letter and by e-mail

PIRA INTERNATIONAL

Cleeve Road, Leatherhead, Surrey, KT22 7RU

Tel: 01372 802050
Fax: 01372 802239
E-mail: infocentre@pira-international.com

Website:
http://www.piranet.com

Enquiries:
Enquiries to: Information Services Manager

Organisation type and purpose:
Consultancy.

Subject coverage:
Pulping and pulp evaluation, paper and board making, water and effluent treatment, printing, imaging, inks, packaging, paper and board testing, printing machinery, package development and testing, management, marketing, publishing, nonwovens, statistical and technical information is available.

Library catalogue:
All or part available in-house

Printed publications:
Packaging Month
Paperbase Abstracts
Press
Imaging Abstracts
Flexible
Brand
Product ID
rfidbase news
Active and intelligent packaging news
Brand protection news
Printed electronics news
Future of printing and packaging series
UK Printing and Publishing Industry Statistics

Electronic and video publications:
Pira database available online

Publications list:
Available online and in print

Access to staff:
Contact by letter, by e-mail and via website. Appointment necessary. Access for members only. Non-members charged.
Hours: Mon to Fri, 0900 to 1700

Access to building, collection or gallery:
Prior appointment required
Special comments: Members only.

PLACE ARTIST DEVELOPMENT, THE

Acronym or abbreviation: TPAD

17 Dukes Road, London, WC1H 9PY

Tel: 020 7121 1040
Fax: 020 7121 1141
E-mail: artistdevelopment@theplace.org.uk

Website:
http://www.theplace.org.uk
Information on The Place and all its functions including Artist Development, London Contemporary Dance School, The Place: Robin Howard Dance Theatre and Richard Alston Dance Company.

Enquiries:
Enquiries to: Assistant
Direct tel: 020 7121 1040

Founded:
1990

Organisation type and purpose:
Membership association (membership is by subscription), present number of members: 1400. Information and advice service for the independent dance profession.

Subject coverage:
Contemporary dance, venues, promoters, dance artists in the UK and Europe, rehearsal spaces for dance in Greater London, information for new dance companies. Contacts for choreographers, dancers and dance managers in the United Kingdom and the rest of the world.

Museum or gallery collection, archive, or library special collection:
Publicity, annual reports etc from Regional Arts Boards, Venues and Festivals, Funding guides and directories, key reports, periodicals

Printed publications:
Information sheets on useful contacts for those in the Independent Dance Sector (eg: platform events, trusts and funds)
Juice (monthly listings magazine)
New York City Pack

Publications list:
Available in print

Access to staff:
Contact by letter, by telephone, by fax, by e-mail, in person and via website. Appointment necessary.
Hours: Tue to Fri, 1000 to 1800

Access to building, collection or gallery:
No prior appointment required

Access for disabled people:
Parking provided, level entry, access to all public areas, toilet facilities

Parent body:
Contemporary Dance Trust Ltd
The Place, 17 Dukes Road, London, WC1H 9PY; tel: 020 7121 1000; fax: 020 7121 1142

PLAID CYMRU – THE PARTY OF WALES

18 Park Grove, Cardiff, CF10 3BN

Tel: 029 2064 6000
Fax: 029 2064 6001
E-mail: post@plaidcymru.org

Website:
http://plaidcymru.org
History, aims and goals, press releases.

Enquiries:
Enquiries to: Communications Officer
Other contacts: Press Officer for press enquiries.

Founded:
1925

Organisation type and purpose:
Membership association (membership is by subscription), present number of members: 10,800. Political party.
To achieve full national status for Wales by electoral means.

Subject coverage:
Politics in Wales.

Museum or gallery collection, archive, or library special collection:
Collections are held on our behalf in the National Library of Wales including the whole party archive extending back to 1925

Printed publications:
Cymru (bilingual – Welsh/English, quarterly)

Microform publications:
Microfilms available from World Microfilms, 2–6 Foscote Mews, London W9 2HH

Electronic and video publications:
CD-ROM available directly

Publications list:
Available in print

Access to staff:
Contact by letter, by telephone, by fax and by e-mail. Appointment necessary.
Hours: Mon to Fri, 0830 to 1700

Access to building, collection or gallery:
No prior appointment required
Special comments: Party Archive kept at the National Library of Wales.

PLAIN LANGUAGE COMMISSION

The Castle, 29 Stoneheads, Whaley Bridge, High Peak, Derbyshire, SK23 7BB

Tel: 01663 733177
Fax: 01663 735135
E-mail: cutts@plainlanguage.demon.co.uk

Website:
http://www.clearest.co.uk
Publications.

Enquiries:
Enquiries to: Director

Founded:
1994

Organisation type and purpose:
Consultancy.

Subject coverage:
Information on the use of plain language in business, government departments, local authorities and the law.

Printed publications:
Lucid Law (Cutts M, £10 direct)
The Oxford Guide to Plain English (Cutts M, £5.99 from bookshops)
Clarifying Eurolaw (Cutts M, £8 direct)
Clarifying EC Regulations (Cutts M & Wagner E, £8 direct)

Publications list:
Available online and in print

Access to staff:
Contact by letter, by telephone, by fax and by e-mail. Appointment necessary.
Hours: Mon to Fri, 0900 to 1700

Access to building, collection or gallery:
No access other than to staff

PLANET RETAIL

Greater London House, Hampstead Road, London NW1 7EJ

Tel: 020 7728 5600
Fax: 020 7728 4999
E-mail: info@planetretail.net

Website:
http://www.planetretail.net

Enquiries:
Enquiries to: Press
Direct e-mail: michael.berggren@planetretail.net

Founded:
1989

Formerly called:
M+M Planet Retail

Organisation type and purpose:
Market research.
On-line database on international retailers.

Subject coverage:
Retail marketing.

Non-library collection catalogue:
All or part available online

Library catalogue:
All or part available online

Printed publications:
Growth Retail Markets Worldwide, Jan 2001 (£200)
Evolution of Retail Structures Worldwide, Jan 2001 (£275)
National Retail Profiles, Dec 2001 including countries of:
Retailing in Western Europe
Retailing in Central and Eastern Europe
Retailing in Latin America
Retailing in Middle East and Africa

continued overleaf

C-Store Retailing: Global Trends and Lessons from Japan, Dec 2001 (£580)
Global Foodservice Concentration, Jan 2001 (£230)
Foodservice Opportunities in Western Europe, Sep 2001

Electronic and video publications:
Online database, market reports, slides and newsletter available at www.planetretail.net

Publications list:
Available online

Access to staff:
Contact by e-mail
Hours: Mon to Fri, 0900 to 1700

Holding Company:
M & M Planet Retail SA
  Avenue Louise 113, 1050 Brussels, Belgium

Other addresses:
M & M Planet Retail
  Dreieichstrasse 59, Frankfurt am Main, D-60594, Germany; tel: + 49 69 96 21 75 0; fax: + 49 69 96 21 75 40

PLANNED ENVIRONMENT THERAPY TRUST ARCHIVE AND STUDY CENTRE

Church Lane, Toddington, Cheltenham, Gloucestershire, GL54 5DQ

Tel: 01242 620125
E-mail: craig@pettarchiv.org.uk

Website:
http://pettarchiv.org.uk

Founded:
1989

Subject coverage:
Archive, library and other materials related to planned environment therapy, therapeutic community, milieu therapy, and progressive, alternative and democratic education more generally.

Access to building, collection or gallery:
Hours: Mon to Thu, 0900 to 1500 by appointment; at other times by special arrangement

PLANTLIFE – THE WILD PLANT CONSERVATION CHARITY

21 Elizabeth Street, London, SW1W 9RP

Tel: 020 7808 0100
Fax: 020 7730 8377
E-mail: enquiries@plantlife.org.uk

Website:
http://www.plantlife.org.uk

Enquiries:
Enquiries to: Public Relations Manager

Founded:
1989

Organisation type and purpose:
International organisation, membership association (membership is by subscription), present number of members: 11,500 individuals, voluntary organisation, registered charity (charity number 1059559).
Wild plant conservation charity.

Subject coverage:
Conservation of wild plants and their habitats in the British Isles, including lichens, bryophytes, algae, fungi.

Printed publications:
Britain's Rare Flowers (Marren P, £24.95)
Commission of Enquiry into Peat and Peatlands (1992, £10)
Death Knell for Bluebells? (£2.50)
Genes, Crops and Superweeds (report, £3)
Guidelines for Rare Plant Wardening (Church J M, £5.50)
Plantlife Magazine

Plantlife Magazine (back numbers when available £1 each)
Plants and the Proposed EC Habitats Directives Report (1990, £2.50)
Protecting Plants and their Habitats under the EC Habitat Directive (Oldfield S, £5.50)
Red Data Books of Britain and Ireland: Stoneworts (Stewart N F and Church J M, £15)
Seeds of Destruction? (£2.50)
The Acid Test for Plants (£2.50)
The Wild Flower Key (Rose F, £9.99)

Access to staff:
Contact by letter
Hours: Mon to Fri, 0900 to 1700

Members:
Botanical Society of Edinburgh
Botanical Society of The British Isles
British Bryophyte Society
British Ecology Society
British Lichen Society
British Phycological Society
British Pteridological Society
Butterfly Conservation Society
Fauna and Flora International
Friends of the Earth
Royal Society for the Protection of Birds
South London Botanical Institute
Wildflower Society

Other address:
Plantlife
  Strome House, Nerth Strome, Lochcarron, Ross-shire, IV54 8YJ; tel: 01520 722588; fax: 01520 722660

PLASTIC PIPE MANUFACTURERS SOCIETY

Acronym or abbreviation: PPMS

89 Cornwall Street, Birmingham, B3 3BY

Tel: 0121 236 1866
Fax: 0121 200 1389

Enquiries:
Enquiries to: Secretary

Founded:
1961

Organisation type and purpose:
Membership association.
To promote the production of consistently high quality pipes and fittings from first class plastic materials. To comply with British/EC standards specifications wherever and whenever such apply to their products.

Subject coverage:
Plastic pipe products and sources.

Access to staff:
Contact by letter, by telephone and by fax
Hours: Mon to Fri, 0900 to 1700

PLASTICS & BOARD INDUSTRIES FEDERATION

Acronym or abbreviation: PBIF

Rock House, Maddacombe Road, Kingskerswell, Newton Abbot, Devon, TQ12 5LF

Tel: 01803 403303
Fax: 01803 873167
E-mail: pbifoffice@aol.com

Website:
http://www.pbif.co.uk
Index of members; index of products and services; news; customer enquiries.

Enquiries:
Enquiries to: Chief Executive

Founded:
1987

Organisation type and purpose:
International organisation, trade association (membership is by subscription), present number of members: 150.

Subject coverage:
High frequency welding of thermoplastics; heat sealing and creasing of polypropylene, converting of board.

Library catalogue:
All or part available in-house

Printed publications:
High Frequency Welding Handbook (£40, available direct)

Access to staff:
Contact by letter, by telephone, by fax, by e-mail, in person and via website. Appointment necessary.
Hours: Mon to Fri, 0900 to 1700

PLASTICS HISTORICAL SOCIETY

Acronym or abbreviation: PHS

31A Maylands Drive, Sidcup, Kent, DA14 4SB

Tel: 020 8302 0684
E-mail: r_chambers@lineone.net

Enquiries:
Enquiries to: Honorary Secretary

Founded:
1986

Organisation type and purpose:
International organisation, learned society, membership association (membership is by subscription), present number of members: 250.
Recording the history of plastics and rubber.

Subject coverage:
History of plastics and rubber, conservation and preservation of plastics and rubbers.

Museum or gallery collection, archive, or library special collection:
Collection of plastics artefacts and historical records

Printed publications:
Newsletter (6 times a year, free to members)
Plastiquarian (2 times a year, free to members)

Access to staff:
Contact by letter
Hours: Mon to Fri, 0900 to 1700

Parent body:
Institute of Materials
  1 Carlton House Terrace, London, SW1Y 5DB; tel: 020 7451 7300; fax: 020 7839 1702

PLAY WALES

Formal name: Play Wales / Chwarae Cymru

Baltic House, Mount Stuart Street, Cardiff, CF10 5FH

Tel: 029 2048 6050
Fax: 029 2048 9359
E-mail: mail@playwales.org.uk

Website:
http://www.playwales.org.uk
http://www.chwaraecymru.org.uk

Enquiries:
Enquiries to: Information Officer

Organisation type and purpose:
Advisory body, membership association, voluntary organisation, registered charity, consultancy.

Subject coverage:
Children's play; to provide or assist in the provision of children's play facilities and services, to offer advice and training.

Museum or gallery collection, archive, or library special collection:
Specialist Library containing books on children's play (theory and practical books), child development, social and political issues related to children

Library catalogue:
All or part available in-house

Printed publications:
The First Claim a framework for playwork quality
  assessment
Order printed publications from: Office Manager

Publications list:
Available in print

Access to staff:
Contact by letter, by telephone, by fax and by e-mail. Appointment necessary.
Hours: Tue to Thu, 1000 to 1400
Special comments: At other times by prior appointment.

Access to building, collection or gallery:
Prior appointment required
Hours: Mon to Fri, 0900 to 1700

Access for disabled people:
Parking provided, ramped entry, toilet facilities

Also at:
Play Wales Chwarae Cymru
  Station House, Bastion Road, Prestatyn
Play Wales Chwarae Cymru
  Units 8/9 Tai Tywyn Business Centre, Sandy
  Lane, LL19 7SF

PLAYBOARD

56–65 York Street, Belfast, BT15 1AA

Tel: 028 9080 3380
Fax: 028 9080 3381
E-mail: information@playboard.co.uk

Website:
http://www.playboard.org/
General playboard information.

Enquiries:
Enquiries to: Chief Executive
Other contacts: Information & Campaigns Officer for general information requests.

Founded:
1985

Organisation type and purpose:
Advisory body, membership association (membership is by subscription), present number of members: 170, voluntary organisation, registered charity (charity number XO139/90), training organisation, consultancy, research organisation.
PlayBoard is the lead agency for children's play in Northern Ireland. It works to promote the child's right to play by providing quality play opportunities for all children, supported by development, policy, information, training and consultancy services.

Subject coverage:
Information relating to children's play and general issues impingeing on children's lives, particularly in Northern Ireland.

Museum or gallery collection, archive, or library special collection:
Reference library on issues relating to children's play and children's lives

Library catalogue:
All or part available in-house

Printed publications:
Action for Play (£5 plus 60p p&p)
Games Not Names (£3 plus 60p p&p)
Gender Matters (£3.50 plus 60p p&p)
Play, Playtime and Playgrounds (£4.50 plus 60p p&p)
Briefing Papers on relationship between play and care; education; the environment; social inclusion (free)
Strategic Plan (free)
Annual Reports (free)
Order printed publications from: Information & Campaigns Officer

Publications list:
Available online and in print

Access to staff:
Contact by letter, by telephone, by fax, by e-mail and via website. Appointment necessary.
Hours: Mon to Thu, 0930 to 1630; Fri, 0930 to 1530

Access for disabled people:
Level entry, toilet facilities
Special comments: Lift to training/meeting rooms.

Armagh Office:
PlayBoard
  Melbourne House, 16 Marlborough Terrace, Russell Street, Armagh, BT61 9AA; tel: 028 3751 5910; fax: 028 3751 5919

Irvinestown Office:
PlayBoard
  Enterprise Park, Market Yard, Mill Street, Irvinestown, BT94 4GR; tel: 028 6862 8825; fax: 028 6862 8825

PLAYER PIANO GROUP

Acronym or abbreviation: PPG

93 Evelyn Avenue, Ruislip, Middlesex, HA4 8AH

Tel: 01895 634288
E-mail: secretary@playerpianogroup.org.uk

Website:
http://www.playerpianogroup.org.uk

Enquiries:
Enquiries to: Honorary Secretary

Founded:
1959

Organisation type and purpose:
Voluntary organisation.

Subject coverage:
Mechanical music, player pianos, pianolas, reproducing pianos, piano rolls, performers, catalogues, sales and exchanges, history of the instrument, its mechanisms, repair and restoration.

Printed publications:
Bulletin (quarterly, available to members only, free)

Linked with sister societies in the:
UK and Germany, Netherlands, USA, Australia

PLIMSOLL PUBLISHING LIMITED

Scotswood House, Teesdale South, Stockton-on-Tees, Cleveland, TS17 6SB

Tel: 01642 626400
Fax: 01642 626410
E-mail: plimsoll@dial.pipex.com

Website:
http://www.plimsoll.co.uk

Enquiries:
Enquiries to: Marketing Officer

Founded:
1986

Organisation type and purpose:
Publishers of financial analysis.

Subject coverage:
Financial analysis of various sectors of UK industry by the analysis of individual players.

Printed publications:
Analysis of a group of companies, covering all sectors, in report form: a one-page analysis of each company in that sector (approximately 700 different industries, available on disc or hardcopy)

Electronic and video publications:
Electronic versions of all analyses are available

Publications list:
Available online and in print

Access to staff:
Contact by letter, by telephone, by fax, by e-mail and via website. Appointment necessary.
Hours: Mon to Fri, 0830 to 1700

Access to building, collection or gallery:
Prior appointment required

Access for disabled people:
Access to all public areas

PLUMPTON COLLEGE

Ditchling Road, Plumpton, Lewes, East Sussex, BN7 3AE

Tel: 01273 890454
Fax: 01273 890071
E-mail: enquiries@plumpton.ac.uk

Website:
http://www.plumpton.ac.uk

Enquiries:
Enquiries to: Librarian
Direct e-mail: anne.boryer@plumpton.ac.uk

Subject coverage:
Agriculture, livestock, equestrian, horticulture, floristry, conservation, wine studies, agricultural mechanics, animal care, forestry.

Library catalogue:
All or part available online

Printed publications:
College prospectus & course leaflets

Access to staff:
Contact by telephone, by fax and by e-mail. Appointment necessary.
Hours: Mon to Thu, 0900 to 2200; Fri, 0900 to 1700

Also at:
Ivyland Farm
  Netherfield, Battle, East Sussex; tel: 01424 838620

Associate college of:
University of Brighton

PLUNKETT FOUNDATION

The Quadrangle, Woodstock, Oxfordshire, OX20 1LH

Tel: 01993 810730
Fax: 01993 810849
E-mail: info@plunkett.co.uk

Website:
http://www.plunkett.co.uk
Services and information.

Enquiries:
Enquiries to: Information Officer
Direct e-mail: k.targett@plunkett.co.uk
Other contacts: Financial Administrator for book purchase.

Founded:
1919

Organisation type and purpose:
International organisation, advisory body, membership association (membership is by subscription), present number of members: 150, registered charity (charity number 313743), public library, training organisation, consultancy, research organisation.
Information centre.
To provide information, advice and consultancy about co-operative enterprise and other member-controlled business models.

Subject coverage:
Co-operative enterprise (all sectors, especially agriculture), farmer-controlled business, international project management, rural enterprise development, co-operative business training and education, co-operative legislation.

Museum or gallery collection, archive, or library special collection:
Co-operative Congress Reports (1869–1931)
Irish Homestead (vol. I to vol. XXX)
Journals
Library of 30,000 books and documents covering all aspects of co-operative enterprise
Research reports

continued overleaf

Sir Horace Plunkett's Diaries (1881–1932) and
Letters
Yearbook of Co-operative Enterprise 1927–1994
(now retitled World of Co-operative Enterprise
1995–2000)

Trade and statistical information:
Detailed data on the trading activity of farmer-
controlled businesses (including co-operatives)
in the UK, covering farm supplies and the
marketing of farm produce.

Non-library collection catalogue:
All or part available in-house

Library catalogue:
All or part available online

Printed publications:
Directory of Agricultural, Co-operatives and Other
Farmer-Controlled Businesses in the UK
Statistics of UK Agricultural Co-operatives and
Farmer-Controlled Businesses

Access to staff:
Contact by letter, by telephone, by fax, by e-mail
and via website. Appointment necessary.
Hours: Mon to Fri, 0900 to 1700

Access to building, collection or gallery:
Prior appointment required

Access for disabled people:
Parking provided, level entry, toilet facilities

PLYMOUTH AND WEST DEVON
RECORD OFFICE

Acronym or abbreviation: PWDRO

Unit 3, Clare Place, Coxside, Plymouth, Devon,
PL4 0JW

Tel: 01752 305940
E-mail: pwdro@plymouth.gov.uk

Enquiries:
Enquiries to: Archivist

Organisation type and purpose:
Local government body. Archive.

Subject coverage:
The records of Plymouth and the west Devon area.

Non-library collection catalogue:
All or part available online and in-house

Access to staff:
Contact by letter, by telephone and by e-mail.
Appointment necessary.
Hours: Tue to Thu, 0930 to 1700; Fri, 0930 to 1600
Special comments: Identification required for visits.

Access for disabled people:
By appointment

PLYMOUTH ATHENAEUM AND
THEATRE

Formal name: Plymouth Athenaeum and Theatre

Derrys Cross, Plymouth, Devon, PL1 2SW

Tel: 01752 266079
E-mail: bussec@btconnect.com

Website:
http://www.plymouthathenaeum.co.uk

Founded:
1812

Organisation type and purpose:
Cultural society and membership organisation
(membership by subscription)

Subject coverage:
Arts, literature, science and technology

Access to staff:
Contact by letter, by telephone, by fax, by e-mail
and via website
Hours: Mon to Fri, 1000 to 1630

PLYMOUTH CITY COUNCIL

Civic Centre, Armada Way, Plymouth, Devon, PL1
2EW

Tel: 01752 668000
Fax: 01752 264819
E-mail: pccmail@plymouth.gov.uk

Website:
http://www.plymouth.gov.uk

Organisation type and purpose:
Local government body.

Access to staff:
Contact by letter, by telephone, by fax, by e-mail
and in person
Hours: Mon to Fri, 0900 to 1700

PLYMOUTH COLLEGE OF ART
AND DESIGN LEARNINNG
RESOURCE CENTRE

Acronym or abbreviation: PCAD

Tavistock Place, Plymouth, Devon, PL4 8AT

Tel: 01752 203412
Fax: 01752 203444
E-mail: pcad@pcad.ac.uk

Website:
hrttp://elibrary.pcad.ac.uk

Enquiries:
Enquiries to: Librarian
Direct e-mail: lharding@pcad.ac.uk

Organisation type and purpose:
Suitable for ages: 16+.
College of further education and higher education.

Subject coverage:
Architecture; colour; communications; design
crafts; fashion; film and television; fine art; graphic
design; industrial design; painting and decorating;
photography; printing; textiles.

Library catalogue:
All or part available online

Printed publications:
Student Study Guide, for art and design students
(£3)

Access to staff:
Contact by telephone and by e-mail. Appointment
necessary.
Hours: Term time: Mon to Thu, 0845 to 1930; Fri,
0845 to 1730
Vacation time: Mon to Fri, 1000 to 1600

Access to building, collection or gallery:
Hours: Mon to Thu, 0845 to 1900; Fri, 0845 to 1700

Affiliated to:
Open University
University of Plymouth

PLYMOUTH LIBRARY SERVICES

Formal name: City of Plymouth Library and
Information Services

Central Library, Drake Circus, Plymouth, Devon,
PL4 8AL

Tel: 01752 305907/8
Fax: 01752 305905
E-mail: ref@plymouth.gov.uk

Website:
http://www.plymouth.gov.uk/libraries
Basic information about the library service in
Plymouth plus additional Plymouth linked
information as added. There will be links to other
web sites and information.
http://www.webopac.plymouth.gov.uk/
PLS – online, library catalogue online, facilities to
reserve items and renew online, directory of
Plymouth clubs and societies; charities; children
and young people's facilities. Plymouth Business
Directory, music information centre, Plymouth
song index.

Enquiries:
Enquiries to: Information Services Manager
Direct e-mail: henders@plymouth.gov.uk

Founded:
1876

Organisation type and purpose:
Local government body, public library.

Subject coverage:
General, technical, naval history, local studies,
music theory, scores and sets of parts, drama,
patents.

**Museum or gallery collection, archive, or library
special collection:**
Day Collection (naval history, previously in the
Gloucester County Library)
Eden Phillpotts collection (local studies
department)
Local Studies Collection
Moxon Collection of Ornithology and Travel
(mainly 19th century)
Music Collection (orchestral parts and scores)
Naval History and Naval Architecture
Naval History Department
Patent Abridgements from 1855
Special indexes: Broderick – History of Devonport;
Honeywill – Submarines; Larn – Shipwrecks of
Devon; Akerman – Dictionary of British Fighting
Ships

Library catalogue:
All or part available online

Printed publications:
Various maps, prints, greeting cards

Access to staff:
Contact by letter, by telephone, by fax, by e-mail,
in person and via website
Hours: Mon to Fri, 0900 to 1900; Sat, 0900 to 1700
Special comments: Patent enquiries, Mon to Fri, 0900
to 1700 only.

Access for disabled people:
Parking provided, level entry, access to all public
areas
Special comments: Lift to 1st Floor.

PLYMOUTH LOCAL AND NAVAL
STUDIES LIBRARY

Plymouth Central Library, Drake Circus,
Plymouth, PL4 8AL

Tel: 01752 305909
E-mail: localstudies@plymouth.gov.uk

Website:
http://www.plymouth.gov.uk/libraries

Enquiries:
Enquiries to: Librarian

Organisation type and purpose:
Local government body, public library.

Subject coverage:
History of Plymouth, West Devon and South East
Cornwall. Family history. Naval history

**Museum or gallery collection, archive, or library
special collection:**
Books and pamphlets, maps, newspapers,
illustrations, family history resources

Library catalogue:
All or part available online

Printed publications:
Selection of books, factsheets, greetings cards and
maps
Order printed publications from: Library or library
website

Publications list:
Available online

Access to staff:
Contact by letter, by telephone, by e-mail, in
person and via website
Hours: Mon to Fri, 0900 to 1900; Sat, 0900 to 1700

Access to building, collection or gallery:
No prior appointment required

Hours: Mon to Fri, 0900 to 1900; Sat 0900 to 1700

Access for disabled people:
Lift to first floor

Member organisation of:
Naval and Maritime Libraries and Archives Group (NMLAG)

PLYMOUTH PROPRIETARY LIBRARY

Alton Terrace, 111 North Hill, Plymouth, Devon, PL4 8JY

Tel: 01752 660515

Enquiries:
Enquiries to: Librarian

Founded:
1810

Organisation type and purpose:
Membership association (membership is by subscription), present number of members: 110, registered charity (charity number 1015700). Private subscription library.

Subject coverage:
General recreational library, nineteenth and twentieth century novels, general non-fiction.

Museum or gallery collection, archive, or library special collection:
Devon and Cornwall local studies section

Library catalogue:
All or part available in-house

Access to staff:
Contact by letter and by telephone. Appointment necessary.
Hours: Mon, Tue, Thu, Fri, 0930 to 1700; Wed, 0930 to 1400; Sat, 0930 too 1230

PMS PUBLICATIONS LIMITED

Formal name: Parliamentary Monitoring Services
Acronym or abbreviation: PMS

19 Douglas Street, Westminster, London, SW1P 4PA

Tel: 020 7233 8283
Fax: 020 7821 9352
E-mail: info@parliamentary-monitoring.co.uk

Enquiries:
Enquiries to: Managing Director

Founded:
1935

Organisation type and purpose:
Research organisation, publishing house.
News agency for politics and government.
To inform clients of what is happening in government and throughout the UK and the EU.

Subject coverage:
Political, parliamentary, local government, European Union.

Museum or gallery collection, archive, or library special collection:
Databases of biographical information on MPs, Peers, top civil servants and local authorities

Printed publications:
European Public Affairs Directory
Parliament and Assemblies of the UK
PMS Guide to Interest Groups
PMS Local Government Companion
PMS Parliamentary Companion
Update Bulletin (weekly)
Parliamentary Bulletin for Local Government Executives (weekly)

Electronic and video publications:
Members of All Parliaments and Assemblies in the UK and European Parliament (CD-ROM)

Publications list:
Available in print

Access to staff:
Contact by letter, by fax and by e-mail. Access for members only.
Hours: Mon to Fri, 0900 to 1700

Also at the same address:
Parliamentary Monitoring Services

POETRY BOOK SOCIETY

Acronym or abbreviation: PBS

4th Floor, 2 Tavistock Place, London, WC1H 9RA

Tel: 020 7833 9247
Fax: 020 7833 5990
E-mail: info@poetrybooks.co.uk

Website:
http://www.poetrybooks.co.uk
Buy books on line; history of PBS.

Enquiries:
Enquiries to: Director

Founded:
1953

Organisation type and purpose:
International organisation, membership association (membership is by subscription), present number of members: c. 2200, registered charity (charity number 313753), suitable for ages: 7+.
A publicly funded membership book club promoting contemporary poetry.

Subject coverage:
Contemporary poetry published in the UK and Eire since 1953; educational resources for 7 to 18 year olds.

Printed publications:
Bulletin (magazine, quarterly, distributed to members)

Electronic and video publications:
CDs

Access to staff:
Contact by letter, by telephone, by fax, by e-mail and via website
Hours: Mon to Fri, 0930 to 1730

POETRY LIBRARY

Royal Festival Hall, South Bank Centre, London, SE1 8XX

Tel: 020 7921 0943 or 0664
Fax: 020 7921 0939
E-mail: info@poetrylibrary.org.uk

Website:
http://www.poetrylibrary.org.uk
Outline of library services, 'lost quotations' noticeboard (discussion group), information lists

Enquiries:
Enquiries to: Poetry Librarian
Direct tel: 020 7921 0940
Other contacts: Assistant Librarians for enquiries.

Founded:
1953

Organisation type and purpose:
National organisation, membership association, present number of members: 21,200, public library, research organisation.
Special arts library.

Subject coverage:
Modern poetry from all English-speaking countries of the world; modern poetry translated from other languages; pre-20th century poetry translated by contemporary English language poets; poetry for children, poetry on tape, video, record, CD and CD-ROM.

Museum or gallery collection, archive, or library special collection:
Alec Craig Bequest
Howard Sargent collection of press cuttings
Images of Poets
Large collection of poetry magazines

Rare modern first editions
SIGNAL collection of children's poetry
Sylvia Townsend Warner Bequest
Tapes, records, videos, CD-ROMs

Non-library collection catalogue:
All or part available in-house

Library catalogue:
All or part available in-house

Printed publications:
Current awareness lists
Lists of UK poetry magazines, bookshops, groups and workshops
Short-title catalogue of Books in the Collection (constitutes a bibliography of poetry published 1912–1980)

Publications list:
Available in print

Access to staff:
Contact by letter, by telephone, by fax, by e-mail, in person and via website
Hours: Tue to Sun, 1100 to 2000

Access for disabled people:
Level entry

Parent body:
Arts Council England
South Bank Board

POETRY SOCIETY

22 Betterton Street, London, WC2H 9BX

Tel: 020 7420 9880
Fax: 020 7240 4818
E-mail: info@poetrysociety.org.uk

Website:
http://www.poetrysociety.org.uk
Reading and writing contemporary poetry.

Enquiries:
Enquiries to: Information Officer

Founded:
1909

Organisation type and purpose:
Membership association, registered charity.
Arts centre for poetry; registered charity supported by the Arts Council.
To promote the study, use and enjoyment of poetry.

Subject coverage:
Poetry and poets, information on writing or publishing poetry, contemporary poetry events, competitions, festivals, teachers' poetry resource.

Services for disabled people:
Induction loop; audio tapes of Poetry Review and Poetry News for blind and partially-sighted members

Printed publications:
Teachers' resources
Poetry News (quarterly)
Poetry Review (quarterly)
Information Pack
Jumpstart Poetry in the Secondary School
Poetry Book for Primary Schools
National Poetry Day teaching materials
Foyle Young Poets of the Year anthologies

Access to staff:
Contact by letter, by telephone, by fax, by e-mail and via website
Hours: Mon to Fri, 1000 to 1800

Access to building, collection or gallery:
Prior appointment required

Access for disabled people:
Lift to basement performance space; toilet facilities; induction loop

POLANI RESEARCH LIBRARY

King's College London School of Medicine at Guy's, King's College and St Thomas', Division of Genetics and Molecular Medicine, 8th Floor Tower Wing, Guy's Campus, London, SE1 9RT

continued overleaf

Tel: 020 7188 3702
Fax: 020 7188 0021
E-mail: lesley.exton@kcl.ac.uk

Website:
http://www.kcl.ac.uk/schools/medicine/dept/
memoge

Enquiries:
Enquiries to: Information Officer

Founded:
1963

Formerly called:
Paediatric Research Unit Library (PRU) (year of
change 1982)

Organisation type and purpose:
University department or institute, research
organisation.
Research laboratory library.

Subject coverage:
Human and medical genetics, genetic counselling,
birth defects.

Library catalogue:
All or part available in-house

Access to staff:
Contact by telephone and by e-mail. Appointment
necessary. All charged.
Hours: Mon to Fri, 0900 to 1700

Access to building, collection or gallery:
Via main entrance to Guy's Hospital

POLICE HISTORY SOCIETY

64 Nore Marsh Road, Wootton Bassett, Wiltshire

Website:
http://www.policehistorysociety.co.uk

Enquiries:
Enquiries to: Honorary Secretary
Other contacts: Membership Secretary for
membership enquiries

Founded:
1985

Organisation type and purpose:
Membership association (membership is by
subscription), present number of members: 400,
registered charity, voluntary organisation (charity
number 295540).
To bring together those interested in the history of
the police and policing. NB The PHS is not
primarily concerned with family historical research
and holds no police personnel records.

Subject coverage:
History of policing; history of crime.

Printed publications:
Annual Journal (free to members, otherwise £5 per
   annum)
Newsletter (free to members 3 or 4 times a year)
Other occasional publications

Access to staff:
Contact by letter and by e-mail
Hours: Mon to Fri, 0900 to 1700
Special comments: SAE for reply essential.

Membership Secretary:
Police History Society
   Foxtrot Oscar, 37 South Lawne, Bletchley, Milton
   Keynes, MK3 6BU; tel: 0161 962 3764

POLICY PRESS

University of Bristol, Fourth Floor, Beacon House,
Queen's Road, Clifton, Bristol, BS8 1QU

Tel: 0117 331 4054
Fax: 0117 331 4093
E-mail: tpp-info@bristol.ac.uk

Website:
http://www.policypress.org.uk

Enquiries:
Enquiries to: Marketing Executive
Direct tel: 0117 331 4096

Other contacts: Director

Founded:
1995

Organisation type and purpose:
Publishing house, publishing policy research.

Subject coverage:
Community care, environment, family policy and
child welfare, criminal justice, ageing, education,
governance, health, housing, labour markets,
urban policy, gender, voluntary sector, welfare and
poverty.

Printed publications:
Books, Research and Policy Reports, Practice
   Guides and Journals, including:
Policy and Politics
Benefits (new)
Order printed publications from: Customer Services,
Marston Book Services, PO Box 269, Abingdon,
Oxfordshire, OX14 4YN; tel. 01235 465500; fax
01235 465556; e-mail direct.orders@marston.co.uk

Electronic and video publications:
Policy and Politics (online)

Publications list:
Available online and in print

Access to staff:
Contact by letter, by telephone, by fax, by e-mail
and via website
Hours: Mon to Fri, 0900 to 1700

Links with:
University of Bristol

POLISH CULTURAL INSTITUTE

Acronym or abbreviation: PCI

34 Portland Place, London, W1B 1HQ

Tel: 0870 774 2300/2
Fax: 020 7637 2190
E-mail: pci@polishculture.org.uk

Website:
http://www.polishculture.org.uk
Details of Institute's events around the country,
past events, events in Poland, Polish language
courses, the library, general information on Polish
culture.

Enquiries:
Enquiries to: Director
Direct tel: 0870 774 2300/2

Organisation type and purpose:
National government body.
Promotion of Polish culture in the UK.

Subject coverage:
Poland and Polish music, film, theatre, literature
and art, Polish history, geography.

**Museum or gallery collection, archive, or library
special collection:**
Library of reference books, video, slides and music
   recordings, newspapers both Polish and English

Trade and statistical information:
Some economic information on Poland.

Non-library collection catalogue:
All or part available online

Library catalogue:
All or part available in-house

Publications list:
Available in print

Access to staff:
Contact by letter, by telephone, by fax, by e-mail
and via website
Hours: Mon to Fri,1000 to 1600

Access to building, collection or gallery:
No prior appointment required
Hours: Mon, Tue, Wed, Fri, 1200 to 1600; Thu, 1600
to 2000

Part of:
Polish Embassy in London

POLISH EMBASSY

Formal name: Embassy of the Republic of Poland

47 Portland Place, London, W1B 1JH

Tel: 0870 7742 700
Fax: 020 7323 4018
E-mail: polishembassy@polishembassy.org.uk

Website:
http://www.polishembassy.org.uk
Website of the Emabassy of Poland in London,
comprehensive information about the Embassy,
Poland and Polish-British relations.
http://www.paiz.gov.pl
Polish Agency of Foreign Investment
http://www.bmb.pl
The promotion of Polish local government with
particular emphasis placed upon the investment
possibilities of districts
http://www.poland.pl
Poland in brief; Polish Archives; Poland on the
web: state and politics, society, geography and
tourism, business and eceonomy, computers and
telecommunications, art and culture, media and
information, science and education, sport and
recreation, lifestyle; views from all round Poland,
maps; Polish Roots: Poland Genealogy Forum,
Dynastic Genealogy, Geneaology & Poland

Enquiries:
Enquiries to: Counsellor (Press & Information)

Organisation type and purpose:
National government body.
Embassy.

Subject coverage:
General enquiries relating to Poland, current
political and economic situation, culture and
tourism, visas etc.

Trade and statistical information:
Trade information from the Commercial Office.

Printed publications:
Press releases on important issues (not on a regular
   basis)

Access to staff:
Contact by letter, by fax, by e-mail and via
website
Hours: Mon to Fri, 0830 to 1630
Special comments: Visa enquiries should be made to
the Consulate General
Tourism enquiries to the Polish National Tourist
Office.

Other addresses:
Commercial Counsellors Office to the Embassy of
the Republic of Poland
   15 Devonshire Street, London, W1N 2AR; tel:
   020 7580 5481; fax: 020 7323 0195
Consulate General of the Republic of Poland
   73 New Cavendish Street, London, W1N 4HQ;
   tel: 0870 7742 800; fax: 020 7323 2320; e-mail:
   consulate@polishconsulate.co.uk; website: www
   .polishconsulate.co.uk
Consulate General of the Republic of Poland
   2 Kinnear Road, Edinburgh, EH3 5PE; tel: 0131
   552 0301; fax: 0131 552 1086; e-mail: edinburgh@
   polishconsulate.org; website: www
   .polishconsulate.org
Polish Cultural Institute
   34 Portland Place, London, W1N 4HQ; tel: 0870
   7742 900; fax: 020 7637 2190; e-mail: pci@
   polishculture.org.uk; website: www
   .polishculture.org

POLISH LIBRARY

238–246 King Street, London, W6 0RF

Tel: 020 8741 0474
Fax: 020 8741 7724
E-mail: polish.library@posk.org

Enquiries:
Enquiries to: Librarian

Founded:
1942

Organisation type and purpose:
Membership association (membership is by subscription), present number of members: 2000+, voluntary organisation, registered charity (charity number 236745), research organisation, publishing house.
Specialised library. Public library circulating service.
Collecting and the dissemination of information, Worldwide, on the subject of Polish emigrés in the UK.

Subject coverage:
Polish culture, history, literature, language, geography, economics, politics, sociology, folklore, arts, philosophy, religious life, militaria.

Museum or gallery collection, archive, or library special collection:
Anglo-Polish relations
Archives of some Polish organisations
Joseph Retinger private papers
Polish emigré publications
Polish underground opposition and Solidarity publications
Works by and about Joseph Conrad

Non-library collection catalogue:
All or part available in-house

Library catalogue:
All or part available in-house

Printed publications:
Annual Report
Bibliographies of books in Polish, or works by Polish scholars, and of books and pamphlets on Katyn
Catalogues of collections and exhibitions
Full list of the publications available from the Library
Joseph Conrad Collection
Polish Library 1942–1979 and 1942–1992
Order printed publications from: e-mail: Polish.library@mailbox.ac.uk

Access to staff:
Contact by letter, by telephone, by fax, by e-mail, in person and via website. Letter of introduction required.
Hours: Mon and Wed, 1000 to 2000; Fri, 1000 to 1700, Sat, 1000 to 1300

Access for disabled people:
Ramped entry, access to all public areas, toilet facilities

Houses the:
Joseph Conrad Society
tel: As for the library

Parent body:
Polish Social and Cultural Association Limited (POSK)
tel: 020 8741 1940; fax: 020 8746 3796; e-mail: admin@posk.org; website: http://www.posk.org

PONTEFRACT REGISTER OFFICE

Old Town Hall, Bridge Street, Pontefract, West Yorkshire, WF8 1PG

Tel: 01977 722670
Fax: 01977 722676

Enquiries:
Enquiries to: Superintendent Registrar

Founded:
1837

Organisation type and purpose:
Local government body, statutory body.

Access to staff:
Contact by letter, by telephone, by fax and in person. Appointment necessary.
Hours: Mon to Fri, 0900 to 1630
Special comments: Sat by prior appointment.

Access to building, collection or gallery:
No prior appointment required

Access for disabled people:
Parking provided, ramped entry

PONTELAND LOCAL HISTORY SOCIETY

Formal name: Ponteland Local History Society

127 Middle Drive, Darras Hall, Newcastle-upon-Tyne, NE20 9DS

E-mail: jmichaeltaylor@btinternet.com

Website:
http://www.ponthistsoc.freeuk.com

Enquiries:
Enquiries to: Secretary
Direct tel: 01661 823880

Founded:
1968

Organisation type and purpose:
Membership association (membership by subscription).
To promote and interest in local history.

Printed publications:
Newsletter (monthly)
Ponte Island News (annually)
Books:
Images of England: Ponteland
Ponteland through the Twentieth Century
Ponteland: One Thousand Years of History
Ponteland: the Garden City

Access to staff:
Contact by letter, by e-mail and via website

Affiliated to:
Association of Northumberland Local History Societies

PONTIFICAL MISSION SOCIETIES

Acronym or abbreviation: MISSION

23 Eccleston Square, London, SW1V 1NU

Tel: 020 7821 9755
Fax: 020 7630 8466
E-mail: director@missio.org.uk

Website:
http://www.missio.org.uk

Enquiries:
Enquiries to: Director

Founded:
1833

Organisation type and purpose:
Registered charity (charity number 1056651).
Support of the Catholic Church in mission areas.

Access to staff:
Contact by letter, by e-mail and via website
Hours: Mon to Fri, 0900 to 1700

PONY CLUB OF GREAT BRITAIN

Formal name: The Pony Club

Stoneleigh Park, Kenilworth, Warwickshire, CV8 2RW

Tel: 024 7669 8300
Fax: 024 7669 6836
E-mail: enquiries@pcuk.org

Website:
http://www.pcuk.org

Enquiries:
Enquiries to: Chief Executive
Other contacts: PA to the Chief Executive

Founded:
1929

Organisation type and purpose:
Membership association (membership is by subscription), registered charity (charity number 1050146), suitable for ages: under 25.
To encourage young people to ride and to learn to enjoy horses and riding: to provide instruction in riding, horsemanship and the proper care of their animals: to promote the highest ideals of sportsmanship, citizenship and loyalty.

Subject coverage:
Running an equestrian-orientated youth organisation; information on all matters relating to equestrianism and horse care for young people.

Printed publications:
A variety of publications including:
Gymkhanas and Rally Games
Instructors Handbook
Keeping a Pony at Grass
Manual of Horsemanship
Training Young Horses
A Young Persons Guide to Showjumping

Publications list:
Available in print

Access to staff:
Contact by letter, by telephone, by fax, by e-mail and via website
Hours: Mon to Fri, 0900 to 1700

Has:
2200 affiliated branches overseas in 17 countries
347 branches and over 400 centres in the UK

POOLE CENTRAL LIBRARY

Dolphin Centre, Poole, Dorset, BH15 1QE

Tel: 01202 262424\ Minicom no. 01202 667113
Fax: 01202 262442
E-mail: centrallibrary@poole.gov.uk

Website:
http://www.boroughofpoole.com/libraries
General description of services, catalogue on the web available soon.

Enquiries:
Enquiries to: Information Services Librarian
Other contacts: Central Library Manager

Founded:
1885

Organisation type and purpose:
Local government body, public library.

Subject coverage:
General information, pottery and ceramics.

Non-library collection catalogue:
All or part available in-house

Library catalogue:
All or part available in-house

Publications list:
Available in print

Access to staff:
Contact by letter, by telephone, by fax, by e-mail, in person and via website
Hours: Mon to Thu, 0900 to 1800; Fri, 0900 to 1900; Sat, 0900 to 1500

Access for disabled people:
Access to all public areas, toilet facilities

Parent body:
Borough of Poole, Cultural Services

POPULATION CONCERN

Studio 325, Highgate Studios, 53–79 Highgate Road, London, NW5 1TL

Tel: 020 7241 8500
Fax: 020 7267 6788
E-mail: info@populationconcern.org.uk

Website:
http://www.populationconcern.org.uk

Enquiries:
Enquiries to: Education Officer

Founded:
1974

Organisation type and purpose:
Registered charity (charity number 1001698).
Originally set up as the international division of the UK FPA; an independent charitable organisation since April 1991.

continued overleaf

Subject coverage:
Reproductive and sexual health, gender, poverty alleviation, young people, population and related issues.

Trade and statistical information:
Data on world population, youth around the world, young people's sexual and reproductive health, and reproductive risk.

Library catalogue:
All or part available in-house

Printed publications:
Annual Report (free)
Newsletter (annually, free)
Introduction (free)
Meeting the Sexual Health Needs of Young People (free)
2001 World Population Data Sheet (£4 each)
Order printed publications from: Education Officer, Population Concern
e-mail: education@populationconcern.org.uk

Electronic and video publications:
Population Dots (video on issues of population)
Population and Development Database (CD-ROM)

Access to staff:
Contact by letter, by telephone, by fax, by e-mail and via website
Hours: Mon to Fri, 0900 to 1700

Collaborates with:
International Planned Parenthood Federation (IPPF)
Marie Stopes International (MSI)

Recognised by the:
United Nations Population Fund (UNFPA)

POPULATION INVESTIGATION COMMITTEE

Acronym or abbreviation: PIC

London School of Economics and Political Science, Houghton Street, London, WC2A 2AE

Tel: 020 7955 7666
Fax: 020 7955 6831
E-mail: pic@lse.ac.uk

Website:
http://www.lse.ac.uk/depts/pic

Enquiries:
Enquiries to: General Secretary

Founded:
1936

Organisation type and purpose:
Professional body, membership association (membership is by election or invitation), present number of members: 11, registered charity (charity number 263783), research organisation.

Subject coverage:
Demography and population studies.

Printed publications:
A Record of Research and Publications 1936–78 (free, but 75p p&p)
Birth Control Practice and Marital Fertility in Great Britain (C. M. Langford, £2 plus £1.75 p&p)
Demographic Estimation for Developing Societies (N. Carrier and J. Hobcraft, £10.00 plus £1.75 p&p)
Population Research in Britain (M. Murphy and J. Hobcraft, £15 incl. p&p)
Population Studies (journal, 1 vol., 3 parts a year, available online at www.popstudies.net)
Supplements to the Journal
The Demography of the British Peerage (T. H. Hollingsworth, 50p plus £1.50 p&p)
The Population Investigation Committee: A Concise History To Mark Its Fiftieth Anniversary (C. M. Langford, £3 incl. p&p)
Towards a Population Policy for the United Kingdom (50p plus £1.50 p&p)
Order printed publications from: Population Investigation Committee, Room PS201, Houghton Street, London, WC2A 2AE, tel: 020 7955 7666, fax: 020 7955 6831, e-mail: pic@lse.ac.uk

Electronic and video publications:
Order electronic and video publications from: http://www.popstudies.net

Publications list:
Available online

Access to staff:
Contact by letter, by telephone, by fax, by e-mail and via website. Appointment necessary.
Hours: Mon to Fri, 1000 to 1600

PORSCHE CLUB GREAT BRITAIN

Acronym or abbreviation: PCGB

Cornbury House, Cotswold Business Village, London Road, Moreton-in-Marsh, Gloucestershire, GL56 0JQ

Tel: 01608 652911
Fax: 01608 652944
E-mail: cluboffice@porscheclubgb.com

Website:
http://www.porscheclubgb.com

Enquiries:
Enquiries to: Club Manager
Other contacts: Publications Manager for Club's Magazine and Publications information.

Founded:
1961

Organisation type and purpose:
Membership association (membership is by subscription), present number of members: c.16,000.

Subject coverage:
All information covering Porsche models manufactured from 1948 to the present day. Provision of display cars. Technical information. Porsche Motorsport.

Museum or gallery collection, archive, or library special collection:
Archive of information, photographs, objects and memorabilia relating to Porsche

Printed publications:
Porsche Post (magazine, monthly)
The Real 928

Access to staff:
Contact by letter, by telephone, by fax, by e-mail and via website. Appointment necessary.
Hours: Mon to Fri, 0900 to 1700

Access to building, collection or gallery:
Access for members only
Hours: Mon to Fri, 0900 to 1700

Access for disabled people:
Ramped entry, toilet facilities

PORTIA CAMPAIGN

Acronym or abbreviation: PORTIA

The Croft, West Common, Bowness-on-Solway, Cumbria, CA7 5AG

Tel: 016973 51820
E-mail: ken_portia@ontel.net.uk

Website:
http://www.portia.org

Enquiries:
Enquiries to: Chairman

Founded:
1971

Organisation type and purpose:
Membership association (membership is by subscription), present number of members: 470, voluntary organisation.
Counselling.

Subject coverage:
Shoplifting allegations, cot-death allegations, risk of baby-snatching, false imprisonment.

Printed publications:
Advice Notes (leaflets, free)

Order printed publications from: Infinity Junction PO Box 64, Neston DO, CH64 0WB, e-mail: http//:www.infinityjunction.com

Electronic and video publications:
The Lynch Mob Syndrome (Internet)

Access to staff:
Contact by letter, by telephone, by fax, by e-mail, in person and via website
Hours: 24 hours

PORTICO LIBRARY AND GALLERY

57 Mosley Street, Manchester, M2 3HY

Tel: 0161 236 6785
Fax: 0161 236 6803
E-mail: librarian@theportico.org.uk

Website:
http://www.theportico.org.uk

Enquiries:
Enquiries to: Librarian

Founded:
1806

Organisation type and purpose:
Independent members' library (membership is by subscription)

Subject coverage:
Travel, biography, topography, novels, poetry, drama, natural philosophy.

Special visitor services:
Group visits by arrangement

Museum or gallery collection, archive, or library special collection:
Mainly 19th-century collection, archives of the Insitution since 1806. Houses publications of the Lancashire and Cheshire Antiquarian Society

Library catalogue:
All or part available in-house

Printed publications:
In-house monographs on topics mainly related to Manchester, the region and the Library's collection, Portico Library histories, exhibition catalogues
Order printed publications from: Librarian

Publications list:
Available online

Access to staff:
Contact by letter, by telephone, by fax, by e-mail, in person and via website

Access to building, collection or gallery:
Via entryphone at Charlotte Street entrance
Hours: Mon to Fri, 0930 to 1630 (or as advertised)
Special comments: Subscription only, open to researchers.

Access for disabled people:
No wheelchair access
Special comments: Located upstairs

Member organisation of:
Association of Independent Libraries
website: http://www.independentlibraries.co.uk

PORTLAND COLLEGE

Nottingham Road, Mansfield, Nottinghamshire, NG18 4TJ

Tel: 01623 499111
Fax: 01623 499133
E-mail: college@portland.ac.uk

Website:
http://www.portland.ac.uk/

Enquiries:
Enquiries to: Admissions Officer
Direct fax: 01623 499134
Direct e-mail: jwilkes@portland.org.uk

Founded:
1950

Organisation type and purpose:
Voluntary organisation, registered charity (charity number 214339).

Subject coverage:
Residential courses for all categories of physically disabled persons, except the totally blind, from 16 years of age upwards; vocational courses in business, technical studies and horticulture; foundation and further education; adult basic education; alternative and augmentative communication skills, unit for head injured (SPAN).

Printed publications:
Prospectus and Annual Report

Access to staff:
Contact by letter, by telephone and by fax. Appointment necessary.
Hours: Mon to Fri, 0900 to 1700

Recognised by the:
British Accreditation Council

PORTSMOUTH & SOUTH EAST HAMPSHIRE CHAMBER OF COMMERCE AND INDUSTRY

Regional Business Centre, Harts Farm Way, Havant, Hampshire, PO9 1HR

Tel: 023 9244 9449
Fax: 023 9244 9444
E-mail: sehants@chamber.org.uk

Website:
http://www.chamber.org.uk
Directory of members, events, news, business opportunities and discussion forum.

Enquiries:
Enquiries to: Information Manager

Founded:
1883

Organisation type and purpose:
Membership association.
Chamber of Commerce.

Subject coverage:
Business information, helpline, export and import advice, documentation, trade missions, training, lobbying and representation.

Trade and statistical information:
Economic survey of members for ABCC quarterly survey.

Printed publications:
Business News (magazine, monthly)

Access to staff:
Contact by telephone and by e-mail
Hours: Mon to Fri, 0900 to 1700

Access to building, collection or gallery:
No prior appointment required
Hours: Mon to Fri, 0900 to 1700

Access for disabled people:
Parking provided, level entry, access to all public areas, toilet facilities

PORTSMOUTH CITY COUNCIL

Acronym or abbreviation: PCC

Civic Offices, Guildhall Square, Portsmouth, Hampshire, PO1 2BG

Tel: 023 9282 2251
E-mail: general@portsmouthcc.gov.uk

Website:
http://www.portsmouthcc.gov.uk

Enquiries:
Enquiries to: Chief Executive
Direct tel: 023 9283 4009

Organisation type and purpose:
Local government body.

Subject coverage:
Services and amenities of the city council.

PORTSMOUTH CITY COUNCIL LIBRARY SERVICE

Portsmouth Central Library, Guildhall Square, Portsmouth, Hampshire, PO1 2DX

Tel: 023 9281 9311
Fax: 023 9283 9855
E-mail: reference.library@portsmouthcc.gov.uk

Enquiries:
Enquiries to: Library Service Manager
Direct e-mail: colin.brown@portsmouthcc.gov.uk

Organisation type and purpose:
Local government body, public library.

Subject coverage:
General reference library, particularly strong in areas of law, patent information, business information, art, local history (Hampshire), naval history, genealogy. European Public Information Centre.

Museum or gallery collection, archive, or library special collection:
Art Monographs
British Government Publications
British Standards
Charles Dickens Collection
Conan Doyle Collection
Genealogical Collection
HMSO Collection (selected subjects, 1972-)
Law Library
Local History Collection
Maps Collection
Naval Collection (12,000 vols)
Patent Abridgements, 1607 to 1992
State Papers (Calendars and Rolls)
Statistics Collection
UK Patent bibliographic data and full text 1993 to date on CD-ROM

Trade and statistical information:
Extensive collection of UK and foreign trade directories.
UK and European statistical information.
Some market research material.

Library catalogue:
All or part available online and in-house

Access to staff:
Contact by letter, by telephone, by fax, by e-mail and in person
Hours: Mon to Fri, 0900 to 1900; Sat, 0930 to 1600
Special comments: Access to historical collections requires proof of name and address.

Member of:
HATRICS Centre
Patent Information Network

PORTSMOUTH MUSEUMS AND RECORDS SERVICE

City Museum and Records Office, Museum Road, Portsmouth, Hampshire, PO1 2LJ

Tel: 02392 827261\ Minicom no. 02392 876550
Fax: 02392 875276
E-mail: searchroom@portsmouthcc.gov.uk

Website:
http://www.portsmouthrecordsoffice.co.uk/
http://www.portsmouthmuseums.co.uk

Enquiries:
Enquiries to: Manager
Other contacts: (1) Commercial Manager; (2) Visitor Services Officer for (1) marketing; (2) group bookings.

Founded:
1972

Organisation type and purpose:
Local government body, museum, art gallery.

Subject coverage:
The Story of Portsmouth; Living in Portsmouth; Fine and Decorative Art Gallery; and The Records Office.

Information services:
Special visitor services: Guided tours. Education services: Group education facilities, resources for Key Stages 1 and 2 and 3. Services for disabled people: For the hearing impaired.

Museum or gallery collection, archive, or library special collection:
17th century furniture
Art Deco Furniture
Frank Dobson Sculptures (terracotta and bronze)
Ceri Richards relief work 'Le Piano'.
Ronal Ossory Dunlop painting 'Still Life with Black Bottle'.
JMW Turner RA watercolour 'Gosport, the Entrance to Portsmouth Harbour' c. 1829
Local History:
Sir Alec Rose (Round the World Yachtsman – artefacts)
Verracahias Ice Cream parlour and artefacts
Records Office contains the official records of the City of Portsmouth from the 14th century, church registers and records, some of which begin in the reign of Henry VIII, and large collections of deposited records of private, commercial, families and other organisations

Access to staff:
Contact by letter, by telephone, by fax and by e-mail

Access to building, collection or gallery:
No prior appointment required
Hours: Museum: daily, 1000 to 1700 except 24 to 26 Dec
Records Office: Mon to Fri, 1000 to 1700, closed on Public Holidays and 24 to 26 Dec

Access for disabled people:
Parking provided, ramped entry, level entry, access to all public areas, toilet facilities
Special comments: Induction loops.

PORTSMOUTH NHS LIBRARY SERVICE

Library, The Quad, Queen Alexandra Hospital, Portsmouth, Hampshire, PO6 3LY

Tel: 023 9228 6039
Fax: 023 9228 6880
E-mail: library.qah@porthosp.nhs.uk

Website:
http://www.porthosp.nhs.uk/library-services.html

Enquiries:
Enquiries to: Library Services Manager

Organisation type and purpose:
National Health Service library.

Subject coverage:
Multi-disciplinary health care

Access to staff:
Contact by letter, by telephone, by fax, by e-mail and via website. Appointment necessary.
Hours: Mon to Fri, 0830 to 1630

Branch libraries:
Education Centre
St Mary's Hospital, Portsmouth, Hampshire, PO6 3AD; tel: 023 9228 6000 ext 4855

Parent body:
Portsmouth Hospitals NHS Trust

POST ABORTION COUNSELLING SERVICE

Acronym or abbreviation: PACS

340 Westbourne Park Road, London, W11 1EQ

Tel: 020 7221 9631
E-mail: abortion@pacs.org.uk

Enquiries:
Enquiries to: Counsellor

Founded:
1986

continued overleaf

Organisation type and purpose:
Advisory body, professional body, registered charity (charity number 802225), training organisation.
Counselling service.
To offer pre-abortion counselling and training for other professionals in the field.

Subject coverage:
The need for counselling as a result of an abortion.

Printed publications:
It's OK to Talk About Abortion (free)

Access to staff:
Contact by letter and by telephone. Appointment necessary. All charged.
Hours: Mon to Fri, 0900 to 2000
Special comments: 24 hour answerphone, counselling all hours by appointment.

Member of:
British Association of Counselling

POST OFFICE VEHICLE CLUB

Acronym or abbreviation: POVC

32 Russell Way, Leighton Buzzard, Bedfordshire, LU7 3NG

Tel: 01525 382129
E-mail: povehclub@aol.com

Website:
http://www.povehclub.org.uk

Enquiries:
Enquiries to: Honorary Secretary
Direct e-mail: povcmembership@btinternet.com

Founded:
1962

Organisation type and purpose:
Membership association.

Subject coverage:
Preservation of Royal Mail and British Telecom vehicles; DVLA appointed for GPO and Post Office vehicles for V765 registration restoration.

Museum or gallery collection, archive, or library special collection:
Books
Photographs
Vehicle data and manuals
Vehicle records

Non-library collection catalogue:
All or part available in-house and in print

Printed publications:
Post Horn (magazine, monthly)
Order printed publications from: 124 Shenstone Avenue, Norton, Stourbridge, West Midlands, DY8 3EJ

Publications list:
Available in print

Access to staff:
Contact by letter, by telephone, by fax, by e-mail and via website. Appointment necessary. Access for members only.
Hours: Mon to Fri, 1900 to 2100; Sat, Sun, 0900 to 1800

POST VINTAGE HUMBER CAR CLUB

Formal name: PVHCC Ltd

1 Hilberry Rise, Berrydale, Northampton, NN3 5ER

Tel: 01604 404363
E-mail: pvhumber.carclub@talk21.com

Website:
http://www.humber.org.uk

Enquiries:
Enquiries to: Director
Other contacts: Secretary

Founded:
1974

Organisation type and purpose:
Membership association (membership is by subscription), present number of members: 700+.
Preservation and enjoyment derived from the ownership and enthusiasm for Humber cars.

Subject coverage:
Humber cars from 1932 to 1976.

Non-library collection catalogue:
All or part available online

Printed publications:
Various publications available (please enquire or see website)

Access to staff:
Contact by letter, by telephone, by e-mail and via website. Appointment necessary.
Hours: Mon to Fri, 0800 to 2200; Sat, Sun, 1000 to 2000

Member organisation of:
Federation of British Historic Vehicle Clubs (FBHVC)

Member organisations:
in more than 20 countries

Parent body:
PVHCC Ltd
1 Hilberry Rise, Northampton, NN3 5ER; tel: 01604 404363

POST-WAR THOROUGHBRED CAR CLUB

Church Villas, 22 Burhill Road, Hersham, Walton on Thames, Surrey, KT12 4JF

Tel: 01932 29101
Fax: 01932 29101

Enquiries:
Enquiries to: Membership Secretary

Founded:
1978

Organisation type and purpose:
Membership association (membership is by subscription), present number of members: 100.
Historic car club.

Subject coverage:
British motor vehicles registered between the years 1945–1974.

Access to staff:
Contact by letter
Hours: Mon to Fri, 0900 to 1700

POSTAL HISTORY SOCIETY

Acronym or abbreviation: PHS

60 Tachbrook Street, London, SW1V 2NA

Tel: 020 7545 7773
Fax: 020 7976 6040
E-mail: home@claireangier.co.uk

Enquiries:
Enquiries to: Membership Secretary

Founded:
1936

Organisation type and purpose:
Learned society (membership is by subscription), present number of members: 416.

Subject coverage:
History of communications by post or telegraph.

Library catalogue:
All or part available in-house

Printed publications:
Postal History (quarterly)
Australian Mails via Suez, 1852–1926 (Kirk)
British Postal Rates 1635–1839 (Sanford & Salt)
British Postal Rates to Europe 1836–76
Devon & Cornwall: a Postal Survey 1500–1791 (Cornelius)

Norwich Post Office 1568–1980 (Sussex)
Official Franking 1800–1840 (Scott)
Royal Mail Steam Packet Co 1842–1879 (Howatt)
Ship Letters (Hendy)
The Bermuda Packet Mails, 1806–1886 (Arnell & Ludington)
Order printed publications from: Publications Officer, Postal History Society
St Andrews Mews, Station Road, Stanley, Ilkeston, Derbyshire, DE7 6FB, tel: 01332 250970, e-mail: nicklynn@standrews85.freeserve.co.uk

Publications list:
Available in print

Access to staff:
Contact by letter, by telephone, by fax and by e-mail
Hours: Mon to Fri, 0900 to 1700

Affiliated to:
Association of British Philatelic Societies Limited
tel: 020 7490 3112

POTATO COUNCIL

4300 Nash Court, John Smith Drive, Oxford Business Park South, Oxford, OX4 2RT

Tel: 01865 714455
Fax: 01865 782200
E-mail: sgerrish@potato.org.uk

Website:
http://www.potato.org.uk

Enquiries:
Enquiries to: Information Resources Manager
Direct tel: 01865 782270
Direct fax: 01865 782283

Founded:
1997

Formerly called:
British Potato Council (year of change 2008)

Organisation type and purpose:
Non-departmental Public Body. Levy funded by the British Potato Industry, providing sponsorship of research and development, knowledge transfer, promotion of British ware and seed potatoes, collection and dissemination of market information and statistics – all activities contributing towards increasing the competitiveness of the British potato industry, and increasing the usage of British potatoes.

Subject coverage:
Potato storage; varieties; pests; diseases; production; marketing; cookery; all aspects, though mainly of UK interest.

Museum or gallery collection, archive, or library special collection:
Some grey literature, collection of published articles going back to 1950s and 1960s on computerised retrieval system

Trade and statistical information:
Data on the production of potatoes in Great Britain and volume of trade throughout the world.
Producer, wholesale and retail prices.
Crop progress reports.

Non-library collection catalogue:
All or part available in-house

Printed publications:
Potato Council Update (newsletter, c.10 a year, sent to all levy payers)
Research and Development Project Reports
Publications for the potato industry, consumers (varieties, cooking), caterers
Order printed publications from: Publications, at the same address, tel: 01865 782222, fax: 01865 782283, e-mail: publications@potato.org.uk

Electronic and video publications:
Many project reports are available on the website

Access to staff:
Contact by letter, by fax and by e-mail.
Appointment necessary.
Hours: Mon to Fri, 0900 to 1700

Special comments: Photocopies cannot be supplied.

Parent body:
Agriculture and Horticulture Development Board (AHDB)
Area 2B, Nobel House, 17 Smith Square, London, SW1P 3JR; tel: 020 7238 3079; e-mail: info@ahdb .org.uk; website: http://www.ahdb.org.uk

POTATO PROCESSORS ASSOCIATION

Acronym or abbreviation: PPA

4a Torphichen Street, Edinburgh, EH3 8JQ

Tel: 0131 229 9415
Fax: 0131 229 9407
E-mail: andrew.jack@sfdf.org.uk

Enquiries:
Enquiries to: Secretary

Organisation type and purpose:
Trade association (membership is by subscription).

Subject coverage:
Potato processing.

Access to staff:
Contact by letter, by telephone, by fax and by e-mail. Appointment necessary.
Hours: Mon to Fri, 0900 to 1700

Member of:
EUITP

POWER GENERATION CONTRACTORS ASSOCIATION

Acronym or abbreviation: PGCA

Westminster Tower, 3 Albert Embankment, London, SE1 7SL

Tel: 020 7793 3040
Fax: 020 7793 1576

Enquiries:
Enquiries to: Director

Organisation type and purpose:
Trade association.

Subject coverage:
Project management and engineering services for utility and industrial power stations, water tube and shell boilers; steam, gas, water and wind turbine generators, condensing and feed heating plant, high integrity pipework, auxiliary and ancillary plant, nuclear engineering, environmental systems, retrofit, refurbishment, repair, maintenance and construction services.

Access to staff:
Contact by fax
Hours: Mon to Fri, 0900 to 1700

Federated in:
BEAMA

POWERFUL INFORMATION

City Discovery Centre, Bradwell Abbey, Milton Keynes, Buckinghamshire, MK13 9AP

Tel: 01908 320033
Fax: 01908 320033

Enquiries:
Enquiries to: Manager
Direct e-mail: lynne@powerfulinformation.org

Founded:
1990

Organisation type and purpose:
Registered charity, suitable for ages: all, training organisation.

Subject coverage:
Environmental information, e.g. habitat protection, energy, transport, pollution and waste management. Capacity Building e.g. organisation development and project management, community development, promoting the

complementary role of specialist and local knowledge. Information provision, supporting local resource centres and exploring the relationship between modern ICT and traditional communication methods.

Access to staff:
Contact by letter, by telephone, by fax and by e-mail. Appointment necessary.
Hours: Mon to Fri, 0900 to 1700

Access for disabled people:
Parking provided, level entry, access to all public areas, toilet facilities

POWERGEN UK PLC

Power Technology, Ratcliffe on Soar, Nottingham, NG11 0EE

Tel: 0115 936 2000
Fax: 0115 936 2711
E-mail: liz.day@powertech.co.uk

Website:
http://www.powertech.co.uk

Enquiries:
Enquiries to: Information Officer
Direct tel: 0115 936 2360
Direct fax: 0115 362 647

Founded:
1989

Organisation type and purpose:
Service industry.
Electricity and gas utility.

Subject coverage:
Environment; wind power; NDT; metallurgy; combustion and fossil fuel; all subjects relating to electricity production, organisation and maintenance; does not include nuclear generation or electricity transmission.

Museum or gallery collection, archive, or library special collection:
CEGB and Powergen reports

Non-library collection catalogue:
All or part available in-house

Library catalogue:
All or part available in-house

Printed publications:
Public information pamphlets on power stations, Powergen departments and types of power production
Ashes to Assets (booklet)

Access to staff:
Contact by letter, by telephone, by fax, by e-mail and via website. Appointment necessary.
Hours: Mon to Fri, 0900 to 1700

Access for disabled people:
Parking provided, level entry, toilet facilities

Head Office:
Powergen plc
Westwood Way, Westwood Business Park, Coventry, CV4 8LG; tel: 01203 424000; fax: 01203 425432

POWYS COUNTY ARCHIVES OFFICE

County Hall, Llandrindod Wells, Powys, LD1 5LG

Tel: 01597 826088
Fax: 01597 826087
E-mail: archives@powys.gov.uk

Website:
http://archives.powys.gov.uk
http://www.powys.gov.uk
Office guide.

Enquiries:
Enquiries to: Manager
Other contacts: Assistant Archivist

Founded:
1991

Organisation type and purpose:
Local government body.
Archives office.

Subject coverage:
Local history of former counties of Breconshire, Montgomeryshire and Radnorshire, 15th century to 20th century.

Museum or gallery collection, archive, or library special collection:
Public Records, incl. Quarter Sessions records
Official Records
Estate and Solicitors' collections
Records of local historical interest, incl. manuscripts and photographs
Census returns (microfiche)
Parish registers (microfilm)
A growing collection of local history books on Powys

Non-library collection catalogue:
All or part available in-house

Library catalogue:
All or part available online and in-house

Printed publications:
Annual Report (£4 inc. p&p)
Guide to the Powys County Archives Office

Access to staff:
Contact by letter, by telephone, by fax and by e-mail. Appointment necessary.
Hours: Tue to Thu, 1000 to 1230 and 1330 to 1700; Fri, 1000 to 1230 and 1330 to 1600; closed at all other times

Part of:
Powys County Council
Recreation, Culture and Countryside

POWYS COUNTY COUNCIL

County Hall, Llandrindod Wells, Powys, LD1 5LG

Tel: 01597 826000
Fax: 01597 826230

Website:
http://www.powys.gov.uk
Council services and information on county.

Enquiries:
Enquiries to: Relevant department

Founded:
1996

Organisation type and purpose:
Local government body.

Subject coverage:
Community services, children, families and lifelong learning, economy and community regeneration, technical and local services.

Access to staff:
Contact by letter, by telephone, by fax, by e-mail and in person
Hours: Mon to Fri, 0900 to 1700

POWYS LIBRARY SERVICE

Library HQ, Cefnllys Lane, Llandrindod Wells, Powys, LD1 5LD

Tel: 01597 826860
Fax: 01597 826872

Website:
http://www.powys.gov.uk/libraries

Enquiries:
Enquiries to: County Librarian

Organisation type and purpose:
Local government body, public library.

Subject coverage:
General.

Museum or gallery collection, archive, or library special collection:
Gregynog Press Collection (at Newtown Area Library)

continued overleaf

Local history collections (relating to Powys and to the former counties of Breconshire, Montgomeryshire and Radnorshire)

Library catalogue:
All or part available online and in-house

Access to staff:
Contact by letter, by telephone, by fax, by e-mail, in person and via website
Hours: HQ: Mon to Fri, 0900 to 1700; for branches, see website

Branches:
within the Recreation and Culture directorate of Powys County Council

POWYS SOCIETY

Flat D, 87 Ledbury Road, London, W11 2AG

Tel: 020 7238 4456 (office); 020 7243 0168 (evening)
E-mail: enquiries@powys-society.org

Website:
http://www.powys-society.org

Enquiries:
Enquiries to: Honorary Secretary
Direct e-mail: chris.thd.thomas@hotmail.co.uk

Founded:
1967

Organisation type and purpose:
Learned society (membership is by subscription), present number of members: 298, registered charity (charity number 801332).
Literary society. Aims to publicise the literary and artistic contribution of all members of the Powys Family, in particular John Cowper (1872–1963), Theodore Francis Powys (1875–1953) and Llewelyn Powys (1884–1939), and their wide circle of friends.

Subject coverage:
Lives and works of the three writers: John Cowper Powys, Theodore Francis Powys and Llewelyn Powys, other members of the Powys family and their circle of friends.

Museum or gallery collection, archive, or library special collection:
Major collections of books, manuscripts and letters, etc. relating to the Powys family, held at the Dorset County Museum, Dorchester, Dorset

Non-library collection catalogue:
All or part available in-house

Library catalogue:
All or part available in-house

Printed publications:
The Powys Journal (annual)
The Powys Society Newsletter (3 times a year)
Other occasional publications
Order printed publications from: Publications Manager, The Powys Society, 23 Cleveland Walk, Bath, BA2 6JW, tel: 01225 469004, e-mail: sm@gotadsl.co.uk

Publications list:
Available in print

Access to staff:
Contact by letter, by telephone, by e-mail and via website
Hours: Mon to Fri, 0900 to 1700

Access to building, collection or gallery:
By arrangement only

PRADER-WILLI SYNDROME ASSOCIATION (U.K.)

Acronym or abbreviation: PWSA(UK)

125A London Road, Derby, DE1 2QQ

Tel: 01332 365676
Fax: 01332 360401
E-mail: admin@pwsa.co.uk

Website:
http://www.pwsa.co.uk

Details of syndrome.

Enquiries:
Enquiries to: Administrator
Other contacts: Welfare Services and Regional Groups Coordinator for welfare queries, new diagnosis

Founded:
1981

Organisation type and purpose:
Voluntary organisation, registered charity (charity number 284583).
Voluntary support group.

Subject coverage:
The Prader-Willi Syndrome, support and information for sufferers and carers.

Library catalogue:
All or part available in-house

Printed publications:
Free information leaflets include:
What is Prader-Willi Syndrome?
So your child has Prader-Willi Syndrome – What Happens Now?
Diagnostic Criteria for PWS
Prader-Willi Syndrome: A handbook for parents and carers of babies and children with PWS (Waters J)
Books for purchase include:
Handbook for parents and carers of adults with PWS (£3 members, £4.50 non members)
Home, School and Community (James T N and Brown R K, 1992, £13.95 members, £15.50 non members)
Kenneth: Living with PWS (book, £10)
Prader-Willi Syndrome: A Practical Guide – Resource materials for teachers (£15)

Electronic and video publications:
Videos (6, for loan)
Prader-Willi Syndrome – Keeping a Balance (video, £8 members, £12 non members)

Publications list:
Available in print

Access to staff:
Contact by letter, by telephone, by fax, by e-mail, in person and via website
Hours: Mon to Fri, 0930 to 1630
Special comments: Answerphone available.

Access to building, collection or gallery:
Prior appointment required

Access for disabled people:
Level entry

PRE-SCHOOL LEARNING ALLIANCE

National Centre, The Fitzpatrick Building, 188 York Way, London, N7 9AD

Tel: 020 7697 2500
Fax: 020 7700 0319
E-mail: info@pre-school.org.uk

Website:
http://www.pre-school.org.uk

Enquiries:
Enquiries to: Information Services
Direct tel: 020 7697 2595

Founded:
1961

Organisation type and purpose:
The Pre-school Learning Alliance is an educational charity specialising in the early years, and a membership association providing practical support to over 15,000 early years settings and contributing to the care and education of over 800,000 young children and their families each year.

Subject coverage:
Products and services include specialist publications, childcare services, quality assurance, campaigning, research, training and family programmes; offers a range of independent

professional information, advice, support and guidance tailored especially to meet the needs of young children and their families, students, early years practitioners and professionals.

Printed publications:
Extensive publications list covers all aspects of running an early-years setting.
Order printed publications from: Online shop: www.pre-school.org.uk/shop; Publications Orderline 0870 603 0062

Publications list:
Available online and in print

Access to staff:
Contact by letter, by telephone, by fax and by e-mail
Hours: Mon to Fri, 0900 to 1700

Constituent bodies:
4 divisional offices, 400 county and branch sub-committees

PRECAST FLOORING FEDERATION

Acronym or abbreviation: PFF

60 Charles Street, Leicester, LE1 1FB

Tel: 0116 253 6161
Fax: 0116 251 4568
E-mail: info@precastfloors.info

Website:
http://www.precastfloors.info

Enquiries:
Enquiries to: Secretary

Organisation type and purpose:
Trade association.

Subject coverage:
Precast concrete flooring units of all types.

Printed publications:
Code of Practice for the Safe Erection of Precast Concrete Flooring
Folder and Data Sheets
Members Product Range

Access to staff:
Contact by letter, by telephone, by fax and by e-mail
Hours: Mon to Fri, 0900 to 1700

Product association of the:
British Precast Concrete Federation

PREHISTORIC SOCIETY

Institute of Archaeology, University College London, 31–34 Gordon Square, London, WC1H 0PY

Website:
http://www.ucl.ac.uk/prehistoric

Enquiries:
Enquiries to: Administrative Assistant
Direct e-mail: prehistoric@ucl.ac.uk

Founded:
1935

Organisation type and purpose:
Learned society.

Subject coverage:
Prehistory.

Printed publications:
Past (newsletter, 3 times a year)
Proceedings of the Prehistory Society (annually)

Access to staff:
Contact by letter
Hours: Mon to Fri, 0900 to 1700

PREMIER CHRISTIAN RADIO

Formal name: Premier – Christian Radio for London

PO Box 13000, London, SW1E 5PP

Tel: 020 7233 6705
Fax: 020 7233 6706
E-mail: premier@premier.org.uk

Website:
http://www.premier.org.uk
Christian Radio.
http://www.radioondemand.net
Archive Christian programming.
http://www.christianityandrenewal.com
Christian magazine.

Enquiries:
Enquiries to: Administrator
Direct e-mail: crystal.callow@premier.org.uk

Founded:
1995

Organisation type and purpose:
Registered charity (charity number 287610).
Radio station.

Subject coverage:
Christian broadcasting and publishing, telephone helpline, internet services via website, Christian resources.

Printed publications:
Newsletter
Programme schedule
Christianity & Renewal (magazine)
Youthwork magazine

Access to staff:
Contact by letter, by telephone, by fax, by e-mail and via website
Hours: Mon to Fri, 0900 to 1700

Access to building, collection or gallery:
No access other than to staff

Publishing subsidiary:
Monarch CCP
PO Box 17911, London, SW1E 5ZR; tel: 020 7316 1450; fax: 020 7316 1453; e-mail: monarchccp@premier.org.uk

Telephone Helpline:
Lifeline
At the same address; tel: 020 7316 0808; e-mail: lifeline@premier.org.uk

PRESBYTERIAN CHURCH OF WALES

Acronym or abbreviation: PCW

Tabernacle Chapel, 81 Merthyr Road, Whitchurch, Cardiff, CF14 1DD

Tel: 029 2062 7465
Fax: 029 2061 6188
E-mail: swyddfa.office@ebcpcw.org.uk

Website:
http://www.ebcpcw.org.uk

Enquiries:
Enquiries to: Manager

Organisation type and purpose:
Registered charity.
Christian church, excepted charity.
To propagate the Gospel of Jesus Christ.

Subject coverage:
The history, organisation and current position of the Presbyterian Church of Wales.

Museum or gallery collection, archive, or library special collection:
The Presbyterian Church of Wales Archive is housed in the National Library, Aberystwyth

Printed publications:
Books
Treasury (English monthly newspaper)
Y Goleuad (Welsh weekly newspaper)
Yearbook and Diary
Order printed publications from: The Manager, Y Bwthyn Press, Lôn Ddewi, Caernarfon, Gwynedd, LL55 1ER, tel: 01286 672018, fax: 01286 677823

Access to staff:
Contact by letter, by telephone, by fax, by e-mail

and via website. Appointment necessary.
Hours: Mon to Fri, 0900 to 1700

PRESBYTERIAN HISTORICAL SOCIETY OF IRELAND

Room 220, Church House, Fisherwick Place, Belfast, BT1 6DW

Tel: 028 9032 2284 ext 258
Fax: 028 9041 7307

Enquiries:
Enquiries to: Library/Assistant Sectretary

Founded:
1907

Organisation type and purpose:
Learned society (membership is by subscription), present number of members: 350, registered charity.
Historical society for the Presbyterian Church in Ireland; the Non-Subscribing Presbyterian Church of Ireland and the Reformed Presbyterian Church of Ireland.

Subject coverage:
History of Presbyterianism and the Presbyterian Churches in Ireland, with congregational, genealogical and biographical information.

Museum or gallery collection, archive, or library special collection:
Books and pamphlets (c. 550 to pre-1851); periodicals; congregational histories; biographies of ministers
Collection of Irish Presbyterian communion tokens
McCahan bequest (historical books and manuscripts)
Microfilm of church records

Printed publications:
A history of congregations of the Presbyterian Church in Ireland, 1610–1982 (1982, supplement only)
Helen Waddell, Presbyterian Medievalist (booklet)
Bulletin (annually)
Fasti of the General Assembly of the Presbyterian Church in Ireland, (1840–1910)
Our Presbyterian Heritage (history) (for purchase)

Access to staff:
Contact by letter, by telephone and in person.
Appointment necessary.
Hours: Mon to Fri, 1000 to 1230; Wed, 1315 to 1530
Special comments: Library for members and introduced visitors.

PRESCRIPTION PRICING AUTHORITY

Acronym or abbreviation: PPA

Bridge House, 152 Pilgrim Street, Newcastle upon Tyne, NE1 6SN

Tel: 0191 232 5270
Fax: 0191 232 5250

Website:
http://www.ppa.org.uk

Enquiries:
Enquiries to: Director of Information Technology
Direct fax: 0191 203 5270
Direct e-mail: douglas.ball@ppa.nhs.uk

Founded:
1911

Organisation type and purpose:
Statutory body.
Information on drugs dispensed and prescribed in England. Details on prescribers and dispensers.
Drug coding and descriptive information.
Authorise and make payment to dispensing contractors in England with regard to NHS prescriptions. Provide prescribing information and systems to NHS bodies and prescribers. Detection and prevention of fraud. Management of Low Income Scheme.

Subject coverage:
Drug prescribing in England, volume of drugs in the UK, updates on drug prices, standard drug file/drug coding systems and information for research groups. Details on prescribing and dispensing contractors.

Printed publications:
Drug file for NHS drugs

Electronic and video publications:
EPACT – Electronic prescribing information access systems
TOOLKIT – Performance indicators

Access to staff:
Contact by letter and by e-mail. Appointment necessary.
Hours: Mon to Fri, 0900 to 1700
Special comments: Access only by appointment.

PRESS ASSOCIATION

Acronym or abbreviation: PA

PA News Library, PA News Centre, Central Park, New Lane, Leeds, West Yorkshire, LS11 5DZ

Tel: 0870 830 6824
Fax: 0870 830 6825
E-mail: newslibrary@pa.press.net

Website:
http://www.palibrary.press.net
Information about the library.

Enquiries:
Enquiries to: News Librarian
Other contacts: Picture Librarian for photo library.

Founded:
1926 (library)

Organisation type and purpose:
National organisation, service industry.
News agency.
Cuttings from all national papers.

Subject coverage:
Archive news material from 1926 to date covering a very wide range of subjects in 15 million press cuttings from all British national newspapers, some back to 1928; domestic news photographs from 1910 to present day.

Museum or gallery collection, archive, or library special collection:
News library
Photo library

Access to staff:
Contact by telephone, by fax, by e-mail and in person. Appointment necessary. All charged.
Hours: Daily, 0700 to 2300

PRESS COMPLAINTS COMMISSION

Acronym or abbreviation: PCC

Halton House, 20–23 Holborn, London, EC1N 2JD

Tel: 020 7831 0022
Fax: 020 7831 0025
E-mail: complaints@pcc.org.uk

Website:
http://www.pcc.org.uk

Enquiries:
Enquiries to: Information and Events Manager
Direct e-mail: pcc@pcc.org.uk

Founded:
1991

Organisation type and purpose:
Independent body founded to oversee the self-regulation of the press, comprising 16 members drawn from the lay public and the press.
Regulation of print media, newspapers and magazines.

continued overleaf

Subject coverage:
Investigation and adjudication of complaints against any newspaper or periodical in the United Kingdom alleged to be in breach of the Code of Practice, where reconciliation between the complainant and the relevant editor has not been achieved; advice on interpretation and improvement to the Code of Practice.

Printed publications:
Code of Practice
Complaints Reports
How to Complain
How the PCC Can Help You – wallet-sized leaflets

Access to staff:
Contact by letter, by telephone, by e-mail and via website
Hours: 0900 to 1730
Special comments: 24-hour Advice Line for use in emergencies only: 07659 152656

Access to building, collection or gallery:
Prior appointment required
Hours: 0930 to 1730

PRESSURE GAUGE AND DIAL THERMOMETER ASSOCIATION

Acronym or abbreviation: PGDT

136 Hagley Road, Edgbaston, Birmingham, B16 9PN

Tel: 0121 454 4141
Fax: 0121 454 4949
E-mail: info@pgdt.org

Website:
http://www.pgdt.org

Enquiries:
Enquiries to: Secretary

Organisation type and purpose:
Trade association.

Subject coverage:
Pressure gauges and pressure measurement, temperature gauges and measurement.

Printed publications:
Buyer's Guide

Access to staff:
Contact by e-mail and via website
Hours: Mon to Fri, 0900 to 1700

PRESTON BOROUGH COUNCIL

PO Box 10, Town Hall, Preston, Lancashire, PR1 2RL

Tel: 01772 906000
Fax: 01772 906195
E-mail: yourcouncil@pbcpr.demon.co.uk

Website:
http://www.preston.gov.uk

Enquiries:
Enquiries to: Public Relations Manager
Direct tel: 01772 906464
Direct e-mail: al.mazzafiore@pbcpr.demon.co.uk

Organisation type and purpose:
Local government body.

Subject coverage:
Local government services.

Printed publications:
Annual Report
Prestonian (Citizens' Newsletter, quarterly)

Access to staff:
Contact by letter and by e-mail
Hours: Mon to Fri, 0900 to 1700

PRESTRESSED CONCRETE ASSOCIATION

Acronym or abbreviation: PCA

4th Floor, 60 Charles Street, Leicester, LE1 1FB

Tel: 0116 253 6161
Fax: 0116 251 4568
E-mail: pca@britishprecast.org

Enquiries:
Enquiries to: Secretary

Organisation type and purpose:
Trade association.

Subject coverage:
Precast pretensioned concrete bridge beams, double tee beams and other precast prestressed units.

Printed publications:
Integral Abutments for Prestressed Beam Bridges (£40)
Prestressed Beam Integral Bridges (1991, £10)
Serviceability limit state aspects of continuous bridges using precast concrete beams (£20)
Simple bridge design using Prestressed Beams (£50)

Access to staff:
Contact by letter, by telephone, by fax and by e-mail
Hours: Mon to Fri, 0900 to 1700

Product association of the:
British Precast Concrete Federation

PRIMARY IMMUNODEFICIENCY ASSOCIATION

Acronym or abbreviation: PiA

Alliance House, 12 Caxton Street, London, SW1H 0QS

Tel: 020 7976 7640
Fax: 020 7976 7641
E-mail: info@pia.org.uk

Website:
http://pia.org.uk

Enquiries:
Enquiries to: Chief Executive
Direct e-mail: david@pia.org.uk

Founded:
1989

Organisation type and purpose:
Membership association (membership is by subscription), present number of members: 2000, voluntary organisation, registered charity (charity number 803217).

Subject coverage:
All primary immunodeficiencies and how they affect individuals.

Publications list:
Available online and in print

Access to staff:
Contact by letter, by telephone, by fax, by e-mail and via website. Appointment necessary.
Hours: Mon to Fri, 0900 to 1700

Member of:
European Patients Primary Immunodeficiency Collaboration (EPPIC)
International Patient of Primary Immunodeficiencies (IPOPI)

PRINCE'S FOUNDATION

Formal name: The Prince's Foundation for the Built Environment
Acronym or abbreviation: PFBE

19–22 Charlotte Road, London, EC2A 3SG

Tel: 020 7613 8500
Fax: 020 7613 8599
E-mail: enquiry@princes-foundation.org

Website:
http://www.princes-foundation.org
Public programme, news, alumni network, project case studies, publications.

Founded:
1998

Formerly called:
The Prince of Wales Institute for Architecture (year of change 2000)

Organisation type and purpose:
Registered charity, consultancy.

Subject coverage:
Architecture, community planning, traditional art, building crafts, Islamic art, environmental building techniques, urban design and regeneration.

Information services:
Architecture and urban design library

Museum or gallery collection, archive, or library special collection:
Library based upon the collections of the late John Julius Stanton and others (access by appointment)
including books on Islamic art, enriched by gift of books from Issam El Said

Printed publications:
Taylor & Green Architects 1938–1943: The Spirit of Place in Modern Housing
Annual Review (free)
Guidance Notes: How to Write a Conservation Plan for a Heritage Industrial Building
John Campbell – Rediscovery of an Arts & Crafts Architect
Regeneration Through Heritage: Industrial Buildings
Sustainable Urban Extensions: Planned through design
The Community Planning Handbook
The Golden City
Urban Villages
VITA Publications:
Fez Occasional Paper
Proportional Rectangles
The Arch in Islamic Architecture
Underneath which Rivers Flow
Unity in Pattern

Publications list:
Available in print

Access to staff:
Contact by letter, by telephone, by fax and by e-mail. Appointment necessary.
Hours: Mon to Fri, 0930 to 1730

Access to building, collection or gallery:
Prior appointment required
Hours: Mon to Fri, 0900 to 1700

Access for disabled people:
Ramped entry, access to all public areas, toilet facilities (fully DDA-compliant)
Hours: Mon to Fri, 0900 to 1700

Links with:
The Prince of Wales' Charitable Foundation
The Prince's Drawing School
The Prince's Regeneration Trust
The Prince's School of Traditional Art

PRINCE'S TRUST, THE

Head Office, 18 Park Square East, London, NW1 4LH

Tel: 020 7543 1234\ Minicom no. 020 7543 1374
Fax: 020 7543 1200
E-mail: info@princes-trust.org.uk

Website:
http://www.princes-trust.org.uk
Information on all programmes and activities.

Enquiries:
Enquiries to: Press Office
Direct tel: 020 7543 1382
Other contacts: Information Officer for research enquiries.

Founded:
1973

Organisation type and purpose:
Registered charity (charity number 1053579).

The Prince's Trust is the UK's leading youth charity, offering 14–30 year olds the training, funding or support they need to gain confidence, improve life skills or get into work.

Subject coverage:
Young people; youth disadvantage; youth unemployment; young people and New Deal; young people and volunteering.

Printed publications:
Various publications including
Annual Review
Yes You Can (booklet)
Abuse and Survival (1998, PAID)
Mapping Disadvantage (PAID)
It's Like That – Young people's hopes and
  aspirations
The Way It Is
Various factsheets
Order printed publications from: Literature
Distribution Service
tel: 020 8957 5190

Electronic and video publications:
Only a Kiss? – helps young people recognise and
  cope with abusive relationships (video, PAID)
Yes You Can – about the Prince's Trust (video)
Yes You Can (audio tape, booklet)
Yes You Can, Work for Yourself (audio tape)

Publications list:
Available in print

Access to staff:
Contact by letter, by telephone and via website
Hours: Mon to Fri, 0900 to 1700

Access to building, collection or gallery:
No prior appointment required
Special comments: Research/information needs in writing to the Information Officer.

Other addresses:
Various offices across the UK
  tel: Freephone 0800 842 842

PRINCIPAL REGISTRY OF THE FAMILY DIVISION (PROBATE DEPARTMENT)

First Avenue House, 42–49 High Holborn, London, WC1V 6NP

Tel: 020 7947 7000
Fax: 020 7947 6946

Website:
http://www.courtservice.gov.uk
Click on forms and leaflets, and probate is towards the end of the list.

Enquiries:
Enquiries to: Manager Probate Department

Organisation type and purpose:
National government body.

Subject coverage:
Wills and grants of probate and administration.

Museum or gallery collection, archive, or library special collection:
All wills in England and Wales since 1858

Printed publications:
How to obtain probate – Form PA2

Access to staff:
Contact by telephone and in person
Hours: Mon to Fri, 1000 to 1630
Special comments: General enquiries only by telephone.

Access for disabled people:
Access to all public areas, toilet facilities

All requests for copies of wills/grants by post:
York Probate Sub-Registry (provide full name of deceased, data of death, locality, where resided, cheque for £5 payable H.M.P.G.)
  Duncombe Place, York, YO1 7EA

PRISON ADVICE AND CARE TRUST

Acronym or abbreviation: PACT

Family Support Services, 254 Caledonian Road, Islington, London, N1 0NG

Tel: 020 7278 3981
Fax: 020 7278 8765
E-mail: familysupport@pact.uk.net

Website:
http://www.imprisonment.org.uk

Enquiries:
Enquiries to: Family Services Manager

Founded:
1974

Organisation type and purpose:
Voluntary organisation, registered charity (charity number 219278).
Gives support advice and help to prisoners' wives, children and any family member or friend who has someone in prison.

Subject coverage:
Welfare benefits, penal systems, 'families and friends' finance, visiting prisons, prison regulations, assisted visits, accommodation. Overnight accommodation for families visiting London prisons/attending trials/appeals.

Museum or gallery collection, archive, or library special collection:
Leaflets, booklets, books and publications relating to penal establishments, rules etc

Printed publications:
PACT information leaflet

Access to staff:
Contact by letter, by telephone, by fax, by e-mail and via website. Appointment necessary.
Hours: Mon to Fri, 0930 to 1700

Liaison with other groups involved in similar work eg:
and various statutory bodies
Federation of Prisoners' Families Support Groups
NACRO
Prison Reform Trust

Other addresses:
All Day Children's Visits
  HMP Holloway, Parkhurst Road, London, N7
  0NU
Holloway Visitors' Centre
  HMP Holloway, Parkhurst Road, London, N7
  0NU; tel: 020 7700 1567
Pentonville Visitors' Centre
  HMP Pentonville, Caledonian Road, London, N7
  8TT; tel: 020 7609 3860

Registered Office and Administration:
PACT
  Lincoln House, 1–3 Brixton Road, London, SW9
  6DE

PRISON OFFICERS' ASSOCIATION

Acronym or abbreviation: POA

Cronin House, 245 Church Street, Edmonton, London, N9 9HW

Tel: 020 8803 0255
Fax: 020 8803 1761

Enquiries:
Enquiries to: General Secretary

Organisation type and purpose:
Trade union, present number of members: 34,000.

Subject coverage:
Trade union view of issues relating to the working and operational conditions of HM Prisons Service.

Access to staff:
Contact by letter. Appointment necessary. Letter of introduction required.
Hours: Mon to Fri, 0900 to 1700

Affiliated to:
EUROFEDOP
TUC

PRISON REFORM TRUST

Acronym or abbreviation: PRT

2nd Floor, 15 Northburgh Street, London, EC1V 0JR

Tel: 020 7251 5070
Fax: 020 7251 5076
E-mail: info@prisonreformtrust.org.uk

Website:
http://www.prisonreformtrust.org.uk

Enquiries:
Enquiries to: Director
Other contacts: Administrator

Founded:
1981

Organisation type and purpose:
National organisation, voluntary organisation, registered charity (charity number 1035525), research organisation.
The work of the Prison Reform Trust is aimed at creating a just, humane and effective penal system.

Subject coverage:
Prison rules, prison regimes, alternatives to custody and sentencing policy.

Museum or gallery collection, archive, or library special collection:
News cuttings
Official reports
Prison statistics
Wide variety of UK and international reports and
  papers

Printed publications:
Prison Report (magazine, quarterly)
Prisoner's information pack (annually, free to
  prisoners and their families)
Plus many other publications

Publications list:
Available online and in print

Access to staff:
Contact by letter and by e-mail
Hours: Mon to Fri, 0900 to 1700

PRISON SERVICE

Headquarters Library, Room 224, Abell House, John Islip Street, London, SW1P 4LH

Tel: 020 7217 5253 or 5452 or 5548
Fax: 020 7217 5209

Enquiries:
Enquiries to: Library Manager

Organisation type and purpose:
National government body.

Subject coverage:
Prisons and penology, penal legislation, building and construction, probation.

Museum or gallery collection, archive, or library special collection:
Annual reports: prison service annual report;
  reports of HM Inspector of Prisons
Monographs and serials on prisons and the prison
  service
Prison service orders and instructions

Trade and statistical information:
Prison statistics England and Wales, statistics of
  offences against prison discipline and
  punishments England and Wales.

Library catalogue:
All or part available in-house

Printed publications:
Prison Service annual report and accounts

Access to staff:
Contact by letter, by telephone and by fax
Hours: Mon to Fri, 0915 to 1700

continued overleaf

Parent body:
Home Office Information and Library Services

PRISON SERVICE COLLEGE LIBRARY

Prison Service College, Newbold Revel, Rugby, Warwickshire, CV23 0TH

Tel: 01788 804119
Fax: 01788 804114
E-mail: catherine.fell@hmps.gsi.gov.uk

Enquiries:
Enquiries to: Librarian

Founded:
1960

Organisation type and purpose:
National government body, training organisation. Central government training establishment.

Subject coverage:
Penology and criminology; history of the prison service in England and Wales; comparative material on penal establishments in other countries; management and training; forensic psychology and psychiatry

Museum or gallery collection, archive, or library special collection:
Miscellaneous 19th-century reports on prison-related matters
Reports of Directors of Convict Prisons
Reports of HM Inspectors of Prisons from 1835
Reports of the Prison Commission/Prison Department from 1878

Library catalogue:
All or part available in-house

Printed publications:
Accessions List (6 a year)
Journals Bulletin (monthly)
Miscellaneous reading lists – produced on request

Access to staff:
Contact by letter, by telephone, by fax and by e-mail. Appointment necessary.
Hours: Mon, 1000 to 2030; Tue to Thu, 0830 to 2030; Fri 0830 to 1400

Parent body:
HM Prison Service
website: http://www.hmprisonservice.gov.uk

PRISONERS ABROAD

Acronym or abbreviation: PA

89–93 Fonthill Road, Finsbury Park, London, N4 3JH

Tel: 020 7561 6820
Fax: 020 7561 6821
E-mail: info@prisonersabroad.org.uk

Website:
http://www.prisonersabroad.org.uk

Founded:
1978

Organisation type and purpose:
International organisation, registered charity (charity number 1093710).
Providing information, advice and support to British citizens held in prison abroad, to their families and when they return to the United Kingdom.

Subject coverage:
Judicial procedures; prisoners' rights; information services; prisoner transfer treaties; extradition; prison conditions; welfare services; aftercare and resettlement; family support.

Printed publications:
Annual Report
Newsletter (3 times a year)

Publications list:
Available online

Access to staff:
Contact by letter, by telephone, by fax, by e-mail, in person and via website
Hours: Mon to Fri, 1000 to 1600

Access for disabled people:
Yes
Hours: Mon to Fri, 1000 to 1600

PRIVATE LIBRARIES ASSOCIATION

Acronym or abbreviation: PLA

Ravelston, South View Road, Pinner, Middlesex, HA5 3YD

E-mail: dchambers@aol.com

Website:
http://www.the-old-school.demon.co.uk/pla.htm

Enquiries:
Enquiries to: Chairman

Founded:
1956

Organisation type and purpose:
Learned society.
Society of book collectors.

Subject coverage:
Book collecting.

Trade and statistical information:
Data on privately printed books worldwide in English.

Printed publications:
Books and monographs, including:
Books on book collecting (irregular)
Miniature Libraries for the Young (Alderson B, 1983, £5)
Printing for Pleasure (Ryder J, £10)
The Private Library (journal, quarterly)
Private Press Books (bibliography, annually)
Apart from the Text (Rota A, £24, an account of the externals of the book: its production and sale over the past two centuries)
Early Lithographed Books (Twyman M, £68.50, a study of the design and production of improper books in the age of the hand press, with a catalogue)
Order printed publications from: Publications Secretary, Claude Cox Books
3 Silent Street, Ipswich, IP1 1TF

Publications list:
Available online and in print

Access to staff:
Contact by letter and by e-mail

In liaison with the:
Library Association

Links with:
Society of Private Printers

PROBATE OFFICES

Local offices:
1st Floor, Crown Building, Rivergate, Peterborough, PE1 1EJ, tel: 01733 562802
Bangor Probate Sub-Registry
Council Offices, Ffordd Gwynedd, Bangor, Gwynedd, LL57 1DT; tel: 01248 362410
Birmingham District Probate Registry
The Priory Courts, 33 Bull Street, Birmingham, B4 6DU; tel: 0121 681 3400
Bodmin Probate Sub-Registry
Market Street, Bodmin, Cornwall, PL31 2JW; tel: 01208 72279
Brighton District Probate Registry
William Street, Brighton, Sussex, BN2 2LG; tel: 01273 684071
Bristol District Probate Registry
Ground Floor, The Crescent Centre, Temple Back, Bristol, BS1 6EP; tel: 0117 9273915
Carlisle Probate Sub-Registry
Courts of Justice, Earl Street, Carlisle, Cumbria, CA1 1DJ; tel: 01228 521751

Carmarthen Probate Sub-Registry
14 King Street, Carmarthen, SA31 1BL; tel: 01267 236238
Chester Probate Sub-Registry
5th Floor, Hamilton House, Hamilton Place, Chester, CH1 2DA; tel: 01244 345082
Exeter Probate Sub-Registry
Finance House, Barnfield Road, Exeter, Devon, EX1 1QR; tel: 01392 274515
Gloucester Probate Sub-Registry
2nd Floor, Combined Court Building, Kimbrose Way, Gloucester, GL1 2DG; tel: 01452 522585
Ipswich District Probate Registry
Haven House, 17 Lower Brook Street, Ipswich, Suffolk, IP4 1DN; tel: 01473 253724
Lancaster Probate Sub-Registry
Mitre House, Church Street, Lancaster, LA1 1HE; tel: 01524 36625
Leeds District Probate Registry
3rd Floor, Coronet House, Queen Street, Leeds, LS1 2BA; tel: 0113 243 1505
Leicester Probate Sub-Registry
5th Floor, Leicester House, Lee Circle, Leicester, LE1 3RE; tel: 0116 2538558
Lincoln Probate Sub-Registry
360 High Street, Lincoln, LN5 7PS; tel: 01522 523648
Liverpool District Probate Registry
Queen Elizabeth II Law Courts, Derby Square, Liverpool, L2 1XA; tel: 0151 236 8264
Maidstone Probate Sub-Registry
The Law Courts, Barker Road, Maidstone, ME18 8EW; tel: 01622 202048
Manchester District Probate Registry
9th Floor, Astley House, 23 Quay Street, Manchester, M2 4AT; tel: 0161 834 4319
Middlesbrough Probate Sub-Registry
Teesside Combined Court Centre, Russell Street, Middlesbrough, Cleveland, TS1 2AE; tel: 01642 340001
Newcastle District Probate Registry
2nd Floor, Plummer House, Croft Street, Newcastle upon Tyne, NE1 6NP; tel: 0191 261 8383
Norwich Probate Sub-Registry
Combined Court Building, Bishopsgate, Norwich, NR3 1UR; tel: 01603 728267
Nottingham Probate Sub-Registry
Butt Dyke House, Park Row, Nottingham, NG1 6GR; tel: 0115 941 4288
Oxford District Probate Registry
Oxford Combined Court Building, St Aldates, Oxford, OX1 1LY; tel: 01865 793 055
Peterborough Probate Sub-Registry
1st Floor
Principal Registry of the Family Division
Probate Department, First Avenue House, 42–49 High Holborn, London, WC1V 6NP; tel: 020 7947 6983
Probate Registry of Wales
PO Box 474, 2 Park Street, Cardiff, CF10 1TB; tel: 029 2037 6479
Sheffield Probate Sub-Registry
PO Box 832, The Law Courts, 50 West Bar, Sheffield, S3 3YR; tel: 0114 281 2596
Stoke on Trent Probate Sub-Registry
Combined Court Centre, Bethesda Street, Hanley, ST1 3BP; tel: 01782 854065
Winchester District Probate Registry
4th Floor, Cromwell House, Andover Road, Winchester, Hampshire, SO23 7EW; tel: 01962 863771
York Probate Office
1st Floor, Castle Chambers, Clifford Street, York, YO1 9RG; tel: 01904 666777

PROCESSORS AND GROWERS RESEARCH ORGANISATION

Acronym or abbreviation: PGRO

The Research Station, Great North Road, Thornhaugh, Peterborough, Cambridgeshire, PE8 6HJ

Tel: 01780 782585
Fax: 01780 783993
E-mail: info@pgro.co.uk

Website:
http://www.pgro.co.uk

Enquiries:
Enquiries to: Director

Founded:
1944

Organisation type and purpose:
Research organisation.

Subject coverage:
Production and harvesting of vegetables, primarily for processing for human consumption; seeds and seed health, general agronomy, evaluation of crop protection materials and techniques, evaluation of new varieties.

Printed publications:
Annual Report
Newsletters, papers & advisory leaflets
Pea Growing Handbook
Pea and Bean Progress (4 times per annum, for members)
Vining Peas in England
Field Bran Handbook

PROCTER & GAMBLE TECHNICAL CENTRES LIMITED

Acronym or abbreviation: P&G

Newcastle Technical Centre, PO Box Forest Hall No 2, Newcastle upon Tyne, NE12 9TS

Tel: 0191 228 1000
Fax: 0191 228 1021

Website:
http://www.uk.pg.com
Publications list

Enquiries:
Enquiries to: Business Information Services Manager
Direct tel: 0191 228 1728

Founded:
1837

Organisation type and purpose:
Manufacturing industry, research organisation. Company technical centre; formerly known as Procter & Gamble Research and Development Laboratories.

Subject coverage:
Soaps and detergents, cleaning products, oils and fats, fatty acids and derivatives, related chemistry and technology.

Non-library collection catalogue:
All or part available in-house

Library catalogue:
All or part available in-house

Publications list:
Available online

Access to staff:
Contact by letter and by fax
Hours: Mon to Fri, 0830 to 1630

Access to building, collection or gallery:
No prior appointment required

PRODUCERS ALLIANCE FOR CINEMA AND TELEVISION

Acronym or abbreviation: PACT

Procter House, 1 Procter Street, Holborn, London, WC1V 6DW

Tel: 020 7067 4367
Fax: 020 7067 4377

Website:
http://www.pact.co.uk

Enquiries:
Enquiries to: Information Manager
Direct e-mail: anish@pact.co.uk

Founded:
1991

Organisation type and purpose:
Trade association.
Represents United Kingdom independent production companies of feature films and broadcast television.

Subject coverage:
Industrial relations within the independent broadcast, television and feature film production industry, copyright, commissioning, financing.

Printed publications:
Art of the Deal
PACT (magazine, monthly, free to members, for sale to non-members)
Members' Directory (annually, £25 to members, £50 to non-members)
Rights Clearance

Publications list:
Available in print

Access to staff:
Contact by telephone. Access for members only.
Hours: Mon to Fri, 0930 to 1800

PROFESSIONAL ASSOCIATION OF NURSERY NURSES

Formal name: VOICE the Union
Acronym or abbreviation: VOICE

2 St James' Court, Friar Gate, Derby, DE1 1BT

Tel: 01332 372337
Fax: 01332 290310
E-mail: triciapritchard@voicetheunion.org.,uk

Website:
http://www.voicetheunion.org.uk

Enquiries:
Enquiries to: Senior Professional Officer
Other contacts: Communications Officer (e-mail: richardfraser@voicetheunion.org.uk)

Founded:
1982

Formerly called:
Professional Association of Nursery Nurses (year of change 2008)

Organisation type and purpose:
Professional body, trade union (membership is by subscription), present number of members: 5,500. Professional association for qualified nursery nurses, nannies and other child carers.

Subject coverage:
Terms and conditions of employment within child care, nannies at home and abroad, contracts, etc., the role of the nursery nurse.

Printed publications:
All you Need to Know About Working as a Nanny
Code of Practice
Role of The Nursery Nurse
Starting a Day Nursery
Variety of booklets and leaflets
Working Together in Powerful Partnership: Nursery Nurses and Teachers
Order printed publications from: e-mail: publications@voicetheunion.org.uk

Publications list:
Available online and in print

Access to staff:
Contact by letter, by telephone, by fax, by e-mail and via website. Appointment necessary. Access for members only.
Hours: Mon to Fri, 0900 to 1700

Access to building, collection or gallery:
Prior appointment required
Hours: Mon to Fri, 0900 to 1700

Access for disabled people:
Parking provided, level entry

Headquarters address:
Voice
at the same address; tel: 01332 372337; fax: 01332 290310; e-mail: hq@voicetheunion.org.uk; website: http://www.voicetheunion.org.uk

PROFESSIONAL BUSINESS AND TECHNICAL MANAGEMENT

Acronym or abbreviation: PBTM

Warwick Corner, 42 Warwick Road, Kenilworth, Warwickshire, CV8 1HE

Tel: 01926 855498
Fax: 01926 513100
E-mail: info@group-ims.com

Website:
http://www.group-ims.com

Enquiries:
Enquiries to: President

Founded:
1983

Organisation type and purpose:
International organisation, professional body (membership is by subscription, qualification), present number of members: 860 in 40 different countries, manufacturing industry, university department or institute, training organisation, professional diploma courses available.

Subject coverage:
Industrial, computing, technological and associated management, education and training.

Printed publications:
Professional Business and Technical Management (3 times a year)

Access to staff:
Contact by letter, by telephone, by fax and by e-mail
Hours: Mon to Fri, 0900 to 1700

Links with:
Academy of Executives and Administrators at the same address
Academy of Multi-Skills at the same address
Institute of Management Specialists at the same address
Institute of Manufacturing at the same address

PROFESSIONAL CLASSES AID COUNCIL

Acronym or abbreviation: PCAC

10 St Christopher's Place, London, W1U 1HZ

Tel: 020 7935 0641

Enquiries:
Enquiries to: Secretary
Other contacts: Deputy Secretary

Founded:
1921

Organisation type and purpose:
National organisation, voluntary organisation, registered charity (charity number 207292).

Subject coverage:
Sources of charitable help to those with a professional background.

Printed publications:
Annual Report

Access to staff:
Contact by letter and by telephone
Hours: Mon to Fri, 0930 to 1700

Access to building, collection or gallery:
No access other than to staff

Administers the:
Guild of Aid for Gentlepeople at the same address

PROFESSIONAL GOLFERS ASSOCIATION

Acronym or abbreviation: PGA

Centenary House, The Belfry, Sutton Coldfield, West Midlands, B76 9PT

continued overleaf

Tel: 01675 470333
Fax: 01675 477888
E-mail: john.yapp@pga.org.uk

Enquiries:
Enquiries to: Finance Director

Founded:
1901

Organisation type and purpose:
Membership association.

Subject coverage:
The game of golf.

Printed publications:
The PGA Professional (magazine, monthly)

Access to staff:
Contact by letter
Hours: Mon to Fri, 0900 to 1700

PROFESSIONAL PHOTOGRAPHIC LABORATORIES ASSOCIATION

Acronym or abbreviation: PPLA

Wisteria House, 28 Fulling Mill Lane, Welwyn, Herts AL6 9NS

Tel: 01438 840367
Fax: 01438 716572
E-mail: pmauk@pmai.org

Website:
http://www.pmai.org

Enquiries:
Enquiries to: Secretary
Other contacts: Administration Manager for office contact.

Founded:
1984

Organisation type and purpose:
Trade association.
To promote and foster excellence in all areas of professional photographic laboratory work.

Subject coverage:
Professional photographic processing (silver halide), digital imaging, inkjet and all normal fields of output.

Printed publications:
Lablink
Laboratory News Report
PPLA (free to members)

Electronic and video publications:
Fact file covering full membership details, terms of business, articles of Association and supplier members (CD-ROM free to members)

Access to staff:
Contact by letter, by telephone, by fax, by e-mail, in person and via website
Hours: Mon to Fri, 0900 to 1700

A section of:
Photo Marketing Association International

Connections with:
British Photographic Association

PRONOVUS LIMITED, THE EAST MIDLANDS BUSINESS INNOVATION CENTRE

Technology Building, Howitt Building, Lenton Boulevard, Nottingham NG7 2BG

Tel: 0115 952 9320
E-mail: admin@pronovus.org.uk

Website:
Summary of Pronovus' activities.

Enquiries:
Enquiries to: Information Officer

Founded:
1990

Organisation type and purpose:
Advisory body.

Non-profit organisation.
Free support to help innovation or technology-based ideas to achieve commercial success.

Subject coverage:
Patent information, technical information, market viability, entrepreneurial ideas, new ideas, idea protection, for individuals and small companies.

Non-library collection catalogue:
All or part available online

Access to staff:
Contact by letter, by telephone, by fax, by e-mail and via website. Appointment necessary.
Hours: Mon to Fri, 0830 to 1730
Special comments: Answerphone out of hours.

PROPERTY CONSULTANTS SOCIETY LIMITED

Acronym or abbreviation: PCS

Basement Office, Surrey Court, Surrey Street, Arundel, West Sussex, BN18 9DT

Tel: 01903 889590
Fax: 01903 883787
E-mail: info@propertyconsultantssociety.org

Website:
http://www.propertyconsultantssociety.org

Enquiries:
Enquiries to: Secretary
Direct e-mail: may-david@btconnect.com

Founded:
1954

Organisation type and purpose:
Professional body (membership is by qualification, election or invitation), present number of members: 600, service industry.

Subject coverage:
Property consultancy.

Printed publications:
Annual Report
Newsletters (occasional, free to members)

Access to staff:
Contact by letter, by telephone, by fax and by e-mail. Access for members only.
Hours: Mon, Wed & Fri
Special comments: Part-time staff only.

PROPERTY PEOPLE PUBLICATIONS LIMITED

232 Great Guildford Business Square, 30 Great Guildford Street, London, SE1 0HS

Tel: 020 7401 2075
Fax: 020 7928 4887
E-mail: edit@ppmagazine.co.uk

Website:
http://www.hera-group.co.uk
Editorial information, recruitment advertising.

Enquiries:
Enquiries to: Managing Director
Other contacts: Editor for editorial enquiries.

Founded:
1997

Organisation type and purpose:
Publishing house.

Subject coverage:
People working in housing, students on full-time housing courses.

Printed publications:
Property People (magazine)

Access to staff:
Contact by letter, by telephone, by fax, by e-mail and via website
Hours: Mon to Fri, 0900 to 1700

PROQUEST INFORMATION AND LEARNING

The Quorum, Barnwell Road, Cambridge, CB5 8SW

Tel: 01223 215512
Fax: 01223 215513
E-mail: marketing@proquest.co.uk

Website:
http://www.proquest.co.uk/
Catalogue, monthly exhibitions list, contacts.

Enquiries:
Enquiries to: Marketing Manager
Direct e-mail: chesterfield@proquest.co.uk

Founded:
1973

Organisation type and purpose:
Publishing house.

Subject coverage:
Bibliographies, library catalogues, reference works to archives, official publications, literature, literary history, newspapers on CD-ROM and the World Wide Web, performing arts, visual arts and architecture, history, economics and statistics, cartography and climate, natural sciences, medical, education, science and technology reference.

Microform publications:
A wide range of microfiche products

Electronic and video publications:
CD-ROMs and online sites of literature, bibliographies, official publications, music and performing arts, and history

Publications list:
Available online and in print

Access to staff:
Contact by e-mail
Hours: Mon to Fri, 0900 to 1700

PROSPECT

Prospect House, 75–79 York Road, London, SE1 7AQ

Tel: 020 7902 6600
Fax: 020 7902 6667
E-mail: enquiries@prospect.org.uk

Website:
http://www.prospect.org.uk
Services to members, aims of union, benefits of membership etc, publications.

Enquiries:
Enquiries to: Assistant General Secretary
Other contacts: Deputy General Secretary

Founded:
1913

Organisation type and purpose:
Trade union (membership is by subscription), present number of members: c. 100,000.
Statutory body responsible to the Secretary of State for Industry.

Subject coverage:
Pay and conditions, market testing, trade unions, public sector pay, privatisation, GCHQ trade union ban, research, health and safety, equal opportunities, air traffic control, PFI.

Printed publications:
Annual Report
Network (journal, monthly, on subscription, members)

Electronic and video publications:
Video

Publications list:
Available in print

Access to staff:
Contact by letter, by telephone, by fax and by e-mail. Appointment necessary.
Hours: Mon to Fri, 0900 to 1700

Access for disabled people:
Ramped entry, access to all public areas, toilet facilities
Special comments: Help with parking can be arranged prior to attendance.

Associated with:
Council of Civil Service Unions (CCSU)
IFATSEA
PSI
TUC

Office at:
Prospect Midlands
Unit 4, Midland Court, Central Park, Leicester Road, Lutterworth, LE17 4PN; tel: 01455 555200; fax: 01455 558711
Prospect North West / North Wales
Unit 1F, Ground Floor, Columbus Quay, Riverside Drive, Liverpool, L3 4DB; tel: 0151 728 9028; fax: 0151 728 9072
Prospect Scotland
Suite 4, 1st Floor, Glenarchy House, 20 Union Street, Edinburgh, EH1 3LR; tel: 0131 558 2660; fax: 0131 558 5280
Prospect South East
Flaxman House, Logmore Lane, Chertsey, Surrey, KT16 9JS; tel: 01932 577007; fax: 01932 567707
Prospect South West / Wales
Newminster House, 27–29 Baldwin Street, Bristol, BS1 1LT; tel: 0117 929 4441; fax: 0117 927 6111

PROSTATE CANCER CHARITY, THE

Acronym or abbreviation: PCC

3 Angel Walk, Hammersmith, London, W6 9HX

Tel: 020 8222 7622
Fax: 020 8222 7639
E-mail: info@prostate-cancer.org.uk

Website:
http://www.prostate-cancer.org.uk
Information on prostate cancer and its treatment.

Enquiries:
Enquiries to: Communications Manager
Direct e-mail: laura@prostate-cancer.org.uk

Founded:
1996

Organisation type and purpose:
National organisation, voluntary organisation, registered charity, research organisation.
Support and information organisation.
Research, support and information.

Subject coverage:
Prostate cancer support and information; information on treatments and their side-effects; general support from counsellors and other sufferers; help for both patients and their families; research into prostate cancer and its treatment.

Printed publications:
Wide range of literature covering all aspects of prostate cancer including:
Factsheets covering issues related to prostate cancer
Prostate Cancer: Everything you need to know (free)
Prostate Cancer – The Facts (free)

Publications list:
Available in print

Access to staff:
Contact by letter, by telephone, by fax, by e-mail, in person and via website
Hours: Mon to Fri, 0900 to 1700
Helpline: Mon to Fri, 1000 to 1600

PROSTATE HELP ASSOCIATION

PHA, Langworth, Lincoln, LN3 5DF

E-mail: philip@bph.org.uk

Website:
http://www.pha.u-net.com

Enquiries:
Enquiries to: Secretary

Founded:
1993

Organisation type and purpose:
Registered charity (charity number 1041372).

Subject coverage:
Prostatitis, BPH and prostatic cancer.

Printed publications:
Newsletters (direct)
Special Reports (direct)
Books (direct)

Electronic and video publications:
Prostrate Cancer (CD-ROM, PC/Mac, direct)

Publications list:
Available in print

Access to staff:
Contact by letter and by e-mail
Hours: Mon to Fri, 0900 to 1700

PSORIASIS ASSOCIATION

Dick Coles House, 2 Queensbridge, Northampton, NN4 7BF

Tel: 08456 760076
Fax: 01604 251621
E-mail: mail@psoriasis-association.org.uk

Website:
http://www.psoriasis-association.org.uk

Enquiries:
Enquiries to: Chief Executive
Other contacts: Information Officer

Founded:
1968

Organisation type and purpose:
Membership organisation providing information and support to people affected by psoriasis, aiming to support people who have psoriasis; to raise awareness of psoriasis; to fund research into causes, treatments and care of psoriasis.

Subject coverage:
Psoriasis, psoriatic arthropathy and all aspects relating to them.

Printed publications:
About the Association
What is psoriasis
Scalp psoriasis
Psoriasis in sensitive areas
Psoriasis in children
UV therapy
Psoriatic Arthritis
PsoTeen – Information for teenagers
Psoriasis – a parents' guide
Quarterly Journal
Order printed publications from: Psoriasis Association, Dick Coles House, 2 Queensbridge, Northampton, NN4 7BF

Electronic and video publications:
PsoKids (CD-ROM for children with psoriasis)
Order electronic and video publications from: Psoriasis Association, Dick Coles House, 2 Queensbridge, Northampton, NN4 7BF

Publications list:
Available in print

Access to staff:
Contact by letter, by telephone, by fax and by e-mail. Appointment necessary.
Hours: Mon to Fri, 0915 to 1645

Links with:
AMRC
APPGS
LTCA
Skin Care Campaign

PSYCHIATRIC REHABILITATION ASSOCIATION

Acronym or abbreviation: PRA SERVICES

Bayford Mews, Bayford Street, Hackney, London, E8 3SF

Tel: 020 8985 3570
Fax: 020 8986 1334
E-mail: admin@praservices.org.uk

Website:
http://www.praservices.org.uk
http://www.c4bh.org.uk

Enquiries:
Enquiries to: Director
Other contacts: Association Secretary

Founded:
1959

Organisation type and purpose:
Membership association (membership is by election or invitation), present number of members: 800, voluntary organisation, registered charity (charity number 227891), training organisation, consultancy.
PRA aims to stimulate the individual recovering from mental health problems towards greater initiative and social awareness. It prepares and encourages the individual to play an active part in the community.

Subject coverage:
PRA is a partnership of patients, relatives, friends and professional workers, and has developed a wide range of community care facilities for people suffering from mental health problems, study of social problems associated with mental illness, geographical incidence of mental illness, lifestyle analysis, training of professional and voluntary workers, group work.

Information services:
E-mail: info@praservices.org.uk

Non-library collection catalogue:
All or part available online and in-house

Printed publications:
Newsletter (quarterly)
Research publications
HUN newsletter (quarterly)

Microform publications:
Tape and slide teaching aids

Electronic and video publications:
Give Us A Chance (video, £13.50)
Forward with Courage (DVD, £15.00)

Access to staff:
Contact by letter, by telephone, by fax, by e-mail and via website. Appointment necessary.
Hours: Mon to Fri, 0900 to 1700

Administers:
Centre for Better Health (C4BH)
Bayford Mews, Bayford Street, London, E8 3SF; tel: 020 8985 3570; fax: 020 8986 1334; e-mail: admin@praservices.org.uk; website: http://www.praservices.org.uk
Et Cetera Gallery (Hackney)
1A Darnley Road, London, E9 6QH; tel: 020 8985 7758; website: http://www.praservices.org.uk
Et Cetera Workshop (Haringey)
Unit 26G3, N17 Studios, 785/788 High Road, London, N17 0DA; tel: 020 8808 5970; fax: 020 8808 5945; e-mail: etceteraworkshop@praservices.org.uk; website: http://www.praservices.org.uk
Hackney Day Centre
1A Darnley Road, London, E9 6QH; tel: 020 8985 4617; e-mail: darnleyroad@praservices.org.uk
Mitchley Industrial Education Unit and Day Centre (Haringey)
Unit 18G, N17 Studios, 784/788 High Road, London, N17 0DA; tel: 020 8808 2833; fax: 020 8880 9075; website: http://www.praservices.org.uk
Southwood Smith Centre (Islington)
Southwood Smith Street, London, N1 0XN; tel: 020 7226 2244; e-mail: swsmithcentre@praservices.org.uk; website: http://www.praservices.org.uk

continued overleaf

Stean Street Industrial Education Unit (Hackney)
13 Stean Street, London, N8 4ED; tel: 020 7254
9103; fax: 020 7254 2691; e-mail: pramembers@
yahoo.co.uk; website: http://www.praservices
.org.uk

Member organisations:
Haringey User Network (HUN) (Haringey)
Unit 26G3, N17 Studios, 784/788 High Road,
London, N17 0DA; tel: 020 8885 1258; e-mail:
info@haringeyusernetwork.org.uk; website:
http://www.haringeyusernetwork.org.uk

PSYCHOTHERAPY CENTRE

67 Upper Berkeley Street, London, W1H 7QX

Tel: 020 7723 6173
E-mail: psychotherapy@the-wordsmith.co.uk

Website:
http://www.the-psychotherapy-centre.org.uk

Enquiries:
Enquiries to: Principal

Founded:
1960

Organisation type and purpose:
International organisation, consultancy, research
organisation, publishing house.
Treatment and referral centre.
Training college.

Subject coverage:
Psychotherapy, emotional problems, neuroses,
compulsions, addictions, relationship problems,
psycho-sexual and marital difficulties, phobias,
anxiety, alcoholism, insomnia, migraine;
parenthood etc.

Printed publications:
Emotional Problems: Different Ways of Dealing
with Them
Enjoy Sex
Enjoy Childbirth
Enjoy Parenthood
Selecting a Psychotherapist
Training in Psychotherapy
The Laius Complex
King Lear – Rejection, Abandonment Projection
and Paranoia
Nervous Symptoms and Problems
Why be Psycho-Analysed before becoming a
Psychotherapist, Hypnotherapist or Counsellor?
How to Assess Therapy Organisations
Two Therapies and After
Experiences of Establishment and Medical
Psychotherapy & Psycho-Analysis
The Psychonaut's Handbook
Financing Your Education, Training or Therapy
The Cycle of Deprivation
Group Therapy: We Tried It
Psychotherapy: Is it Helpful or Harmful?
The Psychocate: A Revolution?
Selected Films, Novels and Poems: A List

Publications list:
Available in print

Access to staff:
Contact by letter and by telephone. Appointment
necessary.
Hours: Mon to Fri, 0900 to 1700

Access to building, collection or gallery:
Prior appointment required

PUBLIC AND COMMERCIAL SERVICES UNION

Acronym or abbreviation: PCS

160 Falcon Road, London, SW11 2LN

Tel: 020 7924 2727
Fax: 020 7924 1847

Website:
http://www.pcs.org.uk
Latest library acquisitions and press cuttings
service.

Enquiries:
Enquiries to: Information Officer
Direct tel: 020 7801 2650
Direct e-mail: info@pcs.org.uk
Other contacts: General Secretary

Founded:
1998

Organisation type and purpose:
Trade union.
Trade Union with its own library.

Subject coverage:
Employment law, health and safety, industrial
relations, civil service, childcare/work life balance,
Civil Service, conditions of service, economic
issues, employment issues, equal opportunities,
Europe, government, health and safety,
international affairs (ie Non-Europe), legislation,
maternity/paternity, organisations, parliament,
partnership, pay, PCS, pensions, professional
management, politics, privatisation – primarily
civil service, private sector, public sector, social
welfare, trade unions, unemployment.

Library catalogue:
All or part available in-house

Printed publications:
PCS View (Union journal, monthly to members)

Access to staff:
Contact by letter, by telephone, by fax and by e-
mail. Access for members only.
Hours: Mon to Fri, 0830 to 1700

Affiliated to:
Council of Civil Service Unions
International Confederation of Free Trade Unions
Public Services International

Member of:
Trades Union Congress
Congress House, Great Russell Street, London,
WC1B 3LS

PUBLIC HEALTH LABORATORY SERVICE – COMMUNICABLE DISEASE SURVEILLANCE CENTRE

Acronym or abbreviation: CDSC

61 Colindale Avenue, London, NW9 5EQ

Tel: 020 8200 6868
Fax: 020 8200 7868

Website:
http://www.phls.co.uk

Enquiries:
Enquiries to: Information Officer
Direct tel: 020 8200 6868 ext 4473
Direct e-mail: eyusuf@phls.org.uk

Organisation type and purpose:
Professional body.
Unit of the Public Health Laboratory Service.
Prevention and control of human communicable
disease through surveillance, epidemiological
investigation, research, teaching and training.

Subject coverage:
Human infectious diseases: prevalence in England
and Wales, and abroad when it is relevant to
England and Wales; control and surveillance of
such disease.

Printed publications:
Communicable Disease Report (weekly)
Communicable Disease and Public Health
(quarterly)

Access to staff:
Contact by letter
Hours: Mon to Fri, 0900 to 1700

Part of:
National Health Service

PUBLIC MONUMENTS AND SCULPTURE ASSOCIATION

Acronym or abbreviation: PMSA

72 Lissenden Mansions, Lissenden Gardens,
London, NW5 1PR

Tel: 020 7485 0566
Fax: 020 7485 0566
E-mail: pmsa@pmsa.org.uk

Website:
http://www.pmsa.org.uk

Enquiries:
Enquiries to: Chief Executive

Founded:
1991

Organisation type and purpose:
Membership association (membership is by
subscription), present number of members: 250,
voluntary organisation, registered charity, suitable
for ages: 18+, consultancy, research organisation.
The promotion, protection and public appreciation
of historic and contemporary public sculpture and
monuments. Preserving Britain's sculptures and
public art for future generations. Save Our
Sculpture project monitors works at risk.
Campaigns for improved conservation and
maintenance. The Association's National
Recording Project, a survey of public works in
Britain, is partially complete: it is a central
information resource for scholars, conservators and
custodians.

Subject coverage:
Art history (sculpture); sculpture conservation;
topographical spread of public works in Britain,
their description, history and condition; British
sculptors; the local and social significance of public
monuments; owners and custodians of same; the
groups involved with public art or similar; either
voluntary or commercial (i.e. commissioning
agencies); regional arts bodies; amenity societies
e.g. Fountain Society/Twentieth Century Society;
listing and planning regulations.

Information services:
Via e-mail

Museum or gallery collection, archive, or library special collection:
Black and white photographs or colour slides of
public sculptures and monuments

Trade and statistical information:
Data on conservation costs; on likely costs of
casting and making sculpture in general.

Non-library collection catalogue:
All or part available online and in print

Printed publications:
Public Sculpture in Britain Series (ongoing):
Public Sculpture of Birmingham
Public Sculpture of the City of London
Public Sculpture of Glasgow
Public Sculpture of Greater Manchester
Public Sculpture of Leicestershire and Rutland
Public Sculpture of Liverpool
Public Sculpture of North-East England
Public Sculpture of Staffordshire
Public Sculpture of Warwickshire and the Black
Country
Public Sculpture of South London (Wandsworth,
Lambeth, Southwark, Lewisham)
Sculpture Journal (twice a year)
Order printed publications from: Simon Bell (for vols)
or Clare Hooper (for journal), Liverpool University
Press, 4 Cambridge Street, Liverpool, L69 7ZU; e-
mail sbell@liverpool.ac.uk, clare.hooper@liverpool
.ac.uk

Electronic and video publications:
PMSA website with NRP database

Publications list:
Available online and in print

Access to staff:
Contact by letter, by telephone, by fax, by e-mail
and in person. Appointment necessary.
Hours: Mon to Fri, 1000 to 1800
Special comments: Notice via e-mail required

Access to building, collection or gallery:
Hours: Mon to Fri, 1000 to 1800

Also at:
Main project at: National Recording Project (NRP)
c/o Conway Library, Courtauld Institute,
Somerset House, The Strand, London, SW2R
0RN; tel: 020 7848 2614; e-mail: jo.darke@
courtauld.ac.uk

PUBLIC RECORD OFFICE OF NORTHERN IRELAND

Acronym or abbreviation: PRONI

66 Balmoral Avenue, Belfast, BT9 6NY

Tel: 028 9025 5905
Fax: 028 9025 5999
E-mail: proni@dcalni.gov.uk

Website:
http://www.proni.gov.uk/index/
research_and_records_held.htm
Publications list.
http://www.proni.gov.uk/
Guide to the Public Record Office of Northern
Ireland.

Enquiries:
Enquiries to: Head of Reader Services

Founded:
1923

Organisation type and purpose:
National government body.
Record office.
To identify, preserve and provide access to
Northern Ireland's archival heritage.

Subject coverage:
Information relating to the political, economic and
social history of Northern Ireland as found in both
official and private records. Genealogy; local
history; government records; non-departmental
public bodies records; academic research.

Museum or gallery collection, archive, or library special collection:
Archives of the Northern Ireland Departments of
government, public bodies and Courts of Law
Papers of private individuals, estate and business
records and church records

Non-library collection catalogue:
All or part available in-house

Printed publications:
Annual Statutory Reports 1991 to 1996/97 (annual),
1997/98 (statutory)
10 Education Facsimiles Packs containing
transcripts of 20 documents with illustrations
and an introduction to provide the historical
context of the documents. Particularly relevant to
higher secondary and the university student of
history
Reports of the Deputy Keeper of the Records 1960–
1989: guides for researchers to potential source
material on many aspects of Irish history from
the sixteenth century
Local History Series including:
Against the Tide: a Calendar of the Papers of Rev J
B Armour, Irish Presbyterian Minister and Home
Ruler, 1869–1914 (McMinn J R B)
Heads and Hearths: the Hearth Money Rolls and
Poll Tax Returns for Co Antrim, 1660–1669,
(Carleton S T)
Lord Shannon's Letters to his Son: a Calendar of
the Letters written by the 2nd Earl of Shannon to
his son, Viscount Boyle 1790–1802 (Hewitt E)
Peep O'Day Boys and Defenders: Selected
Documents on the Co Armagh Disturbances,
1784–1796, (Miller D W)
Settlement and Survival on an Ulster Estate: The
Brownlow Leasebook 1667–1711 (Gillespie R G)
The Fottrell Papers: a calendar of the papers of an
Irish Dominican Provincial captured in 1739
during the penal era (Fenning H)
The Way We Were: Historic Armagh Photographs
from the Allison Collection, (Fitzgerald D and
Weatherup R, available from Friar's Bush Press)
PRONI Guides Series including:
Guide to Cabinet Committees – (at Stormont,
1921–1958)

Guide to Education Records
Guide to County Sources: Armagh
Guide to County Sources: Fermanagh
Guide to County Sources: Monaghan
Guide to Tithe Records
Guide to Probate Records

Publications list:
Available online and in print

Access to staff:
Contact by letter, by telephone, by fax, by e-mail,
in person and via website
Hours: Mon, Tue, Wed, Fri, 0915 to 1645; Thu, 0915
to 2045
Special comments: To facilitate staff training, the
office opens at 1000 on first Thu of each month.
Closed last week of Nov and first week of Dec each
year.

Access for disabled people:
Parking provided, ramped entry, access to all
public areas, toilet facilities
Special comments: Staff assistance if required

Executive Agency of the:
Department of Culture, Arts and Leisure

PUBLIC RELATIONS CONSULTANTS ASSOCIATION LIMITED

Acronym or abbreviation: PRCA

Willow House, Willow Place, London, SW1P 1JH

Tel: 020 7233 6026
Fax: 020 7828 4797
E-mail: katie.goodrum@prca.org.uk

Website:
http://www.prca.org.uk

Enquiries:
Enquiries to: Office Manager

Founded:
1969

Organisation type and purpose:
Trade association (membership is by qualification),
present number of members: 150.

Subject coverage:
Public relations industry, statistics, membership.

Museum or gallery collection, archive, or library special collection:
Archive library

Trade and statistical information:
Case histories
Benchmarking study in PR consultancy industry.

Printed publications:
9 Briefing Papers
25 Educational Guidance Papers
The Public Relations Consultants Year Book
An Insider's Guide to PR
Survival Guides
Order printed publications from: Public Relations
Consultants Association Limited
e-mail: info@prca.org.uk

Publications list:
Available online and in print

Access to staff:
Contact by letter, by telephone, by fax, by e-mail,
in person and via website. Appointment necessary.
Hours: Mon to Fri, 0900 to 1800

Access to building, collection or gallery:
No prior appointment required

PUBLISHERS ASSOCIATION

Acronym or abbreviation: PA

29b Montague Street, London, WC1B 5BW

Tel: 020 7691 9191
Fax: 020 7691 9199
E-mail: mail@publishers.org.uk

Website:
http://www.publishers.org.uk

Enquiries:
Direct tel: 020 7691 9191
Direct e-mail: mail@publishers.org.uk

Founded:
1896

Organisation type and purpose:
Trade association (membership is by subscription).
Organised into core activity and divisions:
International Division, Educational Publishers
Council, Academic and Professional Division,
Electronic Publishers Forum.

Subject coverage:
Matters relating to publishing; not contracts with
authors or the placing of manuscripts.

Museum or gallery collection, archive, or library special collection:
Books about publishing; list available

Trade and statistical information:
Statistical information on publishing.

Printed publications:
Books, pamphlets, electronic information on
publishing, free or for purchase

Electronic and video publications:
See under printed products

Publications list:
Available online and in print

Access to staff:
Contact by letter, by telephone, by fax, by e-mail
and via website. Access for members only. Non-
members charged.
Hours: Mon to Fri, 0930 to 1730

Access to building, collection or gallery:
Prior appointment required

Affiliated to:
Federation of European Publishers
International Publishers Association

PUBLISHERS LICENSING SOCIETY LIMITED

Acronym or abbreviation: PLS

5 Dryden Street, London, WC2E 9NB

Tel: 020 7829 8486
Fax: 020 7829 8488
E-mail: pls@pls.org.uk

Enquiries:
Enquiries to: Manager

Founded:
1981

Organisation type and purpose:
Trade association, present number of members:
1600.

Subject coverage:
Photocopying and digital licensing. Copyright
information relevant to the publishing industry.

Printed publications:
Annual Report
PLS Newsletter

Publications list:
Available in print

Access to staff:
Contact by letter, by telephone, by fax, by e-mail
and via website
Hours: Mon to Fri, 0900 to 1700

Links with:
Association of Learned and Professional Society
Publishers (ALPSP)
South House, The Street, Clapham, Worthing,
Sussex, BN13 3UU; tel: 01903 871686; fax: 01903
871457; e-mail: sec-gen@alsp.org
Copyright Licensing Agency
90 Tottenham Court Road, London, W1T 0LP;
tel: 020 7631 5500; fax: 020 7631 5555; e-mail:
cla@cla.co.uk

continued overleaf

Periodical Publishers Association (PPA)
   Queens House, 28 Kingsway, London, WC2B
   6JR; tel: 020 7404 4166; fax: 020 7404 4167; e-
   mail: info1@ppa.co.uk
Publishers Association (PA)
   29B Montague Street, London, WC1B 5BH; tel:
   020 7691 9191; fax: 020 7691 9199; e-mail: mail@
   publishers.org.uk

PUPPET CENTRE TRUST

Battersea Arts Centre, Lavender Hill, London,
SW11 5TN

Tel: 020 7228 5335
Fax: 020 7228 8863
E-mail: pct@puppetcentre.demon.co.uk

Website:
http://www.puppetcentre.com
General

Enquiries:
Enquiries to: Administrator
Other contacts: Board Member for puppeteers or
related information when the centre is closed.

Founded:
1974

Organisation type and purpose:
Voluntary organisation, registered charity (charity
number 1056021), museum.
To promote the arts of puppetry and animation.

Subject coverage:
Puppetry and animation, serving both the
professional and amateur puppeteer and all those
with a general interest in puppetry and also those
in education.

**Museum or gallery collection, archive, or library
special collection:**
Barry Smith Collection
Erwin Hauser Collection of books on puppetry
Lotte Reiniger collection
Puppetry Archives
Touring exhibitions using Puppet Centre Historical
Collection

Non-library collection catalogue:
All or part available in-house

Library catalogue:
All or part available in-house

Printed publications:
Puppet Centre Education Pack

Electronic and video publications:
Video library to view on site

Publications list:
Available in print

Access to staff:
Contact by letter, by telephone, by fax, by e-mail
and via website. Appointment necessary.
Hours: Wed and Sat, 1400 to 1800 and by
appointment

Access for disabled people:
Ramped entry, access to all public areas, toilet
facilities
Special comments: Lift available

PURBECK DISTRICT COUNCIL

Acronym or abbreviation: PDC

Westport House, Worgret Road, Wareham, Dorset,
BH20 4PP

Tel: 01929 556561
Fax: 01929 552688
E-mail: performanceunit@purbeck-dc.gov.uk

Website:
http://www.purbeck.gov.uk

Organisation type and purpose:
Local government body.

Subject coverage:
Services and functions of the district council.

Access to staff:
Contact by letter, by telephone, by fax, by e-mail,
in person and via website
Hours: Offices: 0845 to 1645; telephone access: 0830
to 1700

PUSEY HOUSE LIBRARY

Formal name: Dr Pusey's Library

Pusey House, 61 St Giles, Oxford, OX1 3LZ

Tel: 01865 278415
E-mail: chapter@puseyhouse.org.uk

Website:
http:www.puseyhouse.org.uk

Enquiries:
Enquiries to: Custodian
Direct tel: 01865 288024
Other contacts: The Archivist for all enquiries
relating to archive holdings

Founded:
1884

Organisation type and purpose:
Theological resource centre and chaplaincy.

Subject coverage:
Patristics, liturgy, church history (especially Oxford
Movement).

**Museum or gallery collection, archive, or library
special collection:**
19th century pamphlets

Non-library collection catalogue:
All or part available in-house

Library catalogue:
All or part available in-house

Microform publications:
Available from World Microfilms, 70 reels, £2750:
The Halifax and Church Sub-Collections
Tractarian Pamphlets at Pusey House

Access to staff:
Contact by letter, by telephone, by e-mail, in
person and via website. Appointment necessary.
Access for members only. Letter of introduction
required. All charged.
Hours: Term time: Mon to Fri, 0900 to 1230 and
1400 to 1630; Sat, by appointment only
Vacation opening: by appointment only

QUALIFICATIONS AND CURRICULUM AUTHORITY

Acronym or abbreviation: QCA

83 Piccadilly, London, W1J 8QA

Tel: 020 7509 5555
Fax: 020 7509 6666
E-mail: info@qca.org.uk

Website:
http://www.qca.org.uk
Recent press releases, list of current publications,
information newsletter.
http://orderline.qca.org.uk/
Publications catalogue.

Founded:
1997

Organisation type and purpose:
National government body, advisory body.
Set up under the 1997 Education Act.
To promote coherence in education and training,
its span of responsibility extends from education
for the under fives to occupational standards and
lifelong learning. QCA's prime duty is to advise the
Secretary of State for Education and Skills.

Subject coverage:
All matters affecting the school curriculum, pupil
assessment and all qualifications available in
publicly-funded education and training (except for
higher education); this includes NVQs, GNVQs, A
Levels, GCSEs and the many other qualifications
available in schools, colleges and publicly funded
training programmes which contribute to the

national occupational standards programme
currently run by the Department for Education and
Skills. Working with the National Training
Organisations, awarding bodies and further and
higher education, and developing a new
regulatory regime which lays down a clear
structure of quality assurance.

Printed publications:
The Monitor (journal)
The QCA has an extensive range of titles covering
national curriculum, schools, NVQ/GNVQs, Key
Stages, statutory tasks, assessment etc

Publications list:
Available online

Access to staff:
Contact by letter, by telephone, by fax, by e-mail
and via website
Hours: Mon to Fri, 0900 to 1700

Parent body:
Department for Education and Skills (DfES)
Sanctuary Buildings, Great Smith Street, London,
SW1P 3BT; tel: 020 7925 5000

QUALITY ASSURANCE AGENCY FOR HIGHER EDUCATION

Acronym or abbreviation: QAA

Southgate House, Southgate Street, Gloucester,
GL1 1UB

Tel: 01452 557000
Fax: 01452 557070
E-mail: comms@qaa.ac.uk

Website:
http://www.qaa.ac.uk

Founded:
1997

Formerly called:
Higher Education Quality Council (year of change
1997)

Organisation type and purpose:
The Quality Assurance Agency for Higher
Education (QAA) was established in 1997 and is an
independent public body funded by subscriptions
from universities and colleges of higher education,
and through contracts with the main higher
education funding bodies. Its principal role is to
safeguard and help to improve the academic
standards and quality of higher education. QAA is
governed by a Board, which has overall
responsibility for the conduct and strategic
direction of its business. It is a company limited by
guarantee (registered charity numbers 1062746 and
SC037786).

Subject coverage:
QAA works with universities and colleges to
define standards for higher education, through a
framework known as the Academic Infrastructure,
which includes the qualifications frameworks for
the UK. QAA also carries out reviews of higher
education institutions against these standards and
publishes their outcomes. It advises governments
on applications for the grant of degree awarding
powers, university title or designation as a higher
education institution.

Printed publications:
Publications include: Review reports, the Code of
practice for the assurance of academic quality
and standards in higher education (10 sections),
higher quality, Directors reports, Annual
reviews, review method handbooks.
Order printed publications from: Linney Direct,
Adams Way, Mansfield, Nottinghamshire, NG18
4FN, tel: 01623 450788, fax: 01623 450481, e-mail:
qaa@linneydirect.com

Publications list:
Available online and in print

Access to staff:
Contact by letter, by telephone, by fax, by e-mail
and via website. Appointment necessary.
Hours: Mon to Fri, 0900 to 1700

QUALITY BRITISH CELERY ASSOCIATION

Acronym or abbreviation: QBCA

133 Eastgate, Louth, Lincolnshire, LN11 9QG

Tel: 01507 602427
Fax: 01507 607165
E-mail: crop.association@pvga.co.uk

Enquiries:
Enquiries to: Membership Secretary

Founded:
1980s

Organisation type and purpose:
National organisation, trade association.

Subject coverage:
Celery production.

QUALITY GUILD

Westwinds, Lambley Bank, Scotby, Carlisle, Cumbria, CA4 8BX

Tel: 01228 631681
E-mail: info@qgbiz.co.uk

Website:
http://www.qualityguild.co.uk

QUALITY IMPROVEMENT AGENCY FOR LIFELONG LEARNING

Acronym or abbreviation: QIA

Friars House, Manor House Drive, Coventry, CV1 2TE

Tel: 0870 162 0632
Fax: 0870 162 0633

Website:
http://www.qia.org.uk/
http://www.lsrc.org.uk

Enquiries:
Enquiries to: Communications Officer
Direct tel: 0870 211 3434
Direct e-mail: gillian.dyer@qia.org.uk

Founded:
2006

Formerly a part of:
the Learning and Skills Development Agency

Organisation type and purpose:
Research organisation.
Quango.

Subject coverage:
Further education, research, teaching and learning.

Museum or gallery collection, archive, or library special collection:
Library catalogue

Non-library collection catalogue:
All or part available in-house

Library catalogue:
All or part available in-house

Printed publications:
Books and Reports
Order printed publications from: Learning and Skills Development Agency
Citadel Place, Tinworth Street, London, SE11 5EF, tel: 020 7840 5400, fax: 020 7840 5401, e-mail: p.fielding@lsda.org.uk

Electronic and video publications:
Books, Journals and Reports

Publications list:
Available in print

QUARRY PRODUCTS ASSOCIATION

Acronym or abbreviation: QPA

156 Buckingham Palace Road, London, SW1W 9TR

Tel: 020 7730 8194
Fax: 020 7730 4355
E-mail: info@qpa.org

Website:
http://www.qpa.org

Enquiries:
Enquiries to: Press and Information Officer
Direct e-mail: clements@qpa.org

Founded:
1997

Organisation type and purpose:
Trade association.

Subject coverage:
Construction aggregates, (ie crushed rock, sand, gravel and slag), asphalt and coated macadam for roads and other surfacing uses, (but not asphalts used in roofing, building and waterproofing), lime for building and industrial uses, agricultural lime (information from ALPC).
Ready mixed concrete technology, production, origins, use, specifications and testing, quality assurance.
Sand and gravel industry, planning, technical, environmental, waste management.

Museum or gallery collection, archive, or library special collection:
Overseas periodicals on bitumen, asphalt, concrete and quarrying from 1930s

Trade and statistical information:
Data on UK and European production of ready mix concrete.

Printed publications:
QPA Statistical Yearbook
General information on quarrying
Technical publications

Access to staff:
Contact by letter, by telephone, by fax and by e-mail
Hours: Mon to Fri, 0900 to 1700

Access to building, collection or gallery:
No access other than to staff

Affiliated to:
European Aggregates Association (UEPG)
European Asphalt Pavement Association
European Ready Mixed Concrete Association

QUEEN ELIZABETH'S FOUNDATION

Acronym or abbreviation: QEF

Leatherhead Court, Woodlands Road, Leatherhead, Surrey, KT22 0BN

Tel: 01372 841100
Fax: 01372 844072
E-mail: cynthia.robinson@qef.org.uk

Website:
http://www.qef.org.uk

Enquiries:
Enquiries to: Chief Executive

Founded:
1934

Organisation type and purpose:
Registered charity (charity number 251051).
To provide services for disabled people.

Subject coverage:
Rehabilitation for brain-damaged people at Banstead Place; mobility information advice and assessment at Carshalton; vocational training residential facilities, at Leatherhead; skills development at Leatherhead

Non-library collection catalogue:
All or part available online and in print

Printed publications:
Annual Report
Leaflets on the various units

Access to staff:
Contact by letter, by telephone and by fax.
Appointment necessary.
Hours: Mon to Fri, 0900 to 1700

Also at:
Banstead, Carshalton, Leatherhead

QUEEN MARGARET UNIVERSITY

Acronym or abbreviation: QMU

Queen Margaret University Drive, Musselburgh, East Lothian, EH21 6UU

Tel: 0131 474 0000
Fax: 0131 474 0001
E-mail: lrchelp@qmu.ac.uk

Website:
http://www.qmu.ac.uk/lb

Founded:
1875

Formerly called:
Queen Margaret University College (year of change 2007)

Organisation type and purpose:
University library

Subject coverage:
Arts therapies; business and management; dietetics and nutrition; events management; nursing; physiotherapy; occupational therapy; radiography; speech therapy; communication studies; podiatry; retailing; drama; hospitality studies; tourism.

Information services:
Access to books, journals and archive for all users.
Network resources subject to user status.

Special visitor services:
Member of Sconul Access; Member of ELISA scheme

Education services:
Information literacy sessions; workshops; sessions for local schools

Services for disabled people:
Assistive technology room available

Museum or gallery collection, archive, or library special collection:
University archive, especially relating to domestic science

Non-library collection catalogue:
All or part available in-house

Library catalogue:
All or part available online

Access to staff:
Contact by letter, by telephone, by e-mail, in person and via website. Appointment necessary.
Hours: Term time: Mon to Fri, 0830 to 2100; Sat and Sun, 0900 to 1700
Vacation: Mon to Fri, 0900 to 1900; Sat and Sun, 0900 to 1700

Access to building, collection or gallery:
Via main reception
Special comments: Visitor card mandatory

Access for disabled people:
Access to all public areas

QUEEN MARY, UNIVERSITY OF LONDON

Acronym or abbreviation: QMW

Mile End Road, London, E1 4NS

Tel: 020 7882 3027
Fax: 020 7882 7525
E-mail: j.e.clarke@qmul.ac.uk

Website:
http://www.qmul.ac.uk

Enquiries:
Enquiries to: Public Relations Manager
Direct tel: 020 7882 5314
Direct fax: 020 7882 5556

continued overleaf

Direct e-mail: n.relph@qmul.ac.uk

Founded:
1887

Organisation type and purpose:
International organisation, university department or institute.
Constituent college of the University of London.
University college providing higher education and offering research opportunities in medicine, science, engineering, arts and law.

Subject coverage:
Medicine, dentistry; science – physics, chemistry, biochemistry, mathematics, astronomy, computer; engineering – electronic, mechanical, civil, materials, aeronautical; arts – English, German, French, Russian, Hispanic studies, history; law; social sciences – economics, geography, politics.

Non-library collection catalogue:
All or part available online

Access to staff:
Contact by letter, by telephone, by fax, by e-mail and via website
Hours: Mon to Fri, 0900 to 1700

QUEEN MARY, UNIVERSITY OF LONDON – DEPARTMENT OF COMPUTER SCIENCE

Acronym or abbreviation: QMUL

Mile End Road, London, E1 4NS

Tel: 020 7882 5217
Fax: 020 8980 6533
E-mail: suew@dcs.qmul.ac.uk

Website:
http://www.dcs.qmul.ac.uk
Courses, research and publications.

Enquiries:
Enquiries to: Research Co-ordinator

Organisation type and purpose:
University department or institute.

Subject coverage:
Computer science.

Publications list:
Available online

Access to building, collection or gallery:
Prior appointment required

QUEEN MARY, UNIVERSITY OF LONDON – MAIN LIBRARY

Acronym or abbreviation: QMUL

Mile End Road, London, E1 4NS

Tel: 020 7882 3300
Fax: 020 8981 0028
E-mail: library-enquiries@qmul.ac.uk

Website:
http://www.mds.qmw.ac.uk/
General home page for School of Medicine and Dentistry (including libraries).
http://www.qmw.ac.uk
Library services and resources.

Enquiries:
Enquiries to: Director of Academic Information Services
Other contacts: Reference Librarian for telephone enquiries.

Organisation type and purpose:
University library, research organisation.
European Documentation Centre.

Subject coverage:
Arts: language and literature – English, Classical, French, German, Italian, Romanian, Russian, Spanish; history, history of art, drama and theatre; engineering: electrical, electronic, aeronautical, civil, mechanical, geomaterials, materials; informatics and mathematical sciences: computer science, mathematical sciences, information

technology, astronomy; physical, biological and basic medical sciences: aquatic biology, microbiology, genetics, ecology, botany, zoology, biochemistry, plant physiology, animal physiology, environmental biology, molecular biology, chemistry (organic, inorganic, physical, structural), physics (astrophysics, mathematical, nuclear, polymer, theoretical, experimental); laws: English law, international law, comparative law, credit and commercial law, legal theory, socio-legal studies, intellectual property law, banking law, international arbitration, international business taxation; social studies: economics, applied econometrics, geography, social analysis, health care, information and planning, political studies, public policy, statistics, operational research, business studies, East London studies.

Museum or gallery collection, archive, or library special collection:
Alumni Collections (St Bartholomew's Hospital, Smithfield)
Alumni Collections (The Royal London Hospital, Whitechapel)
Archives of Westfield College
Camps and Cameron Collection on legal and forensic medicine (written application essential for access)
Constance Maynard Archive
Lyttleton Family Letters and Papers
Manuscripts on the History of Art
People's Palace Archive
Rare book collection (17th and 18th century English and European literature)

Access to staff:
Contact by letter, by telephone, by fax, by e-mail and via website
Hours: Access other than to University members normally restricted to term time: Mon to Fri, 1700 to 2100; Sat, 1000 to 1600 Vacations: Mon to Fri, 0900 to 1700

A college of the:
University of London

Medical Library:
Queen Mary, University of London
Royal London Hospital Medical College, Whitechapel, London, E1 2AD; tel: 020 7882 7112
Queen Mary, University of London
Charterhouse Square, London, EC1M 6BG; tel: 020 7882 6019
Queen Mary, University of London
Medical College of St Bartholomew's Hospital, West Smithfield, London, EC1A 7BE; tel: 020 7601 7853

QUEEN VICTORIA HOSPITAL NHS FOUNDATION TRUST

Acronym or abbreviation: QVH

Library, Holtye Road, East Grinstead, West Sussex, RH19 3DZ

Tel: 01342 414266
Fax: 01342 414005
E-mail: library@qvh.nhs.uk

Website:
http://stlis.thenhs.com/hln/sussex/kqv.asp
Catalogue of items available to members of Queen Victoria Hospital Library.

Enquiries:
Enquiries to: Library Services Manager

Organisation type and purpose:
Staff library.

Subject coverage:
Burns, plastic and reconstructive surgery, hand surgery, oral and maxillofacial surgery, ophthalmic and corneoplastic surgery and nursing.

Library catalogue:
All or part available online

Access to staff:
Contact by letter, by telephone, by fax and by e-mail. Appointment necessary.

Hours: Mon to Fri, 0930 to 1230

Access to building, collection or gallery:
Prior appointment required

QUEEN'S COLLEGE LIBRARY

Oxford, OX1 4AW

Tel: 01865 279130
Fax: 01865 790819
E-mail: library@queens.ox.ac.uk

Website:
http://www.queens.ox.ac.uk

Enquiries:
Enquiries to: Librarian
Direct tel: 01865 279213
Direct e-mail: amanda.saville@queens.ox.ac.uk

Founded:
1341

Organisation type and purpose:
College library.

Subject coverage:
Subject coverage which is likely to be of interest to others lies in those traditional areas, such as theology, philosophy etc, where the library has substantial holdings of older works; theology; philosophy; classics; history, ancient and modern; geography (mainly topography); politics; law; economics; English, French, German, Spanish and Russian languages and literature.

Museum or gallery collection, archive, or library special collection:
Incunabula (280 items)
Manuscripts (560 items, 10th to 20th centuries)
Oakes Collection (American history)
Peet Memorial Library (Egyptology)
Short Title Catalogue Books

Non-library collection catalogue:
All or part available online and in print

Library catalogue:
All or part available online and in-house

Access to staff:
Contact by letter, by telephone, by fax, by e-mail and via website. Appointment necessary. Access for members only.
Hours: Mon to Fri, 0900 to 1700

Access to building, collection or gallery:
Prior appointment required

Access for disabled people:
During staffed hours to ground floor only
Hours: 0900 to 1700

QUEEN'S NURSING INSTITUTE

Acronym or abbreviation: QNI

3 Albemarle Way, Clerkenwell, London, EC1V 4RQ

Tel: 020 7549 1400
Fax: 020 7490 1269
E-mail: mail@qni.org.uk

Website:
http://www.qni.org.uk

Enquiries:
Enquiries to: Director

Founded:
1887

Formerly called:
Queen's Institute of District Nursing (year of change 1973)

Organisation type and purpose:
National organisation, professional body, registered charity (charity number 213128).

Subject coverage:
Community nursing from its foundation in 1887 to the present day.

Museum or gallery collection, archive, or library special collection:
Archival material in connection with district (community) nursing

Printed publications:
Annual Report
Final Reports (by Innovation Award winners)
Newsletter (6 times a year)
QNI leaflet

Microform publications:
Queen's Nurses training records

Electronic and video publications:
Audio tapes, video, disc and CD-ROM

Publications list:
Available online and in print

Access to staff:
Contact by letter, by telephone, by fax, by e-mail and via website. Appointment necessary.
Hours: Mon to Fri, 0900 to 1730

QUEEN'S UNIVERSITY BELFAST – MAIN LIBRARY

Acronym or abbreviation: QUB

Belfast, BT7 1LS

Tel: 028 9097 5023
Fax: 028 9097 3340
E-mail: library@qub.ac.uk

Website:
http://www.qub.ac.uk/lib/
Home page on library services.

Enquiries:
Enquiries to: Director of Information Services
Direct tel: 028 9097 5020
Direct fax: 028 9097 3072
Direct e-mail: n.russell@qub.ac.uj.gormley@qub.ac.uk

Founded:
1845

Organisation type and purpose:
University library.
European Documentation Centre.

Subject coverage:
All subjects with particular strengths in humanities, economics, social science, education, law, theology.

Museum or gallery collection, archive, or library special collection:
Adam Smith Library
Antrim Presbytery Library
Hamilton Harty Music Collection
Helen Waddell Manuscripts
Hibernica Collection
MacDouall Collection (theology)
Sir Robert Hart Manuscripts
Somerville and Ross Manuscripts
Thomas Percy Collection

Non-library collection catalogue:
All or part available online

Library catalogue:
All or part available online

Access to staff:
Contact by letter, by telephone, by fax, by e-mail and via website. Appointment necessary. Non-members charged.
Hours: Mon to Fri, 0900 to 1700

QUEEN'S UNIVERSITY BELFAST – SCIENCE LIBRARY

Acronym or abbreviation: QUB Science Library

Lennoxvale, Belfast, BT9 5EQ

Tel: 028 9097 5441
Fax: 028 9097 4207
E-mail: s.library@qub.ac.uk

Website:
http://www.qub.ac.uk/lib

Online catalogue and library services.

Enquiries:
Enquiries to: Science Librarian
Direct tel: 028 9097 4302
Direct e-mail: k.dick@qub.ac.uk

Founded:
1969

Organisation type and purpose:
University library.
University branch library for science and engineering; the Main Library covers arts and social sciences; the other two branches are the Agriculture Library and the Medical Library.

Subject coverage:
Anatomy; aeronautical engineering; architecture; biochemistry; biology; chemical engineering; chemistry; civil engineering; electrical engineering; geosciences; mechanical engineering; physics; physiology; planning; psychology.

Museum or gallery collection, archive, or library special collection:
British Standards
Queen's University of Belfast collection of doctorate theses

Trade and statistical information:
Collection of manufacturers' trade literature including products made in Northern Ireland.

Library catalogue:
All or part available online

Printed publications:
Various documentation relating to electronic information sources and aspects of the Science Library services

Access to staff:
Contact by letter, by telephone, by fax, by e-mail, in person and via website. Non-members charged.
Hours: Term time: Mon to Fri, 0900 to 2130; Sat, 0900 to 1230. Vacation (approx mid-Jun to Sep): Mon to Fri, 0900 to 1730; Sat, 0900 to 1230

QUEKETT MICROSCOPICAL CLUB

The Natural History Museum, Cromwell Road, London, SW7 5BD

Tel: 020 7938 8921

Website:
http://www.nhm.ac.uk./quekett/
Current activities and information.

Enquiries:
Enquiries to: Honorary Secretary
Direct e-mail: phil.greaves@bllpharma.com

Founded:
1865

Organisation type and purpose:
Learned society.

Subject coverage:
Microscopy.

Printed publications:
Bulletin (twice a year)
The Quekett Journal of Microscopy (twice a year)

Access to staff:
Contact by letter, by telephone, by e-mail and via website
Hours: Mon to Fri, 0900 to 1700

QUILTERS' GUILD OF THE BRITISH ISLES

St Anthony's Hall, Peasholme Green, York, YO1 7PW

Tel: 01904 613242
Fax: 01904 632394
E-mail: info@quiltersguild.org.uk

Website:
http://www.quiltersguild.org.uk

Enquiries:
Enquiries to: Guild Administrator

Founded:
1979

Organisation type and purpose:
International organisation, national organisation, membership association (membership is by subscription), present number of members: 7,000, voluntary organisation, registered charity (charity number 1067361), museum, suitable for all ages, research organisation.
To promote and maintain the crafts of quilting, patchwork and appliqué from an educational base and historical perspective.

Subject coverage:
History of quilting, how to quilt, contemporary quilting, patchwork and appliqué.

Museum or gallery collection, archive, or library special collection:
Book library, slide library, study packs, videos
Heritage Quilt Collection
Quilt collection, historical and contemporary

Library catalogue:
All or part available in-house

Printed publications:
Quilt Studies (£10)
Quilt Treasures (1995)
Nineties Catalogue (£10)
The Quilter (quarterly magazine, free to members, £7 to non-members)

Access to staff:
Contact by letter, by telephone, by fax, by e-mail, in person and via website. Appointment necessary. Non-members charged.
Hours: Mon to Thu, 0900 to 1700; Fri, 0900 to 1700

Access to building, collection or gallery:
Hours: Please contact for current opening hours

Access for disabled people:
Access to all public areas, toilet facilities

R J TALBOTT

Springfields, 10 Sandy Lane, Scalford, Leicestershire, LE14 4DS

Tel: 01664 444668
Fax: 01664 444420
E-mail: rjtalbott@rjtalbott.plus.com

Enquiries:
Enquiries to: Director

Founded:
1986

Organisation type and purpose:
Consultancy.
Specialising in videofilm evidence for courts showing disability related to compensation.

Subject coverage:
Medical videofilm maker.

Printed publications:
Leaflets on services available

Access to staff:
Contact by letter and by fax. Appointment necessary.
Hours: Mon to Fri, 0900 to 1700 (but clients are usually visited)

Access to building, collection or gallery:
No access other than to staff

Access for disabled people:
Parking provided

Associated with:
International Paraplegic Claims Service

RAC LIVE – 1740 LIVE TRAFFIC AND WEATHER INFORMATION

RAC Motoring Services, Great Park Road, Bradley Stoke, Bristol, BS32 4QN

Tel: 1740 from any mobile, (calls cost up to 59p per minute) also on 0906 470 1740 land-line (calls charged at 60p per minute)

continued overleaf

Website:
http://www.rac.co.uk/travelservices/traffic by phone
Information on the 1740 service.
http://www.rac.co.uk
To check the latest traffic information.

Organisation type and purpose:
Membership association (membership is by subscription).
RAC Live is the brand name operated by RAC Trafficmaster Telematics Limited.

Subject coverage:
Live traffic information on your mobile available 24 hours a day:
up to the minute traffic information on over 8000 miles of motorways and major A roads, latest national and local weather forcasts.
After listening to traffic information, talk to an RAC advisor to find an alternative route, plan routes across UK and Europe, provide general UK and European driving information and traffic regulations.

Access to staff:
Contact by telephone
Hours: Mon to Fri, 0700 to 2000; Sat, 0900 to 1700; Sun 0900 to 1700

RAC LIVE – RAC ROUTE MINDER

RAC Motoring Services, Great Park Road, Bradley Stoke, Bristol, BS32 4QN

Tel: 0800 096 1740

Website:
http://www.rac.co.uk/travelservices/route_minder/
To sign up for a free month's trial.

Organisation type and purpose:
Membership association (membership is by subscription).
RAC Live is the brand name operated by RAC Trafficmaster Telematics Limited.

Subject coverage:
Web-based personalised and proactive traffic information service: delivers relevant traffic information alerts via email and text messages, provides unlimited access to colour map that displays live traffic information.

Access to staff:
Contact by telephone
Hours: Mon to Fri, 0800 to 2000; Sat, 0900 1700; Sun, 0900 to 1900

RAC TRAVEL INFORMATION

RAC Live, RAC Motoring Services, Great Park Road, Bradley Stoke, Bristol, BS32 4QN

Tel: 0906 470 1740 (calls charged at 60p per minute)

Website:
http://www.racbusiness.co.uk
http://www.bsm.co.uk
http://www.rac.co.uk
The pages can be used to join the RAC online. Hotel bookings and plans for journeys can be made that take into account traffic conditions and delays. A motorsport section provides members with a virtual tour of British tracks and a diary of events.

Enquiries:
Enquiries to: RAC Travel Information Department

Organisation type and purpose:
Membership association (membership is by subscription).

Subject coverage:
Dynamic traffic updates on the UK motorway and trunk road network: UK and European route information (a charge is made for posted or faxed routes); various UK and European travel related enquiries.

Access to staff:
Contact by telephone

Hours: Advisors available: Mon to Fri, 0700 to 2000; Sat, 0900 to 1700; Sun, 0900 to 2100
Recorded UK road traffic information is 24 hours

RACE WALKING ASSOCIATION

Acronym or abbreviation: RWA

Hufflers, Heard's Lane, Shenfield, Brentwood, Essex, CM15 0SF

Tel: 01277 220687
Fax: 01277 212380
E-mail: racewalkingassociation@btinternet.com

Website:
http://www.racewalkingassociation.btinternet.co.uk
For other pages add: /AboutTheRWA.html; / archivesandrecords.html; /books.html; / clubcontacts.html; /fixtures.html; /moreinfo.html; / news.html; /outsidecontacts.html; / racewalkingrecord.html; /usefullinks.html; (All contents should be obvious from page names) There are several more technical pages.

Enquiries:
Enquiries to: Honorary General Secretary

Founded:
1907

Organisation type and purpose:
Voluntary organisation.
Governing body of race walking.
The development, promotion and control of race walking in England, the Isle of Man and the Channel Islands.

Subject coverage:
Policy; organisation and rules; clubs and athletes; coaches, officials and judging, events; history; relations with other sporting organisations.

Museum or gallery collection, archive, or library special collection:
List of clubs and officials
Lists of events
Minutes

Printed publications:
Fixture List
Handbook
Race Walking Record (monthly)
Race Walking (technique and training)
This Is Race Walking (introduction to race walking)

Electronic and video publications:
Fixture List disc
Handbook disc

Access to staff:
Contact by letter, by telephone, by fax and by e-mail
Hours: Mon to Fri, 0800 to 2300

Access to building, collection or gallery:
No access other than to staff

Area Associations:
Midlands Area RWA
   5 Seven Acres, Home Meadows, Worcester, WR4 0JD; tel: 01905 616718; e-mail: perry.sevenacres@ tinyworld.co.uk
Northern Area RWA
   32 Cedar Walk, Highton Wood Hill, Tromode, Isle of Man; tel: 01624 672009; fax: 01624 672009; e-mail: jpowell@32ceda82.freeserve.co.uk
Southern Area RWA
   74 Southfield Road, Waltham Cross, Hertfordshire, EN8 7HE; tel: 01992 626804

RADCLIFFE SCIENCE LIBRARY

Parks Road, Oxford, OX1 3QP

Tel: 01865 272800
Fax: 01865 272821
E-mail: rsl.enquiries@bodley.ox.ac.uk

Website:
http://www.bodley.ox.ac.uk/
Bodleian Library home page.
http://www.bodley.ox.ac.uk/depts/rsl/

Guide to the Radcliffe Science Library.

Enquiries:
Enquiries to: Keeper of Scientific Books
Direct tel: 01865 272820
Direct fax: 01865 272832
Other contacts: (1) Reader Services Librarian (2) Administrator for (1) bibliographical enquiries (2) admin.

Founded:
1749

Organisation type and purpose:
University library.
Legal deposit library, the science section of the Bodleian Library; the main science library of Oxford University, part of Oxford University Library Services.

Subject coverage:
All pure sciences, mathematics, engineering and medicine.

Museum or gallery collection, archive, or library special collection:
Acland (medical pamphlets and offprints)
Child (pamphlets and offprints on coconuts)
Hardy (mathematical pamphlets and offprints)
Le Gros Clark (anatomical pamphlets and offprints)
Seckerson (pamphlets, offprints and portraits related to eponymous syndromes and diseases)
Tylor (anthropological pamphlets and offprints)
Van Heyningen (pamphlets and offprints in pathology)

Library catalogue:
All or part available online

Access to staff:
Contact by letter, by telephone, by e-mail and via website. Appointment necessary.
Hours: Term time: 0900 to 2200

Access for disabled people:
Level entry, toilet facilities

RADIO MANX LIMITED

PO Box 1368, Broadcasting House, Douglas Head, Douglas, Isle of Man, IM99 1SW, Isle of Man

Tel: 01624 682600
Fax: 01624 682604

Website:
http://www.radiott.com
Information about RadioTT, a concept station oriented to the Isle of Man TT Races.
http://www.manxradio.com
Programme details, research details, personality details and general information about Manx Radio.

Enquiries:
Enquiries to: Managing Director
Direct e-mail: stewartwatterson@manxradio.com
Other contacts: (1) News Editor (2) Sales Director for (1) news releases (2) advertising services.

Founded:
1964

Organisation type and purpose:
Service industry, publishing house.
News and current affairs source – Isle of Man.
Public service broadcaster. Provision of radio advertising services.

Subject coverage:
News and current affairs; information and views – Isle of Man.
Isle of Man advertising market.

Trade and statistical information:
Average listenership base – 80% adult population of Isle of Man. In consequence, very effective, and wide-ranging across all demographics, advertising service.

Printed publications:
Advertising and Research Data
Media Pack

Access to staff:
Contact by letter, by fax, by e-mail and via website
Hours: Mon to Fri, 0900 to 1700

RADISH GROWERS' ASSOCIATION

133 Eastgate, Louth, Lincolnshire, LN11 9QG

Tel: 01507 602427
Fax: 01507 607165
E-mail: crop.association@pvga.co.uk

Enquiries:
Enquiries to: Membership Secretary

Founded:
1980s

Organisation type and purpose:
National organisation, trade association.

Subject coverage:
Radishes.

RADNORSHIRE SOCIETY

Pool House, Discoed, Presteigne, Powys, LD8 2NW

Tel: 01547 560318
E-mail: sadie.cole@virgin.net

Enquiries:
Enquiries to: Hon Secretary

Founded:
1930

Organisation type and purpose:
Learned society (membership is by subscription), present number of members: 450.

Subject coverage:
History, natural history, archaeology of the old county of Radnor.

Printed publications:
The Transactions (annually)

Access to staff:
Contact by letter, by telephone and by e-mail. Appointment necessary. Access for members only.
Hours: Mon to Fri, 0900 to 1700

Access to building, collection or gallery:
No prior appointment required

RADZINOWICZ LIBRARY

Formal name: University of Cambridge – Institute of Criminology, Radzinowicz Library

Sidgwick Avenue, Cambridge, CB3 9DA

Tel: 01223 335386
Fax: 01223 335356
E-mail: crimlib@hermes.cam.ac.uk

Website:
http://www.crim.cam.ac.uk/library

Enquiries:
Enquiries to: Librarian

Founded:
1960

Organisation type and purpose:
University department or institute. Departmental library.

Subject coverage:
Criminology, penology, forensic psychiatry, forensic psychology, deviance, policing, criminal justice (foreign and historical materials are included), criminal law.

Library catalogue:
All or part available online

Electronic and video publications:
Quarterly accessions list
Order electronic and video publications from: http://www.crim.cam.ac.uk/library/pubs.html

Access to staff:
Contact by letter, by telephone, by fax and by e-mail. Appointment necessary. Letter of introduction required.
Hours: Mon to Fri, 0900 to 1600

RAF CENTRE OF AVIATION MEDICINE

Acronym or abbreviation: RAF CAM

RAF Henlow, Henlow, Bedfordshire, SG16 6DN

Tel: 01462 851515
Fax: 01462 851515

Enquiries:
Enquiries to: Librarian
Direct tel: ext 8045
Direct fax: ext 8046
Direct e-mail: hlw-cam-library@henlow.raf.mod.uk
Other contacts: Officer Commanding Centre of Aviation Medicine for non-service personnel who wish to visit the collection.

Organisation type and purpose:
National government body, training organisation, research organisation.

Subject coverage:
Medicine, especially those areas most relevant to aviation; physiology; neurology; psychology; occupational health.

Museum or gallery collection, archive, or library special collection:
Technical reports of British and overseas government agencies relevant to aviation and aviation medicine

Non-library collection catalogue:
All or part available in-house

Library catalogue:
All or part available in-house

Access to staff:
Contact by letter, by telephone, by fax and by e-mail. Appointment necessary.
Hours: Mon to Thu, 0900 to 1630; Fri, 0900 to 1600
Special comments: All non-service personnel must first seek the permission of the Officer Commanding by letter.

Access for disabled people:
Level entry, toilet facilities

RAIL PASSENGERS COUNCIL

Acronym or abbreviation: RPC

Freepost WA 1521, Warrington, WA4 6GP

Tel: 08453 022 022
Fax: 0845 850 1392

Website:
http://www.rail-reg.gov.uk

Enquiries:
Enquiries to: External Relations and Policy Manager

Founded:
1994

Organisation type and purpose:
National government body.
Statutory consumer body of 14 members appointed by the Secretary of State, representing the interests of users of rail services and facilities. The Rail Passengers Committees and the LTUC represent passenger interests locally, the RPC on a national scale.

Subject coverage:
Rail users' consumer matters, monitoring and investigating policies and performance of train and station operators.
For passenger complaints, assessing hardship when stations or lines proposed for closure, see RUCC's and LRPC, which represent passengers' interests locally.

Printed publications:
Annual Report
News Releases

Reports and occasional papers
Series of papers on franchising

Access to staff:
Contact by letter, by telephone, by fax and by e-mail. Appointment necessary.
Hours: Mon to Fri, 0900 to 1700

Affiliated to:
London Transport Users Committee (LTUC)
Rail Passengers Committees (RPC)

Branches at:
East RPC Eastern England
3rd Floor, Stuart House, City Road, Peterborough, Cambridgeshire, PE1 1QF; tel: 01733 312188; fax: 01733 891286
London area See the London Transport Users Committee
Midlands RPC Midlands
6th Floor, The McLaren Building, 35 Dale End, Birmingham, B4 7LN; tel: 0121 212 2133; fax: 0121 236 6945
North East Also has responsibility for Tyne & Wear Metro services
Hilary House, St Saviour's Place, York, YO1 7PJ; tel: 01904 625615; fax: 01904 643026
North West Also has responsibility for Greater Manchester Metrolink services
Third Floor, 82 King Street, Manchester, M2 4WQ; tel: 0161 228 6247; fax: 0161 236 1476
Scotland RPC Scotland
Also has responsibility for shipping services operated by Caledonian MacBrayne
Room 514, Corunna House, 29 Cadogan Street, Glasgow, G2 7AB; tel: 0141 221 7760; fax: 0141 221 3393
South RPC Southern England
3rd Floor, Centric House, 390–391 Strand, London, WC2R 0LY; tel: 020 7240 5308; fax: 020 7240 8923
Wales RPC Wales – Cymru
St David's House, Wood Street, Cardiff, CF10 1ES; tel: 029 2022 7247; fax: 029 2022 3992
West RPC Western England
10th Floor, Tower House, Fairfax Street, Bristol, BS1 3BN; tel: 0117 926 5703; fax: 0117 929 4140

Resourced by:
Office of the Rail Regulator

RAILWAY CORRESPONDENCE AND TRAVEL SOCIETY

Acronym or abbreviation: RCTS

Littlecote, 365 Old Bath Road, Cheltenham, Gloucestershire, GL53 9AH

Tel: 01242 523917
E-mail: peter@littlecote.freeserve.co.uk

Website:
http://www.rcts.org.uk
About the society.

Enquiries:
Enquiries to: Book Publications Sales Manager

Founded:
1928

Organisation type and purpose:
Membership association (membership is by subscription), voluntary organisation.

Museum or gallery collection, archive, or library special collection:
Historic working time-tables collection (for members only)
Photographic portfolio (for members only)

Printed publications:
Definitive histories of the locomotives owned by the four British pre-nationalisation companies and their pre-grouping constituents
Other books of general railway interest
Railway Observer (magazine, monthly, members only)

Publications list:
Available online and in print

Access to staff:
Contact by letter, by e-mail and via website

continued overleaf

Hours: Mon to Fri, 0900 to 1700

Affiliated to:
a number of similar organisations in the UK and overseas

Has:
26 branches within the UK

RAILWAY HERITAGE TRUST

40 Melton Street, London, NW1 2EE

Tel: 020 7557 8090
Fax: 020 7557 9700
E-mail: rht@networkrail.co.uk

Enquiries:
Enquiries to: Executive Director

Founded:
1985

Organisation type and purpose:
Advisory body.
Independent company, sponsored by Network Rail and BRB (Residuary) Ltd, which offers grant aid for the conservation of listed buildings and structures owned by those sponsors.
Heritage funding agency.

Subject coverage:
Repair, restoration and conservation of listed and historic railway buildings and structures owned by Network Rail and BRB (Residuary) Ltd, grant aid for this purpose.

Printed publications:
Annual Report

Access to staff:
Contact by letter, by telephone, by fax and by e-mail. Appointment necessary.
Hours: Mon to Fri, 0900 to 1700

RAILWAY INDUSTRY ASSOCIATION

Acronym or abbreviation: RIA

22 Headfort Place, London, SW1X 7RY

Tel: 020 7201 0777
Fax: 020 7235 5777
E-mail: ria@riagb.org.uk

Website:
http://www.riagb.org.uk

Enquiries:
Enquiries to: Director

Founded:
1875

Organisation type and purpose:
Trade association.

Subject coverage:
Railway equipment, railway infrastructure, standards and specifications.

Printed publications:
BRB/RIA Technical Specifications (13)
Members and Products (directory)

Publications list:
Available in print

Access to staff:
Contact by letter, by telephone, by fax and by e-mail
Hours: Mon to Fri, 0900 to 1700

RAILWAY PRESERVATION SOCIETY OF IRELAND

Acronym or abbreviation: RPSI

Whitehead Excursion Station, Castleview Road, Whitehead, Carrickfergus, Co Antrim, BT38 9NA

Tel: 028 2826 0803
Fax: 028 2826 0803
E-mail: rpsitrains@hotmail.com

Website:
http://www.steamtrainsireland.com

Enquiries:
Enquiries to: Honorary Secretary
Other contacts: Chairman

Founded:
1964

Organisation type and purpose:
Membership association (membership is by subscription), present number of members: 1,100, voluntary organisation, registered charity. Aims to restore, maintain and operate preserved steam locomotives and historic carriages on the main line railways of Ireland.

Subject coverage:
Irish railway preservation, steam locomotives, vintage rolling stock.

Museum or gallery collection, archive, or library special collection:
Irish steam engines and rolling stock

Non-library collection catalogue:
All or part available online

Printed publications:
Journal (to members)
Newsletters (to members)

Access to staff:
Contact by letter, by e-mail and via website.
Appointment necessary.
Hours: Mon to Fri, 0900 to 1300

Access to building, collection or gallery:
On advertised open days, otherwise by prior appointment.

Access for disabled people:
Parking provided, ramped entry

Member organisation of:
Heritage Railway Association (HRA)

RAJAR

Formal name: Radio Joint Audience Research Limited
Acronym or abbreviation: RAJAR

Paramount House, 162–170 Wardour Street, London, W1F 8ZX

Tel: 020 7292 9040
Fax: 020 7292 9041
E-mail: info@rajar.co.uk

Website:
http://www.rajar.co.uk
Quarterly summary of radio listening

Enquiries:
Enquiries to: Managing Director

Founded:
1992

Organisation type and purpose:
Research organisation.
Joint industry research organisation.
Management of UK's agreed system of radio audience measurement.

Subject coverage:
National and local estimates of radio listening analysis by time period and with demographic breakdowns.

Printed publications:
Quarterly Summary of Radio Listening (free)
The Radio Audience (detailed results available quarterly on subscription)

Electronic and video publications:
Electronic access to detailed results available through commercial bureaux

Access to staff:
Contact by letter, by e-mail and via website.
Appointment necessary.
Hours: Mon to Fri, 0930 to 1730

RALEIGH SAFETY SEVEN AND EARLY RELIANT OWNERS CLUB

Acronym or abbreviation: Raleigh/Reliant OC

17 Courtland Avenue, Chingford, London, E4 6DU

Enquiries:
Enquiries to: Secretary

Founded:
1967

Organisation type and purpose:
Membership association (membership is by subscription), present number of members: 180–200.

Subject coverage:
Technical information and spares for all Raleigh motorised vehicles and Reliant vehicles up to the Regal models.

Museum or gallery collection, archive, or library special collection:
Library of Raleigh and Reliant vehicle literature

Printed publications:
Newsletter (quarterly, free to members)

Access to staff:
Contact by letter
Hours: Mon to Fri, 0900 to 1700
Special comments: Stamped addressed envelope with enquiries; Library is open to members only.

RAMBLERS' ASSOCIATION

Acronym or abbreviation: RA

2nd Floor, Camelford House, 89 Albert Embankment, London, SE1 7TW

Tel: 020 7339 8500
Fax: 020 7339 8501
E-mail: ramblers@ramblers.org.uk

Website:
http://www.ramblers.org.uk
Comprehensive source of information on walking in Britain; Ramblers' campaigns, membership and local groups, links to related organisations in Britain and abroad.

Enquiries:
Enquiries to: Information Officer

Founded:
1935

Organisation type and purpose:
National organisation, membership association (membership is by subscription), present number of members: 140,000, voluntary organisation, registered charity (charity number 306089). Encouraging walking, protecting footpaths, campaigning for responsible freedom to roam, defending the beauty of the countryside.

Subject coverage:
Walking; rights of way and footpath law; care of the countryside and preservation of natural beauty; protection of footpaths and provision of access to open country; long-distance footpath information; all matters connected with walking.

Printed publications:
Fact Sheets and Regional Guides
Footpath Worker (quarterly bulletin)
Path Guides and Accommodation Lists
Policy Statements
Walk (quarterly, members)
Rights of Way publications
The Rambler's Yearbook and Accommodation Guide
Research Reports

Publications list:
Available online and in print

Access to staff:
Contact by letter, by telephone, by fax, by e-mail, in person and via website
Hours: Mon to Fri, 1000 to 1700

Access to building, collection or gallery:
No prior appointment required

Access for disabled people:
Parking provided, ramped entry, access to all public areas, toilet facilities

Other addresses:
Ramblers' Association, Scotland (RA Scotland) Kingfisher House, Auld Mart Business Park, Milnathort, Kinross, KY13 9DA; tel: 01577 861222; fax: 01577 861333; e-mail: enquiries@ scotland.ramblers.org.uk
Ramblers' Association, Wales
Ty'r Cerddwyr, High Street, Gresford, Wrexham, LL12 8PT; tel: 01978 855148; fax: 01978 854445; e-mail: cerddwyr@wales.ramblers.org.uk

RAMSGATE LIBRARY

Guildford Lawn, Ramsgate, Kent, CT11 9AJ

Tel: 01843 593532
Fax: 01843 852692

Enquiries:
Enquiries to: Librarian
Other contacts: Heritage Officer

Founded:
1904

Organisation type and purpose:
Local government body, public library.

Subject coverage:
Parish records, census returns, photographs, newscuttings, maps and ephemera relating to the history of Ramsgate.

Museum or gallery collection, archive, or library special collection:
Ramsgate Archive Collections have been moved to the East Kent Archives Centre, Dover
Collections of books, photographs, maps and postcards relating to the history of Ramsgate

Library catalogue:
All or part available in-house

Access to staff:
Contact by letter, by telephone and by fax
Hours: Mon to Thu, 0930 to 1800; Fri, 0930 to 1900; Sat, 0930 to 1700
Special comments: Heritage staff are available to assist on Thursdays.

Access to building, collection or gallery:
No access other than to staff

Parent body:
Kent County Council
Sessions House, County Hall, Maidstone, Kent

RAPE AND SEXUAL ABUSE SUPPORT CENTRE

Acronym or abbreviation: RASASC

PO Box 383, Croydon, Surrey, CR9 2AW

Tel: 020 8683 3311 (Counselling and Office)\ Minicom no. 020 82391124\ 08451 221 331 (Helpline)
Fax: 020 8683 3366
E-mail: info@rasasc.org.uk

Website:
http://www.rasasc.org.uk

Enquiries:
Enquiries to: Director

Founded:
1982

Organisation type and purpose:
Voluntary organisation, registered charity (charity number 1085104), training organisation, consultancy.

Subject coverage:
Support to anyone aged 14 and above who has been raped or sexually abused, however long ago. Support and advice to friends / family / partners, and other agencies working with rape or sexual abuse survivors. External training to other

organisations. Database of other statutory and otherwise relevant organisations for referral. Helpline support for male survivors.

Printed publications:
Leaflets on the service and other related topics (free of charge)

Access to staff:
Contact by letter, by telephone, by fax, by e-mail and via website. Appointment necessary.
Hours: Mon to Fri, 1000 to 1600
Special comments: Helpline: Mon to Fri, 1200 to 1430 and 1900 to 2130; Sat, Sun and bank holidays, 1430 to 1700
Counselling: Mon to Fri 1000 to 1600

Access to building, collection or gallery:
No access other than to staff

Access for disabled people:
Parking provided, level entry, toilet facilities
Special comments: Staff only, at present.
(December 2001)

RAPIER REGISTER

The Smithy, Tregynon, Newtown, Powys, SY16 3EH

Tel: 01686 650396

Enquiries:
Enquiries to: Membership Secretary

Founded:
1953

Organisation type and purpose:
International organisation, membership association (membership is by subscription), present number of members: 150, voluntary organisation.
Motor club catering for the needs of persons owning and driving Lagonda Rapiers and Rapier cars built between 1934 and 1938.

Subject coverage:
General and technical information on Lagonda Rapiers and Rapier cars manufactured between 1934 and 1938. Location of available spare parts for same.

Printed publications:
Newsletter (monthly, free to members)
List of Spares (available to members)

Access to staff:
Contact by letter and by telephone
Hours: Mon to Fri, 0900 to 2200

RAPRA TECHNOLOGY

Shawbury, Shrewsbury, Shropshire, SY4 4NR

Tel: 01939 250383
Fax: 01939 251118
E-mail: publications@rapra.net

Website:
http://www.rapra.net
Website giving access to full range of services and products.
http://www.polymer-books.com
Comprehensive online bookstore for the plastics and rubber industries.

Enquiries:
Enquiries to: Information Resource Librarian
Direct tel: 01939 252458
Direct e-mail: ecooper@rapra.net

Founded:
1920

Organisation type and purpose:
Independent plastics and rubber consultancy; technology and information services; membership association (membership is by subscription); research organisation; publishing house.

Subject coverage:
Rubber, plastics and allied fields, synthesis and applications design, additives, processing, properties and testing, market information,

chemical resistance, industrial hazards, thermal transition, trade names, adhesives, standards and specifications.

Museum or gallery collection, archive, or library special collection:
Porritt and Dawson Collection (on rubbers and plastics)

Non-library collection catalogue:
All or part available online

Library catalogue:
All or part available online

Printed publications:
Cellular Polymers (6 times a year)
Polymers and Polymer Composites (8 times a year)
European Plastics Directory (annual)
International Polymer Science and Technology (monthly)
Progress in Rubber, Plastics and Recycling Technology (quarterly)
RAPRA Abstracts (monthly)
Order printed publications from: Publications Sales

Publications list:
Available online and in print

Access to staff:
Contact by letter, by telephone, by fax, by e-mail and via website. Appointment necessary. Access for members only. All charged.
Hours: Mon to Fri, 0830 to 1630

Access to building, collection or gallery:
Prior appointment required

RAPTOR FOUNDATION

Formal name: Bird of Prey Rescue Centre

The Heath, St Ives Road, Woodhurst, Cambridgeshire, PE28 3BT

Tel: 01487 741140
Fax: 01487 841140
E-mail: heleowl@aol.com

Website:
http://www.homepages.tesco.net/~raptor .foundation
Information about the centre.

Enquiries:
Enquiries to: Director
Other contacts: Founder

Founded:
1989

Organisation type and purpose:
Membership association (membership is by subscription), present number of members: 210, registered charity (charity number 1042085), research organisation.
Care and rehabilitation of raptors.

Trade and statistical information:
Over 350 rescued raptors.

Access to staff:
Contact in person
Hours: 24 hours a day for rescue daily, 1030 to 1700 for visitors

Access for disabled people:
Parking provided, ramped entry, access to all public areas, toilet facilities

RARE BREEDS SURVIVAL TRUST

Acronym or abbreviation: RBST

National Agricultural Centre, Stoneleigh Park, Kenilworth, Warwickshire, CV8 2LG

Tel: 024 7669 6551
Fax: 024 7669 6706
E-mail: enquiries@rbst.org.uk

Website:
http://www.rbst.org.uk

Enquiries:
Enquiries to: Administrator

continued overleaf

Founded:
1973

Organisation type and purpose:
Membership association (membership is by subscription), present number of members: c. 8000, registered charity (charity number 269442). The conservation of rare breeds of farm livestock.

Subject coverage:
Rare breeds of farm livestock.

Non-library collection catalogue:
All or part available in-house

Access to staff:
Contact by letter, by telephone, by fax, by e-mail and via website. Appointment necessary.
Hours: Mon to Fri, 0900 to 1700

Access to building, collection or gallery:
No prior appointment required

RATHBONE

4th Floor, Churchgate House, 56 Oxford Street, Manchester, M1 6EU

Tel: 0161 236 5358
Fax: 0161 238 6356

Website:
http://www.rathbonetraining.co.uk
Information on services.

Enquiries:
Enquiries to: Helpline Co-ordinator
Direct e-mail: advice@rathbonetraining.co.uk
Other contacts: Marketing and External Affairs Manager for overall responsibility for marketing, public relations and information.

Founded:
1969

Formerly called:
Rathbone Training

Organisation type and purpose:
Advisory body, voluntary organisation, registered charity (charity number 287120), training organisation.
Charity is a training provider. Special education advice line to parents and children with special needs.

Subject coverage:
Advice for parents and children with special needs on all aspects of education, statementing, exclusion etc.

Museum or gallery collection, archive, or library special collection:
Elfrida Rathbone archives

Printed publications:
A4 Poster (free)
Advice Line Business cards (free)
Choosing a School (first copy free, 50p each thereafter)
Finding Funding (first copy free, 25p each thereafter)
General Advice Line Leaflet (free)
How to Complain (first copy free, 25p each thereafter)
Making a Statement: The Parent's Guide to the statementing procedure for a child with special educational needs (£5 for professionals and charities, free to parents although they are asked for a £5 donation if they can afford it)
Making a Statement (summary leaflet) (free)
Organisations which can help (first copy free, 50p each thereafter)
Postcard (free)
Proposed Statements (first copy free, 50p each thereafter)
School Admissions (first copy free, 50p each thereafter)
School Exclusions (first copy free, 50p each thereafter)
School Based Stages (first copy free, 50p each thereafter)
SEAL Newsletter (free)

Publications list:
Available in print

Access to staff:
Contact by letter, by telephone, by fax and by e-mail
Hours: Mon to Fri, 1000 to 1600

Development Officer (London & South):
Rathbone Training
260–268 Poplar High Street, London, E14 0BB; tel: 020 7538 2041; fax: 020 7537 9399

Development Officer (Midlands & Wales):
Rathbone Training
1st Floor, Wrekin House, Market Street, Wellington, Telford, Shropshire, TF1 1DT; tel: 01952 245000; fax: 01952 261771

Development Officer (North):
Rathbone Training
165 Cardigan Road, Leeds, LS6 1QL; tel: 0113 278 9333; fax: 0113 278 9870

Director for Scotland:
Rathbone Training
C.I. Building, Scott Street, Motherwell, ML1 1PN; tel: 01698 252326; fax: 01698 251400

RAVENSBOURNE COLLEGE OF DESIGN AND COMMUNICATION LRC

Walden Road, Chislehurst, Kent, BR7 5SN

Tel: 020 8289 4900
Fax: 020 8325 8320
E-mail: lrc@rave.ac.uk

Website:
http://intranet.rave.ac.uk/lrc

Enquiries:
Enquiries to: Director of Information Services
Direct tel: 020 8289 4919
Direct e-mail: s.bowman@rave.ac.uk

Organisation type and purpose:
College of higher education.

Subject coverage:
Broadcasting, fashion design, furniture design, graphic design, moving image, product design, television.

Library catalogue:
All or part available online

Access to staff:
Contact by letter, by telephone, by fax and by e-mail. Appointment necessary.
Hours: Mon to Fri, 0900 to 1700

Funded by:
HEFCE

RAY SOCIETY

Department of Zoology, The Natural History Museum, Cromwell Road, South Kensington, London, SW7 5BD

Tel: 020 7942 5532
Fax: 020 7942 5433
E-mail: nje@nhm.ac.uk

Website:
http://www.books.free-online.co.uk/
Listing of available publications.

Enquiries:
Enquiries to: Honorary Secretary

Founded:
1844

Organisation type and purpose:
Learned society (membership is by subscription), present number of members: 357, registered charity (charity number 208082).

Subject coverage:
Natural history; botany; zoology mainly of Britain and NW Europe but also of wider interest.

Printed publications:
Annual Report (yearly)

Ray Society Volumes (irregular, 164 volumes to date)
Concessionary sales to members of the Ray Society are available through the Honorary Secretary
Order printed publications from: Intercept Limited, PO Box 716, Andover, Hampshire, SP10 1YG, tel: 01264 334748, fax: 01264 334058, e-mail: intercept@andover.co.uk

Microform publications:
For purchase any of Ray Society 'I' publications, see addresses for printed publications
Order microform publications from: Microform Academic Publishers, Microform (Wakefield) Limited, Main Street, East Andsley, Wakefield, WF3 2AT

Publications list:
Available online and in print

Access to staff:
Contact by letter, by telephone, by fax, by e-mail and via website. Appointment necessary.
Hours: Mon to Fri, 0900 to 1700
Special comments: Visitor regulations for the Natural History Museum apply.

Access for disabled people:
Parking provided, ramped entry, access to all public areas, toilet facilities

RAYNAUD'S & SCLERODERMA ASSOCIATION

112 Crewe Road, Alsager, Cheshire, ST7 2JA

Tel: 01270 872776
Fax: 01270 883556
E-mail: info@reynauds.org.uk

Website:
http://www.raynauds.org.uk

Enquiries:
Enquiries to: Chief Executive

Founded:
1982

Organisation type and purpose:
Membership association (membership is by subscription), voluntary organisation, registered charity (charity number 326306), research organisation.

Subject coverage:
Raynaud's, Scleroderma, Vibration White Finger, Sjögren's Syndrome, chilblains, Systemic Lupus Erythematosus, Teenage Raynaud's, Erythromelalgia, advances in research, funding for research.

Printed publications:
Leaflets available on the following:
Chilblains
Erythromelalgia
Raynaud's Phenomenon
Scleroderma
Skin Care
Sjörgren's Syndrome
Systemic Lupus Erythematosus
Teenage Raynaud's
Vibration White Finger
CREST (Limited cutaneous systemic sclerosis)
Localised scleroderma in children
Health Professional booklets on the following:
Oral and Dental Aspects of Scleroderma
Raynaud's and Scleroderma, A Reminder for GP's
The Role of the Nurse in Raynaud's and Scleroderma
The Role of a Podiatrist in Raynaud's and Scleroderma
The Role of the Physiotherapist in Raynaud's and Scleroderma
The Role of the Occupational Therapist in Raynaud's and Scleroderma
Available for purchase are the following books:
Scleroderma Patients Booklet
There Are More Questions Than Answers

Electronic and video publications:
DVDs available for purchase

Publications list:
Available in print

Access to staff:
Contact by letter, by telephone, by fax, by e-mail, in person and via website
Hours: Mon to Fri, 0900 to 1700
Special comments: Answering machine available.

Access for disabled people:
Parking provided, level entry, toilet facilities

RE-SOLV – THE SOCIETY FOR THE PREVENTION OF SOLVENT AND VOLATILE SUBSTANCE ABUSE

Acronym or abbreviation: Re-Solv

30a High Street, Stone, Staffordshire, ST15 8AW

Tel: 01785 817885
Fax: 01785 813205
E-mail: information@re-solv.org

Website:
http://www.re-solv.org

Enquiries:
Enquiries to: Information Officer

Founded:
1984

Organisation type and purpose:
National organisation, membership association (membership is by subscription), registered charity (charity number 326732). Aims to prevent death, suffering and crime that may result as a consequence of solvent and volatile substance abuse. Provides information and support to anyone concerned about or interested in solvent and volatile substance misuse issues.

Subject coverage:
Prevention of solvent and volatile substance abuse.

Information services:
Contact details for other organisations dealing with solvent/volatile substance abuse issues can also be provided.

Trade and statistical information:
Solvent and volatile substance abuse statistics, i.e. mortality statistics.

Printed publications:
Training Pack for Social Services Professionals (£20.00)
Toxic Agents Primary School Pack (£35)
Youth Workers Activities Pack (£20)
Greatest Danger leaflet (£4.50 for 50 copies)
Cupboard leaflet (£15 for 50 copies)
Order printed publications from: via website

Electronic and video publications:
A Loaded Gun (DVD with workbook, £20)
The Silent Killer (DVD with booklet, £10)
Order electronic and video publications from: via website

Publications list:
Available online and in print

Access to staff:
Contact by letter, by telephone, by fax, by e-mail and via website
Hours: Mon to Fri, 0900 to 1700; closed public holidays
Special comments: Answerphone services are in operation outside office hours and provide referral details.

Access to building, collection or gallery:
No access other than to staff

Branches:
Re-Solv North East
7 Burrow Street, South Shileds, Tyne and Wear, NE33 1PP; tel: 0191 497 5522; e-mail: northeast@re-solv.org
Re-Solv Scotland
c/o Fast Forward, 4 Bernard Street, Leith, Edinburgh, EH6 6PP; tel: 07505 000024; e-mail: scotland@re-solv.org

Re-Solv Wales
First Floor, 21A Berriew Street, Welshpool, Powys, SY21 7SQ; tel: 01938 556790; e-mail: wales@re-solv.org

READING BOROUGH COUNCIL

Civic Offices, PO Box 17, The Civic Centre, Reading, Berkshire, RG1 7TD

Tel: 0118 939 0900\ Minicom no. 0118 939 0700
Fax: 0118 958 9770

Website:
http://www.reading.gov.uk
A-Z numbers to contact and much more.

Enquiries:
Enquiries to: Public Relations Manager
Direct tel: 0118 939 0333
Direct fax: 0118 939 0282
Direct e-mail: carl.welham@reading.gov.uk

Founded:
1998

Organisation type and purpose:
Local government body.

Subject coverage:
All aspects of local government.

Printed publications:
A guide to getting around the town – buses
A guide to getting around the town – cyclists
Agenda21
Annual report to tenants
Equalities Annual report
Cllr Posters
Equalities statement
Moving Reading Forward (traffic problems and proposals)
On your Bike
Safer Reading Campaign

Electronic and video publications:
Reading (CD-ROM)

Publications list:
Available in print

Access to staff:
Contact by letter, by telephone, by fax, by e-mail, in person and via website
Hours: Mon to Fri, 0900 to 1700

Access for disabled people:
Parking provided, ramped entry, access to all public areas, toilet facilities

READING CENTRAL LIBRARY

Abbey Square, Reading, Berkshire, RG1 3BQ

Tel: 0118 901 5955
Fax: 0118 901 5954
E-mail: info@readinglibraries.org.uk

Website:
http://www.readinglibraries.org.uk

Enquiries:
Enquiries to: Librarian

Founded:
1883

Organisation type and purpose:
Local government body, public library.

Subject coverage:
General; business information; information on Reading and Berkshire.

Information services:
Internet access provided free of charge at branch libraries

Museum or gallery collection, archive, or library special collection:
Local Studies Library
Mary Russell Mitford collection
Vocal sets collection

Library catalogue:
All or part available online and in-house

Publications list:
Available in print

Access to staff:
Contact by letter, by telephone, by fax, by e-mail, in person and via website
Hours: Mon, Fri, 0900 to 1730; Tue, Thu, 0900 to 1900; Wed, 0900 to 1700; Sat, 0930 to 1700

Access to building, collection or gallery:
No access other than to staff
Hours: Mon, Fri, 0900 to 1730; Tue, Thu, 0900 to 1900; Wed, 0900 to 1700; Sat, 0930 to 1700

Access for disabled people:
Level entry, access to all public areas, toilet facilities

Branch libraries:
Battle Library
Caversham Library
Palmer Park Library
Southcote Library
Tilehurst Library
Whitley Library

Parent body:
Reading Borough Council
Civic Offices, Reading, Berkshire, RG1 7TD; tel: 0118 939 0900

RECORD OFFICE FOR LEICESTERSHIRE, LEICESTER AND RUTLAND

Long Street, Wigston Magna, Leicester, LE18 2AH

Tel: 0116 257 1080
Fax: 0116 257 1120
E-mail: recordoffice@leics.gov.uk

Enquiries:
Enquiries to: Chief Archivist
Other contacts: County Local Studies Librarian for printed material, not archives.

Organisation type and purpose:
Local government body.
Record Office.

Subject coverage:
Local archives and local studies including manuscripts, books, maps, photographs and all other archive material relating to Leicestershire, Leicester and Rutland.

Museum or gallery collection, archive, or library special collection:
Collections include:
Books, magazines and pamphlets on Leicestershire and Rutland
Census returns for Leicestershire and Rutland 1841 to 1901 on microform
Directories and electoral registers
Files of local newspapers
Illustrations of people and places
Oral history tapes and sound recordings
Ordnance Survey maps
Photographs and archive films
Archives of:
Leicestershire and Rutland County Councils
Borough of Leicester (from 1103)
Courts of Quarter Sessions and Petty Sessions
Poor Law Unions
Probate Registry (wills from 1858)
Anglican and nonconformist churches
Archdeaconry of Leicester (including wills and inventories from 1496)
Landed estates and families
Solicitors, commercial firms and manufacturers
Clubs, societies and other organisations
Military, Leicestershire Regiment

Non-library collection catalogue:
All or part available online and in-house

Library catalogue:
All or part available online and in-house

Printed publications:
Service leaflet (free)
Various pamphlets on aspects of the service and the stock

continued overleaf

Microform publications:
Microfiche of items in stock may be ordered

Access to staff:
Contact by letter, by telephone, by fax, by e-mail and in person
Hours: Mon, Tue, Thu, 0915 to 1700; Wed, 0915 to 1930; Fri, 0915 to 1645; Sat, 0915 to 1215
Special comments: Readers ticket required (proof of name and address is necessary).

Access for disabled people:
Parking provided, ramped entry, access to all public areas, toilet facilities

Part funded by:
Leicester City Council and Rutland County Council

Part of the:
Leicestershire County Council's Community Services

RECORD SOCIETY OF LANCASHIRE AND CHESHIRE

John Rylands University of Manchester Library, Oxford Road, Manchester, M13 9PP

E-mail: rslc@lineone.net

Enquiries:
Enquiries to: Council Secretary

Founded:
1878

Organisation type and purpose:
Membership association, registered charity (charity number 500434).
To transcribe and publish original documents relating to the two palatine counties.

Non-library collection catalogue:
All or part available online

Printed publications:
Over 140 volumes including (from vol 110):
A Lancashire weaver's journal, 1856–64, 1872–75 John O'Neil, Low Moor, Clitheroe (ed Brigg M, Vol 122, £7.50)
Index to wills and administrations formerly preserved in the probate registry, Chester, 1826–30 (ed Dickinson R, vol 113, £9)
Odyssey of an Edwardian Liberal: the political diary of Richard Durning Holt, MP (ed Dutton D J, Vol 129, £18)
Stockport probate records, 1578–1619 (eds Philips C B and Smith J H, Vol 124, £15)
The great diurnal of Nicholas Blundell of Little Crosby, 1702–28 (eds Tyrer F and Bagley J J, Vols 110,112,114, set £30)

Microform publications:
Volumes 1 to 109
Order microform publications from: Chadwyck-Healey Limited, The Quorum, Barnwell Road, Cambridge, CB5 8SW, tel: 01223 215512

Publications list:
Available online and in print

Access to staff:
Contact by letter and by e-mail
Hours: Mon to Fri, 0900 to 1700

RECRUITMENT AND EMPLOYMENT CONFEDERATION

Acronym or abbreviation: REC

3rd Floor, Steward House, 16a Commercial Way, Woking, Surrey, GU21 1ET

Tel: 020 7462 3260
Fax: 01483 714979
E-mail: info@rec.uk.com

Website:
http://www.rec.uk.com

Enquiries:
Enquiries to: Chief Executive

Founded:
1930

Organisation type and purpose:
Professional body (membership is by qualification), present number of members: 6000 Corporate, 7000 Individual, service industry, registered charity (charity number 803141), university department or institute, suitable for ages: 18+, training organisation.

Subject coverage:
Employment consultancy and agency practice; employment legislation relevant to employment agencies; professional qualifications in recruitment and employment agency practice.

Printed publications:
Distance learning materials
Recruitment Matters (magazine, for members)

Access to staff:
Contact by letter, by telephone, by fax, by e-mail and via website
Hours: Mon to Fri, 0830 to 1730

Other office:
REC
36–38 Mortimer Street, London, W1W 7RG; tel: 020 7462 3260; fax: 020 7255 2878

REDBRIDGE PUBLIC LIBRARIES

Central Library, Clements Road, Ilford, Essex, IG1 1EA

Tel: 020 8708 2414
Fax: 020 8708 2571
E-mail: central.library@redbridge.gov.uk

Website:
http://www.redbridge.gov.uk

Enquiries:
Enquiries to: Chief Librarian
Other contacts: Local Studies Librarian

Organisation type and purpose:
Public library.

Subject coverage:
General; social problems and services, local history of Redbridge, insurance, youth organisations, public health, family history.

Museum or gallery collection, archive, or library special collection:
Local History including part of the Brand Collection (Ilford and Essex history)

Non-library collection catalogue:
All or part available online and in-house

Library catalogue:
All or part available online

Access to staff:
Contact by letter, by telephone, by e-mail and in person
Hours: Mon to Fri, 0930 to 2000; Sat, 0930 to 1600

REDCAR AND CLEVELAND COUNCIL

Town Hall, Fabian Road, South Bank, Middlesbrough, Cleveland, TS6 9AR

Tel: 01642 444000
Fax: 01642 444584

Enquiries:
Enquiries to: Chief Executive

Organisation type and purpose:
Local government body.
Unitary authority.

Access to staff:
Contact by letter, by telephone and by fax.
Appointment necessary.
Hours: Mon to Fri, 0900 to 1700

REDCAR CENTRAL LIBRARY

Reference Library, Coatham Road, Redcar, Cleveland, TS10 1RP

Tel: 01642 489292

Fax: 01642 492253
E-mail: reference_library@redcar-cleveland.gov.uk

Website:
http://www.redcar-cleveland.gov.uk/libraries/index2.htm
Borough library services, including opening hours.

Enquiries:
Enquiries to: Librarian

Organisation type and purpose:
Local government body.
Public library.

Subject coverage:
General reference collection; local history collection, relating largely to North Yorkshire and East Cleveland area; family history resources.

Museum or gallery collection, archive, or library special collection:
Family History Resources: largely in microform, for East Cleveland area, some national coverage
Local history collection: mainly covering the old North Riding of Yorkshire, East Cleveland and the present borough

Non-library collection catalogue:
All or part available online and in-house

Library catalogue:
All or part available online

Access to staff:
Contact by letter, by telephone, by e-mail, in person and via website
Hours: Mon, Tue, Wed, Fri, 0930 to 1900; Thu, 0930 to 1700; Sat, 0930 to 1230
Special comments: Upstairs, lift available.

Access for disabled people:
Level entry, access to all public areas, toilet facilities

Connections with:
Redcar and Cleveland Borough Council
Chief Executive's Department, Redcar and Cleveland House, Kirkleatham Street, Redcar, TS10 1XX
Teesside Archives
Exchange House, 6 Marton Road, Middlesbrough, TS1 1DB; tel: 01642 248321; fax: 01642 248391; e-mail: teesside_archives@middlesbrough.gov.uk

REDDITCH LIBRARY

15 Market Place, Redditch, Worcestershire, B98 8AR

Tel: 01527 63291
Fax: 01527 68571
E-mail: redditchlib@worcestershire.gov.uk

Enquiries:
Enquiries to: Librarian

Organisation type and purpose:
Local government body, public library.

Subject coverage:
Local history of the Redditch area, including Bordesley Abbey, the needle industry, and Redditch New Town.

Museum or gallery collection, archive, or library special collection:
Needle District Almanacs (annual directories 1873–1936)
Redditch census schedules (1841–91)
Redditch Indicator (from 1859)

Non-library collection catalogue:
All or part available online

Library catalogue:
All or part available online

Access to staff:
Contact by letter
Hours: Mon, Thu, Fri, 0930 to 2000; Tue, Wed, 0930 to 1730; Sat, 0930 to 1730
Special comments: Proof of name and address required.

Parent body:
Worcestershire County Council

REFEREES' ASSOCIATION

1 Westhill Road, Coundon, Coventry,
Warwickshire, CV6 2AD

Tel: 024 7660 1701
Fax: 024 7660 1556
E-mail: ra@footballreferee.org

Website:
http://www.footballreferee.org

Enquiries:
Enquiries to: General Secretary
Direct e-mail: arthur@footballreferee.org

Founded:
1908

Organisation type and purpose:
Membership association (membership is by
subscription), training organisation.

Subject coverage:
Implementation of the laws of association football.
Recruitment and training of referees.

Printed publications:
Refereeing (a joint publication with the FA,
  quarterly)

Access to staff:
Contact by letter, by telephone, by fax and by e-
mail. Appointment necessary.
Hours: Mon to Fri, 0830 to 1630

REFINED SUGAR ASSOCIATION

Acronym or abbreviation: RSA

154 Bishopsgate, London, EC2M 4LN

Tel: 020 7377 2113
Fax: 020 7247 2481
E-mail: durhamn@sugar-assoc.co.uk

Enquiries:
Enquiries to: Secretary

Founded:
1891

Organisation type and purpose:
International organisation, trade association
(membership is by election or invitation), present
number of members: 115.

Subject coverage:
Sugar.

REFRACTORY USERS FEDERATION

Acronym or abbreviation: RUF

5th Floor, Broadway House, Tothill Street, London,
SW1H 9NQ

Tel: 020 7799 2020
Fax: 020 7233 1930

Enquiries:
Enquiries to: Executive Secretary

Founded:
1945

Organisation type and purpose:
Trade association (membership is by subscription),
present number of members: 10.

Subject coverage:
Matters relating to refractory contracting,
industrial relations, terms and conditions of
employment for refractory bricklayers and
labourers, and training.

Printed publications:
Blue Booklet Agreement (for refractory bricklayers)
Red Booklet Agreement (for bricklayers labourers)

Access to staff:
Contact by letter, by telephone and by fax
Hours: Mon to Fri, 0900 to 1700

REFUGEE COUNCIL

Acronym or abbreviation: BRC

240–250 Ferndale Road, Brixton, London, SW9 8BB

Tel: 020 7346 6700
Fax: 020 7346 6701

Website:
http://www.refugeecouncil.org.uk

Enquiries:
Enquiries to: Media Officer
Direct tel: 020 7346 1213
Direct e-mail: hannah.ward@refugeecouncil.org.uk

Organisation type and purpose:
Voluntary organisation, registered charity (charity
number 1014576).

Subject coverage:
Asylum and refugee issues in the UK.

Non-library collection catalogue:
All or part available in-house

Library catalogue:
All or part available in-house

Printed publications:
iNexile (magazine on refugee and asylum issues, 6
  times a year)
Order printed publications from: Publications
Assistant, Refugee Council
at same address, tel: 020 7820 3042

Publications list:
Available online and in print

Access to staff:
Contact by letter, by telephone, by fax, by e-mail
and in person. Appointment necessary.
Hours: Mon to Fri, 1000 to 1700

Access to building, collection or gallery:
No prior appointment required

Member of:
European Council on Refugees and Exiles (ECRE)
Human Rights Documentation Systems
International Refugee Documentation Network
(IRDN)

REGENT'S COLLEGE LIBRARY

Library, Inner Circle, Regent's Park, London, NW1
4NS

Tel: 020 7487 7448

Website:
http://www.regents.ac.uk/library.htm
Library home page.

Enquiries:
Enquiries to: Head Librarian
Direct e-mail: collinsm@regents.ac.uk

Founded:
1985

Organisation type and purpose:
College of higher education.

Subject coverage:
Business, management, psychotherapy and
counselling.

Non-library collection catalogue:
All or part available online

Library catalogue:
All or part available online

Access to staff:
Contact by letter, by telephone and by e-mail.
Appointment necessary. Access for members only.
Hours: Mon to Fri, 0900 to 1700

REGIMENTAL OFFICE ROYAL IRISH REGIMENT

5 Waring Street, Belfast, BT1 2EW

Tel: 028 9023 2086
Fax: 028 9023 2086
E-mail: nirmuseum@yahoo.co.uk

Website:
http://rurmuseum.tripod.com/

Enquiries:
Enquiries to: Curator

Organisation type and purpose:
Professional body.

Subject coverage:
History of the Royal Irish Regiment and the Royal
Ulster Rifles.

REGISTER OF APPAREL AND TEXTILE DESIGNERS

Acronym or abbreviation: RATD

5 Portland Place, London, W1B 1PW

Tel: 020 7636 5577
Fax: 020 7636 7848
E-mail: laurian.daries@ukfe.5portlandplace.org.uk

Enquiries:
Enquiries to: Manager

Founded:
1986

Organisation type and purpose:
Trade association (membership is by subscription),
present number of members: over 400, consultancy.

Subject coverage:
Design; clothing; textiles; printed textiles; woven
textiles; sourcing freelance designers for
manufacturers and retailers in the UK and
overseas; help and advice to freelance designers
who are members of the Register.

**Museum or gallery collection, archive, or library
special collection:**
Library of information relevant to freelance
  designers

Printed publications:
Specialist Services Directory
Newsletter

Publications list:
Available in print

Access to staff:
Contact by letter, by telephone, by fax and by e-
mail. Appointment necessary. Access for members
only.
Hours: Mon to Fri, 0900 to 1700
Special comments: Access only available to members
of the Register of Apparel and Textile Designers.

Access to building, collection or gallery:
No prior appointment required

Parent bodies:
British Clothing Industry Association
  tel: 020 7636 7515
UK Fashion Exports
  tel: 020 7636 5577

REGISTER OF UNUSUAL MICRO-CARS

Acronym or abbreviation: RUM Cars

School House Farm, Boarden Lane, Hawkenbury,
Staplehurst, Kent, TN12 0EB

Tel: 01580 891377
E-mail: jeanrumcars@cs.com

Enquiries:
Enquiries to: Secretary
Other contacts: Editor tel: 01908 321737 for
magazine input.

Founded:
1980

Organisation type and purpose:
National organisation, membership association
(membership is by subscription).

continued overleaf

Subject coverage:
Three and four wheeled post-war (1947 onwards) road going vehicles with engines of 700cc or less, manufactured in small numbers, small electric vehicles and invalid carriages.

Museum or gallery collection, archive, or library special collection:
Sales brochure, contemporary road tests etc, originals and photostats of magazine articles on all kinds of micro-cars

Printed publications:
RUM Car News (magazine, quarterly)

Access to staff:
Contact by letter, by telephone and by e-mail. Appointment necessary.
Hours: any day, before 2030

Access to building, collection or gallery:
Prior appointment required

REGISTERED NURSING HOME ASSOCIATION

Acronym or abbreviation: RNHA

John Hewitt House, Tunnel Lane, Kings Norton, Birmingham, B30 3JN

Tel: 0121 451 1088
Fax: 0121 486 3175
E-mail: info@rnha.co.uk

Website:
http://www.rnha.co.uk

Enquiries:
Enquiries to: Chief Executive

Founded:
1968

Organisation type and purpose:
Advisory body, trade association (membership is by subscription), present number of members: 1400, service industry.
Independent nursing homes, clinics and hospitals registered under the Care Standards Act 2000.

Subject coverage:
Advice and support, including legal advice, to members; assistance to members of the public in looking for a place in a nursing home; lobbying government and other official bodies.

Library catalogue:
All or part available in-house

Printed publications:
Courier-Bulletin (members only)
Nursing Home News (newspaper, members only, 6 times a year)
Operating Manual (guidelines and standard forms, members only)
Reference Book (£50 to non-members)
Special studies

Publications list:
Available in print

Access to staff:
Contact by letter, by telephone, by fax and by e-mail. Appointment necessary.
Hours: Mon to Thur, 0830 to 1630; Fri, 0830 to 1600

Access for disabled people:
Parking provided

Founder member of:
Independent Care Organisations Network (ICON)
Joint Care Council (JCC)

REGISTRAR OF PUBLIC LENDING RIGHT

Acronym or abbreviation: PLR

Richard House, Sorbonne Close, Stockton-on-Tees, TS17 6DA

Tel: 01642 604699
Fax: 01642 615641
E-mail: theregistrar@plr.uk.com

Website:
http://www.plr.uk.com
The registration service; library information; all about PLR; media centre.

Enquiries:
Enquiries to: Registrar's Personal Assistant

Founded:
1979

Organisation type and purpose:
National government body.
Makes payments to authors for loans of their books from public libraries.

Subject coverage:
Public library book issues and associated statistics.

Printed publications:
Writers Talk
Annual Press Release
Annual Report and Accounts
Information for Authors leaflet
Whose Loan is it Anyway, Essays in Celebration of PLR's 20th Anniversary

Publications list:
Available in print

Access to staff:
Contact by letter, by telephone, by fax, by e-mail and via website. Appointment necessary.
Hours: Mon to Thu, 0900 to 1700; Fri, 0900 to 1630

Funded by:
Department for Culture, Media and Sport
tel: 020 7211 6000; fax: 020 7211 6210

REGISTRY TRUST LIMITED

Acronym or abbreviation: RTL

173–175 Cleveland Street, London, W1T 6QR

Tel: 020 7380 0133
Fax: 020 7388 0672
E-mail: info@registry-trust.org.uk

Website:
http://www.registry-trust.org.uk

Enquiries:
Enquiries to: Customer Services Manager

Founded:
1986

Organisation type and purpose:
Registry of Judgments, Orders and Fines (England and Wales)
Register of Decrees (Scotland)
Registers of Judgments (Northern Ireland, Republic of Ireland, Jersey and Isle of Man)

Subject coverage:
Court money judgments

Access to staff:
Contact by letter, by telephone, by e-mail, in person and via website. All charged.
Hours: Mon to Fri, 1000 to 1600

Access to building, collection or gallery:
Hours: Mon to Fri, 1000 to 1600

RELATE

Herbert Gray College, Little Church Street, Rugby, Warwickshire, CV21 3AP

Tel: 01788 573241
Fax: 01788 535007
E-mail: enquiries@relate.org.uk

Website:
http://www.relate.org.uk
Relate centre addresses. Relate bookshop information. Training.

Enquiries:
Enquiries to: Information Officer
Other contacts: Communications Assistant

Founded:
1938

Organisation type and purpose:
Registered charity, training organisation.
Co-ordinates the activities of local marriage guidance centres.

Subject coverage:
Relationship counselling, marriage, family life and personal relationships and educational programmes related to those relationships, sexual problems, divorce, stress and depression.

Printed publications:
Large range of books available through bookshop, Rugby

Access to staff:
Contact by letter, by telephone, by fax and by e-mail. Appointment necessary.
Hours: Mon to Fri, 0900 to 1700

Access to building, collection or gallery:
No access other than to staff

Other addresses:
Local centres in England, Wales and Northern Ireland (see Yellow Pages)

RELATIVES AND RESIDENTS ASSOCIATION

Acronym or abbreviation: RRA

5 Tavistock Place, London, WC1H 9SN

Tel: 020 7692 4302 (admin)
Fax: 020 7916 6093
E-mail: relres@totalise.co.uk

Enquiries:
Enquiries to: Administrator
Other contacts: Advice Line Worker/Co-ordinator for advice offered to callers on the advice line.

Founded:
1992

Organisation type and purpose:
National organisation, membership association (membership is by subscription), voluntary organisation, registered charity (charity number 1020194).

Subject coverage:
Issues relating to long-term care for older people in, or considering admission to, residential or nursing homes. Offers mutual support and advice, facilitates the setting up of groups of relatives in homes. Has a Black and minority ethnic involvement and guides for good practice.

Printed publications:
Involving Relatives and Friends (book, 2001, £10)
As Others See Us (research study including keynote messages, report training pack £26 for members, £29 for non-members, report alone, £10 and £11 respectively, keynote messages £4 for both members and non-members)
Setting Up Relatives' Groups in Homes (1996, £2.50 members, £3 non-members)
Starting up a Local Group (£3 members, £3.50 non-members)
I Have Come to Visit my Wife (Koschland B, 1996, £2 members, £2.50 non-members)
African Caribbean Elders Directory of Sheltered, Very Sheltered Housing, Residential Care Homes & One Nursing Care Unit (£2.50 members, £3 non-members)
Introductory leaflets (free to individuals, bulk copies available to other organisations: 25 for £3, 50 for £6 and 100 for £12)
Changes and Challenges in Later Life (£10 inc. p&p)

Publications list:
Available in print

Access to staff:
Contact by letter, by telephone and by e-mail
Hours: Advice Line: Mon to Fri, 1000 to 1230 and 1330 to 1700
Admin: Mon to Fri, 0900 to 1700

Access to building, collection or gallery:
No access other than to staff

RELIEF FUND FOR ROMANIA

Acronym or abbreviation: RFFR

54–62 Regent Street, London, W1B 5RE

Tel: 020 7733 7018
Fax: 020 7737 4960
E-mail: mail@relieffundforromania.co.uk

Website:
http://www.relieffundforromania.co.uk

Enquiries:
Enquiries to: Executive Director
Other contacts: Project Director for grant
applications.

Founded:
1989

Organisation type and purpose:
International organisation, registered charity
(charity number 1046737).

Subject coverage:
Aid and development for children and adults in
Romania's institutions, focus on medical
improvements, mental health, disabled issues and
groups, funding emerging Romanian NGO sector.

**Museum or gallery collection, archive, or library
special collection:**
Photo library and videos of Romanian institutions
1989 to present day
Press cuttings of socio-political and charity subjects
from 1989 to present

Access to staff:
Contact by letter, by telephone and by fax
Hours: Mon to Fri, 0930 to 1830

RELIGIOUS EDUCATION

University of Birmingham, Selly Oak Campus,
Weoley Park Road, Birmingham, B29 6LL

Tel: 0121 415 8290
Fax: 0121 414 5619
E-mail: g.m.teece@bham.ac.uk

Enquiries:
Enquiries to: Head of Centre
Direct e-mail: c.b.oconnor@bham.ac.uk

Founded:
1974

Formerly called:
Regional Religious Education Centre (Midlands)
(year of change 1994)

Organisation type and purpose:
University department or institute.
To promote good practice in religious education.

Subject coverage:
Multi-faith religious education, moral education,
personal and social development in education,
research and curriculum development.

**Museum or gallery collection, archive, or library
special collection:**
Artefacts
Audio cassettes
Posters
Slides
Videos

Printed publications:
How do I teach RE? (teacher's manual, £10)
How to Write Your School Policy for RE (£10)
Primary Resource packs on Islam and Hinduism
Teacher's manuals on Christianity, Islam and
Judaism (£11.50 each)
Westhill Project: RE 5–16 Teachers and pupils
books and photopacks (major religious and life
themes)

Access to staff:
Contact by letter, by telephone, by fax, by e-mail
and in person. Appointment necessary.
Hours: Mon to Fri, 0900 to 1700

Connections with:
National Association of SACREs (NASACRE)

RELIGIOUS SOCIETY OF FRIENDS (QUAKERS) – BRITAIN YEARLY MEETING

Friends House, 173–177 Euston Road, London,
NW1 2BJ

Tel: 020 7663 1135
Fax: 020 7663 1001
E-mail: library@quaker.org.uk

Website:
http://www.quaker.org.uk
Basic library information, as part of British Quaker
website.

Enquiries:
Enquiries to: Librarian
Direct tel: 020 7663 1135

Founded:
1650s

Organisation type and purpose:
Membership association, present number of
members: c 16,500, voluntary organisation,
registered charity (charity number Exempt from
registration).
Library for the storage and dissemination of
information about Quakers; point of contact for the
Friends Historical Society.

Subject coverage:
Quakers, especially Quaker thought, history and
Quakerism, peace, anti-slavery, conscription.

**Museum or gallery collection, archive, or library
special collection:**
Central archives of the Society in Britain
Digest registers of births, marriages and burials on
microfilm (search fee payable)
Local Quaker archives for London and Middlesex
area
Manuscripts, tracts and pictures
Printed material on Quakers since the mid-17th
century
Records of other bodies with Quaker associations

Non-library collection catalogue:
All or part available online and in-house

Library catalogue:
All or part available in-house

Printed publications:
The following leaflets are also on the Library
website:
Library Rules
Genealogical Sources
Picture Collection
Photocopying and microfilm printouts
The Quaker Calendar – dating of Quaker
documents
Quaker Schools in GB and Ireland
Conscientious Objectors and the Peace Movement
in Britain 1914–1945
Sources: Abolition of the Slave Trade

Microform publications:
Quaker collections on sale by World Microfilms
(London W9 2HH) and Academic Microforms
(Wick, Scotland KW1 4DD)
Early English Books (University Microfilms
International)
Film copies of some central archives
The Quaker Manuscript Collection (World
Microfilms, London)
Quaker Official Correspondence (Academic
Microforms, Wick)
Some MSS collections and other materials available
direct

Access to staff:
Contact by letter, by telephone, by fax and by e-
mail. Letter of introduction required.
Hours: Mon, Tue, Thu, Fri, 1300 to 1700; Wed, 1000
to 1700;
Mon to Fri, 0930 to 1700 for telephone queries
Special comments: Letter of introduction required
for research. Archives and manuscripts under 50
years old are not normally open.

Access for disabled people:
Level entry, toilet facilities

Special comments: Access to library reading room;
access to basement café by lift only.

The main departments are:
Quaker Communications
Quaker Employment and Service
Quaker Finance and Property
Quaker Life
Quaker Peace and Social Witness
Recording Clerk's Office

REMAP

Formal name: Technical Help for Disabled People

D9, Chaucer Business Park, Kemsing, Sevenoaks,
Kent, TN15 6YU

Tel: 0845 130 0456
Fax: 0845 130 0789
E-mail: data@remap.org.uk

Website:
http://www.remap.org.uk
Basic information and area contacts throughout the
UK.

Founded:
1964

Organisation type and purpose:
Registered charity (charity number 1000456). Has
107 branches (panels) across UK.

Subject coverage:
Design, manufacture and supply or adaptation of
equipment to meet the individual needs of a
disabled person when there is no suitable
equipment on the market; no general information.

Printed publications:
Yearbook and leaflets

Publications list:
Available in print

Access to staff:
Contact by letter, by telephone, by fax and by e-
mail
Hours: Mon to Thu, 0930 to 1600; 24-hour
answerphone

REMOTE SENSING AND PHOTOGRAMMETRY SOCIETY, THE

Acronym or abbreviation: RSPSoc

School of Geography, University of Nottingham,
University Park, Nottingham, NG7 2RD

Tel: 0115 951 5435
Fax: 0115 951 5249
E-mail: rspsoc@nottingham.ac.uk

Website:
http://www.rspsoc.org
Home page.

Enquiries:
Enquiries to: Honorary Secretary

Founded:
2001

Organisation type and purpose:
Learned society (membership is by subscription),
present number of members: 1000, registered
charity (charity number 292647).

Subject coverage:
Remote sensing; sensors; platforms; image
processing; interpretation equipment; resource
surveys; applications of remote sensing in land
use, soil mapping, geology, geomorphology,
hydrology, meteorology, oceanography;
monitoring of pollution and natural hazards;
organisations worldwide, photogrammetry.

Printed publications:
Annual Conference Proceedings
Newsletter (quarterly; includes list of publications)
The International Journal of Remote Sensing
The Photogrammetric Record (4 times a year)

continued overleaf

Publications list:
Available online

Access to staff:
Contact by letter, by telephone, by fax and by e-mail
Hours: Mon to Fri, 0900 to 1700

Associate member of:
International Society for Photogrammetry and Remote Sensing
Joint Branch of International Remote Sensing Activities (JOBRESA)

Representation on:
British National Committee for Photogrammetry and Remote Sensing

RENAL ASSOCIATION, THE

Acronym or abbreviation: RA

Secretariat, Durford Mill, Petersfield, Hampshire, GU31 5AZ

Tel: 0870 458 4155
Fax: 0870 442 9940
E-mail: renal@mci-group.com

Website:
http://www.renal.org

Enquiries:
Enquiries to: General Secretary

Founded:
1950

Organisation type and purpose:
Learned society, registered charity (charity number 800733).

Subject coverage:
Research into renal disease, treatment of renal disease.

Printed publications:
Proceedings of the Association's Scientific Meetings are published in Kidney International
Provision of Services for Patients with Renal Failure (£6)
Treatment of Adult Patients with Renal Failure (£6)

Access to staff:
Contact by letter, by telephone, by fax and by e-mail
Hours: Mon to Fri, 0900 to 1700

Affiliated to:
European Renal Association
International Society of Nephrology

RENAULT CLASSIC CAR CLUB

Acronym or abbreviation: RCCC

5 Evesham Walk, Sandhurst, Berkshire, GU47 0YU

Website:
http://www.renaultclassiccarclub.com
Contact information, pictures and descriptions of models covered, links to other sites.

Enquiries:
Enquiries to: Membership Secretary

Founded:
2001

Organisation type and purpose:
International organisation, membership association (membership is by subscription), present number of members: 70.
Restoration and use of rear-engine Renaults, parts supply and advice, general purchase advice, workshop manuals – printed or on CD-ROM.

Subject coverage:
Restoration and use of classic rear-engine Renaults, parts availability, technical information, buying and selling of parts and cars. Anything that will assist members keeping rear-engine Renault cars on the road.

Museum or gallery collection, archive, or library special collection:
Various technical and workshop manuals

Printed publications:
Club Magazine
Workshop Manuals (enquire for prices)

Electronic and video publications:
Workshop Manuals (CD-ROM, enquire for prices)

Access to staff:
Contact by letter, by e-mail and via website
Hours: Mon to Fri, 0900 to 1700

RENFREWSHIRE COUNCIL

Council Headquarters, North Building, Cotton Street, Paisley, Renfrewshire, PA1 1WB

Tel: 0141 842 5000
Fax: 0141 840 3335
E-mail: chiefexec@renfrewshire.gov.uk

Website:
http://www.renfrewshire.gov.uk
Main headings: Welcome to Renfrewshire; The Council; Renfrewshire Magazine; What's On; Contact Us; The Millennium.

Enquiries:
Enquiries to: Chief Executive
Direct tel: 0141 840 3213
Direct fax: 0141 840 3349

Founded:
April 1996

Organisation type and purpose:
Local government body.

Access to staff:
Contact by letter, by telephone, by fax and in person
Hours: Mon to Thu, 0845 to 1645; Fri, 0845 to 1555

RENFREWSHIRE LIBRARY SERVICE

Abbey House, 8A Seedhill Road, Paisley, Renfrewshire, PA1 1AJ

Tel: 0141 840 3003
Fax: 0141 840 3004
E-mail: libraries.els@renfrewshire.gov.uk

Website:
http://www.renfrewshire.gov.uk
Council website, information on services.

Enquiries:
Enquiries to: Libraries Manager

Organisation type and purpose:
Local government body, public library.

Subject coverage:
General reference; local history; local government; community services; welfare; information for the elderly; library automation.

Museum or gallery collection, archive, or library special collection:
Bannatyne Club collection
Gardner collection (books printed in Paisley)
Local newspapers on microfiche
Maitland Club collection
Rowat collection

Library catalogue:
All or part available online and in-house

Access to staff:
Contact by letter, by telephone, by fax, by e-mail, in person and via website
Hours: Mon to Thu, 0900 to 1700; Fri, 0900 to 1600

Parent body:
Renfrewshire Council
Education and Leisure Services

RENOLD PLC

Renold House, Styal Road, Wythenshawe, Manchester, M22 5WL

Tel: 0161 498 4500
Fax: 0161 437 7782
E-mail: enquiry@renold.com

Website:
http://www.renold.com

Enquiries:
Enquiries to: Marketing Manager
Direct tel: 0161 498 4531

Organisation type and purpose:
International organisation, manufacturing industry.

Subject coverage:
All aspects of mechanical power transmission, including: roller chains, wheels and pinions; conveying and elevating chains and wheels; gears; worm gear speed reducers; worm gear sets; spur, helical and spiral bevel gearboxes; shaft mounted gear units; geared motors; variable speed drives, couplings, clutches and brakes; sprag clutches for over-running, indexing and backstopping; vibratory shaker drives; power transmission accessories; machine tools; helical rotors for air compressors.

Museum or gallery collection, archive, or library special collection:
Fully classified catalogue collection of archival material relating to the establishment of the power transmission industry in the UK in the late 19th century

Publications list:
Available in print

Access to staff:
Contact by letter, by telephone, by e-mail and via website
Hours: Mon to Thu, 0900 to 1700; Fri, 0900 to 1600

REPETITIVE STRAIN INJURY AWARENESS

Acronym or abbreviation: RSI Awareness

Keytools Ltd, Abacus House, 1 Spring Crescent, Southampton, SO17 2FZ

Tel: 023 8029 4500
Fax: 023 8029 4501
E-mail: rsia@keytools.co.uk

Website:
http://rsi.org.uk

Enquiries:
Enquiries to: Director

Founded:
1989

Formerly called:
Repetitive Strain Injury Association

Organisation type and purpose:
To provide advice, information and support from those concerned about repetitive strain injury.

Subject coverage:
Repetitive strain injuries.

Information services:
Information website, events, advice, workshops, support groups.

Non-library collection catalogue:
All or part available online

Printed publications:
Factsheets (free)
Order printed publications from: Website (factsheets available for download)

Publications list:
Available online and in print

Access to staff:
Contact by letter, by telephone, by fax, by e-mail and via website
Hours: Mon to Fri, 0900 to 1700

Access to building, collection or gallery:
Prior appointment required

Access for disabled people:
Disabled access available
Special comments: By appointment.

RESCUE – THE BRITISH ARCHAEOLOGICAL TRUST

Acronym or abbreviation: RESCUE

15a Bull Plain, Hertford, SG14 1DX

Tel: 01992 553377
E-mail: rescue@rescue-archaeology.freeserve.co.uk

Website:
http://www.rescue-archaeology.freeserve.co.uk
Basic information.

Enquiries:
Enquiries to: Membership Secretary

Founded:
1972

Organisation type and purpose:
National organisation, membership association
(membership is by subscription), registered charity
(charity number 1064836).
Independent charitable trust.
To promote and foster the discovery, excavation,
preservation, recording and study of archaeology
in Great Britain for the public benefit.

Subject coverage:
Organisation and funding of archaeology
legislation and archaeology, current archaeological
projects and news, recording methods, artefact
excavation and storage methods.

Printed publications:
Competitive Tendering in Archaeology (£2.45
members, £2.95 non-members)
Conference Proceedings
First Aid for Finds (Watkinson. David & Neal,
Virginia, £18 members, £21 non-members)
Recording Standing Buildings (Hutton B, £1.90
members, £2.90 non-members)
Rescuing the Historic Environment (ed Hedley
Swain, £6.50)
A Manual of Archaeological Field Drawing
(Hawker J M, £18 members, £21 non-members)
The Rescue Questionnaire 1990–1991 (Spoerry P,
£2.95 members, £3.45 non-members)
The Southern Feeder: The Archaeology of a Gas
Pipeline (£4)

Publications list:
Available online and in print

Access to staff:
Contact by letter
Hours: Mon, Fri, 0900 to 1700; Wed, morning only;
answerphone when office closed

RESEARCH AND DEVELOPMENT SOCIETY

Acronym or abbreviation: R&D Society

6–9 Carlton House Terrace, London, SW1Y 5AG

Tel: 020 7451 2513
E-mail: rdsociety@royalsociety.org

Website:
http://www.rdsoc.org

Enquiries:
Enquiries to: Administrative Secretary

Founded:
1962

Formerly called:
London Group for the Study of the Administration
of Research and Development (LGARD) (year of
change 1964)

Organisation type and purpose:
Learned society, membership association
(membership by application), present number of
members: 360.

Subject coverage:
Research and development, largely industrial;
R&D management; science policy.

**Museum or gallery collection, archive, or library
special collection:**
Symposium Proceedings (9 vols, 1976–87)

Printed publications:
Newsletter (3 times a year, available by
subscription)

Access to staff:
Contact by letter, by telephone, by fax and by e-
mail
Hours: Mon to Fri, 0900 to 1700

Access to building, collection or gallery:
No access other than to staff

RESEARCH DEFENCE SOCIETY

Acronym or abbreviation: RDS

25 Shaftesbury Avenue, London, W1D 7EG

Tel: 020 7287 2818
Fax: 020 7287 2627
E-mail: rds@rds-net.org.uk

Website:
http://www.rds-online.org.uk/

Enquiries:
Enquiries to: Executive Director

Founded:
1908

Organisation type and purpose:
Membership association, present number of
members: 9800.

Subject coverage:
Experimental research involving the use of
animals; regulations and conditions under which
such work is conducted in the UK; importance of
such experiments to the welfare of mankind and
animals; welfare of laboratory animals; proposed
legislative changes; development of alternative
methods.

Access to staff:
Contact by letter, by telephone, by fax, by e-mail
and via website
Hours: Mon to Fri, 0900 to 1700

RESEARCH INSTITUTE FOR INDUSTRY

Acronym or abbreviation: RIfI

School of Engineering Sciences, University of
Southampton, Southampton, SO17 1BJ

Tel: 023 8059 7052
Fax: 023 8059 7051
E-mail: rifi@soton.ac.uk

Website:
http://www.rifi.soton.ac.uk

Founded:
2002

Organisation type and purpose:
University department or institute, consultancy.
To offer to industry the facilities and expertise of
the School of Engineering Sciences at the
University of Southampton on an applied research
or consultancy basis.

Subject coverage:
Composite fabrication and testing, computational
fluid dynamics, cryogenics, refrigeration and
engineering for low temperatures, electrochemical
engineering, electromechanical systems, energy
systems, erosion and corrosion, fuel cells and
batteries, engineering design and analysis,
engineering materials, experimental mechanics,
failure analysis and mechanical property
determination, finite element analysis, marine
technology and industrial aerodynamics, micro
electro-mechanical systems (MEMS), nano-
indentation, surface engineering and tribology,
software engineering, materials testing,
metallographic examination and analysis, fatigue,
creep fracture, fracture mechanics, corrosion, wear,
surface treatments, heat treatment, welding,
significance of defects, plastics, composites,
electron microscopy, electron microprobe analysis,
failure analysis, machinability and surfacing.

Access to staff:
Contact by letter, by telephone, by fax and by e-
mail. Appointment necessary.
Hours: Mon to Fri, 0900 to 1700

RESEARCH INTO AGEING

Acronym or abbreviation: RiA

207–221 Pentonville Road, London, N1 9UZ

Tel: 020 7239 1895
E-mail: helen.rippon@ageing.org

Website:
http://www.ageing.org/
http://research.helptheaged.org.uk/

Enquiries:
Enquiries to: Head of Research
Direct tel: 020 7239 1896
Direct e-mail: james.goodwin@helptheaged.org.uk
Other contacts: Information and Projects Manager

Founded:
1976

Organisation type and purpose:
Voluntary organisation, registered charity (charity
number 277468), suitable for ages: 45+, research
organisation.
Raises funds to support medical research to
investigate the common diseases and disabilities of
later life.

Subject coverage:
Research into age-related disease and disability.
Makes grants for medical research into diseases of
the older generations; osteoporosis, bone disease
and loss, visual problems in old age, reaction to
drugs, hypothermia, incontinence, loss of smell
and taste, exercise and mobility, dementia
(including Alzheimer's Disease), nutrition, cellular
ageing, urinary incontinence, leg ulcers,
breathlessness, nutrition, pressure sores and the
ageing process itself.

Trade and statistical information:
Ageing epidemiology/demography, health/
diseases in later life.

Printed publications:
Research into Ageing News (newsletter, quarterly)
Annual Report
Exercise for Healthy Ageing (booklet, £5 inc. p&p)
General purpose leaflet (free)
12 Healthy ageing leaflets (free, with a large sae)
Life is for living, and then? (legacy pack, free)
List of sponsored research projects

Electronic and video publications:
More Active More Often: video on chair-based
activity (suggested donation of £10 inc. p&p)

Publications list:
Available in print

Access to staff:
Contact by letter, by telephone, by fax and by e-
mail. Appointment necessary.
Hours: Mon to Fri, 0930 to 1730

Funded by:
Help the Aged
As above

RESTAURANT ASSOCIATION

Acronym or abbreviation: RA

c/o BHA, Queens House, 55–56 Lincoln's Inn
Fields, London, WC2A 3BH

Tel: 0207 404 7744
Fax: 0207 404 7799
E-mail: bha@bha.org.uk

Website:
http://www.ragb.co.uk

Enquiries:
Enquiries to: Commercial Manager
Direct e-mail: pauline.jackson@bha.org.uk
Other contacts: Communications and IT Manager
for publications and website.

continued overleaf

Founded:
1967

Rejoined the British Hospitality Association (broke away to form the Restaurant Association of Great Britain in 1967):
(year of change 2003)

Organisation type and purpose:
National organisation, advisory body, trade association (membership is by subscription), present number of members: 3000, service industry, research organisation, publishing house.

Subject coverage:
Restaurant industry in Britain.

Trade and statistical information:
Size, diversity, performance and trends of restaurant industry in Britain.

Printed publications:
Dine Out (magazine, quarterly, £2.50)
Digest (newsletter, monthly)
Gold Standard Restaurant Industry Report (annually, £95)
Guidance Notes on recent regulation/legislation (time to time)

Access to staff:
Contact by letter, by telephone, by fax and by e-mail
Hours: Mon to Fri, 0900 to 1730

Trading division of:
British Hospitality Association

RESTORMEL BOROUGH COUNCIL

Borough Offices, Penwinnick Road, St Austell, Cornwall, PL25 5DR

Tel: 01726 223300
Fax: 01726 223301
E-mail: rbc@restormel.gov.uk

Website:
http://www.restormel.gov.uk

Enquiries:
Enquiries to: Chief Executive

Founded:
1974

Organisation type and purpose:
Local government body.

Subject coverage:
All local government issues.

Printed publications:
Corporate Plan
Best Value Performance Plan
Housing Srategy
LA21 Strategy
Taking Stock
Order printed publications from: Corporate Policy Officer, Restormel Borough Council Penwinnick Road, St Austell, Cornwall, PL25 5DR, tel: 01726 223514, fax: 01726 223526, e-mail: fbowler@restormel.gov.uk

Access to staff:
Contact by letter, by telephone, by fax, by e-mail, in person and via website. Appointment necessary.
Hours: Mon to Fri, 0900 to 1700

Access for disabled people:
Parking provided, ramped entry, access to all public areas, toilet facilities

Also at:
Tourism & Publicity Offices
Marcus Hill, Newquay, Cornwall, TR7 1AF; tel: 01637 854000; fax: 01637 854044; e-mail: holidaytime@newquay.org.uk

RETAIL INTELLIGENCE WORLDWIDE

Acronym or abbreviation: RIW Research

Richmond Bridge House, 419 Richmond Road, Twickenham, TW1 2EX

Tel: 020 3005 9862
E-mail: monica.woods@riwresearch.com

Website:
http://www.riwresearch.com

Founded:
1975

Organisation type and purpose:
Information broker.
Specialist retail consulting firm.

Subject coverage:
European retailing and consumer goods research service; information available on companies, distribution, food and drink, leisure, DIY, mail order, clothing, convenience stores, CTNs, newsagents, department stores, electrical stores, footwear, furniture, health and beauty, jewellery, opticians, variety stores, off-licences.

Information services:
Specialist desk research service on retail and consumer markets around the world

Museum or gallery collection, archive, or library special collection:
Photographic collection of retailers around the world, over 300,000 images

Trade and statistical information:
Information available for all sectors listed.

Library catalogue:
All or part available in-house

Printed publications:
Shopping Index available on the United Kingdom, France, Germany, Italy, Spain and Ireland

Publications list:
Available in print

Access to staff:
Contact by telephone, by fax and by e-mail
Hours: Mon to Fri, 0900 to 1730

RETAIL MOTOR INDUSTRY FEDERATION

Acronym or abbreviation: RMIF

201 Great Portland Street, London, W1W 5AB

Tel: 020 7580 9122
Fax: 020 7580 6376
E-mail: firstnamelastname@rmif.co.uk

Website:
http://www.rmif.co.uk

Founded:
1913

Organisation type and purpose:
Trade association.

Subject coverage:
UK retail motor industry – sales, service and maintenance of new and used cars, trucks and motorcycles, and associated activities.

Trade and statistical information:
Data on sales and service in the UK motor industry.

Printed publications:
Auto Technician (6 times a year, for members)
Forecourt (monthly, for members)
RM Eye (monthly, for members)

Access to staff:
Contact by letter, by telephone, by fax and by e-mail
Hours: Mon to Fri, 0900 to 1700

Members:
Bodyshop Services Division (BSD)
Cherished Numbers Dealers Association (CNDA)
Independent Garage Division (IGD)
Motorcycle Retailers Association (MRA)
Motorcycle Rider Training Association (MRTA)
National Franchised Dealers Association (NFDA)
Petrol Retailers Association (PRA)
Society of Motor Auctions (SMA)

RETHINK

28 Castle Street, Kingston upon Thames, Surrey, KT1 1SS

Tel: 0845 456 0455
Fax: 020 8547 3862
E-mail: info@rethink.org

Website:
http://www.rethink.org

Founded:
1972

Organisation type and purpose:
Membership association (membership is by subscription), present number of members: 7,500, voluntary organisation, registered charity (charity number 271028). Organisation for people with a severe mental illness, their families and carers; membership £15 pa/£6 unwaged.
To help everyone affected by severe mental illness, including schizophrenia, to recover a better quality of life.

Subject coverage:
Schizophrenia and severe mental illness, the effect it has on people with the condition, on relatives and on friends of sufferers; professional workers caring for service users or clients (not aspects involving clinical or medical judgement); community care.

Printed publications:
Publications on Carers, Complementary Therapy, Creative Writing, Mental Illness, Rights, Treatments, Services and Advice Guides
Order printed publications from: via http://www.mentalhealthshop.rethink.org

Publications list:
Available online and in print

Access to staff:
Contact by letter, by telephone, by fax, by e-mail and via website. Appointment necessary.
Hours: Mon to Fri, 0900 to 1700

Branches:
120 relative/sufferer local support groups and 380 projects (day care, employment or care homes)
NSF Wales
Suite C2, Bratt Britannic House, Llandovey, Neath, West Glamorgan, SA10 6EL; tel: 01792 816600; fax: 01792 813056; e-mail: info@wales.nsf.org.uk
Operations London and East
89 Albert Embankment, London, SE1 7TP; tel: 0845 456 0455; fax: 020 7820 1149; e-mail: info@london.rethink.org
Operations North and Midlands
25A Outram Street, Sutton in Ashfield, Nottinghamshire, NG17 4BA; tel: 01623 551338; fax: 01623 550547
Operations South and South West
Fiarways House, Mountpleasant Industrial Estate, Mountpleasant Road, Southampton, SO4 0QB; tel: 023 8021 0270; fax: 023 8021 0285; e-mail: info@membership.rethink.org
Rethink Advice Service
89 Albert Embankment, London; tel: 020 7840 3188; fax: 020 7820 1149; e-mail: info@nsf.org.uk
Rethink Northern Ireland
Knockbracken Health Care Park, (Wyndhurst) Saintfield Road, Belfast, BT8 8BH; tel: 028 9040 2323; fax: 028 9040 1616; e-mail: info@nireland.nsf.org.uk

Member organisation of:
Disability Alliance
EUFAMI
National Council for Voluntary Organisations

RETREAD MANUFACTURERS ASSOCIATION

Acronym or abbreviation: RMA

PO Box 320, Crewe, Cheshire, CW2 6WY

Tel: 01270 561014
Fax: 01270 668801
E-mail: rma@greentyres.com

Website:
http://www.retreaders.co.uk
Members directory.
http://www.retreaders.org.uk
Information on retreading.

Enquiries:
Enquiries to: Director
Other contacts: (1) Secretary; (2) Technical
Consultant for (1) In Director's absence; (2)
Technical enquiries only, tel 01782 659674.

Founded:
1946

Organisation type and purpose:
National organisation, trade association
(membership is by subscription), present number
of members: 85.

Subject coverage:
Tyre retreading; standards and tyre disposal, tyre
recycling.

Printed publications:
European Regulations for Retreading

Access to staff:
Contact by letter, by telephone, by fax and by e-
mail. Appointment necessary.
Hours: Mon to Fri, 0930 to 1600

Access for disabled people:
Parking provided, access to all public areas, toilet
facilities

Founder member of:
British Tyre Industry Federation
International Organization of Tyre Retreaders
(BIPAVER)
   Retreading Division; tel: 01782 417777; fax:
   01782 417766; e-mail: retreads@ukonline.co.uk
Tyre Industry Council

RETREAT ASSOCIATION

Acronym or abbreviation: RA

The Central Hall, 256 Bermondsey Street, London,
SE1 3UJ

Tel: 020 7357 7736
Fax: 0871 715 1917
E-mail: info@retreats.org.uk

Website:
http://www.retreats.org.uk

Enquiries:
Enquiries to: Director

Founded:
1989

Organisation type and purpose:
Voluntary organisation, registered charity (charity
number 328746). A federation of 6 member groups.
230 retreats and retreat houses in Britain and
Ireland. Provides information to the public, and
support and networking for organisers.

Subject coverage:
Christian spirituality, spiritual direction.

Information services:
Information and resources in connection with
Christian retreats and spiritual direction.

**Museum or gallery collection, archive, or library
special collection:**
Small specialised library on Christian spirituality

Printed publications:
Books
Free leaflets (19) on retreats and their organisation
List of Training Courses in Spirituality and
   Spiritual Direction
RA Mission Statement
Retreats (journal, annually, £5.50 plus p&p)
Order printed publications from: Order direct or
online

Publications list:
Available online and in print

Access to staff:
Contact by letter, by telephone, by fax, by e-mail
and via website. Appointment necessary.

Hours: 0930 to 1730

Access for disabled people:
There is no access for disabled: the offices are at the
top of a 3-storey buildling with no lift

Member of:
Association for Promoting Retreats (APR)
Baptist Union Retreat Group (BURG)
Methodist Retreat Group (MRG)
National Retreat Movement (NRM)
Quaker Retreats Group (QRG)
United Reformed Church Silence and Retreat
Network (URCS&RG)

RETT SYNDROME ASSOCIATION UK

Acronym or abbreviation: RSAUK

Langham House West, Mill Street, Luton,
Bedfordshire LU1 2NA

Tel: 01582 798910
Fax: 01582 724129
E-mail: info@rettsyndrome.org.uk

Website:
http://www.rettsyndrome.org.uk

Enquiries:
Enquiries to: Office Administrator
Other contacts: Family Support Service Manager

Founded:
1985

Organisation type and purpose:
Membership association (membership is by
subscription), voluntary organisation, registered
charity (charity number 327309).

Subject coverage:
Rett syndrome, treatment and care, research, social
support.

**Museum or gallery collection, archive, or library
special collection:**
Pamphlets, books and videos on Rett Syndrome

Printed publications:
Various publications, free of charge, covering all
   aspects of Rett Syndrome including:
Information Packs
Leaflets, which cover varying topics for both
   professionals and carers
Magazine (quarterly)
Rett Syndrome: Adolescence & Adulthood
What is Rett Syndrome? (booklet)
What is RS? (leaflet)

Electronic and video publications:
The Lost Girls (video, £9.99 plus £1 p&p UK)
Silent Angels (video, £12 plus £1 p&p UK)

Publications list:
Available online and in print

Access to staff:
Contact by letter, by telephone, by fax, by e-mail
and in person
Hours: Mon to Fri, 0900 to 1700

RETURNED VOLUNTEER ACTION

Acronym or abbreviation: RVA

76 Wentworth Street, London, E1 7SA

Tel: 020 7247 6406
E-mail: retvolact@lineone.net

Enquiries:
Enquiries to: Membership Officer

Founded:
1963

Organisation type and purpose:
Membership association.

Subject coverage:
Advice and help for prospective and returned
overseas volunteers, understanding of the causes
of poverty and inequality, relationship between
north and south.

**Museum or gallery collection, archive, or library
special collection:**
Newsletters, annual reports, catalogues and other
   information from development-related UK
   groups and campaign organisations, as well as
   NGOs

Printed publications:
Books and booklets including:
For Whose Benefit: Racism and Overseas
   Development Work (£2.50)
Missing Links: Training for Awareness, Analysis
   and Action (£10)
The Only Resource (£2.50)
Thinking about Volunteering Overseas (£2.50)
Handbook for Development Workers Overseas
   (£2.50)
Volunteering and Overseas Development: A Guide
   to Opportunities (£1)
Volunteering Overseas: Personal Perceptions (£3)

Publications list:
Available in print

Access to staff:
Contact by letter and by e-mail. Appointment
necessary.
Hours: By appointment
Special comments: Please phone first.

Links with:
Development Education Association

REUTERS GROUP PLC

85 Fleet Street, London, EC4P 4AJ

Tel: 020 7250 1122
Fax: 020 7542 4064

Website:
http://www.reuters.com
Information on Reuters, news, financial markets,
stock quotes.

Enquiries:
Enquiries to: Director Corporate Communications
Direct tel: 020 7542 4890
Other contacts: Group Archivist for information on
Reuters history.

Founded:
1851

Organisation type and purpose:
International organisation, service industry.

Subject coverage:
Worldwide news coverage of general, political,
cultural, sports, economic, financial and scientific
matters and events; information and quotes on and
from world's money, fixed-income, equity,
commodity and energy markets.

Printed publications:
Annual Report
The Reuters Magazine (publication for Reuters
   clients)

Access to staff:
Contact by letter, by telephone, by fax and by e-
mail
Hours: Mon to Fri, 0900 to 1700

Access to building, collection or gallery:
No access other than to staff

RFCA GREATER LONDON

Formal name: Reserve Forces & Cadets Association
for Greater London

Fulham House, 87 Fulham High Street, London,
SW6 3JS

Tel: 0845 130 7888
E-mail: reception@gl.rfca.mod.uk

Website:
http://www.reserve-forces-london.org.uk

Enquiries:
Enquiries to: Secretary

Founded:
1908

continued overleaf

Organisation type and purpose:
National organisation, membership association (membership is by election or invitation), voluntary organisation.
Voluntary association, financed by central government through the Ministry of Defence.
To look after the interests of the Reserve Forces.

Subject coverage:
Recruiting and housing of the Reserves Forces and Cadets in Greater London.

Access to staff:
Contact by letter, by telephone and via website.
Appointment necessary.
Hours: Mon to Thu, 0900 to 1300, 1400 to 1700; Fri, 0900 to 1300, 1400 to 1600

RHM TECHNOLOGY

Formal name: RHM Technology a trading name of RHM Group Ltd

The Lord Rank Centre, Lincoln Road, High Wycombe, Buckinghamshire, HP12 3QR

Tel: 01494 526191
Fax: 01494 428080

Website:
http://www.rhmtech.co.uk
Information on services offered by RHM Technology.

Enquiries:
Enquiries to: Commercial Manager
Direct tel: 01494 428153
Direct e-mail: david.scott@rhm.com

Founded:
1963

Organisation type and purpose:
Service industry, consultancy.
Science, engineering and information services for the food industry.

Subject coverage:
Food science and technology; cereal chemistry; baking; bread; flour milling, cake, fruit preserves; electron microscopy; microbial biochemistry; food analysis and microbiology; mycotoxin analysis; protein chemistry; process engineering; GM testing and analysis (quantitative).

Library catalogue:
All or part available in-house

Access to staff:
Appointment necessary.
Hours: Mon to Fri, 0900 to 1700

Research and engineering company within:
Rank Hovis McDougall

RHODODENDRON, CAMELLIA AND MAGNOLIA GROUP OF THE RHS

Acronym or abbreviation: The Rhododendron Group

Botallick, Lanreath, Looe, PL13 2PF

Tel: 01503 220215
E-mail: patbucknell@btinternet.com

Website:
http://www.rhodogroup.rhs.org

Enquiries:
Enquiries to: Honorary Secretary

Organisation type and purpose:
International organisation, membership association (membership is by subscription), present number of members: 800.

Subject coverage:
The propagation and cultivation of rhododendrons, camellias and magnolias.

Non-library collection catalogue:
All or part available online

Printed publications:
Rhododendrons with Camellias and Magnolias (yearbook, £11.95, free to members)

Bulletin (3 times a year)

Access to staff:
Contact by letter, by telephone and by e-mail
Hours: Mon to Fri, 0900 to 1700

Parent body:
Royal Horticultural Society
80 Vincent Square, London, SW1P 2PE; tel: 020 7834 4333

RHONDDA CYNON TAFF COUNTY BOROUGH LIBRARIES

Acronym or abbreviation: RCT CBC

Tel: 01443 773204
Fax: 01443 777047

Website:
http://www.rhondda-cynon-taff.gov.uk/libraries
General information.
http://www.rhondda-cynon-taff.gov.uk/photos
Photographic Archive.

Enquiries:
Enquiries to: Principal Librarian
Direct tel: 01685 880060
Direct fax: 01685 881181
Direct e-mail: norma.d.jones@rhondda-cynon-taff .gov.uk

Organisation type and purpose:
Local government body, public library.

Subject coverage:
Local history of Rhondda-Cynon-Taff, music, general.

Library catalogue:
All or part available online

Printed publications:
Cynon Valley Calendar – local events (6 times a year)
Cynon Valley Community Directory (on OPAC 1996, Taff-Ely in preparation)
Older and Bolder, Rhondda Community Directory for the over-50s (on OPAC 1996)

Access to staff:
Contact by letter, by telephone, by fax and by e-mail
Hours: Mon to Fri, 0900 to 1700

Admin Dept.:
Penygraig Library
Tylacelyn Road, Penygraig, Rhondda

Other addresses:
Aberdare Library (Principal Librarian)
Green Street, Aberdare, CF44 7AG; tel: 01685 880050; fax: 01685 881181
Pontypridd Library (Area Librarian-South)
Library Road, Pontypridd; tel: 01443 486850; fax: 01443 493258
The Education Centre (County Borough Librarian)
Grawen Street, Porth, Rhondda; tel: 01443 687666; fax: 01443 680286
Treorchy Library
tel: 01443 773204

Parent body:
Rhondda Cynon Taff County Borough Council
tel: 01443 687666; fax: 01443 680286

RHONDDA CYNON TAFF COUNTY BOROUGH LIBRARIES – ABERDARE

Central Library, Green Street, Aberdare, Mid Glamorgan, CF44 7AG

Tel: 01685 880050
Fax: 01685 881181
E-mail: aberdare.library@rhondda-cynon-taff.gov .uk

Website:
http://www.rhondda-cynon-taff.gov.uk/libraries/ index.htm

Enquiries:
Enquiries to: County Borough Librarian

Organisation type and purpose:
Local government body, public library.

Subject coverage:
General, local history of the Cynon Valley.

Museum or gallery collection, archive, or library special collection:
W W Price Collection (local history)

Non-library collection catalogue:
All or part available in-house

Library catalogue:
All or part available online

Printed publications:
Cynon Valley Community Directory

Access to staff:
Contact by letter, by telephone, by fax, by e-mail and via website
Hours: Mon to Fri, 0900 to 1800; Sat, 0900 to 1300

Access for disabled people:
Ramped entry
Special comments: Lift to Reference Department.

RHONDDA HERITAGE PARK

Lewis Merthyr Colliery, Coed Cae Road, Trehafod, Pontypridd, Rhondda Cynon Taff, CF37 2NP

Tel: 01443 682036
Fax: 01443 687420
E-mail: reception@rhonddaheritagepark.com

Website:
http://www.rhonddaheritagepark.com
General information about the attraction.

Enquiries:
Enquiries to: County Borough Museums Officer, Rhondda Cynon Taff
Other contacts: Marketing Officer for promotion/ public relations.

Founded:
1989

Organisation type and purpose:
Local government body, museum, art gallery, historic building, house or site, suitable for ages: all. Children's play park, shop, restaurant.
Conference facilities available.
Tourist attraction.

Subject coverage:
Heritage, mining. Black Gold includes 3 audiovisual shows telling the history of the Rhondda Valleys and mining. A guided tour with an ex-miner includes a visit to the Grade II listed pit head buildings and a trip to 'pit bottom' to experience life as a miner in the 1950s. A reconstructed village street and art gallery at the visitor centre.

Special visitor services:
Guided tours, materials and/or activities for children.

Education services:
Group education facilities, resources for Key Stages 1 and 2, 3 and 4.

Services for disabled people:
For hearing impaired.

Museum or gallery collection, archive, or library special collection:
Books, photographs, domestic artefacts, shop artefacts
Variety of mining machinery including:
Hand tools, colliers' tools, 1850–1950
Mine rescue, breathing apparatus, smoke helmets
Mining instruments, methonometers, hygrometers, dust sampling equipment, etc.
Large colliery machinery and engines, Lewis Merthyr winding engine, ventilation fans preserved in situ, 1880/1890

Non-library collection catalogue:
All or part available in-house

Electronic and video publications:
Promotional video available for intending group visitors

Access to staff:
Contact by letter and by e-mail. Appointment necessary.
Hours: Mon to Fri, 0900 to 1700

Access to building, collection or gallery:
No prior appointment required
Hours: Daily 1000 to 1800. Closed Dec 25 to 1 Jan inclusive, and Mondays Oct to Easter

Access for disabled people:
Parking provided, ramped entry, level entry, toilet facilities, lift. Access to most areas.

Parent body:
Rhondda Cynon Taff County Borough Council
The Pavilions, Clydach Vale, CF40 2XX; tel: 01443 424000

RHS GARDEN HARLOW CARR

Formal name: The Royal Horticultural Society's Garden Harlow Carr
Acronym or abbreviation: RHS

Crag Lane, Harrogate, North Yorkshire, HG3 1QB

Tel: 01423 565418
Fax: 01423 530663
E-mail: admin-harlowcarr@rhs.org.uk

Enquiries:
Other contacts: Curatorial department for written enquiries on horticulture.

Founded:
1950

Organisation type and purpose:
Membership association (membership is by subscription), present number of members: 365,000, registered charity (charity number 222879), museum.
Educational charity.
Selects shrubs, trees and plants to discover their suitability for northern conditions.

Subject coverage:
Gardening and horticulture, particularly relating to the conditions in the north of England.

Museum or gallery collection, archive, or library special collection:
Four important national plant collections – rheum (rhubarb), fuchsia sect. Quelusia (provisional collection), dryopteris and polypodium (ferns)

Printed publications:
The Garden (monthly)
Harlow Carr Garden (leaflet)

Access to staff:
Contact by letter. Access for members only.
Hours: Mon to Fri, 0900 to 1700

Access for disabled people:
Parking provided, level entry, toilet facilities

RICABILITY

Formal name: Research Institute for Consumer Affairs
Acronym or abbreviation: RICA

30 Angel Gate, City Road, London, EC1V 2PT

Tel: 020 7427 2460\ Textphone no. 020 7427 2469
Fax: 020 7427 2468
E-mail: mail@ricability.org.uk

Website:
http://www.ricability.org.uk
Consumer guides for older and disabled people, covering technology at home, communication, motoring and car information and childcare products for disabled parents
http://www.ricability-digitaltv.org.uk
Independent consumer test reports on digital TV products to help people choose easy-to-use products for the national digital switchover.
http://www.product-reviews.org.uk
Website where disabled people can register their own opinions about good and bad products or services they use.

Enquiries:
Enquiries to: Administrator

Founded:
1991

Organisation type and purpose:
Voluntary organisation, registered charity (charity number 1007726), research organisation.
Independent charity set up by the Consumers' Association. Ricability is the trading name of the Research Institute for Consumer Affairs.
To carry out research and publish unbiased information on products and services used by consumers who are older or disabled.

Subject coverage:
Consumer information, disabled people, older people, carers, disability equipment, disability services, research, information, product testing and assessment, digital televsion, digital switchover, product reviews, online product reviews, assistive technology, car adaptations

Printed publications:
Consumer guides and reports on:
Childcare products, digital tv products, household products, driving with a disability, motoring and mobility, community alarms, phones and product reviews.

Electronic and video publications:
Audio cassette, audio cd, braille and large-print materials available

Publications list:
Available online and in print

Access to staff:
Contact by letter, by telephone, by fax, by e-mail and via website
Hours: Mon to Fri, 0900 to 1700

Access for disabled people:
Access to all public areas, fully adapted toilet
Special comments: Fully accessible and accessible information: tape, braille and large print.

RICARDO UK

Shoreham Technical Centre, Shoreham-by-Sea, West Sussex, BN43 5FG

Tel: 01273 455611
Fax: 01273 464124
E-mail: infoservices@ricardo.com

Website:
http://www.ricardo.com

Enquiries:
Enquiries to: Information Manager
Direct tel: 01273 794230
Direct fax: 01273 794555

Founded:
1915

Organisation type and purpose:
Consultancy.

Subject coverage:
Internal-combustion engineering research, diesel engines, petrol engines, automotive engineering, noise reduction, combustion, exhaust emissions, fuel technology, lubrication, transmissions, finite element stress analysis, computational fluid dynamics, design, vehicle systems, control and electronics.

Library catalogue:
All or part available online

Printed publications:
Components News (details of new powertrain components plans by manufacturers, monthly)
New Engine News (bulletin of new engines and plans by manufacturers, monthly)
Transmissions News (details of new transmissions and plans by manufacturers, monthly)
Alternative Powertrain News
Vehicle Engineering News
Gas Engine News

Electronic and video publications:
Ricardo Powerlink Database – Database of 250,000 references to the literature of the powertrain and vehicle systems (online)
EMLEG – Updating service, covering exhaust emissions legislation (online)

Publications list:
Available online and in print

Access to staff:
Contact by letter, by telephone, by fax, by e-mail and via website. All charged.
Hours: Mon to Fri, 0900 to 1700

Access to building, collection or gallery:
No access other than to staff

Parent body:
Ricardo Group plc
Shoreham Technical Centre, Shoreham-by-Sea, West Sussex, BN43 5FG; tel: 01273 455611; fax: 01273 464124

RICHARD III SOCIETY

4 Oakley Street, Chelsea, London, SW3 5NN

Tel: 01689 823569
E-mail: information@richardiii.net

Website:
http://www.richardiii.net
Home page re Society, research, publication programmes etc.
http://www.r3.org
US Branch site, materials for students, texts, etc.

Enquiries:
Enquiries to: Secretary
Other contacts: Research Officer for research related queries.

Founded:
1924

Organisation type and purpose:
Learned society.

Subject coverage:
Life and times of King Richard III and the social and political history of late 15th century England.

Museum or gallery collection, archive, or library special collection:
Richard III Society Library

Library catalogue:
All or part available in-house

Printed publications:
Catalogues of the Library
The Bulletin (journal, quarterly)
The Ricardian (journal, annual)
Order printed publications from: Membership Dept (also Sales Dept), Time Travellers Limited
Sales Liaison Officer, 42 Pewsey Vale, Forest Park, Bracknell, RG12 9YA

Publications list:
Available online and in print

Access to staff:
Contact by letter, by telephone and by e-mail
Hours: Mon to Fri, 0900 to 1700

RICHARD JEFFERIES SOCIETY

Pear Tree Cottage, Longcot, Oxfordshire, SN7 7SS

Tel: 01793 783040

Website:
http://www.bath.ac.uk/~lissmc/rjeffs.htm
Brief biography, Society details, The Story of My Heart, Pageant of Summer

Enquiries:
Enquiries to: Honorary Secretary
Direct e-mail: r.jefferies_society@tiscali.co.uk

Founded:
1950

continued overleaf

Organisation type and purpose:
Learned society (membership is by subscription),
present number of members: 300, registered
charity (charity number 1042838).
Literary society.

Subject coverage:
Life, writings and associations of Richard Jefferies
(1848–1887), whose principal subjects are: nature,
the Victorian rural scene, agriculture, late Victorian
London, gamekeeping and poaching, spiritual
philosophy.

**Museum or gallery collection, archive, or library
special collection:**
Library of first and early editions of Jefferies'
works, studies and biographies, unpublished
essays and letters issued posthumously,
photographs

Non-library collection catalogue:
All or part available in-house

Printed publications:
Annual Report and Newsletters
List of Booksellers known to have Jefferies' works
   at secondhand
List of Talks and Articles
Leaflets and postcards
Journal (ISSN 0968–4247, one a year)

Access to staff:
Contact by letter, by telephone and by e-mail
Hours: Mon to Sat, 0900 to 1700

Access to building, collection or gallery:
No prior appointment required
Special comments: Richard Jefferies Museum: Wed,
2nd of month, 1000 to 1600; Sun, May to Sept, 1st
and 3rd of month, 1400 to 1700

Affiliated to:
Alliance of Literary Societies
   Rosemary Culley, 22 Belmont Grove, Havant,
   Hampshire, PO9 3PU; tel: 023 9247 5855; fax:
   0870 056 0330; e-mail: rosemary@sndc.demon.co
   .uk

RICHMOND UPON THAMES COLLEGE

Acronym or abbreviation: RUTC

The Library, Egerton Road, Twickenham,
Middlesex, TW2 7SJ

Tel: 020 8607 8355
Fax: 020 8607 8355
E-mail: library@richmond-utcoll.ac.uk

Website:
http://www.richmond-utcoll.ac.uk

Enquiries:
Enquiries to: Librarian
Direct e-mail: Jstauch@richmond-utcoll.ac.uk

Founded:
1977

Subject coverage:
Humanities; social sciences; literature; science;
technology; education; business studies, art and
design.

**Museum or gallery collection, archive, or library
special collection:**
Audiotapes and cassettes; microfiche and
   microfilm
British Standards
CD-ROMs
Slides and filmstrips (over 35,000)

Access to staff:
Contact by letter, by telephone, by e-mail and via
website. Appointment necessary.
Hours: Mon to Thu, 0830 to 1900, Fri, 0830 to 1600

Access to building, collection or gallery:
Prior appointment required

Access for disabled people:
Level entry, toilet facilities
Special comments: No access to first floor

RICHMOND UPON THAMES LIBRARIES AND INFORMATION SERVICES

Education and Childen's Services, Regal House,
London Road, Twickenham, Middlesex, TW1 3QB

Tel: 020 8831 6136
Fax: 020 8891 7904
E-mail: libraries@richmond.gov.uk

Website:
http://www.richmond.gov.uk

Enquiries:
Enquiries to: Head of Libraries and Culture
Other contacts: Assistant Head of Library and
Information Services

Organisation type and purpose:
Local government body, public library.

Subject coverage:
General.

**Museum or gallery collection, archive, or library
special collection:**
Alexander Pope Collection within the Twickenham
   local collection (Twickenham District Library)
Douglas Sladen Collection of correspondence and
   printed ephemera relating to his life and interests
George Vancouver Collection
Hansard, House of Commons and House of Lords
   debates
Other debates and historic journals
Official Journal of the EC
Richmond upon Thames and Barnes local
   collections
Sir Richard Burton Collection of books and other
   items
Telephone Directories (microfiche)
Times (microfilm)
Various statistical sources including many OPCS
   monitors, Annual abstract of Stats, Monthly
   digest of Stats, Regional Trends, Social Trends,
   EUROSTAT, United Nations Statistical Year-
   Book, OECD reports on countries, Europa World
   Year Book, EC publications, please note most of
   these would be held at Central Reference Library
   only

Library catalogue:
All or part available online

Printed publications:
Richmond upon Thames Official Borough Guide
   (every 2 years, £2.50)
The Official Richmond upon Thames Business
   Directory (annually, £7.50)
Other publications include irregular local history
   items

Electronic and video publications:
DVDs available

Access to staff:
Contact by letter, by telephone, by fax, by e-mail,
in person and via website
Hours: Mon to Fri, 0900 to 1700

District libraries at:
East Sheen
Richmond
Teddington
Twickenham

Member of:
SHARE

Other addresses:
Reference and Information Services
   Old Town Hall, Whittaker Avenue, Richmond-
   upon-Thames, Surrey, TW9 1TP; tel: 020 8940
   5529; fax: 020 8940 6899; e-mail: reference
   .services@richmond.gov.uk

RICHMOND: THE AMERICAN INTERNATIONAL UNIVERSITY IN LONDON

Queen's Road, Richmond-upon-Thames, Surrey,
TW10 6JP

Tel: 020 8332 8210

Fax: 020 8332 3050
E-mail: library@richmond.ac.uk

Website:
http://www.richmond.ac.uk
General information about the university.

Enquiries:
Enquiries to: University librarian
Direct tel: 020 8332 8279
Direct e-mail: trewf@richmond.ac.uk

Founded:
1972

Organisation type and purpose:
University library.
Independent American international university, for
liberal arts and professional studies.

Subject coverage:
Business administration, economics, anthropology
and sociology, international business, political
science, international relations, psychology,
women's studies, art history, studio art, theatre
arts, British studies, English literature, history,
French, computer science, mathematical sciences,
communications, environmental studies, modern
languages, philosophy and religion, systems
engineering and management.

**Museum or gallery collection, archive, or library
special collection:**
N J Cann Bequest (history of art)
Harvard Core Collection (gift of Sir Cyril Taylor
   and Roger O Walther)
Asa Briggs Collection (gift of Lord Asa Briggs)

Non-library collection catalogue:
All or part available online

Library catalogue:
All or part available online

Access to staff:
Appointment necessary.
Hours: Mon to Fri, 0900 to 1700

Access for disabled people:
Hours: Mon to Thu, 0900 to 2100; Fri, 0900 to 1700;
Sat, closed; Sun, 1300 to 2300

Other addresses:
Richmond: the American International University
in London
   1 Saint Alban's Grove, Kensington, London, W8
   5PN; tel: 020 7368 8510

RIDER HAGGARD SOCIETY

Acronym or abbreviation: RHS

27 Deneholm, Whitley Bay, Tyne and Wear, NE25
9AU

Tel: 0191 252 4516
Fax: 0191 252 4516
E-mail: rb27allen@blueyonder.co.uk

Website:
http://www.riderhaggardsociety.org.uk

Enquiries:
Enquiries to: Honorary Secretary

Founded:
1984

Organisation type and purpose:
International organisation, learned society
(membership is by subscription), present number
of members: 106.

Subject coverage:
Works by the author Rider Haggard and about
him, his family and any relevant ephemera.

Information services:
On request.

Special visitor services:
On request.

Education services:
Research help.

Non-library collection catalogue:
All or part available online and in print

Printed publications:
Books by Haggard
Books about Haggard
RHS Journals
Guides to Haggard fiction and non-fiction
Order printed publications from: Postal address

Publications list:
Available online and in print

Access to staff:
Contact by letter, by telephone, by e-mail, in person and via website. Appointment necessary.
Hours: Any time

Connections with:
Alliance of Literary Societies (ALS)

RILEY MOTOR CLUB LIMITED

Treelands, 127 Penn Road, Wolverhampton, West Midlands, WV3 0DU

Tel: 01902 773197

Enquiries:
Enquiries to: Honorary Secretary

Founded:
1925

Organisation type and purpose:
Membership association.

Subject coverage:
History of Riley cars, technical information, source of spares, restoration and maintenance.

Access to staff:
Contact by letter and by telephone
Hours: Mon to Fri, 0900 to 1700

RILEY REGISTER

56 Cheltenham Road, Bishops Cleeve, Cheltenham, Gloucestershire, GL52 8LY

Tel: 01242 673598

Website:
http://www.rileyregister.com

Enquiries:
Enquiries to: Membership Secretary

Founded:
1954

Organisation type and purpose:
Membership association (membership is by subscription).

Subject coverage:
One make car club for Rileys up to 1940; sources of spares.

Printed publications:
Bulletin (quarterly)
Newsletter (every 6 weeks)

Access to staff:
Contact by letter and by telephone
Hours: Mon to Fri, 0900 to 1700

RILEY RM CLUB

Y Fachell, Ruthin Road, Gwernymynydd, Mold, Clwyd, CH7 5LQ

Tel: 01352 700427

Enquiries:
Enquiries to: Membership Secretary

Founded:
1969

Organisation type and purpose:
International organisation, membership association (membership is by subscription).

Subject coverage:
Preservation of RM Rileys, spares, technical information and social activities.

Museum or gallery collection, archive, or library special collection:
Archives covering the majority of cars still in existence
Magazines and technical literature
Spare parts for members' cars

Printed publications:
RMemoranda (club magazine)

Access to staff:
Contact by letter and by telephone
Hours: Mon to Fri, 0900 to 1700

RIPON CATHEDRAL LIBRARY

Ripon Cathedral, Ripon, North Yorkshire, HG4 1QR

Tel: 01765 603462

Enquiries:
Enquiries to: Canon Librarian

Subject coverage:
Church history; New Testament; personalities and leaders within the church (mainly 20th century); prayer and spirituality.

Museum or gallery collection, archive, or library special collection:
Higgins Library
Library of Canon A Stephenson
Most of the Cathedral's special collections are housed in the Brotherton Library, Leeds University

Access to staff:
Appointment necessary.
Hours: Mon to Fri, 0900 to 1700

RIPON HISTORICAL SOCIETY

Stone Cottage, Wath-in-Nidderdale, Pateley Bridge, North Yorkshire, HG3 5PL

E-mail: gdl@globalnet.co.uk

Website:
http://www.yorksgen.org.uk

Enquiries:
Enquiries to: Honorary Secretary

Founded:
1986

Organisation type and purpose:
Membership association (membership is by subscription), present number of members: 343+, voluntary organisation.

Subject coverage:
The history of the City of Ripon and the surrounding districts, its heritage and the preservation and protection of items of historic or public interest, family history of the area.

Museum or gallery collection, archive, or library special collection:
Microfilms of many of the records of Ripon (held in six Record Offices) are available in the new Ripon County Library

Printed publications:
The Ripon Historian (quarterly, members)
A Guide to Historical Sources for Ripon and District (ed Hebden J R, £3 plus 40p p&p)
Census Index 1851
Kith and Kin: Nidderdale families 1500–1750 (£7.50 plus 85p p&p)
Thirlway Journal: A record of Life in Early Victorian Ripon (£7.50 plus 85p p&p)
Yorkshire Hearth Tax Lists 1672 and 1673 for the North, East and most of the West Ridings and for York
Indexes to 1822/3 Baines Directory for Yorkshire organised by Wapentakes, NRY in 5 parts, WRY 3 parts to date (£2 each)
Order printed publications from: Publications Officer, Ripon Historical Society
Aldergarth, Galphay, Ripon, North Yorkshire, HG4 3NJ, tel: 01765 658602, e-mail: hebden1name@btopenworld.com

Microform publications:
Monumental Inscriptions:
Farnham; Scotton; Staveley; Arkendale (1 fiche)
Killinghall; Burnt Yates; Padside; Ramsgill (1 fiche)
Methodist Chapels: Harrogate circuit; Gracious Street; Knaresborough; Beamsley; West Tanfield (1 fiche)
High Harrogate: Christ Church; St John (Bilton); St Peter; St Wilfred (2 fiche)
Dacre: Providence chapel; Dacre Banks: Holy Trinity (1 fiche)
Census Index 1851:
Harrogate Area
Knaresborough/Wetherby area
Parish Registers: Ripon, Kirkby Malzeard, Dallowgill, Mickley, Winksley, Sawley, Bishop Thornton, Aldfield, Bishop Monkton, Markington, Skelton-on-Ure, Sharow, North Stainley, Holy Trinity Ripon, Ripon Workhouse

Publications list:
Available in print

Access to staff:
Contact by letter and by e-mail
Hours: Mon to Fri, 0900 to 1700

Family history group:
Ripon, Harrogate & District Family History Group
18 Aspin Drive, Knaresborough, North Yorkshire, HG5 8HH

Membership Secretary:
Ripon Historical Society
Downe, Baldersby, Thirsk, North Yorkshire, YO7 4PP; e-mail: dolonic@cs.com

RNIB NATIONAL LIBRARY SERVICE

Far Cromwell Road, Bredbury, Stockport, Cheshire, SK6 2SG

Tel: 0845 762 6843
Fax: 0161 355 2098
E-mail: cservices@rnib.org.uk

Website:
http://www.rnib.org.uk/library
Provides access to electronic books via OPAC and accessible e-reference materials plus information about NLB services including reader development tools.

Enquiries:
Enquiries to: Marketing Communications Officer
Direct tel: 0161 355 2080
Direct e-mail: megan.gilks@nlbuk.org

Founded:
1882

Organisation type and purpose:
National organisation (membership is by subscription), present number of members: 5000, voluntary organisation, registered charity (charity number 213212), consultancy.
A gateway to free comprehensive library services for those who cannot read print and their intermediaries. Its aim is to enable all visually impaired people to have the same access to library services as sighted people.

Subject coverage:
Library service to blind and partially sighted readers including a range of electronic library services via the internet.

Museum or gallery collection, archive, or library special collection:
Collection of 40,000 titles in Braille including fiction and non-fiction, books for younger readers (aged eight or over) and Braille sheet music.
Giant Print Library (books in 24pt type) for children and young people.
Small collection of large print books covering classics and standard titles
Large collection of Moon titles.

Non-library collection catalogue:
All or part available online

continued overleaf

Library catalogue:
All or part available online and in print

Printed publications:
Annual Review (free)
NLB New Reading (for members, 6 times per annum, in print, Braille, on disk or by email – free)
Focus (newsletter for supporters – free)
NLB Read On (for members, 4 times per annum, in print, Braille, on disk or by email – free)

Electronic and video publications:
Catalogues and lists available on disk (free)

Publications list:
Available online

Access to staff:
Contact by letter, by telephone, by fax, by e-mail and via website. Appointment necessary.
Hours: Mon to Fri, 0900 to 1600

Access to building, collection or gallery:
Prior appointment required

Access for disabled people:
Parking provided, ramped entry, access to all public areas

Links with:
IFLA

RNID

Acronym or abbreviation: RNID

19–23 Featherstone Street, London, EC1Y 8SL

Tel: 0808 808 0123 (Textphone 0808 808 9000)
Fax: 020 7296 8199
E-mail: informationline@mid.org.uk

Website:
http://www.rnid.org.uk

Enquiries:
Enquiries to: Information Line
Direct tel: 0808 808 0123
Direct e-mail: informationline@rnid.org.uk

Founded:
1911

Organisation type and purpose:
Registered charity (charity number 207720), working to change the world for the UK's 9 million deaf and hard of hearing people. Does this with the help of members, by campaigning and lobbying, raising awareness of deafness and hearing loss, providing services and through social, medical and technical research.

Subject coverage:
Deafness, hearing loss, hearing, tinnitus, communication suport, BSL, sign language, lip-reading, campaigns, information, services, and research into deafness and hearing loss.

Museum or gallery collection, archive, or library special collection:
One of Europe's largest library collections of materials on all aspects of deafness and hearing research
Rare pre-1800 book collection on deafness

Library catalogue:
All or part available in-house

Printed publications:
One in Seven (membership magazine)
RNID provides a range of leaflets, factsheets and priced publications on various aspects of deafness, hearing loss and tinnitus

Publications list:
Available online and in print

Access to staff:
Contact by letter, by telephone, by fax, by e-mail and via website. Appointment necessary.
Hours: Mon to Fri, 0900 to 1700

Access to building, collection or gallery:
Unable to provide a drop-in service – please contact the Information Line before visiting
Hours: 0900 to 1700

Access for disabled people:
Toilet facilities, lifts and BSL interpreters
Special comments: Lift from pavement level

Other addresses:
RNID Products
1 Haddonbrook Business Centre, Fallodan Road, Orton Southgate, Peterborough, PE2 6YX; tel: 01733 232607 (textphone 01733 238020); fax: 01733 361161; website: www.rnid.org.uk/shop
RNID Typetalk
PO Box 284, Liverpool, L69 3UZ; tel: 18001 0800 500 888 (textphone users), 0800 7311 888 (hearing people); fax: 0151 709 8119; website: http://www.rnid-typetalk.org.uk

RNID SCOTLAND

Formal name: Royal National Institute for Deaf and Hard of Hearing People (Scotland)
Acronym or abbreviation: RNID Scotland

Empire House, 131 West Nile Street, Glasgow, G1 2RX

Tel: 0141 341 5330\ Minicom no. 0141 341 5347
Fax: 0141 354 0176
E-mail: RNIDScotland@rnid.org.uk

Website:
http://www.rnid.org.uk

Enquiries:
Enquiries to: Regional Communications Officer

Founded:
1966

Organisation type and purpose:
Membership association (membership is by subscription), registered charity (charity number 207720).

Subject coverage:
Information, training, specialist telephone services, assistive devices, communication services unit, employment training and skills service.

Non-library collection catalogue:
All or part available online

Printed publications:
One in Seven (magazine, members)
RNID titles cover a wide range of topics dealing with:
Communications
Hearing Aids
Special equipment
Employment
Education
Benefits
Medical
Tinnitus

Publications list:
Available online and in print

Access to staff:
Contact by letter, by telephone, by fax, by e-mail, in person and via website. Appointment necessary.
Hours: Mon to Fri, 0900 to 1700

Access for disabled people:
Toilet facilities, lift

Head Office:
Royal National Institute for Deaf and Hard of Hearing People
19–23 Featherstone Street, London, EC1Y 8SL; tel: 020 7296 8000; textphone 0808 808 0123 and 0808 808 9000; fax: 020 7296 8199; e-mail: helpline@rnid.org.uk

ROAD OPERATORS SAFETY COUNCIL

Acronym or abbreviation: ROSCO

Cowley House, Watlington Road, Oxford, OX4 6GA

Tel: 01865 775552
Fax: 01865 775552
E-mail: rosco-oxford@supanet.com

Website:
http://www.rosco.org.uk

Enquiries:
Enquiries to: Executive Secretary

Founded:
1955

Subject coverage:
Road safety in the bus and coach industry, accidents and safe driving.

Printed publications:
Safety First (newsletter)

Access to staff:
Contact by letter, by telephone and by fax
Hours: Mon to Fri, 0900 to 1700

ROADPEACE

PO Box 2579, London, NW10 3PW

Tel: 020 8838 5102
Fax: 020 8838 5103
E-mail: info@roadpeace.org

Enquiries:
Enquiries to: Administrator

Founded:
1992

Organisation type and purpose:
Membership association (membership is by subscription), present number of members: 1,200, registered charity (charity number 1087192).

Subject coverage:
Road-traffic victims.

Access to staff:
Contact by letter, by telephone, by fax and by e-mail
Hours: Mon to Fri, 0900 to 1700

ROBENS CENTRE FOR OCCUPATIONAL HEALTH & SAFETY

University of Surrey, 3–4 Huxley Road, Surrey Research Park, Guildford, Surrey, GU2 7RE

Tel: 01483 686690
Fax: 01483 686691
E-mail: cohs@surrey.ac.uk

Website:
http://www.surrey.ac.uk/Robens/rbhome.html

Enquiries:
Enquiries to: Administrator

Founded:
1978

Organisation type and purpose:
University department or institute, consultancy, research organisation.

Subject coverage:
Toxicology, occupational health and hygiene, environmental health, microbiology, analytical chemistry, psychology, ergonomics, human physiology, epidemiology and overseas development.

Printed publications:
Large selection of published journal articles, conference proceedings and reports available

Publications list:
Available in print

Access to staff:
Contact by letter, by fax and by e-mail
Hours: Mon to Fri, 0900 to 1700

Access for disabled people:
Parking provided

ROBERT GORDON UNIVERSITY – GEORGINA SCOTT SUTHERLAND LIBRARY

Garthdee Road, Garthdee, Aberdeen, AB10 7QE

Tel: 01224 263450
Fax: 01224 263460
E-mail: library@rgu.ac.uk

Website:
http://www.rgu.ac.uk/library
http://www.rgu.ac.uk/library/service/special.htm
Details of staff and assistance available to disabled users.

Enquiries:
Enquiries to: Director of Knowledge and Information Services
Direct tel: 01224 263452
Direct fax: 01224 263455

Organisation type and purpose:
University library.

Subject coverage:
Applied science, architecture, art, business management, computer science, engineering (mechanical, electrical, offshore), food and nutrition, health, librarianship, information studies, mathematics, nursing, pharmacy, public administration, social studies, surveying, law, physiotherapy, occupational therapy, radiography, European information, tourism.

Museum or gallery collection, archive, or library special collection:
Art and Architecture Antiquarian collection

Library catalogue:
All or part available online

Access to staff:
Contact by letter, by telephone, by fax, by e-mail, in person and via website
Hours: Details of opening hours during term time and vacations (for the Georgina Scott Sutherland Library and the St Andrew Street Library) are available online

Access for disabled people:
Parking provided, ramped entry, level entry, toilet facilities
Special comments: Details of staff contacts and assistance available can be found online

ROBERT GORDON UNIVERSITY – SCHOOL OF INFORMATION AND MEDIA

Faculty of Management Building, Garthdee Road, Aberdeen, AB10 7QE

Tel: 01224 263900
Fax: 01224 263553
E-mail: sim@rgu.ac.uk

Website:
http://www.rgu.com
Virtual campus, online courses.
http://www.rgu.ac.uk
Courses available; recent research; staff information; links to relevant resources.

Enquiries:
Enquiries to: Head of School
Direct tel: 01224 263901

Founded:
1751

Organisation type and purpose:
University department or institute, training organisation, consultancy, research organisation. The School undertakes teaching and research, consultancy and training in the fields of library and information sciences, publishing, corporate and technical communications, and modern languages.

Printed publications:
From Oct 1999, an increasing range of online course modules at postgraduate level, which can be taken singly or as parts of Masters degree programmes

Electronic and video publications:
Occasional research reports available for downloading free of charge
For details, access the School's Web Pages

Access to staff:
Contact by letter, by telephone, by fax and by e-mail. Appointment necessary. All charged.
Hours: Mon to Fri, 0900 to 1700

Access to building, collection or gallery:
No access other than to staff
Special comments: See separate entry for the University's Library.

ROBINSON COLLEGE LIBRARY

Grange Road, Cambridge, CB3 9AN

Tel: 01223 339100

Enquiries:
Enquiries to: Librarian
Direct tel: 01223 339124

Organisation type and purpose:
University department or institute.
College Library of the University of Cambridge.

Subject coverage:
General, for undergraduate teaching.

Access to staff:
Access for members only.
Hours: Mon to Fri, 0900 to 1700

ROCHDALE LIBRARIES

Wheatsheaf Library, Baillie Street, Rochdale, Lancashire, OL16 1JZ

Tel: 01706 924900
Fax: 01706 924992
E-mail: library.service@rochdale.gov.uk

Website:
http://www.rochdale.gov.uk/
List of addresses, phone numbers, hours of opening, services for visually-impaired people, services for under-5s. Open for learning, British sign language, reminiscence packs, lending. Local studies, reference library, children's services

Enquiries:
Enquiries to: Reference and Information Development Librarian
Direct fax: 01706 924934

Organisation type and purpose:
Local government body, public library.

Subject coverage:
General, local history, international collection on co-operation.

Museum or gallery collection, archive, or library special collection:
Collection of books on the co-operative movement and co-operation (700 items)
Tim Bobbin (John Collier) collection

Non-library collection catalogue:
All or part available online and in-house

Library catalogue:
All or part available online and in-house

Printed publications:
List of periodicals and newspapers held

Access to staff:
Contact by letter, by telephone, by fax, by e-mail and in person
Hours: Mon, 0930 to 1930; Tue to Fri, 0930 to 1730; Sat, 0930 to 1700

Parent body:
Rochdale Metropolitan Borough Council

ROCHFORD DISTRICT COUNCIL

Council Offices, South Street, Rochford, Essex, SS4 1BW

Tel: 01702 546366
Fax: 01702 545737

E-mail: information@rochford.gov.uk

Enquiries:
Enquiries to: Civic and Public Relations Officer
Direct tel: 01702 318144
Direct fax: 01702 318161
Direct e-mail: helen-collins@rochford.gov.uk

Founded:
1974

Organisation type and purpose:
Local government body.

Printed publications:
Official Guide (free, updated every two years)
The Old House (for purchase)
Tourism Guide (free)

Access to staff:
Contact by letter, by telephone, by fax, by e-mail and in person
Hours: Mon to Thu, 0830 to 1700; Fri, 0830 to 1630

ROCKEFELLER MEDICAL LIBRARY

UCL Institute of Neurology, The National Hospital, 23 Queen Square, London, WC1N 3BG

Tel: 020 7829 8709
Fax: 020 7278 5069
E-mail: library@ion.ucl.ac.uk

Website:
http://www.ion.ucl.ac.uk/library

Enquiries:
Enquiries to: Librarian

Founded:
1950

Organisation type and purpose:
University department or institute.
Postgraduate medical institute.

Subject coverage:
Clinical neurology and allied fields, historical neurology, neurosurgery and neuroscience.

Museum or gallery collection, archive, or library special collection:
Historical neurology
Queen Square Collection (of staff publications)
Current Neurology, Neurosurgery and Neuroscience books, journals and multimedia

Non-library collection catalogue:
All or part available online

Library catalogue:
All or part available online

Access to staff:
Contact by letter, by telephone, by fax, by e-mail, in person and via website. Appointment necessary.
Hours: Mon to Fri, 0900 to 1800

Access to building, collection or gallery:
Prior appointment required

Links with:
National Hospital for Neurology and Neurosurgery
University of London

Parent body:
University College London

RODBASTON COLLEGE

Rodbaston, Penkridge, Stafford, ST19 5PH

Tel: 01785 712209
Fax: 01785 715701
E-mail: rodenquiries@rodbaston.ac.uk

Enquiries:
Enquiries to: Reception

Organisation type and purpose:
Suitable for ages: 16+.
College for training and education in the land-based industries.

Subject coverage:
Courses available in areas of study for the land-based industries.

continued overleaf

Access to staff:
Contact by letter
Hours: Mon to Fri, 0900 to 1700

ROEHAMPTON UNIVERSITY

Learning Resources Centre, Roehampton Lane, London, SW15 5SZ

Tel: 020 8392 3770
Fax: 020 8392 3259
E-mail: enquiry.desk@roehampton.ac.uk

Website:
http://www.roehampton.ac.uk
University home page

Enquiries:
Enquiries to: University Librarian and Director of Learning Services
Direct tel: 020 8392 3051
Direct fax: 020 8392 3026
Direct e-mail: s.clegg@roehampton.ac.uk

Founded:
2000

Organisation type and purpose:
University library.

Subject coverage:
English language and literature, modern languages, art, drama, dance studies, theology and religious studies, history, mathematics education, music, film and TV studies, children's literature, arts, therapies, arts management, Education, sociology, social policy and administration, business studies, applied computing, applied consumer studies, retail and product management, anthropology. Biological sciences, health studies, human and social biology, natural resource studies, psychology, counselling, sport studies.

Museum or gallery collection, archive, or library special collection:
Children's Literature Collection
Early Childhood Archive
Froebel Archive

Library catalogue:
All or part available online

Access to staff:
Contact by letter, by telephone, by fax, by e-mail and via website
Hours: Term time: Mon to Thu, 0830 to 2100; Fri, 0830 to 1900; Sat, 1200 to 1700; Sun, 1200 to 1700 Vacations: usually Mon to Fri, 0900 to 1700, but phone to confirm

Affiliated to:
M25 Consortium of HE Libraries
SCONUL
UK Libraries Plus

Other addresses:
Roehampton University
 Froebel College
Roehampton University
 Southlands College
Roehampton University
 Whitelands College
Roehampton University
 Digby Stuart College

ROFFEY PARK INSTITUTE

Forest Road, Horsham, West Sussex, RH12 4TD

Tel: 01293 851644
Fax: 01293 851565
E-mail: info@roffeypark.com

Website:
http://www.roffeypark.com

Enquiries:
Enquiries to: Manager, Learning Resource Centre
Direct tel: 01293 854052
Direct e-mail: lrc@roffeypark.com

Founded:
1946

Organisation type and purpose:
Registered charity (charity number 254591), training organisation, consultancy. Independent management education institute.

Subject coverage:
Manager development, interpersonal relationships, developing the developers, personal effectiveness, assessment centres, self-managed learning, teamwork, organisational and leadership development, human resources.

Library catalogue:
All or part available online and in print

Printed publications:
Newsletter
Brochure
Order printed publications from: Marketing Department

Electronic and video publications:
Research reports (online)

Publications list:
Available online

Access to staff:
Contact by letter, by telephone, by e-mail, in person and via website. Appointment necessary. Access for members only. Non-members charged.

Access to building, collection or gallery:
Hours: Mon to Fri, 0900 to 1700
Special comments: Roffey Park course participants only

ROLLS-ROYCE ENTHUSIASTS' CLUB

Acronym or abbreviation: RREC

The Hunt House, High Street, Paulerspury, Towcester, Northamptonshire, NN12 7NA

Tel: 01327 811788
Fax: 01327 811797
E-mail: admin@rrec.co.uk

Website:
http://www.rrec.co.uk

Enquiries:
Enquiries to: General Secretary

Founded:
1957

Organisation type and purpose:
International organisation, membership association (membership is by subscription), present number of members: 9,500.

Subject coverage:
Rolls-Royce and Bentley archives containing car build records from 1904 onwards.

Printed publications:
R-R EC Advertiser
R-R EC Bulletin

Access to staff:
Contact by letter, by telephone, by fax and by e-mail. Appointment necessary.
Hours: Mon to Fri, 0900 to 1700

ROLLS-ROYCE PLC

Library Services, Rolls-Royce plc, PO Box 31, Victory Road, Derby, DE24 8BJ

Tel: 01332 242424
Fax: 01332 247886

Enquiries:
Enquiries to: Technical Librarian
Direct tel: 01332 248277

Organisation type and purpose:
Manufacturing industry.

Subject coverage:
Gas turbines, aerospace, aerodynamics, mechanical engineering, materials, fluid mechanics, jet propulsion, aero engines.

Printed publications:
R R Heritage Trust Publications historical series, technical series (tel: 01332 248181)
The Jet Engine book (Garry Crook, tel: 01332 246504)

Access to staff:
Contact by letter, by telephone and by fax
Hours: Mon to Fri, 0800 to 1600

ROMANIAN CULTURAL CENTRE

8th Floor, 54–62 Regent Street, London, W1B 5RE

Tel: 020 7439 4052
Fax: 020 7437 5908
E-mail: mail@romanianculturalcentre.org.uk

Website:
http://www.romanianculturalcentre.org.uk

Organisation type and purpose:
An independent association which promotes Romanian cultural programmes and acts as a focus for the Romanian community in Britain.

Subject coverage:
Romanian culture.

ROMANY AND TRAVELLER FAMILY HISTORY SOCIETY

Acronym or abbreviation: RTFHS

c/o Ms. Margaret Montgomery (Secretary), 7 Park Rise, Northchurch, Berkhamsted, Hertfordshire, HP4 3RT

Website:
http://www.rtfhs.org.uk

Organisation type and purpose:
A non-political non-profit self-help group, with membership by subscription.

Subject coverage:
Romany and traveller family history.

Printed publications:
Romany Routes (quarterly journal)

ROOM, THE NATIONAL COUNCIL FOR HOUSING AND PLANNING

RTPI, 41 Botolph Lane, London, EC3R 8DL

Tel: 020 7929 9494
Fax: 020 7929 9490
E-mail: room@rtpi.org.uk

Website:
http://www.room.org.uk

Enquiries:
Enquiries to: External Relations Manager
Other contacts: Assistant Director, Editor of Axis (Journal of Housing, Planning & Regeneration)

Founded:
1900

Organisation type and purpose:
Advisory body, membership association, registered charity.
Campaigning for better housing, planning and regeneration.

Subject coverage:
Housing and planning policy issues, house building and renovation, housing finance, student housing, sheltered housing, community alarms, planning control and policy guidance, regeneration, urban renewal, carbon monoxide/fire control.

Museum or gallery collection, archive, or library special collection:
Historical documents relating to NHPTC

Printed publications:
A Buyers Guide to Retirement Housing (Feb 1995, £4.95)
Axis, the Journal of Housing, Planning and Regeneration (6 times a year)

Best Value for Partnership Housing (Dec 1999, £8.50)
Community Regeneration (June 2001, £5)
Defining Positive Planning (Dec 2000, £5)
Deregulation of the Domestic Energy Market (Aug 1997, £7)
Energy Efficient Design (June 1995, £6)
Financing Partnership Housing (August 1994, £6)
Household Growth – Accommodating Change (Apr 1997, £6)
No Losers-New Users: New Homes from Empty Properties (Sep 1994, £8.50)
Planning Out the Empties (Nov 1998, £5)
Potential Death Traps (Feb 1995, £6)
Regenerating Communities and Neighbourhoods (Apr 1998, £6)
Still Rising High (Feb 1997, £8.50)
Sustaining High Density Living (Dec 1999, £8.50)
Sustainable Living (Jul 2000, £8.50)
Tackling Problem Estates (June 1996, £7)

Publications list:
Available in print

Access to staff:
Contact by letter, by telephone, by fax, by e-mail and via website. Appointment necessary.
Hours: Mon to Fri, 0900 to 1700

Member of:
International Federation of Housing and Planning The Hague, Netherlands

ROSE BRUFORD COLLEGE

Lamorbey Park, Sidcup, Kent, DA15 9DF

Tel: 020 8308 2600
Fax: 020 8308 0542
E-mail: enquiries@bruford.ac.uk

Website:
http://www.bruford.ac.uk

Enquiries:
Enquiries to: Librarian
Direct tel: 020 8308 2626

Founded:
1950

Organisation type and purpose:
A university sector institution.

Subject coverage:
Theatre, literature, drama, music.

Library catalogue:
All or part available in-house

Printed publications:
Library guide
Library information sheets

Access to staff:
Contact by letter, by telephone, by fax, by e-mail and in person. Appointment necessary.
Hours: Mon to Fri, 0900 to 1700

Access to building, collection or gallery:
By appointment
Hours: Mon to Fri, 0900 to 1700

Access for disabled people:
By appointment
Hours: Mon to Fri, 0900 to 1700

ROSKILL INFORMATION SERVICES LIMITED

27a Leopold Road, London, SW19 7BB

Tel: 020 8944 0066
Fax: 020 8947 9568
E-mail: info@roskill.co.uk

Website:
http://www.roskill.com

Enquiries:
Enquiries to: Information Officer
Other contacts: Managing Director

Founded:
1930

Organisation type and purpose:
Consultancy, publishing house.

Subject coverage:
Publish reports on the markets for metals and minerals, covering production, consumption, prices of, and trade in, the materials covered; end-use materials covered include plastics, paints and pigments, paper and pulp.

Trade and statistical information:
Production and consumption information on metals and minerals, e.g. base minerals, precious metals, industrial minerals and ferroalloys.
Statistical information on plastics, paper and pulp, paints and pigments, filler materials etc.

Library catalogue:
All or part available in-house

Printed publications:
Lithium Digest
Roskill's Letter from Japan (monthly)
Roskill's Reports on Metals and Minerals (about 80 on the economics of individual metals and minerals)
Roskill Yearbooks 1996–2000

Publications list:
Available online and in print

Access to staff:
Contact by letter, by telephone, by fax, by e-mail and via website. Appointment necessary.
Hours: Mon to Fri, 0800 to 1700

Access to building, collection or gallery:
No prior appointment required

Affiliated to:
Roskill Consulting Group

Parent body:
Roskill Information Services Limited

ROSPA ADVANCED DRIVERS AND RIDERS

Acronym or abbreviation: RoADAR

Edgbaston Park, 353 Bristol Road, Edgbaston, Birmingham, B5 7ST

Tel: 0121 248 2000
Fax: 0121 248 2001
E-mail: mrae@rospa.com

Website:
http://www.roadar.org

Enquiries:
Enquiries to: Administrator
Direct tel: 0121 248 2099

Organisation type and purpose:
Membership association (membership is by subscription, qualification), registered charity (charity number 207823).

Subject coverage:
Advanced driving; advanced motorcycling; tests and courses; road safety.

Library catalogue:
All or part available in-house

Printed publications:
Care on the Road (newsletter)
Greener Motoring Guide
Essential Minibus Driving
Order printed publications from: Customer Support

Electronic and video publications:
Driver Profiler
Driving for Work film
Driver E-learning
Hazard Perception Challenge
MORR Complete Compliance Tool
Order electronic and video publications from: jbartlett@rospa.com

Publications list:
Available online and in print

Access to staff:
Contact by letter, by telephone, by fax and by e-mail
Hours: Mon to Fri, 0900 to 1700

Access to building, collection or gallery:
Prior appointment required
Hours: Mon to Fri, 0900 to 1700

Access for disabled people:
Toilet facilities

Constituent part of:
Royal Society for the Prevention of Accidents
tel: 0121 248 2000; fax: 0121 248 2001; e-mail: help@rospa.co.uk; website: http://www.rospa .com

ROSPA DRIVER AND FLEET SOLUTIONS

Formal name: Royal Society for the Prevention of Accidents
Acronym or abbreviation: RoSPA

Edgbaston Park, 353 Bristol Road, Edgbaston, Birmingham, B5 7ST

Tel: 0121 248 2000 / 0870 777 2171
Fax: 0121 248 2001 / 0870 777 2199
E-mail: fleetsolutions@rospa.co.uk

Enquiries:
Enquiries to: Administrator
Direct tel: 0121 248 2124
Direct fax: 0121 248 2015
Direct e-mail: dgrady@rospa.co.uk

Organisation type and purpose:
National organisation, professional body, registered charity (charity number 207823), training organisation, consultancy, research organisation, publishing house.
Part of Driver and Fleet Solutions Department of RoSPA.
RoSPA's purpose is to enhance the quality of life by exercising a powerful influence for accident prevention.

Subject coverage:
Training operation in all aspects of defensive driving for companies.

Museum or gallery collection, archive, or library special collection:
General Road Safety/Driving – books, documents etc

Library catalogue:
All or part available in-house

Publications list:
Available in print

Access to staff:
Contact by letter, by telephone and by fax. Appointment necessary. All charged.
Hours: Mon to Fri, 0900 to 1700

Access to building, collection or gallery:
No prior appointment required
Hours: Mon to Fri, 0900 to 1700
Special comments: Library available for reference for members only.

Other offices:
RoSPA Northern Ireland
Nella House, 4 Dargan Crescent, Belfast, BT3 9JP; tel: 028 9050 1160 / 0870 777 2176; fax: 028 9050 1164 / 0870 777 2186
RoSPA Scotland
Livingstone House, 43 Discovery Terrace, Heriot-Watt University Research Park, Edinburgh, EH14 4AP; tel: 0131 449 9378; fax: 0131 449 9379
RoSPA Wales
7 Cleeve House, Lambourne Crescent, Cardiff, CF14 5GP; tel: 029 2025 0600 / 0870 777 2180; fax: 029 2025 0601 / 0870 777 2181

ROSPA NATIONAL SAFE DRIVING AWARDS

Acronym or abbreviation: NSDA

Edgbaston Park, 353 Bristol Road, Edgbaston, Birmingham, B5 7ST

Tel: 0121 248 2000
Fax: 0121 248 2001

continued overleaf

Enquiries:
Enquiries to: Administrator
Direct tel: 0121 248 2106
Direct e-mail: dgrady@rospa.com

Organisation type and purpose:
Voluntary organisation.

Subject coverage:
Safe driving.

Printed publications:
Care on the Road (newsletter)

Access to staff:
Contact by letter, by telephone and by fax
Hours: Mon to Fri, 0900 to 1700

Constituent part of:
Driver and Fleet Solutions – RoSPA

ROTARY INTERNATIONAL IN GREAT BRITAIN AND IRELAND

Acronym or abbreviation: RIBI

Kinwarton Road, Alcester, Warwickshire, B49 6BP

Tel: 01789 765411
Fax: 01789 765570
E-mail: secretary@ribi.org

Website:
http://www.rotary-ribi.org

Enquiries:
Enquiries to: Secretary; CEO
Other contacts: The President

Founded:
1914

Organisation type and purpose:
Membership association.
For charitable, benevolent and philanthropic
purposes.

Subject coverage:
Service to the local, national and international
communities through projects, ideas and physical
assistance, leading to greater international
understanding; scholarships and youth exchanges
in other countries; ethics in business and
professions; the ideal of service.

Printed publications:
Rotary (6 times a year, £1)

Electronic and video publications:
Rotary in Vision (£5 plus p&p)

Access to staff:
Contact by letter, by fax, by e-mail and via
website
Hours: Mon to Fri, 0900 to 1700

Access for disabled people:
Parking provided, ramped entry, toilet facilities

Parent body:
Rotary International
One Rotary Center, 1560 Sherman Avenue,
Evanston, Illinois, 60201, USA; tel: 00 1 847 866
3000; fax: 00 1 847 328 8554

ROTARY OWNERS CLUB

Acronym or abbreviation: ROC

Dunbar, Ingatestone Road, Highwood,
Chelmsford, Essex, CM1 3QU

E-mail: rotaryoc@aol.com

Enquiries:
Enquiries to: Secretary

Organisation type and purpose:
Membership association (membership is by
subscription).

Subject coverage:
Information is pooled on the maintenance of
motorcycles using the Wankel rotary engine,
registers are being compiled of all existing
machines.

**Museum or gallery collection, archive, or library
special collection:**
Copies of owners' manuals, handbook and parts
lists available to members

Printed publications:
The Epitrochoid (club magazine, quarterly, sent
free to members)

Access to staff:
Contact by letter and by e-mail
Hours: Mon to Fri, 0900 to 1700

ROTHAMSTED RESEARCH

Harpenden, Hertfordshire, AL5 2JQ

Tel: 01582 763133
Fax: 01582 760981

Website:
http://www.rothamsted.ac.uk

Enquiries:
Enquiries to: Librarian
Direct e-mail: res.library@bbsrc.ac.uk

Founded:
1843

Organisation type and purpose:
Research organisation.

Subject coverage:
Agricultural research (excluding animal
husbandry, diseases, etc., plant breeding and
agricultural economics); pure research on many
botanical and biochemical aspects of agriculture;
entomology; farms; insecticides and fungicides;
nematology; pedology; plant pathology; soil
microbiology; agricultural computer work;
statistics.

**Museum or gallery collection, archive, or library
special collection:**
Agricultural books, 1471–1840
British Farm Livestock, prints and paintings, 1780–
1910

Library catalogue:
All or part available online

Printed publications:
Annual Report

Access to staff:
Appointment necessary.
Hours: Mon to Fri, 0900 to 1700

Funded by:
Biotechnology and Biological Sciences Research
Council

Links with:
Broom's Barn Experimental Station

ROTHER DISTRICT COUNCIL

Town Hall, Bexhill-on-Sea, East Sussex, TN39 3JX

Tel: 01424 787878
Fax: 01424 787879
E-mail: chiefexec@rother.gov.uk

Website:
http://www.rother.gov.uk

Enquiries:
Enquiries to: Chief Executive

Founded:
1974

Organisation type and purpose:
Local government body.

Subject coverage:
Council issues.

Access to staff:
Contact by letter, by telephone, by fax, by e-mail,
in person and via website. Appointment necessary.
Hours: Mon to Thu, 0830 to 1700; Fri, 0830 to 1630

Access for disabled people:
Ramped entry

Other addresses:
Community Help Point (Battle)
6 Market Street, Battle, East Sussex, TN33 0XB;
tel: 01424 787478; fax: 01424 787479; e-mail:
customerservices@rither.gov.uk
Community Help Point (Bexhill)
Amherst Road, Bexhill-on-Sea, East Sussex; tel:
01424 787999; fax: 01424 787766; e-mail:
customerservices@rither.gov.uk
Community Help Point (Rye)
25 Cinque Ports Street, Rye, East Sussex, TN31
7AD; tel: 01797 222293; fax: 01797 227576; e-
mail: customerservices@rither.gov.uk

ROTHERHAM ARCHIVES AND LOCAL STUDIES SERVICE

Formal name: Rotherham Metropolitan Borough
Council: Archives and Local Studies Service

Central Library, Walker Place, Rotherham, South
Yorkshire, S65 1JH

Tel: 01709 823616
Fax: 01709 823650
E-mail: archives@rotherham.gov.uk

Website:
http://www.rotherham.gov.uk/graphics/Learning/
Archives

Founded:
1986

Organisation type and purpose:
Local government body, public library and archive
repository.

Subject coverage:
The local history of the area of Rotherham MBC.

**Museum or gallery collection, archive, or library
special collection:**
Archival holdings include records of Rotherham
MBC and predecessor local authorities; quarter
sessions and magistrates' courts; hospitals;
nonconformist archives; businesses (including
iron and steel, glass, coal mining, brass founding,
pottery); family and estate records; solicitors.
Local studies holdings include books and
pamphlets; directories; census returns;
newspapers; journals; digital and paper maps.

Non-library collection catalogue:
All or part available online and in-house

Library catalogue:
All or part available online and in-house

Printed publications:
Rotherham's Woodland Heritage (M. Jones,
Rotherwood Press, 1995, ISBN 0903666 86 3,
£6.95)
A History of Rotherham's Roads and Transport (H.
Smith, Rotherham Libraries, 1992, ISBN 0 903666
67 7, £5.95)
A Walk Round Rotherham – the town centre (1994,
Rotherham Libraries, ISBN 0 903666 74 X, £2)
Boyhood Memories of Wath (£3.75)
Rotherham and District Transport, vol. 1 (to 1914)
(C. C. Hall, Rotherwood Press, 1997, ISBN 00
903666 89 8, £18.95)
Rotherham and District Transport, vol. 2 (1914–39)
(C. C. Hall, Rotherwood Press, 1997, ISBN 0
903666 92 8, £16.50)
Rotherham and District Transport, vol. 3 (1940–74)
(in progress)
Rotherham Town Public Houses (P. Satterthwaite,
Rotherham Libraries, 1992, ISBN 0 903666 79 0,
£4.50)
The Saltway Trail (£1.50)

Publications list:
Available online and in print

Access to staff:
Contact by letter, by telephone, by fax, by e-mail
and in person
Hours: Tue, Wed, Fri, 1000 to 1700; Thu, 1300 to
1700; Sat, 0900 to 1300 and 1400 to 1600

ROTHERHAM CENTRAL LIBRARY AND ARTS CENTRE

Walker Place, Rotherham, South Yorkshire, S65 1JH

Tel: 01709 823611
Fax: 01709 823650
E-mail: central.library@rotherham.gov.uk

Website:
http://www.rotherham.gov.uk
Information on RMBC services, community information, business information.

Enquiries:
Enquiries to: Librarian

Organisation type and purpose:
Local government body, public library.

Subject coverage:
General; local history and study of the Rotherham Metropolitan Borough area; South Yorkshire potteries.

Museum or gallery collection, archive, or library special collection:
Mansell (Rotherham) Parish Library
British Standards (CD-ROM)

Library catalogue:
All or part available online and in-house

Printed publications:
Directory of community information

Access to staff:
Contact by letter, by telephone, by fax, by e-mail, in person and via website
Hours: Mon and Thu, 0830 to 2000; Tue, Wed and Fri, 0830 to 1730; Sat, 0900 to 1600

ROUGH FELL SHEEP BREEDERS ASSOCIATION

High Newstead Farm, Jervaulx, Masham, Ripon, North Yorkshire, HG4 4PJ

Tel: 07746 466794
E-mail: roughfell@fsmail.net

Website:
http://www.roughfellsheep.co.uk

Enquiries:
Enquiries to: Secretary

Subject coverage:
Rough Fell sheep.

Publications list:
Available in print

ROUTLEDGE REFERENCE – DIRECTORIES

Albert House, 4th Floor, 1–4 Singer Street, London, EC2A 4BQ

Tel: 020 7017 6000
Fax: 020 7017 6720
E-mail: reference@routledge.co.uk

Website:
http://www.worldwhoswho.com
http://www.routledge.com/reference
http://www.worldoflearning.com
http://www.europaworld.com

Enquiries:
Enquiries to: Marketing Manager
Direct tel: 020 7017 6040
Direct fax: 020 7017 6720
Direct e-mail: mary.sweny@informa.com

Organisation type and purpose:
Publishing house.

Subject coverage:
Geographic, economic and political information on every country in the world; current politics; government; political organisations; diplomatic representation; judicial system; religion; the press; publishers; radio and television; finance; trade and industry; transport; tourism; higher education; the environment; biographies; international organisations.

Printed publications:
Directory titles include:
Africa South of the Sahara (annually)
Aslib Directory of Information Sources in the United Kingdom (every two years)
Central & South-Eastern Europe (annually)
Directory of Human Rights
Directory of University Libraries in Europe
Directory of EU Information Sources
Directory of Trade and Professional Associations in the European Union
Eastern Europe, Russia & Central Asia (annually)
Eastern Europe and the Commonwealth of Independent States (every two years)
Environment Encyclopedia and Directory (irregular)
Europa World Year Book (annually)
European Union Encyclopedia and Directory (annually)
Far East and Australasia (annually)
Guide to EU Information Sources on the Internet
International Directory of Business Information Sources and Services (irregular)
International Directory of Government (annually)
International Foundation Directory (annually)
International Relations Research Directory
International Who's Who (annually)
International Who's Who in Poetry (every two years)
International Who's Who of Authors and Writers (annually)
International Who's Who of Classical Music (annually)
International Who's Who of Popular Music
International Who's Who of Women (every two years)
Middle East and North Africa (annually)
Political & Economic Dictionary of Eastern Europe
South America, Central America and the Caribbean (annually)
South Asia (annually)
Territories of the Russian Federation
USA and Canada (annually)
Western Europe (annually)
Who's Who in International Affairs (every two years)
World of Learning (annually)

Electronic and video publications:
Europa World Plus (online: http://www.europaworld.com)
World Who's Who (online: http://www.worldwhoswho.com)
The Europa World of Learning Online (http://www.worldoflearning.com)

Publications list:
Available online and in print

Access to staff:
Hours: Mon to Fri, 0900 to 1700

Other office:
Taylor & Francis Books (UK)
2 Park Square, Milton Park, Abingdon, Oxfordshire, OX14 4RN; tel: 020 7017 6000; website: http://www.taylorandfrancisgroup.com

Parent body:
Informa plc
4th Floor, 27 Mortimer Street, London, W1; tel: 020 7017 5000; website: http://www.informa.com

ROVER P4 DRIVERS GUILD

32 Arundel Road, Luton, Bedfordshire, LU4 8DY

Tel: 01582 572499
E-mail: colinb@rptdg.freeserve.co.uk

Enquiries:
Enquiries to: Secretary

Founded:
1977

Organisation type and purpose:
International organisation, membership association, voluntary organisation.

Subject coverage:
Historical, technical, spares sourcing and insurance information, advertisements, events related to P4 Rover cars built between 1950 and 1964.

Printed publications:
Overdrive (magazine, 6 times a year)
Yearbook

Access to staff:
Contact by letter and by telephone
Hours: Mon to Fri, 0900 to 1700

ROVER P5 OWNERS CLUB

13 Glen Avenue, Ashford, Middlesex, TW15 2JE

Tel: 01784 258166
Fax: 0117 977 5456
E-mail: membership@roverp5club.org.uk

Website:
http://www.roverp5club.org.uk
Sample of magazine content, services supplied, events calendar, etc.

Enquiries:
Enquiries to: Membership Secretary
Other contacts: Cars for sale register for purchase or sale of Rover P5 car.

Founded:
1985

Organisation type and purpose:
Membership association (membership is by subscription), present number of members: 1100, voluntary organisation.
To enable members to keep their examples of the Rover P5 marque running and in good order so that they can derive the maximum pleasure from owning and driving them.

Subject coverage:
All aspects of Rover P5 cars, buying and selling, technical data, parts supply, maintenance, club regalia.

Museum or gallery collection, archive, or library special collection:
Technical manuals (available to members only)

Printed publications:
Magazine (6 times a year, free to members)

Access to staff:
Contact by letter, by telephone, by fax and by e-mail
Hours: 0900 to 2100, seven days a week

ROWETT RESEARCH INSTITUTE

Acronym or abbreviation: RRI

Greenburn Road, Bucksburn, Aberdeen, AB21 9SB

Tel: 01224 712751
Fax: 01224 715349
E-mail: enquiries@rowett.ac.uk

Website:
http://www.rowett.ac.uk
General background details.

Enquiries:
Enquiries to: Public Relations Manager
Direct tel: 01224 716668
Direct e-mail: s.bird@rowett.ac.uk

Founded:
1913

Organisation type and purpose:
Registered charity, training organisation, consultancy, research organisation.
State-aided animal and human nutrition research centre.

Subject coverage:
Nutrient absorption, nutrient utilisation, trace elements, growth of skeletal and connective tissue, growth and metabolism of skeletal muscle, ruminant science, fermentation biochemistry, lipid metabolism, appetite control, diet related to health and disease states.

continued overleaf

Museum or gallery collection, archive, or library special collection:
Agriculture in the 18th and 19th centuries

Non-library collection catalogue:
All or part available in-house

Library catalogue:
All or part available in-house

Printed publications:
Corporate brochure

Publications list:
Available online

Access to staff:
Contact by letter, by telephone, by fax and by e-mail. Appointment necessary.
Hours: Mon to Fri, 0900 to 1700

Access to building, collection or gallery:
Prior appointment required

Access for disabled people:
Parking provided

Links with:
BBSRC
SEERAD

Subsidiary body:
Rowett Research Services

ROWLANDS LIBRARY

Charles Hastings Education Centre, Worcestershire Royal Hospital, Charles Hastings Way, Worcester, WR5 1DD

Tel: 01905 760601
Fax: 01905 760866
E-mail: rowlands.enquiries@worcsacute.wmids.nhs.uk

Website:
http://www.wkp.nhs.uk

Enquiries:
Enquiries to: Librarian

Founded:
1976

Organisation type and purpose:
National government body.
NHS Hospital Trust.

Subject coverage:
Medicine, nursing, midwifery, mental health, social care, therapies, pathology, public health, health service management.

Museum or gallery collection, archive, or library special collection:
History of Medicine, Royal College of Nursing Resource Centre

Non-library collection catalogue:
All or part available online

Access to staff:
Contact by letter, by telephone, by fax, by e-mail and via website
Hours: Mon to Fri, 0830 to 1700

Access for disabled people:
Parking provided, ramped entry, toilet facilities

ROYAL ACADEMY OF ARTS

Acronym or abbreviation: RA

Library, Burlington House, Piccadilly, London, W1J 0BD

Tel: 020 7300 5737
Fax: 020 7300 5765
E-mail: library@royalacademy.org.uk

Website:
http://www.royalacademy.org.uk
General information on the RA, its history, collections and members, current and forthcoming exhibitions and events.

Enquiries:
Enquiries to: Librarian

Founded:
1768

Organisation type and purpose:
Learned society.

Subject coverage:
Fine arts, British art since 1750, The Royal Academy.

Non-library collection catalogue:
All or part available online and in-house

Library catalogue:
All or part available online and in-house

Access to staff:
Contact by letter, by telephone, by fax, by e-mail and via website. Appointment necessary.
Hours: Tue to Fri, 1000 to 1300 and 1400 to 1700

Access to building, collection or gallery:
Hours: Tue to Fri, 1000 to 1300 and 1400 to 1700

Access for disabled people:
Parking provided, ramped entry, toilet facilities

ROYAL ACADEMY OF DANCE

Acronym or abbreviation: RAD

36 Battersea Square, London, SW11 3RA

Tel: 020 7326 8000
Fax: 020 7924 3129
E-mail: info@rad.org.uk

Website:
http://www.rad.org.uk
http://www.radenterprises.co.uk

Enquiries:
Enquiries to: Marketing
Direct tel: 020 7326 8002
Other contacts: Press and Marketing Manager

Founded:
1920

Organisation type and purpose:
Training, Membership and Examination organisation. To promote knowledge, understanding and practice of dance internationally. International teaching and examining body in classical ballet, incorporating a Faculty of Education for teacher training, a specialised reference library and archives and the home of the Benesh Institute. A global organisation involving approximately 13,000 members resident in 79 countries. The Royal Academy of Dance is a Charity Registered in England No. 312826.

Subject coverage:
Dance and related subjects.

Museum or gallery collection, archive, or library special collection:
Benesh Institute Notation Scores
Books, journals, photographs, pictures, programmes, videos and CD-ROMs

Library catalogue:
All or part available in-house

Printed publications:
Dance Gazette (3 a year)
Annual Report (available on request)
Faculty of Education Prospectus (available on request)
Dancing Around the World (leaflet, for purchase)
Order printed publications from: Royal Academy of Dance Enterprises Ltd; tel. 020 7326 8080; fax 020 7228 6261; e-mail sales@rad.org.uk

Publications list:
Available online

Access to staff:
Contact by letter, by telephone, by fax, by e-mail and via website. Appointment necessary.
Hours: Mon to Thu, 1000 to 1800; Fri, 1000 to 1730

Access to building, collection or gallery:
Prior appointment required

Access for disabled people:
Ramped entry, level entry, toilet facilities

Links with:
Durham University

ROYAL ACADEMY OF DRAMATIC ART

Acronym or abbreviation: RADA

18 Chenies Street, London, WC1E 7PA

Tel: 020 7636 7076
Fax: 020 7323 3865

Website:
http://www.rada.org
Information on current courses, forthcoming productions with online booking, History of RADA and graduate database.

Enquiries:
Enquiries to: Library Manager
Direct tel: 020 7908 4878
Direct e-mail: library@rada.ac.uk

Founded:
1904

Organisation type and purpose:
Registered charity (charity number 312819), suitable for ages: 18 to mid-30s, training organisation.
Academy for professional theatre training, acting and stage management, has 172 full-time students. Provides courses as above and specialist courses in props, electrics, scene painting and wardrobe.

Subject coverage:
Plays, Acting, Voice and Speech, Poetry, Theatre Criticism, Theory of Drama, Theatre History, Technical Theatre Arts, Stage Management, Biography, Costume, Social History, Film.

Museum or gallery collection, archive, or library special collection:
Ivo Currall Bequest (450 books and 46 albums of press cuttings by and about George Bernard Shaw)

Library catalogue:
All or part available in-house

Access to staff:
Contact by letter, by telephone and by e-mail. Appointment necessary. Non-members charged.
Hours: Mon to Wed, 0915 to 1945; Thur, Fri, 1000 to 1830

ROYAL ACADEMY OF ENGINEERING

Acronym or abbreviation: RAEng

29 Great Peter Street, London, SW1P 3LW

Tel: 020 7222 2688
Fax: 020 7233 0054

Website:
http://www.raeng.org.uk

Enquiries:
Enquiries to: Public Relations Manager
Direct tel: 020 7227 0536
Direct fax: 020 7227 7631
Direct e-mail: press@raeng.co.uk

Founded:
1976

Organisation type and purpose:
Membership association (membership is by election or invitation), present number of members: 1170, registered charity (charity number 293074).
The pursuit, encouragement and maintenance of excellence in the whole field of engineering in order to promote the advancement of the science, art and practice of engineering for the benefit of the public.

Subject coverage:
Engineering.

Library catalogue:
All or part available in-house

Publications list:
Available online

Access to staff:
Contact by letter, by telephone, by fax, by e-mail and via website
Hours: Mon to Fri, 0900 to 1700

ROYAL ACADEMY OF MUSIC

Acronym or abbreviation: RAM

Marylebone Road, London, NW1 5HT

Tel: 020 7873 7323
Fax: 020 7873 7322
E-mail: library@ram.ac.uk

Website:
http://www.ram.ac.uk

Enquiries:
Enquiries to: Librarian

Founded:
1822

Organisation type and purpose:
Registered charity, suitable for ages: 18+.

Subject coverage:
Music; especially performance, orchestras, choirs, opera, conducting, history of music.

Museum or gallery collection, archive, or library special collection:
Angelina Goetz Library (full scores)
Robert Spencer Collection (lutenist, 1932–1997, early printed music and manuscripts)
Arthur Sullivan archive (research material, books, scores and serials)
David Munrow Library
G. D. Cunningham Collection (organ music)
Mosco Carner Collection (mss, press cuttings, letters, photographs)
Otto Klemperer Collection (scores and books)
R. J. S. Stevens Savage Collection (early printed music and manuscripts)
Sheet music
Sir Henry Wood Library of orchestral material
Foyle Menuhin Archive

Non-library collection catalogue:
All or part available online

Library catalogue:
All or part available online and in-house

Printed publications:
Annual Prospectus
Library guide
Newsletter
Academy of Music, 1988 Research Publications: The Music Collection of the Royal Academy of Music 1988

Access to staff:
Contact by letter, by e-mail and via website
Hours: 0900 to 1800

Access to building, collection or gallery:
Prior appointment required

ROYAL AERONAUTICAL SOCIETY

Acronym or abbreviation: RAeS

4 Hamilton Place, London, W1J 7BQ

Tel: 020 7670 4362
Fax: 020 7670 4359
E-mail: brian.riddle@aerosociety.com

Website:
http://www.aerosociety.com

Enquiries:
Enquiries to: Librarian

Founded:
1866

Created by the merger of:
Institution of Aeronautical Engineers, Helicopter Association of Great Britain and Society of Licensed Aircraft Engineers and Technologists

Organisation type and purpose:
Learned society, registered charity (charity number 313708).

Subject coverage:
Aeronautics, astronautics, aerospace engineering, aerospace history, space, air law, air power, air transport, guided flight, aerospace propulsion, flight testing, avionics, rotorcraft, aviation medicine, piloting, aerodynamics, aircraft maintenance, aircraft structures and materials. An extensive collection of material relating to the development and recent technical advances in aeronautics, aviation and aerospace technology from the earliest times through to current operations and technology.

Museum or gallery collection, archive, or library special collection:
30,000 books, 1,000 periodical titles, 20,000 technical reports, 200,000 photographs and subscriptions, 200 current journal titles
Extensive collection of aviation photographs, glass lantern slides and lithographs in excess of 200,000
Books, letters, papers and manuscripts of early pioneers, including:
Major B. F. S. Baden-Powell (1860–1937)
Sir George Cayley (1773–1857)
C. G. Grey (1875–1953)
Lawrence Hargrave (1850–1915)
John Stringfellow (1799–1883)
Katharine Wright (1874–1929)
Orville Wright (1871–1948)
Wilbur Wright (1867–1912)
F. S. Barnwell (1880–1938, Design notebooks)
and various papers relating to the long history of the Society.
Cuthbert-Hodgson Collection (ballooning and early aeronautical material)
Maitland Airship Collection
Poynton Collection (early ballooning, etc.)
Air Ministry / Ministry of Aircraft Production Air Publications
Air Accidents Investigations Branch Reports
Advisory Committee for Aeronautics/Aeronautical Research Council (ARC) technical reports
Society of British Aircraft Constructors / Aerospace Companies (SBAC) Minutes 1916–2000
The Air Pilot / UK Aeronautical Information Publication (AIP) August 1948–1999

Library catalogue:
All or part available online

Printed publications:
Aerospace International (monthly)
The Aeronautical Journal (monthly)
The Aerospace Professional (monthly)
Proceedings of Conferences
Publications Index 1897–1977
The National Aerospace Library (B. Riddle, 2007, £4.00)
Letters of the Wright Brothers: Letters of Wilbur, Orville and Katharine Wright in the Royal Aeronautical Society Library (ed. Brian Riddle and Colin Sinnott, 2003)
Pioneers of Flight Exhibition Programme (B. Riddle, 2003)

Access to staff:
Contact by letter, by telephone, by fax, by e-mail, in person and via website. Appointment necessary. Non-members charged.
Hours: Mon to Fri, 1000 to 1700

Branches:
National Aerospace Library
The Hub, Fowler Avenue, IQ Farnborough, GU14 7JP; tel: 01252 701038; 01252 701039; e-mail: hublibrary@aerosociety.com; website: http://www.aerosociety.com/cmspage .asp?cmsitemid=Library_NAL

ROYAL AFRICAN SOCIETY

SOAS, Thornhaugh Street, London, WC1H 0XG

Tel: 020 7898 4390
Fax: 020 7898 4389
E-mail: ras@soas.ac.uk

Enquiries:
Enquiries to: Secretary

Founded:
1901

Organisation type and purpose:
Voluntary organisation, registered charity (charity number 1062764).

Subject coverage:
African affairs.

Printed publications:
African Affairs (quarterly, membership includes subscription)
African Studies Association Newsletter (quarterly with African Affairs)
Occasional Papers

Access to staff:
Contact by telephone
Hours: Mon to Fri, 0900 to 1700

Affiliated with joint members to the:
African Studies Association of the UK at the same address

ROYAL AGRICULTURAL COLLEGE

Acronym or abbreviation: RAC

Library, Stroud Road, Cirencester, Gloucestershire, GL7 6JS

Tel: 01285 652531
Fax: 01285 889844
E-mail: library@rac.ac.uk

Website:
http://www.rac.ac.uk

Enquiries:
Enquiries to: Librarian
Direct tel: 01285 652531 ext 2274

Founded:
1845

Organisation type and purpose:
University library, suitable for ages: 18+.
University sector library.
Undergraduate and postgraduate degrees, research and consultancy in land-based industries and development, and related sectors.

Subject coverage:
Agriculture, forestry, horticulture, land use and management including land law, valuation, building construction, taxation, economics, ecology and conservation, farm woodlands, rural planning; business and management, environment, tourism, property agency, wine and viticulture, equine studies, agribusiness, international rural development.

Museum or gallery collection, archive, or library special collection:
British Deer Society collection
Historical collection of books on agriculture and land management

Trade and statistical information:
Agricultural statistics on trade and production, mainly DEFRA, Food and Agriculture Organisation and Eurostat.

Library catalogue:
All or part available online

Access to staff:
Contact by letter, by telephone, by fax, by e-mail and via website. Appointment necessary. All charged.
Hours: Term time: Mon to Thu, 0900 to 2000; Fri, 0900 to 1700; Sat, 1200 to 1700; Sun, 1300 to 1700
Vacations: Mon to Fri, 0900 to 1700
Special comments: External membership by subscription.

Access for disabled people:
Parking provided, level entry, access to all public areas, toilet facilities, automatic entrance doors

ROYAL AGRICULTURAL SOCIETY OF ENGLAND

Acronym or abbreviation: RASE

National Agricultural Centre, Stoneleigh Park, Kenilworth, Warwickshire, CV8 2LZ

Tel: 024 7669 6969
Fax: 024 7669 6900
E-mail: jaynesp@rase.org.uk

Website:
http://www.rase.org.uk

Enquiries:
Enquiries to: Press Officer
Other contacts: Marketing Manager

Founded:
1840

Organisation type and purpose:
Learned society, voluntary organisation, registered charity.
Transfer of technology and information related to agriculture and the rural economy.

Subject coverage:
Agriculture in general, horticulture, crop husbandry, machinery, livestock husbandry, entomology.

Museum or gallery collection, archive, or library special collection:
Reference library available by appointment

Printed publications:
Annual Journal
Members Newsletter
Surveys

Access to staff:
Contact by letter, by telephone, by fax, by e-mail and via website. Appointment necessary.
Hours: Mon to Fri, 0900 to 1700

Affiliated with French equivalent:
SAF

Affiliated with German equivalent:
DLG

ROYAL AGRICULTURAL SOCIETY OF THE COMMONWEALTH

Acronym or abbreviation: RASC

2 Grosvenor Gardens, London, SW1W 0DH

Tel: 020 7259 9678
Fax: 020 7259 9675
E-mail: rasc@commagshow.org

Website:
http://www.commagshow.org

Enquiries:
Enquiries to: Honorary Secretary

Founded:
1957

Organisation type and purpose:
International organisation, learned society, voluntary organisation, registered charity (charity number 211322).
Promotes agricultural co-operation between the developed and developing Commonwealth countries etc.

Subject coverage:
Practice and science of agriculture, improvement of methods of crop production and breeding of livestock, improvement of efficiency of agricultural implements and machinery.

Printed publications:
Newsletters (4 times a year)
Reports on Biennial Conferences

Access to staff:
Contact by letter, by telephone, by fax and by e-mail. Appointment necessary.
Hours: Mon to Fri, 0930 to 1700

Comprises the:
42 National Agricultural Show Societies in 21 Commonwealth countries

Links with:
Commonwealth Foundation
Commonwealth Secretariat
International Association of Fairs and Expositions (IAFE)
Royal Commonwealth Society (RCS)

ROYAL AIR FORCE COLLEGE

Library, Cranwell, Sleaford, Lincolnshire, NG34 8HB

Tel: 01400 261201 ext 6329
Fax: 01400 261201 ext 6266

Website:
http://www.cranwell.raf.mod.uk
General enquiry service.

Enquiries:
Enquiries to: Librarian

Founded:
1920

Organisation type and purpose:
Central government establishment.

Subject coverage:
Aeronautics, military science and history (especially air power), RAF history, defence studies, current affairs, air warfare, management sciences, computer sciences, engineering (mechanical, electrical, electronic, materials, aeronautical, aerospace), mathematics, logistics, warfare, weapons.

Museum or gallery collection, archive, or library special collection:
College Archives
Part of the library of the late Lord Trenchard
T E Lawrence Collection

Non-library collection catalogue:
All or part available in-house

Library catalogue:
All or part available in-house

Access to staff:
Contact by letter and by telephone. Appointment necessary.
Hours: Mon, Tue, Thu, 0815 to 1700; Wed, Fri, 0815 to 1600

Parent body:
Ministry of Defence – Royal Air Force

ROYAL AIR FORCES ASSOCIATION

Acronym or abbreviation: RAFA

CHQ, 117½ Loughborough Road, Leicester, LE4 5ND

Tel: 0116 266 5224
Fax: 0116 266 5012

Website:
http://www.rafa.org.uk/

Enquiries:
Enquiries to: Secretary General

Organisation type and purpose:
Voluntary organisation, registered charity (charity number 226686).
Incorporated by Royal Charter.

Subject coverage:
Advice and assistance to those who are eligible on all aspects of welfare, pensions, disability awards, civilian employment.

Printed publications:
Air Mail (4 times a year, for members)

Access to staff:
Contact by letter and by telephone. Appointment necessary.
Hours: Mon to Fri, 0900 to 1700

Has:
9 area headquarters within the British Isles

ROYAL ALFRED SEAFARERS' SOCIETY

Acronym or abbreviation: RASS

SBC House, Restmor Way, Wallington, Surrey, SM6 7AH

Tel: 020 8401 2889
Fax: 020 8401 2592
E-mail: royalalfred@btopenworld.com

Enquiries:
Enquiries to: General Secretary

Founded:
1867

Organisation type and purpose:
National organisation, registered charity (charity number 209776).
Providing nursing and residential home care, and sheltered housing for retired seafarers, their dependants and persons who have worked in trades or professions allied to the maritime industry.

Subject coverage:
Information on the subject of long-term care facilities for retired seafarers.

Printed publications:
Annual Report

Access to staff:
Contact by letter, by telephone, by fax and by e-mail
Hours: Mon to Fri, 0900 to 1700

Access to building, collection or gallery:
Prior appointment required
Hours: Mon to Fri, 0900 to 1700

Access for disabled people:
Parking provided, level entry, access to all public areas, toilet facilities

Other addresses:
Royal Alfred Seafarers' Society
Belvedere House, Weston Acres, Woodmansterne Lane, Banstead, Surrey, SM7 3HA; tel: 01737 360106; fax: 01737 353436; e-mail: home.bns@mha.org.uk
Royal Alfred Seafarers' Society
Royal Alfred House, 5–11 Hartington Place, Eastbourne, BN21 3BS; tel: 01323 721828; fax: 01323 431029; e-mail: home.eas@mha.org.uk

ROYAL AND ANCIENT GOLF CLUB OF ST ANDREWS, THE

Acronym or abbreviation: R&A

St Andrews, Fife, KY16 9JD

Tel: 01334 460000
Fax: 01334 460001
E-mail: webmaster@randa.org

Website:
http://www.randa.org
http://www.opengolf.com

Enquiries:
Enquiries to: Secretary

Founded:
1754

Organisation type and purpose:
International organisation (membership is by election or invitation), present number of members: 1800.
Governing Body for the Rules of Golf and Rules of Amateur Status throughout the world (except USA and Canada).

Subject coverage:
Golf, British championships and international matches, rules of golf, rules of amateur status, golf clubs and balls.

Access to staff:
Contact by letter, by telephone, by fax and by e-mail. Appointment necessary.
Hours: Mon to Fri, 0900 to 1700

ROYAL ANTHROPOLOGICAL INSTITUTE OF GREAT BRITAIN AND IRELAND

Acronym or abbreviation: RAI

50 Fitzroy Street, London, W1T 5BT

Tel: 020 7387 0455
Fax: 020 7388 8817
E-mail: admin@therai.org.uk

Website:
http://www.therai.org.uk
Anthropological Index, information on RAI.

Enquiries:
Enquiries to: Director

Founded:
1843

Organisation type and purpose:
International organisation, national organisation, learned society (membership is by election or invitation), present number of members: 1600, voluntary organisation (charity number 246269), suitable for ages: 16+, publishing house.

Subject coverage:
Anthropology.

Museum or gallery collection, archive, or library special collection:
Photograph collection at the Institute
The Library, gifted to the British Museum and held at the Centre for Anthropology in London – access to Fellows

Non-library collection catalogue:
All or part available in-house

Library catalogue:
All or part available in-house

Printed publications:
Anthropological Index to Current Periodicals (available free of charge on the Internet)
Anthropology Today
Journal of the Royal Anthropological Institute (incorporating 'Man')
Order printed publications from: Blackwells Publishers
Journals Dept, 9600 Garsington Road, Oxford, OX4 2DQ, tel: 01865 791100, fax: 01865 791347

Electronic and video publications:
Over 200 videos and films; some for sale and some for hire. Articles from backnumbers of JRAI and Anthropology Today available electronically (for a fee) from JSTOR and Ingenta respectively

Publications list:
Available in print

Access to staff:
Contact by letter, by telephone, by fax and by e-mail. Appointment necessary. Non-members charged.
Hours: Mon to Fri, 930 to 1730

ROYAL ARCHAEOLOGICAL INSTITUTE

Acronym or abbreviation: RAI

Society of Antiquaries, Burlington House, Piccadilly, London, W1J 0BE

Fax: 0116 243 3839
E-mail: admin@royalarchaeolinst.org

Enquiries:
Enquiries to: Administrator

Founded:
1844

Organisation type and purpose:
Learned society (membership is by subscription), present number of members: 1500, registered charity (charity number 226222 ACL), suitable for ages: 18+.

Subject coverage:
Archaeology, art history, architecture.

Printed publications:
Journals (£55 to non-members, some OUP)
Archaeological Journal (annually)
Monographs
Newsletters (free to members)

Publications list:
Available in print

Access to staff:
Contact by letter, by telephone, by fax and by e-mail. Access for members only.
Special comments: Library (Society of Antiquaries).

ROYAL ARMOURIES LIBRARY – LEEDS

Armouries Drive, Leeds, West Yorkshire, LS10 1LT

Tel: 0113 220 1832
Fax: 0113 220 1934
E-mail: enquiries@armouries.org.uk

Website:
http://www.armouries.org.uk

Enquiries:
Enquiries to: Librarian

Organisation type and purpose:
National government body, museum.
Operates under a Board of Trustees appointed by the Secretary of State for Culture, Media and Sport.

Subject coverage:
The Royal Armouries and its collections, the history and development of European and Oriental arms and armour, including firearms, from the middle ages to the present day; the history of the Tower of London and its institutions.

Museum or gallery collection, archive, or library special collection:
A small number of important manuscripts including the earliest known (13th-century) fencing manual, which shows the use of sword and buckler; a 15th-century firework book, which illustrates the manufacture and use of gunpowder; and an account of the jousts between Jehan Chalons of England and Loys de Beul of France at Tours in 1446
Early books on fencing and the art of warfare
Handbooks and manuals on military small arms and artillery
Catalogues of arms and armour sales
Minute books of the Board of Ordnance (microfilm)
Photographs of objects in the Royal Armouries' own collection, of objects in other collections, and of illustrations of arms and armour in art
40,000 books, pamphlets and journals
150,000 black and white photographs
2000 colour transparencies

Access to staff:
Contact by letter, by telephone, by fax and by e-mail
Hours: Library: Mon to Fri, 1030 to 1630, closed bank holidays

Access to building, collection or gallery:
No access other than to staff

Other addresses:
Royal Armouries
HM Tower of London, London, EC3N 4AB; tel: 020 7480 6358; fax: 020 7481 2922
Royal Armouries
Fort Nelson, Down End Road, Fareham, Hampshire, PO17 6AN; tel: 01329 233734; fax: 01329 822092

ROYAL ARMOURIES LIBRARY – LONDON

HM Tower of London, London, EC3N 4AB

Tel: 020 3166 6668
Fax: 020 3166 6678
E-mail: enquiries@armouries.org.uk

Website:
http://www.armouries.org.uk

Enquiries:
Enquiries to: Librarian

Organisation type and purpose:
National government body, museum.
Operates under a Board of Trustees appointed by the Secretary of State for the Environment.

Subject coverage:
History of the Tower of London and its institutions, including the Board of Ordnance, the Menagerie, the Royal Mint at the Tower, history of fortification.

Education services:
Available on tel: 020 3166 6660

Museum or gallery collection, archive, or library special collection:
A small reference collection of books and pamphlets on arms and armour
Collection of Tower-related prints and manuscripts
Photographic reference archive for Tower-related material

Non-library collection catalogue:
All or part available in-house and in print

Library catalogue:
All or part available in-house

Printed publications:
Order printed publications from: Royal Armouries Museum
Armouries Drive, Leeds, LS10 1LT

Access to staff:
Contact by letter, by telephone, by fax and by e-mail. Appointment necessary.
Hours: Library: Mon to Fri, 1000 to 1600 by appointment only

Also at:
Royal Armouries Library
Armouries Drive, Leeds, LS10 1LT; tel: 0113 220 1832

Main Library at:
Royal Armouries Museum, Leeds

Outstation at:
Fort Nelson

ROYAL ARTILLERY HISTORICAL TRUST

Firepower Royal Artillery Museum, Royal Arsenal (West), Warren Lane, Woolwich, London, SE18 6ST

Tel: 020 8855 7755
Fax: 020 8855 7100
E-mail: research@firepower.org.uk

Website:
http://www.firepower.org.uk

Enquiries:
Enquiries to: Honorary Secretary

Organisation type and purpose:
Advisory body.

Subject coverage:
Administration and control of the museum, library, artefacts and archives.

Non-library collection catalogue:
All or part available in-house

Library catalogue:
All or part available in-house

Access to staff:
Contact by letter, by telephone, by fax and by e-mail. Appointment necessary.
Hours: Mon to Fri, 1000 to 1600

Responsible for:
Firepower
James Clavell Library
Firepower, Royal Arsenal (West), Warren Lane, Woolwich, London, SE18 6ST; tel: 020 8855 7755; e-mail: research@firepower.org.uk; website: www.firepower.org.uk
Reserve Collection
Rotunda, Woolwich, London, SE18 4BQ
Royal Artillery Library and Archives

continued overleaf

The Royal Artillery Museum
Royal Arsenal (West), Warren Lane, Woolwich, London, SE18 6ST; tel: 020 8855 7755; fax: 020 8855 7100; e-mail: research@firepower.org.uk; website: www.firepower.org.uk

ROYAL ARTILLERY INSTITUTION

Acronym or abbreviation: RAI

Artillery House, Royal Artillery Barracks, Larkhill, Salisbury, Wiltshire, SP4 8QT

Tel: 01980 845528
Fax: 01980 845210
E-mail: ac-rhqra-regtsec@mod.uk

Enquiries:
Enquiries to: Regimental Secretary

Founded:
1839

Organisation type and purpose:
Professional body.
Regimental institution.

Subject coverage:
History of the Royal Regiment of Artillery 1716 to date; artillery, development, c.1650 onwards; history of army ordnance, especially post-1715, military and campaign history; British Army.

Museum or gallery collection, archive, or library special collection:
Kaye collection of military history
The manuscripts of General Sir Alexander Dickson
Wide range of published and manuscript works on ordnance from 16th century onwards
RA Journals and Minutes of Proceedings of the RAI

Library catalogue:
All or part available in-house

Printed publications:
History of the Royal Regiment of Artillery (6 vols, 1914–55)
Royal Artillery Historical Society Proceedings (annually)
Royal Artillery Journal (2 times a year)
Gunner Magazine (monthly)
Order printed publications from: Property Clerk, Royal Artillery Institution

Access to staff:
Contact by letter, by fax and by e-mail.
Appointment necessary.
Hours: Mon to Fri, 0900 to 1700

Access to building, collection or gallery:
No prior appointment required

Links with:
Firepower, Royal Artillery Museum
Royal Arsenal, Woolwich, London, SE18 6ST; tel: 020 8855 7755; fax: 020 8855 7100; e-mail: info@ firepower.org.uk; website: http://www .firepower.org.uk
James Clavell Library
Firepower, The Royal Artillery Museum, Old Laboratory Office, Royal Arsenal (West), Warren Lane, Woolwich, London, SE18 6ST
Royal Artillery Historical Society
Royal Artillery Barracks, Larkhill, Salisbury, Wiltshire, SP4 8QT; tel: 01980 845367; e-mail: rahs@hqdra.army.mod.ac.uk
Royal Artillery Historical Trust
Old Laboratory Office, Royal Arsenal (West), Warren Lane, Woolwich, London, SE18 6ST; tel: 020 8312 7120; fax: 020 8855 7100; e-mail: marks@firepower.org.uk

ROYAL ARTILLERY LIBRARY

James Clavell Library, Royal Arsenal (West), Warren Lane, Woolwich, London, SE18 6ST

Tel: 020 8312 7125
E-mail: research@firepower.org.uk

Website:
http://www.firepower.org.uk

Enquiries:
Enquiries to: Librarian

Organisation type and purpose:
Independently owned, registered charity.
Part of the Firepower Museum Complex.
To record and promote research into the history of the Royal Artillery and related subjects.

Subject coverage:
Materials on Royal Artillery Regimental History; artillery equipment, armed forces, warfare, tactics, training, fortification, military history, military geography and biography.

Museum or gallery collection, archive, or library special collection:
Books, journals, pamphlets, manuscripts, diaries, maps, plans, drawings, photographs, film and microfiche

Non-library collection catalogue:
All or part available in-house

Printed publications:
History of the Royal Regiment of Artillery (Vols I - VI available, VII in production)

Access to staff:
Contact by letter, by telephone and in person.
Appointment necessary.

Access to building, collection or gallery:
Prior appointment required
Hours: David Evans Reading Room, open for readers Mon to Fri, 1000 to 1600

Linked organisation:
Firepower! Royal Artillery Museum
Royal Regiment of Artillery

Parent body:
Royal Artillery Historical Trust
Royal Artillery Museum, Royal Arsenal (West), Warren Lane, Woolwich, London, SE18 6ST; tel: 020 8312 7120

ROYAL ASIATIC SOCIETY OF GREAT BRITAIN AND IRELAND

14 Stephenson Way, London, NW1 2HD

Tel: 020 7388 4539
E-mail: cl@royalasiaticsociety.org

Website:
http://www.royalasiaticsociety.org

Enquiries:
Enquiries to: Executive Officer
Direct e-mail: cl@royalasiaticsociety.org

Founded:
1823

Organisation type and purpose:
Membership organisation (membership by election).
To provide a forum for those who are interested in the history, languages, cultures and religions of Asia to meet and exchange ideas through lectures, seminars, research and publishing.
Registered charity (charity number 209629)

Subject coverage:
History, languages, cultures and religions of Asia.

Museum or gallery collection, archive, or library special collection:
Library of 80,000 items, including:
Tod Collection (Indian manuscripts and paintings)
Hodgson Collection (Buddhist and Sanskrit manuscripts)
Ram Raz Collection (architectural drawings)
Raffles and Maxwell Collections (Malay manuscripts)
Howell Collection (early photographs of China and Japan)

Non-library collection catalogue:
All or part available in-house

Library catalogue:
All or part available in-house

Printed publications:
Journal of the Royal Asiatic Society (3 times a year)

Order printed publications from: Books published by the Royal Asiatic Society should be ordered from the Society's publishing partner, RoutledgeCurzon, Taylor and Francis Ltd, 2 Park Square, Milton Park, Abingdon, Oxon., OX14 4RN; tel: 020 7017 6000; fax: 020 7017 6699; internet: www.routledge.curzon.com

Publications list:
Available online

Access to staff:
Contact by letter, by telephone, by e-mail and via website. Appointment necessary.

ROYAL ASSOCIATION FOR DEAF PEOPLE

Acronym or abbreviation: RAD

Centre for Deaf People, Walsingham Road, Colchester, Essex, CO2 7BP

Tel: 01206 509509\ Minicom no. 01206 577090
Fax: 01206 769755
E-mail: info@royaldeaf.org.uk

Website:
http://www.royaldeaf.org.uk
Information and advice about the UK Deaf Community.

Enquiries:
Enquiries to: Administrator

Founded:
1841

Organisation type and purpose:
Registered charity (charity number 1081949).
To promote the spiritual, social and general welfare of deaf people.

Subject coverage:
Profound hearing impairment, blindness and deafness, problems of deaf people in psychiatric and sub-normal hospitals, social casework and welfare service, the Church's ministry to and the spiritual and pastoral care of deaf/blind and deaf people.

Publications list:
Available online and in print

Access to staff:
Contact by letter, by telephone, by fax, by e-mail, in person and via website. Appointment necessary.
Hours: Mon to Fri, 0900 to 1700
Special comments: Access also by minicom.

ROYAL ASSOCIATION FOR DISABILITY AND REHABILITATION

Acronym or abbreviation: RADAR

12 City Forum, 250 City Road, London, EC1V 8AF

Tel: 020 7250 3222\ Minicom no. 020 7250 4119 (for the hearing impaired only)
Fax: 020 7250 0212
E-mail: radar@radar.org.uk

Website:
http://www.radar.org.uk

Enquiries:
Enquiries to: Information Officer

Founded:
1977

Organisation type and purpose:
Voluntary organisation, registered charity (charity number 273150).
A major national cross-disability organisation run by and working for disabled people.
Working to end discrimination and to promote the independence of disabled people. Campaigning and advising on: independent living; civil rights; employment; education; housing; mobility; leisure; social security; and access.

Subject coverage:
All aspects of physical disability, except the strictly medical (benefits, employment, education, holidays, housing, legislation, civil rights, mobility, social security, social services).

Printed publications:
Bulletin (monthly)
Books and other publications including:
Access to Teaching (out of print)
Choosing a Wheelchair (out of print)
Disability and Discrimination in Employment (out of print)
Children First – A Guide to the Needs of Children in School (£10.50)
Holidays in Britain & Ireland – A Guide for Disabled People (£8)
National Key Scheme Guide – Accessible toilets for disabled people (£5)
Factsheets

Publications list:
Available online and in print

Access to staff:
Contact by letter, by telephone, by fax, by e-mail and via website
Hours: Information Dept: Mon to Thu, 1000 to 1600
Other depts: 0900 to 1700

Access for disabled people:
Parking provided, ramped entry, level entry, access to all public areas, toilet facilities

Organisation of:
600 local and national bodies

ROYAL ASSOCIATION OF BRITISH DAIRY FARMERS

Acronym or abbreviation: RABDF

Dairy House, Unit 31, Stoneleigh Deer Park, Stareton, Kenilworth, Warwickshire, CV8 2LY

Tel: 0845 458 2711
Fax: 0845 458 2755
E-mail: office@rabdf.co.uk

Website:
http://www.rabdf.co.uk/

Enquiries:
Enquiries to: Press Officer
Direct tel: 01743 344986
Direct e-mail: lizsnaith@btopenworld.com

Founded:
1876

Organisation type and purpose:
Membership association (membership is by subscription), present number of members: 2000, registered charity (charity number 213782). The RABDF organises The European Dairy Farming Event – the United Kingdom's largest specialist event for dairy farmers and the dairy farming industry. The Association also organises conferences, publishes regular newsletters, liaises with Government and is involved in training.

Subject coverage:
Dairy farming and other matters related to dairy cattle.

Printed publications:
Dairy Farming Event Catalogue
RABDF News (quarterly magazine, free to members)

Access to staff:
Contact by letter, by telephone and by fax
Hours: Mon to Fri, 0900 to 1700

Organisers of the:
Dairy Event

ROYAL AUTOMOBILE CLUB LIBRARY

89 Pall Mall, London, SW1Y 5HS

Tel: 020 7747 3398
Fax: 0870 4606285
E-mail: library@royalautomobileclub.co.uk

Website:
http://www.royalautomobileclub.co.uk

Enquiries:
Enquiries to: Librarian
Other contacts: Library Assistant

Founded:
1897

Formerly called:
Automobile Club of Great Britain (and later Ireland) (year of change 1907)

Organisation type and purpose:
Private members club (membership by election), present membership approximately 15,000

Subject coverage:
History of the Royal Autombile Club, history of motoring and motor sport

Museum or gallery collection, archive, or library special collection:
Long runs of motoring periodicals including: Autocar, The Motor, Autosport; motoring books including: racing and production marques and models, biographies, motor sport, technical and legal material; RAC archives including: club handbooks and journals, personal correspondence, membership records, pamphlets, photographs, exhibition programmes, route guides

Non-library collection catalogue:
All or part available online and in-house

Library catalogue:
All or part available in-house

Printed publications:
The Motoring Century: the story of the Royal Automobile Club (available direct, £15 plus p&p)
Badges of the Royal Automobile Club (available direct, £7.95 plus p&p)

Access to staff:
Contact by letter, by telephone, by fax and by e-mail. Appointment necessary. Access for members only. Letter of introduction required.
Hours: Mon to Fri, 0900 to 1700

Access to building, collection or gallery:
Special comments: Researchers only

Member organisation of:
international motoring bodies: FIA, FISA, AIT, MSA

ROYAL BIRMINGHAM SOCIETY OF ARTISTS

Acronym or abbreviation: RBSA Gallery

4 Brook Street, St Paul's, Birmingham, B3 1SA

Tel: 0121 236 4353
Fax: 0121 236 4555
E-mail: secretary@rbsa.org.uk

Website:
http://www.rbsa.org.uk
Information about the gallery, current exhibitions and workshops, joining the RBSA and artist opportunities

Enquiries:
Enquiries to: Honorary Secretary
Other contacts: Honorary Curator for gallery hire.

Founded:
1814

Organisation type and purpose:
Independently owned, professional body (membership is by subscription, election or invitation), present number of members: 460 friends, 83 associates, 105 members, registered charity (charity number 528894), museum, art gallery, workshop facilities, suitable for all ages. To actively encourage the learning, practice and appreciation of fine arts and allied crafts. Fulfilment of a vital community purpose by supporting and showcasing the work of local and national professional artists and crafts people and providing opportunities for amateur artists.

Subject coverage:
Practical fine art and allied crafts. History of the Royal Birmingham Society of Artists. All media are represented, from contemporary to traditional. Biennial exhibition of RBSA Permanent Collection.

Museum or gallery collection, archive, or library special collection:
Bound Exhibition Catalogues continuous from the early years of the Society
Paintings, prints, sculptures etc donated by artists when elected as full members
Documentation, membership register, diploma works and more from the early years onwards

Printed publications:
Exhibition Catalogues
The History of the RBSA to 1928 (Hill J and Midgeley W, pub Society and Cornish Brothers Ltd, via Kynoch Press, Birmingham)
Pre-Raphaelite Birmingham (Hartnell R, pub Studley Brewin Books, 1996)
RBSA Members and Friends Newsletter (3 times a year)

Access to staff:
Contact by letter, by telephone, by fax, by e-mail and in person. Non-members charged.
Hours: Mon to Fri, 1030 to 1730

Access to building, collection or gallery:
No prior appointment required
Hours: Mon to Fri, 1030 to 1730; Sat, 1030 to 1700; Sun, 1300 to 1700
Special comments: Archive that houses the RBSA Collection: by prior appointment.
For exhibitions see website, or phone gallery.

Access for disabled people:
Level entry, access to all public areas, toilet facilities

ROYAL BOTANIC GARDEN EDINBURGH

Acronym or abbreviation: RBGE

Library, 20A Inverleith Row, Edinburgh, EH3 5LR

Tel: 0131 552 7171
Fax: 0131 248 2901
E-mail: library@rbge.org.uk

Website:
http://www.rbge.org.uk/

Enquiries:
Enquiries to: Librarian
Direct tel: 0131 248 2853

Founded:
1670

Organisation type and purpose:
Research organisation.
Administered by a Board of Trustees.

Subject coverage:
Plant taxonomy; amenity horticulture; history and current practice of gardening; landscaping; conservation; botanical illustration; botanical travels and explorations; plant collecting; floras of the world.

Museum or gallery collection, archive, or library special collection:
Archival material, manuscript and printed, relating to the history of plant sciences and particularly to the Garden 1670–, and to the Botanical Society of Edinburgh 1836–.
Correspondence, biographies and portraits of early botanists, horticulturists
Early printed works 1486–, on botany, medicine, agriculture, horticulture
Minute Books of the Royal Caledonian Horticulture Society from 1810
Pre-Linnaean botanical literature

Non-library collection catalogue:
All or part available online

Library catalogue:
All or part available online and in-house

continued overleaf

Printed publications:
The Botanics (The Royal Botanic Garden
   Edinburgh quarterly magazine)
Edinburgh Journal of Botany (3 times a year,
   Cambridge University Press)
British Fungus Flora (irregular, Cambridge
   University Press)
Flora of Bhutan (irregular)
Catalogue of Plants 2001 (at the Royal Botanic
   Garden Edinburgh, eds R. Govier, K. Walter, D.
   Chamberlain et al)
Scottish Wild Plants: their history, ecology and
   conservation (P. Lusby and J. Wright, with
   photographs by S. Clarke, 1996)
The Scottish Garden: a photographic record (B.
   Burbridge, with text by F. Young, 1989)
Guidebooks for Inverleith, Benmore Botanic
   Garden, Logan Botanic Garden, Dawyck Botanic
   Garden

Publications list:
Available online and in print

Access to staff:
Contact by letter, by telephone, by fax, by e-mail,
in person and via website
Hours: Mon to Thu, 0930 to 1630; Fri, 0930 to 1600

Access for disabled people:
Parking provided, access to all public areas, toilet
facilities

Constituent bodies:
Botanical Society for Edinburgh (1872) Botanical
Library
Cleghorn Memorial (1941) Botanical Library
Plinian Society of Edinburgh (1841) Botanical
Library
Wernerian Society (1856) Botanical Library

Funded by:
Scottish Executive Environment – Rural Affairs
Department

ROYAL BOTANIC GARDENS, KEW

Acronym or abbreviation: RBGK

Library, Art and Archives, Royal Botanic Gardens,
Kew, Richmond, Surrey, TW9 3AE

Tel: 020 8332 5414
Fax: 020 8332 5430
E-mail: library@rbgkew.org.uk

Website:
http://www.rbgkew.org.uk
An overview of the programme areas of the Royal
Botanic Gardens, Kew, visitor information, science
publications catalogue, specialist newsletters and
more.
http://www.rbgkew.org.uk/BGCI
Botanic Gardens Conservation International, links
to 450 botanical gardens in over 100 countries.

Enquiries:
Enquiries to: Head of Library, Art and Archives
Direct tel: Archives Enquiries, 020 8332 5476
Direct e-mail: archives@rbgkew.org.uk

Founded:
Library 1852

Organisation type and purpose:
Registered charity, research organisation.
RBG Kew has charitable status and is an exempt
charity under the Charities Act 1960.

Subject coverage:
Botany (plants and fungi of the world), taxonomy,
geography, anatomy, biochemistry, cytology,
molecular biology, economic botany, horticulture,
plant seed physiology, nomenclature, conservation,
RBGK reference collections of living and preserved
plants.

**Museum or gallery collection, archive, or library
special collection:**
150,000 monographs, 4000 serials (1300 current),
   150,000 pamphlets, 200,000 prints and drawings,
   4,600 archival collections
Adams Collection (diatom books)
Botanists Portraits Collection
Darlington Reprint Collection (genetics)

Kewensia and archives (RBG Kew's public records)
Linnaean Collection
Plant Illustrations, including the Church,
   Roxburgh and Tankerville Drawings
RGB Kew also has extensive plant and fungi
   collections: 7 million plant herbarium specimens,
   750,000 fungi specimens, 80,000 economic
   botany specimens, 40,000 living taxa

Library catalogue:
All or part available online

Printed publications:
Annual Report (includes list of staff publications) –
   TSO
Authors of Plant Names
Curtis's Botanical Magazine
Kew Bulletin
Kew Record of Taxonomic Literature relating to
   vascular plants (quarterly)
Papers published in periodicals are listed in RBG
   Kew's Annual Report
Vascular Plant Families and Genera
Volumes on the flora of tropical and other
   countries, and on particular families and genera
   of plants and fungi
Order printed publications from: Orders from
booksellers: Publications Sales, RBG Kew,
Richmond, Surrey, TW9 3AE, tel: 020 8332 5776,
fax: 020 8332 5646, e-mail:
kewscbooks@rbgkew.org.uk
UK Retail Sales: Mail Order Department, Online,
KewBooks.com, c/o Summerfield Books, Main
Street, Brough, Cumbria, CA17 4AX, tel: 01768
341577, fax: 01768 341687, e-mail:
sales@kewbooks.com, website: http://
www.kewbooks.com

Electronic and video publications:
Index Kewensis online as part of IPNI – the
   International Plant Names Index
Electronic Plant Information Centre (ePIC) online –
   Kew's in-house databases including Kew Record

Publications list:
Available online and in print

Access to staff:
Contact by letter, by fax, by e-mail and via
website. Appointment necessary.
Hours: Mon to Fri, 0900 to 1700

Access to building, collection or gallery:
Prior appointment required
Special comments: Only bona-fide researchers.

Access for disabled people:
Parking provided, ramped entry, toilet facilities

Sponsored by:
Department for Environment, Food and Rural
Affairs

ROYAL BRITISH LEGION SCOTLAND

Acronym or abbreviation: RBLS

New Haig House, Logie Green Road, Edinburgh,
EH7 4HR

Tel: 0131 557 2782
Fax: 0131 557 5819
E-mail: rblshq@care4free.com

Website:
http://www.rblscotland.org.uk

Enquiries:
Enquiries to: Press Officer
Direct e-mail: ehfs.pub@btconnect.com

Founded:
1921

Organisation type and purpose:
Membership association (membership is by
subscription), present number of members: 62,000,
voluntary organisation, registered charity (charity
number SCO 03323).

Subject coverage:
Assistance to ex-service men and women in
Scotland, war disability pensions claims, aid
during temporary and chronic illness and

unemployment, assistance in the provision of
surgical appliances, overseas war graves visits for
next-of-kin, provision of sheltered accommodation,
sports competitions, piping competitions,
opportunity to join social club.

Printed publications:
Annual Report
The Scottish Legion News (5 times a year)

Access to staff:
Contact by letter, by telephone, by fax, by e-mail
and in person
Hours: Mon to Fri, 0915 to 1630

Access to building, collection or gallery:
No access other than to staff

Access for disabled people:
Parking provided, level entry, toilet facilities

Includes the:
Earl Haig Fund Scotland
Officers Association Scotland

Member of:
British Commonwealth Ex-services League

ROYAL BRITISH LEGION, THE

48 Pall Mall, London, SW1Y 5JY

Tel. 0345 725725
Fax: 020 7973 7399
E-mail: info@britishlegion.org.uk

Website:
http://www.britishlegion.org.uk
Covers all aspects of the organisation and its
activities.

Enquiries:
Enquiries to: Secretary General
Other contacts: Legionline Coordinator for general
enquiries.

Founded:
1921

Organisation type and purpose:
Membership association (membership is by
qualification), present number of members:
620,000, registered charity (charity number
219279).
To care for, and raise funds for, the disabled and
needy in the ex-service community.

Subject coverage:
War disability pensions and general welfare
benefits applicable to ex-servicemen and women
and their dependants; overseas war graves visits;
the ex-service community generally.

Printed publications:
Annual Report
Legion (journal, 6 times a year)

Access to staff:
Contact by letter, by telephone, by fax, by e-mail
and via website
Hours: Mon to Fri, 0900 to 1700

Access for disabled people:
Level entry, access to all public areas, toilet
facilities

Member of:
British Commonwealth Ex-Services League
Council of British Services and Ex-Services
Organisations
World Veterans Federation

Supports the:
Attendants Company
Disabled Men's Industries Limited
Officers' Association
Royal British Legion Poppy Appeal and Factory
Royal British Legion Women's Section

ROYAL CALEDONIAN CURLING CLUB

Acronym or abbreviation: RCCC

Cairnie House, Ingliston Showground, Newbridge,
Midlothian, EH28 8NB

Tel: 0131 333 3003
Fax: 0131 333 3323
E-mail: office@royalcaledoniancurling.org

Website:
http://www.rccc.org.uk

Enquiries:
Enquiries to: Manager, Finance and Administration
Other contacts: Director of Development for
development of the sport.

Founded:
1838

Organisation type and purpose:
Membership association (membership is by
subscription), present number of members: 15,000,
training organisation.
Governing body for sport of curling in Scotland.

Subject coverage:
The sport and game of curling.

**Museum or gallery collection, archive, or library
special collection:**
Archive films of grand matches
Royal club annuals from 1839 and many rare
books on curling
Various curling artefacts and pictures including
trophies and old curling stones

Printed publications:
Royal Club Annual (yearly £9)
Royal Club Constitution and Rule Book (yearly, £1)
Scottish Curler (monthly, September to April)

Access to staff:
Contact by letter, by telephone, by fax and by e-
mail. Appointment necessary.
Hours: Mon to Fri, 0900 to 1700

ROYAL CAMBRIAN ACADEMY OF ART

Acronym or abbreviation: RCA

Crown Lane, Conwy, LL32 8AN

Tel: 01492 593413
Fax: 01492 593413
E-mail: rca@rcaconwy.org

Website:
http://www.rcaconwy.org

Enquiries:
Enquiries to: Curator

Founded:
1882

Organisation type and purpose:
Membership association (membership is by
election or invitation), present number of
members: 115, registered charity (charity number
219648), art gallery.

Subject coverage:
Past and present members of the Academy since
1882, artists working in Wales.

**Museum or gallery collection, archive, or library
special collection:**
Catalogues of every RCA exhibition since 1882

Printed publications:
Centenary Year (1982) Reference Catalogue (giving
history of the Academy)
Exhibition catalogues
Pembrokeshire (Knapp-Fisher J)
Portraits (Williams K)
The Land and the Sea (Williams K)

Access to staff:
Contact by letter, by telephone, by fax, by e-mail
and via website
Hours: Tue to Sat, 1100 to 1700; Sun, 1300 to 1630
Special comments: No lift to upstairs gallery.

ROYAL CHORAL SOCIETY

Acronym or abbreviation: RCS

Studio 9, 92 Lots Road, London, SW10 0QD

Tel: 020 7376 3718

Fax: 020 7376 3719

Website:
http://www.royalchoralsociety.co.uk
All information about the choir, concerts,
membership, sponsorship

Enquiries:
Enquiries to: Administrator
Direct e-mail: helenbody@royalchoralsociety.co.uk

Founded:
1871

Organisation type and purpose:
Membership association (membership is by
subscription), registered charity.
Choir.

Subject coverage:
Choirs and choral music.

**Museum or gallery collection, archive, or library
special collection:**
Archive material (loaned to the Greater London
Public Record Office)

Printed publications:
Annual brochure

Access to staff:
Contact by letter, by telephone, by fax, by e-mail
and via website
Hours: Mon to Fri, 0900 to 1700

Links with:
NFMS

Subsidiary body:
Friends of the Royal Choral Society

ROYAL COLLEGE OF ART LIBRARY

Acronym or abbreviation: RCA

Kensington Gore, London, SW7 2EU

Tel: 020 7590 4224
Fax: 020 7590 4500
E-mail: library@rca.ac.uk

Website:
Website being redesigned.

Enquiries:
Enquiries to: Library Manager
Direct tel: 020 7590 4225
Direct e-mail: darlene.maxwell@rca.ac.uk
Other contacts: Peter Hassell, Head of Information
& Learning Services

Organisation type and purpose:
Postgraduate college of art, Institution of
University Library status.

Subject coverage:
Art (particularly 20th century), design (industrial,
graphic, fashion, textiles, architecture, interior,
illustration, vehicle), applied arts (ceramics,
metalwork, jewellery), moving image (films,
television, animation), photography, humanities.

**Museum or gallery collection, archive, or library
special collection:**
College Archive
Colour Reference Collection covering many
aspects of colour, including theory, psychology,
symbolism and colour music
Theses Collection

Library catalogue:
All or part available online

Access to staff:
Appointment necessary.
Hours: Term time: Mon to Fri, 0900 to 2100; Sat,
1200 to 1700
Vacations: Mon to Fri, 1000 to 1700

ROYAL COLLEGE OF DEFENCE STUDIES

Acronym or abbreviation: RCDS

37 Belgrave Square, London, SW1X 8NS

Tel: 020 7915 4813
Fax: 020 7915 4800

Website:
http://www.mod.uk.rcds/index.html

Enquiries:
Enquiries to: Librarian

Founded:
1970

Organisation type and purpose:
National government body, learned society
(membership is by election or invitation), present
number of members: 85 current (on site), historic
building, house or site.
Government department.
The house originally known as Sefton House was
built in 1842 by the Marquess of Westminster. It
may be visited on an Open Day.

Subject coverage:
Defence, international relations, politics,
economics, history.

Library catalogue:
All or part available in-house

Printed publications:
Reading Lists
Journal Holdings
New Books Lists
Seaford House Papers (restricted distribution)

Publications list:
Available in print

Access to staff:
Access for members only.
Hours: Mon to Fri, 0900 to 1700
Special comments: Members and OGDs.

Access to building, collection or gallery:
No access other than to staff

Connections with:
Ministry of Defence, London (MOD)

ROYAL COLLEGE OF GENERAL PRACTITIONERS

Acronym or abbreviation: RCGP

14 Princes Gate, Hyde Park, London, SW7 1PU

Tel: 020 7581 3232
Fax: 020 7584 1992
E-mail: library@rcgp.org.uk

Website:
http://www.rcgp.org.uk
General information about the college, its services
and products.

Enquiries:
Enquiries to: Information Manager

Founded:
1952

Organisation type and purpose:
Learned society (membership is by qualification),
present number of members: 19,000, registered
charity (charity number 223106), research
organisation.
Encouraging, fostering, and maintaining the
highest possible standards in general medical
practice.

Subject coverage:
General practice, primary health care, practice
management, family practice.

**Museum or gallery collection, archive, or library
special collection:**
General practice theses
College publications
Primary care journals

Library catalogue:
All or part available online and in-house

Printed publications:
Information Sheets (free)
New Books Listings
Journal Holdings

continued overleaf

Electronic and video publications:
See Catalogue

Publications list:
Available online and in print

Access to staff:
Contact by letter, by telephone, by fax, by e-mail, in person and via website. Appointment necessary. All charged.
Hours: Mon to Fri, 0900 to 1700
Special comments: Book loans to members only.

ROYAL COLLEGE OF GENERAL PRACTITIONERS (SCOTLAND)

Acronym or abbreviation: RCGP SCOTLAND

25 Queen Street, Edinburgh, EH2 1JX

Tel: 0131 260 6800
Fax: 0131 260 6836
E-mail: scottishc@rcgp.org.uk

Enquiries:
Enquiries to: Deputy Chair (Policy)

Organisation type and purpose:
Professional body, membership association (membership is by qualification), present number of members: 3018 (Scotland), registered charity (charity number 223106), research organisation.

Subject coverage:
Academic/quality in General Practice.

Access to staff:
Contact by letter and by e-mail
Hours: Mon to Fri, 0900 to 1700

Other addresses:
Royal College of General Practitioners
14 Princes Gate, Hyde Park, London, SW7 1PU; tel: 020 7581 3232

ROYAL COLLEGE OF MIDWIVES – EDINBURGH

Acronym or abbreviation: RCM

37 Frederick Street, Edinburgh, EH2 1EP

Tel: 0131 225 1633

Enquiries:
Enquiries to: Director

Organisation type and purpose:
Professional organisation.

Subject coverage:
Midwifery.

Access to staff:
Contact by letter
Hours: Mon to Fri, 0900 to 1700

ROYAL COLLEGE OF MIDWIVES – LONDON

Acronym or abbreviation: RCM

15 Mansfield Street, London, W1G 9NH

Tel: 020 7315 3535
Fax: 020 7315 3536
E-mail: info@rcm.org.uk

Website:
http://www.rcm.org.uk/templates/info_centre/index.cfm

Enquiries:
Enquiries to: Information Officer

Founded:
1881

Organisation type and purpose:
Professional body, trade union (membership is by subscription, qualification), present number of members: 37,000, registered charity (charity number 275261), suitable for ages: 21+.
To further the art and science of midwifery.

Subject coverage:
Midwifery: education, profession, training and history; obstetrics; neonatal care; ante-natal care; paediatrics; family planning; role of the midwife in the NHS; sociological and psychological aspects of midwifery; further and higher education.

Museum or gallery collection, archive, or library special collection:
Archives
Marion Rabl Collection
Theses and dissertations in midwifery

Non-library collection catalogue:
All or part available in-house

Library catalogue:
All or part available in-house

Printed publications:
Order printed publications from: The Royal College of Midwives Welsh Board
4 Cathedral Road, Cardiff, CF1 9LJ, tel: 029 2022 8111, e-mail: publications@rcmwelshb.org.uk

Publications list:
Available online and in print

Access to staff:
Contact by letter, by telephone, by fax, by e-mail and via website. Appointment necessary. All charged.
Hours: Mon to Fri, 0900 to 1645
Special comments: Non-members when space permits.

Access to building, collection or gallery:
Prior appointment required

Access for disabled people:
Access to all public areas, toilet facilities

ROYAL COLLEGE OF MUSIC

Acronym or abbreviation: RCM

Library, Prince Consort Road, London, SW7 2BS

Tel: 020 7591 4325
Fax: 020 7589 7740
E-mail: pthompson@rcm.ac.uk

Website:
http://www.rcm.ac.uk
Includes Library web pages and access to that part of the catalogue now online.

Enquiries:
Enquiries to: Librarian
Direct tel: 020 7591 4323

Founded:
1883

Organisation type and purpose:
Academic institution and music conservatoire.

Subject coverage:
Music: books, autograph manuscripts, scores, sheet music, orchestral parts, choral sets, audio-visual materials.

Museum or gallery collection, archive, or library special collection:
Collection of manuscripts of British composers
Heron-Allen Collection of books on the violin
Library of the Concerts of Ancient Music
Library of the Sacred Harmonic Society
Maurice Frost collection
Nicanor Zabaleta archive of harp music
Further listings at www.cecilia-uk.org

Non-library collection catalogue:
All or part available online, in-house and in print

Library catalogue:
All or part available in-house

Printed publications:
Catalogue of the Manuscripts of Herbert Howells in the Royal College of Music Library
Catalogues of the Royal College of Music Library (out of print)
Doane: A Musical Directory for the year 1794 (reprint of original edition)
Hummel: Art of Piano Playing, Part 3 (reprint of original edition)

Royal College of Music Library: guide to services
Where to buy and borrow music

Microform publications:
The Music Collection of the Royal College of Music London (Harvester)
Microfilms of individual works available direct

Access to staff:
Contact by letter, by telephone, by fax, by e-mail and in person
Hours: Term time: Mon to Thu, 0900 to 1900; Fri, 0900 to 1730
Vacations: hours may vary
Special comments: Loans to members only.

Access to building, collection or gallery:
No prior appointment required

ROYAL COLLEGE OF MUSIC FRANK BRIDGE BEQUEST

Royal College of Music, Price Consort Road, London, SW7 2BS

Tel: 020 7591 4340
Fax: 020 7589 7740
E-mail: pbanks@rcm.ac.uk

Website:
http://www.cph.rcm.ac.uk/CPHBridge/Pages/Index.htm
Description of the Bequest's activity, details of grants, and a list of publications and recordings sponsored by the Bequest.

Enquiries:
Enquiries to: Chairman

Founded:
1965

Organisation type and purpose:
Advisory body.

Subject coverage:
Life and music of Frank Bridge (1879–1941).

Museum or gallery collection, archive, or library special collection:
Bridge manuscripts (held in the Library of the Royal College of Music, for access see the entry for the RCM Library)

Publications list:
Available online

Access to staff:
Contact by letter, by telephone, by fax, by e-mail and via website
Hours: Mon to Fri, 0900 to 1700

ROYAL COLLEGE OF NURSING OF THE UNITED KINGDOM

Acronym or abbreviation: RCN

20 Cavendish Square, London, W1G 0RN

Tel: 020 7409 3333
Fax: 020 7647 3420
E-mail: rcn.library@rcn.org.uk

Website:
http://www.rcn.org.uk/

Enquiries:
Enquiries to: Librarian
Direct tel: 020 7647 3610

Organisation type and purpose:
Professional body, trade union.

Subject coverage:
Professional aspects of nursing; nursing practice, management and education; labour relations and legal matters; social services; health services; hospital management.

Museum or gallery collection, archive, or library special collection:
Seymer Collection (historical books on nursing)
Steinberg Collection of Nursing Research Theses

Library catalogue:
All or part available online

Printed publications:
British Nursing Index
Catalogue of the Steinberg Collection
RCN Library Thesaurus of Nursing Terms

Electronic and video publications:
British Nursing Index

Access to staff:
Contact by letter, by telephone, by fax and by e-mail. Non-members charged.
Hours: Mon, Tue, Thu, Fri, 0900 to 1900; Wed, 1000 to 1900; Sat, 0900 to 1700

Access for disabled people:
Ramped entry, toilet facilities

Other addresses:
Royal College of Nursing of the United Kingdom
 Ty Maeth, King George V Drive East, Cardiff, CF4 4XZ; tel: 029 2075 1373
Royal College of Nursing of the United Kingdom
 42 Scottish Board, South Oswald Road, Edinburgh, EH9 2HH; tel: 0131 662 1010
Royal College of Nursing of the United Kingdom
 17 Windsor Avenue, Belfast, BT9 6EE; tel: 01232 668236

ROYAL COLLEGE OF OBSTETRICIANS AND GYNAECOLOGISTS

Acronym or abbreviation: RCOG

27 Sussex Place, Regent's Park, London, NW1 4RG

Tel: 020 7772 6200

Website:
http://www.rcog.org.uk
http://www.rcog.org.uk/library

Enquiries:
Enquiries to: Librarian
Direct tel: 020 7772 6309
Direct fax: 020 7262 8331
Direct e-mail: library@rcog.org.uk

Founded:
1929

Organisation type and purpose:
Professional body (membership is by qualification).

Subject coverage:
Obstetrics, gynaecology and closely related subjects (e.g. female urology, female endocrinology).

Museum or gallery collection, archive, or library special collection:
Large historical collection in subjects as above
Rare books
College archive
Collection of historical instruments including the
 Chamberlen forceps

Non-library collection catalogue:
All or part available in-house

Library catalogue:
All or part available online and in-house

Printed publications:
Short-title catalogue of books printed before 1851
 in the Library of the RCOG (2nd edn)

Publications list:
Available online

Access to staff:
Contact by letter, by telephone, by fax, by e-mail, in person and via website. Appointment necessary.
Hours: Mon to Fri, 0900 to 1800

Administers:
National Collaborating Centre for Women's and Children's Health

Constituent bodies:
Faculty of Sexual and Reproductive Health Care
WellBeing of Women (formerly Birthright)

ROYAL COLLEGE OF OPHTHALMOLOGISTS

17 Cornwall Terrace, London, NW1 4QW

Tel: 020 7935 0702
Fax: 020 7935 9838
E-mail: kathy.evans@rcophth.ac.uk

Website:
http://www.rcophth.ac.uk

Enquiries:
Enquiries to: Chief Executive
Direct tel: 020 7935 0702 ext 33

Founded:
1988

Organisation type and purpose:
Professional body (membership is by subscription, qualification), present number of members: 3027, registered charity (charity number 299872).

Subject coverage:
Ophthalmology.

Printed publications:
EYE (journal)

Publications list:
Available in print

Access to staff:
Contact by letter, by telephone, by fax and by e-mail
Hours: Mon to Fri, 0900 to 1700

Access to building, collection or gallery:
Prior appointment required

ROYAL COLLEGE OF ORGANISTS

Acronym or abbreviation: RCO

PO Box 56357, London, SE16 7XL

Tel: 05600 767208
E-mail: admin@rco.org.uk

Website:
http://www.rco.org.uk

Enquiries:
Enquiries to: General Manager
Other contacts: Director of Academic Development

Founded:
1864

Organisation type and purpose:
International organisation, advisory body, learned society, professional body, registered charity (charity number 312847).
Academic institution, especially examining body.

Subject coverage:
The organ and music for the organ.

Museum or gallery collection, archive, or library special collection:
Houses the library of books, music (mainly organ), manuscripts, records, cassettes and CDs
C. H. Trevor Collection
Cruden Collection
Dalton Bequest
Gordon Phillips Collection
John Ella Bequest
Sowerbutts Collection
T. Lea Southgate Bequest
Tickner Collection

Non-library collection catalogue:
All or part available online

Library catalogue:
All or part available online

Printed publications:
Syllabus of examinations plus other items
RCO Journal (annual collection of learned articles)
RCO Newsletter (3 times a year)

Publications list:
Available in print

Access to staff:
Contact by letter, by telephone, by e-mail and in person. Appointment necessary. Non-members charged.
Hours: Mon to Fri, 1000 to 1700

ROYAL COLLEGE OF PAEDIATRICS AND CHILD HEALTH

Acronym or abbreviation: RCPCH

50 Hallam Street, London, W1W 6DE

Tel: 020 7307 5600
Fax: 020 7307 5601
E-mail: enquiries@rcpch.ac.uk

Website:
http://www.rcpch.ac.uk
General information about the College and College activities.

Enquiries:
Enquiries to: Secretary

Founded:
1928

Organisation type and purpose:
Professional body (membership is by qualification, election or invitation), present number of members: 6500, voluntary organisation, registered charity (charity number 1057744).
Members are paediatricians and other professionals active in the field of child health. The RCPCH forms joint standing committees and working parties with several other professional bodies, for example: the Royal College of Physicians, British Association of Paediatric Surgeons, Association of British Paediatric Nurses, National Association for the Welfare of Children in Hospital, Health Visitors Association, Royal College of Midwives, Royal College of Nursing and Royal College of Obstetricians and Gynaecologists. The RCPCH also engages in consultations with a wide range of organisations including voluntary organisations, for example: Foundation for the Study of Infant Deaths.
To advance the art and science of paediatrics; to raise the standard of medical care for children; to educate and examine those concerned with the health of children; to advance the education of the public in child health.

Subject coverage:
Paediatrics, child health, medical training and research.

Non-library collection catalogue:
All or part available in-house

Printed publications:
Archives of Disease in Childhood (monthly, published jointly with the BMA; on subscription)
Fabricated or Induced Illness by Carers (2002)
Guidelines for the Ethical Conduct of Medical Research Involving Children (1992, free on request)
Manual of Childhood Infections
Medicines for Children
Pocket Medicines for Children (2001, £12.99)
Syllabus and Training Records for GPT and HST (£10 each)
Withholding or Withdrawing Life Saving Treatment in Children (1997, £25)
Order printed publications from: RCPCH Bookclub, Direct Books
FREEPOST (BH1879), Ringwood, Hampshire, BH24 3BR, tel: 01425 471719, e-mail: directbooks@bmbc.com

Electronic and video publications:
The following are available on the website http://www.rcpch.ac.uk:
Fabricated or Induced Illness by Carers (2001)
Specimen exam papers for MRCPCH Part I, Part II and DCH
Guidelines for Good Practice
Newsletter for members (quarterly, sent to all members in hardcopy)

continued overleaf

Publications list:
Available online and in print

Access to staff:
Contact by letter, by telephone, by fax, by e-mail and via website. Appointment necessary.
Hours: Mon to Fri, 0900 to 1700

Strong connections with the:
Confederation of European Specialists in Paediatrics
International Paediatric Association

ROYAL COLLEGE OF PATHOLOGISTS

Acronym or abbreviation: RCPath

2 Carlton House Terrace, St James's, London, SW1Y 5AF

Tel: 020 7451 6700
Fax: 020 7451 6701
E-mail: info@rcpath.org

Website:
http://www.rcpath.org

Enquiries:
Enquiries to: Chief Executive

Founded:
1962

Organisation type and purpose:
Professional body (membership is by subscription, qualification), present number of members: 7500, registered charity (charity number 261035).

Subject coverage:
History of pathology, pathology as a science, histopathology, cytology, medical microbiology, clinical biochemistry, virology, immunology, genetics, forensic pathology, haematology.

Library catalogue:
All or part available in-house

Printed publications:
Journal (quarterly, members)
Various publications
Order printed publications from: Managing Editor, Publications
tel: 020 7451 6730, fax: 020 7451 6701, e-mail: publications@rcpath.org

Publications list:
Available online

Access to staff:
Contact by letter, by telephone, by fax, by e-mail and via website
Hours: Mon to Fri, 0900 to 1700

Access for disabled people:
Ramped entry, toilet facilities

ROYAL COLLEGE OF PHYSICIANS AND SURGEONS OF GLASGOW

Acronym or abbreviation: RCPSG

Library, 232–242 St Vincent Street, Glasgow, G2 5RJ

Tel: 0141 221 6072
Fax: 0141 221 1804
E-mail: library@rcpsg.ac.uk

Website:
http://www.rcpsg.ac.uk
Information on activities, committees, courses run, examinations, library scope and journal holdings.

Enquiries:
Enquiries to: Librarian

Founded:
1698

Organisation type and purpose:
Learned society, professional body (membership is by qualification, election or invitation), present number of members: 8500.

Subject coverage:
Clinical medicine and surgery, history of medicine, history of Glasgow and West of Scotland.

Museum or gallery collection, archive, or library special collection:
Macewen Collection (papers of Sir William Macewen, surgery, late 19th century)
Mackenzie Collection (papers of Dr William MacKenzie, ophthalmology)
Ross Collection (50% of the papers of Sir Ronald Ross, tropical medicine, 19th century)
Glasgow Collection (history of Glasgow and South West Scotland)

Non-library collection catalogue:
All or part available online and in print

Library catalogue:
All or part available online and in-house

Access to staff:
Contact by letter, by telephone, by fax, by e-mail, in person and via website. Appointment necessary.
Hours: Mon to Fri, 0900 to 1700

Access for disabled people:
Access to all public areas, toilet facilities

ROYAL COLLEGE OF PHYSICIANS OF EDINBURGH

Acronym or abbreviation: RCPE

Library, 9 Queen Street, Edinburgh, EH2 1JQ

Tel: 0131 225 7324
Fax: 0131 220 3939
E-mail: library@rcpe.ac.uk

Website:
http://www.rcpe.ac.uk/library/library.html
History of library, library services, manuscript catalogue.

Enquiries:
Enquiries to: Librarian
Other contacts: Information Librarian for literature searches.

Founded:
1681

Organisation type and purpose:
Advisory body, learned society, professional body (membership is by qualification, election or invitation), present number of members: 7000, registered charity (charity number SCO 09465), research organisation.

Subject coverage:
Medicine, particularly clinical medicine (excluding since 1900, surgery and allied sciences); history of medicine, particularly Scottish medicine.

Museum or gallery collection, archive, or library special collection:
J W Ballantyne Pamphlet Collection on foetal pathology
Manuscripts Collection relating to W Cullen and early Edinburgh Medical School
Sir J Y Simpson Collection on gynaecology and obstetrics

Non-library collection catalogue:
All or part available online and in-house

Library catalogue:
All or part available online and in-house

Printed publications:
Catalogue of sixteenth century medical books in Edinburgh libraries (1982)

Publications list:
Available online and in print

Access to staff:
Contact by letter, by telephone, by fax, by e-mail, in person and via website
Hours: Mon to Fri, 0900 to 1700

ROYAL COLLEGE OF PHYSICIANS OF LONDON

Acronym or abbreviation: RCP

Information Centre and Heritage Centre, 11 St Andrews Place, Regent's Park, London, NW1 4LE

Tel: 020 7224 1539\ Minicom no. 020 7486 5687
Fax: 020 7486 3729
E-mail: infocentre@rcplondon.ac.uk

Website:
http://www.rcplondon.ac.uk

Founded:
1518

Organisation type and purpose:
International organisation, professional body (membership is by qualification), registered charity (charity number 210508), suitable for ages: postgraduate, training organisation, research organisation, publishing house. To promote the highest standards of medical practice in order to improve health and healthcare.

Subject coverage:
The Information Centre Library covers the College's work, UK Health Policy and public health. The Heritage Centre covers the history of medicine, medical biography and the history of the College.

Museum or gallery collection, archive, or library special collection:
Archives of the College
Manuscripts (mainly personal papers of physicians)
Portraits and Photographs (mainly of Fellows of the College)
H. M. Barlow Collection of Bookplates
Dorchester Library (2,101 titles left to the College by the Marquis of Dorchester), includes the Wilton Psalter dating from 1250
Evan Bedford Library of Cardiology
Heberden Library of Rheumatology
Willan Library of the British Association of Dermatology

Non-library collection catalogue:
All or part available online and in-house

Library catalogue:
All or part available online and in-house

Printed publications:
Catalogue of Engraved Portraits
Evan Bedford Library of Cardiology Catalogue
Order printed publications from: Publications Department, Royal College of Physicians; tel: 020 7935 1174 ext 358, fax: 020 7486 5425, e-mail: publications@rcplondon.ac.uk

Microform publications:
Annals of the Royal College of Physicians, 1518–1915 (pub. Adam Matthew Publications, Calcot, Reading, 1991)

Publications list:
Available online and in print

Access to staff:
Contact by letter, by telephone, by fax, by e-mail, in person and via website. Appointment necessary.
Non-members charged.
Hours: Mon to Fri, 0900 to 1700

Access to building, collection or gallery:
Some areas open to public. Prior appointment required to access historical collections

Access for disabled people:
Parking provided, level entry, access to all public areas, toilet facilities

ROYAL COLLEGE OF PSYCHIATRISTS

Acronym or abbreviation: RCPsych

17 Belgrave Square, London, SW1X 8PG

Tel: 020 7235 2351
Fax: 020 7245 1231
E-mail: infoservices@rcpsych.ac.uk

Website:
http://www.rcpsych.ac.uk

Enquiries:
Enquiries to: Library and Information Services Manager
Direct tel: 020 7235 2351 ext 138/152
Direct fax: 020 7259 6303

Organisation type and purpose:
Professional body (membership is by qualification).

Subject coverage:
Psychiatry; mental illness and health, history of psychiatry.

Museum or gallery collection, archive, or library special collection:
Antiquarian books on psychiatry

Non-library collection catalogue:
All or part available online and in-house

Library catalogue:
All or part available in-house

Printed publications:
Advances in Psychiatric Treatment (6 times a year, £80)
Books Beyond Words (picture stories, without words, for those with learning difficulties)
Index to Statements, Guidelines and Policy Documents of the College 1971–89 with annual supplements (£2.50)
Books and leaflets for the general public
British Journal of Psychiatry (monthly)
Books for Trainees
Child Psychiatry titles
Clinical Psychiatry titles
College Seminar Series
Public Education Initiatives titles
Service Provision titles
Psychiatric Bulletin (monthly)

Electronic and video publications:
Audio tapes for the general public

Publications list:
Available online and in print

Access to staff:
Contact by letter, by telephone, by fax, by e-mail, in person and via website. Appointment necessary. Access for members only. Letter of introduction required. Non-members charged.
Hours: Mon to Fri, 0930 to 1630

ROYAL COLLEGE OF RADIOLOGISTS

Acronym or abbreviation: RCR

38 Portland Place, London, W1B 1JQ

Tel: 020 7636 4432
Fax: 020 7323 3100
E-mail: enquiries@rcr.ac.uk

Website:
http://www.rcr.ac.uk
Details of all College activities including on-line publications, password-protected members area.

Enquiries:
Enquiries to: Chief Executive

Founded:
1975

Organisation type and purpose:
Professional body (membership is by qualification), present number of members: 7000, registered charity (charity number 211540).

Subject coverage:
Science and practice of clinical radiology, clinical oncology.

Printed publications:
Clinical Oncology (8 times a year)
Clinical Radiology (monthly)
Faculty Reports and Guidelines: Clinical Radiology and Clinical Oncology (publication free, except where price stated)
Large selection of College Reports and Guidelines (publication free, except where price stated)

Publications list:
Available in print

Access to staff:
Contact by letter, by telephone, by fax and by e-mail. Appointment necessary.
Hours: Mon to Fri, 0900 to 1700

ROYAL COLLEGE OF SPEECH AND LANGUAGE THERAPISTS

Acronym or abbreviation: RCSLT

2–3 White Hart Yard, London, SE1 1NX

Tel: 020 7378 1200
Fax: 020 7403 7254

Website:
http://www.rcslt.org
Information about speech and language therapy as a career, etc.

Enquiries:
Enquiries to: Professional Director
Other contacts: Information Officer for general enquiries re: speech and language therapy profession.

Organisation type and purpose:
National organisation, professional body, registered charity (charity number 273724). Examining and registering body.

Subject coverage:
Disorders of human communication.

Printed publications:
Bulletin (monthly, for Members and Associate Members)
International Journal of Language and Communication Disorders

Access to staff:
Contact by letter and by e-mail
Hours: Mon to Fri, 0900 to 1700

Access to building, collection or gallery:
Prior appointment required

Access for disabled people:
Level entry, toilet facilities

Affiliated to:
International Association of Logopaedics and Phoniatrics
Permanent Liaison Committee of Speech Therapists and Logopaedists (EEC)

ROYAL COLLEGE OF SURGEONS OF EDINBURGH

Acronym or abbreviation: RCSEd

The Library, Nicolson Street, Edinburgh, EH8 9DW

Tel: 0131 527 1630
Fax: 0131 557 6406
E-mail: library@rcsed.ac.uk

Website:
http://www.rcsed.ac.uk

Enquiries:
Enquiries to: Librarian
Direct tel: 0131 527 1632

Founded:
1505

Organisation type and purpose:
Membership association (membership is by qualification), registered charity, training organisation, research organisation.

Subject coverage:
Surgery, history of medicine.

Museum or gallery collection, archive, or library special collection:
Records of the institution from 1505

Non-library collection catalogue:
All or part available online and in-house

Library catalogue:
All or part available in-house

Printed publications:
Current journals list (free, from library).
The Surgeon: Journal of the Royal Colleges of Surgeons of Edinburgh and Ireland.
surgeonsnews: The magazine for surgeons everywhere.

Publications list:
Available online

Access to staff:
Contact by letter, by telephone, by fax, by e-mail and via website. Letter of introduction required.
Hours: Mon to Fri, 0900 to 1700

Access for disabled people:
Ramped entry, toilet facilities

ROYAL COLLEGE OF SURGEONS OF ENGLAND

Acronym or abbreviation: RCS

Library, 35–43 Lincoln's Inn Fields, London, WC2A 3PE

Tel: 020 7869 6555
Fax: 020 7405 4438
E-mail: library@rcseng.ac.uk

Website:
http://www.rcseng.ac.uk

Enquiries:
Enquiries to: Librarian
Direct tel: 020 7869 6510

Founded:
1800

Organisation type and purpose:
Learned society, professional body (charity number 212808).

Subject coverage:
Surgery: anaesthesia, dental and oral surgery, ophthalmology, orthopaedics, cardio-vascular surgery, urological surgery, otorhinolaryngology, plastic surgery; anatomy; pathology; physiology; history of medicine with special emphasis on surgery; biomedical engineering.

Museum or gallery collection, archive, or library special collection:
Arthur Keith Collection
Collection of engraved medical portraits
Collection of medical bookplates
Hunter-Baillie Collection of autograph letters and documents including family papers
Lister Collection (Lord Lister's scientific papers)
Papers of Sir Richard Owen, FRS (1804–1892)

Non-library collection catalogue:
All or part available online

Library catalogue:
All or part available online

Printed publications:
Lives of the Fellows of The Royal College of Surgeons of England
Annals of The Royal College of Surgeons of England
Current Periodicals List (via website)

Publications list:
Available online

Access to staff:
Contact by letter, by telephone, by fax, by e-mail and via website. Appointment necessary.
Hours: Mon, Tue, Thu, Fri, 0930 to 1730; Wed, 1000 to 1730
Special comments: Charges may apply to non-members.

ROYAL COLLEGE OF VETERINARY SURGEONS TRUST

Acronym or abbreviation: RCVS

Library and Information Service, Belgravia House, 62–64 Horseferry Road, London, SW1P 2AF

Tel: 020 7202 0752

continued overleaf

Fax: 020 7202 0751
E-mail: library@rcvstrust.org.uk

Website:
http://www.rcvs.org.uk
http://www.rcvslibrary.org.uk

Enquiries:
Enquiries to: Librarian

Founded:
1844

Organisation type and purpose:
Professional body.
Registration and disciplinary body.

Subject coverage:
Veterinary science and surgery, comparative medicine, animal breeding and management.

Museum or gallery collection, archive, or library special collection:
College Archives
Henry Gray Collection (ornithology, late 19th and early 20th centuries)
Historical Collection (books 1514–1850)
J. P. Megnin Collection of drawings, mainly of birds and parasites, and correspondence
Miss Povey Collection of watercolours by Edward Mayhew

Non-library collection catalogue:
All or part available online

Library catalogue:
All or part available online

Publications list:
Available online

Access to staff:
Contact by letter, by telephone, by fax, by e-mail and via website. Appointment necessary. All charged.
Hours: Mon to Fri, 0915 to 1700

Access to building, collection or gallery:
Prior appointment required

ROYAL COMMISSION ON ENVIRONMENTAL POLLUTION

Acronym or abbreviation: RCEP

3rd Floor, 5–8 The Sanctuary, Westminster, London, SW1P 3JS

Tel: 020 7799 8970
Fax: 020 7799 8971
E-mail: enquiries@rcep.org.uk

Enquiries:
Enquiries to: Office Manager
Direct tel: 020 7799 8972

Founded:
1970

Organisation type and purpose:
National government body, advisory body.

Subject coverage:
National and international matters concerning pollution of the environment, further possibilities of danger to the environment, research in this field, transport and the environment, and waste management.

Printed publications:
A Guide to the Commission and its Work
23 reports covering various environmental topics including:
The 'First Report' – A review of the state of the physical environment in Britain at the beginning of the 1970s
Industrial pollution, Air pollution, Nuclear power and the Environment, Agriculture and Pollution, Oil pollution of the Sea, Lead in the Environment, The Release of Genetically Engineered Organisms to the Environment

Publications list:
Available in print

Access to staff:
Contact by letter, by fax, by e-mail and via website
Hours: Mon to Fri, 0900 to 1700

ROYAL COMMISSION ON THE ANCIENT AND HISTORICAL MONUMENTS OF SCOTLAND

Acronym or abbreviation: RCAHMS

John Sinclair House, 16 Bernard Terrace, Edinburgh, EH8 9NX

Tel: 0131 662 1456
Fax: 0131 662 1477
E-mail: info@rcahms.gov.uk

Website:
http://www.rcahms.gov.uk
CANMORE – user access to the National Monuments Record of Scotland database.

Enquiries:
Enquiries to: Chief Executive
Direct e-mail: diana.murray@rcahms.gov.uk

Founded:
1908

Organisation type and purpose:
National government body, national organisation, advisory body, statutory body, registered charity, public library.
Information relating to built heritage of Scotland from the earliest times to the present day.
RCAHMS creates and maintains the above record.

Subject coverage:
Archaeology, architectural history, landscape history, built heritage, ancient monuments, planning, development and urban history, topography, history, industrial archaeology and history of Scotland.

Museum or gallery collection, archive, or library special collection:
Architectural drawings
Books on archaeology, architecture, topography and local history
Manuscripts
National collection of archaeological excavation archives
Papers of many notable Scottish architects
Photographs including aerial photographs
Plans from archaeological excavations and field surveys

Non-library collection catalogue:
All or part available online, in-house and in print

Library catalogue:
All or part available online and in-house

Publications list:
Available online and in print

Access to staff:
Contact by letter, by telephone, by fax, by e-mail, in person and via website
Hours: Mon to Fri, 0930 to 1630

Access to building, collection or gallery:
No prior appointment required

Access for disabled people:
Parking provided, ramped entry, access to all public areas, toilet facilities

Parent body:
The Scottish Executive

ROYAL COMMONWEALTH SOCIETY

Acronym or abbreviation: RCS

18 Northumberland Avenue, London, WC2N 5AP

Tel: 020 7930 6733
Fax: 020 7930 9705
E-mail: info@rcsint.org

Website:
http://www.rcsint.org

Enquiries:
Enquiries to: Head of Public Affairs
Direct tel: 020 7766 9205
Direct e-mail: miles.giljam@rcsint.org

Founded:
1868

Organisation type and purpose:
International organisation, learned society, membership association (membership is by subscription, election or invitation), present number of members: 6500 affiliated to headquarters and 10,000 worldwide, voluntary organisation, registered charity (charity number 226748), art gallery, university library.
International organisation, with 69 self-governing branches and commonwealth societies, operates a private members club, non-governmental organisation.
The RCS promotes, in the UK and internationally, an understanding of the nature and working of the Commonwealth and of the factors that shape the lives of its people and the policies of its governments. Underlying the work of the RCS is the belief that an understanding of the Commonwealth is key to creating successful multicultural societies across the world.

Subject coverage:
The Commonwealth and its members, past and present (virtually all subjects relevant to those countries except scientific and technical); some material on non-Commonwealth countries and on the colonial history of other European countries.

Museum or gallery collection, archive, or library special collection:
Royal Commonwealth Society Collection housed in the Cambridge University Library, West Road, Cambridge, CB3 9DR; includes:
Cobham Collection (on Cyprus)
Photograph Collection

Printed publications:
Annual Report
Meetings & Events Programme (3 times a year)
Newsletter (3 times a year)
Annual Report of the Essay Competition
Occasional reports of seminars and conferences
Various promotional literature
The following are housed in the library at Cambridge:
Biography Catalogue of the Royal Commonwealth Society (1961)
Manuscript Catalogue of the Royal Commonwealth Society (1975)
RCS London Photograph Collection: a unique source of visual documents on Colonial and Commonwealth history (mid-1850s – mid-1980s) on microfiche (Inter Documentation AG, 1987)
Subject Catalogue of the Library of the Royal Empire Society (4 vols, 1930–37)
Subject Catalogue of the Royal Commonwealth Society (7 vols, 1971; supplement, 2 vols, 1977)

Access to staff:
Contact by letter, by telephone, by fax, by e-mail and via website. Appointment necessary.
Hours: Mon to Fri, 0915 to 1715

Access for disabled people:
Ramped entry, toilet facilities

Library housed at:
Cambridge University Library
West Road, Cambridge, CB3 9DR; tel: 01223 333000; fax: 01223 333160

ROYAL CORNWALL AGRICULTURAL ASSOCIATION

Acronym or abbreviation: RCAA

Royal Cornwall Showground, Wadebridge, Cornwall, PL27 7JE

Tel: 01208 812183
Fax: 01208 812713
E-mail: info@royalcornwall.co.uk

Website:
http://www.royalcornwall.co.uk

Enquiries:
Enquiries to: Secretary

Founded:
1793

Organisation type and purpose:
Membership association, registered charity (charity number 250312).
Promotion of agriculture etc.

Subject coverage:
History of the RCAA, general agricultural history of Cornwall.

Museum or gallery collection, archive, or library special collection:
Archives of the Royal Cornwall Agricultural Association

Printed publications:
History of the Royal Cornwall Show (£5 plus p&p)
Show Catalogue (annually £4.00 plus p&p)
Souvenir Programme (£2.30 plus p&p)

Access to staff:
Contact by letter, by telephone, by fax, by e-mail, in person and via website
Hours: Mon to Fri, 0900 to 1700

ROYAL ECONOMIC SOCIETY

Acronym or abbreviation: RES

School of Economics and Finance, University of St Andrews, St Andrews, Fife, KY16 9AL

Tel: 01334 462479
Fax: 01334 462444
E-mail: royaleconsoc@st-andrews.ac.uk

Website:
http://www.res.org.uk

Enquiries:
Enquiries to: RES Administrator
Other contacts: Administrator (for general enquiries); Secretary-General

Founded:
1902

Organisation type and purpose:
Learned society (membership is by subscription).
The promotion and encouragement of the study of economic science.

Subject coverage:
Economics.

Printed publications:
Books, including new editions of economics classics (from Blackwell Publishers, Macmillan and CUP)
Economic Journal (8 times a year)
RES Newsletter quarterly
Order printed publications from: RES Administrator

Electronic and video publications:
Econometrics Journal (online)

Access to staff:
Contact by letter, by telephone, by fax, by e-mail and via website. Appointment necessary.
Hours: Mon to Fri, 1000 to 1600

ROYAL ENFIELD OWNERS CLUB

Acronym or abbreviation: REOC

30–32 Causeway, Burgh-Le-Marsh, Skegness, Lincolnshire, PE24 5LT

Tel: 01754 810119
E-mail: mickseager@mcmail.com

Website:
http://www.royalenfield.org.uk

Enquiries:
Enquiries to: Membership Secretary

Founded:
1978

Organisation type and purpose:
Membership association (membership is by subscription), present number of members: 3,028

Subject coverage:
Royal Enfield motor cycles.

Printed publications:
The Gun Magazine

Access to staff:
Contact by letter, by telephone, by e-mail and via website
Hours: Mon to Fri, 0900 to 1700

ROYAL ENGINEERS LIBRARY

Brompton Barracks, Chatham, Kent, ME4 4UX

Tel: 01634 822416
Fax: 01634 822419

Enquiries:
Enquiries to: Librarian

Founded:
1813

Organisation type and purpose:
Military library.

Subject coverage:
All aspects of military engineering worldwide with specific reference to the Royal Engineers; many non-military fields of early technology e.g. photography.

Museum or gallery collection, archive, or library special collection:
2 volumes of photographs, 1861 North American Boundary Commission
Archival material on the history of the Corps of Royal Engineers and its associated functions since formation
Connolly Papers – manuscript historical records
Large photographic collection dating back to 1855
Many RE World War I war diaries
Sapper magazine on microfiche
Substantial letter book holding

Access to staff:
Contact by letter and by telephone. Appointment necessary.
Hours: Mon, Wed, Fri, 0900 to 1700
Special comments: Closed to telephone calls or visitors on Tue, Thu and public holidays. Charges for copying facilities.

Affiliated to:
Royal Engineers Museum
at the same address

ROYAL ENTOMOLOGICAL SOCIETY

Acronym or abbreviation: RES

The Mansion House, Chiswell Green Lane, St Albans, AL2 3NS

Tel: 01727 899387
Fax: 01727 894797
E-mail: val@royensoc.co.uk

Website:
http://www.royensoc.co.uk

Enquiries:
Enquiries to: Librarian

Founded:
1833

Organisation type and purpose:
International organisation, learned society (membership is by election or invitation), registered charity (charity number 213620), suitable for ages: postgraduate +, research organisation, publishing house.
The improvement and diffusion of entomological science.

Subject coverage:
Entomology: all aspects but in particular taxonomy with reference to the western palaeoarctic region.

Museum or gallery collection, archive, or library special collection:
c.750 journal titles
c.11,000 books
c.30,000 reprints, including the Rothschild collection of siphonaptera reprints (flea)
Archival material
Innumerable monographs
Superb collection of 18th-, 19th- and 20th-century works on insects

Library catalogue:
All or part available in-house

Printed publications:
Agriculture and Forest Entomology (quarterly)
Antenna (house journal of the Society)
Ecological Entomology (quarterly)
Insect Conservation and Diversity
Insect Molecular Biology (quarterly)
Medical and Veterinary Entomology (quarterly)
Physiological Entomology (quarterly)
Systematic Entomology
RES Handbooks for the Identification of British Insects (11 vols, each vol. in several parts)
Symposia proceedings
A Guide to the Archives of the Royal Entomological Society

Publications list:
Available online and in print

Access to staff:
Contact by letter, by telephone, by fax and by e-mail. Appointment necessary. Non-members charged.
Hours: Mon to Thu, 0900 to 1600; Fri, 0900 to 1530

Access to building, collection or gallery:
Prior appointment required
Special comments: Access limited to Fellows and Members, except by appointment

ROYAL ENVIRONMENTAL HEALTH INSTITUTE OF SCOTLAND

Acronym or abbreviation: REHIS

3 Manor Place, Edinburgh, EH3 7DH

Tel: 0131 225 6999
Fax: 0131 225 3993
E-mail: contact@rehis.com

Website:
http://www.rehis.org
Outline of activities, history of REHIS; REHIS, Our People; REHIS news; related organisations.

Enquiries:
Enquiries to: Chief Executive

Founded:
1983

Organisation type and purpose:
Membership association (membership is by qualification), present number of members: 1100, voluntary organisation, registered Scottish charity (charity number SCO 09406).

Subject coverage:
Environmental health in Scotland, education and training in environmental health subjects.

Library catalogue:
All or part available in-house

Printed publications:
Annual Report
Journal
Occasional publications

Access to staff:
Contact by letter and by e-mail
Hours: Mon to Fri, 0900 to 1700

Access to building, collection or gallery:
Prior appointment required

ROYAL FORESTRY SOCIETY

Acronym or abbreviation: RFS

102 High Street, Tring, Hertfordshire, HP23 4AF

Tel: 01442 822028
Fax: 01442 890395
E-mail: rfshq@rfs.org.uk

continued overleaf

Website:
http://www.rfs.org.uk

Enquiries:
Enquiries to: Chief Executive

Founded:
1882

Organisation type and purpose:
Learned society (membership is by subscription).

Subject coverage:
Forestry; arboriculture; careers advice in these fields.

Museum or gallery collection, archive, or library special collection:
Rare forestry books

Printed publications:
Journal of Forestry (quarterly)

Access to staff:
Contact by letter
Hours: Mon to Fri, 0900 to 1700

Access to building, collection or gallery:
No prior appointment required

ROYAL FREE AND UNIVERSITY COLLEGE MEDICAL SCHOOL

Medical Library, Royal Free Hospital, Rowland Hill Street, London, NW3 2PF

Tel: 020 7794 0500
Fax: 020 7794 3534
E-mail: library@rfc.ucl.ac.uk

Website:
http://library.ucl.ac.uk

Enquiries:
Enquiries to: Librarian
Direct tel: 020 7794 0500 ext 3203

Organisation type and purpose:
University library.

Subject coverage:
Medicine, psychiatry and psychology.

Library catalogue:
All or part available online

Access to staff:
Contact by letter. Appointment necessary. Letter of introduction required.
Hours: Mon to Fri, 0900 to 1900;
Sat, 0900 to 1300 (excluding Aug)
Special comments: Members primarily.

Access for disabled people:
Level entry

Parent body:
University College London
 (University of London)

ROYAL GEOGRAPHICAL SOCIETY WITH THE INSTITUTE OF BRITISH GEOGRAPHERS

Acronym or abbreviation: RGS-IBG

1 Kensington Gore, London, SW7 2AR

Tel: 020 7591 3000
Fax: 020 7591 3001
E-mail: enquiries@rgs.org

Website:
http://www.rgs.org

Enquiries:
Enquiries to: Principal Librarian
Direct tel: 020 7591 3041
Direct e-mail: e.rae@rgs.org
Other contacts: Deputy Librarian

Founded:
1830

Organisation type and purpose:
Learned society, professional body (membership is by qualification, election or invitation), present number of members: 14,000, registered charity.

Study groups in the subjects listed below.
Access to the Society's information resources is available in the Foyle Reading Room.

Subject coverage:
Geography, including exploration and travel; cartography, geography of rural and urban areas, medical, transport and population geography, geomorphology, historical geography, quantitative methods, women and geography, planning and geography, industrial activity and area development, biogeography, geography in higher education, social and political geography, transport geography, careers guidance for all geographers, field science training, major research projects overseas.

Non-library collection catalogue:
All or part available online and in-house

Library catalogue:
All or part available online and in-house

Printed publications:
Area (quarterly)
Geographical Journal (quarterly)
Special publications and book series
Transactions of the Institute of British Geographers (quarterly)
Order printed publications from: RGS-IBG Book Series

Publications list:
Available in print

Access to staff:
Contact by letter, by telephone, by fax, by e-mail, in person and via website. Non-members charged.

Access to building, collection or gallery:
Apart from Foyle Reading Room, Members only
Hours: Mon to Fri, 0930 to 1730 (Foyle Reading Room, 1000 to 1700)

Access for disabled people:
Fully accessible

ROYAL GLASGOW INSTITUTE OF THE FINE ARTS, THE

Acronym or abbreviation: RGI

5 Oswald Street, Glasgow, G1 4QR

Tel: 0141 248 7411
Fax: 0141 221 0417
E-mail: rgi@robbferguson.co.uk

Enquiries:
Enquiries to: Secretary

Founded:
1861

Organisation type and purpose:
Membership association (membership is by subscription), present number of members: 1400, registered charity.

Subject coverage:
Promotion of art by means of an open annual exhibition, the third largest in the United Kingdom. The RGI also owns a small gallery for hire for solo or group exhibitions.

Access to staff:
Contact by letter, by telephone and by fax
Hours: Mon to Thu, 0900 to 1600

ROYAL HISTORICAL SOCIETY

Acronym or abbreviation: RHistS

University College London, Gower Street, London, WC1E 6BT

Tel: 020 7387 7532
Fax: 020 7387 7532
E-mail: royalhistsoc@ucl.ac.uk

Website:
http://www.royalhistoricalsociety.org

Enquiries:
Enquiries to: Executive Secretary

Organisation type and purpose:
Learned society, registered charity.

Subject coverage:
History.

Museum or gallery collection, archive, or library special collection:
A collection of about 1,000 pre-1850 books, some of which are part of the bequest of Sir George Prothero (d. 1922), whose papers are also held
Archives of the Society
Archives of the Camden Society

Printed publications:
Annual Bibliography
Studies in History
Camden Series
Guides and Handbooks
Transactions

Access to staff:
Contact by letter, by telephone, by fax and by e-mail
Hours: Mon to Fri, 0900 to 1700

Constituent part of:
University College London

ROYAL HOLLOWAY INSTITUTE FOR ENVIRONMENTAL RESEARCH

Acronym or abbreviation: RHIER

Huntersdale, Callow Hill, Virginia Water, Surrey, GU25 4LN

Tel: 01784 477404
Fax: 01784 477427
E-mail: rhier@rhbnc.ac.uk

Enquiries:
Enquiries to: Project Development Officer
Direct e-mail: s.kandiah-evans@rhul.ac.uk
Other contacts: Director; e.maltby@rhul.ac.uk

Founded:
1994

Organisation type and purpose:
University department or institute.

Subject coverage:
Wetland management, wetland conservation, wetland ecosystem functioning, hydroacoustic methods for fish survey.
Global Biological Diversity Conservation Policy.

Printed publications:
Ecosystem Management: Questions for Science and Society (£15 inc. p&p)
Technical reports and research papers

Access to staff:
Contact by letter and by e-mail
Hours: Mon to Fri, 0900 to 1700

Access to building, collection or gallery:
Prior appointment required

Access for disabled people:
Parking provided

Connections with:
IUCN Commission on Ecosystem Management
Wetland Ecosystems Research Group
 Fish Hydroacoustics Unit; tel: 01784 477404; fax: 01784 477427

Parent body:
Royal Holloway University of London
 tel: 01784 434455

ROYAL HOLLOWAY UNIVERSITY OF LONDON – LIBRARY

Formal name: Royal Holloway and Bedford New College University of London
Acronym or abbreviation: RHUL

Egham, Surrey, TW20 0EX

Tel: 01784 443823
Fax: 01784 477670
E-mail: library@rhul.ac.uk

Website:
http://www.rhul.ac.uk/information-services/
library
Library catalogue, subject guides, recent
acquisitions lists, special collections information

Enquiries:
Enquiries to: Director of Library Services
Other contacts: Information Consultants' Team Co-
ordinator

Founded:
1886

Incorporates the former:
Bedford College London (year of change 1986)

Organisation type and purpose:
University library.
College library of the University of London.

Subject coverage:
Arts, classics, drama, theatre studies and film,
economics, English and American literature,
French, German, Italian language and literature,
history, linguistics, management, medical
sociology, music, sociology, social administration,
social anthropology, Hispanic studies, media arts,
history of women.
Sciences: biochemistry, biology, botany, chemistry,
geography, geology, mathematics, physics,
physiology, psychology and zoology.

**Museum or gallery collection, archive, or library
special collection:**
A. V. Coton collection on dance
Collection on theatre
College Archives
Dawson collection of New Zealand poetry and
prose published since 1900
Dom Anselm Hughes collection on medieval
religious music (includes his personal letters and
papers)
Early printed books from 16th century onwards in
classics; English and French literature; history;
some science, especially botany
Robert Simpson Society Archives comprising
books, scores, records, MS sketches and
miscellanea relating to the composer
Sir Alfred Sherman Papers
Small but significant collection of works by or
about T. E. Lawrence
South East Asia Geology Library

Non-library collection catalogue:
All or part available online

Library catalogue:
All or part available online

Printed publications:
Guide to the Library (free)

Access to staff:
Contact by letter, by telephone, by fax, by e-mail,
in person and via website. Non-members charged.
Special comments: Appointments necessary if
specific specialist help required

Access to building, collection or gallery:
No prior appointment required
Hours: Term time: Mon to Thu, 0900 to 2300; Fri,
0900 to 1900; Sat, 1100 to 1700; Sun, 1300 to 2100.
Vacation: Mon to Fri, 0900 to 1700

Access for disabled people:
Good access to Bedford Library; access to
Founder's and Music Libraries by arrangement

ROYAL HORTICULTURAL SOCIETY

Acronym or abbreviation: RHS

80 Vincent Square, Westminster, London, SW1P
2PE

Tel: 020 7821 3000
Fax: 020 7630 6060

Website:
http://www.rhs.org.uk
http://www.rhs.org.uk/around/shows/chel.asp
Chelsea Flower Show.

Enquiries:
Enquiries to: Librarian
Direct tel: 020 7821 3050
Direct fax: 020 7828 3022
Direct e-mail: library_enquiries@rhs.org.uk
Other contacts: Director RHS Garden for gardening
queries.

Founded:
1804

Organisation type and purpose:
Learned society, professional body, registered
charity, research organisation.

Subject coverage:
Non-commercial horticulture and silviculture, all
plants, trees and shrubs, both ornamental and
culinary, plant pests and diseases, garden design,
history of gardening, floras, botanical art, flower
arranging, to a lesser extent books on systematic
botany, agriculture and forestry.

**Museum or gallery collection, archive, or library
special collection:**
Bunyard Collection of books on fruit (part of the
Lindley Library)
Lindley Library (horticultural and botanical books
from the 16th century to the present)

Library catalogue:
All or part available in-house

Printed publications:
Over 700 publications related to all aspects of
horticulture, list available from RHS Enterprises
Limited, RHS Garden, Wisley, Woking, Surrey
GU23 6QB, tel: 01483 211320, fax: 01483 211003,
Mon to Fri, 0900 to 1730
The Garden (monthly)
The Plantsman (quarterly)
Wisley Handbooks and RHS Associated Series
including:
Advanced and Technical Books
Art, Floral Craft, Indoor Plants and Herbs
Cacti, Succulents and Orchids
Design and History
Flora and Wild Flowers
General Interest
RHS International Register
Specific Plants and Groupings
Trees and Shrubs
Order printed publications from: RHS Enterprises
Ltd, RHS Garden, Wisley, Nr Woking, Surrey,
GU23 6QB, e-mail: mailorder@rhs.org.uk

Electronic and video publications:
30 videos available for purchase including:
Chelsea 1995–2000 (6 videos)
Instructional videos on related topics
Wisley through the Seasons (4 videos)
Rosemoor: a garden in the making (video)

Publications list:
Available in print

Access to staff:
Contact by letter, by telephone, by fax, by e-mail
and in person. Appointment necessary.
Hours: Mon to Fri, 0930 to 1730

Access to building, collection or gallery:
No prior appointment required

Access for disabled people:
Ramped entry, toilet facilities

Other addresses:
RHS Garden
Rosemoor, Great Torrington, Devon, EX38 8PH
RHS Garden
Hyde Hall, Rettendon, Essex
RHS Garden
Wisley, Ripley, Woking, Surrey, GU23 6QB
The Fruit Group of the RHS
at the same address

ROYAL HUMANE SOCIETY

Acronym or abbreviation: RHS

Brettenham House, Lancaster Place, London,
WC2E 7EP

Tel: 020 7836 8155
Fax: 020 7836 8155
E-mail: info@royalhumanesociety.org.uk

Website:
http://www.royalhumanesociety.org.uk

Enquiries:
Enquiries to: Secretary
Direct e-mail: secretary@royalhumanesociety.org.uk

Founded:
1774

Organisation type and purpose:
Charity
Society incorporated by Royal Charter.
Encourages the saving of human life by the giving
of award.

Subject coverage:
Grants non-pecuniary awards for bravery in
saving human life and for the restoration of life by
resuscitation

**Museum or gallery collection, archive, or library
special collection:**
Annual reports and casebooks from 1774 to
present to be held by London Metropolitan
Archives from autumn 2008

Printed publications:
Medals of the Royal Humane Society
Annual Report
Short History of the Royal Humane Society
Saved from a Watery Grave

Access to staff:
Contact by letter, by telephone, by fax and by e-
mail. Appointment necessary. All charged.
Hours: Mon to Thu, 1030 to 1600

ROYAL INCORPORATION OF ARCHITECTS IN SCOTLAND

Acronym or abbreviation: RIAS

15 Rutland Square, Edinburgh, EH1 2BE

Tel: 0131 229 7545
Fax: 0131 228 2188
E-mail: info@rias.org.uk

Website:
http://www.rias.org.uk

Enquiries:
Enquiries to: Secretary

Founded:
1916

Organisation type and purpose:
Professional body, membership association,
consultancy.

Subject coverage:
Architecture, architects and services, history of
architecture.

Printed publications:
Architectural Guides to Scotland
Members' Newsletter (quarterly)

Access to staff:
Contact by letter, by telephone, by fax, by e-mail
and via website. Appointment necessary.
Hours: Mon to Fri, 0900 to 1700

Access to building, collection or gallery:
Hours: Mon to Fri, 0900 to 1700

Branches:
Aberdeen, Dundee, Edinburgh, Glasgow,
Inverness and Stirling

Links with:
Royal Institute of British Architects

ROYAL INSTITUTE OF BRITISH ARCHITECTS

Acronym or abbreviation: RIBA

West Midlands, Birmingham and Midland
Institute, 9 Margaret Street, Birmingham, B3 3SP

Tel: 0121 233 2321

continued overleaf

Fax: 0121 233 4946
E-mail: riba.westmidlands@inst.riba.org

Enquiries:
Enquiries to: Administrator

Organisation type and purpose:
Professional body (membership is by subscription, qualification), present number of members: 1300 in West Midlands, registered charity.

Non-library collection catalogue:
All or part available in-house

Library catalogue:
All or part available in-house

Access to staff:
Contact by letter, by telephone and by fax.
Appointment necessary. Non-members charged.
Hours: Mon to Fri, 0900 to 1700
Special comments: Charges to non-members may be appropriate.

Access to building, collection or gallery:
No prior appointment required
Special comments: Library only open on set days, telephone for details.

ROYAL INSTITUTE OF BRITISH ARCHITECTS (NORTH WEST REGION)

Acronym or abbreviation: RIBA NW

Unit 10, The Tea Factory, 82 Wood Street, Liverpool, L1 4DQ

Tel: 0151 703 0107
Fax: 0151 703 0108
E-mail: riba.northwest@inst.riba.org

Website:
http://www.architecture.com
General information

Enquiries:
Enquiries to: Regional Director

Organisation type and purpose:
Professional body (membership is by subscription).

Subject coverage:
Architecture.

Printed publications:
JCT Contracts and Practice Documents list is available on request
Order printed publications from: RIBA Publications
Construction House, 56–64 Leonard Street, London, EC2A 4LT, tel: 020 7251 0791, fax: 020 7608 2375

Publications list:
Available online and in print

Access to staff:
Contact by letter, by telephone, by fax, by e-mail and in person
Hours: Mon to Fri, 0900 to 1700

Access to building, collection or gallery:
Hours: Mon to Fri, 0900 to 1700

Parent body:
Royal Institute of British Architects (RIBA)
66 Portland Place, London, W1N 4AD

ROYAL INSTITUTE OF INTERNATIONAL AFFAIRS LIBRARY

Acronym or abbreviation: RIIA, Chatham House

Chatham House, 10 St James's Square, London, SW1Y 4LE

Tel: 020 7957 5723
Fax: 020 7957 5710
E-mail: libenquire@chathamhouse.org.uk

Website:
http://www.chathamhouse.org.uk

Founded:
1920

Organisation type and purpose:
International organisation, learned society (membership is by subscription), registered charity, research organisation.
The Royal Institute of International Affairs at Chatham House, London, is one of the world's leading institutes for the analysis of international issues. The Institute is independent of government.

Subject coverage:
International affairs and relations between all states (diplomatic, political, legal, military, economic and financial) since 1918, with special focus on the most recent 30–35 years; international problems and organisations; foreign and defence policies and (on a limited scale) domestic affairs of all countries.

Museum or gallery collection, archive, or library special collection:
British and other government documents relating to foreign policy, 1918 to date
Collection of press cuttings from a wide range of the world's press published in West European languages, closely classified and cross-referenced; the files covering the periods from 1924–August 1939 and 1972–July 1997 (ceased) are at the RIIA (those for September 1939–December 1971 are in the British Library Newspaper Library)
Royal Institute of International Affairs archives by prior application

Library catalogue:
All or part available online

Printed publications:
Chatham House Papers
Classified catalogue of the Library of the RIIA: an introduction (1981)
Briefing Papers
Index to Periodical Articles 1950–78 in the Library of the RIIA (two vols and two supplements)
International Affairs (6 a year)
RIIA Library Thesaurus (1991)
World Today (monthly)

Microform publications:
Classified catalogue of the Library of the RIIA (microfiche)
Index to Periodical Articles 1979–89 in the Library of the RIIA (microfiche edn)

Electronic and video publications:
Briefing papers
Chatham House reports

Publications list:
Available online

Access to staff:
Contact by letter, by e-mail and via website.
Appointment necessary. Letter of introduction required. Non-members charged.
Hours: Mon to Fri, 1000 to 1730
Special comments: Primarily for members.

ROYAL INSTITUTE OF NAVIGATION

Acronym or abbreviation: RIN

1 Kensington Gore, London, SW7 2AT

Tel: 020 7591 3130
Fax: 020 7591 3131
E-mail: info@rin.org.uk

Website:
http://www.rin.org.uk
Navigation information, activities, membership details, library and journal search facilities.

Enquiries:
Enquiries to: Director

Founded:
1947

Organisation type and purpose:
International organisation, advisory body, learned society (membership is by subscription), present number of members: 3500, registered charity (charity number 251512), public library, publishing house.
To unite in one body those interested in navigation and to advance its science and practice, and to promote knowledge in navigation.

Subject coverage:
All aspects of air, sea, vehicle and space navigation; navigation technology, satellite navigation, small craft navigation, general and civil aviation navigation, land navigation, traffic routing, animal navigation, personal navigation, history of navigation, astronomy, bridge design, collision avoidance, weather.

Museum or gallery collection, archive, or library special collection:
Library covering all aspects of navigation

Printed publications:
Journal of Navigation (3 times a year)
Navigation News (6 times a year)

Access to staff:
Contact by letter, by telephone, by fax, by e-mail, in person and via website
Hours: Mon to Fri, 0930 to 1630

Access to building, collection or gallery:
No access other than to staff

Member of:
European Group of Institutes of Navigation (EUGIN)
    tel: + 31 23 540 2485; fax: + 31 23 540 2486; e-mail: navicons@xs4all.nl
International Association of Institutes of Navigation (IAIN)
    tel: 01444 232405; fax: 01444 232405; e-mail: prentpage@aol.com

ROYAL INSTITUTE OF OIL PAINTERS

Acronym or abbreviation: ROI

17 Carlton House Terrace, London, SW1Y 5BD

Tel: 020 7930 6844
Fax: 020 7839 7830
E-mail: press@mallgalleries.com

Website:
http://www.mallgalleries.org.uk

Enquiries:
Enquiries to: Secretary
Other contacts: Marketing and Communications Officer

Founded:
1882

Organisation type and purpose:
Membership association (membership is by election or invitation), present number of members: 68, registered charity (charity number 327615).
To foster and promote the art of oil painting.

Subject coverage:
Oil paintings and painters, annual open exhibition.

Printed publications:
ROI Catalogues available in December exhibition

Access to staff:
Contact by letter, by telephone, by fax, by e-mail and via website. Appointment necessary.
Hours: Mon to Fri, 0930 to 1730

Access to building, collection or gallery:
No access other than to staff
Hours: Mon to Fri, 0930 to 1730

Access for disabled people:
Toilet facilities
Special comments: Stairlift.

Links with:
Federation of British Artists (FBA)
    at the same address

ROYAL INSTITUTE OF PAINTERS IN WATERCOLOURS

Acronym or abbreviation: RI

17 Carlton House Terrace, London, SW1Y 5BD

Tel: 020 7930 6844
Fax: 020 7839 7830
E-mail: press@mallgalleries.com

Website:
http://www.mallgalleries.org.uk

Enquiries:
Enquiries to: Secretary
Other contacts: Marketing and Communications Officer

Founded:
1831

Organisation type and purpose:
Membership association (membership is by election or invitation), present number of members: 78, voluntary organisation, registered charity (charity number 291405).
To foster and promote the art of watercolour painting.

Subject coverage:
Watercolour painting, annual open exhibition.

Printed publications:
RI catalogues available during annual exhibition

Access to staff:
Contact by letter, by telephone, by fax, by e-mail and via website. Appointment necessary.
Hours: Mon to Fri, 0930 to 1730

Access to building, collection or gallery:
No access other than to staff
Hours: Mon to Fri, 0930 to 1730

Access for disabled people:
Toilet facilities
Special comments: Stairlift.

Links with:
Federation of British Artists
at the same address

ROYAL INSTITUTE OF PHILOSOPHY

14 Gordon Square, London, WC1H 0AR

Tel: 020 7387 4130
Fax: 020 7383 4061
E-mail: secretary@royalinstitutephilosophy.org

Website:
http://www.royalinstitutephilosophy.org

Enquiries:
Enquiries to: Secretary

Organisation type and purpose:
Learned society.
To promote the study and discussion of philosophy, arrange and sponsor lectures and conferences.

Subject coverage:
Philosophy: logic, metaphysics, epistemology, ethics, aesthetics, social and political philosophy; the philosophies of science, religion, history, education, mind and language.

Museum or gallery collection, archive, or library special collection:
Bosanquet Collection

Printed publications:
Conference Proceedings (biennial)
Lectures given at the Institute (annual)
Philosophy (quarterly)

Access to staff:
Contact by letter and by e-mail
Hours: Mon to Fri, 0900 to 1700

ROYAL INSTITUTE OF PUBLIC HEALTH

Acronym or abbreviation: RIPH

28 Portland Place, London, W1B 1DE

Tel: 020 7580 2731
Fax: 020 7580 6157
E-mail: info@riph.org.uk

Website:
http://www.riph.org.uk

Enquiries:
Enquiries to: Marketing Communications Officer
Direct tel: 020 7291 8358
Direct e-mail: jknope@riph.org.uk

Founded:
1886

Organisation type and purpose:
Learned society, membership association (membership is by qualification, election or invitation), present number of members: 3000, registered charity (charity number 227746), suitable for ages: 16+, training organisation.

Subject coverage:
Food safety, nutrition, salon hygiene, community care education, health and hygiene, postgraduate training in occupational health.

Printed publications:
Health and Hygiene (journal, quarterly)
Public Health (journal, 6 times a year)
A Handbook of Mortuary Practice & Safety
First Certificate in Food Safety – Student Handbook (1997)
First Certificate in Food Safety – Tutor's Guide (1995)
A Supervisor's Handbook of Food Hygiene and Safety (1998)
HACCP Principles and their Application in Food Safety Training Standards (1995)
Register of Certificated Products
Register of Certificated Training Materials
Symposium Proceedings

Publications list:
Available in print

Access to staff:
Contact by letter, by telephone, by fax and by e-mail
Hours: Mon to Fri, 0900 to 1700

ROYAL INSTITUTION OF CHARTERED SURVEYORS

Acronym or abbreviation: RICS

12 Great George Street, Parliament Square, London, SW1P 3AD

Tel: 0870 333 1600
Fax: 020 7334 3811
E-mail: contactrics@rics.org

Website:
http://www.rics.org
Description of organisation and activities and contact points, press releases, policy submissions listing, Chartered Surveyor Monthly – full text of articles from March 1997, CPD Providers database, RICS Directory of Chartered Surveyors practices database. Details of RICS conferences, research findings, papers and reports. Training and career information.

Enquiries:
Enquiries to: Librarian
Direct fax: 020 7334 3784
Direct e-mail: library@rics.org

Founded:
1868

Organisation type and purpose:
Professional body (membership is by qualification), present number of members: 120,000.

Subject coverage:
Commercial property, leisure property, chartered surveying, property, land, construction, valuation, surveying, town and country planning, construction economics, construction law, housing, agricultural holdings, estate agency, property management, land surveying, hydrographic surveying, landlord and tenant, property tax, quantity surveying, rating, estate management, marine resources.

Museum or gallery collection, archive, or library special collection:
Board of Agriculture Reports, 19th century
Historical Collection (pre-1875) on land, measurement and building economics and topography
Royal Commission Reports, 19th century
Topographical collections

Trade and statistical information:
Construction workload, housing market trend indicator, commercial property market survey, rural market survey and residential lettings.

Library catalogue:
All or part available online

Printed publications:
Knowledge Alert (fortnightly)
RICS Business (monthly)
Chartered Surveyors Directory
New members handbook
Publicity leaflets
RICS Yearbook
Geomatics World
Market Surveys on Residential Property, Commercial Property, Construction, Rural, Residential Lettings
UK Economic Brief
Order printed publications from: Mail Order Department, RICS Books, Surveyor Court, Westwood Way Business Park, Coventry, West Midlands, CV4 8JE, tel: 0870 333 1600, fax: 020 7334 3851, e-mail: mailorder@rics.org, website: ricsbooks.com

Electronic and video publications:
Appraisal and Valuation Manual (CD-ROM and online), isurv Building Surveying, Commercial Property, Construction, Disputes, Environment, Planning, Valuation (all online www.isurv.co.uk)

Publications list:
Available online and in print

Access to staff:
Contact by letter, by telephone, by fax, by e-mail, in person and via website. Non-members charged.
Hours: Mon to Fri, 0930 to 1730
Special comments: Charges made for access to the Library for non-members.

Access for disabled people:
Ramped entry, toilet facilities

Other addresses:
Royal Institution of Chartered Surveyors
Surveyor Court, Westwood Way Business Park, Coventry, CV4 8JE; tel: 0870 333 1600; fax: 020 7334 3811
Royal Institution of Chartered Surveyors
9 Manor Place, Edinburgh, EH3 7DN; tel: 0131 225 7078; fax: 0131 240 0830/31

ROYAL INSTITUTION OF CHARTERED SURVEYORS IN SCOTLAND

Acronym or abbreviation: RICS

9 Manor Place, Edinburgh, EH3 7DN

Tel: 0131 225 7078
Fax: 0131 240 0830
E-mail: edlib@rics.org

Website:
http://www.rics.org/services/library
Library catalogue for members

Enquiries:
Enquiries to: Library Manager

Founded:
1897

Organisation type and purpose:
International organisation, professional body (membership is by qualification), present number of members: 9,000.

continued overleaf

Subject coverage:
Surveying, building construction, property, rural practice.

Library catalogue:
All or part available online

Publications list:
Available online

Access to staff:
Contact by letter, by telephone, by fax, by e-mail, in person and via website. Appointment necessary. Non-members charged.
Hours: Mon to Fri, 0845 to 1700

Also at:
The Librarian, Royal Institution of Chartered Surveyors
12 Great George Street, Parliament Square, London, SW1P 3AD; tel: 020 7334 3714; fax: 020 7334 3784; e-mail: library@rics.org

ROYAL INSTITUTION OF CORNWALL

Acronym or abbreviation: RIC

Courtney Library & Cornish History Research Centre, River Street, Truro, Cornwall, TR1 2SJ

Tel: 01872 272205
Fax: 01872 240514
E-mail: RIC@royalcornwallmuseum.org.uk

Enquiries:
Enquiries to: Librarian

Founded:
1818

Organisation type and purpose:
Learned society, registered charity (charity number 221958).
Private members library with public access to study area. The oldest established Cornish history research centre in the county.

Subject coverage:
Cornwall; all aspects of research into Cornish history.

Museum or gallery collection, archive, or library special collection:
19th- and 20th-century photographs of Cornwall (50,000 items)
Doble Collection (hagiography)
Henderson Collection (manuscripts on history, antiquities, topography, Cornwall)
Manuscripts 13th-19th centuries (c. 30,000 items, Cornish estates and people)
Directories and Newspapers 1798–1951 and 1965–1973 (original files, Cornwall)
Parish registers (microfilms and transcripts)
Shaw Collection (Methodist church history, Cornwall)
Staal Collection (ceramics, glass, clocks)

Non-library collection catalogue:
All or part available in-house

Printed publications:
Journal of The Royal Institution of Cornwall (annually since 1864)
Newsletter of The RIC (2 times a year)
Facsimiles of 19th-century posters from RIC Collection
List of Cornish Parish Registers held by RIC as transcripts, 1992
List of Non-Anglican Registers ... Cornwall, 1999
Sources for Maritime Research
Sources for Newspaper Research ... Cornwall, 2000

Microform publications:
List of Cornish Parish Registers held by RIC on microfilm, 1992

Access to staff:
Contact by letter, by telephone, by fax, by e-mail and in person
Hours: Mon to Sat, 1000 to 1300 and 1400 to 1700
Closed Bank Holidays
Special comments: Non-members may be admitted for the purposes of research.

Access for disabled people:
Lift, ramped entry, access to all public areas, toilet facilities

Links with:
Royal Cornwall Museum and Art Gallery

ROYAL INSTITUTION OF GREAT BRITAIN

Acronym or abbreviation: RI

21 Albemarle Street, London, W1S 4BS

Tel: 020 7409 2992
Fax: 020 7629 3569
E-mail: ri@ri.ac.uk

Website:
http://www.rigb.org/

Enquiries:
Enquiries to: Head of Collections and Heritage
Direct tel: 020 7670 2924
Direct e-mail: fjames@ri.ac.uk

Founded:
1799

Organisation type and purpose:
Learned society (membership is by election or invitation), present number of members: c. 3000. Scientific body.

Subject coverage:
Science for the layman, history and philosophy of science, scientific biography, the social relations of science, solid state and surface chemistry and physics, catalysis, computer molecular modelling.

Museum or gallery collection, archive, or library special collection:
Historic apparatus
Manuscripts of famous scientists connected with The Royal Institution eg H Davy, M Faraday, J Tyndall, J Dewar, W H and W L Bragg, G Porter
Pre-1900 scientific books and periodicals
The Royal Institution Administrative Archives

Non-library collection catalogue:
All or part available in-house

Library catalogue:
All or part available in-house

Printed publications:
Annual report

Microform publications:
J Dewar, 1842–1923, catalogue of papers (1991, pub Chadwyck-Healey)
Journals of T A Hirst (Brock W H et al eds, pub Mansell, 1980)
J Tyndall, 1820–1893 (catalogue of papers, Friday J R ed., pub Mansell, 1974)

Electronic and video publications:
RI Christmas Lectures videotapes (via BBC)

Publications list:
Available in print

Access to staff:
Appointment necessary.
Hours: Mon to Fri, 0900 to 1700

Access for disabled people:
Level entry, toilet facilities

Includes the:
Davy-Faraday Research Laboratory
Library and Archives
Michael Faraday Museum
Royal Institution Centre for the History of Science and Technology

ROYAL INSTITUTION OF NAVAL ARCHITECTS

Acronym or abbreviation: RINA

10 Upper Belgrave Street, London, SW1X 8BQ

Tel: 020 7235 4622
Fax: 020 7245 6959
E-mail: hq@rina.org.uk

Website:
http://www.rina.org.uk
Information on all the Institution's activities, and publications.

Enquiries:
Enquiries to: Information Officer
Direct fax: 020 7259 5912

Founded:
1860

Organisation type and purpose:
International organisation, learned society, professional body (membership is by qualification, election or invitation), registered charity (charity number 211161).

Subject coverage:
Naval architecture, shipbuilding, marine engineering and related subjects.

Non-library collection catalogue:
All or part available online and in print

Printed publications:
Careers Brochure
Marine Technology Monographs
Naval Architect (RINA Journal, 10 times a year)
Occasional Publications
Ship and Boat International (journal, 10 times a year)
Ship Repair and Conversion Technology (journal, quarterly)
Symposia Proceedings
Transactions (annually)
Warship Technology
Order printed publications from: e-mail: publications@rina.org.uk

Electronic and video publications:
Naval Architect (RINA Journal, 10 times a year)
Ship & Boat International (CD-ROM)
Ship Repair and Conversion Technology (journal, quarterly)
Warship Technology

Publications list:
Available online and in print

Access to staff:
Contact by letter, by telephone, by fax, by e-mail and via website. Appointment necessary. Non-members charged.
Hours: Mon to Fri, 0930 to 1700

ROYAL INSTITUTION OF SOUTH WALES

Acronym or abbreviation: RISW

c/o Swansea Museum, Victoria Road, Maritime Quarter, Swansea, West Glamorgan, SA1 1SN

Tel: 01792 653763
Fax: 01792 652585
E-mail: swansea.museum@swansea.gov.uk

Website:
http://www.risw.org.uk

Enquiries:
Enquiries to: Honorary Secretary
Direct tel: 01792 874143
Other contacts: Curator for museum/local history

Founded:
1835

Organisation type and purpose:
Learned society (membership is by subscription), voluntary organisation, registered charity.
Friends of Swansea Museum.

Subject coverage:
Local history and studies of Swansea and surrounding area, including natural history, biography, culture, early photography, archaeology, ceramics (Swansea and District) and local topography.

Printed publications:
Available for purchase directly
Minerva: The Journal of Swansea History (annually, back numbers available)
History of Swansea Vol 2 (Jones W H)

John Humphrey, God's Own Architect (Farmer D)
Welsh Ceramics in Context, Vols 1–2 (ed Gray J)

Publications list:
Available in print

Access to staff:
Contact by letter, by telephone and by e-mail.
Appointment necessary.
Hours: Mon to Fri, 0900 to 1700

Access to building, collection or gallery:
Prior appointment required

Access for disabled people:
Parking provided

ROYAL LANCASHIRE AGRICULTURAL SOCIETY

Acronym or abbreviation: RLAS

South Planks Farm, Garstang Road, Barton,
Preston, Lancashire, PR3 5AB

Tel: 01995 643215
Fax: 01995 640894
E-mail: info@rlas.co.uk

Website:
http://www.rlas.co.uk

Enquiries:
Enquiries to: Secretary

Founded:
1767

Organisation type and purpose:
Membership association (membership is by
subscription), present number of members: 750,
registered charity (charity number 1008403).
Promotion of agriculture. Organisation of three-
day agricultural show.

Subject coverage:
Royal Lancashire Show.

**Museum or gallery collection, archive, or library
special collection:**
History of Society held in County Records Office
Show Journals over many years

Printed publications:
Annual Report (members only)
Annual Schedules/Prize lists (free)
Newsletter (2 times a year, members only)

Access to staff:
Contact by letter, by telephone, by fax, by e-mail,
in person and via website
Hours: Mon to Fri, 0900 to 1700

Access for disabled people:
Access to all public areas

Links with:
Various breed societies

ROYAL LONDON HOSPITAL ARCHIVES AND MUSEUM

The Royal London Hospital, Whitechapel, London,
E1 1BB

Tel: 020 7377 7608
Fax: 020 7377 7401
E-mail: jonathan.evans@bartsandthelondon.nhs.uk

Website:
http://www.bartsandthelondon.nhs.uk
History of the hospital; general guide to archives
and museum.
http://www.a2a.org.uk
Detailed guide to archival holdings.
http://www.aim25.ac.uk
Detailed guide to archival holdings.

Enquiries:
Enquiries to: Archivist

Organisation type and purpose:
National government body, museum, university
department or institute,
suitable for ages: 12+.
Archive.

Subject coverage:
Hospitals, medical and nursing history, dentistry,
orthodontics, forensic medicine, health records.

**Museum or gallery collection, archive, or library
special collection:**
Archives of the Royal London Hospital
Archives of the London Chest Hospital
Archives of the Queen Elizabeth Hospital for
Children
Archives of the London Hospital Medical College
Archives of other hospitals in Tower Hamlets and
Newham
Collections of the British Orthodontic Society
Edith Cavell Collection: Nursing history, artefacts
and archives 1800s-1915
Eva Luckes Collection
London Hospital Surgical Instruments 18th-20th
century
Medical and surgical films
Princess Alexandra School of Nursing: Nursing
history, uniforms, equipment etc.1880–1993

Printed publications:
The Royal London Hospital: A Brief History
(Collins S M, 1995)
London Pride: The Story of a Voluntary Hospital
(Clark-Kennedy A E, 1979)
Emblems, Tokens and Tickets of The London
Hospital and the London Hospital Medical
College (Gibbs D, 1985)
L.H.M.C. 1785–1985 The Story of England's first
Medical School (Ellis J)
The Dental School of The London Hospital Medical
College 1911–1991 (Fish S F, 1991)
Learning to care: A history of nursing and
midwifery education at the Royal London
Hospital, 1740–1983 (Parker E R and Collins S M,
1998)
A History of Radiotherapy at The London Hospital
1896–1996 (Hope-Stone H F, 1999)
Patients are People – Memories of Nursing at 'The
London' 1939–1958 (Broadley M E, 1995)
Patients Come First. Nursing at 'The London'
between the two World Wars (Broadley M E,
1980)
Edith Cavell: Her Life And Her Art – Sa Vie Et Son
Art (Daunton C H G, 1990)
Treves and the Elephant Man (Evans R J, 2003)
Edith Cavell (Evans R J, 2008)

Publications list:
Available online and in print

Access to staff:
Contact by letter, by telephone, by fax, by e-mail,
in person and via website. Appointment necessary.
Hours: Mon to Fri, 1000 to 1630

Access to building, collection or gallery:
Open to the public
Hours: Mon to Fri, 1000 to 1630

Access for disabled people:
Disabled access available
Hours: Mon to Fri, 1000 to 1630

Affiliated to:
Queen Mary University of London

Parent body:
Barts and The London Hospital NHS Trust
Royal London Hospital, London, E1 1BB

ROYAL LONDON SOCIETY FOR THE BLIND

Acronym or abbreviation: RLSB

Dorton House, Seal, Sevenoaks, Kent, TN15 0ED

Tel: 01732 592500
Fax: 01732 592506
E-mail: david.halliday@rlsb.org.uk

Website:
http://www.rlsb.org.uk

Enquiries:
Enquiries to: Marketing and Communications
Director
Direct tel: 07770 947062

Founded:
1838

Organisation type and purpose:
Registered charity (charity number 307892).
A national provider of education, training and
employment for people who are visually impaired.

Subject coverage:
Education of blind or partially-sighted children
aged 3 to 16, further education from 16 upwards,
including mature students, training and
rehabilitation, employment in RLSB industrial
Services, SES scheme, homeworkers.

**Museum or gallery collection, archive, or library
special collection:**
Minutes and official reports on the Society dating
back to its inception in 1838

Printed publications:
Annual Report
Prospectus on school and college
Life Chances (2 times a year)

Electronic and video publications:
Making a will booklet (on tape and Braille)

Access to staff:
Contact by letter, by telephone, by fax and by e-
mail. Appointment necessary.
Hours: Mon to Fri, 0900 to 1700

Member of:
Blindcare
Greater London Fund for the Blind
Opsis

ROYAL MAIL EDUCATION SERVICE

PO Box 145, Sittingbourne, Kent, ME10 1NH

Tel: 01795 437988
Fax: 01795 474871
E-mail: info@edist.co.uk

Enquiries:
Enquiries to: Director

Formerly called:
Post Office Film and Video Library, and Education
Service (year of change 2001)

Subject coverage:
Full range of educational resources – primary,
secondary, higher, supported by video
programmes and other material on all aspects of
Royal Mail, Post Office, Counters and Parcelforce.
Library for GPO classic programmes e.g. 'Night
Mail' on video and many other 1930s subjects. In
addition more recent releases, including videos on
stamps, the Millennium and other subjects.

**Museum or gallery collection, archive, or library
special collection:**
Current Post Office video releases
Archive posters
Classic collection of archive subjects from GPO
film unit (1930s) (on DVD)
Classic video collection

Library catalogue:
All or part available in print

Printed publications:
Teacher's Post

Publications list:
Available in print

Access to staff:
Contact by letter, by telephone, by fax, by e-mail
and in person
Hours: Mon to Fri, 0900 to 1700

Access to building, collection or gallery:
Prior appointment required

ROYAL MARINES ASSOCIATION

Acronym or abbreviation: RMA

Central Office, Building 32, Whale Island,
Portsmouth, Hants, PO2 8ER

continued overleaf

Tel: 023 9265 1519
Fax: 023 9254 7207
E-mail: chiefexec@rma.org.uk

Enquiries:
Enquiries to: Chief Executive

Founded:
1946

Organisation type and purpose:
National organisation, membership association (membership is by subscription, qualification), present number of members: 10,000, registered charity (charity number 206003).
Service charity.

Access to staff:
Contact by letter, by telephone, by fax and by e-mail
Hours: Mon to Fri, 0900 to 1700

ROYAL MEDICAL SOCIETY

Acronym or abbreviation: RMS

Student Centre, Bristo Square, Edinburgh, EH8 9AL

Tel: 0131 650 2672
E-mail: enquiries@royalmedical.co.uk

Website:
http://www.royalmedical.co.uk

Enquiries:
Enquiries to: Secretary

Organisation type and purpose:
Learned society.
Historical, medical students' organisation and library.

Subject coverage:
Edinburgh medical history.

Museum or gallery collection, archive, or library special collection:
Collection of dissertations over last 258 years
Current medical library
Historical medical library
Pathological museum

Printed publications:
RES Medica

Access to staff:
Appointment necessary.
Hours: Mon to Fri, 1200 to 1700

ROYAL MICROSCOPICAL SOCIETY

Acronym or abbreviation: RMS

37–38 St Clements, Oxford, OX4 1AJ

Tel: 01865 248768
Fax: 01865 791237
E-mail: info@rms.org.uk

Website:
http://www.rms.org.uk
Information on the Society and its programme of meetings and courses.

Enquiries:
Enquiries to: Administrator

Founded:
1839

Organisation type and purpose:
Learned society, present number of members: 1500, registered charity (charity number 241990).
To promote the advancement of microscopical science by discussion and publication of research into improvements in the construction and mode of application of microscopes and into those branches of science where microscopy is important.

Subject coverage:
Microscopy.

Museum or gallery collection, archive, or library special collection:
Collection of 18th and 19th century microscopes – housed at the Museum of the History of Science, Broad Street, Oxford

Non-library collection catalogue:
All or part available in print

Printed publications:
Catalogue of the collection
Journal of Microscopy (monthly, £660 a year)
Proceedings of the Royal Microscopical Society (quarterly, £176 a year)
RMS Handbooks Series (1–2 titles a year)

Access to staff:
Contact by letter, by telephone, by fax and by e-mail
Hours: Mon to Fri, 0900 to 1700

Affiliated to:
International Federation of Societies for Histochemistry and Cytochemistry (IFSHC)
International Federation of Societies of Electron Microscopy (IFSEM)

ROYAL MILITARY ACADEMY SANDHURST

Acronym or abbreviation: RMAS

Central Library, Camberley, Surrey, GU15 4PQ

Tel: 01276 412367
Fax: 01276 412359
E-mail: aaorgill@aol.com

Enquiries:
Enquiries to: Librarian

Organisation type and purpose:
Training organisation. Central government military academy.

Subject coverage:
War studies and military history; international affairs; political and social studies; Commonwealth of Independent States and the former republics of the Soviet Union.

Museum or gallery collection, archive, or library special collection:
Le Marchant Collection of manuscripts relating to the foundation of Sandhurst
Letter Books, RMA Woolwich, 1787–1895
Register of Gentlemen Cadets, RMA Woolwich, 1790–1793 and 1799–1939
Registers of Gentlemen Cadets, RMC Sandhurst, 1806–1945
Sandhurst Papers, 1857–1939

Non-library collection catalogue:
All or part available in-house

Library catalogue:
All or part available in-house

Printed publications:
Accessions lists

Access to staff:
Contact by letter, by telephone and by e-mail
Hours: Mon to Thu, 0830 to 1800; Fri, 0830 to 1630
Special comments: Visitors strictly by appointment only.

Part of:
Ministry of Defence

ROYAL NATIONAL COLLEGE FOR THE BLIND

Acronym or abbreviation: RNC

College Road, Hereford, HR1 1EB

Tel: 01432 265725
Fax: 01432 376628
E-mail: info@rncb.ac.uk

Website:
http://www.rncb.ac.uk
Prospectus plus additional information.

Enquiries:
Enquiries to: Marketing Manager
Other contacts: Central Admissions for advice/guidance on enrollment procedures.

Founded:
1872

Organisation type and purpose:
Registered charity (charity number 1000388), training organisation.
Further education and training for people who are blind or partially-sighted.

Subject coverage:
Education of the blind and partially sighted, especially education in music technology, piano tuning and repairing, business studies, remedial therapy, computing, performing arts, tele-tutoring, sport and recreation.

Museum or gallery collection, archive, or library special collection:
Annual Reports dating from foundation of College in 1872
Braille Library

Library catalogue:
All or part available online

Printed publications:
Annual Report
Prospectus (braille, large print and standard print)
Individual course leaflets

Electronic and video publications:
Prospectus on dis, tape and CD
Videos/DVD

Access to staff:
Contact by letter, by telephone, by fax, by e-mail and via website. Appointment necessary.
Hours: Mon to Fri, 0900 to 1700

Access for disabled people:
Parking provided, ramped entry, level entry, toilet facilities

Member of:
Natspec
Opsis

ROYAL NATIONAL INSTITUTE OF THE BLIND

Acronym or abbreviation: RNIB

105 Judd Street, London, WC1H 9NE

Tel: 020 7388 1266
Fax: 020 7388 2034
E-mail: helpline@rnib.org.uk

Website:
http://www.rnib.org.uk

Enquiries:
Enquiries to: Communications Systems Officer
Direct tel: 020 7391 2396
Direct fax: 020 7391 2221
Direct e-mail: julie-crispin@rnib.org.uk

Organisation type and purpose:
Registered charity.

Subject coverage:
Advice, support and information for blind and partially-sighted people. Benefit rights, advice on wills and legacies; production of Braille books, periodicals and music; Talking Books; equipment and games for blind and partially-sighted people and for deaf-blind people; social and employment rehabilitation and training; education including schools and colleges, advisory and training services; residential services; hotels; research into the prevention of blindness; advice on sport, leisure and the arts; health information service, low-vision expertise, consultancy to health authorities on ophthalmic services.

Information services:
Helpline for advice, support and information.

Museum or gallery collection, archive, or library special collection:
Early embossed literature (some 100 items, Alston, Frere, Lucas, Moon, Braille)

Printed publications:
Catalogue of Braille Books
Catalogue of Braille Music
Catalogue of Print Publications
Catalogue of Talking Books
Directory of Agencies for the Blind in the British Isles and Overseas
New Beacon (RNIB Journal)
Product guides (equipment, games etc)

Publications list:
Available online and in print

Access to staff:
Contact by letter, by telephone, by fax, by e-mail and via website
Hours: Mon to Fri, 0900 to 1700

Access for disabled people:
Ramped entry, access to all public areas, toilet facilities

ROYAL NATIONAL INSTITUTE OF THE BLIND – TALKING BOOK SERVICE

UK Customer Service Centre, PO Box 173, Peterborough, PE2 6WS

Tel: 01733 375000
Fax: 01733 375001
E-mail: cservices@rnib.org.uk

Website:
http://www.rnib.org.uk

Enquiries:
Enquiries to: General Customer Services

Founded:
1935

Organisation type and purpose:
Subscription library, registered charity.
Postal library for blind and partially sighted people, of any age, offering a wide range of professionally recorded books (CD) on special easy to use playback equipment.

Subject coverage:
Talking books.

Publications list:
Available online and in print

Access to staff:
Contact by letter, by e-mail and via website
Hours: Library: Mon to Fri, 0845 to 1800; Sat, 0900 to 1600

Access to building, collection or gallery:
No access other than to staff, prior appointment required

Access for disabled people:
Parking provided, level entry, access to all public areas, toilet facilities

ROYAL NATIONAL LIFEBOAT INSTITUTION

Acronym or abbreviation: RNLI

West Quay Road, Poole, Dorset, BH15 1HZ

Tel: 0845 122 6999
Fax: 01202 663366
E-mail: info@rnli.org.uk

Website:
http://www.rnli.org.uk
General information about the service.

Enquiries:
Enquiries to: Media Relations Manager

Founded:
1824

Organisation type and purpose:
Registered charity.

Subject coverage:
Search and rescue at sea, its organisation and statistics; design and construction of lifeboats and their electronic and other equipment; medical and survival techniques and equipment, lifeboat history (since 1824).

Special visitor services:
Library / archive available by appointment.

Museum or gallery collection, archive, or library special collection:
Lifeboat models
Photographic library (lifeboats since c. 1860)
Royal National Lifeboat Collection
Fine art collection
5 museum sites

Printed publications:
Annual Accounts
Educational Resources
Leaflets and posters
RNLI At Work (Annual review)
Storm Force News (quarterly, for children)
The Lifeboat (quarterly)
Order printed publications from: The Publications Dept, at the above address

Electronic and video publications:
Sea Safety Guidelines and DVDs
DVDs for adults and children
Order electronic and video publications from: Film and Image Unit, at the above address

Access to staff:
Contact by letter, by telephone, by fax, by e-mail and via website
Hours: Mon to Fri, 0900 to 1700

Access to building, collection or gallery:
By appointment
Hours: Mon to Fri, 0900 to 1700

Access for disabled people:
Lifts; access to display area and library
Hours: Mon to Fri, 0900 to 1700

Administers:
Chatham Historic Lifeboat Collection
Grace Darling Museum
Henry Blogg Museum
RNLI Whitby Museum
RNLI Zetland Museum

Provides the secretariat for the:
International Lifeboat Federation

ROYAL NATIONAL MISSION TO DEEP SEA FISHERMEN

Shore Street, Fraserburgh, Aberdeenshire, AB43 9BP

Tel: 01346 518388
Fax: 01346 517664

Enquiries:
Enquiries to: The Superintendent

Founded:
1881

Organisation type and purpose:
Registered charity (charity number 24477).

Subject coverage:
Christian missionary and welfare work for fishing communities.

Access to staff:
Contact by letter
Hours: Mon to Fri, 0900 to 1700

ROYAL NATIONAL MISSION TO DEEP SEA FISHERMEN, SCOTLAND

Acronym or abbreviation: Fishermen's Mission

The Fishermen's Mission, Haypark Business Centre, Marchmont Avenue, Polmont, Falkirk, FK2 0NZ

Tel: 01324 716857
Fax: 01324 716423

E-mail: ian.rnmdsf@talk21.com

Enquiries:
Enquiries to: Director Scotland

Founded:
1881

Organisation type and purpose:
Voluntary organisation, registered charity (charity number 232822).

Subject coverage:
The fishing industry; care of fishermen and their families.

Museum or gallery collection, archive, or library special collection:
Records of magazine (Toilers of the Deep) from 1881 onwards

Printed publications:
Fish and Ships (Stanley Pritchard); the story of 100 years of the fishing industry
They Happened to Me (Stanley Pritchard): the world of Charities in the 1950s-70s, plus comments of characters and social life from the 1920s to the late 1970s
Network (2 times a year)

Access to staff:
Contact by telephone
Hours: Mon to Fri, 0900 to 1700

ROYAL NATIONAL ROSE SOCIETY

Acronym or abbreviation: RNRS

Chiswell Green Lane, St Albans, Hertfordshire, AL2 3NR

Tel: 01727 850461
Fax: 01727 850360
E-mail: mail@rnrs.org.uk

Website:
http://www.roses.co.uk

Enquiries:
Enquiries to: Chief Executive

Founded:
1876

Organisation type and purpose:
Membership association (membership is by subscription), present number of members: 15,000, registered charity (charity number 1035848).

Subject coverage:
Roses, cultivation and history etc; trials and exhibitions.

Museum or gallery collection, archive, or library special collection:
Society library including the Courtney Page Library

Printed publications:
How to grow roses (handbook)
Roses to enjoy (directory of cultivars)
The Rose (quarterly, for members only)

Access to staff:
Contact by letter, by telephone, by e-mail and via website
Hours: Mon to Fri, 0900 to 1700

Affiliated to:
World Federation of Rose Societies

ROYAL NAVAL ASSOCIATION

Acronym or abbreviation: RNA

82 Chelsea Manor Street, London, SW3 5QJ

Tel: 020 7352 6764
Fax: 020 7352 7385
E-mail: rna@netcomuk.co.uk

Website:
http://www.royal-naval-association.co.uk

Enquiries:
Enquiries to: General Secretary

continued overleaf

Organisation type and purpose:
Registered charity (charity number 266982).

Access to staff:
Contact by letter and by fax
Hours: Mon to Fri, 0900 to 1700

ROYAL NAVAL VOLUNTEER RESERVE OFFICERS ASSOCIATION

38 Hill Street, London, W1J 5NS

Tel: 020 7493 7672
Fax: 020 7629 7995
E-mail: cdr@navalclub.co.uk

Enquiries:
Enquiries to: Chief Executive

Founded:
1946

Organisation type and purpose:
Membership association (membership is by election or invitation), present number of members: 2600, voluntary organisation.

Subject coverage:
Navy officers.

Access to staff:
Contact by letter, by telephone, by fax and by e-mail. Appointment necessary.
Hours: Mon to Fri, 0900 to 1700

ROYAL NORFOLK AGRICULTURAL ASSOCIATION

Acronym or abbreviation: RNAA

The Showground, Dereham Road, New Costessey, Norwich, Norfolk, NR5 0TT

Tel: 01603 748931
Fax: 01603 748729
E-mail: jpurling@norfolkshowground.com

Enquiries:
Enquiries to: Chief Executive
Other contacts: Show Manager

Founded:
1847

Organisation type and purpose:
Membership association (membership is by subscription), present number of members: 3500, registered charity (charity number 289581). County show organiser. Promotes improvement in breeding of livestock and plants, invention and improvement of agricultural machines and implements, and skills in agriculture, horticulture and allied systems of husbandry.

Subject coverage:
Agricultural shows.

Printed publications:
Annual Report
Royal Norfolk Show Catalogue (annually, £4)
Royal Norfolk Show Programme (annually, £2.50)

Access to staff:
Contact by letter, by telephone, by fax and by e-mail. Appointment necessary.
Hours: Mon to Fri, 0900 to 1700

Access for disabled people:
Parking provided, ramped entry

Affiliated to:
Norfolk Showground Ltd

ROYAL NORTHERN AND UNIVERSITY CLUB

Acronym or abbreviation: RNUC

9 Albyn Place, Aberdeen, AB10 1YE

Tel: 01224 583292
Fax: 01224 571082
E-mail: secretary@rnuc.org.uk

Website:
http://www.rnuc.org.uk

Enquiries:
Enquiries to: Secretary

Founded:
1854

Organisation type and purpose:
Membership association (membership is by election or invitation).

Access to staff:
Contact by letter, by fax and by e-mail
Hours: Mon to Fri, 0900 to 1700

Access for disabled people:
Parking provided, ramped entry

ROYAL NORTHERN COLLEGE OF MUSIC

Acronym or abbreviation: RNCM

124 Oxford Road, Manchester, M13 9RD

Tel: 0161 907 5200
Fax: 0161 273 7611
E-mail: library@rncm.ac.uk

Website:
http://www.rncm.ac.uk
RNCM home page.
http://www.rncm.ac.uk/?_id=218
RNCM Library home page.

Enquiries:
Enquiries to: Librarian
Direct tel: 0161 907 5241
Direct e-mail: anna.smart@rncm.ac.uk

Founded:
1973

Subject coverage:
Music; recordings; musicology.

Museum or gallery collection, archive, or library special collection:
Adolph Brodsky Collection
Arthur Butterworth manuscripts
Dame Eva Turner Collection of songs
Carl Fuchs Collection
Gordon Green Collection
Halifax Collection
Hansen Collection
Horenstein Collection
Ida Carroll Archive
John Golland manuscripts
Philip Newman Collection
John Ogdon manuscripts
Philip Jones Brass Ensemble Archive
Rawsthorne manuscripts
Richard Hall collection
RNCM Collection of Historic Musical Instruments, includes Henry Watson Instrument Collection
Rothwell Collection of wind music
Sir Charles Grove Library
Thomas Pitfield Archive

Non-library collection catalogue:
All or part available online

Library catalogue:
All or part available online

Printed publications:
Library Guides
RNCM News
Programme of Events
Prospectus
Annual Report

Access to staff:
Contact by letter, by telephone, by fax, by e-mail and via website. Appointment necessary.
Hours: Term time: Mon to Thurs, 0900 to 1900; Fri, 0930 to 1700; Sat 0900 to 1300
Vacations: Mon to Fri, 1000 to 1630

Affiliated to:
IAML

ROYAL NORWEGIAN EMBASSY

25 Belgrave Square, London, SW1X 8QD

Tel: 020 7591 5500
Fax: 020 7245 6993
E-mail: emb.london@mfa.no

Enquiries:
Enquiries to: Press and Information Office
Other contacts: Consular Section, Tel: 020 7591 5505 for passports, visas etc.

Organisation type and purpose:
Embassy.

Subject coverage:
Norway.

Printed publications:
Various fact sheets and brochures

Access to staff:
Contact by letter and by telephone
Hours: Mon to Fri, 0900 to 1600
Consular Section: Mon to Fri, 1000 to 1230
Special comments: Telephone enquiries 1000 to 1500 only.

Parent body:
Royal Ministry of Foreign Affairs
   Oslo

ROYAL NUMISMATIC SOCIETY

Acronym or abbreviation: RNS

Department of Coins & Medals, The British Museum, London, WC1B 3DG

Tel: 020 7323 8228
Fax: 020 7323 8171
E-mail: info@numismatics.org.uk

Website:
http://www.numismatics.org.uk
Information on RNS, catalogue of Numismatic Chronicle, society's calendar of meetings, grants/funding opportunities, application form.

Enquiries:
Enquiries to: Honorary Secretary

Founded:
1836

Organisation type and purpose:
Learned society.

Subject coverage:
Numismatics.

Museum or gallery collection, archive, or library special collection:
Joint library with British Numismatic Society

Printed publications:
Coin Hoards (occasional)
Numismatic Chronicle (annually)
Special publications (occasional)

Access to staff:
Contact by letter, by telephone, by fax, by e-mail and via website
Hours: Mon to Fri, 0900 to 1700

Affiliated to:
International Numismatic Commission

ROYAL OBSERVATORY GREENWICH

Acronym or abbreviation: ROG

Park Row, London, SE10 9NF

Tel: 020 8858 4422 or 020 8312 6632
Fax: 020 8312 6734
E-mail: comments@nmm.ac.uk

Website:
http://www.nmm.ac.uk/places/royal-observatory

Founded:
1675

Organisation type and purpose:
National government body, museum, suitable for ages: 7 to adult.

Astronomy information.

Subject coverage:
Modern astronomy.

Information services:
Recorded information, tel: 020 8312 6565

Services for disabled people:
Planetarium shows can be booked in advance for deaf groups and schools using their own sign-interpreter, and Museum runs a programme of signed events. Contact bookings unit, fax: 020 8312 6522, e-mail: bookings@nmm.ac.uk.

Non-library collection catalogue:
All or part available online and in-house

Library catalogue:
All or part available online and in-house

Printed publications:
Astronomy information leaflets (free) and publications
Order printed publications from: Website or direct

Publications list:
Available online and in print

Access to staff:
Contact by letter, by telephone, by fax, by e-mail and via website. Appointment necessary.
Hours: Mon to Fri, 0900 to 1700

Access to building, collection or gallery:
Hours: Mon to Fri, 1000 to 1645; last admission 1630
Special comments: Prior appointment required for reserve collections.

Access for disabled people:
Level access to courtyard, Meridian Line, display of transit instruments and gift shop, complete wheelchair access to new planetarium and education centre, limited wheelchair access to historical buildings of Royal Observatory, level ground floor access and a lift to basement gallery in Flamsteed House, all assistance dogs welcome in museum.
Special comments: No wheelchair access to Octagon Room, 28' telescope and Time & Society gallery.

Site location:
Royal Observatory Greenwich (ROG)
Greenwich Park, London, SE10 8XJ

ROYAL OCEAN RACING CLUB

Acronym or abbreviation: RORC

20 St James's Place, London, SW1A 1NN

Tel: 020 7493 2248 (4 lines)
Fax: 020 7493 5252
E-mail: info@rorc.org.uk

Enquiries:
Enquiries to: General Manager
Direct e-mail: pwm@rorc.org.uk
Other contacts: Accountant Reception for mailings and computers.

Organisation type and purpose:
International organisation, membership association.

Subject coverage:
Ocean racing in general and British ocean racing in particular, long-distance yacht racing, design, building, navigation and sailing of sailing vessels, navigation and seamanship.

Museum or gallery collection, archive, or library special collection:
British ocean racing records since 1925

Printed publications:
Programme of races and current year's rules and regulations (annually)
Results of RORC races (annually)
Seahorse (on offshore racing, 12 times a year)

Access to staff:
Contact by letter, by fax and by e-mail. Letter of introduction required.
Hours: Mon to Fri, 0900 to 1700

Access to building, collection or gallery:
Prior appointment required

Affiliated to:
Offshore Racing Council
Royal Yachting Association

ROYAL OPERA HOUSE

Acronym or abbreviation: ROH

Covent Garden, London, WC2E 9DD

Tel: 020 7304 4000
Fax: 020 7212 9460

Website:
http://www.royaloperahouse.org
http://www.royalopera.org
Repertoire and booking information, background information.
http://www.royalballet.org
Repertoire and booking information, background information.
http://www.artsworld.com

Enquiries:
Enquiries to: Director of Press and Communications
Direct tel: 020 7212 9540
Direct fax: 020 7212 9525
Other contacts: (1) Archivist (2) Mailing List Officer for (1) historical information (2) performance details.

Founded:
1858

Organisation type and purpose:
Registered charity (charity number 211775). The mission of the Royal Opera House is to attract, excite, uplift and inspire the widest possible audiences by performing opera and ballet to the highest international standards at affordable prices, to develop the art forms and to promote their appreciation by people of all ages and backgrounds.

Subject coverage:
The Royal Opera House, The Royal Opera, The Royal Ballet, historical and current; opera and ballet generally.

Museum or gallery collection, archive, or library special collection:
Archive of material relating to The Royal Opera House and its performing companies including: Administration papers, scores and photos
Costumes and set models

Trade and statistical information:
Statistical details relating specifically to the Royal Opera House and its performing companies.

Printed publications:
Annual Report
Educational materials (some free, some charged)
Season Guide
Programmes and Libretti (prices vary)
Booking brochures

Electronic and video publications:
CD/Tape: BMG Conifer, Bedford House, 69–79 Fulham High School, London SW6 3JW, tel: 0171 384 7500, fax; 0171 384 7922
Video/Laser disc: Covent Garden Pioneer, Pioneer House, Hollybush Hill, Stoke Poges, Slough, SL2 4QP, tel: 01753 789661, fax; 01753 789646
Educational CD-ROM in preparation

Access to staff:
Contact by letter, by telephone, by fax and by e-mail
Hours: Mon to Fri, 1000 to 1530
Special comments: No access for personal callers, or to Archive, without appointment.

Access for disabled people:
Ramped entry, level entry, access to all public areas, toilet facilities

Subsidiary body:
The Royal Ballet
at the same address
The Royal Opera
at the same address

ROYAL PAVILION

4–5 Pavilion Buildings, Brighton, East Sussex, BN1 1EE

Tel: 01273 290900
Fax: 01273 292871
E-mail: visitor.services@brighton-hove.gov.uk

Website:
http://www.royalpavilion.org.uk
General information on the Pavilion, prices, etc.

Enquiries:
Enquiries to: Marketing Manager

Founded:
1851

Organisation type and purpose:
Local government body, museum, historic building, house or site.

Subject coverage:
History and conservation of the Royal Pavilion, including interior decorations and Regency gardens.

Museum or gallery collection, archive, or library special collection:
Photographic material
Typescript of the accounts of the Crace Firm of decorators during their time spent in the Pavilion, 1802–1804, 1815–1819, 1820–23
Inventory of the Royal Pavilion, 1828
Abstract of accounts of the various firms working in the Royal Pavilion
Letters
Quantities of letters from or about George, Prince of Wales, Mrs Fitzherbert, or concerning Brighton and the Royal Pavilion, but also including letters by Byron
Also 'Esher' letters, volume containing 56 letters to or concerning the Prince of Wales and Mrs Fitzherbert
Plan Registry – Approximately 800 plans of the Pavilion and the Pavilion Estate
Proceedings of the Pavilion Committee, 1850–1923
Proceedings of the Pavilion and Library Committee, 1924–1974
Proceedings of the Fine Art Sub-Committee, 1901–1941

Non-library collection catalogue:
All or part available in-house

Library catalogue:
All or part available in-house

Printed publications:
Guide Book (£4.99)
Order printed publications from: Commercial Services, Royal Pavilion
at the same address

Access to staff:
Contact by letter, by telephone, by fax, by e-mail and via website. Appointment necessary.
Hours: Mon to Fri, 0900 to 1730. Closed Christmas and Boxing Day
Special comments: No office staff at weekends

Access to building, collection or gallery:
No prior appointment required
Hours: Oct to Mar: Daily, 1000 to 1715 (last admission 1630)
Apr to Sep: Daily, 0930 to 1745 (last admission 1700)
Special comments: Prior appointment required for guided tours etc.

Access for disabled people:
Level entry, toilet facilities ground floor only
Special comments: Wheelchair access to ground floor only. 1st floor is NOT wheelchair accessible.

Parent body:
Brighton & Hove City Council

ROYAL PHARMACEUTICAL SOCIETY OF GREAT BRITAIN

Acronym or abbreviation: RPSGB

1 Lambeth High Street, London, SE1 7JN

continued overleaf

Tel: 020 7735 9141
Fax: 020 7735 7629
E-mail: enquiries@rpsgb.org.uk

Website:
http://www.pharmpress.com
Pharmaceutical press site for info and online ordering.
http://www.pharmj.com
The Pharmaceutical Journal online (full text) site.
http://www.rpsgb.org.uk
The Society's official website.

Enquiries:
Enquiries to: Information Librarian
Direct tel: 020 7572 2300
Direct fax: 020 7572 2499
Direct e-mail: library@rpsgb.org.uk

Founded:
1841

Organisation type and purpose:
Professional body (membership is by qualification), present number of members: 47,000.

Subject coverage:
Pharmacy practice; pharmaceutical science; pharmacology; therapeutics; medicine; toxicology; chemistry and botany.

Museum or gallery collection, archive, or library special collection:
Collection on English and foreign proprietary medicines
Hanbury Library of rare, illustrated, botanical works
Historical collection (including many herbals) from 1485
London, Edinburgh and Dublin Pharmacopoeias from 1618
Records relating to pharmacists from 1841 (comprehensive from 1868 when pharmacists were required to register)

Library catalogue:
All or part available online and in-house

Printed publications:
Publications include:
British National Formulary
BNF for Children
Clarke's Analysis of Drugs and Poisons
Drugs in Use
English Delftware Drug jars
Handbook of Pharmaceutical Excipients
Herbal Medicines
International Journal of Pharmacy Practice (4 a year)
Journal of Pharmacy and Pharmacology (monthly)
Making Medicines: A Brief History of Pharmacy and Pharmaceuticals
Martindale: The Complete Drug Reference
Medicines, Ethics and Practice
Patient Care in Community Practice
Pharmaceutical Journal (weekly)
Pharmacy Law and Ethics
Pharmacy Practice
Stockley's Drug Interactions
Order printed publications from: Pharmaceutical Press, c/o Turpin Distribution, Stratton Business Park, Pegasus Drive, Biggleswade, Bedfordshire, SG18 8TQ; tel: 01767 604971; e-mail: custserv@turpin-distribution.com

Electronic and video publications:
Electronic British National Formulary
Martindale on CD-ROM
Martindale online
MedicinesComplete (online)

Publications list:
Available online and in print

Access to staff:
Contact by letter, by telephone, by fax, by e-mail and via website. Appointment necessary. Non-members charged.
Hours: Mon, Tue, Wed, Fri, 0900 to 1700; Thu, 1000 to 1745

Access to building, collection or gallery:
By prior appointment for non-members

Hours: Thu, 1000 to 1745; Mon to Wed and Fri, 0900 to 1700

Access for disabled people:
Level entry, stairlift

ROYAL PHARMACEUTICAL SOCIETY OF GREAT BRITAIN – SCOTTISH DEPARTMENT

36 York Place, Edinburgh, EH1 3HU

Tel: 0131 556 4386
Fax: 0131 558 8850
E-mail: info@rpsis.com

Enquiries:
Enquiries to: Assistant Secretary

Founded:
1852

Organisation type and purpose:
Professional body.

Subject coverage:
Pharmacy.

Museum or gallery collection, archive, or library special collection:
Collection of rare herbals, pharmacopoeias etc

Access to staff:
Appointment necessary.
Hours: Mon to Fri, 0900 to 1300 and 1400 to 1700

ROYAL PHILATELIC SOCIETY

41 Devonshire Place, London, W1G 6JY

Tel: 020 7486 1044
Fax: 020 7486 0803
E-mail: secretary@rpsl.org.uk

Website:
http://www.rpsl.org.uk

Enquiries:
Enquiries to: Honorary Secretary

Founded:
1869

Organisation type and purpose:
Learned society.

Subject coverage:
Philately.

Access to staff:
Contact by letter, by telephone, by fax, by e-mail and via website. Appointment necessary. Access for members only.
Hours: Mon to Fri, 0930 to 1700

ROYAL PHILHARMONIC SOCIETY

Acronym or abbreviation: RPS

10 Stratford Place, London, W1C 1BA

Tel: 020 7491 8110
Fax: 020 7493 7463
E-mail: admin@royalphilharmonicsociety.org.uk

Website:
http://www.royalphilharmonicsociety.org.uk/lectures.htm
Lectures and debates.
http://www.royalphilharmonicsociety.org.uk/awards.htm
Awards and opportunities.
http://www.royalphilharmonicsociety.org.uk/calendar.htm
Calendar of events

Enquiries:
Enquiries to: General Administrator

Founded:
1813

Organisation type and purpose:
National organisation, membership association, registered charity (charity number 213693).

Administrators of bequests and trusts, and of awards and competitions.

Subject coverage:
History and activities of the Royal Philharmonic Society since its founding in 1813.

Museum or gallery collection, archive, or library special collection:
Society's Archives (correspondence, scores, manuscripts, programmes etc) held at the British Library, London

Printed publications:
Fanfare from The Royal Philharmonic Society (journal, 2 times a year)
RPS Annual Lecture (1 a year)

Access to staff:
Contact by letter, by fax and by e-mail.
Appointment necessary.
Hours: Mon to Fri, 1000 to 1700
Special comments: Prior appointment only.

ROYAL PHOTOGRAPHIC SOCIETY OF GREAT BRITAIN, THE

Acronym or abbreviation: RPS

The Octagon, Milsom Street, Bath, BA1 1DN

Tel: 01225 462841
Fax: 01225 448688
E-mail: rps@rps.org

Website:
http://www.rps.org
Exhibitions, photographic workshops, 'friends'.
Membership information and distinction information.

Enquiries:
Enquiries to: President
Direct tel: 01225 325720
Direct e-mail: john@rps.org

Founded:
1853

Organisation type and purpose:
International organisation, learned society (membership is by subscription, election or invitation), present number of members: 10,000, registered charity (charity number 212684).
To promote the art and science of photography.

Subject coverage:
History and science of photography, specialises in the 19th century.

Museum or gallery collection, archive, or library special collection:
Biographic files on photographers
Dumont Collection (19th century books illustrated with photographs)
Notable collection of rare books and periodicals
Photographic collection (strong in 19th century British photographs and the Photo-Secessionists internationally)

Printed publications:
Bulletins of the specialist groups
Imaging Science Journal (4 times a year)
Photographic Journal (10 times a year)
Regional newsletters

Access to staff:
Contact by letter, by telephone, by fax, by e-mail and via website. Appointment necessary. Non-members charged.
Hours: Mon to Fri; 0930 to 1730, closed 24 Dec to 2 Jan

Access to building, collection or gallery:
No access other than to staff

Has:
16 Regions, and 15 Groups and Chapters abroad

ROYAL PIGEON RACING ASSOCIATION

Acronym or abbreviation: RPRA

The Reddings, Cheltenham, Gloucestershire, GL51
6RN

Tel: 01452 713529
Fax: 01452 857119
E-mail: gm@rpra.org

Website:
http://www.rpra.org

Enquiries:
Enquiries to: General Manager

Founded:
1897

Organisation type and purpose:
Membership association.
Control and administration organisation for the
sport of long-distance pigeon racing.

Subject coverage:
Racing and showing of racing pigeons, racing
pigeons in general, control and supply of rings,
seals, apparatus and appliances.

**Museum or gallery collection, archive, or library
special collection:**
Pigeons in War, Bletchley Park

Printed publications:
British Homing World (weekly)
Yearbook
Order printed publications from: Severn Farm
Industrial Estate, Severn Road, Welshpool, Powys,
SY21 7DF

Access to staff:
Contact by letter, by telephone, by fax and by e-
mail. Appointment necessary.
Hours: Mon to Fri, 0900 to 1700

Affiliated to:
Confederation of Long Distance Racing Pigeon
Unions of Great Britain and Ireland
Fédération Colombophile Internationale
  Brussels

ROYAL PIONEER CORPS ASSOCIATION

c/o 23 Pioneer Regiment Royal Logistic Corps, St
David's Barracks, Graven Hill, Bicester,
Oxfordshire, OX26 6HF

Tel: 01869 360694
Fax: 01869 360695
E-mail: royalpioneercorps@gmail.com

Website:
http://www.royalpioneercorps.co.uk

Enquiries:
Enquiries to: Controller
Direct e-mail: normanbrown@myself.com

Founded:
1942

Organisation type and purpose:
Membership association (membership is by
qualification), present number of members: 3000,
registered charity (charity number 801733),
suitable for ages: 18+.
To relieve needs, stress and hardship of ex-
Pioneers, their wives, widows and dependants.
To foster esprit de corps.

Subject coverage:
Royal Pioneer Corps history.

Printed publications:
Newsletter (2 times a year)

Access to staff:
Contact by letter and by telephone
Hours: Mon to Fri, 0900 to 1700

ROYAL REGIMENT OF FUSILIERS ASSOCIATION LONDON AREA

Acronym or abbreviation: RRF Museum (London)

H M Tower of London, London, EC3N 4AB

Tel: 020 7488 5611
Fax: 020 7481 1093

Enquiries:
Enquiries to: Curator
Direct e-mail: royalfusiliers@fsmail.net
Other contacts: Archivist for research enquiries.

Founded:
1685

Organisation type and purpose:
Membership association (membership is by
subscription, qualification), present number of
members: 1000, registered charity (charity number
255042), museum.
Regimental Museum.

Subject coverage:
Military and social history.

**Museum or gallery collection, archive, or library
special collection:**
Regimental Archives 1685 to 1968

Non-library collection catalogue:
All or part available in-house

Library catalogue:
All or part available in-house

Printed publications:
Museum Guide (£1.50)
Royal Fusiliers in the Great War (£35)
Royal Fusiliers Victoria Crosses (£2.50)

Access to staff:
Contact by letter. Appointment necessary.
Hours: Archivist only: 0900 to 1500
Special comments: Subject to HM Tower of London.

ROYAL SCHOOL FOR DEAF CHILDREN, MARGATE AND WESTGATE COLLEGE FOR DEAF PEOPLE

Acronym or abbreviation: RSDC, Margate

Victoria Road, Margate, Kent, CT9 1NB

Tel: 01843 227561\ Minicom no. 01843 227531
Fax: 01843 227637
E-mail: enquiries@royalschoolfordeaf.kent.sch.uk

Website:
http://www.royalschoolfordeaf.kent.sch.uk
School.
http://www.westgate-college.org.uk
College.
http://members.aol.com/rsdmar/home.htm

Enquiries:
Enquiries to: Director
Other contacts: Bursar, Secretary

Founded:
1792

Organisation type and purpose:
National organisation, registered charity (charity
number 325109), suitable for ages: School: 4 to 16,
College: 16+, consultancy. Non-maintained special
school and specialist college. DfES number
8667017. Education and training of pupils and
students who are deaf.

Subject coverage:
Education of severely to profoundly deaf children
and students. Also educates multiply handicapped
deaf children, including deafblind. Holds historical
records of education of the deaf over the two
centuries. Educational audiology, psychology of
deafness, educational psychology, deafness and
additional disability, speech and language therapy,
communication by sign language, symbol system,
objects etc.

**Museum or gallery collection, archive, or library
special collection:**
Minute books and other records from 1792

Printed publications:
Curriculum – foundation (£15 plus p&p)
Pamphlets and magazine
Prospectus, RSD & Westgate College (annually)
RSDC News (6 times a year)

Electronic and video publications:
RSDC video (22 minutes, PAL and VHS)

Breaking the Sound Barrier – film of the last 209
  years of the Royal School for Deaf Children
  Margate (digital video, £15)

Access to staff:
Contact by letter, by telephone and by fax.
Appointment necessary.
Hours: Mon to Fri, 0900 to 1700

Access to building, collection or gallery:
Prior appointment required for library

Access for disabled people:
Parking provided, ramped entry, toilet facilities

Further education College:
Westgate College for Deaf People
  Sea Road, Westgate on Sea, Thanet, Kent; tel:
  01843 836300; fax: 01843 836300; e-mail:
  enquiries@westgatecollegeadmin.co.uk

Memberships (Professional Bodies):
British Association of Teachers of the Deaf
(BATOD)
NASEN
National Association of Specialist Colleges (FE)
(Charities) (NATSPEC)
National Association of Voluntary Independent
and Non-Maintained Schools (Charities) (NASS)

ROYAL SCHOOL OF CHURCH MUSIC

Acronym or abbreviation: RSCM

19 The Close, Salisbury, Wiltshire, SP1 2EB

Tel: 01722 424848
Fax: 01722 424849
E-mail: enquiries@rscm.com

Website:
http://www.rscm.com
http://www.rscm.com/cat_order.htm
Stock List.
http://www.rscm.com/outreach.htm
Courses and education.

Enquiries:
Enquiries to: Administrator
Other contacts: Publications, tel: 01306 887811; fax:
01306 887240 for musical sales.

Founded:
1927

Organisation type and purpose:
International organisation, membership
association, registered charity, training
organisation, publishing house.
Study and promotion of church music.

Subject coverage:
Church music, liturgy, hymnody.

**Museum or gallery collection, archive, or library
special collection:**
Maurice Frost Collection on hymnology (on
  permanent loan to the Royal College of Music)

Library catalogue:
All or part available in-house

Printed publications:
Church Music (quarterly)
New music and scholarly editions of old music
A large range of hymns, anthems, services and
  other church choral music
Order printed publications from: Music Direct, Royal
School of Church Music
tel: 01306 872811, fax: 01306 877740, e-mail:
musicdirect@rscm.com

Publications list:
Available online and in print

Access to staff:
Contact by letter, by fax, by e-mail and via
website
Hours: Mon to Fri, 0900 to 1700

Access to building, collection or gallery:
Prior appointment required
Hours: Mon to Fri, 0900 to 1700

Access for disabled people:
Parking provided, level entry, toilet facilities

ROYAL SCHOOL OF NEEDLEWORK

Acronym or abbreviation: RSN

Apartment 12a, Hampton Court Palace, Surrey, KT8 9AU

Tel: 020 3166 6932
Fax: 020 8943 4910
E-mail: enquiries@royal-needlework.org.uk

Website:
http://www.royal-needlework.org.uk
Details of the RSN's courses, events and services.

Enquiries:
Enquiries to: Principal
Other contacts: Principal's PA for all enquiries.

Founded:
1872

Organisation type and purpose:
Registered charity (charity number 312774), consultancy.
To care for and preserve antique textiles and to create new works of art. To teach the skills of hand embroidery.

Subject coverage:
All aspects of embroidery and needlework; textiles related skills; art and design related skills; textile restoration and preventive conservation. Training in all aspects of hand embroidery, short courses of 1 to 3 days, 1 year certificated course, 3 year apprenticeship.

Museum or gallery collection, archive, or library special collection:
Books on embroidery, etc
Textile collection

Non-library collection catalogue:
All or part available in-house

Printed publications:
Prospectus (free, yearly)
RSN Friends Newsletter (free with membership)
Royal School of Needlework 'Embroidery Techniques' Book

Electronic and video publications:
CD-ROM

Access to staff:
Contact by letter, by telephone, by fax, by e-mail and via website. Appointment necessary.
Hours: Mon to Fri, 0900 to 1700

Access to building, collection or gallery:
Prior appointment required

Access for disabled people:
Parking provided

ROYAL SCOTTISH ACADEMY

Formal name: Royal Scottish Academy of Painting, Sculpture, Architecture and Printmaking
Acronym or abbreviation: RSA

The Mound, Edinburgh, EH2 2EL

Tel: 0131 225 6671
Fax: 0131 220 6016

Website:
http://www.royalscottishacademy.org
General information, current membership, present and forthcoming exhibitions.

Enquiries:
Enquiries to: Press Officer
Direct e-mail: press@royalscottishacademy.org

Founded:
1826

Organisation type and purpose:
Learned society, professional body (membership is by election or invitation), present number of members: 113, registered charity (charity number SC 004198), art gallery.
Society of elected and nominated Scottish painters, sculptors, architects and printmakers.
The promotion and furtherance of the visual arts in Scotland.

Subject coverage:
Painting, drawing, sculpture, printmaking, architecture and some decorative arts in Scotland.

Museum or gallery collection, archive, or library special collection:
RSA's own archives (minute books, letter collection, photograph collection, etc.) from 1825 onwards
W G Gillies, RSA Bequest (estate of this artist including letters, pictures, catalogues, etc.)

Non-library collection catalogue:
All or part available in-house

Library catalogue:
All or part available in-house

Printed publications:
The Making of The Royal Scottish Academy (Gordon E, £4.95)

Access to staff:
Contact by letter, by telephone, by fax and by e-mail. Appointment necessary.
Hours: Mon to Fri, 1000 to 1300 and 1400 to 1630

Collections and library (only) now located at:
Royal Scottish Academy
The Dean Gallery, 73 Bedford Road, Edinburgh, EH4 3DS; tel: 0131 624 6277

ROYAL SCOTTISH ACADEMY OF MUSIC AND DRAMA

Acronym or abbreviation: RSAMD

100 Renfrew Street, Glasgow, G2 3DB

Tel: 0141 270 8268
Fax: 0141 270 8353
E-mail: library@rsamd.ac.uk

Website:
http://www.rsamd.ac.uk
Library catalogue available online

Enquiries:
Enquiries to: Head of Information Services
Direct e-mail: c.cochrane@rsamd.ac.uk

Founded:
1847

Organisation type and purpose:
HE Academy

Subject coverage:
Music and drama.

Library catalogue:
All or part available online

Access to staff:
Contact by letter, by telephone, by fax, by e-mail, in person and via website
Hours: Mon to Fri, 0900 to 1700

Access to building, collection or gallery:
No prior appointment required

Access for disabled people:
Access to all public areas

ROYAL SCOTTISH AUTOMOBILE CLUB (MOTOR SPORT) LTD

Acronym or abbreviation: RSAC

St James Business Centre, Linwood Road, Paisley, PA3 3AT

Tel: 0141 887 9905
Fax: 0141 887 9906
E-mail: rsac_motorsport@compuserve.com

Website:
http://www.motorsport.co.uk
Motor sport information.
http://www.rsac.co.uk
General club information.

Enquiries:
Enquiries to: Secretary

Founded:
1899

Organisation type and purpose:
Membership association.
Club, for the encouragement of motoring and allied industries and of motor sport.

Subject coverage:
Motoring and motor sport.

Museum or gallery collection, archive, or library special collection:
Hotel Guides
Motoring magazines and other publications from the late 19th century to the present day

Access to staff:
Contact by letter, by telephone, by fax, by e-mail and in person. Appointment necessary. Non-members charged.
Hours: Mon to Fri, 0900 to 1700

Also at the same address:
Royal Scottish Automobile Club (Motor Sport) Limited
tel: 0141 204 4999; fax: 0141 204 4949; e-mail: rsac_motorsport@compuserve.com

Member of:
Alliance Internationale de Tourisme
Standing Joint Committee (AA/RAC/RSAC)

ROYAL SCOTTISH CORPORATION

Formal name: The Scottish Hospital of the Foundation of Charles II
Acronym or abbreviation: ScotsCare

37 King Street, Covent Garden, London, WC2E 8JS

Tel: 020 7240 3718
Fax: 020 7497 0184
E-mail: info@scotscare.com

Website:
http://www.royalscottishcorporation.org.uk
Homepage of Corporation detailing help available.

Enquiries:
Enquiries to: Chief Executive
Other contacts: Welfare Manager for welfare matters.

Founded:
1611

Organisation type and purpose:
Voluntary organisation, registered charity (charity number 207326).

Subject coverage:
Welfare benefits, disability rights, debt advice.

Access to staff:
Contact by letter, by telephone, by fax, by e-mail and via website. Appointment necessary.
Hours: Mon to Fri, 0900 to 1700
Special comments: Callers by strict appointment.

ROYAL SCOTTISH COUNTRY DANCE SOCIETY

Acronym or abbreviation: RSCDS

12 Coates Crescent, Edinburgh, EH3 7AF

Tel: 0131 225 3854
Fax: 0131 225 7783
E-mail: info@rscdshq.freeserve.co.uk

Website:
http://www.rscds.org

Enquiries:
Enquiries to: General Secretary

Founded:
1923

Organisation type and purpose:
International organisation, membership association (membership is by subscription), present number of members: 21,000, registered charity (charity number SC016085), suitable for ages: all.
To promote Scottish Country Dancing and to educate the public therein. To publish instructional dance and music books.

Subject coverage:
Scottish country dances, music, practice and preservation, (not Highland dancing).

Museum or gallery collection, archive, or library special collection:
Library of old music for Scottish country dancing and other related archive material

Printed publications:
Bulletin
Newsbrief
Scottish Country Dances: selection of books with printed music

Electronic and video publications:
Music on CD to accompany RSCDS books
Videos to accompany RSCDS books

Publications list:
Available online and in print

Access to staff:
Contact by letter, by telephone, by fax, by e-mail, in person and via website
Hours: Mon to Fri, 0900 to 1700

Access to building, collection or gallery:
Prior appointment required
Hours: Mon to Fri, 0900 to 1700

Has:
Local associations throughout the world

ROYAL SCOTTISH FORESTRY SOCIETY

Acronym or abbreviation: RSFS

Hagg-on-Esk, Canonbie, Dumfries & Galloway, DG14 0XE

Tel: 013873 71518
Fax: 013873 71418
E-mail: rsfs@lumison.co.uk

Website:
http://www.rsfs.org
History, membership, events diary, news, additional to journal articles.

Enquiries:
Enquiries to: Administrative Director
Other contacts: Editor, Scottish Forestry: editor@rsfs.lumison.co.uk

Founded:
1854

Organisation type and purpose:
National organisation, learned society (membership is by subscription), present number of members: 950, voluntary organisation, registered charity (charity number SCO 02058), suitable for ages: all, publishing house. Independent representative organisation. The advancement of forestry in all its numerous branches.

Subject coverage:
Forestry, woodlands, timber, arboriculture, silviculture, trees, agro forestry, coppicing, community forestry, investment forestry, forestry research, nurseries, forest access, urban forests and trees, social forestry.

Museum or gallery collection, archive, or library special collection:
Books and Journals
Library housed in the University of Edinburgh, Department of Forestry.

Trade and statistical information:
Data on UK forestry.

Printed publications:
Scottish Forestry (quarterly, UK price £13 per issue, overseas £17 per issue)

Electronic and video publications:
Forests For All, Forever (video, 22 mins, with teacher support notes for Scottish schools curriculum 5–14, £7.50)
Scottish Forestry – The Archive 1947–2000 (CD-ROM, single user £100, multi-user £300)

Scottish Forestry – The Archive (CD-ROM, 3 disk set with search engine; single user licence £100, multi-user licence £300)

Access to staff:
Contact by letter, by telephone, by fax, by e-mail and via website. Appointment necessary.
Hours: Mon to Fri, 0900 to 1700

Links with:
CASHEL – A Forest for a Thousand Years Loch Lomond; tel: Forest Manager 01360 870450; fax: 01668 213555; e-mail: info@cashel.org.uk; website: www.CASHEL.org.uk
RSFS Forest Trust Company

ROYAL SCOTTISH GEOGRAPHICAL SOCIETY

Acronym or abbreviation: RSGS

15–19 North Port, Perth, PH1 5LU

Tel: 01738 455050
E-mail: enquiries@rsgs.org

Website:
http://www.geo.ed.ac.uk/rsgs

Enquiries:
Enquiries to: Chief Executive

Founded:
1884

Organisation type and purpose:
Learned society (charity number SCO15599). To further the science of geography.

Subject coverage:
Geography, topography and travel in Scotland.

Museum or gallery collection, archive, or library special collection:
Early maps of Scotland
Geographical journals

Non-library collection catalogue:
All or part available in-house

Library catalogue:
All or part available online

Printed publications:
Early maps of Scotland (2 volume set)
Newsletter (free, 3 times a year)
Scottish Geographical Journal (4 times a year)
Symposium Volumes (annually)

Publications list:
Available online

Access to staff:
Contact by letter, by telephone, by fax, by e-mail and via website. Appointment necessary.
Hours: Mon to Fri, 0900 to 1700

ROYAL SCOTTISH NATIONAL ORCHESTRA

Acronym or abbreviation: RSNO

73 Claremont Street, Glasgow, G3 7JB

Tel: 0141 226 3868
Fax: 0141 221 4317
E-mail: admin@rsno.org.uk

Website:
http://www.rsno.org.uk

Enquiries:
Enquiries to: Information Officer
Direct tel: 0141 225 3571
Direct e-mail: daniel.pollitt@rsno.org.uk

Founded:
1891

Organisation type and purpose:
Registered charity (charity number SCO10702). To perform symphony concerts throughout Scotland.

Subject coverage:
Orchestral music.

Publications list:
Available online and in print

Access to staff:
Contact by letter, by telephone, by fax, by e-mail and via website
Hours: Mon to Fri, 0900 to 1730

ROYAL SOCIETY – ICSU INFORMATION SERVICE

Formal name: The Royal Society for Improving Natural Knowledge

6 Carlton House Terrace, London, SW1Y 5AG

Tel: 020 7451 2500
Fax: 020 7451 2692
E-mail: info@royalsoc.ac.uk

Website:
http://www.codata.org/codata
The CODATA Home Page.
http://www.icsu.org
The ICSU Home Page
http://www.royalsoc.ac.uk

Enquiries:
Enquiries to: ICSU Information Officer
Direct tel: ext 2587
Direct e-mail: ruth.cooper@royalsoc.ac.uk

Founded:
1660

Organisation type and purpose:
Learned society (membership is by election or invitation), present number of members: 1250. The UK National Academy of Science.

Subject coverage:
Information available on all ICSU activities and related journals and publications. Details of union assemblies, conferences and congresses. Advice on travel to ICSU conferences and grants available. Information concerning ICSU projects also available.

Museum or gallery collection, archive, or library special collection:
Archival centre for ICSU related publications such as newsletters, bulletins and journals

Printed publications:
ICSU Focus (newsletter, several times a year, free)

Publications list:
Available online and in print

Access to staff:
Contact by letter, by telephone and via website. Appointment necessary.
Hours: Mon to Fri, 0900 to 1700

Access for disabled people:
Parking provided, level entry, access to all public areas, toilet facilities

ROYAL SOCIETY – LIBRARY

6–9 Carlton House Terrace, London, SW1Y 5AG

Tel: 020 7451 2500
Fax: 020 7930 2170
E-mail: library@royalsociety.org

Website:
http://royalsociety.org

Enquiries:
Enquiries to: Librarian
Direct tel: 020 7451 2606

Founded:
1660

Organisation type and purpose:
Learned society, registered charity (charity number 207043).
The Royal Society is an independent academy promoting the natural and applied sciences. Founded in 1660, the Society has three roles: as the UK academy of science, as a learned society, and as a funding agency. It responds to individual demand with selection by merit not by field.

continued overleaf

Working across the whole range of science, technology and engineering, the Society aims to: strengthen UK science by providing support to excellent individuals; fund excellent research to push back the frontiers of knowledge; attract and retain the best scientists; ensure the UK engages with the best science around the world; support science communication and education, and communicate and encourage dialogue with the public; provide the best independent advice nationally and internationally; promote scholarship and encourage research into the history of science.

Subject coverage:
All sciences, mathematics, statistics, operational research, physics, space research, crystallography, chemistry, engineering, metallurgy, instrumentation, earth sciences, botany, agriculture, zoology, marine biology, physical anthropology, biochemistry, biophysics, physiology, pharmacology, psychology, medicine (non-clinical), molecular biology, genetics, history of science and technology, science education, international scientific relations, science policy.

Museum or gallery collection, archive, or library special collection:
Archives relating to all aspects of the Society and its Fellows
Books and papers by or about Fellows of the Society
Books, manuscripts and items relating to Sir Isaac Newton and other early Fellows
Material on the history of science
Science policy publications

Non-library collection catalogue:
All or part available online, in-house and in print

Library catalogue:
All or part available online

Printed publications:
Review of the Year
Philosophical Transactions of the Royal Society (Series A – Physical, Mathematical, and Series B – Biological)
Proceedings of the Royal Society (Series A and B)
Biology Letters
Journal of the Royal Society Interface
Notes and Records of the Royal Society
Biographical Memoirs of Fellows of the Royal Society
Many occasional publications relating to science policy and science education
Inside Science (quarterly)
Year Book of the Royal Society
List of Fellows of the Royal Society 1660–2007
Obituaries and Biographical Memoirs of Fellows of the Royal Society 1830–2006

Publications list:
Available online

Access to staff:
Contact by letter, by telephone, by fax, by e-mail, in person and via website
Hours: Mon to Fri, 1000 to 1700

Access for disabled people:
Parking provided, disabled lift entry, access to all public areas, toilet facilities

ROYAL SOCIETY FOR ASIAN AFFAIRS

Acronym or abbreviation: RSAA

2 Belgrave Square, London, SW1X 8PJ

Tel: 020 7235 5122
Fax: 020 7259 6771
E-mail: info@rsaa.org.uk

Website:
http://www.rsaa.org.uk

Enquiries:
Enquiries to: Secretary
Direct e-mail: sec@rsaa.org.uk
Other contacts: Editor (editor@rsaa.org.uk, for Asian affairs)

Founded:
1901

Organisation type and purpose:
Learned society (membership is by qualification, election or invitation), present number of members: 1,200 individuals, 30 corporate, registered charity (charity number 212152). To promote greater knowledge and understanding of Asia from the Near and Middle East to Japan.

Subject coverage:
All aspects of Asian affairs.

Museum or gallery collection, archive, or library special collection:
Library of approximately 7,000 books, not available electronically

Library catalogue:
All or part available in-house

Printed publications:
Asian Affairs (3 times a year, subscription £40 a year for individuals, £80 a year for institutions)

Access to staff:
Contact by letter, by telephone, by fax, by e-mail and via website. Appointment necessary. Access for members only.
Hours: Mon to Fri, 0930 to 1700
Special comments: One visit to the library is permitted, after which membership is required

Access to building, collection or gallery:
No prior appointment required
Hours: Mon to Thu, 1000 to 1300 and 1400 to 1600; Fri, 1000 to 1300
Special comments: Prior appointment required for non-members.

ROYAL SOCIETY FOR MENTALLY HANDICAPPED CHILDREN AND ADULTS

Acronym or abbreviation: MENCAP

4 Swan Courtyard, Coventry Road, Birmingham, B26 1BU

Tel: 0121 707 7877
Fax: 0121 707 3019
E-mail: info@mencap.org.uk

Enquiries:
Enquiries to: Head of Advice and Information Service

Founded:
1946

Organisation type and purpose:
National organisation, membership association (membership is by subscription), voluntary organisation, registered charity (charity number 222377).
Mencap is the leading charity working with children and adults with learning disabilities in England, Wales and Northern Ireland. It campaigns to ensure that people with a learning disability have the best possible opportunities to live as full citizens. It aims to influence new legislation and raise the profile of learning disability issues. It undertakes research into issues affecting people with a learning disability.

Subject coverage:
All aspects of learning disabilities, residential, leisure, holiday, welfare, education and training, employment services.

Printed publications:
Range of information leaflets (available from Public Liaison Unit, National Centre)
Viewpoint: The Newspaper of Mencap & Gateway
Order printed publications from: Helpline and Information Unit, MENCAP
123 Golden Lane, London, EC1Y 0RT, tel: 020 7696 6900/6979

Electronic and video publications:
Use the Tube (video)

Publications list:
Available in print

Access to staff:
Contact by letter, by telephone, by fax, by e-mail and via website
Hours: Mon to Fri, 0900 to 1700

Access for disabled people:
Level entry, toilet facilities

ROYAL SOCIETY FOR THE ENCOURAGEMENT OF ARTS, MANUFACTURES AND COMMERCE

Acronym or abbreviation: RSA

8 John Adam Street, London, WC2N 6EZ

Tel: 020 7930 5115
Fax: 020 7839 5805
E-mail: library@rsa.org.uk

Website:
http://www.rsa.org.uk
Main RSA website.
http://www.rsa.org.uk/fellowship/facilities.html
Information on library and archive.

Enquiries:
Enquiries to: Librarian
Direct tel: 020 7451 6874
Direct e-mail: library@rsa.org.uk

Founded:
1754

Organisation type and purpose:
International organisation, membership association (membership is by election or invitation), present number of members: 23,000, registered charity (charity number 212424), research organisation.
Runs conferences and lectures, produces reports relating to education, environment, design, the arts, manufacturing, management.

Subject coverage:
A modern library providing background on the RSA's core concerns: arts, manufacturers and commerce, education, design, environment and management. Also 250 years of archives plus a small library to support access to, and interpretation of, the Society's Archive.

Museum or gallery collection, archive, or library special collection:
Archives of the Society (from 1754 to present). Accessible via AIM25 gateway
Early works (most listed in British Library 18th century catalogue)

Non-library collection catalogue:
All or part available online

Library catalogue:
All or part available online

Printed publications:
RSA Journal (6 issues a year)
Occasional reports relating to RSA project

Publications list:
Available online

Access to staff:
Contact by letter, by telephone, by fax, by e-mail and via website. Appointment necessary.
Hours: Mon to Fri, 0900 to 1700

Access to building, collection or gallery:
Prior appointment required

Access for disabled people:
Ramped entry, access to all public areas, toilet facilities
Special comments: Access has been made by modifications to an 18th century building, so some routes are circuitous.

ROYAL SOCIETY FOR THE PREVENTION OF ACCIDENTS

Acronym or abbreviation: RoSPA

Edgbaston Park, 353 Bristol Road, Birmingham, B5 7ST

Tel: 0121 248 2000
Fax: 0121 248 2001
E-mail: help@rospa.com

Website:
http://www.rospa.com
General information about all aspects of safety;
contact details for publications, products, services
of ROSPA.

Enquiries:
Enquiries to: Information Services Manager
Direct tel: 0121 248 2063/66
Direct e-mail: infocentre@rospa.com

Founded:
1917

Organisation type and purpose:
Membership association (membership is by
subscription), registered charity, training
organisation, consultancy, publishing house.
To save lives and reduce injuries.

Subject coverage:
Occupational health and safety, leisure, road,
home, play (ground) and water safety, safety
education.

Education services:
Training courses.

**Museum or gallery collection, archive, or library
special collection:**
20,000 books and documents
250 journals
British Standards
CD-ROM, Croner, Lawtel
Legislation where relevant to health and safety

Trade and statistical information:
Statistics available, primarily for members
(charges).
Technical and advisory service – members only.

Library catalogue:
All or part available in-house

Printed publications:
Care on the Road (6 times a year)
RoSPA Occupational Safety & Health Journal
(monthly)
OS&H Bulletin (monthly)
Safety Education (termly)
Safety Express (6 times a year)
Staying Alive (3 times a year)

Electronic and video publications:
Range of videos (for purchase)

Publications list:
Available online and in print

Access to staff:
Contact by letter, by telephone and by e-mail.
Appointment necessary.
Hours: Mon to Fri, 0900 to 1600

Access to building, collection or gallery:
Prior appointment required

Access for disabled people:
Parking provided, level entry, access to all public
areas, toilet facilities

Administers the:
RoSPA Advanced Drivers and Riders

Links with:
RoSPA Training Centre
Unit 75, Gravelly Industrial Park, Erdington,
Birmingham, B24 8TL

Offices in:
Wales, Scotland and N Ireland

ROYAL SOCIETY FOR THE PREVENTION OF CRUELTY TO ANIMALS

Acronym or abbreviation: RSPCA

Wilberforce Way, Horsham, West Sussex, RH13
9RS

Tel: 0300 123 4555
Fax: 0300 123 0284

Website:
http://www.rspca.org.uk
General information on the work and activities of
the RSPCA.

Enquiries:
Enquiries to: Information and Records Manager
Direct tel: 0300 123 0188
Direct fax: 0300 123 0188
Direct e-mail: creed@rspca.org.uk

Founded:
1824

Organisation type and purpose:
Registered charity (charity number 219099).

Subject coverage:
Welfare of animals of all types, all aspects, history
of animal welfare in the 19th and 20th centuries,
suppression of cruelty to animals, animal hospitals,
clinics and homes, philosophy and ethics of animal
welfare and animal rights.

**Museum or gallery collection, archive, or library
special collection:**
Complete sets of the Society's publications from
1869: Animal Ways, Animal World and Annual
Reports
Minute Books of the Society

Non-library collection catalogue:
All or part available in-house

Library catalogue:
All or part available in-house

Printed publications:
Animal Life (quarterly)
Animal Action (children's magazine, 6 times a
year)
Booklets, leaflets
Pet care guides
Posters, wall-charts, etc
Scientific reports
Teaching material

Publications list:
Available online

Access to staff:
Contact by letter, by telephone, by fax and by e-
mail. Appointment necessary.
Hours: Mon to Fri, 0930 to 1700

Access for disabled people:
Parking provided, level entry

ROYAL SOCIETY FOR THE PROMOTION OF HEALTH

38a St Georges Drive, London, SW1V 4BH

Tel: 020 7630 0121
Fax: 020 7976 6847
E-mail: rshealth@rshealth.org.uk

Website:
http://www.rsph.org.uk

Enquiries:
Enquiries to: Chief Executive
Direct fax: 020 7828 8913
Other contacts: Managing Editor for journal related
enquiries.

Founded:
1876

Organisation type and purpose:
International organisation, learned society,
registered charity (charity number 215520).
To promote the exchange of knowledge and
experience between health-related professions, to
influence health-related legislation and planning,
to advance the study of health-related subjects.

Subject coverage:
All fields related to medicine, nutrition, hygiene,
pharmaceuticals, planning, architecture, housing,
environment.

**Museum or gallery collection, archive, or library
special collection:**
Essential Food Hygiene

Printed publications:
Essential Food Hygiene (£2.25)
Journal (6 times a year, £55 per annum, free to
members)

Access to staff:
Contact by letter, by telephone, by fax, by e-mail
and in person. Appointment necessary.
Hours: Mon to Fri, 0900 to 1700

Affiliated to:
American Public Health Association
World Federation of Public Health Associations

ROYAL SOCIETY FOR THE PROTECTION OF BIRDS

Acronym or abbreviation: RSPB

The Lodge, Potton Road, Sandy, Bedfordshire,
SG19 2DL

Tel: 01767 680551
Fax: 01767 692365

Website:
http://www.rspb.org.uk

Enquiries:
Enquiries to: Librarian
Direct e-mail: ian.dawson@rspb.org.uk

Founded:
1889

Organisation type and purpose:
Membership association (membership is by
subscription), registered charity (charity number
207076).

Subject coverage:
Birds and birdwatching (but not aviculture);
especially protection and conservation in Britain.

**Museum or gallery collection, archive, or library
special collection:**
W H Hudson Archive

Library catalogue:
All or part available in-house

Printed publications:
Bird Life (6 times a year)
Birds (quarterly)
Wingbeat (6 times a year)
Wild Times (quarterly)
Miscellaneous reports and publications (see
website: www.rspb.org.uk)
Information leaflets and educational material on
birds and wildlife conservation

Publications list:
Available in print

Access to staff:
Appointment necessary.
Hours: Mon to Fri, 0900 to 1700

Member of the global partnership:
BirdLife International

Owns or administers:
over 150 nature reserves in Great Britain and
Northern Ireland

ROYAL SOCIETY FOR THE RELIEF OF INDIGENT GENTLEWOMEN OF SCOTLAND

14 Rutland Square, Edinburgh, EH1 2BD

Tel: 0131 229 2308
Fax: 0131 228 3700

Enquiries:
Enquiries to: Information Officer
Other contacts: General Secretary

Founded:
1847

Organisation type and purpose:
Voluntary organisation, registered charity (charity
number SCO 16095).

continued overleaf

To assist ladies of Scottish birth or education with professional or business backgrounds who exist on low incomes and have limited savings.
Applications from spinsters, widows and divorcees of 50 years or over.

Museum or gallery collection, archive, or library special collection:
Records maintained of ladies who made
    applications to the Fund over many years

Access to staff:
Contact by letter, by telephone, by fax and by e-mail
Hours: Mon to Thu, 0900 to 1700; Fri, 0900 to 1600

ROYAL SOCIETY OF BRITISH ARTISTS

Acronym or abbreviation: RBA

17 Carlton House Terrace, London, SW1Y 5BD

Tel: 020 7930 6844
Fax: 020 7839 7830
E-mail: press@mallgalleries.com

Website:
http://www.mallgalleries.org.uk
http://www.the-rba.org.uk

Enquiries:
Enquiries to: Secretary
Other contacts: Marketing and Communications Officer

Founded:
1824

Organisation type and purpose:
Membership association (membership is by election or invitation), present number of members: 115, registered charity (charity number 294590).

Subject coverage:
British art and artists; annual open exhibition of pictures and sculpture.

Printed publications:
RBA catalogues available during exhibition (May/June)

Access to staff:
Contact by letter, by telephone, by fax, by e-mail and via website. Appointment necessary.
Hours: Mon to Fri, 0930 to 1730

Access to building, collection or gallery:
No access other than to staff
Hours: Mon to Fri, 0930 to 1730

Access for disabled people:
Toilet facilities
Special comments: Stairlift.

Links with:
Federation of British Artists (FBA)
    at the same address

ROYAL SOCIETY OF BRITISH SCULPTORS

Acronym or abbreviation: RBS

108 Old Brompton Road, London, SW7 3RA

Tel: 020 7373 5554
Fax: 020 7370 3721
E-mail: info@rbs.org.uk

Website:
http://www.rbs.org.uk

Enquiries:
Enquiries to: Administrator

Founded:
1904

Organisation type and purpose:
Advisory body, membership association (membership is by election or invitation), present number of members: over 400, registered charity (charity number 2817292), art gallery.

Subject coverage:
Sculpture.

Access to staff:
Contact by letter, by telephone, by fax and by e-mail. Appointment necessary.
Hours: Mon to Fri, 0930 to 1730

Access to building, collection or gallery:
No prior appointment required
Hours: Mon to Fri, 0930 to 1730

ROYAL SOCIETY OF CHEMISTRY – LIBRARY AND INFORMATION CENTRE

Acronym or abbreviation: RSC

Burlington House, Piccadilly, London, W1J 0BA

Tel: 020 7440 8656
Fax: 020 7287 9798
E-mail: library@rsc.org

Website:
http://www.rsc.org

Enquiries:
Enquiries to: Librarian

Founded:
1841

Organisation type and purpose:
Learned society.

Subject coverage:
Alchemy, analytical chemistry, biochemistry, biography, chemical engineering, chemical industry, chemistry, environment, food science and technology, hazards, health and safety at work, inorganic chemistry, organic chemistry, spectrometry and toxicology.

Museum or gallery collection, archive, or library special collection:
Alchemy and chemistry to 1850 (3,000 vols)
Prints and photographs of distinguished chemists (8,000)

Trade and statistical information:
Chemical business statistics on a wide variety of chemicals.

Non-library collection catalogue:
All or part available online and in-house

Library catalogue:
All or part available online and in-house

Printed publications:
Chemistry information resources on the Internet
History of Chemistry sources of information
Periodicals list of the LIC

Publications list:
Available online and in print

Access to staff:
Contact by letter, by telephone, by fax, by e-mail and via website. Appointment necessary. Non-members charged.
Hours: Mon to Fri, 0930 to 1730

Access for disabled people:
Ramped entry

Constituent bodies:
Analytical, Faraday, Dalton, Perkin, Education and Industrial Affairs

ROYAL SOCIETY OF CHEMISTRY – SALES AND CUSTOMER CARE DEPARTMENT

Acronym or abbreviation: RSC

Thomas Graham House, Science Park, Milton Road, Cambridge, CB4 4WF

Tel: 01223 420066
Fax: 01223 426017
E-mail: sales@rsc.org

Website:
http://www.rsc.org

Full publications catalogue plus information of all RSC services, membership, conferences, journals, etc.

Enquiries:
Enquiries to: Sales and Customer Care Department
Direct tel: 01223 432360

Founded:
1980

Organisation type and purpose:
Learned society, professional body (membership is by qualification), present number of members: 47,000, registered charity (charity number 207890), publishing house.

Subject coverage:
Chemistry (all areas, general, organic, analytical); mass spectrometry; biology; biotechnology; biochemistry; food science; nutrition; pesticides; chemical engineering; toxicology; hazards; health and safety; agrochemicals; business information.

Museum or gallery collection, archive, or library special collection:
Library located at Burlington House, Piccadilly, London

Library catalogue:
All or part available online

Printed publications:
A very large number of journals, books and other
    publications including:
Analytical Abstracts
Chemical Communications (flagship journal)
Chemistry World (monthly)
Dictionary of substances and their effects (DOSE) –
    all chemicals described
Lab on a Chip
Green Chemistry
JAAS
Physical Chemistry Chemical Physics
Soft Matter
RSC Journals Super Archive
A large number of books under the headings:
Analytical and Spectroscopy
Agrochemical Science
Educational and Management
Environmental Chemistry
Food Science and Nutrition
Inorganic and Bio-inorganic Chemistry
Organic and Bio-organic Chemistry
Physical, Industrial and Historical Chemistry
Polymers and Materials

Electronic and video publications:
Electronic journals
Videos and CD-ROMs
Software

Publications list:
Available online and in print

Access to staff:
Contact by letter, by telephone, by fax, by e-mail and via website
Hours: Mon to Fri, 0900 to 1700

Member of:
Association of Learned and Professional Society Publishers (ALPSP)

Other address:
Royal Society of Chemistry (RSC)
    Burlington House, Piccadilly, London, W1J 0BA;
    tel: 020 7437 8656; fax: 020 7287 9798

ROYAL SOCIETY OF EDINBURGH

Acronym or abbreviation: RSE

22–26 George Street, Edinburgh, EH2 2PQ

Tel: 0131 240 5000
Fax: 0131 240 5024
E-mail: rse@royalsoced.org.uk

Website:
http://www.royalsoced.org.uk
Details of current activities (meetings, publications, awards) and of offices and staff.

Enquiries:
Enquiries to: Chief Executive

Other contacts: Journals & Archive Officer for
publications and archive information.

Founded:
1783

Organisation type and purpose:
Learned society.

Subject coverage:
Science and literature; arts and humanities; public
administration and business.

**Museum or gallery collection, archive, or library
special collection:**
Charles Piazzi Smyth Archive (now housed at the
Royal Observatory Edinburgh, Blackford Hill,
Edinburgh)
David Hume manuscripts (now housed at the
National Library of Scotland, George IV Bridge,
Edinburgh)
RSE Archive, including Minute Books,
Correspondence etc, held at National Library of
Scotland, George IV Bridge, Edinburgh

Non-library collection catalogue:
All or part available in-house

Library catalogue:
All or part available in-house

Printed publications:
Annual Report (available direct)
Proceedings A – Mathematics (6 times a year)
ReSourcE News – Newsletter (3–4 times a year,
available direct)
Transactions – Earth Sciences (quarterly)
Directory & Sessional Review (formerly Year Book)
Annual Review
Order printed publications from: Customer Services,
CABI Publishing
Wallingford, Oxfordshire, OX10 8DE, tel: 01491
832111, fax: 01491 829292, e-mail: orders@cabi.org

Access to staff:
Contact by letter, by telephone, by fax, by e-mail
and via website. Appointment necessary.
Hours: Mon to Fri, 0900 to 1700

Access for disabled people:
Ramped access, lift access to most rooms, disabled
toilet facilities, induction loop

ROYAL SOCIETY OF LITERATURE OF THE UNITED KINGDOM

Acronym or abbreviation: RSL

Somerset House, Strand, London, WC2R 1LA

Tel: 020 7845 4676
Fax: 020 7845 4679
E-mail: info@rslit.org

Website:
http://www.rslit.org
Pages about the Society's activities, details of how
to join.

Enquiries:
Enquiries to: Secretary
Other contacts: Deputy Secretary

Founded:
1820

Organisation type and purpose:
Learned society (membership is by subscription),
registered charity.

Subject coverage:
The appreciation of literature in English.

Education services:
Monthly lectures.

Printed publications:
Newsletter

Access to staff:
Contact by letter, by telephone, by fax, by e-mail
and via website. Appointment necessary.
Hours: Mon to Thu, 0930 to 1730

Access to building, collection or gallery:
Prior appointment required

Access for disabled people:
Toilet facilities
Special comments: Wheelchair lift available.

ROYAL SOCIETY OF MARINE ARTISTS

Acronym or abbreviation: RSMA

17 Carlton House Terrace, London, SW1Y 5BD

Tel: 020 7930 6844
Fax: 020 7839 7830
E-mail: press@mallgalleries.com

Website:
http://www.mallgalleries.org.uk

Enquiries:
Enquiries to: Secretary
Other contacts: Marketing and Communications
Officer

Founded:
1945

Organisation type and purpose:
Membership association (membership is by
election or invitation), present number of
members: 41, registered charity (charity number
289944).

Subject coverage:
Marine art, annual open exhibition.

Printed publications:
Annual Exhibition Catalogue
Books on marine painting during annual
exhibition

Access to staff:
Contact by letter, by telephone, by fax and by e-
mail. Appointment necessary.
Hours: Mon to Fri, 0930 to 1730

Access to building, collection or gallery:
Prior appointment required
Hours: Mon to Fri, 0930 to 1730

Access for disabled people:
Toilet facilities
Special comments: Stairlift.

Links with:
Federation of British Artists (FBA)
at the same address

ROYAL SOCIETY OF MEDICINE

Acronym or abbreviation: RSM

1 Wimpole Street, London, W1G 0AE

Tel: 020 7290 2940/1/2
Fax: 020 7290 2939

Website:
http://www.rsm.ac.uk

Enquiries:
Enquiries to: Director of Information Services
Direct tel: 020 7290 2931
Direct fax: 020 7290 2976
Direct e-mail: ian.snowley@rsm.ac.uk

Founded:
1805

Organisation type and purpose:
Learned society (membership is by subscription,
qualification, election or invitation), present
number of members: 18,000, registered charity
(charity number 206219), publishing house.

Subject coverage:
Medicine in general, biomedical sciences,
postgraduate biomedical sciences, archives.

**Museum or gallery collection, archive, or library
special collection:**
Chalmers Collection of early medicine
Comfort Collection on gerontology
Historical Medical Collection from 1474
Major periodicals of Europe and America, 19th and
20th centuries

Non-library collection catalogue:
All or part available online

Library catalogue:
All or part available online

Printed publications:
Regular publishing programme of new medical
books
Many journals and other publications
Order printed publications from: Book & Sales
Enquiries, RSM Press
1 Wimpole Street, London, W1G 0AE

Publications list:
Available in print

Access to staff:
Contact by letter, by telephone, by fax, by e-mail,
in person and via website. Access for members
only. Non-members charged.
Hours: Mon to Thur, 0900 to 2030; Fri 0900 to 17.30

Access for disabled people:
Level entry, access to all public areas, toilet
facilities

ROYAL SOCIETY OF MINIATURE PAINTERS, SCULPTORS AND GRAVERS

Acronym or abbreviation: RMS

3 Briar Walk, London, SW15 6UD

Tel: 020 8785 2338
E-mail: tremrod@aol.com

Website:
http://www.royal-minature-society.org.uk

Enquiries:
Enquiries to: Executive Secretary

Founded:
1896

Organisation type and purpose:
International organisation, professional body
(membership is by election or invitation), present
number of members: 160, registered charity
(charity number 291389).
Publicising and educating the public about
miniature painting.

Subject coverage:
All forms of miniature art: painting in all media,
etching, silver-point, sculpture, ceramics, glass
engraving, enamelling, gold and silver work,
jewellery.

**Museum or gallery collection, archive, or library
special collection:**
Diploma collection
Library

Printed publications:
Annual Catalogue and History of the Society
Centenary Book (1995, containing about 220
lifesize colour reproductions of contemporary
members' work)
Order printed publications from: Royal Miniature
Society, at the main address

Access to staff:
Contact by letter, by telephone and by fax.
Appointment necessary.
Hours: Mon to Fri, 0900 to 1700

Access to building, collection or gallery:
No access other than to staff
Hours: Except during the exhibition.

Access for disabled people:
Ramped entry, access to all public areas, toilet
facilities

ROYAL SOCIETY OF MUSICIANS OF GREAT BRITAIN

10 Stratford Place, London, W1C 1BA

Tel: 020 7629 6137
Fax: 020 7629 6137

continued overleaf

Enquiries:
Enquiries to: Secretary

Founded:
1738

Organisation type and purpose:
Membership association (membership is by
election or invitation), present number of
members: 1367, registered charity (charity number
208879).
The world's oldest charity for musicians.
The Society, founded by Handel and over 200 other
musicians to support colleagues and their families
in distress because of illness, accident or old age,
continues to support professional musicians and
their dependants.

Subject coverage:
History of music and musicians, from the 18th
century, from the records of the Society; personal
files of Members; minute books, accounts etc;
much material unavailable elsewhere.

**Museum or gallery collection, archive, or library
special collection:**
Manuscript scores (including marches composed
for the Society by Haydn, Weber, Cipriani Potter,
Bishop and von Winter)

Printed publications:
A History of The Royal Society of Musicians 1738–
1988
Handel in London
List of Members 1738–1984
Arthur Sullivan and the Royal Society of Musicians
of Great Britain, ed Mackie, D

Access to staff:
Contact by letter, by telephone and by fax
Hours: Mon to Fri, 0900 to 1700

Access to building, collection or gallery:
No prior appointment required

ROYAL SOCIETY OF PORTRAIT PAINTERS

Acronym or abbreviation: RP

17 Carlton House Terrace, London, SW1Y 5BD

Tel: 020 7930 6844
Fax: 020 7839 7830
E-mail: press@mallgalleries.com

Website:
http://www.mallgalleries.org.uk
http://www.therp.org.uk

Enquiries:
Enquiries to: Secretary
Other contacts: Marketing and Communications
Officer

Founded:
1891

Organisation type and purpose:
Professional body (membership is by election or
invitation), present number of members: 53,
registered charity (charity number 327460).
To foster and promote the art of portrait painting.

Subject coverage:
Portrait painting and painters, annual open
exhibition.

**Museum or gallery collection, archive, or library
special collection:**
Examples of portrait painters' work on slides,
photographs and some original portrait
paintings

Printed publications:
Annual Exhibition Catalogue (May)
Book containing details and photographs of the
work of some society members

Access to staff:
Contact by letter, by telephone, by fax, by e-mail
and via website. Appointment necessary.
Hours: Mon to Fri, 0930 to 1730

Access to building, collection or gallery:
No access other than to staff

Hours: Mon to Fri, 0930 to 1730

Access for disabled people:
Toilet facilities
Special comments: Stairlift.

Links with:
Federation of British Artists (FBA)
at the same address

ROYAL SOCIETY OF ST GEORGE

Administration Office, 127 Sandgate Road,
Folkestone, Kent, CT20 2BH

Tel: 01303 241795
Fax: 01303 211710
E-mail: info@rssg.u-net.com

Website:
http://www.royalsocietyofstgeorge.com
Complete description of the Society, its history,
current activities, addresses of branches, extracts
from the journal 'England's Standard', forthcoming
events and more.

Enquiries:
Enquiries to: Chairman

Founded:
1894

Organisation type and purpose:
Statutory body (membership is by subscription,
election or invitation), voluntary organisation,
registered charity (charity number 263076).

Printed publications:
England's Standard

Access to staff:
Contact by letter, by telephone, by fax, by e-mail
and via website
Hours: Mon to Thu, 0900 to 1600

Has:
some 100 branches, half of which are overseas

ROYAL SOCIETY OF TROPICAL MEDICINE AND HYGIENE

Acronym or abbreviation: RSTMH

50 Bedford Square, London, WC1B 3DP

Tel: 020 7580 2127
Fax: 020 7436 1389
E-mail: mail@rstmh.org

Website:
http://www.rstmh.org
Introduction, structure, history, the journal,
fellowship, awards and calendar of meetings.

Enquiries:
Enquiries to: Administrator

Founded:
1907

Organisation type and purpose:
Learned society, registered charity (charity number
208204).
To promote and advance the study, control and
prevention of disease in man and other animals in
warm climates, to facilitate discussion and the
exchange of information among those who are
interested in tropical diseases.

Subject coverage:
International health, tropical medicine and
hygiene, tropical veterinary science.

Printed publications:
Transactions of the Royal Society of Tropical
Medicine and Hygiene (12 times a year)
Order printed publications from: Elsevier, Customer
Service Department, PO Box 211, 1000 AE
Amsterdam, The Netherlands; tel. +31 20 485 3757;
fax. +31 20 485 3432; e-mail:
journalscustomerserviceemea@elsevier.com

Publications list:
Available online and in print

Access to staff:
Contact by letter and by e-mail
Hours: Mon to Fri, 0900 to 1700

ROYAL SOCIETY OF ULSTER ARCHITECTS

Acronym or abbreviation: RSUA

2 Mount Charles, Belfast, BT7 1NZ

Tel: 028 9032 3760
Fax: 028 9023 7313
E-mail: info@rsua.org.uk

Enquiries:
Enquiries to: Director

Founded:
1901

Organisation type and purpose:
Professional body (membership is by subscription),
registered charity (charity number NI 00069).

Subject coverage:
Advice on selecting an architect. Advice on
running architectural competitions.

Access to staff:
Contact by letter, by telephone and by fax.
Appointment necessary.
Hours: Mon to Fri, 0900 to 1700

Access for disabled people:
Ramped entry, toilet facilities

ROYAL TOWN PLANNING INSTITUTE

Acronym or abbreviation: RTPI

41 Botolph Lane, London, EC3R 8DL

Tel: 020 7929 9494 (switchboard), 020 7929 9452
(library)
Fax: 020 7929 9490
E-mail: library@rtpi.org.uk

Website:
http://www.rtpi.org.uk
In-house information.
http://www.rtpiconsultants.co.uk
Online directory of planning consultants.
http://www.planningsummerschool.com
Planning Summer School.
http://www.planning.haynet.com
Information from current issues of Planning
magazine.
http://www.planningaid.rtpi.org.uk
Planning Aid.

Enquiries:
Enquiries to: Library and Information Manager
Direct tel: 020 7929 9452

Founded:
1914

Organisation type and purpose:
Professional body, present number of members:
17,500.

Subject coverage:
Urban, regional and rural planning, housing,
transport, conservation, leisure, spatial planning,
recreation, employment, local government.

Non-library collection catalogue:
All or part available online

Library catalogue:
All or part available online

Publications list:
Available online and in print

Access to staff:
Contact by letter, by telephone, by fax, by e-mail
and via website. Appointment necessary.

Access to building, collection or gallery:
Prior appointment required

Access for disabled people:
Access to all public areas (including library), toilet
facilities

Founder member of:
Commonwealth Association of Planners
now about 20 members, secretariat in Canada

Other office:
RTPI in Scotland
57 Melville Street, Edinburgh, EH3 7HL; tel: 0131
226 1959; fax: 0131 226 1909; e-mail: scotland@
rtpi.org.uk

ROYAL TOWN PLANNING INSTITUTE IN SCOTLAND

Acronym or abbreviation: RTPI

57 Melville Street, Edinburgh, EH3 7HL

Tel: 0131 226 1959
Fax: 0131 226 1909
E-mail: scotland@rtpi.org.uk

Website:
http://www.rtpi.org.uk
Policy papers; current news items; member
services.

Enquiries:
Enquiries to: Director

Founded:
1914

Organisation type and purpose:
Professional body (membership is by election or
invitation), present number of members: 1800 in
Scotland, 18,000 in UK, registered charity (charity
number 262865).
To act as the chartered professional body for town
planners and to advance the art and science of
town planning at national, regional and local
levels.

Subject coverage:
Town planning: services to professional planners;
education for planning; policy on national
planning systems and practice; assistance to the
public through Planning Aid Scotland; (the
Institute itself cannot provide advice to the public
on individual planning cases).

Library catalogue:
All or part available in-house

Printed publications:
Planning (incorporating Planning Week, £65)
Scottish Planner (6 times a year, £15)
Order printed publications from: Royal Town
Planning Institute
41 Botolph Lane, London, EC3R 8DL, tel: 020 7929
9494, fax: 020 7929 9490, e-mail: online@rtpi.org.uk

Publications list:
Available in print

Access to staff:
Contact by letter, by telephone, by fax, by e-mail
and via website. Appointment necessary.
Hours: Mon to Fri, 0900 to 1700

Access to building, collection or gallery:
Prior appointment required

Parent body:
RTPI
41 Botolph Lane, London, EC3R 8DL; tel: 020
7929 9494; fax: 020 7929 9490; e-mail: online@rtpi
.org.uk

ROYAL UNITED SERVICES INSTITUTE FOR DEFENCE STUDIES

Acronym or abbreviation: RUSI

Whitehall, London, SW1A 2ET

Tel: 020 7930 5854
Fax: 020 7321 0943
E-mail: defence@rusi.org

Website:
http://www.rusi.org/rusi/

Enquiries:
Enquiries to: Membership Secretary
Other contacts: Librarian, PA to Director

Founded:
1831

Organisation type and purpose:
Membership association, registered charity
(charity number 210639), consultancy, research
organisation.

Subject coverage:
Defence and international security.

Printed publications:
Journal (6 times a year)
Newsbrief (monthly)
Whitehall Papers (6 times a year)
World Defence Systems (3 times a year)

Access to staff:
Contact by letter, by telephone, by fax, by e-mail
and via website. Appointment necessary. Access
for members only.
Hours: Mon to Fri, 0900 to 1700

Access for disabled people:
Toilet facilities

ROYAL VETERINARY COLLEGE ANIMAL CARE TRUST

Acronym or abbreviation: RVC ACT

The Royal Veterinary College, Hawkshead Lane,
Hatfield, Hertfordshire, AL9 7TA

Tel: 01707 666237
Fax: 01707 666382
E-mail: act@rvc.ac.uk

Website:
http://www.rvc.ac.uk/act

Enquiries:
Enquiries to: Director of Fund Raising

Founded:
1982

Organisation type and purpose:
Registered charity (charity number 281571).
To support the work of the Royal Veterinary
College.

Subject coverage:
Education of veterinary students and the treatment
of animals, veterinary science, veterinary surgery,
animal welfare.

Printed publications:
Christmas Gifts Catalogue (annually)
RVC ACT Annual Report
Newsletter (2 times a year)

Access to staff:
Contact by letter, by telephone, by fax, by e-mail
and via website. Appointment necessary.
Hours: Mon to Fri, 0900 to 1700

Parent body:
Royal Veterinary College
University of London, Royal College Street,
London, NW1 0TU; tel: 020 7468 5000; fax: 020
7388 2342

ROYAL VETERINARY COLLEGE LIBRARY

Acronym or abbreviation: RVC

Royal College Street, Camden, London, NW1 0TU

Tel: 020 7468 5161
Fax: 020 7468 5161
E-mail: sjackson@rvc.ac.uk

Website:
http://www.rvc.ac.uk/Services/Libraries/Index.cfm

Enquiries:
Enquiries to: Librarian
Direct tel: 01707 666214
Direct fax: 01707 666214
Other contacts: Deputy Librarian

Founded:
1791

Organisation type and purpose:
University department or institute.

Subject coverage:
Veterinary science and medicine; pre-clinical and
historical material at Royal College Street; current
veterinary material at Hawkshead.

**Museum or gallery collection, archive, or library
special collection:**
Frank Townend Barton Gift
Granville Penn Gift
Historical collection
James Beart Simonds Collection (veterinary
advisor to the Privy Council during the curing of
the cattle disease Rhind Pest in the 19th century)
scrap-books and extensive notes and
photographs
Sir Frederick Smith's Napoleonic manuscripts

Library catalogue:
All or part available online

Printed publications:
College Annual Report
The Historical collections (free)
Library Guide (free)
Prospectus
Services and Price Guide (free)

Microform publications:
James Beart Simonds Collection of scrap-books
(microfilm)

Access to staff:
Appointment necessary.
Hours: Mon to Fri, 0900 to 1700

Other addresses:
Royal Veterinary College Library
Hawkshead House, Hawkshead Lane, North
Mymms, Hatfield, Hertfordshire, AL9 7TA; tel:
01707 666214; fax: 01707 666214; e-mail:
sjackson@rvc.ac.uk

Parent body:
University of London

ROYAL WATERCOLOUR SOCIETY

Acronym or abbreviation: RWS

Bankside Gallery, 48 Hopton Street, London, SE1
9JH

Tel: 020 7928 7521
Fax: 020 7928 2820
E-mail: rws@banksidegallery.com

Website:
http://www.banksidegallery.com

Enquiries:
Enquiries to: Gallery Director

Founded:
1804

Organisation type and purpose:
Learned society (membership is by election or
invitation), present number of members: 90,
registered charity (charity number 258348), art
gallery.

Subject coverage:
Watercolour painting and its history,
contemporary work by members of the Society,
gallery activities.

**Museum or gallery collection, archive, or library
special collection:**
The RWS Diploma collection (1 work from each
member of the society, RWS Archive since its
inception 200 years ago)

Library catalogue:
All or part available in print

Printed publications:
Bankside Bulletin (journal of the Royal
Watercolour Society and the Royal Society of
Painter-Printmakers, quarterly, free to members
and friends, £2 to the public)

Access to staff:
Contact by letter, by telephone, by fax, by e-mail
and via website

continued overleaf

Hours: Mon to Fri, 1100 to 1800

Access to building, collection or gallery:
No prior appointment required

Connected with:
Bankside Gallery, home of the RWS

ROYAL WELSH AGRICULTURAL SOCIETY LIMITED

Acronym or abbreviation: RWAS Ltd

Llanelwedd, Builth Wells, Powys, LD2 3SY

Tel: 01982 553683
Fax: 01982 553563
E-mail: requests@rwas.co.uk

Website:
http://www.rwas.co.uk
Information on the Royal Welsh Show, the Royal Welsh Agricultural Winter Fair, and the Royal Welsh Smallholder and Garden Festival.

Enquiries:
Enquiries to: Secretary

Founded:
1904

Formerly called:
Welsh National Agricultural Society (year of change 1922)

Organisation type and purpose:
International organisation, membership association (membership is by subscription), present number of members: 14,000, voluntary organisation, registered charity (charity number 251232), suitable for ages: all.
To promote agriculture, horticulture, forestry and conservation in Wales.

Subject coverage:
Any matters relating to the Royal Welsh Show, the Royal Welsh Agricultural Winter Fair, and the Royal Welsh Smallholder and Garden Festival.

Printed publications:
Official Show Catalogue
Official Show Programme
Promotional Leaflets
RWAS Journal
Section Schedules

Publications list:
Available online and in print

Access to staff:
Contact by letter, by telephone, by fax, by e-mail and via website. Appointment necessary.
Hours: Mon to Fri, 0845 to 1230 and 1330 to 1700
Special comments: Closed on statutory holidays.

Access for disabled people:
Ramped entry, toilet facilities

ROYAL WELSH COLLEGE OF MUSIC & DRAMA LIBRARY

Acronym or abbreviation: RWCMD

Castle Grounds, Cathays Park, Cardiff, CF10 3ER

Tel: 029 2034 2854
Fax: 029 2039 1304
E-mail: library@rwcmd.ac.uk

Website:
http://www.rwcmd.ac.uk

Enquiries:
Enquiries to: Librarian
Direct tel: 029 2039 1330

Founded:
1947

Formerly called:
Welsh College of Music & Drama (year of change 2002)

Merged with:
University of Glamorgan (year of change 2007)

Organisation type and purpose:
Independent higher education college for training in performing arts.

Subject coverage:
Music, theatre, stage design, stage management, creative music technology and recording, technical stage management, music therapy, art management, acting.

Library catalogue:
All or part available online

Access to staff:
Contact by telephone. Appointment necessary.
Hours: Term time: Mon to Thu, 0830 to 2000; Fri, 0830 to 1800; Sat, 1000 to 1400
Vacation: Mon to Thu, 0900 to 1700; Fri, 0900 to 1630; Sat, closed

Links with:
Cardiff Arts Marketing – Organisation of Arts Organisations in Wales
Incorporated Society of Musicians

ROYAL YACHTING ASSOCIATION

Acronym or abbreviation: RYA

RYA House, Romsey Road, Eastleigh, Hampshire, SO50 9YA

Tel: 023 8062 7400
Fax: 023 8062 9924
E-mail: admin@rya.org.uk

Website:
http://www.rya.org.uk

Enquiries:
Enquiries to: Secretary General
Direct tel: 023 8062 7420
Direct e-mail: rod.carr@ry.org.uk
Other contacts: Chief Executive

Founded:
1875

Formerly called:
Yacht Racing Association (YRA)

Organisation type and purpose:
National government body, membership association (membership is by subscription), present number of members: 88,000.
National governing body for recreational boating in the UK.
Represents recreational boating in the UK.

Subject coverage:
Boating matters relating to sail cruising, sail racing, windsurfing, motor cruising, powerboating, personal watercraft.

Museum or gallery collection, archive, or library special collection:
Minute books of the YRA and RYA meetings 1875-present

Library catalogue:
All or part available in-house

Printed publications:
Range of training booklets, foreign cruising notes, legal information etc
RYA Magazine (4 times per annum)

Electronic and video publications:
A range of videos and CDs covering navigation, boat handling, first aid etc

Publications list:
Available in print

Access to staff:
Contact by letter, by fax and by e-mail.
Appointment necessary.
Hours: Mon to Fri, 0900 to 1700

Access to building, collection or gallery:
Prior appointment required

Access for disabled people:
Ramped entry, access to all public areas

Has:
1500 affiliated clubs and classes, 1500 RYA recognised schools

Houses the:
RYA Sailability
    tel: 02380 647431; fax: 02380 629924; e-mail: info@rya.sailability.org

Links with:
European Boating Association (EBA)
European Sailing Federation (EUROSAF)
International Sailing Federation (ISAF)
Union Internationale Motonautique (UIM)

ROYAL YACHTING ASSOCIATION SCOTLAND

Acronym or abbreviation: RYA Scotland

Caledonia House, Redheughs Rigg, South Gyle, Edinburgh, EH12 9DQ

Tel: 0131 317 7388
Fax: 0131 317 8566
E-mail: admin@ryascotland.org.uk

Enquiries:
Enquiries to: Chairman

Organisation type and purpose:
Training organisation.
National governing body for the sports of sailing, windsurfing, powerboating and personal watercrafting in Scotland.

Printed publications:
An extensive publication list of titles on racing, dinghies, power boats, cruising, course notes, club guides, navigation, seamanship, training, etc
Order printed publications from: Royal Yachting Association
RYA House, Ensign Way, Hamble, Southampton, SO31 4YA, tel: 023 8060 4100, fax: 023 8060 4299

Electronic and video publications:
A range of videos and CDs covering sailing skills, navigation, first aid, etc

Publications list:
Available online and in print

Access to staff:
Contact by letter, by telephone, by fax, by e-mail and in person
Hours: Mon to Fri, 0900 to 1230 and 1315 to 1645

ROYAL ZOOLOGICAL SOCIETY OF SCOTLAND

Acronym or abbreviation: RZSS

Edinburgh Zoo, 134 Corstorphine Road, Corstorphine, Edinburgh, EH12 6TS

Tel: 0131 334 9171/2/3
Fax: 0131 316 4050

Website:
http://www.edinburghzoo.org

Enquiries:
Enquiries to: Visitor Services Manager

Founded:
1909

Organisation type and purpose:
Learned society (membership is by subscription), present number of members: 13,000, registered charity (charity number SCO040604).
To promote, through the preservation of the Society's living collections, the conservation of animal species and wild places through captive breeding, environmental education and scientific research.

Subject coverage:
Zoo management, animals in captivity, Scottish wildlife, aviculture, conservation education.

Museum or gallery collection, archive, or library special collection:
Animal collection held on the International Species Inventory System (ISIS)

Printed publications:
Annual Report

ARKFILE (newsletter, quarterly)
Guide Book to the Zoo
Guidebook for the Highland Wildlife Park

Access to staff:
Appointment necessary.
Hours: Mon to Fri, 0900 to 1700
Special comments: Seasonal opening hours.

Links with:
European Association of Zoos and Aquaria
International Union for Conservation of Nature
and Natural Resources
National Federation of Zoological Gardens of
Great Britain and Ireland
World Zoo Organisation (IUDZG)

Manages:
Highland Wildlife Park
   Kincraig; tel: 01540 651270
Scottish National Zoological Park
   Edinburgh

RSABI

Rural Centre, West Mains of Ingliston, Newbridge,
EH28 8LT

Tel: 0131 472 4166
Fax: 0131 472 4156
E-mail: rsabi@rsabi.co.uk

Website:
http://www.rsabi.org.uk

Enquiries:
Enquiries to: Chief Executive
Other contacts: Welfare Manager for all beneficiary
contact.

Founded:
1897

Formerly called:
Royal Scottish Agricultural Benevolent Institution
(year of change 2005)

Organisation type and purpose:
Voluntary organisation, registered charity (charity
number SC 009828), suitable for all ages.
To assist those in distress who are or have been in
farming, forestry, aquaculture, horticulture and
rural estate work in Scotland and their dependants,
with modest financial grants and in kind, and
welfare assistance tailored to circumstance.

Subject coverage:
Relief of hardship among individuals who have
depended on the land in Scotland.

**Museum or gallery collection, archive, or library
special collection:**
Records of all meetings of subscribers since 1897

Printed publications:
Newsletter (2 times a year)
Annual Report
Pamphlets:
Cook Book
The Centenary of the RSABI
Order printed publications from: from the RSABI

Electronic and video publications:
A Farm for All Seasons (DVD)
A Grain of Truth (DVD)

Publications list:
Available online

Access to staff:
Contact by letter, by telephone, by fax, by e-mail,
in person and via website. Appointment necessary.
Hours: Mon to Fri, 0900 to 1700

RSS CENTRE FOR STATISTICAL EDUCATION

Formal name: Royal Statistical Society
Acronym or abbreviation: RSS

Nottingham Trent University, Burton Street,
Nottingham, NG1 4BU

Tel: 0115 848 4476
Fax: 0115 848 2998

E-mail: rsscse@ntu.ac.uk

Website:
http://science.ntu.ac.uk/rsscse/
Database of available resources. Database of
publications available for purchase.

Enquiries:
Enquiries to: Director
Direct tel: 0115 848 2118
Direct e-mail: Neville.Davies@ntu.ac.uk

Founded:
1995

Organisation type and purpose:
Suitable for ages: all, consultancy, research
organisation.

Subject coverage:
Teaching statistics at all levels and in all contexts.

Library catalogue:
All or part available online

Printed publications:
Teaching Statistics (journal, 3 times a year)

Publications list:
Available online and in print

Access to staff:
Contact by letter, by telephone, by fax and by e-
mail
Hours: Mon to Fri, 0900 to 1700

RUBBER CONSULTANTS

Tun Abdul Razak Research Centre,
Brickendonbury, Hertford, SG13 8NL

Tel: 01992 554657
Fax: 01992 504248
E-mail: rubbercon@tarrc.co.uk

Website:
http://www.rubberconsultants.com

Enquiries:
Enquiries to: Manager

Founded:
1984

Organisation type and purpose:
Consultancy, research organisation.

Subject coverage:
All aspects of the science and technology of natural
and synthetic rubbers and the use of elastomers in
manufactured products, tyre testing, rubber
analysis, earthquake protection using structural
bearings, information on the rubber industry.

**Museum or gallery collection, archive, or library
special collection:**
MORPHS main database

Trade and statistical information:
Statistical information on the rubber trade and the
   international trade in rubber products.

Non-library collection catalogue:
All or part available in-house

Library catalogue:
All or part available in-house

Printed publications:
Journal of Rubber Research
Malaysian Rubber Review
Engineering Design with Natural Rubber
NR Engineering Data Sheets
NR Technical Information Sheets
The natural rubber formulary and property index

Electronic and video publications:
Engineering with Rubber
Natural Rubber Bearings for Earthquake
   Protection (video)

Publications list:
Available online and in print

Access to staff:
Contact by telephone, by fax, by e-mail and via
website. Appointment necessary. All charged.
Hours: Mon to Fri, 0900 to 1700

Access to building, collection or gallery:
Special comments: Appointment required

Consultancy unit of:
Tun Abdul Razak Research Centre

RUGBY BOROUGH COUNCIL

Town Hall, Evereux Way, Rugby, Warwickshire,
CV21 2LB

Tel: 01788 533533
Fax: 01788 533577

Website:
http://www.warwickshire.gov.uk

Enquiries:
Enquiries to: Public Relations Manager

Organisation type and purpose:
Local government body.

Subject coverage:
Council services and amenities; corporate services,
environmental services, finance, housing, legal
services, personnel services, planning
development, tourism, economic development,
technical services, highways, leisure services,
council tax and other payments.

RUGBY FIVES ASSOCIATION

Acronym or abbreviation: RFA

66 Brayburne Avenue, Clapham, London, SW4
6AA

Tel: 020 7627 8303
E-mail: andy.pringle@mac.com

Website:
http://www.rfa.org.uk

Enquiries:
Enquiries to: General Secretary
Direct tel: 07760 172904

Founded:
1927

Organisation type and purpose:
Governing body of the sport.
Promotion of the game and organisation of
regional and national championships.

Subject coverage:
Rules of the game, championship dates and
venues, championship records and past winners,
clubs and playing facilities, manufacturers and
suppliers of gloves and balls.

Printed publications:
Annual Review (annual, free to members)
Annual Newsletter (annual, free to members)
Members' Pocket Book (annual, free to members)

Publications list:
Available in print

Access to staff:
Contact by letter, by telephone, by e-mail and via
website
Hours: No fixed times

RUGBY FOOTBALL UNION

Acronym or abbreviation: RFU

Rugby Road, Twickenham, Middlesex, TW1 1DZ

Tel: 020 8892 2000

Enquiries:
Enquiries to: Sales and Marketing Manager
Direct tel: 020 8831 6737
Direct fax: 020 8891 3254
Direct e-mail: tomhill@rfu.com

Founded:
1871

Formerly called:
England Rugby

Organisation type and purpose:
National organisation, voluntary organisation.

continued overleaf

33 constituent unions.
The promotion of rugby union football.

Subject coverage:
Rugby union football; rugby records.

Printed publications:
England Rugby Magazine
Annual Report

Publications list:
Available online

Access to staff:
Access for members only.
Hours: Mon to Fri, 0900 to 1700

Access to building, collection or gallery:
Prior appointment required

Access for disabled people:
Access to all public areas

Affiliated to:
Committee of Home Unions
Committee of Six Nations (England, Scotland,
Ireland, Wales, France and Italy)
International Rugby Football Board

RUNNYMEDE BOROUGH COUNCIL

Civic Offices, Station Road, Addlestone, Surrey,
KT15 2AH

Tel: 01932 838383
Fax: 01932 855135

Website:
http://www.runnymede.gov.uk

Enquiries:
Enquiries to: Chief Executive
Direct tel: 01932 425500
Direct e-mail: williams@runnymede.gov.uk

Founded:
1974

Organisation type and purpose:
Local government body.

Printed publications:
Annual Report (free)
Borough Guide (free)
Information Directory (£3)
Street Plan (£1)

Access to staff:
Contact by letter, by telephone, by fax and in
person
Hours: Mon to Thu, 0830 to 1700; Fri, 0830 to 1630

Access for disabled people:
Parking provided, level entry, toilet facilities

Parent body:
Surrey County Council

RUNNYMEDE TRUST

7 Plough Yard, Shoreditch, London, EC2A 3LP

Tel: 020 7377 9222
Fax: 020 7377 6622
E-mail: info@runnymedetrust.org

Website:
http://www.runnymedetrust.org

Founded:
1968

Formerly called:
Runnymede Educational Trust, Runnymede
Housing Trust

Organisation type and purpose:
Voluntary organisation, registered charity (charity
number 1063609), research organisation,
publishing house.
Educational charity, research body and social
policy think-tank.
To promote the development of a successful, equal
and culturally diverse society.

Subject coverage:
Social policy issues re multi-ethnicity, race etc. in
the UK and how EU Legislation affects UK
policies.

**Museum or gallery collection, archive, or library
special collection:**
Runnymede Trust Library has been donated to the
Middlesex University, Centre for Racial Equality
Studies

Printed publications:
The Runnymede Bulletin (quarterly)
A Tale of Two Englands: 'race' and violent crime in
the press
A Very Light Sleeper: the persistence & dangers of
antisemitism
Black and Ethnic Minority Young People and
Educational Disadvantage
Civil Renewal, Diversity and Social Capital in a
Multi-Ethnic Britain
Cohesion, Community and Citizenship
Developing Community Cohesion
Equal Respect: ASBOs and race equality
Financial Inclusion and Ethnicity: an agenda for
research and policy action
Guardians of Race Equality
Improving Educational Practice
Islamophobia: a challenge for us all
Perpetrators of Racist Violence and Harassment
Preventing Racist Violence
Re(thinking) 'Gangs'
School Choice and Ethnic Segregation
This is Where I Live: stories and pressures in
Brixton 1996
Why Preferential Policies Can be Fair
Young People in the UK: attitudes and opinions on
Europe, Europeans and the European Union

Publications list:
Available online and in print

Access to staff:
Contact by letter and by e-mail
Hours: Mon to Fri, 0900 to 1700
Special comments: Closed to the public.

Access to building, collection or gallery:
Mon to Fri, 0930 to 1730

Access for disabled people:
Access to all public areas
Special comments: No public access to office except
for scheduled appointments.

Links with:
Commission for the Future of Multi-Ethnic Britain

RUPERT BROOKE SOCIETY & MUSEUM, THE

The Orchard, Grantchester, Cambridgeshire, CB3
9ND

Tel: 01223 845788
Fax: 01223 845862
E-mail: rbs@calan.co.uk

Website:
http://www.rupert-brooke-society.com

Enquiries:
Enquiries to: Curator
Other contacts: Secretary for the RB Society
information.

Founded:
1999

Organisation type and purpose:
International organisation, membership
association (membership is by subscription),
museum, historic building, house or site.
The Museum covers the life history of Rupert
Brooke.
Aims to: foster an interest in the work of Rupert
Brooke, increase knowledge and appreciation of
Rupert Brooke and of the village of Grantchester,
help to preserve places associated with Rupert
Brooke.

Subject coverage:
The life and works of Rupert Brooke.

Printed publications:
A selection of books including:
Forever England, the Life of Rupert Brooke (Read
M)
Old Grantchester, A Sketch book (Willmer E N)
Rupert Brooke & Wilfred Owen (selected and ed
Walter G)
Order printed publications from: The Rupert Brooke
Society

Electronic and video publications:
Rupert Brooke – His Life and Poetry (audiotape,
Hodge D, Read M)

Publications list:
Available in print

Access to staff:
Contact by letter, by telephone, by fax, by e-mail
and via website
Hours: Mon to Fri, 0900 to 1700

Access to building, collection or gallery:
No prior appointment required
Hours: Summer opening usually Mon to Sun,
1000–1600 (phone to confirm opening)

Access for disabled people:
Parking provided
Special comments: ramped entry to tea pavilion,
steps into museum.

RURAL & INDUSTRIAL DESIGN & BUILDING ASSOCIATION

Acronym or abbreviation: RIDBA

ATSS House, Station Road East, Stowmarket,
Suffolk, IP14 1RQ

Tel: 01449 676049
Fax: 01449 770028
E-mail: secretary@ridba.org.uk

Website:
http://www.ridba.org.uk

Enquiries:
Enquiries to: National Secretary

Founded:
1956

Organisation type and purpose:
National organisation, advisory body, trade
association (membership is by subscription),
present number of members: 320.

Subject coverage:
Members have expertise in all aspects of rural &
industrial buildings and cover: planning, design,
new construction (steel, timber, concrete and
traditional), conversion, fitting out, health and
safety, pollution control, education, animal welfare
etc. Regular conferences are organised on subjects
of interest, plus regular visits to interesting and up-
to-date rural & industrial enterprises and an
annual study tour usually in Europe.

**Museum or gallery collection, archive, or library
special collection:**
A full set of past journals and newsletters is held
and members have access to the old Farm
Buildings Centre library at Silsoe College

Trade and statistical information:
Members hold data on all aspects of rural
buildings.

Printed publications:
Countryside Building (4 times a year, annual
subscription £20, free to members)
Order printed publications from: Editor, Ghyll House
Publishing Ltd, ATSS House, Station Road East,
Stowmarket, IP14 1RQ, tel: 01449 676049, fax:
01449 770028, e-mail: tony@ghyllhouse.co.uk

Access to staff:
Contact by letter, by telephone, by fax and by e-
mail. Appointment necessary.
Hours: Mon to Fri, 0900 to 1700

Access to building, collection or gallery:
No access other than to staff

RURAL CRAFTS ASSOCIATION

Heights Cottage, Brook Road, Wormley,
Godalming, Surrey, GU8 5UA

Tel: 01428 682292
Fax: 01428 685969
E-mail: info@ruralcraftsassociation.co.uk

Website:
http://www.ruralcraftsassociation.co.uk

Enquiries:
Enquiries to: Director

Founded:
1970

Organisation type and purpose:
Membership association (membership is by
subscription), present number of members: 600.
To encourage men and women to make and sell
their work and skills, to uphold the quality of work
in whatever price range the craft falls, to provide a
vigorous forum for the sale of members' work, at a
cost they can afford.

Subject coverage:
British craftworkers; contact for members of the
association and for those wishing to and presently
exhibiting in Rural Crafts Association pavilions at
agricultural and equestrian shows, and game fairs
nationwide.

Printed publications:
Year Planner (aims and objectives, activities, shows
during the year; members and interested parties)
Newsletter (members)

Access to staff:
Contact by letter, by telephone, by fax and by e-
mail
Hours: Mon to Fri, 0900 to 1700

Access for disabled people:
Good access at all events
Hours: At all opening times

RURALNET UK

National Rural Enterprise Centre, Stoneleigh Park,
Kenilworth, Warwickshire, CV8 2RR

Tel: 024 7669 6986\ 0845 130 0411
Fax: 024 7669 6770\ 0845 130 0433
E-mail: info@ruralnetuk.org

Website:
http://www.ruralnetuk.org
http://www.ruralnet.org.uk
Support for rural communities and those working
in rural development
http://www.expertsonline.org.uk
Online mentoring service for voluntary sector
organisations and small businesses working in
rural and urban regeneration

Enquiries:
Enquiries to: Chief Executive
Other contacts: Business Development Manager

Founded:
1987

Organisation type and purpose:
Registered charity, training organisation,
consultancy, research organisation.
Deals with information, research and projects that
promote rural business and community enterprise.

Subject coverage:
Rural economic development, employment,
training, ICT, sustainable energy, collaboration.

Library catalogue:
All or part available in-house

Electronic and video publications:
http://www.xpressdigest.org.uk
http://www.inforurale.org.uk

Publications list:
Available online

Access to staff:
Contact by letter, by telephone, by fax, by e-mail,

in person and via website. Appointment necessary.
Hours: Mon to Fri, 0900 to 1700

RUSHCLIFFE BOROUGH COUNCIL

Civic Centre, Pavilion Road, West Bridgford,
Nottinghamshire, NG2 5FE

Tel: 0115 981 9911
Fax: 0115 945 5882
E-mail: customerservices@rushcliffe.gov.uk

Website:
http://www.rushcliffe.gov.uk

Enquiries:
Enquiries to: Public Relations Manager
Direct tel: 0115 9148555
Other contacts: Customer Services Centre for all
enquiries.

Founded:
1974

Organisation type and purpose:
Local government body.

Subject coverage:
Council services and amenities; corporate services,
environmental services, finance, housing, legal
services, personnel services, planning development
and tourism, property and technical services, roads
and transportation, council tax and other
payments.

Publications list:
Available online and in print

Access to staff:
Contact by letter, by telephone, by fax, by e-mail,
in person and via website
Hours: Mon to Fri, 0730 to 1700

Access to building, collection or gallery:
No prior appointment required
Hours: Mon to Fri, 0830 to 1700

Access for disabled people:
Parking provided, level entry, access to all public
areas, toilet facilities

RUSKIN COLLEGE LIBRARY

Walton Street, Oxford, OX1 2HE

Tel: 01865 554331
Fax: 01865 554372
E-mail: library@ruskin.ac.uk

Enquiries:
Enquiries to: Librarian

Founded:
1899

Organisation type and purpose:
Residential college for adult education.

Subject coverage:
Social sciences, labour studies, social work,
community and youth work, women's studies,
history, literature.

**Museum or gallery collection, archive, or library
special collection:**
Abe Lazarus Memorial Library and Archive
Ewan MacColl and Peggy Seeger Archive
Raphael Samuel papers
James and Lucy Middleton Papers

Access to staff:
Appointment necessary.
Hours: Mon to Fri, 0900 to 1700

RUSKIN LIBRARY

Lancaster University, Lancaster, LA1 4YH

Tel: 01524 593587
Fax: 01524 593580
E-mail: ruskin.library@lancaster.ac.uk

Website:
http://www.lancs.ac.uk/users/ruskinlib
Information for visitors, catalogue of collections

Enquiries:
Enquiries to: Curator
Other contacts: Deputy and Assistant Curators

Founded:
1998

Organisation type and purpose:
Art gallery, university library.

Subject coverage:
Art and architecture, history and literature.

**Museum or gallery collection, archive, or library
special collection:**
Whitehouse Collection of manuscripts, books,
photographs and pictures relating to John
Ruskin (1819–1900) and his associates

Non-library collection catalogue:
All or part available online

Library catalogue:
All or part available online

Publications list:
Available online

Access to staff:
Contact by letter, by telephone, by fax, by e-mail,
in person and via website. Appointment necessary.
Hours: Reading Room: Mon to Fri, 1000 to 1630

Access to building, collection or gallery:
No access other than to staff
Hours: Public Gallery: Mon to Sat, 1100 to 1600;
Sun, 1300 to 1600

Access for disabled people:
Ramped entry, access to all public areas, toilet
facilities

RUSKIN SOCIETY OF LONDON

351 Woodstock Road, Oxford, OX2 7NX

Tel: 01865 310987 or 01865 515962

Enquiries:
Enquiries to: Information Officer
Other contacts: Membership Secretary

Founded:
1985

Organisation type and purpose:
International organisation, learned society
(membership is by subscription), present number
of members: 40, suitable for ages: Adults.
The society was founded to promote interest in all
aspects of John Ruskin.

Subject coverage:
Connections or queries about John Ruskin and
19th-century art.

Library catalogue:
All or part available in print

Printed publications:
Ruskin Recalled (published by Ivy Books, £32)
The Ruskin Gazette VI Nos 1 to 12 (annually, free
to members, £13.50 to non-members)
Order printed publications from: Ivy Books, 35
Woodstock Road, Oxford, OX2 7NX

Publications list:
Available in print

Access to staff:
Contact by letter and by telephone. Appointment
necessary.
Hours: Mon to Fri, 0900 to 1700
Special comments: All functions of the society are
held in London.

Affiliated to other literary societies such as:
The British-Italian Society
The Royal Society of Literature

RUSSIAN ORTHODOX CHURCH IN GREAT BRITAIN AND IRELAND, DIOCESE OF SOUROZH

Formal name: Russian Orthodox Patriarchal Church
in Great Britain and Ireland, Diocese of Sourozh

continued overleaf

Cathedral of the Dormition and All Saints, 67
Ennismore Gardens, London, SW7 1NH

Tel: 020 7584 0096
Fax: 020 7584 9864
E-mail: sourozh@mail.ru

Website:
http://www.sourozh.org

Enquiries:
Enquiries to: Diocesan Secretary

Founded:
1962

Organisation type and purpose:
To administer to the Russian Orthodox community
in Great Britain and Ireland. Diocese within the
Russian Orthodox Patriarchate of Moscow.
Registered charity (charity number 254025).

Subject coverage:
Russian Orthodoxy in Great Britain and Ireland.

Access to staff:
Contact by letter and by e-mail

Parent body:
Russian Orthodox Patriarchate of Moscow
website: http://www.mospat.ru

RUSSO-BRITISH CHAMBER OF COMMERCE

Acronym or abbreviation: RBCC

42 Southwark Street, London, SE1 1UN

Tel: 020 7403 1706
Fax: 020 7403 1245
E-mail: office.manager@rbcc.co.uk

Website:
http://www.rbcc.co.uk

Enquiries:
Enquiries to: Office Manager
Direct e-mail: office.manager@rbcc.co.uk

Founded:
1916

Organisation type and purpose:
To facilitate trade between Britain and Russia,
through publications, in-depth regional and
company profiles, exhibitions, conferences and
business advice.

Printed publications:
Newsletter (monthly)

Access to staff:
Contact by letter, by telephone, by fax, by e-mail
and via website

RUTHERFORD APPLETON LABORATORY (STFC)

Chilton, Didcot, Oxfordshire, OX11 0QX

Tel: 01235 445384
Fax: 01235 446403
E-mail: library@rl.ac.uk

Website:
http://www.e-science.stfc.ac.uk/services/library

Organisation type and purpose:
National government body, research organisation.
Formed by Royal Charter in 2007, the Science and
Technology Facilities Council is one of Europe's
largest multidisciplinary research organisations
supporting scientists and engineers world-wide.

Subject coverage:
Elementary particles; computers; lasers; neutron
studies; astrophysics; space research; advanced
engineering; data collection and transmission;
satellites; radio communications; information
technology.

**Museum or gallery collection, archive, or library
special collection:**
ESA reports (UK national repository)

Non-library collection catalogue:
All or part available online

Library catalogue:
All or part available online

Access to staff:
Contact by e-mail. Appointment necessary.
Hours: Mon to Fri, 1000 to 1600

Constituent part of:
Science and Technology Facilities Council (STFC)
website: http://www.scitech.ac.uk/Home.aspx

RUTLAND COUNTY LIBRARY

Catmos Street, Oakham, Rutland, LE15 6HW

Tel: 01572 722918
Fax: 01572 724906
E-mail: libraries@rutland.gov.uk

Website:
http://www.rutland.gov.uk/libraries

Enquiries:
Enquiries to: Librarian

Organisation type and purpose:
Public library.

Subject coverage:
General.

Non-library collection catalogue:
All or part available online

Library catalogue:
All or part available online

Access to staff:
Contact by letter, by telephone, by fax, by e-mail,
in person and via website. Appointment necessary.
Hours: Mon, Wed, Fri, 0900 to 1900; Tue, 0900 to
1700; Thu, 0900 to 1700; Sat, 0900 to 1600

RUTLAND LOCAL HISTORY & RECORD SOCIETY

Acronym or abbreviation: RLHRS

Rutland County Museum, Catmose Street,
Oakham, Rutland, LE15 6HW

Tel: 01572 758440
Fax: 01572 758445
E-mail: enquiries@rutlandhistory.org

Website:
http://www.rutlandhistory.org
Basic details, activities and publication list.

Enquiries:
Enquiries to: Honorary Secretary
Direct tel: via 01572 758440
Direct e-mail: enquiries@rutlandhistory.org

Founded:
1979

Formed from:
Rutland Local History Society, Rutland Record
Society (year of change 1991); Rutland Field
Research Group for Archaeology & History (year
of change 1993)

Organisation type and purpose:
Membership association (membership is by
subscription), registered charity (charity number
700273).
All aspects of the history of the County of Rutland
and the immediate area.

Subject coverage:
History and archaeology of Rutland

Printed publications:
Rutland Record 1–24, Index of nos 1–10
The Oakham Survey 1305 (ed Chinnery A, 1988)
The Rutland Hearth Tax 1665 (ed Bourn J and
Goode A, 1991)
The History of the Hospital of St John the
Evangelist & St Anne in Oakham (Parkin D,
2000)
The 1712 Land Tax Assessments and the 1710 Poll
Book for Rutland (ed Clough, T H McK, 2005)

Common Right and Private Interest: Rutland's
Common Fields and their Enclosure (Ryder I E,
2006)
Tudor Rutland: The County Community under
Henry VIII (ed Cornwall J, 1980)
The Weather Journals of a Rutland Squire –
Thomas Barker's 18th century weather, farming
and countryside records (ed Kington J, 1988)
Stained Glass in Rutland Churches (Sharpling P,
1997)
Time in Rutland: a history and gazetteer of the
bells, scratch dials, sundials and clocks of
Rutland (Ovens R, & Sleath S, 2002)

Publications list:
Available online and in print

Access to staff:
Contact by letter, by telephone, by fax and by e-
mail. Appointment necessary.

Links with:
Rutland County Museum
at the same address

RWE NPOWER PLC

Windmill Hill Business Park, Whitehill Way,
Swindon, Wiltshire, SN5 6PB

Tel: 01793 892565
Fax: 01793 892001

Website:
http://www.rwenpower.com
Company information and news, financial results,
direct sales information.

Enquiries:
Enquiries to: Administrator
Direct e-mail: suzanne.vines@rwenpower.com

Founded:
1990

Organisation type and purpose:
Manufacturing industry, research organisation.
Electricity generation.

Subject coverage:
Power generation (thermal), electrical engineering,
energy, environment, management, fuels.

**Museum or gallery collection, archive, or library
special collection:**
Historical publications on the history of electricity
supply in UK
Reports of former CERL, MEL and BNL
(microform)

Non-library collection catalogue:
All or part available in-house

Library catalogue:
All or part available in-house

Printed publications:
Research Reports

Access to staff:
Contact by letter, by telephone, by fax and by e-
mail. Appointment necessary.
Hours: Mon to Thu, 0830 to 1700; Fri, 0830 to 1600
Special comments: Access is discretionary,
depending on nature of enquiry and other
commitments.

RYEDALE DISTRICT COUNCIL

Acronym or abbreviation: RDC

Ryedale House, Malton, North Yorkshire, YO17
7HH

Tel: 01653 600666
Fax: 01653 696801
E-mail: info@ryedale.gov.uk

Website:
http://www.ryedale.gov.uk

Founded:
1974

Organisation type and purpose:
Local government body.

Subject coverage:
Local government services.

Access to staff:
Contact by letter, by telephone, by fax, by e-mail, in person and via website
Hours: Mon to Thu, 0830 to 1700; Fri, 0830 to 1630

SACKLER LIBRARY

1 St John Street, Oxford, OX1 2LG

Tel: 01865 278088 (enquiries and administration)
Fax: 01865 278098
E-mail: james.legg@saclib.ox.ac.uk

Website:
http://www.saclib.ox.ac.uk
Opening hours, subject coverage, catalogues, special collections.

Enquiries:
Enquiries to: Administrator
Direct e-mail: helen.edwards@ouls.ox.ac.uk
Other contacts: Librarian

Founded:
2001

Formerly called:
Ashmolean Museum Library; Ashmolean Library (year of change 1901–2001)

Organisation type and purpose:
University department or institute.

Subject coverage:
Egyptology; Assyriological and Hittite studies; Altertumswissenschaft; papyrology; numismatics; dies and medals; Western art and architecture; Near Eastern classical and European archaeology; Greek and Latin literature; Byzantine studies; patristics.

Library catalogue:
All or part available online

Access to staff:
Contact by letter, by fax and by e-mail. Letter of introduction required.
Hours: Mon to Fri, 0900 to 2200; Sat, 1000 to 1700

Access for disabled people:
Level entry, toilet facilities, lift

Includes the:
Griffith Institute Library of Egyptology
 tel: 01865 288198 or 278089; e-mail: diane
 .bergman@saclib.ox.co.uk
Heberden Coin Room Library
 tel: as main library; e-mail: diane.bergman@
 saclib.ox.ac.uk
Main Library
 tel: 01865 278092; e-mail: jane.bruder@saclib.ox
 .co.uk
Western Art Library
 tel: 01865 278093/4

SACRO

Formal name: Safeguarding Communities – Reducing Offending

1 Broughton Street, Edinburgh, EH3 6NU

Tel: 0131 624 7270
Fax: 0131 624 7269
E-mail: info@national.sacro.org.uk

Website:
http://www.sacro.org.uk

Founded:
1971

Formerly called:
Scottish Association for the Care and Resettlement of Offenders (SACRO) (year of change 1992); SACRO (year of change 1998)

Organisation type and purpose:
Membership association, present number of members: 50+ full members, 2,204 associate members, voluntary organisation (charity number SCO 16293).

To provide advice, assistance and support to people in conflict, and particularly those in trouble with the law, those at risk of becoming so, and their families, by direct services provided at local level.

Subject coverage:
Criminal justice in Scotland, offenders, mediation, supported accommodation for offenders, alcohol education for probationers, intensive probation programmes, families of offenders, volunteer support, dispute resolution, community mediation, restorative justice.

Printed publications:
See website for list of available publications.
Order printed publications from: Communications Officer

Publications list:
Available online and in print

Access to staff:
Contact by letter, by telephone, by fax, by e-mail and via website. Appointment necessary.
Hours: Mon to Fri, 0900 to 1700

Access to building, collection or gallery:
No prior appointment required
Special comments: Non-catalogued, varied filing types; reference only

SAFETY ASSESSMENT FEDERATION

Acronym or abbreviation: SAFed

Nutmeg House, 60 Gainsford Street, London, SE1 2NY

Tel: 020 7403 0987
Fax: 020 7403 0137
E-mail: info@safed.co.uk

Enquiries:
Enquiries to: Technical Director
Other contacts: Technical Manager for detailed technical information and advice.

Founded:
1995

Formerly called:
Council of Independent Inspecting Authorities (CIIA), Independent Engineering Insurance Committee (IEIC); Associated Offices Technical Committee (AOTC) (year of change 1995)

Organisation type and purpose:
Trade association, present number of members: 8 full, 9 associate.
To represent companies engaged in independent safety inspection, testing and certification of engineering plant and equipment of all types.

Subject coverage:
Engineering inspection and design assessment for plant such as boilers, pressure vessels, lifts, cranes, electrical equipment etc, including welding; NDT techniques; export of engineering plant.

Printed publications:
Fact Sheet: Potential Hazards Created by Water Hammer in Steam Systems (set of ten, £3)
Guidelines for the Periodic Testing and Examination of Fixed Low Voltage Electrical Installations at Quarries (£25)
Lifts Guidelines on the Thorough Examination and Testing of Lifts (£100)
Shell Boilers – Guidelines for the Examination of Longitudinal Seams of Shell Boilers (£30)
Shell Boilers – Guidelines for the Examination of Shell-to-Endplate and Furnace-to-Endplate Welded Joints (£30)
The Use of Accredited Inspection Bodies (£5)
Welding Procedures and Welding Guidelines on Approval Testing (£20)

Publications list:
Available in print

Access to staff:
Contact by letter, by telephone, by fax and by e-mail
Hours: Mon to Fri, 0900 to 1700

UK member of:
Confédération Européenne d'Organismes de Prévention et de Contrôle (CEOC)

SAIL TRAINING INTERNATIONAL

Acronym or abbreviation: STI

5 Mumby Road, Gosport, Hampshire, PO12 1AA

Tel: 023 9258 6367
Fax: 023 9258 4661
E-mail: office@sailtraininginternational.org

Website:
http://www.tallshipsraces.com
http://www.sailtraininginternational.com
http://www.ista.co.uk

Enquiries:
Enquiries to: Media Publications Manager
Direct e-mail: corinne.hitching@
sailtraininginternational.org
Other contacts: Business Director

Founded:
1956

Organisation type and purpose:
International organisation.
Operating as a subsidiary of a registered charity, for the development and education of young people through sail training.
Organisers of the Tall Ships Races.

Subject coverage:
Ocean sailing, sail training, race planning, race organisation, event management, adventure activities.

Printed publications:
Tall Ships

Access to staff:
Contact by letter, by telephone, by fax and by e-mail
Hours: Mon to Fri, 0900 to 1700

Parent body:
Sail Training Association
 2A The Hard, Portsmouth, Hampshire, PO1 3PT; tel: 023 9283 2055

SAILORS' FAMILIES' SOCIETY

Newland, Cottingham Road, Hull, HU6 7RJ

Tel: 01482 342331
Fax: 01482 447868
E-mail: info@sailors-families.org.uk

Enquiries:
Enquiries to: Chief Executive

Founded:
1821

Organisation type and purpose:
Voluntary organisation.

Subject coverage:
Welfare and care of seafarers and their families. Respite care for disadvantaged children.

SAILORS' SOCIETY

Sailors' Society, 350 Shirley Road, Southampton, Hampshire, SO15 3HY

Tel: 023 8051 5950
Fax: 023 8051 5951
E-mail: admin@sailors-society.org

Website:
http://www.biss.org.uk

Enquiries:
Enquiries to: PR/Fundraising Manager
Direct tel: 023 8063 0789
Direct fax: 023 8063 1789

Founded:
1818

Organisation type and purpose:
Registered charity (charity number 237778).

continued overleaf

International Christian charity working amongst seafarers, particularly merchant seamen.

Subject coverage:
Welfare of seafarers.

Museum or gallery collection, archive, or library special collection:
Bound copies of past magazines of Society going back to early 19th century when the Society was founded

Printed publications:
Annual Review (free)
Chart & Compass (annually, free)
Quayways; Magazine of Chaplain's Department (annually, free)

Access to staff:
Contact by letter, by telephone, by fax, by e-mail and in person. Appointment necessary.
Hours: Mon to Fri, 0900 to 1700

Member of:
International Christian Maritime Association
Merchant Navy Welfare Board

Sister societies in:
Canada, New Zealand, South Africa, Ghana and Belgium

SAINT-GOBAIN GYPSUM

GTC – Information Centre, Gypsum Technical Building, East Leake, Loughborough, Leicestershire, LE12 6JS

Tel: 0115 945 1652
Fax: 0115 945 1678
E-mail: liz.redfern@saint-gobain.com

Enquiries:
Enquiries to: Head of Information Services

Organisation type and purpose:
Manufacturing industry.

Subject coverage:
Gypsum and plaster technology

Non-library collection catalogue:
All or part available in-house

Library catalogue:
All or part available in-house

Access to staff:
Contact by letter, by telephone, by fax, by e-mail and in person
Hours: Mon to Fri, 0900 to 1630

Access to building, collection or gallery:
No access other than to staff, no prior appointment required

Parent body:
Compagnie de Saint-Gobain
Les Miroirs, 18 avenue d'Alsace, 92096 La Defense, Paris, France

SAINT-GOBAIN QUARTZ LTD

PO Box 6, Neptune Road, Wallsend, Tyne and Wear, NE28 6DG

Tel: 0191 262 5311
Fax: 0191 263 8040
E-mail: quartz.sales@saint-gobain.com

Website:
http://www.quartz.saint-gobain.com

Enquiries:
Enquiries to: Sales Manager
Direct tel: 0191 259 8315

Founded:
1906

Formerly called:
TSL Group PLC; TSL Thermal Syndicate PLC; Thermal Syndicate Ltd.

Organisation type and purpose:
Manufacturing industry.

Subject coverage:
Transparent and opaque fused quartz, synthetic transparent, translucent fused silica, ingot, plate, rod tube and machined components for fibre optics, semiconductors, heating and lighting, optical aerospace, foundry, chemical, laboratory and refractory industries.

Non-library collection catalogue:
All or part available online

Printed publications:
Catalogues, brochures, datasheets

Publications list:
Available online

Access to staff:
Contact by letter, by telephone, by fax, by e-mail and via website. Appointment necessary.
Hours: Mon to Thu, 0800 to 1615; Fri, 0800 to 1400

Access to building, collection or gallery:
No access other than to staff

SAINTPAULIA AND HOUSEPLANT SOCIETY

33 Church Road, Newbury Park, Ilford, Essex, IG2 7ET

Tel: 020 8590 3710

Enquiries:
Enquiries to: Honorary Secretary

Founded:
1956

Organisation type and purpose:
International organisation, membership association (membership is by qualification).

Subject coverage:
Houseplants, especially saintpaulias; interests of the small or amateur grower in the home.

Library catalogue:
All or part available in-house

Printed publications:
Bulletin (quarterly)
The following leaflets are available from the Secretary at 20p each. Please pay with stamps and enclose an sae
Artificial Light for Houseplants
Begonias
Gesneriads (2 leaflets)
How to Care for Your Pot Plants
Indoor Ferns
Philodendrons and their Relatives
Propagation in the Home
Saintpaulias (African violets) in the Home
Streptocarpus (Cape Primrose)
Tradescantias and their Relatives

Access to staff:
Contact by letter and by telephone
Hours: Mon to Fri, 0900 to 1700

Affiliated to:
African Violet Society of America
American Gloxinia and Gesneriad Society
Gesneriad Society International
Royal Horticultural Society

SALFORD CITY LIBRARIES

Minerva House, Pendlebury Road, Swinton, Manchester, M27 4EQ

Tel: 0161 778 0123
Fax: 0161 728 6145
E-mail: robin.culpin@salford.gov.uk

Enquiries:
Enquiries to: Librarian

Founded:
1974

Organisation type and purpose:
Local government body, public library.

Subject coverage:
General, local history, working class movement, labour movement, James Nasmyth (the engineer).

Museum or gallery collection, archive, or library special collection:
Boothstown Horticultural and Botanical Collection (18th century material)
Cowan Collection (theology, 17th century)
Davies Collection (theology, history and literature and political pamphlets of 17th-19th centuries)
Photography Collection
Trinity Collection (theology, 17th-19th centuries)
Working Class Movement Library, banners, pottery and medallions
Workshops Manuals Collection

Printed publications:
Information leaflets on local topics with bibliographies
Various local history publications at various prices

Access to staff:
Contact by letter, by telephone, by fax, by e-mail, in person and via website. Appointment necessary.
Hours: Mon to Fri, 0900 to 1700

Comprises the:
17 libraries of the City of Salford, Eccles, Irlam, Swinton and Worsley

SALFORD LOCAL HISTORY LIBRARY

Peel Park Avenue, Salford, Greater Manchester, M5 4WU

Tel: 0161 736 2649
Fax: 0161 745 9490
E-mail: salford.museum@salford.gov.uk

Website:
http://www.lifetimes.org.uk
Information on social and local history library

Enquiries:
Enquiries to: Librarian

Organisation type and purpose:
Local government body, public library, suitable for ages: 12+.

Subject coverage:
Local history including census returns, parish registers, documents, maps, and photographs chronicling the history of Salford City.

Access to staff:
Contact by letter, by telephone, by fax, by e-mail and in person
Hours: Mon to Fri, 0900 to 1700

Access to building, collection or gallery:
No prior appointment required
Hours: Mon to Fri, 1000 to 1700

Parent body:
Salford Museums Heritage Service
at same address

SALFORD TOURIST INFORMATION CENTRE

Acronym or abbreviation: Salford TIC

1 The Quays, Salford, Greater Manchester, M50 3SQ

Tel: 0161 848 8601
Fax: 0161 872 3848
E-mail: tic@salford.gov.uk

Website:
http://www.visitsalford.info

Enquiries:
Enquiries to: Manager

Founded:
2000

Organisation type and purpose:
Local government body.

Subject coverage:
Tourist information. Local information, leaflets, Greater Manchester, arts, theatre, small souvenir shop, local history books, maps, postcards, videos, souvenirs, accommodation bookings, boat trips.

Special visitor services:
Free access to tourism websites.

Services for disabled people:
Hearing loop at desk, easy access for wheel chair users, front desk and internet desk correct height for wheelchair users.

Printed publications:
Many books and videos on local history including:
Manchester, This Good Old Town (£6)
Mersey Ferry Guide (£1.99)
My Kind of People (Wadlon M, £2)
My Salford (Armstrong A, £4.95)
Recollections of Salford (£5.95)
free self guided walks leaflets

Electronic and video publications:
Bygone Manchester (video)
Bygone Salford (video)
Manchester Ship Canal Vols 1 and 2 (video)

Publications list:
Available in print

Access to staff:
Contact by letter, by telephone, by fax, by e-mail, in person and via website
Hours: Tue to Fri 1000 to 1715; Sat 1000 to 1600; Sun and Bank Holidays 1100 to 1700; closed Mon

Access for disabled people:
Parking provided, level entry, access to all public areas
Special comments: No disabled toilet facilities inside TIC but available in The Lowry

Administered by:
Salford City Council

SALISBURY & DISTRICT COUNCIL FOR VOLUNTARY SERVICE

Acronym or abbreviation: Salisbury CVS

42 Salt Lane, Salisbury, Wiltshire, SP1 1EG

Tel: 01722 421747
Fax: 01722 415544
E-mail: salisbury.cvs@ruralnet.org.uk

Enquiries:
Enquiries to: Chief Executive

Founded:
1973

Organisation type and purpose:
Registered charity (charity number 1019716). Local development agency for community and voluntary activity.

Access to staff:
Contact by e-mail
Hours: Mon to Fri, 0930 to 1630

Access to building, collection or gallery:
Prior appointment required

Access for disabled people:
Ramped entry, toilet facilities

Connected with:
National Association of Councils for Voluntary Service (NACVS)

SALISBURY COLLEGE

The Learning Resources Centre, Southampton Road, Salisbury, Wiltshire, SP1 2LW

Tel: 01722 344325/344243\ Minicom no. 01722 344307
Fax: 01722 344345
E-mail: library@salisbury.ac.uk

Website:
http://www.salisbury.ac.uk

Enquiries:
Enquiries to: Learning Resources Coordinator
Direct e-mail: janet.beauchamp@salisbury.ac.uk
Other contacts: Library Learning Assistants for general enquiries regarding bookstock and loans.

Organisation type and purpose:
Suitable for ages: 16+.
College Learning Resources Centre.

Subject coverage:
Computing and administration, management studies, basic and key skills, built environment, foundation studies, technology and science, information technology, performing arts, humanities, social sciences, fashion, art and design, graphics, film, TV and media, health and social care, food and hospitality, tourism, leisure and recreation, construction crafts, hairdressing, beauty therapy, business studies, teacher education.

Non-library collection catalogue:
All or part available online and in-house

Library catalogue:
All or part available online and in-house

Access to staff:
Contact by letter, by telephone, by fax, by e-mail, in person and via website. Appointment necessary. Non-members charged.
Hours: Mon, 8.30–5.30; Tue to Thu, 0830 to 1945; Fri, 1000 to 1615;

Access for disabled people:
Parking provided, access to all public areas, toilet facilities

SALMONS TICKFORD REGISTER

Acronym or abbreviation: STR

24 Woodland Rise West, Sheringham, Norfolk, NR26 8PF

Tel: 01263 824045
E-mail: mynard.revarg@tiscali.co.uk

Enquiries:
Enquiries to: Secretary and Registrar
Direct e-mail: mynard@telinco.co.uk

Founded:
1998

Organisation type and purpose:
Membership association.
No charge for membership.
To provide information on Salmons and Tickford bodied motor cars.

Subject coverage:
Salmons and Tickford bodied cars.

Museum or gallery collection, archive, or library special collection:
Collection of photographs of Salmons/Tickford cars, printed brochures, original manuscripts etc

Non-library collection catalogue:
All or part available in-house and in print

Printed publications:
Register of surviving cars
Salmons and Sons the Tickford Coachbuilders
Order printed publications from:
mynard.revarg@tiscali.co.uk

Publications list:
Available in print

Access to staff:
Contact by letter, by telephone, by e-mail and in person. Appointment necessary. Letter of introduction required.
Hours: Sun to Sat, 0900 to 2100

SALTERS' CHEMISTRY CLUB, THE

Salters' Hall, 4 Fore Street, London, EC2Y 5DE

Tel: 020 7628 5962
Fax: 020 7638 3679
E-mail: club@salters.co.uk

Website:
http://www.salters.co.uk

Enquiries:
Enquiries to: Administrator

Founded:
1991

Organisation type and purpose:
Voluntary organisation, registered charity.

Subject coverage:
Promotion of chemistry in schools by establishing school-based chemistry clubs.

Printed publications:
Newsletter

Access to staff:
Contact by letter, by telephone, by fax and by e-mail
Hours: Mon to Fri, 0900 to 1700

Parent body:
The Salters' Institute
 tel: 020 7628 5962; fax: 020 7638 3679; e-mail: institute@salters.co.uk

SALTERS' COMPANY

Formal name: The Worshipful Company of Salters

Salters' Hall, 4 Fore Street, London, EC2Y 5DE

Tel: 020 7588 5216
Fax: 020 7638 3679
E-mail: clerk@salters.co.uk

Website:
http://www.salters.co.uk

Enquiries:
Enquiries to: Clerk

Founded:
1394

Organisation type and purpose:
Membership association, present number of members: 195. A livery company of the City of London with charitable interests.

Subject coverage:
Promoting careers in chemistry and the chemical industries through its flagship charity The Salters' Institute.

Access to staff:
Contact by letter, by telephone, by fax and by e-mail. Appointment necessary. Access for members only.
Hours: Mon to Fri, 0900 to 1700

Access for disabled people:
Toilet facilities

Also at the same address:
Salters' Chemistry Camps
Salters' Chemistry Club
Salters' Institute
The Charities of Nicholas & Beamond
The James' Smiths' Alms House Charity
The Salters' Charities
The Salters' Charity for the Relief of Need

An investment subsidiary at the same address:
The Salters' Management Company Limited

SALTERS' INSTITUTE

Salters' Hall, 4 Fore Street, London, EC2Y 5DE

Tel: 020 7628 5962
Fax: 020 7638 3679
E-mail: institute@salters.co.uk

Website:
http://www.salters.co.uk

Enquiries:
Enquiries to: Institute Manager

Founded:
1918

Formerly called:
Salters' Institute of Industrial Chemistry

continued overleaf

Organisation type and purpose:
Membership association, registered charity.

Subject coverage:
Award of Salters' Prizes to final year undergraduates in chemistry or chemical engineering; to Salters' A level chemistry candidates; limited information on research subjects undertaken by Salters Fellows and Scholars; grants for school chemistry libraries and chemistry equipment; no other help given at undergraduate level.

Access to staff:
Contact by letter, by telephone, by fax and by e-mail
Hours: Mon to Fri, 0900 to 1700

Parent body:
The Salters' Company
  tel: 020 7588 5216; fax: 020 7638 3679

SALVAGE ASSOCIATION

Acronym or abbreviation: SA

4th Floor, Holland House, 1–4 Bury Street, London, EC3A 5AW

Tel: 0207 648 9650
Fax: 0207 929 5564
E-mail: enquiries@bmtmarinerisk.com

Website:
http://www.wreckage.org
Publications including International Directory.

Enquiries:
Enquiries to: Director, Business Development
Direct tel: 020 7648 9652
Other contacts: Chief Executive; Managing Director

Founded:
1856

Organisation type and purpose:
International organisation, professional body, membership association (membership is by election or invitation), service industry, consultancy.
Marine survey and risk management.
From offices around the world, the SA's surveyors, marine engineers and master mariners are on call; being involved in loss prevention and pre-risk assessment, they travel constantly to ships that are in trouble.

Subject coverage:
Marine surveying and consultancy, insurance loss prevention, marine damage assessment, marine casualty investigation.

Printed publications:
Salvage Lines (newsletter quarterly)

Access to staff:
Contact by letter, by telephone, by fax, by e-mail and via website
Hours: Mon to Fri, 0900 to 1730

Has:
offices worldwide

Other address:
The Salvage Association
  Axe & Bottle Court, 70 Newcomen Street, London, SE1 1YT; tel: 020 7234 9120; fax: 020 7234 9168/9169; e-mail: salvage@wreckage.org

Parent body:
British Maritime Technology Limited (BMT)
  Orlando House, 1 Waldegrave Road, Teddington, TW11 8LZ; tel: 020 8943 5544; fax: 020 8943 5347; e-mail: enquiries@bmtmail.com

SALVATION ARMY

United Kingdom Territory, Territorial Headquarters, 101 Newington Causeway, London, SE1 6BN

Tel: 020 7367 4500
Fax: 020 7367 4728
E-mail: thq@salvationarmy.org.uk

Website:
http://www.salvationarmy.org.uk

Enquiries:
Enquiries to: Press Officer
Direct e-mail: sarah.miller@salvationarmy.org.uk
Other contacts. Media contacts, Media and Press Officer tel no: 020 7367 4700

Founded:
1865

Organisation type and purpose:
Voluntary organisation.
Part of the worldwide Christian church, providing social welfare in 108 countries.

Subject coverage:
Evangelism; health; social welfare; housing; education; prison welfare; agriculture; emergency aid; refugees; child care; handicapped ministries; leprosaria; care of the aged; community aid; agricultural development; family tracing; feeding programmes; educational programmes.

Museum or gallery collection, archive, or library special collection:
Historical information and archive material at The Heritage Centre, tel: 0171 387 1656

Printed publications:
146 Publications Worldwide, in the UK:
The Salvationist
The War Cry
Kids Alive Children's newspaper

Electronic and video publications:
Videos re work of Army from audio-visual department, HQ

Access to staff:
Contact by letter, by telephone and by fax. Appointment necessary.
Hours: Mon to Fri, 0815 to 1630
Special comments: No personal callers without prior appointment.

SALVATION ARMY FAMILY TRACING SERVICE

101 Newington Causeway, King's Cross, London, SE1 6BN

Tel: 020 7367 4747
E-mail: family.tracing@salvationarmy.org.uk

Website:
http://www.salvationarmy.org.uk/familytracing

Enquiries:
Enquiries to: Director

Founded:
1885

Formerly called:
Salvation Army Investigation Department

Organisation type and purpose:
International organisation, registered charity, voluntary organisation.
A service for endeavouring to trace members of family with whom contact has been lost for some reason, whether recently or in the distant past, for reconciliation purposes only.
Adoption searches are not accepted.

Subject coverage:
Tracing missing relatives for the purposes of reconciliation only; counselling for this need (enquiries for friends, adoption, estate, divorce, family tree or business reasons are NOT accepted).

Printed publications:
Annual Review and Statistics
Information leaflets and brochures

Access to staff:
Contact by letter and by telephone. All charged.
Hours: Mon to Fri, 0830 to 1545
Special comments: Enclose an sae for a reply.

Parent body:
Salvation Army THQ
  101 Newington Causeway, London, SE1 6BN

SAMARITANS

The Upper Mill, Kingston Road, Ewell, Surrey, KT17 2AF

Tel: 020 8394 8300
Fax: 020 8394 8301
E-mail: admin@samaritans.org

Website:
http://www.samaritans.org.uk

Founded:
1953

Organisation type and purpose:
Voluntary organisation, registered charity (charity number 219432). Samaritans is available 24 hours a day to provide confidential emotional support for people who are experiencing feelings of distress or despair, including those which may lead to suicide

Subject coverage:
Suicide and emotional support

Museum or gallery collection, archive, or library special collection:
Books and leaflets on related subjects
Small collection of books on suicide, parasuicide (epidemiology, prevention, intervention)

Trade and statistical information:
Suicide statistics – national and international.

Printed publications:
Annual Report
General Information leaflet (free)
Suicide figures (annually, free)

Access to staff:
Contact by letter, by telephone, by e-mail, in person and via website
Hours: Mon to Fri, 0900 to 1700 (admin only). 24-hour access to volunteers
Special comments: Confidential emotional support by phone: 08457 908090; by e-mail: jo@samaritans.org; by letter: Chris, PO Box 90 90, Stirling, FK8 2SA

Access to building, collection or gallery:
For individual branches, see website

Access for disabled people:
Please see website

SAMB

Formal name: Scottish Association of Master Bakers
Acronym or abbreviation: SAMB

4 Torpichen Street, Edinburgh, EH3 8JQ

Tel: 0131 229 1401
Fax: 0131 229 8239
E-mail: master.bakers@samb.co.uk

Enquiries:
Enquiries to: Chief Executive

Founded:
1891

Organisation type and purpose:
Trade association (membership is by subscription).

Subject coverage:
The baking industry.

Printed publications:
Year Book (£128)

Access to staff:
Contact by letter
Hours: Mon to Fri, 0900 to 1700

SANDWELL AND WEST BIRMINGHAM HOSPITALS NHS TRUST

Acronym or abbreviation: SWBH

Clinical Library, Sandwell General Hospital, Lyndon, West Bromwich, West Midlands, B71 4HJ

Tel: 0121 507 3587 ext. 3587
Fax: 0121 507 3586
E-mail: clinical.library@swbh.nhs.uk

Enquiries:
Enquiries to: Librarian

Formerly called:
Sandwell General Hospital

Organisation type and purpose:
Hospital.

Subject coverage:
Medicine.

Library catalogue:
All or part available in-house

Access to staff:
Contact by letter, by telephone, by fax and by e-mail
Hours: Mon to Fri, 0830 to 1700

Also at:
Sandwell and West Birmingham Hospitals NHS Trust
    Bevan Library, City Hospital, Dudley Road, Winson Green, Birmingham B18 4HQ; tel: 0121 507 5245; e-mail: bevan.library@swbh.nhs.uk

SANDWELL COLLEGE

Learning Centre, Wednesbury Campus, Woden Road South, Wednesbury, West Midlands, WS10 0PE

Tel: 0121 556 6000, from 0800 to 2000; 505 6000, any other time
Fax: 0121 253 6069

Website:
http://www.sandwell.ac.uk
College web page.

Enquiries:
Enquiries to: Learning Centre Manager (for each campus)
Direct tel: ext 6615

Founded:
1986

Formerly called:
Warley College, West Bromwich College

Includes the former:
Warley College

Organisation type and purpose:
College of further and higher education.
Headquarters for the 3 sites of the college:
Wednesbury, West Bromwich and Smethwick.

Subject coverage:
Foundry technology; metallurgy; welding; marketing; business economics; management; motor vehicle technology; production and mechanical engineering; photography (the College lists over 130 subjects, but excludes agriculture).

Museum or gallery collection, archive, or library special collection:
Diecasting Society Library
Library of the National Foundry College

Non-library collection catalogue:
All or part available in-house

Access to staff:
Contact by letter, by telephone and in person
Hours: Mon to Thu, 0830 to 2000; Fri, 1000 to 1500
Special comments: Reference only, no loans.

Access for disabled people:
Ramped entry, access to all public areas, toilet facilities

Also at:
Smethwick Campus
    Crochelts Lane, Smethwick, West Midlands
West Bromwich Campus
    High Street, West Bromwich, West Midlands

SANDWELL COMMUNITY HISTORY AND ARCHIVES SERVICE

Acronym or abbreviation: CHAS

Smethwick Library, High Street, Smethwick, West Midlands, B66 1AA

Tel: 0121 558 2561
Fax: 0121 555 6064
E-mail: archives.service@sandwell.gov.uk

Website:
http://www.archives.sandwell.gov.uk

Founded:
1988

Organisation type and purpose:
Local government body, record office.

Subject coverage:
Local history of area now covered by Metropolitan Borough of Sandwell.

Museum or gallery collection, archive, or library special collection:
Records of churches, schools, organisations, businesses, families and individuals within Sandwell Metropolitan Borough. Notable collections include:
Public records, e.g. magistrates' court, quarter sessions court, coroner's court, hospitals and health authority
Business records, including Patent Shaft Steelworks of Wednesbury, T. W. Camm, Stained Glass Manufacturer of Smethwick, Chance Bros Ltd of Smethwick
Records of the Deanery of Warley and its churches
Records of the Boroughs of Oldbury, Rowley Regis, Smethwick, Tipton, Warley, Wednesbury and West Bromwich

Non-library collection catalogue:
All or part available online and in-house

Library catalogue:
All or part available online

Access to staff:
Contact by letter, by telephone, by fax, by e-mail, in person and via website. Appointment necessary.
Hours: Mon, Wed, Fri, 1000 to 1800; Tue, 1030 to 1800; Thu, closed; Sat, 0930 to 1600

Access for disabled people:
Level entry, access to all public areas

Parent body:
Sandwell Metropolitan Borough Council
    Council House, Oldbury, Warley

SANDWELL METROPOLITAN BOROUGH COUNCIL

Sandwell Information Service, Sandwell Central Library, High Street, West Bromwich, West Midlands, B70 8DZ

Tel: 0121 569 4911
Fax: 0121 525 9465
E-mail: information.service@sandwell.gov.uk

Website:
http://www.libraries.sandwell.gov.uk

Enquiries:
Enquiries to: Information Librarian
Other contacts: Information Manager for all information services.

Organisation type and purpose:
Local government body, public library.

Subject coverage:
General; local history, business, European, local council and community.

Non-library collection catalogue:
All or part available in-house

Library catalogue:
All or part available online and in-house

Access to staff:
Contact by letter, by telephone, by fax, by e-mail, in person and via website
Hours: Mon, Fri, 0930 to 1900; Tue, 0930 to 1800; Wed, 1030 to 1800; Thu, 0930 to 1300; Sat, 0900 to 1600

Access for disabled people:
Level entry

SANE

Formal name: Schizophrenia – A National Emergency
Acronym or abbreviation: SANE

1st Floor, Cityside House, 40 Adler Street, London, E1 1EE

Tel: 020 7375 1002
Fax: 020 7375 2162
E-mail: info@sane.org.uk

Website:
http://www.sane.org.uk
What is SANE? (background information on the charity and its aims), what is SANELINE? Research carried out by SANE, supporting SANE and how to make donations.

Enquiries:
Enquiries to: Communications Officer
Direct tel: 020 7422 5557
Direct e-mail: info@saneline.org
Other contacts: Press Officer

Founded:
1986

Organisation type and purpose:
National organisation, voluntary organisation, registered charity (charity number 296572), training organisation, research organisation.
SANE campaigns to combat the prejudice and intolerance surrounding mental illness, and improve attitudes and services for individuals coping with mental health problems and their families.
SANELINE is a national mental health helpline providing information and support for people with mental health problems and those who support them.

Subject coverage:
Greater public awareness of all mental health problems.

Printed publications:
Alcohol, Drugs and Mental Illness
Anxiety Phobia and Depression
Community Care and Schizophrenia: The Need for Social Research
Depression and Manic Depression
Medical Methods of Treatment
Psychological Methods of Treatment
Schizophrenia: The Forgotten Illness
Schizophrenia92: Catch 22 (Wallace M)
The Forgotten Illness I, II & III
Understanding Clozapine Treatment

Publications list:
Available online and in print

Access to staff:
Contact by letter, by telephone, by fax and by e-mail. Appointment necessary.
Hours: Mon to Fri, 0900 to 1700
Special comments: SANELINE (helpline), 1300 to 2300 every day.

Access to building, collection or gallery:
Prior appointment required

Access for disabled people:
Parking provided

Has one satellite:
Prince of Wales Research Centre (POWIC), Oxford

SANGAT ADVICE CENTRE

Sancroft Road, Harrow, HA3 7NS

Tel: 020 8427 0659
Fax: 020 8863 2196
E-mail: info@sangat.org.uk

Website:
http://www.asiansinharrow.org

Founded:
1997

continued overleaf

Organisation type and purpose:
A not-for-profit company limited by guarantee, providing the local Asian community with advice and advocacy in such matters as legal rights, housing, debt, welfare benefits, immigration and discrimination.

Access to building, collection or gallery:
Hours: Mon to Fri, 0900 to 1700

Access for disabled people:
Accessible for people with mobility problems

SARUM COLLEGE LIBRARY

19 The Close, Salisbury, Wiltshire, SP1 2EE

Tel: 01722 424803
Fax: 01722 338508
E-mail: library@sarum.ac.uk

Website:
http://www.sarum.ac.uk then click Library
Includes library catalogue

Enquiries:
Enquiries to: Librarian
Other contacts: Bookshop Supervisor (tel. 01722 326899)

Founded:
1860

Formerly called:
Salisbury and Wells Theological College Library

Organisation type and purpose:
Registered charity (charity number 309501). Ecumenical centre for theological education, subscription library.

Subject coverage:
Theology, church history, spirituality, biblical studies

Museum or gallery collection, archive, or library special collection:
Bishop Hamilton's Library
19th-century theology, including the Markham Bequest of 276 bound vols of pamphlets
Sowter Clerical Library, some 12,000 vols including local history
Some 6,000 books of historical theology (17th–19th centuries)
Christian Socialist Archive supported by the Christian Socialist Movement
Jubilee Trust Archive
Michael Vasey papers
Tom Baker papers

Non-library collection catalogue:
All or part available online

Library catalogue:
All or part available online and in-house

Printed publications:
Guide to Library Services

Access to staff:
Contact by letter, by telephone, by fax, by e-mail and via website. Appointment necessary. All charged.
Hours: Mon to Fri, 0900 to 1700

SAVE BRITAIN'S HERITAGE

Acronym or abbreviation: SAVE

70 Cowcross Street, London, EC1M 6EJ

Tel: 020 7253 3500
Fax: 020 7253 3400
E-mail: save@btinternet.com

Website:
http://www.savebritainsheritage.org
Information on the organisation, publications, news, database of buildings at risk.

Enquiries:
Enquiries to: Secretary

Founded:
1975

Organisation type and purpose:
National organisation, membership association, present number of members: 800, voluntary organisation, registered charity (charity number 269129), research organisation, publishing house. Charitable trust supported by Friends.
Campaign group for historic buildings threatened by neglect or demolition.

Subject coverage:
Demolished, threatened or neglected historic buildings; new uses for old buildings and conversions.

Publications list:
Available online and in print

SCARBOROUGH BOROUGH COUNCIL

Town Hall, St Nicholas Street, Scarborough, North Yorkshire, YO11 2HG

Tel: 01723 232323
Fax: 01723 354979
E-mail: customerfirst@scarborough.gov.uk

Website:
http://www.scarborough.gov.uk
General, contact, members, economic development.

Enquiries:
Enquiries to: Office Manager
Direct tel: 01723 232570
Direct e-mail: janet.deacon@scarborough.gov.uk

Founded:
1974

Organisation type and purpose:
Local government body.

Subject coverage:
All local government services.

Access to staff:
Contact by letter, by telephone, by fax, by e-mail, in person and via website
Hours: Mon to Fri, 0830 to 1700

SCARBOROUGH LIBRARY

Formal name: Scarborough Library and Information Centre

Vernon Road, Scarborough, North Yorkshire, YO11 2NN

Tel: 0845 034 9516
Fax: 01723 353893
E-mail: scarborough.library@northyorks.gov.uk

Website:
htttp://www.northyorks.gov.uk

Founded:
1930

Organisation type and purpose:
Local government body, public library.

Subject coverage:
General, local studies relating to Scarborough, the Yorkshire coast, North York Moors, Vale of Pickering and Yorkshire Wolds.

Museum or gallery collection, archive, or library special collection:
Censuses 1841–1901
Local newspapers 1839-
GRO indexes 1837–1997

Non-library collection catalogue:
All or part available online

Library catalogue:
All or part available online

Access to staff:
Contact by letter, by telephone, by fax, by e-mail and in person
Hours: Mon, Tue, Fri, 0900 to 1800; Wed, 1000 to 1800; Thu, 0900 to 2000; Sat, 0900 to 1700; Sun, 1100 to 1600
Special comments: Closed Public Holidays.

Access for disabled people:
Ramped entry

Parent body:
North Yorkshire County Library
Grammar School Lane, Northallerton, North Yorkshire, DL6 1DF; tel: 01609 767829; fax: 01609 780793

SCHERING HEALTH CARE LIMITED

The Brow, Burgess Hill, West Sussex, RH15 9NE

Tel: 01444 232323
Fax: 01444 246613

Website:
http://www.schering.co.uk

Enquiries:
Enquiries to: Medical Information Department

Organisation type and purpose:
Pharmaceuticals manufacturer.

Subject coverage:
Medicine, especially endocrinology, diagnostic radiology, cardiovascular medicine and surgery, dermatology, neurophysiology and pharmacology, urology, obstetrics and gynaecology.

Printed publications:
Annotated Bibliographies
Patient information leaflets on acne, oral contraceptives, menopause, colposcopy, CT, MRI

Access to staff:
Contact by letter and by telephone
Hours: Mon to Fri, 0900 to 1700
Special comments: Schering Health Care Limited operates under the association of British Pharmaceutical Industry's code of practice and is unable to enter into correspondence with individual patients concerning their treatment.

SCHOOL LIBRARY ASSOCIATION

Acronym or abbreviation: SLA

Unit 2, Lotmead Business Village, Wanborough, Swindon, Wiltshire, SN4 0UY

Tel: 01793 791787
Fax: 01793 791786
E-mail: info@sla.org.uk

Website:
http://www.sla.org.uk

Enquiries:
Enquiries to: Chief Executive

Founded:
1937

Organisation type and purpose:
International organisation, advisory body, professional body (membership is by subscription), registered charity (charity number 313660 & SC039453), suitable for ages: 5 to 19, training organisation, publishing house. Branches throughout the United Kingdom
To support the development of school libraries, through advocacy, advice, training and publications.

Subject coverage:
School librarianship and information literacy, children's literature and literacy.

Printed publications:
The School Librarian (quarterly, free to members)
info@SLA (newsletter, quarterly, free to members)
Annotated booklists and practical guidelines to help those running a school library

Publications list:
Available online and in print

Access to staff:
Contact by letter, by telephone, by fax and by e-mail. Appointment necessary.
Hours: Mon to Fri, 0900 to 1700

Links with:
Cilip

Member organisation of:
IASL
IFLA

SCHOOL OF DEVELOPMENT STUDIES

Acronym or abbreviation: DEV/ODG

University of East Anglia, Norwich, Norfolk, NR4 7TJ UK

Tel: 01603 592807
Fax: 01603 451999
E-mail: dev.general@uea.ac.uk

Website:
http://www.uea.ac.uk/dev/odg/
Details of consultancy activities, research experience and training courses
http://www.uea.ac.uk/publink/intro.shtml
Publications Link – faculty publications since 1996; commercially published books, articles in academic journals, some work is available to download from the website.
http://www.uea.ac.uk/dev/
Details of School, faculty information, research, publications, courses available, application forms.

Enquiries:
Enquiries to: General Office

Founded:
1973

Organisation type and purpose:
University department or institute, suitable for ages: 18+, consultancy, research organisation. Teaching, research and consultancy in international development.

Subject coverage:
International development and related academic disciplines, including: gender and social development, literacy and development, globalisation and transition, livelihoods and well-being, natural resources and environment, Latin America, South Asia.

Printed publications:
'Development' (annual newsletter), prospectuses and brochures

Publications list:
Available online

Access to staff:
Contact by letter, by telephone, by fax, by e-mail and via website. Appointment necessary.
Hours: Mon to Fri, 0900 to 1700

Access to building, collection or gallery:
Open during Staff Hours

Access for disabled people:
Ramped entry

Attached consultancy group:
Overseas Development Group (ODG)
University of East Anglia, Norwich, Norfolk, NR4 7TJ UK; tel: 0603 592813; fax: 01603 591170; e-mail: odg.gen@uea.ac.uk

SCHOOL OF MEDITATION

158 Holland Park Avenue, London, W11 4UH

Tel: 020 7603 6116
E-mail: info@schoolofmeditation.org

Website:
http://www.schoolofmeditation.org

Enquiries:
Enquiries to: Administrator

Founded:
1961

Organisation type and purpose:
Membership association (membership is by subscription), present number of members: 700, registered charity (charity number 292171), suitable for ages: 18 to 80.

Subject coverage:
Technique of meditation as passed down through the Vedantic tradition; philosophical background.

Access to staff:
Contact by letter, by telephone and by e-mail. Appointment necessary.
Hours: Mon to Fri, 0930 to 1600

Parent body:
Society for Spiritual Development

SCHOOL OF ORIENTAL AND AFRICAN STUDIES

Acronym or abbreviation: SOAS

Thornhaugh Street, Russell Square, London, WC1H 0XG

Tel: 020 7637 2388
Fax: 020 7898 4159
E-mail: libenquiry@soas.ac.uk

Website:
http://www.soas.ac.uk/library/
Online resources, opening hours, subject guide, other library guides and access to the rest of SOAS website.
http://www.soas.ac.uk/archives/home.html
Information on archives.
http://lib.soas.ac.uk
Library online catalogue.

Enquiries:
Enquiries to: Librarian
Direct tel: 020 7898 4150
Other contacts: Archivist

Founded:
1916

Organisation type and purpose:
University library.

Subject coverage:
Asian and African studies in the humanities and social sciences, with special emphasis on anthropology, ethnography, history, language, literature, economics, law, politics, sociology, philosophy, religion and art (particularly Chinese); covering the following areas and regions: Africa, Near and Middle East and Israel, Central Asia, South Asia, South East Asia, East Asia, Oceania.

Museum or gallery collection, archive, or library special collection:
Major collections of missionary and business archives relating to Asia and Africa

Printed publications:
International African Bibliography (quarterly, pub Mansell)
Guide to archives and manuscript collections in the Library, compiled by Rosemary Seton, July 1994
Library Catalogue, 1963, 28 vols Supplement, 1968, 16 vols Supplement, 1973, 16 vols Supplement, 1979, 19 vols (pub G K Hall)
Library Guide and various specialist guides

Microform publications:
Library catalogue supplement, 1978–1989, microfiche (pub IDC)

Publications list:
Available in print

Access to staff:
Contact by fax, by e-mail and via website. Access for members only.
Hours: Term time and Christmas and Easter vacations: Mon to Thu, 0900 to 2045; Fri, 0900 to 1900; Sat, 0930 to 1700
Summer vacation: Mon to Fri, 0900 to 1700; Sat, 0930 to 1700
Special comments: Occasional visits allowed for consultation. Non-members of the school may apply for library membership, but a charge may be made and a letter of introduction is required.

Parent body:
University of London

SCHOOL SCIENCE SERVICE

41 Orchard Bank, Edinburgh, EH4 2DS

Tel: 0131 332 9886
Fax: 0131 332 7447
E-mail: anne@sciencesleuth.co.uk

Website:
http://www.sciencesleuth.co.uk

Enquiries:
Enquiries to: Managing Director
Other contacts: Secretary for Bookings Manager.

Founded:
1989

Formerly called:
The Science Sleuth Shop, Science Sleuth

Organisation type and purpose:
Service industry, consultancy.
Practical science workshops for schools, museums and festivals.

Subject coverage:
Educational equipment and resources packaged together for use in Primary School Science. The Science Sleuth visits schools, museums and science festivals with story-based science investigations, science toys.

Trade and statistical information:
World data on science sleuth investigations for primary schools.

Printed publications:
The Science Sleuth – Sense Investigations for Primary 1 to 3
The Science Sleuth – Chemistry and biology experiments for Primary 4 to 7
School Science Resources on a variety of subjects including electricity, magnetism and materials

Publications list:
Available in print

Access to staff:
Contact by letter, by telephone, by fax, by e-mail and via website
Hours: Mon to Fri, 0900 to 1700

Access to building, collection or gallery:
No access other than to staff

Close links with:
Science Sleuth: Colour Chemistry: DC Electricity: Magnetism: Senses Investigations for science festivals or school visits
tel: 0131 332 7447; fax: 0131 332 7447; e-mail: anne@sciencesleuth.co.uk
The Association for Science Education (ASE) College Lane, Hatfield, AL10 9AA

Other address:
The Science Sleuth Shop (Science Sleuth)
41 Orchard Bank, Edinburgh, EH4 1HN; tel: 0131 332 7447; fax: 0131 332 7447; e-mail: anne@sciencesleuth.co.uk

SCHUBERT SOCIETY OF BRITAIN

The German YMCA, 35 Craven Terrace, London, W2 3EL

Tel: 020 7723 9276
Fax: 020 7706 2870
E-mail: y-services@german-ymca.org.uk

Website:
http://www.german-ymca.org.uk/schubert.htm
Recital dates and programme offered.

Enquiries:
Enquiries to: Programme Secretary
Direct tel: 020 7723 5684
Direct e-mail: u.bauer@german-ymca.org.uk

Founded:
1957

continued overleaf

Organisation type and purpose:
Music Society.
To help young musicians on threshold of a professional career. Recitals given third Sunday of month, 3pm from Oct to May (except Dec) at Lancaster Hall, Lancaster Hall Hotel, Craven Terrace, London W2 to include at least one work by Franz Schubert.

Subject coverage:
Recitals.

Printed publications:
Recital Programmes via mailing list

Publications list:
Available online and in print

Access to staff:
Contact by letter, by telephone, by fax, by e-mail and via website
Hours: Mon to Fri, 0900 to 1700

Access for disabled people:
Level entry
Special comments: Toilets accessible but not adapted for extra support etc.

SCI

Formal name: Society of Chemical Industry
Acronym or abbreviation: SCI

International Headquarters, 14–15 Belgrave Square, London, SW1X 8PS

Tel: 020 7598 1500
Fax: 020 7598 1545
E-mail: secretariat@soci.org

Website:
http://www.thesupplyline.org
Electronic version of Supply Line magazine.
http://www.tomorrows-leaders.net
Tomorrow's Leaders, SCI's online leadership project for young managers worldwide
http://www.chemind.org
Electronic version of Chemistry & Industry magazine.
http://www.soci.org
SCI on the web, the e-Society.

Enquiries:
Enquiries to: Marketing and Publicity Manager
Direct tel: 020 7598 1572
Direct fax: 020 7598 1279
Direct e-mail: lynn.cole@soci.org
Other contacts: General Secretary

Founded:
1881

Formerly called:
Society of Chemical Industry

Organisation type and purpose:
International organisation, learned society (membership is by subscription), present number of members: 6500, registered charity (charity number 206883).

Subject coverage:
The science research, investment and industrial interface. Chemical technology and biotechnology, pest management, materials, agriculture, food, fine and heavy chemicals manufacture, environmental protection, corporate management, whole company direction, discovery, marketing and distribution, natural and economic sciences, engineering, law and medicine.

Museum or gallery collection, archive, or library special collection:
The Society's publications (starting 1881)

Printed publications:
Chemistry & Industry (24 times a year)
SCI News (monthly)
The Supply Line (monthly)
Environmental Science & Technology Meetings
Food Science & Technology Meetings
Publisher of:
Journal of Chemical Technology & Biotechnology
Journal of the Science of Food and Agriculture
Pest Management Science

Polymer International

Publications list:
Available online and in print

Access to staff:
Contact by letter, by telephone, by fax, by e-mail and via website. Appointment necessary.
Hours: Mon to Fri, 0900 to 1700

SCIENCE & SOCIETY PICTURE LIBRARY

North Entrance, Science Museum, Exhibition Road, South Kensington, London, SW7 2DD

Tel: 020 7942 4400
Fax: 020 7942 4401
E-mail: piclib@nmsi.ac.uk

Website:
http://www.scienceandsociety.co.uk

Organisation type and purpose:
Represents the collections of the Science Museum, the National Railway Museum and the National Museum of Photography, Film and Television, and other related collections.

Subject coverage:
Science and people's applications of science.

Museum or gallery collection, archive, or library special collection:
More than 150 image collections from within and outside the museums' own core collections, including 70,000 online records and 40,000 digital images. Themes: entertainment and media; medicine and health; natural world; personalities; places; science and technology; society and wars; trade and industry; transport

SCIENCE AND ADVICE FOR SCOTTISH AGRICULTURE

Formal name: Science and Advice for Scottish Agriculture (Rural Payments and Inspections Directorate)
Acronym or abbreviation: SASA

Roddinglaw Road, Edinburgh, EH12 9FJ

Tel: 0131 244 8873
Fax: 0131 244 8940
E-mail: library@sasa.gsi.gov.uk

Website:
http://www.sasa.gov.uk

Enquiries:
Enquiries to: Librarian
Direct tel: 0131 244 8826

Founded:
1992

Organisation type and purpose:
National government body, research organisation. Provides scientific research and advice to the Scottish Government, Environment and Rural Affairs Department.

Subject coverage:
Seed testing, seed potato classification, plant health, nematology, crop entomology, control of pests, pesticide usage, analytical chemistry, plant varieties, diagnostics and molecular biology.

Trade and statistical information:
Pesticide usage surveys for Scotland.

Library catalogue:
All or part available in-house

Printed publications:
SASA Scientific Review 1997–2003
SASA Annual Report

Publications list:
Available online

Access to staff:
Contact by letter, by telephone, by fax, by e-mail and via website. Appointment necessary.
Hours: Mon to Fri, 0900 to 1700

Access to building, collection or gallery:
Prior appointment required

Access for disabled people:
Parking provided, level entry, toilet facilities

Parent body:
Scottish Government, Rural Payments and Inspections Directorate
Robb's Loan, Edinburgh, EH14 1TW; tel: 0131 244 6024; fax: 0131 244 6116; website: http://www.scotland.gov.uk

SCIENCE FICTION FOUNDATION COLLECTION

Acronym or abbreviation: SFF

Sydney Jones Library, University of Liverpool, PO Box 123, Liverpool, L69 3DA

Tel: 0151 794 2696
Fax: 0151 794 2681
E-mail: asawyer@liverpool.ac.uk

Website:
http://www.SFHsfhub.ac.uk

Enquiries:
Enquiries to: Librarian
Direct tel: 0151 794 3142

Founded:
1970

Organisation type and purpose:
Learned society, university library, research organisation. Aims to support and encourage research into science fiction.

Subject coverage:
Science fiction and related literary genres, their history and criticism.

Library catalogue:
All or part available online

Printed publications:
Foundation: the review of science fiction (3 times a year)

Access to staff:
Contact by letter, by telephone, by e-mail and via website. Appointment necessary.
Hours: Mon to Fri, 0915 to 1645

Funded by:
Science Fiction Foundation
website: http://www.sf-foundation.org

Links with:
British Science Fiction Association
website: http://www.bsfa.co.uk/bsfa

SCIENCE OXFORD

1–5 London Place, St Clements, Oxford, OX4 1BD

Tel: 01865 728953
E-mail: info@scienceoxford.com

Website:
http://www.scienceoxford.com

Organisation type and purpose:
Administered by the Oxford Trust. A registered charity (no. 292664) and a company limited by guarantee (no. 1898691). Science Oxford offers exhibitions, a hands-on science gallery and conference facilities.

Subject coverage:
Science.

Information services:
Information Centre.

Access to building, collection or gallery:
Hours: exhibitions open Mon to Fri, 1000 to 1600; science gallery open Sat in term-time and Mon to Sat during local school holidays

SCIENCE PHOTO LIBRARY LIMITED

Acronym or abbreviation: SPL

327–329 Harrow Road, London, W9 3RB

Tel: 020 7432 1100
Fax: 020 7286 8668
E-mail: info@sciencephoto.com

Website:
http://www.sciencephoto.com
The whole collection of more than 200,000 images
is available to search online and download.

Founded:
1979

Organisation type and purpose:
Service industry. Provider of science photographs.

Subject coverage:
Science photographs.

Non-library collection catalogue:
All or part available online

Access to staff:
Contact by telephone, by fax, by e-mail and via
website. Appointment necessary. All charged.
Hours: Mon to Fri, 0930 to 1800

Member of:
British Association of Picture Libraries and
Agencies (BAPLA)

SCIENTIFIC AND MEDICAL NETWORK

Gibliston Mill, Colinsburgh, Leven, Fife, KY9 1JS

Tel: 01333 340490
E-mail: dl@scimednet.org

Website:
http://www.scimednet.org

Enquiries:
Enquiries to: Programme Director
Other contacts: Secretary

Founded:
1973

Organisation type and purpose:
International organisation, membership
association (membership is by subscription,
election or invitation), present number of
members: 2600, registered charity (charity number
295267).

Subject coverage:
Science and spirituality, consciousness studies.

Printed publications:
Network (3 times a year, subscription £24)
Research Directory (for private use)

Electronic and video publications:
Large selection of audio cassettes and videos of
talks and conferences
Members' Directory (for private use)

Publications list:
Available online and in print

Access to staff:
Contact by letter, by telephone, by fax, by e-mail
and via website
Hours: Mon to Fri, 0900 to 1700

Access for disabled people:
Parking provided, level entry

SCIENTIFIC APPARATUS RECYCLING SCHEME

Acronym or abbreviation: SARS

Department of Biochemistry and Molecular
Biology, University College London, London,
WC1E 6BT

Tel: 020 7679 2169
Fax: 020 7679 7193
E-mail: p.campbell@biochemsitry.ucl.ac.uk

Organisation type and purpose:
International organisation, voluntary organisation.

The purpose of SARS is to collect and despatch
scientific equipment, books and journals surplus to
the requirements of Western European countries to
biochemists in need in Central and Eastern Europe.

Parent body:
Federation of European Biochemical Societies
(FEBS)

SCIENTIFIC COMMITTEE ON ANTARCTIC RESEARCH

Acronym or abbreviation: SCAR

SCAR Secretariat, Scott Polar Research Institute,
Lensfield Road, Cambridge, CB2 1ER

Tel: 01223 336550
Fax: 01223 336549
E-mail: info@scar.org

Website:
http://www.scar.org

Enquiries:
Enquiries to: Executive Director

Founded:
1958

Organisation type and purpose:
International organisation (membership is by
election or invitation), present number of
members: 31 full members, 4 associates, 8
international scientific unions.
Members are National Academic Societies, e.g. The
Royal Society (UK).
To initiate, promote and co-ordinate scientific
research in Antarctica and to provide scientific
advice to the Antarctic Treaty System.

Subject coverage:
Antarctic biology, geodesy and geographic
information, glaciology, human biology and
medicine, physics and chemistry of the
atmosphere, solar-terrestrial and astrophysical
research, geosciences, environment and
conservation, global change, astronomy,
oceanography.

Publications list:
Available online and in print

Access to staff:
Contact by e-mail
Hours: Mon to Fri, 0900 to 1700

Member organisations:
National Scientific Academies of Argentina,
Australia, Belgium, Brazil, Bulgaria, Canada, Chile,
People's Republic of China, Denmark (associate
mem.), Ecuador, Finland, France, Germany, India,
Italy, Japan, Republic of Korea, Malaysia,
Netherlands, New Zealand, Norway, Pakistan
(associate mem.), Peru, Poland, Portugal (associate
mem.), Romania (associate mem.), Russia, South
Africa, Spain, Sweden, Switzerland, Ukraine,
United Kingdom, Uruguay, USA

Parent body:
International Council of Scientific Unions (ICSU)
ICSU Secretariat, 5 rue Auguste Vacquerie, 75016
Paris, France; tel: + 33 1 45 25 03 29; fax: + 33 1 42
88 94 31; e-mail: secretariat@icsu.org; website:
http://www.icsu.org

SCIENTIFIC EXPLORATION SOCIETY

Acronym or abbreviation: SES

Highgrove, Clifton Road, Amersham,
Buckinghamshire

E-mail: ses@ses-explore.org

Website:
http://www.ses-explore.org
General activities of the SES; expeditions; science;
community aid.

Enquiries:
Enquiries to: Executive Director

Founded:
1969

Organisation type and purpose:
International organisation, membership
association (membership is by subscription,
election or invitation), present number of
members: 500, voluntary organisation, registered
charity (charity number 267410), consultancy,
research organisation.
The running of expeditions for the benefit of
scientific research, conservation, education,
community and medical aid.

Subject coverage:
Scientific research, conservation, community and
medical aid in developing countries, education,
environmental protection, the welfare of wildlife.

**Museum or gallery collection, archive, or library
special collection:**
A comprehensive library of slides is kept from
worldwide expeditions and expedition reports

Trade and statistical information:
Advice relating to the running of expeditions.

Non-library collection catalogue:
All or part available in-house

Printed publications:
Expeditions – the experts' way (Blashford-Snell J
and Ballantine A, £2)
In The Eye of The Wind (Chapman R, £5)
SESAME (newsletter, free to members)
Mammoth Hunt (Blashford-Snell J with Lenska R,
£15)
Operation Raleigh, Adventure Challenge
(Blashford-Snell J with Tweedy A, £5)
Operation Raleigh, The Start of An Adventure
(£10)
Various publications and expedition reports
Voyage of Discovery (Mitchell A, £10)
Kota Mama (Blashford-Snell J and Snailham R)
Order printed publications from: ses@ses-explore.org

Electronic and video publications:
Promotional Video (£5)

Access to staff:
Contact by letter, by e-mail and via website
Hours: Mon to Fri, 0900 to 1700

Access to building, collection or gallery:
None

SCOLIOSIS ASSOCIATION UK

Acronym or abbreviation: SAUK

4 Ivebury Court, 323–327 Latimer Road, London,
W10 6RA

Tel: 020 8964 5343/1166
Fax: 020 8964 5343
E-mail: sauk@sauk.org.uk

Website:
http://www.sauk.org.uk

Enquiries:
Enquiries to: Information Officer

Founded:
1981

Organisation type and purpose:
Membership association, present number of
members: 3500, voluntary organisation, registered
charity (charity number 285290).
Offers sufferers a chance to share experience of the
physical, emotional and social aspects of scoliosis.

Subject coverage:
Scoliosis (ie lateral spinal curvature); information
about all aspects of scoliosis, but not individual
medical advice.

Printed publications:
Legacy Leaflet (free)
A Twist of Fate (£3)
Clothes to Suit (£3)
Newsletter (twice a year, to members)
Newsletter Index (covers 11 years, with list of
reprints available, 20p to 50p)
Schools Fact Sheet (free)

continued overleaf

Scoliosis (handbook, £5.50)

Electronic and video publications:
Videos available for purchase or loan

Publications list:
Available in print

Access to staff:
Contact by letter, by telephone, by fax, by e-mail and via website
Hours: Mon to Fri, 1000 to 1730

Links with:
International Federation of Scoliosis Associations

SCOOTACAR REGISTER

18 Holman Close, Aylsham, Norwich, Norfolk, NR11 6DD

Tel: 01263 733861
E-mail: scootacar@btinternet.com

Website:
http://www.scootacar.org.uk

Enquiries:
Enquiries to: Secretary

Founded:
1980

Organisation type and purpose:
Membership association.
To locate and register all Scootacars.

Subject coverage:
Micro cars, bubble cars, location and registration of Scootacars.

Museum or gallery collection, archive, or library special collection:
Photographs
Register of all known cars
Service bulletins
Spares and component numbers
Workshop manuals

Trade and statistical information:
Production figures.
Chassis numbers.
Engine numbers.
Number of cars located.

Printed publications:
Scootabout (newsletter, 2 times a year, £5 annual subscription)

Electronic and video publications:
Videos (available for hire)

Access to staff:
Contact by letter, by telephone and by e-mail
Hours: Mon to Fri, 0900 to 1700

SCOPE

6 Market Road, London, N7 9PW

Tel: 020 7619 7100
Fax: 020 7619 7360

Website:
http://www.scope.org.uk
Information on cerebral palsy, therapies, education etc.
Information on SCOPE campaigns etc.
Publications list.

Enquiries:
Enquiries to: Library & Information Officer
Direct tel: 020 7619 7340
Direct e-mail: information@scope.org.uk

Founded:
1952

Formerly called:
Spastics Society

Organisation type and purpose:
Voluntary organisation, registered charity (charity number 208231).

To ensure that all people with cerebral palsy and related disabilities, their families and carers have access to properly resourced services that meet their needs and full rights to control their own lives.

Subject coverage:
Cerebral palsy; attitudes to disability; discrimination against disabled people; education and employment of disabled people.
Equipment, legislation related to disability; statistics on disability.

Museum or gallery collection, archive, or library special collection:
Complete run of Developmental Medicine & Child Neurology
Full set of Classics in Developmental Medicine
Full set of Clinics in Developmental Medicine

Trade and statistical information:
Disability related statistics eg numbers of disabled people and their income/expenditure, equipment needs etc.

Non-library collection catalogue:
All or part available in-house

Library catalogue:
All or part available in-house

Printed publications:
Disability Now (newspaper, monthly, £1.80)
Other publications (education, conductive education and therapies, parent information leaflets, campaigns and research) include:
A lot to say (Morris J, 2002)
Advocating for Equality
Right From The Start
Focusing on Cerebral Palsy (2001)
Polls Apart
Ready, willing and disabled (2003)
Speak for Yourself (Ford J, 2000)
Stop Press (Cooke C, Daone L, and Morris G, 2000)
That Kind of Life (Morris J, 2002)
Order printed publications from: Library and Information Unit, SCOPE
at the same address, tel: 020 7619 7342, fax: 020 7619 7360, e-mail: information@scope.org.uk

Electronic and video publications:
Disability awareness videos (available for free loan or purchase £15)
All titles can be made available on tape
Order electronic and video publications from:
Education Distribution Service (AV material), SCOPE
Unit 2, Drywall Estate, Castle Road, Marston, Sittingbourne, Kent, ME10 3RL, tel: 01795 427614, fax: 01795 474871

Publications list:
Available online and in print

Access to staff:
Contact by letter, by telephone, by fax, by e-mail, in person and via website
Hours: Helpline (0808 8003333): Mon to Fri, 0900 to 2100; Sat to Sun, 1400 to 1800

Access to building, collection or gallery:
Prior appointment required
Hours: Mon to Fri, 0900 to 1700
Special comments: Prior appointment required for access to library.

Access for disabled people:
Access to all public areas

Has:
a network of local offices around England and Wales providing support
over 200 local groups around England and Wales

Helpline:
Cerebral Palsy Helpline
PO Box 833, Milton Keynes, Buckinghamshire, MK12 5NY; tel: 0808 800 3333; fax: 01908 321051; e-mail: cphelpline@scope.org.uk

SCOPE – RESPONSE

PO Box 833, Milton Keynes, Buckinghamshire, MK12 5NY

Tel: 0808 800 3333 / text SCOPE plus message to 80039
Fax: 01908 321051
E-mail: response@scope.org.uk

Website:
http://www.scope.org.uk
Information about cerebral palsy and Scope, sevices and publications.

Organisation type and purpose:
National disability organisation. About cerebral palsy. For disabled people achieving equality. Registered charity (charity number 208231). Helpline provides free and confidential information, advice and support about cerebral palsy, disability issues and Scope services.

Subject coverage:
Cerebral palsy and associated disabilities.

Printed publications:
A range of publications including:
Cerebral Palsy Helpline (leaflet)
Series of factsheets around cp, therapies and disability issues.
Multilingual Leaflet
SCOPE for You (leaflet)
Parent Information Leaflets
Factsheets available in large print or Braille on request
Order printed publications from: Scope, CP Helpline, P.O. Box 833, Milton Keynes MK12 5NY, tel: 01908 321049 (Publications Line)

Electronic and video publications:
Information in other languages (Audio tape)
Scope videos available

Publications list:
Available online and in print

Access to staff:
Contact by letter, by telephone, by fax, by e-mail and via website
Hours: Mon to Fri, 0900 to 1900; Sat, 1000 to 1400; Sun, closed.

Service run by:
SCOPE (formerly The Spastics Society)

SCOTCH WHISKY ASSOCIATION

Acronym or abbreviation: SWA

20 Atholl Crescent, Edinburgh, EH3 8HF

Tel: 0131 222 9200
Fax: 0131 222 9237
E-mail: contact@swa.org.uk

Website:
http://www.scotch-whisky.org.uk
General information and statistics on Scotch Whisky.

Enquiries:
Enquiries to: Director of Government and Consumer Affairs
Other contacts: Press & Media Relations Manager for press enquiries

Founded:
1943

Organisation type and purpose:
Trade association.
Promotion and protection of Scotch Whisky.

Subject coverage:
Scotch whisky trade worldwide; statistical and industry information.

Printed publications:
Publicity materials
Questions and answers (handbook, for sale)
Statistical report (annually, for sale)

Access to staff:
Contact by letter, by telephone, by fax, by e-mail and via website

London Office:
Scotch Whisky Association
14 Cork Street, London, W1S 3NS; tel: 020 7629 4384; fax: 020 7493 1398

SCOTLAND IS

Suite 41, Geddes House, Kirkton North,
Livingston, EH54 6GU

Tel: 01506 472200
Fax: 01506 460615
E-mail: info@scotlandis.com

Website:
http://www.scotlandis.com

Enquiries:
Enquiries to: Membership Liaison Manager
Direct e-mail: karen.meechan@scotlandis.com
Other contacts: General Manager

Founded:
2000

Formerly called:
IMAS, Internet Society (ISOC), Scottish Software
Federation (SSF) (year of change 2000)

Organisation type and purpose:
Trade association (membership is by subscription),
present number of members: 300 companies.
Representative trade organisation for the ICT
industry in Scotland. Members encompass a wide
cross-section of companies covering the users,
academia, developers, applications providers and
service providers.
To make the software industry in Scotland
collectively successful.

Subject coverage:
Computer software.

Printed publications:
Switched On (newsletter, available through
   info@scotlandis.com)
Directory of Member Companies 2002 (£35 plus
   VAT)

Electronic and video publications:
Members Directory (CD-ROM, available with hard
   copy £35 plus VAT)

Publications list:
Available online and in print

Access to staff:
Contact by letter, by telephone, by fax, by e-mail
and via website
Hours: Mon to Fri, 0900 to 1700

Access to building, collection or gallery:
Prior appointment required

Access for disabled people:
Parking provided, ramped entry

Grampian Office:
Scotland IS
   The Software Centre, Aberdeen Science and
   Technology Park, Campus 2, Balgowie Drive,
   Bridge of Don, Aberdeen, AB22 8GU; tel: 01224
   332182; fax: 01224 332082; e-mail: info@
   scotlandis.com

SCOTLAND'S GARDENS SCHEME

Acronym or abbreviation: SGS

42A Castle Street, Edinburgh, EH2 3BN

Tel: 0131 226 3714
E-mail: sgsgardens@btconnect.com

Enquiries:
Enquiries to: Director

Founded:
1931

Organisation type and purpose:
Registered charity (charity number SCO 11337).
Opening gardens to the public for a range of
charities.

Subject coverage:
Opening dates for gardens which open under the
scheme in Scotland each year.

Printed publications:
Gardens of Scotland (annual, for purchase)

Access to staff:
Contact by letter, by telephone, by fax and by e-
mail
Hours: Mon to Fri, 0900 to 1700

Access to building, collection or gallery:
No access other than to staff

SCOTT BADER COMPANY LIMITED

Wollaston, Wellingborough, Northamptonshire,
NN29 7RL

Tel: 01933 663100
Fax: 01933 666608
E-mail: stuart_reeves@scottbader.com

Enquiries:
Enquiries to: Information Officer

Founded:
1920

Organisation type and purpose:
Manufacturing industry.

Subject coverage:
Plastics, synthetic resins, their manufacture and
technical applications (specifically unsaturated
polyester resins, emulsion and solution polymers),
polyesters, reinforced plastics, surface coatings for
paper, textiles and other materials, adhesives and
thickeners.

Museum or gallery collection, archive, or library special collection:
Ernest Bader's Archives, founder of the company
   and pioneer in common ownership of companies

Printed publications:
Technical trade literature on polymers, polyesters
   and their applications in end-use markets

Access to staff:
Appointment necessary.
Hours: Mon to Fri, 0830 to 1700

SCOTT OWNERS' CLUB, THE

Acronym or abbreviation: SOC

Walnut Cottage, Abbey Lane, Aslockton,
Nottinghamshire, NG13 9AE

Tel: 01949 851027
Fax: 01949 851027

Website:
http://www.scottownersclub.org
Marque history, membership application details,
technical information.

Enquiries:
Enquiries to: Public Relations Officer
Other contacts: (1) Membership Secretary; (2)
Machine Registrar; (3) Archivist

Founded:
1958

Organisation type and purpose:
Membership association (membership is by
subscription), present number of members: 650.
To promote interest in Scott and Silk motorcycles
and to provide a spares scheme, library,
photographic archives, technical information, a
machine register, badges, transfers (decals), and
mutual support to members.

Subject coverage:
Scott motorcycles made 1908–1951, Birmingham
Scott 1957–1972, Silk Scott 1970s-1980s and the Silk
motorcycle which followed.

Museum or gallery collection, archive, or library special collection:
Collections of period photographs, some factory
   records, engineering drawings, technical
   information and machine register

Printed publications:
Yowl (club magazine, 6 times a year, for members)

Electronic and video publications:
CD-ROMs – under development

Access to staff:
Contact by letter, by telephone and by fax
Hours: Mon to Fri, 0900 to 1700
Special comments: Enclose SAE if written reply is
required.
No access to facilities without membership.

SCOTT POLAR RESEARCH INSTITUTE

Acronym or abbreviation: SPRI

Lensfield Road, Cambridge, CB2 1ER

Tel: 01223 336552
Fax: 01223 336549
E-mail: enquiries@spri.cam.ac.uk

Website:
http://www.spri.cam.ac.uk

Enquiries:
Enquiries to: Librarian and Keeper
Direct e-mail: library@spri.cam.ac.uk
Other contacts: Information Assistant for general
library enquiries.

Founded:
1920

Organisation type and purpose:
Museum, university department or institute.

Subject coverage:
Polar regions; Arctic regions; Antarctic regions
including the Falkland Islands; Russian North;
snow and ice studies; glaciology; cold regions in
general; whaling; sealing; exploration.

Museum or gallery collection, archive, or library special collection:
Polar Archives

Non-library collection catalogue:
All or part available online, in-house and in print

Library catalogue:
All or part available online

Printed publications:
Catalogue of the Scott Polar Research Institute
   Library
Polar Record (quarterly)
Polar and Glaciological Abstracts (3 times a year)
Universal Decimal Classification for use in Polar
   Libraries

Electronic and video publications:
Arctic and Antarctic regions CD-ROM
Polar Pac CD-ROM

Publications list:
Available in print

Access to staff:
Contact by letter, by telephone, by fax, by e-mail,
in person and via website. Appointment necessary.
Hours: Mon to Fri, 0900 to 1300 and 1400 to 1730

Access to building, collection or gallery:
Hours: Mon to Fri, 0900 to 1715; Sat, 1430 to 1600

Department of the:
University of Cambridge

Houses the:
International Glaciological Society
   tel: 01223 355974; e-mail: igsoc@igsoc.org
Scientific Committee on Antarctic Research
(SCAR)
   tel: 01223 336550; fax: 01223 336549; e-mail:
   info@scar.org
World Data Centre for Glaciology, Cambridge
   tel: 01223 336565; fax: 01223 336549; website:
   wdcgc.spri.cam.ac.uk

SCOTTISH ACCIDENT PREVENTION COUNCIL

Acronym or abbreviation: SAPC

Livingstone House, 43 Discovery Terrace,
Edinburgh, EH14 4AP

Tel: 0131 449 9379
Fax: 0131 449 9380

continued overleaf

E-mail: secretary@sapc.org.uk

Enquiries:
Enquiries to: Secretary

Founded:
1931

Organisation type and purpose:
Membership association (membership is by subscription), voluntary organisation, registered charity.

Subject coverage:
Home, road, water and leisure safety.

Access to staff:
Contact by letter, by telephone and by e-mail.
Appointment necessary.
Hours: Mon to Fri, 0900 to 1700

Allied to:
RoSPA
at the same address

SCOTTISH AGRICULTURAL COLLEGE – AUCHINCRUIVE

Acronym or abbreviation: SAC

Auchincruive, Ayr, KA6 5HW

Tel: 01292 525209
Fax: 01292 525211
E-mail: libraryau@sac.ac.uk

Website:
http://www.sac.ac.uk

Enquiries:
Enquiries to: Librarian
Direct tel: 01292 525208

Founded:
1896

Formerly called:
West of Scotland College of Agriculture (year of change 1990)

Organisation type and purpose:
Research organisation, consultancy.
Higher education. Independent body funded by the Scottish Office.

Subject coverage:
Science and economics of agriculture, horticulture, biotechnology, dairying, milk and milk products, poultry husbandry, agricultural engineering, food sciences, water pollution, conservation, environmental science, countryside recreation, tourism and leisure.

Museum or gallery collection, archive, or library special collection:
Historical collection on agriculture and horticulture

Non-library collection catalogue:
All or part available online

Library catalogue:
All or part available online

Printed publications:
Advisory leaflets, etc.
Annual Report
Order printed publications from: Publications Unit, SAC, Kings Buildings, West Mains Road, Edinburgh, EH9 3JG, tel: 0131 535 4000

Publications list:
Available in print

Access to staff:
Contact by telephone, by fax and by e-mail.
Appointment necessary.
Hours: Term time: Mon to Fri, 0845 to 2045; Sat, Sun, 1100 to 1700
Vacations: Mon to Thu, 0845 to 1715; Fri, 0845 to 1645

Access to building, collection or gallery:
No prior appointment required

Links with:
University of Glasgow

SCOTTISH AGRICULTURAL COLLEGE – EDINBURGH

Acronym or abbreviation: SAC

West Mains Road, Edinburgh, EH9 3JG

Tel: 0131 535 4000
Fax: 0131 535 4246

Website:
http://www.sac.ac.uk/
SAC home page with library details.

Enquiries:
Enquiries to: Librarian
Direct tel: 0131 535 4116
Direct e-mail: m.mullay@ed.sac.ac.uk

Founded:
1990

Formed from:
East of Scotland College of Agriculture, Scottish Agricultural Colleges

Formerly called:
Edinburgh School of Agriculture

Organisation type and purpose:
consultancy, research organisation.

Subject coverage:
All aspects of agriculture excluding fisheries; agricultural economics, farming and engineering; animal nutrition and production; applied plant science; crop production and protection; pests; microbiology; organic and soil science; veterinary medicine; environment; rural affairs.

Museum or gallery collection, archive, or library special collection:
Early agricultural texts

Library catalogue:
All or part available online

Printed publications:
Library Guide

Electronic and video publications:
AGDEX – in-house bibliographic database indexing the popular farming press

Publications list:
Available in print

Access to staff:
Contact by letter and by e-mail. Appointment necessary.
Hours: Term time: Mon to Thu, 0845 to 2100; Fri, 0845 to 1700; Sat, Sun, 1000 to 1700
Vacations: Mon to Fri, 0845 to 1700

Combines the:
Institute of Ecology and Resource Management, University of Edinburgh
Scottish Agricultural College

Other addresses:
Scottish Agricultural College
Craibstone Estate, Auchincruive, Ayrshire

SCOTTISH AMATEUR MUSIC ASSOCIATION

Acronym or abbreviation: SAMA

18 Craigton Crescent, Alva, Clackmannanshire, FK12 5DS

Tel: 01259 760249
E-mail: secretary@sama.org.uk

Website:
http://www.sama.org.uk

Enquiries:
Enquiries to: Honorary Secretary

Founded:
1956

Organisation type and purpose:
Membership association (membership is by election or invitation), registered charity (charity number SCO 14503).

Subject coverage:
The encouragement and stimulation of amateur music-making in Scotland, mainly through summer courses.

Printed publications:
The Gentle Jacobite (a play with music for young people)

Publications list:
Available in print

Access to staff:
Contact by letter, by telephone and by e-mail
Hours: Not always available

SCOTTISH AMATEUR SWIMMING ASSOCIATION

Acronym or abbreviation: SASA

National Swimming Academy, University of Stirling, Stirling, FK9 4LA

Tel: 01786 466520
Fax: 01786 466521
E-mail: info@scottishswimming.com

Website:
http://www.scottishswimming.com

Enquiries:
Enquiries to: Director of Administration
Direct e-mail: e.mackenzie@scottishswimming.com

Founded:
1888

Organisation type and purpose:
Membership association (membership is by subscription), voluntary organisation.
National governing body of the sport.

Subject coverage:
Speed swimming, masters' swimming, synchronised swimming, long distance swimming, water polo.

Printed publications:
Swimming 2000 (magazine, 6 times a year, £7.50)
Scottish Learn to Swim Syllabus (£29.99)
Adult and Child Syllabus (£35)

Access to staff:
Contact by letter, by telephone and by e-mail
Hours: Mon to Thu, 0830 to 1700; Fri, 0830 to 1600

Access to building, collection or gallery:
No prior appointment required

Access for disabled people:
Parking provided, level entry, access to all public areas, toilet facilities

Links with:
Fédération Internationale de Natation Amateur (FINA)
Avenue de Beaumont 9, Lausanne, CH-1012, Switzerland

SCOTTISH AND NORTHERN IRELAND PLUMBING EMPLOYERS' FEDERATION

Acronym or abbreviation: SNIPEF

2 Walker Street, Edinburgh, EH3 7LB

Tel: 0131 225 2255
Fax: 0131 226 7638
E-mail: info@snipef.org

Website:
http://www.snipef.org
Benefits of using SNIPEF member firms, displays a list of member firms in Scotland and Northern Ireland, membership details available to potential new member firms, history of the Federation.

Enquiries:
Enquiries to: Information Officer

Founded:
1923

Organisation type and purpose:
Trade association (membership is by subscription, qualification), present number of members: 950, service industry.
The national association for all types of firms involved in the plumbing and domestic heating industry in Scotland and Northern Ireland.

Subject coverage:
Customers using SNIPEF members can contact the Federation for advice relating to any plumbing and heating work undertaken by a member firm. In the event that a dispute arises, the customer can contact the Federation, who will advise them on the operation of their complaints procedure through their Code of Fair Trading, which is recognised by the Office of Fair Trading.

Printed publications:
Plumb Heat (trade journal, 4 issues a year, free to members, non-members £20, overseas surface mail £30)
SNIPEF Year book (free to member firms and non-commercial organisations, otherwise £25)

Access to staff:
Contact by letter, by telephone, by fax, by e-mail, in person and via website
Hours: Mon to Thu, 0900 to 1700; Fri, 0900 to 1630

SCOTTISH ANGLERS NATIONAL ASSOCIATION

Acronym or abbreviation: SANA

The National Game Angling Centre, The Pier, Loch Leven, Kinross, Scotland, KY13 8UF

Tel: 01577 861116
Fax: 01577 864769
E-mail: admin@sana.org.uk

Website:
http://www.sana.org.uk

Enquiries:
Enquiries to: Administrator
Other contacts: Secretary

Founded:
1985

Organisation type and purpose:
National organisation, advisory body, membership association (membership is by subscription), service industry, voluntary organisation.
Governing body for the sport of game fishing in Scotland.

Subject coverage:
Game fishing, especially in Scotland.

Printed publications:
Annual report
Annual newsletter

Access to staff:
Contact by letter, by telephone, by e-mail and via website
Hours: 0930 to 1300
Special comments: Answering machine available.

SCOTTISH ASIAN ACTION COMMITTEE

Acronym or abbreviation: SAAC

39 Napiershall Street, Glasgow, G20 6EZ

Tel: 0141 341 0025
Fax: 0141 341 0020
E-mail: secretary@saac.freeserve.co.uk

Enquiries:
Enquiries to: Secretary
Other contacts: Development Officer

Founded:
1981

Organisation type and purpose:
Voluntary organisation.

To provide information and advice to black and ethnic minority communities in Scotland. To combat racism and discrimination through campaigning.

Subject coverage:
Black and Asian communities in Scotland, racism, work and equal opportunities, community groups, racial equality standards.

Printed publications:
Newsletter (quarterly)
Annual Report

Access to staff:
Contact by telephone, by fax, by e-mail and in person
Hours: Mon to Fri, 1000 to 1600

SCOTTISH ASSOCIATION FOR MARINE SCIENCE

Acronym or abbreviation: SAMS

Dunstaffnage Marine Laboratory, Dunbeg, Oban, Argyll, PA37 1QA

Tel: 01631 559000
Fax: 01631 559001
E-mail: innfo@sams.ac.uk

Website:
http://www.sams.ac.uk

Enquiries:
Enquiries to: Librarian
Direct tel: 01631 559217
Direct e-mail: olga.kimmins@sams.ac.uk
Other contacts: Director

Founded:
1896

Formerly called:
Scottish Marine Biological Association (SMBA) (year of change 1990)

Organisation type and purpose:
Learned society (membership is by subscription), registered charity (charity number SCO 09206), research organisation.

Subject coverage:
Marine biology, marine ecology, marine chemistry and oceanography.

Library catalogue:
All or part available in-house

Printed publications:
Annual Report

Access to staff:
Contact by letter, by fax and by e-mail
Hours: Mon to Fri, 0900 to 1700
Special comments: SAMS members only. Other bona fide scientists by prior appointment.

Access to building, collection or gallery:
Prior appointment required

Connections with:
Natural Environment Research Council

SCOTTISH ASSOCIATION FOR MARINE SCIENCE

Acronym or abbreviation: SAMS

Dunstaffnage Marine Laboratory, Oban, Argyll, PA37 1QA

Tel: 01631 559000
Fax: 01631 559001
E-mail: info@sams.ac.uk

Website:
http://www.sams.ac.uk/

Enquiries:
Enquiries to: Activities Manager
Direct e-mail: anuschka.miller@sams.ac.uk

Organisation type and purpose:
Research organisation.

Subject coverage:
Marine aquaculture, fish culture, shellfish culture, fish biology, marine science

Non-library collection catalogue:
All or part available online and in-house

Library catalogue:
All or part available in-house

Printed publications:
Technical reports on project research work undertaken

Publications list:
Available online and in print

Access to staff:
Contact by letter, by telephone, by fax and by e-mail. Appointment necessary.
Hours: Mon to Fri, 0900 to 1700
Special comments: Access to members of fishing and aquaculture industry only.

Access to building, collection or gallery:
Prior appointment required

Access for disabled people:
Ramped entry, toilet facilities

Headquarters:
Sea Fish Industry Authority
 18 Logie Hill, Logie Green Road, Edinburgh, EH7 4HG; tel: 0131 558 3331; fax: 0131 558 1442
Sea Fish Technology
 Sea Fish House, St Andrews Dock, Hull, HU3 4QE; tel: 01482 327837; fax: 01482 223310

Parent body:
Sea Fish Industry Authority
 SFIA; tel: 0131 558 3331; fax: 0131 558 1442

SCOTTISH ASSOCIATION FOR PUBLIC TRANSPORT

Acronym or abbreviation: SAPT

11 Queen's Crescent, Glasgow, G4 9BL

Tel: 07760 381729
E-mail: sapt@btinternet.com

Enquiries:
Enquiries to: Secretary

Founded:
1972

Formerly called:
Scottish Railway Development Association (SRDA) (year of change 1962–1972)

Organisation type and purpose:
National organisation, membership association (membership is by subscription), present number of members: 150, voluntary organisation.
National organisation (Scotland).
Supporting public transport and environmental improvement.

Subject coverage:
All modes of public transport in Scotland; policy and finance; transport-related environmental issues.

Printed publications:
Annual Report
Newsletter (quarterly)
Study papers

Access to staff:
Contact by letter, by telephone and by e-mail
Hours: Mon to Fri, 0900 to 1700

Member of:
Environmental Transport Association
TRANSform Scotland
 tel: 0131 467 7714; fax: 0131 554 8656; e-mail: campaigns@transformscotland.org.uk
Transport 2000

SCOTTISH ATHLETICS LIMITED

Caledonia House, Redheughs Rigg, South Gyle, Edinburgh, EH12 9DQ

Tel: 0131 317 7320

continued overleaf

Fax: 0131 317 7321
E-mail: admin@scottishathletics.org.uk

Website:
http://www.scottishathletics.org.uk

Enquiries:
Enquiries to: General Manager
Other contacts: Press Officer for media relations.

Founded:
1992

Formed from:
Scottish Amateur Athletics Federation (SAAF),
Scottish Womens Amateur Athletics Federation
(SWAAF)

Formerly called:
Scottish Athletics Federation (SAF) (year of change
2000)

Organisation type and purpose:
Membership association (membership is by
subscription), present number of members: 6500,
voluntary organisation.
National sports governing body.
Management, promotion and development of
athletics in Scotland.

Subject coverage:
Track and field athletics, hill, road and cross-
country running, Scottish heavy events, athletics
development packages and support from 5 years
upwards, coaching courses and examinations.

**Museum or gallery collection, archive, or library
special collection:**
Athletics memorabilia

Printed publications:
Awards booklets
Information leaflet and packs
Membership Information
Newsletter (4 times a year, members only)

Access to staff:
Contact by letter, by telephone, by fax, by e-mail
and via website. Appointment necessary.
Hours: Mon to Fri, 0900 to 1700

Affiliated to:
Commonwealth Games Council for Scotland
    tel: 0131 336 1924
UK Athletics
    tel: 0121 456 5098; fax: 0121 456 4998

SCOTTISH BIBLE SOCIETY

7 Hampton Terrace, Edinburgh, EH12 5XU

Tel: 0131 337 9701
Fax: 0131 337 0641
E-mail: colin.hay@scottishbiblesociety.org

Website:
http://www.scottishbiblesociety.org

Enquiries:
Enquiries to: Chief Executive
Direct e-mail: elaine.duncan@scottishbiblesociety
.org

Founded:
1809

Formerly called:
National Bible Society of Scotland (year of change
2000)

Organisation type and purpose:
Registered charity (charity number SCO10767)

Non-library collection catalogue:
All or part available online and in print

Printed publications:
Catalogue
Word at Work (magazine)
Read and Pray around the World

Publications list:
Available in print

Access to staff:
Contact by letter, by telephone, by fax and by e-
mail
Hours: Mon to Fri, 0900 to 1700

SCOTTISH BORDERS ARCHIVE AND LOCAL HISTORY CENTRE

Library Headquarters, St Mary's Mill, Selkirk,
Borders, TD7 5EW

Tel: 01750 20842
Fax: 01750 22875
E-mail: archives@scotborders.gov.uk

Website:
http://www.scottishborders.gov.uk/libraries

Enquiries:
Enquiries to: Archivist
Other contacts: Librarian: Archives/Local History/
Reference

Organisation type and purpose:
Local government body, public library.
Archive.

Subject coverage:
Local history of the Scottish Borders.

**Museum or gallery collection, archive, or library
special collection:**
Andrew Lang Collection
Census returns 1841–1901 (microfilm)
Craig Brown Collection (local history)
IGI for the whole world
Index to christenings and marriages in the pre-1855
    old parish records for each county in Scotland
    (microfiche)
Information on pre-1975 counties of
    Roxburghshire, Berwickshire, Peebleshire,
    Selkirkshire
James Hogg Collection
Local business records
Local newspapers (many on microfilm)
Maps and plans
Postcards
Pre-1855 parish records covering the counties of
    Roxburghshire, Berwickshire, Peebleshire,
    Selkirkshire
Sir Walter Scott Collection

Non-library collection catalogue:
All or part available in-house

Library catalogue:
All or part available in-house

Access to staff:
Contact by letter, by telephone, by fax, by e-mail
and in person
Hours: Mon to Thu, 0900 to 1300 and 1400 to 1700;
Fri, 0900 to 1300 and 1400 to 1530
Special comments: Closed access collection (visitors
must make a prior appointment to consult
microfilm).

Access for disabled people:
Parking provided, ramped entry

Parent body:
Scottish Borders Council

SCOTTISH BORDERS COUNCIL

Acronym or abbreviation: SBC

Council Headquarters, Newtown St Boswells,
Melrose, Roxburghshire, TD6 0SA

Tel: 01835 824000
Fax: 01835 825001
E-mail: enquiries@scotborders.gov.uk

Website:
http://www.scotborders.org.uk.
Information on all aspects of the Scottish Borders
http://www.scotborders.gov.uk
Information about Scottish Borders Council

Enquiries:
Enquiries to: Head of Communications
Direct tel: 01835 825008
Direct fax: 01825 825059

Founded:
1996

Formed from reorganisation of:
Berwickshire District Council, Borders Regional
Council, Ettrick and Lauderdale District Council,
Roxburgh District Council, Tweeddale District
Council (year of change 1996)

Organisation type and purpose:
Local government body.

Subject coverage:
Services and amenities; corporate services,
education, environmental services, finance,
housing, legal services, personnel services,
planning development and tourism, property and
technical services, roads and transportation, social
services, council tax and other payments,
registration of births, death and marriages, leisure
and recreation, cleansing, environmental health
and trading standards.

Access to staff:
Contact by letter, by telephone, by fax, by e-mail,
in person and via website
Hours: Mon to Thu, 0845 to 1700; Fri, 0845 to 1545

Access for disabled people:
Parking provided, ramped entry, access to all
public areas

SCOTTISH BOWLING ASSOCIATION

Acronym or abbreviation: SBA

National Centre for Bowling, Northfield, Hunters
Avenue, Ayr, KA8 9BL

Tel: 01292 294623
Fax: 01292 294623

Enquiries:
Enquiries to: Secretary

Founded:
1892

Organisation type and purpose:
Membership association.
National Association controlling the level green
game of lawn bowls.

Subject coverage:
All matters relative to level green lawn bowls.

Printed publications:
Bowls for Beginners
Laws of the Game
Newsletter (annually, for clubs)
Year Book (annually)

Access to staff:
Contact by letter, by telephone, by fax and in
person
Hours: Mon to Fri, 0900 to 1630

Associated to:
British Isles Bowls Council (BIBC)
World Bowls Board (WBB)

SCOTTISH BRAILLE PRESS

Craigmillar Park, Edinburgh, EH16 5NB

Tel: 0131 662 4445
Fax: 0131 662 1968
E-mail: info.sbp@royalblind.org

Website:
http://www.royalblind.org

Enquiries:
Enquiries to: Customer Service

Founded:
1881

Organisation type and purpose:
Voluntary organisation, registered charity (charity
number SC 017167), publishing house.
Printers and publishers of Braille, and suppliers of
audio, large-print material, tactile diagrams and
material on disk.

Subject coverage:
Publishing literature and educational textbooks in
Braille, audio and large print.

Non-library collection catalogue:
All or part available online and in print

Printed publications:
A number of weekly and monthly magazines
Publications list is also available in braille
Large selection of books available for purchase, direct, including:
Adult fiction
Catalogue of Braille books
Catalogue of Braille magazines
Children's fiction
Educational texts
Homecraft
Music and musical literature
Religion

Electronic and video publications:
CD-ROM

Publications list:
Available online and in print

Access to staff:
Contact by letter, by telephone, by fax, by e-mail, in person and via website
Hours: Mon to Thu, 0830 to 1630; Fri, 0830 to 1300

Access to building, collection or gallery:
No prior appointment required

Access for disabled people:
Parking provided, ramped entry, access to all public areas, toilet facilities

Associated with:
Royal Blind Asylum and School

SCOTTISH BREAST CANCER CAMPAIGN

PO Box 26191, Dunfermline, Fife, KY11 3YG

Tel: 0131 623 0037
Fax: 0131 623 0037
E-mail: enquiries@scottishbreastcancercampaign.org

Enquiries:
Enquiries to: Convener
Direct tel: 01383 826112
Direct e-mail: moira@scottishbreastcancercampaign.org
Other contacts: Vice Convener tel no: 0131 623 0037 for general.

Founded:
1993

Organisation type and purpose:
Membership association (membership is by subscription), present number of members: 90.
Pressure group and support group.

Subject coverage:
Breast cancer services in Scotland.
Campaign for increased state resources for; treatment and care for patients and their families and partners, research into the causes (including environmental factors), development and treatment, counselling and the promotion of local self-help groups.

Printed publications:
Annual Report
News-sheet (4 times a year)
Occasional leaflets

Access to staff:
Contact by letter, by fax and by e-mail
Hours: No office, contact should be made as indicated

SCOTTISH BUILDING

Acronym or abbreviation: SBEF

Crichton House, 4 Crichton's Close, Holyrood, Edinburgh, EH8 8DT

Tel: 0131 556 8866
Fax: 0131 558 5247
E-mail: info@scottish-building.co.uk

Website:
http://www.scottish-building.co.uk

Enquiries:
Enquiries to: Communications and Marketing Manager
Direct e-mail: lynsey@scottish-building.co.uk

Formerly called:
Scottish Building Employers' Federation (SBEF) (year of change 2000)

Organisation type and purpose:
Trade association.

Subject coverage:
Building construction industry, legislation and contracts, education and training, single market, health and safety, industrial relations, technical, environmental.

Printed publications:
Bulletin (fortnightly, members and subscribers)
Building Matters (quarterly)
Directory of Members
Memoranda on specific subjects

Publications list:
Available online and in print

Access to staff:
Contact by letter, by telephone, by fax and by e-mail
Hours: Mon to Thu, 0900 to 1700; Fri, 0900 to 1630

Access to building, collection or gallery:
Prior appointment required

Access for disabled people:
Parking provided, ramped entry, toilet facilities

Affiliated to:
Building Employers' Confederation
Building Guarantee Scheme (Scottish Administration)

SCOTTISH BUSINESS INFORMATION SERVICE

Acronym or abbreviation: SCOTBIS

National Library of Scotland, George IV Bridge, Edinburgh, EH1 1EW

Tel: 0131 225 8488
Fax: 0131 623 3809
E-mail: enquiries@scotbis.com

Website:
http://www.scotbis.com
Provides a guide to the resources and services available from the Scottish Business Information Service

Enquiries:
Enquiries to: Head of Business Information

Founded:
1989

Organisation type and purpose:
National organisation.
National business information service.

Subject coverage:
Business information, company information, market research, statistics, news information, business journals.

Trade and statistical information:
Extensive industry and trade data held.

Non-library collection catalogue:
All or part available online and in-house

Library catalogue:
All or part available online and in-house

Access to staff:
Contact by letter, by telephone, by fax, by e-mail, in person and via website. Appointment necessary.
Hours: Mon, Tues, Thurs, Fri 0930 to 1700; Wed 1000 to 1700.
Special comments: Access to business resources in person available via the General Reading Room of the National Library of Scotland.

Other addresses:
National Library of Scotland
George IV Bridge, Edinburgh, EH1 1EW

SCOTTISH CANOE ASSOCIATION

Acronym or abbreviation: SCA

Caledonia House, South Gyle, Edinburgh, EH12 9DQ

Tel: 0131 317 7314
Fax: 0131 317 7319
E-mail: general.office@canoescotland.com

Website:
http://www.scot-canoe.org
General on sport.

Enquiries:
Enquiries to: Administrator

Founded:
1939

Organisation type and purpose:
Membership association (membership is by subscription), voluntary organisation.
Governing body of the sport.

Subject coverage:
Canoeing.

Non-library collection catalogue:
All or part available online

Printed publications:
Scottish Whitewater (£15.95)
Scottish Canoe Touring (£14.95)

Access to staff:
Contact by letter, by fax, by e-mail and via website
Hours: Mon to Fri, 0830 to 1330

Federal agreement with:
British Canoe Union
    tel: 0115 982 1100
Canoe Association for Northern Ireland
Welsh Canoeing Association

SCOTTISH CENTRE FOR CHILDREN WITH MOTOR IMPAIRMENTS

Acronym or abbreviation: SCCMI

Craighalbert Centre, 1 Craighalbert Way, Cumbernauld, Strathclyde, G68 0LS

Tel: 01236 456100
Fax: 01236 736889
E-mail: sccmi@craighalbert.org.uk

Website:
http://www.craighalbert.org.uk

Enquiries:
Enquiries to: Director
Other contacts: Administrative Officer

Founded:
1991

Organisation type and purpose:
Registered charity (charity number SC 008428), suitable for ages: 0–8.
Special needs school.

Subject coverage:
Children with motor impairments.

Access to staff:
Contact by letter, by telephone, by fax and by e-mail. Appointment necessary.
Hours: Mon to Thu, 0830 to 1700; Fri, 0830 to 1600

Access for disabled people:
Fully accessible

SCOTTISH CHAMBER ORCHESTRA LIMITED

Acronym or abbreviation: SCO

4 Royal Terrace, Edinburgh, EH7 5AB

continued overleaf

Tel: 0131 557 6800
Fax: 0131 557 6933
E-mail: info@sco.org.uk

Website:
http://www.sco.org.uk

Enquiries:
Enquiries to: Finance Director
Direct tel: 0131 478 8345
Direct e-mail: les@sco.org.uk

Founded:
1974

Formed from:
Scottish Baroque Ensemble, Scottish Philharmonia Society (year of change 1981)

Organisation type and purpose:
Professional body (membership is by election or invitation), registered charity (charity number SCO 15039).
Company Limited by Guarantee.
To promote interest in and appreciation of classical music throughout Scotland.

Subject coverage:
Orchestral music.

Printed publications:
Brochure
Concerts in Scotland
Recordings catalogue

Electronic and video publications:
Discography

Publications list:
Available online

Access to staff:
Contact by letter, by e-mail and via website
Hours: Mon to Fri, 0930 to 1730

SCOTTISH CHILD LAW CENTRE

Acronym or abbreviation: SCLC

54 East Cross Causeway, Edinburgh, EH8 9HD

Tel: 0131 667 6333
Fax: 0131 662 1713
E-mail: enquiries@sclc.org.uk

Enquiries:
Enquiries to: Administrator
Other contacts: Director

Founded:
1988

Organisation type and purpose:
National organisation, membership association (membership is by subscription), present number of members: 350, registered charity, training organisation. Advice Service, provides training and publications.

Subject coverage:
All aspects of law relating to children and young people in Scotland up to age 18; family, childcare, abduction and education law, divorce, residence, contact, children's rights, youth offenders and access to files.

Printed publications:
Various leaflets
Fact Sheet Pack
SCLC's Guide to the Children (Scotland) Act 1995 (£10)
At What Age Can I Go To See The Doctor? (50p)
Your Views in Court (50p)
Young People and Alcohol (50p)
ASBOs (50p)
Police Power (50p)
What Happens if I am Taken to the Police Station (50p)

Publications list:
Available in print

Access to staff:
Contact by letter, by telephone, by fax and by e-mail

Hours: Mon to Fri, 0930 to 1600

Access to building, collection or gallery:
No access other than to staff

SCOTTISH CHRISTIAN ALLIANCE LTD

3 Nethercairn Place, Newton Mearns, Glasgow, G77 5SZ

Tel: 0141 571 3804
E-mail: the.director@scottishchristianalliance.org

Enquiries:
Enquiries to: Director

Founded:
1993

Formerly called:
Christian Alliance (Scotland) Ltd

Incorporates the former:
YWCA of Scotland; Keychange Scotland Ltd (year of change 1997)

Organisation type and purpose:
Voluntary organisation, Scottish charity registered with OSCR and relevant local projects also registered with Care Commission.

Subject coverage:
Provision of housing support services

Printed publications:
Annual Report
Newsletters
Publicity material

Access to staff:
Contact by letter, by telephone and by e-mail
Hours: Mon to Fri, 0900 to 1700

SCOTTISH CHURCH HISTORY SOCIETY

Acronym or abbreviation: SCHS

16 Murrayburn Park, Edingburgh, EH14 2PX

Tel: 0131 442 3772
E-mail: virginia.russell@uas.gov.uk

Enquiries:
Enquiries to: Honorary Secretary

Founded:
1922

Organisation type and purpose:
Learned society.

Subject coverage:
History of the Church in Scotland.

Printed publications:
Records (annually)
Select Critical Bibliographies

Access to staff:
Contact by letter and by e-mail
Hours: Mon to Fri, 0900 to 1700

SCOTTISH COMMUNITY DRAMA ASSOCIATION

Acronym or abbreviation: SCDA

5 York Place, Edinburgh, EH1 3EB

Tel: 0131 557 5552
Fax: 0131 557 5552
E-mail: headquarters@scda.org.uk

Website:
http://www.scda.org.uk
History of the association. Services available. What's on around Scotland.

Enquiries:
Enquiries to: Administrative Assistant
Other contacts: Chairman for information on website.

Founded:
1926

Organisation type and purpose:
Membership association, registered charity (charity number SC021397), training organisation. Promotes all aspects of amateur/community theatre in Scotland. Open to all amateur clubs and interested individuals.

Subject coverage:
Information on all theatre arts, related subjects, details of theatre libraries for hire of scripts, theatre arts for the amateur in Scotland. Professional assistance with amateur productions, workshops etc.

Museum or gallery collection, archive, or library special collection:
Five libraries of play scripts situated in major cities in Scotland

Non-library collection catalogue:
All or part available in-house

Printed publications:
Scene (house magazine, quarterly, free to members, non-members £1)

Access to staff:
Contact by letter, by telephone, by fax, by e-mail, in person and via website
Hours: Mon, 0900 to 1700; Tue, Fri, 1300 to 1700; Wed, 1000 to 1200 and 1300 to 1700; Thu, 1000 to 1200

Affiliated to:
Central Council for Amateur Theatre
International Amateur Theatre Association

SCOTTISH CONSERVATION BUREAU

Room G20, Longmore House, Salisbury Place, Edinburgh, EH9 1SH

Tel: 0131 668 8668
Fax: 0131 668 8669
E-mail: hs.conservation.bureau@scotland.gov.uk

Enquiries:
Enquiries to: Bureau Manager

Founded:
1980

Organisation type and purpose:
National government body.
To provide information, advice and support to those concerned with the conservation of historic artefacts and cultural property in Scotland.

Subject coverage:
Conservation of historic objects and buildings in Scotland, careers in conservation, technical information on conservation.

Museum or gallery collection, archive, or library special collection:
Database of careers information
Database of restorers and conservators working in Scotland
Database of suppliers of conservation materials
Library of conservation books, videos, photographic material, samples

Library catalogue:
All or part available in-house

Printed publications:
Architects in Conservation (together with RIAS)
Books on stonecleaning
Conservation publications on:
Repair of Historic Buildings in Scotland (£9)
Scottish Conservation Bureau leaflet (free)
Scottish Conservation Handbook (£2.50)
Technical Advice Notes (13 titles, various prices)
Working in Conservation/Training in Conservation (£5)

Publications list:
Available in print

Access to staff:
Contact by letter, by telephone, by fax and by e-mail. Appointment necessary.
Hours: Mon to Fri, 0900 to 1700

Part of:
Historic Scotland

SCOTTISH CONSERVATIVE PARTY

Acronym or abbreviation: SCUP

83 Princes Street, Edinburgh, EH2 2ER

Tel: 0131 247 6890
Fax: 0131 247 6891
E-mail: info@scottishconservatives.com

Enquiries:
Enquiries to: Chairman

Organisation type and purpose:
Advisory body, membership association
(membership is by subscription).
Political organisation.

Subject coverage:
Scottish Conservative Party: history, organisation,
membership, statements, policies.

Access to staff:
Contact by letter, by telephone, by fax and by e-
mail. Appointment necessary.
Hours: Mon to Fri, 0900 to 1700

SCOTTISH CONSUMER COUNCIL

Acronym or abbreviation: SCC

Royal Exchange House, 100 Queen Street,
Glasgow, G1 3DN

Tel: 0141 226 5261 \ Minicom no. 0141 226 8459
Fax: 0141 221 0731
E-mail: scc@scotconsumer.org.uk

Website:
http://www.scotconsumer.org.uk

Enquiries:
Enquiries to: Director

Founded:
1975

Organisation type and purpose:
National government body.
Set up by the government in 1975 to promote the
interests of Scottish consumers, particularly those
experiencing disadvantage in society.

Subject coverage:
Consumer issues including access to information,
advice, debt, education, food, health, housing,
legal matters, local authorities, rural problems,
social security, transport, social services,
environmental affairs, food and diet, disability
issues.

Printed publications:
Annual Report
Code on Openness
Reports, policy papers and consumer information
leaflets on various issues

Publications list:
Available online and in print

Access to staff:
Contact by letter, by telephone, by fax, by e-mail
and via website. Appointment necessary.
Hours: Mon to Fri, 0900 to 1700

Part of:
National Consumer Council
20 Grosvenor Gardens, London, SW1W 0DH; tel:
020 7730 3469; fax: 020 7730 0191

SCOTTISH COT DEATH TRUST

Acronym or abbreviation: SCDT

Royal Hospital for Sick Children, Yorkhill,
Glasgow, G3 8SJ

Tel: 0141 357 3946
Fax: 0141 334 1376
E-mail: contact@sidscotland.org.uk

Website:
http://www.sidscotland.org.uk

Enquiries:
Enquiries to: Executive Director

Founded:
1985

Organisation type and purpose:
Registered charity (charity number SCO 03458).

Subject coverage:
Bereavement after cot death, advice on reducing
the risks of cot death, information on cot death
research.

Education services:
Training for health professionals

Printed publications:
Newsletter (2 times a year)
Information leaflets are available for parents,
funeral directors, police officers, health visitors,
doctors and the public (free)
Facts about Cot Death

Access to staff:
Contact by letter, by telephone, by fax and by e-
mail
Hours: Mon to Thu, 0900 to 1700; Fri, 0900 to 1600

Access for disabled people:
Parking provided, ramped entry

Links with:
SIDS International

SCOTTISH COUNCIL FOR SINGLE HOMELESS

Acronym or abbreviation: SCSH

Wellgate House, 200 Cowgate, Edinburgh, EH1
1NQ

Tel: 0131 226 4382
Fax: 0131 225 4382
E-mail: enquiries@scsh.org.uk

Website:
http://www.scsh.co.uk
General.

Enquiries:
Enquiries to: Director
Direct e-mail: robert@scsh.org.uk

Founded:
1974

Organisation type and purpose:
Voluntary organisation.
To highlight needs of homeless people, including
young people, and offer practical ideas and
information to tackle homelessness.

Subject coverage:
Homelessness, benefits, community care, housing,
education.

Printed publications:
Streets Ahead (guide for young people)
My Space My Place (young person's guide)
My Space My Place (workers toolkit)
Moving towards independence (the carer's guide)
I'd like to go to college (access to further education)
But what about me? (stock transfer and
homelessness)

Publications list:
Available online and in print

Access to staff:
Contact by letter, by telephone, by fax, by e-mail
and via website. Appointment necessary.
Hours: Mon to Fri, 0900 to 1700
Special comments: Top floor office, lift available.

SCOTTISH COUNCIL FOR VOLUNTARY ORGANISATIONS

Acronym or abbreviation: SCVO

Mansfield Traquair Centre, 15 Mansfield Place,
Edinburgh, EH3 6BB

Tel: 0131 556 3882
Fax: 0131 556 0279
E-mail: enquiries@scvo.org.uk

Website:
http://www.scvo.org.uk

Enquiries:
Enquiries to: Information Service
Direct tel: 0800 169 0022

Founded:
1943

Organisation type and purpose:
Voluntary organisation, recognised Scottish charity
(charity number SC003558).

Subject coverage:
Weekly news and current affairs, research, policy
and lobbying, conferences and seminars, training
courses, information and publications, computer
software, office supplies, payroll bureau, pensions,
insurance for the sector, project development,
Charity Giving Scotland and Give As You Earn,
and direct links with Councils for Voluntary
Service and national networks.

Printed publications:
Directories, reports, statistics, handbooks, policy
papers, workpacks, consultative documents, etc.
Third Force News (weekly)

Publications list:
Available online and in print

Access to staff:
Contact by letter, by telephone, by fax, by e-mail,
in person and via website. Appointment necessary.
Hours: Mon to Fri, 1000 to 1600

Access for disabled people:
Fully accessible

SCOTTISH COUNCIL OF INDEPENDENT SCHOOLS

Acronym or abbreviation: SCIS

21 Melville Street, Edinburgh, EH3 7PE

Tel: 0131 220 2106
Fax: 0131 225 8594
E-mail: information@scis.org.uk

Website:
http://www.scis.org.uk
Information for parents, public and press on
independent, fee-paying schools in Scotland,
including profiles of all member schools.

Enquiries:
Enquiries to: Director

Founded:
1990

Organisation type and purpose:
Advisory body, membership association
(membership is by qualification), present number
of members: 80 schools, registered charity (charity
number SC 018033), suitable for ages: 2 to 18,
consultancy.
Key aims are to: provide information, advice and
guidance to parents; advance education via
curriculum development and the training of
teachers; advise member schools and their
governing bodies about educational developments
and legislation affecting independent schools (e.g.
education, taxation, welfare, health and safety);
and to communicate and negotiate with the
Scottish Parliament, the Government, public and
private bodies on behalf of the independent sector.

Trade and statistical information:
Information and data on independent schools in
Scotland.

Library catalogue:
All or part available in-house

Printed publications:
Directory of Independent Schools in Scotland
(annual, free)
Scottish Independent Schools' Exam Results (free)
What is SCIS? (leaflet, free)
Questions to Consider When Visiting a School
(free)
A Guide to the Admissions Process (free)
Boarding Schools in Scotland (free)

continued overleaf

Meeting the Cost of School Fees (free)

Publications list:
Available online and in print

Access to staff:
Contact by letter, by telephone, by fax, by e-mail,
in person and via website. Appointment necessary.
Hours: Mon to Fri, 0900 to 1700

SCOTTISH COUNCIL ON DEAFNESS

Acronym or abbreviation: SCoD

Suite 62, 1st Floor, Central Chambers, 93 Hope
Street, Glasgow, G2 6LD

Tel: 0141 248 2474\ Textphone: 0141 248 2477
Fax: 0141 248 2479
E-mail: admin@scod.org.uk

Website:
http://www.scod.org.uk

Enquiries:
Enquiries to: Information Officer

Founded:
1927

Organisation type and purpose:
Organisation for deaf issues in Scotland.
Represents 90 organisations working with and on
behalf of deaf Sign Language users, deafened,
deafblind and hard of hearing people. The
membership provides an effective working
partnership between the voluntary sector, social
work and education departments, NHS Trusts,
health boards and the Government. Registered
charity (charity number SC016957).

Subject coverage:
All aspects of deafness, e.g. deaf Sign Language
users, hard of hearing, deafened, deafblind,
agencies for deaf people, employment, voluntary
help, advice and information.

Printed publications:
Annual Report
History
Range of Leaflets
Scottish Directory of Relevant Service Providers

Publications list:
Available online and in print

Access to staff:
Contact by letter, by telephone, by fax, by e-mail,
in person and via website. Appointment necessary.
Hours: Mon to Fri, 0900 to 1600

Links with:
organisations working with deaf, hard of hearing
and deafblind people.

SCOTTISH CRICKET UNION

Acronym or abbreviation: SCU

National Cricket Academy, MES Sports Centre,
Ravelston, Edinburgh, EH4 3NT

Tel: 0131 313 7420
Fax: 0131 313 7430
E-mail: admin.scu@btinternet.com

Website:
http://www.scu.org.uk
General information and results service on Scottish
cricket.
http://www.btinternet.com/~sncl
Scottish National Cricket League: results and
league tables.

Enquiries:
Enquiries to: Chief Executive

Founded:
1909

Organisation type and purpose:
National government body, advisory body
(membership is by subscription), present number
of members: 800 members, 168 clubs, training
organisation, consultancy.

Governing body of cricket in Scotland.

Subject coverage:
Scottish cricket at domestic and international level.

Printed publications:
Newsletter (annually, free)
SCU coaching cards (£10)
The guide to Scottish cricket (annually, £6)

Access to staff:
Contact by letter, by telephone, by fax, by e-mail
and in person
Hours: Mon to Fri, 0900 to 1700

Affiliated to:
International Cricket Council

SCOTTISH CROP RESEARCH INSTITUTE

Acronym or abbreviation: SCRI

Mylnefield, Invergowrie, Dundee, DD2 5DA

Tel: 01382 562731
Fax: 01382 562426
E-mail: library@scri.ac.uk

Website:
http://www.scri.ac.uk

Enquiries:
Enquiries to: Librarian

Founded:
1922

Organisation type and purpose:
Learned society, registered charity (charity number
SCO 11854), research organisation.

Subject coverage:
All facets of crop research in the northern
hemisphere. Plant genetics and breeding, plant
biotechnology and molecular biology, plant
physiology and agronomy, plant pathology and
crop protection, biochemistry and plant analyses,
biomathematics, potatoes, barley and soft fruit.
Biodiversity and sustainability in managed arable
ecosystems.

**Museum or gallery collection, archive, or library
special collection:**
Pethybridge Collection on potato pathology, 1870–
1930
Special collections of research literature on
raspberries and potatoes now closed

Library catalogue:
All or part available in-house

Printed publications:
Annual Report

Access to staff:
Appointment necessary.
Hours: Mon to Fri, 0900 to 1700

Constituent part of:
Scottish Research Institutes

Funded by:
Scottish Government

SCOTTISH CULTURAL PRESS & SCOTTISH CHILDREN'S PRESS

Acronym or abbreviation: SCP

Unit 6, Newbattle Abbey Business Park, Newbattle
Road, Dalkeith, Midlothian, EH22 3LJ

Tel: 0131 660 6366
Fax: 0870 285 4846
E-mail: info@scottishbooks.com

Website:
http://www.scottishbooks.com
Publication list.

Enquiries:
Direct tel: 0131 660 4666

Founded:
1992

Subject coverage:
Children's Scottish fiction and non-fiction
including history, literature, poetry, environmental
history, biography, Scottish language and folk
tradition.

Printed publications:
Ally Frazer Stories, a selection of historical
adventures (Cameron I, £3.99)
Columba: Iona & the Spread of Christianity (Mac
Laverty B, £2.99)
Discover Scotland's History: guide to Scottish
history for children (Cameron A D, £12.99)
Selection of fiction, poetry and children's writing
Selection of Scots language books
Teach the Bairns to Cook: Traditional Scottish
recipes (Ashworth L, £5.95)
Touching the Past Archaeology 5–14 (Curtis N & E
ed, £4.95)
Order printed publications from: tel: 0131 660 4666,
fax: 0870 285 4846

Publications list:
Available online

Access to staff:
Contact by letter, by telephone, by fax, by e-mail
and via website. Appointment necessary.
Hours: Mon to Fri, 1000 to 1600
Special comments: By appointment only.

Access to building, collection or gallery:
No access to building.

SCOTTISH CYCLING

Acronym or abbreviation: SC

The Velodrome, London Road, Edinburgh, EH7
6AD

Tel: 0131 652 0187
E-mail: info@scottishcycling.com

Website:
http://www.scottishcycling.com

Enquiries:
Enquiries to: Administrator

Founded:
1889

Organisation type and purpose:
Membership association (membership is by
subscription), present number of members: 2000.
Governing body for cycle sport in Scotland.

Subject coverage:
Cycle sport, road racing, mountain biking, track
racing, time trialing, cyclo cross, coaching.

Printed publications:
Handbook (annually, £7.50)

Publications list:
Available in print

Access to staff:
Contact by letter, by telephone, by e-mail, in
person and via website. Appointment necessary.
Hours: Mon to Fri, 0900 to 1700

Member of:
British Cycling (BC)
National Cycling Centre, Stuart Street,
Manchester, M11 4DQ; tel: 0870 871 2000; e-mail:
info@britishcycling.org

SCOTTISH DANCE TEACHERS' ALLIANCE

Acronym or abbreviation: SDTA

101 Park Road, Glasgow, G4 9JE

Tel: 0141 339 8944
Fax: 0141 357 4994
E-mail: sdta@btconnect.com

Enquiries:
Enquiries to: Executive Secretary

Founded:
1934

Organisation type and purpose:
International organisation, professional body (membership is by qualification).

Subject coverage:
Highland, ballet, theatre, ballroom, Latin American Baton, rock 'n roll, disco dancing, line dancing and cheer dance.

Printed publications:
SOBHD Text Book
Syllabi and textbooks for all branches of dancing

Electronic and video publications:
Tape/disc/video for purchase directly

Access to staff:
Contact by letter, by telephone, by fax and by e-mail
Hours: Mon to Fri, 0900 to 1700

Access to building, collection or gallery:
No access other than to staff, no prior appointment required

Access for disabled people:
Parking provided, ramped entry, level entry, toilet facilities

Links with:
SOBHD and BCD/WD&DSC

SCOTTISH DECORATORS FEDERATION

Acronym or abbreviation: SDF

Castlecraig Business Park, Players Road, Stirling, FK7 7SH

Tel: 01786 448838
Fax: 01786 450541
E-mail: info@scottishdecorators.co.uk

Website:
http://www.scottishdecorators.co.uk

Enquiries:
Enquiries to: Chief Executive

Founded:
1878

Organisation type and purpose:
Trade association (membership is by qualification), service industry.

Subject coverage:
Painting and decorating.

Museum or gallery collection, archive, or library special collection:
Historical collection

Printed publications:
Newsletters
Year Book

Access to staff:
Contact by letter, by telephone and by fax
Hours: Mon to Fri, 0900 to 1700

Member of:
National Specialist Contractors Council (NSCC)

SCOTTISH DEVELOPMENT INTERNATIONAL

Acronym or abbreviation: SDI

150 Broomielaw, Glasgow, G2 8LU

Tel: 0141 228 2828
E-mail: michelle.cowan@scotent.co.uk

Website:
http://www.scottishdevelopmentinternational.com
Full details of services on offer to inward investors and trade investors.

Enquiries:
Enquiries to: Information Officer

Founded:
2001

Formerly called:
Locate in Scotland (LIS), Scottish Trade International (STI) (year of change 2001)

Organisation type and purpose:
International organisation.

Access to staff:
Contact by letter, by telephone, by e-mail and via website
Hours: Mon to Fri, 0900 to 1700

National and international offices:
offices in Brussels, Düsseldorf, Italy, Paris, USA, Tokyo, Seoul, Taipei, Singapore, China, India, Russia, Azerbaijan, UAE
SDI
  Dover House, Whitehall, London, SW1A 2AU; tel: 020 7839 2117; fax: 020 7839 2975

SCOTTISH DISABILITY SPORT

Acronym or abbreviation: SDS

Fife Sports Institute, Viewfield Road, Glenrothes, Fife, KY6 2RB

Tel: 01592 415700
Fax: 01592 415710
E-mail: ssadsds@aol.com

Website:
http://www.scottishdisabilitysport.com

Enquiries:
Enquiries to: Administrator

Founded:
1962

Formerly called:
Scottish Sports Association for Disabled People (SSAD)

Organisation type and purpose:
Voluntary organisation.

Subject coverage:
Sport and recreation for people with disabilities.

Transitional office:
Scottish Disability Sport
  Caledonian House, South Gyle, Edinburgh, EH12 9DQ; tel: 0131 317 1130; fax: 0131 317 1075; e-mail: ssadsds2@aol.com

SCOTTISH DRUGS FORUM

Acronym or abbreviation: SDF

91 Mitchell Street, Glasgow, G1 3LN

Tel: 0141 221 1175
Fax: 0141 248 6414
E-mail: enquiries@sdf.org.uk

Website:
http://www.sdf.org.uk

Enquiries:
Enquiries to: Information Officer
Other contacts: Regional Manager (for specific drugs issues)

Founded:
1986

Organisation type and purpose:
Membership association (membership is by subscription), voluntary organisation, registered charity (charity number 106295).
National policy and information agency working in partnership with others to co-ordinate effective responses to drug use in Scotland.

Subject coverage:
Information on drugs issues, information about all (national) drugs projects and groups in Scotland, leaflets and brochures for anyone interested in drugs issues.

Information services:
Library of material relevant to drug use in Scotland

Special visitor services:
Visits by appointment

Printed publications:
SDF Bulletin (including Volatile Substances Focus, 10 times a year, free to members, subscription rate for non-members)
Policy Statements (single copies free, charges for multiples)
Survivor's Guide to Drugs and Clubbing
Methadone at Work – guidance for employers
Methadone Leaflet
Order printed publications from: via website publications order form

Electronic and video publications:
Where to get help for a drug problem (online)

Publications list:
Available online and in print

Access to staff:
Contact by letter, by telephone, by fax, by e-mail, in person and via website. Appointment necessary.

Access to building, collection or gallery:
Hours: Mon to Fri, 0900 to 1700

Access for disabled people:
lift is wheelchair accessible
Special comments: no disabled toilet

Also at:
Scottish Drugs Forum
  139 Morrison Street, Edinburgh, EH3 8AJ; tel: 0131 221 9300; fax: 0131 221 1556

SCOTTISH ENGINEERING

105 West George Street, Glasgow, G2 1QL

Tel: 0141 221 3181
Fax: 0141 204 1202
E-mail: consult@ScottishEngineering.org.uk

Website:
http://www.ScottishEngineering.org.uk

Enquiries:
Enquiries to: Secretary

Founded:
1865

Formerly called:
Scottish Engineering Employers' Association

Organisation type and purpose:
Advisory body, professional body (membership is by subscription), present number of members: 400, manufacturing industry, consultancy.

Subject coverage:
Employee relations; terms and conditions of employment; employment law and industrial tribunals; health and safety; training and development.

Trade and statistical information:
Wage and salary surveys.

Printed publications:
Members Briefings
Quarterly Review

Access to staff:
Contact by letter, by telephone and by fax. Appointment necessary. Non-members charged.
Hours: Mon to Fri, 0900 to 1700

Links with:
Engineering Employers' Federation

SCOTTISH ENTERPRISE

Acronym or abbreviation: SE

5 Atlantic Quay, 150 Broomielaw, Glasgow, G2 8LU

Tel: 0141 248 2700
Fax: 0141 221 3217
E-mail: network.helpline@scotent.co.uk

Website:
http://www.scottish-enterprise.com

Enquiries:
Enquiries to: Manager, Knowledge Exchange
Direct tel: 0141 228 2268
Direct e-mail: gail.rogers@scotent.co.uk

Founded:
1991

continued overleaf

Formed from:
Scottish Development Agency, Training Agency

Formerly called:
Scottish Development Agency (SDA) (year of change 1991)

Organisation type and purpose:
National government body.
Economic development of Scotland.

Subject coverage:
Company data, market data, sectoral data, economic data, county data, government publications, in-house reports.

Museum or gallery collection, archive, or library special collection:
Internally generated research

Access to staff:
Contact by letter
Hours: Mon to Fri, 0900 to 1700

Access to building, collection or gallery:
No access other than to staff

SCOTTISH ENVIRONMENT LINK

Acronym or abbreviation: LINK

2 Grosvenor House, Shore Road, Perth, Tayside, PH2 8BD

Tel: 01738 630804
Fax: 01738 643290
E-mail: enquiries@scotlink.org

Website:
http://www.scotlink.org
Home page.
http://www.scotlink.org/pub.htm
Publications list.

Enquiries:
Enquiries to: Information Officer

Founded:
1987

Formerly called:
Scottish Wildlife and Countryside Link (SWCL)

Still known as:
Scottish LINK

Organisation type and purpose:
Membership association, Scottish company limited by guarantee and without a share capital, and a Scottish charity (number SC000296).
Voluntary organisations working together to care for and improve Scotland's environment for people and nature.
Liaison body for 30 of the main voluntary environmental organisations in Scotland.

Subject coverage:
Environmental sustainability in Scotland.

Non-library collection catalogue:
All or part available online

Printed publications:
Publications on a variety of environmental issues, conference proceedings, reports, audits, campaign briefings

Publications list:
Available online and in print

Access to staff:
Contact by letter, by telephone, by fax and by e-mail
Hours: Mon to Fri, 0900 to 1600

SCOTTISH ENVIRONMENT PROTECTION AGENCY

Acronym or abbreviation: SEPA

Erskine Court, The Castle Business Park, Stirling, FK9 4TR

Tel: 01786 457700
Fax: 01786 446885
E-mail: enquiries@sepa.org.uk

Website:
http://www.sepa.org.uk

Enquiries:
Enquiries to: Information Scientist
Direct e-mail: alison.mackinnon@sepa.org
Other contacts: Press Officer for press enquiries.

Founded:
1996

Formed from:
Her Majesty's Industrial Pollution Inspectorate (HMIPI), The River Protection Boards (RPB) for Forth, Highland, North East, Solway, Tay, Tweed

Formerly called:
Clyde River Purification Board (RPB) (year of change 1996)

Organisation type and purpose:
Statutory body.

Subject coverage:
Environmental regulation, air quality, radioactive substances, water quality, pollution, sustainable development, compliance with EU environmental directives.

Museum or gallery collection, archive, or library special collection:
Environment
Scotland & Northern Ireland Forum on Environmental Research – library of publications: guidance document, statistics, air quality, water quality, radioactive substances
Organisation/Government reports
Legal information – environment

Trade and statistical information:
Statistics: bathing waters; water quality.

Non-library collection catalogue:
All or part available in-house

Library catalogue:
All or part available in-house

Printed publications:
Corporate & Environmental Reports
Information leaflets
Technical papers
Order printed publications from: Publications Officer

Publications list:
Available online

Access to staff:
Contact by telephone, by e-mail and via website.
Appointment necessary.
Hours: Mon to Fri, 0900 to 1700

Access to building, collection or gallery:
Prior appointment required

Access for disabled people:
Level entry

Other offices:
SEPA East Region HQ
 Clearwater House, Heriot Watt Research Park, Avenue North, Riccarton, Edinburgh, EH14 4AP; tel: 0131 449 7296; fax: 0131 449 7277
SEPA Head Office
 Erskine Court, The Castle Business Park, Stirling, FK9 4TR; tel: 01786 457700; fax: 01786 446885
SEPA North Region HQ
 Graesser House, Fodderty Way, Dingwall Business Park, Dingwall, IV15 9XB; tel: 01349 862021; fax: 01349 863987
SEPA West Region HQ
 SEPA West, 5 Redwood Crescent, Peel Park, East Kilbride, Glasgow, G74 5PP; tel: 01355 574200; fax: 01355 574688

SCOTTISH EXECUTIVE

Information Management Unit, Y Spur, Saughton House, Edinburgh, EH11 3XD

Tel: 0131 244 4556
Fax: 0131 244 4545
E-mail: selibrary@scotland.gsi.gov.uk

Website:
http://www.scotland.gov.uk

Enquiries:
Enquiries to: Information Officer
Direct e-mail: selibrary@scotland.gsi.gov.uk

Formerly called:
Scottish Office (year of change 1999)

Organisation type and purpose:
National government body.
Library and information service, serving the Scottish Executive.

Subject coverage:
Scottish administration, education, health, crime, police, prisons, social work, transport.

Non-library collection catalogue:
All or part available in-house

Library catalogue:
All or part available in-house

Printed publications:
The Scottish Executive Publications List
Order printed publications from: Astron or Blackwells Bookshop, Edinburgh

Publications list:
Available online and in print

Access to staff:
Appointment necessary.
Hours: Mon to Fri, 0900 to 1700

Access for disabled people:
Access to all public areas

SCOTTISH FEDERATION OF HOUSING ASSOCIATIONS LIMITED

Acronym or abbreviation: SFHA

38 York Place, Edinburgh, EH1 3HU

Tel: 0131 556 5777
Fax: 0131 557 6028
E-mail: sfha@sfha.co.uk

Website:
http://www.sfha.co.uk
Current news service, job-search service, information on membership, details of conferences, training, publications, links to related websites.

Enquiries:
Enquiries to: Administrator
Direct tel: 0131 473 6224
Direct e-mail: smorton@sfha.co.uk

Founded:
1976

Organisation type and purpose:
Trade association (membership is by subscription).
Representative body for Registered Social Landlords in Scotland.

Subject coverage:
Information on Scottish Registered Social Landlords, housing policy and practice.

Printed publications:
Briefing Papers on topics such as homelessness, community care, regenerating communities, legislation
Codes of Conduct
Housing Focus (journal, 10 times a year, annual subscription, free to members, £95 non-members)
Guidance Booklets on topics such as contracts for care, stock transfers guidance manual (also with computerised spreadsheet model), internal management plans, planned maintenance and repairs
Raising Standards series of best practice guidance
Model Agreements on tenancy, occupancy, leasing
SCORE (periodic reports, and annual digest)

Access to staff:
Contact by letter, by telephone, by fax, by e-mail and via website. Appointment necessary.
Hours: Mon to Fri, 0900 to 1700

Access to building, collection or gallery:
No access other than to staff

Access for disabled people:
Ramped entry
Special comments: Wheelchair lift (external).

Other addresses:
Scottish Federation of Housing Associations
24 Mauchline Place West, Dundee, DD4 8HS; tel:
01382 510656; fax: 01382 510990
Scottish Federation of Housing Associations
4th Floor, Pegasus House, 375 West George
Street, Glasgow, G2 4LW; tel: 0141 332 8113; fax:
0141 332 9684

SCOTTISH FEDERATION OF SEA ANGLERS

Acronym or abbreviation: SFSA

Unit 6, Evans Business Centre, Mitchelston Drive,
Mitchelston Industrial Estate, Kirkaldy, Fife, KY1
3NB

Tel: 01592 657520
Fax: 01592 657520

Website:
http://www.sfsa.freeserve.co.uk

Founded:
1961

Organisation type and purpose:
Membership association (membership is by
subscription).
Recognised by Sportscotland as the governing
body for the sport of sea fishing in Scotland.

Subject coverage:
Sea fishing.

Printed publications:
2006 Handbook (for purchase)

Access to staff:
Contact by letter, by telephone, by fax and in
person. Appointment necessary.
Hours: Mon, Tue, Thu, Fri, 0930 to 1300

Links with:
Sea Angling Liaison Committee of Great Britain
and Ireland (SALC)
tel: 0626 331 330

SCOTTISH FOOD AND DRINK FEDERATION

Acronym or abbreviation: SFDF

4a Torphichen Street, Edinburgh, EH3 8JQ

Tel: 0131 229 9415
Fax: 0131 229 9407
E-mail: flora.mclean@sfdf.org.uk

Website:
http://www.sfdf.org.uk

Enquiries:
Enquiries to: Director

Founded:
1999

Organisation type and purpose:
Trade association (membership is by subscription).

Subject coverage:
Food and drink manufacturing in Scotland.

Access to staff:
Contact by letter, by telephone, by fax, by e-mail
and via website. Appointment necessary. Access
for members only.
Hours: Mon to Fri, 0900 to 1700

Constituent part of:
Food and Drink Federation

SCOTTISH FOOTBALL ASSOCIATION LIMITED

Acronym or abbreviation: SFA

Hampden Park, Glasgow, G42 9AY

Tel: 0141 616 6000

Fax: 0141 616 6001
E-mail: info@scottishfa.co.uk

Website:
http://www.scottishfa.co.uk

Enquiries:
Enquiries to: Chief Executive

Founded:
1873

Organisation type and purpose:
Governing body for football in Scotland.

Subject coverage:
Player registrations, the laws of the game,
coaching, refereeing, general and specific football
matters of public interest.

**Museum or gallery collection, archive, or library
special collection:**
Old documents, minute books etc are now housed
in the Scottish Football Museum at Hampden
Park
Various football trophies and mementos

Printed publications:
SFA Annual Report (free)
SFA Handbook (annually, £12 inc. p&p)

Electronic and video publications:
Various coaching videos (available via football
development department)

Access to staff:
Contact by letter, by telephone, by fax and by e-
mail
Hours: Mon to Fri, 0900 to 1700

Member of:
Fédération Internationale de Football Association
(FIFA)
Union Des Associations Européennes de Football
(UEFA)

SCOTTISH FOOTBALL LEAGUE, THE

Acronym or abbreviation: SFL

Hampden Park, Glasgow, G42 9EB

Tel: 0141 620 4160
Fax: 0141 620 4161
E-mail: info@scottishfootballleague.com

Enquiries:
Enquiries to: Secretary

Founded:
1890

Subject coverage:
Administration, marketing, promotion, fostering
and development of association football, especially
via the SFL championship, league cup, and league
challenge cup competitions.

**Museum or gallery collection, archive, or library
special collection:**
Minute Books 1890–2006
Registration Books 1898–2006
SFL results, appearances, attendances, etc
Various historical documents pertaining to
association football

Printed publications:
Scottish Football League Fixture Booklet (annually)
Scottish Football League Handbook (annually)
The Scottish Football League Review (annually)

Access to staff:
Contact by letter, by telephone and by fax
Hours: Mon to Fri, 0900 to 1700; Sat, 0930 to 1200

SCOTTISH FUNDING COUNCIL

Formal name: Scottish Further and Higher
Education Funding Council
Acronym or abbreviation: SFC

Donaldson House, 97 Haymarket Terrace,
Edinburgh, EH12 5HD

Tel: 0131 313 6500
Fax: 0131 313 6501

E-mail: info@sfc.ac.uk

Website:
http://www.sfc.ac.uk
Circular letters, council reports, teaching quality
assessment reports, council publications, news
releases

Enquiries:
Enquiries to: Head of Communications
Direct tel: 0131 313 6612
Direct e-mail: communications@sfc.ac.uk

Founded:
2005

Replaced:
Scottish Further Education Council and Scottish
Higher Education Funding Council (year of
change 2005)

Organisation type and purpose:
National government body, advisory body,
funding body, supporting universities and colleges
in the provison of high quality learning and
internationally competitive research.

Subject coverage:
Funding policies, guidance on the provision of
learning and teaching, further and higher
education in Scotland.

Trade and statistical information:
Data on numbers of students and staff at further
and higher education institutions in Scotland;
data on income and expenditure of further and
higher education institutions in Scotland.

Printed publications:
Annual Report
Corporate Plan
Circular Letters
Consultation Papers
Ad hoc reports

Publications list:
Available online

Access to staff:
Contact by letter, by telephone, by e-mail and via
website
Hours: Mon to Fri, 0900 to 1700

SCOTTISH GAELIC TEXTS SOCIETY

Acronym or abbreviation: SGTS

c/o McLeish Carswell, 29 St Vincent Place,
Glasgow, G1 2DT

Tel: 0141 248 4134
Fax: 0141 226 3118

Enquiries:
Enquiries to: Honorary Secretary

Founded:
1934

Organisation type and purpose:
Learned society (membership is by subscription),
registered charity.

Subject coverage:
Scottish Gaelic literature generally, but especially
learned texts hitherto unpublished or requiring
revision.

Printed publications:
Texts as they become available (list from the
Society)

Publications list:
Available in print

Access to staff:
Contact by letter
Hours: Mon to Fri, 0900 to 1700

Grant-aided by:
three universities

SCOTTISH GAMES ASSOCIATION

Acronym or abbreviation: SGA

continued overleaf

24 Florence Place, Perth, Tayside, PH1 5BH

Tel: 01738 627782
Fax: 01738 639622
E-mail: andrew@highlandgames.org.uk

Website:
http://www.highlandgames-sga.com

Enquiries:
Enquiries to: Honorary Secretary

Founded:
1946

Organisation type and purpose:
Professional body.
National Governing body.

Subject coverage:
Professional activities and participation in most games and sports in Scotland.

Printed publications:
Annual year book – normally available in February
Order printed publications from: The Secretary, Scottish Games Association

SCOTTISH GENEALOGY SOCIETY

15 Victoria Terrace, Edinburgh, EH1 2JL

Tel: 0131 220 3677
Fax: 0131 220 3677
E-mail: info@scotsgenealogy.com

Website:
http://www.scotsgenealogy.com
Information on society, membership and sales.

Enquiries:
Enquiries to: Honorary Secretary

Founded:
1953

Organisation type and purpose:
Learned society.
Genealogy and Family History Library.

Subject coverage:
Scottish family history and genealogy.

Museum or gallery collection, archive, or library special collection:
Card indexes relating to several families including Stirling and Mackay
Largest Scottish collection of unpublished lists of monumental (graveyard) inscriptions

Library catalogue:
All or part available in-house

Printed publications:
A large range of publications on genealogy, local and family history under the headings armed forces, Burgh Records, Castles of Scotland, Census 1841, 1851, 1861; Directories, Emigrants & Immigrants, Jacobites, Mariners and Ships, People & Poll Tax Lists of 1696, Sources and Guides, Trades and Professions, Vital Records, Wills and Testaments
Monumental Inscriptions (32 volumes)
The Scottish Genealogist (journal, quarterly, free to members)

Microform publications:
Edinburgh Directories (microfiche)
Some Census indexes
Members' Interests

Electronic and video publications:
Inquisitionum Retornatum ad Capellam Domini Regis Quae in Publicis Archives Scotiae (ed Thomson T, CD-ROM)
Decennial Indexes to the Services of Heirs in Scotland, 1700–1859 (CD-ROM)
The Scots Peerage (ed Paul J B, CD-ROM)

Publications list:
Available in print

Access to staff:
Contact by letter, by fax, by e-mail, in person and via website
Hours: Mon, Tue, Thu, 1030 to 1730; Wed, 1030 to 2030; Sat, 1000 to 1700

Member of:
Scottish Association of Family History Societies

SCOTTISH GLADIOLUS SOCIETY

Acronym or abbreviation: SGS

63 Gardiner Road, Edinburgh, EH4 3RL

Tel: 0131 332 3681

Enquiries:
Enquiries to: Secretary

Founded:
1972

Organisation type and purpose:
National organisation, membership association (membership is by subscription), present number of members: 40, voluntary organisation, research organisation.

Subject coverage:
To promote the cultivation, exhibition, research and hybridisation of Gladioli. Contribute towards Gladioli interest in both Britain and overseas and generally support Scottish Flower Shows and Scottish Horticulture with exhibits, expert show judges and lecturers.

Other address:
British Gladiolus Society (BGS)
Honorary Correspondence Secretary, 197 Aston Clinton Road, Aylesbury, Buckinghamshire, HP22 5AD

SCOTTISH GROCERS' FEDERATION

222–224 Queensferry Road, Edinburgh, EH4 2BN

Tel: 0131 343 3300
Fax: 0131 343 6147

Enquiries:
Enquiries to: Chief Executive

Founded:
1918

Organisation type and purpose:
Trade association (membership is by subscription).

Printed publications:
Retail News (to members, monthly)

Access to staff:
Contact by letter, by telephone, by fax and in person. Access for members only.
Hours: Mon to Fri, 0900 to 1700

SCOTTISH GROCERY TRADE EMPLOYERS' ASSOCIATION

222–224 Queensferry Road, Edinburgh, EH4 2BN

Tel: 0131 343 3300
Fax: 0131 343 6147

Enquiries:
Enquiries to: Chief Executive

Organisation type and purpose:
Membership association (membership is by subscription), present number of members: c. 700.

Access to staff:
Contact by letter, by telephone and by fax.
Appointment necessary. Access for members only.
Hours: Mon to Fri, 0900 to 1700

Parent body:
Scottish Grocers' Federation

SCOTTISH HEALTH SERVICE CENTRE

Acronym or abbreviation: SHSC

Health Management Library, Crewe Road South, Edinburgh, EH4 2LF

Tel: 0131 275 7760
Fax: 0131 315 2369

E-mail: library@shsc.csa.scot.nhs.uk

Website:
http://www.healthmanagementonline.co.uk
Library Website

Enquiries:
Enquiries to: Librarian

Founded:
1965

Formerly called:
Common Services Agency – Management Education and Training Division (MET), Scottish Health Service Management Development Group (MDG); NHS in Scotland Development Group (DG) (year of change 1998)

Organisation type and purpose:
National government body. Library and information service for NHS in Scotland staff.

Subject coverage:
National Health Service, health services planning, administration, management, social welfare.

Library catalogue:
All or part available in-house

Printed publications:
Library Current Awareness Bulletin (monthly)
Periodicals List (annually)
Training Materials List (annually)

Publications list:
Available online and in print

Access to staff:
Contact by letter, by telephone, by fax, by e-mail and via website
Hours: Mon to Thu, 0830 to 1700; Fri, 0830 to 1630

Access to building, collection or gallery:
No prior appointment required

Access for disabled people:
Ramped entry

Part of the:
Common Services Agency for the NHS in Scotland

SCOTTISH HISTORIC BUILDINGS TRUST

Acronym or abbreviation: SHBT

11 Atholl Crescent Lane, Edinburgh, EH3 8ET

Tel: 0131 656 0700
Fax: 0131 656 0701
E-mail: shbt@conservationtrust.co.uk

Website:
http://www.conservationtrust.co.uk/shbt/

Enquiries:
Enquiries to: Chairman

Founded:
1986

Organisation type and purpose:
Registered charity.
Building preservation trust.
Acquisition, repair and reuse of buildings of architectural or historic importance throughout Scotland.

Subject coverage:
Management and techniques of building conservation.

Museum or gallery collection, archive, or library special collection:
Books, journals, reports, slides etc on building conservation

Printed publications:
Annual Report and Accounts (£2)
Building Archaeology Reports (individually priced)

Access to staff:
Contact by letter, by telephone and by fax.
Appointment necessary.
Hours: Mon to Fri, 0900 to 1800

Special comments: Information only available to registered charities and other non-profit making organisations.

Member of:
UK Association of Preservation Trusts
Clarevill House, 26–27 Oxendon Street, London, SW1Y 4EL; tel: 020 7930 1629; fax: 020 7930 0295

SCOTTISH HISTORY SOCIETY

Acronym or abbreviation: SHS

Dr Katie Stevenson, School of History, University of St Andrews, St Katharine's Lodge, The Scores, St Andrews, KY16 9AL

Tel: 01337 831996
E-mail: kcs7@st-andrews.ac.uk

Website:
http://www.scottishhistorysociety.org

Enquiries:
Enquiries to: Honorary Secretary

Organisation type and purpose:
Learned society. Publication of documents relevant to Scottish history.

Subject coverage:
Scottish history.

Publications list:
Available online and in print

SCOTTISH HUMAN RIGHTS CENTRE

Acronym or abbreviation: SHRC

146 Holland Street, Glasgow, G2 4NG

Tel: 0141 332 5960
Fax: 0141 332 5309
E-mail: info@scottishhumanrightscentre.org.uk

Website:
http://www.scottishhumanrightscentre.org.uk
An overview of advice, research, scrutiny of legislational reports to the United Nations on Human Rights. There are also useful links to other sites and the text of the Scottish Declaration of Human Rights.

Enquiries:
Enquiries to: Administrator
Other contacts: Advice and Information Officer for advice on human rights issues.

Founded:
1970

Formerly called:
Scottish Council for Civil Liberties (SCCL) (year of change 1997)

Organisation type and purpose:
Membership association (membership is by subscription), voluntary organisation.
Campaigning for the promotion and defence of human rights in Scotland.

Subject coverage:
Promote Human Rights in Scotland.

Museum or gallery collection, archive, or library special collection:
European Court of Human Rights Reports

Library catalogue:
All or part available in-house

Printed publications:
Wide variety of briefing papers
Rights (newsletter, six times a year, available to members)

Publications list:
Available in print

Access to staff:
Contact by letter, by telephone, by fax, by e-mail and via website
Hours: Mon to Fri, 1400 to 1700

Access to building, collection or gallery:
Prior appointment required

Affiliated to:
International Federation of Human Rights (FIDH)

SCOTTISH HUNTINGTON'S ASSOCIATION

Thistle House, 61 Main Road, Elderslie, Johnstone, Renfrewshire, PA5 9BA

Tel: 01505 322245
Fax: 01505 382980
E-mail: sha-admin@hdscotland.org

Enquiries:
Enquiries to: Administrator

Founded:
1989

Organisation type and purpose:
Voluntary organisation, registered charity.

Subject coverage:
Huntington's Disease.

Publications list:
Available in print

Access to staff:
Contact by telephone
Hours: Mon to Fri, 0900 to 1700

SCOTTISH INLAND WATERWAYS ASSOCIATION

Acronym or abbreviation: SIWA

Clifton Staithe, Newbridge, Midlothian, EH28 8LQ

Tel: 0131 333 1231

Enquiries:
Enquiries to: Chairman

Organisation type and purpose:
National government body (membership is by subscription), voluntary organisation.
National organisation to further use of canals in Scotland.

Subject coverage:
Scottish canals.

Access to staff:
Contact by letter and by telephone
Hours: Mon to Fri, 0900 to 1700

SCOTTISH JEWISH ARCHIVES CENTRE

Garnethill Synagogue, 129 Hill Street, Glasgow, G3 6UB

Tel: 0141 332 4911
Fax: 0131 332 4911
E-mail: info@sjac.org.uk

Website:
http://www.sjac.org.uk

Enquiries:
Enquiries to: Director
Direct e-mail: rvlkaplan@googlemail.com

Founded:
1987

Organisation type and purpose:
Registered charity, museum, research organisation.

Subject coverage:
History of Jews in Scotland.

Non-library collection catalogue:
All or part available in-house

Library catalogue:
All or part available in-house

Publications list:
Available online

Access to staff:
Contact by letter, by e-mail and in person.
Appointment necessary.
Hours: Monthly Sun, 1400 to 1600. Fri morning, by appointment.

SCOTTISH JU-JITSU ASSOCIATION

Acronym or abbreviation: SJJA

House of Samurai, 3 Dens Street, Dundee, DD4 6BU

Tel: 01382 458262
Fax: 01382 458262
E-mail: scottishjujitsu@aol.com

Website:
http://www.sjja.eu

Enquiries:
Enquiries to: Executive Administrator
Other contacts: Technical Director, Events Director, Communications Director

Founded:
1979

Organisation type and purpose:
National organisation, membership association (membership is by subscription).
Governing body of sport.
To regulate, control and educate in the sport and art of ju-jitsu.

Subject coverage:
Information on ju-jitsu clubs throughout Scotland.
International ju-jitsu organisations and ko ryu (traditional systems) organisations.

Museum or gallery collection, archive, or library special collection:
Coaching videos (only available to members), 'The Essentials' (Robert G. Ross)

Non-library collection catalogue:
All or part available in-house

Library catalogue:
All or part available in-house

Printed publications:
Newsletter (6 times a year, free to members)

Electronic and video publications:
EMBU – paired competition format compulsory moves (video)
The Syllabus – Series of five videos depicting association curriculum

Access to staff:
Contact by letter, by telephone, by fax, by e-mail and via website. Appointment necessary. Access for members only.
Hours: Mon, Wed and Fri, 1100 to 2200; Tue and Thu, 1100 to 1500; Sat, 1100 to 1300

Access to building, collection or gallery:
No prior appointment required
Hours: Mon to Fri, 1830 to 2200

Member organisation of:
British Association of Sport and Exercise Sciences
tel: 0113 8126162; fax: 0113 8126163; website: http://www.bases.org.uk
Scottish Schools Sports Association
tel: 0141 353 3215; fax: 0141 353 3815

SCOTTISH LANDOWNERS' FEDERATION

Acronym or abbreviation: SLF

Stuart House, Eskmills Business Park, Musselburgh, Midlothian, EH21 7PB

Tel: 0131 653 5400
Fax: 0131 653 5401
E-mail: slfinfo@slf.org.uk

Enquiries:
Enquiries to: Director

Founded:
1906

Organisation type and purpose:
Membership association (membership is by subscription), present number of members: 3500.

Subject coverage:
Land use advice, legal advice on land management to members only.

continued overleaf

Printed publications:
Landowning in Scotland (journal, six times a year, free to members)

Access to staff:
Contact by letter, by telephone, by fax and by e-mail
Hours: Mon to Thu, 0800 to 1700; Fri, 0800 to 1630

SCOTTISH LANGUAGE DICTIONARIES LIMITED

Acronym or abbreviation: SLD

27 George Square, Edinburgh, EH8 9LD

Tel: 0131 650 4149
Fax: 0131 650 4149
E-mail: mail@scotsdictionaries.org.uk

Website:
http://www.scotsdictionaries.org.uk
General information on SNDA, information for schools.

Enquiries:
Enquiries to: Director

Founded:
2002

Formerly called:
Scottish National Dictionary Association Ltd, A Dictionary of the Older Scottish Tongue (year of change 2002)

Organisation type and purpose:
Membership association, present number of members: 150, registered charity (charity number SC 032910), research organisation, lexicography.

Subject coverage:
The multi-volume dictionaries of Scots language, which include historical and regional principles, 12th century to 2005; study of Scottish language; information on Scots language to the present day. Smaller, related publications.

Education services:
Outreach, teaching packs, schools website: http://www.scuilwab.org.uk

Museum or gallery collection, archive, or library special collection:
Word collection in electronic database, in addition to published dictionaries

Printed publications:
Concise Scots Dictionary
Dictionary of Scottish Building
Grammar Broonie
Newsletter (2 times a year, members)
Pocket Scots Dictionary
Scots School Dictionary
The Concise English-Scots Dictionary
The Scottish National Dictionary
The Scots Thesaurus
The Scottish National Dictionary (10 volumes)
The Compact SND (2 volumes)
A Dictionary of the Older Scottish Tongue
Say it in Scots Series
Order printed publications from: Amazon via website: http://www.scotsdictionaries.org.uk

Electronic and video publications:
Cannie Spell (Scots spellchecker on disk)
Electronic Scots School Dictionary (CD-ROM)

Publications list:
Available in print

Access to staff:
Contact by letter, by telephone, by fax, by e-mail, in person and via website. Appointment necessary.
Hours: Mon to Fri, 0900 to 1700
Special comments: Visits by prior appointment only. Hours in the office are variable in the afternoon. Please leave message on answerphone. Mornings fully covered.

SCOTTISH LAW COMMISSION

Acronym or abbreviation: SLC

140 Causewayside, Edinburgh, EH9 1PR

Tel: 0131 668 2131
Fax: 0131 662 4900
E-mail: info@scotlawcom.gov.uk

Website:
http://www.scotlawcom.gov.uk

Enquiries:
Enquiries to: Librarian

Founded:
1965

Organisation type and purpose:
National government body, statutory body. Law Reform Agency. A statutory body set up under the Law Commissions Act 1965.

Subject coverage:
Responsible for keeping under review the law of Scotland and making recommendations for reform.

Museum or gallery collection, archive, or library special collection:
Law reform publications from throughout the world

Non-library collection catalogue:
All or part available in-house

Library catalogue:
All or part available in-house

Printed publications:
Discussion papers
Reports
Order printed publications from: Stationery Office

Publications list:
Available online

Access to staff:
Contact by letter, by telephone and by e-mail. Appointment necessary.
Hours: Mon to Fri, 0900 to 1700

Access to building, collection or gallery:
prior appointment required

SCOTTISH LEGAL ACTION GROUP

Acronym or abbreviation: SCOLAG

148 Muirdrum Avenue, Glasgow, G52 3AP

Tel: 05600 727138
Fax: 05600 727138
E-mail: admin@scolag.org

Website:
http://www.scolag.org

Founded:
1975

Organisation type and purpose:
Membership association (membership is by subscription).

Non-library collection catalogue:
All or part available online

Printed publications:
SCOLAG Legal Journal (monthly by subscription)

Access to staff:
Contact by letter, by telephone, by fax, by e-mail and via website
Hours: Mon to Fri, 0900 to 1700

SCOTTISH LEGAL AID BOARD

44 Drumsheugh Gardens, Edinburgh, EH3 7SW

Tel: 0131 226 7061 \ Helpline 0845 122 8686
Fax: 0131 220 4878
E-mail: general@slab.org.uk

Website:
http://www.slab.org.uk
Information on legal aid in Scotland.

Enquiries:
Enquiries to: Senior Communications Officer

Founded:
1986

Formerly called:
Legal Aid Assessment Office of the Scottish Home and Health Department, The Legal Aid Central Committee of the Law Society of Scotland (year of change 1987)

Organisation type and purpose:
Public body that manages legal aid in Scotland.

Subject coverage:
Expenditure on legal aid in Scotland; volumes of legal aid applications and grants in Scotland.

Non-library collection catalogue:
All or part available online and in print

Printed publications:
Leaflets for the public
Annual Report
Annual Review
Corporate Plan
Various publications for the legal profession

Publications list:
Available online

Access to staff:
Contact by letter, by telephone, by fax, by e-mail and via website. Appointment necessary.
Hours: Mon to Fri, 0900 to 1700

Sponsor body:
Scottish Executive Justice Department
St Andrews House, Regents Road, Edinburgh; tel: 0131 244 2200

SCOTTISH LIBERAL DEMOCRATS

Acronym or abbreviation: SLD

4 Clifton Terrace, Edinburgh, EH12 5DR

Tel: 0131 337 2314
Fax: 0131 337 3566
E-mail: scotlibdem@cix.co.uk

Website:
http://www.scotlibdems.org.uk

Enquiries:
Enquiries to: Administrator

Founded:
1989

Formerly called:
Scottish Liberal Party, Scottish Social and Liberal Democrats, SDP (Scotland)

Organisation type and purpose:
Membership association (membership is by subscription).
Party political organisation.

Subject coverage:
Local government elections, national elections, Scottish Liberal Democrat policies.

Museum or gallery collection, archive, or library special collection:
Gladstone's Midlothian speeches
Liberal Democrat policy papers

Trade and statistical information:
Election statistics.

Affiliated to:
Liberal Democrats

SCOTTISH LIBRARY AND INFORMATION COUNCIL

1st Floor, Building C, Brandon Gate, Leechlee Road, Hamilton, ML3 6AU

Tel: 01698 458888
Fax: 01698 283170
E-mail: slic@slainte.org.uk

Website:
http://www.slainte.org.uk/slic
Information about the council and its activities, plus access to information about Scottish libraries.

Enquiries:
Enquiries to: Director

Founded:
1991

Organisation type and purpose:
Advisory body, registered charity.

Subject coverage:
All library and information service issues; networking, internet, social inclusion, open learning, further education, college libraries, higher education, school libraries, public libraries, special libraries, performance indicators.

Printed publications:
SLIC Subscription Newsletter (online/ free)
SLIC Annual Review Resources (online – free/ hardcopy – free plus p&p)
Services Supporting Learning: A service Development Quality Toolkit (online – free/ hardcopy – free plus p&p)
Making a Difference: Libraries, ICT and Social Inclusion (online – free/ hardcopy – free plus p&p)

Publications list:
Available in print

Access to staff:
Contact by letter, by telephone, by fax and by e-mail. Appointment necessary.
Hours: Mon to Fri, 0900 to 1700

SCOTTISH LOCAL GOVERNMENT INFORMATION UNIT

Acronym or abbreviation: SLGIU

Room 507, Baltic Chambers, 50 Wellington Street, Glasgow, G2 6HJ

Tel: 0141 226 4636
Fax: 0141 221 8786
E-mail: slgiu@btinternet.com

Enquiries:
Enquiries to: Director

Founded:
1985

Organisation type and purpose:
Local government body, present number of members: 27 full members & 6 associate members, research organisation.

Subject coverage:
General information related to the local government including reorganisation, compulsory competitive tendering, community care, housing, education, European Community, local government finance.

Museum or gallery collection, archive, or library special collection:
General library of information materials on local government

Printed publications:
Publications include:
A Guide to Local Government Education Issues
A Guide to the Children (Scotland) Act 1995
A Guide to the Local Government etc. (Scotland) Act 1995
Housing Issues in Scotland
Scottish Local Government (10 times a year)
The Changing Role of Councillors
The Scottish Local Government Handbook (£12 inc. p&p)

Publications list:
Available in print

Access to staff:
Appointment necessary.
Hours: Mon to Fri, 0900 to 1700

Access to building, collection or gallery:
Prior appointment required

SCOTTISH LOW PAY UNIT

Unit 30, Ladywell Business Centre, 94 Duke Street, Glasgow, G4 0UW

Tel: 0845 602 3802

Fax: 0141 552 8837
E-mail: unit@scotlpu.org.uk

Enquiries:
Enquiries to: Director

Founded:
1989

Organisation type and purpose:
Campaigning, research and advice on low pay and employment rights.

Non-library collection catalogue:
All or part available online

Access to staff:
Contact by letter, by telephone, by fax and by e-mail
Hours: Mon to Fri, 0930 to 1700

Access to building, collection or gallery:
No access other than to staff

SCOTTISH MASK AND PUPPET CENTRE

Formal name: Scottish Mask and Puppet Centre (The Garret Mask & Puppet Centre Trust Ltd)
Acronym or abbreviation: SMPC

8–10 Balcarres Avenue, Glasgow, G12 0QF

Tel: 0141 339 6185
Fax: 0141 576 0112
E-mail: info@scottishmaskandpuppetcentre.co.uk

Website:
http://www.scottishmaskandpuppetcentre.co.uk
History, aims and objects, HDN Course – professional training, news and events, membership, festival agenda, publications, education and workshops, puppeteers across Scotland, Film and FX Gallery, behind the mask, exhibitions, master classes, contact us.

Enquiries:
Enquiries to: Administrator
Other contacts: Exhibitions Curator: malcolm .knight@scottishmaskandpuppetcentre.co.uk

Founded:
1981

Organisation type and purpose:
International organisation, advisory body, professional body, membership association (membership is by subscription), voluntary organisation, registered charity (charity number SCO 14379), training organisation, consultancy, research organisation.
To promote, maintain and develop the ancient art of puppets, masks and performing objects; to seek recognition for the medium as an art form in its own right; to dignify the profession; to network internationally.

Subject coverage:
Masks, puppets, performing objects, exhibitions, workshops, performances, networking, commissions, (no loan or hire), collections, publications.

Museum or gallery collection, archive, or library special collection:
Malcolm Knight Collection of Puppets and Masks
James Arnott Library
Claude Schumacher Library
The Miles Lee Collection of Puppets
The Caricature Theatre Collection
Harry Vernon Punch and Judy Set
Wayang Golek ASEP Collection

Non-library collection catalogue:
All or part available in-house

Library catalogue:
All or part available in-house

Printed publications:
IFCPA Festival Agenda (for purchase)
Masks and Puppets (newsletter, free)
Material suppliers list (free)
Puppeteers across Scotland (free)
Starting a puppet company (free)

Publications list:
Available online and in print

Access to staff:
Contact by letter, by telephone, by fax, by e-mail and via website. Appointment necessary.
Hours: Mon to Fri, 1000 to 1600; Sat, 1300 to 1700

Access to building, collection or gallery:
Prior appointment required
Hours: Mon to Wed, 1300 to 1600; Sat, 1330 to 1600

Access for disabled people:
Parking provided, ramped entry, toilet facilities
Special comments: Induction loop provided for theatre.

SCOTTISH MASSAGE THERAPISTS ORGANISATION LIMITED

Acronym or abbreviation: SMTO

24 Ellon Road, Bridge of Don, Aberdeen, AB23 8BX

Tel: 01224 822956
Fax: 01224 822960
E-mail: smto@scotmass.co.uk

Enquiries:
Enquiries to: Chairman
Other contacts: General Secretary

Founded:
1992

Organisation type and purpose:
Professional body.

Subject coverage:
Massage, clinical aromatherapy, remedial and sports massage, manipulative therapy, reflexology, on-site seated massage, advanced remedial massage therapy.

Printed publications:
Free brochure on all courses
On The Massage Scene (journal, 3 times a year for members or for £2.50)

Access to staff:
Contact by letter, by telephone, by fax, by e-mail, in person and via website. Appointment necessary.
Hours: Mon to Fri, 0900 to 1700

SCOTTISH MOTOR MUSEUM TRUST

Motoring Heritage Centre, Loch Lomond Outlets, Main Street, Alexandria, Dumbartonshire, G83 0UG

Tel: 01389 607 862
Fax: 01389 607 862
E-mail: info@motoringheritage.co.uk

Website:
http://www.motoringheritage.co.uk
http://www.visitlochlomond.org

Enquiries:
Enquiries to: Honorary Secretary

Founded:
1995

Formerly called:
Argyll Motor Museum

Organisation type and purpose:
Voluntary organisation, registered charity (charity number SCO 28515), museum, historic building, house or site, suitable for ages: 5+.

Subject coverage:
Scottish motoring industry.

Information services:
Library available for reference.

Special visitor services:
Guided tours, materials and/or activities for children.

Museum or gallery collection, archive, or library special collection:
Collection of cine-film on Scottish motoring

continued overleaf

Film archive of Scottish motoring
Motor cars of Scottish origin
Photographic archive of Scottish transport 1890 to
present day

Non-library collection catalogue:
All or part available in print

Library catalogue:
All or part available in print

Electronic and video publications:
Video tapes

Access to staff:
Contact by letter, by telephone, by fax, by e-mail,
in person and via website
Hours: Mon to Fri, 0930 to 1730

Access to building, collection or gallery:
No prior appointment required
Hours: Daily, 0930 to 1730

Access for disabled people:
Parking provided, ramped entry, access to all
public areas, toilet facilities

Museum:
Motoring Heritage Centre
at same address

SCOTTISH MOTOR NEURONE DISEASE ASSOCIATION

76 Firhill Road, Glasgow, G20 7BA

Tel: 0141 945 1077
Fax: 0141 945 2578
E-mail: info@scotmnd.co.uk

Website:
http://www.scotmnd.org.uk

Enquiries:
Enquiries to: Information Officer – Librarian

Founded:
1981

Organisation type and purpose:
Voluntary organisation, registered charity (charity
number SCO 02662).
Aims to ensure that people with Motor Neurone
Disease secure the care and support they need.
Activites: a network of MND Care Team Specialists
throughout Scotland; specialist equipment loan
service; family information evenings, library and
information service; study days for health and
social care professionals; small grants to
individuals in need; counselling service; holiday
caravan

Subject coverage:
Motor Neurone Disease/Amyotrophic Lateral
Sclerosis; palliative care; carers; bereavement;
disability issues; carers' issues; community care;
complementary medicine; health care; charity
management.

Information services:
Library and Information Service for patients/
families, and health and social care professionals

Education services:
MND Study Days for health professionals

Library catalogue:
All or part available online

Printed publications:
Aware (quarterly newsletter)
Annual Report
Factsheets
Many publications downloadable from website

Publications list:
Available online and in print

Access to staff:
Contact by letter, by telephone, by fax, by e-mail,
in person and via website
Hours: Mon to Fri, 0900 to 1700; out-of-hours
answerphone
Special comments: Information Officer works part-
time so appointment necessary

Access to building, collection or gallery:
No prior appointment required

Hours: Mon to Fri, 0900 to 1700
Special comments: Library: by appointment only

Access for disabled people:
Parking provided, level entry, toilet facilities, fully
accessible

Links with:
International Alliance of MND/ALS Associations
Scottish Health Information Network (SHINE)
Scottish Health Libraries Catalogue (SHELCAT)

SCOTTISH MOTOR TRADE ASSOCIATION LIMITED

Acronym or abbreviation: SMTA

Palmerston House, 10 The Loan, South
Queensfield, EH30 9NS

Tel: 0131 331 5510
Fax: 0131 331 4296
E-mail: info@smta.co.uk

Website:
http://www.smta.co.uk
Services available, news bulletins, membership
details, links to related sites.

Enquiries:
Enquiries to: Membership Secretary
Direct e-mail: bill.dunn@smta.co.uk

Founded:
1903

Organisation type and purpose:
Advisory body, trade association (membership is
by subscription), present number of members:
1000, training organisation, research organisation.

Subject coverage:
Employment and personnel issues, health and
safety, taxation and VAT, legal information,
technical information, Scotsure Insurance Co.,
SMTA (Trading Partners) Ltd.

**Museum or gallery collection, archive, or library
special collection:**
Scottish Motor Show Brochures (1905 to date)
Members Bulletin (monthly)

Trade and statistical information:
New vehicle sales – Scotland.

Access to staff:
Contact by letter, by telephone, by fax, by e-mail,
in person and via website. Appointment necessary.
Access for members only.
Hours: Mon to Fri, 0900 to 1700

Access to building, collection or gallery:
No access other than to staff
Hours: Mon to Fri, 0900 to 1700

SCOTTISH MUSEUMS COUNCIL

Acronym or abbreviation: SMC

County House, 20–22 Torphichen Street,
Edinburgh, EH3 8JB

Tel: 0131 229 7465
Fax: 0131 229 2728
E-mail: inform@scottishmuseums.org.uk

Website:
http://www.scottishmuseums.org.uk
Information about the Scottish Museums Council
and museums in Scotland.

Enquiries:
Enquiries to: Information Officer
Direct tel: 0131 538 7435
Direct fax: 0131 229 2728

Founded:
1964

Formerly called:
Council for Museums and Galleries in Scotland

Organisation type and purpose:
National organisation, membership association,
present number of members: 200, registered
charity (charity number SCO 15593).

SMC is the membership organisation for local
museums and galleries in Scotland. SMC's mission
is 'to achieve the best possible museum and gallery
provision in Scotland for the public benefit'.

Subject coverage:
Museums; museology; museography; heritage
studies; leisure; tourism; all especially as applied to
Scotland.

**Museum or gallery collection, archive, or library
special collection:**
General information on Scottish museums

Trade and statistical information:
Data on the number and nature of museums in
Scotland.

Library catalogue:
All or part available in-house

Publications list:
Available online

Access to staff:
Contact by letter, by telephone, by fax, by e-mail
and via website
Hours: Mon to Fri, 0900 to 1700
Special comments: Prior appointment is required.
Limited service for non-members.

Affiliated to:
Scottish Arts Council
Scottish Executive Education Department
(Government sponsoring body)
Scottish Library and Information Council

SCOTTISH NATIONAL FEDERATION FOR THE WELFARE OF THE BLIND

Acronym or abbreviation: SNFWB

5 Balmashanner Rise, Forfar, Angus, DD8 1PD

Tel: 01307 460359
Fax: 01307 460359
E-mail: snfwb@care4free.net

Enquiries:
Enquiries to: Honorary Secretary

Founded:
1917

Organisation type and purpose:
Voluntary organisation, registered charity (charity
number SC 002185).
Parent body for numerous organisations, including
local authorities in Scotland, concerned with the
welfare of blind and partially sighted people.

Subject coverage:
Social work, education and employment services
for the blind and partially sighted.

Printed publications:
Annual Report

Access to staff:
Contact by letter, by telephone, by fax and by e-
mail
Hours: Mon to Fri, 0900 to 1700

SCOTTISH NATIONAL INSTITUTION FOR THE WAR BLINDED

Acronym or abbreviation: SNIWB, LINBURN

PO Box 500, Gillespie Crescent, Edinburgh, EH10
4HZ

Tel: 0131 229 1456
Fax: 0131 229 4060
E-mail: enquiries@rbas.org.uk

Enquiries:
Enquiries to: Secretary and Treasurer

Founded:
1915

Organisation type and purpose:
Voluntary organisation, registered charity (charity
number SC002652).

Training, employment and aftercare for Scottish ex-services visually impaired.

Subject coverage:
Care and welfare of blind and visually impaired ex-servicemen and women, setting up of specialised workshops, grants.

Printed publications:
Annual Report

Publications list:
Available in print

Access to staff:
Contact by letter, by telephone, by fax and by e-mail. Appointment necessary.
Hours: Mon to Fri, 0900 to 1300 and 1400 to 1700

Access to building, collection or gallery:
No access other than to staff

Access for disabled people:
Parking provided, level entry

Links with:
Royal Blind Asylum and School
at the same address

SCOTTISH NATIONAL PARTY

Acronym or abbreviation: SNP

107 McDonald Road, Edinburgh, EH7 4NW

Tel: 0131 525 8900
Fax: 0131 525 8901
E-mail: snp.hq@snp.org.uk

Website:
http://www.snp.org
About, information, policy, people, join and donations, online shop

Enquiries:
Enquiries to: Policy and information officer
Direct tel: 0131 525 8908

Founded:
1934

Organisation type and purpose:
Membership association (membership is by subscription). Political party.

Subject coverage:
Party policy and information on Scottish independence in Europe.

Printed publications:
Ad hoc publications

Access to staff:
Contact by letter, by telephone, by fax, by e-mail, in person and via website. Appointment necessary.
Hours: Mon to Fri, 0900 to 1700

SCOTTISH NATIONAL SPORTS CENTRE CUMBRAE

Isle of Cumbrae, Millport, Ayrshire, KA28 0HQ

Tel: 01475 530757
Fax: 01475 530013
E-mail: cumbraecentre@sportscotland.org.uk

Website:
http://www.nationalcentrecumbrae.org.uk

Enquiries:
Enquiries to: Principal

Founded:
1974

Organisation type and purpose:
National government body, advisory body, registered charity, training organisation.
To train instructors in watersports, to train the National Sailing Squads, to offer high level instruction in watersports to all.

Subject coverage:
All aspects of watersport; cruising, dinghy racing, catamaran sailing, windsurfing, sailing, canoeing, power boat racing, sub aqua.

Printed publications:
Brochure (available, direct by phone)

Publications list:
Available in print

Access to staff:
Contact by letter, by telephone, by fax, in person and via website
Hours: Mon to Fri, 0900 to 1700

Access for disabled people:
Parking provided, ramped entry, toilet facilities
Hours: Mon to Fri, 0900 to 1700

Part of the:
Scottish Sports Council Trust Company
Caledonian House, South Gyle, Edinburgh; tel: 0131 317 7200; fax: 0131 317 7202; website: www .sportscotland.org.uk

SCOTTISH NATIONAL SWEET PEA, ROSE & CARNATION SOCIETY

57 Dalfarson Avenue, Dalmellington, Ayrshire, KA6 7TX

Tel: 01292 551526

Website:
http://www.snsprcs.org.uk
Sweet pea trial results, international rose trial results, tips and information.

Enquiries:
Enquiries to: Chairman
Other contacts: General Secretary

Founded:
1919

Organisation type and purpose:
National organisation (membership is by subscription), present number of members: 110, voluntary organisation, registered charity.

Subject coverage:
Information on cultivating and exhibiting sweet peas, roses and carnations.

Access to staff:
Contact by letter and by e-mail
Hours: Mon to Fri, 0900 to 1700

Other addresses:
President/Chairman
7 Dalfarson Avenue, Dalmellington, Ayrshire, KA6 7TX; tel: 01292 551526

SCOTTISH NATURAL HERITAGE – EDINBURGH

Acronym or abbreviation: SNH

12 Hope Terrace, Edinburgh, EH9 2AS

Tel: 0131 447 4784
Fax: 0131 446 2277

Website:
http://www.snh.org.uk

Enquiries:
Enquiries to: Public Relations Department
Direct tel: 0131 446 2270
Direct fax: 0131 446 2279

Founded:
1992

Formerly called:
Countryside Commission for Scotland, Nature Conservancy Council

Organisation type and purpose:
National government body, advisory body. Works with Scotland's people to care for Scotland's natural heritage.

Subject coverage:
All aspects of the environment, including wildlife, but not building conservation.

Printed publications:
Advisory Publications, Occasional Papers, Policy Documents and Research Publications

Annual Report (free)
Ancient Woodlands in Scotland (free)
Cairngorms: A Landscape Fashioned by Geology (£2)
Earth Heritage
Education and teacher's resources
Farming land management and landscape
Focus on Firths (free)
General Interest Series includes:
Grants information
Leaflets on the main areas in Scotland (free)
National Nature Reserve Leaflets (free)
Progress and Plans (free)
Scotland's Natural Heritage (magazine, 2 times a year, free)
Scotland's Wildlife: Bats (£1.50)
Who We Are and Where We Are: leaflet listing the network of SNH HQ, Regional and Area offices' addresses, contact names and telephone numbers (free)
Wildlife and habitats
Order printed publications from: Publications Department, Scottish Natural Heritage
Battleby, Redgorton, Perth, PH1 3EW, tel: 01738 444177, fax: 01738 444180

Publications list:
Available in print

Access to staff:
Contact by letter, by telephone, by fax and in person. Appointment necessary.
Hours: Mon to Thu, 0830 to 1700; Fri, 0830 to 1630

Access to building, collection or gallery:
No prior appointment required

Access for disabled people:
Parking provided

East Areas:
Scottish Natural Heritage Forth and Borders
Laundry House, Dalkeith Country Park, Dalkeith, Midlothian, EH22 2NA; tel: 0131 654 2466; fax: 0131 654 2477
Scottish Natural Heritage Grampian
16–17 Rubislaw Terrace, Aberdeen, AB1 1XE; tel: 01224 642863; fax: 01224 635020
Scottish Natural Heritage Tayside
Battleby, Redgorton, Perth, PH1 3EW; tel: 01783 444177; fax: 01783 442060

North Areas:
Scottish Natural Heritage East Highland
Foddety Way, Dingwall Business Park, Dingwall, IV15 9XB; tel: 01349 865333; fax: 01349 865609
Scottish Natural Heritage North Highland
Main Street, Golspie, Sutherland, KW10 6TG; tel: 01408 633602; fax: 01408 633071
Scottish Natural Heritage Northern Isles
Ground Floor, Stewart Building, Alexandra Wharf, Lerwick, Shetland, ZE1 0LL; tel: 01595 693345; fax: 01595 692565
Scottish Natural Heritage West Highland
The Governor's House, The Parade, Fort William, Inverness-shire, PH33 6BA; tel: 01397 704716; fax: 01397 700303
Scottish Natural Heritage Western Isles
32 Francis Street, Stornoway, Isle of Lewis, HS1 2ND; tel: 01851 705258; fax: 01851 704900

West Areas:
Scottish Natural Heritage Argyll & Stirling
The Beta Centre, Innovation Park, University of Stirling, Stirling, FK9 4NF; tel: 01786 450362; fax: 01786 451974
Scottish Natural Heritage Dumfries & Galloway
Carmont House, The Crichton, Bankend Road, Dumfries, DG1 4ZF; tel: 01387 247010; fax: 01387 259247
Scottish Natural Heritage Strathclyde and Ayrshire
Caspian House, Mariner Court, Clydebank Business Park, Clydebank, G81 2NR; tel: 0141 951 4488; fax: 0141 951 8948

SCOTTISH NATURAL HERITAGE – INVERNESS

Great Glen House, Leachkin Road, Inverness, IV3 8NW

continued overleaf

Tel: 01463 725294
E-mail: library@snh.gov.uk

Website:
http://www.snh.org.uk
A variety of information on Scottish National
Heritage.

Enquiries:
Enquiries to: Librarian

Founded:
1992

Formerly called:
Countryside Commission for Scotland, Nature
Conservancy Council

Organisation type and purpose:
National government body.
Library.

Subject coverage:
All aspects of nature and landscape conservation,
land use and recreation especially in relation to
Scotland's natural heritage.

Library catalogue:
All or part available in-house

Printed publications:
The following available direct or via website:
Annual Report (free)
A Landscape Fashioned by Geology, booklets for:
Arran and the Clyde Islands, East Lothian and
the Borders, Edinburgh, Skye, Cairngorms, Loch
Lomond to Stirling, Orkney and Shetland (£1.50
to £2 each)
Operational and Corporate Plan (free)
Scotland's Natural Heritage (magazine, 3 times a
year, free)
Numerous other publications covering the natural
heritage of Scotland, wildlife and habitats, Sites
of Special Scientific Interest, earth heritage,
education and teachers' resources, research and
technical, access and recreational, farming and
land management
Order printed publications from: Scottish National
Heritage Publishing
Battleby, Redgorton, Perth, PH1 3EW, tel: 01738
627921, e-mail via website: http://www.snh.org.uk

Publications list:
Available online and in print

Access to staff:
Contact by letter. Appointment necessary.
Hours: Mon to Thu, 0900 to 1700; Fri, 0900 to 1630

Access for disabled people:
Ramped entry, toilet facilities

SCOTTISH NATURAL HISTORY LIBRARY

Acronym or abbreviation: SNHL

Foremount House, Kilbarchan, Renfrewshire,
PA10 2EZ

Tel: 01505 702419

Enquiries:
Enquiries to: Chairman
Other contacts: Honorary Librarian

Founded:
1972

Organisation type and purpose:
Learned society, registered charity (charity number
SCO 42142), research organisation.
Specialist library.

Subject coverage:
All aspects of Scottish natural history.

Museum or gallery collection, archive, or library special collection:
The largest separate collection of Scottish natural
history books and journals in existence anywhere
in the world. Some 150,000 items, including
some 400 periodicals. Several specialised Scottish
collections which have been presented to the
library

Non-library collection catalogue:
All or part available in-house

Library catalogue:
All or part available in-house

Printed publications:
The Scottish Naturalist (founded 1871) (3 times a
year, annual subscription £35)

Access to staff:
Contact by letter and by telephone
Hours: Mon to Fri, 0900 to 1700

Access to building, collection or gallery:
Prior appointment required

Works in co-operation with the:
British Library
National Library of Scotland
Natural History Museum
Royal Museum of Scotland
Society for the History of Natural History

SCOTTISH OFFICIAL BOARD OF HIGHLAND DANCING

Acronym or abbreviation: SOBHD

Heritage House, 32 Grange Loan, Edinburgh, EH9
2NR

Tel: 0131 668 3965
Fax: 0131 662 0404
E-mail: admin@sobhd.net

Enquiries:
Enquiries to: Administrator

Founded:
1950

Organisation type and purpose:
International organisation, professional body
(membership is by election or invitation).
Governing body.

Subject coverage:
Highland dancing governing body.

Museum or gallery collection, archive, or library special collection:
Collection of books on the subject

Printed publications:
Constitution and Rule Book (£4.95)
Text Book Highland Dancing (£10.90)
Examining body items include:
BATD National Book (£4.95)
SDTA National Book (£3.95)
UKA National Book (£3.95)

Publications list:
Available in print

Access to staff:
Contact by letter, by telephone, by fax and by e-mail. Appointment necessary.
Hours: Mon to Fri, 0900 to 1700

SCOTTISH OPERA

39 Elmbank Crescent, Glasgow, G2 4PT

Tel: 0141 248 4567
Fax: 0141 221 8812

Website:
http://www.scottishopera.org.uk
Preview new season's performances, find out
about special ticket offers and forthcoming events.

Enquiries:
Direct tel: 0141 248 4567

Founded:
1962

Organisation type and purpose:
National organisation, registered charity (charity
number 37531).

Access to staff:
Contact by letter, by telephone, by fax, by e-mail
and in person. Appointment necessary.

Hours: Mon to Fri, 0930 to 1730

Access to building, collection or gallery:
No access other than to staff

SCOTTISH ORNITHOLOGISTS' CLUB

Acronym or abbreviation: SOC

The Scottish Birdwatching Resource Centre,
Waterston House, Aberlady, East Lothian, EH32
0PY

Tel: 01875 871330
Fax: 01875 871035
E-mail: mail@the-soc.org.uk

Website:
http://www.the-soc.org.uk

Enquiries:
Enquiries to: SOC Development Manager
Other contacts: Admin Officer

Founded:
1936

Organisation type and purpose:
Membership association (membership is by
subscription), present number of members: 2500,
voluntary organisation, registered charity (charity
number CR38075), publishing house.
To encourage ornithology in Scotland.

Subject coverage:
Conservation and research into birds in Scotland,
ornithology in general.

Museum or gallery collection, archive, or library special collection:
Extensive ornithological reference library (The
George Waterston Library)

Library catalogue:
All or part available in-house

Printed publications:
Raptor Round Up (annually, free to members)
Scottish Bird News (quarterly, free to members)
Scottish Bird Report (annually, free to members)
Scottish Birds (once a year, free to members or on
subscription)

Access to staff:
Contact by letter, by telephone and by e-mail.
Appointment necessary.
Hours: Mon to Fri, 0900 to 1700
Special comments: Please phone beforehand.

Access to building, collection or gallery:
Prior appointment required

Has:
14 branches throughout Scotland

SCOTTISH PARACHUTE CLUB

Strathallan Airfield, Auchterarder, Perthshire, PH3
1LA

Tel: 01764 662 572
E-mail: andy@afrew.fsnet.co.uk

Website:
http://www.skydivestrathallan.co.uk
Parachuting courses.

Enquiries:
Enquiries to: General Secretary

Founded:
1960

Organisation type and purpose:
National organisation, membership association
(membership is by subscription), present number
of members: 70, voluntary organisation, training
organisation.

Subject coverage:
Parachute training courses for beginners to
experienced jumpers.

Access to staff:
Contact by letter, by telephone, by e-mail, in
person and via website. All charged.

Hours: Fri, 1700 to 2100; Sat, Sun, 0900 to 2100

Access to building, collection or gallery:
No prior appointment required

Access for disabled people:
Parking provided, level entry

Connections with:
British Parachute Association (BPA)
Wharf Way, Glenparva, Leicester, LE2 9TF; tel:
0116 278 5271; fax: 0116 247 7662
Scottish Sport Parachute Association (SSPA)
Strathallan Airfield, Auchterarder, Perthshire,
PH3 1BE; tel: 01698 812 443

SCOTTISH PARENT TEACHER COUNCIL

Acronym or abbreviation: SPTC

53 George Street, Edinburgh, EH2 2HT

Tel: 0131 226 4378/1917
Fax: 08707 065814
E-mail: sptc@sptc.info

Website:
http://www.sptc.info
Current newsletter; insurance information,
responses to consultations.

Enquiries:
Enquiries to: Information Officer
Other contacts: Administrator, Convenor

Founded:
1948

Organisation type and purpose:
Membership association, registered charity.
Educational organisation, open to PAs/PTAs and
others with an interest in education in Scotland.

Subject coverage:
Information about PTAs/PAs in Scotland, Parent/
teacher relationships and general information
about Scottish education.

Printed publications:
Backchat Newsletter (approx 7 times a year, free to
members)
Leaflets on constitutions, devolved school
management, charitable status and setting up
PTAs

Access to staff:
Contact by letter, by telephone, by fax, by e-mail
and via website
Hours: Mon, Tue and Thu, 0900 to 1500; Wed and
Fri, 0900 to 1230

SCOTTISH PARTNERSHIP FOR PALLIATIVE CARE

Acronym or abbreviation: SPPC

1a Cambridge Street, Edinburgh, EH1 2DY

Tel: 0131 229 0538
Fax: 0131 228 2967
E-mail: office@palliativecarescotland.org.uk

Website:
http://www.palliativecarescotland.org.uk

Enquiries:
Enquiries to: Director

Founded:
1991

Formerly called:
Scottish Partnership Agency for Palliative and
Cancer Care (SPAPCC) (year of change 2001)

Organisation type and purpose:
Registered charity (charity number SCO 17979).

Subject coverage:
Palliative care, specialist palliative care, hospices.

Printed publications:
See website http://
www.palliativecarescotland.org.uk

Access to staff:
Contact by letter, by telephone, by fax and by e-mail
Hours: Mon to Fri, 0900 to 1700

Access to building, collection or gallery:
No public access to building

Members include:
more than 50 voluntary and statutory bodies

SCOTTISH PHARMACEUTICAL FEDERATION

Acronym or abbreviation: SPF

135 Wellington Street, Glasgow, G2 2XD

Tel: 0141 221 1235
Fax: 0141 248 5892
E-mail: spf@npanet.co.uk

Website:
http://www.npa.co.uk

Enquiries:
Enquiries to: Secretary

Founded:
1919

Organisation type and purpose:
Trade association (membership is by subscription),
present number of members: 1040.
Trade association for owners of community
pharmacies in Scotland.

Access to staff:
Contact by letter, by telephone, by fax and by e-mail
Hours: Mon to Fri, 0900 to 1700

Affiliated to:
The National Pharmaceutical Association
Mallinson House, 38–42 St Peters Street, St
Albans, Hertfordshire, AL1 3NP; tel: 01727
832161; fax: 01727 840858; e-mail: npa@npa.co
.uk

SCOTTISH POETRY LIBRARY

Acronym or abbreviation: SPL

5 Crichton's Close, Edinburgh, EH8 8DT

Tel: 0131 557 2876
Fax: 0131 557 8393
E-mail: Librarian1@spl.org.uk

Website:
http://www.spl.org.uk
General information on the Scottish Poetry Library
and its activities, including events, outreach and
education. Links, online catalogue, Scottish Poetry
Index and enquiry service. Digital essay Poets'
Pub, poets' biographies and European Poetry
Information Centre information including
translation workshops. Canadian and New
Zealand poetry exchanges, poets' A-Z, poet of the
month, poetry news, poetry reading room with
online discussions and reading group resources.

Enquiries:
Enquiries to: Librarian

Founded:
1984

Organisation type and purpose:
Membership association (membership is by
subscription), present number of members: 750,
registered charity (charity number SCO 23311),
public library.
Borrowing is free to the general public.

Subject coverage:
20th century Scottish poetry written in English,
Scots and Gaelic; older Scottish poetry; substantial
international collection of poetry from Britain,
Europe and the rest of the world.

**Museum or gallery collection, archive, or library
special collection:**
Edwin Morgan Archive

Non-library collection catalogue:
All or part available online

Library catalogue:
All or part available online

Printed publications:
Free publicity brochure
Lists and bibliographies
Scottish Poetry Index Series, indexing Scottish
poetry periodicals, 1952–1992
SPL Poetry Reader (2 a year)
Handsel: Scottish Poems for Welcoming and
Naming Babies
Lament: Scottish Poems for Funerals and
Consolations
Handfast: Scottish Poems for Weddings and
Affirmations
Intimate Expanses : XXV Scottish Poems 1978–2002
100 Favourite Scottish Poems
The Weaver's Task: a Gaelic Sampler
The Thing that Mattered Most: Scottish poems for
children
Poems United: A Commonwealth Anthology

Electronic and video publications:
The Jewel Box: Contemporary Scottish Poems (CD)

Access to staff:
Contact by letter, by telephone, by fax, by e-mail,
in person and via website
Hours: Mon to Fri, 1100 to 1800; Sat, 1300 to 1700

Access to building, collection or gallery:
Hours: Mon to Fri, 1100 to 1800; Sat, 1300 to 1700

Access for disabled people:
Level entry, access to all public areas, toilet
facilities

Supported by:
Scottish Arts Council and others

SCOTTISH PRE-SCHOOL PLAY ASSOCIATION

Acronym or abbreviation: SPPA

21 Granville Street, Glasgow, G3 7EE

Tel: 0141 221 4148
Fax: 0141 221 6043
E-mail: info@sppa.org.uk

Website:
http://www.sppa.org.uk

Enquiries:
Enquiries to: Membership Services Officer

Founded:
1966

Formerly called:
Scottish Pre-School Playgroups Association

Organisation type and purpose:
Membership association (membership is by
subscription), present number of members: 1300,
voluntary organisation, registered charity (charity
number SC003725), training organisation.
SPPA supports community-based early years
education and childcare services for children and
families.

Subject coverage:
Setting up, maintaining and supporting
playgroups, toddler groups, family centres, under-
fives groups; parental involvement; adult
education; fieldwork; integrated working in the
field of under-fives and their families;
constitutional matters relating to voluntary-
governed groups; integration of children with
additional learning needs; early learning; play
provision and child development.

Trade and statistical information:
Annual facts and figures relating to the association
and to groups.

Non-library collection catalogue:
All or part available online

Printed publications:
Information packs
First Five (magazine)

continued overleaf

Publications and visual aids list available
(constitutional, training and play titles etc)

Electronic and video publications:
Video library

Publications list:
Available in print

Access to staff:
Contact by letter, by telephone, by fax and by e-mail
Hours: Mon to Fri, 0900 to 1630

Links with:
Association of Shetland Playgroups
CALA (Highland)
Irish PPA
Northern Ireland PPA
Orkney Pre-School Play Association
PLA (England)
Wales PPA

SCOTTISH PRINT EMPLOYERS FEDERATION

Acronym or abbreviation: SPEF

48 Palmerston Place, Edinburgh, EH12 5DE

Tel: 0131 220 4353
Fax: 0131 220 4344
E-mail: info@spef.org.uk

Website:
http://www.spef.org.uk

Enquiries:
Enquiries to: Director

Founded:
1910

Formerly called:
Society of Master Printers of Scotland (SMPS) (year of change 1991)

Organisation type and purpose:
Trade association (membership is by subscription).

Subject coverage:
Employee relations; training; health and safety; commercial information.

Access to staff:
Contact by letter, by telephone and by fax.
Appointment necessary.
Hours: Mon to Fri, 0900 to 1700

Links with:
Intergraf (International Confederation for Printing and Allied Industries)

SCOTTISH PUBLIC SERVICES OMBUDSMAN

Acronym or abbreviation: SPSO

4 Melville Street, Edinburgh, EH3 7NS

Tel: 0800 377 7330
Fax: 0800 377 7331
E-mail: ask@spso.org.uk

Website:
http://www.spso.org.uk

Enquiries:
Enquiries to: Ombudsman

Founded:
2002

Organisation type and purpose:
Statutory body.
Appointed by the Crown on the recommendation of the Scottish Parliament.
To investigate complaints from members of the public about local government, registered social landlords, NHS and Scottish administration.

Access to staff:
Contact by letter, by telephone, by fax, by e-mail and in person. Appointment necessary.
Hours: Mon, Wed to Fri, 0900 to 1700; Tue, 1000 to 1700

SCOTTISH PUBLISHERS ASSOCIATION

Acronym or abbreviation: SPA

Scottish Book Centre, 137 Dundee Street, Edinburgh, EH11 1BG

Tel: 0131 228 6866
Fax: 0131 228 3220
E-mail: enquiries@scottishbooks.org

Website:
http://www.scottishbooks.org
http://www.scottishbooksdirect.com

Enquiries:
Enquiries to: Member Services and Marketing Manager
Direct e-mail: allan@scottishbooks.org

Founded:
1974

Organisation type and purpose:
Trade association (membership is by subscription).

Subject coverage:
Publishing, contracts and copyright, training, trade fairs, publicity and marketing, information provision.

Printed publications:
Directory of Publishing in Scotland 1998 (£9.99)
Newsletter (monthly, members only)
Training in Publishing (annual brochure detailing publishing training)
Order printed publications from: Scottish Book Source 50 Cambuslang Road, Cambuslang, Glasgow, G32 8NB, tel: 0131 229 6800, fax: 0131 229 9070

Access to staff:
Contact by letter, by e-mail and via website.
Access for members only.
Hours: Mon to Fri, 0930 to 1730

Access to building, collection or gallery:
Prior appointment required

Access for disabled people:
Ramped entry

SCOTTISH QUALIFICATIONS AUTHORITY

Acronym or abbreviation: SQA

The Optima Building, 58 Robertson Street, Glasgow, G2 8DQ

Tel: 0845 279 1000
Fax: 0845 213 5000
E-mail: customer@sqa.org.uk

Website:
http://www.sqa.org.uk
Information on Scottish Qualifications Authority and its functions.

Enquiries:
Enquiries to: Customer Contact Centre
Direct tel: 0141 242 2291
Direct fax: 0141 242 2219
Direct e-mail: mike.haggerty@sqa.org.uk

Founded:
1 April 1997

Formed from:
Scottish Examination Board (SEB), Scottish Vocational Educational Council (SCOTVEC)

Organisation type and purpose:
Suitable for ages: all.

Subject coverage:
Education qualifications in Scotland.

Publications list:
Available online and in print

Access to staff:
Contact by letter, by telephone, by fax, by e-mail and via website
Hours: Mon to Fri, 0900 to 1700

Other addresses:
Scottish Qualifications Authority
Ironmills Road, Dalkeith, Midlothian, EH22 1LE;
tel: 0131 663 6601

SCOTTISH RAILWAY PRESERVATION SOCIETY

Acronym or abbreviation: SRPS

The Station, Union Street, Bo'ness, West Lothian, EH51 9AQ

Tel: 01506 825855
Fax: 01506 828766
E-mail: enquiries@srps.org.uk

Website:
http://www.srps.org.uk
Activities of the organisation.

Enquiries:
Enquiries to: Honorary Secretary
Direct tel: 01506 843207

Founded:
1963

Organisation type and purpose:
Membership association (membership is by subscription), present number of members: 1300, voluntary organisation, registered charity (charity number SCO02375), museum.
Railway preservation and operation.

Subject coverage:
Railway preservation, restoration of steam locomotives and rolling stock, and their operation; Scottish railways and their historical development; Bo'ness and Kinneil Railway; locations for filming of steam-hauled trains of appropriate vintage; the preservation and display, in work if appropriate, of artefacts pertaining to Scottish railways.

Museum or gallery collection, archive, or library special collection:
Builders plates for study
Railway artefacts ranging from railway buildings to locomotives (etc)
Small collection of books on practical aspects of railways and rolling stock, also photographs

Printed publications:
Blastpipe (magazine, quarterly, free to members or on subscription)
Bo'ness & Kinneil Railway Guide
Other publications as needed

Access to staff:
Contact by letter, by telephone, by fax and by e-mail. Appointment necessary.
Hours: Mon to Fri, 1000 to 1600

Access for disabled people:
Parking provided, ramped entry, toilet facilities

Links with:
Heritage Railway Association (HRA)
tel: 01707 643568; fax: 01707 643568

SCOTTISH REFUGEE COUNCIL

Acronym or abbreviation: SRC

Wellgate House, 200 Cowgate, Edinburgh, EH1 1NQ

Tel: 0131 225 9994
Fax: 0131 225 9997
E-mail: info@scottishrefugeecouncil.org.uk

Website:
http://www.scottishrefugeecouncil.org.uk

Enquiries:
Enquiries to: Information Officer
Other contacts: Manager/Policy Development Officer for local services referrals.

Founded:
1985

Organisation type and purpose:
Advisory body, voluntary sector organisation, registered charity (charity number SC008639). To assist and advise local authorities and other

agencies on all refugee and related issues by providing training, seminars and briefings and assisting with policy development.
To provide advice, information and assistance to asylum seekers and refugees in Scotland. To promote a strategic response to refugee needs. To campaign to ensure Scotland plays a role in meeting the UK's legal and humanitarian obligations under the 1951 UN Convention on Refugees.

Subject coverage:
Provides advice, information and legal representation to asylum seekers and refugees in Scotland including information on asylum law and procedures, employment, housing, education, health and welfare.

Printed publications:
Finding Asylum (newsletter, quarterly, for members)
Annual Report (printed in December)
Briefings (regular updates)
Information Pack for agencies (printed or online)

Publications list:
Available in print

Access to staff:
Contact by letter, by telephone, by fax, by e-mail and via website. Appointment necessary.
Hours: Mon to Fri, 0900 to 1700

Access for disabled people:
Ramped entry, access to all public areas, toilet facilities

Head Office:
Scottish Refugee Council
94 Hope Street, Glasgow, G2 6QA; tel: 0141 248 9799; fax: 0141 243 2499

SCOTTISH RIGHTS OF WAY AND ACCESS SOCIETY

Acronym or abbreviation: ScotWays

24 Annandale Street, Edinburgh, EH7 4AN

Tel: 0131 558 1222
Fax: 0131 558 1222
E-mail: info@scotways.com

Website:
http://www.scotways.com
Access news (e.g., restrictions imposed in emergencies), membership information, history of society.

Enquiries:
Enquiries to: Secretary
Other contacts: Membership Secretary; Field Officer for membership applications; access problems.

Founded:
1845

Formerly called:
Scottish Rights of Way Society, date of change, 26 November 1999

Organisation type and purpose:
National organisation, advisory body, membership association (membership is by subscription), present number of members: 2569, voluntary organisation, registered charity (charity number SC 015460), consultancy, research organisation, publishing house.
To safeguard public access, including public rights of way in Scotland.

Subject coverage:
Public access in Scotland; access to the countryside, responsibility in association with Scottish Natural Heritage for constant updating of National Catalogue of Rights of Way. Signposting routes. Legal advice on access, publications of maps and guides, lectures on access matters, mediation service, bridge maintenance.

Museum or gallery collection, archive, or library special collection:
Maps and other records of rights of way in Scotland held in 37 volumes and on 122 special 1:50,000 scale maps. Copies available, ask for a quotation of individual routes/maps

Trade and statistical information:
Data on access routes, especially rights of way, for every local authority area in Scotland, by class of usage (foot, horse, bicycle) and by legal category (asserted, claimed, other).

Printed publications:
Most publications at 25% discount to members
Annual Report and Newsletters (annually)
Case Law Studies (£5)
Lochaber Walks (set of 8 leaflets with maps describing 10 walks, 50p)
Rights of Way: A Guide to the Law in Scotland (£5)
Rights of Way: The Authority of Case Law (£5)
Scottish Hill Tracks (4th ed, 1999, £16)
Scottish Hill Tracks Map (free)
Various leaflets (free)
The Military Roads in Scotland (Taylor W, 208pp, £9.95)
The Drove Roads of Scotland (Haldane A R B, 266pp, £9.99)
New Ways Through the Glens (Haldane A R B, £7.99)

Publications list:
Available online and in print

Access to staff:
Contact by letter, by telephone, by fax, by e-mail and via website. Appointment necessary. Non-members charged.
Hours: Mon to Fri, 0900 to 1300

Access for disabled people:
Level entry, access to all public areas

SCOTTISH RUGBY UNION

Acronym or abbreviation: SRU

Murrayfield, Edinburgh, EH12 5PJ

Tel: 0131 346 5000
Fax: 0131 346 5001
E-mail: feedback@sru.org.uk

Website:
http://www.sru.org.uk
News, results, facts and figures, games and competitions.

Enquiries:
Enquiries to: Chief Executive

Founded:
1924

Organisation type and purpose:
International organisation, advisory body, statutory body, membership association.
Governing body of rugby in Scotland.

Subject coverage:
Promotion and development of rugby union football in Scotland.

Museum or gallery collection, archive, or library special collection:
Library and museum (closed due to redevelopment of stadium)

Printed publications:
Calendar (annually)
Coaching brochures (series)
Coaching handbook (annually)
Handbook (annually)
Lawbook (annually)

Access to staff:
Contact by letter, by telephone, by fax, by e-mail and via website
Hours: Mon to Fri, 0900 to 1700

Member of:
International Rugby Board

SCOTTISH SALMON PRODUCERS ORGANISATION

Acronym or abbreviation: SSPO

Durn, Isla Road, Perth, Tayside, PH2 7HG

Tel: 01738 587000
Fax: 01738 621454
E-mail: enquiries@scottishsalmon.co.uk

Website:
http://www.scottishsalmon.co.uk

Enquiries:
Enquiries to: Chief Executive
Direct e-mail: spatten@scottishsalmon.co.uk
Other contacts: Communications Director for all PR and marketing issues.

Founded:
2006

Organisation type and purpose:
Trade association (membership is by qualification), present number of members: 50 companies.
To promote production of farmed Scottish salmon.

Subject coverage:
Farming and production of Scottish salmon.

Trade and statistical information:
Salmon production data, import and export data.

Printed publications:
Corporate brochure
Variety of consumer information

Publications list:
Available in print

Access to staff:
Contact by letter
Hours: Mon to Fri, 0900 to 1700

SCOTTISH SALMON SMOKERS ASSOCIATION

Acronym or abbreviation: SSSA

20 Beaufort Road, Inverness, IV2 3NP

Tel: 01463 712902
Fax: 01463 712902
E-mail: sssa@ecosse.net

Enquiries:
Enquiries to: Secretary

Founded:
1987

Organisation type and purpose:
Trade association, membership association (membership is by subscription), present number of members: 19.

Access to staff:
Contact by letter, by fax and by e-mail
Hours: Mon to Fri, 0900 to 1700

SCOTTISH SCHOOL OF REFLEXOLOGY, THE

Acronym or abbreviation: SSR

11 Stonefield Park, Ayr, KA7 4HS

Tel: 01292 440730
Fax: 01292 440750

Website:
http://www.reflexscott.co.uk
School training prospectus and reservation form.

Enquiries:
Enquiries to: Principal

Founded:
1985

Organisation type and purpose:
Suitable for ages: 18+, training organisation.
To provide training in knowledge and physical skills to professional level.

continued overleaf

Subject coverage:
Reflexology and anatomy, physiology, pathology.
Magnets and their therapeutic uses, nutritional
herbology.

Printed publications:
Arthritis Relief of Pain Naturally (Bell W D)
Introduction to Nutrition (Bell W D)
Reflexology and the Christian (Bell W D)
Reflexology Foot Charts

Electronic and video publications:
Reflexology Methods (Video, available to purchase
for Graduates only)

Publications list:
Available in print

Access to staff:
Contact by letter, by telephone and by fax
Hours: Mon to Thu, 0930 to 1300 and 1415 to 1700;
Fri, 0930 to 1300; Sat and Sun, closed

SCOTTISH SCHOOLS EQUIPMENT RESEARCH CENTRE LIMITED

Acronym or abbreviation: SSERC

St Mary's Land, 23 Holyrood Road, Edinburgh,
EH8 8AE

Tel: 01383 626070
Fax: 01383 842793
E-mail: sts@sserc.org.uk

Website:
http://www.sserc.org.uk
Summary of services, publications price list,
sample pages, graphics, etc.

Enquiries:
Enquiries to: Chief Executive Officer
Direct e-mail: fred.young@sserc.org.uk

Founded:
1965

Organisation type and purpose:
Local government body, advisory body,
membership association (membership is by
subscription), present number of members: 32
corporate, 100+ individual, registered charity
(charity number SCO 17884), training organisation,
consultancy, research organisation.
Educational organisation, health and safety
consultancy.
Testing house and laboratory, advisory,
consultancy and training services.

Subject coverage:
Technical aspect of science and technology
equipment for education, relevant British
standards, health and safety literature relevant to
science and technology in particular and to
education in general; advice, information, training
and consultancy on purchase, testing and use
(including safety, maintenance and repair) of
educational equipment.

**Museum or gallery collection, archive, or library
special collection:**
Selected British and EN standards
Specialised science and technology education
journals

Printed publications:
Bulletin, Science and Technology Equipment
(journal, quarterly)
Science and Technology Equipment News
(quarterly)
Specialised one offs on IT applications, health and
safety in education etc
Various leaflets and booklets

Electronic and video publications:
Graphics relevant to science and technology CD-
ROM, Acorn Archimedes platform, Apple Mac,
PC (metafiles); Science Graphics on application
Hazardous Chemicals: An interactive manual for
science education (CD-ROM version, 2nd ed.)

Publications list:
Available online

Access to staff:
Contact by e-mail and via website. Appointment
necessary. Non-members charged.
Hours: Mon to Fri, 0900 to 1700
Special comments: Usually only available to
members.

Also trading as:
SSERCSOFT
STS (Science, Technology and Safety) Support
Services

SCOTTISH SCREEN ARCHIVE

Acronym or abbreviation: SSA

39–41 Montrose Avenue, Hillington Park,
Glasgow, G52 4LA

Tel: 0845 366 4600
Fax: 0845 366 4601
E-mail: archive@scottishscreen.com

Website:
http://www.scottishscreen.com
Home page.
http://www.pads.ahds.ac.uk:81/SFTACatalogue
.html
Selected catalogue.

Enquiries:
Enquiries to: Librarian
Direct tel: 0141 337 7407
Direct e-mail: ann.beaton@scottishscreen.com
Other contacts: (1) Access and Admin. Assistant; (2)
Production Library Administrator; (3) Curator for
(1) Enquiries Broadcasters/general; (2) Public/
academic research; (3) Educational.

Founded:
1976

Formed from:
Scottish Screen; Scottish Film and Television
Archive (SFTA) (year of change 2001)

Formerly called:
Scottish Film Archive (year of change 1997)

Organisation type and purpose:
National government body.
Archive.
To locate and preserve moving images made in or
about Scotland.

Subject coverage:
Non-fiction film material relating to Scotland
including documentaries, newsreels, educational,
advertising and promotional, industrial,
broadcasts and amateur film.

**Museum or gallery collection, archive, or library
special collection:**
Film and documentation on the films of Scotland
Committee 1938 to 1982
Upper Clyde Shipbuilders 1926 to 1971

Non-library collection catalogue:
All or part available online, in-house and in print

Library catalogue:
All or part available in-house

Printed publications:
Scottish Film Archive Catalogue (1st ed., free plus
p&p)
To Speak Its Pride – the work of the Films of
Scotland Committee 1938 to 1982, A Scottish
Film Monograph (£5 plus p&p)
With an Eye to the Future – A Scottish Film
Monograph (Alexander D and Cooper B,
Documentary Film Makers, £5 plus p&p)

Electronic and video publications:
Seawards the Great Ships (video, £12.99)
Young At Heart (video, £12.99)
The Rugged Island and Eriskay (video, £12.99)
The Face of Scotland and Wealth of a Nation
(video, £12.99)
Various other videos by mail order

Access to staff:
Contact by letter, by telephone, by fax and by e-
mail. Appointment necessary.
Hours: Mon to Fri, 0900 to 1700

Parent body:
Scottish Screen
249 West George Street, Glasgow, G2 4QE; tel:
0141 302 1700; fax: 0141 302 1711; e-mail: info@
scottishscreen.com

SCOTTISH SECONDARY TEACHERS' ASSOCIATION

Acronym or abbreviation: SSTA

14 West End Place, Edinburgh, EH11 2ED

Tel: 0131 313 7300
Fax: 0131 346 8057
E-mail: info@ssta.org.uk

Enquiries:
Enquiries to: General Secretary

Founded:
1945

Organisation type and purpose:
Trade union (membership is by qualification),
present number of members: 8000.

Subject coverage:
Education in secondary schools in Scotland;
general education in Scotland.

Access to staff:
Contact by letter, by telephone, by fax and by e-
mail. Appointment necessary.
Hours: Mon to Thu, 0900 to 1645; Fri, 0900 to 1615

SCOTTISH SENSORY CENTRE

Acronym or abbreviation: SSC

Moray House School of Education, Holyrood
Road, Edinburgh, EH8 8AQ

Tel: 0131 651 6501\ Minicom no. 0131 651 6067
Fax: 0131 651 6502
E-mail: sscmail@education.ed.ac.uk

Website:
http://www.ssc.education.ed.ac.uk
http://www.ssc.education.ed.ac.uk/library/list
.html
Catalogue.

Enquiries:
Enquiries to: Resource Library Manager
Direct tel: 0131 651 6069
Other contacts: Administrator

Founded:
1991

Created by the merger of:
Scottish Centre for Education of the Deaf (SCED),
Visual Impairment Centre (VIC) (year of change
1991)

Organisation type and purpose:
Advisory body, public library.
Training organisation.
Educational organisation.
To promote and disseminate effective practices and
innovation in the education of children and young
people with sensory impairments.

Subject coverage:
All aspects of sensory impairment including visual
impairment, deaf education, dual sensory
impairment and special educational needs.

Information services:
Postal Lending Library for members; information
enquiries from the public; primary documents
available online

**Museum or gallery collection, archive, or library
special collection:**
Resource library contains over 3,000 books, videos,
audio cassettes and teaching packs (available for
loan to library members)

Library catalogue:
All or part available online, in-house and in print

Printed publications:
Booklet (listing courses, seminars, workshops and open days available free of charge from the Centre)
Centre Newsletter (2 times a year)
Sensory Series (conference proceedings, etc.)
Autism and Visual Impairment Conference (£5 plus £1.50 p&p)
Cerebral Palsy and Visual Impairment in Children: Experience of Collaborative Practice in Scotland (£10 incl. p&p)
Empowerment '97 International conference on Deaf Education (£3.50 incl. p&p)
Empowering Young Deaf and VI People (free)
Managing Change in Visual Impairment Education (£3.50 incl. p&p)
Mobility Education: a Gateway to Learning, Putting Skills in Context (£1.50 incl. p&p)
Moving Through: Stages of the educational journey for deaf children and young people in North Ayrshire – A Parent/Carer Guide (free)
Promoting Social Inclusion of Pupils with Visual Impairment in Mainstream Schools in Scotland (£4.50 incl. p&p)
Self Evaluation by Peripatetic Sensory Services: Quality Assurance in Education Authority Peripatetic Sensory Services (£5 plus £1 p&p)
Video for Visually Impaired Learners (printed version, £10 incl. p&p)
Visual Impairment: Partnership, Networking and Support, Proceedings of the Conference, Sept. 1993 (£3 plus £1.50 p&p)
Order printed publications from: Resource Library Manager, Scottish Sensory Centre; tel. 0131 651 6069; e-mail sscmail@education.ed.ac.uk

Electronic and video publications:
The Crowded Cottage (in British Sign Language, CD-ROM, free)
IT the VI Way (video)
Let the Fingers do the Reading (video)
Let Me See (video)
Movement, Gesture and Sign (video)
Show Me How to Do It (video)
Video for Visually Impaired Learners (CD-ROM, free)
Vision for Doing (online only)

Publications list:
Available online and in print

Access to staff:
Contact by letter, by telephone, by fax, by e-mail and in person. Appointment necessary.
Hours: Mon to Fri, 0930 to 1300 and 1400 to 1630

Access for disabled people:
Parking provided, ramped entry and lifts, toilet facilities

Links with:
Moray House School of Education
University of Edinburgh; website: http://www.education.ed.ac.uk

SCOTTISH SNOOKER LIMITED

Acronym or abbreviation: SSL

c/o Baillie, 59 Locher Avenue, Houston, Renfrewshire, PA6 7NX

Tel: 07814 150064
E-mail: scottishsnooker147@yahoo.co.uk

Website:
http://www.scottishsnooker.co.uk
Website of Scottish Snooker – The National Governing Body for Snooker in Scotland.

Enquiries:
Enquiries to: Administrator

Founded:
2001

Created by the merger of:
Scottish Billiards & Snooker Association (SBSA), and Scottish Snooker Association (SSA) (year of change 2001)

Organisation type and purpose:
National government body, national organisation, advisory body, statutory body, membership association (membership is by subscription), present number of members: 200, voluntary organisation, training organisation, consultancy.

Subject coverage:
Snooker.

Access to staff:
Contact by letter, by telephone and by e-mail
Hours: Mon to Fri, 0900 to 1700

SCOTTISH SOCIETY FOR AUTISM

Hilton House, Alloa Business Park, Whins Road, Alloa, Clackmannanshire, FK10 3SA

Tel: 01259 720044
Fax: 01259 720051
E-mail: autism@autism-in-scotland.org.uk

Website:
http://www.autism-in-scotland.org.uk
Information on autism, training and conference services available.

Enquiries:
Enquiries to: Chief Executive

Founded:
1968

Formerly called:
Scottish Society for Autistic Children (SSAC) (year of change 1999)

Organisation type and purpose:
Voluntary organisation, registered charity (charity number SC009068).
To ensure the provision of the best possible education, care, support and opportunities for those of all ages with autism, to support families, improve understanding, and develop best practice amongst carers, professionals and society at large.

Subject coverage:
Autism and Aspergers Syndrome.

Printed publications:
Magazine (members)
Various books related to autism
Newsletters
Information on services for adults, children, respite and training

Publications list:
Available in print

Access to staff:
Contact by letter, by telephone, by fax, by e-mail and via website. Appointment necessary.
Hours: Mon to Thu, 0900 to 1700; Fri, 0900 to 1630

Access for disabled people:
Level entry, access to all public areas, toilet facilities

SCOTTISH SOCIETY FOR CONSERVATION AND RESTORATION

Acronym or abbreviation: SSCR

Chantstown, Tartraven, Bathgate Hills, West Lothian, EH48 4NP

Tel: 01506 811777
Fax: 01506 811777
E-mail: admin@sscr.demon.co.uk

Website:
http://www.sscr.demon.co.uk
Information regarding SSCR, its activities and events.

Enquiries:
Enquiries to: Administrator

Founded:
1977

Organisation type and purpose:
International organisation, learned society, professional body (membership is by subscription), present number of members: 400, voluntary organisation, registered charity (charity number SC017185), suitable for ages: 18+, publishing house.
The purpose of the Society is to improve public knowledge, methods and working standards needed to protect, preserve and to maintain the condition of any work of art or structure of important historic interest and value.

Subject coverage:
All aspects of object conservation and restoration.

Printed publications:
SSCR Journal (3 times a year, members only)
Papers from conferences on: resins ancient and modern, paper and textiles, conservation of furnishing textiles, environmental control and monitoring, decorative wood, conservation and restoration of materials

Publications list:
Available online and in print

Access to staff:
Contact by letter, by telephone, by fax, by e-mail and via website. Appointment necessary.
Hours: Mon to Thu, 1300 to 1700

Member of:
European Confederation for Conservator-Restorers' Organizations (ECCO)
International Institute for Conservation (IIC)
United Kingdom Institute for the Conservation of Historic and Artistic Works (UKIC)

SCOTTISH SOCIETY FOR PSYCHICAL RESEARCH

Acronym or abbreviation: SSPR

5 Church Wynd, Kingskettle, By Cupar, Fife, KY15 7PS

Tel: 01337 830387
Fax: 01337 830387
E-mail: archie.lawrie@ukgateway.net

Enquiries:
Enquiries to: Honorary Secretary

Founded:
1987

Organisation type and purpose:
Learned society, registered charity (charity number SCO 20421), research organisation.

Subject coverage:
All types of phenomena known as paranormal or parapsychological, ghosts, poltergeists.

Museum or gallery collection, archive, or library special collection:
CD and tape library (members only)

Printed publications:
PSI report (newsletter, 9 times a year, £10 a year; as at Jan 2007)

Electronic and video publications:
Tapes of lectures (£3.50)

Access to staff:
Contact by letter, by telephone, by fax and by e-mail
Hours: 0900 to 2100, later in an emergency

SCOTTISH SOCIETY FOR THE PREVENTION OF CRUELTY TO ANIMALS

Acronym or abbreviation: Scottish SPCA

Braehead Mains, 603 Queensferry Road, Edinburgh, EH4 6EA

Tel: 0131 339 0222
Fax: 0131 339 4777
E-mail: enquiries@scottishspca.org

continued overleaf

Website:
http://www.scottishspca.org
Locations of animal welfare centres; emergency telephone numbers for reporting an animal in distress; inspectorate; education; membership and volunteering.

Enquiries:
Enquiries to: Public Relations Director
Other contacts: Press Officer

Founded:
1839

Formerly called:
Aberdeen APCA, Glasgow Dog and Cat Home

Organisation type and purpose:
National organisation, advisory body, membership association (membership is by subscription), voluntary organisation, registered charity (charity number SC 006467), suitable for ages: Nursery to Adult.
Main aim is to prevent animal cruelty and to encourage kindness and humanity in their treatment.

Subject coverage:
Prevention of cruelty to animals, animal care, the law regarding animals, education in kind and humane treatment.

Printed publications:
Animal Express (Junior members magazine, quarterly)
Annual Report
Information sheets and leaflets
SSPCA News (members magazine, 6 times a year)

Access to staff:
Contact by letter, by telephone, by fax and by e-mail. Appointment necessary.
Hours: Mon to Fri, 0900 to 1700

Member of:
Eurogroup and World Society for the Protection of Animals (WSPA)

SCOTTISH SOCIETY OF THE HISTORY OF MEDICINE

Acronym or abbreviation: SSHM

13 Craiglea Drive, Edinburgh, EH10 5PB

Tel: 0131 447 2572
E-mail: nigel@malcolm-smith43.wanadoo.co.uk

Website:
http://www.st-andrews.ac.uk/~sshm/

Enquiries:
Enquiries to: Honorary Secretary

Founded:
1948

Organisation type and purpose:
Learned society (membership is by subscription), present number of members: 200.

Subject coverage:
History of medicine.

Museum or gallery collection, archive, or library special collection:
Dr Haldane P Tait's book collection is held in the Royal College of Physicians Library, Queen Street, Edinburgh. (subject Paediatrics and Public Health)

Printed publications:
Report of Proceedings

Access to staff:
Contact by letter, by telephone and by e-mail
Hours: Mon to Fri, 0900 to 1700

Affiliated to:
British Society for the History of Medicine

SCOTTISH SPINA BIFIDA ASSOCIATION

Acronym or abbreviation: SSBA

The Dan Young Building, 6 Craighalbert Way, Cumbernauld, G68 0LS

Tel: 01236 794500
Fax: 01236 736435

Website:
http://ourworld.compuserve.com/homepages/ssbahq
http://www.ssba.org.uk/

Enquiries:
Enquiries to: family Support Service
Direct tel: 01236 794516
Direct fax: 01236 736435
Direct e-mail: familysupport@ssba.org.uk

Founded:
1965

Organisation type and purpose:
Membership association, present number of members: 3500, registered charity (charity number SCO13328).
To increase public awareness and understanding of spina bifida and/or hydrocephalus. Aims to secure provision for the needs of those with spina bifida and/or hydrocephalus and those of their families.

Subject coverage:
Spina bifida, hydrocephalus and allied disorders.

Printed publications:
Leaflets and booklets including:
Hydrocephalus
Hydrocephalus and You
Incontinence
Medical Aspects
Orthopaedic Aspects
Points for Parents
Pregnancy, Folic Acid and You
Scoliosis
Spina Bifida Occulta
Spina Bifida and Pregnancy
The Learner Driver with Spina Bifida and/or Hydrocephalus
Standard Information Pack

Publications list:
Available in print

Access to staff:
Contact by letter, by telephone, by fax, by e-mail, in person and via website
Hours: Mon to Fri, 0900 to 1700

Family Support Service:
Scottish Spina Bifida Association
6 Blackie Street, Glasgow, G3 8TN; tel: 0645 11 11 12 (lo-call routes); fax: 0141 339 8658

Fundraising Office:
Scottish Spina Bifida Association
14 Manse Road, Motherwell, ML1 2PW; tel: 01698 258854; fax: 01698 258854

SCOTTISH SPORTS ASSOCIATION

Acronym or abbreviation: SSA

Caledonia House, South Gyle, Edinburgh, EH12 9DQ

Tel: 0131 339 8785
Fax: 0131 339 5168
E-mail: joanne@info-ssa.org.uk

Enquiries:
Enquiries to: Executive Administrator
Other contacts: Chairman

Founded:
1992

Formerly called:
Confederation of National Governing Bodies of Scottish Sport (year of change 1992)

Organisation type and purpose:
Membership association (membership is by election or invitation), present number of members: 78.
To represent the interests of Scottish Sports Governing Bodies.

Subject coverage:
Governing Bodies of sport in Scotland.

Printed publications:
Annual Report
Operational Plan
Running Sport Scotland literature
Saltire (seasonal members information brochure)
Who We Are, What We Do

Access to staff:
Contact by letter, by telephone, by fax and by e-mail
Hours: Mon to Thu, 0900 to 1700

Access for disabled people:
Parking provided, level entry, access to all public areas, toilet facilities

SCOTTISH SQUASH LIMITED

Caledonia House, 1 Redheughs Rigg, South Gyle, Edinburgh, EH12 9DQ

Tel: 0131 317 7343
Fax: 0131 317 7734
E-mail: scottishsquash@aol.com

Enquiries:
Enquiries to: Administration Manager

Formerly called:
Scottish Squash Rackets Association (SSRA)

Organisation type and purpose:
Membership association.

Subject coverage:
Player rankings, events, sources of finance, advice on construction and maintenance, equipment, rules, coaching, training courses, refereeing, history of squash, playing records, fitness.

Electronic and video publications:
Videos on coaching and events

Affiliated to:
European Squash Rackets Federation (ESRF)
World Squash Federation (WSF)

SCOTTISH SUB-AQUA CLUB

Acronym or abbreviation: SSAC

The Cockburn Centre, 40 Bogmoor Place, Glasgow, G51 4TQ

Tel: 0141 425 1021
Fax: 0141 425 1021
E-mail: hqssac@ssac.demon.co.uk

Website:
http://www.scotsac.com
Details of SSAC and its services.

Enquiries:
Enquiries to: Administrator

Founded:
1953

Organisation type and purpose:
Membership association (membership is by subscription), present number of members: 1900. National governing body of the sport.

Subject coverage:
Information on history of diving, dive training methods, diving equipment, salvage methods, underwater medicine, dive sites, construction of ships, underwater life, marine archaeology, video on diving, underwater sport.

Museum or gallery collection, archive, or library special collection:
Library of 760 books on diving etc

Printed publications:
Advanced dive training manual
Dive logbook
Dive Training Schedule
Introductory Dive Training Manual
Scottish Diver Magazine

Publications list:
Available in print

Access to staff:
Contact by letter, by telephone, by fax, by e-mail and via website
Hours: Mon to Thu, 0900 to 1700; Fri, 0900 to 1630

Access for disabled people:
Level entry, toilet facilities

SCOTTISH TEXT SOCIETY

Acronym or abbreviation: STS

27 George Square, Edinburgh, EH8 9LD

Tel: 0115 951 5922
Fax: 0115 951 5924
E-mail: editorialsecretary@scottishtextsociety.org

Website:
http://www.scottishtextsociety.org

Enquiries:
Enquiries to: Editorial Secretary

Founded:
1882

Organisation type and purpose:
Learned society, publishing house.
To further the study and teaching of Scottish literature, its language and history, in particular by publishing editions of original texts.

Subject coverage:
Scottish literature especially, although not exclusively, of the medieval and early modern period.

Non-library collection catalogue:
All or part available online

Library catalogue:
All or part available in-house

Printed publications:
List of all the publications (over 120) since 1883, some of which are now out of print, of Scottish poetry and histories, etc.
Recent annual vols include:
The Song Repertoire of Amelia and Jane Harris (ed. E. Lyle, K. McAlpine, A. McLucas)
Older Scots Vowels (A. J. Aitken and C. MacAfee)
The Poems of Walter Kennedy (ed. N. Meier)
The Shorter Poems of Gavin Douglas (ed. P. Bawcutt)
David Hume of Godscroft, The History of the House of Angus (ed. D. Reid)
Order printed publications from: Boydell and Brewer Ltd, PO Box 9, Woodbridge, Suffolk, IP12 3DF; tel. 01394 610600; fax 01394 610316; e-mail trading@boydell.co.uk

Publications list:
Available online and in print

Access to staff:
Contact by letter, by e-mail and via website. Appointment necessary.
Hours: Mon to Fri, 0900 to 1700

Also at:
Scottish Text Society
c/o Editorial Secretary, 27 George Square, Edinburgh, EH8 9LD

SCOTTISH TOURIST GUIDES ASSOCIATION

Acronym or abbreviation: STGA

Norrie's House, 18b Broad Street, Stirling, FK8 1EF

Tel: 01786 447784
Fax: 01786 447784
E-mail: info@stga.co.uk

Website:
http://www.stga.co.uk

Enquiries:
Enquiries to: Administrator
Other contacts: Booking Secretary for booking guides.

Founded:
1959

Organisation type and purpose:
Professional body (membership is by subscription, qualification), present number of members: 320, service industry, suitable for ages: 25 to 75.

Subject coverage:
Specialised knowledge of Scotland past and present.
Guides are available to conduct tours throughout Scotland.

Printed publications:
List of members: a list of qualified guides, services, Gaelic and other language guides, driver guides
Guide List 2001

Publications list:
Available in print

Access to staff:
Contact by letter, by telephone, by fax, by e-mail and via website. Appointment necessary.
Hours: Mon to Fri, 0900 to 1700
Special comments: Please provide sae for reply.

Centralised booking service:
STGA booking service
tel: 01786 451953; fax: 01786 451953; e-mail: bookings@stga.co.uk

SCOTTISH TRAMWAY AND TRANSPORT SOCIETY

Acronym or abbreviation: STTS

PO Box 78, Glasgow, G3 6ER

Enquiries:
Enquiries to: General Secretary
Direct tel: 0141 445 3883
Direct e-mail: hughmc@87gv.freeserve.co.uk

Founded:
1951

Organisation type and purpose:
Voluntary organisation.

Subject coverage:
Scottish tramways, trolleybuses and omnibuses.
Glasgow Underground Railway, Strathclyde and Lothian Electric Trains.

Museum or gallery collection, archive, or library special collection:
R B Parr photographic collection
Scottish Road Public Transport photographic collection

Printed publications:
Green Cars to Hurlford
Scottish Transport Magazine (annually)
The Glasgow Tramcar (Stewart I G, 1994 ed., £16.95)
The Glasgow Horse Tramways 1872–1902 (Robertson S J T)

Electronic and video publications:
Aberdeen Trams (video, 1994, £19)
Dundee Trams (video, 1996, £16)
Glasgow Trams Part One (video, 1992, £22)
Glasgow Trams Part Two (video, 1993, £22)
Look Back at Glasgow's Trams and Trolleybuses

Publications list:
Available in print

Access to staff:
Contact by letter, by telephone and by e-mail
Hours: Mon to Fri, 0900 to 1700

Affiliated to:
AMTUIR (France)
Tramway Museum Society
Transport Trust

SCOTTISH TRANSPORT STUDIES GROUP

Acronym or abbreviation: STSG

26 Palmerston Place, Edinburgh, EH12 5AL

Tel: 0870 350 4202
E-mail: enquiries@stsg.org

Website:
http://www.stsg.org
Background information on STSG. Updated list of contacts.

Enquiries:
Enquiries to: Chairman
Other contacts: Organiser

Founded:
1984

Organisation type and purpose:
Membership association (membership is by subscription), present number of members: 100, registered charity.
To stimulate interest in, and awareness of, the transport function and its importance for the Scottish economy; to encourage contacts between operators, public bodies, users, academia and other organisations and individuals with interests in transport in a Scottish context; to issue publications and organise conferences and seminars related to transport policy and research.

Subject coverage:
Transport policy in Scotland.

Non-library collection catalogue:
All or part available online and in print

Library catalogue:
All or part available online and in print

Printed publications:
Scottish Transport Review (quarterly, free to members)
Annual Report and Research Review (free to members)
Occasional Papers (free to members)

Publications list:
Available online

Access to staff:
Contact by letter, by telephone, by fax, by e-mail and via website
Hours: Mon to Fri, 0900 to 1700

SCOTTISH UNIVERSITIES ENVIRONMENTAL RESEARCH CENTRE

Acronym or abbreviation: SUERC

Scottish Enterprise Technology Park, Rankine Avenue, East Kilbride, South Lanarkshire, G75 0QF

Tel: 01355 270139, 270102
Fax: 01355 229898
E-mail: director@suerc.gla.ac.uk

Website:
http://www.gla.ac.uk/suerc

Enquiries:
Enquiries to: Director
Direct tel: 01355 223332

Founded:
2002

Formerly called:
Scottish Universities Research and Reactor Centre (year of change 2002)

Subject coverage:
Environmental research.

Access to staff:
Contact by letter, by telephone, by fax, by e-mail, in person and via website

SCOTTISH URBAN ARCHAEOLOGICAL TRUST

Acronym or abbreviation: SUAT

55 South Methven Street, Perth, Tayside, PH1 5NX

Tel: 01738 622393
Fax: 01738 631626

Website:
http://www.suat.demon.co.uk

continued overleaf

Enquiries:
Enquiries to: Director

Founded:
1982

Organisation type and purpose:
Registered charity, research organisation, consultancy.
Archaeological research.

Subject coverage:
Urban archaeology in Scotland, general archaeology in Scotland.

Access to staff:
Contact by letter, by telephone and by fax.
Appointment necessary.
Hours: Mon to Fri, 0830 to 1630

Member of:
Council for British Archaeology
Council for Scottish Archaeology
Tayside and Fife Archaeological Committee

SCOTTISH WATER

Castle House, 6 Castle Drive, Carnegie Campus, Dunfermline, Fife, KY11 8GG

Tel: 0845 601 8855
E-mail: customer.service@scottishwater.co.uk

Website:
http://www.scottishwater.co.uk

Enquiries:
Enquiries to: Customer Services

Formed from:
East of Scotland Water (ESW), North of Scotland Water (NoSWA), West of Scotland Water (W'SWA), date of change, 1 April 2002

Subject coverage:
Land analysis, environment management, risk analysis, engineering consultancy, water and waste water analysis, waste management, pipeline installation, water charges, recreation, site surveys and site investigation, education.

Library catalogue:
All or part available in-house

Printed publications:
Information leaflets available on request
Household charges
Code of Practice
Annual Report

Access to staff:
Contact by letter, by telephone, by e-mail and via website
Hours: Mon to Fri, 0900 to 1700

Access to building, collection or gallery:
No access other than to staff

Access for disabled people:
Parking provided, level entry, toilet facilities

SCOTTISH WATER – EDINBURGH

Acronym or abbreviation: SW

55 Buckstone Terrace, Fairmilehead, Edinburgh, EH10 6XH

Tel: 0845 601 8855
Fax: 0131 445 5040
E-mail: customer.services@scottishwater.co.uk

Website:
http://www.scottishwater.co.uk
General information about Scottish Water and its services. Major sections include business and domestic services.

Enquiries:
Enquiries to: Customer Service Adviser
Direct tel: 0845 601 8855
Direct e-mail: customer.services@scottishwater.co.uk
Other contacts: Corporate Communications for press enquiries.

Founded:
2002

Organisation type and purpose:
Statutory body.

Subject coverage:
Supply of water and waste water services to the whole of Scotland

Museum or gallery collection, archive, or library special collection:
Small library of books and reports relating to water and waste water services and the water industry.
For internal use only.

Library catalogue:
All or part available in-house

Printed publications:
Annual Report and Accounts
Conditions of Contract – Purchase of Goods and Services Various leaflets
(All the above available electronically)

Publications list:
Available online

Access to staff:
Contact by letter, by telephone, by fax, by e-mail, in person and via website. Appointment necessary.
Hours: Mon to Fri, 0900 to 1700

Access for disabled people:
Hours: Mon to Fri, 0900 to 1700

Area Offices:
Inverness Area Office and Stores
  31 Henderson Drive, Longman North, Inverness, IV1 1TR; tel: 0845 601 8855; e-mail: customer.services@scottishwater.co.uk
Scottish Water
  Bullion House, Invergowrie, Dundee, DD2 5BB; tel: 0845 601 8855; e-mail: customer.services@scottishwater.co.uk
Scottish Water
  Kingshill House, Arnhall Business Park, Westhill, Aberdeen, AB32 6UF; tel: 0845 601 8855; e-mail: customer.services@scottishwater.co.uk
Scottish Water
  419 Balmore Road, Glasgow, G22 6NU; tel: 0845 601 8855; e-mail: customer.services@scottishwater.co.uk

Head Office:
Scottish Water
  Castle House, 6 Castle Drive, Carnegie Campus, Dunfermline, KY11 8GG; tel: 0845 601 8855; e-mail: customer.services@scottishwater.co.uk

Subsidiary body:
Scottish Water Scientific
  Heriot-Watt Research Park, Avenue North, Edinburgh, EH14 4AP; tel: 0845 601 8855; e-mail: customer.services@scottishwater.co.uk

SCOTTISH WATER SKI ASSOCIATION

Acronym or abbreviation: SWSA

Townhill Country Park, Townhill, Dunfermline, Fife, KY12 0HT

Tel: 01383 620123
Fax: 01383 620122
E-mail: info@swsc.fsbusiness.co.uk

Website:
http://www.waterskiscotland.co.uk

Enquiries:
Enquiries to: Administrator
Other contacts: National Co-ordinator for first point of contact.

Founded:
1960

Formerly called:
(SWSA) (year of change 1998)

Organisation type and purpose:
Membership association (membership is by subscription), present number of members: 250, voluntary organisation.

To teach and instruct water skiing and wakeboarding including good driving practice.

Subject coverage:
All aspects relating to the sports of water skiing and waterboarding.

Non-library collection catalogue:
All or part available online

Library catalogue:
All or part available online

Access to staff:
Contact by letter, by fax and by e-mail
Hours: Tue to Fri, 1300 till Dusk; Sat, Sun, 1000 till Dusk
Special comments: Closed Monday.

Access to building, collection or gallery:
No prior appointment required

Access for disabled people:
Parking provided, ramped entry, level entry, access to all public areas, toilet facilities

SCOTTISH WIDER ACCESS PROGRAMME

Acronym or abbreviation: SWAPWest

300 Cathedral Street, Glasgow, G1 2TG

Tel: 0141 553 2471
Fax: 0141 552 6090
E-mail: swapwest@btconnect.com

Website:
http://www.swap2highereducation.com

Enquiries:
Enquiries to: Director

Founded:
1987

Organisation type and purpose:
Membership association (membership is by subscription), present number of members: 30, registered charity (charity number SCO 25833), suitable for adults.

Subject coverage:
All aspects of education for adults with few or no formal qualifications.

Access to staff:
Contact by letter, by telephone, by fax, by e-mail and via website
Hours: Mon to Fri, 0900 to 1700

SCOTTISH WILDLIFE TRUST

Acronym or abbreviation: SWT

Cramond House, 3 Kirk Cramond, off Cramond Glebe Road, Edinburgh, EH4 6HZ

Tel: 0131 312 7765
Fax: 0131 312 8705
E-mail: enquiries@swt.org.uk

Website:
http://www.swt.org.uk

Enquiries:
Enquiries to: Receptionist
Other contacts: Communications Manager for press and media

Founded:
1964

Organisation type and purpose:
Advisory body, membership association (membership is by subscription), present number of members: 31,000, voluntary organisation, registered charity (charity number SC005792), training organisation, consultancy, publishing house.
Campaigning environment body, land managers.
The protection of all forms of Scottish wildlife and the Scottish environment.

Subject coverage:
Conservation of all forms of wildlife in Scotland, land use for wildlife interest, biological surveying, environmental education, reserves management, practical land management.

Non-library collection catalogue:
All or part available in-house

Library catalogue:
All or part available in-house

Printed publications:
Annual Review (free)
Information leaflets
Scottish Wildlife (magazine, 3 times a year, free to members)
Biodiversity Facts and Figures report

Access to staff:
Contact by letter, by telephone, by fax, by e-mail and via website. Appointment necessary.
Hours: Mon to Fri, 0900 to 1700

Administers:
123 reserves, including three visitor centres

Links with:
People's Postcode Lottery
Scottish Environment Link
Scottish National Heritage
The Scottish Executive
Wildlife Trusts Partnership

SCOTTISH WOMEN'S AID

2nd Floor, 132 Rose Street, Edinburgh, EH2 3JD

Tel: 0131 226 6606
Fax: 0131 226 2996
E-mail: contact@scottishwomensaid.org.uk

Website:
http://www.scottishwomensaid.org.uk

Organisation type and purpose:
Membership association, voluntary organisation, registered charity (charity number SC001099), training organisation.

Subject coverage:
Information, support and refuge for women, children and young people who have been affected by domestic abuse.

Printed publications:
Children, Young People and Domestic Abuse (30p)
Hello (welcome magazine for young children, statutory organisations £2, voluntary organisations £1)
Posters for children and young people (Rights, £1; Hello, £2; I am important, £2)
Respect (30p)
Welcome (magazine for young people, £2, statutory organisations; £1, voluntary organisations)
Young People Say (£5, voluntary organisations £4)
Your Rights (leaflet pack, £6 plus 50p p&p or singularly at 60p)

Publications list:
Available online and in print

Access to staff:
Contact by letter, by telephone, by fax, by e-mail and via website. Appointment necessary.
Hours: Mon to Fri, 1000 to 1600; except Tue, 1300 to 1600

Access for disabled people:
Parking provided, ramped entry, level entry, access to all public areas, toilet facilities

Has:
network of 39 local groups throughout Scotland

SCOTTISH WOMEN'S FOOTBALL

Acronym or abbreviation: SWF

Hampden Park, Glasgow, G42 9DF

Tel: 0141 620 4580
Fax: 0141 620 4581
E-mail: swf@scottish-football.com

Enquiries:
Enquiries to: Executive Administrator

Founded:
1972

Formerly called:
Scottish Women's Football Association

Organisation type and purpose:
Membership association (membership is by subscription), present number of members: 3000.

Subject coverage:
Women's football.

Printed publications:
Match Fit (quarterly magazine)

Access to staff:
Contact by letter, by telephone, by fax and by e-mail. Appointment necessary.
Hours: Mon to Fri, 0900 to 1700

SCOTTISH WOMEN'S RURAL INSTITUTES

Acronym or abbreviation: SWRI

42 Heriot Row, Edinburgh, EH3 6ES

Tel: 0131 225 1724
Fax: 0131 225 8129
E-mail: swri@swri.demon.co.uk

Website:
http://www.swri.org.uk

Enquiries:
Enquiries to: General Secretary

Founded:
1917

Organisation type and purpose:
Membership association (membership is by subscription), present number of members: 26,000, voluntary organisation, registered charity (charity number SCO 11901), suitable for ages: 12+, training organisation, consultancy.

Subject coverage:
Cookery, crafts, village history.

Museum or gallery collection, archive, or library special collection:
Village Histories Collection (histories of many villages in Scotland)

Printed publications:
Scottish Home and Country (monthly)

Access to staff:
Contact by letter, by telephone, by fax, by e-mail and in person
Hours: Mon to Thu, 0900 to 1700; Fri, 0900 to 1530

Access to building, collection or gallery:
No access other than to staff, prior appointment required

Member of:
Associated Country Women of the World

SCOTTISH WRESTLING ASSOCIATION

Acronym or abbreviation: SWA

SWA Administrator, 26A Watchmeal Crescent, Faifley, Glasgow, G81 5ED

Tel: 01389 381532
E-mail: scottishwrestling@hotmail.com

Enquiries:
Enquiries to: Administrator

Formerly called:
Scottish Amateur Wrestling Association (SAWA) (year of change 2000)

Organisation type and purpose:
National organisation, membership association.

Subject coverage:
All wrestling, including Cumberland, in Scotland, starting up clubs, coaching, training programmes, tournaments.

Printed publications:
Wrestling award courses (leaflet, free)
Wrestling at the Grassroots (leaflet, free)
Annual Tournament Calendar

Access to staff:
Contact by letter, by telephone and by e-mail
Hours: By appointment via telephone/email.
Special comments: Personal Callers: Tue and Fri, 1000 to 1500 only by appointment via telephone/ email.

Affiliated to:
International Federation of Wrestling Associations (FILA)
Scottish Sports Association (SSA)

SCOTTISH YOUTH HOSTELS ASSOCIATION

Acronym or abbreviation: SYHA

7 Glebe Crescent, Stirling, FK8 2JA

Tel: 01786 891400
Fax: 01786 891333
E-mail: syha@syha.org.uk

Website:
http://www.syha.org.uk
Information on all youth hostels in Scotland, travel details, activity holidays, etc.

Enquiries:
Enquiries to: Public Relations Manager
Direct e-mail: marketing@syha.org.uk

Founded:
1931

Organisation type and purpose:
Voluntary organisation, registered charity (charity number SCO 13138).

Subject coverage:
Low cost holiday accommodation for all ages; recreational and activity holidays for young people; holiday itineraries using youth hostels.

Printed publications:
Annual Report
General information leaflets
Scottish Hosteller (magazine, 2 times a year)
Hostel Guide (annual, free)

Access to staff:
Contact by letter, by telephone, by fax, by e-mail, in person and via website
Hours: Mon to Fri, 0900 to 1700

Access to building, collection or gallery:
No prior appointment required

Affiliated to:
International Youth Hostels Federation

SCOTTISH YOUTH THEATRE

Acronym or abbreviation: SYT

105 Brunswick Street, Glasgow, G1 1TF

Tel: 0141 552 3988
Fax: 0141 552 7615
E-mail: info@scottishyouththeatre.org

Website:
http://www.scottishyouththeatre.org

Enquiries:
Enquiries to: Marketing Officer
Direct e-mail: sophie@scottishyouththeatre.org

Founded:
1976

Organisation type and purpose:
Registered charity (charity number SCO 14283), suitable for ages: 3 to 25.
National arts organisation.
Giving children and young people in Scotland the opportunity to reach their creative potential through a quality theatre arts experience.

continued overleaf

Subject coverage:
Theatre, arts, drama, theatrical training, directing, acting, movement, choreography, technical theatre/stage management, musical theatre.

Access to staff:
Contact by letter, by telephone, by e-mail, in person and via website
Hours: Mon to Fri, 1000 to 1730

Funded by:
Glasgow City Council (GCC)
Scottish Arts Council (SAC)

Member of:
Federation of Scottish Theatres (FST)
Independent Theatre Council (ITC)

SCOUT ASSOCIATION

Gilwell Park, Bury Road, Chingford, London, E4 7QW

Tel: 0845 300 1818
Fax: 020 8433 7103
E-mail: scoutbase@scoutbase.org.uk

Website:
http://www.scoutbase.org.uk
Information available on all aspects of scouting, both home and abroad.

Enquiries:
Enquiries to: Public Relations Officer

Founded:
1907

Organisation type and purpose:
International organisation, membership association, present number of members: 554,440 members in the UK, registered charity.

Subject coverage:
Scout training; outdoor pursuits, skills training and service to the community; needs of the physically handicapped and slow learners; youth education.

Museum or gallery collection, archive, or library special collection:
Archives of 90 years of scouting

Printed publications:
Fact sheets on history or activities
Handbooks and manuals on outdoor pursuits
Publications on scout training and leader training
Scouting (magazine, monthly)

Electronic and video publications:
Rules and fact sheets (CD-ROM)

Publications list:
Available online

Access to staff:
Contact by letter, by telephone, by fax, by e-mail and via website. Appointment necessary.
Hours: Mon to Fri, 0800 to 2000; Sat 0900 to 1200

Close association with the:
Guides Association

Member of:
National Council for Voluntary Youth Services
World Scout Bureau in Geneva

SCOUTS SCOTLAND

Formal name: The Scottish Council The Scout Association

Fordell Firs, Hillend, near Dunfermline, Fife, KY11 7HQ

Tel: 01383 419073
Fax: 01383 414892
E-mail: shq@scouts-scotland.org.uk

Enquiries:
Enquiries to: Chief Executive

Organisation type and purpose:
Membership association (membership is by subscription), present number of members: 43,828, registered charity (Scottish Charity No. SC017511), training organisation.

The physical, intellectual, social and spiritual development of young people.

Subject coverage:
Development programmes and outdoor activities for young people; training of voluntary adult leaders.

Printed publications:
Scottish Scout News (newsletter 5 times a year)

Access to staff:
Contact by letter, by telephone, by fax, by e-mail and via website
Hours: Mon to Fri, 0900 to 1700
Special comments: Prior appointment recommended.

Affiliated to:
Scout Association UK
  Gilwell Park, Chingford, London, E4 7QW; tel: 020 8433 7100; fax: 020 8433 7103; e-mail: scout .association@scout.org.uk

SCREENWRITERS' WORKSHOP

Acronym or abbreviation: SW

Euroscript Ltd, 64 Hemingford Road, London, N1 1DB

Tel: 07958 244 656
E-mail: ask@euroscript.co.uk

Website:
http://www.lsw.org.uk/
Details of upcoming seminars, workshops and industry events with members-only online magazine on screenwriting.

Enquiries:
Enquiries to: Administrator
Direct e-mail: screenoffice@tiscali.co.uk

Founded:
1983

Formerly called:
London Screenwriters Workshop (LSW) (year of change 1998)

Organisation type and purpose:
National organisation, membership association (membership is by subscription), present number of members: 800 approx, training organisation. To train writers of cinema and TV scripts and offer industry information and networking opportunities.

Subject coverage:
Screenwriting for cinema and TV.
Information on writing and marketing scripts.

Access to staff:
Contact by letter, by telephone, by e-mail and via website. Appointment necessary.
Hours: Mon to Fri, 0900 to 1700
Special comments: By arrangement or at times of advertised meetings, workshops and seminars.

SCRIPTURE UNION

Acronym or abbreviation: SU

207–209 Queensway, Bletchley, Milton Keynes, Buckinghamshire, MK2 2EB

Tel: 01908 856000
Fax: 01908 856111
E-mail: info@scriptureunion.org.uk

Website:
http://www.scriptureunion.org.uk
news from Scripture Union's various ministries across England and Wales

Enquiries:
Enquiries to: Chief Executive

Founded:
1867

Organisation type and purpose:
International organisation, voluntary organisation, registered charity (charity number 213422), training organisation.

Christian missionary society, member of the Evangelical Alliance.
Evangelising and discipling children, young people and families through school work, missions, holidays, bible ministries, training and resources.

Subject coverage:
Christian outreach to children, young people and families through schools, churches, holidays and missions. Development for church members through training, publications and other resources.

Printed publications:
The Life (magazine, 4 times a year)
A wide range of titles covering many subjects and
  age ranges:
Up to six years old
Six to eleven year olds
Eleven years plus
School books and resources
Working with children
Bible readings for groups/adults
The Christian Life
Order printed publications from: Scripture Union Mail Order
PO Box 5148, MLO, Milton Keynes, MK2 2YX, tel: 01980 856006, fax: 01980 856020, e-mail: subs@ scriptureunion.org.uk

Publications list:
Available in print

Access to staff:
Contact by letter, by telephone, by fax, by e-mail and via website
Hours: Mon to Fri, 0900 to 1700

Access to building, collection or gallery:
No prior appointment required

SEA FISH INDUSTRY AUTHORITY

Acronym or abbreviation: SEAFISH

18 Logie Mill, Logie Green Road, Edinburgh, EH7 4HS

Tel: 0131 558 3331
Fax: 0131 558 1442
E-mail: seafish@seafish.co.uk

Website:
http://www.seafish.co.uk
The work of each department; quality award schemes; publications list with prices; recipes.
http://www.seafish.co.uk/education
Information on fish industry and fish as food, for schools.

Founded:
1981

Formed from:
Herring Industry Board (HIB) and White Fish Authority (WFA)

Organisation type and purpose:
Advisory body, statutory body, training organisation, consultancy, research organisation. Statutory body; accountable to the Department for Environment, Food and Rural Affairs for broad activities, but funded largely by the fish industry. The Authority works with the fish industry to meet the demands of consumers, to raise standards throughout the industry, to improve the efficiency and unity of the industry, and to secure a prosperous future for all fish industry sectors. The Authority is the Industry Designated Body for training within all sectors of the fish industry, and provides a forum for discussion between sectors.

Subject coverage:
Fishery economics; fish industry statistics (trade, landings, consumption, employment etc), infrastructure economics; fishery management; fish stocks and their assessment; marketing of fish within the UK and abroad; quality assurance throughout the fish industry; technology of fish processing; safety and legal compliance surveys of fishing vessels; grants and loans to the fish industry; EU legislation, and perspective on the

UK fish industry; training of workers in all industry sectors; studies of fishing gear behaviour; mariculture.

Museum or gallery collection, archive, or library special collection:
Collection of fisheries statistical publications from Europe, North America, and also international in scope

Trade and statistical information:
Data on UK imports and exports of fish and fish products, data on fish landings into the UK, data on household consumption of fish and fish products in the UK, data on fish landings and trade of European and North American countries (variable information in this case)

Non-library collection catalogue:
All or part available in-house

Library catalogue:
All or part available in-house

Printed publications:
Variety of papers concerning aspects of Seafish Marketing
Annual Reports and accounts
Variety of industry sector newsletters
European Supplies Bulletin (quarterly, plus one data issue annually, UK £85 a year)
Household Fish Consumption in Great Britain (quarterly, UK £75 a year)
Key Indicators (quarterly, UK £35 a year)
UK Trade Bulletin (monthly, UK £35 a year)
Leaflets on the fishing industry, species of fish and fish recipes (free)
Marine Survey: Rules of Construction Series
Variety of economics research papers and seafish technology reports

Electronic and video publications:
Publications Guide (also available by e-mail)

Publications list:
Available online and in print

Access to staff:
Contact by letter, by telephone, by fax, by e-mail and via website. Appointment necessary.
Hours: Mon to Fri, 0900 to 1700

Access to building, collection or gallery:
No prior appointment required

Access for disabled people:
Ramped entry, toilet facilities

Branches at:
Sea Fish Industry Authority
Humber Seafood Institute, Origin Way, Europarc, Grimsby, DN37 9TU; tel: 01472 252300; fax: 01472 268792; e-mail: seafish@ seafish.co.uk

SEAFACS INFORMATION AND RESEARCH

Acronym or abbreviation: SIR

PO Box 317, Welwyn Garden City, Hertfordshire, AL8 6DP

Tel: 01707 334192
E-mail: seafacs@sir.co.uk

Website:
http://www.sir.co.uk

Enquiries:
Enquiries to: Manager

Founded:
1985

Organisation type and purpose:
Consultancy.

Subject coverage:
Shipping, marine insurance, commodities.

Access to staff:
Contact by letter, by telephone, by e-mail and via website. All charged.

Hours: Mon to Fri, 0900 to 1700

Access to building, collection or gallery:
No access other than to staff

SEASONAL AFFECTIVE DISORDER ASSOCIATION

Acronym or abbreviation: SADA

PO Box 989, Steyning, West Sussex, BN44 3HG

Tel: 01903 814942 (recorded message)
Fax: 01903 879939

Website:
http://www.sada.org.uk
Information about SAD and the Association.

Enquiries:
Enquiries to: Administrator

Founded:
1987

Organisation type and purpose:
Membership association (membership is by subscription), present number of members: c. 1800, voluntary organisation, registered charity (charity number 800917).

Subject coverage:
Depression related to lack of sunlight.

Printed publications:
Information leaflet, (free with sae)
Information Pack (£5)
Turning the Spotlight on SAD – The Patient Perspective (£2)

Publications list:
Available in print

Access to staff:
Contact by letter and by fax
Hours: Mon to Fri, 0900 to 1700

SEDGEMOOR DISTRICT COUNCIL

Bridgwater House, King Square, Bridgwater, Somerset, TA6 3AR

Tel: 01278 435435
Fax: 01278 446412

Enquiries:
Enquiries to: Media Relations Officer

Organisation type and purpose:
Local government.

SEFTON LIBRARY AND INFORMATION SERVICES

Pavilion Buildings, 99–105 Lord Street, Southport, Merseyside, PR8 1RJ

Tel: 01704 533133
Fax: 0151 934 2370
E-mail: library.service@leisure.sefton.gov.uk

Website:
http://www.sefton.gov.uk

Enquiries:
Enquiries to: Head of Library and Information Services

Founded:
1974

Organisation type and purpose:
Local government body, public library.

Library catalogue:
All or part available online

Access to staff:
Contact by letter, by telephone, by fax, by e-mail, in person and via website. Appointment necessary.

Access for disabled people:
Ramped entry

Parent body:
Sefton Metropolitan Borough Council

SELDEN SOCIETY

School of Law, Queen Mary University of London, Mile End Road, London, E1 4NS

Tel: 020 7882 5136
Fax: 020 8981 8733
E-mail: selden-society@qmul.ac.uk

Website:
http://www.selden-society.qmul.ac.uk

Enquiries:
Enquiries to: Secretary

Founded:
1887

Organisation type and purpose:
Learned society (membership is by subscription), present number of members: 1,700, registered charity (charity number 211536), research organisation, publishing house.
Promotion of research into history of English law, and of legal profession, institutions, etc.

Subject coverage:
History of English law and legal institutions, legal literature and records, palaeography, bibliography, history of the legal profession, legal biography; translation, transcription and evaluation of legal manuscripts.

Museum or gallery collection, archive, or library special collection:
Own publications 1887–2006

Printed publications:
Annual Report
Annual Series and Supplementary Series (over 140 volumes of early law reports, courts' records, legal treatises, etc.)
Centenary Guide to Publications (1987) with history of the Society, etc.
Published lectures
Publications, List of Members and Rules (handbook)

Publications list:
Available online and in print

Access to staff:
Contact by letter, by telephone, by fax, by e-mail and via website. Appointment necessary.
Hours: Mon, Tue, Thu, 0900 to 1700

SELECT

Formal name: The Electrical Contractors' Association of Scotland
Acronym or abbreviation: ECAofS

The Walled Garden, Bush Estate, Midlothian, EH26 0SB

Tel: 0131 445 5577
Fax: 0131 445 5548
E-mail: admin@select.org.uk

Website:
http://www.select.org.uk

Enquiries:
Enquiries to: Head of External Affairs

Founded:
1900

Organisation type and purpose:
Trade association (membership is by qualification). To represent the electrical, electronic and communications systems industry. To advance and promote members interests. To respond to the key strategic issues facing the industry and the Association.

Subject coverage:
Electrical installation, safety and security systems, information technology, telecommunications, electronics, industrial relations and employment law matters; commercial and contractual matters; education, training and health and safety matters; management; marketing, technical advice and on-site inspections.

Printed publications:
Annual Report

continued overleaf

Cabletalk (magazine, 6 times a year)
Contract Manual
Members' Directory (annually)

Publications list:
Available in print

Access to staff:
Contact by letter, by telephone, by fax, by e-mail and in person
Hours: Mon to Fri, 0900 to 1700
Special comments: Charges to non-members under certain circumstances.

Access for disabled people:
Parking provided, level entry, access to all public areas, toilet facilities

Member of:
International Association of Electrical Contractors (AIE)
Specialist Engineering Contractors Group

Subsidiary body:
Scottish Electrical Contractors Insurance Company

SELEX SENSORS AND AIRBORNE SYSTEMS LTD

300 Capability Green, Luton, LU1 3PG

Tel: 01582 886135
Fax: 01582 795861
E-mail: dawn.couzens@selex-sas.com

Website:
http://www.baesystems.com
Corporate website.

Enquiries:
Enquiries to: Site Data Manager
Other contacts: Information Resources Officers for departmental staff.

Formerly called:
BAE Systems Avionics Ltd; GEC Marconi Ltd (year of change 1998); Marconi Electronic Systems (year of change 1999)

Organisation type and purpose:
International organisation, manufacturing industry.

Subject coverage:
Defence electronics, aerospace engineering and technology.

Non-library collection catalogue:
All or part available in-house

Library catalogue:
All or part available in-house

Access to staff:
Contact by letter, by telephone, by fax and by e-mail
Hours: Mon to Thu, 0845 to 1715; Fri, 0845 to 1645
Special comments: No personal visitors. Some information restricted to employees only.

Part of:
BAE Systems

SENSE

11–13 Clifton Terrace, Finsbury Park, London, N4 3SR

Tel: 020 7272 7774\ Minicom no. 020 7272 9648
Fax: 020 7272 6012
E-mail: enquiries@sense.org.uk

Website:
http://www.sense.org.uk/information
Publications and archived Talking Sense articles.
http://www.sense.org.uk/large
Large text version of the website.
http://www.sense.org.uk/deafblind
Information specifically for deafblind people.
http://www.sense.org.uk
Home page.

Enquiries:
Enquiries to: Information Officer

Founded:
1955

Organisation type and purpose:
National organisation, membership association (membership is by qualification, election or invitation), voluntary organisation, registered charity (charity number 289868).
A partnership of organisations working in the field of disability, education, social and medical services.

Subject coverage:
Rubella: the disease and the damage it can cause to an unborn child whose mother contracts the disease during pregnancy; rubella immunisation for schoolchildren, schoolgirls and non-immune adult women; immunisation against all childhood diseases. Deafblindness (dual sensory impairment); sensory impairment with multiple disabilities; Usher syndrome and other conditions leading to deafblindness, CHARGE syndrome.

Museum or gallery collection, archive, or library special collection:
Press cuttings on subject of deafblindness
Regional surveys of deaf-blind population and services
Research material on rubella in pregnancy

Printed publications:
Fact sheets, leaflets, booklets, reports and proceedings (some free, some for sale)
Communication and Advocacy Training Pack (Voluntary Service Team, 2000)
Sense Annual Review
Living with Usher Syndrome (leaflet, free)
Dbl Review (newsletter, 2 times a year)
Good Sense: The National Deafblind and Rubella Association 1955–1995, a history
Making Contact, A Good Practice Guide: How to Involve and Communicate with a Deafblind Person (Hicks G, 1996)
Talking Sense (magazine, 3 times a year)

Electronic and video publications:
All publications on tape and disc

Publications list:
Available online and in print

Access to staff:
Contact by letter, by telephone, by fax, by e-mail and via website
Hours: Mon to Fri, 0900 to 1730
Special comments: Limited wheelchair access. Disabled parking not available.

Access to building, collection or gallery:
No prior appointment required
Hours: Mon to Fri, 0900 to 1730

Access for disabled people:
Level entry, toilet facilities
Special comments: Lift to two floors

Partnership including the:
MENCAP
National Deaf Children's Society
RNIB
RNID

SEQUAL TRUST

3 Ploughman's Corner, Wharf Road, Ellesmere, Shropshire, SY12 0EJ

Tel: 01691 624222
Fax: 01691 624222
E-mail: enquiries@thesequaltrust.co.uk

Website:
http://www.thesequaltrust.org.uk

Enquiries:
Enquiries to: Charity Manager
Direct e-mail: liz@thesequaltrust.co.uk

Founded:
1969

Organisation type and purpose:
Membership association (membership is by subscription), registered charity (charity number 260119).

To raise funds to provide communication aids to disabled children and adults on a permanent free loan basis.

Subject coverage:
Communication aids for those with speech, movement or learning difficulties.

Services for disabled people:
Provision of communication aids for those with speech, movement or learning disabilities.

Printed publications:
The Sequal Newsletter (annual)

Publications list:
Available in print

Access to staff:
Contact by letter, by telephone, by fax and by e-mail
Hours: Mon to Fri, 0900 to 1630

Access to building, collection or gallery:
No visits necessary

SERA

Formal name: Socialist Environment and Resources Association
Acronym or abbreviation: SERA

1 London Bridge, Downstream Building, London SE1 9BG

Tel: 020 7022 1985
E-mail: enquiries@sera.org.uk

Website:
http://www.serauk.org.uk

Enquiries:
Enquiries to: National Co-ordinator

Founded:
1973

Organisation type and purpose:
National organisation, membership association (membership is by subscription), present number of members: 1500, voluntary organisation.

Subject coverage:
Environmental issues, politics (Labour party), pollution, green economics, trade union issues.

Printed publications:
New Ground (magazine journal of Green Socialism, two times a year)

Access to staff:
Contact by letter, by telephone and by e-mail
Hours: Mon to Fri, 1000 to 1800

Affiliated to:
Labour Party

SERIES 2 CLUB LTD

PO Box 41, Manchester, M43 7WZ

E-mail: secretary@series2club.co.uk

Website:
http://www.series2club.org.uk
Historical, pictorial, contacts.

Enquiries:
Enquiries to: Membership Secretary

Founded:
1985

Organisation type and purpose:
Membership association (membership is by subscription), present number of members: 800.

Subject coverage:
Land Rover Series II 1958–1971, restoration, operation, history, registration enquiries (DVLA Registered Club).

Museum or gallery collection, archive, or library special collection:
Technical manuals

Printed publications:
Magazine (quarterly)

Access to staff:
Contact by letter. Non-members charged.
Hours: Mon to Fri, 1700 to 2000

Member of:
Association of Rover Clubs
Federation of British Historic Vehicle Clubs

SERVICES CENTRAL LIBRARY

Acronym or abbreviation: SCL

The ACC Memorial Hall, Thornhill Road,
Aldershot, Hampshire, GU11 2BG

Tel: 01252 349839
Fax: 01252 349836
E-mail: scl@alibs.detsa.co.uk

Enquiries:
Enquiries to: Librarian

Organisation type and purpose:
National government body.

Subject coverage:
General, particularly computing, law and
management, no military stock.

Library catalogue:
All or part available in-house

Printed publications:
Subject bibliographies of stock holding

Access to staff:
Contact by letter. Appointment necessary. Access
for members only.
Hours: Mon to Fri, 0900 to 1630

Links with:
Army Library Service
   Upavon, Pewsey, Wiltshire

SESAME INSTITUTE UK

Acronym or abbreviation: Sesame

Christchurch, 27 Blackfriars Road, London, SE1
8NY

Tel: 020 7633 9690
E-mail: sesameinstituteuk@btinternet.com

Enquiries:
Enquiries to: Director

Founded:
1964

Organisation type and purpose:
Advisory body, professional body (membership is
by subscription), registered charity (charity
number 263155), suitable for ages: 22+, training
organisation.
Recognised by the National Health Service,
Department for Education and the British
Association for Drama Therapists.
Promotes drama and movement in therapy.

Subject coverage:
Drama and movement as therapy in work with the
mentally and physically sick and the physically
handicapped, training in such special skills, direct
patient services.

Printed publications:
Newsletter (quarterly)
Bring White Beads When You Call on the Healer
   (Lindkvist M)
Discovering the Self Through Drama and
   Movement Therapy – The Sesame Approach
   (Pearson J)
Report of Project at Smith Hospital (autistic
   children) and at Goodmayes Hospital
   (schizophrenic patients)

Microform publications:
Films and videos of Sesame Projects showing the
   use of drama with schizophrenic, severely
   subnormal and autistic children and adults

Publications list:
Available in print

Access to staff:
Contact by letter, by telephone and by e-mail.
Appointment necessary.
Hours: Tue, 1000 to 1700; Thu, Fri, 1000 to 1700
Special comments: No disabled access.

Affiliated to:
MENCAP
MIND

Member of:
European Consortium for Arts Therapies
Education

SEVENOAKS DISTRICT COUNCIL

Council Offices, Argyle Road, Sevenoaks, Kent,
TN13 1HG

Tel: 01732 227000
Fax: 01732 740693
E-mail: communications@sevenoaks.gov.uk

Website:
http://www.sevenoaks.gov.uk
Basic information on authority, expanding into site
containing varied information on Sevenoaks area.

Enquiries:
Enquiries to: Communications Officer
Other contacts: Chief Executive

Organisation type and purpose:
Local government body.

Subject coverage:
Planning and building control, car parking, council
tax collection, environmental health, housing
benefits, recycling, refuse collection, community
and environmental services

Publications list:
Available in print

Access to staff:
Contact by letter, by telephone, by fax, by e-mail,
in person and via website
Hours: Mon to Thu, 0845 to 1700; Fri, 0845 to 1645

Access for disabled people:
Parking provided, level entry, toilet facilities

Local Sub-offices at:
Edenbridge Local Office and Tourist Information
Centre
   Stangrove Park, Edenbridge, Kent; tel: 01732
   868110; fax: 01732 868114; e-mail:
   edenbridgetic@sevenoaks.gov.uk
Swanley Library and Contact Centre
   London Road, Swanley, Kent; tel: 01322 614660;
   fax: 01322 665082; e-mail: information@
   sevenoaks.gov.uk

SEWELLS INFORMATION & RESEARCH

Media House, Lynchwood, Peterborough Business
Park, Peterborough, Cambridgeshire, PE2 6EA

Tel: 01733 468000
Fax: 01733 468349
E-mail: sewells@emap.com

Website:
http://www.sewells.co.uk

Enquiries:
Enquiries to: Information Manager
Direct tel: 01733 468290
Direct fax: 01773 468349
Direct e-mail: eric.carnell@emap.com
Other contacts: Production Manager for
subscriptions and publishing enquiries.

Founded:
1962

Organisation type and purpose:
Advisory body, membership association
(membership is by subscription), service industry,
training organisation, research organisation,
publishing house.
Automotive research information and
publications.

Subject coverage:
Motor trade management, motor industry in the
UK and overseas, statistics, vehicle retailing
companies and manufacturers.

Trade and statistical information:
UK and European motor industry information and
   Best Practice publications.

Printed publications:
Aftersales Management (monthly)
Automotive Marketing Review (bi-monthly)
Automotive Digest (weekly)
Automotive Finance (monthly)
Dealer Principal (monthly)
Digital Dealer (monthly)
Fleet Dealer (monthly)
Sales Management (monthly)
Used Car Dealer (monthly)
Management Guides
New Vehicle Registrations
Statistical Reports on Franchise Networks
Weekly Digests of Abstracts

Publications list:
Available online and in print

Access to staff:
Contact by letter, by telephone, by fax and by e-
mail. Non-members charged.
Hours: Mon to Fri, 0900 to 1730

SEXUAL HEALTH AND REPRODUCTIVE CARE

Acronym or abbreviation: SHARC

25 Warwick Road, Coventry, CV1 2EZ

Tel: 024 7696 1300
Fax: 024 7696 1339

Enquiries:
Enquiries to: Information Officer
Other contacts: Manager, Clinical Medical Officer,
Senior Nurse

Founded:
1990

Formerly called:
Well Woman Clinic, Well Women's Services,
Women's Health and Information Centre

Organisation type and purpose:
Local government body.
Medical services, information service, support
groups.

Subject coverage:
Women's health, contraception, family planning,
health information, pregnancy.
Specialist genetic, sickle cell and thalassaemia
services, chlamydia screening for ages 16–24.

Access to staff:
Contact by letter, by telephone, by fax and in
person. Appointment necessary.
Hours: Mon to Thu, 0830 to 1900; Fri, 0830 to 1630;
Sat 1300 to 1630
Special comments: Appointments for clinical
services.

Access for disabled people:
Parking provided, ramped entry, access to all
public areas, toilet facilities
Special comments: Hearing loop, magnifier.

Parent body:
Coventry Primary Care Trust
   Parkside House, Quinton Road, Coventry, West
   Midlands, CV1 2NJ; tel: 024 7655 3344

SHAFTESBURY AND DISTRICT HISTORICAL SOCIETY

Gold Hill, Shaftesbury, Dorset, SP7 8JW

Tel: 01747 852157
E-mail: sdhs@waitrose.com

Website:
http://www.shaftesburyheritage.org.uk

continued overleaf

Enquiries:
Enquiries to: Honorary Secretary
Direct tel: 01747 851950

Founded:
1946

Organisation type and purpose:
Membership association, voluntary organisation, registered charity (charity number 229883). Local history society and museum.

Subject coverage:
Local history of Shaftesbury and district.

Museum or gallery collection, archive, or library special collection:
Significant parts of the museum collection:
Anglo-Saxon coins of the Shaftesbury mint
Dorset buttons
Costumes with Shakespeare origins
Maps
Lace-making
Victorian social history
World Wars I and II personal mementoes
Photographs and postcards (incl. 700 slides)
John Rutter's scrap album (19th-century)
Other exhibits include Byzant (ritual token), medieval alabaster panel, a 1744 fire engine, 2 church bells (16th- & 17th-century), a church font, 1919 Sale of Shaftesbury catalogue.
Small library of local reference books

Non-library collection catalogue:
All or part available in-house

Library catalogue:
All or part available in-house

Printed publications:
History of The Dorset Button
Museum leaflet
Shaftesbury Guide

Access to staff:
Contact by letter, by telephone, by e-mail, in person and via website. Appointment necessary. Non-members charged.

Access to building, collection or gallery:
Apr to Oct (museum open season); library by appointment only

Member of:
Area Museum Council for the South West
Dorset Museums Association

SHAKESPEARE BIRTHPLACE TRUST RECORDS OFFICE

Henley Street, Stratford-upon-Avon, Warwickshire, CV37 6QW

Tel: 01789 201816 or 204016
Fax: 01789 296083
E-mail: records@shakespeare.org.uk

Website:
http://www.shakespeare.org.uk
Introductory information on Records Office page within the Website with summary information on the major collections, specialist subjects (e.g., family history sources, poor law records, sources for property history etc) and services.

Enquiries:
Enquiries to: Head of Archives and Local Studies

Founded:
1847

Organisation type and purpose:
Registered charity (charity number 209302). Charitable trust.

Subject coverage:
Local history for Stratford-upon-Avon and Warwickshire, and the adjoining areas of Gloucestershire, Worcestershire and Oxfordshire, Shakespeare biography, genealogy of Stratford families, Elizabethan and Jacobean history, (source material for the foregoing subjects is mainly unprinted, but is supplemented by printed books, photographs, drawings etc). Shakespeare memorabilia, furniture, local history, crafts and agriculture, archaeological material.

Museum or gallery collection, archive, or library special collection:
Books, documents, photographs, prints and drawings, newspapers, films and video
Borough Collection (items relating to law and order, civic regalia and furniture, 15th to 19th century)
David Garrick Collection (costume, pewter and other personal effects belonging to Garrick, commemorative material relating to the Garrick Jubilee in 1769)
Records of early Stratford antiquarians and Shakespeare biographers
Records of leading Warwickshire families
Records of the Stratford-upon-Avon Corporation
Parish and nonconformist registers for Stratford-upon-Avon
Parish register transcripts for most of South Warwickshire and neighbouring parishes in Gloucestershire and Worcestershire
Monumental inscriptions for the same area
Local newspapers, with an index of obituaries, 1860–1913

Non-library collection catalogue:
All or part available online and in-house

Library catalogue:
All or part available online and in-house

Printed publications:
Shakespeare in the Stratford Records (Bearman R, out of print, new ed in prep)
John Hall and his Patients: The Medical Practice of Shakespeare's Son-in-Law (Lane J, 1996, 378pp)
Family Life in Shakespeare's England: Stratford-upon-Avon, 1570–1630 (Jones J, 1996, 172pp)
The Civil War in Stratford-upon-Avon: Conflict and Community in South Warwickshire, 1642–1646 (Tennant P, 1996, 202pp)
The History of an English Borough: Stratford-upon-Avon, 1196–1996 (ed Bearman R, 1997, 218pp)
Compton Verney: A History of the House and its Owners (ed Bearman R, 2000, 188pp)
Stoneleigh Abbey: The House, Its Owners, Its Lands (ed Bearman R, 2004, 290pp)

Publications list:
Available in print

Access to staff:
Contact by letter, by telephone, by fax, by e-mail, in person and via website
Hours: Mon, Tue, Thu, Fri, 0930 to 1700; Wed, 0930 to 1900; Sat, 0930 to 1230

Access for disabled people:
Ramped entry, access to all public areas, toilet facilities
Special comments: Advance notice for wheelchair users preferred.

Maintains the:
Shakespeare Centre Library

SHAKESPEARE CENTRE LIBRARY

Henley Street, Stratford-upon-Avon, Warwickshire, CV37 6QW

Tel: 01789 204016
Fax: 01789 296083
E-mail: library@shakespeare.org.uk

Website:
http://www.shakespeare.org.uk/main/3/339
Royal Shakespeare Company Performance Database of productions and production personnel from 1879.
http://www.shakespeare.org.uk
Shakespeare's life and houses, library and archives, museums department, education department, diary of events.

Enquiries:
Enquiries to: Head of Library & Information Resources
Direct tel: 01789 201838 (Direct line)
Direct e-mail: sylvia.morrisk@shakespeare.org.uk

Founded:
1850

Organisation type and purpose:
Registered charity (charity number 209302), research organisation.
Research library of the Shakespeare Birthplace Trust.

Subject coverage:
Shakespeare (texts, versions, translations, criticism etc); Shakespeareana; English stage history, especially Shakespearean; early modern British social history; topography of Warwickshire; RSC.

Museum or gallery collection, archive, or library special collection:
Archives of the Shakespeare Memorial Theatre 1879–1960 and of the Royal Shakespeare Company 1961 to date
Joe Cocks Studio Collection (photographs of RSC productions 1969–1991)
Stoker Collection (material relating to Henry Irving at the Lyceum Theatre)
Holte Photographic Collections (photographs of RSC productions 1950s-1981)
Reg Wilson Collection (photographs of RSC productions 1961–1997)

Non-library collection catalogue:
All or part available online and in-house

Library catalogue:
All or part available online and in-house

Microform publications:
Shakespeare prompt books (microfilm, Harvest Microfilm, 1988, now marketed by Primary Source Media)
Bram Stoker collection on Henry Irving (Harvest Microfilm, 1988, now marketed by Primary Source Media)
Shakespeare at Stratford-upon-Avon (microfiche)

Access to staff:
Contact by letter, by fax, by e-mail and in person
Hours: Mon, Tue, Thu, Fri, 1000 to 1700; Wed, 1000 to 1900; Sat, 0930 to 1230; Closed 23 to 26 Dec inclusive, all Bank Holidays and the preceding Saturdays
Special comments: ID with address for general use. Letter of introduction required for access to special collections not available in surrogate form.

Access to building, collection or gallery:
No prior appointment required except for video viewing.
Special comments: Letter of introduction required for the use of some materials.

Access for disabled people:
Access to all public areas, toilet facilities
Special comments: Wheelchair lift to front door. Parking 50 metres.

Houses the:
International Shakespeare Association

Incorporates the:
Royal Shakespeare Company Archive and Library

SHAKESPEARE INSTITUTE LIBRARY

Information Services, University of Birmingham, Mason Croft, Church Street, Stratford-upon-Avon, Warwickshire, CV37 6HP

Tel: 0121 414 9525
Fax: 01789 292021
E-mail: silib@bham.ac.uk

Website:
http://www.is.bham.ac.uk/shakespeare

Enquiries:
Enquiries to: Librarian
Other contacts: Secretary for student admissions and enquiries.

Founded:
1951

Organisation type and purpose:
University library, university department or institute.
Postgraduate research institute.

Subject coverage:
Shakespeare; English literature 1475 to 1640;
theatre history.

Museum or gallery collection, archive, or library special collection:
Archive of New Shakespeare Theatre Company
Archive of the Renaissance Theatre Company
Early English books 1475–1640 (microform)
Three centuries of English and American plays
  (microform)

Library catalogue:
All or part available online

Printed publications:
Brochure on facilities
Shakespeare libraries in the West Midlands

Access to staff:
Contact by letter. Letter of introduction required.
Hours: Mon to Thu, 0900 to 2000; Fri and Sat, 0900
to 1700; Sun, 1000 to 1700
Special comments: Only members and visitors with
valid library cards may be admitted after 1700 and
on Saturday and Sunday. Letter of introduction
required by non-members of the University.

Parent body:
Information services
  The University of Birmingham, Edgbaston,
  Birmingham, B15 2TT

SHAP WORKING PARTY ON WORLD RELIGIONS IN EDUCATION

Acronym or abbreviation: SHAP

National Society's RE Centre, Church House, Great
Smith Street, London, SW1P 3NZ

Tel: 020 7898 1495
Fax: 020 7898 1493
E-mail: mike.berry@natsoc.org.uk

Website:
http://dspace.dial.pipex.com/nsrec

Enquiries:
Enquiries to: Secretary

Founded:
1969

Organisation type and purpose:
Advisory body, professional body (membership is
by election or invitation), training organisation,
consultancy.
Concerned with providing accurate information
about world religions for schools and institutions
of higher education, police, hospitals, prisons, etc.

Subject coverage:
Religious education and teaching, the world's
major religions.

Printed publications:
Calendar of Festivals (annually)
Journal (annually)
Festivals in World Religions
Handbook of World Religions

Publications list:
Available in print

Access to building, collection or gallery:
Prior appointment required
Hours: Mon to Fri, 0900 to 1630

Access for disabled people:
Ramped entry, access to all public areas, toilet
facilities

Associated with:
European Association of World Religions in
Education (EAWRE)

SHAPE

Deane House Studios, 27 Greenwood Place,
London, NW5 1LB

Tel: 0845 521 3457\ Minicom no. 020 7424 7368
Fax: 0845 521 3458
E-mail: info@shape-uk.co.uk

Website:
http://www.shapearts.org.uk

Enquiries:
Enquiries to: Chief Executive
Direct e-mail: mhairi@shapearts.org.uk

Founded:
1976

Organisation type and purpose:
Advisory body, membership association, voluntary
organisation, registered charity (charity number
279184), training organisation.
Ticket Scheme: reduced price tickets and volunteer
escorts/drivers for London arts and entertainment
events for disabled people or those over 70 years of
age. Shape in Education: training for deaf and
disabled artists to work in education settings.
Shape Training: accredited training courses and
placement in all aspects of arts management and
practice. Training Support Network for young
disabled and deaf people wishing to enter arts
industries. Advice and information on training and
employment. Local Arts Development: workshops,
projects and events for disabled people, people
with learning difficulties, mental health system
survivors and older people. Deaf Arts Programme:
national programme of projects and events
promoting deaf arts and equal access to the arts for
deaf and hard of hearing people. Advice,
Information and Consultancy on all aspects of arts
and disability.
Shape opens up access to the arts, enabling greater
participation by disabled and older people.

Subject coverage:
Disability arts, deaf arts, training courses, ticket
scheme with reduced price tickets and volunteer
drivers, training placements and accredited
courses in arts management.

Museum or gallery collection, archive, or library special collection:
Arts related archives specific to Shape, disability
arts

Printed publications:
Disability Arts and Culture Papers

Access to staff:
Contact by letter, by telephone, by fax and by e-
mail
Hours: Mon to Fri, 1000 to 1800

Affiliated to:
Shape network, a federation of independent
disability arts organisations

Other addresses:
Shape in Hammersmith and Fulham
  Polish Arts and Cultural Centre, 238–246 Kings
  Street, Hammersmith, London, W6 0RF; tel: 020
  8741 7548 (answer machine) 020 8563 2894
  (minicom); fax: 020 8741 6375
Shape in Islington
  Room G15, c/o LBI, Arts and Heritage
  Department, Islington Town Hall, Upper Street,
  London, N1 1UD; tel: 020 7527 3850; fax: 020
  7477 3856
Shape in Wandsworth
  BAC, Lavender Hill, London, SW11 5TS; tel: 020
  7924 5287; fax: 020 7978 2507

SHARK ANGLING CLUB OF GREAT BRITAIN

Acronym or abbreviation: SACGB

The Quay, Looe, Cornwall, PL13 1DX

Tel: 01503 262642
Fax: 01503 262642
E-mail: enquiries@sharkanglingclubofgreatbritain
.org.uk

Enquiries:
Enquiries to: Secretary

Organisation type and purpose:
National organisation, membership association
(membership is by subscription), present number
of members: 400.

Subject coverage:
Shark fishing.

Access to staff:
Contact by letter, by telephone, by fax, by e-mail
and in person
Hours: 7 days a week.

Access to building, collection or gallery:
No prior appointment required

SHAW SOCIETY

C/o Alan Knight, 10 Compston Road, London, N1
2PA

Tel: 020 7226 4266

Website:
http://www.shawsociety.org.uk

Enquiries:
Enquiries to: Honorary Secretary
Direct e-mail: anthnyellis@aol.com

Founded:
1941

Organisation type and purpose:
Membership association (membership is by
subscription), present number of members: c. 300,
voluntary organisation.

Subject coverage:
Life and works of Bernard Shaw.

Other addresses:
Membership Secretary
  1 Buckland Court, 37 Belsize Park, London, NW3
  4EB; tel: 020 7794 7014; fax: 020 7431 0816; e-
  mail: shawsociety@blueyonder.co.uk
Newsletter Editor
  C/o Philip Riley, 11 Founders House, Aylesford
  Street, London, SW1V 3QE; tel: 020 7630 1675; e-
  mail: commonroom04@yahoo.com

SHEFFIELD AND DISTRICT FAMILY HISTORY SOCIETY

5 Old Houses, Piccadilly Road, Chesterfield,
Derbyshire, S41 0EH

E-mail: secretary@sheffieldfhs.org.uk

Website:
http://www.sheffieldfhs.org.uk
Aims of the society, area covered, membership
information, officers, meetings and activities,
publications, members email addresses, related
links, maps back to 1600.

Enquiries:
Enquiries to: Honorary Secretary

Founded:
1977

Organisation type and purpose:
Membership association (membership is by
subscription), present number of members: 1050,
voluntary organisation, suitable for ages: all.
To promote, for the benefit and education of the
public, the study of genealogy, family history and
local history in the County of South Yorkshire.

Subject coverage:
Family history, local (Sheffield and District) history,
census records, parish records.

Library catalogue:
All or part available in print

Printed publications:
The Flowing Stream (journal, quarterly, free to
  members)
The Small Guide to Parishes in the Sheffield Area
The Small Guide to Nonconformists in Sheffield
Researching Your Family History in Sheffield
Sheffield Ancestors
Sheffield's Volunteer Armies
Changes in Sheffield Street Names 1871
Order printed publications from: Sheffield and
District Family History Society
17 Firshill Road, Sheffield, S4 7BB

continued overleaf

Microform publications:
Bradfield Poor Law Documents (microfiche)
Hill Top Chapel and Christ Church Attercliffe, indexed transcript of the Baptism Registers 1719–1840, Marriage Registers 1734–1753 and Bishops Transcripts 1693–4 (microfiche)
Militia Men of the Barnsley District 1806 (details of 3,322 men in 40 townships that comprised the Staincross Wapentake, lying to the north and west of Sheffield) (microfiche)
St Mary's Ecclesfield, indexed transcript of Marriage Registers 1622–1840 and Banns 1653–1655, 1754–1775 (Marriages missing 14 miscellaneous years between 1665 and 1692) (microfiche)
St Nicholas Bradfield Marriages 1723–1840 (microfiche)
St Peter's Church Tankersley, indexed transcript of Baptisms, Marriages and Burials 1598–1840, Intent of Marriage 1653–1657 and Banns 1754–1810 (Registers 1650/1–1661 are missing. 1662 - 1677 have been compiled from Bishops Transcripts) (microfiche)
Hearth Tax Returns for South Yorks, 1672 (microfiche)
Militia Men of the Barnsley District (microfiche)
Burngreave Cemetery Consecrated Section Monumental Inscriptions (microfiche)
Burngreave Cemetery General Section Monumental Inscriptions (microfiche)
St Thomas Church Brightside Monumental Inscriptions (microfiche)
St Phillip's Churchyard and Wardsend Cemetery Monumental Inscriptions (microfiche)
Christ Church Dore Churchyard Monumental Inscriptions

Electronic and video publications:
Burial Transcript and Index All Saints, Ecclesall, 1789–1903 (CD)
Burial Transcript and Index All Saints Rotherham 1813–1854 (CD)
Burial Transcript and Index St Mary Greasbrough 1813–1858 (CD)
Burial Transcript and Index Attercliffe Cemetery 1859–1960 (CD)
Burial Transcript and Index Darnall Cemetery 1859–1901 (CD)
Burial Transcript and Index Revel Lane Cemetery, Woodhouse 1875 -1949 (CD)
Burial Transcript and Index Beauchief Abbey 1813–1988 (CD)
Burial Transcript and Index Christ Church Fulwood 1839–1908 (CD)
Burial Transcript and Index St James Norton 1813–1947 (CD)
Burial Transcript and Index Christ Church Attercliffe 1813–1902 (CD)
Burial Transcript and Index Christ Church Stannington 1830–1932 (CD)
Burial Transcript and Index St Mary Bolsterstone 1813–1856 (CD)
Burial Transcript and Index St Nicholas Bradfield 1813–1899 (CD)
Burial Transcript and Index Church of the Ascension Oughtibridge 1843–1942 (CD)
Burial Transcript and Index St Mary Walkley 1880–1901 (CD)
Burial Transcript and Index Holy Trinity Darnall 1846–1866 (CD)
Burial Transcript and Index Christ Church Pitsmoor 1850–1931(CD)
Burial Transcript and Index, St Lawrence Tinsley 1813–1901(CD)
Burial Transcript and Index Holy Trinity Wicker 1859 only Burials (CD)
Burial Transcript and Index St George's Portobello 1830–1899 (CD)
Burial Transcript and Index St John Chapeltown 1860–1971 (CD)
Burial Transcript and Index Christ Church Dore 1829–1967 (CD)
Burial Transcript and Index Cholera Burial Ground 1832 (CD)
Burial Transcript and Index St Mary Ecclesfield 1813–1909 (CD)
Burial Transcript and Index St Paul's Church 1813–61 (city centre) (CD)

Burial Transcript and Index St Thomas Brightside 1854–1901 (CD)
Burial Transcript and Index Christ Church Gleadless 1839–1953
Burial Transcript and Index Christ Church Heeley 1848–1906
Burial Transcript and Index St James 1813–55 (city centre)
Burial Transcript and Index St John Park 1830–1908
Burial Transcript and Index St Mary's (Bramall Lane) 1830–1908 (CD)
Burial Transcript and Index St Peter & St Paul (Cathedral) 1813–55 (CD)
Burial Transcript and Index St Philip's 1829–1918 (including Wardsend Cemetery 1857–1905) (CD)
Burial Transcript and Index St Thomas Crookes 1859–1973 (CD)
Burial Transcript and Index Wadsley 1835–1903 (7/5/1891–11/1/1895 records missing) (CD)
Burial Transcript and Index Tinsley Park Cemetery 1882–1973 (CD)
1831 Census Transcript and Index Nether Hallam
1891 Census Transcript and Index Sheffield North, Sheffield West, Sheffield Park, Sheffield South, Ecclesall Bierlow, Nether Hallam, Norton, Upper Hallam, Attercliffe cum Darnall, Brightside Bierlow (CD)
1861 Census Index for Sheffield, Rotherham and Bradfield (CD)
Bradfield Parish Church of St Nicholas Monumental Inscriptions (CD)
Christ Church Heeley Index of Baptisms 1848–1895 (disk)
St James Norton, indexed transcript of Marriages 1559–1837 (disk)
St Mary the Virgin Beighton, indexed transcript of Marriages 1645–1837 (disk)

Publications list:
Available online and in print

Access to staff:
Contact by letter, by e-mail and via website
Hours: Library: Mon to Thu, 0930 to 1730; Fri, closed; Sat, 0900 to 1300 and 1400 to 1630

Library facility held at:
Sheffield Archives
52 Shoreham Street, Sheffield, S1 4SP; tel: 0114 203 9395

Member of:
Federation of Family History Societies (FFHS)

SHEFFIELD ARCHIVES

52 Shoreham Street, Sheffield, South Yorkshire, S1 4SP

Tel: 0114 203 9395
Fax: 0114 203 9398
E-mail: archives@sheffield.gov.uk

Website:
http://www.sheffield.gov.uk/archives

Enquiries:
Enquiries to: Duty Archivist

Organisation type and purpose:
Local government body.

Subject coverage:
Family and estate records, church records (Church of England, Roman Catholic and Nonconformist), business archives, local authority and public records, trade union archives, antiquarian collections, political party records, societies and institutional records.

Museum or gallery collection, archive, or library special collection:
Collections include:
Arundel Castle Manuscripts (Sheffield, Derbyshire, and Nottinghamshire estates of the Dukes of Norfolk)
Business records of industrial history of the area, coal mining, iron and steel, cutlery, silver plate, professional firms, institutions and clubs
Correspondence and papers of Edward Carpenter (1844–1929)
Diocesan records for the Archdeaconry of Sheffield

Papers of the Earls of Wharncliffe
Papers of the Spencer Stanhope and Vernon Wentworth families and estates
Records of the Roman Catholic Diocese of Hallam
Wentworth Woodhouse Muniments (includes the papers of Thomas Wentworth, Earl of Strafford, 2nd Marquis of Rockingham and Edmund Burke)

Non-library collection catalogue:
All or part available online and in print

Printed publications:
A History of Sheffield Castle and Markets (£3.99)
Catalogue of the Arundel Castle Manuscripts in the Sheffield City Libraries (£15)
Diamonds in Brown Paper (£3.95)
Guide to the Fairbank Collection (£1)
Guide to the Manuscript Collections Supplement 1950–1976 (£7)
Essays in the Economic and Social History of South Yorkshire (£2.50)
Local Colour (£1)
Lyceum (£2)
Manuscript Collections in the Sheffield City Libraries (£2.50)
On the Knife Edge (£6.95)
Sheffield Walkabout (£4.95)
Sheffield Official Guide (£1.95)
Sir Francis Chantrey (£1)
The Sword of Sheffield (£1.50)
Family History Guides – listings of the sources available in the Archives (all seven £5 plus £1 p&p UK):
Census Returns, 1841, 1851, 1861, 1871 and 1881 listed alphabetically by place, covers the whole of South Yorkshire. 1981 – Sheffield, Ecclesall, Bierlow, Rotherham and Wortley registration districts
Monumental Inscriptions listed alphabetically by place, both Anglican and Non-conformist records included
Bishop's Transcripts, listed alphabetically by place, covers the whole of South Yorkshire
Parish Registers, Anglican registers from parishes in the Archdeaconry of Sheffield, listed alphabetically by place: Part 1 those in the Archives, Part 2 those churches which keep their own; both with dates
Copies of Parish Registers Held by Other Record Offices, listed alphabetically by place, covers parts of South Yorkshire and Derbyshire
Nonconformist Registers
Registers of Burials in Churchyards, Chapel Yards and Cemeteries, covers the whole of South Yorkshire and includes Anglican churchyards, nonconformist chapelyards and local authority cemeteries

Publications list:
Available online

Access to staff:
Contact by letter, by telephone, by fax, by e-mail and in person
Hours: Mon, 1000 to 1730; Tue to Thu, 0930 to 1730; Fri, closed; Sat, 0900 to 1300 and 1400 to 1700
Special comments: Users of the searchroom must obtain a reader's ticket, two official proofs of identity required on first visit. Access is suitable for disabled persons and wheelchairs.

Access for disabled people:
Level entry, access to all public areas, toilet facilities

SHEFFIELD ASSAY OFFICE

Guardians Hall, 137 Portobello Street, Sheffield, South Yorkshire, S1 4DS

Tel: 0114 275 5111
Fax: 0114 275 6473
E-mail: richj@assayoffice.co.uk

Website:
http://www.assayoffice.co.uk/resource.htm
Information about library and archives
http://www.assayoffice.co.uk
Services provided, history, contact details, etc.
http://www.assayoffice.co.uk/info.htm

List of publications and ordering details

Enquiries:
Enquiries to: Librarian
Other contacts: Laboratory Manager

Founded:
1773

Organisation type and purpose:
Statutory, non-profit making body, UKAS accredited laboratory.

Subject coverage:
Jewellery design, silverware design, principally European but worldwide coverage; precious metal assaying including historical material; some information on non-ferrous mining and metallurgy; hallmarking records for Sheffield.

Museum or gallery collection, archive, or library special collection:
Catalogues and records from various silversmithing firms no longer in existence (mainly local)
Daybooks from 1773 to 1830 and 1932 to the present
Office records from 1773

Trade and statistical information:
Hallmarking figures for UK, produced by British Hallmarking Council.

Non-library collection catalogue:
All or part available in-house

Library catalogue:
All or part available in-house

Printed publications:
Bradbury's Book of Hallmarks
Old Silver Platers and their Marks (£25 plus p&p)
Sheffield Assay Office Register 1773/1909 (£9.95 plus p&p)

Access to staff:
Contact by letter, by telephone, by fax, by e-mail and via website. Appointment necessary. Non-members charged.
Hours: Mon to Fri, 0900 to 1400

Access to building, collection or gallery:
No prior appointment required

Access for disabled people:
Parking provided, ramped entry, access to all public areas

SHEFFIELD CITY COUNCIL

Formal name: City of Sheffield Metropolitan District Council
Acronym or abbreviation: SCC

Howden House, 1 Union Street, Sheffield, S1 2HH

Tel: 0114 272 6444
Fax: 0114 273 5003
E-mail: firstpoint@sheffield.gov.uk

Website:
http://www.sheffield.gov.uk/

Enquiries:
Enquiries to: Media Relations Manager
Direct tel: 0114 2736604
Direct fax: 0114 273 4652
Direct e-mail: katie.harrison@sheffield.gov.uk

Founded:
1897

Organisation type and purpose:
Local government body.

Subject coverage:
Information about Sheffield, trade, tourism, entertainment, sport, education, social services, housing, parks, environmental health, highways, markets, planning, transport and all other local government services in Sheffield.

Printed publications:
Official Guide to Sheffield (£2)
Official Street Guide to Sheffield (£2)

Access to staff:
Contact by letter, by telephone, by fax, by e-mail and in person
Hours: Mon to Fri, 0900 to 1700

SHEFFIELD FIRST FOR INVESTMENT

Acronym or abbreviation: SF4I

1 St James Row, Sheffield, South Yorkshire, S1 2EU

Tel: 0114 223 2345
Fax: 0114 223 2346
E-mail: info@makeitinsheffield.com

Website:
http://www.makeitinsheffield.com
Information on Sheffield for potential investors, and services provided by Sheffield First for Investment

Enquiries:
Enquiries to: Enquiry Management Officers

Organisation type and purpose:
Local government body.
Provides a single point of contact for inward investment, relocation and business development enquiries.

Subject coverage:
Industrial and commercial property, sources of financial assistance, the development climate, local partner organisations, statistical information on Sheffield, local labour market and economy.

Trade and statistical information:
Database of available industrial and commercial property.
General information and statistics on Sheffield.

Printed publications:
Promotional brochures and other material from a variety of local organisations and estate agents

Access to staff:
Contact by letter, by telephone, by fax, by e-mail and via website. Appointment necessary.
Hours: Mon to Fri, 0900 to 1700

Parent body:
Sheffield City Council

SHEFFIELD GALLERIES & MUSEUMS TRUST

Leader House, Surrey Street, Sheffield, South Yorkshire, S1 2LH

Tel: 0114 278 2600
Fax: 0114 278 2604
E-mail: info@sheffieldgalleries.org.uk

Website:
http://www.sheffieldgalleries.org.uk

Founded:
1998

Organisation type and purpose:
Local government body, registered charity (charity number 1068850).
Administrative body.

Subject coverage:
Galleries and Museums Trust has management responsibility for five musems and galleries in Sheffield, including responsibility for policies, forward planning and performance.

Access to staff:
Contact by letter, by telephone, by fax, by e-mail and via website. Appointment necessary.
Hours: Mon to Fri, 0900 to 1730

Access for disabled people:
Toilet facilities
Special comments: Parking in Surrey Street, one step at door, phone prior to visit if assistance required.

Jointly funded by:
Sheffield City Council and the Arts Council of England

Trust sites:
Bishops' House
  Meersbrook Park, Norton Lees Lane, Sheffield, South Yorkshire, S8 9BE; tel: 0114 278 2600; fax: 0114 278 2604
Graves Art Gallery
  Surrey Street, Sheffield, South Yorkshire, S1 1XZ; tel: 0114 273 5158; fax: 0114 273 4705
Mappin Art Gallery
  Weston Park, Sheffield, South Yorkshire, S10 2TP; tel: 0114 278 2600; fax: 0114 275 0957
Millennium Galleries
  Arundel Gate, Sheffield, South Yorkshire, S1 2PP; tel: 0114 278 2600; fax: 0114 278 2604
Sheffield City Museum
  Weston Park, Sheffield, South Yorkshire, S10 2TP; tel: 0114 278 2600; fax: 0114 275 0957

SHEFFIELD HALLAM UNIVERSITY

Acronym or abbreviation: SHU

City Campus, Pond Street, Sheffield, South Yorkshire, S1 1WB

Tel: 0114 225 3581
Fax: 0114 225 4985

Website:
http://www.shu.ac.uk

Founded:
1843

Organisation type and purpose:
University department or institute.

Printed publications:
Prospectuses (undergraduate and postgraduate)
Course leaflets
Visitors' Guide
Sports Club Guide
Happening at Hallam
Annual Report

Electronic and video publications:
Undergraduate Prospectus (CD-ROM)
Student Life at the University (video)

Publications list:
Available online and in print

Access to staff:
Contact by letter
Hours: Mon to Fri, 0900 to 1700

Access for disabled people:
Access to all public areas

SHEFFIELD HALLAM UNIVERSITY LEARNING AND IT SERVICES

Acronym or abbreviation: SHU

Howard Street, Sheffield, South Yorkshire, S1 1WB

Tel: 0114 225 3333
Fax: 0114 225 3859
E-mail: learning.centre@shu.ac.uk

Website:
http://www.shu.ac.uk/services/lits/index.html

Organisation type and purpose:
University library

Subject coverage:
Adsetts Centre, City Campus: computing, sciences, engineering, built environment, business, management, tourism, hospitality, food, social sciences, history, English, languages, TESOL (Teaching English to Speakers of Other Languages), education, performing arts, communication studies, art, design, fashion, photography, film and media studies, metalwork and jewellery.
Collegiate Learning Centre: health, nursing, midwifery, occupational and physical therapies, paramedicine, radiotherapy and oncology, radiography, operating department practice, sports studies, psychology, social work, social sciences, law and criminology.

continued overleaf

Museum or gallery collection, archive, or library special collection:
Adsetts Centre:
Corvey collection (18th- and 19th-century books in English)
18th- and 19th-century books on art and design
Archives of Sheffield School of Art 1843–1969
David Morgan Rees collection (photographs of Yorkshire crafts)
Festival of Britain collection
George Fullard drawings
Photographs of the Miners' strike 1984–85
Public art research archive
Collegiate Learning Centre:
European Documentation Centre

Library catalogue:
All or part available online

Access to staff:
Contact by letter, by telephone, by fax, by e-mail, in person and via website. Appointment necessary.

Access to building, collection or gallery:
Hours: Term time: Mon to Thu, 0845 to 2100; Fri, 0845 to 2100; Sat, 1000 to 1700; Sun, 1000 to 1700
Special comments: 24-hour opening for Sheffield Hallam University students operates during term time.

Access for disabled people:
Ramped entry, access to all public areas, toilet facilities

Also at:
Collegiate Learning Centre
Sheffield, S10 2BP; tel: 0114 225 3333; fax: 0114 225 2476

SHEFFIELD LIBRARIES, ARCHIVES AND INFORMATION SERVICES – ARTS AND SOCIAL SCIENCES AND SPORTS SECTION

Central Library, Surrey Street, Sheffield, South Yorkshire, S1 1XZ

Tel: 0114 273 4747
Fax: 0114 273 5009
E-mail: artsandsport.library@sheffield.gov.uk

Website:
http://www.sheffield.gov.uk/in-your-area/libraries

Enquiries:
Enquiries to: Librarian

Organisation type and purpose:
Local government body, public library.

Subject coverage:
Social sciences including sociology, politics, education and careers, parliamentary and local government information, social welfare, charities and voluntary sector; the arts, leisure including travel and maps, sport and mountaineering, history, language and literature, census, statistics, government publications, abstracts and indexes.

Museum or gallery collection, archive, or library special collection:
Physical Education Association's sport collection
Climbing and Mountaineering
Funder Finder: charitable trusts database
International Genealogy Index Great Britain and Ireland
Sheffield Philatelic Society Library (on deposit)

Non-library collection catalogue:
All or part available online and in-house

Library catalogue:
All or part available online and in-house

Microform publications:
British Trades Union Histories (Harvester Press)
Tom Harrison Mass Observation Archive

Access to staff:
Contact by letter, by telephone, by fax, by e-mail and in person
Hours: Mon, 1000 to 2000; Tue, Thu, Fri, 0930 to 1730; Wed, 0930 to 2000; Sat, 0930 to 1730

Parent body:
Sheffield City Council

SHEFFIELD LIBRARIES, ARCHIVES AND INFORMATION SERVICES – BUSINESS SCIENCE AND TECHNOLOGY LIBRARY

Central Library, Surrey Street, Sheffield, South Yorkshire, S1 1XZ

Tel: 0114 273 4736/7 or 4743
Fax: 0114 273 5009
E-mail: businessandtech.library@sheffield.gov.uk

Website:
http://www.sheffield.gov.uk/libraries
http://www.hip.sheffield.gov.uk
Online catalogue.

Enquiries:
Enquiries to: Information Services Officer

Founded:
1934

Organisation type and purpose:
Local government body, public library.

Subject coverage:
Business and commercial information on companies, products, suppliers, importers, exporters, trade names. Company information (general and financial information on local, UK and foreign companies); UK telephone directories. All aspects of science and technology, pure and applied, industry related matters, innovation, trade and technical journals and reports. Official publications, official and non-official national, European and international statistics. Historic and current collection of patents. Current and historic collection of British and world-wide standards and specifications. Metallic materials identification service provided via the World Metal Index (WMI), part of a collection of standards and specifications; trade literature and technical journals on both ferrous and non-ferrous metal. Over 200,000 individual grades are included, both current and historical. MI-21 (Metals Information for the 21st century), a collaboration between the WMI and the Welding Institute (TWI), providing an information resource on metallic materials and welding consumables.

Information services:
24-hour access to search the currently available 20,000 MI-21 World Metal Index datasheets online, by subscription at http://www.mi-21.com.

Museum or gallery collection, archive, or library special collection:
British directories
FAME company database
Company annual reports
Kompass Worldwide (online)
British Standards (online and paper collection of withdrawn and superseded British Standards)
Foreign and international standards
Company financial data, patents, standards, trademarks (online)
Local company and local economic data
Motor vehicle workshop manuals
Market research databases (online)
Radio and TV servicing data
UK patents 1617 to present
Intellectual property information

Library catalogue:
All or part available in-house

Access to staff:
Contact by letter, by telephone, by fax, by e-mail and in person

Access to building, collection or gallery:
Hours: Mon, 1000 to 2000; Tue, Thu, Fri, 0930 to 1730; Wed, 0930 to 2000; Sat, 0930 to 1730
Special comments: Charges may apply for certain services, e.g. photocopying and printing

Includes the:
World Metal Index

Member organisation of:
BSI
European Public Information Centre
PatLib UK

Parent body:
Sheffield City Council

SHEFFIELD LIBRARIES, ARCHIVES AND INFORMATION SERVICES – CENTRAL MUSIC AND VIDEO LIBRARY

Central Library, Surrey Street, Sheffield, South Yorkshire, S1 1XZ

Tel: 0114 273 47323
Fax: 0114 273 5009
E-mail: musicandav@sheffield.gov.uk

Website:
http://www.sheffield.gov.uk/musicandvideo

Enquiries:
Enquiries to: Librarian
Other contacts: Library and Information Assistant

Organisation type and purpose:
Local government body, public library.

Subject coverage:
Music (books, scores, sets of orchestral parts and vocal scores, sound recordings), music reference services; DVD lending collection.

Museum or gallery collection, archive, or library special collection:
Bayreuth Collection (Wagner)
Whitworth Collection (organs and organ building)
Both collections now incorporated into the total stock

Non-library collection catalogue:
All or part available online

Library catalogue:
All or part available online and in-house

Printed publications:
Catalogue of Orchestral Sets
Catalogue of Vocal Sets

Access to staff:
Contact by letter, by telephone, by fax, by e-mail and in person
Hours: Mon, 1000 to 2000; Tue, Thu, Fri, Sat, 0930 to 1730; Wed, 0930 to 2000

Access to building, collection or gallery:
Hours: Mon, 1000 to 2000; Tue, Thu, Fri, Sat, 0930 to 1730; Wed, 0930 to 2000

Links with:
Yorkshire and Humberside Joint Library Services

SHEFFIELD LIBRARIES, ARCHIVES AND INFORMATION SERVICES – LOCAL STUDIES LIBRARY

Central Library, Surrey Street, Sheffield, South Yorkshire, S1 1XZ

Tel: 0114 273 4753
Fax: 0114 273 5009
E-mail: local.studies@dial.pipex.com

Website:
http://www.picturesheffield.com
Historical image library of Sheffield photographs.
http://www.local.studies/dial.pipex.com
Sample of Sheffield Time Machine only.

Enquiries:
Enquiries to: Senior Local Studies Librarian

Organisation type and purpose:
Public library.

Subject coverage:
History, geography etc of Sheffield Metropolitan District and surrounding area, articles of local interest in newspapers and periodicals, 19th century ED returns, 1971/81/91 Small Area Statistics (local census data), trade directories, newspapers, electoral registers.

Museum or gallery collection, archive, or library special collection:
Census records 1841, 51, 61, 71, 81 for Sheffield and parts of South Yorkshire and North Derbyshire on microfilm; 1891 and 1901 on microfiche (name indexes for Sheffield 1841–81)
Ephemera such as playbills, notices, leaflets
Film and video of scenes of life in Sheffield (some access restrictions for preservation reasons)
Map collection (historic and modern)
Newspapers (files of local papers on microfilm)
Oral history recordings
Photographic collection of 60,000 local images
Sheffield street and trade directories from 1774 to 1974

Library catalogue:
All or part available in-house

Printed publications:
Sheffield History Reporter (6 times a year, free, £2 UK subscription to cover p&p)

Electronic and video publications:
Sheffield Time Machine: A Virtual Tour of Historic Sheffield (CD-ROM, £20)

Publications list:
Available in print

Access to staff:
Contact by letter, by telephone, by fax, by e-mail and in person
Hours: Mon, 1000 to 2000; Tue to Sat, 0930 to 1730

SHEFFIELD, PEAK DISTRICT & SOUTH YORKSHIRE CPRE

The Stables, 22A Endcliffe Crescent, Sheffield, South Yorkshire, S10 3EF

Tel: 0114 2665822
Fax: 0114 2685514
E-mail: mail@cprepeakandsyorks.org.uk

Website:
http://www.cprepeakandsyorks.org.uk
Details of current campaigns, information about countryside development in the Peak District and South Yorkshire area.

Enquiries:
Enquiries to: Director
Other contacts: Administrative Secretary for general.

Founded:
1924

Organisation type and purpose:
National organisation, membership association (membership is by subscription), present number of members: 1000, registered charity (charity number 227429).
Countryside protection society.

Subject coverage:
Countryside protection, countryside planning, sustainable development, green belts, transport, forestry, National parks, architecture, quarrying.

Publications list:
Available online

Access to staff:
Contact by letter, by telephone, by fax, by e-mail and via website. Appointment necessary.
Hours: Mon to Fri, 0900 to 1700

Access to building, collection or gallery:
No prior appointment required
Hours: Mon to Fri, 0900 to 1700

Access for disabled people:
Ramped entry

National Office:
CPRE
Warwick House, 25 Buckingham Palace Road, London, SW1W 0PP; tel: 020 7976 6433; fax: 020 7976 6373

SHELL GLOBAL SOLUTIONS (UK), INFORMATION CENTRE

Cheshire Innovation Park, Poole Lane, Ince, Chester, Cheshire, CH1 3SH

Tel: 0151 373 5900
Fax: 0151 373 5230
E-mail: cip.library@shell.com

Website:
http://www.shellglobalsolutions.com

Enquiries:
Enquiries to: Information Specialist
Direct tel: 0151 373 5476
Direct e-mail: eddie.carter@shell.com
Other contacts: Librarian; Archivist for reference and archive enquiries.

Founded:
1940

Organisation type and purpose:
Shell Global Solutions is part of the Royal Dutch / Shell Group and provides business and operational consultancy to the energy industry and petrochemicals industry worldwide; these services are available both to Shell and non-Shell companies. The Information Centre provides a full range of library, information and archive services to Shell Global Solutions Staff.

Subject coverage:
Applicational research and development of fuels, lubricants and other petroleum products; combustion; lubrication; environment; analysis and measurement.

Non-library collection catalogue:
All or part available in-house

Library catalogue:
All or part available in-house

Printed publications:
Small journals and book collections

Access to staff:
Contact by letter, by telephone, by e-mail and in person
Hours: Mon to Fri, 0900 to 1700

Access to building, collection or gallery:
Staff only except by prior appointment
Hours: Mon to Fri, 0900 to 1600
Special comments: Access to Library and Information Services, normally restricted to Shell Global Solutions Staff; is available to 3rd parties by agreement.

Access for disabled people:
Hours: Mon to Fri, 0900 to 1700

SHELL SERVICES INTERNATIONAL

Business Information Centre, Shell Centre, London, SE1 7NA

Tel: 020 7934 1234
Fax: 020 7934 7679

Enquiries:
Enquiries to: Archivist
Direct tel: 020 7934 2328
Other contacts: Head of Business Information Centre

Organisation type and purpose:
Industrial company.

Subject coverage:
Business aspects of the energy and petrochemical industries worldwide.

Trade and statistical information:
Extensive statistical collection.

SHELL UK LTD

1 Altens Farm Road, Nigg, Aberdeen, AB12 3FY

Tel: 01224 882000
E-mail: tullosic-enquiries@shell.com

Enquiries:
Enquiries to: Information Adviser
Direct tel: 01224 882032

Organisation type and purpose:
International organisation.
Oil and gas company.

Subject coverage:
Oil, gas, exploration, production and operation procedures, offshore safety, offshore engineering.

Access to staff:
Contact by telephone and by e-mail
Hours: Mon to Fri, 0830 to 1630

Access to building, collection or gallery:
Not open to the public.

SHELLFISH ASSOCIATION OF GREAT BRITAIN

Acronym or abbreviation: SAGB

Fishmongers' Hall, London Bridge, London, EC4R 9EL

Tel: 020 7283 8305
Fax: 020 7929 1389
E-mail: SAGB@shellfish.org.uk

Website:
http://www.shellfish.org.uk

Enquiries:
Enquiries to: Secretary
Other contacts: Director

Founded:
1903

Organisation type and purpose:
Trade association.
Represents the UK Shellfish industry.

Subject coverage:
Shellfish stocks, biology, markets, storage, handling and quality.

Printed publications:
Papers of the Annual Conference

Access to staff:
Contact by letter, by telephone, by fax, by e-mail and via website. Non-members charged.
Hours: Mon to Fri, 0900 to 1700

Links with:
Association of Scottish Shellfish Growers

SHERLOCK HOLMES SOCIETY OF LONDON

15 Copperfield Court, 146 Worple Road, Wimbledon, London, SW20 8QA

Tel: 020 8879 0332
E-mail: c.cooke@dsl.pipex.com

Website:
http://www.sherlock-holmes.org.uk

Enquiries:
Enquiries to: Secretary

Founded:
1951

Organisation type and purpose:
Membership association.

Subject coverage:
Study of the life, work and times of Sherlock Holmes and Dr Watson, with more than a passing interest in the same of Sir Arthur Conan Doyle.

Printed publications:
Occasional other publications on the Society's expeditions
Sherlock Holmes Journal (twice a year, for members only)

Access to staff:
Contact by letter, by telephone and by e-mail
Hours: Mon to Fri, 0900 to 1700

SHETLAND ARCHIVES

Formal name: Shetland Museum and Archives

Hay's Dock, Lerwick, Shetland, ZE1 0WP

Tel: 01595 695057 and 01595 741554
Fax: 01595 696729
E-mail: info@shetlandmuseumandarchives.org.uk

Enquiries:
Enquiries to: Archivist

Founded:
1976

Organisation type and purpose:
Trust administering Museum and Archives for local authority Archives office.

Subject coverage:
Shetland.

Museum or gallery collection, archive, or library special collection:
Archival and some printed historical matter all concerning Shetland; microfilm copies of demographic records concerning Shetland, and of virtually all newspapers with Shetland news, 1830s onwards

Non-library collection catalogue:
All or part available in-house

Printed publications:
Shetland Documents 1195–1579 (Lerwick, 1999)
Shetland Documents 1580–1611 (Lerwick, 1994)
Order printed publications from: Shetland Museum and Archives

Access to staff:
Contact by letter, by telephone, by fax, by e-mail and in person
Hours: Mon to Fri, 1000 to 1630; Sat, 1000 to 1300

Access for disabled people:
Parking provided, ramped entry, access to all public areas, toilet facilities

Administered by:
Shetland Amenity Trust
Garthspool, Lerwick, Shetland; tel: 01595 694688

SHETLAND FAMILY HISTORY SOCIETY

Acronym or abbreviation: SFHS

6 Hillhead, Lerwick, Shetland, ZE1 0EJ

E-mail: secretary@shetland-fhs.org.uk

Website:
http://www.shetland-fhs.org.uk
Society information and contacts.

Enquiries:
Enquiries to: General Secretary
Other contacts: Membership Secretary for joining information and application

Founded:
1991

Organisation type and purpose:
Membership association (membership is by subscription), present number of members: 850, registered charity (charity number SCO 20018). A focus to share, collate and disseminate genealogical data of Shetland Island families.

Subject coverage:
Genealogy of Shetland families, emigration worldwide, family trees, monumental inscriptions, research sources available locally.

Non-library collection catalogue:
All or part available in-house

Library catalogue:
All or part available in-house

Printed publications:
Shetland Surnames, Beattie A M (£5 plus p&p)
Coontin Kin (journal, quarterly £2 plus p&p)
Members Interests Directory, fifth edn, (£2 plus p&p)
Monumental Inscription Booklets (£3 each, £4 inc. p&p)

Shetland Pre-1855 Parish Sources for Family Historians (Beattie A M, £3.50 plus p&p)

Electronic and video publications:
Shetland Censuses 1745/1841, 1851/61, 1871/81, 1891/1901 (CD-ROM, members: £9 plus p&p, non-members: £12 plus p&p)

Access to staff:
Contact by letter, by e-mail, in person and via website. Appointment necessary.
Hours: Mon to Sat, 1400 to 1600; Mon and Thu, 1900 to 2100

Access for disabled people:
Level entry

Links with:
Scottish Association of Family History Societies

SHETLAND ISLANDS COUNCIL

Acronym or abbreviation: SIC

Town Hall, Hillhead, Lerwick, Shetland, ZE1 0HB

Tel: 01595 693535
Fax: 01595 744509
E-mail: sic@sic.shetland.gov.uk

Website:
http://www.shetland.gov.uk

Enquiries:
Enquiries to: Chief Executive

Founded:
1974

Organisation type and purpose:
Local government body.

Subject coverage:
Local government services.

Access to staff:
Contact by letter, by telephone, by fax, by e-mail and in person
Hours: Mon to Thur, 0900 to 1700; Fri, 0900 to 1600

SHETLAND LIBRARY

Lower Hillhead, Lerwick, Shetland, ZE1 0EL

Tel: 01595 743868
Fax: 01595 694430
E-mail: shetlandlibrary@sic.shetland.gov.uk

Website:
http://www.shetland-library.gov.uk
Library catalogue, current events and features.

Founded:
1950

Organisation type and purpose:
Local government body, public library.

Subject coverage:
All aspects of Shetland, including its geography, agriculture and local history.

Museum or gallery collection, archive, or library special collection:
Local newspapers (on microfilm)

Non-library collection catalogue:
All or part available online

Library catalogue:
All or part available online

Printed publications:
Court Book of Shetland 1615–1629 (Donaldson G, £8.50)
Da Vaam O, Da Skynbow – Stories of Shetland Music (Morton, T, £5.99)
MacDiarmid in Shetland (Graham L and Smith B, £7.95)
Voes & Sounds (De Luca C, £6.50)
Wast wi da Valkyries (De Luca C, £8.99)
The Placenames of Shetland (Jacobsen J, out-of-print)

Access to staff:
Contact by letter, by telephone, by fax, by e-mail and via website. Appointment necessary.

Hours: Mon, Thu, 0930 to 2000; Tue, Wed, Fri, Sat, 0930 to 1700

Access for disabled people:
Ramped entry, access to all public areas, toilet facilities

SHETLAND PONY STUD-BOOK SOCIETY

Acronym or abbreviation: SPSBS

22 York Place, Perth, Tayside, PH2 8EH

Tel: 01738 623471
Fax: 01738 442274
E-mail: elaineward@shetlandponystudbooksociety.co.uk

Website:
http://www.shetlandponystudbooksociety.co.uk

Enquiries:
Enquiries to: Breed Secretary

Founded:
1891

Organisation type and purpose:
Membership association (membership is by subscription), present number of members: 2000, registered charity (charity number 38044). Breed society. Maintains records and gives advice on registered Shetland Ponies.

Subject coverage:
All subjects concerning Shetland ponies including registrations, pedigrees, performance, exports, welfare, society sales, showing, publications.

Museum or gallery collection, archive, or library special collection:
The Shetland Pony Stud-Book (101 volumes)

Printed publications:
Magazine (annually)
Studbook (annually)

Publications list:
Available online and in print

Access to staff:
Contact by letter, by telephone, by fax and by e-mail. Appointment necessary.
Hours: Mon to Fri, 0900 to 1700
Special comments: Telephone answered 1100 to 1500 daily.

SHINGLES SUPPORT SOCIETY

Acronym or abbreviation: SSS

41 North Road, London, N7 9DP

Tel: 020 7607 9661
E-mail: info@herpes.org.uk

Website:
http://www.herpes.org.uk/shingles.htm

Enquiries:
Enquiries to: Director

Founded:
1985

Organisation type and purpose:
patient support group

Subject coverage:
information on drug treatments a GP can prescribe and self-help therapies

Printed publications:
Information pack

Publications list:
Available online and in print

Access to staff:
Contact by letter, by telephone and by e-mail. Appointment necessary.
Hours: Mon to Fri, 1000 to 1800

Access to building, collection or gallery:
Prior appointment required

Access for disabled people:
Level entry

Parent body:
Herpes Viruses Association (HVA)
same address

SHIPPING GUIDES LIMITED

75 Bell Street, Reigate, Surrey, RH2 7AN

Tel: 01737 242255
Fax: 01737 222449
E-mail: sgl@shipping-guides.co.uk

Website:
http://www.portinfo.co.uk

Enquiries:
Enquiries to: Managing Director
Other contacts: Director Information Services

Founded:
1970

Organisation type and purpose:
Advisory body, publishing house.
Nautical Advisers.

Subject coverage:
Marine publishers, port information, marine
manuals, nautical information, nautical advisers,
atlases, maps, books and CDs.

Printed publications:
Guide to Port Entry (2001/2002, £255 UK, £275
overseas)
Guide to Tanker Ports (updated every 8 weeks)
The Shipping World's Map (£20 UK, £25 overseas)
The Ships Atlas (9th ed., 2002, £70 UK, £75
overseas)

Electronic and video publications:
The Guide on CD

Publications list:
Available in print

Access to staff:
Contact by letter, by telephone, by fax, by e-mail
and in person
Hours: Mon to Fri, 0900 to 1700

SHOOTERS' RIGHTS ASSOCIATION

Acronym or abbreviation: SRA

PO Box 3, Cardigan, Ceredigion, SA43 1BN

Tel: 01239 698607
Fax: 01239 698614
E-mail: richard.law@btinternet.com

Enquiries:
Enquiries to: Secretary

Founded:
1984

Organisation type and purpose:
International organisation, membership
association (membership is by subscription),
present number of members: 4500, voluntary
organisation, training organisation.
For persons who hold firearm or shotgun
certificates, are registered dealers, or who are
interested in taking up shooting as a pastime.

Subject coverage:
Firearms licensing; legal problems arising from the
possession and use of firearms.

Museum or gallery collection, archive, or library special collection:
Reports about firearms legislation in the UK,
including the unpublished Blackwell & McKay
Reports

Printed publications:
Newsletter (free to members, for sale to others)
Special Reports (irregular)

Access to staff:
Contact by letter, by telephone, by fax and by e-mail. Appointment necessary.

Hours: Mon to Fri, 0900 to 1700

Access to building, collection or gallery:
Prior appointment required

SHOP AND DISPLAY EQUIPMENT ASSOCIATION

Acronym or abbreviation: sdea

24 Croydon Road, Caterham, Surrey, CR3 6YR

Tel: 01883 348911
Fax: 01883 343435
E-mail: enquiries@sdea.co.uk

Website:
http://www.shopdisplay.org

Enquiries:
Enquiries to: Administration Manager

Founded:
1947

Organisation type and purpose:
Trade association.

Subject coverage:
Sourcing manufacturers and suppliers of
shopfittings and retail display equipment.

Information services:
Information regarding suppliers of shopfittings
and retail display equipment

Printed publications:
sdea Directory of Shopfittings and Display
(annually, £10)

Access to staff:
Contact by letter, by telephone, by fax, by e-mail
and via website
Hours: Mon to Fri, 0900 to 1700

Access to building, collection or gallery:
No access other than to staff

SHORTHORN CATTLE SOCIETY

National Agricultural Centre, Stoneleigh Park,
Kenilworth, Warwickshire, CV8 2LG

Tel: 024 7669 6549
Fax: 024 7669 6729
E-mail: shorthorn@shorthorn.freeserve.co.uk

Website:
http://www.shorthorn.co.uk

Enquiries:
Enquiries to: General Secretary
Other contacts: Secretary

Founded:
1822

Organisation type and purpose:
Membership association (membership is by
subscription), present number of members: 1100,
registered charity (charity number 213216).
To keep up a herd book and breed standard, to
provide and promote information and advice,
genetics and general support for members and
supporters of the breed.

Subject coverage:
Shorthorn cattle including membership,
registration, classification, semen, breed publicity
and general information.

Museum or gallery collection, archive, or library special collection:
Coates' Herd Books
Year Book and Journals
Photographs

Trade and statistical information:
Wordwide Trade for livestock, semen and
embryos.

Printed publications:
Dairy Shorthorns (video available for clubs and
associations)
Information leaflets and brochures
Genetic Sales list
Journal (2 times a year)

Electronic and video publications:
Northern Beef Shorthorns (video, to purchase)

Access to staff:
Contact by letter, by telephone, by fax, by e-mail
and in person
Hours: Mon to Fri, 0900 to 1600

Access for disabled people:
Parking provided

SHREWSBURY COLLEGE OF ARTS & TECHNOLOGY

Learning Resource Centre, London Road,
Shrewsbury, Shropshire, SY2 6PR

Tel: 01743 342342
Fax: 01743 342343
E-mail: carolinet@shrewsbury.ac.uk

Website:
http://www.shrewsbury.ac.uk

Enquiries:
Enquiries to: Team Leader – Learning Resources
Direct tel: 01743 342354
Direct e-mail: lrlrc@shrewsbury.ac.uk

Organisation type and purpose:
Suitable for ages: 16+.
College of further education with some HE
provision.

Subject coverage:
All areas of further education including
accounting, administration, art and design, beauty
and holistic therapies, business, care, childcare,
computing and IT, construction, engineering,
fashion, hairdressing, hospitality and catering, law,
media, motor vehicle, music and performing arts,
public services, sports and recreation, travel and
tourism.

Museum or gallery collection, archive, or library special collection:
Technical indexes

Non-library collection catalogue:
All or part available in-house

Library catalogue:
All or part available in-house

Access to staff:
Contact by letter, by telephone, by fax, by e-mail,
in person and via website. Appointment necessary.
Non-members charged.
Hours: Mon to Fri, 0900 to 1700

Access for disabled people:
Parking provided, ramped entry, access to all
public areas, toilet facilities

Constituent bodies:
Radbrook College Campus
Radbrook Road, Shrewsbury, Shropshire SY3
9BL; tel: 01743 342642; e-mail: rblrc@shrewsbury
.ac.uk

SHREWSBURY SCHOOL LIBRARY

The Schools, Shrewsbury, Shropshire, SY3 7BA

Tel: 01743 280595
Fax: 01743 243107
E-mail: archivist@shrewsbury.org.uk

Website:
http://www.shrewsbury.org.uk
See archives. Brief history of library, images of
manuscripts, books and bindings.

Enquiries:
Enquiries to: Taylor Librarian and Archivist

Founded:
1606

Organisation type and purpose:
Independent school library.

Subject coverage:
General, for a school library.

continued overleaf

Museum or gallery collection, archive, or library special collection:
Collection of bookbindings, 12th to 20th centuries, and private press books
Collection on early science, natural history and medicine, documented from 1607
Grammar School Library dating from 1606, 7500 vols including medieval manuscripts, incunabula, and books of the 16th and 17th centuries
Letters of Charles Darwin
Manuscripts and watercolours relating to Samuel (Erewhon) Butler
Moser collection of 19th century watercolours
Photographic archive c. 1860 to the present
School and Governing Body Archives, 1552 to the present

Library catalogue:
All or part available in-house

Access to staff:
Contact by letter, by fax and by e-mail. Appointment necessary. Letter of introduction required.
Hours: Mon to Fri, 0900 to 1700

SHRIEVALTY ASSOCIATION TRADING AS 'THE HIGH SHERIFFS' ASSOCIATION OF ENGLAND & WALES

Formal name: The High Sheriffs' Association of England and Wales

PO Box 198, Letchworth Garden City, SG6 3ZQ

Tel: 01462 629914
Fax: 01462 618247
E-mail: secretary@highsheriffs.com

Enquiries:
Enquiries to: Honorary Secretary

Founded:
1971

Organisation type and purpose:
Membership association (membership is by election or invitation).
To promote and strengthen the Office of High Sheriff in England and Wales.

Subject coverage:
History and current activities of High Sheriffs in the Counties of England and Wales, relating to ceremonial matters. The prevention of crime and particularly juvenile crime through 'National Crimebeat', and debt and money management through 'DebtCredt', both of which are Charities established by the Association.

Printed publications:
The High Sheriff (magazine, 2 times a year)

Access to staff:
Contact by letter, by telephone, by fax and by e-mail. Appointment necessary.
Hours: Mon to Fri, 0900 to 1700

Other addresses:
Shrievalty Association
Heritage House, PO Box 21, Baldock, Hertfordshire, SG7 5SH; tel: 01462 896688; fax: 01462 896677

SHROPSHIRE ARCHAEOLOGICAL AND HISTORICAL SOCIETY

Acronym or abbreviation: SAHS

Lower Wallop Farm, Westbury, Shrewsbury, Shropshire, SY5 9RT

Tel: 01743 891215
Fax: 01743 891805
E-mail: walloparch@farming.co.uk

Enquiries:
Enquiries to: Honorary Secretary

Founded:
1877

Organisation type and purpose:
Learned society (membership is by subscription), present number of members: 431 individual and 51 institutional members.

Subject coverage:
Local history and archaeology of Shropshire, parish registers.

Museum or gallery collection, archive, or library special collection:
J H Smith watercolours of Shropshire churches c. 1840

Library catalogue:
All or part available in-house

Printed publications:
Newsletter (2 times a year)
Monographs (irregular)
Parish Register Transcripts (over 80, from the present or former Diocese of St Asaph, Hereford and Lichfield, some indexes only)
Transactions (annually)
New Series (1931 onwards)
From Volume 60 onwards the volumes are not divided into parts
Volume 59 part 2 (£2), part 3 (£3)
Volumes 60 to 75 (various prices)
Shropshire Field Names (Foxall H D G, £2.50)
The Wealth of Shrewsbury in the Early 14th Century – 6 Local Subsidy Rolls 1297–1322: Text and Commentary (ed Cromarty D & R, £13)
The Cartulary of Lilleshall Abbey (ed Rees U, £25)
Shrewsbury Abbey (ed Baker N, £26.50)

Access to staff:
Contact by letter, by telephone, by fax, by e-mail and in person
Hours: Tue, 1000 to 2100; Wed, Fri, 1000 to 1700; Thu, 1000 to 1300; Sat, 1000 to 1600

Access to building, collection or gallery:
No prior appointment required

Access for disabled people:
Parking provided, level entry, access to all public areas, toilet facilities

Incorporating the:
Shropshire Parish Register Society

Member of:
Council for British Archaeology

The Society's Library is housed at the:
Shropshire Records and Research Centre
tel: 01743 255350; fax: 01743 255355; e-mail: research@shropshire-cc.gov.uk

SHROPSHIRE ARCHIVES

Castle Gates, Shrewsbury, Shropshire, SY1 2AQ

Tel: 01743 255350
Fax: 01743 255355
E-mail: archives@shropshire.gov.uk

Website:
http://www.shropshirearchives.org.uk

Enquiries:
Enquiries to: Head of Archives

Founded:
1885

Organisation type and purpose:
Local government body, public library. Record office.

Subject coverage:
Records and printed works relating to the County of Shropshire; local history, archaeology, genealogy, etc.

Museum or gallery collection, archive, or library special collection:
Archives of Anglican Parishes, Nonconformist Churches, Poor Law Unions, Schools, Quarter Sessions, etc.
Estate Records
J. H. Smith watercolours of Shropshire churches c.1840
Lily F. Chitty Collection (archaeology)
Local Authority Records

Photographic Archive (from 1842)
Prints, drawings and watercolours
Shrewsbury newspapers from 1772
Shropshire censuses 1841–91
Solicitors' Archives

Non-library collection catalogue:
All or part available in-house

Library catalogue:
All or part available in-house

Printed publications:
List of Methodist Registers
List of Other Nonconformist and Roman Catholic Registers
List of Original Parish Registers
Family History Guide: An A to Z guide to sources at Shropshire Archives

Microform publications:
Shropshire Directories 1822–1941

Publications list:
Available online

Access to staff:
Contact by letter, by telephone, by fax, by e-mail, in person and via website
Hours: Tue, 1000 to 2100; Wed, Fri, 1000 to 1700; Sat, 1000 to 1600; Thu, 1000 to 1300

Access for disabled people:
Parking provided

Houses the library of the:
Shropshire Archaeological and Historical Society

Parent body:
Shropshire County Council

SHROPSHIRE CHAMBER OF COMMERCE & ENTERPRISE LTD

Acronym or abbreviation: SCCE

Trevithick House, Stafford Park 4, Telford, Shropshire, TF3 3BA

Tel: 01952 208200
Fax: 01952 208208
E-mail: enquiries@shropshire-chamber.co.uk

Website:
http://www.shropshire-chamber.co.uk

Enquiries:
Enquiries to: Membership / Policy Executive

Organisation type and purpose:
Membership association, training organisation.
To offer complete business solutions, to members and non-members.

Subject coverage:
Business services, advice, information.

Library catalogue:
All or part available in-house

Printed publications:
Business Directory
Labour Market Report
Monthly Bulletin
Solutions (magazine)

Access to staff:
Contact by letter, by telephone, by fax, by e-mail, in person and via website. Appointment necessary.
Hours: Mon to Fri, 0900 to 1700
Special comments: Shropshire businesses and members only.

Access to building, collection or gallery:
No access other than to staff, prior appointment required

Access for disabled people:
Parking provided, ramped entry, toilet facilities

Links with:
British Chambers of Commerce
Confederation of West Midlands' Chambers of Commerce
Small Business Service

SHROPSHIRE COUNTY LIBRARIES

Reference Library, 1A Castle Gates, Shrewsbury, Shropshire, SY1 2AQ

Tel: 01743 255380
Fax: 01743 255383
E-mail: ris.enquiries@shropshire.gov.uk

Website:
http://www.shropshire.gov.uk/library.nsf

Enquiries:
Enquiries to: Librarian

Organisation type and purpose:
Local government body, public library.

Subject coverage:
Business information service, law, community information, project information for local schools and colleges, European information.

Library catalogue:
All or part available online

Printed publications:
General Leaflet
Online Reference Library leaflet

Publications list:
Available online

Access to staff:
Contact by letter, by telephone, by fax, by e-mail, in person and via website
Hours: Mon, Wed, Fri, 0930 to 1700; Tue and Thu, 0930 to 2000; Sat, 0900 to 1700; Sun, 1300 to 1600

Access for disabled people:
Parking provided, toilet facilities

Member organisation of:
European Information Relay

Parent body:
Shropshire County Council, Community Services

SHROPSHIRE COUNTY LIBRARY SERVICE

Shirehall, Abbey Foregate, Shrewsbury, Shropshire, SY2 6ND

Tel: 01743 255000
Fax: 01743 255050
E-mail: libraries@shropshire-cc.gov.uk

Website:
http://www.shropshire.gov.uk/library.nsf
http://www.literaryheritage.org.uk
http://www.shropshireroots.org.uk

Enquiries:
Enquiries to: Librarian

Organisation type and purpose:
Local government body, public library.

Subject coverage:
Music, recorded sound and drama collections, (Library, Castle Gates, Shrewsbury); local government and government publications (Reference Library, Castle Gates, Shrewsbury); European (EC) Information (Reference Library, Castle Gates, Shrewsbury); Shropshire local studies, extensive coverage of Shropshire and the Welsh Marches (Shropshire Archives, Castle Gates, Shrewsbury).

Museum or gallery collection, archive, or library special collection:
Shropshire Parochial Libraries (10,000 early printed and rare volumes) (Shropshire Archives)
West Midlands creative literature collection (Shrewsbury Library)

Library catalogue:
All or part available online

Printed publications:
Disaster Plans
Guide to School Services
Stock Policy

Publications list:
Available in print

Access to staff:
Contact by letter, by telephone, by fax and by e-mail. Appointment necessary.
Hours: Mon to Thu, 0900 to 1700; Fri, 0900 to 1600

Area libraries at:
Bridgnorth, Oswestry, Shrewsbury

Part of:
Shropshire County Council, Community Services Department

SHROPSHIRE FAMILY HISTORY SOCIETY

Acronym or abbreviation: SFHS

Redhillside, Ludlow Road, Church Stretton, Shropshire, SY6 6AD

E-mail: secretary@sfhs.org.uk

Website:
http://www.sfhs.org

Enquiries:
Enquiries to: Honorary Secretary
Other contacts: Membership Secretary for membership applications.

Founded:
1979

Organisation type and purpose:
Membership association (membership is by subscription), present number of members: 2,000, voluntary organisation, registered charity (charity number 514014).

Subject coverage:
Family history, research, transcription and indexing of historical records such as parish registers, census returns and monumental inscriptions in the county of Shropshire.

Education services:
Talks/courses on Family History Topics. Voluntary presence in Shropshire Archives to assist the public.

Museum or gallery collection, archive, or library special collection:
1881 Census transcript and index for England and Wales (microfiche)
British Section of the IGI (microfiche)
Early trade directories (microfiche)
Members' Interests (database)
Original Parish Registers Shropshire (microfiche)
Parish Registers of Shropshire (almost complete set of the printed vols)
Quarter Sessions (database)
Shrewsbury Wills from 1858 (database)
Shropshire Monumental Inscriptions (database)
Shropshire Strays (online)

Printed publications:
Census Indexes for 1821, 1831, 1841 (few), 1851 (nearly 200), 1861, 1871, 1881, 1891 (few)
Directory of Members' Interests
Journal (quarterly, members)
Transcripts of Monumental Inscriptions (about 250 sites, some available in microfiche)
Transcripts of registers (particularly nonconformist, for Church of England see Shropshire Archaeological and Historical Society)
Order printed publications from: Shropshire Family History Society, 68 Oakley Street, Belle Vue, Shrewsbury, Shropshire, SY3 7JZ

Electronic and video publications:
Shropshire Burials Index (CD-ROM, edn 4)
Shropshire Marriage Index (CD-ROM, edn 1)
Shropshire Quarter Sessions Index (CD-ROM)
Wrockwardine Poor Law Papers (CD-ROM)
Order electronic and video publications from: Shropshire Family History Society, 19 Upper Bar, Newport, Shropshire, TF10 7EH

Publications list:
Available online and in print

Access to staff:
Contact by letter, by e-mail and via website
Hours: Mon to Fri, 0900 to 1700

Special comments: Please enclose an sae for reply to letters.

Access to building, collection or gallery:
Library access for members only.

Also at:
Membership Secretary
Shropshire Family History Society, 18 Gorse Lane, Bayston Hill, Shrewsbury, SY3 0JL; e-mail: monica@emery18g.1com43.net

SIBTHORP LIBRARY

Bishop Grosseteste University College, Lincoln, LN1 3DY

Tel: 01522 583790
Fax: 01522 530243
E-mail: library-enquiries@bishopg.ac.uk

Website:
http://www.bishopg.ac.uk/library
General library information.

Enquiries:
Enquiries to: Director of Library and Knowledge Services
Direct tel: 01522 583744

Founded:
1862

Organisation type and purpose:
Membership association (membership is by qualification), present number of members: 1526. Library of the Church of England college of higher education, principally training teachers, with 3 humanities first degrees, and several foundation degrees.

Subject coverage:
Teaching studies; education: history, geography, English literature, drama, theology, music, art, children's literature, early education, heritage.

Museum or gallery collection, archive, or library special collection:
Tom Baker Collection – local historical interest
John Tomlinson Collection

Non-library collection catalogue:
All or part available online and in-house

Library catalogue:
All or part available online and in print

Access to staff:
Contact by letter, by telephone, by fax, by e-mail and in person
Hours: Term time: Mon to Thu, 0830 to 2030; Fri, 0830 to 1900; Sat, 1000 to 1600; Sun, 1330 to 1700

Access for disabled people:
Ramped entry

Constituent school of the:
University of Leicester

Member of:
UK Libraries Plus

SICKLE CELL AND THALASSAEMIA FOUNDATION

Acronym or abbreviation: SSCATF

A. C. E. Business Centre, 110–120 Wicker, Sheffield, South Yorkshire, S3 8JD

Tel: 0114 275 3209
Fax: 0114 279 6870
E-mail: sscatf1@btconnect.com

Website:
http://www.sscatf-8m.com

Enquiries:
Enquiries to: Chairman
Other contacts: Health Officer for health issues specific to the services offered.

Founded:
1997

continued overleaf

Subject coverage:
Information and advice about Sickle Cell and
Thalassaemia. Where to get treatment, to be
screened, symptoms of the disorder, applying for
financial or other support, respite care, genetic
counselling, etc.

Printed publications:
A wide range of leaflets about the services and
about the disorders – Sickle Cell and
Thalassaemia in Urdu, Somali, Bangladeshi,
Arabic, Mandarin Chinese and English
A wide range of text books and booklets

Access to staff:
Contact by letter, by telephone, by fax, by e-mail,
in person and via website. Appointment necessary.
Hours: Mon to Fri, 0900 to 1700

Access to building, collection or gallery:
No prior appointment required
Hours: Mon to Fri, 0700 to 1700; Sat, 0900 to 1700

Access for disabled people:
Parking provided, level entry, access to all public
areas, toilet facilities

SICKLE CELL SOCIETY

54 Station Road, London, NW10 4UA

Tel: 020 8961 7795
Fax: 020 8961 8346
E-mail: sicklecellsoc@btinternet.com

Website:
http://www.sicklecellsociety.org

Enquiries:
Enquiries to: Director
Direct e-mail: sickleinfo.line@btinternet.com
Other contacts: Finance Manager; Fundraising
Manager

Founded:
1979

Organisation type and purpose:
Voluntary organisation, registered charity (charity
number 1046631), suitable for ages: all.

Subject coverage:
Information on sickle cell disorders, financial
assistance, educational grants, holiday and
recreational opportunities.

Printed publications:
Not Another Lazy Child (1 copy free)
Nursing Children with Sickle Cell Disorders (1
copy free)
A guide for parents, guardians and families (1
copy free)
Sickle Cell do you Know? (£2)
Living with Sickle Pain (£2)

Publications list:
Available online and in print

Access to staff:
Contact by letter, by telephone, by fax, by e-mail,
in person and via website
Hours: Mon to Fri, 0900 to 1700

Access to building, collection or gallery:
No prior appointment required
Hours: Mon to Fri, 0900 to 1700

Other address:
Brent Sickle Link
25 High Street, Harlesden, NW10; tel: 020 8961
6090

SIGHT SAVERS INTERNATIONAL

Acronym or abbreviation: SSI

Grosvenor Hall, Bolnore Road, Haywards Heath,
West Sussex, RH16 4BX

Tel: 01444 446600
Fax: 01444 446688
E-mail: generalinformation@sightsavers.org

Website:
http://www.sightsavers.org

About sight savers, about blindness and the
blinding diseases, about where SSI works.

Enquiries:
Enquiries to: Internal Communications Manager
Direct tel: 01444 446661
Direct e-mail: kbirrell@sightsaversint.org

Founded:
1950

Organisation type and purpose:
International organisation, registered charity
(charity number 207544).
To prevent and cure blindness in the developing
world, to provide training for incurably blind
children and adults, and to train local staff.

Subject coverage:
Ophthalmology, community ophthalmology
education, prevention and cure of blindness in
developing countries, training of ophthalmic
personnel, training of personnel working with
visually handicapped people, education of blind
children and rehabilitation for blind adults.

**Museum or gallery collection, archive, or library
special collection:**
Small resource centre of books, articles, journals,
slides and photos primarily for internal use but
available for reference by the public by
appointment

Non-library collection catalogue:
All or part available in-house

Printed publications:
Annual accounts
Annual review
Sight Savers News (newsletter, for supporters, 3
times a year)
Try to See it my Way Pack (£8 plus p&p)

Electronic and video publications:
Videos (for loan or free)

Publications list:
Available in print

Access to staff:
Contact by letter, by telephone, by fax, by e-mail
and via website. Appointment necessary.
Hours: Mon to Fri, 0900 to 1700

Access to building, collection or gallery:
Prior appointment required
Hours: Mon to Fri, 0900 to 1630

Has consultative status with the:
United Nations

In collaboration with the:
World Health Organisation

Links with:
International Agency for the Prevention of
Blindness
International Council for the Education of the
Visually Handicapped
World Blind Union

SIGNET LIBRARY

Society of Writers to HM Signet, Parliament
Square, Edinburgh, EH1 1RF

Tel: 0131 225 4923
Fax: 0131 220 4016
E-mail: library@wssociety.co.uk

Website:
http://www.signetlibrary.co.uk
Details of history, contacts and developments.

Enquiries:
Enquiries to: Librarian

Founded:
1594

Organisation type and purpose:
Professional body (membership is by
qualification), present number of members: 1000.

Subject coverage:
Law, particularly Scots law; Scottish history and
genealogy.

**Museum or gallery collection, archive, or library
special collection:**
Court of Session Papers (2500 vols)
Roughead Collection of trials (500 vols)

Non-library collection catalogue:
All or part available online and in-house

Library catalogue:
All or part available in-house

Access to staff:
Contact by letter. Appointment necessary. Access
for members only. Non-members charged.
Hours: Mon to Fri, 0930 to 1630

Access for disabled people:
Level entry

SIKH EDUCATIONAL ADVISORY SERVICES

Guru Guru House, 42 Park Avenue, Leeds, West
Yorkshire, LS15 8EW

Tel: 0113 260 2484

Enquiries:
Enquiries to: Director General
Direct tel: 07973 286585

Founded:
1984

Organisation type and purpose:
Advisory body, professional body, suitable for
ages: all, training organisation, consultancy.
Spiritual counselling.

Subject coverage:
Religion, culture, Sikh education, stories, drama,
dance, music, language, exhibitions, training.

Electronic and video publications:
Stories from Sikh traditions. Price list available

Publications list:
Available in print

Access to staff:
Contact by letter and by telephone
Hours: Sun to Sat, 0700 to 2100

Access to building, collection or gallery:
Prior appointment required

Access for disabled people:
Parking provided, level entry, toilet facilities

SILK ASSOCIATION OF GREAT BRITAIN

Acronym or abbreviation: SAGB

5 Portland Place, London, W1B 1PW

Tel: 020 7636 7788
Fax: 020 7636 7515
E-mail: sagb@dial.pipex.com

Website:
http://www.silk.org.uk

Enquiries:
Enquiries to: Secretary

Organisation type and purpose:
Trade association.

Subject coverage:
All aspects of silk, silk trade and promotion.

**Museum or gallery collection, archive, or library
special collection:**
Samples and literature about silk for teachers,
graduates and school children

Trade and statistical information:
Silk in UK.

Printed publications:
Serica (newsletter, quarterly)

Electronic and video publications:
The History of Silk (video)

Access to staff:
Contact by letter, by fax and by e-mail
Hours: Mon to Fri, 0900 to 1700

Incorporated when the:
Silk and Man-made Fibre Users Association was liquidated

Member of:
British Apparel & Textile Confederation
International Silk Association

SILSOE RESEARCH INSTITUTE

Wrest Park, Silsoe, Bedfordshire, MK45 4HS

Tel: 01525 860000
Fax: 01525 860156
E-mail: library.sri@bbsrc.ac.uk

Website:
http://www.sri.bbsrc.ac.uk
Website for the Institute.

Enquiries:
Enquiries to: Head of Information Services

Founded:
1947

Organisation type and purpose:
Research organisation.
Research organisation of the Biotechnology and Biological Sciences Research Council.

Subject coverage:
Agricultural engineering; physical sciences; robotics; instrumentation; electronics; tractor and farm vehicle design; ergonomics; farm buildings; milking machinery; animal waste treatment; crop drying and storage; food engineering; greenhouses; appropriate technology; cultivation.

Printed publications:
SRI News (quarterly newsletter)
Biennial Report

Publications list:
Available online

Access to staff:
Appointment necessary.
Hours: Mon to Fri, 0900 to 1700

Parent body:
Biotechnology and Biological Sciences Research Council

SILVER SOCIETY

Box 246, 2 Lansdowne Row, London, W1J 6HL

E-mail: secretary@thesilversociety.org

Website:
http://www.thesilversociety.org

Enquiries:
Enquiries to: Secretary

Founded:
1958

Organisation type and purpose:
Learned society (membership is by election or invitation), present number of members: 400, registered charity (charity number 279352).
To encourage an interest in the craft of the gold and silversmith, past and present.

Subject coverage:
Silver; silversmiths; silver workers; gold; goldsmiths; goldworking; plate; plate working/ workers; plated wares (Sheffield plate and electroplate); design and designers; social history (as regards the use of gold, silver and plated wares); biographical information on the above.

Printed publications:
The Silver Society Journal (annually, £15)

Publications list:
Available online

Access to staff:
Contact by letter, by telephone and by fax

Editor:
Silver Society
e-mail: editor@thesilversociety.org

SIMPLIFIED SPELLING SOCIETY

Acronym or abbreviation: SSS

23 Albion Street, New Brighton, Wirral, Merseyside, CH45 9LE

Tel: 0151 327 5837
E-mail: bjhughes71@hotmail.com

Website:
http://www.spellingsociety.org
Aims, texts of leaflets including membership application form, digest of publications.

Enquiries:
Enquiries to: Secretary

Founded:
1908

Organisation type and purpose:
Learned society (membership is by subscription), voluntary organisation, research organisation.
Working for planned change in English spelling for the benefit of learners and users everywhere.

Subject coverage:
Modernisation and simplification of English spelling, English spelling systems, literacy, English language teaching, linguistics, psychology of writing systems, lexicography, typography.

Museum or gallery collection, archive, or library special collection:
Historical collection of Society material (Mont Follick Collection) in Library of Manchester University, Department of General Linguistics

Printed publications:
Bibliography of English language and spelling reform
Cut Spelling Handbook (1992, £10)
Journal (occasional)
New Spelling 90 (1991, £5)
Newsletter (quarterly)
Regularity and Irregularity in English Spelling (1997, £2)
Spelling Reform in Context (1991, £2)

Access to staff:
Contact by letter, by telephone, by e-mail and via website. Appointment necessary.
Hours: Any day, 0900 to 2200

Links with:
British Dyslexia Association
Initial Teaching Alphabet Federation
UK Reading Association

SINGAPORE HIGH COMMISSION

9 Wilton Crescent, London, SW1X 8SP

Tel: 020 7235 8315
Fax: 020 7245 6583
E-mail: schlondon@singcomm.demon.co.uk

Website:
http://www.singstat.gov.sg
Statistics on Singapore
http://www.sgnews.info
News on Singapore
http://www.gov.sg
Singapore Government website.

Enquiries:
Enquiries to: Information Officer
Other contacts: Second Secretary (Information)

Organisation type and purpose:
National government body.

Subject coverage:
Singapore in general.

Printed publications:
Singapore
Singapore Facts and Pictures

Electronic and video publications:
Visit website

Access to staff:
Contact by letter, by telephone and by e-mail
Hours: Mon to Fri, 0900 to 1700

Connections with:
Trade Development Board
53 Monument Street, London, EC3R 8BU; tel: 020 7626 1717; fax: 020 7626 1711

Links to:
Contact Singapore
5 Regent Street, Lower Ground Floor, London, SW1 4LR; tel: 020 7321 5600; website: www .contactsingapore.org.sg

SINGER OWNERS CLUB

Acronym or abbreviation: SOC

11 Ermine Rise, Great Casterton, Stamford, Lincolnshire, PE9 4AJ

Tel: 01780 762740
E-mail: martyn@singeroc.free-online.co.uk

Website:
http://www.singerownersclub.co.uk
Guide to the Singer Owners Club and Singer vehicles from 1880–1970.

Enquiries:
Enquiries to: Secretary

Founded:
1951

Organisation type and purpose:
Membership association (membership is by subscription), present number of members: 800.

Subject coverage:
Singer motor cars and motor cycles 1876–1970, history of George Singer and the Singer motor companies and Rootes group.

Museum or gallery collection, archive, or library special collection:
Photographs and documentation on all Singer models

Printed publications:
The Singer Owner (six times a year – free to members)

Access to staff:
Contact by letter, by telephone, by e-mail and via website
Hours: Mon to Fri, 1900 to 2200

SINO-HIMALAYAN PLANT ASSOCIATION

81 Parlaunt Road, Slough, Berkshire, SL3 8BE

Tel: 01753 542823
Fax: 01753 543823

Enquiries:
Enquiries to: Secretary

Founded:
1991

Organisation type and purpose:
Membership association (membership is by subscription).

Subject coverage:
Sino-Himalayan, i.e. Himalayan and Chinese, mountain plants.

Museum or gallery collection, archive, or library special collection:
P N Kohli Memorial Herbarium of Himalayan plant pressed specimens and Memorial Himalayan Garden

Printed publications:
Newsletter

Access to staff:
Contact by letter

SINTO – THE INFORMATION PARTNERSHIP FOR SOUTH YORKSHIRE AND NORTH DERBYSHIRE

c/o Learning Centre, Sheffield Hallam University, Collegiate Crescent, Sheffield, South Yorkshire, S10 2BP

Tel: 0114 225 5739/40
Fax: 0114 225 2476
E-mail: c.j.clayton@shu.ac.uk

Website:
http://www.sinto.org.uk

Enquiries:
Enquiries to: Director

Founded:
1933

Created by the merger of:
Board for Library and Information Services in Sheffield and SINTO (year of change 1991)

Formerly called:
Scheme for the Interchange of Technical Publications; Sheffield Interchange Organisation; Sheffield Information Organisation

Organisation type and purpose:
Membership association (membership is by subscription).
To promote and develop library and information services through co-operation, planning and partnership. SINTO is the Library and Information Plan (LIP) for South Yorkshire and North Derbyshire.

Subject coverage:
Access to resources of member libraries with emphasis on business, science and technology.

Printed publications:
Directory of SINTO Members
Learners' Guide to Libraries in South Yorkshire
Subject Guides to Libraries (details on request)

Electronic and video publications:
Fines and Charges in Public Libraries in England and Wales (CD-ROM, annually)

Access to staff:
Contact by letter, by telephone, by fax, by e-mail and via website. Appointment necessary.
Hours: Mon to Fri, 0900 to 1700

SIR ARTHUR SULLIVAN SOCIETY

Acronym or abbreviation: SASS

Unit 4, Mount Pleasant Ecological Park, Porthtowan, Truro, TR4 8HL.

Tel: 07969 559213
E-mail: shturnbull@aol.com

Enquiries:
Enquiries to: Secretary
Other contacts: Membership Secretary

Founded:
1977

Organisation type and purpose:
International organisation, learned society, membership association (membership is by subscription), present number of members: 450, voluntary organisation, registered charity (charity number 274022), suitable for ages: all, research organisation, publishing house.
Promotion of the music of Arthur Sullivan.

Subject coverage:
All aspects of the life, career and work of Sir Arthur Sullivan (1842–1900), performances and recordings of his music, musical criticism.

Museum or gallery collection, archive, or library special collection:
Library of performing material for music by Sullivan, including the only extant orchestral parts for a number of major orchestral works (notably Victoria and Merrie England; L'Ile Enchantée; Thespis; The Merry Wives of Windsor); full choral and orchestral material for

the Martyr of Antioch (Cantata); Kenilworth (Masque); On Shore and Sea (Cantata); also vocal, choral scores for operas Haddon Hall and The Chieftain

Printed publications:
78 rpm Record Discography (sale)
CD-Discography (free to members only, annually)
Illustrated Booklets (commemorating the centenaries of operas and other works by Sullivan, sale)
Magazine (free to members, sale to non-members, 2 times a year)
Newsletter (free, members only, 2 times a year)
Opera Libretti (sale)
Yearbook (free, members only, annual)
Order printed publications from: The Sales Officer, Sir Arthur Sullivan Society
Fuchsia Cottage, Main Road, Colwich, ST17 0XE.
e-mail: elaineatsass@aol.com

Electronic and video publications:
CD recordings (sale)

Publications list:
Available online and in print

Access to staff:
Contact by letter, by telephone, by e-mail and via website. Appointment necessary.
Hours: Preferred hours for telephone calls: Mon to Fri, 1000 to 2000; any time at weekends

Access to building, collection or gallery:
By appointment

Other addresses:
Membership Secretary
71 The Heights, Foxgrove Road, Beckenham, BR3 5BZ

SIR ERNEST CASSEL EDUCATIONAL TRUST

199 West Malvern Road, Malvern, Worcestershire, WR14 4BB

Tel: 01684 572437
E-mail: casseltrust@sherborn.demon.co.uk

Enquiries:
Enquiries to: Secretary
Direct e-mail: casseltrust@sherborn.demon.co.uk

Founded:
1919

Organisation type and purpose:
Registered charity.
Educational grant-awarding body.

Subject coverage:
Overseas research grants in the humanities (administered by the British Academy) for more junior teaching members of faculties; Mountbatten Memorial grants to Commonwealth students taking higher education courses in the UK who run into unforeseen financial difficulties in their final year; grants to organisations in the field of adult and higher education.

Access to staff:
Contact by letter, by telephone and by e-mail
Hours: Mon to Fri, 0900 to 1700

SIR NORMAN CHESTER CENTRE FOR FOOTBALL RESEARCH

Acronym or abbreviation: SNCCFR

Department of Sociology, University of Leicester, Leicester, LE1 7RH

Tel: 0116 252 2741
Fax: 0116 252 2746
E-mail: footballresearch@le.ac.uk

Enquiries:
Enquiries to: Administrator

Founded:
1987

Organisation type and purpose:
University department or institute, research organisation.

Subject coverage:
Football.

Publications list:
Available in print

Access to staff:
Contact by letter and by e-mail. Appointment necessary.
Hours: Mon to Fri, 0900 to 1700

Access to building, collection or gallery:
No prior appointment required
Hours: Mon to Fri, 0930 to 1700

SIRSIDYNIX

The Chequers, St Mary's Way, Chesham, Buckinghamshire, HP5 1LL

Tel: 01494 777666
Fax: 01494 777555
E-mail: sales@sirsidynix.co.uk

Website:
http://www.sirsidynix.co.uk
European contact details.

Enquiries:
Enquiries to: Sales Director
Direct e-mail: nick.dimant@sirsidynix.co.uk

Founded:
1990

Organisation type and purpose:
Consultancy.
European sales and support office for the Unicorn library automation system.

Subject coverage:
Software for libraries and information handlers.

Access to staff:
Contact via website
Hours: Mon to Fri, 0900 to 1730

SKI CLUB OF GREAT BRITAIN

The White House, 57–63 Church Road, Wimbledon, London, SW19 5SB

Tel: 020 8410 2000
Fax: 020 8410 2001
E-mail: skiers@skiclub.co.uk

Website:
http://www.skiclub.co.uk

Enquiries:
Enquiries to: Information Officer

Founded:
1903

Organisation type and purpose:
Membership association.
Promoting skiing and snowboarding.

Subject coverage:
Recreational skiing, ski mountaineering, ski touring, resorts and holidays, snow conditions, history of skiing, statistics.

Printed publications:
Range of skiing factsheets available
List of dry ski slopes
Ski and Board (club magazine, 5 issues during the skiing season, free to members, for sale to others)

Access to staff:
Contact by letter, by telephone, by fax, by e-mail, in person and via website. Appointment necessary.
Access for members only.
Hours: Mon to Fri, 0900 to 1730 (summer); 0900 to 1800 (winter)

Access to building, collection or gallery:
Prior appointment required
Hours: Mon to Fri, 0900 to 1730

Special comments: Other events held in the library.

Access for disabled people:
Ramped entry, level entry, access to all public areas, toilet facilities

SKILL: NATIONAL BUREAU FOR STUDENTS WITH DISABILITIES

Acronym or abbreviation: Skill

Chapter House, 18–20 Crucifix Lane, London, SE1 3JW

Tel: 020 7450 0620; 0800 328 5050 (information); 0800 068 2422 (textphone)
Fax: 020 7450 0650
E-mail: info@skill.org.uk

Website:
http://www.skill.org.uk

Enquiries:
Enquiries to: Information and Services Manager

Founded:
1974

Organisation type and purpose:
Advisory body, membership association (membership is by subscription), present number of members: 1,000, voluntary organisation, registered charity (charity number 801971, also registered in Scotland number SC039212), suitable for ages: 16+.
Aims to promote opportunities for people with any kind of impairment in 16+ education, training, transition to employment and volunteering.

Subject coverage:
Information and advice for people with disabilities or learning difficulties, their families, friends and people working with them, regarding post-16 education and training.

Printed publications:
Notes and Quotes: Skill's student newsletter
The Skill Journal: articles concerning current developments and projects
The Skill Newsletter: news and information for people working in post-16 education and training
A variety of information booklets and publications including:
Into Teaching
Guides for Disabled Students
Guides to National Policy
Into Higher Education 2009
Order printed publications from: http://www.skill.org.uk/shop/shop.asp

Electronic and video publications:
Information sheets and publications are available in audio and disk format, and online
Order electronic and video publications from: info@skill.org.uk

Publications list:
Available online and in print

Access to staff:
Contact by letter, by telephone, by fax, by e-mail and via website
Hours: Information Service helpline: Tue, 1130 to 1330; Thu, 1330 to 1530

Access to building, collection or gallery:
No access other than to staff

Access for disabled people:
Parking provided, ramped entry, level entry, access to all public areas, toilet facilities

Branches:
Skill Northern Ireland
Unit 2, Jennymount Court, North Derby Street, Belfast, BT15 3HN; tel: 028 9028 7000; fax: 028 9028 7002; e-mail: info@skillni.org.uk; website: http://www.skillni.org.uk
Skill Scotland
Norton Park, 57 Albion Road, Edinburgh, EH7 5QY; tel: 0131 475 2348; fax: 0131 475 2397; e-mail: admin@skillscotland.org.uk; website: http://www.skill.org.uk/scotland

Skill Wales
Skill Wales, Suite 14, 2nd Floor, The Executive Centre, Temple Court, Cathedral Road, Cardiff, CF11 9HA; tel: 029 2078 6506; e-mail: admin@skillwales.org.uk; website: http://www.skill.org.uk/wales

SKIN, HIDE AND LEATHER TRADERS ASSOCIATION

Acronym or abbreviation: SHALTA

Douglas House, Douglas Road, Melrose, Roxburghshire, TD6 9QT

Tel: 01896 822233
Fax: 01896 823344
E-mail: offices@andaco.com

Enquiries:
Enquiries to: Secretary General

Founded:
1916

Organisation type and purpose:
Trade association.

Subject coverage:
Trade in hides, skins and leather both nationally and internationally, contractual information, overseas trade missions.

Access to staff:
Contact by letter, by telephone and by fax
Hours: Mon to Fri, 0900 to 1700

Member of:
International Council of Hides, Skins and Leather Traders Associations
Union Européenne des Négociants en Cuir et Peaux Brutes

SKIPTON LIBRARY

High Street, Skipton, North Yorkshire, BD23 1JX

Tel: 01756 792926
Fax: 01756 798056
E-mail: skipton.library@northyorks.gov.uk

Enquiries:
Enquiries to: Librarian
Other contacts: Information Librarian for reference, local and family history.

Founded:
1909

Organisation type and purpose:
Public library.

Subject coverage:
General reference and information sources, including business information and local history material for the Craven area.

Museum or gallery collection, archive, or library special collection:
Petyt Collection of material on 17th century history and theology

Non-library collection catalogue:
All or part available in-house

Library catalogue:
All or part available in-house

Access to staff:
Contact by letter, by telephone, by fax, by e-mail and in person
Hours: Mon, Wed and Thu, 0930 to 1900; Fri, 0930 to 1700; Sat, 0930 to 1600; Tue, closed

Parent body:
North Yorkshire County Library
21 Grammar School Lane, Northallerton, North Yorkshire, DL6 1DF; tel: 01609 780780; fax: 01609 780793

SKYCOL PUBLICATIONS

12 Nithsdale Road, Liverpool, L15 5AX

Enquiries:
Enquiries to: Archivist

Founded:
1974

Organisation type and purpose:
Research organisation, publishing house.

Subject coverage:
Morris Marina and Ital (1971–84 cars); motorsport in the North-west (especially Aintree, history); aviation in the North-west (especially English Electric/Napier); the Standard-Triumph factories of Liverpool.

Museum or gallery collection, archive, or library special collection:
Triumph cars prototypes register (factory documents)
Triumph Liverpool No 1 Plant, factory layout plan
Race-by-race data of Motorsport at Aintree 1954 to present day (cars and motorcycles)
Race-by-race data of Motorsport at Oulton Park 1953 to 1966 (cars only)

Printed publications:
Order printed publications from: John G Lawson (for full publications list), Skycol Publications at the same address

Publications list:
Available in print

Access to staff:
Contact by letter. Appointment necessary. All charged.
Hours: Mon to Fri, 0900 to 1700

SLOUGH BOROUGH COUNCIL

Acronym or abbreviation: SBC

Town Hall, Bath Road, Slough, Berkshire, SL1 3UQ

Tel: 01753 552288\ Minicom no. 01753 875030
Fax: 01753 692499

Website:
http://www.slough.gov.uk
What the council offers, services.

Enquiries:
Enquiries to: Chief Executive

Organisation type and purpose:
Local government body.

Access to staff:
Contact by telephone
Hours: Mon to Fri, 0900 to 1645

Other addresses:
Wellington House

SLOUGH LIBRARIES

85 High Street, Slough, SL1 1EA

Tel: 01753 535166
Fax: 01753 825050
E-mail: library@slough.gov.uk

Website:
http://www.slough.gov.uk/libraries

Enquiries:
Enquiries to: Information Services Librarian
Direct tel: 01753 787511

Organisation type and purpose:
Local government body, public library.

Subject coverage:
Slough local studies collection; general information; business information; EU information; Slough Community Information Database, careers and education.

Library catalogue:
All or part available online and in-house

Access to staff:
Contact by letter, by telephone, by fax, by e-mail and in person
Hours: Mon, Thu, 0900 to 1700; Tue, Fri, 0900 to 1900; Wed, 0930 to 1900; Sat, 0900 to 1600

Access for disabled people:
Ramped entry

SMALL BUSINESS BUREAU LIMITED

Acronym or abbreviation: SBB

Curzon House, Church Road, Windlesham, Surrey, GU20 6BH

Tel: 01276 452010
Fax: 01276 451602
E-mail: info@sbb.org.uk

Website:
http://www.smallbusinessbureau.org.uk

Enquiries:
Enquiries to: Managing Director

Founded:
1976

Organisation type and purpose:
Membership association (membership is by subscription).
Lobbying organisation.

Subject coverage:
Small and medium size businesses.

Printed publications:
Small Business News (4 times a year)

Access to staff:
Contact by letter, by telephone, by fax and by e-mail
Hours: Mon to Fri, 0900 to 1700

SMALL ENTERPRISE RESEARCH TEAM

Acronym or abbreviation: SERTeam

Open University Business School, Open University, Walton Hall, Milton Keynes, Buckinghamshire, MK7 6AA

Tel: 01908 655831 / 020 8560 3004
Fax: 01908 655898 / 020 8560 3004
E-mail: oubs-sbrt@open.ac.uk

Website:
http://www.serteam.co.uk
Publications and links to other small business organisations.

Enquiries:
Enquiries to: Secretary

Founded:
1984

Organisation type and purpose:
Registered charity (charity number 1100928), university department or institute, research organisation.
Educational research charity.

Subject coverage:
Management issues, exporting, regional differences, business services, BS5750, small business policy, small business economy. Further education and colleges report, computers in rural small firms across Europe.

Non-library collection catalogue:
All or part available in print

Library catalogue:
All or part available in print

Printed publications:
Some 30 books, reports and research monographs including:
Behind the Veneer of Success: Propensities for UK Franchisor Failure
Enterprise in Britain (out of print)
Ethnic Minorities in Business (1998, £30)
Lloyds Bank/SBRT Quarterly Small Business Management Report (vol. 4, 1996 through to current Volume 10)
NatWest/SBRT Quarterly Survey of Small Business in Britain (vol.16, 2000)
NatWest/SBRT Survey of Exporters (back issues only, discontinued 2000)
Register of Small Business Researchers (hard copy plus disk with the register in Microsoft Access v4, £50)
Risk Capital for Small Firms (guidebook, 1988)

SME Database
The Making of Entrepreneurs
The role of the small firm in the UK economy: Hot Stereotypes and Cool Assessments
Work Status and Self-Employment in the British Construction Industry

Publications list:
Available online and in print

Access to staff:
Contact by telephone, by fax and by e-mail
Hours: Mon to Fri, 0900 to 1700

Access to building, collection or gallery:
No prior appointment required

Other addresses:
Small Enterprise Research Team
45 Clydesdale Close, Isleworth, London, TW7 6ST; tel: 020 8568 3004; fax: 020 8568 3004; e-mail: b.porter-blake@open.ac.uk

SMALLPEICE ENTERPRISES LIMITED

27 Newbold Terrace East, Leamington Spa, Warwickshire, CV32 4ES

Tel: 01926 336423
Fax: 01926 450679
E-mail: train@smallpeice.co.uk

Website:
http://www.smallpeice.co.uk
Course descriptions, dates, prices.

Enquiries:
Enquiries to: Marketing Assistant

Founded:
1966

Organisation type and purpose:
Professional body, registered charity, training organisation, consultancy.
Training Centre.
Smallpeice combines over 30 years training experience and specialist industry focus to provide a total training service for engineering and manufacturing companies nationwide.

Subject coverage:
Design engineering, Six Sigma; Lean Manufacturing; Autocad; project management; management skills; public courses nationwide; in-company bespoke training; corporate development partnership; strategic conferences; facilitation and consultancy; one-to-one training; ICT-based training partnerships.

Non-library collection catalogue:
All or part available online

Publications list:
Available in print

Access to staff:
Contact by letter, by telephone, by fax, by e-mail and via website
Hours: Mon to Fri, 0830 to 1730

Parent body:
The Smallpeice Trust
tel: 01926 333200; fax: 01926 333202

SNACK, NUT AND CRISP MANUFACTURERS ASSOCIATION LIMITED

Acronym or abbreviation: SNACMA

37–41 Bedford Row, London, WC1R 4JH

Tel: 020 7611 4660
Fax: 020 7611 4661
E-mail: esa@esa.org.uk

Website:
http://www.esa.org.uk

Enquiries:
Enquiries to: Director General

Founded:
1983

Organisation type and purpose:
Trade association.

Subject coverage:
Snack industry and products; nutritional data; statistics.

Printed publications:
Periodic distribution of material of educational nature to schools

Access to staff:
Contact by letter, by telephone, by fax, by e-mail and via website. Appointment necessary.
Hours: Mon to Fri, 0900 to 1700

Member of:
Food and Drink Federation
tel: 020 7836 2460
Potato Processors Association

SNOWDONIA SOCIETY

Formal name: Snowdonia Society – Cymdeithas Eryri
Acronym or abbreviation: SS/CE

Ty Hyll (The Ugly House), Capel Curig, Betws-y-Coed, Conwy, LL24 0DS

Tel: 01690 720287
Fax: 01690 720247
E-mail: info@snowdonia-society.org.uk

Website:
http://www.snowdonia-society.org.uk
Broad range of information about the Society, updated regularly

Enquiries:
Enquiries to: Dan James, Operations Director

Founded:
1968

Organisation type and purpose:
Membership association (membership is by subscription), present number of members: 2700, voluntary organisation, registered charity (charity number 253231).
Conservation society for Snowdonia, aiming to protect the landscape of Snowdonia.

Subject coverage:
Planning, administration and conservation of the Snowdonia National Park and district, transport, wildlife, flora.

Museum or gallery collection, archive, or library special collection:
Files on past issues within Snowdonia

Printed publications:
The Old Cottages of Snowdonia (out of print)
Annual Report (members free, non-members £1)
Snowdonia Society/Cymdeithaseryri (2 times a year, members, free; non-members £1)
The Old Churches of Snowdonia (Out of print)
Back issues of Society magazine

Access to staff:
Contact by letter, by telephone, by fax, by e-mail and via website. Appointment necessary.
Hours: Mon to Fri, 0900 to 1700

Access to building, collection or gallery:
No prior appointment required
Hours: Mon to Fri, 0930 to 1700

Affiliated to:
Council for National Parks

SNOWSPORT ENGLAND

Acronym or abbreviation: SSE

Area Library Building, Queensway Mall, The Cornbow, Halesowen, West Midlands, B63 4AJ

Tel: 0121 501 2314
Fax: 0121 585 6448
E-mail: info@snowsportengland.org.uk

Website:
http://www.snowsportengland.org.uk

Enquiries:
Enquiries to: Chief Executive

Founded:
1978

Formerly called:
English Ski Council (year of change 2004)

Organisation type and purpose:
Governing body for skiing in England.

Subject coverage:
English skiers and skiing, membership scheme, coaching awards scheme, promotion of events, design and development of ski slopes.

Printed publications:
Dry Ski Slopes List
National Coaching Scheme Information booklet
SAE required for booklet and list

Publications list:
Available in print

Access to staff:
Contact by letter and by e-mail
Hours: Mon to Fri, 0900 to 1700

Access to building, collection or gallery:
Prior appointment required

Access for disabled people:
Parking provided, ramped entry, access to all public areas

Grant-aided by:
Sport England

SNOWSPORT GB

Hillend, Biggar Road, Edinburgh, EH10 7EF

Tel: 0131 445 7676
Fax: 0131 445 4949
E-mail: info@snowsportgb.com

Website:
http://www.snowsportgb.com/

Enquiries:
Enquiries to: CEO
Other contacts: Administration Manager

Founded:
1964

Organisation type and purpose:
National organisation.
National governing body of the sport.
The management and promotion of Britain's top international snowsports competitors and the co-ordination of UK activities.

Subject coverage:
Disciplines of Alpine, Nordic and Freestyle skiing, snowboarding.

Printed publications:
Media Guide
Rule books

Access to staff:
Contact by letter, by telephone and by e-mail
Hours: Mon to Fri, 0900 to 1700

SOCIAL CARE INSTITUTE FOR EXCELLENCE

Acronym or abbreviation: SCIE

1st Floor, Goldings House, Hay's Lane, London, SE1 2HB

Tel: 020 7089 6840
Fax: 020 7089 6841
E-mail: info@scie.org.uk

Website:
http://www.scie.org.uk
http://www.scie-socialcareonline.org.uk
Social Care Online
http://www.researchweb.org.uk
ResearchWeb: Scottish social care research
http://www.scie-peoplemanagement.org.uk
People Management
http://www.researchregister.org.uk

Research Register for Social Care

Enquiries:
Enquiries to: Director of Knowledge Management

Founded:
2001

Formerly called:
National Institute for Social Work (year of change 2001)

Organisation type and purpose:
Voluntary organisation; research commissioning body

Subject coverage:
Social welfare policy; personal social services; social care.

Non-library collection catalogue:
All or part available online

Printed publications:
Wide variety of publications available
Order printed publications from: http://www.scie.org.uk/publications/ordering/index.asp

Electronic and video publications:
Social Care Online
ResearchWeb
Research Register for Social Care

Publications list:
Available online and in print

Access to staff:
Contact by e-mail and via website
Hours: Mon to Fri, 1000 to 1700

Access to building, collection or gallery:
No prior appointment required
Hours: Mon to Fri, 1000 to 1700

Access for disabled people:
Parking provided, access to all public areas, toilet facilities

SOCIAL HISTORY SOCIETY

Acronym or abbreviation: SHS

Furness College, Bailrigg, Lancaster, LA1 4YG

Tel: 01524 592547
Fax: 01524 846102
E-mail: l.persson@lancaster.ac.uk

Website:
http://socialhistory.org.uk/
Society information, conference information, links.

Enquiries:
Enquiries to: Administrative Secretary

Founded:
1976

Organisation type and purpose:
Learned society.

Subject coverage:
The history of society in all times and places.

Printed publications:
Culture and Social History Journal (4 times a year)

Access to staff:
Contact by letter, by telephone, by fax, by e-mail and via website. Appointment necessary.
Hours: Tue, 0930 to 1630; Wed, 1330 to 1630; Fri, 0930 to 1700

Access for disabled people:
Parking provided, level entry, access to all public areas, toilet facilities

Affiliated to:
Association of Learned Societies in the Social Sciences

SOCIAL RESEARCH ASSOCIATION

Acronym or abbreviation: SRA

PO Box 33660, London, N16 6WE

Tel: 020 8880 5684

Fax: 020 8880 5684
E-mail: admin@the-sra.org.uk

Website:
http://www.the-sra.org.uk
Membership, careers, job adverts, training days, annual conference details and seminars.

Enquiries:
Enquiries to: Administrator

Founded:
1978

Organisation type and purpose:
Membership association.

Subject coverage:
Application and development of social research, methodology, funding, training and policy.

Printed publications:
Directory of members
Newsletter (quarterly)
Commissioning Social Research: a Practical Guide
Ethical Guidelines

Access to staff:
Contact by letter, by telephone, by fax, by e-mail and via website. Appointment necessary.
Hours: Mon to Fri, 0900 to 1700

Affiliated to:
ALSISS
ARCISS
SCASS

SOCIAL, EMOTIONAL AND BEHAVIOURAL DIFFICULTIES ASSOCIATION

Acronym or abbreviation: SEBDA

Room 211, The Triangle, Exchange Square, Manchester, M4 3TR

Tel: 0161 240 2418
Fax: 0161 838 5601
E-mail: admin@sebda.org

Website:
http://www.sebda.org/

Enquiries:
Enquiries to: Office Services Manager

Formerly called:
Association of Workers for Children with Emotional and Behavioural Difficulties (AWCEBD); Association of Workers for Maladjusted Children

Organisation type and purpose:
Membership association (membership is by subscription), registered charity (charity number 258730), training organisation, consultancy.

Subject coverage:
Educational and therapeutic care of disturbed children, staff training and support, emotional and behavioural difficulties, policy development.

Printed publications:
Journal
Newsletter
Prospectus

Electronic and video publications:
EBD schools database

Publications list:
Available in print

Access to staff:
Contact by letter, by telephone, by fax, by e-mail and via website
Hours: Response to telephone enquiries 1000 to 1600

Access to building, collection or gallery:
Prior appointment required

Access for disabled people:
Parking provided, level entry, toilet facilities

Member of:
National Childrens' Bureau

continued overleaf

Special Educational Needs National Advisory Council
Young Minds (successor to Child Guidance Trust)

SOCIALIST HEALTH ASSOCIATION

Acronym or abbreviation: SHA

22 Blair Road, Manchester, M16 8NS

Tel: 0870 013 0065
E-mail: admin@sochealth.co.uk

Website:
http://www.sochealth.co.uk
Information about related organisations, campaigns, current topics, glossary of acronyms, legal materials.

Enquiries:
Enquiries to: Director

Founded:
1930

Formerly called:
Socialist Medical Association (year of change 1980)

Organisation type and purpose:
Membership association (membership is by subscription), present number of members: 650, voluntary organisation.
Political campaigning.

Subject coverage:
Structure and accountability of the National Health Service, community care, local authority health responsibilities, health promotion, politics of health, mental health services, primary health care, health inequalities, public health.

Museum or gallery collection, archive, or library special collection:
Archives (held at the Brynmor Jones Library, University of Hull)

Printed publications:
Annual Report
Discussion papers
Socialism and Health (3 times a year)

Publications list:
Available in print

Access to staff:
Contact by letter, by telephone, by e-mail and via website
Hours: Any reasonable hour

Access to building, collection or gallery:
Prior appointment required

Access for disabled people:
Ramped entry

Affiliated to:
Labour Party

SOCIALIST INTERNATIONAL WOMEN

Acronym or abbreviation: SIW

Maritime House, Old Town, Clapham, London, SW4 0JW

Tel: 020 7627 4449
Fax: 020 7720 4448
E-mail: socintwomen@gn.apc.org

Website:
http://www.socintwomen.org

Enquiries:
Enquiries to: General Secretary
Direct fax: 020 7498 1293

Founded:
1907

Organisation type and purpose:
International organisation.

Subject coverage:
Women; human rights; development; disarmament.

Printed publications:
Women and Politics (magazine, quarterly)

Has:
131 member organisations in different countries
7 fraternal and associated organisations world-wide

SOCIÉTÉ JERSIAISE

7 Pier Road, St Helier, Jersey, JE2 4XW, Channel Islands

Tel: 01534 758314 (office); 730538 (library); 633398 (photo archive)
Fax: 01534 888262
E-mail: library@societe-jersiaise.org

Website:
http://www.societe-jersiaise.org

Enquiries:
Enquiries to: Librarian
Other contacts: Photographic Administrator (for photographic archive)

Founded:
1873

Organisation type and purpose:
Learned society.

Subject coverage:
Local history, natural history with sections on zoology, ornithology, botany, garden history, entomology, marine biology, archaeology, geology, numismatics, transport and industrial archaeology, bibliography, archives, genealogy, mycology.

Museum or gallery collection, archive, or library special collection:
Manuscripts, archival documents, correspondence, family papers, ephemera, newspapers, photographs, periodicals and rare books related to Jersey

Non-library collection catalogue:
All or part available online and in-house

Library catalogue:
All or part available online and in-house

Printed publications:
Annual Bulletin (since 1875)
Channel Island Family History Journal
Many publications on historical topics and people, old maps, memoirs and natural history
1851 Census of Jersey
1871 Census of Jersey
A range of publications for children

Electronic and video publications:
Jersey Moving Memories (video)
John Jean's Maritime Jersey (video)
Naturally Jersey (video)
cassettes, CDs

Publications list:
Available online and in print

Access to staff:
Contact by letter, by telephone, by fax, by e-mail, in person and via website
Hours: Mon to Fri, 0900 to 1700

Links with:
Jersey Archives Service
    tel: 01534 633303; fax: 01534 633301
Jersey Museums Service
    The Weighbridge, St Helier, Jersey, JE2 3NF; tel: 01534 633330; fax: 01534 633301

SOCIETY AND COLLEGE OF RADIOGRAPHERS

Acronym or abbreviation: SCOR

Quartz House, 207 Providence Square, London, SE1 2EW

Tel: 020 7740 7200
Fax: 020 7740 7204
E-mail: info@sor.org

Website:
http://www.sor.org

A range of professional and industrial relations information, members' section.

Enquiries:
Enquiries to: Admin Assistants
Other contacts: Director of Professional Development for professional matters

Organisation type and purpose:
Trade union, present number of members: 18,000.

Subject coverage:
Radiography and related careers.

Education services:
Education for radiographers and related careers.

Printed publications:
Available free or for purchase direct

Publications list:
Available online and in print

Access to staff:
Contact by letter, by telephone, by fax, by e-mail, in person and via website. Appointment necessary.
Hours: Mon to Fri, 0900 to 1700

Access for disabled people:
Parking provided, access to all public areas, toilet facilities

SOCIETY FOR ADVANCED LEGAL STUDIES

Acronym or abbreviation: SALS

17 Russell Square, London, WC1B 5DR

Tel: 020 7862 5865
Fax: 020 7862 5855
E-mail: sals@sas.ac.uk

Website:
http://www.iats.sas.ac.uk/SALS/society.htm

Enquiries:
Enquiries to: Secretary

Founded:
1997

Organisation type and purpose:
Learned society (membership is by subscription, qualification).

Access to staff:
Contact by e-mail
Hours: Mon to Fri, 0900 to 1700

SOCIETY FOR ANGLO-CHINESE UNDERSTANDING

Acronym or abbreviation: SACU

2 Lawnswood Avenue, Poulton-le-Fylde, Lancashire, FY6 7ED

Tel: 01253 894582

Website:
http://www.sacu.org

Enquiries:
Enquiries to: Information Officer

Founded:
1965

Organisation type and purpose:
Membership association, registered charity.
To promote Anglo-Chinese understanding and friendship.

Subject coverage:
China and Chinese culture; current events; calligraphy and brush painting (not specialised business or academic information).

Printed publications:
China Now
Newsletter

Access to staff:
Contact by letter and by telephone
Hours: Mon to Fri, 0900 to 1700

SOCIETY FOR APPLIED MICROBIOLOGY

Acronym or abbreviation: sfam

Bedford Heights, Brickhill Drive, Bedford, MK41 7PH

Tel: 01234 326661
Fax: 01234 326678
E-mail: info@sfam.org.uk

Website:
http://www.sfam.org.uk
Information on membership, meetings, publications.

Enquiries:
Enquiries to: Office Manager
Direct e-mail: alison@sfam.org.uk

Founded:
1931

Organisation type and purpose:
International organisation, learned society (membership is by subscription), registered charity (charity number 326509).

Subject coverage:
All aspects of applied bacteriology and microbiology.

Printed publications:
Environmental Microbiology (bi-monthly, pub Blackwell Science)
Journal of Applied Microbiology (monthly, pub Blackwell Science)
Letters in Applied Microbiology (monthly, pub Blackwell Science)
Order printed publications from: Blackwell Science Osney Mead, Oxford, OX2 0EL, tel: 01865 206206

Electronic and video publications:
Journals (available online via Blackwell Science)

Publications list:
Available online and in print

Access to staff:
Contact by letter, by telephone, by fax, by e-mail and via website
Hours: Mon to Fri, 0900 to 1700

Member of:
Federation of European Microbiological Societies
Institute of Biology
International Union of Microbiological Societies

SOCIETY FOR ARMY HISTORICAL RESEARCH

Acronym or abbreviation: SAHR

c/o National Army Museum, Royal Hospital Road, London, SW3 4HT

Enquiries:
Enquiries to: Honorary Treasurer
Direct tel: 020 3227 0156
Direct fax: 020 3227 0156
Direct e-mail: guysayle@hotmail.com

Founded:
1921

Organisation type and purpose:
Learned society (membership is by subscription), present number of members: 1000.
Military historical research.

Subject coverage:
History of British and Commonwealth armies and their ancillary formations. Members' articles/research published in quarterly journal.

Printed publications:
Index to the Journal (vols 1–68)
Journal of the Society (commenced publication in 1921, quarterly)
Special Numbers

Access to staff:
Contact by letter and by telephone. Access for members only.
Hours: Mon to Fri, 0900 to 1700

SOCIETY FOR CARDIOTHORACIC SURGERY IN GREAT BRITAIN AND IRELAND

Acronym or abbreviation: SCTS

35–43 Lincoln's Inn Fields, London, WC2A 3PE

Tel: 020 7869 6893
Fax: 020 7869 6890
E-mail: sctsadmin@scts.org

Website:
http://www.scts.org
Details of members, events and general information of the Society.

Enquiries:
Enquiries to: Society Administrator

Organisation type and purpose:
Professional body.

Subject coverage:
Thoracic and cardiac surgery.

Access to staff:
Contact by e-mail
Hours: Mon to Wed, 0800 to 1400; Thur, 0930 to 1430

SOCIETY FOR CO-OPERATION IN RUSSIAN AND SOVIET STUDIES

Acronym or abbreviation: SCR

320 Brixton Road, London, SW9 6AB

Tel: 020 7274 2282
Fax: 020 7274 3230
E-mail: ruslibrary@scrss.co.uk

Website:
http://www.scrss.fsnet.co.uk
Information on lectures and film shows; Russian courses in Russia; society information; photo library; SCR Russian Information Guide.

Enquiries:
Enquiries to: Librarian

Founded:
1924

Organisation type and purpose:
Membership association (membership is by subscription), present number of members: 750 and 25 affiliated universities/organisations, voluntary organisation, research organisation.
To facilitate contacts and understanding between the peoples of the UK and the former Soviet Union through language courses, information, library etc.

Subject coverage:
Russian history including pre-revolutionary and Soviet history, geography, literature, art, theatre, film, ballet, music, education, sport, social sciences (including ethnography), economics, law.

Museum or gallery collection, archive, or library special collection:
Andrew Rothstein Collection (early Soviet documents and pamphlets)
Archive material of the SCR (founded 1924)
Huntly Carter Bequest (early Soviet theatre and architecture photographs)
Children's library
Elsie Timbey Collection (pre-revolutionary and early Soviet photography and books)
Newspaper cuttings files on all subjects plus many others maintained, mainly Russian press in translation

Trade and statistical information:
Statistics, in cuttings files.
Texts in Russian and English of some laws.
Statistical, economic and political data available in variety of subjects.

Non-library collection catalogue:
All or part available in-house

Printed publications:
SCR Information Digest (3 times a year)
SCR Russian Information Guide (annually)

Access to staff:
Contact by letter, by telephone, by fax and by e-mail. Appointment necessary. Non-members charged.
Hours: Mon to Fri, 1000 to 1300 and 1400 to 1800

Access for disabled people:
Parking provided, level entry, toilet facilities
Special comments: Prior notice required for parking.

SOCIETY FOR COMPANION ANIMAL STUDIES

Acronym or abbreviation: SCAS

10B Leny Road, Callander, Perthshire, FK17 8BA

Tel: 01877 330996
Fax: 01877 330996

Website:
http://www.scas.org.uk
Details of membership and main aims of SCAS.

Enquiries:
Enquiries to: Executive Director

Founded:
1979

Organisation type and purpose:
Membership association (membership is by subscription), present number of members: 400, voluntary organisation, registered charity (charity number 1070938), suitable for ages: 18+.

Subject coverage:
Relationship between people and their companion animals; potential therapeutic value in treating psychological problems, mental illness, impaired health, promotion of responsible pet ownership to ensure quality of life of a pet and owner. Training in providing support for bereaved pet owners.

Museum or gallery collection, archive, or library special collection:
Library for reference in research at general and academic level
Requests by phone and letter only

Non-library collection catalogue:
All or part available in print

Library catalogue:
All or part available in-house

Printed publications:
Death of an Animal Friend (1990, £2.50, also on audio cassette)
Enriching our Lives (A celebration of the first 20 years of SCAS, £5.50 inc. p&p)
Guidelines for Development and Delivery of Animal Assisted Activity and Therapy Projects (£5 inc. p&p)
Guidelines for the Introduction of Pets into Nursing Homes and other Institutions (1990, £2.50)
Pet Loss and Support for Bereaved Pet Owners (£1.50 inc. p&p)
SCAS Journal (quarterly, £1)

Electronic and video publications:
A Kind Goodbye (video, £10 inc. p&p)

Publications list:
Available online and in print

Access to staff:
Contact by letter, by telephone, by fax and by e-mail. Non-members charged.
Hours: Mon to Fri, 0900 to 1700

Founder member in 1992 of:
International Association of Human/Animal Interaction Organisations (IAHAIO)

Informal links with:
AFIRAC
  France
and other members of IAHAIO
DELTA Society
  USA
Organisations having similar interests and concerns in the UK and abroad
Pet Fostering Service
  Scotland; tel: 01877 331496

continued overleaf

The Blue Cross
(Pet Bereavement Support Service 0800 096
6606); tel: 01993 822651; fax: 01993 823083

SOCIETY FOR COMPUTERS AND LAW

Acronym or abbreviation: SCL

10 Hurle Crescent, Clifton, Bristol, BS8 2TA

Tel: 0117 923 7393
Fax: 0117 923 9305
E-mail: ruth.baker@scl.org

Website:
http://www.scl.org

Enquiries:
Enquiries to: General Manager

Founded:
1973

Organisation type and purpose:
National organisation, professional body,
membership association (membership is by
subscription), present number of members: 2500,
registered charity (charity number 266331).

Subject coverage:
Information technology law, information
technology for lawyers.

Printed publications:
Computers & Law (6 times a year, by subscription)
Magazine

Access to staff:
Contact by letter, by telephone, by fax, by e-mail
and via website. Appointment necessary.
Hours: Mon to Fri, 0900 to 1700
Special comments: Prior appointment only.

Access to building, collection or gallery:
Prior appointment required
Hours: Mon to Fri, 0900 to 1700

Access for disabled people:
Level entry

SOCIETY FOR DANCE RESEARCH

Laban Centre London, Laurie Grove, New Cross,
London, SE14 6NH

Tel: 020 8692 4070 ext 120
Fax: 020 8694 8749 or 8691 3792
E-mail: sdr1@tinyworld.co.uk

Enquiries:
Enquiries to: Administrative Secretary
Direct tel: 01903 742019

Founded:
1982

Organisation type and purpose:
Learned society (membership is by subscription),
present number of members: 170, voluntary
organisation, registered charity, research
organisation.
British based organisation, which promotes and
fosters the quality and scope of scholarship and
research in all forms of dance.

Subject coverage:
Dance.

Printed publications:
Dance Research (2 times a year)
Newsletter (2 times a year)
Society sponsored reports (occasional)

Access to staff:
Contact by letter, by telephone and by e-mail
Hours: Mon to Fri, 0900 to 1700
Special comments: Please contact by telephone or fax
and leave message.

SOCIETY FOR EARTHQUAKE AND CIVIL ENGINEERING DYNAMICS

Acronym or abbreviation: SECED

Institution of Civil Engineers, One Great George
Street, London, SW1P 3AA

Tel: 020 7222 7722
Fax: 020 7222 7500

Enquiries:
Enquiries to: Secretary
Direct tel: 020 7655 2238
Direct fax: 020 7799 1325
Direct e-mail: caroline.howe@ice.org.uk

Organisation type and purpose:
Learned society.

Subject coverage:
Earthquakes and engineering; seismology; blast,
vibration and impact; soil dynamics and
foundation engineering.

Printed publications:
Conference proceedings
Directory of UK practitioners (free)
Earthquake Engineering and Structural Dynamics
– Journal of the International Association for
Earthquake Engineering (published Wiley)
Earthquake reports

National section of the:
International Association for Earthquake
Engineering

SOCIETY FOR EDITORS AND PROOFREADERS

Acronym or abbreviation: SfEP

Erico House, 93–99 Upper Richmond Road,
London, SW15 2TG

Tel: 020 8785 5617
Fax: 020 8785 5618
E-mail: administration@sfep.org.uk

Website:
http://www.sfep.org.uk

Enquiries:
Enquiries to: Administrator
Direct e-mail: executive@sfep.org.uk
Other contacts: PR Co-ordinator for press enquiries.

Founded:
1988

Organisation type and purpose:
Professional body (membership is by subscription),
present number of members: c.1,300, training
organisation.
Upholding editorial excellence.

Subject coverage:
Copy-editing and proofreading, editorial project
management, editorial training, editorial
standards. The profession is involved in a wide
range of subject areas including: modern
languages, business, finance and economics,
medicine, music, reference, technical writing,
science and computing.

Printed publications:
Newsletter (6 times a year, by subscription,
members only)
Directory of Members' Services (annually, free to
members, cover price £15 but up to two copies
free to bona fide users of freelance editorial
services)

Electronic and video publications:
Directory of Members' Services (available online)

Access to staff:
Contact by letter, by e-mail and via website
Hours: 0930 to 1600
Special comments: Personal attendance not
encouraged.

SOCIETY FOR ENDOCRINOLOGY

17–18 North Court, The Courtyard, Woodlands,
Bradley Stoke, Bristol, BS32 4NQ

Tel: 01454 642200
Fax: 01454 642222
E-mail: info@endocrinology.org

Website:
http://www.endocrinology.org
Society home pages, ordering information, journal
abstracts and contents, full text for institutional
subscribers.

Enquiries:
Enquiries to: Society Services Manager

Founded:
1946

Organisation type and purpose:
Learned society, registered charity (charity number
266813), publishing house.
To promote the advancement of public education
in endocrinology.

Subject coverage:
Endocrinology; hormones.

Printed publications:
Endocrine-Related Cancer (quarterly)
Journal of Endocrinology (monthly)
Journal of Molecular Endocrinology (6 times a
year)
The Endocrinologist (newsletter, quarterly)
Order printed publications from: Portland Press Ltd
Commerce Way, Colchester, Essex, CO2 8HP, tel:
01206 796351, fax: 01206 799331, e-mail: sales@
portlandpress.co.uk

Electronic and video publications:
Online versions of journals

Publications list:
Available online

Access to staff:
Contact by letter
Hours: Mon to Fri, 0900 to 1700

Subsidiary body:
BioScientifica Ltd
16 The Courtyard, Woodlands, Bradley Stoke,
Bristol, BS32 4NQ; tel: 01454 642200; fax: 01454
642222; e-mail: info@endocrinology.org

SOCIETY FOR FOLK LIFE STUDIES

Snibston Discovery Park, Ashby Discovery Park,
Ashby Road, Coalville, Leicestershire, LE67 2LN

Tel: 01530 278468
Fax: 01530 813301
E-mail: smastoris@leics.gov.uk

Website:
http://www.folklife.org.uk
General description of society, lists of articles in
Folklife Journal

Enquiries:
Enquiries to: Secretary

Founded:
1961

Organisation type and purpose:
Learned society (membership is by subscription),
present number of members: c. 500, voluntary
organisation.

Subject coverage:
Traditional ways of life in Great Britain and
Ireland, folk life, popular culture, ethnology.

Printed publications:
Journal of Folk Life Studies (annually)
Newsletter (annually)
Order printed publications from: Society for Folk Life
Studies, Welsh Folk Museum
St Fagan's, Cardiff, CF5 6XB, tel: 029 2056 9441, fax:
029 2057 8413

Access to staff:
Contact by letter, by telephone, by fax, by e-mail
and via website
Hours: Mon to Fri, 0900 to 1700

SOCIETY FOR GENERAL MICROBIOLOGY

Acronym or abbreviation: SGM

Marlborough House, Basingstoke Road, Spencers Wood, Reading, Berkshire, RG7 1AG

Tel: 0118 988 1800
Fax: 0118 988 5656
E-mail: admin@sgm.ac.uk

Website:
http://www.sgm.ac.uk
Society, membership, subscriptions, forthcoming scientific meetings, publications, availability of publications electronically, external relations and grants, careers, training, microbiology for schools.
http://www.sgmjournals.org
Online journals.

Enquiries:
Enquiries to: Deputy Chief Executive
Direct tel: 0118 988 1809
Direct e-mail: j.hurst@sgm.ac.uk
Other contacts: Chief Executive

Founded:
1945

Organisation type and purpose:
International organisation, learned society (membership is by subscription), present number of members: 5,500, registered charity (charity number 264017), publishing house.
Represents the interests of microbiologists world-wide, particularly in the United Kingdom.

Subject coverage:
Microbiology, virology, biotechnology in response to requests from the general public, academia, industry, government and all levels of education. Careers and training in microbiology.

Printed publications:
Careers in microbiology (free)
International Journal of Systematic and Evolutionary Microbiology (monthly)
Journal of General Virology (monthly)
Microbiology (monthly)
Microbiology Today (quarterly)
Journal of Medical Microbiology (monthly)

Electronic and video publications:
Online journals

Publications list:
Available in print

Access to staff:
Contact by letter, by telephone, by fax, by e-mail and via website. Appointment necessary.
Hours: Mon to Fri, 0900 to 1700

Links with:
Federation of European Microbiology Societies
International Union of Microbiology Societies

SOCIETY FOR INDIVIDUAL FREEDOM

Acronym or abbreviation: SIF

PO Box 744, Bromley, Kent, BR1 4WG

Tel: 01424 713737
Fax: 01424 713737
E-mail: chairman@individualist.org.uk

Website:
http://www.individualist.org.uk
Details on SIF.Tell It.

Enquiries:
Enquiries to: Chairman
Other contacts: President

Founded:
1940

Organisation type and purpose:
Membership association, voluntary organisation.
Lobbying group.
Campaigning for personal freedom.

Subject coverage:
Personal freedom, reducing state control and taxation, fostering free enterprise.

Printed publications:
The Power to Destroy: a study of the British Taxation System (D Myddelton)

The Individual (newsletter)

Publications list:
Available in print

Access to staff:
Contact by letter, by telephone, by e-mail and via website
Hours: Also evenings

SOCIETY FOR INTERNATIONAL FOLK DANCING

Acronym or abbreviation: SIFD

5 South Rise, Carshalton, SM5 4PD

Tel: 020 8395 1400
E-mail: mail@sifd.org

Website:
http://www.sifd.org

Enquiries:
Enquiries to: Publicity Officer

Founded:
1946

Organisation type and purpose:
Membership association (membership is by subscription), present number of members: 400, voluntary organisation, registered charity (charity number 284509), suitable for all ages.
Voluntary society.
Support and co-ordination of work of local bodies.

Subject coverage:
Traditional folk dances of many countries, especially European; costume and music of those countries.

Printed publications:
Newsletter (monthly, members only)
Instruction books
History of Society for International Folk Dancing
Order printed publications from: Publications Secretary, Society for International Folk Dancing, 5 South Rise, Carshalton, Surrey, SM5 4PD, tel: 020 8395 1400

Electronic and video publications:
Music tapes, CDs and a video

Publications list:
Available online

Access to staff:
Contact by letter, by telephone, by e-mail and via website
Hours: Variable

Also at:
63 affiliated and associated UK groups
Society for International Folk Dancing
  6 Leveson Crescent, Balsall Common, Coventry, CV7 7DR; tel: 01676 534112
West Midlands Branch

Links with:
Central Council for Physical Recreation (CCPR)
  Francis House, Francis Street, London, SW1P 1DE; tel: 020 8828 3163; fax: 020 8630 8820

SOCIETY FOR ITALIC HANDWRITING

Acronym or abbreviation: SIH

205 Dyas Avenue, Great Barr, Birmingham, B42 1HN

Tel: 0121 358 0032
Fax: 0121 358 0032
E-mail: nickthenibs@netscapeonline.co.uk

Enquiries:
Enquiries to: Secretary

Founded:
1952

Organisation type and purpose:
Learned society (membership is by subscription), present number of members: 500, registered charity (charity number 287889R).

To sustain the interest in italic handwriting and to secure the advancement of education in relation to handwriting.

Subject coverage:
Italic handwriting and Renaissance calligraphy.

Printed publications:
A Simple Guide to Italic Handwriting (Winters N, £6 plus £1 p&p)
Writing Matters (formerly the Journal and the Newsletter, 3 times a year to members)

Electronic and video publications:
Good Handwriting Initiative: School's Pack (CD-ROM and copy sheets, £14.50 inc. p&p)

Access to staff:
Contact by letter and by e-mail
Hours: Mon to Fri, 0900 to 1700

Connections with:
Society of Scribes and Illuminators

SOCIETY FOR LIBYAN STUDIES

Institute of Archaeology, 31–34 Gordon Square, London, WC1H 0PY

E-mail: shinleystrong@btconnect.com

Website:
http://britac3.britac.ac.uk/institutes/libya/index .html
Information about the Society, lists of publications, lecture programme, subscription rate, etc.

Enquiries:
Enquiries to: General Secretary

Founded:
1969

Organisation type and purpose:
Learned society.

Subject coverage:
Libyan life and culture, particularly archaeology, history, Islamic law, geography and geomorphology.

Museum or gallery collection, archive, or library special collection:
Specialist works on Libya, including the Goodchild Library

Printed publications:
Annual Journal, Report and Monographs
Publications include:
Excavations at Sidi Khrebish, Bengazi
Farming the Desert: The UNESCO Libyan Valleys Archaeological Survey
The Christian Monuments of Cyrenaica
The Severan Buildings of Leptis Magna
The Archaeology of Fazzan
The Libyan Desert
Natural Resources and Cultural Heritage
Travellers in Libya

Publications list:
Available online and in print

Access to staff:
Contact by letter and by e-mail
Hours: Mon to Fri, 0900 to 1700

SOCIETY FOR LINCOLNSHIRE HISTORY AND ARCHAEOLOGY

Acronym or abbreviation: SLHA

Jews' Court, 2 & 3 Steep Hill, Lincoln, LN2 1LS

Tel: 01522 521337
Fax: 01522 521337
E-mail: slha@lincolnshirepast.org.uk

Website:
http://www.lincolnshirepast.org.uk

Enquiries:
Enquiries to: Administrator

Founded:
1974

continued overleaf

Organisation type and purpose:
Learned society, membership association
(membership is by subscription), present number
of members: 600, voluntary organisation,
registered charity (charity number 504766),
suitable for ages: all.
To promote interest in and the study of all aspects
of Lincolnshire history.

Subject coverage:
Lincolnshire history, archaeology, industrial
archaeology, topography, architecture, dialect etc.

**Museum or gallery collection, archive, or library
special collection:**
Library for members (at Jews' Court)
Periodicals and valuable material on deposit at the
  Lincolnshire Archives Office

Library catalogue:
All or part available in-house

Printed publications:
Bulletin (quarterly)
Diary Dates (quarterly)
Lincolnshire History and Archaeology (annually)
Lincolnshire Past and Present (quarterly)

Publications list:
Available in print

Access to staff:
Contact by letter, by telephone, by fax, by e-mail
and in person. Appointment necessary. Access for
members only.
Hours: Mon to Thu, 1000 to 1300
Special comments: Library open to members only.

Trading company is:
Lincolnshire Heritage Limited
  at the main address; tel: 01522 532280; fax: 01522
  521337

SOCIETY FOR LOW
TEMPERATURE BIOLOGY

Acronym or abbreviation: SLTB

The General Secretary, c/o Jon Green, Genómica
Funcional, CIC-Biogune, Parque Tecnológico de
Vizcaya, Edificio 801A, 1pl., 48160-Derio, Spain

Tel: +34 944 061 326
Fax: +34 944 061 301
E-mail: jgreen@cicbiogune,es

Website:
http://www.sltb.info
Information about the society, list of committee
members.

Enquiries:
Enquiries to: Treasurer
Direct e-mail: mcurry@lincoln.ac.uk

Founded:
1964

Organisation type and purpose:
International organisation, learned society.

Subject coverage:
Biological effects of low temperature; preservation
of cells, tissues, organs, in both plant and animal
kingdoms; preservation of genetic stock (plants);
adaptation to cold; cryosurgery.

Printed publications:
Newsletter (3 times a year, free to members)

Access to staff:
Contact by letter, by fax, by e-mail and via
website
Hours: Mon to Fri, 0900 to 1700

SOCIETY FOR
MUCOPOLYSACCHARIDE
DISEASES

Acronym or abbreviation: MPS

MPS House, Repton Place, White Lion Road,
Amersham, Buckinghamshire, HP7 9LP

Tel: 0845 389 9901
Fax: 0845 389 9902

E-mail: mps@mpssociety.co.uk

Website:
http://www.mpssociety.co.uk

Enquiries:
Enquiries to: Chief Executive

Founded:
1982

Organisation type and purpose:
International organisation, membership
association (membership is by qualification),
present number of members: 1500, voluntary
organisation, registered charity (charity number
287034).
Members who qualify are: those having MPS,
parent or carer.
Provides support and advocacy to individuals and
their families affected by MPS diseases, brings
about public awareness and raises funds for
furthering research.

Subject coverage:
Mucopolysaccharide and related diseases; clinical
management, gene research, education, home
adaptations, welfare benefits, specialist clinics,
social events.

Printed publications:
Series of booklets produced by parents and doctors
  to provide guidance for families and
  professionals caring for individuals suffering
  from MPS (£2 each)
Order printed publications from: http://
www.mpssociety.co.uk

Publications list:
Available online and in print

Access to staff:
Contact by letter, by telephone, by fax, by e-mail
and via website. Appointment necessary.
Hours: Mon to Fri, 0900 to 1700
Out-of-hours helpline: Mon to Fri, 1700 to 2200;
Sat, Sun, 0700 to 2200

Access to building, collection or gallery:
Prior appointment preferred.
Hours: Mon to Fri, 0900 to 1700
Special comments: Subject to adequate staffing.

Access for disabled people:
Level entry
Special comments: Limited access to ground floor
only.

SOCIETY FOR POPULAR
ASTRONOMY

Acronym or abbreviation: SPA

Dept DIS, 36 Fairway, Keyworth, Nottingham,
NG12 5DU

E-mail: info@popastro.com

Website:
http://www.popastro.com

Enquiries:
Enquiries to: Honorary Secretary
Other contacts: Editor Popular Astronomy
Magazine for material for review.

Founded:
1953

Organisation type and purpose:
Membership association (membership is by
subscription), present number of members: 3000.
To encourage the study and understanding of
astronomy, particularly for beginners of all ages
and those who prefer a less technical approach.

Subject coverage:
Astronomy.

Printed publications:
News circulars (6 times a year)
Popular Astronomy (quarterly)

Electronic and video publications:
Electronic News Bulletins (via e-mail, may be
  requested through website)

Access to staff:
Contact by letter and by e-mail
Hours: Mon to Fri, 0900 to 1700
Special comments: Please send sae with postal
enquiries.

Editor:
Popular Astronomy Magazine
  4a Halimote Road, St Dennis, St Austell, PL26
  8BH

SOCIETY FOR POST-MEDIEVAL
ARCHAEOLOGY, THE

Acronym or abbreviation: SPMA

Department of Medieval and Later Antiquities,
British Museum, London, WC1B 3DG

Tel: 0191 482 1037
E-mail: cranstone@btinternet.com

Website:
http://www.spma.org.uk/

Enquiries:
Enquiries to: Honorary Secretary
Direct fax: 0191 487 2343

Founded:
1966

Organisation type and purpose:
Learned society, registered charity (charity number
281651).

Subject coverage:
Archaeology in the period of European and
Colonial history ranging from the close of the
Middle Ages up to the twentieth century.

Printed publications:
Newsletter
Post-Medieval Archaeology (annually)
Monograph series

Access to staff:
Contact by letter, by fax and by e-mail
Hours: Mon to Fri, 0900 to 1700

Links with:
Society for Historical Archaeology
  USA

Other address:
Secretary
  267 Kells Lane, Low Fell, Gateshead, NG9 5HU

SOCIETY FOR PROMOTING
CHRISTIAN KNOWLEDGE

Acronym or abbreviation: SPCK

36 Causton Street, London, SW1P 4ST

Tel: 020 7592 3900
Fax: 020 7592 3939
E-mail: spck@spck.org.uk

Website:
http://www.spck.org.uk
Details of all SPCK's activities and services.

Enquiries:
Enquiries to: General Secretary
Direct e-mail: publicity@spck.org.uk

Founded:
1698

Organisation type and purpose:
Membership association (membership is by
election or invitation), present number of
members: 800, registered charity (charity number
231144), publishing house.
To promote Christian knowledge.

**Museum or gallery collection, archive, or library
special collection:**
Archives of SPCK publications from 1698 (held at
  Cambridge University Library)

Printed publications:
Annual Report

A wide variety of books on church mission and ministry, prayer and meditation, personal growth and relationships, biblical studies and education etc
Order printed publications from: Mail Order, SPCK, 36 Steep Hill, Lincoln, LN2 1LU, tel: 0845 7626747, fax: 01522 534484, e-mail: mailorder@spck.org.uk
SPCK, Holy Trinity Church, Marylebone Road, London, NW1 4DU, tel: 020 7643 0382, fax: 020 7643 0391, e-mail: sales@spck.org.uk

Publications list:
Available in print

Access to staff:
Contact by letter
Hours: Mon to Fri, 0900 to 1700

Subsidiary bodies:
Azure Books
at the same address
Sheldon Press
at the same address
Triangle Books
at the same address

SOCIETY FOR PSYCHICAL RESEARCH

Acronym or abbreviation: SPR

49 Marloes Road, Kensington, London, W8 6LA

Tel: 020 7937 8984
Fax: 020 7937 8984

Website:
http://www.spr.ac.uk

Enquiries:
Enquiries to: Secretary

Founded:
1882

Organisation type and purpose:
International organisation, learned society (membership is by election or invitation), present number of members: 1000, voluntary organisation, registered charity (charity number 207325), suitable for ages: 16+, research organisation. To advance the understanding of events and abilities commonly described as psychic or paranormal, without prejudice and in a scientific manner. Houses one of the largest libraries in Europe of psychic material.

Subject coverage:
Inquiry into the reality and nature of paranormal cognition by means of experiments, and by collecting and analysing accounts of spontaneously occurring incidents that appear to be of this nature. The Society operates without prejudice and can offer no corporate view or opinion.

Museum or gallery collection, archive, or library special collection:
Archival material and rare books

Non-library collection catalogue:
All or part available in-house

Library catalogue:
All or part available in-house

Printed publications:
Journal and Newsletter (quarterly)
Objects and Activities (leaflet)
Proceedings (irregular)

Publications list:
Available online and in print

Access to staff:
Contact by letter, by telephone, by fax and in person. Access for members only. Non-members charged.
Hours: Tue, Wed, Thu, 1300 to 1700 for personal callers

Access to building, collection or gallery:
No prior appointment required
Hours: Library: Tue, Wed, Thu, 1300 to 1700
Special comments: Free to members, no appointment required for access to library.

SOCIETY FOR RENAISSANCE STUDIES

School of Arts, Communication and Culture, Nottingham Trent University, Nottingham, NG11 8NS

Tel: 01158 483020

Website:
http://www2.sas.ac.uk/srs/Default.htm

Enquiries:
Enquiries to: Honorary Secretary
Direct e-mail: claire.jowitt@ntu.ac.uk

Founded:
1967

Organisation type and purpose:
International organisation, learned society (membership is by subscription), present number of members: 800, Registered charity (charity number 1025890). Promotion of Renaissance studies.

Subject coverage:
Art, history, literature and philosophy of the Renaissance.

Printed publications:
Biennial Bulletin (free to members)
Journal (Blackwell, subscription at discount to members)
List of Research Interests of Members
Occasional Papers
Renaissance Studies (journal)
Order printed publications from: Journals Marketing, Blackwell Publishing, 9600 Garsington Road, Oxford OX4 2DQ

Access to staff:
Contact by letter, by telephone, by e-mail and via website
Hours: Mon to Fri, 0900 to 1700

Affiliated to:
Institutes for the Study of the Renaissance
International Federation of Societies

SOCIETY FOR REPRODUCTION & FERTILITY

Acronym or abbreviation: SSF

SRF Business Office, Procon Conferences Ltd, Tattersall House, East Parade, Harrogate, North Yorkshire, HG1 5LT

Tel: 01423 564488
Fax: 01423 701433
E-mail: srfsecretariat@procon-conferences.co.uk

Website:
http://www.srf-reproduction.org/

Enquiries:
Enquiries to: Secretary

Founded:
1950

Organisation type and purpose:
Learned society.

Subject coverage:
Reproductive biology, fertility and infertility in animals and man.

Printed publications:
Newsletter (members only)
Reproduction (journal)

Access to staff:
Contact by letter, by e-mail and via website
Hours: Mon to Fri, 0900 to 1700

SOCIETY FOR RESEARCH IN THE PSYCHOLOGY OF MUSIC AND MUSIC EDUCATION

Acronym or abbreviation: SEMPRE

Institute of Education, 20 Bedford Way, London, WC1H 0AL

Tel: 020 7612 6740

Fax: 020 7612 6741
E-mail: membership@sempre.org.uk

Website:
http://www.srpmme.u-net.com/subs.html

Enquiries:
Enquiries to: Membership Secretary

Founded:
1973

Organisation type and purpose:
Learned society.

Subject coverage:
Psychology of music; music education; music education research; music psychology research; music perception psychology; child development (music); music therapy; social psychology of music.

Printed publications:
Psychology of Music (journal, twice a year)

Access to staff:
Contact by letter
Hours: Mon to Fri, 0900 to 1700

Affiliated to:
International Society for Music Education
UK Council for Music Education and Training

SOCIETY FOR THE HISTORY OF ALCHEMY AND CHEMISTRY

Acronym or abbreviation: SHAC

Applied Sciences, Anglia Ruskin University, East Road, Cambridge, CB1 1PT

Tel: 01223 363271 ext 2380
Fax: 01223 417711
E-mail: jhudson@bridge.anglia.ac.uk

Website:
http://www.open.ac.uk/Arts/HST/SHAC/index.html
How to join the society, Ambix – contents of current issue, forthcoming meetings, members of society's council.

Enquiries:
Enquiries to: Honorary Secretary

Founded:
1937

Organisation type and purpose:
Learned society.

Subject coverage:
History of alchemy and chemistry.

Printed publications:
Ambix (journal, 3 times a year, on subscription)

Access to staff:
Contact by letter, by telephone and by e-mail
Hours: Mon to Fri, 0900 to 1700

SOCIETY FOR THE HISTORY OF NATURAL HISTORY

Acronym or abbreviation: SHNH

c/o Natural History Museum, Cromwell Road, London, SW7 5BD

Tel: 020 7887 5261
Fax: 020 7887 5391
E-mail: secretary@shnh.org

Website:
http://www.shnh.org
Objectives, how to join, publications, council members list, forthcoming meetings, news and updates.

Enquiries:
Enquiries to: Honorary Secretary
Other contacts: Treasurer for sale of publications.

Founded:
1936

continued overleaf

Organisation type and purpose:
Learned society, professional body (membership is
by subscription), present number of members: 650,
registered charity (charity number 210355).
Promotes the study of all branches of the history of
natural history including biographical and
bibliographical studies.

Subject coverage:
History of botany, geology, zoology and other
subjects included in the broad term 'natural
history'.

Printed publications:
Archives of Natural History (3 times a year)
Essai sur la Géographie des Plantes (1807)
   (Alexander von Humboldt, 1959, £5)
Newsletter (2 times a year)
A guide to the official archives of The Natural
   History Museum, London 1998 (Thackray J, £25)
Order printed publications from: Society for the
History of Natural History, c/o Natural History
Museum, Cromwell Road, London, SW7 5BD

Publications list:
Available online

Access to staff:
Contact by letter, by e-mail and via website. Non-
members charged.
Hours: Mon to Fri, 0900 to 1600

Close links with:
The Natural History Museum

SOCIETY FOR THE PROMOTION OF HELLENIC STUDIES

Acronym or abbreviation: SPHS

Senate House, Malet Street, London, WC1E 7HU

Tel: 020 7862 8730
Fax: 020 7862 8731
E-mail: office@hellenicsociety.org.uk

Website:
http://www.hellenicsociety.org.uk

Enquiries:
Enquiries to: Executive Secretary

Founded:
1879

Organisation type and purpose:
Learned society.

Subject coverage:
Greek art, archaeology, architecture, history,
literature, law, politics, religion, philosophy,
language, and science of the Minoan, Mycenaean
and Hellenic world and the Byzantine Empire, and
modern periods.

**Museum or gallery collection, archive, or library
special collection:**
Library which (together with the Institute of
   Classical Studies library) contains some 78,867
   monographs and pamphlets and some 15,592
   bound vols of periodicals. 526 current periodicals
   taken
Slides collection of some 6,500 images
Wood donation of the Diaries of Robert Wood and
   his companions with the sketch books of G. B.
   Borra

Printed publications:
Archaeological Reports (annually)
Journal of Hellenic Studies (annually)
Occasional publications

Publications list:
Available online and in print

Access to staff:
Contact by letter, by telephone and by e-mail.
Access for members only.
Hours: Mon to Fri, 0900 to 1700

Constituent part of:
Hellenic and Roman Societies

Links with:
Institute of Classical Studies Library

SOCIETY FOR THE PROMOTION OF ROMAN STUDIES

Acronym or abbreviation: SPRS

Senate House, Malet Street, London, WC1E 7HU

Tel: 020 7862 8727
Fax: 020 7862 8728
E-mail: office@romansociety.org

Website:
http://icls.sas.ac.uk/library/home.htm
Library information
http://www.romansociety.org
Activities of the Roman Society, including lectures,
grants and publications.

Enquiries:
Enquiries to: Secretary

Founded:
1910

Organisation type and purpose:
Learned society (membership is by subscription),
present number of members: 2,600, registered
charity (charity number 210644).

Subject coverage:
Archaeology, architecture, art, history, language,
religion, philosophy, law, politics, science and
literature of Rome and the Roman Empire to about
AD 700; Roman Britain.

**Museum or gallery collection, archive, or library
special collection:**
Library which (together with the Institute of
   Classical Studies Library) contains some 85,000
   monographs and pamphlets and some 16,000
   bound vols of periodicals. 560 current periodicals
   taken
Slides collection of some 6,700
Wood donation of the diaries of Robert Wood and
   his companions with the sketch-books of G. B.
   Borra

Library catalogue:
All or part available online

Printed publications:
Journal of Roman Studies and Britannia
Monograph Series

Electronic and video publications:
Journal of Roman Studies and Britannia (CD-ROM,
   2002–06, available for purchase by members
   only)

Publications list:
Available online and in print

Access to staff:
Contact by letter, by telephone, by fax, by e-mail
and in person. Access for members only.
Hours: Mon to Fri, 0930 to 1730

Links with:
Co-ordinating Committee for Classics
Fédération Internationale des Études Classiques

SOCIETY FOR THE PROTECTION OF ANCIENT BUILDINGS

Acronym or abbreviation: SPAB

37 Spital Square, London, E1 6DY

Tel: 020 7377 1644
Fax: 020 7247 5296
E-mail: info@spab.org.uk

Website:
http://www.spab.org.uk

Enquiries:
Enquiries to: Archivist
Other contacts: Promotions Officer for media
enquiries

Founded:
1877

Organisation type and purpose:
Advisory body, learned society, membership
association (membership is by subscription),
charitable company (company number 5743962,

charity number 111 3753, Scottish charity number
SC 039244), suitable for ages: adults, training
organisation, publishing house.

Subject coverage:
Repair and protection of historic buildings,
building conservation in general.

**Museum or gallery collection, archive, or library
special collection:**
Manuscript archive of society's work since 1877,
   about 15,000 files available to researchers by
   appointment, mills cases held by Mills Archive
   Trust, Reading

Library catalogue:
All or part available in-house

Printed publications:
Quarterly magazine (members only)
SPAB technical pamphlets
SPAB information sheets
A range of publications on building conservation
   and preservation are available from the Society

Publications list:
Available online and in print

Access to staff:
Contact by letter, by telephone, by e-mail and via
website. Appointment necessary.
Hours: Technical Helpline: Mon to Fri, 0930 to 1230
Special comments: Archivist is part-time.

Access to building, collection or gallery:
No prior appointment required
Hours: 0930 to 1730

SOCIETY FOR THE PROTECTION OF ANIMALS ABROAD

Acronym or abbreviation: SPANA

14 John Street, London, WC1N 2EB

Tel: 020 7831 3999
Fax: 020 7831 5999
E-mail: hq@spana.org

Website:
http://www.spana.org

Enquiries:
Enquiries to: Chief Executive

Founded:
1923

Organisation type and purpose:
International organisation, advisory body,
professional body (membership is by election or
invitation), present number of members: 192,
voluntary organisation, registered charity (charity
number 209015). Aims to improve standards of
animal care wherever the need arises.

Access to staff:
Contact by letter, by telephone, by fax, by e-mail
and via website
Hours: Mon to Fri, 0900 to 1700

Members of:
IUCN

SOCIETY FOR THE PROTECTION OF UNBORN CHILDREN

Acronym or abbreviation: SPUC

3 Whitacre Mews, Stannary Street, London, SE11
4AB

Tel: 020 7091 7091
Fax: 020 7820 3131
E-mail: information@spuc.org.uk

Website:
http://www.spuc.org.uk
Information on abortion, euthanasia, foetal
development, pro-life campaigns, embryo
research, etc.

Enquiries:
Enquiries to: General Secretary
Direct e-mail: paultully@spuc.org.uk

Other contacts: Regional development officers for provision of educational services to schools, voluntary groups etc

Founded:
1966

Organisation type and purpose:
National organisation, membership association (membership is by subscription), present number of members: 46,000, voluntary organisation, suitable for ages: 12+, research organisation. Parliamentary lobby group.
To affirm, defend and promote the existance and value of human life from the moment of conception, and to defend and protect human life especially in the areas of abortion, handicap, euthanasia, embryo experiments and population control. To examine existing or proposed laws, legislation or regulations relating to abortion and to support or oppose such as appropriate.

Subject coverage:
Abortion, human pre-natal development, abortion side-effects, social effects of abortion legislation, handicap, eugenics, euthanasia, infertility treatment and research, human embryo experimentation and population control, cloning, abortifacients (morning after pill, RU486, 'emergency contraception'), mental incapacity legislation, post-abortion syndrome.

Museum or gallery collection, archive, or library special collection:
Press cuttings and parliamentary debates, questions, speeches etc relating to abortion, euthanasia, embryo research

Printed publications:
Pro-Life Times (journal, every other month, 25p)
SPUC – Our Aims, Ethics and Activities (50p)

Electronic and video publications:
Video and audio tapes relating to various of the subjects listed

Publications list:
Available in print

Access to staff:
Contact by letter, by telephone, by fax, by e-mail and via website. Appointment necessary.
Hours: Mon to Fri, 0900 to 1730

Access to building, collection or gallery:
Prior appointment required

Access for disabled people:
Parking provided, ramped entry, level entry, access to all public areas, toilet facilities

Affiliated to:
International Right to Life Federation
  Via Niccolò V 44, 00165 Rome, Italy

Associated with:
SPUC Educational Research Trust
  address as the SPUC

Subsidiary body:
British Victims of Abortion
  tel: 0141 226 5407

SOCIETY FOR THE PROTECTION OF UNBORN CHILDREN – SCOTLAND

Acronym or abbreviation: SPUC Scotland

75 Bothwell Street, Glasgow, G2 6TS

Tel: 0141 221 2094
Fax: 0141 225 3696
E-mail: info@spucscotland.org

Website:
http://spucscotland.org/

Enquiries:
Enquiries to: Director
Other contacts: Development Officer for matters to do with branches.

Organisation type and purpose:
Membership association (membership is by subscription), present number of members: 4500, voluntary organisation.
The protection of all human life from conception to natural death.

Subject coverage:
Abortion, cloning, euthanasia.

Printed publications:
Pro-Life Times (4 page magazine, once every other month)
Various information leaflets

Electronic and video publications:
Videos and Tapes on Abortion, Cloning, Euthanasia, Population

Access to staff:
Contact by letter, by telephone, by fax, by e-mail and in person. Appointment necessary.
Hours: Mon to Fri, 0900 to 1700

Access to building, collection or gallery:
No prior appointment required

SOCIETY FOR THE SOCIAL HISTORY OF MEDICINE

Acronym or abbreviation: SSHM

Department of History, University of Aberdeen, Aberdeen, AB24 3FX

Tel: 01224 272456
Fax: 01224 272203
E-mail: o.walsh@abdn.ac.uk

Website:
http://www.sshm.org

Enquiries:
Enquiries to: Honorary Secretary
Direct tel: 01224 273884

Founded:
1970

Organisation type and purpose:
Learned society (membership is by subscription), registered charity (charity number 278414).

Subject coverage:
Social history of medicine; history of health care and policy.

Printed publications:
Guide to Members' Research and Interests (1995, new edition in preparation)
Social History of Medicine (journal, 3 times a year, Oxford Journals)
Studies in the Social History of Medicine (Book Series, pub Routledge, variable number of publications a year)

Access to staff:
Contact by letter, by telephone, by fax, by e-mail and via website
Hours: Mon to Fri, 0900 to 1700

SOCIETY FOR THEATRE RESEARCH

Acronym or abbreviation: STR

The Theatre Museum, 1E Tavistock Street, London, WC2E 7PR

E-mail: e.cottis@btinternet.com

Website:
http://www.str.org.uk
Prospectus information, list of current lectures, list of members' research interests, online research award form.

Enquiries:
Enquiries to: Honorary Secretary
Direct e-mail: e.cottis@btinternet.com

Founded:
1948

Organisation type and purpose:
Learned society (membership is by subscription), present number of members: 750, registered charity (charity number 266186), publishing house.

Subject coverage:
History and technique of the British theatre, and allied entertainments.

Museum or gallery collection, archive, or library special collection:
The Society's library was amalgamated with that of the Theatre Museum in 1987

Printed publications:
Theatre Notebook (journal, 3 issues per annual volume)
Publications include Journals and Memoirs, Biographies, books on Stage Conditions, on Theatres, Reference Books and others.

Publications list:
Available online and in print

Access to staff:
Contact by letter, by e-mail and via website
Hours: Not applicable

Also at:
Society for Theatre Research
  PO Box 3214, Brighton, BN2 1LU

Institutional Friends member of:
Theatres Advisory Council (TAC)
Theatres Trust

SOCIETY FOR UNDERWATER TECHNOLOGY

Acronym or abbreviation: SUT

80 Coleman Street, London, EC2R 5BJ

Tel: 020 7382 2601
Fax: 020 7382 2684
E-mail: info@sut.org

Website:
http://www.sut.org.uk
General information about SUT.

Enquiries:
Enquiries to: Executive Secretary
Other contacts: Press and Publications Officer for media or publications enquiries.

Founded:
1966

Organisation type and purpose:
International organisation, learned society (membership is by subscription), present number of members: 1600, registered charity (charity number 256659).
Multidisciplinary learned society bringing together individuals and organisations from industry, government and academia with a common interest in underwater technology, marine science and engineering.

Subject coverage:
Marine science and technology applied to: submersible robotic design and operation, diving technology and physiology, scientific diving, underwater acoustics, subsea engineering systems and operations, naval architecture and offshore structures, environmental forces, offshore site investigation, ocean resources, marine pollution and environment, marine biology and archaeology, oceanography, instrumentation, education and training.

Museum or gallery collection, archive, or library special collection:
SUT reference material lodged in the IMarE Marine Information centre

Printed publications:
Advances in Underwater Technology, Ocean Science and Offshore Engineering (conference proceedings series, 34 volumes)
Oceans of Opportunity (careers information pack)
Other collected papers and conference proceedings
SUT News (newsletter, 8 times a year)
Underwater Technology (journal, quarterly)

continued overleaf

Electronic and video publications:
Oceans of Opportunities (careers video, £6
including p&p)

Access to staff:
Contact by letter, by fax, by e-mail and via
website
Hours: Mon to Fri, 0900 to 1700

Other addresses:
Aberdeen Office
 Innovation Centre, Exploration Drive, Offshore
 Technology Park, Bridge of Don, Aberdeen,
 AB23 8GX; tel: 01224 823637; fax: 01224 820236
Southampton branch
 Southampton Oceanography Centre, Empress
 Dock, Southampton

Parent body for:
Underwater Science Group

SOCIETY OF AFGHAN RESIDENTS IN THE UK

Acronym or abbreviation: SAR

West Acton Community Centre, Churchill
Gardens, Acton, London, W3 0JN

Tel: 020 8993 8168
Fax: 020 8993 2129

Enquiries:
Enquiries to: Chairman
Direct tel: 07947 777705
Direct e-mail: saruk@btconnect.com

Founded:
1982

Organisation type and purpose:
National organisation, advisory body, membership
association (membership is by subscription,
qualification, election or invitation), present
number of members: 700, voluntary organisation,
registered charity (charity number 800460), public
library.
Refugee community organisation.

Subject coverage:
Housing, health, law, welfare benefits,
immigration, education, employment.

**Museum or gallery collection, archive, or library
special collection:**
Press cuttings relevant to Afghanistan

Printed publications:
Annual Report
Introductory leaflet
Magazine in Pashto/Dari languages (monthly, 60
pp)

Access to staff:
Contact by letter, by telephone, by fax, by e-mail
and in person
Hours: Mon to Fri, 0900 to 1600

Access to building, collection or gallery:
Mon to Fri, 0900 to 1600

Access for disabled people:
Hours: Mon to Fri, 0900 to 1600

Other address:
Offices in Birmingham, Harrow and Northampton

SOCIETY OF ANTIQUARIES OF LONDON

Burlington House, Piccadilly, London, W1J 0BE

Tel: 020 7734 0193
Fax: 020 7287 6967
E-mail: library@sal.org.uk

Website:
http://www.sal.org.uk
Brief details of organisation. Link to on-line
catalogue of printed books acquired since 1988.

Enquiries:
Enquiries to: Librarian
Direct tel: 020 7479 7084

Founded:
1707

Organisation type and purpose:
Learned society.

Subject coverage:
Archaeology; architectural history; British
topography; art history mostly of decorative arts;
heraldry; history (mainly British).

**Museum or gallery collection, archive, or library
special collection:**
Broadsides, proclamations, Civil War tracts
Incunabula
Jackson Collection (Wiltshire)
Manuscripts, photographs and portraits
Prattinton Collection (Worcestershire)
Prints and drawings (18th and 19th centuries)
Rubbings of all the pre-1700 monumental brasses
 in Britain
Willson Collection (Lincolnshire)

Library catalogue:
All or part available online

Printed publications:
Antiquaries Journal
Archaeologia
Occasional Papers
Reports of the Research Committee

Microform publications:
Medieval and Renaissance Manuscripts from the
 Society of Antiquaries of London (research
 publications)

Access to staff:
Contact by letter, by telephone, by fax and by e-
mail. Appointment necessary.
Hours: Mon to Fri, 1000 to 1700
Special comments: Closed August.

SOCIETY OF ANTIQUARIES OF NEWCASTLE UPON TYNE

The Black Gate, Castle Garth, Newcastle upon
Tyne, NE1 1RQ

Tel: 0191 261 5390
E-mail: socantiqs@nc.ac.uk

Enquiries:
Enquiries to: Membership Secretary

Founded:
1813

Organisation type and purpose:
Learned society (membership is by subscription),
present number of members: 750, registered
charity (charity number 230888).

Subject coverage:
History and archaeology of Durham,
Northumberland and Newcastle upon Tyne.

**Museum or gallery collection, archive, or library
special collection:**
Library of some 30,000 volumes

Non-library collection catalogue:
All or part available in-house

Library catalogue:
All or part available in-house

Printed publications:
Archaeologia Aeliana (the Society's journal,
 annually)
Newsletter (twice a year)
Guidebooks
Monograph series
Excavations at South Shields Roman Fort Vol 1
 (Bidwell P and Speak S, 1994, £35)
Newcastle Chamberlains' Accounts 1508–1511 (ed
 Fraser C M, 1986 £5)
Whisky Smuggling on the Border (Philipson J,
 1991, £1.50)

Publications list:
Available online and in print

Access to staff:
Contact by letter, by telephone and by fax.
Appointment necessary.

Hours: Library: Wed, 1400 to 1600; Thu, 1700 to
1900; Sat, 1000 to 1200: answerphone at other times
Special comments: Many stairs and no lift.

Links with:
The Literary and Philosophical Society of
Newcastle upon Tyne
 23 Westgate Road, Newcastle upon Tyne, NE1
 1SE; tel: 0191 232 0192

SOCIETY OF ANTIQUARIES OF SCOTLAND

Royal Museum, Chambers Street, Edinburgh, EH1
1JF

Tel: 0131 247 4115
Fax: 0131 247 4163
E-mail: f.ashmore@nms.ac.uk

Website:
http://www.socantscot.org
Introduction to the Society, grant information,
publications and Fellow information.

Enquiries:
Enquiries to: Director
Other contacts: Publications Assistant for
monograph sales and publicity.

Founded:
1780

Organisation type and purpose:
Learned society (membership is by election or
invitation), present number of members: 3500,
registered charity (charity number SC010240).

Subject coverage:
History and archaeology of Scotland.

**Museum or gallery collection, archive, or library
special collection:**
Archaeologia Scotica (irregularly from the Society's
 foundation until 1851)

Library catalogue:
All or part available in-house

Printed publications:
Monograph series (irregularly from 1982 to date)
Proceedings of the Society of Antiquaries of
 Scotland (annually from 1855 to date)
Order printed publications from: Publications
Administrator, Society of Antiquaries of Scotland
at the same address, tel: 0131 247 4145, e-mail: r
.lancaster@nms.ac.uk

Publications list:
Available online and in print

Access to staff:
Contact by letter and by telephone. Appointment
necessary.
Hours: Mon to Fri, 0900 to 1700
Special comments: Staff work part time – office may
be unsupervised at certain times.

SOCIETY OF ARCHER-ANTIQUARIES

Acronym or abbreviation: SAA

29 Batley Court, Oldland, South Gloucestershire,
BS30 8YZ

Tel: 0117 932 3276
Fax: 0117 932 3276
E-mail: bogaman@btinternet.com

Website:
http://www.societyofarcher-antiquaries.org

Enquiries:
Enquiries to: Honorary Secretary

Founded:
1956

Organisation type and purpose:
International organisation, learned society
(membership is by subscription), present number
of members: 350, registered charity, consultancy,
research organisation.

Subject coverage:
General and specialised information on the history of archery, Asiatic archery, English archery, crossbows, Middle Eastern archery, ethnographical archery, literature and constructional information, bowery, fletchery, legends and practices.

Museum or gallery collection, archive, or library special collection:
Library and display room

Non-library collection catalogue:
All or part available in-house

Library catalogue:
All or part available in-house

Printed publications:
A Guide to the Crossbow
Journal of the Society of Archer-Antiquaries
Arrowhead (newsletter booklet)

Access to staff:
Contact by letter, by telephone and via website. Appointment necessary.
Hours: Mon to Fri, 1800 to 2000; Sat, Sun, 1000 to 1800

Access to building, collection or gallery:
Prior appointment required
Hours: Two Sundays a year

Access for disabled people:
Special comments: Limited disabled access.

Associated with:
HM Armories, Leeds
Royal Toxophilite Society
Simon Foundation at Manchester University

SOCIETY OF ARCHIVISTS

Acronym or abbreviation: SOA

Prioryfield House, 20 Canon Street, Taunton, Somerset, TA1 1SW

Tel: 01823 327030
Fax: 01823 271719
E-mail: societyofarchivists@archives.org.uk

Website:
http://www.archives.org.uk
Society web page.

Enquiries:
Enquiries to: Executive Secretary

Founded:
1947

Organisation type and purpose:
Professional body (charity number 1041063).

Subject coverage:
Archives, records management, archives conservation.

Printed publications:
Journal (2 times a year)
Newsletter (monthly)
Members of the Society mailing only

Publications list:
Available online and in print

Access to staff:
Contact by letter, by telephone, by fax and by e-mail. Appointment necessary.
Hours: Mon to Fri, 0830 to 1630

Affiliated to:
International Council on Archives

SOCIETY OF AUTHORS

Acronym or abbreviation: SOA

84 Drayton Gardens, London, SW10 9SB

Tel: 020 7373 6642
Fax: 020 7373 5768
E-mail: info@societyofauthors.org

Website:
http://www.societyofauthors.org
Information about membership benefits, information for interest groups within the Society.

Enquiries:
Enquiries to: General Secretary

Founded:
1884

Organisation type and purpose:
Trade union.

Subject coverage:
Specialist groups within the Society serve the needs of broadcasters, literary translators, educational writers, medical writers, children's writers, information also on literary agents, publishers, royalties, contracts, authors' rights, public lending right.

Printed publications:
Quick Guides (on topics such as copyright and libel)
The Author (quarterly, £35 a year; free to members)

Publications list:
Available online and in print

Access to staff:
Contact by e-mail and via website. Appointment necessary. Access for members only. Letter of introduction required.
Hours: Mon to Thu, 0930 to 1730; Fri, 0930 to 1700

Member of:
British Copyright Council
European Writers Congress
International Confederation of Societies of Authors and Composers
National Book Committee

SOCIETY OF BOOKBINDERS

Acronym or abbreviation: SOB

2 Lower Faircox, Henfield, West Sussex, BN5 9UT

Tel: 01273 491811
E-mail: nat.secretary@societyofbookbinders.com

Website:
http://www.societyofbookbinders.com
All information appertaining to the Society of Bookbinders re: national and regional organisation and events, education and training information, exhibitions of members' work.

Enquiries:
Enquiries to: Honorary Secretary
Other contacts: Membership Secretary for membership enquiries

Founded:
1974

Organisation type and purpose:
Professional body, trade association, membership association (membership is by subscription), present number of members: 650, registered charity (charity number 1032108), training organisation.

Subject coverage:
All information appertaining to bookbinding.

Printed publications:
Bookbinder (journal, annually)
Educational Leaflets
National Newsletters
Order printed publications from: Society of Bookbinders
Little Broxham, Four Elms Road, Four Elms, Kent, TN8 6LR, e-mail: publications@ societyofbookbinders.com

Publications list:
Available online

Access to staff:
Contact by letter, by telephone, by e-mail and via website
Hours: Mon to Fri, 1000 to 1600

Access to building, collection or gallery:
No access other than to staff

Membership Secretary:
Society of Bookbinders
102 Hetherington Road, Shepperton, Middlesex, TW17 0SW; tel: 01746 763896; e-mail: membership@societyofbookbinders.com

SOCIETY OF BORDER LEICESTER SHEEP BREEDERS

Greenend, St Boswells, Melrose, Roxburghshire, TD6 9ES

Tel: 01835 824207
Fax: 01835 824207
E-mail: info@borderleicesters.co.uk

Website:
http://www.borderleicesters.co.uk
Facts and history of Border Leicester Sheep.

Enquiries:
Enquiries to: Membership Secretary

Founded:
1900

Organisation type and purpose:
Membership association (membership is by subscription), present number of members: 250, registered charity (charity number SCO 00011). Pedigree sheep breeding.

Subject coverage:
Border Leicester Sheep Society, pedigree information and records.

Printed publications:
For members only

Publications list:
Available in print

Access to staff:
Contact by letter, by telephone, by fax and in person
Hours: Mon to Fri, 0800 to 2100

Access to building, collection or gallery:
No access other than to staff

SOCIETY OF BOTANICAL ARTISTS

Acronym or abbreviation: SBA

1 Knapp Cottages, Wyke, Gillingham, Dorset, SP8 4NQ

Tel: 01747 825718
Fax: 01747 826835

Website:
http://www.society-botanical-artists.org

Enquiries:
Enquiries to: Executive Secretary
Direct tel: 01747 852718
Direct e-mail: pam@soc-botanical-artists.org

Founded:
1985

Organisation type and purpose:
International organisation, professional body (membership is by election or invitation), present number of members: 190, registered charity (charity number 1047162).
Publicising and educating the public about botanical painting.

Subject coverage:
Botanical painting.

Printed publications:
Annual exhibition catalogue
The Art of Botanical Painting

Access to staff:
Contact by letter, by telephone and by fax. Appointment necessary.
Hours: Mon to Fri, 0900 to 1700

Access for disabled people:
Ramped entry, access to all public areas, toilet facilities

SOCIETY OF BRITISH AEROSPACE COMPANIES LIMITED

Acronym or abbreviation: SBAC

Salamanca Square, 9 Albert Embankment, London, SE1 7SP

Tel: 020 70914500
Fax: 020 7091 4545
E-mail: post@sbac.co.uk

Website:
http://www.sbac.co.uk

Founded:
1916

Organisation type and purpose:
Trade association (membership is by subscription), present number of members: 180 direct members.
To represent and promote the whole of the UK aerospace industry.

Subject coverage:
UK aerospace industry, standards, airworthiness requirements, Farnborough International Exhibition and Flying Display, research and development, best practice, lobbying matters, co-ordinates United Kingdom participation at aerospace exhibitions overseas, promotes (within the DTI) high level trade missions overseas.

Trade and statistical information:
United Kingdom aerospace statistics.

Printed publications:
Annual Aerospace Statistics
Annual Reports

Electronic and video publications:
What's New in UK Aerospace
Membership capabilities (CD-ROM from SBAC)

Access to staff:
Contact by e-mail
Hours: Mon to Fri, 0915 to 1730

Key Sectorial Group:
British Airports Group (BAG)

SOCIETY OF BRITISH GAS INDUSTRIES

Acronym or abbreviation: SBGI

36 Holly Walk, Leamington Spa, Warwickshire, CV32 4LY

Tel: 01926 334357
Fax: 01926 450459
E-mail: mail@sbgi.org.uk

Website:
http://www.gasjobs.org.uk
An online job search facility for the gas industry.
http://www.sbgi.org.uk
Comprehensive list of products and services supplied by members. Information on forthcoming events in the United Kingdom and overseas. Useful contact details and relevant industry news.

Enquiries:
Enquiries to: Director

Founded:
1905

Organisation type and purpose:
Trade association (membership is by subscription), present number of members: 170 companies.

Subject coverage:
Gas industry, products and services providers, manufacturers and contractors, gas suppliers/shippers and transporters.

Printed publications:
Directory of Products and Services (annual, free)
Gas Business (journal, quarterly, free)
Review of Activities (annual, free)

Access to staff:
Contact by letter, by telephone, by fax, by e-mail and via website
Hours: Mon to Fri, 0900 to 1700

SOCIETY OF BRITISH WATER & WASTEWATER INDUSTRIES

Acronym or abbreviation: SBWWI

38 Holly Walk, Leamington Spa, Warwickshire, CV32 4HY

Tel: 01926 831530
Fax: 01926 831931
E-mail: hq@sbwwi.co.uk

Website:
http://www.sbwwi.co.uk

Enquiries:
Enquiries to: Executive Director

Founded:
1986

Organisation type and purpose:
Trade association (membership is by subscription, election or invitation), present number of members: 70 companies.
A forum for UK manufacturers and contractors who supply the water industry.
Water industry specific, disseminates information, liaises with water companies and other bodies to help members serve the industry better.

Subject coverage:
Product standards and approval, regulations, training, product suppliers, contractor services providers.

Museum or gallery collection, archive, or library special collection:
OFWAT Reports
Water industry standards

Printed publications:
A Decade of British Service to Water Companies 1986–1996
Directory of Products and Services (free)

Access to staff:
Contact by letter, by telephone, by fax, by e-mail and via website
Hours: Mon to Fri, 0900 to 1700

Affiliated to:
Euro-Automatic Meter Reading Association (E-AMRA)
    tel: 01926 330935; fax: 01926 330935; e-mail: hq@e-amra.com
Utility Contractors Associations Federation (UCAF)

SOCIETY OF CABLE TELECOMMUNICATION ENGINEERS

Acronym or abbreviation: SCTE

Fulton House Business Centre, Fulton Road, Wembley Park, Middlesex, HA9 0TF

Tel: 020 8902 8998
Fax: 020 8903 8719
E-mail: office@scte.org.uk

Website:
http://www.scte.org.uk

Enquiries:
Enquiries to: Secretary

Founded:
1945

Organisation type and purpose:
Learned society.

Subject coverage:
Cable telecommunications.

Printed publications:
Cable Telecommunication Engineering
Broadband
Members Handbook

Access to staff:
Appointment necessary.
Hours: Mon to Fri, 0900 to 1700

SOCIETY OF COLLEGE, NATIONAL AND UNIVERSITY LIBRARIES

Acronym or abbreviation: SCONUL

102 Euston Street, London, NW1 2HA

Tel: 020 7387 0317
Fax: 020 7383 3197
E-mail: info@sconul.ac.uk

Website:
http://www.sconul.ac.uk

Enquiries:
Enquiries to: Secretary

Founded:
1950

Organisation type and purpose:
International organisation, professional body.

Subject coverage:
British academic libraries; advisory committees on: buildings, copyright, health services, information systems and services, performance indicators, publications, scholarly communication, staffing.

Trade and statistical information:
Data on funding and activities of university libraries.

Printed publications:
Annual Library Statistics
Performance indicators for university libraries: a practical guide
The management of integrated Learning Resources
SCONUL Annual Review
Working papers on a range of topics including:
Architects' briefs
Development plans
Management issues: finance, general concerns, in-house research, staff
Staff development and appraisal, training

Publications list:
Available online and in print

Access to staff:
Contact by letter, by telephone, by fax, by e-mail and via website. Appointment necessary.
Hours: Mon to Fri, 0900 to 1700

SOCIETY OF CONSULTING MARINE ENGINEERS AND SHIP SURVEYORS

Acronym or abbreviation: SCMS

202 Lambeth Road, London, SE1 7JW

Tel: 020 7261 0869
Fax: 020 7261 0871
E-mail: sec@scmshq.org

Website:
http://www.scmshq.org

Enquiries:
Enquiries to: Secretary

Founded:
1920

Organisation type and purpose:
Learned society.
An MCA appointed certifying authority.

Subject coverage:
The interests of consulting engineers, naval architects and ship surveyors; shipbuilding, maritime authorities' activities.

Printed publications:
List of Members (annually)

Access to staff:
Contact by letter, by telephone, by fax and by e-mail
Hours: Mon to Fri, 0900 to 1700

Access to building, collection or gallery:
Prior appointment required

SOCIETY OF COSMETIC SCIENTISTS

Acronym or abbreviation: SCS

GT House, 24–26 Rothesay Road, Luton, Bedfordshire, LU1 1QX

Tel: 01582 726661
Fax: 01582 405217
E-mail: ifscc.scs@btconnect.com

Website:
http://www.scs.org.uk

Enquiries:
Enquiries to: Secretary-General

Founded:
1948

Organisation type and purpose:
Learned society.

Subject coverage:
Cosmetic science.

Printed publications:
International Journal of Cosmetic Science (6 times a year)

Access to staff:
Contact by letter, by telephone, by fax and by e-mail
Hours: Mon to Fri, 0900 to 1700

Affiliated to, and providing the secretariat for, the:
International Federation of Societies of Cosmetic Chemists
    tel: 01582 726661; fax: 01582 405217; e-mail: ifscc.scs@btconnect.com

SOCIETY OF DAIRY TECHNOLOGY

Acronym or abbreviation: SDT

PO Box 12, Appleby in Westmorland, CA16 6HH

Tel: 01768 354034
Fax: 01768 352546
E-mail: execdirector@sdt.org

Website:
http://www.sdt.org

Enquiries:
Enquiries to: Executive Director

Founded:
1943

Organisation type and purpose:
Learned society (membership is by election or invitation), present number of members: 580, registered charity (charity number 1081615). Education, training and information transfer in dairy sciences and technology.

Subject coverage:
Dairy science, dairy technology and dairy research, including husbandry, engineering and education.

Printed publications:
International Journal of Dairy Technology (quarterly)
7 Technical publications/manuals include:
CIP: Cleaning in Place (2nd ed., 1990)
Membership of the Society of Dairy Technology
Cream Processing Manual (2nd ed.)
Milk Fat: Production, Technology and Utilization (1991)
Milk and Whey Powders (1980)
Pasteurizing Plant Manual (1983)
Short-Shelf-Life Products (1986)
The UK Milk Marketing Boards: A Concise History

Publications list:
Available online and in print

Access to staff:
Contact by letter, by telephone, by fax, by e-mail and via website
Hours: Mon to Fri, 0900 to 1700

Access to building, collection or gallery:
No access other than to staff

SOCIETY OF DESIGNER CRAFTSMEN

Acronym or abbreviation: SDC

24 Rivington Street, London, EC2A 3DU

Tel: 020 7739 3663
Fax: 020 7739 3663
E-mail: info@societyofdesignercraftsmen.org.uk

Website:
http://www.societyofdesignercraftsmen.org.uk/

Enquiries:
Enquiries to: Hon. Secretary
Other contacts: Carol Naylor for Chairman.

Founded:
1888

Organisation type and purpose:
National organisation, advisory body, membership association (membership is by election or invitation), present number of members: 750, registered charity (charity number 328202), training organisation, consultancy.

Subject coverage:
Information on contemporary practitioners in the following crafts: basketry, calligraphy, ceramics, furniture-making, glass-engraving, jewellery, lettering, metalwork, printmaking, sculpture, silversmithing, stained glass making, textiles, toymaking, woodworking.

Museum or gallery collection, archive, or library special collection:
Archives of the Arts and Crafts Exhibition Society and the Society of Designer Craftsmen, housed at the Victoria and Albert Museum

Printed publications:
Exhibition Catalogues
Newsletters (5 times a year, for members)

Access to staff:
Contact by letter, by telephone and by e-mail.
Appointment necessary. Access for members only.
Hours: Mon, Wed, Fri, 1400 to 1700

Access to building, collection or gallery:
Prior appointment required

Access for disabled people:
Level entry

Founded in 1888 by:
William Morris and Walter Crane

SOCIETY OF EDITORS

University Centre, Granta Place, Mill Lane, Cambridge, CB2 1RU

Tel: 01223 304080
Fax: 01223 304090
E-mail: info@societyofeditors.org

Website:
http://www.societyofeditors.org

Enquiries:
Enquiries to: Executive Director
Other contacts: Administrator for administrative matters

Founded:
1946

Organisation type and purpose:
Professional body, over 400 members.
The Society has members in local, regional and national newspapers, magazines, broadcasting, new media, journalism education and media law. The Society provides collective consultation and representation.

Subject coverage:
Collective consultation and representation on all matters of editorial concern including editorial freedom, independence, standards and training, legislation concerning the media. Provision of contacts for media consultancy.

Access to staff:
Contact by letter, by telephone, by fax, by e-mail and via website

Hours: Office hours and 24-hour contact

Access to building, collection or gallery:
No access other than to staff

SOCIETY OF ENGINEERS (INCORPORATED)

Acronym or abbreviation: SOE

Guinea Wiggs, Nayland, Colchester, Essex, CO6 4NF

Tel: 01206 263332
Fax: 01206 262624
E-mail: chiefexecutive@society-of-engineers.org.uk

Website:
http://www.society-of-engineers.org.uk
Details of membership, awards, exams, etc.

Enquiries:
Enquiries to: Chief Executive

Founded:
1854

Organisation type and purpose:
International organisation, professional body (membership is by qualification and experience). To promote the interests of multi-disciplinary engineers worldwide and to provide a forum for discussion; to examine engineers in art and science to ensure that they can apply their theoretical knowledge to practical situations.

Subject coverage:
All branches of civil, electrical and mechanical engineering.

Printed publications:
Engineering World (journal, quarterly)
Membership and exam information
Publications list available

Access to staff:
Contact by letter, by telephone, by fax and by e-mail
Hours: Mon to Thurs, 0900 to 1730

SOCIETY OF ENVIRONMENTAL ENGINEERS

Acronym or abbreviation: SEE

The Manor House, High Street, Buntingford, Hertfordshire, SG9 9AB

Tel: 01763 271209
Fax: 01763 273255
E-mail: office@environmental.org.uk

Website:
http://www.environmental.org.uk

Enquiries:
Enquiries to: Chief Executive

Founded:
1959

Organisation type and purpose:
Learned society.
Licensed Member of the Engineering Council (UK).

Subject coverage:
Climatic contamination control, packaging, vibration shock and noise product assurance and reliability, electromagnetic compatibility.

Printed publications:
Environmental Engineering (quarterly)
Proceedings of Symposia
Test House Directory

Access to staff:
Contact by e-mail
Hours: Mon to Fri, 0900 to 1700

Access to building, collection or gallery:
No access other than to staff

Access for disabled people:
Ramped entry, toilet facilities

SOCIETY OF EVENT ORGANISERS

Acronym or abbreviation: SEO

29a Market Square, Biggleswade, Bedfordshire,
SG18 8AQ

Tel: 01767 316255
Fax: 01767 316430

Website:
http://www.seoevent.co.uk

Enquiries:
Enquiries to: Manager

Founded:
1996

Organisation type and purpose:
Trade association.

Subject coverage:
The running of events.

Printed publications:
Newsletters (email, free)

SOCIETY OF FLORISTRY LIMITED

Acronym or abbreviation: SOF

Meadowside, Hall Road, West Bergholt,
Colchester, Essex, CO6 3DU

Tel: 0870 241 0432
Fax: 0870 241 0432
E-mail: info@societyoffloristry.org

Enquiries:
Enquiries to: Secretary

Founded:
1951

Organisation type and purpose:
Professional body (membership is by subscription,
qualification), present number of members: 1164.
A non-profit making organisation, founded with
the sole purpose of raising the standards of
floristry worldwide.

Subject coverage:
Professional floristry, careers information.

Printed publications:
Please enquire for publication details

Publications list:
Available in print

Access to staff:
Contact by letter, by telephone and by fax
Hours: Mon to Fri, 0900 to 1300

SOCIETY OF FOOD HYGIENE TECHNOLOGY, THE

Acronym or abbreviation: SOFHT

The Granary, Middleton House Farm, Tamworth
Road, Middleton, Staffs, B78 2BD

Tel: 01827 872500
Fax: 01827 875800
E-mail: admin@sofht.co.uk

Website:
http://www.sofht.co.uk
Full details of the Society, its activities, publications
and membership.

Enquiries:
Enquiries to: Administrator
Direct e-mail: claudetteschlitter@sofht.co.uk

Founded:
1979

Organisation type and purpose:
Learned society (membership is by subscription),
present number of members: 750.
Dedicated to improving food hygiene and safety
within the food industry.

Subject coverage:
Food hygiene, hygiene technology, hygiene
training, food technology, food science, food safety.

Printed publications:
Hygiene in Focus Technical Manual (free to
members, £52.50 non members)
Magazine (3 times a year)

Publications list:
Available online and in print

Access to staff:
Contact by letter, by telephone, by fax, by e-mail
and via website
Hours: Mon to Fri, 0900 to 1700

Access to building, collection or gallery:
No access other than to staff

SOCIETY OF GARDEN DESIGNERS

Acronym or abbreviation: SGD

Katepwa House, Ashfield Park Avenue, Ross-on-
Wye, Herefordshire, HR9 5AX

Tel: 01989 566695
Fax: 01989 567676
E-mail: info@sgd.org.uk

Website:
http://www.sgd.org.uk

Enquiries:
Enquiries to: Administrator

Founded:
1981

Organisation type and purpose:
Professional body.
Promotion of professional standards in garden
design.

Subject coverage:
Garden design, accreditation of garden designers,
information about journal, visits, events organised
by society (some open to public).

Printed publications:
Garden Design Journal (10 a year, £6 per copy)
Register of Designers and their Profiles (free)

Publications list:
Available online

Access to staff:
Contact by letter, by telephone, by fax, by e-mail
and via website

Access to building, collection or gallery:
Prior appointment required
Hours: Mon to Fri, 0900 to 1700 (closed bank
holidays)

Links with:
Royal Horticultural Society

SOCIETY OF GENEALOGISTS

Acronym or abbreviation: SoG

14 Charterhouse Buildings, Goswell Road,
London, EC1M 7BA

Tel: 020 7251 8799
Fax: 020 7250 1800
E-mail: info@sog.org.uk

Website:
http://www.sog.org.uk
http://www.britishorigins.net
Indexes and genealogical data
http://www.findmypast.com/home.jsp
Indexes and genealogical data

Enquiries:
Enquiries to: Librarian
Direct tel: 020 7702 5485
Direct e-mail: library@sog.org.uk
Other contacts: Genealogy Officer

Founded:
1911

Organisation type and purpose:
Learned society, present number of members:
c.13,000, registered charity (charity number
233701), training organisation, publishing house.

Educational Charity.
To promote and encourage the study of genealogy
and heraldry.

Subject coverage:
Genealogy, biography, family history, heraldry,
history and topography world-wide, but with
emphasis on Great Britain, Ireland, former British
Colonies, America and Europe.

Education services:
Advice sessions in person or by telephone; lectures,
courses and visits; publications

Services for disabled people:
Portable hearing loop

**Museum or gallery collection, archive, or library
special collection:**
Australasian Civil Registration indexes to c.1900
Bank of England Wills 1717–1845
Bernau index to pre-1800 Chancery records, etc.
(microfilm)
Boyd's Inhabitants of London 16th–18th centuries
primarily
Boyd's London Burials (adult males, 1538–1853)
Boyd's Marriage Index (c.12% of pre-1837 English
marriages)
Civil Service Irreplaceable Evidences of Age
c.1855–c.1939
Estate Duty will indexes 1796–1857 (microfilm)
Family Histories c.15,000
General Register Office, Birth, Marriage and Death
Indexes (England and Wales 1837–1925, Scotland
1855–1920) (microfiche and microfilm)
Great Western Railway Probate (Stock Transfer)
Registers 1835–1932
Indexes to Scottish Baptisms and Marriages 1558–
1854 (microfiche)
International Genealogical Index (c.400m. world-
wide entries, CD-ROM and online)
Monumental inscriptions (c.7,000)
Pallot Marriage Index 1780–1837 (online)
Parish Register transcripts (c.10,000)
Teachers' Registration Council Registers 1902–48
Times births, marriages and deaths
announcements 1816–1920 and indexes 1785–
1920 (microfilm)
Palmer's index to The Times 1790–1905 (CD-ROM)
Trinity House Petitions 1780–1890 (microfilm)
Vital Records Indexes for British Isles, Western
Europe, Scandinavia, North America, Middle
America covering millions of baptisms and
marriages between 1538 and 1905 (CD-ROM)
Principal Probate Registry will indexes 1858–1930
(microfilm)
Vicar General Marriage Allegations 1660–1851
(microfilm)
Faculty Office Marriage Allegations 1715–1851
(microfilm)
Marriage licence and will indexes
1841–1901 census indexes for England, Wales and
Scotland and some overseas

Non-library collection catalogue:
All or part available online, in-house and in print

Library catalogue:
All or part available online and in-house

Printed publications:
Full Publications List available from the Society
(some 50 titles listed)
Genealogists' Magazine (quarterly)
Order printed publications from: Bookshop Manager,
Society of Genealogists Enterprises; tel. 020 7702
5480; e-mail sales@sog.org.uk

Microform publications:
Many on microfiche

Publications list:
Available online and in print

Access to staff:
Contact by letter, by telephone, by fax, by e-mail,
in person and via website. Non-members charged.
Hours: Tue, Wed, Fri, Sat, 1000 to 1800; Thu, 1000 to
2000
Special comments: Individual staff work a shift
system and may not be available during all
opening hours

Access to building, collection or gallery:
Hours: Tue, Wed, Fri, Sat, 1000 to 1800; Thu, 1000 to 2000
Special comments: No pens, bags, coats, mobile phones or pagers allowed in the library.

Access for disabled people:
Level entry, access to all public areas, toilet facilities
Special comments: Lift will not take larger wheelchairs.

Member organisation of:
British Genealogical Record Users Committee
Federation of Family History Societies
   PO Box 8857, Lutterworth, LE17 9BJ; tel: 01455
   203133; e-mail: info@ffhs.org.uk; website: http://
   www.ffhs.org.uk/index.php

SOCIETY OF GLASS TECHNOLOGY

Acronym or abbreviation: SGT

Unit 9, Twelve O'Clock Court, 21 Attercliffe Road, Sheffield, South Yorkshire, S4 7WW

Tel: 0114 263 4455
Fax: 0114 263 4411
E-mail: info@sgt.org

Website:
http://www.sgt.org.
Links, information services, consultants, journal contents pages

Enquiries:
Enquiries to: Librarian
Direct tel: 0114 222 7307
Direct fax: 0114 279 6406
Other contacts: Managing Editor (for information)

Founded:
1916

Organisation type and purpose:
International organisation, learned society, membership association (membership is by subscription), present number of members: 900, registered charity (charity number 237438), publishing house.
Education charity promoting the use of glass of any and every kind by holding conferences, promoting exchange, publishing books and journals.
Supports student exchanges around the world.

Subject coverage:
Glass science and manufacture, history, art, design and use of glass.

Non-library collection catalogue:
All or part available online

Library catalogue:
All or part available online

Printed publications:
Glass Technology (6 a year)
Physics and Chemistry of Glasses (journal, 6 a
   year)
Coloured Glasses (W. A. Weyl)
Conference Proceedings
Glass Furnaces; design, construction and
   operations (translation from German by W. Trier)
Stones and Cord in Glass (C. Clark-Monks and J.
   M. Parker)
Basic Optical Stress Measurement in Glasses (R. J.
   Hand and H. W. McKenzie)
Raw Materials for Glass Melting (B.
   Simmingsköld)
The Art of Glass (A. Neri)
Bosc D'Antic on Glass-Making (M. Cable)
Early Nineteenth Century Glass Technology in
   Austria and Germany (M. Cable)
Apsley Pellatt on Glass Making (M. Cable)
Bontemps on Glass Making (M. Cable)
Old English Glass Houses (F. Buckley)
The Window Glass Makers of Saint Helens (R.
   Parkin)
Glass Blowing (C. Bray)
Ceramics and Glass: A Basic Technology (C. Bray)
Practising Stained Glass Safely (M. Stanton Harris)
Glass to Metal Seals (I. Donald)

Refractories in the Glass Industry
Fundamentals of Inorganic Glasses (A. Varshneya)

Electronic and video publications:
ICG 2001 International Congress on Glass –
   collection of invited papers and extended
   abstracts from the meeting (CD-ROM)
Looking Through Glass (DVD)

Publications list:
Available online and in print

Access to staff:
Contact by letter, by telephone, by fax, by e-mail and via website. Appointment necessary. Access for members only. Letter of introduction required.
Hours: Mon, 0900 to 1700; Wed, 0900 to 1300

Constituent part of:
University of Sheffield
   St Georges Library, Mappin Street, Sheffield, S1
   4DT; tel: 0114 222 7307; fax: 0114 279 6406

Member organisation of:
International Commission on Glass
   website: http://www.icglass.org

SOCIETY OF HOMEOPATHS

11 Brookfield, Duncan Close, Moulton Park, Northampton, NN3 6WL

Tel: 0845 450 6611
Fax: 0845 450 6622
E-mail: info@homeopathy-soh.org

Website:
http://www.homeopathy-soh.org

Founded:
1978

Organisation type and purpose:
Professional body.

Subject coverage:
Homoeopathy.

Printed publications:
Annual Report
Information leaflets
Newsletter (quarterly)
Register of Professional Homoeopaths
The Homoeopath (quarterly)

Publications list:
Available in print

Access to staff:
Contact by letter, by telephone, by fax, by e-mail and via website
Hours: Mon to Fri, 0800 to 1630

Member of:
European Council for Classical Homoeopathy
(ECCH)
International Council for Classical Homoeopathy
(ICCH)

SOCIETY OF INDEXERS

Acronym or abbreviation: SI

Woodbourn Business Centre, 10 Jessell Street, Sheffield, S9 3HY

Tel: 0114 2449561
Fax: 0114 2449563
E-mail: admin@indexers.org.uk

Website:
http://www.socind.demon.co.uk

Enquiries:
Enquiries to: Administrator

Founded:
1957

Organisation type and purpose:
Professional body (membership is by subscription).

Subject coverage:
Guidance and support on professional and technical indexing matters for members, publishers and authors; indexing of books, periodicals and other publications; information storage and

retrieval, manual, computer-assisted or fully automated; the foregoing techniques in virtually all fields of academic subject specialisation; improvement of standards; training course for indexing.

Printed publications:
Occasional papers in indexing
Newsletter (quarterly)
The Indexer (2 times a year)
Training in Indexing: Units A-D

Publications list:
Available online and in print

Access to staff:
Contact by letter, by telephone, by fax and by e-mail
Hours: Mon to Fri, 0930 to 1630

Affiliated bodies:
American Society of Indexers
Association of Southern African Bibliographers
and Indexers
Australian Society of Indexers
China Society of Indexers
Indexing & Abstracting Society of Canada

SOCIETY OF JEWELLERY HISTORIANS

Acronym or abbreviation: SJH

Department of Scientific Research, The British Museum, London, WC1B 3DG

Fax: 01588 620558
E-mail: jewelleryhistorians@yahoo.co.uk

Website:
http://www.societyofjewelleryhistorians.org.uk

Enquiries:
Enquiries to: Membership Secretary

Founded:
1977

Organisation type and purpose:
Learned society (membership is by subscription), present number of members: 500, registered charity (charity number 282160), suitable for ages: all.

Subject coverage:
History and development of the craft and craftspeople connected with the manufacture, design and processes concerning jewellery.

Printed publications:
Gems and Jewellery (bulletin, quarterly, members)
Jewellery Studies (journal, free to members,
   available for purchase)

Publications list:
Available online and in print

Access to staff:
Contact by letter, by fax and by e-mail

SOCIETY OF LEATHER TECHNOLOGISTS AND CHEMISTS LIMITED

Acronym or abbreviation: SLTC

49 North Park Street, Dewsbury, West Yorkshire, WF13 4LZ

Tel: 01924460864
Fax: 01924 460864

Website:
http://www.iultcs.org

Enquiries:
Enquiries to: Membership Secretary
Direct e-mail: office@sltc.org

Founded:
1897

Organisation type and purpose:
Learned society.

continued overleaf

Subject coverage:
Leather manufacture, science, technology and testing.

Printed publications:
Journal (6 times a year)
Leather Technologists Pocket Book
Official Methods Analysis
Society handbook

Access to staff:
Contact by e-mail

Founder member of:
International Union of Leather Technologists & Chemists Societies (IULTCS)

SOCIETY OF LEY HUNTERS, THE

Acronym or abbreviation: SOL

7 Mildmay Road, Romford, Havering, Essex, RM7 7DA

Tel: 01708 732362 leyhunter@ntlworld.com
E-mail: leyhunter@ntlworld.com

Website:
http://www.leyhunter.com
Information on ley lines and research references.

Enquiries:
Enquiries to: Secretary
Other contacts: Chairman 01425 273517 for media.

Founded:
2000

Organisation type and purpose:
International organisation, membership association (membership is by subscription), voluntary organisation, research organisation.

Subject coverage:
Ley lines, Neolithic archaeology, alignments, landscape, folklore, pre-Christian religious sites, pre-literacy farming calenders and energy line nodes.

Museum or gallery collection, archive, or library special collection:
Archive of researched alignments

Access to staff:
Contact by letter and by telephone
Hours: Mon to Fri, 0900 to 1700
Special comments: Letter preferred, voluntary staff availability varies.

Access to building, collection or gallery:
No access other than to staff

Member of:
Stone Circle Webring

SOCIETY OF LICENSED CONVEYANCERS, THE

Chancery House, 110 High Street, Croydon, Surrey, CR9 1PF

Tel: 020 8681 1001
Fax: 020 8681 6001

Enquiries:
Enquiries to: Chief Executive

Founded:
1988

Organisation type and purpose:
Professional body (membership is by qualification), present number of members: 350, service industry.

Subject coverage:
Licensed conveyancing, residential conveyancing and related matters.

Trade and statistical information:
Licensed conveyancers' fees and market share in England and Wales.

Printed publications:
The Licensed Conveyancer (journal, 4 times a year, £20)

Access to staff:
Contact by letter, by telephone and by fax
Hours: Mon to Fri, 1000 to 1800

Access to building, collection or gallery:
No access other than to staff

Subsidiary:
SLC Lawyer's Services (Provision of seminars, stationery, books etc to non-members)
At the same address; tel: 020 8603 5560; fax: 020 8681 6001; e-mail: slccroydon@netscapeonline.co.uk

SOCIETY OF LOCAL COUNCIL CLERKS

No.8 The Crescent, Taunton, Somerset, TA1 4EA

Tel: 01823 253646
Fax: 01823 253681
E-mail: admin@slcc.co.uk

Website:
http://www.slcc.co.uk/

Enquiries:
Enquiries to: External Affairs Officer
Direct tel: 01603 871153
Direct fax: 01603 871153
Direct e-mail: alanfairchild@cawston-pc.gov.uk

Organisation type and purpose:
Local government body.

Access to staff:
Contact by letter, by telephone, by fax and by e-mail
Hours: Mon to Fri, 0900 to 1700

SOCIETY OF LONDON ART DEALERS

Acronym or abbreviation: SLAD

Ormond House, 3 Duke of York Street, London, SW1Y 6JP

Tel: 020 7930 6137
Fax: 020 7321 0685
E-mail: sladoffice@aol.com

Website:
http://www.slad.org
List of members. Individual virtual galleries.

Enquiries:
Enquiries to: Director General

Founded:
1932

Organisation type and purpose:
Trade association.
To promote and protect the good name and the interests of the art trade.

Subject coverage:
Advice on areas of specialisation of London's art dealers.

Printed publications:
Directory of members (annual)

Access to staff:
Contact by letter, by telephone, by fax and by e-mail
Hours: Mon to Thu, 1000 to 1730

Members:
British Art Market Federation

SOCIETY OF LONDON THEATRE

Acronym or abbreviation: SOLT

32 Rose Street, London, WC2E 9ET

Tel: 020 7557 6700
Fax: 020 7557 6799
E-mail: enquiries@solttma.co.uk

Website:
http://www.OfficialLondonTheatre.co.uk
London Theatre Guide news, information and tickets online.

Enquiries:
Enquiries to: Development Manager (Press/Statistics)
Other contacts: Head of Publications for show information.

Founded:
1908

Organisation type and purpose:
Trade association.
Representing theatre managers, owners and producers in the major West End London Theatres.

Subject coverage:
Industrial relations and legal advice, publications, audience research, promotions, theatre tokens, the Laurence Olivier Awards and the Leicester Square half-price ticket booth.

Museum or gallery collection, archive, or library special collection:
London Theatre guides since 1921
Audience data since 1981
Production information

Trade and statistical information:
Trade news for the media and travel trade (by subscription).
Annual box office data report, audience research.

Printed publications:
Disabled Access Guide to London's West End Theatres (free)
London Theatre Guide (free)
Theatre list (fortnightly, £30 a year UK)

Access to staff:
Contact by letter, by telephone, by fax, by e-mail and via website. Appointment necessary.
Hours: Mon to Fri, 1000 to 1800

Access to building, collection or gallery:
No access other than to staff

SOCIETY OF LONDON TOASTMASTERS

Acronym or abbreviation: SOLT

148 Park Crescent, Erith, Kent, DA8 3DY

Tel: 01322 341465
Fax: 01322 402619
E-mail: toastmasters@topfunctions.com

Website:
http://www.societyoflondontoastmasters.co.uk

Enquiries:
Enquiries to: Honorary Secretary

Founded:
1953

Organisation type and purpose:
Membership association (membership is by qualification, election or invitation), present number of members: 25, service industry, training organisation.
To provide toastmasters, announcers for formal functions, conferences, exhibitions, etc.

Subject coverage:
Art of the professional toastmaster, and master of ceremonies, the organisation and running of banquets, conferences, receptions, wedding receptions, etc.

Museum or gallery collection, archive, or library special collection:
Large collection of banquet invitations, photographs and menus; books and manuscripts on banqueting protocol held by individual members

Access to staff:
Contact by letter, by telephone, by fax, by e-mail and via website
Hours: Any reasonable time

Access to building, collection or gallery:
No access other than to staff

SOCIETY OF MARITIME INDUSTRIES LIMITED

Acronym or abbreviation: SMI

4th Floor, 30 Great Guildford Street, London, SE1 0HS

Tel: 020 7928 9199
E-mail: info@maritimeindustries.org

Enquiries:
Enquiries to: Chief Executive
Direct e-mail: ce@maritimeindustries.org

Founded:
1966

Organisation type and purpose:
Trade association.

Subject coverage:
Marine equipment for both merchant and naval ships ranging from main engines, auxiliaries, bridge, radar, galley and deck fittings. Also covers the offshore industry and pollution control equipment. Facilitation of overseas port development investment opportunities. Marine science and technology. Oceanology.

Printed publications:
Guide to Suppliers
Market Information
Members Directory

Access to staff:
Contact by letter, by telephone and by e-mail
Hours: Mon to Fri, 0900 to 1700

Subsidiaries:
Association of British Offshore Industries
    e-mail: aboi@maritimeindustries.org
Association of Marine Scientific Industries
    e-mail: amsi@maritimeindustries.org
British Marine Equipment Association
    e-mail: bmea@maritimeindustries.org
British Naval Equipment Association
    e-mail: bnea@maritimeindustries.org
British Oil Spill Control Association
    e-mail: bosca@maritimeindustries.org
Ports and Terminals Group
    e-mail: ptga@maritimeindustries.org

SOCIETY OF MARTIAL ARTS

Acronym or abbreviation: SMA

PO Box 34, Manchester, M9 8DN

Tel: 0161 702 1660
Fax: 0161 702 1660
E-mail: registrar@societyofmartialarts.co.uk

Website:
http://www.societyofmartialarts.co.uk

Enquiries:
Enquiries to: Registrar
Other contacts: President for founder of the society.

Founded:
1994

Organisation type and purpose:
International organisation, professional body (membership is by qualification), present number of members: 50, research organisation.

Subject coverage:
Martial arts education.

Printed publications:
Conference Abstracts
International Journal of Martial Art Research

Access to staff:
Contact by letter, by telephone, by fax and by e-mail
Hours: Mon to Fri, 0900 to 1700

Access to building, collection or gallery:
No access other than to staff, prior appointment required

Connections with:
College of Higher Education of Martial Arts (CHEMA)
    e-mail: principal@chema.co.uk

SOCIETY OF MASTER SHOE REPAIRERS LIMITED

Acronym or abbreviation: SOMSR

St Crispin's House, 21 Station Road, Desborough, Kettering, Northamptonshire, NN14 2SA

Tel: 01536 760374
Fax: 01536 762348
E-mail: info@somsr.com

Website:
http://www.somsr.com
List of members (searchable database)

Enquiries:
Enquiries to: General Secretary

Founded:
1963

Organisation type and purpose:
Trade association.

Subject coverage:
Shoe repair, shoe care, independent shoe repairers in the UK, training.

Printed publications:
Shoe Service (journal, monthly, £12 pa, free to members)
Guide to the Code of Practice for Shoe Repairs (free)

Access to staff:
Contact by letter, by telephone and by fax. Appointment necessary.
Hours: Mon to Fri, 0900 to 1700

SOCIETY OF METAPHYSICIANS LIMITED

Acronym or abbreviation: SofM

Archers Court, Stonestile Lane, The Ridge, Hastings, East Sussex, TN35 4PG

Tel: 01424 751577
Fax: 01424 751577
E-mail: newmeta@btinternet.com

Website:
http://www.metaphysicians.org.uk
e-mail enquiry form and society application form. Statement of policy, history.
http://www.btinternet.com/~newmeta/index/home.html
Second hand book sales list, etc.

Enquiries:
Enquiries to: Managing Director
Other contacts: Founder President

Founded:
1944

Organisation type and purpose:
International organisation, advisory body, professional body (membership is by qualification, election or invitation), present number of members: 2298, voluntary organisation, suitable for ages: all, training organisation, consultancy, research organisation, publishing house.

Subject coverage:
Neometaphysics (study and application of fundamental laws), includes all physical and non-physical sciences, parapsychology, paraphysics, esoterics, psychic science, biofeedback systems, bioenergics, psycho-kinetics, neopsychological studies, healing, energy and mind-based, human aura, development of infinitely based administrative systems, alternative medicine.

Museum or gallery collection, archive, or library special collection:
Full research data, photographs etc on Aura Viewing including complementary colour method, electro-deposition and corona discharge
Bibliography and equipment
Paraphysics, Psychic Science

Trade and statistical information:
World manufactures of aura imaging and radiesthetic equipment.

Non-library collection catalogue:
All or part available online

Library catalogue:
All or part available online, in-house and in print

Printed publications:
Abstracts
Bibliographies
Catalogues of current works, rare reprints and special issues
Journals
Neo-Metaphysical Digest (journal)
Newsletters
Research Projects
Reprints

Publications list:
Available in print

Access to staff:
Contact by letter, by telephone, by fax, by e-mail and via website. Appointment necessary.
Hours: Mon to Fri, 0900 to 1400

Access for disabled people:
Parking provided, access to all public areas, toilet facilities

Also at:
Istituto Italiano di Ricerche Metafisiche
    via Ritmeyer 6-I34/32, Trieste, Italy; fax: 0039 40 224206; e-mail: istmeta@tin.it

Links with:
Metaphysical Research Group
    tel: 01424 751577; fax: 01424 751577; e-mail: newmeta@btinternet.com

SOCIETY OF MODEL SHIPWRIGHTS

Acronym or abbreviation: SMS

5 Lodge Crescent, Orpington, Kent, BR6 0QE

Tel: 01689 827213

Enquiries:
Enquiries to: Honorary Secretary

Founded:
1974

Organisation type and purpose:
Membership association (membership is by election or invitation), present number of members: 85, suitable for ages: all.
The society is devoted to the research into and the construction of accurate scale models of vessels.

Subject coverage:
All matters relating to the construction of scale models of sailing and powered vessels of any period.

Access to staff:
Contact by letter and by telephone
Hours: Sun to Sat, 0900 to 2200

SOCIETY OF NURSERY NURSING, THE

Acronym or abbreviation: SNN

40 Archdale Road, East Dulwich, London, SE22 9HJ

Tel: 020 8693 0555
Fax: 07092 342170

Enquiries:
Enquiries to: Chief Executive

Founded:
1991

Organisation type and purpose:
Professional body (membership is by subscription, qualification, election or invitation), suitable for ages: 18+.

Subject coverage:
Child care education and training.

Printed publications:
Code of Ethics

continued overleaf

Prospectus and Syllabus

Access to staff:
Contact by letter, by telephone, by fax, by e-mail and in person. Appointment necessary.
Hours: Mon to Fri, 0900 to 1700

SOCIETY OF OPERATIONS ENGINEERS

Acronym or abbreviation: SOE

22 Greencoat Place, London, SW1P 1PR

Tel: 020 7630 1111
Fax: 020 7630 6677
E-mail: soe@soe.org.uk

Website:
http://www.iplante.org.uk
http://www.irte.org.uk
http://www.soe.org.uk

Enquiries:
Enquiries to: Chief Executive

Founded:
2000

Organisation type and purpose:
International organisation, learned society, professional body (membership is by election or invitation), present number of members: 18,500, registered charity (charity number 1081753).

Subject coverage:
Plant engineering, maintenance, engineering surveying, and inspection, road transport engineering.

Printed publications:
Guides
Transport Engineer (12 times a year, free to members, non-members by subscription)
The Plant Engineer (6 times a year, free to members, non-members by subscription)
Operations Engineer (10 times a year, free to members)

Publications list:
Available online

Access to staff:
Contact by letter and by e-mail. Appointment necessary. Access for members only.
Hours: Mon to Fri, 0900 to 1700

SOCIETY OF ORTHOPAEDIC MEDICINE

Acronym or abbreviation: SOM

PO Box 204, Woolton, L25 7WA

Tel: 0845 680 1608
Fax: 0845 680 1618
E-mail: admin@somed.org

Website:
http://www.somed.org
About the Society, courses, conferences, research grants, journal abstracts.

Founded:
1979

Organisation type and purpose:
International organisation, learned society (membership is by qualification), present number of members: 1400, registered charity, training organisation.

Subject coverage:
Orthopaedic Medicine, Musculoskeletal Medicine.

Printed publications:
Journal: International Musculoskeletal Medicine (free to members, for purchase to non-members)

Access to staff:
Contact by letter, by telephone, by fax, by e-mail and via website
Hours: Mon to Fri, 0900 to 1700

Access to building, collection or gallery:
No access other than to staff

Connections with:
British Institute of Musculoskeletal Medicine
Chartered Society of Physiotherapy
Middlesex University
Society of Apothecaries

SOCIETY OF PENSION CONSULTANTS

Acronym or abbreviation: SPC

St Bartholomew House, 92 Fleet Street, London, EC4Y 1DG

Tel: 020 7353 1688
Fax: 020 7353 9296
E-mail: john.mortimer@spc.uk.com

Website:
http://www.spc.uk.com

Enquiries:
Enquiries to: Secretary

Founded:
1958

Organisation type and purpose:
Membership association (membership is by subscription, qualification, election or invitation), present number of members: 124 organisations. Representative body for the providers of the advice and services needed to provide pensions (occupational and personal) and other benefits. Its members include pension and actuarial consultants, legal and accounting firms, insurance companies, investment houses and third-party administrators.

Subject coverage:
Occupational pension schemes, personal pension schemes and other employee benefit schemes, interests of organisations involved in providing advice and/or services in connection with the setting up or running of pension schemes.

Printed publications:
Newsletter (for members only)
Annual report

Access to staff:
Contact by letter, by telephone, by e-mail and via website. Appointment necessary.
Hours: Mon to Fri, 0900 to 1700

Member organisation of:
Occupational Pension Schemes Joint Working Group

SOCIETY OF PLOUGHMEN LIMITED

Quarry Farm, Loversall, Doncaster, South Yorkshire, DN11 9DH

Tel: 01302 852469
Fax: 01302 859880
E-mail: info@ploughmen.co.uk

Website:
http://www.ploughmen.co.uk

Enquiries:
Enquiries to: Secretary

Founded:
1972

Organisation type and purpose:
Membership association (membership is by subscription), registered charity (charity number 1062780).
To promote and encourage the art, skill and science of ploughing the land.

Subject coverage:
Ploughing.

Printed publications:
Handbook for Championships (September/October)
Newsletter (twice a year, members)

Access to staff:
Contact by letter, by telephone, by fax, by e-mail and via website

Hours: Mon to Fri, 0930 to 1630

Links with:
World Ploughing Organisation

SOCIETY OF PROFESSIONAL ENGINEERS

Acronym or abbreviation: SPE

St Mary House, 15 St Mary Street, Chippenham, Wiltshire, SN15 3WD

Tel: 01249 655398
Fax: 01249 443602
E-mail: soc.prof.eng@asi.org.uk

Enquiries:
Enquiries to: Office Co-ordinator

Founded:
1969

Organisation type and purpose:
Professional body.

Subject coverage:
Maintains a register of well qualified professional engineers of whatever discipline. Protects, enhances and promotes the status of the professional engineer and promotes the concept of this title throughout the world. Acts as the secretariat and provider of licences and registration cards to suitably qualified professional engineers on behalf of the UIDIP for the English speaking countries of the world.
UIDIP is currently on hold until further notice.

Printed publications:
The Professional Engineer (quarterly bulletin, free to members, £2 per issue to non-members)

Access to staff:
Contact by letter, by telephone, by fax and by e-mail
Hours: Mon to Fri, 0900 to 1700

Member of:
Union Internationale des Ingenieurs Professionnels – Currently on hold until further notice (UIDIP)
66 rue de la Rochefoucauld, Paris, F-75009, France

Twinned with the:
Bundesverband der Berufsingenieure Deutschlands (BDI)
Germany; tel: 01249 655398
Société Nationale des Ingénieurs Professionnels France (IPF)
tel: 01249 655398
South African Society for Professional Engineers (SASPE)

SOCIETY OF RADIOGRAPHERS

Acronym or abbreviation: SoR

207 Providence Square, Mill Street, London, SE1 2EW

Tel: 020 7740 7200
Fax: 020 7740 7204
E-mail: info@sor.org

Website:
http://www.sor.org
A range of professional and industrial relations information, members section.

Enquiries:
Enquiries to: Chief Executive
Direct tel: 020 7740 7202
Direct e-mail: richarde@sor.org
Other contacts: Director of Professional Development for professional matters.

Founded:
1920

Organisation type and purpose:
Trade union, present number of members: 18,000.

Printed publications:
Available free or for purchase, direct

Electronic and video publications:
CPD Portfolio (free to members)

Publications list:
Available online and in print

Access to staff:
Contact by letter, by telephone, by fax, by e-mail, in person and via website. Appointment necessary.
Hours: Mon to Fri, 0900 to 1700

Access to building, collection or gallery:
Hours: Mon to Fri, 0900 to 1700

Access for disabled people:
Parking provided, access to all public areas, toilet facilities

SOCIETY OF RECORDER PLAYERS

Acronym or abbreviation: SRP

Linkside, 21 Bereweeke Avenue, Winchester, SO22 6BH

E-mail: secretary@srp.org.uk

Website:
http://www.srp.org.uk

Enquiries:
Enquiries to: Secretary

Founded:
1937

Organisation type and purpose:
Membership association (membership is by subscription), present number of members: 1,500, voluntary organisation, registered charity (charity number 282751/SC038422), suitable for all ages.

Subject coverage:
Recorder playing.

Printed publications:
The Recorder Magazine (quarterly)
Teachers' Guide to the Recorder

Access to staff:
Contact by letter, by e-mail, in person and via website
Hours: Mon to Fri, 0900 to 1700

Also at:
50 regional branches

SOCIETY OF SALES AND MARKETING, THE

Acronym or abbreviation: SSAM

40 Archdale Road, East Dulwich, London, SE22 9HJ

Tel: 020 8693 0555
Fax: 07092 342170
E-mail: info@ssocm.co.uk

Enquiries:
Enquiries to: Chief Executive

Founded:
1980

Organisation type and purpose:
International organisation, advisory body, professional body (membership is by subscription, qualification, election or invitation).

Subject coverage:
Professional body for those interested in selling and sales management, marketing, retailing and international trade.

Printed publications:
Code of Ethics
Journal
Prospectus and syllabus

Access to staff:
Contact by letter, by telephone, by fax, by e-mail and in person. Appointment necessary.
Hours: Mon to Fri, 0900 to 1700

SOCIETY OF SCRIBES AND ILLUMINATORS

Acronym or abbreviation: SSI

The Art Workers Guild, 6 Queen's Square, London, WC1N 3AT

Tel: 015242 51534
Fax: 015242 51534
E-mail: scribe@calligraphyonline.org

Website:
http://www.calligraphyonline.org

Enquiries:
Enquiries to: Honorary Secretary

Founded:
1921

Organisation type and purpose:
International organisation, professional body (Fellowship by election, Lay Membership by subscription); present number of members: 550, suitable for ages: 16+.
To perpetuate a tradition of craftsmanship in the production of manuscript books and documents; to encourage and influence calligraphy and fine lettering.

Subject coverage:
Crafts of writing and lettering, production of manuscript books and documents, fine lettering and calligraphy, lists of calligraphy courses, exhibitions, materials and availability, advice on all aspects of calligraphy and lettering.

Museum or gallery collection, archive, or library special collection:
Rare calligraphy books
Reference library
Small permanent exhibition, with historical and modern pieces

Printed publications:
Journal (for members only, twice a year)
Newsletter (3 a year)
Order printed publications from: via website

Access to staff:
Contact by letter, by telephone, by fax, by e-mail and via website
Hours: Mon to Fri, 0900 to 1700

Access to building, collection or gallery:
No access to building

SOCIETY OF SHOE FITTERS, THE

Acronym or abbreviation: SSF

3 Burystead Place, Wellingborough, Northamptonshire, NN8 1AH

Tel: 01933 229005
Fax: 01933 225009
E-mail: ssf@britfoot.com

Website:
http://www.shoefitters-uk.org
Foot health and general interest.

Founded:
1959

Organisation type and purpose:
National organisation, advisory body, professional body, trade association (membership is by qualification), present number of members: 250, training organisation.
A non-profit making society who train people to become professional shoe fitters, advice provided to the public on feet and footwear, general assistance to the shoe trade.

Subject coverage:
Shoe fitting, foot health, location of qualified shoe fitters.

Printed publications:
Foothealth Leaflets

Access to staff:
Contact by letter, by telephone, by fax and by e-mail
Hours: Mon to Fri, 0900 to 1700

SOCIETY OF SOLICITORS IN THE SUPREME COURTS OF SCOTLAND

Acronym or abbreviation: SSC

SSC Library, Parliament House, 11 Parliament Square, Edinburgh, EH1 1RF

Tel: 0131 225 6268
Fax: 0131 225 2270
E-mail: enquiries@ssclibrary.co.uk

Enquiries:
Enquiries to: Librarian

Founded:
1784

Organisation type and purpose:
Learned society (membership is by subscription), present number of members: 300.

Subject coverage:
Scottish legal material, statutes, law reports, SIs, textbooks, (comprehensive); English legal materials, statutes, law reports, SIs, limited selection of textbooks. Scots law in all its branches; UK law where it is common to Scotland and England.

Museum or gallery collection, archive, or library special collection:
Court of Session and High Court of Justiciary Opinions from 1982 to date (open unreported and indexed on database from 1991)
Session papers 1750–1954

Library catalogue:
All or part available in-house

Access to staff:
Contact by letter. Appointment necessary. Access for members only. Non-members charged.
Hours: Mon to Fri, 0930 to 1600

SOCIETY OF SPORTS THERAPISTS

Acronym or abbreviation: SST

16 Royal Terrace, Glasgow G3 7NY

Tel: 0845 6002613
Fax: 0141 3325335
E-mail: admin@society-of-sports-therapists.org

Website:
http://www.society-of-sports-therapists.org

Enquiries:
Enquiries to: Chairman
Direct e-mail: webmaster@society-of-sports
-therapists.org
Other contacts: Secretary

Founded:
1989

Organisation type and purpose:
National government body, advisory body, professional body (membership is by subscription, qualification), present number of members: 1500+, training organisation, consultancy.
To provide a professional and educational identity for sports therapists.

Subject coverage:
Sports injury management, treatment and rehabilitation.

Museum or gallery collection, archive, or library special collection:
Fact sheets, newsletters, book lists and course and conference details

Access to staff:
Contact by letter, by telephone, by fax, by e-mail and via website. Appointment necessary.
Hours: Mon to Fri, 1000 to 1500

Subsidiary body:
Sports Rehab & Education
tel: 0141 221 1494; fax: 0141 221 1525

SOCIETY OF ST GREGORY

Acronym or abbreviation: SSG

continued overleaf

76 Great Bushey Drive, London, N20 8QL

Tel: 020 8445 5724
E-mail: chairman@ssg.org.uk

Website:
http://www.ssg.org.uk

Enquiries:
Enquiries to: Chairman

Founded:
1929

Organisation type and purpose:
Membership association (membership is by subscription), voluntary organisation, training organisation.

Subject coverage:
Roman Catholic worship and church music.

Museum or gallery collection, archive, or library special collection:
Church Music
Church Music Association Music Library, 1955–1972
Complete sets, 1929 to date:
Life and Worship
Liturgy
Music and Liturgy

Printed publications:
Music and Liturgy (4 times a year)

Access to staff:
Contact by letter, by telephone, by e-mail and via website
Hours: Any reasonable time.

SOCIETY OF VOLUNTARY ASSOCIATES

Acronym or abbreviation: SOVA

1st Floor, Chichester House, 37 Brixton Road, London, SW9 6DZ

Tel: 020 7793 0404
Fax: 020 7735 4410
E-mail: london@sova.org.uk

Website:
http://www.sova.org.uk/

Enquiries:
Enquiries to: Manager
Direct tel: 0114 282 3187
Direct fax: 0114 282 3292
Direct e-mail: mail@sova.org.uk

Founded:
1975

Organisation type and purpose:
National organisation, voluntary organisation, registered charity (charity number 1073877), training organisation, consultancy.
To involve local communities in community safety, crime reduction and offenders' rehabilitation.

Subject coverage:
Volunteers within the criminal justice system, partnerships between statutory and voluntary agencies, community action, community safety and community support for ex-offenders.

Museum or gallery collection, archive, or library special collection:
Reports on SOVA projects

Printed publications:
Annual Report
Selection of free leaflets
Volunteer Newsletter

Access to staff:
Contact by telephone and by e-mail
Hours: Mon to Fri, 0900 to 1700

Affiliated to:
National Council for Voluntary Organizations

SOCIETY OF WEDDING AND PORTRAIT PHOTOGRAPHERS LIMITED

Acronym or abbreviation: SWPP

Colomendy House, Ivale Road, Denbigh, Clwyd, LL16 3DF

Tel: 01745 815030
E-mail: enquiries@swpp.co.uk

Enquiries:
Enquiries to: Chief Executive

Founded:
1988

Organisation type and purpose:
Trade association.

Subject coverage:
Training and support in wedding portrait photography and videoing.

Printed publications:
Professional portrait photography (T Hansen, £25)
The A-Z of Wedding photography (T Hansen, £25)
Variety of manuals and videos covering all aspects of wedding photography and videoing

Electronic and video publications:
Barrie Thomas CD-ROMs:
Master Class (£39)
Digital Printing and Presentation (£39)

Publications list:
Available in print

Access to staff:
Contact by letter, by telephone and by fax.
Appointment necessary.
Hours: Mon to Fri, 0900 to 1700

SOCIETY OF WILDLIFE ARTISTS

Acronym or abbreviation: SWLA

17 Carlton House Terrace, London, SW1Y 5BD

Tel: 020 7930 6844
Fax: 020 7839 7830
E-mail: press@mallgalleries.com

Website:
http://www.mallgalleries.org.uk

Enquiries:
Enquiries to: Secretary
Other contacts: Marketing and Communications Officer

Founded:
1964

Organisation type and purpose:
Membership association (membership is by election or invitation), present number of members: 78, registered charity (charity number 328717).

Subject coverage:
Wildlife art as painting, drawings and sculpture, its exhibition and promotion.

Printed publications:
Catalogue of the annual exhibition

Access to staff:
Contact by letter, by telephone, by fax, by e-mail and via website. Appointment necessary.
Hours: Mon to Fri, 0930 to 1730

Access to building, collection or gallery:
No access other than to staff
Hours: Mon to Fri, 0930 to 1730

Access for disabled people:
Toilet facilities
Special comments: Stairlift.

Links with:
Federation of British Artists
at the same address

SOCIETY OF WOMEN ARTISTS, THE

Acronym or abbreviation: SWA

1 Knapp Cottages, Wyke, Gillingham, Dorset, SP8 4NQ

Tel: 01747 825718
Fax: 01747 826835
E-mail: pamhenderson@dial.pipex.com

Website:
http://www.society-women-artists.org.uk

Enquiries:
Enquiries to: Executive Secretary

Founded:
1855

Organisation type and purpose:
International organisation, membership association (membership is by election or invitation), present number of members: 150, registered charity (charity number 298241).

Subject coverage:
Art and women artists; annual exhibition of paintings, drawings, prints and sculpture.

Museum or gallery collection, archive, or library special collection:
Archive of Art and Design, Victoria and Albert Museum, Blythe House, 23 Blythe Road, London W14 0QF

Access to staff:
Contact by letter, by telephone, by fax and by e-mail
Hours: Mon to Fri, 0900 to 1700

Access to building, collection or gallery:
No prior appointment required
Special comments: Archives are kept by the Victoria and Albert Museum's Archive of Art and Design.

SOCIETY OF WOOD ENGRAVERS

Acronym or abbreviation: SWE

The Old Governor's House, Norman Cross, Peterborough, PE7 3TB

Tel: 01733 242833
Fax: 01733 242833
E-mail: g.waddington@dial.pipex.com

Website:
http://www.woodengravers.co.uk

Enquiries:
Enquiries to: General Secretary

Founded:
1920

Organisation type and purpose:
International organisation, membership association.
Artists' exhibiting society and international contact organisation.

Subject coverage:
Printmaking, relief printmaking, wood engraving, its practice, current practitioners and its history.

Museum or gallery collection, archive, or library special collection:
Society archives

Printed publications:
Newsletter (6 times a year)
Occasional fine print books on wood engraving

Access to staff:
Contact by letter, by telephone, by fax and by e-mail
Hours: Mon to Fri, 1000 to 1700

SOG LIMITED

PO Box 13, The Heath, Runcorn, Cheshire, WA7 4QF

Tel: 01928 511888
Fax: 01928 567979
E-mail: heath_library@sog.ltd.uk

Website:
http://www.sog.ltd.uk

Enquiries:
Enquiries to: Librarian
Direct tel: 01928 513438
Direct fax: 01928 513334

Organisation type and purpose:
Service industry.
Facilities management & specialist services.

Subject coverage:
Chlor-alkali; chlorine and inorganic derivatives; caustic soda; electrochemistry and electrochemical technology, water, sewage and effluent treatment chemicals. Processes; chlorinated hydrocarbons and derivatives; cleaning and degreasing solvents; refrigerants; CFC alternatives, fluorinated hydrocarbons and derivatives, chlorine containing monomers and polymers; PVC; fluorine containing monomers and polymers; PTFE.

Non-library collection catalogue:
All or part available in-house

Library catalogue:
All or part available in-house

Publications list:
Available in print

Access to staff:
Contact by letter, by telephone, by fax, by e-mail and via website. Appointment necessary. Access for members only. All charged.
Hours: Mon to Fri, 0830 to 1200 and 1230 to 1630

Access to building, collection or gallery:
Prior appointment required

SOIL ASSOCIATION, THE

Acronym or abbreviation: SA

Bristol House, 40–56 Victoria Street, Bristol, BS1 6BY

Tel: 0117 929 0661
Fax: 0117 314 5000

Website:
http://www.soilassociation.org

Enquiries:
Enquiries to: Information Officer
Direct tel: 0117 914 2444

Founded:
1946

Organisation type and purpose:
Membership association (membership is by subscription), registered charity.

Subject coverage:
Organic food and farming, responsible forestry, agriculture.

Printed publications:
Living Earth (membership magazine, 3 times a year, £18)
Organic Farming (journal, quarterly, £15)

Publications list:
Available online and in print

Access to staff:
Contact by letter, by telephone, by fax and in person. Appointment necessary.
Hours: Mon to Fri, 0900 to 1730

Wholly owned subsidiary of:
Soil Association Certification Limited
at the same address; tel: 0117 914 2405; fax: 0117 925 2504; e-mail: cert@soilassociation.org

SOIL MECHANICS

Acronym or abbreviation: SML

Glossop House, Hogwood Lane, Finchampstead, Wokingham, Berkshire, RG40 4QW

Tel: 0118 932 8888
Fax: 0118 932 8383
E-mail: library@esgl.co.uk

Website:
http://www.esgl.co.uk

Enquiries:
Enquiries to: Librarian
Direct tel: 0118 932 4459

Founded:
1943

Organisation type and purpose:
Service industry, consultancy.

Subject coverage:
Soil mechanics, rock mechanics, geology, geotechnical engineering, site investigation, vibration and dynamics, earthquake engineering, seismicity.

Museum or gallery collection, archive, or library special collection:
Results of site investigations throughout the United Kingdom and some overseas localities (microform and scans)

Non-library collection catalogue:
All or part available in-house

Library catalogue:
All or part available in-house

Access to staff:
Contact by telephone, by fax, by e-mail and in person. Appointment necessary. Non-members charged.
Hours: Mon to Fri, 0900 to 1700

Access to building, collection or gallery:
Prior appointment required
Hours: Mon to Fri, 0900 to 1700

Access for disabled people:
Parking provided, level entry, access to all public areas, toilet facilities

Constituent bodies:
CL Associates (CLA)
at the same address
Exploration Associates (EA)
at the same address
TES Bretby
at the same address

Parent body:
Environmental Services Group Limited (ESGL)
at the same address

SOLAR ENERGY SOCIETY

Acronym or abbreviation: UK-ISES

School of Technology, Oxford Brookes University, Headington Campus, Gipsy Lane, Oxford, OX3 0BP

Tel: 01865 484367
Fax: 01865 484263
E-mail: ukises@brookes.ac.uk

Website:
http://www.thesolarline.com

Enquiries:
Enquiries to: Administrator

Founded:
1974

Organisation type and purpose:
Learned society.

Subject coverage:
Solar energy.

Printed publications:
Conference Proceedings (list available)
Solar News (4 times a year)
Refocus (6 times a year)
Heating Water by the Sun: a layman's guide to the use of flat-plate solar collectors for domestic water heating and for heating swimming pools (3rd ed 2000)
Solar Electricity: a layman's guide to the generation of electricity by the direct conversion of solar energy (1999)
Solar Energy Today (1981)
Set of 6 factsheets by the Society for the Solar Trust

Publications list:
Available online and in print

Access to staff:
Contact by e-mail
Hours: Mon to Fri, 0900 to 1700

Access to building, collection or gallery:
No prior appointment required

Section of:
International Solar Energy Society
Freiburg, Germany; tel: + 49 761 4590652; fax: + 49 761 4590699; e-mail: info@ises.org

SOLAR TRADE ASSOCIATION

Acronym or abbreviation: STA

National Energy Centre, Davy Avenue, Knowlhill, Milton Keynes, Buckinghamshire, MK5 8NG

Tel: 01908 442290
Fax: 01908 665577
E-mail: enquiries@solar-trade.org.uk

Website:
http://www.solar-trade.org.uk

Enquiries:
Enquiries to: Chief Executive

Founded:
1974

Organisation type and purpose:
Trade association (membership is by election or invitation), present number of members: 170, manufacturing industry, service industry, training organisation, consultancy.
National enquiry centre.

Subject coverage:
Solar industry and solar energy utilisation from the commercial point of view, commercial and domestic water heating, swimming pool heating, passive solar design, solar controllers.

Trade and statistical information:
National sales of solar systems.
International sales of solar systems.

Printed publications:
Booklet outlining fundamentals of solar heating and lighting (free)
Membership list (free)

Access to staff:
Contact by letter, by telephone, by fax and by e-mail
Hours: Mon to Fri, 0900 to 1700

Member of:
European Solar Thermal Industries Federation (ESTIF)
The Micropower Council

SOLDIER MAGAZINE

Parsons House, Ordnance Road, Aldershot, Hampshire, GU11 2DU

Tel: 01252 347353
Fax: 01252 347358
E-mail: mail@soldiermagazine.co.uk

Website:
http://www.soldiermagazine.co.uk

Enquiries:
Enquiries to: Archive/Information manager
Direct tel: 01252 355056
Direct e-mail: rkusionowicz@soldiermagazine.co.uk

Founded:
1945

Organisation type and purpose:
National government body, publishing house.

Subject coverage:
The British Army, especially post-1945.

Museum or gallery collection, archive, or library special collection:
Magazine archive of every issue printed since 19th March 1945

continued overleaf

Photo archive of photographs used in issues of British Army subjects, in colour, and black and white
Crown copyright of photographs taken by Soldier Magazine staff

Library catalogue:
All or part available in-house

Printed publications:
Soldier Magazine (monthly, £2.50)

Access to staff:
Contact by letter, by telephone, by fax, by e-mail and in person. Appointment necessary.
Hours: Mon to Fri, 0900 to 1600

Access to building, collection or gallery:
Prior appointment required

Access for disabled people:
Parking provided

SOLDIERS, SAILORS, AIRMEN AND FAMILIES ASSOCIATION – FORCES HELP

Acronym or abbreviation: SSAFA Forceshelp

19 Queen Elizabeth Street, London, SE1 2LP

Tel: 020 7403 8783
Fax: 020 7403 8815
E-mail: management@ssafa.org.uk
Website:
http://www.ssafa.org.uk
Connections to Army, Navy, Air Force welfare and ex-service charities.

Enquiries:
Enquiries to: Welfare Advisors
Other contacts: Director of Welfare & Housing

Founded:
1885

Organisation type and purpose:
Voluntary organisation, registered charity (charity number 210760).
Armed Forces National Charity.
Support for serving and ex-service men, women and their families in need.

Subject coverage:
Welfare of Armed Service and ex-Service families and dependants.

Museum or gallery collection, archive, or library special collection:
Small resource library containing up-to-date benefit, housing and welfare advice leaflets and literature

Non-library collection catalogue:
All or part available in-house

Library catalogue:
All or part available in-house

Printed publications:
OnTarget (2 times a year, available for interested persons)
SSAFA News & Views (2 times a year, available to all branches, volunteers and interested persons)
SSAFA Scope (4 times a year, in-house, newsletter for professional and volunteer staff)
In Touch (4 times a year, in-house, update for professional and volunteer staff)

Access to staff:
Contact by letter, by telephone, by fax, by e-mail and via website. Appointment necessary.
Hours: Mon to Fri, 0915 to 1700

Has:
102 Branches throughout the UK and Ireland. Can also be contacted through Citizens Advice Bureaux

SOLICITORS BENEVOLENT ASSOCIATION

Acronym or abbreviation: SBA

1 Jaggard Way, London, SW12 8SG

Tel: 020 8675 6440

Fax: 020 8675 6441
E-mail: solben@btclick.com

Website:
http://www.sba.org.uk

Enquiries:
Enquiries to: Secretary

Founded:
1858

Organisation type and purpose:
Professional body (membership is by election or invitation), present number of members: 17,000, registered charity (charity number 208878).

Access to staff:
Contact by letter, by telephone, by fax and by e-mail
Hours: Mon to Fri, 0930 to 1730

SOLICITORS FAMILY LAW ASSOCIATION

Acronym or abbreviation: SFLA

PO Box 302, Orpington, Kent, BR6 8QX

Tel: 01689 850227
Fax: 01689 855833
E-mail: sfla@btinternet.co.uk

Website:
http://www.sfla.co.uk
Seminars, guidance on family law.
http://www.sfla.org.uk
Seminars, guidance on family law.

Enquiries:
Enquiries to: Administrative Director

Founded:
1982

Organisation type and purpose:
Membership association (membership is by subscription, qualification, election or invitation), present number of members: 5000, voluntary organisation.

Subject coverage:
All solicitor members deal with family law in a constructive rather than aggressive approach to resolving problems flowing from relationship breakdown. The public can contact the Association to receive a list of local members.

Printed publications:
The SFLA Guide to Good Practice for Solicitors Acting for Children (5th ed., 1997, £5)
Precedents for Consent Orders (book 5th ed., 1998, £40 members, £50 non-members)
Precedents – Separation and Pre-Marital Agreements 2001 (book, 1998, £45 members, £60 non-members)
Fairness for Families (free to members)
International Aspects of Family Law – The SFLA Guide to Good Practice and Procedure (£35 members, £45 non-members)

Electronic and video publications:
Please state which WP system when ordering disks:
Precedents for Consent Orders (disk 5th ed., 1998, £20 members, £26 non-members, footnotes not included)
Precedents – Separation and Pre-Marital Agreements 2001 (disk, £25 members, £30 non-members)

Publications list:
Available in print

Access to staff:
Contact by letter, by telephone, by fax and by e-mail
Hours: Mon to Fri, 0900 to 1700

SOLID FUEL ASSOCIATION

Acronym or abbreviation: SFA

7 Swanwick Court, Alfreton, Derbyshire, DE55 7AS

Tel: 01773 835400
Fax: 01773 834351
E-mail: sfa@solidfuel.co.uk

Website:
http://www.solidfuel.co.uk

Enquiries:
Enquiries to: General Secretary

Founded:
1994

Organisation type and purpose:
National organisation, advisory body, trade association (membership is by subscription), present number of members: 38.

Subject coverage:
Utilisation of natural and manufactured solid fuels in domestic heating. Installation and maintenance of solid fuel domestic heating appliances.

Publications list:
Available online

Access to staff:
Contact by letter, by telephone, by fax, by e-mail and via website
Hours: Mon to Fri, 0900 to 1700

Access to building, collection or gallery:
No access other than to staff

SOLIHULL CENTRAL LIBRARY

Homer Road, Solihull, West Midlands, B91 3RG

Tel: 0121 704 6965
Fax: 0121 704 6991

Enquiries:
Enquiries to: Head of Community Services, Libraries, Arts & Lifelong Learning
Direct tel: 0121 704 6945
Direct e-mail: nward@solihull.gov.uk
Other contacts: Head of Information & Local Studies Manager; email: dgill@solihull.gov.uk; tel: 0121 704 6808

Organisation type and purpose:
Public library.

Non-library collection catalogue:
All or part available online and in-house

Library catalogue:
All or part available online and in-house

Access to staff:
Contact by letter, by telephone, by fax and by e-mail
Hours: Mon, 0900 to 2000; Tue, 0900 to 1800; Wed, 1000 to 1800; Thu, 0900 to 2000; Fri, 0900 to 1800; Sat, 0900 to 1700

Access to building, collection or gallery:
No prior appointment required

Access for disabled people:
Level entry, access to all public areas, toilet facilities

Other branches at:
Balsall Common
283 Kenilworth Road, Balsall Common, CV7 7EL; tel: 01676 532590; fax: 01676 530119
Castle Bromwich
Hurst Lane North, Castle Bromwich, B36 0EY; tel: 0121 747 3708; fax: 0121 748 5919
Chelmsley Wood
Stephenson Drive, Chelmsley Wood, B37 5TA; tel: 0121 788 4380; fax: 0121 788 4391
Hampton in Arden
39 Fentham Road, Hampton in Arden, B92 0AY; tel: 01675 442629; fax: 01675 443608
Hobs Moat
Ulleries Road, Solihull, West Midlands, B92 8EE; tel: 0121 743 4592; fax: 0121 743 2473
Kingshurst
Marston Drive, Kingshurst, B37 6BD; tel: 0121 770 3451; fax: 0121 770 9388
Knowle
Chester House, High Street, Knowle, B93 0LL; tel: 01564 775840; fax: 01564 770953

Marston Green
  Land Lane, Marston Green, B37 7DQ; tel: 0121 779 2131; fax: 0121 770 1565
Meriden
  The Green, Meriden, CV7 7LN; tel: 01676 522717; fax: 01676 521146
Olton
  169a Warwick Road, Olton, B92 7AW; tel: 0121 706 3038; fax: 0121 708 0549
Shirley
  Church Road, Shirley, B90 2AY; tel: 0121 744 1076; fax: 0121 744 5047

SOLIHULL CHAMBER OF INDUSTRY AND COMMERCE

142 Lode Lane, Solihull, West Midlands, B91 2HP

Tel: 0121 704 6406
Fax: 0121 704 8259
E-mail: solihull@birminghamchamber.org.uk

Enquiries:
Enquiries to: Information Officer

Organisation type and purpose:
Membership association (membership is by subscription).

Subject coverage:
Business services.

Access to staff:
Contact by letter, by telephone and by fax. Appointment necessary.
Hours: Mon to Fri, 0900 to 1700

Associate of:
Birmingham Chamber of Commerce (BCI)
  75 Harborne Road, Birmingham, B15 3DH; tel: 0121 454 6171

SOLIHULL COLLEGE

Blossomfield Road, Solihull, West Midlands, B91 1SB

Tel: 0121 678 7000
Fax: 0121 678 7200
E-mail: library@solihull.ac.uk

Website:
http://www.solihull.ac.uk
On-line catalogue, useful internet sites.

Enquiries:
Enquiries to: Library and Learning Centre Manager
Direct tel: 0121 678 7205

Organisation type and purpose:
College of further and higher education.

Subject coverage:
Education; business studies; art and design; leisure; travel and tourism; hotel and catering studies; teacher training (further education); counselling; humanities; social sciences.

Library catalogue:
All or part available online

Access to staff:
Contact by letter, by telephone and by e-mail. Appointment necessary.
Hours: Term time: Mon to Thu, 0830 to 2030; Fri, 0830 to 1630; Sat, 0930 to 1300
Vacations: Mon to Fri, 0900 to 1700

SOLIHULL LIBRARIES AND ARTS

Central Library, Homer Road, Solihull, West Midlands, B91 3RG

Tel: 0121 704 6977
Fax: 0121 704 6212
E-mail: infols@solihull.gov.uk

Website:
http://www.solihull.gov.uk/wwwlib
Information about all library services

Enquiries:
Enquiries to: Head of Information and Local Studies
Direct tel: 0121 704 6808

Direct e-mail: dgill@solihull.gov.uk

Organisation type and purpose:
Local government body, public library.

Subject coverage:
General library, information and reference service. Local and family history resources relating to the area covered by the present Metropolitan Borough of Solihull.

Museum or gallery collection, archive, or library special collection:
British Small Arms (BSA) Archives Collection (motorcycles and small arms)
Joiner Collection of Photographs (local history)

Printed publications:
A select list of sources relating to Solihull Local Studies Collection (1999, £1.50 plus p&p)
Looking back at Solihull (1987, £4.95 plus p&p)
Shirley – a pictorial history (1993, £11.95 plus p&p)
Solihull – a pictorial history (1991, £11.95 plus p&p)
Stately Homes of Solihull (2001, £4.75 plus p&p)
Order printed publications from: Local Studies Librarian, Solihull Libraries and Arts at same address

Access to staff:
Contact by letter, by telephone, by fax and in person
Hours: Mon, Tue, 0900 to 1730; Wed, 1000 to 1730; Thu, Fri, 0900 to 2000; Sat, 0900 to 1700

Access for disabled people:
Level entry, access to all public areas, toilet facilities
Special comments: Disabled parking in Church Hill car park, Special needs parking bays in adjacent underground car park with lifts to Library level.

Parent body:
Solihull Metropolitan Borough Council

SOMERSET AND WESSEX EATING DISORDERS ASSOCIATION

Acronym or abbreviation: SWEDA

Strode House, 10 Leigh Road, Street, Somerset, BA16 0HA

Tel: 01458 448611
Fax: 01458 448611
E-mail: admin@swedauk.org

Website:
http://www.swedauk.org

Enquiries:
Enquiries to: Manager
Other contacts: Administrator

Founded:
1997

Organisation type and purpose:
Membership association, voluntary organisation, registered charity (charity number 1056441), suitable for ages: 18+, training organisation.
A charity based on the ethos of being user-led and encouraging self-help and improvement. SEDA aims to reach out to all affected by eating disorders, sufferers, carers and professionals.

Subject coverage:
Eating disorders, helpline and website for sufferers and carers, training and consultation on eating disorders, awareness raising.

Access to staff:
Contact by letter, by telephone, by e-mail, in person and via website. Appointment necessary.
Hours: Administrator: Mon to Fri, 0900 to 1300
Special comments: answerphone at all other times

Access to building, collection or gallery:
Prior appointment required
Hours: Wed, 1000 to 1300

SOMERSET ARCHAEOLOGICAL AND NATURAL HISTORY SOCIETY

Acronym or abbreviation: SANHS

c/o Somerset Studies Library, Paul Street, Taunton, Somerset, TA1 3XZ

Tel: 01823 340300
Fax: 01823 340301
E-mail: office@sanhs.org

Website:
http://www.sanhs.org

Enquiries:
Enquiries to: Honorary Librarian
Other contacts: somstud@somerset.gov.uk

Founded:
1849

Organisation type and purpose:
Learned society, registered charity (charity number 201929).

Subject coverage:
History, archaeology and natural history of the pre-1974 county of Somerset.

Museum or gallery collection, archive, or library special collection:
Pigott and Braikenridge Collections (Somerset drawings)
Tite Collection (Somerset books)

Library catalogue:
All or part available in-house

Printed publications:
Beetles of Somerset
Flora of Somerset
Decorated medieval floor tiles of Somerset
The Taunton Dissenting Academy
Somerset Archaeology and Natural History (annual vol. from 1849)

Access to staff:
Contact by letter, by telephone, by fax, by e-mail and in person
Hours: Mon, Tue, Thu, 0930 to 1730; Wed, Fri, 0930 to 1900; Sat, 0930 to 1600

Constituent part of:
Council for British Archaeology

SOMERSET ARCHIVE AND RECORD SERVICE

Somerset Record Office, Obridge Road, Taunton, Somerset, TA2 7PU

Tel: 01823 278805
Fax: 01823 325402
E-mail: archives@somerset.gov.uk

Website:
http://www.somerset.gov.uk
Guide to holdings, details of services.

Enquiries:
Enquiries to: Archivist

Founded:
1929

Organisation type and purpose:
Local government body.
Archive service.

Subject coverage:
Historic records of the county of Somerset, churches, societies, businesses and individuals.

Non-library collection catalogue:
All or part available online

Library catalogue:
All or part available online

Printed publications:
Your Somerset Family (£2)
Your Somerset House (£2)

Microform publications:
Images of original records held, especially parish records

continued overleaf

Electronic and video publications:
Guide to Holdings (CD-ROM)

Publications list:
Available online

Access to staff:
Contact by letter, by telephone, by fax and by e-mail. Appointment necessary.
Hours: Mon, 1400 to 1650; Tue to Thu, 0900 to 1650; Fri, 0900 to 1620; Sat, 0915 to 1215
Special comments: Not open every Saturday.

Access to building, collection or gallery:
Prior appointment required

Access for disabled people:
Ramped entry, access to all public areas, toilet facilities

Parent body:
Somerset County Council

SOMERSET COLLEGE OF ARTS AND TECHNOLOGY

Acronym or abbreviation: SCAT

Wellington Road, Taunton, Somerset, TA1 5AX

Tel: 01823 366331
Fax: 01823 366418
E-mail: enquiries@somerset.ac.uk

Website:
http://www.somerset.ac.uk
General college information and course search.

Enquiries:
Enquiries to: Information Officer

Founded:
1974

Organisation type and purpose:
Suitable for ages: FE & HE.

Subject coverage:
Art and design, performing arts, business and management studies, information technology, catering and hospitality, hairdressing and beauty therapy, community and caring services, construction, automotive engineering, engineering technology, humanities, science, access studies, A levels, health studies, leisure and tourism, sports-related courses, courses for students with learning difficulties/disabilities, adult education classes, commercial courses.

Library catalogue:
All or part available in-house

Printed publications:
The following prospectuses are available free on request:
Adult Education and Part-time Prospectus
Further Education Prospectus
Higher Education Prospectus

Publications list:
Available online and in print

Access to staff:
Contact by letter, by telephone, by fax, by e-mail, in person and via website
Hours: Mon to Fri, 0900 to 1700

Access for disabled people:
Parking provided, toilet facilities

SOMERSET COUNSELLING CENTRE

Acronym or abbreviation: SCC

38 Belvedere Road, Taunton, Somerset, TA1 1HD

Tel: 01823 337049
E-mail: info@scctaunton.org.uk

Website:
http://www.wpf.org.uk
http://www.scctaunton.org.uk

Enquiries:
Enquiries to: Centre Manager

Other contacts: Counselling Service Manager for referral for counselling.

Founded:
1990

Organisation type and purpose:
Voluntary organisation, registered charity (charity number 1038975), training organisation. Counselling service and training courses.

Subject coverage:
Counselling Service. Assessment and weekly open-ended therapeutic counselling, sliding scale of fees. Training Workshops

Printed publications:
Information pamphlets (free)

Access to staff:
Contact by letter, by telephone, by e-mail and via website
Hours: Mon, Wed, Fri, Receptionist usually available 1000 to 1500
Special comments: 24 hours answerphone, calls returned within one working day.

Access for disabled people:
Toilet facilities

Affiliated to:
Westminster Pastoral Foundation (WPF)
23 Kensington Square, London, W8 5HN; tel: 020 7361 4864; fax: 020 7361 4860; e-mail: counselling@wpf.org.uk

SOMERSET COUNTY FEDERATION OF WOMEN'S INSTITUTES

11 Trull Road, Taunton, Somerset, TA1 4PT

Tel: 01823 284261
Fax: 01823 322545
E-mail: wiltonlodge@somersetwi.fsbusiness.co.uk

Website:
http://www.somersetwi.fsbusiness.co.uk
Events, etc.

Enquiries:
Enquiries to: County Secretary

Founded:
1918

Organisation type and purpose:
National organisation, membership association (membership is by subscription), present number of members: 5500, voluntary organisation, registered charity (charity number 1022578), training organisation.

Access to staff:
Contact by letter, by telephone, by fax and by e-mail
Hours: Mon, Tue, Wed, 0930 to 1245 and 1315 to 1530

Access for disabled people:
Parking provided, level entry

SOMERSET ENVIRONMENTAL RECORDS CENTRE

Acronym or abbreviation: SERC

Tonedale Mill, Wellington, Somerset, TA20 0AW

Tel: 01823 664450
Fax: 01823 652411
E-mail: info@somerc.com

Website:
http://www.somerc.com
Example Biodiversity data, publications list, IHS, biological recording.

Founded:
1989

Organisation type and purpose:
Advisory body, training organisation, consultancy.

Subject coverage:
Environmental topics specific to Somerset; wildlife, biodiversity, flora, fauna, geological, protected species, habitats, wildlife sites.

Museum or gallery collection, archive, or library special collection:
Site specific and location records of more than 4000 sites

Printed publications:
Publications – see website

Electronic and video publications:
IHS Integrated Habitat System (CD-ROM)

Access to staff:
Contact by telephone and by e-mail
Hours: Mon to Fri, 0900 to 1700
Special comments: Charges made for some services.

Affiliated to:
National Federation of Biological Recording

Parent body:
Somerset Wildlife Trust

SOMERSET FEDERATION OF YOUNG FARMERS CLUB

Acronym or abbreviation: Somerset YFC

The Old School, School Road, Weston Zoyland, Bridgwater, Somerset, TA7 0LN

Tel: 01278 681711
Fax: 01278 691912
E-mail: admin@somersetyfc.org.uk

Website:
http://www.somersetyfc.org.uk

Enquiries:
Enquiries to: Federation Co-ordinator

Founded:
1934

Organisation type and purpose:
Membership association (membership is by subscription), present number of members: 800, registered charity (charity number 273051).

Subject coverage:
Agriculture, rural youth work, social education.

Publications list:
Available in print

Access to staff:
Contact by letter, by telephone, by fax, by e-mail, in person and via website. Non-members charged.
Hours: Mon to Fri, 0900 to 1700

Access for disabled people:
Parking provided, level entry, access to all public areas, toilet facilities

Affiliated to:
National Federation of Young Farmers Clubs (NFYFC)
Stoneleigh Park, Stoneleigh, Warwickshire, CV8 2LG; tel: 024 7685 7200; fax: 024 7685 7229; e-mail: post@nfyfc.org.uk; website: www.nfyfc.org .uk

SOMERSET LIBRARIES

Enquiry Centre, Paul Street, Taunton, Somerset, TA1 3XZ

Tel: 01823 336370
Fax: 01823 272178
E-mail: enquiry@somerset.gov.uk

Website:
http://www.foursite.somerset.gov.uk
Library catalogue.

Enquiries:
Enquiries to: Librarian

Organisation type and purpose:
Public library.

Library catalogue:
All or part available online

Access to staff:
Contact by letter, by telephone, by fax and by e-mail
Hours: Mon, Tue, Thu, 0930 to 1800; Wed, Fri, 0930 to 1900; Sat, 0930 to 1600

Parent body:
Library Administration Centre
  Mount Street, Bridgwater, Somerset, TA6 3ES;
  tel: 01278 451201; fax: 01278 452787

SOMERSET STUDIES LIBRARY

The Library, Paul Street, Taunton, Somerset, TA1 3XZ

Tel: 01823 340300
Fax: 01823 340301
E-mail: somstud@somerset.gov.uk

Website:
http://www.librarieswest.org.uk
Library catalogue (combined with the rest of the public libraries in Somerset and four neighbouring authorities).

Enquiries:
Enquiries to: Librarian

Founded:
1973

Organisation type and purpose:
Public library.

Subject coverage:
History, archaeology, genealogy and natural history of historic county of Somerset.

Library catalogue:
All or part available online

Access to staff:
Contact by letter, by telephone, by fax, by e-mail and in person
Hours: Mon, Tue, Thu, 0930 to 1730; Wed, Fri, 0930 to 1900; Sat, 0930 to 1600

SOMERVILLE COLLEGE LIBRARY

Oxford, OX2 6HD

Tel: 01865 270694
Fax: 01865 270620
E-mail: library@somerville.ox.ac.uk

Enquiries:
Enquiries to: Librarian

Founded:
1879

Organisation type and purpose:
University department or institute.
College of Oxford University.

Subject coverage:
Main subjects read in the University.

Museum or gallery collection, archive, or library special collection:
Amelia B Edwards Library and Manuscript
  Collection
John Stuart Mill Library
Margaret Kennedy correspondence
Percy Withers Library and family correspondence
Vernon Lee (Violet Paget) correspondence

Non-library collection catalogue:
All or part available in-house

Library catalogue:
All or part available in-house

Access to staff:
Contact by letter, by telephone, by fax and by e-mail. Appointment necessary. Letter of introduction required.
Hours: Mon to Fri, 0900 to 1700

SONS OF DIVINE PROVIDENCE

Acronym or abbreviation: SDP

13 Lower Teddington Road, Hampton Wick,
Kingston Upon Thames, Surrey, KT1 4EU

Tel: 020 8977 5130
Fax: 020 8977 0105

Website:
http://www.sonsofdivineprovidence.org/literature

Enquiries:
Enquiries to: Senior Administrator

Founded:
1952

Organisation type and purpose:
Registered charity (charity number 1088675).

Subject coverage:
Charitable company running two care homes for the elderly, three residential care homes for people with learning disabilities, a horticultural training centre and units of independent accommodation.

Publications list:
Available online

Access to staff:
Contact by letter, by telephone and via website.
Appointment necessary.
Hours: Mon to Fri, 0900 to 1700

SORIS

PO Box 1108, Berkhamsted, Hertfordshire, HP4 2XW

Tel: 01442 870310
Fax: 0870 7059037
E-mail: cdrew@soris.org

Website:
http://www.soris.org

Enquiries:
Enquiries to: Principal Consultant

Founded:
1980

Formerly a part of:
Chemical Industries' Association (year of change 2001); Chemical Industry Regional Centre of Excellence (CIRCE Ltd) (year of change 2005)

Formerly called:
SORIS Ltd (year of change 1992)

Organisation type and purpose:
International organisation, trade association (membership is by subscription), service industry, research organisation.
Provides chemical market intelligence, soft information and tailored introductions.

Subject coverage:
Chemical intelligence and information-broking for chemistry-using industries.

Museum or gallery collection, archive, or library special collection:
Special Chemical Return to 1993

Printed publications:
Newsletter (monthly for subscribers)

Access to staff:
Contact by letter, by telephone, by fax, by e-mail and via website. Appointment necessary. Non-members charged.
Hours: Mon to Fri, 0900 to 1700

Links with:
Chemical Business Network Group
Chemical Industries Association
Chemical Industry Consultants Association
Chemical Innovation Knowledge Transfer
Network
Chemicals North West
Royal Society of Chemistry
Society of Chemical Industry
Yorkshire Chemical Focus

SOUND RESEARCH LABORATORIES LIMITED

Acronym or abbreviation: SRL

Head Office & Laboratory, Holbrook Hall, Little
Waldingfield, Sudbury, Suffolk, CO10 0TH

Tel: 01787 247595
Fax: 01787 248420
E-mail: srl@soundresearch.co.uk

Website:
http://www.soundresearch.co.uk

Enquiries:
Enquiries to: Managing Director

Founded:
1967

Organisation type and purpose:
Consultancy.

Subject coverage:
Acoustics, noise and vibration control, traffic noise, vehicle noise, auditoria acoustics, industrial noise control, laboratory testing, product development.

Printed publications:
Airflow and Acoustic Measurements (lecture
  manual)
Basic Vibration Control (lecture manual)
Industrial Noise Control (lecture manual)
Mechanical Services Noise Control (lecture
  manual)
Noise Control in Industry (book)
Noise Control in Mechanical Services (book)
Practical Building Acoustics (lecture manual)
Technical reports

Access to staff:
Contact by letter, by telephone, by fax and by e-mail
Hours: Mon to Fri, 0900 to 1700

Access to building, collection or gallery:
No access other than to staff

Access for disabled people:
Parking provided, level entry, toilet facilities

SOUTH AFRICA HOUSE LIBRARY

South African High Commission, Trafalgar Square,
London, WC2N 5DP

Tel: 020 7451 7299
Fax: 020 7451 7289
E-mail: london.general@foreign.gov.za

Website:
http://www.gov.za
South African government portal.
http://www.safrica.info
Official gateway for tourists, immigrants, investors, citizens, South Africans abroad and a wide range of general information.
http://www.artslink.co.za
Arts and cultural events in South Africa.
http://www.southafricahouse.com
General items of relevance to people in Britain on government activity in South Africa. Information includes topical issues, business and economic information, and matters relating to South African passports, visas and residence permits. Also has websites relevant to links between Britain and South Africa.

Enquiries:
Enquiries to: Librarian

Organisation type and purpose:
Government (South Africa).

Subject coverage:
South Africa.

Printed publications:
South Africa Yearbook (to organisations, schools etc only)

Electronic and video publications:
South Africa Yearbook (past Yearbooks in pdf
  format only)
Order electronic and video publications from: http://www.info.gov.za/aboutsa/index.htm as text version or http://www.gcis.gov.za/docs/publications/yearbook/index.html for pdf format

Access to staff:
Contact by letter and by fax
Hours: Mon to Fri, 0900 to 1300 and 1345 to 1700

continued overleaf

Special comments: Fax should be marked Attention Reference Library.

Access to building, collection or gallery:
No access other than to staff
Special comments: Library not on open access, written enquiries only.

SOUTH AFRICAN TOURISM

5–6 Alt Grove, Wimbledon, London, SW19 4DZ

Tel: 020 8971 9351
Fax: 020 8944 6705
E-mail: info@south-african-tourism.org

Website:
http://www.south-african-tourism.org
Order publications
http://www.southafrica.net

Enquiries:
Enquiries to: Information Officer

Organisation type and purpose:
National government body.

Subject coverage:
South African tourism, business travel, special interest tours, conferences and exhibitions, incentives.

Museum or gallery collection, archive, or library special collection:
Film and photographs (colour and black-and-white) libraries

Trade and statistical information:
Tourist data on South Africa.

Printed publications:
South African Tourism Factfiler 2002
Highlights Map 2002

Electronic and video publications:
Photographs available from photo library on website

Access to staff:
Contact by letter, by telephone, by fax, by e-mail, in person and via website
Hours: Mon to Fri, 0900 to 1700
Special comments: Appointments by prior arrangement.

Access for disabled people:
Level entry, toilet facilities

SOUTH AYRSHIRE LIBRARIES

Formal name: South Ayrshire Library and Information Service

Carnegie Library, 12 Main Street, Ayr, KA8 8ED

Tel: 01292 286385
Fax: 01292 611593
E-mail: carnegie.library@south-ayrshire.gov.uk

Website:
http://www.south-ayrshire.gov.uk/libraries/
General information about the library service.

Enquiries:
Enquiries to: Development Officer – Libraries Manager
Direct tel: 01292 288820
Direct fax: 01292 619019
Direct e-mail: jean.inness@south-ayrshire.gov.uk

Organisation type and purpose:
Local government body, public library.

Subject coverage:
General, local history of Kyle and Carrick, and South Ayrshire, Robert Burns.

Museum or gallery collection, archive, or library special collection:
Ayrshire (Kyle and Carrick from 1975)
Robert Burns Collection

Non-library collection catalogue:
All or part available in-house

Library catalogue:
All or part available in-house

Printed publications:
Local history pamphlets and illustrations
Ayr Memories (£4.95)
Girvan Memories (£4.95)
Troon Memories (£4.95)
History of Prestwick (£18)
History of Ayr (£14.95)
Prestwick in the 40's (£5)
Old Parish Records Ayr 1766–1820 (£6.50)
Tarbolton Churchyard Monumental Inscriptions (£4.95)
Smuggling & The Ayrshire Economic Boom (£4)
Order printed publications from: Enterprise Officer, South Ayrshire Council
Library HQ, 26 Green Street, Ayr, KA8 8ED, tel: 01292 288820, fax: 01292 619019, e-mail: jean.inness@south-ayrshire.gov.uk

Publications list:
Available in print

Access to staff:
Contact by letter, by telephone, by fax, by e-mail and in person. Appointment necessary.
Hours: Mon, Tue, Thu, Fri, 0900 to 1930; Wed, Sat, 0900 to 1700

Access for disabled people:
Ramped entry, access to all public areas, toilet facilities

SOUTH BEDFORDSHIRE DISTRICT COUNCIL

The District Offices, High Street North, Dunstable, Bedfordshire, LU6 1LF

Tel: 01582 472222
Fax: 01782 474009 or 01582 474058

Website:
http://www.southbeds.gov.uk
Information for residents, visitors to and businesses in South Bedfordshire, about District Council services and local information.

Enquiries:
Enquiries to: Chief Executive
Direct tel: 01582 474047
Direct e-mail: jon.ruddick@southbeds.gov.uk

Organisation type and purpose:
Local government body.

Subject coverage:
Local government services: administrative, technical, financial, planning and estates, environmental health and housing.

Printed publications:
Council Plan (full and summary, annual)
Informaction (residents magazine)
Housing matters (tenants magazine)

Access to staff:
Contact by letter, by telephone, by fax, by e-mail and in person
Hours: Mon to Thu, 0900 to 1700; Fri, 0900 to 1645

Access to building, collection or gallery:
Mon to Thu, 0900 to 1700; Fri, 0900 to 1645

Access for disabled people:
Hours: Mon to Thu, 0900 to 1700; Fri, 0900 to 1645

SOUTH BUCKS DISTRICT COUNCIL

Council Offices, Windsor Road, Slough, Berkshire, SL1 2HN

Tel: 01753 533333\ Minicom no. 01753 676251
Fax: 01753 731803
E-mail: sbdc@southbucks.gov.uk

Website:
http://www.southbucks.gov.uk

Enquiries:
Enquiries to: Chief Executive

Organisation type and purpose:
Local government body.

Subject coverage:
All usual local government subjects.

Access to staff:
Contact by letter, by telephone, by fax, by e-mail and in person
Hours: Mon to Wed, 0900 to 1730; Thu to Fri, 0900 to 1700

SOUTH DERBYSHIRE DISTRICT COUNCIL

Acronym or abbreviation: SDDC

Civic Offices, Civic Way, Swadlincote, Derbyshire, DE11 0AH

Tel: 01283 221000\ Minicom no. 01283 595849
Fax: 01283 595964
E-mail: civic.offices@south-derbys.gov.uk

Website:
http://www.south-derbys.gov.uk

Enquiries:
Enquiries to: Customer Services
Direct fax: 01283 595854
Direct e-mail: customer.services@south-derbys.gov.uk

Organisation type and purpose:
Local government body.

Subject coverage:
All aspects of local government.

Access to staff:
Contact by letter, by telephone, by fax, by e-mail and via website
Hours: Mon to Fri, 0900 to 1700

Access for disabled people:
Parking provided, ramped entry, level entry, access to all public areas, toilet facilities

SOUTH EAST AREA LIBRARIES INFORMATION CO-OPERATIVE

Acronym or abbreviation: SEAL

Central Library, Townley Road, Bexleyheath, Kent, DA6 7HJ

Tel: 020 8303 7777 ext. 3450
Fax: 020 8304 7058
E-mail: david.bowles@bexley.gov.uk

Enquiries:
Enquiries to: Secretary

Founded:
1969

Organisation type and purpose:
Local information co-operative.

Subject coverage:
The organisation promotes co-operation between all types of libraries located in the London Boroughs of Bexley, Bromley, Greenwich, Lewisham and Southwark, the Medway Council area and the County of Kent. It is not a direct information provider.

Printed publications:
Annual Report and Directory of Members
(circulated to member organisations)

Access to staff:
Contact by letter, by telephone, by fax and by e-mail
Hours: Mon to Fri, 0930 to 1730

SOUTH EAST ENGLAND TOURIST BOARD

Acronym or abbreviation: SEETB

40 Chamberlayne Road, Eastleigh, Hampshire, SO50 5JH

Tel: 023 8062 5400
E-mail: customerservices@tourismse.com

Website:
http://www.southeastengland.uk.com

Tourist information (accommodation, events, attractions etc)
http://www.tourismsoutheast.com
Tourism statistics, business advice.
http://www.southeastwalks.com
Walking holidays/activities.
http://www.southeastgardens.co.uk
Gardens open to the public.

Enquiries:
Enquiries to: Company Secretary

Founded:
1973

Organisation type and purpose:
Advisory body, membership association (membership is by subscription), service industry.

Subject coverage:
Tourist information on accommodation, visitor attractions, events of special interest and conference venues in South East England i.e. Kent, Surrey, East and West Sussex.

Trade and statistical information:
Tourism volumes and values, hotel occupancies and tourism investments in the area.

Printed publications:
Annual Report
Bed and Breakfast Touring Map (annual, free)
Group Organisers' Guide (annual, free)
Regional Tourism Strategy
Various publications and brochures produced (mainly free of charge)

Access to staff:
Contact by letter, by telephone, by fax and by e-mail
Hours: Mon to Fri, 0900 to 1700

SOUTH EAST LONDON ARMY CADET FORCE

Formal name: Army Cadet Force
Acronym or abbreviation: ACF

Hollyhedge House, Wat Tyler Road, Blackheath, London, SE3 0QZ

Tel: 020 8692 4066
Fax: 020 8694 0566
E-mail: ceoseacf@reserve-forces-london.mod.uk

Enquiries:
Enquiries to: Executive Officer

Organisation type and purpose:
National organisation, voluntary organisation, suitable for ages: 12 to 18.
The Army Cadet Force is a National Voluntary Youth Organisation. It is sponsored by the Army and provides challenging military, adventurous, and community activities. Its aim is to inspire young people to achieve success in life with a spirit of service to the Queen, their country and their local community, and to develop in them the qualities of a good citizen.

Subject coverage:
Adventurous and challenging activities, leadership, character training, work for the community, understanding of the Army and its place in national life.

Printed publications:
Army Cadet National (quarterly, via ACFA, Duke of York's HQ)
Order printed publications from: ACFA, Holderness House, 51–61 Clifton Street, London, EC2A 4DW
South East London ACF
Hollyhedge House, Wat Tyler Road, Blackheath, SE3 0QZ

Publications list:
Available online

Access to staff:
Contact by letter, by telephone, by fax and by e-mail
Hours: Mon to Fri, 0900 to 1700

Links with:
Department for Education and Employment
National Council for Voluntary Youth Services

Territorial Army Volunteer Reserve
Supports the:
Cadet Force which is sponsored by the Army

SOUTH GLOUCESTERSHIRE COUNCIL

Council Offices, Castle Street, Thornbury, Gloucestershire, BS35 1HF

Tel: 01454 868686\ Minicom no. 01454 863055
Fax: 01454 863855
E-mail: mailbox@southglos.gov.uk

Website:
http://www.southglos.gov.uk

Enquiries:
Enquiries to: Public Relations Manager
Direct tel: 01454 863890
Direct fax: 01454 865046
Direct e-mail: stella_parkes@southglos.gov.uk

Founded:
1996

Organisation type and purpose:
Local government body.

Subject coverage:
Local government services.

Printed publications:
All available on the website

Access to staff:
Contact by letter, by telephone, by fax, by e-mail and via website
Hours: Mon to Thu, 0845 to 1700; Fri 0845 to 1630

Access to building, collection or gallery:
No prior appointment required
Hours: Mon to Thu, 0845 to 1700; Fri 0845 to 1630

Access for disabled people:
Parking provided, ramped entry, level entry, access to all public areas, toilet facilities

SOUTH KENT COLLEGE

Shorncliffe Road, Folkestone, Kent, CT20 2TZ

Tel: 01303 858340
Fax: 01303 858400
E-mail: webmaster@southkent.ac.uk

Website:
http://www.southkent.ac.uk

Enquiries:
Enquiries to: Learning Resources Manager
Direct tel: 01304 244341
Direct e-mail: paul.north@southkent.ac.uk

Organisation type and purpose:
College of further education.

Subject coverage:
Business studies, management, mechanical engineering, electrical and electronic engineering, building, education, social sciences, humanities, sciences, information technology, media studies, catering, health and social care, hairdressing and beauty.

Library catalogue:
All or part available in-house

Access to staff:
Contact in person
Hours: Mon to Thu, 0845 to 1930; Fri, 0845 to 1615
Special comments: May be closed during vacations, so enquire first

Access for disabled people:
Parking provided, level entry, toilet facilities

Also at:
South Kent College
Jemmett Road, Ashford, Kent, TN23 4RJ; tel: 01233 655573; fax: 01233 655501
South Kent College
Maison Dieu Road, Dover, CT16 1DH; tel: 01304 244344; fax: 01304 244301

SOUTH KESTEVEN DISTRICT COUNCIL

Acronym or abbreviation: SKDC

Council Offices, St Peters Hill, Grantham, Lincolnshire, NG31 6PZ

Tel: 01476 406080
Fax: 01476 406000
E-mail: d.nicholls@skdc.com

Website:
http://www.skdc.com

Enquiries:
Enquiries to: Public Relations Manager
Direct tel: 01476 406128
Other contacts: Customer Services Manager

Founded:
1974

Organisation type and purpose:
Local government body.

Subject coverage:
All aspects of local government.

Printed publications:
District Line (council newsletter)
Best Value Performance Plan
L A 21 document
Welland Partnership Strategy

Publications list:
Available in print

Access to staff:
Contact by letter, by telephone, by fax, by e-mail and via website. Appointment necessary.
Hours: Mon to Thu, 0845 to 1715; Fri, 0845 to 1645

Access for disabled people:
Ramped entry, toilet facilities

Connections with:
East Midlands Regional Local Government Association (EMRLGA)
The Belvoir Suite, Council Offices, Nottingham Road, Melton Mowbray, Leicestershire, LE13 0UL

Member of:
East Midlands Regional Assembly
Federation of Economic Development Authorities
FEDA Administrator, 36 Sheep Street, Shipston-on-Stour, Warwickshire, CU36 4AE
Lincolnshire Development Partnership
The Chief Executive, Central Support Team, Lincolnshire County Council, Lincoln
Lincolnshire Local Government Association
The Chief Executive, Lincolnshire County Council, Lincoln
Local Government Association
Local Government House, Smith Square, London, SW1P 3HZ

Other addresses:
Bourne Area Office
Town Hall, North Street, Bourne, PE10 9EA; tel: 01476 406071
Market Deeping Area Office
89 High Street, Market Deeping, PE6 8ED; tel: 01476 406070
Stamford Area Office
1 Maiden Lane, Stamford, PE9 2AZ; tel: 01476 406072

SOUTH LANARKSHIRE COUNCIL

Council Building, Almada Street, Hamilton, South Lanarkshire, ML3 0AA

Tel: 01698 454444
Fax: 01698 454275

Enquiries:
Enquiries to: Chief Executive
Other contacts: Public Relations Manager

Founded:
1996

Organisation type and purpose:
Local government body.

continued overleaf

Councillors by election 67. Staff 15,000 by appointment.
Unitary Council.

Subject coverage:
Local government.

Trade and statistical information:
South Lanarkshire statistical information; South Lanarkshire statistical profile contains information on area's characteristics: physical, population, housing, economy and education.

Access to staff:
Contact by letter, by telephone and by fax. Appointment necessary.
Hours: Mon to Thu, 0845 to 1645; Fri, 0845 to 1615

Member of:
Convention of Scottish Local Authorities (COSLA) Edinburgh

Principal Offices:
Atholl House
Churchill Avenue, East Kilbride, G74 1LU; tel: 01355 806000
Civic Centre
Andrew Street, East Kilbride, G74 1AB; tel: 01355 806000
Royal Burgh House
380 King Street, Rutherglen, G73 1DB; tel: 0141 613 5000
South Vennel
Lanark, ML11 7JT; tel: 01555 673000

SOUTH LANARKSHIRE COUNCIL ARCHIVES AND INFORMATION MANAGEMENT SERVICE

30 Hawbank Road, College Milton, East Kilbride, South Lanarkshire, G74 5EX

Tel: 01355 239193
Fax: 01355 242365
E-mail: archives@southlanarkshire.gov.uk

Website:
http://www.southlanarkshire.gov.uk/gateway
Summary of records held
http://www.scan.org.uk
Collection catalogue

Enquiries:
Enquiries to: Archivist

Founded:
1997

Organisation type and purpose:
Local government archive.

Subject coverage:
Local, family, social, economic and administrative history of South Lanarkshire.

Museum or gallery collection, archive, or library special collection:
Archives of South Lanarkshire Council and predecessor local authorities and public corporations
Deposited archives of business, voluntary organisations and associations in South Lanarkshire

Non-library collection catalogue:
All or part available online

Access to staff:
Contact by letter, by telephone, by fax and by e-mail. Appointment necessary.
Hours: Mon to Fri, 0930 to 1630; other times by arrangement
Special comments: All visits by appointment only.

SOUTH LANARKSHIRE LIBRARY SERVICE

Education Resources, Council Offices, Almada Street, Hamilton, South Lanarkshire, ML3 0AE

Tel: 01698 454545
Fax: 01698 454465
E-mail: diana.barr@southlanarkshire.gov.uk

Website:
http://www.southlanarkshire.gov.uk
http://www.slc-learningcentres.org.uk
http://www.library.southlanarkshire.gov.uk
Library catalogue.

Enquiries:
Enquiries to: Manager
Direct tel: 01698 454412
Other contacts: Information Services Co-ordinator (tel. 01698 452220)

Founded:
1996

Organisation type and purpose:
Local government body, public library.

Subject coverage:
General, history and topography of South Lanarkshire, health and safety, government statistics and other publications.

Museum or gallery collection, archive, or library special collection:
Audio archives, jazz, classical, contemporary
Barbour health and safety microfile
Genealogical index
Statutory government publications
Vehicle technical information
Collection on Robert Owen and New Lanark (Lanark Library)
William Smellie Collection (obstetrics, midwifery)
Collection on the estates of the Dukes of Hamilton (Hamilton Library)
Lace making (Hamilton Library)

Non-library collection catalogue:
All or part available online and in-house

Library catalogue:
All or part available online

Printed publications:
Book lists of local history

Access to staff:
Contact by letter, by telephone, by fax and by e-mail
Hours: Mon to Fri, 0900 to 1700

Parent body:
South Lanarkshire Council

SOUTH LONDON BOTANICAL INSTITUTE

Acronym or abbreviation: SLBI

323 Norwood Road, London, SE24 9AQ

Tel: 020 8674 5787
Fax: 020 8674 5787
E-mail: info@slbi.org.uk

Website:
http://www.slbi.org.uk

Enquiries:
Enquiries to: Chairman

Founded:
1910

Organisation type and purpose:
Learned society (membership is by subscription), present number of members: 275, registered charity (charity number 214251).
Education in botany. Small botanic garden, library and herbarium.

Subject coverage:
General botany, seed plants, pteridophytes, bryophytes, lichens.

Education services:
WEA classes and primary school groups (pre-book)

Museum or gallery collection, archive, or library special collection:
Extensive herbarium, British and European, including the Beeby and Palmer Collection from the Orkneys and Shetlands, seed collection, pteridophytes, bryophytes, lichen and marine algae
Historic floras; 35mm slide collection

Taxonomic library: British and European floras, British county floras

Library catalogue:
All or part available in-house

Printed publications:
Gazette (3 to 4 times a year, free)
Order printed publications from: Administrator

Access to staff:
Contact by letter, by telephone, by fax and by e-mail. Appointment necessary.
Hours: Thu, 1000 to 1600, or by appointment

Access to building, collection or gallery:
Prior appointment required, except on Thu

Access for disabled people:
Garden accessible for wheelchairs

SOUTH NORFOLK DISTRICT COUNCIL

South Norfolk House, Swan Lane, Long Stratton, Norwich, Norfolk, NR15 2XE

Tel: 01508 533633
Fax: 01508 533695

Website:
http://www.south-norfolk.gov.uk
Tourism, economic development/business, local services and news.

Enquiries:
Enquiries to: Chief Executive
Direct tel: 01508 533601
Direct fax: 01508 533619
Direct e-mail: sdinneen@s-norfolk.gov.uk
Other contacts: Community Information Officer for general information (not advertising).

Organisation type and purpose:
Local government body.

Subject coverage:
District Council Services.

Printed publications:
The Link (community magazine, half yearly)

Access to staff:
Contact by letter, by telephone, by fax, by e-mail, in person and via website
Hours: Mon to Thu, 0845 to 1700; Fri, 0845 to 1615

Access for disabled people:
Parking provided, level entry, access to all public areas, toilet facilities

SOUTH NORTHAMPTONSHIRE DISTRICT COUNCIL

Acronym or abbreviation: SNC

Council Offices, Springfields, Towcester, Northamptonshire, NN12 6AE

Tel: 01327 350211
Fax: 01327 359219

Website:
http://www.southnorthants.gov.uk

Enquiries:
Enquiries to: Head of Community and Leisure Development
Direct tel: 01327 322340
Direct fax: 01327 322332
Other contacts: Chief Executive

Founded:
1974

Organisation type and purpose:
Local government body.

Subject coverage:
Council services and amenities; corporate services, education, environmental services, finance, housing, legal services, personnel services, planning development, property and technical services, roads and transportation, social work, council tax and other payments, leisure and tourism.

Printed publications:
Council Guide book
Year book

Access to staff:
Contact by letter, by telephone, by fax and in person
Hours: Mon to Fri, 0900 to 1700

SOUTH NOTTINGHAM COLLEGE

Greythorn Drive, West Bridgford, Nottingham, NG2 5GA

Tel: 0115 914 6400
Fax: 0115 914 6444

Enquiries:
Enquiries to: Curriculum Support Manager
Direct tel: 0115 914 6418
Direct e-mail: wilsonp@snc.ac.uk

Founded:
1971

Organisation type and purpose:
Suitable for ages: 16+.
College of further education.

Subject coverage:
Printing.

Non-library collection catalogue:
All or part available online and in-house

Library catalogue:
All or part available online and in-house

Access to staff:
Contact by letter, by telephone, by fax and by e-mail. Appointment necessary.
Hours: Mon to Thu, 0830 to 1930; Fri, 0830 to 1600
Special comments: Academic term time only.

Access for disabled people:
Parking provided, ramped entry, access to all public areas, toilet facilities

Associate college of:
Nottingham Trent University

Other addresses:
Charnwood site
  tel: 0115 914 6300; fax: 0115 914 6333

SOUTH OXFORDSHIRE DISTRICT COUNCIL

Acronym or abbreviation: SODC

Benson Lane, Crowmarsh Gifford, Wallingford, Oxfordshire, OX10 8HQ

Tel: 01491 823000
Fax: 01491 823104

Website:
http://www.southoxon.gov.uk

Enquiries:
Enquiries to: Public Relations Officer
Direct tel: 01491 823748
Direct fax: 01491 823420

Founded:
1974

Organisation type and purpose:
Local government body.

Subject coverage:
Information relating to council issues can be obtained from the multitude of sources available.

Museum or gallery collection, archive, or library special collection:
Documentation, in general, may be viewed but not taken

Printed publications:
Outlook (magazine for all residents of the district)

Access to staff:
Contact by letter, by telephone, by fax, by e-mail and in person. Appointment necessary.

Hours: Mon to Thu, 0830 to 1700; Fri, 0830 to 1630

Access for disabled people:
Parking provided, level entry, toilet facilities

SOUTH RIBBLE BOROUGH COUNCIL

Civic Centre, West Paddock, Leyland, Lancashire, PR25 1DH

Tel: 01772 421491
Fax: 01772 622287
E-mail: info@southribble.gov.uk

Website:
http://www.south-ribblebc.gov.uk

Enquiries:
Enquiries to: Public Relations Officer
Direct tel: 01772 625312
Direct e-mail: communications@southribble.gov.uk

Founded:
1974

Organisation type and purpose:
Local government body.

Subject coverage:
Council services and amenities; corporate services, environmental services, finance, housing, legal services, personnel services, planning development and tourism, property and technical services, roads and transportation, council tax and other payments.

Printed publications:
Forward (newspaper, quarterly, free to residents)

Access to staff:
Contact by letter, by telephone, by fax and by e-mail
Hours: Mon to Thu, 0830 to 1715; Fri, 0830 to 1645

Access for disabled people:
Parking provided, level entry, access to all public areas, toilet facilities

SOUTH SHROPSHIRE DISTRICT COUNCIL

Acronym or abbreviation: SSDC

Stone House, Corve Street, Ludlow, Shropshire, SY8 1DG

Tel: 01584 813000
Fax: 01584 813127
E-mail: reception@southshropshire.gov.uk

Website:
http://www.southshropshire.gov.uk/

Enquiries:
Enquiries to: Chief Executive
Direct tel: 01584 813201
Direct fax: 01584 813120
Direct e-mail: gcbiggs_ssdc@btconnect.com

Founded:
1974

Organisation type and purpose:
Local government body.

Access to staff:
Contact by letter, by telephone, by fax, by e-mail, in person and via website
Hours: Mon to Thu, 0840 to 1715; Fri, 0840 to 1630

Access for disabled people:
Parking provided, toilet facilities

SOUTH SOMERSET DISTRICT COUNCIL

Council Offices, Brympton Way, Yeovil, Somerset, BA20 2HT

Tel: 01935 462462
Fax: 01935 462503
E-mail: info@southsomerset.gov.uk

Website:
http://www.southsomerset.gov.uk
500 pages of information about the district, the council and local services and facilities, designed for the local community, businesses and visitors.

Enquiries:
Enquiries to: Communications Manager
Direct tel: 01935 462122

Founded:
1974

Organisation type and purpose:
Local government body.

Subject coverage:
Long distance walking routes in South Somerset, circular walks, cycle routes, horse trails in South Somerset, business premises and opportunities available in South Somerset.

Trade and statistical information:
Statistical information about South Somerset.

Printed publications:
News and Views
Taxing Times
Contact Points

Access to staff:
Contact by letter, by telephone, by fax, by e-mail and in person. Appointment necessary.
Hours: Mon to Fri, 0900 to 1700

SOUTH TYNESIDE COLLEGE – HEBBURN

Acronym or abbreviation: STC

Mill Lane, Hebburn, Tyne and Wear, NE31 2ER

Tel: 0191 427 3614
Fax: 0191 427 3555

Website:
http://www.stc.ac.uk
College website.

Enquiries:
Enquiries to: Assistant Librarian

Founded:
1984

Subject coverage:
Mechanical engineering, health studies, performing arts, welding, automobile engineering, social work, child care, health and safety, management, sports, leisure and tourism.

Museum or gallery collection, archive, or library special collection:
British Standards on CD-ROM
Bound Copies of Hansard 1988–1999

Library catalogue:
All or part available in-house

Access to staff:
Contact by letter, by telephone and by fax
Hours: Mon, Wed, 0900 to 2000; Tue, Thu, 0900 to 1700; Fri, 0900 to 1630

Access for disabled people:
Parking provided, ramped entry

Other Campus at:
South Tyneside College
  St Georges Avenue, South Shields, Tyne & Wear, NE34 6ET; tel: 0191 427 3606; fax: 0191 427 3643

SOUTH TYNESIDE COLLEGE – SOUTH SHIELDS

St Georges Avenue, South Shields, Tyne and Wear, NE34 6ET

Tel: 0191 427 3500
Fax: 0191 427 3535
E-mail: margaret.haram@stc.ac.uk

Enquiries:
Enquiries to: Librarian
Direct tel: 0191 427 3605

continued overleaf

Organisation type and purpose:
Post-compulsory education, 14–16 provision
College of further and higher education.

Subject coverage:
Sixth form, teacher education, business and
professional studies, hairdressing and beauty
therapies, health care and early years, nautical
studies, marine engineering, general engineering

Library catalogue:
All or part available in-house

Access to staff:
Contact by letter, by telephone and by e-mail
Hours: Term time: Mon to Fri, 0830 to 2000
Vacations: Mon to Fri, 0900 to 1700

Access for disabled people:
Parking provided, ramped entry, level entry, access
to all public areas, toilet facilities

SOUTH TYNESIDE LIBRARY

Central Library, Prince George Square, South
Shields, Tyne and Wear, NE33 2PE

Tel: 0191 427 1818
Fax: 0191 427 8085
E-mail: reference.library@southtyneside.gov.uk

Website:
http://www.southtyneside.info/
learningandleisure/libraries.asp

Enquiries:
Enquiries to: Libraries Manager
Direct tel: 0191 424 7880
Direct e-mail: mark.freeman@southtyneside.gov.uk

Created by the merger of:
Jarrow, Hebburn, Whitburn, South Shields and
Boldon Libraries

Organisation type and purpose:
Local government body, public library.

Subject coverage:
General public library information service, local
history of South Tyneside, the Jarrow March, slum
clearance, sailing ships, shipbuilding.

**Museum or gallery collection, archive, or library
special collection:**
Jarrow March Collection
Kelly Collection; posters from a South Shields
    jobbing printer c.1790 to c.1880
Manuscripts and local history: Fox, Wallis and
    Flagg collections
Photograph collections of South Shields: Willetts,
    Flagg, Parry, Grimes, Cleet, Peterson and Shields
    Gazette

Library catalogue:
All or part available online

Printed publications:
Various publications including:
A Victorian Village School: Mr Grundy at
    Whitburn (S. Reeder, £2.95)
History of Hebburn 1894–1994 (£2.25)
Notes on the History of Shipbuilding in South
    Shields 1746–1946 (A. C. Flagg, £5.50)
Preservation of Life from Shipwreck: Trilogy on the
    history of the lifeboat (B. Whitaker, 3 vols, £5.50
    each)
South Shields Then and Now (£3.50)
The Borough of South Shields (G. Hodgson, £27
    incl. p&p, out of print)
Order printed publications from: Information and
Education Co-ordinator, at the same address; tel.
0191 424 7865; fax 0191 455 8085; e-mail hildred
.whale@s-tyneside-mbc.gov.uk

Publications list:
Available in print

Access to staff:
Contact by letter, by telephone, by fax, by e-mail,
in person and via website
Hours: Mon to Thu, 0900 to 1900; Fri, 0900 to 1700;
Sat, 0900 to 1600

Member organisation of:
MLA (NE)

SOUTH WARWICKSHIRE EDUCATION CENTRE

Education Centre Library, John Turner Building,
Warwick Hospital, Lakin Road, Warwick, CV34
5BW

Tel: 01926 495321 ext 4287
Fax: 01926 400895
E-mail: veronica.mitchell@swarkhosp-tr.wmids.nhs
.uk

Website:
http://www.swec.org.uk

Enquiries:
Enquiries to: Medical Librarian

Organisation type and purpose:
Hospital.

Subject coverage:
Medicine and related disciplines.

Library catalogue:
All or part available in-house

Access to staff:
Contact by letter, by telephone, by fax, by e-mail
and via website. Appointment necessary.
Hours: Mon, Wed, 0900 to 1700; Tue, Thu, 0900 to
2000; Fri, 0900 to 1630

Access to building, collection or gallery:
Prior appointment required

Access for disabled people:
Parking provided, level entry, access to all public
areas, toilet facilities

SOUTH WEST COAST PATH ASSOCIATION

Acronym or abbreviation: SWCPA

Bowker House, Lee Mill Bridge, Ivybridge, Devon,
PL21 9EF

Tel: 01752 896237
Fax: 01752 893654
E-mail: info@swcp.org.uk

Website:
http://www.swcp.org.uk
Photo tour of South West Coast Path, Association
history, Association literature, latest news of the
Coast Path.

Enquiries:
Enquiries to: Honorary Secretary

Founded:
1973

Organisation type and purpose:
Advisory body, membership association
(membership is by subscription), present number
of members: 5000, voluntary organisation,
registered charity (charity number 266754).
To promote interest in, and the use of, the coast
path. To improve standards of waymaking and
maintenance.

Subject coverage:
The 630 miles of the South West Coast Path, from
Minehead to Poole Harbour via Land's End.

**Museum or gallery collection, archive, or library
special collection:**
8000 Colour slides of coastal scenery along 630
    miles of coast path
Digital archive of 4000 images of the South West
    Coast Path

Printed publications:
Annual Guide (£8.00 plus £2 p&p to a UK address,
    free to members; £3.50 p&p to non-UK)
55 Path Description leaflets of short sections (£1
    each inc. p&p)

Publications list:
Available online and in print

Access to staff:
Contact by letter, by telephone, by fax, by e-mail,
in person and via website. Appointment necessary.
Hours: Any reasonable time

Access to building, collection or gallery:
No prior appointment required
Hours: Mon to Fri, 0900 to 1300

Access for disabled people:
Yes

SOUTH WESTERN REGIONAL LIBRARY SERVICE

Acronym or abbreviation: SWRLS

c/o Library Headquarters, Ridgewood Centre, 244
Station Road, Yate, South Gloucestershire, BS37
4AF

Tel: 01454 865782
Fax: 01454 863309
E-mail: martin.burton@southglos.gov.uk

Website:
http://www.swrls.org.uk

Enquiries:
Enquiries to: Director
Direct tel: 07504 047625
Direct e-mail: desk2@csndesk.eclipse.co.uk

Founded:
1937

Organisation type and purpose:
Charity aimed at developing library cooperation
across the South West of England
Regional library system.

Subject coverage:
General; co-operative library service providing
access to material held by members.

Printed publications:
Annual Report

Access to staff:
Contact by e-mail

SOUTHAMPTON AND FAREHAM CHAMBER OF COMMERCE AND INDUSTRY

Bugle House, 53 Bugle Street, Southampton, SO14
2LF

Tel: 023 8022 3541
Fax: 023 8022 7426
E-mail: info@soton-chamber.co.uk

Website:
http://www.soton-chamber.co.uk

Enquiries:
Enquiries to: Information Officer

Founded:
1851

Organisation type and purpose:
Membership association (membership is by
subscription), present number of members: 1500.
Chamber of Commerce.

Subject coverage:
Business enquiries, business training, events and
seminars, export documentation and advice,
French desk, China desk, lobbying/representation.

**Museum or gallery collection, archive, or library
special collection:**
Business directories
Reference books

Printed publications:
Membership directory (yearly)
Gateway (journal, monthly)
Business South Magazine (incorporating Chamber
    of Commerce News Pages (publ Echo
    Newspaper))

Access to staff:
Contact by letter, by telephone, by fax, by e-mail,
in person and via website. Appointment necessary.
Access for members only. Non-members charged.
Hours: Mon to Fri, 0900 to 1700

Access to building, collection or gallery:
No prior appointment required

SOUTHAMPTON CITY ARCHIVES OFFICE

Civic Centre, Southampton, SO14 7LY

Tel: 023 8083 2251
Fax: 023 8083 2156
E-mail: city.archives@southampton.gov.uk

Enquiries:
Enquiries to: Archivist

Founded:
1953

Organisation type and purpose:
Local government body.

Subject coverage:
Southampton records date from 1199, family and local history.

Museum or gallery collection, archive, or library special collection:
Maritime Records: Crew lists 1863–1913; Central Index of Merchant Seamen, 1918–1941
Business Records: Many local firms' records are held here
Family Records: Southampton Parish Records 1552 to date
Local Government – The Council and its predecessors including the harbour and records of justice

Non-library collection catalogue:
All or part available in-house

Printed publications:
Many guides, histories and maps including:
Information Leaflet
Southampton Papers Nos 1–10
Southampton Records 1: A Guide to the Records of Southampton Corporation and Absorbed Authorities (1964, £1)
Sources for Family History in Southampton Archives Office with map showing parish boundaries (£3)
Town Directory – Southampton in 1620 and the Mayflower
Southampton Crew Lists 1863–1913 (printed on request)
Archives Teaching Pack Southampton in the Second World War (£15, to schools £12)
Set of Maps of different dates showing the historical development of the City 1611 to 1802 (£3)

Publications list:
Available in print

Access to staff:
Contact by letter, by telephone, by fax, by e-mail, in person and via website
Hours: Tue to Fri, 0930 to 1630
Special comments: One late evening each month, by prior appointment, contact office staff for details. Member of CARN system.

Access for disabled people:
Parking provided, level entry, toilet facilities

SOUTHAMPTON CITY COUNCIL

Civic Centre, Southampton, SO14 7LY

Tel: 023 8022 3855\ Minicom no. 023 8083 2798
Fax: 023 8023 4537
E-mail: webmaster@southampton.gov.uk

Website:
http://www.southampton.gov.uk
Website for Southampton, covering all aspects of the city.

Enquiries:
Direct fax: 023 8023 4527
Other contacts: Head of Marketing and Information Division for head of information services.

Organisation type and purpose:
Local government body.

Subject coverage:
All information about Southampton, its services and amenities, history, heritage, highways, leisure, events, local housing, social services, education, libraries etc.

Museum or gallery collection, archive, or library special collection:
Art gallery
Large variety of accessible information (on request)
Library service including reference

Trade and statistical information:
Electoral register, grant schemes in the local area, local business, tourism and historic information, general city information.

Printed publications:
Annual Report (free)
Southampton City News (6 times a year, free)
Southampton Commercial and Industrial Property Register (6 times a year, free)
Wide variety of leaflets and brochures

Electronic and video publications:
Electoral register (on disk, available for purchase)

Access to staff:
Contact by letter, by telephone, by fax, by e-mail and via website
Hours: Mon to Fri, 0900 to 1700
Special comments: 24 hour emergency hotline 01703 233344.

Also:
Education Services
4th Floor, Frobisher House, Commercial Road, Southampton; tel: 023 8083 2771
Valuation and Estates Services
Marlands House, Civic Centre Road, Southampton, SO14 7PR; tel: 023 8083 2879

SOUTHAMPTON CITY COUNCIL – CULTURAL SERVICES

Civic Centre, Southampton, SO14 7LP

Tel: 023 8022 3855
Fax: 023 8033 7593
E-mail: s.dawtry@southampton.gov.uk

Website:
http://www.southampton.gov.uk/leisure
http://www.southampton.gov.uk
Services provided by the council, leisure services in the city, etc.

Enquiries:
Enquiries to: Manager
Direct tel: 023 8083 2768
Direct e-mail: s.harrington@southampton.gov.uk

Founded:
1912

Organisation type and purpose:
Local government body.

Subject coverage:
Archaeology, particularly British and North European; fine art, particularly 20th century; maritime history; Southampton local history.

Museum or gallery collection, archive, or library special collection:
Buchanan Collection (needlework tools and accessories)
Chipperfield Bequest
Hull-Grundy Gift (jewellery)
Jeffress Bequest
Sandell Collection (miscellaneous)
Smith Bequest
Various local history collections

Non-library collection catalogue:
All or part available in-house

Printed publications:
Various publications on: aspects of the Art Gallery, archaeology, social history (oral and maritime)

Publications list:
Available in print

Access to staff:
Contact by letter, by telephone, by fax, by e-mail and via website. Appointment necessary.
Hours: Mon to Fri, 0900 to 1700

SOUTHAMPTON CITY COUNCIL – HERITAGE ARTS AND ENTERTAINMENT MANAGEMENT

Civic Centre, Southampton, SO14 7LP

Museums and Galleries:
God's House Tower Archaeology Museum
Hawthorns Urban Wildlife Centre
John Hamsard Gallery
The University, Southampton, SO9 5NH
Southampton City Art Gallery
Southampton Hall of Aviation
Southampton Maritime Museum
Tudor House Museum

SOUTHAMPTON CITY COUNCIL – LIBRARIES

Southampton Central Library, Civic Centre, Southampton, SO14 7LW

Tel: 023 8083 2462
Fax: 023 8033 6305
E-mail: reference.library@southampton.gov.uk

Website:
http://www.southampton.gov.uk/libraries

Enquiries:
Enquiries to: Libraries Manager
Direct tel: 023 8083 2219
Other contacts: Local Studies and Maritime Librarian, Business Librarian

Founded:
1889

Organisation type and purpose:
Local government body, public library.

Subject coverage:
General public library with a reference stock of over 100,000 items; specialisations are: UK and international commerce, shipping (especially ocean liners) and marine transport, nautical almanacs and chronology, standards and specifications, genealogy, Hampshire studies, business and commercial information, British and foreign trade directories, statistics, British Government publications, art monographs, European Union, information, law reports, English history, careers and education, community information.

Museum or gallery collection, archive, or library special collection:
Bowen collection (maritime)
British Government publications
British Standards
European Union (European Public Information Centre)
Hampshire Collection (particularly Southampton)
Maritime Collection (including a collection on the Titanic disaster and ocean-going liners)
Pitt collection (17th- and 18th-century scientific books: restricted access)

Library catalogue:
All or part available online

Printed publications:
Catalogue of the Pitt Collection
Genealogical Sources (1989)
Saints: the glory games (2005)
Shirley: Nuisances and Services (2002)
Southampton Ships (1978)
Titanic Victims and Survivors (2002)
Titanic Voices (2007)
Various leaflets describing collections

Electronic and video publications:
Plimsoll: photographs of Southampton's history (for purchase online)
Southampton Area Census 1871 (CD-ROM, 2003)

Publications list:
Available in print

continued overleaf

Access to staff:
Contact by letter, by telephone, by fax, by e-mail, in person and via website
Hours: Mon to Fri, 0930 to 1900; Sat, 0930 to 1600

Constituent bodies:
Level 1 European Public Information Centre
   tel: 023 8083 2958
Southern Area European Information Centre
   tel: 023 8083 2866

Parent body:
Southampton City Council

SOUTHAMPTON SOLENT UNIVERSITY

Acronym or abbreviation: SSU

East Park Terrace, Southampton, SO14 0RJ

Tel: 023 8031 9000
Fax: 023 8022 2259

Website:
http://www.solent.ac.uk/library
Southampton Solent University home page.
http://www.solent.ac.uk
Information on the university, library and sources of information.

Enquiries:
Enquiries to: Deputy University Librarian
Direct tel: 023 8031 9248
Direct e-mail: enquiries@solent.ac.uk

Founded:
1964

Formerly called:
Southampton Institute

Organisation type and purpose:
University department.

Subject coverage:
Accountancy, business studies, e-commerce, law, management, computing, information systems, CAD/CAM, naval architecture, yacht and boat design, condition monitoring, electronics, construction, graphic design, fashion, maritime studies, leisure management, fine art, media communications, film studies.

Museum or gallery collection, archive, or library special collection:
Multimedia collection (video cassettes/DVDs, audio tapes)
Godden collection (antiques and fine art periodicals and sale catalogues)
Ken Russell Collection (film)
Maritime History collection, including Captain Cooper's Letters and Reports, 1922–56
Slide collection (Art & Design)

Library catalogue:
All or part available online

Printed publications:
Yacht and Boat Design: select list of references (irregular)

Access to staff:
Contact by letter, by telephone, by fax, by e-mail, in person and via website
Hours: Term time: Mon to Thu, 0830 to 2230; Fri, 0830 to 1900; Sat, 0900 to 1700; Sun, 1300 to 1700

Access for disabled people:
Level entry, access to all public areas, toilet facilities.

Branch at:
Warsash Library
   Newtown Road, Warsash, Southampton, SO31 9ZL; tel: 01489 576161; fax: 01489 573988

Membership to:
Hatrics Southern Information Network
   81 North Walls, Winchester, SO23 8BY; tel: 01962 826650; fax: 01962 826615; e-mail: HatricsHQ@ hants.gov.uk; website: www.hants.gov .uk?hatrics/index.html

SOUTHBROOK COMMUNITY MENTAL HEALTH TEAM

Acronym or abbreviation: SCMHT

1 Southbrook Road, London, SE12 8LH

Tel: 020 8318 1330
Fax: 020 8297 1448

Enquiries:
Enquiries to: Manager

Founded:
1978

Organisation type and purpose:
Community Mental Health Team.
Provides support and advice for clients with mental health problems who live within the catchment area of Central and East Lewisham.

Subject coverage:
Mental health.

Access to staff:
Contact by letter, by telephone and in person
Hours: Mon to Fri, 0900 to 1700
Special comments: Residents of Central and East Lewisham only.

Access for disabled people:
Ramped entry, level entry, toilet facilities

Parent body:
Lewisham Social Care and Health
South London and Maudsley NHS/MH Trust

SOUTHEND-ON-SEA BOROUGH LIBRARIES

Southend Library, Victoria Avenue, Southend-on-Sea, Essex, SS2 6EX

Tel: 01702 534100\ Minicom no. 01702 600579
Fax: 01702 469241
E-mail: library@southend.gov.uk

Website:
http://www.southend.gov.uk/library

Enquiries:
Enquiries to: Libraries Services Manager

Organisation type and purpose:
Local government body, public library.

Subject coverage:
Large general library.

Services for disabled people:
Induction loops, magnifying aids and electronic reading machines.

Museum or gallery collection, archive, or library special collection:
Focal point photographic gallery
Specialist collections for local history

Trade and statistical information:
General collection of statistics and trade directories.

Non-library collection catalogue:
All or part available online and in-house

Library catalogue:
All or part available online

Access for disabled people:
Parking provided, level entry, access to all public areas, toilet facilities

Links with:
Essex County Libraries
Thurrock Borough Council library services

Member organisation of:
CO-EAST

SOUTHERN AFRICA BUSINESS ASSOCIATION

Acronym or abbreviation: SABA

Queensland House, 393 Strand, London, WC2R 0JQ

Tel: 020 7836 9980

Fax: 020 7836 6001
E-mail: martinhogg@saba.co.uk

Website:
http://www.saba.co.uk
Information about SABA, links to some members' websites.

Enquiries:
Enquiries to: Membership Secretary

Founded:
1995

Organisation type and purpose:
Trade association (membership is by subscription), present number of members: over 130.
To promote investment into the Southern African region and trade within the region.

Subject coverage:
Information on investment effectiveness in the countries of the region: South Africa, Zimbabwe, Mozambique, Zambia, Botswana, Namibia, Malawi, Swaziland, Angola, Lesotho.
General information about the political and economic situation and prospects in each country, investment required, trade agreements.

Printed publications:
Confidential Bulletin (monthly, for members only)
Country Profiles (twice a year)

Publications list:
Available in print

Access to staff:
Contact by letter, by telephone, by fax, by e-mail and via website. Appointment necessary. Non-members charged.
Hours: Mon to Fri, 1000 to 1600

Access to building, collection or gallery:
Prior appointment required

Access for disabled people:
Level entry

SOUTHERN AND SOUTH EAST ENGLAND TOURIST BOARD, THE

Acronym or abbreviation: STB

40 Chamberlayne Road, Eastleigh, Hampshire, SO50 5JH

Tel: 023 8062 5400
Fax: 023 8062 0010
E-mail: info@tourismse.com

Website:
http://www.tourismsoutheast.com

Enquiries:
Enquiries to: Managing Director

Founded:
1977

Organisation type and purpose:
Membership association (membership is by subscription), present number of members: 1600, service industry.
Promotion and development of tourism.

Subject coverage:
Tourism.

Printed publications:
A wide variety of publications aimed at providing information and advice on tourism in the South East of England

Access to staff:
Contact by letter, by telephone, by fax and by e-mail
Hours: Mon to Thu, 0830 to 1700; Fri, 0830 to 1630

SOUTHERN BRICK FEDERATION LIMITED

Brick Development Association, 26 Store Street, London, WC1E 7BT

Tel: 020 7323 7030
Fax: 020 7580 3795
E-mail: brick@brick.org.uk

Enquiries:
Enquiries to: Secretary

Founded:
1970

Organisation type and purpose:
Trade association.

Subject coverage:
Clay brickmakers in the South of England.

Access to staff:
Contact by letter, by telephone, by fax and by e-mail
Hours: Mon to Fri, 0900 to 1700

Links with:
Brick Development Association
tel: 020 7323 7030; fax: 020 7580 3795; e-mail: brick@brick.org.uk
British Ceramic Confederation
tel: 01782 744631; fax: 01782 744102; e-mail: bcc@ceramfed.co.uk
British Ceramic Research Limited
tel: 01782 746476; fax: 01782 412331; e-mail: info@ceram.co.uk

SOUTHERN EDUCATION AND LIBRARY BOARD

Acronym or abbreviation: SELB

Library Headquarters, 1 Markethill Road, Armagh, BT60 1NR

Tel: 028 3752 5353
Fax: 028 3752 6879

Website:
http://www.selb.org
Address and opening hours of branch libraries, staff listing.

Enquiries:
Enquiries to: Chief Librarian
Direct tel: 028 3752 0702

Founded:
1974

Organisation type and purpose:
Local government body, public library.
Schools library service.

Subject coverage:
General, local history, Irish studies.

Museum or gallery collection, archive, or library special collection:
Crosslé Collection of manuscripts of local Newry families
Irish and local studies collection
Irish folk music record collection

Printed publications:
Annual Report
Bibliographies of Resources available for Northern Ireland Curriculum for Primary Schools
Catalogue of 16mm films (irregular)
Catalogue of video cassettes for education and general interest (yearly)
Public Service Information Bulletin (in collaboration with the other 4 Education and Library Boards) (monthly)
Selected list of recent publications for post-primary schools

Access to staff:
Contact by letter, by telephone, by fax and in person
Hours: Mon to Fri, 0900 to 1700

Access for disabled people:
Parking provided, level entry, access to all public areas, toilet facilities

SOUTHERN WATER

Southern House, Yeoman Road, Worthing, West Sussex, BN13 3NX

Tel: 01903 264444
Fax: 01903 691435

Website:
http://www.southernwater.co.uk
News desk, making water work, providing a quality service, caring for the environment, becoming WaterWise, Water Wise gardening, Bewl Water reservoir.

Enquiries:
Enquiries to: Head of Communications

Organisation type and purpose:
Service industry.

Subject coverage:
Water supply, sewerage services.

Access to staff:
Contact by letter and by fax
Hours: Mon to Fri, 0900 to 1700

Has links with:
Scottish Power

SOUTHGATE COLLEGE

Library and Learning Resources Service, High Street, Southgate, London, N14 6BS

Tel: 020 8982 5123
Fax: 020 8982 5118

Website:
http://www.southgate.ac.uk
Information about the college and its services.

Enquiries:
Enquiries to: Library & Learning Resources Manager
Other contacts: Learning Resources Co-ordinators

Founded:
1963

Organisation type and purpose:
Suitable for ages: 16+.
General further education.

Subject coverage:
General and vocational, including: business, catering, clothing, design, engineering, health and social care, leisure.

Library catalogue:
All or part available in-house

Access to staff:
Contact by letter, by telephone and by e-mail
Hours: Term time only, Mon to Thu, 0900 to 2000; Fri, 0900 to 1630
Special comments: Reference use, for print materials only.

Access to building, collection or gallery:
Prior appointment required

Access for disabled people:
Parking provided, level entry

SOUTHWARK LIBRARY AND INFORMATION SERVICES

15 Spa Road, Bermondsey, London, SE16 3QW

Tel: 020 7525 3920 or 3716/7
Fax: 020 7525 1505
E-mail: adrian.olsen@southwark.gov.uk

Enquiries:
Enquiries to: Librarian
Direct tel: 020 7525 1577
Other contacts: Libraries Development Manager

Founded:
1800s

Organisation type and purpose:
Local government body, public library.

Subject coverage:
General, modern fiction in Swedish, Norwegian and Finnish; local studies; computers and data processing.

Museum or gallery collection, archive, or library special collection:
Greater London Audio Specialisation Scheme (mainly black disc): composers, Berlioz and Messaien; jazz artists, JOO-LED; music minus 1; folk music of SE Asia (at Spa Road)
Joint fiction reserves (English, including play sets by authors whose surnames come within the ranges BAJ-BEL (BOS-CAP and RDA-SHV up to and including 1987 only)) (at Spa Road)
Local history and archives collection relating to the London Borough of Southwark (including civil but not parish records)
Local Studies Library (at John Harvard Library, Borough High Street)
London Special Collection Dewey Nos. 000–009 (at Newington Library)
Mother tongue collection – Bengali, Hindi, Punjabi, Gujerati, Urdu, Chinese, Turkish, Greek, Vietnamese (based at various libraries)
Swedish, Norwegian and Finnish fiction (at Rotherhithe Library)

Library catalogue:
All or part available online and in-house

Printed publications:
Histories of particular areas or aspects of the Borough (irregular)
Occasional specialist booklists (irregular)
Reprinted Ordnance Survey maps of Southwark
Order printed publications from: Local Studies Librarian, London Borough of Southwark
Local Studies Library, 211 Borough High Street, London, SE1 1JA, tel: 020 7403 3507, fax: 020 7403 8633

Access to staff:
Contact by letter, by telephone, by fax and by e-mail. Appointment necessary.
Hours: Mon to Fri, 0900 to 1700

Parent body:
Southwark Environment and Leisure Department Chatelaine House, 186 Walworth Road, London SE17 1JJ; tel: 020 7525 5000

SOUTHWARK LOCAL HISTORY LIBRARY

211 Borough High Street, London, SE1 1JA

Tel: 020 7403 3507
Fax: 020 7403 8633
E-mail: local.studies.library@southwark.gov.uk

Website:
http://www.southwark.gov.uk/DiscoverSouthwark/LocalStudiesLibrary

Enquiries:
Enquiries to: Archivist

Organisation type and purpose:
Local government body, public library.
Local history library and archive for London Borough of Southwark area.

Subject coverage:
Local history and current affairs of London Borough of Southwark area. Includes extensive sources of interest to family historians with ancestors from the area and the archives of local authorities previous to the present London Borough of Southwark and of other organisations, institutions and individuals.

Museum or gallery collection, archive, or library special collection:
The Library Collection includes: printed published books, periodicals, illustrations, maps, cuttings and ephemera, sound recordings, videos
The Archives comprise: the official records of the London Borough of Southwark and its predecessors, the metropolitan boroughs and vestries, and unofficial deposited records of local organisations, institutions, businesses and individuals

Library catalogue:
All or part available online and in print

continued overleaf

Printed publications:
Guide to the Archives in Southwark Local Studies
    Library (Humphrey S)
London Borough of Southwark's Neighbourhood
    Histories (illustrated pocket histories of the
    communities within the London Borough of
    Southwark):
The story of Bermondsey (covers the parishes of St
    Olaves, St John Horselydown and St Mary,
    Bermondsey) (Boast M)
The story of Camberwell (Boast M)
The story of Dulwich (Boast M)
The story of Peckham and Nunhead (Beasley J)
The story of Rotherhithe (Humphrey S)
The story of Walworth (covers the parish of St
    Mary, Newington, the Elephant & Castle and the
    Old Kent Road) (Boast M)
The story of the Borough (covers the parish of St
    George the Martyr, Trinity Newington and
    Borough High Street) (Boast M)
The story of Bankside (covers the parish of St
    Saviour, Christ Church and part of St George
    Martyr) (Reilly L and Marshall G)
Southwark; an illustrated history (an overview of
    Southwark's history, lavishly illustrated with
    over 100 views) (Reilly L)
Family history in Southwark (a concise
    introduction to tracing Southwark ancestors)
    (Reilly L)
Below Southwark (46 page booklet, showing the
    story of Southwark revealed by excavations over
    the last 30 years) (Cowan C)
Several others, please apply for prices and postage

Publications list:
Available online and in print

Access to staff:
Contact by letter, by telephone, by fax, by e-mail
and in person
Hours: Mon, Thu, 0930 to 2000; Tue, Fri, 0930 to
1700; Sat, 0930 to 1300, Wed, closed

Access to building, collection or gallery:
No prior appointment required

Access for disabled people:
Level entry, access to all public areas, toilet
facilities

SOUTHWELL MINSTER LIBRARY

The Minster Office, Trebeck Hall, Bishop's Drive,
Southwell, Nottinghamshire, NG25 0JP

Tel: 01636 812649

Enquiries:
Enquiries to: Cathedral Librarian & Archivist
Direct tel: 01636 812123
Direct fax: 01636 812904
Direct e-mail: mail@southwellminster.prestel.co.uk

Organisation type and purpose:
Cathedral library.

Subject coverage:
Genealogy, Bishop's transcripts and marriage
licences for Nottinghamshire, theology, history,
music, Southwell Minster, its history and archives.

**Museum or gallery collection, archive, or library
special collection:**
Bishop's Transcripts for Nottinghamshire from
    1600
Southwell Minster Archive manuscripts from 1600

Access to staff:
Contact by letter and by telephone. Appointment
necessary.
Hours: Mon to Fri, 0900 to 1700

Access to building, collection or gallery:
No prior appointment required

SPA BUSINESS ASSOCIATION

Acronym or abbreviation: SpaBA

c/o Pennyhill Park Hotel, London Road, Bagshot,
Surrey, GU19 5EU

Tel: 01276 478647

Fax: 01276 478635
E-mail: info@spabusinessassociation.co.uk

Website:
http://www.spabusinessassociation.co.uk
UK and Irish Spas and spa-related businesses, links
to individual members' sites.

Enquiries:
Enquiries to: General Secretary
Other contacts: Chair, Medical Advisory Committee

Founded:
2004

Organisation type and purpose:
Advisory body, trade association (membership is
by subscription), present number of members: 120,
training organisation, consultancy, research
organisation.
Promotion of businesses in the spa sector, and of
the benefits of using spas for health and wellbeing.

Subject coverage:
Spas in the UK and Ireland. Spa Heritage and
Tourism. Networking meetings for members and
non-members. Quality Standards in spas and
promotional campaigns for members.

Printed publications:
Full range of advisory services on Spa regeneration
Glossary of European Spa Terminology
Newsletter
e-newsletter (monthly)

Access to staff:
Contact by letter, by telephone, by fax, by e-mail
and via website
Hours: Mon to Fri, 0900 to 1700

Affiliated to:
European Spas Association
    1, Avenue de la Renaissance, 1000 Bruxelles,
    Belgium; tel: +32 2733 2661

SPANISH EMBASSY COMMERCIAL OFFICE

66 Chiltern Street, London, W1M 1PR

Tel: 020 7467 2330
Fax: 020 7487 5586
E-mail: buzon.oficial@londres.ofcomes.mcx.es

Website:
http://www.mcx.es/londres

Enquiries:
Enquiries to: Information Officer

Organisation type and purpose:
National government body.
Embassy department.

Subject coverage:
General information on Spain: commercial or
investment, specific department promoting export
into Spain, foods and wines from Spain, consumer
goods, industrial products and services.

Trade and statistical information:
General statistical information on trade and
    investment to and from Spain.

Printed publications:
Information material (booklets, brochures, list of
    companies etc, available by letter, fax or email to
    the Information Officer)

Access to staff:
Contact by letter, by telephone, by fax, by e-mail
and via website
Hours: Mon to Thu, 0900 to 1700; Fri, 0900 to 1500
Special comments: Requests in writing.

Access to building, collection or gallery:
No access other than to staff

Access for disabled people:
Access to all public areas

Connections with:
ICEX
    PO Castellana 14–16, 28046 Madrid; tel: 00 34 91
    349 3500; fax: 00 34 91 431 6128; website: http://
    www.icex.es

Parent body:
Spanish Embassy
    39 Chesham Place, London, SW1X 8SB; tel: 020
    7235 5555; fax: 020 7259 5392; e-mail:
    embespuk@mail.mae.es

SPANISH TOURIST OFFICE

Acronym or abbreviation: OET

22–23 Manchester Square, London, W1U 3PX

Tel: 020 7486 8077
Fax: 020 7486 8034
E-mail: info.londres@tourspain.es

Website:
http://www.colarioja.es
Regional website for La Rioja.
http://www.comadrid.es
Regional website for Madrid.
http://www.murcia-turismo.es
Regional website for Murcia.
http://www.Tourspain.co.uk
Spanish Tourist Office website.
http://www.andalucia.org
Regional website for Andalucia.
http://www.turismo.cantabria.es
Regional website for Cantabria.
http://www.jccm.es
Regional website for Castilla – La Mancha.
http://www.jcyl.es
Regional website for Castilla Y León.
http://www.gencat.es
Regional website for Cataluña.
http://www.staragon.com
Regional website for Aragon.
http://www.srt.es
Regional website for Asturias.
http://www.caib.es
Regional website for Baleares.
http://www.gobcan.es
Regional website for Canarias.
http://www.juntaex.es
Regional website for Extremadura.
http://www.estancias.es
Accommodation at Spanish historic
establishments.
http://www.Tourspain.es
Up to date information on Turespaña.
http://www.mcu.es
Cultural events.
http://www.cybermundi.es/vanatur
Rural tourism accommodation.
http://www.ciudad-ceuta.com
Regional website for Ceuta.
http://www.melilla500.com
Regional website for Melilla.
http://www.tourgalicia.es
Regional website for Galicia.
http://www.cfnavarra.es
Regional website for Navarra.
http://www.euskadi.net
Regional website for País Vasco.
http://www.gua.es
Regional website for Comunidad Valenciana.

Enquiries:
Enquiries to: Information Officer

Organisation type and purpose:
National government body.
Tourist information office.

Subject coverage:
Tourist information about Spain.

**Museum or gallery collection, archive, or library
special collection:**
Photographs and slides

Printed publications:
Tourist leaflets on Spanish regions

Electronic and video publications:
Videos on tourist resorts and tourist related
    matters

Access to staff:
Contact by letter, by telephone, by fax, by e-mail,
in person and via website
Hours: Mon to Fri, 0915 to 1615

Parent body:
Turespaña
José Lazaro Galdiano 6, 28036 Madrid, Spain; tel: 00 34 91 343 3500

SPARTAN OWNERS' CLUB

Acronym or abbreviation: SOC

28 Ashford Drive, Ravenshead, Nottingham, NG15 9DE

Tel: 01623 409351
Fax: 01623 409352

Website:
http://www.spartan-oc.demon.co.uk

Enquiries:
Enquiries to: Secretary

Founded:
1978

Organisation type and purpose:
Membership association (membership is by subscription), present number of members: 350–400, suitable for ages: 17+.
To bring together owners, builders and enthusiasts of the Spartan car.

Subject coverage:
All aspects of the Spartan kit car.

Printed publications:
Spartacus (journal, quarterly, members)

Access to staff:
Contact by letter, by telephone, by fax and via website
Special comments: Telephone between 1800 and 2000 only.

SPEAKABILITY

1 Royal Street, London, SE1 7LL

Tel: 020 7261 9572 (Administration)
Fax: 020 7928 9542
E-mail: speakability@speakability.org.uk

Website:
http://www.speakability.org.uk

Enquiries:
Enquiries to: Chief Executive

Founded:
1979

Organisation type and purpose:
National organisation, voluntary organisation, registered charity (charity number 295094).

Subject coverage:
Dysphasia/aphasia, speech and language problems after stroke, head injury or neurological condition.
Supporting people with aphasia/dysphasia and their carers and friends, through its information service and national network of groups.
Influencing individuals and organisations in order to improve services for people with aphasia.

Museum or gallery collection, archive, or library special collection:
Database of information for people with aphasia, carers and professionals

Printed publications:
Books, posters, leaflets, factsheets, charter for people with aphasia
Lost for Words – an introductory booklet
Speaking Up – twice yearly newsletter
Workbook for Carers, Dr Marshall J, Carlson E, Moir D

Electronic and video publications:
Tapes, Teaching Pack (including video and slides) for medical professionals (written by professionals)
Speaking Up About Aphasia (video) presented by Andrew Marr (the BBC's Chief Political Editor)

Publications list:
Available in print

Access to staff:
Contact by letter, by telephone, by fax, by e-mail and via website
Hours: Helpline: 080 8808 9572 – Mon to Fri, 1000 to 1600
24-hour answerphone

Associated with:
Association Internationale Aphasie (AIA)
Association of Speech & Language Therapists
British Aphasiology Society (BAS)

Has:
national network of support groups

SPECIAL EDUCATION CONSORTIUM

8 Wakely Street, London, EC1V 7QE

Tel: 020 7843 6334 / 6060
Fax: 020 7843 6313
E-mail: cdc@ncb.org.uk

Enquiries:
Enquiries to: SEC Co-ordinator

Organisation type and purpose:
Advisory body, voluntary organisation, registered charity (charity number 258825).
To protect and promote the interests of disabled children and children with special educational needs during the passage of legislation which may affect them.

Subject coverage:
Special educational needs and disability – policy, practice and legislation in this field.

Access to staff:
Contact by letter, by telephone, by fax and by e-mail
Hours: Mon to Fri, 0900 to 1700

Access to building, collection or gallery:
Prior appointment required

Access for disabled people:
Ramped entry, level entry, toilet facilities

Registered under the auspices of:
The Council for Disabled Children at The National Children's Bureau

SPECIAL EDUCATIONAL NEEDS TRIBUNAL

Acronym or abbreviation: SENT

50 Victoria Street, London, SW1H 0NW

Tel: 020 7925 6902
Fax: 020 7926 6926
E-mail: tribunalqueries@sent.gsi.gov.uk

Website:
http://www.sentribunal.gov.uk
How to appeal and other guidance for parties.

Enquiries:
Enquiries to: Secretary

Founded:
1994

Organisation type and purpose:
Statutory body.

Subject coverage:
Appeals by parents against local decisions about children's special educational needs.

Trade and statistical information:
Volume of SEN appeals by type, nature of SEN and local authority area.

Printed publications:
How to Appeal (booklet)
Annual Reports
Order printed publications from: DfES Publications Centre, Special Educational Needs Tribunal PO Box 5050, Sherwood Park, Annersley, Nottingham, NG15 0DJ, tel: 0845 602 2260, fax: 0845 603 3360, e-mail: dfes@prolog.uk.com

Electronic and video publications:
Right to be Heard (video)

Order electronic and video publications from: SENT
As main address

Access to staff:
Contact by letter, by telephone, by fax, by e-mail and via website
Hours: Mon to Fri, 0900 to 1700

Access to building, collection or gallery:
Prior appointment required

SPECIAL OLYMPICS GREAT BRITAIN

Acronym or abbreviation: SOGB

6–8 Great Eastern Street, London, EC2A 3NT

Tel: 020 7247 8891
Fax: 020 7247 2393
E-mail: karen.wallin@sogb.org.uk

Website:
http://www.sogb.org.uk

Enquiries:
Enquiries to: Administrator
Direct e-mail: peju.oriunuta@sogb.org.uk
Other contacts: Chief Operating Officer

Founded:
1978

Organisation type and purpose:
International organisation, national government body, membership association, present number of members: 30,000, registered charity (charity number 800329), suitable for all ages, training organisation.
To provide year round training and competition in Olympic sports for all with a mental handicap.

Subject coverage:
Sport for people with learning disabilities.

Printed publications:
General information packs
Information leaflets
Special Olympics Summer Sports Rules
Special Olympics Winter Sports Rules
Skill Guides to 23 different sports
Starter packs for new groups

Electronic and video publications:
New Gymnastics Artistic (video and audio cassette)
New Gymnastics Rhythmic (video and audio cassette)
Floor Hockey

Publications list:
Available in print

Access to staff:
Contact by letter, by telephone, by fax, by e-mail and in person. Appointment necessary. Letter of introduction required.
Hours: Mon to Fri, 0900 to 1700

Access to building, collection or gallery:
Prior appointment required

Parent body:
Special Olympics International
1133 19th Street NW, Washington, DC 20036–3604, USA

SPECIALIST CHEESEMAKERS' ASSOCIATION

Acronym or abbreviation: SCA

17 Clerkenwell Green, London, EC1R 0DP

Tel: 020 7253 2114
Fax: 020 7608 1645
E-mail: info@specialistcheesemakers.co.uk

Website:
http://www.specialistcheesemakers.co.uk

Enquiries:
Enquiries to: Secretary

Founded:
1989

continued overleaf

Organisation type and purpose:
Membership association (membership is by subscription), present number of members: 260.

Subject coverage:
Representation of the interests of specialist cheesemakers, providing a link between cheesemakers, retailers and wholesalers, providing promotional opportunities and own hygiene scheme.

Printed publications:
Specialist Cheesemakers Code of Best Practice
The Guide to the Finest Cheeses of Britain and Ireland (£5.95)

Publications list:
Available online

Access to staff:
Contact by letter, by telephone, by fax, by e-mail and via website
Hours: Mon to Fri, 0900 to 1700

Access to building, collection or gallery:
No access other than to staff

SPELTHORNE BOROUGH COUNCIL

Council Offices, Knowle Green, Staines, Middlesex, TW18 1XB

Tel: 01784 451499\ Minicom no. 01784 446423
Fax: 01784 463356
E-mail: customer.services@spelthorne.gov.uk

Website:
http://www.spelthorne.co.uk
General page.

Enquiries:
Enquiries to: PR & Communications Officer
Direct fax: 01784 446297
Direct e-mail: a.creek@spelthorne.gov.uk

Organisation type and purpose:
Local government body.

Subject coverage:
Local government services.

Printed publications:
Bulletin (community magazine, six times a year)

Publications list:
Available online and in print

Access to staff:
Contact by letter, by telephone, by fax, by e-mail, in person and via website
Hours: Mon to Fri, 0900 to 1700

Access for disabled people:
Parking provided, ramped entry, toilet facilities

Parent body:
Surrey County Council

SPINAL INJURIES ASSOCIATION

Acronym or abbreviation: SIA

SIA House, 2 Trueman Place, Oldbrook, Milton Keynes, MK6 2HH

Tel: 0845 678 6633
Fax: 0845 070 6911
E-mail: sia@spinal.co.uk

Website:
http://www.spinal.co.uk

Enquiries:
Enquiries to: Executive Director

Founded:
1974

Organisation type and purpose:
National organisation, advisory body, membership association (membership is by subscription), present number of members: 5,500, voluntary organisation, registered charity (charity number 1054097), consultancy, publishing house. Self-help group.

Subject coverage:
Paraplegia, tetraplegia, the spinal cord injured, wheelchair living, self-help aids, personal care, mobility, employment, integration, welfare benefits, sexuality, continence, parenthood, aids and equipment, pain, and a Message Board and Chat Room.

Information services:
Signposts services provided by SIA plus a Chat Room for spinal cord injured people.

Library catalogue:
All or part available online and in print

Printed publications:
A variety of Factsheets
Books for Younger Children and Teenagers
Forward Magazine
Moving Forward: The Guide to Living with Spinal Cord Injury
Directory of Personal Injury Solicitors
Books for medical and healthcare professionals

Electronic and video publications:
Wheelchair Skills (DVD)
Fitness (DVD)
Physiotherapy (DVD)

Publications list:
Available online and in print

Access to staff:
Contact by letter, by telephone, by fax, by e-mail and via website. Appointment necessary.
Hours: Mon to Fri, 0930 to 1630

Access to building, collection or gallery:
Hours: 0900 to 1700

Access for disabled people:
Parking provided, level entry, access to all public areas, toilet facilities

Links with:
Scottish Spinal Cord Injuries Association
some 136 other bodies

SPINAL INJURIES SCOTLAND

Acronym or abbreviation: SIS

Festival Business Centre, 150 Brand Street, Glasgow, G51 1DH

Tel: 0141 314 0056
Fax: 0141 427 9258
E-mail: info@sisonline.org

Enquiries:
Enquiries to: Chief Executive

Founded:
1960

Organisation type and purpose:
National organisation, membership association (membership is by subscription), present number of members: c. 700, voluntary organisation, registered charity (charity number SC 015405). Specifically for spinally injured people, their families, friends and carers.

Subject coverage:
Access, accessible holiday information, manufacturers and suppliers of equipment etc.

Printed publications:
Newsline (quarterly, free to members)

Access to staff:
Contact by letter, by telephone, by fax and in person
Hours: Mon to Thu, 0930 to 1700; Fri, 0930 to 1700

Access to building, collection or gallery:
No prior appointment required

Access for disabled people:
Parking provided, level entry, access to all public areas, toilet facilities

Acts in association with the:
Spinal Injuries Association

SPINAL RESEARCH

Formal name: International Spinal Research Trust

Unit 8a, Bramley Business Centre, Station Road, Bramley, Guildford, Surrey, GU5 0AZ

Tel: 01483 898786
Fax: 01483 898763
E-mail: info@spinal-research.org

Website:
http://www.spinal-research.org
General details about spinal research.

Enquiries:
Enquiries to: Chief Executive
Other contacts: Head of Fundraising

Founded:
1981

Organisation type and purpose:
International organisation, registered charity (charity number 281325), research organisation. Spinal Research exists to fund research with the sole aim of finding a treatment for paralysis caused by spinal cord injury.

Subject coverage:
Research into ending the permanence of paralysis caused by spinal cord injury.

Printed publications:
Annual report (free)
Annual Review (free)
Newsletter (2 times a year, free)
Research digest (twice a year, free)

Electronic and video publications:
Connections (video)

Access to staff:
Contact by letter, by telephone, by fax, by e-mail, in person and via website
Hours: Mon to Fri, 0900 to 1730

Access to building, collection or gallery:
No prior appointment required

Access for disabled people:
Parking provided, level entry, access to all public areas, toilet facilities

SPLIT SCREEN VAN CLUB

Acronym or abbreviation: SSVC

Old Mills Cottage, Old Mills Road, Elgin, Moray, IV30 1YH

Tel: 01343 550639
E-mail: cjtasker@hotmail.com

Website:
http://www.ssvc.org.uk
Full information, links, forum, contacts for Committee.

Enquiries:
Enquiries to: Information Officer
Other contacts: President/Membership Secretary; email: president@ssvc.org.uk for membership.

Founded:
1983

Organisation type and purpose:
National organisation, membership association (membership is by subscription), present number of members: 1100.
To preserve and celebrate these unique vintage Volkswagen vans and also the expertise needed to maintain and restore them.

Subject coverage:
Split screen Volkswagen vans, their history, restoration and maintenance.

Museum or gallery collection, archive, or library special collection:
Details of over 500 vans and their histories are collated on the van register.

Printed publications:
Split Screen Scene – packed with photographs, technical articles and advice, restoration hints, van profiles, members anecdotes, letters and classifieds (magazine, 6 times a year)
Order printed publications from: Membership Secretary or via website
e-mail: membership@ssvc.org.uk

Access to staff:
Contact by letter, by telephone, by e-mail and via website
Hours: Mon to Fri, 0900 to 1700

SPORT ENGLAND

3rd Floor Victoria House, Bloomsbury Square, London, WC1B 4SE

Tel: 020 7273 1551
Fax: 020 7383 5740

Website:
http://www.sportengland.org

Enquiries:
Enquiries to: Information Centre
Direct e-mail: jordan.russell@sportengland.org

Founded:
1997

Organisation type and purpose:
National government body. Receives an annual grant-in-aid from the Department for Culture, Media and Sport and in turn distributes grants; 9 regional offices and 5 national sports centres.

Subject coverage:
Sport and physical recreation: administration; grants; design, planning and provision of facilities; technical and architectural factors; development of sport in general; sport for specific groups e.g. unemployed, children etc; governing bodies; sports science and medicine, sports sociology, legislation, sports psychology; individual sports, sporting events.

Museum or gallery collection, archive, or library special collection:
700 Journals
30,000 books and journal articles
Small video collection

Library catalogue:
All or part available in-house

Printed publications:
Best of British Sport (1992, £10)
Injuries in Sport and Exercise (1993, £25)
Planning obligations for sport and recreation – a guide for negotiation and action (£10)
Recreation management (information sheet, free)
Research and technical papers
Select bibliographies on many aspects of sport and its facilities
The development of sporting talent 1997: how do performers make it to the top (research report 1997, £5)
Order printed publications from: Sport England PO Box 255, Wetherby, West Yorkshire, LS23 7LZ, tel: 0870 521 0255, fax: 0870 521 0266

Publications list:
Available online and in print

Access to staff:
Contact by letter, by telephone, by e-mail, in person and via website. Appointment necessary.
Hours: Mon to Fri, 1330 to 1600
Special comments: Postgraduate students only.

Access for disabled people:
Toilet facilities

Regional Sports Councils are:
East Midlands Region
  Grove House, Bridgford Road, West Bridgford, Nottinghamshire, NG2 6AP; tel: 0115 982 1887; fax: 0115 945 5236
East Region
  Crescent House, 19 The Crescent, Bedford, MK40 2QP; tel: 01234 345222; fax: 01234 359046

London Region
  PO Box 480, Crystal Palace National Sports Centre, Ledrington Road, London, SE19 2BQ; tel: 020 8778 8600; fax: 020 8676 9812
North East Region
  Aykley Heads, Durham, DH1 5UU; tel: 0191 384 9595; fax: 0191 384 5807
North West Region
  Astley House, Quay Street, Manchester, M3 4AE; tel: 0161 834 0388; fax: 0161 835 3678
South East Region
  51A Church Street, Caversham, Reading, Berkshire, RG4 8AX; tel: 0118 948 3311; fax: 0118 947 5935
South West Region
  Ashlands House, Ashlands, Crewkerne, Somerset, TA18 7LQ; tel: 01460 73491; fax: 01460 77263
West Midlands Region
  1 Hagley Road, Five Ways, Edgbaston, Birmingham, B16 8TT; tel: 0121 456 3444; fax: 0121 456 1583
Yorkshire Region
  4th Floor, Minerva House, East Parade, Leeds, LS1 5PS; tel: 0113 243 6443; fax: 0113 242 2189

SPORT HORSE BREEDING OF GREAT BRITAIN

Acronym or abbreviation: SHB(GB)

96 High Street, Edenbridge, Kent, TN8 5AR

Tel: 01732 866277
Fax: 01732 867464
E-mail: office@sporthorsegb.co.uk

Website:
http://www.sporthorsegb.co.uk

Enquiries:
Enquiries to: General Secretary

Founded:
1884

Organisation type and purpose:
Advisory body, membership association (membership is by subscription), present number of members: c. 4000, registered charity.
To develop and improve the breeding of the British sport horse.

Subject coverage:
Horse breeding, registration and shows.

Museum or gallery collection, archive, or library special collection:
Stud Books

Library catalogue:
All or part available in-house

Access to staff:
Contact by letter, by telephone, by fax and by e-mail
Hours: Mon to Fri, 0900 to 1700

SPORTING FIATS CLUB

Acronym or abbreviation: SFC

Elms Farm, Long Clawson, Melton Mowbray, Leicestershire, LE14 4NG

Tel: 01664 822395
E-mail: webmaster@sportingfiatsclub.com

Website:
http://www.sportingfiatsclub.com
Meetings, events, activities and links.

Enquiries:
Enquiries to: Membership Secretary
Other contacts: Chairman for organisational, alliance or regulatory enquiries.

Founded:
1978

Organisation type and purpose:
Membership association (membership is by subscription), present number of members: 500.
To further interest in and enjoyment of Fiat motor cars, worldwide, centred in the UK.

Subject coverage:
Fiat cars.

Printed publications:
Magazine (biannual, glossy)
Newsletter
Books (available through merchandising officer)

Electronic and video publications:
Videos
Photographs (usually in JPEG format)

Access to staff:
Contact by letter, by telephone, by e-mail and via website
Hours: Mon to Fri, 1000 to 2200

Affiliated to:
Group B Car Club
Motor Sport Association
XI/9 Owners Club

SPORTS INDUSTRIES FEDERATION, THE

Acronym or abbreviation: TSIF

Federation House, National Agricultural Centre, Stoneleigh Park, Kenilworth, Warwickshire, CV8 2RF

Tel: 024 7641 4999
Fax: 024 7641 4990
E-mail: admin@sportslife.org.uk

Website:
http://www.sports-life.com

Enquiries:
Enquiries to: Head of Membership & Development
Other contacts: Chief Executive

Founded:
1920

Organisation type and purpose:
Trade association, membership association (membership is by subscription).

Subject coverage:
Lists of suppliers of sports equipment and capital goods equipment. Playground safety guidelines, information on British and European standards relevant to sports industry.

Trade and statistical information:
Data on imports and exports of sports equipment between the United Kingdom and the European Union and non-European Union Countries.
Quarterly United Kingdom sports trends and surveys.
Statistics relating to tennis court construction, sports surfaces, angling trade and play equipment.

Publications list:
Available online

Access to staff:
Contact by letter, by telephone, by fax, by e-mail and via website
Hours: Mon to Fri, 0900 to 1700

Access to building, collection or gallery:
Prior appointment required

Access for disabled people:
Parking provided, toilet facilities

Houses the:
Angling Trade Association
Golf Ball Manufacturers Conference

SPORTS TURF RESEARCH INSTITUTE, THE

Acronym or abbreviation: STRI

St Ives Estate, Bingley, West Yorkshire, BD16 1AU

Tel: 01274 565131
Fax: 01274 561891
E-mail: info@stri.co.uk

Website:
http://www.stri.co.uk

continued overleaf

Details of our organisation and the full range of services we offer including details of the book catalogue and publications with order forms for publishing.

Enquiries:
Enquiries to: External Affairs Manager
Other contacts: Chief Executive

Founded:
1929

Organisation type and purpose:
International organisation, advisory body, professional body (membership is by subscription), training organisation, consultancy, research organisation, publishing house.
The STRI is the leading independent organisation in turf grass research and agronomy. Our aims are to carry out research and promote innovation; provide advisory and consultancy services; educate and inform through training and publications.

Subject coverage:
Drainage of sports fields and golf courses, design and construction of golf courses and sports fields, specifications for drainage and construction, irrigation, advisory work including maintenance and management programmes on any sports surface, artificial surfaces, research into turf problems, training courses, publications and books.

Museum or gallery collection, archive, or library special collection:
Library on turf-related publications including rare publications and journals

Library catalogue:
All or part available in-house

Printed publications:
Annual Review (STRI)
Journal of Turfgrass Science (annually)
International Turfgrass Bulletin (4 times a year)
Turfax (US publication, 6 times a year)
Turfgrass Seed (Information booklet, annually)
Miscellaneous books and publications on turf management including:
Cricket Grounds: The Evolution, Maintenance & Construction of Natural Turf Cricket Tables and Outfields (Evans R D C)
International Turf Management Handbook (Aldous D, 1999)
The Care of the Golf Course (Perris J and Evans R D C, 2nd ed., 1996)
The Turfgrass Disease Handbook (Couch H B, 2000)
Winter Games Pitches: The Construction & Maintenance of Natural Turf Pitches for Team Games (Evans R D C, 1994)

Electronic and video publications:
Golf Course Ecology (Video)
Golf Greenkeepers Training Course – Theory Notes (CD-ROM, £85 plus VAT plus p&p)
The Bowling Green Maintenance Video (Evans R D C)
Turfgrass Diseases – Diagnosis and Management (CD-ROM)

Publications list:
Available online and in print

Access to staff:
Contact by letter, by telephone, by fax, by e-mail and via website. Appointment necessary.
Hours: Mon to Fri, 0900 to 1700

Access to building, collection or gallery:
Prior appointment required

Access for disabled people:
Parking provided, level entry

Links with:
All Sports Governing Bodies including:
Association of Independent Research & Technology Organisations (AIRTO)
Football Association
Royal & Ancient Golf Club of St Andrews
Sport England
Sports Council

SPORTSCOTLAND

Caledonia House, South Gyle, Edinburgh, EH12 9DQ

Tel: 0131 317 7200
Fax: 0131 317 7202
E-mail: library@sportscotland.org.uk

Website:
http://www.sportscotland.org.uk

Enquiries:
Enquiries to: Information Officer

Founded:
1972

Organisation type and purpose:
Non-departmental public body.
The national agency for sport in Scotland.

Subject coverage:
Sport in Scotland, physical recreation, facilities, coaching, sports and associated organisations contacts, participation statistics, sports sponsorship, drugs in sport.

Museum or gallery collection, archive, or library special collection:
10,000 books and 120 current journals

Trade and statistical information:
Data on sports facilities located in Scotland, data on countryside recreation sites located in Scotland, National Lottery-funded projects for sport in Scotland.

Library catalogue:
All or part available online and in-house

Printed publications:
Advisory information and research in a wide range of sports aspects, over 150 titles

Publications list:
Available online

Access to staff:
Contact by letter, by telephone, by fax, by e-mail and via website. Appointment necessary.
Hours: Mon to Fri, 0900 to 1700

Access to building, collection or gallery:
Prior appointment required
Hours: Mon to Fri, 0900 to 1700

Access for disabled people:
Parking provided, level entry

Funded by:
Central Government under Royal Charter

SPORTSCOTLAND NATIONAL CENTRE INVERCLYDE

Burnside Road, Largs, Ayrshire, KA30 8RW

Tel: 01475 674666
Fax: 01475 674720
E-mail: john.kent@sportscotland.org.uk

Website:
http://www.sportscotland.org.uk

Enquiries:
Enquiries to: Manager
Other contacts: Office Manager for bookings.

Founded:
1970

Organisation type and purpose:
National government body, registered charity.
Residential Sports Centre.
Provision of sport facilities for National Teams, clubs, society of coaches, education groups, schools, colleges, sportspeople, conference and commercial seminars.

Subject coverage:
Sports coaching and awards, educational field work, fitness testing, sports science and medicine, residential sports coaching. Corporate team building, sports days and events.

Trade and statistical information:
United Kingdom market for residential sports training for elite athletes, clubs, sports groups and corporate activities.

Printed publications:
Brochure on the centre, its services and attractions

Electronic and video publications:
Video available of the Centre, showing all the facilities

Publications list:
Available online and in print

Access to staff:
Contact by letter, by telephone, by fax, by e-mail and via website. Appointment necessary. All charged.
Hours: Mon to Sun, 0800 to 2300

Access to building, collection or gallery:
Prior appointment required

Access for disabled people:
Parking provided, ramped entry

Parent body:
SportScotland
tel: 0131 317 7200; fax: 0131 317 7202

SPRAYED CONCRETE ASSOCIATION

Acronym or abbreviation: SCA

Tournai Hall, Evelyn Woods Road, Aldershot, Hampshire GU11 2LL

Tel: 01252 357842
Fax: 01252 357831
E-mail: lauren.fairley@sca.org.uk

Website:
http://www.sca.org.uk

Enquiries:
Enquiries to: Secretary

Founded:
1976

Organisation type and purpose:
Trade association, present number of members: 41.
Contractors, manufacturers and others involved in sprayed concrete. Operates, through CITB, a certificate scheme for operatives.

Subject coverage:
Sprayed concrete, gunite, shotcrete.

Printed publications:
Introduction to Sprayed Concrete
Directory of Members
EFNARC specification for sprayed concrete

Publications list:
Available online and in print

Access to staff:
Contact by letter, by telephone, by fax, by e-mail and via website
Hours: Mon to Fri, 0900 to 1700

SPRU (SCIENCE AND TECHNOLOGY POLICY RESEARCH)

The Freeman Centre, University of Sussex, Falmer, Brighton, East Sussex, BN1 9QE

Tel: 01273 686758
Fax: 01273 685865
E-mail: b.a.merchant@sussex.ac.uk

Website:
http://www.sussex.ac.uk/spru/library
Information about library and information services.
http://www.sussex.ac.uk/spru
Research, teaching, library, information, publications and activities of SPRU.
http://sprulib.central.sussex.ac.uk
SPRU library catalogue.

Enquiries:
Enquiries to: Information Officer
Direct tel: 01273 678178
Direct e-mail: m.e.winder@sussex.ac.uk
Other contacts: Information Services Manager

Founded:
1966

Organisation type and purpose:
University department or institute, research organisation.

Subject coverage:
Economics of technical change, technology and innovation management, science and technology indicators, research evaluation, technology transfer, technology in developing countries, energy policy, national science and technology policies, environmental and social implications of technical change, chemical, biological and nuclear arms control. Sectors studied include: energy, electronics, information and communications technologies, weapons, building, automobiles, mining, food, chemicals, pharmaceuticals, biotechnology, complex systems.

Museum or gallery collection, archive, or library special collection:
Specialist science and technology policy collection, including a large holding of grey literature, and a core science and technology policy journals collection

Trade and statistical information:
Statistics, particularly on R & D expenditure and funding, and science and technology.

Printed publications:
Various Brochures describing research or teaching programmes
Order printed publications from: e-mail: spru_library@sussex.ac.uk

Access to staff:
Hours: Mon to Fri, 0900 to 1300 and 1400 to 1700
Special comments: Charges to non-academic non-members.

Houses the former:
Armaments and Disarmaments Information Unit

SSCCI LTD

Ridings House, Ridings Park, Eastern Way, Cannock, Staffordshire, WS11 2FJ

Tel: 01543 460050
Fax: 01543 462822

Enquiries:
Enquiries to: Chief Executive

Founded:
1994

Formerly called:
East Mercia Chamber of Commerce and Industry (EMCCI)

Organisation type and purpose:
Service industry, training organisation, consultancy.

Subject coverage:
Business information, international trade and documentation, training, health and safety consultancy, quality consultancy, environmental consultancy, late payment of debt and financial business reports.

Museum or gallery collection, archive, or library special collection:
Comprehensive library of UK and international business directories

Access to staff:
Contact by letter
Hours: Mon to Fri, 0830 to 1730

ST ALBANS CITY AND DISTRICT COUNCIL

District Council Offices, Civic Centre, St Peter's Street, St Albans, Hertfordshire, AL1 3JE

Tel: 01727 8662100
Fax: 01727 8662100

Website:
http://www.stalbans.gov.uk
Local information including record offices, repositories, local researchers.

Enquiries:
Enquiries to: Public Relations Officer

Organisation type and purpose:
Local government body.

Subject coverage:
Local government services.

ST ANDREWS COMMUNITY LIBRARY

Church Square, St Andrews, Fife, KY16 9NN

Tel: 01334 412685
Fax: 01334 413029
E-mail: standrews.library@fife.gov.uk

Enquiries:
Enquiries to: Library Supervisor

Formerly called:
Hay Fleming Library

Organisation type and purpose:
Local government body, public library.

Non-library collection catalogue:
All or part available online and in-house

Library catalogue:
All or part available online and in-house

Access to staff:
Contact by letter, by telephone, by fax and by e-mail
Hours: Mon, Fri, Sat, 0930 to 1700; Tue, Wed, Thu, 0930 to 1900

Access for disabled people:
Ramped entry, lift to first floor.

Branch library of:
Fife Council Library

ST ANNE'S COLLEGE

Library, Woodstock Road, Oxford, OX2 6HS

Tel: 01865 274810
Fax: 01865 274899
E-mail: library@st-annes.ox.ac.uk

Website:
http://www.lib.ox.ac.uk/libraries/guides/ann.html

Enquiries:
Enquiries to: Librarian
Direct e-mail: david.smith@st-annes.ox.ac.uk

Founded:
1879

Organisation type and purpose:
University department or institute.
College library.

Subject coverage:
Most undergraduate subjects in arts, social sciences and sciences, education and anthropology.

Museum or gallery collection, archive, or library special collection:
Handover Bequest (typography and history of printing)

Library catalogue:
All or part available online

Access to staff:
Contact by letter. Appointment necessary.
Hours: Mon to Fri, 0900 to 1700

Access to building, collection or gallery:
Only by appointment after prior application to Librarian

Parent body:
University of Oxford

ST BRIDE LIBRARY

Bride Lane, Fleet Street, London, EC4Y 8EE

Tel: 020 7353 4660
Fax: 020 7583 7073
E-mail: library@stbridefoundation.org

Enquiries:
Enquiries to: Librarian

Founded:
1891

Organisation type and purpose:
Public reference library.

Subject coverage:
Printing (history and technology) and related subjects (paper, binding, graphic design, typography, typefaces, calligraphy, illustration, printmaking, publishing, bookselling, social and economic aspects of printing and book trades). The collection comprises books, printing types, antique presses, photographs, etc.

Museum or gallery collection, archive, or library special collection:
Historical collection dealing with printing, publishing, graphic design and related subjects, early technical manuals, trade literature, manufacturers' prospectuses, type specimens, trade serials, directories, prints, drawings and artefacts
Archives and Collections
Broadside Collection (18th century songsheets, 19th century broadsides, chapbooks)
Eric Gill Collection (drawings for printing types and stone cut inscriptions)
Leaflets, broadsides, union reports on printing trade relations from 1785
Manuals and periodicals on shorthand (about 3000 items)
Printing tools and equipment
Prints, drawings and manuscripts

Trade and statistical information:
Data on the printing trade, and also on paper and publishing.

Library catalogue:
All or part available online and in-house

Access to staff:
Contact by letter, by telephone, by fax, by e-mail and in person
Hours: Tue, 1200 to 1730; Wed, 1200 to 1900; Thu, 1200 to 1730
Special comments: Reference library.

Parent body:
St Bride Foundation
St Bride Library, Bride Lane, Fleet Street, London, EC4Y 8EE; tel: 020 7353 4660; fax: 020 7583 7073; e-mail: library@stbrideinstitute.org; website: www.stbride.org

ST CHRISTOPHER'S HOSPICE

Halley Stewart Library, 51–59 Lawrie Park Road, Sydenham, London, SE26 6DZ

Tel: 020 8768 4660
Fax: 020 8776 9345
E-mail: d.brady@stchristophers.org.uk

Website:
http://www.stchristophers.org.uk

Enquiries:
Enquiries to: Librarian

Founded:
1980 (Library)

Organisation type and purpose:
Voluntary organisation, registered charity (charity number 210667).
Hospice library (includes information and education facilities).
Hospice for people with advanced disease.

Subject coverage:
All aspects of hospice and palliative care; death and dying, ethical issues, bereavement, children's books on these topics.

continued overleaf

Museum or gallery collection, archive, or library special collection:
In-house database on the subject (c.10,000 items – mainly books, articles and grey literature)

Library catalogue:
All or part available in-house

Printed publications:
Mail order bookshop
Wide range of books available on:
Bereavement, death and dying, ethics and euthanasia, hospice care, motor neurone disease, pastoral care, psychosocial aspects, symptom control, terminal care
Some St Christopher's publications available on bereaved children

Publications list:
Available in print

Access to staff:
Contact by letter, by telephone, by fax and by e-mail. Appointment necessary.
Hours: Mon to Fri, 0900 to 1700

Access for disabled people:
Parking provided, ramped entry, toilet facilities

Links with:
Hospice Information

ST DEINIOL'S RESIDENTIAL LIBRARY

Hawarden, Flintshire, CH5 3DF

Tel: 01244 532350
Fax: 01244 520643
E-mail: librarian@st-deiniols.org

Website:
http://www.st-deiniols.org

Enquiries:
Enquiries to: Librarian

Founded:
1896

Organisation type and purpose:
Residential research library founded by the Rt Hon. W. E. Gladstone.

Subject coverage:
Victorian studies; history; theology; philosophy; literature; church history; Franciscan studies.

Museum or gallery collection, archive, or library special collection:
Benson Collection (books on Judaism)
Gladstoniana (W. E. Gladstone)
Glynne-Gladstone Collection (over 250,000 manuscripts, family letters, estate, household and business papers)
Moorman Franciscan Collection (Bishop John R. H. Moorman)
Pamphlet Collection (over 40,000 from the late 17th century onwards)
Pre-1800 Collection (biblical studies, philosophy, church history, European history)

Library catalogue:
All or part available online and in-house

Printed publications:
Bibliographies of special collections, etc.

Access to staff:
Contact by letter, by telephone, by fax, by e-mail, in person and via website. Letter of introduction required. All charged.
Hours: External readers: Mon to Sat, 0900 to 1830: resident readers: daily, 0900 to 2200
Special comments: All users must provide a testimonial; non-resident readers must purchase an annual ticket; reference only

ST DUNSTAN'S – AN INDEPENDENT FUTURE FOR BLIND EX-SERVICE MEN & WOMEN

12–14 Harcourt Street, London, W1H 4HD

Tel: 020 7723 5021
Fax: 020 7262 6199
E-mail: pressoffice@st.dunstans.org.uk

Enquiries:
Enquiries to: Head of Public Relations

Founded:
1915

Formerly called:
St Dunstan's Blind ex-Service Men and Women; St Dunstan's Caring for Men and Women Blinded in the Service of their Country

Organisation type and purpose:
Registered charity (charity number 216227).
To provide an independent future through rehabilitation and training for blind ex-service men and women.

Printed publications:
Annual Brochure
Annual Report
Bi-annual Newsletter

Access to staff:
Contact by letter and by telephone
Hours: Mon to Fri, 0900 to 1700

ST EDMUNDSBURY BOROUGH COUNCIL

Borough Offices, Angel Hill, Bury St Edmunds, Suffolk, IP33 1XB

Tel: 01284 763233\ Minicom no. 01284 757023
Fax: 01284 757124
E-mail: stedmundsbury@stedsbc.gov.uk

Website:
http://www.stedmundsbury.gov.uk
The heart of East Anglia – a fine place to live, work and visit.
Council services, press releases, accommodation, events etc.
http://www.stedmundsbury.gov.uk/moyses.htm
Museums Service

Enquiries:
Enquiries to: Chief Executive

Founded:
1974

Organisation type and purpose:
Local government body.

Subject coverage:
Local government within St Edmundsbury Borough. Council services, tourist information, economic development.

Printed publications:
Best Value Performance Plan
Community Spirit

Access to staff:
Contact by letter, by telephone, by fax, by e-mail and via website
Hours: Mon to Thu, 0900 to 1700; Fri, 0900 to 1600

Access for disabled people:
Parking provided, ramped entry, level entry, toilet facilities

Other offices:
St Edmundsbury Borough Council
St Edmundsbury House, Western Way, Bury St Edmunds, Suffolk, IP33 3YS; tel: 01284 763233; fax: 01284 757378
St Edmundsbury Borough Council
Council Offices, Lower Downs Slade, Haverhill, Suffolk, CB9 9EE; tel: 01440 702271; fax: 01440 702397

ST FRANCIS LEPROSY GUILD

Acronym or abbreviation: SFLG

73 St Charles Square, London, W10 6EJ

Tel: 020 8969 1345
Fax: 020 8969 3272
E-mail: enquiries@stfrancisleprosy.org

Enquiries:
Enquiries to: General Secretary

Founded:
1895

Organisation type and purpose:
Membership association (membership is by subscription), registered charity (charity number 208741), voluntary organisation.
Raising funds for the assistance of Catholic priests, brothers and sisters working among leprosy sufferers whatever their nationality or creed.

Subject coverage:
Care for leprosy patients; assistance in the provision of food, drugs, wheelchairs, artificial limbs, hospital equipment and surgical instruments, etc.; information on the leprosy projects and centres assisted.

Printed publications:
Annual Review (free)

Access to staff:
Contact by letter and by e-mail
Hours: Mon to Fri, 1000 to 1700

ST HELENS COLLEGE LIBRARY

Brook Street, St Helens, Merseyside, WA10 1PZ

Tel: 01744 733766
Fax: 01744 623007

Website:
http://www.sthelens.ac.uk

Enquiries:
Enquiries to: Head of Information and Library Services
Direct tel: 01744 623225
Direct e-mail: library@sthelens.ac.uk

Formerly called:
St Helens Community College

Organisation type and purpose:
College of further education.

Subject coverage:
Business studies; office technology; management; computer-aided design and manufacture; art and design, health and social care.

Non-library collection catalogue:
All or part available online

Library catalogue:
All or part available online

Printed publications:
College Prospectus
Order printed publications from: Student Services, St Helens College
at the same address

Access to staff:
Contact via website. Appointment necessary.
Non-members charged.
Hours: Term time: Mon to Thu, 0845 to 2000; Fri, 0845 to 1600; Sat, 1000 to 1500; Sun, 1000 to 1400
Vacations: Mon to Thu, 0900 to 1700; Fri, 0900 to 1600

Access for disabled people:
Access to all public areas

The College houses the:
St Helens School of Management Studies, a constituent of the North West Regional Management Centre

ST HELENS LIBRARIES

Central Library, Gamble Institute, Victoria Square, St Helens, Merseyside, WA10 1DY

Tel: 01744 456989
Fax: 01744 20836
E-mail: criu@sthelens.gov.uk

Enquiries:
Enquiries to: Librarian

Organisation type and purpose:
Local government body, public library.

Subject coverage:
Local history, glass.

Museum or gallery collection, archive, or library special collection:
Sir Thomas Beecham Archive Collection, not the original library of the conductor

Access to staff:
Contact by telephone
Hours: Mon, Wed, 0900 to 2000; Tues, Thurs, Fri, 0900 to 1700; Sat, 0900 to 1600

Access for disabled people:
Access to all public areas

ST HILDA'S COLLEGE LIBRARY

Cowley Place, Oxford, OX4 1DY

Tel: 01865 276884
Fax: 01865 276816

Website:
http://www.sthildas.ox.ac.uk/information/history/archive.htm
http://www.sthildas.ox.ac.uk/information/library/index.htm

Enquiries:
Enquiries to: Librarian
Direct tel: 01865 276848
Direct e-mail: maria.croghan@st-hildas.ox.ac.uk
Other contacts: Archivist for access to the archives and related queries.

Founded:
1893

Organisation type and purpose:
University department or institute.
College library.

Subject coverage:
General undergraduate collection, languages, literature, history, philosophy, theology, geography, politics, economics, biology, physiology, medicine, physics, chemistry, engineering, fine art, music.

Museum or gallery collection, archive, or library special collection:
College archive
History of Women's University Education
Maconchy manuscripts, original music manuscripts of Dame Elizabeth Maconchy (20th century composer)

Non-library collection catalogue:
All or part available in-house

Library catalogue:
All or part available online

Access to staff:
Appointment necessary.
Hours: Mon to Fri, 0900 to 1700

Access for disabled people:
Hours: Mon to Fri, 0900 to 1700

Parent body:
University of Oxford

ST JAMES'S UNIVERSITY HOSPITAL

Medical Library, Level 3, Clinical Sciences Building, Beckett Street, Leeds, West Yorkshire, LS9 7TF

Tel: 0113 2065638
Fax: 0113 2064682

Website:
http://www.leeds.ac.uk/library
Information on all resources available at Leeds University Libraries, including catalogue, databases and other electronic resources.

Enquiries:
Enquiries to: Librarian

Formerly called:
St James's and Seacroft University Hospital

Organisation type and purpose:
University library.

Subject coverage:
Medicine; health care management.

Non-library collection catalogue:
All or part available online

Library catalogue:
All or part available online

Access to staff:
Contact by letter, by telephone and in person.
Access for members only.
Hours: Mon to Thu, 0830 to 1800; Fri, 1000 to 1700

Parent body:
University of Leeds

ST JOHN'S COLLEGE LIBRARY

3 South Bailey, Durham, DH1 3RJ

Tel: 0191 334 3500
E-mail: johns.library@durham.ac.uk

Website:
http://www.dur.ac.uk/st-johns.college

Enquiries:
Enquiries to: Librarian
Direct tel: 0191 334 3891
Direct e-mail: richard.briggs@durham.ac.uk
Other contacts: Assistant Librarian

Founded:
1909

Organisation type and purpose:
College library.

Subject coverage:
Mostly theology, some other subject areas.

Library catalogue:
All or part available online

Access to staff:
Contact by letter and by e-mail. Appointment necessary. Non-members charged.
Hours: Mon to Fri, 0900 to 1400
Special comments: Telephone calls morning only

Access to building, collection or gallery:
Prior appointment required

Parent body:
University of Durham

ST JOHN'S INSTITUTE OF DERMATOLOGY

The Calnan Library, St Thomas' Hospital, Lambeth Palace Road, London, SE1 7EH

Tel: 020 7928 9292 ext 1313
Fax: 020 7928 1428
E-mail: patricia.tharratt@kcl.ac.uk

Enquiries:
Enquiries to: Librarian

Founded:
1947

Formerly called:
Institute of Dermatology

Organisation type and purpose:
University department or institute.
Postgraduate medical school library.

Subject coverage:
Dermatology, dermatopathology, some pathology.

Museum or gallery collection, archive, or library special collection:
As well as the latest books and journals, there is a small pre-1900 collection on skin and its diseases, including atlases

Library catalogue:
All or part available in-house

Access to staff:
Appointment necessary.
Hours: Mon to Fri, 0930 to 1730

Parent body:
Guy's, King's and St Thomas' Schools of Medicine, Dentistry and Biomedical Sciences

ST KITTS TOURISM AUTHORITY

10 Kensington Court, London, W8 5DL

Tel: 020 7376 0881
Fax: 020 7937 6742

Website:
http://www.stkitts-tourism.com

Enquiries:
Enquiries to: Manager
Other contacts: Sales Representative

Founded:
1989

Formerly called:
St Kitts and Nevis Department of Tourism

Organisation type and purpose:
National government body.
Tourism promotion.

Subject coverage:
Travel and tourism information for St Kitts and Nevis, also basic investment information.

Trade and statistical information:
Statistical information on tourism arrivals to St Kitts and Nevis.
Relevant cost of a holiday (accommodation, meals and activities).

Printed publications:
Maps and Posters
Promotional Literature
The Secret Caribbean
The Traveller Tourist Guide (free annually)

Publications list:
Available in print

Access to staff:
Contact by telephone
Hours: Mon to Fri, 0930 to 1730

Access to building, collection or gallery:
No prior appointment required

Parent body:
St Kitts and Nevis Department of Tourism
PO Box 132, Basseterre, St Kitts, West Indies

ST LUCIA TOURIST BOARD

Lower Ground Floor, 1 Collingham Gardens, London, SW5 0HW

Tel: 0870 900 7697
Fax: 0207 341 7001

Website:
http://www.bandweb.co.uk/dolphin
Dolphin divers, St Lucia.
http://www.stlucia.org
Tourist board official site.
http://www.interknowledge.com/st-lucia
Tourist information.
http://www.stluciajazz.com
St Lucia jazz festival.
http://www.ansechastanet.com
Anse Chastanet Hotel/diving St Lucia.

Enquiries:
Enquiries to: Information Officer
Direct tel: 020 7431 3675
Direct e-mail: sonia.joseph@axissm.com
Other contacts: Sales Executive

Founded:
1986

Organisation type and purpose:
National Tourist Office.

Subject coverage:
General information on the island, hotels, dining out and places to visit. Incentive groups welcome.

Museum or gallery collection, archive, or library special collection:
Slide library, brochures, posters

continued overleaf

Access to staff:
Contact by letter, by telephone, by fax, by e-mail, in person and via website
Hours: Mon to Fri, 0930 to 1730

ST MARY'S COLLEGE

Acronym or abbreviation: SMUC

Learning Resources Centre, Waldegrave Road, Strawberry Hill, Twickenham, Middlesex, TW1 4SX

Tel: 020 8240 4097
Fax: 020 8240 4270

Enquiries:
Enquiries to: Public Services Manager
Direct e-mail: enquiry@smuc.ac.uk

Founded:
1850

Organisation type and purpose:
University library, university department or institute.

Subject coverage:
Drama, education, English language and Literature, film and television, geography, history, Irish studies, management and business studies, media arts, physical theatre, sociology, sport sciences and theology.

Library catalogue:
All or part available online

Access to staff:
Contact by letter, by telephone, by fax, by e-mail and in person. Appointment necessary.
Hours: 0900 to 2100, term time only

Funded by:
HEFC

ST MARY'S UNIVERSITY COLLEGE LIBRARY (BELFAST)

191 Falls Road, Belfast, BT12 6FE

Tel: 028 9032 7678
Fax: 028 9033 3719

Website:
http://www.stmarys-belfast.ac.uk/
General information, academic information, services, partnerships, student information, what's new.

Enquiries:
Enquiries to: Librarian
Direct e-mail: j.morrissey@stmarys-belfast.ac.uk

Founded:
1900

Formerly called:
St Mary's College Library (Belfast)

Incorporates the former:
St Joseph's College of Education

Organisation type and purpose:
University library, university department or institute.
University College of The Queen's University Belfast.
Education of teachers for the Catholic education system in Northern Ireland, education of teachers for Irish medium education, BA degree in Liberal Arts.

Subject coverage:
Education; religious education; art; physical education; English; drama; history; geography; Celtic; music; mathematics; ICT; science; business studies; European Studies, Irish Medium, technology and design.

Library catalogue:
All or part available online

Access to staff:
Appointment necessary.
Hours: Mon to Thu, 0900 to 2100; Fri, 0900 to 1700, (term time)

Special comments: Students from other universities may use the library for study purposes if there is sufficient space. They must show a current students union card and sign the visitors book.

Constituent college of the:
Queen's University
tel: 028 9032 7678; e-mail: j.morrissey@stmarys-belfast.ac.uk

ST MUNGO'S COMMUNITY HOUSING ASSOCIATION

Formal name: St Mungo Community Housing Association Limited
Acronym or abbreviation: St Mungo's

Griffin House, 2nd Floor, 161 Hammersmith Road, London, W6 8BS

Tel: 020 8762 5500
Fax: 020 8762 5501
E-mail: info@mungos.org

Website:
http://www.mungos.org

Enquiries:
Enquiries to: Information Officer
Direct tel: 020 8762 5500

Founded:
1969

Organisation type and purpose:
Voluntary organisation.
Housing Association No. LH0279. Industrial and Provident Society No. 20598R.
Homelessness charity.

Subject coverage:
Providing hostels and care homes; offering long-term and intensive support for the single homeless. Rough sleeping, subgroups of single homeless people (mental health problems, substance misuse, the elderly, women, multiple/complex needs), employment and training for single homeless people, services and facilities for homeless people in London.

Non-library collection catalogue:
All or part available in-house

Printed publications:
Leaflets about St Mungo's services (various, free, available direct)
In-Reach: Services for the homeless (1 every 1 to 2 years, free, available direct)
Annual Report (free, available direct)
Order printed publications from: Information Department

Access to staff:
Contact by letter, by telephone and by e-mail
Hours: Mon to Fri, 0900 to 1700

Access to building, collection or gallery:
No access other than to staff

ST PAUL'S CATHEDRAL LIBRARY

The Chapter House, St Paul's Churchyard, London, EC4M 8AE

Tel: 020 7246 8342
E-mail: library@stpaulscathedral.org.uk

Website:
http://www.stpauls.co.uk

Enquiries:
Enquiries to: Librarian

Organisation type and purpose:
Private Cathedral library.

Subject coverage:
17th-century theology.

Museum or gallery collection, archive, or library special collection:
Bishop Sumner Collection of 19th-century tracts and pamphlets (6,348 items)
Sacheverell Controversy (233 items)

Access to staff:
Contact by letter, by telephone and by e-mail.
Appointment necessary.
Hours: Mon, Tue, 0900 to 1700; Fri, 1330 to 1700

The archive of Dean and Chapter is deposited at:
Guildhall Library
Aldermanbury, London, EC2V 7HH; tel: 020 7332 1863; e-mail: manuscripts.guildhall@cityoflondon.gov.uk; website: http://www.history.ac.uk/gh

ST PAUL'S SCHOOL LIBRARY

Lonsdale Road, Barnes, London, SW13 9JT

Tel: 020 8746 5413
Fax: 020 8746 5353
E-mail: librarian@stpaulsschool.org.uk

Enquiries:
Enquiries to: Librarian
Direct e-mail: librarian@stpaulsschool.org.uk

Founded:
1509

Organisation type and purpose:
School library.

Subject coverage:
General subjects, particularly history and history of the school.

Museum or gallery collection, archive, or library special collection:
Rare Books Collection (in particular material on John Colet, William Lily, John Milton, G K Chesterton, Laurence Binyon and Edward Thomas)

Library catalogue:
All or part available in-house

Printed publications:
Guides to Research Techniques
Guides to Subject Areas of the Library
The History of St Paul's Library

Access to staff:
Contact by letter, by telephone, by fax and by e-mail. Appointment necessary. Letter of introduction required.
Hours: Mon to Fri, 0800 to 1630
Special comments: Restricted access during school holidays.

ST VINCENT AND THE GRENADINES TOURIST OFFICE

Acronym or abbreviation: SVGTO

10 Kensington Court, London, W8 5DL

Tel: 020 7937 6570
Fax: 020 7937 3611
E-mail: svgtourismeurope@aol.com

Website:
http://www.svgtourism.com

Enquiries:
Enquiries to: Manager

Organisation type and purpose:
National Tourist Office.

Subject coverage:
General information on St. Vincent and the Grenadines, including various types of accommodation, places to go, things to see, sports activities available, climate and all the relevant information required when travelling to the islands.

Printed publications:
Ins and Outs (magazine)
Holiday Bequia (brochure)
Accommodation Guide
Life in St Vincent and the Grenadines

Access to staff:
Contact by letter, by telephone, by fax, by e-mail and in person. Appointment necessary.
Hours: Mon to Fri, 0930 to 1700

Access to building, collection or gallery:
No prior appointment required
Hours: Mon to Fri, 0900 to 1630

STAFF AND EDUCATIONAL DEVELOPMENT ASSOCIATION

Acronym or abbreviation: SEDA

Woburn House, 20–24 Tavistock Square, London, WC1H 9HF

Tel: 020 7380 6767
Fax: 020 7387 2655
E-mail: office@seda.ac.uk

Website:
http://www.seda.ac.uk

Enquiries:
Enquiries to: Administrator

Founded:
1993

Organisation type and purpose:
Professional body (membership is by subscription).

Subject coverage:
Staff and educational development.

Printed publications:
Innovations in Education and Training
  International (IETI, journal, quarterly)
Educational Developments Magazine (quarterly)
Variety of SEDA papers and specials

Publications list:
Available in print

Access to staff:
Contact by letter, by telephone, by fax, by e-mail
and via website
Hours: Mon to Fri, 0900 to 1700

Access to building, collection or gallery:
Prior appointment required

STAFFORD BOROUGH COUNCIL

Acronym or abbreviation: SBC

Civic Centre, Riverside, Stafford, ST16 3AQ

Tel: 01785 619000
Fax: 01785 619119

Website:
http://www.staffordbc.gov.uk

Enquiries:
Enquiries to: Chief Executive
Direct e-mail: chiefexecutive@staffordbc.gov.uk

Founded:
1974

Organisation type and purpose:
Local government body.

Subject coverage:
Local government services.

Access to staff:
Contact by letter, by fax and by e-mail.
Appointment necessary.
Hours: Mon to Fri, 0900 to 1700

Access to building, collection or gallery:
No prior appointment required

STAFFORDSHIRE ARCHAEOLOGICAL AND HISTORICAL SOCIETY

Acronym or abbreviation: SAHS

6 Lawson Close, Aldridge, Walsall, West Midlands, WS9 0RX

Tel: 01922 452230
E-mail: sahs@sahs.uk.net

Website:
http://www.sahs.uk.net

General aims of the Society, list of meetings for
current season, membership secretary's name and
address.

Enquiries:
Enquiries to: Membership Secretary
Direct e-mail: frances@fefox.fsnet.co.uk

Founded:
1959

Formerly called:
Lichfield Archaeological and Historical Society
(year of change 1961); Lichfield and South
Staffordshire Archaeological and Historical Society
(year of change 1995)

Organisation type and purpose:
Learned society (membership is by subscription),
present number of members: 203, registered
charity (charity number 500586), suitable for ages:
16+, publishing house.
Presently conducting a landscape survey of
Shenstone Parish.

Subject coverage:
Local history of Staffordshire, in particular South
Staffordshire, archaeology of Staffordshire,
concentrating on Lichfield and Tamworth areas.

Museum or gallery collection, archive, or library special collection:
Transactions of 17 similar societies in UK and
  abroad held at Lichfield Joint Record Office

Library catalogue:
All or part available online, in-house and in print

Printed publications:
Contents of Transactions Volumes I–XLII
Index to Transactions Volumes I–XXXIV and
  XXXV–XXXIX
Newsletter (3 or 4 times a year)
Transactions (2 times a year, free to members, back
  numbers at various prices, apply to Membership
  Secretary)

Electronic and video publications:
All Transactions now on disc (£50)
Index can be supplied on a disc, but only in its
  published form, not as a database
Order electronic and video publications from:
Membership Secretary

Publications list:
Available online and in print

Access to staff:
Contact by letter, by telephone, by e-mail and via
website
Hours: Any time up to 2200

Links with:
Birmingham and District Local History
Association
Council for British Archaeology

STAFFORDSHIRE LIBRARY AND INFORMATION SERVICES DEPARTMENT

Information Services, Shire Hall Library, Market
Street, Stafford, ST16 2LG

Tel: 01785 278350\ Minicom no. 01785 278347
Fax: 01785 278599
E-mail: information.service@staffordshire.gov.uk

Website:
http://www.talisweb.staffordshire.gov.uk
http://www.staffordshire.gov.uk
15,000 pages approximately, county council
information, education and training in county,
what's on, vacancies, links to other information
databases, online electronic tourism brochure.

Enquiries:
Enquiries to: Service Adviser: Knowledge
Management, IT & Funding
Direct tel: 01785 278352
Direct fax: 01785 278319
Direct e-mail: lynne.stanley@staffordshire.gov.uk

Organisation type and purpose:
Local government body, public library.

Subject coverage:
Staffordshire, music, coal mining, brewing,
industry, playsets.

Museum or gallery collection, archive, or library special collection:
British Standards
Government publications
National Joint Fiction Reserve KB-KEL, KIN-KZ,
  LAR-LED, LIA-LOD, MAM-MARN, MAY-MAZ

Library catalogue:
All or part available online

Printed publications:
Local studies, publications and reprints

Access to staff:
Contact by letter, by telephone, by fax, by e-mail
and via website
Hours: Mon to Fri, 0900 to 1700

Member of:
European Information Association
Midlands On-line User Group
The Library Partnership West Midlands (TLPWM)

Parent body:
Staffordshire County Council

STAFFORDSHIRE MOORLANDS DISTRICT COUNCIL

Acronym or abbreviation: SMDC

Moorlands House, Stockwell Street, Leek,
Staffordshire, ST13 6HQ

Tel: 01538 483483
Fax: 01538 483474

Website:
http://www.staffsmoorlands.gov.uk

Enquiries:
Enquiries to: Chief Executive
Direct tel: 01538 483400
Direct fax: 01538 483423
Direct e-mail: simon.baker@staffsmoorlands.gov.uk
Other contacts: PR & Media Communications
Officer for press contact.

Founded:
1974

Organisation type and purpose:
Local government body.

Subject coverage:
Local government services: council tax, national
non-domestic rates, benefits, housing strategy,
tourism, regeneration, industrial and commercial
property management, markets, waste collection,
street cleaning and public conveniences, waste
minimisation and recycling, environmental health,
local agenda 21, development control, building
conservation, building control, engineering
services, car parks, CCTV, leisure services,
countryside management.

Museum or gallery collection, archive, or library special collection:
Permanent collection of artistic and historical
  artefacts from across Staffordshire Moorlands

Non-library collection catalogue:
All or part available online and in print

Library catalogue:
All or part available in print

Printed publications:
Various publications about local government
  services
The Moorlands Messenger (newspaper, quarterly,
  distributed free to every household)
Order printed publications from: Public Relations &
Media Communications Officer
tel: 01538 483538, fax: 01538 483423, e-mail: charles
.malkin@staffsmoorlands.gov.uk

Electronic and video publications:
The Moorlands Messenger – Council's quarterly
  newspaper (audio tape, distributed free to
  around 200 visually impaired subscribers)

continued overleaf

Publications list:
Available in print

Access to staff:
Contact by letter, by telephone, by fax, by e-mail, in person and via website. Appointment necessary.
Hours: Mon to Thu, 0900 to 1715; Fri, 0900 to 1645

Access for disabled people:
Parking provided, level entry, toilet facilities

Other addresses:
Biddulph Councils Connect
Biddulph Town Hall, Biddulph, Stoke-on-Trent, Staffordshire, ST8 6AR; tel: 01782 297837; fax: 01782 297846; e-mail: biddulph.connect@ staffsmoorlands.gov.uk
Cheadle Councils Connect
15–17A High Street, Cheadle, Stoke-on-Trent, Staffordshire, ST10 1AA; tel: 01538 483860; fax: 01538 757495; e-mail: cheadle.connect@ staffsmoorlands.gov.uk

STAFFORDSHIRE PARISH REGISTERS SOCIETY

Acronym or abbreviation: SPRS

82 Hilport Avenue, Newcastle under Lyme, Staffordshire, ST5 8QT

Tel: 01782 859078
E-mail: secretary@sprs.org.uk

Website:
http://www.staffs.prs.freeserve.co.uk

Enquiries:
Enquiries to: Honorary Secretary

Founded:
16 January 1900

Organisation type and purpose:
Learned society (membership is by subscription), present number of members: over 150, registered charity (charity number 517646), suitable for ages: all, publishing house.

Subject coverage:
The Society was formed to preserve the contents of the parochial registers in Staffordshire by transcribing and printing them. The long-term aim is to publish all the registers down to 1837 for the county of Staffordshire.

Printed publications:
Nearly 120 volumes of registers have been published and usually two volumes are published each year
Order printed publications from: Honorary Secretary

Microform publications:
All out-of-print registers are on microfiche
Order microform publications from: Birmingham & Midland Society for Genealogy & Heraldry 121 Rowood Drive, Damson Wood, Solihull, West Midlands, B92 9LJ, e-mail: mhbmsgh@aol.com

Publications list:
Available online and in print

Access to staff:
Contact by letter and by e-mail

STAFFORDSHIRE RECORD OFFICE

Eastgate Street, Stafford, ST16 2LZ

Tel: 01785 278379\ Minicom no. 01785 278376
Fax: 01785 278384
E-mail: staffordshire.record.office@staffordshire .gov.uk

Website:
http://www.staffordshire.gov.uk/archives/
Access arrangements and general description of holdings. Reprographic and research order forms.

Enquiries:
Enquiries to: Head of Archive Services

Founded:
1947

Organisation type and purpose:
Local government body.
To locate, collect and preserve archive collections relating to past life and activity in the county of Staffordshire and to make these collections available to the public.

Subject coverage:
Archives, local history.

Museum or gallery collection, archive, or library special collection:
Major archive collections relating to the History of Staffordshire

Non-library collection catalogue:
All or part available online

Printed publications:
Family History Pack for Beginners (rev 2005, £4.50 plus p&p)
Advanced Family History Pack (rev 2005, £5.50 plus p&p)
Guide to Parish Registers and Bishop's Transcripts (download free from website)
Nonconformist Registers (£4.50 plus p&p)
Maps: Parish, County and Ordnance Survey

Microform publications:
Staffordshire Parish Registers (fiche)

Publications list:
Available online and in print

Access to staff:
Contact by letter, by telephone, by fax, by e-mail and in person
Hours: Mon, Tue, Thu, 0900 to 1700; Wed, 0900 to 2000; Fri, 0930 to 1630; Sat, 0900 to 1600

Access to building, collection or gallery:
Prior appointment required
Special comments: Reader's ticket required.

Access for disabled people:
Parking provided, ramped entry, access to all public areas, toilet facilities

Other addresses:
Lichfield Record Office
The Friary, Lichfield, WS13 6QG; tel: 01543 510720; e-mail: lichfield.record.office@ staffordshire.gov.uk
Stoke on Trent City Archives
Hanley Library, Bethesda Street, Hanley, Stoke-on-Trent, Staffordshire; tel: 01782 238420; e-mail: stoke.archives@stoke.gov.uk

STAFFORDSHIRE RECORD SOCIETY

William Salt Library, Eastgate Street, Stafford, ST16 2LZ

E-mail: matthew.blake@btinternet.com

Enquiries:
Enquiries to: Honorary Secretary

Founded:
1879

Organisation type and purpose:
Learned society (membership is by subscription), present number of members: 300, registered charity.
Publication of historical records relating to the county of Staffordshire.

Subject coverage:
Archives, records and history of Staffordshire.

Printed publications:
Collections for a history of Staffordshire (for members, on sale to the public)

Microform publications:
Microfiche of the collections
Order microform publications from: Chadwyck-Healey, The Quorum, Barnwell Road, Cambridge, CB5 8SW

Access to staff:
Contact by letter and by e-mail

STAFFORDSHIRE UNIVERSITY – SCHOOL OF ART AND DESIGN

College Road, Stoke-on-Trent, Staffordshire, ST4 2DE

Tel: 01782 294812

Website:
http://www.staffs.ac.uk/slide_library
Currently being updated.

Enquiries:
Enquiries to: Librarian
Direct e-mail: h.r.brown@staffs.ac.uk

Founded:
c1970

Organisation type and purpose:
University department or institute.
Slide Library.

Museum or gallery collection, archive, or library special collection:
Slide library of about 250,000 slides

Access to staff:
Contact by letter, by telephone and by e-mail. Appointment necessary. Non-members charged.
Hours: Mon to Fri, 0900 to 1230 and 1330 to 1600

Access for disabled people:
Ramped entry, access to all public areas, toilet facilities
Special comments: Lift to 4th Floor.

STAFFORDSHIRE UNIVERSITY – THOMPSON LIBRARY

Information Services, Thompson Library, College Road, Stoke-on-Trent, Staffordshire, ST4 2XS

Tel: 01782 294443
Fax: 01782 295799

Website:
http://www.staffs.ac.uk

Enquiries:
Enquiries to: Head of Resources Management
Direct tel: 01782 294961
Direct e-mail: d.j.parkes@staffs.ac.uk

Organisation type and purpose:
University library, university department or institute.

Subject coverage:
Art, law, sciences, social sciences, business, humanities, design, ceramics, engineering, electrical engineering, computing.

Museum or gallery collection, archive, or library special collection:
Arts Archive
Badminton Collection (Badminton Library of Sports and Pastimes)
Centre for the History of Psychology (CHOP) Collection (1600-)
Dorothy Thompson Collection (Chartism 1800-)
Eysenck Collection (H J Eysenck)
Iris Strange Collection (Campaign for pensions for British war widows, mainly WWII)
Mining Archive (worldwide)
Riley Collection
ROAPE (Review of African Studies) Collection
Solon Collection (literature on ceramics)
Staffordshire Film Archive (history of the county and key events)

Library catalogue:
All or part available online

Access to staff:
Contact by letter, by telephone, by e-mail, in person and via website. Non-members charged.
Hours: Mon to Fri, 0900 to 1700

Access to building, collection or gallery:
Hours: (term-time only) Mon to Fri, 0900 to 2000; Sat and Sun, 1300 to 1800

STAG OWNERS CLUB

Acronym or abbreviation: SOC

c/o The Membership Secretary, The Old Rectory, Aslacton, Norfolk, NR15 2JN

Tel: 01379 677735
Fax: 01379 677363
E-mail: membership@stag.uk.net

Website:
http://www.stag.org.uk
Overview of club and activities.

Enquiries:
Enquiries to: Membership Secretary

Founded:
1979

Organisation type and purpose:
Membership association (membership is by subscription), present number of members: 5000, voluntary organisation.
To further interest in the Triumph Stag motor car.

Subject coverage:
The Triumph Stag.

Printed publications:
Magazine (monthly, members only)

Access to staff:
Contact by letter, by telephone, by e-mail and via website
Hours: Mon to Fri, 0900 to 1700

STAGE MANAGEMENT ASSOCIATION

Acronym or abbreviation: SMA

55 Farringdon Road, London, EC1M 3JB

Tel: 020 7242 9250
Fax: 020 7242 9303
E-mail: admin@stagemanagementassociation.co.uk

Website:
http://www.stagemanagementassociation.co.uk
Information about SMA, training, publications, events, message board.

Enquiries:
Enquiries to: Administrator

Founded:
1954

Organisation type and purpose:
National organisation, professional body (membership is by application), present number of members: 620, training organisation.
Theatre and television stage management.

Subject coverage:
Supporting and representing stage management in the UK.

Printed publications:
Company Manager's Notes (£3.50, £5 non members inc. p&p)
List of members free for engagements (monthly free)
A Stage Manager's Guide to:
The West End Theatre Agreement 2002 (£2, £3.50 non members inc. p&p)
The Subsidised Repertory Agreement 2003 (£2, £3.50 non members inc. p&p)
The Commercial Contract 2003 (£2, £3.50 non members inc. p&p)
Stage Management Notes (£4, £6 non members inc. p&p)
Stage Management: a career guide
SMA Guide to Props and Propping (£4.50, £7 non members inc. p&p)

Publications list:
Available online and in print

Access to staff:
Contact by letter, by telephone, by fax, by e-mail and via website. Appointment necessary.
Hours: Mon to Fri, 1000 to 1600

Access to building, collection or gallery:
No access other than to staff

Connections with:
National Council for Drama Training (NCDT)

In constant correspondence with the:
Stage Managers' Association
 USA
Theatrical Management Association (TMA)

Links with:
Association of British Theatre Technicians (ABTT)
British Actors Equity Association
Independent Theatre Council (ITC)
Most theatre organisations
Save London's Theatres Campaign
Theatres Trust

STANDARD VANGUARD OWNERS CLUB

7 Priory Close, Wilton, Salisbury, Wiltshire, SP2 0LD

Tel: 01722 503101

Enquiries:
Enquiries to: Secretary

Founded:
1989

Organisation type and purpose:
Membership association (membership is by subscription).

Subject coverage:
Standard Vanguard cars, preservation and restoration.

Access to staff:
Contact by letter and by telephone. Appointment necessary.
Hours: 1000 to 2200, any day

STANDING COMMITTEE ON OFFICIAL PUBLICATIONS

Acronym or abbreviation: SCOOP

ISG, SCOOP, c/o CILIP, 7 Ridgmount Street, London, WC1E 7AE

Tel: 020 7255 0500
Fax: 020 7255 0501
E-mail: scoop@nurcombe.com

Website:
http://www.cilip.org.uk/isg

Enquiries:
Enquiries to: Secretary

Founded:
1971

Organisation type and purpose:
Professional body.
To improve access to UK official information.

Subject coverage:
Official publications and information in the UK.

Printed publications:
Directory of Specialists in Official Publications (£7)
Proceedings of seminars and conferences (for sale)
Publicity leaflet (free of charge)
Refer: The Journal of the ISG (£20 subscription)
Order printed publications from: Publications Secretary, SCOOP, 42 Moors Lane, Darnhall, Winsford, Cheshire, CW7 1JX, tel: 01606 558242, e-mail: scoop@nurcombe.com

Publications list:
Available in print

Access to staff:
Contact by letter, by telephone and by e-mail
Hours: Mon to Fri, 0900 to 1700

Sub-group of the:
Library Association's Information Service Group

STANDING CONFERENCE OF PRINCIPALS

Acronym or abbreviation: SCOP

20 Tavistock Square, Woburn House, London, WC1H 9HB

Tel: 020 7387 7711
Fax: 020 7387 7712
E-mail: info@scop.ac.uk

Enquiries:
Enquiries to: Executive Secretary
Other contacts: Chairman

Founded:
1978

Organisation type and purpose:
National organisation, membership association (membership is by subscription), registered charity (charity number 1012218), research organisation.

Subject coverage:
Higher education issues relating specially to colleges of higher education in England and Northern Ireland.

Publications list:
Available online

Access to staff:
Contact by letter, by telephone, by fax and by e-mail
Hours: Mon to Fri, 0900 to 1700

STANDING CONFERENCE ON LIBRARY MATERIALS ON AFRICA

Acronym or abbreviation: SCOLMA

c/o Commonwealth Secretariat, Marlborough House, Pall Mall, London, SW1Y 5HX

Tel: 020 7747 6253
Fax: 020 7747 6168
E-mail: scolma@hotmail.com

Website:
http://www.lse.ac.uk/library/scolma
Details of SCOLMA and its publications, details on membership, including subscriptions, for full membership and for the SCOLMA journal.

Enquiries:
Enquiries to: Chairman

Founded:
1962

Organisation type and purpose:
Learned society, registered charity (charity number 325086).
African studies.

Subject coverage:
Location of materials relating to African studies, for the following countries and areas: Algeria, Angola, Ascension Island, Benin, Botswana, Burundi, Cameroon, Canary Islands, Cape Verde Islands, Central Africa, Chad, Congo (Brazzaville), Democratic Republic of Congo, Djibouti, Ethiopia, Gabon, Gambia, Ghana, Guinea, Guinea-Bissau, Ivory Coast, Kenya, Lesotho, Liberia, Libya, Madagascar, Madeira, Malawi, Mali, Mauritania, Mauritius, Morocco, Mozambique, Namibia, Niger, Nigeria, Principe, Rwanda, St Helena, St Tomé, Senegal, Seychelles, Sierra Leone, Somalia, South Africa, Sudan, Swaziland, Tanzania, Togo, Tristan da Cunha, Tunisia, Uganda, Upper Volta, Western Sahara, Zimbabwe.

Publications list:
Available online and in print

Access to staff:
Contact by letter, by telephone, by e-mail and in person
Hours: Mon to Fri, 0900 to 1700

STAR PUBLISHERS DISTRIBUTORS

112 Whitfield Street, London, W1T 5EE

Tel: 020 7380 0622
Fax: 020 7419 9169
E-mail: indbooks@aol.com

continued overleaf

Organisation type and purpose:
Bookshop.

Subject coverage:
A bookshop exclusively devoted to Indian books.
Latest Indian publications (in English, Hindi, Urdu
and Punjabi) on art, architecture, fine arts (music,
dance, films etc), travel, history, politics, social
sciences, business and economics, women's
studies, religion and philosophy, reference and
encyclopaedias, language and literature, general
subjects, and books for children.

Printed publications:
Bulletin (quarterly)
Catalogue (annually)

Parent body:
Star Publications
   New Delhi, India

STAR, STARLING, STUART & BRITON REGISTER

New Wood Lodge, 2A Hyperion Road, Stourton,
Stourbridge, West Midlands, DY7 6SB

Tel: 01384 374329

Website:
http://www.localhistory.scit.wlv.ac.uk/museum/
transport/cars/staregister/starreg01.htm

Enquiries:
Enquiries to: Registrar

Founded:
1964

Organisation type and purpose:
Membership association (membership is by
election or invitation), present number of
members: 200.
To promote the restoration and preservation of
vehicles manufactured by the Star and Briton
Companies of Wolverhampton, England.

Subject coverage:
Historical and technical information service on
Star, Stirling, Stuart and Briton cars and
commercial vehicles of Wolverhampton.

**Museum or gallery collection, archive, or library
special collection:**
Catalogues, drawings, instructional handbooks
   and original order specifications on vehicles
Magazine and book references to companies and
   products, 1869 to 1932

Trade and statistical information:
Order books and statistical data on production
   between 1927 and 1932.
Data prior to 1927 being compiled.

Printed publications:
List of existing vehicles and current owners (free to
   members)

Access to staff:
Contact by letter, by telephone and in person
Hours: Mon to Fri, 0900 to 1700

STATE OF SOUTH AUSTRALIA

The Australia Centre, Strand, London, WC2B 4LG

Tel: 020 7836 3455
Fax: 020 7887 5332
E-mail: info@south-aus.org

Enquiries:
Enquiries to: Agent General
Direct tel: 020 7887 5124

Founded:
1858

Organisation type and purpose:
Government trade and investment office.

Publications list:
Available in print

Access to staff:
Contact by letter, by telephone, by fax and by e-
mail

Hours: Mon to Fri, 0900 to 1700

Access for disabled people:
Level entry, toilet facilities

STATIONERS' AND NEWSPAPER MAKERS' COMPANY

Stationers' Hall, Ave Maria Lane, London, EC4M
7DD

Tel: 020 7248 2934
Fax: 020 7489 1975
E-mail: admin@stationers.org

Website:
http://www.stationers.org

Enquiries:
Enquiries to: The Clerk

Founded:
1403

Organisation type and purpose:
Membership association (membership is by
election or invitation).
City of London Livery Company.

**Museum or gallery collection, archive, or library
special collection:**
Company Archives (1554 to present)

Access to staff:
Contact by letter, by telephone, by fax and by e-
mail

STATIONERY OFFICE, THE

Acronym or abbreviation: TSO

St Crispins, Duke Street, Norwich, NR3 1PD

Tel: 01603 622211
E-mail: customer.services@tso.co.uk

Website:
http://www.clicktso.com
http://www.thestationeryoffice.com

Enquiries:
Enquiries to: Press Officer
Direct tel: 01603 622211
Other contacts: Deputy Manager

Founded:
privatised 1996

Organisation type and purpose:
National organisation, publishing house.
Retail bookshops, information provider.

Subject coverage:
Official and regulatory information.

**Museum or gallery collection, archive, or library
special collection:**
The Stationery Office publications
Ordnance Survey
HSE publications
British Standards Distributor including Print on
   Demand Service

Printed publications:
Various publications available via
   www.clicktso.com, mail order, from shop

Publications list:
Available online

Access to staff:
Contact by letter, by telephone, by fax, by e-mail,
in person and via website
Hours: Mon, Wed, Thu, Fri, 0900 to 1730; Tue, 0930
to 1730; Sat, 1000 to 1500

Access to building, collection or gallery:
No prior appointment required

Access for disabled people:
Level entry

Other addresses:
TSO Bookshop
   9–21 Princess Street, Manchester, M60 8AS; tel:
   0161 834 7201

TSO Bookshop
   18–19 High Street, Cardiff, CF10 1PT; tel: 029
   2039 5548

Other offices:
TSO Birmingham
   68–69 Bull Street, Birmingham, B4 6AD; tel: 0121
   236 9696
TSO Head Office
   St Crispins, Duke Street, Norwich; tel: 0870 600
   5522
TSO Head Office
   51 Nine Elms Lane, London, SW8 5DR; tel: 0870
   600 5522
TSO Northern Ireland
   16 Arthur Street, Belfast, BT1 4GD; tel: 028 9023
   8451
TSO Scotland
   71 Lothian Road, Edinburgh, EH3 9AZ; tel: 0870
   606 5566

STATISTICAL SERVICES CENTRE

Acronym or abbreviation: SSC

University of Reading, Harry Pitt Building, PO Box
240, Reading, Berkshire, RG6 6FN

Tel: 0118 378 8025
Fax: 0118 975 3169
E-mail: l.e.turner@reading.ac.uk

Website:
http://www.reading.ac.uk/ssc/

Enquiries:
Enquiries to: Executive Assistant

Founded:
1982

Organisation type and purpose:
Training organisation, consultancy.

Subject coverage:
Statistical consultancy, statistical training/courses,
statistical computing, database management
systems.

Electronic and video publications:
Statistical software package INSTAT (a teaching
   package, free)

Publications list:
Available online

Access to staff:
Contact by letter, by telephone, by fax, by e-mail
and via website. Appointment necessary. All
charged.
Hours: Mon to Fri, 0900 to 1700

Access for disabled people:
Access to all public areas, toilet facilities
Special comments: Lift

Parent body:
University of Reading

STATUTE LAW SOCIETY

Acronym or abbreviation: SLS

Institute of Advanced Legal Studies, 17 Russell
Square, London, WC1B 5DR

Tel: 020 7862 5875
Fax: 020 7862 5855
E-mail: statute.law@sas.ac.uk

Enquiries:
Enquiries to: Secretary

Founded:
1968

Organisation type and purpose:
Learned society, registered charity (charity number
261226).

Subject coverage:
Statute law and legislation.

Printed publications:
Statute Law Review (pub. OUP)

Access to staff:
Contact by letter, by telephone and by fax
Hours: Mon to Fri, 0900 to 1700

STAUNTON SOCIETY, THE

98 Cole Park, Twickenham, Middlesex, TW1 1JA

Tel: 020 8744 2868
Fax: 020 8742 2311

Enquiries:
Enquiries to: General Secretary

Founded:
1993

Organisation type and purpose:
Learned society, membership association (membership is by election or invitation), present number of members: 80.
To further the importance of chess as an educational sport; to provide support and illumination to young players; to make public the achievements of past national figures such as Howard Staunton.

Subject coverage:
The life and works of Howard Staunton (1810–1874), chess player, editor of Shakespeare. Editor of The Great Schools of England, education in the endowed schools. Chess play, historical and contemporary. British chess players 19th and 20th century and foreign nationals who have played here over time.

Museum or gallery collection, archive, or library special collection:
Limited number of Staunton books. Memorabilia

Printed publications:
Staunton Society Newsletter

Access to staff:
Contact by letter, by telephone and by fax
Hours: Sat & Sun inclusive

STEAM BOAT ASSOCIATION OF GREAT BRITAIN

Acronym or abbreviation: SBA

Avoca Cottage, School Lane, Niton, Isle of Wight, PO38 2BP

Tel: 01983 730664

Website:
http://www.steamboat.org.uk

Enquiries:
Enquiries to: Honorary Secretary

Founded:
1972

Organisation type and purpose:
Membership association (membership is by subscription), present number of members: over 1000.
A society to foster and encourage steamboating and building, development, preservation and restoration of steam boats and steam machinery.

Subject coverage:
Small steam boats and steam launches; other steam machinery.

Museum or gallery collection, archive, or library special collection:
Archive collection

Printed publications:
Journal (quarterly)

Access to staff:
Contact by letter and by telephone
Hours: Any reasonable time.

STEEL CONSTRUCTION INSTITUTE

Acronym or abbreviation: SCI

Silwood Park, Buckhurst Road, Ascot, Berkshire, SL5 7QN

Tel: 01344 636525
Fax: 01344 636570
E-mail: library@steel-sci.com

Website:
http://www.steel-sci.org
Information relating to the work of the Steel Construction Institute and services provided to the construction industry.

Enquiries:
Enquiries to: Librarian

Founded:
1986

Organisation type and purpose:
Research organisation.

Subject coverage:
Use of steel in construction onshore and offshore; steel properties, related standards and codes of practice (UK, European and American); steel buildings, bridges, tunnels, offshore platforms.

Printed publications:
A large number of books on topics including: Stainless Steel, Steel and the Environment, Steel Below Ground, Steel Bridges, Offshore Engineering, Light Gauge Steel
Handbooks and Commentaries to BS Codes
New Steel Construction (6 times a year)
Steel Construction Yearbook

Publications list:
Available in print

Access to staff:
Contact by letter, by telephone, by fax, by e-mail and via website. Appointment necessary. Access for members only. Non-members charged.
Hours: Mon to Fri, 0900 to 1700

STEEL WINDOW ASSOCIATION

Acronym or abbreviation: SWA

The Building Centre, 26 Store Street, London, WC1E 7BT

Tel: 020 7637 3571
Fax: 020 7637 3572
E-mail: info@steel-window-association.co.uk

Website:
http://www.steel-window-association.co.uk
List of member companies; specifier's guide to steel windows.

Enquiries:
Enquiries to: Director

Founded:
1967

Organisation type and purpose:
Trade association (membership is by subscription), present number of members: 25.

Subject coverage:
Steel window manufacture, supply and installation, technical advice and information.

Printed publications:
Fact Sheets
List of member companies
Specifier's Guide to Steel Windows (6th ed.)

Access to staff:
Contact by letter, by telephone, by fax, by e-mail, in person and via website. Appointment necessary.
Hours: Mon to Fri, 0900 to 1700

STEPHENSON COLLEGE, COALVILLE

Thornborough Road, Coalville, Leicestershire, LE67 3TN

Tel: 01530 836136
Fax: 01530 814253
E-mail: Deniser@stephensoncoll.ac.uk

Website:
http://www.stephensoncoll.ac.uk

Enquiries:
Enquiries to: Learning Resources Manager
Direct tel: 01530 836136 ext 181

Formerly called:
Coalville Technical College (year of change 1997)

Organisation type and purpose:
Suitable for ages: 16+, training organisation. Further education establishment.

Subject coverage:
Business and management; motor vehicle technology; engineering; access to higher education; construction, information technology, health and social care; hair and beauty; early years

Non-library collection catalogue:
All or part available in-house

Library catalogue:
All or part available in-house

Printed publications:
New Book Lists (occasional)

Access to staff:
Contact by letter, by telephone, by fax and by e-mail. Appointment necessary. Access for members only.
Hours: Mon to Thu, 0830 to 2100; Fri, 0830 to 1700

Access for disabled people:
Parking provided, access to all public areas

STERILISED SUTURE MANUFACTURERS ASSOCIATION

Acronym or abbreviation: SSMA

Ethicon Limited, PO Box 408, Bankhead Avenue, Edinburgh, EH11 4HE

Tel: 0131 453 5555
Fax: 0131 453 6011

Enquiries:
Enquiries to: Honorary Secretary
Other contacts: Chairman of the Technical Committee for matters of a technical nature or if the Hon Secretary is unavailable.

Organisation type and purpose:
Trade association (membership is by qualification, election or invitation), present number of members: 3, voluntary organisation.

Subject coverage:
Production and supply of surgical sutures.

Access to staff:
Contact by letter, by telephone and by fax
Hours: Mon to Fri, 0900 to 1700

Affiliated to:
European Association of the Surgical Suture Industry (EASSI)
tel: 49 69 2556 1338; fax: 49 69 2556 1471

STEVENAGE BOROUGH COUNCIL

Acronym or abbreviation: SBC

Daneshill House, Danestrete, Stevenage, Hertfordshire, SG1 1HN

Tel: 01438 242242
Fax: 01438 242566

Website:
http://www.stevenage.gov.uk

Enquiries:
Enquiries to: Public Relations Manager

Organisation type and purpose:
Local government body.

Subject coverage:
Local government services.

STEVENAGE BUSINESS INITIATIVE

Acronym or abbreviation: SBI

Business & Technology Centre, Bessemer Drive, Stevenage, Hertfordshire, SG1 2DX

Tel: 0845 078 0600
Fax: 01438 310001
E-mail: enquiries@sbi-herts.co.uk

Website:
http://www.sbi-herts.co.uk

Enquiries:
Enquiries to: Information Officer

Founded:
1983

Organisation type and purpose:
Service industry.
Enterprise agency, free start-up business advice service.

Subject coverage:
Business advice.

Access to staff:
Contact by letter, by telephone, by fax, by e-mail, in person and via website. Appointment necessary.
Hours: Mon to Thu, 0830 to 1730; Fri, 0830 to 1700

STEWART SOCIETY

53 George Street, Edinburgh, EH2 2HT

Tel: 0131 220 4512
Fax: 0131 220 4512
E-mail: info@stewartsociety.org

Website:
http://www.stewartsociety.org

Enquiries:
Enquiries to: Librarian

Founded:
1899

Organisation type and purpose:
International organisation, learned society (membership is by subscription), present number of members: 614, voluntary organisation, registered charity (charity number SC 000692), museum, research organisation.

Subject coverage:
Stewart and general Scottish history, Stewart genealogy.

Museum or gallery collection, archive, or library special collection:
Family papers, old books and family trees pertaining to the Stewarts and Stuarts
Members' library

Non-library collection catalogue:
All or part available in-house

Library catalogue:
All or part available in-house

Printed publications:
The Stewarts (magazine, annually)
Stewart News (newsletter)

Publications list:
Available in print

Access to staff:
Contact by letter, by telephone, by fax, by e-mail, in person and via website. Appointment necessary.
Hours: Mon to Fri, 0900 to 1300

STILLBIRTH AND NEONATAL DEATH CHARITY

Acronym or abbreviation: SANDS

28 Portland Place, London, W1B 1LY

Tel: 020 7436 7940
Fax: 020 7436 3715
E-mail: support@uk-sands.org

Website:
http://www.uk-sands.org

Description of services; how to contact SANDS; publications list; stillbirth; neonatal death and baby loss.

Enquiries:
Enquiries to: Administrator

Founded:
1981

Organisation type and purpose:
Membership association (membership is by subscription), present number of members: 970, voluntary organisation, registered charity (charity number 299679).
To support parents when their baby dies at or soon after birth. Training for professionals.

Subject coverage:
Death of a baby at or soon after birth (stillbirth, neonatal death), pregnancy losses. Incidence of stillbirth and neonatal death in the UK. Causes of stillbirth and neonatal death. Support and care of families affected, funerals for infants.

Museum or gallery collection, archive, or library special collection:
Wide collection on stillbirth, neonatal loss and pregnancy losses

Trade and statistical information:
UK stillbirth and neonatal mortality statistics.

Printed publications:
Pregnancy Loss and the Death of a Baby:
Guidelines for professionals
SANDS Newsletter (3 times a year)
Information leaflets (7 titles, 10p each)
When a baby dies
What has to be done
Saying Goodbye to your baby
Books and leaflets for families and health professionals

Publications list:
Available online and in print

Access to staff:
Contact by letter, by telephone, by fax, by e-mail and via website
Hours: Mon to Fri, 0930 to 1700
Special comments: No disabled access.

Access to building, collection or gallery:
Prior appointment required

STILTON CHEESE MAKERS' ASSOCIATION

Acronym or abbreviation: SCMA

PO Box 384A, Surbiton, Surrey, KT5 9YL

Tel: 020 8255 1334
Fax: 020 8255 1335
E-mail: stilton@stiltoncheese.com

Website:
http://www.stiltoncheese.com

Enquiries:
Enquiries to: Stilton Information Bureau
Direct tel: 0161 923 4994
Direct fax: 0161 923 4760
Direct e-mail: enquiries@stiltoncheese.com

Founded:
1936

Organisation type and purpose:
Trade association (membership is by qualification), present number
of members: 5, manufacturing industry.
Promotion of Stilton cheese
Protection of Stilton certification trade marks.

Subject coverage:
Stilton cheese: all matters including trade mark, manufacture, methods of storing and serving, sources of supply.

Printed publications:
Recipe leaflets and cards
Order printed publications from: Stilton Information Bureau, c/o BRAZEN, Brazen House, Great Ancoats Street, Manchester, M4 5AJ

Access to staff:
Contact by letter, by telephone and by e-mail
Hours: Mon to Fri, 0900 to 1700

Links with:
Dairy UK
93 Baker Street, London, W1U 6RL; tel: 020 7486 7244; fax: 020 7487 4734

STIRLING COUNCIL ARCHIVE SERVICE

Acronym or abbreviation: SCAS

5 Borrowmeadow Road, Springkerse Industrial Estate, Stirling, FK7 7UW

Tel: 01786 450745
Fax: 01786 433005
E-mail: archive@stirling.gov.uk

Website:
http://www.stirling.gov.uk/index/access-info/archives.htm

Enquiries:
Enquiries to: Archivist

Founded:
1996

Organisation type and purpose:
Local government body.
Archive.

Subject coverage:
Manuscript sources relating to the area administered by Stirling Council.

Non-library collection catalogue:
All or part available online and in-house

Access to staff:
Contact by letter, by telephone, by fax, by e-mail, in person and via website
Hours: Mon to Wed, 0930 to 1630

Access for disabled people:
Level entry

STIRLING COUNCIL LIBRARIES

Administrative Headquarters, Borrowmeadow Road, Springkerse Industrial Estate, Stirling, FK7 7TN

Tel: 01786 432383
Fax: 01786 432395
E-mail: libraryheadquarters@stirling.gov.uk

Website:
http://www.stirling.gov.uk

Enquiries:
Enquiries to: Libraries and Archives Manager
Direct tel: 01786 443398

Founded:
1975

Organisation type and purpose:
Local government body, public library.

Subject coverage:
Local history of the Stirling District (Stirling County to 1975); general.

Museum or gallery collection, archive, or library special collection:
Local and Scottish History Collections
Stirling Journal and Advertiser, local newspaper from 1820–1970
Stirling Observer local newspaper from June 1970
Thomson Collection (theology)

Library catalogue:
All or part available online and in-house

Publications list:
Available online and in print

Access to staff:
Contact by letter and by telephone
Hours: Mon to Fri, 0900 to 1700

Access to building, collection or gallery:
No prior appointment required

Access for disabled people:
Parking provided, ramped entry, access to all public areas

STOCKPORT ARCHIVE SERVICE

Central Library, Wellington Road, Stockport, Cheshire, SK1 3RS

Tel: 0161 474 4530\ Minicom no. 0161 474 4541
Fax: 0161 474 7750
E-mail: localheritagelibrary@stockport.gov.uk

Enquiries:
Enquiries to: Archivist

Organisation type and purpose:
Local government body, public library.

Subject coverage:
Stockport archives, family history, local history.

Museum or gallery collection, archive, or library special collection:
Christy & Co (hat manufacturers) records
Stockport Sunday School records

Non-library collection catalogue:
All or part available in-house

Access to staff:
Contact by letter, by telephone, by fax, by e-mail and in person. Appointment necessary.
Hours: Mon, Tue, 1000 to 2000; Wed, Thu, 0900 to 1700; Fri, 0900 to 2000; Sat, 0900 to 1600
Special comments: Records held in outstore require advance notice.

Access for disabled people:
Lift

STOCKPORT COLLEGE

Wellington Road South, Stockport, Cheshire, SK1 3UQ

Tel: 0161 958 3471
Fax: 0161 958 3469
E-mail: TheLearningCentre@stockport.ac.auk

Website:
http://www.stockport.ac.uk
Information on college facilities and courses offered.

Enquiries:
Enquiries to: Learning Centre Circulation and Operations Manager

Organisation type and purpose:
College of further and higher education. Takes students aged 14–16 and 16+.

Subject coverage:
Art and design; applied social sciences; building and civil engineering; electrical, mechanical and production engineering; general education; management and business studies; science; computing; nursing; travel and tourism; catering.

Museum or gallery collection, archive, or library special collection:
College archives
Video recordings (2500) and DVDs

Non-library collection catalogue:
All or part available online

Library catalogue:
All or part available online

Access to staff:
Contact in person
Hours: Term time: Mon to Thu, 0830 to 2000; Fri, 0830 to 1700
Vacations: Mon to Fri, 0900 to 1700
Special comments: Reference only for non-members (printed materials only).

Access to building, collection or gallery:
Special comments: Please report to main reception as a visitor

Access for disabled people:
Access to all public areas

STOCKSCOTLAND

The Croft Studio, Croft Roy, Crammon Brae, Tain, Ross-shire, IV19 1JG

Tel: 01862 892298
Fax: 01862 892298
E-mail: info@stockscotland.com

Website:
http://www.stockscotland.com
10,000 image catalogue.

Enquiries:
Enquiries to: Proprietor

Founded:
1992

Organisation type and purpose:
Photographic Library.

Subject coverage:
Contemporary images of the highlands and islands of Scotland. Photographs available for landscape, tourism, industry, agriculture, transport, fisheries etc.

Library catalogue:
All or part available online

Printed publications:
Catalogue (free)
Showcard brochure (free)

Electronic and video publications:
CD-ROM catalogue (normally free)

Access to staff:
Contact by letter, by telephone, by fax, by e-mail and via website. Appointment necessary. All charged.
Hours: Mon to Fri, 0900 to 1700

STOCKTON-ON-TEES BOROUGH COUNCIL

PO Box 11, Municipal Buildings, Church Road, Stockton-on-Tees, Cleveland, TS18 1LD

Tel: 01642 393939
Fax: 01642 393092

Website:
http://www.stockton.gov.uk
Service details, councillors details, events, facts and figures.

Enquiries:
Enquiries to: Personnel and Communications Officer

Organisation type and purpose:
Local government body.

Subject coverage:
Stockton-on-Tees borough services and amenities.

Access to staff:
Contact by letter, by telephone, by fax, by e-mail and in person
Hours: Mon to Fri, 0900 to 1700

STOKE-ON-TRENT CLASSIC CAR CLUB

19 Nashe Drive, Blurton, Stoke-on-Trent, Staffordshire, ST3 2HD

Tel: 01782 323167
E-mail: malcolm@classiccarclub.freeserve.co.uk

Enquiries:
Enquiries to: Secretary
Other contacts: Chairman

Founded:
2000

Access to staff:
Contact by letter and by telephone
Hours: Mon to Fri, 0900 to 1700

STOKE-ON-TRENT COLLEGE

Cauldon Campus, Stoke Road, Shelton, Stoke-on-Trent, Staffordshire, ST4 2DG

Tel: 01782 208208
Fax: 01782 603504

Website:
http://www.stokecoll.ac.uk

Enquiries:
Enquiries to: Learning Resources Manager
Other contacts: Cataloguer

Founded:
1947

Organisation type and purpose:
Suitable for ages: 16+.
College of further and higher education.

Subject coverage:
Building construction, management, office skills, social sciences, science, catering, hairdressing, beauty, computer-aided engineering.

Museum or gallery collection, archive, or library special collection:
Construction and Property Information Centre

Library catalogue:
All or part available online

Printed publications:
Welcome to the LRC

Access to staff:
Contact by letter, by telephone, by fax, by e-mail and in person
Hours: Term time: Mon to Thu, 0830 to 2100; Fri, 0830 to 1800; Sat, 0900 to 1300

Access to building, collection or gallery:
No access other than to staff

Access for disabled people:
Parking provided, ramped entry, level entry, access to all public areas, toilet facilities

Associated with:
Forum for Information Resources in Staffordshire (FIRST)

Includes the:
Construction and Property Information Centre

STOKE-ON-TRENT LIBRARIES, INFORMATION AND ARCHIVES

City Central Library, Information Department, Bethesda Street, Hanley, Stoke-on-Trent, Staffordshire, ST1 3RS

Tel: 01782 238431/32/33
Fax: 01782 238434
E-mail: central.library@swift.gov.uk

Website:
http://www.stoke.gov.uk/libraries

Enquiries:
Enquiries to: Librarian

Organisation type and purpose:
Public library.

Subject coverage:
General information; ceramics; local history and archives, especially Stoke-on-Trent and Staffordshire; European Public Information Centre (EPIC).

Museum or gallery collection, archive, or library special collection:
British Standards (online)
Ceramics
Local history collection and archives

Non-library collection catalogue:
All or part available online

Library catalogue:
All or part available online

continued overleaf

Access to staff:
Contact by letter, by telephone, by fax, by e-mail and in person
Hours: Mon, Tues, Wed, Thurs, 0900 to 1930; Fri, 0900 to 1700; Sat, 0900 to 1600

Parent body:
Stoke-on-Trent Libraries, Information and Archives
City Central Library, Bethesda Street, Hanley, Stoke-on-Trent, ST1 3RS; tel: 01782 238455; fax: 01782 238499; e-mail: central.library@swift.stoke .gov.uk

STOKE-ON-TRENT TOURISM GROUP

Trentham Business Centre, Bellringer Road, Trentham Lakes South, Trentham, Stoke-on-Trent, Staffordshire, ST4 8HH

Tel: 01782 232786
Fax: 01782 232910
E-mail: tourism@stoke.gov.uk

Website:
http://www.stoke.gov.uk/tourism

Enquiries:
Enquiries to: Manager

Organisation type and purpose:
Local government body.

Subject coverage:
Tourism in the Stoke-on-Trent area and The Potteries.

Access to staff:
Contact by letter
Hours: Mon to Fri, 0900 to 1700

STORAGE AND HANDLING EQUIPMENT DISTRIBUTORS' ASSOCIATION

Acronym or abbreviation: SHEDA

Heathcote House, 136 Hagley Road, Edgbaston, Birmingham, B16 9PN

Tel: 0121 454 4141
Fax: 0121 454 4949
E-mail: enquiries@sheda.org.uk

Website:
http://sheda.org.uk

Enquiries:
Enquiries to: General Secretary

Founded:
1978

Organisation type and purpose:
National organisation, trade association (membership is by qualification), present number of members: 60.

Subject coverage:
Sources of supply of storage equipment and distributors.

Printed publications:
Newsletters and publications

Access to staff:
Contact by letter, by telephone, by fax, by e-mail and via website
Hours: Mon to Fri, 0900 to 1700

Links with:
Storage Equipment Manufacturers Association (SEMA)

STORAGE EQUIPMENT MANUFACTURERS ASSOCIATION

Acronym or abbreviation: SEMA

The National Metalforming Centre, 47 Birmingham Road, West Bromwich B70 6PY

Tel: 0121 601 6350
Fax: 0121 601 6387

E-mail: enquiry@sema.org.uk

Website:
http://www.sema.org.uk

Enquiries:
Enquiries to: Information Officer

Founded:
1970

Organisation type and purpose:
Trade association.

Subject coverage:
Storage equipment, racking, shelving etc.

Printed publications:
Code of Practice for the Design of Low Rise Static Steel Shelving
Code of Practice for the Design of Static Racking
Code of Practice for the Use of Static Racking
Guide to the Conduct of Palley Racking Surveys
Guideline No. 2 Guide to Erection Tolerances for Static Racking
SEMA Guide to the Building Regulations Guideline No. 5 Guide to the Design and Installation of Mobile Shelving
Terms and Descriptions of Storage Equipment (terminology)

Electronic and video publications:
CDM Regulations – Storage Industry Interpretation (2000, CD-ROM)
Guidelines for Specifier's of Static Steel Racking and Shelving (2000, CD-ROM)

Access to staff:
Contact by letter, by telephone, by fax and by e-mail
Hours: Mon to Fri, 0900 to 1700

Member of:
British Materials Handling Federation
tel: 0121 200 2100; fax: 0121 200 1306; e-mail: enquiry@bmhf.org.uk

STOURBRIDGE LIBRARY

Crown Centre, Stourbridge, West Midlands, DY8 1YE

Tel: 01384 812945
Fax: 01384 812946
E-mail: stourbridge.library@dudley.gov.uk

Website:
http://www.dudley.gov.uk/libraries
Online catalogue, news, book reviews.

Enquiries:
Enquiries to: Locality Manager
Direct tel: 01384 812951

Organisation type and purpose:
Local government body, public library.

Subject coverage:
Local history of Stourbridge and the surrounding area, tourist information.

Museum or gallery collection, archive, or library special collection:
County Express (local newspaper) 1856 to present, almost all on rollfilm
Stourbridge Census Returns 1841–1901
Stourbridge local history: books, maps, photographs, pamphlets, manuscripts, posters, newspapers

Library catalogue:
All or part available online

Access to staff:
Contact by letter, by telephone, by fax, by e-mail, in person and via website

Access to building, collection or gallery:
Hours: Mon, 0930 to 1900; Tue to Fri, 0900 to 1900; Sat, 0900 to 1700; Sun 1000 to 1400

Access for disabled people:
Level entry

Parent body:
Dudley Libraries
St James's Road, Dudley

STOURPORT LIBRARY

County Buildings, Worcester Street, Stourport-on-Severn, Worcestershire, DY13 8EH

Tel: 01299 822866
Fax: 01299 827464
E-mail: stourportlib@worcestershire.gov.uk

Website:
http://www.worcestershire.gov.uk

Enquiries:
Enquiries to: Librarian

Founded:
1969

Organisation type and purpose:
Public library.

Subject coverage:
General public stock, local history of Stourport, small canal collection.

Museum or gallery collection, archive, or library special collection:
Local information about Stourport

Access to staff:
Contact by letter, by telephone, by e-mail and in person
Hours: Mon, Tue, Thu, 0930 to 1730; Fri, 0930 to 2000; Sat, 0930 to 1730; Wed, closed

Access to building, collection or gallery:
No prior appointment required

Access for disabled people:
Parking provided, ramped entry, level entry, access to all public areas

STRATEGIC PLANNING SOCIETY, THE

Acronym or abbreviation: SPS

17 Portland Place, London, W1N 3AF

Tel: 020 7636 7737
Fax: 020 7323 1692
E-mail: enquiries@sps.org.uk

Website:
http://www.sps.org.uk
Dissemination and sharing of strategic management information, news, tools and society events.

Enquiries:
Enquiries to: Administration Manager
Direct fax: 020 7636 7737
Direct e-mail: a.claase@sps.org.uk
Other contacts: Marketing Manager email: h .stones@sps.org.uk

Founded:
1967

Organisation type and purpose:
Learned society, professional body (membership is by subscription), present number of members: 4000, registered charity (charity number 253879), training organisation.
The Society aims to foster and promote research and best practice in strategic thought and action for the success of individual members and organisations.

Subject coverage:
Strategic management and planning knowledge, applications, techniques and a specialist membership advisory network; conferences and workshops; specialist discussion groups.

Trade and statistical information:
Index of published material relating to strategic management.

Printed publications:
Long Range Planning (journal, 6 times a year)
Strategy (journal, 6 times a year)

Access to staff:
Contact by letter, by telephone, by fax, by e-mail and via website. Appointment necessary.
Hours: Mon to Fri, 0900 to 1700

STRATFORD LIBRARY

12 Henley Street, Stratford-upon-Avon,
Warwickshire, CV37 6PZ

Tel: 01789 292209
Fax: 01789 268554
E-mail: stratfordlibrary@warwickshire.gov.uk

Enquiries:
Enquiries to: Information Officer
Direct e-mail: emmasparkes@warwickshire.gov.uk

Organisation type and purpose:
Local government body, public library.

Subject coverage:
General collection ranging from material for young
children to studies at undergraduate levels. No
special subject areas.

**Museum or gallery collection, archive, or library
special collection:**
South Warwickshire census returns 1841–1891 held
on microfilm
Stratford Herald on microfilm

Access to staff:
Contact by letter, by telephone, by fax, by e-mail
and in person
Hours: Mon, Fri, 0930 to 1900; Tue and Wed, 0930
to 1730; Sat 0930 to 1600; Sun, 1000 to 1400

Parent body:
Warwickshire County Council Department of
Libraries and Heritage

STREETBIKE DRAG CLUB

17 Southampton Road, London, NW5 4JS

Tel: 020 7485 0473
Fax: 020 7813 0198

Enquiries:
Enquiries to: Chairman

Founded:
1989

Organisation type and purpose:
Membership association (membership is by
subscription).
To promote street bike drag races.

STRESSWATCH SCOTLAND

23 Campbell Street, Kilmarnock, Ayrshire, KA1
4HL

Tel: 01563 570886
Fax: 01563 570886
E-mail: info@stresswatchscotland.org

Website:
http://www.stresswatchscotland.org

Enquiries:
Enquiries to: Administrator
Other contacts: Development Director

Founded:
1984

Organisation type and purpose:
Membership association (membership is by
subscription), present number of members: 90,
voluntary organisation, registered charity (charity
number SC004456), suitable for ages: 18+.

Subject coverage:
Phobias, stress, anxiety, panic attacks.

Printed publications:
Annual Report
Serenity (newsletter, quarterly, £10, a year, £5
concession (unemployed, pensioners))
Numerous books including:
Don't Panic
Fight your Phobia and Win
Positive Thinking

Electronic and video publications:
Agoraphobic pack (audio tapes)
Anxiety pack (audio tapes)
Phobic pack (audio tapes)

Publications list:
Available in print

Access to staff:
Contact by letter, by telephone, by fax, by e-mail
and via website
Hours: Mon to Fri, 0900 to 1200

Affiliated to:
Scottish Council for Voluntary Organisations

Connections with:
numerous local support groups

STRODE COLLEGE & THEATRE

Church Road, Street, Somerset, BA16 0AB

Tel: 01458 844410
Fax: 01458 844415

Website:
http://www.strode-college.ac.uk

Enquiries:
Enquiries to: Head of Learning Resources
Direct tel: 01458 844400 ext 303
Direct e-mail: cbull@strode-college.ac.uk
Other contacts: Learning Centre Manager for
catalogue enquiries, membership.

Founded:
1973

Organisation type and purpose:
Suitable for ages: 16+.
Further education college.

Subject coverage:
Business studies, engineering, secretarial and office
studies, health and beauty, hairdressing, drama,
languages, leisure and tourism, media studies;
degree studies in politics, psychology, sociology,
philosophy, art and design, sport, social care,
childhood studies, information technology,
performing arts, complementary therapies.

Library catalogue:
All or part available online and in-house

Access to staff:
Contact by letter, by telephone and by fax.
Appointment necessary. Access for members only.
Hours: Mon to Thu, 0830 to 2045; Fri, 0830 to 1700;
Sat, 0900 to 12.45

Access for disabled people:
Parking provided, level entry, access to all public
areas, toilet facilities

STROKE ASSOCIATION, THE

Acronym or abbreviation: TSA

Stroke House, 240 City Road, London, EC1V 2PR

Tel: 020 7566 0300; helpline: 0845 303 3100
Fax: 020 7490 2686
E-mail: info@stroke.org.uk

Website:
http://www.stroke.org.uk

Enquiries:
Enquiries to: Stroke Information Services

Founded:
1899

Organisation type and purpose:
Registered charity (charity number 211015).
Concerned with combating stroke in people of all
ages; funds research into prevention, treatment
and better methods of rehabilitation, and helps
stroke patients and their families directly through
its Rehabilitation and Support Services, including
communication support, family and carer support,
information services and welfare grants.
Campaigns, educates and informs to increase
knowledge of stroke.

Subject coverage:
Stroke research, conditions and welfare of
sufferers.

Printed publications:
Stroke News (3 times a year)

six leaflets
40 factsheets
Order printed publications from: Publications
Distribution, The Stroke Association, 16
Orlingbury Road, Little Harrowden, Northants,
NN9 5BH; tel. 01933 403963; fax 01933 403616

Electronic and video publications:
Comprehensive range of information booklets,
factsheets and resource sheets (all free online)
Order electronic and video publications from: http://
www.stroke.org.uk/information/our_publications/
factsheets/az_list_of_factshee.html

Publications list:
Available online and in print

Access to staff:
Contact by letter and by telephone
Hours: Telephone helpline: Mon to Fri, 0900 to 1700

STROUD DISTRICT COUNCIL

Ebley Mill, Stroud, Gloucestershire, GL5 4UB

Tel: 01453 766321\ Minicom no. 01453 754949
Fax: 01453 750932
E-mail: information@stroud.gov.uk

Website:
http://www.stroud.gov.uk

Enquiries:
Enquiries to: Principal Marketing Officer
Direct tel: 01453 754385
Direct fax: 01453 754942

Founded:
1974

Organisation type and purpose:
Local government body.

Subject coverage:
Stroud district, services and amenities.

Access to staff:
Contact by letter, by telephone, by fax, by e-mail,
in person and via website. Appointment necessary.
Hours: Mon to Thu, 0845 to 1700; Fri, 0845 to 1630

Access for disabled people:
Parking provided, level entry, access to all public
areas, toilet facilities

STRUCTURAL PRECAST
ASSOCIATION

Acronym or abbreviation: SPA

60 Charles Street, Leicester, LE1 1FB

Tel: 0116 253 6161
Fax: 0116 251 4568
E-mail: spa@britishprecast.org

Website:
http://www.structural-precast-association.org.uk

Enquiries:
Enquiries to: Secretary

Founded:
1995

Organisation type and purpose:
Trade association.

Subject coverage:
Precast concrete structural components for
building.

Printed publications:
SPANews (newsletter)
Members Products data folder
Code of Practice for the Safe Erection of Precast
Concrete Frameworks

Access to staff:
Contact by letter, by telephone, by fax and by e-
mail
Hours: Mon to Fri, 0900 to 1700

Parent body:
British Precast Concrete Federation

STUDENT CHRISTIAN MOVEMENT OF GREAT BRITAIN

Acronym or abbreviation: SCM

Unit 308F, The Big Peg, 120 Vyse Street, The Jewellery Quarter, Birmingham B18 6NF

Tel: 0121 200 3355
E-mail: scm@movement.org.uk

Website:
http://www.movement.org.uk

Enquiries:
Enquiries to: Administrator
Other contacts: Groups Worker for info on events and setting up groups.

Founded:
1889

Organisation type and purpose:
National organisation, membership association, registered charity (charity number 241896), suitable for ages: 16 to 30 (approx).
SCM endeavours to present students in further and higher education with an understanding of the Christian Faith which is enquiring, ecumenical and related to all aspects of life. SCM currently supports a network of around 65 groups across Britain.

Subject coverage:
Introductions to theology, liberation theology, prophecy, feminist theology, Bible studies, sexuality, spirituality, ecumenism, social action, responsibility, politics.

Non-library collection catalogue:
All or part available online

Printed publications:
Common People (Community)
F Word
Fleshing out Faith
God Made Simple
Just Love: sexuality
Movement (termly)
No More Mr Nice Guy
Raging In The Streets
SCM Publications and Resources Guide (free)
Significant Others
The Dying Game (Death)

Publications list:
Available online and in print

Access to staff:
Contact by letter, by telephone, by fax, by e-mail and via website. Appointment necessary.
Hours: Mon to Fri, 0900 to 1630

Access to building, collection or gallery:
No prior appointment required

Access for disabled people:
Level entry

Affiliated to:
Church Together in Britain and Ireland
 tel: 020 7523 2139
Churches Together in England
 tel: 020 7332 8230
World Student Christian Federation
 tel: + 31 20 675 4921; e-mail: europe@wscf.xs4all.nl

Has:
Local groups

STUDENTS PARTNERSHIP WORLDWIDE

Acronym or abbreviation: SPW

Faith House, 2nd Floor, 7 Tufton Street, London, SW1P 3QB

Tel: 020 7222 0138
Fax: 020 7233 0008
E-mail: info@spw.org

Website:
http://www.spw.org

Information regarding volunteering in Africa and Asia; country-specific information, SPW's approach, application, support; information about SPW's partners.

Enquiries:
Enquiries to: Operations Manager

Founded:
1985

Subject coverage:
Volunteering; development; education; environment; health; youth development in rural Africa and Asia; community development; non-governmental organisation, focus on HIV/AIDS awareness, nutrition, sanitation; method is youth-to-youth approach through informal activities.

Non-library collection catalogue:
All or part available online and in-house

Library catalogue:
All or part available online and in-house

Printed publications:
Newsletter (free)
Information Pack (free)
Brochure (free)
Annual Report (free)
Information leaflets (free)
Posters (free)

Electronic and video publications:
SPW video of volunteering programmes in Africa

Access to staff:
Contact by letter, by telephone, by fax, by e-mail and via website. Appointment necessary.
Hours: Mon to Fri, 0900 to 1800

Access to building, collection or gallery:
No access other than to staff

Links with:
Duke of Edinburgh
HELP
SAFE

SUBTERRANEA BRITANNICA

Acronym or abbreviation: SB

c/o CNHSS Ltd, 96A Brighton Road, South Croydon, Surrey, CR2 6AD

Tel: 020 8688 3593

Website:
http://www.subbrit.org.uk

Enquiries:
Enquiries to: Membership Secretary

Founded:
1974

Organisation type and purpose:
Learned society (membership is by subscription), voluntary organisation.
Researches concerning the archaeology and history of man-made and man-used underground space. Mainly (but not exclusively) United Kingdom and Europe.

Subject coverage:
Man-made and man-used underground space of all kinds and all periods – especially miscellaneous (non coal/non metal) mines, tunnels, ice houses, souterrains, deneholes, rockcut cellars, shelters, underground military structures etc.

Museum or gallery collection, archive, or library special collection:
Correspondence concerning underground sites of all kinds and periods
County files including notes, surveys, newscuttings, offprints, pamphlets
Printed books relating to this subject

Library catalogue:
All or part available in-house

Printed publications:
Subterranea Britannica Guides 1 to 6, include:
The Geological Literature as a Source for Industrial History
Underground Industrial Archaeology in Kent

Wells in Kent
Deneholes and Chalkwells
The Germans' World War II V-weapons sites in France
Why Go Underground for Mineral Sources?
Newsletter (1–3 times per annum)
Bulletin Subterranea Britannica (irregularly, for sale)

Publications list:
Available in print

Access to staff:
Contact by letter and by telephone. Appointment necessary.
Hours: Sun to Sat, at any reasonable hour
Special comments: Specific research enquiries only.

Access to building, collection or gallery:
Special comments: The past chairman's personal files/library can be accessed by prior arrangement only.

Links with:
Association for Industrial Archaeology
Council for British Archaeology
National Association of Mining History Organisations

Secretary/Enquiries:
Subterranea Britannica
 14 Maple Close, Sandford, Wareham, Dorset, BH20 7QD; tel: 01929 553872

Secretary/Membership:
Subterranea Britannica
 13 Highcroft Cottages, London Road, Swanley, Kent, BR8 8DB; tel: 01322 408081

SUFFOLK ACRE

Formal name: Suffolk ACRE (Action with Communities in Rural England)
Acronym or abbreviation: ACRE

Suffolk Community Resource Centre, Suffolk House, 2 Wharfedale Road, Ipswich, Suffolk, IP1 4JP

Tel: 01473 242500
Fax: 01473 242530
E-mail: info@suffolkacre.org.uk

Enquiries:
Enquiries to: Chief Executive

Founded:
1937

Organisation type and purpose:
Membership association, present number of members: 2000, voluntary organisation, registered charity (charity number 1062038).
Representative and advisory body for the voluntary social services sector in Suffolk; with a membership of a very large number of voluntary and statutory bodies and individuals.
Community development in rural areas of Suffolk.

Subject coverage:
Welfare and quality of life in Suffolk; local communities; Parish Council procedures; village hall regulations; playing fields; job creation programmes; crafts; horticulture, charities acts.

Printed publications:
A-Z Fundraising Ideas
Conducting a Village Appraisal
Information Circulars and Newsletters and Packs (list available)
Village Halls Catalogue

Publications list:
Available in print

Access to staff:
Contact by letter, by telephone, by fax and by e-mail
Hours: Mon to Fri, 0900 to 1700

Access for disabled people:
Parking provided, ramped entry, access to all public areas, toilet facilities

Affiliated to:
ACRE

SUFFOLK CHAMBER OF COMMERCE, INDUSTRY AND SHIPPING INCORPORATED

Felaw Maltings, South Kiln, 42 Felaw Street, Ipswich, Suffolk, IP2 8SQ

Tel: 01473 680600
Fax: 01473 603888
E-mail: info@suffolkchamber.co.uk

Website:
http://www.suffolkchamber.co.uk

Enquiries:
Enquiries to: Business Information Co-ordinator
Direct tel: 01473 694800
Direct e-mail: wendy@suffolkchamber.co.uk

Founded:
1884

Organisation type and purpose:
Membership association (membership is by subscription), present number of members: 1400, service industry.
Chamber of commerce.

Subject coverage:
International trade, exporting, business information, business credit checking, personnel assistance.

Museum or gallery collection, archive, or library special collection:
Extensive business library

Printed publications:
SI Trader (newsletter, monthly, members of Suffolk International Trade Association)
Suffolk Business (magazine, monthly, free to members)

Access to staff:
Contact by letter, by telephone, by fax, by e-mail, in person and via website
Hours: Mon to Fri, 0900 to 1700

Affiliated to:
Association of British Chambers of Commerce

SUFFOLK COASTAL DISTRICT COUNCIL

Melton Hill, Woodbridge, Suffolk, IP12 1AU

Tel: 01394 383789; 01394 444211 (minicom)
Fax: 01394 385100
E-mail: scdc@suffolkcoastal.gov.uk

Website:
http://www.suffolkcoastal.gov.uk

Enquiries:
Enquiries to: Communications Manager
Direct tel: 01394 444361
Direct fax: 01394 444690
Direct e-mail: viv.hotten@suffolkcoastal.gov.uk

Founded:
1974

Organisation type and purpose:
Local government body.

Subject coverage:
Local government services, including local planning, environmental protection, housing, recreation and leisure, recycling and waste management, food safety and tourism.

Special visitor services:
Tourist Information Centres at Felixstowe, Woodbridge and Aldeburgh

Printed publications:
CoastLine (magazine)

Publications list:
Available online and in print

Access to staff:
Contact by letter, by telephone, by fax, by e-mail, in person and via website
Hours: Mon to Thu, 0845 to 1715; Fri, 0845 to 1645

Access to building, collection or gallery:
Hours: Mon to Thu, 0845 to 1715; Fri, 0845 to 1645

Access for disabled people:
Parking provided, level entry, toilet facilities

Also at:
Suffolk Coastal District Council (local area office)
91 Undercliffe Road, Felixstowe; tel: 01394 276766

SUFFOLK COLLEGE

Library, Rope Walk, Ipswich, Suffolk, IP4 1LT

Tel: 01473 296585
Fax: 01473 230054

Website:
http://www.suffolk.ac.uk
Details of courses available.

Enquiries:
Enquiries to: Librarian
Direct tel: 01473 296586

Founded:
1961

Organisation type and purpose:
Suitable for ages: Further and Higher.
College of higher and further education.

Subject coverage:
Computing; engineering; management; construction; social work; nursing; sociology; catering; graphic design; biology; education; midwifery; chemistry; CAD/CAM; personnel management; psychology; business studies; art.

Non-library collection catalogue:
All or part available online

Library catalogue:
All or part available online

Printed publications:
Library Guide

Access to staff:
Contact by letter. Appointment necessary.
Hours: Mon to Fri, 0900 to 1700

Associate college of:
University of East Anglia

SUFFOLK HORSE SOCIETY

The Market Hill, Woodbridge, Suffolk, IP12 4LP

Tel: 01394 380643
Fax: 01394 610058
E-mail: sec@suffolkhorsesociety.org.uk

Website:
http://www.suffolkhorsesociety.org.uk

Enquiries:
Enquiries to: Administrator

Founded:
1877

Organisation type and purpose:
Registered charity (charity number 220756).

Subject coverage:
Breed society for the Suffolk Punch heavy horse.

Museum or gallery collection, archive, or library special collection:
Collections held in the Suffolk Horse Museum

Printed publications:
Stud Book (annually)

Access to staff:
Contact by letter, by telephone, by fax, by e-mail and via website. Appointment necessary.
Hours: Mon to Fri, 0900 to 1700

SUFFOLK LIBRARIES

Endeavour House, 8 Russell Road, Ipswich, Suffolk, IP1 2BX

Tel: 01473 265086
Fax: 01473 216843
E-mail: help@suffolklibraries.co.uk

Website:
http://www.suffolk.gov.uk/LeisureAndCulture/Libraries/SuffolkLibrariesDirect
Fully searchable library catalogue.
http://www.suffolk.gov.uk/leisureandculture/libraries
Information about library and Record Office services in Suffolk. It includes a Web version of the library catalogue and community information (Suffolk InfoLink).

Enquiries:
Enquiries to: Information Officer
Direct tel: 01473 583727
Direct e-mail: Roger.McMaster@libher.suffolkcc.gov.uk
Other contacts: Head of Service Delivery

Founded:
1974

Organisation type and purpose:
Local government body, public library.

Subject coverage:
General; local studies; local government; business information; European Reference Centre and Relay point. Community Legal Service quality mark holder. IAG services accredited by Guidance Accreditation Board.

Museum or gallery collection, archive, or library special collection:
Benjamin Britten Collection (all published works up to 1973); at Lowestoft Central Library
Cullum Collection (family library of a 19th century gentleman, George Milner-Gibson-Cullum) at Bury St Edmunds Record Office
Fitzgerald Collection at Woodbridge Library
Horse Racing Collection (mainly flat racing; sporting reminiscences; history and anatomy of the horse; steeplechasing; includes the Racing Calendar from 1774 and the Bloodstock Breeders Review from 1912) at Newmarket Branch Library, 1A, The Rookery, Newmarket
Ipswich Old Town Library, including incunabula and manuscripts and rare works from the 16th and 17th centuries at Ipswich School by appointment only
Local Studies Collections at: Suffolk Record Office, 77 Raingate Street, Bury St Edmunds; Central Library, Lowestoft; Woodbridge Branch, New Street, Woodbridge (collection on Sutton Hoo); Suffolk Record Office, Gatacre Road, Ipswich
Seckford Collection (local history of East Anglia, with emphasis on a Woodbridge locality; includes the manuscript of a multi-volume work, Suffolk Moated Houses) at Woodbridge Branch Library

Non-library collection catalogue:
All or part available online

Library catalogue:
All or part available online

Printed publications:
Opening Hours of Libraries and Record Offices in Suffolk (leaflet)

Access to staff:
Contact by letter, by telephone, by fax, by e-mail, in person and via website
Hours: Mon to Fri, 0900 to 1700

SUFFOLK LOCAL HISTORY COUNCIL

Suffolk Community Resource Centre, 2 Wharfdale Road, Ipswich, Suffolk, IP1 4JP

Tel: 01473 242540
E-mail: admin@slhc.org.uk

Website:
http://www.suffolklocalhistorycouncil.org.uk

Enquiries:
Enquiries to: Honorary Secretary

Founded:
1953

continued overleaf

Organisation type and purpose:
Membership association (membership is by subscription), voluntary organisation, registered charity (charity number 294270).

Subject coverage:
Local history of Suffolk.

Non-library collection catalogue:
All or part available online

Printed publications:
Recorders' Booklet (in pack form)
SLHC Calendar of Events (2 times a year)
Suffolk Local History Council Newsletter (2 times a year)
Suffolk Review (2 times a year)

Publications list:
Available online

Access to staff:
Contact by letter
Hours: Mon to Fri, 0900 to 1700
Special comments: Variable, not daily.

SUFFOLK RECORD OFFICE

77 Raingate Street, Bury St Edmunds, Suffolk, IP33 2AR

Tel: 01284 352352
E-mail: bury.ro@libher.suffolkcc.gov.uk

Website:
http://www.suffolk.gov.uk/sro

Enquiries:
Enquiries to: Public Service Manager
Direct tel: 01284 352355

Founded:
1974

Organisation type and purpose:
Local government body.

Subject coverage:
Local history, local studies, family history.

Museum or gallery collection, archive, or library special collection:
Records of local authorities, ecclesiastical bodies, families, societies, organisations, businesses and estates relating primarily to Suffolk, 12th to 20th centuries

Non-library collection catalogue:
All or part available online and in-house

Library catalogue:
All or part available online

Printed publications:
Notes for Searchers: free leaflets on source material for popular areas of research and on major collections (also online)
Guide to Genealogical Sources: parts 1–9 (1998–2000)
Order printed publications from: Suffolk Record Office, Gatacre Road, Ipswich, Suffolk, IP1 2LQ; tel: 01473 584542, fax: 01473 584533, e-mail: ipswich.ro@libher.suffolkcc.gov.uk

Microform publications:
Parish Registers (fiche)
Order microform publications from: Suffolk Record Office, Gatacre Road, Ipswich, Suffolk, IP1 2LQ; tel: 01473 584542, fax: 01473 584533, e-mail: ipswich.ro@libher.suffolkcc.gov.uk

Access to staff:
Contact by letter, by telephone, by fax, by e-mail and in person
Hours: Bury St Edmunds and Ipswich: Mon to Sat, 0900 to 1700
Lowestoft: Mon, Wed, Thu, Fri, 0915 to 1730; Tue, 0900 to 1900; Sat, 0900 to 1700; Sun 1000 to 1600 (no original documents produced on Sunday)
Special comments: CARN ticket required for access to original material.

Also at:
Suffolk Record Office
Gatacre Road, Ipswich, Suffolk, IP1 2LQ; tel: 01473 584541; fax: 01473 584533; e-mail: ipswich .ro@libher.suffolkcc.gov.uk

Suffolk Record Office
Central Library, Clapham Road, Lowestoft, Suffolk, NR32 1DR; tel: 01502 405357; fax: 01502 405350; e-mail: lowestoft.ro@libher.suffolkcc.gov .uk

Parent body:
Suffolk County Council
Endeavour House, Russell Road, Ipswich, IP1 2BX; tel: 01473 583000

SUGAR ASSOCIATION OF LONDON

Acronym or abbreviation: SAL

154 Bishopsgate, London, EC2M 4LN

Tel: 020 7377 2113
Fax: 020 7247 2481
E-mail: durhamn@sugar-assoc.co.uk

Enquiries:
Enquiries to: Secretary

Founded:
1882

Organisation type and purpose:
International organisation, trade association (membership is by election or invitation), present number of members: 130.

Printed publications:
Information Brochure (free)
Book of Rules and Regulations (£60)

Access to staff:
Contact by letter, by telephone and by fax. All charged.
Hours: Mon to Fri, 0900 to 1700

SUGAR BUREAU, THE

6 Catherine Street, London, WC2B 5JS

Tel: 020 7379 6830
Fax: 020 7836 4113
E-mail: info@sugar-bureau.co.uk

Website:
http://www.sugar-bureau.co.uk
Latest research into diet and health for health professionals; publications ordering.

Enquiries:
Enquiries to: Information Manager

Founded:
1964

Organisation type and purpose:
Trade association.

Subject coverage:
Information on sugar (the generic product), diet and health, consumers and the media.

Printed publications:
Nutrition in Practice (for dietitians, health professionals, GP practice nurses, twice a year)
Order printed publications from: See website (resources now mainly online)

Publications list:
Available online

Access to staff:
Contact by letter, by telephone and by e-mail. Appointment necessary.
Hours: Mon to Fri, 0900 to 1700

Access to building, collection or gallery:
No access

Member of:
European Sugar Manufacturers Committee (CEFS)
Food and Drink Federation
World Sugar Research Organisation

SUGAR TRADERS ASSOCIATION OF THE UNITED KINGDOM

Acronym or abbreviation: STAUK

Czarnikow Group Limited, 24 Chiswell Street, London, EC1Y 4SG

Tel: 020 7972 6631
Fax: 020 7972 6699
E-mail: dclark@czarnikow.com

Website:
http://www.sugartraders.co.uk

Enquiries:
Enquiries to: Honorary Secretary

Founded:
1952

Organisation type and purpose:
Trade association (membership is by subscription, election or invitation), present number of members: 12.
To promote, develop and protect the international trade in sugar.

Subject coverage:
Raw cane sugar; beet white sugar.

Access to staff:
Contact by telephone and by fax. Access for members only.
Hours: Mon to Fri, 0900 to 1700

Member organisation of:
ASSUC aisbl, European Association of Sugar Traders
Boite 24, 32 Square Ambiorix, 1000 Brussels, Belgium; tel: +32 (2) 7366873; fax: +32 (2) 7326766; e-mail: assuc@assuc.eu

SUN CHEMICAL LIMITED

Cray Avenue, St Mary Cray, Orpington, Kent, BR5 3PP

Tel: 01689 894000
Fax: 01689 894051

Website:
http://www.sunchemical.com

Enquiries:
Enquiries to: Manager, Information Department
Direct tel: 01689 894208
Direct e-mail: barry.hermiston@eu.sunchem.com

Founded:
1877

Formerly called:
Coates Brothers plc; Coates Lorilleux International

Organisation type and purpose:
Manufacturing industry.

Subject coverage:
Printing inks and printing processes.

Access to staff:
Appointment necessary.
Hours: Mon to Fri, 0900 to 1700

SUNBEAM RAPIER OWNERS CLUB

Acronym or abbreviation: SROC

Wayside, Depmore Lane, Frodsham, Cheshire, WA6 6UD

Tel: 01928 788583
E-mail: kingston@wayside53.freeserve.co.uk

Website:
http://www.sroc.org.uk
All relevant information about the Club.

Enquiries:
Enquiries to: Membership Secretary
Other contacts: The Editor: sunbeams92@aol.com for magazine advertising.

Founded:
1979

Organisation type and purpose:
Membership association (membership is by subscription), present number of members: 450–500.

Subject coverage:
Sunbeam Rapier cars, details of spare parts availability, technical advice, details and dates of club events, details of cars for sale, objectives of the club.

Printed publications:
Magazine (quarterly)

Access to staff:
Contact by letter, by telephone, by e-mail and via website
Hours: Mon to Fri, 1800 to 2200; Sat and Sun, 0900 to 1700

Member of:
Association of Rootes Car Clubs (ARCC)
tel: 01993 878471

SUNBEAM TIGER OWNERS CLUB

8 Villa Real Estate, Consett, Co Durham, DH8 6BJ

Tel: 01207 508296
Fax: 01207 582297

Enquiries:
Enquiries to: Membership Secretary

Founded:
1976

Organisation type and purpose:
International organisation, membership association (membership is by subscription).

Subject coverage:
Sunbeam Tiger cars.

Access to staff:
Contact by letter and by telephone
Hours: Mon to Fri, 0900 to 1700

SUNBEAM VENEZIA TOURING MILANO

Briarstone House, 51 Cheadle Road, Uttoxeter, Staffordshire, ST14 7BX

Tel: 01889 568346
Fax: 01889 568346

Enquiries:
Enquiries to: General Secretary
Direct tel: 00 1 603 675 6622
Direct e-mail: laars@cyberportal.net

Founded:
1969

Organisation type and purpose:
Membership association (membership is by subscription), present number of members: 10, voluntary organisation, training organisation, consultancy, research organisation.

Subject coverage:
Full and general information club for Rootes, full history of car manufacturers Touring Milano; special mark Sunbeam Venezia, diesel powered cars and transport; technical advice and spares manufacturing.

Museum or gallery collection, archive, or library special collection:
Lord Rootes collection, some paperwork, touring, liquidator, body-builders 1963–5
Photographs, handbooks, spares

Printed publications:
Instruction Books
Parts List
Technical Information
Work Shop Manual

Access to staff:
Contact by letter and by e-mail. Appointment necessary. Non-members charged.
Hours: Mon to Fri, 0900 to 1700

Archives and technical details:
Sunbeam Venezia Touring Milano
RR 3 Box 33, Cornish, New Hampshire, NH 03745, USA; tel: 00 1 603 675 6622; e-mail: jaars@cyberportal.net

SUNBED ASSOCIATION

Acronym or abbreviation: TSA

Chess House, 105 High Street, Chesham, Buckinghamshire, HP5 1DE

Tel: 01494 785941
Fax: 01494 786791
E-mail: info@sunbedassociation.org.uk

Website:
http://www.sunbedassociation.org.uk

Enquiries:
Enquiries to: Chief Executive

Founded:
1995

Organisation type and purpose:
Trade association (membership is by subscription), present number of members: 25 manufacturing industry and 1500 service industry.

Subject coverage:
Manufacture and use of sunbeds.

Museum or gallery collection, archive, or library special collection:
Standards for the manufacture and use of sunbeds

Trade and statistical information:
Comprehensive industry statistics, training programme.

Printed publications:
Industry Statistics
List of Members
Training programme

Access to staff:
Contact by letter, by telephone, by fax and by e-mail
Hours: Mon to Fri, 0900 to 1700

SUNDERLAND CITY COUNCIL, COMMUNITY & CULTURAL SERVICES DIRECTORATE

City Library and Arts Centre, Fawcett Street, Sunderland, Tyne and Wear, SR1 1RE

Tel: 0191 514 1235
Fax: 0191 514 8444
E-mail: libraries@sunderland.gov.uk

Website:
http://www.sunderland.gov.uk/libraries

Organisation type and purpose:
Local government body, art gallery, public library.

Subject coverage:
General, local studies, commercial and technical fields, and art.

Museum or gallery collection, archive, or library special collection:
Bob Mason Collection (maritime history)
Local collection on Sunderland and County Durham (8000 volumes, 12,000 illustrations, 2000 maps)

Non-library collection catalogue:
All or part available online, in-house and in print

Library catalogue:
All or part available online

Printed publications:
Cyril Barton VC (£6.99)
Frances Fisher RIP (£6.99)
Out All Out (£3)
Sunderland Builds the Ships (£1.95)
Sunderland in the Blitz
The Likes of Us (£4.99)
Washington Then & Now (£3.99)

Electronic and video publications:
The Barbary Coast (talking book, £6.50)

Publications list:
Available in print

Access to staff:
Contact by letter, by telephone, by fax and by e-mail
Hours: Mon to Fri, 0900 to 1700

Access for disabled people:
Access to all public areas

Part of:
NETWORK

SUNDERLAND VOLUNTEER LIFE BRIGADE

Acronym or abbreviation: SVLB

The Watch House, Pier View, Roker, Sunderland, Tyne and Wear, SR6 0PR

Tel: 0191 5672579
Fax: 0191 5292651
E-mail: sunderland.vlb@tiscali.co.uk

Website:
http://www.communigate.co.uk/ne/svlb/index.phtml
The history of the brigade, other information and publications.

Enquiries:
Enquiries to: Secretary
Direct tel: 07754 461728
Direct e-mail: sonia_spence@hotmail.com
Other contacts: Treasurer

Founded:
1877

Organisation type and purpose:
Professional body, present number of members: 15 active members, voluntary organisation, registered charity (charity number 1041849), museum, historic building, house or site, suitable for ages: all, training organisation.
Coastal search and cliff rescue.

Subject coverage:
Volunteer Life Brigade Search and Rescue Unit and its history, 100 years of Life Saving on the Coast of Sunderland.

Museum or gallery collection, archive, or library special collection:
Model ships and historical photographs

Printed publications:
Include leaflets and postcards

Publications list:
Available online and in print

Access to staff:
Contact by letter, by telephone, by fax, by e-mail, in person and via website. Appointment necessary.
Hours: Mon to Fri, 0900 to 1700

Links with:
RNLI Coastguard

SUPPLY CHAIN KNOWLEDGE CENTRE

Acronym or abbreviation: SCKC

Cranfield Centre for Logistics & Supply Chain, Cranfield School of Management, Cranfield, Bedfordshire, MK43 0AL

Tel: 01234 754931
Fax: 01234 754930
E-mail: sckc@cranfield.ac.uk

Website:
http://www.sckc.info
http://www.logisticsweb.co.uk
Automated database of logistics information searchable by keyword and freetext.
http://www.ila.co.uk
International Logistics Abstracts.

Enquiries:
Enquiries to: Knowledge Manager

Founded:
1970

Organisation type and purpose:
University department or institute.
Information centre (logistics).

continued overleaf

Subject coverage:
Logistics, supply chain management, materials handling, warehouse design including cold stores, physical distribution, pallet testing, freight transport, ergonomics.

Museum or gallery collection, archive, or library special collection:
Extensive collection of 35mm slides of materials handling equipment

Printed publications:
Supply Chain Practice (quarterly)
International Logistics Abstracts (6 times a year)

Electronic and video publications:
Automated database of logistics information searchable by keyword and freetext

Publications list:
Available online and in print

Access to staff:
Contact by e-mail and via website. Appointment necessary. Access for members only. Non-members charged.
Hours: Mon to Fri, 0900 to 1730

Division of:
Cranfield Centre for Logistics & Supply Chain

SUPREME COURT LIBRARY

Queen's Building, Royal Courts of Justice, Strand, London, WC2A 2LL

Tel: 020 7947 6587
Fax: 020 7947 6661

Enquiries:
Enquiries to: Librarian
Direct tel: 020 7947 7198

Founded:
1972

Organisation type and purpose:
National government body.
Department for Constitutional Affairs Library and Information Services.
Primarily for the use of the Judiciary and Officials of the Royal Courts of Justice.

Subject coverage:
English law; some coverage of the Commonwealth and EC law.

Museum or gallery collection, archive, or library special collection:
Old editions of legal textbooks
Transcripts of the Determinations of the Immigration Appeal Tribunal
Transcripts of the judgements of the Court of Appeal (Civil Division, 1951 to date)

Library catalogue:
All or part available in-house

Access to staff:
Contact by letter and by fax. Appointment necessary.
Hours: Mon to Fri, 1000 to 1630; during legal vacations 0930 to 1630

Access for disabled people:
Special comments: Access provided throughout the library and court buildings

SURF LIFE SAVING ASSOCIATION OF GREAT BRITAIN

Acronym or abbreviation: SLSA GB

19 Southernhay West, Exeter, EX1 1PJ

Tel: 01392 218007
Fax: 01392 217808
E-mail: mail@slsgb.org.uk

Website:
http://www.surflifesaving.org.uk/

Enquiries:
Enquiries to: Executive Officer

Founded:
1955

Organisation type and purpose:
Membership association, voluntary organisation, registered charity (charity number 1015668), training organisation.

Subject coverage:
Life-saving on beaches with surf, training, awards.

Printed publications:
Advanced Resuscitation Guidelines
Competition Manual
Examinations and Awards Manual
IRB Coaching Manual
Professional Surf – Lifeguard Teaching Module
SLSA GB Manual

Access to staff:
Contact by letter, by telephone and by fax.
Appointment necessary.
Hours: Mon to Fri, 0900 to 1700

SURFACE ENGINEERING ASSOCIATION

Acronym or abbreviation: SEA

Federation House, 10 Vyse Street, Birmingham, B18 6LT

Tel: 0121 237 1123
Fax: 0121 237 1124
E-mail: finishes@waverider.co.uk

Website:
http://www.sea.org.uk
Surface Engineering Association home page.
http://www.bstsa.org.uk
British Surface Treatment Suppliers Association home page.

Enquiries:
Enquiries to: General Manager

Founded:
1887

Organisation type and purpose:
Trade association (membership is by subscription), present number of members: 400, manufacturing industry, consultancy.
To promote the interests of the UK surface engineering activity.

Subject coverage:
Metal finishing, coating metal, putting metal coatings on other products, supply of materials or services to companies, sub-contractors for finishing, surface engineering, surface coating materials, economics, health and safety, environmental issues.

Museum or gallery collection, archive, or library special collection:
Standards for surface engineering

Trade and statistical information:
Some data on value of the surface engineering industry.

Printed publications:
Newsletter (quarterly, free of charge to members)
Buyers Guide to Surface Finishing (free of charge to members)
Proceedings of Electroless Nickel Conferences 1987 and 1991 (p.o.a.)
Safer Chromium Finishing (members: £10, non-members: £12)
Waste Minimisation Guide (members: £25, non-members: £75)

Electronic and video publications:
Electroless Nickel Plating (video £15 plus VAT)
Electroplating in Automobile Construction (CD-ROM £5 plus VAT)

Publications list:
Available in print

Access to staff:
Contact by letter, by telephone, by fax, by e-mail and via website. Appointment necessary.
Hours: Mon to Fri, 0900 to 1700
Special comments: Some services – members only.

Access for disabled people:
Level entry, access to all public areas, toilet facilities

Affiliated to:
CETS
METCOM

Member of:
The British Jewellery and Giftware Federation (BJGF)

SURREY ARCHAEOLOGICAL SOCIETY

Castle Arch, Guildford, Surrey, GU1 3SX

Tel: 01483 532454
Fax: 01483 532454
E-mail: info@surreyarchaeology.org.uk

Website:
http://www.surreyarchaeology.org.uk

Enquiries:
Enquiries to: Honorary Secretary

Founded:
1854

Organisation type and purpose:
Learned society.
To promote the study of archaeology and antiquities within the historic county of Surrey.

Subject coverage:
Archaeological, antiquarian or historical material relating to historic county of Surrey including building records, records and manuscripts, cartographic and pictorial material, ceramics, ecclesiastical history and industrial history.

Museum or gallery collection, archive, or library special collection:
The Society's collections, research material and library are housed at Castle Arch

Non-library collection catalogue:
All or part available online and in-house

Library catalogue:
All or part available online and in-house

Printed publications:
Purchased directly from Society

Publications list:
Available online and in print

Access to staff:
Contact by letter, by telephone, by fax, by e-mail, in person and via website. Appointment necessary. Non-members charged.
Hours: Mon to Fri, 1030 to 1630
Special comments: Non-members first visit free, subsequent visits £8.00 each

Access to building, collection or gallery:
Prior appointment required

SURREY COMMUNITY ACTION

Acronym or abbreviation: SCA

Astolat, Coniers Way, New Inn Lane, Burpham, Guildford, Surrey, GU4 7HL

Tel: 01483 566072
Fax: 01483 440508 or 0870 0566147
E-mail: info@surreyca.org.uk

Website:
http://www.surreyca.org.uk
Full details of Surrey Community Action and all its projects; Directory search facility.

Enquiries:
Enquiries to: Information Officer

Founded:
1950

Organisation type and purpose:
Membership association (membership is by subscription), present number of members: 600, voluntary organisation, registered charity (charity number 1056527).

Independent registered charity working with communities to strengthen voluntary action. To enhance the quality of life for people in Surrey by promoting, supporting and strengthening voluntary action.

Subject coverage:
Local charities and voluntary groups including village halls and good neighbour car schemes. Volunteering and voluntary transport schemes. Local training. Rural communities in Surrey. Local grant schemes and funding sources.

Printed publications:
Directories (all online via website):
Surrey Health and Social Care
Community Transport
Village & Community Halls
Guidelines: Volunteering, Care groups, Committee procedures

Access to staff:
Contact by letter, by telephone, by fax, by e-mail, in person and via website. Appointment necessary.
Hours: Mon to Fri, 0900 to 1700

Access for disabled people:
Parking provided, level entry, access to all public areas, toilet facilities

SURREY COUNTY ARCHAEOLOGICAL UNIT

Acronym or abbreviation: SCAU

Surrey History Centre, Goldsworth Road, Woking, Surrey, GU21 1ND

Tel: 01483 518777
Fax: 01483 594637
E-mail: archaeology.scau@surreycc.gov.uk

Website:
http://www.surreycc.gov.uk/archaeology

Enquiries:
Enquiries to: Unit Manager
Other contacts: Archaeological Project Officer, tel: 01483 594630 for general

Founded:
1991

Organisation type and purpose:
Local government body, professional body.

Subject coverage:
Archaeological information for Surrey.

Museum or gallery collection, archive, or library special collection:
Archive of archaeological material from a number of sites in Surrey

Printed publications:
Publications on application, for purchase direct or through Surrey Archaeological Society

Access to staff:
Contact by letter, by telephone and by e-mail. Appointment necessary.
Hours: Mon to Fri, 0800 to 1600

Access to building, collection or gallery:
Prior appointment required

Access for disabled people:
Parking provided, level entry, access to all public areas, toilet facilities

Parent body:
Surrey County Council
County Hall, Kingston upon Thames; tel: 020 8541 8800; fax: 020 8541 9004

SURREY COUNTY COUNCIL LIBRARIES

Surrey County Council, Room 356, County Hall, Kingston upon Thames, Surrey, KT1 2DY

Tel: 01483 543599
Fax: 01483 543597
E-mail: libraries@surreycc.gov.uk

Website:
http://www.surreycc.gov.uk/libraries

Library catalogue:
All or part available online

Access to staff:
Contact by letter, by telephone, by fax, by e-mail, in person and via website

SURREY GUILD OF CRAFTSMEN

Acronym or abbreviation: SGC

Surrey Guild Craft Gallery, 1 Moushill Lane, Milford, Godalming, Surrey, GU8 5BH

Tel: 01483 424769
E-mail: enquiries@surreyguild.co.uk

Enquiries:
Enquiries to: Administrator

Organisation type and purpose:
Membership association.

Subject coverage:
Craftworkers in the county; craft activities and techniques; professional craftsmen in Surrey.

Printed publications:
Directory of members and associates (annually)
Newsletter (approximately quarterly)

Access to staff:
Contact by e-mail. Appointment necessary. Access for members only. Letter of introduction required.

Access to building, collection or gallery:
Hours: Mon to Sun, 1030 to 1700

Access for disabled people:
Special comments: Assistance provided, please telephone before visiting

Member of:
South East Arts Association

SURREY HEATH ARCHAEOLOGICAL & HERITAGE TRUST

Acronym or abbreviation: SHAHT

Archaeology Centre, 4–10 London Road, Bagshot, Surrey, GU19 5HN

Tel: 01276 451181

Founded:
1988

Organisation type and purpose:
Learned society (membership is by subscription), present number of members: 200, voluntary organisation, registered charity (charity number 299409), museum, suitable for ages: 9 to 75, training organisation, research organisation.

Subject coverage:
Archaeology of Borough of Surrey Heath; mesolithic to post-industrial revolution.

Non-library collection catalogue:
All or part available in-house

Library catalogue:
All or part available in-house

Access to staff:
Contact by letter and by telephone
Hours: By appointment

Access to building, collection or gallery:
No prior appointment required

SURREY HEATH BOROUGH COUNCIL

Acronym or abbreviation: SHBC

Surrey Heath House, Knoll Road, Camberley, Surrey, GU15 3HD

Tel: 01276 707100
Fax: 01276 707177
E-mail: enquiries@surreyheath.gov.uk

Website:
http://www.surreyheath.gov.uk

Enquiries:
Enquiries to: Chief Executive

Founded:
1974

Organisation type and purpose:
Local government body.

Subject coverage:
Local authority, housing, planning, environmental health, recreation, council tax, benefits.

Printed publications:
Borough Guide (£3)
Directory of Local Organisations (£15)

Access to staff:
Contact by letter, by telephone, by fax, by e-mail, in person and via website
Hours: Mon to Thu, 0830 to 1730; Fri, 0900 to 1700

Access for disabled people:
Parking provided, ramped entry, level entry, toilet facilities

Link with:
Surrey County Council

SURREY HERITAGE

Surrey History Centre, 130 Goldsworth Road, Woking, Surrey, GU21 6ND

Tel: 01483 518737
Fax: 01483 518738
E-mail: shs@surreycc.gov.uk

Website:
http://www.surreycc.gov.uk/surreyhistoryservice
Details of services and events, searchable catalogues of holdings, research guides.

Enquiries:
Enquiries to: Surrey History Centre Helpdesk
Other contacts: Head of Heritage (for matters of overall policy and complaints)

Founded:
1998

Created by the merger of:
Surrey Record Office, Surrey Local Studies Library, Guildford Muniment Room (year of change 1998)

Organisation type and purpose:
Local government body.
County archives and local studies library.

Subject coverage:
Surrey records and history, including material on churches, houses, schools, businesses, charitable institutions (reformatories, asylums, etc.), local government and local legal institutions (i.e. quarter sessions and petty sessions), urban growth and housing development, railways and other public undertakings, family and estate papers; not matters dealt with by central government or heavy industries.

Museum or gallery collection, archive, or library special collection:
John Broadwood and Sons Ltd, piano manufacturers: records
Barclay collection of watercolours by John Hassell (1767–1825)
Dennis Specialist Vehicles Ltd, makers of fire engines, buses and other specialist vehicles: records
Photographs of Surrey by Francis Frith
Papers relating to C. L. Dodgson (Lewis Carroll) and of Dodgson family
Goulburn family of Betchworth: papers, including Henry Goulburn (1784–1856), politician
Gertrude Jekyll (1843–1932), garden designer of Munstead: papers including garden designs
More and More-Molyneux family of Loseley House: papers, particularly relating to Tudor and Stuart Surrey
Queen's Royal Surrey Regiment and predecessors, including Queen's Royal Regiment (West Surrey) and East Surrey Regiment: records

continued overleaf

IGI complete

Non-library collection catalogue:
All or part available online and in-house

Library catalogue:
All or part available online

Printed publications:
Guide to parish register holdings
Information sheets (mostly for family history and
house history)
Surrey History Service (descriptive leaflet)

Microform publications:
Some fiche and films copies available through
bureaux at request of Surrey Heritage; no filming
service at present

Publications list:
Available online

Access to staff:
Contact by letter, by telephone, by fax, by e-mail
and via website. Appointment necessary.

Access to building, collection or gallery:
Hours: Tue, Wed, Fri, 0930 to 1700; Thu, 0930 to
1930; Sat, 0930 to 1600
Special comments: CARN tickets, Surrey Library
cards or ID required

Access for disabled people:
Parking provided, ramped entry, access to all
public areas, toilet facilities

SURREY PERFORMING ARTS LIBRARY

Denbies Wine Estate, London Road, Dorking,
Surrey, RH5 6AA

Tel: 01306 887509
Fax: 01306 875074
E-mail: performing.arts@surreycc.gov.uk

Website:
http://www.surreycc.gov.uk/libraries

Enquiries:
Enquiries to: Senior Librarian

Founded:
1981

Organisation type and purpose:
Local government body, public library.

Subject coverage:
Performing arts including, music, drama, theatre,
arts, dance and cinema.

Museum or gallery collection, archive, or library special collection:
Audio and video collections within the subject
areas
Performance materials; sets of plays, vocal scores,
orchestral parts, chamber music parts

Non-library collection catalogue:
All or part available online

Library catalogue:
All or part available online

Access to staff:
Contact by letter, by telephone, by fax, by e-mail
and in person
Hours: Tue and Fri, 1000 to 1700; Thu, 1000 to 2000;
Sat, 0930 to 1300; Mon and Wed, closed

Access for disabled people:
Level entry, access to all public areas

Parent body:
Surrey County Council

SURREY RECORD SOCIETY

c/o Surrey History Centre, 130 Goldsworth Road,
Woking, Surrey, GU21 6ND

Tel: 01483 518754
Fax: 01483 518738

Enquiries:
Enquiries to: Honorary Secretary

Founded:
1913

Organisation type and purpose:
Learned society (membership is by subscription).
The Society exists to publish records relating to the
historic county of Surrey, which includes the
parishes of South London as far east as
Rotherhithe.

Subject coverage:
Surrey history and genealogy. No research
undertaken.

Printed publications:
Transcripts, translations and abstracts of texts
ranging in date from the twelfth to the
nineteenth century, and in subject from central,
county and municipal government to
ecclesiastical, manorial, industrial and military
history. Manuscript sources held in repositories
in and outside the county are thus made
accessible
35 volumes to date, not all in print, but including:
Vol VII The Pipe Roll for 1295, Surrey membrane
(ed Mills M H, paperback reprint 1968)
Vol XV Surrey Manorial Accounts (ed Briggs H M,
paperback reprint, 1968)
Vol XXVIII Kingston upon Thames Register of
Apprentices 1563–1703 (ed Daly A, 1974)
Vol XXXIII Minutes of the Board of Directors of the
Reading, Guildford and Reigate Railway
Company (ed Course E, 1988, members £12.50,
non-members £15, overseas £17.50)
Vol XXXIV Parson and Parish in Eighteenth-
Century Surrey: Replies to Bishops' Visitations
(ed Ward W R, £15 UK)
Vol XXXV The 1851 Religious Census: Surrey
(transcribed by Webb C and Robinson D, £25
UK)
Vol XXXVI Gunpowder Mills: Documents of the
17th and 18th centuries (ed Crocker, Crocker,
Fairclough and Wilks, 2000, £15 plus £2 p&p UK)
For full list, visit website http://
www.surreycc.gov.uk/surreyhistorycentre

Access to staff:
Contact by letter
Hours: Mon to Fri, 0900 to 1700

SURVEY FORCE LIMITED

Algarve House, 140 Borden Lane, Sittingbourne,
Kent, ME9 8HW

Tel: 01795 423778
Fax: 01795 423778
E-mail: surveyforce@yahoo.com

Enquiries:
Enquiries to: Director
Other contacts: Sales Managers

Founded:
1974

Organisation type and purpose:
International organisation, service industry,
consultancy, research organisation.

Subject coverage:
Market research in chemical, pharmaceutical,
health care, electronics, computer, IT, optical,
elastomers, rubbers, plastics, food and drink,
diagnostics (instrumentation and reagents).

Museum or gallery collection, archive, or library special collection:
Market research studies (over 500) covering world,
EU, USA, Japan etc, regularly updated

Trade and statistical information:
Computers – World.
Health care – World and USA.
Pharmaceutical USA, Japan, World.
Electronics – EC, UK, USA, Japan.
Optical – Italy, France, UK, USA.
Elastomers – Europe; USA.
Chemical – World.
IT – World.

Non-library collection catalogue:
All or part available in print

Printed publications:
Over 500 market research studies regularly
updated

Electronic and video publications:
Some reports available on CD-ROM
Most databases available on disk

Publications list:
Available in print

Access to staff:
Contact by letter, by telephone, by fax and by e-
mail. Appointment necessary.
Hours: Mon to Fri, 0900 to 1700

Access to building, collection or gallery:
Prior appointment required

SUSSEX COUNTY CRICKET CLUB

Eaton Road, Hove, East Sussex, BN3 3AN

Tel: 01273 827100
Fax: 01273 771549

Website:
http://www.sussexcricket.co.uk

Enquiries:
Enquiries to: Business Manager
Direct tel: 01273 827102
Direct e-mail: Russell@sussexcricket.co.uk

Founded:
1839

Organisation type and purpose:
Membership association (membership is by
subscription), present number of members: c. 5000.
Sporting organisation.

Subject coverage:
History of the clubs and its players.

Access to staff:
Contact by letter, by telephone, by fax and via
website
Hours: Mon to Fri, 0900 to 1700

SUSSEX INDUSTRIAL ARCHAEOLOGY SOCIETY

Acronym or abbreviation: SIAS

42 Falmer Avenue, Saltdean, Brighton, East Sussex,
BN2 8FG

Tel: 01273 271330
E-mail: ronald@martin42.fsnet.co.uk

Website:
http://www.sussexias.co.uk

Enquiries:
Enquiries to: General Secretary
Other contacts: Treasurer for financial matters.

Founded:
1968

Organisation type and purpose:
Membership association (membership is by
subscription), present number of members: 350,
voluntary organisation, registered charity (charity
number 267159), research organisation.

Subject coverage:
Sussex industrial archaeology, mills, brickmaking,
railways, ice houses, breweries.

Museum or gallery collection, archive, or library special collection:
Records of industrial archaeology sites in Sussex

Printed publications:
Newsletter (quarterly, 50p)
Sussex Industrial History (annually, £4.25, p&p
75p, back numbers available)

Publications list:
Available in print

Access to staff:
Contact by letter, by telephone and by e-mail
Hours: 0800 to 2300

SUSSEX PAST

Formal name: Sussex Archaeological Society

Bull House, 92 High Street, Lewes, East Sussex, BN7 1XH

Tel: 01273 486260
Fax: 01273 486990
E-mail: admin@sussexpast.co.uk

Website:
http://www.sussexpast.co.uk
Properties open to the public, research, details of organisation and membership.

Enquiries:
Enquiries to: Public Relations Manager
Direct tel: 01273 487188
Direct e-mail: pro@sussexpast.co.uk

Founded:
1846

Organisation type and purpose:
Learned society, registered charity, museum.

Subject coverage:
Sussex archaeology, local history and historic properties.

Special visitor services:
Guided tours.

Education services:
Group education facilities.

Museum or gallery collection, archive, or library special collection:
Artefacts relating to archaeology and history
Collection of prints, pictures, books related to Sussex
Manuscripts

Printed publications:
Sussex Past & Present (magazine, 3 times a year)
Sussex Archaeological Collections (annually, to members or on subscription)

Access to building, collection or gallery:
Prior appointment required
Hours: Mon to Sat, 1000 to 1700; Sun, 1100 to 1700
Special comments: Library: 01273 405738
Museum: 01273 405739

Affiliated to:
Council for British Archaeology

Sussex Past sites:
Anne of Cleves House Museum
52 Southover High Street, Lewes, East Sussex, BN7 1JA; tel: 01273 474610
Fishbourne Roman Palace and Museum
Salthill Road, Fishbourne, Chichester, West Sussex, PO19 3QR; tel: 01243 785859; fax: 01243 539266; e-mail: adminfish@sussexpast.co.uk
Lewes Castle & Museums
169 High Street, Lewes, East Sussex, BN7 1YE; tel: 01273 486290; e-mail: castle@sussexpast.co.uk
Marlpins Museum
High Street, Shoreham-by-Sea, West Sussex, BN43 5NN; tel: 01273 462994
Michelham Priory
Upper Dicker, Hailsham, East Sussex, BN27 3QS; tel: 01323 844224
The Priest House
North Lane, West Hoathly, East Grinstead, West Sussex, RH19 4PP; tel: 01342 810479; e-mail: priest@sussexpast.co.uk

SUSSEX RECORD SOCIETY

Barbican House, High Street, Lewes, East Sussex, BN7 1YE

Tel: 01273 486290

Enquiries:
Enquiries to: Secretary
Direct tel: 01243 533911
Direct fax: 01243 533959
Direct e-mail: wilkinson@newnet.co.uk

Founded:
1901

Organisation type and purpose:
Learned society.

Subject coverage:
Publication of texts relating to the history and topography of Sussex.

Printed publications:
Annual Report
Annual volumes
Newsletter (annually, for members)

Microform publications:
Volumes 1–61 (available on microfiche from Chadwyck-Healey)

Publications list:
Available in print

Access to staff:
Contact by letter, by telephone and by fax
Hours: Mon to Fri, 0900 to 1700

SUSTAIN: THE ALLIANCE FOR BETTER FOOD FARMING

Acronym or abbreviation: Sustain

94 White Lion Street, London, N1 9PF

Tel: 020 7837 1228
Fax: 020 7837 1141
E-mail: sustain@sustainweb.org

Website:
http://www.sustainweb.org

Enquiries:
Enquiries to: Co-ordinator

Founded:
1985

Created by the merger of:
National Food Alliance, and Sustainable Agriculture Food and Environment Alliance (year of change 1999)

Organisation type and purpose:
Membership association (membership is by application or invitation), present number of members: around 100, voluntary organisation, registered charity (charity number 1018643). Umbrella group.

Subject coverage:
All aspects of food along the length of the food chain including environment, nutrition, farming, fair trade, animal welfare.

Printed publications:
Digest Newsletter (annual subscription, quarterly, for national members)
The Jellied Eel (annual subscription, quarterly, for London Food Link members)
A wide range of publications are available online
Order printed publications from: via http://www.sustainweb.org/publications

Publications list:
Available online

Access to staff:
Contact by letter, by telephone, by fax, by e-mail and via website. Appointment necessary. Non-members charged.
Hours: Mon to Fri, 0900 to 1800

Access to building, collection or gallery:
Prior appointment required

Member organisations:
around 100 member organisations

SUSTRANS

Formal name: Sustainable Transport

2 Cathedral Square, College Green, Bristol, BS1 5DD

Tel: 0117 926 8893
Fax: 0117 929 4173
E-mail: info@sustrans.org.uk

Website:
http://www.sustrans.org.uk

Information about the National Cycle Network, safe routes to schools and Sustrans. Includes list of publications.

Enquiries:
Enquiries to: Information Officer
Direct e-mail: press@sustrans.org.uk

Founded:
1978

Organisation type and purpose:
Registered charity (charity number 326550). Campaigns for and builds cycle and pedestrian routes.

Subject coverage:
The designing and building of traffic-free routes for cyclists, pedestrians and wheelchair users, the National Cycle Network, the need for a new sustainable transport policy which lessens dependence on the motor car.

Museum or gallery collection, archive, or library special collection:
About 400 design and policy studies on walking and particularly cycling facilities

Printed publications:
Recent publications include:
Annual Report
Information Sheets (free)
Making Ways for the bicycle; A Guide to Traffic-Free Path Construction (1994, £10)
National Cycle Network Route Maps
Safe Routes to Schools: various
The National Cycle Network: Guidelines and Practical Details; Issue 2 (1997, £29.50 plus p&p)
Order printed publications from: Sustrans Information Service
PO Box 21, Bristol, BS99 2HA, e-mail: info@sustrans.org.uk

Publications list:
Available online and in print

Access to staff:
Contact by letter, by telephone, by fax, by e-mail and via website. Appointment necessary.
Hours: Mon to Fri, 0900 to 1700

Head Office:
35 King Street, Bristol, BS1 4DZ; tel: 0117 926 8893; fax: 0117 929 4173

Regions:
North East
Rockwood House, Barn Hill, Stanley, Co Durham, DH9 8AN; tel: 01207 281259; fax: 01207 28113
Northern Ireland
McAvoy House, 17A Ormeau Avenue, Belfast, BT2 8HD; tel: 028 9043 4569; fax: 028 9043 4556
Scotland
162 Fountainbridge, Edinburgh, EH3 9RX; tel: 0131 624 7660; fax: 0131 624 7764

SUTTON AND EAST SURREY WATER PLC

London Road, Redhill, Surrey, RH1 1IJ

Tel: 01737 772000
Fax: 01737 766807

Website:
http://www.waterplc.com

Enquiries:
Enquiries to: Press Officer
Direct tel: 01372 460111
Direct fax: 01372 470955
Direct e-mail: stuart.hyslop@surreyhouseuk.com

Organisation type and purpose:
Service industry.

Printed publications:
Pipelines (magazine, two times a year, Spring and Autumn, free to customers)
The Wonderful World of Water: H2O

Access to staff:
Contact by letter, by telephone, by fax and by e-mail

continued overleaf

Hours: Mon to Fri, 0830 to 1700

Access to building, collection or gallery:
Prior appointment required

Access for disabled people:
Level entry

SUTTON COLDFIELD LIBRARY

45 Lower Parade, Sutton Coldfield, West Midlands,
B72 1XX

Tel: 0121 464 2274
Fax: 0121 464 0173
E-mail: sutton.coldfield.lending.library@
birmingham.gov.uk

Enquiries:
Enquiries to: Librarian
Direct tel: 0121 464 0164

Organisation type and purpose:
Public library.

Subject coverage:
Separate reference library, children's library and
music library and a substantial local history
section.

Non-library collection catalogue:
All or part available online

Library catalogue:
All or part available online

Printed publications:
Societies and Organisations in Sutton Coldfield
Sutton Coldfield (Baxter M)
Sutton Coldfield: the Second Selection (Baxter M)

Access to staff:
Contact by letter, by telephone, by fax, by e-mail,
in person and via website
Hours: Mon, Wed, Fri, 0900 to 1800; Tue, Thu, 0900
to 2000; Sat, 0900 to 1700

Access for disabled people:
Toilet facilities

SUTTON LIBRARY AND HERITAGE SERVICES

Central Library, St Nicholas Way, Sutton, Surrey,
SM1 1EA

Tel: 020 8770 4700\ Minicom no. 020 8770 4779
Fax: 020 8770 4777
E-mail: sutton.information@sutton.gov.uk

Website:
http://www.sutton-libraries.gov.uk/uhtbin/webcat
List of libraries, services, 'search the catalogue'
facility.

Enquiries:
Enquiries to: Librarian

Organisation type and purpose:
Local government body, public library.

Subject coverage:
General, including genealogy and heraldry, local
studies.

**Museum or gallery collection, archive, or library
special collection:**
Croydon Airport Collection
River Wandle Collection

Library catalogue:
All or part available online

Printed publications:
Range of local history publications including:
All our Yesterdays: A pictorial record of the
  London Borough of Sutton over the last century
  (2nd ed, Bradley I et al)
Courts of the Manors of Bandon and Beddington
  1498–1552 (Gowans H ed)
Croydon Airport and the Battle of Britain, 1939–
  1940 (Bogle J, Cluett D and Learmouth B)
Croydon Airport: The Australian Connection:
  Flights and other links between Croydon Airport
  and Australia (Cluett D)

Discovering Sutton's Heritage: The story of five
  parishes (Cluett D)
Nonsuch: Pearl of the Realm: Henry VIII's fantastic
  palace (Lister L)
The Story of Little Woodcote and Woodcote Hall
  (Cunningham M)

Publications list:
Available in print

Access to staff:
Contact by letter, by telephone, by fax, by e-mail
and in person
Hours: Mon, closed; Tue to Fri, 0900 to 2000; Sat,
0900 to 1700; Sun, 1400 to 1700

Access for disabled people:
Ramped entry, access to all public areas, toilet
facilities

SUZY LAMPLUGH TRUST

National Centre for Personal Safety, Hampton
House, 20 Albert Embankment, London, SE1 7TJ

Tel: 020 7091 0014
Fax: 020 7091 0015
E-mail: info@suzylamplugh.org

Website:
http://www.suzylamplugh.org
Complete personal safety information and
resources.

Founded:
1986

Organisation type and purpose:
Advisory body, voluntary organisation, registered
charity (charity number 802567), suitable for ages:
all, training organisation, consultancy, research
organisation.
The leading authority on personal safety.
To reduce violence and aggression in society and
help everyone – men, women and children – to
gain the knowledge and confidence they need to
live safer lives.

Subject coverage:
Personal safety, indoors, outdoors, and in the
workplace.

Non-library collection catalogue:
All or part available online

Library catalogue:
All or part available in-house

Printed publications:
Living Safely – Personal Safety in Your Daily Life
  (booklet, versions for adults, teenagers and
  people with disabilities)
Think Safety (booklet for teenagers) Both of these
  publications will be sent free on receipt of a sae.
Think Safety Green (£2.50 p&p)
Books and videos for schools, children, and young
  people, personal safety at work
Research Reports

Electronic and video publications:
Personal Safety At Work (video)
Home Safe (video and pack)
Well Safe (video and pack)
World Wise (video and pack)

Publications list:
Available online and in print

Access to staff:
Contact by letter, by telephone and by fax.
Appointment necessary.
Hours: Mon to Fri, 0900 to 1700

SWALE BOROUGH COUNCIL

Acronym or abbreviation: SBC

Swale House, East Street, Sittingbourne, Kent,
ME10 3HT

Tel: 01795 424341
Fax: 01795 417217

Website:
http://www.swale.gov.uk

Enquiries:
Enquiries to: Public Relations Manager
Direct tel: 01795 417400
Direct fax: 01795 417382
Direct e-mail: kimevans@swale.gov.uk

Founded:
1974

Organisation type and purpose:
Local government body.

Subject coverage:
Local government.

Access to staff:
Contact by letter, by telephone, by fax and by e-
mail
Hours: Mon to Fri, 0900 to 1700

SWALEDALE SHEEP BREEDERS ASSOCIATION

The Shooting Lodge, High Shipley, Eggleston,
Barnard Castle, Co Durham, DL12 0DP

Tel: 01833 650516
Fax: 01833 650516
E-mail: jstephenson@swaledale-sheep.com

Subject coverage:
Breeders and breeding of Swaledale Sheep.

SWANSEA CITY AND COUNTY COUNCIL

County Hall, Swansea, West Glamorgan, SA1 3SN

Tel: 01792 636000
Fax: 01792 637206
E-mail: bob.cuthill@swansea.gov.uk

Website:
http://www.swansea.gov.uk

Enquiries:
Enquiries to: Information Officer
Direct tel: 01792 636737

Founded:
1996

Organisation type and purpose:
Local government body.

Subject coverage:
Policy issues, demography including census of the
population, local statistics and modernising local
government agenda.

Access to staff:
Contact by letter, by telephone, by fax, by e-mail
and via website. Appointment necessary.
Hours: Mon to Fri, 0830 to 1700

Access for disabled people:
Parking provided, ramped entry, level entry, toilet
facilities

SWANSEA INSTITUTE OF HIGHER EDUCATION

Acronym or abbreviation: SIHE

Townhill Road, Swansea, West Glamorgan, SA2
0UT

Tel: 01792 481000
Fax: 01792 208683
E-mail: enquiry@sihe.ac.uk

Website:
http://www.sihe.ac.uk

Enquiries:
Enquiries to: Head of Library and Learning Support
Services
Direct tel: 01792 481240
Direct fax: 01792 298017
Direct e-mail: t.lamb@sihe.ac.uk

Organisation type and purpose:
Library.

Subject coverage:
Art, stained glass, education – primary teacher training, humanities, construction, business, management, law, tourism, leisure, health care, transport, engineering, manufacturing design, optoelectronics computing, safety in leisure pursuits, motor sport, applied design.

Access to staff:
Non-members charged.
Hours: Mon to Thu, 0845 to 2100; Fri, 0845 to 1630; Sat, 1000 to 1600

Associated college of:
University of Wales

Other addresses:
Swansea Institute of Higher Education
Mount Pleasant, Swansea, SA1 6ED; tel: 01792 481000

SWANSEA TRIBOLOGY SERVICES LIMITED

Acronym or abbreviation: STS Ltd

5 Penrice Court, Fenrod Business Park, Enterprise Park, Swansea, West Glamorgan, SA6 8QW

Tel: 01792 799036
Fax: 01792 799034
E-mail: oiltest@trib.co.uk

Website:
http://www.trib.co.uk

Enquiries:
Enquiries to: Laboratory Director

Founded:
1996

Organisation type and purpose:
International organisation, manufacturing industry, service industry, training organisation, consultancy, research organisation, laboratory.

Subject coverage:
Tribology, condition monitoring, wear debris monitors, oil analysis, maintenance.

Publications list:
Available in print

Access to staff:
Contact by letter, by telephone, by fax, by e-mail, in person and via website. Appointment necessary.
Hours: Mon to Fri, 0900 to 1630

SWANSEA UNIVERSITY – LIBRARY & INFORMATION SERVICES

Singleton Park, Swansea, SA2 8PP

Tel: 01792 295175
Fax: 01792 295851
E-mail: library@swansea.ac.uk

Website:
http://www.swan.ac.uk/lis
Description of Library & Information Services: gateway to other information sources; on-line exhibitions.

Enquiries:
Enquiries to: Director of Library and Information Services

Founded:
1920

Organisation type and purpose:
University library.

Subject coverage:
Humanities, economic and social sciences, physical, natural and engineering sciences, education, business studies, law, history of South Wales coalfield.

Museum or gallery collection, archive, or library special collection:
Archives of the South Wales coalfield and other local archives
British Standards

Strong collections in history, mathematics, Celtic studies, Welsh writers in English

Non-library collection catalogue:
All or part available online and in-house

Library catalogue:
All or part available online

Printed publications:
Guides and leaflets for library users

Microform publications:
University of Wales Swansea Theses can be supplied at a charge.

Access to staff:
Contact by letter, by telephone, by fax, by e-mail and in person
Hours: Term time: Sun to Thu, 0800 to 0200; Fri, Sat, 0800 to 2000
Vacations: Mon to Thu 0800 to 2000; Fri, Sat, 0800 to 1700; Sun, closed
Special comments: Different hours apply in branch libraries.

Access to building, collection or gallery:
No prior appointment required

Access for disabled people:
Ramped entry, access to all public areas, toilet facilities
Special comments: Special facilities for users with visual impairment.

SWEDENBORG SOCIETY

Swedenborg House, 20–21 Bloomsbury Way, London, WC1A 2TH

Tel: 020 7405 7986
E-mail: james@swedenborg.org.uk

Website:
http://www.swedenborg.org.uk
Introduction to the function of the Swedenborg Society, the life, work and influence of Emanuel Swedenborg. Online bookshop. News and events. Library catalogue (partial).

Enquiries:
Enquiries to: Librarian
Other contacts: Secretary

Founded:
1810

Organisation type and purpose:
Learned society (membership is by subscription, election or invitation), present number of members: 850, registered charity (charity number 209172), publishing house.
The Swedenborg Society was established for the purpose of printing and publishing the works of Emmanuel Swedenborg.

Subject coverage:
Life and works of Emanuel Swedenborg and related material.

Museum or gallery collection, archive, or library special collection:
Complete works of Swedenborg; all languages and all editions; original archival items re society, Swedenborg, the New Church; collateral works
Completely catalogued reference library
Separate lending library

Non-library collection catalogue:
All or part available online

Library catalogue:
All or part available online and in-house

Printed publications:
Annual Report
Journal
Catalogue: a wide range of books available – theological, Latin editions, facsimile reproductions of first editions, miscellaneous books and booklets
Order printed publications from: http://www.swedenborg.org.uk

Publications list:
Available online and in print

Access to staff:
Contact by letter, by telephone, by e-mail and via website. Appointment necessary.
Hours: Mon to Fri, 0930 to 1700

Access to building, collection or gallery:
Prior appointment required for use of library; please bring ID and proof of address

Links with:
similar bodies world-wide
The Library and Archives of The General Conference of the New Church at the same address

SWEDISH CHAMBER OF COMMERCE FOR THE UNITED KINGDOM

Sweden House, 5 Upper Montagu Street, London, W1H 2AG

Tel: 020 7224 8001
Fax: 020 7224 8884
E-mail: info@scc.org.uk

Website:
http://www.swedish-chamber.org.uk

Enquiries:
Enquiries to: Director

Founded:
1906

Organisation type and purpose:
Membership association (membership is by subscription), present number of members: 500.

Subject coverage:
General information dealing with British-Swedish trade.

Trade and statistical information:
Data on British-Swedish trade.

Printed publications:
Link Magazine (monthly, free)
Swedish Chamber of Commerce Trade Directory (annually, £79 incl. p&p)

Access to staff:
Contact by letter, by fax, by e-mail, in person and via website. Non-members charged.
Hours: Mon to Fri, 0900 to 1730

SWIFT CLUB

The Croft, Ash Green, Surrey, GU12 6HD

Tel: 01252 344402
Fax: 01252 311187

Enquiries:
Enquiries to: Honorary Secretary

Founded:
1985

Organisation type and purpose:
Membership association (membership is by subscription), present number of members: 67, voluntary organisation.

Subject coverage:
Technical advice on Swift cars produced by the Swift Motor Co. of Coventry between 1901 and 1931.

Printed publications:
Magazine and Newsletter (members only)

Access to staff:
Contact by letter, by telephone, by fax and by e-mail. Appointment necessary.
Hours: Mon to Sun, 0900 to 2200

SWINDON BOROUGH COUNCIL

Civic Offices, Euclid Street, Swindon, Wiltshire, SN1 2JH

Tel: 01793 463000\ Minicom no. 01793 436659
Fax: 01793 463930

continued overleaf

Website:
http://www.swindon.gov.uk

Enquiries:
Enquiries to: Chief Executive
Direct tel: 01793 463010
Direct fax: 01793 463930
Direct e-mail: gjones@swindon.gov.uk

Organisation type and purpose:
Local government body.

Subject coverage:
Local government.

Access to staff:
Contact by letter, by telephone and by fax
Hours: Mon to Fri, 0900 to 1630

SWINDON BOROUGH COUNCIL LIBRARIES

4th Floor, Premier House, Station Road, Swindon, Wiltshire, SN1 1TZ

Tel: 01793 466035
Fax: 01793 466484
E-mail: ajordan@swindon.gov.uk

Enquiries:
Enquiries to: Library Services Manager

Organisation type and purpose:
Local government body, public library.

Subject coverage:
General, railways.

Museum or gallery collection, archive, or library special collection:
Great Western Railway collection
Richard Jefferies manuscript collection
Swindon and Wiltshire local studies

Library catalogue:
All or part available online

Access to staff:
Contact by letter, by telephone, by fax, by e-mail and in person. Appointment necessary. Access for members only.
Hours: Mon to Fri, 0900 to 1700; Sat, 0930 to 1600

Access to building, collection or gallery:
No prior appointment required

Access for disabled people:
Ramped entry, level entry

Parent body:
Swindon Borough Council

Sponsor for:
WILCO

SWISS COTTAGE CENTRAL LIBRARY

88 Avenue Road, London, NW3 3HA

Tel: 020 7974 6522\ Minicom no. 020 7974 6513
Fax: 020 7974 6532
E-mail: swisscottagelibrary@camden.gov.uk

Enquiries:
Enquiries to: Librarian
Other contacts: Lending, Audiovisual and Music

Organisation type and purpose:
Local government body, public library.

Subject coverage:
General reference library, philosophy; psychology; selected official publications.

Museum or gallery collection, archive, or library special collection:
Maps
Selected official publications of United Kingdom (some EU)
KnowUK
DNB
Xrefer
Newsbank
Times Digital 1785–1985
Hampstead and Highgate Express 1980–

Trade and statistical information:
Selected British official statistics, some EU statistics.

Library catalogue:
All or part available online

Access to staff:
Contact by telephone, by e-mail and in person
Hours: Mon 1000 to 1900; Tue, Wed and Fri, 1000 to 1800; Thu, 1000 to 2000; Sat, 1000 to 1700; Sun, 1100 to 1600

Access for disabled people:
Level entry, access to all public areas, toilet facilities

Parent body:
London Borough of Camden, Culture and Enviroment
   Crowndale Centre, 218 Eversholt Street, London, NW1 1BD

SWISS EMBASSY

16–18 Montagu Place, London, W1H 2BQ

Tel: 020 7616 6000
Fax: 020 7724 7001
E-mail: vertretung@lon.rep.admin.ch

Website:
http://www.swissembassy.org.uk

Enquiries:
Enquiries to: Secretary

Subject coverage:
Switzerland: general, commercial, cultural and educational matters.

SWITZERLAND TOURISM

30 Bedford Street, London, WC2E 9ED

Tel: 020 7420 4900
Fax: 00800 100 200 31
E-mail: info.uk@myswitzerland.com

Website:
http://www.myswitzerland.com
Information, reservations and interaction.

Enquiries:
Enquiries to: Marketing Services

Founded:
1875

Organisation type and purpose:
International organisation.

Access to staff:
Contact by letter, by telephone, by fax and by e-mail
Hours: Mon to Fri, 0900 to 1700

Access to building, collection or gallery:
No access other than to staff, prior appointment required

Access for disabled people:
Ramped entry, toilet facilities

SYBIL CAMPBELL COLLECTION

c/o Mr David Farley, University of Winchester, West Hill, Winchester, Hampshire, SO22 4NR

Fax: 01962 827479
E-mail: scl@britishlibrary.net

Website:
http://pages.britishlibrary.net/scl

Founded:
1927
Crosby hall Library

Subject coverage:
Women's writing and history in the nineteenth and twentieth centuries, women's education and their personal libraries, (auto)biography, women in wartime (including refugees), early twentieth century philosophy, literary criticism, poetry and travel.

Museum or gallery collection, archive, or library special collection:
Library of 8,000 items

Non-library collection catalogue:
All or part available online and in-house

Library catalogue:
All or part available online and in-house

Electronic and video publications:
Order electronic and video publications from: Seminar Monographs (online)

Access to staff:
Contact by letter, by telephone, by fax and by e-mail. Appointment necessary.

Parent body:
University of Winchester

Part of:
The British Library

TALIS INFORMATION LIMITED

Knights Court, Solihull Parkway, Birmingham Business Park, B37 7YB

Tel: 0870 400 5000
Fax: 0870 400 5001
E-mail: info@talis.com

Website:
http://www.talis.com
Information, news, web opacs.

Enquiries:
Direct e-mail: press@talis.com

Founded:
1969

Organisation type and purpose:
UK's leading provider of library management systems and also provides solutions to manage academic course resources, digitised image collections, and maintain a unique database containing over 19 million bibliographical records.

Subject coverage:
Library automation, library services, unity web, network services, information delivery services, Talislist – guided learning environment, training and consultancy, Invisage – digital content management, OPAC.

Museum or gallery collection, archive, or library special collection:
BLCMP Database of 17 million bibliographic records
Unityweb

Printed publications:
Product Literature for all products

Electronic and video publications:
Talis library automation system
Talis Invisage
Talis List
Talis Message
OPAC
Acquisitions and cataloguing services
Ztarget
Management Information
Circulation & ILL
Talis Inquire
TalisBase database
EDI Gateway services
Unityweb

Access to staff:
Contact by letter, by telephone, by fax, by e-mail and via website. Appointment necessary.
Hours: Mon to Fri, 0900 to 1700

TALKING NEWSPAPER ASSOCIATION OF THE UNITED KINGDOM

Acronym or abbreviation: TNAUK

National Recording Centre, 10 Browning Road, Heathfield, East Sussex, TN21 8DB

Tel: 01435 866102

Fax: 01435 865422
E-mail: info@tnauk.org.uk

Website:
http://www.tnauk.org.uk

Enquiries:
Enquiries to: Director

Founded:
1974

Organisation type and purpose:
Membership association (membership is by subscription), registered charity (charity number 293656).

Subject coverage:
Recording of over 200 national newspapers and magazines on audio tape, audio CD, Daisy CD's, E-text CD-ROM, Website download and email for visually impaired and disabled people.

Printed publications:
Guide to tape services for the handicapped (£7)
Talking Newspaper News (in-house magazine, quarterly)

Electronic and video publications:
Information tape and disk

Publications list:
Available online and in print

Access to staff:
Contact by letter, by telephone, by fax, by e-mail and in person
Hours: Mon to Fri, 0900 to 1700

Umbrella organisation for:
over 500 local talking newspaper groups who record local newspapers
tel: 01435 866102; fax: 01435 865422; e-mail: info@tnauk.org.uk

TALL SHIPS YOUTH TRUST

Acronym or abbreviation: STA

2A The Hard, Portsmouth, Hampshire, PO1 3PT

Tel: 023 9283 2055
Fax: 023 9281 5769
E-mail: info@tallships.org

Website:
http://www.tallships.org

Enquiries:
Enquiries to: PR & Events Manager
Other contacts: Reservations Supervisor for voyage enquiry.

Founded:
1956

Formerly called:
STA Schooners (year of change 1995); International STA (year of change 1999); Sail Training Association (year of change 2004)

Organisation type and purpose:
Voluntary organisation, registered charity (charity number 314229), training organisation.
The Tall Ships Youth Trust is dedicated to the personal development of young people, aged 16–25, through the experience of tall ship sailing, aboard one of our Brigs, 'Stavros S Niarchos' and 'Prince William'. Similar opportunities are available on adult voyages (18–75). Voyages are available in the UK, Europe, Caribbean, Mediterranean and transatlantic

Subject coverage:
Tall Ships' Voyages and Cutty Sark Tall Ships' Races, personal development of 16 to 25 year olds.
Adult Voyages for 18–75 year olds.
Day Sails for 18–75 year olds.

Trade and statistical information:
World's largest and leading sail training organisation.

Printed publications:
Aloft (3 times a year, free of charge)

Electronic and video publications:
Tall Ships Youth Trust (Video, DVD, available for purchase)

Access to staff:
Contact by letter, by telephone, by fax, by e-mail, in person and via website
Hours: Mon to Fri, 0900 to 1700

Member of:
Association of Sea Training Organisations
Duke of Edinburgh's Award
tel: 01753 727400; fax: 01753 810666; e-mail: info@theaward.org
Royal Yachting Association
tel: 023 8062 7400; website: www.rya.org

TALLOW CHANDLERS' COMPANY, THE

Formal name: Worshipful Company of Tallow Chandlers

4 Dowgate Hill, London, EC4R 2SH

Tel: 020 7248 4726
Fax: 020 7236 0844
E-mail: clark@tallowchandlers.org

Website:
http://www.tallowchandlers.org

Enquiries:
Enquiries to: Clerk

Founded:
1462

Organisation type and purpose:
Membership association.
City of London Livery Company.

Subject coverage:
Tallow and candles, tallow trade, oils and fats

Museum or gallery collection, archive, or library special collection:
Company documents from 1456

Access to staff:
Contact by letter
Hours: Mon to Fri, 0900 to 1700

TALYLLYN RAILWAY

Wharf Station, Tywyn, Gwynedd, LL36 9EY

Tel: 01654 710472
Fax: 01654 711755
E-mail: enquiries@talyllyn.co.uk

Website:
http://www.tallyn.co.uk
Timetables, special events, routes, locomotives.

Enquiries:
Enquiries to: Secretary
Direct e-mail: secretary@talyllyn.co.uk
Other contacts: Managing Director

Founded:
1865

Organisation type and purpose:
Voluntary organisation, museum.
Preservation Society.

Subject coverage:
Narrow gauge railways; Welsh slate industry history; narrow gauge railway modelling; maintenance of narrow gauge railways, steam and diesel. The Talyllyn runs from Tywyn Wharf to Nant Gwernol and was opened in 1865. The Narrow Gauge Railway Museum is at Tywyn.

Museum or gallery collection, archive, or library special collection:
Archives in conjunction with Gwynedd County Council
6 steam locomotives
A large collection of items from British and Irish narrow gauge lines.

Printed publications:
Timetable, guide, handbook, group travel organisers' guide

Microform publications:
16mm film (for hire)

Electronic and video publications:
Videos (for purchase)

Access to staff:
Contact by letter, by telephone, by fax, by e-mail and in person
Hours: Mon to Fri, 0900 to 1700

TAMBA

Formal name: Twins and Multiple Births Association

2 The Willows, Gardner Road, Guildford, Surrey, GU1 4PG

Tel: 0870 770 3305
Fax: 0870 770 3303
E-mail: enquiries@tamba.org.uk

Website:
http://www.tamba.org.uk

Enquiries:
Enquiries to: Administrator

Founded:
1978

Formerly called:
Twins Clubs Association

Organisation type and purpose:
Membership association (membership is by subscription), present number of members: 6000, registered charity (charity number 1076478).

Subject coverage:
Multiple births (two three, four or more) families; professional support for parents and carers; ante-natal and post-natal aspects of management; network of local twin clubs for parents; fertility treatment, bereavements; one parent families; special needs groups; education of twins and higher multiples. Super Twins (for families of triplets or more).

Museum or gallery collection, archive, or library special collection:
Educational references
Medical references to twins and higher multiples

Printed publications:
Ante-Natal booklet: Expecting more than one (£4.50)
Leaflets covering the early years, school and bereavement
Information for professionals
Personal experience leaflets
Twins & Multiple Births: The Essential Parenting Guide from Pregnancy to Adulthood

Electronic and video publications:
DVDs, videos

Publications list:
Available in print

Access to staff:
Contact by letter, by telephone and by fax
Hours: Mon to Fri, 0930 to 1700
Special comments: Out of hours answerphone.

TAMESIDE ARCHIVES SERVICE

Formal name: Tameside Local Studies and Archives

Tameside Local Studies and Archives Centre, Central Library, Old Street, Stalybridge, Ashton-under-Lyne, OL6 7SG

Tel: 0161 342 4242
Fax: 0161 342 4245
E-mail: archives@tameside.gov.uk

Website:
http://www.tameside.gov.uk/history
Brief summary of services offered by Tameside Local Studies Library.

Enquiries:
Enquiries to: Archivist
Other contacts: Local Studies Librarian

continued overleaf

Founded:
1976

Organisation type and purpose:
Local government body.

Subject coverage:
Local public, business, religions, family and regimental records.

Museum or gallery collection, archive, or library special collection:
Manchester Regiment Archives

Non-library collection catalogue:
All or part available in-house

Library catalogue:
All or part available in-house

Printed publications:
Guide to Tameside Archives Service (£12.95, plus £2.20 p&p)
House History (free)
The Manchester Regiment Archive Collection (free)
Family History (free)
Archives for Family History (free)

Access to staff:
Contact by letter, by telephone, by fax, by e-mail, in person and via website
Hours: Mon, Tue, Thu, 0900 to 2000; Wed, Fri, 0900 to 1700; Sat, 0900 to 1600

Access for disabled people:
Disabled access available
Hours: As above

Parent body:
Tameside Borough Council
    Wellington Road, Ashton-under-Lyne

TAMESIDE LIBRARIES INFORMATION SERVICE

Tameside Central Library, Old Street, Ashton-under-Lyne, Lancashire, OL6 7SG

Tel: 0161 342 2031
Fax: 0161 330 4762
E-mail: information.direct@tameside.gov.uk

Website:
http://www.tameside.gov.uk/libraries
Council site with links to library services.

Enquiries:
Enquiries to: Librarian

Organisation type and purpose:
Local government body, public library.

Subject coverage:
General.

Museum or gallery collection, archive, or library special collection:
European Public Information Relay
HMSO publications

Non-library collection catalogue:
All or part available online

Library catalogue:
All or part available online

Access to staff:
Contact by letter, by telephone, by fax, by e-mail and in person
Hours: Mon, Tue, Thu, 0900 to 2000; Wed, Fri, 0900 to 1700; Sat, 0900 to 1600

Parent body:
Tameside Metropolitan Borough Council, Education and Cultural Services

TAMESIDE LOCAL GOVERNMENT INFORMATION SERVICE AND MEMBERS SERVICES

Level B, Council Offices, Wellington Road, Ashton-under-Lyne, Lancashire, OL6 6DL

Tel: 0161 342 8355
Fax: 0161 342 2102
E-mail: tameside-reflib@mcr1.poptel.org.uk

Enquiries:
Enquiries to: Democratic Services Officer
Direct tel: 0161 342 3020

Founded:
1982

Organisation type and purpose:
Local government body.

Subject coverage:
Local government.

Library catalogue:
All or part available in-house

Parent body:
Tameside Metropolitan Borough Council
    Borough Solicitor

TAMESIDE LOCAL STUDIES ARCHIVES CENTRE

Central Library, Old Street, Ashton-under-Lyne, OL6 7SP

Tel: 0161 342 4242
Fax: 0161 342 4245
E-mail: archives@tameside.gov.uk

Website:
http://www.tameside.gov.uk
Brief summary of services offered.

Enquiries:
Enquiries to: Local Studies Librarian
Other contacts: Archivist

Founded:
1976

Organisation type and purpose:
Local government body, public library.

Subject coverage:
Local history and topography of Tameside area, and background material on Lancashire and Cheshire.

Museum or gallery collection, archive, or library special collection:
Manchester Regiment archive collection
Manchester Studies tape collection (oral history interviews recorded c. 1974–1984)

Non-library collection catalogue:
All or part available in-house

Printed publications:
Ashton and Mossley in Archive Photographs (pub Tempus)
Ashton Munitions Explosion (£1.00)
Cotton in Ashton (£1.00)
Denton in Old Photographs (£1.00)
Dukinfield in Old Photographs (£1.00)
Flickering Memories: a history of the cinemas of Ashton (£3)
Folklore of Tameside (£6.99)
General leaflet (2001, free)
Home Front (£3)
Longdendale and Glossopdale in Archive Photographs (£9.99)
Looking Back At Series: books containing a mixture of articles on various aspects of life in the towns including Ashton, Victorian Ashton, Hyde and Stalybridge
Lands and Lordships (volume 6)
The History of Tameside: series of volumes covering the history of the nine towns from earliest times up to World War ll, including:
Tameside Before 1066 (volume 1, £9.95)
Tameside 1066–1700 (volume 2, £9.95)
Tameside in Transition (£9.95)
Tameside 1700–1930 (volume 3, £12.95)
The Buildings of Tameside (volume 5, £13.95)
The People Who Made Tameside (volume 4, £11.95)
Tracing the History of Your House (2001, free)
Tracing Your Family Tree (2001, free)
Victorian Ashton (£1)
Writings of a Nineteenth Century Working Man (£4.50)
Portland Basin (£7.50)

Publications list:
Available in print

Access to staff:
Contact by letter, by telephone, by fax, by e-mail, in person and via website
Hours: Mon, Tue, Thu, 0900 to 2000; Wed, Fri, 0900 to 1700

Part of:
Sustainable Communities
    Community and IT Services, Council Offices, Wellington Road, Ashton-under-Lyne, OL6 6DL

TAMWORTH BOROUGH COUNCIL

Marmion House, Lichfield Street, Tamworth, Staffordshire, B79 7BZ

Tel: 01827 709709
Fax: 01827 709271
E-mail: enquiries@tamworth.gov.uk

Website:
http://www.tamworth.gov.uk

Enquiries:
Enquiries to: Public Relations Officer

Organisation type and purpose:
Local government body.

TANDRIDGE DISTRICT COUNCIL

Station Road East, Oxted, Surrey, RH8 0BT

Tel: 01883 722000
Fax: 01883 722015
E-mail: the.council@tandridge.gov.uk

Website:
http://www.tandridgedc.gov.uk
http://www.tandridge.gov.uk

Enquiries:
Enquiries to: Information Officer

Organisation type and purpose:
Local government body.

Access to staff:
Contact by letter, by telephone, by fax, by e-mail and via website. Appointment necessary.
Hours: Mon to Thu, 0900 to 1700; Fri, 0900 to 1630

Access for disabled people:
Level entry

Parent body:
Surrey County Council

TAUNTON DEANE BOROUGH COUNCIL

The Deane House, Belvedere Road, Taunton, Somerset, TA1 1HE

Tel: 01823 356356\ Minicom no. 01823 356356
Fax: 01823 356329
E-mail: public.relations@tauntondeane.gov.uk

Website:
http://www.tauntondeane.gov.uk/tourism
Tourism, accommodation and local events.

Enquiries:
Enquiries to: Public Relations Manager
Direct tel: 01823 356407

Organisation type and purpose:
Local government body.

Subject coverage:
Local agenda 21 and domestic energy efficiency information for residents of Taunton Deane in addition to normal local authority functions.

Access to staff:
Contact by letter, by telephone, by fax, by e-mail, in person and via website
Hours: Mon to Thu, 0830 to 1730; Fri, 0830 to 1700

Access for disabled people:
Parking provided, level entry, toilet facilities

TAUNTON TOURIST INFORMATION CENTRE

Library, Paul Street, Taunton, Somerset, TA1 3XZ

Tel: 01823 336344
Fax: 01823 340308
E-mail: tauntontic@tauntondeane.gov.uk

Website:
http://www.somerset.gov.uk/libraries

Enquiries:
Enquiries to: Manager

Founded:
1974

Organisation type and purpose:
Local government body.
To provide a wide range of information on the local area and the UK.

Subject coverage:
Tourist information on Taunton and Somerset, holiday information on the whole of the UK, local walks and cycle rides, theatre, gallery and cinema information, local bus and train information. Bookings can be made for National Express coaches, Berrys Coaches, local theatres, local concerts and events, Ticketmaster and YHA membership.

Museum or gallery collection, archive, or library special collection:
Reference books for visitors: hotel and other accommodation, various guides and travel information

Printed publications:
Mini Guide and Heritage Trail (free)
Publications relating to the area – local walks, local cycle trails, maps and books
Taunton Deane Visitor Guide (free)

Electronic and video publications:
Videos of local interest

Access to staff:
Contact by letter, by telephone, by fax, by e-mail, in person and via website
Hours: Mon to Sat, 0930 to 1700; Sun (July and Aug), 1100 to 1500

Access for disabled people:
Access to all public areas

Parent body:
Somerset County Council
Library Headquarters, Mount Street, Bridgewater, Somerset, TA6 3LF; tel: 01278 451201; fax: 01278 452787

TAVISTOCK INSTITUTE OF HUMAN RELATIONS

Acronym or abbreviation: TTI

30 Tabernacle Street, London, EC2A 4UE

Tel: 020 7417 0407
Fax: 020 7417 0566
E-mail: central.admin@tavinstitute.org

Website:
http://www.tavinstitute.org

Enquiries:
Enquiries to: Operations Manager

Founded:
1947

Organisation type and purpose:
Advisory body, registered charity (charity number 209706), training organisation, research organisation.
Independent social science research.

Subject coverage:
Human relations, community care, community organisations, voluntary action, social welfare, employment, vocational training, telematics, action research, group relations training, organisational change and development, evaluation and review.

Printed publications:
Annual Review

Occasional Papers

Publications list:
Available in print

Access to staff:
Contact by letter. Appointment necessary.
Hours: Mon to Fri, 0930 to 1730

Access to building, collection or gallery:
Prior appointment required

Access for disabled people:
Access to all public areas, toilet facilities

TAVISTOCK LIBRARY

Tavistock Centre, 120 Belsize Lane, London, NW3 5BA

Tel: 020 7435 7111
Fax: 020 7447 3734
E-mail: adouglas@tavi-port.org

Website:
http://www.tavi-port.org

Enquiries:
Enquiries to: Librarian
Direct tel: 020 7447 3868

Founded:
1947

Organisation type and purpose:
Training organisation.
NHS Trust Library.

Subject coverage:
Psychoanalysis, psychotherapy, psychology, psychiatry, human relations, marital studies, social work and social welfare.

Non-library collection catalogue:
All or part available online

Library catalogue:
All or part available online

Access to staff:
Contact by telephone, by fax, by e-mail and via website. Appointment necessary. Non-members charged.
Hours: Mon to Thu, 0930 to 1930; Fri, 1030 to 1730
Special comments: Limited access for non-members in term time.

Access for disabled people:
Parking provided, level entry, access to all public areas, toilet facilities

Parent body:
Tavistock and Portman NHS Trust
tel: 020 7435 7111

TAVISTOCK SUBSCRIPTION LIBRARY

Court Gate, Guildhall Square, Tavistock, Devon, PL19 0AE

Tel: 01822 612352
E-mail: jackwalkerstar@aol.com

Enquiries:
Enquiries to: Honorary Secretary

Founded:
1799

Organisation type and purpose:
Membership association (membership is by subscription, election or invitation), historic building, house or site.
Independent library.

Subject coverage:
Tavistock (Devon) local books and information.

Museum or gallery collection, archive, or library special collection:
Tavistock and District

Library catalogue:
All or part available in-house and in print

Printed publications:
Various publications available for purchase

Publications list:
Available in print

Access to staff:
Contact by letter, by telephone and by e-mail. Appointment necessary.
Hours: Mon to Fri, 0900 to 1700

Access to building, collection or gallery:
Prior appointment required

Access for disabled people:
Level entry

Also at:
Honorary Secretary, Tavistock Subscription Library
9 Manor Road, Tavistock, Devon, PL19 0PL; tel: 01822 612352; e-mail: jackwalkerstar@aol.com

Member organisation of:
Independent Library Association

TAXBRIEFS LIMITED

2–5 Benjamin Street, London, EC1M 5QL

Tel: 020 7250 0967
Fax: 020 7251 8867
E-mail: info@taxbriefs.co.uk

Website:
http://www.taxbriefs.co.uk
Details of products, conferences, hot tips and a full listing of publications.

Enquiries:
Enquiries to: Director

Founded:
1975

Organisation type and purpose:
Publishing house.

Subject coverage:
Finance information on pensions, life assurance, taxation.

Library catalogue:
All or part available online and in print

Printed publications:
AFPC Case Studies for G10, G20, G30, G60 and H15
AFPC Manuals for G10, G20, G30, G60, G70 and H25
Financial Timesaver
FP3 Case Study Workbook
Life Assurance and Pensions Handbook
Professional Adviser's Factfile
Report Planner Manual
Stakeholder and Personal Pensions Workbook
The Facts of Life and Health Insurance
The Basic Principles of Tax

Electronic and video publications:
Report Planner (CD-ROM to accompany manual)

Publications list:
Available online and in print

Access to staff:
Contact by letter, by telephone, by fax, by e-mail and via website
Hours: Mon to Fri, 0900 to 1730

Access to building, collection or gallery:
Prior appointment required

TAY VALLEY FAMILY HISTORY SOCIETY

Acronym or abbreviation: TVFHS

Family History Research Centre, 179–181 Princes Street, Dundee, DD4 6DQ

Tel: 01382 461845
Fax: 01382 455532
E-mail: tvfhs@tayvalleyfhs.org.uk

Website:
http://www.tayvalleyfhs.org.uk

Enquiries:
Enquiries to: Honorary Secretary

continued overleaf

Organisation type and purpose:
Membership association (membership is by subscription), present number of members: 2,000, registered charity.

Subject coverage:
Family histories, pedigrees, research interests of members, unpublished birth, marriage and death information, census information 1841–91 and collection of monumental inscriptions, all in the counties of Angus, Fife, Kinross and Perth.

Museum or gallery collection, archive, or library special collection:
Extensive collection of family history materials for the counties of Angus, Fife, Kinross and Perth

Library catalogue:
All or part available online

Printed publications:
Books to help family historians in the counties of Angus, Fife, Kinross and Perth
Census Name Indexes 1851 for Angus, Fife, Kinross and Perth
Journal (3 times a year)
Monumental Inscriptions of Local Cemeteries

Microform publications:
Census Indexes: 1841 Dundee and Angus; 1851 Kinross; 1851 parts of Fife (microfiche)

Publications list:
Available in print

Access to staff:
Contact by letter, by telephone, by e-mail, in person and via website. Non-members charged.

Access to building, collection or gallery:
Hours: Mon, Tue, Wed, Fri, 1000 to 1600; Sat, 1000 to 1300; Thu, 1000 to 1600 and 1900 to 2100
Special comments: Charge £2 per hour for non-members.

Access for disabled people:
Level entry, toilet facilities

TAYLOR INSTITUTION LIBRARY

University of Oxford, St Giles', Oxford, OX1 3NA

Tel: 01865 278158
Fax: 01865 278165
E-mail: enquiries@taylib.ox.ac.uk

Website:
http://www.taylib.ox.ac.uk
Access hours etc.

Enquiries:
Enquiries to: Information Officer
Direct tel: 01865 278162
Direct e-mail: liz.baird@taylib.ox.ac.uk

Founded:
1848

Organisation type and purpose:
University department or institute. The Taylor Institution is Oxford University's centre for the teaching of modern European languages. The building houses two libraries (both under the same management): the Taylor Institution (Main) Library, used mainly by post-graduate/academic researchers; and the Taylor Institution Modern Languages Faculty Library, used mainly by undergraduates. The Taylor Bodleian Slavonic and Modern Greek Library is housed nearby (47 Wellington Square).

Subject coverage:
Medieval and modern continental European (and related) languages and literature, predominantly Spanish and Portuguese, German, French, and Italian; included are those of modern Latin America, the literature of Canada, and North and sub-Saharan Africa; also Linguistics; film studies; Celtic; and Dutch, Yiddish, and Afrikaans. Also, at 47 Wellington Square, Russian and other Slavonic (and related) languages, and modern Greek, languages and literature.

Museum or gallery collection, archive, or library special collection:
Butler Clarke Collection (Spanish books)
Dante Collection (Italian)
Dawkins Collection (Byzantine and modern Greek books)
Fiedler Collection of German literary, philological and historical works
Finch Collection of literary and linguistic works printed in the 16th, 17th and 18th centuries (Italian and other)
Martin Collection (Spanish and Portuguese books)
Nevill Forbes and W R Morfill Collections of Slavonic books
Rudler Collection of French books (particularly Benjamin Constant items and early 20th century French writers)
Besterman Voltaire Bequest: collection of works relating to Voltaire and the French Enlightenment with a world locational index of 18th century editions of Voltaire
Whitechapel and Schweizer Collections of Yiddish Literature
Collection of European writers' letters and manuscripts
Strachan Collection of French 19th-century 'livres d'artiste'

Non-library collection catalogue:
All or part available online and in print

Library catalogue:
All or part available online

Printed publications:
Catalogues of some of the special collections

Access to staff:
Contact by letter, by fax, by e-mail and via website. Appointment necessary. Letter of introduction required.
Hours: See website for details www.taylib.ox.ac.uk

Access to building, collection or gallery:
Visitors are advised to check the library's website beforehand for times of access.

Parent body:
University of Oxford

Taylor Bodleian Slavonic and Modern Greek Library is housed at:
Bodleian Slavonic and Modern Greek Library, University of Oxford
47 Wellington Square, Oxford, OX1 2JF; tel: 01865 270464; fax: 01865 270469; e-mail: enquiries@taslib.ox.ac.uk

TAYLOR NELSON SOFRES PLC

Westgate, London, W5 1UA

Tel: 020 8967 0007
E-mail: enquiries@tnsofres.com

Website:
http://www.tnsofres.com

Enquiries:
Enquiries to: Director of Social and Political Research
Direct tel: 020 8332 8551
Direct fax: 020 8332 1090

Organisation type and purpose:
Service industry, research organisation.
Engaged in all forms of social and commercial survey research.

Subject coverage:
Marketing information – continuous and custom research in over 80 countries. Specialist expertise in IT, telecoms, healthcare, automotive, TV, media, internet, consumer.

Access to staff:
Contact by letter, by telephone, by e-mail and via website
Hours: Mon to Fri, 0900 to 1730

Access to building, collection or gallery:
No access other than to staff

Member of:
BMRA
Gallup International Association

MRS

Parent body:
SOFRES

TEACHER SCIENTIST NETWORK

Acronym or abbreviation: TSN

John Innes Centre, Norwich Research Park, Colney, Norwich, Norfolk, NR4 7UH

Tel: 01603 450000
Fax: 01603 450015
E-mail: ts.network@bbsrc.ac.uk

Website:
http://www.tsn.org.uk

Enquiries:
Enquiries to: Co-ordinator

Founded:
1994

Organisation type and purpose:
Membership association (membership is by qualification), present number of members: 250, suitable for ages: 5–18.
Collaboration between teachers of science and professional scientists in the Norfolk area, to enhance science in schools.

Subject coverage:
Science education (from 5 to 18 years), networking teachers of science and professional scientists.

Printed publications:
Newsletter (periodic)
Occasional papers

Publications list:
Available online

Access to staff:
Contact by letter, by telephone, by fax, by e-mail and via website. Appointment necessary.
Hours: Mon to Fri, 0900 to 1700

TEARFUND

100 Church Road, Teddington, Middlesex, TW11 8QE

Tel: 020 8977 9144
Fax: 020 8943 3594
E-mail: enquiry@tearfund.org

Website:
http://www.tearfund.org

Enquiries:
Enquiries to: Supporter Enquiries Team

Founded:
1968

Organisation type and purpose:
International organisation, registered charity (charity number 265464).
Relief and development charity.

Subject coverage:
Development, overseas aid, evangelical church.

Library catalogue:
All or part available in-house

Printed publications:
Tearfund produce a range of titles under the following headings:
Books and booklets
Leaflets and magazines
Resource packs
Youth and young people

Electronic and video publications:
Videos, CDs, DVDs and audio cassettes

Publications list:
Available in print

Access to staff:
Contact by letter, by telephone, by e-mail and via website
Hours: Mon to Fri, 0900 to 1700

Other addresses:
Tearfund Ireland
23 University Street, Belfast, BT7 1FY; tel: 028
9032 4940; fax: 028 9023 6930
Tearfund Scotland
Challenge House, 29 Canal Street, Glasgow, G4
0AD; tel: 0141 332 3621; fax: 0141 400 2980

TECHGNOSIS

PO Box 154, Manchester, M20 3AL

Tel: 0161 445 9757
Fax: 0161 434 2913

Website:
http://www.techgnosis-uk.com
Guides to e-commerce, IT security products and
services; IT market databases

Enquiries:
Enquiries to: Director

Founded:
1988

Organisation type and purpose:
Publishing house, research organisation.
IT information provider.

Subject coverage:
Information technology; computing; computer
security; software development;
telecommunications; office automation, IT end-
user profiles; e-commerce.

Electronic and video publications:
Computer Services Index
Guide to Electronic Commerce Products and
Services
Guide to IT Security Products and Services
The National Computer Index

Publications list:
Available in print

Access to staff:
Contact by letter, by telephone and by fax.
Appointment necessary. All charged.
Hours: Mon to Fri, 0900 to 1700

TECHNICAL HELP TO EXPORTERS

Acronym or abbreviation: THE

British Standards Institution, 389 Chiswick High
Road, London, W4 4AL

Tel: 020 8996 7474
Fax: 020 8996 7048
E-mail: the@bsi-global.com

Website:
http://www.bsi.org.uk

Enquiries:
Enquiries to: Business Development Manager

Organisation type and purpose:
Training organisation, consultancy, research
organisation, publishing house.

Subject coverage:
Overseas technical laws, regulations, standards
and certification requirements; interpretation and
translation of overseas technical requirements;
assistance with technical problems and research
projects; assistance in obtaining test certificates or
approval for products in overseas markets; UK
testing and inspection of goods for export.

**Museum or gallery collection, archive, or library
special collection:**
Library of over 500,000 foreign laws, regulations,
national and non-national standards (BSI library)

Printed publications:
Range of technical publications on engineering
(Europe and International), pressure vessels,
electronic products and general subjects

Electronic and video publications:
BSI Standards Electronic Catalogue (CD-ROM)

PERINORM (database of standards and
regulations, PERINORM Europe and
PERINORM International, CD-ROM)

Access to staff:
Contact by letter, by telephone, by fax and by e-
mail. All charged.
Hours: Mon to Fri 0900 to 1700

TECHNOLOGY INNOVATION CENTRE, THE

Acronym or abbreviation: tiC

Millennium Point, Curzon Street, Birmingham, B4
7XG

Tel: 0121 331 5400
Fax: 0121 331 5401
E-mail: enquiries@tic.ac.uk

Website:
http://www.tic.ac.uk/learningcentre
Links to catalogue, workshops and learning
resources provided.
http://www.tic-online.com/shortcourses
Details the part-time and evening only courses
offered.

Enquiries:
Enquiries to: Librarian
Direct tel: 0121 202 2500
Direct e-mail: james.dean@tic.ac.uk

Founded:
2000

Organisation type and purpose:
International organisation, professional body,
suitable for ages: 18+, training organisation,
consultancy, research organisation.

Subject coverage:
Manufacturing, mechanical engineering,
operations management, computer technology,
electronics and communication engineering,
automotive engineering.

Non-library collection catalogue:
All or part available online

Library catalogue:
All or part available online

Access to staff:
Contact by letter, by telephone, by fax, by e-mail,
in person and via website. Appointment necessary.
Hours: Mon to Fri, 0830 to 1900; Sat, Sun, 1000 to
1600

Access for disabled people:
Access to all public areas, toilet facilities

Parent body:
University of Central England (UCE)
Perry Barr, Birmingham, B42 2BU; tel: 0121 331
5000

TEESSIDE ARCHIVES

Exchange House, 6 Marton Road, Middlesbrough,
Cleveland, TS1 1DB

Tel: 01642 248321
Fax: 01642 248391
E-mail: teesside_archives@middlesbrough.gov.uk

Enquiries:
Enquiries to: Archivist

Founded:
1974

Organisation type and purpose:
Local government body.

Subject coverage:
Archives relating to Middlesbrough, Hartlepool,
Stockton on Tees and Redcar and Cleveland
Boroughs (formerly Cleveland County).

Access to staff:
Contact by letter, by telephone, by fax and by e-
mail. Appointment necessary.

Hours: Mon, Wed, Thu, 0900 to 1700; Tue, 0900 to
2100; Fri, 0900 to 1630

Access for disabled people:
Access to all public areas, toilet facilities

TEESWATER SHEEP BREEDERS ASSOCIATION

Wodencroft, Cotherstone, Barnard Castle, Co
Durham, DL12 9UQ

Tel: 01833 650032
Fax: 01833 650909
E-mail: wodencroft@freenet.co.uk

Enquiries:
Enquiries to: Secretary

Founded:
1949

Organisation type and purpose:
Membership association (membership is by
subscription).

Subject coverage:
Teeswater sheep.

TELECOMMUNICATIONS USERS' ASSOCIATION

Acronym or abbreviation: TUA

Woodgate Studios, 2–8 Games Road, Barnet,
Hertfordshire, EN4 9HN

Tel: 020 8449 8844
Fax: 020 8447 4901
E-mail: tua@dial.pipex.com

Website:
http://www.tua.co.uk

Enquiries:
Enquiries to: Chairman

Founded:
1964

Organisation type and purpose:
Independent membership association
(membership is by subscription), service industry,
training organisation, consultancy, research
organisation. Provides information and services to
members whilst promoting open competition
worldwide.

Subject coverage:
Telecommunications and related industries; open
telecommunications environment; to lobby and
monitor quality of service; consultancy service to
members.

Printed publications:
Factline via FAX broadcast (monthly)
Infocus (newsletter, 4 times a year)
Specialist Research Reports
Telecommunications Users' Association (2 times a
year)
TUA Calling Card

Electronic and video publications:
Factline via FAX broadcast (monthly, available as
electronic delivery e-factline, PDF format)

Access to staff:
Contact by letter, by telephone, by fax, by e-mail
and via website. Access for members only.
Hours: Mon to Fri, 0900 to 1700

TELEPHONE PREFERENCE SERVICE

Acronym or abbreviation: TPS

DMA House, 70 Margaret Street, London, W1W
8SS

Tel: 020 7291 3320
Fax: 020 7323 4226
E-mail: tps@dma.org.uk

Website:
http://www.tpsonline.org.uk

continued overleaf

http://www.dma.org.uk

Enquiries:
Enquiries to: Administrator

Founded:
1995

Organisation type and purpose:
Self-regulatory body.
Provide individuals with the opportunity to register not to receive direct marketing telephone calls.

Subject coverage:
Restriction on unsolicited sales and marketing telephone calls to individuals.

Printed publications:
Consumer leaflet and application form
Industry subscriber pack

Electronic and video publications:
TPS file (download from web-site, diskette or electronic transfer, CD-ROM)

Access to staff:
Contact by letter, by telephone, by fax, by e-mail and via website. Appointment necessary.
Hours: Mon to Fri, 0900 to 1700
Special comments: Charges made to all subscribers (companies making telephone calls).

Affiliated to:
Direct Marketing Association (DMA)
tel: 020 7291 3300; fax: 020 7523 4226; e-mail: dma@dma.org.uk
OFTEL
tel: 020 7434 8700; fax: 020 7434 8893

TELEPHONES FOR THE BLIND FUND

7 Huntersfield Close, Reigate, Surrey, RH2 0DX

Tel: 01737 248032
Fax: 01737 248032

Website:
http://www.tftb.org.uk

Enquiries:
Enquiries to: Hon Secretary

Founded:
1967

Organisation type and purpose:
Voluntary organisation (charity number 255155).

Subject coverage:
Grants towards the provision of telephones for registered blind people. Referrals must be made through Social Services.

Access to staff:
Contact by letter, by telephone and by fax
Hours: Mon to Fri, 1000 to 1600
Special comments: No access to premises allowed.

TELEVISION TRUST FOR THE ENVIRONMENT

Acronym or abbreviation: TVE

21 Elizabeth Street, London, SW1W 9RP

Tel: 020 7901 8855
Fax: 020 7901 8856
E-mail: tve@tve.org.uk

Website:
http://www.tve.org
Information on TVE and publications, list of films available through TVE.

Enquiries:
Enquiries to: Distribution Manager
Direct tel: 020 7901 8834
Direct e-mail: distribution@tve.org.uk

Founded:
1984

Organisation type and purpose:
International organisation, registered charity.

Film, video and television producer and distributor.
To inform and educate on environmental, health, human rights and developmental issues.

Subject coverage:
Environment, health, development, human rights, women's issues.

Non-library collection catalogue:
All or part available online

Printed publications:
Specialist subject bulletins on varying issues produced irregularly. To receive copies contact Distribution Manager

Electronic and video publications:
A large number of videos for purchase by broadcasters, non-governmental organisations, government organisations, educational institutions, community, women's groups etc

Publications list:
Available in print

Access to staff:
Contact by letter, by telephone, by fax, by e-mail and via website. Appointment necessary.
Hours: Mon to Fri, 0930 to 1800

Access to building, collection or gallery:
No access other than to staff

Access for disabled people:
No wheelchair access – premises on first floor with narrow stairs.

Affiliated to:
United Nations Environment Programme
WWF UK

Has connections with:
57 other organisations throughout the world

TELFORD LIBRARY

St Quentin Gate, Telford, Shropshire, TF3 4JG

Tel: 01952 382918
Fax: 01952 382937
E-mail: telford.library@telford.gov.uk

Website:
http://library.telford.gov.uk

Enquiries:
Enquiries to: Librarian

Organisation type and purpose:
Public library.

Library catalogue:
All or part available online and in-house

Access to staff:
Contact by letter, by telephone, by fax, by e-mail and in person
Hours: Mon 1000 to 1800; Tue, Wed, Fri, 0930 to 1800; Thu 0930 to 2000; Sat 0930 to 1700

Access for disabled people:
Level entry, access to all public areas, toilet facilities

Parent body:
Telford & Wrekin Council

TEMPLETON COLLEGE

Kennington, Oxford, OX1 5NY

Tel: 01865 422500
Fax: 01865 422501
E-mail: infocent@templeton.ox.ac.uk

Website:
http://www.templeton.ox.ac.uk

Enquiries:
Enquiries to: Information Centre Manager

Founded:
1965

Organisation type and purpose:
Management studies college.

Subject coverage:
Management studies in general; retailing (Oxford Centre of Retail Management); employee relations; information management; food and drink industry; human resource management; industrial relations.

Printed publications:
See website for publications

Publications list:
Available online

Access to staff:
Contact by letter, by telephone and by e-mail
Hours: Mon to Fri, 0830 to 1700

Access to building, collection or gallery:
Prior appointment required
Special comments: Restricted, please ring for information.

Access for disabled people:
Parking provided, ramped entry

Member of:
British Business Schools Librarians Group
European Business Schools Librarians Group

TENANT FARMERS ASSOCIATION

Acronym or abbreviation: TFA

5 Brewery Court, Theale, Reading, Berkshire, RG7 5AJ

Tel: 0118 930 6130
Fax: 0118 930 3424
E-mail: tfa@tfa.org.uk

Website:
http://www.tfa.org.uk

Enquiries:
Enquiries to: Events and Communications Co-ordinator
Other contacts: Membership Co-ordinator

Founded:
1981

Organisation type and purpose:
Trade association (membership is by subscription), present number of members: 4,000.
Provides advice, information and a strong lobby for British tenant farmers.

Subject coverage:
Agricultural tenancies, agricultural policy, tenant farming, landlord/tenant affairs in rural areas.

Trade and statistical information:
Agricultural rent databank (available to tenants only).

Printed publications:
TFA News (6 times a year, members only)
Briefing Notes (weekly, members only)
Guidance Notes (as required, members only)

Access to staff:
Contact by letter, by telephone, by fax, by e-mail and via website. Appointment necessary.
Hours: Mon to Fri, 0900 to 1700
Special comments: Full benefits only available to members.

Access to building, collection or gallery:
No prior appointment required

TENDRING DISTRICT COUNCIL

Town Hall, Station Road, Clacton-on-Sea, Essex, CO15 1SE

Tel: 01255 425501
Fax: 01255 253139
E-mail: Email form on website

Website:
http://www.tendringdc.gov.uk

Enquiries:
Enquiries to: Chief Executive

Organisation type and purpose:
Local government body.

Printed publications:
Civic Newspaper (quarterly)
Annual Report
Citizens Guide

Access to staff:
Contact by letter, by telephone, by fax, by e-mail, in person and via website
Hours: Mon to Fri, 0900 to 1700

Access for disabled people:
Ramped entry, toilet facilities

TENNIS AND RACKETS ASSOCIATION, THE

Acronym or abbreviation: The T&RA

c/o The Queens Club, Palliser Road, West Kensington, London, W14 9EQ

Tel: 020 7386 3447/8
Fax: 020 7385 7424
E-mail: ceo@tennis-rackets.net

Website:
http://www.real-tennis.com

Enquiries:
Enquiries to: Chief Executive

Founded:
1907

Organisation type and purpose:
Membership association (membership is by subscription), present number of members: 2450, suitable for ages: all.
Governing body of the sports of real tennis and rackets.
To administer and control the games of Tennis (Real Tennis) and Rackets.

Subject coverage:
Real tennis and Rackets (not to be confused with lawn tennis and squash rackets); rules; location of courts; history of the games, championships, sponsorship, development, membership, publicity, fixtures, international liaison.

Printed publications:
Annual and Spring Reports
Historical records back to 18th century

Access to staff:
Contact by letter, by fax and by e-mail.
Appointment necessary.
Hours: Mon to Fri, 0900 to 1700

Member of:
CCPR
Sport England

TENNYSON RESEARCH CENTRE

Central Library, Free School Lane, Lincoln, LN2 1EZ

Tel: 01522 510800
Fax: 01522 575011
E-mail: grace.timmins@lincolnshire.gov.uk

Website:
http://www.lincolnshire.gov.uk

Enquiries:
Enquiries to: Librarian

Founded:
1964

Organisation type and purpose:
Research organisation.
Research unit.

Subject coverage:
Life and work of Alfred, Lord Tennyson.

Museum or gallery collection, archive, or library special collection:
Tennyson Collection: includes family libraries, 9,000 letters, manuscripts of the poet's work, family papers, illustrations, proofs, biographical and critical material, including

Family Libraries: Some 350 volumes from the library of Tennyson's father, George Clayton Tennyson, giving an indication of the books Tennyson would have used as a child, when taught by his father. Approximately 2000 books from Tennyson's own library, reflecting his many interests and often annotated by the poet.
Family Papers: Family diaries and notebooks including a journal kept by Tennyson's wife, Emily; household books and publishers accounts.
Illustrations: Portraits and other illustrative material on Tennyson, his family, contemporaries and places associated with them, including a number of photographs by Julia Margaret Cameron.
Letters to and from Tennyson and other members of the family. Several thousand letters from eminent Victorians including Browning, Gladstone, Lear and Fitzgerald
Manuscripts: The most complete autograph manuscript of In Memoriam
Plays: Queen Mary, Harold, Becket, The Foresters and an acting copy of The Cup.
Proofs: Approximately 200 proofs of Tennyson's poetry, a number being significantly corrected in the poet's hand
Biography and Criticism: A comprehensive collection of books and articles, both contemporary and modern, dealing with his life and works
Tennyson's works: An almost complete set of first and other important editions of poetry
Usher Gallery: A display of personalia from the Tennyson Research Centre Collection can be seen in the Tennyson Room at the Usher Gallery, Lindum Road, Lincoln. Items displayed include Tennyson's coat and hat, family photographs, cartoons etc.

Non-library collection catalogue:
All or part available in-house and in print

Printed publications:
Monographs and occasional papers (Tennyson Society)
Tennyson in Lincoln, vols 1 and 2 (Tennyson Society)
Tennyson Research Bulletin (Tennyson Society, annually)

Access to staff:
Contact by letter, by telephone, by fax and by e-mail. Appointment necessary.
Hours: Mon to Fri, 0930 to 1700

Access for disabled people:
Ramped entry, toilet facilities

Parent body:
Lincolnshire County Council
County Offices, Newland, Lincoln, LN1 1YL; tel: 01522 553207; fax: 01522 552811; e-mail: library .support@lincolnshire.gov.uk

TENOVUS, THE CANCER CHARITY

43 The Parade, Cardiff, CF24 3AB

Tel: 029 2048 2000
Fax: 029 2048 4199
E-mail: post@tenovus.com

Website:
http://www.tenovus.com

Enquiries:
Enquiries to: Public Relations Manager

Founded:
1943

Organisation type and purpose:
Registered charity (charity number 1054015).

Subject coverage:
Cancer research and patient care.

Museum or gallery collection, archive, or library special collection:
Library holds information on over 200 cancers and support organisations

Trade and statistical information:
Data on cancer in the UK and in Europe.

Printed publications:
Publications free of charge

Publications list:
Available online and in print

Access to staff:
Contact by letter, by telephone, by fax and by e-mail
Hours: Mon to Fri, 0900 to 1700

Access for disabled people:
Parking provided, level entry, toilet facilities

TERRENCE HIGGINS TRUST

Acronym or abbreviation: THT

314–320 Gray's Inn Road, London, WC1X 8DP

Tel: 020 7812 1600; helpline: 0845 122 1200
Fax: 020 7812 1601
E-mail: info@tht.org.uk

Website:
http://www.tht.org.uk

Enquiries:
Enquiries to: Information Officer

Founded:
1982

Organisation type and purpose:
Registered charity, voluntary organisation (charity number 288527).

Subject coverage:
HIV and AIDS, sexual health

Printed publications:
A range of leaflets on HIV and Sexual Health, Gay and Lesbian information
Printed products available from Information Department (single copies are free, bulk copies for purchase)

Publications list:
Available online and in print

Access to staff:
Contact by letter, by telephone, by fax, by e-mail, in person and via website
Hours: Mon to Fri, 0930 to 1730

TETRONICS LIMITED

A2 Marston Gate, Stirling Road, South Marston Business Park, Swindon, Wiltshire, SN3 4DE

Tel: 01793 238 500
Fax: 01793 832 533
E-mail: info@tetronics.com

Website:
http://www.tetronics.com

Enquiries:
Enquiries to: Marketing Manager

Founded:
1964

Organisation type and purpose:
Manufacturing industry.
Research and development organistion.

Subject coverage:
Plasma equipment and furnaces, nanopowders, metal melting and heating, new waste treatment processes, melting of incineration ashes, treatment of steel works dusts and hazardous wastes, refractory metal melting.

Access to staff:
Contact by letter, by telephone, by fax and by e-mail
Hours: Mon to Fri, 0900 to 1700

TEXTILE INSTITUTE

Formal name: The Textile Institute

continued overleaf

International Headquarters, 1st Floor, St James's Building, Oxford Street, Manchester, M1 6FQ

Tel: 0161 237 1188
Fax: 0161 236 1991
E-mail: tiihq@textileinst.org.uk

Website:
http://www.textileinstitute.org

Enquiries:
Enquiries to: Professional Affairs Administrator
Direct e-mail: escott@textileinst.org.uk

Founded:
1910

Organisation type and purpose:
Professional body.

Subject coverage:
Textiles worldwide; textile technology; floorcovering; clothing; industrial textiles; knitting; weaving; design and marketing; finishing, fibre science, footwear.

Non-library collection catalogue:
All or part available in-house

Library catalogue:
All or part available in-house

Printed publications:
International Textile Calendar (12 times a year)
Journal of the Textile Institute (quarterly)
Textile Progress (quarterly)
Textile Terms and Definitions
Textiles (quarterly)

Publications list:
Available in print

Access to staff:
Contact by letter, by telephone, by fax, by e-mail and via website. Appointment necessary. All charged.
Hours: Mon to Fri, 0900 to 1700

Access to building, collection or gallery:
Prior appointment required

TEXTILE SERVICES ASSOCIATION

Acronym or abbreviation: TSA

Unit 7, Churchill Court, 58 Station Road, North Harrow, Middlesex, HA2 7SA

Tel: 020 8863 7755
Fax: 020 8861 2115
E-mail: tsa@tsa-uk.org

Enquiries:
Enquiries to: Chief Executive

Founded:
1886

Organisation type and purpose:
Trade association (membership is by subscription), present number of members: 600.

Subject coverage:
Developments within the dry-cleaning, laundry and textile rental industry, national and EC legislation affecting the industry e.g. health and safety, workwear etc. NVQs in the textile rental industry.

Printed publications:
A Guide to Workwear Rental (free)
Annual Report and Accounts
Bulletin (monthly, for members)
Career Choices – The Textile Care Industry (careers leaflet, free)
Educational Publications Leaflet for the Laundry and Dry Cleaning Industry (members only)
Fabric and Garment Care
Godly Adjunct (history of the association)
Health, Safety & Environment Management Guidelines
Suede and Leather Care and Cleaning
TSA Code of Practice Booklet
TSA Membership Handbook (members only)
What Your Drycleaner Can Do For You (leaflet for dry cleaning customers, free)

Publications list:
Available in print

Access to staff:
Contact by letter, by telephone, by fax, by e-mail and via website. Non-members charged.
Hours: Mon to Fri, 0900 to 1800

Affiliated to:
International Committee for Textile Care (CINET)

Works closely with:
Guild of Cleaners and Launderers
  Cheshire; tel: 0161 483 4655
SATRA
  Kettering, Northamptonshire; tel: 01536 410000

TFPL LIMITED

Acronym or abbreviation: TFPL

160 Queen Victoria Street, 2nd Floor, London, EC4V 4BF

Tel: 020 7332 6000
Fax: 0870 333 7131

Website:
http://www.tfpl.com
Information about TFPL, job vacancies, training courses, news, knowledge management, Intranets, records management and conferences.

Enquiries:
Enquiries to: Managing Director
Direct e-mail: nicky.smith@tfpl.com

Founded:
1987

Organisation type and purpose:
Service industry, training organisation, consultancy, research organisation, publishing house.
Recruitment and the provision of temporary and contract information staff.
To provide specialist services to the global information market.

Subject coverage:
Employment trends and opportunities for information specialists, training courses and seminars, recruitment, consultancy, European Information World and market research, seminars and conferences.

Printed publications:
Intranet Management: A TFPL Guide to Best Practice
Skills for Knowledge Management
Who's Who in the European Information World (annually)
Who's Who in the UK Information World (annually)

Publications list:
Available in print

Access to staff:
Contact by letter, by telephone, by fax, by e-mail, in person and via website
Hours: Mon to Fri, 0800 to 1800

THAI EMBASSY

Formal name: Royal Thai Embassy

29–30 Queen's Gate, London, SW7 5JB

Tel: 020 7589 2944
Fax: 020 7823 9695
E-mail: thaiduto@btinternet.com

Website:
http://www.thaiembassyuk.org.uk

Enquiries:
Enquiries to: Information Officer
Direct tel: 020 7225 5520
Direct e-mail: thaiembassy.pr@btconnect.com

Organisation type and purpose:
Embassy.

Subject coverage:
Thailand: government, history, culture, society, economy, arts, language, religion, travel.

Museum or gallery collection, archive, or library special collection:
The Embassy's collection is small and mostly in Thai language, though there are a few useful reference books in English

Trade and statistical information:
Contact the Office of Commercial Affairs.

Access to staff:
Contact by letter, by telephone, by fax and by e-mail. Appointment necessary.
Hours: Mon to Fri, 0930 to 1230 and 1400 to 1700
Special comments: Closed on Thai holidays and UK public holidays.

Access to building, collection or gallery:
No prior appointment required

Access for disabled people:
Toilet facilities

Also at:
Office of Commercial Affairs
11 Hertford Street, Mayfair, London, W1Y 7DX; tel: 020 7493 5749; fax: 020 7493 7416; e-mail: thaicomuk@dial.pipex.com; website: http://www.thaitrade.com
Office of Economics and Financial Affairs
3rd Floor, 29–30 Queen's Gate, London, SW7 5JB; tel: 020 7589 7266; fax: 020 7589 2624
Office of Educational Affairs
28 Prince's Gate, London, SW7 1QF; tel: 020 7584 4538; fax: 020 7823 9896; e-mail: info@oealondon.com

THAMES ROWING COUNCIL – LOWER RIVER

Acronym or abbreviation: TRC

45 Sterne Street, London, W12 8AB

Tel: 020 8743 8596

Enquiries:
Enquiries to: Honorary Secretary

Organisation type and purpose:
Membership association (membership is by qualification), voluntary organisation.
Co-ordinating sports body.
To encourage participation in the sport of rowing.

Subject coverage:
Rowing river users, the river Thames.

Access to staff:
Contact by letter
Hours: Mon to Fri, 0900 to 1700

Parent body:
Amateur Rowing Association

THAMES VALLEY CHAMBER OF COMMERCE AND INDUSTRY

Commerce House, 2–6 Bath Road, Slough, Berkshire, SL1 3SB

Tel: 01753 870518
Fax: 01753 524644
E-mail: enquiries@thamesvalleychamber.co.uk

Website:
http://www.thamesvalleychamber.co.uk
General information on products/services, events diary, training course diary.
http://www.euro-info.org.uk
European information centres national site.

Enquiries:
Enquiries to: Information Officer
Direct tel: 01753 870530

Founded:
1927

Organisation type and purpose:
Membership association.
Chamber of Commerce.

Subject coverage:
Business, local and European Information Centre.

Printed publications:
Business Voice (6 times a year)
Europe Matters (6 times a year)

Access to staff:
Contact by letter, by telephone, by fax, by e-mail and via website. Appointment necessary.
Hours: Mon to Thu, 0900 to 1700; Fri, 0900 to 1500
Special comments: Charges for some services.

Hosts:
Thames Valley European Information Centre at the same address

THAMES VALLEY UNIVERSITY

Acronym or abbreviation: TVU

St Mary's Road, London, W5 5RF

Tel: 020 8579 5000

Website:
http://www.tvu.ac.uk
Information about Thames Valley University.

Enquiries:
Enquiries to: Head of Learning and Research Support
Direct tel: 020 8231 2678
Direct fax: 020 8231 2402
Direct e-mail: johniwolstenholme@tvu.ac.uk
Other contacts: SMR, LRC Manager for Learning Resource Provision.

Founded:
1993

Organisation type and purpose:
University library, university department or institute.

Subject coverage:
Business, management, accountancy, law, health sciences, humanities, languages, hospitality, music, information studies, technology, art and design, built environment, sports science.

Non-library collection catalogue:
All or part available online

Library catalogue:
All or part available online

Printed publications:
In-house products only

Publications list:
Available online

Access to staff:
Contact by letter, by telephone, by fax and by e-mail. Appointment necessary. Access for members only.
Hours: St Mary's Road; term-time: Mon to Thu, 0830 to 2200; Fri to Sun, 0830 to 1800
Special comments: Reciprocal arrangements with similar institutions. Members only primarily, visitors by prior appointment.

Access to building, collection or gallery:
Prior appointment required
Special comments: 24 hour access to IT facilities during term time – Ealing only

Access for disabled people:
Parking provided, ramped entry, level entry, access to all public areas, toilet facilities

Member of:
M25 Group
SCONUL

Other departments at:
Faculty of Health and Human Sciences
  Westel House, 32 Uxbridge Road, London, W5 2BZ; tel: 020 8280 5043; fax: 020 8280 5045
Paul Hamlyn Learning Resource Centre
  Wellington Street, Slough, Berkshire, SL1 1YG; tel: 01753 697536; fax: 01753 574264
Wolfson School of Health, Sciences Learning Resource Centre
  Royal Berkshire Hospital, Reading, RG1 5AN; tel: 0118 322 7661; fax: 0118 322 8675

THAMES VALLEY UNIVERSITY – LEARNING RESOURCE CENTRE

Acronym or abbreviation: TVU

St Mary's Road, Ealing, London, W5 5RF

Tel: 020 8231 2248
Fax: 020 8231 2631
E-mail: lrs@tvu.ac.uk

Website:
http://www.tvu.ac.uk

Enquiries:
Enquiries to: Head of Learning Resources
Direct tel: 020 8231 2678
Direct e-mail: john.wolstenholme@tvu.ac.uk
Other contacts: Director of Information Services for all ICT within the University.

Founded:
1992

Organisation type and purpose:
Learned society, professional body (membership is by qualification), university library, training organisation, research organisation.
Learning Resource Service.

Subject coverage:
Management, including marketing, purchasing, business, accounting, languages, hospitality management, law, music, media, health sciences.

Library catalogue:
All or part available online

Publications list:
Available online

Access to staff:
Contact by letter, by telephone, by fax, by e-mail and via website. Appointment necessary. Access for members only.
Hours: TVU Ealing and PH: Mon to Thu, 0830 to 2200; Fri, Sat, Sun, 0830 to 1800
WIHS Ealing: Mon to Thu, 0830 to 1900; Fri, 1000 to 1700; Sat, 1100 to 1600
Reading: Mon, 1000 to 1930; Tue to Fri, 0830 to 1930; Sat, 0900 to 1300
Special comments: TVU Ealing and PH: Computer access only 2200 to 0600
UK+, SCONUL and M25 Schemes, Shorter hours in vacations, please telephone first.

Access to building, collection or gallery:
Prior appointment required

Access for disabled people:
Parking provided, level entry, access to all public areas, toilet facilities

Location:
Paul Hamlyn Learning Resource Centre
  Wellington Street, Slough, Berkshire, SL1 1YG; tel: 01753 697536; fax: 01753 697538
Wolfson Institute of Health Sciences Learning Resource Centre
  Wexham Park Hospital, Slough, Berkshire, SL2 4HL; tel: 01753 634343; fax: 01753 634344
Wolfson Institute of Health Sciences Learning Resource Centre
  Royal Berkshire Hospital, Reading, RG1 5AN; tel: 0118 987 7661; fax: 0118 986 8675
Wolfson Institute of Health Sciences Learning Resource Centre
  Westel House, 32 Uxbridge Road, Ealing, London, W5 2BS; tel: 020 8280 5043; fax: 020 8280 5045

THE-SRDA

Formal name: The Systems Reliability Data Association
Acronym or abbreviation: the-SRDA

Thomson House, Risley, Warrington, Cheshire, WA3 6AT

Tel: 01925 254249
Fax: 01925 254569
E-mail: the-srda@sercoassurance.com

Website:
http://www.the-srda.net

Access to component reliability data online, plus information about data sources, tools and techniques, publications, technical meetings and training courses of interest to safety, reliability and risk professionals.

Enquiries:
Enquiries to: Manager

Founded:
2001

Organisation type and purpose:
Membership association, consultancy.
Providing services to members for annual subscription.

Subject coverage:
Risk assessment, consequence analysis and safety management, reliability analysis and availability management (cross-industry).

Trade and statistical information:
Component reliability data bank online at www.the-srda.net (is available to members only).

Printed publications:
SRDA report series

Publications list:
Available online

Part of:
Serco Ltd

THEATRES TRUST

22 Charing Cross Road, London, WC2H 0QL

Tel: 020 7836 8591
Fax: 020 7836 3302
E-mail: info@theatrestrust.org.uk

Website:
http://www.theatrestrust.org.uk
Newsletter articles, advice notes, general information about the work of The Trust.

Enquiries:
Enquiries to: Resources Officer
Direct e-mail: paul.connolly@theatrestrust.org.uk
Other contacts: Planning and Architecture Adviser for planning/architectural advice

Founded:
1976

Organisation type and purpose:
Non-departmental public body, statutory body.
To promote the better protection of theatres.

Subject coverage:
History and design of theatre buildings, their planning and architecture.

Museum or gallery collection, archive, or library special collection:
Planning applications relating to theatres in England, Wales and Scotland since 1976, photos

Non-library collection catalogue:
All or part available in-house

Library catalogue:
All or part available in-house

Printed publications:
Advice notes (free)
Annual Report (free)
Theatres Trust Newsletter (subscribers only)
Encore: Strategies for Theatre Renewal
Pilot Study of the Condition of Theatres in England
Theatres: A Guide to Theatre Conservation from English Heritage

Publications list:
Available online and in print

Access to staff:
Contact by letter, by telephone, by fax, by e-mail and via website. Appointment necessary.
Hours: Mon to Fri, 0900 to 1700

Access to building, collection or gallery:
No prior appointment required

Access for disabled people:
No disabled access

continued overleaf

Special comments: Steps and narrow lift.

Close links with:
Theatres Trust Charitable Fund
  at the same address

THEATRO TECHNIS

26 Crowndale Road, London, NW1 1TT

Tel: 020 7387 6617
Fax: 020 7383 2545
E-mail: info@theatrotechnis.com

Website:
http://www.theatrotechnis.com

Enquiries:
Enquiries to: Co-ordinator

Founded:
1967

Organisation type and purpose:
Advisory body, registered charity (charity number 2808859).
Target/client group: the Greek Cypriot community and other English-speaking communities.

Subject coverage:
Centre for the Cypriot community offering a range of cultural and social activities including multilingual and multicultural theatre. Advice service covering housing, welfare rights, law, language, family life, advocacy, interpreting and translation services.

Access to staff:
Contact by letter, by telephone, by fax and by e-mail. Appointment necessary.
Hours: Mon to Fri, 1000 to 1700

Access to building, collection or gallery:
No access other than to staff

Access for disabled people:
Ramped entry, toilet facilities

THEOSOPHICAL SOCIETY IN ENGLAND

Acronym or abbreviation: TSIE

50 Gloucester Place, London, W1U 8EA

Tel: 020 7935 9261
Fax: 020 7935 9543
E-mail: office@theosoc.org.uk

Enquiries:
Enquiries to: National President

Founded:
1888

Organisation type and purpose:
International organisation, membership association, universal brotherhood.

Subject coverage:
Theosophy, religion, meditation, philosophy, occultism, mysticism.

Museum or gallery collection, archive, or library special collection:
Library of 10,000 vols, bound theosophical magazines.

Printed publications:
Insight (journal, quarterly, free to members, non-members annual fee: UK £9, international £14)

Electronic and video publications:
Cassettes (over 1,000) of past lectures are available

Publications list:
Available in print

Access to staff:
Contact by letter, by telephone, by fax and by e-mail. Appointment necessary.

Access to building, collection or gallery:
No prior appointment required
Hours: Tue to Fri, 1400 to 1830
Special comments: Members and subscribers; some meetings members only

Also at:
sections and lodges in over 60 countries

Parent body:
Theosophical Society
  Adyar, Madras, 600020, India

THERAPY TRAINING COLLEGE

Acronym or abbreviation: LCH

PO Box 10500, Birmingham, B14 4WB

Tel: 0121 430 3336
E-mail: hypnosis@lesserian.co.uk

Website:
http://www.lesserian.co.uk
http://www.lesserian.co.uk/courses.htm
Training courses available.
http://www.lesserian.co.uk/recommen.htm
Publications.
http://www.lesserian.co.uk/syllabus.htm
Course syllabus.

Enquiries:
Enquiries to: Director
Direct e-mail: courses@lesserian.co.uk

Founded:
1979

Organisation type and purpose:
Training organisation.
Training in the curative use of hypnosis.

Subject coverage:
The curative use of hypnosis, hypnotherapy and licensed to use 'Lesserian' Trademark.

Printed publications:
Details of training courses
Course Prospectus
Hypnotherapy Explained (Lesser D, £12.95 inc. p&p)
The Book of Hypnosis (Lesser D, £12.95 inc. p&p)

Electronic and video publications:
Training Course, content, methods explained
  (Video and DVD available, free)

Publications list:
Available online and in print

Access to staff:
Contact by letter, by telephone, by e-mail and via website. Appointment necessary.
Hours: Mon to Thu, 0900 to 1800

THERMAL ENGINEERING INTERNATIONAL LIMITED

Acronym or abbreviation: Tei

PO Box 80, Calder Vale Road, Wakefield, West Yorkshire, WF1 5YS

Tel: 01924 780000
Fax: 01924 201901
E-mail: enquiries@tei.co.uk

Website:
http://www.tei.co.uk

Enquiries:
Enquiries to: Director
Direct e-mail: maddisond@tei.co.uk
Other contacts: Technical Director for Ruislip office.

Founded:
1997

Organisation type and purpose:
International organisation, manufacturing industry, service industry, consultancy.
Design, engineering and commissioning services for utility, industrial and marine boiler plants.

Subject coverage:
Steam boiler plant design and engineering and commissioning for utility, industrial and marine industries.

Museum or gallery collection, archive, or library special collection:
British, European and USA Standards

Printed publications:
Brochures

Access to staff:
Contact by letter, by telephone, by fax and by e-mail. Appointment necessary.
Hours: Mon to Fri, 0730 to 1230 and 1400 to 1700

Head office:
Thermal Engineering International Limited
  Mechanical Services Division, PO Box 80, Calder Vale Road, Wakefield, West Yorkshire, WF1 5PF;
  tel: 01924 780000; fax: 01924 201901

THERMAL INSULATION CONTRACTORS ASSOCIATION

Acronym or abbreviation: TICA

TICA House, Arlington Way, Yarm Road Business Park, Darlington, Co Durham, DL1 4QB

Tel: 01325 466704
Fax: 01325 487691
E-mail: enquiries@tica-acad.co.uk

Website:
http://www.tica-acad.co.uk

Enquiries:
Enquiries to: Chief Executive

Founded:
1959

Organisation type and purpose:
Trade association, present number of members: 90.
Advisory services for members and representation of their interests.

Subject coverage:
Thermal insulation contracting, hot and cold insulation in power stations, oil refineries, chemical plant and marine projects, including pipework, plant, ductwork, storage tanks etc, the insulation of heating and ventilation in schools, hospitals, offices and other buildings, asbestos control and removal, firms undertaking such work, technical information, health, safety and training.

Publications list:
Available online and in print

Access to staff:
Contact by letter, by telephone, by fax, by e-mail, in person and via website. Non-members charged.
Hours: Mon to Thu, 0830 to 1700; Fri, 0830 to 1530

Access for disabled people:
Parking provided

Affiliated to:
Fédération Européenne des Syndicats d'Enterprises d'Isolation (FESI)
World Insulation and Acoustics Congress Organisation (WIACO)

Subsidiary bodies:
Asbestos Control and Abatement Division (ACAD)
  tel: 01325 466704; fax: 01325 487691; e-mail: enquiries@tica-acad.co.uk
Insulation and Environmental Training Agency
  tel: 01325 466704; fax: 01325 487691; e-mail: ieta@tica-acad.co.uk

THERMAL INSULATION MANUFACTURERS AND SUPPLIERS ASSOCIATION

Acronym or abbreviation: TIMSA

Tournai Hall, Evelyn Woods Road, Aldershot, Hampshire, GU11 2LL

Tel: 01252 357844
Fax: 01252 357831
E-mail: timsa@associationhouse.org.uk

Website:
http://www.timsa.org.uk

Enquiries:
Enquiries to: Secretary

Founded:
1978

Organisation type and purpose:
Trade association, present number of members: 36. Represents major manufacturers, specialist suppliers and distributors and consultants in the UK thermal insulation industry.

Subject coverage:
Promotes the correct use and application of thermal insulation and ancillary materials.

Printed publications:
List of Members
Technical Guidance Notes

Publications list:
Available in print

Access to staff:
Contact by letter, by telephone, by fax, by e-mail and via website
Hours: Mon to Fri, 0900 to 1700

THERMAL SPRAYING AND SURFACE ENGINEERING ASSOCIATION, THE

Acronym or abbreviation: TSSEA

18 Hammeton Way, Wellesbourne, Warwick, CV35 9NT

Tel: 01789 842822
Fax: 01789 842229
E-mail: thermal.sprayers@btinternet.com

Enquiries:
Enquiries to: General Secretary

Founded:
1934

Organisation type and purpose:
International organisation, advisory body, trade association (membership is by subscription), service industry, consultancy.

Subject coverage:
Surface coatings on metals or other substrates of other metals, ceramics and cermets.

Printed publications:
Brochures
Directory of members
Technical information sheets

Access to staff:
Contact by letter, by telephone, by fax and by e-mail. Appointment necessary.
Hours: Mon to Fri, 0900 to 1700

Affiliated to:
The Institute of Materials (IOM)
1 Carlton House Terrace, London, SW1Y 5DB

THOMAS HARDY SOCIETY

PO Box 1438, Dorchester, Dorset, DT1 1YH

Tel: 01305 251501
Fax: 01305 251501
E-mail: info@hardysociety.org

Website:
http://www.hardysociety.org

Enquiries:
Enquiries to: Honorary Secretary

Founded:
1968

Organisation type and purpose:
Membership association (membership is by subscription), present number of members: 1,500. Literary society.

Subject coverage:
Life and work of Thomas Hardy; country associated with Hardy's writing.

Museum or gallery collection, archive, or library special collection:
Comprehensive collection of books by Hardy and all literary criticism held at Dorset County Library, Dorchester
Important Hardy collections at Dorset County Museum, Dorchester

Printed publications:
Books and pamphlets (18 titles, list available)
The Thomas Hardy Journal (3 times a year)
Tour Guides to the Hardy Country

Publications list:
Available in print

Access to staff:
Contact by letter, by telephone, by fax, by e-mail, in person and via website. Appointment necessary.
Hours: Mon to Thu, 1400 to 1600

THOMAS LOVELL BEDDOES SOCIETY

9 Amber Court, Belper, Derbyshire, DE56 1HG

Tel: 01773 828066
Fax: 01773 828066
E-mail: john@beddoes.demon.co.uk

Website:
http://www.phantomwooer.org

Enquiries:
Enquiries to: Chair

Founded:
1994

Organisation type and purpose:
International organisation, learned society (membership is by subscription, election or invitation), present number of members: 100, registered charity (charity number 1041402), research organisation, publishing house.
To research Beddoes' life, times and work and encourage relevant publications. To further the reading and appreciation of his works by a wider public. To liaise with other groups and organisations. To plan events to further the aims.

Subject coverage:
Life and works of Thomas Lovell Beddoes (1803–1849).

Museum or gallery collection, archive, or library special collection:
Works of Thomas Lovell Beddoes

Non-library collection catalogue:
All or part available online, in-house and in print

Printed publications:
Newsletter (annually, by membership or £5 each)
Other Publications

Electronic and video publications:
Poems and Songs (audio tape, £5)

Publications list:
Available online and in print

Access to staff:
Contact by letter, by telephone, by fax, by e-mail and in person
Hours: Mon to Fri, 0900 to 1700

Access to building, collection or gallery:
Prior appointment required

Connections with:
Alliance of Literary Societies (ALS)
Secretary, 22 Belmont Grove, Havant, Hampshire, PO9 3PU; tel: 01926 337874

THOMAS PAINE SOCIETY

c/o Stuart Hill, 14 Park Drive, Forest Hall, Newcastle, NE12 9JP

E-mail: stuart.hill23@ntlworld.com

Website:
http://www.thomaspainesocietyuk.org.uk

Organisation type and purpose:
Membership association (membership is by subscription). Promotes the recognition of Thomas Paine's contribution to the cause of freedom and seeks to spread a knowledge of his work and activities with a view to encouraging the growth of a similar spirit of constructive criticism in every aspect of public life.

Subject coverage:
The work and activities of Thomas Paine.

Printed publications:
Journal of Radical History

THOMAS PLUME'S LIBRARY

C/o Maldon Town Council, Town Hall, Market Hill, Maldon, Essex, CM9 4PZ

Tel: 01621 854850
Fax: 01621 854850
E-mail: info@thomasplumeslibrary.co.uk

Enquiries:
Enquiries to: Librarian

Founded:
1704

Subject coverage:
C17th theology, natural philosophy, chemistry, medicine, physics, mathematics, and astronomy.

Museum or gallery collection, archive, or library special collection:
Thomas Plume Collection of 10,000 vols

Printed publications:
Catalogue
The Intentions of Thomas Plume
Postcards
Greetings card

Access to staff:
Contact by letter, by telephone, by fax, by e-mail and in person
Hours: Tue to Thu, 1400 to 1600; Sat, 1000 to 1200; Mon, Fri, closed

Access to building, collection or gallery:
Hours: As access to staff
Special comments: Spiral staircase to 1st floor

Access for disabled people:
No disabled access

THOMAS TALLIS SOCIETY

Acronym or abbreviation: TTS

13 Albury Street, London, SE8 3PT

Tel: 020 8691 8337
Fax: 020 8691 8337

Website:
http://www.thomas-tallis-society.org.uk/
http://www.classical-artists.com/tcc

Enquiries:
Enquiries to: Administrator

Founded:
1965

Organisation type and purpose:
Choral society.

Subject coverage:
The music of Thomas Tallis. The choir performs mainly classical music of all periods. Specialising in programmes to suit different venues, themes.

Printed publications:
Brochure (annually)
Newsletter

Access to staff:
Contact by letter, by telephone and by fax
Hours: Mon to Fri, 0900 to 1700

Connections with:
Tallis Chamber Choir (TCC)
13 Albury Street, London, SE8 3PT; tel: 020 8691 8337

THOMPSON HENRY LIMITED

London Road, Sunningdale, Berkshire, SL5 0EP

Tel: 01344 624615
Fax: 01344 626120
E-mail: thl@thompsonhenry.co.uk

Enquiries:
Enquiries to: Manager
Direct e-mail: t.thompson@thompsonhenry.co.uk

Founded:
1972

Organisation type and purpose:
Service industry.

Subject coverage:
Publications and services of the US publishers represented.

Electronic and video publications:
CD-Matters: a CD-ROM subscription service

Access to staff:
Contact by letter and by e-mail
Hours: Mon to Fri, 0900 to 1700

UK agent for:
BIOSIS
Britannica
CABI Publishing
Gale Group
H W Wilson Company
LexisNexis Academic & Library Solutions
Online Inc

THOMSON REUTERS ZOOLOGICAL LTD

Enterprise House, Innovation Way, Heslington, York, YO10 5NY

Tel: 020 7433 4590
Fax: 020 7433 4589

Website:
http://www.thomsonreuters.com
http://www.organismnames.com
Taxonomic name information for life science research
http://www.biologybrowser.com
Resource index for biodiversity and zoology

Enquiries:
Enquiries to: Director, Operations and Development
Direct e-mail: nigel.robinson@thomsonreuters.com

Founded:
1864

Formerly called:
BIOSIS UK

Organisation type and purpose:
Provider of information services and solutions for professionals in life sciences

Subject coverage:
Life sciences – bibliographic data, zoology.

Printed publications:
Zoological Record (annual bibliography)

Electronic and video publications:
Zoological Record (updated monthly)
Index to Organism Names
Biology Browser
Order electronic and video publications from: Thomson Reuters sales office

Publications list:
Available online

Access to staff:
Contact by letter, by telephone, by fax, by e-mail and via website
Hours: Mon to Fri, 0900 to 1700

Access to building, collection or gallery:
No access other than to staff

Parent body:
Thomson Reuters
  77 Hatton Garden, London, EC1N 8JS; website: http://www.thomsonreuters.com

THORESBY SOCIETY

Formal name: Thoresby Society – The Leeds Historical Society

Claremont, 23 Clarendon Road, Leeds, West Yorkshire, LS2 9NZ

Tel: 0113 247 0704
E-mail: secretary@thoresby.org.uk

Website:
http://www.thoresby.org.uk
The Society's history, programmes of lectures, publications

Enquiries:
Enquiries to: Honorary Secretary (for general enquiries)
Other contacts: Librarian (for research enquiries – library@thoresby.org.uk)

Founded:
1889

Organisation type and purpose:
Historical society (membership is by subscription), present number of members: 500, registered charity (charity number 227526).

Subject coverage:
Local history of Leeds and surrounding areas.

Museum or gallery collection, archive, or library special collection:
Books, pictures, maps and plans, archives

Non-library collection catalogue:
All or part available online and in-house

Library catalogue:
All or part available in-house

Printed publications:
Thoresby Society Publications (annually, 82 vols 1891–2007). The publications cover a wide variety of subjects on local industrial, social and political history.
The parish registers of Leeds Parish Church have been transcribed and published up to 1776 by the Society, but are currently out of print. They are indexed and contain baptism, marriage and burial entries
Order printed publications from: The Society, by post (address above) or by e-mail distribution@thoresby .org.uk

Publications list:
Available online and in print

Access to staff:
Contact by letter, by telephone, by e-mail and via website. Appointment necessary. Non-members charged.
Hours: Tue and Thu, 1000 to 1400; phone messages can be left at other times

Access to building, collection or gallery:
Hours: Tue and Thu, 1000 to 1400

Access for disabled people:
Parking provided; toilet facilities
Special comments: Library is on first floor, but there is no lift

THREE RIVERS DISTRICT COUNCIL

Acronym or abbreviation: TRDC

Three Rivers House, Northway, Rickmansworth, Hertfordshire, WD3 1RL

Tel: 01923 776611
Fax: 01923 896119
E-mail: stuart.marlton@threerivers.gov.uk

Website:
http://www.3rivers.gov.uk

Enquiries:
Enquiries to: Public Relations Manager
Direct tel: 01923 727255
Direct fax: 01923 727258

Founded:
1974

Organisation type and purpose:
Local government body.

Subject coverage:
All local services and amenities covering the Rickmansworth, South Oxhey, Carpenders Park, Chorleywood, Sarratt, Abbots Langley, Moor Park and Maple Cross area, allotments, cemeteries, electoral registration, environmental health, parking, concessionary public transport fares, housing, museums and arts, local planning, building control and development control, council tax and business rates collection, sports and recreation.

Printed publications:
Accommodation Guide (free)
Halls for Hire (free)
How to Contact Your Councillor (free)
Places of Worship (free)
Three Rivers District Guide (free)
Three Rivers Map (free)
Three Rivers Times Magazine (free)

Access to staff:
Contact by letter, by telephone, by fax, by e-mail, in person and via website. Appointment necessary.
Hours: Mon to Thu, 0830 to 1730; Fri, 0830 to 1700

Access for disabled people:
Parking provided, level entry, access to all public areas, toilet facilities

THRIVE

The Geoffrey Udall Centre, Beech Hill, Reading, Berkshire, RG7 2AT

Tel: 0118 988 5688
Fax: 0118 988 5677
E-mail: info@thrive.org.uk

Website:
http://www.thrive.org.uk

Enquiries:
Enquiries to: Information Officer
Direct e-mail: jan.duncan@thrive.org.uk

Founded:
1978

Organisation type and purpose:
Membership association (membership is by subscription), present number of members: 730, voluntary organisation, registered charity (charity number 277570), suitable for all ages; training organisation, consultancy. To research, educate and promote the use and advantages of gardening for people with a disability.

Subject coverage:
Disability and gardening. Activities focus on promoting the benefits of gardening to individuals and organisations, as well as teaching techniques and practical applications so that anyone with a disability can take part in and benefit from gardening.

Special visitor services:
Two gardens (call office for details)

Museum or gallery collection, archive, or library special collection:
Library containing comprehensive collection on therapeutic horticulture

Printed publications:
Come Gardening (for blind gardeners, quarterly)
Growthpoint (magazine, quarterly)
Children's Gardening
Gardening is for Everyone

Publications list:
Available online and in print

Access to staff:
Contact by letter, by telephone, by fax, by e-mail and via website. Appointment necessary.
Hours: Mon to Fri, 0900 to 1700

Links with:
Coventry University
numerous professional and voluntary bodies
Royal Horticultural Society

THURROCK AND BASILDON COLLEGE

Woodview Campus, Grays, Essex, RM16 2YR

Tel: 01375 362691
Fax: 01375 373356
E-mail: lbarker@tab.ac.uk

Enquiries:
Enquiries to: Librarian

Founded:
1959

Organisation type and purpose:
College of further education.

Subject coverage:
Management and business studies, office and information technology, hotels and catering, tourism and leisure, language, hair and beauty technology, motor vehicle studies, art and design, caring, pre-school education, vocational.

Library catalogue:
All or part available in-house

Access to staff:
Contact by telephone and in person
Hours: Mon, 0845 to 2130; Tue to Thu, 0845 to 1800; Fri, 0845 to 1645

Access for disabled people:
Parking provided, level entry, toilet facilities

Other address:
Thurrock and Basildon College
Nethermayne Campus, Basildon, Essex, SS16 5NN; tel: 01268 461614

THURROCK UNITARY COUNCIL

Civic Offices, New Road, Grays, Essex, RM17 6SL

Tel: 01375 652652
Fax: 01375 652785

Enquiries:
Enquiries to: Head of Corporate Communications
Direct tel: 01375 652016
Direct fax: 01375 652874
Direct e-mail: methorne@thurrock.gov.uk

Organisation type and purpose:
Local government body.

Subject coverage:
Local government, residential services, regeneration, environmental conservation.

Printed publications:
Thurrock Magazine
corporate literature

Access to staff:
Contact by letter, by telephone and by fax
Hours: Mon to Fri, 0900 to 1700

Access to building, collection or gallery:
Hours: Mon to Fri, 0830 to 1700

Access for disabled people:
Hours: Mon to Fri, 0830 to 1700

TILE ASSOCIATION

Acronym or abbreviation: TTA

Forum Court, 83 Copers Cope Road, Beckenham, Kent, BR3 1NR

Tel: 020 8663 0946
Fax: 020 8663 0949
E-mail: info@tiles.org.uk

Website:
http://www.tiles.org.uk

Enquiries:
Enquiries to: Executive Officer

Founded:
2000

Organisation type and purpose:
Trade association.

Subject coverage:
Generic information on wall and floor tiling.

Printed publications:
Technical literature

Access to staff:
Contact by letter, by telephone, by fax, by e-mail and via website. Appointment necessary.
Hours: Mon to Fri, 0900 to 1700

Member of:
European Union of Tile Fixers' Associations (EUF)
National Specialist Contractors Council (NSCC)

TILES AND ARCHITECTURAL CERAMICS SOCIETY

Acronym or abbreviation: TACS

'Oakhurst', Cocknage Road, Rough Close, Stoke on Trent, ST3 7NN

Tel: 0151 207 0001
E-mail: kathbertadams@hotmail.com

Website:
http://www.tilesoc.org.uk
Information about the society, information about the tiles, location index and gazetteer project.

Enquiries:
Enquiries to: Secretary

Founded:
1981

Organisation type and purpose:
Advisory body, learned society (membership is by subscription), present number of members: 367, registered charity (charity number 289090), research organisation, publishing house.
The study and protection of tiles and architectural ceramics.

Subject coverage:
All areas of historical and contemporary tile production and functional applications, as well as tile collecting and tile conservation, architectural ceramics.

Printed publications:
Publications list currently being revised
Brightening the Long Days, hospital tile pictures
Fired Earth: 1000 Years of Tiles in Europe: Exhibition catalogue
Glazed Expressions (magazine, 3 times a year)
Journal (annual)
Newsletter (quarterly)

Publications list:
Available online and in print

Access to staff:
Contact by letter and by e-mail
Hours: Mon to Fri, 0900 to 1700

TILLENDOVE PICTURE LIBRARY

Bowood, Ewell House Grove, Epsom, Surrey, KT17 1NT

Tel: 07831 598018
Fax: 020 8394 2247
E-mail: tillendove@mailbox.co.uk

Website:
http://www.tillendove.co.uk

Enquiries:
Enquiries to: Partner

Founded:
1993

Organisation type and purpose:
Service industry.
Press photography library.

Subject coverage:
Press photography.

Museum or gallery collection, archive, or library special collection:
Photographs of celebrities, film, TV and music
Photographs of public figures

Non-library collection catalogue:
All or part available online and in-house

Publications list:
Available in print

Access to staff:
Contact by letter, by telephone, by fax and by e-mail. All charged.
Hours: Mon to Fri, 0900 to 1700

Access to building, collection or gallery:
No access other than to staff

TIMBER PACKAGING AND PALLET CONFEDERATION

Acronym or abbreviation: TIMCON

840 Melton Road, Thurmaston, Leicester, LE4 8BN

Tel: 0116 264 0579
Fax: 0116 264 0141
E-mail: timcon@associationhq.org.uk

Website:
http://www.timcon.org

Enquiries:
Enquiries to: Executive Secretary

Organisation type and purpose:
Trade association.

Subject coverage:
Wooden cases and pallets; export packing; technical, legislative, environmental and industrial relations matters in the industry.

Printed publications:
Be Sure with Wood
Code of Practice
Directory of Members
Pallet Buyers Guide

Access to staff:
Contact by letter, by telephone, by fax, by e-mail and via website
Hours: Mon to Fri, 0900 to 1700

Access to building, collection or gallery:
Prior appointment required

Access for disabled people:
Access to all public areas

TIMBER TRADE FEDERATION

Acronym or abbreviation: TTF

The Building Centre, 26 Store Street, London, WC1E 7BT

Tel: 020 3205 0067
E-mail: ttf@ttf.co.uk

Website:
http://www.ttf.co.uk/

Enquiries:
Enquiries to: Director General

Founded:
1892

Organisation type and purpose:
Trade association.

Access to staff:
Contact by letter, by telephone and by e-mail. Appointment necessary. Non-members charged.
Hours: Mon to Fri, 0900 to 1700

Access to building, collection or gallery:
No prior appointment required

TNS MEDIA INTELLIGENCE LIMITED

Formal name: The Media Monitoring Service

6th Floor, 292 Vauxhall Bridge Road, London, SW1V 1AE

Tel: 0870 202 0100
Fax: 0870 202 0110
E-mail: tnsmi_sales@tnsofres.com

continued overleaf

Website:
http://www.tellex.press.net

Enquiries:
Enquiries to: Marketing & Communications
Manager
Direct tel: 020 7963 7638
Direct fax: 020 7963 7609

Founded:
1954

Formerly called:
Parker Bishop Limited, TNS Tellex Limited (year of
change 2002)

Organisation type and purpose:
Service industry.
Broadcast reporting service monitoring over 350
television and radio stations throughout the UK; a
service providing selective broadcast information
to the communications industry including: PR
agencies, advertising and design agencies,
manufacturing and marketing companies, service
companies, government organisations, financial
PR agencies and companies.

Subject coverage:
Mainly news and current affairs, although any
item or station can be monitored with a detailed
brief supplied by the client with reasonable notice.

Printed publications:
Blue Book of British Broadcasting (annually in
March)
Burgundy Book of European Broadcasting
(annually in September)
Order printed publications from: Publications
Department
at the same address, tel: 020 7566 3108

Access to staff:
Contact by letter, by telephone, by fax, by e-mail
and via website. Appointment necessary.
Hours: Sales office: Mon to Fri, 0700 to 1900

Other addresses:
TNS Media Intelligence
    Manchester; tel: 0161 228 6922
TNS Media Intelligence
    Durham; tel: 0191 386 6767
TNS Media Intelligence
    Leeds; tel: 0113 243 4233
TNS Media Intelligence
    Peterborough, Cambridgeshire; tel: 01733 896776
TNS Media Intelligence
    Cardiff; tel: 029 2039 5313
TNS Media Intelligence
    Worthing, West Sussex; tel: 01903 212731
TNS Media Intelligence
    Edinburgh; tel: 0131 226 2612

Subsidiary of:
Taylor Nelson Sofres plc

TOASTMASTERS FOR ROYAL OCCASIONS

12 Little Bornes, Alleyn Park, Dulwich, London,
SE21 8SE

Tel: 020 8670 5585/ 8424
Fax: 020 8670 0055

Enquiries:
Enquiries to: President

Founded:
1980

Organisation type and purpose:
Professional body, training organisation.

Subject coverage:
Royal visits, state banquets etc, in Britain and
overseas; all aspects of the preparation and
organisation of these events.

Access to staff:
Contact by letter, by telephone, by fax and by e-
mail
Hours: Mon to Fri, 0900 to 1700

Member of:
Guild of International Professional Toastmasters
    at the same address

TOASTMASTERS OF GREAT BRITAIN

12 Little Bornes, Alleyn Park, Dulwich, London,
SE21 8SE

Tel: 020 8670 5585
Fax: 020 8670 0055

Website:
http://www.ivorspencer.com

Enquiries:
Enquiries to: Chief Executive

Founded:
1980

Organisation type and purpose:
Advisory body, professional body.

Subject coverage:
Organisation of royal events, banquets,
conferences, and other ceremonies for firms and
public bodies.

Access to staff:
Contact by letter, by telephone, by fax and by e-
mail. Access for members only.
Hours: Mon to Fri, 0900 to 1700

Member of:
Guild of Professional Toastmasters

TOBACCO MANUFACTURERS' ASSOCIATION

Acronym or abbreviation: TMA

5th Floor, Burwood House, 14/16 Caxton Street,
London, SW1H 0ZB

Tel: 020 7544 0100
Fax: 020 7544 0117
E-mail: information@the-tma.org.uk

Website:
http://www.the-tma.org.uk

Enquiries:
Enquiries to: Information and Media Manager
Direct tel: 020 7544 0108

Founded:
1940

Organisation type and purpose:
Trade association.

Subject coverage:
Tobacco industry; smoking issues.

Non-library collection catalogue:
All or part available online, in-house and in print

Access to staff:
Contact by letter, by telephone, by fax and by e-
mail
Hours: Mon to Fri, 0900 to 1700

Access to building, collection or gallery:
No access other than to staff

TOC H

3rd Floor, Wing House, Britannia Street, Aylesbury,
Buckinghamshire, HP20 1QS

Tel: 01296 331099
Fax: 01296 331135
E-mail: info@toch.org.uk

Website:
http://www.toch.org.uk
Information about the movement. Information on
projects and events.

Enquiries:
Enquiries to: Director

Founded:
1915

Organisation type and purpose:
Membership association, present number of
members: 3061, voluntary organisation, registered
charity (charity number 211042).
Christian-based, but open to people of all walks of
life and faith.

To break down social, racial and cultural barriers
by challenging individuals' perceptions of others
and the divisions which exist in society.

Subject coverage:
Voluntary work, personal and community service.

**Museum or gallery collection, archive, or library
special collection:**
Archive of Toc H books and photographs

Printed publications:
Royal Charter 1971
Point Three (6 times a year)
Projects and Activities Brochure

Publications list:
Available in print

Access to staff:
Contact by letter, by telephone and by fax
Hours: Mon to Fri, 0900 to 1700

TOGETHER (MACA)

Formal name: Together (The Mental After Care
Association)
Acronym or abbreviation: MACA

12 Old Street, London, EC1V 9BE

Tel: 020 7780 7300
Fax: 020 7780 7301
E-mail: contactus@together-uk.org

Website:
http://www.together-uk.org/
General and local services listings.

Enquiries:
Enquiries to: Press and Publications Officer
Direct e-mail: claire-monger@together-uk.org

Founded:
1879

Organisation type and purpose:
National organisation, voluntary organisation,
registered charity (charity number 211091).
Probably the earliest organisation of its kind,
established from 1879.
To provide high quality services for people with
mental health needs and their carers and to
influence policy and practice in relation to mental
health.

Subject coverage:
Services in the community, hospitals and prisons
for people with mental health needs and their
carers.

**Museum or gallery collection, archive, or library
special collection:**
Archives of the Association dating back to 1879,
    now held at the Wellcome Trust, London

Library catalogue:
All or part available in-house

Printed publications:
Annual Report
Annual Review
General Information Brochure
Leaflets

Access to staff:
Contact by letter, by telephone, by fax, by e-mail
and via website. Appointment necessary.
Hours: Mon to Fri, 0900 to 1730
Special comments: For staff, council members and
service users only. No wheelchair access. No public
access to library.

Regional Offices:
MACA Development Areas (North, Midlands and
Scotland)
    3 Fieldhouse Road, Rochdale, Lancashire, OL12
    0AD; tel: 01706 640 027; fax: 01706 640 027; e-
    mail: maca-midlandsandnorth@maca.org.uk
MACA London and East
    89 Turners Hill, Cheshunt, Hertfordshire, EN8
    9BN; tel: 01992 622 000; fax: 01992 622 621; e-
    mail: maca-londonandeast@maca.org.uk

MACA South
94b High Street, Epsom, Surrey, KT19 8BJ; tel: 01372 722 970; fax: 01372 722 980; e-mail: maca .south@maca.org.uk

TOLKIEN SOCIETY

8 Queens Lane, Eynsham, Witney, OX2 4HL

E-mail: tolksoc@tolkiensociety.org

Website:
http://www.tolkiensociety.org
Information about the Society, sales catalogue, information request service, articles, seminars

Enquiries:
Enquiries to: Membership Secretary
Direct e-mail: membership@tolkiensociety.org
Other contacts: Archivist – archives@tolkiensociety.org for access to the Society's archives.

Founded:
1969

Organisation type and purpose:
International organisation, learned society (membership is by subscription), present number of members: 1,245, voluntary organisation, registered charity (charity number 273809).

Subject coverage:
J R R Tolkien, life and works, associated authors, the Inklings etc.

Museum or gallery collection, archive, or library special collection:
Archives of Tolkien-related material including newspaper cuttings, fanzines, merchandise and foreign editions

Non-library collection catalogue:
All or part available in-house

Printed publications:
Amon Hen (bulletin, 6 times a year)
The Best of Amon Hen 1 (£5)
Digging Potatoes, Growing Trees Vol 1, Vol 2 and Vol 3 (£5 each)
First and Second Ages (£5)
Mallorn (journal, annually)
Proceedings of the 1992 Tolkien Centenary Conference (£15pb; £40 hb)
The Ways of Creative Mythologies (£10)
Tolkien, the Sea and Scandinavia (£5)
Travel and Communication in Tolkien's Worlds (£5)
Sindarin Lexicon (£5)
Order printed publications from: Tolkien Society Trading Ltd
8 Chantry Lane, Westbury, Wiltshire, BA13 3BS, tel: 01373 822884, fax: 01373 865001, e-mail: sales@ tolkiensociety.org

Access to staff:
Contact by letter and by e-mail. Appointment necessary.
Hours: Mon to Fri, 0900 to 1700
Special comments: By special appointment and not usually made on weekends.

Access to building, collection or gallery:
Prior appointment required

Affiliated to:
The Alliance of Literary Societies

Has:
23 affiliated local groups (Smials)

TONBRIDGE AND MALLING BOROUGH COUNCIL

Gibson Building, Gibson Drive, Kings Hill, West Malling, Kent, ME19 4LZ

Tel: 01732 844522
Fax: 01732 842170
E-mail: executive.services@tmbc.gov.uk

Website:
http://www.tmbc.gov.uk

Enquiries:
Enquiries to: Media and Communications Manager
Direct tel: 01732 876009
Direct fax: 01732 876004
Direct e-mail: linda.moreau@tmbc.gov.uk

Organisation type and purpose:
Local government body.

Printed publications:
A wide range of literature including:
Tonbridge and Malling – A Guide to Services (free to 47,000 homes)
Leisure guide and other service specific literature (free)
Here and Now (newspaper, free to 47,000 homes)

Access to staff:
Contact by letter, by telephone, by fax, by e-mail and in person
Hours: Mon to Fri, 0830 to 1700

Access for disabled people:
Parking provided, level entry, toilet facilities

TONSIL

Formal name: The Ongoing Singing Liaison Group

35 Old Lynn Road, Wisbech, Cambridgeshire, PE14 7AJ

E-mail: enquiries@tonsil.org.uk

Website:
http://www.tonsil.org.uk/

Enquiries:
Enquiries to: Secretary
Direct e-mail: philliptolley@colcanto.co.uk

Founded:
1988

Organisation type and purpose:
Registered charity. Represents 14 organisations promoting choral singing, supporting over 25,000 member choirs and over 500,000 singers

Subject coverage:
Singing Days, Singing Projects and Animation Schemes, Training for Animateurs and Singing Leaders.

Access to staff:
Contact by letter, by telephone, by fax, by e-mail and via website. Appointment necessary.
Hours: Mon to Fri, 0930 to 1500

Member of:
European Federation of Young Choirs

TOOL AND TRADES HISTORY SOCIETY

Acronym or abbreviation: TATHS

Woodbine Cottage, Budleigh Hill, East Budleigh, Budleigh Salterton, Devon, EX9 7DT

Tel: 01395 443030
E-mail: membership@taths.org.uk

Enquiries:
Enquiries to: Membership Secretary

Founded:
1983

Organisation type and purpose:
International organisation, learned society (membership is by subscription), present number of members: 500, registered charity (charity number 290474).
To advance the education of the general public in the history and development of hand tools and their use, and of the people and trades that used them.

Subject coverage:
Hand tools; traditional trades using hand tools e.g. blacksmiths, thatchers, coopers, all woodworking trades, furniture-making, clockmaking, jewellery-making, some building trades, medical and scientific instruments.

Library catalogue:
All or part available in print

Printed publications:
Newsletter (quarterly)
The Tool Chest of Benjamin Seaton (1797)
Tools & Trades (journal)
Reprint of Trade Catalogue of James John and Isaac Fussell
Reprint 1787 Directory of Sheffield

Publications list:
Available in print

Access to staff:
Contact by letter, by telephone, by e-mail and via website
Hours: Mon to Fri, 0900 to 1700

Connections with:
Early American Industries Association (same field in USA)

TORBAY COUNCIL

Town Hall, Castle Circus, Torquay, Devon, TQ1 3DR

Tel: 01803 201201
Fax: 01803 292677
E-mail: webmaster@torbay.gov.uk

Website:
http://www.torbay.gov.uk

Enquiries:
Enquiries to: Public Relations Manager
Direct tel: 01803 208850
Direct fax: 01803 208844
Direct e-mail: public.relations@torbay.gov.uk

Founded:
1998

Formerly called:
Torbay Borough Council

Organisation type and purpose:
Local government body.

Subject coverage:
Local government services.

Printed publications:
Torbay View

Access to staff:
Contact by letter, by telephone, by fax, by e-mail and via website
Hours: Mon to Thu, 0840 to 1715; Fri, 0840 to 1615

Access to building, collection or gallery:
No access other than to staff

TORBAY LIBRARY SERVICES

Torquay Library, Lymington Road, Torquay, Devon, TQ1 3DT

Tel: 01803 208305
Fax: 01803 208307
E-mail: tqreflib@torbay.gov.uk

Website:
http://www.torbay.gov.uk/index/education/ libraries.htm

Enquiries:
Enquiries to: Head of Library Services

Organisation type and purpose:
Local government body, public library.

Subject coverage:
Devon local studies collection, particularly information on Torbay.

Museum or gallery collection, archive, or library special collection:
Devon local studies collection
Census returns on microfilm (local area only)
Cuttings file
Maps
Newspapers (microfilm)

Non-library collection catalogue:
All or part available online

continued overleaf

Library catalogue:
All or part available online

Access to staff:
Contact by letter, by telephone, by fax, by e-mail and in person
Hours: Main Library and Local Studies Library Mon, Wed, Fri, 0930 to 1900; Tue, 0930 to 1700; Thu, 0930 to 1300; Sat, 0930 to 1600

Access for disabled people:
Ramped entry, lift to first floor.

Parent body:
Torbay Council
e-mail: tqreflib@torbay.gov.uk; website: http://www.torbay.gov.uk/index/education/libraries.htm

TORFAEN COUNTY BOROUGH COUNCIL

Civic Centre, Pontypool, Gwent, NP4 6YB

Tel: 01495 762200
Fax: 01495 755513

Website:
http://www.torfaen.gov.uk

Enquiries:
Enquiries to: Chief Executive
Direct tel: 01495 766069
Direct fax: 01495 766059

Founded:
1 April 1996

Organisation type and purpose:
Local government body.

Printed publications:
Torfaen Guide
Torfaen A-Z of Streets & Services

Access to staff:
Contact by letter
Hours: Mon to Fri, 0900 to 1700

Other office at:
Torfaen County Borough Council
County Hall, Croesyceiliog, Cwmbran

TORFAEN LIBRARY AND INFORMATION SERVICE

Pendragon House, General Rees Square, Cwmbran, NP44 1AH

Tel: 01633 628941
Fax: 01633 628935
E-mail: Christine.george@torfaen.gov.uk

Website:
http://www.torfaen.gov.uk/en/leisure/property.php/mid=42

Enquiries:
Enquiries to: Cultural Services Manager
Direct e-mail: cwmbran.library@torfaen.gov.uk

Founded:
1996

Organisation type and purpose:
Local government body, public library.

Subject coverage:
General, local studies, advice and self help, bibliotherapy.

Non-library collection catalogue:
All or part available online

Library catalogue:
All or part available online

Publications list:
Available in print

Access to staff:
Contact by letter, by telephone, by fax and by e-mail
Hours: Mon to Fri, 0900 to 1700

Access for disabled people:
Toilet facilities

Parent body:
Torfaen County Borough Council

TORIT DCE, DONALDSON DUST COLLECTION GROUP

Humberstone Lane, Thurmaston, Leicester, LE4 8HP

Tel: 0116 269 6161
Fax: 0116 269 3028
E-mail: toritdce.uk@mail.donaldson.com

Website:
http://www.btrenvironmental.co.uk

Enquiries:
Enquiries to: UK Sales Manger
Other contacts: Marketing Officer for publications.

Founded:
1919

Formerly called:
BTR Environmental Limited; Dust Control Equipment Limited (DCE) (year of change 1998)

Organisation type and purpose:
Manufacturing industry.

Subject coverage:
Design, manufacture, installation and commissioning of industrial dust control equipment; unit collectors; insertable filters; automatic reverse jet filters; tubular bag filters; complete plant installations; compact venting filters; centralised vacuum cleaning systems.

Museum or gallery collection, archive, or library special collection:
Complete Product Literature

Printed publications:
Full literature set available on request (free)

Electronic and video publications:
Product CD-ROM
Product video

Publications list:
Available online

Access to staff:
Contact by letter, by telephone, by fax, by e-mail and via website. Appointment necessary.
Hours: Mon to Thu, 0830 to 1700; Fri, 0830 to 1545

Access to building, collection or gallery:
Prior appointment required

TORNADO AND STORM RESEARCH ORGANIZATION

Acronym or abbreviation: TORRO

TCO (Thunderstorm) Division, PO Box 84, Oxford, OX1 4NP

Tel: 01865 483761
Fax: 01865 483937
E-mail: jonathan.webb@torro.org.uk

Website:
http://www.torro.org.uk

Enquiries:
Enquiries to: Director
Direct e-mail: torro@brookes.ac.uk
Other contacts: Director, Geography Unit, Oxford Brookes University, Gipsy Lane, Oxford

Founded:
1924

Formerly called:
Thunderstorm Census Organisation (year of change 1982)

Organisation type and purpose:
Research organisation.
Organisation for data collection, consultancy and research.

Subject coverage:
Thunderstorm frequency in Great Britain, geographical distribution in Great Britain, research into damaging lightning incidents, historical data

collection, thunderstorm climatology, rainfall and temperature extremes, damaging hailstones and point rainfalls.

Museum or gallery collection, archive, or library special collection:
Database for tornadoes, damaging hailstorms, thunderstorms (UK)
Information on temperature and rainfall extremes
Thunderstorm reports and relevant press cuttings 1925 to date

Printed publications:
Monthly summaries of thunderstorm activity (published in the Journal of Meteorology, UK)
Research papers at periodic intervals (price on application)

Publications list:
Available in print

Access to staff:
Contact by letter, by e-mail and via website
Hours: Mon to Fri, 0900 to 1700

Parent body:
Tornado and Storm Research Organisation (TORRO)
Geography Unit, Oxford Brookes University, Gipsy Lane, Oxford

TORRIDGE DISTRICT COUNCIL

Acronym or abbreviation: TDC

Riverbank House, Bideford, Devon, EX39 2QG

Tel: 01237 428700
Fax: 01237 478849

Website:
http://www.torridge.gov.uk

Enquiries:
Enquiries to: Chief Executive

Founded:
1974

Organisation type and purpose:
Local government body.

TOTAL FINA ELF EXPLORATION UK PLC

Acronym or abbreviation: TFEEUK

Crawpeel Road, Altens Industrial Estate, Aberdeen, AB12 3FG

Tel: 01224 297000
Fax: 01224 298000

Enquiries:
Enquiries to: Librarian

Formerly called:
Elf Exploration UK plc (EEUK), Total Oil Marine (TOM) (year of change 2000)

Organisation type and purpose:
Commercial company.

Subject coverage:
Oil, gas, exploration and production.

Library catalogue:
All or part available in-house

TOURETTES ACTION

Formal name: Tourette Syndrome (UK) Association (Tourettes Action)

Southbank House, Black Prince Road, London, SE1 7SJ

Tel: 0845 458 1252 (helpline)
E-mail: help@tourettes-action.org.uk

Website:
http://www.tourettes-action.org.uk

Enquiries:
Enquiries to: Chief Executive
Direct tel: 020 7793 2356
Direct e-mail: jmkidd@tourettes-action.org.uk

Founded:
1980

Organisation type and purpose:
National organisation, advisory body, membership association (membership is by subscription, qualification, election or invitation), present number of members: 650, voluntary organisation, registered charity (charity number 1003317). The object of the Association is the relief of persons who have the neurological movement disorder Gilles de la Tourette Syndrome.

Subject coverage:
Tourette Syndrome, a neurological disorder causing motor and vocal tics

Information services:
Helpline; information pack available on request.

Printed publications:
General Information Pack
Booklets for teachers
Booklets for doctors (forthcoming)
Newsletter (quarterly)
Factsheet on Tourette Syndrome
Order printed publications from: From helpline

Electronic and video publications:
E-mail news bulletins

Publications list:
Available online and in print

Access to staff:
Contact by letter, by telephone, by e-mail and via website
Hours: Mon to Fri, 0900 to 1700

Access to building, collection or gallery:
No access other than to staff

TOURISM AUSTRALIA

Acronym or abbreviation: TA

Australia Centre, Australia House, 6th Floor, Melbourne Place/Strand, London, WC2B 4LG

Tel: 020 7438 4601
Fax: 020 7240 6690
E-mail: tjarman@tourism.australia.com

Website:
http://www.australia.com
Over 10,000 pages of travel-related information on Australia.
http://www.tourism.australia.com

Enquiries:
Enquiries to: Marketing
Direct e-mail: amallard@tourism.australia.com
Other contacts: PR Manager, Advertising Manager

Formerly called:
Australian Tourist Commission (year of change 2004)

Organisation type and purpose:
National government body.
To promote tourism to Australia.

Subject coverage:
Australian travel trade contacts and Australian tourism in general.

Museum or gallery collection, archive, or library special collection:
Image library
Tourism Research
Video footage library

Trade and statistical information:
Statistical details on Australian tourism, arrival statistics.

Printed publications:
Australia Travel Guide (also available in German, French, Italian and Dutch)

Electronic and video publications:
Image Collection on CD-ROM
Video Footage

Access to staff:
Contact by letter, by telephone, by fax, by e-mail and via website

Hours: Mon to Fri, 0900 to 1700

Access to building, collection or gallery:
No prior appointment required

Other addresses:
Main office London, representative offices throughout Europe

TOURISM FOR ALL

c/o Vitalise, Shap Road Industrial Estate, Shap Road, Kendal, Cumbria, LA9 6NZ

Tel: 0845 124 9971
Fax: 01539 735567
E-mail: info@tourismforall.org.uk

Enquiries:
Enquiries to: Manager
Other contacts: Head of Consultancy Services for consultancy service of the charity.

Founded:
1981

Created by the merger of:
Holiday Care, the Tourism for All Consortium and IndividuALL

Formerly called:
Holiday Care Service (HCS)

Organisation type and purpose:
Voluntary organisation, registered charity (charity number 279169), consultancy, research organisation.

Subject coverage:
The UK's central source of information for disabled people and carers wishing to take a holiday break.

Publications list:
Available in print

Access to staff:
Contact by letter, by telephone, by fax, by e-mail and in person
Hours: Mon to Fri, 0900 to 1700

Access for disabled people:
Access to all public areas, toilet facilities

TOURISM NEW ZEALAND

Acronym or abbreviation: TNZ

New Zealand House, 80 Haymarket, London, SW1Y 4TQ

Tel: 020 7930 1662
Fax: 020 7839 8929

Website:
http://www.newzealand.com

Enquiries:
Enquiries to: Office Manager
Direct e-mail: alisac@tnz.govt.nz

Organisation type and purpose:
National government body.
Government department of New Zealand.

Subject coverage:
Accommodation, transport, sights, vehicle hire, special events, outdoor activities, general tourism information, coach tours re New Zealand.

Printed publications:
New Zealand Motivator Brochure

Access to staff:
Contact by letter, by fax and via website

Member of:
Association of National Tourist Office Representatives
UK Chapter of the Pacific Asia Travel Association

TOURISM SOCIETY

Trinity Court, 34 West Street, Sutton, Surrey, SM1 1SH

Tel: 020 8661 4636
Fax: 020 8661 4637

E-mail: admin@tourismsociety.org

Website:
http://www.tourismsociety.org
Brief history of the society, membership grades, fees, benefits, current event calendar.

Enquiries:
Enquiries to: Executive Director
Other contacts: Conference Co-ordinator for forthcoming events.

Founded:
1977

Organisation type and purpose:
Professional body (membership is by subscription), present number of members: 1300, service industry, suitable for ages: 15+.
Links tourism sectors, enhances members' professionalism and is the leading tourism network.

Subject coverage:
Education and training in tourism; tourism management, current issues, news.

Printed publications:
Tourism (journal, quarterly)

Publications list:
Available in print

Access to staff:
Contact by letter, by telephone, by fax and by e-mail. Access for members only.
Hours: Mon to Fri, 0900 to 1700

Sub-groups are:
The Scottish Chapter
Tourism Society Consultants Group

TOWER HAMLETS LIBRARIES

Bancroft Library, 227 Bancroft Road, London, E1 4DQ

Tel: 020 8980 4366
Fax: 020 8983 4510

Website:
http://www.towerhamlets.gov.uk
Staff and services.

Enquiries:
Enquiries to: Head of Libraries

Organisation type and purpose:
Local government body, public library.

Subject coverage:
General, local history, art, music, languages, general and American literature.

Museum or gallery collection, archive, or library special collection:
Art Library (Whitechapel Library)
Chinese and Vietnamese literature (4200 volumes Limehouse Library)
Collection of books in Asian languages (Indian, 12,500 volumes Whitechapel Library)
Inner London Special Collection: General and American literature (Limehouse Library)(closed)
Inner London Special Collections: French, German and Portuguese literature (Limehouse Library)
Joint Fiction Reserve: authors OP-PIC (closed), ST-SZ (current, 7000 volumes, Limehouse Library)
Local History Library, including the Bolt Collection on sailing and early steamships (Bancroft Library)
Music and foreign language records (Whitechapel Library)
Play-Reading sets (Whitechapel Library)
Sound recordings (all main libraries, totalling 55,000)

Library catalogue:
All or part available in-house

Printed publications:
Tower Hamlets Libraries Periodical (current)
Union List of Telephone Directories held by central London Reference Libraries (1999)
List of Local History publications – available from the Bancroft Library

continued overleaf

Publications list:
Available in print

Access to staff:
Contact by letter, by telephone, by fax, by e-mail and in person
Hours: Mon, Tue, Thu, 0900 to 2000; Wed, closed; Fri, 0900 to 1800; Sat, 0900 to 1700

Has:
11 branch libraries

Reference & Information Service:
Tower Hamlets Libraries
  Bethnal Green Library, Cambridge Heath Road, London, E2 0HL; tel: 020 8980 3902 or 6274; fax: 020 8981 6129; e-mail: 100633.624@compuserve.com

TOWNSWOMEN

Formal name: Townswomen's Guilds
Acronym or abbreviation: TG

Tomlinson House, 1st Floor, 329 Tyburn Road, Erdington, Birmingham, B24 8HJ

Tel: 0121 326 0400
Fax: 0121 326 1976
E-mail: tghq@townswomen.org.uk

Website:
http://www.townswomen.org.uk
Site maintained by head office, giving information on all current Townswomen's Guilds campaigns, activities, structure, aims and objectives.

Enquiries:
Enquiries to: National Secretary
Direct e-mail: joanne@townswomen.org.uk
Other contacts: Public Affairs Officer, Press Officer

Founded:
1928

Formerly called:
National Union of Townswomen's Guilds

Organisation type and purpose:
Membership association (membership is by subscription), registered charity (charity number 306072R).
75,000 members in nearly 1500 Guilds grouped in 114 Federations campaign on national and regional issues.
Organise national and regional events and conferences, national sport and leisure events and competitions.

Subject coverage:
Education in citizenship for women, current affairs, leadership, sports, environment, consumer affairs, women's health, Europe; current campaigns include the National Lottery, genetically modified food, transport, long-term care, energy conservation, carers, part-time workers.

Museum or gallery collection, archive, or library special collection:
Archives of the Townswomen's Guilds

Printed publications:
Annual Report
Guide to Personal Safety 1996
Townswomen's Guild: Factfile
Townswoman Magazine (4 times a year, for members)
Understanding Genetics 1996
Who Cares in the Long Term? (report on long term care for the elderly, 1997)

Access to staff:
Contact by letter, by telephone, by fax, by e-mail and via website. Appointment necessary.
Hours: Mon to Fri, 0900 to 1700

Member of:
Associated Countrywomen of the World
Women's National Commission

TOYHORSE SOCIETY

Acronym or abbreviation: THI

Howick Farm, The Haven, Billingshurst, West Sussex, RH14 9BQ

Tel: 01403 822639
Fax: 01403 822014

Enquiries:
Enquiries to: President/Director
Direct e-mail: tikadorian@yahoo.co.uk

Founded:
1992

Formerly called:
British Miniature Horse Society (BMHS)

Organisation type and purpose:
International organisation, membership association (membership is by subscription), present number of members: 100, suitable for ages: 5+, training organisation.
To register the stock of miniature horses; foreign bloodline department formed in 1995. To advise on the welfare of miniature horses and arrange seminars for instruction on training, welfare, showing and exhibiting of miniature horses.

Subject coverage:
Welfare of miniature horses, training for driving etc.

Museum or gallery collection, archive, or library special collection:
AMHA Stud Books
BMHS newsletters, books
BMHS Register
MAFF newsletters
SPSBS Stud Books

Printed publications:
Newsletter (for members)
Information leaflets

Access to staff:
Contact by letter, by telephone and by fax. Appointment necessary.
Hours: Mon to Fri, 0900 to 1700
Special comments: Charges to non-members for more than basic information.

TOYOTA ENTHUSIASTS' CLUB

Acronym or abbreviation: TEC

11 St Georges Crescent, Gravesend, Kent, DA12 4AR

Tel: 01474 746911

Enquiries:
Enquiries to: Membership Secretary
Other contacts: Newsletter Editor for information.

Founded:
1991

Organisation type and purpose:
Membership association (membership is by subscription).

Subject coverage:
Information on spares and services for all UK import Toyota Models, technical information and vehicle valuation.

Museum or gallery collection, archive, or library special collection:
Comprehensive range of motoring literature on all models of Toyota, both domestic and overseas, road tests, sales brochures and historical references

Printed publications:
Newsletter (quarterly, 40 pages A4)
Tec Topics (free to members, others £2 per copy plus p&p)
Order printed publications from: Newsletter Editor, Toyota Enthusiasts Club
71 Park Road, Chorley, Lancashire, PR7 1QZ, tel: 01257 415795

Access to staff:
Contact by letter and by telephone
Hours: 1900 to 2200, everyday

TR REGISTER

Formal name: TR Owners Club Ltd

1B Hawksworth, Southmead Industrial Park, Didcot, Oxfordshire, OX11 7HR

Tel: 01235 818866
Fax: 01235 818867
E-mail: office@tr-register.co.uk

Website:
http://www.tr-register.co.uk
Club information.

Enquiries:
Enquiries to: General Manager

Founded:
1970

Organisation type and purpose:
Membership association.
Car enthusiast's club.

Subject coverage:
Triumph TR series cars, car register, build records, technical data.

Museum or gallery collection, archive, or library special collection:
Books and archives
Material on TR sports cars

Printed publications:
TR Action (Club magazine, free to members or £2 each to non-members, 8 times a year)

Access to staff:
Contact by letter, by telephone, by fax and by e-mail. Access for members only.
Hours: Mon to Fri, 0900 to 1700

TRADA TECHNOLOGY LIMITED

Acronym or abbreviation: TTL

Stocking Lane, Hughenden Valley, High Wycombe, Buckinghamshire, HP14 4ND

Tel: 01494 569600
Fax: 01494 565487
E-mail: information@trada.co.uk

Website:
http://www.tradatechnology.co.uk
http://www.trada.co.uk

Enquiries:
Enquiries to: Manager, TRADA Information Centre
Other contacts: Special technical enquiry line for enquiries of a technical nature.

Formerly called:
Timber Research and Development Association (TRADA)

Organisation type and purpose:
International organisation (membership is by subscription), training organisation, consultancy, research organisation.
Contracted by TRADA to provide research and information services.

Subject coverage:
Timber research and most aspects of timber utilisation (excluding paper and furniture), with particular reference to timber in construction, fire, finishes, timber engineering, design; testing of structures and components; timber buildings; training; wood-based sheet materials; pallets and packaging; preservation; timber drying. Product conformity services; quality assurance; health and safety; environmental services to a wide-range of industries as well as information services and training courses.

Museum or gallery collection, archive, or library special collection:
Compliance with health and safety and environmental legislation
Construction industry information
Construction products directive-related European directives
Information on timber and wood-based products
Standards

Printed publications:
Newsletter (members only)
TRADA Updata (Awareness services on standards)

Electronic and video publications:
Timber – an architectural resource
Timberwise CD-ROM
Timberworks (CD-ROM)

Publications list:
Available in print

Access to staff:
Contact by letter, by telephone, by fax and by e-mail
Hours: Mon to Fri, 0900 to 1700

Other offices:
TRADA Technology Limited
    Stirling; tel: 01786 462122; fax: 01786 474412

Sister company:
BMTRADA Certification Limited
    tel: 01494 569700; fax: 01494 565487
Chiltern International Fire
    tel: 01494 569800; fax: 01494 564895
FIRA International Ltd
    tel: 01438 777700; fax: 01438 777800

TRADE MARK OWNERS ASSOCIATION LIMITED

Acronym or abbreviation: TMOA

Sea Containers House, 20 Upper Ground, London, SE1 9PD

Tel: 020 7902 7100
Fax: 020 7902 7111
E-mail: trademarks@tmoa.com

Website:
http://www.tmoa.com/trademarks.html

Enquiries:
Enquiries to: General Secretary
Other contacts: Managing Director

Founded:
1886

Organisation type and purpose:
Service industry.
Trade mark agents.

Subject coverage:
Advisors for trademark registrations, searches, renewals, infringements etc, worldwide.

Access to staff:
Contact by letter, by telephone, by fax and by e-mail
Hours: Mon to Fri, 0900 to 1800

TRADE MARKS, PATENTS AND DESIGNS FEDERATION

Acronym or abbreviation: TMPDF

Fifth Floor, 63–66 Hatton Garden, London, EC1N 8LE

Tel: 020 7242 3923
Fax: 020 7242 3924
E-mail: admin@tmpdf.org.uk

Website:
http://www.tmpdf.org.uk

Enquiries:
Enquiries to: Administrator

Founded:
1920

Organisation type and purpose:
Membership association (membership is by subscription, qualification, present number of members: 50, manufacturing industry, service industry.
Spokesman for industry on intellectual property (patents, trade marks, designs and copyright).

Subject coverage:
Industry views on trade marks, patents, copyright and industrial designs.

Access to staff:
Contact by letter, by telephone and by e-mail
Hours: Mon to Fri, 1030 to 1800

TRADES UNION CONGRESS

Acronym or abbreviation: TUC

Congress House, 23–28 Great Russell Street, London, WC1B 3LS

Tel: 020 7636 4030
Fax: 020 7636 0632
E-mail: info@tuc.org.uk

Website:
http://www.tuc.org.uk

Enquiries:
Enquiries to: Information Manager
Direct fax: 020 7467 1273

Founded:
1868

Organisation type and purpose:
Trade union.

Subject coverage:
Trade unions, TUC policy, international and overseas trade unions.

Library catalogue:
All or part available in-house

Printed publications:
Annual Report
TUC Budget Submission (annually)
TUC Directory (annually)
TUC General Council Report (annually)
A large number of publications on trade union issues, employment and the law, working conditions, equal rights for women and black workers and other minorities, health and safety, personal injury law, disability rights, pensions, Europe and international issues, learning and skills and TUC history
Order printed publications from: Publications Department, Trades Union Congress
at the same address, tel: 020 7467 1294, fax: 020 7636 0632, e-mail: smills@tuc.org.uk

Electronic and video publications:
Videos

Publications list:
Available online and in print

Access to staff:
Contact by letter, by telephone, by fax, by e-mail and via website
Hours: Mon to Fri, 0915 to 1700
Special comments: Not open to the public. TUC Archive Library at London Metropolitan University accessible by appointment.

Member of:
European Trade Union Confederation
International Confederation of Free Trade Unions

TUC Library Collection:
London Metropolitan University Learning Centre
    236–250 Holloway Road, London, N7 6PP; tel: 020 7753 3184; fax: 020 7753 3191; e-mail: c .coates@londonmet.ac.uk

TRADES UNION CONGRESS LIBRARY COLLECTIONS

Acronym or abbreviation: TUC Library Collections

London Metropolitan University, Learning Centre, 236–250 Holloway Road, London, N7 6PP

Tel: 020 7133 2260
Fax: 020 7133 2529
E-mail: tuclib@londonmet.ac.uk

Website:
http://www.londonmet.ac.uk/services/sas/library-services/tuc/
http://catalogue.londonmet.ac.uk/search~S7
TUC Library Collections OPAC
http://www.tuc.org.uk
Trades Union Congress

Enquiries:
Enquiries to: Librarian
Direct e-mail: c.coates@londonmet.ac.uk

Founded:
1922

Organisation type and purpose:
Trade union, university library.
Research collection.

Subject coverage:
Trade unions, economic, political and social history, industrial relations, collective bargaining, international affairs, industrial history, education, women's history, colonial policy.

Museum or gallery collection, archive, or library special collection:
General Strike Collection
Gertrude Tuckwell Collection (women's trade unionism and welfare, 1890–1921)
London Trades Council Records
Marjorie Nicholson Papers (colonial affairs)
Workers' Educational Association Library and Archive

Non-library collection catalogue:
All or part available online

Library catalogue:
All or part available in-house

Microform publications:
Microfilm for purchase:
Committee Minutes and Papers 1922–53
General Council Minutes 1921–46
Gertrude Tuckwell Collection 1890–1920
Parliamentary Committee Minutes 1888–1921
The Mining Crisis and the General Strike 1925–26
TUC Annual Congress Reports 1869–2001
TUC Pamphlets and Leaflets 1887–1972
TUC Periodicals and Serials 1918–77
TUC publications in Britain and Europe since 1945, collection
Women's Trade Union League Papers 1875–1921

Access to staff:
Contact by letter, by telephone, by fax, by e-mail and via website. Appointment necessary.
Hours: Mon to Fri, 0900 to 1700
Special comments: Letter of introduction required for undergraduates.

Access to building, collection or gallery:
Prior appointment required

Access for disabled people:
Toilet facilities, ramped entry to main building, level entry to collections.

Member organisation of:
International Association of Labour History Institutions (IALHI)

Parent body:
Trades Union Congress
    Congress House, Great Russell Street, London, WC1B 3LS; tel: 020 7636 4030

TRADING STANDARDS INSTITUTE

Acronym or abbreviation: TSI

1 Sylvan Court, Sylvan Way, Southfields Business Park, Basildon, Essex, SS15 6TH

Tel: 0870 872 9000
Fax: 0870 872 9025
E-mail: institute@tsi.org.uk

Website:
http://www.tradingstandards.gov.uk
General information and information about courses.

Enquiries:
Enquiries to: Chief Executive

Founded:
1881

continued overleaf

Formerly called:
Institute of Weights and Measures Administration; Institute of Trading Standards Administration (ITSA) (year of change 2000)

Organisation type and purpose:
Professional body (membership is by qualification).
Society for local government officers in trading standards departments.

Subject coverage:
Consumer and trade protection legislation, description of legal requirements, consumer trends, enforcement interests.

Printed publications:
Directory of Trading Standards Officers in UK (6 times a year)
The Trading Standards Today (journal, monthly)

Access to staff:
Contact by letter, by telephone, by fax and by e-mail. Appointment necessary. Access for members only.
Hours: Mon to Fri, 0900 to 1700

Access for disabled people:
Access to all public areas

TRAFFIC INTERNATIONAL

Acronym or abbreviation: TRAFFIC

219a Huntingdon Road, Cambridge, CB3 0DL

Tel: 01223 277427
Fax: 01223 277237
E-mail: traffic@traffic.org

Website:
http://www.traffic.org

Enquiries:
Enquiries to: Executive Director

Founded:
1976

Organisation type and purpose:
International organisation, registered charity (charity number 1076722).

Subject coverage:
Wildlife trade monitoring, the trade and utilisation of wild plants and animals.

Library catalogue:
All or part available online, in-house and in print

Printed publications:
See Publications section on http://www.traffic.org
Order printed publications from: Information & Publication Officer, TRAFFIC International, tel: 01223 277427, e-mail: susan.vivian@traffic.org

Publications list:
Available online and in print

Access to staff:
Contact by letter, by telephone, by fax, by e-mail and via website
Hours: Mon to Fri, 0900 to 1700

Access to building, collection or gallery:
No prior appointment required

Supported by:
World Conservation Union (IUCN)
WWF

TRAFFIC RESEARCH CENTRE

Formal name: Centre for Transport Engineering and Land Use Planning
Acronym or abbreviation: TRC CENTELUP

12 Flamsteed Road, Cambridge, CB1 3QU

Tel: 01223 248444 (answer after 7 rings)

Enquiries:
Enquiries to: Director

Founded:
1982

Formed from:
Arthur Henderson Consultants (year of change 1982)

Formerly called:
Centre for Transport Engineering and Land Use Planning

Organisation type and purpose:
Advisory body, learned society, registered charity (charity number 284449), university library, research organisation.
Charitable research trust.
To research and improve safety standards for pedestrians and all road users, improve the efficiency and convenience of all forms of transport for the movement of passengers and freight with particular reference to rail, air and sea terminals.

Subject coverage:
Traffic engineering, transport planning, highway layout, highway and traffic safety, education, law enforcement, urban junction design, transport systems appraisal, transport economics.

Museum or gallery collection, archive, or library special collection:
Denys Mumby Collection in Transport Economics
London Airport Rapid Transit; Guided Bus concept established 1964

Printed publications:
Design Sheets: loose-leaf system to follow (restricted circulation)

Access to staff:
Contact by letter and by telephone. Appointment necessary.
Hours: Mon to Fri, 0900 to 1700
Special comments: Reference only.

TRAFFORD MBC

Acronym or abbreviation: Trafford Libraries

Lifelong Learning Directorate, Bibliographical Services, Davyhulme Library Site, Hayeswater Road, Davyhulme, Greater Manchester, M41 7BL

Tel: 0161 912 2882
Fax: 0161 912 2895
E-mail: libraries@trafford.gov.uk

Website:
http://www.trafford.gov.uk/encompass
Community information database.

Enquiries:
Enquiries to: Librarian

Founded:
1974

Formerly called:
Trafford MBC Education, Arts and Leisure Department, Recreation and Culture Division

Organisation type and purpose:
Local government body, public library.

Subject coverage:
Local government information, business information and European information at Altrincham library, local studies centre at Sale Library. General public library stock at Altrincham, Urmston, Sale and Stretford libraries. Community and leisure information database and bibliographical services.

Museum or gallery collection, archive, or library special collection:
Photo database (digitised photos)
Cruikshank Collection (some 50 examples of the illustrator's work, housed at Altrincham, access strictly by prior appointment)

Non-library collection catalogue:
All or part available in-house

Printed publications:
Various local history publications
Order printed publications from: Bibliographical Services
As main address

Electronic and video publications:
EnCompass (community information database, online)

Access to staff:
Contact by letter, by telephone, by fax, by e-mail and in person
Hours: Mon to Fri, 0830 to 1630

Access to building, collection or gallery:
Prior appointment required

Access for disabled people:
Parking provided, ramped entry

TRANSLATORS ASSOCIATION

84 Drayton Gardens, London, SW10 9SB

Tel: 020 7373 6642
Fax: 020 7373 5768
E-mail: info@societyofauthors.org

Website:
http://www.societyofauthors.org
Criteria for membership, aims and services.

Enquiries:
Enquiries to: Secretary

Founded:
1958

Organisation type and purpose:
Trade association, trade union (membership is by subscription, election or invitation), present number of members: 480.
Specialist section of the Society of Authors, its members are literary translators whose translations of full length foreign works have already been published in the UK.

Subject coverage:
Interests and problems of translators whose work has been published or produced commercially in the UK, general and legal advice on marketing of work, rates of remuneration, contractual arrangements.

Printed publications:
Guidelines for Translators of Dramatic Works (members only)
In Other Words (journal, twice a year, available to non-members on subscription)
Quick Guide to Literary Translation (£2 inc. p&p)
Specimen Contract (members only)

Access to staff:
Contact by letter and by telephone. Access for members only.
Hours: Mon to Thu, 0930 to 1730; Fri, 0930 to 1700

Affiliated to:
Conseil Européen des Associations de Traducteurs Littéraires
Fédération Internationale de Traducteurs

Parent body:
The Society of Authors
at the same address

TRANSPORT & GENERAL WORKERS UNION

Acronym or abbreviation: TGWU (NCTS)

Northern Carpet Trades' Section, 22 Clare Road, Halifax, West Yorkshire, HX1 2HX

Tel: 01422 360492
Fax: 01422 321146

Enquiries:
Enquiries to: Regional Industrial Organiser
Direct e-mail: nhalton@tgwu.org.uk

Founded:
1892

Organisation type and purpose:
Trade union, present number of members: 2000.

Subject coverage:
Organisation in the carpet industry, staff and shop floor; history; industrial relations.

Museum or gallery collection, archive, or library special collection:
Archives held in Calderdale Central Library (Archives Department)

Printed publications:
Catalogue of historical documents, available in Calderdale Central Library (archives department)
Annual Report
Newsletter (occasional)

Access to staff:
Contact by letter, by telephone, by fax and by e-mail. Appointment necessary. Access for members only.
Hours: Mon to Thur, 0845 to 1645; Fri 0445 to 1545

Access to building, collection or gallery:
No prior appointment required

Affiliated to:
General Federation of Trade Unions (GFTU)
National Affiliation of Carpet Trade Unions (NACTU)
Trades Union Congress

TRANSPORT 2000

The Impact Centre, 12–18 Hoxton Street, London, N1 6NG

Tel: 020 7613 0743
Fax: 020 7613 5280

Website:
http://www.transport2000.org.uk

Enquiries:
Enquiries to: Administrator

Founded:
1973

Organisation type and purpose:
Membership association (membership is by election or invitation), present number of members: 42, voluntary organisation.
Concerned with transport issues; membership consists of a variety of environmental or amenity groups, trade unions and industry in the transport sector.
Campaigns for environmentally sensitive transport policies.

Subject coverage:
General transport policy issues – railways, buses, cycling, walking, freight transport, roads and traffic, land use and planning, environmental impact and pollution associated with transport, public transport.

Printed publications:
Briefings and Information Sheets
Information pack (send sae)
Transport Report (4 times a year)
A range of books and reports under the headings:
General Transport Policy
Planning Issues
Guides for Public Activism
Walking and Cycling
Resources for Teachers
Health and Road Safety
Public Transport
Roads
Freight
Rail Privatisation
Green Travel Plans

Publications list:
Available in print

Access to staff:
Contact by letter. Appointment necessary.
Hours: Mon to Fri, 0930 to 1230 and 1330 to 1630

Access to building, collection or gallery:
Prior appointment required

TRANSPORT ASSOCIATION

Peter Acton Associates, 185 Great Tattenhams, Epsom Downs, Surrey, KT18 5RA

Tel: 01737 362232

Fax: 01737 352323
E-mail: secretary@trans-assoc.co.uk

Website:
http://www.trans-assoc.co.uk

Enquiries:
Enquiries to: Secretary

Founded:
1953

Organisation type and purpose:
Trade association (membership is by election or invitation), present number of members: 50+ companies.

Subject coverage:
Road transport.

Access to staff:
Contact by letter, by e-mail and via website
Hours: Mon to Fri, 0900 to 1700

TRANSPORT FOR LONDON

Acronym or abbreviation: TfL

Windsor House, 42–50 Victoria Street, London, SW1H 0TL

Tel: 020 7941 4500
Fax: 020 7941 4572
E-mail: enquiries@tfl.gov.uk

Website:
http://www.transportforlondon.gov.uk
All information on London's Transport and its subsidiaries.

Enquiries:
Enquiries to: Head of Customer Services
Direct tel: 020 7918 4040 Underground; 020 7918 4300 Buses
Direct fax: 020 7918 4093 Underground; 020 7918 3999 Buses
Direct e-mail: Underground: customerservices@email.lul.co.uk;
Other contacts: Buses: customerservices@tfl-buses.co.uk

Founded:
3 July 2000

Formerly (as a holding company):
London Transport (LRT) (LT), date of change, 3 July 2000

Formerly called:
London Underground Limited (LUL), date of change, 3 July 2000

Organisation type and purpose:
Local government body.
TfL is London's integrated transport body. Its role is to implement the Mayor's transport strategy for London and manage the transport services for which the Mayor is responsible.

Subject coverage:
Public transport in London and its operation today.

Museum or gallery collection, archive, or library special collection:
Historic records held by London's Transport Museum

Printed publications:
Annual Report

Publications list:
Available online

Access to staff:
Contact by letter, by telephone, by fax, by e-mail and via website
Hours: Mon to Fri, 0900 to 1700
Special comments: 24 Hours London Travel Information 020 7222 1234.

Access to building, collection or gallery:
No access other than to staff

Historic records:
London's Transport Museum
Covent Garden, London, WC2E 7BB; tel: 020 7379 6344; fax: 020 7836 4118; e-mail: resourcec@ltmuseum.co.uk

Link:
London Underground Limited
55 Broadway, London, SW1H 0BD; tel: 020 7222 5600; fax: 020 7918 3134; e-mail: customerservices@email.lul.co.uk

Responsible to the:
Mayor of London
Romney House, 43 Marsham Street, London, SW1P 3PY; tel: 020 7983 4100; e-mail: enquire@london.gov.uk

Subsidiary bodies:
Docklands Light Railway
Castor Lane, London, E14 0DS; tel: 020 7363 9700
London Buses
172 Buckingham Palace Road, London, SW1W 9TN; tel: 020 7222 5600; fax: 020 7918 3999; e-mail: customerservices@TfL-buses.co.uk
London River Services
Tower Pier, Lower Thames Street, London, EC3N 4DT; tel: 020 7941 2400
Street Management
Windsor House, 42–50 Victoria Street, London, SW1H 0TL; tel: 020 7343 5000; website: www.streetmanagement.org.uk
Victoria Coach Station Limited
164 Buckingham Place, London, SW1W 9TP; tel: 020 7730 3466; website: www.transportforlondon.gov.uk/vcs

TRANSPORT TRUST

202 Lambeth Road, London, SE1 7JW

Tel: 020 7928 6464
Fax: 020 7928 6565
E-mail: hq@thetransporttrust.org.uk

Website:
http://www.thetransporttrust.org.uk

Enquiries:
Enquiries to: Director General
Other contacts: Chairman

Founded:
1965

Organisation type and purpose:
National organisation, membership association (membership is by subscription), present number of members: 1500, voluntary organisation, registered charity (charity number 280943).
To promote and encourage the permanent preservation and where necessary the restoration of transport items of historical or technical interest for the benefit of the nation.

Subject coverage:
Preservation and restoration of all forms of transport: veteran and vintage cars, aircraft, locomotives, all old ships and canal craft plus inland waterway boats etc, cycles, mail and public coaches, buses, trams, trolley buses, military vehicles.

Museum or gallery collection, archive, or library special collection:
An extensive library and archives relating to Britain's transport heritage. Library and archives held at Ironbridge Museum, Shropshire (Tel: 01952 432141)

Library catalogue:
All or part available in-house

Printed publications:
Digest (4 times a year)
List of Transport Museums and Preserved Railways (annually)

Access to staff:
Contact by letter, by telephone, by fax, by e-mail and via website
Hours: Mon to Fri, 0900 to 1700
Special comments: 24 hour answerphone.

Access to building, collection or gallery:
Prior appointment required
Hours: Mon to Fri, 0900 to 1700

Access for disabled people:
Parking provided, ramped entry, access to all public areas, toilet facilities

TREE COUNCIL

51 Catherine Place, London, SW1E 6DY

Tel: 020 7828 9928
Fax: 020 7828 9060
E-mail: info@treecouncil.org.uk

Website:
http://www.treecouncil.org.uk

Enquiries:
Enquiries to: Director General

Founded:
1974

Organisation type and purpose:
Registered charity.
Company limited by guarantee; promotional, educational and information body; a list of members follows this entry.

Subject coverage:
Trees in the United Kingdom.

Printed publications:
Native Trees and Shrubs for Wildlife (£1)
How to do a Tree Survey (£1)
Select Bibliography on Trees and Woodlands 1984 (free)
Taking Care – Why pay twice for a tree – Tree Planting and Care (free)
Teacher's Handbook – Working with Trees (£6.50, Linden Publications)
Tree Council Forum Notes including: Trees and Property Development; Old trees; Street Trees; Tree Related Subsidence – What are the issues? (£2.50 each title)
Trees of Britain Poster (£2)
Tree News (2 times a year)
The Good Seed Guide (£3.50)
Trees Love Care (leaflet, free)

Electronic and video publications:
Trees of Britain (CD-ROM £19.95, from Main Publishing, City House, 16 City Road, Winchester SO23 8SD tel: 01962 870680)

Access to staff:
Contact by letter, by telephone, by fax, by e-mail and via website
Hours: Mon to Fri, 0900 to 1700

Consultative Members:
Common Ground
Convention of Scottish Local Authorities
Countryside Agency
Countryside Council for Wales
Department for the Environment, Food and Rural Affairs
Department of the Environment for Northern Ireland
Department of Transport, Local Government and the Regions
English Heritage
English Nature
Forestry Commission
Highways Agency
Joint Nature Conservation Committee
Learning Through Landscapes
Ministry of Defence
Scottish Natural Heritage

Full Members:
Ancient Tree Forum
Arboricultural Association
Arid Lands Initiative
British Trust for Conservation Volunteers (BTCV)
Civic Trust
Country Land and Business
Department of Transport, Local Government to the Regions
Forestry & Timber Association
Groundwork Foundation
Horticultural Trades Association
Institute of Chartered Forests
Institute of Horticulture
International Tree Foundation
Landscape Institute
National Association of Tree Officers
National Forest Company
National Memorial Arboretum
National Trust

National Urban Forestry Unit
Royal Agricultural Society of England
Royal Forestry Society of England, Wales & Northern Ireland
Royal Horticultural Society
Royal Institution of Chartered Surveyors
Royal Society for Nature Conservation
Royal Society for the Protection of Birds
Royal Town Planning Institute
Tree Advice Trust
Woodland Trust

TREVITHICK SOCIETY

PO Box 62, Camborne, TR14 7ZN

Tel: 01209 716811
E-mail: k.rickard@trevithick-society.org.uk

Enquiries:
Enquiries to: Honorary Secretary
Direct tel: 01209 711685
Direct e-mail: gbwilson@macace.net

Founded:
1934

Organisation type and purpose:
Membership association (membership is by subscription), present number of members: 450.

Subject coverage:
Industrial archaeology in Cornwall, mines and mining, Cornish engines and engine houses and other restorations, explosives, transport.

Museum or gallery collection, archive, or library special collection:
Collection of artefacts at Geevor Mining Museum, Pendeen, Penzance, and at King Edward Mine, Camborne School of Mines, Cornish mines and engines, Pool, Redruth
Drawings and plans relating to Cornish engines and mines lodged with the County Record Office, Truro

Printed publications:
Journal (annually)
Newsletter (quarterly)

Publications list:
Available in print

Access to staff:
Contact by letter
Hours: Mon to Fri, 0900 to 1700

TRIDENT & ROCKET THREE OWNERS CLUB

Acronym or abbreviation: TR3OC

6 Beechnut Drive, Darby Green, Camberley, Surrey, GU17 0DJ

Tel: 01252 861259
E-mail: graham.r@talktalk.net

Website:
http://www.tr3oc.org
Worldwide contact with owners, problems discussed. News, views and sales, also wanted section.

Enquiries:
Enquiries to: Secretary

Founded:
1979

Organisation type and purpose:
International organisation, membership association (membership is by subscription), present number of members: 1100, voluntary organisation, suitable for ages: all.

Subject coverage:
3 cylinder pushrod engined machines manufactured by Triumph and BSA between 1968 and 1976 and other machines fitted with these engines; technical information and other areas of interest.

Museum or gallery collection, archive, or library special collection:
Technical data of original machines and developments, including factory records
All published material concerning the 3 cylinder machines

Printed publications:
Triple Echo (6 times a year)
Triple Service Notes (available from Merchandise Secretary)

Access to staff:
Contact by letter, by telephone and by e-mail
Hours: Mon to Fri, 0830 to 2200
Special comments: No visits to Committee Members addresses.

Affiliated to:
BMF

TRIDENT CAR CLUB

23 Matlock Crescent, Cheam, Sutton, Surrey, SM3 9SS

Tel: 020 8644 9029
Fax: 020 8641 5359
E-mail: trident.carclub@virgin.net

Enquiries:
Enquiries to: Chairman

Founded:
1980

Organisation type and purpose:
International organisation, membership association (membership is by subscription), present number of members: 31.
Membership open to owners and those interested in Trident cars.

Subject coverage:
Trident cars, technical knowledge, information and experience.

Printed publications:
Magazine/newsletter (quarterly, members)

TRINIDAD AND TOBAGO HIGH COMMISSION

42 Belgrave Square, London, SW1X 8NT

Tel: 020 7245 9351
Fax: 020 7823 1065
E-mail: tthc@btconnect.com

Website:
http://www.highcommission.co.uk
Specific information, trade, tourism on Trinidad and Tobago
http://www.discovertrinidad.com
General information on Trinidad
http://www.discovertobago.com
General information on Tobago

Enquiries:
Enquiries to: Information Officer

Organisation type and purpose:
National government body.
Diplomatic mission.

Subject coverage:
Trinidad and Tobago trade and commerce; imports and exports, petroleum industry, natural gas industry, culture.

Printed publications:
Newsletter (monthly, £10 a year)

Access to staff:
Appointment necessary.
Hours: Mon to Fri, 0900 to 1700

TRINITY & ALL SAINTS COLLEGE

Library, Brownberrie Lane, Horsforth, Leeds, West Yorkshire, LS18 5HD

Tel: 0113 283 7100
Fax: 0113 283 7200
E-mail: e.brush@leedstrinity.ac.uk

Website:
http://www.tasc.ac.uk/iss/library.htm
Brief details of Library services. Access to TAS
Library catalogue.

Enquiries:
Enquiries to: Librarian
Direct tel: 0113 283 7246
Direct e-mail: l.murphy@leedstrinity.ac.uk

Founded:
1966

Organisation type and purpose:
University library.

Subject coverage:
Education; communication and media studies;
business and management; social and
environmental studies: psychology; English,
French and Spanish language and literature;
economics; history; music; sport, health and
leisure; sociology; theology; public media;
journalism.

**Museum or gallery collection, archive, or library
special collection:**
Yorkshire Local History Collection

Library catalogue:
All or part available online

Access to staff:
Contact by letter, by telephone and by e-mail
Hours: Mon to Fri, 0900 to 1700

Access to building, collection or gallery:
No access other than to staff
Hours: Term time: Mon to Thu, 0900 to 2045; Fri,
0900 to 1745; Sat, 1300 to 1645; Sun, 1400 to 2045

Affiliated to:
University of Leeds

TRINITY COLLEGE LIBRARY

Cambridge, CB2 1TQ

Tel: 01223 338488
Fax: 01223 338532
E-mail: trin-lib@lists.cam.ac.uk

Website:
http://www.trin.cam.ac.uk

Enquiries:
Enquiries to: Librarian

Founded:
1546

Organisation type and purpose:
College library in the University of Cambridge.

Subject coverage:
Subjects covered by the special collections.

**Museum or gallery collection, archive, or library
special collection:**
Papers include: R A Butler, J G Frazer, Otto Frisch,
Lord Macaulay, R M Milnes, Lord Houghton, D
H Robertson, Henry Sidgwick, Piero Sraffa,
Alfred, Lord Tennyson, G P Thomson, William
Whewell, Ludwig Wittgenstein
Some catalogues available on www
Capell Collection of Shakespeareana*.
Incunabula (c. 750 items)
Medieval manuscripts (c. 1500 items)*.
Newton Library
Oriental manuscripts*.
Rothschild Collection of 18th century literature*.
* indicates that a printed catalogue exists

Access to staff:
Contact by letter, by fax, by e-mail and via
website. Appointment necessary. Letter of
introduction required.
Hours: Mon to Fri, 0900 to 1700

TRINITY COLLEGE LIBRARY
(BRISTOL)

Stoke Hill, Bristol, BS9 1JP

Tel: 0117 968 2803
Fax: 0117 968 7470

Website:
http://www.trinity-bris.ac.uk

Enquiries:
Enquiries to: Librarian

Founded:
1971

Formed by the amalgamation of:
Clifton Theological, Dalton House Colleges;
Tyndale Hall (year of change 1971)

Organisation type and purpose:
Theological College.

Subject coverage:
Theology; religion; ecclesiastical history; the
Church of England; history; philosophy; ethics;
comparative religion.

Library catalogue:
All or part available in-house

Access to staff:
Contact by letter, by telephone, by fax and by e-
mail. Non-members charged.
Hours: Mon to Fri, 0900 to 1700
Special comments: Closed Sat and Sun.

Affiliated to:
University of Bristol, which validates the College's
degrees

Links with:
Church of England

TRINITY COLLEGE OF MUSIC

Acronym or abbreviation: TCM

Jerwood Library of the Performing Arts, King
Charles Court, Old Royal Naval College,
Greenwich, London, SE10 9JF

Tel: 020 8305 3950
Fax: 020 8305 9444
E-mail: library@tcm.ac.uk

Website:
http://www.tcm.ac.uk
General information.
http://sirsi3.tcm.ac.uk/uhtbin/webcat
Online catalogue.
http://www.musicpreserved.org.uk
Music preserved.
http://www.mander-and-mitchenson.co.uk
Mander & Mitchenson Theatre Collection.

Enquiries:
Enquiries to: Head Librarian
Other contacts: (1) Director, Mander & Mitchenson
Theatre Collection (2) Library Assistant, Centre for
Young Musicians Library for (1) access to the
Collection (2) queries relating to the CYM Library.

Founded:
1872

Organisation type and purpose:
Suitable for ages: 18+.
Specialist college library for students of music and
the performing arts.

Subject coverage:
Music, history of the British theatre.

**Museum or gallery collection, archive, or library
special collection:**
Music Preserved (historic recordings of live
  performances)
Antonio de Almeida Collection
Barbirolli Collection
Sir Frederick Bridge Library
Centre for Young Musicians Library
Christopher Wood Collection
Frank Cordell Collection
Filmharmonic Archive
Lionel Tertis Collection
Mander & Mitchenson Theatre Collection
Shura Cherkassky Collection
William Lovelock Collection

Non-library collection catalogue:
All or part available in-house

Library catalogue:
All or part available online

Printed publications:
Library guides (available free of charge)

Access to staff:
Contact by letter, by telephone and by e-mail.
Appointment necessary.
Hours: Term time: Mon to Thu, 0900 to 1900; Fri,
0900 to 1700
Special comments: Out of term, please telephone.

Access to building, collection or gallery:
Prior appointment required

Access for disabled people:
Parking provided, ramped entry, access to all
public areas, toilet facilities

Centre for Young Musicians Library:
Trinity College of Music
  at same address; tel: 020 8305 3952; e-mail: tony
  .lynes@googlemail.com

TRIUMPH 2000/2500/2.5 REGISTER

10 Gables Close, Chalfont St Peter, Gerrards Cross,
Buckinghamshire, SL9 0PR

Tel: 01494 582673
E-mail: t2000register@compuserve.com

Website:
http://www.t2000register.org.uk

Enquiries:
Enquiries to: Secretary

Founded:
1981

Organisation type and purpose:
International organisation, membership
association (membership is by subscription),
present number of members: 900.

Subject coverage:
Triumph 2000, 2500 and 2.5 cars manufactured
between 1963 and 1977.

Printed publications:
Six Appeal

Access to staff:
Contact by letter, by telephone, by fax and by e-
mail
Hours: Evenings and weekends

TRIUMPH MAYFLOWER CLUB

19 Broadway North, Walsall, West Midlands, WS1
2QG

Tel: 01922 633042
E-mail: johnchoaker@btinternet.com

Website:
http://www.triumphmayflowerclub.com

Enquiries:
Enquiries to: Membership Secretary

Founded:
1975

Organisation type and purpose:
Membership association (membership is by
subscription), present number of members: 152.

Subject coverage:
Workings, both mechanical and non-mechanical, of
the Triumph Mayflower; history of Triumph
Mayflower; general information and statistics
regarding cars still in existence; technical
information, sources of spares.

**Museum or gallery collection, archive, or library
special collection:**
Archive of material on the Triumph Mayflower

Printed publications:
Flowerpower (magazine, quarterly)

Publications list:
Available in print

continued overleaf

Access to staff:
Contact by letter and by telephone
Hours: Mon to Fri, 1700 to 1930

TRIUMPH RAZOREDGE OWNERS CLUB

62 Seaward Avenue, Barton-on-Sea, Hampshire, BH25 7HP

Tel: 01425 618074
E-mail: davidwickens@clara.net

Enquiries:
Enquiries to: Secretary General

Founded:
1975

Organisation type and purpose:
Membership association (membership is by subscription), present number of members: 220.

Subject coverage:
Triumph Razoredge saloons manufactured between 1946 and 1954, spare parts, technical information.

Printed publications:
Magazine (6 times a year, free to members)

Access to staff:
Contact by letter, by telephone and by e-mail
Hours: Mon to Fri, 0900 to 1700

Member of:
Historic Vehicle Clubs Committee

TRIUMPH ROADSTER CLUB

Acronym or abbreviation: TRC

15 Lower Hill Road, Epsom, Surrey, KT19 8LS

Tel: 01372 812141
Fax: 01372 812141
E-mail: webmaster@triumphroadster.org.uk

Website:
http://www.triumphroadster.org.uk
Club services and e-mail contact addresses.

Enquiries:
Enquiries to: Secretary

Founded:
1960

Organisation type and purpose:
International organisation, membership association (membership is by subscription), present number of members: 500.
Club for the preservation of Triumph Roadster motor cars (1946–49 18TR and 20TR only).

Subject coverage:
Technical information related to the preservation and restoration of 1946–49 Triumph Roadster models 18TR and 20TR, including sources of replacement components, advice on purchase and registration mark authentication.

Printed publications:
Technical Manual and Restoration Guide
User Manual

Publications list:
Available online

Access to staff:
Contact by letter, by telephone, by fax, by e-mail and via website. Appointment necessary.
Hours: Mon to Fri, 0900 to 1700

Affiliated to:
Federation of British Historic Vehicle Clubs (FBHVC)
Elton House, Church Lane, Tydd St Giles, Wisbech, Cambridgeshire, PE13 5LA; tel: 01945 871295; fax: 01945 870528; e-mail: admin@fbhvc .co.uk; website: www.fbhvc.co.uk

TRIUMPH SPORTS SIX CLUB

Acronym or abbreviation: TSSC LTD

Freepost, Lubenham, Market Harborough, Leicestershire, LE16 9TF

Tel: 01858 434424
Fax: 01858 431936
E-mail: tssc@tssc.org.uk

Website:
http://www.tssc.org.uk

Enquiries:
Enquiries to: Executive Director
Direct e-mail: trudi@tssc.org.uk

Founded:
1977

Organisation type and purpose:
Membership association (membership is by subscription), present number of members: 9,000. Classic car club.

Non-library collection catalogue:
All or part available in-house

Library catalogue:
All or part available in-house

Printed publications:
Accessories Catalogue
The Courier (magazine, monthly, £2.25, free to members)

Publications list:
Available in print

Access to staff:
Contact by letter, by telephone, by fax, by e-mail, in person and via website
Hours: Mon to Fri, 0900 to 1700

Access to building, collection or gallery:
No access other than to staff
Hours: Mon to Fri, 0900 to 1700

Access for disabled people:
Ramped entry, access to all public areas, toilet facilities

TRL LTD

Formal name: Transport Research Laboratory

TRL Library and Information Centre, Crowthorne House, Nine Mile Ride, Wokingham, Berks, RG40 3GA

Tel: 01344 770203
Fax: 01344 770193
E-mail: info@trl.co.uk

Website:
http://www.trl.co.uk

Enquiries:
Enquiries to: Librarian
Direct e-mail: sbenjamin@trl.co.uk
Other contacts: Document Supply (tel. 01344 770783)

Founded:
1933

Formerly called:
Road Research Laboratory (year of change 1972); Transport and Road Research Laboratory (TRRL) (year of change 1992); Transport Research Laboratory (TRL) (year of change 1992)

Organisation type and purpose:
Consultancy. Provides consultancy on transport, civil engineering, vehicle safety, vehicles and environment both in the UK and overseas.

Subject coverage:
Planning, design, construction and maintenance of roads and highway structures, particularly bridges and tunnels; safe and convenient movement of people and goods, including the layout of roads and traffic networks, control of traffic flow, study of road accidents and methods of reducing their frequency and severity; transport-planning and land-use strategies; existing and projected passenger and freight transport systems; environmental effects; new transport technology, intelligent transport, crash testing, traffic software, vehicle safety.

Printed publications:
Advisory leaflets (free)
Application Guides
Contractor Reports
Current Topics in Transport (bibliographies)
KWIC Indexes to Report Titles
Laboratory Reports
Research Reports
Supplementary Reports
TRL Publications Catalogue (revised annually, free)
TRL Reports (current series)
Order printed publications from: Via website, or from IHS, tel. 01344 328039; e-mail trl@ihs.com

Microform publications:
All TRL's publications to end of 1994

Electronic and video publications:
New Reports (CD-ROM)
Selections from TRL's database

Publications list:
Available online and in print

Access to staff:
Contact by letter, by telephone, by fax, by e-mail and via website. Appointment necessary. All charged.

Access to building, collection or gallery:
Prior appointment required
Hours: Mon to Fri, 0900 to 1700
Special comments: Discounts to academic and non-commercial organisations; one-day visit charge £30.

Access for disabled people:
Access to all public areas, toilet facilities

Links with:
Transport Research Foundation
Crowthorne House, Nine Mile Ride, Wokingham, Berkshire RG40 3GA; tel: 01344 773131; fax: 01344 770356; e-mail: enquiries@trl .co.uk; website: http://www.trl.co.uk

TROON @ AYRSHIRE FAMILY HISTORY SOCIETY

c/o MERC, Troon Public Library, South Beach, Troon, Ayrshire, KA10 6EF

E-mail: info@troonayrshirefhs.org.uk

Website:
http://www.troonayrshirefhs.org.uk
Details of the society, list of publications for sale, membership application form.

Enquiries:
Enquiries to: Secretary

Founded:
1989

Formerly called:
Troon and District Family History Society

Organisation type and purpose:
Membership association, voluntary organisation. Family History research.

Subject coverage:
Family history in the Troon and surrounding area of Ayrshire.

Printed publications:
Death and Burial Records in South Ayrshire
Dundonald Burial Register
Irvine 1820 Census Index (booklet)
Monumental Inscriptions for the Parishes of: Ayr, Craigie, Coylton, Dailly, Dundonald, Girvan, Kirkoswald, Prestwick & Monkton, St Quivox & Newton on Ayr and Symington Parishes
Sources of Family History in Ayrshire
Galston Census, 1801, 1811, 1821 and 1831
Galston militia 1799 and 1801 with servicemen's letters of 1918
St. Quivox 1821 Census Index
OPR Death & Burial Indexes for Auchinleck, Ballantrae & Girvan, Dalrymple, Irvine, Mauchline, Stair, Symington and Tarbolton

Microform publications:
Irvine Census 1820 – full transcription & Index (set of 2 fiche)
Supplemental Register of births from Kilmarnock 1855 (set of two fiche)

Publications list:
Available online and in print

Access to staff:
Contact by letter and by e-mail
Hours: Mon to Fri, 0900 to 1700

TROPICAL HEALTH AND EDUCATION TRUST

Acronym or abbreviation: THET

210 Euston Road, London, NW1 2BE

Tel: 020 679 7127/8/9
Fax: 020 7679 8190
E-mail: info@thet.org

Enquiries:
Enquiries to: Project Coordinator

Founded:
1988

Organisation type and purpose:
Registered charity (charity number 800567).
To develop capacity for healthcare in Africa through collaboration with training institutions in Africa and the UK.

Subject coverage:
Training for healthcare in Africa.

Non-library collection catalogue:
All or part available in-house

Printed publications:
Annual Review
Newsletter

Access to staff:
Contact by letter, by fax and by e-mail.
Appointment necessary.
Hours: Mon to Fri, 0900 to 1700

Access to building, collection or gallery:
Prior appointment required

Access for disabled people:
Ramped entry

TT SUPPORTERS CLUB

50 Lyndhurst Road, Birmingham, B24 8QS

Tel: 0121 686 3799
Fax: 0121 686 8700

Website:
http://www.ttsupportersclub.com

Enquiries:
Enquiries to: Information Officer

Subject coverage:
The Manx motor cycle TT races.

TUBEROUS SCLEROSIS ASSOCIATION

Acronym or abbreviation: TSA

PO Box 12979, Barnt Green, Birmingham, B45 5AN

Tel: 0121 445 6970
Fax: 0121 445 6970
E-mail: diane.sanson@tuberous-sclerosis.org

Website:
http://www.tuberous-sclerosis.org

Enquiries:
Enquiries to: Head of Administration
Other contacts: TS Specialist Advisers, Appeals and Publicity Officer for advice regarding support and publicity

Founded:
1977

Organisation type and purpose:
Membership association (membership is by subscription), present number of members: 1500, voluntary organisation, registered charity (charity number 1039549).

Subject coverage:
Tuberous sclerosis, epilepsy, mental handicap, autism, behaviour generally, psychotic behaviour, renal problems, symptoms, genetic counselling.

Printed publications:
Annual Report
Clinical Guide-lines
Factsheets on relevant topics (40 titles)
Medical Brochure (2001)
TalkingShop (newsletter for mildly affected adults)
TSA Scan (newsletter)
What the teacher of a TS Child should know
Your Child with TS – What Happens Next

Electronic and video publications:
CD-ROMs
3 Videos for hire or purchase

Publications list:
Available online and in print

Access to staff:
Contact by letter, by telephone, by fax, by e-mail and via website
Hours: Mon to Fri, 0900 to 1700

Links with:
Disability Alliance
1st Floor, Universal House, 88–94 Wentworth Street, London, E1 7SA; tel: 020 7247 8776
Genetics Interest Group
Unity 4D, Leroy House, 436 Essex Road, London, N1 3QP; tel: 020 7704 3141; fax: 020 7359 1447
Neurological Alliance
PO Box 31287, London, NW2 6NL; tel: 020 7831 7522; fax: 020 7831 7522
Tuberous Sclerosis International
Prins Bernhardlaan 36, Bilthoven, NL-3722 AG, The Netherlands

TUN ABDUL RAZAK RESEARCH CENTRE

Acronym or abbreviation: TARRC

Brickendonbury, Hertford, SG13 8NL

Tel: 01992 584966
Fax: 01992 554837
E-mail: general@tarrc.tcom.co.uk

Website:
http://www.tcom.co.uk/tarrc/
Provides an overview of products and services available. Included is a publications list, together with an on-line ordering facility.

Enquiries:
Enquiries to: Head of Information

Founded:
1938

Formerly called:
Malaysian Rubber Producers' Research Association (MRPRA)

Organisation type and purpose:
Trade association, research organisation.

Subject coverage:
Rubber, especially natural rubber, rubber products.

Museum or gallery collection, archive, or library special collection:
History of Rubber
MORPHS main database 100,000 documents (mainly on microfilm)
Photographs

Trade and statistical information:
SMR Monthly Statistical Bulletin.
Quarterly Statistical Bulletin.

Printed publications:
Journal of Rubber Research (quarterly)
Malaysian Rubber Review (quarterly)
Rubber Developments (2 times a year)

Books, market research and technical reports, monographs, information packs for schools
MRPRA Publications 1938–1991: author bibliographies
Natural rubber engineering data sheets

Electronic and video publications:
Natural Rubber Bounces On (video)
Naturally its Rubber (video)
see also Rubber Consultants

Publications list:
Available in print

Access to staff:
Contact by letter, by fax, by e-mail and via website. Appointment necessary.
Hours: Mon to Fri, 0900 to 1700
Special comments: Charges made to some users.

Parent body:
Malaysian Rubber Research and Development Board
PO Box 10508, Kuala Lumpur, 50716, Malaysia

TUNBRIDGE WELLS BOROUGH COUNCIL

Town Hall, Tunbridge Wells, Kent, TN1 1RS

Tel: 01892 526121\ Minicom no. 01892 545449
Fax: 01892 534227
E-mail: info@tunbridgewells.gov.uk

Website:
http://www.tunbridgewells.gov.uk
Comprehensive site informing users of services and attractions within Tunbridge Wells locality.

Organisation type and purpose:
Local government body.
Local authority.

Subject coverage:
Local government services.

Publications list:
Available online and in print

Access to staff:
Contact by letter, by telephone, by fax, by e-mail, in person and via website
Hours: Mon to Fri, 0900 to 1700

Access to building, collection or gallery:
No prior appointment required

Access for disabled people:
Parking provided, level entry, access to all public areas, toilet facilities

TUNBRIDGE WELLS FAMILY HISTORY SOCIETY

Yew Tree Byre, Yew Tree Lane, Rotherfield, East Sussex, TN6 3QP

Tel: 01892 852334
E-mail: veronicasiddall@hotmail.co.uk

Website:
http://www.tunwells-fhs.co.uk

Enquiries:
Enquiries to: Secretary

Founded:
1991

Organisation type and purpose:
Membership association (membership is by subscription), present number of members: 250.
To promote genealogical studies and family history, particularly in the Tunbridge Wells area.

Subject coverage:
Family history research in Tunbridge Wells area for members.

Printed publications:
Journal (three times a year, for members)
Other publications include:
Memorials and other Inscriptions St Mark's Church, Broadwater Down, Tunbridge Wells
Tonbridge Area, incl. Tunbridge Wells
Census Index 1851, A–L and M–Z

continued overleaf

Speldhurst Church CD Burials 1558–1837 and
other records
Frant Church CD of parish records,
Census returns for 1801, 1821, 1831, 1841 and 1851
for some East Sussex Parishes (fiche or hard
copy)
Rolls of Honour and War Memorials in some East
Sussex and Kent Villages
Local history books including:
Crowborough – Bygone Crowborough (M. Payne
and L. Batchelor)
Place Names of Kent (J. Glover)
Groombridge – An Illustrated History of the
Village
Royal Tunbridge Wells (R. Farthing)
Southborough and High Brooms (C. McCooey)
Order printed publications from: Tunbridge Wells
Family History Society, 16 Hydehurst Close,
Crowborough, East Sussex, TN6 1EN

Electronic and video publications:
1891 Census Index for the Tunbridge Wells Area
RG12/0676–0683 (£5.50 plus p&p)

Publications list:
Available in print

Access to staff:
Contact by letter, by e-mail and via website
Hours: Mon to Fri, 0900 to 1700
Special comments: Evenings (private residence)

TUNNEL LINING MANUFACTURERS ASSOCIATION

Acronym or abbreviation: TLMA

60 Charles Street, Leicester, LE1 1FB

Tel: 0116 253 6161
Fax: 0116 251 4568
E-mail: info@britishprecast.org

Enquiries:
Enquiries to: Secretary

Organisation type and purpose:
Trade association.

Subject coverage:
Tunnel linings.

Parent body:
British Precast Concrete Federation

TURKISH CYPRIOT CULTURAL ASSOCIATION

14a Graham Road, Hackney, London, E8 1BZ

Tel: 020 7249 7410
Fax: 020 7241 5643
E-mail: turk.cultural@btinternet.com

Enquiries:
Enquiries to: Chairman
Other contacts: Co-ordinator

Founded:
1977

Organisation type and purpose:
Membership association (membership is by
subscription), present number of members: About
400, voluntary organisation, registered charity
(charity number 285799).

Subject coverage:
Social and cultural problems of the Turkish
community and the Turkish Cypriot community in
particular.

Access to staff:
Contact by letter and by telephone
Hours: Tue to Fri, 1000 to 1700

Access to building, collection or gallery:
No access other than to staff
Hours: Mon to Fri, 1000 to 1700

TURKISH EMBASSY

Education Counsellor's Office, Tigris House, 256
Edgware Road, London, W2 1DS

Tel: 020 7724 1511
Fax: 020 7724 9989

Enquiries:
Enquiries to: Education Counsellor

Organisation type and purpose:
National government body.
Education for Turkish students.

Subject coverage:
Advice and guidance to Turkish students in UK;
Turkish education system and scholarships offered
by the Turkish government.

Access to staff:
Contact by letter, by telephone and by fax
Hours: Mon to Fri, 0930 to 1630, by telephone; Mon
to Fri, 0930 to 1330, in person

Unit of the:
Turkish Ministry of National Education in Turkey

TURKISH TOURIST OFFICE

Acronym or abbreviation: TTO

4th Floor, 29–30 St James's Street, London, SW1A
1HB

Tel: 020 78397778
Fax: 020 7925 1388
E-mail: info@gototurkey.co.uk

Website:
http://www.gototurkey.co.uk
General, regional, practical.

Enquiries:
Enquiries to: Public Relations Officer
Direct e-mail: tourismturkey.mediauk@fd.com

Formerly called:
Turkish Information Office

Organisation type and purpose:
National government body.
Section of the Turkish Embassy.

Subject coverage:
Tourist information on Turkey.

Printed publications:
Brochures, posters, slides, films, and video
cassettes
General holiday guide
List of tour operators

Access to staff:
Contact by letter, by telephone, by fax, by e-mail,
in person and via website
Hours: Mon to Fri, 0930 to 1730

Affiliated to:
Ministry of Tourism in Turkey
tel: +312 212 8300; fax: +312 212 8391; e-mail:
tanitma@turizm.gov.tr

TURNER LIBRARY, THE

Whitefield Schools and Centre, Macdonald Road,
Walthamstow, London, E17 4AZ

Tel: 020 8531 8703
Fax: 020 8527 0907
E-mail: lib@whitefield.org.uk

Website:
www.whitefield.org.uk

Enquiries:
Enquiries to: Librarian
Direct tel: 020 8531 8703 ext 150

Organisation type and purpose:
Membership association (membership is by
subscription), service industry.
Professional library, with national and
international membership, for all who have an
interest in special educational needs; based at
Whitefield Special School, the largest special school
in the United Kingdom.
Current awareness service by post.

Subject coverage:
All aspects of special educational needs:
curriculum; management; policy; legislation;
syndromes and disorders; integration; support
teaching.

**Museum or gallery collection, archive, or library
special collection:**
Large periodical collection of national and
international journals relating to special
education, early years education and curriculum

Printed publications:
Current awareness bulletin (6 times a year, with
back-up photocopying service on subscription)

Access to staff:
Contact by letter, by telephone, by fax, by e-mail
and in person. Non-members charged.
Hours: Mon, Thu, 0900 to 1830; Tue, Wed, 0900 to
1700; Fri, 0900 to 1630,
August, Half terms, Easter: Tue, Wed, Thu, 0900 to
1600, closed all other days. Please check opening
hours before visiting during holiday periods
Special comments: Closed for two weeks at
Christmas & New Year.

TURNER REGISTER

21 Ellsworth Road, High Wycombe,
Buckinghamshire, HP11 2TU

Tel: 01494 445636

Enquiries:
Enquiries to: Registrar

Founded:
1960

Organisation type and purpose:
Membership association.

Subject coverage:
Information relating to design, manufacture,
restoration and maintenance of Turner sports and
racing cars manufactured by Mr J H Turner in
Wolverhampton 1949–1966.

**Museum or gallery collection, archive, or library
special collection:**
Copies of original works publications
Manufacturing records of vehicles built
Road Tests from motoring journals

Printed publications:
Club Newsletter (11 times a year, members only)

Access to staff:
Contact by letter
Hours: Mon to Fri, 0900 to 1700

Parent body:
Fairthorpe Sports Car Club (Turner Register)
9 Lynhurst Crescent, Hillingdon, Middlesex,
UB10 9EF

TURNER SOCIETY

BCM Box Turner, London, WC1N 3XX

Website:
http://www.turnersociety.org.uk

Enquiries:
Enquiries to: Chairman

Founded:
1975

Organisation type and purpose:
Learned society (membership is by subscription),
present number of members: c. 400, registered
charity (charity number 269832).
To further interest in the life and work of J M W
Turner RA.

Subject coverage:
The life, work and influence of J M W Turner, RA.

Printed publications:
Turner Society News (3 times a year)

Access to staff:
Contact by letter

TWI LTD

Granta Park, Great Abington, Cambridgeshire, CB21 6AL

Tel: 01223 899000
Fax: 01223 894342
E-mail: library@twi.co.uk

Website:
http://www.twi.co.uk

Enquiries:
Enquiries to: Manager, Information Services
Direct e-mail: linda.dumper@twi.co.uk
Other contacts: Technical Enquiry Services;
weldasearch@twi.co.uk

Founded:
1968

Formerly called:
British Welding Research Association, Institute of Welding (year of change 1968); The Welding Institute (year of change 1991)

Organisation type and purpose:
International organisation, professional body, training organisation, consultancy, research organisation.

Subject coverage:
Technology and practice of welding; brazing; soldering; thermal cutting; weld surfacing; metal spraying; inspection and non-destructive testing; QA systems; welding design; welding and joining metallurgy and materials science; performance of welded assemblies (failure, fatigue, brittle fracture, corrosion); fabrication and construction; quality control; joining of plastics and ceramics; adhesives.

Museum or gallery collection, archive, or library special collection:
Materials identification
Trade literature on welding equipment and consumables

Library catalogue:
All or part available online and in-house

Printed publications:
Connect
Welding Abstracts (abstracts journal, monthly)

Electronic and video publications:
Software programmes (c.15)
WELDASEARCH (online file on QUESTEL/ORBIT, Dialog, CINECA (Italy), FIZ-TECHNIK and via CSA web-based search services and through the TWI website at http://www.twi.co.uk)

Publications list:
Available in print

Access to staff:
Contact by letter, by telephone, by fax, by e-mail and via website. Appointment necessary. Access for members only.
Hours: Mon to Thu, 0830 to 1630; Fri, 0830 to 1615

Constituent bodies:
Certification Scheme for Welding and Inspection Personnel (CSWIP)
Institute of Rail Welding (IORW)
School of Applied Non-Destructive Testing (SANDT)
School of Welding Technology (SWT)
Welding and Joining Society (WJS)

TYNDALE HOUSE BIBLICAL STUDIES RESEARCH CENTRE

Tyndale House, 36 Selwyn Gardens, Cambridge, CB3 9BA

Tel: 01223 566601
Fax: 01223 566608
E-mail: librarian@tyndale.cam.ac.uk

Website:
http://www.tyndale.cam.ac.uk
Details of the library, facilities and staff. Access to other libraries and centres for biblical research.

Enquiries:
Enquiries to: Librarian

Direct tel: 01223 566604

Founded:
1940s

Organisation type and purpose:
Registered charity, university department or institute, research organisation, publishing house.

Subject coverage:
Biblical studies and research; theology.

Museum or gallery collection, archive, or library special collection:
Maps of Palestine
The library is said to contain one of the best collections of books and electronic resources on biblical studies in the world

Library catalogue:
All or part available online

Printed publications:
Tyndale Bulletin (twice a year)

Access to staff:
Contact via website. Appointment necessary. Letter of introduction required.
Hours: Mon to Fri, 0900 to 1730

Parent body:
Universities and Colleges Christian Fellowship

TYNE AND WEAR ARCHIVES SERVICE

Acronym or abbreviation: TWAS

Blandford House, Blandford Square, Newcastle upon Tyne, NE1 4JA

Tel: 0191 277 2248
Fax: 0191 230 2614
E-mail: twas@gateshead.gov.uk

Website:
http://www.tyneandweararchives.org.uk

Enquiries:
Enquiries to: Chief Archivist

Founded:
1974

Organisation type and purpose:
Local government body.
Archives service.

Subject coverage:
Tyne and Wear, shipbuilding, family history, other aspects of the North-East.

Museum or gallery collection, archive, or library special collection:
Records of many organisations, industries and individuals relating to Tyne and Wear

Non-library collection catalogue:
All or part available online and in-house

Library catalogue:
All or part available online and in-house

Printed publications:
Newcastle upon Tyne Charters (out of print)
Combination and Confederacy Chartist Pack (£2)
Guide to Sources for Family Historians
Index to 1851 Census of Northumberland (£4)
Newcastle Quayside – Heart of a City Pack (£5)
Pressgangs and Privateers (£6.95)
South Shields in the Nineteenth Century Pack (£2)
Sunderland Builds the Ships (£1.95)
Tyne and Wear at Work (£2.95)

Electronic and video publications:
A History of Newcastle (video, £12.99)
Gateshead – A Journey Through Time (video, £12.99)
Newcastle – A Journey Through Time (video, £12.99)

Access to staff:
Contact by letter, by telephone, by fax, by e-mail, in person and via website
Hours: Mon, Wed to Fri, 0900 to 1700; Tue, 0900 to 2030; first Sat every month, 0900 to 1700

Special comments: Appointments are essential for Tue evening.

Access for disabled people:
Parking provided, ramped entry, level entry, access to all areas, toilet facilities

TYNE METROPOLITAN COLLEGE

The Library, Embleton Avenue, Wallsend, Tyne and Wear, NE28 9NJ

Tel: 0191 229 5301
Fax: 0191 229 5243
E-mail: gillian.rutherford@tynemet.ac.uk

Website:
http://www.tynemet.ac.uk

Enquiries:
Enquiries to: Head of Library Resources
Direct e-mail: mark.callan@tynemet.ac.uk

Organisation type and purpose:
Suitable for ages: 14+
College of further education.

Subject coverage:
All areas covered particularly international baccalaureate, A-levels, art and design, media, engineering, hairdressing

Trade and statistical information:
FEFC documents.

Non-library collection catalogue:
All or part available online

Library catalogue:
All or part available online and in-house

Printed publications:
Library user guide (annually)

Access to staff:
Contact by letter, by telephone, by fax and by e-mail. Appointment necessary. Access for members only.
Hours: Mon to Thu, 0900 to 2000; Fri, 0900 to 1600; Sat, 1000 to 1300
Vacations: 0900 to 1600

TYNEDALE COUNCIL

Hexham House, Hexham, Northumberland, NE46 3NH

Tel: 01434 652200\ *Minicom no.* 01434 652323
Fax: 01434 652420
E-mail: enquiries@tynedale.gov.uk

Website:
http://www.tynedale.gov.uk
Tourist information, economic development information.

Enquiries:
Enquiries to: Chief Executive
Other contacts: Public Relations and Marketing Officer for sources of information about the council.

Founded:
1974

Organisation type and purpose:
Local government body.
District Council.

Subject coverage:
Public information about the work of the Tynedale Council.

Printed publications:
Annual Report
A-Z Council Services
Local Performance Plan
Tynedale Community Plan

Access to staff:
Contact by letter, by telephone, by fax, by e-mail, in person and via website
Hours: Mon to Thu, 0830 to 1700; Fri, 0830 to 1630

TYNWALD LIBRARY

Legislative Buildings, Finch Road, Douglas, Isle of Man, IM1 3PW, Isle of Man

Tel: 01624 685520
Fax: 01624 685522
E-mail: library@tynwald.org.im

Website:
http://www.tynwald.org.im

Enquiries:
Enquiries to: Librarian
Other contacts: Research Officer: tel no: 01624 685521; e-mail research@tynwald.org.im for parliamentary research (members of Tynwald only)

Founded:
1975

Formerly called:
Central Reference Library (year of change 1987)

Organisation type and purpose:
National government body.
Parliamentary library.
To provide a comprehensive source of information and documentation relevant to the work of the Legislature of the Isle of Man.

Subject coverage:
General reference collection especially social sciences, Manx affairs, law, parliament, executive government, sale of official documents.

Museum or gallery collection, archive, or library special collection:
Documents produced by the Isle of Man
 Government (Civil Service)
Laws of the Isle of Man
Parliamentary papers considered by the
 Legislature of the Isle of Man
Report of the Official Proceedings: Isle of Man
 (Hansard)

Trade and statistical information:
Isle of Man Digest of Economic and Social Statistics
 (annual)
Isle of Man Government Policy Review (annual).

Non-library collection catalogue:
All or part available in-house

Library catalogue:
All or part available in-house

Printed publications:
Publications include:
Reports and Bills laid before the Legislature
Acts of Tynwald
Statutory Documents of the Isle of Man
Tynwald Calendar
Tynwald Ceremony (booklet, annual)
Isle of Man Orders in Council (2nd ed, 1996)
Chronological Table of Acts of Parliament
 extending to the Isle of Man

Access to staff:
Contact by letter, by telephone, by fax, by e-mail, in person and via website. Appointment necessary.
Hours: Mon to Fri, 0900 to 1700

Access for disabled people:
Parking provided, toilet facilities, lifts

Parent body:
Clerk of Tynwald's Department
 at the same address; tel: 01624 685000; fax: 01624
 685004; e-mail: enquiries@tynwald.org.in

UACE

Formal name: Universities Association for
Continuing Education
Acronym or abbreviation: UACE

University of Cambridge, Board of Continuing Education, Madingley Hall, Madingley, Cambridge, CB3 8AQ

Tel: 01954 280279
Fax: 01954 280200
E-mail: mer1000@cam.ac.uk

Website:
http://www.uace.org.uk
Publications list; membership list.

Enquiries:
Enquiries to: Secretary
Direct e-mail: sm120@cam.ac.uk

Formerly called:
Polytechnic Association for Continuing Education (PACE), Universities Council for Adult and Continuing Education

Organisation type and purpose:
Professional body.
Consultative body for universities and university colleges; information centre for continuing and adult education; liaison and collaborative body with, for example, the Department for Education and Skills.
Co-ordinating policy development for the whole field of continuing education at university level in the UK; acting as a source of information and, where appropriate, pressure on Universities UK, Department for Education and Skills.

Subject coverage:
Continuing education, continuing vocational education, part-time student and non-standard student matters in HE, FE/HE links, access and other flexible entry routes, flexible study patterns in higher education, research in continuing education, European and international links in CE development and research, CE provision to counter educational disadvantage (including targeted work with specific groups such as minority ethnic communities, disabled people, unwaged people, socio-economically disadvantaged groups, universities in their relations with the community, workers' education).

Trade and statistical information:
Statistical information available on all aspects of
 CE provision in the higher education sector in
 the UK.

Printed publications:
Annual Report
Membership List
Newsletters
Range of scholarly and good practice
 documentation

Publications list:
Available online and in print

Access to staff:
Contact by e-mail
Hours: Mon to Fri, 0900 to 1700

Access to building, collection or gallery:
No access other than to staff

UCL HUMAN COMMUNICATION SCIENCE LIBRARY

Acronym or abbreviation: UCL, NICeST

NICeST: National Information Centre for Speech-Language Therapy, UCL Dept of Human Communication Science, Chandler House, 2 Wakefield Street, London, WC1N 1PF

Tel: 020 7679 4207
Fax: 020 7713 0861
E-mail: hcs.library@ucl.ac.uk

Website:
http://www.ucl.ac.uk/Library/hcslib.shtml
http://www.ucl.ac.uk/HCS/HCSlibrary
Information about the library, library guides, various databases (members only), links to other speech and language therapy sites.

Enquiries:
Enquiries to: Librarian
Direct e-mail: s.russell@ucl.ac.uk

Organisation type and purpose:
University department or institute.

Subject coverage:
Speech, language, and communication disorders; speech and language therapy.

Museum or gallery collection, archive, or library special collection:
Tests and assessments used in clinics and schools;
 Historical collection of books and pamphlets

Non-library collection catalogue:
All or part available online

Library catalogue:
All or part available online and in-house

Access to staff:
Contact by telephone, by e-mail and via website. Appointment necessary. Access for members only. Non-members charged.
Hours: Mon to Thu, 0915 to 1900; Fri, 1000 to 1900
Special comments: Vacations, please telephone.

Part of:
UCL Library Services
UCL Medical School

UCL INSTITUTE OF CHILD HEALTH LIBRARY

Acronym or abbreviation: ICH

30 Guilford Street, London, WC1N 1EH

Tel: 020 7242 9789 ext 2424
Fax: 020 7831 0488
E-mail: library@ich.ucl.ac.uk

Website:
http://www.ich.ucl.ac.uk/library

Enquiries:
Enquiries to: Librarian and Deputy Librarian
Other contacts: Assistant Librarian (for SOURCE collection)

Founded:
1945

Organisation type and purpose:
University department or institute.

Subject coverage:
Paediatrics, diseases of children, SOURCE collection covers disability, mother and child health, HIV/AIDS, poverty and health in less developed countries.

Museum or gallery collection, archive, or library special collection:
SOURCE collection: an international information support centre designed to strengthen the management, use and impact of information in health and disability. Jointly owned by ICH, Healthlink Worldwide and Handicap International.

Non-library collection catalogue:
All or part available online

Library catalogue:
All or part available online

Access to staff:
Contact by letter, by telephone, by fax, by e-mail, in person and via website. Appointment necessary.
Hours: Mon to Fri, 0900 to 1800

Access for disabled people:
Ramped entry, access to all public areas, toilet facilities
Special comments: Chairlifts

Constituent part of:
University College London
 tel: 020 7679 7700; fax: 020 7679 7373; e-mail:
 library@ucl.ac.uk

Links with:
Hospital for Sick Children
 Great Ormond Street, London; tel: 020 7405 9200;
 fax: 020 7829 8643; e-mail: info@gosh.nhs.uk

UFO MONITORS EAST KENT

Acronym or abbreviation: UFOMEK

23 Brabner Close, Folkestone, Kent, CT19 6LW

Tel: 07968 583435 / 07091 020078
E-mail: astratech@supanet.com

Website:
http://www.homestead.com/kentufowatch/
homepage.html
http://www.homestead.com/kentufowatch/ufomek
.html

Enquiries:
Enquiries to: Director of Research and
Investigations

Founded:
Dec 1995

Formerly called:
National UFO Research Centre

Organisation type and purpose:
National organisation, voluntary organisation,
research organisation.
Investigation and research into aerial phenomena.

Subject coverage:
Information on investigations and research into
aerial phenomena in the county of Kent, first and
foremost, and nationally in the regions of the UK.

Access to staff:
Contact by letter, by telephone, by e-mail and via
website
Hours: Sun to Sat, 0900 to 2100

Access to building, collection or gallery:
No access other than to staff

Connections with:
UFO-Trek Information Service
UFO-Trek, c/o 23 Brabner Close, Folkestone,
Kent, CT19 6LW; tel: 07091 020078

UK CLEANING PRODUCTS INDUSTRY ASSOCIATION

Acronym or abbreviation: UKCPI

1st Floor, Century House, High Street, Tattenhall,
Cheshire, CH3 9RJ

Tel: 01829 770055
Fax: 01829 770101
E-mail: ukcpi@ukcpi.org

Enquiries:
Enquiries to: Secretary

Founded:
1939

Organisation type and purpose:
Trade association.

Subject coverage:
Effect of detergents on the environment, human
health and safety; regulations affecting the
cleaning products industry; history of the UK soap
industry.

Trade and statistical information:
Basic consumption statistics.

Printed publications:
A–Z of Detergents
Health and Hygiene
Cleaning with Care (Guide for Local Authorities)

Access to staff:
Contact by letter, by telephone, by fax and by e-
mail
Hours: Mon to Fri, 0900 to 1730

Links with:
Chemical Industries Association

Member organisation of:
Association Internationale de la Savonnerie et de la
Détergence (AISE)

UK COLLEGE FOR COMPLEMENTARY HEALTHCARE STUDIES

Acronym or abbreviation: UK College

St Charles Hospital, Exmoor Street, London, W10
6DZ

Tel: 020 8964 1206
Fax: 020 8964 1207

E-mail: info@ukcollege.com

Website:
http://www.ukcollege.com

Enquiries:
Enquiries to: Administrator
Other contacts: Principal or Director for areas of
expertise.

Founded:
1985

Formerly called:
UK Training College for Hypnotherapy and
Counselling

Organisation type and purpose:
Suitable for ages: Mature students 19+, training
organisation.
For complementary healthcare.

Subject coverage:
Accredited courses for complementary therapies;
BTEC, City and Guilds and VTCT, massage,
hypnotherapy, reflexology, counselling, first aid,
and aromatherapy, NLP one and two day
introductory courses.

**Museum or gallery collection, archive, or library
special collection:**
Register of Practitioners in United Kingdom
(telephone only for nearest one in location)

Library catalogue:
All or part available in-house

Printed publications:
Prospectus

Access to staff:
Contact by letter, by telephone, by fax, by e-mail
and via website. Appointment necessary.
Hours: Mon to Fri, 0900 to 1700

Access to building, collection or gallery:
Prior appointment required

Access for disabled people:
Parking provided, access to all public areas, toilet
facilities

UK CORD BLOOD IMMUNOLOGY GROUP

Acronym or abbreviation: UKCBIG

PO Box 3079, Barnet, Hertfordshire, EN5 4ZD

Tel: 0709 216 5730
Fax: 0709 211 4307
E-mail: sharacohen@euroscicon.com

Enquiries:
Enquiries to: Chairman
Direct e-mail: chairman@ukcbig.org.uk

Founded:
2000

Organisation type and purpose:
National organisation, learned society. To bring
together people working with, or interested in,
cord blood.

Subject coverage:
Science, immunology, transplantation, biology,
research.

Access to staff:
Contact by letter, by e-mail and via website
Hours: Mon to Fri, 0900 to 1700

Access to building, collection or gallery:
No access other than to staff

UK DATA ARCHIVE

Acronym or abbreviation: UKDA

University of Essex, Wivenhoe Park, Colchester,
Essex, CO4 3SQ

Tel: 01206 872143
Fax: 01206 872003
E-mail: help@esds.ac.uk

Website:
http://www.data-archive.ac.uk

Enquiries:
Enquiries to: Helpdesk

Founded:
1967

Formerly called:
ESRC Data Bank, ESRC Survey Archive; ESRC
Data Archive (year of change 1996); The Data
Archive (year of change 2000)

Organisation type and purpose:
University department or institute.
To preserve, maintain and disseminate research
data.

Subject coverage:
The UK Data Archive (UKDA) acquires, preserves,
disseminates and promotes data, including digital
data in the social sciences and humanities.
The UKDA provides resource discovery and
support for secondary use of quantitative and
qualitative data in research, teaching and learning
as a lead partner of the Economic and Social Data
Service (ESDS). The UKDA hosts AHDS History,
provides preservation services for other data
organisations and facilitates international data
exchange.

**Museum or gallery collection, archive, or library
special collection:**
The UKDA houses several thousand datasets of
interest to researchers, students and teachers in
the HE/FE sectors and from many disciplines.
Datasets cover the full range of the social
sciences and most aspects of social and economic
study.

Non-library collection catalogue:
All or part available online and in-house

Printed publications:
UKDA News (newsletter, quarterly, free, online or
printed copy)

Publications list:
Available online

Access to staff:
Contact by letter, by telephone, by fax, by e-mail,
in person and via website. Appointment necessary.
Hours: Mon to Fri, 0900 to 1700

Funded by:
Economic and Social Research Council (ESRC)
Joint Information Systems Committee (JISC)
University of Essex

UK FASHION EXPORTS

Acronym or abbreviation: UKFE

5 Portland Place, London, W1B 1PW

Tel: 020 7636 5577
Fax: 020 7636 7848
E-mail: info@ukfashionexports.com

Website:
http://www.ukfashionexports.com
Full description of aims and activities of UK
Fashion Exports and of the services available to
members and non-members.

Enquiries:
Enquiries to: Executive Director

Founded:
1940

Formed by the amalgamation of:
British Knitting Export Council (BKEC), Clothing
Export Council of Great Britain (CECGB) (year of
change 1984)

Formerly called:
British Knitting and Clothing Export Council
(BKCEC) (year of change 2000)

Organisation type and purpose:
Trade association (membership is by subscription).
To promote the export from UK of all clothing and
fashion-related accessories.

continued overleaf

Subject coverage:
Export markets and marketing, export statistics, export procedures and tariffs, information on overseas markets for clothing (members only), general information, to potential buyers of British clothing etc, all relevant details of appropriate UK suppliers.

Museum or gallery collection, archive, or library special collection:
Library of commercial information available to member companies (directories, export regulations, buyer information, trade journals (UK and foreign) etc)

Trade and statistical information:
Via associated organisations in the British Apparel and Textile Confederation, details of production in UK, numbers employed etc.

Library catalogue:
All or part available in-house

Printed publications:
Annual Report and Accounts
The BKCEC Exporter (monthly bulletin, free to members only)
The Fashion Buyer's Guide to Britain (formerly British Apparel Directory; free to overseas buyers or agents)
Various promotional leaflets

Access to staff:
Contact by letter, by telephone, by fax, by e-mail and via website. Appointment necessary.
Hours: Mon to Fri, 0900 to 1800

Affiliated to:
British Apparel and Textile Confederation at the same address
British Clothing Industry Association at the same address

Subsidiary body:
Apparel Marketing Services (Export) Ltd at the same address

UK HYDROGRAPHIC OFFICE

Acronym or abbreviation: UKHO

Admiralty Way, Taunton, Somerset, TA1 2DN

Tel: 01823 337900
Fax: 01823 284077
E-mail: via website www.ukho.gov.uk

Website:
http://www.ukho.gov.uk

Enquiries:
Enquiries to: Archives Research Manager
Direct tel: 01823 337900 ext 3409
Direct e-mail: research@ukho.gov.uk

Founded:
1795

Organisation type and purpose:
National government body, research organisation. Producer of navigational charts and related publications.
An appointed place of deposit for its own records under the Public Records Act 1958.

Subject coverage:
Navigation; hydrographic surveying; geodesy; photogrammetry; cartography; geophysics; oceanography; meteorology; shipping and ports.

Museum or gallery collection, archive, or library special collection:
Archives of hydrographic surveys, Admiralty Charts, navigational information, books, letters

Non-library collection catalogue:
All or part available in-house

Library catalogue:
All or part available in-house

Printed publications:
Catalogue of Admiralty Charts and other hydrographic publications available via worldwide network of agents
Order printed publications from: List of agents for UKHO publications available on website

Microform publications:
Microform copies of historical material available for purchase directly, subject to copyright restrictions

Electronic and video publications:
Some data may be purchased in electronic format where held subject to copyright restrictions

Access to staff:
Contact by letter, by telephone, by fax and by e-mail. Appointment necessary.
Hours: Mon to Fri, 0930 to 1630

Access to building, collection or gallery:
Prior appointment required

Access for disabled people:
Parking provided, toilet facilities, level access, lift to Research Room

A Trading Fund Agency within the:
Ministry of Defence

UK INNOVATION RELAY CENTRES

Avon:
Bristol
tel: 0117 221 016

Cambridgeshire:
Cambridge
tel: 01954 261199

Hampshire:
Farnborough
tel: 01252 394607

Kent:
Canterbury
tel: 01227 763414

Merseyside:
St Helens
tel: 01744 453366

Northern Ireland:
Belfast
tel: 028 9052 9475
Belfast
tel: 028 9049 1031

Oxfordshire:
Oxford
tel: 01865 784888

Scotland:
Aberdeen
tel: 01224 211500
Glasgow
tel: 0141 946 0500
Glasgow
tel: 0141 221 0999
Inverness
tel: 01463 715400
Sterling
tel: 01786 448333

South Yorkshire:
Barnsley
tel: 01226 249590

Tyne & Wear:
Sunderland
tel: 0191 383 3336

Wales:
Cardiff
tel: 029 2082 8739

West Midlands:
Coventry
tel: 024 7683 8140

UK JEEP CLUB

Jeep Books Ltd/Jeep Promotions Ltd, 5 Chestnut Avenue, Wheatley Hills, Doncaster, South Yorkshire, DN2 5SW

Tel: 01302 739000
Fax: 01302 739001
E-mail: info@jeepworld.co.uk

Website:
http://www.jeepworld.co.uk

Enquiries:
Enquiries to: Editor

Founded:
1990

Formerly called:
C J Jeep Club UK, Jeep Club UK

Organisation type and purpose:
Membership association (membership is by subscription), voluntary organisation.

Subject coverage:
Jeeps for sale, jeep parts new and used, suppliers, insurance, technical advice, information, events, everything for real jeeps from 1941 Willys to new CJs, Wranglers and Cherokees.

Museum or gallery collection, archive, or library special collection:
Many books, magazines, manuals for helping club members, but not for loan

Non-library collection catalogue:
All or part available online, in-house and in print

Library catalogue:
All or part available in-house and in print

Printed publications:
Magazine (6 times a year)

Publications list:
Available online

Access to staff:
Contact by letter, by telephone, by e-mail and via website
Hours: Mon to Fri, 0900 to 1700

UK LUBRICANTS ASSOCIATION LTD

Acronym or abbreviation: BLF

Berkhamsted House, 121 High Street, Berkhamsted, Hertfordshire, HP4 2DJ

Tel: 01442 230589
Fax: 01442 259232
E-mail: enquiries@ukla.org.uk

Website:
http://www.ukla.org.uk

Enquiries:
Enquiries to: Executive Director

Founded:
1921

Organisation type and purpose:
Trade association.

Subject coverage:
Lubrication and additives, all aspects of manufacture, distribution and marketing of lubricants.

Printed publications:
Exposure to Hard Metals in Metalworking Fluids during Machining Operations
Lube (Association magazine)
Membership Handbook
Membership Lists

Access to staff:
Contact by letter, by fax, by e-mail and via website
Hours: Mon to Fri, 0900 to 1700

UK MAJOR PORTS GROUP

Acronym or abbreviation: UKMPG

4th floor, Carthusian Court, 12 Carthusian Street, London, EC1M 6EZ

Tel: 020 7260 1785
Fax: 020 7260 1785
E-mail: richardbird@ukmajorports.org.uk

Website:
http://www.ukmajorports.org.uk

Enquiries:
Enquiries to: Executive Director

Founded:
1993

Formerly called:
British Ports Federation (year of change 1992)

Organisation type and purpose:
Trade association.

Subject coverage:
Policy issues affecting the major ports arising from UK Government, European Commission or other action.

Printed publications:
Brochure (free)

Access to staff:
Contact by letter, by telephone, by fax and by e-mail
Hours: Mon to Fri, 0900 to 1700

UK NATIONAL COMMITTEE FOR THE PREVENTION OF ALCOHOL AND DRUG DEPENDENCY

Acronym or abbreviation: NCPA

BUC Office, Stanborough Park, Watford, Hertfordshire, WD25 9JZ

Tel: 01923 665553
Fax: 01923 893212

Enquiries:
Enquiries to: Executive Director

Organisation type and purpose:
Membership association (membership is by election or invitation), registered charity (charity number 1008129).

Printed publications:
Cannabis and Mental Function (£2 plus pp)

Access to staff:
Contact by letter, by telephone and by fax
Hours: Fri, 0900 to 1200

Affiliated to:
International Commission for the Prevention of Alcoholism and Drug Dependency (an NGO of the WHO and UN)
12501 Old Columbia Pike, Silver Spring, MD20904, USA

UK SOCIETY OF INVESTMENT PROFESSIONALS

Acronym or abbreviation: UKSIP

21 Ironmonger Lane, London, EC2V 8EY

Tel: 020 7796 3000
Fax: 020 7796 3333
E-mail: uksipstaff@uksip.org

Website:
http://www.uksip.org

Enquiries:
Enquiries to: Chief Executive
Other contacts: (1) Director of Finance; (2) Director of Education and IT

Founded:
2000

Formerly called:
Institute of Investment Management and Research (IIMR) (year of change 2000)

Organisation type and purpose:
National organisation, professional body (membership is by qualification), present number of members: 4400.
To set standards in profession of fund management and investment research.

Subject coverage:
Techniques of investment; stocks and shares and other securities; investment analysis; portfolio management. Careers in investment analysis and fund management.

Printed publications:
Headline Earnings (booklet)
Investment Management Certificate Training Manual
Journal (monthly)
Past Examination Papers and Examiners Reports
Career Booklet

Publications list:
Available in print

Access to staff:
Contact by letter, by telephone, by fax, by e-mail and via website
Hours: Mon to Fri, 0930 to 1730

Member society of the:
Association for Investment Management & Research (AIMR)
tel: 00 1 434 951 5489

UK SPORTS ASSOCIATION FOR PEOPLE WITH LEARNING DISABILITY

Acronym or abbreviation: UKSAPLD

Ground Floor, Leroy House, 436 Essex Road, London, N1 3QP

Tel: 0870 770 2464
Fax: 0870 770 2466
E-mail: info@uksportsassociation.org

Website:
http://www.canninghouse.com
http://www.disable.info.com
http://www.fimdsupport.co.uk
http://www.smartchange.org
http://www.wizziwiz.co.uk

Enquiries:
Enquiries to: National Director, for administrative, accounts, general information

Founded:
1980

Formerly called:
UK Sports Association for People with Mental Handicap

Organisation type and purpose:
National organisation, membership association, registered charity (charity number 1050767).

Subject coverage:
Co-ordination, promotion and development of sport and recreation for all people with learning disability (mental handicap) throughout UK; regional and local contacts. UK representative in International Arena as member of International Sports Federation for Persons with Intellectual Disability (INAS-FID).

Museum or gallery collection, archive, or library special collection:
Booklists
Regional and local contacts

Printed publications:
Information Bulletin (quarterly, £8 a year)
Coaching People with Learning Disability (£5)
Photographic Library available – For cost, contact office

Publications list:
Available in print

Access to staff:
Contact by letter, by telephone, by fax and by e-mail. Appointment necessary.
Hours: Mon to Fri, 1000 to 1700

Access for disabled people:
Parking possibly provided, access to all public areas, toilet facilities

UK STEEL

Broadway House, Tothill Street, London, SW1H 9NQ

Tel: 020 7222 7777
Fax: 020 7222 2782

E-mail: steel@eef.org.uk

Website:
http://www.uksteel.org.uk

Enquiries:
Enquiries to: Director
Direct tel: 020 7654 1519
Direct e-mail: irodgers@eef.org.uk

Founded:
1967

Organisation type and purpose:
Trade association for the UK steel industry, representing the industry to policy and opinion formers, promoting the industry and the importance of steel to the public, and providing information and services to its members.

Subject coverage:
UK steel industry, including its structure, performance (nationally and internationally) and its contribution to the UK economy and everyday life. Specialist knowledge of steel production, processing and steel products; steel standards and steel sourcing; environmental issues relating to the production, processing and recyclability of steel; legislation and representation to government in the United Kingdom, Europe and elsewhere; international trade in steel; other issues affecting steel companies such as transport and haulage, careers in the UK steel industry, and health and safety.

Trade and statistical information:
Key statistics for the United Kingdom steel industry available free; other statistics (United Kingdom, Europe, world-wide) available on request and online.

Printed publications:
Annual Review (2007, free)
Member Companies (free)
Key Statistics (free)
Steel Specifications – contains detailed information about the chemical, mechanical and physical properties of steels specified in British, European and other standards together with details of UK steel industry producers (11th edn, approx. £90)

Electronic and video publications:
SteelSpec (online version of Steel Specifications, subscriptions start at £90 per year)

Publications list:
Available online

Access to staff:
Contact by letter, by telephone, by fax and by e-mail
Hours: Mon to Fri, 0900 to 1700

Also at:
UK Steel
Swinden House, Rotherham, S60 3AR; tel: 01709 362288; fax: 01709 724999; e-mail: rruddlestone@eef.org.uk

Constituent bodies:
ISSB Limited
1 Carlton House Terrace, London, SW1Y 5DB; tel: 020 7343 3900; fax: 020 7343 3902; e-mail: enquiries@issb.co.uk

Member organisation of:
Energy Intensive Users Group (EIUG)
Broadway House, Tothill Street, London, SW1H 9NQ; tel: 020 7654 1536; fax: 020 7222 2782

Sponsor of:
Challenge of Materials Gallery
Science Museum, Exhibition Road, London, SW7 2DD; tel: 020 7938 8000

UK STEEL ASSOCIATION

Reinforcement Manufacturing Product Group, Millbank Tower, 21–24 Millbank, London, SW1P 4QP

Tel: 020 7343 3150
Fax: 020 7343 3190
E-mail: enquiries@uksteel.org.uk

continued overleaf

Website:
http://www.uksteel.org.uk
Links to member companies' sites, buyers guide, general information on steel, press releases, etc.

Enquiries:
Enquiries to: Head of Commercial Services

Formerly called:
British Reinforcement Manufacturers Association; British Iron & Steel Producers Association, Reinforcement Manufacturing Product Group (BISPA) (year of change 1997)

Organisation type and purpose:
Trade association.

Subject coverage:
Iron and steel reinforcement products.

Publications list:
Available online

Access to staff:
Contact by e-mail and via website
Hours: Mon to Fri, 0900 to 1700

UK THALASSAEMIA SOCIETY

Acronym or abbreviation: UKTS

19 The Broadway, Southgate Circus, London, N14 6PH

Tel: 020 882 0011
Fax: 020 8882 8618
E-mail: office@ukts.org

Website:
http://www.ukts.org

Enquiries:
Enquiries to: Honorary Secretary

Founded:
1976

Subject coverage:
Information on thalassaemia.

Printed publications:
Books, posters and leaflets including:
What is Thalassaemia
Management protocol for the treatment of thalassaemia patients
Information for people who have haemoglobin H disease
Standards for the Clinical Care of Children and Adults with Thalassaemia in the UK

Access to staff:
Contact by letter, by telephone, by fax, by e-mail, in person and via website
Hours: Mon to Fri, 0900 to 1700

Access for disabled people:
Level entry

UK TRADE & INVESTMENT

Acronym or abbreviation: UKTI

Kingsgate House, 66–74 Victoria Street, London, SW1E 6SW

Tel: 020 7215 8000
Fax: 020 7828 1281

Website:
http://www.ukinvest.gov.uk/

Enquiries:
Enquiries to: Information Officer

Founded:
1977

Formerly called:
Invest-UK, Trade Partners UK, Invest in Britain Bureau (year of change 2003)

Organisation type and purpose:
National government body.
Unit of the Department of Trade and Industry and Foreign and Commonwealth Office.
The major role of UKTI is to assist and encourage overseas companies with internationally mobile manufacturing and service sector projects to locate their activities in this country. Particularly interested in securing those projects which bring long-term jobs or which introduce new technologies or management techniques and which improve the UK's competitive manufacturing position. UKTI works in partnership with national development agencies in Scotland, Wales and Northern Ireland and the English regional development agencies.

Subject coverage:
The Government's main inward investment agency in the United Kingdom, assisting firms with all aspects of locating or relocating a business or expanding existing facilities. UKTI offers a one-stop advisory service in drawing together information from government and public agencies, and can put together a complete package of locations, financial incentives, employment, taxation, entry clearance and immigration, company formation, training, research assistance and product sector advice. The service is both free and confidential.

Trade and statistical information:
Comparison statistics for above subjects between UK and EU countries.

Printed publications:
Operations Review
Flagship Brochure
Briefing in Britain
Sector Brochures
Information Sheets
Order printed publications from: DTI Publications tel: 0870 150 2500, fax: 0870 150 2333, e-mail: publications@dti.gsi.gov.uk

Microform publications:
Some material available through the DTI Library, tel: 020 7215 5000

Publications list:
Available online and in print

Access to staff:
Contact by letter, by telephone, by fax, by e-mail and via website
Hours: Mon to Fri, 0900 to 1700

Parent body:
Department of Trade and Industry

UK TRADE & INVESTMENT INFORMATION CENTRE

Kingsgate House, 66–74 Victoria Street, London, SW1E 6SW

Tel: 020 7215 8000
Fax: 020 7215 2482
E-mail: diane.brodie@uktradeinvest.gov.uk

Website:
http://www.tradepartners.gov.uk/ information_centre
Provides information on the Trade Partners UK Information Centre as well as links with other sites around the world of interest to exporters.
https://www.uktradeinvest.gov.uk

Enquiries:
Enquiries to: Librarian

Founded:
1962

Formerly called:
Export Market Information Centre (EMIC) (year of change 2000); Trade Partners UK Information Centre (year of change 2004)

Organisation type and purpose:
National government body.
Trade Partners UK is the Government's network that helps UK companies trade internationally.

Subject coverage:
Exporting from the United Kingdom. Official statistics from overseas, governmental and international sources on trade, production, general economic indicators, prices, employment and social fields; development plans; bibliographies of statistical information, multilateral development aid database and documentation.

Museum or gallery collection, archive, or library special collection:
Market research reports, country profiles, development plans and inward investment
Statistical data and trade directories from round the world, providing information on potential agents, distributors and other overseas contacts
Unique set of mail order catalogues from round the world

Trade and statistical information:
Comprehensive range of trade statistics (UK and worldwide).
Production data, general economic information, size, shore and structure of overseas markets for products, industries and services.

Non-library collection catalogue:
All or part available online

Library catalogue:
All or part available online

Printed publications:
Guide to CD-ROM databases and commercial internet services
A Brief Guide to the Trade Partners UK Information Centre
A User's Guide to the Trade Partners UK Information Centre

Electronic and video publications:
20 internet databases

Access to staff:
Contact by telephone, by fax, by e-mail, in person and via website
Hours: Mon to Fri, 0900 to 1730 for telephone enquiries

Access for disabled people:
Access to all public areas, toilet facilities

UK TRADE AND INVESTMENT, HONG KONG AND MACAO DESK

Acronym or abbreviation: UKTI

Bay 960, Kingsgate House, 66–74 Victoria Street, London, SW1E 6SW

Tel: 020 7215 8095
Fax: 020 7215 4074
E-mail: michael.opoku@ukti.gsi.gov.uk

Website:
http://www.uktradeinvest.gov.uk

Enquiries:
Enquiries to: Country Manager

Formerly a part of:
Department of Trade and Industry (DTI) (year of change 2007)

Organisation type and purpose:
National government body.
Trade promotion.

Subject coverage:
Exporting to Hong Kong, prospects for investment and other forms of commercial co-operation.

Publications list:
Available in print

Access to staff:
Contact by letter, by telephone, by fax and by e-mail
Hours: Mon to Fri, 0900 to 1700

Access for disabled people:
Access to all public areas

Constituent part of:
BERR

UK YOUTH

3rd Floor, Lancaster House, 33 Islington High Street, London, N1 9LH

Tel: 0845 862 0155
Fax: 0845 862 0155
E-mail: info@ukyouth.org

Website:
http://www.ukyouth.org
Youth work, projects, magazines, publications, etc.

Enquiries:
Enquiries to: Chief Executive
Direct tel: 0845 862 0157
Direct e-mail: jo@ukyouth.org

Founded:
1911

Formerly called:
National Association of Youth Clubs; Youth Clubs
UK (YCUK) (year of change 1999)

Organisation type and purpose:
Voluntary organisation, registered charity (charity
number 306066).

Subject coverage:
Youth, youth work and services.

Non-library collection catalogue:
All or part available online and in print

Library catalogue:
All or part available online and in print

Printed publications:
Videos catalogue
UK Youth (magazine, quarterly)
ninety-five per cent (magazine, quarterly)
Books, booklets, action packs, posters, including:
Actual Reality – a programme for young people
    beyond 2000: the report
Foundations – the guide to running a youth group
Making Connections – the role of youth work
Perspectives on Young Carers
The Art of Youth Work
Understanding Anger – a group work programme
Youth Listens – training & support for peer
    mentors

Electronic and video publications:
Videos (over 50 titles)

Publications list:
Available online and in print

Access to staff:
Contact by letter, by telephone, by fax, by e-mail
and via website. Appointment necessary.
Hours: Mon to Fri, 0900 to 1700

Access to building, collection or gallery:
Prior appointment required

Access for disabled people:
Level entry

Affiliated to:
European Confederation of Youth Club
Organisations (ECYC)
    Ornevej 45, Copenhagen NV, DK-2400,
    Denmark; tel: 00 45 38 10 80 38
National Council for Voluntary Organisations
National Council for Voluntary Youth Services

Has:
3 divisions (Scotland, Wales and Northern Ireland)
43 local associations of youth clubs

UK-IDF

c/o Dairy UK, 93 Baker Street, London W1U 6QQ

Tel: 0207 467 2621
Fax: 0207 487 4734
E-mail: iwakeling@dairyuk.org

Website:
http://www.ukidf.org/
Publications.

Enquiries:
Enquiries to: Secretary

Founded:
1950

Formerly called:
United Kingdom Dairy Association

Organisation type and purpose:
Membership association (membership is by
subscription).
UK National Committee of the International Dairy
Federation.

Subject coverage:
Hygiene, dairy technology, economics, analytical
techniques, nutrition and education.

Printed publications:
IDF bulletins and special issues

Access to staff:
Contact by letter, by telephone, by fax and by e-
mail
Hours: Mon to Fri, 0900 to 1700

UKAEA

Formal name: United Kingdom Atomic Energy
Authority
Acronym or abbreviation: UKAEA

Fusion Library, Culham Science Centre, Abingdon,
Oxfordshire, OX14 3DB

Tel: 01235 466347
Fax: 01235 466507
E-mail: helen.bloxham@ukaea.org.uk

Website:
http://www.ukaea.org.uk

Enquiries:
Enquiries to: Librarian

Founded:
1961

Organisation type and purpose:
National government body, research organisation.
Fusion research and development.

Subject coverage:
Nuclear fusion, plasma physics.

**Museum or gallery collection, archive, or library
special collection:**
UKAEA Fusion Reports
JET Reports

Non-library collection catalogue:
All or part available online and in-house

Library catalogue:
All or part available in-house

Electronic and video publications:
Order electronic and video publications from: via
website

Publications list:
Available online

Access to staff:
Contact by letter, by telephone, by fax, by e-mail,
in person and via website. Appointment necessary.
Access for members only. Non-members charged.
Hours: Mon to Fri, 0815 to 1630

Access to building, collection or gallery:
Prior appointment required

UKAEA CULHAM DIVISION (INCORPORATING JET)

Formal name: United Kingdom Atomic Energy
Authority (UKAEA)
Acronym or abbreviation: UKAEA

Abingdon, Oxfordshire, OX14 3DB

Tel: 01235 464190
Fax: 01235 463706
E-mail: chris.carpenter@ukaea.org.uk

Website:
http://www.jet.efda.org
http://www.fusion.org.uk
Descriptive information including pictures/
diagrams of sites and work done.

Enquiries:
Enquiries to: Public Relations Manager

Founded:
1978

Organisation type and purpose:
International organisation, research organisation.
JET is funded by the EU member states fusion
research organisations under the European Fusion
Development Agreement (EFDA). JET is operated
on behalf of the research organisations by UKAEA.
Undertakes research into nuclear fusion as a long-
term non-CO2 producing future source of energy.

Subject coverage:
Thermonuclear fusion for peaceful purposes,
especially energy production, plasma physics.

**Museum or gallery collection, archive, or library
special collection:**
Annual reports, annual progress reports and
    detailed scientific reports in the various fields of
    relevance to fusion research

Printed publications:
Fusion for the Future – technology for today

Publications list:
Available online and in print

Access to staff:
Contact by letter, by telephone, by fax, by e-mail
and via website. Appointment necessary.
Hours: Mon to Fri, 0830 to 1630

Access to building, collection or gallery:
Prior appointment required

Access for disabled people:
Parking provided, ramped entry

UKCISA: THE COUNCIL FOR INTERNATIONAL STUDENT AFFAIRS

9–17 St Albans Place, London, N1 0NX

Tel: 020 7107 9922
Fax: 020 7288 4360

Website:
http://www.ukcisa.org.uk

Enquiries:
Enquiries to: Membership Secretary

Founded:
1968

Formerly called:
UKCOSA: The Council for International Education

Organisation type and purpose:
Advisory body, membership association
(membership is by subscription), voluntary
organisation, registered charity (charity number
1095294), training organisation, consultancy,
research organisation.
To promote the interests of international students.

Subject coverage:
All matters affecting international students in the
UK.

Trade and statistical information:
Comparative statistics on international students.

Printed publications:
Good Practice publications
Guidance Notes for Students (21 titles)
Research reports
Manual
Order printed publications from: Publications Officer,
UKCOSA
e-mail: publications@ukcosa.org.uk

Electronic and video publications:
Onyx: the electronic guide to regulations and
    procedures for international students
CD-ROM
Videos

Publications list:
Available online and in print

Access to staff:
Contact by letter, by telephone, by fax, by e-mail
and via website
Hours: Telephone: 020 7354 5210: Mon to Fri, 1300
to 1600

UKERNA

Formal name: United Kingdom Education and
Research Networking Association
Acronym or abbreviation: UKERNA

Atlas Centre, Chilton, Didcot, Oxfordshire, OX11
0QS

Tel: 01235 822212
Fax: 01235 822397
E-mail: service@ukerna.ac.uk

Website:
http://www.ja.net/
Holds information about JANET, the UK's
academic and research network.
http://www.ukerna.ac.uk

Enquiries:
Enquiries to: Customer Service Director

Founded:
1993

Organisation type and purpose:
Statutory body.
UKERNA is responsible for the coordination and
management of the networking programme of the
UK education and research community known as
JANET.

Subject coverage:
Internetworking for the UK academic and research
community, multiservice networking, information
superhighway for education, managing the JANET
network.

Printed publications:
Annual Report
Networking Programme Report
UKERNA News (3 times a year)

Access to staff:
Contact by letter, by telephone, by fax and by e-
mail. Appointment necessary.
Hours: Mon to Fri, 0800 to 1800

Affiliated to:
JISC, HEFCE
    Northavon House, Coldharbour Lane, Bristol,
    BS16 1QD

UKOLN

Library and Learning Centre, University of Bath,
Claverton Down, Bath, BA2 7AY

Tel: 01225 386580
Fax: 01225 386838
E-mail: ukoln@ukoln.ac.uk

Website:
http://www.ukoln.ac.uk

Enquiries:
Enquiries to: Resource Co-ordinator
Direct tel: 01225 386250
Direct e-mail: s.lewis@ukoln.ac.uk
Other contacts: Events Manager for conference
organisation.

Founded:
1977

Organisation type and purpose:
Advisory body, research organisation.

Subject coverage:
Use of national and international computer
networks for library and information work, e-mail
and other value-added network services, network
publishing, information resources available on
national and international networks. Use of
bibliographic records for acquisitions, cataloguing
and issue systems, online access, public access to
library files, resource-sharing schemes, subject
access, user studies, other related areas of study.

Printed publications:
Research reports
UKOLN Newsletter (free)

Electronic and video publications:
Ariadne (online)

Access to staff:
Contact by letter, by telephone, by e-mail and via
website
Hours: Mon to Fri, 0900 to 1700

Funded by:
European Union Project Funding
Joint Information Systems Committee of the
Higher and Further Education Funding Councils
Museums, Libraries and Archives Council (MLA)

Supported by:
University of Bath

UKSPACE

Acronym or abbreviation: SBAC

Salamanca Square, 9 Albert Embankment, London,
SE1 7SP

Tel: 020 7091 4500
Fax: 020 7091 4545

Website:
http://www.sbac.co.uk

Enquiries:
Enquiries to: Policy and Communications
Direct e-mail: mark.watson@sbac.co.uk

Founded:
1975

Formerly called:
United Kingdom Industrial Space Committee
(UKISC)

Organisation type and purpose:
National organisation, trade association, present
number of members: 40. Represents the collective
interests of its member companies in increasing
space and space-related business, and their share
of the home and export markets.

Subject coverage:
UK Space Industry – policy and capability. Links to
specialist sources.

Access to staff:
Contact by letter
Hours: Mon to Fri, 0900 to 1700

Access to building, collection or gallery:
No access other than to staff

Connections with:
Federation of the Electronics Industry
    Russell Square House, London, WC1B 5EE; tel:
    020 7331 2000
Society of British Aerospace Companies (SBAC)
    60 Petty France, London, SW1H 9EU; tel: 020
    7227 1000

UKSPILL ASSOCIATION

PO Box 21, Over Wallop, Stockbridge, Hampshire,
SO20 8WY

Tel: 0870 4868980
Fax: (0870 4863235
E-mail: info@ukspill.org

Website:
http://www.ukspill.org

Enquiries:
Enquiries to: Director

Founded:
1981

Organisation type and purpose:
Trade association.

Subject coverage:
All aspects of the prevention, control and clean-up
of marine, inland and industrial pollution, both in
the UK and overseas.

Access to staff:
Contact by letter
Hours: Mon to Fri, 0900 to 1700

ULSTER COLLEGE OF MUSIC

13 Windsor Avenue, Belfast, BT9 6EE

Tel: 028 9038 1314

Website:
http://www.ulstercollegeofmusic.com

Enquiries:
Enquiries to: Administrator
Direct e-mail: annestafford@btinternet.com
Other contacts: Chairman

Founded:
1966

Organisation type and purpose:
College of Music.
The training of musicians on all instruments and
voice, or vocal and instrumental tuition.

Subject coverage:
All aspects of the profession of music.

Library catalogue:
All or part available in-house

Access to staff:
Contact by letter, by telephone, by e-mail, in
person and via website
Hours: Mon to Fri, 1400 to 2030; Sat, 0900 to 1700

Access for disabled people:
Toilet facilities
Special comments: Disabled access to ground and
first floor only.

ULSTER HISTORICAL FOUNDATION

Acronym or abbreviation: UHF

12 College Square East, Belfast, BT1 6DD

Tel: 028 9033 2288
Fax: 028 9023 9885
E-mail: enquiry@uhf.org.uk

Website:
http://www.uhf.org.uk
http://www.ancestryireland.com
http://www.booksireland.org.uk

Enquiries:
Enquiries to: Executive Director
Direct e-mail: fintan@uhf.org.uk

Founded:
1956

Organisation type and purpose:
Voluntary organisation, registered charity (charity
number XN48460), research organisation,
publishing house. Genealogical research,
computerisation of historical records, publications.

Subject coverage:
Genealogical research for all of Ireland, history of
Ulster, particularly migration to and from, Irish
Genealogical Project (for the computerisation of all
pre-1900 church and civil records in Ireland),
designated centre for Co. Antrim and Co. Down
(including Belfast).

**Museum or gallery collection, archive, or library
special collection:**
Completed searches regarding Ulster families
    (over 10,000)

Printed publications:
Directory of Irish Family History Research
    (Subscribers' interest list, annually, some back
    volumes available)
Familia: Ulster Genealogical Review (annually,
    some back volumes available)
Newsletter (annually)
Gravestone Inscription Series (28 volumes some in
    hardcopy, some also as fiche, some only as fiche)
Historical series includes:
Essays in Scotch-Irish History (ed Green E R R)
A Century of Northern Life – The Irish News & 100
    Years of Ulster History 1890s-1990s
A Past Apart: Studies in the History of Catholic
    Belfast (1996)
Buildings of County Antrim
Clergy of Connor

Clergy of Down and Dromore
Down Cathedral: The Church of St Patrick of
Down (Rankin J F)
How to Trace Your Irish Ancestry (free)
Merchants in Plenty
New Light at the Cape of Good Hope
Nine Ulster Lives
Northern Ireland and the Second World War (1995)
Peoples Champion
Presbyterians and The Irish Language (Blaney R)
Private Life and Public Fortune: Macartney of
Lisanaire (Roebuck P ed.)
Scottish Migration to Ulster in the Reign of James I
(rev 1999, Perceval-Maxwell M)
Two Acres of Irish History: A Study Through Time
of Friars Bush and Belfast (Phoenix E)
The Famine in Ulster (Kinealy C and Parkhill T)
Ulster Emigration to Colonial America 1718–1775
(Dickson R J, 2nd reprint 1996)
Ulster Libraries, Archives, Museums & Ancestral
Heritage Centres: A visitors guide (O'Neill R K,
£6.99 plus £1.50 p&p)
Other publications out of print:
Penal Era and Golden Age: Essays in Irish history
1690–1800
Plantation Acres: A Historical Study of the Irish
Land Surveyor and His Maps (Andress J H)
Scottish Covenanters and Irish Confederates

Microform publications:
Gravestone Inscription Series for Co. Down and
Co. Antrim including Belfast (All 27 volumes of
the series in microfiche, £6 per individual volume
inc. p&p)

Publications list:
Available online and in print

Access to staff:
Contact by letter, by telephone, by fax, by e-mail,
in person and via website
Hours: Mon to Fri, 0930 to 1730

Access to building, collection or gallery:
No prior appointment required
Hours: Mon to Fri, 0900 to 1730

Links with:
Federation of Family History Societies
Irish Family History Foundation
Irish Genealogical Project
Ulster Genealogical and Historical Guild

ULSTER UNIONIST PARTY

Acronym or abbreviation: UUP

First Floor, 174 Albertbridge Road, Belfast, BT5
4GS

Tel: 028 9046 3299
Fax: 028 9045 6899
E-mail: uup@uup.org

Website:
http://www.uup.org
General party information; history, policies,
objectives, documents, press statements, election
results, contact details for elected representatives.

Enquiries:
Enquiries to: Administrator
Direct tel: 028 9046 3201
Direct e-mail: hazel.legge@uup.org

Founded:
1905

Organisation type and purpose:
Membership association (membership is by
subscription).
Political party.

Access to staff:
Contact by letter, by telephone, by fax, by e-mail
and via website
Hours: Mon to Fri, 0900 to 1700

ULSTER WILDLIFE TRUST

Acronym or abbreviation: UWT

Ulster Wildlife Centre, 3 New Line, Crossgar,
Downpatrick, Co Down, BT30 9EP

Tel: 028 4483 0282
Fax: 028 4483 0888
E-mail: ulsterwt@cix.co.uk

Website:
http://www.ulsterwildlife.org

Enquiries:
Enquiries to: Development Manager
Direct e-mail: ulsterwt@uwtdevelopment.fsnet.co
.uk
Other contacts: Membership Secretary for
membership issues.

Founded:
1978

Organisation type and purpose:
Registered charity.

Subject coverage:
Conservation, biodiversity, planning, waste
minimalisation, environmental education.

**Museum or gallery collection, archive, or library
special collection:**
Irish Hare back catalogue
Various environmental and conservation texts

Printed publications:
Irish Hare (magazine)
Network World (magazine)

Publications list:
Available online and in print

Access to staff:
Contact by letter, by telephone, by fax and by e-
mail. Appointment necessary.
Hours: Mon to Fri, 0900 to 1700

Access to building, collection or gallery:
Prior appointment required
Special comments: Library, members only.

Access for disabled people:
Parking provided, level entry, access to all public
areas, toilet facilities

Member of:
The Wildlife Trust
The Kiln, Waterside, Mather Road, Newark,
Nottinghamshire, NG24 1WT; tel: 01636 677711;
fax: 01636 67001; e-mail: info@wildlifetrust.org

Other addresses:
Ulster Wildlife Trust Farm
142 Glendun Road, Glendun, West Antrim,
BT44; tel: 028 2176 1403; fax: 028 2176 1403; e-
mail: ulsterwt@glendunfarm.fsnet.co.uk
Ulster Wildlife Trust in West Belfast
438 Falls Road, Belfast; fax: 028 9031 4772; e-
mail: ulsterwt@bogmeadows.fsnet.co.uk

UNICEF UK

Formal name: United Nations Children's Fund
Acronym or abbreviation: UNICEF

Africa House, 64–78 Kingsway, London, WC2B
6NB

Tel: 020 7405 5592
Fax: 020 7405 2332
E-mail: helpdesk@unicef.org.uk

Website:
http://www.unicef.org.uk
Information on UNICEF and situation of children;
video clips; interviews.

Enquiries:
Enquiries to: Information Department

Founded:
1947

Organisation type and purpose:
International organisation, registered charity
(charity number 1072612).
Fund raising and advocacy organisation,
supporting the work of UNICEF in over 160
countries. Helping to provide basic services for
children and promoting children's rights.

Subject coverage:
Health, children's rights, child labour, nutrition,
water and sanitation, children in conflict,
education, aid and development work for the
improvement of conditions for mothers and
children in developing countries; children's issues
and rights in the industrialised world.

**Museum or gallery collection, archive, or library
special collection:**
Photographs (black and white) and colour
transparencies
UNICEF international publications, board papers,
speeches

Trade and statistical information:
Statistics on child births, deaths, performance,
malnutrition, immunisation, primary education,
maternal deaths.

Printed publications:
A large number of publications on child rights,
economic policies, local government, urban
children in difficult circumstances
Annual Report
Financial Statement
News in Brief (monthly)
Publicity material
Resources for Schools (a series of publications and
videos for Key Stage 1 to adult)
The Progress of Nations (annually)
The State of the World's Children (annually)
Order printed publications from: UNICEF
Unit 1, Rignals Lane, Chelmsford, Essex, CM2
8TU, tel: 01245 476315, fax: 01245 477394

Publications list:
Available in print

Access to staff:
Contact by letter, by telephone, by fax, by e-mail
and via website
Hours: Mon to Fri, 0930 to 1730

Access to building, collection or gallery:
No access other than to staff

Parent body:
United Nations

UNION OF MUSLIM ORGANISATIONS OF UK AND EIRE

Acronym or abbreviation: UMO

109 Campden Hill Road, London, W8 7TL

Tel: 020 7221 6608 or 7229 0538
Fax: 020 7792 2130 (on request)

Enquiries:
Enquiries to: Secretary-General
Other contacts: Assistant Secretary.

Founded:
1970

Organisation type and purpose:
National organisation, membership association
(membership is by subscription), present number
of members: 214, voluntary organisation.
Voluntary religious organisation, representative
body of the Muslim community in UK and Eire.
To co-ordinate the activities of Muslim
organisations in the UK and Eire, to negotiate with
government departments and serve the religious
rights of the British Muslim community.

Subject coverage:
Islam; Islamic education; social and cultural
aspects of British Muslim life, including
youth activities in the UK; current Mosque projects
dealing with any problems faced by Muslim
students or workers in the observance of their
religions duties.

Printed publications:
Islamic books
Press releases issued after major events

Publications list:
Available in print

continued overleaf

Access to staff:
Contact by letter, by telephone and by fax.
Appointment necessary.
Hours: Mon to Fri, 0900 to 1700

Has as members:
Local Muslim organisations in UK and Eire

Houses the:
National Muslim Education Council and the UMO
Youth Council of UK and Eire
   tel: 020 7221 6608; fax: 020 7792 2130 (on request)
UMO Board of Ulama, UK
UMO Trust

UNION OF SHOP, DISTRIBUTIVE AND ALLIED WORKERS

Acronym or abbreviation: USDAW

188 Wilmslow Road, Fallowfield, Manchester, M14
6LJ

Tel: 0161 224 2804
Fax: 0161 257 2566
E-mail: enquiries@usdaw.org.uk

Website:
http://www.usdaw.org.uk

Enquiries:
Enquiries to: Head of Media and Communications
(applications to use library and archive facilities
need to be in writing)

Organisation type and purpose:
Trade union, present number of members: 340,000.
The Supervisory, Administrative and Technical
Association (SATA) is the white collar section.

Subject coverage:
Trade union activity and industrial relations
matters in retail and wholesale distribution and
associated sectors of food and chemical processing
and the catering and hairdressing trades; wages
councils; shopping hours and Sunday trading;
history of USDAW and earlier shopworker unions.

**Museum or gallery collection, archive, or library
special collection:**
Copies of Union journals: New Dawn, The Shop
   Assistant, Dawn and Usdaw Today, Agenda,
   Arena, Network
Union's Official Records since the 1880s

Printed publications:
Network (6 times a year)
Arena (4 times a year)

Access to staff:
Contact by letter, by telephone, by fax, by e-mail
and via website. Appointment necessary.
Hours: Mon to Fri, 0900 to 1700

UNISON

Information Unit, 1 Mabledon Place, London,
WC1H 9AJ

Tel: 0845 355 0845
Fax: 0845 355 0845

Website:
http://www.unison.org.uk/catalogue
UNISON Publications catalogue.
Online catalogue.
http://www.unison.org.uk
Information on UNISON.

Enquiries:
Enquiries to: Information Officer
Direct tel: 020 7551 1736
Direct fax: 020 7551 1164

Founded:
1993

Organisation type and purpose:
Trade union, present number of members:
1,275,000.

Subject coverage:
Trade union and industrial relations, pay and
conditions, public services.

Printed publications:
See website
Order printed publications from: UNISON
Communications
tel: 020 7551 1115

Publications list:
Available online and in print

Access to staff:
Contact by letter, by telephone, by fax and by e-
mail. Appointment necessary.
Hours: Mon to Fri, 0900 to 1700

Affiliated to:
Labour Party
Public Services International
Trades Union Congress
   website: www.tuc.org.uk

UNIT FOR LANDSCAPE MODELLING

Acronym or abbreviation: Air Photo Library

University of Cambridge, Sir William Hardy
Building, Tennis Court Road, Cambridge, CB2 1QB

Tel: 01223 764377
Fax: 01223 764381
E-mail: library@uflm.cam.ac.uk

Website:
http://www.uflm.cam.ac.uk

Enquiries:
Enquiries to: Librarian

Founded:
1945

Organisation type and purpose:
University library.

Subject coverage:
Indexed collection of 500,000 vertical and oblique
aerial photographs of United Kingdom and Ireland
from 1945 onwards. Smaller collection of air
photographs of France, the Netherlands and
Denmark taken from 1966 to 1974. Emphasis on
areas of ecological, historical and archaeological
interest.

Non-library collection catalogue:
All or part available online and in-house

Library catalogue:
All or part available in-house

Access to staff:
Contact by letter, by telephone, by fax, by e-mail
and in person
Hours: Mon to Thu, 0900 to 1700; Fri, 0900 to 1600

Access to building, collection or gallery:
Appointment required

UNIT FOR RESEARCH INTO CHANGING INSTITUTIONS

Acronym or abbreviation: URCHIN

115 Poplar High Street, London, E14 0AE

Tel: 020 7987 3600
Fax: 020 7515 8627
E-mail: info@meridian.org.uk

Website:
http://www.meridian.org.uk

Enquiries:
Enquiries to: Executive Director

Founded:
1981

Organisation type and purpose:
Registered charity (charity number 284542),
research organisation.
To carry out research into ways to implement and
advance the capacity of society and its associated
institutions to adapt to change in a functional and
realistic manner.

Subject coverage:
Management of change, organisational learning,
psychoanalysis, social dynamics, pre- and
perinatal psychology, primal integration.

Non-library collection catalogue:
All or part available online

Library catalogue:
All or part available online

Printed publications:
All publications free and online

Publications list:
Available online and in print

Access to staff:
Contact by letter
Hours: Mon to Fri, 0900 to 1700

UNITARIAN GENERAL ASSEMBLY

Formal name: General Assembly of Unitarian and
Free Christian Churches
Acronym or abbreviation: GAUFCC

Essex Hall, 1–6 Essex Street, London, WC2R 3HY

Tel: 020 7240 2384
Fax: 020 7240 3089
E-mail: ga@unitarian.org.uk

Website:
http://www.unitarian.org.uk
Publicity material, list of congregations with
addresses and service times, forthcoming events,
affiliated groups and periodicals.

Enquiries:
Enquiries to: Information Officer

Founded:
1928

Organisation type and purpose:
Membership association, registered charity
(charity number 250788).
Religious, Unitarianism.
Spreads information about liberal religion and
provides support services for member groups.

Subject coverage:
Current British Unitarian beliefs and practices;
liberal religious ideas and principles; personalised
weddings, baptisms, child namings and funerals;
liberal religious movements abroad, blessings of
same-sex relationships.

**Museum or gallery collection, archive, or library
special collection:**
Year Books, 1870 to date

Printed publications:
Directory
Handbook (every 3 years)
Other occasional publications

Publications list:
Available in print

Access to staff:
Contact by letter, by telephone, by fax, by e-mail
and via website. Appointment necessary. Access
for members only.
Hours: Mon to Fri, 0900 to 1700
Special comments: Please telephone first.

Affiliated to:
International Association for Religious Freedom
(IARF)
   2 Market Street, Oxford, OX1 3EF; tel: 01865
   202744; fax: 01865 202746; e-mail: iarf@interfaith
   -center.org

UNITARIAN HISTORICAL SOCIETY

Acronym or abbreviation: UHS

223 Upper Lisburn Road, Belfast, BT10 0LL

Tel: 0131 667 4360

Enquiries:
Enquiries to: Honorary Secretary
Direct e-mail: a.steers.1@research.gla.ac.uk

Founded:
1916

Organisation type and purpose:
Learned society (membership is by subscription), present number of members: 200.

Subject coverage:
Unitarian history.

Museum or gallery collection, archive, or library special collection:
For library, see Dr Williams's Library

Printed publications:
Transactions of the Unitarian Historical Society (annually)

Access to staff:
Contact by letter and by e-mail
Hours: Mon to Fri, 0900 to 1700

Associated with:
General Assembly of Unitarian and Free Christian Churches

UNITED KINGDOM ACCREDITATION SERVICE

Acronym or abbreviation: UKAS

21–47 High Street, Feltham, Middlesex, TW13 4UN

Tel: 020 8917 8400
Fax: 020 8917 8500
E-mail: info@ukas.com

Website:
http://www.ukas.com
General information about UKAS and its purpose.

Enquiries:
Enquiries to: Head of Corporate Communications
Direct tel: 020 8917 8554
Direct fax: 020 8917 8754
Direct e-mail: mca@ukas.com

Founded:
1995

Organisation type and purpose:
Statutory body, service industry.
Accreditation of conformity assessment bodies.

Subject coverage:
Interpretation and clarification of conformity assessment standards; calibration: electrical (dc, lf, rf and microwave), mechanical, fluids, thermal, radiological, thermal conductivity, acoustics, humidity, force, mass, accelerometry, magnetic, pressure, hardness, optical, fibre; testing: acoustical, ballistic, biological, chemical, corrosion, dimensional, electrical, EMC, environmental, fire, geological, health and hygiene, information technology, mechanical, metallurgical, NDDT, performance, physical, safety.

Printed publications:
Directory of Accredited Laboratories

Access to staff:
Contact by letter, by telephone, by fax, by e-mail and via website
Hours: Mon to Fri, 0900 to 1700

UNITED KINGDOM AGRICULTURAL SUPPLY TRADE ASSOCIATION

Acronym or abbreviation: UKASTA

21 Arlington Street, London, SW1A 1RN

Tel: 020 7495 9100
Fax: 020 7495 9150
E-mail: enquiries@ukasta.org.uk

Website:
http://www.ukasta.org.uk

Enquiries:
Enquiries to: Company Secretary
Direct e-mail: jeremy.smith@ukasta.org.uk

Founded:
1917

Organisation type and purpose:
Trade association (membership is by subscription), present number of members: 370.
To represent the interests of the agricultural supply industry.

Subject coverage:
Manufacturers of animal feedstuffs, agricultural merchants, feed, seed, fertilisers, agrochemicals and forage additives, public understanding of modern food and farming methods, the agricultural supply industry, legislation in Whitehall, Westminster and Brussels, insurance and financial services for the industry.

Non-library collection catalogue:
All or part available online

Printed publications:
Contracts Pack (£44.06 inc. VAT and p&p, members only)
Good Training Policy and Practice
UKASTA Green Book (£3)
Various contracts to cover the range of products (for sale, members only)
Various health and safety publications and Codes of Practice
Yearbook (£15 members only)
Publications on standard conditions of sale, product safety, safety of drivers

Publications list:
Available in print

Access to staff:
Contact by letter, by fax, by e-mail and via website. Appointment necessary. Non-members charged.
Hours: Mon to Fri, 0915 to 1715

Affiliated to:
ANGO
COCERAL
COSEMCO
FEFAC
UCEPPCEE

UNITED KINGDOM ALLIANCE

Acronym or abbreviation: UKA

176 Blackfriars Road, London, SE1 8ET

Tel: 07985 011029

Enquiries:
Enquiries to: General Secretary

Founded:
1853

Organisation type and purpose:
Membership association (membership is by subscription), present number of members: 500, voluntary organisation, registered charity (charity number 293067).
Education in respect of alcohol and drug abuse.

Subject coverage:
Advising on the dangers of alcohol and drug abuse.

Access to staff:
Contact by letter
Hours: Mon to Fri, 0900 to 1700

Access to building, collection or gallery:
No access other than to staff

UNITED KINGDOM ASSOCIATION OF MANUFACTURERS OF BAKERS' YEAST

Acronym or abbreviation: UKAMBY

6 Catherine Street, London, WC2B 5JJ

Tel: 020 7420 7109
Fax: 020 7836 0580
E-mail: grace.foyle@fdf.org.uk

Enquiries:
Enquiries to: Executive Secretary

Organisation type and purpose:
Trade association (membership is by subscription), manufacturing industry.

Subject coverage:
Bakers' yeast, legislative developments.

Printed publications:
Annual Report

Access to staff:
Contact by letter, by fax and by e-mail
Hours: Mon to Fri, 0900 to 1700

Member of:
Food & Drink Federation

UNITED KINGDOM ASTRONOMY TECHNOLOGY CENTRE

Acronym or abbreviation: UK ATC

The Library, Royal Observatory, Blackford Hill, Edinburgh, EH9 3HJ

Tel: Switchboard 0131 668 8100 \ Library 0131 668 8395
Fax: 0131 668 8264
E-mail: user@roe.ac.uk

Website:
http://www.roe.ac.uk/atc/library
Astronomical literature

Enquiries:
Enquiries to: Librarian
Direct tel: 0131 668 8395
Direct e-mail: library@roe.ac.uk

Founded:
1896

Organisation type and purpose:
Research organisation.

Subject coverage:
National centre for the design and production of state-of-the-art astronomical instrumentation and associated technology, in collaboration with UK organisations and/or overseas partners.

Museum or gallery collection, archive, or library special collection:
Crawford Collection of historical books and manuscripts on astronomy, and related subjects from 13th to late 19th century, c. 15,000 items

Non-library collection catalogue:
All or part available online

Library catalogue:
All or part available online

Printed publications:
Annual Report of the James Clerk Maxwell Telescope
Annual Report of the United Kingdom Infrared Telescope
JCMT Newsletter (irregular)
Research and Facilities/Royal Observatory, Edinburgh (1981-)
Spectrum (quarterly)
Supplement to the Catalogue of the Crawford Library of the Royal Observatory, Edinburgh (1977)

Publications list:
Available in print

Access to staff:
Contact by letter, by telephone, by fax, by e-mail, in person and via website. Appointment necessary.
Hours: Mon to Fri, 0900 to 1730
Special comments: Not open to the public

Funded by:
Science & Technology Facilities Council
Polaris House, North Star Avenue, Swindon, SN2 1SZ; website: http://www.scitech.ac.uk

UNITED KINGDOM CENTRE FOR ECONOMIC AND ENVIRONMENTAL DEVELOPMENT

Acronym or abbreviation: UK CEED

continued overleaf

Suite 1, Priestgate House, 3–7 Priestgate, Peterborough, Cambridgeshire, PE1 1JN

Tel: 01733 311644
Fax: 01733 312782
E-mail: info@ukceed.org

Website:
http://www.ukceed.org
Company description and information on project areas.

Enquiries:
Enquiries to: Information Officer

Founded:
1984

Organisation type and purpose:
National organisation, registered charity (charity number 289469), research organisation.

Subject coverage:
All aspects of environmental economics including energy, coastal, marine, leisure, packaging, sustainable development, land use planning, nuclear, business ethics and corporate environmental reporting, and information and communication technologies; public participation; tourism.

Non-library collection catalogue:
All or part available online and in print

Printed publications:
Conference proceedings
UK CEED Bulletin (4 times a year)
UK CEED Discussion Papers (irregular)
Atmospheric Emissions from Private Motor Vehicles (1995)
Cleaner Technology (1992)
Digital Futures – Living in a Dot-Com World (Feb 2001)
Inland, Coastal and Estuarine Waters Magazine (bi-monthy, by subscription)
Leicestershire Rural Partnership Citizen's Jury on Rural Issues (May 2001)
Monitoring and Retrievability of Radioactive Waste (I) (Dec 2000)
Monitoring and Retrievabililty of Radioactive Waste (II) (Feb 2001)
Signposting the Sustainable Development Strategy (1994)
The Impacts of Recreation on Marine Special Areas of Conservation (mSAC) (Mar 2000)

Access to staff:
Contact by letter, by telephone, by fax, by e-mail and via website
Hours: Mon to Fri, 0900 to 1700

UNITED KINGDOM CERTIFICATION AUTHORITY FOR REINFORCING STEELS

Acronym or abbreviation: UK CARES

Pembroke House, 21 Pembroke Road, Sevenoaks, Kent, TN13 1XR

Tel: 01732 450000
Fax: 01732 455917
E-mail: general@ukcares.com

Website:
http://www.ukcares.com

Enquiries:
Enquiries to: Company Secretary
Direct e-mail: colinnicholson@ukcares.com

Founded:
1983

Organisation type and purpose:
Third party certification body.

Subject coverage:
Reinforcing steels.

Printed publications:
List of approved firms

Publications list:
Available online and in print

Access to staff:
Contact by letter, by telephone, by fax and by e-mail
Hours: Mon to Fri, 0900 to 1700

UNITED KINGDOM CLINICAL PHARMACY ASSOCIATION

Acronym or abbreviation: UKCPA

Alpha House, Countesthorpe Road, Wigston, Leicestershire, LE18 4PJ

Tel: 0116 277 6999
Fax: 0116 277 6272
E-mail: admin@ukcpa.com

Website:
http://www.ukcpa.org

Founded:
1981

Organisation type and purpose:
Advisory body, professional body (membership is by subscription), present number of members: 2000+, training organisation. Promotes pharmaceutical care for the benefit of patients.

Subject coverage:
Clinical pharmacy, education and training, quality and risk management, critical care, care of the elderly, surgery, infection management, respiratory, cardiac, diabetes, emergency care, IT, leadership development, pain management, community, gastroenterology/hepatology.

Printed publications:
Clinical Pharmacy Models of Care
Newsletter (quarterly, free to members)
Symposia abstract booklets (free to members)

Publications list:
Available in print

Access to staff:
Contact by letter, by telephone, by fax, by e-mail and via website
Hours: Mon to Fri, 0900 to 1700

UNITED KINGDOM FLIGHT SAFETY COMMITTEE

Acronym or abbreviation: UKFSC

Graham Suite, Fairoaks Airport, Chobham, Woking, Surrey, GU24 8HX

Tel: 01276 855193
Fax: 01276 855195
E-mail: ukfsc@freezone.co.uk

Website:
http://www.ukfsc.co.uk

Enquiries:
Enquiries to: Chief Executive

Founded:
1959

Organisation type and purpose:
Advisory body, professional body (membership is by subscription, election or invitation), present number of members: 85, voluntary organisation. To improve aviation safety.

Subject coverage:
Aviation safety.

Information services:
Website and magazine

Education services:
Flight Safety Familiarisation Course

Trade and statistical information:
Aviation safety articles and statistics.

Library catalogue:
All or part available in-house

Printed publications:
Focus on Commercial Aviation Safety (FOCUS)

Publications list:
Available online

Access to staff:
Contact by letter, by telephone, by fax and by e-mail
Hours: Mon to Fri, 0900 to 1630

UNITED KINGDOM FORTIFICATIONS CLUB

Acronym or abbreviation: UKFC

4 Mablethorpe Road, Wymering, Portsmouth, Hampshire, PO6 3LJ

Tel: 023 9238 7794

Website:
http://www.mysite.freeserve.com/ukfc

Enquiries:
Enquiries to: Chairman
Direct tel: 023 9238 7794 (24 hours)
Other contacts: Webmaster for Internet enquiries email Peter.Cobb@btopenworld.com.

Founded:
1972

Organisation type and purpose:
International organisation, membership association (membership is by subscription), voluntary organisation, research organisation.

Subject coverage:
All types of fortification within UK and certain other nations overseas from 2,500 BC to the present day; specifically Iron Age hill and promontory forts, Romano-British camps, forts and towers etc; castle construction; Tudor fortifications: Martello towers and 18th and 19th century fortifications; Georgian and Victorian defences and armoured works; coast artillery, anti-aircraft artillery and field fortifications from both World Wars; Northern Ireland defences; airfield layouts and offshore fortified structures (any period); 130 different subject groupings.

Museum or gallery collection, archive, or library special collection:
Cobb Family Archive
Rare books on fortifications, military archaeology and nautical matters
Slide and photographic archives
UKFC Central Archive (over 115 subjects in many volumes)
W E J Parker Archive (Gosport)

Non-library collection catalogue:
All or part available in print

Library catalogue:
All or part available in-house

Printed publications:
Book and reports on general and particular sites include:
ALDIS, newsletter (free to members; at cost plus postage to non-members)
Muster of Archive/Additions to UKFC collections (annually, free to members)
Solent Papers (on sale only)

Publications list:
Available online and in print

Access to staff:
Contact by letter, by telephone, by e-mail and in person. Appointment necessary.
Hours: Mon to Sat, 0800 to 1130 and 2100 to 2230; Sun and bank holidays, 0830 to 2100

Access to building, collection or gallery:
Prior appointment required

Connections with:
Airfield Research Group
CAMP
  USA
CDSG
  USA
Coast Defence Study Group
Kent Defence Research Group
  tel: 01304 205885
Palmerston Forts Society
  tel: 023 9258 6575

Pill Box Study Group
  tel: 01502 710149; e-mail: gkdesignresearch@
  tiscali.co.uk
Society for Army Historical Research

UNITED KINGDOM HOME CARE ASSOCIATION

Acronym or abbreviation: UKHCA

Group House, 52 Sutton Court Road, Sutton, SM1 4SL

Tel: 020 8288 1551
Fax: 020 8288 1550
E-mail: enquiries@ukhca.co.uk

Website:
http://www.ukhca.co.uk

Enquiries:
Enquiries to: Information Officer

Founded:
1988

Organisation type and purpose:
National professional and representative association for the independent, voluntary, and statutory homecare sector, representing 1600 organisations.

Subject coverage:
Domiciliary care, community care, social services, health and safety, contracting services and training, welfare of clients and welfare of care workers.

Printed publications:
Choosing Care in Your Home (leaflet, members only)
UKHCA Careworker handbook (£5.99 members, £8.99 non-members)
The Code of Practice (members only)
Costing Mode (online, free to members and non-members)
Who Cares Now?

Publications list:
Available in print

Access to staff:
Contact by letter, by telephone, by fax and by e-mail
Hours: Mon to Fri, 0900 to 1700

Access to building, collection or gallery:
No access other than to staff

Affiliated to:
Care Forum Wales
CCC
NCVO

UNITED KINGDOM ISLAMIC MISSION

Al Furqan School, 27 Arlington Street, Glasgow, G3 6DT

Tel: 0141 331 1119
Fax: 0141 332 2811
E-mail: ukimgla@yahoo.co.uk

Website:
http://www.ukim.org

Enquiries:
Enquiries to: Information Officer
Other contacts: President

Founded:
1920

Organisation type and purpose:
Membership association (membership is by subscription), present number of members: 45, voluntary organisation.
Provides information, training and resources on Islam/Muslims.

Subject coverage:
Islam/Muslim religion and culture.

Printed publications:
Zeal (magazine)
Islamic books (some free, mostly for purchase)

Publications list:
Available in print

Access to staff:
Contact by letter, by telephone, by fax, by e-mail and in person. Appointment necessary.
Hours: 1230 to 1630

Also at:
United Kingdom Islamic Mission
  19 Carrington Street, Glasgow, G4 6AJ

UNITED KINGDOM PASSPORT SERVICE

Acronym or abbreviation: UKPS

Globe House, 89 Eccleston Square, London, SW1V 1PX

Tel: 0870 521 0410

Website:
http://www.passport/gov.uk
How to obtain a British passport.

Enquiries:
Enquiries to: Private Office of Headquarters of UKPS
Direct tel: 020 7901 2428

Organisation type and purpose:
National government body.
Executive agency of the Home Office; 7 regional offices.

Subject coverage:
Issue of UK passports to British citizens, British Dependent Territories citizens, British Nationals (Overseas); British Overseas citizens, British Subjects and British Protected Persons.

Museum or gallery collection, archive, or library special collection:
Records of all UK passport issues including those issued at British Consular posts abroad (at Hayes)

Printed publications:
Advice leaflets (free)

Access to staff:
Contact by letter and by telephone. Appointment necessary.
Hours: Mon to Fri, 0830 to 1800; Sat, 0900 to 1500
Special comments: Prior appointment is required – 0870 521 0410.

Regional Offices:
Belfast Passport Office
  tel: 0870 521 0410
Durham Passport Office
  tel: 0870 521 0410
Glasgow Passport Office
  tel: 0870 521 0410
Liverpool Passport Office
  tel: 0870 521 0410
London Passport Office
  tel: 0870 521 0410
Newport Passport Office
  tel: 0870 521 0410
Peterborough Passport Office
  tel: 0870 521 0410

UNITED KINGDOM PETROLEUM INDUSTRY ASSOCIATION LIMITED

Acronym or abbreviation: UKPIA

Quality House, Quality Court, Chancery Lane, London, WC2A 1HP

Tel: 020 7269 7600
Fax: 020 7269 7608
E-mail: info@ukpia

Website:
http://www.ukpia.com

Enquiries:
Enquiries to: Director General

Founded:
1978

Organisation type and purpose:
Trade association.

Subject coverage:
The downstream oil industry (supply, refining and distribution of petroleum products in the UK and Northern Ireland).

Publications list:
Available online

Access to staff:
Contact by telephone and via website

Close liaison with:
Europia
Institute of Petroleum
Oil & Gas UK
other organisations serving the petroleum field

UNITED KINGDOM SCIENCE PARK ASSOCIATION, THE

Acronym or abbreviation: UKSPA

Chesterford Research Park, Little Chesterford, Saffron Walden, Essex, CB10 1XL

Tel: 01779 532050
Fax: 01779 532049
E-mail: info@ukspa.org.uk

Website:
http://www.ukspa.org.uk

Enquiries:
Enquiries to: UKSPA Administrator
Other contacts: Business Development Manager

Founded:
1984

Organisation type and purpose:
Membership Association.

Subject coverage:
UK science parks; tenant companies of UK science parks; science parks finance, premises, types of business.

Printed publications:
Annual Report
The Planning, Development and Operation of Science Parks, 2nd edn, 2006 (£50 plus p&p)
Research (economic) main report
Science Park Directory – 14th edition (£50 plus p&p)
Evaluation of the Past and Future Economic Contribution of the UK Science Park Movement (report)

Publications list:
Available online and in print

Access to staff:
Contact by letter, by telephone, by fax and by e-mail. Appointment necessary.
Hours: Mon to Fri, 0900 to 1700

Affiliated to:
AURIL (Association for University Research and Industry Links)
  Queens University Belfast, Lanyon North, University Road, Belfast, BT7 1NN; tel: 028 9027 2588; fax: 028 9027 2570; website: www.auril.org.uk
International Association of Science Parks (IASP)

UNITED KINGDOM TRANSPLANT CO-ORDINATORS ASSOCIATION

Acronym or abbreviation: UKTCA

PO Box 6300, Birmingham, B15 2RN

Tel: 07071 223171
Fax: 07071 223171
E-mail: alex@uktca.org.uk

Enquiries:
Enquiries to: The Secretariat

Founded:
1983

continued overleaf

Organisation type and purpose:
Professional body (membership is by subscription), registered charity (charity number 1065609).
To increase transplantation and organ donation within the UK and Eire.

Subject coverage:
Transplantation and organ donation.

Access to staff:
Contact by letter, by telephone, by fax and by e-mail
Hours: Mon to Fri, 0900 to 1700

UNITED KINGDOM VINEYARDS ASSOCIATION

Acronym or abbreviation: UKVA

PO Box 985, Bottisham, Cambridge, CB5 9WW

Tel: 01223 813812
E-mail: info@ukva.org.uk

Enquiries:
Enquiries to: General Secretary

Founded:
1996

Organisation type and purpose:
Trade association.
Central body for the affiliated regional associations.

Subject coverage:
The growth of the wine trade and the cultivation of vines and making of wine in the United Kingdom; negotiation with central and local government in matters such as planning, rating and taxation, and EC and its wine regulations; the interchange of technical and other information concerning wine or the vine; Quality wine scheme for English and Welsh Wine; and the annual competition and awards for the English and Welsh Wine of the Year.

Printed publications:
Grape Press (2 times a year, for members)

Access to staff:
Contact by letter, by telephone, by fax and by e-mail. Appointment necessary.
Hours: Mon to Fri, 0900 to 1700

Affiliated to the:
National Farmers Union
Wine and Spirit Association of Great Britain

UNITED KINGDOM WAREHOUSING ASSOCIATION

Acronym or abbreviation: UKWA

Walter House, 418–422 Strand, London, WC2R 0PT

Tel: 020 7836 5522
Fax: 020 7438 9379
E-mail: dg@ukwa.org.uk

Website:
http://www.ukwa.org.uk

Enquiries:
Enquiries to: Membership Secretary

Founded:
1944

Organisation type and purpose:
Trade association.

Subject coverage:
Public warehousing information in the UK, warehousing standards, European legislation.

Printed publications:
BS5750 Quality Manuals
Newsletter (monthly)
Warehousing Manual

Access to staff:
Appointment necessary.
Hours: Mon to Fri, 0900 to 1700

Member of:
European Warehousing and Logistics Confederation
International Federation of Warehousing Logistics Associations

UNITED LIBRARY

Old Coates House, 32 Manor Place, Edinburgh, EH3 7EB

Tel: 0131 225 4911
E-mail: tisec@scotland.anglican.org

Enquiries:
Enquiries to: Librarian

Founded:
1995

Subject coverage:
Theology, counselling.

Library catalogue:
All or part available in-house

Access to staff:
Contact by letter, by telephone, by e-mail and in person. Non-members charged.
Hours: Tue to Fri, 0900 to 1230
Special comments: Annual subscription for borrowing to non-members.

Combined library from:
Scottish Congregational College
Scottish Episcopal Theological College
St Colm's College (Church of Scotland) Pastoral Foundation

Parent body:
Scottish Episcopal Church
tel: 0131 225 6357; fax: 0131 346 7247

UNITED LODGE OF THEOSOPHISTS

Acronym or abbreviation: ULT

62 Queens Gardens, London, W2 3AL

Tel: 020 7723 0688
Fax: 020 7262 8639
E-mail: ult@ultlon.freeserve.co.uk

Website:
http://www.ultlon.freeserve.co.uk

Enquiries:
Enquiries to: Information Officer

Founded:
1925

Organisation type and purpose:
International organisation, voluntary organisation.

Subject coverage:
Theosophy and comparative religions, psychic powers in man and philosophies.

Museum or gallery collection, archive, or library special collection:
19th-century magazines on theosophy: Lucifer, Theosophy and other now extinct publications

Non-library collection catalogue:
All or part available online, in-house and in print

Library catalogue:
All or part available in-house and in print

Printed publications:
Theosophy Magazine
Pamphlets, books and magazines

Publications list:
Available online and in print

Access to staff:
Contact by letter, by telephone, by fax, by e-mail, in person and via website. Appointment necessary. Letter of introduction required.
Hours: Mon to Fri, 1000 to 1400; at other times by appointment

Access to building, collection or gallery:
Prior appointment required
Hours: by appointment on Wed and Sun

UNITED NATIONS ASSOCIATION OF GREAT BRITAIN AND NORTHERN IRELAND

Acronym or abbreviation: UNA-UK

3 Whitehall Court, London, SW1A 2EL

Tel: 020 7766 3444
Fax: 020 7930 5893
E-mail: info@una-uk.org

Website:
http://www.una.org.uk

Enquiries:
Enquiries to: Deputy Director
Direct tel: 020 7766 3469
Direct e-mail: southgate@una.org.uk
Other contacts: Head of Advocacy, Executive Director

Founded:
1945

Organisation type and purpose:
Voluntary organisation.
Educational and lobbying body.

Subject coverage:
United Nations' activities and international affairs, especially United Nations and conflict, human rights, environment and development.

Museum or gallery collection, archive, or library special collection:
Current UN documents and material relating to 1996

Printed publications:
Briefings (4 times a year, on particular UN interests; 8pp A4 usually)
New World (journal primarily for members and others interested in UN, every 3 months)

Publications list:
Available online and in print

Access to staff:
Contact by letter, by telephone and by e-mail.
Appointment necessary.
Hours: Mon to Fri, 1000 to 1600

Links with:
UNA Trust

Member of:
World Federation of UNAs
Which has consultative status grade 1 with United Nations Economic and Social Council

UNITED NATIONS HIGH COMMISSIONER FOR REFUGEES

Acronym or abbreviation: UNHCR

21st Floor, Millbank Tower, 21–24 Millbank, London, SW1P 4QP

Tel: 020 7828 9191
Fax: 020 7630 5349

Website:
http://www.unhcr.ch
Refugee statistics, section for teachers, country information.
http://www.ukforunhcr.com
Website of national charitable organisation.
Information on UK issues.

Enquiries:
Enquiries to: Information Assistant

Founded:
1951

Organisation type and purpose:
International organisation.
To assist and protect asylum seekers and refugees.

Subject coverage:
Information on refugee situations worldwide, refugee statistics, work of UNHCR and type of assistance provided to refugees.

Museum or gallery collection, archive, or library special collection:
Photographs

Trade and statistical information:
Statistics on refugees.

Printed publications:
REFUGEES Magazine (quarterly)
Variety of books, posters, leaflets, educational
  resources
The State of the World's Refugees – In search of
  Solutions (every 2 years)

Electronic and video publications:
Videos available on loan, list available includes:
UNHCR: A Global View
Educational Videos available to schools include:
To Feel At Home

Access to staff:
Contact by letter, by telephone and by fax.
Appointment necessary.
Hours: Mon to Thu, 0900 to 1730; Fri, 0900 to 1500

Parent body:
United Nations

UNITED NATIONS INFORMATION CENTRE, LONDON

Acronym or abbreviation: UNIC-London

Millbank Tower, (21st Floor), 21 – 24 Millbank,
London, SW1P 4QH

Tel: 020 7630 1981
Fax: 020 7976 6478
E-mail: info@uniclondon.org

Website:
http://www.unitednations.org
UNIC London website

Enquiries:
Enquiries to: Librarian
Direct tel: 020 7630 2716
Direct e-mail: kdavies@uniclondon.org
Other contacts: Information Assistant for collection
of photographs and videos for loan.

Founded:
1947

Organisation type and purpose:
International organisation.

Subject coverage:
Activities of the United Nations, social sciences,
crime, drug abuse, role of women, children,
peacekeeping, human rights, environment.

Trade and statistical information:
Production information, social and economic
statistics and statistics on trade, population,
agriculture, mortality and AIDS.

Printed publications:
Order printed publications from: Stationery Office,
who are agents for distribution of all United
Nations publications in the United Kingdom

Publications list:
Available in print

Access to staff:
Contact by letter, by telephone, by fax, by e-mail
and via website. Appointment necessary.
Hours: Mon to Thu, 0900 to 1300 and 1400 to 1700

Access to building, collection or gallery:
Prior appointment required

One of the:
70 Information Centres of the United Nations

UNITED REFORMED CHURCH

Acronym or abbreviation: URC

86 Tavistock Place, London, WC1H 9RT

Tel: 020 7916 2020
Fax: 020 7916 2121
E-mail: urc@urc.org.uk

Website:
http://www.urc.org.uk

Enquiries:
Enquiries to: General Secretary

Founded:
1972

Organisation type and purpose:
Membership association.
Christian Church.

Subject coverage:
United Reformed Church affairs and history.

**Museum or gallery collection, archive, or library
special collection:**
United Reformed Church Historical Society
  Library (now at Westminster College, Madingley
  Road, Cambridge CB3 0AA)

Printed publications:
Journal of the URC History Society
Reform (monthly except August)
Year Book

Publications list:
Available in print

Access to staff:
Contact by e-mail. Appointment necessary.
Hours: Mon to Fri, 0900 to 1630

Member of:
Churches Together in Britain and Ireland
Churches Together in England
World Alliance of Reformed Churches
World Council of Churches

Partner in:
Council for World Mission

UNITED REFORMED CHURCH HISTORY SOCIETY

Acronym or abbreviation: URCHS

Westminster College, Madingley Road,
Cambridge, CB3 0AA

Tel: 01223 741300
Fax: 01223 300765
E-mail: mt212@cam.ac.uk

Enquiries:
Enquiries to: Administrator

Founded:
1972

Incorporates the former:
Congregational Historical Society, Presbyterian
Historical Society of England and Churches of
Christ Historical Society

Organisation type and purpose:
Learned society (membership is by subscription),
present number of members: 250.

Subject coverage:
Denominational church history, in particular that
of the United Reformed Church in England and
Wales, the Congregational Church of England and
Wales and the Presbyterian Church of England.

**Museum or gallery collection, archive, or library
special collection:**
Library of Presbyterian Church of England and
  central/organisational archives of the church
Carruthers Collection
17th-century dissenting pamphlets

Non-library collection catalogue:
All or part available in-house

Library catalogue:
All or part available online and in-house

Printed publications:
Journal (2 times a year)

Access to staff:
Contact by letter, by telephone, by fax and by e-
mail. Appointment necessary. Non-members
charged.
Hours: Mon to Wed, 0930 to 1530

Access for disabled people:
Hours: Mon to Wed, 0930 to 1530

UNITED SOCIETY FOR CHRISTIAN LITERATURE

Acronym or abbreviation: USCL

36 Causton Street, London, SW1P 4ST

Tel: 020 7592 3900
Fax: 020 7592 3929
E-mail: info@feedtheminds.org

Enquiries:
Enquiries to: Information Officer

Founded:
1799

Organisation type and purpose:
Registered charity (charity number 226512).

Subject coverage:
Christian literature in developing countries,
including development of publishing houses
through training, etc., training of pastors and
ministers.

**Museum or gallery collection, archive, or library
special collection:**
Lutterworth Press archive, held at SOAS, London

Printed publications:
Annual Report
Information Sheet

Access to staff:
Contact by letter, by telephone, by fax and by e-
mail. Appointment necessary.
Hours: Mon to Fri, 0900 to 1700

Links with:
Feed the Minds
  at the same address

UNITED SOCIETY FOR THE PROPAGATION OF THE GOSPEL

Acronym or abbreviation: USPG

Partnership House, 157 Waterloo Road, London,
SE1 8XA

Tel: 020 7803 3422
Fax: 020 7928 2371
E-mail: enquiries@uspg.org.uk

Website:
http://www.uspg.org.uk
http://shop.uspg.org.uk/acatalog/
Publications

Enquiries:
Enquiries to: Donor Care Coordinator
Other contacts: Archivist (archive@uspg.org.uk) for
archival and historical enquiries.

Founded:
1965

Organisation type and purpose:
Voluntary organisation, registered charity (charity
number 234518).
USPG is an Anglican mission agency with a
successful 300-year track record of enabling people
to grow spiritually, to thrive physically and to have
a voice in an unjust world.

Subject coverage:
Anglican church life and mission in many areas of
the world, predominantly but not exclusively in
the Commonwealth.
The archive contains the records of USPG and its
predecessor Societies from 1701 onwards,
including information about former missionaries
of the Societies.

**Museum or gallery collection, archive, or library
special collection:**
Joint library collection with the Church Mission
  Society
Photograph library (current collection of prints,
  slides and digital images)
The Archives from 1965, plus all files on individual
  missionaries from the mid-19th century onwards
The Archives to 1965 are at the Rhodes House
  Library, South Parks Road, Oxford OX1 3RG and
  these include:
The historic library collection

continued overleaf

Photographs to the 1950s
Records of the Society for the Propagation of the
Gospel, 1701 to 1965
Records of the Universities' Mission to Central
Africa, 1859 to 1965
Records of the Cambridge Mission to Delhi, 1877
to 1968

Non-library collection catalogue:
All or part available in-house

Library catalogue:
All or part available online and in-house

Printed publications:
Born Among Us (resource pack, £18)
The Christ We Share (resource pack, £18)
Three Centuries of Mission: The United Society for
the Propagation of the Gospel, 1701 -2001
(O'Connor D et al, hb £25, pb £12.50)
From Shore to Shore (£5.99)
Transmission (quarterly)
USPG Prayer Diary (quarterly)

Microform publications:
A number of SPG and UMCA archive series are
available on microfilm (from Microform
Academic Publishers, Main Street, East Ardsley,
Wakefield, WF3 2AT, tel: 01924 825700, website:
http//www.microform.co.uk)

Electronic and video publications:
The Life We Share (resource pack, £10)
Rethinking Mission at www.rethinkingmission.org

Publications list:
Available online

Access to staff:
Contact by letter, by telephone, by fax and by e-
mail. Appointment necessary.
Hours: Mon to Fri, 0900 to 1700

Member of:
Global Mission Network
tel: 020 7654 7232; fax: 020 7654 7222; e-mail:
ccom@ctbi.org.uk
Partnership for World Mission (PWM)
tel: 020 7803 3201; fax: 020 7633 0185; e-mail:
pwm@c-of-e.org.uk

UNITED SYNAGOGUE AGENCY FOR JEWISH EDUCATION

Acronym or abbreviation: AJE

Bet Meir Building, 44b Albert Road, Hendon,
London, NW4 2SG

Tel: 020 8457 9700
Fax: 020 8457 9707
E-mail: info@aje.org.uk

Website:
http://www.aje.org.uk
Full Agency for Jewish Education information,
publications, catalogue and order facility.

Enquiries:
Enquiries to: Resource Centre Manager
Direct tel: 020 8457 9717
Direct e-mail: resources@aje.org.uk

Founded:
1995

Formed from:
United Synagogue Board of Religious Education;
Institute of Jewish Education (year of change 1995)

Formerly called:
Agency for Jewish Education (year of change 2004)

Organisation type and purpose:
Membership association, registered charity,
training organisation, publishing house.
Education resource centre.

Subject coverage:
All aspects of Jewish Studies teaching, training and
information.

**Museum or gallery collection, archive, or library
special collection:**
Education Library containing books on Jewish
Studies and teaching methodology

Printed publications:
The Jewish Educator (journal)
Wide variety of teaching resources including
curriculum guidance, posters, maps, charts and
resource packs

Publications list:
Available online

Access to staff:
Contact by letter, by telephone, by fax, by e-mail,
in person and via website. Appointment necessary.
Non-members charged.
Hours: Mon to Thu, 0900 to 1700; Fri, 0900 to 1300

UNITED WORLD COLLEGE OF THE ATLANTIC LIMITED

Acronym or abbreviation: UWCA

St Donat's Castle, Llantwit Major, Vale of
Glamorgan, CF61 1WF

Tel: 01446 799000
Fax: 01446 799013
E-mail: principal@uwcac.uwc.org

Website:
http://www.atlanticcollege.org
Prospectus and student views.

Enquiries:
Enquiries to: Principal
Other contacts: Bursar

Founded:
1962

Organisation type and purpose:
International organisation, registered charity.
International understanding through education
and service.

Subject coverage:
International baccalaureate, international
education, emergency sea rescue services,
community service, environmental monitoring
(marine).

Printed publications:
Extramural centre prospectus
Handbook
Prospectus

Access to staff:
Contact by letter, by telephone, by fax, by e-mail
and via website. Appointment necessary.
Hours: Mon to Fri, 0830 to 1630

Affiliated to:
United World Colleges (International)
Lynton House, Tavistock Square, London,
WC1H 9SX; tel: 020 7388 2066; fax: 020 7388
3166; e-mail: uwcio@uwc.org

UNITED WORLD COLLEGES (INTERNATIONAL)

Formal name: The United World Colleges
(International) Ltd
Acronym or abbreviation: UWC

Second floor, 1721 Emerald Street, London, WC1N
3QN

Tel: 020 7269 7800
Fax: 020 7405 4374
E-mail: uwcio@uwc.org

Website:
http://www.uwc.org
Overview of the UWC International Movement.

Enquiries:
Enquiries to: Executive Director
Other contacts: Communications Co-ordinator

Founded:
1962

Organisation type and purpose:
International organisation, membership
association (membership is by qualification),
present number of members: 33,000, voluntary
organisation, registered charity (charity number
313690), suitable for ages: 16 to 19.

The UWC International Office is a co-ordinating
office for an international educational movement.
The aims of the movement are international
education for responsible citizenship with
emphasis on service, peace, justice, international
understanding and environmental concern.

Printed publications:
College Prospectuses and Publications
UWC United World Magazine
UWC: An Overview

Electronic and video publications:
UWC Promotional Video – Preparing Tomorrow's
International Leaders

Access to staff:
Contact by letter, by telephone, by fax and by e-
mail
Hours: Mon to Fri, 0900 to 1730
Special comments: Closed weekends and holidays.

A member college is:
United World College of the Atlantic
St. Donat's Castle, Llantwit Major, Vale of
Glamorgan, CF61 1WF; tel: 01446 799000; fax:
01446 799013; e-mail: principal@uwcac.uwc.org

Has:
12 Member Colleges
132 National Committees

UNIVERSITIES AND COLLEGES ADMISSIONS SERVICE

Acronym or abbreviation: UCAS

Rosehill, New Barn Lane, Cheltenham,
Gloucestershire, GL52 3LZ

Tel: 01242 544879\ Minicom no. 01242 544942
Fax: 01242 544954

Website:
http://www.ucas.com
Higher education, getting into university or
college, university/college details, course research,
statistical information, press releases.

Enquiries:
Enquiries to: Director of Outreach Department
Direct e-mail: j.johnson@ucas.ac.uk
Other contacts: Applicant enquiries tel no: 0870
1122211 for information and advice on application
to higher education.

Founded:
1993

Organisation type and purpose:
Higher education admissions service. Managed by
representatives of universities and schools.

Subject coverage:
Applications for admission to full-time and
sandwich first degree, diploma HND, HNC, and
Certificate of Higher Education courses at United
Kingdom universities (not Open University) and in
most colleges of higher education; also manages
separate systems for diplomas in social work,
nursing and midwifery, and for postgraduate
teacher training; promotion of opportunities
available in higher education.

Trade and statistical information:
Application statistics and related information on
access to higher education.

Printed publications:
GTTR Guide for Applicants
Mature Students Guide to Higher Education
NMAS Application Form
NMAS Handbook
Parents' Guide to Higher Education
University and College Entrance: The Official
Guide
UCAS Annual Report
UCAS Application Form
UCAS Directory
Order printed publications from: tel: 01242 544610, e-
mail: distribution@ucas.ac.uk

Electronic and video publications:
Electronic Applications System (disc)
Study Link UK (CD-ROM)

UCAS Directory (formerly UCAS Handbook)

Access to staff:
Contact by letter, by telephone, by fax, by e-mail and via website
Hours: Mon to Fri, 0900 to 1700

Access for disabled people:
Parking provided, level entry

Other branch at:
UCAS Scottish Office
tel: 0131 6670958

UNIVERSITIES FEDERATION FOR ANIMAL WELFARE

Acronym or abbreviation: UFAW

The Old School House, Brewhouse Hill, Wheathampstead, Hertfordshire, AL4 8AN

Tel: 01582 831818
Fax: 01582 831414
E-mail: ufaw@ufaw.org.uk

Website:
http://www.ufaw.org.uk

Enquiries:
Enquiries to: Secretary
Other contacts: (1) Scientific Officer; (2) Editorial Assistant; (3) Development Officer for (1) grants; (2) Animal Welfare journal; (3) general scientific information.

Founded:
1926

Organisation type and purpose:
Membership association (membership is by subscription), present number of members: 900, registered charity (charity number 207996), research organisation.
Extensive publications and educational aids on animal welfare.
Promotion of human behaviour towards wild and domestic animals in the UK and abroad.

Subject coverage:
Care and management of laboratory, farm, wild, zoo and companion animals, humane killing, pest control, control of animals in the wild.

Printed publications:
Animal Welfare (journal, quarterly)
Annual Report
Information leaflets
News Sheet (annually)
Proceedings of Symposia
What Should We Do About Animal Welfare? (Appleby M)
Animal Welfare A Cool Eye Towards Eden (Webster A J F)

Electronic and video publications:
Videos

Publications list:
Available in print

Access to staff:
Contact by letter, by telephone, by fax and by e-mail. Appointment necessary.
Hours: Mon to Fri, 0900 to 1600

Access to building, collection or gallery:
Prior appointment required

UNIVERSITY AND COLLEGE UNION (SCOTLAND)

Acronym or abbreviation: UCU (Scotland)

6 Castle Street, Edinburgh, EH2 3AT

Tel: 0131 226 6694
Fax: 0131 226 2066
E-mail: edinburgh@ucu.org.uk

Website:
http://www.ucu.org.uk

Enquiries:
Other contacts: Research Officer
Association of University Teachers (Scotland)

Organisation type and purpose:
Trade union.

Subject coverage:
Professional and trade union interests of academic and academically-related staff in Scottish Universities; University teaching, quality assurance and research in Scotland.

Access to staff:
Contact by letter, by telephone, by fax and by e-mail. Appointment necessary.
Hours: Mon to Fri, 0900 to 1645

Affiliated to:
Scottish Trades Union Congress

UNIVERSITY ASSOCIATION FOR CONTEMPORARY EUROPEAN STUDIES

Acronym or abbreviation: UACES

UACES Secretariat, King's College London, Strand, London, WC2R 2LS

Tel: 020 7240 0206
Fax: 020 7240 0206
E-mail: admin@uaces.org

Website:
http://www.uaces.org
Information on Association, its activities, register of courses and publications and links to other relevant sites.

Enquiries:
Enquiries to: Executive Director

Founded:
1970

Organisation type and purpose:
International organisation, professional body (membership is by subscription), present number of members: 800, registered charity (charity number 274470).

Subject coverage:
Contemporary European studies, European integration, European Union.

Printed publications:
Contemporary European Studies (series)
Journal of Common Market Studies: The European Union Annual Review 2000/2001
Negotiating a European Energy Policy: Role Play Simulation (George S, Haythorne D and Wright P, 1995, £5)
Register of Courses in European Studies 1998/2000 in UK Universities and University Colleges (biennial, £6) now on website
Register of Current Research in European Integration 1999/2001 in the UK (biennial, £10)
Order printed publications from: Contemporary European Studies Series, Sheffield Academic Press, c/o Orca Book Services, Stanley House, 3 Fleets Lane, Poole, Dorset, BH15 3AJ, tel: 01202 665 432, fax: 01202 666 219
For Journal of Common Market Studies/The EU: Annual Review, Contemporary European Studies Series, Blackwell Publishers, PO Box 805, 108 Cowley Road, Oxford, OX4 1FH, tel: 01865 244083, fax: 01865 381381, e-mail: jnlinfo@blackwellpublishers.co.uk

Electronic and video publications:
UACES Online Essays

Publications list:
Available online and in print

Access to staff:
Contact by letter, by fax, by e-mail and via website
Hours: Mon to Fri, 0900 to 1700

UNIVERSITY COLLEGE FALMOUTH LIBRARY

Woodlane, Falmouth, Cornwall, TR11 4RA

Tel: 01326 213815
Fax: 01326 213827

E-mail: library@falmouth.ac.uk

Website:
http://www.falmouth.ac.uk

Enquiries:
Enquiries to: Head of Library and Information Services
Direct tel: ext 3815
Direct e-mail: dawn.lawrence@falmouth.ac.uk

Formerly called:
Falmouth School of Art and Design

Organisation type and purpose:
University department or institute.

Subject coverage:
Fine art, photography, contemporary crafts, graphic design, textile design, fashion design, 3D/spatial design illustration and media studies, film, garden design

Museum or gallery collection, archive, or library special collection:
35,000 books/exhibition catalogues
230 current journal subjects in art, design and media studies
Journals Collection – extensive range of contemporary international art and design titles
Broadcasting; journalism, media collection
Illustrated books and graphic novels special collection
Contemporary artists catalogues
Video library (art, film, general)
Cornwall artists

Printed publications:
Journals listing
Library Guide

Electronic and video publications:
Newsletter

Access to staff:
Contact by letter, by telephone, by e-mail and via website. Appointment necessary.
Hours: Term time: Mon to Thu, 0900 to 2000; Fri, 0900 to 1700; Sat, 1000 to 1800
Vacations: Mon to Fri, 0900 to 1700

Access for disabled people:
level entry, access to all public areas, toilet facilities

UNIVERSITY COLLEGE LONDON – BARTLETT LIBRARY

5th Floor, Wates House, 22 Gordon Street, London, WC1H 0QB

Tel: 020 7679 4900
Fax: 020 7679 7373
E-mail: library@ucl.ac.uk

Website:
http://www.ucl.ac.uk/library
Library services, opening hours, catalogue etc for all UCL library sites.

Enquiries:
Enquiries to: Librarian

Organisation type and purpose:
University library.

Subject coverage:
Architecture, town planning, construction management, development planning.

Library catalogue:
All or part available online

Access to staff:
Appointment necessary.
Hours: Term time: Mon, Thu, 0930 to 2000; Tue, Wed, Fri, 0930 to 1900; Sat, 0930 to 1630; Vacation: Mon to Fri, 0930 to 1900

Part of:
University College London Library
tel: 020 7679 2000; fax: 020 7679 7373; e-mail: library@ucl.ac.uk

UNIVERSITY COLLEGE LONDON – CRUCIFORM LIBRARY

Acronym or abbreviation: UCL

Cruciform Building, Gower Street, London, WC1E 6BT

Tel: 020 7679 6079
Fax: 020 7679 6981
E-mail: clinscilib@ucl.ac.uk

Website:
http://www.ucl.ac.uk/library/crucilib.shtml

Enquiries:
Enquiries to: Librarian

Founded:
1907

Organisation type and purpose:
University department or institute.

Subject coverage:
Clinical medicine, urology

Library catalogue:
All or part available online

Access to staff:
Contact by letter, by telephone, by e-mail, in person and via website. Appointment necessary. Non-members charged.
Hours: Mon to Fri, 0900 to 1700

Access for disabled people:
Ramped entry, toilet facilities
Special comments: Internal lift.

Part of:
Royal Free and University College Medical School
UCL Library Services

UNIVERSITY COLLEGE LONDON – JEWISH STUDIES LIBRARY

Acronym or abbreviation: UCL

Gower Street, London, WC1E 6BT

Tel: 020 7679 7700
Fax: 020 7679 7373
E-mail: library@ucl.ac.uk

Website:
http://www.ucl.ac.uk/library

Enquiries:
Enquiries to: Jewish Studies Librarian
Direct tel: 020 7679 2598
Direct e-mail: v.freedman@ucl.ac.uk

Founded:
1826

Incorporates the former:
Mocatta Library

Organisation type and purpose:
University library.
Library of the Jewish Historical Society of England.

Subject coverage:
Jewish history, Hebrew and Semitic languages, Bible, Rabbinic literature, mysticism, Jewish philosophy, Hebrew literature and Yiddish language and literature.

Services for disabled people:
Alternative-format leaflets, catalogue terminal with large-format keyboard and screen, book fetching service, induction loop, visual magnifiers.

Museum or gallery collection, archive, or library special collection:
Abramsky Collection
Albert Hyamson Collection
Altmann Collection
Asher Myers Collection
F. D. Mocatta Collection
Lucien Wolf Genealogical Papers
Moses Gaster Papers
Schachar Collection (of Hassidism)
William Margulies Yiddish Library

Library catalogue:
All or part available online

Printed publications:
The Gaster Papers (1976, occasional publications no. 2)
Order printed publications from: library@ucl.ac.uk

Access to staff:
Contact by letter, by telephone, by fax, by e-mail and in person

Access to building, collection or gallery:
Membership required (see website for details). Appointment required for access to special collections.
Hours: Term time: Mon to Thu, 0845 to 2230; Fri, 0845 to 1900; Sat, 1100 to 1745; Sun, 1100 to 2100; summer vacation: Mon to Fri, 0845 to 1900

Access for disabled people:
Building accessible (entrance, lift); some items inaccessible, but can be fetched by staff; toilet facilities

Constituent part of:
University College London

UNIVERSITY COLLEGE LONDON – JOINT LIBRARY, INSTITUTE OF OPHTHALMOLOGY

Bath Street, London, EC1V 9EL

Tel: 020 7608 6814
Fax: 020 7608 6814
E-mail: ophthlib@ucl.ac.uk

Website:
http://www.ucl.ac.uk/ioo/library
Library website, contact details, journals list, access to catalogue.

Enquiries:
Enquiries to: Librarian
Direct tel: 020 7608 6815
Direct e-mail: d.heatlie@ucl.ac.uk

Founded:
1947

Organisation type and purpose:
University department or institute.
Post-graduate and medical research.

Subject coverage:
Ophthalmology and visual sciences, clinical optics (postgraduate only).

Museum or gallery collection, archive, or library special collection:
Long runs of journals in European languages
Collection of Historical Works on ophthalmology, optics and visual science
E Nettleship Papers
Sydney Harry Stephenson books (with historical collection)

Non-library collection catalogue:
All or part available online

Printed publications:
Institute Annual Report

Access to staff:
Contact by letter, by telephone, by fax and by e-mail. Appointment necessary. Non-members charged.
Hours: Mon to Fri, 0900 to 1700
Special comments: Limited service provided which is not available directly to visitors (postal, telephone, fax enquiries). Will charge cost of handling and postage.

Joint Library of:
Moorfields Eye Hospital

Part of:
University College London

UNIVERSITY COLLEGE LONDON – LIBRARY OF THE INSTITUTE OF ARCHAEOLOGY

31–34 Gordon Square, London, WC1H 0PY

Tel: 020 7679 7485
Fax: 020 7383 2572

E-mail: library@ucl.ac.uk

Website:
http://library.ucl.ac.uk/

Enquiries:
Enquiries to: Institute Librarian
Direct e-mail: r.kirby@ucl.ac.uk
Other contacts: Library Admission Officer for requests for use of library, cost and access.

Organisation type and purpose:
University library, university department or institute.

Subject coverage:
Archaeology, particularly general prehistoric, pre-Columbian Latin American, Roman Provinces, Egyptology, pre-Islamic Western Asiatic, Medieval European; environmental archaeology, scientific basis of archaeology; technology and conservation of archaeological material; museology, museum studies and cultural heritage studies.

Museum or gallery collection, archive, or library special collection:
Tylecote Collection (archaeometallurgy)
The following have been relocated to The Special Collection Library services at University College:
The Edwards Collection of Egyptology
Air survey photographs of Near Eastern sites
De Navarro Collection (books and journals dealing with La Tène period)
Margaret Wood Collection (English architectural history)
Records of Near Eastern excavations

Library catalogue:
All or part available online

Printed publications:
Archaeology International (annually)
Papers from The Institute of Archaeology

Access to staff:
Contact by letter, by telephone and by e-mail. Appointment necessary. Non-members charged.
Hours: Mon to Fri, 0900 to 1700

Houses the:
Institute for Archaeometallurgical Studies

Part of:
University College London Library

UNIVERSITY COLLEGE LONDON – LIBRARY OF THE INSTITUTE OF ORTHOPAEDICS

Royal National Orthopaedic Hospital, Brockley Hill, Stanmore, Middlesex, HA7 4LP

Tel: 020 8909 5351
Fax: 020 8909 5390
E-mail: orthlib@ucl.ac.uk

Enquiries:
Enquiries to: Institute Librarian

Founded:
1946

Organisation type and purpose:
University department or institute.
To form a special collection on orthopaedics.

Subject coverage:
Orthopaedics.

Museum or gallery collection, archive, or library special collection:
Historical orthopaedic books

Non-library collection catalogue:
All or part available online

Library catalogue:
All or part available online

Access to staff:
Contact by letter, by telephone, by fax, by e-mail and in person. Appointment necessary.
Hours: Mon to Fri, 0930 to 1730

Access to building, collection or gallery:
Mon to Fri, 0930 to 1730

Part of:
University College London Library
University College London Medical School

UNIVERSITY COLLEGE LONDON – LIBRARY SERVICES

Gower Street, London, WC1E 6BT

Tel: 020 7387 7700
Fax: 020 7380 7373
E-mail: library@ucl.ac.uk

Website:
http://www.ucl.ac.uk/library

Enquiries:
Enquiries to: Director of Library Services
Direct tel: 020 7380 7834
Direct e-mail: p.ayris@ucl.ac.uk

Founded:
1826

Organisation type and purpose:
University library.

Subject coverage:
American history, anthropology, archaeology, architecture, art (fine art and history of art), biological sciences, Celtic, classical studies, clinical sciences, comparative philology, computer science, Dutch, economics, Egyptology, earth sciences, engineering, English, film studies, geography, German, Hebrew, history, human rights, Jewish studies, Latin American studies, law, library, archive and information studies, life sciences, linguistics, London history, mathematical sciences, medical sciences, management, philosophy, phonetics, physical sciences, planning, politics, psychology, public policy, Romance languages, Scandinavian studies, science and technology studies, Slavonic and East European studies.

Museum or gallery collection, archive, or library special collection:
Libraries of learned societies housed in the College Library (some in Special Collections – see later entry):
British Society of Franciscan Studies
Folklore Society
Gaelic Society
Geologists Association
Hertfordshire Natural History and Field Club
Huguenot Society
Jeremy Bentham Society
Jewish Historical Society of England
London Mathematical Society (now incorporated into the maths collections)
Malacological Society
Mocatta Library of Anglo-Judaica
Philological Society
Royal Historical Society
Royal Statistical Society
Viking Society for Northern Research (now incorporated into the Scandinavian collections)

Non-library collection catalogue:
All or part available in-house

Library catalogue:
All or part available online

Access to staff:
Contact by letter, by telephone, by fax, by e-mail and in person
Hours: Various: see website

College of the:
University of London

Houses the::
RNID Library for deaf and hard of hearing people

UNIVERSITY COLLEGE LONDON – SPECIAL COLLECTIONS

Acronym or abbreviation: UCL

Library Services, Gower Street, London, WC1E 6BT

Tel: 020 7679 5197
Fax: 020 7679 5157
E-mail: spec.coll@ucl.ac.uk

Website:
http://www.ucl.ac.uk/Library/special-coll/index.shtml
General information, site information, directory of special collections and library catalogue.

Enquiries:
Enquiries to: Archivist

Organisation type and purpose:
University library.

Subject coverage:
Special collections from the medieval to the present day covering a wide range of subjects. Highlights include the C K Ogden and Graves Libraries of rare books, incunabula and medieval manuscripts, rich in the fields of science, language and literature; 19th century collections, notably Jeremy Bentham's manuscripts and the papers of Lord Brougham, renowned in the field of social, political, legal and educational reform, as well as particular strengths in medical and scientific innovation; and 20th century professorial manuscripts, literary collections and papers, notably the Orwell Archive and the Little Magazines collection.

Museum or gallery collection, archive, or library special collection:
Some of the more important special collections are:
G C Allen Papers
Bagehot Notebooks
Bank of London and South America archives
Arnold Bennett Papers
Bentham Collection and Manuscripts (Jeremy Bentham 1748–1832)
Joseph Black lecture notes (chemistry)
John Bright letters (1811–1889)
Brougham Papers (Lord Brougham, 1778–1868)
Carswell Drawings
Chadwick
Dante Collection
De Morgan Papers (mathematics)
Early Renaissance Manuscripts
Flaxman Collection (drawings)
Folklore Society Collection and Archives
Sir Ambrose Fleming Papers
Gaelic Society Collection
Hugh Gaitskell Papers
Graves Library
Haldane Papers
Hertfordshire Natural History Society
Laurence Housman Collection (1865–1959)
Hume Tracts
Incunabula
Jewish Studies
Johnston Lavis Collection
Josephus Collection
James Joyce Collection
Learned Society Libraries
London History Collection
London Mathematical Society Archive
Kathleen Lonsdale Papers
Malacological Society
Medieval Manuscripts
Moses Montefiore Collection and family papers
Charles Kay Ogden Library and Papers (including Basic English)
George Orwell Archive
Mervyn Peake Manuscripts
L. S. Penrose Papers
Piranesi Collection (Books)
William Ramsey Papers
Rossetti Letters
Routledge & Kegan Paul Archives
John Russell Papers
Lord Odo Russell Collection
Julia Strachey Papers
Thane Papers
Underground Presses
David M S Watson Papers (palaeontology, zoology, geology)
Sir Arthur Smith Woodward Papers (palaeontology)
J Z Young Papers
Zola Letters

Non-library collection catalogue:
All or part available online, in-house and in print

Library catalogue:
All or part available online and in-house

Access to staff:
Contact by letter, by telephone, by fax, by e-mail, in person and via website. Appointment necessary.
Hours: Mon to Thu, 0930 to 1700; Fri, 0930 to 1645
Closed Sat and Sun

Access to building, collection or gallery:
Prior appointment required
Hours: Mon to Thu, 0930 to 1700, Fri 0930 to 1645
Closed Sat and Sun
Special comments: Admission is by UCL ID and/or by completing a reader application form for consultation for manuscripts and archives.

UNIVERSITY COLLEGE PLYMOUTH ST MARK AND ST JOHN LIBRARY LTD

Acronym or abbreviation: UCP Marjon Library

Derriford Road, Plymouth, Devon, PL6 8BH

Tel: 01752 636700
Fax: 01752 636720
E-mail: wevans@marjon.ac.uk

Website:
http://www.marjon.ac.uk
General information about the institution and the prospectus.
http://www.marjon.ac.uk/library

Enquiries:
Enquiries to: Head of Library
Direct tel: 01752 636700 ext. 4206
Direct fax: 01752 636712
Other contacts: Librarian for general enquiries.

Founded:
1840

Organisation type and purpose:
Registered charity (charity number 312929). College of higher education.

Subject coverage:
Education, curriculum development, history; geography and literature, urban studies, African studies, USA census data, media studies including film studies, public relations, theology.

Museum or gallery collection, archive, or library special collection:
College archive material 1840 to the present

Library catalogue:
All or part available online

Access to staff:
Contact by letter, by telephone, by fax, by e-mail and via website. Appointment necessary. Non-members charged.
Hours: Term time: Mon to Thu, 0830 to 2000; Fri, 0830 to 2000; Sat and Sun, 1000 to 1645. Summer holidays: Mon to Fri, 0900 to 1700

Access for disabled people:
Parking provided, ramped entry, toilet facilities, lifts

UNIVERSITY HOSPITAL LEWISHAM

The Robin Stott Library, Education Centre, Lewisham High Street, London, SE13 6LH

Tel: 020 8333 3030 ext 6454
Fax: 020 8333 3247
E-mail: library@uhl.nhs.uk

Enquiries:
Enquiries to: Library Manager
Direct tel: 020 8333 3439
Direct e-mail: jane.coyte@uhl.nhs.uk

Founded:
1969

Organisation type and purpose:
Trust hospital, multidisciplinary library.
To provide all Trust staff with the evidence base of health care.

continued overleaf

Subject coverage:
Medicine and subjects allied to medicine, the
National Health Service and health services in
general.

Library catalogue:
All or part available in-house

Electronic and video publications:
CINAHL database
Medline database
The Cochrane Library database

Access to staff:
Contact by letter, by telephone, by fax, by e-mail
and in person. Appointment necessary.
Hours: Term time: Mon to Thu, 0900 to 1900; Fri,
0900 to 1700
Vacations: Mon to Fri, 0900 to 1700

UNIVERSITY HOSPITALS BRISTOL NHS FOUNDATION TRUST

Acronym or abbreviation: UHBristol

University Hospitals, Bristol Learning Resource
Centre, Education Centre, Upper Maudlin Street,
Bristol, BS2 8AE

Tel: 0117 342 0105
Fax: 0117 917 0161
E-mail: elizabeth.jordan@uhbristol.nhs.uk

Website:
http://www.uhbristol.nhs.uk/library

Enquiries:
Enquiries to: Learning Resource Services Manager
Direct tel: 0117 342 0102
Direct e-mail: learningresources@uhbristol.nhs.uk

Founded:
1957

Organisation type and purpose:
Libraries of a teaching hospital.

Subject coverage:
All health-related information.

Museum or gallery collection, archive, or library special collection:
Richard Smith Bibliographical Collection of
Manuscripts (medicine in Bristol in the 18th and
19th centuries; housed in the Bristol City
Archives)

Non-library collection catalogue:
All or part available online

Library catalogue:
All or part available online

Printed publications:
Learning Resource Services User's Guide

Access to staff:
Appointment necessary.
Hours: Mon to Fri, 0900 to 1700

Access to building, collection or gallery:
Prior appointment required

Access for disabled people:
Access to all public areas

Also at:
Bristol Eye Hospital
Bristol General Hospital
Bristol Haematology and Oncology Centre
St Michael's Hospital

UNIVERSITY OF ABERDEEN – DIRECTORATE OF INFORMATION SYSTEMS AND SERVICES: HISTORIC COLLECTIONS, SPECIAL LIBRARIES AND ARCHIVES

King's College, Aberdeen, AB24 3SW

Tel: 01224 272598
Fax: 01224 273891
E-mail: speclib@abdn.ac.uk

Website:
http://www.abdn.ac.uk/historic
Introductory, searchable database of descriptive
lists of manuscripts, library catalogue, digitised
resources.

Enquiries:
Enquiries to: Reading Room Manager

Founded:
1495

Formerly called:
Aberdeen University Library, Department of
Special Collections and Archives (year of change
1997)

Organisation type and purpose:
University library.

Subject coverage:
Humanism, renaissance science and medicine,
maps, Jacobitism, travel and transport, North-East
Scotland.

Museum or gallery collection, archive, or library special collection:
Gregory Collection (early science and medicine)
Local Collection (NE Scotland)
Local Estate Papers
Macbean Jacobite Collection
O'Dell Railway Collection
Taylor Psalmody Collection
Theological Library

Non-library collection catalogue:
All or part available online and in print

Library catalogue:
All or part available online

Access to staff:
Contact by letter, by telephone, by fax, by e-mail,
in person and via website
Hours: Mon to Fri, 0930 to 1630

Access for disabled people:
Ramped entry

UNIVERSITY OF ABERDEEN – QUEEN MOTHER LIBRARY

Meston Walk, Aberdeen, AB24 3UE

Tel: 01224 273600
Fax: 01224 273956
E-mail: library@abdn.ac.uk

Website:
http://www.abdn.ac.uk/
Information about the University, departments,
courses and research, information for prospective
students, graduates, visitors and businesses.

Enquiries:
Enquiries to: Librarian
Direct tel: 01224 273321

Founded:
1495

Incorporates the:
Northern College of Education, Aberdeen Campus
Library, date of change, 1 December 2001;
MacRobert Library, date of change, August 2001

Organisation type and purpose:
University library.

Subject coverage:
All subjects covered by the Colleges of Arts and
Social Sciences (Divinity, History and Philosophy;
Education; Language & Literature; Law; Social
Sciences; Business School),
Life Sciences and Medicine (Biological Sciences,
Medical Sciences, Medicine, Psychology),
Physical Sciences (Engineering & Physical Sciences,
Geosciences)

Museum or gallery collection, archive, or library special collection:
Aberdeen Harbour Board
Archives and Local Collection (history of the
University and of the North East of Scotland)
Biesenthal Collection (Hebraica)
Celtic literature

European Documentation Centre
George Washington Wilson (Victorian and
Edwardian Photographic Archive)
Gregory Collection (history of science and
medicine)
Macbean Collection (Jacobites)
Melvin Collection (classics)
Music Scores
O'Dell Collection (railways)
Taylor Collection (psalmody)
Victorian Literature Collection

Non-library collection catalogue:
All or part available online

Library catalogue:
All or part available online

Access to staff:
Contact by letter, by telephone, by fax, by e-mail
and in person. Appointment necessary.
Hours: Term time: Mon to Thur, 0900 to 2200; Fri
0900 to 2000; Sat 0900 to 2200; Sun 1100 to 2200
Vacations: Mon to Fri, 0900 to 1700

Includes the:
Medical Library, Foresterhill
tel: 01224 552488; fax: 01224 685157
Queen Mother Library
tel: 01224 273600; fax: 01224 273956; e-mail:
library@abdn.ac.uk
Special Libraries and Archives, Historic Collections
at King's College
tel: 01224 272598; fax: 01224 273891
Taylor Library
tel: 01224 272601; fax: 01224 273893

UNIVERSITY OF ABERTAY DUNDEE

Acronym or abbreviation: UAD

Kydd Building, 40 Bell Street, Dundee, DD1 1HG

Tel: 01382 308000
Fax: 01382 308877
E-mail: infodesk@abertay.ac.uk

Website:
http://www.abertay.ac.uk
Library: details on academic schools: Steps theatre
information.

Enquiries:
Enquiries to: Information Officer
Direct tel: 01382 308080
Direct fax: 01382 308081
Direct e-mail: iro@abertay.ac.uk

Founded:
1888

Organisation type and purpose:
International organisation, advisory body,
membership association, university library,
university department or institute, suitable for
ages: all, training organisation, consultancy,
research organisation, publishing house. To
provide a high quality learning and scholarly
environment for students and staff and to
contribute to the development of local companies
and the regional economy.

Subject coverage:
Accountancy, behavioural science, biology and
biotechnology, building sciences, business studies;
civil, mechanical, electronic, electrical engineering;
chemistry, sciences, social science, mathematics,
computing sciences, economics, law,
environmental technology, forest product
technology, information management, law and
European business law, nursing, physics,
psychology, quantity surveying, travel and
tourism, sport, golf tourism, sports coaching,
Japanese, construction management, chemistry,
French, German, Spanish, computer games
technology, computer arts, management, forensic
psychobiology, sport science, internet
communications, mechatronics, software
engineering, sociology, financial services, taxation,
commercialisation, urban water technology,
tourism, hospitality management, marketing,

forensic sciences, food and consumer services, animation, health and exercise, web design, communication, counselling.

Non-library collection catalogue:
All or part available online

Library catalogue:
All or part available online

Printed publications:
A.D. Alumni (magazine, annual)
Abertay Beacon newsletter (quarterly, free)
Abertay Sociology Papers
Conference proceedings
Guide to Finance (free)
Guide for International Students (free)
Guide to sport and recreation (free)
School proceedings
Undergraduate and postgraduate leaflets (free)
Undergraduate and postgraduate prospectus (free)

Electronic and video publications:
CD-ROM
Video

Publications list:
Available online and in print

Access to staff:
Contact by letter, by telephone, by fax, by e-mail and via website. Appointment necessary.
Hours: Mon to Fri, 0845 to 1700

Access to building, collection or gallery:
No access other than to staff
Hours: Term time: Mon to Thu, 0830 to 2200; Fri, 0830 to 2100; Sat, 1000 to 1700; Sun, 1200 to 1700. Vacations: Mon to Fri, 0845 to 1700
Special comments: External membership required for non-members

Access for disabled people:
Parking provided, ramped entry, level entry, toilet facilities

UNIVERSITY OF BATH

Library and Learning Centre, Claverton Down, Bath, BA2 7AY

Tel: 01225 385000
Fax: 01225 386229
E-mail: library@bath.ac.uk

Website:
http://www.bath.ac.uk/library

Enquiries:
Enquiries to: Office of the University Librarian
Direct tel: 01225 826084

Founded:
1966

Organisation type and purpose:
University library.

Subject coverage:
Architecture; biological sciences; chemical engineering; chemistry; economics; education; electrical and electronic engineering; management; materials science; mathematics; mechanical engineering; French, German, Italian, Russian and Spanish, modern European studies; modern languages; pharmacy and pharmacology; physics; psychology; social and policy studies; statistics; sports science; medical sciences; computer science.

Museum or gallery collection, archive, or library special collection:
Holburne of Menstrie Museum and Crafts Study Centre Library
Pitman Collection (shorthand and phonographic systems, initial teaching alphabet)
Royal Bath & West & Southern Counties Society Library
Watkins/Hudson Industrial Archaeology Collection

Trade and statistical information:
European Documentation Centre and other statistical compilations.

Non-library collection catalogue:
All or part available online

Library catalogue:
All or part available online

Access to staff:
Contact by letter, by telephone, by fax, by e-mail and via website. Appointment necessary.
Hours: Term-time: Mon to Fri, 0900 to 2000
Special comments: See: www.bath.ac.uk/library

Access for disabled people:
Level entry, access to all public areas, toilet facilities

UNIVERSITY OF BEDFORDSHIRE

Park Square, Luton, Bedfordshire, LU1 3JU

Tel: 01582 734111
Fax: 01582 489325

Website:
http://www.beds.ac.uk
Prospectus information.
http://www.lrweb.beds.ac.uk
Learning resources information and gateway to resources

Enquiries:
Enquiries to: Librarian
Direct tel: 01582 489312
Direct e-mail: tim.stone@luton.ac.uk

Founded:
2006

Organisation type and purpose:
University library.

Subject coverage:
Business; health care and social studies; management; media studies, nursing, psychology, biology and geology.

Non-library collection catalogue:
All or part available online

Library catalogue:
All or part available online

Access to staff:
Contact by letter
Hours: Mon to Thu, 0830 to 2200

Access to building, collection or gallery:
Prior appointment required

Access for disabled people:
Level entry, access to all public areas, toilet facilities

UNIVERSITY OF BIRMINGHAM – EDUCATION LIBRARY

Edgbaston, Birmingham, B15 2TT

Tel: 0121 414 4869
Fax: 0121 471 4691
E-mail: library@bham.ac.uk

Website:
http://www.is.bham.ac.uk/education/
Location and opening hours; enquiries; staff; admissions and borrowing arrangements of the library; services for users with disabilities; subject resources; services to distance learners.

Enquiries:
Enquiries to: Librarian

Organisation type and purpose:
University library.

Subject coverage:
Education, special education, education management, educational psychology, curriculum subjects particularly: religious education, English, maths, geography, history, modern languages, science, physical education.

Museum or gallery collection, archive, or library special collection:
Archives of the British Association of Teachers of the Deaf (BATOD)

Access to staff:
Contact by letter, by telephone, by fax and by e-

mail. Appointment necessary.
Hours: Mon to Fri, 0900 to 1700

UNIVERSITY OF BIRMINGHAM – INFORMATION SERVICES

Edgbaston, Birmingham, B15 2TT

Tel: 0121 414 5817
Fax: 0121 471 4691
E-mail: library@bham.ac.uk

Website:
http://www.is.bham.ac.uk/publications/index.htm
Index page for all publications produced by Information Services.
http://www.is.bham.ac.uk/
Home page for Information Services, leading to Information Services website and full details of all facilities and services offered.

Enquiries:
Enquiries to: Director of Information Services
Direct tel: 0121 414 5828
Other contacts: Head of Special Collections

Founded:
1880

Formerly called:
University of Birmingham Library

Organisation type and purpose:
University library.

Subject coverage:
All subjects taught and researched at the University of Birmingham. Arts: American studies; ancient history and archaeology; Canadian studies; classical studies (Latin, classical and modern Greek, Byzantine and Ottoman studies); drama and theatre arts; Dutch; English; film studies; fine art; French studies; German studies; history; Italian; linguistics; Middle and Near Eastern ancient history; music; philosophy; Romanian; Russian and other Slavonic languages (e.g. Czech, Polish, Serbo-Croat); Scandinavian (Danish, Icelandic, Norwegian, Swedish); Spanish and Portuguese (including Latin America); theology; cultural studies; West African studies; commerce and social sciences: accounting and finance; business; development administration; economic and social history; economics; education; international studies; local government studies; management; political science; Russian and East European studies; social administration; social policy; social work; sociology; urban and regional studies; law (all in the Harding Law Library); medicine (all in the Barnes Medical Library): anaesthetics; anatomy; cancer studies; general practice; geriatric medicine; haematology; immunology; intensive care; medical microbiology; medicine; neurology; neurosurgery; nursing studies; obstetrics and gynaecology; occupational health; paediatrics and child health; pathology; pharmacology; physiology; psychiatry; rheumatology; public health and epidemiology; social medicine; surgery; dentistry (all in the Ronald Cohen Dental Library, in the Birmingham Dental Hospital); physical education and recreation; sports science; science and engineering as follows: biochemistry; computer science; earth sciences; mathematics and statistics; physics; space research; chemistry; biological sciences (including botany, environmental health, genetics, microbiology, zoology and comparative physiology); psychology; geography; manufacturing and mechanical engineering; civil engineering; electronic and electrical engineering; chemical engineering; metallurgy and materials; minerals engineering.

Museum or gallery collection, archive, or library special collection:
Main Library (Heslop Room)
Alma Tadema Collection
Birmingham and West Midlands general local history (including Canal Collection, Cannock Chase Colliery Collection, Priestley Collection,

continued overleaf

Seward Letters, Slade-Baker Correspondence, West Midland Group on Post-War Planning and Reconstruction Papers)

British business and economic history of the eighteenth to twentieth centuries (including British Cotton Growing Association Papers, Cadbury Papers, Canal Collection, Cannock Chase Colliery Collection, Nineteenth century Industry Collection)

British Nonconformist history (including Catholic Apostolic Church Collection, Dale Papers, Martineau Collection, Weatherhead Archive)

British Recusant history (including Jerningham Letters, Little Malvern Court Collection)

Church of England history in the nineteenth and twentieth centuries (including Dr Ernest William Barnes, Bishop of Birmingham 1924–1953 Papers, Church Missionary Society Papers, Church Pastoral Aid Society Papers, Stafford Letters)

English literature and drama (including Edgeworth Letters, Marsh Letters, Harriet Martineau Collection, Mill Collection, Modern Poetry Collection, Nicoll Collection, Reed Collection, Seward Letters, Theatre Collection, Wedgwood Collection (philology), Francis Brett Young Collection, David Lodge papers, Noel Coward collection)

English political and related archives of the nineteenth and twentieth centuries (including Lord Avon Papers, Chamberlain Papers (Arthur Neville, Joseph and Sir Joseph Austen), Dale Papers, Dawson Papers, Dixon Letters, Masterman Papers)

General theology and Church history (including Bengeworth Library, Hetherington Library, St Mary's Warwick Parish Library, Thomas Wigan Library of 17th and 18th century literature and theology)

History of The University of Birmingham

History of science (including Priestley Collection)

Printing history (including Baskerville Collection, Birmingham School of Printing Collection, Bodoni Collection of Early Italian Books, English Special Period 1660–69, Foulis Collection, Kelmscott Press Collection, Mandeville Press Collection, Sceptre Press Collection, Shakespeare Head Press Collection)

Russian history of the late nineteenth and early twentieth centuries (including Dolgorukov Papers, Pashkov Papers, Shishkin Papers)

West Africana (including Bradbury Papers, British Cotton Growing Association Papers, Cadbury Papers (mainly photographs of archaeological interest), Church Missionary Society Papers, Matacong Island Papers)

Archives of special educational associations (National Special Schools Union, National Association of Teachers of the Deaf)

Other English general local and family history (including Jerningham Letters, Mingana collection of Middle Eastern historical manuscripts, Mytton Papers, Shaw Letters, Stafford Letters)

Barber Fine Art Library

Art and architecture topography

Items related to specific works of art in the Barber Collection

Sale catalogues and the history of collecting

Barber Music Library

Barber Opera Archive

Early 20th century classical recordings

English and European instrumental music (including Feeney Collection, Shaw-Hellier Collection)

English and European musical treatises and libretti of the seventeenth and eighteenth centuries

English and European vocal music of the seventeenth and eighteenth centuries (including Shaw-Hellier Collection)

Granville Bantock Collection

Barnes Library

History of medicine (including Birmingham Medical Institute Historical Collection, William Withering Collection)

Baykov Library (European Resource Centre)

History and social sciences of pre- and, especially, post-Revolutionary Russia and of Ukraine, Poland, Hungary and most of the republics of the former Soviet Union (including Pares Collection)

Sports history (especially Olympic Games and athletics, including Abrahams Collection)

Sports science

The Ronald Cohen Dental Library

History of dentistry

Education Library

Children's books, c. 1790–1970

History of education

Mathematics textbooks

Harding Law Library

History of English law

Shakespeare Institute Library

Corelli Collection

18th to 20th century editions of Shakespeare

English Renaissance literature

History of drama and the theatre (including Press Cuttings Collection)

Sources and analogues for Shakespeare's plays

Non-library collection catalogue:
All or part available online and in print

Library catalogue:
All or part available online

Printed publications:
Information Services Bulletin (3 times a year)
Large number of User Guides to specific subjects and/or services (print and web versions)
Heslopian (once a year)
Vision (once a year)

Publications list:
Available online

Access to staff:
Contact by letter, by telephone, by fax, by e-mail, in person and via website. Appointment necessary. All charged.
Hours: Mon to Fri, 0900 to 1700

Access to building, collection or gallery:
Special comments: ID required for non-members; limited number of visits per year

Access for disabled people:
Parking provided, level entry, access to all public areas, toilet facilities

UNIVERSITY OF BIRMINGHAM – ORCHARD LEARNING RESOURCES CENTRE

Hamilton Drive, Weoley Park Road, Selly Oak, Birmingham, B29 6QW

Tel: 0121 415 2255
Fax: 0121 415 2273
E-mail: olrc@bham.ac.uk

Website:
http://www.olrc.bham.ac.uk
Catalogue of books and serials. Summary of subjects covered. List of relevant CD-ROMs and websites.

Enquiries:
Enquiries to: Manager
Direct tel: 0121 414 8598
Direct e-mail: d.n.vuong@bham.ac.uk

Founded:
1997

Formerly called:
Selly Oak Colleges Central Library, Westhill College of Higher Education

Organisation type and purpose:
University department or institute.

Subject coverage:
Art in general, community care and service, dance and movement, design, disability, educational studies, English language, English literature, history, Islamics, leisure, physical education, religious education, Christian ministry, missiology, theology, youth studies, youth work and services, counselling.

Christian theology; Bible; Islam and Christian-Muslim relations; Judaism; world religions; community welfare; social work; overseas development studies; church overseas; church history; mission studies; English as a foreign language; peace studies; Syriac studies; education; Quaker studies (in Woodbrooke College).

Museum or gallery collection, archive, or library special collection:
Harold W Turner Collection of New Religious Movements
Mingana Collection of Islamic and Syriac Manuscripts
Rare books 1475–1830
Rendel Harris Collection of Greek papyri

Printed publications:
Catalogues of the special collections
Alphonse Mingana 1878–1937 (Samir Samir Khali, Selly Oak Colleges, 1990)
The Mingana and Related Collections (Hunt L, Selly Oak Colleges, 1997)

Microform publications:
Mingana Collection of Oriental Manuscripts (for purchase)
Harold Turner Collection of New Religious Movements (for purchase)

Access to staff:
Contact by letter, by fax, by e-mail and via website. Appointment necessary.
Hours: Mon to Fri, 0900 to 1700

Access to building, collection or gallery:
Prior appointment required
Hours: Mon to Fri, 0900 to 1700

Access for disabled people:
Parking provided, toilet facilities

Parent body:
University of Birmingham
Information Services, Main Library, Edgbaston, Birmingham, B15 2TT; tel: 0121 414 5805; fax: 0121 471 4691; e-mail: library@bham.ac.uk

UNIVERSITY OF BOLTON

Deane Road, Bolton, Lancashire, BL3 5AB

Tel: 01204 903160
Fax: 01204 903166
E-mail: k.senior@bolton.ac.uk

Website:
http://www.bolton.ac.uk
Links to library information at http://www.bolton.ac.uk/learning.

Enquiries:
Enquiries to: Head of Library
Direct tel: 01204 903563
Other contacts: Margaret Wright Library Administrator

Founded:
1982

Formerly called:
Bolton Art College, Bolton College of Education (Technical), Bolton Institute of Technology, Bolton Institute of Higher Education (year of change 2005)

Organisation type and purpose:
Educational institution.

Subject coverage:
Textiles, business studies, psychology, electrical, mechanical and civil engineering, teacher education (FE/HE), art and design.

Library catalogue:
All or part available online

Publications list:
Available online

Access to staff:
Contact via website. Non-members charged.
Hours: Mon to Fri, 0845 to 2100; Sat, 0930 to 1230

Access for disabled people:
Access to all public areas, toilet facilities

Member organisation of:
SCONUL NoWAL

UNIVERSITY OF BRADFORD –
LEARNING SUPPORT SERVICES

Richmond Road, Bradford, West Yorkshire, BD7 1DP

Tel: 01274 233301\ Minicom no. 01274 233687
Fax: 01274 233398
E-mail: Library@bradford.ac.uk

Website:
http://www.brad.ac.uk/lss/library
News, services, catalogue.

Enquiries:
Enquiries to: Librarian
Direct e-mail: p.m.ketley@bradford.ac.uk

Founded:
1966

Organisation type and purpose:
University Library.

Museum or gallery collection, archive, or library special collection:
Arthur Raistrick Map Collection
Calvin Wells Collection (archaeological sciences)
Commonweal Collection – non-violence and peace
History of Dyeing Collection
History of Pharmacy Collection
Mitrinovic Library
WR Mitchell Collection (the 'Dalesman' archive)
The Joel M Halpern Balkan Collection
The Waddington – Feather Collection (Yorkshire dialect and poetry)
JB Priestley Collection

Library catalogue:
All or part available online

Access to staff:
Contact by letter
Hours: Mon to Fri, 0845 to 1730

Access for disabled people:
Level entry, access to all public areas, toilet facilities

Includes the:
Health Studies Library
tel: 01274 236375; fax: 01274 236470
J B Priestley Library
Yvette Jacobson Library (Management Library)
tel: 01274 234401; fax: 01274 234398

UNIVERSITY OF BRIGHTON –
EASTBOURNE SITE

The Queenwood Library, Darley Road, Eastbourne, East Sussex, BN20 7UN

Tel: 01273 643822
Fax: 01273 643825
E-mail: askqueenwood@brighton.ac.uk

Website:
http://library.brighton.ac.uk

Enquiries:
Enquiries to: Information Services Manager
Direct tel: 01273 643820
Other contacts: User Services Librarian (for most appropriate opening hours, membership queries)

Founded:
1992

Organisation type and purpose:
University library.

Subject coverage:
Physical education, dance, sports and exercise science, leisure and sports studies/management; physiotherapy, occupational therapy, nursing, podiatry.
Management, tourism, hospitality studies, food studies (Queenwood Library)
Nursing (Eastbourne District General Hospital Health Sciences Library).

Access to staff:
Contact by letter and by telephone. Appointment necessary.
Hours: Mon to Fri, 0900 to 1730

Access for disabled people:
Parking provided, ramped entry, access to all public areas, toilet facilities

Also at:
Eastbourne District General Hospital Health Sciences Library
King's Drive, Eastbourne, East Sussex, BN21 2UD; tel: 01323 417400 ext 4048

UNIVERSITY OF BRIGHTON –
GRAND PARADE SITE

St Peter's House Library, 16–18 Richmond Place, Brighton, BN2 9NA

Tel: 01273 643221
Fax: 01273 607532
E-mail: asksph@brighton.ac.uk

Website:
http://library.brighton.ac.uk
Library catalogue.
http://www.brighton.ac.uk
Opening hours, services.

Enquiries:
Enquiries to: Enquiry Desk Team

Founded:
1992

Organisation type and purpose:
University library.

Subject coverage:
Art and design history, fine arts, graphic design, photography, fashion and textiles, crafts, performing arts, humanities.

Library catalogue:
All or part available online

Printed publications:
Guides to Library Services (free)

Access to staff:
Contact by letter, by telephone, by fax, by e-mail, in person and via website

Access to building, collection or gallery:
Hours: Term time: Mon to Thu, 0900 to 2000; Fri, 0900 to 1800; Sat, 1300 to 1700; Sun, 1300 to 1700
Vacations: Mon to Fri, 0900 to 1700

Access for disabled people:
Ground floor enquiries area only

UNIVERSITY OF BRISTOL –
LIBRARY

Tyndall Avenue, Bristol, BS8 1TJ

Tel: 0117 928 8000
Fax: 0117 925 5334
E-mail: library@bristol.ac.uk

Website:
http://www.bristol.ac.uk/is/

Enquiries:
Enquiries to: Librarian
Other contacts: Special Collections Librarian

Organisation type and purpose:
University library, with 13 branch libraries.

Subject coverage:
Arts, law, social sciences, science, medicine, engineering and education.

Museum or gallery collection, archive, or library special collection:
British philosophers
Business histories
Courtesy Books
Early English novels
Early mathematics
Early medical works (including some on spas and mineral waters)
European Documentation Centre

Eyles Collection of early geology
Family papers (Dorset and West Indies, 1650–1948)
General Election Addresses (acquired with the purchase of the National Liberal Club Library)
Historical chemistry
I K Brunel's papers
Landscape gardening
Penguin Publishing Archives
Sir Allen Lane Collection of Penguin Books, most of them signed by their authors
Somerset Miners Association papers
West Indies papers
Wiglesworth Ornithological Library

Non-library collection catalogue:
All or part available online and in-house

Library catalogue:
All or part available online and in-house

Access to staff:
Contact by letter, by telephone, by fax and by e-mail. Appointment necessary.
Hours: Special Collections: Mon to Wed, 0915 to 1845; Thu, 0945 to 1845; Fri, 0915 to 1645

Department of:
Information Services (includes Library and Computing Services)

UNIVERSITY OF BUCKINGHAM
LIBRARY

Hunter Street, Buckingham, MK18 1EG

Tel: 01280 814080
Fax: 01280 820312
E-mail: library@buckingham.ac.uk

Website:
http://www.buckingham.ac.uk/library

Enquiries:
Enquiries to: Assistant Librarian
Direct tel: 01280 820218

Founded:
1976

Organisation type and purpose:
University library.

Subject coverage:
Law, politics, economics, accounting and finance, management, history, English and modern languages, information systems, psychology.

Museum or gallery collection, archive, or library special collection:
Denning Law Library

Library catalogue:
All or part available online

Printed publications:
Denning Law Journal

Access to staff:
Contact by letter, by telephone, by fax, by e-mail and in person
Hours: Mon to Fri, 0900 to 1700

UNIVERSITY OF CAMBRIDGE –
BALFOUR AND NEWTON
LIBRARIES OF THE DEPARTMENT
OF ZOOLOGY

Downing Street, Cambridge, CB2 3EJ

Tel: 01223 336600
Fax: 01223 336676
E-mail: library@zoo.cam.ac.uk

Website:
http://www.zoo.cam.ac.uk/library/index.html
Admissions, opening times, contacts, exam papers, reprints, theses, print journals, facilities, disabled access, rules.

Enquiries:
Enquiries to: Librarian
Direct tel: 01223 336648
Direct e-mail: library@zoo.cam.ac.uk
Other contacts: Academic Librarian for letter of application to use library.

continued overleaf

Organisation type and purpose:
University department or institute.
Departmental library. Balfour Library founded
1883, Newton Library founded 1907.

Subject coverage:
Zoology and ecology.

Museum or gallery collection, archive, or library special collection:
Newton Collection (ornithology and natural history)
Strickland Collection (ornithology)

Non-library collection catalogue:
All or part available online

Library catalogue:
All or part available online and in-house

Access to staff:
Contact by letter, by telephone, by fax, by e-mail and via website. Appointment necessary. Letter of introduction required.
Hours: Mon to Fri, 0830 to 1700
Special comments: Membership is restricted to members of Cambridge University. Application for access by others by letter to the Academic Librarian.

Access to building, collection or gallery:
Please telephone in advance of your visit
Hours: Mon to Fri, 0830 to 1700

Access for disabled people:
Lift, wheelchair accessible, disabled parking, toilet facilities available
Hours: Mon to Fri, 0830 to 1700
Special comments: Please telephone in advance of your visit

UNIVERSITY OF CAMBRIDGE – BETTY AND GORDON MOORE LIBRARY

Wilberforce Road, Cambridge, CB3 0WD

Tel: 01223 765670
Fax: 01223 765678
E-mail: moore-library@lib.cam.ac.uk

Website:
http://www.lib.cam.ac.uk/bgml

Enquiries:
Enquiries to: Librarian

Founded:
2001

Incorporates the former:
Department of Applied Mathematics and Theoretical Physics Library, Department of Pure Mathematics and Mathematical Statistics Library, Wishart Library

Organisation type and purpose:
University library.

Subject coverage:
Mathematics, physics, astronomy, computer science, materials science and engineering.

Museum or gallery collection, archive, or library special collection:
University collections for mathematics, physics, astronomy, computer science, materials science and engineering.

Library catalogue:
All or part available online

Access to staff:
Contact by letter, by telephone, by e-mail, in person and via website. Appointment necessary.
Hours: Mon to Fri, 0900 to 1700; Sat, 0900 to 1300

Parent body:
University of Cambridge Library

UNIVERSITY OF CAMBRIDGE – BOTANIC GARDEN

Cory Lodge, Bateman Street, Cambridge, CB2 1JF

Tel: 01223 336265

Fax: 01223 336278
E-mail: enquiries@botanic.cam.ac.uk

Website:
http://www.botanic.cam.ac.uk

Enquiries:
Enquiries to: Information Officer
Direct tel: 01223 336265
Direct e-mail: enquiries@botanic.cam.ac.uk

Founded:
1762

Organisation type and purpose:
University department or institute.
Sub-department library, of the Department of Plant Sciences.

Subject coverage:
Taxonomy of vascular plants; horticulture; the history of botany and horticulture; information on plants within the Garden.

Museum or gallery collection, archive, or library special collection:
Indexed collection of living plants
Library of books on horticulture and botany
Nurserymen's catalogues
Slide collection of plants

Publications list:
Available in print

Access to staff:
Contact by letter and by telephone. Appointment necessary.
Hours: Mon to Fri, 0900 to 1700

Houses the:
Cory Library

UNIVERSITY OF CAMBRIDGE – CENTRAL SCIENCE LIBRARY

Arts School, Bene't Street, Cambridge, CB2 3PY

Tel: 01223 334742
Fax: 01223 334748

Website:
http://www.lib.cam.ac.uk/CSL/

Enquiries:
Enquiries to: Librarian
Direct tel: 01223 334744
Direct e-mail: mlw1003@cam.ac.uk

Founded:
1820

Organisation type and purpose:
University library.

Subject coverage:
Biological, Chemical, Earth and Environmental Sciences.

Museum or gallery collection, archive, or library special collection:
19th century scientific books
Biffen Collection on plant breeding (reprints)
Buttress Collection (books and journals on agriculture, formerly the library of the Department of Applied Biology)
Marshall Collection on animal reproduction (reprints)

Non-library collection catalogue:
All or part available online

Library catalogue:
All or part available online

Access to staff:
Contact by letter, by e-mail and via website. Appointment necessary.
Hours: Mon to Fri, 0900 to 1700

Originally the library, but still houses the offices, of the:
Cambridge Philosophical Society

Parent body:
Cambridge University Library

UNIVERSITY OF CAMBRIDGE – CENTRE OF MIDDLE EASTERN AND ISLAMIC STUDIES

Acronym or abbreviation: CMEIS

Sidgwick Avenue, Cambridge, CB3 9DA

Tel: 01223 335110
Fax: 01223 335103
E-mail: secretary@cmeis.cam.ac.uk

Website:
http://www.cmeis.cam.ac.uk
History of the centre/lectures/activities.
http://www.lib.cam.ac.uk/catalogues/opac/union.shtml
Catalogue

Enquiries:
Enquiries to: Secretary
Direct tel: 01223 335103
Direct fax: 01223 335110
Direct e-mail: oriental-library@lists.cam.ac.uk
Other contacts: Director

Founded:
1960

Formerly called:
Centre for Middle Eastern Studies (CMES) (year of change 1999)

Organisation type and purpose:
University department or institute, consultancy.
Fostering understanding of Middle Eastern culture and politics.

Subject coverage:
Modern history, culture, politics and economics of the Middle East with special reference to the Arabian peninsula and Yemen.

Museum or gallery collection, archive, or library special collection:
Some personal collections of rare papers and photographs

Trade and statistical information:
Stocks some Middle Eastern trade and statistical information.

Library catalogue:
All or part available online

Printed publications:
Arabian Studies, vol. VII

Access to staff:
Contact by letter, by telephone, by fax, by e-mail and via website
Hours: Mon to Fri, 0900 to 1700
Special comments: Questions and queries can usually be answered by mail; could be of use to traders, politicians and academics.

Library now administered as part of:
Faculty of Oriental Studies

UNIVERSITY OF CAMBRIDGE – COLMAN LIBRARY OF THE DEPARTMENT OF BIOCHEMISTRY

Tennis Court Road, Cambridge, CB2 1QW

Tel: 01223 333600
Fax: 01223 333345
E-mail: librarian@bioc.cam.ac.uk

Website:
http://www.bio.cam.ac.uk/dept/biochem/ColmanLibrary/index.html

Enquiries:
Enquiries to: Librarian
Direct tel: 01223 333613

Founded:
1924

Organisation type and purpose:
University department or institute.

Subject coverage:
Biochemistry.

Museum or gallery collection, archive, or library special collection:
Departmental papers
Departmental archives

Non-library collection catalogue:
All or part available online

Library catalogue:
All or part available online

Printed publications:
List of Research Projects (Postgraduate Prospectus)

Access to staff:
Contact by telephone, by fax, by e-mail and in person. Appointment necessary. Access for members only.
Hours: Mon to Thu, 0830 to 1700; Fri, 0830 to 1600
Special comments: Non-members by arrangement.

Access to building, collection or gallery:
Card needed
Hours: Mon to Thu, 0830 to 1700; Fri, 0830 to 1600

Access for disabled people:
Hours: Mon to Thu, 0830 to 1700; Fri, 0830 to 1600

UNIVERSITY OF CAMBRIDGE – HADDON LIBRARY OF THE FACULTY OF ARCHAEOLOGY AND ANTHROPOLOGY

Downing Street, Cambridge, CB2 3DZ

Tel: 01223 333505/6
Fax: 01223 333503
E-mail: haddon-library@lists.cam.ac.uk

Website:
http://haddon.archanth.cam.ac.uk
Library guide and Cambridge Union Catalogue.

Enquiries:
Enquiries to: Librarian

Founded:
1920

Organisation type and purpose:
University department or institute.

Subject coverage:
Archaeology; biological anthropology; social anthropology.

Museum or gallery collection, archive, or library special collection:
Burkitt Collection: archaeology (Europe)
Bushnell Collection: archaeology (Americas)
Clarke bequest (archaeology)
De Navarro Collection: archaeology (Europe)
Frazer bequest (anthropology)
McBurney bequest (archaeology)
McBurney Collection: archaeology and anthropology (world-wide)
Offprints
Pitt-Rivers Collection: archaeology and anthropology (19th century)
Rare books collection: c.600 vols, archaeology and anthropology (17th to 19th centuries)

Library catalogue:
All or part available online

Access to staff:
Contact by letter, by telephone, by fax, by e-mail and in person. Appointment necessary. Letter of introduction required.
Hours: Mon to Fri, 0900 to 1700

Constituent bodies:
Cambridge Antiquarian Society Library

UNIVERSITY OF CAMBRIDGE – INSTITUTE OF ASTRONOMY LIBRARY

Acronym or abbreviation: IoA

The Observatories, Madingley Road, Cambridge, CB3 0HA

Tel: 01223 337548
Fax: 01223 337523

E-mail: ioalib@ast.cam.ac.uk

Website:
http://www.ast.cam.ac.uk/~ioalib/homepage.html
Online catalogue of holdings; information about the library; resource listings.

Enquiries:
Enquiries to: Departmental Librarian
Direct tel: 01223 337537

Founded:
1823

Formerly called:
Institute of Theoretical Astronomy, Library of the Observatories (year of change 1972)

Organisation type and purpose:
University department or institute.
Departmental library.

Subject coverage:
Astronomy and astrophysics.

Museum or gallery collection, archive, or library special collection:
John Couch Adams Collection of astronomy books, mostly pre-1850

Library catalogue:
All or part available online

Access to staff:
Contact by letter, by telephone and by e-mail. Appointment necessary.
Hours: Mon to Fri, 0900 to 1700

UNIVERSITY OF CAMBRIDGE – JOINT LIBRARY OF THE FACULTY OF CLASSICS AND MUSEUM OF CLASSICAL ARCHAEOLOGY

Sidgwick Avenue, Cambridge, CB3 9DA

Tel: 01223 335154
Fax: 01223 335409
E-mail: library@classics.cam.ac.uk

Website:
http://www.classics.cam.ac.uk/library
Guide to in-house/local resources and other classical resources.

Enquiries:
Enquiries to: Librarian

Founded:
1982

Created by the merger of:
Faculty of Classics Library and Museum of Classical Archaeology Library (year of change 1982)

Organisation type and purpose:
University department or institute.
Teaching and research needs of the Faculty of Classics.

Subject coverage:
Classics, Greek and Latin literature, ancient history, ancient philosophy, classical philology, classical archaeology, classical art, palaeography, epigraphy and modern Greek.

Museum or gallery collection, archive, or library special collection:
J. E. Sandys Collection (classical books)
Owen Collection (ancient philosophy books)
Sir Ellis Minns Collection (palaeography)
Sir Stephen Gaselee Collection (palaeography)
William Martin Leake Collection (classical books and notebooks)

Non-library collection catalogue:
All or part available online

Library catalogue:
All or part available online

Printed publications:
Guide to the Museum of Classical Archaeology (£4)

Access to staff:
Contact by letter, by telephone and by e-mail. Appointment necessary. Letter of introduction required.
Hours: Mon to Fri, 0900 to 1700; Sat (term time) 0900 to 1300

Access for disabled people:
Level entry, access to all public areas, toilet facilities

UNIVERSITY OF CAMBRIDGE – KANTHACK & NUTTALL LIBRARY OF THE DEPARTMENT OF PATHOLOGY

Tennis Court Road, Cambridge, CB2 1QP

Tel: 01223 333690
Fax: 01223 333346
E-mail: librarian@path.cam.ac.uk

Website:
http://www.path.cam.ac.uk/~library

Enquiries:
Enquiries to: Librarian
Direct tel: 01223 333698
Direct fax: 01223 333698
Other contacts: Library administrator

Formed from:
Molteno Institute, Parasitology Library

Formerly called:
Nuttall Library

Organisation type and purpose:
University department or institute.

Subject coverage:
Pathology; microbiology; virology; immunology; parasitology; oncology.

Non-library collection catalogue:
All or part available online and in-house

Access to staff:
Contact by letter and by telephone. Appointment necessary. Access for members only.
Hours: Mon to Fri, 0900 to 1600
Special comments: Non-members by prior arrangement.

Access for disabled people:
Ramped entry, toilet facilities

UNIVERSITY OF CAMBRIDGE – LIBRARY AND INFORMATION SERVICE OF THE FACULTY OF EDUCATION

184 Hills Road, Cambridge, CB2 8PQ

Tel: 01223 767700
E-mail: library@educ.cam.ac.uk

Website:
http://www.educ.cam.ac.uk

Enquiries:
Enquiries to: Librarian

Founded:
2001

Formerly called:
Department of Education, Institute of Education (year of change 1997); School of Education (year of change 2001)

Organisation type and purpose:
University department or institute.

Subject coverage:
Education, educational research, children with special needs, in-service training of teachers and related subjects, e.g. psychology, philosophy, sociology.

Museum or gallery collection, archive, or library special collection:
Audiovisual material on in-service teacher education

continued overleaf

Collections of school textbooks and books on teaching method in the fields of English, classics, modern languages, science (general), physics, chemistry, biology, mathematics, history, geography
Source material on history of education now transferred to Cambridge University Library

Library catalogue:
All or part available online

Printed publications:
Library Guide (annually, free)

Access to staff:
Contact by letter, by telephone, by e-mail and in person
Hours: Mon to Fri, 0930 to 1700

Parent body:
University of Cambridge

UNIVERSITY OF CAMBRIDGE – LIBRARY OF THE DEPARTMENT OF CHEMISTRY

Formal name: Department of Chemistry Library

Lensfield Road, Cambridge, CB2 1EW

Tel: 01223 336300
Fax: 01223 336362
E-mail: library@ch.cam.ac.uk

Website:
http://www.library.ch.cam.ac.uk

Enquiries:
Enquiries to: Librarian
Direct tel: 01223 336329
Other contacts: Deputy Librarian

Organisation type and purpose:
University department or institute.

Subject coverage:
Inorganic, organic, physical and theoretical chemistry.

Library catalogue:
All or part available online

Access to staff:
Contact by letter, by telephone, by fax, by e-mail and via website. Appointment necessary. Letter of introduction required.
Hours: Mon to Fri, 0800 to 1630

UNIVERSITY OF CAMBRIDGE – LIBRARY OF THE DEPARTMENT OF EARTH SCIENCES

Downing Street, Cambridge, CB2 3EQ

Tel: 01223 333429
Fax: 01223 333450
E-mail: libraryhelp@esc.cam.ac.uk

Website:
http://www.esc.cam.ac.uk
List of publications written by department members from the beginning of 1993. There is also a list of recent abstracts. Both the publications list and the abstracts list are updated daily.
Parts of most of the collections are available through this site.
Links to university on-line journals.

Enquiries:
Enquiries to: Librarian

Founded:
1980

Formed by the amalgamation of:
Departments of Geology, Mineralogy & Petrology and Geodesy & Geophysics (year of change 1980)

Organisation type and purpose:
University department or institute.

Subject coverage:
Earth sciences, palaeontology, mineralogy, geophysics, mineral physics.

Museum or gallery collection, archive, or library special collection:
Black Collection
Collection of geological reprints
Collection of mineralogical reprints
Godwin Collection
Extensive geological map collection
W A Dear Collection
Bullard Collection
R G West Collection
Sedgwick Collection
Bulman Collection
Harker Collection
N F Hughes Collection
Macfadyen Collection
Tilley Collection
Whittington Collection
Collection of geophysics offprints

Non-library collection catalogue:
All or part available online and in-house

Library catalogue:
All or part available online

Printed publications:
Annual Report, which includes a bibliography of work published by members of the department

Access to staff:
Contact by letter, by telephone, by fax, by e-mail and via website. Letter of introduction required.
Hours: Term time: Mon to Fri, 0900 to 1700, Sat, 1000 to 1300
Vacations: closed Sat
Bullard Laboratory Library is only staffed for one hour a day

Other address:
Bullard Laboratory Library
 Madingley Road, Cambridge

UNIVERSITY OF CAMBRIDGE – LIBRARY OF THE DEPARTMENT OF GENETICS

Downing Street, Cambridge, CB2 3EH

Tel: 01223 333973
Fax: 01223 333992
E-mail: library@gen.cam.ac.uk

Website:
http://www.gen.cam.ac.uk/Library
Homepage with information about the library, the Department of Genetics and links to genetics resources on the WWW.

Enquiries:
Enquiries to: Librarian
Direct e-mail: caa30@mole.bio.cam.ac.uk

Organisation type and purpose:
University department or institute.

Subject coverage:
Genetics; cytology; parts of biochemistry, cell biology.

Museum or gallery collection, archive, or library special collection:
Drosophila offprint collection
Offprints of papers by past Department members

Access to staff:
Contact by letter, by telephone, by fax, by e-mail and via website. Appointment necessary.
Hours: Mon to Fri, 0900 to 1700

UNIVERSITY OF CAMBRIDGE – LIBRARY OF THE DEPARTMENT OF GEOGRAPHY

Sir William Hardy Building, Downing Place, Cambridge, CB2 3EN

Tel: 01223 333399
Fax: 01223 333392

Website:
http://www.lib.cam.ac.uk

University library home page with access to catalogue. The department is part of the Union Catalogue. Periodicals listed in Union list of Serials. Clark Collection and offprints accessed via card catalogue.

Enquiries:
Enquiries to: Librarian
Direct tel: 01223 333391
Direct e-mail: rcc23@hermes.cam.ac.uk

Organisation type and purpose:
University department or institute.

Subject coverage:
Geography and its related subjects: ecology, sociology, cultural studies, economics, politics, history and historical geography, cartography, statistics, research techniques, glaciology, some geology, geomorphology, hydrology, climatology, environmental science, environmental policy etc; remote sensing, geographical information systems, urban planning, substantial regional collections covering India, Africa, North and South America, Soviet and post-Soviet Russia.

Museum or gallery collection, archive, or library special collection:
Clark Collection (primarily 18th and 19th century books on travel and exploration)

Non-library collection catalogue:
All or part available online and in-house

Library catalogue:
All or part available online

Access to staff:
Contact by letter, by telephone, by e-mail and in person
Hours: Term time: Mon to Fri, 0845 to 1800; Sat, 0845 to 1245
Vacations: Mon to Thu, 0900 to 1300 and 1400 to 1630; Fri, 0900 to 1300 and 1400 to 1530, Sat, closed
Special comments: Visitors by prior appointment during term time. Vacation hours may vary, phone in advance.

UNIVERSITY OF CAMBRIDGE – LIBRARY OF THE DEPARTMENT OF PHYSIOLOGY, DEVELOPMENT AND NEUROSCIENCE

Acronym or abbreviation: PDN Library

Downing Street, Cambridge, CB2 3EG

Tel: 01223 333899
Fax: 01223 333840
E-mail: library@pdn.cam.ac.uk

Website:
http://www.pdn.cam.ac.uk/library

Enquiries:
Enquiries to: Librarian
Direct tel: 01223 333821

Created by the merger of:
School of Anatomy Library and Department of Physiology Library (year of change 2006)

Organisation type and purpose:
University department or institute.

Subject coverage:
Physiology, human and veterinary anatomy, embryology, developmental biology, neurobiology.

Museum or gallery collection, archive, or library special collection:
Boyd histological collection (slides), embryological collection, compiled by Professor J. D. Boyd. History of physiology.

Non-library collection catalogue:
All or part available in-house

Library catalogue:
All or part available online, in-house and in print

Access to staff:
Contact by letter, by telephone, by fax and by e-mail. Appointment necessary. Letter of introduction required.
Hours: Mon to Fri, 0900 to 1230, 1400 to 1700

Special comments: Advanced notice required for consultations

Access to building, collection or gallery:
Prior appointment required
Hours: Mon to Fri, 0900 to 1230, 1330 to 1700
Special comments: Prior appointment required for Library and Collections.

Access for disabled people:
Fully accessible

UNIVERSITY OF CAMBRIDGE – LIBRARY OF THE DEPARTMENT OF PLANT SCIENCES

Downing Street, Cambridge, CB2 3EA

Tel: 01223 333900
Fax: 01223 333953
E-mail: lib1@cus.cam.ac.uk or rs10018@cus.cam.ac.uk

Enquiries:
Enquiries to: Librarian
Direct tel: 01223 333930

Formerly called:
Botany School University of Cambridge

Organisation type and purpose:
University department or institute.

Subject coverage:
All aspects of plant sciences: genetics, biochemistry, physiology, ecology and taxonomy, excluding agriculture and forestry but including quaternary vegetation.

Museum or gallery collection, archive, or library special collection:
Early herbals
Simpson Collection of local floras

Access to staff:
Contact by letter, by telephone, by fax and by e-mail. Appointment necessary.
Hours: Mon to Fri, 0900 to 1700

UNIVERSITY OF CAMBRIDGE – LIBRARY OF THE DEPARTMENT OF VETERINARY MEDICINE

Madingley Road, Cambridge, CB3 0ES

Tel: 01223 337600
Fax: 01223 337610

Website:
http://www.vet.cam.ac.uk

Enquiries:
Enquiries to: Librarian
Direct tel: 01223 337633
Direct e-mail: lel1000@hermes.cam.ac.uk

Founded:
1955

Organisation type and purpose:
University department or institute.

Subject coverage:
Veterinary medicine.

Museum or gallery collection, archive, or library special collection:
Rare book collection

Library catalogue:
All or part available online

Printed publications:
Library Users Guide (free)
List of new accessions (quarterly, free)

Access to staff:
Contact by letter, by telephone, by fax and by e-mail. Appointment necessary.
Hours: Mon to Fri, 0900 to 0430

Access to building, collection or gallery:
Special comments: Card access only

UNIVERSITY OF CAMBRIDGE – LIBRARY OF THE EXPERIMENTAL PSYCHOLOGY LABORATORY

Downing Street, Cambridge, CB2 3EB

Tel: 01223 333554
Fax: 01223 333564
E-mail: library@psychol.cam.ac.uk

Enquiries:
Enquiries to: Librarian

Organisation type and purpose:
University department or institute.
Teaching and research unit of the University of Cambridge.

Subject coverage:
Experimental psychology and psychopathology.

Museum or gallery collection, archive, or library special collection:
McCurdy Psychopathology Library (1900-, about 1000 books)
Oldfield Collection (material on vision, 1900–1940, about 100 books)

Access to staff:
Appointment necessary.
Hours: Mon to Fri, 0930 to 1700 during full term
Special comments: Please telephone for an appointment outside full term.

UNIVERSITY OF CAMBRIDGE – LIBRARY OF THE FACULTY OF ARCHITECTURE AND HISTORY OF ART

1 Scroope Terrace, Trumpington Street, Cambridge, CB2 1PX

Tel: 01223 332953
Fax: 01223 332960
E-mail: mb151@cam.ac.uk

Website:
http://www.arct.cam.ac.uk/library.html
Library guide and catalogue

Enquiries:
Enquiries to: Librarian

Organisation type and purpose:
University department or institute.

Subject coverage:
Architecture; history of art; architecture and design.

Museum or gallery collection, archive, or library special collection:
16th–19th-century architectural special collection
19th- and 20th-century architectural periodicals, mainly European

Library catalogue:
All or part available online

Access to staff:
Contact by letter
Hours: Term time: 0915 to 1730
Vacation: opening hours vary, but usually 0930 to 1230 and 1430 to 1730

UNIVERSITY OF CAMBRIDGE – LIBRARY OF THE FACULTY OF DIVINITY

West Road, Cambridge, CB3 9BS

Tel: 01223 763040
Fax: 01223 763003
E-mail: library@divinity.cam.ac.uk

Website:
http://www.divinity.cam.ac.uk/library.html
http://www.lib.cam.ac.uk/newton
Catalogue

Enquiries:
Enquiries to: Librarian

Founded:
1879

Organisation type and purpose:
University department or institute.

Subject coverage:
Theology, ecclesiastical history, biblical studies, Judaism, Islam, Hinduism, Buddhism, ethics, philosophy of religion, psychology of religion, sociology of religion, science and religion, patristics, liturgy.

Museum or gallery collection, archive, or library special collection:
Feltoe Bequest (liturgy)
Lightfoot Bequest (library of Bishop J. B. Lightfoot 1828–89)

Non-library collection catalogue:
All or part available online

Library catalogue:
All or part available online

Access to staff:
Contact by letter and by e-mail. Appointment necessary. Access for members only.
Hours: Term time: Mon to Fri, 0900 to 1700
Vacations: Mon to Fri, 0900 to 1255 and 1400 to 1630

Access to building, collection or gallery:
Prior appointment required

Access for disabled people:
Access to all public areas

UNIVERSITY OF CAMBRIDGE – LIBRARY OF THE ORIENTAL STUDIES

Formal name: University of Cambridge – Faculty of Asian and Middle Eastern Studies Library
Acronym or abbreviation: FAMES

Sidgwick Avenue, Cambridge, CB3 9DA

Tel: 01223 335111/2
Fax: 01223 335110
E-mail: library@ames.cam.ac.uk

Website:
http://www.ames.cam.ac.uk/faclib/index.html
http://www.ames.cam.ac.uk

Enquiries:
Enquiries to: Librarian

Founded:
1935

Organisation type and purpose:
University department or institute.
Faculty library; the collection of the Middle East Centre.

Subject coverage:
Chinese, Japanese, Sanskrit, modern Indian languages, Persian, Turkish, Arabic, Hebrew; Egyptology, Assyriology, Indian history and archaeology, coverage of the language, literature, history, religion and general culture of all countries of the Middle and Far East Indian sub-continent and Central Asia (but excluding south-east Asia).

Museum or gallery collection, archive, or library special collection:
I. B. Horner Collection (paper and letters, etc.)
Israel Abrahams Collection (Rabbinics)
Lattimore Collection on Central Asia and Mongolia
Marshall Collection of Indian photographs (5,000 items on Indian monuments and antiquities)
Middle East Centre Library (modern Middle East – especially the Arabian peninsula and Yemen)
Queens' College Oriental Collection
W. Lockhart Collection (Persian)
Wheeler Collection (700 photographs of Indian archaeology)

Non-library collection catalogue:
All or part available online

Library catalogue:
All or part available online

continued overleaf

Access to staff:
Contact by letter, by telephone, by e-mail and via website. Appointment necessary.
Hours: Mon to Fri, 0900 to 1730

UNIVERSITY OF CAMBRIDGE – MATERIALS SCIENCE AND METALLURGY LIBRARY

New Museums Site, Pembroke Street, Cambridge, CB2 3QZ

Tel: 01223 334300 (dept); 01223 334318 (library)
Fax: 01223 334567
E-mail: library@msm.cam.ac.uk

Website:
http://www.msm.cam.ac.uk/library

Enquiries:
Enquiries to: Librarian

Organisation type and purpose:
University department or institute.

Subject coverage:
Metallurgy, materials science. National and local library services and information.

Non-library collection catalogue:
All or part available online

Library catalogue:
All or part available online

Access to staff:
Contact by letter, by telephone, by fax, by e-mail and in person. Appointment necessary.
Hours: 24-hour access for members of department
Special comments: Non-members of the department during library office hours, 0930 to 1500.

Access to building, collection or gallery:
No access other than to staff
Hours: Mon to Fri, 0930 to 1300 and 1330 to 1500
Special comments: Closed Fri during vacations. Visitors from outside Cambridge by appointment for reference only.

Access for disabled people:
Access to library on 4th floor via user-operated lifts.

UNIVERSITY OF CAMBRIDGE – MILL LANE LIBRARY OF THE DEPARTMENT OF LAND ECONOMY

Acronym or abbreviation: DLE

8 Mill Lane, Cambridge, CB2 1RX

Tel: 01223 337110
Fax: 01223 337130
E-mail: wt10000@cus.cam.ac.uk

Website:
http://www.landecon.cam.ac.uk/library/library
.htm
http://www.landecon.cam.ac.uk
http://www.lib.cam.ac.uk/catalogues/opac/union
.shtml
Catalogue.

Enquiries:
Enquiries to: Librarian
Direct e-mail: wt10000@cam.ac.uk

Founded:
1950

Organisation type and purpose:
University department or institute.

Subject coverage:
Agriculture economics, architecture, environmental policy and law, forestry, housing, land economics, land law, land tenure, land values, regional economics, rural development, town and country planning.

Non-library collection catalogue:
All or part available online

Library catalogue:
All or part available online

Printed publications:
Handbook of the Department
Research and Publications (annually)

Publications list:
Available in print

Access to staff:
Contact by letter, by telephone, by e-mail, in person and via website
Hours: Mon to Fri, 0900 to 1700
Special comments: No disabled access.

UNIVERSITY OF CAMBRIDGE – MODERN AND MEDIEVAL LANGUAGES LIBRARY

Acronym or abbreviation: MML Library

Sidgwick Avenue, Cambridge, CB3 9DA

Tel: 01223 335041
Fax: 01223 335062
E-mail: mmllib@hermes.cam.ac.uk

Website:
http://www.mml.cam.ac.uk/library

Enquiries:
Enquiries to: Librarian
Direct tel: 01223 335047
Direct e-mail: aec25@cam.ac.uk

Organisation type and purpose:
University department or institute.

Subject coverage:
Most Continental European languages and literatures (no Greek); Germanic, Romance and Slavonic groups; linguistics, cinema, literary theory; DVDs and videos.

Museum or gallery collection, archive, or library special collection:
Beit Library (German research material)

Library catalogue:
All or part available online

Printed publications:
Annual Report
Readers' Guide

Access to staff:
Contact by letter, by telephone, by fax, by e-mail and in person
Hours: Term time: Mon to Fri, 0900 to 1900; Sat, 1000 to 1600; Vacations: Mon to Fri, 0900 to 1700

Access to building, collection or gallery:
Hours: Term time: Mon to Fri, 0900 to 1900; Sat, 1000 to 1600; Vacations: Mon to Fri, 0900 to 1700

UNIVERSITY OF CAMBRIDGE – RAYLEIGH LIBRARY OF THE DEPARTMENT OF PHYSICS

C.J.J. Thomson Avenue, Madingley Road, Cambridge, CB3 0HE

Tel: 01223 337414
Fax: 01223 363263
E-mail: nh240@hermes.cam.ac.uk

Website:
http://www.phy.cam.ac.uk/library

Enquiries:
Enquiries to: Librarian

Organisation type and purpose:
University department or institute.
Departmental library

Subject coverage:
Physics, meteorology.

Museum or gallery collection, archive, or library special collection:
Maxwell Collection
Napier Shaw Meteorology Library (books and periodicals)
Rayleigh Library (books and periodicals)
History of science

Non-library collection catalogue:
All or part available in-house

Library catalogue:
All or part available online

Access to staff:
Contact by letter, by telephone, by fax, by e-mail, in person and via website. Appointment necessary.
Hours: Mon to Fri, 0900 to 1700

Access for disabled people:
Parking provided

UNIVERSITY OF CAMBRIDGE – SQUIRE LAW LIBRARY

10 West Road, Cambridge, CB3 9DZ

Tel: 01223 330077
Fax: 01223 330057
E-mail: dfw1003@cus.cam.ac.uk

Website:
http://www.lib.cam.ac.uk

Enquiries:
Enquiries to: Librarian
Other contacts: Deputy Librarian

Founded:
1904

Organisation type and purpose:
University library.

Subject coverage:
English, Scottish and Irish Law; legal history; Roman law; US law; comparative law; international law; Commonwealth law.

Museum or gallery collection, archive, or library special collection:
Commonwealth Law Reform Commissions
International Law Treaty Series
Nominate Reports, pre-1800 Law Books and Manuscripts

Library catalogue:
All or part available online

Printed publications:
Guides to the Library and its Collections (Commonwealth, European Communities, International, American) are available in the Library

Access to staff:
Contact by letter, by telephone, by e-mail and via website. Letter of introduction required.
Hours: Mon to Fri, 0900 to 1700

Access for disabled people:
Toilet facilities

Part of:
Cambridge University Library

UNIVERSITY OF CAMBRIDGE – THE MARSHALL LIBRARY OF ECONOMICS

Sidgwick Avenue, Cambridge, CB3 9DB

Tel: 01223 335217
Fax: 01223 335475
E-mail: marshlib@econ.cam.ac.uk

Website:
http://www.econ.cam.ac.uk/marshlib

Enquiries:
Enquiries to: Librarian
Direct tel: 01223 335215

Organisation type and purpose:
University department or institute, research organisation.
Research library.

Subject coverage:
Economics, statistics.

Non-library collection catalogue:
All or part available online and in-house

Printed publications:
Monograph Series and Occasional Papers (pub.
  CUP)
Working papers

Access to staff:
Contact by letter, by telephone, by fax, by e-mail
and in person
Hours: Mon to Fri, 0900 to 1700

Access for disabled people:
Access to all public areas, toilet facilities

UNIVERSITY OF CAMBRIDGE – WHIPPLE LIBRARY OF THE DEPARTMENT OF HISTORY AND PHILOSOPHY OF SCIENCE

Free School Lane, Cambridge, CB2 3RH

Tel: 01223 334547
Fax: 01223 334554
E-mail: hpslib@hermes.cam.ac.uk

Website:
http://www.hps.cam.ac.uk/library/Fpage.html

Enquiries:
Enquiries to: Librarian
Direct e-mail: tje25@cam.ac.uk

Founded:
1944

Organisation type and purpose:
University department or institute.
Departmental library attached to the Department
of History and Philosophy of Science.

Subject coverage:
History and philosophy of science and of medicine,
scientific instruments and instrument makers,
history of medicine.

**Museum or gallery collection, archive, or library
special collection:**
Phrenology Collection
Scientific works of 16th-19th centuries
Works of Robert Boyle
Foster Pamphlet Collection (physiology)

Library catalogue:
All or part available online

Access to staff:
Appointment necessary.
Hours: Term time: 0930 to 1730
Vacations: 0930 to 1700

Access for disabled people:
Special comments: lift, Library on 1st floor, narrow
aisles, limited access for wheelchairs, please
telephone or email in advance of your visit

UNIVERSITY OF CENTRAL LANCASHIRE

Acronym or abbreviation: LLRS

Library and Learning Resource Services, Preston,
Lancashire, PR1 2HE

Tel: 01772 892261
Fax: 01772 892937
E-mail: k.r.ellard@uclan.ac.uk

Website:
http://www.uclan.ac.uk/library/libhom.1.htm
Library mission statement, opening hours,
services, staff names, subject specialist information,
FAQs.

Enquiries:
Enquiries to: Head of Library and Learning
Resource Services
Other contacts: Head of Information Services

Organisation type and purpose:
University library, suitable for ages: 18+.

Subject coverage:
Social sciences; nursing and midwifery; education;
humanities; accountancy; business; management;
astronomy; biology; chemistry; mathematics;
physics; computing science; electrical and

electronic engineering; mechanical engineering;
production engineering; construction and urban
studies.

**Museum or gallery collection, archive, or library
special collection:**
Illustrated Books Collection
Joseph Livesey Collection (temperance)
Local history collections
Preston Incorporated Law Society Library

Non-library collection catalogue:
All or part available online

Printed publications:
Miscellaneous library subject guides and IT guides

Access to staff:
Contact by letter, by telephone, by fax, by e-mail
and via website. Appointment necessary. Non-
members charged.
Hours: Term time: Mon to Thu, 0830 to 2300; Fri,
0830 to 2000; Sat, Sun, 1000 to 1800
Vacations: Mon, Wed, Fri, 0845 to 1700; Tue, Thu,
0845 to 2000; Sat, 1200 to 1800

Access to building, collection or gallery:
Prior appointment required
Special comments: Access to non-members by prior
arrangement in writing or Lancashire County
Library members via library card.

Access for disabled people:
Ramped entry, access to all public areas

UNIVERSITY OF CHESTER

Parkgate Road, Chester, Cheshire, CH1 4BJ

Tel: 01244 511000 (university); 511234 (learning and
information services)
Fax: 01244 511300 (university); 511325 (learning
and information service)
E-mail: lis.helpdesk@chester.ac.uk

Website:
http://www.chester.ac.uk/lr
Details of learning resources, including library
services, catalogue access

Enquiries:
Enquiries to: Customer Services Manager

Founded:
1839

Formerly called:
Chester College of Higher Education (year of
change 2003); University College Chester (year of
change 2005)

Organisation type and purpose:
University library.

Subject coverage:
Art, education, biological science, business and
management, computing, drama, English
literature, history, geography, languages,
mathematics, nursing and midwifery, social work,
sports science, religious studies, psychology,
journalism, media and communications, law,
graphic design, nutrition and dietetics.

Information services:
Helpdesk and reference services

Services for disabled people:
Adjustable tables, specialist software

**Museum or gallery collection, archive, or library
special collection:**
310,000-vol. academic library

Non-library collection catalogue:
All or part available online

Library catalogue:
All or part available online and in-house

Electronic and video publications:
DVDs, videos

Access to staff:
Contact by letter, by telephone, by e-mail and in
person

Hours: Term time: Mon to Thu, 0830 to 2100; Fri,
0830 to 2000; Sat, Sun, 1200 to 1800
Vacations: Mon, Tue, Thu, Fri, 0900 to 1730; Wed,
0900 to 2000

Access for disabled people:
Ramped entry, toilet facilities, lift

UNIVERSITY OF CHICHESTER LIBRARY

Acronym or abbreviation: UoC

Bishop Otter Campus, College Lane, Chichester,
West Sussex, PO19 6PE

Tel: 01243 816089
Fax: 01243 816096

Website:
http://www.chi.ac.uk/info/lrc.cfm

Enquiries:
Enquiries to: Head of Library Services
Direct tel: 01243 816090
Direct e-mail: s.robertson@chi.ac.uk

Founded:
1977

Created by the merger of:
Bishop Otter College and Bognor Regis College
(year of change 1977)

Formerly called:
West Sussex Institute of Higher Education (year of
change 1995); Chichester Institute of Higher
Education (year of change 1999); University
College Chichester (year of change 2005)

Organisation type and purpose:
University library.

Subject coverage:
History, English, theology, media studies, fine art,
music, dance, performing arts, childhood and
youth studies, counselling, social work, sport
studies, sport science, sport therapy, physical
education, adventure education, management

**Museum or gallery collection, archive, or library
special collection:**
Otter Gallery
Chichester Theological Collection
Ted Walker Archive
Dance Videos
Children's Resources (Bognor)
Gerard Young Collection (Bognor local history)
  (Bognor)
Bishop Kemp Collection (Bognor)
John Fines Collection (Bognor)

Trade and statistical information:
Social and health statistics

Library catalogue:
All or part available online

Access to staff:
Contact by letter, by telephone, by fax, by e-mail,
in person and via website. Appointment necessary.
Hours: Term time: Mon to Thu, 0845 to 2145; Fri,
0845 to 1700; Sat, 1000 to 1700; Sun, 1000 to 1700
Vacation: Mon to Fri, 0900 to 1700

Access to building, collection or gallery:
No prior appointment required
Hours: Term time: Mon to Thu, 0845 to 2145; Fri,
0845 to 1700; Sat, 1000 to 1700; Sun, 1000 to 1700
Vacation: Mon to Fri, 0900 to 1700
Special comments: Half-hour only parking, 0800 to
1700

Access for disabled people:
Parking provided, ramped entry, level entry, lift,
access to all public areas, toilet facilities

Branch libraries:
Bognor Regis Campus Library
  Upper Bognor Road, Bognor Regis, West Sussex,
  PO21 1HR; tel: 01243 812099; fax: 01243 812081

UNIVERSITY OF CUMBRIA

Learning and Information Services, Harold Bridges Library, University of Cumbria, Bowerham Road, Lancaster, LA1 3JD

Tel: 01524 384243
Fax: 01524 384588

Website:
http://www.cumbria.ac.uk/services/lis/home.aspx

Enquiries:
Enquiries to: Head of Learning and Information Services
Direct tel: 01524 384238
Other contacts: Site Library Managers for Ambleside, Carlisle Fusehill Street, Lancaster; Campus Library Managers for Carlisle Brampton Road, Newton Rigg Libraries

Founded:
1964

Created by the merger of:
St Martin's College, Cumbria Institute of the Arts, Cumbria campuses of University of Central Lancashire (year of change 2007)

Formerly called:
University College of St Martin, Lancaster (year of change 1998)

Incorporates the former:
Charlotte Mason College, Ambleside (year of change 1996)

Organisation type and purpose:
Multi-site university library.

Subject coverage:
Education, humanities, health studies, management, nursing, radiography, occupational therapy and midwifery, social studies, outdoor studies

Museum or gallery collection, archive, or library special collection:
Large collection of children's books, and teaching and learning materials
Local studies collection (Lancashire, Cumbria and Yorkshire)
Religious and moral studies collection.

Non-library collection catalogue:
All or part available online

Library catalogue:
All or part available online

Access to staff:
Contact by telephone, by fax, by e-mail and in person
Hours: Mon to Fri, 0900 to 1700

Access to building, collection or gallery:
No prior appointment required

Access for disabled people:
Parking provided, ramped entry, access to all public areas, toilet facilities

Also at:
The Library, University of Cumbria
   Fusehill Street, Carlisle, CA1 2HH; tel: 01228 616218; fax: 01228 616263; e-mail: libcarfs@ cumbria.ac.uk
The Library, University of Cumbria
   Rydal Road, Ambleside, Cumbria, LA22 9BB; tel: 015314 30274; fax: 015394 30371; e-mail: libamb@ cumbria.ac.uk
The Library, University of Cumbria
   Newton Rigg, Penrith, Cumbria, CA11 0AH; tel: 01768 893503; fax: 01768 893506; e-mail: libpen@ cumbria.ac.uk
The Library, University of Cumbria
   Brampton Road, Carlisle, Cumbria, CA3 9AY; tel: 01228 400312; fax: 01228 514491; e-mail: libcarbr@cumbria.ac.uk

Associated health-related libraries in:
Westmoreland and Cumbria

Funded by:
Health Authorities
HEFCE
TTA

UNIVERSITY OF DUNDEE – LIBRARY

Small's Wynd, Dundee, DD1 4HN

Tel: 01382 344087
Fax: 01382 229190
E-mail: library@dundee.ac.uk

Website:
http://www.dundee.ac.uk/library/
Library catalogue, library services, library tour, bibliographic and related resources.

Enquiries:
Enquiries to: Librarian
Direct tel: 01382 344082
Direct e-mail: j.m.bagnall@dundee.ac.uk

Organisation type and purpose:
University library.

Subject coverage:
Arts, art and design, social sciences, education, environmental studies, law, medicine, dentistry, nursing, science, engineering and applied science including architecture.

Museum or gallery collection, archive, or library special collection:
Brechin Diocesan Library
Joan Auld Memorial Collection
Kinnear Allan Ramsay Collection
Kinnear Local Collection
Leng Collection (Scottish philosophical writers)
Nicoll Collection (books on the fine arts)
Thoms mineralogical collection
William Lyon Mackenzie Collection (Canadiana)

Printed publications:
Catalogue of Allan Ramsay Collection (1990)
Guides to Library Services
University Education in Dundee, 1881–1981: a pictorial history (1982, £3.50)

Microform publications:
University theses on request subject to copyright restrictions

Access to staff:
Contact by letter, by telephone, by fax and by e-mail
Hours: Mon to Fri, 0900 to 1700

UNIVERSITY OF DUNDEE – NINEWELLS LIBRARY

Ninewells Hospital and Medical School, Dundee, DD1 9SY

Tel: 01382 632519
Fax: 01382 566179
E-mail: ninewells-library@dundee.ac.uk

Website:
http://www.dundee.ac.uk/library
Library pages including access to catalogue.

Formed from merger of:
Aberdeen College of Education, Dundee College of Education (year of change 1987)

Formerly called:
Northern College of Education (year of change 2001)

Subject coverage:
Education; psychology; educational technology; community education; social work; children's literature; open learning.

Library catalogue:
All or part available online

Access to staff:
Contact by letter, by telephone, by e-mail and via website
Hours: Term time: Mon to Thu, 0900 to 2100; Fri, 0930 to 1700; Sat, 0900 to 1200
Vacations: Mon to Thu, 0900 to 1700; Fri, 0930 to 1700

Access to building, collection or gallery:
No prior appointment required

UNIVERSITY OF EAST ANGLIA – LIBRARY

Acronym or abbreviation: UEA Library

University of East Anglia, Norwich, Norfolk, NR4 7TJ

Tel: 01603 592434
Fax: 01603 591010
E-mail: library@uea.ac.uk

Website:
http://www.lib.uea.ac.uk

Enquiries:
Enquiries to: Library Director
Direct tel: 01603 592382
Direct e-mail: nicholas.lewis@uea.ac.uk

Founded:
1963

Organisation type and purpose:
University library.

Subject coverage:
Social sciences and the humanities; history; law; education; development studies; biological, chemical, environmental, mathematical, physical and computing sciences; accounting; management; information systems; health sciences; film studies; medicine; pharmacy.

Museum or gallery collection, archive, or library special collection:
Abbott Collection (English literature)
European Documentation Centre (Selective)
Holloway Collection of Contemporary Culture Records
Illustrated Books
Ketton-Cremer Collection (local history)
Pritchard Archive
Zuckerman Archive

Non-library collection catalogue:
All or part available online

Library catalogue:
All or part available online

Access to staff:
Contact by letter, by telephone, by fax, by e-mail, in person and via website
Hours: Mon to Fri, 0900 to 1700
Special comments: Reference only to non-registered borrowers.

Access for disabled people:
Level entry, access to all public areas, toilet facilities

Links with:
Centre for Environment, Fisheries and Agriculture Sciences (CEFAS)
   Lowestoft
Institute of Food Research (Norwich)
John Innes Centre
Norfolk and Norwich University Hospital
Norwich University College of the Arts
   Norwich, Norfolk
Otley College
   Ipswich
Suffolk New College
   Ipswich
University Campus Suffolk
West Suffolk College

Member organisation of:
ANGLES (formerly NINES)

UNIVERSITY OF EAST ANGLIA – SCHOOL OF ENVIRONMENTAL SCIENCES

Acronym or abbreviation: ENV, UEA

University Plain, Norwich, Norfolk, NR4 7TJ

Tel: 01603 592994
Fax: 01603 593035
E-mail: j.darch@uea.ac.uk

Website:
http://www.uea.ac.uk/env/

Enquiries:
Enquiries to: Research Administrator

Organisation type and purpose:
University department or institute.

Subject coverage:
Environmental sciences, atmospheric chemistry, climatic change, climatic modelling, wind energy, ecology, geophysics, oceanography, health, planning, risk assessment, cost-benefit analysis, environmental assessment and appraisal, geology, geomorphology, quaternary period, global environmental change, air-sea interactions, GIS, waste management, hydrology and hydrogeology, estuaries, soils and land use planning.

Printed publications:
Annual Report
CERM working papers
Climatic Research Unit Research Publications (occasional)
Centre for Social and Economic Research on the Global Environment (CSERGE) (working papers)

Electronic and video publications:
Climatic Monitor (online)
Various items available online or CD-ROM, for purchase

Publications list:
Available online and in print

Access to staff:
Contact by letter, by fax, by e-mail and via website. Appointment necessary.
Hours: Mon to Fri, 0900 to 1700

Includes the:
Centre for Environmental Risk
tel: 01603 593129; fax: 01603 507719; e-mail: n .pidgeon@uea.ac.uk
Centre for Social and Economic Research on the Global Environment (CSERGE)
tel: 01603 592551; fax: 01603 250588; e-mail: n.k .turner@uea.ac.uk
Climatic Research Unit
tel: 01603 593647; fax: 01603 507784; e-mail: j .palativiof@uea.ac.uk
Tyndall Centre for Climate Change

UNIVERSITY OF EAST LONDON – BARKING LEARNING RESOURCE CENTRE

Acronym or abbreviation: UEL

Longbridge Road, Dagenham, Essex, RM8 2AS

Tel: 020 8223 2614
Fax: 020 8223 2804

Enquiries:
Enquiries to: Customer Services Manager
Direct tel: ext 2620
Direct e-mail: m.davies@uel.ac.uk

Organisation type and purpose:
University library.

Subject coverage:
Education, humanities in general, social sciences, management, law, literature, architecture, art and design, business studies, economics, accounting, computing, land surveying, engineering, science, health and rehabilitation services.

Museum or gallery collection, archive, or library special collection:
Times and Financial Times on microfilm

Access to staff:
Contact by letter, by telephone and by fax
Hours: Mon to Fri, 0900 to 1700

UNIVERSITY OF EAST LONDON – DOCKLANDS LEARNING RESOURCE CENTRE

Acronym or abbreviation: UEL

University Way, London, E16 2RD

Tel: 020 8223 3434

Fax: 020 8223 7497
E-mail: J.A.Preece@uel.ac.uk

Website:
http://www.uel.ac.uk

Enquiries:
Enquiries to: Manager

Founded:
1999

Organisation type and purpose:
University department or institute, suitable for ages: 18+.

Subject coverage:
Fine art, art theory and history, contemporary art, design history, graphics, photography, film history, textiles, psychology, fashion, cultural studies, third world studies, refugee studies, literature, history, gender studies, new technology, media studies, communication studies.

Museum or gallery collection, archive, or library special collection:
William Morris collection

Access to staff:
Contact by telephone and by e-mail. Appointment necessary. Access for members only.
Hours: Mon to Fri, 0900 to 1700

Access to building, collection or gallery:
Prior appointment required
Special comments: No prior appointment required for members of UEL, UK Libraries Plus, M25 Scheme and Newham Leisure Card Holders.

Access for disabled people:
Parking provided, ramped entry, level entry, access to all public areas, toilet facilities

UNIVERSITY OF EAST LONDON – LIBRARY

Acronym or abbreviation: UEL

Longbridge Road, Dagenham, Essex, RM8 2AS

Tel: 020 8223 3000\ Minicom no. 020 8223 2853
Fax: 020 8590 7799

Website:
http://www.uel.ac.uk
School information, prospectus and course information, departmental information.

Enquiries:
Enquiries to: Head of Library
Direct tel: 020 8223 2317

Organisation type and purpose:
University library.

Subject coverage:
Mathematics, physics, chemistry, biology, psychology, paramedical sciences, art, architecture, design, science, education, IT, social work, law, health, business, engineering, economics.

Printed publications:
Prospectus (free)

Electronic and video publications:
Prospectus (CD-ROM, online copy available)

Access to staff:
Contact by letter, by telephone, by fax and by e-mail
Hours: Mon to Fri, 0900 to 2100

Access for disabled people:
Parking provided, ramped entry, access to all public areas, toilet facilities

UNIVERSITY OF EAST LONDON – STRATFORD LEARNING RESOURCE CENTRE

Acronym or abbreviation: UEL

Holbrook Annexe, Holbrook Road, Stratford, London, E15 3EA

Tel: 020 8223 3251
Fax: 020 8223 3296

Website:
http://www.uel.ac.uk/library

Enquiries:
Enquiries to: Manager
Direct e-mail: s.p.lyes@uel.ac.uk

Organisation type and purpose:
University library.

Subject coverage:
Architecture, building, planning.

Museum or gallery collection, archive, or library special collection:
Collection of architectural slides
Collection on architecture (RIBA trade literature)

Library catalogue:
All or part available online

Access to staff:
Contact by letter, by telephone, by e-mail and via website. Appointment necessary.
Hours: Mon to Thu, 0900 to 1900; Fri, 0900 to 1700
Vacations have varying opening hours

Access to building, collection or gallery:
Prior appointment required

Access for disabled people:
Level entry

UNIVERSITY OF EDINBURGH – CENTRE FOR EDUCATIONAL SOCIOLOGY

Acronym or abbreviation: CES

St John's Land, Holyrood Road, Edinburgh, EH8 8AQ

Tel: 0131 651 6238
Fax: 0131 651 6239
E-mail: ces@ed.ac.uk

Website:
http://www.ces.ed.ac.uk
Information about the Centre, personnel, projects and publications.

Enquiries:
Enquiries to: Administrator
Direct tel: 0131 651 6238
Direct e-mail: ces@ed.ac.uk

Founded:
1972

Organisation type and purpose:
University department or institute, research organisation.

Subject coverage:
Education, training, youth labour market, transitions to adulthood, information systems.

Library catalogue:
All or part available in-house

Publications list:
Available online and in print

Access to staff:
Contact by letter, by telephone, by fax, by e-mail, in person and via website. Appointment necessary.
Hours: Mon to Fri, 0900 to 1700

Access for disabled people:
Access to all public areas, toilet facilities

UNIVERSITY OF EDINBURGH – UNIVERSITY LIBRARY

Acronym or abbreviation: EUL

George Square, Edinburgh, EH8 9LJ

Tel: 0131 650 3384
Fax: 0131 667 9780
E-mail: library@ed.ac.uk

Website:
http://www.lib.ed.ac.uk/
Library Online, Information about the library, post-1984 catalogue, links to databases, electronic journals and electronic reference material.

continued overleaf

Enquiries:
Enquiries to: Director of Library Services
Direct tel: 0131 650 3409, IS Helpdesk (lending services); 0131 650 3384, general enquiries
Direct fax: 0131 650 3380, administration; 6863, special collections
Other contacts: Director of University Collections, e-mail: john.scally@ed.ac.uk

Founded:
1580

Organisation type and purpose:
University library.
The books acquired by the Library between its foundation in 1580 and the publication of its 3-volume printed catalogue in 1918–23, especially during the period 1710–1837 when it was a library of copyright deposit, now represent a significant historical research resource in most branches of the humanities, especially on the history of Scotland and the United Kingdom, European history and literature, and the Commonwealth and British expansion overseas. The Library also has significant collections of early printed books, and mediaeval and modern Western and Oriental manuscripts. It is a European Documentation Centre, and this facility is focused on the Law and Europa Library.

Subject coverage:
The Library serves the needs of the 3 University Colleges and Schools within them: College of Humanities and Social Science; College of Medicine and Veterinary Medicine; College of Science and Engineering. It holds general academic collections in all these fields as well as in-depth collections in many of them.
Astronomy (Royal Observatory), botany (Darwin Library), chemistry (Chemistry Library), engineering and geology (Robertson Engineering and Science Library), forestry (Darwin Library), genetics (Darwin Library), mathematics, computer science and physics (James Clerk Maxwell Library), zoology (Darwin Library).
Medicine and medical sciences, dentistry, psychiatry, community medicine (Main Library).
European Union, German public law and political organisation (Law and Europa Library).
Scottish ethnology, folklore, folk tales, oral traditions, customs and belief, literature, dialectology, material culture, ethnomusicology, song, place-names, social history and organisation, urban ethnology, ethnology of religion, emigrant traditions (Scottish Studies Library).
Christianity and Church history, biblical studies, theology, patristics, Church missions, non-Christian religions in relation to Christianity (New College Library),
education, psychology, English Language Teaching, physical education, movement, leisure studies, sports science and recreational management (Moray House Library), veterinary anatomy, biochemistry, medicine, parasitology, pathology, pharmacology, physiology; animal health and reproduction (Royal (Dick) School of Veterinary Studies Library).

Museum or gallery collection, archive, or library special collection:
Named special collections, with year of acquisition, include:
Lord Abercromby, 1924 (archaeology, ethnology, linguistics)
Auden, 1982 (W H Auden and associated writers of the 1930s)
John Stuart Blackie, 1895 (Greek)
Blondal, 1950 (Icelandic studies)
Bruce, 1921 (oceanography and Polar studies)
Cameron, 1889 (Celtic studies and theology)
Hugh Cleghorn, 1895 (Indian forestry, land use and botany)
Compton, 1997 (American history)
Corson, 1989 (Sir Walter Scott)
Cumming, 1939 (Italian studies)
William Drummond of Hawthornden, 1620–30 (English, Latin, Italian, French and Spanish literature)
East Asian Studies
Will Foret Archive (Scottish studies)

Geikie, 1915 (geology)
Halliwell-Phillipps, 1866, 1872 (Shakespeare, 17th and 18th century English drama)
W B Hodgson, 1880 (economics)
Jameson Collection (mineralogy)
Berriedale Keith, 1944 (Indian literature, history and politics and the constitutional history of the British Commonwealth)
Kennedy-Fraser, c. 1950 (Scottish music, dance, history and literature)
Arthur Koestler, 1985 (literature)
David Laing, 1878 (3000 Scottish charters, mediaeval and modern manuscripts on Scottish history and literature, early Scottish music texts, and letters of artists)
Kenneth Leighton Manuscripts (music)
John Levy archive (oriental music) (Scottish Studies)
Clement Littill, 1580 (theology)
Lyell Collection (geology)
Mackinnon, 1924 (Celtic studies and theology)
Sir John Murray, 1921 (zoology, geography, geology)
James Nairn, 1678 (theology, philosophy, history and literature)
Penguin Books 1935–1985
Adam Smith, 18th century (literature, classics, political economy, science)
Serjeant, 1996 (Middle East)
Dugald Stewart, 18th-19th centuries (political economy, moral philosophy, mathematics)
James Thin, 1880 (hymnology)
Sir Donald F Tovey, 1940 (music scores and books)
Weiss, 1948 (books on Beethoven)
Watt, 1997 (Arabic)
Un-named special collections:
18th- and 19th-century books on agriculture
Audio-visual Archive (Scottish Studies)
Bundesgesetzblatt
Cases of the European Court of Human Rights
Collection of early printed books on music theory
Debates of the European Parliament
Ecumenical Collection (includes all World Council of Churches and British Council of Churches publications)
European Courts Reports (English, French, German and Dutch language)
Historical collections of Scottish churchmen (books, pamphlets and portraits)
Historical collection of veterinary science, nucleus of which belonged to the school's founder, William Dick
Manuscript collections (mainly Scottish church history, including Thomas Chalmers, 1780–1847, archive of c. 20,000 letters)
Official Journal of the European Union (Communities) (C and L series)
Photographic Archive (Scottish studies)
Sound Archive (10,000 tapes, Scottish studies)
Verhandlungen des Deutschen Bundestages
Libraries of the:
Dumfries Presbytery
Edinburgh Geological Society
Edinburgh Mathematical Society
Lothian Health Services Archives
Royal Physical Society
Royal Scottish Forestry Society
University of Edinburgh Archives
Manuscripts of various scientific societies
Subject specialisations:
African studies
Canadian studies
History of medicine and science
Landscape architecture
New Zealand studies
Scandinavian studies
Modern Scottish and English literature
Scottish studies
South Asian studies
The Church of Scotland
The Scottish Enlightenment
The University of Edinburgh
Poets and writers:
W H Auden
George Mackay Brown
Thomas and Jane Welsh Carlyle
Thomas Chalmers
Helen B Cruikshank

Christopher Murray Grieve ('Hugh MacDairmid')
Norman McCaig
James Leslie Mitchell ('Lewis Grassic Gibbon')
John Middleton Murry
Poets of Scottish Literary Renaissance
Sydney Goodsir Smith
Sir Walter Scott
John Wain
Size of collections: The Library holds over 3,400,000 printed volumes and pamphlets, as well as many manuscripts and archives of international importance. Largest University library in Scotland. Its electronic data, including full-text journals and other resources which are now core to its collections, are accessible across the University network and increasingly off-campus.

Non-library collection catalogue:
All or part available online

Library catalogue:
All or part available online

Printed publications:
Publications list available on request
Catalogue of manuscripts, printed music and books on music up to 1850 in the Main Library
Catalogue of the Printed Books in the Library of the University, 3 vols (1918–1923)
Index to [post-mediaeval Western] manuscripts, 2 vols and supplement to 1978
Library Guide 9, Library services for external users (free)
Pre-1985 catalogues: Main Library Guard-Book catalogue 1580–1984 available in situ and on microfiche.
Catalogues of older material are still in manual form in most Faculty Libraries
Scottish Studies (annual volume)
Union list of Current Serials received in Edinburgh University Library and some other research libraries in Edinburgh
Small range of publications available on request
Order printed publications from: Publications, Edinburgh University Library
George Square, Edinburgh, EH8 9LS, tel: 0131 651 1438, fax: 0131 650 3380, e-mail: library@ed.ac.uk

Electronic and video publications:
The Library Catalogue (online)

Access to staff:
Contact by letter, by telephone, by fax, by e-mail and via website. Appointment necessary. Letter of introduction required. Non-members charged.
Hours: Semester Time: Main Library, Mon to Thu, 0830 to 2200; Fri, 0830 to 1900; Sat, 0900 to 1700; Sun, 1200 to 1900; most other major College & School Libraries, Mon to Thu, 0900 to 2200; Fri, Sat 0900 to 1700; Sun, 1200 to 1700;
Vacations: Main Library, Mon to Thurs, 0830 to 2000; Fri, 0830 to 1700; Sat, 1000 to 1300
Special comments: Members of the University of Edinburgh have full access as of right. They may borrow free of charge and are charged for photocopying, photography and inter-library loans.
External users may be charged for access (consultation and/or borrowing), photocopying, photography and inter-library loans.
Undergraduate students from other European Union HEIs during EUL vacations may have access for reference purposes free of charge on production of their own current ID cards. They may have borrowing facilities on payment of the current external fee. During term-time they are admitted only by prior arrangement with their own institutions' librarians. Postgraduate students are admitted at all times.
Staff, postgraduate students and undergraduate students from overseas HEIs, including members of Universitas 21, Coimbra, and other groups, will be charged external fees for borrowing unless they are official academic visitors to the University.
Advanced Higher Students, School students and equivalent project-based course students may have access to the Library for consultation purposes free of charge, provided that prior arrangements have

been made between each School and the University Library. Other school students are not normally admitted to the Library.

Corporate membership is available on application and by subscription.

Prices, which may be adjusted at any time, are available on request or through Library Online at www.lib.ed.ac.uk

Access for disabled people:
Parking provided, ramped entry, level entry, access to all public areas, toilet facilities
Special comments: These facilities apply to the Main Library. On other sites the provision will vary.

College of Medicine and Veterinary Medicine:
Easter Bush Veterinary Centre Library (including CTVM – Centre for Tropical Veterinary Medicine Library)
   Senior Library Assistant, Edinburgh Bush Veterinary Centre, Easter Bush, Roslin, Midlothian, EH25 9RG; tel: 0131 650 6405; fax: 0131 650 6594
Main Library
   Medical Librarian, University Main Library, George Square, Edinburgh, EH8 9LJ; tel: 0131 650 3690; fax: 0131 650 3381
Medical Library
   Senior Library Assistant, Western General Hospital, Crewe Road South, Edinburgh, EH4 2XU; tel: 0131 537 2299
Psychiatry Library
   Please contact Main Library; tel: 0131 650 3409
Royal (Dick) School of Veterinary Studies Library
   Veterinary Librarian, Summerhall, Edinburgh, EH9 1QH; tel: 0131 650 6175; fax: 0131 650 6593

College of Science and Engineering:
Artificial Intelligence Library now in Main Library
   Edinburgh University Main Library, George Square, Edinburgh EH8 9LJ; tel: 0131 650 3409
Darwin Library
   Biological Sciences Librarian, Darwin Building, The King's Buildings, West Mains Road, Edinburgh, EH9 3JU; tel: 0131 650 5784
James Clerk Maxwell Library
   Physical Sciences Librarian, James Clerk Maxwell Building, The King's Buildings, West Mains Road, Edinburgh, EH9 3JZ; tel: 0131 650 5206
Robertson Engineering and Science Library
   Engineering and Informatics Librarian, The King's Buildings, West Mains Road, Edinburgh, EH9 3JF; tel: 0131 650 5666
School of Chemistry, Chemistry Library
   Please contact Darwin Library; tel: 0131 650 5784
Science Libraries
   Science Librarian, The King's Buildings, West Mains Road, Edinburgh, EH9 3JU; tel: 0131 650 5205; fax: 0131 650 6702; e-mail: ScienceLib@ed .ac.uk

Moray House School of Education:
Moray House Library
   Dalhousie Land, St John Street, Edinburgh, EH8 8AQ; tel: 0131 651 6193; fax: 0131 557 3458

School of Arts, Culture and Environment:
Reid Music Library in Main Library, Special Collections
   5th Floor, Edinburgh University Library, George Square, Edinburgh EH8 9LJ; tel: 0131 650 8379; fax: 0131 650 6863; e-mail: special.collections .library@ed.ac.uk; website: http://www.lib.ed.ac .uk/resources/collections/specdivision/

School of Divinity:
New College Library
   New College Librarian, School of Divinity, Mound Place, Edinburgh, EH1 2LU; tel: 0131 650 8957; fax: 0131 650 6579

School of Law:
Law and Europa Library (European Documentation Centre)
   Law Librarian, Old College, South Bridge, Edinburgh, EH8 9YL; tel: 0131 650 2044; fax: 0131 650 6343

School of Literatures, Languages and Cultures:
Scottish Studies Library
   School of Scottish Studies, 27–29 George Square, Edinburgh, EH8 9LD; tel: 0131 650 3060; fax: 0131 650 6536; e-mail: Scottish.Studies@ed.ac.uk

UNIVERSITY OF ESSEX LIBRARY

Formal name: The Albert Sloman Library, University of Essex

Wivenhoe Park, Colchester, Essex, CO4 3SQ

Tel: 01206 873333
Fax: 01206 872289
E-mail: librarian@essex.ac.uk

Website:
http://libwww.essex.ac.uk
Catalogues and library guides.

Enquiries:
Enquiries to: Librarian

Founded:
1963

Organisation type and purpose:
University library.

Subject coverage:
Biology, computing science, electronics, health sciences, mathematics, psychology; art, history, language and linguistics, literature and philosophy; accounting and financial management, business studies, economics, government, law, psychoanalysis, sociology. Special emphasis on Latin America, USA and the former Soviet Union.

Museum or gallery collection, archive, or library special collection:
Archives of Mrs Mary Whitehouse, CBE
Archives of SCOPE-ENUWAR (Scientific Committee on Problems of the Environmental Consequences of Nuclear War)
Archives of the National Viewers' and Listeners' Association
Archives of the Rowhedge Ironworks Company (1904–1964)
Archives of the Social Democratic Party (SDP)
Lord Rogers of Quarrybank (SDP papers)
Archives of the Tawney Society (the SDP 'Think Tank')
Bassingbourn Parish Library
Bean Collection on William Blake
Donald Davie Archive
Edgell Rickword Collection
European Documentation, from 1977
S E Finer Papers (UK transport policy)
George Goddeck Archive (psychoanalysis)
Hervey Benham Sound Archive (local history)
Historical Collection of the Royal Statistical Society
David Kerr Papers (UK health policy)
Letters of T E Lawrence
Levene/Sky Television Political interviews Video Archive
Nolan Committee Papers (Committee of Standards of Conduct in Public Life) 1995–1997
Letters, papers and diaries of Henri and Sophie Gaudier Brzeska
Letters, papers and diaries of John Hassall
National Social Policy and Social Change Archive (QUALIDATA)
Library of the Essex Society for Archaeology and History
Papers and printed books of the Colchester and Coggeshall Meetings of the Society of Friends
Papers of Enid Balint (psychoanalysis)
Papers (1992–93) of the Boundary Commission for England
Papers and Diaries of S L Bensusan
Papers of Lord Alport (Rhodesia, House of Lords, Colchester and Essex)
Papers of Lord Brimelow (Yalta Repatriation Agreement)
Papers on the Third London Airport controversy
Paul Sieghart Human Rights Archive
Russell Collection Family Archive
Sigmund Freud Collection (psychoanalysis)
Sir Vincent Evans Collection (European Court of Human Rights)

Watergate Collection
Windscale Inquiry Papers, 1977 (Nuclear reactor fuel reprocessing)
Margery Allingham / Philip Youngman Carter literary archives
Charter88 Archives (civil, political and human rights)
Bernie Hamilton Archive (human rights)
Colchester Medical Society Library (historical books)

Library catalogue:
All or part available online

Printed publications:
English Law 2001
European Documentation 2001
Guide to the Latin American Collection 2001
Human Rights 2001
Guides and bibliographies
Microforms 1998
Library guide 2000/01

Publications list:
Available online and in print

Access to staff:
Contact by letter and by fax. Appointment necessary. Letter of introduction required.
Hours: Term time: Mon to Fri, 0800 to 2200; Sat, 0900 to 1800; Sun, 1400 to 1900
Vacations: Mon to Fri, 0900 to 1730

Access for disabled people:
Level entry, access to all public areas, toilet facilities

UNIVERSITY OF EXETER – CAMBORNE SCHOOL OF MINES

Acronym or abbreviation: CSM

Pool, Redruth, Cornwall, TR15 3SE

Tel: 01209 714866
Fax: 01209 719677
E-mail: libcsm@csm.ex.ac.uk

Enquiries:
Enquiries to: Librarian
Direct e-mail: jfoote@csm.ex.ac.uk

Formerly called:
Camborne School of Mines

Organisation type and purpose:
University department or institute.
Education and research in mining engineering, extractive metallurgy, industrial geology, surveying and minerals resource management, environmental management.

Subject coverage:
Metalliferous mining, mineral processing, extractive metallurgy, industrial geology, surveying, minerals resource management, environmental and waste management, mined land reclamation.

UNIVERSITY OF EXETER – LAW LIBRARY

Amory Building, Rennes Drive, Exeter, Devon, EX4 4RJ

Tel: 01392 263356
Fax: 01392 263196

Website:
http://www.library.ex.ac.uk/internet
European studies and law pages on the Exeter library resources page.

Enquiries:
Enquiries to: Librarian
Direct e-mail: p.c.overy@ex.ac.uk

Founded:
1974

Organisation type and purpose:
University library.

Subject coverage:
English, European and international law.

continued overleaf

Museum or gallery collection, archive, or library special collection:
European Documentation Centre: European Commission publications

Trade and statistical information:
EU Statistics.

Non-library collection catalogue:
All or part available online

Library catalogue:
All or part available online

Access to staff:
Contact by letter, by telephone and by e-mail.
Appointment necessary.
Hours: Mon to Fri, 0900 to 1700

Member of:
European Information Association

UNIVERSITY OF EXETER – ST LUKE'S CAMPUS LIBRARY

Heavitree Road, Exeter, Devon, EX1 2LU

Tel: 01392 264785
Fax: 01392 264784
E-mail: roy.davies@ex.ac.uk

Website:
http://www.ex.ac.uk/library

Enquiries:
Enquiries to: Librarian
Direct tel: 01392 264782

Founded:
1837

Formerly called:
Institute of Education

Organisation type and purpose:
University library, university department or institute.
Library of university faculty.

Subject coverage:
Education, social work, exercise and sport science.

Museum or gallery collection, archive, or library special collection:
National curriculum archive

Non-library collection catalogue:
All or part available online

Library catalogue:
All or part available online

Access to staff:
Contact by letter, by telephone, by fax, by e-mail, in person and via website
Hours: Term time: Mon to Thu, 0900 to 2100; Fri, 0900 to 1715; Sat, 0900 to 1700, Sun 1400 to 1800
Vacations: Mon to Fri, 0900 to 1715, Sat 1300 to 1700, Sun 1400 to 1800

Access for disabled people:
Parking provided, level entry, toilet facilities, lift, stair-lift

Parent body:
University of Exeter Library

UNIVERSITY OF EXETER – UNIVERSITY LIBRARY

Stocker Road, Exeter, Devon, EX4 4PT

Tel: 01392 263869
Fax: 01392 263871
E-mail: library@exeter.ac.uk

Website:
http://www.as.exeter.ac.uk/library
Details of academic services and staff.

Enquiries:
Enquiries to: Assistant Director, Collections and Research Support

Founded:
1855

Organisation type and purpose:
University library. Serving the community as well as the university staff and students.

Subject coverage:
Arts, law, social studies, science and technology.

Museum or gallery collection, archive, or library special collection:
Arabic and Gulf Studies
Audio-visual resources
Books and recordings related to American music, especially popular music
Dan Davin book collection of New Zealand literature
Imperial Institute collection of photographs
Bill Douglas Centre for Film Studies
Crediton, Ottery St Mary and Totnes Parish Libraries
Dodderidge Collection
Ghana Collection (Scolma Area Specialization Plan)
MSS Collections (West Country authors)
Syon Abbey Collection

Non-library collection catalogue:
All or part available online

Library catalogue:
All or part available online

Access to staff:
Contact by letter, by telephone, by fax and by e-mail. Appointment necessary.
Hours: Mon to Fri, 0900 to 1700

Includes the:
Devon and Exeter Institution Library
Exeter University (St Luke's) Library

UNIVERSITY OF GLAMORGAN

Learning Resources Centre, Pontypridd, Rhondda Cynon Taff, CF37 1DL

Tel: 01443 482625\ Minicom no. 01443 482322
Fax: 01443 482629
E-mail: smorgan1@glam.ac.uk

Website:
http://www.glam.ac.uk/lrc/home.htm
Information; including learning resources centre guide, news, guide to selected internet resources, staff directory, connection to the OPAC.

Enquiries:
Enquiries to: Librarian
Direct e-mail: lrc@glam.ac.uk
Other contacts: Head of Learning Resources Centre

Organisation type and purpose:
University library.

Subject coverage:
Mathematics; computer science; physics; chemistry; life sciences; geology; chemical, civil, mechanical, manufacturing, electrical and electronic engineering; information technology; building; quantity surveying; estate management; law; politics; public administration; behavioural and communication studies; accountancy; business studies and management; arts and humanities; statistics; safety; languages; nursing and midwifery.

Museum or gallery collection, archive, or library special collection:
Centre for the Study of Welsh Writing in English Collection

Printed publications:
Learning Resources Centre Guide
Specialised publications, on particular facilities, services, databases
Some publications are available via the Learning Resource Centre's WWW pages

Access to staff:
Contact by letter, by telephone, by fax and by e-mail
Hours: Mon to Fri, 0900 to 1700

UNIVERSITY OF GLASGOW – ARCHIVE SERVICES

77–87 Dumbarton Road, Glasgow, G11 6PW

Tel: 0141 330 5515
Fax: 0141 330 4158
E-mail: dutyarch@archives.gla.ac.uk

Website:
http://www.archives.gla.ac.uk
http://www.archives.gla.ac.uk/news/pubsales.html
Publications in print

Enquiries:
Enquiries to: Duty Archivist

May still be looked for as:
Glasgow University Archives & Business Records Centre; Business Records Centre (year of change 2000)

Organisation type and purpose:
University department or institute.
Archive repository.

Subject coverage:
Higher education archives and history, business archives, retail, shipbuilding, engineering and textiles archives, Scottish culture, Scottish history.

Museum or gallery collection, archive, or library special collection:
Glasgow University Archives from 1451
Greater Glasgow Health Board Archive
Scottish Brewing Archives
Scottish Business Archives

Non-library collection catalogue:
All or part available online and in-house

Library catalogue:
All or part available in-house

Printed publications:
Source Lists

Access to staff:
Contact by letter, by telephone, by fax, by e-mail, in person and via website. Appointment necessary.
Hours: Mon, 1330 to 1700; Tue, Wed, Fri, 0930 to 1700; Thu, 0930 to 2000 (appointment essential)

Access for disabled people:
Parking provided, access to all public areas, toilet facilities

Searchroom:
Glasgow University Archive Services
13 Thurso Street, Glasgow, G11 6PE

UNIVERSITY OF GLASGOW – DIVISION OF VIROLOGY

Institute of Virology, Church Street, Glasgow, G11 5JR

Tel: 0141 330 4017 or 4029
Fax: 0141 337 2236

Website:
http://www.vir.gla.ac.uk/staff.shtml
Summaries of current research.

Enquiries:
Enquiries to: Joint Heads of Division
Direct tel: 0141 330 4029

Founded:
1958

Formerly called:
Institute of Virology (year of change 1994)

Organisation type and purpose:
University department or institute.

Subject coverage:
Herpes virus genomic and evolutionary biology, herpes virus gene control and latency, herpes virus genome replication, viral structure and assembly; antivirals, vaccines and immunological reagents; eukaryotic mRNA processing in virus infected cells; genomic and functional analysis of bunyavirus; molecular biology of hepatitis B virus; molecular biology of hepatitis C virus, molecular biology of RSV, molecular biology of picorna viruses.

Printed publications:
Research results are published in the primary
scientific journals

Access to staff:
Contact by letter, by telephone, by fax and by e-
mail
Hours: Mon to Fri, 0900 to 1700
Special comments: Books and journals not available
for outside loan.

Access to building, collection or gallery:
Prior appointment required

Access for disabled people:
Ramped entry

Parent body:
Medical Research Council
University of Glasgow

UNIVERSITY OF GLASGOW – LANGUAGE CENTRE LIBRARY

Acronym or abbreviation: UGLC

Hetherington Building, Bute Gardens, Glasgow,
G12 8RS

Tel: 0141 330 4117
Fax: 0141 330 4114
E-mail: lc-librarian@arts.gla.ac.uk

Website:
http://www.glasgow.ac.uk/services/
languagecentre/library

Enquiries:
Enquiries to: Librarian

Founded:
1985

Organisation type and purpose:
University department or institute.

Subject coverage:
Language learning and linguistics through
audiovisual and multimedia; in French, Spanish,
Portuguese, German, Italian, Russian languages;
materials in over 35 other languages.

Non-library collection catalogue:
All or part available online

Library catalogue:
All or part available online

Printed publications:
Library guide

Access to staff:
Contact by letter, by telephone, by fax, by e-mail
and in person
Hours: Term time: Mon to Thu, 0930 to 2000; Fri,
0900 to 1645. Vacation: Mon to Fri, 0930 to 1645
Special comments: Please phone as opening times
vary

Access for disabled people:
Ramped entry, toilet facilities

UNIVERSITY OF GLASGOW – UNIVERSITY LIBRARY

Hillhead Street, Glasgow, G12 8QE

Tel: 0141 330 6704/5
Fax: 0141 330 4952
E-mail: library@lib.gla.ac.uk

Website:
http://www.lib.gla.ac.uk/index.html
Library catalogue, news and information;
bibliographic, reference and network resources
and exhibition information.

Enquiries:
Enquiries to: Head of Enquiry Service
Direct e-mail: enquiries@lib.gla.ac.uk
Other contacts: Keeper of Special Collections

Founded:
1451

Organisation type and purpose:
University library.

Subject coverage:
Social sciences, humanities and medicine;
administrative medicine; adult and continuing
education; anaesthesia; ancient Near Eastern
history; Arabic and Islamic studies; archaeology;
architecture; art history; bibliography; cardiac
surgery; cartography; Celtic; child and adolescent
psychiatry; child health; clinical medicine; clinical
physics; clinical surgery; community medicine;
constitutional law and history; Czech; dental
medicine; dermatology; drama; ecclesiastical
history; economic history; economics; education;
emblem studies; English language and literature;
European Community; financial studies; fine art;
forensic medicine; French; general practice
(medicine); geography; geriatric medicine;
German; Greek; haematology; Hebrew and Semitic
languages; Hispanic studies; history; immunology;
industrial relations; infectious diseases;
international economic studies; Italian; Latin; Latin
American studies; law; linguistics and phonetics;
logic; media studies; medical genetics; medicine;
music; neurology; neuropathology; neurosurgery;
nursing studies; obstetrics and gynaecology;
oncology; ophthalmology; orthopaedics;
otolaryngology; pathology; pharmacology;
philosophy; plastic surgery; Polish; politics;
psychological medicine; psychology; religious
studies; Russian; Scottish history; Scottish
literature; social and economic research; social
administration and social work; sociology; Soviet
and East European studies; surgery; theology;
veterinary medicine; science and technology;
aeronautics and fluid mechanics; agriculture;
anatomy; animal developmental biology; animal
nutrition; astronomy; bacteriology and
immunology; biochemistry; biology; botany; cell
biology; chemical physics; chemistry; civil
engineering; computing science; conveyancing;
economics; electronics and electrical engineering;
genetics; geology; history of science; management
studies; mathematics; mechanical engineering;
mercantile law; microbiology; naval architecture;
ocean engineering; parasitology; pathology;
physics; physiology; statistics; taxation;
topographic science; virology; zoology.

**Museum or gallery collection, archive, or library
special collection:**
Blau (200 vols, 16th-century Hebrew books)
Bourgeois (2,000 vols on philology)
Broady and Bisset (2,000 left-wing pamphlets)
Caricatures (3,000 French political caricatures of
the Commune and Franco-Prussian war)
Eadie (8,000 vols of biblical studies and early
printing)
Euing (15,000 vols including 400 black-letter
ballads, 15th- and 16th-century books)
Euing Music (5,300 vols of scores, early printed
music, history of music)
Farmer (the library of Henry George Farmer
comprising 1,600 printed vols and 600 MSs with
special emphasis on oriental and military music)
Ferguson (8,000 vols on alchemy, chemistry,
witchcraft, gypsies and secret societies)
Gemmell (90 vols on the Dance of Death)
Geological Society of Glasgow: foreign periodicals
Hamilton (8,000 vols on philosophy)
Hepburn (300 vols mainly of 19th-century English
literature)
Hunterian (10,000 vols including 534 incunabula,
649 MSs, especially strong in history of medicine
and anatomy)
Institution of Engineers and Shipbuilders in
Scotland: Library
Kelvin (papers relating to Lord Kelvin, William
Thomson)
MacColl (6,000 letters to and from the art critic and
poet, D. S. MacColl)
McGrigor (650 vols and 1,000 pamphlets on
Palestine)
Mearns (3,000 vols on hymnology)
Morgan (papers of the poet, Edwin Morgan)
Munro (300 vols of editions of Sir Thomas Browne)
Murray (15,000 vols on bibliography and history of
the West of Scotland)
Ogilvie (1,700 vols of 17th-century material and
civil war pamphlets)
Robertson (1,000 vols on oriental languages)

Scottish Theatre Archive (playscripts,
programmes, press cuttings, financial records,
photographs, plans, taped interviews and
correspondence)
Simson, Robert, mathematical library (850 vols of
early mathematics and astronomy)
Smith (350 vols mostly of rare Glasgow pamphlets)
Spencer (111 vols of books and MSs relating to the
Darien Scheme)
Stevenson (900 vols on Semitic languages,
literature and archaeology)
Stirling Maxwell (2,000 vols of emblem and fête
books)
Tischendorf (2,500 vols on biblical studies,
codicology and topography from the library of
Konstantin von Tischendorf)
Veitch (600 vols of medieval philosophy)
Walker-Arnott Botanical Collection
Whistler (3,300 vols of letters, MSs and papers of
James McNeill Whistler)
Wright (the papers of Harold Wright, mainly
concerning late 19th- and early 20th-century
British artists and print-makers)
Wylie (1,000 vols on the history and antiquities of
Glasgow)

Non-library collection catalogue:
All or part available online

Library catalogue:
All or part available online

Printed publications:
A guide to the major collections in the Department
of Special Collections
Cell Biology, Molecular Biology and Genetics
Directory of British Government publications in
GUL
Kelvin Papers: Index to the Manuscript Collection
of William Thomson, Baron Kelvin
St Mungo's Bairns – some notable Glasgow
students down the centuries
Starting Research in... (series)
The Book as a Modern Artefact
Whistler, MacColl, Wright: art history papers,
1850–1950, in GUL

Microform publications:
Guardbook catalogue (fiche)
Presentation of Medical and Scientific Theses
According to British Standard 4821:1972 (tape/
slide guide)
Serials list (fiche)

Publications list:
Available in print

Access to staff:
Contact by letter, by telephone, by fax, by e-mail,
in person and via website. Appointment necessary.
Hours: Mon to Fri, 0900 to 1955; Sat, 1300 to 1655

Access to building, collection or gallery:
Hours: Mon to Sun, 0715 to 2000
Special comments: Special Collections: Mon to Fri,
0900 to 1700; Sat, 0900 to 1230

Access for disabled people:
Level entry, access to all public areas, toilet
facilities
Special comments: Emergency egress when lifts not
in use by protected stairwells only. Refuge areas
available on levels 4 to 11

UNIVERSITY OF GLOUCESTERSHIRE

Acronym or abbreviation: UoG

The Park Campus, Cheltenham, Gloucestershire,
GL50 2QF

Tel: 01242 714275

Website:
http://aleph.glos.ac.uk
Online catalogue.
http://www.glos.ac.uk

Enquiries:
Enquiries to: Head of Learning and Information
Services
Direct e-mail: amathie@glos.ac.uk

continued overleaf

Other contacts: Senior Information Adviser (Archives) for access to archive collections.

Founded:
1834

Incorporates the former:
Cheltenham Mechanical Institute (year of change 1834); Gloucester Mechanical Institute (year of change 1840); Church Training College, Cheltenham (year of change 1847); St Paul's College of Education (year of change 1920); St Mary's College of Education (year of change 1920); Gloucestershire College of Education (year of change 1967); College of St Paul and St Mary (year of change 1979); Higher Education Section, Gloucestershire College of Arts and Technology (year of change 1980); Cheltenham and Gloucester College of Higher Education (year of change 1990)

Organisation type and purpose:
University library.
University, providing Foundation degrees, undergraduate and taught postgraduate degrees, research programmes.

Subject coverage:
Advertising; animal biology; animation and interactive media; biology; business and management; creative writing; criminology; digital film; education; English language; English literature; environmental policy and management; film and media; fine art – painting and drawing; geography; graphic design; health studies; history; illustration; IT and computing; journalism; landscape architecture; law; leisure, tourism, hospitality and events management; photography; playwork; popular music; psychology; public relations; publishing; religion, philosophy, ethics; social work; sociology; sports and exercise science; sports development and coaching; teacher training; television and radio production.

Museum or gallery collection, archive, or library special collection:
Bristol and Gloucestershire Archaeological Society Library
College archive, 1840–
Gloucestershire Poets, Writers and Artists collection: Dymock Poets Archive and Study Centre – L. Abercrombie; E. Thomas; R. Frost; W. Gibson; R. Brooke; J. Drinkwater; James Elroy Flecker; Ivor Gurney; W. H. Davies; U. A. Fanthorpe.
Paul Oliver Collection of African-American Music.
Local Heritage Initiative Archive.
History of physical education
Whittington Press – private press, founded 1972

Non-library collection catalogue:
All or part available online

Library catalogue:
All or part available online

Access to staff:
Contact by letter, by telephone, by e-mail, in person and via website. Appointment necessary. Non-members charged.
Hours: Mon to Fri, 0900 to 1700

Access to building, collection or gallery:
Hours: Mon to Fri, 0900 to 1700

Access for disabled people:
Parking provided, ramped entry, toilet facilities

UNIVERSITY OF GREENWICH – INFORMATION SERVICES AND LIBRARY, WOOLWICH CAMPUS/ GREENWICH CAMPUS

Queen Mary Court, Old Royal Naval College, Park Row, Greenwich, London, SE10 9LS

Tel: 020 8331 8000 (switchboard)

Website:
http://www.gre.ac.uk/offices/ils/ls

Enquiries:
Enquiries to: Head of Learning Services
Direct tel: 020 8331 8196
Direct fax: 020 8331 9084

Direct e-mail: a.e.murphy@gre.ac.uk

Founded:
1891

Incorporates the former:
Dartford College of Education (year of change 1972); Avery Hill College (year of change 1985); Garnett College (year of change 1989); Thames College of Health Care Studies, Thames Polytechnic (year of change 1993); Natural Resources Institute (year of change 1996)

Organisation type and purpose:
University library.

Subject coverage:
Architecture and landscape architecture, built environment, civil engineering, surveying, construction management, biology, chemistry, pharmaceutical science, pharmacy, business and management, computing, IT, earth sciences, engineering, environmental sciences, natural resources, humanities, law, mathematics, statistics, education, social sciences, health, sport science, maritime studies.

Museum or gallery collection, archive, or library special collection:
Sidney Keyes Archive
Institutional archives of Woolwich Polytechnic, Thames Polytechnic, Dartford College of Education, Avery Hill College of Education, Garnett College

Library catalogue:
All or part available online

Publications list:
Available online

Access to staff:
Contact by fax, by e-mail and via website. Appointment necessary. Non-members charged.

Access to building, collection or gallery:
Hours: Term time: hours vary across campuses, usually: Mon to Thu, 0830 to 2100; Fri, 0900 to 1700; Sat and Sun, 1100 to 1700; vacation: Mon to Fri, 0900 to 1700; (see website for details)

Access for disabled people:
Parking provided, ramped entry, level entry, toilet facilities

Branch libraries:
University of Greenwich
  Drill Hall Library, North Road, Chatham Maritime, Kent, ME4 4TB; tel: 01634 883278; fax: 01634 883567; e-mail: v.g.malone@gre.ac.uk
University of Greenwich
  Dreadnought Library, Maritime Greenwich Campus, 30 Park Row, Greenwich, London, SE10 9LS; tel: 020 8331 7788; fax: 020 8331 7775; e-mail: t.harland@gre.ac.uk
University of Greenwich
  Avery Hill Campus Library, Bexley Road, London, SE9 2PQ; tel: 020 8331 9656; fax: 020 8331 8756; e-mail: r.m.moon@gre.ac.uk

UNIVERSITY OF GREENWICH – LIBRARY

Central Avenue, Chatham Maritime, Chatham, Kent, ME4 4TB

Tel: 020 8331 9617
Fax: 020 8331 9837
E-mail: info@greenwich.ac.uk

Website:
http://www.gre.ac.uk:8080/www-bin/ www_talis32
Library catalogue.
http://www.greenwich.ac.uk
General university information.

Enquiries:
Enquiries to: Librarian
Direct tel: 01634 883419

Founded:
1894

Formerly called:
Centre of Overseas Pest Research, Land Resources Department, Natural Resources Institute Library, Overseas Development Natural Resources Institute, Tropical Products Institute

Organisation type and purpose:
University library, consultancy, research organisation.
Formerly owned by Department for International Development.
Principal aim is to alleviate poverty and hardship in developing countries by increasing the productivity of their renewable resources.

Subject coverage:
Agriculture including: tropical agriculture, forestry and fisheries, land resource assessment, tropical environment, soil science, pests and pest control, water resources, tropical diseases and vectors of tropical diseases, climatology, use of natural resources in developing countries, geography, geology, environmental sciences, engineering.

Library catalogue:
All or part available online

Printed publications:
A wide range of titles on crops, fisheries, food storage, forestry, land resources, soils and water, livestock etc
Order printed publications from: NRI Catalogue Services, CABI
Wallingford, Oxfordshire, OX10 8DE

Publications list:
Available in print

Access to staff:
Appointment necessary.
Hours: Term time: 0900 to 2100

Headquarters:
University of Greenwich
  Southwood House, Avery Hill Road, Eltham, London, SE9 2UG; tel: 020 8331 8000; fax: 020 8331 8145; e-mail: info@greenwich.ac.uk

UNIVERSITY OF HERTFORDSHIRE

Learning & Information Services, College Lane, Hatfield, Hertfordshire, AL10 9AB

Tel: 01707 284678
Fax: 01707 284670
E-mail: lisadmin@herts.ac.uk

Website:
http://www.herts.ac.uk/lis
http://www.voyager.herts.ac.uk
Collection catalogue
http://www.herts.ac.uk/uhpress
Publication list

Enquiries:
Enquiries to: Dean of Learning & Information Services

Founded:
1952

Formerly called:
Hatfield Polytechnic

Organisation type and purpose:
University library.

Subject coverage:
Accounting, art, biosciences, careers and employment information, computing, design, economics, education, engineering, film and theatre, health, history, law, linguistics, literature, management, marketing, mathematics, midwifery, music, nursing, paramedic sciences, pharmacy, philosophy, physical sciences, physiotherapy, psychology, radiography, social care, social sciences, sports science, technology, tourism

Non-library collection catalogue:
All or part available online

Library catalogue:
All or part available online

Printed publications:
Order printed publications from: UH Press

tel: 01707 284681

Publications list:
Available online and in print

Access to building, collection or gallery:
No prior appointment required
Hours: Mon to Fri, 0830 to 2200; Sat, Sun, 1100 to 1800
Special comments: Visual ID required for issue of Visitors Day Pass.

Access for disabled people:
Parking provided, level entry, toilet facilities

UNIVERSITY OF HUDDERSFIELD – LIBRARY AND COMPUTING CENTRE

Queensgate, Huddersfield, West Yorkshire, HD1 3DH

Tel: 01484 422288
Fax: 01484 517897
E-mail: s.a.white@hud.ac.uk

Website:
http://www.hud.ac.uk/cls
Catalogue and e-resources

Enquiries:
Enquiries to: Head of Library Services
Direct tel: 01484 472784
Other contacts: Director of Computing and Library Services

Founded:
1841

Organisation type and purpose:
University library.

Subject coverage:
Architecture, art and design, drama, English, history, hospitality and logistics, chemistry, computing, education, engineering, law, management, marketing, media, music, paramedical subjects including podiatry, social sciences, social work, teacher training, textiles

Museum or gallery collection, archive, or library special collection:
Colne Valley Constituency Labour Party archives
G. H. Wood Collection (free trade, women's employment, co-operative movement)
Huddersfield Labour Party archives
Huddersfield Mechanics Institute archives
Rugby League archive
Wesley Historical Society (Yorkshire)
Engineering Industry archives

Non-library collection catalogue:
All or part available online

Library catalogue:
All or part available online

Access to staff:
Contact by letter, by telephone, by fax, by e-mail, in person and via website

Access to building, collection or gallery:
Access via Student Centre, 4th Floor, Central Services Building
Hours: Term time: Mon to Thu, 0800 to 2400; Fri, 0800 to 2100; Sat, 0930 to 2100; Sun, 1300 to 2100
Vacations: Mon to Thu, 0845 to 2000; Fri, 0845 to 1700
Special comments: Personal reference use only

Access for disabled people:
Level entry, toilet facilities

UNIVERSITY OF HULL – ACADEMIC SERVICES LIBRARIES

Brynmor Jones Library, Cottingham Road, Hull, East Yorkshire, HU6 7RX

Tel: 01482 466581
Fax: 01482 466205
E-mail: libhelp@hull.ac.uk

Website:
http://www.hull.ac.uk/lib

Enquiries:
Enquiries to: Director of Academic Services and Librarian
Direct tel: 01482 465436
Direct e-mail: r.g.heseltine@hull.ac.uk

Founded:
1927

Organisation type and purpose:
University library.

Subject coverage:
Arts, humanities, social sciences, law, pure sciences, applied physics, electronic engineering, education, health sciences.

Museum or gallery collection, archive, or library special collection:
South-East Asia Collection
Labour history
Contemporary papers of political and social interest
Local archives

Non-library collection catalogue:
All or part available in-house

Library catalogue:
All or part available online

Access to staff:
Contact by letter, by telephone, by fax, by e-mail and via website. Appointment necessary.
Hours: Mon to Fri, 0900 to 1700

Access to building, collection or gallery:
Hours: Mon to Thu, 0830 to 2200; Fri, 0830 to 2100; Sat, 0900 to 2100; Sun, 1300 to 2100 (term-time hours)

Access for disabled people:
Ramped entry, toilet facilities

UNIVERSITY OF KENT – TEMPLEMAN LIBRARY

Canterbury, Kent, CT2 7NU

Tel: 01227 764000
Fax: 01227 823984
E-mail: library-enquiry@ukc.ac.uk

Website:
http://www.library.ukc.ac.uk/library
Library web catalogue.
http://www.library.ukc.ac.uk/librarycollections.htm
Links to special collections, EDC.
http://www.library.ukc.ac.uk/cartoons
Centre for the study of Cartoons and Caricatures (with searchable image database).
http://www.library.ukc.ac.uk/library/bysubject.htm
Library guides by subject.
http://www.library.ukc.ac.uk/special
Weatherill Papers.

Enquiries:
Enquiries to: Director of Information Services and Librarian
Direct tel: 01227 823565
Direct e-mail: m.m.coutts@ukc.ac.uk
Other contacts: Deputy Librarian

Founded:
1963

Organisation type and purpose:
University library.

Subject coverage:
Humanities: drama and theatre studies; English and American literature; history; classical and archaeological studies, comparative literature; Colonial and Post-Colonial studies, Medieval and Tudor studies; American studies; French, German, Italian, Spanish, linguistics and English language; philosophy, theology and religious studies; applied ethics; propaganda; history of science; modern cultural studies; European culture and languages; cartoons and caricature.

Sciences: chemistry; physics; biosciences; biotechnology; space sciences and astrophysics; materials research; medicine and health sciences; psychotherapy; computing; electronics; mathematics and statistics.
Social Sciences: accounting; anthropology; business; economics; law; politics and international relations; psychology; social and public policy; social work; sociology; conservation and ecology; social anthropology and computing; European regional and transport economics; health behaviour; group processes; health services; urban and regional studies; women's studies; geography; European studies.

Museum or gallery collection, archive, or library special collection:
British Chess Federation Library
Cartoons: 20th century cartoons and caricatures
Drama and Theatre:
Frank Pettingell Collection (19th century, texts, mss, playbills)
Melville Collection (1870–1930: typescripts, playbills, theatre records, memorabilia)
Reading-Raynor Collection (texts: biographical, critical, historical)
Richard Fawkes Collection (material on Dion Boucicault)
English Literature:
John Crow Collection
Bonamy Dobree Collection
T S Eliot Collection
Modern Poetry Collection
History of Science:
Maddison Collection of the History of Science
Miscellaneous:
Weatherill Collection (papers of the Speaker of the House of Commons)
C P Davies Wind- and Water-mill Collection
Muggeridge Collection of Windmill Photographs
Lloyd George Collection (signed copies from his library)
European Documentation Centre
Madagascar (formerly SCOLMA SPECIALISATION)
Slide Collection (135,000 slides, chiefly fine arts)
Microfilm Collection:
British Sessional Papers 1801–1969 (microcard)
Landmarks of Science (microcard)
Three Centuries of Drama (microcard)

Non-library collection catalogue:
All or part available online

Library catalogue:
All or part available online

Printed publications:
Centre for the study of Cartoons and Caricatures (see list of publications at website)

Microform publications:
Pettingell (microfilms from Research Publications Inc)

Electronic and video publications:
Cartoons (database at website)
Weatherill Papers (at website)

Publications list:
Available online and in print

Access to staff:
Contact by letter, by telephone, by fax, by e-mail, in person and via website. Appointment necessary. Non-members charged.
Hours: Mon to Fri, 0900 to 1700
Special comments: Limited availability in evenings and at weekends.

Access to building, collection or gallery:
No access other than to staff
Hours: Term time: Mon to Fri, 0845 to 2200; Sat, Sun, 1100 to 2200
Vacations: Mon to Fri, 0900 to 1900; Sat, 1100 to 1900; Sun, closed

Access for disabled people:
Level entry, access to all public areas, toilet facilities

UNIVERSITY OF LEEDS – BRETTON HALL CAMPUS LIBRARY

West Bretton, Wakefield, West Yorkshire, WF4 4LG

Tel: 01924 830261
Fax: 01924 832077
E-mail: library@library.leeds.ac.uk

Website:
http://www.leeds.ac.uk
All college information.
http://www.bretton.ac.uk/library/front.htm
Library's web pages with FAQs, virtual tour,
services and OPAC.

Enquiries:
Enquiries to: Librarian
Other contacts: Assistant Archivist for National Arts
Education Archive.

Organisation type and purpose:
University department or institute, suitable for
ages: 18+.

Subject coverage:
Education, visual and performing arts, arts
education.

Access to staff:
Contact by letter, by telephone, by fax and by e-
mail. Appointment necessary.
Hours: Term time: Mon to Thu, 0830 to 1700 (self-
service to 2100); Fri, 0830 to 1700; Sat, 0900 to 1700
(self-service only)
Vacations; Mon to Fri, 0900 to 1700

UNIVERSITY OF LEEDS – DEPARTMENT OF ARABIC AND MIDDLE EASTERN STUDIES

Leeds, West Yorkshire, LS2 9JT

Tel: 0113 343 3421
Fax: 0113 343 3517
E-mail: a.spellman@leeds.ac.uk

Enquiries:
Enquiries to: Secretary

Organisation type and purpose:
University department.

Subject coverage:
Arabic language; Islamic religion and culture;
Mediterranean studies and culture.

Printed publications:
Middle East Sources (Netton I R, available via
publisher Curzon Press)

Access to staff:
Contact by letter, by telephone, by fax and by e-
mail
Hours: Mon to Fri, 0900 to 1700

UNIVERSITY OF LEEDS – EDUCATION COLLECTION

University Library, Leeds, West Yorkshire, LS2 9JT

Tel: 0113 233 5517
Fax: 0113 233 5539
E-mail: libjms@library.novell.leeds.ac.uk

Website:
http://www.leeds.ac.uk/library/library.html
Information on all the university's libraries.

Enquiries:
Enquiries to: Assistant Librarian

Organisation type and purpose:
University library.

Subject coverage:
Education, psychology, teaching methods of
curricular subjects.

**Museum or gallery collection, archive, or library
special collection:**
W B Thompson Collection of Greek and Latin
school textbooks
Historical collection of biology school textbooks

19th century educational sources and texts

Printed publications:
British Education Index, (annually from 1986,
contact British Education Index at this address)
British Education Thesaurus (1st ed., 1988, 2nd ed.,
1991, contact British Education Index at this
address)
Improved Visibility: an international bibliography
on the education of women and girls 1978–1989
(LISE Publications 1991 £8)

Electronic and video publications:
International Eric CD-ROM (contact British
Education Index at this address)

Access to staff:
Contact by letter and by e-mail. Appointment
necessary.
Hours: Mon to Fri, 0900 to 1700

UNIVERSITY OF LEEDS – UNIVERSITY LIBRARY

Leeds, West Yorkshire, LS2 9JT

Tel: 0113 343 5501
Fax: 0113 343 3556
E-mail: library@library.novell.leeds.ac.uk

Website:
http://www.leeds.ac.uk/library/spcoll/
Information on special collections.
http://www.leeds.ac.uk/library/library.html
Information on library services, contacts, holdings.

Enquiries:
Enquiries to: Librarian
Direct tel: 0113 343 5663

Founded:
1874

Organisation type and purpose:
University library.

Subject coverage:
Agriculture; Arabic; architecture; astronomy;
bibliography; biology; biophysics; botany;
ceramics; chemical engineering and technology;
chemistry; China and Chinese studies; civil
engineering; classical studies; dentistry; dyes and
dyeing; economics; education; electrical
engineering; engineering in general; English; food
science and technology; French; fuels and fuel
technology; geography and topography; geology;
German; history; Italian; law; leather and
leatherwork; linguistics; mathematics; mechanical
engineering; medicine; metallurgy; meteorology;
mines and mining; music; numismatics;
palaeontology; philosophy; physics; politics;
Portuguese; psychology; Russian; science;
seismology; Semitics; Slavonic studies; social
sciences; Spanish; technology in general; textiles;
theology; translations; transport; Yorkshire;
zoology.
Law Library: English, European, Commonwealth
and American Law, criminology, police studies.

**Museum or gallery collection, archive, or library
special collection:**
All Souls' College and Chaston Chapman
Collections of early science
Anglo-French Collection (French books reflecting
the influence of Great Britain on France to 1850)
Blanche Leigh, J F Preston and Camden Collections
(historical books on cookery and domestic
management)
Brotherton Collection (rare books and MSS,
especially on English literature of the 17th, 18th
and 19th centuries and on Romany literature)
Business archives of the West Yorkshire wool
textile industry (18th to 20th centuries)
European Documentation Centre
Icelandic Collection
Leeds and West Riding Medico-Chirurgical Society
Collection
Leeds Philosophical and Literary Society Library
Leeds Russian Archive (literary and historical
MSS)
Liddle Collection of First World War archive
materials

Medical classics, originally of the library of the old
Infirmary
19th and 20th century educational sources, texts
and archives
Quaker literature
Ripon Cathedral Library, and archives of the Dean
and Chapter
Roth Collection of Judaica
W B Thompson Collection of Greek and Latin
school textbooks
Wentworth-Woolley Hall estate papers (16th to
20th centuries)
Whitaker Collection of Atlases (mainly of the
British Isles)
Yorkshire Geological Society Library
Yorkshire Quaker Archives (17th to 20th centuries)

Non-library collection catalogue:
All or part available online and in print

Library catalogue:
All or part available online

Printed publications:
The Brotherton Collection, University of Leeds; its
contents described with illustrations of fifty
books and manuscripts (£20)
Current periodicals in the University Libraries
Duplicated handlists of many of the Special
Collections
German literature printed in the 17th and 18th
centuries
Icelandic Collection
Printed catalogues of some of the collections

Electronic and video publications:
British Education Index

Publications list:
Available in print

Access to staff:
Contact by letter. Non-members charged.
Hours: Mon to Fri, 0900 to 1700

Access for disabled people:
Access to all public areas

UNIVERSITY OF LEICESTER – CLINICAL SCIENCES LIBRARY

Robert Kilpatrick Clinical Sciences Building, PO
Box 65, Leicester Royal Infirmary, Leicester, LE2
7LX

Tel: 0116 252 3104
Fax: 0116 252 3107
E-mail: clinlib@leicester.ac.uk

Website:
http://www.le.ac.uk/library/clinical/clinlib.htm

Enquiries:
Enquiries to: Clinical Sciences Librarian
Direct tel: 0116 252 3100
Direct e-mail: jd1@leicester.ac.uk

Founded:
1978

Organisation type and purpose:
University library.
Hospital library of the Medical School of the
University of Leicester.

Subject coverage:
Medicine, health, nursing, midwifery and
professions allied to medicine and social care

Non-library collection catalogue:
All or part available online

Library catalogue:
All or part available online

Access to staff:
Contact by letter, by telephone, by fax, by e-mail,
in person and via website. Appointment necessary.
Hours: Mon to Fri, 0900 to 2100; Sat, 0900 to 1800;
Sun, 1400 to 1800

Access to building, collection or gallery:
No prior appointment required
Hours: 24-hour access

Special comments: Outside of staffed hours, access for University of Leicester staff and students, and NHS staff only

Access for disabled people:
Level entry, access to all public areas, toilet facilities

Links with:
other hospital libraries in the region

UNIVERSITY OF LEICESTER – EDUCATION LIBRARY

21 University Road, Leicester, LE1 7RF

Tel: 0116 252 3739
Fax: 0116 252 3653
E-mail: edlib@leicester.ac.uk

Website:
http://www.le.ac.uk/library/

Enquiries:
Enquiries to: Librarian

Founded:
1949

Organisation type and purpose:
University library.

Subject coverage:
Initial teacher training; education theory; primary, secondary school and further education levels.

Museum or gallery collection, archive, or library special collection:
19th century children's fiction and school primers Resource Collection

Access to staff:
Contact by letter, by telephone, by fax, by e-mail and in person
Hours: Term time: Sep to Jun: Mon to Thu, 0900 to 2100; Fri, Sat, 0900 to 1700
Vacations: Jul to Aug: Mon to Fri, 0900 to 1700

Affiliated to:
Libraries of Institutes and Schools of Education

UNIVERSITY OF LEICESTER – MAIN LIBRARY

Box 248, University Road, Leicester, LE1 9QD

Tel: 0116 252 2043
Fax: 0116 252 2066
E-mail: libdesk@le.ac.uk

Website:
http://www.le.ac.uk/library/

Enquiries:
Enquiries to: Enquiry service
Direct tel: 0116 252 2043

Organisation type and purpose:
University library.

Subject coverage:
Archaeology; art history; astronomy; biological sciences; chemistry; computing; economic and social history; economics; engineering; English; French; genetics; geography; geology; German; history; Italian; law; local history; management; mass communications; mathematics; microbiology; museum studies; physics; politics; pre-clinical medicine; psychology; social work; sociology; zoology.

Museum or gallery collection, archive, or library special collection:
Burrows Collection (20th Century music)
English local history
European documentation
Fairclough Collection (17th century)
Leicester Medical Society
Mathematical Association Library
Orton Papers

Non-library collection catalogue:
All or part available online

Library catalogue:
All or part available online

Access to staff:
Contact by letter, by telephone, by fax, by e-mail, in person and via website. Appointment necessary. Letter of introduction required. Non-members charged.
Hours: Sep to Jun: Mon to Fri, 0900 to 2100; Sat, 0900 to 1700; Sun, 1200 to 1800
Jul and Aug: Mon to Fri, 0900 to 1700; Sat 0900 to 1700

Access to building, collection or gallery:
Hours: Sep to Jun: Mon to Fri, 0800 to 0000; Sat, Sun, 0900 to 0000
Jul and Aug: Mon to Fri, 0900 to 1730; Sat 0900 to 1800

Branch library:
Clinical Sciences Library
School of Education Library

UNIVERSITY OF LINCOLN, UNIVERSITY LIBRARY

Brayford Pool, Lincoln, LN6 7TS

Tel: 01522 886664
Fax: 01522 886311
E-mail: acquisitions@lincoln.ac.uk

Website:
http://www.lincoln.ac.uk

Enquiries:
Enquiries to: Head of Library and Learning Resources
Direct tel: 01522 886310
Direct e-mail: manderson@lincoln.ac.uk

Formerly called:
University of Lincolnshire and Humberside

Organisation type and purpose:
University library.

Subject coverage:
Accountancy, architecture, art and design, building, business, communications, criminology, design, economics, electrical engineering, English, environment, film, finance, food management, history, housing, humanities, languages, law, literature, management, marketing, media studies, photography, politics, printing, printmaking, psychology, radio, social policy, social science, social work, sociology, statistics and tourism.

Access to staff:
Contact via website

Member organisation of:
UK Libraries Plus

UNIVERSITY OF LIVERPOOL – UNIVERSITY LIBRARY

PO Box 123, Liverpool, L69 3DA

Tel: 0151 794 2674
Fax: 0151 794 2681

Website:
http://www.liv.ac.uk/library

Enquiries:
Enquiries to: Librarian
Direct tel: 0151 794 2673
Other contacts: Head of Special Collections and Archives

Organisation type and purpose:
University library.

Subject coverage:
The main holdings in humanities, social sciences and special collections are housed in the Sydney Jones Library; those in science, medicine, engineering, veterinary and dental science and archives are in the Harold Cohen Library; there are departmental libraries in education, law, archaeology, chemistry, civic design, continuing education, geology, music, oceanography, physics, marine biology (Port Erin, Isle of Man), veterinary science (Leahurst, Wirral).

Museum or gallery collection, archive, or library special collection:
Blake Collection (items by and about William Blake)
Brunner Papers (letter-books, accounts, diaries, etc. of Sir John Brunner, 1842–1919, including material on chemical industry)
Campbell Brown Collection (414 books of the 16th-19th centuries, on alchemy and chemistry)
Comte Collection (Positivism)
Fraser Collection (includes about 900 items on tobacco art, English literature, Scottish books, positivism, phrenology, some manuscript material)
Grace Collection (158 books on mathematics, printed 17th-19th centuries)
Manuscript collections of Joseph Blanco White, Charles Booth, John and Katharine Bruce Glasier, Josephine Butler
Noble Collection (fine printed and limited editions of English books of the late 19th and early 20th centuries and many examples of the private presses)
Peers Collection (Spanish Civil War)
Rathbone Papers (family and business papers of the Rathbones, Greenbank, Liverpool, 18th-20th centuries)
Rendall Collection (a. Marcus Aurelius; b. Shakespeare controversy)
Robert Graves Collection
Salisbury Collection (340 scientific books of the 19th century, mostly English)
Science Fiction Foundation Collection (books and magazines of science fiction and fantasy, including critical works and journals. Much foreign-language material, including the Myers Collection of Russian SF; manuscript and archive material of a number of SF writers; pseudo-science material including the Flat Earth Society Papers. c. 25,000 items)
Scott-MacFie Collection (works on Romany and Gypsy lore, books, manuscripts, broadsides, prints, photographs, sheet music, records and tape)
Simey Collection (women in society)
Stapledon Collection (philosophy and science fiction)
Merseyside Poets Collection (manuscripts, first drafts)
Thomson Collection (114 bound volumes of c. 1200 English pamphlets, 1689–1789)
Un-named collections on the history of medicine, 19th century documents of the US Congress, Latin American topography, selected modern poets
Whale Collection (309 books and pamphlets of the 19th-20th centuries on finance and banking)

Library catalogue:
All or part available online

Printed publications:
User guides to main libraries

Access to staff:
Contact by letter, by telephone, by e-mail and in person
Hours: Special collections and archives, Mon to Fri, 0930 to 1645
Special comments: Visitors by appointment for special collections and archives.

Access for disabled people:
Ramped entry, access to all public areas, toilet facilities

UNIVERSITY OF LONDON – GERMANIC STUDIES LIBRARY

29 Russell Square, London, WC1B 5DP

Tel: 020 7862 8967
Fax: 020 7862 8970
E-mail: igslib@sas.ac.uk

Enquiries:
Enquiries to: Librarian

Founded:
1950

continued overleaf

Organisation type and purpose:
University library.

Subject coverage:
German language and literature of all periods (including Austria and Switzerland).

Museum or gallery collection, archive, or library special collection:
Friedrich Gundolf Archive
Lexicography, dialect dictionaries and grammars
Priebsch-Closs Collection (first and early edns of 18th- and early 19th-century authors)
Reference library of some 100,000 vols and 300 current periodicals

Library catalogue:
All or part available online

Access to staff:
Contact by letter, by telephone, by fax, by e-mail and in person
Hours: Mon to Fri, 0945 to 1730

Access to building, collection or gallery:
Hours: Mon to Fri, 0945 to 1745

Constituent part of:
University of London Research Library Services

UNIVERSITY OF LONDON – INTERNATIONAL SCHOOL EFFECTIVENESS AND IMPROVEMENT CENTRE

Acronym or abbreviation: ISEIC

Institute of Education, 20 Bedford Way, London, WC1H 0AL

Tel: 020 7612 6347/6323/6409
Fax: 020 7612 6344
E-mail: iseic.admin@ioe.ac.uk

Website:
http://www.ioe.ac.uk/iseic

Enquiries:
Enquiries to: Administrator

Founded:
1994

Organisation type and purpose:
Membership association (membership is by subscription), present number of members: 1100, university department or institute, research organisation.
Research and consultancy.

Subject coverage:
ISEIC brings together academics and professionals involved in research and development work in the fields of school effectiveness and improvement. It engages in consultancy work for LEAs and schools, and runs NSIN, the National School Improvement Network.

Printed publications:
Research Matters Series
NSIN Newsletter
Books and articles on school effectiveness and improvement topics

Publications list:
Available online and in print

Access to staff:
Contact by telephone, by fax and by e-mail. Non-members charged.
Hours: Mon to Fri, 0900 to 1700

Subsidiary body:
National School Improvement Network (NSIN) at the same address

UNIVERSITY OF NORTHAMPTON

Park Campus, Boughton Green Road, Northampton, NN2 7AL

Tel: 01604 735500
Fax: 01604 718819

Website:
http://library.northampton.ac.uk

Enquiries:
Enquiries to: Director of Information Services
Direct tel: 01604 892045
Direct e-mail: Hilary.Johnson@northampton.ac.uk

Organisation type and purpose:
University .

Subject coverage:
Whole range of social sciences and humanities, education, history of Northamptonshire, American studies, health studies, nursing, leather technology, waste management.

Museum or gallery collection, archive, or library special collection:
Collection of the National Leathersellers Centre
Osborne Robinson Collection of posters (1890 onwards) (School of Art and Design)
AEA Technology Wastes Management Collection

Library catalogue:
All or part available online

Access to staff:
Contact by letter, by telephone, by fax and by e-mail. Appointment necessary.
Hours: Term time: Mon to Fri, 0830 to 2200; Sat, 1000 to 1700; Sun, 1300 to 1700

Access for disabled people:
Access to all public areas, toilet facilities

Other address:
Avenue Campus
St George's Avenue, Northampton, NN2 6JD

UNIVERSITY OF NOTTINGHAM – DJANOGLY LEARNING RESOURCE CENTRE

Jubilee Campus, Nottingham, NG8 1BB

Website:
http://www.nottingham.ac.uk/library

Organisation type and purpose:
University library.

Subject coverage:
Business, education, computer studies.

UNIVERSITY OF NOTTINGHAM – GEORGE GREEN LIBRARY OF SCIENCE AND ENGINEERING

University Park, Nottingham, NG7 2RD

Tel: 0115 951 4570
Fax: 0115 951 4578

Website:
http://www.nottingham.ac.uk/library/
List of staff contacts.

Enquiries:
Enquiries to: Librarian
Direct tel: 0115 951 4572

Organisation type and purpose:
Constituent part of the University library.

Subject coverage:
Botany; chemical engineering; chemistry; civil engineering; computer science; electrical and electronic engineering; geology; manufacturing engineering; materials science; mathematics; mechanical engineering; metallurgy; mineral resources engineering; pharmacy; physics; psychology; remote sensing; theoretical mechanics; zoology.

Museum or gallery collection, archive, or library special collection:
British Standards
Porter Collection (on ornithology)

Trade and statistical information:
International metal statistics.

Branch library:
Nottingham University
Chemistry Library

UNIVERSITY OF NOTTINGHAM – GREENFIELD MEDICAL LIBRARY

Queen's Medical Centre, Nottingham, NG7 2UH

Tel: 0115 970 9441
Fax: 0115 970 9449
E-mail: library-medical-enquiries@nottingham.ac.uk

Website:
http://www.nottingham.ac.uk/is/locations/library/greenfield

Enquiries:
Enquiries to: Medical Librarian
Direct e-mail: wendy.stanton@nottingham.ac.uk

Founded:
1968

Organisation type and purpose:
University library.

Subject coverage:
Biochemistry; child health; community health; human anatomy; genetics; medicine; obstetrics and gynaecology; nursing; midwifery; pathology; physiology; pharmacology; psychiatry; surgery; therapeutics; anaesthetics; chemical pathology; chest medicine; dermatology; geriatrics; haematology; histopathology; learning disabilities; neurology; ophthalmology; paediatrics; radiology; rheumatology.

Museum or gallery collection, archive, or library special collection:
F H Jacob History of Medicine Collection

Library catalogue:
All or part available online

Access to staff:
Contact by letter, by telephone, by fax, by e-mail, in person and via website. Non-members charged.
Hours: Mon to Fri, 0800 to 2300

Access for disabled people:
Ramped entry, toilet facilities

Other affiliated libraries:
School of Nursing Library
Mansfield
School of Nursing Library
Derby

Serves the:
Nottingham University
Faculty of Medicine and Health Sciences
University Hospital NHS Trust
Queens Medical Centre

UNIVERSITY OF NOTTINGHAM – HALLWARD LIBRARY

University Park, Nottingham, NG7 2RD

Tel: 0115 951 4557
Fax: 0115 951 4558

Website:
http://www.nottingham.ac.uk/library

Enquiries:
Enquiries to: Librarian

Organisation type and purpose:
University library.

Subject coverage:
American studies (literature and history), archaeology, architecture, art history, child development, classics, economic, industrial and social history, economics, education, including adult education, educational psychology, English language and literature, film and cinema, French language and literature, geography, German language and literature, Hispanic studies (Spanish, Catalan, Portuguese), history, insurance, local government and administration, management, money and banking, music, philosophy; planning and development, politics, Slavonic studies, including Russian, Yugoslav, Serbian, Croatian and Slovene; social administration, social work, sociology, textile history, theology, trade unions and Viking studies.

Museum or gallery collection, archive, or library special collection:
Archive of newspaper cuttings (approximately 750,000 cuttings) relating to the politics, social, economic and cultural conditions in Germany (especially East Germany) 1946–1981
Holdings from former East German library (Diesdorf, Magdeburg)
Mellish Collection (meteorology)
Waldheim: A Commission of Enquiry – documentary research material collected by Thames Television for a television programme June 1988
Large collection of microforms, mainly in the arts and humanities
Large collection of CD-ROMs

Trade and statistical information:
Large collection of UK government and international statistics.

Library catalogue:
All or part available online

Printed publications:
Introductory guide and index to archive of newspaper cuttings

Microform publications:
Large numbers mainly in the arts and humanities

Electronic and video publications:
Large collection of CD-ROMs and web-based products

Branch library of:
Nottingham University
Music Library

UNIVERSITY OF NOTTINGHAM – JAMES CAMERON GIFFORD LIBRARY

Sutton Bonington Campus, Loughborough, Leicestershire, LE12 5RD

Tel: 0115 951 6390
Fax: 0115 951 6389
E-mail: suzanna.rogers@nottingham.ac.uk

Website:
http://www.nottingham.ac.uk/is

Enquiries:
Enquiries to: Librarian
Direct e-mail: library-biosciences-enquiries@nottingham.ac.uk

Organisation type and purpose:
University library.

Subject coverage:
Agriculture, horticulture, farm management, food science and microbiology, animal and plant biochemistry and physiology, environmental biology, soil science, applied biology, animal production, nutrition and dietetics, veterinary medicine and science.

Library catalogue:
All or part available online

Printed publications:
Guides to services and resources

Publications list:
Available online

Access to staff:
Contact by letter and by e-mail
Hours: Mon to Fri, 0900 to 1700

Constituent part of:
University of Nottingham Information Services

UNIVERSITY OF NOTTINGHAM – MANUSCRIPTS AND SPECIAL COLLECTIONS

King's Meadow Campus, Lenton Lane, Nottingham, NG7 2NR

Tel: 0115 951 4565
Fax: 0115 8468651
E-mail: mss-library@nottingham.ac.uk

Website:
http://www.nottingham.ac.uk/mss
Reader services, including opening hours, manuscripts and special collections, holdings descriptions, catalogues, online resources, e-learning and skills resources.

Enquiries:
Enquiries to: Keeper of Manuscripts and Special Collections

Organisation type and purpose:
University library.

Museum or gallery collection, archive, or library special collection:
Manuscript and Archive Collections:
Includes local ecclesiastical, industrial and trade union collections, substantial collections of local family papers, records of the Severn-Trent Water Authority and its forerunners from the 17th century; records of the General Hospital and other Nottingham hospitals
Manuscript collections in Restoration verse, William of Orange and the 1688 Revolution, the Jacobite Rising of 1745, the American War of Independence, the Peninsular War, the Crimean War, 18th- and 19th-century British and Irish politics and foreign affairs, India of the early 19th century, British colonies of the mid-19th century, history of nonconformity, draining of the Fens, the 17th-century naturalists John Ray and Francis Willoughby
D. H. Lawrence Collection (literary papers, books)
Germany 1946–1981: Archive of Newspaper Cuttings (in German)
Mellish Collection (meteorological papers)
Printed Books Collections:
Benedikz Collection (Icelandic literature, mainly in Icelandic)
Briggs Collection (educational books before 1851)
Cambridge Drama Collection (English plays 1750–1850)
Cambridge Shakespeare Collection (edns of Shakespeare's plays)
East Midlands Collection (Derbyshire, Leicestershire, Lincolnshire, Nottinghamshire, Rutland)
F. H. Jacob History of Medicine Collection
French Revolution Collection
Nottingham Medico-Chirurgical Society Collection
Oakham and Elston Parochial Libraries (17th century)
Parker Woodward Collection (on the Bacon-Shakespeare controversy)

Non-library collection catalogue:
All or part available online

Library catalogue:
All or part available online

Printed publications:
Archives Teaching Units, based on the manuscript collections
Catalogues of the Manuscripts Collections
Children in War: Reminiscences of the Second World War
D. H. Lawrence Exhibition Catalogues (1980 and 1985)
Politics and Society in Germany, Austria and Switzerland (vols 2 to 5)
Mender of disorders: court and community in the Archdeaconry of Nottingham, 1560–1756 (Kate Holland, ed., 2004)

Microform publications:
Soviet War Posters, c.1940–1945
The Tass Poster Series from the Hallward Library, University of Nottingham
Guide with fiche/film (1992, Adam Matthew Publications)

Electronic and video publications:
D. H. Lawrence at the University of Nottingham (DVD, video, 2003)

Publications list:
Available online

Access to staff:
Contact by letter, by telephone, by fax, by e-mail

and via website. Appointment necessary.
Hours: Mon to Fri, 0900 to 1700
Special comments: Reader card issued at the discretion of the Keeper.

UNIVERSITY OF OXFORD – BALFOUR LIBRARY (PITT RIVERS MUSEUM)

School of Anthropology and Museum Ethnography, South Parks Road, Oxford, OX1 3PP

Tel: 01865 270928
Fax: 01865 270943
E-mail: librarian@prm.ox.ac.uk

Website:
http://www.lib.ox.ac.uk/olis
OLIS, union catalogue
http://www.prm.ox.ac.uk

Enquiries:
Enquiries to: Librarian
Direct tel: 01865 270939
Direct e-mail: library@prm.ox.ac.uk
Other contacts: Director of the Museum

Founded:
1882

Organisation type and purpose:
Museum, university library, suitable for ages: 18+.

Subject coverage:
Anthropology, ethnology, prehistoric archaeology, material culture, museum studies, ethnomusicology, visual anthropology (including ethnographic film and photography), ethnographic art.

Museum or gallery collection, archive, or library special collection:
Books owned by Henry Balfour, first curator of the Museum, and General Pitt Rivers (incomplete)
Collection of over 100,000 anthropological photographs from c.1850 onwards
Collections of papers of Henry Balfour, E. B. Tyler, W. Baldwin Spencer and others who have made important contributions to the history of anthropology and archaeology (separate Manuscript and Photographic Archive – see website)
Ellen Ettlinger Bequest of books on folklore
June Bedford collection of books on ethnographic art

Non-library collection catalogue:
All or part available online

Library catalogue:
All or part available online and in-house

Printed publications:
Annual Report
Catalogue of the Australian Collections
Catalogue of the Native American Collection
Monograph series
Occasional papers on technology, archaeology, miscellaneous publications
The Origin and Development of the Pitt Museum

Publications list:
Available online and in print

Access to staff:
Contact by letter, by telephone, by fax and by e-mail. Appointment necessary.
Hours: Vacations: 0900 to 1230 and 1400 to 1600; closed August
For Christmas and Easter hours, please phone or e-mail
Special comments: Reference only for non-members of the University.

Access for disabled people:
Parking provided

Links with:
Institute of Social and Cultural Anthropology
Tylor Library, University of Oxford

UNIVERSITY OF OXFORD – COMPUTING LABORATORY

The Library, Wolfson Building, Parks Road, Oxford, OX1 3QD

Tel: 01865 273838
Fax: 01865 273839
E-mail: library@comlab.ox.ac.uk

Website:
http://www.comlab.ox.ac.uk/
Information about courses, research and personnel with links to other parts and Oxford University.

Enquiries:
Enquiries to: Librarian
Direct tel: 01865 273837
Direct e-mail: Gordon.Riddell@comlab.ox.ac.uk

Organisation type and purpose:
University department or institute, research organisation.

Subject coverage:
Scientific computation including formal methods, numerical analysis and computational fluid dynamics, and general computing science.

Library catalogue:
All or part available online

Printed publications:
PRG Research Reports

Access to staff:
Appointment necessary.
Hours: Mon to Fri, 0900 to 1700

Subsidiary body:
Centre for Requirements and Foundations
Numerical Analysis Group (NAGp)
Programming Research Group (PRG)

UNIVERSITY OF OXFORD – DEPARTMENT OF EARTH SCIENCES

Parks Road, Oxford, OX1 3PR

Tel: 01865 272000
Fax: 01865 272072
E-mail: jennyc@earth.ox.ac.uk

Enquiries:
Enquiries to: Librarian
Direct tel: 01865 272050

Organisation type and purpose:
University department or institute.

Subject coverage:
Earth sciences; geology; geodesy; mineralogy; geochemistry; geophysics; oceanography; stratigraphy; tectonics; crystallography; petrology; sedimentology.

Museum or gallery collection, archive, or library special collection:
Collection of reprints
Wager, Lawrence Rickard (1904–1965) collection

Access to staff:
Contact by letter, by telephone, by fax and by e-mail. Appointment necessary. Letter of introduction required.
Hours: Term time; Mon to Thu, 0900 to 1730; Fri, 0900 to 1630
Vacations; Mon to Thu, 0900 to 1730

Access to building, collection or gallery:
No prior appointment required
Special comments: Bodleian Readers Card required

Access for disabled people:
Toilet facilities
Special comments: One step at entrance

UNIVERSITY OF OXFORD – DEPARTMENT OF EDUCATION LIBRARY

Acronym or abbreviation: OUDE-L

15 Norham Gardens, Oxford, OX2 6PY

Tel: 01865 274028
Fax: 01865 274027
E-mail: kate.williams@education.ox.ac.uk

Website:
http://www.education.ox.ac.uk/library

Enquiries:
Enquiries to: Librarian
Direct e-mail: library@education.ox.ac.uk

Formerly called:
Department of Educational Studies Library (year of change 2007)

Organisation type and purpose:
University department or institute.

Subject coverage:
Education; educational psychology; sociology of education; applied social sciences; methodology of teaching of subjects in the secondary school curriculum.

Museum or gallery collection, archive, or library special collection:
Histories of individual schools and universities
Pre-1918 government publications on education

Library catalogue:
All or part available online

Access to staff:
Contact by letter, by telephone, by fax and by e-mail
Hours: Termtime: Mon to Thu, 0845 to 2030; Fri, 0845 to 1900; Sat, 1300 to 1700; Sun, 1200 to 1600
Vacation: Mon to Thu, 0900 to 1730; Fri, 0900 to 1700

Access to building, collection or gallery:
Prior appointment required

Access for disabled people:
Parking provided
Special comments: Steps are a big problem for mobility impaired at present.

UNIVERSITY OF OXFORD – DEPARTMENT OF PHYSICS

Denys Wilkinson Building, Keble Road, Oxford, OX1 3RH

Tel: 01865 273333
Fax: 01865 273418

Website:
http://www2.physics.ox.ac.uk/library/default.asp

Enquiries:
Enquiries to: Librarian
Direct tel: 01865 273421
Direct e-mail: library@physics.ox.ac.uk

Organisation type and purpose:
University department or institute.

Subject coverage:
Theoretical and observational cosmology, galactic astronomy, stellar and interstellar physics, telescopes and instrumentation, nuclear physics, particle physics.

Museum or gallery collection, archive, or library special collection:
Astronomical library (not open to the public)

Library catalogue:
All or part available in-house

Publications list:
Available in print

Access to staff:
Access for members only.
Hours: Mon to Fri, 1400 to 1700

Access to building, collection or gallery:
No access other than to staff

Access for disabled people:
Level entry, access to all public areas, toilet facilities

UNIVERSITY OF OXFORD – ENGINEERING SCIENCE LIBRARY

Department of Engineering Science, Parks Road, Oxford, OX1 3PJ

Tel: 01865 273193
Fax: 01865 273010
E-mail: library@eng.ox.ac.uk

Website:
http://www.eng.ox.ac.uk/home.html
General information on department and its research.

Enquiries:
Enquiries to: Librarian
Direct e-mail: anne.greig@eng.ox.ac.uk

Organisation type and purpose:
University department or institute.

Subject coverage:
Engineering.

Printed publications:
OUEL Reports (Departmental reports)
Annual summaries of current research projects

Access to staff:
Contact by letter, by telephone and by e-mail.
Appointment necessary.
Hours: Mon to Fri, 0900 to 1700

Parent body:
Oxford University

UNIVERSITY OF OXFORD – ENGLISH FACULTY LIBRARY

St Cross Building, Manor Road, Oxford, OX1 3UQ

Tel: 01865 271050
Fax: 01865 271054

Website:
http://www.lib.ox.ac.uk
Oxford University libraries home page.
http://users.ox.ac.uk/~enginfo/
Library home page.

Enquiries:
Enquiries to: Librarian
Direct tel: 01865 271051
Direct e-mail: susan.usher@efl.ox.ac.uk

Founded:
1914

Organisation type and purpose:
University library.

Subject coverage:
English language and literature; Old Norse language and literature.

Museum or gallery collection, archive, or library special collection:
E H W Meyerstein's published books and manuscripts
Old Norse: working libraries of E O G Turville-Petre, W P Ker, G Vigfússon, and F York Powell (the last two on loan from Christ Church)
Wilfred Owen Collection (his library, some manuscripts and memorabilia)

Access to staff:
Contact by letter, by telephone, by fax and by e-mail. Appointment necessary.
Hours: Termtime: Mon to Fri, 0930 to 1900, Sat 0930 to 1230
Vacations: Mon to Fri, 0930 to 1700
Special comments: Visitors from other academic institutions may normally use the library for reference purposes in the vacations only.

Access for disabled people:
Parking provided, ramped entry, level entry, access to all public areas, toilet facilities

UNIVERSITY OF OXFORD – MODERN LANGUAGES FACULTY LIBRARY

Taylor Institution, St Giles, Oxford, OX1 3NA

Tel: 01865 278152
E-mail: library@modern-languages-library.oxford
.ac.uk

Website:
http://www.ox.ac.uk
Oxford University home page.
http://users.ox.ac.uk/~mlflinfo/index.html
Home page – some details of publications and
information, including classification, layout and
services; it also links to other web pages of interest
to modern linguists.
http://www.lib.ox.ac.uk
Oxford University libraries home page.

Enquiries:
Enquiries to: Librarian
Direct tel: 01865 278155
Direct e-mail: gordon.robson@mlfl.ox.ac.uk
Other contacts: Deputy Librarian for Spanish and
Portuguese.

Founded:
1960

Organisation type and purpose:
University department or institute.

Subject coverage:
Modern European languages and literature;
general linguistics, German, French, Italian,
Spanish, Portuguese, Latin American, Catalan,
Occitan; European cinema.

**Museum or gallery collection, archive, or library
special collection:**
Collection of European Newspapers (in original
form). This collection is to be disposed of owing
to lack of space. Any request from libraries for
any part of it will be welcome.
Recordings on audio and video cassette of
European literary, historical and cultural works,
and cinema

Non-library collection catalogue:
All or part available online

Library catalogue:
All or part available online

Printed publications:
Library Rules and Information

Access to staff:
Contact by letter, by telephone, by e-mail and in
person. Letter of introduction required.
Hours: Term time: Mon to Fri, 0900 to 1800
Vacations: 0900 to 1300 and 1400 to 1730
Summer: 0900 to 1300 and 1400 to 1700

UNIVERSITY OF OXFORD –
MUSIC FACULTY LIBRARY

St Aldate's, Oxford, OX1 1DB

Tel: 01865 276148
Fax: 01865 286260
E-mail: library@music.ox.ac.uk

Website:
http://www.bodley.ox.ac.uk/oxlip
Catalogue of library holdings
http://www.music.ox.ac.uk/library

Enquiries:
Enquiries to: Librarian

Founded:
c.1950

Organisation type and purpose:
University library.

Subject coverage:
Music (western classical tradition).

**Museum or gallery collection, archive, or library
special collection:**
Byzantine music
Flute music
Howes folk music collection
Music from the Oxford University Music Society
Library

Non-library collection catalogue:
All or part available online

Library catalogue:
All or part available online and in-house

Printed publications:
Library guide (free)

Access to staff:
Contact by telephone, by e-mail and in person
Hours: Term time: Mon to Fri, 0930 to 1730; Sat,
1000 to 1300
Vacations: shorter hours
Special comments: Non-university members have
reference-only access at the discretion of library
staff.

UNIVERSITY OF OXFORD –
PHYSICAL AND THEORETICAL
CHEMISTRY LABORATORY

South Parks Road, Oxford, OX1 3QZ

Tel: 01865 275400
Fax: 01865 275410
E-mail: jacob.klein@chem.ox.ac.uk

Website:
http://physchem.ox.ac.uk
General information on department.

Enquiries:
Enquiries to: Head of Department
Direct tel: 01865 275402

Organisation type and purpose:
University department or institute.

Subject coverage:
Physical, theoretical and computational chemistry.

Access to staff:
Contact by letter, by telephone, by fax, by e-mail
and via website
Hours: Mon to Fri, 0900 to 1700

UNIVERSITY OF OXFORD –
PLANT SCIENCES LIBRARY AND
OXFORD FOREST INFORMATION
SERVICE

Oxford University Library Services, South Parks
Road, Oxford, OX1 3RB

Tel: 01865 275087
Fax: 01865 275095
E-mail: enquiries@plantlib.ox.ac.uk

Website:
http://www.plantlib.ox.ac.uk/
Home page for Plant Sciences Library.

Enquiries:
Enquiries to: Plant Sciences Librarian
Direct tel: 01865 275080
Direct e-mail: roger.mills@ouls.ox.ac.uk
Other contacts: Reader Services Librarian for all
subject enquiries.

Founded:
1621

Organisation type and purpose:
University library.
Formal agreement with CAB International to
acquire forestry material for abstracting and to
provide a document delivery service.

Subject coverage:
Forestry and related subjects; plant and soil
sciences in relation to agriculture; botany;
biochemistry; genetics; ecology; taxonomy;
physiology, molecular biology.

**Museum or gallery collection, archive, or library
special collection:**
Sibthorpian and Sherard Collections (historic
botanical works);
World forestry literature from 1822

Non-library collection catalogue:
All or part available online and in-house

Library catalogue:
All or part available online

Printed publications:
O.F.I. Occasional Papers
Tropical Forestry Papers

Microform publications:
Books of historical interest – on microfilm
Catalogue of World Forestry Literature – on
microfilm
Conference and Congress Proceedings – on
microfilm
Theses – on microfilm

Electronic and video publications:
Tree CD-ROM (pub. Silver Platter)

Publications list:
Available online

Access to staff:
Contact by letter, by telephone, by fax, by e-mail,
in person and via website
Hours: Mon to Fri, 0900 to 1730

Access for disabled people:
Access to all public areas, toilet facilities

Parent body:
University of Oxford

UNIVERSITY OF OXFORD –
REGENT'S PARK COLLEGE
LIBRARY

Pusey Street, Oxford, OX1 2LB

Tel: 01865 288120
Fax: 01865 288121
E-mail: library@regents.ox.ac.uk

Website:
http://library.ox.ac.uk
Main College Library, David Nicholls Collection
and part of Angus Library on OLIS
http://www.lib.ox.ac.uk/libraries/guides/REG.html
Brief details.
http://www.lib.ox.ac.uk/olis/
Angus Library holdings are gradually being added
to OLIS.
http://www.rpc.ox.ac.uk/
Information on Regent's Park College and various
links.

Enquiries:
Enquiries to: Librarian
Direct tel: 01865 288142
Direct e-mail: sue.mills@regents.ox.ac.uk
Other contacts: The Archivist (in the Librarian's
absence), Assistant Librarian

Founded:
1810

Organisation type and purpose:
Registered charity (charity number 309710).
Permanent Private Hall of the University of
Oxford.
The Angus library also houses the library of the
Baptist Union of Great Britain and the archives of
the Baptist Missionary Society.

Subject coverage:
Baptist history.

**Museum or gallery collection, archive, or library
special collection:**
Baptist Historical Society, library
Baptist Missionary Society Archives
Baptist Union of Great Britain: minute books, some
records, library
David Nicholls Collection: separate location from
both libraries
4000 books on theology, church and state, politics,
philosophy, Caribbean studies (especially Haiti)

Non-library collection catalogue:
All or part available online and in-house

Library catalogue:
All or part available in-house

Printed publications:
Angus Library, conditions of use
Sources for the study of Baptist History (offprint
from the Baptist Quarterly, xxxiv, 6 April 1992,
£2)

continued overleaf

Microform publications:
200 35mm reels

Electronic and video publications:
Photographs, glass slides, audiotapes, videos

Publications list:
Available online

Access to staff:
Contact by letter, by telephone, by fax and by e-mail. Appointment necessary. Letter of introduction required.
Hours: Mon to Fri, 0930 to 1600
Special comments: College Library: members only
Angus Library: by appointment, with references.

Access to building, collection or gallery:
Hours: Mon to Fri, 0900 to 1700

UNIVERSITY OF OXFORD – SCHOOL OF GEOGRAPHY AND THE ENVIRONMENT LIBRARY

Mansfield Road, Oxford, OX1 3TB

Tel: 01865 271919
Fax: 01865 271929

Website:
http://www.geog.ox.ac.uk/facilities/library/index
.html
General library guide.

Enquiries:
Enquiries to: Librarian
Direct tel: 01865 271911
Direct e-mail: linda.atkinson@geog.ox.ac.uk

Founded:
1887

Organisation type and purpose:
University library.

Subject coverage:
Geography and allied subjects, mountaineering, map collection.

Museum or gallery collection, archive, or library special collection:
Oxford Mountaineering Library
Radcliffe Meteorological Collection held within School of Geography and access for visitors is via the Library

Non-library collection catalogue:
All or part available online

Library catalogue:
All or part available online

Access to staff:
Contact by letter, by telephone, by fax, by e-mail and in person. Appointment necessary.
Hours: Term time: Mon to Fri, 0930 to 1800
Vacations: Mon to Fri, 0900 to 1700

Access for disabled people:
Ramped entry, toilet facilities

UNIVERSITY OF OXFORD – SOCIAL SCIENCE LIBRARY

Manor Road Building, Manor Road, Oxford, OX1 3UL

Tel: 01865 271093
Fax: 01865 271072
E-mail: library@ssl.ox.ac.uk

Website:
http://www.ssl.ox.ac.uk

Founded:
2004

Organisation type and purpose:
University library.

Subject coverage:
Criminology, economics, international development, politics and international relations, Russian and East European studies, social policy and social work, socio-legal studies, sociology

Museum or gallery collection, archive, or library special collection:
120,000 vols, 1,000 journal and serial subscriptions
Economics and international development working papers from 200 institutions
African and Latin American collections

Trade and statistical information:
Data on all international trade.

Library catalogue:
All or part available online

Access to staff:
Contact by letter, by telephone, by fax, by e-mail and via website. Appointment necessary. Access for members only.
Hours: Mon to Fri, 0900 to 1730

Access to building, collection or gallery:
Term time: Mon to Thu, 0900 to 2200; Fri, 0900 to 1900; Sat, 1000 to 1800; Sun, 1200 to 1800
Vacation: Mon to Fri, 0900 to 1900; Sat, 1000 to 1600; Sun, closed

Access for disabled people:
Ramped entry, wide doorway, toilet facilities

UNIVERSITY OF OXFORD – ZOOLOGY LIBRARY

Oxford University Library Services, Tinbergen Building, South Parks Road, Oxford, OX1 3PS

Tel: 01865 271141
Fax: 01865 271142
E-mail: enquiries.zoo@ouls.ox.ac.uk

Website:
http://www.ouls.ox.ac.uk/isbes/catalogues/
zoology
Online catalogue
http://www.lib.ox.ac.uk/olis
Catalogue of offprints

Enquiries:
Enquiries to: Librarian

Founded:
1860

Organisation type and purpose:
University department or institute.

Subject coverage:
Zoology, ecology, ornithology, genetics, cell biology, molecular biophysics, animal behaviour, biochemistry, entomology, parasitology, epidemiology, evolution.

Museum or gallery collection, archive, or library special collection:
British Falconers' Club Library
Ornithological notebooks and diaries of 19th- and 20th-century ornithologists
Special collections in ornithology and ecology
Wytham Wood research publications and surveys

Non-library collection catalogue:
All or part available online

Library catalogue:
All or part available online

Printed publications:
Library guide
Publications List of Department's Ornithological Research
Publications List of Departmental Research
Publications List of Research in Wytham Wood

Access to staff:
Contact by letter, by telephone, by fax, by e-mail and via website. Appointment necessary.
Hours: Mon to Fri, 0900 to 1700

Constituent bodies:
Alexander Library of the Edward Gray Institute (ornithology, specialised reference only)
    tel: 01865 271143; fax: 01865 271142; e-mail: sophie.wilcox@ouls.ox.ac.uk
Main Library (general zoology, lending)
    tel: 01865 291141/2; fax: 01865 271141/2; e-mail: enquiries.zoo@ouls.ox.ac.uk

UNIVERSITY OF PLYMOUTH

University Library, Drake Circus, Plymouth, Devon, PL4 8AA

Tel: 01752 232310
Fax: 01752 232340

Website:
http://www.plymouth.ac.uk/library
Opening hours, access to catalogue, information for visitors and Associate Membership scheme.

Enquiries:
Enquiries to: Head of Customer Services
Direct tel: 01752 232352
Direct e-mail: libraryservices@plymouth.ac.uk

Organisation type and purpose:
University library.

Subject coverage:
Agriculture, architecture, art and design, computing, civil engineering, economics, education, electronic engineering, English literature, environmental sciences, geography, geology, health services, history, law; life sciences, management, marine sciences, mathematics, mechanical engineering, medicine, petroleum geology, politics, psychology, shipping, social work, sociology, transport.

Trade and statistical information:
UK Core Statistical Data.

Library catalogue:
All or part available online

Access to staff:
Contact by letter, by telephone, by e-mail and via website
Hours: Mon to Fri, 0900 to 1700
Special comments: See website for detailed opening hours.
Reference only except for Associate Membership scheme.
Limited access to electronic information.

Other libraries:
University of Plymouth
    The Library, Douglas Avenue, Exmouth, Devon, EX8 2AT; tel: 01395 265331; fax: 01395 265337
University of Plymouth
    The Library, Earl Richards Road North, Exeter, Devon, EX2 6AS; tel: 01392 415060; fax: 01392 415053

UNIVERSITY OF PORTSMOUTH

Frewen Library, Cambridge Road, Portsmouth, Hampshire, PO1 2ST

Tel: 023 9284 3228
Fax: 023 9284 3233
E-mail: library@port.ac.uk

Website:
http://www.port.ac.uk
General information on the University of Portsmouth, courses, departments, library information services.

Enquiries:
Enquiries to: Librarian

Organisation type and purpose:
University library.

Subject coverage:
Business studies; economics; management; law and criminology; engineering and technology; computing; environmental studies; social sciences; physical and life sciences; health studies; psychology; marine resources; languages and area studies; literature; history; art and design; European studies; media studies.

Museum or gallery collection, archive, or library special collection:
Bolton collection (history of architecture)
European Documentation Centre

Library catalogue:
All or part available online

Access to staff:
Contact by letter, by telephone, by fax, by e-mail, in person and via website. Non-members charged.
Hours: Mon to Fri, 0900 to 2045; Sat, Sun, 1000 to 1600.
See website for holiday and vacation hours.

Access to building, collection or gallery:
No prior appointment required

Access for disabled people:
Level entry, access to all public areas, toilet facilities

UNIVERSITY OF READING – BULMERSHE LIBRARY

Woodlands Avenue, Reading, Berkshire, RG6 1HY

Tel: 0118 378 8652
Fax: 0118 378 8651
E-mail: g.connell@reading.ac.uk

Website:
http://www.library.rdg.ac.uk/about/bulmershe/index.html
http://www.reading.ac.uk/library/using/sites/lib-bulmershe.asp

Enquiries:
Enquiries to: Faculty Team Manager

Founded:
1964

Organisation type and purpose:
University library.

Subject coverage:
Education and related social sciences, community health, social work, drama, film, history, children's literature, and music.

UNIVERSITY OF READING – CENTRE FOR STRESS RESEARCH

Room 6, Building 44, London Road, Reading, Berkshire, RG1 5AQ

Tel: 0118 975 6059

Enquiries:
Enquiries to: Director
Direct tel: 0118 969 4780

Founded:
1988

Organisation type and purpose:
Training organisation, consultancy, research organisation.

Subject coverage:
Stress management strategies as applicable to both individuals and organisations.

Printed publications:
Human Factors in Safety (pub. Gower, 1995)
Making Decisions. How to (1998)
Manual for Leisure-consulting (pub. Kirkfield, 1993)
The Stress Manual (Peter Francis, 1991)
Successful Problem-solving (pub. Foulsham, 1989)
Overcoming Depression (2000)

Access to staff:
Contact by letter and by telephone. Appointment necessary.
Hours: Mon to Fri, 0900 to 1300

UNIVERSITY OF READING – DEPARTMENT OF FOOD BIOSCIENCES

PO Box 226, Whiteknights, Reading, Berkshire, RG6 6AP

Tel: 0118 378 8722
Fax: 0118 931 0080
E-mail: r.a.wilbey@reading.ac.uk

Website:
http://www.rdg.ac.uk

Enquiries:
Enquiries to: Librarian

Founded:
1892

Organisation type and purpose:
University department or institute.

Subject coverage:
Food, science and technology, nutrition, biotechnology, industrial microbiology and fermentation technology.

Museum or gallery collection, archive, or library special collection:
McLachlan Library (food science and technology)

Access to staff:
Contact by e-mail
Hours: Mon to Fri, 0900 to 1700

UNIVERSITY OF READING – EUROPEAN DOCUMENTATION CENTRE

Acronym or abbreviation: EDC

Main Library, Whiteknights, PO Box 223, Reading, Berkshire, RG6 6AE

Tel: 0118 378 8782
Fax: 0118 378 2335
E-mail: library-edc@reading.ac.uk

Website:
http://www.library.reading.ac.uk

Enquiries:
Enquiries to: EDC Librarian

Founded:
1967

Organisation type and purpose:
University library.

Subject coverage:
European Communities, European Union.

Museum or gallery collection, archive, or library special collection:
Collection of European Communities and European Union published material, donated for the use of the University and local community

Non-library collection catalogue:
All or part available online

Access to staff:
Contact by letter, by telephone, by fax and by e-mail. Appointment necessary.
Hours: Mon to Fri, 0900 to 1700 and evenings and weekends during term time

Access to building, collection or gallery:
No prior appointment required

Access for disabled people:
Parking provided, access to all public areas

UNIVERSITY OF READING LIBRARY

Whiteknights, PO Box 223, Reading, Berkshire, RG6 6AE

Tel: 0118 378 8770
Fax: 0118 378 6636
E-mail: library@reading.ac.uk

Website:
http://www.reading.ac.uk/library

Enquiries:
Enquiries to: Circulation Services Manager

Founded:
1926

Organisation type and purpose:
University library.

Subject coverage:
Agriculture (including history), archaeology, classics, community studies, contemporary European studies, economics, education, English, fine art, French, physical sciences, earth sciences, biological sciences, geography, German history, history of art, Italian, land management, law, linguistics, medieval studies, music, philosophy, politics, psychology, sociology, typography and graphic communication.

Museum or gallery collection, archive, or library special collection:
Agricultural history
Farm Records
Publishers' and Printers' Archives
Children's Collection (and H. M. Brock)
Cole Library (history of zoology, comparative anatomy and early medicine)
Finzi Collections of English Literature and Music
Henley Parish Library (history, philosophy and literature)
Isotype Collection (statistical information in graphic form)
Music (printed by lithography) and Victorian music covers
Overstone Library (economics, literature, history and travel)
Papers of Lord and Lady Astor
Printed ephemera
Printing history (including Robert Gibbings)
Samuel Beckett Archive
Stenton Library (medieval history)
Turner Collection (French Revolution)

Non-library collection catalogue:
All or part available in-house

Library catalogue:
All or part available online

Printed publications:
Beckett at Reading: Catalogue of the Beckett manuscript collection
Catalogue of the collection of children's books, 1617–1939
Cole Library of Early English Medicine and Zoology (catalogue)
Historical Farm Records

Publications list:
Available online

Access to staff:
Contact by letter, by telephone and by e-mail
Hours: See information online

Access to building, collection or gallery:
No prior appointment required at Main and Bulmershe Libraries
Special comments: Prior appointment advisable to visit University archives and special collections at Special Collections Services, Redlands Road

Access for disabled people:
Parking provided, ramped entry, level entry, access to all public areas, toilet facilities

Branch libraries:
Bulmershe Library
Bulmershe Court, Earley, Reading, Berkshire, RG6 1HY; tel: 0118 378 8652; fax: 0118 378 8651

Links with:
Special Collections Services
University of Reading, Redlands Road, Reading, RG1 5EX; tel: 0118 378 6660; fax: 0118 378 5632; e-mail: specialcollections@reading.ac.uk; website: http://www.reading.ac.uk/special-collections

UNIVERSITY OF SALFORD, INFORMATION AND LEARNING SERVICES DIVISION

Acronym or abbreviation: ILS

The Crescent, Salford, Manchester, M5 4WT

Tel: 0161 295 2444
Fax: 0161 295 6624
E-mail: ils-servicedesk@salford.ac.uk

Website:
http://www.ils.salford.ac.uk
http://www.salford.ac.uk

Founded:
1967

continued overleaf

Formerly called:
Information Services Division (ISD) (year of change 2008)

Organisation type and purpose:
University library, information and learning services

Subject coverage:
Art and design; built environment; business; computing, science and engineering; English, sociology, politics and contemporary history; environment and life sciences; health and social care; law; media, music and performance

Museum or gallery collection, archive, or library special collection:
Arthur Hopcraft Archive
Badnall Papers
Bartington Hall Papers
Bridgewater Estates Archive
British Election Campaign Material
Changing Face of Salford Collection
Dockray Collection
Duke of Bridgewater Archive
English Velvet and Cord Dyers' Association Archive
Lancashire and Yorkshire Railway Drawings
Phil May and Leo Cheney Cartoons
Mather Papers
Oldham and Son Ltd Archive
Revans Collection
Salford Technical and Engineering Association Archive
Stanley Houghton Collection
University of Salford Local Collection
Walter Greenwood Collection
Willink Archive

Trade and statistical information:
General statistics issued by UK government departments.

Non-library collection catalogue:
All or part available online

Library catalogue:
All or part available online

Electronic and video publications:
Guides available (http://www.ils.salford.ac.uk)

Access to staff:
Contact by letter, by telephone, by fax, by e-mail and via website. Appointment necessary.

Access to building, collection or gallery:
Hours: Term time main library: Mon to Thu, 0830 to 2000; Fri, 0830 to 1700; Sat, 1000 to 1600; Sun, 1200 to 1800.
Visit website for other library opening times.

Access for disabled people:
All libraries have ramp access, toilet facilities, lift

UNIVERSITY OF SHEFFIELD

Department of Information Studies, Regent Court, 211 Portobello Street, Sheffield, South Yorkshire, S1 4DP

Tel: 0114 222 2630
Fax: 0114 278 0300
E-mail: dis@sheffield.ac.uk

Website:
http://www.shef.ac.uk/is
Information about the Department, its staff, its programmes of study and its research.
http://www.shef.ac.uk/is/publications
Provides information about publications produced by the Department.

Enquiries:
Enquiries to: Head of Department
Direct tel: 0114 222 2632
Direct e-mail: s.m.corrall@sheffield.ac.uk
Other contacts: Departmental Administrator

Founded:
1963

Organisation type and purpose:
University department or institute.

Subject coverage:
The department offers a number of taught degree programmes both at graduate (PGCert, PGDip, MA, MSc, MRes, MPhil, PhD) and undergraduate (BA and BSc) level, in the areas of librarianship, digital library management, information literacy, information management, legal information management, information systems, chemoinformatics and health informatics. In addition the Department has an internationally renowned research profile within which two main research groups operate: Computational Informatics; and Library and Information Management. The research areas of study undertaken by these groups include: chemoinformatics; information retrieval; information systems; libraries and information society; knowledge and information management; health informatics; and educational informatics.

Information services:
Consultancy in all aspects of library and information management and information systems.

Education services:
Training in all aspects of library and information management and information systems. Occasional short courses. Bespoke training by arrangement.

Printed publications:
Occasional reports

Electronic and video publications:
Research reports

Publications list:
Available online

Access to staff:
Contact by letter, by telephone, by fax, by e-mail and via website
Hours: Mon to Fri, 0900 to 1700

Access for disabled people:
Ramped entry, toilet facilities

UNIVERSITY OF SHEFFIELD – LIBRARY

Western Bank, Sheffield, South Yorkshire, S10 2TN

Tel: 0114 222 7200
Fax: 0114 222 7290
E-mail: library@sheffield.ac.uk

Website:
http://www.shef.ac.uk/library

Enquiries:
Enquiries to: Director of Library Services

Organisation type and purpose:
University library.

Subject coverage:
Arts; pure and life sciences; applied sciences; social sciences; engineering; medicine and dentistry; law; architectural studies; educational studies.

Museum or gallery collection, archive, or library special collection:
Collection of books on glass
Firth Collection of 19th century ballads
Firth Collection of Civil War pamphlets
Hans Krebs Archives
Innes Smith collection of medical illustrations
Japanese and Korean Collection
Papers of Samuel Hartlib, W S Hewins and A J Mundella
Royal Infirmary donation of medical books
Sir Thomas Beecham Archive

Library catalogue:
All or part available online

Electronic and video publications:
Hartlib Papers (CD-ROM, pub. UMI)

Access to staff:
Contact by letter, by e-mail, in person and via website
Hours: Mon to Thu, 0900 to 2130; Fri and Sat, 0900 to 1700; Sun, 1400 to 1800

Access for disabled people:
Parking provided, ramped entry, toilet facilities

Consists of:
Health Sciences Library
   tel: 0114 271 2030; fax: 0114 278 0923; e-mail: hsl.rhh@sheffield.ac.uk
St George's Library (engineering, management studies, and computing science)
   tel: 0114 222 7301; fax: 0114 222 7290; e-mail: sgl@sheffield.ac.uk
Western Bank Library
   tel: 0114 222 7200; fax: 0114 222 7200; e-mail: library@sheffield.ac.uk

UNIVERSITY OF SHEFFIELD – METALS ADVISORY CENTRE

Acronym or abbreviation: SUMAC

Department of Engineering Materials, Sir Robert Hadfield Building, Mappin Street, Sheffield, South Yorkshire, S1 3JD

Tel: 0114 222 5497
Fax: 0114 222 5493
E-mail: sumac@sheffield.ac.uk

Website:
http://www.sumac.group.shef.ac.uk
Promotional and services information.

Enquiries:
Enquiries to: Senior Consultant

Founded:
1981

Organisation type and purpose:
Advisory body, professional body, university department or institute, consultancy, research organisation.

Subject coverage:
Metal component failures, materials selection, mechanical testing, chemical analysis, electron microscopy, materials consultancy service. Machinery, vehicle and structural malfunction. Engineering Measurements on operating machinery and plant.

Access to staff:
Contact by letter, by telephone, by fax and by e-mail. Appointment necessary.
Hours: Mon to Fri, 0900 to 1700

Access to building, collection or gallery:
Prior appointment required

Access for disabled people:
Parking provided, level entry, access to all public areas, toilet facilities

UNIVERSITY OF SHEFFIELD – THE INSTITUTE FOR LIFELONG LEARNING

Acronym or abbreviation: TILL

196–198 West Street, Sheffield, South Yorkshire, S1 4ET

Tel: 0114 222 7000
Fax: 0114 222 7001
E-mail: till@sheffield.ac.uk

Website:
http://www.shef.ac.uk/till

Enquiries:
Enquiries to: Publicity Officer
Direct tel: 0114 222 7009
Direct e-mail: k.wainwright@sheffield.ac.uk

Organisation type and purpose:
University library, university department or institute, research organisation.
To make the resources of the university available to the public, with a focus on continuing, part-time and flexible education for adults.

Subject coverage:
Archaeology, arts, computing and information technology, creative writing, earth sciences, education, film, health, humanities, history,

language (French and Spanish), literature, music, natural science, religious studies, theatre studies, social and political studies, botanical illustration, local studies; also part-time degree and certificate courses.

Printed publications:
Part-time Degrees and Certificates brochure – named awards (free)
Courses for Everyone brochure – general programme (free)
Order printed publications from: via http:// coursesforeverone.co.uk

Access to staff:
Contact by letter, by telephone, by fax, by e-mail and in person. Appointment necessary.
Hours: Mon to Fri, 0930 to 1640

Access to building, collection or gallery:
Customers via West Street Reception area
Hours: Mon to Fri, 0930 to 1630

UNIVERSITY OF SOUTHAMPTON LIBRARY

University Road, Highfield, Southampton, SO17 1BJ

Tel: 023 8059 2180
Fax: 023 8059 3007
E-mail: libenqs@soton.ac.uk

Website:
http://www.soton.ac.uk/library
Guide to services and information resources.

Enquiries:
Enquiries to: Librarian

Organisation type and purpose:
University library.

Subject coverage:
All subjects covered by the faculties and departments of the university

Museum or gallery collection, archive, or library special collection:
Cope Collection on Hampshire and the Isle of Wight (Hartley)
European Documentation Centre (Hartley)
Ford Collection of British Official Publications (Hartley)
Parkes Library on relations between the Jewish and non-Jewish peoples (Hartley)
Perkins Agricultural Library (British and Irish writers on agriculture published before 1901) (Hartley)
Manuscript collections, principally of 19th and 20th Centuries (Hartley) including:
Papers of the first Duke of Wellington
The Palmerston papers
The Mountbatten papers
The Broadlands collections

Non-library collection catalogue:
All or part available online

Printed publications:
Archive lists, Catalogues and Guides Series
Isle of Wight Photographers 1840–1940
Users' Guides

Publications list:
Available online

Access to staff:
Contact by letter, by telephone, by fax, by e-mail and in person
Hours: Mon to Fri, 0900 to 1700
Special comments: Library collections available for reference only.
Evening and weekend opening at selected sites.
Visitors by prior appointment at the National Oceanographic Library and the Winchester School of Art.

Includes the:
Avenue Library
tel: 023 8059 5405; e-mail: alengs@soton.ac.uk
Biomedical Sciences Library
tel: 023 8059 4215; fax: 023 8059 3251; e-mail: bslenqs@soton.ac.uk

Hartley Library
Highfield Campus; tel: 023 8059 2180; fax: 023 8059 3007; e-mail: libenqs@soton.ac.uk
Health Services Library
tel: 023 8079 6547; e-mail: hslib@soton.ac.uk
National Oceanographic Library
Southampton Oceanographic Centre; tel: 023 8059 6111; fax: 023 8059 6115; e-mail: nol@soc.soton.ac.uk
Parkes Library
tel: 023 8059 3335; fax: 023 8059 3007; e-mail: libenqs@soton.ac.uk
Winchester School of Art Library
tel: 023 8059 6982; e-mail: wsa@soton.ac.uk

UNIVERSITY OF ST ANDREWS LIBRARY

Formal name: University Library, University of St Andrews

North Street, St Andrews, Fife, KY16 9TR

Tel: 01334 462281
Fax: 01334 462282
E-mail: lis.library@st-andrews.ac.uk

Website:
http://www-library.st-andrews.ac.uk
General information about the library and its services.

Enquiries:
Enquiries to: Director of Library Services
Direct tel: 01334 462301
Direct e-mail: j.purcell@st-andrews.ac.uk

Founded:
1411

Organisation type and purpose:
University library.

Subject coverage:
Subjects of the Faculties of Arts, Divinity, Science and Medicine.

Museum or gallery collection, archive, or library special collection:
Large collection of United Kingdom and European community statistical publications
16th century books (c. 3500 items)
Andrew Lang Collection
Beveridge Collection (includes bee culture)
Bible Collection
Buchanan Collection (George Buchanan's works)
Copyright deposit collection, 1710–1837
Donaldson Collection (classics)
Finzi Collection (18th century music scores)
Forbes Collection (early and rare science works)
Incunabula (150 items)
MacGillivray Collection (Celtic history and literature)
Mackay Collection (mathematics)
Manuscripts (over 100,000)
Photographs and prints (c. 300,000)
Runciman Collection
Simson and Wedderburn Collection (early medical books)
STC items (over 1000 titles)
Valentine Collection (photographs and postcards)
von Hugel Collection (theology and philosophy)

Non-library collection catalogue:
All or part available online

Library catalogue:
All or part available online

Printed publications:
Dundee in 1793 and 1833: the First And Second Statistical Accounts
Living in St Andrews
Sheriffs of Scotland
St Andrews in 1793 and 1838: the First and Second Statistical Accounts
The Carved Stones of St Andrews
The Coins of St Andrews
The University of St Andrews: a Short History

Publications list:
Available in print

Access to staff:
Contact by letter, by telephone, by fax and by e-mail. Appointment necessary.
Hours: Mon to Fri, 0845 to 0000; Sat, 0900 to 1700; Sun, 1300 to 0000
Vacations: Mon to Fri, 0900 to 2000

Access to building, collection or gallery:
University ID required or sign in at Security Desk

Access for disabled people:
Level entry, access to all public areas, lift, toilet facilities

Member organisation of:
Consortium of European Research Libraries
Scottish Confederation of University and Research Libraries
Tayside and Fife Library Information Network

UNIVERSITY OF STIRLING LIBRARY

Library, Andrew Miller Building, University of Stirling, Stirling, FK9 4LA

Tel: 01786 467227
Fax: 01786 466866
E-mail: library@stir.ac.uk

Website:
http://www.external.stir.ac.uk
http://www.is.stir.ac.uk
Library catalogue and holdings information

Enquiries:
Enquiries to: Director of Information Services
Other contacts: University Librarian

Founded:
1967

Organisation type and purpose:
University library.

Subject coverage:
General academic subjects (no engineering).

Museum or gallery collection, archive, or library special collection:
Lindsay Anderson Archive
Drummond Collection (religious tracts)
Early English Books (STC I) microfilm set
Howietoun Fish Farm Archive
John Grierson Archive (papers relating to the documentary film movement)
Leighton Library (personal collection of Archbishop Leighton 1611–84, 4,000 vols, 16th to 19th centuries)
MacLeod Collection (Scottish theatrical history)
Sir Walter Scott and Scottish authors contemporary with Scott
Tait Collection (left wing political pamphlets)
Watson Collection (labour history)

Trade and statistical information:
General statistical reference section.

Non-library collection catalogue:
All or part available online

Library catalogue:
All or part available online

Printed publications:
John Grierson Archive Occasional Papers
Tait Pamphlet Collection: a checklist (1983)
Checklist of newspapers and periodicals in the Tait and Watson Collections: Stirling University Library (1990)
Two glossaries by Robert Burns: the glossaries to the Edinburgh and Kilmarnock Poems reproduced in facsimile (1987)
Inchnadamph and other poems (Norman MacCaig, 1978)
Rob Stene's dream (David Reid ed., 1989)
Catalogue of manuscripts: Leighton Library (Gordon Willis, 1981)
The Stirling Tract Enterprise and the Drummonds (Mike Cormack, 1984)
J. D. Fergusson at Stirling: an illustrated catalogue with an introduction by Guy Peploe (1991)

continued overleaf

Order printed publications from: Library Office, University of Stirling Library, Andrew Miller Building, University of Stirling, Stirling, FK9 4LA

Publications list:
Available online

Access to staff:
Contact by letter, by telephone, by fax, by e-mail, in person and via website. Appointment necessary. Non-members charged.
Hours: Mon to Fri, 0900 to 1700

Access to building, collection or gallery:
From June 2009 a major redevelopment of the Library building will be taking place. Please contact library@stir.ac.uk for information about access to the building and collections during that time
Hours: Please check website for current opening hours

Access for disabled people:
Lift access to all floors

Also at:
Highland Health Sciences Library
   University of Stirling – Highland Campus, Centre for Health Science, Old Perth Road, Inverness, IV2 3JH; tel: 01463 255600 (ext. 7600); fax: 01463 255605; e-mail: hhsl-inverness@stir.ac.uk

UNIVERSITY OF STRATHCLYDE – ANDERSONIAN LIBRARY

Curran Building, 101 St James Road, Glasgow, G4 0NS

Tel: 0141 548 3701
Fax: 0141 552 3304
E-mail: librarian@strath.ac.uk

Website:
http://www.lib.strath.ac.uk/library/index.htm

Enquiries:
Enquiries to: Director of Library Services
Direct tel: 0141 548 4619
Direct e-mail: k.a.davis@strath.ac.uk

Founded:
1964

Organisation type and purpose:
University library.

Subject coverage:
All subjects studied in the Faculties of Science, Engineering, Arts and Social Sciences, Education and in the Strathclyde Business School.

Museum or gallery collection, archive, or library special collection:
Aldred Collection (pamphlets on anarchism)
Anderson Collection (Founder's Library, 1726–1796)
British Standards on Microfiche
Jordanhill Archive (Scottish Education)
Laing Collection (mathematics, 17th-19th centuries)
Major British Company Reports
Robertson Collection (West of Scotland)
Royal Scottish Geographical Society Library
Strathclyde collection (publications by University Staff or Departments)
Young Collection (alchemy, chemistry, pharmacy, 16th-19th centuries)

Non-library collection catalogue:
All or part available online

Library catalogue:
All or part available online

Printed publications:
Annual Report
Guides to Library Services

Access to staff:
Contact by e-mail
Hours: Mon to Fri, 0900 to 1700

Access for disabled people:
Access to all public areas

Special comments: Lift access to all floors of Andersonian Library.

Includes the:
Jordanhill Library
   tel: 0141 950 3300; fax: 0141 950 3150; e-mail: jordanhill.library@strath.ac.uk
Law Library
   tel: 0141 548 3293; e-mail: chirsty@law.strath.ac.uk

UNIVERSITY OF STRATHCLYDE – ARCHIVES

McCance Building, 16 Richmond Street, Glasgow, G1 1XQ

Tel: 0141 548 2497
E-mail: archives@strath.ac.uk

Website:
http://www.strath.ac.uk/archives

Enquiries:
Enquiries to: Archivist

Organisation type and purpose:
University department or institute.

Subject coverage:
Archive of the official records of the University of Strathclyde and its antecedents.

Museum or gallery collection, archive, or library special collection:
Institutional archives of the University of Strathclyde and its antecedent institutions back to 1796. Also institutional archives of Jordanhill College and its antecedent institutions back to 1828. Other archival collections such as Patrick Geddes Papers.

Non-library collection catalogue:
All or part available online and in-house

Printed publications:
Catalogue of the Papers of Sir Patrick Geddes
Order printed publications from: University Archivist

Access to staff:
Contact by letter, by telephone, by e-mail and in person
Hours: Wed to Fri, 0900 to 1300 and 1400 to 1700

Access to building, collection or gallery:
Hours: Wed to Fri, 0900 to 1300 and 1400 to 1700

Access for disabled people:
Ramped entry; lift

UNIVERSITY OF STRATHCLYDE – GRADUATE SCHOOL OF ENVIRONMENTAL STUDIES

Acronym or abbreviation: GSES

Graham Hills Building, 50 Richmond Street, Glasgow, G1 1XN

Tel: 0141 548 4078
Fax: 0141 548 3489
E-mail: g.s.e.s@strath.ac.uk

Website:
http://www.strath.ac.uk/Departments/GSES/
Course details, general information on department, staff, etc.

Enquiries:
Enquiries to: Director
Direct e-mail: p.h.booth@strath.ac.uk

Founded:
1992

Organisation type and purpose:
University department or institute.

Subject coverage:
Environmental issues.

Printed publications:
Course Details (free)

Publications list:
Available online and in print

Access to staff:
Contact by letter, by telephone, by fax and by e-mail. Appointment necessary.
Hours: Mon to Fri, 0900 to 1700

UNIVERSITY OF STRATHCLYDE – JORDANHILL LIBRARY

76 Southbrae Drive, Glasgow, G13 1PP

Tel: 0141 950 3300
Fax: 0141 950 3150
E-mail: jordanhill.library@strath.ac.uk

Website:
http://www.strath.ac.uk/jhlibrary
http://www.strath.ac.uk/archives/cat/jhill/cat.html

Enquiries:
Enquiries to: Librarian

Founded:
1828

Organisation type and purpose:
University library.

Subject coverage:
Teacher education, social work, community education, sport and leisure, community arts, speech therapy, children's literature, Scottish and Gaelic language and literature, music, journalism.

Museum or gallery collection, archive, or library special collection:
ADES Archive 1920–96 (Association of Directors of Education in Scotland)
AV Media collection (20,000 items)
College archive, including material on constituent bodies, from foundation of the Glasgow Infant School (1828) and Glasgow Normal Seminary (1837) including Hamilton College of Education archives 1966–81
Educational papers of Robert Rusk and Marjorie Cruickshank

Non-library collection catalogue:
All or part available online

Library catalogue:
All or part available online

Printed publications:
Library user leaflets (annually)
College History – Teaching the Teachers: The History of Jordanhill College of Education 1828–1993

Access to staff:
Contact by letter, by telephone, by fax, by e-mail, in person and via website. Appointment necessary.
Hours: Term time: Mon to Thu, 0900 to 2100; Fri and Sat, 0900 to 1700; Sun, 1100 to 1700
Vacations: Mon to Fri, 0900 to 1700; Sat, 0900 to 1200; Sun, 1100 to 1700

Access for disabled people:
Parking provided, ramped entry, access to all public areas
Special comments: Toilet facilities outside library.

UNIVERSITY OF SUNDERLAND – ASHBURNE LIBRARY

Ashburne House, Backhouse Park, Ryhope Road, Sunderland, Tyne and Wear, SR2 7EF

Tel: 0191 515 2119
Fax: 0191 515 3166
E-mail: jan.dodshon@sunderland.ac.uk

Website:
http://www.library.sunderland.ac.uk/
Library information and catalogue.

Enquiries:
Enquiries to: Librarian

Organisation type and purpose:
University library.

Subject coverage:
Art history, design history, sculpture, ceramics, illustration, design, glass, painting, printmaking, photography, model making.

Museum or gallery collection, archive, or library special collection:
40,000 books
Slide collection of 60,000 slides

Non-library collection catalogue:
All or part available online

Library catalogue:
All or part available online

Access to staff:
Contact by letter, by telephone and by e-mail.
Appointment necessary. Non-members charged.
Hours: Term Time: Mon, Tue, 0900 to 2100; Wed, Thu, 0900 to 2000; Fri, 0900 to 1700, Sat, 1000 to 1300
Vacation: Mon to Fri, 0900 to 1700
Special comments: Charges to non-members for borrowing; open to general public for reference.

Access to building, collection or gallery:
No prior appointment required
Hours: As before

Access for disabled people:
Parking provided
Special comments: Library on 1st floor – no lift.

UNIVERSITY OF SUNDERLAND – MURRAY LIBRARY

Information Services, The Murray Library, Chester Road, Sunderland, Tyne and Wear, SR1 3SD

Tel: 0191 515 2900
Fax: 0191 515 2904
E-mail: andrew.mcdonald@sunderland.ac.uk

Website:
http://www.library.sunderland.ac.uk

Enquiries:
Enquiries to: Director
Direct tel: 0191 515 2905
Direct fax: 0191 515 3914
Other contacts: Assistant Director Information Services

Organisation type and purpose:
University library.

Subject coverage:
Art and design, education, business management, law, humanities, social studies, computing, mathematics, science, engineering, technology, pharmacy, health studies, environmental studies.

Printed publications:
Prospectus

Access to staff:
Contact by letter, by fax and by e-mail
Hours: Term time: Mon to Thu, 0830 to 2200; Fri, 0830 to 2100; Sat 0945 to 1800; Sun 0945 to 1800
Vacations: Mon to Fri, 0900 to 1700

UNIVERSITY OF SURREY

Acronym or abbreviation: UniS

University Library, Guildford, Surrey, GU2 7XH

Tel: 01483 683325
Fax: 01483 689500
E-mail: library-enquiries@surrey.ac.uk

Website:
http://talis-prism.lib.surrey.ac.uk/TalisPrism/
Library catalogue.
http://portal.surrey.ac.uk:7778/portal/
page?_pageid=734,1&_dad=portal&_schema=
PORTAL
Library name-page.

Enquiries:
Enquiries to: The Librarian

Organisation type and purpose:
University library.

Subject coverage:
Biomedical sciences, biochemistry, toxicology, nutrition, chemical engineering, environmental strategy, civil engineering, electronic engineering (including satellite research), computing science,

mechanical engineering, physics, chemistry, microbiology, economics, sociology, law, dance studies, statistics, politics, psychology, hotel, catering and tourism management, linguistics, music, mathematics, materials science, industrial and environmental health, nursing and midwifery, occupational health and safety, biomedical engineering, translation, sound recording.

Museum or gallery collection, archive, or library special collection:
European Documentation Centre (catalogue online)
National Resource Centre for Dance
E H Shepard Archive, original drawings and manuscripts

Non-library collection catalogue:
All or part available online

Library catalogue:
All or part available online

Access to staff:
Contact by telephone, by e-mail and via website
Hours: During Semester: Mon to Fri, 0830 to 2100; Sat, 1400 to 1800; Sun, 1400 to 1800
Special comments: Hours alter during vacations – see library website.

Access for disabled people:
Parking provided, toilet facilities

Connections with:
M25 Consortium of Higher Education Libraries
Surrey and Sussex Libraries in Co-operation (SASLIC)
UK Libraries Plus Scheme

UNIVERSITY OF SUSSEX

The Library, Falmer, Brighton, East Sussex, BN1 9QL

Tel: 01273 678163
Fax: 01273 678441
E-mail: library@sussex.ac.uk

Website:
http://www.sussex.ac.uk/library

Enquiries:
Enquiries to: Librarian
Other contacts: Head of Special Collections (tel. 01273 678157, e-mail library.specialcoll@sussex.ac.uk, for access to special collections, mss and rare books)

Founded:
1962

Incorporates the former:
Education Library

Organisation type and purpose:
University library.

Subject coverage:
All arts and social sciences, applied science and technology, biological sciences, mathematics, physical sciences, molecular science, economics (including commerce).

Museum or gallery collection, archive, or library special collection:
Special Collections: manuscripts, archives and rare books
Allsop Collection (correspondence, notes and drafts of Kenneth Allsop)
Baker Collection of Fine Books (mainly 19th century, some 180 titles)
Caffyn Books (first and other editions of works by Shelley, and some critical and biographical studies, some 28 items, together with copies of 22 letters from Shelley and other non-printed material)
Carrington Collection (papers of C. E. Carrington and others c.1935–79 on Rudyard Kipling)
Charleston Collection (personal correspondence of members of the Bloomsbury Group)
Common Wealth Collection (papers of the British political organisation 1940 onwards)
Crowther Collection (on scientific journalism and politics, 1920–74)

Benn W. Levy Collection (collection of Benn Wolfe Levy on politics and the theatre, c.1930–70)
Eugene Shulkind Commune collection (periodicals, newspapers, monographs, posters and cartoons from and about the Paris Commune, 1871, some 2,500 items)
Gorer Collection (papers, correspondence, photographs, notebooks, c.1930–80, of Geoffrey Gorer, social anthropologist)
Gregory Collection (papers of Sir Richard Gregory, astronomer and editor of 'Nature' on scientific affairs and journalism, c.1880–1952)
Hogarth Press Collection (items from Leonard Woolf's file collection of Hogarth Press books, augmented by purchases and gifts)
James Stevenson Collection (Baron Stevenson of Holmbury, 1873–1926)
John Hilton Bureau Collection (papers, press-cuttings, written evidence for official enquiries, etc., of the John Hilton Bureau, News of the World Ltd, 1945–68)
Kingsley Martin Collection (correspondence, diaries, notes, pamphlets and press cuttings 1910–69)
Kipling Collection (correspondence, literary manuscripts, press cuttings, drawings, photographs, India and England 1870–1940 of Rudyard Kipling and John Lockwood Kipling, on deposit from the National Trust)
Leonard Woolf Collection (papers of Leonard Woolf on literary, political, domestic and personal affairs c.1890–1969)
Leys Collection (papers of Professor C. T. Leys on the politics and administration of Uganda, 1962–66)
Madge Papers (early poetry, notebooks and correspondence of Charles Madge, 1920–96)
Mass-Observation Archive (see separate entry)
Matusow Collection I (correspondence, press cuttings, court reports, diaries, photographs, tape recordings and films particularly on the politics of the McCarthy period 1950–55)
Matusow Collection II (USA underground ephemera, alternative society material, and Harvey Matusow personalia 1960s–80s)
Monks House Collection (literary papers and correspondence 1900–42 of Virginia Woolf and associated collection of Virginia Woolf books)
Muir/Norden archive (radio comedy scripts and notes 1948–70)
New Statesman Collection (editorial correspondence, drafts, business papers, etc., from the files of The New Statesman 1943–88)
Pledge Collection (papers on the history of science and knowledge, 1919–60, of Humphrey Thomas Pledge, Assistant Keeper and then Keeper of the Science Museum Library)
Reckitt Collection (papers, correspondence and press cuttings of Maurice Benington Reckitt on religion in politics and social questions, and Christian socialism 1915–70)
Rolph Collection (papers of C. H. Rolph including correspondence, news cuttings, etc., relating to Kingsley Martin and The New Statesman)
Rosey Pool Collection (papers, correspondence, photographs, music, etc., on black American literature 1945–70)
Stamp Collection (papers on geographical subjects, especially land use, 1910–65, of Sir Laurence Dudley Stamp, Director of the Land-Use Survey (International Geographical Union))
Travers Collection (mainly 15th- and 16th-century printed books, some 350 titles)
Wartime Social Survey Collection (papers, principally interviews and survey reports, on economic and social conditions in Britain, 1940–41)
World Parliament Association Collection (papers, photographs, minutes, reports, correspondence and programmes, mostly on federalism and world government)

Non-library collection catalogue:
All or part available online

Library catalogue:
All or part available online

Printed publications:
All Special Collections catalogues available online

continued overleaf

General helpsheets and information leaflets available in-house to support use of library

Publications list:
Available online

Access to staff:
Contact by letter, by telephone, by fax, by e-mail, in person and via website
Hours: Term time: 24-hour access from 0845 Mon to 1930 Sat; Sun, 1230 to 1930
Vacations: Mon, Wed, Thu, Fri, 0900 to 1730; Tue, 0900 to 2000; Sat, closed; Sun, 1300 to 1800

UNIVERSITY OF SUSSEX SPECIAL COLLECTIONS

The Library, University of Sussex, Brighton, East Sussex, BN1 9QL

Tel: 01273 678157
Fax: 01273 678441
E-mail: library.specialcoll@sussex.ac.uk

Website:
http://www.sussex.ac.uk/library/speccoll

Enquiries:
Enquiries to: Special Collections Manager

Founded:
1964

Organisation type and purpose:
To provide public access to and care for the archives, manuscripts, rare books and art works of the University of Sussex, including the Mass-Observation Archive which is a registered charity. The Mass-Observation Archive continues to operate as a research unit specialising in the collection of autobiographical accounts of everyday life in Britain.

Subject coverage:
The University of Sussex holds a number of internationally acclaimed archival, manuscript and rare book collections, mostly relating to 20th-century literary, political and social history.

Museum or gallery collection, archive, or library special collection:
Over 80 collections, including:
Several Rare Book collections (Travis and Baker)
Bloomsbury related collections, including the Monks House Papers (Virginia Woolf)
Archive of Rudyard Kipling
Eugene Schulkind Paris Commune Collection
New Statesman Archive
Mass-Observation Archive: 1937 to mid-1950s
Mass-Observation Archive (phase 2) from 1981 to the present
Related collections of diaries, letters, personal collections and photographs

Non-library collection catalogue:
All or part available online

Printed publications:
Mass-Observation Archive publications include:
Occasional Papers Series (12 titles) includes:
Beneath the Mourning Veil: Mass Observation and the Death of Diana (J. Thomas, 2002)
Damned Anecdotes and Dangerous Confabulations: Mass Observation as Life History (D. Sheridan, 1996)
Health, Sickness and the Work Ethic (H. Busby, 2000)
Observing the Other: Mass Observation and Race (T. Kushner, 1995)
Order printed publications from: All original Mass-Observation book publications and selected collections 1937–55 by
theme available from Adam Matthew Publications.

Electronic and video publications:
Mass-Observation File Report Sequence (Primary Media Services)

Publications list:
Available online and in print

Access to staff:
Contact by letter, by telephone, by fax, by e-mail and in person. Appointment necessary.

Access to building, collection or gallery:
ID required (including photograph and address); visits to Special Collections by appointment only
Hours: Mon to Thu, 0915 to 1700
Special comments: Charges made to some non-academic users.

Access for disabled people:
Level entry, toilet facilities. Assistive technology available in reading room.

Links with:
University of Sussex Library
tel: 01273 678163; fax: 01273 678441; website: http://www.sussex.ac.uk/library

UNIVERSITY OF THE ARTS LONDON – CHELSEA

Millbank, London, SW1P 4JU

Tel: 020 7514 7751
Fax: 020 7514 7778
E-mail: enquiries@chelsea.arts.ac.uk

Website:
http://www.linst.ac.uk/library
London Institute Library catalogue, includes online catalogue

Enquiries:
Enquiries to: Head of Learning Resources
Direct tel: 020 7514 7750 ext 7773

Founded:
1890

Formerly called:
Chelsea College of Art and Design; Chelsea School of Art

Organisation type and purpose:
University department or institute. Partnered with Camberwell College of Arts, Central Saint Martins College of Art and Design, London College of Communication, London College of Fashion and Wimbledon College of Art.

Subject coverage:
Fine art; modern art history; applied arts; design and design history; women's art.

Museum or gallery collection, archive, or library special collection:
Archives of the College
African-Caribbean, Asian and African Art in Britain Archive
Artists' books
Artists' Multiples
European and American Art and Design History from 1850
Exhibition catalogues
Jean Spencer Archive
Kurt Schwitters Archive
Modern Art Periodicals
Women's International Art Club Archive

Non-library collection catalogue:
All or part available online

Library catalogue:
All or part available online

Printed publications:
Periodicals List
Public Art Bibliography

Microform publications:
Contemporary Art Slide Scheme (subscription service)

Access to staff:
Appointment necessary.
Hours: Mon to Fri, 0900 to 1700

Part of:
University of the Arts London

UNIVERSITY OF THE WEST OF ENGLAND – FRENCHAY CAMPUS (BOLLAND) LIBRARY

Acronym or abbreviation: UWE

Coldharbour Lane, Bristol, BS16 1QY

Tel: 0117 328 2404
Fax: 0117 328 2407
E-mail: library.admin@uwe.ac.uk

Website:
http://www.uwe.ac.uk/library

Enquiries:
Enquiries to: Head of Library Services
Direct tel: 0117 328 2406
Direct e-mail: catherine.rex@uwe.ac.uk

Formerly called:
Bristol Polytechnic (year of change 1992)

Organisation type and purpose:
University library.

Subject coverage:
Nursing and allied health professions (Glenside, Hartpury)
Architecture, languages, law, management, social sciences, built environment, business, mathematics, computing, education, engineering, applied science, psychology, environmental health, geography, information science (Frenchay Campus (Bolland) Library)
History, literature, cultural studies, drama, music therapy (St Matthias)
Animal and land sciences, sports sciences (Hartpury)
Art, media and design (Bower Ashton)

Library catalogue:
All or part available online

Access to staff:
Contact by letter, by telephone, by fax, by e-mail, in person and via website. Non-members charged.
Hours: Term time: Mon to Thu, 0900 to 2000; Fri, 0900 to 1900; Sat, 1000 to 1600
Vacations: Mon to Thu, 0900 to 1700; Fri, 0900 to 1630; Sat, 0930 to 1300
Special comments: No charges for use of the library for reference.

Branch libraries:
Bower Ashton
UWE Library Services, Kennel Lodge Road, Bristol, BS3 2JT; tel: 0117 328 4750; fax: 0117 328 4745
Glenside
UWE Library Services, Blackberry Hill, Stapleton, Bristol, BS16 1DD; tel: 0117 328 8404; fax: 0117 328 8402
St Matthias
UWE Library Services, Oldbury Court Road, Fishponds, Bristol, BS16 2JP; tel: 0117 328 4472
The Frank Parkinson Learning Resources Centre
UWE Library Services, Hartpury College, Hartpury House, Gloucester, GL19 3BE; tel: 01452 702160; fax: 01452 702161

UNIVERSITY OF THE WEST OF SCOTLAND

Acronym or abbreviation: UWS

Paisley, Renfrewshire, PA1 2BE

Tel: 0141 848 3758
Fax: 0141 848 3761
E-mail: library@paisley.ac.uk

Website:
http://www.uws.ac.uk
Access to online catalogues

Enquiries:
Enquiries to: University Librarian
Direct tel: 0141 848 3750
Direct fax: 0141 887 0812
Direct e-mail: gordon.hunt@uws.ac.uk

Founded:
2007

Created by the merger of:
University of Paisley and Bell College Hamilton (year of change 2007)

Organisation type and purpose:
University library, university department or institute.

Subject coverage:
Computing, land economics, business economics, mathematics, physics, chemistry, biology, electronics, electrical engineering, mechanical engineering, industrial engineering, civil engineering, chemical engineering, applied social studies, information technology, management, nursing and health care.

Museum or gallery collection, archive, or library special collection:
Aviation history collection
Norman Buchan parliamentary papers
Collection of material on Scottish railways including maps
Hugh MacDiarmid collection
L. F. Richardson archive
IUP 19th-century government papers
SLGIU Scottish Poll Tax Archive
Hugh McMahon EU Papers
West of Scotland Community Relations Council Archive
Scottish Milk Marketing Board Archive
20th-century American literature archive and collection
Stuart Harvey Papers

Non-library collection catalogue:
All or part available online

Library catalogue:
All or part available online

Printed publications:
Calendar of Scottish Railway Maps
Forward by Degrees: the University of Paisley 1897–1997
L. F. Richardson Calendar
Paisley Poets: A Critical Re-appraisal
Renfrewshire Studies

Access to staff:
Contact by letter, by telephone, by fax and by e-mail. Appointment necessary.
Hours: Term time: 0900 to 2100
Special comments: Enquiries involving the use of special information units, to the Director of the Technology and Business Centre; reference and lending services available to external users without charge; fees charged for bibliographic work, online searches, loans from other libraries and telecommunications services.

Access for disabled people:
Level entry, access to all public areas, toilet facilities
Special comments: Parking available.

Also at:
Ayr Campus
Beech Grove, Ayr, KA8 0SR; tel: 01292 886345; fax: 01292 886006; e-mail: margo.stewart@paisley.ac.uk
Dumfries Campus
The Crichton Library, Dumfries and Galloway College Building, Bankend Road, Dumfries, DG1 4FD; tel: 01387 734275; e-mail: avril.goodwin@uws.ac.uk
Hamilton Campus
Almada Street, Hamilton, ML3 0JB; tel: 01698 283100; e-mail: john.burke@uws.ac.uk
Royal Alexandra Hospital Library
Corsebar Road, Paisley, PA2 9PN; tel: 0141 580 4757; fax: 0141 887 4962

Constituent bodies:
Ayrshire Management Centre
tel: 01292 886400; fax: 01292 886401; e-mail: amc-info@paisley.ac.uk
Biotechnology Transfer Centre
e-mail: biology@paisley.ac.uk
Centre for Alcohol and Drug Studies
tel: 0141 848 3140
Centre for Gerontology and Health Studies
tel: 0141 848 3771; fax: 0141 848 3891; e-mail: m.gilhooly@paisley.ac.uk
Centre for Particular Characterization and Analysis
tel: 0141 848 3241; fax: 0141 848 3204

Comhairle: The Scottish Centre for European Public Sector Studies
tel: 0141 848 3351; fax: 0141 848 3395; e-mail: comhairle@paisley.ac.uk
Electromagnetic Compatibility Centre
tel: 0141 848 3419; fax: 0141 848 3404; e-mail: emcc@paisley.ac.uk
Land Value Information Unit
tel: 0141 848 3747; fax: 0141 848 9799; e-mail: lviu@paisley.ac.uk
Materials and Components Development and Testing Association
tel: 0141 848 3000
Microelectronics in Business Centre
tel: 0141 848 3419; fax: 0141 848 3404; e-mail: mib-ee@paisley.ac.uk
Scottish Property Network
tel: 0141 561 7300; fax: 0141 561 7319; e-mail: spn@paisley.ac.uk
Technology and Business Centre
tel: 0141 848 3302; fax: 0141 848 3542; e-mail: brian.cross@paisley.ac.uk

UNIVERSITY OF THE WEST OF SCOTLAND – AYR CAMPUS

Acronym or abbreviation: UWS Ayr

Beech Grove, Ayr, KA8 0SR

Tel: 01292 886000
Fax: 01292 886006

Website:
http://www.uws.ac.uk/schoolsdepts/library

Enquiries:
Enquiries to: Librarian
Direct tel: 01292 886345
Direct fax: 01292 886288
Direct e-mail: libraryayr@uws.ac.uk

Founded:
1965

Created by the merger of:
University of Paisley and Bell College (year of change 2007)

Formerly called:
Craigie College of Education (year of change 1993)

Organisation type and purpose:
University library.

Subject coverage:
Education, educational psychology, children's books, nursing, health care studies, management and business studies, media studies, film studies, commercial music, digital art.

Museum or gallery collection, archive, or library special collection:
Scottish Poetry Library (branch)
West of Scotland Development Education Centre (collection)

Non-library collection catalogue:
All or part available online

Library catalogue:
All or part available online

Access to staff:
Contact by letter, by telephone, by e-mail, in person and via website
Hours: Term time: Mon to Thu, 0900 to 2050; Fri, Sat, 0900 to 1650
Vacations: Mon to Sat, 0900 to 1650

Branch of:
University of the West of Scotland
Robertson Trust Library and Learning Resources, High Street, Paisley, PA1 2BE; tel: 0141 848 3000; e-mail: library@uws.ac.uk

UNIVERSITY OF ULSTER

Acronym or abbreviation: UU

Information Services Department, Cromore Road, Coleraine, Co Londonderry, BT52 1SA

Tel: 08700 400 700

Website:
http://www.ulster.ac.uk/
University's home page.
http://www.ulster.ac.uk/library/
Library's home page, library online catalogue, staff, services, facilities, news and announcements.
Connect to the University of Ulster Library Catalogue and other library catalogues in the UK.

Enquiries:
Enquiries to: Director of Information Services

Founded:
1984

Formed by the merger of:
New University of Ulster, Ulster Polytechnic (year of change 1984)

Organisation type and purpose:
University library.

Subject coverage:
Economics, social administration, social organisation, social anthropology, conflict studies, media studies, education, English, Irish, French, German and, Spanish languages and literature, linguistics, classics, history, business studies, nursing, psychology, geography, environmental studies, communication studies, biological and biomedical sciences and surface science.

Museum or gallery collection, archive, or library special collection:
Denis Johnston Manuscripts
E N Carrothers Collection of Bookplates
English linguistics collection, microfiche
European Documentation Centre
Francis Stewart Archive of literary manuscripts
Headlam-Morley Collection, library of books, pamphlets and manuscripts relating to World War I and the Peace Treaty
Henry Davis gift of incunabula, fine bindings etc
Henry Morris Irish Collection
Irish Travelling People: Resource Collection
John Hewitt Library
Paul Ricard Library relating to World War II
Shiels plays
Stelfox Natural History Collection

Non-library collection catalogue:
All or part available in-house

Library catalogue:
All or part available online

Printed publications:
Guides to the use of the library and services

Access to staff:
Contact by letter, by telephone, by fax, by e-mail and via website. Appointment necessary. Letter of introduction required.
Hours: Term time: Mon to Fri, 0845 to 2200; Sat, 0100 to 1700
Vacations: Mon to Fri, 0900 to 1700; Sat, closed

Access for disabled people:
Parking provided, ramped entry, level entry, toilet facilities

Other campuses at:
Belfast campus
York Street, Belfast, BT15 1ED; tel: 08700 400 700
Jordanstown campus
Shore Road, Newtownabbey, Co Antrim, BT37 0BQ; tel: 08700 400 700
Magee campus
Northland Road, Londonderry, BT48 7JL; tel: 08700 400 700

UNIVERSITY OF WALES CENTRE FOR ADVANCED WELSH AND CELTIC STUDIES

Acronym or abbreviation: CAWCS

National Library of Wales, Aberystwyth, Ceredigion, SY23 3HH

Tel: 01970 636543
Fax: 01970 639090
E-mail: cawcs@wales.ac.uk

continued overleaf

Website:
http://www.wales.ac.uk/cawcs
Details of research undertaken at the Centre, publications, fora, seminars, conferences.

Enquiries:
Enquiries to: Director
Other contacts: Administrative Officer for publications.

Organisation type and purpose:
Research organisation.
Research, Welsh and Celtic study.

Subject coverage:
Language, literature, history and culture of Wales and the other Celtic countries.

Museum or gallery collection, archive, or library special collection:
Library books and periodicals – mainly Celtic- and Welsh-language material

Library catalogue:
All or part available in-house

Printed publications:
See website for full list of publications
Centre Research Papers (29 papers)
Memorial Lectures (T. H. Parry-Williams)
Poets of the Nobility Series (36 vols)
Poets of the Princes Series (8 vols, University of Wales Press)
The Effects of Tourism on the Welsh Language in North-West Wales (D. Phillips, C. Thomas)
Wales and the Welsh 2000: proceedings of the Millennium Conference of the University of Wales Centre for Advanced Welsh and Celtic Studies (ed. G. Jenkins)

Publications list:
Available online and in print

Access to staff:
Contact by letter, by telephone, by fax and by e-mail. Appointment necessary.
Hours: Mon to Fri, 0900 to 1700

Access for disabled people:
Level entry, toilet facilities

Constituent part of:
University of Wales

UNIVERSITY OF WALES COLLEGE OF MEDICINE

Acronym or abbreviation: UWCM

Department of Library Services, Sir Herbert Duthie Library, Heath Park, Cardiff, CF14 4XN

Tel: 029 2074 2874
Fax: 029 2074 3651
E-mail: brattelra@cf.ac.uk

Website:
http://voyager.uwcm.ac.uk
Library catalogue

Enquiries:
Enquiries to: Director of Library Services
Direct fax: 029 2074 3574
Direct e-mail: pritchard@cf.ac.uk

Founded:
1931

Formerly called:
Welsh National School of Medicine Library

Incorporates the former:
Combined Training Institute, Institute of Healthcare Studies, South East Wales Institute of Nursing and Midwifery

Organisation type and purpose:
University library.
NHS library.

Subject coverage:
Medicine; dentistry; nursing (including relevant sociology and social sciences); basic medical sciences; professions allied to medicine; library and information sciences (especially academic medical and life sciences).

Museum or gallery collection, archive, or library special collection:
Health and Safety
Historical collection (medicine and some dentistry)

Non-library collection catalogue:
All or part available online and in-house

Library catalogue:
All or part available online

Printed publications:
AWHILES Handbook
Guide to the Use of Dental Literature
New acquisitions list, periodicals lists
UWCM Information Services Guides

Access to staff:
Contact by letter, by telephone, by fax and by e-mail. Appointment necessary.
Hours: Duthie Library: Oct to July, Sep: Mon to Fri, 0900 to 2100; Sat, 0900 to 1700
Aug: Mon to Fri, 0900 to 1900; Sat, 0900 to 1230
Special comments: Full library service provided to NHS employees in South Glamorgan; extension services to NHS employees throughout Wales; fee for some services for external users. Certain services to staff and students of Welsh HE institutions.

Access for disabled people:
Parking provided, level entry, access to all public areas
Special comments: NB Located within hospital building.

Branch libraries:
University of Wales College of Medicine Library, School of Nursing Studies, Grounds of St Cadoc's Hospital, Caerleon, Newport, NP6 1XR; tel: 01633 430346 ext 224; fax: 01633 430717; e-mail: caerleonlib@cf.ac.uk
University of Wales College of Medicine Library, School of Nursing & Healthcare Studies, Ty Dewi Sant Building, Haeth Park, Cardiff, CF4 4XN; tel: 029 2074 2387; fax: 029 2075 6431; e-mail: healthlib@cf.ac.uk
University of Wales College of Medicine Sir Herbert Duthie Medical Library, Heath Park, Cardiff, CF14 4XN; tel: 029 2074 2875; fax: 029 2074 3651; e-mail: duthielib@cf.ac.uk
University of Wales College of Medicine Library, Postgraduate Medical Centre, Whitchurch Hospital, Whitchurch, Cardiff, CF4 7XB; tel: 029 2069 3101 ext 6382; fax: 029 2052 0170; e-mail: whitlib@cf.ac.uk
University of Wales College of Medicine Dental Library, Heath Park, Cardiff, CF4 4XY; tel: 029 2074 2523; fax: 029 2074 3651; e-mail: dentlib@cf.ac.uk
University of Wales College of Medicine The Violet Hughes Library, Velindre Hospital, Whitchurch, Cardiff, CF4 7XL; tel: 029 2061 5888; fax: 029 2031 6927; e-mail: bernadette.coles@velindre-tr.wales.nhs.uk
University of Wales College of Medicine Cochrane Library, Llandough & Community NHS Trust, Penarth, South Glamorgan, CF6 1XX; tel: 029 2071 1711 ext 5497; e-mail: cochranelib@cf.ac.uk

Constituent college of the:
University of Wales

Members of:
All-Wales Health Information and Libraries Extension Service (AWHILES)
Libraries for Nursing
National Acquisitions Group
NHS Regional Librarians Group
One Network-all-Wales Health Library and Information Group
Standing Conference of National University Libraries
UK Serials Group
University Medical School Librarians Group
Welsh Higher Education Libraries' Forum (WHELF)

UNIVERSITY OF WALES INSTITUTE, CARDIFF

Acronym or abbreviation: UWIC

Western Avenue, Llandaff, Cardiff, CF5 2YB

Tel: 029 2041 6244
Fax: 029 2041 6908

Website:
http://www.uwic.ac.uk/library/

Enquiries:
Enquiries to: Head of Library Division
Direct tel: 029 2041 6240
Direct e-mail: priley@uwic.ac.uk

Founded:
1976

Organisation type and purpose:
University department or institute.

Subject coverage:
Business; computing; food science and technology; education; art education; physical education; human movement and sport studies; art and design; applied sciences; health and social sciences; product and engineering design.

Library catalogue:
All or part available online

Printed publications:
Bullying – a positive response (1991)

Access to staff:
Contact by letter, by telephone, by fax, by e-mail and via website. Letter of introduction required.
Hours: Mon to Fri, 0900 to 2030; Sat, 0900 to 1300

Access to building, collection or gallery:
Prior appointment required

Access for disabled people:
Parking provided, level entry, access to all public areas, toilet facilities

Other addresses:
Colchester Avenue Library, UWIC
Colchester Avenue, Cardiff, CF3 7XR; tel: 029 2041 6241
Cyncoed Library, UWIC
Cyncoed Road, Cardiff, CF23 6XD; tel: 029 2041 6242
Howard Gardens Library, UWIC
Howard Gardens, Cardiff, CF24 1SP; tel: 029 2041 6243

UNIVERSITY OF WALES, LAMPETER

Lampeter, Ceredigion, SA48 7ED

Tel: 01570 424997
E-mail: library@lamp.ac.uk

Website:
http://www.lamp.ac.uk/founders_library
Home page of Founders' Library (pre-1850 collections) with access and contact information.
http://www.lamp.ac.uk/library/
Library home page with library information and links to online bibliographic resources and to information about University of Wales, Lampeter.

Enquiries:
Enquiries to: Library Administrator
Direct e-mail: j.bracher@lamp.ac.uk

Founded:
1822

Formerly called:
St David's University College Library

Organisation type and purpose:
University library.

Subject coverage:
Anthropology, archaeology, classics, film and media, German, history, informatics, philosophy, theology and religious studies, Welsh.

Museum or gallery collection, archive, or library special collection:
Early Welsh periodicals

MSS collection includes 15th century Books of Hours and other service books
Pre-1850 material (over 20,000 volumes) includes Tract Collection (printed catalogue published 1975), Incunabula (ca. 60 items representing most early centres of printing)
Welsh Bibles, prayerbooks etc

Library catalogue:
All or part available online

Printed publications:
Exhibition guides and other occasional items
Notes for readers, revised annually

Access to staff:
Contact by letter, by telephone, by fax, by e-mail, in person and via website
Hours: Term time: Mon to Thu, 0900 to 2145; Fri, 0900 to 1945; Sat, 1300 to 1645; Sun, 1300 to 1645
Vacations: Mon to Fri, 0900 to 1645

Access for disabled people:
Parking provided, level entry, toilet facilities
Special comments: Ask at counter for access to lift between floors.

Constituent Institution of the:
University of Wales

UNIVERSITY OF WALES, NEWPORT

Library and Information Services, Caerleon Campus, PO Box 179, Newport, Gwent, NP18 3YG

Tel: 01633 432101
Fax: 01633 432105
E-mail: lis@newport.ac.uk

Website:
http://www.library.newport.ac.uk
Provides access to catalogue, location maps, user guides and useful internet links.

Enquiries:
Enquiries to: Librarian
Direct tel: 01633 432103
Direct fax: 01633 432920
Direct e-mail: lesley.may@newport.ac.uk

Founded:
1974

Formerly called:
Gwent College of Higher Education Library (year of change 1995); University of Wales College, Newport (year of change 2004)

Organisation type and purpose:
University library.

Subject coverage:
Art and design, interactive arts, documentary photography, archaeology, education, humanities, environmental science, business, accountancy, human resource management, counselling, technology, computing, electrical and electronic engineering, mechatronics, sports studies, psychology, social sciences.

Museum or gallery collection, archive, or library special collection:
David Hurn collection of documentary photography materials
Newport Survey Collection of photographic images

Trade and statistical information:
General statistics for Wales.
Education statistics.

Non-library collection catalogue:
All or part available online

Library catalogue:
All or part available online

Printed publications:
How to study successfully
Library and Learning Resources Annual Report
Making References Using Harvard
Various guides to subjects

Access to staff:
Contact by letter, by telephone, by fax, by e-mail and via website. Appointment necessary.

Hours: Term time: Mon to Thu, 0900 to 2100; Fri 0930 to 1700; Sat, Sun 1300 to 1700
Special comments: Access to electronic databases may be restricted.

Other addresses:
Library and Information Services
Allt yr yn Campus, PO Box 180, Newport, NP20 5XR; tel: 01633 432310; fax: 01633 432343; e-mail: dawne.leatherdale@newport.ac.uk

UNIVERSITY OF WARWICK – MAIN LIBRARY

Coventry, Warwickshire, CV4 7AL

Tel: 024 7652 2026
Fax: 024 7652 4211
E-mail: library@warwick.ac.uk

Website:
http://www.warwick.ac.uk/services/library
Library information, including staff contacts.
http://www.warwick.ac.uk/services/library/mrc/mrc.html
Information on the Modern Records Centre.

Founded:
1965

Organisation type and purpose:
University library.

Subject coverage:
Social sciences including law; humanities (Western languages only); trade unions, pressure groups and radical political movements; statistics; biological sciences; chemistry; molecular sciences; computer science; engineering; economics; environmental studies; mathematics; physics; business studies; United Kingdom official publications; European Documentation Centre; statistical series.

Services for disabled people:
Fetch and carry service.

Museum or gallery collection, archive, or library special collection:
Economics and Management Working Papers
Employers Records collections
French Theatre 18th-19th centuries
Modern Records Centre tel no: 024 7652 4219 (collection of British trade union (eg NUR), and employers' records, and records relating to pressure groups and political movements; they include the CBI and TUC archives and the private papers of Sir Victor Gollancz)
Statistics Collection (current and historical)

Non-library collection catalogue:
All or part available online

Printed publications:
Guides to the Modern Records Centre
Modern Records Centre Information Bulletin (quarterly)

Access to staff:
Contact by letter, by telephone, by fax, by e-mail, in person and via website
Hours: Term time: Mon to Sun, 0830 to 2130
Opening times may vary during vacations and the summer term
Special comments: Members of the public may access the Library for reference provided they show photographic proof of ID and proof of address.

Access to building, collection or gallery:
Hours: Term time: Mon to Sun, 0830 to 0000
Opening times may vary during vacations and the summer term
Special comments: Visitor access during staff access hours

Access for disabled people:
Parking provided, lift, toilet facilities
Hours: As above

UNIVERSITY OF WESTMINSTER

Headquarter Building, 309 Regent Street, London, W1B 2UW

Tel: 020 7911 5000
Fax: 020 7911 5858
E-mail: admissions@wmin.ac.uk

Website:
http://www.wmin.ac.uk
Course information, events/open days, job vacancies.

Enquiries:
Enquiries to: Marketing Officer
Direct tel: 020 7911 5862
Direct fax: 020 7911 5788
Direct e-mail: davenpo@wmin.ac.uk

Founded:
1838

Formerly called:
Royal Polytechnic Institution (year of change 1882); Regent Street Polytechnic (year of change 1970); Polytechnic of Central London (PCL) (year of change 1992)

Organisation type and purpose:
University department or institute, suitable for ages: 18+,
teaching and research organisation.

Subject coverage:
Business, management, psychology and social sciences, biosciences, computer sciences, integrated health and complementary therapies, English and linguistics, architecture and the built environment, communications, languages, law, media, arts and design, electronics.

Library catalogue:
All or part available in-house

Printed publications:
Individual course brochures
Annual Review
Prospectuses (undergraduate and post graduate)
Financial Statements
Order printed publications from: Marketing and Development (for list),
Westminster Press Publications
4th Floor, 9–18 Euston Centre, London, NW1 3ET
Westminster Press Publications, Marylebone Books
Marylebone Campus, 35 Marylebone Road, NW1 5LS, tel: 020 7911 5046

Access to staff:
Contact by letter, by telephone, by fax, by e-mail and via website
Hours: Mon to Fri, 0900 to 1700
24 hr telephone enquiry service

Access for disabled people:
Facilities differ at each site, please contact for details
Special comments: Contact Disabilities Officer for further details.

Other Campus at:
Cavendish Campus
115 New Cavendish Street, London, W1W 6UW
Harrow Campus
Watford Road, Northwich Park, Harrow, London, HA1 3TP
Marylebone Campus
35 Marylebone Road, London, NW1 5LS

UNIVERSITY OF WESTMINSTER – INFORMATION SYSTEMS & LIBRARY SERVICES

115 New Cavendish Street, London, W1W 6UW

Tel: 020 7911 5095
Fax: 020 7911 5093

Website:
http://www.westminster.ac.uk/library
Information on libraries and their services, plus links to Information Systems and Computing.

continued overleaf

Enquiries:
Enquiries to: Director, Information Systems &
Library Services
Other contacts: Library Managers for campus-
related enquiries.

Founded:
1839

Formed by the merger of:
Holborn College of Law, Languages and
Commerce, Regent Street Polytechnic

Formerly called:
Polytechnic of Central London (PCL) (year of
change 1992)

Organisation type and purpose:
University library, on 4 campuses.

Subject coverage:
Planning, architecture, construction, tourism,
transport, business management and economics, at
35 Marylebone Road, NW1 5LS (tel. no. for this site
and the following sites 020 7911 5000 ext 3047)
Women's studies, economics, economic history,
law, politics, psychology, sociology, and languages,
civil rights, criminology, EC and Commonwealth
law, English law, international law, sociology of
law at 4 -12 Little Titchfield Street, London, W1P
7FW, ext 2516
Art and design, communications, film, radio and
television, journalism, mass media, computing,
photography, business management, engineering,
at Harrow Learning Resources Centre, ext 5954
Technical and scientific subjects including
mathematics, computing, chemistry, biological
sciences, electronic engineering, systems
engineering at 115 New Cavendish Street, W1M
8JS ext 3628.

**Museum or gallery collection, archive, or library
special collection:**
University Archive: record of predecessor
institutions including Royal Polytechnic
Institution (1838 – 1881), Regent Street
Polytechnic (1881 – 1970), the Polytechnic of
Central London (1970 – 1992). Access by
appointment

Non-library collection catalogue:
All or part available in-house

Library catalogue:
All or part available online

Access to staff:
Appointment necessary. Access for members only.
Non-members charged.
Hours: Term time: Mon to Fri, 0915 to 2100; Sat,
Sun, 1100 to 1700
Vacations: Mon to Fri, 0915 to 1700
Special comments: Members only: plus M25, Access
schemes members and UK Libraries Plus members.

Access for disabled people:
Ramped entry
Special comments: Otherwise varies from campus to
campus.

UNIVERSITY OF WINCHESTER

Formal name: Martial Rose Library

Sparkford Road, Winchester, Hampshire, SO22
4NR

Tel: 01962 827306
Fax: 01962 827443
E-mail: libenquiries@winchester.ac.uk

Website:
http://www.winchester.ac.uk/library

Enquiries:
Enquiries to: Librarian

Formerly called:
King Alfred's College (year of change 2005)

Organisation type and purpose:
University library.

Subject coverage:
Art, biology, design and technology, drama,
education, English, environmental studies,
geography, history, human movement studies,
mathematics, music, religious studies, psychology,
television studies, archaeology, learning
difficulties, American studies, Japanese studies,
business studies, sports studies, leisure
management, tourism.

Library catalogue:
All or part available online

Printed publications:
Guide to the Library

Access to staff:
Contact by letter, by telephone, by e-mail and via
website
Hours: Mon to Fri, 0900 to 1700

Access for disabled people:
Access to all public areas

UNIVERSITY OF WOLVERHAMPTON – LEARNING CENTRE

Telford Campus, Priorslee, Telford, Shropshire,
TF2 9NT

Tel: 01902 323983
Fax: 01902 323985

Website:
http://www.wlv.ac.uk/lib
Access to catalogues and access information.

Enquiries:
Enquiries to: Librarian
Direct tel: 01902 312672

Founded:
1992

Formerly called:
Wolverhampton Polytechnic

Organisation type and purpose:
University library.

Subject coverage:
Business and management, social work,
engineering design.

Trade and statistical information:
United Kingdom statistics.

Library catalogue:
All or part available online

Access to staff:
Contact in person
Hours: Term time: Mon to Fri, 0900 to 2200; Sat &
Sun, 1330 to 1730. Vacations: Mon to Fri, 1000 to
1700
Special comments: No staff or counter access until
1100.
Visitors must check in at Reception for Identity
Day Pass.

Access for disabled people:
Parking provided, level entry, access to all public
areas, toilet facilities

UNIVERSITY OF WORCESTER

Peirson Building, Henwick Grove, Worcester, WR2
6AJ

Tel: 01905 855338
Fax: 01905 855197
E-mail: a.hannaford@worc.ac.uk

Website:
http://www2.worc.ac.uk/ils/

Enquiries:
Enquiries to: Director of Information and Learning
Services
Other contacts: Customer Services Manager for use
of library.

Subject coverage:
Education, humanities, social sciences,
environmental science, health, nursing, midwifery,
sport studies, business, IT, digital media.

Library catalogue:
All or part available online

Publications list:
Available online

Access to staff:
Contact by telephone, by e-mail and via website.
Appointment necessary.
Hours: Mon to Fri, 0900 to 1700
Special comments: Longer opening hours during
semester, check with library.

Access to building, collection or gallery:
No prior appointment required

Access for disabled people:
Level entry, access to all public areas, toilet
facilities

UNIVERSITY OF YORK

J B Morrell and Raymond Burton Libraries,
Heslington, York, YO10 5DD

Tel: 01904 433873
Fax: 01904 433866
E-mail: lib-enquiry@york.ac.uk

Website:
http://www.york.ac.uk/services/library
Includes notes on all libraries in University of York,
including King's Manor Library, their contents and
opening hours. It also leads to the York Subject
Tree, linking in turn to home pages for
Departments in the University.

Enquiries:
Enquiries to: Director of the University Library and
Archives
Direct e-mail: lib-enquiry@york.ac.uk

Founded:
1962

Organisation type and purpose:
University library and archives.

Subject coverage:
Economics; politics; psychology; sociology; social
administration; social work; archaeology;
education; English and related literature; history;
language and linguistics; music; philosophy;
biochemistry; biology; chemistry; computer
science; electronics; mathematics; physics;
architecture; history of art; health sciences;
medicine; environment; law; theatre; film;
television (J B Morrell and Raymond Burton
Libraries). Architecture in general; architectural
history and conservation in particular;
conservation of historic parks and gardens;
continuing education for
architectural and related professions (King's Manor
Library).

**Museum or gallery collection, archive, or library
special collection:**
Copland Collection (scores composed by Aaron
   Copland)
Cooper Abbs Collection (library of an 18th century
   clergyman)
Dyson Collection (English literature of the 17th,
   18th and early 19th centuries)
Eliot Collection (20th century English literature
   first editions)
Halifax Parish Library (17th century parish library)
Milner-White Collection (English detective stories)
Milnes-Walker Collection (medicine)
Mirfield Collection (theology pre-1800)
Peggy Janiurek Collection (children's literature)
Poetry Society Library (poetry)
Raymond Burton Yorkshire Collection (books on
   Yorkshire)
Smith Collection (British engraving and painting in
   18th and 19th century)
Slaithwaite Collection (18th century theology)
York Medical Society Library (medicine)

Non-library collection catalogue:
All or part available online

Library catalogue:
All or part available online

Printed publications:
Library Guides (updated as required)

Access to staff:
Contact by letter, by telephone, by fax, by e-mail, in person and via website
Hours: Term time opening: Mon to Thurs, 0630 to 2400; Fri, 0830 to 2100; Sat, Sun, 1000 to 2100
Special comments: Vacation opening hours vary: see website

Subsidiary library:
King's Manor Library (formerly, up to 1996, the library of the Institute of Advanced Architectural Studies)
Exhibition Square, York, YO1 7EP; tel: 01904 433969; fax: 01904 433949

UPKEEP

Formal name: Upkeep – The Trust for Training and Education in Building Repairs and Maintenance

1st Floor, The Building Centre, 26 Store Street, London, WC1E 7BT

Tel: 020 7631 1677
Fax: 020 7631 1699
E-mail: info@upkeep.org.uk

Website:
http://www.upkeep.org.uk

Enquiries:
Enquiries to: Director

Founded:
1983

Formerly called:
The Building Conservation Trust

Organisation type and purpose:
Registered charity (charity number 277351), educational charity
Operates the Upkeep Exhibition, provides training courses and publishes materials about buildings. To promote good practice and public education in the maintenance and improvement of buildings.

Subject coverage:
Maintenance and refurbishment of buildings, training and education in building maintenance.

Museum or gallery collection, archive, or library special collection:
Upkeep Exhibition

Printed publications:
Guide to the Exhibition

Access to staff:
Contact by letter, by telephone, by fax, by e-mail and via website. Appointment necessary.
Hours: Mon to Fri, 0900 to 1700

Access to building, collection or gallery:
Reception: 0900 to 1700

UPPER NORWOOD JOINT LIBRARY

Acronym or abbreviation: UNJL

Westow Hill, Upper Norwood, London, SE19 1TJ

Tel: 020 8670 2551
Fax: 020 8670 5468
E-mail: jsavage@uppernorwodd.akhter.com

Enquiries:
Enquiries to: Chief Librarian

Founded:
1898

Organisation type and purpose:
Local government body, public library.

Subject coverage:
History of both Crystal Palaces (Hyde Park and Norwood); the Great Exhibition 1851, the history of Norwood (especially Upper Norwood). Gerald Massey, 1828–1907 (Victorian Chartist, poet, Spiritualist and Egyptologist), Chartist Movement.

Museum or gallery collection, archive, or library special collection:
Material relating to Gerald Massey (1828 – 1907), Victorian Chartist, poet, spiritualist and Egyptologist
Gerald Massey collection
Oral history collection of taped interviews (c.60) with people who remember Crystal Palace, collected by the Crystal Palace Foundation
The J B Wilson Collection: materials and photographs of the Norwood Area, particularly West Norwood, collected by J B Wilson (d. 1949)

Non-library collection catalogue:
All or part available in-house

Library catalogue:
All or part available in-house

Access to staff:
Contact by letter, by telephone, by fax, by e-mail and in person
Hours: Mon, 1000 to 1900; Tue, Thu, Fri, 0900 to 1900; Sat, 0900 to 1700; Wed and Sun, closed

Access to building, collection or gallery:
Hours: Mon, 1000 to 1900; Tue, Thu, Fri, 0900 to 1900; Sat, 0900 to 1700; Wed and Sun, closed

Access for disabled people:
Disabled access available

Jointly financed by the:
London Boroughs of Croydon and Lambeth

URBAN AND ECONOMICAL DEVELOPMENT GROUP

Acronym or abbreviation: URBED

41 Old Birley Street, Manchester, M16 5RF

Tel: 0161 226 5078
Fax: 0161 226 7307
E-mail: urbed@urbed.co.uk

Website:
http://www.urbed.co.uk
General material on activities of the organisation.

Enquiries:
Enquiries to: Director

Founded:
1976

Organisation type and purpose:
National organisation, consultancy, research organisation.
Urban Regeneration Consultants.

Subject coverage:
Town centres, housing, sustainable development and urban regeneration.

Museum or gallery collection, archive, or library special collection:
Library of 4000 journals, books and publications of sustainable urban development

Library catalogue:
All or part available in-house

Printed publications:
Sun Dial (newsletter, quarterly)
Building the 21st Century Home (Architectural Press 1999)
Building to Last (21st Century Homes) Joseph Rowntree Foundation, 1995
But Would You Live There (Urban Task Force 1999)
Tomorrow a Peaceful Path to Urban Returns (Friends of the Earth, 1998)

Publications list:
Available in print

Access to staff:
Contact by letter, by telephone, by fax and by e-mail. Appointment necessary.

Hours: Mon to Fri, 0900 to 1700

Other addresses:
Urban and Economical Development Group
19 Store Street, London, WC1E 7DH; tel: 020 7436 8050; fax: 020 7436 8083; e-mail: n.falk@urbed.co.uk

URBAN WILDLIFE PARTNERSHIP

The Kiln, Waterside, Mather Road, Newark, Nottinghamshire, NG24 1WT

Tel: 01636 670092/93
Fax: 01636 670001
E-mail: uwp@wildlife-trusts.cix.co.uk

Enquiries:
Enquiries to: Honorary Secretary

Founded:
1985

Formerly called:
Fairbrother Group (UWP)

Organisation type and purpose:
Membership association (membership is by subscription), present number of members: 152 organisations, voluntary organisation, registered charity.
Network of Urban Wildlife Organisations.
The UWP is a network of organisations working to create a better future for wildlife and people.

Subject coverage:
Urban nature conservation, community action.

Printed publications:
Briefings (6 times a year, free to members)
Urban Wildlife (newsletter, quarterly, free to members)

Access to staff:
Contact by letter, by telephone, by fax and by e-mail. Appointment necessary.
Hours: Mon to Fri, 0900 to 1700

Affiliated to:
Wildlife Trusts

Has:
46 member organisations

UROSTOMY ASSOCIATION

Acronym or abbreviation: UA

Central Office, 18 Foxglove Avenue, Uttoxeter, Staffordshire, ST14 8UN

Tel: 0845 241 2159; 01889 563191
E-mail: info.ua@classmail.co.uk

Website:
http://www.uagbi.org

Enquiries:
Enquiries to: National Secretary
Direct e-mail: secretary.ua@classmail.co.uk

Founded:
1971

Organisation type and purpose:
Voluntary organisation, registered charity (charity number 270600).

Subject coverage:
The Urostomy Association aims to assist all who are about to undergo, or have undergone surgery resulting in the diversion or removal of the bladder with such information, help and support as may be necessary to assist them to resume as full a life as possible with every confidence.

Information services:
Leaflets about urinary diversion

Special visitor services:
Trained and CRB-checked visitors available

Printed publications:
Journal (3 times a year)
Membership information (leaflet)
Information request (leaflet)
What is a Urostomy? (leaflet)
Travel advice (leaflet)

continued overleaf

Active living (leaflet)
Coping with urinary infections (leaflet)
How you can help the UA with a legacy (leaflet)
Neo-bladder/reconstruction – An alternative to
   Urostomy (leaflet)
Understanding problems that may occur (leaflet)
Sexual Matters (Male and Female, leaflet)
Travel Hints (leaflet)
Suprapubic catheter (leaflet)
Continent Diversion (leaflet)
Order printed publications from: Central Office, 18
Foxglove Avenue, Uttoxeter, Staffordshire, ST14
8UN; tel. 08452 412159, 01889 563191; e-mail
secretary.ua@classmail.co.uk

Electronic and video publications:
Living with a Urostomy (video, £8.95)
Problem Solving for Urostomates (£8.95)
Recorded version of Journal
Order electronic and video publications from: Central
Office, 18 Foxglove Avenue, Uttoxeter,
Staffordshire, ST14 8UN; tel. 08452 412159, 01889
563191; e-mail secretary.ua@classmail.co.uk

Publications list:
Available in print

Access to staff:
Contact by letter, by telephone, by e-mail, in
person and via website. Appointment necessary.
Hours: Mon to Fri, 0900 to 1730

Access to building, collection or gallery:
By appointment only

Links with:
International Ostomy Association

US-UK FULBRIGHT COMMISSION

Fulbright House, 62 Doughty Street, London,
WC1N 2JZ

Tel: 020 7404 6994
Fax: 020 7404 6874
E-mail: education@fulbright.co.uk

Website:
http://www.fulbright.co.uk

Enquiries:
Enquiries to: Educational Adviser

Founded:
1948

Also:
US-UK Educational Commission

Organisation type and purpose:
Anglo-American scholarship organisation
(Fulbright grants). Specialised US education library
and resource centre.
To promote educational and cultural exchanges
between the United States and the United
Kingdom. Advisory service on all aspects of
education in the USA.

Subject coverage:
Education in the US at all levels and for most
disciplines; exchanges for British students.

**Museum or gallery collection, archive, or library
special collection:**
Application forms for US admissions tests (SAT,
   GRE, GMAT, TOEFL, USMLE, LSAT, MCAT,
   ACT) and test preparation books
Reference collection of US education directories

Printed publications:
A Few Things You Should Know Before You Go
   (1999–2000 ed., £5.50)
Postgraduate Study in the United States (£5)
Undergraduate Study in the United States (£3.50)
Postgraduate Test Review Publications
Undergraduate Test Review Publications

Electronic and video publications:
TOEFL Test Preparation Kit (2nd ed)

Publications list:
Available online and in print

Access to staff:
Contact by letter and via website
Hours: Mon, 1330 to 1900; Wed and Fri, 1330 to
1700

USHAW COLLEGE LIBRARY

Ushaw College, Durham, DH7 9RH

Tel: 0191 373 8516
E-mail: alistair.macgregor@ushaw.ac.uk

Website:
http://www.ushaw.ac.uk

Enquiries:
Enquiries to: Librarian

Founded:
1808

Organisation type and purpose:
Library of a Roman Catholic Seminary.

Subject coverage:
Recusant history, church councils, medieval church
history, English civil law to 1840. Liturgy.

**Museum or gallery collection, archive, or library
special collection:**
18th century lectures from English College, Douai
John Lingard's Correspondence with Newsham
   and Wiseman
Lisbon Collection (Archives of English College,
   Lisbon, 1628–1971)
Printed books from Durham Priory
Weld Bank Parish Library

Non-library collection catalogue:
All or part available in-house

Library catalogue:
All or part available in-house

Printed publications:
In Illo Tempore

Access to staff:
Contact by letter
Hours: Tue, Wed, Thu, 0900 to 1530

Access for disabled people:
Parking provided, toilet facilities

Associated with:
University of Durham

UTTLESFORD DISTRICT COUNCIL

London Road, Saffron Walden, Essex, CB11 4ER

Tel: 01799 510510\ Minicom no. 01799 5104129
Fax: 01799 510510
E-mail: postroom@uttlesford.gov.uk

Enquiries:
Enquiries to: Chief Executive

Founded:
1974

Organisation type and purpose:
Local government body

Subject coverage:
Local government services

Access to staff:
Contact by letter, by telephone, by fax, by e-mail,
in person and via website. Appointment necessary.
Hours: Mon to Thur, 0900 to 1700, Fri 0900 to 1630

VALE OF GLAMORGAN COUNCIL

Civic Offices, Holton Road, Barry, Vale of
Glamorgan, CF63 4RU

Tel: 01446 700111
Fax: 01446 421479
E-mail: civ@valeofglamorgan.gov.uk

Website:
http://www.valeofglamorgan.gov.uk

Organisation type and purpose:
Local government body.

VALE OF GLAMORGAN RAILWAY COMPANY LIMITED

Acronym or abbreviation: VOGR

Barry Island Station, Romanwell Road, Barry
Island, Vale of Glamorgan, CF62 5TII

Tel: 01446 748816
Fax: 01446 749018
E-mail: valeofglamrai@hotmail.com

Website:
http://www.valeglamrail.co.uk
Information on Barry Island Steam Railway and
Heritage Centre

Enquiries:
Enquiries to: Librarian and Archivist

Founded:
1994

Organisation type and purpose:
Museum, historic building, house or site, suitable
for ages: all.
Steam Heritage Centre for pleasure and
educational purposes.

Subject coverage:
General railway history (especially South Wales
railways), history and information on the
Woodham Locomotive Scrapyard.

Information services:
Library available for reference

Special visitor services:
Guided tours, materials and/or activities for
children.

Education services:
Group education facilities, resources for Key
Stages 1 and 2.

Services for disabled people:
Displays and/or information at wheelchair height.

**Museum or gallery collection, archive, or library
special collection:**
Reference library
Railwayiana
Victorian Station Building
Steam and diesel locomotives
Coaches, including a Taff Vale Railway one of 1874
   being restored
Cranes, steam and hand operated
Woodham collection (photos and scrapbooks)

Library catalogue:
All or part available in-house

Printed publications:
Barry Island Steam Railway and Heritage Centre
   Handbook (£4.99)
Barry Island Steam Railway and Heritage Centre
   Colouring Book (99p)
Steam Heritage Centre, Barry Island Station,
   Timetable and Information 2002/2003 Events
   (free)

Access to staff:
Contact by letter, by telephone, by fax, by e-mail,
in person and via website

Access for disabled people:
Parking provided, level entry, access to all public
areas, toilet facilities
Special comments: Ramped entry to coaches

Affiliated to the:
Council for Museums in Wales

VALE OF WHITE HORSE DISTRICT COUNCIL

The Abbey House, Abbey Close, Abingdon,
Oxfordshire, OX14 3JE

Tel: 01235 520202
Fax: 01235 554960

Website:
http://www.oxfordshire.gov.ukio.idc-ioid=6.htm/

Organisation type and purpose:
Local government body.
District council.

Subject coverage:
Waste collection and recycling, housing register, homelessness, planning, building control, leisure facilities, housing benefit, council tax collection, non-domestic rates, car parks, electoral registration.

Access to staff:
Contact by letter, by telephone, by fax, by e-mail and in person
Hours: Mon to Fri, 0845 to 1700

Access for disabled people:
Ramped entry, access to all public areas, toilet facilities

VALUES INTO ACTION

Acronym or abbreviation: VIA

Oxford House, Derbyshire Street, London, E2 6HG

Tel: 020 7729 5436
Fax: 020 7729 7797
E-mail: general@viauk.org

Website:
http://www.viauk.org
Membership, publications, current work.

Enquiries:
Enquiries to: Manager
Other contacts: Administrator

Founded:
1971

Formerly called:
Campaign for People with Mental Handicaps (CPMH) (year of change 1989)

Organisation type and purpose:
Membership association (membership is by subscription), voluntary organisation, registered charity (charity number 1057249), training organisation, research organisation.
VIA is committed to achieving laws, services and public attitudes which will allow people with learning difficulties to become valued citizens.

Subject coverage:
Learning difficulties, research training.

Printed publications:
A range of publications including:
The Principle of Normalisation
One Law for All
Setting up a Tenants' Group
The Cost of Opportunity

Electronic and video publications:
It's My House: Your Rights as a Tenant (video)
Make Your Move – video guide to independent
  living (Holman A, 1998)
Telesafe 2 video resource pack
Good Support (DVD)
Mission Possible – DVD about Mental Capacity
  Act made by and for people with learning
  difficulties

Publications list:
Available online and in print

Access to staff:
Contact by letter, by telephone, by fax and by e-mail. Appointment necessary.
Hours: Mon to Fri, 0930 to 1630

VANGUARD 3 OWNERS CLUB

14 Kennet Rise, Axford, Marlborough, Wiltshire, SN8 2EZ

Tel: 01672 520154

Enquiries:
Enquiries to: General Secretary

Founded:
1990

Organisation type and purpose:
Membership association (membership is by subscription).

Subject coverage:
Technical information and sources of spares for Vanguard 3 cars.

Museum or gallery collection, archive, or library special collection:
Factory workshop manuals
Technical Bulletins

Printed publications:
Newsletter (quarterly)

Access to staff:
Contact by letter and by telephone
Hours: Mon to Fri, 0900 to 1700, also evenings and weekends

VARIETY CLUB OF GREAT BRITAIN

93 Bayham Street, London, NW1 0AG

Tel: 020 7428 8100
E-mail: info@varietyclub.org.uk

Website:
http://www.varietyclub.org.uk

Enquiries:
Enquiries to: Chief Executive

Founded:
October 1949

Organisation type and purpose:
Registered charity (charity number 209259).
Has 53 chapters in 14 countries and ten regional offices in the UK.
To give financial help to projects and individual disadvantaged children. Recipients include hospitals, schools, youth groups and individuals. The club helps to provide equipment such as Sunshine Coaches (minibuses), mobility equipment or other specialised equipment for disabled or disadvantaged children.

Subject coverage:
Support for disabled and disadvantaged children.

Parent body:
Variety Clubs International
  350 Fifth Avenue, Suite 1119, New York, 10118, USA; tel: 00 1 212 695 3818; fax: 00 1 212 695 3857; e-mail: vci@interport.net

VAUGHAN LIBRARY

Harrow School, High Street, Harrow on the Hill, Middlesex, HA1 3HT

Tel: 020 8872 8278
Fax: 020 8872 8013
E-mail: mek@harrowschool.org.uk

Website:
http://www.harrowschool.org.uk
Whole school information with library link.

Enquiries:
Enquiries to: Librarian
Other contacts: Archivist for school history.

Founded:
1863

Organisation type and purpose:
Suitable for ages: 13 to 18.
Independent school library.

Subject coverage:
General.

Museum or gallery collection, archive, or library special collection:
Aldine Collection
Byron Collection
Churchill Collection
Harrow School Archive
Sheridan Collection

Non-library collection catalogue:
All or part available online

Library catalogue:
All or part available online

Access to staff:
Contact by letter and by e-mail. Appointment necessary.
Hours: Mon to Fri, 0830 to 1830

VAUXHALL CONVERTIBLE CAR CLUB

Acronym or abbreviation: VCCC

47 Brooklands Close, Luton, Bedfordshire, LU4 9EH

Tel: 01582 573269
E-mail: ronnie.goddard@ntlworld.com

Website:
http://www.vccc.org.uk
Club information.

Enquiries:
Enquiries to: Membership Secretary

Founded:
1990

Formerly called:
Vauxhall Cavalier Convertible Club

Organisation type and purpose:
Membership association, voluntary organisation. Independent organisation to promote the use of Vauxhall convertible cars.

Subject coverage:
All aspects of Vauxhall convertible cars; conversion of Cavalier, Astra and Nova cars; agreed value insurance.

Printed publications:
Convertible correspondence (magazine)
Newsletter
Order printed publications from: Regalia Officer,
Vauxhall Convertible Car Club
28 Deans Meadow, Dagnall, Berkhamstead, Hertfordshire, HP4 1RW, e-mail: tonycoates@btinternet.com

Access to staff:
Contact by letter and by telephone
Hours: Mon to Fri, 0900 to 1700

VAUXHALL DROOP SNOOT GROUP

Acronym or abbreviation: DSG

17 Priors Road, Tadley, Hampshire, RG26 4QJ

Tel: 0118 981 5238

Website:
http://come.to/droop.snoot.group

Enquiries:
Enquiries to: Information Officer
Other contacts: Public Relations Manager

Founded:
1981

Organisation type and purpose:
International organisation, membership association (membership is by subscription), present number of members: 350–400, voluntary organisation. Performance/classic car owners.

Subject coverage:
Vauxhall Firenza, Magnum, HP Firenza, Sportshatch, and HS/HSR Chevette vehicle data and specification; production history; competition history; original vehicle data and authentication data; modification/technical material; spares schedules and information; vehicle insurance validations.

Trade and statistical information:
Vauxhall performance, race and rally cars 1970–1985.

Non-library collection catalogue:
All or part available in-house

Printed publications:
The Droop Snoot Noos (quarterly)

continued overleaf

Microform publications:
Available for viewing only

Publications list:
Available in print

Access to staff:
Contact by letter and by telephone
Hours: Mon to Fri, 1930 to 2230

Links with:
Vauxhall Bedford Opel Association (VBOA)

Publicity Office:
Vauxhall Droop Snoot Group
11 New Road, Sands, High Wycombe, Bucks,
HP12 4LH; tel: 01494 525948

VAUXHALL OWNERS CLUB (1903–1957)

Acronym or abbreviation: VOC

1 Horseshoe Drive, Red Lodge, Bury St Edmunds,
Suffolk, IP28 8ER

Tel: 01638 751275
E-mail: roychilders@onetec.com

Website:
http://www.vauxhallownersclub-1903-1957.co.uk
Membership, magazine, events and contact details.

Enquiries:
Enquiries to: Membership Secretary

Founded:
1976

Organisation type and purpose:
Membership association (membership is by
subscription), present number of members: 400.

Subject coverage:
Details of 1903–1957 Vauxhall cars, advice on
restoration and use, spares scheme.

**Museum or gallery collection, archive, or library
special collection:**
Some sales brochures, technical data and house
magazines

Printed publications:
Newsletter (monthly)
Register

Access to staff:
Contact by letter and by telephone
Hours: Evenings and weekends

VAUXHALL VIVA OWNERS CLUB

The Thatches, Snetterton North End, Snetterton,
Norwich, Norfolk, NR16 2LD

Tel: 01953 498818
E-mail: adrian@vivaclub.freeserve.co.uk

Website:
http://www.vivaclub.freeserve.co.uk

Enquiries:
Enquiries to: Membership Secretary

Founded:
1982

Organisation type and purpose:
Membership association (membership is by
subscription), present number of members: 1000,
voluntary organisation.

Subject coverage:
Vauxhall Viva motorcars.

Printed publications:
Viva Owners Club Newsletter (quarterly)

Access to staff:
Contact by letter, by telephone, by fax and by e-
mail. Appointment necessary. Access for members
only.
Hours: Mon to Fri, 0900 to 1730 only

Member of:
Vauxhall/Bedford/Opel Association (VBOA)

VEGAN SOCIETY

Donald Watson House, 7 Battle Road, St Leonards-
on-Sea, East Sussex, TN37 7AA

Tel: 01424 427393
Fax: 01424 717064
E-mail: info@vegansociety.com

Website:
http://www.vegansociety.com
News, information, catalogue, membership,
contact/links.

Enquiries:
Enquiries to: Information Officer
Other contacts: Fundraising Officer, Email:
fundraising@vegansociety.com for adverts,
trademark licensing, legacies.

Founded:
1944

Organisation type and purpose:
Membership association (membership is by
subscription), present number of members: 4500,
registered charity (charity number 279228).
Provides information on all aspects of veganism –
including nutrition and health – to the public,
schools, media, healthcare professionals, caterers,
food manufacturers etc.

Subject coverage:
Vegan diets, animal welfare, land use, nutrition,
environment, health.

Non-library collection catalogue:
All or part available online

Printed publications:
The Animal-Free Shopper (shopping guide), Plant
Based Nutrition and Health (nutrition guide),
Vegan Passport (travel / language guide), Vegan
Stories (lifestyle book), Why Vegan? (booklet),
The Vegan (quarterly magazine)
Books, cookbooks, leaflets, pamphlets and booklets

Electronic and video publications:
Leaflets, booklets, website

Publications list:
Available online and in print

Access to staff:
Contact by letter, by telephone, by fax, by e-mail
and via website. Appointment necessary.
Hours: Mon to Fri, 0900 to 1700

Access to building, collection or gallery:
Prior appointment required

VEGETARIAN SOCIETY OF THE UNITED KINGDOM

Acronym or abbreviation: VSUK

Parkdale, Dunham Road, Altrincham, Cheshire,
WA14 4QG

Tel: 0161 925 2000
Fax: 0161 926 9182
E-mail: info@vegsoc.org

Website:
http://www.vegsoc.org

Enquiries:
Enquiries to: Information Officer

Founded:
1847

Formed by the amalgamation of:
London Vegetarian Society, Vegetarian Society

Organisation type and purpose:
Membership association (membership is by
subscription), present number of members: 18,000,
registered charity (charity number 259358),
consultancy.

Subject coverage:
Vegetarianism.

**Museum or gallery collection, archive, or library
special collection:**
Collection of books on vegetarianism and Society
Journals dating back to 1848

Printed publications:
Leaflets on the movement
The Vegetarian (magazine, quarterly)

Electronic and video publications:
Food Without Fear (video)
Devour the Earth (video)
Vegetarian Nutrition (GCSE) (video)

Access to staff:
Contact by letter, by telephone, by fax, by e-mail
and via website. Appointment necessary.
Hours: Mon to Fri, 0900 to 1700

Access to building, collection or gallery:
Prior appointment required

Access for disabled people:
Ramped entry, toilet facilities

Affiliated to:
International Vegetarian Union (IVU)

VEHICLE AND OPERATOR SERVICES AGENCY

Acronym or abbreviation: VOSA

Berkeley House, Croydon Street, Bristol, BS5 0DA

Tel: 0117 954 3200
Fax: 0117 954 3212
E-mail: enquiries@vosa.gov.uk

Website:
http://www.vosa.gov.uk/
General information about the work of Vehicle
Inspectorate and the services it provides. Details of
addresses and telephone numbers of regional
offices; publications; complaints procedure;
training courses.

Enquiries:
Enquiries to: Agency Secretariat

Founded:
2003

Created by the merger of:
the Vehicle Inspectorate and the Traffic Area
Network Division of the Department for Transport

Organisation type and purpose:
National government body.

Subject coverage:
Conducting statutory testing of lorries, coaches
and buses; supervising the MOT scheme; carrying
out roadside checks and other spot checks to
ensure vehicles comply with legal standards and
regulations; undertaking specialised vehicle
inspections; investigating accidents and defects,
and overseeing vehicle recall campaigns.

Printed publications:
A wide range of leaflets and general information
are available from local VI offices and in html
and pdf versions on the Internet.
About twenty technical manuals and instruction
for the testing of all vehicles
Order printed publications from: Vehicle Inspectorate
PO Box 12, Swansea, SA1 1BP, tel: 01792 454320

Electronic and video publications:
A series of twenty videos to support its education
and development programme

Publications list:
Available online and in print

Access to staff:
Contact by letter, by telephone, by fax, by e-mail,
in person and via website
Hours: Mon to Fri, 0900 to 1700

VEHICLE BUILDERS AND REPAIRERS ASSOCIATION LIMITED

Acronym or abbreviation: VBRA

Belmont House, Finkle Lane, Gildersome, Leeds,
West Yorkshire, LS27 7TW

Tel: 0113 253 8333
Fax: 0113 238 0496

E-mail: vbra@vbra.co.uk

Website:
http://www.vbra.co.uk

Enquiries:
Enquiries to: Director General

Founded:
1914

Organisation type and purpose:
Trade association.
1300 members engaged in vehicle building and repairing industry. To ensure VBRA membership is recognised as a sign of the professional builder and repairer. To develop membership criteria, profitability and relationships with key industry players. To improve communications within the industry. To provide membership benefits and assistance.

Subject coverage:
Working conditions and wages in the vehicle body building industry, material and data relating to commercial vehicle body building and body repair, car body repair, market research.

Printed publications:
Body (magazine, 10 times a year, free to members, £4.50 per issue for non-members)

Electronic and video publications:
TIPS (online, tips on vehicle repair, updated quarterly, members free, non-members £120)

Access to staff:
Contact by letter, by telephone, by fax, by e-mail and via website. Appointment necessary. Non-members charged.
Hours: Mon to Fri, 0830 to 1630

Access for disabled people:
Ramped entry

Affiliated to:
International Association of Vehicle Body Builders and Repairers (AIRC)

VEHICLE CERTIFICATION AGENCY

Acronym or abbreviation: VCA

VCA2, Room G1, Eastgate Office Centre, Bristol, BS5 6XX

Tel: 0117 952 4126
Fax: 0117 952 4103

Website:
http://www.vca.gov.uk

Enquiries:
Enquiries to: Librarian

Organisation type and purpose:
National government body.

Subject coverage:
National testing and certification service for new models of road and agricultural vehicles and vehicle parts, administers the compulsory national vehicle type approval schemes and the European whole vehicle approval schemes.

Access to staff:
Contact by letter and by e-mail
Hours: Mon to Fri, 0900 to 1700

Access to building, collection or gallery:
No access other than to staff

Executive Agency of:
Department of Transport, Local Government to the Regions
   e-mail: enquiries@vca.gov.uk

VELOCETTE OWNERS CLUB

12A Hampton Close, Newport, Shropshire, TF10 7RB

Website:
http://www.velocetteowners.com

Enquiries:
Enquiries to: Public Relations Officer

Founded:
1957

Organisation type and purpose:
Membership association (membership is by subscription), present number of members: 1,700.

Subject coverage:
Velocette motorcycles.

Access to staff:
Contact by letter
Hours: Mon to Fri, 0900 to 1700

VERE HARMSWORTH LIBRARY

Rothermere American Institute, 1a South Parks Road, Oxford, OX1 3UB

Tel: 01865 282700
Fax: 01865 282709
E-mail: vhl@ouls.ox.ac.uk

Website:
http://www.ouls.ox.ac.uk/vhl

Enquiries:
Enquiries to: Librarian

Founded:
2002

Organisation type and purpose:
University library, university department or institute.

Subject coverage:
History of the USA, political, economic and social.

Library catalogue:
All or part available online

Access to staff:
Contact by letter, by telephone, by fax, by e-mail, in person and via website
Hours: Oct to Jun: Mon to Fri, 0900 to 1900; Sat, 0900 to 1300
Jul to Sep: Mon to Fri, 0900 to 1700

Access for disabled people:
Level entry, access to all public areas, toilet facilities

Parent body:
Oxford University Library Services

VERIFICATION RESEARCH, TRAINING AND INFORMATION CENTRE

Acronym or abbreviation: VERTIC

Development House, 56–64 Leonard Street, London EC2A 4LT,

Tel: 020 7065 0880
Fax: 020 7065 0890
E-mail: info@vertic.org

Website:
http://www.vertic.org/
Monthly newsletter 'Trust and Verify' and summary of VERTIC and current activities pages, VERTIC briefing papers available free on-line.

Enquiries:
Enquiries to: Information Officer
Direct e-mail: rocio.escauriaza@vertic.org

Founded:
1986

Formerly called:
Verification Technology Information Centre (VERTIC) (year of change 1998)

Organisation type and purpose:
International organisation, registered charity (charity number 1073051), consultancy, research organisation.
Non-Governmental Organisation.

Subject coverage:
Research on verification and confidence-building measures in international treaties and agreements, spanning arms control and disarmament, conflict resolution and the environment; nuclear testing; greenhouse gas emissions, climate change.

Museum or gallery collection, archive, or library special collection:
Library containing books, journals, news clippings, documents, papers and Hansard on all research areas dating from 1985

Printed publications:
Annual Reports 'VERTIC Matters' 1986 to 1995

Microform publications:
Trust and Verify (6 times a year, £20 individuals, £25 organisations)
Verification: The VERTIC Year Book (1997 edition, 2000 edition)
VERTIC Briefing Papers (occasional papers)
VERTIC Research Reports (occasional papers)

Electronic and video publications:
Trust and Verify (available free on website, or by email on request)

Publications list:
Available online and in print

Access to staff:
Contact by letter, by telephone, by fax, by e-mail and via website. Appointment necessary.
Hours: Mon to Fri, 1000 to 1730
Special comments: Charges for photocopies, free access to the library.

Access to building, collection or gallery:
No prior appointment required

VERNACULAR ARCHITECTURE GROUP

Acronym or abbreviation: VAG

Ashley, Willows Green, Chelmsford, Essex, CM3 1QD

Tel: 01245 361408

Website:
http://www.vag.org.uk
Information on group and links to other compatible sites.

Enquiries:
Enquiries to: Honorary Secretary

Founded:
1952

Organisation type and purpose:
Learned society, registered charity (charity number 279839).

Subject coverage:
Vernacular (smaller traditional) architecture, particularly in the UK.

Printed publications:
Bibliography of Vernacular Architecture (irregularly, 4 vols. to date)
Newsletter (2 times a year)
Vernacular Architecture (annually)

VETERAN CAR CLUB OF GREAT BRITAIN

Acronym or abbreviation: VCC

Jessamine Court, 15 High Street, Ashwell, Hertfordshire, SG7 5NL

Tel: 01462 742818
Fax: 01462 742997
E-mail: hq@vccofgb.co.uk

Website:
http://www.vccofgb.co.uk

Enquiries:
Enquiries to: Secretary

Founded:
1930

continued overleaf

Organisation type and purpose:
International organisation, membership association (membership is by subscription, election or invitation), present number of members: 1600.

Subject coverage:
Preservation and use of Veteran and Edwardian cars manufactured before 1919.

Museum or gallery collection, archive, or library special collection:
Early motoring period literature

Library catalogue:
All or part available in-house

Printed publications:
Club magazine (6 times a year)

Access to staff:
Contact by letter and by fax. Appointment necessary. Access for members only. Letter of introduction required.
Hours: Mon to Fri, 0930 to 1700

VETERINARY LABORATORIES AGENCY

Acronym or abbreviation: VLA

Woodham Lane, New Haw, Addlestone, Surrey, KT15 3NB

Tel: 01932 341111
Fax: 01932 347046
E-mail: enquiries@vla.defra.gsi.gov.uk

Website:
http://www.vla.gov.uk

Enquiries:
Enquiries to: Librarian
Direct tel: 01932 357314
Direct fax: 01932 357608

Founded:
1995

Organisation type and purpose:
National government body, consultancy, research organisation.
To provide consultancy, surveillance, research, laboratory services and products to promote animal health and welfare and to minimise hazards associated with animals which are important to public health and the environment.

Subject coverage:
Investigation and control of diseases of commercial farm animals, animal husbandry, biochemistry, veterinary science and medicine, life sciences as related to animals.

Museum or gallery collection, archive, or library special collection:
10,000 books, 40,000 bound periodicals, 300 current subscriptions, 10,000 pamphlets, 300 annual reports, collection of staff papers, 3,000 slides

Trade and statistical information:
Statistics on outbreaks of animal diseases in the United Kingdom

Library catalogue:
All or part available in-house

Printed publications:
VLA Annual Report
Library New Books List (quarterly)
Veterinary Surveillance Report – VIDA
Salmonella in Livestock Production in Great Britain

Electronic and video publications:
Library Current Awareness Bulletin (weekly e-mail)

Publications list:
Available in print

Access to staff:
Appointment necessary. Non-members charged.
Hours: Mon to Fri, 0900 to 1645

Also at:
central research facility at Weybridge
network of 15 regional laboratories

Constituent part of:
Department for Environment, Food and Rural Affairs (DEFRA)

VICTIM SUPPORT

National Centre, Hallam House, 56–60 Hallam Street, London, W1W 6JL

Tel: 020 7268 0200
Fax: 020 7268 0210
E-mail: contact@victimsupport.org.uk

Website:
http://www.victimsupport.org.uk

Enquiries:
Enquiries to: Information Officer
Direct tel: 020 7268 0281
Direct e-mail: info@victimsupport.org.uk
Other contacts: Library/Information Officer for arrangements to use library resources

Founded:
1974

Organisation type and purpose:
Voluntary organisation, registered charity (charity number 298028).
Provides emotional support, information and practical help to victims and witnesses of crime and their families. Raises awareness of victims' rights and the effects of crime.

Subject coverage:
Services for victims of crime, effects of crime, victims' rights, victims in the criminal justice system, victim policy.

Trade and statistical information:
Statistics of referrals to Victim Support by crime. Statistics on use of the Witness Service and Victim Supportline.

Non-library collection catalogue:
All or part available in-house

Library catalogue:
All or part available in-house

Printed publications:
View (twice yearly)

Access to staff:
Contact by letter, by telephone, by fax, by e-mail and via website. Appointment necessary.
Hours: Mon to Fri, 0900 to 1730
Special comments: Access to the collection for reference by postgraduates and professional users only, and by prior appointment with the Library/Information Officer.

Access to building, collection or gallery:
Prior appointment required

Affiliated to:
European Forum for Victim Services
National Council for Voluntary Organisations
Volunteering England
World Society of Victimology

Victim Support has:
a Witness Service in every Crown Court and magistrate's court in England and Wales
about 400 local Victim Support services throughout England, Wales and N Ireland

VICTIM SUPPORT SCOTLAND

Acronym or abbreviation: VSS

15–23 Hardwell Close, Edinburgh, EH8 9RX

Tel: 0131 668 4486
Fax: 0131 662 5400
E-mail: info@victimsupportsco.org.co.uk

Website:
http://www.victimsupport.sco.org.uk

Enquiries:
Enquiries to: Head of Communications and Fundraising

Direct tel: 0131 662 5409
Direct fax: 0131 662 8209
Direct e-mail: david.sinclair@victimsupportsco.org.uk
Other contacts: Communications Officer

Founded:
1985

Organisation type and purpose:
Registered charity (charity number SC002138). Helping the victims and witnesses of crime.

Subject coverage:
Information on help available to victims of crime. Practical and emotional support and essential information.

Publications list:
Available online and in print

Access to staff:
Contact by letter, by telephone, by fax, by e-mail and via website. Appointment necessary.
Hours: Mon to Fri, 0900 to 1700

Also at:
32 local victim-support branches and witness service offices
15–23 Hardwell Close, Edinburgh, EH8 9RX; tel: 0131 668 4486; website: http://www.victimsupportsco.org.uk

VICTORIA COLLEGE EXAMINATIONS

Acronym or abbreviation: VCM

52 Bedford Row, London, WC1R 4LR

Tel: 020 7405 6483
Fax: 020 7405 6483
E-mail: vcmexams@aol.com

Website:
http://www.vcmexams.com

Enquiries:
Enquiries to: Chief Executive

Founded:
1890

Organisation type and purpose:
Examining body in music and speech.

Subject coverage:
Examinations in music and speech.

Printed publications:
College Noticeboard
Music for VCM Exams in American Organ Playing
Music for VCM Exams in Clarinet Playing
Music for VCM Exams in Electronic Organ Playing
Music for VCM Exams in Flute Playing
Music for VCM Exams in Guitar Playing
Music for VCM Exams in Keyboard Playing
Music for VCM Exams in Pianoforte Playing
Music for VCM Exams in Pipe Organ Playing
Music for VCM Exams in Recorder Playing
Music for VCM Exams in Singing
Music for VCM Exams in Violin Playing
Music ofr VCM Exams in Harpsichord Playing
Music for VCM Exams in Ukelele Playing
Music for Exams in Ocarina Playing
Past Papers Theory of Music/Speech Exams

Publications list:
Available in print

Access to staff:
Contact by letter, by telephone, by fax and by e-mail
Hours: All times

Access to building, collection or gallery:
No access other than to staff

Constituent bodies:
College of Violinists
London Music Press (publications department of Victoria College)

Member organisation of:
Association of British Choral Directors (ABCD)
European Piano Teachers Association (EPTA)
European Recorder Teachers Association (ERTA)

European String Teachers Association (ESTA)
Music Education Council (MEC)
Society of Teachers of Recorder Players (STRP)
Society of Teachers of Speech and Drama (STSD)

VICTORIA COUNTY HISTORY

Formal name: Victoria History of the Counties of England

C/o Victoria History of the Counties of England, Institute of Historical Research, University of London, Senate House, Malet Street, London, WC1E 7HU

Tel: 020 7862 8770
Fax: 020 7862 8749
E-mail: kerry.whitston@asa.ac.uk

Website:
http://www.victoriacountyhistory.ac.uk

Enquiries:
Enquiries to: Publications Assistant
Direct e-mail: william.peck@sas.ac.uk

Founded:
1899

Organisation type and purpose:
To produce an encyclopaedic national history in a series of volumes which cover, county by county, and parish by parish, the general and detailed history of England from earliest times to the present

Printed publications:
County volumes
Parish volumes

Electronic and video publications:
Order electronic and video publications from: Text of some vols available online at www.british-history.ac.uk

Publications list:
Available online

Access to staff:
Contact by letter, by telephone and by e-mail

VICTORIA INSTITUTE OR PHILOSOPHICAL SOCIETY OF GREAT BRITAIN

Acronym or abbreviation: VI

c/o The Secretary to the Trustees, 41 Marne Avenue, Welling, Kent, DA16 2EY

Tel: 020 8303 0465
Fax: 020 8303 0465

Website:
http://www.faithandthought.org.uk

Enquiries:
Enquiries to: Honorary Treasurer
Direct tel: 01279 422661
Direct e-mail: johnbuxton@tesco.net
Other contacts: Editor for publication and material reviews:110 Flemming Avenue, Leigh-on-Sea, Essex, SS9 3AX, tel: 01702 475110

Founded:
1865

Operating as:
Faith and Thought

Organisation type and purpose:
Learned society (membership is by subscription), registered charity (charity number 285871). Faith and thought.

Subject coverage:
The interface between science (increasing knowledge) and the Christian revelation contained in the Holy Bible, investigating apparent contradictions and seeking reconciliation.

Museum or gallery collection, archive, or library special collection:
Back numbers of Faith and Thought, its predecessor the Journal of the Transactions of the Victoria Institute 1867 to 1989 and its successor Science and Christian Belief from 1989

Printed publications:
Brochure
Faith and Thought Bulletin (2 times a year)
Science and Christian Belief (published jointly with Christians in Science, 2 times a year)

Access to staff:
Contact by letter and by telephone
Hours: Mon to Fri, 0900 to 1700
Special comments: The society does not have regular opening times.

Editor (also for book reviews):
Faith & Thought
110 Flemming Avenue, Leigh-on-Sea, Essex, SS9 3AX; tel: 01702 475110; e-mail: reg@luhman.freeserve.co.uk

Editorial Consultant:
Victoria Institute or Philosophical Society of Great Britain
185 Wickham Road, Croydon, Surrey, CR0 8TF; tel: 020 8654 4887

In association with:
Christians in Science
The Secretary, 4 Sackville Close, Sevenoaks, Kent, TN13 3QD; tel: 01732 451907; fax: 01732 464253; e-mail: cberry@centrenet.co.uk

VICTORIAN SOCIETY

1 Priory Gardens, Bedford Park, London, W4 1TT

Tel: 020 8994 1019
Fax: 020 8747 5899
E-mail: library@victoriansociety.org.uk

Website:
http://www.victoriansociety.org.uk

Enquiries:
Enquiries to: Administrator

Founded:
1958

Organisation type and purpose:
Statutory body, learned society, registered charity (charity number 1081435).
Pressure group.
Campaigns for the Victorian and Edwardian historic environment and promotes public understanding of the architecture and decorative arts of the period.

Subject coverage:
19th- and early 20th-century architectural history, conservation legislation and protection of historic buildings, conservation and refurbishment advice, care for Victorian houses.

Museum or gallery collection, archive, or library special collection:
Case files relating to individual buildings that have been the subject of listed building consent applications

Non-library collection catalogue:
All or part available in-house

Library catalogue:
All or part available in-house

Printed publications:
Care of Victorian Houses
Reports, books, conference papers
Journal

Publications list:
Available online and in print

Access to staff:
Contact by letter, by telephone and by e-mail.
Appointment necessary.

Access to building, collection or gallery:
Prior appointment required

VIDEO PERFORMANCE LIMITED

Acronym or abbreviation: VPL

1 Upper James Street, London, W1F 9DE

Tel: 020 7534 1400
Fax: 020 7534 1414

Founded:
1984

Organisation type and purpose:
Trade association, present number of members: 800.
Music video licensing.

Subject coverage:
Music videos.

Access to staff:
Contact by letter, by telephone, by fax and by e-mail
Hours: Mon to Fri, 0900 to 1700

Trading division:
Music Mall
at the same address; tel: 020 7534 1444; fax: 020 7534 1440; e-mail: info@musicmall.co.uk

VIKING SOCIETY FOR NORTHERN RESEARCH

Department of Scandinavian Studies, University College London, Gower Street, London, WC1E 6BT

Tel: 020 7679 7176
Fax: 020 7679 7750
E-mail: vsnr@ucl.ac.uk

Website:
http://www.nolt.ac.uk/~aezjj/homepage.html

Enquiries:
Enquiries to: Honorary Secretary

Founded:
1892

Organisation type and purpose:
Learned society.

Subject coverage:
Old Norse literature; medieval Scandinavian literature, languages and history; the history and culture of The North (the Viking Age, Viking settlements in British Isles, runes etc).

Museum or gallery collection, archive, or library special collection:
Viking Society Library (now housed as part of the University College Collection)

Printed publications:
Dorothea Coke Memorial Lectures (occasional publication, free to members)
Saga Book (free to members)
Text series and books covering history, sagas, and other Viking-related subjects

Publications list:
Available in print

Access to staff:
Contact by letter, by telephone, by fax, by e-mail and in person
Hours: Mon to Fri, 1100 to 1700

Links with:
Scottish Society for Northern Studies

VINTAGE AUSTIN REGISTER LTD

The Briars, Four Lane Ends, Oakerthorpe, Alfreton, Derbyshire, DE55 7LH

Tel: 01773 831646
E-mail: frank.smith7@tesco.net

Enquiries:
Enquiries to: Honorary Secretary

Founded:
1958

Organisation type and purpose:
Membership association, voluntary organisation.

continued overleaf

Subject coverage:
Information on all Austin motor cars produced between 1906 and 1930.

Museum or gallery collection, archive, or library special collection:
Handbooks, spares lists, sales brochures for most Austin motor cars 1906–1930

Printed publications:
VAR Newsletter (monthly, free to members)
The Vintage Austin Magazine (quarterly, free to members)

Access to staff:
Contact by letter, by telephone and by e-mail
Hours: Mon to Fri, 0900 to 1700

VINTAGE GLIDER CLUB

Acronym or abbreviation: VGC

Arewa, Shootersway Lane, Berkhamsted, Hertfordshire, HP4 3NP

Tel: 01442 873258
Fax: 01442 873258
E-mail: geoffmoore@madasafish.com

Website:
http://www.vintagegliderclub.org.uk

Enquiries:
Enquiries to: Membership Secretary

Founded:
1972

Organisation type and purpose:
International organisation, membership association (membership is by subscription), present number of members: 800 internationally, museum.
Museum – flying, restoration.

Subject coverage:
History of gliding since the early 1920s, plans of vintage gliders, whereabouts of vintage gliders, gliding museums, dates of rallies and similar events.

Museum or gallery collection, archive, or library special collection:
Collection of photographs
Construction plans of gliders especially Slingsby drawings held at Lasham Airfield and microfilm covering a wider range including Slingsby

Printed publications:
Technical Articles
Vintage (Glider) News (3 times a year)

Access to staff:
Contact by letter, by fax, by e-mail and via website
Hours: 24-hour answerphone and fax

Associated with:
British Gliding Association

VINTAGE MOTOR CYCLE CLUB LIMITED

Acronym or abbreviation: VMCC

Allen House, Wetmore Road, Burton on Trent, Staffordshire, DE14 1TR

Tel: 01283 495102
Fax: 01283 510547
E-mail: library@vmcc.net

Website:
http://www.vmcc.net
Membership details, history, section details.

Enquiries:
Enquiries to: Librarian

Founded:
1946

Organisation type and purpose:
International organisation, membership association (membership is by subscription), present number of members: 15,573, suitable for ages: all, research organisation.

Subject coverage:
Information on motorcycling and motorcycles with related accessories from 1890s to the present. Preservation and use of motorcycles over 25 years old.

Museum or gallery collection, archive, or library special collection:
Complete sets of Motorcycle, Motorcycling etc.; Ariel, BSA, Norton, Royal Enfield (early), Scott, Triumph, Velocette (early) and late Zenith works records; other collections held; handbooks, technical information etc.
Photograph collection

Non-library collection catalogue:
All or part available online and in-house

Library catalogue:
All or part available online and in-house

Printed publications:
Magazine (monthly, members)

Publications list:
Available online and in print

Access to staff:
Contact by letter, by telephone, by fax, by e-mail, in person and via website
Hours: Mon to Thu, 0900 to 1730; Fri 0900 to 1600

Access to building, collection or gallery:
Hours: Mon to Thu, 0900 to 1730; Fri, 0900 to 1600
Special comments: Library and archives situated on first floor, no lift access.

Access for disabled people:
Access to ground floor; no lift access to first floor.

Affiliated Member of:
Auto Cycle Union
 tel: 01788 566400; fax: 01788 573585; e-mail: admin@acu.org.uk
Federation of British Historic Vehicle Clubs

Associated Member of:
Royal Automobile Club

VINTAGE SPORTS-CAR CLUB LIMITED

Acronym or abbreviation: VSCC

The Old Post Office, West Street, Chipping Norton, Oxfordshire, OX7 5EL

Tel: 01608 644777
Fax: 01608 644888
E-mail: info@vscc.co.uk

Enquiries:
Enquiries to: Secretary

Founded:
1934

Organisation type and purpose:
Membership association.

Subject coverage:
General and specialised information on pre-war cars and historic racing cars; mechanical data, history and whereabouts of existing cars; specialist firms; racing and competitions up to the last war; addresses of one-make and other clubs specialising in old cars in the UK and abroad; emphasis on vintage cars made 1919–1930.

Museum or gallery collection, archive, or library special collection:
Book library
Film library

Printed publications:
Bulletin (quarterly)
Circular (monthly)

Access to staff:
Contact by letter, by fax and by e-mail
Hours: Mon to Fri, 0900 to 1700

Access to building, collection or gallery:
No prior appointment required
Hours: Mon to Fri, 0900 to 1700
Special comments: Wednesday preferred.

Member of:
Fédération Internationale des Voitures Anciennes
Federation of British Historic Vehicle Clubs

VINTNERS' COMPANY

Vintners' Hall, Upper Thames Street, London, EC4V 3BG

Tel: 020 7236 1863
Fax: 020 7236 8177
E-mail: theclerk@vintnershall.co.uk

Website:
http://www.vintnershall.co.uk

Enquiries:
Enquiries to: The Clerk

Founded:
1363

Organisation type and purpose:
Membership association (membership is by election or invitation).
City of London Livery Company.

Access to staff:
Contact by letter, by telephone, by fax, by e-mail and via website

VIOLA DA GAMBA SOCIETY

Acronym or abbreviation: VdGS

56 Hunters Way, Dringhouses, York, YO24 1JJ

Tel: 01904 706959
Fax: 01904 706959
E-mail: admin@vdgs.demon.co.uk

Website:
http://www.vdgs.org.uk

Enquiries:
Enquiries to: Administrator

Founded:
1948

Organisation type and purpose:
International organisation, learned society (membership is by subscription), present number of members: 525, voluntary organisation, registered charity (charity number 258544), publishing house, research organisation.

Subject coverage:
Printed and manuscript sources of music for viols, particularly English sources; limited information on instruments and on original treatises on playing technique.

Printed publications:
The Viol (quarterly)
Membership List (annually)
Music for Viols
Newsletter (quarterly)
Thematic Index of Music for Viols (6 vols)

Electronic and video publications:
Online Journal

Access to staff:
Contact by letter, by telephone, by fax, by e-mail, in person and via website
Hours: afternoons and weekends

Links with:
Lute Society
Viola da Gamba Society of America

VIRGINIA WOOLF SOCIETY OF GREAT BRITAIN

Acronym or abbreviation: VWSGB

Fairhaven, Charnleys Lane, Banks, Southport, Merseyside, PR9 8HJ

Tel: 01704 225232
E-mail: stuart.n.clarke@btinternet.com

Website:
http://www.virginiawoolfsociety.co.uk
Society web page.

Enquiries:
Enquiries to: Membership Secretary

Founded:
1998

Organisation type and purpose:
Learned society (membership is by subscription), present number of members: 400. Literary society.

Subject coverage:
Virginia Woolf and the Bloomsbury Group.

Printed publications:
Annual Virginia Woolf Birthday Lectures
Virginia Woolf Bulletin (3 times a year)
Society Postcards (set of 5 costs £2, £2.50 overseas inc. p&p)

Publications list:
Available online

Access to staff:
Contact by e-mail
Hours: Mon to Fri, 0900 to 1700

VISIBILITY

2 Queen's Crescent, St George's Cross, Glasgow, G4 9BW

Tel: 0141 332 4632
Fax: 0141 353 2981
E-mail: info@visibility.org.uk

Website:
http://www.visibility.org.uk
Outline of Society services.

Enquiries:
Enquiries to: Operational Director
Direct tel: 0141 572 0744
Direct e-mail: val@visibility.org.uk
Other contacts: Chief Executive Officer for organisational issues, funding, promotion and advertising.

Founded:
1859

Formerly called:
Glasgow & West of Scotland Society for the Blind; Mission To The Outdoor Blind

Organisation type and purpose:
Voluntary organisation, registered charity (charity number SCO 009738).
To support the independence of people with a visual impairment by providing information, welfare rights, home support, social and recreational opportunities, and volunteer support. To raise awareness of the issues of people who are visually impaired. Research.

Subject coverage:
Visual impairment and issues of concern to those working with people with sight impairment. Awareness of visual impairment/access issues for employers/service providers.

Trade and statistical information:
Data on registration in West of Scotland.

Printed publications:
Annual Report (free)
Information newsletter (free)
Project Leaflets (free)

Electronic and video publications:
Other printed information available on audio tape, disc, braille

Access to staff:
Contact by letter, by telephone, by fax and by e-mail. Appointment necessary.
Hours: Mon to Thu, 0900 to 1700; Fri, 0900 to 1630

Access to building, collection or gallery:
No prior appointment required

Access for disabled people:
Ramped entry, access to all public areas, toilet facilities

Members of:
National Association of Local Societies for the Visually Impaired (NALSVI)
tel: 01582 391848
SCVO

VISIT CORNWALL

Acronym or abbreviation: VC

Pydar House, Pydar Street, Truro, Cornwall, TR1 1EA

Tel: 01872 322900
Fax: 01872 322919
E-mail: tourism@cornwallenterprise.co.uk

Website:
http://www.cornwalltouristboard.co.uk

Enquiries:
Enquiries to: Administrator
Other contacts: Head of Marketing
Cornwall Tourist Board

Organisation type and purpose:
Tourism.

Subject coverage:
Marketing and promotion of Cornwall as a tourism destination.

Trade and statistical information:
Various surveys giving statistical information on aspects of tourism in Cornwall.

Printed publications:
Accommodation brochures
Activity brochures/maps
Gardens of Cornwall Open Guide
Cornwall Guide
Walking in Inspirational Cornwall

Access to staff:
Contact by letter, by telephone, by fax and by e-mail
Hours: Answerphone out of office hours

Parent body:
Cornwall Enterprise
Pydar House, Pydar Street, Truro, Cornwall, TR1 1EA; tel: 01872 322800

VISIT FINLAND

Formal name: Visit Finland, Finland Trade Centre UK

177–179 Hammersmith Road, London, W6 8BS

Tel: 020 8600 7260 (trade and press only)

Website:
http://www.visitfinland.com/uk
Travel information on Finland.

Organisation type and purpose:
National government body, professional body.
National tourist board, promoting Finland in the UK and Ireland.
Working closely with local travel trade and press.

Subject coverage:
Travelling to and in Finland; tourism facilities in Finland; addresses and contacts within the travel trade in Finland; timetables; packages available; statistics; tourist attractions.

Museum or gallery collection, archive, or library special collection:
Brochures, posters
Photographic library
Video films available on loan

Trade and statistical information:
Statistics on tourism to and in Finland.

Non-library collection catalogue:
All or part available online

Library catalogue:
All or part available online

Printed publications:
Summer and Winter brochures, lists of tour operators, activities and events
Order printed publications from: Website

Electronic and video publications:
Videos

Access to staff:
Contact via website. Appointment necessary.
Special comments: Not open to public. Visitors by prior appointment only.

Access to building, collection or gallery:
Prior appointment required
Hours: Mon to Fri, 0900 to 1700

Parent body:
Finnish Tourist Board
PO Box 625, Helsinki, 00101, Finland; tel: + 358 9 4176911; fax: + 358 9 41769399; e-mail: mek@mek.fi

VISIT LONDON

5th Floor, 1 Warwick Row, London, SW1E 5ER

Tel: 020 7234 5800
Fax: 020 7234 5751
E-mail: enquiries@visitlondon.com

Website:
http://www.visitlondon.com

Enquiries:
Enquiries to: Information Officer

Organisation type and purpose:
Tourist Board.

Subject coverage:
What to see, and where to go and stay in London.

Printed publications:
London Breaks
London for the Travel Trade
Where to stay and what to do
Where to stay on a Budget

Publications list:
Available online and in print

Access to staff:
Contact by letter, by telephone, by fax, by e-mail and via website

VISIT SWEDEN

Sweden House, 5 Upper Montagu Street, London, W1H 2AG

Tel: 020 7108 6168
Fax: 020 7724 5872
E-mail: uk@visitsweden.com

Website:
http://www.visitsweden.com

Enquiries:
Enquiries to: Director
Direct tel: 020 7870 5601
Direct e-mail: semmy.rulf@visitsweden.com

Organisation type and purpose:
National government body.
Tourist office.

Subject coverage:
All aspects of travel to and in Sweden, including ferry routes, airlines, suggested holiday areas.

Access to staff:
Contact by letter, by telephone, by fax, by e-mail and via website
Hours: Mon to Fri, 0900 to 1700

VISITDENMARK

55 Sloane Street, London, SW1X 9SY

Fax: 020 7259 5955
E-mail: london@visitdenmark.com

Website:
http://www.visitdenmark.com

Founded:
1948

Organisation type and purpose:
National tourist board.

continued overleaf

Subject coverage:
Travel and tourism to and in Denmark.

Museum or gallery collection, archive, or library special collection:
Tourist information, brochures, images, posters

Trade and statistical information:
Information for educational purposes is obtainable from the Press and Cultural Department of the Royal Danish Embassy.

Printed publications:
Tourist brochures are free, please contact VisitDenmark for further information

Access to staff:
Contact by letter, by fax, by e-mail and via website

Links with:
VisitDenmark
    Islands Brygge 43 – 3, 2300 Copenhagen S, Denmark

VISITGUERNSEY

PO Box 23, St Peter Port, Guernsey, GY1 3AN, Channel Islands

Tel: 01481 726611
Fax: 01481 721246
E-mail: enquiries@visitguernsey.com

Website:
http://www.visitguernsey.com

Founded:
1946

Organisation type and purpose:
Local government body.
Tourist office.

Subject coverage:
All aspects of the tourism and conference business of the Bailiwick of Guernsey.

Trade and statistical information:
Data on the number of visitors to the Island each year.

Electronic and video publications:
Image Library (CD-ROM)

Access to staff:
Contact by letter, by telephone, by fax, by e-mail and via website
Hours: Mon to Fri, 0900 to 1700

Access for disabled people:
Ramped entry, toilet facilities

Parent body:
States of Guernsey
    Sir Charles Frossard House, La Charroterie, St Peter Port, GY1 1FH, Guernsey

VISITSCOTLAND

Fairways Business Park, Deer Park Avenue, Livingston, EH54 8AF

Tel: 01506 832213
E-mail: info@visitscotland.com

Website:
http://www.visitscotland.com

Enquiries:
Enquiries to: Information Services Manager

Formerly called:
Scottish Tourist Board (STB)

Organisation type and purpose:
National government body.

Subject coverage:
Tourism: development, marketing, research, tourist information.

Printed publications:
Accommodation guides (4 titles)
Information fact sheets
Promotional leaflets
Research publications

Access to staff:
Contact by letter, by telephone, by fax, by e-mail and via website
Hours: Mon to Fri, 0900 to 1700

VISITSCOTLAND (HIGHLANDS)

Peffery House, Strathpeffer, Ross-shire, IV14 9HA

Tel: 01997 421160
Fax: 01997 421168
E-mail: info@visitscotland.com

Website:
http://www.visithighlands.com

Enquiries:
Enquiries to: Chief Executive

Founded:
1996

Created by the merger of:
Aviemore and Spey Tourist Board, Caithness Tourist Board, Fort William and Lochaber Tourist Board, Inverness, Loch Ness and Nairn Tourist Board, Isle of Skye Tourist Board, Ross and Cromarty Tourist Board, Sutherland Tourist Board (year of change 1996)

Organisation type and purpose:
Statutory body.
Tourism marketing.

Subject coverage:
Tourism in the Highlands of Scotland.

Trade and statistical information:
Data on volume and value of tourism in the Highlands.

Printed publications:
Freedom of the Highlands (brochure, free)

Electronic and video publications:
Tourism and the Arts in the Highlands of Scotland (CD-ROM)

Access to staff:
Contact by letter, by telephone, by fax and by e-mail
Hours: Mon to Fri, 0900 to 1700

Access for disabled people:
Level entry, toilet facilities

VISITSCOTTISHBORDERS

VisitScotland, Ocean Point One, 94 Ocean Drive, Edinburgh, EH6 6JH

Tel: 01750 20555
Fax: 01750 21886
E-mail: sbtb@scot-borders.co.uk

Website:
www.visitscottishborders.com
Wide range of consumer tourism related material.
http://www.scot-borders.co.uk

Enquiries:
Enquiries to: Chief Executive
Direct tel: 01750 23800
Direct e-mail: rgraham@scot-borders.co.uk
Other contacts: Director of Customer Marketing; Director of Development

Founded:
1982

Formed from:
Borders Regional Council (Tourism Division), Borders Tourist Association (year of change 1983)

Formerly called:
Scottish Borders Tourist Board (year of change 2006)

Organisation type and purpose:
Statutory body, membership association (membership is by subscription), present number of members: 994.
Area Tourist Board.

Subject coverage:
Tourism in the Scottish Borders, the attractions, activities, accommodation, business advice, marketing, statistics and research.

Museum or gallery collection, archive, or library special collection:
Collection includes 10,000 slide transparencies of the Scottish Borders

Trade and statistical information:
Data on visitor statistics, market research, and tourism revenue, wide range of local statistical data on local and national tourism.

Library catalogue:
All or part available in-house

Printed publications:
Annual Report and Statement of Accounts
Variety of general guides and leaflets, including:
Angling Guide
Borders Historic Route Guide
Cycling Guide
Freedom of Fairways (golf)
Gardens Guide
Meeting and Incentives Guide
Scottish Borders Holiday Planner (annually)
Scottish Borders Essential Guide (annually)
Shopping Guide
Walking Guide
Welcome leaflet

Publications list:
Available online and in print

Access to staff:
Contact by letter, by telephone, by fax, by e-mail, in person and via website. Appointment necessary.
Hours: Mon to Thu, 0900 to 1700; Fri, 0900 to 1630
Special comments: Tourist information centre opening times vary according to the time of the year.

Access to building, collection or gallery:
No prior appointment required

Access for disabled people:
Parking provided, ramped entry, access to all public areas

Tourist Information Centres:
Coldstream
    Town Hall, 76 High Street, Coldstream, TD12 4DH; tel: 01890 882607; e-mail: coldstream@scot-borders.co.uk
Eyemouth
    Auld Kirk, Market Square, Eyemouth, TD14 5HE; tel: 01890 750678; e-mail: eyemouth@scot-borders.co.uk
Hawick
    Drumlanrig's Tower, Tower Knowe, Hawick, TD9 9EN; tel: 01450 327457; fax: 01450 373993; e-mail: hawick@scot-borders.co.uk
Jedburgh
    Murrays Green, Jedburgh, TD8 6BE; tel: 01835 863688 or 863435; fax: 01835 864099; e-mail: info@scot-borders.co.uk
Kelso
    Town House, The Square, Kelso, TD5 7HF; tel: 01573 223464; e-mail: kelso@scot-borders.co.uk
Melrose
    Abbey House, Abbey Street, Melrose, Roxburghshire, TD6 LG; tel: 01896 822555; e-mail: melrose@scot-borders.co.uk
Peebles
    High Street, Peebles, EH45 8AG; tel: 01721 720138; fax: 01721 724401; e-mail: peebles@scot-borders.co.uk
Selkirk
    Halliwells House, Selkirk, TD7 4BL; tel: 01750 20054; e-mail: selkirk@scot-borders.co.uk

VITAL INFORMATION LIMITED

Stowe Castle Business Park, Buckingham, MK18 5AB

Tel: 01280 827078
Fax: 01280 827077
E-mail: maggie@vitalinformation.co.uk

Website:
http://www.vitalinformation.co.uk

Enquiries:
Enquiries to: Director

Founded:
1984

Organisation type and purpose:
Information Business

Subject coverage:
Life sciences; biology; medicine; veterinary medicine; agriculture; food science; environmental sciences; biotechnology; pharmaceuticals; toxicology; diagnostics; health care; general news services.

Access to staff:
Contact by letter, by telephone, by fax, by e-mail and via website. Appointment necessary. All charged.
Hours: Mon to Fri, 0900 to 1730

VOCATIONAL AWARDS INTERNATIONAL LIMITED

Acronym or abbreviation: VAI

3rd Floor, Eastleigh House, Market Street, Eastleigh, Hampshire, SO50 9FD

Tel: 01243 842064
Fax: 01243 842489
E-mail: info@vtct.org.uk

Website:
http://www.vtct.org.uk

Enquiries:
Enquiries to: Information Officer
Other contacts: Head of Quality Assurance, telephone: 023 8068 4500 for training centres as opposed to individual enquiries.

Founded:
1986

Formerly a division of:
International Health and Beauty Council (year of change 1986)

Organisation type and purpose:
International organisation.
Promotes qualifications of Vocational Training Charitable Trust (VTCT) internationally.

Subject coverage:
Availability of qualifications for beauty, hairdressing, health and fitness and complementary therapies. Also centres providing training.

Printed publications:
Publications only available to approved training centres
List of approved centres for training is available on website

Access to staff:
Contact by letter
Hours: Mon to Fri, 0900 to 1700

Parent body:
Vocational Training Charitable Trust
at the same address; tel: 023 8068 4500; fax: 023 8065 1493

VOICE OF THE LISTENER AND VIEWER

Acronym or abbreviation: VLV

101 King's Drive, Gravesend, Kent, DA12 5BQ

Tel: 01474 352835
Fax: 01474 351112
E-mail: vlv@btinternet.com

Website:
http://www.vlv.org.uk

Enquiries:
Enquiries to: Chairman

Founded:
1983

Incorporated:
Broadcasting Research Unit (Archive) (BRU) (year of change 1990); Voice of the Listener (VOL) (year of change 1991); British Action for Children's Television (Archive) (BACTV) (year of change 1995)

Organisation type and purpose:
Membership association (membership is by subscription), present number of members: 2500, voluntary organisation, registered charity (charity number 296207), research organisation, publishing house.
To support high quality, independence and diversity in broadcasting; to maintain the principle of public service in broadcasting; and to represent the interests of listeners and viewers, citizens and consumers in broadcasting.

Subject coverage:
Radio and television, broadcasting policy, children's radio and television educational broadcasting, public service broadcasting in the UK, Europe and worldwide.

Museum or gallery collection, archive, or library special collection:
British Action for Children's Television (BACTV) Archive, 1988–1995
Broadcasting Research Unit (BRU) Archive, 1980–1991
Voice of the Listener and Viewer Archive, 1984-.

Non-library collection catalogue:
All or part available online and in print

Library catalogue:
All or part available in-house

Printed publications:
Response to Radio Authority, Independent Television Commission and Broadcasting Standards Commission Consultations
Conference reports
Responses to UK Government, Council of Europe and European Commission Consultations
Information sample pack (free)
Newsletter (quarterly)
Order printed publications from: Publications Secretary

Electronic and video publications:
Newsletter (quarterly, on audio tape, mainly for the blind)
Audio tapes of conference proceedings

Publications list:
Available online and in print

Access to staff:
Contact by letter, by telephone, by fax and by e-mail
Hours: Mon to Fri, 0900 to 1700

Access to building, collection or gallery:
Prior appointment required

VOICE: THE UNION FOR EDUCATION PROFESSIONALS

2 St James' Court, Friar Gate, Derby, DE1 1BT

Tel: 01332 372337
Fax: 01332 290310 or 292431
E-mail: enquiries@voicetheunion.org.uk

Website:
http://www.pat.org.uk
News, booklets, factsheets, information packs, surveys; information or actual copies available online.

Enquiries:
Enquiries to: General Secretary
Other contacts: Communications Officer for media – pressoffice@voicetheunion.org.uk.

Founded:
1970

Formerly called:
Professional Association of Teachers (PAT) (year of change 2008)

Incorporates the former:
Professional Association of Nursery Nurses (PANN) (year of change 2008)

Organisation type and purpose:
Professional body, trade union (membership is by subscription), present number of members: 38,000. Teachers, lecturers, education support staff and childcarers.

Subject coverage:
Matters of interest to the teaching and child care professions at all levels and in all sectors.

Printed publications:
Your Voice (4 times a year)
Advice booklets, factsheets and information packs on pay and conditions, education and childcare practice
Some publications available free online (some to members only, some to all)
Order printed publications from: e-mail: publications@voicetheunion.org.uk

Publications list:
Available online and in print

Access to staff:
Contact by letter, by telephone, by fax, by e-mail and via website. Appointment necessary. Access for members only.
Hours: Mon to Fri, 0900 to 1700

Access to building, collection or gallery:
Prior appointment required
Hours: Mon to Fri, 0900 to 1700

Access for disabled people:
Parking provided, level entry

Also at:
Voice (Scotland)
4–6 Oak Lane, Edinburgh, EH12 6XH; tel: 0131 317 8282; fax: 0131 317 8111; e-mail: scotland@voicetheunion.org.uk

VOLKSWAGEN TYPE 2 OWNERS' CLUB

Acronym or abbreviation: VWT20C

57 Humphrey Avenue, Charford, Bromsgrove, Worcestershire, B60 3JD

Tel: 01527 872194
Fax: 01527 872194
E-mail: philshawvw@cs.com

Website:
http://www.vwt2oc.org.uk
http://www.vanfest.org

Enquiries:
Enquiries to: Honorary Club Secretary

Founded:
1991

Organisation type and purpose:
International organisation, advisory body, membership association (membership is by subscription), present number of members: 2500, voluntary organisation.

Subject coverage:
Volkswagen Type 2 vehicles, advice and help given to members with any related problem.

Museum or gallery collection, archive, or library special collection:
Wide range of printed information concerning Volkswagen Type 2 vehicles

Library catalogue:
All or part available in-house

Printed publications:
Magazine (6 times a year, members)

Access to staff:
Contact by letter, by telephone, by fax, by e-mail, in person and via website. Appointment necessary.
Hours: 7 days, 1000 to 2200

VOLUNTARY EUTHANASIA SOCIETY

Acronym or abbreviation: VES

13 Prince of Wales Terrace, London, W8 5PG

Tel: 020 7937 7770
Fax: 020 7376 2648
E-mail: info@ves.org.uk

Website:
http://www.ves.org.uk
Up-to-date news, background information and articles on end-of-life issues. Information on campaign.

Founded:
1935

Formerly called:
EXIT (year of change 1982)

Organisation type and purpose:
Voluntary organisation.
Promoting living wills, campaigning to change the law so that a competent incurably ill adult who is suffering unbearably can choose medical assistance to die.

Subject coverage:
Voluntary euthanasia, advance directives, living wills, patients' rights, physician-assisted suicide, refusal of medical treatment.

Museum or gallery collection, archive, or library special collection:
Newsletters of World Federation Members
Press cuttings and articles
Extensive collection of books and journal articles

Printed publications:
Information pack
Information leaflets on voluntary euthanasia
Living Wills and Physician Assisted Suicide
VES newsletter (3 times a year)
Living Wills

Access to staff:
Contact by letter, by telephone, by fax, by e-mail and via website
Hours: Mon to Fri, 1000 to 1600
Special comments: Visitors strictly by prior appointment.

Access to building, collection or gallery:
No prior appointment required
Hours: Mon to Fri, 1000 to 1600

Affiliated to:
World Federation of Right to Die Societies

VOLUNTARY SERVICE BUREAU

Acronym or abbreviation: VSB

34 Shaftesbury Square, Belfast, BT2 7DB

Tel: 02890 200850
Fax: 02890 200860
E-mail: info@vsb.org.uk

Website:
http://www.vsb.org.uk/

Enquiries:
Enquiries to: Co-ordinator

Founded:
1968

Organisation type and purpose:
Volunteer Centre for Belfast, Castlereagh, North Down and Ards. Provides support for volunteers and around 600 organisations working with volunteers.

Subject coverage:
Information on volunteer opportunities throughout Northern Ireland.

Access to staff:
Contact by letter, by telephone, by fax, by e-mail, in person and via website. All charged.
Hours: Mon to Fri, 0900 to 1700

Other branches:
VSB North Down & Ards
  91 High Street, Bangor, BT20 5BD; tel: 02891
  270486; fax: 02891 275335; e-mail: lorraine@vsb
  .org.uk

VOLUNTARY SERVICE OVERSEAS

Acronym or abbreviation: VSO

317 Putney Bridge Road, London, SW15 2PN

Tel: 020 8780 7200\ Minicom no. 020 8780 7440
Fax: 020 8780 7300
E-mail: enquiry@vso.org.uk

Website:
http://www.vso.org.uk
Job information, campaigns and events, information provision, publishing working papers, magazine, overseas programmes, fundraising events.

Enquiries:
Enquiries to: Enquiries Unit
Direct tel: 020 8780 7500
Direct fax: 020 8780 7207

Founded:
1958

Organisation type and purpose:
International organisation, present number of members: 1939, voluntary organisation, registered charity (charity number 313757).
Development agency that works through volunteers to tackle disadvantage in developing communities worldwide.

Subject coverage:
Advice on volunteering opportunities with VSO.

Publications list:
Available online and in print

Access to staff:
Contact by letter, by telephone, by fax, by e-mail and via website
Hours: Enquiries unit: Mon to Fri, 0900 to 1700

Access to building, collection or gallery:
No prior appointment required
Hours: Library: Mon to Fri, 0900 to 1700; Sat, 1000 to 1630

Access for disabled people:
Ramped entry, toilet facilities

VOLUNTEER CENTRE

Formal name: Centre for Community Action, Volunteering & Employment Initiatives
Acronym or abbreviation: VC

4th Floor, 84 Miller Street, Glasgow, G1 1DT

Tel: 0141 226 3431
Fax: 0141 221 0716
E-mail: info@volunteerglasgow.org

Website:
http://www.volunteerglasgow.org
Information on all the services provided.
Soon – online database of volunteering opportunties.

Enquiries:
Enquiries to: Information Officer

Founded:
1970

Organisation type and purpose:
Membership association (membership is by election or invitation), present number of members: 99, registered charity (charity number SCO 05462).
A catalogue of volunteering opportunities available in Glasgow. A resource library of publications relating to volunteering and issues affecting the voluntary sector.
The Centre aims to improve the quality of life for the people of Glasgow by offering opportunities to use and develop their skills in volunteering, training and personal development. In addition,

the Centre works in neighbourhoods to develop informal care and support services with vulnerable families and individuals; and in partnership with charitable trusts, local authorities and other organisations to deliver community care services.

Subject coverage:
Volunteering, good practice in working with volunteers, befriending, carers, employment issues for voluntary and community organisations, community care, employment training for physically disabled people, health and wellbeing.

Museum or gallery collection, archive, or library special collection:
Resource library of books and documents relating to volunteering, the voluntary sector, health and social care, community care, disability, health and safety, employment, education etc
Catalogue of voluntary opportunities for potential volunteers

Non-library collection catalogue:
All or part available online

Printed publications:
Newsletter for volunteers (2 times a year, free)
Newsletter for organisations that involve volunteers (2 times a year)
A Guide to Good Practice on Employment and Management Issues for Voluntary Organisations (ISBN 1 87175901 3, £19 plus £1.95 p&p)
Good practice factsheets for organisations involving volunteers (free)

Access to staff:
Contact by letter, by telephone, by fax, by e-mail, in person and via website
Hours: Mon to Thu, 0900 to 1700; Fri, 0900 to 1600

Access to building, collection or gallery:
No access other than to staff

VOLUNTEERING ENGLAND

Acronym or abbreviation: VE

Regents Wharf, 8 All Saints Street, London, N1 9RL

Tel: 0845 305 6979
Fax: 020 7520 8910
E-mail: volunteering@volunteeringengland.org

Website:
http://www.volunteering.org.uk/

Enquiries:
Enquiries to: Head of Information

Founded:
2004

Created by the merger of:
the Consortium on Opportunities for Volunteering, the National Centre for Volunteering and Volunteer Development England. Subsequently merged with Student Volunteering England (in 2007).

Organisation type and purpose:
Voluntary organisation, registered charity (charity number 1102770).
National development agency for volunteering.

Subject coverage:
Information, training and support to organisations who work with volunteers, campaign on public policy.

Museum or gallery collection, archive, or library special collection:
Largest library on volunteering in the UK

Library catalogue:
All or part available in-house

Printed publications:
Volunteering (magazine, 10 times a year, UK £20)
Many leaflets and books including:
Managing Volunteers
The 1997 National Survey of Volunteering in the UK
Volunteering in Europe: Opportunities and challenges for the 90s

Working With Volunteers (4 booklets, personnel
 issues, recruitment and selection, training,
 support)
Order printed publications from: MJF Data
Management
River House, Riverside Way, Uxbridge, UB8 2YF,
tel: 01895 909050, fax: 01895 909060

Publications list:
Available in print

Access to staff:
Contact by letter, by telephone, by fax and by e-
mail. Appointment necessary.
Hours: Mon to Fri, 1000 to 1700

Access to building, collection or gallery:
Prior appointment required

Access for disabled people:
Access to all public areas, toilet facilities

VOLVO ENTHUSIASTS CLUB

Acronym or abbreviation: VEC

127 Kidderminster Road, Wribbenhall, Bewdley,
Worcestershire, DY12 1JE

Tel: 01872 553740 or 01425 476425
Fax: 01872 553740 (phone first)

Website:
http://www.volvo1800.co.uk
http://www.volvoenthusiastsclub.co.uk

Enquiries:
Enquiries to: Chairman/Founder

Founded:
1989

Organisation type and purpose:
International organisation, membership
association (membership is by subscription),
present number of members: 1500, voluntary
organisation.
To encourage ownership, interest, preservation
and correct maintenance of all Volvos over 15 years
old or out of production, and to serve as a source
of technical information and parts through a
friendly family style club.

Subject coverage:
Historic and technical information on all Volvo
cars, buses and trucks over 15 years old, spares
location and availability, restoration advice, guide
to purchase, classic Volvo historical data P1800
(Saint Volvo), 120 (Amazon) etc, international
register, historic rally-race preparation-information
and data-race/rally register.

**Museum or gallery collection, archive, or library
special collection:**
Complete Volvo production data for P1800 1961–
 63 – first 6000 vehicles built by Jensen
Sales brochures – P1800, 120 etc
Technical library – Volvo workshop manuals, parts
 lists etc
Homologation papers 120, 1800-PV-140 etc
Volvo special tuning data B18/B20 engines and
 vehicles fitted with these units
Volvo special tools

Trade and statistical information:
Production data pre 1990 – rolling over 15 years,
all models.
Production data from original records of P1800
1961–1963.
Current vehicle values and trends.

Printed publications:
Buyers Guides for each model covered by the Club
Club Magazine (quarterly, free to members)
List of Cars For Sale or Wanted
Volvo Enthusiasts Club Magazine

Access to staff:
Contact by letter and by telephone. Non-members
charged.
Hours: Mon to Fri, 0900 to 1700

VOLVO OWNERS CLUB

18 Macaulay Avenue, Portsmouth, Hampshire,
PO6 4NY

Tel: 023 9238 1494
Fax: 023 9238 1494
E-mail: membership@volvoclub.org.uk

Website:
http://www.Volvoclub.org.uk
Information relating to the Club.

Enquiries:
Enquiries to: Membership Secretary

Organisation type and purpose:
Membership association (membership is by
subscription), present number of members: 5000.
Club for owners and enthusiasts of Volvo cars.

Subject coverage:
All aspects of the ownership and maintenance of
Volvo cars.

Access to staff:
Contact by letter, by telephone, by fax, by e-mail
and via website
Hours: Mon to Sun

VTCT

Third Floor, Eastleigh House, Market Street,
Eastleigh, Hampshire, SO50 9FD

Tel: 023 8068 4500
Fax: 023 8065 1493
E-mail: info@vtct.org.uk

Website:
http://www.vtct.org.uk

Enquiries:
Enquiries to: Customer Service Department
Direct e-mail: customerservice@vtct.org.uk
Other contacts: Head of Quality Assurance for
potential training centres.

Founded:
1986

Formed from:
International Health and Beauty Council (IHBC)
(year of change 1986)

Organisation type and purpose:
International organisation, registered charity
(charity number 295192). Awarding body (service
sector). National and international qualifications in
hairdressing, beauty, fitness, sport, holistic and
complementary therapies. Supportive
qualifications in business organisation, customer
service and keyskills.

Subject coverage:
Availability of National and Scottish vocational
qualifications (NVQs and S/NVQs) and
international qualifications in beauty, hairdressing,
holistic and complementary, fitness and sports
therapies. Courses are provided across the British
Isles, primarily in Colleges of Further Education.

Access to staff:
Contact by letter, by telephone and by e-mail
Hours: Mon to Fri, 0900 to 1700
Special comments: No visitors in person.

VW OWNERS' CLUB GB

Acronym or abbreviation: VWOC (GB)

PO Box 7, Burntwood, Walsall, West Midlands,
WS7 2SB

E-mail: info@vwocgb.com

Website:
http://www.vwocgb.com
Technical information, vehicle age verification,
online membership, articles, adverts and
discounts.

Founded:
1953

Organisation type and purpose:
Membership association (membership is by
subscription), present number of members: 1,000,
voluntary organisation.
To provide a focal group for all enthusiasts of
Volkswagen Group vehicles both old and modern.
Also to obtain from associated trades any financial
benefits possible for members.

Subject coverage:
VW cars including all Volkswagen Group
Companies.

Access to staff:
Contact by letter, by e-mail and via website
Hours: Mon to Fri, 0900 to 1700

WADHAM COLLEGE

The Library, Oxford, OX1 3PN

Tel: 01865 277900
E-mail: library@wadham.ox.ac.uk

Enquiries:
Enquiries to: Librarian

Founded:
1613

Organisation type and purpose:
University department or institute.
College library.

Subject coverage:
General undergraduate material; Spanish (16th
and 17th centuries); Persian.

**Museum or gallery collection, archive, or library
special collection:**
16th-century theology (2,000 vols)
16th- and 17th-century Spanish books (1,000 vols)
Persian and Arabic manuscripts (800 items)
Persian lithographs (200 items)
Printed books in Persian, Arabic and European
 languages on Persian classical literature and
 history, up to the end of the Constitutional
 Persian Revolution in 1911

Non-library collection catalogue:
All or part available online and in-house

Library catalogue:
All or part available online and in-house

Access to staff:
Contact by letter, by telephone and by e-mail.
Appointment necessary.
Hours: Mon to Fri, 0900 to 1700

Parent body:
University of Oxford

WAKEFIELD COLLEGE

Margaret Street, Wakefield, West Yorkshire, WF1
2DH

Tel: 01924 789789\ Minicom no. 01924 789270
Fax: 01924 789340
E-mail: staffmember@wakcoll.ac.uk

Website:
http://www.wakcoll.ac.uk

Enquiries:
Enquiries to: Marketing Manager
Direct tel: 01924 789162
Direct fax: 01924 789362

Formerly called:
Wakefield District College

Organisation type and purpose:
Suitable for ages: 16+.
Further Education College.

Subject coverage:
GCSEs, 'A' levels, GNVQs, HNDs, HNCs, NVQs,
computer studies, languages, health, child and
social care, hospitality, leisure and tourism,
business and secretarial, building, technology,
CAD/CAM, art, drama, media, graphics, adult
education, engineering, hair and beauty, sport
studies, public services, horticulture.

continued overleaf

Printed publications:
Corporate Business Courses Literature – Service to
    Business
Full Time Prospectus (full time courses for young
    people)
Part Time Prospectus
HE Prospectus

Electronic and video publications:
Full Time and HE Courses (CD-ROM, free)

Publications list:
Available in print

Access to staff:
Contact by letter
Hours: Mon to Fri, 0900 to 1700

Access to building, collection or gallery:
No prior appointment required
Special comments: Report to main reception.

Access for disabled people:
Parking provided, ramped entry, access to all
public areas, toilet facilities

Connections with:
Learndirect Learning Centre
    tel: 01924 789333; e-mail: c.furbisher@wakcoll.ac
    .uk

Other Campuses:
Hemsworth SkillsBank
    Bank Street, Hemsworth, West Yorkshire, WF9
    4JX; tel: 01924 789789 Minicom: 01977 619784;
    fax: 01977 619480
Thornes Park Campus
    Thornes Park, Horbury Road, Wakefield, West
    Yorkshire, WF2 8QZ; tel: 01924 789789 Minicom:
    01924 789800; fax: 01924 789821
Whitwood Campus
    Four Lane Ends, Castleford, West Yorkshire,
    WF10 5NF; tel: 01924 789789 Minicom: 01924
    789431; fax: 01924 789478

WAKEFIELD HISTORICAL SOCIETY

19 Pinders Grove, Wakefield, WF1 4AH

E-mail: kate@airtime.co.uk

Website:
http://www.wakefieldhistoricalsoc.org.uk

Enquiries:
Enquiries to: President

Founded:
1924

Organisation type and purpose:
To bring together those with an interest in local or
national history

Access to staff:
Contact by letter, by e-mail and via website

WAKEFIELD LIBRARIES AND INFORMATION SERVICE

Library Headquarters, Balne Lane, Wakefield,
West Yorkshire, WF2 0DQ

Tel: 01924 302210\ Typetalk 01924 302210
Fax: 01924 302245
E-mail: lib.admin@wakefield.gov.uk

Website:
http://www.wakefield.gov.uk/libraries
Policy documents, description of service, service
point addresses and opening hours, performance
indicators.

Enquiries:
Enquiries to: Libraries & Information Services
Manager

Founded:
1974

Organisation type and purpose:
Local government body, public library.

Subject coverage:
General, local and family history.

Museum or gallery collection, archive, or library special collection:
British Official Publications, 1974 onwards all
    parliamentary and selected non-Parliamentary
British Standards
Cryer Collection
J S Fletcher Collection
George Gissing Collection
Henry Moore Collection
Local and Family History (District and Yorkshire)
    Collection
School Library Service including:
    books, posters, audio cassettes, videos
Yorkshire Libraries & Information collections:
Junior out-of-print fiction reserve
Medical Library Services
Music and drama services (single copies and sets of
    plays and music)
Provincial Fiction Reserve (N-S section)
Regional Fiction reserve (A-M and T-Z)

Non-library collection catalogue:
All or part available in-house

Library catalogue:
All or part available in-house

Printed publications:
Yorkshire and Humberside Joint Healthcare
    Service Union List of Periodical Holdings

Access to staff:
Contact by letter, by telephone, by fax, by e-mail
and via website
Hours: Mon to Fri, 0900 to 1700

Access for disabled people:
Parking provided, level entry, toilet facilities

Administers:
Yorkshire Libraries & Information (YLI)
    tel: 01924 302210; fax: 01924 302245; e-mail:
    kholliday@wakefield.gov.uk

WALES COUNCIL FOR VOLUNTARY ACTION

Acronym or abbreviation: WCVA

Cyngor Gweithredu Gwirfoddol Cymru, Baltic
House, Mount Stuart Square, Cardiff, CF10 5FH

Tel: 029 2043 1700\ Minicom no. 029 2043 1702
Fax: 029 2043 1701
E-mail: help@wcva.org.uk

Website:
http://www.wcva.org.uk

Enquiries:
Enquiries to: WCVA Helpdesk
Direct tel: 0870 607 1666

Founded:
1934

Organisation type and purpose:
Trade union (membership is by subscription),
present number of members: 1,750 approx, service
industry, voluntary organisation, registered charity
(charity number 218093).
Promotes and supports voluntary action and
community development in Wales.

Subject coverage:
Information relating to the voluntary sector in
Wales; legal matters, funding advice, Europe and
European funding, training, community care,
contracting, volunteering matters, community
development, voluntary sector liaison with the
National Assembly for Wales.

Museum or gallery collection, archive, or library special collection:
Comprehensive collection of material relating to
    the voluntary sector, with particular emphasis on
    Wales

Trade and statistical information:
Database of voluntary organisations in Wales.

Library catalogue:
All or part available in-house

Printed publications:
Best Value and the voluntary sector: A Guide
    (2001, £5)
Dance with the Dragon – A guide to devolution in
    Wales for UK voluntary organisations (bilingual,
    1999, £5)
Faith and hope don't run charities (trustees do) – a
    practical guide for voluntary members of
    management committees (1999, £10)
National Voluntary Organisations in Wales:
    Directory 2000 (2000, £10)
Wales Funding Handbook 2000 (£17)
Wales voluntary sector almanac 2002 – Key facts
    and figures
Wales voluntary sector almanac 2002 – Mapping
    the sector
Briefing and consultation documents
Information sheets
Network Wales (newsletter, fortnightly)
Order printed publications from: WCVA Publications,
WCVA
At the same address, tel: 029 2043 1723, fax: 029
2043 1701, e-mail: publications@wcva.org.uk

Electronic and video publications:
Disc version (customised) of Directory of
    Voluntary Organisations in Wales: National
    contacts

Publications list:
Available in print

Access to staff:
Contact by letter, by telephone, by fax, by e-mail
and via website. Appointment necessary. Non-
members charged.
Hours: Mon to Fri, 0900 to 1700

Access for disabled people:
Parking provided, ramped entry, access to all
public areas, toilet facilities

Other addresses:
Mid Wales Office
    Ladywell House, Newtown, Powys, SY16 1JB
North Wales Office
    13 Wynnstay Road, Colwyn Bay, Conwy, LL29
    8NB; tel: 01492 539800; fax: 01492 539801

WALES EURO INFO CENTRE

Acronym or abbreviation: WEIC

UWCC, Guest Building, PO Box 430, Cardiff, CF24
0DE

Tel: 029 2022 9525
Fax: 029 2022 9740
E-mail: info@weic.demon.co.uk

Website:
http://www.waleseic.org.uk

Enquiries:
Enquiries to: Information Officer

Founded:
1989

Organisation type and purpose:
European information centre.
To provide SMEs with European information and
advice to help them take full advantage of the
Single Market.

Subject coverage:
European information, business, legislation,
statistics etc.

Museum or gallery collection, archive, or library special collection:
Complete collection of EC documentation: some
    gaps in the Eurostats collection

Trade and statistical information:
EC statistical information.
Basic market information.
EU legislation.
Public Procurement.
Grantfinder.
Business Conditions.
Business Co-operation offers

Access to staff:
Contact by letter, by telephone and by e-mail.
Appointment necessary. Non-members charged.
Hours: Mon to Fri, 0900 to 1700

Access for disabled people:
Level entry

Parent bodies:
Commission of the European Communities
    DG Enterprise
Flint County Council
University of Wales, Cardiff

WALES TOURIST BOARD

Acronym or abbreviation: WTB

Brunel House, 2 Fitzalan Road, Cardiff, CF24 0UY

Tel: 029 2049 9909
Fax: 029 2048 5031

Website:
http://www.visitwales.com
Product, statistical and grant aid information for
Wales, a gateway to information on visiting Wales,
Wales as a nation and the work of the Wales
Tourist Board.

Enquiries:
Enquiries to: Information Development Officer
Direct tel: 029 2047 5277
Direct e-mail: kathryn.newton@tourism.wales.gov
.uk

Organisation type and purpose:
National government body.
Statutory body.

Subject coverage:
Development, marketing and advisory functions
relating to tourism in Wales, events, attractions,
activities, holidays and accommodation.

Trade and statistical information:
Data on the number of overseas visitors, domestic
    visitors, visitors to attractions in Wales.

Printed publications:
Events Listings
Maps
Promotional publications
Tourist guides

Electronic and video publications:
Heritage of a Nation (video)
Homecoming 2000 (video)
Rugby World Cup (video)
The Wonder of Wales (video)
Welcome to Wales (CD-ROM)
Voices from Wales (CD)

Publications list:
Available in print

Access to staff:
Contact by letter, by telephone, by fax and by e-
mail
Hours: Mon to Fri, 0900 to 1700

Associated with:
British Tourist Authority

WALLCOVERINGS SECTOR COUNCIL

Acronym or abbreviation: WMA

British Coatings Federation, James House, Bridge
Street, Leatherhead, Surrey, KT22 7EP

Tel: 01372 360660
Fax: 01372 376069
E-mail: alison.brown@bcf.co.uk

Enquiries:
Enquiries to: Administrator

Founded:
2005

Created by the merger of:
Wallcovering Manufacturers' Association of Great
Britain Limited (f. 1970) and British Coatings
Federation (year of change 2005)

Organisation type and purpose:
Trade association, membership association
(membership is by subscription, election or
invitation), present number of members: 15.

Subject coverage:
Wallcovering manufacture, product standards,
pattern book names.

Trade and statistical information:
Statistics (very selective distribution).

Access to staff:
Contact by letter, by fax and by e-mail
Hours: Mon to Fri, 0900 to 1700

WALLPAPER HISTORY SOCIETY

Acronym or abbreviation: WHS

c/o Victoria and Albert Museum, South
Kensington, London, SW7 2RL

Tel: 020 7942 2560

Enquiries:
Enquiries to: Secretary
Direct tel: 020 8977 4978

Founded:
1986

Organisation type and purpose:
Research organisation.

Subject coverage:
History of wallpaper, bibliography, specialist
conservation sources, manufacturers specialising
in the production of reproduction historic papers,
details of museums and archives holding
wallpapers.

**Museum or gallery collection, archive, or library
special collection:**
Please note that the Society itself holds no
    collections, though it has members and contacts
    in institutions which do have collections of
    wallpaper

Printed publications:
Wallpaper History Review

Access to staff:
Contact by letter and by telephone
Hours: Mon to Fri, 0900 to 1700

WALMSLEY SOCIETY

April Cottage, 1 Brand Road, Hampden Park,
Eastbourne, East Sussex, BN2 9PX

Tel: 01323 506447

Website:
http://www.walmsleysoc.org

Enquiries:
Enquiries to: Honorary Secretary
Other contacts: Membership Secretary for
membership enquiries only

Founded:
1985

Organisation type and purpose:
International organisation (membership is by
subscription). Literary society. To promote and
encourage an appreciation of the literary and
artistic heritage left by Leo and J Ulric Walmsley.

Subject coverage:
Appreciation of the work of Leo Walmsley (author)
and the work of James Ulric Walmsley (artist).

**Museum or gallery collection, archive, or library
special collection:**
Various items and information applicable to the
    aims of the society

Printed publications:
Society Journal (two a year, members free, £3 non-
members)
Various booklets (prices on application)
Reprints by publisher of some of Leo Walmsley's
books (price on application)
Order printed publications from: Walmsley Society, 55
Red Hall Drive, Leeds, West Yorksire, LS14 1EJ

Electronic and video publications:
Turn of The Tide (video, £13.95 incl p&p, J Arthur
Rank's first feature film based on Leo Walmsley's
book 'Three Fevers')

Publications list:
Available online and in print

Access to staff:
Contact by letter, by telephone and via website
Hours: Anytime within reason

Member of:
The Alliance of Literary Societies

Other addresses:
Membership Secretary (letter only)
21 The Crescent, Hipperholme, Halifax,
Yorkshire, HX3 8NQ

WALSALL HOSPITAL NHS TRUST

Manor Hospital Postgraduate Medical Centre,
Medical Library, Moat Road, Walsall, West
Midlands, WS2 9PS

Tel: 01922 721172

Enquiries:
Enquiries to: Librarian

WALSALL LOCAL HISTORY CENTRE

Essex Street, Walsall, West Midlands, WS2 7AS

Tel: 01922 721305
Fax: 01922 634954
E-mail: localhistorycentre@walsall.gov.uk

Website:
http://www.walsall.gov.uk/localhistorycentre

Enquiries:
Enquiries to: Archivist/Local Studies Officer

Founded:
1986

Formerly called:
Walsall Archives Service

Organisation type and purpose:
Local government body, public library. Record
office, archive and local studies library.

Subject coverage:
All aspects of the history of Walsall Metropolitan
Borough and its constituent towns: Aldridge,
Bloxwich, Brownhills, Darlaston, Willenhall and
Walsall. Photographic, map, oral history,
ephemera, newspapers, printed materials, archives
and family history.

Non-library collection catalogue:
All or part available online and in-house

Library catalogue:
All or part available online and in-house

Printed publications:
A large number of publications, many with
photographs, on the Black Country, its people,
industry and history
Many books on specific areas including:
Aldridge, Bloxwich, Brownhills, Caldmore and
Palfrey, Darlaston, Pheasey, Streetly, Walsall,
Willenhall

Publications list:
Available online and in print

Access to staff:
Contact by letter, by telephone, by fax, by e-mail,
in person and via website
Hours: Mon, closed; Tue and Thu, 0930 to 1730;
Wed, 0930 to 1900; Fri, 0930 to 1700; Sat, 0930 to
1300

Access for disabled people:
Ramped entry, access to all public areas, toilet
facilities

WALTHAM FOREST ARCHIVES AND LOCAL STUDIES LIBRARY

Vestry House Museum, Vestry Road, Walthamstow, London, E17 9NH

Tel: 020 8509 1917
E-mail: vestry.house@walthamforest.gov.uk

Website:
http://www.walthamforest.gov.uk/index/leisure/local-history.htm

Enquiries:
Enquiries to: Archivist
Other contacts: Local Studies Librarian

Founded:
Late 1970s

Organisation type and purpose:
Local government body, public library.

Subject coverage:
History and development of the area covered by the London Borough of Waltham Forest (comprising the former boroughs of Chingford, Leyton and Walthamstow).

Museum or gallery collection, archive, or library special collection:
Records of Waltham Forest Deanery (including parish records)

Non-library collection catalogue:
All or part available in-house

Library catalogue:
All or part available in-house

Printed publications:
Victoria County History (extracts from the Victoria History of the Counties of England – A History of Essex Vol. V and Vol. VI, extracts for Chingford and Leyton, published by LBWF)
War over Walthamstow (Ross Wyld, LBWF)
Alfred Hitchcock: From Leytonstone to Hollywood (Nigel Sadler and Victoria Coxon)
Walthamstow Historical Society Publications:
Waltham Forest Revisited, 1910–1940
Some Old Walthamstow Houses
A Brief History of Courtenay Warner and the Warner Estate
Bullseyes
Chingford Historical Society Publications:
Chingford As It Was
Chingford in History
The Chingflier (extracts from the Chingford Royal Naval Air Station magazine, WWI)
Waltham Forest Oral History Society Publications:
Walthamstow Village
We Want Winns
Jenny Hammond – the life of a Labour Councillor
One Door Closes, Another Opens
Order printed publications from: Linda Weston at Vestry House Museum, Vestry Road, Walthamstow, London E17 9NH, tel: 020 8509 1917

Publications list:
Available in print

Access to staff:
Contact by letter, by telephone, by e-mail and in person. Appointment necessary.
Hours: By prior appointment; Thu, Fri and Sat, 1000 to 1300 and 1400 to 1700

Access for disabled people:
Stairs to Searchroom (located in a listed building), but appointments can take place in an accessible ground floor room by prior arrangement.

WALTHAM FOREST COLLEGE

Library, Forest Road, Walthamstow, London, E17 4JB

Tel: 020 8501 8501
Fax: 020 8501 8302
E-mail: library@waltham.ac.uk

Enquiries:
Enquiries to: Learning Resources Manager
Direct tel: 020 8501 8026
Direct e-mail: pauline.nash@waltham.ac.uk

Founded:
1938

Subject coverage:
Business studies, management, office technology, computing, electrical and electronic engineering, manufacturing, automobile engineering, art and design, fashion technology, caring, health studies, counselling, ESOL, EFL, catering, meat technology, travel and tourism, hotel management, performing arts, media studies, general education, science, beauty therapy, hairdressing, built environment.

Library catalogue:
All or part available in-house

Access to staff:
Contact by letter, by telephone, by fax and by e-mail. Appointment necessary.
Hours: Mon to Thu, 0845 to 1900; Fri, 0845 to 1600

WALTHAM FOREST HEALTHCARE LIBRARY

Acronym or abbreviation: WXUHT

Whipps Cross Hospital, Leytonstone, London, E11 1NR

Tel: 020 8535 6860
Fax: 020 8535 6973
E-mail: library@whippsx.nhs.uk

Website:
http://www.libnel.nhs.uk

Enquiries:
Enquiries to: Librarian
Direct tel: 020 8535 6860
Direct e-mail: angela.head@whippsx.nhs.uk

Organisation type and purpose:
Multidisciplinary NHS Trust Library.
To meet the information needs of health and social care staff based in the local health economy

Subject coverage:
General Medical and healthcare library with NHS management and social care

Non-library collection catalogue:
All or part available online

Library catalogue:
All or part available online and in-house

Access to staff:
Contact by letter, by telephone, by fax, by e-mail, in person and via website. Non-members charged.
Hours: Mon, Thu, 0830 to 1900; Tue, Wed, Fri, 0830 to 1700

Access for disabled people:
Lift access, toilet facilities

WALTHAM FOREST LIBRARIES AND CULTURAL SERVICES

Central Library, High Street, London, E17 4JN

Tel: 020 8496 3305
Fax: 020 8496 1101
E-mail: wf.libs@lbwf.gov.uk

Website:
http://www.lbwf.gov.uk
Waltham Forest Council's home page.

Enquiries:
Enquiries to: Head of Libraries and Cultural Services
Direct tel: 020 8520 8522
Direct e-mail: penny.charlish-jackson@walthamforest.gov.uk
Other contacts: Bibliographical Services Manager, tel no: 020 8529 8291

Formerly called:
Waltham Forest Arts and Leisure Department

Organisation type and purpose:
Local government body, public library.

Subject coverage:
General; domestic arts and sciences.

Museum or gallery collection, archive, or library special collection:
Laser subject specialisation, Dewey 640–649, 663–664, 338.47663–338.47664
William Morris Collection

Access to staff:
Contact by letter, by telephone, by fax, by e-mail, in person and via website
Hours: Mon to Fri, 0900 to 1700

WALTHAMSTOW HISTORICAL SOCIETY

Vestry House Museum, Vestry Road, London, E17 9NH

Tel: 020 8509 1917
E-mail: ellingham@clara.co.uk

Website:
http://www.walthamstowhistoricalsociety.org

Enquiries:
Enquiries to: Publications Secretary

Founded:
1914

Formerly called:
Walthamstow Antiquarian Society (year of change 1986)

Organisation type and purpose:
Membership association, registered charity (charity number 277823).
Local history society.

Subject coverage:
Local history of Walthamstow and Waltham Forest.

Publications list:
Available in print

WANDSWORTH LIBRARIES

Department of Leisure & Amenity Services, Wandsworth Town Hall, Wandsworth High Street, London, SW18 2PU

Tel: 020 8871 8536
Fax: 020 8871 7630
E-mail: libraries@wandsworth.gov.uk

Website:
http://www.wandsworth.gov.uk

Enquiries:
Enquiries to: Librarian

Organisation type and purpose:
Local government body, public library.
12 libraries and reference service.

Museum or gallery collection, archive, or library special collection:
Early children's books (tel: 0181 871 7090)
Edward Thomas Collection
G A Henty Collection
William Blake Collection
World War One and Two

Library catalogue:
All or part available online

Access to staff:
Contact by letter, by telephone, by fax, by e-mail and in person
Hours: Mon to Fri, 0900 to 1700

WANDSWORTH LOCAL HISTORY SERVICE

Battersea Library, 265 Lavender Hill, London, SW11 1JB

Tel: 020 8871 7753
Fax: 020 7978 4376

Website:
http://www.wandsworth.gov.uk
Summary of holdings and services, opening hours, (part of Wandsworth Museums website).

Enquiries:
Enquiries to: Local History Archivist
Direct e-mail: localhistory@wandsworth.gov.uk
Other contacts: Senior Librarian for local history.

Organisation type and purpose:
Public library.

Museum or gallery collection, archive, or library special collection:
Local history library for Wandsworth area; photograph collection
Archives of London Borough of Wandsworth and predecessor authorities, local institutions and societies including WWII records, electoral registers
Microfilm resources: Census returns 1841 to 1901 (local area); IGI (1992 edition) for England; local newspapers c.1853 to 1990s (some gaps); maps of local area mid-17th century to present day
Cuttings collections of Mayors of Wandsworth circa 1950s to 1960s
Cuttings collections of Alfred Hurley, proprietor of Tooting and Balham Gazette 1900 to 1947
Wandsworth Scrapbooks circa 1880 to 1939
Slides of local area (approx. 3000) loan service
Wandsworth Museum holds original watercolours and prints; printed ephemera and photograph collections
Battersea Scrapbooks 1901–1939

Non-library collection catalogue:
All or part available in-house

Library catalogue:
All or part available online

Printed publications:
Modern reproductions of postcards and paintings; maps and prints (prices available on application)
Local history publications produced by local authors etc (also on sale)

Access to staff:
Contact by letter, by telephone, by fax, by e-mail, in person and via website
Hours: Tue, Wed, 1000 to 2000; Fri, 1000 to 1700; Sat, 0900 to 1300

WAR WIDOWS' ASSOCIATION OF GREAT BRITAIN

c/o 48 Pall Mall, London, SW1Y 5JY

Tel: 0845 241 2189
E-mail: info@warwidowsassociation.org.uk

Website:
http://www.warwidowsassociation.org.uk

Enquiries:
Enquiries to: Secretary

Founded:
1971

Organisation type and purpose:
Membership association (membership is by subscription), present number of members: 5,500, voluntary organisation, registered charity (charity number 1002656).
The improvement of War Widows' Pensions and the regulations pertaining to them. Support for War Widows. Not grant-making.

Subject coverage:
War Widows' pensions; associated DSS benefits.

Printed publications:
Courage

Publications list:
Available in print

Access to staff:
Contact by letter, by telephone, by e-mail and via website
Hours: Mon to Fri, 0900 to 1700

WARBURG INSTITUTE

Woburn Square, London, WC1H 0AB

Tel: 020 7862 8949
Fax: 020 7862 8955

E-mail: warburg@sas.ac.uk
Website:
http://www.warburg.sas.ac.uk

Enquiries:
Enquiries to: Secretary

Founded:
1921

Organisation type and purpose:
University department or institute.
Postgraduate research institute.

Subject coverage:
History of the classical tradition: those elements of European thought, literature, art and institutions which derive from the ancient world.

Education services:
Postgraduate degrees.

Museum or gallery collection, archive, or library special collection:
Library (305,000 vols) on the classical tradition
Collection of photographs, primarily designed for the study of iconography
Archive

Non-library collection catalogue:
All or part available online and in-house

Library catalogue:
All or part available online

Printed publications:
Journal of the Warburg and Courtauld Institutes (annually, £105 plus p&p)
Fritz Saxl (1890–1948, a biographical memoir, reprint 1998, £5)
Journals (set of six vols 32–37 plus index, £30 plus p&p)
Studies, studies and texts, colloquia and surveys (lists available at end of each issue of the above Journal)
Legal Documents of the Hellenistic World (eds M. J. Geller and H. Maehler, with A. D. E. Lewis, 1995, £30)
Order printed publications from: e-mail: warburg.books@sas.ac.uk

Publications list:
Available online and in print

Access to staff:
Contact by letter, by telephone, by fax, by e-mail, in person and via website. Letter of introduction required.
Hours: Mon to Fri, 1000 to 1800

Access to building, collection or gallery:
Access to library by library ticket
Hours: Mon to Fri, 1000 to 1800; Sat opening varies

Access for disabled people:
Ramped entry front and rear, access to all public areas, toilet facilities
Special comments: Lift access to floors other than ground floor and basement.

Houses the library of:
British Numismatic Society
  tel: 020 7862 8951 (part time)
Folklore Society
  tel: 020 7862 8564 (part time)
Royal Numismatic Society

Parent body:
University of London, School of Advanced Study
  tel: 020 7862 8659; fax: 020 7862 8657

WARRINGTON BOROUGH COUNCIL

Town Hall, Warrington, Cheshire, WA1 1UH

Tel: 01925 444400
Fax: 01925 442138

Website:
http://www.warrington.gov.uk

Enquiries:
Enquiries to: Head of Communications
Direct tel: 01925 442042
Direct fax: 01925 442024

Direct e-mail: bwilliams@warrington.gov.uk

Organisation type and purpose:
Local government body.

Subject coverage:
Council services and amenities; corporate services, education, environmental services, finance, housing, legal services, personnel services, planning development and tourism, property and technical services, roads and transportation, social work, council tax and other payments.

Printed publications:
Contacting the Council (free)
Warrington News (4 times a year)
Warrington Official Handbook (free)
Warrington Official Street Guide

Access to staff:
Contact by letter, by telephone and by fax.
Appointment necessary.
Hours: Mon to Fri, 0900 to 1700

WARRINGTON CHAMBER OF COMMERCE AND INDUSTRY

International Business Centre, Delta Crescent, Westbrook, Warrington, Cheshire, WA5 7WQ

Tel: 01925 715150
Fax: 01925 715159
E-mail: info@warrington-chamber.co.uk

Website:
http://www.warrington-chamber.co.uk
Details of Chamber activities.

Enquiries:
Enquiries to: Chief Executive

Founded:
1876

Organisation type and purpose:
Trade association. Provides advice and guidance on matters of commercial and industrial concern.

Subject coverage:
Export documentation and advice; seminars and training; language provision; general information in fields of industrial and commercial interest.

Printed publications:
Annual members' handbook
Newspaper (quarterly, free to members)
News-sheets (monthly, free to members)

Access to staff:
Contact by letter, by telephone, by fax, by e-mail and via website. Appointment necessary.
Hours: Mon to Thu, 0900 to 1700; Fri, 0900 to 1630

Member of the:
Association of Cheshire Chambers
Association of North West Chambers of Commerce
North Cheshire, Wirral and North Wales Consortium of Chambers of Commerce

WARRINGTON COLLEGIATE

Winwick Road Campus, Winwick Road, Warrington, Cheshire, WA2 8QA

Tel: 01925 494422
Fax: 01925 494422
E-mail: swatkiss@warrington.ac.uk

Website:
http://www.warrington.ac.uk
Information about the college, library catalogue, links to other organisations.

Founded:
1979

Formerly called:
North Cheshire College

Organisation type and purpose:
Further and higher education.

continued overleaf

Subject coverage:
Construction, engineering, business studies, leisure, media, performing arts and sports studies, travel and tourism, creative arts, health and social care, hairdressing, beauty therapy, holistics.

Museum or gallery collection, archive, or library special collection:
Lewis Carroll

Library catalogue:
All or part available online and in-house

Access to staff:
Contact by letter and by telephone
Hours: Mon to Thu, 0845 to 2000; Fri, 0845 to 1630
Winwick Campus: Sat, 0900 to 1300

Access for disabled people:
Parking provided, ramped entry, access to all public areas, toilet facilities

WARRINGTON LIBRARY

Museum Street, Warrington, Cheshire, WA1 1JB

Tel: 01925 442889\ Minicom no. 01925 442890
Fax: 01925 411395
E-mail: library@warrington.gov.uk

Website:
http://www.warrington.gov.uk/libraries

Enquiries:
Enquiries to: Information Services Manager

Founded:
1848

Organisation type and purpose:
Local government body, public library.

Subject coverage:
Soap industry and manufacture, wire manufacture, welding, general.

Museum or gallery collection, archive, or library special collection:
Substantial body of material held on local area in terms of local and family history including: a large collection of manuscripts and archives; local studies books and pamphlets; photographs and other images; voters' lists; maps; ephemera; microform copies of censuses, newspapers, and parish and other church records

Library catalogue:
All or part available online

Access to staff:
Contact by letter, by telephone, by fax, by e-mail, in person and via website
Hours: Mon to Thu, 0900 to 1800; Fri, 0900 to 1700; Sat, 0900 to 1600

Access to building, collection or gallery:
No prior appointment required

Access for disabled people:
Disabled access to main entrance, access to all public areas

Parent body:
Warrington Borough Council Libraries, Heritage and Learning Service
website: http://www.warrington.gov.uk

WARWICKSHIRE COLLEGE

Warwick New Road, Leamington Spa, Warwickshire, CV35 5JE

Tel: 01926 318000
Fax: 01926 318111
E-mail: enquiries@warkscol.co.uk

Website:
http://www.warkscol.ac.uk

Enquiries:
Enquiries to: Admission
Direct tel: 0800 7836767
Other contacts: The Principal

Founded:
1949

Organisation type and purpose:
Training and education. Further and higher education.

Subject coverage:
Art and design, building and construction, business, accounting and management studies, caring, nursing and social welfare, computing and administration, engineering technology, agriculture, horticulture, machinery, equine studies, animal care, business studies, education, training, media, music, performing arts, veterinary nursing, arboriculture, spa management, English as a foreign language, English as a second language, GCE A levels, GCSEs, hairdressing and beauty therapy, hospitality and catering, languages, motor vehicle technology, sports studies, leisure and tourism, return to learn courses, adult basic education and programmes for students with learning difficulties and disabilities.

Printed publications:
Prospectus (free)

Publications list:
Available online and in print

Access to staff:
Contact by letter, by telephone, by fax, by e-mail, in person and via website
Hours: Mon to Fri, 0900 to 1700

WARWICKSHIRE COLLEGE – MORETON MORRELL CENTRE

Formal name: Warwickshire College Royal Leamington Spa and Moreton Morrell

Moreton Morrell, Warwick, CV35 9BL

Tel: 01926 318278
Fax: 01926 318300
E-mail: librarymm@warkscol.ac.uk

Website:
http://www.warkscol.ac.uk
Select student intranet

Enquiries:
Enquiries to: Librarian

Founded:
1949

Formerly called:
Warwickshire College of Agriculture (year of change 1996)

Organisation type and purpose:
Suitable for ages: Further and Higher Education. College for land-based industries.

Subject coverage:
Agriculture; agricultural engineering; amenity and commercial horticulture; business studies; equine studies; horse management and horse business management; small animal care; green-keeping; landscaping; woodland and estate maintenance; animal care; pre-veterinary nursing; arboriculture; countryside and rural affairs; human sports science.

Museum or gallery collection, archive, or library special collection:
LOOI Horticultural Library
British Horse Society Library

Non-library collection catalogue:
All or part available in-house

Library catalogue:
All or part available in-house

Printed publications:
Equine Business Guide 2002 (4th ed.)
Equine distance learning materials (Equi Study)
Order printed publications from: Equi Study
at the same address, tel: 01926 318340

Electronic and video publications:
EQUIRY, computerised index of library-held equine periodical articles

Access to staff:
Contact by letter, by telephone, by fax, by e-mail and via website. Appointment necessary. Non-members charged.
Hours: Term time: Mon to Thu, 0830 to 2200; Fri, 0830 to 1700; Sat, 1000 to 1600
Vacations: Mon to Fri, 0915 to 1645
Special comments: One free visit, then have to become members; charges to non-members.

Access for disabled people:
Level entry, access to all public areas, toilet facilities

Other site at:
Warwickshire College
Leamington Centre, Warwick New Road, Leamington Spa, Warwickshire, CV32 5JE; tel: 01926 318000; fax: 01926 318111

WARWICKSHIRE COUNTY RECORD OFFICE

Priory Park, Cape Road, Warwick, CV34 4JS

Tel: 01926 738959
Fax: 01926 738969
E-mail: recordoffice@warwickshire.gov.uk

Website:
http://www.warwickshire.gov.uk/
countyrecordoffice
http://www.a2a.org.uk
Catalogue of part of the collection online

Enquiries:
Enquiries to: Head of Archive Service

Founded:
1933

Organisation type and purpose:
Local government body.
Record office.
To collect, preserve and make accessible the historic records of the County.

Subject coverage:
Warwickshire historical records (largely excluding Birmingham and Coventry).

Museum or gallery collection, archive, or library special collection:
Warwickshire Historical Manuscripts
Warwickshire Local History Library (printed works)
Warwickshire Map Collection
Warwickshire Photograph Collection
Small reference library of books on Warwickshire

Non-library collection catalogue:
All or part available online and in-house

Library catalogue:
All or part available in-house

Printed publications:
Parish Register and Census Holdings (1992, £1.50)

Access to staff:
Contact by letter, by telephone, by fax, by e-mail, in person and via website
Hours: Tue, Wed, Thu, 0900 to 1730; Fri, 0900 to 1700; Sat, 0900 to 1230
Special comments: Identification required.

Access to building, collection or gallery:
Special comments: Members and public must be in possession of a CARN reader's ticket or bring proof of ID including name, address and signature to obtain a ticket

Access for disabled people:
Limited parking provided (please phone to reserve a space), access to all public areas, readers' tea room, toilet facilities

Parent body:
Warwickshire County Council

WARWICKSHIRE FAMILY HISTORY SOCIETY

7 Mersey Road, Bulkington, Nuneaton, Warwickshire, CV12 9QB

E-mail: chairman@wfhs.org.uk

Website:
http://www.wfhs.org.uk

Enquiries:
Enquiries to: Chairman

Founded:
1986

Organisation type and purpose:
Membership association (membership is by subscription).

Subject coverage:
Family history and genealogy, in particular of Warwickshire.

Museum or gallery collection, archive, or library special collection:
IGI
Census 1881

Printed publications:
Leaflet detailing the publications of the Society, some of which are on disc
WFHS Pamphlets including Bedworth Inclosure 1861; Shipston upon Stour – short history and 1874 Directory; Warwickshire Poor Law Unions; School Admission Registers.
Blue Coat School, Coventry (£2.50 plus 35p p&p)
Canal Miscellanea (£3.50 plus 60p p&p)
Early Admission registers for Nuneaton Charity Schools (a must for Nuneaton tracers)(£2.50 plus 90p p&p)
General Baptist Registers – Salem Births 1785 – 1837 (Longford, Foleshill)(£2 plus 35p p&p)
I remember Coventry's War – a compilation of memories, facts and archival information. (£2 plus 60p p&p)
It grew by Industry – The story of Bedworth (limited quantity)(£3 plus 60p p&p)
Warwickshire Militia Lists 1758–60 (including Birmingham but not Coventry, £2.50 plus 60p p&p)
Order printed publications from: Publications, Warwickshire Family History Society
26 Flude Road, Binley Woods, Coventry, CV7 9AQ

Publications list:
Available online and in print

Access to staff:
Contact by letter and by e-mail
Hours: Mon to Fri, 0900 to 1700

Access for disabled people:
Parking provided

WARWICKSHIRE LIBRARY AND INFORMATION SERVICE

Barrack Street, Warwick, CV34 4TH

Tel: 01926 412164
Fax: 01926 412165
E-mail: librarieslearningandculture@warwickshire.gov.uk

Website:
http://www.warwickshire.gov.uk/libraries

Enquiries:
Enquiries to: Head of Libraries, Learning and Culture

Founded:
1920

Formerly called:
Warwickshire County Library

Organisation type and purpose:
Local government body, public library.

Subject coverage:
General information service, tourist information, local history.

Museum or gallery collection, archive, or library special collection:
George Eliot Collection at Nuneaton library
Local History collections at Warwick, Leamington, Nuneaton and Rugby libraries
Michael Drayton Collection at Nuneaton library

Warwickshire collection at Warwick Library
Music and Drama Collection at Warwick Library

Non-library collection catalogue:
All or part available in-house

Library catalogue:
All or part available online and in-house

Printed publications:
Current periodicals list
Information leaflets

Access to staff:
Contact by letter, by telephone, by fax, by e-mail, in person and via website
Hours: Mon to Fri, 0900 to 1700

Access to building, collection or gallery:
No access other than to staff

Branch libraries:
in 34 locations

Parent body:
Warwickshire County Council

WARWICKSHIRE LOCAL HISTORY SOCIETY

Acronym or abbreviation: WLHS

until 17 March 2009: 9 Willes Terrace, Leamington Spa, Warwickshire, CV31 1DL

Tel: 01926 429671

Enquiries:
Enquiries to: Honorary Secretary

Founded:
1965

Organisation type and purpose:
Learned society (membership is by subscription), present number of members: 222, voluntary organisation.

Subject coverage:
Warwickshire history.

Printed publications:
Bulletin (2–3 times a year)
Warwickshire History (2 times a year)
Order printed publications from: Warwickshire Local History Society
28 Lillington Road, Leamington Spa, Warwickshire, CV32 5YY, tel: 01926 422628

Publications list:
Available in print

Access to staff:
Contact by letter
Hours: Mon to Fri, 0900 to 1700

Member of:
British Association for Local History

WASTE WATCH

96 Tooley Street, London, SE1 2TH

Tel: 020 7089 2100
Fax: 020 7403 4802
E-mail: info@wastewatch.org.uk

Website:
http://www.wastewatch.org.uk
http://www.nrf.org.uk
The UK Recycled Products Guide

Enquiries:
Enquiries to: Waste Watch Wasteline
Direct tel: 0870 243 0136

Founded:
1991

Organisation type and purpose:
Voluntary organisation, registered charity (charity number 1005417).
To promote and support action on waste reduction and recycling.

Subject coverage:
Recycling, waste management, waste reduction, recycled products.

Printed publications:
Community Recycling (4th ed, 1999, £4.95)
Educational resources (free for sae)
Information sheets (free set for three 1st class stamps plus A4 sae)
The National Recycling Directory (6th ed., Nov 2001, £37.50)
Work at Waste at School (1997, £5.50)
Work at Waste at Work (£9.95)

Publications list:
Available online and in print

Access to staff:
Contact by letter, by telephone, by fax and via website. Appointment necessary.
Hours: Mon to Fri, 1000 to 1700

Access to building, collection or gallery:
No prior appointment required

Part funded by:
Department of the Environment's Environmental Action Fund

WATER MANAGEMENT SOCIETY

Acronym or abbreviation: WMSoc

6 Sir Robert Peel Mill, Tolson's Enterprise Park, Fazeley, Tamworth, B78 3QD

Tel: 01827 289558
Fax: 01827 250408
E-mail: wmsoc@btconnect.com

Website:
http://www.wmsoc.org.uk
Membership.
Training courses, conferences – both online booking.
Publications – online ordering.

Enquiries:
Enquiries to: Information Officer

Founded:
1975

Organisation type and purpose:
Professional body, membership association (membership is by qualification), present number of members: 565.

Subject coverage:
Specification, selection and operating of equipment and systems applied to the use and re-use of water; cooling systems; cooling towers; air conditioning plants; heat exchangers; de-aeration; boiler and condensate systems; hot water systems; effluents and wastes from water preparation processes; recovery systems; environmental aspects and optimisation of available supplies of water; water audits; risk assessment of water services; in-house treatment for reducing effluent costs; current legislation.

Printed publications:
Conference papers, codes of practice, technical literature
Waterline (journal, quarterly, free to members; available on subscription also)

Publications list:
Available in print

Access to staff:
Contact by letter, by telephone, by fax, by e-mail and via website
Hours: Mon to Fri, 0900 to 1600

Access to building, collection or gallery:
No access other than to staff

WATER UK

1 Queen Anne's Gate, London, SW1H 9BT

Tel: 020 7344 1844
Fax: 020 7344 1866
E-mail: info@water.org.uk

Website:
http://www.water.org.uk

continued overleaf

Enquiries:
Enquiries to: Chief Executive

Founded:
1998

Formerly called:
Water Companies Association (WCA), Water Services Association (WSA) (year of change 1998)

Organisation type and purpose:
Trade association.
Water UK is the industry association that represents water and waste water service suppliers at national and European level.

Subject coverage:
Water and wastewater services.

Printed publications:
Publications include:
Water (magazine, fortnightly)

Publications list:
Available online and in print

Access to staff:
Contact by letter, by e-mail and via website
Hours: Mon to Fri, 0900 to 1700

Members of the Association are:
24 water and wastewater companies in England and Wales
Northern Ireland Water Service
    website: www.water.org.uk
Scottish Water
    website: see water uk website

WAVENEY DISTRICT COUNCIL

Town Hall, High Street, Lowestoft, Suffolk, NR32 1HS

Tel: 01502 562111
Fax: 01502 589327
E-mail: webmaster@waveney.gov.uk

Website:
http://www.waveney.gov.uk

Enquiries:
Enquiries to: Chief Executive
Direct tel: 01502 523210

Organisation type and purpose:
Local government body.

Printed publications:
Each department provides many leaflets on its own areas (eg housing, planning)
A-Z of Services
Councillor Information booklet

Access to staff:
Contact by letter, by telephone, by fax, by e-mail, in person and via website
Hours: Mon to Thu, 0900 to 1700; Fri, 0900 to 1630

Local Offices at:
Beccles District Office
    6 Market Street, Beccles, Suffolk, NR34 9QD; tel: 01502 713113; fax: 01502 713113
Bungay District Office
    Broad Street, Bungay, Suffolk, NR35 1EE; tel: 01986 892176
Halesworth District Office
    London Road, Halesworth, Suffolk, IP9 8LW; tel: 01986 873162; fax: 01986 874516
Tourist Information
    Town Hall, Southwold, Suffolk, IP18 6EF; tel: 01502 722366

WAVERLEY CARE HIV AND HEPATITIS C INFORMATION SERVICE

Waverley Care, 24 Abbeymount, Edinburgh, EH8 8EJ

Tel: 0131 661 0982
Fax: 0131 652 1780
E-mail: info@waverleycare.org

Website:
http://www.waverleycare.org

Enquiries:
Enquiries to: Information Worker
Other contacts: Manager, Waverley Care SOLAS

Founded:
1991

Organisation type and purpose:
Voluntary organisation, registered charity (charity number SCO 036500).
HIV and Hepatitis C information and support.

Subject coverage:
Supporting the HIV and Hepatitis C community in Scotland

Electronic and video publications:
Newletter (pdf, online)

Access to staff:
Contact by letter, by telephone, by fax, by e-mail, in person and via website
Hours: Mon to Fri, 0900 to 1700

Access to building, collection or gallery:
No prior appointment required
Hours: Mon to Fri, 0830 to 1530

Access for disabled people:
Ramped entry
Special comments: Wheelchair access to ground floor only

Constituent bodies:
Waverley Care Milestone Respite Unit
    113 Oxgangs Road North, Edinburgh, EH14 1EB; tel: 0131 441 6989

Parent body:
Waverley Care
    Old Coates House, 32 Manor Place, Edinburgh, EH3 7EB; tel: 0131 226 2206; fax: 0131 226 2209

WAX CHANDLERS' COMPANY

Formal name: Worshipful Company of Wax Chandlers

Wax Chandlers' Hall, Gresham Street, London, EC2V 7AD

Tel: 020 7606 3591/2
Fax: 020 7600 5462
E-mail: info@waxchandlershall.co.uk

Website:
http://www.waxchandlershall.co.uk
Banqueting, meeting and reception facilities and history, charities.

Enquiries:
Enquiries to: Clerk
Other contacts: Beadle for bookings for meetings and banquets.

Founded:
Before 1371

Organisation type and purpose:
Membership association, service industry.
City of London livery company, provider of banqueting and meeting facilities.

Museum or gallery collection, archive, or library special collection:
The Company's archive is lodged at Guildhall Library, London, EC2 and is open for public inspection

Printed publications:
A chronology of the history of the Company, and a brochure on hall letting facilities (available for download via website)

Access to staff:
Contact by letter, by telephone, by fax, by e-mail and in person
Hours: Mon to Fri, 0900 to 1700

WEALDEN IRON RESEARCH GROUP

2 West Street Farm Cottages, Maynards Green, Heathfield, Sussex, TN21 0DG

Tel: 01435 812506

E-mail: wirghonsec@hotmail.com

Website:
http://www.wealdeniron.org.uk

Founded:
1968

Subject coverage:
The extinct iron industry of the Weald of Sussex, Kent and Surrey.

Printed publications:
Wealden Iron
Newsletter

Publications list:
Available online

Access to staff:
Contact by letter, by telephone, by e-mail, in person and via website

WELFARE STATE INTERNATIONAL

Lanternhouse, The Ellers, Ulverston, Cumbria, LA12 0AA

Tel: 01229 581127\ Minicom no. 01229 587146
Fax: 01229 581232
E-mail: info@welfare-state.com

Website:
http://www.welfare-state.org

Enquiries:
Enquiries to: Centre Manager
Direct e-mail: alec@welfare-state.com
Other contacts: Artistic Director

Founded:
1968

Organisation type and purpose:
International organisation, registered charity (charity number 265461), art gallery, suitable for ages: all, consultancy, research organisation, publishing house.
Artist-led company pioneering the arts of celebration and ceremony.

Subject coverage:
Arts of celebration.

Special visitor services:
Guided tours.

Education services:
Group education facilities.

Printed publications:
The Dead Good Funerals Book (£9.50 plus p&p)
The Dead Good Guide to Namings & Baby Welcoming Ceremonies (£7.50 plus p&p)
The Dead Good Time Capsule Book (£6.95 plus p&p)
Engineers of the Imagination (£12.99 plus p&p)
Eyes on Stalks (£14.99 plus p&p)

Access to staff:
Contact by letter, by telephone, by fax, by e-mail and via website. Appointment necessary.
Hours: Mon to Fri, 0900 to 1700

Access for disabled people:
Parking provided, level entry, access to all public areas, toilet facilities

WELL DRILLERS ASSOCIATION

Acronym or abbreviation: WDA

PO Box 4595, Nuneaton, Warwicks, CV11 9DX

Tel: 07885 957 9583
E-mail: david.s.duke@gmail.com

Website:
http://www.welldrillers.org.uk

Enquiries:
Enquiries to: Executive Secretary
Other contacts: Chairman and Treasurer

Founded:
pre-1940

Organisation type and purpose:
Trade association.
Association of water well drillers in the United Kingdom

Subject coverage:
Water-well drilling, pump installation and maintenance.

Printed publications:
Guidance Notes for the Construction of Boreholes for Water Supply
Membership list

Access to staff:
Contact by letter, by telephone and by e-mail
Hours: Mon to Fri, 0900 to 1800

WELLCHILD

16 Royal Crescent, Cheltenham, Gloucestershire, GL50 3DA

Tel: 01242 530007
Fax: 01242 530008
E-mail: info@wellchild.org.uk

Website:
http://www.wellchild.org.uk

Enquiries:
Enquiries to: Chief Executive

Founded:
1977

Organisation type and purpose:
Registered charity (charity no. 289600).
To raise funds for medical research into childhood diseases and illnesses and provide information and support to sick children and their families

Subject coverage:
Medical grants programme.

Printed publications:
General
Newsletter
Leaflets on events
Annual Review
Helpline leaflet

Access to staff:
Contact by letter, by telephone, by fax, by e-mail and via website. Appointment necessary.
Hours: Mon to Fri, 0900 to 1700

WELLCOME LIBRARY

183 Euston Road, London, NW1 2BE

Tel: 020 7611 8722
Fax: 020 7611 8369
E-mail: library@wellcome.ac.uk

Website:
http://library.wellcome.ac.uk

Enquiries:
Enquiries to: User Services Manager
Other contacts: Librarian

Founded:
1949

Organisation type and purpose:
Registered charity (charity number 210183), research organisation.

Subject coverage:
Medicine and its role in society, past and present, including popular science, biomedical ethics and the public understanding of science.

Museum or gallery collection, archive, or library special collection:
Over 600,000 books and journals
13,000 original letters and facsimiles of letters by Florence Nightingale, Lord Lister and Melanie Klein
Records of numerous organisations and bodies involved in medical science and health care
Autograph Letters (100,000)
Books from the library of William Morris (including 67 incunabula)

Ethnology and travel c.1800 to c.1940; thereafter medically oriented ethnology and anthropology
Incunabula (over 600 items); early printed books (over 7,000 pre-1641; over 66,000 1641–1850), including about 11,000 items from the Library of the Medical Society of London
Library of the Royal Society of Health
Library of the Society for the Study of Addiction
Microforms (1,600)
Asian collection of 12,000 MSS in 43 eastern languages including Sanskrit, Arabic, Persian, Hebrew, Chinese, Japanese, (c.70 microfilm rolls in oriental languages); 3,000 items printed in Oriental scripts and topographical and other works relevant to oriental studies in Western languages; American Collection including medical imprints from the Hispanic and Portuguese American Empires 1557–1833 and from the British Colonies in America 1720–1820; also material on Amerindian medicine, manuscripts and much reference material, especially bibliographies
200,000 prints, drawings; paintings and photographs, from the Orient to the Americas, (middle ages to present)
Western Manuscripts (9,000)

Non-library collection catalogue:
All or part available online, in-house and in print

Library catalogue:
All or part available online

Printed publications:
Catalogue of Arabic Manuscripts on Medicine and Science in the Wellcome Historical Medical Library
Catalogue of Incunabula in the Wellcome Historical Medical Library
Catalogue of Medical Americana in the Library of the Wellcome Institute for the History of Medicine
Catalogue of Persian Manuscripts in the Library of the Wellcome Institute for the History of Medicine
Catalogue of Portraits of Doctors and Scientists in the Wellcome Institute
Catalogue of Printed Books in the Wellcome Historical Medical Library: Vol. I, Books printed before 1641; Vol. II, Books printed from 1641 to 1850 A–E; Vol. III, Books printed from 1641 to 1850 F–L; Vol. IV, Books printed from 1641 to 1850 M–R; Vol. V, Books printed from 1641 to 1850 S–Z (forthcoming).
Catalogue of Western Manuscripts on Medicine and Science in the Wellcome Historical Medical Library: Vol. I, Manuscripts written before 1650 AD; Vol. II, Manuscripts written after 1650 AD (2 vols)
Handlist of Sanskrit and Prakrit manuscripts in the library of the Wellcome Institute for the History of Medicine, vol. I
Medical History (quarterly with annual monograph supplement)
Order printed publications from: Mrs Tracy Tillotson, tel. 020 7611 8486, fax 020 7611 8369, e-mail t .tillotson@wellcome.ac.uk

Publications list:
Available online and in print

Access to staff:
Contact by letter, by telephone, by fax, by e-mail, in person and via website
Hours: Mon, Tue, Wed, Fri, 1000 to 1800; Thu, 1000 to 2000; Sat, 1000 to 1600

Funded by:
Wellcome Trust

Links with:
University College London

WELLCOME LIBRARY – MOVING IMAGE AND SOUND COLLECTION

183 Euston Road, London, NW1 2BE

Tel: 020 7611 8766
Fax: 020 7611 8577

E-mail: misc@wellcome.ac.uk

Website:
http://library.wellcome.ac.uk

Enquiries:
Enquiries to: Curator

Formerly called:
Wellcome Trust Medical Film and Video Library

Organisation type and purpose:
Research organisation.

Subject coverage:
Moving image and sound materials illustrating the evolution of medicine and health over the last 100 years. A primary source in the study of the use of media as a communication tool in medical science and practice.

Museum or gallery collection, archive, or library special collection:
Approx 3,000 film items, 3,000 video items and 2,000 sound items. Mostly available for reference only with a limited number of titles for loan and/ or licensing.

Non-library collection catalogue:
All or part available online and in-house

Library catalogue:
All or part available online

Electronic and video publications:
60 Wellcome Trust copyright videos (VHS/DVD PAL or NTSC for purchase)

Publications list:
Available online

Access to staff:
Contact by letter, by telephone, by fax, by e-mail, in person and via website. Appointment necessary.
Hours: Mon to Fri, 0900 to 1700

Access to building, collection or gallery:
Hours: Mon, Tue, Wed, Fri, 1000 to 1800; Thu, 1000 to 2000; Sat, 1000 to 1600

Access for disabled people:
Fully accessible

WELLCOME TRUST MEDICAL PHOTOGRAPHIC LIBRARY

210 Euston Road, London, NW1 2BE

Tel: 020 7611 8348
Fax: 020 7611 8577
E-mail: photolib@wellcome.ac.uk

Website:
http://www.wellcome.ac.uk/mpl

Enquiries:
Direct e-mail: photolib@wellcome.ac.uk

Formerly called:
Wellcome Library for the History and Understanding of Medicine

Organisation type and purpose:
Research organisation.

Subject coverage:
Images of medical and social history, photographs of clinical medicine and biomedical sciences.

Museum or gallery collection, archive, or library special collection:
Over 160,000 images of medical and social history; 17,000 photos of modern clinical medicine and biomedical sciences

Non-library collection catalogue:
All or part available online and in-house

Library catalogue:
All or part available online

Publications list:
Available online and in print

Access to staff:
Contact by letter, by telephone, by fax, by e-mail and via website. Appointment necessary.
Hours: Mon to Fri, 0930 to 1730

continued overleaf

Access to building, collection or gallery:
Prior appointment required
Hours: Mon to Fri, 0930 to 1730

WELLINGBOROUGH BOROUGH COUNCIL

Council Offices, Swanspool House, Wellingborough, Northamptonshire, NN8 1BP

Tel: 01933 229777
Fax: 01933 231629
E-mail: customerservices@wellingborough.gov.uk
Website:
http://www.wellingborough.gov.uk/

Organisation type and purpose:
Local government body.

WELLS AND WALSINGHAM LIGHT RAILWAY

Acronym or abbreviation: WWLR

Wells-Next-the-Sea, Norfolk, NR23 1QB

Tel: 01328 710631

Enquiries:
Enquiries to: Owner
Direct tel: 01328 711630

Founded:
1982

Organisation type and purpose:
Membership association (membership is by subscription), present number of members: 120.

Subject coverage:
Steam railway preservation.

Printed publications:
Guide to Line (obtainable by post or visit)

Access to staff:
Contact by letter, by telephone and in person
Hours: Mon to Fri, 0900 to 1700

WELSH ADVISORY COMMITTEE ON TELECOMMUNICATIONS

Acronym or abbreviation: WACT

4 The Science Park, Aberystwyth, Ceredigion, SY23 3AH

Fax: 01970 636414
E-mail: wact@acts.org.uk
Website:
http://www.acts.org.uk

Enquiries:
Enquiries to: Secretary

Founded:
1984

Formerly called:
OFTEL

Organisation type and purpose:
Advisory body, statutory body.
Under the Telecommunications Act 1984 duty to advise the Director General of Telecommunications on any subject concerning regulation of the industry.

Subject coverage:
Representation of the needs of users of telecommunications services and equipment in Wales to those who run and control the industry; telecommunications services and equipment complaints and queries in Wales.

Printed publications:
Annual Reports

Access to staff:
Contact by letter, by fax, by e-mail and via website
Hours: Mon to Fri, 0900 to 1700

Access to building, collection or gallery:
No access other than to staff

WELSH AMATEUR SWIMMING ASSOCIATION

Acronym or abbreviation: WASA

Wales National Pool, Sketty Lane, Swansea, SA2 8QG

Tel: 01792 513636
Fax: 01792 513637
E-mail: secretary@welshasa.co.uk
Website:
http://www.welshasa.co.uk

Enquiries:
Enquiries to: Head of Administration

Founded:
1897

Organisation type and purpose:
Membership association (membership is by subscription), present number of members: 9500, voluntary organisation.
Recognised as the governing body for swimming in Wales and to promote the sport throughout Wales and to develop members' potential to represent Wales and Great Britain at European and World levels in swimming, diving and water polo.

Subject coverage:
Amateur swimming, diving and water polo.

Access to staff:
Contact by letter, by telephone, by fax and by e-mail
Hours: Mon to Fri, 0900 to 1600

WELSH ASSEMBLY GOVERNMENT – CENTRAL REGISTER OF AERIAL PHOTOGRAPHY FOR WALES

Statistical Division, Room G-073a, Crown Offices, Cathays Park, Cardiff, CF10 3NQ

Tel: 029 2082 3819
Fax: 029 2082 3080
E-mail: aerialphotoofficer@wales.gsi.gov.uk

Enquiries:
Enquiries to: Aerial Photographs Officer

Organisation type and purpose:
National government body. Central government department.

Subject coverage:
The Central Register aims to index all vertical air survey coverage of Wales flown by the Royal Air Force, Ordnance Survey, commercial air survey companies and other air survey organisations. The Register is a comprehensive source of information about the aerial photography of Wales and advises all interested users. Customers need to supply a map or OS National Grid Reference of their area of interest to perform a cover search.

Museum or gallery collection, archive, or library special collection:
The Aerial Photographs Library holds an extensive collection of photographs covering Wales at various dates and scales. The base of the collection is the national 1:10,000 aerial survey flown 1945–52 by the RAF. To this has been added other RAF photographs including the 1969 and 1981 small-scale national surveys; Ordnance Survey 1958–2002; Medmenham 1940–45; and Meridian 1952–83. The Welsh Assembly has continued to update the collection which now includes extensive coverage in colour 1983–97. Some oblique and infrared photos are held of the Welsh coastline and also MAFF/ADAS (black and white and colour) from the 1970s–80s.
Full cover of Wales by Getmapping (1999–2000), COWI (2006) is available to view in colour on screen.

Printed publications:
Reprints of some of the collection are available for sale

Access to staff:
Contact by letter, by telephone, by fax and by e-mail. Appointment necessary.
Hours: Mon to Fri, 0900 to 1700

Access to building, collection or gallery:
Prior appointment required
Special comments: Hand luggage will be liable to search and x-ray to meet security requirements

Access for disabled people:
Parking provided, level entry, toilet facilities

WELSH ASSOCIATION OF MOTOR CLUBS

Acronym or abbreviation: WAMC

General Secretary, 63 Maes y Sarn, Pentyrch, Cardiff, CF15 9QR

Tel: 029 2089 1314
E-mail: secretary@wamcweb.com
Website:
http://www.wamcweb.com/

Enquiries:
Enquiries to: Press Officer
Direct e-mail: wamc.pressoffice@wamcweb.com

Founded:
1957

Organisation type and purpose:
National government body, membership association (membership is by qualification), present number of members: 100.

Subject coverage:
Motor sport in Wales.

Printed publications:
Annual Year Book

Access to staff:
Contact by letter, by telephone and by fax
Hours: Mon to Fri, 1800 to 2100; Sat, Sun, 1000 to 1800

Associated with:
MSA
Motorsport House, Colnbrook, Slough, Berkshire, SL3 0HG

WELSH BLACK CATTLE SOCIETY

13 Bangor Street, Caernarfon, Gwynedd, LL55 1AP

Tel: 01286 672391
Fax: 01286 672022
E-mail: welshblack@btclick.com
Website:
http://www.welshblackcattlesociety.org

Enquiries:
Enquiries to: Chief Executive
Direct fax: 01267 290263

Founded:
1904

Organisation type and purpose:
International organisation (membership is by subscription, qualification, election or invitation), present number of members: 960, registered charity (charity number 244415/acl).

Subject coverage:
Breeding of Welsh Black cattle.

Printed publications:
Annual Herdbook (£22)

Access to staff:
Contact by letter, by telephone, by fax, by e-mail and in person. Appointment necessary. All charged.
Hours: Mon to Fri, 0900 to 1700

Other office:
Welsh Black Cattle Society
Royal Welsh Showground, Llanelwedd, Builth Wells, Powys, LD2 3NJ; tel: 01982 551111; fax: 01982 551333

WELSH BOOKS COUNCIL

Distribution Centre, Unit 16, Glan Yr Afon
Enterprise Park, Llanbadarn Fawr, Aberystwyth,
Ceredigion, SY23 3AQ

Tel: 01970 624455
Fax: 01970 625506
E-mail: distribution.centre@wbc.org.uk

Website:
http://www.gwales.com
Complete online catalogue and ordering facility.
http://www.wbc.org.uk
Welsh Books Council's website (including
bestseller lists, pdf's of latest catalogues).

Enquiries:
Enquiries to: Head of Administration and Public
Relations
Direct e-mail: elwyn.jones@cllc.org.uk
Other contacts: (1) Distribution Centre Manager; (2)
Head of Children's Books Department for (1)
visiting the Distribution Centre; (2) visiting the
Children's Books Collection.

Founded:
1961

Organisation type and purpose:
National organisation, trade association.

Subject coverage:
Welsh Language and Welsh-Interest books and
magazines, books for learning Welsh, books for
children (Welsh and Welsh Interest).

**Museum or gallery collection, archive, or library
special collection:**
Complete collection of Welsh Language and Welsh
Interest Children's Books published during
previous 10 years and which are still in print

Printed publications:
Subject catalogues, brochures, leaflets
Order printed publications from: Head of Marketing,
Welsh Books Council
Castell Brychan, Aberystwyth, Ceredigion, SY23
2JB, tel: 01970 624151, fax: 01970 625385

Publications list:
Available online

Access to staff:
Contact by letter, by telephone, by fax, by e-mail
and via website. Appointment necessary.
Hours: Mon to Thu, 0900 to 1700; Fri, 0900 to 1430
Special comments: Only account holders at
Distribution Centre may purchase titles during
visit.

Access to building, collection or gallery:
Prior appointment required

Access for disabled people:
Parking provided, level entry

Other Addresses:
Welsh Books Council/Cyngor Llyfrau Cymru
(CLLC)
Castell Brychan, Aberystwyth, Ceredigion, SY23
2JB; tel: 01970 624151; fax: 01970 625385; e-mail:
castellbrychan@cllc.org.uk

WELSH CENTRE FOR INTERNATIONAL AFFAIRS

Acronym or abbreviation: WCIA

Temple of Peace, Cathays Park, Cardiff, CF10 3AP

Tel: 029 2022 8549
Fax: 029 2064 0333
E-mail: centre@wcia.org.uk

Website:
http://www.wcia.org.uk

Enquiries:
Enquiries to: Director
Direct e-mail: stephenthomas@wcia.org.uk
Other contacts: Executive Officer for requests for
information.

Founded:
1973

Formerly called:
Welsh League of Nations Union, Welsh National
Council of the United Nations Association (UNA
Wales)

Organisation type and purpose:
International organisation, membership
association (membership is by subscription),
present number of members: 550, voluntary
organisation, suitable for ages: 15+.
To promote public awareness of international
affairs.

Subject coverage:
International political, economic and social affairs;
international affairs generally including the UN
and its agencies, EU and European affairs,
Commonwealth, disarmament, development,
UNICEF, humanitarian.

**Museum or gallery collection, archive, or library
special collection:**
Good library covering international politics
between the wars (1918–1939)

Printed publications:
Annual Report
Newsletter (3 times a year)
Special papers on international affairs
The Temple of Peace and Health 1938–1998: Its
Impact on Wales and the World (Davies W R,
1998)

Publications list:
Available in print

Access to staff:
Contact by letter, by telephone, by fax and by e-
mail. Appointment necessary.
Hours: Mon to Fri, 0900 to 1700

Access to building, collection or gallery:
No prior appointment required

WELSH COLLEGE OF HORTICULTURE

Holywell Road, Northop, Mold, Flintshire, CH7
6AA

Tel: 01352 841000
Fax: 01352 841031
E-mail: info@wcoh.ac.uk

Website:
http://www.wcoh.ac.uk

Enquiries:
Enquiries to: Information Centre

Founded:
1953

Organisation type and purpose:
Suitable for ages: 16+, training organisation.
College offering courses in land-based subjects for
students aged 16+.

Subject coverage:
Floristry, landscape design and construction; turf
management, market gardening, biological control,
equine studies, environmental studies, small
animal care, IT, garden centre practices, crop
production, nursery stock production, machinery.

**Museum or gallery collection, archive, or library
special collection:**
Distance learning courses in floristry and
management

Printed publications:
Prospectus (on application)

Access to staff:
Contact by letter, by telephone and by fax.
Appointment necessary.
Hours: Mon to Fri, 0900 to 1700

Access to building, collection or gallery:
Prior appointment required

Access for disabled people:
Parking provided, ramped entry, level entry, access
to all public areas, toilet facilities

WELSH FOLK DANCE SOCIETY

Acronym or abbreviation: WFDS/CDdWC

Cymdeithas Ddawns Werin Cymru, Ffynnonlwyd,
Trelech, Carmarthen, SA33 6QZ

Tel: 01994 484496
E-mail: dafydd.evans@ic24.net

Website:
http://www.welshfolkdance.org.uk

Enquiries:
Enquiries to: Honorary Secretary

Founded:
1949

Organisation type and purpose:
Membership association (membership is by
subscription), present number of members: 264
individuals, 20 groups, voluntary organisation,
registered charity (charity number 1023817).
To promote traditional dance and music.

Subject coverage:
Welsh folk dancing and music.

**Museum or gallery collection, archive, or library
special collection:**
Library at the Welsh Folk Museum, St Fagans,
Cardiff of early dance manuals and notations

Printed publications:
Annual Report
Dance and Music notations and books
Dawns (magazine, annually)
Newsletters
Order printed publications from: Sales Point,
Cymdeithas Ddawns Werin Cymru/Welsh Folk
Dance Society, Palas Print, 10 Stryd y Plas,
Caernarfon, Gwynedd, LL55 1RR; tel. 01286
674631; e-mail siop@palasprint.com

Electronic and video publications:
CD and DVD

Publications list:
Available online and in print

Access to staff:
Contact by letter, by telephone, by e-mail and via
website
Hours: Mon to Fri, 0900 to 1700

Affiliated to:
Welsh Amateur Music Federation
Welsh Arts Council

Librarian:
Welsh Folk Dance Society
8 St Cyre's Road, Penarth, South Glamorgan

WELSH LANGUAGE SOCIETY

Pen Roc, Rhodfa'r Môr, Aberystwyth, Ceredigion,
SY23 2AZ

Tel: 01970 624501
Fax: 01970 627122
E-mail: swyddfa@cymdeithas.com

Website:
http://www.cymdeithas.com
Online version of the quarterly magazine, together
with information on all aspects of the society's
work.

Enquiries:
Enquiries to: Administrative Officer
Other contacts: Assembly Campaigns Officer

Founded:
1962

Organisation type and purpose:
Voluntary organisation.
Political pressure group.
To campaign for the Welsh language and Welsh
communities.

Subject coverage:
Welsh language: its future and campaigns to
secure its future; socio-linguistic planning and
education; official status of the Welsh language.

continued overleaf

Printed publications:
Manifesto (in Welsh and English)
Tafod y Ddraig (quarterly)
Various policy documents, leaflets etc

Access to staff:
Contact by letter, by fax, by e-mail and via
website. Appointment necessary.
Hours: Mon to Fri, 0930 to 1730

WELSH TEACHERS' UNION

Acronym or abbreviation: UCAC

Pen Roc, Rhodfa'r Môr, Aberystwyth, Ceredigion,
SY23 2AZ

Tel: 01970 639950
Fax: 01970 626765
E-mail: ucac@athrawon.com

Website:
http://www.athrawon.com

Enquiries:
Enquiries to: General Secretary

Founded:
1940

Organisation type and purpose:
Trade union (membership is by subscription),
present number of members: c.4,800.
As well as safeguarding the rights of teachers and
lecturers and ensuring fair salaries, pensions and
conditions of employment, UCAC has always
campaigned for an independent education system
for Wales.

**Museum or gallery collection, archive, or library
special collection:**
Archive, University of Cardiff

Publications list:
Available online

Access to staff:
Contact by letter, by telephone, by fax and by e-
mail. Appointment necessary. Non-members
charged.
Hours: Mon to Thu, 0900 to 1700; Fri, 0900 to 1600
Special comments: Office is closed for a fortnight
over Christmas, on St David's Day and during
August; emergency tel. number on office
answerphone.

Access for disabled people:
limited disabled access

WELWYN HATFIELD BOROUGH COUNCIL

Council Offices, Welwyn Garden City,
Hertfordshire, AL8 6AE

Tel: 01707 357000
Fax: 01707 357257

Website:
http://www.welhat.gov.uk
General service information.

Enquiries:
Enquiries to: Customer Services Officer
Direct fax: 01707 357480

Founded:
1974

Organisation type and purpose:
Local government body.

Printed publications:
Welwyn Hatfield Life (external, quarterly)

Publications list:
Available in print

Access for disabled people:
Parking provided, level entry

WELWYN HATFIELD BUSINESS INITIATIVE LIMITED

Acronym or abbreviation: WHBI

Weltech Centre, The Ridgeway, Welwyn Garden
City, Hertfordshire, AL7 2AA

Tel: 01707 377377
Fax: 01707 335000
E-mail: dougking@whbi.co.uk

Website:
http://www.whbi.co.uk

Enquiries:
Enquiries to: Manager

Founded:
1994

Formerly called:
Business Link Hertfordshire (year of change 2000)

Organisation type and purpose:
Advisory body.
Support to start up businesses.

Subject coverage:
Impartial, objective advice, guidance and
information on business issues, particularly those
wishing to start a business.

Access to staff:
Contact by letter, by telephone, by fax, by e-mail,
in person and via website. Appointment necessary.
Hours: Mon to Fri, 0900 to 1700

Access for disabled people:
Parking provided, ramped entry, toilet facilities

WENDY WARR AND ASSOCIATES

6 Berwick Court, Holmes Chapel, Cheshire, CW4
7HZ

Tel: 01477 533837
Fax: 01477 533837
E-mail: wendy@warr.com

Website:
http://www.warr.com

Enquiries:
Enquiries to: Principal Consultant

Founded:
1992

Organisation type and purpose:
Consultancy.

Subject coverage:
Chemical information, scientific, technical and
medical information systems, competitive
intelligence. Electronic publishing. Virtual
communities. Drug discovery.

Printed publications:
About 60 learned publications including nine
books
Reports as commissioned by clients

Publications list:
Available online and in print

Access to staff:
Contact by letter, by telephone, by fax, by e-mail,
in person and via website
Hours: Mon to Fri, 0900 to 1700

WENSLEYDALE LONGWOOL SHEEP BREEDERS' ASSOCIATION

Acronym or abbreviation: WLSBA

Breed Secretary, Coffin Walk, Sheep Dip Lane,
Princethorpe, Rugby, Warwickshire, CV23 9SP

Tel: 01926 633439

Website:
http://www.wensleydale-sheep.com
Breed characteristics, history, sales and news items.

Enquiries:
Enquiries to: Membership Secretary
Direct tel: 01388 777852

Founded:
1890

Organisation type and purpose:
Membership association (membership is by
subscription), present number of members: 210.
Breeding and promotion of Wensleydale sheep.

Subject coverage:
Breed characteristics and sales of Wensleydale
sheep.

Printed publications:
Breed brochure (free)
Journal (£2.50)

Access to staff:
Contact by letter and by telephone
Hours: Mon to Fri, 0900 to 1700

WESLEY HISTORICAL SOCIETY

Acronym or abbreviation: WHS

7 Haugh Shaw Road, Halifax, HX1 3AH

Tel: 01422 250780
E-mail: johnahargreaves@blueyonder.co.uk

Website:
http://www.wesleyhistoricalsociety.org.uk

Enquiries:
Enquiries to: General Secretary
Direct e-mail: jandclenton@blueyonder.co.uk
Other contacts: Registrar (for membership);
Librarian (for access to collections); Editor (for offer
of articles, advertising rates)

Founded:
1893

Organisation type and purpose:
Learned society (membership is by subscription),
present number of members: 850, registered
charity (charity number 283012). To promote the
study of the history and literature of all branches of
Methodism, to accumulate exact knowledge, and
to provide a medium of intercourse on all related
subjects.

Subject coverage:
Methodist history, literature, Methodism,
Methodist portraits. No genealogical Methodist
records held.

**Museum or gallery collection, archive, or library
special collection:**
Bretherton Collection
Reference library housed at Westminster Institute
of Education. Contact library before visiting

Non-library collection catalogue:
All or part available online and in-house

Library catalogue:
All or part available online and in-house

Printed publications:
Annual Lecture (published separately on occasion,
depending on the subject)
Annual listings of Methodist historical literature
Proceedings (3 times a year, free to members, with
index to each vol., 6 issues per vol.)
Order printed publications from: c/o The Registrar,
Wesley Historical Society, 15 Foxlands Drive,
Lloyd Hill, Penn, Wolverhampton, WV4 5NB

Publications list:
Available in print

Access to staff:
Contact by letter, by telephone and by e-mail.
Appointment necessary. Non-members charged.
Hours: Mon to Fri, 0900 to 1700
Special comments: Check library opening times with
WHS Library (tel: 01865 488319).

Access to building, collection or gallery:
Prior appointment required

Access for disabled people:
Please telephone in advance to make arrangements

Branches:
17 local branches
c/o Local Branches Secretary, Wesley Historical
Society, 50 Well Oak Park, Dryden Road, Exeter,
Devon, EX2 5BB; e-mail: rthorne@fish.co.uk

Library:
Wesley Historical Society Library
  Westminster Institute of Education, Harcourt
  Hill Campus, Oxford Brookes University,
  Oxford, OX2 9AT; e-mail: peter@forsaith-oxon
  .demon.co.uk; website: http://opac.brookes.ac
  .uk:8001/wes

WEST DUNBARTONSHIRE COUNCIL

Garshake Road, Dumbarton, Strathclyde, G82 3PU

Tel: 01389 737000
Fax: 01389 737070
E-mail: wdcmgr@post.allmac.co.uk

Website:
http://www.west-dunbarton.gov.uk

Enquiries:
Enquiries to: Public Relations Manager
Direct tel: 01389 737296
Direct fax: 01389 737578
Direct e-mail: joe.cox@west-dunbarton.gov.uk

Founded:
April 1996

Organisation type and purpose:
Local government body.

Subject coverage:
All local government services.

Non-library collection catalogue:
All or part available online

Printed publications:
Publications on request

Publications list:
Available in print

Access to staff:
Contact by letter, by telephone, by e-mail and via
website
Hours: Mon to Fri, 0900 to 1700

Access for disabled people:
Parking provided, ramped entry, toilet facilities

WEST DUNBARTONSHIRE LIBRARIES

Headquarters, Levenford House, Helenslee Road,
Dumbarton, Strathclyde, G82 4AH

Tel: 01389 608041
Fax: 01389 608044

Enquiries:
Enquiries to: Service Manager
Direct e-mail: graham.hopner@west-dunbarton.gov
.uk
Other contacts: pat.malcolm@west-
dunbarton.gov.uk

Founded:
1996

Organisation type and purpose:
Local government body, public library.

Subject coverage:
General and local history of Dunbartonshire, Clyde
shipbuilding, sewing machine manufacture, textile
industry

Museum or gallery collection, archive, or library special collection:
West-Dunbartonshire Archives
Singer sewing machines, Dennystown Forge,
  Dumbarton Burgh Council minutes, 1599–1975
Thompson Collection (local history)
Watchmeal Collection (local history)

Non-library collection catalogue:
All or part available online and in-house

Library catalogue:
All or part available online and in-house

Printed publications:
Local history books and pamphlets including:

Beardmore Built: The Rise and Fall of a Clydeside
  Shipyard (Ian Johnston, £9.95)
Clydebank in Old Picture Postcards (£4)
History of The Parish of West or Old Kilpatrick
  (John Bruce, £7.95)
Marchstones in the Kilpatrick Hills (Dr R A
  Rankine)
Historic Dumbarton, Scottish Burgh Survey (E.
  Patricia Dennison & Russel Coleman, £14.95)

Electronic and video publications:
Clydebank – Building on the Past (video, £10)
Clydebank Memories (Singer, video, £10)
From Canoes to Cunarders (video, £8)
Music for a Christmas Evening VI (video, £5)

Access to staff:
Contact by letter, by telephone, by fax, by e-mail,
in person and via website. Appointment necessary.
Hours: Mon to Fri, 0830 to 1615
Special comments: Telephone switchboard operates
from Mon to Fri, 0830 to 1615.

Affiliated to:
Glasgow & West of Scotland Family History
Society
Library Association
Scottish Genealogy Society
Scottish History Society
Scottish Library and Information Council
Scottish Local Government Information Unit
Scottish Museum Council
Scottish Poetry Library
Scottish Records Association

WEST GLAMORGAN ARCHIVE SERVICE

Acronym or abbreviation: WGAS

Civic Centre, Oystermouth Road, Swansea, West
Glamorgan, SA1 3SN

Tel: 01792 636589
Fax: 01792 637130
E-mail: westglam.archives@swansea.gov.uk

Website:
http://www.swansea.gov.uk/
westglamorganarchives
Description of service including online guide,
locations, opening times and facilities.

Enquiries:
Enquiries to: Archivist

Organisation type and purpose:
Local government body.
Archive service.

Subject coverage:
Local and family history in West Glamorgan.

Museum or gallery collection, archive, or library special collection:
Usual local authority holdings

Non-library collection catalogue:
All or part available online, in-house and in print

Printed publications:
Various books and booklets, including:
Annual Reports of the West Glamorgan County
Archivist
A Guide to the Collections
Recent publications include:
Historic Swansea
George Orlean Delamotte: A South Wales Sketch
  Album c1816–1835
Rhossili: The Land, Landscape and People

Publications list:
Available online and in print

Access to staff:
Contact by letter, by telephone, by fax, by e-mail
and in person
Hours: Tue, 0900 to 1900; Wed to Fri, 0900 to 1700;
Sat, 1000 to 1600 (Family History Centre only)

Access for disabled people:
Parking provided, ramped entry, level entry, access
to all public areas, toilet facilities

Also at:
Neath Archives Access Point
  The Mechanics Institute, 4 Church Place, Neath,
  SA11 3LL; tel: 01639 620139
Port Talbot Archives Access Point
  Aberafan Library, Port Talbot, SA13 1PB; tel:
  01639 763430

WEST HERTS COLLEGE

Cassio Campus Teaching and Learning Resources
Service, Langley Road, Watford, Hertfordshire,
WD7 4YH

Tel: 01923 812231
Fax: 01923 812232
E-mail: anne.h@westherts.ac.uk

Website:
http://colleges.herts.ac.uk/
Voyager.

Enquiries:
Enquiries to: Learning Resources Manager
Direct tel: 01923 812200

Formerly called:
Cassio College (year of change 1991)

Organisation type and purpose:
Suitable for ages: 16+.
College of further and higher education.

Subject coverage:
Catering, retail and distribution services, travel
and tourism, NVQ business administration,
GNVQ business and finance, social and
community courses, hairdressing, A levels and
GCSEs, languages.

Library catalogue:
All or part available online

Printed publications:
Occasional booklists

Publications list:
Available online

Access to staff:
Contact by letter, by telephone and by fax.
Appointment necessary.
Hours: Mon, 0845 to 1700; Tue to Thu, 0845 to 2000;
Fri, 0845 to 1630
College Holidays: Mon to Thu, 0900 to 1230 and
1330 to 1700; Fri, 0900 to 1230 and 1330 to 1630
Special comments: Phone to make prior
appointment, required because of security checks.

Access to building, collection or gallery:
No prior appointment required

Access for disabled people:
Parking provided
Special comments: Library on first floor, no lift –
arrangements can be made for access to learning
centre (ground floor).

WEST KENT COLLEGE

Acronym or abbreviation: WKC

Brook Street, Tonbridge, Kent, TN9 2PW

Tel: 01732 358101\ Minicom no. 01732 350763
Fax: 01732 771415
E-mail: marketing@wkc.ac.uk

Enquiries:
Enquiries to: Admissions Officer
Direct tel: 01732 358101
Direct fax: 01732 771415

Organisation type and purpose:
Training organisation.

Subject coverage:
Further and higher education, training courses for
business and commerce, professional development
courses.

Printed publications:
Order printed publications from: Student Services
at the same address, tel: 01732 358101, fax: 01732
771415, e-mail: enquiries@wkc.ac.uk

continued overleaf

Access to staff:
Contact by letter, by telephone, by fax, by e-mail,
in person and via website
Hours: Mon to Fri, 0900 to 1730

In association with:
University of Greenwich

WEST LANCASHIRE DISTRICT COUNCIL

52 Derby Street, Ormskirk, Lancashire, L39 2DF

Tel: 01695 577177
Fax: 01695 585082

Website:
http://www.westlancsdc.gov.uk

Enquiries:
Enquiries to: Public Relations Manager
Direct tel: 01695 585011
Direct fax: 01695 585220
Direct e-mail: public.relations@westlancsdc.gov.uk

Founded:
1974

Organisation type and purpose:
Local government body.

Subject coverage:
Policy issues, public relations, leisure, planning,
housing, economic development, finance and
council tax, civic administration, building control,
contract services, environmental health, refuse
collection.

Printed publications:
Citizens Guide and Visitors Guide
Information on council services

Access to staff:
Contact by letter, by telephone, by fax, by e-mail,
in person and via website
Hours: Mon to Fri, 0900 to 1700

Access for disabled people:
Parking provided

WEST LOTHIAN COUNCIL

Libraries Department, Connolly House, Hopefield
Road, Blackburn, West Lothian, EH47 7HZ

Tel: 01506 776336
Fax: 01506 776345
E-mail: library.info@westlothian.gov.uk

Website:
http://www.westlothian.gov.uk/libraries
Online catalogue.

Enquiries:
Enquiries to: Library Services Manager

Founded:
1996

Organisation type and purpose:
Local government body, public library.

Subject coverage:
General, local studies, local government

**Museum or gallery collection, archive, or library
special collection:**
Local history, local government

Non-library collection catalogue:
All or part available online

Library catalogue:
All or part available online

Access to staff:
Contact by letter, by telephone, by fax, by e-mail
and in person
Hours: Mon to Thu, 0900 to 1700; Fri, 0900 to 1600

WEST LOTHIAN COUNCIL ARCHIVES AND RECORDS CENTRE

9 Dunlop Square, Deans Industrial Estate,
Livingston, EH54 8SB

Tel: 01506 773770
Fax: 01506 773775
E-mail: archive@westlothian.gov.uk

Website:
http://www.westlothian.gov.uk/tourism/
libservices/ves/

Enquiries:
Enquiries to: Archivist
Other contacts: Local History Librarian for
genealogy enquiries, secondary (published)
sources.

Founded:
1995

Formerly called:
Lothian Regional Council (West Lothian Area),
West Lothian District Council (year of change
1996); Livingston Development Corporation (year
of change 1997)

Organisation type and purpose:
Local government body.
Archive Office.

Subject coverage:
New town development (Livingston) in West
Lothian.
Archives of local government.

**Museum or gallery collection, archive, or library
special collection:**
Livingston Development Corporation Collection
  (computerised finding aid)

Access to staff:
Contact by letter, by telephone and by fax.
Appointment necessary.
Hours: Mon to Thu, 0900 to 1700; Fri, 0900 to 1600

Access to building, collection or gallery:
Prior appointment required

WEST MIDLANDS REGIONAL MUSEUMS COUNCIL

Acronym or abbreviation: WMRMC

Harris Industrial Estate, Hanbury Road, Stoke
Prior, Bromsgrove, Worcestershire, B60 4AD

Tel: 01527 872258
Fax: 01527 576960
E-mail: wmrmc@wm-museums.co.uk

Website:
http://www.wm-museum.co.uk
Information for museums in the West Midlands.
http://www.wm-museums.co.uk/pub/

Enquiries:
Enquiries to: Chief Executive

Founded:
1982

Formerly called:
West Midlands Area Museums Service (WMAMS)
(year of change 1997)

Organisation type and purpose:
National government body, advisory body,
membership association (membership is by
subscription, qualification), present number of
members: 93, registered charity (charity number
513708).
Provision of advice, support, advocacy to
museums in the region.

Subject coverage:
Museum practice and philosophy; library.

Library catalogue:
All or part available in-house

Publications list:
Available online

Access to staff:
Contact by letter, by telephone, by fax, by e-mail
and via website
Hours: Mon to Fri, 0900 to 1700

Access to building, collection or gallery:
Prior appointment required

Access for disabled people:
Parking provided, access to all public areas, toilet
facilities

WEST OF SCOTLAND VW CLUB

Formal name: West of Scotland Volkswagen Club

20 Greenlaw Avenue, Paisley, Renfrewshire, PA1
3RD

Tel: 0141 889 6914

Enquiries:
Enquiries to: Chairman
Other contacts: Membership Secretary for Club
information.

Founded:
1963

Organisation type and purpose:
Advisory body, membership association
(membership is by subscription), present number
of members: 200, consultancy.
Social gatherings, motoring events, helping
members with technical and mechanical problems
regarding their vehicles.

Subject coverage:
General or technical information regarding
Volkswagen vehicles, and other relevant makes of
vehicles in the V.A.G. group, e.g. Audi.

Printed publications:
Club newsletter (5 times a year, members only)

Access to staff:
Contact by letter and by telephone
Hours: Mon to Fri, 0900 to 2300
Special comments: All services and information for
members only.

Memberships:
Harold Cameron
  8 Allander Drive, Torrance, Glasgow, G64 4LG;
  tel: 01360 622766

WEST OXFORDSHIRE DISTRICT COUNCIL

Council Offices, Woodgreen, Witney, Oxfordshire,
OX28 1NB

Tel: 01993 702941
Fax: 01993 770255
E-mail: enquiries@westoxon.gov.uk

Enquiries:
Enquiries to: Chief Executive
Other contacts: Visitor and Information Centre
Manager for publications.

Organisation type and purpose:
Local government body.

Subject coverage:
Information for visitors to the district of West
Oxfordshire.

Printed publications:
Leaflets on places of interest, places to visit etc
  within the District of West Oxfordshire

Access to staff:
Contact by letter, by telephone, by fax, by e-mail,
in person and via website
Hours: Mon to Thu, 0830 to 1730; Fri, 0830 to 1700

Access for disabled people:
Parking provided, ramped entry, level entry, toilet
facilities

Other offices:
West Oxfordshire District Council
  26 Church Green, Witney, Oxfordshire, OX28
  4AU; tel: 01993 702941; fax: 01993 770155

WEST RIDING TRADE PROTECTION ASSOCIATION

Acronym or abbreviation: WRTPA

Protection House, 16–17 East Parade, Leeds, West Yorkshire, LS1 2BS

Tel: 0113 243 2561
Fax: 0113 244 3901
E-mail: wrtpa@cwcom.net

Website:
http://www.wrtpa.com

Enquiries:
Enquiries to: General Manager
Other contacts: Company Secretary

Founded:
1848

Organisation type and purpose:
Membership association (membership is by subscription), present number of members: 4500. Credit information and debt recovery agency.

Subject coverage:
Debt recovery specialists in both UK and overseas, company monitoring, tracing agents, business and credit information specialists.

Printed publications:
Brochure (available free, on request)

Publications list:
Available in print

Access to staff:
Contact by letter, by telephone, by fax, by e-mail, in person and via website. Appointment necessary. Access for members only.
Hours: Mon to Fri, 0900 to 1700

WEST SURREY FAMILY HISTORY SOCIETY

Acronym or abbreviation: WSFHS

21 Sheppard Road, Basingstoke, Hampshire, RG21 3HT

Tel: 01256 358454
E-mail: secretary@wsfhs.org

Website:
http://www.surreyweb.org.uk/wsfhs/index.html
All society details, list of publications, etc.
http://www.wsfhs.org

Enquiries:
Enquiries to: Secretary
Direct e-mail: secretary@wsfhs.org

Founded:
1974

Organisation type and purpose:
Membership association (membership is by subscription), present number of members: 1200, voluntary organisation, registered charity (charity number 278091-R), research organisation.
To collect, index, co-ordinate, publish and make accessible, in the interests of genealogy, any documents or records relating to the ancient County of Surrey; to promote their preservation; to encourage the study of genealogy.

Subject coverage:
Genealogy.

Non-library collection catalogue:
All or part available online, in-house and in print

Printed publications:
Handbook (members only)
Research aids, records, maps, including:
A List of Books and Articles about London, Middlesex and Metropolitan Surrey Places (£2.50 plus 40p p&p)
A List of Surrey Parishes – Ancient and Modern (£1 plus 26p p&p)
Index to Archdeaconry Court of Surrey Wills, 1752–1858 (2nd ed, £3.20)
Surrey Genealogy and Records (£2.50 plus 40p p&p)
Order printed publications from: Publications Officer, West Surrey Family History Society
17 Lane End Drive, Knaphill, Woking, Surrey, GU21 2QQ

Microform publications:
Census and hearth tax records, monumental inscriptions, Surrey early wills, including:
1851 Census Index of Western Surrey (£10)
1861 Census Index for 13 areas
Transcriptions and indexes of parishes registers (over 80)(£1.20 to £5.20)
Archdeaconry Court of Surrey Early Wills (fiche)

Electronic and video publications:
Surrey Poor Law (CD-ROM)

Publications list:
Available online and in print

Access to staff:
Contact by letter, by e-mail and via website
Hours: Mon to Fri, 0900 to 1700
Special comments: Some charges to non-members.

Access for disabled people:
check in advance

WEST SUSSEX COUNTY COUNCIL

County Hall, West Street, Chichester, West Sussex, PO19 1RQ

Tel: 01243 777100
Fax: 01243 777950
E-mail: webmaster@westsussex.gov.uk

Website:
http://www.westsussex.gov.uk
Information about the County Council and the county of West Sussex.

Enquiries:
Enquiries to: News Manager
Direct tel: 01243 777117
Direct fax: 01243 777266
Direct e-mail: nigel.galloway@westsussex.gov.uk

Founded:
1889

Organisation type and purpose:
Local government body.

Access to staff:
Contact by letter, by telephone, by fax, by e-mail, in person and via website
Hours: Mon to Fri, 0900 to 1700

Access for disabled people:
Parking provided, toilet facilities
Special comments: Lift into the building

WEST SUSSEX LIBRARY SERVICE

Worthing Reference Library, Richmond Road, Worthing, BN11 1HD

Tel: 01903 704824
Fax: 01903 821902
E-mail: worthing.reference.library@westsussex.gov.uk

Website:
http://www.westsussex.gov.uk

Enquiries:
Enquiries to: Information Librarian

Organisation type and purpose:
Local government body, public library.

Subject coverage:
Local history; art; folklore; ornithology; zoology; business information sources; law; government publications, European information, Family History.

Non-library collection catalogue:
All or part available online

Library catalogue:
All or part available online

Access to staff:
Contact by letter, by telephone, by fax, by e-mail and in person
Hours: Mon to Fri, 0900 to 1930; Sat, 0900 to 1700

Access for disabled people:
Ramped entry

Links with:
Society of Sussex Librarians

WEST SUSSEX RECORD OFFICE

Acronym or abbreviation: WSRO

County Hall, Chichester, West Sussex, PO19 1RN

Tel: 01243 753600
Fax: 01243 533959
E-mail: records.office@westsussex.gov.uk

Website:
http://www.westsussex.gov.uk/ccm/navigation/libraries-and-archives/record-office/
General introduction to the office.

Enquiries:
Enquiries to: Archivist

Founded:
1946

Organisation type and purpose:
Local government body, research organisation.

Subject coverage:
1200 years of the County's history, including the Diocese of Chichester, and the county's landed estates (especially Goodwood, Petworth, Cowdray and Wiston), family papers including Richard Cobden, WS Blunt, and the Wilberforce and Maxse families, and the Royal Sussex Regiment.

Museum or gallery collection, archive, or library special collection:
Garland Photographic Collection (70,000 photographs)
South East Film and Video Archive
William Blake (Crookshank Collection)

Non-library collection catalogue:
All or part available online, in-house and in print

Library catalogue:
All or part available in-house

Printed publications:
Some 70 publications including:
A Catalogue of the Records of the Bishop, Archdeacons and Former Exempt Jurisdictions (compiled by Steer F W £15)
Cinema West Sussex: The First Hundred Years (Eyles A et al, £15.95)
Genealogists Guide to the West Sussex Record Office (Wilkinson P M, reprinting 2002)
Petworth House Archives Vol 1 (Steer F W ed, £10)
The Goodwood Estate Archives Vol 1 (Steer F W ed, £15)
The Royal Sussex Regiment: A Catalogue of Records (Readman A E ed, £25)
West Sussex Local History Mini Guides to Sources, 15 titles (£1 each)
West Sussex Census Returns 1841–1901
The Wiston Archives (Booker J M L ed, £15)
General Register Office Indexes

Microform publications:
Copies of West Sussex Parish Registers (microfiche)

Electronic and video publications:
Scanned images of West Sussex photographs, pictures and documents (prints or disk)

Access to staff:
Contact by letter, by telephone, by fax, by e-mail, in person and via website
Hours: Mon to Fri, 0915 to 1645; Sat, 0915 to 1230 and 1330 to 1630
Special comments: A valid County Archives Research Network Ticket is required to use the search room. This is available free of charge on proof of identity on arrival.

Access for disabled people:
Ramped entry, access to all public areas, toilet facilities

Parent body:
West Sussex County Council
County Hall, Chichester, PO19 1RG; tel: 01243 777100; fax: 01243 777952

WEST THAMES COLLEGE

London Road, Isleworth, Middlesex, TW7 4HS

Tel: 020 8326 2308
Fax: 020 8569 7787
E-mail: library.services@west-thames.ac.uk

Website:
http://www.west-thames.ac.uk

Enquiries:
Enquiries to: Library Services Manager
Direct tel: 020 8326 2310
Direct e-mail: karen.kelly@west-thames.ac.uk

Formerly called:
Hounslow Borough College

Organisation type and purpose:
Further education.

Subject coverage:
Psychology; social sciences; education; computing; language; art; literature; history; biography; art history; graphic design; architecture, physics, chemistry, catering, hairdressing and beauty, health and care, ESOL (English for Speakers of Other Languages), business studies, engineering, construction trade skills, biology.

Museum or gallery collection, archive, or library special collection:
Collection relating to Joseph Banks

Library catalogue:
All or part available in-house

Printed publications:
Course Prospectus

Publications list:
Available in print

Access to staff:
Contact by letter, by telephone, by fax and by e-mail
Hours: Mon, Fri, 0845 to 1600; Tue, Wed, Thu, 0845 to 2000

Access to building, collection or gallery:
Prior appointment required

Access for disabled people:
Parking provided, ramped entry, toilet facilities
Special comments: Lifts

WEST YORKSHIRE ARCHAEOLOGY ADVISORY SERVICE

Acronym or abbreviation: WYAAS

Registry of Deeds, Newstead Road, Wakefield, West Yorkshire, WF1 2DE

Tel: 01924 306797
Fax: 01924 306810
E-mail: wysmr@wyjs.org.uk

Website:
http://www.arch.wyjs.org.uk

Enquiries:
Enquiries to: SMR Officer, for information on archaeological sites and findspots and some historic buildings

Organisation type and purpose:
Local government body, advisory body, suitable for ages: all.
Provision of advice to local authorities on archaeological matters.

Subject coverage:
The area served by the Metropolitan Districts of Bradford, Calderdale, Kirklees, Leeds and Wakefield.
All aspects of the archaeology of the area, for all periods up to and including the 'Cold War'. The SMR is interested in all new discoveries of sites, artefacts, cartographic, photographic and documentary sources.
Planning and research enquiries, site management and heritage issues. The service includes a Historic Buildings Officer and an outreach Education Officer. The SMR includes a reference library, the

principal oblique aerial photographic collection for West Yorkshire, a number of significant archaeological surveys, as well as details of all known sites, find spots and archaeological monuments within the five Metropolitan Districts. The SMR is interested in liaising with other local and national groups and with individuals who possess information on archaeological sites and historic buildings within West Yorkshire.

Printed publications:
Newsletter (2 times a year, free with A4 sae)
A number of other publications concerning archaeology of West Yorkshire
West Yorkshire: An Archaeological Survey to AD 1500 (£19.50, p&p £7.25)
Yorkshire Archaeology Series:
1. Kirkstall Abbey Vol 1 (£4.50 plus p&p £2)
2. Wrenthorpe Potteries (£5.50 plus p&p £2.50)
3. Dalton Parlours (£8.50 plus p&p £4.25)
4. Roman Castleford Vol 1 The Small Finds (£24 inc. p&p)
5. Roman Castleford Vol 2 The Structural and Environmental Evidence (£26 inc. p&p)
6. Roman Castleford Vol 3 The Pottery (£26 inc. p&p)
Kirkstall Abbey Guest House (£1.50 plus p&p 50p)
The Story of Roman Castleford (£1.50 plus p&p 50p)
Medieval Churches in West Yorkshire (£9.95 plus p&p £3.50)
Order printed publications from: Resources, West Yorkshire Archaeology Service
PO Box 30, Nepshaw Lane South, Morley, Leeds, LS27 0UG, tel: 0113 383 6404

Electronic and video publications:
Some Archaeological Information via Email

Publications list:
Available in print

Access to staff:
Contact by letter, by telephone, by fax and by e-mail. Appointment necessary.
Hours: Mon to Fri, 1000 to 1700 by appointment only

WEST YORKSHIRE ARCHIVE SERVICE – BRADFORD

Acronym or abbreviation: WYAS

Bradford Central Library, Prince's Way, Bradford, BD1 1NN,

Tel: 01274 435099
E-mail: bradford@wyjs.org.uk

Website:
http://www.archives.wyjs.org.uk

Enquiries:
Enquiries to: Principal Archivist

Founded:
1982

Organisation type and purpose:
Local government body.
Record office.

Subject coverage:
Primary source material for historical and other purposes.

Museum or gallery collection, archive, or library special collection:
Local authority records, parish and nonconformist records, family and estate records, business records, political and trade union records, etc

Printed publications:
Guide to the Bradford District Archives (to purchase)
Information leaflets ie the West Yorkshire Archive Service and Bradford District Archives (free)
Guide for Family Historians (to purchase)

Publications list:
Available online

Access to staff:
Appointment necessary.

Hours: Mon, Tue, Thu, Fri, 0930 to 1300 and 1400 to 1700; closed on Wed; open alternate Thu evenings, to 2000

Part of:
West Yorkshire Archive Service

Supported by:
Metropolitan District Councils of Bradford, Calderdale, Kirklees, Leeds and Wakefield

WEST YORKSHIRE ARCHIVE SERVICE – CALDERDALE

Central Library, Northgate, Halifax, West Yorkshire, HX1 1UN

Tel: 01422 392636
Fax: 01422 341083
E-mail: calderdale@wyjs.org.uk

Website:
http://www.archives.wyjs.org.uk
Leaflets, general information etc, database of collections.

Enquiries:
Enquiries to: Senior Archivist
Direct tel: 01422 392635
Direct e-mail: psewell@wyjs.org.uk

Founded:
1983

Formerly a separate body:
Calderdale District Archive Service from 1964 to 1983

Organisation type and purpose:
Local government body.
A county-wide archive service.

Subject coverage:
Primary source material for historical and other purposes.

Museum or gallery collection, archive, or library special collection:
Local authority records, nonconformist records, family and estate records, business records, charities and societies records, political and trade union records etc

Non-library collection catalogue:
All or part available online, in-house and in print

Printed publications:
Calderdale Archives 1964–1989: an illustrated guide to Calderdale District Archives 1990, supplement 1990–1998
Information leaflets re the West Yorkshire Archive Service and Collections and User Guides (free)
See also entry for Service HQ at Wakefield

Publications list:
Available online and in print

Access to staff:
Contact by letter, by telephone, by fax, by e-mail, in person and via website. Appointment necessary.
Hours: Mon, Tue, Thu, Fri, 1000 to 1730; Wed, closed

Access for disabled people:
Parking provided, level entry, access to all public areas

Part of:
West Yorkshire Archive Service

Supported by:
Metropolitan District Councils of Bradford, Calderdale, Kirklees, Leeds and Wakefield

WEST YORKSHIRE ARCHIVE SERVICE – KIRKLEES

Central Library, Princess Alexandra Walk, Huddersfield, West Yorkshire, HD1 2SU

Tel: 01484 221966
Fax: 01484 518361
E-mail: enq@wyashq.demon.co.uk

Website:
http://www.archives.wyjs.org.uk

Enquiries:
Enquiries to: Archivist

Founded:
1982

Organisation type and purpose:
Local government body.

Subject coverage:
Primary source material for historical and other purposes relating to the Kirklees District.

Museum or gallery collection, archive, or library special collection:
Local authority records, nonconformist records, family and estate records, business records (especially textile industry), society records etc

Non-library collection catalogue:
All or part available online

Printed publications:
Leeds Archives 1938–1988: an illustrated guide to Leeds District Archives
Information leaflets re the West Yorkshire Archive Service and Kirklees District Archives (free)
Kirklees Archives 1959–1989 (guide, supplement 1989–1995)
Sources of information at Kirklees Archives on specific topics
Order printed publications from: Publication Sales Office, West Yorkshire Archive Service HQ Registry of Deeds, Newstead Road, Wakefield, WF1 2DE, tel: 01924 305982, fax: 01924 305983, e-mail: wakefield@wyjs.org.uk

Microform publications:
See WYAS Wakefield Headquarters

Publications list:
Available online and in print

Access to staff:
Appointment necessary.
Hours: Mon, Thu, 1000 to 1700; Tue, 1000 to 2000; Fri, 1000 to 1300
Closed Wed

Other addresses:
West Yorkshire Archive Service (WYAS) Headquarters, Registry of Deeds, Newstead Road, Wakefield, WF1 2DE; tel: 01924 305980; fax: 01924 305983; e-mail: wakefield@wyjs.org.uk

Part of:
West Yorkshire Archive Service

Supported by:
Metropolitan District Councils of Bradford, Calderdale, Kirklees, Leeds and Wakefield

WEST YORKSHIRE ARCHIVE SERVICE – LEEDS

Acronym or abbreviation: WYAS

2 Chapeltown Road, Sheepscar, Leeds, West Yorkshire, LS7 3AP

Tel: 0113 214 5814
Fax: 0113 214 5815
E-mail: leeds@wyjs.org.uk

Website:
http://www.archives.wyjs.org.uk
Office leaflet style pages providing brief summary of records held and access details.

Enquiries:
Enquiries to: Senior Archivist

Founded:
1938

Organisation type and purpose:
Local government body.
Archive service.

Subject coverage:
Primary source material for historical and other purposes.

Museum or gallery collection, archive, or library special collection:
Local authority records

Parish and nonconformist records; family and estate records; business records; voluntary bodies, charities and societies records, political and trade union records, manorial records, tithe records, solicitors and estate agents papers
Major deposited collections:
Family and estate archives including:
Baines family of Leeds
Gascoigne family of Parlington
Earl of Mexborough
Earl of Harewood
Ingilby family of Ripley Castle
Lane Fox family of Bramham Park
Newby Hall Estate
Nostell Priory
Ramsden family of Byram
Samuel Smiles papers
Studley Royal Estate including Fountains Abbey
Temple Newsam
Business records, including:
T and M Bairstow
British Coal
Burton Group
Joshua Tetley
John Wilson
Yorkshire Patent Steam Waggon Co

Non-library collection catalogue:
All or part available online, in-house and in print

Printed publications:
Around Leeds: archive photographs (Young M and Payne D, 1995, £8.99 plus £1.50 p&p)
Information leaflets re. the West Yorkshire Archive Service and collections and user guides (free)
Leeds Archives 1938–1988 (guide)
Leeds in the News: Britain in Old Photographs (Harrison B, £8.99 plus £1.50 p&p)
Order printed publications from: Sue Pad, WYAS, Wakefield, Newstead Road, Wakefield, WF1 2DE

Microform publications:
Various Parish Registers of West Yorkshire and beyond.
Order microform publications from: Sue Pad, WYAS, Wakefield, Newstead Road, Wakefield, WF1 2DE

Publications list:
Available online and in print

Access to staff:
Contact by letter, by telephone, by fax, by e-mail, in person and via website. Appointment necessary.
Hours: Mon, Tue, Thu and Fri 0930 to 1700, restricted service 1200 to 1400; closed Wed; closed to the public for the first full week of every month.

Part of:
West Yorkshire Archive Service

Supported by:
Metropolitan District Councils of Bradford, Calderdale, Kirklees, Leeds and Wakefield

WEST YORKSHIRE ARCHIVE SERVICE – WAKEFIELD

Acronym or abbreviation: WYAS

Registry of Deeds Building, Newstead Road, Wakefield, West Yorkshire, WF1 2DE

Tel: 01924 305980
Fax: 01924 305983
E-mail: wakefield@wyjs.org.uk

Website:
http://www.archives.wyjs.org.uk
Introduction to offices, publications, information for family historians, events.

Enquiries:
Enquiries to: Senior Archivist, Wakefield
Direct tel: 01924 305988
Direct e-mail: wakefield@wyjs.org.uk

Organisation type and purpose:
Local government body.
Archive service.

Subject coverage:
Primary source material for historical and other purposes including administration at county, district and parish levels, religion, law and order, education, health, historical geography, transport, property rights, rights of way, industry.

Museum or gallery collection, archive, or library special collection:
Manuscript documentation on the West Riding and on Wakefield District from the Middle Ages to the present day
West Riding Quarter Sessions records; local authority records including former West Riding County Council and West Yorkshire Metropolitan County Council. West Riding Registry of Deeds records; records of public bodies and utilities; county-wide records; Wakefield Diocesan parish records and records of public bodies; nonconformist records; family and estate records; business records; charities and societies records; courts, coroners, estates, schools, probate registry, hospitals, political and trade union records etc

Trade and statistical information:
1971 Census of distribution maps.
1960 Land utilisation maps.
19th and 20th century records of businesses.

Non-library collection catalogue:
All or part available online and in print

Library catalogue:
All or part available online and in print

Printed publications:
Guide for Family Historians, a list of parish and nonconformist and other related records held by the West Yorkshire Archive Service (3rd edition, £2.99 + £2.50 p&p)
Information leaflets re the West Yorkshire Archive Service and Wakefield Headquarters (free)
Bradford Archives 1974–1995: an illustrated guide to Bradford District Archives (1996, 220pp, £4 plus £2 p&p)
Calderdale Archives 1964–1989: an illustrated guide to Calderdale District Archives (1990, 120pp, £4 plus £2 p&p)
Calderdale Archives, Supplement 1990–1998 (1999, 87pp, £1 plus 50p p&p)
Kirklees Archives 1959–1989: an illustrated guide to Kirklees District Archives (1989, 80pp, £4 plus £1 p&p)
Leeds Archives 1938–1988: an illustrated guide to Leeds District Archives (1989, 72pp £4 plus £1 p&p)
Order printed publications from: Administration Officer, West Yorkshire Archive Service at the same address, tel: 01924 305982, e-mail: spad@wyjs.org.ukuk

Microform publications:
Microfiche of parish registers etc (for sale)
Order microform publications from: Administration Officer, as above

Publications list:
Available online and in print

Access to staff:
Contact by letter, by telephone, by fax, by e-mail, in person and via website. Appointment necessary.
Hours: Mon, 0930 to 2000; Tue, Thu, 0930 to 1700; 2nd Sat in month, 0930 to 1300; closed Wed, Fri, Sun
Special comments: CARN tickets required.
Appointment recommended as the searchrooms can get very busy.

Access for disabled people:
Parking provided
Special comments: Disabled access not available; wheelchair users have to be lifted into building or if able to walk a little use handrails by steps.

Supported by:
Metropolitan District Councils of Bradford, Calderdale, Kirklees, Leeds and Wakefield

continued overleaf

Works under the guidance of the:
Lord Chancellor's Department with regard to
public records
Master of the Rolls with regard to tithe and
manorial records

WESTCOUNTRY STUDIES LIBRARY

Acronym or abbreviation: WSL

Exeter Central Library, Castle Street, Exeter,
Devon, EX4 3PQ

Tel: 01392 384216
Fax: 01392 384228
E-mail: westcountry.library@devon.gov.uk

Website:
http://www.devon.gov.uk/localstudies

Enquiries:
Enquiries to: Westcountry Studies Librarian

Founded:
1870

Formerly called:
Royal Albert Memorial; Exeter City Library (year
of change 1974)

Organisation type and purpose:
Local government body, public library. Main local
studies collection for Devon Library and
Information Services. Reference library.

Subject coverage:
All aspects of Devon and the adjoining counties,
past and present.

**Museum or gallery collection, archive, or library
special collection:**
Brooking Rowe collection (local history, brass
  rubbings, bookplates)
Burnet Morris index on Devon history
Devon and Cornwall Record Society (collections
  and unpublished transcripts, available to
  members; membership can be taken out in the
  library)
Devon Folk Life Register
Heber Mardon Collection of Napoleonic
  illustrations
Pike Ward collection (Iceland)
Pocknell collection of shorthand books

Non-library collection catalogue:
All or part available online

Library catalogue:
All or part available in-house

Printed publications:
Publications include:
Abbots Bickington to Zeal Monachorum: a handlist
  of parish histories compiled on the occasion of
  the centenary of parish councils 1994
An Index of Brass Rubbings in the Westcountry
  Studies Library 1991 (Andrew G, also on web)
Devon Bibliography (1985 to date, annually, also
  on web since 1999)
Devon's Testimony of War (1995)
Devon Topographical Prints 1660–1870: a
  catalogue and guide
Facsimiles of maps
In Pursuit of Devon's History (Maxted I, Devon
  Books 1997, partly on web)
Resource Guides: three series of leaflets on
  genealogy, house history, parish history etc,
  giving details of resources available for local
  studies research in Devon (also on web)
The Devon Collection of Children's Books 1692–
  1849 (Moon M, also on web)
Various handlists and guides to resources (many
  also on web)

Microform publications:
Microfiche of early trade directories from 1791
  onwards and some other historical sources
  (details available on request)

Electronic and video publications:
Extracts from local studies database in dBase or
  ASCII format can be provided on request on disc
  or can be downloaded from the web

Publications list:
Available online

Access to staff:
Contact by letter, by telephone, by e-mail, in
person and via website
Hours: Mon and Fri, 0930 to 1800; Tue and Thu,
0930 to 1900; Wed, 1000 to 1700; Sat, 0930 to 1600

Branch library:
North Devon Local Studies Centre
  Tuly Street, Barnstaple, Devon, EX32 7EJ; tel:
  01271 388607

Parent body:
Devon Library and Information Services
  Devon County Council; tel: 01392 384315

WESTERKIRK PARISH LIBRARY

Bentpath, Langholm, Dumfriesshire, DB13 0PB

Enquiries:
Enquiries to: Chairman of the Trustees
Direct tel: 013873 70201
Other contacts: Mrs M. Sanderson, Chairman of the
Trustees: Westerkirk Schoolhouse, Langholm
DG13 0PB, tel: 013873 70201

Founded:
1793

Organisation type and purpose:
Library.
Registered Scottish charity (charity number
SCO20308)

Subject coverage:
Parish records

**Museum or gallery collection, archive, or library
special collection:**
8,000 books (mid-18th century to the present)

Access to staff:
Contact by letter and by telephone. Appointment
necessary.

Access to building, collection or gallery:
Hours: 1st Mon of month, 1900 to 2000 (by
appointment with staff)

WESTERN ISLES LIBRARIES

19 Cromwell Street, Stornoway, Isle of Lewis, HS1
2DA

Tel: 01851 708631
Fax: 01851 708676

Website:
http://www.cne-siar.gov.uk
Details of services provided by the library can be
found from the Council's home page.

Enquiries:
Enquiries to: Chief Librarian
Direct tel: 01851 708641
Other contacts: Senior Librarian Adult Services,
Senior Librarian Youth Services

Organisation type and purpose:
Local government body, public library.

Subject coverage:
General, local history, Gaelic.

**Museum or gallery collection, archive, or library
special collection:**
An Comunn Gaidhealach collection of Gaelic and
  Highland language and history
Donald MacDonald Papers
Gaelic Collection including recorded sound,
  language, learning, books and periodicals
Local history of the Western Isles
Morrison Manuscripts
School Board minute books
School log books
T B Macaulay photographs collection

Library catalogue:
All or part available online

Access to staff:
Contact by letter, by telephone, by fax and in
person

Hours: Mon to Wed, 1000 to 1700; Thu and Fri, 1000
to 1800; Sat, 1000 to 1700

Access for disabled people:
Access to all public areas, toilet facilities

Parent body:
Comhairle Nan Eilean Siar (formerly Western Isles
Islands Council)

WESTERN KURDISTAN ASSOCIATION

Palingswick House, 241 King Street, London, W6
9LP

Tel: 020 8748 7874
Fax: 020 8741 6436
E-mail: info@westernkurdistan.org.uk

Website:
http://www.westernkurdistan.org.uk

Organisation type and purpose:
Community centre for Kurdish refugees, offering
help in matters such as immigration, welfare,
housing and health, and courses in English
language and other subjects. Administers a
Kurdish museum, library and archive.

Education services:
Courses in English language, use of computers, use
of the Internet, media and film-making.

**Museum or gallery collection, archive, or library
special collection:**
Historical and cultural archive of the Kurdish
  community

Access to building, collection or gallery:
Hours: Mon to Fri 1000 to 1700
Special comments: Access to archive is by
appointment only.

WESTMINSTER (ROMAN CATHOLIC) DIOCESAN ARCHIVES

16a Abingdon Road, Kensington, London, W8 6AF

Tel: 020 7938 3580

Enquiries:
Enquiries to: Administrator

Organisation type and purpose:
Diocesan archive.

Subject coverage:
History of England's post-reformation Roman
Catholic community.

Non-library collection catalogue:
All or part available in-house

Library catalogue:
All or part available in-house

Access to staff:
Contact by letter and by telephone. Appointment
necessary.
Hours: Tue, Wed, Thu, 1000 to 1600

Access to building, collection or gallery:
Prior appointment required
Hours: Tue, Wed, Thu, 1000 to 1600
Special comments: The Archive is private. Letter of
introduction required.

WESTMINSTER ABBEY

Library and Muniment Room, London, SW1P 3PA

Tel: 020 7654 4830
Fax: 020 7654 4827
E-mail: library@westminster-abbey.org

Website:
http://www.westminster-abbey.org/library
For general information on Westminster Abbey
and virtual tour, library pages.

Enquiries:
Enquiries to: Librarian
Direct tel: 020 7654 4826

Other contacts: Keeper of the Muniments for muniments.

Founded:
1623

Organisation type and purpose:
Abbey church library and archives collection.

Subject coverage:
History of Westminster Abbey and its precincts, coronations, St Margaret's Westminster.

Museum or gallery collection, archive, or library special collection:
c. 14,000 early printed books
c. 70,000 documents relating to the Abbey since 1066
Collection of books on the history of Westminster Abbey
Collection of illuminated and other medieval manuscripts
Collection of Pamphlets belonging to William Camden (1551–1623)
K H Oldaker Collection of English Bookbindings, 1655–1920
Langley collection of prints and drawings
Large photographic collection
Music Collection (mainly late 16th and 17th centuries)

Non-library collection catalogue:
All or part available in print

Library catalogue:
All or part available in-house

Printed publications:
Westminster Abbey Record Series Vol 1 (1997-) – In progress, 4 volumes published to date

Microform publications:
Early music and manuscript collections available from World Microfilms, POB 35488, St John's Wood, London NW8 6WD

Access to staff:
Contact by letter, by telephone, by fax, by e-mail and via website. Appointment necessary.
Hours: Mon to Fri, 1000 to 1300 and 1400 to 1645

Access for disabled people:
Medieval building with staircases. Please consult staff about alternative arrangements for access to library materials

WESTMINSTER COLLEGE LIBRARY (CAMBRIDGE)

Madingley Road, Cambridge, CB3 0AA

Tel: 01223 741084
Fax: 01223 300765

Website:
http://www.westminster.cam.ac.uk
Brief description of the college and courses.

Enquiries:
Enquiries to: Librarian
Direct tel: 01223 741093
Direct e-mail: cr248@cam.ac.uk

Founded:
1844

Formed by the amalgamation of:
Presbyterian theological college and a Congregational College

Formerly called:
Cheshunt College, Westminster College

Organisation type and purpose:
Suitable for ages: 18+. Preparation of men and women for the Christian ministry.

Subject coverage:
Theological and Biblical studies, particularly Reformed theology and church history, philosophy of religion, Christian ethics and pastoral studies.

Museum or gallery collection, archive, or library special collection:
Archives of the Countess of Huntingdon's colleges and chapels

Archive material of the Ecclesiastical History Society of the United Reformed Church
Elias Library of Hymnology
Lewis and Gibson Collection of manuscripts from the Cairo Synagogue Genizah (complements the University Library's Taylor-Schechter Collection)
Library of the Ecclesiastical History Society of the United Reformed Church
Todd Collection of liturgical works

Non-library collection catalogue:
All or part available online and in-house

Library catalogue:
All or part available online

Access to staff:
Contact by letter and by e-mail. Appointment necessary. Letter of introduction required. Non-members charged.
Hours: Mon to Fri, 0900 to 1700
Special comments: Open to members of the Cambridge Theological Federation, ministers of the United Reformed Church and approved external members only.

Parent body:
United Reformed Church

WESTMINSTER LIBRARIES AND ARCHIVES

Charing Cross Library, 4 Charing Cross Road, London, WC2H 0HF

Tel: 020 7641 6573
Fax: 020 7641 6551

Website:
http://www.westminster.gov.uk/index/libraries.cfm

Enquiries:
Enquiries to: Westminster Libraries Manager
Direct e-mail: a.stevens@dial.pipex.com
Other contacts: Archives Centre for full list of current publications tel no: 020 7641 5180.

Formerly called:
Westminster City Archives and Libraries

Organisation type and purpose:
Local government body.
Public library and archive.

Subject coverage:
Local studies and archives at City of Westminster Archives; music at Westminster Music Library; art and design, official publications, EU at Westminster Reference Library.

Museum or gallery collection, archive, or library special collection:
Archive and local history collections (City of Westminster Archives)
Ashbridge Collection (City of Westminster Archives)
Gillow Archives (furniture design history, Victoria Library)
Sherlock Holmes Collection (Marylebone Library)

Non-library collection catalogue:
All or part available online

Library catalogue:
All or part available online

Printed publications:
Contact Archives Centre tel: 020 7641 5180 for full list
Artisans and Avenues: A History of the Queen's Park Estate (E McDonald and D J Smith, 2nd ed., 1990)
Blitz over Westminster: City of Westminster Civil Defence bomb incident photographs 1940–1944 (R Harrison, City of Westminster Libraries, 1990)
Catalogue of Orchestral Sets held at Westminster Music Library
Greetings cards: 18th Century Westminster Views
Old Westminster Parish Maps from John Strype's 1755 edition of John Stow's Survey of London
Pineapples and Pantomimes: A History of Church Street and Lisson Green (E McDonald and D J Smith, 1992)

The Contents of a Lumber Room – A catalogue of the Sherlock Holmes Collection

Publications list:
Available in print

Access to staff:
Contact by letter, by telephone and by e-mail
Hours: Mon to Fri, 0900 to 1700
Special comments: Please telephone individual sites for opening hours and to establish restrictions on access.

Headquarters:
Westminster City Hall, Victoria Street, London, SW1E 6QP; tel: 020 7641 2496

Other addresses:
Charing Cross Library
Charing Cross Road, London, WC2H 0HG; tel: 020 7641 4628
Church Street Library
Church Street, London, NW8 8EU; tel: 020 7641 5479
City of Westminster Archives Centre
10 St Ann's Street, London, SW1T 2XR; tel: 020 7641 5180
Maida Vale Library
Sutherland Avenue, London, W9 2QT; tel: 020 7641 3659
Marylebone Library
Marylebone Road, London, NW1 5PS; tel: 020 7641 1037
Mayfair Library
25 South Audley Street, London, W1Y 5DJ; tel: 020 7641 4903
Paddington Library
Porchester Road, London, W2 5DU; tel: 020 7641 4475
Pimlico Library
Rampayne Street, London, SW1V 2PU; tel: 020 7641 2983
Queen's Park Library
666 Harrow Road, London, W10 4NE; tel: 020 7641 4575
St James's Library
62 Victoria Street, London, SW1E 6QP; tel: 020 7641 2989
St John's Wood Library
20 Circus Road, London, NW8 6PD; tel: 020 7641 5087
Victoria Library
160 Buckingham Palace Road, London, SW1W 9UD; tel: 020 7641 4287
Westminster Music Library
Victoria Library, 160 Buckingham Palace Road, London, SW1W 9UD; tel: 020 7641 4292
Westminster Reference Library
St Martin's Street, London, WC2H 7HP; tel: 020 7641 4636

Parent body:
Westminster City Council

WESTMINSTER PROPERTY OWNERS ASSOCIATION

Acronym or abbreviation: WPOA

7th Floor, 1 Warwick Row, London, SW1E 5ER

Tel: 020 7630 1782
Fax: 020 7630 8344

Enquiries:
Enquiries to: Director
Direct e-mail: douglas@bpf.org.uk

Founded:
1988

Organisation type and purpose:
Trade association.

Subject coverage:
Property in Westminster.

Access to staff:
Contact by letter, by telephone and by e-mail
Hours: Mon to Fri, 0900 to 1700

Affiliated to the:
British Property Federation

WESTMINSTER REFERENCE LIBRARY

35 St Martins Street, London, WC2H 7HP

Tel: 020 7641 4634/4636/4638
Fax: 020 7641 4606
E-mail: westreflib@dial.pipex.com

Website:
http://www.westminster.gov.uk/libraries/search
Catalogue.
http://www.westminster.gov.uk/libraries/libraries/
westref
Information about the library.

Enquiries:
Enquiries to: Manager
Direct tel: 020 7641 5260
Direct e-mail: tarathoon@dial.pipex.com

Formerly called:
Westminster Central Reference Library

Organisation type and purpose:
Local government body, public library.

Subject coverage:
A general public reference library specialising in the following key areas:
Business: market research, business directories and international telephone directories, company information.
Official Publications: HMSO publications since 1947, Parliamentary papers since 1906, Hansard since 1803, EU Official Publications.
Arts: covering art, fine arts, painting, drawing, sculpture, ceramics, glassware, coins, tapestry, carpets, furniture, jewellery, interior design, costume, goldsmiths' work, silverware, arms and armour, architecture, antiques, collecting, cinema, film, theatre, radio and television and dance.

Museum or gallery collection, archive, or library special collection:
EU Depository Library

Trade and statistical information:
Wide range of UK, EU and International statistics.

Non-library collection catalogue:
All or part available online

Library catalogue:
All or part available online

Access to staff:
Contact by letter, by telephone, by fax, by e-mail, in person and via website
Hours: Mon to Fri, 1000 to 2000; Sat, 1000 to 1700
Special comments: Reference library.

Also at:
Marylebone Information Service (MIS)
109–117 Marylebone Road, London, NW1 5PS;
tel: 020 7641 1031; fax: 020 7641 1028; e-mail: m.i
.s@dial.pipex.com

Parent body:
Westminster City Council

WESTON COLLEGE

Learning Resources Centre, Knightstone Road, Weston-super-Mare, Somerset, BS23 2AL

Tel: 01934 411411
Fax: 01934 411410
E-mail: college@weston.ac.uk

Website:
http://www.weston.ac.uk
College home page.

Enquiries:
Enquiries to: Librarian
Direct tel: 01934 411409
Direct e-mail: lrc@weston.ac.uk

Formerly called:
Weston-Super-Mare College of Further Education

Organisation type and purpose:
Further Education.

Subject coverage:
General, psychology, sociology, social sciences, catering, hairdressing, electronics, engineering, business, care, art, leisure, drugs information base, computer studies, information technology, music technology, sciences, languages, EFL, humanities, education, sign language.

Museum or gallery collection, archive, or library special collection:
Drugs information base

Printed publications:
General information (opening hours, borrowing rights)
CD guides
Subject guides
Web site guides

Access to staff:
Contact by letter, by telephone, by fax, by e-mail, in person and via website
Hours: Term time: Mon to Thu, 0845 to 2100, Fri, 0845 to 1700
Vacations: Mon to Fri, 0900 to 1700

Access for disabled people:
Parking provided, ramped entry, toilet facilities

Also at:
Weston College 6th Form Library
Loxton Road, Weston-super-Mare, Somerset; tel: 01934 411615

WEYMOUTH COLLEGE

Library, Cranford Avenue, Weymouth, Dorset, DT4 7LQ

Tel: 01305 208820
Fax: 01305 208912
E-mail: library@weymouth.ac.uk

Website:
http://www.weymouth.ac.uk

Enquiries:
Enquiries to: Librarian

Founded:
1985

Organisation type and purpose:
Further Education College with some HE courses.

Subject coverage:
Art, biology, classics, business studies, careers, catering, chemistry, computer studies, conservation, construction, engineering, geography, hairdressing, history, literature, maths, physics, physical education, recreation management, sociology, tourism, education, religion, stone carving, beauty, dance, drama, music, management, public services

Museum or gallery collection, archive, or library special collection:
Fleet Study archive

Library catalogue:
All or part available online and in-house

Printed publications:
Resource lists of library stock

Access to staff:
Contact by letter, by telephone, by fax, by e-mail and in person
Hours: Term time: Mon to Thu, 0830 to 2000; Fri, 0830 to 1700; Sat, Sun, closed
Vacations: daily, 0830 to 1700

Access for disabled people:
Level entry, access to all public areas, toilet facilities

WHALE AND DOLPHIN CONSERVATION SOCIETY

Acronym or abbreviation: WDCS

Brookfield House, 38 St Paul Street, Chippenham, Wiltshire, SN15 1LY

Tel: 01249 449500

Fax: 01249 449501
E-mail: info@wdcs.org

Website:
http://www.bluetravel.co.uk
WDCS travel wing/conservation holidays (out of the blue).
http://www.wdcs.org
WDCS homepage.

Founded:
1987

Organisation type and purpose:
Registered charity (charity number 1014705). The global voice for the protection of whales, dolphins and their environment.

Subject coverage:
Conservation of all species of whale, dolphin and porpoise.

Printed publications:
Journey Under the Sea – Getting to Know Orcas and Other Whales, Dolphins and Porpoises (education pack for Key Stages 1–3, includes video and poster)
Various on captivity, fisheries, oil and gas, UK cetaceans, sightings and strandings, whale watching and whaling available as PDF Files from websites

Access to staff:
Contact by letter, by telephone, by fax, by e-mail and via website
Hours: Mon to Fri, 0900 to 1700

WHEELYBOAT TRUST, THE

North Lodge, Burton Park, Petworth, West Sussex, GU28 0JT

Tel: 01798 342222
Fax: 01798 342222
E-mail: wheelyboats@tiscali.co.uk

Website:
http://www.wheelyboats.org
Work of the Trust, wheelyboat locations list.

Enquiries:
Enquiries to: Director

Founded:
1984

Formerly called:
Handicapped Anglers Trust – Boating for the Disabled

Organisation type and purpose:
Registered charity (charity number 292216). Promoting solutions for access by disabled people to fisheries, waterways and other bodies of water.

Subject coverage:
Access by disabled people to fisheries and other waterways. Disability Discrimination Act 1995 – advice on implications of the act on fisheries and other waterways.

Access to staff:
Contact by letter, by telephone, by fax and by e-mail
Hours: Mon to Fri, 0900 to 1700

Access to building, collection or gallery:
No access other than to staff

WHERNSIDE MANOR

Formal name: Whernside Manor Bunkhouses

Cave and Fell Centre, Dent, Sedburgh, Cumbria, LA10 5RE

Tel: 01539 625213
E-mail: whernsidemanor@aol.com

Website:
http://www.whernsidemanor.com

Enquiries:
Enquiries to: Manager

Founded:
2000

Changed ownership (year of change 2000)

Organisation type and purpose:
Historic building, house or site.

Subject coverage:
Caving, walking.

Printed publications:
Leaflets available on request

Access to staff:
Contact by letter. Appointment necessary.
Hours: Mon to Fri, 0900 to 1700

Access to building, collection or gallery:
Prior appointment required

WHICHINTRO.COM

18 Thayer Street, London, W1U 3JY

Tel: 020 7935 6408
Fax: 020 7486 3817
E-mail: info@whichintro.com

Website:
http://www.whichintro.com
Database providing comprehensive details of
every organisation offering introductions; advice
and guidance to individuals considering joining an
agency.

Enquiries:
Enquiries to: Information Officer

Founded:
1970

Formerly called:
Society of Marriage Bureaux (SMB) (year of change
1999)

Organisation type and purpose:
National organisation (membership is by
subscription), service industry, research
organisation.
Searchable database on all organisations in UK
offering introduction services; plus advice and
guidance on selecting and using such agencies.

Subject coverage:
Joining a marriage bureau or introductory agency,
things to be aware of and alert to, general
information about the industry, objective comment
on proposed legislation and news items.
Comprehensive information on fees, methodology,
specialisms and location of introduction agencies.

**Museum or gallery collection, archive, or library
special collection:**
Many brochures from introduction agencies
Various books on marriage and finding partners

Trade and statistical information:
Number of active agencies; membership numbers;
agencies ceasing to trade; new agencies.

Printed publications:
Happily Ever After, advising 30-something young
women on relationships (book, available from
website)

Electronic and video publications:
Codes of conduct
Watchdog (leaflet, available online to subscribers)

Access to staff:
Contact by letter, by telephone, by e-mail and via
website
Hours: Mon to Fri, 0900 to 1700 by telephone.

WHITAKER

Woolmead House West, Bear Lane, Farnham,
Surrey, GU9 7LG

Tel: 01252 742500
Fax: 01252 742501

Enquiries:
Enquiries to: Sales Manager

Organisation type and purpose:
Publishing house.

Subject coverage:
Bibliographic files of English language books
published in the UK and over 70 other countries
which are or were in print and those which are
forthcoming.

Trade and statistical information:
Data on the publication of English language titles
published in the UK or with a stock holding
distributor in the UK.

Printed publications:
The Bookseller (weekly)
Directory of Publishers (annually)
Whitaker's Almanack (annually)
Whitaker's Books in Print (annually)

Microform publications:
ISBN Listing (fiche)
New and Forthcoming (weekly fiche)
Out-of-Print (fiche)
Whitaker's Books in Print (annual fiche)
Whitaker's Book List (fiche)

Electronic and video publications:
BookBank (CD-ROM)
BookBank OP (CD-ROM)
BookBank with SABIP (CD-ROM)
BookBank with ThorpeROM (includes database of
Australasian books) (CD-ROM)
Global BookBank (finder) (CD-ROM)
Global BookBank, Premium (CD-ROM)
Whitaker's Books in Print (magnetic tape)

Access to staff:
Contact by letter, by telephone, by fax and by e-
mail
Hours: Mon to Fri, 0900 to 1700

Associated with:
BookTrack Limited
tel: 01252 542555; e-mail: booktrack.info@
booktrack.co.uk
Teleordering Limited

Connections with:
Standard Book Numbering Agency Limited
12 Dyott Street, London, WC1A 1DF

WHITBY PICTORIAL ARCHIVES HERITAGE CENTRE

Flowergate, Whitby, North Yorkshire, YO21 3BA

Tel: 01947 821364
Fax: 01947 821436
E-mail: info@whitbyarchives.freeserve.co.uk

Website:
http://www.freeserve.co.uk/whitbyarchives
Details of archives services, list of items for sale or
research, links to other sites.

Enquiries:
Enquiries to: Director
Other contacts: Manager

Founded:
1985

Organisation type and purpose:
Membership association (membership is by
subscription), museum, suitable for ages: all,
research organisation.
Charitable Trust, tourist facility.

Subject coverage:
Local, general, family history of Whitby and North
Yorkshire, directories, birth, marriage and death
records, extensive photographic collection,
documents, local records and ephemera. Growing
collection of artefacts and historic objects, maps.
New exhibition: The Warring 40s Team, authentic
1940s, educational and entertaining. Rohilla
Exhibition.
A full range of photographic and 'on paper'
general history files, all filed by subject. These
include many census records, parish registers, lists
of trades and professional people, monumental
inscriptions, ships and school records and many
more. Resource material may be consulted in
person or by mail order.

Information services:
Archives available for reference. Local and family
history research service either by the enquirer, or
on their behalf. Local history advice given.

Special visitor services:
Guided tours, materials and/or activities for
children.

Education services:
Group education facilities, resources for Key
Stages 1 and 2, 3 and 4.

**Museum or gallery collection, archive, or library
special collection:**
Photographs, memorabilia and artefacts collected
mainly from local sources to mark Whitby's long
and distinguished history
Documentary collection, includes photos, maps,
documents and oral history tapes
Family history department with collection of North
Yorkshire family trees and related material
Genealogical information and lists
Historic photograph collection of Whitby in
particular and North Yorkshire in general
The Warring 40s Team

Trade and statistical information:
Local population data and statistics, related
information regarding the history of the area,
genealogical and photographic records, maps.

Non-library collection catalogue:
All or part available in print

Printed publications:
Whitby Directory 1781, 1784 & 1798 (£4.50)
Whitby Directory 1834 (£4.50)
Whitby Directory 1840 (£4.50)
Whitby Directory 1849 (£4.50)
Local history series of booklets (photographic
copies available)
Oral history tapes – interviews with old residents
(copies may be ordered)
Whitby Archives

Electronic and video publications:
1899 list of Whitby residents (disc)
Other genealogical diskettes available
Videos for sale

Publications list:
Available online and in print

Access to staff:
Contact by letter, by telephone, by fax, by e-mail,
in person and via website. All charged.
Hours: Summer: Mon to Fri; 1030 to 1600; Sat, Sun,
1100 to 1500
Winter: Mon to Sun, 1100 to 1500
Special comments: Research facilities restricted at
weekends.

Access to building, collection or gallery:
No prior appointment required
Hours: Apr to Oct: Mon to Fri, 1000 to 1600
Nov to Mar: Mon to Fri, 1100 to 1500
Special comments: Appointment advised for
research using collections. Collection and file room
may be closed some Sat, Sun.

Access for disabled people:
Level entry, toilet facilities
Special comments: Access to all areas except café.
Disabled chairlift to lower floor.

Parent body:
Whitby Pictorial Archives Trust (WPAT)

WHITWELL LOCAL HISTORY GROUP

10 Jubilee Road, Whitwell, Nottinghamshire, S80
4PL

Tel: 01909 723230
E-mail: wlhg@hopkins-uk.co.uk

Website:
http://www.wlhg.co.uk

Enquiries:
Enquiries to: Secretary

continued overleaf

Founded:
1986

Education services:
Contact with local school.

Printed publications:
Whitwell Miscellany (journal, occasional)
Whitwell, A Parish History

Access to staff:
Contact by letter, by telephone, by e-mail and via website

WIENER LIBRARY

Formal name: Wiener Library Institute of Contemporary History

4 Devonshire Street, London, W1W 5BH

Tel: 020 7636 7247/8
Fax: 020 7436 6428
E-mail: info@wienerlibrary.co.uk

Website:
http://www.wienerlibrary.co.uk

Enquiries:
Enquiries to: Librarian
Other contacts: Senior Librarian

Founded:
1933

Formerly called:
Institute of Contemporary History and Wiener Library; Jewish Central Information Office

Organisation type and purpose:
Registered charity, charity number 313015. Research library, open to the public. Extensive archive on the Holocaust and Nazi era, with a collection of over 1m. items.

Subject coverage:
Holocaust, Third Reich, Fascism, Neo-Fascism, German-Jewish history, Exile studies, Antisemitism

Museum or gallery collection, archive, or library special collection:
Books and pamphlets (c.60,000)
Periodicals (c.3,000 titles and 140 current subscriptions)
Document collections (c.1,300)
Eyewitness Accounts (of survivors of the Holocaust)
Photo Archive (over 10,000)
Press Archive

Non-library collection catalogue:
All or part available online

Library catalogue:
All or part available online

Printed publications:
Newsletter (twice a year)

Access to staff:
Contact by letter, by telephone, by fax, by e-mail, in person and via website. Letter of introduction required.
Hours: Mon to Fri, 1000 to 1715

Access to building, collection or gallery:
Hours: Mon to Fri, 1000 to 1715

Links with:
Institute of Contemporary History

WIGAN ARCHIVES SERVICE

Town Hall, Leigh, Lancashire, WN7 1DY

Tel: 01942 404430
Fax: 01942 404425
E-mail: heritage@wlct.org

Enquiries:
Enquiries to: Archivist

Founded:
1968

Formerly called:
Wigan Record Office

Organisation type and purpose:
Local government body.

Museum or gallery collection, archive, or library special collection:
Archive

Non-library collection catalogue:
All or part available online, in-house and in print

Printed publications:
Guide to the Archives
Genealogical Services

Access to staff:
Contact by letter, by telephone, by fax, by e-mail and in person. Appointment necessary.
Hours: Tue to Thu, 1000 to 1300 and 1400 to 1630

Access to building, collection or gallery:
Prior appointment required
Hours: To view documents: Tue to Thu, 1000 to 1300 and 1400 to 1630

Access for disabled people:
Access to all public areas

Parent body:
Wigan Leisure and Culture Trust
 Department of Leisure; tel: 01942 244991

WIGAN HERITAGE SERVICE

The History Shop, Library Street, Wigan, Lancashire, WN1 1NU

Tel: 01942 828128
Fax: 01942 827645
E-mail: heritage@wlct.org

Enquiries:
Enquiries to: Visitor Services Manager
Other contacts: Collection Department Manager for collections.

Founded:
1992

Organisation type and purpose:
Local government body, museum, suitable for ages: 12+.

Subject coverage:
Local history – all types, genealogy.

Services for disabled people:
Displays and/or information at wheelchair height.

Museum or gallery collection, archive, or library special collection:
Social and industrial history
Family history, parish records, census material

Access to staff:
Contact by letter, by telephone, by fax, by e-mail and in person

Access to building, collection or gallery:
No prior appointment required
Hours: Mon, 1000 to 1900; Tue to Fri, 1000 to 1700; Sat, 1000 to 1300

Access for disabled people:
Ramped entry, toilet facilities
Special comments: Access to ground floor only.

WIGAN LIBRARY

College Avenue, Wigan, Lancashire, WN1 1DQ

Tel: 01942 827621
Fax: 01942 827640
E-mail: wigan.library@wlct.org

Website:
http://www.wlct.org

Enquiries:
Enquiries to: Information Services Officer
Direct tel: 01942 827619
Other contacts: Information Services Co-ordinator

Organisation type and purpose:
Public library.

Subject coverage:
General subjects.

Museum or gallery collection, archive, or library special collection:
All the following collections now in the Wigan History Shop (heritage service) or the Central Reserve Store, Leigh Library
Dootson Collection (Lancashire and local history at Leigh Library)
Eckersley Collection and Leyland Collections (personal, general collections at Hindley Library)
Fine Bindings Collection
Incunabula Collection

Non-library collection catalogue:
All or part available online

Library catalogue:
All or part available online

Access to staff:
Contact by letter, by telephone, by fax, by e-mail, in person and via website
Hours: Mon, 1000 to 1830; Tues, Wed, Thu, 0930 To 1830; Fri, 0930 to 1700; Sat, 1000 to 1600
Special comments: Prior arrangement required to consult the Dootson Collection.

Access for disabled people:
Ramped entry, toilet facilities

Parent body:
Wigan Leisure & Culture Trust
 Loire Drivem Robon Park, Wigan, WN5 0UL; tel: 01942 828508

WILCO

Central Library, Regent Circus, Swindon, Wiltshire, SN1 1QG

Tel: 01793 463796/7
Fax: 01793 541319
E-mail: rtrayhurn@swindon.gov.uk

Website:
http://www.wilco.org.uk

Enquiries:
Enquiries to: Secretary
Other contacts: Treasurer

Founded:
1974

Formerly called:
Wiltshire Libraries in Co-operation

Organisation type and purpose:
Local government body, membership association (membership is by election or invitation), present number of members: 20 Full, 10 Associate. Library co-operative scheme between public, government, academic, research and industrial libraries.

Subject coverage:
Business, commercial and industrial information, standards, journals, reports, serials, monographs, in a wide range of business topics.

Non-library collection catalogue:
All or part available online

Access to staff:
Contact by telephone, by fax and by e-mail.
Access for members only.
Hours: Mon to Fri, 0930 to 1900; Sat, 0930 to 1600

WILDFOWL & WETLANDS TRUST

Acronym or abbreviation: WWT

Slimbridge, Gloucestershire, GL2 7BT

Tel: 01453 891900
Fax: 01453 890827
E-mail: information@wwt.org.uk

Website:
http://www.wwt.org.uk

Enquiries:
Enquiries to: Managing Director
Direct e-mail: marketing@wwt.org.uk

Founded:
1946

Formerly called:
Wildfowl Trust

Organisation type and purpose:
Registered charity (charity number 1030884).
Trust for conservation, education, and research. 8
visitors centres throughout the UK.

Subject coverage:
Conservation of: wildfowl and their habitat,
mainly geese, ducks and swans but also
considerable data on other waterfowl; wildfowl
populations, behaviour, migration, nutrition and
disease; breeding of wildfowl; Wetlands; ponds,
streams, lakes, rivers, marshes, bogs, wet
meadows, ecology, management, conservation,
aviculture.

**Museum or gallery collection, archive, or library
special collection:**
Library of books and documents on wildfowl and
Wetlands

Printed publications:
Wildfowl and Wetlands (4 times a year, free to
members)
Wildfowl: an annual collection of scientific papers

Publications list:
Available in print

Access to staff:
Contact by letter, by telephone and by fax
Hours: Mon to Fri, 0900 to 1700

Other addresses:
London Wetland Centre
 Queen Elizabeth's Walk, Barnes, London, SW13
 9WT; tel: 020 8409 4400; e-mail: info.london@
 wwt.org.uk
National Wetlands Centre for Wales
 Penclacwydd, Llwynhendy, Llanelli, Dyfed,
 SA14 9SH; tel: 01554 741087
National Wetlands Centre Wales
 Llanelli Centre, Penclacwydd, Llwynhendy,
 Llanelli, SA14 9SH; tel: 01554 741087; fax: 01554
 744101; e-mail: info.llanelli@wwt.org.uk
Wildfowl & Wetlands Trust
 Castle Espie, Ballydrain Road, Comber, Co
 Down, BT23 6EA; tel: 028 9187 4146; fax: 028
 9187 3857; e-mail: info.castleespie@wwt.org.uk
Wildfowl & Wetlands Trust
 Pintail House, Hundred Foot Bank, Welney,
 Wisbech, Cambridgeshire, PE14 9TN; tel: 01353
 860711; fax: 01353 860711; e-mail: info.welney@
 wwt.org.uk
Wildfowl & Wetlands Trust
 Martin Mere, Burscough, Ormskirk, Lancashire,
 L40 0TA; tel: 01704 895181; fax: 01704 892343; e-
 mail: info.martinmere@wwt.org.uk
Wildfowl & Wetlands Trust
 District 15, Washington, Tyne & Wear, NE38 8LE;
 tel: 0191 416 5454; fax: 0191 416 5801; e-mail: info
 .washington@wwt.org.uk
Wildfowl & Wetlands Trust
 Mill Road, Arundel, West Sussex, BN18 9PB; tel:
 01903 883355; fax: 01903 884834; e-mail: info
 .arundel@wwt.org.uk
Wildfowl & Wetlands Trust
 Eastpark Farm, Caerlaverock, Dumfriesshire,
 DG1 4RS; tel: 01387 770200; fax: 01387 770539; e-
 mail: info.caerlaverock@wwt.org.uk

Subsidiary body:
Wetlands Advisory Service Limited
 Slimbridge, Gloucestershire, GL2 7BT; tel: 01453
 891905; fax: 01453 890827; e-mail: was@wwt.org
 .uk
Wildfowl & Wetlands Trust (Property) Ltd

WILDLIFE TRUSTS

The Kiln, Mather Road, Waterside, Newark,
Nottinghamshire, NG24 1WT

Tel: 01636 677711
Fax: 01636 670001
E-mail: info@wildlife-trusts.cix.co.uk

Website:
http://www.wildlifetrust.org

Enquiries:
Enquiries to: Information Officer

Founded:
1912

Formerly called:
Royal Society for Nature Conservation

Organisation type and purpose:
Voluntary organisation, registered charity (charity
number 207238).
The protection of local countryside and wildlife
inhabitants.

Subject coverage:
Nature conservation, protection and enhancement
of species and habitats in the UK; wildlife
legislation; history of nature conservation;
environmental education; membership and work
of Wildlife Trusts.

Printed publications:
Annual Report and Accounts
Annual Review
Natural World (3 times a year, members only)
A variety of leaflets, newsletters (free of charge)
Many books for sale including:
Guide to Nature Reserves in Bedfordshire and
 Cambridgeshire
The Wildlife Trusts' Nature Reserves Guide

Publications list:
Available in print

Access to staff:
Contact by letter, by e-mail and via website
Hours: Mon to Fri, 0900 to 1700

Member of:
European Environment Bureau
International Union for the Conservation of Nature
Wildlife Link

Regional Offices:
Avon Wildlife Trust
 Wildlife Centre, 32 Jacob's Wells Road, Bristol,
 BS8 1DR; tel: 0117 926 8018; fax: 0117 929 7273;
 e-mail: avonwt@cix.compulink.co.uk
Berkshire, Buckinghamshire & Oxfordshire
Wildlife Trust
 The Lodge, 1 Armstrong Road, Littlemore,
 Oxford, OX4 4XT; tel: 01865 775476; fax: 01865
 711301; e-mail: bbowt@cix.co.uk
Brecknock Wildlife Trust
 Lion House, Bethel Square, Brecon, Powys, LD3
 7AY; tel: 01874 625708; fax: 01874 625708; e-mail:
 brecknockwt@cix.co.uk
Cheshire Wildlife Trust
 Grebe House, Reaseheath, Nantwich, Cheshire,
 CW5 6DG; tel: 01270 610180; fax: 01270 610430;
 e-mail: cheshirewt@cix.co.uk
Cornwall Wildlife Trust
 Five Acres, Aller, Truro, Cornwall, TR4 9DJ; tel:
 01872 273939; fax: 01872 225476; e-mail: cornwt@
 cix.co.uk
Cumbria Wildlife Trust
 Brockhole, Windermere, Cumbria, LA23 1LJ; tel:
 015394 48280; fax: 015394 48281; e-mail:
 cumbriawt@cix.co.uk
Derbyshire Wildlife Trust
 East Mill, Bridgefoot, Belper, Derby, DE56 1XH;
 tel: 01773 881188; fax: 01773 821826; e-mail:
 derbywt@cix.co.uk
Devon Wildlife Trust
 Shirehampton House, 35–37 St David's Hill,
 Exeter, Devon, EX4 4DA; tel: 01392 279244; fax:
 01392 433221; e-mail: devonwt@cix.co.uk
Dorset Wildlife Trust
 Brooklands Farm, Forston, Dorchester, DT2
 7AA; tel: 01305 264620; fax: 01305 251120; e-
 mail: dorsetwt@cix.co.uk
Durham Wildlife Trust
 Rainton Meadows, Chilton Moor, Houghton-le-
 Spring, Tyne & Wear, DH4 6PU; tel: 0191 584
 3112; fax: 0191 584 3934; e-mail: durhamwt@cix
 .co.uk
Essex Wildlife Trust
 Abbotts Hall Farm, Great Wigborough,
 Colchester, Essex, CO5 7RZ; tel: 01621 862960;
 fax: 01621 862990; e-mail: admin@essexwt.org.uk

Glamorgan Wildlife Trust
 Nature Centre, Fountain Road, Tondu, Bridgend,
 Mid Glamorgan, CF32 0EH; tel: 01656 724100;
 fax: 01656 729880; e-mail: glamorganwt@cix.co
 .uk
Gloucestershire Wildlife Trust
 Dulverton Building, Robinswood Hill Country
 Park, Reservoir Road, Gloucester, GL4 6SX; tel:
 01452 383333; fax: 01452 383334; e-mail: gmcg@
 cix.co.uk
Gwent Wildlife Trust
 16 White Swan Court, Church Street,
 Monmouth, Gwent, NP25 3NY; tel: 01600
 715501; fax: 01600 715832; e-mail:
 gwentwildlife@cix.co.uk
Hampshire & Isle of Wight Wildlife Trust
 Woodside House, Woodside Road, Eastleigh,
 Hampshire, SO50 4ET; tel: 02380 613636; fax:
 02380 688900; e-mail: hampswt@cix.co.uk
Herefordshire Nature Trust
 Lower House Farm, Ledbury Road, Tupsley,
 Hereford, HR1 1UT; tel: 01432 356872; fax: 01432
 275489; e-mail: herefordwt@cix.co.uk
Hertfordshire & Middlesex Wildlife Trust
 Grebe House, St Michael's Street, St Albans,
 Hertfordshire, AL3 4SN; tel: 01727 858901; fax:
 01727 854542; e-mail: hertswt@cix.co.uk
Kent Wildlife Trust
 Tyland Barn, Sandling, Maidstone, Kent, ME14
 3BD; tel: 01622 662012; fax: 01622 671390; e-mail:
 kentwildlife@cix.co.uk
Lancashire Wildlife Trust
 Cuerden Park Wildlife Centre, Shady Lane,
 Bamber Bridge, Preston, PR5 6AU; tel: 01772
 324129; fax: 01772 628849
Leicestershire & Rutland Wildlife Trust
 Longfellow Road, Knighton Fields, Leicester,
 LE2 6BT; tel: 01162 702999; fax: 01162 709555; e-
 mail: leicswt@cix.compulink.co.uk
Lincolnshire Wildlife Trust
 Banovallum House, Manor House Street,
 Horncastle, Lincolnshire, LN9 5HF; tel: 01507
 526667; fax: 01507 525732; e-mail: lincstrust@cix
 .compulink.co.uk
London Wildlife Trust
 Harling House, 47–51 Great Suffolk Street,
 London, SE1 0BS; tel: 020 7261 0447; fax: 020
 7261 0538; e-mail: londonwt@cix.compulink.co
 .uk
Manx Wildlife Trust
 Conservation Centre, The Courtyard, Tynwald
 Mills, St Johns, Isle of Man; tel: 01624 801985;
 fax: 01624 801022; e-mail: manxwt@cix.co.uk
Montgomeryshire Wildlife Trust
 Collott House, 20 Severn Street, Welshpool,
 Powys, SY21 7AD; tel: 01938 555654; fax: 01938
 556161; e-mail: montwt@cix.compulink.co.uk
Norfolk Wildlife Trust
 72 Cathedral Close, Norwich, Norfolk, NR1 4DF;
 tel: 01603 625540; fax: 01603 630593; e-mail:
 nwt@cix.compulink.co.uk
North Wales Wildlife Trust
 376 High Street, Bangor, Gwynedd, LL57 1YE;
 tel: 01248 351541; fax: 01248 353192; e-mail:
 nwwt@cix.compulink.co.uk
Northumberland Wildlife Trust
 The Garden House, St Nicholas Park, Jubilee
 Road, Newcastle upon Tyne, NE3 3XT; tel: 0191
 284 6884; fax: 0191 284 6794; e-mail:
 northwdlife@cix.compulink.co.uk
Nottinghamshire Wildlife Trust
 The Old Ragged School, Brook Street,
 Nottingham, NG1 1EA; tel: 0115 958 8242; fax:
 0115 924 3175; e-mail: nottswt@cix.compulink.co
 .uk
Radnorshire Wildlife Trust
 Warwick House, High Street, Llandrindod Wells,
 Powys, LD1 6AG; tel: 01597 823298; fax: 01597
 823274; e-mail: radnorshirewt@cix.compulink.co
 .uk
Scottish Wildlife Trust
 Crammond House, Kirk Crammond, Crammond
 Glebe Road, Edinburgh, EH4 6NS; tel: 0131 312
 7765; fax: 0131 312 8705; e-mail: scottishwt@cix
 .compulink.co.uk

continued overleaf

Sheffield Wildlife Trust
37 Stafford Road, Sheffield, S2 2FS; tel: 0114 263 4335; fax: 0114 263 4345; e-mail: sheffieldwt@cix.co.uk

Shropshire Wildlife Trust
193 Abbey Foregate, Shrewsbury, Shropshire; tel: 01743 284280; fax: 01743 284281; e-mail: shropshirewt@cix.co.uk

Somerset Wildlife Trust
Fyne Court, Broomfield, Bridgwater, Somerset, TA5 2EQ; tel: 01823 451587; fax: 01823 451671; e-mail: somwt@cix.co.uk

Staffordshire Wildlife Trust
Coutts House, Sandon, Staffordshire, ST18 0DN; tel: 01889 508534; fax: 01889 508422; e-mail: staffswt@cix.co.uk

Suffolk Wildlife Trust
Brooke House, The Green, Ashbocking, Ipswich, Suffolk, IP6 9JY; tel: 01473 890089; fax: 01473 890165; e-mail: suffolkwt@cix.co.uk

Surrey Wildlife Trust
School Lane, Pirbright, Woking, Surrey, GU24 0JN; tel: 01483 488055; fax: 01483 486505; e-mail: surreywt@cix.co.uk

Sussex Wildlife Trust
Woods Mill, Shoreham Road, Henfield, West Sussex, BN5 9SD; tel: 01273 492630; fax: 01273 494500; e-mail: sussexwt@cix.co.uk

Tees Valley Wildlife Trust
Bellamy Pavilion, Kirkleatham Old Hall, Kirkleatham, Redcar, Cleveland, TS10 5NW; tel: 01642 759900; fax: 01642 480401; e-mail: clevelandwt@cix.co.uk

Ulster Wildlife Trust
3 New Line, Crossgar, Co Down, BT30 9EP; tel: 028 9083 0282; fax: 028 9083 0888; e-mail: ulsterwt@cix.co.uk

Warwickshire Wildlife Trust
Brandon Marsh Nature Centre, Brandon Lane, Coventry, CV3 3GW; tel: 01203 302912; fax: 01203 639556; e-mail: warkswt@cix.co.uk

Wildlife Trust for Bedfordshire, Cambridgeshire, Northamptonshire and Peterborough
3B Langford Arch, London Road, Sawston, Cambridge, CB2 4EE; tel: 01223 712400; fax: 01223 712412; e-mail: cambswt@cix.co.uk

Wildlife Trust for Birmingham & Black Country
Unit 310, Jubilee Trade Centre, 130 Pershore Street, Birmingham, B5 6ND; tel: 0121 666 7474; fax: 0121 622 4443; e-mail: urbanwt@cix.co.uk

Wildlife Trust: West Wales
7 Market Street, Haverfordwest, Dyfed, SA61 1NF; tel: 01437 765462; fax: 01437 767163; e-mail: wildlife@wildlife-wales.org.uk

Wiltshire Wildlife Trust
Elm Tree Court, Long Street, Devizes, Wiltshire, SN10 1NH; tel: 01380 725670; fax: 01380 729017; e-mail: wiltswt@cix.co.uk

Worcestershire Wildlife Trust
Lower Smite Farm, Smite Hill, Hindlip, Worcester, WR3 8SZ; tel: 01905 754919; fax: 01905 755868; e-mail: worcswt@cix.co.uk

Yorkshire Wildlife Trust
10 Toft Green, York, YO1 6JT; tel: 01904 659570; fax: 01904 613467; e-mail: yorkshirewt@cix.co.uk

The national association of UK's:
Urban Wildlife Groups
Wildlife Trusts
Wildlife Watch (the junior branch)

WILDLIFE WATCH

The Kiln, Waterside, Mather Road, Newark, Nottinghamshire, NG24 1WT

Tel: 0870 036 7711
Fax: 0870 036 0101
E-mail: watch@wildlife-trusts.cix.co.uk

Website:
http://www.wildlifetrusts.org/watch

Enquiries:
Enquiries to: Development Officer
Direct e-mail: arawson@wildlife-trusts.cix.co.uk
Other contacts: Membership Officer

Founded:
1971

Formerly called:
Watch Trust for Environmental Education, Wildlife WATCH

Organisation type and purpose:
Membership association (membership is by subscription), present number of members: 20,000, voluntary organisation, registered charity (charity number 207238), suitable for ages: 7 to 14.
Junior Branch of The Wildlife Trust.
To encourage young people to investigate and help solve environmental problems.

Subject coverage:
Nature conservation, environmental education, activities and projects, advice to teachers and educationalists, site interpretation via local Wildlife Trusts.

Printed publications:
Wildlife Extra – An A4 children's magazine that folds out to a full colour poster (£1.20)
Wildlife Extra – Compost Café: Composting and the life in your compost heap (£1.20)
Wildlife Extra – Butterfly Bonanza: A look at how to attract butterflies to your garden (£1.20)
Wildlife Extra – Pondemonium: Taking action for amphibians (£1.20)
Wildlife Extra – Water For Life: How to avoid wasting water (£1.20)
Wildlife Extra – Twilight Zone: Bat stars of the night sky (£1.20)
Wildlife Extra – Snug as Bugs – The winter survival challenge of minibeasts (£1.20)
Watchword (magazine, £1.80)
Ready For Action? (leaflet on Wildlife Watch and its club for animal fans etc, children aged 8–14, SAE)
Watch Activity Books (£5 each, £22.50 for set of 5)
Young Voices – Turning ideas into action (£7.50)
Rescuing Ratty (1999, free)
Various factsheets (free, 5 or more a donation of £1 towards postage)

Publications list:
Available in print

Access to staff:
Contact by letter, by telephone, by fax, by e-mail and via website. Appointment necessary.
Hours: Mon to Fri, 0900 to 1700

WILKIE COLLINS SOCIETY

Acronym or abbreviation: WCS

Flat 3, Merton House, 36 Belsize Park, London, NW3 4EA

E-mail: apogee@apgee.co.uk

Website:
http://www.wilkie-collins.info/ wilkie_collins_society.htm

Enquiries:
Enquiries to: Chairman
Other contacts: Membership Secretary (paul@paullewis.co.uk)

Founded:
1980

Organisation type and purpose:
International organisation, membership association (membership is by subscription), present number of members: 145.
To foster interest in the life and works of Wilkie Collins.

Subject coverage:
Wilkie Collins: biographical, literary works.

Printed publications:
Reprints of out-of-print Collins short pieces (free with membership or for separate purchase)
Journal (annually, free with membership or for separate purchase)
Newsletters (3 times a year, free with membership or for separate purchase)
Order printed publications from: Membership Secretary, Wilkie Collins Society, 4 Ernest Gardens, London, W4 3QU; e-mail paul@paullewis.co.uk

Publications list:
Available in print

Access to staff:
Contact by letter and by e-mail
Hours: Mon to Fri, 0900 to 1700

Links with:
Alliance of Literary Societies

WILLIAM COBBETT SOCIETY

3 Park Terrace, Tillington, Petworth, Sussex, GU23 9AE

Tel: 01798 342008
E-mail: williamcobbett@fsmail.net

Enquiries:
Enquiries to: Chairman
Other contacts: Honorary Membership Secretary for details of membership.

Founded:
1976

Organisation type and purpose:
Learned society.

Subject coverage:
Life, times and writings of William Cobbett, 1763–1835.

Museum or gallery collection, archive, or library special collection:
Complete set of Cobbett's State Trials
Complete set of political registers 1802–31
Large collection of books by and about Cobbett

Printed publications:
Cobbett's New Register
Anne Cobbett's Account of the Family

Access to staff:
Contact by letter, by telephone and by e-mail
Hours: Mon to Fri, 0900 to 1700

Also at:
Honorary Membership Secretary
Boynell House, Outlands Lane, Curdridge, Southampton, SO30 2HD; tel: 01489 782453

WILLIAM HARVEY LIBRARY

GETEC, George Eliot Hospital NHS Trust, College Street, Nuneaton, Warwickshire, CV10 7DJ

Tel: 024 7686 5464
Fax: 02476 865218
E-mail: library@geh.nhs.uk

Enquiries:
Enquiries to: Library Services Manager
Other contacts: Clinical Librarian

Formerly called:
George Eliot Postgraduate Education Centre Library (year of change 2006)

Organisation type and purpose:
National Health Service.

Subject coverage:
Medicine, nursing, allied health, mental health, health management.

Library catalogue:
All or part available online

Access to staff:
Access for members only. Non-members charged.
Hours: Mon to Thu, 0830 to 1700; Fri, 0830 to 1630

Access to building, collection or gallery:
Hours: Mon to Fri, 0800 to 1700
Special comments: outside normal opening hours access is by staff swipe card

Access for disabled people:
Toilet facilities

WILLIAM MORRIS SOCIETY

Kelmscott House, 26 Upper Mall, Hammersmith, London, W6 9TA

Tel: 020 8741 3735
Fax: 020 8748 5207
E-mail: william.morris@care4free.net

Website:
http://www.morrissociety.org
Information on Morris's life and work, including photographs and links to related sites.

Enquiries:
Enquiries to: Curator

Founded:
1956

Formerly called:
Kelmscott Fellowship, William Morris Society

Organisation type and purpose:
Learned society (membership is by subscription), present number of members: 1500, voluntary organisation, registered charity (charity number 261437), museum.

Subject coverage:
The life and works of William Morris, his associates and successors in art, craft, design, literature and politics.

Museum or gallery collection, archive, or library special collection:
Library of work by and about William Morris, his associates and followers

Non-library collection catalogue:
All or part available in-house

Library catalogue:
All or part available in-house

Printed publications:
Journal (twice a year, members only)
A range of titles on William Morris, his life and works including:
A History of Kelmscott House (Poulson C, 1989, 50p)
Red House – A Guide (1993, £3.95)
The Story of Kormak, the Son of Ogmund (Morris, William & Magnusson, Eirikir, £10)
Three William Morris Songs for soprano and piano (1990, £3)
William Morris and the Printed Book (Kelmscott Lecture, 1986, £5)

Publications list:
Available in print

Access to staff:
Contact by letter, by telephone, by fax, by e-mail, in person and via website
Hours: Thu and Sat, 1400 to 1700

Access to building, collection or gallery:
No access other than to staff
Hours: Thu & Sat, 1400 to 1700

Access for disabled people:
Level entry, toilet facilities

WILLIAM REED PUBLISHING LIMITED

Broadfield Park, Crawley, West Sussex, RH11 9RT

Tel: 01293 613400
Fax: 01293 610322

Website:
http://www.products-online.co.uk
http://www.william-reed.co.uk

Enquiries:
Enquiries to: Information Officer

Founded:
1862

Organisation type and purpose:
Publishing house.

Subject coverage:
Food and drink manufacturing, retailing, distribution, food and drink industry, petrol forecourt shops, shopping centres; some European coverage.

Museum or gallery collection, archive, or library special collection:
Complete runs of journals published eg The Grocer 1865 to date, Off Licence News, Convenience Store, Forecourt Trader, Shopping Centre

Trade and statistical information:
Food Marketing Database.

Printed publications:
Directories, Guides and Reports on the food, drink and retail industries, including:
Food & Drink From Britain Buyers Guide
Shopping Centre & Retail Directory
The Grocer Food & Drink Manufacturers & Suppliers
The Grocer Directory of Non Food Manufacturers & Suppliers
The Mardek Guide to the UK Catering Industry
The Mardek Guide to the UK Grocery Retailers
The Grocer (weekly £60 a year)
Order printed publications from: website http://www.products-online.co.uk

Publications list:
Available online and in print

Access to staff:
Contact by telephone and by e-mail. Appointment necessary. All charged.
Hours: Mon to Fri, 1100 to 1600

WILLIAM SALT LIBRARY

19 Eastgate Street, Stafford, ST16 2LZ

Tel: 01785 278372
Fax: 01785 278414
E-mail: william.salt.library@staffordshire.gov.uk

Website:
http://www.staffordshire.gov.uk/salt.htm

Enquiries:
Enquiries to: Librarian

Founded:
1872

Organisation type and purpose:
Registered charity (charity number 528570). The library aims to preserve printed books, manuscripts, pamphlets and illustrative material relating to Staffordshire for future generations.

Subject coverage:
Staffordshire local history.

Museum or gallery collection, archive, or library special collection:
Collections relating to Staffordshire history, including parish and family histories, topographical histories, pictorial collections, pamphlets, newspapers, periodicals, manuscripts and notes

Non-library collection catalogue:
All or part available online and in-house

Library catalogue:
All or part available online and in-house

Access to staff:
Contact by letter, by telephone, by fax, by e-mail, in person and via website

Access to building, collection or gallery:
No prior appointment required
Hours: Tue to Thu, 0900 to 1300 and 1400 to 1700; Fri, 0930 to 1300 and 1400 to 1630; first Sat in each month, 0900 to 1300; closed Mon
Special comments: Reader's ticket is required. No children under age of 11 unless accompanied by an adult. Reader registration system is in operation.

Links with:
Staffordshire Record Office
Eastgate Street, Stafford, ST16 2LZ; tel: 01785 278379; fax: 01785 278384

WILLIAM SNYDER PUBLISHING ASSOCIATES

5 Five Mile Drive, Oxford, OX2 8HT

Tel: 01865 513186
Fax: 01865 513186
E-mail: snyderpub@aol.com

Website:
http://www.hoovers-europe.com

Enquiries:
Enquiries to: Managing Director

Founded:
1992

Organisation type and purpose:
Publishing house.

Subject coverage:
Distributer of business, health and general reference publications

Library catalogue:
All or part available online and in print

Printed publications:
International business directories, mainly from America, and some from UK, Europe and the world
Titles covering international business
Europe's 15,000 Largest Companies (also on CD-ROM)
Asia's 10,000 Largest Companies (also on CD-ROM)
UK's 5,000 Largest Companies (also on CD-ROM)
Europe's Largest Banks Corporate Snapshots

Electronic and video publications:
Europe's 15,000 Largest Companies (for use on user's own databases, wordprocessing or spreadsheets)

Publications list:
Available online and in print

Access to staff:
Contact by letter, by telephone, by fax, by e-mail and via website

WILTSHIRE & SWINDON USERS NETWORK

Formal name: Wiltshire Community Care User Involvement Network
Acronym or abbreviation: WCCUIN

The Bentley Centre, Stratton Road, Marshgate, Swindon SN1 2SH

Tel: 01793 616 333
E-mail: swindon.wsun@virgin.net

Website:
http://www.wsun.co.uk/

Enquiries:
Enquiries to: Semington Office
Direct tel: 01380 871800
Direct e-mail: adminwsun@btconnect.com

Founded:
November 1993

Organisation type and purpose:
Voluntary organisation.
Service-user controlled organisation.

Subject coverage:
User involvement in all aspects of community care.

Printed publications:
I am in Control – a report of user-controlled research into disabled people's views of Wiltshire Independent Living Fund (£5)
From Bobble Hats to Red Jackets – A history of the first 5 years of Wiltshire and Swindon Users Network (Evans, C C)
Tall oaks from little acorns – an account of user participation in care management training (Evans and Hughes, £3.50)
The Trowbridge Experience – A guide to involving older people and their carers in planning of local health and social core services

Publications list:
Available in print

continued overleaf

Access to staff:
Contact by letter
Hours: Mon to Fri, 0900 to 1700

WILTSHIRE AND SWINDON RECORD OFFICE

Libraries Hall, Bythesea Road, Trowbridge, Wiltshire, BA14 8BS

Tel: 01225 713139
Fax: 01225 713715
E-mail: wsro@wiltshire.gov.uk

Enquiries:
Enquiries to: Archivist

Founded:
1947

Non-library collection catalogue:
All or part available online and in-house

Access to staff:
Contact by letter
Hours: Mon to Fri, 0915 to 1700

WILTSHIRE ARCHAEOLOGICAL AND NATURAL HISTORY SOCIETY

Acronym or abbreviation: WANHS

Wiltshire Heritage Museum, 41 Long Street, Devizes, Wiltshire, SN10 1NS

Tel: 01380 727369
Fax: 01380 722150
E-mail: wanhs@wiltshireheritage.org.uk

Website:
http://www.wiltshireheritage.org.uk
Website database of collections and information about exhibitions and events.

Enquiries:
Enquiries to: Director
Direct e-mail: david.dawson@wiltshireheritage.org.uk

Founded:
1853

Organisation type and purpose:
Learned society (membership is by subscription), present number of members: c.1000, registered charity (charity number 1080096), museum.

Subject coverage:
Archaeology, natural history and local history of the county of Wiltshire; prehistoric, Roman and medieval antiquities; family history, biological records etc.

Information services:
Research library, with extensive collections about the archaeology, history and natural history of Wiltshire.

Services for disabled people:
Library is on the first floor, and so is not easily accessible to those with mobility impairments, but there is a dedicated research area on the ground floor that is accessible.

Museum or gallery collection, archive, or library special collection:
Designated as being of national significance, with important archaeological collections, particularly the Bronze Age, as well as natural history and art collections

Non-library collection catalogue:
All or part available online, in-house and in print

Library catalogue:
All or part available in-house

Printed publications:
Wiltshire Archaeological and Natural History Magazine – the County archaeological journal
Trilithon newsletter and annual reports
A range of other monographs about the history and archaeology of the County
Order printed publications from: Website and direct from the museum

Publications list:
Available online

Access to staff:
Contact by letter, by telephone, by e-mail and via website
Hours: Mon to Fri, 0900 to 1700

Access to building, collection or gallery:
Hours: Mon to Sat, 1000 to 1700; Sun, 1200 to 1600
Special comments: Library open Tue to Fri, 1000 to 1700; Sat, 1000 to 1300 and 1400 to 1700; closed first Sat of every month

WILTSHIRE ASSOCIATION OF LOCAL COUNCILS

Acronym or abbreviation: WALC

Wyndhams, St Josephs Place, Devizes, Wiltshire, SN10 1DD

Tel: 01380 729549
Fax: 01380 728476
E-mail: office@wiltshire-alc.org.uk

Website:
http://www.wiltshire-alc.org.uk/

Enquiries:
Enquiries to: County Secretary
Direct tel: 01380 729549
Other contacts: Local Councils' Adviser

Organisation type and purpose:
Advisory body, membership association (membership is by subscription), present number of members: 220.

Access to staff:
Contact by letter and by e-mail
Hours: Mon to Fri, 0930 to 1530

WILTSHIRE COLLEGE LACKHAM

Library & Learning Resources, Lacock, Chippenham, Wiltshire, SN15 2NY

Tel: 01249 466800
Fax: 01249 444474
E-mail: lackham@wiltscoll.ac.uk

Website:
http://www.wiltscoll.ac.uk

Enquiries:
Enquiries to: Manager Library and Learning Resources
Direct tel: 01249 466814
Direct e-mail: obrihn@wiltscoll.ac.uk

Founded:
1946

Formed by the merger of:
Lackham College of Agriculture Library; Lackham College Library (year of change 2001)

Organisation type and purpose:
College of further education.

Subject coverage:
Agriculture; agricultural economics, horticulture, small animal care, land-based industries, equine studies.

Non-library collection catalogue:
All or part available online

Library catalogue:
All or part available online

Access to staff:
Contact by telephone and by e-mail
Hours: Mon, to Thu, 0845 to 1700; Fri, 1000 to 1700

Access to building, collection or gallery:
Prior appointment required

Access for disabled people:
Lift, toilet facilities

Other addresses:
Wiltshire College Chippenham
Cocklebury Road, Chippenham, Wiltshire, SN15 3QD; tel: 01249 464644; e-mail: chippenham@wiltscoll.ac.uk

Wiltshire College Trowbridge
College Road, Trowbridge, Wiltshire, BA14 0ES; tel: 01225 766241; e-mail: trowbridge@wiltscoll.ac.uk

WILTSHIRE COUNTY COUNCIL LIBRARIES AND HERITAGE

Library Headquarters, Community Services Department, Bythesea Road, Trowbridge, Wiltshire, BA14 8BS

Tel: 01225 713701
Fax: 01225 713993
E-mail: libraryenquiries@wiltshire.gov.uk

Website:
http://www.wiltshire.gov.uk
Library catalogue, CI database.

Enquiries:
Enquiries to: Information Manager

Organisation type and purpose:
Local government body, public library.

Subject coverage:
Archaeology of Wiltshire; Christology; conservation of moveable objects of archaeological and historical significance; museums and museology; Wiltshire local studies; European information.

Museum or gallery collection, archive, or library special collection:
David Long Collection
Early English Children's Books
Tatham Collection of Girls' School Stories
Wiltshire Collection

Library catalogue:
All or part available online

Electronic and video publications:
Community Information Database with over 9,000 contact names and addresses
Sites and Monuments Database
Museum Objects Database

Access to staff:
Contact by letter, by telephone, by fax, by e-mail, in person and via website
Hours: Admin: Mon to Fri, 0900 to 1700

Access to building, collection or gallery:
No prior appointment required

Branch libraries:
Chippenham Public Library
tel: 01249 650536; fax: 01249 443793
Devizes Public Library
tel: 01380 726878; fax: 01380 722161
Salisbury Public Library
tel: 01722 324145; fax: 01722 413214

Parent body:
Wiltshire County Council

WILTSHIRE EDUCATION & LIBRARIES

Salisbury Library and Galleries, Market Place, Salisbury, Wiltshire, SP1 1BL

Tel: 01722 324145
Fax: 01722 413214

Website:
http://www.wiltshire.gov.uk
Full county website.
http://www.wiltshire.gov.uk/library
Online catalogue, renewals, reservations and information.

Enquiries:
Enquiries to: District Librarian
Direct tel: 01722 330606
Direct e-mail: chrisharling@wiltshire.gov.uk
Other contacts: Art Curator, tel: 01722 410614; Reference and Local Studies Library, tel: 01722 411098

Formerly called:
Wiltshire Library and Museum Service

Organisation type and purpose:
Local government body, art gallery, public library.

Subject coverage:
History of Salisbury and Wiltshire; arts; general subjects.

Museum or gallery collection, archive, or library special collection:
Edwin Young Watercolour collection – Victorian watercolours of Salisbury
Creasey Collection of contemporary art
Robin Tonner Collection – 1930s Children's Art
Edgar Barclay Collection – Victorian paintings of Stonehenge
Jerram Collection of Bellringing Books (Guild of Campanologists Collection of books and documents, many hand-annotated, formerly in the Sowter Clerical Library)
John Creasey Literary Museum

Library catalogue:
All or part available online

Printed publications:
Business Key leaflet, and many others
For under 5s: What's On? and Education Fact Sheets (free)

Access to staff:
Contact by letter, by telephone, by fax, in person and via website
Hours: Mon to Fri, 0900 to 1700

Access for disabled people:
Level entry
Special comments: Level entry via side entrance.

Member of:
WILCO

Parent body:
Wiltshire County Council

WILTSHIRE FAMILY HISTORY SOCIETY

10 Castle Lane, Devizes, Wiltshire, SN10 1HJ

E-mail: society@wiltshirefhs.co.uk

Website:
http://www.wiltshire.fhs.co.uk
http://www.genfair.com

Enquiries:
Other contacts: Membership Secretary; Research Co-ordinator

Founded:
1981

Organisation type and purpose:
Membership association (membership is by subscription), present number of members: 2600, voluntary organisation, registered charity (charity number 290284), suitable for ages: adults, research organisation.

Subject coverage:
Family and local history in Wiltshire.

Non-library collection catalogue:
All or part available online and in-house

Library catalogue:
All or part available in-house

Printed publications:
Wiltshire Family History Society Journal
Local Censuses in Wiltshire
Parish Registers

Microform publications:
Bishop's Marriage Licence Bonds
Parish Registers
Wiltshire Apprentices
Early Censuses (various in the period 1695–1887)
1851 Census Surname Index
Wiltshire Strays

Publications list:
Available online and in print

Access to staff:
Contact by letter and by e-mail. Appointment necessary. All charged.

Hours: Variable

Access to building, collection or gallery:
Prior appointment required
Hours: By arrangement

Access for disabled people:
Special comments: By arrangement.

WILTSHIRE LIBRARIES AND HERITAGE

Libraries and Heritage Branch, Corporate & Library Services Department, Bythesea Road, Trowbridge, Wiltshire, BA14 8BS

Tel: 01225 713700
Fax: 01225 713993
E-mail: libraryenquiries@wiltshire.gov.uk

Enquiries:
Enquiries to: Head of Libraries and Heritage Branch

Organisation type and purpose:
Local government body.
Museums Service.

Subject coverage:
Wiltshire County Historic Photograph Collection.

Museum or gallery collection, archive, or library special collection:
Wiltshire County Historic Photograph Collection, 35,000 records
Museum Objects Database, 155,000 records

Non-library collection catalogue:
All or part available in-house

Library catalogue:
All or part available online and in-house

Electronic and video publications:
Museum Objects Database, 155,000 records
Historic Photograph Database, 35,000 records

Access to staff:
Contact by letter, by telephone, by fax and by e-mail
Hours: Mon to Fri, 0900 to 1700

Access to building, collection or gallery:
No prior appointment required
Hours: Mon, Thu, Fri, 0900 to 1900; Tue, 0900 to 1700; Wed, 1000 to 1700; Sat, 0900 to 1600

Access for disabled people:
Parking provided, level entry, access to all public areas, toilet facilities

Parent body:
Wiltshire County Council

WILTSHIRE MUSIC CENTRE

Formal name: Wiltshire Music Centre Trust Limited

Ashley Road, Bradford-on-Avon, Wiltshire, BA15 1DZ

Tel: 01225 860110, Box Office, 01225 860100
Fax: 01225 860111
E-mail: enquiries@wiltsmusiccentre.fsnet.co.uk

Enquiries:
Enquiries to: Administrator

Organisation type and purpose:
Registered charity (charity number 1026160).
Purpose-built concert hall and music centre.
Music education, performance, recording and creation.

Subject coverage:
The Wiltshire Music Centre Trust has three closely related objectives: the advancement of music education for all ages and levels of ability, in and around the county of Wiltshire, placing the work of young musicians at the heart of this programme; the development of a high quality, varied and stimulating programme in terms of the scope of activity, breadth of musical cultures and range of people involved; to work with artists, other arts organisations and arts development agencies to achieve sustainable growth in participation, the development of audiences and of the art form.

Printed publications:
Available, free

Publications list:
Available in print

Access to staff:
Contact by letter, by telephone, by fax, by e-mail and in person
Hours: Mon to Fri, 0900 to 1700

Access for disabled people:
Parking provided, ramped entry, level entry, toilet facilities
Special comments: Infrared sound relay system; access to all areas on Ground Floor.

WILTSHIRE RECORD SOCIETY

Acronym or abbreviation: WRS

Wiltshire and Swindon History Centre, Cocklebury Road, Chippenham, SN15 3QN

Tel: 01249 705500
Fax: 01249 705527
E-mail: stevenhobbs@wiltshire.gov.uk

Enquiries:
Enquiries to: Secretary

Founded:
1936

Organisation type and purpose:
Learned society.
Originated as a branch of the Wiltshire Archaeological and Natural History Society but autonomous since 1964.

Subject coverage:
The publication of Wiltshire's historical archives.

Printed publications:
Vol. of edited historical records (60 to date, annually)

Publications list:
Available in print

WIMBLEDON COLLEGE OF ART

Main Building, Merton Hall Road, London, SW19 3QA

Tel: 020 7514 9641
Fax: 020 7514 9642

Website:
http://www.wimbledon.arts.ac.uk/
Learning Resources Centre information (Library, Slide Library, IT Centre) and link to Library catalogue.

Enquiries:
Enquiries to: Head of Learning and Information Resources
Direct tel: 020 8408 5039
Direct e-mail: pjennett@wimbledon.ac.uk

Founded:
1963

Formerly called:
Wimbledon School of Art (year of change 2006)

Organisation type and purpose:
Independent art school.

Subject coverage:
Fine art, art history, scenography, costume history, dramatic literature.

Museum or gallery collection, archive, or library special collection:
Books, journals and video tapes, slides, CD-ROM databases

Library catalogue:
All or part available online

Access to staff:
Contact by letter, by telephone, by fax and by e-mail. Appointment necessary.
Hours: Mon to Thu, 1000 to 2030; Fri, 1000 to 1930

Access to building, collection or gallery:
Prior appointment required

continued overleaf

Hours: Mon to Thu, 1000 to 2030; Fri, 1000 to 1930

Access for disabled people:
Parking provided

Parent body:
University of the Arts London

WIMBLEDON LIBRARY

Wimbledon Hill Road, London, SW19 7NB

Tel: 020 8274 5759 (central reference library)
Fax: 020 8944 6804
E-mail: wimbledon.library@merton.gov.uk

Enquiries:
Enquiries to: Librarian
Other contacts: Library and Service Manager for
specifically reference matters.

Organisation type and purpose:
Public library.

Subject coverage:
General.

**Museum or gallery collection, archive, or library
special collection:**
Local studies – materials for the study of
Wimbledon, Mitcham, Morden and Merton at
Local Studies Centre

Non-library collection catalogue:
All or part available online and in-house

Library catalogue:
All or part available in-house

Printed publications:
Order printed publications from: Local Studies
Centre, Morden Library
London Road, Morden, Surrey, SM4 5DX, tel: 020
8545 3239, fax: 020 8545 4037

Access to staff:
Contact by letter, by telephone, by fax, by e-mail
and in person
Hours: Mon, Tue, Thu, Fri, 0930 to 1900; Wed, 0930
to 1300; Sat, 0930 to 1700

Access to building, collection or gallery:
No prior appointment required

Access for disabled people:
Level entry, toilet facilities

Central reference library for:
Merton Library Service

Local studies centre at:
Morden Library
Merton Civic Centre, London Road, Morden,
Surrey, SM4 5DX; tel: 020 8545 3239; fax: 020
8545 4037

WINCHESTER CITY COUNCIL

City Offices, Colebrook Street, Winchester,
Hampshire, SO23 9LJ

Tel: 01962 840222
Fax: 01962 841365
E-mail: info@winchester.gov.uk

Website:
http://www.winchester.gov.uk
Information on council services.

Enquiries:
Enquiries to: Information Officer

Organisation type and purpose:
Local government body.
Provision of local government services to 110,000
residents in the City Council district, which covers
250 sq miles.

Access to staff:
Contact by letter, by telephone, by fax, by e-mail,
in person and via website
Hours: Mon to Fri, 0900 to 1700

WINCHESTER MUSEUMS

Historic Resources Centre, 75 Hyde Street,
Winchester, Hampshire, SO23 7DW

Tel: 01962 848269
Fax: 01962 848299
E-mail: museums@winchester.gov.uk

Website:
http://www.winchester.gov.uk/heritage

Enquiries:
Enquiries to: Curator
Direct tel: 01962 848396
Direct e-mail: gdenford@winchester.gov.uk
Other contacts: Head of Cultural Services

Founded:
1847

Formerly called:
South Eastern Museums Service

Organisation type and purpose:
Local government body, museum, art gallery,
historic building, house or site, suitable for ages:
all.

Subject coverage:
The Historic Resources Centre, is the headquarters
of Winchester Museums Service. It houses reserve
collections of archaeology, topographical art and
photographs. The Museums education and finds
identification services are based at the Historic
Resource Centre as is the Sites and Monuments
Record for the area. There is a small display area
for the temporary exhibitions programme.

Special visitor services:
Materials and/or activities for children.

Education services:
Group education facilities, resources for Key
Stages 1 and 2 and Further or Higher Education.

**Museum or gallery collection, archive, or library
special collection:**
Archaeology and local history of Winchester and
District including topographical prints,
photographs and numismatics
Books relating to the history of Winchester and its
district

Non-library collection catalogue:
All or part available online and in-house

Library catalogue:
All or part available in-house

Printed publications:
Winchester Museums Service Newsletter
Various books, booklets and leaflets, maps, prints
and posters
Winchester Museums Service Information for
Teachers (1 copy free per school, additional
copies £1, available from Keeper of Education,
HRC)

Electronic and video publications:
Bygone Winchester (video, £12.99)

Publications list:
Available online and in print

Access to staff:
Contact by letter, by telephone, by fax, by e-mail,
in person and via website. Appointment necessary.
Hours: Mon to Fri, 0900 to 1700

Access for disabled people:
Parking provided, level entry, toilet facilities
Special comments: Level entry to ground floor areas.

Other museums or galleries:
Guildhall Gallery
The City Museum
Westgate Museum

WINE AND SPIRIT ASSOCIATION, THE

Acronym or abbreviation: WSA

International Wine and Spirit Centre, 39–45
Bermondsey Street, London SE1 3XF

Tel: 020 7089 3877

Fax: 020 7089 3870

Website:
http://www.wsa.org.uk
Information on the WSA. Links with other relevant
organisations.

Enquiries:
Enquiries to: Press Officer
Direct e-mail: gavin@wsta.co.uk

Founded:
1824

Formerly called:
Wine and Spirit Association of Great Britain and
Northern Ireland (year of change 1999)

Organisation type and purpose:
Trade association (membership is by subscription).
To represent shippers and distributors of wine and
imported spirits and producers of English/Welsh
wines, British Wines and Designer Drinks (not
exceeding 5.5%).

Subject coverage:
Wine and spirit trade.

Printed publications:
The following available by purchase directly:
A Code of Practice, for bulk transportation of
wines and spirits
Checklists (authoritative source of guidance to
European wine and spirit legislation)
Everyday Methods of Analysis for Wine

Publications list:
Available online and in print

Access to staff:
Contact by telephone, by e-mail and via website.
Appointment necessary. Access for members only.
Non-members charged.
Hours: Mon to Fri, 0915 to 1715

Access to building, collection or gallery:
Prior appointment required
Hours: Mon to Fri, 0915 to 1715

Affiliated to:
Comité Européen de Vins
Brussels, Belgium; tel: 00 322 2309970
European Federation of Wine & Spirit Importers
and Distributors, London (EFWSID)
London; tel: 020 7248 5377; fax: 020 7489 0322; e-
mail: efwsid@wsa.org.uk
FIVS
Paris, France; tel: 00 331 4268 8248

WINSTON CHURCHILL MEMORIAL TRUST

15 Queen's Gate Terrace, London, SW7 5PR

Tel: 020 7584 9315
Fax: 020 7581 0410
E-mail: office@wcmt.org.uk

Website:
http://www.wcmt.org.uk

Founded:
1965

Organisation type and purpose:
Registered charity (charity number 313952).
To provide Travelling Fellowships overseas for
British citizens resident in the United Kingdom

Access to staff:
Contact by letter, by telephone, by fax, by e-mail
and via website
Hours: Mon to Thu, 0930 to 1700; Fri, 0930 to 1600

WIRE PRODUCTS ASSOCIATION

Riverside House, Bow Industrial Park, Carpenters
Road, London, E15 2DZ

Tel: 020 8525 7100
Fax: 020 8525 7124
E-mail: wpa@brundle.com

Enquiries:
Enquiries to: President
Direct e-mail: rbrundle@hotmail.com

Organisation type and purpose:
Trade association.

Subject coverage:
Distribution of nails and agricultural wire products.

Access to staff:
Contact by letter
Hours: Mon to Fri, 0900 to 1700

WIRELESS FOR THE BEDRIDDEN

159a High Street, Hornchurch, Essex, RM11 3YD

Tel: 01708 621101 or Freephone: 0800 182137
Fax: 01708 620816
E-mail: info@w4b.org.uk

Enquiries:
Enquiries to: Chief Executive

Founded:
1939

Organisation type and purpose:
Registered charity (charity number 207400). To provide radio and television sets to the housebound, disabled and elderly who cannot afford to buy or rent for themselves.

Subject coverage:
Provision of radio and television facilities for the needy, elderly, disabled, handicapped or housebound.

Access to staff:
Contact by letter, by telephone, by fax and by e-mail
Hours: Mon to Fri, 0830 to 1630

WIRRAL ARCHIVES SERVICE

Wirral Museum, Hamilton Square, Birkenhead, Wirral, CH41 5BR

Tel: 0151 666 3903
E-mail: archives@wirral-libraries.net

Enquiries:
Enquiries to: Archivist
Other contacts: Information Services Librarian

Founded:
1974

Organisation type and purpose:
Public library.

Subject coverage:
Deposit for public records: schools, hospitals, local government and Poor Law. Business and private records. Antiquarian collections.

Museum or gallery collection, archive, or library special collection:
Archives of local hospitals
Cammell Laird Shipbuilders archive
Local government records
Macclesfield Collection
Poor Law Records
School records
Unichema Chemicals Limited (Price's Patent Candle Company)

Non-library collection catalogue:
All or part available in-house

Library catalogue:
All or part available in-house

Access to staff:
Contact by letter, by telephone, by fax, by e-mail and in person
Hours: Thu, Fri, 1000 to 1700; Sat, 1000 to 1300

Access for disabled people:
Ramped entry, access to all public areas

WIRRAL LIBRARIES

Acronym or abbreviation: WIZ

Central Library, Borough Road, Birkenhead, Merseyside, CH41 2XB

Tel: 0151 652 6106/7/8 ext 7
Fax: 0151 653 7320
E-mail: birkenhead.ref@wirral-library.net

Website:
http://www.wirral-libraries.net

Enquiries:
Enquiries to: Librarian
Other contacts: Information Services Librarian.

Founded:
1856

Created by the merger of:
Birkenhead, Bebington, Wallasey and Cheshire County Library Services, Wirral (year of change 1974)

Organisation type and purpose:
Local government body, public library.

Subject coverage:
General public library stock range.

Museum or gallery collection, archive, or library special collection:
Birkenhead Photographic Survey 1900–1920 and 1971–1974
Hopps Paintings of Wallasey 1910–1950
Macclesfield Collection
Price Collection (Price's Patent Candle Company and Model Village records 1840–1960)
Priestley Collection of Photographs 1890–1930
Wirral and Cheshire Photographic Survey 1900–1910
Wirral Borough Council Public Records 1833 to date
Wirral Photographic Survey, 1974-to date

Non-library collection catalogue:
All or part available in-house

Library catalogue:
All or part available online

Access to staff:
Contact by letter, by telephone, by fax, by e-mail and in person. Appointment necessary.
Hours: Mon, Tue, Thu, 0900 to 2000; Fri and Sat, 0900 to 1700; closed Wed and Sun

Access to building, collection or gallery:
Mon, Tue, Thu, 0900 to 2000; Fri and Sat, 0900 to 1700; closed Wed and Sun

Access for disabled people:
Ramped entry only; limited disabled access to Reference Department; no ground floor toilets

WIRRAL METROPOLITAN COLLEGE

Carlett Park, Eastham, Merseyside, CH62 0AY

Tel: 0151 551 7866
Fax: 0151 551 7751

Website:
http://www.wmc.ac.uk

Enquiries:
Enquiries to: Information Officer
Direct tel: 0151 551 7751
Direct e-mail: pat.roberts@wmc.ac.uk

Organisation type and purpose:
Suitable for ages: 16+.
College of further education.

Subject coverage:
Management, engineering, social sciences, sciences.

Access to staff:
Contact by letter, by telephone, by fax, by e-mail, in person and via website
Hours: Mon to Fri, 0900 to 1700

Other sites:
International Business and Management Centre
Europa Boulevard, Conway Park, Birkenhead, L41 4NT; tel: 0151 551 7067
Wirral Metropolitan College
Borough Road, Birkenhead, L42 9QD; tel: 0151 551 7476

WIRRAL METROPOLITAN COLLEGE – TWELVE QUAYS CAMPUS

Acronym or abbreviation: Wirral Met

Shore Road, Birkenhead, Merseyside, CH41 1AG

Tel: 0151 551 7476
Fax: 0151 551 7476
E-mail: steve.cropper@wmc.ac.uk

Website:
http://www.wmc.ac.uk
General description of WMC and its facilities.

Enquiries:
Enquiries to: Senior Librarian

Founded:
2003

Organisation type and purpose:
Further Education College

Subject coverage:
Construction, engineering, caring professions, leisure, tourism and catering, humanities, sciences

Non-library collection catalogue:
All or part available in-house

Library catalogue:
All or part available online, in-house and in print

Access to staff:
Contact by letter, by telephone, by fax and by e-mail. Appointment necessary.
Hours: Mon to Thu, 0845 to 2000; Fri, 0845 to 1600
Special comments: Reference use of collections only.

Access for disabled people:
Electric doors, lifts

Other addresses:
Wirral Metropolitan College Library
Carlett Park Campus, Eastham, Wirral, CH62 0AY; tel: 0151 551 7866

WISE VEHICLE PROGRAMME

Formal name: Women into Science and Engineering
Acronym or abbreviation: WISE

Nottingham Trent University, Burton Street, Nottingham, NG1 4BU

Tel: 0115 848 2101
Fax: 0115 947 2780
E-mail: joyce.bullimore@ntu.ac.uk

Enquiries:
Enquiries to: Operational Manager

Founded:
1992

Organisation type and purpose:
Suitable for ages: 13 to 14 (girls).

Subject coverage:
Women's education.

Access to staff:
Contact by letter, by fax and by e-mail
Hours: Mon to Fri, 0900 to 1600

WITAN INTERNATIONAL COLLEGE

Library, London Road, Reading, Berkshire, RG1 5AQ

Tel: 0118 920 9321 (Library)
Fax: 0118 931 0137

Website:
http://www.gyosei.ac.uk
http://www.witancollege.org/

Enquiries:
Enquiries to: Librarian
Direct tel: 0118 9209321
Direct e-mail: chris@witancollege.org

Founded:
1989

continued overleaf

Formerly called:
Gyosei International College in the UK (year of change 2004)

Organisation type and purpose:
Higher education: provision of UK university-validated graduate and postgraduate courses. Suitable for ages: 18+.

Subject coverage:
Japanese culture.

Museum or gallery collection, archive, or library special collection:
Books in English about Japanese culture, business and management
Large collection of books in Japanese

Library catalogue:
All or part available in-house

Access to staff:
Contact by letter, by telephone and by e-mail
Hours: Mon to Fri, 0900 to 1700

WJEC

245 Western Avenue, Cardiff, CF5 2YX

Tel: 029 2026 5000
Fax: 029 2057 5894
E-mail: info@wjec.co.uk

Website:
http://www.wjec.co.uk/publicat.html
Publications programme.

Enquiries:
Enquiries to: Chief Executive

Founded:
1948

Organisation type and purpose:
Registered charity (charity number 3150875). Until local government reorganisation in 1996, it was a body established under a statutory order following the 1944 Education Act. Now established as a company limited by guarantee and a charity. The WJEC provides a range of educational services; as an awarding body offering a range of academic and vocational qualifications; support of these qualifications through in-service training for teachers (INSET); support for the Welsh language and culture through the work of the National Language Unit of Wales; and support in relation to the expressive arts, including the administration of the National Youth Orchestra of Wales and the National Youth Theatre of Wales.

Subject coverage:
Examinations at GCE, AEA, GCSE and Entry level, Key Skills, Welsh Baccalaureate, INSET, National Language Unit teaching resources, Welsh for Adults, Welsh Language INSET scheme, Expressive Arts support of National Youth Orchestra of Wales (NYOW), and National Youth Theatre of Wales (NYTW).

Printed publications:
Examinations catalogue of past question papers, marking schemes, specifications and other related materials in print form
Order printed publications from: WJEC Bookshop tel: 029 2026 5112

Electronic and video publications:
Online catalogue of educational publications and teaching resources (available from the National Language Unit)

Access to staff:
Contact by letter, by telephone, by fax, by e-mail, in person and via website. Appointment necessary.
Hours: Mon to Fri, 0900 to 1700

Access for disabled people:
Parking provided, ramped entry

WM ENTERPRISE

Formal name: West Midlands Enterprise Ltd

Wellington House, 31–34 Waterloo Street, Birmingham, B2 5TJ

Tel: 0121 236 8855
Fax: 0121 233 3942
E-mail: mail@wm-enterprise.co.uk

Enquiries:
Enquiries to: Marketing Manager

Founded:
1981

Formerly called:
West Midlands Enterprise Board (WMEB)

Organisation type and purpose:
Consultancy, socio-economic research organisation.
Venture capital provider.

Subject coverage:
All aspects of the management of local and regional economic development within the UK, Europe and Asia, development of small and medium sized enterprises, business start-up and marketing support.

Access to staff:
Contact by letter, by telephone, by fax and by e-mail
Hours: Mon to Fri, 0900 to 1700

WOKING BOROUGH COUNCIL

Civic Offices, Gloucester Square, Woking, Surrey, GU21 1YL

Tel: 01483 755855
Fax: 01483 768746

Website:
http://www.woking.gov.uk
Tourism and leisure information, location maps, council information (e.g., list of services, telephone numbers). Links to local websites, business information, vacant commercial property.

Enquiries:
Enquiries to: Public Relations Manager
Direct tel: 01483 743022
Direct fax: 01483 743055
Other contacts: Business Liaison Officer for business enquiries.

Founded:
1895

Organisation type and purpose:
Local government body.

Subject coverage:
Economic information, population characteristics, vacant sites and business in the area, and tourist information.

Museum or gallery collection, archive, or library special collection:
Photographic library of Woking

Printed publications:
Business Contacts in Woking
Commercial and Industrial Property Register
Discovering Ponds – a guide to encourage primary and secondary schools to use ponds as an educational resource
Economical Development Plan for Woking
Employment Sites Register
The Council Tax 1996–1997 and A-Z of Services for Woking Borough
The Woking Magazine
Where to Stay Guide
Where to Eat Guide
Woking – A visitors' guide to the town centre
Woking Business to Business Directory – lists over 800 local companies

Electronic and video publications:
Information video on the borough of Woking

Publications list:
Available in print

Access to staff:
Contact by letter, by telephone and by fax. Appointment necessary.
Hours: Mon to Fri, 0900 to 1700 (telephone enquiries)
Mon to Fri, 0900 to 1645 (personal enquiries)

Twin town with:
Amstelveen
   Amstelveen, The Netherlands
Le Plessis Robinson
   France

WOKINGHAM LIBRARIES AND INFORMATION SERVICE

Shute End, Wokingham, Berkshire, RG40 1WN

Tel: 0118 974 6261; 0118 974 6276
Fax: 0118 974 6259
E-mail: libraries@wokingham.gov.uk

Website:
http://www.wokingham.gov.uk/libraries
Library catalogues

Founded:
1998

Formerly a part of:
Berkshire County Council (year of change 1998)

Organisation type and purpose:
Public library.

Subject coverage:
General (public library network).

Library catalogue:
All or part available online

Access to staff:
Contact by letter, by telephone, by fax, by e-mail, in person and via website
Hours: Library opening hours vary

Branch libraries:
Aborfield Container Library
   Parish Council Car Park, Swallowfield Road, Arborfield Cross; tel: 07801 664520
Lower Earley Library
   Chalfont Close, Chalfont Way, Lower Earley; tel: 0118 931 2150; fax: 0118 975 0162
Maiden Erlegh Library
   Maiden Erlegh Drive, Earley; tel: 0118 966 6630; fax: 0118 966 6630
Spencers Wood Library
   Basingstoke Road, Spencers Wood; tel: 0118 988 4771; fax: 0118 988 4771
Twyford Library
   Polehampton Close, Twyford; tel: 0118 934 0800; fax: 0118 934 5399
Wargrave Library
   Woodclyffe Hostel, Church Street, Wargrave; tel: 0118 940 4656; fax: 0118 940 4656
Winnersh Library
   Robin Hood Lane, Winnersh; tel: 0118 974 7979; fax: 0118 974 7989
Woodley Library
   Headley Road, Woodley; tel: 0118 940 0304; fax: 0118 969 9807

Headquarters address:
Wokingham Library
   Denmark Street, Wokingham; tel: 0118 978 1368; fax: 0118 989 1214

WOLFSON CENTRE FOR MAGNETICS TECHNOLOGY

Cardiff School of Engineering, Cardiff University, PO Box 925, Newport Road, Cardiff, CF24 0YF

Tel: 029 2087 6729
Fax: 029 2087 6729
E-mail: wolfson@cf.ac.uk

Website:
http://www.cf.ac.uk/engin/research/wolfson

Enquiries:
Enquiries to: Director

Founded:
1969

Organisation type and purpose:
University department or institute.
University research centre; formerly Wolfson Centre for the Technology of Soft Magnetic Materials.

Subject coverage:
Applications and performance of magnetic materials.

Printed publications:
List of published papers
List of research projects

Publications list:
Available online and in print

Access to staff:
Contact by letter, by telephone, by fax, by e-mail and via website. Appointment necessary.
Hours: Mon to Fri, 0900 to 1700

Access to building, collection or gallery:
Prior appointment required

Access for disabled people:
Parking provided, ramped entry, level entry, toilet facilities

WOLFSON ELECTROSTATICS, UNIVERSITY OF SOUTHAMPTON

Department of Electronics and Computer Science, University of Southampton, Southampton, SO17 1BJ

Tel: 023 8055 2266
Fax: 023 8059 3015
E-mail: wolfson@soton.ac.uk

Website:
http://www.soton.ac.uk/~wolfson

Enquiries:
Enquiries to: Technical Director

Founded:
1971

Formerly called:
Wolfson Electrical Engineering Consultancy Service (year of change 1987); Wolfson Electrostatics Advisory Unit (year of change 1990)

Organisation type and purpose:
University department or institute, consultancy, research organisation.

Subject coverage:
Electrostatic hazard analysis, explosion prevention and protection, loss prevention, classification of flammable materials, safety audits, electrostatic applications including: liquid and dry powder coatings, precipitation and electrostatic separation, high voltage testing.

Access to staff:
Contact by letter, by telephone, by fax and by e-mail. Appointment necessary.
Hours: Mon to Fri, 0900 to 1700

Access for disabled people:
Level entry, toilet facilities
Special comments: Lifts

WOLFSON FOUNDATION

8 Queen Anne Street, London, W1G 9LD

Tel: 020 7323 5730
Fax: 020 7323 3241

Website:
http://www.wolfson.org.uk

Enquiries:
Enquiries to: Executive Secretary

Founded:
1955

Organisation type and purpose:
Registered charity (charity number 206495).

Subject coverage:
Funding of charities or exempt charities such as universities in areas such as medicine and health care, research, science, technology and education, arts and the humanities.

Printed publications:
Annual Report

Access to staff:
Contact by letter
Hours: Mon to Fri, 0900 to 1700

Sister trust:
Wolfson Family Charitable Trust
  tel: 020 7323 5730; fax: 020 7323 3241

WOLFSON HEAT TREATMENT CENTRE

Acronym or abbreviation: WHTC

Federation House, 10 Vyse Street, Birmingham, B18 6LT

Tel: 0121 237 1122
Fax: 0121 237 1124
E-mail: derek.close@sea.org.uk

Website:
http://www.sea.org.uk/whtc

Enquiries:
Enquiries to: Information Officer
Direct tel: 0121 237 1122

Founded:
1973

Organisation type and purpose:
Subscription service for information, advice centre on heat treatment of metals, consultancy, courses.

Subject coverage:
Heat treatment of metals, metallurgy, materials standards and specifications, consultancy, failure investigations and reports, heat treatment courses, conferences, safety in heat treatment, heat treatment processes and equipment, location of contract heat treatment facilities for engineering companies.

Museum or gallery collection, archive, or library special collection:
Library of heat treatment books
Trade literature, equipment suppliers

Trade and statistical information:
Data on heat treatment equipment suppliers and
  suppliers of consumables to the trade.

Printed publications:
Heat Treatment of Metals (journal, quarterly)

Publications list:
Available in print

Access to staff:
Contact by letter, by telephone and by e-mail. Appointment necessary. Access for members only. Non-members charged.
Hours: Mon to Fri, 0800 to 1600
Special comments: Free to subscribers, consultancy fee for non-subscribers

Associated with:
Surface Engineering Association

WOLFSON MICROELECTRONICS LIMITED

Westfield House, 26 Westfield Road, Edinburgh, EH11 2QB

Tel: 0131 272 7000
Fax: 0131 272 7001
E-mail: europe@wolfsonmicro.com

Website:
http://www.wolfsonmicro.com
Full site information, publications

Enquiries:
Enquiries to: Product Marketing Engineer

Founded:
1985

Organisation type and purpose:
Manufacturing industry.
Design and manufacture of semiconductor devices.

Subject coverage:
Integrated circuit design and manufacture for consumer, PC, audio and imaging applications.

Non-library collection catalogue:
All or part available online

Printed publications:
Data sheets

Access to staff:
Contact by letter, by telephone, by fax, by e-mail and via website
Hours: Mon to Fri, 0900 to 1700

Access for disabled people:
Access to all public areas
Special comments: Level entrance at back of building

Associated with:
Edinburgh University

WOLFSON UNIT FOR MARINE TECHNOLOGY AND INDUSTRIAL AERODYNAMICS

Acronym or abbreviation: WUMTIA

University of Southampton, Southampton, SO17 1BJ

Tel: 023 8058 5044
Fax: 023 8067 1532
E-mail: wumtia@soton.ac.uk

Website:
http://www.wolfsonunit.com
Services, products and personnel.

Enquiries:
Enquiries to: Secretary

Founded:
1968

Organisation type and purpose:
Commercial consultancy and research organisation, using skills, knowledge and facilities of university; feedback of commercial problems to academics.

Subject coverage:
Towing tank testing of ship models; wind tunnel testing of sailing vessel rigs, keels, superstructures, buildings, road vehicles; computer program bureau service in hydrostatics and stability, ship motions and propulsion, model testing; trials data acquisition; computer modelling; material testing/ failure analysis; feasibility studies; expert witnesses.

Electronic and video publications:
Software for Naval Architects including
  hydrostatics and stability, ship motions,
  powering and propulsion, lines fairing (for sale)

Access to staff:
Contact by letter, by telephone, by fax, by e-mail, in person and via website
Hours: Mon to Fri, 0900 to 1700

Parent body:
University of Southampton, Department of Ship Science

WOLSELEY 6/80 & MORRIS OXFORD CLUB

21 Bates Lane, Weston Turville, Aylesbury, Bucks, HP22 5SL

Tel: 01296 614065
E-mail: brianspost1@myway.com

Enquiries:
Enquiries to: Membership Secretary

Founded:
1977

Organisation type and purpose:
Membership association (membership is by subscription).

Subject coverage:
Technical information and sources of spares for Wolseley 6/80 and Morris Oxford cars.

continued overleaf

Museum or gallery collection, archive, or library special collection:
A small collection of workshop manuals and technical data

Printed publications:
News sheet (quarterly)

Access to staff:
Contact by letter, by telephone, by e-mail and in person
Hours: Sun to Sat, 0900 to 2200
Special comments: Enclose an sae for reply.

WOLVERHAMPTON ARCHIVES AND LOCAL STUDIES

Acronym or abbreviation: WALS

42–50 Snow Hill, Wolverhampton, West Midlands, WV2 4AG

Tel: 01902 552480\ Minicom no. 01902 552479
Fax: 01902 552481
E-mail: wolverhamptonarchives@dial.pipex.com

Website:
http://www.wolverhampton.gov.uk/archives
http://www.wolverhampton.gov.uk/library/archives.htm
Information on holdings and services; opening hours; details of postal search service; leaflets; (leaflets available in PDF format); location map.

Enquiries:
Enquiries to: City Archivist

Founded:
1978

Organisation type and purpose:
Local government body, suitable for ages: 8+.
Archive repository.
To ensure the long-term preservation of the City's documentary heritage and to encourage and develop the use of these materials by the general public and within the council itself.

Subject coverage:
Archive and local studies material, local history, genealogy.

Non-library collection catalogue:
All or part available in-house

Library catalogue:
All or part available in-house

Printed publications:
Education Service leaflet
Family History Fact Sheets – brief guides for beginners – records of births, marriages and deaths, census returns and parish registers etc (£1)
Family History Forms pack (£1.50)
General information leaflet
Guide to Church of England Parish Registers
Guide to Nonconformist Registers and Roman Catholic Registers
Guide to the Contents of Wolverhampton Archives and Local Studies (£4.99)
Map of Wolverhampton 1750 (surveyed by Taylor I, £2.50)
Mapping the Past – Wolverhampton 1577–1986 (£4.50)
Tracing your Army Ancestors
Tracing your family tree leaflet
Town Centre Timeline – A Guide to Using the Story of Wolverhampton's past as a Source for National Curriculum History (1997, £6)

Electronic and video publications:
Bilston in the 19th Century (CD-ROM, £6.99)

Publications list:
Available online and in print

Access to staff:
Contact by letter, by telephone, by fax, by e-mail, in person and via website
Hours: Mon, Tue, Fri, 1000 to 1700; Wed, 1000 to 1900; Thu closed; 1st and 3rd Sat in the month, 1000 to 1700

Access for disabled people:
Ramped entry, access to all public areas, toilet facilities

WOLVERHAMPTON LIBRARIES AND INFORMATION SERVICES

Central Library, Snow Hill, Wolverhampton, West Midlands, WV1 3AX

Tel: 01902 552025\ Minicom no. 01902 552020
Fax: 01902 552024
E-mail: libraries@wolverhampton.gov.uk

Website:
http://www.wolverhampton.gov.uk/libraries
Locations, opening hours, catalogue, readers' and writers' groups, links to council information and useful websites

Enquiries:
Enquiries to: Information Officer (Reference)

Organisation type and purpose:
Local government body, public library.

Subject coverage:
General information in all fields, materials in Asian languages, materials of African-Caribbean interest.
On-line resources: business information, newspapers, European information, Wolverhampton local history; popular and classical music on CD; educational and instructional videos and DVDs; music scores.

Special visitor services:
Public internet access at all service points

Library catalogue:
All or part available online and in-house

Printed publications:
Directories of local organisations

Access to staff:
Contact by letter, by telephone, by fax, by e-mail, in person and via website
Hours: Mon to Thu, 0900 to 1900; Fri and Sat, 0900 to 1700

Access to building, collection or gallery:
No prior appointment required

Access for disabled people:
Ramped entry, toilet facilities, adaptive technologies on PCs

Has:
19 service points throughout the City

Links with:
MLA, BCLiP, CIlip and SCL

WOLVERHAMPTON MEDICAL INSTITUTE

Bell Library, New Cross Hospital, Wolverhampton, West Midlands, WV10 0QP

Tel: 01902 695322
Fax: 01902 723037
E-mail: jean.paterson@rwh-tr.nhs.uk

Enquiries:
Enquiries to: Medical Librarian

Founded:
1971

Formerly called:
South Staffordshire Medical Centre Library

Organisation type and purpose:
A group of medical libraries in the NHS including the Eye Infirmary Library, Wolverhampton.

Subject coverage:
Medicine, dentistry, veterinary surgery, pharmacy, ophthalmology, physiotherapy, nursing.

Access to staff:
Contact by letter, by telephone, by fax and by e-mail
Hours: Mon to Wed, 0830 to 1700; Thu, 0830 to 1830; Fri, 0830 to 1630

WOMEN AGAINST RAPE

Acronym or abbreviation: WAR

Crossroads Women's Centre, 230a Kentish Town Road, London, NW5 2AB

Tel: 020 7482 2496\ Minicom no. 020 7482 2496
Fax: 020 7209 4761
E-mail: war@womenagainstrape.net

Website:
http://www.womenagainstrape.net

Enquiries:
Enquiries to: Secretary

Founded:
1976

Organisation type and purpose:
Voluntary organisation.
Pressure group.
To campaign for reform of the law and legal system with respect to violence against women and children.

Subject coverage:
Counselling, legal advice, support for women and girls who have been raped or sexually assaulted, compensation and other resources for recovery and the prevention of violence against women and children. Help with reporting attacks, legal action, testifying in court, health referrals, rehousing, claiming benefits and compensation, including for immigrant wives facing domestic violence and refugees who are rape survivors seeking asylum.

Printed publications:
Ask Any Woman
Rape in the Media
The Power to Refuse
The Rapist Who Pays the Rent

Publications list:
Available in print

Access to staff:
Contact by letter, by telephone, by fax and by e-mail
Hours: Telephone open, Mon to Fri, 1330 to 1600
Centre opening hours, Tue and Wed, 1200 to 1600; Thu, 1700 to 1900
Special comments: Letters should be addressed to PO Box 287, London NW6 5QU.

Other address:
Women Against Rape
 PO Box 287, London, NW6 5QU

WOMEN IN FILM AND TELEVISION

Acronym or abbreviation: WFTV

4th Floor, Unit 2 Wedgwood Mews, 12–13 Greek Street, London, W1D 4BB

Tel: 020 7287 1400
Fax: 020 7287 1500
E-mail: info@wftv.org.uk

Website:
http://www.wftv.org.uk

Enquiries:
Enquiries to: Administrator
Direct e-mail: administrator@wftv.org.uk

Founded:
1990

Organisation type and purpose:
Trade association (membership is by qualification), present number of members: 1,000.

Access to staff:
Contact by letter, by telephone and by e-mail
Hours: Mon to Fri, 1000 to 1800

WOMEN'S AID FEDERATION OF ENGLAND

Acronym or abbreviation: Women's Aid

PO Box 391, Bristol, BS99 7WS

Tel: 0117 944 4411
Fax: 0117 924 1703
E-mail: info@womensaid.org.uk

Website:
http://www.womensaid.org.uk

Enquiries:
Enquiries to: Information Officer

Founded:
1974

Organisation type and purpose:
Membership association (membership is by subscription), present number of members: 120 full, 280 associate, voluntary organisation, registered charity (charity number 1054154). Co-ordinate work of refuges in England, campaigning and lobbying on behalf of women and children. Provides Freephone 24 hour national domestic violence helpline: 0808 2000 247. Run in partnership between Women's Aid and Refuge.

Subject coverage:
Domestic violence in the form of physical violence, sexual abuse and psychological abuse, and related issues: housing, social security, legal rights, women's rights, children.

Library catalogue:
All or part available in-house

Printed publications:
Many books and leaflets including:
Children, Domestic Violence and Refuges: a study of needs and responses (£14.50)
Getting Free from Domestic Violence – language leaflets for women available in eleven different languages
Children Living with Domestic Violence (1994, £17)
It's Just a Domestic (£4.50)
Posters
The Gold Book: The Women's Aid Directory of Domestic Violence Refuge and Helpline Services 2005 (£25)
Strengthening Diversity: Good practice in delivering domestic violence services to Black women and children (£12)
It hurts me too – Children's experiences of domestic violence and refuge life (£7)

Publications list:
Available online and in print

Access to staff:
Contact by letter, by telephone, by fax, by e-mail and via website
Hours: Office: 1000 to 1600 only by telephone
Helpline: 24 hours

Access to building, collection or gallery:
No access other than to staff

Access for disabled people:
Ramped entry

Has:
over 160 member Refuge Groups in England

WOMEN'S DESIGN SERVICE

Acronym or abbreviation: WDS

52–54 Featherstone Street, London, EC1Y 8RT

Tel: 020 7490 5210
Fax: 020 7490 5212
E-mail: info@wds.org.uk

Website:
http://www.wds.org.uk

Enquiries:
Enquiries to: Director

Founded:
1986

Organisation type and purpose:
Advisory body, membership association (membership is by election or invitation), voluntary organisation, registered charity (charity number 801282), public library, consultancy, research organisation.

Information and research on women's needs in the built environment.

Subject coverage:
Women's issues relating to the urban environment, including: architecture, planning, design, safety, transport, work environments, childcare, housing, tenant participation, access, disability, technical aid hazards, regeneration.

Museum or gallery collection, archive, or library special collection:
EX-GLC reports
EX-LPAC reports
Reports of proceedings of London Women and Planning Forum

Printed publications:
Accessible Offices (£5.50)
At Women's Convenience (£6.50)
Designing Housing for Older Women (£6.50)
Disability and Regeneration (£18)
Good Practice Manual on Tenant Participation (£8)
Housing for Independence (£18)
It's Not All Swings and Roundabouts (£6.50)
Making Safer Places (£15)
Removing the Goalposts (£18)
Shoppers' Creches (£6.50)
Thinking Of Small Children – Access, Provision and Play (£3.50)
Women's Safety On Housing Estates (£6.50)
Many broadsheets on related subjects are also available (£2 or £3 each)

Publications list:
Available in print

Access to staff:
Contact by letter, by telephone, by fax, by e-mail, in person and via website
Hours: Mon to Fri, 1000 to 1700

Access to building, collection or gallery:
Prior appointment required

Access for disabled people:
Ramped entry, toilet facilities

WOMEN'S EDUCATION IN BUILDING

Acronym or abbreviation: WEB

12 Malton Road, London, W10 5UP

Tel: 020 8968 9139
Fax: 020 8964 0255

Enquiries:
Enquiries to: Occupational Guidance Officer
Direct e-mail: jatinder@webuilding1.org.uk
Other contacts: Trades Training Manager, for information about construction training.

Founded:
1984

Organisation type and purpose:
Voluntary organisation, training organisation. To provide training for women in the construction industry, offering free courses and childcare assistance.

Subject coverage:
Women in the construction industry, carpentry and joinery, electrics, plumbing, painting and decorating.

Trade and statistical information:
Largest construction skills training centre for women in Europe.

Printed publications:
Annual Report (free)

Access to staff:
Contact by letter, by telephone, by fax and by e-mail. Appointment necessary.
Hours: Mon to Fri, 0900 to 1700

Access for disabled people:
Parking provided, level entry, toilet facilities

Also at:
Women's Education in Building
24 Quebec Way, Surrey Quays, London, SE16 1LF; tel: 020 7740 3199; fax: 020 7740 3201

Links with:
Women and Manual Trades (WAMT)
52–54 Featherstone Street, London, EC1 8RT; tel: 020 7251 9192

WOMEN'S EMPLOYMENT ENTERPRISE & TRAINING UNIT

Acronym or abbreviation: WEETU

2 Redwell Street, Norwich, NR2 4SN

Tel: 01603 230625
Fax: 01603 776426
E-mail: admin@weetu.org

Website:
http://www.weetu.org

Enquiries:
Enquiries to: Chief Executive

Founded:
1988

Organisation type and purpose:
Voluntary organisation, training organisation. To help women deal with economic change, and to improve access to and experience of employment and training, as well as providing information and advice on these issues.

Subject coverage:
Adult guidance: women (all ages); women returners; women's self employment; existing network for women who run their own businesses.

Access to staff:
Contact by letter, by telephone, by fax and by e-mail
Hours: Mon to Fri, 0900 to 1700

WOMEN'S ENGINEERING SOCIETY

Acronym or abbreviation: WES

2 Queen Anne's Gate Buildings, Dartmouth Street, London, SW1H 9BP

Tel: 020 7233 1974
Fax: 020 7233 1973
E-mail: info@wes.org.uk

Website:
http://www.wes.org.uk
Society news, views, information, publicity, some job vacancies, etc.

Enquiries:
Enquiries to: Secretary
Other contacts: President

Founded:
1920

Organisation type and purpose:
Professional body, registered charity (charity number 1008913).
To promote the study and practice of engineering among women.

Subject coverage:
Engineering, all levels, all fields, particularly relating to women's careers, bursaries, career breaks, equal opportunities, continuing professional development.

Trade and statistical information:
Data on women in engineering.

Printed publications:
Free leaflets publicising the society and its activities
The Woman Engineer (journal, quarterly by subscription £20 pa UK, £25 overseas, or free to members)

Access to staff:
Contact by letter, by telephone, by fax, by e-mail and via website

continued overleaf

Hours: Not Friday

Affiliated to:
International Conference of Women Engineers &
Scientists (ICWES)
Verena Holmes Lecture Fund

WOMEN'S ENVIRONMENTAL NETWORK

Acronym or abbreviation: WEN

Real Nappy Project, PO Box 30626, London, E1
1TZ

Tel: 020 7481 9004
Fax: 020 7481 9144
E-mail: info@wen.org.uk

Website:
http://www.wen.org.uk
See nappy pages from subjects page 3.

Enquiries:
Enquiries to: Project Worker
Other contacts: Project Assistant for second-hand
nappy exchange.

Founded:
2000

Subject coverage:
Information on the environmental impact and the
economic, social and health aspects of disposable
nappies. Life cycle analyses and other studies on
environmental impacts of real versus disposable
nappies.

Trade and statistical information:
Nappy waste statistics in the UK, and other
information relating to the environment, health
and economics. List of retailers and businesses
(including non-profit) who provide washable
cotton nappies for home washing or via nappy
laundry delivery service.

Library catalogue:
All or part available online

Printed publications:
WEN Nappy Briefing
Real Nappy Project Leaflet
Preventing Nappy Waste (Report 1996)
Health Professionals' Pack
Local Authorities' Information Pack
Parents' Information Pack
Real Nappy Activists' Pack
Information Packs available only by post, on
receipt of a large SAE with two 1st or 2nd class
stamps
Order printed publications from: Real Nappy
Association
PO Box 3704, London, SE26 4RX

Publications list:
Available online and in print

Access to staff:
Contact by letter, by telephone, by fax, by e-mail
and via website. Appointment necessary.
Hours: Mon to Fri, 1000 to 1800

Access to building, collection or gallery:
Prior appointment required

Access for disabled people:
Level entry

WOMEN'S FARM AND GARDEN ASSOCIATION

Acronym or abbreviation: WFGA

175 Gloucester Street, Cirencester, Gloucestershire,
GL7 2DP

Tel: 01285 658339
E-mail: admin@wfga.org.uk

Enquiries:
Enquiries to: Organiser

Founded:
1899

Organisation type and purpose:
Membership association (membership is by
subscription), present number of members: 550,
registered charity (charity number 212527),
training organisation. Association for professional
women in all aspects of agriculture and
horticulture. To provide advice and practical
training in horticulture. To represent women in
agriculture and horticulture.

Subject coverage:
Careers advice for women in agriculture and
horticulture; national, European and international
information on women's affairs. Practical
horticultural training.

**Museum or gallery collection, archive, or library
special collection:**
Archives covering 100 years

Non-library collection catalogue:
All or part available in-house

Printed publications:
Careers in Agriculture and Horticulture (set of 15
fact sheets, £3)
Role of Women in British Agriculture (£2)
The Hidden Workforce: a self-help guide to
Safeguards and Benefits for Women (£2)
Women Rule the Plot, the story of the 100 year
fight to establish Women's place in farm and
garden (£16.95 +£2 p&p)
Order printed publications from: Available from the
office in Cirencester

Access to staff:
Contact by letter, by telephone and by e-mail
Hours: Mon to Fri, 0900 to 1700

WOMEN'S FOOD AND FARMING UNION

Acronym or abbreviation: WFU

WFU National Office, The National Rural
Enterprise Centre, Stoneleigh Park, Warwickshire,
CY8 2LZ

Tel: 024 7669 3171
Fax: 024 7669 3181
E-mail: admin@wfu.org.uk

Website:
http://www.wfu.org.uk
WFU news and activities, policies and official
responses, CEC information.

Enquiries:
Enquiries to: President
Direct tel: 01469 588257
Direct fax: 01469 588740
Direct e-mail: janet.godfrey@godfrey.uk.com
Other contacts: Administrator for policy
administration.

Founded:
1979

Formerly called:
Women's Farming Union (year of change 1997)

Organisation type and purpose:
Membership association (membership is by
subscription), voluntary organisation, suitable for
ages: 18+, training organisation, research
organisation.
To link consumer and producer.

Subject coverage:
All aspects of food production, the concerns of
consumers, the cooperation between industries
related to food and farming; monitors production
methods, scientific developments, retail products
and the presentation of food in the market place.

Electronic and video publications:
A Woolly Tale (video, available for purchase)

Access to staff:
Contact by letter, by telephone, by e-mail and via
website
Hours: Mon to Fri, 0900 to 1700

Access to building, collection or gallery:
Prior appointment required

Access for disabled people:
Access to all public areas

Other addresses:
Women's Farming Union
The Grove, Wootton, Ulceby, North Lincolnshire,
DN39 6SF; tel: 01469 588257; fax: 01469 588740;
e-mail: janet.godfrey@godfrey.uk.com

WOMEN'S HEALTH

52 Featherstone Street, London, EC1Y 8RT

Tel: 020 7251 6333\ Minicom no. 020 7490 5489
Fax: 020 7608 0928
E-mail: womenshealth@pop3.poptel.org.uk

Website:
http://www.womenshealthlondon.org.uk

Enquiries:
Enquiries to: Information Officer

Founded:
1982

Formerly called:
Women's Health and Reproductive Rights
Information Centre

Organisation type and purpose:
National organisation, membership association
(membership is by subscription), voluntary
organisation, registered charity (charity number
296002), research organisation.
Health information organisation.
To provide health information that enables women
to make informed decisions about their health.

Subject coverage:
Women's health: menstruation, menopause,
gynaecology; abortion, hysterectomy, fibroids,
polycystic ovaries, pelvic inflammatory disease.

**Museum or gallery collection, archive, or library
special collection:**
Over 5700 books, cuttings, reports on women's
health issues

Printed publications:
Newsletter (quarterly, by subscription)
Publications list of over 50 titles (send sae)
Leaflets on various aspects of women's health
describe a problem or situation and give
practical solutions, plus leaflets for women with
learning difficulties

Electronic and video publications:
Leaflets are all available on tape

Publications list:
Available online and in print

Access to staff:
Contact by letter, by telephone, by fax and by e-
mail. Appointment necessary.
Hours: Office: Mon to Fri, 0900 to 1700
Helpline enquiries: Mon to Fri, 0930 to 1330

Access for disabled people:
Parking provided, ramped entry, toilet facilities

WOMEN'S HEALTH CONCERN

Acronym or abbreviation: WHC

4–6 Eton Place, Marlow, Buckinghamshire, SL7
2QA

Tel: 01628 478473
Fax: 01628 482743
E-mail: advice@womens-health-concern.org

Website:
http://www.womens-health-concern.org

Enquiries:
Enquiries to: Chief Executive
Direct e-mail: info@womens-health-concern.org

Founded:
1979

Organisation type and purpose:
Registered charity (charity number 279651).
Provides advice and counselling about the
menopause, and information about, and treatment
for, sexual health and gynaecological conditions.

Subject coverage:
Women's sexual and gynaecological problems and
other health matters.

Education services:
Professional development seminars (see website)

Electronic and video publications:
Series of factsheets (online)

Publications list:
Available online

Access to staff:
Contact by letter, by telephone, by e-mail and via
website
Hours: Mon to Fri, 0900 to 1700

Access to building, collection or gallery:
No access other than to staff

WOMEN'S INTERNATIONAL LEAGUE FOR PEACE AND FREEDOM

Acronym or abbreviation: WILPF

UK Section, Tindlemanor, 52/54 Featherstone
Street, London, EC1Y 8RT

Tel: 020 7250 1968
E-mail: office@ukwilpf.org.uk

Website:
http://www.ukwilpf.org.uk

Enquiries:
Enquiries to: Secretary
Other contacts: Office Manager

Founded:
1915

Subject coverage:
National and international lobbying, campaigning
and networking on all issues affecting peace, civil
liberties and human rights, status of all women,
disarmament.

**Museum or gallery collection, archive, or library
special collection:**
Archives of Women's Peace Movement are held in
the Women's Library, London Guildhall
University and the Bradford Peace Museum

Printed publications:
Annual Report
Peace and Freedom News
Various reports of seminars, etc.

Publications list:
Available in print

Access to staff:
Contact by letter, by telephone, by e-mail and via
website
Hours: Mon to Fri, 0900 to 1700
Special comments: For a written reply an sae is
required.

Parent body:
WILPF
Case Postale 28, Geneva 20, 1211, Switzerland;
tel: +41 22919 7080; fax: +41 22919 7081; e-mail:
wilpf@iprolink.ch; website: http://www.wilpf.int
.ch

WOMEN'S INTERNATIONAL SQUASH PLAYERS ASSOCIATION

Acronym or abbreviation: WISPA

27 Westminster Palace Gardens, Artillery Row,
London, SW1P 1RR

Tel: 020 7222 1667
Fax: 020 7976 8778
E-mail: wispahq@aol.com

Website:
http://www.wispa.net

Enquiries:
Enquiries to: Administrator

Founded:
1983

Organisation type and purpose:
International organisation, professional body
(membership is by subscription), present number
of members: 300.

Subject coverage:
To promote and administer professional squash for
women; to promote squash as a game; to advise
and assist squash promoters / media / players /
officials on all aspects of the game.

Access to staff:
Contact by letter, by telephone, by fax, by e-mail
and via website
Hours: Mon to Fri, 0900 to 1700

WOMEN'S LEAGUE OF HEALTH AND BEAUTY

Acronym or abbreviation: WLHB

6 Station Parade, Sunningdale, Berkshire, SL5 0EP

Tel: 01344 874787
Fax: 01344 873887
E-mail: tfi@thefitnessleague.com

Website:
http://www.thefitnessleague.com

Enquiries:
Enquiries to: Administrator

Founded:
1930

Formerly called:
The Fitness League (year of change 1999)

Trading as:
Health and Beauty Exercise

Organisation type and purpose:
Membership association (membership is by
subscription), present number of members: 14,000,
registered charity (charity number 226127).
To promote health through exercise.

Printed publications:
Magazine (3 times a year, free to members)
Various leaflets

Electronic and video publications:
MANFIT (exercise video)

Access to staff:
Contact by letter, by telephone, by e-mail and via
website
Hours: Mon to Fri, 1000 to 1600

WOMEN'S LIBRARY

London Metropolitan University, Old Castle Street,
London, E1 7NT

Tel: 020 7320 2222
Fax: 020 7320 2333
E-mail: moreinfo@thewomenslibrary.ac.uk

Website:
http://www.thewomenslibrary.ac.uk
Home page.

Enquiries:
Enquiries to: Librarian
Direct tel: 020 7320 3515
Direct e-mail: enquirydesk@thewomenslibrary.ac
.uk
Other contacts: (1) Archivist (2) Curator for (1) non-
published material, manuscripts, etc (2) pictorial
material.

Founded:
1926

Formed from:
Fawcett Library, London Guildhall University
(year of change 2001)

Formerly called:
The Fawcett Society (year of change 2001)

Organisation type and purpose:
Membership association, university library.

Subject coverage:
Women's studies and women's history, particularly
in Britain and the Commonwealth.

**Museum or gallery collection, archive, or library
special collection:**
Archives of many feminist organisations and of
some individual women
Cavendish Bentinck Library
Josephine Butler Society Library
Sadd Brown Library

Non-library collection catalogue:
All or part available online

Library catalogue:
All or part available online

Printed publications:
Information leaflet
Newsletter (4 times a year)

Access to staff:
Contact by letter, by telephone, by fax, by e-mail,
in person and via website
Hours: Mon, closed; Tue, Wed and Fri, 0930 to 1700;
Thu, 0930 to 2000; Sat, 1000 to 1600

Access to building, collection or gallery:
No prior appointment required
Hours: Mon, closed; Tue, Wed and Fri, 0930 to 1700;
Thu, 0930 to 2000; Sat, 1000 to 1600

Access for disabled people:
Access to all public areas, toilet facilities

WOMEN'S NATIONAL COMMISSION

Acronym or abbreviation: WNC

1st Floor, Cabinet Office, 35 Great Smith Street,
London, SW1P 3BQ

Tel: 020 7276 2555
Fax: 020 7276 2563
E-mail: wnc@cabinet-office.x.gsi.gov.uk

Website:
http://www.thewnc.org.uk

Enquiries:
Enquiries to: Director
Direct e-mail: jveitch@cabinet-office.x.gsi.gov.uk

Founded:
1969

Organisation type and purpose:
Advisory body, membership association.
Advisory body funded and staffed, but not
controlled, by the government; composed of
women's organisations, including national
organisations, women's sections of major political
parties, trade unions, professional and business
bodies, churches.

Subject coverage:
Helsinki fund, women's organisations, public
appointments, women returners, older women,
women's point of view contributed to the
deliberations of Government, in, for example,
health and social services, education, prostitution,
illegitimacy, family law, income tax. International
work on women's equality, particularly on
CEDAW and CSW. Advice on women's
organisations in the UK and contact between them
and Government.

Printed publications:
Future Female
Growing Up Female in the UK
National Agenda for Action
Reports of Working Parties
WNC Business Report 1999/01
Women's Organisations in United Kingdom 1997
Women in Public Life
World Conference Against Racism (WACR)

continued overleaf

Publications list:
Available online and in print

Access to staff:
Contact by letter, by fax, by e-mail and via website. Appointment necessary.
Hours: Mon to Fri, 0900 to 1700

WOMEN'S SPORTS FOUNDATION

Acronym or abbreviation: WSF

3rd Floor, Victoria House, Bloomsbury Square, London, WC1B 4SE

Tel: 020 7273 1740
Fax: 020 7273 1981
E-mail: info@wsff.org.uk

Website:
http://www.wsf.org.uk
Role and function of Women's Sports Foundation, current news, student pages, links to other organisations.

Enquiries:
Enquiries to: Head of Communications
Direct tel: 020 7273 1744
Other contacts: Membership & Administrative Officer for routine enquiries, resource orders, membership applications.

Founded:
1984

Organisation type and purpose:
Advisory body, membership association (membership is by subscription), present number of members: 450.
To develop and promote women's sport.

Subject coverage:
Women's sport, participation, careers, coaching, media contacts, funding and sponsorship, resources (posters and photographs). Single sex sport and leisure provision.

Museum or gallery collection, archive, or library special collection:
Range of resources and publications on women's sport

Trade and statistical information:
Data on women's involvement in sport.

Printed publications:
A Booklet on Careers in Sport and Recreation for Women and Girls (1994, £2)
Careers in Sport (1997, £3 plus £1.75 p&p)
Factsheets (1998–1999, £1)
Photographic displays for hire
Poster Set (1999, £10)
Single Sex Sport Provision (1998, free)
Syllabus Guide (2000, £20)
Women and Coaching Information Pack (1994, free with sae for 98p)
Women and Sport Information Pack (Mar 2000, £2)

Electronic and video publications:
Time of Change (video, 1995, £7.50 plus £5 p&p)
Women and Sport (VHS video, 22 mins)

Publications list:
Available online and in print

Access to staff:
Contact by letter, by e-mail and via website
Hours: Mon to Fri, 0900 to 1700

Access to building, collection or gallery:
No prior appointment required

WOMENAID INTERNATIONAL

Acronym or abbreviation: WAI

3 Whitehall Court, Whitehall, London, SW1A 2EL

Tel: 020 7976 1032
Fax: 020 7839 2929
E-mail: womenaid@womenaid.org

Website:
http://www.womenaid.org/infocalendar
http://www.womenaid.org/ukat
http://www.womenaid.org/caucasus

http://www.womenaid.org

Enquiries:
Enquiries to: Director

Founded:
1988

Formerly called:
Women of the World, WomenAid

Organisation type and purpose:
Voluntary organisation, registered charity (charity number 299224).
Humanitarian aid and development.

Subject coverage:
Humanitarian aid, development, human rights, environmental health, specialist work: anti-trafficking of women and children.

Museum or gallery collection, archive, or library special collection:
Information and resource library

Printed publications:
Information leaflets (free)
Research papers (chargeable)

Access to staff:
Contact by letter, by telephone, by fax, by e-mail and via website
Hours: Mon to Fri, 1000 to 1800

Access to building, collection or gallery:
Prior appointment required

WOOD BUREAU

PO Box 9, Farnborough, Hampshire, GU14 6WE

Tel: 01252 522545
Fax: 01252 522546
E-mail: enquiries@woodbureau.co.uk

Website:
http://www.woodbureau.co.uk

Organisation type and purpose:
Voluntary organisation.
Wood awareness campaign.

Subject coverage:
The promotion of a better understanding of wood, as a basic fibre, common and vital to many and varied industries, to encourage a rational approach to the utilisation of both wood fibre and the forest resource.

WOOD GREEN ANIMAL SHELTERS

Acronym or abbreviation: WGAS

King's Bush Farm, London Road, Godmanchester, Cambridgeshire, PE29 2NH

Tel: 08701 904090
Fax: 01480 832815
E-mail: info@woodgreen.org.uk

Website:
http://www.woodgreen.org.uk
Official site for the charity.
http://www.woodgreenenterprises.co.uk
Official site for the trading company.

Enquiries:
Enquiries to: Fundraising Department
Other contacts: Communications Manager for media enquiries, PR and fundraising.

Founded:
1924

Organisation type and purpose:
Registered charity (charity number 298348).
Animal Welfare organisation.

Subject coverage:
Animal Rehoming Charity, Animal welfare, protection, surgery and veterinary services.

Printed publications:
Annual Review
Animals Matter (3 a year)

WAGS – for junior members (quarterly, free to members, 50p to non-members)

Publications list:
Available online

Access to staff:
Contact by letter, by telephone, by fax, by e-mail, in person and via website
Hours: 24-hour service, 365 days a year; visitors, open 1000 to 1600

Access for disabled people:
Parking provided, ramped entry, toilet facilities

Affiliated to:
Wood Green Enterprises Ltd
    King's Bush Farm, London Road, Godmanchester, Cambridgeshire, PE29 2NH; tel: 08701 904090; e-mail: tina.jeffery@woodgreen.org.uk; website: http://www.woodgreen.org.uk

Other addresses:
Wood Green Animal Shelter
    601 Lordship Lane, Wood Green, London, N22 5LG; tel: 08701 904440; fax: 020 8889 0245; e-mail: info@woodgreen.org.uk; website: http://www.woodgreen.org.uk
Wood Green Animal Shelter
    Chishill Road, Heydon, Royston, Hertfordshire, SG8 8PN; tel: 08701 909099; fax: 01763 838824; e-mail: info@woodgreen.org.uk; website: http://www.woodgreen.org.uk

WOOD PANEL INDUSTRIES FEDERATION

Acronym or abbreviation: WPIF

28 Market Place, Grantham, Lincolnshire, NG31 6LR

Tel: 01476 563707
Fax: 01476 579314
E-mail: enquiries@wpif.org.uk

Website:
http://www.wpif.org.uk

Enquiries:
Enquiries to: Director General

Founded:
1995

Organisation type and purpose:
Trade association (membership is by subscription), present number of members: 25.

Subject coverage:
Industrial, professional or DIY use of particle boards, chipboard, oriented strand board and medium density fibreboard (MDF); fire and building regulations; design and application data; fixing methods; finishing techniques.

Trade and statistical information:
Data on the imports of particle boards and fibreboards into the UK.
UK production.

Publications list:
Available in print

Access to staff:
Contact by letter, by telephone, by fax, by e-mail and in person. Appointment necessary.
Hours: Mon to Fri, 0900 to 1700

Member organisation of:
BWF
CEI-BOIS
CPA
EPF
FIRA
TRADA
TTF
WPA

WOODBROOKE QUAKER STUDY CENTRE

1046 Bristol Road, Selly Oak, Birmingham, B29 6LJ

Tel: 0121 472 5171

Fax: 0121 472 5173
E-mail: library@woodbrooke.org.uk

Website:
http://www.woodbrooke.org.uk/woodbrooke
Contains library pages.

Enquiries:
Enquiries to: Librarian
Other contacts: Director

Founded:
1903

Organisation type and purpose:
Registered charity (charity number 313816).
Adult religious educational college for Quakers
and others.

Subject coverage:
Quaker studies, theology.

Museum or gallery collection, archive, or library special collection:
Bevan Naish Library of 17th and 18th century
Quaker books and pamphlets
Powicke Collection of Richard Baxter books

Non-library collection catalogue:
All or part available in-house

Library catalogue:
All or part available in-house

Printed publications:
The Woodbrooke Journal (occasional)

Access to staff:
Contact by letter, by telephone, by fax and by e-mail. Appointment necessary.
Hours: Variable, please enquire

WOODLAND HERITAGE CENTRE

Brokerswood Country Park, Westbury, Wiltshire,
BA13 4EH

Tel: 01373 822238
Fax: 01373 858474

Enquiries:
Enquiries to: Education Officer
Direct e-mail: woodland.park@virgin.net

Founded:
1971

Formerly called:
Phillip's Countryside Museum; Woodland
Heritage Museum (year of change 1997)

Organisation type and purpose:
Registered charity (charity number L246167),
museum, suitable for ages: all, but primarily 5 to
11.

Subject coverage:
Forestry and forest management, forests for leisure
and recreation, public participation in forestry,
natural history, botany, flora, fauna, ornithology,
ecology and conservation of woodland.

Museum or gallery collection, archive, or library special collection:
Barber Collection of Birds' Eggs of the World
(approximately 2000 species)

Printed publications:
Details of educational facilities (on request)

Access to staff:
Contact by letter, by fax and by e-mail
Hours: Mon to Fri, 0900 to 1700
Special comments: Opening dependent on season,
please phone in advance.

Access to building, collection or gallery:
Prior appointment required
Hours: Mon to Fri, 1000 to 1600; Sat, Sun, 1100 to
1600
Winter: Mon to Fri, 1000 to 1600; Sat, Sun, 1200 to
1600

WOODLAND TRUST, THE

Autumn Park, Dysart Road, Grantham,
Lincolnshire, NG31 6LL

Tel: 01476 581111
Fax: 01476 590808

Website:
http://www.woodland-trust.org.uk
Electronic versions of most Trust publications,
including annual reports, press releases, policy
information, Woodfinder, etc.

Enquiries:
Enquiries to: Information Manager
Direct e-mail: library@woodland-trust.org.uk

Founded:
1972

Organisation type and purpose:
Membership association (membership is by
subscription), present number of members: c.
100,000, voluntary organisation, registered charity
(charity number 294344).
Woodland conservation and creation.

Subject coverage:
Conservation and planting of native broadleaved
woodland.

Museum or gallery collection, archive, or library special collection:
Photographic collection relating to Trust properties

Printed publications:
Newsletter (for members)
Woodland Trust directory of Trust woodlands

Access to staff:
Contact by letter, by telephone, by fax, by e-mail
and via website
Hours: Mon to Fri, 0900 to 1700

WORCESTER COLLEGE OF TECHNOLOGY

Deansway, Worcester, WR1 2JF

Tel: 01905 725555
Fax: 01905 725600
E-mail: library@wortech.ac.uk

Website:
http://www.wortech.ac.uk

Enquiries:
Enquiries to: Head of Library and Study Centres
Direct tel: 01905 725578
Direct e-mail: kgardner@wortech.ac.uk

Organisation type and purpose:
Further Education College

Subject coverage:
General education, construction, business studies,
hospitality, engineering, electronics, science,
mathematics, caring, art and design, local
government, personnel, law, accountancy, leisure
studies.

Library catalogue:
All or part available online and in-house

Access to staff:
Contact by letter, by telephone, by e-mail, in
person and via website. Appointment necessary.
Hours: Term time: Mon to Thu, 0830 to 2100; Fri,
0830 to 1700; Sat, 0930 to 1230
Vacations: 0900 to 1600

Access for disabled people:
Ramped entry, access to all public areas

WORCESTERSHIRE ARCHAEOLOGICAL SERVICE

Woodbury Hall, University College, Worcester,
Henwick Grove, Worcester, WR2 9AJ

Tel: 01905 855455
Fax: 01905 855035
E-mail: archaeology@worcestershire.gov.uk

Website:
http://www.worcestershire.gov.uk/archaeology
Information, guidance on planning applications,
sites to visit, directory of local people.

Enquiries:
Enquiries to: Archaeology Officer

Founded:
1974

Organisation type and purpose:
Local government body, professional body, public
library, university department or institute.

Subject coverage:
Archaeology in general and of Worcestershire in
particular, historic buildings, aerial photographs,
industrial archaeology, archaeological excavation
archives and archaeological finds.

Non-library collection catalogue:
All or part available in-house

Library catalogue:
All or part available in-house

Printed publications:
Archaeology Newsletter (quarterly)
Archaeology Service Reports (on excavations and
fieldwork) (c. 60 p.a.)
Information leaflets (various)

Publications list:
Available in print

Access to staff:
Contact by letter, by telephone, by fax and by e-mail
Hours: Mon to Fri, 1000 to 1630

Access to building, collection or gallery:
No prior appointment required

Parent body:
Worcestershire County Council

WORCESTERSHIRE ARCHAEOLOGICAL SOCIETY

The Commandery, Sidbury, Worcester, WR1 2HU

Tel: 01905 361820
Fax: 01905 361822
E-mail: tbridges@cityofworcester.gov.uk

Enquiries:
Enquiries to: Librarian
Direct tel: 01905 361827
Other contacts: Museum Collections Manager for
library and Honorary Librarian.

Organisation type and purpose:
Learned society (membership is by subscription).

Subject coverage:
Archaeology, architecture, history.

Non-library collection catalogue:
All or part available in-house

Library catalogue:
All or part available in-house

Printed publications:
Worcestershire Archaeological Society's
Transactions
The Recorder
Order printed publications from: Honorary Editor,
Worcestershire Archaeological Society
14 Scobell Close, Pershore, Worcestershire, WR10
1QJ, tel: 01905 766353

Access to staff:
Contact by letter, by telephone and by e-mail.
Appointment necessary.
Hours: Mon, 1000 to 1700 or by arrangement

Access to building, collection or gallery:
Prior appointment required

Access for disabled people:
Parking provided, level entry, toilet facilities

Connections with:
Worcester City Museums
At the same address; tel: 01905 361820

WORCESTERSHIRE LIBRARIES AND LEARNING

Libraries and Learning, County Hall, Spetchley Road, Worcester, WR5 2NP

Tel: 01905 822819
Fax: 01905 766930
E-mail: kkirk@worcestershire.gov.uk

Website:
http://www.worcestershire.gov.uk/libraries

Enquiries:
Enquiries to: Strategic Libraries and Learning Manager

Founded:
1920

Organisation type and purpose:
Local government body, public library.
22 branch libraries.

Subject coverage:
General, local history (all libraries), carpet and textile industry (at Kidderminster); needle industry (at Redditch), business information (particularly at Worcester, Kidderminster and Redditch).

Museum or gallery collection, archive, or library special collection:
Carpets and Textile Collection (Kidderminster)
A. E. Housman and L. Housman Collection (Bromsgrove)
Needle Industry (Redditch)
Stuart Period Collection (Worcester)
Willis Bund Collection (local studies material, Worcester)

Library catalogue:
All or part available online

Access to staff:
Contact by letter, by telephone, by fax, by e-mail, in person and via website. Appointment necessary.

Access to building, collection or gallery:
Prior appointment required
Hours: Headquarters: office hours; Branch libraries have various opening hours including some evenings and some hours on Sat

Member organisation of:
SCL – West Midlands
TLP – West Midlands

Parent body:
Worcestershire County Council

WORCESTERSHIRE RECORD OFFICE

County Hall, Spetchley Road, Worcester, WR5 2NP

Tel: 01905 766351\ Minicom no. 01905 766399
Fax: 01905 766363
E-mail: recordoffice@worcestershire.gov.uk

Website:
http://www.worcestershire.gov.uk/records
General information concerning Worcestershire County Council, including Record Office and heritage function.

Enquiries:
Enquiries to: Archivist

Founded:
1947

Organisation type and purpose:
Local government body.

Subject coverage:
Local authority, Quarter Sessions, Petty Sessions, hospital, coroners, schools, parish, Diocesan and privately deposited records relating to Worcestershire.

Museum or gallery collection, archive, or library special collection:
Worcestershire photographic survey

Non-library collection catalogue:
All or part available in-house

Library catalogue:
All or part available online

Printed publications:
General information (leaflet, free)
House Hunting at the Worcestershire Record Office (leaflet, free)
Worcestershire Research Service (leaflet, free)
Local History at Worcestershire Library and History Centre (leaflet, free)
Using the Worcestershire Library and History Centre for Family History Research (leaflet, free)
The Photographic Survey (leaflet, free)

Publications list:
Available in print

Access to staff:
Contact by letter, by telephone, by fax, by e-mail, in person and via website
Hours: Mon, Fri, 0930 to 1900; Tue to Thu, 0930 to 1730; Sat 0930 to 1600

Access to building, collection or gallery:
No prior appointment required
Special comments: Reader's ticket required for consultation of original documents.

Access for disabled people:
Parking provided, ramped entry

Branch office known as:
Worcestershire Library and History Centre (WLHC)
Trinity Street, Worcester, WR1 2PW; tel: 01905 765922; fax: 01905 765925; e-mail: wlhc@worcestershire.gov.uk

WORK FOUNDATION, THE

Peter Runge House, 3 Carlton House, London SW1Y 5DG

Tel: 0870 165 6700
Fax: 0870 165 6701
E-mail: contactcentre@theworkfoundation.com

Website:
http://www.theworkfoundation.com

Enquiries:
Enquiries to: Information Officer

Organisation type and purpose:
Membership association, registered charity, training organisation, consultancy, research organisation.
Promoting best practice at work.

Subject coverage:
Conditions of employment, health and safety, training, leadership, equal opportunities, employment law, communication at work, total quality.

Printed publications:
A large range of books in all aspects of people management and development

Electronic and video publications:
Right First Time (video)
Say the Right Thing (video)
Team Briefing for the 21st Century (video)
Wish You Were Here (video)

Publications list:
Available in print

Access to staff:
Appointment necessary. Non-members charged.
Hours: Mon to Fri, 0900 to 1700

WORKERS' EDUCATIONAL ASSOCIATION

Acronym or abbreviation: WEA

Third Floor, 70 Clifton Street, London, EC2A 4HB

Tel: 020 7426 3450
Fax: 020 7426 3451
E-mail: national@wea.org.uk

Website:
http://www.wea.org.uk

Enquiries:
Enquiries to: Marketing Manager
Direct e-mail: mflemmer@wea.org.uk

Founded:
1903

Organisation type and purpose:
International organisation, national organisation, statutory body, membership association (membership is free), present number of members: 18,000, voluntary organisation, registered charity (charity number 314001), suitable for ages: adults; training organisation, research organisation. Workers' Educational Association is one national association in England and Scotland, organised into 13 districts in England and 1 Scottish association and over 650 branches, meeting the educational and training needs of 100,000 adult students each year.

Subject coverage:
Adult education, day, evening, weekend courses in a wide range of subjects, in liberal academic studies, women's studies, trade union studies, workplace learning, partnership work, etc.

Museum or gallery collection, archive, or library special collection:
The WEA Archive is held at London Metropolitan University

Non-library collection catalogue:
All or part available in print

Library catalogue:
All or part available in print

Printed publications:
Annual Review
Best Practice (annual)
Bibliography on Adult Education
Financial/Trustees Statement
Other reports, minutes and training manuals (full listing in the Archive Catalogue)
Archive Catalogue

Publications list:
Available in print

Access to staff:
Contact by letter, by telephone, by fax, by e-mail, in person and via website. Appointment necessary.
Hours: Mon to Fri, 0915 to 1645

Access to building, collection or gallery:
No prior appointment required
Hours: Archive by appointment only, Mon to Fri, 0915 to 1645

Also at:
WEA Brussels Office
rue Royale 207, Brussels 1210, Belgium; tel: +32 2 223 5552; fax: +32 2 223 5555; e-mail: wealtc@pophost.eunet.be
WEA East Midlands
39 Mapperley Road, Mapperley Park, Nottingham, NG3 5AQ; tel: 0115 962 8400; fax: 0115 962 8401; e-mail: eastmidland@wea.org.uk
WEA Eastern Region
Cintra House, 12 Hills Road, Cambridge, CB2 1JP; tel: 01223 350978; fax: 01223 300911; e-mail: eastern@wea.org.uk
WEA London Region
4 Luke Street, London, EC2A 4XW; tel: 020 7426 1950; fax: 020 7729 9821; e-mail: london@wea.org.uk
WEA National Archive
London Metropolitan University, Learning Centre, 236 Holloway Road, London, N7 6PP; tel: 020 7753 3184; fax: 020 7753 3191; e-mail: c.coates@unl.ac.uk
WEA North East
21 Portland Terrace, Jesmond, Newcastle upon Tyne, NE2 1QQ; tel: 0191 212 6100; fax: 0191 212 6101; e-mail: northeast@wea.org.uk
WEA North West
Suite 405, The Cotton Exchange Building, Old Hall Street, Liverpool, L3 9JR; tel: 0151 243 5340; fax: 0151 243 5359; e-mail: northwest@wea.org.uk

WEA Scottish Association
  Riddle's Court, 322 Lawnmarket, Edinburgh,
  EH1 2PG; tel: 0131 226 3456; fax: 0131 220 0306;
  e-mail: scotland@wea.org.uk
WEA South West
  Bradninch Court, Castle Street, Exeter, EX4 3PL;
  tel: 01392 490970; fax: 01392 490330; e-mail:
  southwest@wea.org.uk
WEA Southern Region
  57 Riverside, 2 Sir Thomas Longley Road,
  Rochester, Kent, ME2 4DP; tel: 01634 298600;
  fax: 01634 298601; e-mail: southern@wea.org.uk
WEA West Midlands
  Fourth Floor, Lancaster House, 67 Newhall
  Street, Birmingham, B3 1NQ; tel: 0121 237 8120;
  fax: 0121 237 8121; e-mail: westmidlands@wea
  .org.uk
Yorkshire and Humber
  6 Woodhouse Square, Leeds, LS3 1AD; tel: 01132
  453304; fax: 01132 450883; website: http://
  yorkshumberwea.org.uk

Member organisation of:
ADSET
Council for Educational Advance
Development Education Association (DEA)
European Regional Organisation of IFWEA
(EURO-WEA)
International Broadcasting Trust (IBT)
International Federation of Workers' Education
Associations
Local Authorities Women's Network
National Council for Voluntary Organisations
National Institute of Adult Continuing Education
Women's Training Network (EU-IRIS)

WORKING CLASS MOVEMENT LIBRARY

Acronym or abbreviation: WCML

Jubilee House, 51 The Crescent, Salford,
Manchester, M5 4WX

Tel: 0161 736 3601
Fax: 0161 737 4115
E-mail: enquiries@wcml.org.uk

Website:
http://www.wcml.org.uk
Online catalogue of books and archival material

Enquiries:
Enquiries to: Library Manager

Founded:
1963

Organisation type and purpose:
Registered charity (charity number 1115731),
public library, historic building, house or site,
suitable for ages: adults/students.
To assist in the study and research of labour
history, the working class and political struggles
from 1770 to the present day.

Subject coverage:
Trade unions, campaigns for change, poverty and
social conditions, politics, economics, working
class education, Co-operative Movement.

Museum or gallery collection, archive, or library special collection:
Records from brushmakers, shipwrights,
  boilermakers and other unions
Papers from Benny Rothman, Angela Tuckett, Jim
  Allen, Eddie and Ruth Frow
Papers relating to the International Brigade in the
  Spanish Civil War, with a specific focus on
  volunteers from the North West of England

Non-library collection catalogue:
All or part available online and in-house

Library catalogue:
All or part available online and in-house

Printed publications:
Shelf Life (quarterly bulletin for Friends of the
  Library)
Publications include:
Chartism in Salford (£1.95)
Political Women, their participation 1800–1850 (E.
  Frow and R. Frow, £5)

The General Strike in Salford in 1911 (E. Frow and
  R. Frow, £1.50)
Essays in Insurrection (E. Frow and R. Frow, £3)
Karl Marx in Manchester (E. Frow and R. Frow, £1)
Frederick Engels in Manchester and The Condition
  of the Working Class in England in 1844 (E. Frow
  and R. Frow, £1.50)
Order printed publications from: WCML

Microform publications:
Nelson Gazette, 1928–1962
Order microform publications from: Microform
Academic Publishers, Main Street, East Ardsley,
Wakefield, WF3 2AP

Publications list:
Available online

Access to staff:
Contact by letter, by telephone, by fax, by e-mail
and via website. Appointment necessary.
Hours: Tue to Fri, 1000 to 1700; third Sat of the
month, 1000 to 1600

Access to building, collection or gallery:
Prior appointment required
Hours: Tue to Fri, 1000 to 1700; third Sat of the
month, 1000 to 1600

Access for disabled people:
Parking provided, ramped entry, toilet facilities

Administered by:
Board of Trustees
  at the same address

WORLD AHLUL BAYT ISLAMIC LEAGUE

Acronym or abbreviation: WABIL

19 Chelmsford Square, London, NW10 3AP

Tel: 020 8459 8475
Fax: 020 8451 7059
E-mail: wabil@wabil.com

Website:
http://www.cealpha1.swan.ac.uk
Information on Islam, Quran, Islamic books,
history, lives of Islam's personalities.
http://www.wabil.com

Enquiries:
Enquiries to: Secretary General
Direct tel: 020 8459 6051
Direct e-mail: mmusawi@gmail.com
Other contacts: Public Relations Officer

Founded:
1983

Organisation type and purpose:
International organisation, voluntary organisation,
registered charity (charity number 291922).

Subject coverage:
Islam, Shiaism, jurisprudence, scholars' welfare in
poor countries, books, charity.

Printed publications:
Ahlul Bayt Journal (available in English, Arabic
  and French)
Ja'fari Observer

Electronic and video publications:
Islamic & Educational Subjects available (CD-
ROM)

Publications list:
Available in print

Access to staff:
Contact by letter, by fax and by e-mail
Hours: Mon to Fri, 0900 to 1700

WORLD ARABIAN HORSE ORGANIZATION

Acronym or abbreviation: WAHO

Newbarn Farmhouse, Forthampton,
Gloucestershire, GL19 4QD

Tel: 01684 274455
Fax: 01684 274422

E-mail: waho@compuserve.com

Website:
http://www.waho.org

Enquiries:
Enquiries to: Executive Secretary

Founded:
1972

Organisation type and purpose:
International organisation, membership
association, present number of members: 54
member countries, 1000 individual associate
members, registered charity.

Subject coverage:
Arabian horses.

Printed publications:
Members Directory

Access to staff:
Contact by letter, by telephone, by fax, by e-mail
and via website. Appointment necessary.
Hours: Mon to Fri, 0900 to 1700

WORLD BOWLS LIMITED

SportScotland, Caledonia House, 1 Redheughs
Rigg, South Gyle, Edinburgh, EH12 9DQ

Tel: 0131 317 9764
Fax: 0131 317 9765
E-mail: worldbows@btconnect.com

Website:
http://www.worldbowlsltd.co.uk

Enquiries:
Enquiries to: Chief Executive Officer

Founded:
1907

Formed by the amalgamation of:
International Womens Bowling Board (IWBB),
World Bowls Board (WB'), date of change, 1 Jul
2001

Formerly called:
International Bowling Board (IBB) (year of change
1992)

Organisation type and purpose:
International organisation, advisory body,
membership association (membership is by
subscription), present number of members: 53
National Authorities.
Governing body of the sport.

Subject coverage:
International competition, laws of game,
manufacture and testing of bowls, standards for
bowling green surfaces.

Printed publications:
Constitution and By-Laws (free)
Joint Laws of the Game (£1.50)
Performance Standard for Artificial Flat Green
  Bowls Surfaces (£10)

Electronic and video publications:
Umpiring and Marking Skills DVD price £10.00

Access to staff:
Contact by letter, by telephone, by fax and by e-
mail
Hours: Mon to Fri, 0900 to 1700

Access for disabled people:
Parking provided, level entry, access to all public
areas, toilet facilities

WORLD CANCER RESEARCH FUND

Acronym or abbreviation: WCRF

19 Harley Street, London, W1G 9QJ

Tel: 020 7343 4200
Fax: 020 7343 4201

Website:
http://www.wcrf.org.uk
http://www.wcrfhealthcheck.org

continued overleaf

Enquiries:
Enquiries to: Supporter Services Department
Direct tel: 020 7343 4205
Direct e-mail: wcrf@wcrf.org.uk

Founded:
1990

Organisation type and purpose:
Registered charity (charity number 1000739),
suitable for ages: all, research organisation.
To raise awareness of cancer as a preventable
disease; to provide advice for healthy living; to
translate scientific research findings into accessible
form; to motivate individuals to change to
healthier diets and lifestyles; to provide supporter
services.

Subject coverage:
Diet, nutrition, physical activity and cancer.

Printed publications:
A series of booklets and fact sheets available free
(although donations to cover postage and
printing gratefully received) including:
Cancer Process Series
Children's Series
Children's Newsletters (3 times a year)
Community Series
Healthcare Professional Series
Series One: Booklets on Food Nutrition and the
Prevention of Cancer
Series One: Factsheets: 14 diet and health
recommendations
Series Two: Booklet and Leaflets: Finding Out
About Cancer
Series Three: Healthy Eating
WRCF Newsletters (quarterly)

Publications list:
Available in print

Access to staff:
Contact by letter, by telephone, by fax and via
website. Appointment necessary.
Hours: Mon to Fri, 0900 to 1730

Access to building, collection or gallery:
No access other than to staff

Affiliated to:
American Institute for Cancer Research
World Cancer Research Fund
Netherlands

WORLD CONFEDERATION FOR PHYSICAL THERAPY

Acronym or abbreviation: WCPT

Fourth Floor, Charles House, 375 Kensington High
Street, London, W14 8QH

Tel: 020 7471 6765
Fax: 020 7471 6766
E-mail: info@wcpt.org

Website:
http://www.wcpt.org

Enquiries:
Enquiries to: Secretary-General

Founded:
1951

Organisation type and purpose:
International organisation, professional body
(membership is by qualification), present number
of members: 92, registered charity (charity number
234307).
WCPT is a confederation of 92 national
professional associates around the world. It aims to
improve global health care by representing
physical therapists (physiotherapists)
internationally, enabling information exchange and
co-operation among physical therapists across the
world, and encouraging high standards of
research, education and practice in physical
therapy.

Printed publications:
Single copies of most publications are free of
charge to member organisations

Newsletter (available by subscription, £16 for 2
years, 8 issues)

Publications list:
Available online and in print

Access to staff:
Contact by letter and by e-mail. Appointment
necessary.
Hours: Mon to Fri, 0900 to 1700

Access to building, collection or gallery:
No prior appointment required

WORLD CURLING FEDERATION

Acronym or abbreviation: WCF

74 Tay Street, Perth, Tayside, PH2 8NP

Tel: 01738 451 630
Fax: 01738 451 641
E-mail: wcf@dial.pipex.com

Website:
http://www.worldcurling.org

Enquiries:
Enquiries to: Secretary-General
Other contacts: Media Relations Officer

Founded:
1966

Formerly called:
International Curling Federation (ICF) (year of
change 1991)

Organisation type and purpose:
International organisation, membership
association.
Represents 44 member associations and promotes
the sport of curling world-wide.

Subject coverage:
The sport of curling world-wide, details of
participants and performance, venues of World
and World Junior Curling Championships since
1959, organisation of all World and World
Wheelchair Curling Championships.

Printed publications:
Coaching Manuals (various)
WCF Constitution and By-Laws
WCF Rules of Curling and Competition
Curling Ice-Making Manual
Order printed publications from: World Curling
Federation, 74 Tay Street, Perth, PH2 8NP

Publications list:
Available in print

Access to staff:
Contact by letter, by telephone, by fax and by e-
mail. Appointment necessary.
Hours: Mon to Fri, 0900 to 1700

Access for disabled people:
Ramped entry

WORLD EDUCATION DEVELOPMENT GROUP

Acronym or abbreviation: WEDG

98A Broad Street, Canterbury, Kent, CT1 2LU

Tel: 01227 766552
Fax: 01227 766552
E-mail: info@wedg.org.uk

Website:
http://www.wedg.org.uk

Enquiries:
Enquiries to: Projects Leader
Other contacts: Development Education Co-
ordinator

Founded:
1987

Organisation type and purpose:
Development Education Centre

Subject coverage:
TWEDG engages with schools, universities,
community groups and other educators in East
Kent to promote global education and make issues
such as sustainable development, social justice and
human rights accessible to all. Provides training, a
resources centre, workshops, assemblies, support
and advice through projects.

**Museum or gallery collection, archive, or library
special collection:**
A variety of material for educational use in
geography, RE, English, science, etc.
Reference information on Peace, Human Rights,
Environment and Development including
teachers' packs

Non-library collection catalogue:
All or part available online

Printed publications:
Dolls Defying Discrimination
Young Diasporas – Longing and Belonging
Order printed publications from: WEDG

Electronic and video publications:
Videos and slides

Access to staff:
Contact by letter, by telephone, by fax, by e-mail
and via website. Appointment necessary. Non-
members charged.
Hours: Wed, 1400 to 1800; first Sat of month, 1100
to 1300; by appointment at other times

Access to building, collection or gallery:
No access other than to staff, no prior appointment
required
Hours: Wed, 1400 to 1800; first Sat of month, 1100
to 1300

Access for disabled people:
Ramped entry

Links with:
Kent and the Wider World
website: http://www.commonwork.org/kww/
default.htm
PIDEC
website: http://www.pestalozzi.org.uk

Member organisation of:
DEA
CAN Mezzanine, 32–36 Loman Street, London,
SE1 0EH; website: http://www.dea.org.uk
Local4Global
website: http://www.local4global.org.uk

WORLD EMERGENCY RELIEF

Acronym or abbreviation: WER

20 York Buildings, London, WC2N 6JU

Tel: 020 7839 3854
Fax: 020 7839 8202
E-mail: info@wer-uk.org

Website:
http://www.wer-uk.org
Details of charity operation and accounts.

Enquiries:
Enquiries to: Executive Director
Direct e-mail: alex@wer-uk.org

Founded:
1994

Organisation type and purpose:
Registered charity (charity number 1045672).

Access to staff:
Contact by letter and by e-mail
Hours: Mon to Fri, 0900 to 1700

Access for disabled people:
Access to all public areas

WORLD ENERGY COUNCIL

Acronym or abbreviation: WEC

5th Floor, Regency House, 1–4 Warwick Street,
London, W1B 5LT

Tel: 020 7734 5996
Fax: 020 7734 5926

Website:
http://www.worldenergy.org
Publication list

Enquiries:
Enquiries to: Information Officer

Founded:
1924

Formerly called:
World Energy Congress

Organisation type and purpose:
International organisation, membership
association, registered charity (charity number
1086559).
To promote the sustainable supply and use of
energy for the greatest benefit of all.

Subject coverage:
Energy (all forms, fossil, renewables, nuclear),
provision and use thereof, energy-related issues
including environmental, efficiency and
conservation, economic and social development,
financing, technology, policy.

**Museum or gallery collection, archive, or library
special collection:**
Small energy library

Trade and statistical information:
Triennial surveys of energy resources and national
energy databases
Special publications, e.g. WEC Commission report,
renewable energy resources, combined heat and
power schemes

Printed publications:
For purchase:
Survey of Energy Resources 2001 £25
Renewable Energy in South Asia: Status and
Prospects £15
Drivers of the Energy Scene 2004 (PDF only) £55
Drivers of the Energy Scene 2004 (CD package) £70
Drivers of the Energy Scene 2004 (hardcopy
volume) £95
Renewable Energy Projects Handbook (PDF) £20
Comparison of Energy Systems Using Life Cycle
Analysis £45
Regulating District Heating and Cogeneration in
Central and Eastern Europe (Hard Copy) £40
Regulating District Heating and Cogeneration in
Central and Eastern Europe (PDF version) £25
Energy Market Reforms: Lessons Learned and
Next Steps (Hard Copy) £100
Energy Market Reforms: Lessons Learned and
Next Steps (PDF version) £75
Comparison of Energy Systems Using Life Cycle
Analysis (PDF version) £30
Energy Efficiency: A Worldwide Review (Hard
Copy) £75
Energy Efficiency: A Worldwide Review (PDF
version) £55
Performance of Generating Plant: New Realities,
New Needs (Hard Copy) £85
Performance of Generating Plant: New Realities,
New Needs (PDF version) £60
Sustainable Global Energy Development: The Case
of Coal (Hard Copy) £70
Sustainable Global Energy Development: The Case
of Coal (PDF version) £60
Energy End-Use Technologies for the 21st Century
(PDF version) £75
Energy End-Use Technologies for the 21st Century
(Hard Copy) £100
Comparación de los Sistemas Energéticos
Utilizando Evaluación del Ciclo de Vida (PDF)
£30
Global Energy Perspectives (1998) £15
Online:
Déclaration 2004 du CME: Réflexions sur la
dynamique des marchés du pétrole et du gaz
naturel (also in hard copy)
Electricity Market Design and Creation in Asia
Pacific Report 2001
Energy & Climate Change Working Paper 2004
Energy Efficiency Policies and Indicators Report
2001

Energy for Tomorrow's World – Acting Now!
Report 2000
Energy Markets in Transition: The Latin American
and Caribbean Experience Report 2001
Energy Technologies for the 21st Century Report
Living in One World (also in hard copy)
Mensaje del CME para 2003: Cuotas de la Energía
Performance of Generating Plant Report 2001
Performance of Thermal Generating Plant (PTGP)
Monographs Report 1998
Potentiel de développement intégré de l'énergie au
plan régional en Afrique Report 2003
Pricing Energy in Developing Countries Report
2001
Renewable Energy in South Asia Report 2000 (also
in hard copy)
Report on COP-5: A Bonn Outcome or Bad?
Climate Change Report No. 13, 1999
Report on COP-6: Lack of Progress at COP 6
Climate Change Report No. 14, 2000
Restructuring and Privatizing the Coal Industries
in Central and Eastern Europe and the CIS
Report 2000 (also in hard copy)
Survey of Energy Resources Report 2001 (also on
CD)
The Benefits and Deficiencies of Energy Sector
Liberalisation Report 1998
The Challenge of Rural Energy Poverty in
Developing Countries Report 1999
The Potential for Regionally Integrated Energy
Development in Africa Report 2003
Towards Local Energy Systems: Revitalizing
District Heating and Co-Generation in Central
and Eastern Europe
WEC Statement 2001: Pricing Energy in
Developing Countries – Summary Only
WEC Statement 2002: Energy for People, Energy
for Peace Only
WEC Statement 2003: Renewable Energy Targets
Only
WEC Statement 2004: Reflections on the Dynamics
of Oil and Natural Gas Markets (also in hard
copy)
Order printed publications from: London Office,
WEC
at the same adddress, e-mail: info@worldenergy
.org

Electronic and video publications:
All Publications available on the Council's website
Survey of Energy Resources (online 1998, 2001,
CD-ROM)
Energy for Tomorrow's World – Acting Now
(online 2000)
Living in One World (online 2001)
Renewables in S Asia (online 2001)
The Challenge of Rural Energy Poverty (online
1999)

Publications list:
Available online and in print

Access to staff:
Contact by letter, by telephone, by fax and by e-
mail. Appointment necessary.
Hours: Mon to Fri, 1000 to 1600

Has:
96 affiliated national energy associations
worldwide

WORLD HERITAGE

Heritage House, 25 High West Street, Dorchester,
Dorset, DT1 1UW

Tel: 01305 269741
Fax: 01305 268885
E-mail: info@world-heritage.org.uk

Website:
http://www.dinosaur-museum.org.uk
http://www.world-heritage.co.uk
http://www.tutankhamun-exhibition.co.uk
http://www.teddybearmuseum.co.uk
http://www.terracottawarriors.co.uk

Enquiries:
Enquiries to: Manager

Founded:
1989

Organisation type and purpose:
Museum.
A consortium of independent museums and
exhibitions. Also operates literature distribution
and tourism services, and Teddy Bear fairs.

Subject coverage:
Egyptology, dinosaurs, fossils, geology, teddy
bears, tourism, museum management, terracotta
warriors, photography.

Printed publications:
Wide selection of books produced by other
publishers, available by mail order or direct from
one of the museum shops
Main themes of books: Egyptology, dinosaurs,
teddy bears (price lists available)

Access to staff:
Contact by letter, by telephone, by fax, by e-mail
and via website. Appointment necessary.
Hours: Mon to Fri, 0900 to 1700

Branch museums:
Dinosaur Museum
  Icen Way, Dorchester, DT1 1EW; tel: 01305
  269880; fax: 01305 268885; e-mail: info@
  thedinosaurmuseum.com; website: http://www
  .thedinosaurmuseum.com
Dorset Teddy Bear Museum
  Eastgate, cnr of High East Street and Salisbury
  Street, Dorchester, DT1 1JU; tel: 01305 266040;
  fax: 01305 268885; e-mail: info@
  teddybearmuseum.co.uk; website: http://www
  .teddybearmuseum.co.uk
Terracotta Warriors Museum
  Salisbury Street, Dorchester, Dorset, DT1 1JU;
  tel: 01305 266040; fax: 01305 268885; e-mail:
  info@terracottawarriors.co.uk; website: http://
  www.terracottawarriors.co.uk
Tutankhamun Exhibition
  High West Street, Dorchester, DT1 1UW; tel:
  01305 269571; fax: 01305 268885; e-mail: info@
  tutankhamun-exhibition.co.uk; website: http://
  www.tutankhamun-exhibition.co.uk

WORLD NUCLEAR ASSOCIATION

Acronym or abbreviation: WNA

Carlton House, 22a St James's Square, London,
SW1Y 4JH

Tel: 020 7451 1520
Fax: 020 7839 1501
E-mail: wna@world-nuclear.org

Website:
http://www.world-nuclear.org
All aspects of uranium and nuclear energy
industries, including forthcoming conferences,
statistics, information papers.

Founded:
1975

Organisation type and purpose:
International organisation, trade association
(membership is by subscription), present number
of members: 120, research organisation.

Subject coverage:
Uranium: supply and demand, geology, mining,
processing, laws and regulations, trade, safety,
environmental issues; nuclear power: status worldwide, technology.

Trade and statistical information:
Uranium production statistics, international by
country; nuclear energy statistics, international
by country.

Non-library collection catalogue:
All or part available in-house

Printed publications:
Pocket Guides (free) on:
Nuclear Power Reactor Characteristics
Uranium: From Mine to Mill
Nuclear Power: Energy and the Environment
Market Report (every 2 years, price on application)
Order printed publications from: Via website

Electronic and video publications:
Information papers (online)

continued overleaf

Symposium proceedings (online)

Publications list:
Available online and in print

Access to staff:
Contact by letter, by telephone, by fax, by e-mail and via website. Appointment necessary.
Hours: Mon to Fri, 1000 to 1600

Access to building, collection or gallery:
Hours: Mon to Fri, 0930 to 1700

WORLD PARROT TRUST

Acronym or abbreviation: WPT

Glanmor House, Hayle, Cornwall, TR27 4HB

Tel: 01736 751026
Fax: 01736 751028
E-mail: uk@worldparrottrust.org

Website:
http://www.parrots.org

Enquiries:
Enquiries to: Administrator
Other contacts: Chairman

Founded:
1989

Incorporates the former:
Paradise Park (wildlife sanctuary)

Organisation type and purpose:
International organisation, membership association (membership is by subscription), present number of members: 2,116, registered charity (charity number 800944).
Conservation and welfare of parrots.

Subject coverage:
Parrot conservation projects, the welfare of pet parrots and aviculture.

Printed publications:
Parrot Action Plan 2000–2005
Leaflets on pet care welfare
PsittaScene (quarterly newsletter, free to members or £3 each)

Access to staff:
Contact by letter, by telephone, by fax, by e-mail and via website
Hours: Mon to Fri, 0900 to 1700

Links with:
Paradise Park
   tel: 01736 751026; fax: 01736 751028

WORLD PHEASANT ASSOCIATION

Acronym or abbreviation: WPA

7–9 Shatesbury Street, Fordingbridge, Hampshire, SP6 1JF

Tel: 0118 984 5140
Fax: 0118 984 3369
E-mail: office@pheasant.org.uk

Website:
http://www.pheasant.org.uk

Enquiries:
Enquiries to: Administrator
Other contacts: Director

Founded:
1975

Formerly called:
WPA International (WPA)

Organisation type and purpose:
International organisation, membership association, voluntary organisation, registered charity (charity number 271203).

Subject coverage:
Conservation, breeding and management of galliformes (pheasants, grouse, quail etc) field studies.

Trade and statistical information:
Data on the status and distribution of galliformes worldwide.

Printed publications:
Annual Review
WPA News (2 a year)

Electronic and video publications:
Under development (bibliographic database)

Publications list:
Available online and in print

Access to staff:
Contact by letter, by telephone, by fax and by e-mail. Appointment necessary.
Hours: Mon to Fri, 0900 to 1700

Access for disabled people:
Parking provided, level entry, access to all public areas, toilet facilities

Specialist group for:
Birdlife International

WORLD PLOUGHING ORGANIZATION

Acronym or abbreviation: WPO

26 Gable Avenue, Cockermouth, Cumbria, CA13 9BU

Tel: 01900 825686
Fax: 01900 68736

Website:
http://www.worldploughing.org

Enquiries:
Enquiries to: Treasurer

Founded:
1952

Organisation type and purpose:
Voluntary organisation.

Subject coverage:
Standards of ploughmanship, the rules for ploughing, competition ploughing as an incentive to good husbandry of the soil, soil tillage demonstrations and machinery exhibition.

Printed publications:
WPO Bulletin of News and Information (annually)
WPO Contest Handbook (annually)

Access to staff:
Contact by letter
Hours: Mon to Fri, 0900 to 1700

WORLD PROFESSIONAL BILLIARDS AND SNOOKER ASSOCIATION LIMITED

Acronym or abbreviation: WPBSA

Suite 2/1, Albert House, 111–117 Victoria Street, Bristol, BS1 6AX

Tel: 0117 317 8200
Fax: 0117 317 8300
E-mail: enq@worldsnooker.com

Website:
http://www.worldsnooker.com

Enquiries:
Enquiries to: Company Secretary

Organisation type and purpose:
Membership association.
Governing body of the games.

Subject coverage:
Details of the professional and amateur games of billiards and snooker.

Museum or gallery collection, archive, or library special collection:
Books and records of snooker and billiards from the commencement of the games in 1887 and founding of a formal Snooker and Billiards Association in that year

Access to staff:
Contact by letter
Hours: Mon to Fri, 0900 to 1700

WORLD SIKH FOUNDATION

33 Wargrave Road, South Harrow, Middlesex, HA2 8LL

Tel: 020 8864 9228
E-mail: bablibharara@hotmail.com

Enquiries:
Enquiries to: Secretary
Direct e-mail: worldsikhfoundation@hotmail.com

Founded:
1960

Formerly called:
Sikh Cultural Society of Great Britain (year of change 1993)

Organisation type and purpose:
International organisation, learned society (membership is by subscription), present number of members: 850, voluntary organisation, registered charity (charity number 1054913), publishing house.
Religious society.
To spread message of Sikhism worldwide.

Subject coverage:
The Sikh religion.

Printed publications:
Pamphlets
Sikh Courier International (journal)

Access to staff:
Contact by letter and by telephone
Hours: Mon to Fri, 0900 to 1700

Also at the same address:
Guru Nanak Foundation UK

WORLD SOCIETY FOR THE PROTECTION OF ANIMALS

Acronym or abbreviation: WSPA

89 Albert Embankment, London, SE1 7TP

Tel: 020 7587 5000
Fax: 020 7793 0208
E-mail: wspa@wspa.org.uk

Website:
http://www.wspa.org.uk

Enquiries:
Enquiries to: Supporter Services

Founded:
1980

Formerly called:
ISPA; WFPA (year of change 1980)

Organisation type and purpose:
Membership association, present number of members: 953 member societies in 154 countries, registered charity (charity number 1081849).
Animal welfare charity.

Subject coverage:
Wildlife, companion animals, farm animals, animal welfare legislation, disaster relief, humane education, animal protection.

Printed publications:
Annual Report
Membership Communication Material
Ongoing Animal Reports

Electronic and video publications:
Campaign videos

Publications list:
Available in print

Access to staff:
Contact by letter, by telephone, by fax and by e-mail. Appointment necessary.
Hours: Mon to Fri, 0900 to 1700

Access for disabled people:
Parking provided, ramped entry, toilet facilities

Also at:
World Society for the Protection of Animals
90 Eglington Avenue East, Suite 960, Toronto, Ontario, M4P 2Y3, Canada; tel: +1 416 369 0044; fax: +1 416 369 0147; e-mail: wspa@wspa.ca; website: http://www.wspa.ca
World Society for the Protection of Animals
Mall Paseo las Flores Business Center, 5th floor, Apdo Postal 516–3000, Heredia, Costa Rica; tel: +506 2562 1200; fax: +506 2562 1225; e-mail: info@wspala.org; website: http://wspa.or.cr
World Society for the Protection of Animals
PO Box 105476, Dar es Salaam, Tanzania; tel: +255 22 270 1032; fax: +255 22 270 1033; e-mail: enquiries@wspaafrica.org; website: http://www.wspa-international.org
World Society for the Protection of Animals
Lincoln Plaza, Suite 201, 89 South Street, Boston 02111, USA; tel: +1 617 896 9214; fax: +1 617 737 4404; e-mail: wspa@wspausa.org; website: http://www.wspa-usa.org
World Society for the Protection of Animals
19th Floor, Olympia Thai Tower, 444 Ratchadaphisek Road, Huay Kwang, Bangkok 10310, Thailand; tel: +66 2 513 0475; fax: +66 2 513 0477; e-mail: thailand.enquiries@wspa-asia.org; website: http://www.wspa-international.org
World Society for the Protection of Animals
GPO Box 3294, Sydney, NSW 2001, Australia; tel: +61 2 9902 8000; fax: +61 2 9906 1166; e-mail: wspa@wspa.org.au; website: http://www.wspa.org.au
World Society for the Protection of Animals
Av. Princesa Isabel, 323 – 8 andar, Copacabana, 22011–901, Rio de Janeiro, Brazil; tel: +55 21 3820 8200; fax: +55 21 3820 8229; e-mail: wspabrasil@wspabr.org; website: http://www.wspabrasil.org
World Society for the Protection of Animals
501B, Dong Wai Diplomatic Building, No. 23, Dongzhimen Wai Avenue, Beijing 100600, People's Republic of China; tel: +86 10 85325211 – 8008; fax: +86 10 85324211; e-mail: alyceyu@wspa-asia.org; website: http://www.wspa-international.org
World Society for the Protection of Animals
Carrera 13 #29–21 Of. 234, Manzana 1, Parque Central Bavaria, Bogotá, Colombia; tel: +571 288 8829; fax: +571 232 1361; e-mail: wspa@wspa.org.co; website: http://www.wspa-international.org
World Society for the Protection of Animals
Kaiserstrasse 22, 53113, Bonn, Germany; tel: +49 228 956 3455; fax: +49 228 956 3454; e-mail: info@wspa.de; website: http://www.wspa.de
World Society for the Protection of Animals
Benoordenhoutseweg 23, 2596 BA Den Haag, The Netherlands; tel: +31 70 314 2800; fax: +31 70 314 2809; e-mail: info@wspa.nl; website: http://www.wspa.nl
World Society for the Protection of Animals
Private Bag 93220, Parnell 1151, Auckland, New Zealand; tel: +64 9 309 3901; fax: +64 9 336 1947; e-mail: wspa@wspa.org.nz; website: http://www.wspa.org.nz
World Society for the Protection of Animals
Vesterbrogade 34, 1, 1620 Copenhagen V, Denmark; tel: +45 33 93 7212; fax: +45 33 93 7210; e-mail: info@wspa.dk; website: http://www.wspa.dk

Links with:
United Nations (consultative status)

Member organisation of:
Eurogroup for Animal Welfare

WORLD SQUASH FEDERATION LIMITED

Acronym or abbreviation: WSF

6 Havelock Road, Hastings, East Sussex, TN34 1BP

Tel: 01424 429245
Fax: 01424 429250
E-mail: squash@worldsquash.org

Website:
http://www.squash.org
The Internet Squash Federation.

Enquiries:
Enquiries to: Chief Executive
Other contacts: Executive Assistant

Founded:
1967

Formerly called:
International Squash Rackets Federation (ISRF) (year of change 1992)

Organisation type and purpose:
International organisation.

Subject coverage:
The sport of squash, court, clothing, ball, racket specifications; rules, refereeing, coaching, world championships.

Access to staff:
Contact by letter, by telephone, by fax, by e-mail and via website. Appointment necessary.
Hours: Mon to Fri, 0900 to 1700

WORLD UNION FOR PROGRESSIVE JUDAISM EUROPEAN BOARD

Acronym or abbreviation: WUPJ

Sternberg Centre for Judaism, 80 East End Road, London, N3 2SY

Tel: 020 8349 3779
Fax: 020 8343 5699
E-mail: europeanjudaism@directmail.org

Enquiries:
Enquiries to: Administrator

Founded:
1926

Organisation type and purpose:
International organisation (membership is by election or invitation), registered charity (charity number 253000).
Nurture and develop progressive Jewish communities in Europe.

Printed publications:
European Eye (newsletter, quarterly)

Access to staff:
Contact by letter, by fax and by e-mail
Hours: Mon to Thu, 1030 to 1600

Parent body:
World Union for Progressive Judaism
13 King David Street, Jerusalem, 9101, Israel; tel: 00 972 26203 447; fax: 00 972 26203 446; e-mail: wupjis@netvision.net.il

WORLD WAR TWO RAILWAY STUDY GROUP

17 Balmoral Crescent, West Molesey, Surrey, KT8 1QA

Tel: 020 8783 1024
E-mail: tcane@ww2rsg.u-net.com

Website:
http://www.2rsg.org

Organisation type and purpose:
Membership association.
Research into the use of railways in World War II.

Subject coverage:
Use of railways in World War Two, mainly UK railways and the overseas use of railways by British forces. Topics include civil engineering, ambulance trains, rail guns etc.

Printed publications:
Newsletter 4–5 times a year

WORLD'S POULTRY SCIENCE ASSOCIATION UK BRANCH

Acronym or abbreviation: WPSA

Woodlands, Bradfield St Clare, Bury St Edmunds, Suffolk, IP30 0EQ

Tel: 01284 386520
Fax: 01284 386520
E-mail: wpsa@hotmail.co.uk

Website:
http://www.wpsa-uk.com
Details of membership, meetings and publications.

Enquiries:
Enquiries to: Honorary Secretary

Founded:
1946

Organisation type and purpose:
Membership association (membership is by subscription), present number of members: 280, voluntary organisation, registered charity (charity number 803616).
To promote the spread and exchange of information on poultry science and the poultry industry.

Subject coverage:
Poultry science and technology, poultry industry.

Printed publications:
Membership Directory
Newsletter (3 times a year)
Poultry Science Symposia (every two years)
World's Poultry Science Journal (4 times a year)

Publications list:
Available online

Access to staff:
Contact by letter, by telephone, by fax, by e-mail and via website. Access for members only.
Hours: variable part time

Access to building, collection or gallery:
No

Parent body:
World's Poultry Science Association (WPSA)
tel: + 31 55 506 6534; fax: + 31 55 506 4858; e-mail: wpsa@xs4all.nl; website: www.wpsa.com

WORLDAWARE

Echo House, Ullswater Crescent, Coulsdon, Surrey, CR5 2HR

Tel: 020 8763 2555
Fax: 020 8763 2888
E-mail: info@worldaware.org.uk

Website:
http://www.worldaware.org.uk
Organisational information and online ordering of education materials.
http://www.globaleye.org.uk
Interactive facility for schools and teachers.

Enquiries:
Enquiries to: Director

Founded:
1966

Formerly called:
Centre for World Development Education (CWDE) (year of change 1991)

Organisation type and purpose:
Registered charity (charity number 273260), suitable for ages: 5–18, training organisation, consultancy, research organisation, publishing house.

Subject coverage:
All aspects of world development, especially Britain's aid to, and trade and interdependence with, developing countries.

Museum or gallery collection, archive, or library special collection:
Library of educational materials for teachers and students on developing countries and global issues

Printed publications:
Global Eye (magazine for students 5–16, 3 times a year, also see website)

continued overleaf

Range of books, packs, factsheets and software for primary and secondary schools providing ideas for study and information on many countries and natural areas (for purchase by mail order, also see website)

Electronic and video publications:
Videos and CD-ROMs available

Publications list:
Available online and in print

Access to staff:
Contact by letter, by telephone, by fax, by e-mail and via website
Hours: Mon to Fri, 0900 to 1700

Access for disabled people:
Parking provided

WORLDSCALE ASSOCIATION (LONDON) LIMITED

Acronym or abbreviation: Worldscale

Copenhagen House, 5–10 Bury Street, London, EC3A 5AT

Tel: 020 7456 6600
Fax: 020 7456 6601
E-mail: wscale@worldscale.co.uk

Website:
http://www.worldscale.co.uk
As per published book but extended dataset (approximately 4 times as much).

Enquiries:
Enquiries to: Managing Director

Founded:
1962

Organisation type and purpose:
Consultancy.

Subject coverage:
Standard of reference for nominal freight scale to the oil tanker industry.

Trade and statistical information:
Nominal oil tanker freight rates for worldwide trade.

Printed publications:
Worldscale Schedule (annual, book)

Publications list:
Available in print

Access to staff:
Contact by letter, by telephone, by fax and by e-mail. Appointment necessary.
Hours: Mon to Fri, 0930 to 1730
Special comments: Services offered on an annual subscription basis.

Joint publishers:
Worldscale Association (NYC) Inc
116 John Street, Suite 620, New York, NY 10038, USA; tel: + 1 212 422 2786; fax: +1 212 344 4169; e-mail: worldscale@worldscale-usa.com; website: www.worldscale-usa.com

WORSHIPFUL COMPANY OF ACTUARIES

3rd Floor, Cheapside House, 138, Cheapside, London, EC2V 6BW

Tel: 020 7776 3880
E-mail: clerk@actuariescompany.co.uk

Website:
http://www.actuariescompany.co.uk

Enquiries:
Enquiries to: The Clerk

Founded:
1979

Organisation type and purpose:
Membership association (membership is by election or invitation).
City of London Livery Company.

To extend recognition and understanding of the work of actuaries within the City and beyond, through educational and charitable works.

Access to staff:
Contact by letter, by telephone, by e-mail and via website

WORSHIPFUL COMPANY OF ARBITRATORS

13 Hall Gardens, Colney Heath, St Albans, Hertfordshire, AL4 0QF

Tel: 01727 826578
Fax: 01727 822652
E-mail: clerk@arbitratorscompany.org

Website:
http://www.arbitratorscompany.org

Enquiries:
Enquiries to: The Clerk
Direct tel: 01727 826578
Direct e-mail: clerk@arbitratorscompany.org

Founded:
1981

Organisation type and purpose:
Membership association (membership is by election or invitation).
City of London Livery Company. Promotes arbitration and interest in arbitration of the City of London, and supports education in the field of arbitration through charitable works.

Access to staff:
Contact by letter, by telephone, by fax, by e-mail and via website. Non-members charged.

WORSHIPFUL COMPANY OF ARMOURERS & BRASIERS

Armourers' Hall, 81 Coleman Street, London, EC2R 5BJ

Tel: 020 7374 4000
Fax: 020 7606 7481

Enquiries:
Enquiries to: The Clerk

Founded:
1322

Organisation type and purpose:
Livery company.

Access to staff:
Contact by letter
Hours: Mon to Fri, 0900 to 1700

Access to building, collection or gallery:
No access other than to staff

WORSHIPFUL COMPANY OF BAKERS

Bakers' Hall, Harp Lane, London, EC3R 6DP

Tel: 020 7623 2223
Fax: 020 7621 1924
E-mail: clerk@bakers.co.uk

Website:
http://www.bakers.co.uk

Founded:
c. 12th century

Organisation type and purpose:
Membership association (membership is by election or invitation).
City of London Livery Company.

Access to staff:
Contact by letter, by telephone, by fax, by e-mail and via website

WORSHIPFUL COMPANY OF BARBERS, THE

Acronym or abbreviation: The Barbers' Company

Barber-Surgeons' Hall, Monkwell Square, Wood Street, London, EC2Y 5BL

Tel: 020 7606 0741
Fax: 020 7606 3857

Website:
http://www.barberscompany.org

Enquiries:
Enquiries to: The Clerk

Founded:
1308

Organisation type and purpose:
Learned society (membership is by election or invitation).
City of London Livery Company.

Subject coverage:
Surgery (up to 1745) and barbery.

Printed publications:
Newsletter (issued to members)

Access to staff:
Contact by letter
Hours: Mon to Fri, 0930 to 1700

Access to building, collection or gallery:
No access other than to staff

WORSHIPFUL COMPANY OF BASKETMAKERS

29 Ingram House, Park Road, Hampton Wick, Kingston upon Thames, Surrey, KT1 4BA

Tel: 020 8943 2343
Fax: 020 8977 6793
E-mail: clerk@basketmakersco.org

Website:
http://www.basketmakersco.org

Enquiries:
Enquiries to: The Clerk
Direct tel: 020 8943 2343
Direct fax: 020 8977 6793
Direct e-mail: clerk@basketmakersco.org

Founded:
1569

Organisation type and purpose:
Membership association (membership is by election or invitation).
City of London Livery Company.

Access to staff:
Contact by letter, by telephone, by fax, by e-mail and via website

WORSHIPFUL COMPANY OF BLACKSMITHS

48 Upwood Road, Lee, London, SE12 8AN

Tel: 020 8318 9684
Fax: 020 8318 9687
E-mail: hammerandhand@supanet.com

Website:
http://www.blacksmithscompany.org.uk

Enquiries:
Enquiries to: Clerk

Founded:
1325

Organisation type and purpose:
Membership association.
City of London Livery Company.

Subject coverage:
The blacksmith craft.

Printed publications:
History of the Company – booklet and leaflet
Directory of Blacksmiths in the UK

Access to staff:
Contact by letter
Hours: Mon to Fri, 0900 to 1700

WORSHIPFUL COMPANY OF BOWYERS

Archer House, Vicarage Crescent, London, SW11 3LF

E-mail: clerk@bowyers.com

Website:
http://www.bowyers.com/public

Enquiries:
Enquiries to: The Clerk
Direct e-mail: clerk@bowyers.com

Founded:
1363

Organisation type and purpose:
Membership association (membership is by election or invitation).
City of London Livery Company.
Registered charity (charity number 270702).

Access to staff:
Contact by letter and by e-mail

WORSHIPFUL COMPANY OF BRODERERS

Ember House, 35–37 Creek Road, East Molesey, Surrey, KT8 9BE

Tel: 020 8941 3116
Fax: 020 8979 5934

Enquiries:
Enquiries to: Clerk
Direct e-mail: office@newbycrouch.co.uk

Founded:
1400

Organisation type and purpose:
City of London Livery Company.

Subject coverage:
The Worshipful Company of Broderers.

Printed publications:
History notes of the Worshipful Company of Broderers and 'Plain Dealing Fellows' (Squadron Leader P R Levy MBE, £20)

Access to staff:
Contact by letter, by telephone, by fax and by e-mail
Hours: Mon to Fri, 0900 to 1730

WORSHIPFUL COMPANY OF BUILDERS' MERCHANTS

4 College Hill, London, EC4R 2RB

Tel: 020 7329 2189
E-mail: wcobm@aol.com

Enquiries:
Enquiries to: The Clerk
Direct e-mail: wcobm@aol.com

Organisation type and purpose:
Membership association (membership is by election or invitation).
City of London Livery Company.

Access to staff:
Contact by letter, by telephone and by e-mail

WORSHIPFUL COMPANY OF BUTCHERS

Acronym or abbreviation: Butchers' Company

Butchers' Hall, 87 Bartholomew Close, London, EC1A 7EB

Tel: 020 7606 4106
Fax: 020 7606 4108

Enquiries:
Enquiries to: Clerk to the Company

Founded:
1198

Organisation type and purpose:
Learned society (membership is by election or invitation), present number of members: 690.

Subject coverage:
City Livery Companies, City of London.

Library catalogue:
All or part available in-house

Printed publications:
Butchers' Company brochure

Access to staff:
Contact by letter, by telephone, by fax and by e-mail. Appointment necessary.
Hours: Mon to Fri, 0900 to 1700

Access to building, collection or gallery:
Prior appointment required
Hours: Mon to Fri, 0900 to 1700

Access for disabled people:
Ramped entry, access to all public areas, toilet facilities

WORSHIPFUL COMPANY OF CARMEN

Five Kings House, 1 Queen Street Place, London EC4R 1QS

Tel: 020 7489 8289
Fax: 020 7236 3313
E-mail: enquiries@thecarmen.co.uk

Website:
http://thecarmen.co.uk

Enquiries:
Enquiries to: Clerk
Direct e-mail: theclerk@thecarmen.co.uk

Founded:
1517

Organisation type and purpose:
Membership association (membership is by election or invitation), present number of members: 550, voluntary organisation.
City of London Livery Company.

Printed publications:
Carr and Carman (Birch C, available for purchase, direct)

Access to staff:
Contact by letter, by telephone, by fax, by e-mail, in person and via website. Appointment necessary. Letter of introduction required. All charged.
Hours: Mon to Fri, 0900 to 1700

WORSHIPFUL COMPANY OF CHARTERED ACCOUNTANTS IN ENGLAND AND WALES

The Rustlings, Valley Close, Studham, Dunstable, Bedfordshire, LU6 2QN

Tel: 01582 872070
E-mail: clerk@wccaew.org.uk

Website:
http://www.wccaew.org.uk

Enquiries:
Enquiries to: The Clerk
Direct tel: 01582 872070
Direct e-mail: clerk@wccaew.org.uk

Founded:
1977

Organisation type and purpose:
Membership association (membership is by election or invitation).
City of London Livery Company.
To foster the profession of accountancy and to provide social intercourse and mutual information between members of the Institute of Chartered Accountants in England and Wales.

Access to staff:
Contact by letter, by telephone, by e-mail and via website

WORSHIPFUL COMPANY OF CHARTERED ARCHITECTS

82A Muswell Hill Road, London, N10 3JR

Tel: 020 8292 4893
Fax: 020 8292 4893
E-mail: coleadams@architects-livery-company.org

Website:
http://www.architects-livery-company.org

Enquiries:
Enquiries to: The Clerk
Direct tel: 020 8292 4893
Direct fax: 020 8292 4893
Direct e-mail: coleadams@architects-livery-company.org

Founded:
1988

Organisation type and purpose:
Membership association (membership is by election or invitation). City of London Livery Company. To advance the profession of architecture, to act as an independent forum for fellowship and exchange of ideas between members.

Access to staff:
Contact by letter, by telephone, by fax, by e-mail and via website

WORSHIPFUL COMPANY OF CHARTERED SECRETARIES AND ADMINISTRATORS

Saddlers' House, 3rd Floor, 40 Gutter Lane, London, EC2V 6BR

Tel: 020 7726 2955
E-mail: clerk@wccsa.org.uk

Website:
http://www.wccsa.org.uk

Enquiries:
Enquiries to: Clerk

Organisation type and purpose:
Membership association (membership is by election or invitation).
City of London Livery Company.

Access to staff:
Contact by letter, by telephone and by e-mail

WORSHIPFUL COMPANY OF CLOCKMAKERS

The Salters' Hall, Fore Street, London EC2Y 5DE

Tel: 020 7638 5500
Fax: 020 7638 5522
E-mail: clockmakersco@aol.com

Website:
http://www.clockmakers.org

Enquiries:
Enquiries to: Clerk

Founded:
1631

Organisation type and purpose:
Membership association (membership is by election or invitation), present number of members: 480, registered charity (charity number 275380), museum.

Subject coverage:
Antiquarian horology – in particular clockmaking in London.

Museum or gallery collection, archive, or library special collection:
Fine horological library (founded 1813) consisting of books and manuscripts, together with a collection of clocks and watches, which were also originally (1817) intended for reference purposes

Non-library collection catalogue:
All or part available in print

continued overleaf

Printed publications:
Photographs of the Collection from Bridgemans
   Art Library

Access to staff:
Contact by letter, by telephone, by fax and by e-
mail. Appointment necessary.
Hours: Mon, Wed, Fri, 1000 to 1600

Clockmakers' Museum is at the:
Guildhall Library
   Aldermanbury, London, EC2P 2EJ; tel: 020 7332
   1865

WORSHIPFUL COMPANY OF COACHMAKERS AND COACH-HARNESS MAKERS OF LONDON

Elm Tree Cottage, Bottom House Farm Lane,
Chalfont St Giles, Buckinghamshire

Tel: 07971 017255
Fax: 01494876728

Website:
http://www.coachmakers.co.uk

Enquiries:
Enquiries to: The Clerk
Direct e-mail: gerry@thebunns.com

Founded:
1677

Organisation type and purpose:
Membership association (membership is by
election or invitation).
City of London Livery Company.

Access to staff:
Contact by letter, by telephone, by fax and via
website

WORSHIPFUL COMPANY OF CONSTRUCTORS

Ragby House, 157 Sidney Road, Walton on
Thames, Surrey, KT12 3SA

Tel: 01932 253212
E-mail: m.kearsley1@ntworld.com

Website:
http://www.constructorscompany.co.uk

Enquiries:
Enquiries to: The Clerk

Founded:
1990

Organisation type and purpose:
Membership association (membership is by
election or invitation).
City of London Livery Company.
To bring together those professionally qualified
individuals concerned with all aspects of building
design, execution, management, vision and
economic appraisal within the framework of
Guildery and Livery in the City of London.

Access to staff:
Contact by letter, by telephone and by e-mail

WORSHIPFUL COMPANY OF COOKS

Coombe Ridge, Thursley Road, Churt, Farnham,
Surrey, GU10 2LQ

Tel: 01428 606670
E-mail: clerk@cookslivery.org.uk

Website:
http://www.cookslivery.org.uk

Enquiries:
Enquiries to: The Clerk
Direct tel: 01428 606670
Direct e-mail: clerk@cookslivery.org.uk

Founded:
1482

Organisation type and purpose:
Membership association (membership is by
election or invitation).
City of London Livery Company.
To support the City, the modern catering trade and
charitable activities.

Access to staff:
Contact by letter, by telephone and by e-mail

WORSHIPFUL COMPANY OF COOPERS

Coopers' Hall, 13 Devonshire Square, London,
EC2M 4TH

Tel: 020 7247 9577
Fax: 020 7377 8061
E-mail: clerk@coopers-hall.co.uk

Website:
http://www.coopers-hall.co.uk

Enquiries:
Enquiries to: The Clerk
Direct e-mail: clerk@coopers-hall.co.uk

Founded:
1501

Organisation type and purpose:
Membership association (membership is by
election or invitation).
City of London Livery Company.

Access to staff:
Contact by letter, by telephone, by fax, by e-mail
and via website

WORSHIPFUL COMPANY OF CORDWAINERS

Acronym or abbreviation: Cordwainers Company

8 Warwick Court, Gray's Inn, London, WC1R 5DJ

Tel: 020 7242 4411
Fax: 020 7242 3366

Enquiries:
Enquiries to: The Clerk (Chief Executive)
Direct e-mail: office@cordwainers.org

Founded:
1272

Organisation type and purpose:
Membership association (membership is by
election or invitation), present number of
members: 161.
City Livery Company.

**Museum or gallery collection, archive, or library
special collection:**
Archives and records are held in The Guildhall
   Library

Access to staff:
Contact by letter
Hours: Mon to Fri, 0930 to 1730

Access to building, collection or gallery:
Prior appointment required

WORSHIPFUL COMPANY OF CURRIERS

Hedgerley, The Leaze, Ashton Keynes, Wiltshire,
SN6 6PE

Tel: 01285 861017
E-mail: clerk@curriers.co.uk

Website:
http://www.curriers.co.uk

Enquiries:
Enquiries to: The Clerk

Founded:
1367

Granted Royal Charter of Incorporation:
(year of change 1605)

WORSHIPFUL COMPANY OF CUTLERS

Cutlers' Hall, Warwick Lane, London, EC4M 7BR

Tel: 020 7248 1866
E-mail: clerk@cutlerslondon.co.uk

Website:
http://www.cutlerslondon.co.uk

Enquiries:
Enquiries to: The Clerk
Direct tel: 020 7248 1866
Direct e-mail: clerk@cutlerslondon.co.uk

Founded:
1416

Organisation type and purpose:
Membership association (membership is by
election or invitation).
City of London Livery Company.

**Museum or gallery collection, archive, or library
special collection:**
Cutlery
Medals

Access to staff:
Contact by letter, by telephone, by e-mail and via
website

WORSHIPFUL COMPANY OF DISTILLERS

71 Lincoln's Inn Fields, London, WC2A 3JF

Tel: 020 7405 7091
E-mail: chughes@bcmw.co.uk

Enquiries:
Enquiries to: The Clerk

Organisation type and purpose:
Membership association (membership is by
election or invitation).
City of London Livery Company.

Access to staff:
Contact by letter, by telephone and by e-mail

WORSHIPFUL COMPANY OF DYERS

Dyers Hall, 11–13 Dowgate Hill, London, EC4R
2ST

Tel: 020 7236 7197
Fax: 020 7248 0774
E-mail: clerk@dyerscompany.com

Website:
http://www.dyerscompany.co.uk

Enquiries:
Enquiries to: The Clerk

Founded:
1471

Organisation type and purpose:
Membership association (membership is by
election or invitation).
City of London Livery Company.

Access to staff:
Contact by letter, by telephone, by fax, by e-mail
and via website

Organisation type and purpose (top right):
City of London Livery Company.
Membership association (membership is by
election or invitation).
Historical, charitable, social

Access to staff:
Contact by letter, by telephone, by e-mail and via
website

WORSHIPFUL COMPANY OF ENGINEERS

Wax Chandlers' Hall, 6 Gresham Street, London, EC2V 7AD

Tel: 020 7726 4830
Fax: 020 7726 4820
E-mail: clerk@engineerscompany.org.uk

Website:
http://www.engineerscompany.org.uk

Enquiries:
Enquiries to: The Clerk

Organisation type and purpose:
Membership association (membership is by election or invitation).
City of London Livery Company.
To promote the development and advancement of the science, art and practice of engineering through a series of lectures, events and visits.

Access to staff:
Contact by letter, by telephone, by fax, by e-mail and via website

WORSHIPFUL COMPANY OF ENVIRONMENTAL CLEANERS

Acronym or abbreviation: WCEC

6 Grange Meadow, Elmswell, Bury St Edmunds, IP30 9GE

Tel: 01359 242947
Fax: 01359 242947
E-mail: michael.bizley@environmental-cleaners.com

Website:
http://www.environmental-cleaners.com

Enquiries:
Enquiries to: Clerk of the Company

Founded:
1986

Organisation type and purpose:
Membership association (membership is by election or invitation).
City of London Livery Company.
To encourage and maintain high standards of practice and integrity through social and professional exchange, while supporting and promoting education, training and research projects within the industry

Access to staff:
Contact by letter, by telephone, by fax, by e-mail and via website

WORSHIPFUL COMPANY OF FAN MAKERS

Skinners' Hall, 8 Dowgate Hill, London, EC4R 2SP

Tel: 020 7329 4633
Fax: 020 7329 4633
E-mail: clerk@fanmakers.com

Website:
http://www.fanmakers.com

Enquiries:
Enquiries to: The Clerk
Direct tel: 020 7329 4633
Direct e-mail: clerk@fanmakers.com

Founded:
1709

Organisation type and purpose:
Membership association (membership is by election or invitation).
City of London Livery Company.

Museum or gallery collection, archive, or library special collection:
Collection of 250 fans

Access to staff:
Contact by letter, by telephone, by fax, by e-mail and via website

WORSHIPFUL COMPANY OF FARMERS

Red Copse End, Red Copse Lane, Boars Hill, Oxford, OX1 5ER

Tel: 01865 321580
E-mail: clerk@wcfarmers.freeserve.co.uk

Enquiries:
Enquiries to: The Clerk
Direct tel: 01865 321580
Direct e-mail: clerk@wcfarmers.freeserve.co.uk

Founded:
1952

Organisation type and purpose:
Membership association (membership is by election or invitation).
City of London Livery Company.

Access to staff:
Contact by letter, by telephone and by e-mail

WORSHIPFUL COMPANY OF FARRIERS

19 Queen Street, Chipperfield, Kings Langley, Hertfordshire, WD4 9BT

Tel: 01923 260747
Fax: 01923 261677
E-mail: theclerk@wcf.org.uk

Website:
http://www.wcf.org.uk

Enquiries:
Enquiries to: Clerk

Organisation type and purpose:
Membership association.
City of London Livery Company.

Access to staff:
Contact by letter, by telephone and by fax
Hours: Mon to Fri, 0900 to 1700

WORSHIPFUL COMPANY OF FELTMAKERS

Formal name: The Worshipful Company of Feltmakers of London

Clerk to the Trustees, Post Cottage, Greywell, Hook, Hampshire, RG29 1DA

Website:
http://www.feltmakers.co.uk/

Enquiries:
Enquiries to: The Clerk

Founded:
1604

Organisation type and purpose:
Membership association (membership is by election or invitation).
City of London Livery Company.

Access to staff:
Contact by letter, by telephone and by e-mail

Administers:
The Feltmakers Charitable Foundation (Charity No. 259906)

WORSHIPFUL COMPANY OF FIREFIGHTERS

20 Aldermanbury, London, EC2V 7GF

Tel: 020 7600 1666
Fax: 020 7600 1666
E-mail: clerk@firefighterscompany.org

Website:
http://www.firefighterscompany.org

Enquiries:
Enquiries to: The Clerk

Founded:
1988

Formerly called:
The Company of Firefighters, The Guild of Firefighters

Organisation type and purpose:
Membership association (membership is by subscription, election or invitation), present number of members: 155, registered charity. Livery company.

Subject coverage:
Firefighting and associated products, industry and activities.

Trade and statistical information:
Fire fighting and protection.

Access to staff:
Contact by letter
Hours: Mon to Fri, 0900 to 1700

WORSHIPFUL COMPANY OF FISHMONGERS

Acronym or abbreviation: The Fishmongers' Company

Fishmongers' Hall, London Bridge, London, EC4R 9EL

Tel: 020 7626 3531
Fax: 020 7929 1389
E-mail: clerk@fishhall.co.uk

Website:
http://www.fishhall.co.uk

Enquiries:
Enquiries to: The Clerk
Other contacts: Chief Fisheries Inspector for Billingsgate Market or other trade enquiries.

Founded:
1272

Organisation type and purpose:
Membership association (membership is by election or invitation), present number of members: 750.
Quality control, health and hygiene inspection service at Billingsgate Market.

Library catalogue:
All or part available in-house

Printed publications:
Fishmongers' Company Cook Book
Order printed publications from: Fishmongers' Hall

Publications list:
Available in print

Access to staff:
Contact by letter, by telephone, by fax and by e-mail. Appointment necessary.
Hours: Mon to Fri, 0900 to 1700

Access to building, collection or gallery:
Prior appointment required

Connections with:
Gresham's School
  Holt, Norfolk, NR25 6EA; tel: 01263 713271

WORSHIPFUL COMPANY OF FLETCHERS

Farmers' and Fletchers' Hall, 3 Cloth Street, EC1A 7LD

Tel: 020 7600 2204
Fax: 020 7606 4971
E-mail: ff@chesterboyd.co.uk

Website:
http://www.fletchers.org.uk

Enquiries:
Enquiries to: The Clerk
Direct e-mail: fletchersclerk@aol.com

Founded:
1371

Organisation type and purpose:
Membership association (membership is by election or invitation).

continued overleaf

City of London Livery Company.

Access to staff:
Contact by letter, by telephone, by fax and by e-mail

WORSHIPFUL COMPANY OF FOUNDERS

Founders' Hall, Number One, Cloth Fair, London, EC1A 7JQ

E-mail: founderscompany@aol.com

Website:
http://www.foundersco.org.uk

Enquiries:
Enquiries to: The Clerk
Direct tel: 01273 858700
Direct fax: 01273 858900
Direct e-mail: founderscompany@aol.com

Organisation type and purpose:
Membership association (membership is by election or invitation).
City of London Livery Company.
To promote technical education and research in founding

Access to staff:
Contact by letter, by telephone, by fax and by e-mail

WORSHIPFUL COMPANY OF FRAMEWORK KNITTERS, THE

86 Park Drive, Upminster, Essex, RM14 3AS

Tel: 01708 510439
Fax: 01708 510439
E-mail: clerk@frameworkknitters.co.uk

Website:
http://www.frameworkknitters.co.uk

Enquiries:
Enquiries to: Clerk to the Company

Founded:
1713

Organisation type and purpose:
Membership association (membership is by election or invitation), present number of members: 215.
A City of London livery company.

Printed publications:
A history of the company

Access to staff:
Contact by letter, by telephone, by fax, by e-mail, in person and via website. Appointment necessary.
Hours: Upminster: Mon to Fri, 0900 to 1700
Oadby: Mon to Fri, 0930 to 1330

Access to building, collection or gallery:
Prior appointment required
Special comments: Archives are deposited at the Guildhall Library.

Subsidiary:
Framework Knitters Homes
Corah House, Framework Knitters Cottages, Stoughton Road, Oadby, Leicestershire, LE2 4FQ; tel: 01162 712171; fax: 01162 713894; e-mail: fwkcottages@oadby.fs.business.co.uk

WORSHIPFUL COMPANY OF FRUITERERS

Chapelstones, 84 High Street, Codford St Mary, Warminster, Wiltshire, BA12 0ND

Tel: 01985 850682
E-mail: clerk@fruiterers.org.uk

Website:
http://www.fruit-baskets.co.uk/asp/default.asp

Enquiries:
Enquiries to: The Clerk
Direct tel: 01985 850682
Direct e-mail: clerk@fruiterers.org.uk

Founded:
1463

Organisation type and purpose:
Membership association (membership is by election or invitation).
City of London Livery Company.
To promote excellence across all sectors of the fruit industry and to support education and research within it.

Access to staff:
Contact by letter, by telephone, by fax and by e-mail

WORSHIPFUL COMPANY OF FUELLERS

26 Merrick Square, London, SE1 4JB

E-mail: clerk@fuellers.co.uk

Website:
http://www.fuellers.co.uk

Enquiries:
Enquiries to: The Clerk
Direct tel: 020 7234 0760
Direct e-mail: clerk@fuellers.co.uk

Organisation type and purpose:
Membership association (membership is by election or invitation).
City of London Livery Company.
To foster the business of persons involved in providing energy for the home, industry, commerce and export.

Access to staff:
Contact by letter, by telephone, by e-mail and via website

WORSHIPFUL COMPANY OF FURNITURE MAKERS

Furniture Makers' Hall, 12 Austin Friars, London, EC2N 2HE

Tel: 020 7256 5558
Fax: 020 7256 5155
E-mail: clerk@furnituremakers.org.uk

Website:
http://www.furnituremakers.org.uk

Enquiries:
Enquiries to: The Clerk

Founded:
1951

Organisation type and purpose:
Membership association (membership is by election or invitation).
City of London Livery Company.
To foster both the craft and the industry of furniture-making, marketing and retailing in the United Kingdom.

Access to staff:
Contact by letter, by fax, by e-mail and via website

WORSHIPFUL COMPANY OF GARDENERS OF LONDON

25 Luke Street, London, EC2A 4AR

Tel: 020 7953 2321
E-mail: clerk@gardenerscompany.org.uk

Website:
http://www.gardenerscompany.org.uk

Enquiries:
Enquiries to: The Clerk
Direct tel: 020 7953 2321
Direct e-mail: clerk@gardenerscompany.org.uk

Organisation type and purpose:
Membership association (membership is by election or invitation).
City of London Livery Company.

To promote the art and practice of good gardening throughout the country and especially in the London area, to support charitable activities connected with horticulture or the City of London, and to beautify the City of London by encouraging the display of flowers and foliage.

Access to staff:
Contact by letter, by telephone, by e-mail and via website

WORSHIPFUL COMPANY OF GIRDLERS

Girdlers' Hall, Basinghall Avenue, London, EC2V 5DD

Tel: 020 7638 0488
E-mail: clerk@girdlers.co.uk

Enquiries:
Enquiries to: The Clerk
Direct e-mail: clerk@girdlers.co.uk

Founded:
1327

Organisation type and purpose:
Membership association (membership is by election or invitation).
City of London Livery Company.

Access to staff:
Contact by letter, by telephone, by e-mail and via website

WORSHIPFUL COMPANY OF GLASS SELLERS

57 Witley Court, Coram Street, London, WC1N 1HD

Tel: 020 7837 2231
Fax: 020 7837 2231
E-mail: info@glass-sellers.co.uk

Website:
http://www.glass-sellers.co.uk

Enquiries:
Enquiries to: The Honorary Clerk
Direct tel: 020 7837 2231
Direct e-mail: info@glass-sellers.co.uk

Founded:
1664

Organisation type and purpose:
Membership association (membership is by election or invitation).
City of London Livery Company.
To stimulate interest in glass in all its aspects and to carry out charitable works, with special emphasis on education.

Access to staff:
Contact by letter, by telephone, by fax, by e-mail and via website

WORSHIPFUL COMPANY OF GLAZIERS AND PAINTERS OF GLASS

Acronym or abbreviation: Glaziers Company

Glaziers' Hall, 9 Montague Close, London Bridge, London, SE1 9DD

Tel: 020 7403 6652
Fax: 020 7403 6652
E-mail: info@worshipfulglaziers.com

Website:
http://www.worshipfulglaziers.com

Enquiries:
Enquiries to: Clerk
Direct e-mail: clerk@worshipfulglaziers.com

Founded:
1638

Organisation type and purpose:
City of London Livery Company.

Membership association (membership is by election or invitation), present number of members: 300.

Subject coverage:
Advice on stained glass, particularly on conservation of historic glass.

Museum or gallery collection, archive, or library special collection:
Library on stained glass

Library catalogue:
All or part available in-house

Access to staff:
Contact by letter, by telephone, by fax and by e-mail. Appointment necessary.
Hours: Mon to Fri, 1000 to 1600

Access for disabled people:
Ramped entry, access to all public areas, toilet facilities

WORSHIPFUL COMPANY OF GLOVERS

Cherry Tree Cottage, 73 Clapham Manor Street, London, SW4 6DS

E-mail: clerk@thegloverscompany.org

Website:
http://www.thegloverscompany.org

Enquiries:
Enquiries to: The Clerk
Direct e-mail: clerk@thegloverscompany.org

Founded:
1349

Organisation type and purpose:
Membership association (membership is by election or invitation).
City of London Livery Company.

Access to staff:
Contact by letter, by e-mail and via website

WORSHIPFUL COMPANY OF GOLD AND SILVER WYRE DRAWERS

Bee Cottage, North Heath, Chieveley, Berkshire, RG20 8UA

Tel: 01635 247014
Fax: 01635 247014
E-mail: clerk@gswd.co.uk

Website:
http://www.gswd.co.uk

Enquiries:
Direct tel: 01635 247014
Direct fax: 01635 247014
Direct e-mail: clerk@gswd.co.uk

Founded:
1423

Organisation type and purpose:
Membership association (membership is by election or invitation).
City of London Livery Company.

Access to staff:
Contact by letter, by telephone, by fax, by e-mail and via website

WORSHIPFUL COMPANY OF GOLDSMITHS

Goldsmiths' Hall, Foster Lane, London, EC2V 6BN

Tel: 020 7606 7010
Fax: 020 7606 1511
E-mail: library@thegoldsmiths.co.uk

Website:
http://www.thegoldsmiths.co.uk
Basic information on the Goldsmiths' Company, history and publications.

Enquiries:
Enquiries to: Librarian
Other contacts: Assistant to the Librarian for special responsibility for A-V material.

Founded:
1327

Organisation type and purpose:
Membership association (membership is by qualification), present number of members: 1500. The Goldsmiths' Company is one of the Twelve Great Livery Companies of the City of London with its roots in the trade guilds of the Middle Ages.
It is responsible for:
operating the London Assay Office which hallmarks precious metal articles, gold, silver and platinum,
promoting excellence in design and craftmanship of silver and jewellery, through exhibitions and other projects,
administering charitable trusts to help the disadvantaged and specific areas of education.

Subject coverage:
Assaying and hallmarking of precious metals, gold plate, silver and jewellery, antique and modern, regalia.

Museum or gallery collection, archive, or library special collection:
Archives of the Company from 1334
Photographic collection
Slide collection
Twining Collection (books on regalia)
A unique collection of antique and modern silver, modern jewellery and modern art medals

Non-library collection catalogue:
All or part available in-house

Library catalogue:
All or part available in-house

Printed publications:
Hallmark: A History of the London Assay Office (Forbes J S)
Unravelling the Mystery: The Story of the Goldsmiths' Company in the C20th (Jenkins P)
Treasures of the C20th (Ransome Wallis R)
Goldsmiths' Review (annually)
Variety of catalogues and booklets

Microform publications:
Film loan collection (list available)

Electronic and video publications:
Video loan collection (list available)

Publications list:
Available online and in print

Access to staff:
Contact by letter, by telephone, by fax and by e-mail. Appointment necessary.
Hours: Mon to Fri, 1000 to 1645

Access to building, collection or gallery:
Prior appointment required

Access for disabled people:
Disabled entrance, bathroom facilities, street parking
Special comments: Parking subject to availability. Entry assisted by a device and staff.

Subsidiary body:
London Assay Office

WORSHIPFUL COMPANY OF GROCERS

Grocers' Hall, Princes Street, London, EC2R 8AD

Tel: 020 7606 3113
Fax: 020 7600 3082
E-mail: clerk@grocershall.co.uk

Website:
http://www.grocershall.co.uk

Enquiries:
Enquiries to: The Clerk

Founded:
c. 12th century

Organisation type and purpose:
Membership association (membership is by election or invitation).
City of London Livery Company.

Access to staff:
Contact by letter, by telephone, by fax, by e-mail and via website

WORSHIPFUL COMPANY OF GUNMAKERS

Proof House, 48–50 Commercial Road, London, E1 1LP

Tel: 020 7481 2695
E-mail: clerk@gunmakers.org.uk

Enquiries:
Enquiries to: The Clerk
Direct tel: 020 7481 2695
Direct e-mail: clerk@gunmakers.org.uk

Founded:
1637

Organisation type and purpose:
Membership assocation (membership is by election or invitation).
City of London Livery Company.

Access to staff:
Contact by letter, by telephone, by e-mail and via website

WORSHIPFUL COMPANY OF HACKNEY CARRIAGE DRIVERS

25 The Grove, Parkfield Latimer, Buckinghamshire, HP5 1VE

Website:
http://www.wchcd.com

Enquiries:
Enquiries to: The Clerk

Founded:
2004

Organisation type and purpose:
Membership association (membership is by election or invitation).
City of London Livery Company.
To raise public awareness of the extremely high standards of the London Hackney Carriage trade and industry.

Access to staff:
Contact by letter

WORSHIPFUL COMPANY OF HORNERS

C/o The Clergy House, Hide Place, London, SW1P 4NJ

Tel: 020 7834 1575
E-mail: horners.clerk@btinternet.com

Website:
http://www.horners.org.uk

Enquiries:
Enquiries to: The Clerk
Direct tel: 020 7834 1575
Direct e-mail: horners.clerk@btinternet.com

Organisation type and purpose:
Membership association (membership is by election or invitation).
City of London Livery Company.

Access to staff:
Contact by letter, by telephone and by e-mail

WORSHIPFUL COMPANY OF INFORMATION TECHNOLOGISTS

39A Bartholomew Close, London, EC1A 7JN

continued overleaf

Tel: 020 7600 1992
Fax: 020 7600 1991
E-mail: info@wcit.org.uk

Website:
http://www.wcit.org.uk

Enquiries:
Enquiries to: The Clerk
Direct e-mail: michael@wcit.org.uk

Founded:
1992

Organisation type and purpose:
Membership association (membership is by
election or invitation).
City of London Livery Company.

Access to staff:
Contact by letter, by telephone, by fax, by e-mail
and via website

Access for disabled people:
Yes

WORSHIPFUL COMPANY OF INNHOLDERS

Innholders' Hall, 29–30 College Street, London,
EC4R 2RH

Tel: 020 7236 6703
Fax: 020 7236 0059
E-mail: mail@innholders.co.uk

Enquiries:
Enquiries to: Information Officer

Founded:
1514

Organisation type and purpose:
Voluntary organisation.

Access to staff:
Contact by letter, by telephone, by fax and by e-
mail
Hours: Mon to Fri, 0900 to 1700

Access to building, collection or gallery:
No access other than to staff

Access for disabled people:
Limited – please enquire prior to visit

WORSHIPFUL COMPANY OF INSURERS

The Insurance Hall, 20 Aldermanbury, London,
EC2V 7HY

Tel: 020 7600 4006
Fax: 020 7972 0153
E-mail: enquiries@wci.org.uk

Website:
http://www.wci.org.uk

Enquiries:
Enquiries to: The Clerk

Founded:
1970

Organisation type and purpose:
Membership association (membership is by
election or invitation).
City of London Livery Company.
To foster the business of Insurers and to provide
social intercourse and mutual information between
members of that business

Access to staff:
Contact by letter, by telephone, by fax, by e-mail
and via website

WORSHIPFUL COMPANY OF IRONMONGERS, THE

Ironmongers' Hall, Shaftesbury Place, Barbican,
London, EC2Y 8AA

Tel: 020 7606 2726
Fax: 020 7600 3519

E-mail: beadle@ironhall.co.uk

Enquiries:
Enquiries to: The Clerk
Other contacts: Hall Manager for conferences and
facilities hire.

Founded:
1463

Organisation type and purpose:
Membership association (membership is by
election or invitation), voluntary organisation.

Access to staff:
Contact by letter, by telephone and by e-mail
Hours: Mon to Fri, 0900 to 1700

Access to building, collection or gallery:
Prior appointment required

Access for disabled people:
Ramped entry, access to all public areas, toilet
facilities

WORSHIPFUL COMPANY OF JOINERS AND CEILERS

75 Meadway Drive, Horsell, Woking, Surrey, GU21
4TF

Fax: 01483 720098
E-mail: info@joinersandceilers.co.uk

Website:
http://www.joinersandceilers.co.uk

Enquiries:
Enquiries to: The Clerk
Direct fax: 01483 720098
Direct e-mail: info@joinersandceilers.co.uk

Organisation type and purpose:
Membership association (membership is by
election or invitation).
City of London Livery Company.

Access to staff:
Contact by letter, by telephone, by e-mail and via
website

WORSHIPFUL COMPANY OF LAUNDERERS

Launderers' Hall, 9 Montague Close, London, SE1
9DD

Enquiries:
Enquiries to: The Clerk
Direct tel: 020 7378 1430

Organisation type and purpose:
Membership association (membership is by
election or invitation).
City of London Livery Company.

Access to staff:
Contact by letter

WORSHIPFUL COMPANY OF LEATHERSELLERS

Acronym or abbreviation: Leathersellers

Leathersellers Hall, St Helen's Place, London,
EC3A 6DQ

Tel: 020 7330 1444
Fax: 020 7330 1445
E-mail: enquiries@leathersellers.co.uk

Website:
http://www.leathersellers.co.uk
Background on Company activities.

Enquiries:
Enquiries to: Chief Executive

Founded:
1444

Organisation type and purpose:
National organisation, membership association
(membership is by election or invitation), present
number of members: 150, voluntary organisation,
registered charity (charity number 278072).

Investment company and grant giving foundation.

Subject coverage:
History of leather trade, history of livery
companies.

Library catalogue:
All or part available in-house

Access to staff:
Contact by letter, by telephone and by e-mail
Hours: Mon to Fri, 0900 to 1700

Access to building, collection or gallery:
Prior appointment required
Hours: Mon to Fri, 1000 to 1600
Special comments: Bona fide researchers only.

WORSHIPFUL COMPANY OF LIGHTMONGERS

Crown Wharf, 11A Coldharbour, Blackwall Reach,
London, E14 9NS

Tel: 020 7515 9055
Fax: 020 7538 5466
E-mail: clerk@lightmongers.org.uk

Website:
http://www.lightmongers.org.uk

Enquiries:
Enquiries to: The Clerk
Direct tel: 020 7515 9055
Direct e-mail: clerk@lightmongers.org.uk

Founded:
1967

Organisation type and purpose:
Membership association (membership is by
election or invitation).
City of London Livery Company.

Access to staff:
Contact via website

WORSHIPFUL COMPANY OF LORINERS

8 Portland Square, Wapping, London, E1W 2QR

Tel: 020 7709 0222
E-mail: clerk@loriner.co.uk

Website:
http://www.loriner.co.uk

Enquiries:
Enquiries to: The Clerk
Direct e-mail: clerk@loriner.co.uk

Founded:
1261

Organisation type and purpose:
Membership association (membership is by
election or invitation).
City of London Livery Company.
To maintain manufacturing standards in the trade
and the encouragement of the proper use of bits,
spurs, stirrups, buckles, bridles, saddle trees and
other metal parts of horse tack, together with
support for the Mayoralty of the City of London
and good fellowship amongst the Livery.

Access to staff:
Contact by letter, by telephone and by e-mail

WORSHIPFUL COMPANY OF MAKERS OF PLAYING CARDS

Acronym or abbreviation: WCMPC

Flat 5, 15 Greycoat Place, London, SW1P 1SB

Tel: 020 7799 3556
Fax: 020 7799 3557

Enquiries:
Enquiries to: Archivist
Other contacts: Clerk

Founded:
1628

Organisation type and purpose:
Membership association (membership is by
election or invitation).
City of London Livery Company and with its own,
separate Charitable Trust.

Subject coverage:
Origins of playing cards world-wide, their
manufacture, history, use and games, also ancillary
items such as card games, tarot cards etc.

**Museum or gallery collection, archive, or library
special collection:**
Famous and large collection of playing cards, kept
(on permanent loan) at the Guildhall Library.
Prior notice is required for an examination of
most exhibits

Printed publications:
Small history booklet available to genuinely
interested enquirers

Access to staff:
Contact by letter, by telephone, by fax and by e-
mail
Hours: Mon to Fri, 0900 to 1700

WORSHIPFUL COMPANY OF MANAGEMENT CONSULTANTS

Copperfield, The Ridgeway, Cranleigh, Surrey,
GU6 7HR

Tel: 01483 271459
E-mail: clerk@wcomw.org.uk

Website:
http://www.comc.org.uk

Enquiries:
Enquiries to: The Clerk
Direct tel: 01483 271459
Direct e-mail: clerk@wcomc.org.uk

Founded:
1993

Organisation type and purpose:
Membership association (membership is by
election or invitation).
City of London Livery Company.

Access to staff:
Contact by letter, by telephone and by e-mail

WORSHIPFUL COMPANY OF MARKETORS

13 Hall Gardens, Colney Heath, St Alban's,
Hertfordshire, AL4 0QF

Tel: 01727 824446
Fax: 01727 822652
E-mail: clerk@marketors.org

Website:
http://www.marketors.co.uk

Enquiries:
Enquiries to: The Clerk
Direct tel: 01727 824446
Direct e-mail: clerk@marketors.org

Founded:
1978

Organisation type and purpose:
Membership association (membership is by
election or invitation).
City of London Livery Company.
To promote excellence in marketing practice and
education, support for the interests of the City of
London as well as fellowship amongst its
members.

Access to staff:
Contact by letter, by telephone, by fax, by e-mail
and via website

WORSHIPFUL COMPANY OF MASONS, THE

22 Cannon Hill, Southgate, London, N14 6LG

Tel: 020 8882 9520
Fax: 020 8882 9520
E-mail: clerk@masonslivery.co.uk

Website:
http://www.masonslivery.co.uk

Enquiries:
Enquiries to: Clerk

Founded:
1472

Organisation type and purpose:
City of London Livery Company.

Subject coverage:
City of London, stonemasonry.

Access to staff:
Contact by letter, by telephone, by fax and by e-
mail
Hours: Mon, Wed, Fri, 0900 to 1700

WORSHIPFUL COMPANY OF MERCERS

Acronym or abbreviation: Mercers' Company

Mercers' Hall, Ironmonger Lane, London, EC2V
8HE

Tel: 020 7726 4991
Fax: 020 7600 1158
E-mail: mail@mercers.co.uk

Website:
http://www.mercers.co.uk

Enquiries:
Enquiries to: Archivist and Curator
Direct tel: 020 7776 7244
Direct e-mail: janer@mercers.co.uk

Founded:
1394

Organisation type and purpose:
Membership association (membership is by
election or invitation), present number of
members: 300+.
City of London Livery Company.
Fraternity, corporate body and charitable
foundation.

Subject coverage:
History of the Mercers' Company and its
associated trusts and charities.

**Museum or gallery collection, archive, or library
special collection:**
Mercers' Company archives 1347 to present and art
collection.

Non-library collection catalogue:
All or part available in-house

Library catalogue:
All or part available in-house

Printed publications:
General information booklets and bibliographies
available free of charge

Publications list:
Available in print

Access to staff:
Contact by letter, by telephone, by fax, by e-mail
and via website. Appointment necessary.
Hours: Wed to Fri, 0930 to 1700

Access to building, collection or gallery:
No access other than to staff; prior appointment
required

Access for disabled people:
Level entry, toilet facilities

WORSHIPFUL COMPANY OF MUSICIANS

6th Floor, 2 London Wall Buildings, London,
EC2M 5PP

Tel: 020 7496 8980
Fax: 020 7588 3633

Website:
http://www.wcom.org.uk
General information on the livery and details of
awards and grants.

Enquiries:
Enquiries to: Clerk
Other contacts: Deputy Clerk; email: deputyclerk@
wcom.org.uk

Founded:
1500

Organisation type and purpose:
Membership association (membership is by
election or invitation), registered charity.

Subject coverage:
Grants.

**Museum or gallery collection, archive, or library
special collection:**
Archives deposited at the Guildhall Library

Access to staff:
Contact by letter and by e-mail
Hours: Mon to Fri, 0900 to 1700

WORSHIPFUL COMPANY OF NEEDLEMAKERS

5 Staple Inn, London, WC1V 7QH

Tel: 020 7242 5031

Enquiries:
Enquiries to: The Clerk
Direct tel: 020 7242 5031
Direct e-mail: michael@hobsonarditti.com

Founded:
1656

Organisation type and purpose:
Membership association (membership is by
election or invitation).
City of London Livery Company.

Access to staff:
Contact by letter, by telephone and by e-mail

WORSHIPFUL COMPANY OF PAINTER-STAINERS

Acronym or abbreviation: Painter-Stainers' Company

Painters' Hall, 9 Little Trinity Lane, London, EC4V
2AD

Tel: 020 7236 6258
Fax: 020 7236 0500
E-mail: beadle@painters-hall.co.uk

Website:
http://www.painters-hall.co.uk
Brief history and details of Painters' Hall. Basic
listing and details of the various rooms available
for hire at Painters' Hall.

Enquiries:
Enquiries to: Clerk
Direct tel: 020 7236 7070
Direct fax: 020 7236 7074
Direct e-mail: clerk@painters-hall.co.uk

Founded:
1268

Formed by the amalgamation of:
Worshipful Company of Stainers (year of change
1268–1502); Worshipful Company of Painters
(year of change 1283–1502)

Organisation type and purpose:
Membership association (membership is by
election or invitation), present number of
members: 542, registered charity (charity number
200001), museum, historic building, house or site,
suitable for ages: 16+.
Livery company.

Subject coverage:
Historical details of the Company and its
membership.

continued overleaf

Museum or gallery collection, archive, or library special collection:
Assorted paintings and silver of varying degrees of interest
Charters and other documents of historical interest

Non-library collection catalogue:
All or part available in-house

Access to staff:
Contact by telephone, by fax and by e-mail.
Appointment necessary.
Hours: Mon to Fri, 0900 to 1700

Access to building, collection or gallery:
Prior appointment required

Access for disabled people:
Access to all public areas, toilet facilities

WORSHIPFUL COMPANY OF PATTENMAKERS

3 The High Street, Sutton Valence, Kent, ME17 3AG

Tel: 01622 842440
E-mail: rwmurfin@btinternet.com

Website:
http://www.pattenmakers.co.uk

Enquiries:
Enquiries to: The Clerk
Direct tel: 01622 842440
Direct e-mail: rwmurfin@btinternet.com

Founded:
c. 14th century

Organisation type and purpose:
Membership association (membership is by election or invitation).
City of London Livery Company.

Access to staff:
Contact by letter, by telephone, by e-mail and via website

WORSHIPFUL COMPANY OF PAVIORS

3 Ridgemount Gardens, Enfield, Middlesex, EN2 8QL

Tel: 020 8366 1566
E-mail: clerk@paviorscompany.org.uk

Website:
http://www.paviors.org.uk

Enquiries:
Enquiries to: The Clerk
Direct tel: 020 8366 1566
Direct e-mail: clerk@paviorscompany.org.uk

Founded:
1479

Organisation type and purpose:
Membership association (membership is by election or invitation).
City of London Livery Company.

Access to staff:
Contact by letter, by telephone and by e-mail

WORSHIPFUL COMPANY OF PEWTERERS

Acronym or abbreviation: The Pewterers' Company

Pewterers' Hall, Oat Lane, London, EC2V 7DE

Tel: 020 7397 8190
Fax: 020 7600 3896
E-mail: clerk@pewterers.org.uk

Website:
http://www.pewterers.org.uk

Enquiries:
Enquiries to: Clerk (Chief Executive)
Direct e-mail: clerk@pewterers.org.uk

Founded:
1474

Organisation type and purpose:
Membership association (membership is by election or invitation), present number of members: 230, voluntary organisation.
City of London Livery Company.
Custodians of the history of pewter and the pewter trade. Promote pewter and the trade, particularly through youth education.

Subject coverage:
All aspects of antique and modern pewter.

Museum or gallery collection, archive, or library special collection:
A unique collection of antique pewterware
Comprehensive records of pewter and pewterers since the company's first charter in 1474

Printed publications:
Englefields – Two Centuries of Pewtering in London (1996)
History of British Pewter
Short History of the Worshipful Company of Pewterers of London and a Catalogue of Pewterware in its Possession (1968)
Supplementary Catalogue of Pewterware (1979)
Shire Album, Pewter
Techniques of Pewtersmithing (1984)

Access to staff:
Contact by letter, by telephone and by fax.
Appointment necessary.
Hours: Mon to Fri, 0900 to 1700

Headquarters of the:
Association of British Pewter Craftsmen
tel: 0114 266 3084; fax: 0114 267 0910
European Pewter Union
tel: 020 7606 9363; fax: 020 7600 3896; e-mail: epu@pewterers.org.uk

WORSHIPFUL COMPANY OF PLAISTERERS

1 London Wall, London, EC2Y 5JU

Tel: 020 7796 4333
Fax: 020 7796 4334
E-mail: clerk@plaistererslivery.co.uk

Website:
http://www.plaistererslivery.co.uk

Enquiries:
Enquiries to: The Clerk
Direct tel: 020 7796 4333
Direct e-mail: clerk@plaistererslivery.co.uk

Founded:
1501

Organisation type and purpose:
Membership association (membership is by election or invitation).
City of London Livery Company.

Access to staff:
Contact by letter, by telephone, by fax and by e-mail

WORSHIPFUL COMPANY OF PLUMBERS

Acronym or abbreviation: WCP

Wax Chandlers' Hall, 6 Gresham Street, London, EC2V 7AD

Tel: 020 7796 2468
Fax: 020 7796 2468
E-mail: clerk@plumberscompany.org.uk

Website:
http://www.plumberscompany.org

Enquiries:
Enquiries to: Clerk

Founded:
1365

Organisation type and purpose:
Membership association.

City of London Livery Company.

Subject coverage:
Plumbing.

Museum or gallery collection, archive, or library special collection:
Records back to 1365 deposited in the Guildhall Museum

Printed publications:
Short History of Company 1365–1988

Access to staff:
Contact by letter
Hours: Mon to Fri, 0900 to 1700

Connections with:
CORGI (for registered gas fitters)
Institute of Plumbing (for registered plumbers)

WORSHIPFUL COMPANY OF SADDLERS

40 Gutter Lane, Cheapside, London, EC2V 6BR

Tel: 020 7726 8661
Fax: 020 7600 0386
E-mail: clerk@saddlersco.co.uk

Enquiries:
Enquiries to: Clerk

Founded:
early 12th century

Organisation type and purpose:
City of London Livery Company.
Support of trade of saddlery, support of education and charity.

Non-library collection catalogue:
All or part available in-house

Library catalogue:
All or part available in-house

Access to staff:
Contact by letter, by telephone, by fax and by e-mail. Appointment necessary.
Hours: Mon to Fri, 0900 to 1700

WORSHIPFUL COMPANY OF SCIENTIFIC INSTRUMENT MAKERS

Glaziers Hall, 9 Montague Close, London, SE1 9DD

Tel: 020 7407 4832
Fax: 020 7407 1565
E-mail: theclerk@wcsim.co.uk

Website:
http://www.wcsim.co.uk

Enquiries:
Enquiries to: The Clerk
Direct tel: 020 7407 4832
Direct e-mail: theclerk@wcsim.co.uk

Founded:
1956

Organisation type and purpose:
Membership association (membership is by election or invitation).
City of London Livery Company.

Access to staff:
Contact by letter, by telephone, by fax, by e-mail and via website

WORSHIPFUL COMPANY OF SCRIVENERS

HQS Wellington, Temple Stairs, Victoria Embankment, London, WC2R 2PN

Tel: 020 7240 0529
Fax: 020 7497 0645
E-mail: clerk@scriveners.org.uk

Website:
http://www.scriveners.org.uk

Enquiries:
Enquiries to: Clerk

Founded:
1373

Formerly called:
Mysterie of the Writers of the Court Letter

Organisation type and purpose:
Professional body, membership association (membership is by election or invitation), present number of members: 200, registered charity. Livery company of the City of London. Regulating the standards of notaries intending to practise in the City of London.

Subject coverage:
The profession of public notary principally within the City of London, its history and regulation.

Museum or gallery collection, archive, or library special collection:
History and former membership of the company, for which all records are deposited in the City of London Guildhall Library, Aldermanbury, London, EC2P 2EJ

Printed publications:
Regulations and Syllabuses (occasional, free to firms of Scriveners' notaries and to intending apprentices)
Scriveners' Apprentices Examinations (for London notaries) – Rules

Access to staff:
Contact by letter
Hours: Mon, Wed and Thu, 1000 to 1700

WORSHIPFUL COMPANY OF SHIPWRIGHTS

Ironmongers' Hall, Shaftesbury Place, London, EC2Y 8AA

Tel: 020 7606 2376
Fax: 020 7600 8117

Website:
http://www.shipwrights.co.uk

Enquiries:
Enquiries to: Clerk
Direct e-mail: clerk@shipwrights.co.uk

Founded:
pre 1199

Organisation type and purpose:
Membership association (membership is by election or invitation), present number of members: 460, registered charity (charity number 262043 313249).
City of London Livery Company.

Subject coverage:
History of the company.

Access to staff:
Contact by letter, by telephone, by fax and by e-mail. Appointment necessary.
Hours: Mon to Fri, 0900 to 1700

WORSHIPFUL COMPANY OF SKINNERS

Skinners' Hall, 8 Dowgate Hill, EC4R 2SP

Tel: 020 7236 5629
E-mail: beadle@skinners.org.uk

Website:
http://www.skinnershall.co.uk

Enquiries:
Enquiries to: The Clerk
Direct tel: 020 7236 5629
Direct e-mail: beadle@skinners.org.uk

Organisation type and purpose:
Membership association (membership is by election or invitation).
City of London Livery Company.
To increase the prosperity of the Company and to support Skinners' schools.

Access to staff:
Contact by letter, by telephone and by e-mail

WORSHIPFUL COMPANY OF SPECTACLE MAKERS

Formal name: Also known as The Spectacle Makers Company
Acronym or abbreviation: SMC

Apothecaries' Hall, Black Friars Lane, London, EC4V 6EL

Tel: 020 7236 2932
Fax: 020 7329 3249
E-mail: clerk@spectaclemakers.com

Website:
http://www.spectaclemakers.com
Training courses, history.

Enquiries:
Enquiries to: Clerk

Founded:
1629

Organisation type and purpose:
Professional body.
City of London Livery Company.

Subject coverage:
Livery company, optical technicians, optics, history of the company.

Museum or gallery collection, archive, or library special collection:
Company Records
Library, city history, histories of livery companies

Printed publications:
Programmed Learning Booklet
The Barrow Lectures (Fay and Bennett)
Worshipful Company of Spectacle Makers (Frank Law)

Access to staff:
Contact by letter
Hours: Mon to Fri, 0900 to 1700

WORSHIPFUL COMPANY OF TALLOW CHANDLERS

Tallow Chandlers Hall, 4 Dowgate Hill, London, EC4R 2SH

Tel: 020 7248 4726
Fax: 020 7236 0844
E-mail: clerk@tallowchandlers.org

Website:
http://www.tallowchandlers.org

Founded:
c. 1300

Organisation type and purpose:
Membership association (membership is by election or invitation).
City of London Livery Company.

Access to staff:
Contact by letter, by telephone, by fax and by e-mail

WORSHIPFUL COMPANY OF TAX ADVISERS

191 West End Road, Ruislip, HA4 6LD

Tel: 01895 625817
E-mail: clerk@taxadvisers.org.uk

Website:
http://www.taxadvisers.org.uk

Enquiries:
Enquiries to: The Clerk
Direct tel: 01895 625817
Direct e-mail: clerk@taxadvisers.org.uk

Founded:
1995

Organisation type and purpose:
Membership association (membership is by election or invitation).
City of London Livery Company.

Access to staff:
Contact by letter, by telephone and by e-mail

WORSHIPFUL COMPANY OF TIN PLATE WORKERS ALIAS WIRE WORKERS

Acronym or abbreviation: Tin Plate Workers' Company

Highbanks, Ferry Road, Surlingham, Norfolk, NR14 7AR

Tel: 0845 643 9967
E-mail: clerk@tinplateworkers.co.uk

Website:
http://www.tinplateworkers.co.uk

Enquiries:
Enquiries to: The Clerk

Founded:
1670

Organisation type and purpose:
Membership association (membership is by election or invitation).
City of London Livery Company.

Printed publications:
The Lanthorn (newsletter, annually)

Access to staff:
Contact by letter, by telephone and by e-mail

WORSHIPFUL COMPANY OF TOBACCO PIPE MAKERS AND TOBACCO BLENDERS

Hackhurst Farm, Lower Dicker, Hailsham, East Sussex, BN27 4BP

Tel: 01323 844267
Fax: 01323 441199
E-mail: nickhp@prhack.demon.co.uk

Enquiries:
Enquiries to: Clerk

Founded:
1619/1954

Organisation type and purpose:
Membership association (membership is by election or invitation), present number of members: 200.
City of London Livery Company.
Charitable.

Subject coverage:
Tobacco products, pipes.

WORSHIPFUL COMPANY OF TURNERS OF LONDON

182 Temple Chambers, Temple Avenue, London, EC4Y 0HP

Tel: 020 7353 9595
Fax: 020 7353 9933
E-mail: clerk@turnersco.com

Website:
http://www.turnersco.com

Enquiries:
Enquiries to: The Clerk

Founded:
1604

Organisation type and purpose:
Membership association (membership is by election or invitation).
City of London Livery Company.
To promote the craft of turning, to participate in the life of the City of London and to support related charities.

continued overleaf

Access to staff:
Contact by letter, by telephone, by fax, by e-mail and via website

WORSHIPFUL COMPANY OF TYLERS AND BRICKLAYERS

30 Shelley Avenue, Tiptree, Essex, CO5 0SF

Tel: 01621 816592
E-mail: tandbclerk@aol.com

Website:
http://www.tylersandbricklayers.co.uk

Enquiries:
Enquiries to: The Clerk
Direct tel: 01621 816592

Founded:
1568

Organisation type and purpose:
Membership association (membership is by election or invitation).
City of London Livery Company.

Access to staff:
Contact by letter, by telephone and by e-mail

WORSHIPFUL COMPANY OF UPHOLDERS

C/o K.E.S. Limited, 46 Quail Gardens, Selsdon, South Croydon, Surrey, CR2 8TF

Tel: 020 8651 3303
Fax: 020 8651 3454
E-mail: clerk@codyranch.co.uk

Website:
http://www.upholders.co.uk

Enquiries:
Enquiries to: The Clerk
Direct tel: 020 8651 3303
Direct fax: 020 8651 3454
Direct e-mail: clerk@codyranch.co.uk

Founded:
1626

Organisation type and purpose:
Membership association (membership is by election or invitation).
City of London Livery Company.

Access to staff:
Contact by letter, by telephone, by fax and by e-mail

WORSHIPFUL COMPANY OF WATER CONSERVATORS

The Lark, 2 Bell Lane, Worlington, Bury St Edmunds, Suffolk, IP28 8SE

Tel: 01638 510 626
Fax: 01638 510 626
E-mail: clerk@waterconservators.org

Website:
http://www.waterconservators.org

Enquiries:
Enquiries to: The Clerk
Direct tel: 020 8421 0305
Direct e-mail: clerk@waterconservators.org

Founded:
1994

Organisation type and purpose:
Membership association (membership is by election or invitation).
City of London Livery Company.
To promote the development and advancement of the science, art and practice of water and environmental management and the various scientific subjects related thereto.

Access to staff:
Contact by letter, by telephone, by fax and by e-mail

WORSHIPFUL COMPANY OF WAX CHANDLERS

Wax Chandlers Hall, 6 Gresham Street, London, EC2V 7AD

Tel: 020 7726 0710
Fax: 020 7600 5462
E-mail: enquiries@waxchandlershall.co.uk

Website:
http://www.waxchandlershall.co.uk

Enquiries:
Enquiries to: The Clerk
Direct e-mail: cler@chandlers.ndonet.com

Organisation type and purpose:
Membership association (membership is by election or invitation).
City of London Livery Company.

Museum or gallery collection, archive, or library special collection:
Archive held by Guildhall Library (open access)

Access to staff:
Contact by letter, by telephone, by fax and by e-mail

WORSHIPFUL COMPANY OF WEAVERS

Saddlers' House, Gutter Lane, London, EC2V 6BS

Tel: 020 7606 1155
Fax: 020 7606 1119
E-mail: weavers@weavers.org.uk

Website:
http://www.weavers.org.uk

Enquiries:
Enquiries to: Clerk

Founded:
1130

Organisation type and purpose:
Membership association (membership is by election or invitation), present number of members: 150.
City of London Livery Company.

Subject coverage:
History of the company.

Museum or gallery collection, archive, or library special collection:
The company's historical records and admission records are deposited at Guildhall Library

Printed publications:
The Weavers Company in the City of London (booklet)

Microform publications:
Microfilms of company's records (through World Microfilms)

Publications list:
Available in print

Access to staff:
Contact by letter
Hours: Mon to Fri, 0900 to 1700

WORSHIPFUL COMPANY OF WHEELWRIGHTS, THE

7 Glengall Road, Bexleyheath, Kent, DA7 4AL

Tel: 020 8306 5119
Fax: 020 8979 5934
E-mail: enquiries@wheelwrights.org

Website:
http://www.wheelwrights.org

Enquiries:
Enquiries to: Clerk

Founded:
1670

Organisation type and purpose:
Membership association (membership is by election or invitation), present number of members: 220.

Subject coverage:
The craft of wheelwrighting. List of working wheelwrights in the United Kingdom.

Printed publications:
The Worshipful Company of Wheelwrights of the City of London 1670–1970 (Bennett, E; 1970, £3 plus p&p)
Making a Wheel (Wright J and Hurford R, 1997, The Rural Development Commission, £10 plus p&p)

Access to staff:
Contact by letter, by e-mail and via website
Hours: Mon to Fri, 0900 to 1700

WORSHIPFUL COMPANY OF WOOLMEN

Brewer's Hall, Aldermanbury Square, London, EC2V 7HR

Tel: 020 7606 1301
Fax: 020 7796 3557
E-mail: woolmensclerk@brewershall.co.uk

Website:
http://www.woolmen.com

Enquiries:
Enquiries to: The Clerk
Direct e-mail: woolmensclerk@brewershall.co.uk

Founded:
c. 12th century

Organisation type and purpose:
Membership association (membership is by election or invitation).
City of London Livery Company.

Access to staff:
Contact by letter, by telephone, by fax and by e-mail

WORSHIPFUL COMPANY OF WORLD TRADERS

Acronym or abbreviation: World Traders

13 Hall Gardens, Colney Heath, St Albans, Herts, AL4 0QF

Tel: 01727 822181
E-mail: clerk@world-traders.org

Website:
http://www.world-traders.org

Enquiries:
Enquiries to: Clerk

Founded:
2000

Organisation type and purpose:
Membership association (membership is by election or invitation).
City of London Livery Company.

Access to staff:
Contact by telephone and by e-mail

Access to building, collection or gallery:
No access

WORSHIPFUL SOCIETY OF APOTHECARIES OF LONDON

Apothecaries' Hall, Black Friars Lane, London, EC4V 6EJ

Tel: 020 7236 1189
Fax: 020 7329 3177
E-mail: clerk@apothecaries.org

Website:
http://www.apothecaries.org
Information on the Society and the Hall, details of all Society examinations.

Enquiries:
Enquiries to: The Clerk

Founded:
1617

Organisation type and purpose:
Learned society.
City of London Livery Company.

Subject coverage:
History of the Society, membership lists since 1617, medical historical matters, non-university medical examination and licensing matters, the following examinations: Licentiate in Medicine and Surgery of the Society of Apothecaries, Diploma in the History of Medicine, Mastership in Medical Jurisprudence, Diploma in Medical Jurisprudence, Diploma in Genito-Urinary Medicine, Diploma in the Philosophy of Medicine, Diploma in Sports Medicine, Diploma in Musculo-Skeletal Medicine, Diploma in Medical Care of Catastrophes, Diploma in Regulatory Toxicology.

Museum or gallery collection, archive, or library special collection:
Medical examination matters from 1815
Some records from 1617 to date

Access to staff:
Contact by letter, by telephone, by fax and by e-mail. Appointment necessary.
Hours: Mon to Fri, 0900 to 1700

Access to building, collection or gallery:
Prior appointment required

Access for disabled people:
Ramped entry, access to all public areas

Links with:
Faculty of the History and Philosophy of Medicine and Pharmacy

WORTHING BOROUGH COUNCIL

Town Hall, Chapel Road, Worthing, West Sussex, BN11 1HA

Tel: 01903 239999\ Minicom no. 01903 204500
Fax: 01903 236552
E-mail: enquiries@worthing.gov.uk

Website:
http://www.worthing.gov.uk

Enquiries:
Enquiries to: Public Relations Manager

Founded:
1890

Organisation type and purpose:
Local government body.

Subject coverage:
Two tier authority. Provider of public services within Worthing Borough.

Access to staff:
Contact by letter, by telephone, by fax, by e-mail and via website
Hours: Mon to Fri, 0900 to 1700

Access for disabled people:
Parking provided, ramped entry, toilet facilities

WOTTON-UNDER-EDGE HISTORICAL SOCIETY

Wotton-under-Edge Heritage Centre, The Chipping, Wotton-under-Edge, Gloucestershire, GL12 7AD

Tel: 01453 521541
E-mail: info@wottonheritage.com

Website:
http://www.wottonheritage.com
Information provided on opening hours, displays and collections held at the Centre

Enquiries:
Enquiries to: Honorary Curator & Librarian
Other contacts: Administrator

Founded:
1945

Organisation type and purpose:
Membership association, present number of members: 70, voluntary organisation, registered charity (charity number 291936), museum, suitable for ages: all.

Subject coverage:
Local history of Wotton-under-Edge and adjoining parishes, local family history, Wotton-under-Edge and adjoining parishes, tourist information point.

Information services:
Tourist Information Point

Education services:
Education packs available for loan to local schools

Services for disabled people:
Displays and/or information at wheelchair height.

Museum or gallery collection, archive, or library special collection:
Books, documents, manuscripts, pictures, photographs and artefacts, all in computerised database
Parish registers and 1891 census on microfiche and 1881 census on CD-ROM

Non-library collection catalogue:
All or part available in-house

Printed publications:
Annual Journal

Microform publications:
Parish registers and 1891 census (microfiche)

Electronic and video publications:
1881 census (CD-ROM)

Publications list:
Available online

Access to staff:
Contact by letter, by telephone, by e-mail and in person

Access to building, collection or gallery:
No prior appointment required
Hours: Tue to Fri, 1000 to 1300 and 1400 to 1700 (1600 in winter); Sat, 1000 to 1300
Some Sun in summer, 1430 to 1700
Special comments: Charges made for the use of research facilities only.

Access for disabled people:
Parking provided, level entry, access to all public areas, toilet facilities

WOUND CARE SOCIETY

Acronym or abbreviation: WCS

PO Box 170, Huntingdon, Cambridgeshire, PE29 1PL

Tel: 01480 434401
Fax: 01480 434401
E-mail: wound.care.society@talk21.com

Enquiries:
Enquiries to: Administrator

Founded:
1987

Subject coverage:
WCS is a charitable organisation concerned with all aspects of wound care. It is a registered charity which provides educational material to nursing professionals.

Printed publications:
Educational Booklets (available for purchase, £2.50 per booklet)

Access to staff:
Contact by letter, by telephone, by fax, by e-mail and via website
Hours: 24 hours Answer Machine

Access to building, collection or gallery:
No access other than to staff

WPF COUNSELLING AND PSYCHOTHERAPY

Formal name: Westminster Pastoral Foundation Counselling and Psychotherapy
Acronym or abbreviation: WPF

23 Kensington Square, London, W8 5HN

Tel: 020 7361 4800
Fax: 020 7361 4808
E-mail: counselling@wpf.org.uk

Website:
http://www.wpf.org.uk
Counselling service, training department.

Enquiries:
Enquiries to: Secretary
Other contacts: Appointments Office tel no: 020 7361 4803

Founded:
1970

Organisation type and purpose:
Registered charity (charity number 273434), training organisation, consultancy.
Counselling service.
To provide affordable counselling and psychotherapy, to train counsellors and psychotherapists.

Subject coverage:
Counselling and psychotherapy.

Access to staff:
Contact by telephone
Hours: Mon to Fri, 0900 to 1700

Access for disabled people:
Parking provided, ramped entry, toilet facilities

Affiliated Counselling Centres:
WPF Counselling and Psychotherapy
23 Kensington Square, London, W8 5HN; tel: 020 7361 4864

WRC PLC

Acronym or abbreviation: WRc

Frankland Road, Blagrove, Swindon, Wiltshire, SN5 8YF

Tel: 01793 865000
Fax: 01793 865001
E-mail: solutions@wrcplc.co.uk

Website:
http://www.wrcplc.co.uk

Enquiries:
Enquiries to: Librarian

Formerly called:
Water Research Centre (WRc)

Organisation type and purpose:
Consultancy, research organisation.

Subject coverage:
Water supply, drinking water analysis, environmental chemistry, microbiology, quality and health matters, legislation; water pollution; solid wastes and sewage sludge disposal; ecotoxicology; water and waste water treatment; sewage treatment and disposal; sludge treatment; processes automation and control; sewers and sewerage; water mains; marine and freshwater studies including modelling; computing; Water Byelaws Advisory Service.

Printed publications:
Annual Report
Order printed publications from: Publications Department, WRc Information Resources, Frankland Road, Blagrove, Swindon, Wiltshire, SN5 8YF, tel: 01793 865138, fax: 01793 514562, e-mail: sales@webookshop.com; website: http://www.webookshop.com

Access to staff:
Contact by letter, by telephone, by fax, by e-mail and via website
Hours: Mon to Fri, 0930 to 1630

continued overleaf

Access to building, collection or gallery:
No access other than to staff

Other address:
WRc-NSF
  Henley Road, Memenham, Marlow,
  Buckinghamshire, SL7 2HD; tel: 01491 571531;
  fax: 01491 579094; e-mail: solutions@wrcplc.co
  .uk

WREXHAM COUNTY BOROUGH COUNCIL

Acronym or abbreviation: WCBC

Guildhall, Wrexham, Clwyd, LL11 1AY

Tel: 01978 292000
Fax: 01978 292106

Website:
http://www.wrexham.gov.uk

Enquiries:
Enquiries to: Public Relations Manager
Direct tel: 01978 292275
Direct fax: 01978 292252
Direct e-mail: sue.wynjones@wrexham.gov.uk

Founded:
1996

Organisation type and purpose:
Local government body.

Printed publications:
Connect – Local residents magazine (2 times a
  year)
Order printed publications from: Publicity Officer
tel: 01978 292274, fax: 01978 292252, e-mail: kesah
.trowell@wrexham.gov.uk

Electronic and video publications:
See website

Access to staff:
Contact by letter, by telephone, by fax, by e-mail,
in person and via website. Appointment necessary.
Hours: Mon to Thu, 0845 to 1715; Fri, 0845 to 17.45

Access to building, collection or gallery:
No prior appointment required
Hours: Vary

Access for disabled people:
Parking provided

WRITERS GUILD OF GREAT BRITAIN

Acronym or abbreviation: WGGB

430 Edgware Road, London, W2 1EH

Tel: 020 7723 8074
Fax: 020 7706 2413
E-mail: admin@writersguild.org.uk

Website:
http://www.writersguild.org.uk

Enquiries:
Enquiries to: General Secretary

Founded:
1957

Organisation type and purpose:
Professional body, trade union, present number of
members: 2000.

Subject coverage:
Professional writing in TV, radio, films, theatre,
books and multimedia.

Printed publications:
Writers' Newsletter (6 times a year, £25 annual
  subscription)

Access to staff:
Contact by letter, by telephone, by fax, by e-mail
and via website. Appointment necessary.
Hours: Mon to Fri, 0930 to 1730

Incorporates the:
Theatre Writers Union

WRITTLE COLLEGE

Chelmsford, Essex, CM1 3RR

Tel: 01245 424200
Fax: 01245 420456
E-mail: info@writtle.ac.uk

Website:
http://www.writtle.ac.uk

Enquiries:
Enquiries to: Librarian

Founded:
1893

Formerly called:
Writtle Agriculture College (year of change 1993)

Organisation type and purpose:
Local government body, university library. Higher
Education College.

Subject coverage:
Agriculture; agricultural engineering; horticulture
(amenity and commercial); agricultural
diversification; plant and animal science; soil
science; farm and horticultural enterprise
management, equine science.

**Museum or gallery collection, archive, or library
special collection:**
Collection of 18th and 19th century books on
  agriculture and horticulture
Video collection

Library catalogue:
All or part available in-house

Printed publications:
Weekly accessions lists

WWF-UK

Acronym or abbreviation: WWF

Panda House, Weyside Park, Godalming, Surrey,
GU7 1XR

Tel: 01483 426444
Fax: 01483 426409

Website:
http://www.wwf.org.uk
Website updated frequently.
http://www.wwflearning.org.uk

Enquiries:
Enquiries to: Supporter Relations

Founded:
1961

Formerly called:
World Wildlife Fund (WWF) (year of change 1986);
Worldwide Fund for Nature (WWF) (year of
change 2001)

Organisation type and purpose:
International organisation, registered charity
(charity number 201707).
To conserve species of animals and plants and their
habitats, and to reconcile the needs of people with
the conservation of the natural environment upon
which they depend.

Subject coverage:
Climate change, forests, freshwater, marine and
coasts, rare species, toxics, agriculture, plants,
tourism, economics, trade and investment,
international development, oil, gas and mining,
UK social change.

Library catalogue:
All or part available in-house

Printed publications:
UK Factsheets: A selection of 30 factsheets on the
  most often-requested topics
Specialist Reports
WWF Annual Review
Action (magazine, members, quarterly)
Order printed publications from: Education resources
only, WWF-UK
Education Distribution, PO Box 963, Slough, SL2
3RS, tel: 01753 643104, fax: 01753 646553

Electronic and video publications:
Computerised data bulletins (educational
  software): for 7 to 11 years: Exploring Coasts,
  Exploring Farms, Exploring Rivers, Exploring
  Towns and Cities
Computerised data bulletins (educational
  software): for 13 to 16 years
Climate Chaos (for teachers)
Stimulus (video pack 11 to 16 yrs)

Publications list:
Available online and in print

Access to staff:
Contact by letter, by telephone, by fax and by e-
mail. Appointment necessary.
Hours: Mon to Fri, 0900 to 1700
Special comments: Library use by appointment.

Access to building, collection or gallery:
Prior appointment required

Access for disabled people:
Parking provided

Affiliated to:
International Union for Conservation of Nature
and Natural Resources (IUCN)

Other addresses:
WWF Cymru
  Room 313, Baltic House, Mount Stuart Square,
  Cardiff, CF10 5FH; tel: 029 2045 4970; fax: 029
  2045 1306; e-mail: wwf-uk-wales@wwf.org.uk
WWF Northern Ireland
  13 West Street, Carrickfergus, Co Antrim, BT38
  7AR; tel: 028 9335 5166; fax: 028 9336 4448; e-
  mail: wwf-uk-ni@wwf.org.uk
WWF Scotland
  Little Dunkeld, Dunkeld, Perthshire, PH8 0AD;
  tel: 01887 820449

Parent body:
WWF International
  Avenue du Mont Blanc, Gland, CH-1196,
  Switzerland

WYRE BOROUGH COUNCIL

Civic Centre, Breck Road, Poulton-le-Fylde,
Lancashire, FY6 7PU

Tel: 01253 891000
Fax: 01253 899000

Website:
http://www.wyrebc.gov.uk

Enquiries:
Enquiries to: Corporate Support Officer
Direct tel: 01253 887503
Direct fax: 01253 887499

Founded:
1974

Organisation type and purpose:
Local government body.

Subject coverage:
Provision of local government services by a district
council, council tax; environmental health, health
and safety, housing, transport, sport, leisure and
recreation, planning, personnel and management
services, tourism.

Printed publications:
Index of free leaflets available to the public

Publications list:
Available in print

Access to staff:
Contact by letter, by telephone and by e-mail
Hours: Mon to Fri, 0900 to 1700

Access for disabled people:
Parking provided, ramped entry, level entry, access
to all public areas, toilet facilities

XENOPHON

98 Cambridge Gardens, London, W10 6HS

Tel: 020 8968 1360
E-mail: wolstan-dixie@hotmail.co.uk

Enquiries:
Enquiries to: Information Officer

Founded:
1979

Organisation type and purpose:
Learned society (membership is by election or invitation).

Subject coverage:
Recreational and historical cryptography, i.e. codes, ciphers, cryptanalysis, signs, signals, secret and hidden artificial languages and their recovery.

Museum or gallery collection, archive, or library special collection:
Books
Pamphlets
Magazines
Grey Literature
Press Clippings

Printed publications:
Crypt (newsletter, irregular)
Wordpattern Dictionary

Electronic and video publications:
Decrypting programs
IBM PC encrypting
Random text program
Wordsearch programs

Access to staff:
Contact by letter, by telephone and by e-mail. Non-members charged.
Hours: Mon to Fri, 1000 to 1800

XR OWNERS CLUB

Acronym or abbreviation: XROC

9 Cope Place, Earls Court Road, Kensington, London, W8 6AA

Tel: 020 7937 7595
E-mail: info@xroc.co.uk

Website:
http://www.interford.co.uk
http://www.xrownersclub.co.uk
Membership information.
http://www.xroc.co.uk

Enquiries:
Enquiries to: National Co-ordinator
Direct e-mail: john@xroc.co.uk

Founded:
1983

May be looked for as:
Ford XR Owners Club

Organisation type and purpose:
Car Club.

Subject coverage:
Ford XR2, XR3, XR4, XR6 and XR8 information, supersport register, classic car insurance, technical information and national day track event.

Printed publications:
Xtra (magazine, 5 times a year, members)

Access to staff:
Contact by letter, by telephone, by fax, by e-mail and via website
Hours: Mon to Fri, 1000 to 1900; Sat, 1000 to 1600

Access to building, collection or gallery:
No access other than to staff

YACHT BROKERS, DESIGNERS AND SURVEYORS ASSOCIATION

Acronym or abbreviation: YBDSA

The Glass Works, Penns Road, Petersfield, Hants, GU32 2EW

Tel: 01730 710425
Fax: 01730 710423
E-mail: info@ybdsa.co.uk

Website:
http://www.ybdsa.co.uk

Information on the Association including membership

Enquiries:
Enquiries to: Chief Executive
Direct e-mail: jane@ybdsa.co.uk
Other contacts: Certifying Authority Secretary for MCA Code vessel work.

Founded:
1912

Organisation type and purpose:
National organisation, professional body (membership is by qualification, election or invitation), present number of members: 300. Training and maintaining of standards, support of small craft surveyors and designers and yacht brokers

Subject coverage:
Brokerage, surveying and designing of yachts and small craft; training; tonnage measurement as required for registration by the Department of Trade; certification under the MCA Small Commercial Vessel Code; registration and its benefits; codes of practice; forms of contract.

Library catalogue:
All or part available in-house

Printed publications:
Brochures, leaflets and rules
Training Pack Block I (£75)
Sample Report Pack (£10)

Publications list:
Available online and in print

Access to staff:
Contact by letter, by telephone, by fax, by e-mail, in person and via website. Appointment necessary.
Hours: Mon to Fri, 0900 to 1700

Access to building, collection or gallery:
Prior appointment required

Access for disabled people:
Parking provided

Sister bodies:
Association of Brokers and Yacht Agents (ABYA)
Professional Charter Association (PCA)
Yacht Designers and Surveyors Association (YDSA)

YACHT DESIGNERS AND SURVEYORS ASSOCIATION

Acronym or abbreviation: YDSA

The Glass Works, Penns Road, Petersfield, Hampshire, GU32 2EW

Tel: 01730 710425/710490
Fax: 01730 710423
E-mail: info@ybdsa.co.uk

Website:
http://www.ybdsa.co.uk

Enquiries:
Enquiries to: Chief Executive
Direct e-mail: jane@ybdsa.co.uk

Founded:
1912

Organisation type and purpose:
Professional body (membership is by election or invitation), present number of members: 125.

Subject coverage:
Surveyors and designers of small craft.

Museum or gallery collection, archive, or library special collection:
Wide selection of books relating to small craft, dating back to early 20th century

Library catalogue:
All or part available in-house

Printed publications:
Membership list (free, enclose A5 sae, or see website)

Access to staff:
Contact by letter, by telephone, by fax, by e-mail, in person and via website. Appointment necessary.
Hours: Mon to Fri, 0900 to 1700

Access to building, collection or gallery:
Prior appointment required
Hours: Mon to Fri, 0900 to 1700

Access for disabled people:
Some parking

YEMEN EMBASSY

57 Cromwell Road, London, SW7 2ED

Tel: 020 7584 6607
Fax: 020 7584 3759

Enquiries:
Enquiries to: Information Officer

Organisation type and purpose:
National government body.

Subject coverage:
The Yemen.

Access to staff:
Contact by letter, by telephone and by fax
Hours: Mon to Fri, 0900 to 1700

YMCA ENGLAND

Formal name: Young Men's Christian Associations of England
Acronym or abbreviation: YMCA

National Council of YMCAs, 640 Forest Road, London, E17 3DZ

Tel: 020 8520 5599
Fax: 020 8509 3190
E-mail: info@england.ymca.org.uk

Website:
http://www.ymca.org.uk
Information on housing and the other work carried out by the YMCA.

Enquiries:
Enquiries to: Senior Media Officer
Direct tel: 020 7061 3324
Direct fax: 0845 873 6644
Direct e-mail: press@england.ymca.org.uk

Founded:
1844

Organisation type and purpose:
International organisation, membership association, voluntary organisation, registered charity (charity number 212810), training organisation.

Subject coverage:
Youth and community work; Mentoring for young people; Rehabilitation of young offenders; Sport, Health, Exercise and Fitness; Education and training for young people; youth homelessness; residential facilities for young people; adult education; outdoor education; drugs education, extended schools.

Museum or gallery collection, archive, or library special collection:
Archive material, photographs and memorabilia relating to the history of the YMCA

Printed publications:
Anniversary Review (12pp history booklet, 1844–1994)
Annual Report
Annual Review
Publications relating to specific projects
Unity (newsletter, 4 times a year)
Y Care International's annual review, booklet on Street Children and educational material. (Y Care International is the international development agency of the English, Scottish, Welsh and Irish national councils of YMCAs)
YMCA in Focus
YMCA World (3 times a year)

continued overleaf

Electronic and video publications:
Chasing the Bandwagon (video and teaching pack for drugs education)
Videos about the YMCA's work (for loan)

Publications list:
Available in print

Access to staff:
Contact by letter, by telephone, by fax and by e-mail. Appointment necessary.
Hours: Mon to Fri, 0900 to 1730

Access to building, collection or gallery:
Hours: Mon to Fri, 0900 to 1700

Branch office:
YMCA Metropolitan Region
53 Parker Street, London, WC2B 5PT

Has:
160 local YMCA Associations

Member of:
National Council for Voluntary Youth Services

YORK ARCHAEOLOGICAL TRUST

Formal name: York Archaeological Trust for Excavation and Research Limited
Acronym or abbreviation: YAT

Cromwell House, 13 Ogleforth, York, YO1 7FG

Tel: 01904 663000
Fax: 01904 640024
E-mail: postmaster@yorkarchaeology.co.uk

Website:
http://www.yorkarchaeology.co.uk
http://www.vikingjorvik.com
Information on Jorvik Viking Centre.

Enquiries:
Enquiries to: Director
Direct tel: 01904 663001
Direct fax: 01904 663024
Direct e-mail: pvaddyman@yorkarchaeology.co.uk
Other contacts: Head of Finance and Administration for administrative matters.

Founded:
1972

Organisation type and purpose:
Membership association (membership is by election or invitation), present number of members: c. 100, registered charity (charity number 509060), museum, suitable for ages: all, research organisation, publishing house.

Subject coverage:
Archaeology of York and its region; Roman, Anglo Saxon, Viking and medieval archaeology, Jorvik Viking Centre, Archaeological Resource Centre, Barley Hall Medieval Centre, archaeological techniques, visitors' centre and attraction development and management; collections management, maintenance and archaeological artefact conservation, waterlogged archaeological materials.

Museum or gallery collection, archive, or library special collection:
Air photographic collections for Yorkshire
Archaeological picture library, with worldwide coverage but specialisation in York, Britain and Viking topics
Artefacts and excavation records relating to the archaeology of York 1972 onwards
CD-ROM on Viking and other subjects
Exhibited collections in Jorvik Viking Centre (Viking age) and of replicas in Barley Hall (medieval)

Printed publications:
Annual Report
Yorkshire Archaeology Today Vol 1 ongoing
The Archaeology of York Vols 1–21 ongoing

Microform publications:
Archive materials (copies of certain site records)

Electronic and video publications:
Facing the Past (video)
Roman Britain (CD-ROM)

World of the Vikings (CD-ROM)

Publications list:
Available online and in print

Access to staff:
Contact by letter, by telephone, by fax, by e-mail, in person and via website. Appointment necessary.
Hours: Mon to Fri, 0900 to 1700

Access for disabled people:
Level entry, access to all public areas, toilet facilities
Special comments: Visitor Centres: Disabled access available to most areas.
Other Offices: Conditions vary.

Connections with:
Archaeological Resource Centre (ARC)
St Saviour's Church, St Saviour Gate, York, YO1 8NN; tel: 01904 643211
JORVIK
Coppergate, York, YO1 9WT; tel: 01904 543400; fax: 01904 627097; e-mail: enquiries@vikingjorvik.com

YORK COLLEGE

Acronym or abbreviation: YC

Tadcaster Road, Dringhouses, York, YO24 1UA

Tel: 01904 770400
Fax: 01904 770499

Website:
http://www.yorkcollege.ac.uk

Enquiries:
Enquiries to: Customer Services
Direct e-mail: customer-services@yorkcollege.ac.uk
Other contacts: Marketing Manager, 01904 770543

Founded:
1827

Formed by the merger of:
York College of Further and Higher Education (YCFHE), York Sixth Form College (YSFC) (year of change 1999)

Organisation type and purpose:
Suitable for ages: 16+, training organisation, consultancy.

Subject coverage:
Art and design, business, catering, computing, construction, engineering, hair and beauty, health and social care, sport and leisure, fashion, performing arts and A-Levels, etc.

Non-library collection catalogue:
All or part available in-house

Library catalogue:
All or part available in-house

Printed publications:
Branding Information
Prospectuses: Full Time, Higher Education, Part-time (annually, free)
Annual Report

Access to staff:
Contact by letter, by telephone, by fax, by e-mail and via website. Appointment necessary.
Hours: Mon to Thu, 0830 to 1930; Fri, 0830 to 1800

Access for disabled people:
Parking provided, ramped entry, level entry, toilet facilities

Sixth Form Site:
York College
Sim Balk Lane, York; tel: 01904 704141

YORK COUNCIL FOR VOLUNTARY SERVICE

Acronym or abbreviation: York CVS

Priory Street Centre, 15 Priory Street, York, YO1 6ET

Tel: 01904 621133
Fax: 01904 630361
E-mail: yorkcvs@yorkcvs.org.uk

Website:
http://www.yorkcvs.org.uk/
Citizen's Guide entries, Voluntary Voice articles, topical information.

Enquiries:
Enquiries to: Information & Development Manager

Founded:
1939

Organisation type and purpose:
Registered charity (charity number 225087).
York CVS provides information and advice on issues which are common to all charities and voluntary groups – fundraising, legal constitutions, volunteering, accounts etc.

Subject coverage:
How to set up and run a voluntary group or charity.

Museum or gallery collection, archive, or library special collection:
Books and pamphlets relating to issues concerning the voluntary sector

Printed publications:
Citizen's Guide (annually updated directory of local voluntary groups)
Voluntary Voice (newsletter, 10 times a year)

Access to staff:
Contact by letter, by telephone, by fax, by e-mail and in person. Appointment necessary.
Hours: Mon to Fri, 0900 to 1630

Access for disabled people:
Parking provided, ramped entry, level entry, access to all public areas, toilet facilities
Special comments: Hearing loops in meeting rooms

YORK HOSPITAL

Health Library and Information Service, 3rd Floor, Administration Block, York Hospital, Wigginton Road, York, YO31 8HE

Tel: 01904 726712
Fax: 01904 675583
E-mail: hslibydh@york.ac.uk

Enquiries:
Enquiries to: Librarian

Founded:
1971

Organisation type and purpose:
Health library.

Subject coverage:
Medicine, nursing, management and all health-related subjects.

Library catalogue:
All or part available online

Printed publications:
Journal holdings
Library guide

Access to staff:
Contact by letter, by telephone, by fax, by e-mail, in person and via website. Appointment necessary.
Letter of introduction required. Non-members charged.
Hours: Mon to Thu, 0830 to 2000; Fri, 0830 to 1700; Sat, 1000 to 1300

Also at:
Bootham Park Library

At the same address:
Bootham Park Hospital Library

Parent bodies:
York Hospitals NHS Trust

YORK MINSTER LIBRARY AND ARCHIVES

Dean's Park, York, YO1 7JQ

Tel: 01904 625308 (library); 01904 611118 (archives)
Fax: 01904 611119
E-mail: jsp5@york.ac.uk

Website:
http://www.yorkminster.org/learning/library
-archives-conservation

Enquiries:
Enquiries to: Librarian
Other contacts: Archivist, e-mail archivist@
yorkminsterlibrary.org.uk

Founded:
627

Formerly called:
York Minster Library

Organisation type and purpose:
Registered charity.
Cathedral library and archives.

Subject coverage:
Church history, history of York Minster and its
attendant bodies (but not the archdiocese),
medieval manuscripts, illuminated manuscripts,
literature, theology, religious art and architecture,
religious literature (poetry, drama), York and
Yorkshire local history, historical bibliography,
music (religious and secular).

**Museum or gallery collection, archive, or library
special collection:**
Library: General Collection; Old Library
collections, including items from the collections
of Revd Dr Marmaduke Fothergill (d. 1731) and
Canon T. F. Simmons (d. 1884); Yorkshire
collections, including the Hailstone Collection
(printed matter; Edward Hailstone (d. 1890)) and
the Foot-Walker Collection; and Yorkshire Parish
Library collections.
Archives: Minster archives, from c.1148, including
the archives of the Vicars Choral (1252–1936) and
the Minster School; small archives of other
organisations; personal papers; manuscript
collections (MSS XVI and MSS Add.), from late
10th century; music manuscripts, 16th–20th
centuries; Hailstone Collection (chiefly
documents and manuscript material, 12th–19th
centuries); modern media, including
photographs, and video and sound recordings.

Non-library collection catalogue:
All or part available in-house

Library catalogue:
All or part available online

Printed publications:
A Catalogue of the Printed Music Published before
1850 in York Minster Library (D. Griffiths, 1977)
A Catalogue of Music Manuscripts in York Minster
Library (D. Griffiths, 1982)
A Catalogue of the Printed Books in the Library of
the Dean and Chapter of York (J. Raine, York,
1896)
Probate Inventories of the York Diocese, 1350–1500
(P. M. Stell trans., York Archaeological Trust,
2006)

Access to staff:
Contact by letter, by telephone, by fax, by e-mail
and via website. Appointment necessary. Letter of
introduction required.
Hours: Mon to Fri, 0900 to 1700

Access for disabled people:
One parking space, by appointment; lift to first
floor reading room; ground floor toilet facilities

Administered by:
Dean and Chapter of York
tel: 01904 557200; website: http://yorkminster.org

Links with:
University of York

YORK ST JOHN UNIVERSITY COLLEGE

Lord Mayors' Walk, York, YO31 7EX

Tel: 01904 716700
Fax: 01904 612512
E-mail: library@yorksj.ac.uk

Website:
http://www.yorksj.ac.uk/library

Library home page. Library catalogue. Information
on services, database and Internet links, on-line
guides and publications, academic programmes,
academic departments and conference facilities.

Enquiries:
Enquiries to: Librarian
Other contacts: Archivist for enquiries concerning
College Archives.

Founded:
1841

Formed by the amalgamation of:
Ripon College, St John's College, York (year of
change 1975)

Formerly known as:
College of Ripon and York St John (year of change
2001)

Organisation type and purpose:
University department or institute, suitable for
ages: 18+.
College of higher education.

Subject coverage:
Applied social sciences, art, design and technology,
English, history, management studies, physical
education, psychology, theology and religious
studies, personal and professional development,
film, TV, literature and theatre studies, health
studies, leisure and tourist management,
occupational therapy, physiotherapy, sports and
exercise science, teaching studies.
Postgraduate courses in humanities, teaching
studies, professional and management studies,
social, environmental, health and life sciences,
international education.

**Museum or gallery collection, archive, or library
special collection:**
College Archive
Comenius Centre (language teaching materials)
Rees-Williams Collection of 19th century children's
literature
Religious Education Centre
School library resource collections
Yorkshire Film Archive

Library catalogue:
All or part available online

Printed publications:
Bibliographies on Religious Education
Library guides for most subject areas

Access to staff:
Contact by letter, by telephone, by fax, by e-mail,
in person and via website. Non-members charged.
Hours: Term time: Mon to Thu, 0845 to 2130; Fri,
0845 to 1900; Sat, 0900 to 1700; Sun, 1400 to 1900
Vacations: Mon to Fri, 0900 to 1700

Access for disabled people:
Level entry

Degrees and diplomas validated by:
University of Leeds

Incorporating:
David Hope Religious Education Centre
York Outreach Comenius Centre
Yorkshire Film Archive

YORKSHIRE ARCHAEOLOGICAL SOCIETY

Acronym or abbreviation: YAS

Claremont, 23 Clarendon Road, Leeds, West
Yorkshire, LS2 9NZ

Tel: 0113 245 7910
Fax: 0113 244 1979
E-mail: yas@wyjs.org.uk

Website:
http://www.users.globalnet.co.uk/~gdl/yasfhs.htm
Family History Section

Enquiries:
Enquiries to: Librarian
Other contacts: Assistant Librarian

Founded:
1863

Organisation type and purpose:
Learned society (membership is by subscription),
registered charity (charity number 224083).

Subject coverage:
Historical sciences, including archaeology, local
history, genealogy, with particular emphasis on
Yorkshire but some material on the North of
England and England in general.

**Museum or gallery collection, archive, or library
special collection:**
Archival material on Yorkshire, 12th to 20th
century, including the Wakefield Court Rolls and
parish register transcripts
Large collection of national and international
periodicals
The archives of the Yorkshire Archaeological
Society are administered in conjunction with the
West Yorkshire Archive Service
Extensive collection of books, maps, photographs
etc on Yorkshire

Non-library collection catalogue:
All or part available in-house

Library catalogue:
All or part available in-house

Printed publications:
Maps and Plans
Wakefield Court Rolls Series
Y.A.S. Parish Register Section
Y.A.S. Record Series
Yorkshire Archaeological Journal (annually)
Yorkshire Archaeological Reports

Microform publications:
Parish registers available on microfiche (details on
application)
Indexes of wills available (microfiche)

Publications list:
Available in print

Access to staff:
Contact by letter, by telephone, by fax, by e-mail
and in person
Hours: Tue and Wed, 1400 to 2030; Thu, Fri, 1000 to
1730; Sat, 0930 to 1700
Special comments: Appointment necessary for visit
to archives.

Access for disabled people:
Parking provided
Special comments: Limited access for disabled.

**Separate subscription sections at the same
address:**
Family History and Population Studies Section
Industrial History Section
Local History Section
Medieval Section
Parish Register Section
Prehistory Research Section
Roman Antiquities Section

YORKSHIRE DIALECT SOCIETY

Acronym or abbreviation: YDS

51 Stepney Avenue, Scarborough, North Yorkshire,
YO12 5BW

Website:
http://www.ydsociety.org.uk
General information about the Society's aims,
meetings, publications, etc.

Enquiries:
Enquiries to: Honorary Secretary

Founded:
1897

Organisation type and purpose:
International organisation, membership
association (membership is by subscription),
present number of members: 500.
The study, publication, recording and research of
dialects, mainly Yorkshire.

Subject coverage:
Yorkshire dialects.

continued overleaf

Printed publications:
Summer Bulletin (annually, free to members)
Transactions (annually, free to members)
Many books and anthologies including:
The Yorkshire Dictionary of Dialect, Tradition and
Folklore (Kellett A)

Electronic and video publications:
Tapes and records

Publications list:
Available in print

Access to staff:
Contact by letter
Hours: Mon to Fri, 0900 to 1700

YORKSHIRE GEOLOGICAL SOCIETY

Acronym or abbreviation: YGS

19 Thorngate, Barnard Castle, Co Durham, DL12
8QB

Tel: 01833 638893
E-mail: tjm4@tutor.open.ac.uk

Website:
http://www.yorkgeolsoc.org.uk
Society news.

Enquiries:
Enquiries to: General Secretary

Founded:
1837

Organisation type and purpose:
Learned society (membership is by subscription),
present number of members: 794 all sections,
voluntary organisation, registered charity.

Subject coverage:
Geology.

Printed publications:
Circular of the Yorkshire Geological Society
Occasional Publications
Proceedings of the Yorkshire Geological Society

Access to staff:
Contact by letter, by telephone, by e-mail and via
website
Hours: Mon to Fri, 0900 to 1800

Affiliated to:
Geologist's Association

YORKSHIRE PHILOSOPHICAL SOCIETY

Acronym or abbreviation: YPS

The Lodge, Museum Gardens, York, YO1 7DR

Tel: 01904 656713
Fax: 01904 656713
E-mail: info@yorksphilsoc.org.uk

Website:
http://www.yorksphilsoc.org.uk

Enquiries:
Enquiries to: Honorary Editor
Other contacts: Clerk to the Society (for general
information and membership)

Founded:
1822

Organisation type and purpose:
Learned society (membership is by subscription,
election or invitation), present number of
members: 500, registered charity (charity number
529709).

Subject coverage:
Natural history, science, archaeology and history of
York, Yorkshire and elsewhere.

**Museum or gallery collection, archive, or library
special collection:**
Records and publications of the Society from 1822

Printed publications:
Annual Reports from 1825 to 2007 (£1.50 each)

An Index to the Articles and Obituaries in the
Annual Reports 1823–1995 (£2.50, £1.50 to
members)
A Brief Index to the Annual Reports 1995–2005
(price on enquiry)
BAAS jubilee poster of 1881 (black and white print,
£5)
The Gardens of the Yorkshire Philosophical Society
(colour print, £15, £12.50 to members)
Philosophers and Provincials: The Yorkshire
Philosophical Society from 1822 to 1844 (A. D.
Orange, £2, £1.50 to members)
Sir George Cayley 1773–1857, the inventor or the
aeroplane (Leonard S. Rivet, 50p)
St Mary's Abbey and the City of York (Dr Jane
Burton, £1.50, £1 to members)
The Mythical Norman Element in the 1822
Bishophill (York) find of Anglo-Saxon Coins
(Michael Dolley, 50p)
York Observatory (leaflet, 25p)
Yorkshire People and Places: A Millennium
Celebration (eds, Sylvia Hogarth and Veronica
Wallace, 2001, £7.50)
Postage extra on all publications

Publications list:
Available in print

Access to staff:
Contact by letter, by telephone, by fax, by e-mail,
in person and via website
Hours: Mon, Fri, 1000 to 1330; Wed, 1000 to 1600

YORKSHIRE TOURIST BOARD

Acronym or abbreviation: YTB

312 Tadcaster Road, York, YO24 1GS

Tel: 01904 707961
Fax: 01904 701414
E-mail: info@ytb.org.uk

Website:
http://www.yorkshirevisitor.com
Consumer site for planning a visit to Yorkshire
http://www.yorkshiretouristboard.net
Business to business site
http://www.venueyorkshire.com
Conference and venue site
http://www.grouptravelyorkshire.com
site for group travel

Enquiries:
Enquiries to: Marketing Assistant

Formerly called:
Yorkshire and Humberside Tourist Board

Organisation type and purpose:
Regional tourist board.

Subject coverage:
General tourist information for Yorkshire.

Printed publications:
Yorkshire Visitor Guide 2005
Conference & Venue Guide

Publications list:
Available online

Access to staff:
Contact by letter, by telephone, by fax and by e-
mail
Hours: Mon to Fri, 0900 to 1730

Access for disabled people:
Parking provided, ramped entry, level entry, access
to all public areas, toilet facilities

YOUNGMINDS

Formal name: YoungMinds, the Children's Mental
Health Charity

48–50 St John Street, London, EC1M 4DG

Tel: 020 7336 8445
Fax: 020 7336 8446
E-mail: enquiries@youngminds.org.uk

Website:
http://www.youngminds.org.uk

Founded:
1992

Organisation type and purpose:
Voluntary organisation, registered charity (charity
number 1016968).
Umbrella group of professional bodies.

Subject coverage:
Parents and professionals with concerns about the
mental health or emotional wellbeing of a child.

Printed publications:
Booklets for Young People
Leaflets including:
Bullying – Why it Matters
Children and Young People Get Depressed Too
Why do Young Minds Matter?
Worried about a Young Person's Eating Problems?
Resource Sheets
YoungMinds Magazine
YoungMinds Directory of Services

Publications list:
Available online and in print

Access to staff:
Contact by letter, by telephone, by fax, by e-mail
and via website
Hours: Mon to Fri, 0930 to 1730

Access to building, collection or gallery:
Prior appointment required

YOUTH CYMRU

Unit 5, Ty Nant Court, Morganstown, Cardiff,
CF15 8LW

Tel: 029 2081 4335
E-mail: mailbox@youthcymru.org.uk

Website:
http://www.youthcymru.org.uk

Enquiries:
Enquiries to: Chief Executive

Founded:
1934

Organisation type and purpose:
National organisation, membership association
(membership is by subscription, qualification),
present number of members: 200+ Youth Groups,
voluntary organisation, registered charity (charity
number 524480).

Subject coverage:
All aspects of youth and community work.

Printed publications:
Ad hoc papers and information sheets
Conference Report
Training Programme
Annual Report
Corporate Plan
Newsletters (quarterly)

Access to staff:
Contact by letter, by telephone, by fax, by e-mail
and via website. Appointment necessary.
Hours: Mon to Fri, 0845 to 1615

Access to building, collection or gallery:
Prior appointment required

Access for disabled people:
Parking provided, ramped entry, level entry, access
to all public areas, toilet facilities

YOUTH HOSTELS ASSOCIATION (ENGLAND AND WALES)

Acronym or abbreviation: YHA

Trevelyan House, Dimple Road, Matlock,
Derbyshire, DE4 3YH

Tel: 01629 592600
Fax: 01629 592702

Website:
http://www.yha.org.uk

Enquiries:
Enquiries to: Print & Publications Assistant
Direct tel: 01629 592778
Direct e-mail: lizevans@yha.org.uk

Organisation type and purpose:
Membership association, registered charity (charity number 301657). Provides budget accommodation throughout England and Wales.

Subject coverage:
Hostelling and outdoor activities, particularly for young people of limited means.

Printed publications:
Hostel Factsheets and information booklets
Triangle YHA Magazine (twice a year)
YHA Accommodation Guide (listing all hostels) and YHA map

Access to staff:
Contact by telephone and by e-mail
Hours: Mon to Fri, 0900 to 1700

Access for disabled people:
Parking provided, ramped entry, access to all public areas, toilet facilities

YOUTH LINK SCOTLAND

Central Hall, West Tollcross, Edinburgh, EH3 9BP

Tel: 0131 229 0339
Fax: 0131 229 0339
E-mail: info@youthlink.co.uk

Website:
http://www.youthlink.co.uk
Overview of Youthlink Scotland's activities. Links to member organisation websites.

Enquiries:
Enquiries to: Administrator
Direct e-mail: rdambrosio@youthlink.co.uk

Founded:
1942

Formerly called:
Scottish Standing Conference of Voluntary Youth Organisations (SSCVYO) (year of change 1996)

Organisation type and purpose:
Voluntary organisation.
Umbrella/intermediary organisation supporting voluntary youth organisations.

Subject coverage:
Range of youth issues and related topics such as funding, charity law, peer education, youth work and sustainable development, sport and the arts.

Museum or gallery collection, archive, or library special collection:
Catalogue currently being developed

Printed publications:
Wide range of publications, leaflets etc. related to youth work including own publications
Annual Report

Publications list:
Available in print

Access to staff:
Contact by letter, by telephone, by fax, by e-mail and via website. Appointment necessary. Non-members charged.
Hours: Mon to Fri, 0900 to 1700

Members include:
51 youth organisations

ZEPHYR & ZODIAC MKIV OWNERS CLUB

94 Claremont Road, Rugby, Warwickshire, CV21 3LU

Tel: 01788 574884

Enquiries:
Enquiries to: Treasurer

Founded:
1983

Organisation type and purpose:
Membership association (membership is by subscription), present number of members: 210, voluntary organisation.

Subject coverage:
All aspects of Zephyr and Zodiac MkIV cars.

Printed publications:
Quarterly magazine

Access to staff:
Contact by letter and by telephone
Hours: Evenings and weekends

ZINC INFORMATION CENTRE

Acronym or abbreviation: ZINC

Wrens Court, 56 Victoria Road, Sutton Coldfield, West Midlands, B72 1SY

Tel: 0121 362 1201
Fax: 0121 355 8727
E-mail: zincinfocentre@hdg.org.uk

Enquiries:
Enquiries to: Director

Founded:
2001

Ceased trading:
Zinc Development Association, date of change, October 2000

Organisation type and purpose:
Trade association.

Subject coverage:
Worldwide uses of zinc, lead and cadmium and their products, statistics and economics, toxicity of lead and cadmium, pollution control methods.

Printed publications:
Publications and films on zinc

Access to staff:
Contact by letter, by telephone, by fax and by e-mail
Hours: Mon to Fri, 0900 to 1700

Operated in conjunction with the:
Galvanizers Association

ZOOLOGICAL SOCIETY OF GLASGOW AND WEST OF SCOTLAND

Secretary: George W.H. Thomson, Morrisbank, Bathgate, EH48 1JU

Tel: 0845 108 1426
Fax: 0845 108 1426
E-mail: george@thomsons.org

Website:
http://www.glasgowzoopark.org.uk
Current and historical information on zoos in Glasgow.

Enquiries:
Enquiries to: Secretary

Founded:
1936

Organisation type and purpose:
Membership association (membership is by election or invitation), present number of members: 200, registered charity (charity number SCO 02651).

Subject coverage:
Zoo biology, biodiversity, environment.

Museum or gallery collection, archive, or library special collection:
Books and photographs

Printed publications:
Annual Report (£10)

Access to staff:
Special comments: Volunteer staff only

Access to building, collection or gallery:
Prior appointment required

ZOOLOGICAL SOCIETY OF LONDON

Acronym or abbreviation: ZSL

Library, Regent's Park, London, NW1 4RY

Tel: 020 7449 6293
Fax: 020 7586 5743
E-mail: library@zsl.org

Website:
http://www.zsl.org

Enquiries:
Enquiries to: Librarian

Founded:
1826

Organisation type and purpose:
Learned society (membership is by subscription), present number of members: 25,000, registered charity (charity number 208728), research organisation.
ZSL aims to achieve and promote the world-wide conservation of animals and their habitats.

Subject coverage:
Zoology, animal conservation, zoo management.

Museum or gallery collection, archive, or library special collection:
Archives of ZSL
Current journals on all aspects of zoology, animal conservation and zoos
An extensive photographic collection covering the diversity of nature with special emphasis on endangered and extinct animals
Library specialising in historical taxonomy (200,000 vols)
Unique collection of works of Gould, Wolf, Tickell, Reeves, Lear and Elliott

Non-library collection catalogue:
All or part available online and in-house

Library catalogue:
All or part available online and in-house

Printed publications:
Animal Conservation (journal, quarterly, Blackwells)
Conservation Biology Series (Blackwells)
International Zoo Yearbook
Journal of Zoology (monthly, Blackwells)
Wild About
Nomenclator Zoologicus

Access to staff:
Appointment necessary.
Hours: Mon to Fri, 0930 to 1730

Access to building, collection or gallery:
Photographic ID and proof of address required

Access for disabled people:
Special comments: Reading Room accessed via steps or small lift. Facilities are available to use the online catalogue and consult material elsewhere if the Reading Room cannot be accessed.

Parent body:
Institute of Zoology
London Zoo
Whipsnade Wild Animal Park

ZURICH RISK ENGINEERING UK

Zurich Risk Engineering UK, Park House, Bristol Road South, Rubery, Birmingham, B45 9AH

Tel: 0121 698 5810
E-mail: riskengineering@zurich.co.uk

Enquiries:
Enquiries to: Librarian

Formerly called:
Zurich Risk Services; Eagle Star Insurance Company

Organisation type and purpose:
Service industry.

Access to staff:
Contact by letter
Hours: Mon to Fri, 0900 to 1700

Access to building, collection or gallery:
No access other than to staff

Index of
Abbreviations and Acronyms

The abbreviations and acronyms listed here are cross-referenced by page number to their respective organisations in the Main Directory.

ADSA	Automatic Door Suppliers Association Limited, *page 90*
ADSS	Association of Directors of Social Services, *page 69*
AEA	Academy of Executives and Administrators, *page 8*
AEA	Action on Elder Abuse, *page 12*
AEA	Agricultural Engineers Association, *page 19*
AEA	Association of Electoral Administrators, *page 69*
AECC	Anglo European College of Chiropractic, *page 33*
AEDC BAS	Antarctic Environmental Data Centre, *page 36*
AEF	Aviation Environment Federation, *page 91*
AEMC	Association of Eastern Motor Clubs, *page 69*
AENA Ltd	All England Netball Association Limited, *page 23*
AEO	Association of Event Organisers Limited, *page 70*
AEP	Association of Electricity Producers, *page 70*
AES	Agricultural Economics Society, *page 19*
AES	Audio Engineering Society Ltd, *page 87*
AEWM	Association for Education Welfare Management, *page 53*
AFA	Amateur Football Alliance, *page 27*
AFA	Association of Flight Attendants, *page 70*
AFCS	Asian Family Counselling Service, *page 50*
AFK	Action for Kids, Charitable Trust, *page 11*
AfME	Action for ME, *page 11*
AFPE	Association for Physical Education, *page 56*
AFPP	Association for Perioperative Practice, *page 55*
AFS	Alcohol Focus Scotland, *page 22*
AFS	Association of Friendly Societies, *page 70*
AFTUK	Anne Frank Trust UK, *page 35*
AGBC(SE)	Association of Grace Baptist Churches (SE), *page 71*
AGBU	Armenian General Benevolent Union (London), *page 44*
AGF	Anglo German Foundation for the Study of Industrial Society, *page 33*
AGIP	Association for Group and Individual Psychotherapy, *page 53*
AGR	Association of Graduate Recruiters, *page 71*
AGRA	Association of Genealogists and Researchers in Archives, *page 70*
AGS	Alpine Garden Society, *page 25*
AGS	Architectural Glazing Services, *page 41*
AGS	Association of Geotechnical and Geoenvironmental Specialists, *page 71*
AGW	Association of Golf Writers, *page 71*
AHDS	Association of Head Teachers and Deputes in Scotland, *page 71*
AHF	Architectural Heritage Fund, *page 41*
AHGTC	Ancient and Honourable Guild of Town Criers, *page 31*
AHL	Anglo-Hellenic League, *page 34*
AHPB	Association for Humanistic Psychology in Britain, *page 53*
AHS	Antiquarian Horological Society, *page 37*
AHS	Arab Horse Society, *page 38*
AHSS	Architectural Heritage Society of Scotland, *page 42*
AHT	Animal Health Trust, *page 35*
AI	Amnesty International (United Kingdom), *page 30*
AIA	Anglo-Israel Association, *page 34*
AIA	Association for Industrial Archaeology, *page 53*
AIA	Association of International Accountants, *page 72*
AIAI	Artificial Intelligence Applications Institute, *page 46*
AIC	Agricultural Industries Confederation, *page 20*
AICS	Association of Independent Computer Specialists, *page 71*
AIIC	AIIC (United Kingdom and Ireland Region), *page 20*
AIIT	MaceCorp Limited, *page 742*
AIL	Association of Independent Libraries, *page 72*

AILLSTTB	Argyll, the Isles, Loch Lomond, Stirling & Trossachs Tourist Board, *page 43*
AILU	Association of Laser Users, *page 73*
AIM	Association of Independent Museums, *page 72*
AIR	Alliance of Independent Retailers, *page 25*
Air Photo Library	Unit for Landscape Modelling, *page 1164*
AIS	Association of Interior Specialists Limited, *page 72*
AITO	Association of Independent Tour Operators Limited, *page 72*
AIYF	Aberdeen International Youth Festival, *page 5*
AJA	Anglo Jewish Association, *page 33*
AJE	United Synagogue Agency for Jewish Education, *page 1170*
AJR	Association of Jewish Refugees in Great Britain, *page 73*
AKA	Association of Ki Aikido, *page 73*
ALCD	Association of Law Costs Draftsmen, *page 73*
ALCI	Association of Landscape Contractors of Ireland (Northern Region), *page 73*
ALCL	Association of London Chief Librarians, *page 74*
ALCS	Association for Low Countries Studies in Great Britain and Ireland, *page 54*
ALCS	Authors' Licensing & Collecting Society Limited, *page 89*
ALFED	Aluminium Federation, *page 26*
ALG	Association of London Government, *page 74*
ALHA	Avon Local History and Archaeology, *page 91*
ALIS	Aberdeenshire Library and Information Service, *page 6*
ALL	Association for Language Learning, *page 54*
ALL	Association for Latin Liturgy, *page 54*
ALPSP	Association of Learned and Professional Society Publishers, *page 74*
ALS	Alliance of Literary Societies, *page 25*
ALT	Association for Learning Technology, *page 54*
ALT	Association of Law Teachers, *page 73*
ALUPRO	Aluminium Packaging Recycling Organisation, *page 26*
ALVA	Association of Leading Visitor Attractions, *page 74*
AMA(UK)	Ahmadiyya Muslim Association (UK), *page 20*
AMBARWA	Embassy of Rwanda, *page 427*
AMED	Association for Management Education and Development, *page 55*
Amicus–CPHVA	Community Practitioners and Health Visiting Association, *page 337*
AMOC	Aston Martin Owners Club Limited, *page 85*
AMPS	Association of Manufacturers of Power Generating Systems, *page 74*
AMR	Association of Muslim Researchers, *page 75*
AMRC	Association of Medical Research Charities, *page 75*
AMRCO Ltd	Association of Motor Racing Circuit Owners Ltd, *page 75*
AMS	Academy of Multi-Skills, *page 8*
AMS	Ancient Monuments Society, *page 31*
AMS	Association of Muslim Schools, *page 75*
AMSPAR	AMSPAR Limited, *page 30*
ANC	Association of Noise Consultants, *page 76*
ANCC	All Nations Christian College, *page 24*
ANESFHS	Aberdeen and North East Scotland Family History Society, *page 4*
ANLHS	Association of Northumberland Local History Societies, *page 76*
ANMW	Association of Newspaper and Magazine Wholesalers, *page 76*
ANSA	Association of Nurses in Substance Abuse, *page 76*
ANTOR	Association of National Tourist Office Representatives, *page 76*
ANTS	Anglo-Norman Text Society, *page 34*
AOC	Aromatherapy Council, *page 45*
AoC	Association of Colleges, *page 66*
AOI	Association of Illustrators, *page 71*
AOP	Association of Optometrists, *page 76*
AOP	Association of Photographers Limited, *page 77*
AoR	Association of Reflexologists (UK), *page 80*

AYME	Association of Young People with ME, *page 84*	BAILER	British Association for Information and Library Education and Research, *page 146*
B S Society	Bram Stoker Society, The, *page 132*		
B&NES	Bath and North East Somerset Council, *page 100*	BAL	British Architectural Library, *page 143*
		BALH	British Association for Local History, *page 146*
B-SBT	BritishSerbian Benevolent Trust, *page 228*	BALI	British Association of Landscape Industries, *page 151*
BA	Bicycle Association of Great Britain Limited, *page 111*	BAMA	British Aerosol Manufacturers' Association, *page 139*
BA	Booksellers Association of the UK & Ireland Limited, *page 127*	BAMS	British Art Medal Society, *page 143*
BAAC	British Association of Aviation Consultants, *page 149*	BANS	British Association of Numismatic Societies, *page 151*
BAAL	British Association for Applied Linguistics, *page 144*	BAP	British Association for Psychopharmacology, *page 147*
BAALPE	British Association of Advisers and Lecturers in Physical Education, *page 148*	BAP	British Association of Psychotherapists, *page 152*
BAAP	British Association of Audiological Physicians, *page 148*	BAPAM	British Association for Performing Arts Medicine, *page 146*
BAAS	British Association for American Studies, *page 144*	BAPC	British Association for Print and Communication, *page 147*
BAAT	British Association of Art Therapists, *page 148*	BAPC	British Aviation Preservation Council, *page 154*
BABi	British American Business Inc, *page 141*	BAPH	British Association of Paper Historians, *page 151*
BAC	British Accreditation Council, *page 139*		
BAcC	British Acupuncture Council, *page 139*	BAPIS	Leeds City Libraries – Business and Patent Information Services, *page 704*
BACCH	British Association for Community Child Health, *page 145*	BAPLA	British Association of Picture Libraries and Agencies, *page 151*
BACD	British Association of Conference Destinations, *page 149*	BAPM	British Association for Perinatal Medicine, *page 147*
BACEE	British Association for Central and Eastern Europe, *page 145*	BAPN	British Association for Paediatric Nephrology, *page 146*
BACFI	Bar Association for Commerce, Finance and Industry, The, *page 96*	BAPT	British Association for Psychological Type, *page 147*
BACG	British Association for Crystal Growth, *page 145*	BAPW	British Association of Pharmaceutical Wholesalers, *page 151*
BACM-TEAM	British Association of Colliery Management, Technical, Energy and Administrative Management, *page 149*	BAR	British Agents Register, *page 140*
		BAR	British Association of Removers, *page 152*
		Bar Council	General Council of the Bar of England and Wales, *page 511*
BACO	British Academic Conference in Otolaryngology, *page 138*	BARC	British Automobile Racing Club Limited, *page 154*
BACP	British Association for Counselling & Psychotherapy, *page 145*	BARLA	British Amateur Rugby League Association, *page 140*
BACR	British Association for Cancer Research, *page 144*	BAS	Berkshire Archaeological Society, *page 107*
BACS	British Association for Canadian Studies, *page 144*	BAS	British Antarctic Survey, *page 142*
		BAS	British Arachnological Society, *page 143*
BACS	British Association for Chemical Specialities, *page 145*	BAS	Buckinghamshire Archaeological Society, *page 235*
BACS	Business Archives Council of Scotland, *page 239*	BAS	Bureau of Analysed Samples Limited, *page 237*
BACSA	British Association for Cemeteries in South Asia, *page 144*	BASA	British Adhesive and Sealants Association, *page 139*
BACUP 'NAT'	Bacup Natural History Society, *page 93*	BASC	Birmingham Automotive Safety Centre, *page 114*
BAD	British Association of Dermatologists, *page 149*		
BADA	British Antique Dealers' Association, *page 142*	BASES	British Association of Sports and Exercise Sciences, *page 153*
BADC	British Academy of Dramatic Combat, *page 138*	BASI	British Association of Snowsports Instructors, *page 152*
BADCO	British Association of Domiciliary Care, *page 150*		
BADN	British Association of Dental Nurses, *page 149*	BASICS	British Association for Immediate Care, *page 146*
BADth	British Association of Dramatherapists, *page 150*	BASO~ACS	British Association of Surgical Oncology, *page 153*
BAEM	British Association for Emergency Medicine, *page 146*	BASP	British Association of Ski Patrollers (BASP UK LTD), *page 152*
BAF	British Abrasives Federation, *page 138*	BASPCAN	British Association for the Study and Prevention of Child Abuse and Neglect, *page 148*
BAFA	British Arts Festivals Association, *page 143*		
BAFD	British Association of Fastener Distributors, *page 150*	BASRT	British Association for Sexual and Relationship Therapy, *page 147*
BAFE	British Approvals for Fire Equipment, *page 143*	bassac	British Association of Settlements and Social Action Centres, *page 152*
BAFM	British Association of Friends of Museums, *page 150*		
BAFRA	British Antique Furniture Restorers Association, *page 142*	BASW	British Association of Social Workers, *page 153*
		BAT	British American Tobacco, *page 141*
BAFTA	British Academy of Film and Television Arts, *page 139*	BATC	British Apparel & Textile Confederation, *page 142*
BAGCD	British Association of Green Crop Driers Limited, *page 150*	BATD	British Association of Teachers of Dancing, *page 153*
BAGMA	British Agricultural & Garden Machinery Association, *page 140*	BATOD	British Association of Teachers of the Deaf, *page 153*
BAHA	British Activity Holiday Association, *page 139*	BAUS	British Association of Urological Surgeons, *page 154*
BAHS	British Agricultural History Society, *page 140*		

BExA	British Exporters Association, *page 169*	
BFA	British Footwear Association, *page 172*	
BFA	British Franchise Association, *page 172*	
BFBB	British Federation of Brass Bands, *page 170*	
BfBi	Brewing, Food & Beverage Industry Suppliers Association, *page 135*	
BFBS	Bible Society, *page 111*	
BFC	British Falconers' Club, *page 169*	
BFC	British Fashion Council, *page 170*	
BFCMA	British Flue and Chimney Manufacturers' Association, *page 171*	
BfD	Bees for Development, *page 105*	
BFI	British Film Institute – National Library, *page 170*	
BFLSBA	Bluefaced Leicester Sheep Breeders Association, *page 122*	
BFPA	British Fluid Power Association, *page 171*	
BFPSA	British Fire Protection Systems Association Limited, *page 171*	
BFRMC	British Friends of Rambam Medical Centre, *page 172*	
BFS	British Fluoridation Society, *page 171*	
BFS	British Flute Society, *page 172*	
BFS	British Fuchsia Society, The, *page 172*	
BFSS	British and Foreign School Society, *page 141*	
BFWG	British Federation of Women Graduates, *page 170*	
BG	British Gymnastics, *page 175*	
BGA	British Gear Association, *page 172*	
BGA	British Geotechnical Association, *page 174*	
BGA	British Gliding Association, *page 174*	
BGA	British Glove Association, *page 174*	
BGA	British-German Association, *page 228*	
BGAS	Bristol and Gloucestershire Archaeological Society, *page 136*	
BGMC	British Glass Manufacturers Confederation, *page 174*	
BGRB	British Greyhound Racing Board Limited, *page 175*	
BGS	Board of Graduate Studies, *page 123*	
BGS	British Geological Survey, *page 173*	
BGS	British Geological Survey – Marine Operations and Engineering, *page 173*	
BGS	British Geological Survey – Research Knowledge Services, *page 173*	
BGS	British Geriatrics Society, *page 174*	
BGS	British Goat Society, *page 175*	
BGS	British Grassland Society, *page 175*	
BGTW	British Guild of Travel Writers, *page 175*	
BH & HPA Ltd	British Holiday and Home Parks Association, *page 178*	
BHA	British Hardmetal Association, *page 176*	
BHA	British Homeopathic Association, *page 178*	
BHA	British Horseball Association, *page 179*	
BHA	British Hospitality Association, *page 179*	
BHA	British Humanist Association, *page 179*	
BHA	British Hypnotherapy Association, *page 180*	
BHAB	British Helicopter Advisory Board Limited, *page 177*	
BHAVAN	Institute of Indian Culture (Bharatiya Vidya Bhavan), *page 617*	
BHCA	British Health Care Association, *page 176*	
BHCT	Brougham Hall Charitable Trust, *page 232*	
BHF	British Heart Foundation, *page 177*	
BHF	British Horological Federation, *page 178*	
BHI	British Horological Institute, *page 178*	
BHI	British Horological Institute Ltd, *page 179*	
BHL	Bromley House Library, *page 230*	
BHMA	British Herbal Medicine Association, *page 177*	
BHMA	British Holistic Medical Association, *page 178*	
BHPA	British Hang Gliding and Paragliding Association, *page 176*	
BHPS	British Hedgehog Preservation Society, *page 177*	
BHRS	Bedfordshire Historical Record Society, *page 105*	
BHS	Baptist Historical Society, *page 95*	
BHS	British Herpetological Society, *page 178*	
BHS	British Horse Society, *page 179*	

BHTA	British Healthcare Trades Association, *page 176*	
BIA Scotland	Bio Industry Association Scotland, *page 112*	
BIAA	British Institute at Ankara, *page 181*	
biab online	biab online – the British and Irish Archaeological Bibliography, *page 110*	
BIAC	British Institute of Agricultural Consultants, *page 182*	
BIALL	British and Irish Association of Law Librarians, *page 141*	
BIB	Brunel Institute for Bioengineering, *page 232*	
Bib Dev	British Library – Bibliographic Development, *page 188*	
BIBA	British Insurance Brokers' Association, *page 185*	
BIBF	British and Irish Basketball Federation, *page 142*	
BICSc	British Institute of Cleaning Science, *page 182*	
BICTA	British Investment Casting Trade Association, *page 186*	
BIEA	British Institute in Eastern Africa, *page 182*	
BIFA	British International Freight Association, *page 186*	
BIFCA	British Industrial Furnace Constructors Association, *page 180*	
BIFHE	Belfast Institute of Further and Higher Education, *page 106*	
BIFM	British Institute of Facilities Management, *page 182*	
BIG	British Institute of Graphologists, *page 183*	
BIH	British Institute of Homeopathy, *page 183*	
BIHR	British Institute of Human Rights, *page 183*	
BII	British Institute of Innkeeping, *page 183*	
BIICL	British Institute of International and Comparative Law, *page 183*	
BIIT	British Institute of Industrial Therapy, *page 183*	
BILA	British Insurance Law Association, *page 185*	
BILD	British Institute for Learning & Development, *page 181*	
BILD	British Institute of Learning Disabilities, *page 184*	
BIMM	British Institute of Musculoskeletal Medicine, *page 184*	
BINDT	British Institute of Non-destructive Testing, *page 184*	
BIOH	British Institute of Occupational Hygienists, *page 184*	
BIOS	British and Irish Orthoptic Society, *page 142*	
BIOS	British Institute of Organ Studies, *page 184*	
BIOSS	BIOSS International, *page 113*	
BIPA	British Imaging and Photographic Association, *page 180*	
BIPEA	British Independent Plastic Extruders' Association, *page 180*	
BIPP	British Institute of Professional Photography, *page 185*	
BIR	British Institute of Radiology, *page 185*	
Birmingham Focus	Birmingham Focus on Blindness, *page 116*	
BIS	British Infection Society, *page 181*	
BIS	British Interplanetary Society, *page 186*	
BIS	British Iris Society, *page 186*	
BISA	British International Studies Association, *page 186*	
BITA	British Industrial Truck Association, *page 181*	
BITA	British Interior Textiles Association, *page 185*	
BITC	Business in the Community, *page 239*	
BIVDA	British In Vitro Diagnostic Association, *page 180*	
BIWF	British-Israel-World Federation, *page 228*	
BJA	British Jewellers' Association, *page 187*	
BJC	British Judo Council, *page 187*	
BJL	Bodleian Japanese Library, *page 124*	
BJPL	British Jigsaw Puzzle Library, *page 187*	
BKA	British Korfball Association, *page 187*	
BKKU	British Kenpo Karate Union, *page 187*	
BKPA	British Kidney Patient Association, *page 187*	
BL	British Library – Business and Intellectual Property Centre, *page 188*	
BL	British Library – Eccles Centre for American Studies, *page 189*	
BL	British Library – Map Collections, *page 191*	

BRUFMA	British Rigid Urethane Foam Manufacturers' Association Limited, *page* 210	BSSAA	British Snoring and Sleep Apnoea Association Limited, *page* 213
BSA	Birmingham School of Acting, *page* 118	BSSC	British Shooting Sports Council, *page* 212
BSA	Boarding Schools' Association, *page* 123	BSSM	British Society for Strain Measurement, *page* 216
BSA	British Society of Aesthetics, *page* 216	BSSPD	British Society for the Study of Prosthetic Dentistry, *page* 216
BSA	British Society of Audiology, *page* 217		
BSA	British Sociological Association, *page* 219	BSSS	British Society of Soil Science, *page* 218
BSA	British Stammering Association, *page* 219	BSY GROUP	British School of Yoga, *page* 211
BSA	British Surfing Association, *page* 220	BTA	British Tinnitus Association, *page* 221
BSA	Building Societies Association, *page* 237	BTA	British Trout Association, *page* 222
BSA	Business Services Association, *page* 244	BTCV	BTCV – Wallingford, *page* 234
BSA	Business Software Alliance, *page* 245	BTCV Scotland	British Trust for Conservation Volunteers Scotland, *page* 222
BSA at NIACE	Basic Skills Agency at NIACE, *page* 99		
BSACI	British Society for Allergy and Clinical Immunology, *page* 214	BTF	British Thyroid Foundation, *page* 221
BSAFWDC	BSA Front-Wheel Drive Club, *page* 232	BTG	British Toymakers Guild, *page* 222
BSAS	British Society of Animal Science, *page* 217	BTHA	British Toy & Hobby Association Limited, *page* 222
BSAT	British Sporting Art Trust, *page* 219		
BSAVA	British Small Animal Veterinary Association, *page* 213	BTMA	British Textile Machinery Association, *page* 221
		BTMA	British Turned Parts Manufacturers Association, *page* 223
BSBI	Botanical Society of the British Isles, *page* 128	BTO	British Trust for Ornithology, *page* 223
BSC	British Safety Council, *page* 211	BTS	British Tarantula Society, *page* 221
BSCA	British Schools Cycling Association, *page* 212	BTS	British Trolleybus Society, *page* 222
BSCB	British Society for Cell Biology, *page* 214	BTS	British Tunnelling Society, *page* 223
BSCC	British Society for Clinical Cytology, *page* 214	BTS	Business and Trade Statistics Limited, *page* 239
BSD	British Society of Dowsers, *page* 217	BUAV	British Union for the Abolition of Vivisection, *page* 224
BSDA	British Soft Drinks Association Limited, *page* 219		
		BUC	British Union Conference of Seventh-day Adventists, *page* 223
BSDB	British Society for Developmental Biology, *page* 214		
		BUFORA	British Unidentified Flying Object Research Association, *page* 223
BSDR	British Society for Dental Research, *page* 214		
BSES Expeditions	British Schools Exploring Society, *page* 212	BUFVC	British Universities Film & Video Council, *page* 224
BSF	British Sikh Federation, *page* 213		
BSF	British Softball Federation, *page* 219	BURA	British Urban Regeneration Association, *page* 224
BSFA	British Science Fiction Association Limited, *page* 212		
		Bury Metro	Metropolitan Borough of Bury, *page* 767
BSG	British Society for Geomorphology, *page* 214	BUSA	British Universities Sports Association, *page* 224
BSG	British Society of Gastroenterology, *page* 217		
BSG	British Society of Gerontology, *page* 217	BUSWE	British Union of Social Work Employees, *page* 224
BSGA	British Schools Gymnastic Association, *page* 212		
		Butchers' Company	Worshipful Company of Butchers, *page* 1265
BSGA	British Sign & Graphics Association, *page* 213	BVA	British Veterinary Association, *page* 225
BSH	British Society for Haematology, *page* 215	BVA	British Video Association, *page* 225
BSH	British Society of Hypnotherapists, *page* 218	BVA	British Voice Association, *page* 226
BSHAA	British Society of Hearing Aid Audiologists, *page* 218	BVAMA	British Valve & Actuator Association, *page* 225
		BVS	Battery Vehicle Society, *page* 101
BSHP	British Society for the History of Pharmacy, *page* 216	BVSS	British Vendeen Sheep Society, *page* 225
		BWA	Bitumen Waterproofing Association (UK) Ltd, *page* 119
BSHS	British Society for the History of Science, *page* 216		
		BWBF	British Wireless for the Blind Fund, *page* 227
BSI	British Society for Immunology, *page* 215	BWCMG	British Watch and Clockmakers Guild, *page* 226
BSI	British Suzuki Institute, *page* 220	BWLA	British Weight Lifters Association Limited, *page* 226
BSI	BSI Product Services, *page* 233		
BSIA	British Security Industry Association Limited, *page* 212	BWMA	British Weights and Measures Association, *page* 226
BSIA	British Starch Industry Association, *page* 220	BWPA	British Women Pilots' Association, *page* 227
BSIF	British Safety Industry Federation, *page* 211	BWRC	British Wildlife Rescue Centre, *page* 227
BSJA	British Show Jumping Association, *page* 213	BWSF	British Wheelchair Sports Foundation, *page* 227
BSMDH (MET&S)	British Society for Medical and Dental Hypnosis, *page* 215	BYC	British Youth Council, *page* 228
		CA	Classical Association, *page* 320
BSMFD	British Society for Mercury Free Dentistry, *page* 215	CA	Consumers' Association, *page* 346
		CA	Croquet Association, *page* 364
BSMGP	British Society of Master Glass Painters, *page* 218	CA	Cruising Association, *page* 366
		CAA	Cement Admixtures Association, *page* 266
BSMT	British Society for Music Therapy, *page* 215	CAA	Cinema Advertising Association Limited, *page* 312
BSNR	British Society of Neuroradiologists, *page* 218		
BSO	British School of Osteopathy, *page* 211	CAA	Civil Aviation Authority, *page* 318
BSP	British Society for Parasitology, *page* 215	CAA	Club for Acts and Actors, *page* 322
BSP	British Society of Periodontology, *page* 218	CAABU	Council for the Advancement of Arab-British Understanding, *page* 356
BSPB	British Society of Plant Breeders Limited, *page* 218		
		CAAT	Campaign Against Arms Trade, *page* 252
BSR	British Society for Rheumatology, *page* 216	Cab	Christians Abroad, *page* 308
BSRD	British Society for Restorative Dentistry, *page* 216	CAB	Council for Aluminium in Building, *page* 354
		CABE	Christian Association of Business Executives, *page* 307
BSRIA	Building Services Research and Information Association, *page* 237		
BSS	Botanical Society of Scotland, *page* 128	CABI	CAB International, *page* 246
BSS	British Standards Society, *page* 219	CAC	Central Arbitration Committee, *page* 267
BSS-Do	British School of Shiatsu-Do, *page* 211	CAC	Citizens Advice Cymru, *page* 314

GIMA	Garden Industry Manufacturers Association (1999) Limited, *page 509*		HAT Archive	History of Advertising Trust Archive, *page 569*
GLAD	Greater London Action on Disability, *page 530*		HBC	Havant Borough Council, *page 548*
Glaziers Company	Worshipful Company of Glaziers and Painters of Glass, *page 1268*		HBMC or EH	English Heritage, *page 436*
			HBP	Housebuilder Publications, *page 578*
GLCRT	Gray Cancer Institute, *page 529*		HBS	Havergal Brian Society, *page 548*
GLIS (UK)	Germanischer Lloyd Industrial Services (UK) Limited, *page 516*		HC	Hairdressing Council, *page 542*
			HCA	Hall-Carpenter Archives, *page 543*
GLTA	Glued Laminated Timber Association, *page 524*		HCA	Holiday Centres Association, *page 571*
GMCRO	Greater Manchester County Record Office, *page 531*		HCC	Hospital Chaplaincies Council, *page 576*
			HCC	Hungarian Cultural Centre, *page 583*
GMCVO	Greater Manchester Centre for Voluntary Organisation, *page 531*		HCGB	Hovercraft Club of Great Britain Limited, *page 578*
GMG	Guardian Newspapers Limited, *page 534*		HCIMA	Hotel and Catering International Management Association, *page 577*
GNI Int	Guild of Naturopathic Iridologists International, *page 536*		HCIO	House of Commons Information Office, *page 577*
GNTO	German National Tourist Office, *page 516*		HCIS	British Library – Health Care Information Service, *page 190*
GOC	General Optical Council, *page 512*			
GofHT	Guild of Handicraft Trust, *page 536*		HCKC	Hillman Commer & Karrier Club, *page 567*
GOONS	Guild of One-Name Studies, *page 536*		HCSA	Hospital Consultants and Specialists Association, *page 576*
GOsC	General Osteopathic Council, *page 512*			
GOT	Guild of Taxidermists, *page 537*		HCST	H C Starck Limited, *page 541*
GPDA	Gypsum Products Development Limited, *page 540*		HCVS	Historic Commercial Vehicle Society, *page 567*
			HDA	Health Development Agency, *page 551*
GPI	George Padmore Institute, *page 515*		HDA	Huntington's Disease Association, *page 584*
GPMU	Graphical, Paper and Media Union, *page 528*		HDC	Horticultural Development Company, *page 575*
GPV	Guild of Professional Videographers, *page 537*		HDRA	Home Decoration Retailers Association, *page 572*
GRA	Greeves Riders Association, *page 533*			
GRCA	Glassfibre Reinforced Concrete Association, *page 522*		HEBS	Health Education Board for Scotland, *page 552*
			HECSU	Graduate Prospects Ltd, *page 527*
Greater Mersyside LSC	Greater Merseyside Learning and Skills Council, *page 531*		HEFCE	Higher Education Funding Council for England, *page 564*
GRO	Gwent Record Office, *page 540*		HEFCW	Higher Education Funding Council for Wales, *page 564*
GROS	General Register Office for Scotland, *page 512*			
GSA	Glasgow School of Art, *page 522*		Henry George Foundation	Henry George Foundation of Gt Britain Limited, *page 556*
GSEIS	Graduate School of European and International Studies, *page 528*		Herefordshire Council	County of Herefordshire District Council, *page 359*
GSES	University of Strathclyde – Graduate School of Environmental Studies, *page 1202*		HESA	Higher Education Statistics Agency, *page 565*
			HFAN (UK)	Health for All Network (UK) Ltd, *page 552*
GSG	Good Schools Guide, *page 526*		HFBG	Historic Farm Buildings Group, *page 567*
GSMD	Guildhall School of Music and Drama, *page 538*		HFHS	Herefordshire Family History Society, *page 559*
GT	Gender Trust, *page 510*		HFHS	Highland Family History Society, *page 565*
GTA	Gun Trade Association Limited, *page 539*		HFMA	Health Food Manufacturers' Association, *page 552*
GTC Scotland	General Teaching Council for Scotland, *page 513*			
			HGWS	H G Wells Society, The, *page 541*
GTCW	General Teaching Council for Wales, *page 513*		HHA	Historic Houses Association, *page 567*
GTMA	Gauge and Tool Makers' Association, *page 510*		HHC	Holistic Health College, *page 572*
GTPU	Guys' and St Thomas' Poisons Unit, Guy's and St Thomas' NHS Foundation Trust, *page 539*		HIE	Highlands & Islands Enterprise, *page 566*
			HKTB	Hong Kong Tourism Board, *page 574*
GTT Ltd	Growth Through Training (GTT) Limited, *page 533*		HLBC	Canning House Library, *page 256*
			HLF	Heritage Lottery Fund, *page 560*
GVA	Gin and Vodka Association, *page 517*		HLIS	Hampshire Library and Information Service – Farnborough, *page 545*
GWCT	Game and Wildlife Conservation Trust, *page 508*			
GWL	Glasgow Women's Library, *page 522*		HLN	Hounslow Library Network, *page 577*
GWP	Guild of Photographers (United Kingdom), *page 537*		HLR	Historic Lotus Register, *page 568*
			HLRO	Parliamentary Archives, *page 912*
GWS	Great Western Society Limited, *page 530*		HLS	Huntingdon Life Sciences, *page 583*
H&D FHS	Huddersfield and District Family History Society, *page 580*		HLSI	Highgate Literary and Scientific Institution, *page 565*
H.E.A.R.T UK	Hyperlipidaemia Education & Atherosclerosis Research Trust UK, *page 585*		HMBCE	English Heritage (South West Region), *page 439*
			HMC	Headmasters' and Headmistresses' Conference, *page 550*
HA	Historical Association, *page 568*			
HA	Huntingdonshire Archives, *page 583*		HMC&E	HM Customs and Excise – Library and Information Service, *page 570*
HABIA	Hair and Beauty Industry Authority (HABIA), *page 542*		HMLR	HM Land Registry, *page 570*
			HMNAO	HM Nautical Almanac Office, *page 571*
HAC	Help Advisory Centre, *page 556*		HMRS	Historical Model Railway Society, *page 569*
HACSG	Hyperactive Children's Support Group, *page 584*		HMS	Historical Metallurgical Society Limited, *page 569*
HAE	Hire Association Europe, *page 567*			
HALS	Hampshire Archives and Local Studies, *page 543*		HMSTC	Hertfordshire Multiple Sclerosis Therapy Centre, *page 562*
			HNHS	Hertfordshire Natural History Society, *page 562*
HALS	Hertfordshire Archives and Local Studies, *page 562*		HOS	Housing Ombudsman Service, *page 578*
Hants Field Club	Hampshire Field Club and Archaeological Society, *page 545*		HOT	Hawk and Owl Trust, *page 549*
			HP CDS	Hewlett-Packard CDS, *page 563*
HAPPA	Horses and Ponies Protection Association, *page 575*		HPA	Health Protection Agency, *page 553*
HAT	History of Advertising Trust, *page 569*		HPA	Health Protection Agency – Centre for Infections, *page 553*

ISOA   International Support Vessel Owners Association, *page 655*
ISP   Institute of Sales Promotion, *page 628*
ISPAL   Insitute for Sport, Parks and Leisure, *page 598*
ISPE   Institute of Swimming Pool Engineers Limited, *page 629*
ISR   International Star Registry, *page 654*
ISRM   Institute of Sport and Recreation Management, *page 629*
ISS   Institute of Sports Sponsorship, *page 629*
ISSB   ISSB Limited, *page 667*
ISSMGE   International Society for Soil Mechanics and Geotechnical Engineering, *page 654*
ISSO   International Swaminarayan Satsang Organisation, *page 655*
IST   Institute of Spring Technology Limited, *page 629*
ISTA   International Steel Trade Association, *page 655*
ISTD   Imperial Society of Teachers of Dancing, *page 590*
IStructE   Institution of Structural Engineers, *page 635*
ISTT   International Society for Trenchless Technology, *page 654*
ISVR   Institute of Sound and Vibration Research, *page 628*
ITC   International Tea Committee Limited, *page 656*
ITC Ltd   Individual Travellers Co Ltd, *page 594*
ITDG   Intermediate Technology Development Group Limited, *page 636*
ITEC   International Therapy Examination Council, *page 656*
ITF   International Transport Workers' Federation, *page 657*
ITF   International Tree Foundation, *page 657*
ITI   Institute of Translation and Interpreting (ITI), *page 630*
ITI   International Theatre Institute Limited, *page 656*
ITL   Imperial Tobacco Limited, *page 590*
ITMA   Institute of Trade Mark Attorneys, *page 630*
ITOPF   International Tanker Owners Pollution Federation Limited, *page 656*
ITS   Institute for Transport Studies, *page 602*
ITS   Irish Texts Society, *page 662*
ITT   Institute of Travel and Tourism, *page 630*
ITTF   International Table Tennis Federation, *page 656*
IUA   International Underwriting Association, *page 657*
IVCA   International Visual Communication Association, *page 657*
IVE   Institute of Vitreous Enamellers, *page 631*
IVehE   Institute of Vehicle Engineers, *page 630*
IVS   International Voluntary Service, *page 658*
IVS   International Voluntary Service (North), *page 658*
IWA   Inland Waterways Association, *page 597*
IWA   International Water Association, *page 658*
IWC   International Whaling Commission, *page 658*
IWCOC   Isle of Wight Chamber of Commerce and Industry, *page 665*
IWCT   International Wildlife Coalition Trust, *page 658*
IWFS   International Wine & Food Society, *page 658*
IWH   Institute of Women's Health, *page 631*
IWM   Imperial War Museum, *page 590*
IWPPA   Independent Waste Paper Processors Association, *page 593*
IWR   Information World Review, *page 596*
IWSc   Institute of Wood Science, *page 631*
IYF   International Youth Foundation of Great Britain, *page 659*
IZAUK   International Zen Association (United Kingdom), *page 659*
JACT   Joint Association of Classical Teachers, *page 676*
JAMPRO   Jamaica Trade Commission, *page 668*
Jane's   Jane's Information Group, *page 669*
JBD   Jewish Blind and Disabled, *page 672*
JBS   Josephine Butler Society, *page 678*
JBSoc   John Buchan Society, *page 674*

JCCI   Japanese Chamber of Commerce and Industry in the United Kingdom, *page 670*
JCCL   Junior Chamber of Commerce for London, *page 679*
JCLI   Joint Council for Landscape Industries, *page 676*
JCWI   Joint Council for the Welfare of Immigrants, *page 676*
JDA   Jewellery Distributors' Association, *page 672*
JDRF   Juvenile Diabetes Research Foundation, *page 680*
JEB   Jewish Education Bureau, *page 672*
JEC   Jaguar Enthusiasts' Club, *page 668*
JEC   Jewel & Esk College, *page 671*
JEECS   Jewish East End Celebration Society, *page 672*
JET   Joint Educational Trust, *page 676*
JETRO   JETRO London, *page 671*
JHSE   Jewish Historical Society of England, *page 673*
JIB   Joint Industry Board for the Electrical Contracting Industry, *page 677*
JIB   Jordan Information Bureau, *page 678*
JIC   John Innes Centre and Sainsbury Laboratory, *page 674*
JICC   Japanese Embassy, *page 670*
JIMA   John Innes Manufacturers Association, *page 675*
JKJ Society   Jerome K Jerome Society, *page 670*
JMC   Jewish Marriage Council, *page 673*
JMF Soc   John Meade Falkner Society, *page 675*
JMI   Jewish Music Institute, *page 673*
JMTC   Johnson Matthey Technology Centre, *page 676*
JNCC   Joint Nature Conservation Committee, *page 677*
JNTO   Japan National Tourist Organization, *page 669*
JOAC   Jupiter Owners Auto Club, *page 679*
John Cabot CTC John Cabot City Technology College, *page 674*
JPR   Institute for Jewish Policy Research, *page 600*
JRF   Joseph Rowntree Foundation, *page 678*
JRULM   John Rylands University Library of Manchester, *page 675*
JRULM   Methodist Archives and Research Centre, *page 767*
JSCSC   Joint Services Command & Staff College Library, *page 677*
JTSMA   Jennifer Trust for Spinal Muscular Atrophy, *page 670*
JVC   JVC Professional Europe Limited, *page 680*
JVDC   Justice for all Vaccine-Damaged Children, *page 680*
K&ESR   Kent and East Sussex Railway, *page 682*
KABCA   Kaolin and Ball Clay Association, *page 680*
KAS   Kent Archaeological Society, *page 682*
KC   Kirklees College – Huddersfield Centre, *page 688*
KCC Libraries and Archive Kent County Council Libraries and Archives, *page 682*
KCL   King's College London – St Thomas' Hospital Medical Library, *page 686*
KCL   King's College London – Stamford Street Information Services Centre, *page 686*
KFAT   National Union of Knitwear, Footwear and Apparel Trades, *page 853*
KFHS   Kent Family History Society, *page 683*
KIAD   Kent Institute of Art and Design at Maidstone, *page 683*
KIB   Kodály Institute of Britain, *page 689*
KIF   Knitting Industries' Federation, *page 688*
KNTO   Korea National Tourism Organization, *page 689*
KSGB   Kite Society of Great Britain, *page 688*
KSL   Kate Sharpley Library, *page 681*
L&I   List and Index Society, *page 716*
L&SWLFHS   Liverpool & SW Lancashire Family History Society, *page 718*
LA   Libertarian Alliance, *page 710*
LA   Lincolnshire Archives, *page 715*
LA   Lymphoma Association, *page 741*
LAACTSA   Local Authority Action for Southern Africa, *page 721*
LACA   Local Authority Caterers Association, *page 722*

LSC or LSCKM	Learning and Skills Council for Kent and Medway, *page 702*
LSF	London Sports Forum for Disabled People, *page 737*
LSHTM	London School of Hygiene and Tropical Medicine, *page 735*
LSJ	London School of Journalism Limited, *page 735*
LSN	Learning and Skills Development Network, *page 702*
LSNI	Law Society of Northern Ireland, *page 699*
LSO	London Symphony Orchestra Limited, *page 737*
LSP	London School of Publishing, *page 735*
LSRA	Lead Smelters and Refiners Association, *page 701*
LSSA	London Subterranean Survey Association, *page 737*
LSt	London School of Theology, *page 735*
LTA	Lawn Tennis Association, *page 699*
LTB	London Tourist Board and Convention Bureau, *page 738*
LTBP	London Tanker Brokers' Panel Limited, *page 737*
LTGF	London Thames Gateway Forum of Voluntary and Community Organisations, *page 737*
LTL	Learning Through Landscapes, *page 703*
LTS	Lands Tribunal for Scotland, *page 696*
LTS	Learning and Teaching Scotland, *page 702*
LTS	London Theological Seminary, *page 738*
LTS	London Topographical Society, *page 738*
LURS	London Underground Railway Society, *page 738*
LVSC	London Voluntary Service Council, *page 739*
LYA	Lancashire Youth Association, *page 694*
M&LFHS	Manchester and Lancashire Family History Society, *page 747*
MA	Magistrates' Association, *page 744*
MA	Mathematical Association, *page 755*
MA	Metamorphic Association, *page 766*
MA	Museums Association, *page 789*
MAA	Migraine Action Association, *page 772*
MAC	Mastic Asphalt Council, *page 754*
MACA	Together (MACA), *page 1142*
Macaulay Institute	Macaulay Land Use Research Institute, *page 742*
MACP	Manipulation Association of Chartered Physiotherapists, *page 750*
MAF (UK)	Mission Aviation Fellowship (UK), *page 776*
MAFVA	Miniature AFV Association, *page 774*
MAGB	Maltsters Association of Great Britain, *page 746*
MALS	Manchester Archives and Local Studies, *page 747*
MALSC	Medway Archives and Local Studies Centre, *page 760*
MAMA	Meet a Mum Association, *page 761*
MARQUES	Association of European Brand Owners, *page 70*
MAS	Medical Advisory Service, *page 757*
MASTA	Medical Advisory Services for Travellers Abroad, *page 757*
MAVIS	Mobility Advice and Vehicle Information Service, *page 777*
MBF	Multiple Births Foundation, *page 787*
MBR	Department of the Environment for Northern Ireland, *page 383*
MBS	Manchester Business School, *page 748*
MBSGB	Musical Box Society of Great Britain, *page 790*
MCA	Management Consultancies Association, *page 747*
MCA	Maritime and Coastguard Agency, *page 752*
MCA	McTimoney Chiropractic Association, *page 756*
MCA	Medical Council on Alcohol, The, *page 757*
MCAS	Menzies Centre for Australian Studies, *page 763*
MCC	Motor Cycling Club Limited, *page 784*
MCCC	Midlands Club Cricket Conference, *page 771*
MCG	Major Contractors Group, *page 745*
MCI	Motor Cycle Industry Association Limited, *page 783*

MCOC	Morris Cowley & Oxford Owners Club, *page 782*
MCPS	Mechanical-Copyright Protection Society Limited, *page 756*
MCRH	Manchester Centre for Regional History, *page 748*
MCS	Marine Conservation Society, *page 751*
MCU	Modern Churchpeople's Union, *page 778*
MDC	Muscular Dystrophy Campaign, *page 788*
MDF	MDF The Bipolar Organisation, *page 756*
MDHA	Masters of Deerhounds Association, *page 754*
MDS	Macular Disease Society, *page 743*
MDU	Medical Defence Union Limited, *page 758*
MEA	ME Association, *page 756*
MEC	Masterfoods Education Centre, *page 754*
MEC	Matra Enthusiasts' Club UK, *page 755*
MEC	Middle East Centre Library and Archives, *page 769*
MEC	Music Education Council, *page 790*
MEDASSET	Mediterranean Association to Save the Sea Turtles, *page 760*
MEEMA	Marine Engine and Equipment Manufacturers Association, *page 751*
MELCOM(UK)	Middle East Libraries Committee (UK), *page 769*
MENCAP	Royal Society for Mentally Handicapped Children and Adults, *page 1000*
MENSA	British Mensa Limited, *page 197*
Mercers' Company	Worshipful Company of Mercers, *page 1271*
MERL	Museum of English Rural Life, *page 789*
Mersey Television	Mersey Television Group, The, *page 764*
MES	Minerals Engineering Society, *page 774*
MET	Muslim Educational Trust, *page 790*
Met Office Library	National Meteorological Library and Archive, *page 832*
MF	Morris Federation, *page 782*
MFC	Multi-Faith Centre, *page 787*
MGA	Mushroom Growers' Association, *page 790*
MGCGB	Moto Guzzi Club GB, *page 783*
MGOC(NI)	MG Owners' Club (Northern Ireland), *page 769*
MGS	Manchester Geographical Society, *page 749*
MGS	Mediterranean Garden Society, *page 760*
MHEA	Materials Handling Engineers Association, *page 754*
MHF	Mental Health Foundation, *page 762*
MHM	Mental Health Media, *page 763*
MHRA	Medicines and Healthcare Products Regulatory Agency, *page 760*
MHRA	Modern Humanities Research Association, *page 778*
MHS	Merioneth Historical and Record Society, *page 764*
MI-21 WMI	MI-21 World Metal Index, *page 769*
MIA	Maritime Information Association, *page 752*
MIA	Mortar Industry Association, *page 783*
MIB	Motor Insurers' Bureau, *page 784*
MIDA	Malaysian Industrial Development Authority, *page 746*
MidAIG	Midlands Agricultural Information Group, *page 771*
MIDC	Morris Marina/Ital Drivers' Club, *page 782*
MiH	Council for Music in Hospitals, The, *page 355*
MIHS	Merseyside Industrial Heritage Society, *page 764*
MIL	Missionary Institute London, *page 776*
MILLS	Manchester Law Library, *page 749*
MinSoc	Mineralogical Society of Great Britain and Ireland, *page 774*
MIR	Medical Indemnity Register, *page 758*
MIRA	MIRA Limited, *page 775*
MIRO	Mineral Industry Research Organisation, *page 773*
MIRRC/Thatcham	Motor Insurance Repair Research Centre, *page 784*
MIS	Mobility Information Service – Shrewsbury, *page 777*
MISSION	Pontifical Mission Societies, *page 929*
MKC	Milton Keynes Council, *page 773*

MKCOC   Milton Keynes & North Bucks Chamber of
             Commerce, *page 772*
MLA   Marine Leisure Association, *page 751*
MLA   Master Locksmiths Association, *page 754*
MLA   Museums, Libraries and Archives
             Council, *page 789*
MLA South East Museums, Libraries and Archives South
             East, *page 789*
MLA Yorkshire   Museums, Libraries and Archives
             Yorkshire, *page 790*
MLIS   Monmouthshire Libraries and Information
             Service, *page 779*
MLS   Magic Lantern Society, *page 744*
MLTS   Mountain Leader Training Scotland, *page 785*
MMA   Music Masters' and Mistresses'
             Association, *page 790*
MML Library University of Cambridge – Modern and
             Medieval Languages Library, *page 1182*
MMMA   Metalforming Machinery Makers Association
             Limited, *page 766*
MMOC   Mini Marcos Owners Club, *page 774*
MMS   Methodist Missionary Society, *page 767*
MMTO   Maria Montessori Training
             Organisation, *page 751*
MND Association Motor Neurone Disease Association, *page 784*
MNH   Manx National Heritage Library, *page 750*
MNTO   Moroccan National Tourist Office, *page 781*
MOC   Messerschmitt Owners Club, *page 765*
MOD   Ministry of Defence Information and Library
             Service – Glasgow, *page 775*
MOD   Ministry of Defence Information and Library
             Service – Whitehall Information and Library
             Centre, *page 775*
MORI   Ipsos MORI, *page 660*
MOS   Men of the Stones, *page 762*
MOTA   Mail Order Traders' Association, *page 745*
MPA   Master Photographers Association of Great
             Britain, *page 754*
MPAGB   Modern Pentathlon Association of Great
             Britain, The, *page 779*
MPMA   Metal Packaging Manufacturers
             Association, *page 766*
MPS   Medical Protection Society, *page 759*
MPS   Society for Mucopolysaccharide
             Diseases, *page 1072*
MPS Specialist Metropolitan Police Economic Specialist Crime
  Crime OCU OCU, *page 768*
MPU   Medical Practitioners Union, *page 758*
MRC   Mathematics Research Centre, *page 755*
MRC   Mountain Rescue Council, *page 785*
MRC CTU   Medical Research Council – Cancer Division,
             MRC Clinical Trials Unit, *page 759*
MRC HGU   MRC Human Genetics Unit, *page 786*
MRC HNR   MRC Collaborative Centre for Human
             Nutrition Research, *page 785*
MRC-CBU   Medical Research Council – Cognition and
             Brain Sciences Unit, *page 759*
MRS   Market Research Society, *page 752*
MRU   Mycobacterium Reference Unit, *page 791*
MSA   Margarine and Spreads Association, *page 750*
MSA   Motor Sports Association, The, *page 784*
MSB   Metropolitan Society for the Blind, *page 768*
MSDRL   Merck, Sharp and Dohme Research
             Laboratories, *page 763*
MSF   Médecins Sans Frontières, *page 756*
MSG   Mesemb Study Group, *page 765*
MSGB   Manorial Society of Great Britain, *page 750*
MSI   MSI Marketing Research for Industry, *page 786*
MSIF   Multiple Sclerosis International
             Federation, *page 787*
MSRC   Multiple Sclerosis Resource Centre, *page 787*
MSRG   Medieval Settlement Research Group, *page 760*
MSS   Multiple Sclerosis Society, *page 788*
MSSL   Mullard Space Science Laboratory, *page 787*
MTCBC   Merthyr Tydfil County Borough
             Council, *page 764*
MTTA   Machine Tool Technologies
             Association, *page 742*

MTW   Maidstone & Tunbridge Wells NHS
             Trust, *page 745*
MU   Mothers' Union, *page 783*
MU   Musicians' Union, *page 790*
MUTA   Made-Up Textiles Association
             Limited, *page 743*
MVT   Military Vehicle Trust, *page 772*
MWC   Mental Welfare Commission for
             Scotland, *page 763*
MWF   Medical Women's Federation, *page 759*
MYA   Model Yachting Association, *page 778*
N.A.P.P.   National Association for Patient
             Participation, *page 798*
NA   National Archives – Chancery Lane, *page 795*
NA   Northern Arc Limited, *page 881*
NAAC   National Association of Agricultural
             Contractors, *page 800*
NAAPS   National Association of Adult Placement
             Services, *page 800*
NAAS   Nerine and Amaryllid Society, *page 859*
NABIC   National Association of Bank & Insurance
             Customers, *page 800*
NABMA   National Association of British Market
             Authorities, *page 800*
NAC   National Association of Choirs, *page 801*
NACAB   National Association of Citizens Advice
             Bureaux, *page 801*
NACC   National Association for Colitis and Crohn's
             Disease, *page 797*
NACC   National Autocycle and Cyclemotor Club
             Ltd, *page 808*
NACCAN   Association of Christian Communities and
             Networks, *page 66*
NACCC   National Association of Child Contact
             Centres, *page 800*
NACF   Art Fund, *page 45*
NACOA   National Association for Children of
             Alcoholics, *page 797*
NACS   National Association of Chimney
             Sweeps, *page 800*
NACT   National Association of Clinical
             Tutors, *page 801*
NADFAS   National Association of Decorative & Fine Arts
             Societies, *page 801*
NADP   National Association of Deafened
             People, *page 801*
NAEA   Lawrence Batley Centre for the National Arts
             Education Archive (Trust), *page 699*
NAEE (UK)   National Association for Environmental
             Education (UK), *page 797*
NAEIAC   National Association of Educational
             Inspectors, Advisers and
             Consultants, *page 802*
NAFBAE   National Association of Farriers, Blacksmiths
             and Agricultural Engineers, *page 802*
NAFD   National Association of Funeral
             Directors, *page 802*
NAG   National Acquisitions Group, *page 794*
NAG   National Association of Goldsmiths of Great
             Britain and Ireland, *page 802*
NAGC   National Association for Gifted
             Children, *page 797*
NAHC   National Anti-Hunt Campaign, *page 795*
NAHCF   National Association of Hospital &
             Community Friends, *page 802*
NAHWT   National Association of Health Workers for
             Travellers, *page 802*
NAITA   National Association of Independent Travel
             Agents, *page 803*
NAL   National Art Library, *page 796*
NALC   National Association of Ladies'
             Circles, *page 803*
NALC   National Association of Laryngectomee
             Clubs, *page 803*
NALC   National Association of Local
             Councils, *page 803*
NALD   National Association for Literature
             Development, *page 798*

NALI	National Association of the Launderette Industry Limited, *page 806*
NAMB	National Association of Master Bakers, *page 804*
NAME	National Association of Music Educators, *page 804*
NAMHO	National Association of Mining History Organisations, *page 804*
NAMLC	National Association of Master Letter Carvers, *page 804*
NAMM	National Association of Memorial Masons, *page 804*
NAO	National Audit Office, *page 808*
NAPCE	National Association for Pastoral Care in Education, *page 798*
NAPE	National Association for Primary Education, *page 798*
NAPF	National Association of Pension Funds, *page 804*
NAPGC	National Association of Public Golf Courses, *page 805*
NAPL	National Association of Licensed Paralegals, *page 803*
NAPS	National Association for Premenstrual Syndrome, *page 798*
NAPV	National Association of Prison Visitors, *page 805*
NARPD	National Association for the Relief of Paget's Disease, *page 799*
NAS	National Archives of Scotland, *page 796*
NAS	National Association of Self Employed, *page 805*
NAS	National Association of Shopfitters, *page 806*
NAS	National Autistic Society, *page 808*
NAS	Noise Abatement Society, *page 868*
NASC	National Access & Scaffolding Confederation, *page 794*
NASCH	National Association of Swimming Clubs for the Handicapped, *page 806*
NASEN	National Association for Special Educational Needs, The, *page 799*
NASGP	National Association of Sessional GPs, *page 806*
NASS	National Ankylosing Spondylitis Society, *page 795*
NASS	National Association of Steel Stockholders, *page 806*
NASUWT	National Association of Schoolmasters and Union of Women Teachers, *page 805*
NASUWT	National Association of Schoolmasters and Union of Women Teachers – Hillscourt Education Centre, *page 805*
NAT	National AIDS Trust, *page 794*
NATCECT	National Centre for English Cultural Tradition, *page 811*
NATD	National Association of Teachers of Dancing, *page 806*
NATD	National Association of Tool Dealers, *page 806*
NATE	National Association for the Teaching of English, *page 799*
NATLL	National Association of Toy and Leisure Libraries, *page 807*
NatSCA	Natural Sciences Collections Association, *page 857*
NAVCA	National Association for Voluntary and Community Action, *page 799*
NAVH	Norfolk Association of Village Halls, *page 869*
NAW	National Association of Widows, *page 807*
NAWC	National Association of Women's Clubs, *page 807*
NAWP	National Association of Women Pharmacists, *page 807*
NAWT	National Animal Welfare Trust, *page 794*
NAYO	National Association of Youth Orchestras, *page 808*
NAYT	National Association of Youth Theatres, *page 808*
NBA	National Beef Association, *page 809*
NBA	National Blood Authority, *page 809*
NBF	National Bed Federation, *page 809*

NBGW	National Botanic Garden of Wales, The, *page 810*
NBI	National Benevolent Institution, *page 809*
NBPC	National Birds of Prey Centre, *page 809*
NCA	National Council on Archives, *page 817*
NCAPTC	Norfolk County Association of Parish & Town Councils, *page 869*
NCB	National Children's Bureau, *page 812*
NCC	National Caravan Council Limited, *page 810*
NCC	National Computing Centre Limited, *page 814*
NCCF	National Consumer Credit Federation, *page 814*
NCCPG	National Council for the Conservation of Plants and Gardens, *page 815*
NCDC	North Cornwall District Council, *page 871*
NCDS	National Council for the Divorced and Separated, *page 815*
NCDT	National Council for Drama Training, *page 814*
NCEC	National Chemical Emergency Centre, *page 812*
NCEM	National Centre for Early Music, *page 811*
NCF	National Consumer Federation, *page 814*
NcfeD	National Centre for Eating Disorders, *page 811*
NCFS	National Campaign for Firework Safety, *page 810*
NCHA	National Care Association, *page 810*
NCHP	National College of Hypnosis and Psychotherapy, *page 814*
NCNE	National Campaign for Nursery Education, *page 810*
NCOB	Nuffield Council on Bioethics, *page 891*
NCOPO	National Council of Pakistani Organisations (UK), *page 816*
NCPA	Norfolk County Petanque Association, *page 869*
NCPA	UK National Committee for the Prevention of Alcohol and Drug Dependency, *page 1159*
NCS	National Chrysanthemum Society, *page 813*
NCSS	National Council for School Sports, *page 815*
NCT	Norfolk Church Trust Limited, *page 869*
NCTC	National Collection of Type Cultures, *page 813*
NCTEPO	National Centre for Training and Education in Prosthetics and Orthotics, *page 812*
NCTJ	National Council for the Training of Journalists, *page 815*
NCUACS	National Cataloguing Unit for the Archives of Contemporary Scientists, *page 811*
NCVCCO	National Council of Voluntary Child Care Organisations, *page 816*
NCVO	National Council for Voluntary Organisations, *page 816*
NCVYS	National Council for Voluntary Youth Services, *page 816*
NCW	National Council of Women of Great Britain, *page 816*
NCYPE	National Centre for Young People with Epilepsy, *page 812*
NDAF	National Disability Arts Forum, *page 818*
NDBMOC	North Devon British Motorcycle Owners Club, *page 871*
NDCS	National Deaf Children's Society, *page 817*
NDFS	National Deposit Friendly Society Limited, *page 818*
NDL	National Debtline, *page 817*
NDNA	National Day Nurseries Association, *page 817*
NDRO	North Devon Record Office, *page 871*
NEA	National Energy Action, *page 819*
NEA	National Exhibitors Association, *page 819*
NEAC	New English Art Club, *page 861*
NEBOSH	National Examination Board in Occupational Safety and Health, *page 819*
NEC	National Extension College Trust Limited, *page 820*
NECC	North East Chamber of Commerce, Trade & Industry, *page 872*
NECPWA	North-East Club for Pre-War Austins, *page 879*
NEELB/NELS	North Eastern Education and Library Board, *page 873*
NEF	National Energy Foundation, *page 819*
NEMA	National Early Music Association, *page 818*

REC	Recruitment and Employment Confederation, *page 954*
REHIS	Royal Environmental Health Institute of Scotland, *page 985*
REOC	Royal Enfield Owners Club, *page 985*
RES	Royal Economic Society, *page 985*
RES	Royal Entomological Society, *page 985*
RESCUE	RESCUE – The British Archaeological Trust, *page 959*
RFA	Rugby Fives Association, *page 1007*
RFFR	Relief Fund for Romania, *page 957*
RFS	Royal Forestry Society, *page 985*
RFU	Rugby Football Union, *page 1007*
RGI	Royal Glasgow Institute of the Fine Arts, The, *page 986*
RGS-IBG	Royal Geographical Society with the Institute of British Geographers, *page 986*
RHIER	Royal Holloway Institute for Environmental Research, *page 986*
RHistS	Royal Historical Society, *page 986*
RHS	RHS Garden Harlow Carr, *page 963*
RHS	Rider Haggard Society, *page 964*
RHS	Royal Horticultural Society, *page 987*
RHS	Royal Humane Society, *page 987*
RHUL	Royal Holloway University of London – Library, *page 986*
RI	Royal Institute of Painters in Watercolours, *page 989*
RI	Royal Institution of Great Britain, *page 990*
RIA	Railway Industry Association, *page 950*
RiA	Research Into Ageing, *page 959*
RIAS	Royal Incorporation of Architects in Scotland, *page 987*
RIBA	Royal Institute of British Architects, *page 987*
RIBA NW	Royal Institute of British Architects (North West Region), *page 988*
RIBI	Rotary International in Great Britain and Ireland, *page 970*
RIC	Royal Institution of Cornwall, *page 990*
RICA	Ricability, *page 963*
RICS	Royal Institution of Chartered Surveyors, *page 989*
RICS	Royal Institution of Chartered Surveyors in Scotland, *page 989*
RIDBA	Rural & Industrial Design & Building Association, *page 1008*
RIfI	Research Institute for Industry, *page 959*
RIIA, Chatham House	Royal Institute of International Affairs Library, *page 988*
RIN	Royal Institute of Navigation, *page 988*
RINA	Royal Institution of Naval Architects, *page 990*
RIPH	Royal Institute of Public Health, *page 989*
RISW	Royal Institution of South Wales, *page 990*
RIW Research	Retail Intelligence Worldwide, *page 960*
RLAS	Royal Lancashire Agricultural Society, *page 991*
RLHRS	Rutland Local History & Record Society, *page 1010*
RLSB	Royal London Society for the Blind, *page 991*
RMA	Retread Manufacturers Association, *page 960*
RMA	Royal Marines Association, *page 991*
RMAS	Royal Military Academy Sandhurst, *page 992*
RMIF	Retail Motor Industry Federation, *page 960*
RMS	Royal Medical Society, *page 992*
RMS	Royal Microscopical Society, *page 992*
RMS	Royal Society of Miniature Painters, Sculptors and Gravers, *page 1003*
RNA	Royal Naval Association, *page 993*
RNAA	Royal Norfolk Agricultural Association, *page 994*
RNC	Royal National College for the Blind, *page 992*
RNCM	Royal Northern College of Music, *page 994*
RNHA	Registered Nursing Home Association, *page 956*
RNIB	Royal National Institute of the Blind, *page 992*
RNLI	Royal National Lifeboat Institution, *page 993*
RNRS	Royal National Rose Society, *page 993*
RNS	Royal Numismatic Society, *page 994*
RNUC	Royal Northern and University Club, *page 994*
RoADAR	RoSPA Advanced Drivers and Riders, *page 969*
ROC	Rotary Owners Club, *page 970*
ROG	Royal Observatory Greenwich, *page 994*
ROH	Royal Opera House, *page 995*
ROI	Royal Institute of Oil Painters, *page 988*
RORC	Royal Ocean Racing Club, *page 995*
ROSCO	Road Operators Safety Council, *page 966*
RoSPA	RoSPA Driver and Fleet Solutions, *page 969*
RoSPA	Royal Society for the Prevention of Accidents, *page 1000*
RP	Royal Society of Portrait Painters, *page 1004*
RPC	Rail Passengers Council, *page 949*
RPRA	Royal Pigeon Racing Association, *page 996*
RPS	Royal Philharmonic Society, *page 996*
RPS	Royal Photographic Society of Great Britain, The, *page 996*
RPSGB	Royal Pharmaceutical Society of Great Britain, *page 995*
RPSI	Railway Preservation Society of Ireland, *page 950*
RRA	Relatives and Residents Association, *page 956*
RREC	Rolls-Royce Enthusiasts' Club, *page 968*
RRF Museum (London)	Royal Regiment of Fusiliers Association London Area, *page 997*
RRI	Rowett Research Institute, *page 971*
RSA	Refined Sugar Association, *page 955*
RSA	Royal Scottish Academy, *page 998*
RSA	Royal Society for the Encouragement of Arts, Manufactures and Commerce, *page 1000*
RSAA	Royal Society for Asian Affairs, *page 1000*
RSAC	Royal Scottish Automobile Club (Motor Sport) Ltd, *page 998*
RSAMD	Royal Scottish Academy of Music and Drama, *page 998*
RSAUK	Rett Syndrome Association UK, *page 961*
RSC	Devon Library Services – Railway Studies Library, *page 388*
RSC	Royal Society of Chemistry – Library and Information Centre, *page 1002*
RSC	Royal Society of Chemistry – Sales and Customer Care Department, *page 1002*
RSCDS	Royal Scottish Country Dance Society, *page 998*
RSCM	Royal School of Church Music, *page 997*
RSDC, Margate	Royal School for Deaf Children, Margate and Westgate College for Deaf People, *page 997*
RSE	Royal Society of Edinburgh, *page 1002*
RSFS	Royal Scottish Forestry Society, *page 999*
RSGS	Royal Scottish Geographical Society, *page 999*
RSI Awareness	Repetitive Strain Injury Awareness, *page 958*
RSL	Royal Society of Literature of the United Kingdom, *page 1003*
RSM	Royal Society of Medicine, *page 1003*
RSMA	Royal Society of Marine Artists, *page 1003*
RSN	Royal School of Needlework, *page 998*
RSNO	Royal Scottish National Orchestra, *page 999*
RSPB	Royal Society for the Protection of Birds, *page 1001*
RSPCA	Royal Society for the Prevention of Cruelty to Animals, *page 1001*
RSPSoc	Remote Sensing and Photogrammetry Society, The, *page 957*
RSS	RSS Centre for Statistical Education, *page 1007*
RSTMH	Royal Society of Tropical Medicine and Hygiene, *page 1004*
RSUA	Royal Society of Ulster Architects, *page 1004*
RTA	British Rose Trade Association, *page 210*
RTBI	National Association of Round Tables of Great Britain and Ireland, *page 805*
RTFHS	Romany and Traveller Family History Society, *page 968*
RTL	Registry Trust Limited, *page 956*
RTPI	Royal Town Planning Institute, *page 1004*
RTPI	Royal Town Planning Institute in Scotland, *page 1005*
RTTC	Cycling Time Trials, *page 370*
RUF	Refractory Users Federation, *page 955*
RUKBA	IndependentAge (formerly the Royal United Kingdom Beneficent Association), *page 593*
RUM Cars	Register of Unusual Micro-Cars, *page 955*

RUSI	Royal United Services Institute for Defence Studies, *page 1005*	SBAC	Society of British Aerospace Companies Limited, *page 1078*
RUTC	Richmond Upon Thames College, *page 964*	SBAC	UKspace, *page 1162*
RVA	Returned Volunteer Action, *page 961*	SBB	Small Business Bureau Limited, *page 1066*
RVC	Royal Veterinary College Library, *page 1005*	SBC	Scottish Borders Council, *page 1024*
RVC ACT	Royal Veterinary College Animal Care Trust, *page 1005*	SBC	Slough Borough Council, *page 1065*
		SBC	Stafford Borough Council, *page 1109*
RWA	Race Walking Association, *page 948*	SBC	Stevenage Borough Council, *page 1113*
RWAS Ltd	Royal Welsh Agricultural Society Limited, *page 1006*	SBC	Swale Borough Council, *page 1126*
		SBEF	Scottish Building, *page 1025*
RWCMD	Royal Welsh College of Music & Drama Library, *page 1006*	SBGI	Society of British Gas Industries, *page 1078*
		SBI	Stevenage Business Initiative, *page 1114*
RWS	Royal Watercolour Society, *page 1005*	SBRC	Biological Records Centre & Ludlow Museum, *page 113*
RYA	Royal Yachting Association, *page 1006*		
RYA Scotland	Royal Yachting Association Scotland, *page 1006*	SBWWI	Society of British Water & Wastewater Industries, *page 1078*
RZSS	Royal Zoological Society of Scotland, *page 1006*		
SA	Salvage Association, *page 1014*	SC	Glasgow Caledonian University Library in the Saltire Centre, *page 520*
SA	Soil Association, The, *page 1087*		
SAA	Society of Archer-antiquaries, *page 1076*	SC	Scottish Cycling, *page 1028*
SAAC	Scottish Asian Action Committee, *page 1023*	SCA	Scottish Canoe Association, *page 1025*
SABA	Southern Africa Business Association, *page 1098*	SCA	Specialist Cheesemakers' Association, *page 1101*
SAC	Scottish Agricultural College – Auchincruive, *page 1022*	SCA	Sprayed Concrete Association, *page 1104*
		SCA	Surrey Community Action, *page 1122*
SAC	Scottish Agricultural College – Edinburgh, *page 1022*	SCAR	Scientific Committee on Antarctic Research, *page 1019*
SACGB	Shark Angling Club of Great Britain, *page 1053*	SCAS	Society for Companion Animal Studies, *page 1069*
SACU	Society for Anglo-Chinese Understanding, *page 1068*	SCAS	Stirling Council Archive Service, *page 1114*
SADA	Seasonal Affective Disorder Association, *page 1049*	SCAT	Somerset College of Arts and Technology, *page 1090*
SAFed	Safety Assessment Federation, *page 1011*	SCAU	Surrey County Archaeological Unit, *page 1123*
SAGB	Shellfish Association of Great Britain, *page 1057*	SCC	Scottish Consumer Council, *page 1027*
SAGB	Silk Association of Great Britain, *page 1062*	SCC	Sheffield City Council, *page 1055*
SAHR	Society for Army Historical Research, *page 1069*	SCC	Somerset Counselling Centre, *page 1090*
SAHS	Shropshire Archaeological and Historical Society, *page 1060*	SCCE	Shropshire Chamber of Commerce & Enterprise Ltd, *page 1060*
SAHS	Staffordshire Archaeological and Historical Society, *page 1109*	SCCMI	Scottish Centre for Children with Motor Impairments, *page 1025*
SAIF	National Society of Allied and Independent Funeral Directors, The, *page 842*	SCDA	Scottish Community Drama Association, *page 1026*
SAL	Sugar Association of London, *page 1120*	SCDT	Scottish Cot Death Trust, *page 1027*
Salford TIC	Salford Tourist Information Centre, *page 1012*	SCHS	Scottish Church History Society, *page 1026*
Salisbury CVS	Salisbury & District Council for Voluntary Service, *page 1013*	SCI	Steel Construction Institute, *page 1113*
		SCIE	Social Care Institute for Excellence, *page 1067*
SALS	Society for Advanced Legal Studies, *page 1068*	SCIS	Scottish Council of Independent Schools, *page 1027*
SAMA	Scottish Amateur Music Association, *page 1022*	SCKC	Supply Chain Knowledge Centre, *page 1121*
SAMS	Scottish Association for Marine Science, *page 1023*	SCL	Services Central Library, *page 1051*
		SCL	Society for Computers and Law, *page 1070*
SAMS	Scottish Association for Marine Science, *page 1023*	SCLC	Scottish Child Law Centre, *page 1026*
SANA	Scottish Anglers National Association, *page 1023*	SCM	Student Christian Movement of Great Britain, *page 1118*
SANDS	Stillbirth and Neonatal Death Charity, *page 1114*	SCMA	Stilton Cheese Makers' Association, *page 1114*
		SCMHT	Southbrook Community Mental Health Team, *page 1098*
SANHS	Somerset Archaeological and Natural History Society, *page 1089*	SCMS	Society of Consulting Marine Engineers and Ship Surveyors, *page 1078*
SAPC	Scottish Accident Prevention Council, *page 1021*	SCO	Scottish Chamber Orchestra Limited, *page 1025*
SAPT	Scottish Association for Public Transport, *page 1023*	SCoD	Scottish Council on Deafness, *page 1028*
		SCOLAG	Scottish Legal Action Group, *page 1034*
SAR	Society of Afghan Residents in the UK, *page 1076*	SCOLMA	Standing Conference on Library Materials on Africa, *page 1111*
SARS	Scientific Apparatus Recycling Scheme, *page 1019*	SCONUL	Society of College, National and University Libraries, *page 1078*
SASA	Science and Advice for Scottish Agriculture, *page 1018*	SCOOP	Standing Committee on Official Publications, *page 1111*
SASA	Scottish Amateur Swimming Association, *page 1022*	SCOP	Standing Conference of Principals, *page 1111*
		SCOR	Society and College of Radiographers, *page 1068*
SASS	Sir Arthur Sullivan Society, *page 1064*	SCOTBIS	Scottish Business Information Service, *page 1025*
SAUK	Scoliosis Association UK, *page 1019*		
SAVE	Save Britain's Heritage, *page 1016*	ScotsCare	Royal Scottish Corporation, *page 998*
SB	Subterranea Britannica, *page 1118*	Scottish SPCA	Scottish Society for the Prevention of Cruelty to Animals, *page 1043*
SBA	Scottish Bowling Association, *page 1024*		
SBA	Society of Botanical Artists, *page 1077*	ScotWays	Scottish Rights of Way and Access Society, *page 1041*
SBA	Solicitors Benevolent Association, *page 1088*		
SBA	Steam Boat Association of Great Britain, *page 1113*	SCP	Scottish Cultural Press & Scottish Children's Press, *page 1028*

SMI	Society of Maritime Industries Limited, *page 1083*	SPMA	Society for Post-Medieval Archaeology, The, *page 1072*
SML	Soil Mechanics, *page 1087*	SPPA	Scottish Pre-School Play Association, *page 1039*
SMPC	Scottish Mask and Puppet Centre, *page 1035*	SPPC	Scottish Partnership for Palliative Care, *page 1039*
SMS	Society of Model Shipwrights, *page 1083*	SPR	Society for Psychical Research, *page 1073*
SMTA	Scottish Motor Trade Association Limited, *page 1036*	SPRI	Scott Polar Research Institute, *page 1021*
SMTO	Scottish Massage Therapists Organisation Limited, *page 1035*	SPRS	Society for the Promotion of Roman Studies, *page 1074*
SMUC	St Mary's College, *page 1108*	SPRS	Staffordshire Parish Registers Society, *page 1110*
SNACMA	Snack, Nut and Crisp Manufacturers Association Limited, *page 1066*	SPS	Strategic Planning Society, The, *page 1116*
SNC	South Northamptonshire District Council, *page 1094*	SPSBS	Shetland Pony Stud-book Society, *page 1058*
		SPSO	Scottish Public Services Ombudsman, *page 1040*
SNCCFR	Sir Norman Chester Centre for Football Research, *page 1064*	SPTC	Scottish Parent Teacher Council, *page 1039*
SNFWB	Scottish National Federation for the Welfare of The Blind, *page 1036*	SPUC	Society for the Protection of Unborn Children, *page 1074*
SNH	Scottish Natural Heritage – Edinburgh, *page 1037*	SPUC Scotland	Society for the Protection of Unborn Children – Scotland, *page 1075*
SNHL	Scottish Natural History Library, *page 1038*	SPW	Students Partnership Worldwide, *page 1118*
SNIPEF	Scottish and Northern Ireland Plumbing Employers' Federation, *page 1022*	SQA	Scottish Qualifications Authority, *page 1040*
SNIWB, LINBURN	Scottish National Institution for the War Blinded, *page 1036*	SRA	Shooters' Rights Association, *page 1059*
		SRA	Social Research Association, *page 1067*
SNN	Society of Nursery Nursing, The, *page 1083*	SRC	Scottish Refugee Council, *page 1040*
SNP	Scottish National Party, *page 1037*	SRL	Sound Research Laboratories Limited, *page 1091*
SoA	Broadcasting Group of the Society of Authors, *page 229*	SROC	Sunbeam Rapier Owners Club, *page 1120*
SOA	Society of Archivists, *page 1077*	SRP	Society of Recorder Players, *page 1085*
SOA	Society of Authors, *page 1077*	SRPS	Scottish Railway Preservation Society, *page 1040*
SOAS	School of Oriental and African Studies, *page 1017*	SRU	Scottish Rugby Union, *page 1041*
		SS/CE	Snowdonia Society, *page 1066*
SOB	Society of Bookbinders, *page 1077*	SSA	Scottish Screen Archive, *page 1042*
SOBHD	Scottish Official Board of Highland Dancing, *page 1038*	SSA	Scottish Sports Association, *page 1044*
SOC	Scott Owners' Club, The, *page 1021*	SSAC	Scottish Sub-Aqua Club, *page 1044*
SOC	Scottish Ornithologists' Club, *page 1038*	SSAFA Forcehelp	Soldiers, Sailors, Airmen and Families Association – Forces Help, *page 1088*
SOC	Singer Owners Club, *page 1063*	SSAM	Society of Sales and Marketing, The, *page 1085*
SOC	Spartan Owners' Club, *page 1101*	SSBA	Scottish Spina Bifida Association, *page 1044*
SOC	Stag Owners Club, *page 1111*	SSC	Scottish Sensory Centre, *page 1042*
SODC	South Oxfordshire District Council, *page 1095*	SSC	Society of Solicitors in the Supreme Courts of Scotland, *page 1085*
SOE	Society of Engineers (Incorporated), *page 1079*	SSC	Statistical Services Centre, *page 1112*
SOE	Society of Operations Engineers, *page 1084*	SSCATF	Sickle Cell and Thalassaemia Foundation, *page 1061*
SOF	Society of Floristry Limited, *page 1080*	SSCR	Scottish Society for Conservation and Restoration, *page 1043*
SOFHT	Society of Food Hygiene Technology, The, *page 1080*	SSDC	South Shropshire District Council, *page 1095*
SofM	Society of Metaphysicians Limited, *page 1083*	SSE	Snowsport England, *page 1066*
SoG	Society of Genealogists, *page 1080*	SSERC	Scottish Schools Equipment Research Centre Limited, *page 1042*
SOGB	Special Olympics Great Britain, *page 1101*	SSF	Society for Reproduction & Fertility, *page 1073*
SOL	Society of Ley Hunters, The, *page 1082*	SSF	Society of Shoe Fitters, The, *page 1085*
SOLT	Society of London Theatre, *page 1082*	SSG	Society of St Gregory, *page 1085*
SOLT	Society of London Toastmasters, *page 1082*	SSHM	Scottish Society of the History of Medicine, *page 1044*
SOM	Society of Orthopaedic Medicine, *page 1084*		
Somerset YFC	Somerset Federation of Young Farmers Club, *page 1090*	SSHM	Society for the Social History of Medicine, *page 1075*
SOMSR	Society of Master Shoe Repairers Limited, *page 1083*	SSI	Sight Savers International, *page 1062*
SoR	Society of Radiographers, *page 1084*	SSI	Society of Scribes and Illuminators, *page 1085*
SOVA	Society of Voluntary Associates, *page 1086*	SSL	Scottish Snooker Limited, *page 1043*
SPA	Scottish Publishers Association, *page 1040*	SSLRC	National Soil Resources Institute, *page 842*
SPA	Society for Popular Astronomy, *page 1072*	SSMA	Sterilised Suture Manufacturers Association, *page 1113*
SPA	Structural Precast Association, *page 1117*	SSPO	Scottish Salmon Producers Organisation, *page 1041*
SPAB	Society for the Protection of Ancient Buildings, *page 1074*	SSPR	Scottish Society for Psychical Research, *page 1043*
SpaBA	Spa Business Association, *page 1100*	SSR	Scottish School of Reflexology, The, *page 1041*
SPANA	Society for the Protection of Animals Abroad, *page 1074*	SSS	Shingles Support Society, *page 1058*
SPC	Society of Pension Consultants, *page 1084*	SSS	Simplified Spelling Society, *page 1063*
SPCK	Society for Promoting Christian Knowledge, *page 1072*	SSSA	Scottish Salmon Smokers Association, *page 1041*
SPE	Society of Professional Engineers, *page 1084*	SST	Society of Sports Therapists, *page 1085*
SPEF	Scottish Print Employers Federation, *page 1040*	SSTA	Scottish Secondary Teachers' Association, *page 1042*
SPF	Scottish Pharmaceutical Federation, *page 1039*		
SPHS	Society for the Promotion of Hellenic Studies, *page 1074*	SSU	Southampton Solent University, *page 1098*
SPL	Science Photo Library Limited, *page 1018*	SSVC	Split Screen Van Club, *page 1102*
SPL	Scottish Poetry Library, *page 1039*		

VC	Visit Cornwall, *page 1217*
VC	Volunteer Centre, *page 1220*
VCA	Vehicle Certification Agency, *page 1213*
VCC	Veteran Car Club of Great Britain, *page 1213*
VCCC	Vauxhall Convertible Car Club, *page 1211*
VCM	Victoria College Examinations, *page 1214*
VdGS	Viola da Gamba Society, *page 1216*
VE	Volunteering England, *page 1220*
VEC	Volvo Enthusiasts Club, *page 1221*
VERTIC	Verification Research, Training and Information Centre, *page 1213*
VES	Voluntary Euthanasia Society, *page 1220*
VGC	Vintage Glider Club, *page 1216*
VI	Victoria Institute or Philosophical Society of Great Britain, *page 1215*
VIA	Values into Action, *page 1211*
VLA	Veterinary Laboratories Agency, *page 1214*
VLV	Voice of the Listener and Viewer, *page 1219*
VMCC	Vintage Motor Cycle Club Limited, *page 1216*
VOC	Vauxhall Owners Club (1903–1957), *page 1212*
VOGR	Vale of Glamorgan Railway Company Limited, *page 1210*
VOICE	Professional Association of Nursery Nurses, *page 939*
VOSA	Vehicle and Operator Services Agency, *page 1212*
VPL	Video Performance Limited, *page 1215*
VSB	Voluntary Service Bureau, *page 1220*
VSCC	Vintage Sports-Car Club Limited, *page 1216*
VSO	Voluntary Service Overseas, *page 1220*
VSS	Victim Support Scotland, *page 1214*
VSUK	Vegetarian Society of the United Kingdom, *page 1212*
VWOC (GB)	VW Owners' Club GB, *page 1221*
VWSGB	Virginia Woolf Society of Great Britain, *page 1216*
VWT20C	Volkswagen Type 2 Owners' Club, *page 1219*
WABIL	World Ahlul Bayt Islamic League, *page 1259*
WACT	Welsh Advisory Committee on Telecommunications, *page 1230*
WAHO	World Arabian Horse Organization, *page 1259*
WAI	WomenAid International, *page 1256*
WALC	Wiltshire Association of Local Councils, *page 1246*
WALS	Wolverhampton Archives and Local Studies, *page 1252*
WAMC	Welsh Association of Motor Clubs, *page 1230*
WANHS	Wiltshire Archaeological and Natural History Society, *page 1246*
WAR	Women Against Rape, *page 1252*
WASA	Welsh Amateur Swimming Association, *page 1230*
WCBC	Wrexham County Borough Council, *page 1276*
WCCUIN	Wiltshire & Swindon Users Network, *page 1245*
WCEC	Worshipful Company of Environmental Cleaners, *page 1267*
WCF	World Curling Federation, *page 1260*
WCIA	Welsh Centre for International Affairs, *page 1231*
WCML	Working Class Movement Library, *page 1259*
WCMPC	Worshipful Company of Makers of Playing Cards, *page 1270*
WCP	Worshipful Company of Plumbers, *page 1272*
WCPT	World Confederation for Physical Therapy, *page 1260*
WCRF	World Cancer Research Fund, *page 1259*
WCS	Wilkie Collins Society, *page 1244*
WCS	Wound Care Society, *page 1275*
WCVA	Wales Council for Voluntary Action, *page 1222*
WDA	Well Drillers Association, *page 1228*
WDCS	Whale and Dolphin Conservation Society, *page 1240*
WDS	Women's Design Service, *page 1253*
WEA	Workers' Educational Association, *page 1258*
WEB	Women's Education in Building, *page 1253*
WEC	World Energy Council, *page 1260*
WEDG	World Education Development Group, *page 1260*
WEETU	Women's Employment Enterprise & Training Unit, *page 1253*
WEIC	Wales Euro Info Centre, *page 1222*
WEN	Women's Environmental Network, *page 1254*
WER	World Emergency Relief, *page 1260*
WES	Women's Engineering Society, *page 1253*
WFDS/CDdWC	Welsh Folk Dance Society, *page 1231*
WFGA	Women's Farm and Garden Association, *page 1254*
WFTV	Women in Film and Television, *page 1252*
WFU	Women's Food and Farming Union, *page 1254*
WGAS	West Glamorgan Archive Service, *page 1233*
WGAS	Wood Green Animal Shelters, *page 1256*
WGGB	Writers Guild of Great Britain, *page 1276*
WHBI	Welwyn Hatfield Business Initiative Limited, *page 1232*
WHC	Women's Health Concern, *page 1254*
WHS	Wallpaper History Society, *page 1223*
WHS	Wesley Historical Society, *page 1232*
WHTC	Wolfson Heat Treatment Centre, *page 1251*
Wigan Council	Metropolitan Borough of Wigan, *page 768*
WILPF	Women's International League for Peace and Freedom, *page 1255*
Wirral Met	Wirral Metropolitan College – Twelve Quays Campus, *page 1249*
WISE	WISE Vehicle Programme, *page 1249*
WISPA	Women's International Squash Players Association, *page 1255*
WIZ	Wirral Libraries, *page 1249*
WKC	West Kent College, *page 1233*
WLHB	Women's League of Health and Beauty, *page 1255*
WLHS	Warwickshire Local History Society, *page 1227*
WLSBA	Wensleydale Longwool Sheep Breeders' Association, *page 1232*
WMA	Wallcoverings Sector Council, *page 1223*
WMRMC	West Midlands Regional Museums Council, *page 1234*
WMSoc	Water Management Society, *page 1227*
WNA	World Nuclear Association, *page 1261*
WNC	Women's National Commission, *page 1255*
Women's Aid	Women's Aid Federation of England, *page 1252*
World Traders	Worshipful Company of World Traders, *page 1274*
Worldscale	Worldscale Association (London) Limited, *page 1264*
WPA	World Pheasant Association, *page 1262*
WPBSA	World Professional Billiards and Snooker Association Limited, *page 1262*
WPF	WPF Counselling and Psychotherapy, *page 1275*
WPIF	Wood Panel Industries Federation, *page 1256*
WPO	World Ploughing Organization, *page 1262*
WPOA	Westminster Property Owners Association, *page 1239*
WPSA	World's Poultry Science Association UK Branch, *page 1263*
WPT	World Parrot Trust, *page 1262*
WRc	WRc plc, *page 1275*
WRS	Wiltshire Record Society, *page 1247*
WRTPA	West Riding Trade Protection Association, *page 1234*
WSA	Wine and Spirit Association, The, *page 1248*
WSF	Women's Sports Foundation, *page 1256*
WSF	World Squash Federation Limited, *page 1263*
WSFHS	West Surrey Family History Society, *page 1235*
WSL	Westcountry Studies Library, *page 1238*
WSPA	World Society for the Protection of Animals, *page 1262*
WSRO	West Sussex Record Office, *page 1235*
WTB	Wales Tourist Board, *page 1223*
WUMTIA	Wolfson Unit for Marine Technology and Industrial Aerodynamics, *page 1251*
WUPJ	World Union for Progressive Judaism European Board, *page 1263*
WWF	WWF-UK, *page 1276*
WWLR	Wells and Walsingham Light Railway, *page 1230*
WWT	Wildfowl & Wetlands Trust, *page 1242*

Subject Index

Entries in the Subject Index refer the reader to the page numbers of full entries in the Main Directory.

butchery

Bute

Butler, _Lord_ Richard Austen (1902–1982)

Butler, Josephine Elizabeth (1828–1906)

Butler, Samuel (1835–1902)

butlers

butterflies and moths

– special collection

Butterworth, Arthur

Butterworth, George Sainton Kaye (1885–1916)

buttonhooks

buttons

Byron, _Lord_ George Gordon (1788–1824)

– special collection

Byzantine studies

Subject Index

ASLIB DIRECTORY of INFORMATION SOURCES